The New Grove® Dictionary of
Jazz

The New Grove® Dictionary of Jazz

Edited by

Barry Kernfeld

ST. MARTIN'S PRESS
NEW YORK

THE NEW GROVE® DICTIONARY OF JAZZ

The New Grove® Dictionary of Jazz
edited by Barry Kernfeld, in two volumes, 1988

Reprinted 1991

This edition, in one volume, published 1994 in the United Kingdom by the Macmillan Press Limited,
London and in the United States of America by St. Martin's Press, New York.

Reprinted 1995, 1996

First published in two volumes in 1988 by the Macmillan Press Limited, London
and Grove's Dictionaries of Music Inc., New York.

Parts of this dictionary originally appeared in

The New Grove Dictionary of Music and Musicians®
edited by Stanley Sadie, in twenty volumes, 1980

The New Grove® Dictionary of Musical Instruments
edited by Stanley Sadie, in three volumes, 1984

The New Grove® Dictionary of American Music
edited by Stanley Sadie and H. Wiley Hitchcock, in four volumes, 1986

A catalogue record for this book is available from
The British Library.

ISBN 0-333-63231-1

Library of Congress Cataloging-in-Publication Data
is available upon request.

ISBN 0-312-11357-9

Printed in Hong Kong

Contents

Editor
Barry Kernfeld

Consultant Editor
Alyn Shipton

Managing Editor
Rosemary Roberts

Series Editor
Stanley Sadie

Publishers' Note

This one-volume edition of *The New Grove Dictionary of Jazz* is an unaltered reprint of the two-volume hardback first published in 1988. Immediately on its appearance, this dictionary was recognized by jazz-lover, scholar and librarian alike as a monumental and indispensable reference book. As in any field of lexicography, the editorial stance taken by the editor and publishers found its critics, but the book has become – for all those who have regular access to it – the first and most comprehensive point of enquiry on all matters to do with jazz, its musicians, musical language, performance practice, instrumentation and history. As with any hardback set, aimed predominantly at an institutional market, the original edition was beyond the means of many enthusiasts and general readers. This edition is intended to make a widely acknowledged standard work available to the broadest possible public.

Jazz itself has not stood still since 1988, and there have been recent developments that are not covered here, as well as the emergence of a new generation of young musicians. Equally, this reprint does not address the two most significant areas of change in the field of jazz studies: the continuing discoveries of jazz scholars, and the deaths of many of the men and women who shaped jazz in the first place. Fortunately, there have been few enough new discoveries of genuine importance that the majority of entries here remain the definitive dictionary articles on their subjects. Less fortunately, the death toll among musicians has pervaded almost every area of the book. It has been heaviest among pioneers like Danny Barker (also a contributor), Garvin Bushell, Wild Bill Davison, Roy Eldridge, Bud Freeman, Adelaide Hall, Art Hodes, Andy Kirk, Freddie Moore, Sammy Price and Jabbo Smith. Equally, it has affected the founders of bop such as Art Blakey, Kenny Drew, Billy Eckstine, Dizzy Gillespie and Sarah Vaughan, as well as musicians beyond category, such as Miles Davis, Stan Getz, and Sun Ra. A full list of death dates is included on pages xxx–xxxii of this volume.

The New Grove Dictionary of Jazz is reissued in this form as the most comprehensive dictionary of jazz ever published, containing essays by many of the world's best jazz writers and scholars. Its unique blend of clearly presented information, selected recordings, bibliographical data and critical assessments make it unrivalled in the field of jazz studies. Since publication, the dictionary has not been superseded by any other work and therefore, although not updated or revised, this edition brings to the general reading public the book hailed by *Library Journal* as "supplementing and updating all extant jazz reference works."

Preface

Genesis and development of *The New Grove Dictionary of Jazz.* Early in 1982, shortly after I was asked to contribute articles on jazz to *The New Grove Dictionary of American Music*, I began to consider the possibility of creating a dictionary of jazz in the Grove tradition. Although there were already several fine biographical dictionaries of jazz musicians, there seemed to be a need for a comprehensive work in which the breadth and rigorous methodology that characterize the Grove projects could be applied for the first time to jazz. At the annual meeting of the American Musicological Society at Louisville, Kentucky, in November 1983 I suggested the idea to Stanley Sadie and he invited me to submit a formal proposal to the publishers of the Grove Dictionaries, the London firm of Macmillan. The following March I sent a proposal, which was immediately accepted, and through the spring and summer I developed a general plan with the help of Dr. Sadie and Alyn Shipton, then Music Publisher at Macmillan. Work began in earnest in the autumn.

Originally this was to have been a one-volume, 500-page work, consisting of articles on individuals, groups, and styles of jazz, as well as selected terms and theoretical topics. During its production, however, I realized that a rounded coverage of the music required us to add many other areas. As a consequence the book has more than doubled in size and now includes a comprehensive treatment of terminology and theory, articles on musical instruments, record labels, festivals, venues, films, institutions, and individuals who are not performers, and also an extensive bibliography – none of which formed part of my initial conception.

Grove and jazz. In *The New Grove Dictionary of Music and Musicians,* published in 1980, jazz took its place in the context of a worldwide coverage of all aspects of art music, popular music, and ethnic traditions; there were substantial articles on jazz and related styles of music, and more than 175 articles on jazz musicians. *The New Grove Dictionary of American Music* provided the opportunity to present a fuller picture of a music that is American in its origins and substantially so in its development; more than 400 articles in that dictionary covered musicians and styles of jazz. With *The New Grove Dictionary of Jazz* the process of expansion takes a significant leap. It is the largest dictionary of the music ever published; it contains the broadest coverage of the subject to appear in one work and seeks to give detailed attention to all periods and styles of jazz from many countries, in an effort to counteract the factionalism noticeable in some jazz literature.

The distinguished predecessors of this dictionary in the Grove series established principles of lexicographical organization and scholarly presentation that have never before been applied to jazz. While the purpose of an encyclopedic work is to reflect the current understanding of its subject and not to initiate research, it is important to note that a large amount of information is published for the first time here, and that many of the major articles present new thinking on the ways in which jazz may be approached. Contributors and editors alike have attempted an unprecedented biographical and discographical accuracy through a rigorous assessment of data taken from books, periodicals, liner notes, questionnaires, transcriptions of oral histories, telephone interviews, advertisements, press kits, and many other sources. Aiming to make generally available the materials of jazz research on which a few scholars have hitherto held a monopoly, the dictionary includes extensive bibliographies supplemented by references to the holdings of oral history collections. And finally, as befits a Grove dictionary, close and wide-ranging attention is paid to the music itself: numerous musical terms are precisely defined, musical structures, procedures, and styles are described in detail, and there are informed analytical surveys (with music examples) of such theoretical topics as forms, harmony, and improvisation.

According to the original plan for the dictionary about a quarter of the material was to have drawn on articles already published in *The New Grove Dictionary of Music and Musicians* and *The New Grove Dictionary of American Music*. With the expansion of the work has come a greater independence from the earlier dictionaries, so that in its final form about 90% of the material is new. The two dozen or so articles on non-American musicians previously published in *The New Grove* have been extensively revised and updated, and have had recording-lists and bibliographies added to them. 400 articles from the American dictionary are incorporated here; most have been revised, some extensively so. Of special note is James Lincoln Collier's fine essay **Jazz**, which has been reconsidered in the light of recent research and expanded to cover jazz internationally; its inclusion represents a new departure for the Grove dictionaries, in none of which until now has the title been defined in a single entry. Articles on instruments in this dictionary frequently summarize the organological definitions given in *The New Grove Dictionary of Musical Instruments*, but in all other respects are newly written, since they deal exclusively with aspects of usage in jazz.

Contents and scope. Quite apart from Collier's article, the work as a whole constitutes a definition of jazz because of the subjects it does and does not include. It is shaped generally by two points of view, one expansive, the other restrictive. The first arises from the broad development of the music during the scant century of its existence: a music principally of black-American creation, jazz is now an international music; accordingly somewhat more than a quarter of the book concerns non-American subjects. The second seeks to establish useful limits to a definition of jazz in its relationships with other genres. Such relationships are discussed in surveys of, for example, blues, brass bands, Latin jazz, and ragtime. There are also articles on individuals such as Eubie Blake, Bessie Smith, Johnny Mercer, Ray Charles, and Jeff Beck, whose careers, though focused on (respectively) ragtime and musical theater, blues, popular song, soul music, and rock music, include significant associations with jazz musicians or a connection with certain jazz styles. But musicians such as Scott Joplin, Blind Lemon Jefferson, George Gershwin, Aretha Franklin, and Jimi Hendrix are not included because they are not directly associated with jazz. I have met with some resistance to this editorial policy from respected advisers and contributors who have argued for casting the net widely, but in consultation with my colleagues on the editorial team I have chosen not to heed their advice. I believe that a view of jazz that incorporates vaudeville, ragtime, blues, gospel music, country music, pop, folk music, rhythm-and-blues, rock-and-roll, soul music, hard rock, funk, salsa . . . obscures the musical characteristics that distinguish these genres from one another and from jazz.

Proceeding from these premises I constructed a coverage of jazz based on interdependent categories of articles. The categories, broadly, are these: individuals, groups and bands, styles, topics and terms, instruments, record companies and labels, and institutions.

In most areas the dictionary has an interlocking hierarchical structure that allows it to be used in different ways by readers with different needs. For example, the key article **Jazz** would lead the reader to articles on the three dozen or so central styles and substyles of jazz throughout its history and on related styles such as blues, Latin jazz, and ragtime; each article on a style would in turn direct him or her to entries on its principal exponents, and from there to the entries on important sidemen and soloists. Taking another direction, the reader might begin with the companion article **Bands** (also by Collier) and work out from there to entries on various types of ensemble, individual groups, and finally individual performers; or to instruments and from those to the definitions of instrumental effects and thence to **Notation**, where the various attempts to fix a principally improvised music in written form are summarized. Similar routes might be followed from other starting points.

By contrast, readers more familiar with the music might begin from the bottom of the hierarchy, seeking information on a less important style or an obscure term, and be led finally to theoretical articles such as **Beat**, **Forms**, **Harmony**, and **Improvisation**, which break new grounds discussing such fundamental issues. A group of articles that will be of particular interest to the record collector and the discographer centers on **Recording** and **Discography**. The first of these discusses technical and historical developments, the second explains the systematic study of sound recordings and surveys the literature; both are interrelated with many short entries defining terms of particular importance. A complete listing of the several hundred record companies and labels that have their own entries in the dictionary is given at the end of **Recording**.

A number of important articles in the dictionary relate only peripherally to the central framework, and it may therefore be as well to draw special attention to their presence. **Films** provides a comprehensive survey of the uses of jazz in motion pictures and television. The dictionary contains several entries that consist principally of lists. **Festivals** gives detailed information on some 200 events held throughout the world (there are also individual entries on the 15 most important jazz festivals), and **Nightclubs and other venues** offers short descriptions of more than 900 venues that have fostered the performance of jazz; these two articles (each with its own index) represent the first attempt at a historical and international coverage of these subjects. **Libraries and archives** describes public and private collections of materials pertaining to jazz. Because this dictionary deals with a relatively circumscribed area of music it has been possible to compile a comprehensive bibliography of books and periodicals, which is presented as Appendix 1.

Categories of article. Some account should be given of the criteria for inclusion of entries in the dictionary and the character and content of articles in the different categories outlined above.

Individuals. Of the more than 3000 individuals on whom articles appear in the dictionary, selected in collaboration with a group of international advisers, the large majority are performing musicians, but there are also entries on composers, arrangers, record producers, writers, editors, discographers, and impresarios.

In general a performer merits inclusion in the dictionary if he or she has formed a lasting affiliation with a jazz musician of international renown, has recorded regularly, and has recorded as a soloist. Every effort has been made to include in each article on a performer at least one citation of a recording that represents his or her playing. Many articles have lists of such representative recordings (see Introduction, §9, below).

Groups and bands. Wherever possible, information on an ensemble appears in the entry on its leader. For reasons of lexicographical propriety this is always the case with a group whose name coincides with its leader's: the Count Basie Orchestra is accordingly discussed under the heading **Basie, Count**, not under **Count Basie Orchestra** (and no cross-reference is included under the latter name). In all other cases the principles governing the inclusion of an article on a group are commensurate with those for individuals. In addition it should be noted that in this area there are many instances of the brief definition and cross-reference (see Introduction, §6, below), which guide the reader from the name of a group to the article on its leader or members, where information on its activities may be found.

Topics and terms. Besides the sweeping surveys of major theoretical topics – under the headings **Arrangement**, **Beat**, **Forms**, **Harmony**, **Improvisation**, **Notation**, and **Transcription (i)** – the dictionary contains more than 200 definitions of musical terms. The criterion for inclusion here is that a term be peculiar to jazz, or have a particular meaning in jazz, or be so commonly found in connection with jazz that its omission would be perverse. In the case of the many entries on instrumental effects and techniques, recorded examples are cited, and music examples are given where appropriate.

Instruments. This area of the dictionary is one in which a comprehensive rather than a selective coverage has been attempted. It has been our purpose to include entries on all musical instruments found in jazz and to illustrate their use by the citing of recorded examples. The only exceptions to this policy of inclusion are homemade and "found" instruments and noise-makers, and certain non-Western instruments occasionally employed by musicians who have introduced elements of "world music" into their playing.

Each article on an instrument or family of instruments begins with an organological description, indicating the compass and explaining significant aspects of the playing technique. Full organological details appear in *The New Grove Dictionary of Musical Instruments* and are not included here, except where some aspect of the instrument's development is peculiar to jazz or has affected the way in which it is used; sometimes jazz research has thrown new light on lesser-known instruments and in these cases, too, fuller information about construction and playing technique is given. The main subject matter of these articles, however, is the use of musical instruments in jazz.

Entries are included under the names of all the members of instrumental families, giving brief definitions and directing the reader to the family name; the generic articles **Bass**, **Electronic keyboards**, and **Percussion** also provide a useful means of locating many articles on instruments. The instruments that form the equipment of the jazz drummer are dealt with as a group in the article **Drum set**. In addition to entries on instruments there is a comprehensive discussion of mutes and there are brief definitions of devices used in amplified music.

Record companies and labels. The entries on record companies and primary and subsidiary labels, more than 350 in number, represent the first published attempt at a balanced historical and geographical survey of the commercial development of the recording of jazz. Although the 78 r.p.m. era is well covered in the literature, information on the later period is not readily available. In this category the criteria for inclusion are not at all the same as in the areas of individuals and groups, since importance cannot here be measured according to prominence or longevity. Nearly every major enterprise appears but so do many smaller ones, and the latter are often as interesting and sometimes as significant as the former. The very smallness of an operation often gave it the freedom to make innovative recordings, and some of the landmarks in the repertory are preserved on labels that issued only a small number of titles.

Institutions. Besides the detailed lists of festivals and libraries referred to above, there are entries on many different kinds of institution devoted to furthering jazz scholarship and performance. They include educational organizations, concert series, musicians' collectives, and societies dedicated to the promotion of jazz worldwide. (Student institutions and fan clubs are not included.)

Acknowledgments. The preparation of a reference work of this nature necessarily involves not only the authors and the editorial staff, whose contributions are easily identified, but a large number of others – advisers, research assistants, scholars, enthusiasts, musicians, and promoters (all of whom answer appeals for help), secretarial and clerical assistants, production staff, typesetters, and printers. Those to whom I owe particular thanks are named below: to the many others whom it is impossible to acknowledge individually I should like to extend my warm thanks for their careful and willing work on behalf of the dictionary.

Contributors and advisers. First and foremost I wish to express my gratitude to the authors who have written the dictionary, whose specialized knowledge and expert understanding of the music in all its aspects make the work what it is. Many of them have generously exceeded all claims of scholarly obligation in their readiness to help us in numerous ways: by alerting us to material that merits inclusion, by warning us of possible errors, by supplying – often unasked – information that enabled us to keep our entries up to date, and by patiently answering our many questions. Authors are named at the ends of individual entries (see also Introduction, §12, below), and a list of contributors, together with the titles of the entries they wrote, is printed at the end of the dictionary.

The team of advisers on the international coverage of the dictionary was headed by Rainer E. Lotz. He directed my attention to potential advisers and contributors in different countries, proposed lists of subjects for each, and himself wrote many articles on players working in areas outside the geographical mainstream of the music. Those who took up the task of shaping the treatment of jazz in different countries were Simon Adams (England), Cristóbal Díaz Ayala (Cuba), Heidi Boulton (Germany), Omar García Brunelli (Argentina), André Clergeat (France), Gerhard Conrad (Czechoslovakia), Laureano Fernández (Argentina), Charles Fox (England), Tony Gould (Australia), Pekka Gronow (Scandinavia), Max Harrison (England), A. J. B. Johnson (Australia), Erik Kjellberg (Sweden), Wolfram Knauer (Germany and Poland), Michel Laplace (France), Adriano Mazzoletti (Italy), Mark Miller (Canada), Walter Ojakäär (USSR), Alfredo Papo (Spain), Robert Pernet (Belgium), Jeff Pressing (Australia), Klaus Schulz (Austria), Vidar Vanberg (Norway), Wim van Eyle (Netherlands), Erik Wiedemann (Denmark), and Valerie Wilmer (England). Bill Russell and Mike Hazeldine advised us on early jazz, Heinrich-Lukas Lindenmaier on free jazz, and Bert Noglik on free jazz in Eastern Europe. Some 265 articles on early jazz musicians are based on John Chilton's impeccable scholarship, as represented in the *Who's Who of Jazz* (London, rev. and enlarged 4/1985) (see also Introduction, §12, below). Mark Gardner identified and wrote articles on about 60 record companies and labels in the period after 1950, and Howard Rye gave help in the same area for the early and swing periods. A number of our advisers, notably Lawrence E. Koch, Howard Rye, Scott Yanow, and Frank Driggs, supplied citations of representative recordings for many lesser-known figures. Curtis Jerde provided material for the entry **Libraries and archives** and also information concerning oral history holdings.

Editors and assistants. Stanley Sadie, the series editor of the Grove dictionaries and architect of the fine tradition of lexicography that began with *The New Grove*, assisted in planning the book; much of its breadth is owed to his penetrating questions about my initial plans and his guidance as we later expanded the coverage. Further, his contribution as the head of a team of editors trained in a meticulous and scholarly methodology is deeply felt.

The editorial team of the *The New Grove Dictionary of American Music* developed a language and a format for the presentation of aspects of jazz within a Grove dictionary. Of particular importance were the contributions of the editors, H. Wiley Hitchcock and Stanley Sadie, the editorial coordinator, Susan Feder, and the adviser on jazz, J. Bradford Robinson.

The consultant editor, Alyn Shipton, until July 1987 also the Music Publisher of the Macmillan Press, is responsible for much of the plan of the book. He also made an extensive contribution to the shaping of individual articles, particularly in the areas of early jazz, swing, and musical instruments. In his capacity as Music Publisher he steered the book through all but its last stages; his support and patient commitment to our common aim to achieve a comprehensive and accurate work have been crucial to the success of the project. Rosemary Roberts, the dictionary's tireless managing editor, supplied much of the precision and depth of thought that we tried to apply to the planning and execution of individual entries. Her insights into subtle distinctions among related ideas, her telling questions about the meaning of complex statements on music, and her editorial expertise were all invaluable.

Among the editorial staff I should like to single out Caroline Richmond, who participated in the planning of the book, edited major articles, in July 1987 took responsibility under the direction of the Production Manager, David Robertson, for the dictionary's production to a demanding schedule, and in April 1988 assumed the role of managing editor. Other text editors were Anthony Marks, who also edited and prepared the music examples, Fred Kameny, Helen Jeffrey, Fiona Little, Alan Mitchell, and Tracey Smith; Helen Ottaway was the illustrations and captions editor. Many good qualities which may be found in the dictionary are in large measure due to the care and attention to detail shown by all members of this editorial team.

The staff of research and clerical helpers required to support and coordinate a project of this size is considerable. I would first thank our principal researcher, Howard Rye, who answered almost every question we sent him, no matter how obscure, and made many suggestions for improving the dictionary; his enthusiasm and perseverance are responsible for accurate data in many areas. He also wrote articles on some 150 record companies and labels and on lesser-known musicians. Other expert research help was given by William S. Brockman, who, together with Elisabeth Cook, Laura McCann, David Cladel, and Dorothy DeVal, dealt with bibliographical and other queries; I should like also to thank my father, Bernard Kernfeld, whose vigilance in combing San Francisco newspapers kept us abreast of developments on the West Coast throughout the project. Of great importance to the thorough coverage of the dictionary were Anita Prewitt, Dave Smyth, and Ronald M. Radano, who researched and wrote hundreds of articles on lesser-known musicians, principally in bop and later styles. Paul Laird prepared the international list of jazz festivals and contributed in various areas during the final stages of editing. Jeff Cooper and my assistants in the State College office, Marjory Sente, Kathy Zager, and Melady Kehm, indexed biographies and obituaries in countless books and periodicals. And finally the State College staff and Michael Durnin in London deserve the thanks of the whole editorial team for efficiently maintaining the dictionary's administrative systems, which were greatly complicated by the separation of the two offices.

Others. The success of a research network such as we established for this project depends heavily on the willing cooperation of librarians and archivists. I am more indebted than I can say to the staff of the Institute of Jazz Studies at Rutgers – notably Dan Morgenstern, Ed Berger, and Marie Griffin – who patiently fielded countless queries from our researchers and contributors. Phil Schaap generously gave his time as an independent adviser. I offer my sincere thanks as well to Daniel Zager, the music librarian of the Pennsylvania State University until spring 1987, and Carol Watson, Walter Wells, and other staff members, all of whom gave me ready access to the library's holdings and called my attention to important sources of information.

I should like to acknowledge with thanks the contribution of those who have supplied illustrations for the dictionary, chiefly the picture librarian Frank Driggs and the photographer David Redfern. (Acknowledgment of the copyright holders of illustrations and music examples is to be found at the end of the dictionary.)

Edwards Brothers, of Ann Arbor, Michigan, typeset the dictionary with the skill and accuracy which, during many years of collaboration, the Grove staff has come to appreciate.

The dictionary's computerized management system was devised and maintained by Doug Bruce, Jr., of the William Byrd Press, Richmond, Virginia, to whom I am grateful for his ready help.

Finally I wish to pay tribute to the publishers, the Macmillan Press Ltd. of London, who have supported the project through the various stages of its development with a steady confidence in our ability to bring it successfully to completion.

* * *

On a personal note, I should like to thank my loving wife Sally McMurry, whose support in every way made this book possible.

BARRY KERNFELD
State College, PA, May 1988

Introduction

1. Alphabetization. 2. Usages. 3. Article headings. 4. Article definitions. 5. Article structure. 6. Cross-references. 7. Oral history material. 8. Work-lists. 9. Recording-lists. 10. Transcriptions. 11. Bibliographies. 12. Authors. 13. Transliteration.

1. ALPHABETIZATION. Entries are ordered alphabetically according to their headings (see §3 below), which are interpreted as though they were continuous, ignoring spaces, hyphens, ampersands, apostrophes, accents, modifications, and diacritical marks, and all parenthesized and bracketed material; vowels carrying the umlaut in German and its equivalent in other northern European languages are read as a, o, and u, not ae, oe, and ue. These rules apply up to the comma, then again after it. Where two headings are identical except for their capitalization (ignoring parenthesized and bracketed material), the entry with the upper-case heading is placed first. Where two headings are identical in all respects (ignoring parenthesized and bracketed material), the entries are ordered chronologically and distinguished by lower-case roman numerals in parentheses. The prefixes "Mac" and "Mc" are alphabetized as "Mac"; "St." and "Mr." are alphabetized as though spelled out ("Saint" and "Mister"). Headings containing numerals are ordered as though the numerals were spelled out. Some of these points are illustrated by the following sequences of headings:

ARC
Arc
Arcadian Serenaders
ARC–BRC
Archer, Tony [Anthony John]

Dejan, Harold [Duke]
DeJohnette, Jack
De Kers [De Keersmaeker], **Robert**
Delamont, Gordon (Arthur)
Delaney, Jack (Michael)
De La Rosa, Frank [Francisco Esteban, Jr.]
Delaunay, Charles

Johnson, Howard (William) [Swan] **(i)**
Johnson, Howard (Lewis) (ii)
Johnson, James P(rice)
Johnson, Jimmie [James Leroy, Jr.]
Johnson, J. J. [James Louis]
Johnson, Money [Harold]
Johnson, Ollie [Oliver]
Johnson, (James) Osie
Johnson, Otis

McGriff, Jimmy [James Harrell, Jr.]
Machito [Grillo, Frank Raul]
McIntyre, Ken(neth Arthur)
McKay, Cliff(ord John)
Mackay, Dave [David Owen]
Mackel, Billy [John William]
McKenna, Dave [David J.]

Olympia
Olympia Brass Band
Olympia Orchestra
Omer, Jean
101 Ranch
100 Club
Ones
Ono, Shunzo
Onward Brass Band (i)
Onward Brass Band (ii)

In ambiguous cases, especially personal names that include particles, an effort has been made to establish first the personal preference of the subject and second the conventional usage. Such entries therefore appear where the majority of readers of the dictionary will expect to find them.

2. USAGES. In the editing of this dictionary every effort has been made to achieve consistency of presentation. Usages in such matters as italicization and capitalization will become evident (as far as that is necessary) to readers of the dictionary and do not need explanation here. Orthography, terminology, and punctuation generally follow American practices. Abbreviations are confined to those listed on pp. xxiii–xxix.

Some of the editorial usages in the dictionary are explained below.

Dates. Methods of citing dates that are approximate or conjectural are outlined in §3 below. Here it should be mentioned that when a period is delineated in the form *c*1940–58 the dates 1940 and 1958 are both approximate, whereas the form *c*1940–1958 indicates that only the first date is approximate.

Pitch notation. The dictionary uses a modified version of the Helmholtz system: middle C is *c'*, the successive octaves above are *c''*, *c'''*, etc., and the successive octaves below are *c*, *C*, *C'*, *C''*, etc. Octaves are reckoned from C upwards. Pitch classes are shown in roman type, specific pitches in italic.

Place names. For the current names of cities the orthography of *The Times Atlas of the World: Comprehensive Edition* (London, 1977 edn) is followed, except in cases where a city has a well-established name form in English (e.g., Munich, Florence, Vienna). Except for the largest cities, places in the USA are identified by a state and those in the rest of the world by a country, unless the context makes this unnecessary; every effort has been made to identify small places (i.e., those that do not appear in *The Times Atlas*) by naming the nearest larger place. Where a place name has changed in the course of history an attempt has generally been made to call it by the name current at the time under discussion; at the first occurrence its present name may be supplied in parentheses if this seems helpful. (For the practices followed in article headings, see §3 below.)

Institutional names. In references to institutions the correct name form is used for the time under discussion. Thus what is now the Juilliard School is referred to as the Institute of Musical Art or the Juilliard Graduate School where the period concerned is before 1946; similarly what started as the Newport Jazz Festival is referred to as the Newport Jazz Festival New York, the Kool Newport Jazz Festival, the Kool Jazz Festival, or the JVC Jazz Festival New York as the period under discussion dictates.

Titles. In the texts of articles the titles of pieces are italicized. In recording-lists titles of albums are given in italic type, titles of singles and individual tracks in roman type; in work-lists all titles of single works are given in roman. In English-language titles the initial letters of main words are generally capitalized, except where a title consists of the incipit or principal line of a song text (in which case only proper nouns have capital initials); in titles in other languages capitalization follows the orthography used in running prose.

3. ARTICLE HEADINGS.

Individuals. Articles on people begin with their names and places and dates of birth and death:

Bostic, Earl (*b* Tulsa, OK, 25 April 1913; *d* Rochester, NY, 28 Oct 1965).

The first part of the heading, excluding parenthetical and bracketed material, shows (in inverted form) the name of the subject as he or she is most commonly known. Parentheses and brackets in headings perform different and specific functions. In general, parts of a name that are not always used are shown in parentheses, alternative names (in inverted form) in brackets; semicolons are used between alternative names where commas might cause confusion. The examples given here illustrate this system, and the reader will often find more complex name forms discussed in the texts of articles.

Wynn, Al(bert (L.)) – known as Al Wynn, or, less often, as Albert Wynn; full name Albert L. Wynn

Abriani, John [Giovanni] – given name Giovanni Abriani; known as John Abriani

Bailey [née Rinker], **Mildred** – known as Mildred Bailey; maiden name Mildred Rinker

Lunceford, Jimmie [Jimmy, James Melvin] – known as Jimmie (sometimes spelled Jimmy) Lunceford; given name James Melvin Lunceford

Aiken [Aitken], **Gus** [Augustine] – known principally as Gus Aiken but also as Gus Aitken, Augustine Aiken, and Augustine Aitken (i.e., either form of forename is found with either form of surname)

Raeburn [Raden], **Boyd(e Albert)** – known principally as Boyd Raeburn, but also professionally as Boyd Raden; given name Boyde Albert Raeburn

West, Doc [Hal, Harold] – known as Doc West, or, less often, Hal West; full name Harold West

Howard, Paul (Leroy) [Ox Blood] – known as Paul Howard or by the nickname Ox Blood; given name Paul Leroy Howard

Gardner, Jack [Francis Henry; Jumbo Jack] – known as Jack Gardner or by the nickname Jumbo Jack; given name Francis Henry Gardner

Clarke, Kenny [Kenneth Spearman; Klook; Klook-mop; Salaam, Liaquat Ali] – known as Kenny Clarke or by the nicknames Klook or Klook-mop; Muslim name, Liaquat Ali Salaam; given name Kenneth Spearman Clarke

Hodges, Johnny [Hodge, John(ny); Hodge, Cornelius; Jeep; Rabbit] – known principally as Johnny Hodges, but also professionally as John or Johnny Hodge, or by the nicknames Jeep and Rabbit; given name Cornelius Hodge

Because nicknames are common in jazz, quotation marks are used sparingly, but they are sometimes employed to distinguish a descriptive nickname from a more conventional given name or nickname:

Chittison, Herman "Ivory" – known as Herman "Ivory" Chittison; given name Herman Chittison

Hines, Earl (Kenneth) [Earl "Fatha," Fatha] – known principally as Earl Hines, or, less often, as Earl "Fatha" or Fatha Hines; given name Earl Kenneth Hines

Davis, Eddie "Lockjaw" [Davis, Eddie [Edward]; Lockjaw] – known principally as Eddie "Lockjaw" Davis, or, less often, as Eddie Davis or as Lockjaw alone; given name Edward Davis

People known by a sobriquet that cannot be interpreted as consisting of a surrogate forename and surname are entered under the first element of the name:

Sun Ra [Blount, Herman ("Sonny"); Bourke, Sonny; Le Sony'r Ra]

When three or more members of a family merit entries the articles on them are grouped under the family name. The entries are ordered chronologically (according to date of birth) and numbered, and the names of members are given in uninverted form:

Brunies. Family of musicians.
(1) Henny [Henry] **Brunies**
(2) Merritt Brunies
(3) Abbie [Albert] **Brunies**
(4) Georg(e Clarence) Brunis [Brunies]
(5) Little Abbie [Albert] **Brunies**

Where two people bear the same name (which for this purpose means the same name in bold type, excluding parenthesized and bracketed material) each heading concludes with a lower-case roman numeral, determined chronologically according to date of birth:

Thomas, Joe [Brother Cornbread] **(i)**
Thomas, Joe [Joseph, Jr.] **(ii)**

Places and dates of birth and death are given where they are known; where nothing is known, nothing is stated. Except for the largest cities, places in the USA are identified by a state (in abbreviated form – for these abbreviations see pp. xxiii–xxv) and those in the rest of the world by a country. In all other respects the practice followed for citing place names in headings is the same as that in the texts of articles (see §2 above). Where a date is approximate the abbreviation *c* ("circa") is used. Where any part of the information is conjectural a question-mark is used, placed close to the statement it qualifies, or spaced where it qualifies the entire series of statements that follows. The examples given here clarify the methods of showing approximate and conjectural information:

(*b* New York, 1900; *d* ?Los Angeles, 3 Jan 1970) – born in New York in 1900 (day and month not known); died conjecturally in Los Angeles on 3 January 1970.

(*b* New York, ?Oct 1900 . . .) – born in New York in 1900, conjecturally in October

(*b* New York, 21 Oct ?1900 . . .) – born in New York on 21 October, conjecturally in 1900

(*b* New York, 21 ?Oct 1900 . . .) – born in New York on the 21st day of a month, conjecturally October, in 1900

(*b* ? New York, 1900 . . .) – born conjecturally in New York, conjecturally in 1900

Others. The headings of articles on subjects other than individuals follow the same principles, in so far as they apply, with one exception. In headings consisting of initials, readability dictates that the normal practice of enclosing unused parts of a name in parentheses be abandoned in favor of a clearer presentation. Thus

UHCA [United Hot Clubs of America]

is preferred to

U(nited) H(ot) C(lubs of) A(merica)

4. ARTICLE DEFINITIONS. All articles begin with a statement defining or describing the subject. Articles on individuals, groups, and (where relevant) institutions begin with a statement of nationality, if other than American, and a description. An individual is regarded as American if he or she took American citizenship or was naturalized; reference to a person's immigration, taking of citizenship, or naturalization is normally made in the text.

The word or words of description account, essentially, for the subject's being entered in the dictionary. In all cases the definition is intended to indicate only principal activities, meanings, etc. This restriction has a particular bearing on articles on individuals: someone who is noted as a tenor saxophonist but engages in other activities is not normally described as (for example) "tenor saxophonist, alto saxophonist, soprano saxophonist, flutist, composer, arranger, and pianist"; supplementary activities may be referred to in the text. Similarly, the opening statement of an article on a term does not seek to give every meaning of it, but is confined to the most commonly found or the broadest usage; other meanings are introduced in the course of the article. Articles on genres and instruments normally begin with a general definition of the subject, which is elaborated in the opening section; where appropriate the definition is followed by a statement of the terms of reference of the article, which draws attention to the manner in which the subject pertains specifically to jazz.

For any individual who has no entry in the dictionary, but who is mentioned in the text of an article, every effort has been made to add a description identifying the individual – for example, as a trumpeter and bandleader.

5. ARTICLE STRUCTURE. The longer articles in the dictionary are divided into sections, each with its own heading. The simplest division is into sections bearing arabic numerals and headed in large and small capitals (e.g., 1. LIFE. 2. MUSIC). Sections of this kind may be grouped under headings bearing upper-case roman numerals, and may be further divided into subsections headed in italic type and numbered with lower-case roman numerals or (at the lowest level) letters. A list of "contents" is given at the start of all subdivided articles. The following illustrate the levels of subdivision and the lay-out of the contents list and section headings:

Drum set. [general definition]

I. Components. II. Use.

I. Components

1. General. 2. Bass drum. 3. Snare drum. 4. Tom-tom. 5. Cymbals. 6. Cowbell and other metal instruments. 7. Woodblock and temple block. 8. Drumsticks and brushes. 9. Timpani. 10. Washboard. 11. Electronic devices.

1. GENERAL.

Harmony (i). [general definition]

1. Terminology and theory: (i) Introduction (ii) Intervals and chords (iii) Dissonance (iv) Inversion and voicing (v) Chord progressions (vi) Extensions of tonality and modal harmony. 2. History.

1. TERMINOLOGY AND THEORY.

(i) Introduction. . . .

(v) Chord progressions.

(a) Notation.

6. CROSS-REFERENCES. Cross-references appear in large and small capitals, the large capital showing the initial letter of the entry referred to. If the reference is in running prose it takes the form

Hot Five. Recording group led by LOUIS ARMSTRONG in Chicago from 1925 .

If the reference is more explicit (it may consist of a sentence or parenthetical statement) it includes the word *"see"* or words *"see also"* and the heading referred to is given (where relevant) in inverted form:

For further recordings and bibliography *see* ARMSTRONG, LOUIS.
See also JAZZ (i), §§V, 6; VI, 2, 4, and fig.6; HARMONY (i), §1(vi), Table 2, and §2; and TRUMPET, §§5 and 6.

(It should be noted that the words "see" and "see also" are always italicized in cross-references; where they appear in roman type, the reference is to a different part of the same entry or to a publication listed in the bibliography.) In all cross-references the heading of the article referred to is given exactly as it appears in the dictionary, excluding parenthesized material (except for lower-case roman numerals) and bracketed material.

Cross-references are of two basic kinds. First, there are those cross-reference entries that direct the reader to the heading under which the information being sought is located. Simple cross-references have been included to help the reader who first looks under a different orthography or formulation, or an alternative name:

Gojkovic, Dusan. *See* GOYKOVICH, DUSKO.

Glissandi, Arpeggio. Pseudonym used by CASPER REARDON.

Many cross-reference entries include, for the benefit of the reader who does not require fuller information, a brief definition:

Head. The theme on which a jazz performance is based (*see* FORMS, §1); the term is normally applied to a popular song used for this purpose. The repeat of the head at the end of the performance is sometimes referred to as the OUT CHORUS.

Hammond organ. An electronic organ developed in 1933–4 by the American engineers Laurens Hammond (1895–1973) and John M. Hanert (*b* 1909). For a discussion of its use in jazz *see* ORGAN, §2.

The other type of cross-reference occurs within an article. Some references of this kind are placed at the ends of articles or sections of articles, directing the reader to another entry where further information relevant to the subject may be found: these may, as appropriate, embody such formulas as *"see also"* or "for a fuller discussion *see*." Many further cross-references are found in running text, but none is provided to an entry that could be expected to appear in this dictionary unless it contains material to which attention needs particularly to be drawn. The intention is to direct the reader to places where he or she can, but might not expect to, find further information on the topic that is first looked up. Thus the article "Bop" need not contain cross-references to the entries on Charlie Parker and Dizzy Gillespie, although these of course contain material relevant to the history of bop; it does, however, carry cross-references to entries on related forms or subgenres (for example, "Cool jazz" and "Soul jazz") which are separately considered.

Where an illustration, table, or music example is relevant to more than one entry, an appropriate cross-reference is included.

7. ORAL HISTORY MATERIAL. At the end of the text of an article on an individual there may appear a note in small type drawing attention to the existence of oral history material in one or more major collections. A list of the abbreviations for libraries, archives, and museums used in such notes appears on p. xxix.

8. Work-lists. Because the principal medium of preservation of jazz compositions is the recording, work-lists (i.e., lists of compositions in printed or manuscript form) are given for comparatively few individuals in this dictionary. Work-lists are normally categorized by genre or medium, and works are listed chronologically within categories. Dates are those of composition unless otherwise indicated. Instrumentation and manuscript sources are shown in abbreviated form; lists of the abbreviations used may be found on pp. xxiii–xxv.

9. Recording-lists. The dictionary includes nearly 2000 lists of representative recordings, exemplifying the work of performers, arrangers, and composers. These generally stand in place of the work-lists found in earlier Grove dictionaries, and fill the same function of identifying the principal sources that preserve the music. The lists are, in every sense, selective, not comprehensive. It is intended that they be used in conjunction with standard discographies and record catalogues.

(i) Elements of a citation. In accordance with the scholarly principle of citing original sources, every effort has been made to identify the first issue of each recording listed; reissues are cited only in exceptional circumstances. The main elements of a citation are: the name of the leader(s); the title; the year of recording; the name of the record label; the issue number. (Abbreviations for the names of record labels may be found on pp. xxvi–xxvii.)

(a) Name of leader. Recordings are, as far as possible, cited by the name under which they were issued, whether the name of a single leader (as is predominantly the case), the names of more than one leader, or the name of a group. For the sake of practicality, however, no more than four leaders are named in any citation: where a group has five or more leaders the citation normally appears under the group's name.

(b) Title. Single titles and the titles of individual tracks on albums appear in roman type, album titles in italic type. Where discrepancies occur among versions of a title (there may be as many as four different versions of an album title – for example, one each on the front, the spine, and the back of the liner, and one on the label on the disc), we have endeavored to use the title that appears on the front of the liner.

(c) Issue information. As explained above, it is our aim to cite the first issue of all recordings. There are cases, however, where it is difficult to identify the first issue. In instances of simultaneous issue in different countries, the data cited are those pertaining to the issue in the country where the recording was made, or where the record label is based, as appropriate. In instances of simultaneous issue before 1943 on associated American labels (as, for example, on labels belonging to the American Record Company), the data cited are normally those pertaining to the first label listed in the standard source, Brian Rust's *Jazz Records, 1897–1942* (1961, rev. and enlarged 5/1983). In instances of simultaneous, or nearly simultaneous, issue in different formats (78 r.p.m. single, 45 r.p.m. EP, and 10- or 12-inch 33 1/3 r.p.m. LP), if the first issue cannot be identified an album is cited in preference to a single, and a single in preference to an EP; such instances arise chiefly in recordings issued in the early 1950s. In instances of simultaneous monophonic and stereophonic issue, the data cited are those pertaining to the latter; such instances normally occur with albums issued between the late 1950s and the mid-1960s.

Prefixes and suffixes to issue numbers are generally omitted unless they are required to identify recordings uniquely.

(ii) Structure and organization of a list. Recording-lists are ordered strictly chronologically according to the date of recording, insofar as that may be determined. Lists may cite selected recordings of performances, arrangements, or compositions. The first type, which occurs most frequently, carries the heading "Selected Recordings." If the subject is the leader on every item cited, no subheading appears. Otherwise the list is categorized, usually under one or more of the following side-headings:

As unaccompanied soloist:
Duos:
As leader:
As sideman:

These categories may be further subdivided as appropriate:

As sideman with D. Ellington:
As sideman with others:

In the "As leader" category the formula "with . . ." indicates that the recording was issued jointly under the names of the subject of the article and at least one other; in this case the names of the joint leaders apply to all following citations until canceled by a semicolon. In all other instances the name of the leader, duo partner, etc., applies until canceled by another name.

As leader: *Johnny One-note* (1954, Beth. 25); with T. Akiyoshi: *Toshiko-Mariano Quartet* (1960, Can. 9012), *Toshiko-Mariano Quartet* (1963, Takt Jazz 12); *A Jazz Portrait of Charlie Mariano* (1963, Regina 286)

As sideman: J. R. Morton: Kansas City Stomps (1928, Vic. 38010); C. Hawkins: Crazy Rhythm (1937, Swing 1); Out of Nowhere (1937, HMV K8511); E. Brunner: I double dare you (1938, Swing 30)

One of two formulas is used to cite an individual track or several tracks on an album: "incl." indicates that the subject performs on a majority of the tracks on the album, "on" that the subject performs on fewer than half of the tracks on the album; in both cases the track (or tracks) named is (are) particularly representative.

Recordings of representative arrangements and compositions may be dealt with in one of two ways. Where a list of selected recordings includes important arrangements or compositions by the subject of the article, an asterisk, keyed to an appropriately worded legend at the head of the list (e.g., * – composed by Monk), precedes each title concerned. When an arranger or composer has little or no significance as a performer, or where a list of selected recordings does not coincide with or comprehend a list of the subject's arrangements or compositions, separate lists of these are given. Such lists carry the headings "Selected Arrangements" and "Recorded Compositions" and use the subheadings "As leader" and "Recorded by" as appropriate. In other respects they follow the practices outlined above.

10. Transcriptions. A list of significant collections of transcriptions of a musician's work is given for some very prominent players. Individual transcriptions and anthologies are not normally cited.

11. Bibliographies. Most articles in the dictionary include one or more bibliographical citations of items for further reading. The bibliographies are not intended to represent complete lists of literature on the topic, but rather the most useful, informative sources. General histories of jazz are not normally cited unless they contain material of special importance or are a principal source of information on the subject in question. General discographies are not cited. (For full citations of all such works the reader should consult the comprehensive bibliography of jazz presented as Appendix 1.) For figures on whom little or nothing has been published, ephemeral items such as newspaper articles or album liner notes are often cited (in the latter case dates of issue, not of recording, are given, and appear after, rather than before, the issue number).

Bibliographies are arranged chronologically according to year of first publication (chronologically within categories where a bibliography is subdivided, as are the longest ones); items published in the same year are listed alphabetically by author, those by the same author, by title. However, certain standard works of reference are cited at the head of a list, in abbreviated form and alphabetical order. (Bibliographical abbreviations are explained on p.xxviii.)

The procedures of citation are broadly speaking self-evident, but it may nevertheless be helpful to outline here the main principles. For books the place(s) and date of first publication are given, as is the date of the latest edition; intermediate editions are cited only if they were revised, enlarged, translated, or photographically reprinted (such reprints are denoted by *R* and are normally cited only when at least ten years have elapsed between the date of first publication and the date of the reprint). Volume numbers, both for multivolume books and for periodicals, are shown in lower-case roman numerals. Issue numbers for periodicals are shown in arabic numerals. Where periodicals have volume numbers but are not through-paginated by volume, both volume and fascicle numbers are given, separated by a solidus (e.g., xiv/3). Initial page numbers only are given for articles in periodicals and other specific references, except where the item concerned extends to more than 30 pages, in which case a terminal page number is supplied. Dissertations and theses are so identified, the institution to which such a work is submitted is named, and the date of acceptance is given.

Lists of writings, which appear in all appropriate entries, are organized according to the same principles as bibliographies. Such lists are as a rule selective and limited to the author's publications in book form and to especially influential essays in periodicals. An item prefaced by "ed.:" is edited by the subject.

12. Signatures. The names of authors appear, in the form each has chosen, at the ends of the articles to which they apply. Where authorship is joint or multiple, this is indicated, and where appropriate, the contribution of each author is shown by reference to sections of a numbered

article or to different parts of an article (text, recording-list, etc.). Where two or more names appear separated only by a comma, the entire authorship is joint or the contributions are fused to a degree where it would be impractical to show how responsibility is divided. A signature in the form

JOHN DOE (with MARY BROWN)

means that John Doe is the principal author but Mary Brown contributed material that the author or the editors of the dictionary felt was appropriate for acknowledgment.

A signature in the form

JOHN DOE/MARY BROWN

indicates that an article written by John Doe for an earlier *New Grove* dictionary has been revised and updated by Mary Brown. A signature in the form

JOHN DOE/R

signifies editorial revision and updating of such an article, or the deletion of material irrelevant to this dictionary.

A number of articles carry the note

based on *ChiltonW*

in place of a signature. This indicates that biographical data have been taken from John Chilton's *Who's Who of Jazz* (London, Macmillan, rev. 4/1985) and supplemented and updated by a member or members of the editorial team to form the article as it appears in this dictionary.

Unsigned articles, which are mostly on lesser-known musicians, were compiled by members of the editorial team from various sources.

13. Transliteration. The transliteration of Cyrillic script in this dictionary essentially follows the system used in *The New Grove.*

General Abbreviations

a	alto
AB	Bachelor of Arts
ABC	American Broadcasting Company
acc.	accompaniment, accompanied by
addn	addition
AFM	American Federation of Musicians
AFRS	Armed Forces Radio Service
AFR&TS	Armed Forces Radio & Television Service
AK	Alaska
AL	Alabama
a.m.	ante meridiem (Lat.: before noon)
appx	appendix
AR	Arkansas
arr.	arrangement, arranged (by/for)
ARSC	Association for Recorded Sound Collections
AS	American Samoa
ASCAP	American Society of Composers, Authors, and Publishers
Assn	Association
Aug	August
aut.	autumn
AZ	Arizona
b	bass
b	born
BA	Bachelor of Arts
bar	baritone
BBC	British Broadcasting Corporation
BM	Bachelor of Music
BME; BMEd	Bachelor of Music Education
BMI	Broadcast Music, Inc.
BMus	Bachelor of Music
Bros.	Brothers
BS	Bachelor of Science
c	cent(s)
c	circa
CA	California
CBC	Canadian Broadcasting Corporation
CBE	Commander of the Order of the British Empire
cf	confer (Lat.: compare)
chap.	chapter
cl	clarinet

CM	Northern Mariana Islands (US Trust Territory of the Pacific Islands)
cm	centimeter(s)
CO	Colorado
Co.	Company; County
c/o	care of
collab.	collaborator, collaborated (with)
colln	collection
comp.	compiler, compiled (by)
conc.	concerto
contd	continued
Corp.	Corporation
CT	Connecticut
CUNY	City University of New York
Cz	Czech
d	died
Dan.	Danish
db	double bass
DC	District of Columbia
DE	Delaware
Dec	December
Den.	Denmark
dir.	director, directed (by)
diss.	dissertation
DMA	Doctor of Musical Arts
Dr.	Doctor
ed.	editor, edited (by)
edn	edition
e.g.	exempli gratia (Lat.: for example)
elec	electric
Eng.	English
ens	ensemble
EP	extended-play (record)
esp.	especially
etc.	et cetera (Lat.: and so on)
ex(x).	example, examples
f	following (page)
f	forte
facs.	facsimile
Feb	February
ff	following (pages)

ff	fortissimo
fff	fortississimo
fig.	figure [illustration]
FL	Florida
Fr.	French
GA	Georgia
Ger.	German
GU	Guam
HI	Hawaii
hpd	harpsichord
Hung.	Hungarian
IA	Iowa
ibid.	ibidem (Lat.: in the same place)
ID	Idaho
i.e.	id est (Lat.: that is)
IL	Illinois
IN	Indiana
Inc.	Incorporated
inc.	incomplete
incl.	includes, including
inst.	instrument, instrumental
intl	international
It.	Italian
Jan	January
Jap.	Japanese
Jr.	Junior
km	kilometer(s)
KS	Kansas
KY	Kentucky
LA	Louisiana
LP	Long-play (record)
Ltd.	Limited
MA	Massachusetts; Master of Arts
MB	Bachelor of Music
MBE	Member of the Order of the British Empire
MD	Maryland
ME	Maine
MEd	Master of Education
mf	mezzo-forte
MFA	Master of Fine Arts
MGM	Metro–Goldwyn–Mayer
MI	Michigan
MIDI	Musical Instrument Digital Interface
MM; MMus	Master of Music
Mme	Madame
MN	Minnesota
MO	Missouri
mp	mezzo-piano
MPhil	Master of Philosophy
Mr.	Mister
MS	Mississippi; manuscript; Master of Science
MT	Montana
MusB	Bachelor of Music
nar	narrator
NBC	National Broadcasting Company
NC	North Carolina
ND	North Dakota
n.d.	no date (of publication)
NE	Nebraska
NEA	National Endowment for the Arts
NH	New Hampshire
NJ	New Jersey
NM	New Mexico
no.	number
Nor.	Norwegian
Nov	November
n.p.	no place (of publication)
n.pub.	no publisher
nr	near
NV	Nevada
NY	New York (state)
OBE	Officer of the Order of the British Empire
Oct	October
OH	Ohio
OK	Oklahoma
op. cit.	opere citato (Lat.: in the work cited)
OR	Oregon
orch	orchestra
orig.	original
ORTF	Office de Radiodiffusion-Télévision Française
p	piano
p.	page
PA	Pennsylvania
PBS	Public Broadcasting System
pf	piano(forte)
PhD	Doctor of Philosophy
p.m.	post meridiem (Lat.: after noon)
PO	Philharmonic Orchestra; Post Office
Pol.	Polish
Port.	Portuguese
pp	pianissimo
pp.	pages
ppp	pianississimo
PR	Puerto Rico
pseud.	pseudonym
pt	part
pubd	published (by)
pubn	publication
qnt	quintet
qt	quartet
R	(editorial) revision [in signature]
R	photographic reprint
RAAF	Royal Australian Air Force
RAF	Royal Air Force
RAI	Radio Audizioni Italiane (Italy)
repr.	reprinted
Rev.	Reverend
rev.	revision, revised (by)
RI	Rhode Island
RIAS	Rundfunk im amerikanischen Sektor
RKO	Radio–Keith–Orpheum
RO	Radio Orchestra
Rom.	Romanian
r.p.m.	revolution(s) per minute
Russ.	Russian

S.	San, Santa, Santo
$	dollar(s)
sax	saxophone
SC	South Carolina
SD	South Dakota
Sept	September
ser.	series
sf, *sfz*	sforzando, sforzato
SFSR	Soviet Federated Socialist Republic
SO	Symphony Orchestra
Sp.	Spanish
spr.	spring
Sr.	Senior
SS	steamship
SSR	Soviet Socialist Republic
St.; Ste.	Saint, Sainte
str	string(s)
sum.	summer
SUNY	State University of New York
suppl.	supplement, supplementary
Swed.	Swedish
sym.	symphony
t	tenor
TN	Tennessee
tpt	trumpet
trans.	translation, translated (by)
transcr.	transcription, transcribed (by/for)
trbn	trombone
TV	television
TX	Texas
U.	University
UCLA	University of California, Los Angeles
UHF	ultra-high frequency
UK	United Kingdom of Great Britain and Northern Ireland
unacc.	unaccompanied
UNESCO	United Nations Educational, Scientific, and Cultural Organization
unpubd	unpublished
US	United States [adjective]
USA	United States of America
USO	United Service Organizations
USSR	Union of Soviet Socialist Republics
UT	Utah
v	voice
VA	Virginia
VHF	very high frequency
VI	Virgin Islands
vol.	volume
VT	Vermont
vv	voices
WA	Washington
WI	Wisconsin
win.	winter
WPA	Works Progress Administration
WV	West Virginia
WY	Wyoming

Discographical Abbreviations

This list contains all abbreviations devised editorially for recording citations; acronyms adopted by companies for use as label names are not included.

AAFS	Archive of American Folksong (Library of Congress)
A&M Hor.	A&M Horizon
ABC-Para.	ABC-Paramount
AH	Artists House
Ala.	Aladdin
AM	American Music
Amer.	America
AN	Arista Novus
Ant.	Antilles
Ari.	Arista
Asy.	Asylum
Atl.	Atlantic
Aut.	Autograph
Bak.	Bakton
Ban.	Banner
Bay.	Baystate
BB	Black and Blue
Bb	Bluebird
Beth.	Bethlehem
BH	Bee Hive
BL	Black Lion
BN	Blue Note
Bruns.	Brunswick
BS	Black Saint
BStar	Blue Star
Can.	Candid
Cap.	Capitol
Car.	Caroline
Cat.	Catalyst
Cen.	Century
Chi.	Chiaroscuro
Cir.	Circle
CJ	Classic Jazz
Cob.	Cobblestone
Col.	Columbia
Com.	Commodore
Conc.	Concord
Cont.	Contemporary
Contl	Continental
CP	Charlie Parker
CW	Creative World
Del.	Delmark
Dis.	Discovery
Dra.	Dragon
EB	Electric Bird
Elec.	Electrola
Elek.	Elektra
Elek. Mus.	Elektra Musician
EmA	EmArcy
ES	Elite Special
Eso.	Esoteric
Ev.	Everest
EW	East Wind
Ewd	Eastworld
Fan.	Fantasy
FaD	Famous Door
FD	Flying Dutchman
FDisk	Flying Disk
Fel.	Felsted
Fon.	Fontana
Fre.	Freedom
FW	Folkways
Gal.	Galaxy
Gen.	Gennett
GM	Groove Merchant
Gram.	Gramavision
GTJ	Good Time Jazz
HA	Hat Art
Hal.	Halcyon
Har.	Harmony

Harl.	Harlequin
HH	Hat Hut
ImA	Improvising Artists
IC	Inner City
Imp.	Impulse!
IndN	India Navigation
Isl.	Island
JAM	Jazz America Marketing
Jlgy	Jazzology
Jlnd	Jazzland
Jub.	Jubilee
Jwl	Jewell
Jzt.	Jazztone
Key.	Keynote
Kt.	Keytone
Lib.	Liberty
Lml.	Limelight
Lon.	London
Mdsv.	Moodsville
Mel.	Melodiya
Mer.	Mercury
Met.	Metronome
Metro.	Metrojazz
MJR	Master Jazz Recordings
Mlst.	Milestone
Mlt.	Melotone
Moers	Moers Music
MonE	Monmouth–Evergreen
Mstr.	Mainstream
Musi.	Musicraft
Nat.	National
NewJ	New Jazz
Norg.	Norgran
OK	Okeh
Omni.	Omnisound
PAct	Pathé Actuelle
PAlt	Palo Alto
Para.	Paramount
Parl.	Parlophone
Per.	Perfect
Phi.	Philips
Phon.	Phontastic
PJ	Pacific Jazz
PL	Pablo Live
Pol.	Polydor
Prog.	Progressive
Prst.	Prestige
PT	Pablo Today
PW	Paddle Wheel
Qual.	Qualiton
Reg.	Regent
Rep.	Reprise
Rev.	Revelation
Riv.	Riverside
Roul.	Roulette
RR	Red Records
RT	Real Time
Sack.	Sackville
Sat.	Saturn
SE	Strata-East
Sig.	Signature
Slnd	Southland
SN	Soul Note
SolS	Solid State
Son.	Sonora
Spot.	Spotlite
Ste.	Steeplechase
Sto.	Storyville
Sup.	Supraphon
TE	Toshiba Express
Tei.	Teichiku
Tel.	Telefunken
The.	Theresa
Tim.	Timeless
TL	Time–Life
Tran.	Transition
20C	20th Century
20CF	20th Century-Fox
UA	United Artists
Upt.	Uptown
Van.	Vanguard
Var.	Variety
Vars.	Varsity
Vic.	Victor
VJ	Vee-Jay
Voc.	Vocalion
WB	Warner Bros.
WP	World Pacific
Xan.	Xanadu

Bibliographical Abbreviations

ARJS	*Annual Review of Jazz Studies*
ARSCJ	*Association for Recorded Sound Collections Journal*
BHcF	*Bulletin du Hot Club de France*
CBY	*Current Biography Yearbook* (New York, 1940–)
ChartersJ	S. B. Charters: *Jazz: New Orleans, 1885–1957; an Index to the Negro Musicians of New Orleans* (Belleville, NJ, 1958, rev. 2/1963/*R*1983 as *Jazz: New Orleans, 1885–1963: an Index to the Negro Musicians of New Orleans*)
ChiltonW	J. Chilton: *Who's Who of Jazz: Storyville to Swing Street* (London, 1970, rev. and enlarged 4/1985)
CI	*Crescendo International*
CK	*Contemporary Keyboard*
DB	*Down Beat*
DF	*Discographical Forum*
FeatherE	L. Feather: *The Encyclopedia of Jazz* (New York, 1955, rev. and enlarged 2/1960/*R*1984)
Feather '60s	L. Feather: *The Encyclopedia of Jazz in the Sixties* (New York, 1966/*R*1986)
Feather–Gitler '70s	L. Feather and I. Gitler: *The Encyclopedia of Jazz in the Seventies* (New York, 1976/*R*1987)
Fn	*Footnote*
GoldJL	R. S. Gold: *A Jazz Lexicon: an A–Z Directory of Jazz Terms* (New York, 1964, rev. 2/1975 as *Jazz Talk*)
GP	*Guitar Player*
GroveI	S. Sadie, ed.: *The New Grove Dictionary of Musical Instruments* (London, 1984)
Grove6	S. Sadie, ed.: *The New Grove Dictionary of Music and Musicians* (London, 1980)
GroveAM	S. Sadie and H. W. Hitchcock, eds.: *The New Grove Dictionary of American Music* (New York, 1986)
IAJRCJ	*International Association of Jazz Record Collectors Journal*
IM	*International Musician*
IMSCR	*International Musicological Society Congress Report* (1930–)
JB	*Jazz Beat*
J&B	*Jazz & Blues*
J&P	*Jazz and Pop*
JF [intl edn]	*Jazz Forum* [international edition]
JF [Pol. edn]	*Jazz Forum* [Polish edition]
Jf	*Jazzforschung/Jazz Research*
Jh	*Jazz hot, Jazz-hot*
JJ	*Jazz Journal*
JJI	*Jazz Journal International*
JJS	*Journal of Jazz Studies*
JM	*Jazz Monthly*
Jm	*Jazz magazine* (Paris)
JP	*Jazz-Podium*
JR	*The Jazz Review*
JSN	*Jazz Spotlite News*
JT	*Jazz Times* (Washington, 1980–)
MD	*Modern Drummer*
MM	*Melody Maker*
MR	*The Mississippi Rag*
PJ	*Le point du jazz*
ReclamsJ	C. Bohländer and K. H. Holler: *Reclams Jazzführer* (Stuttgart, Germany, 1970, rev. and enlarged 2/1977)
RS	*Rolling Stone*
SJ	*Swing Journal*
SL	*Second Line*
Sv	*Storyville*
VV	*Village Voice*

Library Abbreviations

The abbreviations used in this dictionary for the names of American libraries are those established by the Catalog Publication Division of the Library of Congress and published in *Symbols of American Libraries* (Washington, rev. 12/1980). Only those abbreviations that appear in the dictionary (where they are always printed in italic type) are listed here.

ATaT	USA, Talladega, AL, Talladega College
CaQMG	Canada, Montreal, Quebec, Concordia University, Sir George Williams Campus
CtY	USA, New Haven, CT, Yale University
DLC	USA, Washington, DC, Library of Congress
GBLnsa	Great Britain, London, National Sound Archive of the British Library
ICJic	USA, Chicago, IL, Jazz Institute of Chicago
ICU	USA, Chicago, IL, University of Chicago
InU-Atm	USA, Bloomington, IN, Indiana University Archives of Traditional Music
LNT	USA, New Orleans, LA, Tulane University
MoKmh	Kansas City, MO, Kansas City Museum of History
MoU-St	USA, St. Louis, MO, University of Missouri
NjR	USA, Newark, NJ, Rutgers, the State University of New Jersey
NjR (JOHP)	USA, Newark, NJ, Rutgers, the State University of New Jersey: Jazz Oral History Project
NNC	USA, New York, NY, Columbia University
NN-Sc	USA, New York, NY, Schomburg Collection, New York Public Library
NOnj	Norway, Oslo, Norsk Jazzarkiv
SSsv	Sweden, Stockholm, Svenskt Visarkiv, Centralinstitution för Vis- och Folkmusikforskning
TNF	USA, Nashville, TN, Fisk University
TxU	USA, Austin, TX, University of Texas

Death Dates and Corrigenda

The following is principally a list of death dates and places for the subjects of biographical entries, the majority having occurred since publication of the dictionary. A brief second list offers corrections to article headings, excepting Louis Armstrong's proper birthdate, a fact of such importance that the article itself has been corrected. The lists have been prepared by the editor, Barry Kernfeld, and the consultant editor, Alyn Shipton, with the assistance of Howard Rye and Steve Voce. No contributors of original entries should be held accountable if by any chance this process has introduced errors.

DEATH DATES

Abdul-Malik, Ahmed (*d* Long Branch, NJ, 2 Oct 1993)
Adams, George (Rufus) (*d* New York, 14 Nov 1992)
Alexander, Mousey (*d* Longwood, FL, 9 Oct 1988)
Alvarez, Chico (*d* Las Vegas, 1 Aug 1992)
Auld, Georgie (*d* Palm Springs, CA, 8 Jan 1990)

Bailey, Pearl (Mae) (*d* Philadelphia, 17 Aug 1990)
Bales, Burt(on Frank) (*d* San Francisco, 26 Oct 1989)
Barefield, Eddie (Emmanuel) (*d* New York, 4 Jan 1991)
Barker, Danny (*d* New Orleans, 13 March 1994)
Barnet, Charlie (*d* San Diego, 4 Sept 1991)
Barron, Bill (*d* Middletown, CT, 21 Sept 1989)
Bauzá, Mario (*d* New York, 11 July 1993)
Beal, Charlie (*d* San Diego, Aug 1991)
Benford, Tommy (*d* Mount Vernon, NY, 24 March 1994)
Benskin, Sammy (*d* 26 Aug 1992)
Blackburn, Lou (*d* Berlin, 6 June 1990)
Blackwell Ed(ward Joseph) (*d* Hartford, CT, 7 Oct 1992)
Blakeney, Andy (*d* Baldwin Park, CA, 12 Feb 1992)
Blakey, Art (*d* New York, 16 Oct 1990)
Boone, Lester (*d* New York, 4 July 1989)
Bowles, Russell (*d* Lancaster, PA, 5 July 1991)
Bradley, Will (*d* Flemington, NJ, 15 July 1989)
Briggs, Arthur (*d* Chantilly, France, 15 July 1991)
Brown, Lawrence (*d* Los Angeles, 5 Sept 1988)
Brun, Philippe (*d* Paris, 14 Jan 1994)
Budwig, Monty (Rex) (*d* Los Angeles, 9 March 1992)
Burke, Ed(ward) (*d* East Elmhurst, NY, 19 April 1988)
Burrell, Duke (*d* Los Angeles, 5 Aug 1993)
Bushell, Garvin (Payne) (*d* Las Vegas, 31 Oct 1991)
Butler, Billy (*d* Teaneck, NJ, 20 March 1991)

Calhoun, Eddie (*d* Paradise Lake, MI, *c*1993)
Callender, Red (*d* Saugus, CA, 8 March 1992)
Carisi, Johnny (*d* New York, 3 Oct 1992)
Carter, John (Wallace) (*d* Inglewood, CA, 31 March 1991)
Cary, Dick (*d* Glendale, CA, 6 April 1994)
Castle, Lee (*d* Hollywood, FL, 16 Nov 1990)
Chiboust, Noël (*d* France, 17 Jan 1994)
Christy, June (*d* Los Angeles, 21 June 1990)
Clare, Alan (George) (*d* London, 29 Nov 1993)
Clayton, Buck (*d* New York, 8 Dec 1991)
Cobb(s), Arnett(e Cleophus) (*d* Houston, 24 March 1989)
Comfort, Joe (*d* Los Angeles, 29 Oct 1988)
Cook, Junior (*d* New York, 4 Feb 1992)
Cooper, Bob (*d* Hollywood, 5 Aug 1993)
Crosby, Bob (*d* La Jolla, CA, 9 March 1993)

Davis, Miles (Dewey, III) (*d* Santa Monica, CA, 28 Sept 1991)
Davis, Walter (Jr.) (*d* New York, 2 June 1990)
Davison, Wild Bill (*d* Santa Barbara, CA, 14 Nov 1989)
Deuchar, Jimmy (*d* Dundee, Scotland, 9 Sept 1993)
De Villers, Michel (*d* France, 25 Oct 1992)
Dixon, Eric (*d* New York, 19 Oct 1989)
Drew, Kenny (*d* Copenhagen, 4 Aug 1993)

Eardley, Jon (*d* Germany, late March 1991)
Eckstine, Billy (*d* Pittsburgh, 8 March 1993)
Eldridge, (David) Roy (*d* Valley Stream, NY, 26 Feb 1989)
Ertegun, Nesuhi (*d* New York, 15 July 1989)

Fairweather, Al(astair) (*d* Edinburgh, 21 June 1993)

Fox, Charles (Richard Jeremy) (*d* Weymouth, England, 9 May 1991)
Freeman, Bud (*d* Chicago, 15 March 1991)

Gaillard, Slim (*d* London, 26 Feb 1991)
Garrett, Donald (Rafael) (*d* Champaign, IL, 14 Aug 1989)
Getz, Stan(ley) (*d* Malibu, CA, 6 June 1991)
Gillespie, Dizzy (*d* Englewood, NJ, 6 Jan 1993)
Gluskin, Lud (*d* Palm Springs, CA, 17 Oct 1989)
Gordon, Dexter (Keith) (*d* Philadelphia, 25 April 1990)
Greenlee, Charles (*d* Springfield, MA, 23 Jan 1993)
Grimes, Tiny (*d* New York, 4 March 1989)

Hall, Adelaide (*d* London, 7 Nov 1993)
Hardman, Bill (*d* Paris, 5 Dec 1990)
Harris, Beaver (*d* New York, 22 Dec 1991)
Harris, Bill (ii) (*d* Washington, DC, 6 Dec 1988)
Haughton, Chauncey (*d* Tarrytown, NY, 1 July 1989)
Hawkins, Erskine (Ramsey) (*d* Willingboro, NJ, 11 Nov 1993)
Heard, J(ames) C(harles) (*d* Royal Oak, MI, 27 Sep 1988)
Henderson, Horace (W.) (*d* Denver, 29 Aug 1988)
Herfurt, Skeets (*d* New Orleans, 17 April 1992)
Heywood, Eddie (*d* Miami Beach, FL, 2 Jan 1989)
Hodes, Art(hur W.) (*d* Harvey, IL, 4 March 1993)
Holley, Major (Quincy, Jr.) (*d* Maplewood, NJ, 25 Oct 1990)
Holmes, Groove (*d* St. Louis, 29 June 1991)
Hood, Bill (*d* Oregon, *c*Dec 1992)
Hultcrantz, Tjorbörn (*d* Stockholm, 17 Jan 1994)
Hutchenrider, Clarence (Behrens) (*d* New York, 18 Aug 1991)

Inge, Edward (Frederick) (*d* Buffalo, NY, 8 Oct 1988)

Jacquet, (Robert) Russell (*d* Los Angeles, 28 Feb 1990)
Jenkins, John (Jr.) (*d* New York, *c*June 1993)
Johnson, Howard (William) (i) (*d* New York, 28 Dec 1991)
Johnson, Lem(uel Charles) (*d* New York, 1 April 1989)
Jones, (Ronald) Max(well) (*d* Chichester, England, 1 Aug 1993)
Jones, Reunald (Sr.) (*d* Los Angeles, CA, 26 Feb 1989)
Jones, Rufus (*d* Las Vegas, 25 April 1990)
Jordan, Clifford (Laconia, Jr.) (*d* New York, 27 March 1993)
Jordan, Steve (*d* Alexandria, VA, 13 Sept 1993)

Kincaide, (Robert) Deane (*d* St. Cloud, FL, 14 Aug 1992)
Kirk, Andy (*d* New York, 11 Dec 1992)
Klink, Al(bert) (*d* Bradenton, FL, 7 March 1991)
Kohlman, Freddie (*d* New Orleans, 29 Sept 1990)

Landers, Wes(ley) (*d* New York, 23 Feb 1993)
Larsson, Rolf (*d* Stockholm, 5 May 1991)
Letman, Johnny (*d* New York, 17 July 1992)
Lewis, Mel (*d* New York, 2 Feb 1990)
Lim, Harry (*d* New York, 27 July 1990)
Lind, Ove (*d* Sweden, 16 April 1991)
Lowe, Sammy (*d* New York, 10 March 1993)

McCall, Steve (*d* 5 or 24 May 1989)
McGregor, Chris (*d* Agen, France, 26 May 1990)
McPartland, Jimmy (*d* Port Washington, NY, 13 Mar 1991)
MacPherson, (John) Fraser (*d* Vancouver, Canada, 28 Sept 1993)
Mastren, Al (*d* Troy, NY, 2 Feb 1992)
Miller, Eddie (*d* Van Nuys, CA, 1 April 1991)
Miller, Sing (*d* New Orleans, 18 May 1990)
Mills Brothers. Herbert Mills (*d* Las Vegas, 12 April 1989)
Minerve, Geezil (*d* New York, 4 June 1992)
Mitchell, Red (*d* Salem, OR, 8 Nov 1992)
Mondello, Toots (*d* New York, 15 Nov 1992)
Monterose, J.R. (*d* Utica, NY, 26 Sept 1993)
Moore, Billy (*d* Copenhagen, 28 Feb 1989)
Moore, Eddie (*d* Oakland, CA, 21 May 1990)
Moore, Freddie (*d* New York, 3 Nov 1992)
Moore, Gerry (*d* Twickenham, England, 30 Jan 1993)
Moore, Mel(vin) (*d* 26 Feb 1989)
Morrow, George (Washington) (*d* Orlando, FL, 26 May 1992)

Napoleon. (1) Phil Napoleon (*d* Miami, 30 Sept 1990)
Nelson, Louis (*d* New Orleans, 5 April 1990)
Nerem, Bjarne (*d* Oslo, 1 April 1991)
Newborn, Phineas (Jr.) (*d* Memphis, 26 May 1989)
Newman, Joe (*d* New York, 4 July 1992)
Nistico, Sal(vatore) (ii) (*d* Berne, Switzerland, 3 March 1991)
Noone, Jimmie, Jr. (*d* San Diego, 29 March 1991)
Norman, Fred (*d* New York, 19 Feb 1993)

Osborne, Mary (*d* Bakersfield, CA, 4 March 1992)

Palmer, Singleton (*d* St. Louis, 8 March 1993)
Patrick, Pat (*d* Moline, IL, 31 Dec 1991)
Pierce, Nat(haniel) (*d* Los Angeles, 10 June 1992)
Pillars, Hayes (*d* Richmond Heights, MO, 11 Aug 1992)
Price, Sammy (*d* New York, 14 April 1992)
Pukwana, Dudu (*d* London, 29 June 1990)

Quill, Gene (*d* Atlantic City, NJ, Jan 1989)

Rae, Johnny (*d* San Francisco, 4 Sept 1993)
Ramirez, Ram (*d* New York, 11 Jan 1994)
Randolph, Zilner T(renton) (*d* Chicago, 2 Feb 1994)
Remler, Emily (*d* Sydney, Australia, 4 May 1990)
Roberts, Howard (Mancel) (*d* Seattle, 28 June 1992)
Robinson, Ikey (L.) (*d* Chicago, 25 Oct 1990)
Ross, Ronnie (*d* London, 12 Dec 1991)
Rostaing, Hubert (*d* Paris, 10 June 1990)
Rouse, Charlie (*d* Seattle, 30 Nov 1988)
Russell, Bill (*d* New Orleans, 9 Aug 1992)
Russell, Johnny (*d* New York, 26 July 1991)

Schilperoort, Peter (*d* The Hague, 17 Nov 1990)
Schwindt, Christian (*d* Finland, 12 Oct 1992)
Scott, Raymond (*d* North Hills, CA, 8 Feb 1994)
Sears, Al(bert Omega) (*d* New York, 23 March 1990)
Shaw, Arnold (*d* Las Vegas, 26 Sept 1989)
Shaw, Woody (*d* New York, 9 May 1989)
Shihab, Sahib (*d* Tennessee, 24 Oct 1989)
Shirley, Jimmy (*d* New York, 3 Dec 1989)
Silva, Michael (*d* France, 1990)
Smith, Buster (*d* Dallas, 10 Aug 1991)
Smith, Jabbo (*d* New York, 16 Jan 1991)
Stauffer, Teddy (*d* 27 Aug 1991)
Stoller, Alvin (*d* Los Angeles, 19 Oct 1992)
Sun Ra (*d* Birmingham, AL, 30 May 1993)

Tee, Richard (Edward) (*d* New York, 21 July 1993)
Thelin, Eje (*d* Stockholm, 18 May 1990)
Turner, Bruce (*d* Newport Pagnell, England, 28 Nov 1993)
Turner, Joe (i) (*d* Montreuil, France, 21 July 1990)
Tyler, Charles (Lacy) (*d* Toulon, France, 27 June 1992)

Vauchant(-Arnaud), Léo (*d* Hamptonville, NC, April 1991)
Vaughan, Sarah (Lois) (*d* Los Angeles, 3 April 1990)
Ventura, Charlie (*d* Pleasantville, NJ, 17 Jan 1992)

Waits, Freddie (*d* New York, 18 Nov 1989)
Wallington, George (*d* New York, 15 Feb 1993)
Walton, Greely (*d* 9 Oct 1993)
Watters, Lu(cious) (*d* Santa Rosa, CA, 5 Nov 1989)
Werner, Lasse (*d* Stockholm, 7 Feb 1992)
Wilkins, Dave (*d* London, 26 Nov 1990)
Williams, Martin (*d* Alexandria, VA, 11 or 12 April 1992)
Williams, Sandy (*d* New York, 25 March 1991)
Wilson, Phillip (Sanford) (*d* New York, 1 April 1992)
Woodyard, Sam(uel) (*d* Paris, 20 Sept 1988)
Wright, Frank (*d* Germany,17 May 1990)
Wright, Leo (Nash) (*d* Vienna, 4 Jan 1991)

Zappa, Frank (*d* Los Angeles, 4 Dec 1993)
Zardis, Chester (*d* New Orleans, 14 Aug 1990)

CORRIGENDA

Abdul-Malik, Ahmed [Tim, Jonathan; not Gill, Sam]
Ak Laff, Pheeroan (*b* Detroit, 27 Jan 1955)
Bellson, Louie (*b* Rock Falls, IL, 6 July 1924)
Christian, Charlie (*b* Dallas, 29 July 1916)
Dodds, Johnny [not John M.]
Dutrey, Honore (*b* New Orleans, 1894)
Gaillard, Slim (*b* Santa Clara, Cuba)
Hall. (1) Edward (Blainey) Hall (Sr.) (*b* 9 June 1860; *d* 8 July 1933) **(4) Clarence Hall** (*b* 19 Feb 1903; *d* 29 Sept 1969)
Hall, Al(fred Wesley) (*b* 8 March 1915)
Hemphill, Julius (*b* 24 Jan 1938)
Hightower, Willie (H.) (*b* Nashville, 23 Oct 1889)
Holiday, Billie [Fagan, Eleanora; Harris, Elinore; Lady Day] (*b* Philadelphia, 7 April 1915)
Humphrey. Professor Jim Humphrey (*d* 25 Nov 1935) **Willie (Eli) Humphrey (Sr.)** (*b* 24 May 1879)
Kaye, Cab [Quaye, Augustus Kwamlah] (*b* London, 3 Sept 1921)
Kesterton [Kesterson], Bob
Lee, Julia (*b* 13 Oct 1903)
Machito (*b* Tampa, FL)
Morehouse, Chauncey (*d* Medford, NJ, 31 Oct 1980)
Noone, Jimmie, Jr. [James Fleming] (*b* Chicago, 21 April 1938)
Pepper, Art(hur Edward, Jr.) (*d* 15 June 1982)
Pope, Odean. Tenor saxophonist and bandleader.
Sayles, George (*d* 1955 or 1956)
Shoffner, Bob (*b* 30 April 1900)
Smith, Willie "the Lion" [Bertholoff, William Henry Joseph Bonaparte]
Swallow, Steve (*b* New York)
Taylor, Billy (ii) (*b* 21 July 1921)
Thomas, Joe [Joseph William; Brother Cornbread] **(i)**
Yancey, Jimmy (*b* 20 Feb 1898)

A

AACM. *See* ASSOCIATION FOR THE ADVANCEMENT OF CREATIVE MUSICIANS.

Aaltonen, Juhani (*b* Kouvola, Finland, 12 Dec 1935). Finnish tenor and alto saxophonist and flutist. He played in a sextet led by the trumpeter Heikki Rosendahl in Inkeroinen in the 1950s. He moved to Helsinki in 1961 and worked frequently as a studio musician. At the same time he made a name as a lyrical free-jazz and jazz-rock soloist, recording with Eero Koivistoinen (1969–73), Edward Vesala (from 1969), and Heikki Sarmanto (1969, 1972), and as a leader (from 1974). He also played with the Nordic All Stars (1971–2), Arild Andersen's quartet in Norway (late 1970s), and the New Music Orchestra in Helsinki (from 1975). Aaltonen's playing may be heard to advantage on his album *Etiquette* (1974, Love 119).

BIBLIOGRAPHY

A. Granholm: *Finnish Jazz* (Helsinki, 1974, rev. and enlarged by M. Konttinen 2/1982, rev. and enlarged by J.-P. Vuorela 3/1986), 8

J. Sermila: "Juhani Aaltonen," *JF* [intl edn], no.42 (1976), 52 [incl. discography]

PEKKA GRONOW

A&M Horizon. Name by which the record label HORIZON is sometimes known.

Aaron, Abe [Alvin] (*b* Toronto, 27 Jan 1910; *d* Jan 1970). Reed player. He played alto saxophone and recorded with Jack Teagarden (1942). After moving to Hollywood he performed and recorded with Horace Heidt (1943–5, 1948–9) and Skinnay Ennis (1945–8). He toured Europe and Asia and recorded with Les Brown, first on clarinet and alto saxophone (1950–3), then on tenor and baritone saxophones (1953–64). He also made recordings in Los Angeles as a bass clarinetist with Billy Usselton (including *His First Album*, 1956, Kapp 1051).

BIBLIOGRAPHY

FeatherE

Obituary, *Orkester journalen*, xxxix/3 (1971), 5

Aarons, Al(bert N.) (*b* Pittsburgh, 23 March 1932). Trumpeter and flugelhorn player. He studied music in Pittsburgh (1948–50) and privately (1951–2), then played with Yusef Lateef (1956–7) and Barry Harris (1957) in Detroit. He played with Wild Bill Davis (1961), then toured and recorded with Count Basie (1961–9), and recorded with Frank Wess (1962) and Frank Foster (1963). After moving to Los Angeles in 1969 he worked in television and recorded commercial jazz with Milt Jackson (1969), Bobby Bryant (1971), Sarah Vaughan (1971–2, 1974), Ella Fitzgerald (1972, 1978, 1982), the Capp–Pierce Juggernaut (1978, 1981), and Zoot Sims (1979). He also played with the bandleader Henry Mancini (from 1971), Buddy Collette (from 1973), Gerald Wilson (1985–6), and as a leader with sidemen such as Collette, Gildo Mahones, Earl Palmer, and Andy Simpkins. Aarons's style is exemplified by a recording he made on his own record label as a sideman for Buddy Collette, *Now and Then* (1973, Legend 1004). (*Feather–Gitler '70s*)

Abbey, Leon (Alexander) (*b* Minneapolis, 7 May 1900; *d* Minneapolis, 15 Sept 1975). Bandleader and violinist. He began his career playing light and classical music as a member of J. Rosamond Johnson's orchestra (1920–25). In 1925 he recorded as a soloist with Clara Smith (*If only you knowed*, Col. 14058) and began to lead his own band. The following year he directed the Savoy Bearcats, reorganizing the group for a tour of Brazil, Argentina, and Uruguay in 1927; he also took a band to England. Between 1928 and 1939 he toured extensively in Europe and visited India twice. After returning to the USA he organized a band in 1940 for Ethel Waters, toured with a small group, and then settled in Chicago, where he played regularly with a trio until 1964. Although he was not a jazz soloist, Abbey employed excellent sidemen, including Fletcher Allen, Emile Christian, Bill Coleman, Peter DuConge, and Crickett Smith. His jazz recordings as a leader remain unissued except for *Whoa Babe*, recorded in Copenhagen in 1938 and first issued on *Jazz and Hot Dance in Denmark* (Harl. 2024, 1986).

BIBLIOGRAPHY

B. Englund: "Leon Abbey and his Recordings," *Sv*, no.49 (1973), 7

R. Gulliver: "Leon Abbey," *Sv*, no.73 (1977), 4

H. Rye: "Visiting Firemen, 8," *Sv*, no.108 (1983), 207

M. Clausen: "'Swing-time 1938' in the North," *Sv*, no.121 (1985), 10

——: "Leon Abbey in Denmark, 1939," *Sv*, no.125 (1986), 168

RAINER E. LOTZ

Abdul-Malik, Ahmed [Gill, Sam] (*b* New York, 30 Jan 1927). Double bass and 'ūd player. He grew up in the multiracial environment of Brooklyn, and studied African and Middle-Eastern music as well as violin and double bass. As a double bass player he worked with Art Blakey (1948), Randy Weston (1954–7), Thelonious Monk (1957–8), Herbie Mann (1961), Earl

Hines (1964), and Ken McIntyre (1971), and performed at jazz festivals in Montreux, Switzerland, and New York. He took his Muslim name in the mid-1950s. He played the 'ūd, a Middle-Eastern lute, on a tour of South America that was sponsored by the US State Department (1961), and at one of the first important African jazz festivals, at Tangier, Morocco (1972); he also recorded on this instrument with John Coltrane (1961) and Hamiet Bluiett (1977). From 1970 he has taught at New York University; he also teaches in the department of African Studies at Brooklyn College, CUNY. In recognition of his achievements in bringing the influence of Middle-Eastern music to jazz, Abdul-Malik was given BMI's "Pioneer in Jazz Award" in 1984.

SELECTED RECORDINGS

As leader: *Jazz Sahara* (1958, Riv. 287); *The Music of Ahmed Abdul-Malik* (1961, NewJ 8266); *Ahmed Abdul-Malik/Sounds of Africa* (1961–2, NewJ 8282)

As sideman: R. Weston: *Get Happy with the Randy Weston Trio* (1955, Riv. 203); T. Monk: *Thelonious in Action* (1957, Riv. 262); *Misterioso* (1958, Riv. 279)

BIBLIOGRAPHY

Feather '60s

B. Coss: "The Philosophy of Ahmed Abdul-Malik," *DB*, xxx/15 (1963), 14

JOHN CURRY

Abene, Mike [Michael Christian Joseph] (*b* New York, 2 July 1942). Pianist, arranger, and composer. He performed and recorded at the Newport Jazz Festival in Marshall Brown's International Youth Band (1958) and studied composition at the Manhattan School of Music (1959–61). He played piano with Don Ellis (1960–61), Maynard Ferguson (1961–5), for whom he also wrote arrangements, and Buddy Rich (1963). From the mid-1960s he played regularly in New York at the Half Note (with the double bass player Rudy Braff, 1965–7), Bradley's (1972–5), Sweet Basil (1978), and Freddy's (with the singer Barbara Rankin, 1984). He has written arrangements for the trombonists Grover Mitchell, David Taylor, and Jim Pugh, and the popular singer Liza Minnelli, and produced and played piano on albums recorded for Stash by the singers Peggy King (1983), Earl Coleman (1984), and Anita Gravine (1984); he composed the score to the film *Goodbye, New York* (1984).

SELECTED RECORDINGS

As unaccompanied soloist: *You must have been a Beautiful Baby* (1984, Stash 249)

As sideman: M. Ferguson: *Si si M.F.* (1962, Roul. 52084); C. Tjader: *Solar Heat* (1968, Skye 1)

SELECTED ARRANGEMENTS

Recorded by M. Ferguson: on *The Blues Roar* (1964, Mstr. 6045), Mary Ann

Recorded by Burt Collins and J. Shepley: *Time, Space and the Blues* (*c*1971, MTA 2)

BIBLIOGRAPHY

Feather–Gitler '70s

G. Hoefer: "Newport Youth Band: Marshall Brown's Talent Incubator," *DB*, xxxiv/19 (1967), 19

W. F. Lee: "Michael Christian Joseph (Mike) Abene," *People in Jazz: Jazz Keyboard Improvisors of the 19th and 20th Centuries* (Hialeah, FL, 1984)

GREGORY E. SMITH

Abercrombie, John (L.) (*b* Port Chester, NY, 16 Dec 1944). Guitarist. He attended the Berklee College of Music in Boston from 1962 to 1966, during which time he also toured with Johnny Hammond. After moving to New York in 1969 he played first in Chico Hamilton's group and later with Billy Cobham's jazz-rock group Spectrum, where he attracted widespread attention. From 1974, when his highly regarded trio recording *Timeless* was issued, he has preferred a subdued, "chamber" jazz style of performance, either working with his own small groups, including the trio Gateway with Dave Holland and Jack DeJohnette (1975–7) and a notable quartet (1978–*c*1981), or as a much sought-after sideman. He has made important contributions to ensembles led by DeJohnette and has taken part in numerous sessions, mostly for the ECM label. Although not primarily an innovator, Abercrombie makes imaginative use of distorting devices such as the phase shifter and volume pedal with the electric guitar (and occasionally electric mandolin) and has explored the possibilities offered by the guitar synthesizer. His distinctive personal style combines elements from bop to free jazz and his sensitive control of tone-color is particularly apparent in his duo performances with Ralph Towner.

SELECTED RECORDINGS

Duos with R. Towner: *Sargasso Sea* (1976, ECM 1080); *Five Years Later* (1981, ECM 1207)

As leader: *Timeless* (1974, ECM 1047); *Gateway* (1975, ECM 1061); *Gateway 2* (1977, ECM 1105); *Characters* (1977, ECM 1117); *M* (1980, ECM 1191); *Night* (1984, ECM 1272); *Current Events* (1985, ECM 1311)

As sideman: B. Cobham: *Crosswinds* (1974, Atl. 7300); J. DeJohnette: *Sorcery* (1974, Prst. 10081); *Untitled* (1976, ECM 1074); *New Directions* (1978, ECM 1128)

BIBLIOGRAPHY

C. Berg: "John Abercrombie's Six-string Stylistic Summit," *DB*, xliii/4 (1976), 16

T. Schneckloth: "John Abercrombie: a Direction of his Own," *DB*, xlvi/4 (1979), 16

J. Ferguson: "John Abercrombie: Testing the Thresholds of Jazz," *GP*, xx/11 (1986), 58 [incl. discography]

B. Milkowski: "John Abercrombie: Seduced by Synths," *DB*, liii/9 (1986), 17 [incl. discography]

B. Riedinger: "John Abercrombie: Guitar with no Bounds," *JT* (Feb 1988), 5

J. BRADFORD ROBINSON

Abney, (John) Don(ald) (*b* Baltimore, 10 March 1923). Pianist. He studied piano at the Manhattan School of Music. After playing french horn in an army band he returned to New York, where he worked with Snub Mosley (1948), Wilbur De Paris (1948–9), Kai Winding (1951), Chuck Wayne (1952), Sy Oliver, and Louie Bellson (1954, 1957); he also recorded with Eddie South (1947) and Louis Armstrong (1951). From 1954 to 1957 he toured and recorded with Ella Fitzgerald, and from 1958 to 1959 was accompanist to Carmen McRae. Abney worked as a staff musician for NBC and CBS, then in 1962 moved to Los Angeles, where he worked with Benny Carter and played in a concert with Stan Kenton's Neophonic Orchestra (1966). Later he toured with his own trio (1969–71) and with Pearl Bailey (1971–4).

SELECTED RECORDINGS

As sideman: L. Bellson: *Louis Bellson Quintet* (1954, Norg. 1011); B. Carter: *Benny Carter Plays Pretty* (1955, Norg. 1015); E. Fitzgerald: *Ella and Billie at Newport* (1957, Verve 8234); B. Carter: *Additions to Further Definitions* (1966, Imp. 9116)

BIBLIOGRAPHY

FeatherE; *Feather '60s*; *Feather–Gitler '70s*

ANDREW JAFFE

Abrams, Lee [Abramson, Leon] (*b* New York, 6 Jan 1925). Drummer, brother of Ray Abrams. After serving in the army (1943–6) he played and made recordings (including *Lover come back to me*, 1946, Decca 24119) with Roy Eldridge (1946–7), and also recorded with Joe Thomas (iv). He worked on 52nd Street in the mid-1940s with Coleman Hawkins, J. J. Johnson, and Eddie "Lockjaw" Davis (with whom he recorded in 1950), then played in Eddie Heywood's trio and Andy Kirk's orchestra (both 1948). After touring with Hot Lips Page he rejoined Heywood, performed and recorded with Illinois Jacquet (1951–2), played with Oscar Pettiford (1952), and worked with Lester Young (1952–3). He also recorded in bop trios led by Wynton Kelly (1951), Duke Jordan (1954), and Al Haig (1954). He appeared with Joe Albany in the film *Joe Albany . . . a Jazz Life* (1980); he also led workshops and taught jazz in Brooklyn. In the 1980s he performed in his brother's big band. (*FeatherE*)

Abrams, Muhal Richard [Abrahams, Richard] (*b* Chicago, 19 Sept 1930). Pianist, composer, and administrator. He studied piano from the age of 17, attended the Chicago Musical College for four years, and first worked professionally in 1948. He wrote arrangements for the saxophonist King Fleming from 1950, and from 1957 played hard bop in Walter Perkins's group MJT + 3, for which he also wrote arrangements and compositions. For several years he played with leading soloists during their visits to Chicago, including Miles Davis, Max Roach, Sonny Rollins, and Johnny Griffin. Of greater importance was his role in forming the Experimental Band (1961), one of the earliest free-jazz groups, and the ASSOCIATION FOR THE ADVANCEMENT OF CREATIVE MUSICIANS (1965), a musicians' cooperative. As the association's first president he encouraged young musicians to become familiar with the entire history of jazz and at the same time to experiment with new forms; he exerted a profound influence on such performers as Lester Bowie, Anthony Braxton, and George Lewis (ii). After moving to New York around 1977 he performed and recorded as an unaccompanied soloist, worked in duos with Lewis, Braxton, Leroy Jenkins, and Amina Claudine Myers, and led small groups and a big band. In the mid-1980s he fulfilled a commission by the Kronos String Quartet. In the late 1980s he led a quintet that included the reed player John Purcell and the trumpeter Stanton Davis. Abrams's work as a pianist reflects his interest in music of many genres, including stride piano (especially the music of James P. Johnson), free jazz, and 20th-century art music. He plays clarinet in addition to his principal instrument.

SELECTED RECORDINGS

As unaccompanied soloist: *Afrisong* (1975, Trio–Whynot 7121); *Spiral* (1978, AN 3007)

Duos: with M. Favors: *Sightsong* (1975, BS 0003); with A. Braxton: *Duets* (1976, Ari. 4101); with L. Jenkins: *Lifelong Ambitions* (1977, BS 0033); with A. C. Myers: *Duet* (1981, BS 0051)

As leader: *Levels and Degrees of Light* (1967, Del. 413); *Young at Heart, Wise in Time* (1969, Del. 423); *1–OQA+19* (1977, BS 0017); *Lifea blinec* (1978, AN 3000); *Spihumonesty* (1979, BS 0032); *Mama and Daddy* (1980, BS 0041); *Blues Forever* (1981, BS 0061); *Rejoicing with the Light* (1983, BS 0071)

As sideman: Art Ensemble of Chicago: *Fanfare for the Warriors* (1973, Atl. 1651)

BIBLIOGRAPHY

Feather–Gitler '70s

J. Litweiler: "Chicago's Richard Abrams: a Man with an Idea," *DB*, xxxiv/20 (1967), 23

T. Martin: "The Chicago Avant-garde," *JM*, no.157 (1968), 12

E. Jost: *Free Jazz* (Graz, Austria, 1974)

R. Townley: "Profile: Muhal Richard Abrams," *DB*, xli/14 (1974), 34

V. Wilmer: *As Serious as your Life: the Story of the New Jazz* (London, 1977, rev. 1980)

J.-E. Berendt: *Photo-Story des Jazz* (Frankfurt am Main, 1978; Eng. trans., New York and London, 1979)

J. De Muth: "Muhal Richard Abrams: Jazz Innovator, Founder of the A.A.C.M.," *CK*, iv/5 (1978), 20

B. McRae: "Avant Courier: Beyond the Mainstream: Muhal Richard Abrams," *JJI*, xxxiii/4 (1980), 25

G. Giddins: "Something Else Again," *Rhythm-a-ning: Jazz Tradition and Innovation in the '80s* (New York, and Oxford, England, 1985) [colln of previously pubd articles], 23

LEE JESKE/R

Abrams, Ray [Abramson, Raymond] (*b* New York, 23 Jan 1920). Tenor saxophonist, brother of Lee Abrams. In the early 1940s he played in the resident band at Monroe's Uptown House, which accompanied Coleman Hawkins in performances and on the first studio recordings of bop (16 February 1944); he remained with the group when it became the core of Dizzy Gillespie's first big band in 1945. The following year he recorded with Kenny Clarke and (during a tour of Europe) Don Redman; his solo playing is well represented on Redman's *For Europeans Only* (1946, Ste. 6020–21). His own band (formed 1947) recorded with the singer Billy Stewart (1947, 1949) and under Abrams's name (1948); Fats Navarro and Coleman Hawkins were among his sidemen. After playing with Andy Kirk (1947–8) he re-joined Gillespie and recorded with Cecil Payne (both 1949). He toured and made recordings with Hot Lips Page (1949–50, including *Miss Larceny Blues*, 1950, Col. 30204), worked with Roy Eldridge (1952), and performed and recorded with Bill Harris (i), Buddy DeFranco, and Gillespie (all 1952), and Terry Gibbs (1953). He later taught jazz in Brooklyn, and in the 1980s led his own big band. (*FeatherE*)

Abriani, John [Giovanni] (*b* San Girolamo di Lusiana, province of Vicenza, Italy, 15 May 1898; *d* Milan, Aug 1960). Italian bandleader, saxophonist, and violinist. He was brought up in Switzerland, where he formed a café orchestra with his brother Felice, who played banjo and violin. From 1925 to 1932 he toured Italy, Germany, and Switzerland and made several recordings as a leader for Homocord (1927–8, including *Just Once Again*, 2514, and *Say it with a Red Rose*, 2524, both 1928), in which Arthur Briggs may have taken part. Abriani held an engagement in Calcutta from 1932 to 1934, during which time he recorded for HMV's Twin label. After returning to Europe he toured (1934–9) and made further recordings (1937–9), and then settled in Italy. Although he was not himself a jazz soloist, he often employed excellent jazz players as his sidemen. (A. Mazzoletti: *Il jazz in Italia: dalle origini al dopoguerra*, Rome, 1983)

RAINER E. LOTZ

Accordion. A portable keyboard instrument of the reed organ family. It consists of a bass button keyboard played with the left hand, which also operates a bellows, and a treble keyboard (with piano keys or buttons) played by the right. The instrument is suspended by straps from the player's shoulders.

The accordion has a long, undistinguished history in jazz. The obscure player Charles Melrose provides an early example of jazz accordion solos on the recording *Wailing Blues/Barrel House Stomp* (1930, Voc. 1503) by the Cellar Boys, a sextet that also comprised Wingy Manone, Frank Teschemacher, Bud Freeman, Frank Melrose, and George Wettling. Buster Moten played second piano and accordion as a member of Bennie Moten's orchestra; his solo on *Moten's Blues* (1929, Vic. 38072) demonstrates that the instrument's sweet sound fails to capture the raw emotions of the blues. Another obscure jazz accordionist was Jack Cornell, who recorded with Irving Mills (1929, 1930). In Europe, where the musical traditions more often allowed the instrument to be used in ensembles doubling as dance bands and jazz bands, there emerged accordionists of some importance; these included Kamil Behounek, who recorded as a soloist in 1936, Toivo Kärki, Nisse Lind and the Swiss pianist and accordionist Buddy Bertinat, who belonged to the Original Teddies (1936–48) and also played accordion on many recordings with his own swing quartets and quintets (1940–48).

The first jazz accordionist to become well-known was Joe Mooney, who led an acclaimed swing quartet at clubs on 52nd

Street in New York (1946–7). Other swing accordionists included Mat Mathews, a member of the Dutch group the Millers (1947–50), and Art van Damme (*b* Norway, MI, 9 April 1920). The pianist George Shearing plays fine bop solos on the accordion on the recording *Cherokee/Four Bars Short* (1949, Dis. 107), and there were a number of important bop accordionists in the 1950s and early 1960s, including Mathews (after his move to the USA), van Damme (who continued to lead a bop group into the 1980s), Leon (Robert) Sash (*b* Chicago, 19 Oct 1922), Pete Jolly, and Tommy Gumina. The accordion has no place in jazz-rock and is virtually unused in free jazz, although the Willem Breuker Kollektief has employed it to humorous effect.

BARRY KERNFELD

Acea, John (Adriano) (*b* Philadelphia, 11 Oct 1917). Pianist. From the late 1930s he played trumpet with Sam Price and tenor saxophone with Don Bagley. After moving to New York he performed and recorded as a pianist with Eddie "Lockjaw" Davis (1947–8), Dizzy Gillespie (1949–50), and Illinois Jacquet (1952–4). He recorded with James Moody (1951) and Al Sears (1952), and played briefly with Cootie Williams. He also made recordings with Joe Newman (1954, 1957; including *Blues for Slim*, on the album *Joe Newman and his Band*, 1954, Van. 8007) and Eddie Jefferson (1959). (*FeatherE*)

Ace of Hearts. Record label. It was established by British Decca (*see* DECCA) in 1961, and became known for low-priced reissues of early jazz and popular music, and swing. Most items on Ace of Hearts were drawn from the back catalogue of American Decca and from recordings made for Brunswick and Vocalion before 1932, though the last few jazz issues in the series of more than 150 LPs had first been released by Commodore. Ace of Clubs, an associated label, put out items made in Europe, including important jazz recordings by such American musicians resident there as Coleman Hawkins and Benny Carter.

Acheson, Merv(yn Fletcher) (*b* Sydney, 31 March 1922; *d* Sydney, 11 Aug 1987). Australian saxophonist, clarinetist, and bandleader. He began to play saxophone in 1933 and joined George Fuller, before working as a freelance musician and in wartime entertainment units. After the war he played in nightclubs and pit orchestras, and in coffee lounges in Melbourne (1948), then worked in Sydney with George Trevare and as a freelance musician. From 1955 he led bands in Sydney hotels including the Criterion (1958–65), the Windsor Castle, and the Bellevue. He played with bands led by Dick Hughes (1979–85) and Alan Geddes (1984–6) and led his own group at the Canberra Hotel in Paddington, Sydney, before retiring because of ill health (1986). His playing, which is chiefly in dixieland and swing styles, is heard to advantage on *Merv Acheson 60th Birthday Concert* (1982, MBS Jazz 1). He also worked as a music journalist and held positions of responsibility in the Australian Musicians' Union.

BIBLIOGRAPHY

A. Bisset: *Black Roots, White Flowers: a History of Jazz in Australia* (Sydney, 1979), 85
B. Johnson: "Acheson, Mervyn Fletcher (Merv)," *The Oxford Companion to Australian Jazz* (Melbourne, Australia, 1987)

BRUCE JOHNSON

Acoustical [acoustic] **recording.** A term applied to early techniques of sound recording (and playback), which employed only mechanical means; it is also used of the cylinders and discs produced by these means. *See* RECORDING, §§I, 1, and II, 2.

Action jazz. Term used originally by the jazz critic Don Heckman to describe FREE JAZZ.

Actuelle. Record label, established in 1920, on which PATHÉ first issued lateral-cut discs in the USA; the company began using the name in other countries the following year.

Acuña, Alex [Alejandro; Neciosup-Acuña, Alejandro] (*b* Pativilca, Peru, 12 Dec 1944). Peruvian drummer and percussionist. He learned trumpet and piano with his father, but is self-taught as a drummer. At the age of 16 he became a studio musician in Lima and in 1964 he was engaged by the dance-band leader Perez Prado to work in Las Vegas. From 1966 to 1975 he played in bands and worked as a studio musician in Puerto Rico, Las Vegas, and Los Angeles. From 1975 to 1977 he played with Weather Report, first as a percussionist (October 1975 to April 1976), then as the drummer (April 1976 to October 1977; for illustration *see* ZAWINUL, JOE); he recorded two albums with the group, one of which was the highly successful *Heavy Weather* (1976, Col. PC34418). He formed his own group, Koinonia, in 1980. He also worked with Lee Ritenour and recorded with (among others) Clare Fischer (1978–9), Ella Fitzgerald (1980), Tania Maria (1983), Chick Corea and the guitarist Paco De Lucia (1984), and the rock singer Joni Mitchell (1985). His style is influenced by Peruvian traditional music, Latin rhythms, and the playing of Elvin Jones and Tony Williams; Acuña is highly regarded for his ability as a Latin-jazz and jazz-rock drummer.

BIBLIOGRAPHY

M. Rozek: "Alex Acuña: Transcending all Influences," *MD*, vi/3 (1982), 12

CATHERINE COLLINS

Adams, George (Rufus) (*b* Covington, GA, 29 April 1940). Tenor saxophonist and flutist. As a teenager he attended Clark College, Atlanta, where he was taught by Wayman Carver; while studying in Cleveland in the early 1960s he worked in organ trios, playing a hybrid of rhythm-and-blues and jazz. He settled in New York in 1968 and from 1969 to 1973 worked with Roy Haynes, recording with him around 1972. He then played with Art Blakey, Charles Mingus (1973–6), Gil Evans (1975–8), and McCoy Tyner (1976–9). In 1975, while touring Europe with Mingus's band, he made his first recordings under his own name with some fellow sidemen. In 1979 he became the leader with the pianist Don Pullen of a quartet which often included Dannie Richmond, who was formerly the drummer in Mingus's group. Adams is best known for his saxophone playing, which has gradually assumed a very recognizable style; it draws on the work of John Coltrane, Albert Ayler (who was based in Cleveland when Adams was there), Ben Webster, and Paul Gonsalves. His flute playing displays a similar eclectic approach. From the time he worked with Mingus, Adams has occasionally indulged in blues singing.

SELECTED RECORDINGS

As leader: with D. Richmond: *Hand to Hand* (1980, SN 1007); with D. Pullen: *Life Line* (1981, Tim. 154)
As sideman: R. Haynes: *Senyah* (*c*1972, Mstr. 351); C. Mingus: *Mingus Moves* (1973, Atl. 1653); *Changes* (1974, Atl. 1677–8); G. Evans: *There Comes a Time* (1975, RCA APL1-1057)

BIBLIOGRAPHY

G. Pellicciotti and D. Soutif: "George Adams," *Jm*, no.233 (1975), 24
L. Jeske: "George Adams has Arrived," *DB*, xlvi/17 (1979), 32 [incl. discography]

C. Sheridan: "Young Men Ascending: some Notes on Chico Freeman and George Adams," *JJI*, xxxiii/10 (1980), 26 [incl. discography]
B. Priestley: *Mingus: a Critical Biography* (London, Melbourne, Australia, and New York, 1982), 196

BRIAN PRIESTLEY

Adams, Pepper [Park, III] (*b* Highland Park, MI, 8 Oct 1930; *d* New York, 10 Sept 1986). Baritone saxophonist. As a child he moved with his family to Rochester, New York, where he played tenor saxophone and clarinet with local bands (1944) and worked with Ben Smith; he modeled his early style after that of Coleman Hawkins. He was inspired by the example of Harry Carney to take up the baritone saxophone, and after moving to Detroit he worked professionally from 1947 with Barry Harris, Frank Foster, and others. He served in the US Army (1951–3), then returned to Detroit, where as a member of the house band at the Bluebird he accompanied Sonny Stitt, Wardell Gray, and Miles Davis; he also played in Kenny Burrell's group. In January 1956 he moved to New York; during the following years he belonged to big bands led by Stan Kenton, Maynard Ferguson (with whom he toured the USA), Benny Goodman, Lionel Hampton, and Thelonious Monk (whom he accompanied at Town Hall, New York, 1959) and worked with Charles Mingus. Between 1958 and 1962 he led quintets with Donald Byrd; among those who played with the groups as sidemen were the pianists Bobby Timmons, Duke Pearson, and Herbie Hancock, the double bass player Doug Watkins, and the drummers Elvin Jones, Lex Humphries, Harold Jones, and Jimmy Cobb. He belonged to the Thad Jones–Mel Lewis Orchestra from 1965 to 1976 (for illustration *see* JONES, fig.1*b*), recorded with David Amram, and in the late 1970s toured Britain and the Continent. In the 1980s he took part in a tribute to Count Basie in Nice, France, and recorded with Kenny Wheeler. Adams used stylistic devices more often associated with black players; these included adventurous harmonies, a gruff tone, and a large sound.

Oral history material in *GBLnsa*.

SELECTED RECORDINGS

As leader: *10–4 at the 5-Spot* (1958, Riv. 1104); *Pepper Adams Plays Charles Mingus* (1963, Jazz Workshop 219); with Z. Sims: *Encounter* (1968, Prst. 7677); *Ephemera* (1974, Spot. 6); *Julian* (1975, Enja 2060); *Reflectory* (1979, Muse 5182); *The Master* (1980, Muse 5213); *Urban Dreams* (1981, Palo Alto 8009)

BIBLIOGRAPHY

J. Tynan: "Doctor Pepper: Valuable Detroit Internship Helped Adams Find himself," *DB*, xxiv/22 (1957), 17
G. Lees: "Pepper Adams," *DB*, xxx/12 (1963), 18
P. Adams: "Being Unpopular is Great Fun!," *CI*, x/3 (1971), 26
A. J. Smith: "The Essence of Spice," *DB*, xliv/18 (1977), 18
P. Hanson: "Pepper Adams: Detroit Roots," *JJI*, xxxiii/1 (1980), 30
L. Jeske: "Pepper Adams," *DB*, xlix/8 (1982), 28
P. Danson: "Pepper Adams," *Coda*, no.191 (1983), 4 [interview]
G. Carner: "Pepper Adams," *Cadence*, xii (1986), no.1, p.13; no.2, p.5; no.3, p.11; no.4, p.5

LEE JESKE/R

Adde, Leo (*b* New Orleans, 21 April 1904; *d* New Orleans, March 1942). Drummer. He first played cigar box in a spasm duo with Raymond Burke (1914). Later he was a member of Abbie Brunies's Halfway House Orchestra (1923–5), with which he made recordings in 1925 (including *Golden Leaf Strut*, OK 40327), and the New Orleans Frolickers led by the pianist Johnny Miller (1925–30), with which he recorded in 1928. He also recorded with the cornetist Johnny Bayersdorffer (1924) and the re-formed New Orleans Rhythm Kings (1925). In 1930 he joined the Melody Masters, led by Leon Prima and Sharkey Bonano; the band moved to New York later that year under new leadership. (A. Rose and E. Souchon: *New Orleans Jazz: a Family Album*, Baton Rouge, LA, 1967, rev. 2/1978, rev. and enlarged 3/1984)

MIKE HAZELDINE

Adderley, Cannonball [Julian Edwin] (*b* Tampa, FL, 15 Sept 1928; *d* Gary, IN, 8 Aug 1975). Alto saxophonist and bandleader, brother of Nat Adderley. The nickname "Cannonball" was a childhood corruption of "cannibal," describing his large appetite. He played alto saxophone in Florida bands from around 1942 and directed a high-school band in Fort Lauderdale for more than two years from September 1948. After serving in army bands from 1950 to 1953 he resumed teaching until 1955. He then moved to New York, intending to play with his brother,

Members of Miles Davis's sextet at a recording session for Columbia, 2 April 1958: (left to right) John Coltrane (tenor saxophone), Cannonball Adderley (alto saxophone), Davis (trumpet), and Bill Evans (ii) (piano)

and to begin graduate studies at New York University. Instead, a chance jam session led to his joining Oscar Pettiford's band and signing a recording contract.

The Adderley brothers formed a promising quintet in January 1956, but in September the following year the group was forced to disband because of financial difficulties. Adderley then replaced Sonny Rollins in the Miles Davis Quintet in October 1957. He stayed in Davis's famous sextets, playing with John Coltrane (see illustration), until September 1959, when he formed a second quintet with his brother. This group, which played soul jazz and bop, remained intact until 1975, achieving considerable success. At various times the members included George Duke, Victor Feldman, Joe Zawinul (who composed their hit tune *Mercy, mercy, mercy*), Louis Hayes, and Roy McCurdy. From January 1962 to July 1965 the group expanded to form a sextet with the addition of Yusef Lateef and later Charles Lloyd on reed instruments. Articulate and effective as a teacher, Adderley led the quintet at college workshops in the late 1960s and early 1970s, speaking on the musical and sociological aspects of jazz.

A masterful, confident improviser, Adderley was called "the new Bird" because his début in 1955 occurred shortly after Charlie Parker's death. This unfortunate label caused resentment among the press and public, and set him unattainable standards. Although he at times imitated Parker (as did all bop alto saxophonists), his first bop recordings reveal more chromatic and continuous lines and a more cutting tone than Parker's; on other early recordings he played and composed in a simple blues- and gospel-oriented style. His approach to improvisation changed significantly while he was with Davis, who taught him to use silence effectively, and again during the mid-1960s when he incorporated elements of free jazz. From 1969 he also performed on soprano saxophone. A collection of materials relating to his life and career is held in the Black Archives Research Center and Museum of Florida A&M University in Tallahassee, Florida; *see* LIBRARIES AND ARCHIVES, §2.

Oral history material in *NjR*.

SELECTED RECORDINGS

As leader: *Presenting Cannonball Adderley* (1955, Savoy 12018); *Somethin' Else* (1958, BN 1595); *Portrait of Cannonball Adderley* (1958, Riv. 269); *Things are Getting Better* (1958, Riv. 286); *The Cannonball Adderley Quintet in San Francisco* (1959, Riv. 311); *Them Dirty Blues* (1960, Riv. 1170); *At the Lighthouse* (1960, Riv. 9355), incl. Sack o' Woe; *African Waltz* (1961, Riv. 9377); *Nippon Soul* (1963, Riv. 9477); *Live!* (1964, Cap. ST2399); *Mercy, Mercy, Mercy! Live at "the Club"* (1966, Cap. ST2663); *Country Preacher* (1969, Cap SKA0404); *Inside Straight* (1973, Fan. 9435)

As sideman with M. Davis: *Milestones* (1958, Col. CL1193); *Jazz Track* (1957–8, Col. CL1268); *Miles and Monk at Newport* (1958, Col. CL2178); *Jazz at the Plaza* (1958, Col. C32470); *Kind of Blue* (1959, Col. CL1355)

BIBLIOGRAPHY

I. Gitler: "Julian 'Cannonball' Adderley," *Jazz: a Quarterly of American Music*, no.3 (1959), 197; no.4 (1959), 289

J. Adderley: "Paying Dues: the Education of a Combo Leader," *JR*, iii/4 (1960), 12

D. DeMicheal: "The Responsibilities of Success: Cannonball," *DB*, xxix/13 (1962), 13

F. Postif: "Julian 'Cannonball' Adderley," *Jh*, no.184 (1963), 17

J. Ginibre: "Les frères amis à la question," *Jm*, no.131 (1966), 18

B. Quinn: "The Well Rounded 'Ball'," *DB*, xxxiv/23 (1967), 17

C. Albertson: "Cannonball the Communicator," *DB*, xxxvii/1 (1970), 12

P. Wilson: "Conversing with Cannonball," *DB*, xxxix/12 (1972), 12

B. Priestley: "Cannonball: from the Soul," *MM* (4 Nov 1972), 48

"Farewell Cannonball," *SJ*, xxix/12 (1975), 248 [discography]

W. van Eyle: "Cannonball Adderley discografie," *Jazz Press*, no.37 (1977), 14; no.38 (1977), 7; no.40 (1977), 19; no.43 (1977), 6 [addns and corrections]

D. Baker: *The Jazz Style of Cannonball Adderley* (Lebanon, IN, 1980)

B. Kernfeld: *Adderley, Coltrane, and Davis at the Twilight of Bebop: the Search for Melodic Coherence (1958–59)* (diss., Cornell U., 1981) [incl. transcrs.]

J. Winter: "Julian Cannonball Adderley," *Coda*, no.186 (1982), 4

J. Kawrza: "Julian 'Cannonball' Adderley (1928–1975): seine Improvisationstechnik in der Zeit seines Schaffens bei Miles Davis," *Jf*, xviii (1986), 9 [incl. transcrs.]

BARRY KERNFELD

Adderley, Nat(haniel, Sr.) (*b* Tampa, FL, 25 Nov 1931). Cornetist and composer, brother of Cannonball Adderley. He took up trumpet as a teenager after World War II, and began his career playing with local bands in Florida. After changing to cornet (1950) he played in an army band during military service (1951–3). His first important association was with Lionel Hampton (1954–5); in 1956 he joined the influential small group led by his brother. While Cannonball played with Miles Davis (1957–9) Nat worked with J. J. Johnson and Woody Herman; he then joined his brother's second group and remained with it until the latter's death in 1975. Thereafter he toured Europe, both as a leader and a member of larger ensembles (1976). He has recorded frequently with his own quintet, and has also led seminars at Harvard.

One of the few contemporary soloists on cornet, Adderley has begun to emerge from the shadow of his more famous brother. His style successfully combines lyricism with the directness and immediacy of hard bop. He is a skilled composer; his pieces include *Work Song* and *Jive Samba*. His musical about the folk hero John Henry, *Shout up a Morning*, which he began in collaboration with his brother, was performed on Broadway in 1986. His son, the pianist and keyboard player Nat Adderley, Jr. (*b* Quincy, FL, 22 May 1955), began performing and recording with Cannonball Adderley as a teenager, and has worked as a producer and accompanist for such soul singers as Luther Vandross and Aretha Franklin.

Oral history material in *NjR*.

SELECTED RECORDINGS

As leader: *Work Song* (1960, Riv. 1167); *That's Right!* (1960, Riv. 9330); *Autobiography* (1964–5, Atl. 1439); *The Scavenger* (1968, Mlst. 9016); *Hummin'* (1976, Little David 1012); *On the Move* (1982, The. 117)

As sideman with C. Adderley: *Jazz Workshop Revisited* (1962, Riv. 9444), incl. Jive Samba; *Mercy, Mercy, Mercy! Live at "the Club"* (1966, Cap. ST2663); *Phenix* (1975, Fan. 79004)

BIBLIOGRAPHY

N. Adderley: "Cannon and I," *Metronome*, lxxvii/12 (1960), 18

B. Gardner: "The Biggest Little Brother: an Appreciation of Nat Adderley," *DB*, xxxiii/3 (1966), 22

L. Lyons: "Nat Adderley: Standing out on his Own," *DB*, xliii/19 (1976), 14 [incl. discography]

J. Carey: "Nat Adderley: On the Move," *JT* (1983), Sept, 7

SCOTT DEVEAUX

Addison, Bernard (S.) [Bernie] (*b* Annapolis, MD, 15 April 1905). Acoustic guitarist. In the early 1920s he worked around Washington as a banjoist, at one point leading a group with Claude Hopkins. After moving to New York he performed and recorded with Louis Armstrong (1930) and Fletcher Henderson (1933–4); it was during his association with Armstrong that the guitar became his principal instrument. Addison was an excellent rhythm guitarist; during his illustrious career he also made recordings with Jelly Roll Morton (1930), Bubber Miley (1930), and Coleman Hawkins (1933–4) and accompanied the Mills Brothers (1936–8); he worked as a leader on various occasions, sharing with Freddie Jenkins the leadership of a recording session in 1935. Later he played and recorded with Stuff Smith (1938–9) and Sidney Bechet (1940), recorded again with Hawkins and Armstrong (both 1940), and after completing military service during World War II recorded again with Bechet (1947), with the popular singing group the Ink Spots (1950s), and with Eubie Blake (1958). In later years he was active as a teacher.

SELECTED RECORDINGS

As leader: I Can't Dance/Toledo Shuffle (1935, Bb 6174); with P. Brown: *Pete's Last Date* (1961, 77 SEU52)

As sideman: J. R. Morton: Little Lawrence/Harmony Blues (1930, Vic. 38135); L. Armstrong: My Sweet/I can't believe that you're in love with me (1930, OK 41415); F. Henderson: Yeah Man!/King Porter's Stomp (1933, Voc. 2527); C. Hawkins: Jamaica Shout/Heartbreak Blues (1933, OK 41566); S. Smith: My Thoughts/My Blue Heaven (1939, Var. 8081); S. Bechet: Shake it and Break it/Wild Man Blues (1940, Vic. 26640)

BIBLIOGRAPHY

ChiltonW

WARREN VACHÉ, SR.

Addleman, Bonnie (Jean). *See* WETZEL, BONNIE.

Adler, Larry [Lawrence] (*b* Baltimore, ? 10 Feb 1914). Harmonica player. He first recorded as a leader in London in 1934, and from that date participated in hundreds of sessions, working with many prominent jazz musicians. He also appeared in several films; in *Many Happy Returns* (1934) he played with Duke Ellington's orchestra. He made recordings with Stephane Grappelli and Django Reinhardt in Paris (1938) and with John Kirby's orchestra in New York (1944, including *Blues in the Night*, Decca 23254). From 1934 he lived in London, although he toured extensively; in 1959 he returned to the USA and worked with Ellis Larkins. The two musicians remained associated into the 1980s, and in 1986 performed to critical acclaim in New York. Adler is perhaps the world's best-known harmonica player, and as well as jazz his repertory includes classical music (some of it written especially for him) and popular songs. He has also recorded as a pianist and singer and has been active as a teacher, composer, and arranger.

BIBLIOGRAPHY

FeatherE
L. Adler: *It Ain't Necessarily So* (London, 1984) [autobiography]
G. Giddins: "Ghost Story," *VV*, xxxi (21 Jan 1986), 70

Adulyadej, Bhumibol. *See* BHUMIBOL ADULYADEJ.

AEC. *See* ART ENSEMBLE OF CHICAGO.

Aerts, Jos(eph) [Josse] (*b* Antwerp, Belgium, 11 Nov 1903; *d* Keerbergen, Belgium, 9 Sept 1973). Belgian drummer. He first performed as a child in revues, and in the 1920s he worked with local bands in Antwerp and Ostend. He then became a member of the big band led by Chas Remue (1929) and played with Gus Deloof (1931) and an orchestra led by the Dutch bandleader Jack de Vries (1932). In 1936 he joined a newly formed big band led by Stan Brenders; he worked with this group, which was the official jazz orchestra of Belgian radio, until the end of World War II. Later he played for various bandleaders, including Fud Candrix, Deloof, and Jean Omer, and worked as a freelance musician throughout Belgium. Among the musicians with whom he recorded were Remue (1929), Jack and Louis de Vries (1933), Brenders (1938–43), the pianist Johnny Jack (1939–40), Eddie Tower (1940–46), John Ouwerx (1941–2), the clarinetist Jack Lowens (1942), Jean Robert (1942), Hubert Rostaing (1942), Candrix (1945–51), the Peter Sisters (1952), the clarinetist and alto saxophonist Louis Billen (1952), and David Bee (1956).

ROBERT PERNET

Affinity. Record label. It was founded in London in 1977 by Jean Luc Young on behalf of Charly Records Limited. During the first ten years of its existence Affinity reissued some 220 albums; most of the material was drawn from the catalogues of BYG, Capitol, Pacific Jazz, MCA (including many items originally put out on Impulse!), Columbia, and Bethlehem, and it also initiated new recordings by Don Weller and John Stevens. One of its most successful reissues was Serge Chaloff's album *Blue Serge*, which became a substantial hit and encouraged the company to re-release Chaloff's *Boston Blow-up*, another LP previously unavailable in the UK. Much of Affinity's material has been made available elsewhere under licensing arrangements with other companies. Affinity was among the first independent labels to embrace the compact disc format, and its releases on compact disc include a series of box sets by major solo artists, comprehensively annotated and including a number of important vintage performers.

MARK GARDNER

AFJS. *See* AMERICAN FEDERATION OF JAZZ SOCIETIES.

African thumb piano. *See* LAMELLAPHONE.

Afro-Cuban jazz [cubop]. A jazz style, created from a fusion of bop with traditional Cuban elements, that arose in the 1940s, primarily in the work of Dizzy Gillespie; it is distinguished from the more general LATIN JAZZ by the specific influence of Cuban dance, folk, and popular idioms. Although a Latin-American or Caribbean influence (Jelly Roll Morton called it the "Latin tinge") is discernible in jazz from the late 19th century, the earliest use of Cuban elements is traceable only to Alberto Socarras and Mario Bauzá in the late 1930s. Notable examples of recordings exhibiting such elements are Woody Herman's *Bijou* (subtitled *Rhumba à la Jazz*, 1945, Col. 36861) and Charlie Barnet's *New Redskin Rumba* (1946, Cardinal 25001). However, Afro-Cuban jazz became a clearly defined style and acquired an international following only when Gillespie, who had been influenced by Bauzá, began to collaborate with the outstanding Cuban percussionist Chano Pozo. For Gillespie, Bauzá, and others, the main impulse for the Afro-Cuban movement came from their feeling that American jazz of the 1930s and 1940s, being essentially monorhythmic, needed the kind of enrichment that an infusion of Afro-Cuban polyrhythms would provide.

Gillespie's big band made several notable recordings in the late 1940s, including Pozo's compositions *Manteca* (1947, Vic. 203023), *Afro-Cuban Suite* (on the album of the same name, 1948, Swing 33301), and *Guarachi guaro* (1948, Vic. 203370), and George Russell's *Cubana be/Cubana bop* (1947, Vic. 203145); these pieces, which feature Pozo's conga drumming, were the first to integrate authentic Afro-Cuban polyrhythmic concepts with the bop idiom. Soon other big bands began to make recordings in the Afro-Cuban style; Stan Kenton's *Machito* (1947, Cap. 900), *Peanut Vendor* (1947, Cap. 904), *Cuban Episode* (1950, Cap. 28000), and *Twenty Three Degrees North, Eighty Two Degrees West* (1952, Cap. 3134), and Machito's *Cubop City* (1948, Roost 502), *Afro Cuban Jazz Suite* (1950, Clef 505), *Kenya* (1957, Roul. 52006), and *Afro-jazziac* (on the album *With Flute to Boot*, 1958, Roul. 52026) are noteworthy examples. Smaller groups also contributed significantly to the new genre, in particular those led by Tadd Dameron (*Jahbero*, 1948, BN 559), Charlie Parker (*My Little Suede Shoes*, 1951, Mer./Clef 11093), and Bud Powell (*Un poco loco*, 1951, BN 1577).

Gillespie's band continued to perform Afro-Cuban jazz throughout the 1950s, and recorded such titles as *Manteca Suite* (on the album *Afro*, 1954, Norg. 1003) and *Gillespiana* (1960, Verve 8394). A number of prominent Cuban percussionists were active during the same period; among these were Candido Camero, Armando Peraza (who made recordings with George Shearing, notably *Poodle Mambo* on the album *Latin Escapade*, 1956, Cap. T737), and Mongo Santamaria, who recorded the albums *Yambu* (1958, Fan. 3267) and *Mongo* (1959, Fan. 3291) with his own band.

While the impact of Afro-Cuban jazz began to wane in jazz circles by the end of the 1950s, Cuban and other Caribbean-oriented musicians, coming under the influence of modern jazz, maintained the fusion of the two genres, but with a slight shift of emphasis towards the Cuban side of the equation. Ray Barretto, Eddie Palmieri, Bobby Paunetto, and Santamaria helped further to "Latinize" Afro-Cuban jazz and thereby also to broaden its scope and definition.

BIBLIOGRAPHY

F. Ortiz: *La africanía de la música folklórica de Cuba* (Havana, 1950) [incl. transcrs.]

M. W. Stearns: *The Story of Jazz* (New York, 1956, rev. and enlarged 2/1958, enlarged 1970)

J. S. Roberts: *Black Music of Two Worlds* (New York, Washington, and London, 1972), chap.8

——: *The Latin Tinge: the Impact of Latin American Music on the United States* (New York, and Oxford, England, 1979), chap.5

GUNTHER SCHULLER

AFRS [Armed Forces Radio Service]. Broadcasting and recording organization, and record label. The organization was established in 1942 as the Radio Section of the Special Service Division of the US War Department; this title appears in full on the earliest discs issued on the label, made before the name AFRS was adopted late in 1943. The service was formed to broadcast to American military bases abroad; the recording department provided fully produced radio programs for this purpose, at first on 16-inch transcription discs, later (from the mid-1950s) on tape. The AFRS became the largest recording enterprise in history. In 1953 it was renamed the Armed Forces Radio and Television Service (AFR&TS); it has remained in operation into the late 1980s.

Much of the organization's material has consisted of copies of commercially issued recordings, which are released in such series as the Basic Music Library and the Gold Label Library. Nevertheless, some series have contained recordings of broadcasts made first on commercial radio stations, or of live performances specially commissioned by the AFRS. These were particularly prevalent in the 1940s, when demand was at its peak (during World War II) and the supply of commercial material was restricted because of recording bans. Such series as Spotlight Bands, One Night Stand, GI Jive, and Command Performance include recordings of hundreds of live performances by jazz and big bands which form an extensive documentation of great value. Especially notable is the Jubilee Series, started in October 1942, which at first contained only performances by black musicians and ran to 365 transcriptions before being discontinued in 1950. Many of these were introduced by the comedian Ernie "Bubbles" Whitman, and included material by the big bands of Duke Ellington, Count Basie, Benny Carter, Lionel Hampton, and Lucky Millinder, as well as items by smaller groups and soloists. (A brief revival of the series in 1952–3 during the war in Korea is of lesser importance.)

Many other sequences of AFRS recordings include items of jazz interest, and one, A Date with the Duke (1945–6), consists entirely of material by Duke Ellington – 79 transcriptions of broadcasts made for the US Treasury Department. Concert performances by Louis Armstrong were issued in the series Here's to Veterans. A collection of more than 150,000 discs made by AFRS and AFR&TS is in the Library of Congress in Washington; *see* LIBRARIES AND ARCHIVES, §2.

BIBLIOGRAPHY

T. S. DeLay, Jr.: *An Historical Study of the Armed Forces Radio Service to 1946* (diss., U. of Southern California, 1951)

J. Valburn and B. Aaslund: "A Look at the Date with the Duke Transcriptions," *Discographer*, ii/1 (1969)

R. E. Lotz: *The AFR & TS (Gold Label) Transcription Library: a Label Listing* (Menden, Germany, 1978)

R. E. Lotz and U. Neuert: *The AFRS "Jubilee" Transcription Programs: an Exploratory Discography* (Frankfurt am Main, Germany, 1985)

Afterbeat. Any beat of the bar other than the first beat, or downbeat; *see* BEAT, §4(i).

Ahead of the beat. Expression used to describe the performance of a player or singer who places notes slightly before the beat, as articulated by the rhythm section or implied by the playing of the rest of the ensemble; *see* BEAT, §2.

Aho, Erkki (*b* Lapinjärvi, nr Lovisa, Finland, 10 Dec 1918). Finnish trumpeter and trombonist. He began his career in dance bands in the late 1930s in Helsinki; he played with Eugen Malmstén and others. During World War II he led a band that introduced the big-band swing style to Finland; as the Rytmi-orkesteri it made a series of recordings in 1944, including a version of W. C. Handy's *St. Louis Blues* (Rytmi 2052). Aho later abandoned jazz and played trumpet in the Tampere SO (1963–71). (O. Häme: *Rytmin voittokulku* [The triumph of rhythm] (Helsinki, 1949), 159)

PEKKA GRONOW

Ahola, Sylvester [Hooley] (*b* Gloucester, MA, 24 May 1902). Trumpeter. After playing in the brass band of the local Finnish-American temperance society, he became a professional dance-band musician in Boston. In 1925 he moved to New York to play with the violinist and bandleader Paul Specht. From 1927 he lived in London, where he performed with the Savoy Orpheans and Ambrose and his Orchestra, and played in many studio groups. He moved back to the USA in 1931 and worked as a studio musician in New York, then returned to Gloucester in 1940. Ahola was much admired for his technique, pure tone, and imaginative solos, but he never recorded jazz as a leader. His solos are scattered through the hundreds of recordings he made with obscure and often indifferent studio groups. From the 1970s his work was the subject of renewed interest among record collectors.

SELECTED RECORDINGS

As sideman: P. Specht: Static Strut (1926, Col. 627D); Rhythmic Eight: Can't help lovin' dat man (1928, Zonophone 5185); Arcadians Dance Orchestra: When I met Connie in the cornfield (1929, Zonophone 5429); P. Lewis: That's a plenty (1929, Decca F1573); Night Club Kings: Someone (1930, HMV B5776); B. Ambrose: A girlfriend of a boyfriend of mine (1930, HMV B5909)

BIBLIOGRAPHY

B. Rust: "An American in London," *Vintage Jazz Mart* (1966), June, p.4; Sept, p.5; Nov, p.6; (1967), Feb, p.4; July, p.4

W. Vaché, Sr.: "Hooley," *MR*, vii/12 (1980), 1

P. Gronow: "Ethnic Recordings: an Introduction," *Ethnic Recordings in America: a Neglected Heritage: Washington 1977* (Washington, 1982) [pubn of the American Folklife Center, Library of Congress], 10

PEKKA GRONOW

Aiken [Aitken], **Gus** [Augustine] (*b* Charleston, SC, 26 July 1902; *d* New York, April 1973). Trumpeter. He was brought up in the Jenkins' Orphanage in Charleston, South Carolina, where he received extensive musical tuition; he also toured with the orphanage bands. In about 1921 he moved to New York, and later toured with the Black Swan Masters under the direction of Fletcher Henderson. He recorded with Ethel Waters (1921), Perry Bradford (1923), Charlie Johnson (1930), the Mills Blue Rhythm Band (1930), Luis Russell (1931), Elmer Snowden (1932), and Lucky Millinder (*c*1934). He worked regularly with Russell from 1934 (remaining with the band under Louis Armstrong's leadership), then in 1937 joined a band led by Alberto Socarras. In 1941 he recorded four titles, including *Swing Parade* (Vic. 27574), with Sidney Bechet. After a brief period with Budd Johnson (1944) he worked in New York as a freelance musician; he played with Jimmy Archey (*c*1951), and in the 1960s led his own band. Aiken's elder brother Gene "Bud" Aiken (*d* 21 Aug 1927), who was also a member of the Jenkins' Orphanage bands, played trombone and trumpet. (J. Chilton: *A Jazz Nursery: the Story of the Jenkins' Orphanage Bands*, London, 1980)

based on *ChiltonW*

Air. Free-jazz trio. In 1971 the alto saxophonist Henry Threadgill was asked to arrange music by the ragtime composer Scott Joplin for a theater production at Columbia College, Chicago; with the drummer Steve McCall and the double bass player Fred Hopkins he formed a cooperative trio called Reflection to perform the material (which was eventually recorded in 1979, on the trio's seventh album). Reflection broke up in 1972, but when McCall returned in 1975 from a period in Europe it was re-formed in New York under the name Air. The trio recorded its first album that year and subsequently toured Europe, Japan, and the USA; by 1986 it had made 11 recordings. During the 1980s McCall was replaced by Pheeroan Ak Laff (1982), and later by Andrew Cyrille (by 1985), and the group re-formed again as New Air. Threadgill, who composed most of the group's repertory, performed in *Air Mail* (1980, BS 0049) on the hubkaphone, a percussion instrument that he built from hubcaps. Air is unusual, even within the domain of free jazz, for the equality of the members' roles in the ensemble. Like Albert Ayler's trio of 1964 and to a greater extent than the Revolutionary Ensemble, the group has avoided the traditional divisions of solo and accompaniment.

For further recording details *see* THREADGILL, HENRY.

BIBLIOGRAPHY

J. B. Litweiler: "Air: Impossible to Pigeonhole," *DB*, xliii/21 (1976), 22
B. McRae: "Avant Courier: Air," *JJI*, xxxvi/6 (1983), 6

HOWARD MANDEL

Air check [air shot]. A recording made from a broadcast, usually by an enthusiast using a recorder in his home. The term is normally used of recordings made during the era of the 78 r.p.m. disc. *See* TRANSCRIPTION (ii); *see also* RECORDING, §II, 3.

Airto. *See* MOREIRA, AIRTO.

Ajax. Record company and label. The company was established by the Compo Co. of Lachine, Canada, which marketed records through its subsidiary, the Ajax Record Co. of Chicago. Although the label name was registered as a trademark in 1921, issue is not thought to have begun until October 1923; it ceased in the summer of 1925. The label was used to put out race records, most of which were made in New York; a few, however, were recorded in the company's studios in Montreal, and some were leased from Pathé and Plaza. The recordings provide important evidence of the jazz and vaudeville blues styles prevalent in New York at the time.

BIBLIOGRAPHY

W. C. Allen: "Discomania, 53: Ajax," *JJ*, ix (1956), no.7, p.56; no.8, p.30; x (1957), no.7, p.8; no.10, p.29; xi/3 (1958), 7
J. Godrich and R. M. W. Dixon: *Blues and Gospel Records, 1902–1942* (Hatch End, nr London, 1964, rev. 2/1969, rev. and enlarged 3/1982 as R. M. W. Dixon and J. Godrich: *Blues and Gospel Records, 1902–1943*), 25
C. Kendziora: "Behind the Cobwebs: Ajax," *Record Research*, no.74 (1966), 6
R. M. W. Dixon and J. Godrich: *Recording the Blues* (London, 1970), 32
B. Rust: *The American Record Label Book* (New Rochelle, NY, 1978), 13

Akiyoshi, Toshiko (*b* Dairen, China, 12 Dec 1929). Composer, pianist, and bandleader. She studied classical music and turned to jazz only in 1947 after moving to Japan. There she was discovered by visiting American jazz musicians, among them Oscar Peterson, who urged her to take up a career in the USA. After studying at the Berklee College of Music in Boston (1956–9) she became an active and highly regarded bop pianist, especially in groups with Charlie Mariano (who was at that time her husband), and with Charles Mingus (1962). In 1973 she founded a large rehearsal band in Los Angeles with Lew Tabackin, whom she married. Its first album, *Kogun*, was commercially successful in Japan, and the group attracted increasing popularity and critical acclaim until, by 1980, it was generally regarded as the leading big band in jazz; among its sidemen have been Gary Foster, Dick Spencer, and Bobby Shew. The band allowed Akiyoshi to cultivate her gifts as a composer, and she has written a number of rich, subtle scores in the modern big-band tradition of Gil Evans and Thad Jones and Mel Lewis, often incorporating elements from Japanese music. Her compositions, several of which have been published by Toba Music, Hollywood, include *Kogun*, *American Ballad*, *Long Yellow Road*, and *Sumi-e*. (Scores by her are in the George P. Vanier Library of Concordia University, Montreal; *see* LIBRARIES AND ARCHIVES, §2.) She has continued to develop as a pianist, playing in a delicate, accurate bop style, and in 1984 she was the subject of a documentary film, *Toshiko Akiyoshi: Jazz is my Native Language*. By 1985 she and Tabackin had disbanded their group and Akiyoshi had formed a new big band, Toshiko Akiyoshi's New York Jazz Orchestra.

For illustration *see* TABACKIN, LEW.

SELECTED RECORDINGS

Small group: *Toshiko's Piano* (1953, Norg. 22); with C. Mariano: *Mariano–Toshiko Quartet* (1963, Takt 12); *Dedications* (1976, 1977, Disco Mate 5001, 5006); *Toshiko Akiyoshi Plays Billy Strayhorn* (1978, Disco Mate 5011); *Finesse* (1978, Conc. 69), incl. American Ballad

Big band: with L. Tabackin: *Kogun* (1974, RCA JPL1-0236); *Long Yellow Road* (1974–5, RCA JPL1-1350); *Tales of a Courtesan* (1975, RCA JPL1-0723); *Road Time* (1976, RCA CLP2-2242); *Insights* (1976, RCA AFL1-2678); *Sumi-e* (1979, Insights 6061); *Tanuki's Night Out* (1981, JAM 006)

BIBLIOGRAPHY

"Toshiko Akiyoshi Discography," *SJ*, xxviii/12 (1974), 76
L. Feather: "East Meets West or Never the Twain Shall Cease," *DB*, xliii/11 (1976), 16
——: "Toshiko Akiyoshi: Contemporary Sculptress of Sound," *DB*, xliv/17 (1977), 13
C. Sheridan: "The Manchurian Candidate," *JJI*, xxxii/1 (1979), 6
G. Endress: *Jazz Podium: Musiker über sich selbst* (Stuttgart, Germany, 1980), 174
L. Feather: "Akiyoshi/Tabackin," *The Passion for Jazz* (New York, 1980), 109
——: "Toshiko Akiyoshi," *CK*, vii/9 (1980), 58
P. Rothbart: "Toshiko Akiyoshi," *DB*, xlvii/8 (1980), 14
C. Kuhl: "Akiyoshi & Tabackin: Interview," *Cadence*, viii/7 (1982), 8
L. Lyons: *The Great Jazz Pianists, Speaking of their Lives and Music* (New York, 1983), 250
N. Sodetani: "She's a Jazzy, Japanese Pianist," *San Francisco Examiner* (19 Jan 1986), 40

J. BRADFORD ROBINSON

Ak Laff, Pheeroan [Maddox, Paul] (*b* Detroit, 1955). Drummer. He played free jazz with Jay Hoggard in 1975. His work in New Haven, Connecticut, with Leo Smith's group New Dalta Ahkri led to long associations with Oliver Lake and Anthony Davis: in New York he performed and recorded as a member of Lake's trio with Michael Gregory Jackson (1978–9), as a member of the quartet led by Davis and James Newton (1978–9), and with Davis's Episteme (from 1981) and Lake's reggae group Jump Up (from 1983). He also recorded with Amina Claudine Myers (1979) and Baikida Carroll (1982) and performed and recorded with Henry Threadgill's AIR (from 1982). From 1982 he was active as a leader (recording *Fits like a Glove*, Gram. 8207, in 1983) and soloist.

BIBLIOGRAPHY

R. Riggins: "Pheeroan Ak Laff," *Coda*, no.186 (1982), 8
C. Stern: "Pheeroan Ak Laff: Groovin' Free," *MD*, viii/5 (1984), 14

Alabama Washboard Stompers. Name under which the personnel of the WASHBOARD RHYTHM KINGS also recorded.

Albalat, Sebastià (*b* Spain, *c*1905; *d* after 1949). Spanish tenor saxophonist. He learned music as a youth, but preferred to improvise rather than study conventionally. At the age of 20 he traveled to New York; he later moved to Paris and then to Berlin, where he played mainly tangos and Latin-American music. After returning to Spain at the beginning of the 1930s he worked with the best jazz bands in Barcelona. He continued to play during the 1940s and was considered one of the finest Spanish saxophonists. *Leonor/Si yo tocara bien la concertina* (Odeon 203952), which he recorded as a leader around 1944, offer good examples of his style.

ALFREDO PAPO

Albam, Manny [Emmanuel] (*b* Samaná, Dominican Republic, 24 June 1922). Arranger and composer. He was brought up in New York, where he first played (usually baritone saxophone) and wrote arrangements for Don Joseph (1940), Muggsy Spanier (1941), Bob Chester (1942), Georgie Auld (1942–5), Charlie Spivak, and Boyd Raeburn (1943–5). Following army service (1945–6) he undertook similar work for Sam Donahue (1947), Charlie Barnet (1948–9), Jerry Wald (1949), and others. In 1951 he gave up playing to concentrate on arranging and composing. He achieved considerable success during the 1950s and 1960s with several albums recorded as the director of his own studio bands, and also with his arrangements for prominent jazz musicians, including leaders of small groups (Terry Gibbs, Hal McKusick, Gerry Mulligan, Dizzy Gillespie, Al Cohn, and Stan Getz), and big bands (Count Basie, Woody Herman, Stan Kenton, Buddy Rich) as well as singers (Sarah Vaughan, Carmen McRae, Dakota Staton). From 1958 to 1960 Albam studied with Tibor Serly, and from 1964 became active in jazz education, teaching at the Eastman School's summer arranging workshops and at Glassboro State College. His compositions, which appeal to a broad public, include large-scale pieces for jazz band (such as *The Blues is Everybody's Business* and the suite *Soul of the City*) as well as chamber music (much of it written for the tuba player Harvey Phillips) and music for films and television; manuscript scores of his works are in the holdings of the BMI Archives in New York. One of the most important mainstream jazz arrangers of the 1950s and 1960s, Albam never lost touch with the qualities of swing and blues in his writing.

RECORDED COMPOSITIONS
(selective list)

The Blues is Everybody's Business (1957, Coral 59101); *Soul of the City* (*c*1966, SolS 18009)

SELECTED ARRANGEMENTS

As leader: *The Jazz Workshop* (1955, RCA LPM1211); *The Drum Suite* (1956, RCA LPM1279); *Manny Albam and his Orchestra* (1961, RCA LSA2432); *Jazz Goes to the Movies* (1962, Imp. 19); *Brass on Fire* (*c*1966, SolS 18000)
Recorded by others: on W. Herman: *Road Band* (1955, Cap. T658), Captain Ahab; H. McKusick: *In a 20th-century Drawing Room* (1955, RCA LPM1164); J. Newman: *I'm Still Swingin'* (1955, RCA LPM1198); T. Gibbs: *Vibes on Velvet* (1955, EmA 36064)

BIBLIOGRAPHY

FeatherE
L. Feather: "One Manny's Opinion," *DB*, xxiv/4 (1957), 33
D. Cerulli: "Manny Albam," *BMI: the Many Worlds of Music* (1968), May, 12
"A Gallery of Composers," *BMI: the Many Worlds of Music* (1981), no.3, p.22

STEVEN STRUNK

Albany, Joe [Albani, Joseph] (*b* Atlantic City, NJ, 24 Jan 1924; *d* New York, 12 Jan 1988). Pianist. He studied accordion as a child and took up piano in high school. He moved to the West Coast when he was 17 and in 1942 joined Leo Watson's group, heard Art Tatum, and met Lester Young. After playing with Benny Carter (1943) and Georgie Auld he met Charlie Parker (New York, 1944); the two men lived together and took drugs together. In 1945 Albany worked again with Auld and then performed with Boyd Raeburn. In 1946 he played with Parker in Los Angeles, but was dismissed owing to an argument; the same year he recorded four sides with Young, and his reputation rested on these alone until a recording of a rehearsal with Warne Marsh was issued in 1957. In the late 1950s he wrote songs for Anita O'Day, and in 1963 played with Charles Mingus at the Village Gate, New York. He lived for a period in Europe, then returned to the USA and played in New York in the late 1970s. Among the pianists who influenced Albany were Tatum, Count Basie and, later, Bud Powell and Thelonious Monk. In the 1940s he sought to imitate Tatum, but, by his own admission, lacked the skill. He effectively transferred Parker's melodic style to the keyboard, constructing long, drawn-out lines; he became noted for his renditions of ballads and, in later years, for his fluent left-hand technique. He is a highly respected musician but rarely heard, because his career was checkered by decades of drug addiction and periods of time spent in prison. He is the subject of Carole Langer's documentary film, *Joe Albany . . . a Jazz Life* (1980).

Oral history material in *NjR*.

SELECTED RECORDINGS

As unaccompanied soloist: *At Home Alone* (1971, Rev. 25)
As leader: *The Right Combination* (1957, Riv. 270); *Proto-Bopper* (1972, Rev. 16); *Birdtown Birds* (1973, Ste. 1003); *Bird Lives* (1979, Inter. 7723); *Portrait of an Artist* (1982, Elek. Mus. 60161), incl. Confirmation
As sideman: G. Auld: Honey/Stompin' at the Savoy (1945, Guild 135); L. Young: New Lester Leaps in (1946, Ala. 137); Lester's Bebop Boogie (1946, Ala. 138)

BIBLIOGRAPHY

Feather–Gitler '70s
R. Russell: "The Legendary Joe Albany," *JR*, ii/3 (1959), 18
I. Gitler: "Portrait of a Legend: Joe Albany," *DB*, xxx/28 (1963), 20
J. Shaw: "Joe Albany: Out of the Wilderness," *Mainstream*, no.1 (1974), 12
H. Pekar: "Joe Albany," *Coda*, xii/5 (1975), 10
D. Tarrant and C. Evans: "Joe Albany Discography," *Journal of Jazz Discography*, no.4 (1979), 2
L. Jeske: "Profile: Joe Albany," *DB*, xlvii/6 (1980), 54

ANDRÉ BARBERA

Albert, Don [Dominique, Albert] (*b* New Orleans, 5 Aug 1908; *d* San Antonio, Jan 1980). Trumpeter and bandleader, nephew of Natty Dominique. He was active in New Orleans and the Southwest during the 1920s and toured with one of Alphonso

Trent's bands (1925) and Troy Floyd (1926–9). Throughout the 1930s and 1940s he was based in Texas and led his own touring band, which launched the careers of Alvin Alcorn, Louis Cottrell, Jr., and Herb Hall. Albert played only occasionally himself, preferring to manage and lead the band and write arrangements for it; he recorded his arrangement of *Rockin' and Swingin'* in 1936 (Voc. 3401). In the 1950s he settled in San Antonio and until the mid-1970s played with small groups. His later work may be heard on *Echoes of New Orleans* (1962, Slnd 239).

Oral history material in *LNT*.

BIBLIOGRAPHY

ChiltonW

F. Driggs: "Don Albert," *JM*, v/5 (1959), 4

D. Allen: "Don Albert and his Ten Pals," *Sv*, no.31 (1970), 18 [incl. discography]

R. Russell: *Jazz Style in Kansas City and the Southwest* (Berkeley, CA, and elsewhere, 1971/*R*1983)

A. McCarthy: *Big Band Jazz* (New York and London, 1974)

LAWRENCE KOCH

Album. A term applied in popular-music usage to a long-playing disc of any kind (normally a 12-inch disc) or, latterly, to a cassette or compact disc; also the collection of musical numbers or the continuous piece recorded on the disc, cassette, or compact disc. The term was first used of recordings in the era of 78 r.p.m. discs when sets of records (carrying, for example, the separate items recorded on a single session, or a long piece running over several discs) were sold in album-like containers consisting of individual liners bound between hard covers. Since the discs were also available separately they carried separate matrix and issue numbers but sometimes the albums had issue numbers of their own. From around 1950 the word was used of the long-playing microgroove disc on which a similar group of numbers or a continuous performance was recorded; a "double" or "triple" album consists of two or three such discs issued in a folder. *See also* Recording, §I, 3.

Alcorn, Alvin (Elmore) (*b* New Orleans, 7 Sept 1912). Trumpeter. He was taught music theory by his brother Oliver (*b* New Orleans, 3 Aug 1910; *d* New Orleans, 1981), a clarinetist and alto saxophonist. In the late 1920s and early 1930s he worked in New Orleans with his own group, with the violinists Clarence Desdune and A. J. Piron, and with the Sunny South Syncopators. Then from 1932 to 1937 he toured with Don Albert's band. Apart from a period of army service during World War II he continued to play with bands in New Orleans, notably those of Sidney Desvigne, Papa Celestin, and Alphonse Picou, until the mid-1950s, when he worked in California with Kid Ory. Alcorn made some of his finest recordings while with Ory's band; he also appeared in the film *The Benny Goodman Story* (1955) and toured Europe (1956) with the group. He then returned to New Orleans and performed regularly with various bands into the 1980s. He made several more tours of Europe – with the New Orleans All Stars (1966), as a soloist (1973, 1974, 1976), and with Chris Barber's Jazz Band (1978) – and one of Australia (1973); he also appeared in the film *Live and Let Die* (1973).

Alcorn's technique is quite equal to the lead and solo work he attempts, but he is at his best when leading an ensemble. He favors the middle range of the instrument and plays with a well-rounded tone and controlled vibrato; he also uses mutes in a creative manner. His style is economical and contained rather than hot or overtly emotional.

Alcorn's son Sam (Samuel) is also a trumpeter.

Oral history material in *LNT*.

SELECTED RECORDINGS

As leader: [untitled] (1970, The Right to Profit and all that Jazz Again [unnumbered]), incl. Bogalusa Strut, Sugar Blues; *An Original New Orleans Jazz Brunch* (1976, Sandcastle 1030)

As sideman: K. Ory: *Kid Ory's Creole Jazz Band 1954* (1954, GTJ 12004); *The Legendary Kid* (1955, GTJ 12016); on Eureka Brass Band: *The Love–Jiles Ragtime Orchestra and the Eureka Brass Band* (1959, 1968, Sounds of New Orleans 1), Nearer my God to thee

BIBLIOGRAPHY

ChiltonW; FeatherE

A. Rose and E. Souchon: *New Orleans Jazz: a Family Album* (Baton Rouge, LA, 1967, rev. 2/1978, rev. and enlarged 3/1984)

P. Van Vorst: Liner notes, *Alvin Alcorn and his New Orleans Jazz Band* (New Orleans 7205, 1975)

ALAN BARRELL

Aldebert, Louis (J.) (*b* Ismā' ilīya, Egypt, 8 June 1931). French singer and pianist. He studied music in Paris and played piano with Don Byas (1955) and Stephane Grappelli (1957). He was a singer with the Blue Stars (1955–6), toured and recorded with the Double Six (1959–65), and played in a session with Jon Hendricks and others in 1965. He was married to the singer Monique Dozo (*b* Monaco, 5 May 1931; later known as Monique Aldebert-Guérin), who had sung with Bernard Peiffer (1947) and performed in Paris clubs with Byas, Django Reinhardt, Bobby Jaspar, the Double Six (with which she recorded in 1959 and 1964), and Bill Coleman (1966). After moving to the USA in 1967, they settled first in Las Vegas, where they appeared in revues, and then in Los Angeles (1969). They sang in local clubs, made concert appearances with their own small vocal groups, and recorded with the Crusaders (1979); Monique was also active as a studio musician in films, television, and radio. Besides their performing activities, the Aldeberts have written a number of songs and made vocal arrangements of jazz tunes. (*Feather–Gitler '70s*)

Alemán, Oscar (Marcelo) (*b* Resistencia, Argentina, 20 Feb 1909; *d* Buenos Aires, 10 Oct 1980). Argentinian guitarist. He took up guitar in his teens and in 1924 he formed a guitar duo with Gaston Bueno Lobo. In the late 1920s the dancer Harry Fleming engaged the duo (known as Los Lobos) to play in Spain. By 1931 Alemán was in Paris leading the Baker Boys, who accompanied the popular singer Josephine Baker; he then played regularly with Freddy Taylor's Swing Men from Harlem (1933–5) and led a band with Frank "Big Boy" Goudie at Le Chantilly. Alemán returned in 1941 to Buenos Aires, where he continued to play and record.

Alemán made his first jazz recordings in the mid-1930s: he played in sessions with Taylor (1935), Bill Coleman (1936), Eddie Brunner (1938), and Danny Polo (1939). As a leader he recorded in Europe in 1939–40 and in Buenos Aires steadily from the early 1940s to the end of the 1970s. He was one of the most competent and inventive swing guitarists. Like Django Reinhardt, to whom he is often compared, he employed a classical "finger-picking" technique in the right hand, but his playing was more linear than Reinhardt's and he produced a fuller, heavier sound; his improvisations were colored by South American dance music.

SELECTED RECORDINGS

As unaccompanied soloist: Nobody's Sweetheart/Whispering (1938, HMV X6213)

As leader: Sweet Sue (1938, HMV X6212); Just a Little Swing (1939, Swing 213); Sweet Georgia Brown (1941, Odeon 45780); *Oscar Alemán y sus cinco caballeros* (1965, Impacto 14014); *Alemán '72* (1972, Redondel 10508)

As sideman: B. Coleman: Joe Louis Stomp/Coquette (1936, HMV K7705)

BIBLIOGRAPHY

M. Abell: "Oscar Alemán: 'l'enfant terrible'," *Doctor Jazz*, no.45 (1970–71), 4

C. Delaunay: "Un guitariste méconnu: Oscar Alemán," *Jh*, no.283 (1972), 25
J. Evensmo: *The Guitars of Charlie Christian, Robert Normann, Oscar Alemán (in Europe)* (n.p. [Oslo], n.d. [?1976]) [discography]
M. Grosz and L. Cohn: Liner notes, *Giants of Jazz: the Guitarists* (TL 12, 1980), 33
T. Mooney: "Oscar Alemán: Swing Guitarist," *JJI*, xxxv (1982), no.4, p.10; no.5, p.14
M. Pahls: Liner notes, *Oscar Alemán: Swing Guitar Legend* (Rambler 106, 1982)

GARY CARNER

Aless, Tony [Alessandrini, Anthony] (*b* Garfield, NJ, 22 Aug 1921). Pianist and leader. He played with Bunny Berigan (*c*1938) and performed and recorded with Teddy Powell (1941–2). After serving in the army he appeared briefly with Charlie Spivak and played and recorded with Woody Herman (1945–6); he also recorded with Georgie Auld (1945), Flip Phillips (1945), Chubby Jackson (1945, 1947, 1950), Neal Hefti (1946–7), Charlie Parker (1948, 1953), and Stan Getz (1950); his playing is well represented on Jackson's *"Mom" Jackson* (1947, MGM 10354). Later he performed on radio and in 1955 recorded with George Handy and Seldon Powell and as the leader of a group playing his own compositions (*Long Island Suite*, Roost 2202). (*FeatherE*)

Alexander, Charlie [Charles] (*b* Cincinnati, *c*1904; *d* California, *c*1970). Pianist. He studied music and played in theater orchestras in Cincinnati. After moving to Chicago he worked with Johnny and Baby Dodds and in 1927–8 made a number of recordings under the former's leadership, including *Blue Piano Stomp* (1928, Vic. 21554). He was house pianist at Bert Kelly's Stables, then in spring 1931 joined Louis Armstrong's big band. The following year, after Armstrong's group disbanded, he returned to Chicago to work for a while before settling in California. (K. G. zur Heide: "Footnotes, 29: Charlie Alexander," *Fn*, viii/6 (1977), 31)

based on *ChiltonW*

Alexander, Monty [Montgomery Bernard] (*b* Kingston, Jamaica, 6 June 1944). Jamaican pianist. He moved to Miami in 1961 and began working in local clubs, and in 1967 traveled to New York, where he played at Minton's Playhouse and other establishments. For five summer seasons he worked with Milt Jackson and Ray Brown, recording with both musicians. He then formed his own trio, with which he toured Europe in 1974 and 1980; the group's appearance at the Montreux International Jazz Festival in 1976 was particularly successful. Alexander has absorbed several mainstream styles, in which he is a skilled performer; Art Tatum, Oscar Peterson, Erroll Garner, and Nat "King" Cole have been major influences on his work. His Jamaican heritage has imparted a Caribbean flavor to his music, as may be heard on *Cobilimbo*, and he has also recorded several rhythm-and-blues tunes. He is noted for his highly rhythmic approach and melodic and harmonic inventiveness derived from mainstream jazz.

SELECTED RECORDINGS

As leader: *Here Comes the Sun* (1971, MPS 2120913); *Montreux Alexander* (1976, MPS 68170); with M. Jackson: *Soul Fusion* (1977, Pablo 2310804); *Cobilimbo* (1977, MPS 68188); *Jamento* (1978, Pablo 2310826); *Facets* (1979, Conc. 108); *Triple Treat* (1982, Conc. 193)

BIBLIOGRAPHY

S. Quaver: "Monty Alexander . . . and All that Sinful Jazz," *CI*, xiii/6 (1975), 9
D. Spitzer: "Profile: Monty Alexander," *DB*, xlii/9 (1975), 26
L. Tomkins: "The Monty Alexander Story," *CI*, xiii/10 (1975), 6; contd as "The Philosophy of Swing: Expounded by Monty Alexander," xiii/11 (1975), 14; contd as "Monty Alexander Says the Piano is an Orchestra," xiii/12 (1975), 6
L. Lyons: "Monty Alexander: Spirited Jamaican Jazz Pianist," *CK*, iv/8 (1978), 14 [incl. discography]
M. Hennessey: "Europajazz," *JT* (1984), July, 8
——: "Alexander the Great," *JJI*, xxxix/11 (1986), 6 [incl. discography]

PAUL RINZLER

Alexander, Mousey [Mousie; Elmer] (*b* Gary, IN, 29 June 1922). Drummer. He worked as a dixieland drummer with Jimmy McPartland in Chicago (1948–50) and in 1952 he moved to New York, where he performed and recorded for a year as a member of Marian McPartland's bop trio. After spending three years with the Sauter–Finegan Orchestra he played briefly with Johnny Smith (1955–6), with whom he also recorded (1955, 1957, 1959–60). He belonged to Benny Goodman's band for four years from 1956, but between engagements with Goodman played and recorded with other leaders, among them Bud Freeman (1958) and Buck Clayton (1960), and performed at Eddie Condon's club in New York. After 1965 he worked intermittently with a quintet led by Al Cohn and Zoot Sims, toured with the popular singer Paul Anka (1966), and played with Goodman's sextet (1966–7, 1972). He led his own trio (1968–9) and quartet (1974), played with James Moody (1972), Sonny Stitt (1972), and Sy Oliver (1973), and performed and recorded with Clark Terry (1969–72), Lee Konitz (1971, 1972), and Sims (1977, 1978). In the mid- to late 1970s he recorded often for the Famous Door label. He was partly paralyzed by a stroke in 1980.

SELECTED RECORDINGS

As leader: *The Mouse Roars* (1979, FaD 130)
As sideman: B. Clayton: *Buck and Buddy* (1960, Swingville 2017); L. Konitz: *Spirits* (1971, Mlst. 9038); B. Goodman: *On Stage with Benny Goodman and his Sextet* (1972, Lon. 44182–3); Z. Sims: *Warm Tenor* (1978, Pablo 2310831)

BIBLIOGRAPHY

FeatherE; *Feather–Gitler '70s*
"It's All Starting to Come Alive Again, Opines Mousey Alexander," *CI*, x/12 (1972), 14

RICK MATTINGLY

Alexandria, Lorez [Nelson [née Turner], Dolorez Alexandria] (*b* Chicago, 14 Aug 1929). Singer. She grew up in a musical family, and sang gospel music at churches during the 1940s and early 1950s; she was also a member of a choral group that performed spirituals, jubilee music, comedy numbers, and other secular songs, which influenced her subsequent choice of repertory as a soloist. Later she sang at clubs in Chicago with the pianist King Fleming and others, and recorded four albums (1957–9). She performed with Ramsey Lewis in 1958 during an engagement at the Cloister which lasted seven months. Thereafter Alexandria began to concentrate on mainstream jazz and popular music; she recorded six albums in the early 1960s, using such sidemen as Lewis's trio and members of Count Basie's orchestra (1960), Howard McGhee (1962), and Wynton Kelly's trio (1964). After moving to Los Angeles in 1964 she performed on television and at clubs and concerts on the West Coast. She has continued to perform and record regularly into the 1980s, often with such distinguished musicians as Gildo Mahones.

SELECTED RECORDINGS

This is Lorez Alexandria with the King Fleming Quartet (1957, King 542); *Deep Roots* (1960, Argo 682); *A Woman Knows* (1978, Dis. 800); *Harlem Butterfly* (*c*1984, Dis. 905)

BIBLIOGRAPHY

Feather '60s
J. Tynan: "Lorez Alexandria," *DB*, xxxi/1 (1964), 18
P. Elmwood: "Jazz with a Blues Gospel Touch," *San Francisco Examiner* (24 Oct 1986), §D, p.17

MARTY HATCH

Members of John Coltrane's quartet at the Newport Jazz Festival, July 1966: (left to right) Jimmy Garrison (double bass), Rashied Ali (drums), and Coltrane (soprano saxophone)

Ali, Rashied [Patterson, Robert] (*b* Philadelphia, 1 July 1935). Drummer. He studied in Philadelphia at the Granoff School and worked with various rhythm-and-blues bands and occasionally with jazz groups. In 1963 he visited Japan with Sonny Rollins and moved to New York, where he worked with Pharoah Sanders, Bill Dixon, Paul Bley, Sun Ra, Albert Ayler, and Sunny Murray. He began an important association in 1965 with John Coltrane, with whom he traveled again to Japan in 1966, and after Coltrane's death in 1967 he worked first with Alice Coltrane, then as a leader. He helped to organize the New York Musicians' Festival in the summer of 1972 and took a leading part in a movement among jazz musicians to retain control over their careers and be economically self-sufficient. Around 1973 he formed Survival Records, through which he issued his own recordings, and opened a "loft" club, Ali's Alley, which remained in existence until the summer of 1979. In the mid-1970s he also took part with Milford Graves and Andrew Cyrille in a series of concerts called "Dialogue of the Drums." A propulsive drummer influenced by Elvin Jones, Ali is best known for his playing with Coltrane (see illustration), who praised his ability to play "multi-directional rhythms" and his willingness to grant improvisational freedom to the soloist. His brother Muhammad Ali (*b* Philadelphia, 1936), also a drummer, has performed and recorded with Ayler, Archie Shepp, and Frank Wright.

SELECTED RECORDINGS

Duos: with J. Coltrane: *Interstellar Space* (1967, Imp. 9277); with F. Lowe: *Duo Exchange* (1973, Survival 101)

As leader (all recorded for Survival): *New Directions in Modern Music* (1973, 103); *Moon Flight* (1975, 109)

As sideman with J. Coltrane: *Meditations* (1965, Imp. 9110); *Cosmic Music* (1966, Coast Recorders 4950); *Live at the Village Vanguard Again* (1966, Imp. 9124); *Concert in Japan* (1966, Imp. 9246-2); *Jupiter Variations* (1967, Imp. 9360)

As sideman with others: A. Shepp: *On this Night* (1965, Imp. 97); J. McLean: *'Bout Soul* (1967, BN 84284)

BIBLIOGRAPHY

V. Wilmer: "Dialogue of the Drummers," *Coda*, xi/6 (1974), 2 [interview]

——: *As Serious as your Life: the Story of the New Jazz* (London, 1977, rev. 1980)

H. Howland: "Rashied Ali: the Will to Survive," *MD*, viii/7 (1984), 27

MICHAEL ULLMAN

Alix, May (i). Pseudonym of ALBERTA HUNTER.

Alix, May [Liza Mae] **(ii)** (*b* Chicago, 31 Aug 1904). Singer. She worked in Chicago as a cabaret artist with Jimmie Noone (*c*1922), Carroll Dickerson (at the Sunset Cafe), and in a duo with Ollie Powers. She recorded two titles with Louis Armstrong's Hot Five – *Big Butter and Egg Man* and *Sunset Cafe Stomp* (1926, OK 8423) – and six with Noone (1929–30). In the late 1920s she toured Europe. She continued to perform in New York and Chicago until the early 1940s, when ill health forced her to retire.

based on *ChiltonW*

Allan, Jan (Bertil) (*b* Falun, Sweden, 7 Nov 1934). Swedish trumpeter. He studied piano from the age of six and became involved in jazz at 14, when he took up the trumpet. He first played professionally in Motala (1951), then moved to Stockholm, where he played in dance bands at the Nalen. He was a member of the quartet led by the double bass player Georg Riedel and in 1954 with Riedel joined the newly formed quintet the Modern Swedes, in which he played trumpet and piano. After working with Carl-Henrik Norin (1955–7) he led a quartet with Rolf Billberg (1960–63) and his own jazz orchestras (1963–8), which progressed stylistically from popular music modeled on that of the trumpeter Herb Alpert to the bossa nova of Sergio Mendes and the jazz-rock of Blood, Sweat and Tears. Allan's first album as a leader (*Jan Allan '70*, 1970) won awards in Sweden. He was active as a freelance musician into the mid-1970s, notably with the Swedish Radiojazzgruppen; he also played with visiting Americans, including Thad Jones, Bob Brookmeyer, John Lewis, and Warne Marsh. In 1982 he joined Riedel's Trio con Tromba, with which he has toured in Europe. Allan is a thoughtful improviser who delivers light phrases with a warm, soft tone, aided by a strong embouchure and admirably controlled technique.

SELECTED RECORDINGS

As leader (all recorded for Four Leaf Clover): *Jan Allan '70* (1970, 5035); with B. Shew: *Dialogic* (1982, 5061)

As sideman with Trio con Tromba: *Fusion* (1982, Phono suecia 1)

BIBLIOGRAPHY

Feather–Gitler '70s

O. Lindholm: "Jan Allan fick 'Grammis – 70'," *Orkester journalen*, xxxviii (1970), Oct, 9

L. O. Westin: "Allan, Jan," *Cappelens musikkleksikon*, ed. K. Michelsen (Oslo 1978)

KEN RATTENBURY

Allen, Charlie (*b* Jackson, MS, 25 Sept 1908; *d* Chicago, 19 Nov 1972). Trumpeter. He grew up in Chicago, where he played with the trombonist Hugh Swift (1925), Dave Peyton and Doc Cook (both 1927), and Clifford "Klarinet" King (1928). He later rejoined Cook, after which he performed and recorded with Earl Hines (1931–4, 1937; for illustration *see* HINES, EARL) and Duke Ellington (1935); he recorded no solos, however. During the 1940s and 1950s he worked with several bands, mainly in Chicago, and was also active as a music teacher.

based on *ChiltonW*

Allen, David. *See* ALLYN, DAVID.

Allen, Ed(ward Clifton) (*b* Nashville, 15 Dec 1897; *d* New York, 28 Jan 1974). Trumpeter. He took up piano and cornet as a youth in St. Louis. After some early professional work in Seattle (1916) he played frequently on Mississippi riverboats, both under Charlie Creath and as the leader of his own band on the SS *Capitol* (1922); he then worked in New Orleans until May 1923. In 1924 he moved to Chicago, where he joined Earl Hines. The following year, while in a touring show with Joe Jordan's band, he went to New York, and later worked there with various groups, recording frequently with Clarence Williams (1927–37). From the late 1930s he played predominantly in taxi dance halls. Ill-health forced him to cease full-time playing in 1963.

Allen made particular use in his early work of the cackle-like muted timbre employed by contemporary jazz cornetists, and produced a pleasant tone with a wa-wa mute; his playing on the open instrument, however, revealed a poor tone quality. He had a weak melodic sense and the rhythmic stiffness in his playing characterized many of Williams's recordings.

SELECTED RECORDINGS

As sideman: Barrel House Five: Mama stayed out (1929, QRS R7059); Somedo and some don't (1929, QRS R7019); C. Williams: Saturday Night Jag (1929, Para. 12870)

BIBLIOGRAPHY

ChiltonW

N. R. Ortiz-Oderigo: "A proposito de Ed. Allen," *Ritmo y melodia*, iv (1947), Oct

D. Hague: "Ed Allen," *JJ*, xi/1 (1958), 7

R. Powell: "The Miracle Trumpet of Ed Allen," *JJ*, xiv/6 (1961), 15

E. Townley: "Blues for Ed Allen," *JJ*, xxvii/3 (1974), 12

T. Lord: *Clarence Williams* (Chigwell, England, 1976)

BOB ZIEFF

Allen, Fletcher (B.) (*b* LaCrosse, WI, 25 July 1905). Saxophonist and clarinetist. He went to New York with Lloyd Scott's band (1926) and performed and recorded there with Scott and his brother Cecil (1927). He then joined Leon Abbey, with whom he traveled to Europe and recorded (1928) in England. He remained in Europe, toured with Louis Armstrong (making another visit to Britain, 1932), played and recorded in Paris with Freddy Taylor (1935), and worked in India with Abbey (1936). Allen also arranged music and led his own band for long periods; in 1938 he made recordings in Paris as a leader (including *Fletcher's Stomp*, Swing 29) and with Benny Carter and Willie Lewis. After a trip to Egypt with the Harlem Rhythmakers (late 1938) he returned in 1940 to the USA. He took up baritone saxophone in the late 1940s and worked in New York with various leaders, among them Fred "Taxi" Mitchell (1970–71).

based on *ChiltonW*

Allen, Gene [Sufana, Eugene] (*b* East Chicago, IN, 5 Dec 1928). Baritone saxophonist and bass clarinetist. He studied piano and clarinet from the age of eight, played with Louis Prima

Members of Henry "Red" Allen's band at the Metropole in New York, May 1955: (left to right) Allen (trumpet), Buster Bailey (clarinet), and Herb Flemming (trombone)

(1944–7) and Tex Beneke (1951–3), and performed and recorded with Claude Thornhill (1949–50), the Sauter–Finegan Orchestra (at intervals from 1953 to 1961), and Tommy Dorsey's last orchestra. He toured and recorded with Benny Goodman (1958, 1962) and Gerry Mulligan (1957, 1960–2); he also recorded with Manny Albam (1958, 1961–2) and Woody Herman (1959, 1962). Allen worked principally as a baritone saxophonist in big bands, including one that accompanied Thelonious Monk in concert in 1963. A typical solo by Allen can be heard on *Finegan's Wake* from the Sauter–Finegan Orchestra's album *Inside Sauter–Finegan* (1953, RCA LPM1003). (*FeatherE*)

Allen, Henry, Sr. (*b* New Orleans, 1877; *d* New Orleans, 11 Jan 1952). Cornetist, father of Henry "Red" Allen. For more than 40 years he was the leader of the Allen Brass Band in New Orleans.

MARCEL JOLY

Allen, Henry "Red" [Red; Allen, Henry (James, Jr.)] (*b* New Orleans, 7 Jan 1908; *d* New York, 17 April 1967). Trumpeter. He learned trumpet in New Orleans in the brass band of his father, Henry Allen, Sr. After playing in various New Orleans groups, including that of George Lewis (i), he went to St. Louis in 1927 to join King Oliver. He traveled with Oliver to New York, where he recorded with Clarence Williams. In 1928–9 he played in Fate Marable's Mississippi riverboat bands; during this period he was discovered by representatives of the Victor company, who were searching for a jazz trumpeter to offset the tremendous success of Louis Armstrong on the Okeh label. Brought to New York, Allen immediately recorded four sides in July 1929 for Victor with members of Luis Russell's band. These performances were sensationally received among jazz musicians, and Allen immediately began a long engagement as lead trumpeter in Russell's band (1929–32), followed by similar terms with Fletcher Henderson (1933–4) and the Mills Blue Rhythm Band (1934–7; for illustration *see* MILLS BLUE RHYTHM BAND). Here, and in many small-group studio recordings under his own leadership, Allen established himself as a leading soloist of the early swing period, setting standards for big-band trumpet playing.

In 1937 Allen returned to Russell's band, which was then being used to accompany Louis Armstrong. Removed from his role as a soloist, and perhaps troubled by the new swing style of Roy Eldridge and others, he lost some of his power and direction. After leaving Armstrong in 1940 he took part in the burgeoning traditional-jazz movement, recording in New Orleans formats with Jelly Roll Morton, Sidney Bechet, and his own sextets. In the late 1940s and 1950s he regained his momentum and became a dominant figure in the mainstream jazz movement, leading his own groups and recording prolifically with musicians such as Coleman Hawkins, Buster Bailey, Kid Ory, Pee Wee Russell, and J. C. Higginbotham. He held a long residency at the Metropole, New York, from 1954 to 1965 (see illustration), and undertook several tours of Europe in the 1960s.

Like that of many swing trumpeters, Allen's early style was very similar to Louis Armstrong's; he had heard Armstrong in his father's band in New Orleans and mastered to perfection the same technical prowess and rhythmic freedom (the two musicians are indistinguishable in their joint solo on *I ain't got nobody*, 1929). Later, with Russell's band and especially with Henderson, Allen developed a personal manner characterized by a fluid, legato articulation, a remarkably free concept of rhythm in which he seemed to ignore the fixed pulse, a wide dynamic range, and above all a large arsenal of timbral effects (lip trills, smears, rips, glissandos, spattered notes, and growls). In later years he further explored these effects to such an extent that, in the 1960s, he drew the attention of free-jazz players looking for alternatives to the uniform sonority of bop trumpet playing. Although famous in the 1930s for his flamboyant middle- and high-register solos, in the 1950s he cultivated an expressive, quasivocal manner in the low register as a complement to his jazz singing. Gradually he came to reject his swing legacy and concentrate on the New Orleans ensemble format and repertory, particularly the blues, of which he was an outstanding interpreter.

See also TRUMPET, §4.

SELECTED RECORDINGS

As leader: It should be you/Biff'ly Blues (1929, Vic. 38073); Feeling Drowsy/Swing Out (1929, Vic. 38080); Sugar Hill Function (1930, Vic. 38140); Body and Soul (1935, Voc. 2965); Get the Mop (1946, Vic. 201808); *Ride, Red, Ride in Hi-fi* (1957, RCA LPM1509); *Stormy Weather* (1957–8, Jazz Groove 002); *Feeling Good* (1965, Col. CS9247)

As sideman: L. Armstrong: I ain't got nobody (1929, OK 8756); L. Russell: Song of the Swanee (1930, OK 8780); K. Oliver: Stingaree Blues (1930, Vic. 23009); S. Hughes: Sweet Sorrow Blues (1933, Decca 5101); F. Henderson: Wrappin' it up (1934, Decca 157); Mills Blue Rhythm Band: Ride, Red, Ride (1935, Col. 3087D); T. Wilson: Sentimental and Melancholy (1937, Bruns. 7844); S. Bechet: Egyptian Fantasy (1941, Vic. 27337)

BIBLIOGRAPHY

A. J. McCarthy: "Henry Allen," *JM*, iii/12 (1958), 29

V. Wilmer: "Henry 'Red' Allen," *JM*, x/4 (1964), 8 [interview]

D. Ellis: "Henry (Red) Allen is the Most Avant-garde Trumpet Player in New York City," *DB*, xxxii/2 (1965), 13

W. Balliett: "The Blues is a Slow Story," *Such Sweet Thunder* (Indianapolis, 1966); repr. in *Improvising: Sixteen Jazz Musicians and their Art* (New York, 1977)

J. Chilton: "Henry 'Red' Allen," *Sv*, no.5 (1966), 5

M. Jones: "Red: Financially Quartets are Good, but a Couple More Horns Would Help," *MM* (26 Feb 1966), 8

L. Tomkins: "Henry 'Red' Allen," *Crescendo*, iv/7 (1966), 16 [interview]

M. Williams: "Henry Red," *Jazz Masters of New Orleans* (New York and London, 1967/*R*1978)

H. Allen and A. J. McCarthy: "The Early Years," *JM*, no.180 (1970), 2

J. R. T. Davies and L. Wright: "The Allen Victors," *Sv*, no.34 (1971), 131

J. Evensmo and P. Borthen: *The Trumpet and Vocal of Henry Red Allen, 1927–1942* (n.p. [Oslo], n.d. [?1977]) [discography]

F. Hoffman: *Henry "Red" Allen (Jan. 7th 1908 – Apr. 17th 1967)/J. C. Higginbotham (May 11th 1906 – May 26th 1973): Compiled Negro-press Material about Bands with Henry Red Allen, 1927–1940* (MS, Berlin, 1979, rev. 1982) [unpubd typescript]

——: *Henry "Red" Allen (Jan. 7th 1908 – Apr. 17th 1967)/J. C. Higginbotham (May 11th 1906 – May 26th 1973): Discography, 1927–1968: Excerpt out a Future "Red Allen Bio-Disco"* (MS, Berlin, 1982) [unpubd typescript]

——: *Henry "Red" Allen in England, 1964, 1966, 1967: an Excerpt out a Future Henry "Red" Allen Bio-Disco, 1908–1967* (MS, Berlin, n.d.) [unpubd typescript]

M. L. Hester: "Henry 'Red' Allen," *MR*, xii/1 (1984), 7

J. BRADFORD ROBINSON

Allen, Marshall (*b* Louisville, KY, 25 May 1924). Alto saxophonist. He played with the pianist Art Simmons in Paris (1949–50) and toured Europe with James Moody. After moving to Chicago in 1951 he met Sun Ra, with whom he played, toured, and recorded from 1956 into the 1980s. He also recorded with Paul Bley (1964). Besides his principal instrument, Allen plays flute, oboe, and other winds; he performs a piccolo solo on *A House of Beauty* from Sun Ra's *The Heliocentric Worlds of Sun Ra*, ii (1965, ESP 1017). (V. Wilmer: *As Serious as your Life: the Story of the New Jazz*, London, 1977, rev. 1980)

Allen, Moses (*b* Memphis, 1907; *d* New York, 2 Feb 1983). Double bass and tuba player, and singer. At Le Moyne College, Memphis, he played in a band with Jimmy Crawford. Both men recorded two titles in 1927 with the Chickasaw Syncopators (Col. 14301D); *Chickasaw Stomp* includes an example of Allen's half-spoken, half-sung vocal "preaching." Allen joined Jimmie Lunceford's orchestra in summer 1928 (for illustration *see* LUNCEFORD, JIMMIE), and four years later changed from tuba to double bass. He left Lunceford in summer 1942 to run a store in New York, but continued to play part-time to the end of the 1960s. He was one of the earliest double bass players to experiment with an amplified instrument.

based on *ChiltonW*

Allen, Red. *See* ALLEN, HENRY "RED."

Allen, Sam (*b* Middleport, OH, 30 Jan 1909; *d* California, Sept 1963). Pianist. At the age of ten he played for silent films. He joined Dave Nelson, recording with him in 1931, then worked as second pianist in James P. Johnson's orchestra. From 1932 to 1937 he performed and recorded with Teddy Hill; a good example of his playing may be heard on *China Boy* (1937, Bb 6941). While on a tour of Europe in 1937 he recorded in Paris with Dicky Wells, and the following year he recorded in New York with Slim (Gaillard) and Slam (Stewart). Later he worked with Stuff Smith (1938–40) and played as a soloist in Washington. After moving to California he led his own trio and worked as accompanist to the singer Billie Heywood.

based on *ChiltonW*

Allen, Steve [Stephen Valentine Patrick William] (*b* New York, 16 Dec 1921). Pianist and singer. His parents were vaudeville performers, and he traveled extensively as a child; he played piano from an early age, though his musical training was mainly informal. He began a professional career as a disc jockey on radio during the 1940s, then turned to television in the 1950s. He established himself as a comedian, and often played piano on his shows, improvising jazz and singing his own songs; among the musicians who appeared with him regularly was Terry Gibbs. His most popular program was "The Tonight Show," which became a nationwide success, and in 1957 he produced the series "Jazz Scene USA." Allen performed the title role in the film *The Benny Goodman Story* (1955). He made a number of recordings in the 1950s, using such sidemen as Charlie Shavers, Urbie Green, Gibbs, Mundell Lowe, Gus Bivona, Milt Hinton, and Gary Peacock; his playing is well represented by the album *Allen's All Stars* (1958, EmA 36138). He also wrote music for television and films.

BIBLIOGRAPHY

"Steve Allen: Man in Motion," *DB*, xxv/23 (1958), 16
S. Allen: *Mark it and Strike it* (New York, 1960)
——: *Bigger than a Breadbox* (New York, 1967)
"Allen, Steve," *CBY 1982*

MARK TUCKER/R

Allen, Walter C(arl) (*b* New York, 2 Nov 1920; *d* Point Pleasant, NJ, 23 Dec 1974). Writer. Although an engineer by profession (PhD, Rutgers, 1964) and a teacher of ceramics engineering at Rutgers (1964–74), he was involved in jazz discography throughout his life. He wrote bio-discographies of King Oliver and Fletcher Henderson, the latter being an exhaustive and definitive study. He published and distributed these books as part of his own Jazz Monograph Series, which also included important works by Samuel B. Charters, Brian Rust, and others. As a further means of disseminating information, he produced annually *Allen's Poop Sheet*, a catalogue of books related to jazz (1958–74), which was sent to subscribers. He served on the advisory committee of the Institute of Jazz Studies at Rutgers and organized annual conferences on discography there (1968–74). His son, Daniel Allen, is the author of *Bibliography of Discographies*, ii: *Jazz* (New York and London, 1981).

WRITINGS
(selective list)

with B. Rust: *King Joe Oliver* (Belleville, NJ, 1955) [completely rev. version by L. Wright and others (Chigwell, England, 1987)]
ed.: *Studies in Jazz Discography*, i (New Brunswick, NJ, 1971) [proceedings of *Discographical Research*, i *New Brunswick, NJ, 1968*; *Discographical Research*, ii *New Brunswick, NJ, 1969*; *Preservation and Extension of the Jazz Heritage: New Brunswick, NJ, 1969*]
Hendersonia: the Music of Fletcher Henderson and his Musicians: a Bio-discography (Highland Park, NJ, 1973)
"Discographical Musicology," *JJS*, i/2 (1974), 27

BIBLIOGRAPHY

M. Tucker: "Remembering Walter C. Allen (1920–1974)," *I.S.A.M. Newsletter*, xvi/1 (1986), 4

DANIEL ZAGER

Alley, Vernon (Creede) (*b* Winnemucca, NV, 26 May 1915). Double bass player. He performed and made recordings with Lionel Hampton on double bass and electric bass guitar (1940–42; including *Attitude*, 1940, Vic. 27316) and with Count Basie (1942–3). After serving in the navy he settled in San Francisco, where he led bands (into the 1980s) and acted as the host of radio and television programs. He recorded with a dixieland band led by Jack Sheedy (1949), and with the guitarist Nick Esposito (1949), Flip Phillips (1952), and Charlie Mariano (1953); he also performed and recorded with Jimmy Witherspoon and Ralph Sutton (both 1959). (*ChiltonW*; *FeatherE*)

All-in. The final chorus of a lively piece, collectively improvised in a loud, spirited manner (*see* FORMS, §2); the term is associated with early styles of jazz.

Allison, Mose (John, Jr.) (*b* Tippo, MS, 11 Nov 1927). Pianist, singer, and songwriter. He grew up in the Mississippi Delta region, where boogie-woogie piano and the blues were formative influences. He started piano lessons in the first grade, learned trumpet in high school, played piano in the army, and studied English at Louisiana State University (BA 1950). After playing in a trio which toured Louisiana and Texas, Allison moved with his family to New York and performed with Al Cohn, Zoot Sims, Gerry Mulligan, and Stan Getz (1956–8). In the late 1950s he recorded several albums for Prestige. He toured Europe in 1959 and played in London in 1966. Throughout the 1960s and 1970s Allison performed most frequently in a trio with double bass and drums, and recorded extensively for Atlantic; he began recording for Elektra in 1982.

Allison's songs have become popular on account of their ironic, often biting, wit; among the finest are *Parchman Farm* and *Tell me Something*. He performs these in a sophisticated, blues-inflected style, and has also recorded successful versions of songs written by others, including Duke Ellington's *Do nothing till you hear from me*. His piano playing reflects his interest in the entire range of jazz styles and in classical music.

Oral history material in *LNT*.

SELECTED RECORDINGS

Back Country Suite (1957, Prst. 7091); *Local Color* (1957, Prst. 7121); *Creek Bank* (1958, Prst. 7152); *Transfiguration of Hiram Brown* (1960, Col. CS8248); *Swingin' Machine* (1961, Atl. 1398); *Mose Alive!* (1966, Atl. 1450), incl. Parchman Farm; *Hellow There, Universe* (1970, Atl. 1550); *Western Man* (1971, Atl. SD1584), incl. Tell me Something; *Middle Class White Boy* (1982, Elek. 60125); *Lessons in Living* (1982, Elek. 60237-1)

BIBLIOGRAPHY

D. Cerulli: "Country-style Jazz," *DB*, xxv/9 (1958), 19
L. Tomkins: "Speaking my Mind," *Crescendo*, iv/8 (1966), 16

J. Delehant: "Mose Allison: Country Sophisticate," *DB*, xxxv/21 (1968), 18
Jagajivan: "Mose Discloses," *DB*, xxxix/9 (1972), 16
M. Rozek: "Mose Allison: Can a White Man Sing the Blues?," *Different Drummer*, i/8 (1974), 11
B. Ness: "Mose Allison: Interview," *Coda*, xii/5 (1975), 6
D. F. Truitt: "Mose Allison: Interview," *Cadence*, viii/9 (1982), 11
D. Waddington: "Mose Allison," *JJI*, xl/2 (1987), 22 [incl. discography]

PHILIP GREENE

Allyn [Allen], **David** (*b* Hartford, CT, 19 July 1923). Singer. He first performed and recorded with Jack Teagarden's big band (1940–42). From 1944 he worked with Boyd Raeburn, sometimes singing complicated arrangements by George Handy; his style is well represented by *I only have eyes for you*, which he recorded with Raeburn in 1946 (Jwl 10002). (By this time he was using both forms of his surname.) Also in 1946 he recorded as a leader, accompanied by a quintet that included Lucky Thompson. Later he was associated with Paul Smith (1949), Johnny Mandel, Stan Kenton, and Count Basie. He sang at clubs, including those on the Playboy Club circuit (1960–64), then from 1968 was less active in music for a period during which he worked with drug addicts in New York and Los Angeles. In 1975, however, he resumed recording in New York, making the album *Don't Look Back* (Xan. 101) in a duo with the pianist Barry Harris; later he recorded again as a leader in Los Angeles (1975, 1981).

BIBLIOGRAPHY

FeatherE; *Feather–Gitler '70s*

ERIC THACKER

Almeida, Laurindo (*b* São Paulo, 2 Sept 1917). Brazilian acoustic guitarist. He was a staff guitarist on radio in Rio de Janeiro and led his own orchestra. In Los Angeles he was a soloist in Stan Kenton's orchestra (1947–9); after settling in California he worked for 25 years in films and television. He remained active in jazz, however, and led quartets with saxophone, double bass, and drums. The first of these, to which Bud Shank belonged, made recordings that prefigured the mixing of bossa nova elements with jazz in the 1960s; another included Gary Foster. In the late 1960s he accompanied his wife, the singer Deltra Eamon, in recitals, and continued to perform as a soloist and with various symphony orchestras. In 1974 he formed the L. A. FOUR with Shank, Chuck Flores (replaced by Shelly Manne, who was in turn replaced by Jeff Hamilton), and Ray Brown; later he performed in a duo with Shank and in a trio with Larry Coryell and the classical guitarist Sharon Isbin. Almeida wrote the guitar methods *Guitar Tutor in Three Courses* (New York, 1957) and *Contemporary Moods for Classical Guitar* (New York, 1970).

SELECTED RECORDINGS

As leader: *Laurindo Almeida Quartet Featuring Bud Shank* (1954, PJ 7, 13); of L. A. Four (with R. Brown, S. Manne, and B. Shank): *The L. A. Four Scores!* (1975, Conc. 8); *The Laurindo Almeida Trio* (1984, Conc. 238); *Concierto Aranjuez* (1985, EW 35JDBP51)
As sideman with S. Kenton: Lament (1947, Cap. 172); Journey to Brazil (1947, Cap. 631); *Lush Interlude* (1958, Cap. ST1130); *Artistry in Voices and Brass* (1963, Cap. ST2132), incl. Solitaire

BIBLIOGRAPHY

FeatherE; *Feather–Gitler '70s*
C. Easton: *Straight Ahead: the Story of Stan Kenton* (New York, 1973)
L. Tomkins: "Laurindo Almeida," *CI*, xviii (1979–80), no.1, p.20; no.2, p.16
W. F. Lee: *Stan Kenton: Artistry in Rhythm* (Los Angeles, 1980) [incl. discography]

WILLIAM F. LEE III

Alpert, Trigger [Herman] (*b* Indianapolis, 3 Sept 1916). Double bass player. He studied music at Indiana University (1938–9). He played with the bandleader Alvino Rey in New York in 1940 and from 1940 to 1944 toured and recorded with Glenn Miller (for illustration *see* MUTE, fig.3), playing both in New York and with his forces band. After working briefly with Tex Beneke and taking part in a radio show with Benny Goodman, he recorded with Bud Freeman, Ella Fitzgerald, Muggsy Spanier, and Roy Eldridge (all 1945), and Louis Armstrong, Ray McKinley, and Bernie Leighton (all 1946). He worked with Frank Sinatra (1946–50) and Woody Herman's quintet (1947) and recorded with Jerry Jerome (1947). He worked for CBS in New York (1950–62), during which time he recorded with Artie Shaw (1950, 1953), Coleman Hawkins (1952), the Sauter–Finegan Orchestra (1952–3, 1955), Mundell Lowe (1954–6), Don Elliott (*c*1958), Gene Krupa (1962), and Buddy Rich (1962). In 1956 he made his only recording as a leader, with a septet that included Zoot Sims, Al Cohn, and Urbie Green. He ceased to work as a musician in 1970 and pursued a career as a photographer.

SELECTED RECORDINGS

As leader: *Trigger Happy!* (1956, Riv. 225)
As sideman: G. Miller: *Army Air Force Band* (1943–4, RCA LPM6700); M. Lowe: *Guitar Moods* (1956, Riv. 208); D. Kincaide: *The Solid South* (1959, Ev. 5064)

BIBLIOGRAPHY

FeatherE; *Feather '60s*
G. T. Simon: *Glenn Miller and his Orchestra* (New York, 1974)

Alston, Ovie [Overton] (*b* Washington, *c*1906). Trumpeter and singer. After working in New York with the trombonist Bill Brown (1928–30) he performed and recorded with Claude Hopkins (1931–6); a good example of his playing may be heard on *I would do anything for you* (1932, Col. 2665D). He then formed his own big band, which held residencies at various clubs in New York, including the Roseland Ballroom (1939–41, 1942–7) and the Baby Grand Café (1948–52). The band was led by Noble Sissle and Eubie Blake during service tours in 1941–2. Alston recorded as a leader in 1938 and again in 1946, and continued to work with his band into the 1950s.

based on *ChiltonW*

Altena [Van Regteren, Van Regteren Altena], **Maarten** (*b* Amsterdam, 22 Jan 1943). Dutch double bass player and composer. He studied at the Sweelinck Conservatory in Amsterdam (1961–7) and played with Marion Brown, Theo Loevendie, Burton Greene, Willem Breuker, the Instant Composers Pool, Steve Lacy, Derek Bailey, and Guus Janssen. He worked as a leader from 1975 and also performed as an unaccompanied soloist. In 1977 he formed a record company, Claxon, and in the early 1980s toured the USA, Canada, and South America. He was awarded the Dutch National Jazz Prize in 1978. Altena's playing can be heard to advantage on Brown's album *Porto novo* (1967, Pol. 583724). His compositions include *Rondedans* and *Quick Step* (both recorded for Claxon on albums of the same name, 1985, 15; 1986, 16), *Papa Oewa*, and *Buona notte*. (G. Rouy: "Maarten Altena: 'vers l'indépendance'," *Jm*, no.295 (1981), 32)

For illustrations *see* JAZZ (i), fig.9, and LACY, STEVE.

WIM VAN EYLE

Altered chord. A chord in which elements other than the root, third, or seventh are inflected by a semitone, appearing therefore to be "borrowed" from the tonic minor if the prevailing key is major, or the tonic major if the prevailing key is minor, or from another scale altogether. Such inflection usually brings the element melodically closer to its resolution. *See* HARMONY (i), §1(ii).

Alternate fingering. *See* FALSE FINGERING.

Alto (i). In general musical terminology the vocal part or range lying below the soprano and above the tenor; the word is also used as a qualifying adjective to distinguish those members of certain families of instruments (especially wind) that play in that range (for example, alto clarinet, alto flute, etc.; *see* CLARINET and FLUTE). In jazz argot "alto" is used alone to mean the alto saxophone (*see* SAXOPHONE), and occasionally to mean the player of that instrument.

Alto (ii). Record label established by BORIS ROSE in the early 1970s.

Alto clarinet. The alto instrument of the clarinet family, normally pitched in E♭; *see* CLARINET, §§1 and 5.

Alto flute. A flute pitched in G, a 4th below the soprano instrument; *see* FLUTE, §§1 and 4.

Alto [tenor] **horn.** The alto instrument of the SAXHORN family, pitched in E♭; it normally plays the alto part but occasionally plays tenor.

Alto saxophone. The alto instrument of the saxophone family, pitched in E♭; the compass of the standard instrument is *d♭-a♭″*, though many alto saxophones have a key for concert *a″*. *See* SAXOPHONE, §3.

Altschul, Barry (*b* New York, 6 Jan 1943). Drummer. After teaching himself initially he studied with Charli Persip from 1960. In 1964 he met Paul Bley, with whom he worked regularly until 1970 and occasionally into the 1980s; at the same time he belonged to the Jazz Composers Guild and the Jazz Composer's Orchestra Association (1964–8), played more conventional jazz in Europe (for ten months, 1967–8), and studied with Sam Ulano (1969). Early in 1970, with Chick Corea, Dave Holland, and Anthony Braxton, he formed the group Circle, which recorded his composition *Lookout Farm* the following year. After Circle disbanded in 1972 Altschul recorded *Conference of the Birds* with Holland, Braxton, and Sam Rivers; he also played with Holland in Braxton's quartet (1974–6) and Rivers's trio (1974–8). From 1978 he taught drumming, led groups that included Ray Anderson and Mark Helias as sidemen, and was himself a sideman for a variety of musicians. David Himmelstein describes Altschul's music as "freebop" (in his liner notes to *You can't Name your Own Tune*, 1977), which aptly connotes its rhythmic drive and wide stylistic range.

SELECTED RECORDINGS

As leader: *You can't Name your Own Tune* (1977, Muse 5124); *Another Time/Another Place* (1978, Muse 5176); *Brahma* (1980, Sack. 3023); *Irina* (1983, SN 1065)

As sideman: P. Bley: *Closer* (1965, ESP 1021); Circle: *Paris Concert* (1971, ECM 1018–9), incl. Lookout Farm; D. Holland: *Conference of the Birds* (1972, ECM 1027); A. Braxton: *Five Pieces 1975* (1975, Ari. 4064); S. Rivers: *The Quest* (1976, RR 106)

BIBLIOGRAPHY

M. Cuscuna: "Barry Altschul: Mister Joy," *J&P*, vii/4 (1968), 16
P. Keepnews: "Traps in the South Bronx," *DB*, xlii/3 (1975), 14 [incl. discography]
C. J. Safane: "Barry Altschul," *Coda*, no.168 (1979), 11 [incl. discography]
H. L. Lindenmaier: "Barry Altschul: Interview," *Cadence*, vi/6 (1980), 5
L. Jeske: "Barry Altschul's Drum Role," *DB*, xlix/2 (1982), 17 [incl. discography]

DAVID WILD

Altschul, Mike (*b* Los Angeles, 27 Dec 1945). Tenor saxophonist. After attending California State University, Los Angeles (1963–7), he toured with Stan Kenton (1967–9), with whom he also recorded (*Stan Kenton Conducts the Jazz Compositions of Dee Barton*, 1967, Cap. ST2932). In 1969 he performed with Nat Adderley and Bobby Bryant, played and recorded with Don Ellis, and began an association with Gerald Wilson that continued intermittently for several years. He also performed with Louie Bellson, Terry Gibbs, Duke Pearson, and Frank Zappa, and in television orchestras. (*Feather–Gitler '70s*)

Alvarez, Chico [Alfred] (*b* Montreal, 3 Feb 1920). Trumpeter. He was brought up in Inglewood, California, and studied piano and violin for ten years before taking up trumpet. He was a soloist with Stan Kenton from 1941 to 1943, served in the US Army (1943–6), then rejoined Kenton, with whom he remained until 1951 except for a brief period in the late 1940s when he played with Red Norvo, Benny Carter, and Charlie Barnet. He then opened a music store in Hermosa Beach, California, and worked as a trumpeter and arranger for Latin bands. From 1958 to 1982 he accompanied Ella Fitzgerald, Sarah Vaughan, and others at a number of hotels in Las Vegas, including the Flamingo, where he played for eight years. Later he formed the Las Vegas Jazz Band and in 1985 was a featured performer at the Sacramento (California) Dixieland Jubilee. Although he was primarily a section player, Alvarez performed solos in several of the bands to which he belonged in the 1930s and 1940s, besides Kenton's; he played in a swing style that was strongly influenced by the work of Roy Eldridge.

SELECTED RECORDINGS
(all as sideman with S. Kenton)

on *The Kenton Era* (1940–54, Cap. WDX569), St. James Infirmary; The Nango (1941, Decca 4037); Cocktails for Two (1946, Cap. B252); Machito (1947, Cap. 408)

BIBLIOGRAPHY

FeatherE
C. Easton: *Straight Ahead: the Story of Stan Kenton* (New York, 1973)
W. F. Lee: *Stan Kenton: Artistry in Rhythm* (Los Angeles, 1980) [incl. discography]

WILLIAM F. LEE III

Alvaro, Romero (*b* Genoa, Italy, 1908). Italian pianist, singer, and violinist. He played in Genoa with Tullio Mobiglia and others (1927–33). From 1934 he played piano and violin in a small band led by Kramer Gorni in Milan, which made several recordings, including *Anime gemelle* (1935, Fonit 7214) and *Una spagnola di nola* (1936, Fonit 7373); he also played with Piero Cottiglieri. He left Gorni and in the 1940s formed the Quintetto Fantasma, with which he recorded. Later he retired from jazz to write pop music. Alvaro was an inventive pianist and violinist whose career was hampered by an eccentric personality. His fellow musicians felt that when he was inclined to play he had no equal in Italy.

ADRIANO MAZZOLETTI

Alvin, Danny [Viniello, Daniel Alvin] (*b* New York, 29 Nov 1902; *d* Chicago, 6 Dec 1958). Drummer and bandleader. He began playing professionally in New York with Aunt Jemima (Edith Wilson) (1918) and recorded there with Sophie Tucker (1919–22). His jazz career centered on Chicago, where he performed with Jules Buffano (1922), Charlie Straight, Elmer Schoebel, and Frankie Quartell (with whom he recorded in 1924); he later worked in commercial bands and briefly as a bandleader, before joining Art Hodes in 1933. In 1936 he returned to New York to work with musicians who were profiting by the revival of interest in dixieland. He moved back to Chicago in 1947 and formed the Kings of Dixieland in 1949, which played at Alvin's Club Basin Street and recorded in the 1950s. Alvin's playing, based on Sbarbaro's ragtime style, displays much of the comic play-acting characteristic of dixieland drummers. This is especially true of his recordings as a bandleader where he creates a wash of rhythmic sound, which sometimes bears little relationship to what his sidemen play.

SELECTED RECORDINGS

As leader: *Club Basin Street* (1958, Stepheny 4002), incl. South Rampart Street Parade, The Sheik of Araby
As sideman: A. Hodes: Maple Leaf Rag (1944, BN 505)

BIBLIOGRAPHY

ChiltonW
J. Tracy: "Alvin Adds to Dixie Revival," *DB*, xvii/11 (1950), 2
B. Aurthur: "Drummer Danny," *Selections from the Gutter: Jazz Portraits from 'The Jazz Record'*, ed. A. Hodes and C. Hansen (Berkeley, CA, Los Angeles, and London, 1977), 139

T. DENNIS BROWN

Alvis, Hayes (Julian) (*b* Chicago, 1 May 1907; *d* New York, 29 Dec 1972). Tuba and double bass player. He began playing drums, but while working with Jelly Roll Morton (1927–8) he changed to tuba and double bass, learning the rudiments from Lawson Buford and Quinn Wilson respectively. From 1928 to 1930 he played tuba with Earl Hines, with whom he recorded his arrangement *Blue Nights* (1929, Vic. 38096). After moving to New York with Jimmie Noone (1931) Alvis performed on double bass and tuba with the Mills Blue Rhythm Band (1931–4, 1936) and for a time acted as the group's road manager; he plays one of the earliest recorded double bass solos on *Rhythm Spasm* (1932). From the mid-1930s he worked with Duke Ellington (1935–8), Benny Carter (1939–40), Joe Sullivan (1940, 1942), Louis Armstrong (1940–42), in an army band led by Sy Oliver (1943–5), and with the pianist Dave Martin (1946–7). After a long-term engagement as a house musician at the Café Society, New York, he worked as a freelance musician with several players, including Wilbur De Paris (1958). In 1970 he toured and recorded in Europe with Jay McShann and Tiny Grimes.

SELECTED RECORDINGS

As sideman: Mills Blue Rhythm Band: Rhythm Spasm (1932, Mlt. 12418); D. Ellington: Cotton (1935, Bruns. 7526); Truckin' (1935, Bruns. 7514); Clarinet Lament (1936, Bruns. 7650); Oh Babe! Maybe Someday (1936, Bruns. 7667); R. Stewart: Back Room Romp/Tea and Trumpets (1937, Var. 618); Love in my Heart/Sugar Hill Shim-sham (1937, Var. 664)

BIBLIOGRAPHY

ChiltonW; *FeatherE*
J. Simmen: "Hayes Alvis," *BHcF*, no.150 (1965), 7 [interview]
——: "The Story of Hayes Alvis," *JJ*, xix/5 (1966), 13
C. Carrere: "Pitter Panther Patter: les bassistes de Duke Ellington," *Jh*, no.316 (1975), 10

JOHNNY SIMMEN

Ambrose, Bert (*b* London, 1897; *d* Leeds, England, 18 June 1971). English bandleader. His family emigrated when he was a youth to the USA, and he later worked in New York as music director at the Club de Vingt (1917–20) and Clover Gardens (1922), in addition to making several recordings for Columbia (1923). However, from the 1920s he was active almost exclusively in London, where he was music director at the Embassy Club (1920–26) and the Mayfair Hotel (1927–33). From 1927 his band regularly included American musicians, such as Sylvester Ahola, Danny Polo, and the singer Sam Browne, and from the same year it performed regularly at the London Palladium and made several recordings. In 1928 the BBC began to broadcast a fortnightly program from the Mayfair Hotel, and by autumn the following year Ambrose had become a national figure. From 1933 to 1936 he was again at the Embassy Club, then moved back to the Mayfair before becoming manager and bandleader at Ciro's Club (1937). In 1938–9 he led an octet, while still occasionally working with full band. Ambrose re-formed his band at the Mayfair in December 1939, but his activities were curtailed the following year owing to ill-health. He resumed theater tours with his octet in July 1941, and continued to lead bands until 1956, when he concentrated on management. His band displayed flair and discipline and employed a team of skilled arrangers which included Lew Stone and Sid Phillips; it was the most highly rated British ensemble of its period.

SELECTED RECORDINGS

(all recorded for Decca)

Embassy Stomp (1935, F5375); B'wanga (1935, F5529); Copenhagen (1935, F5696); Champagne Cocktail (1936, F6282); Cotton Pickers' Congregation (1937, F6458)

BIBLIOGRAPHY

A. McCarthy: *The Dance Band Era: the Dancing Decades from Ragtime to Swing, 1910–1950* (London, 1971/*R*1982)
B. Amstell and R. T. Deal: *Don't Fuss, Mr. Ambrose: Memoirs of a Life Spent in Popular Music* (Tunbridge Wells, England, 1986) [autobiography of Billy Amstell]

DIGBY FAIRWEATHER

Ambrosetti, Flavio (*b* Lugano, Switzerland, 8 Oct 1919). Swiss alto saxophonist and vibraphonist, father of Franco Ambrosetti. An engineer by profession, he has never been a full-time musician. He made his first recordings in 1943 with Rio de Gregori and with his own group, and in 1949 played and recorded swing and bop with Gil Cuppini and Hazy Osterwald. Thereafter he played in various Swiss groups and also worked as a leader, recording in Italy and other European countries. His quintet in the mid-1960s included his son Franco, George Gruntz, Daniel Humair, and a number of different double bass players; it appeared at many festivals and broadcast on radio and television. This group became the nucleus of the Concert Jazz Band, a larger ensemble, which toured Europe in 1972 and recorded with such Americans as Dexter Gordon and Phil Woods (1972). It recorded again in 1976. (*FeatherE*; *Feather–Gitler '70s*)

Ambrosetti, Franco (*b* Lugano, Switzerland, 10 Dec 1941). Swiss trumpeter and flugelhorn player, son of Flavio Ambrosetti. He first learned piano and began playing trumpet at the age of 17. In 1964 he recorded with Gato Barbieri under the leadership of the Italian double bass player Giorgio Azzolini and also made his first recording with George Gruntz, with whom he remained associated into the 1980s; the following year he made his first recording as a leader. He won first prize in the trumpet category at a competition sponsored by Friedrich Gulda in 1966 and was a founding member, with his father and Daniel Humair, of Gruntz's Concert Jazz Band in 1972. Among those who have recorded with Ambrosetti as sidemen are Benny Wallace (1978), Phil Woods (1981), Mike Brecker and Kenny Kirkland (1983), and Dave Holland (1985).

SELECTED RECORDINGS

(all recorded for Enja)

Close Encounter (1978, 3017); *Wings* (1983, 4068); *Franco Ambrosetti* (1985, 4096)

BIBLIOGRAPHY

Feather '60s; Feather–Gitler '70s

I. Carr: "Ambrosetti, Franco," in I. Carr, D. Fairweather, and B. Priestley: *Jazz: the Essential Companion* (London, 1987)

PETER SCHWALM

American Federation of Jazz Societies [AFJS]. Organization formed to facilitate communication between jazz societies throughout the USA and to encourage the preservation and performance of jazz on a national level. It was founded in 1985 at a convention in Savannah, Georgia, attended by representatives of 15 state, regional, and local jazz societies. The founding societies and clubs consisted of more than 2,000 individual members, and by 1987 the AFJS was composed of 80 constituent organizations with a total membership estimated at around 50,000. In cooperation with its member groups, the AFJS offers educational projects, booking facilities for jazz events, and various other services; it has received a grant from the NEA to pursue its programs and has begun several cooperative ventures with the National Association of Jazz Educators and the Berklee College of Music. The organization published its newsletter *Federation Jazz* bimonthly during the first year of its existence.

American Jazz Orchestra. Big band. A nonprofit organization dedicated to the performance of standards from the big-band repertory, it was founded in New York by John Lewis, Roberta Swann, and Gary Giddins, who also serves as its artistic director. At its first performance in spring 1986 the ensemble played works by Fletcher Henderson, Duke Ellington, Jimmie Lunceford, Count Basie, and Dizzy Gillespie. Its first concert of 1987 was devoted to the compositions of Benny Carter.

BIBLIOGRAPHY

A. Duncan: "The American Jazz Orchestra: the Dream Becomes a Reality," *JT* (May 1986), 12

G. Giddins: "Weather Bird: an Orchestra is Born," *VV*, xxxi (6 May 1986), 86

I. Gitler: "The American Jazz Orchestra: Repertory Revisited," *JT* (July 1986), 7

G. Santoro: "Jazz," *The Nation*, ccxliv (21 March 1987), 374

THOMAS OWENS

American Music. Record company and label. The company was established by BILL RUSSELL and operated successively from his homes in Pittsburgh, Canton (Missouri), Chicago, and New Orleans. The first issues were made in 1944, and drew on material Russell had been recording since 1942. The catalogue contained mostly New Orleans jazz by such musicians as Bunk Johnson, George Lewis (i), and Wooden Joe Nicholas; the extent to which Russell's direction affected the type of material remains the subject of considerable controversy. 57 recordings were released on 78 r.p.m. discs; these included piano solos by Dink Johnson and a short series of reissues of jazz and blues recorded by Paramount in the 1920s. Issue continued on LPs, both of new recordings and previously released material, until 1957. Thereafter extensive reissue of the catalogue was undertaken by Storyville, and from 1973 a comprehensive series of LPs drawn from American Music's catalogue was put out on the Japanese label Dan.

BIBLIOGRAPHY

W. Russell: Liner notes, Wooden Joe Nicholas: *A Nite at Artesian Hall* (American Music 640, *c*1952)

B. King: "A Reassessment of New Orleans Jazz on American Music Records," *JM*, v (1959), no.1, p.2; no.2, p.6

M. Slatter: "A Portrait of William Russell," *JJ*, xii/9 (1959), 28

E. Lambert: "William Russell's New Orleans Recordings: Some Notes and Reflections," *JM*, no.183 (1970), 3

D. Pawson: "American Music on the 'Dan' Label: the Unissued Material," *Fn*, vii/1 (1975), 3

E. Kraut: *The Revival: Documents of the American Music Sessions, 1940–45* (Arcegno, nr Ascona, Switzerland, 1986) [exhibition catalogue, Festa New Orleans Music, Ascona; texts in Ger. and It.]

American Record Company [ARC]. Record company. It was formed in August 1929 by the merger of three smaller organizations: the Plaza Music Company (which owned the labels Jewel, Domino, Oriole, Banner, and Regal), the Pathé Phonograph and Radio Corporation (which owned Pathé, Actuelle, and Perfect), and the Cameo Record Corporation (which owned Cameo, Romeo, and Lincoln). Many of these labels were used to issue cheap records. The American Record Company was purchased in October 1930 by Consolidated Film Industries, which in December 1931 also bought the Brunswick Record Corp. from Warner Bros. (*see* BRUNSWICK). Although formally they remained independent, ARC and Brunswick were effectively operated as one enterprise. In August 1934 the company also acquired the labels Columbia and Okeh, but relinquished them shortly thereafter. ARC was by this time using the label names Brunswick and Vocalion and issuing cheaper records on Perfect, Oriole, Romeo, Banner, and Melotone. The entire organization was purchased in February 1938 by the Columbia Broadcasting System (*see* COLUMBIA), which soon discontinued the cheap labels and in 1940 changed the names of the major ones from Brunswick to Columbia and from Vocalion to Okeh. The name ARC itself appeared only on the labels of certain series aimed at specific limited markets such as theaters. The recording activities of John Hammond during the 1930s were conducted through ARC.

BIBLIOGRAPHY

J. Godrich and R. M. W. Dixon: *Blues & Gospel Records, 1902–1942* (Hatch End, nr London, 1964, rev. 2/1969, rev. and enlarged 3/1982 as R. M. W. Dixon and J. Godrich: *Blues & Gospel Records, 1902–1943*), 22

W. Allen, P. Armagnac, and C. Kendziora: "Plaza–A.R.C.: a Clarification," *Matrix*, no.70 (1967), 4

R. M. W. Dixon and J. Godrich: *Recording the Blues* (London, 1970), 67

W. C. Allen and M. Brooks: "The 'TO' Series of the American Record Company," *Sv*, no.38 (1971), 56

J. Beaton and H. Rye: "More on the ARC TO- Series," *Sv*, no.75 (1978), 102

Aminata Moseka. *See* LINCOLN, ABBEY.

Ammons, Albert (C.) (*b* Chicago, 23 Sept 1907; *d* Chicago, 2 Dec 1949). Pianist, father of Gene Ammons. After playing as a soloist and with various bands in Chicago he formed a sextet, the Rhythm Kings, in 1934. With this ensemble he recorded his version of Pine Top Smith's *Boogie Woogie*, which he called *Boogie Woogie Stomp* (1936). He later became identified with that piano blues style. From 1938 he was active in New York, first in piano trios with Meade "Lux" Lewis and Pete Johnson, and later in a duo with Johnson, with whom he made a series of recordings in 1941. Ammons's early solos *Boogie Woogie Stomp*, *Bass Gone Crazy*, and *Suitcase Blues* were frequently based on the styles of his predecessors, but his later work was quite individual.

For illustration *see* BLUES, fig.2.

SELECTED RECORDINGS

As unaccompanied soloist: Shout for Joy (1939, Voc. 4608); Boogie Woogie Stomp/Boogie Woogie Blues (1939, BN 2); Suitcase Blues/Bass Goin' Crazy (1939, BN 21); Bass Gone Crazy/Monday Struggle (1939, Solo Art 12000); Albert's Special Boogie/The Boogie Rocks (1944, Com. 617)

Duos with P. Johnson: Boogie Woogie Man/Walkin' the Boogie (1941, Vic. 27505)

As leader: Boogie Woogie Stomp (1936, Decca 749)

BIBLIOGRAPHY

W. Russell: "Boogie Woogie," *Jazzmen*, ed. F. Ramsey, Jr., and C. E. Smith (New York, 1939/*R*1977), 183

M. Harrison: "Boogie Woogie," *Jazz: New Perspectives on the History of Jazz*, ed. N. Hentoff and A. J. McCarthy (New York, 1959/*R*1974), 105–37

Y. Bruynoghe: "Albert Ammons," in S. Dance and others: *Jazz Era: the 'Forties* (London, 1961/*R*1985), 48

J. Hopes: "Boogie Woogie Man: a Bio-discography of Albert Ammons," *J&B*, i/6 (1971), 5

L. Feather: "Piano Giants of Jazz: Albert Ammons," *CK*, vii/2 (1981), 70 [incl. transcr.]

M. Williams: "Cuttin' the Boogie," *Jazz Heritage* (New York and Oxford, England, 1985) [colln of previously pubd interviews], 160

MARTIN WILLIAMS/R

Ammons, Gene [Eugene; Jug] (*b* Chicago, 14 April 1925; *d* Chicago, 6 Aug 1974). Tenor saxophonist and bandleader, son of Albert Ammons. He studied music at Du Sable High School under Captain Walter Dyett, and at the age of 18 left Chicago with the band led by the trumpeter King Kolax. He then joined Billy Eckstine's innovative big band as its principal bop soloist (1944; for illustration *see* ECKSTINE, BILLY). From 1947 he began leading small groups and recording under his own name, using such sidemen as Junior Mance and Gene Wright. After playing briefly with Woody Herman's big band (mid-1949) he returned exclusively to leading small groups, working from 1950 to 1952, and frequently thereafter, in partnership with Sonny Stitt. Ammons became a leading exponent of the impassioned blend of bop and black gospel preaching known as soul jazz. Problems with drugs then disrupted his career, although he was allowed to continue playing in jail (1958–60, 1962–9). His term in prison coincided with the rise of soul music as a commercial genre, and after his release his improvisations, now accompanied by electric instruments, were more popular than ever before.

SELECTED RECORDINGS

As leader: *The Happy Blues* (1956, Prst. 7039); *Boss Tenor* (1960, Prst. 7180); *Soul Summit* (1962, Prst. 7234); *The Boss is Back* (1969, Prst. 7739); *Together Again for the Last Time* (1973, Prst. 10100)

As leader with S. Stitt: Blues Up and Down (1950, Birdland 6005); Woofin' and Tweetin' (1955, Prst. 45166); *Boss Tenor* (1960, Verve 68426)

As sideman: B. Eckstine: Blowin' the blues away (1944, De Luxe 2001); W. Herman: More Moon (1949, Cap. 682)

BIBLIOGRAPHY

M. Crawford: "Jug Ain't Changed," *DB*, xxviii/17 (1961), 24

B. Porter and F. Gibson: "Gene Ammons: a Discography," *DF*, no.6 (1968), 11; no.7 (1968), 10

M. Walker and T. Williams: "Private Recordings," *DF*, no.5 (1968), 11; no.13 (1969), 2; no.16 (1970), 2

L. Feather: "The Rebirth of Gene Ammons," *DB*, xxxvii/12 (1970), 12

J. Burns: "Gene Ammons," *JJ*, xxiii/4 (1970), 22

Obituary, *DB*, xli/16 (1974), 11

BARRY KERNFELD

Amram, David (Werner, III) (*b* Philadelphia, 17 Nov 1930). Composer and french horn player. After attending the Oberlin College Conservatory (1948) and serving in the army in Europe he worked as a horn player in Paris, where in 1955 he recorded with Lionel Hampton and as a leader. He moved later that year to New York, performed with Charles Mingus and Oscar Pettiford's band (1956), and led a group with the tenor saxophonist George Barrow that recorded in 1957 and performed regularly at the Five Spot in 1963–5. During the following years he became well-known as a composer of orchestral and instrumental works, incidental music (in particular for the New York Shakespeare Festival), and film scores. He was the first composer-in-residence of the New York PO (1966–7) and he conducted concerts for children and workshops at which he played and discoursed enthusiastically on folk music, especially that of Latin America, and jazz. In 1977 he performed on a cruise ship that visited Cuba. Amram's activities may seem peripheral to jazz, but his horn battle with Julius Watkins on Pettiford's *Two French Fries* is impressive, and his Triple Concerto for Woodwind, Brass, and Jazz Quintets and Orchestra (1970; recorded in 1974 on RCA ARL1-0459) is of a higher quality than many third stream compositions.

SELECTED RECORDINGS

As leader: with G. Barrow: *Jazz Studio Six* (1957, Decca 8558); *Havana/New York* (1977, Flying Fish 057)

As sideman: L. Hampton: *Lionel Hampton and his New French Sound* (1955, Barclay 84004–5); O. Pettiford: *Orchestra in Hi Fi* (1956, ABC-Para. 135), incl. Two French Fries

BIBLIOGRAPHY

FeatherE; *Feather '60s*; *Feather–Gitler '70s*

D. Amram: *Vibrations: the Adventures and Musical Times of David Amram* (New York, 1968)

"Amram, David (Werner)," *CBY 1969*

BRIAN PRIESTLEY

Amstell, Billy [William] (*b* London, 20 Aug 1911). English clarinetist and saxophonist. He took up piano at the age of ten and then taught himself alto saxophone from the age of 13. He began playing professionally in Glasgow, but moved to London, where he worked with the violinist and bandleader Jack Harris (1930). In 1931 he played with the bandleader Roy Fox; in September of that year he joined Bert Ambrose, and after changing to tenor saxophone became a principal soloist with the band (1932). Amstell worked again with Harris (1939), then with the bandleader Geraldo (1943–5), and later rejoined Ambrose. He spent six years in the dance orchestra of the BBC, after which he worked as a session musician with such leaders as George Chisholm. In the 1980s Amstell has concentrated on playing clarinet and has made recordings with his own quartet (including *Session after Midnight*, 1980, Zodiac 1010). He has written numerous compositions and arrangements; his solo tenor saxophone style may be heard on Ambrose's recording of Amstell's composition *Tootin' Around* (1939, first issued on *Champagne Cocktail*, Ace of Clubs ACL1246).

BIBLIOGRAPHY

B. Amstell: "When We were Gods in Ambrosian Fields," *MM*, xxiv (24 Jan 1948), 3; contd as "When Jimmy Dorsey was at the Kit Kat" (31 Jan 1948), 3; contd as "When the U.S. Listened to Us" (7 Feb 1948), 2

J. Godbolt: *A History of Jazz in Britain, 1919–50* (London, Melbourne, Australia, and New York, 1984)

B. Amstell and R. T. Deal: *Don't Fuss, Mr. Ambrose: Memoirs of a Life Spent in Popular Music* (Tunbridge Wells, England, 1986)

B. Deal: "Billy's Bounce," *JJI*, xxxix/1 (1986), 12

NEVIL SKRIMSHIRE

Amy, Curtis (Edward) (*b* Houston, 11 Oct 1929). Tenor and soprano saxophonist and leader. He learned to play clarinet as a child, took up tenor saxophone while playing in an army band, and studied music education at Kentucky State College (BS 1952). He worked as a schoolteacher in Tennessee, performed in clubs in the Midwest, and in 1955 moved to Los Angeles, where he recorded with Dizzy Gillespie (1955), the pianist Onzy Matthews (1962–5), and Roy Ayers (1963); he also performed and recorded with Gerald Wilson (1965–6). From 1960 to about 1966 he led modal-jazz groups that included Ayers, Bobby Hutcherson, Victor Feldman, Jimmy Owens, and Kenny Barron as sidemen; among the recordings he made as a leader is *Groovin' Blue* (1961, PJ 19).

BIBLIOGRAPHY

Feather '60s

J. Tynan: "Curtis Amy: Gettin' into it," *DB*, xxix/30 (1962), 22 [interview]

Andersen, Arild (*b* Lilleström, Norway, 27 Oct 1945). Norwegian double bass player. He studied double bass with Karel Netolicka and the lydian chromatic concept of tonal organization with its originator, George Russell. From 1967 he played at festivals in Norway, including that of Molde, at which he was heard by Don Cherry in 1968; his first engagement outside Norway was with Cherry at the Berliner Jazztage later that year. From 1969 to 1973 he worked in various groups with Jan Garbarek, and at the same time appeared at festivals in Bologna, Italy, with Russell (1969); Antibes–Juan-les-Pins, France, with Stan Getz (1970); Kongsberg, Norway, with Sonny Rollins; Berlin with Garbarek's trio (1972); Yugoslavia with Karin Krog (1973); and Molde with Sam Rivers's trio and Paul Bley. He also played in New York in 1972 with Bley, Rivers, Joe Farrell, Dave Friedman, Barry Altschul, Steve Kuhn, and Sheila Jordan. From the autumn of 1973 he belonged to a quartet led by the guitarist Jon Eberson while continuing to work with Bley. He worked with the singer Radka Toneff from the mid-1970s and recorded as the leader of quartets that included as his sidemen the tenor saxophonist Knut Riisnaes, the pianist Jon Balke, and the drummer Paal Thowsen (1975); Thowsen, Juhani Aaltonen, and the keyboard player Lars Jansson (1977, 1978); Charlie Mariano, Edward Vesala, and Jasper van 't Hof (1980); and Kenny Wheeler, Paul Motian, and the pianist Steve Dobrogosz (1981). From 1981 he worked occasionally with Alphonse Mouzon; the same year he recorded with Mouzon, John Taylor, and Bill Frisell at the festival in Molde. He led a quintet, Masqualero, with Jon Christensen in the 1980s in which Balke, the tenor saxophonist Tore Brunborg, and the trumpeter Nils Petter Molvaer worked as sidemen; the group toured England and the Continent, made recordings (1983, 1985), and performed at the Village Vanguard in New York (1986). In 1986 Andersen toured the Continent and appeared at the Kongsberg festival with Mouzon and the guitarist Frode Alnaes, and performed with Masqualero in Molde. He received the Buddy Award from the Norwegian Jazz Federation in 1969.

SELECTED RECORDINGS

(recorded for ECM unless otherwise indicated)

As leader: *Clouds in my Head* (1975, 1059); *Green Shading into Blue* (1978, 1127); with J. Christensen: *Masqualero* (1983, Odin 08), *Bande à part* (1985, 1319)

As sideman: D. Cherry: *Eternal Rhythm* (1968, Saba MPS15204); J. Garbarek: *The Esoteric Circle* (c1969, FD 10125); *Afric Pepperbird* (1970, 1007); B. Stenson: *Underwear* (1971, 1012); J. Garbarek: *Triptykon* (1972, 1029); R. Toneff: *Winter Poem* (1977, Sonet 1439)

BIBLIOGRAPHY

Feather–Gitler '70s

P. Brodowski: "An Andersen Tale," *JF* [intl edn], no.37 (1975), 37 [incl. discography]

C. Smith: "A Profile of the Norwegian Bassist Arild Andersen," *JJI*, xli/1 (1988), 12

RANDI HULTIN

Anderson, Andy [Andrew; Jug] **(i)** (*b* New Orleans, 12 Aug 1912; *d* ?New Orleans, 1982 or early 1983). Trumpeter. He made recordings in New Orleans as a leader (1939, 1942), including his own composition *Chant of the Tuxedos* (1939, first issued on *Dance New Orleans Style 1937–41*, Mono 12), and also in Chicago with George Lewis (i) (1959–60). From the late 1950s to the early 1970s he played and recorded with the Young Tuxedo Brass Band and the Olympia Brass Band, making a tour of Europe with the latter in 1968.

Oral history material in *LNT*.

BARRY KERNFELD

Anderson, Andy (ii). *See* ANDERSON, ED.

Anderson, Cat [William Alonzo] (*b* Greenville, SC, 12 Sept 1916; *d* Norwalk, CA, 29 April 1981). Trumpeter. He grew up in the Jenkins' Orphanage in Charleston, South Carolina, playing in its famous student bands and receiving a thorough training in the rudiments of music. In the early 1930s, while still a teenager, he formed the Carolina Cotton Pickers, a touring group consisting of orphanage students like himself. After leaving the Cotton Pickers in 1935 he played in the big bands of Claude Hopkins, Lionel Hampton (1942), and others before attracting the attention of Duke Ellington, who immediately engaged him for his orchestra as a high-note specialist (1944). After leading his own band from 1947 to 1949, in 1950 Anderson rejoined Ellington and remained with the group until 1959, taking a prominent part in many of Ellington's "suites" of that period. He became a member of Ellington's band again in 1961, playing intermittently until 1971, but thereafter worked as a freelance on the West Coast, and joined Ellington only for special occasions. Anderson's celebrated high-note forays (he could effortlessly strike c'''') tended to overshadow his outstanding abilities as a section leader, and as a jazz soloist with an uninhibited, good-humored style and remarkable precision of execution. He published a teaching manual, *The Cat Anderson Trumpet Method: Dealing with Playing in the Upper Register* (Los Angeles, 1973).

For illustration *see* ELLINGTON, DUKE, fig.2.

SELECTED RECORDINGS

As leader: Swingin' the Cat (1947, Apollo 771); Cat's Boogie/For Jumpers Only (1947, Apollo 774); Cat's in the Alley (1949, Gotham 174); *Cat on a Hot Tin Horn* (1958, EmA 36142)

As sideman with D. Ellington: A Gatherin' in a Clearin' (1946, Vic. 474281); Trumpet No End (1946, Musi. 484); *Such Sweet Thunder* (1957, Col. CL1033), incl. Madness in Great Ones; *Afro-Bossa* (1962–3, Rep. 6069), incl. The Eighth Veil; *Concert in the Virgin Isles* (1965, Rep. 6185), incl. Jungle Kitty

BIBLIOGRAPHY

"Interviews with the Men Beside Duke Ellington," *Jazz Statistics*, no.8 (1959), 9

S. Dance: *The World of Duke Ellington* (London and New York, 1970/*R*1981) [colln of previously pubd articles and interviews], 144

"Un trompette de Duke Ellington: Cat Anderson parle des concerts de musique sacrée," *BHcF*, no.195 (1970), 3

J. Chilton: *A Jazz Nursery: the Story of the Jenkins' Orphanage Bands of Charleston, South Carolina* (London, 1980)

Obituary, G. Colombé, *JJI*, xxxiv/7 (1981), 15

E. Lambert: "Cat Anderson: a Resumé of his Recorded Work," *JJI*, xxxv (1982), no.6, p.16; no.7, p.10

J. BRADFORD ROBINSON

Anderson, Ed(ward) [Andy] (*b* Jacksonville, FL, 1 July 1910). Trumpeter. He played in Florida with Luckey Roberts and traveled with him in 1926 to New York, where he worked with the drummer George Howe and Luis Russell and performed and recorded with Jelly Roll Morton (1927–8). He also recorded occasionally with Clarence Williams (1927–9). After playing with Benny Carter, Charlie Johnson, and Bingie Madison he joined the Mills Blue Rhythm Band (1930), and between 1931 and 1934 made several recordings with the group (including *Doin' the Shake*, 1932, Per. 15634). Anderson was a member of Charlie Turner's Arcadians when that band was led by Fats Waller (1935). Later he played with Hazel Scott (1939), Joe Sullivan (1939–41), and Frankie Newton (1941), then ceased to be a full-time musician.

based on *ChiltonW*

Anderson, Ernestine (Irene) (*b* Houston, 11 Nov 1928). Singer. She performed with the rhythm-and-blues bands of Russell Jacquet (1943) and the drummer Johnny Otis (1947–9). While working with Lionel Hampton (1952–3), she met Gigi Gryce, with whom she recorded in 1955. The following year she made a successful tour with Rolf Ericson's group in Sweden, where she also recorded *Hot Cargo* with Harry Arnold's band. The critic Ralph Gleason introduced her to audiences in the USA, where she was well received. At the beginning of the 1960s, however, her popularity began to decline and she moved to England in 1965. After returning to the USA in the mid-1970s, she made recordings for Concord with Hank Jones (1976, 1983), Ray Brown (1979), Monty Alexander (1979–80), and her own quartet (1984). Anderson's vocal warmth, bluesy intensity, and refined musical taste are well represented in the series of recordings she made for Mercury.

Oral history material in *GBLnsa*.

SELECTED RECORDINGS

As leader: *Hot Cargo* (1956, Met. 15015); *Ernestine Anderson* (1958, Mer. 20400); *Moanin', Moanin', Moanin'* (1960, Mer. 60242); *Hello Like Before* (1976, Conc. 31); *Live at the Concord Jazz Festival, 1979* (1979, Conc. 102); *When the Sun Goes Down* (1984, Conc. 263)

As sideman: on G. Gryce: *Gigi Gryce Orchestra and Quartet* (1955, Signal 1201), The One I Love, Social Call

BIBLIOGRAPHY

FeatherE; *Feather '60s*

LAWRENCE KOCH

Anderson, Fred(, Jr.) (*b* Monroe, LA, 22 March 1929). Tenor saxophonist. He studied theory and was influenced by the music of Lester Young, Coleman Hawkins, and Gene Ammons, and later Ornette Coleman. In the 1960s he was a founding member of the Association for the Advancement of Creative Musicians in Chicago and led a number of its groups; he also recorded as a sideman with Joseph Jarman (1966–7). In 1974 he toured Europe with his own quintet, which included Douglas Ewart, and in 1978 performed in Germany with a new group, another quintet, among the members of which were Ewart and George Lewis (ii). In Germany he also recorded with the group Neighbors (1979), led by the Austrian composer, conductor, and pianist Dieter Glawischnig. Anderson was among the first avant-garde performers to emerge from Chicago, where he exerted an important influence on younger musicians.

SELECTED RECORDINGS

As leader: *Another Place* (1978, Moers 01058)

As sideman: on J. Jarman: *Song for* (1966, Del. 410), Little Fox Run, Adam's Rib; Neighbors: *Accents* (1979, EMI 06632854)

BIBLIOGRAPHY

S. Friedman and L. Birnbaum: "Fred Anderson: AACM's Biggest Secret," *DB*, xlvi/5 (1979), 20

E. Jost: *Jazzmusiker: Materialen zur Soziologie der afro-amerikanischen Musik* (Frankfurt am Main, Germany, Berlin, and Vienna, 1982)

DAVID G. SUCH

Anderson, Ivie (Marie) [Ivy] (*b* Gilroy, CA, 10 July 1905; *d* Los Angeles, 28 Dec 1949). Singer. She studied in Washington and began performing in Los Angeles around 1921. She sang at the Cotton Club, New York, in 1925 and after touring with the revue *Shuffle Along* she returned to Los Angeles, where she performed with Paul Howard and the drummers Curtis Mosby and Sonny Clay. In 1928 she worked with Clay in Australia and toured the USA as a solo singer. After a short period with Earl Hines (1930) she worked with Duke Ellington (1931–42), and she appeared with the Marx brothers in the film *A Day at the Races* (1937), in which she sang *All God's chillun got rhythm*. She continued to perform until the late 1940s. Anderson was the most versatile of the singers who worked with Ellington. She was the first to record *It don't mean a thing* (1932), which was peculiarly suited to her relaxed sense of rhythm; on this recording she alternates a penetrating, nasal voice with gruff, exuberant scat singing that recalls Louis Armstrong's style. By contrast, her voice on *I got it bad and that ain't good* (1941) is low pitched and beautifully rounded, and her use of blues inflections adds a depth of emotion rivaling that found in performances by Billie Holiday.

SELECTED RECORDINGS

As sideman with D. Ellington: It don't mean a thing (1932, Bruns. 6265); Raisin' the Rent (1933, Bruns. 6571); Stormy Weather (1933, Bruns. 6600); I'm Satisfied (1933, Bruns. 6638); Solitude (1940, Col. 35427); Mood Indigo (1940, Col. 35427); I got it bad and that ain't good (1941, Vic. 27531); Rocks in my Bed (1941, Vic. 27639)

BIBLIOGRAPHY

ChiltonW

P. E. Miller: "Ivie joined the Duke for four weeks, stays with band for 12 years," *DB*, ix/14 (1942), 31

B. Ulanov: *Duke Ellington* (New York, 1946/*R*1975)

D. Ellington: *Music is my Mistress* (Garden City, NY, 1973), 122

S. Placksin: *American Women in Jazz, 1900 to the Present: their Words, Lives, and Music* (New York, 1982), 113

SCOTT FREDRICKSON

Anderson, John (H., Jr.) (*b* Birmingham, AL, 31 Jan 1921; *d* Birmingham, 18 Aug 1974). Trumpeter. He attended the Los Angeles Conservatory and the Westlake College of Music, played with Tiny Bradshaw (1941), and belonged to a navy band (1942–6). From 1946 he worked as a freelance on the West Coast, performing with Benny Carter and recording as a soloist on Buddy Collette's album *Tanganyika Jazz* (1956, Dig 101); he also performed and recorded with Earl Bostic (1957), recorded with Nat "King" Cole (1958), and led West Coast jazz groups that included Collette, Curtis Counce, and Britt Woodman as sidemen. From 1959 to 1960 he toured and recorded with Count Basie; later he toured with Ray Charles and recorded as the leader of a big band (1966). He is often confused (particularly in discographies) with another trumpeter named John Anderson, who performed and recorded with Stan Kenton (1945–7).

BIBLIOGRAPHY

FeatherE; *Feather–Gitler '70s*

R. Gordon: *Jazz West Coast: the Los Angeles Jazz Scene of the 1950s* (London and New York, 1986)

Anderson, Ray (*b* Chicago, 1952). Trombonist. He grew up with George Lewis (ii) and studied with Frank Tirro and Dean Hay; having taken part in a summer jazz workshop sponsored by the University of Illinois, he played in funk and jazz-rock groups while attending Macalester College for a year. He rehearsed with the saxophonist Keshavan Maslak and the drummers Charles Moffett and Stanley Crouch in California before moving to New York in 1972. Later he produced concerts with Maslak while rehearsing with a group that included Lewis, Anthony Davis, and others in New Haven, Connecticut. In 1977 he replaced Lewis in Anthony Braxton's quartet and began working with Barry Altschul. He performed in the Roscoe Mitchell–Leo Smith Orchestra at the Moers Festival in 1979 and toured Europe in 1980 with his own group. He also leads a funk group, Slickaphonics, with Mark Helias.

SELECTED RECORDINGS

As leader: *Harrisburg Half-life* (1980, Moers 01074); *Right Down your Alley* (1984, SN 1087); of Slickaphonics: *Humatonic Energy* (1984, Teldec 626128)

As sideman: B. Altschul: *Another Time/Another Place* (1978, Muse 5176); *For Stu* (1979, SN 1015); A. Braxton: *Seven Compositions, 1978* (1979, Moers 01066); R. Mitchell: *Sketches from Bamboo* (1979, Moers 02024)

BIBLIOGRAPHY

S. Loupien and G. Rouy: "Ray Andersen [*sic*]," *Jm*, nos.266–7 (1978), 42

B. Shoemaker: "Boning up for the Future," *DB*, xlix/7 (1982), 21 [incl. discography]

D. Soutif: "Le free funk de Slickaphonics," *Jm*, no.314 (1983), 36
M. Wangler: "Slickaphonics," *JP*, xxxiv/1 (1985), 18

DAVID WILD

Anderson's Annex. Nightclub in New Orleans, also known as Tom Anderson's Annex; *see* NIGHTCLUBS AND OTHER VENUES.

Andre, Wayne (*b* Manchester, CT, 17 Nov 1931). Trombonist. He performed and recorded with Charlie Spivak (1950–51), the Sauter–Finegan Orchestra (1955–6), and Woody Herman (1956), and played on sessions with Kai Winding's septet (1956–8). He also composed and arranged for Winding; he plays a solo in his own piece *Nutcracker* on Winding's *Trombone Sound* (1956, Col. CL936). He then studied at the Manhattan School of Music (BA 1962). He toured and recorded with Gerry Mulligan (1960) and with Benny Goodman in the USSR (1962). He continued to be associated with Goodman, playing intermittently in the orchestra and the septet, until the late 1970s; he may be heard as a member of Goodman's band on *Darn that Dream* from *The King Direct to Disc* (1979, Cen. 1150). He played again with Mulligan (1963), and with Quincy Jones (1964–7), the Thad Jones–Mel Lewis Orchestra (1966), and Clark Terry (1967). As a studio musician in New York he recorded in big bands accompanying Art Farmer (1959), Sarah Vaughan (1964), Wes Montgomery (1965–8), Chick Corea (1975), Dexter Gordon (1977), Jaco Pastorius (1982), and many others. In 1984 he formed a septet, the members of which included Ron McClure.

Andreozzi, Eduardo (*b* São Paulo, 1892; *d* Rio de Janeiro, 1979). Brazilian bandleader, violinist, and saxophonist. He studied music in Rio de Janeiro (1917–19) and directed his own dance orchestra, gradually changing its repertory from Latin American music to jazz. He recorded prolifically on the Odeon label (1919–24) and although he did not perform as a soloist he became one of the pioneers of jazz in Brazil. While touring Europe (1924–34) he played for a time with the dancer and bandleader Grégor Kélékian. He made several recordings for Grammophon in Berlin (including *Everything is hotsy totsy now*, 1926, Grammophon 20338, and *Big Bad Bill*, 1926, Grammophon 20340), some of which show to advantage the hot trumpet playing of Mickey Diamond and the blue blowing on kazoo of Sydney Sterling. (R. E. Lotz: "Eduardo Andreozzi: the Jazz Pioneer from Brazil," *Sv*, no.122 (1985–6), 62 [incl. discography])

RAINER E. LOTZ

Andrus, Chuck [Charles E., Jr.] (*b* Holyoke, MA, 17 Nov 1928). Double bass player. After attending the Manhattan School of Music, he performed with Charlie Barnet (1953), Terry Gibbs (1954), Claude Thornhill (1954–5), and Bernard Peiffer (1956), and recorded with Herbie Mann (1955), the drummer Jim Chapin (1955), and the trumpeter Don Stratton (1956). From 1961 to 1965 he toured the USA and Europe and recorded with Woody Herman; he later worked as a freelance musician in the New York area. A telling example of Andrus's playing is his solo on *Satin Doll* from Herman's album *Herman 1964* (1963, Phi. 118). (*FeatherE*; *Feather '60s*)

Anna Marie. *See* LINCOLN, ABBEY.

Anthony, Bill (*b* New York, 28 March 1930). Double bass player. He played with Georgie Auld (1951), Jimmy Dorsey (1953), Gerry Mulligan (1954), and Claude Thornhill (1956), and performed and recorded with Buddy DeFranco (1950–51), Charlie Spivak (1952), and Stan Getz (1954–5). He also recorded with Bob Brookmeyer (1954) and Zoot Sims (1956). His creative rhythm playing is well represented by *We'll be together again* from *Stan Getz at the Shrine Auditorium* (1954, Norg. 2000) and Brookmeyer's *Bob Brookmeyer Quartet* (1954, PJ 16).

BIBLIOGRAPHY

FeatherE
R. Gordon: *Jazz West Coast: the Los Angeles Jazz Scene of the 1950s* (London and New York, 1986), 100

Anthony [Antonini], **Ray(mond)** (*b* Bentleyville, PA, 20 Jan 1922). Trumpeter and bandleader. He first played professionally in the late 1930s, then worked with bands led by Glenn Miller (1940–41; for illustration *see* MUTE, fig.3) and Jimmy Dorsey (1942). During World War II he led a navy band for two years. After being discharged he formed a band in 1946 which had a hit single, *Bunny Hop*, in 1952. This started a national dance craze that contributed considerably to Anthony's success. As well as continuing to record he performed with his band on television (1953–5) and in several films, including *The Girl can't Help it* (1957). He also appeared without the band in other films, including *The Five Pennies* (1959), a biography of Red Nichols in which he portrayed Jimmy Dorsey. After 1960 he reduced his band to a sextet. Anthony's trumpet playing possesses a warm lower register and a lyricism reminiscent of Harry James, and his band performs mainly commercially-oriented arrangements which imitate the sound of Miller's orchestra.

His brother Leo Anthony (Lee Roy Antonini) (*b* Dover, OH, 19 Aug 1925), a baritone saxophonist and bandleader, played in Ray Anthony's band (1946–53), then led his own, which performed in a style that was aimed mainly at audiences of pop and rhythm-and-blues.

SELECTED RECORDINGS

(all recorded for Capitol)

Harlem Nocturne (1950, 1249); Bunny Hop (?1952, 2427); Slaughter on Tenth Avenue (1952, 72085); Dragnet (1953, 2562)

BIBLIOGRAPHY

FeatherE
H. Holly: "Anthony Band a Solid Hit in First West Coast Date," *DB*, xvii/23 (1950), 8
G. T. Simon: *The Big Bands* (New York, 1967, rev. and enlarged 2/1971, rev. 3/1974, 4/1981), 466
D. Meeker: *Jazz in the Movies: a Guide to Jazz Musicians, 1917–77* (London, 1977, rev. 2/1981)

WAYNE SCHNEIDER

Antibes–Juan-les-Pins Jazz Festival [Festival International du Jazz Antibes–Juan-les-Pins]. Festival held annually from 1960 in Juan-les-Pins, near Antibes, France; it was known until around 1975 as the Festival Mondial du Jazz Antibes–Juan-les-Pins. The musicians were engaged in the early 1960s by Henri Goldgran and later, during the 1970s, the festival was directed by Norbert Gamsohn. It takes place over ten days in July and offers performances of most styles of jazz, from swing to free jazz and jazz-rock, by internationally recognized musicians, many of whom also play at the JVC Grande Parade du Jazz in Nice, which immediately precedes the festival at Juan-les-Pins. Most concerts take place at La Pinède, an outdoor arena that seats 4000. From its inception the festival has included performances by prominent American and European musicians; Charles Mingus appeared at the festival during his first European tour (1960) and the popularity of Ray Charles on the continent was established by his early performances at Antibes–Juan-les-Pins. The album *Miles Davis in Europe* was recorded at the festival in 1963. Among the musicians who played at the festival in 1985 were Charles, Jack DeJohnette, Lionel Hampton, Herbie Hancock, Keith Jarrett, and the Modern Jazz Quartet.

PAUL R. LAIRD

Antillean jazz. A term used to refer to a type of jazz, current in the swing era, that incorporated elements of the music of the francophone Caribbean, in particular the Martinique beguine. The music of Martinique, and to a lesser extent of Guadeloupe and Haiti, shares several characteristics with that of Creole New Orleans; it was therefore natural that the practitioners of these styles should associate when they came into contact with one another in Paris in the 1920s. Over the next 30 years musicians from the Caribbean took part in recording sessions devoted to jazz, and expatriate Afro-Americans made recordings of Caribbean music. Some elements of jazz are evident in the work of Alexandre Stellio and Félix Valvert, but the earliest jazz recordings to show the distinctive Creole coloration are by a band led by Flavius Notte (for example, *'Tain't no Sin*, 1931, Ultraphone AP121). Further notable recordings in the style were made by Sam Castandet, André Siobud, Bertin Salnave, Robert Mavounzy, the trumpeter Abel Beauregard, and the guitarist and pianist Claude Martial. Antillean jazz was particularly popular during the Nazi occupation of Paris, when the black French nationals from the Antilles were the only substantial group of Afro-Americans in the city; a major entrepreneurial role was played by Fredy Jumbo, a German-speaking drummer from Togo, whose *Swing 42* (1942, Pol. 524794), recorded with Siobud and Mavounzy as sidemen, is a fine example of the style.

BIBLIOGRAPHY

M. W. Stearns: *The Story of Jazz* (New York, 1956, rev. and enlarged 2/1958, enlarged 1970)

A. Boulanger: Liner notes, *Jazz and Hot Dance in Martinique* (Harl. HQ2018, 1985)

Antolini, Charly (*b* Zurich, ?*c*1935). Swiss drummer. He began his career in 1956 in Paris, where he worked with Bill Coleman (recording in Zurich, 1957), Albert Nicholas (recording in Zurich, 1958), and various French musicians. Between 1957 and 1961 he belonged to the Swiss dixieland group the Tremble Kids (with which he recorded in 1957, 1961–3, and 1971–5) and worked with other European groups. After moving in 1962 to Stuttgart, Germany, he played for five years in the big band of the Süddeutscher Rundfunk under Erwin Lehn and recorded in Germany with Wolfgang Dauner (1964), Eugen Cicero (1965–7, 1970), Stuff Smith (1967), and Baden Powell (1967), and as a leader (from 1966). He worked as a studio musician in Cologne from 1969 to 1971 and also belonged to Kurt Edelhagen's big band, with which he toured the USSR. Later he performed with Lionel Hampton (1980) and Benny Goodman (1981). A good example of Antolini's work is his recording *Bop Dance* (1981, Jazz Publications 8202). (S. Goodwin: "The Drummers of West Germany: Charly Antolini," *MD*, xi/6 (1987), 27)

PETER SCHWALM

Apex Club. The name of several nightclubs, notably one in Chicago; *see* NIGHTCLUBS AND OTHER VENUES. The club gave its name to the Apex Club Orchestra, which performed there from autumn 1926 under the leadership of JIMMIE NOONE.

Apollo Theatre. Theater in Harlem, New York; the name was subsequently adopted by performance venues in other American cities. *See* NIGHTCLUBS AND OTHER VENUES.

Appleton, Joe (*b* Jamaica, *c*1900; *d* after 1954). Jamaican tenor saxophonist, clarinetist, and bandleader. He moved to Great Britain around 1924 and performed in dance bands there and in Europe until the early 1930s. He played in London with West Indian jazz musicians, including Leslie Thompson's Emperors of Jazz (1936), and in 1937 he led his own band. In the 1940s he worked mainly with Cyril Blake and also with Jiver Hutchinson (1944–5). Appleton's clarinet playing may be heard on *Muscat Ramble* (Amiga 1165), which he recorded with Rex Stewart in Berlin in 1948. He again performed as a bandleader in London from 1952 to 1954.

JOHN COWLEY, HOWARD RYE

Appleyard, Peter (*b* Cleethorpes, England, 26 Aug 1928). Canadian vibraphonist of English birth. After playing drums in English dance bands and in orchestras of the Royal Canadian Air Force he moved first to Bermuda, then to Toronto (1951), where after taking up the vibraphone he worked in nightclubs and in radio and television with Calvin Jackson (recording in 1954–5) and as a leader (from 1957). In the 1970s he toured occasionally with Benny Goodman and in 1972 took part in the recording of *On Stage with Benny Goodman and his Sextet* (Lon. 44182–3); he also recorded several albums of jazz and pop as a leader (including *Peter Appleyard Presents*, 1977, Salisbury 001) and was the host of a television series, "Peter Appleyard Presents" (1977–9). He recorded with Peanuts Hucko in 1979 and in 1985 formed a band of former sidemen of Goodman in order to perform the latter's repertory. (M. Miller: "Appleyard, Peter," *Encyclopedia of Music in Canada*, ed. H. Kallmann, G. Potvin, and K. Winters (Toronto, Buffalo, and London, 1981) [incl. discography])

MARK MILLER

Arbello, Fernando (*b* Ponce, PR, 30 May 1907; *d* Puerto Rico, 26 July 1970). Trombonist. He first worked in New York with Wilbur De Paris (1928), June Clark (1929–30), Claude Hopkins, and Bingie Madison. In the early 1930s he performed and made recordings with Hopkins (it is probable that he is the trombone soloist on *Chasing all the blues away*, 1934, Decca 441), Chick Webb (1934–5), Fletcher Henderson (1935–6), and Billy Hicks (1937, including *Joe the Bomber/Fade out*, Var. 601). Thereafter he played briefly with Lucky Millinder, Edgar Hayes, and Fats Waller. After another short period with Hopkins, Arbello worked with Benny Carter and Zutty Singleton (both 1940), Henderson (1941), and Marty Marsala (1941–2). He was a member of Jimmie Lunceford's band from 1942 to 1946, then in the 1950s led his own band; he also recorded with Rex Stewart in Boston (1953). From 1960 he performed with Machito. Later he moved back to Puerto Rico and in 1969 he again led his own group.

based on *ChiltonW*

ARC. *See* AMERICAN RECORD COMPANY.

Arc. Record label established by TREVOR WATTS in 1983.

Arcadian Serenaders. Group of New Orleans musicians, originally known as the Crescent City Jazzers, which performed at the Arcadia Ballroom, St. Louis, during the 1920s. Among the personnel who recorded with the ensemble were Wingy Manone (1924) and Sterling Bose (1925).

ARC–BRC. Acronym used to represent the combined operations of the AMERICAN RECORD COMPANY and BRUNSWICK when the two organizations were owned by Consolidated Film Industries in the 1930s.

Archer, Tony [Anthony John] (*b* London, 14 July 1939). English double bass player. After a general musical education at school he took up double bass, and in 1961 he joined a group led by Don Rendell, with which he recorded during the same year. Archer played and recorded with trios led by the pianists Roy Budd and Eddie Thompson (1970) and then worked with Tony Lee for many years, accompanying visiting musicians at Ronnie Scott's, among other engagements. He has performed with Harold McNair and John Dankworth, and in the 1980s he was a member of the group Best of British Jazz, which includes Kenny Baker and the trombonist Don Lusher. His playing may be heard to advantage on *Blue Bossa* from Lee's album *British Jazz Artists* (1976, Lee Lambert 3416).

NEVIL SKRIMSHIRE

Archey, Jimmy [James H.] (*b* Norfolk, VA, 12 Oct 1902; *d* Amityville, NY, 16 Nov 1967). Trombonist. He began instruction at the age of 12 and studied music at the Hampton Institute (1915–19). During the 1920s he worked with various bands in New York and occasionally left the city to tour with revues. He joined King Oliver in late 1929 and recorded with him the following year. For most of the period 1931–7 he was with Luis Russell (Russell and Louis Armstrong were collaborating during this time), then, after playing with Willie Bryant, he joined Benny Carter in 1939. He worked as a freelance with several bands during the 1940s and played with such notable leaders as Coleman Hawkins, Cab Calloway, Claude Hopkins, Noble Sissle, and Mezz Mezzrow. In December 1948 he began a long residency with a group at the Savoy Café in Boston; at that time the group was led by Bob Wilber, but Archey assumed its leadership in April the following year. He toured Europe with a six-piece group (1952) and led another in the film *Jazz Dance* (1954). From the mid-1950s he played with Mezzrow (1954–5), Earl Hines (1955–62), Muggsy Spanier, and others.

Archey was a strong practitioner of a style, initiated by his contemporary Jimmy Harrison, in which a new emphasis was placed on the trombone as a melodic instrument. He developed this style throughout his long career, making use of an extended range and a powerful attack.

SELECTED RECORDINGS

As leader: *Jimmy Archey with Michael Attenoux Orchestra* (1955, Barclay 84001), incl. Sensation, Texas Moaner Blues, That's a-plenty, Tiger Rag

As sideman: K. Oliver: St. James Infirmary/When you're smiling (1930, Vic. 22298); H. Allen: Roamin'/Patrol Wagon Blues (1930, Vic. 23006); T. Parenti: Grace and Beauty/Praline (1947, Cir. [USA] 1030); A. Hunter: *Alberta Hunter with Lovie Austin's Blues Serenaders* (1961, Riv. 9418), incl. Downhearted Blues, Moanin' Low, Now I'm satisfied, St. Louis Blues; E. Hines: *A Monday Date* (1961, Riv. 9398), incl. Bill Bailey, Lonesome Road

BIBLIOGRAPHY

ChiltonW; *FeatherE*

LAWRENCE KOCH

Archiv für Populäre Musik. Archive devoted to jazz, blues, and popular music in Bremen, Germany; *see* LIBRARIES AND ARCHIVES, §2.

Archiwum Standardów Jazzowych [Archives of Jazz Standards]. Archive founded in Sopot, Poland, in 1981; *see* LIBRARIES AND ARCHIVES, §2.

Arco. Record label. It was owned by the American Record Company, and run by Irving Berman. The label continued the policies of Berman's earlier labels Regis and Manor, but is especially noteworthy for its issue on double-sided 78 r.p.m. discs of recordings of jam sessions that took place at Jazz at the Philharmonic concerts of the mid-1940s. The operation appears to have lasted only for a few months in 1950. ("Regis–Manor–Arco," *Blues Research*, no.15 (n.d. [?1966]), 2)

Ardley, Neil (Richard) (*b* Wallington, England, 26 May 1937). English composer. After graduating from Bristol University (1959) he studied arranging and composition with Raymond Premru (1960–61) and Bill Russo (1962). From 1964 to 1968 he directed the New Jazz Orchestra, an ensemble that provided a forum for its members to perform their own compositions; among the musicians in the group were Harry Beckett, Jack Bruce, Ian Carr, Mike Gibbs, Jon Hiseman, Don Rendell, Barbara Thompson, and Norma Winstone. Several of these musicians played in the occasional orchestra that Ardley subsequently led under his own name (1969–81). He wrote music for both orchestras, notably the multimovement work *Kaleidoscope of Rainbows*, which was recorded on an album of the same name in 1976 (Gull 1018). He has concentrated in the 1980s on writing books, among them *Music: an Illustrated Encyclopedia* (London, 1986). Ardley's compositions are adventurous in style, using themes derived from many different musical sources. In his later works he has combined acoustic instruments with electronics.

BIBLIOGRAPHY

M. C. King: "British Jazzmen, no.3: Neil Ardley," *JJ*, xxiii/9 (1970), 14
R. Cotterrell, ed.: *Jazz Now: the Jazz Centre Society Guide* (London, 1976)
I. Carr, D. Fairweather, and B. Priestley: *Jazz: the Essential Companion* (London, 1987)

SIMON ADAMS

Argo. Record label. It was established in Chicago in 1955 by the brothers Phil and Leonard Chess as a division of their company Chess. Apart from incidental sessions by Gene Ammons, Leo Parker, and Al Hibbler, the parent company was principally concerned with blues, but it entered the jazz market seriously with Argo's earliest recordings in 1955. Among the first musicians to record for Argo were James Moody, Ahmad Jamal, and Ramsey Lewis, all three of whom remained for several years and provided the catalogue with several extremely successful albums. The label was also used to issue the first recordings of Barry Harris and Ira Sullivan, as well as material by the Jazztet, Kenny Burrell, Illinois Jacquet, Budd Johnson, Gene Ammons, Max Roach, Red Rodney, and many others. Issue continued prolifically into the 1970s; the catalogue was one of the most extensive and important of all the independent labels in Chicago, and included some excellent mainstream jazz and bop.

In 1965 the name Argo was changed to Cadet after objections by the longer-established record company Argo in England. Issue and recording continued unchanged, however, until Leonard Chess died in 1971. Thereafter the entire catalogue was bought by GRT, which in 1975 sold it to All Platinum; Chess's masters eventually passed to Sugar Hill, a division of Roulette. Reissue programs from Chess's catalogues, including that of Argo, have been instituted in several countries; previously unreleased material by Dodo Marmarosa and others was made available for issue in Italy as late as 1986. (M. Ruppli: *The Chess Labels: a Discography*, Westport, CT, and London, 1983)

MARK GARDNER

Arista. Record company and label. The company was formed in New York in 1974 by Clive Davis. Its catalogue included three jazz series, all directed by Steve Backer, and each issued on a separate label. Anthony Braxton, the Brecker Brothers, and Gil Scott-Heron were the most important artists on the Arista label itself. The Arista–Freedom label was mostly used to reissue free-jazz recordings first released not only on the English label Freedom, but also on such other European labels as Black Lion, Debut, Fontana, and Polydor; these included Albert Ayler's key recordings of 1964, as well as important albums by Charles Tolliver, Cecil Taylor, Oliver Lake, and Randy Weston. Also put out on Arista–Freedom were several notable new recordings by Roswell Rudd and Archie Shepp. The Arista–Novus label, founded in 1978, presented new material by such free-jazz musicians and ensembles as Muhal Richard Abrams, Lake, Henry Threadgill, and Air, as well as an album by John Scofield. In 1975 Backer acquired the rights to the Savoy label and initiated an extensive series of reissues from that catalogue; he also acquired GRP (Grusin–Rosen Productions), and began putting out its jazz-rock albums. After 1980 the company's importance declined; its catalogue has remained available into the late 1980s, but recording of new sessions has ceased. Arista sold Savoy to Muse around 1985. Backer later joined RCA, under the auspices of which he revived the Novus label. (M. Ullman: *Jazz Lives: Portraits in Words and Pictures* (Washington, 1980), 215)

Arkansas Travelers. Recording group led in the late 1920s by RED NICHOLS.

Armed Forces Radio Service. *See* AFRS.

Armstrong [née Hardin], **Lil(lian)** (*b* Memphis, 3 Feb 1898; *d* Chicago, 27 Aug 1971). Pianist, singer, and composer. After studying music at Fisk University she moved to Chicago (1917), where she worked as a song plugger. She performed with Freddie Keppard, led her own band at Dreamland (*c*1920), and played with King Oliver (1921–4). As a member of Oliver's band she met Louis Armstrong, whom she married in 1924 and whom she encouraged to leave Oliver for Fletcher Henderson; in 1925 Armstrong joined the group that his wife was by then leading in Chicago. Lil Armstrong's encouragement made an important contribution to the development of Louis' career. She wrote songs for Armstrong's recording groups the Hot Five (which also recorded as Lil's Hot Shots) and Hot Seven and played and sang in many of the sessions (1925–7). In 1926 she organized the NEW ORLEANS WANDERERS, a recording group for Columbia. Thereafter she resumed her studies and was awarded a teacher's diploma from the Chicago Musical College (1928) and a postgraduate degree from the New York College of Music (1929); at the same time she toured with Freddie Keppard (*c*1928) and recorded with Johnny Dodds (1928, 1929). In the 1930s she led several bands in New York and Chicago, among them an all-female group, and she appeared as a soloist in two revues. She parted from Armstrong in 1931 and they were eventually divorced in 1938. As a session pianist for Decca in New York (from the late 1930s) she recorded with various musicians, among them Henry "Red" Allen. After returning to Chicago in the 1940s she continued to perform, record, and write music. She made a number of tours, including one of Europe (1952). She died while playing at a concert in memory of Louis Armstrong in Chicago. Lil Armstrong was remarkable for her insight, ambition, and talent for organization, which helped Louis Armstrong to launch his career and thus exercised no small influence on the development of jazz. Her playing is noted for its strong rhythmic force, which supports and drives on the ensemble.

For illustrations *see* ARMSTRONG, LOUIS, fig.1, and OLIVER, KING.

SELECTED RECORDINGS

As leader: Drop that Sack (1926, Voc. 1037); of New Orleans Wanderers: Gate Mouth (1926, Col. 698D); Harlem on Saturday Night (1938, Decca 2234); *Lil Hardin Armstrong and her Orchestra* (1961, Riv. 9401)

As sideman: Louis Armstrong: You're next (1926, OK 8299); J. Dodds: Indigo Stomp (1929, Vic. 23396); H. Allen: Canal Street Blues (1940, Decca 18092)

RECORDED COMPOSITIONS

(selective list)

Recorded by Louis Armstrong: Jazz Lips/Skid-dat-de-dat (1926, OK 8436)

Recorded by J. Dodds: Heah me Talkin' (1929, Vic. 38541)

BIBLIOGRAPHY

ChiltonW

M. Jones: "Lil Armstrong: Royalties and the Old Songs," *MM* (8 April 1967), 8

M. Jones and J. Chilton: *Louis: the Louis Armstrong Story, 1900–1971* (London, 1971), 67

Obituaries: *Fn*, iii/1 (1971), 10; *SL*, xxiii (aut. 1971), 33

S. Placksin: *American Women in Jazz, 1900 to the Present: their Words, Lives, and Music* (New York, 1982), 58

J. L. Collier: *Louis Armstrong: an American Genius* (New York, 1983, London, 1984, as *Louis Armstrong: a Biography*), 111

L. Dahl: *Stormy Weather: the Music and Lives of a Century of Jazzwomen* (London, Melbourne, Australia, and New York, 1984)

MIKE HAZELDINE

Armstrong, Louis [Dippermouth, Pops, Satchelmouth, Satchmo] (*b* New Orleans, 4 Aug 1901; *d* New York, 6 July 1971). Trumpeter and singer. His musical presence, technical mastery, and imaginative genius so overwhelmed jazz musicians of his day that he became their principal model, leaving an indelible imprint on the music.

1. LIFE. It was long believed that Armstrong was born on 4 July 1900, but following the discovery of his baptismal record at the Sacred Heart of Jesus Church, the correct date has now been established. His father was a laborer named Willie Armstrong, his mother a domestic and probably a part-time prostitute called Mary Albert, but known to her son as Mayann. Armstrong was born in a cabin in a dilapidated black slum in the Back o' Town section of New Orleans. His father abandoned the family around the time of Armstrong's birth, and shortly afterwards his mother moved into a nearby area reserved for black prostitutes. After spending his first few years with his paternal grandmother, Josephine Armstrong, he returned to his mother in "Black Storyville", a tawdry, run-down neighborhood of brothels, cribs, seedy dance halls, and honky-tonks, frequented by black laborers and some Whites. Here Armstrong grew up, hearing in the dance halls and clubs around him the blues and the new "hot" music then emerging from ragtime.

He was brought up without a father in deepest poverty, wearing little more than rags and eating the cheapest of food, occasionally even scavenging for refuse in garbage cans. His mother, although warm and loving, was irresponsible, and frequently left Armstrong and his younger sister to the kindness of strangers for days at a time. He grew up deprived both physically and emotionally to an exceptional degree, and the experience left him scarred with a deep-seated, lifelong sense of insecurity.

He began singing in a barbershop quartet, which, over several years, amounted to an excellent course in ear training. Sometime in his early teens he was sentenced to the Home for Colored Waifs – not, as once believed, for firing a pistol on New Year's Eve, but for more general delinquency. While in the home he joined the band and eventually was given a cornet.

With this band he played customary band music of the day – marches, rags, and sentimental songs. When he was released from the home about two years later he was determined to become a musician. Using borrowed instruments, he began sitting in at the honky-tonks around his home, playing mainly the blues and the few songs in his slowly expanding repertory.

Throughout his life Armstrong habitually put himself under the wing of a tough, aggressive older man. One of these was the strong-minded King Oliver, then considered to be the best jazz cornetist in New Orleans. Armstrong, a genius who invented his own methods, owed little musically to Oliver or anyone else; but Oliver's sponsorship provided him with opportunities to play in public and so to develop his musical personality. When Oliver left for Chicago in 1918 during the general migration of Blacks to the North, Armstrong took his place in a band led by Kid Ory, then regarded as the leading jazz band in the city. In 1918 he married a prostitute named Daisy, beginning a stormy and short-lived relationship. By 1919 he was working in clubs and also on riverboats, the floating dance halls which traveled from town to town on the Mississippi every summer. This experience in particular contributed towards Armstrong's development as a professional musician who could read and play any music required of him.

In 1922 Oliver invited Armstrong to Chicago to play second cornet in his band, which was then working at a black dance hall called Lincoln Gardens. This Creole Jazz Band had an extraordinary impact on musicians in the Chicago area, and through it Armstrong began to draw their attention. At this time he also made his first recordings with Oliver's group. In 1924 he married the band's pianist, Lil Hardin. (He subsequently married Alpha Smith and then Lucille Wilson.) Shortly thereafter, at his wife's urging, he left Oliver, and in autumn 1924 he moved to New York to join the Fletcher Henderson Orchestra, one of the leading black dance bands in the city. Through his work as jazz specialist with this band he soon became known to musicians; they quickly recognized in him the pre-eminent player of the new "hot" music, and his influence began to be felt.

Armstrong returned to Chicago in November 1925, and, with his Hot five (see fig.1), immediately began recording a series of more than 60 performances that were to transform jazz. Issued under a variety of names, their effect on musicians and jazz enthusiasts was instantaneous and profound; few performers, either in or outside jazz, entirely escaped their influence. During this period Armstrong changed from cornet to the more brilliant trumpet. One of the series, *Heebie Jeebies*, was his first recording as a scat singer, and its success led to his singing being given greater prominence (*see also* Scat singing).

In 1929 Armstrong's record director, Tommy Rockwell, took him to New York. There he played and sang in the Broadway show *Hot Chocolates* by Andy Razaf and Fats Waller, where he attracted attention singing *Ain't Misbehavin'* (*see also* Dickerson, carroll). From this point, at the expense of his career as a jazz musician, he began to concentrate on appearing as a popular entertainer. In part he did this at the urging of Rockwell, and more especially under the influence of another strong figure in his life – Joe Glaser, who managed him from 1935. But in part Armstrong was drawn to show business through an insatiable hunger for applause, rooted in the insecurities formed in his early years. Under Glaser's guidance he became the first Black to appear regularly in feature-length films and to have a sponsored radio show; by the late 1930s he was a nationwide star. Until 1947 he worked with a big band, for many years using the group led by Luis Russell, playing music of an increasingly commercial nature. Then, with the collapse of the big-band movement after World War II, Glaser organized for him a small, more jazz-oriented group, the All Stars. At

1. Louis Armstrong's Hot Five, Chicago, 1925: (left to right) Armstrong (cornet), Johnny St. Cyr (banjo), Johnny Dodds (clarinet and alto saxophone), Kid Ory (trombone), and Lil Armstrong (piano)

first the group was truly an all-star band, and included Earl Hines (see fig.2), Jack Teagarden, Sid Catlett, and Barney Bigard. But as it became clear that Armstrong was the attraction, Glaser began to use journeyman players, some of whom were unknown to the jazz public before their appearances with Armstrong. At times the All Stars played good jazz, but more frequently the band was simply a showcase for Armstrong's singing of popular songs. The public found him a winning and attractive personality, and, helped by shrewd management, by the mid-1950s he was one of the best-known entertainers in the

2. Louis Armstrong (right) with Earl Hines, c1949

world; he appeared in almost 50 popular films (*see* FILMS, §§I, 2, 4(ii); II, 1, 4). The US State Department sponsored him on numerous international tours, earning him the title "Ambassador Satch." He suffered a heart attack in 1959, and from then on recurrent health problems forced him gradually to curtail his trumpet playing and eventually his singing as well. His death produced headlines in newspapers throughout the world. His personal archive was donated under the provisions of the will of his wife, Lucille Armstrong, to Queens College, Flushing, New York, in 1987; *see* LIBRARIES AND ARCHIVES, §2.

2. MUSIC. Armstrong's recordings may be divided into three groups: those with New Orleans-style bands (up to 1928), those with big dance bands (from 1928 to 1947), and finally those of his return to the New Orleans format (from 1947 until his death). In his first recorded solo, with Oliver's band on *Chimes Blues* (1923), he merely played a preset melody. However, during the same session he recorded his first important jazz solo, on *Froggie Moore*; here Armstrong did not entirely depart from the melody, but already he was producing the "swing" that so delighted his contemporaries. The origins of swing are still obscure, but even if Armstrong did not invent this phenomenon, he "swung" more than anyone else of his time – an important quality that attracted other players to his style. Armstrong's swing was created by at least four devices: a terminal vibrato which begins after the note has been struck; a division of a quarter-note into two eighth-notes of varying but decidedly unequal duration; a constant displacement of accent, so that the music seems alternately to move towards and away from the listener; and a placement of notes fractionally in front of or behind the beat. This last trait later became increasingly significant in Armstrong's playing.

This sense of swing is also apparent in Armstrong's recordings with Henderson, where in addition he began to abandon fixed melody for pure invention. His improvisations are not simply random, for the parts always combine to form unified wholes: on Henderson's *Go 'long mule* (1924) he played three parallel figures over the first six bars (ex.1); in *Copenhagen* (1924) he placed parallel figures over the first two segments of the blues strain and a contrasting one over the last segment. This ability to construct an entire dramatic form, along with his powerful swing, astonished musicians from the start. During his stay with Henderson, Armstrong accompanied many blues singers; his recording of *St. Louis Blues* (1925) with Bessie Smith is particularly fine. He also recorded many numbers in the New Orleans style for Clarence Williams. Some of these featured Sidney Bechet, notably a driving rendition of *Cake Walkin' Babies* (1924) which is considered a classic of the genre, and *Texas Moaner Blues* (1924), the finest extant example of the blues as played in the honky-tonks of Storyville.

All the foregoing recordings, however, must be seen as precursors to the Hot Fives which, because of their profound effect on later music, are one of the most important bodies of recordings in 20th-century music. They provide an astonishing record of Armstrong's musical growth – his quick, electric climb to artistic maturity. Four trends are evident: a steady improvement in his technical skills; a growing confidence in the value of what he had to say; a progressive turning away from paraphrase to fresh invention; and a steady increase in emotional depth.

The Hot Fives may be divided into four groups. The initial group of 26 recordings (made from 12 November 1925 to 27 November 1926, with cornet, clarinet, trombone, piano, and banjo) are basically in the New Orleans style. However, as the series progressed, Armstrong came more to the fore as a soloist and, following the success of his scat singing on *Heebie Jeebies*, as a singer as well. It was not his singing but the sequence of breaks which most impressed musicians on *Cornet Chop Suey*. They are set over 16 bars of stop-time accompaniment. The first eight bars are cut neatly into two-bar segments, each appearing to comment or reflect on the preceding one. In the second eight bars the figures are cut more unevenly, enhancing the effect of a musical dialogue. Nonetheless Armstrong had not yet reached his musical maturity: he sometimes fumbled notes, and a mood of cheerfulness predominates throughout the series.

A second group of recordings was cut between 7 and 14 May 1927 by the Hot Five, this time augmented by drums and tuba, and issued under the name of Louis Armstrong and his Hot Seven. These performances include more solo playing at the expense of the ensemble, and show Armstrong moving even further away from paraphrase. On *Potato Head Blues*, the most celebrated of this group, he again played a solo over stop-time accompaniment, throwing long figures, at first regular in length but then increasingly varied, over the punctuation of the band. He also created short stretches of countermelody where the

Ex.1 From *Go 'long mule* (1924, Col. 228D); transcr. G. Schuller

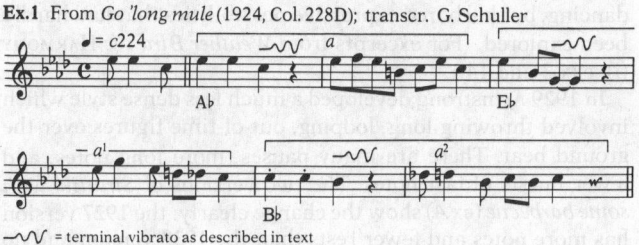

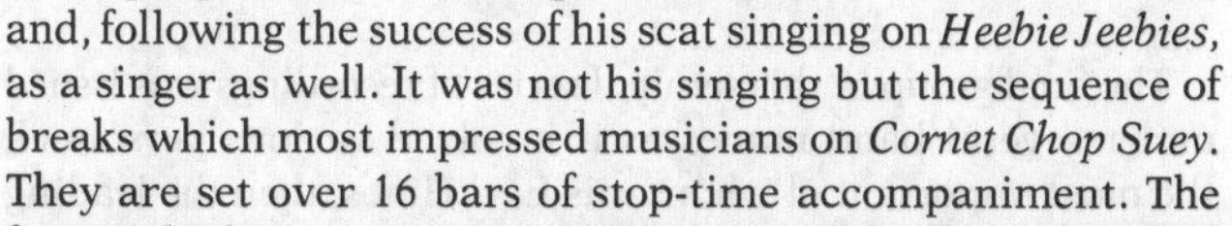

= terminal vibrato as described in text

accents fall away from the standard 4/4 pattern, for example at the beginning of the last eight bars of the solo and in the coda. His playing is more confident, and radiates variety and novelty.

The third group in the series returns to the original Hot Five band for nine sides made in September and December of 1927. Armstrong produced many brilliant moments in these performances, including a delicate solo on *Savoy Blues* and a fine bravura solo on *Struttin' with some barbecue.* The masterpiece of the set, however, is *Hotter than that,* possibly the most exuberant recorded performance in jazz. The piece opens with a boisterous introduction, and leaps immediately into a fervent trumpet solo. Later in the piece is a chorus of Armstrong's scat singing, the second half of which consists of a string of hemiolas over three-beat groups in the 4/4 accompaniment – an experiment in polymeters that foreshadows jazz performances of 30 years later (ex.2). By this point in his career Armstrong possessed the finest technique of any trumpeter in jazz, a reckless confidence, and an extraordinarily rich melodic imagination.

Ex.2 From *Hotter than that* (1927, OK 8535); transcr. J. B. Robinson

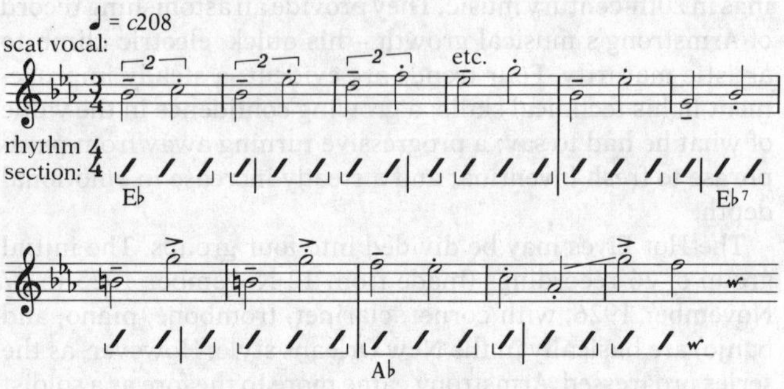

The final group in this seminal series of recordings was issued under several band names as it involved various personnel, the most important of whom was Earl Hines, then the leading jazz pianist. Armstrong had deepened emotionally: there is brooding melancholy in *Tight like this,* playfulness in *Weather Bird,* tragic sadness in *West End Blues.* This last is considered by many critics to be the greatest of Armstrong's recorded performances. It opens with a long rising and falling introduction, containing shifts in tempo and meter. Then follows a simple statement of the theme, which grows denser and rises at the end in a figure that echoes the introduction. There is a poignant vocal exchange with the clarinet, then a final chorus which Armstrong begins by holding a single high B♭ for nearly four bars, creating unbearable tension. This finally breaks into a sequence of desperate descending figures, followed by a long swirl to a quiet completion and resignation in the coda (ex.3). *West End Blues* is built on a series of climaxes, each higher than its predecessor. It has a unity of form and feeling rare in jazz, and was recognized immediately by the jazz community as a work of genius. It made clear once and for all that jazz was not a simple music meant to accompany drinking and dancing, but harbored expressive possibilities that had hardly been explored. (For excerpts from *Weather Bird see* HARMONY (i), exx.3 and 14.)

In 1929 Armstrong developed a much less dense style which involved throwing long, looping, out-of-time figures over the ground beat. There are many pauses, more long notes, and fewer bursts of fast notes. The two versions of *Struttin' with some barbecue* (ex.4) show the change clearly: the 1927 version has more notes and fewer rests than the 1938 version and no

Ex.3 From *West End Blues* (1928, OK 8597); transcr. G. Schuller

notes longer than a dotted quarter, whereas the later version has many half- and whole-notes, besides being taken in a higher key to display Armstrong's upper register. This new economy of style resulted in part from chronic lip problems and overwork. Armstrong at times used this spare method to great effect, as for example in *Sweethearts on Parade* (1930), whose novel introduction seems to double back on itself, and *Mahogany Hall Stomp* (1929), where in the second chorus of his second solo he created counter-meters which flow back and forth across the bar lines. Nonetheless, his work from this point on represents a gradual but inexorable decline. Far too often he indulged in meaningless high-register riffs which excited audiences of the time but lacked the passion and musical interest of his performances with the Hot Five. Yet even here there are gems to be discovered: *Star Dust* (1931), a fine example of his spare method; *I double dare you* (1938), in which the lines are cut obliquely to the shape of the tune; and the big-band version of *Struttin' with some barbecue* (1938), which he turned into a mere skeleton of the song. And whatever his excesses Armstrong always swung, and frequently created more pure jazz from straightforward statements of mediocre tunes than lesser players could produce from much better material.

Ex.4

(a) From *Struttin' with some barbecue* (1927, OK 8566); transcr. G. L. Collier

(b) From *Struttin' with some barbecue* (1938, Decca 1661); transcr. G. L. Collier

During these years Armstrong's singing style also changed. On his early recordings with the Hot Five he used his natural gravelly voice, but later he adopted a smoother, lighter tone in the style of the crooners. By the mid-1930s, however, thickening of the vocal chords made it difficult for him to produce a smooth sound, and he reverted to his natural voice. (For a more detailed discussion of Armstrong's style as a singer *see* SINGING, esp. §4.)

In 1947 Armstrong returned to a small-band format with the All Stars, which he led until shortly before his death, although he continued to record occasionally with large studio orchestras. His formal recordings tended to be commercialized. However, a great deal of music from informal concerts and broadcasts is available; although quite uneven and often replete with showy and well-worn phrases, it is nevertheless sometimes filled with Armstrong's former passion. Among the best recordings from this period is a collection of new versions of his classic performances called *Satchmo: a Musical Autobiography* (1956–7, Decca 155). At times in these he reaches the heights he attained in the originals, as in *See See Rider* and *King of the Zulus*.

Armstrong's greatest significance lies in his music up to about 1936, after which, although he continued to play brilliant jazz at times, he became primarily a popular entertainer. His first achievement was his incessant, intense swing, of which he was the consummate master and prime exemplar. Second was the originality and passion of his musical invention, through which the listener seemed directly to sense the artist's personality. Finally, through his example, he turned jazz from an ensemble to a soloist's music. His approach was so remarkable that Armstrong became the model for virtually all jazz musicians of his time.

Oral history material in *LNT*, *NjR*.

See also BLUES, §3; JAZZ (i), §III, 3; and TRUMPET, §§2 and 3; for further illustrations *see* CATLETT, SID; JAZZ (i), fig.2; OLIVER, KING; NIGHTCLUBS AND OTHER VENUES, fig.3; and TEAGARDEN.

SELECTED RECORDINGS

Duo with E. Hines: Weather Bird (1928, OK 41454)

As leader of the Hot Five, Hot Seven: Heebie Jeebies (1926, OK 8300); Cornet Chop Suey (1926, OK 8320); Skid-dat-de-dat (1926, OK 8436); Big Butter and Egg Man (1926, OK 8423); Willie the Weeper (1927, OK 8482); Potato Head Blues (1927, OK 8503); S.O.L. Blues (1927, Col. 35661); Gully Low Blues (1927, OK 8474); Struttin' with some barbecue (1927, OK 8566); I'm not Rough (1927, OK 8551); Hotter than that/Savoy Blues (1927, OK 8535); A Monday Date (1928, OK 8609); Fireworks (1928, OK 8597); West End Blues (1928, OK 8597); Save it pretty mama (1928, OK 8657); Muggles (1928, OK 8703); Tight like this (1928, OK 8649)

As leader of big bands: Mahogany Hall Stomp (1929, OK 8680); Ain't Misbehavin' (1929, OK 8714); When you're smiling (1929, OK 8729); Sweethearts on Parade (1930, Col. 2688D); Star Dust (1931, OK 41530); Between the devil and the deep blue sea (1932, OK 41550); I gotta right to sing the blues (1933, Vic. 24233); Struttin' with some barbecue (1938, Decca 1661); I double dare you (1938, Decca 1636)

As leader of the All Stars: Rockin' Chair/Save it pretty mama (1947, Vic. 40-4004); I surrender, dear/Baby, won't you please come home (1950, Decca 9-27190); Basin Street Blues (1954, Decca 29102); *Louis Armstrong Plays W. C. Handy* (1954, Col. CL591), incl. St. Louis Blues, Yellow Dog Blues; *Satch Plays Fats* (1955, Col. CL708), incl. Black and Blue, Honeysuckle Rose; Hello Dolly (1963, Kapp 573)

As sideman: K. Oliver: Chimes Blues/Froggie Moore (1923, Gen. 5135); F. Henderson: Go 'long mule (1924, Col. 228D); C. Williams: Texas Moaner Blues (1924, OK 8171); F. Henderson: Copenhagen (1924, Voc. 14926); Mandy make up your mind (1924, Para. 20367); Red Onion Jazz Babies: Cake Walkin' Babies (1924, Gen. 5627); Bessie Smith: St. Louis Blues (1925, Col. 14064D); Reckless Blues (1925, Col. 14056D); Trixie Smith: Railroad Blues (1925, Para. 12262); Clara Smith: Shipwrecked Blues (1925, Col. 14077D); F. Henderson: Sugar Foot Stomp (1925, Col. 395D); Chippie Hill: Lonesome Weary Blues (1926, OK 8453)

TRANSCRIPTIONS

125 Jazz Breaks for Cornet (Chicago, 1927)
Louis Armstrong's 50 Hot Choruses for Cornet (Chicago, 1927)
L. Castle: *Louis Armstrong's Immortal Trumpet Solos* (New York, 1947)
A Jazz Master (New York, 1961) [20 solos]

BIBLIOGRAPHY

DISCOGRAPHIES, ETC.

Satchmo: Collector's Copy (Hollywood, CA, 1971) [iconography]
J. G. Jepsen: *A Discography of Louis Armstrong: 1923–1971* (Copenhagen, 1973)
B. Englund: "A Louis Armstrong Filmography," *Coda*, xii/3 (1975), 5; addns and corrections by K. Stratemann, xii/4 (1975), 32
K. Stratemann: "Louis Armstrong: a Filmo-discography," *IAJRCJ*, x–xi (aut. 1977–aut. 1978)
H. Westerberg: *Boy from New Orleans: Louis "Satchmo" Armstrong, on Records, Films, Radio and Television* (Copenhagen, 1981) [incl. discography]

LIFE AND WORKS STUDIES

L. Armstrong: *Swing that Music* (New York, 1936)
R. Goffin: *Louis Armstrong: le roi du jazz* (Paris, 1947; Eng. trans., 1947/*R*1977 as *Horn of Plenty*)
H. Panassié: *Louis Armstrong* (Paris, 1947)
L. Armstrong: *Satchmo: my Life in New Orleans* (New York, 1954; Ger. trans., Zurich, 1977)
D. Halberstam: "A Day with Satchmo," *JJ*, x/8 (1957), 1
P. Studer and J. Failows: "Louis Armstrong réenregistre les 'Hot Five'," *BHcF*, no.65 (1957), 3
——: "Les enregistrements 'Decca' de Louis Armstrong," *BHcF*, no.66 (1957), 5
B. Wood: "Honteuses attaques contre Louis Armstrong," *BHcF*, no.70 (1957), 7
D. Houlden: "All Stars Past and Present," *JJ*, xi/3 (1958), 3
G. E. Lambert: "Louis Armstrong Today," *JM*, v/4 (1959), 10
A. McCarthy: *Louis Armstrong* (London, 1960); repr. in *Kings of Jazz*, ed. S. Green (South Brunswick, NJ, and New York, 1978)
M. Williams: "Satchmo and the Soloist," *JJ*, xviii/6 (1965), 5
M. Williams: *Jazz Masters of New Orleans* (New York and London, 1967/*R*1978)
F. Romary: "Struttin' with some Louis," *Sv*, no.15 (1968), 5
B. Kumm: "Louis Armstrong: Reflections on King Oliver and the Cotton Club," *Sv*, no.19 (1968), 9
H. Panassié: *Louis Armstrong* (Paris, 1969; Eng. trans., New York, 1971)
M. Jones, J. Chilton, and L. Feather: *Salute to Satchmo* (London, 1970)
S. Traill: "Back o' Louis," *JJ*, xxiii/7 (1970), 24
M. Williams: *The Jazz Tradition* (New York, 1970, rev. 2/1983)
T. Zwicky: "Louis and some West Coast Friends," *Sv*, no.29 (1970), 176
R. Meryman: *Louis Armstrong: a Self-portrait* (New York, 1971)
M. Jones and J. Chilton: *Louis: the Louis Armstrong Story, 1900–1971* (London, 1971)
H. Panassié: "Souvenirs sur Louis Armstrong," *BHcF*, no.211 (1971), 7
M. Gautier and H. Panassié: "Louis Armstrong," *BHcF*, no.219 (1972), 3
Coda, xi/2 (1973) [special issue]
B. Englund: "Louis Armstrong in Scandinavia, 1933," *Sv*, no.49 (1973), 23
G. M. Colombe: "How do they Age so well?: Louis's Last Half Dozen," *JJ*, xxvii/1 (1974), 22
"Louis: by his Friends," *Sv*, no.59 (1975), 180
R. Hoskins: *Louis Armstrong: Biography of a Musician* (Los Angeles, 1979) [incl. list of films and discography]
W. Mauro: *Louis Armstrong: il re del jazz* (Milan, 1979)
H. Rye: "Visiting Firemen, 2: Louis Armstrong," *Sv*, no.89 (1980), 184
J. L. Collier: *Louis Armstrong: an American Genius* (New York, 1983, London, 1984, as *Louis Armstrong: a Biography*)
G. Giddins, ed.: "Armstrong at 85," *VV*, xxx (27 Aug 1985), 65 [special section]
M. Pinfold: *Louis Armstrong* (Tunbridge Wells, England, and New York, 1987) [incl. discography]

ANALYTICAL AND SPECIALIST STUDIES

F. Ramsey, Jr., and C. E. Smith, eds.: *Jazzmen* (New York, 1939/*R*1977)
J. Slawe: *Louis Armstrong: zehn monographische Studien* (Basle, 1953)
A. Hodeir: *Hommes et problèmes du jazz, suivi de La religion du jazz* (Paris, 1954; Eng. trans., rev. Hodeir, as *Jazz: its Evolution and Essence*, New York, 1956/*R*1975)
M. Edey: "Louis Armstrong," *JR*, ii/7 (1959), 28
R. Hadlock: *Jazz Masters of the Twenties* (New York, 1965/*R*1985)
W. Austin: *Music in the 20th Century, from Debussy through Stravinsky* (New York, 1966)
G. Schuller: *Early Jazz: its Roots and Musical Development* (New York, 1968), 89–133
H. Pleasants: *The Great American Popular Singers* (New York, 1974)
H. D. Caffey: "The Musical Style of Louis Armstrong," *JJS*, iii/1 (1975), 72 [incl. transcrs.]
C. Albertson and J. S. Wilson: Liner notes, *Giants of Jazz* (TL 01, 1978)

JAMES LINCOLN COLLIER

Arnet, Jan (*b* Prague, 1934). Czechoslovak double bass player. He first studied violin and trombone (1945–52), then double bass and theory (1957). In the early to mid-1960s he recorded many albums in Prague with Zdenek Bartak's big band, Karel Vlach (1962–3), Karel Velebný's quartet and quintet (1962–5), Jan Konopasek (1963), and the pianist Milan Dvořák (1964); in 1965 he toured and recorded with the Reduta Quintet. In West Germany and France he played with Leo Wright and Booker Ervin. In 1966 he moved to the USA, where he worked as a producer, arranger, conductor, and performer. He played with Elvin Jones, Tony Scott, Howard McGhee, and Attila Zoller, and recorded with Sonny Stitt (1966), Chico Hamilton (*c*1967, *c*1974), and Ervin (1968). As a member of Art Blakey's Jazz Messengers (1969–70) he toured Japan, where the group recorded *Jazz Messengers '70* (1970, Cat. 7902). He has also lectured and written articles on jazz, and was for a time a commentator for the radio network Voice of America. (*Feather–Gitler '70s*)

ERIC THACKER

Arnold [Persson], **Harry** (*b* Hälsingborg, Sweden, 7 Aug 1920; *d* Stockholm, 11 Feb 1971). Swedish bandleader, arranger, and saxophonist. He led a big band in Malmö (1942–9), belonged to Thore Ehrling's band in Stockholm (1949–52), and worked in studios. From 1956 to 1965 he was the leader of Radiobandet (the Swedish Radio Big Band), which achieved considerable success in the USA under the name Jazztone Mystery Band. The ensemble played in a modernized swing style, included such prominent Swedish musicians as Arne Domnérus, Bengt Hallberg, Bjarne Nerem, Åke Persson, Carl-Henrik Norin, Egil Johansson, and Georg Riedel, and made several recordings with such guest soloists as Benny Bailey, Nat Adderley, and Coleman Hawkins; in 1958 Quincy Jones wrote several fine arrangements for the band.

SELECTED RECORDINGS

This is Harry and the Mystery Band (1957, Met. MLP15006), incl. Six-ten, Stand by (This is Harry); *Quincy's Home Again* (1958, Met. MLP15010), incl. The Midnight Sun Never Sets, Room 608; *Harry Arnold Guest Book* (1960–61, Met. MLP15081), incl. Frosty Summer, On the Sunny Side of the Street

BIBLIOGRAPHY

"Mannen bakom orkestern" [The man behind the orchestra], *Estrad*, vii/1 (1945), 11

"Svenskt stjärnalbum" [Swedish star-album], *Orkester journalen*, xiv/7 (1946), 5

B. Englund: "Arnold, Harry," *Sohlmans musiklexikon* (Stockholm, rev. and enlarged 2/1975–9 ed. H. Åstrand)

E. Kjellberg: *Svensk jazzhistoria: en översikt* [Swedish jazz history: an overview] (Stockholm, 1985)

ERIK KJELLBERG

Arnold, Horacee [Horace Emmanuel] (*b* Wayland, KY, 25 Sept 1937). Drummer. He began playing drums in 1957 while stationed in Los Angeles as a member of the US Coast Guard. After taking a stage name by adding a silent "e" to his forename he played in Dave Baker's big band (1959), with Roland Kirk (1959–60) and Charles Mingus (1960), and in a trio with Cecil McBee and the pianist Kirk Lightsey (1960). He worked in New York with Henry Grimes and the pianist Hassan Ibn Ali (1961–2), in 1962 toured Asia with Alvin Ailey's dance company and played with Bud Powell, and worked with Hugh Masekela and Miriam Makeba (1963–5). In 1965–6 he studied composition with Heiner Stadler, and guitar and composition with Hy Gubenick and Ralph Towner, and in 1967 he formed the Here and Now Company, which at various times included Karl Berger, Sam Rivers, Robin Kenyatta, Joe Farrell, and Mike Lawrence. He led the company until 1970, then performed and recorded as the leader of other groups in the early 1970s; he also performed with Return to Forever and Stan Getz (1973) and toured Japan with Archie Shepp (1978). With the drummers Billy Hart and Freddie Waits he formed Colloquium III in the late 1970s, which led workshops at the New York Drummers' Collective; in the 1980s he taught at William Paterson College of New Jersey, worked as a freelance, and performed in a trio with Dave Friedman.

SELECTED RECORDINGS

As leader: *Tribe* (1972, Col. KC32150); *Tales of the Exonerated Flea* (*c*1973, Col. KC32869)

As sideman: R. Kenyatta: *Until* (1966–7, Vortex 2005); C. Corea: *Is* (1969, SolS 18055); A. Shepp: *Live in Tokyo* (1978, Denon 7538); B. Harper: *Billy Harper Quintet in Europe* (1979, SN 1001)

BIBLIOGRAPHY

J. Welch: "Horacee Arnold: Turning Kids onto Jazz," *DB*, xxxvii/18 (1970), 11

M. Hohman: "Profile: Horacee Arnold," *DB*, xli/21 (1974), 36

B. Primack: "Drummers Colloquium III: Multiple Percussionists," *DB*, xlvi/17 (1979), 25

C. Iero: "Colloquium III," *MD*, iv/1 (1980), 12

L. Jeske: "Horacee Arnold: Examining the Values," *MD*, viii/11 (1984), 24

ED HAZELL

Arodin [Arnondrin], **Sidney (J.)** (*b* Westwego, LA, 29 March 1901; *d* New Orleans, 6 Feb 1948). Clarinetist and composer. He played on Mississippi riverboats with Johnny Stein, then moved in 1922 to New York, where he performed with the Original New Orleans Jazz Band until 1925. He worked in San Antonio with the New Orleans Rhythm Masters (1926) and in New Orleans with the Halfway House Orchestra and Monk Hazel, for whom he also occasionally played tin whistle (1928). Between tours with the trombonist Sunny Clapp (1929) and the New Orleans Swing Kings (1930) he participated in the renowned recording session by the JONES AND COLLINS ASTORIA HOT EIGHT. After working in Kansas City during summer 1933 Arodin returned to New York the following year with Louis Prima's band; he also played there with Wingy Manone and the New Orleans Rhythm Kings. During 1939 and 1940 he led his own group in New Orleans, but in 1941 became ill and as a result worked only sporadically until his death. Arodin was highly respected by his colleagues. He wrote several songs, many of which relate to the Mississippi; the best known of these is *Lazy River* (1930), written in collaboration with Hoagy Carmichael.

SELECTED RECORDINGS

As sideman: Johnnie Miller: Panama/Dipper Mouth Blues (1928, Col. 1546D); M. Hazel: Sizzling the Blues/High Society (1928, Bruns. 4181); Jones and Collins Astoria Hot Eight: Astoria Strut/Duet Stomp (1929, Vic. 38576); New Orleans Rhythm Kings: San Antonio Shout/Tin Roof Blues (1934, Decca 161); Ostrich Walk/Original Dixieland One-step (1934, Decca 229)

BIBLIOGRAPHY

ChiltonW

D. Perry: "Up the Lazy River: Sidney Arodin: his Life and Records," *Jazzfinder*, i/3 (1948), 11 [incl. discography]

J. Simmen: "Wylie Avenue Blues: Homage to a Wonderful Clarinet Player: Sidney J. Arodin," *Sv*, no.37 (1971), 28

RAYMOND J. GARIGLIO

Arrangement. The reworking or recomposing of a musical composition or some part of it (such as the melody) for a medium or ensemble other than that of the original; also the resulting version of the piece.

1. Definition and scope. 2. To 1930. 3. The swing era. 4. After 1945. 5. Conclusion.

1. DEFINITION AND SCOPE. The term "arrangement" has acquired a special meaning in jazz within the concept of arrangement as it is applied in a variety of ways in the broader field of music in general. In a sense all jazz performance, insofar as it is

improvised and constantly renewed, constitutes a form of arranging; that is, the performers rearrange the basic material in ever new variations and forms. In that broadest sense an extemporization on a popular standard by Louis Armstrong (e.g., *Star Dust*, 1931, OK 41530), Eric Dolphy (e.g., *Stormy Weather* on Charles Mingus's album *Mingus!*, 1960, Can. 9021), or John Coltrane (e.g., *My Favorite Things* on the album of the same name, 1960, Atl. 1361) is a one-time arrangement, to be once again re-arranged in a different form in the next performance of the same material.

But in a narrower sense the term "arrangement" in jazz has come to mean a written-down, fixed, often printed and published version of a composition, usually arranged for one of the various standard jazz ensembles (jazz orchestra, big band, small group, etc.). Such arrangements range from strictly practical versions, primarily designed to serve commercial interests and wider professional dissemination – as in the "stock arrangements" of the 1930s and 1940s – to highly creative recompositions, which transform the basic material in a specific style or manner, in itself marked by a striking originality which may even surpass the quality of the original material. In the latter category it is the arranger's musical imagination and skill in terms of, for example, harmonic invention or orchestrational resourcefulness that will inform the final product much more than the original piece on which it is based.

There are thus parallels to the various concepts of arrangement applicable in Western classical music. An arrangement that is merely a reinstrumentation of an existing work (e.g., a symphony by Mozart arranged for a small ensemble of flute, violin, cello, and piano; or Liszt's arrangements for piano of Beethoven's symphonies) is very similar to the straightforward dance-band and jazz-orchestra arrangements made by the thousand (and often published as stock arrangements) in the 1930s and 1940s. On the other hand, a rather substantial reworking, not only in instrumentation but in aspects of harmony, melody, and even continuity (such as Rimsky-Korsakov's recasting of Musorgsky's opera *Boris Godunov*), finds its parallel in jazz in such arrangements as those by Duke Ellington of Philip Braham's *Limehouse Blues* (1931, Vic. 22743) and his own *A Gypsy without a Song* (1938, Bruns. 8186), by Eddie Sauter of Arthur Johnston's *My Old Flame* (recorded by Benny Goodman, 1941, Col. 36754), and by Gil Evans of Chummy McGregor's *Moon Dreams* and Gershwin's *Porgy and Bess* (both for Miles Davis, respectively on *Classics in Jazz*, 1949–50, Cap. H459, and *Porgy and Bess*, 1958, Col. CL1274). In jazz, therefore, the arranger's task can cover a wide spectrum of options, ranging from a strict, unadorned rendering of a tune or popular song (as in the vast majority of "commercial" arrangements) to the most inventive recomposing of such material, and all manner of gradations in between.

Just as the relationship between the arrangement and the original composition varies greatly from piece to piece, so the role of the arranger and his relationship to the material and its performance vary greatly from one case to another. Some composers make arrangements of their own or (less commonly) others' works for their own or (less commonly) others' bands (e.g., Duke Ellington, Jelly Roll Morton, Benny Carter, John Lewis, and Gerry Mulligan); but many arrangers are not themselves composers (e.g., Bill Challis, Sy Oliver, Fletcher Henderson, Ray Conniff, and Eddie Durham). Some arrangers are also bandleaders (e.g., Isham Jones, Henderson, Glenn Miller, and Artie Shaw), while others work for bands on any of a number of possible bases (as a sideman, a staff arranger, and freelance). The permutations of these functions are numerous and there has often been considerable overlap among the categories.

One other type of arrangement, which jazz shares with blues, rock, and other kinds of popular music, is the so-called "head arrangement." Such "arrangements" are generally not written down (though in some cases they are partially written or sketched out in notation) but are assembled instead from the ideas (as it were, out of the heads) of an entire band or perhaps some of its leading members. Widespread in jazz, this form of arrangement results from a conceptually simple yet technically complex combining of players' suggestions, the working out of individual parts in rehearsals, intuitive spontaneous contributions, memorization, and, sometimes, the group leader's final arbitration concerning all these elements. Many of the finest arrangements by orchestras such as Count Basie's and Duke Ellington's were achieved in this collective, collaborative way.

In the early history of jazz, a music then largely improvised by players who in most instances could not read musical notation, the concept of arrangement was considered by many musicians and critics at worst a contradiction in terms and at best antithetical to the spirit and essence of jazz. But as arrangers and composers such as Don Redman, Duke Ellington, John Nesbitt, Bill Challis, and Jesse Stone began successfully to translate the prevailing improvisational styles into distinctive orchestral ensemble concepts, arrangements achieved an artistic validity of their own, becoming increasingly a central, integral part of the developing jazz tradition. Moreover, from a practical point of view, as jazz ensembles grew in size, as reading skills improved, as the repertory expanded, and as jazz practice turned from collective improvisation to a more solo-oriented approach, the written arrangement became a virtual necessity, within which improvisational spontaneity could be preserved and integrated.

2. To 1930. The earliest arrangements that can be associated with jazz (at least some forms of it) were made in the late 1910s and early 1920s by orchestra leaders such as James Reese Europe, Art Hickman, Isham Jones, and Sammy Stewart, and composer–arrangers such as Jelly Roll Morton and Ferde Grofé, as well as for some of the more successful "polite" dance orchestras in New Orleans. Jones was a particularly imaginative arranger, achieving with his relatively small orchestras (ten players in 1922, for example) a maximum of timbral and ensemble effect by the use of ingeniously varied voicings and instrumental combinations (as exemplified by *My Honey's Lovin' Arms*, 1922, Bruns. 2301, and *Farewell Blues*, 1923, Bruns. 2406). Indeed, Jones (and Grofé with Paul Whiteman's band) must be credited with elaborating and standardizing the basic dance-band and jazz-orchestra instrumentation, which continued in jazz virtually unchanged until the mid-1940s: it consisted of three choirs of instruments – reeds (saxophones and clarinets), brass, and a rhythm section (piano, drums, banjo or guitar, and double bass or tuba).

King Oliver's Creole Jazz Band in Chicago and Sam Morgan's orchestra in New Orleans, relying principally on ensemble improvisations (with an occasional interpolated solo accompanied by the rhythm section), basically eschewed written-down arrangements, although occasionally certain ensemble passages might be evolved as head arrangements (a case in point is the stop-time passage accompanying the clarinet solo on Oliver's two recordings made in 1923 of *Dippermouth Blues*, Gen. 5132 and OK 4918).

The most outstanding and influential pioneer arrangers in jazz in the 1920s were (in chronological order) Don Redman (with Fletcher Henderson's orchestra), Jelly Roll Morton (with his recording group the Red Hot Peppers), Duke Ellington (with his own orchestra), John Nesbitt (with McKinney's Cotton Pickers), and Bill Challis (with Paul Whiteman's orchestra). Redman certainly helped to elaborate and establish that basic orchestral style of jazz characterized by the call-and-response alternation of instrumental choirs (reeds and brass) and the integration of solos in a larger ensemble context; Redman also introduced a specialty of his own, the prominent use of a trio of clarinets. Redman's ensemble scoring consisted in essence of jazz solos translated into multiple-part harmonizations, usually in parallel voicings. Morton's outstanding contributions as an arranger, on the other hand, lay in his virtuoso handling of improvised solos so as to integrate them stylistically and formally with the essential character of the underlying composition, his ability to preserve the spirit of collective spontaneity, and the achievement of an astonishing timbral and orchestrational diversity with only seven players; he was also exceptional in his insistence on painstaking rehearsing, which was virtually unknown in jazz of the mid-1920s. Table 1 shows the structure (based on two different themes) and salient details of the instrumentation of Morton's *Black Bottom Stomp* (1926, Vic. 20221); it well illustrates the balance between improvised and arranged material, the contrast of full ensemble sound and various solo combinations, and the aforementioned timbral and sonoric variety he could achieve with small resources.

Ellington, undoubtedly the greatest arranger (and composer) jazz has ever known, evolved a unique approach to orchestral writing and sound, profoundly influenced in the early stages of his career by the highly individual instrumental styles of some of his players, notably the trumpeters Bubber Miley and Arthur Whetsol, the trombonist Tricky Sam Nanton, the baritone saxophonist Harry Carney, and the clarinetist Barney Bigard. In such works as *East St. Louis Toodle-o* (1926, Voc. 1064), *Black and Tan Fantasy* (1927, Bruns. 3526), *The Mooche* (1928, OK 8623), *Old Man Blues* (1930, Bb 6450), and *Mood Indigo* (1930, Bruns. 4952) Ellington was able to produce orchestral scores that brought together composition and arrangement in a highly creative symbiosis never before achieved in jazz, and which, as it developed in the ensuing years, remained completely distinctive for nearly two decades.

Table 1 Structure and instrumentation of *Black Bottom Stomp* (1926, Vic. 20221) composed and arranged by Jelly Roll Morton

Structural divisions	intro	A1	A2			
Instrumentation	*full ens (vamp)	full ens (arranged)	tpt	full ens	tpt	full ens
Number of bars	‖: 4 :‖	‖: 8 :‖	4	4	4	4

A3	modulating interlude	B1				B2	
cl (acc. banjo)	full ens	full ens	tpt break	trbn break	full ens	cl solo	†full ens
16	4	6	1	1	12	18	2
		20				20	

B3		B4	B5	B6		
pf solo (without rhythm section)	†full ens	tpt solo (stop-time acc.)	banjo solo	full ens	drum break	full ens
18	2	20	20	6	2	12
20				20		

B7			coda
full ens (prominent tom-tom)	trbn break	full ens (prominent tom-tom)	full ens (prominent tom-tom)
6	2	12	2
20			

*Full ens: cornet, cl, trbn, pf, banjo, db, drums

†Full ens break: 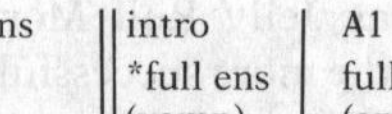

Table 2 Structure and instrumentation of *Put it there* (1928, Vic. 38025) arranged by John Nesbitt and recorded by McKinney's Cotton Pickers

Structural divisions	intro	1	2	3 [4]
Instrumentation	sax section, tuba	full ens	brass	pf solo
Number of bars	2	12	12	‖: 2 + 12 :‖

5	6 (material from intro)		7	8 (material from intro)				
sax section, tuba		trbn solo	sax section	full ens	pf solo	full ens	pf solo	full ens
12	2	12	12	2	2	2	2	2

9 (material from intro)						10 (material from intro)	
full ens	a sax solo	trbn solo	tpt solo	t sax solo	full ens		full ens
2	2	2	2	2	4	2	12

Nesbitt drew inspiration in his remarkable arrangements and compositions for McKinney's Cotton Pickers from both Redman and Ellington. Table 2 (*Put it there*, 1928, Vic. 38025) shows the considerable textural and thematic variety he achieved, his generally variational approach to form and continuity, and structures that are at times almost mosaic-like (as in choruses 8 and 9).

Challis's arranging for Whiteman was inspired both by the trumpeter Bix Beiderbecke and by the work of contemporary classical composers such as Ravel and Stravinsky; his scores are, though in their own quite different way, as distinctive as Ellington's. In the late 1920s Challis and Grofé were able to draw upon the remarkably versatile talents of the larger than usual Paul Whiteman Orchestra: in 1928 the orchestra had 21 players (six reeds, four trumpets, four trombones, tuba, string bass, banjo, piano, and four violins) – an ensemble that offered unprecedentedly copious doubling capacities in the reeds. (In a number of arrangements as many as 26 different wind instruments were played by six musicians in the course of $3\frac{1}{2}$ minutes.)

3. The swing era. The fundamentals of jazz arranging having been established by 1930, the swing era – especially after the phenomenal success of Benny Goodman's orchestra in 1935, and the resultant emergence of hundreds of jazz and dance bands – witnessed an unprecedented proliferation of diverse arranging styles. The jazz orchestra stabilized at 14 or 15 players, typically three trumpets, three trombones, four (later five) saxophones, and four rhythm instruments. Two major arranging styles were current: that of the Henderson brothers, Fletcher and Horace, as represented in Goodman's orchestra, and that of Count Basie's orchestra, which was based in Kansas City. Fletcher Henderson had taken over the duty of arranging for his own orchestra after Redman left to join McKinney's Cotton Pickers, but when Henderson's operation failed in 1934 Goodman engaged Henderson as his chief arranger and asked him to re-create his earlier arrangements, such as *Blue Skies* (1935, Vic. 25136), *King Porter Stomp* (which Goodman recorded as *King Porter*, 1935, Vic. 25090; *see* Forms, §3), and *Down South Camp Meeting* (1936, Vic. 25387); Goodman's recordings

Table 3 Structure and instrumentation of Count Basie's *Texas Shuffle* (1938, Decca 2030) arranged by Herschel Evans

Structural divisions	intro	1	2	3	4			5			6
		aaba	*aaba*	*aaba*	*aa*	*b*	*a*	*aa*	*b*	*a*	*aa*
Number of bars	4	32	32	32	16	8	8	16	8	8	16
Instrumentation								cl obbligato	8	cl obbligato	cl obbligato
				cl solo	trbn solo	t sax solo	trbn solo	muted tpt punctuations	8	muted tpt punctuations	muted tpt punctuations
			tpt solo	muted tpt punctuations	muted tpt punctuations (varied)			trbn (riff)	8	trbn (riff)	trbn (riff)
			sax (riff)	trbn (riff)	sax (riff varied)			sax (riff)	8	sax (riff)	sax (riff)
	pf (unacc.)	rhythm section	rhythm section	rhythm section	rhythm section			rhythm section	pf solo, rhythm section	rhythm section	rhythm section
Dynamics		p	mp	mf	f			ff			p

thus brought black orchestral jazz to a vast new white audience for the first time. Basie's band set a much looser style, more oriented towards improvised solos, and in its early days relied heavily on head arrangements and the frequent use of riffs, though it also occasionally employed written-out scores by Buster Smith, Jimmy Mundy, Andy Gibson, and Herschel Evans. Table 3 shows how the structure of Evans's arrangement for Basie of *Texas Shuffle* (1938, Decca 2030) builds up over the work's six choruses, and how its solos are integrated with and accompanied by a variety of interrelated motifs (riffs).

Apart from Ellington, the most creative arranger of the 1930s was Sy Oliver, who set the basic style of Jimmie Lunceford's orchestra. Like Ellington, Oliver was a masterly orchestral colorist, as *Dream of you* (1934, Decca 765), *Babs* (1935, Decca 576), *Organ Grinder's Swing* (1936, Decca 908), and *For Dancers Only* (1937, Decca 1340; ex.1 p.36) demonstrate. His economical scores (*Organ Grinder's Swing* is a good example, see Table 4) allow for a maximum of swing and solo participation, as well as highly original, richly varied orchestral textures.

Virtually every major orchestra had by the early 1930s its own staff of arrangers: Chick Webb was served by Edgar Sampson and Charlie Dixon, Andy Kirk by Mary Lou Williams and Earl Thompson, Cab Calloway by Foots Thomas (brother of Joe Thomas (ii)) and Harry White, and Earl Hines by Jimmy Mundy and Budd Johnson. By the late 1930s, in the wake of Goodman's great popular and artistic success, the competition among white swing bands led to a frantic search for a clearly identifiable style. This was usually achieved by the arranger,

Table 4 Structure and instrumentation of Jimmie Lunceford's *Organ Grinder's Swing* (1936, Decca 908) arranged by Sy Oliver

Structural divisions	1 (E♭ major)		2 (G major)	
Instrumentation	tpt, trbn, cl trio (acc. temple blocks)	growl tpt solo (acc. bar sax, rhythm section)	celesta solo (acc. temple blocks)	gui solo (acc. soft sax section, rhythm section)
Number of bars	8 (4 + 4)	8	8 (4 + 4)	8
	12-bar blues		12-bar blues	

3 (G major)		4 [5] (G major)	6 (E♭ major)	
cl solo (acc. soft sax section)	tpt solo (P. Webster)	muted tpt solo (S. Oliver)	tpt, trbn, cl trio (acc. temple blocks)	growl tpt solo (acc. bar sax, rhythm section)
4	8	: 8 :	8 (4 + 4)	8
12-bar blues			12-bar blues	

though a few bandleaders, such as Glenn Miller (himself a talented arranger), Goodman, Charlie Barnet, and Artie Shaw, were actively involved in setting their orchestras' idioms. Others, such as Tommy Dorsey and Harry James, had to rely on their arrangers to effect a distinctive, recognizable style (Oliver and Axel Stordahl worked for Dorsey, Leroy Holmes and Dave Matthews for James).

In the meantime Ellington and his favorite instrument – his orchestra – forged ahead, consolidating their earlier achievements and refining an orchestral conception in which composition and arrangement were inextricably and uniquely linked. Through countless experiments and continual probing and expanding of his orchestra's resources, in works such as *Daybreak Express* (1933, Vic. 24501), *Delta Serenade* (1934, Vic. 24755), *Moonglow* (1934, Bruns. 6987), *Reminiscing in Tempo* (1935, Bruns. 7546), *Echoes of Harlem* (1936, Bruns. 7650), *Azure* (1937, Master 131), *Diminuendo in Blue/Crescendo in Blue* (1937, Bruns. 8004), *A Gypsy without a Song* (1938, Bruns. 8186), and *Blue Light* (1938, Bruns. 8297), Ellington had created by 1940 a perfection and unity of style that led to the ultimate masterpieces of the early 1940s, beginning with *Ko-Ko* (1940, Vic. 26577), *Cotton Tail* (1940, Vic. 26610), *Dusk* (1940, Vic. 26677), *Take the "A" Train* (1941, Vic. 27380), Billy Strayhorn's *Chelsea Bridge* (1941, Vic. 27740), *Moon Mist* (1942, Vic. 27856), and *Main Stem* (1942, Vic. 20-1556).

The turn of the decade saw the emergence of three major arranging talents: Billy Strayhorn began to work with Duke Ellington in 1939, Eddie Sauter (who had earlier worked for Red Norvo) joined Benny Goodman in the same year, and Buster Harding began to work as a freelance with Count Basie in 1940 (he later joined Goodman, 1941, and Artie Shaw, 1944). During this period, the height of the big-band era, the arranger became pre-eminent in jazz. As one who developed concepts, set the style, and inspired the musicians, he had become in many cases more important than the titular leader of the band. Thus in jazz the arrangement took on an importance far beyond the composition. In the best examples, improvisation and arrangement stimulated and complemented each other; in lesser manifestations the arrangement eventually drove out improvisation, and as arrangements became increasingly formulaic (a trend typified by the use of call-and-response in Henderson's scores for Goodman and the use of riffs by Basie's orchestra) jazz orchestral styles atrophied and the essential spontaneity of jazz was seriously undermined and threatened.

4. After 1945. But as swing evolved into bop and modern jazz, young arrangers such as Ralph Burns (with Woody Herman's

Ex.1 Fourth chorus of Jimmie Lunceford's *For Dancers Only* (1937, Decca 1340) arranged by Sy Oliver; transcr. G. Schuller (all parts notated at sounding pitch)

seminal band, Herman's Herd, of 1944–6), Gerald Valentine and Tadd Dameron (with Billy Eckstine's band of the mid-1940s), Dameron, John Lewis, and Gil Fuller (with Dizzy Gillespie's orchestra), Gerry Mulligan (with Gene Krupa, Elliott Lawrence, and Stan Kenton), Pete Rugolo and Bill Russo (with Kenton), George Williams (with Krupa), Quincy Jones (with Lionel Hampton), and George Handy, Eddie Finckel, and Johnny Richards (with Boyd Raeburn) began to translate the newly emerging solo improvisational language of Parker and Gillespie into orchestral terms. At the same time the size of the jazz ensemble (though not the style of the music) returned to the small-group settings typical of early jazz before the advent of the big band – the trio, the quartet, and the quintet – which did not necessarily require the services of an arranger. Indeed as jazz practice also turned increasingly to composition, in which more often than not the composer was himself the arranger and the specific arrangement or instrumentation was inherent in the original conception of the composition, the type of arranging that flourished in the swing era played a much smaller role.

Composition and arrangement have, on the other hand, functioned in highly integrated, inseparable ways in the work of such groups as the Modern Jazz Quartet, many of the so-called West Coast groups of the 1950s (led by Gerry Mulligan, Shorty Rogers, Jimmy Giuffre, and others), and Charles Mingus's workshop of 1955 and his later quintets with musicians such as Jimmy Knepper, Eric Dolphy, Dannie Richmond, and Jackie McLean. But it is almost impossible to speak of arranging, in its traditionally notated, elaborate sense, in the work of Miles Davis's various quintets, John Coltrane's quartet, Ornette Coleman's small groups, Art Blakey's Jazz Messengers, Horace Silver's and Max Roach's quintets, and the many hundreds of other small ensembles active in jazz after 1950.

As jazz evolved from the music of the late swing and big-band era into bop, with the return of small groups, new compositions gradually took over from popular songs and show tunes (the heart of the jazz repertory in the 1920s and 1930s) and became the most pervasive creative impetus in jazz. And since many modern jazz players are not only composers, creating original, often completely written-out compositions, but also outstanding improvisers (whose activity may be seen as extemporaneous composition) the need for an independent arranger became obsolete. It is unthinkable that great improvisers and virtuoso players such as Charlie Parker and Dizzy

Ex.2 Miles Davis's *Boplicity* (1949, Cap. 60011) arranged by Gil Evans; transcr. G. Schuller (all parts notated at sounding pitch)

Gillespie should need an arranger or should need to write out an arrangement of one of their pieces. At most they might write out the theme statement (or "head"), which is usually played in unison, with the three-piece rhythm section improvising its own accompaniment. Some discussion as to the sequence of improvised solos might follow and that would be the extent of the "arrangement." In larger groups – septets, octets, nonets – of course, arrangements might still be necessary, but as indicated earlier, very often such arranging is already embodied in the original conception of the composition or is evolved in the form of a head arrangement.

Other possibilities may be heard in the recordings of Jimmy Giuffre's various trios of the 1950s and 1960s, which offer a number of approaches, ranging from "totally free" improvisations (virtually unpredetermined) to skimpily sketched-out formats or entirely through-composed pieces. Still another variant is exemplified by Lennie Tristano's trio of 1946, in which the guitarist played written-out or previously memorized melodic lines and the double bass player played partly improvised variations on the existing harmonic progression of the given piece, while the pianist, Tristano, wove free-roving, mostly atonal improvisations (to some extent prepared beforehand) around the lines of the other two players.

Unique among arrangers is Gil Evans. Beginning with his early work for Claude Thornhill's orchestra (1941–8) and Miles Davis's seminal nonet (on the recordings of 1949–50, which were later issued under the title "Birth of the Cool") Evans elevated arranging virtually to the art of composition. His work is marked by a rich sonoric palette (often including the use of flutes and instruments with darker timbres such as the orchestral horn and the tuba; ex.2), unusually skillful use of contrapuntal lines (rare in jazz), and warmly radiant harmonizations. In his uniquely creative transformations of jazz standards (as on his own album *New Bottle, Old Wine,* 1958, WP 1246), of traditional music (as on Davis's *Sketches of Spain,* 1959–60, Col. CS8271), and of Gershwin's opera *Porgy and Bess* (on Davis's album of the same name, 1958, Col. CL1274) Evans perfected the art of recomposition, while at the same time retaining the spontaneous improvisatory essence of jazz and achieving a rare integration of arranged and improvised elements.

With the demise of the big bands in the late 1940s (for both economic and musical reasons), arranging for large orchestral formations became a relatively rare function in jazz. The few orchestras that continued in existence, such as Ellington's, Basie's, and Herman's, drew upon the superior arranging talents of, for example, Ernie Wilkins, Neal Hefti, Quincy Jones, and

Thad Jones (who worked with Basie), but very little of truly innovative achievement in arranging concepts can be claimed after 1960.

5. Conclusion. Although arranging as a separate art and craft has lost much of its primacy in jazz in recent decades, it survives in various ad hoc situations (such as the occasional big-band recording date, jazz festivals, radio and television features treating orchestral jazz, etc.). Arranging flourishes more consistently in the fields of popular music, Broadway musicals, music for films and television, accompaniments for singers, and even pieces for the larger rock groups. Among the more outstanding arrangers in these fields outside but related to jazz have been the three great pioneers of symphonic arrangements of popular songs in the 1930s and 1940s, André Kostelanetz, Morton Gould, and David Rose, as well as Michel Legrand, Jeremy Lubbock, Henry Mancini, Mantovani, Billy May, and Nelson Riddle.

A special area of jazz arranging is represented by the transcribing from recordings of jazz masterpieces of the past and their arrangement for new forces; of this kind are, for instance, Hall Overton's arrangements for large jazz orchestra of pieces recorded by Thelonious Monk's quartet and quintet, and the arranged harmonizations by the group Supersax of improvisations by Charlie Parker.

For discussion of associated topics *see* Forms, Harmony (i), Improvisation, and Notation, and articles on individual musical instruments.

BIBLIOGRAPHY

G. Miller: *Glenn Miller's Method for Orchestral Arranging* (New York, 1943)
L. Feather: *The Book of Jazz: a Guide to the Entire Field* (New York, 1957, 2/1965 as *The Book of Jazz from Then till Now: a Guide to the Entire Field*)
W. Russo: *Composing for the Jazz Orchestra* (Chicago and London, 1961)
H. Mancini: *Sounds and Scores: a Practical Guide to Professional Orchestration* (n.p., 1962, 2/1973) [incl. disc]
W. Russo: *Jazz Composition and Orchestration* (Chicago and London, 1968, rev. 2/1975)
G. Schuller: *Early Jazz: its Roots and Musical Development* (New York, 1968)
D. Baker: *Arranging and Composing for the Small Ensemble: Jazz, R & B, Jazz-rock* (Chicago, 1970)
M. Berger, E. Berger, and J. Patrick: *Benny Carter: a Life in American Music* (Metuchen, NJ, and London, 1982)

GUNTHER SCHULLER

Art Ensemble of Chicago [AEC]. Free-jazz quintet. Its members are Roscoe Mitchell and Joseph Jarman (reed instruments, vibraphone, marimba, and unusual winds such as whistles, conch shells, etc.), Lester Bowie (brass instruments, harmonica, celeste, kelp horn, etc.), Malachi Favors (double bass, zither, melodica, banjo), and Don Moye ("sun percussion"). All vocalize and all play percussion instruments, including drums from several continents (especially Africa), cymbals, gongs, bells, woodblocks, sirens, bicycle horns, etc.

This eclectic and theatrical ensemble evolved gradually from Mitchell's group and, more generally, from the spirit of cooperative discovery encouraged in Chicago's Experimental Band (formed 1961) and formalized in the Association for the advancement of creative musicians (1965). It was officially formed in Paris in 1969 as a "drummer-less" (but not percussion-less) quartet consisting of Mitchell, Jarman, Bowie, and Favors, with Moye joining in 1970. While based in France the ensemble performed on television and radio, recorded 11 albums and three film scores, and presented hundreds of government-sponsored concerts throughout Western Europe. Upon returning to the USA in 1971 the members decided, for financial reasons, to restrict their performances to profitable

Art Ensemble of Chicago: performing at the Roundhouse Arts Centre, London, during Camden Jazz Week, 1979

events such as large concerts, jazz festivals, and university workshops. In 1975 extended club engagements and a tour of the West Coast brought them considerable recognition. Thereafter, they were able to collaborate sporadically and to cultivate individual projects without undermining the group's popularity, which grew in the late 1970s and early 1980s with the release of albums from a major international recording company (ECM) and its own label (AECO). In the mid-1980s the group has continued to perform on occasion in France, and in 1980 and 1984 it made extensive tours of the USA, the latter to promote its recording titled, rather prematurely, *The Third Decade*.

The Art Ensemble of Chicago developed within the free-jazz tradition, the principal instruments being trumpet, alto saxophone, double bass, and drums. Its members are virtuoso, experimental improvisers in this tradition who liberally use dissonance, nontempered intonation, noise, fast flurries of saxophone melody, dense textures, and irregular rhythms. However, their motto, "Great Black Music – Ancient to Modern," more accurately describes the breadth of their music than the term "free jazz." Their performances combine theatricality – costumes, make-up, dance, pantomime, comedy, parody, absurd dialogue, playlets – with musics from Africa (drum choirs), black America (blues, gospel, pop, jazz), and Europe (waltzes, marches). This diversity is further magnified by an economical, sensitive use of the tone colors of several hundred standard, exotic, and invented instruments, and by an ever-changing mélange of original compositions, individual features, and collective improvisation. These widely varying actions and sounds might appear at any time within a performance, yet years of rehearsal have enabled each member to react immediately to his fellows, the result being spontaneous and yet immanently coherent musical structures.

SELECTED RECORDINGS

A Jackson in your House (1969, BYG 529302); *People in Sorrow* (1969, Pathé 2C062-10523); *Message to our Folks* (1969, BYG 529328); *Reese and the Smooth Ones* (1969, BYG 529329); *Les stances à Sophie* (1970, Pathé 2C062-11365); *Phase One* (1970, Amer. 6116); *With Fontella Bass* (1970, Amer. 6117); *Live at Mandel Hall* (1972, Trio 6022-3); *Bap-tizum* (1972, Atl. 1639); *Kabalaba* (1974, AECO 004); *Nice Guys* (1978, ECM 1126); *Full Force* (1980, ECM 1167); *Urban Bushmen* (1980, ECM 1211-2); *The Third Decade* (1984, ECM 1273)

BIBLIOGRAPHY

E. Jost: *Free Jazz* (Graz, Austria, 1974)
L. Birnbaum: "Art Ensemble of Chicago: 15 Years of Great Black Music," *DB*, xlvi/9 (1979), 15
R. Palmer: "Art Ensemble of Chicago Takes Jazz to the Stage," *RS*, no.303 (1 Nov 1979), 9
R. Zabor: "Profile: the Art Ensemble," *Musician, Player and Listener*, no.17 (1979), 39
C. Gans: "Art Ensemble of Chicago: Nice Guys Finish First," *JF* [intl edn], no.68 (1980), 33 [incl. discography]
P. Kemper: "Zur Funktion des Mythos im Jazz der 70er Jahre: soziokulturelle Aspekte eines musikalischen Phänomens dargestellt an der ästhetischen Konzeption des 'Art Ensemble of Chicago'," *Jf*, xiii (1981), 45
J. Litweiler: "The Art Ensemble of Chicago: Adventures in the Urban Bush," *DB*, xlix/6 (1982), 19 [incl. discography]
P. Carles: "De l'AACM à ECM: l'Art Ensemble," *Jm*, no.320 (1983), 52
E. Janssens and H. de Craen: *Art Ensemble of Chicago Discography: Unit and Members* (Brussels, 1983) [incl. list of compositions]
J. Rockwell: "Jazz, Group Improvisation, Race and Racism," *All American Music: Composition in the Late Twentieth Century* (New York, 1983), 164
P. Keepnews: "Art Ensemble's Tour Celebrates 'Third Decade'," *Billboard*, xcvi (6 Oct 1984), 33
J. Litweiler: *The Freedom Principle: Jazz after 1958* (New York, 1984), 172
G. Lock: "Windy City Warriors," *The Wire*, no.9 (1984), 26 [incl. discography]
G. Giddins: *Rhythm-a-ning: Jazz Tradition and Innovation in the '80s* (New York, and Oxford, England, 1985) [colln of previously pubd articles], 194
D. Palmer: "20th Anniversary for an Unusual Jazz Ensemble," *New York Times* (14 April 1985), §II, p.24

BARRY KERNFELD

Artists House. Record company and label. The company was established in 1977 in New York by John Snyder. A short-lived continuation of the project Snyder had begun with HORIZON, it offered high-quality recordings and sophisticated liner notes. Snyder involved many musicians with whom he had worked at Horizon – Ornette Coleman, Paul Desmond, Charlie Haden, Jim Hall, Thad Jones, Mel Lewis – and several of the recordings were made during the earlier association (1975–6). Artists House also put out James "Blood" Ulmer's first and most important jazz recording (1978). Around 10 albums were released between 1977 and 1979; each included an eight-page pamphlet which contained recording details, biographical information, a discography, and music examples, including transcriptions of improvised solos from the recording. It was the company's policy to allow musicians total control over their projects, from supervision of the sessions to selection of artwork for album liners. Each musician retained ownership of the rights to the music; as a result a leader or composer could earn up to three times as much in royalties as might be received under contract with a more conventional company. No sessions were organized after 1978. (M. Ullman: *Jazz Lives: Portraits in Words and Pictures* (Washington, 1980), 141)

Arto. Record company and label. It was owned by the Standard Music Roll Company of Orange, New Jersey, and was based in New York. Arto was one of the first companies to record vaudeville blues musicians; shortly after its foundation it organized sessions for Lucille Hegamin (about November 1920). The label was also used to issue a large number of recordings by the Original Memphis Five. Much of the company's catalogue was also issued on the subsidiary labels Globe, Bell, and Hy-tone, and masters, including those by Hegamin, were exchanged with the New York Recording Laboratories and the Bridgeport Die & Machine Co. Arto also owned a pressing plant; this was used by Nordskog for the manufacture of three items by Kid Ory's band, the first recordings by a black band from New Orleans. The company ceased to operate late in 1922; although the subsidiaries Globe and Bell were continued, few of their later issues were of importance in jazz.

BIBLIOGRAPHY

M. Wyler: *A Glimpse of the Past: an Illustrated History of Some Early Record Companies that Made Jazz History* (West Moors, England, 1957)
R. M. W. Dixon and J. Godrich: *Recording the Blues* (London, 1970), 10
B. Rust: *The American Record Label Book* (New Rochelle, NY, 1978)

Arvanitas, Georges (*b* Marseilles, France, 13 June 1931). French pianist and organist. After working in Marseilles with traditional jazz bands he moved in the early 1950s to Paris, where he worked as a freelance for several years with Jimmy Archey (1955), Bill Coleman (1958), Dexter Gordon (*c*1959–60), Sonny Stitt, Donald Byrd, and many others. Around this time he formed his own group, and was the resident pianist at the Blue Note for two years. He also played with Buck Clayton and Don Byas (both 1962) and Sonny Criss (1963). He spent some months in New York in 1964–5, where he worked with Ted Curson and Yusef Lateef; in 1966 he made a second visit to the USA. He formed a trio in Paris with the double bass player Jacky Samson and the drummer Charles Saudrais. Either with this ensemble or alone Arvanitas performed and recorded as an accompanist to visiting Americans, including Art Farmer and Dexter Gordon (1967), Buddy Tate and Bill Coleman (1968), Slide Hampton (1968, 1972), Anita O'Day (1970), and Curson (1970, 1971). In 1972 he worked with Robin Kenyatta, toured Japan with Michel Legrand, and performed in Italy with Criss and Stitt. He continues to work with his trio and as an accompanist; he has played with Pepper Adams (1977, 1982), Curson (1980), and Dizzy Gillespie and James Moody (1985). Arvanitas's style has its roots in bop and the styles that succeeded it; he cites Bud Powell and Bill Evans (ii) as major influences upon his work.

SELECTED RECORDINGS

As leader: *Soul Jazz* (1960, Col. FPX193); *Space Ballad* (1970, Saravah 10012); *Anniversary* (c1976, AFA 5019)

As sideman: B. Webster: *Makin' Whoopee* (1972, Spot. 09); D. Gordon: *College of Education* (1973, Futura 412054); P. Adams: *Live in Europe* (1977, Impro 02)

BIBLIOGRAPHY

Feather '60s; *Feather–Gitler '70s*
"Georges Arvanitas: Closing the Gap," *DB*, xxxii/8 (1965), 19
C. Carriere: "Le saga d'Arva," *Jh*, no.295 (1973), 8

PAUL RINZLER (with MICHEL LAPLACE)

Ash, Vic(tor) (*b* London, 9 March 1930). English clarinetist, tenor saxophonist, and flutist. In the early 1950s he worked with Kenny Baker (1951–3) and was a principal soloist with Vic Lewis's orchestra (1953–6). He led his own quartet (1956–8) and sextet (1958–60), with which he made several recordings (including *Vic Ash Quartet*, 1956, Nixa 1032 [EP]). With Harry Klein he led the Jazz Five (1960–63), which often performed as the support group for such visiting American musicians as Miles Davis, Dizzy Gillespie, and Dave Brubeck. One of the pioneers of modern jazz clarinet in Great Britain, Ash was the leading clarinetist at this time; for eight years he was voted best player on his instrument in *Melody Maker* polls. He played with Ray Charles (1961) and John Dankworth (1963–5) and from 1966 to 1969 he worked in Bermuda. After returning to England he continued to perform jazz occasionally but worked mostly as a session musician; he also played with various popular singers, including Frank Sinatra and Shirley MacLaine. (*FeatherE*)

DIGBY FAIRWEATHER

Ashby, Dorothy (Jeanne) (*b* Detroit, 6 Aug 1932; *d* Santa Monica, CA, 13 April 1986). Harpist and leader. She studied music education at Wayne State University, and in 1957 performed with Louis Armstrong and Woody Herman. She recorded as a leader of trios and quartets, which included Frank Wess, Gene Wright, Art Taylor, Roy Haynes, Jimmy Cobb, and Richard Davis (1957–65). In the early 1960s she was host of a radio program in Detroit, and in the mid-1970s, after moving to California, she played in studio orchestras on albums by Sonny Criss and Stanley Turrentine. Ashby was the only important bop harpist; her playing is well represented on the album *Soft Winds* (1961, Jazzland 961).

BIBLIOGRAPHY

FeatherE; *Feather '60s*
S. Placksin: *American Women in Jazz, 1900 to the Present: their Words, Lives, and Music* (New York, 1982), 239

Ashby, Harold (Kenneth) (*b* Kansas City, MO, 27 March 1925). Tenor saxophonist. From 1946 he worked with Tommy Douglas and the singer Walter Brown in Kansas City, then in the early 1950s moved to Chicago, where he played with a number of blues bands. In 1957 he went to New York and played with the trumpeters Milt Larkin and Mercer Ellington; he also deputized occasionally for Duke Ellington. He recorded with Ben Webster (1958), Johnny Hodges (1960), Paul Gonsalves (1961), and Lawrence Brown (1965). He became a regular member of Duke Ellington's orchestra in 1968 and, although he replaced the clarinet virtuoso Jimmy Hamilton, continued to be principal tenor saxophone soloist, taking up clarinet for ensemble parts only. Ashby remained with the band until February 1975, working after Ellington's death under Mercer Ellington. Thereafter he worked as a freelance in New York and played at jazz festivals in the USA and Europe. In 1984 he presented his own concert at St. Peter's Church, New York, with the assistance of an NEA grant. Although the influence of Webster may be detected in his playing, Ashby has an individual style and is a thorough craftsman; he makes more use than most mainstream players of the higher register of the tenor saxophone.

Oral history material in *CtY*.

SELECTED RECORDINGS

(all as sideman with D. Ellington)

Duke Ellington's 70th Birthday Concert (1969, SolS 19000), incl. B. P., Just squeeze me; *New Orleans Suite* (1970, Atl. 1580), incl. Thanks for the beautiful land on the delta; *The Afro-Eurasian Eclipse* (1971, Fan. 9498), incl. Chinoiserie; *Togo Brava Suite* (1971, UA 92), incl. Naturellement; *Eastbourne Performance* (1973, RCA APL1-1023), incl. I can't get started

BIBLIOGRAPHY

S. Dance: *The World of Duke Ellington* (London and New York, 1970/R1981) [colln of previously pubd articles and interviews], 231
D. Ellington: *Music is my Mistress* (Garden City, NY, 1973), 403
A. Balalas: "Harold 'Al' Ashby," *BHcF*, no.262 (1978), 3
E. Cook: "Harold Ashby," *JJI*, xxxviii/12 (1985), 8 [interview]
C. Deffaa: "Harold Ashby: Remembering Duke and Ben," *MR*, xii/6 (1985), 7

EDDIE LAMBERT

Ashby, Irving (C.) (*b* Somerville, MA, 29 Dec 1920; *d* Perris, CA, 22 April 1987). Guitarist. A member of a musical family, he began to study guitar at the age of nine. After declining a scholarship from the New England Conservatory, he played in local bands until Lionel Hampton engaged him; he was a member of Hampton's big band from 1940 to 1942 and then played with Eddie Beal in Los Angeles. In 1947 he replaced Oscar Moore in Nat "King" Cole's trio, with which he stayed until 1952; after leaving Cole he joined Oscar Peterson's group and took part with it in the first European tour of Norman Granz's Jazz at the Philharmonic. From the early 1950s he worked as a freelance in and around Los Angeles and taught, both privately and at the University of California, Riverside.

Besides his few recordings as a leader (1946, *c*1957, 1976), Ashby made many as a sideman, with, among others, Fats Waller (1943), Lester Young, Charles Mingus, and Ivie Anderson (all 1946), Erroll Garner (1947), Illinois Jacquet (1955), Willie Smith (1965), and Count Basie and Joe Turner (ii) (both 1973). Influenced principally by Charlie Christian, Ashby improvised single-note lines in a swinging, bluesy style, and was an excellent rhythm guitarist.

SELECTED RECORDINGS

As leader: *Memoirs* (1976, Accent 5091)

As sideman: L. Hampton: Altitude (1941, Vic. 27316); Fiddle-dee-dee (1941, Vic. 27364); N. Cole: Bop Kick (1949, Cap. 641); O. Peterson: Blue Moon (1952, Clef 89009); on *The History of an Artist* (1972–4, Pablo 2625702), You can depend on me, This is where it's at (1972); C. Basie: *Basie Jam* (1973, Pablo 2310718)

BIBLIOGRAPHY

FeatherE; *Feather '60s*; *Feather–Gitler '70s*
H. Sieders: "Irving Ashby: Playing with the Greats," *GP*, viii/9 (1974), 10

GARY CARNER

Ashton, Bill [William Michael Allingham] (*b* Blackpool, England, 6 Dec 1936). English bandleader. He began playing saxophone and organized two jazz bands while studying at Oxford University (1955–62), and in the early 1960s he performed in several clubs in London. In 1965 he formed the London Schools Jazz Orchestra, which was later known as the London Youth Jazz Orchestra and then the National Youth Jazz Orchestra; it became a professional organization in 1974 and is the only full-time big band of its kind in Great Britain. Much of the music it performs is written by its members. It has toured with Shorty Rogers (1982, 1983) and John Dankworth (1986) and has made a large number of recordings, among them *Full Score* (1985, NYJO 005). Ashton has written several songs and instrumental compositions and he continues to work as the band's music director; he was made an MBE for his services to youth and music in 1978.

BIBLIOGRAPHY

L. Tomkins: "NYJO: the Success Story of a British Big Band," *CI*, xx/6 (1982), 6
R. Palmer: "NYJO," *JJI*, xxxviii/5 (1985), 16 [interview]

DIGBY FAIRWEATHER

Asmussen, Svend (*b* Copenhagen, 28 Feb 1916). Danish violinist and singer. He began playing violin at the age of seven. He left the Academy of Arts in Copenhagen, where he studied sculpture, when the death of his father necessitated his going to work, and in 1933 made his début playing at the Apollo Theater in Copenhagen. The following year he formed a group, along the lines of Joe Venuti's Blue Four, which made its first recordings in 1935. Asmussen played with the Mills Brothers (1937) and Fats Waller (1938) when they toured Denmark. He disbanded his sextet in 1943 to work as an actor and comedian,

Svend Asmussen during a concert given with Benny Goodman's band at Snape Maltings Concert Hall, near Aldeburgh, England, 4 October 1981

but resumed his musical activities after World War II. Benny Goodman attempted at least twice during the 1950s to bring Asmussen's group to the USA to perform for American audiences, but the country's immigration laws at the time prevented any such tour from taking place. Asmussen played and sang in pop-oriented groups with the singer Alice Babs (1958–1963, 1969–72, 1974) and the guitarist Ulrik Neumann (to the mid-1960s), and on many occasions performed with Stuff Smith during the latter's tours of Europe. His style is individual, though it reveals a debt to that of Venuti. His many recordings show that he lacked Smith's biting attack, but that his tone was characterized by a veiled, almost muted, quality.

SELECTED RECORDINGS

Duos with U. Neumann: *Danish Import* (1961, WB 1408)
As leader: Tiger Rag/My Blue Heaven (1935, HMV 1327); Sweet Sue/Limehouse Blues (1940, Odeon 448); It don't mean a thing/My Old Man (1944, Tono 4329); *Rhythm is our Business* (1955, Angel 60010); of Violin Summit (with S. Grappelli, J.-L. Ponty, and S. Smith): *Violin Summit* (1966, Saba 15099); *Amazing Strings* (1974, MPS 20223736)
As sideman: D. Ellington: *Jazz Violin Session* (1963, Atl. 1688)

BIBLIOGRAPHY

Feather '60s; *Feather–Gitler '70s*
"The Talk of the Town," *New Yorker*, xxxi (30 April 1955), 24
D. Morgenstern: "Jazz Fiddle," *DB*, xxxiv/3 (1967), 16
M. Glaser and S. Grappelli: *Jazz Violin* (New York and elsewhere, 1981) [incl. transcrs.]

DAVID FLANAGAN

Association for the Advancement of Creative Musicians [AACM]. A nonprofit organization devoted to black avant-garde jazz. It is based in Chicago. The AACM grew out of the Experimental Band, a large free-jazz ensemble established by Muhal Richard Abrams in 1961. Founded on 8 May 1965 (with Abrams as president), the AACM provided a framework for sympathetic rehearsals and public performances of new works. Its members were required to contribute original compositions, to give a solo recital, and to maintain high moral standards. In addition, experienced players trained the younger musicians.

In its early years the AACM sponsored local recording sessions led by Abrams, Roscoe Mitchell, Joseph Jarman, Anthony Braxton, or Lester Bowie (the organization's second president); it also produced a weekly radio show and presented concerts and jam sessions in the ghetto's Abraham Lincoln Center or at the University of Chicago. In 1969 Braxton, Leroy Jenkins, Leo Smith, Steve McCall, and the members of the ART ENSEMBLE OF CHICAGO settled temporarily in Paris, thereby bringing the methods and goals of the AACM to new international affiliations. Later the organization held a festival in New York (1977) and continued to flourish in Chicago: many of its members received grants from the NEA and the Illinois Arts Council, and new talent emerged – notably Chico Freeman, George Lewis (ii), and the group Air. In a genre traditionally dominated by individual performers, the AACM has proved to be a lasting, historically significant cooperative venture.

See also FESTIVALS.

BIBLIOGRAPHY

"Jazz Musicians Group in Chicago Growing," *DB*, xxxiii/15 (1966), 11
T. Martin: "The Chicago Avant-garde," *JM*, no.157 (1968), 12
E. Jost: *Free Jazz* (Graz, Austria, 1974)
"AACM," *SJ*, xxix/8 (1975), 231 [discography]
B. Smith: "CAC/AACM," *Coda*, no.140 (1975), 6
G. Giddins: "Inside Free Jazz: the AACM in New York," *VV*, xxii (30 May 1977), 46
V. Wilmer: "Chicago's Alternative Society," *As Serious as your Life: the Story of the New Jazz* (London, 1977, rev. 1980)
J. DeMuth: "15 Years of the AACM," *JF* [intl edn], no.68 (1980), 28
K. Muni: "AACM: Continuing the Tradition," *Be-bop and Beyond*, iv/2 (1986), 8 [incl. discography]

BARRY KERNFELD

Assunto. Family of musicians.

(1) Papa Jac [Jacinto A.] **Assunto** (*b* Lake Charles, LA, 1 Nov 1905; *d* New Orleans, 5 Jan 1985). Trombonist and banjoist. He began learning drums but then changed to trombone and banjo and played in groups in and around Jennings, Louisiana. He moved to New Orleans, where he received instruction from a local bandleader and worked in dance and vaudeville bands. He studied business administration at Tulane University (BA 1929) and ceased full-time performing in 1933. After receiving the BA in music education from Loyola University (1947) he began teaching. In 1955 his sons (2) Freddie and (3) Frank invited him to join their group, the DUKES OF DIXIELAND, in Chicago and Las Vegas. He toured the USA with the band, but after Freddie's death (1966) he left it to resume his career as a teacher.

For recording-list *see* DUKES OF DIXIELAND.

BIBLIOGRAPHY

Obituary, E. Anderson, *New Orleans Times-Picayune* (8 Jan 1985)

(2) Freddie [Fred J.] **Assunto** (*b* Jennings, LA, 3 Dec 1929; *d* Las Vegas, NV, 21 April 1966). Trombonist, son of (1) Papa Jac Assunto. When he was young he was taught by his father and in 1946 he and his brother Frank formed a dixieland band. He worked in various clubs in New Orleans and Las Vegas, then in 1949, with his brother, he formed the DUKES OF DIXIELAND. He married the group's singer, Betty Owens. He continued to play with the band until his death, though he performed only infrequently from 1965 because of illness.

For recording-list *see* DUKES OF DIXIELAND.

BIBLIOGRAPHY

Feather '60s
Obituary, *SL*, xvii (1966), May–June, 55

(3) Frank (Joseph) Assunto (*b* New Orleans, 29 Jan 1932; *d* New Orleans, 25 Feb 1974). Trumpeter, son of (1) Papa Jac Assunto. He was taught by his father, and after organizing a dixieland band with his brother Freddie in 1946 he worked in several clubs. He formed the DUKES OF DIXIELAND with his brother in 1949 and continued to play with them until his death. During the group's tour of South-east Asia he performed with Bhumibol Adulyadej.

For recording-list *see* DUKES OF DIXIELAND.

BIBLIOGRAPHY

FeatherE; *Feather '60s*
Obituary, B. Shearman, *New Orleans Times-Picayune* (18 April 1974)
Obituary, *SL*, xxvi (spr. 1974), 29

KARL KOENIG

Astaire, Fred [Austerlitz, Frederick] (*b* Omaha, NE, 10 May 1899; *d* Los Angeles, 22 June 1987). Dancer, singer, and actor. He toured in vaudeville shows from the age of seven with his sister Adele. From 1916 to 1932 (when the latter married) the duo appeared regularly in shows on Broadway; thereafter Astaire began a partnership with the dancer Ginger Rogers and achieved substantial success in films and on stage, television, and radio. In 1935 he was placed third (after Bill Robinson and Jack Donahue) in a dancing contest. The film *Broadway Melody of 1940* includes excellent examples of his tap-dancing. Astaire often toured the USA, Canada, and England, and recorded frequently as a singer and tap-dancer. He may be heard accompanied by a small group on the album *The Fred Astaire Story* (1952, Clef 1001-4); he also made recordings with Benny Goodman (1940).

As a youth Astaire studied ballroom, tap-, and ballet dancing; later he combined elements of all these genres to form his highly individual, rhythmic style. He also composed popular songs, including *I'm building up to an awful letdown*, which was recorded by Red McKenzie in 1936 (Decca 667).

BIBLIOGRAPHY

F. Astaire: *Steps in Time* (New York, 1959/*R*1981)
"Astaire, Fred," *CBY 1964*
M. Stearns and J. Stearns: *Jazz Dance: the Story of American Vernacular Dance* (New York and London, 1968)
S. Green and B. Goldberg: *Starring Fred Astaire* (New York, 1973)
B. Thomas: *Astaire: the Man, the Dancer* (New York, 1984)

RAINER E. LOTZ

Astoria Hot Eight. *See* JONES AND COLLINS ASTORIA HOT EIGHT.

Atco. Record company and label. The company was established in 1955 as a subsidiary of Atlantic. Although the label was chiefly devoted to popular music, it was also used to issue jazz; many of its recordings were produced by Nesuhi Ertegun and Gary Kramer. Among the most important musicians in the catalogue was King Curtis, who recorded five albums for the label; other notable issues were of work by Harry Arnold, Herb Geller, Helen Merrill, Betty Carter, and Vi Redd. Roland Hanna's first recording as a leader was made for Atco. Though the company recorded jazz only intermittently for around ten years, it remained involved with the music thereafter. By 1973 it had acquired the catalogue of Flying Dutchman, which it continued to distribute until about 1976.

MARK GARDNER

Atkins, Boyd (*b* Paducah, KY, *c*1900; *d* ? Chicago, after 1960). Saxophonist and violinist. He was brought up in St. Louis, where he played with Dewey Jackson and Fate Marable (*c*1923). He then moved to Chicago, led his own band, and worked with Earl Hines (1925) and Louis Armstrong (1927). His composition *Heebie Jeebies* was made famous by Armstrong's recording (1926, OK 8300), but he himself recorded only once, on saxophones and clarinet under Armstrong (*Chicago Breakdown*, 1927, Col. 36376). During the 1930s Atkins led his own groups and worked with a number of lesser-known bands in Chicago and (from 1934) Minneapolis; in 1940 he played with Eddie South. Thereafter he led his own bands in Peoria, Illinois, and Chicago, and was also active as an arranger.

For illustration *see* NIGHTCLUBS AND OTHER VENUES, fig.3.

based on *ChiltonW*

Atlantic. Record company and label. The company was founded in New York by Herb Abramson and Ahmet Ertegun in 1947; both men were jazz and blues enthusiasts and the label was used primarily to issue Afro-American music. Among the jazz musicians to record prolifically for the organization in the late 1940s were Tiny Grimes and Erroll Garner. From the early 1950s records began to appear that were intended specifically for jazz enthusiasts, rather than for the race market. These included items made in France by Sidney Bechet, Don Byas, and Dizzy Gillespie and leased from Blue Star for release in the USA, and the results of sessions by Wilbur De Paris and Jimmy Yancey; the former became one of the company's most important musicians.

In 1953 Abramson left the company for military service; he was replaced by Jerry Wexler, who became the principal architect of Atlantic's considerable commercial success. This was largely due to its recordings of musicians whose work encompassed jazz, blues, and rhythm-and-blues, such as Joe Turner (ii), Ray Charles, and, from the 1960s, the singer Aretha Franklin. Ertegun's brother Nesuhi joined the organization in 1955, and supervised artists and repertory for the LP catalogue; under his direction the company became further involved with jazz, organizing sessions by Lennie Tristano (1955, 1962), Lee Konitz (1955–7), and Charles Mingus (intermittently 1956–61, 1973–8). Atlantic also recorded albums by the Modern Jazz Quartet, and sessions under the leadership of the quartet's members Milt Jackson and John Lewis; the ensemble remained with the company until 1981.

Abramson returned to Atlantic in 1955 and took responsibility for the company's newly established label ATCO; shortly thereafter, however, he left to become a freelance producer.

From this time until the early 1960s the company recorded much avant-garde jazz, including work by Ornette Coleman and John Coltrane. But by the middle of the decade the label was primarily known for soul music; in 1966, at the height of the company's success in this field, it founded the Vortex label for the release of jazz records. It was used to issue albums by Dave Pike and Robin Kenyatta, and, most importantly, Chick Corea's and Keith Jarrett's first albums as leaders. In 1967 the company was bought by Warner Bros., which in turn was purchased two years later by the Kinney Corp.; Ahmet and Nesuhi Ertegun, however, continued to direct Atlantic. Among the musicians who recorded for the label from this period into the mid-1970s were Eddie Harris, Charles Lloyd, Yusef Lateef, Carmen McRae, Jarrett, Les McCann, Gary Burton, and Roland Kirk. Jean-Luc Ponty began an important association with the label in 1975. The following year the company began its first systematic program of reissues, "That's Jazz"; in 1986 it commenced another reissue series, "Atlantic Jazz."

BIBLIOGRAPHY

C. Gillett: *Making Tracks: Atlantic Records and the Growth of a Multi-billion-dollar Industry* (London, 1975)
P. A. Grendysa: *Atlantic Master Book #1* (Milwaukee, 1975)
M. Jones: "Jerry Wexler," *MM*, l (15 Feb 1975), 39
——: "That's Jazz – that's Nesuhi," *MM*, li (24 July 1976), 36
M. Ruppli: *Atlantic Records: a Discography* (Westport, CT, and London, 1979)
P. Grendysa: "Birth of a Legend: the Atlantic Label," *Record Collector's Monthly*, no.4 (1982), 1

Audiophile. Record company and label. Founded by the recording engineer E. D. Nunn in 1947, the company was dedicated to making recordings of dixieland jazz, and aimed to achieve the best possible sound quality. It was notable for its use of monophonic recording techniques in the belief that they gave higher fidelity than stereophonic. By 1966 control of the company had passed to Jim Cullum of San Antonio, who used the label to issue recordings by his own Happy Jazz Band and other dixieland groups. In the mid-1970s the rights to the label name and back catalogue, excluding the items recorded by Cullum, were purchased by George H. Buck's company Jazzology. Under this ownership, the Audiophile label has been used mainly for popular music and lighter styles of jazz. ("Jazzology Acquires Audiophile Records," *CRC Newsletter*, iii/1–2 (1977), 2)

Auer, Pepsi [Josef] (*b* Munich, 14 June 1928). German pianist. After playing accordion in a youth orchestra in 1936, he taught himself vibraphone and worked in American clubs in Munich in 1945. He changed to piano in 1949 and played with Freddie Christmann's group from 1954, becoming its leader in 1956. Over the next three years he worked with the jazz ensemble of Hessischer Rundfunk in Frankfurt am Main; he also toured with Freddie Brocksieper (1957–8) and the German All Stars (1958). Having at first shown a liking for the cool idiom, at the beginning of the 1960s his style grew closer to that of Horace Silver and Bud Powell. During this decade Auer played with Stan Getz, Eric Dolphy, Don Menza, Benny Bailey, Miriam Klein, and others. From 1962 he worked as a studio musician, composer, and arranger. Despite his importance among German pianists of the 1950s, Auer never recorded as a leader.

SELECTED RECORDINGS

As sideman: A. Mangelsdorff: *Albert Mangelsdorff und seine Frankfurt All Stars* (1958, Jzt. 1246); E. Dolphy: *The Berlin Concerts* (1961, Enja 3007–9); M. Klein: *Honeysuckle Rose* (1964, Sup. 33561)

BIBLIOGRAPHY

ReclamsJ

GÜNTHER HUESMANN

Auer [Boucher], **Vera** (*b* Vienna, 20 April 1919). Austrian vibraphonist and accordionist. A niece of the violinist Leopold Auer, she studied piano in Vienna. Her earliest jazz playing was influenced by Attila Zoller, who moved from Hungary to Austria in 1948. Auer formed the Vera Auer Combo, which included Zoller, and worked for Österreichische Radioverkehrs AG (RAVAG). After moving to Frankfurt am Main, Germany (1954), she played with Donald Byrd and Art Taylor and performed at various jazz festivals in Germany (1955, 1956, 1959). She married an American (1959) and moved to the USA (1960), where she joined the quintets of Dave Burns and Cal Massey (1962) and also played with J. J. Johnson, Ted Curson, Zoot Sims, and Sonny Red. She later recorded as the leader of a bop quintet with Richard Williams (*Positive Vibes*, 1977, Honey Dew 6621), and in 1982 she led a quintet at the Wiener Jazzfrühling.

KLAUS SCHULZ

Auld, Georgie [Altwerger, John] (*b* Toronto, 19 May 1919). Tenor saxophonist. He first played professionally on alto saxophone, but changed to the tenor instrument because of Coleman Hawkins's influence. He led his own band at Nick's, New York, and played with Bunny Berigan (1937–8) and Artie Shaw (1938–40); he led Shaw's band briefly after the latter's first retirement, then played for a short time with Jan Savitt before joining Benny Goodman's orchestra and sextet in 1940 (for illustration *see* GOODMAN, BENNY). After a second period with Shaw, Auld served in the army (1943). He led his own big band for a period (1943–6) though his career was interrupted by recurrent illness. Dizzy Gillespie and Erroll Garner played on the band's early recordings and later Serge Chaloff, Joe Albany, Stan Levey, and Al Porcino were among the regular sidemen. Al Cohn, Neal Hefti, and Tadd Dameron wrote arrangements for the band and Sarah Vaughan sang on its recording of Dameron's version of *A Hundred Years from Today* (1946). In 1949 Auld led a ten-piece group that played in a style influenced by bop. He also appeared as an actor on Broadway. After playing with Count Basie's octet (1950) and his own small band (1950–51) he worked for ten years as a freelance. During the 1960s and 1970s he formed several short-lived bands, and achieved great success in Japan, touring there frequently. He appeared in the film *New York, New York* (1977) and was also the principal soloist on the soundtrack, playing in an energetic swing style. He continued to perform regularly into the 1980s; his later recordings are in a romantic idiom. Auld is a superb craftsman and has kept pace with the stylistic developments of a half-century while maintaining an individual, readily identifiable sound.

SELECTED RECORDINGS

As leader: Pick-up Boys (1944, Apollo 754); Taps Miller (1944, Apollo 359); Stomping at the Savoy (1945, Guild 135); A Hundred Years from Today (1946, Musi. 15072); You've got me jumpin'/Nashooma (1949, Dis. 116)

As sideman: B. Berigan: Mahogany Hall Stomp (1937, Vic. 25622); A. Shaw: One Night Stand (1939, Bb 10202); B. Goodman: Good Enough to Keep (Air Mail Special) (1941, Col. 36099); L. Brown: *Aurex Jazz Festival '83* (1983, Ewd 80267)

BIBLIOGRAPHY

ChiltonW
J. Tracy: "No More Big Bands for me, Says Georgie Auld," *DB*, xviii/12 (1951), 2
H. Holly: "Even Record Click Can't Lure Auld back to Music," *DB*, xix/4 (1952), 9
J. Burns: "Lesser Known Bands of the Forties: Gene Krupa and Georgie Auld," *JM*, no.160 (1968), 8
A. McCarthy: *Big Band Jazz* (New York and London, 1974), 272

DAVE GELLY

Aura. *See* RULLY, AURA.

Aurora. Record label. It was established by the T. Eaton Co. Ltd., a Canadian mail-order house. Items released in June 1931 in a 22000 series were drawn from the catalogues of Brunswick and Melotone and included recordings by King Oliver and Duke Ellington. Although labeled "made in Canada," the records were in fact manufactured by Brunswick in the USA. A later series, the 36100s, drawn from Victor's catalogue and pressed at that company's plant in Montreal, contained recordings by such musicians as Dave Nelson, Fess Williams, and Hoagy Carmichael, all issued under pseudonyms.

BIBLIOGRAPHY

M. Wyler: *A Glimpse of the Past: an Illustrated History of Some Early Record Companies that Made Jazz History* (West Moors, England, 1957)

A. Robertson: "The Rare Canadian Aurora Label," *Record Research*, nos.219–20 (1986), 1

Austin, Cuba (*b* Charleston, WV, *c*1906; *d* ? Baltimore, after 1960). Drummer. He worked initially as a tapdancer. He played occasionally with William McKinney's Synco Jazz Band and in 1926, when McKinney ceased playing to concentrate on managing the group (renamed MCKINNEY'S COTTON PICKERS), became a full-time member. He made a number of recordings with the band, including (under the name the Chocolate Dandies) *Birmingham Breakdown* (1928, OK 8668) and *Four or Five Times* (1928, OK 8627). After the band split into two factions in 1931 Austin took over as leader of the Original Cotton-Pickers, with which he toured extensively until 1934. He then settled in Baltimore and ran his own business, though he continued to play part-time with orchestras led by the pianist Rivers Chambers, and also with his own trio. (J. Chilton: *McKinney's Music: a Bio-discography of McKinney's Cotton Pickers*, London, 1978)

based on *ChiltonW*

Austin, Lovie [née Calhoun, Cora] (*b* Chattanooga, TN, 19 Sept 1887; *d* Chicago, 10 July 1972). Pianist. After studying music at Roger Williams and Knoxville colleges she toured extensively on the vaudeville circuit, sometimes leading her own band (1923). She then settled in Chicago, where she recorded frequently and worked in various theaters, arranging much of her own music. From the late 1940s she played in a dancing school. During the mid-1920s she was the house pianist for Paramount; she recorded under her own name with the Blues Serenaders and with female blues singers, including Ida Cox, Alberta Hunter, and Ma Rainey, providing sturdy and even-pulsed, yet rolling and rhythmic accompaniments (some of the singers went on to record in New York with bands led by Fletcher Henderson). Her groups usually consisted of a trio in which she was joined by a cornetist and a clarinetist (Tommy Ladnier, Bob Shoffner, Jimmy O'Bryant, and Johnny Dodds played regularly with her); sometimes she added another wind player or a drummer. She was not a solo improviser but maintained a fullness of sound in her playing while achieving a variety of ensemble textures through the use of stop-time, arranged block harmony, and passages of collective improvisation that occasionally required all the musicians to play in double-time.

SELECTED RECORDINGS

As leader: Heebie Jeebies (1925, Para. 12283); Frog Tongue Stomp (1926, Para. 12361)

As sideman: I. Cox: Graveyard Dream Blues (1923, Para. 12044); Edmonia Henderson: Traveling Blues (1924, Para. 12095); M. Rainey: Lucky Rock Blues (1924, Para. 12215)

BIBLIOGRAPHY

D. Stewart-Baxter: "Lovie Austin Discography," *Playback*, ii (1949), Aug, 14

G. Hoefer: "Lovie Austin still Active as a Pianist in Chicago," *DB*, xvii/12 (1950), 11

C. Hillman: "Paramount Serenaders, 1923–1926," *Sv* (1976), no.67, p.8; no.68, p.52; (1977), no.69, p.91; no.70, p.149; no.72, p.227; no.73, p.29; no.74, p.67; (1978), no.75, p.84 [incl. discography]

S. Placksin: *American Women in Jazz, 1900 to the Present: their Words, Lives, and Music* (New York, 1982), 43

M. Unterbrink: *Jazz Women at the Keyboard* (Jefferson, NC, and London, 1983)

L. Dahl: *Stormy Weather: the Music and Lives of a Century of Jazzwomen* (New York, 1984), 25

BOB ZIEFF

Austin High School Gang. Name given to an informal group of midwestern musicians whose principal members had attended Austin High School in Chicago in the early 1920s; *see* CHICAGO JAZZ.

For illustration *see* TESCHEMACHER, FRANK.

Australian Jazz Quartet. Ensemble formed in December 1954 by the reed players Errol Buddle and Dick Healey, the pianist Bryce Rohde, and the drummer and vibraphonist Jack Brokensha. It first recorded in New York in 1955; thereafter its members played with a succession of other musicians (including Frank Capp, Osie Johnson, and Nick Stabulas), working latterly as a quintet and occasionally as a sextet. The group disbanded after touring Australia in 1958.

Autograph. Record label. It was established by MARSH LABORATORIES in 1925 and existed only until the following year. Its catalogue was made up of two series, both of which contained recordings made by the parent company. One, an unnumbered series, included items thought to have been custom pressings; the other, a numbered series for which the label is chiefly remembered, was used to issue important early recordings by Jelly Roll Morton. Distribution was confined to the Chicago area.

Autrey, Herman (*b* Evergreen, AL, 4 Dec 1904; *d* New York, 14 June 1980). Trumpeter and singer. He studied alto horn from 1913 but changed to trumpet in 1918. In 1923 he moved to Pittsburgh, where he performed with local bands; he also toured extensively, mostly in the South, and temporarily worked as a bandleader in Florida. After playing in Boston he moved to Washington, then three years later settled in Philadelphia, where he worked mainly with the bandleader George "Doc" Hyder. In late 1933, while playing with the pianist Charlie Johnson at Smalls' Paradise in New York, he caught the attention of Fats Waller; Autrey may be heard on most of Waller's recordings, both with sextet and big band, between 1934 and 1939, and again in 1941–2. When Waller had solo engagements Autrey played (mostly as first trumpet) with Fletcher Henderson, Charlie Turner, Luis Russell, and Claude Hopkins. In the early 1940s he worked frequently with Stuff Smith, then from 1945 he led his own group for a long residency at the Musical Bar, Philadelphia. A serious automobile accident in 1954 curtailed his activities, but from 1960 to 1969 he was a member of the SAINTS AND SINNERS. He continued to perform, though often only as a singer, into the 1970s.

Autrey was a forceful trumpeter who had an intense admiration for the work of Louis Armstrong; his engaging style of singing was reminiscent of Waller, with whom he shared an extraordinary appetite for life and a great sense of humor. His recordings with Waller demonstrate the extent to which he understood and reacted to a leader's requirements.

Oral history material in *NjR* (JOHP).

SELECTED RECORDINGS

As leader with Bob Gordon: *Finger Poppin'* (1971–2, Jezebel 101)

As sideman: F. Waller: Dinah (1935, Vic. 25471); 12th Street Rag (1935, Vic. 25087); Lounging at the Waldorf (1936, Vic. 25430); Latch on (1936, Vic. 25471); Two Sleepy People (1938, Bb 10000); Anita (1939, Bb 10369); Saints and Sinners: *Saints and Sinners in Europe* (1968, MPS 15174), incl. Sugar

BIBLIOGRAPHY

ChiltonW; *FeatherE*; *Feather '60s*; *Feather–Gitler '70s*
H. Panassié: "Herman Autrey," *JJ*, viii/12 (1955), 1
A. Persiany: "Herman Autrey," *BHcF*, no.151 (1965), 3
G. W. Kay: "Herman Autrey Recalls the Early Days," *JJ*, xxii/10 (1969), 10
J. Simmen: "Herman Autrey," *BHcF*, no.331 (1985), 1; no.332 (1985), 10; no.333 (1985), 14; no.334 (1986), 4; no.335 (1986), 6; no.336 (1986), 8; no.337 (1986), 11; no.338 (1986), 5; no.339 (1986), 1

JOHNNY SIMMEN

Ava. Record company and label. The company was founded by Fred Astaire in Hollywood in 1962, and recorded several jazz albums by Victor Feldman, Muggsy Spanier, Herbie Steward, Ben Tucker, and others. The recordings were produced by Jackie Mills and distributed by MGM, which later bought the company.

MARK GARDNER

Avakian, George (*b* Armavir, Russian SFSR, 15 March 1919). Record producer and writer of Armenian descent. He grew up in New York, played piano (from 1930), and studied English literature at Yale University (BA 1941); while a student he began to work as a jazz critic for *Tempo* (1937). He was later a contributing editor on jazz to *Mademoiselle* and *Pic* (1946–8), contributed to *Esquire's 1947 Jazz Book* and, with W. E. Schaap, revised and enlarged Charles Delaunay's *Hot Discography* for its first American edition (1948). He also contributed to *Down Beat* and *Metronome* and wrote numerous liner notes for jazz albums. Avakian produced the pioneering documentary jazz album, *Chicago Jazz* (1939–40), for Decca, and in early 1940 began to work for Columbia, where he established a series of jazz reissues. After four years of military service he returned to Columbia as a full-time record producer for jazz and popular music; he was also director of the international department, and later head of the popular album department. In 1956 he published a listeners' guide to Columbia's jazz recordings entitled *Jazz from Columbia: a Complete Jazz Catalog*. He left Columbia in 1958 to join World-Pacific and later worked for Warner Bros. and RCA, where he was mainly involved with popular music. Avakian organized the first jazz reissues on LP and in sets of LPs, and produced the first recording of a performance at a festival (from the Newport Jazz Festival in 1954); he was also among the earliest producers to utilize the technique of splicing different takes. Among the best-selling recordings he generated were albums by Louis Armstrong, Erroll Garner, and Benny Goodman. He also played an important role in the early careers of Dave Brubeck, Miles Davis, Keith Jarrett, and Sonny Rollins. (L. Feather: *The New Yearbook of Jazz*, New York, 1958)

Avant-garde jazz. A term used synonymously in the 1960s with FREE JAZZ. In the 1970s and 1980s many musicians have preferred the label "avant-garde," since the word "free" is misleading: in many instances their music is highly organized. As free jazz has become more familiar and has been absorbed into the standard repertory, however, the term "avant-garde" has ceased to describe the genre accurately; moreover, the use of an alternative term obscures the many streams linking the free-jazz musicians of the 1980s with the pioneers Ornette Coleman, Cecil Taylor, Albert Ayler, and John Coltrane.

Ax(e). In jazz argot originally (from about 1950) a saxophone, later any musical instrument. (*GoldJL*)

ROBERT WITMER

Axen, Bent (*b* Copenhagen, 12 Aug 1925). Danish pianist. From 1949 to 1958 he played with commercially oriented groups and recorded with such musicians as the baritone saxophonist Max Brüel (1955). He led the group Jazz Quintet '60 (1959–63), belonged to the Danish Radiojazzgruppen (1961–7), and recorded with both ensembles, as a leader (1959–61), and with several American musicians on their visits to Denmark, including Eric Dolphy (1961), Brew Moore (1962), and Don Byas (1964). From 1967 he worked principally as a music director and composer for theaters in Copenhagen and only occasionally in jazz. Axen was the leading jazz pianist in Denmark in the years following World War II; his style, which owes something to the work of Bill Evans (ii), is heard to advantage on his album *Let's Keep the Message* (1960, Debut 133), in particular its title track.

ERIK WIEDEMANN

Ayers, Roy (E., Jr.) (*b* Los Angeles, 10 Sept 1940). Vibraphonist. He studied keyboard instruments, clarinet, and singing with his mother, then concentrated on vibraphone from his late teens. After attending college for a brief period he played West Coast jazz with Gerald Wilson (recording in 1965–6), Teddy Edwards, Curtis Amy (recording in 1962), Chico Hamilton, Hampton Hawes, Jack Wilson (recording in 1963–4 and 1966–7), and Phineas Newborn. He performed with Herbie Mann at the Lighthouse in Hermosa Beach, near Los Angeles, and from 1966 to 1970 toured and recorded with Mann, who produced three of Ayers's albums. In 1970 he formed the group Ubiquity, which played what he described as an amalgam of jazz, blues, rhythm-and-blues, pop, bossa nova, and Latin music; in the late 1970s the influence of disco could be discerned in his work.

SELECTED RECORDINGS

West Coast Vibes (1963, UA 6325); *Virgo Vibes* (1967, Atl. 1488); *Mystic Voyage* (1976, Pol. 6057); *Vibrations* (1977, Pol. 6091); *No Stranger to Love* (1980, Pol. 6246)

BIBLIOGRAPHY

Feather '60s; *Feather–Gitler '70s*

GARY THEROUX

Ayler, Albert (*b* Cleveland, 13 July 1936; *d* ?New York, between 5 and 25 Nov 1970). Tenor saxophonist and leader, brother of Donald Ayler. At the age of seven he began three years of lessons on alto saxophone with his father, a violinist and tenor saxophonist. He played professionally in rhythm-and-blues bands by his mid-teens, and toured with Little Walter and his Jukes at the age of 16. In 1959 he began a three-year term in army concert bands, during which time he changed to tenor saxophone. He occasionally played in Paris clubs while stationed in France in 1960–61. After his discharge he remained in Europe, leading a bop trio for eight months in Sweden (one performance, in 1962, was recorded) and playing with Cecil Taylor in winter 1962–3 in Copenhagen, where he also led a studio recording. He moved to New York in 1963. There he performed infrequently with Taylor and made another obscure LP recording in winter 1963–4. After returning to Cleveland briefly, owing to lack of work, in summer 1964 he formed a quartet in New

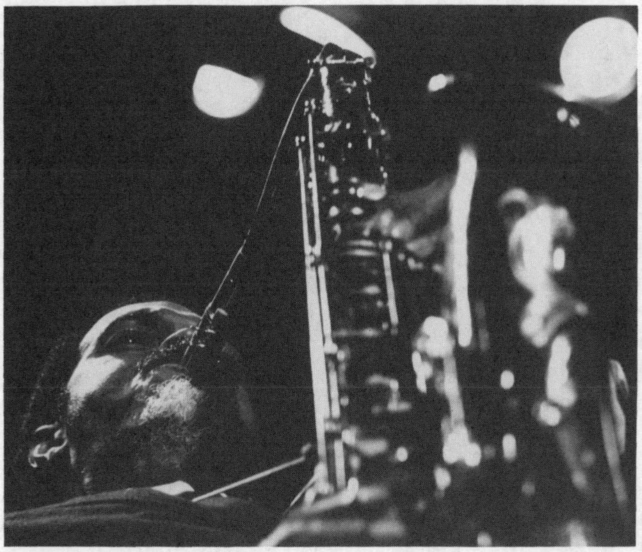

Albert Ayler, London, 1966

York with Don Cherry, Gary Peacock, and Sunny Murray. This group toured Europe in late 1964.

Ayler was never to find a steady audience for his radical music – his group appeared perhaps only three times in 1965 – and, although his albums were well received by the critics, he remained poor. He made no effort to clarify his music for his listeners, actively discouraging musical interpretations of his recordings and instead stressing their social and spiritual issues; the inconsistent and confusing titles to his pieces further obscured his work (see Litweiler). Nevertheless, in studios and New York clubs (1965–8), at the Newport Jazz Festival (1966), on a brief European tour (November 1966), and for college concerts he was able to assemble faithful sidemen. His groups included his brother, one or two double bass players, such as Peacock and Henry Grimes, the drummers Murray, Milford Graves, or Beaver Harris, and Cal Cobbs on piano or harpsichord. Only Cobbs remained in Ayler's new rhythm-and-blues groups of 1969–70. On 5 November 1970, shortly after having returned from a tour of Europe with his quintet, Ayler was reported missing in New York; his body was found in the East River on 25 November.

Ex.1 From the title track of *Ghosts* (1964, Debut 144); transcr. B. Kernfeld

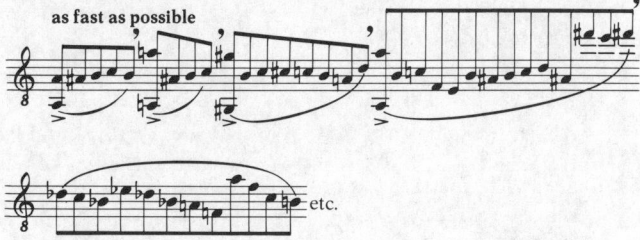

Ayler's extraordinary music of the mid-1960s was difficult and controversial. Without losing its identity as jazz, it rejected most of the conventions of the prevailing bop and free styles. According to Jost (who alone has surveyed his career analytically), Ayler often replaced tempered melody with sweeping flourishes; he combined these "sound-spans" (Jost) with sudden low-pitched honks and a wide, sentimental vibrato (ex.1). His recordings of 1962–3 in Scandinavia were unsuccessful because of the stylistic gulf between the "in-tune" bop accompanists and the "out-of-tune" saxophone. By contrast, Peacock and Murray provided sympathetic accompaniments to Ayler's highly original playing. Their recordings (1964) juxtapose difficult collective improvisation and Ayler's simple, rhythmically square, frequently tonal themes. Sometimes these two factors are interrelated, as in the gradual deformation of the folk-like melody in several versions of *Ghosts* (1964). More often, however, the brief themes serve as foils for lengthy, exciting improvisations in which the group, avoiding predictable sounds, achieves remarkably varied textures and rhythms (as in *Spirits* on the album *Spiritual Unity*, or *Ay* and *Itt* on *New York Eye and Ear Control*).

Soon after the performance of *Bells* in May 1965 the balance shifted from improvisation to composition. Three tracks on *Spirits Rejoice* emphasize thematic material: the title track (representative of Ayler's growing preference for marches) includes numerous repetitions of a theme that incorporates bits of the *Marseillaise*; *Holy Family* consists of rhythm-and-blues riffs; and *Angels* is a strange ballad delivered to the accompaniment of harpsichord, bowed double bass, and cymbal rolls. Later, in a new version of *Ghosts* (1967), the players never depart from thematic statements. This striving for simplicity, augmented by pressure from the record company Impulse! to increase his sales, led Ayler to return to rhythm-and-blues in the late 1960s. Unfortunately, his late rhythm-and-blues songs and his singing were dull, and his last two albums received little attention.

See also BLUES, §12.

SELECTED RECORDINGS

My Name is Albert Ayler (1963, Debut 140); *Spirits* (1964, Debut 146); *Spiritual Unity* (1964, ESP 1002), incl. Ghosts, Spirits; *New York Eye and Ear Control* (1964, ESP 1016), incl. Ay, Itt; *Ghosts* (1964, Debut 144); *Bells* (1965, ESP 1010); *Spirits Rejoice* (1965, ESP 1020), incl. Angels, Holy Family; *Lörrach/Paris* (1966, HH 3500); *Albert Ayler in Greenwich Village* (1966–7, Imp. 9155), incl. Ghosts; *Love Cry* (1967, Imp. 9165); *New Grass* (1968, Imp. 9175); *Music is the Healing Force of the Universe* (1969, Imp. 9191)

BIBLIOGRAPHY

N. Hentoff: "The Truth is Marching In," *DB*, xxxiii/23 (1966), 16 [interview]
V. Wilmer: "Albert and Don Ayler," *JM*, xii/10 (1966), 11
P. Burke: "Albert Ayler: a Preliminary Checklist of Concert/Club etc. Appearances," *Discographical Forum*, nos.12–15 (1969)
E. Raben: *A Discography of Free Jazz* (Copenhagen, 1969)
Obituary, *DB*, xxxviii/1 (1971), 8
E. Jost: *Free Jazz* (Graz, Austria, 1974)
V. Wilmer: "Albert Ayler: Spiritual Unity," *As Serious as your Life: the Story of the New Jazz* (London, 1977, rev. 1980)
M. Rissi and H. Hollenstein: "Albert Ayler Discography," *Jazz 360°*, no.32 (1980), 12
J. Litweiler: "Albert Ayler," *DB*, xlix/2 (1982), 45
M. Hames: *Albert Ayler, Sunny Murray, Cecil Taylor, Byard Lancaster, and Kenneth Terroade on Disc and Tape* (Ferndown, Dorset, England, 1983)
B. Smith and B. Case: "The Truth is Marching In," *The Wire*, no.3 (1983), 12

BARRY KERNFELD

Ayler, Donald (*b* Cleveland, 5 Oct 1942). Trumpeter, brother of Albert Ayler. He attended the Cleveland Institute and performed locally with Charles Tyler. From 1965 to 1968 he played and recorded in New York and Europe with his brother, and in 1966 he performed at Lincoln Center in New York with John Coltrane. He returned to Cleveland and from around 1973 performed only occasionally. He later formed a septet, which in 1981 visited Italy and made a three-record album, *In Florence* (Frame 2001–3).

BIBLIOGRAPHY

Feather '60s
N. Hentoff: "The Truth is Marching In," *DB*, xxxiii/23 (1966), 16 [interview]
B. Rusch: "Donald Ayler: Interview," *Cadence*, v/2 (1979), 14

Azimuth. Trio formed by JOHN TAYLOR in 1977.

B

Babasin, Harry (*b* Dallas, 19 March 1921). Double bass player and cellist. He learned cello and double bass in his teens and later studied at North Texas State College. During the early 1940s he toured with territory bands in the Midwest and traveled to New York, where he performed with Gene Krupa, Boyd Raeburn, and Charlie Barnet (all 1945). He then moved to the West Coast and worked again with Raeburn (1945–6) and with Benny Goodman's big band and small group (1946–7). Shortly after leaving Goodman he made a number of recordings with Dodo Marmarosa (1947), which are important for his introduction of pizzicato on cello. In 1948 Babasin toured with Woody Herman (for illustration *see* HERMAN, WOODY, fig.1*b*) and began to work in recording studios in Hollywood; he also appeared in a number of films, including *A Song is Born* (1948). He was a founder of a small record company, NOCTURNE, which recorded his own group (1954) and others. From 1956 he played cello as the leader of the Jazzpickers, and in 1959 he performed briefly with Harry James. Later he attended San Fernando Valley State College and received an MA in composition (1961), and during the 1960s he worked as a freelance and played in a duo with the pianist Phil Moody.

SELECTED RECORDINGS

As leader: How about you?/Saunders Meanders (1952, PJ 603); Night and Day/'S wonderful (1952, Dis. 163); *Harry Babasin Quintet* (1954, Nocturne 3); *The Jazzpickers* (1957, Mode 119); *For Moderns Only* (1957, EmA 36111); *Command Performance* (1957, EmA 36123)

As sideman: B. Goodman: Cherokee/Love is just around the corner (1947, Cap. 15166); D. Marmarosa: Bopmatism/Tradewinds (1947, Dial 752)

BIBLIOGRAPHY

FeatherE; *Feather '60s*

LAWRENCE KOCH

Babbington, Roy (*b* Kempston, England, 8 July 1940). English bass player. A self-taught musician, he became fully professional in 1958 and played for various leaders in clubs and ballrooms. In 1969 he moved to London, where he worked as a session musician; among the groups with which he recorded were those led by Ian Carr (1972–3), Mike Westbrook (1973), and Keith Tippett (1970–73). He was a member of SOFT MACHINE (*c*1974–1976), accompanied many visiting American musicians, and played for several productions at the National Theatre. He has recorded with Harry Beckett (1977) and Graham Collier and Barbara Thompson (both 1978). In the 1980s Babbington has performed regularly with the BBC Radio Orchestra and several of Stan Tracey's groups (recording from 1980). His playing is featured on *The Firmament* from Tracey's album *Genesis* (1987, Steam 114).

BIBLIOGRAPHY

K. Dallas: "Soft Machine," *MM*, l (5 April 1975), 18 [incl. individual biographies]

R. Cotterrell, ed.: *Jazz Now: the Jazz Centre Society Guide* (London, 1976), 109

NEVIL SKRIMSHIRE

Babs [Sjöblom [née Nilson]], **Alice** (*b* Kalmar, Sweden, 26 Jan 1924). Swedish singer. She made her début on radio at the age of 14 and her first recordings at 15, appeared in the film *Swing it Magistern* (1940), and performed at the Paris Jazz Fair in 1949. In the 1950s she achieved success as a popular singer in Germany and elsewhere, then resumed her career in jazz as a member of the trio Swe-Danes with Svend Asmussen and Ulrik Neumann (1958–63). From 1963 she performed and recorded with Duke Ellington in Europe and New York; from the 1960s she also sang classical music. She made recordings as a leader into the 1970s but was active only occasionally in the following decade. Babs was the first Swedish jazz singer to project a genuine sense of swing; she won acclaim for her clear articulation, her reliable intonation (particularly in the upper register), and her facility for improvisation. Her private collection of recordings and other materials is now in the Svenskt Visarkiv, Stockholm; *see* LIBRARIES AND ARCHIVES, §2.

SELECTED RECORDINGS

As leader: Dedicated to you (1940, Son. 3637); Blues in the Night (1942, HMV X6789); It's a hundred to one (1944, HMV X7069); *Alice and Wonderland* (1959, Telestar 11025); *Music with a Jazz Flavour* (1973, Bluebell 120); *Far Away Star* (1974–6, Phon. 7511)

As sideman with D. Ellington: *Serenade to Sweden* (1963, Rep. 5024)

BIBLIOGRAPHY

S. Dance: *The World of Duke Ellington* (London and New York, 1970/*R*1981), 226

F. Hedman, K. Liliedahl, and L. Zackrisson: *Alice Babs* (Stockholm, 1973) [discography]

F. Hedman: *Alice Babs: berättelsen om artisten Alice "Babs" Nilson* [Alice Babs: the story of the artist Alice "Babs" Nilson] (Stockholm, 1975)

ERIK KJELLBERG

Back. In jazz argot to accompany, whence "backing" and "background," meaning "accompaniment." The words are applied to all kinds of accompanying, ranging from basic comping by the rhythm section to elaborate arrangements played behind a soloist or solo section in a big band. Because of the character of many accompaniments, "to back" is often understood more specifically to mean to play fills, riffs, and countermelodies.

ROBERT WITMER

Backbeat. A term applied to the second and fourth beats of a 4/4 or 12/8 bar; *see* BEAT, §4(i).

Bacon, Louis (*b* Louisville, KY, 1 Nov 1904; *d* New York, 8 Dec 1967). Trumpeter and singer. He played with Zinky Cohn in Harbor Springs, Michigan (1926), then in 1928 moved to New York. He played with Bingie Madison (1928), recorded with Bessie Smith (1930) and Louis Armstrong (1932), and performed and recorded with Chick Webb (1930–?1934), Benny Carter (1932, 1939), Duke Ellington (1933–?1934), and Armstrong (1935–8). He toured Europe with Willie Lewis, and recorded as a leader in Paris (1939) and with Lewis in Zurich (1941). In 1941 he returned to the USA, where he played and recorded with Cootie Williams (1942) and Garvin Bushell (1944). After a long illness he worked as a vocal coach and recorded as a singer with Wilbur De Paris (1960). Bacon's playing can be heard to advantage on *Jam with Bacon/Big Wig in the Wigwam* (1939, Swing 75) by Freddy Johnson and his Orchestra, and on Smith's *Keep it to yourself/New Orleans Hop Scop Blues* (1930, Col. 14516D).

BIBLIOGRAPHY

ChiltonW
J. Simmen: "Louis Bacon–Henry Mason," *JJ*, xxi/2 (1968), 12

Bacsik, Elek (*b* Budapest, 22 May 1926). Hungarian guitarist. He is a cousin of Django Reinhardt. He studied classical violin and played gypsy music in Budapest, but later changed to jazz guitar. He first recorded in 1943 in a big band led by the alto saxophonist Géza Szabó and the trumpeter József Quitter. He toured Europe and Lebanon with Mihály Tabányi's band. In 1959 he moved to Paris, where he recorded with visiting American musicians, among them the pianist Art Simmons and Quentin Jackson (both 1959), Lou Bennett (1960), and Dizzy Gillespie (1962). He also made recordings with his own groups (1962–3, including *The Electric Guitar of the Eclectic Elek Bacsik*, 1962, Fon. 680221ML). After emigrating to the USA in 1966 he worked with Teresa Brewer (1967–74) and again recorded as a leader (1974–5); his violin playing can be heard on *Bird and Dizzy: a Musical Tribute* (1975, FD BDL1-1082). He performed at the Newport Jazz Festival (1974) and at the Olympic Games Jazz Festival in Los Angeles (1984). (*Feather '60s; Feather–Gitler '70s*)

GÉZA GÁBOR SIMON, RAINER E. LOTZ

Baden Powell [de Aquino, Roberto Baden Powell] (*b* Rio de Janeiro, 6 Aug 1937). Brazilian guitarist and leader. His father and grandfather were both prominent Brazilian musicians, and he began playing professionally at the age of 15. He first achieved fame through his work with the poet Vinicius de Moraes, who wrote lyrics for many of Baden Powell's compositions. In 1962 he recorded in a duo with Herbie Mann. At the suggestion of Joachim Berendt he recorded as a leader (1966) and later toured Europe. He continued to make recordings throughout the 1970s, including an album in the bossa nova style, *La grande réunion* (1974, Festival 634), with Stephane Grappelli. Although he has spent much time in Europe, he returns regularly to Brazil to perform and record. He has also worked in the USA with Stan Getz. (M. J. Summerfield: *The Jazz Guitar: its Evolution and its Players* (Gateshead, England, 1978), 163 [incl. discography])

Badini, Gérard (*b* Paris, 16 April 1931). French tenor saxophonist, clarinetist, and leader. He studied classical singing as a child and took up the clarinet in 1950. After playing traditional jazz with the soprano saxophonist Michel Attenoux (1952) he belonged to Claude Bolling's trio (1955) and toured Europe, Africa, and the Middle East with Bolling and with Jazz aux Champs Elysées, led by the pianist Jack Dieval. From 1958 his principal instrument was the tenor saxophone, which he played for many years with Bolling and in studios. In 1973 he formed the Swing Machine, a quartet in which his sidemen were Raymond Fol, Michel Gaudry, and Bobby Durham (replaced after Badini visited the USA in 1974–5 by Sam Woodyard, who was in turn replaced by Sonny Payne in 1976). Later he lived in New York (1977–9), led a small group, and taught in Paris (from 1982). In 1984 he formed the Super Swing Machine, a big band. Badini has gained recognition for his warm tone in ballads and his fierce drive in faster pieces; his playing is in the tradition of Coleman Hawkins, Ben Webster, and Paul Gonsalves.

SELECTED RECORDINGS

As leader: *The Swing Machine* (1975, BStar 80701); *French Cooking* (1980, Vogue 502607)
As sideman: C. Bolling: *Bolling's Band's Blowing* (1963, Phi. 77965); C. Anderson and C. Bolling: *Cat Anderson, Claude Bolling and Co* (1965, Phi. 77731), incl. The Twins; P. Gonsalves and F. Guin: *Avec les swingers et les Four Bones* (1969, Riviera 521137), incl. Darn that Dream, Jumpin' at the Woodside; H. Humes: *Sneakin' Around* (1974, BB 33083), incl. Every now and then

BIBLIOGRAPHY

J. H. Klee: "Hot from Paris," *MR*, iv/12 (1977), 9
F. Billard and G. Rouy: "Le B.A. Ba de Badini," *Jm*, no.306 (1982), 48
P. Bourdin: "Les débuts du big band de Badini," *Jh*, no.415 (1984), 50 [interview]
P. Carles: "Le big band à Badini," *Jm*, no.326 (1984), 25

ANDRÉ CLERGEAT

Badrena, Manolo (*b* Puerto Rico, *c*1952). Puerto Rican percussionist. He worked as a freelance with Art Blakey and toured with the Rolling Stones. From 1976 to 1977 he was a member of Weather Report (for illustration *see* ZAWINUL, JOE), with which he recorded three albums, including *Heavy Weather* (1976, Col. PC34418). He then worked with Steve Khan (1981), Spyro Gyra (*c*1982–1983), Bill Evans (iii) (1983), and Carla Bley (1983–4). (K. Dallas: "Weather Report," *MM*, lii (29 Oct 1977), 56)

BAG. *See* BLACK ARTISTS GROUP.

Bagley, Don(ald Neff) [Bags] (*b* Salt Lake City, 18 July 1927). Double bass player. He played with Shorty Sherock and Wingy Manone (1945). He attended Los Angeles City College (1945–50), where he studied double bass, composition, and arranging. From 1950 to 1953, and thereafter on an intermittent basis, he toured and recorded with Stan Kenton; in 1954 he began leading his own group. Bagley also recorded in Los Angeles with Nat "King" Cole (1950), Maynard Ferguson (1950), and Dexter Gordon (1952), and in Stockholm and Paris with Zoot Sims, Lars Gullin, and a sextet led by Frank Rosolino and Åke Persson (all 1953). Between 1956 and 1967 he worked chiefly with Kenton and Les Brown, but also recorded (1957–8) as a leader of bands that included Jimmie Rowles, Shelly Manne, and Phil Woods, and as a sideman with Pete Fountain (1959) and Ben Webster (1961). *Jazz on the Rocks* (1958, Reg. 6061), an album made with Woods, shows Bagley's playing to advantage. From 1976 to 1984 he played with Burt Bacharach. He wrote compositions and arrangements for television and films and worked and recorded with many popular singers.

BIBLIOGRAPHY

FeatherE
R. Gordon: *Jazz West Coast: the Los Angeles Jazz Scene of the 1950s* (London and New York, 1986)

Bags. Nickname of MILT JACKSON.

Bahula, (Sebothane) Julian (*b* Johannesburg, 13 March 1938). South African percussionist. He was a popular drummer in the band Molombo, one of the foremost groups playing *kwela* (a style of jazz close to urban popular music performed in the South African townships); the other members were the flutist Abe Cindi and the guitarist Philip Tabane. He moved to London in 1973 and formed the group Jabula, which played an amalgam of African music and rock; in 1977 this joined forces with a band led by Dudu Pukwana to form Jabula/Spear, which recorded the album *Thunder in our Hearts* (1977, Car. 2009). Later Bahula worked to promote African music in London, while also playing occasionally with the group Jazz Afrika and with a new group under the name Jabula. In the late 1980s he played with Dick Heckstall-Smith in the band Electric Dream.

BIBLIOGRAPHY

R. Cotterell, ed.: *Jazz Now: the Jazz Centre Society Guide* (London, 1976)
C. de Ledesma: "Afro Jazz: Evolution and Revolution," *The Wire*, no.12 (1985), 26, esp. 38

CHARLES DE LEDESMA

Bailey, Benny [Ernest Harold] (*b* Cleveland, 13 Aug 1925). Trumpeter. After learning piano and flute he took up trumpet and studied at the Cleveland Conservatory of Music and privately with George Russell. In the early 1940s he played with the tenor saxophonist Bull Moose Jackson and the drummer and singer Scatman Crothers; thereafter he toured with Jay McShann and played with Teddy Edwards. He joined Dizzy Gillespie's big band in 1947 and toured Europe with it the following year. After leaving Gillespie he was one of the principal soloists with Lionel Hampton's orchestra (1948-53). In 1953 Bailey settled in Europe; he lived for several years in Sweden and became an important musician there. He was a member of Harry Arnold's band (1957–9), recorded with Stan Getz (1958), and joined Quincy Jones (1959). After returning briefly to the USA in 1960 he moved to Germany, where he worked with many big bands and smaller ensembles. In 1961 he performed and recorded with Eric Dolphy in Berlin. He was a soloist with the Clarke–Boland Big Band from the early 1960s to 1973, and in 1969, with Les McCann, he gave an acclaimed performance at the Montreux International Jazz Festival. After playing with George Gruntz in the mid-1970s he worked in radio bands. In 1986 he joined the Paris Reunion Band, which toured Europe and the USA.

Bailey's playing is distinctive and powerful; he possesses a bright, forceful tone and a remarkable range. His solos are both exciting and inventive.

SELECTED RECORDINGS

As leader: *Big Brass* (1960, Can. 9011); *Islands* (1976, Enja 2082); *East of Isar* (1978, Ego 4010); *Grand Slam* (1978, Jazzcraft 8)
As sideman: L. Hampton: Cool Train (1951, MGM 10979); *Oh Rock!* (1951, MGM 3386), incl. Air Mail Special; K. Clarke and F. Boland: *Live at Ronnie Scott's* (1969, MPS 22297284); Upper Manhattan Jazz Society: *The Upper Manhattan Jazz Society* (1981, Enja 4090)

BIBLIOGRAPHY

FeatherE; *Feather '60s*; *Feather–Gitler '70s*
J. Shaw: "Benny Bailey: a Lifetime in Big Bands," *JJ*, xxiii/4 (1970), 12
L. Lysted: "Meet Benny Bailey," *DB*, xl/3 (1973), 16
P. Sullivan: "Benny Bailey," *JJ*, xxx/4 (1977), 8
N. Hentoff: Liner notes, *Grand Slam* (Jazzcraft 8, 1978)
G. Endress: "Benny Bailey," *JP*, xxxiv/8 (1985), 3

ROLAND BAGGENAES

Bailey, Buster [William C.] (*b* Memphis, 19 July 1902; *d* New York, 12 April 1967). Clarinetist. As a teenager he played in the orchestra led by W. C. Handy. In 1919 he settled in Chicago and worked with Erskine Tate and King Oliver, then in 1924 moved to New York to join Fletcher Henderson's band. His considerable technique on clarinet meant that he was featured on many of Henderson's recordings during the years from 1924 to 1937, though he also played with Noble Sissle (1929, in Europe; 1931–3) and the Mills Blue Rhythm Band (1934–5). Later he worked with John Kirby (1937–46), Wilbur De Paris (1947–9), Henry "Red" Allen (1950–51), and Big Chief Moore (1952–3), and from 1954 performed mostly with Allen's group. From 1961 to 1963 he was with Wild Bill Davison, after which he joined the Saints and Sinners; he spent the last two years of his life as a member of Louis Armstrong's All Stars.

While Bailey was in Henderson's band, the ruggedness of Johnny Dodds's and Sidney Bechet's improvisations exerted an effect on his classically trained approach, but later, with Kirby's sextet, his playing became smoother. One of the best demonstrations of his exceptionally fast fingering is heard on *Man with a horn goes berserk* (1938). Bailey remained a master

Buster Bailey (clarinet) and Russell Procope (alto saxophone) during a performance by John Kirby's band at the Randalls Island (New York) Jazz Festival, May 1938

technician until the end of his life. While he rarely "swung" in the manner of the great jazz clarinetists and his playing lacked passion, his solos were always fluent and tuneful.

For further illustrations *see* ALLEN, HENRY "RED," Jazz (i), fig.2, and KIRBY, JOHN.

SELECTED RECORDINGS

As leader: Afternoon in Africa/Dizzy Debutante (1937, Var. 668); Man with a horn goes berserk (1938, Voc. 4564); Am I Blue? (1940, Vars. 8333); *All about Memphis* (1958, Fel. 7003)

As sideman with F. Henderson: Jackass Blues (1926, Col. 654D); St. Louis Blues (1927, Har. 451H); King Porter Stomp (1928, Col. 1543D); Shanghai Shuffle (1934, Decca 158)

As sideman with others: Clarence Williams: Everybody loves my baby (1924, OK 8181); Bessie Smith: Jazzbo Brown from Memphis Town (1926, Col. 14133D); Clarence Williams: Yama Yama Blues/Church Street Sobbin' Blues (1927, OK 8525); N. Sissle: Tiger Rag (1933), first issued on untitled album (Ristic SAL); L. Hampton: Rhythm, rhythm (1937, Vic. 25586); J. Kirby: 9:20 Special (1945, Asch 3571); Dixie All Stars: *Dixiecats* (1957, Roul. 25015), incl. Tin Roof Blues

BIBLIOGRAPHY

S. Dance: Liner notes, *All about Memphis* (Fel. 7003, 1959)
Obituary, *DB*, xxxiv/10 (1967), 13
A. McCarthy and others: *Jazz on Record: a Critical Guide to the First 50 Years: 1917–1967* (London, 1968), 13

JOHN CHILTON

Bailey, Colin (*b* Swindon, England, 9 July 1934). English drummer. He is said to have toured with the Australian Jazz Quartet, visiting the USA in 1960–61, but by other accounts the group disbanded in 1958. He recorded with the pianists Bill Benham and Bryce Rohde in 1960 in Australia, and again with Rohde in 1962 after moving to the USA. He performed and recorded with Vince Guaraldi (1962–3), Clare Fischer (1962–4), and Victor Feldman (1964), and recorded with Joe Pass (1963–4). In 1964–5 he made a tour of Japan with Benny Goodman, during which he recorded the album *Made in Japan* (1964, Cap. ST2282), and played on television with Terry Gibbs. After touring with George Shearing (1966–7) he performed with Pass, Gibbs, Ray Brown, Chet Baker, João Gilberto, and Feldman, and recorded with Feldman (1967, 1977) and Blossom Dearie (1975). In the mid-1980s he played regularly in Richie Cole's quartet on the West Coast. (*Feather '60s*; *Feather–Gitler '70s*)

Bailey, Dave [Samuel David] (*b* Portsmouth, VA, 22 Feb 1926). Drummer and administrator. After serving as a pilot in World War II he studied drumming in New York and played with Johnny Hodges, Charles Mingus, Lou Donaldson, Curtis Fuller, and Horace Silver; he is best known for his work with Gerry Mulligan (1954–68; for illustration *see* RECORDING, fig.5) and with Clark Terry and Bob Brookmeyer (in the 1960s). While touring South America in 1959 he learned Brazilian bossa nova rhythms, which he demonstrated to other American musicians before the style became popular in the 1960s. In 1969 he interrupted his career in music to work as a pilot and flight instructor; from 1973 he was active as a teacher and administrator. He is the executive director of the JAZZMOBILE in New York.

SELECTED RECORDINGS

As leader: *One Foot in the Guitar* (1960, Epic 17008); *Gettin' into Something* (1960, Epic 17011); *Bash!* (1961, Jazzline 33-01)

As sideman: G. Mulligan: *What is there to Say* (1958–9, Col. CL1307); C. Fuller: *South American Cooking* (1961, Epic 17020); L. Donaldson: *Here 'tis* (1961, BN 4066); C. Terry: *Tonight* (1964, Mstr. 6043)

BIBLIOGRAPHY

M. Jones: "A Drummer must Join the Group," *MM*, xxxviii (18 May 1963), 6
A. J. Smith: "Jazzmobile: Billy Taylor and Dave Bailey, Magnetizing the Arts," *DB*, xliv/20 (1977), 14 [interview]
——: "A Jazz Odyssey," *Jazz Magazine*, iii/4 (1979), 52

J. KENT WILLIAMS

Bailey, Derek (*b* Sheffield, England, 29 Jan 1932). English guitarist. His grandfather and uncle were both professional musicians, and Bailey was first involved in commercial music and conventional jazz. In 1966 he moved to London to play free jazz with John Stevens, Evan Parker, Paul Rutherford, and others. He joined the Spontaneous Music Ensemble, and from 1968 to 1973 belonged to Tony Oxley's sextet; together they explored technical innovations and new sound resources, Oxley on acoustic and amplified percussion and Bailey on acoustic and electric guitars. In 1970 Bailey formed the trio Iskra 1903 with Rutherford and Barry Guy, and founded the record label Incus with Oxley and Evan Parker. From 1976 he led the group Company (for illustration *see* JAZZ (i), fig.9), which, with changing personnel, has played in Europe, the Americas, Africa, and Japan. While continuing to perform in duos and small groups, he has also appeared as a soloist. A creative and highly original improviser, Bailey has influenced a generation of guitarists in Europe and North America. His book *Improvisation: its Nature and Practice in Music* (Ashbourne, England, 1980; Ger. trans., Hofheim, Germany, 1986) treats perceptively the relationships among different traditions of improvisation.

Oral history material in *GBLnsa*.

SELECTED RECORDINGS

As unaccompanied soloist: *Solo Guitar* (1971, Incus 2); *Aida* (1980, Incus 40)

Duos: with H. Bennink: [untitled album] (1969, ICP 004); with D. Holland: *Improvisations for Cello and Guitar* (1971, ECM 1013ST)

As leader with E. Parker: *The Topography of the Lungs* (1970, Incus 1)

As sideman: T. Oxley: *The Baptised Traveller* (1969, CBS 52664); M. Schoof: *European Echoes* (1969, FMP 0010); T. Oxley: *Ichnos* (1969–70, RCA SF8215); Music Improvisation Company: *The Music Improvisation Company* (1970, ECM 1005); Iskra 1903: *Iskra 1903* (1970–72, Incus 3–4); B. Guy: *Ode for Jazz Orchestra* (1972, Incus 6–7)

See also COMPANY.

BIBLIOGRAPHY

I. Carr: *Music Outside: Contemporary Jazz in Britain* (London, 1973)
B. McRae: "Best of British, no.2: Derek Bailey," *JJI*, xxxi/3 (1978), 19
S. Britt: *The Jazz Guitarists* (Poole, England, 1984)
T. Gaudynski: "Derek Bailey: Interview," *Cadence*, x/7 (1984), 11
K. Ansell: "Keeping the Right Company with Derek Bailey," *The Wire*, no.15 (1985), 33

ROGER T. DEAN

Bailey, Donald (Orlando) [Donald "Duck"] (*b* Philadelphia, 26 March 1934). Drummer. He is largely self-taught as a musician; among those who influenced his style were Max Roach, Art Blakey, and Philly Joe Jones. He worked with local groups around Philadelphia, played for eight years with Jimmy Smith (from 1956), and in the mid-1960s moved to Los Angeles, where he performed and recorded with Hampton Hawes, Harold Land, Blue Mitchell, Mundell Lowe, Bobby Bryant, Jimmie Rowles, and others. While living for five years in Japan he performed and recorded with such musicians as Sadao Watanabe, and after returning to the USA in 1982 he worked with Carmen McRae and Sarah Vaughan. Later he settled in Oakland, California, where he worked as a freelance and led a group with which he played harmonica. Bailey has a smooth, graceful style, a light touch, and a keen sense of time; his use of complex rhythms is well illustrated by his work with Hawes.

SELECTED RECORDINGS
(all as sideman)

As drummer: J. Smith: *Jimmy Smith Plays Fats Waller* (1962, BN 84100); H. Hawes: *The Seance* (1966, Cont. 7621); M. Lowe: *California Guitar* (1974, FaD 102); S. Most: *Flute Flight* (1976, Xan. 141); S. Rowles and J. Rowles: *Tell it Like it is* (1984, Conc. 249)

As harmonica player: B. Bryant: *Earth Dance* (1969, PJ 20154)

BIBLIOGRAPHY

FeatherE; *Feather '60s*; *Feather–Gitler '70s*
H. Siders: "Drum Shticks," *DB*, xl (1973), no.5, p.15; no.6, p.18

J. KENT WILLIAMS

Bailey, Judy [Judith Mary] (*b* Auckland, New Zealand, 3 Oct 1935). New Zealand pianist and composer. After arriving in Sydney in 1960 she quickly became a prominent studio musician. She led a succession of trios and larger groups, and worked with many important Australian players, including Don Burrows and Errol Buddle. Her compositional output increased considerably during the 1970s; she wrote film scores and music for children, and also became active as a teacher. She participated in performances of Don Banks's *Nexus* for jazz quintet and orchestra, and made several recordings, including *Colours* (1976, Eureka 103) with her quartet, and *Judy Bailey: Solo* (1977, Eureka 107) as an unaccompanied soloist. In the 1980s she has undertaken several tours of Asia.

BIBLIOGRAPHY

Judy Bailey, Australian Composers (Sydney, 1981) [incl. discography; pubn of Australia Music Centre]
M. Williams: *The Australian Jazz Explosion* (London and elsewhere, 1981)
E. Myers: "An Improvised Career," *APRA* [journal of the Australasian Performing Right Association], iv/1 (1986), 6
B. Johnson: "Bailey, Judith Mary," *The Oxford Companion to Australian Jazz* (Melbourne, Australia, 1987)

JEFF PRESSING (with JOHN WHITEOAK)

Bailey [née Rinker], **Mildred** (*b* Tekoa, WA, 27 Feb 1907; *d* Poughkeepsie, NY, 12 Dec 1951). Singer and pianist. She was educated in Spokane, Washington, and began her career on the West Coast as a cinema pianist and radio performer. In 1929 she made her first recording (with Eddie Lang), and from then until 1933 sang with the band led by Paul Whiteman, to whom she was introduced by her brother, Al Rinker, a member of Whiteman's Rhythm Boys vocal trio. On radio, she sang for the shows of George Jessel and Willard Robison (1934–5) and with Benny Goodman (1939). From 1936 to 1939 Bailey performed Eddie Sauter's arrangements in Red Norvo's band. During the 1930s she was known as the "Rockin' Chair Lady" because of her renditions of Hoagy Carmichael's song *Rockin' Chair*, though from 1933 to 1945 she was married to Norvo, (for illustration *see* NORVO, RED), and the couple were referred to as "Mr. and Mrs. Swing." Despite recurrent illness after 1940, Bailey continued to perform.

Bailey was the first white singer to absorb and master the jazz-flavored phrasing, enunciation, embellishments, improvisatory fervor, and swinging rhythm of her black contemporaries, notably Ethel Waters, Bessie Smith, and Billie Holiday. She was essentially a jazz musician and at her best when inspired by a band of the finest players (her associates included Bunny Berigan, Chu Berry, Jimmy and Tommy Dorsey, Goodman, Coleman Hawkins, Johnny Hodges, Gene Krupa, Norvo, and Teddy Wilson); she often used her voice as if it were the lead instrument, and was a skilled scat singer.

SELECTED RECORDINGS

Rockin' Chair (1932, Vic. 24117); Someday Sweetheart/When day is done (1935, Voc. 3057); Willow Tree/Honeysuckle Rose (1935, Decca 18109); Arkansas Blues (1939, Voc. 4801); Fools rush in/From Another World (1940, Col. 35463)

BIBLIOGRAPHY

B. Esposito: "That Rockin' Chair Lady," *JJ*, xxv/2 (1972), 2
S. Dance: *The World of Swing* (New York, 1974) [colln of previously pubd interviews], 391
H. Pleasants: *The Great American Popular Singers* (London, 1974), 143
M. Pinfold: "Dead, but not Remembered," *JJI*, xxx/12 (1977), 12
L. Gourse: *Louis' Children: American Jazz Singers* (New York, 1984), 100

RAYMONDE S. KRAMLICH/R, HENRY PLEASANTS

Bailey, Pearl (Mae) (*b* Newport News, VA, 29 March 1918). Singer. She performed with Noble Sissle's band in the mid-1930s and with Cootie Williams and Count Basie in the early 1940s. Her solo début, in New York at the Village Vanguard (1944), followed by an engagement at the Blue Angel (1944–5), led to an association with Cab Calloway. She first appeared on Broadway in *St. Louis Woman* (1946), in which her style was compared by critics with that of Ethel Waters; she achieved notable successes with her renditions of *Legalize my Name* and *It's a woman's prerogative*. She also took part in a number of films, including *Carmen Jones* (1954), *That Certain Feeling* (1956), and *St. Louis Blues* (1958). In 1952 Bailey married Louie Bellson, with whom she worked and recorded regularly throughout the 1960s. She earned a Special Tony Award in 1968 for her performance in an all-black version of *Hello, Dolly!*. Although she announced her retirement in 1976 to serve as a member of the American delegation to the United Nations, she later resumed concert and television appearances, and also made a number of international tours.

While with Calloway's band, Bailey developed a comical, offhand style of performance that incorporated a patter of droll asides. She always relied on subtle variation of phrasing and intonation rather than indulging in bravura scat singing.

SELECTED RECORDINGS

Tired (1946, Col. 36837); Legalize my Name/It's a woman's prerogative (1946, Col. 36969); That's good enough for me/Row, row, row (1946, Col. 37280); Takes Two to Tango (1952, Coral 60817); *Pearl Bailey* (1953, Coral 57037); *The One and Only Pearl Bailey Sings* (1956, Mer. 20187)

BIBLIOGRAPHY

FeatherE; *Feather '60s*; *Feather–Gitler '70s*
P. Bailey: *The Raw Pearl* (New York, 1968)
——: *Talking to Myself* (New York, 1971)

ARNOLD SHAW

Baker, Chet [Chesney Henry] (*b* Yale, OK, 23 Dec 1929; *d* Amsterdam, 13 May 1988). Trumpeter and singer. He first encountered jazz while playing in army bands, and by the time of his discharge in 1951 his distinctive, reticent style was fully developed. In 1952 he played briefly with Charlie Parker before beginning an important association with Gerry Mulligan in the latter's celebrated "pianoless" quartet. His performances with the group, particularly his ballad rendition of *My Funny Valentine*, brought him instant fame; his clear tone and subdued, lyrical manner – he rarely played louder than *mezzo-forte* and sometimes restricted his melodic span to less than an octave – immediately became hallmarks of West Coast cool jazz, and were widely imitated. After leaving Mulligan in 1953 Baker rejoined Parker briefly and then led his own groups. He continued to dominate domestic and international jazz opinion polls for the next few years. Thereafter, owing largely to the effects of drug addiction, his career became erratic, being interrupted at one point by a prison sentence in Italy for drug-related offenses (1960–61). In the 1970s he resumed playing regularly, particularly in ensembles without piano or drums, and by the mid-1980s he was again much in demand for club performances and recording dates.

SELECTED RECORDINGS

Duos with P. Bley: *Diane* (1985, Ste. 1207)
As leader: Maid in Mexico (1953, PJ 605); *Chet Baker Sings* (1954, PJ 11); *Chet Baker Big Band* (1956, PJ 1229); *Quartet: Russ Freeman, Chet Baker* (1956, PJ 1232); *Chet Baker in New York* (1958, Riv. 281); *Comin' on with the Chet Baker Quintet* (1965, Prst. 7478); *Cool Burnin'* (1965, Prst. 7496); *The Touch of your Lips* (1979, Ste. 1122); *Someday my Prince Will Come* (1979, Ste. 1180); *Chet Baker Live: 'Round Midnight* (1981, Cir. [G] 25); *Blues for a Reason* (1984, Criss 1010); *Chet Baker Trio* (1985, Enja 5005)
As sideman with G. Mulligan: Line for Lyons/Carioca (1952, Fan. 522); My Funny Valentine/Bark for Barksdale (1952, Fan. 525)

BIBLIOGRAPHY

A. Morgan: "Chet Baker," *JM*, ix/4 (1963), 7
I. Gitler: "Chet Baker's Tale of Woe," *DB*, xxxi/20 (1964), 22

M. James: "A Case of Mistaken Identity," *JM*, no.173 (1969), 4
G. Gautherin and A. Tercinet: "Discographie de Chet Baker," *Jh*, no.327 (1976), 12
B. Rusch: "Chet Baker: Interview," *Cadence*, iv/7 (1978), 3
L. Tomkins: "Chet Baker: The Man who Came Back – Better then Ever," *CI*, xvii/10 (1979), 20
G. Endress: *Jazz Podium: Musiker über sich selbst* (Stuttgart, Germany, 1980)
M. Hawthorn: "Chet Baker," *DB*, xlviii/10 (1981), 24
R. Cook and G. Rouy: "Chet Baker: Walking on Eggshells," *The Wire*, no.21 (1985), 31
H. H. Lerfeldt and T. Sjøgren: *Chet: the Discography of Chesney Henry Baker* (Copenhagen, 1985)
Obituary, S. Voce, *The Independent* (16 May 1988)

J. BRADFORD ROBINSON

Baker, David (Nathaniel) [Dave] (*b* Indianapolis, 21 Dec 1931). Trombonist, cellist, composer, writer, and educator. He studied at Indiana University (BMEd 1953, MMEd 1954) and worked for a doctorate while touring with various big bands, including that of Lionel Hampton. He played on the West Coast with Stan Kenton (1956) and Maynard Ferguson (1957), led his own big band in Indianapolis (1958–9), and then played in experimental small groups led by George Russell (1959–62) and in Quincy Jones's orchestra (1961). Baker was a highly promising trombonist until 1962, when the effects of an injury sustained in 1953 forced him to abandon his instrument. He took up the cello (recording with Charles Tyler in 1967), but by the 1970s was playing trombone again. He recorded on trombone with Bill Evans (ii) in an orchestra directed by Russell in 1972.

Baker has composed many works for various jazz and classical ensembles, and combinations of the two, including *Levels*, a concerto for solo double bass, jazz band, wind, and strings (1973), which was nominated for a Pulitzer Prize. He has written extensively on jazz and has produced several innovative textbooks and analyses of jazz works; he has published numerous transcriptions of improvisations in the journal *Down Beat* and also in his own books. Baker is head of the jazz department in the School of Music, Indiana University, and has served on many panels and commissions dealing with jazz, including those of the John F. Kennedy Center for the Performing Arts, the State Department, and the NEA. In the late 1980s he was president of the National Jazz Service Organization.

SELECTED RECORDINGS

As leader: *David Baker's 21st Century Bebop Band* (*c*1984, Laurel 503); *RSVP* (1985, Laurel 504)
As sideman: John Lewis: *The Golden Striker* (1960, Atl. 1334); G. Russell: *Jazz in the Space Age* (1960, Decca 79219); *Stratusphunk* (1960, Riv. 9341); *Ezz-thetics* (1961, Riv. 9375)

RECORDED COMPOSITIONS

(selective list; all recorded by Baker as leader)

Le chat qui pêche (*c*1975, Louisville 751); *Concerto for Flute, String Quartet, and Jazz Band* (*c*1984, Laurel 125)

WRITINGS

Arranging and Composing for the Small Ensemble: Jazz, R & B, Jazz-rock (Chicago, 1970)
Jazz Styles & Analysis: Trombone: a History of Jazz Trombone via Recorded Solos, Transcribed and Annotated (Chicago, 1973) [incl. transcrs.]
ed. with L. M. Belt and H. C. Hudson: *The Black Composer Speaks* (Metuchen, NJ, and London, 1978)
The Jazz Style of Cannonball Adderley: a Musical and Historical Perspective (Lebanon, IN, 1980) [incl. transcrs.]
The Jazz Style of John Coltrane: . . . (Lebanon, 1980) [incl. transcrs.]
The Jazz Style of Miles Davis: . . . (Lebanon, 1980) [incl. transcrs.]
The Jazz Style of Sonny Rollins: . . . (Lebanon, 1980) [incl. transcrs.]
with P. Coker: *Vocal Improvisation: an Instrumental Approach* (Lebanon, IN, 1981) [incl. discography]
The Jazz Style of Clifford Brown: . . . (Hialeah, FL, 1982) [incl. transcrs.]
The Jazz Style of Fats Navarro: . . . (Hialeah, 1982) [incl. transcrs.]

BIBLIOGRAPHY

FeatherE; *Feather '60s*; *Feather–Gitler '70s*
M. Bourne: "Defining Black Music," *DB*, xxxvi/19 (1969), 14 [interview]
T. Schneckloth: "Guardians of the Musical Future: a Gallery of Contemporary Music Educators," *DB*, xliv/20 (1977), 16
J. Browne: Interview, *JSN*, ii/4 (1982), 107
L. Tomkins: "David Baker: Integrating String Players and Jazz," *CI*, xxiv/11 (1987), 26

PAUL RINZLER

Baker, Kenny [Kenneth] (*b* Withernsea, England, 1 March 1921). English trumpeter and flugelhorn player. He began his career in London in 1939. A versatile, technically brilliant player, he worked and recorded with numerous bands in styles ranging from sweet dance music to hot jazz: his principal associations were with the bandleader and arranger Lew Stone (1941), George Chisholm (1944), and Ted Heath (1944–9); he was one of the original members of Heath's orchestra, its lead trumpeter and jazz soloist, and responsible for many of the arrangements and compositions that set its strong, energetic style. He then worked in radio, television, and films, and assembled his own group, Kenny Baker's Dozen, for the BBC radio program "Let's Settle for Music" (1951–9); he also played with the Melody Maker Allstars (1957–8). He recorded with Benny Goodman (1969) and Chisholm (1971, 1973), and took part in Johnny Patrick's re-creations on record of the music of Harry James (1976). In 1976 he formed the Best of British Jazz with Betty Smith and the trombonist Don Lusher, and in the 1980s he took part in revivals of Ted Heath's music and played solo trumpet on the soundtracks of the television programs "The Beiderbecke Affair" and "The Beiderbecke Tapes." A highly professional and dependable mainstream musician, Baker is a fluent improviser with a strong feeling for melody.

SELECTED RECORDINGS

As leader: *Kenny Baker's Half-Dozen* (1957, Nixa 10), incl. How's this?; *Date with the Dozen* (1957, Nixa 19020), incl. Too Cool for the Blues; *Baker Plays McHugh* (1958, Nixa 517), incl. Exactly like you
As sideman: First English Public Jam Session: Tea for Two (1941, HMV B9249); T. Heath: Opus One (1944, Decca F8512); Twilight Time/First Jump (1945, Decca F8578); B. Goodman: *London Date* (1969, Phi. 6308023); G. Chisholm: *George Chisholm* (1973, Gold Star 1500001); British All-Stars: *The Very Best of British Jazz* (1983, Polyphonic 501), incl. Sweet Sue

BIBLIOGRAPHY

FeatherE; *Feather–Gitler '70s*
M. Jones: "If you Want to Play Jazz, Go Commercial, Says Poll-top Trumpeter Kenny Baker," *MM*, xxix (28 Nov 1953), 3
G. London: "Kenny Baker," *Beat*, i/1 (n.d. [1956]), 20
M. Burman: "I'll Stick to Jazz, Says Kenny Baker," *MM*, xxxiii (28 June 1958), 5
M. Marr: "Kenny Baker Question Time," *Crescendo*, i/2 (1962), 28
H. Nash: "Trumpet Involuntary," *Sounding Brass and the Conductor*, v/2 (1976), 43
L. Tomkins: "Blowing the Bugle for Britain: Kenny Baker," *CI*, xxiv/8 (1987), 20

KEN RATTENBURY

Baker, Shorty [Harold J.] (*b* St. Louis, 26 May 1914; *d* New York, 8 Nov 1966). Trumpeter. His first instrument was the drums; he first played trumpet in the late 1920s in the band of his brother, the trombonist Winfield Baker. After working in the early 1930s with Fate Marable and Erskine Tate he played with Don Redman (1936–8), Duke Ellington (briefly in 1938, and at intervals from 1942 to 1962), Teddy Wilson's big band (1939–40), Andy Kirk (1940–42), and Mary Lou Williams, whom he married in 1942. He worked for several years as a freelance in New York and on the East Coast, and in 1952 played again with Wilson; from 1954 to 1955 he belonged to Johnny Hodges's orchestra. From 1959 he worked in New York as the leader of a quartet and as a sideman at the Metropole; he also made recordings with Doc Cheatham and Bud Freeman. As a section player Baker was known for his careful dynamics and phrasing; in his solo work he displayed a fine, pure tone and an elegant lyricism. Ellington described Baker's playing in his autobiography: "With his phenomenal phrasing and tone control he was an immense asset. He ad-libbed hot or blues . . . His way of playing a melody was absolutely personal, and he had no bad notes at all."

SELECTED RECORDINGS

As sideman: D. Ellington: first issued on *Duke Ellington Carnegie Hall Concert: January 1943* (1943, Prst. 34004), A Portrait of Florence Mills (Black Beauty); Time's a-wastin' (1945, Vic. 201718); Trumpet No End (Blue Skies) (1946, Musi. 484); *Masterpieces* (1950, Col. ML4418), incl. Mood Indigo, The Tattooed Bride; J. Hodges: Burgundy Walk (1954, Norg. 122); On the Sunny Side of the Street (1954, Norg. 131); D. Ellington: *All American in Jazz* (1962, Col. CS8590), incl. We Speak the Same Language

BIBLIOGRAPHY

ChiltonW
J. Postgate: "The St. Louis Sound," *JM*, [no.158] (1964), 2
S. Dance: *The World of Duke Ellington* (London and New York, 1970/R1981) [colln of previously pubd articles and interviews], 164
D. Ellington: *Music is my Mistress* (Garden City, NY, 1973), 221

KEN RATTENBURY

Bakton. Record label. It was established by Randy Weston in New York in 1966, and was used to issue only one album, recorded by Weston's sextet. The masters of this material were later sold to Atlantic and reissued.

MARK GARDNER

Balaban, Red [Leonard J.] (*b* Chicago, 22 Dec 1929). Double bass and tuba player and leader. From 1955 to 1966 he played double bass periodically in Florida. He then moved to New York, where he played tuba and double bass at Your Father's Mustache, a traditional-jazz club, accompanying Wild Bill Davison, Eddie Condon, Gene Krupa, and others. He also performed with Dick Wellstood and Kenny Davern, and as a leader. He became the owner of Eddie Condon's club in 1975, from which time he led its house band, Balaban and Cats; the group's regular members included Vic Dickenson, Ed Polcer, Herb Hall, Warren Vaché, and Connie Kay. The club closed in 1985. Balaban's playing can be heard on his recording *A Night at the New Eddie Condon's* (1975, CJ 17).

BIBLIOGRAPHY

Feather–Gitler '70s
J. H. Klee: "Balaban and Cats," *MR*, v/3 (1978), 1

Baldock, Kenny [Ken(neth Ernest)] (*b* London, 5 April 1932). English double bass player. He played piano from the age of six, then studied piano and double bass at the Guildhall School of Music and Drama in London. He played in Peter King's quartet at Annie's Room (1964) and with John Dankworth's orchestra (1965–73). In 1972 he appeared with Oscar Peterson at the Montreux International Jazz Festival, and the following year, while touring with an all-star group led by Freddy Randall and the clarinetist Dave Shepherd, played there with Peterson and recorded under Teddy Wilson and Barney Kessel; he is heard to advantage on Kessel's album *Summertime in Montreux* (1973, Pol. 2460210). Thereafter Baldock led his own sextet, which included Henry Lowther (1973), played in Ronnie Scott's quartet with Louis Stewart (1975–7), then led small groups (1977–81), with the electric guitarist Phil Lee and the pianist John Horler as sideman. He has also backed many American visitors to London at Ronnie Scott's club and in 1983 was awarded an Arts Council grant for his composition *Kosen Rufu*. He teaches privately and at a summer school in Barry in Wales. (R. Cotterrell, ed.: *Jazz Now: the Jazz Centre Society Guide*, London, 1976)

NEVIL SKRIMSHIRE

Bales, Burt(on Frank) (*b* Stevensville, MT, 20 March 1916). Pianist and bandleader. In San Francisco he played traditional jazz with Turk Murphy (1942) and Lu Watters (1943) and performed and recorded with Bunk Johnson (1943–4). From 1947 to the early 1950s he performed and recorded with Murphy and Bob Scobey and in 1949 he rejoined Watters. He led his own bands from 1944 to 1949 and recorded as a leader in 1949, 1950, and 1957. As a soloist he made recordings in 1949 (*After Hours Piano*, GTJ 19) and around 1955, and played at clubs in San Francisco in 1954–66 and from 1975 into the 1980s.

BIBLIOGRAPHY

ChiltonW; *FeatherE*; *Feather–Gitler '70s*
P. Elwood: "S. F.'s Greatest Saloon Pianist Still Going Strong," *San Francisco Examiner* (26 Dec 1985), §E, p.1

Ball, Kenny [Kenneth Daniel] (*b* London, 22 May 1930). English trumpeter and bandleader. He played trumpet from the age of 15 and first worked professionally two years later. In the early 1950s he played dixieland with several bands, notably those of Charlie Galbraith and the drummer Eric Delaney, and in 1953 he joined the band of Sid Phillips, with which he played a highly stylized brand of dixieland characterized by elaborate arrangements. He recorded as a leader from 1957, and after leaving Phillips's group worked briefly as a freelance and belonged to the band of Terry Lightfoot; in November 1958 he formed the Jazzmen, with which he made several recordings that achieved great popularity (*Samantha*, 1961; *Midnight in Moscow*, 1961; *So do I*, 1962) and many tours, including one of the USSR in the early 1980s. Ball's full, muscular tone and strong sense of melody display the influence not only of Armstrong but also of Bunny Berigan and Bix Beiderbecke; in his performances he reveals a warm, extroverted personality.

SELECTED RECORDINGS

As leader: Breezing Along with the Breeze, Riverboat Shuffle/St. James' Infirmary, Struttin' with Some Barbeque (1957, Tempo EXA83) [EP]; Dardanella/Tin Roof Blues (1958, Parl. 8733); Samantha (1961, Pye 2040); Midnight in Moscow (1961, Pye 2049); So do I (1962, Pye 2056); *The Kenny Ball Show* (1962, Pye 342); *Kenny Ball in Berlin* (1968, Fon. 13169)
As sideman with G. Chisholm: When the Saints Go Marching In/Lollie Rag (1958, Esquire 10519)

BIBLIOGRAPHY

S. Race: Liner notes, *The Kenny Ball Show* (Pye 342, 1962)
R. Cotterrell, ed.: *Jazz Now: the Jazz Centre Society Guide* (London, 1976)

KEN RATTENBURY

Ball, Ronnie [Ronald] (*b* Birmingham, England, 22 Dec 1927). English pianist. He led sessions in London with Ronnie Scott (1951) and Harry Klein (1952), and also recorded as leader of his own group (1951–2). After moving to New York in 1952 he studied with Lennie Tristano and worked with Chuck Wayne, Dizzy Gillespie, and Lee Konitz (1953–5). In 1956 he recorded with Kenny Clarke, Hank Mobley, Art Pepper, and as leader (*All about Ronnie*, Savoy 12075), and in 1956–7 also performed and recorded in New York and California with Warne Marsh. Thereafter he worked with Buddy Rich (1957), Kai Winding, Gene Krupa (both 1958), Roy Eldridge (1959–60), and Chris Connor (1961–3). In 1961 he recorded with a group that included Al Cohn, Kenny Dorham, and Zoot Sims in Rio de Janeiro. (*FeatherE*)

Ballad. In jazz and popular music a slow, sentimental love-song; the ballad forms an important part of the jazz repertory, particularly in the swing era. Ballads are generally cast in 32-bar song form (*see* FORMS, §1(i)(a)) and 4/4 or 12/8 meter; they are performed at a relaxed tempo, in a soft, intimate style, and lack the rhythmic drive and intensity of four-beat jazz. The word is often used, loosely, of any slow piece, regardless of its form, style, or subject matter. (P. Clayton and P. Gammond: *Jazz: A–Z*, Enfield, nr London, 1986)

ROBERT WITMER

Ballamy, Iain (Mark) (*b* Guildford, England, 20 Feb 1964). English tenor, alto, and soprano saxophonist. He played alto saxophone from the age of 14, and later took up the tenor saxophone. From 1983 he led a quintet (which included Django Bates), re-forming it in November 1983 as the Iains; in the same year he joined Graham Collier's workshop band, which later developed into the group LOOSE TUBES. He became a member of the Voice of God Collective, led by the electric guitarist Billy Jenkins, in 1985, and in December that year recorded with Gil Evans for the film *Absolute Beginners*. With Bill Bruford's jazz-rock group Earthworks, which he joined in March 1986, Ballamy recorded the album *Earthworks* (1986, Editions EG 48), which provides a good example of his playing. He tours extensively, has taken part in workshops at events such as the New Jazz Meeting at Baden-Baden (1985), and occasionally teaches privately. From the mid-1980s onwards he has also composed extensively.

Oral history material in *GBLnsa*.

BIBLIOGRAPHY

N. Coleman: "Iain Ballamy," *The Wire*, no.25 (1986), 32

DIGBY FAIRWEATHER

Ballard, Butch [George Edward] (*b* Camden, NJ, 26 Dec 1917). Drummer. He played with Fats Waller and performed and recorded with Cootie Williams (1942). After navy service he recorded with Williams and Louis Armstrong (both 1946), worked with Illinois Jacquet, and toured and recorded with Eddie "Lockjaw" Davis (1947–8). He joined Mercer Ellington (1948), then played and made recordings with Count Basie (1949, including *The Slider*, Vic. 20-3542). In 1950 he toured Europe with Duke Ellington, recording in Paris with Shorty Baker, Ernie Royal, Nelson Williams, and Johnny Hodges (all sidemen with Ellington), and recorded in the USA with Arnett Cobb; he rejoined Ellington in 1953, and played further sessions with Basie and Davis in 1957. He then led his own band, mainly in Philadelphia, where, from the early 1980s, he has concentrated on teaching.

BIBLIOGRAPHY

ChiltonW; *FeatherE*
S. Geller and J. E. Maberry: "Portraits: Butch Ballard," *MD*, vi/4 (1982), 82

Ballew, Smith (*b* Palestine, TX, 21 Jan 1902; *d* Fort Worth, 2 May 1984). Singer and bandleader. He led his own band in Dallas (*c*1925) and also toured Texas, then briefly led the Wolverines. In 1928 he worked as a banjoist in New York, but from 1929 specialized as a singer. He made a large number of recordings with such musicians as the Dorsey Brothers (1928–9), Irving Mills, the Goofus Five, Ben Pollack (all 1929), the California Ramblers, Joe Venuti, Frankie Trumbauer (all 1929–30), the violinist Ben Selvin (1929–31), Duke Ellington (1930, including *Nine Little Miles from Ten-Ten-Tennessee*, Vic. 22586), Red Nichols and Benny Goodman (both 1931), and as a leader (1929–31, 1934). During the early 1930s his band held many residencies in New York, and Ballew also led an all-star group which included Bunny Berigan and Glenn Miller. Later he appeared in many films.

BIBLIOGRAPHY

R. Houston and R. Ringo: "A Visit to Smith Ballew," *Sv*, no.59 (1975), 164
J. Peterson: "Smith Ballew," *SL*, xxvii (1975), aut., 40 [interview]

based on *ChiltonW*

Balliett, Whitney (L.) (*b* New York, 17 April 1926). Writer. After graduating from Cornell University (BA 1951) he joined the staff of the *New Yorker*. For the *Saturday Review* (1953–7) and then for the *New Yorker* he contributed reviews of jazz concerts, recordings, and books, as well as interviews with jazz musicians; many of these articles have been reprinted in a continuing series of books. He has also published poetry. In 1957 he conceived the idea and was adviser for a television program, "The Sound of Jazz," broadcast live by CBS. Balliett's writings are eloquent and highly stylized. His interviews portray his subjects with dignity, and his reviews often create effects that parallel those of the music being discussed. At his best, in an assessment of style or a description of an improvisation, Balliett has provided insights more penetrating than many formal musical analyses.

WRITINGS

(*selective list; all collns of previously pubd articles and/or reviews*)

The Sound of Surprise (New York, 1959/*R*1978)
Dinosaurs in the Morning (Philadelphia, 1962)
Such Sweet Thunder (Indianapolis, 1966)
Ecstasy at the Onion (New York and Indianapolis, 1971)
Alec Wilder and his Friends (Boston, 1974)
New York Notes: a Journal of Jazz, 1972–1975 (Boston, 1976)
Improvising: Sixteen Jazz Musicians and their Art (New York, 1977)
Night Creature: a Journal of Jazz, 1975–1980 (New York, 1981)
Jelly Roll, Jabbo and Fats (New York, and Oxford, England, 1983)

BARRY KERNFELD

Balliu, Rudy (*b* Ghent, Belgium, 3 Aug 1941). Belgian clarinetist. He took up the trumpet in 1957, played with the Roof Jazzband, and in 1960 formed the Hot Six (soon renamed the COTTON CITY JAZZ BAND); in 1965 he changed to clarinet. While working as a leader he made recordings with such players of traditional jazz as Louis Nelson, Alton Purnell, Emanuel Sayles, and Kid Thomas, and in 1971 with the Australian group the Yarra Yarra Band; he also toured with Barry Martyn's revue *A Night in New Orleans* (1974). With the pianist Walter De Troch and the double bass player Paul Gevaert he left the Cotton City Jazzband in 1977 to form the Society Serenaders and the Original Flemish Ragtime Orchestra. In 1983 he made recordings as a leader (*Rudy Balliu's Society Serenaders with Kid Thomas Valentine*, 1983, Eustachius 003) and with the New Black Eagle Jazz Band. Balliu plays a style of traditional jazz strongly influenced by the work of Lorenzo Tio, Jr.

BIBLIOGRAPHY

W. Eysselinck: Liner notes, *The Cotton Club Jazzband* (Alpha 7001,1969)
T. Dash: "The Rudi Balliu Society Serenaders," *Fn*, ix/2 (1977–8), 22

MARCEL JOLY

Baltazar, Gabe [Gabriel Ruiz, Jr.] (*b* Hilo, HI, 1 Nov 1929). Alto saxophonist. He performed with Howard Rumsey in 1960, then from 1960 to 1965 toured as lead alto saxophonist and soloist with Stan Kenton; he recorded six albums with the group, including *Stan Kenton's West Side Story* (1961, Cap. ST1609). He also worked with the pianist Onzy Matthews (1963–4), Ralph Peña (1964), and Terry Gibbs (1965), then played and recorded with Gil Fuller (1965–6) and Oliver Nelson (1966–7). After returning to Hawaii he began leading the Royal Hawaiian Band in 1969. He recorded as leader of his own big band in 1979.

BIBLIOGRAPHY
Feather '60s
W. F. Lee: *Stan Kenton: Artistry in Rhythm* (Los Angeles, 1980) [incl. discography], 276

'Bama State Collegians. Band at Alabama State Teachers College of which ERSKINE HAWKINS became the leader in the early 1930s.

Bandleader. The musician who leads, "fronts," or organizes a band. A bandleader may also be a singer, instrumentalist, or conductor; *see* BANDS, §3(a).

Band man. A member of a band; the term may also be used more specifically of a sideman who works strictly as a section player without taking any solos.

Bandoneon. A type of button accordion or concertina often used in South America. Its best-known exponent in jazz is DINO SALUZZI.

Bands. The word "band" is used to denote many types of instrumental ensemble; it is thought to originate in the medieval Latin *bandum* ("banner," also "company" or "crowd"). In jazz the term is used of any group of musicians exceeding two in number (a "duo"), but is most frequently applied to larger ensembles for which the terms "big band," "dance band," and "orchestra" have often been used interchangeably; a smaller group may also be described as a "dance band" or "orchestra." In American schools the term "stage band" is used as a synonym for "big band."

1. Definitions. 2. Instrumentation. 3. Personnel. 4. Historical development.

1. DEFINITIONS. Jazz bands, broadly speaking, may be divided into two categories: smaller groups which play music that is largely improvised; and larger groups, in which a substantial amount of the music performed is previously arranged, either worked out in rehearsal and memorized, or actually played from written scores. The determining factor in general is the number of melody instruments in the ensemble: it is widely believed that not more than three or four such instruments can successfully improvise together, and that groups containing a larger number of them must play arranged parts. However, the small groups that played "improvised" music in New Orleans during the early years of the 20th century in fact worked out a substantial proportion of each piece in advance, as was also the case with such later small groups as Artie Shaw's Gramercy Five. Conversely, a few large avant-garde groups, for example, those led by Sun Ra, allow as many as 20 instruments to improvise simultaneously. Nevertheless, it is generally true that the music of bands with four or more melody instruments will largely be arranged, and those with three or fewer largely improvised. The terms "small group" and "combo" are applied to an ensemble of any size up to about nine players.

Some kinds of band are named according to their instrumentation and are associated with particular periods, places, or types of jazz: these are dealt with in their own articles (*see* BRASS BAND, JUG BAND, STRING BAND, and WASHBOARD BAND); the term SPASM BAND also denotes instrumentation, though less precisely, since it refers to a band made up of any homemade instruments. Other kinds of band are named according to a style, such as "dixieland" and "swing" bands. Groups of between five and eight musicians playing traditional or dixieland music frequently adopted names that included the words "Jazz Band."

2. INSTRUMENTATION. A basic division between melody (or "frontline") and accompanying (or "rhythm") instruments is integral to the concept of ensembles playing in most styles except free jazz. The term "front line" comes from the brass-band tradition, and in New Orleans jazz groups came to mean the wind instruments: trumpet or cornet, clarinet and (less often) saxophone, and trombone; one or more of these might sometimes be replaced or supplemented by a violin or a singer. The principal rhythm instruments are piano, guitar or banjo, a bass instrument (usually double bass or tuba, occasionally bass saxophone, or perhaps simply a piano on which a bass line is provided), and drum set; all the rhythm instruments may also be called on to play a melody line. While the term "front line" is applied less frequently to later styles of jazz, the combination of wind instrument(s) plus rhythm section, or (in many trios and some quartets) the rhythm section alone, remains the basis for the small jazz group. From the above, it may be seen that the instrumentarium of jazz is fairly restricted; the use and role of individual instruments is discussed in articles concerning those instruments.

The instrumentation of big bands (with the exception of such free-jazz ensembles as Muhal Richard Abrams's Experimental Band and the Jazz Composer's Orchestra) has not changed significantly from the 1920s. An underlying principle has been the disposition of instruments in homogeneous "sections": brass (trumpets and trombones); reed (saxophones; also clarinets and, occasionally, flutes); and rhythm (piano, guitar, double bass (later electric bass guitar), and drums). Early big bands consisted of 2 or 3 trumpets, 1 or 2 trombones, 3 saxophones, and rhythm section. By the late 1940s such bands as the Kenton and Herman orchestras made use of as many as 5 trumpets, 4 trombones (3 tenor, 1 bass), 5 saxophones (2 alto, 2 tenor, 1 baritone), and rhythm section; Ellington's band at one point supported 6 trumpets. The ensemble was built on the counterbalancing of the brass and reed sections in passages for the full band, interspersed with substantial solos; in general, one section answered the other, or punctuated its playing with simple repetitive riffs that were more rhythmic than harmonic in function.

3. PERSONNEL. Although the instrumentation of a band varies according to its size and style, as well as the period of time in which it is or has been active, some terms connected with the various roles of members of bands have become standard. The most widely used of these are described below.

(a) Leader. The musician who leads, "fronts," or organizes a band. The leader is usually in charge of the band, but he may employ a music director (Don Redman worked in Fletcher Henderson's orchestra in this capacity in the 1920s). The leader may also engage a "front man," who may sing, dance, or conduct, or perhaps do nothing more than look handsome. However, leaders more usually front their own bands, especially if they are also principal soloists (e.g., Benny Goodman, Woody Herman, Don Ellis, Thad Jones). Some bands have made use of a "guest leader" – a famous musician who lends his name to the group for the duration of his tenure (a notable example being Louis Armstrong, who was nominally the leader of Carroll Dickerson's band for several months). Certain groups have more than one leader ("co-leaders"); others, such as all-star groups and collective ensembles, have no leader.

(b) Sideman. Any member of a band other than the leader.

(c) Soloist. Any musician who plays a solo. In smaller groups, all the members will act as soloists, whereas in big bands, some

sidemen serve only as section players. A principal soloist is a player who may act entirely in a solo capacity or who may also perform within the body of the orchestra. Musicians who fulfilled the latter role include Buck Clayton and Harry Edison, who were principal trumpet soloists in Count Basie's band in the late 1930s: in ensemble work these men played second or third trumpet parts, leaving the more technically demanding lead parts to Ed Lewis or Al Killian, who almost never took solos.

(d) Lead player. The leader of a section. The lead trumpeter, trombonist, and alto saxophonist play the highest-pitched line in their respective sections and are responsible for determining how the other musicians in their section articulate their lines. Lead players are not generally expected to be the most formidable soloists in a big band (though, like Johnny Hodges, they may be excellent improvisers), but are prized for their technical skill.

(e) Session [studio] *musician.* A freelance musician who performs with a group for recording purposes only. An entire band might be organized from among such players for a specific recording project, or a single musician may be drafted into an otherwise regularly constituted group.

(f) Chair. A term applied to any individual musician's part within an ensemble; hence a new player coming into a band took over, for example, the "second trumpet chair," or the "bass chair."

(g) Substitute [sub; deputy, dep]. A musician employed on an occasional or short-term basis to take the place of a regular member of a band. Amongst musicians, the terms "subbing," "deputizing," and "depping" are used to describe the occupation of such players.

4. Historical development

(i) Early New Orleans bands. The jazz that was developing in New Orleans in the years after 1900 was of four differing kinds and was played by four types of band. There was of course a considerable amount of overlap, for instrumentation was never firmly fixed, and many players worked in more than one type of band.

There was, first, the famous marching or street band, which early jazz histories took to be the prototypical jazz band (*see* Brass band). These groups bore a superficial resemblance to the large military bands that dominated American music in the latter decades of the 19th century. How much jazz they played is uncertain; it is probable that their repertories, in the earliest days at least, included ragtime with some blues inflections, and that the jazz content increased over the years towards 1915.

A second type of jazz band existing in New Orleans during this period was the small, informal, and quite rough group that worked particularly in the honky-tonks of the black brothel district around Liberty and Perdido streets. The instrumentation of these bands was various and unpredictable: they frequently consisted solely of a guitar (or piano) and a single melody instrument; some also included a snare drum or bass, but almost any combination of melody and rhythm instruments, up to four or at most five, occurred. The musicians in these "tonk" or "stink" bands were badly paid, even by the standards of that time and place, and were low in status; like the members of street bands, they were rough players and apprentices. Their repertories ran heavily towards the blues, which the prostitutes in the tonks wanted for the "slow drag" dances they performed to seduce customers, and a few simple tunes like *Down in Jungle Town* and *Bill Bailey.* Some of the most important early jazz players, notably Louis Armstrong and Sidney Bechet, were apprentices in the tonk bands, and it is thought by some authorities that the amalgamation of the blues and ragtime that was critical to the making of jazz took place in such groups. Something about the music they played may be inferred from *Texas Moaner Blues* (1924, OK 8171) by Clarence Williams's Blue Five, a quintet that included both Armstrong and Bechet.

A third type of band was the "society" band. These groups, such as the bands led by A. J. Piron and John Robichaux, worked at prestigious locations like Tranchina's restaurant (see fig.1) and gambling rooms on Lake Pontchartrain, which attracted wealthy Whites. The musicians in these bands, some of whom later became known as jazz musicians, were mainly the better schooled black Creoles. They played a good deal of arranged music for dancing, some of it possibly jazz, and usually made use of a violin and one or two saxophones.

It was the fourth type of band, however, that proved to be the model for the earliest jazz bands. These were more organized bands, whose principal function was to play for dances, on advertising wagons, and at picnics for both Blacks and Whites. They usually numbered the better black and black Creole players among their members, and they were the groups that the apprentices aspired to join: Bunk Johnson's Original Superior Orchestra, the Imperial Orchestra, the Eagle Band (see fig.2), and various groups led by Buddy Bolden, Buddy Petit, Kid Ory, King Oliver, and others. The basic instrumentation of such groups was violin, cornet, clarinet, trombone, guitar, double bass, and a drum set of snare and bass. Contrary to what is widely believed, these bands did not usually include a tuba, banjo, or second cornet; however, instrumentation varied according to the exigencies of the moment in what was, after all, a relatively informal musical setting.

Developing almost in parallel with the black dance bands were the white jazz groups, many of them organized by Papa Jack Laine; these included such players as Nick LaRocca, Larry Shields, Leon Roppolo, and the Brunies brothers, who later had considerable influence on other jazz musicians. Although the white bands were drawing on the repertories of the black bands for much of their music, the players came out of a somewhat different musical tradition from that of the Blacks. Where the latter tended to play parallel lines in the homophonic tradition that derived from African music, the Whites drew upon the military-band style exemplified by John Philip Sousa, in which trombones supplied connecting links between the melodic phrases played by the cornet, and the clarinet played obbligato figures above. Too much should not be made of this distinction, for Blacks shared in the military-band tradition, but the difference was real.

(ii) Dissemination from New Orleans and the rise of symphonic jazz. Although jazz bands had been moving out of New Orleans as early as, perhaps, 1910, they went to play mainly in mining camps, the saloons and gambling houses of San Francisco's Barbary Coast, and similar places, and their impact was limited. In 1915 and 1916 white bands led by Tom Brown and Johnny Stein achieved considerable success in Chicago cabarets. Stein's band (without Stein himself) went to New York in January 1917 and, as the Original Dixieland Jass Band, was enormously successful. Its instrumentation consisted of cornet, trombone, clarinet, piano, and drums, and the musicians played in the more contrapuntal military-band style. The success of

1. A. J. Piron's orchestra at Tranchina's restaurant, Spanish Fort, New Orleans, c1923: (left to right) Peter Bocage (trumpet), John Lindsay (trombone), Louis Cottrell, Sr. (drums), Louis Warnecke (alto saxophone), Lorenzo Tio, Jr. (tenor saxophone, clarinet), Steve Lewis (piano), Charles Bocage (banjo), and Piron (violin)

2. The Eagle Band, New Orleans, c1916: (left to right) Big Eye Louis Nelson (clarinet), Abbe "Chinee" Foster (drums), Frankie Dusen (trombone, leader), Buddy Petit (trumpet), Lorenzo Staulz (guitar), and Dandy Lewis (double bass)

this group made it the model for the jazz bands that sprang up to play the exciting, and popular, new music. The violin, which had hitherto been carried because violinists could usually read music, and could therefore teach the other men new songs, was now seen as superfluous, and was abandoned. The banjo, which became fashionable after 1918, superseded the guitar in the rhythm section, and the double bass, which was difficult to record, was replaced by the tuba. From about 1915 to the early 1920s the standard American jazz band, which had evolved from the black New Orleans dance bands, consisted of cornet, trombone, clarinet, piano, banjo, tuba, and drum set.

The rise of jazz in the USA was fueled in considerable measure by a concomitant boom in a new form of social dancing. Before about 1910 the most widely performed dances were waltzes and quick-steps. By 1912, however, these were being replaced by a number of less sedate new dances, such as the Texas Tommy and the Grizzly Bear, which had developed initially in honky-tonks and low-class cabarets. Jazz, coming along just behind the dance boom, was seen as the ideal music to complement the new, more suggestive, steps; very quickly music and dance became associated to a degree that the term "jazz" was used indiscriminately to mean either, and it cannot be emphasized too much that jazz music was seen initially by the mass American audience as dance music.

Sometime in the years after about 1916, FERDE GROFÉ, working in San Francisco with the band led by the drummer Art Hickman, began writing "arrangements" in which he made use of the new jazz sonorities and rhythms. Hitherto, dance bands had usually repeated a melody in more or less the same fashion for as long as necessary. Grofé's new idea was to change the orchestration of a song at points along the way, now allowing one instrument to play a solo, now harmonizing the instruments in different combinations. In particular, he employed Hickman's two-piece saxophone "section" as a unit, frequently balancing it against other instruments in a broadly contrapuntal fashion. This concept of playing off the various sections of a dance band against one another became basic to big-band writing. In 1919 PAUL WHITEMAN, who had received a classical training, took Grofé into his new orchestra and encouraged him to elaborate on what he had done for Hickman. Whiteman called the new music, which combined elements drawn from jazz and classical music, "symphonic jazz," and proclaimed himself "King of Jazz."

Although jazz had been generally popular in the USA, there were elements in society that disliked it for its associations with rough dance halls and brothels. The new symphonic jazz was seen as having risen above these "low" origins, and was immediately declared a great new art form. Whiteman's popularity was immense; increased income enabled him to enlarge his orchestra, allowing Grofé even greater scope to develop his concept of playing off various sections of the ensemble against one another.

(iii) The big-band boom. During the early 1920s symphonic jazz swept everything before it. Musicians quickly saw that the path to success was being taken by Whiteman, not the New Orleans groups, and young bandleaders like Duke Ellington, Fletcher Henderson, Jean Goldkette, Red Nichols, and others moved away from the New Orleans style and formed big bands that played arrangements. The pattern may also be seen in the recordings made by Louis Armstrong's Hot Five (1925–8); the earliest of these are wholly in the New Orleans mode, but by the last of the series Armstrong was essentially the principal player in a group performing dance-band arrangements. The older type of band lingered on – Jelly Roll Morton was still working in the New Orleans idiom in the 1930s – but big bands were predominant.

Paradoxically, even as Whiteman's popularity was at its peak (in the second half of the 1920s), leadership in the style was beginning to shift to others. Both out of personal taste, and because they were discovering that American audiences wanted it, other bandleaders (notably Henderson and his music director Don Redman; Goldkette and his arranger Bill Challis; the Casa Loma Orchestra and its principal arranger Gene Gifford; Ben Pollack, Nichols, and Ellington) were producing a hotter, "jazzier" version of symphonic jazz. The arrangements used by these bands provided more opportunities for jazz soloists to perform, and, more significantly, the arranged passages themselves made greater use of jazz sonorities and rhythms. The rhythm sections in these groups also contributed a greater sense of swing to the ensemble than did those of Whiteman and similar bands.

By the end of the 1920s it was evident that the hotter bands had a strong following in the USA. Although, on balance, it was probably true that the "sweet" bands, as they came to be called, were more popular than the hot ones, the difference was not substantial. Even Whiteman recognized the trend, and in 1927 he raided Goldkette's band for some of its finest hot soloists (Bix Beiderbecke and Frankie Trumbauer) and its arranger, Challis, in order to compete with the hotter bands. The formulation of the big jazz band, which dominated the music from the early 1920s until the late 1940s, was thus a two-stage process: first, in the creation by Grofé, Hickman, Whiteman, and others of symphonic jazz; and second, the production of a hotter version of the music by a new wave of bandleaders.

Big bands gradually grew in size, and by the early 1930s most were carrying 3 trumpets, 3 trombones, 3 or 4 saxophones, and a four-piece rhythm section. The expansion meant that, rather than functioning as part of the brass section, the trombones could be treated autonomously; arrangers could make greater use of contrasting sonorities and employ thicker harmonic textures. In about 1930 the banjo and tuba were abandoned in favor of the guitar and double bass, both of which had been included in the rhythm sections of the New Orleans groups. The latter instruments were capable of producing a sharper attack and a brighter sound, and could also be played more rapidly.

The economic slump that followed the crash of the stock market in 1929 brought about a collapse of the nightclub and recording business. Despite the setbacks, however, some big bands managed to thrive – a notable example being Duke Ellington's orchestra. Then, in 1935, another band, led by Benny Goodman, suddenly captured the popular imagination and shot to prominence. Goodman's band was modeled on previous large ensembles, especially the Casa Loma Orchestra and the bands led by Pollack and Henderson. A swing-band boom began, with at first dozens, and later scores, of big dance bands competing for fans. The amount of good jazz performed by such groups varied markedly from one to the next, but almost all of them played with a jazz beat (in which all four beats of a measure were given equal weight) and included musicians who were hot soloists. Among the foremost of these bands were those led by Ellington (see fig.3), Goodman, Count Basie, Jimmie Lunceford, Charlie Barnet, Bob Crosby, Woody Herman, and Chick Webb.

The size of large bands increased steadily between 1935 and

3. *Duke Ellington's orchestra at either the Oriental Theatre or the Chicago Theatre, Chicago, 1940: (front row, left to right) Fred Guy (guitar), Ellington (piano), Jimmy Blanton (double bass); (middle row) Juan Tizol (valve trombone), Tricky Sam Nanton and Lawrence Brown (trombones), Johnny Hodges, Barney Bigard, Ben Webster, Otto Hardwick, and Harry Carney (saxophones), Wallace Jones (trumpet), Rex Stewart (cornet), Ray Nance (trumpet); (back) Sonny Greer (drums)*

1945, and a standard instrumentation of 4 trumpets, 4 trombones, 4 saxophones, and rhythm section was established. Later five saxophones became common, and eventually as many as nine or ten brass instruments were included. Leaders and arrangers – notably Boyd Raeburn – experimented with the addition of french horns, flutes, violins, timpani, and other instruments drawn from the symphony orchestra. However, the concept of playing off various sections of the group against one another remained the essential formula of big-band writing.

(iv) Small swing groups. In 1933, after the lifting of Prohibition, the nightclub industry began a resurgence. For a variety of reasons the new clubs tended to be smaller rooms where the clientele was expected to listen to jazz, as at a concert. Because, unlike the former large cabarets, these clubs could not always accommodate the popular big swing bands, their managers were forced to depend on solo pianists, trios, quartets, and similar small groups. Swing remained the popular music of the time, however, and thus there came into being a new type of small jazz band. This group was composed of one to three melody instruments and a rhythm section. The favored front line was trumpet and alto or tenor saxophone, while use of the trombone and clarinet decreased rapidly; the rhythm section almost always included piano and drum set, with guitar and/or double bass being added as circumstances provided. Sometimes a small swing band consisted of a single melody instrument played by a prominent musician whose name would draw an audience and who would be supported by relatively anonymous rhythm players. These groups were transient, sometimes existing only for recording purposes as, for example, a number of ensembles led in the mid-1930s by Teddy Wilson.

Jazz bands of this type had of course existed before, both in New Orleans and elsewhere: Jimmie Noone, for instance, led a group in Chicago in the 1920s that consisted of clarinet and alto saxophone and a four-piece rhythm section. At that period, however, the New Orleans format predominated, whereas from the mid-1930s the small four- to six-piece band was the standard.

A further impetus towards the small jazz band was the creation, in 1935, of the Benny Goodman Trio, which consisted of clarinet, piano, and drums. Goodman frequently made a feature in his programs of this "band-within-a-band" by using it to play a special set, a practice that lent a greater variety of texture to the music. At the same time the small group allowed solo musicians more freedom to express themselves than was possible within the confines of a formal arrangement. Goodman gradually built up the trio, adding vibraphone, electric guitar, and other instruments, until it became established as a sextet (see fig.4, p.62), and the success of his groups inspired other leaders to form similar units. Woody Herman's Woodchoppers, Bob Crosby's Bob Cats, Tommy Dorsey's Clambake Seven, and an array of groups drawn from Ellington's band recorded some of the most significant jazz of the period. Although the big bands remained more popular with the general public, the small groups gained considerable support, and such recordings as *Jeep's Blues* by Johnny Hodges, *Body and Soul* by Coleman Hawkins, and *After you've gone* by Goodman's trio became, in jazz terms, hits.

Interest in small jazz bands was intensified by the growing

critical opinion that big-band jazz was not the true music. There had not been universal approval at the replacement of the small New Orleans jazz band by the large dance orchestra. During the 1920s a number of jazz enthusiasts in the USA began writing knowledgably about their subject and producing a rudimentary jazz criticism. The early critics – R. D. Darrell, John Hammond, Carl Van Vechten, Abbe Niles, Charles Edward Smith and others – never really approved of Whiteman's concept of symphonic jazz, which they felt did not capture the essence of the music; some of them did not even like the hotter music produced by Henderson, Ellington, and the rest, and insisted that only the older, wholly improvised music was the true jazz. This view helped to spark a revival of the New Orleans band, now rigidly defined as trumpet (or cornet), clarinet, trombone, and a four-piece rhythm section; sometimes a tenor saxophone was included. The dixieland revival groups of Eddie Condon, Lu Watters, and Turk Murphy achieved considerable popular success throughout the 1940s and into the 1950s, and brought in their train a host of amateur and semiprofessional groups, many of them formed on college campuses, which kept the form alive into the 1980s.

At the close of World War II the majority of the big bands collapsed, mostly for economic reasons. For a while Stan Kenton achieved some popular success with a huge dance band that eventually comprised more than 20 instruments and performed a repertory that drew on many devices from classical music. But, as was the case with Whiteman's orchestra, many critics felt that Kenton's band had sacrificed jazz feeling for innovation, and its importance faded. Other leaders, such as Ellington, Basie, and Herman, continued to lead big bands in the old manner, but these groups were no longer in the forefront of jazz development.

(v) Bop bands. In the early 1940s, with the development of bop, another type of small band emerged. By about 1950 its instrumentation had become almost as rigid as that of the dixieland band, consisting of two or at most three melody instruments over a rhythm section of piano, double bass, and drum set. The front line almost invariably comprised trumpet and tenor saxophone; sometimes an alto saxophone was added or, as in the case of Charlie Parker's groups, replaced the tenor instrument. With the move towards greater freedom for the melody instruments and a reduction in the harmonic structure provided by the rhythm section, the rhythm guitar became an encumbrance. The clarinet fell into disuse, partly because it was seen by many Blacks as an instrument played by Whites, and partly because a number of reed players preferred the sonorities of the saxophone. The trombone, which was difficult to play at the speeds often required in bop, also lost favor, although a few trombonists who became accomplished players at fast tempos, such as J. J. Johnson, remained in demand. By the time hard bop evolved, the line-up of trumpet, tenor saxophone, piano, double bass, and drums was almost mandatory – exemplified by Art Blakey's Jazz Messengers (see fig.5), one of the most popular of the hard-bop bands. Even many of the early bands of the avant-garde experimentalists – for example, those of Ornette Coleman and Albert Ayler – took this form. Although bop developed essentially as a small-band genre, there were a few bop big bands, notably those led in the late 1940s by Dizzy Gillespie. There were also some continuing experiments during this period with middle-sized bands, notably the nonet led by Miles Davis that made a series of recordings subsequently known as the "Birth of the Cool." This group created unusual tone colors in arrangements by Gil Evans, Gerry Mulligan, and others by making use of such instruments as french horn and tuba.

(vi) Jazz-rock and other fusion groups. The 1950s was a period of stability for jazz musicians; work was plentiful, and a few players, including Dave Brubeck, Miles Davis, and, eventually, John Coltrane, became wealthy and celebrated. In the early 1960s, however, with the sudden fame of the Beatles and the appearance of rock groups like the Doors, the Rolling Stones, and Jefferson Airplane, jazz had to compete with other forms

4. Benny Goodman's sextet at the Waldorf-Astoria Hotel in New York, January 1940: (left to right) Lionel Hampton (vibraphone), Artie Bernstein (double bass), Goodman (clarinet), Nick Fatool (drums), Charlie Christian (guitar), and Johnny Guarnieri (piano)

5. Art Blakey's Jazz Messengers at the Café Bohemia, New York, 29 January 1956: (left to right) Sam Dockery (piano), Jackie McLean (alto saxophone), Spanky De Brest (double bass), Bill Hardman (trumpet), and Blakey (drums)

of popular music. By 1969 there were only six jazz clubs in New York, where earlier there had been some two dozen. By way of response, a number of jazz musicians began to meet the competition by adopting some of the devices of rock. In particular, they made use of the instruments employed in rock bands: electric guitars, electric bass guitars, electric and electronic pianos, and synthesizers, as well as an array of signal processors. The instrumentation of jazz-rock groups was drawn from both types of music – the electric and electronic instruments from rock, and the melody instruments, particularly trumpets and saxophones, from jazz. The format for such bands was more varied than those of the dixieland and bop bands. The number of melody instruments was fairly arbitrary, but there was almost always an electronic keyboard, electric guitar, electric bass guitar, and drum set; sometimes there were additional guitars. Although some of the jazz-rock bands, notably Blood, Sweat and Tears (see fig.6, p.64), worked from written arrangements in the manner of the big bands, most of them improvised, often quite freely, within a memorized head arrangement or set routine.

The net effect of the fusion of jazz and rock was to make at least some of the electronic instruments standard in jazz bands. The guitar, which (with a few notable exceptions) had fallen into disuse as a rhythm instrument during the ascendancy of bop, was restored in its electric form; the electric piano and even the synthesizer sometimes replaced what was coming to be called the "acoustic" piano; and the double bass, preferred to the electric bass guitar on account of its more subtle qualities, was almost always amplified. The electric guitar still fulfilled a role in the rhythm section, but it also functioned as a melody instrument and occasionally as the principal melody instrument in the group.

Closely following the rise of jazz-rock was a series of experiments with other forms of fusion, in which either jazz or rock (or both) was melded with ethnic musics, especially Latin American and Indian music. This inevitably meant the introduction of a number of non-Western and exotic instruments, such as tablā, sitar, berimbau, and bongos.

(vii) Free-jazz groups. If fusion music effected substantial changes to the form of the jazz band, the experiments of a second generation of free-jazz players brought still more. The first free-jazz bands followed the standard small-band form: Ornette Coleman's earliest group consisted of trumpet and alto saxophone plus rhythm section, and Cecil Taylor's first important band comprised soprano saxophone, piano, double bass, and drums. But the new wave of avant-garde musicians that came to the fore in the late 1960s and the 1970s, among them Leroy Jenkins, Anthony Braxton, and Muhal Richard Abrams, concluded that, just as the earlier experimentalists had dispensed with bar-lines, Western harmonies, and even the tempered scale, so they were free to utilize whatever instruments and noise-makers they wished. On the album *Numbers 1 & 2* (1967, Nessa 1), Lester Bowie's quartet made use of bells, kazoo, whistle, gourd, kelp horn, and steer horn in addition to conventional jazz instruments; Braxton's trio played accordion, bells, harmonica, recorder, string instruments, bottles, kazoo, musette, and slide whistle on his recording *Three Compositions of New Jazz* (1968, Del. 415). By the 1970s Bowie, Braxton, and other members of the AACM were at times employing scores, if not hundreds, of unusual items, which they labeled collectively "little instruments." Avant-garde musicians also began to ignore the limitation of size that had been apparent in jazz groups since the demise of the big bands. Sun Ra frequently presented bands that included 20 musicians or more, many of them playing exotic instruments.

By the 1980s free-jazz musicians were moving back towards the mainstream and tending to employ a more basic jazz instrumentation of a few melody instruments plus electric guitar, which were supported by a rhythm section that frequently included piano as well as double bass and drums. At the same time it was widely conceded that jazz had become splintered: no longer did one given style and its requisite type of band predominate, as had generally been the case. Instead a variety of forms coexisted, and dixieland bands, big swing bands, small swing groups, bop groups, and avant-garde ensembles all continued to perform. Jazz-rock remained a major genre, probably

6. Blood, Sweat and Tears, late 1960s

outstripping other forms of jazz in popularity; in particular, the recordings by Miles Davis's groups sold millions of copies and brought Davis to the forefront of popular music. Nevertheless, the small jazz band consisting of a few melody instruments, predominantly trumpets and saxophones, over a rhythm section remained the standard, being used by many of the best-known young jazz musicians, including Wynton and Branford Marsalis, Scott Hamilton, Warren Vaché, and the Brecker brothers.

BIBLIOGRAPHY

J.-E. Berendt: *Das Jazzbuch: Entwicklung und Bedeutung der Jazzmusik* (Frankfurt am Main, Germany, 1953, rev. 2/1959 as *Das neue Jazzbuch*, Eng. trans., New York, 1962; rev. and enlarged 5/1981 as *Das grosse Jazzbuch: von New Orleans bis Jazz Rock*, Eng. trans. as *The Jazz Book: from New Orleans to Fusion and Beyond*, Westport, CT, 1982)

L. Feather: *The Book of Jazz: a Guide to the Entire Field* (New York, 1957, 2/1965 as *The Book of Jazz from Then till Now: a Guide to the Entire Field*)

G. T. Simon: *The Big Bands* (New York, 1967, rev. and enlarged 2/1971, rev. 3/1974, 4/1981)

G. Schuller: *Early Jazz: its Roots and Musical Development* (New York, 1968)

G. Fernett: *Swing Out: Great Negro Jazz Bands* (Midland, MI, 1970)

A. McCarthy: *Big Band Jazz* (New York and London, 1974)

F. Tirro: *The Jazz Combo from ODJB to the MJQ* (Urbana, IL, 1977)

J. L. Collier: *The Making of Jazz: a Comprehensive History* (New York and London, 1978)

F. Driggs and H. Lewine: *Black Beauty, White Heat: a Pictorial History of Classic Jazz, 1920–1950* (New York, 1982)

JAMES LINCOLN COLLIER

Bang, Billy [Walker, William Vincent] (*b* Mobile, AL, 20 Sept 1947). Violinist and composer. He grew up in Spanish Harlem in New York, and studied violin briefly in his youth. He later became acquainted with the music of such progressive black musicians as John Coltrane and Ornette Coleman, and realized that he could express his views on racial injustice through musical creativity. In 1968 he resumed playing violin and by 1972 was working as a professional musician in New York; he also studied with Leroy Jenkins. He played his first solo concert in 1977 at the end of a brief tour of Europe; thereafter he made annual European tours. Also in 1977, following a series of sessions at La Mama, an experimental theater in New York, he formed a chamber jazz group, the String Trio of New York, with the electric guitarist James Emery and John Lindberg; he was the leader of this ensemble until 1986. In the late 1970s he formed a quintet. He has also played in Ronald Shannon Jackson's Decoding Society and with Sonny Sharrock in the funk and free-jazz band Material. The incisive attack and rough, bluesy tone that characterize Bang's style have led critics to compare his playing with that of Stuff Smith, Ray Nance, and Ornette Coleman.

SELECTED RECORDINGS

As unaccompanied soloist: *Distinction without a Difference* (1979, HH 4)

Duos with D. Charles: *Bangception* (1982, Hat Music 3512)

As leader: *Sweet Space* (1979, Anima 1002); *Rainbow Gladiator* (1981, SN 1016); *Invitation* (1982, SN 1036)

As leader of String Trio of New York (with J. Emery and J. Lindberg): *First String* (1979, BS 0031); *Common Goal* (1981, BS 0058)

BIBLIOGRAPHY

B. Rusch: "Billy Bang: Interview," *Cadence*, vi/11 (1980), 5

L. Jeske: "Billy Bang," *DB*, xlviii/9 (1981), 26 [incl. discography]

B. McRae: "Avant Courier," *JJI*, xxxv/7 (1982), 20

F. Davis: "Violin Madness (John Blake and Billy Bang)," *In the Moment: Jazz in the 1980s* (New York, and Oxford, England, 1986) [colln of previously pubd articles], 67

K. Whitehead: "String Trio of New York: a decade of Perseverance," *DB*, liv/11 (1987), 26 [incl. discography]

DAVID FLANAGAN

Banjo. A plucked string instrument with a long guitar-like neck and a circular soundtable of tautly stretched vellum, skin, or plastic against which the bridge is pressed by the strings. Although unfretted instruments exist, the modern banjo is normally fitted with frets and strung with steel wire strings. Three types of banjo are common in jazz: the five-string banjo in G or C (tuned *g'-d-g-b-d'* and *g'-c-g-b-d'* respectively), the four-string tenor banjo (tuned *c-g-d'-a'*), and the six-string "guitar banjo," which has the same tuning as a guitar (*E-A-d-g-b-e'*).

The role of the banjo in early jazz grew out of its use in both blues and ragtime. Paul Oliver has pointed out the general unsuitability of the staccato-sounding banjo as an accompanying instrument for country blues singers and has suggested that the two principal blues exponents to record, Papa Charlie Jackson (who employed the relatively rare six-string instrument) and Gus Cannon (who played the G banjo), were bridging the gap between the 19th-century songster tradition and the country blues; both musicians used a technique involving retuning to a chord ("crossed notes") to facilitate finger-picking patterns. In Jackson's work (notably *Long Gone Lost John*, 1928, Para. 12602), especially in his links between choruses, some of the fingering patterns that later emerged in the jazz playing of Lonnie Johnson are identifiable. Cannon may be heard exhorting his fellow players (the Jug Stompers) to "Rag it!" in the instrumental choruses of *Money never runs out* (1930, Vic. 23262); here and elsewhere (such as in his duets as "Banjo Joe" with the guitarist Blind Blake) Cannon uses the incisive banjo to play single-string ragtime-oriented phrases over guitar or banjo accompaniment.

Ragtime banjo playing, exemplified in the recordings of such virtuoso musicians as Vess L. Ossman, Harry Reser, Phil Russell, and, in particular, Fred Van Eps, involved the speedy execution of syncopated patterns; later the tradition of "novelty" solo banjo playing further developed the virtuoso possibilities of the instrument.

During the classic jazz period the role of the banjo was generally a chordal one; in ensemble work it was played on each beat of the bar, and recordings from the 1920s show that there was no difference in the way tenor, G, or six-string instruments were used. The style is well represented by Johnny St. Cyr in his recordings with Louis Armstrong's Hot Five and Hot Seven, where, except for occasional four- or eight-bar bridge passages, stop-time choruses, and his own remarkably accomplished solos, he complements the looser accompaniment of Lil Hardin on piano by keeping a propulsive beat going throughout. St. Cyr was equally at home on the six-string banjo (Armstrong's *The King of the Zulus*, 1926, OK 8396), on tenor banjo (Jelly Roll Morton's *The Chant*, 1926, Vic. 20221), and on guitar (Armstrong's *Willie the Weeper*, 1927, OK 8482). On *The Chant* (which Gunther Schuller has analyzed in detail) he produces a typical solo: a single-string line played on the lower strings and redolent of elements of standard tailgate trombone or double bass line clichés is juxtaposed with apposite chords on the upper strings. These chords generally, though not invariably, fall on the second and fourth beats of the bar, so the impression gained approaches that of the left-hand part of a piano rag. Interestingly, in his work with Morton, St. Cyr carried this solo style into his ensemble playing to a greater degree than he did when performing with Armstrong; in the chorus after his solo on *The Chant*, for example, he may be heard continuing the same line of thought. St. Cyr was perhaps the pre-eminent banjoist in early jazz, and his work on the above recordings, together with such pieces as *Hum and Strum* (recorded with Doc Cook, 1928, Col. 1430D), show something of why he was the New Orleans player most in demand in Chicago for session work.

The New Orleans tradition was a strong one. An early and influential figure was William Penn (*d c*1946), who taught Emanuel Sayles. The latter made some fine recordings as a member of the Jones and Collins Astoria Hot Eight; *Astoria Strut* (1929, Vic. 38576), in particular, shows his gift for carrying a melodic line. Sayles continued to perform into the

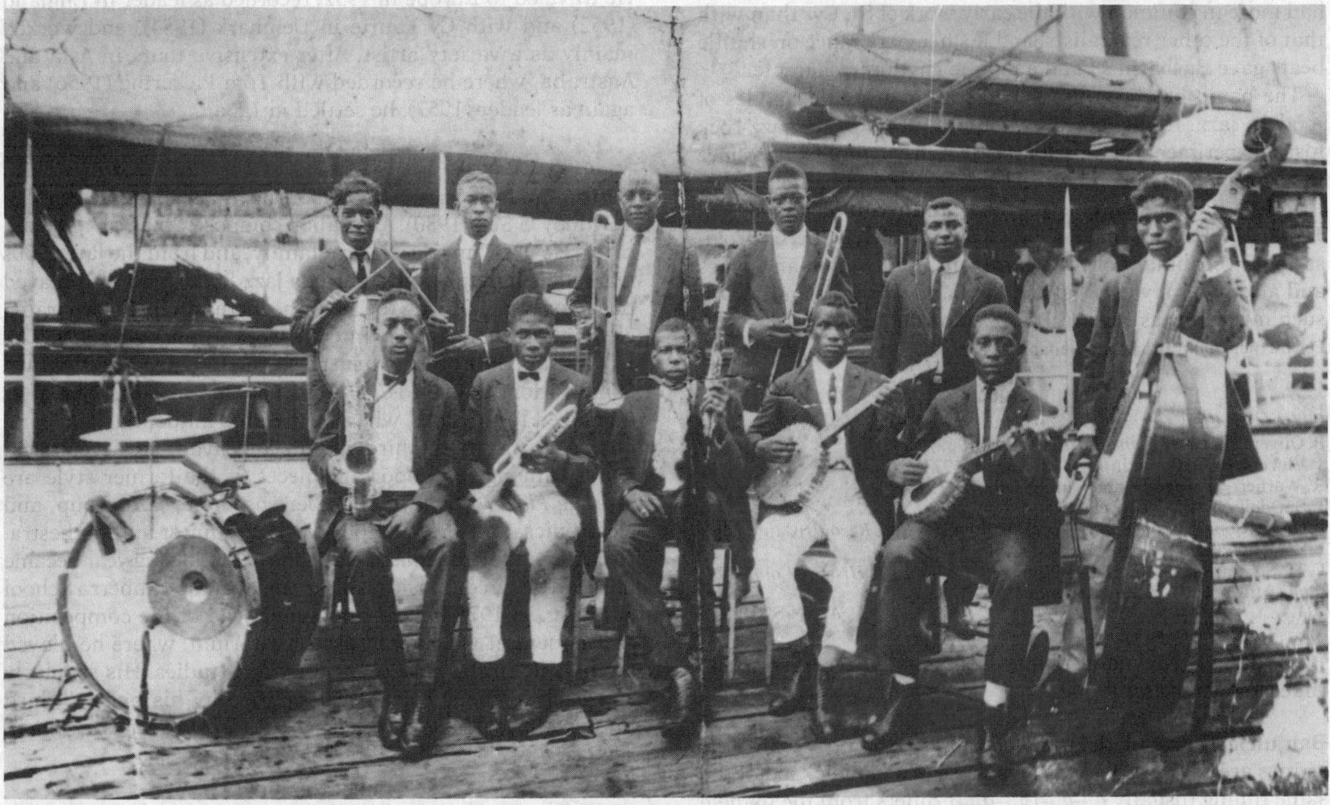

Members of the Original Tuxedo Orchestra and the Young Tuxedo Orchestra aboard Admiral Jahncke's yacht, New Orleans, 10 June 1923: (seated, left to right) Henry Julien (alto saxophone), Sam "Bush" Hall (trumpet), Willard Thourny (clarinet), Lawrence and John Marrero (banjos); (standing) Abbe "Chinee" Foster and Milford Dolliole (drums), William "Baba" Ridgley and Bob Thomas (trombones), Duck Ernest Johnson and Eddie Marrero (double basses)

1980s, and his late recordings under musicians associated with Preservation Hall confirm that he retained his style throughout his long career. Other important early figures were Bill Johnson (i) (who made some significant recordings with King Oliver), John Marrero, and Ikey Robinson. Marrero's work with Papa Celestin's Tuxedo Jazz Orchestra may be heard to advantage on *Station Calls* (1926, Col. 636D). Robinson's solo and ensemble playing on Jabbo Smith's *Jazz Battle* (1929, Bruns. 4244) is to some extent an example of a synthesis of all early styles: he executes runs, glissandos, and rolls or trills, all of which form a logical and consistent part in his construction of solos, with consummate ease. Like St. Cyr, Robinson manages to provide propulsion and achieve a sense of swing in a drumless rhythm section without the clanking monotony obtained by banjoists in later styles of traditional jazz.

With the dawn of the big-band era in the early 1930s, the banjo gave way relatively quickly to the guitar, although some big-band musicians – notably Fred Guy with Duke Ellington (*Echoes of the Jungle*, 1931, Vic. 22743) and Morris White with Cab Calloway – made their mark on banjo before changing instruments.

The banjo re-emerged in the 1940s with the revival of traditional jazz. Among the significant players of the instrument in New Orleans during this period were Lawrence Marrero (with George Lewis (i) and Bunk Johnson), Danny Barker (with Paul Barbarin), and Creole George Guesnon (*b* New Orleans, 25 May 1907; *d* New Orleans, 5 May 1968) (with Kid Howard and Capt. John Handy). Marrero's work on tenor banjo was widely imitated, as was the single-string solo playing of Guesnon. Barker's more complex style on the six-string instrument, which was heavily cross-fertilized with swing guitar playing, had more in common with the early work of St. Cyr than with that of the other revivalists, and his heavy reliance on shuffle beats gave Barbarin's band a unique rhythmic character.

The banjo has been little used in bop and other styles of modern jazz. It has, however, found a place in the jazz-rock fusion experiments of Chris Barber, whose rhythm section since the 1960s has included both electric guitar and banjo playing together. Barber's banjoists, Eddie Smith, Stu Morrison, and Johnny McCallum, have successively extended the improvisational vocabulary of the instrument into rhythm-and-blues and also other styles of jazz in the band's performances with such musicians as Russell Procope and John Lewis.

For further illustrations *see* BEIDERBECKE, BIX; LANG, EDDIE; and WATTERS, LU.

BIBLIOGRAPHY

G. Schuller: *Early Jazz: its Roots and Musical Development* (New York, 1968)
P. Oliver: *The Story of the Blues* (London, 1969), 27
J. Vincent: "The Banjo in Jazz," *JJ*, xxx/3 (1977), 20
R. Warner: "On Banjos and Guitars," *Sv*, no.73 (1977), 31
J. S. Odell: "Banjo," *GroveI*
P. Oliver: *Songsters and Saints: Vocal Traditions on Race Records* (Cambridge, England, and elsewhere, 1984), 119
L. H. Schreyer: "The Banjo in Ragtime," *Ragtime: its History, Composers, and Music*, ed. J. E. Hasse (London, 1985), 54

ALYN SHIPTON

Banjo Ike(y). Nickname of IKEY ROBINSON; he was also sometimes known as Banjo Joe.

Banjulele [banjo ukulele, ukulele banjo]. A banjo of which the strings are of the same length as those of a ukulele, and of the same tuning (usually *a'–d'–f♯'–b*). It differs from the ukulele in that its tone is more strident. One of few musicians to use the banjulele as a jazz instrument was the English singer Al Bowlly.

JULIAN F. V. VINCENT

Bank, Danny [Daniel Bernard] (*b* New York, 17 July 1922). Baritone saxophonist. He studied saxophone, clarinet, and flute. From 1942 to 1944 and again in 1948–9 he worked with Charlie Barnet, making several recordings (including *Cu-ba*, 1949, Cap. 15417). He toured and recorded with Benny Goodman (1945–6), played with Paul Whiteman (1946–7), recorded with Mel Powell (1946), then performed and recorded with Jimmy Dorsey (1947–8), Artie Shaw (1949–50), and Tommy Dorsey (1950–51). From 1951 he worked mainly with studio big bands in New York, recording for Charlie Parker (1952), Dizzy Gillespie (1954–5), Cannonball Adderley (1956), Miles Davis and Gil Evans (1957–62, often as a bass clarinetist), Johnny Hodges (1966–7, 1970), Louis Armstrong (1970), and many others. He continued to work as a freelance into the 1980s, playing clarinets, flute, and piccolo, as well as baritone saxophone, and performed again with Goodman in 1986.

BIBLIOGRAPHY

FeatherE
T. Baron: "Danny Bank," *Rythme et musique* (May 1974), 8 [interview, incl. discography]
C. Barnet and S. Dance: *Those Swinging Years* (Baton Rouge, LA, 1984)

Banks, Billy [William] (*b* Alton, IL, *c*1908; *d* Tokyo, 19 Oct 1967). Singer. From April to August 1932 he recorded in New York with an all-star pickup band known variously as Billy Banks and his Orchestra, the RHYTHMAKERS, and Billy Banks's Chicago Rhythm Kings. *Oh! You Sweet Thing* (1932, Vic. 24148) provides an example of his delightful scat singing. In 1932 Banks also recorded with the Mills Blue Rhythm Band and played at Connie's Inn. He joined Noble Sissle around 1934, then from 1938 to 1948 was resident at the Diamond Horseshoe. He traveled to Europe in 1952, recorded as leader in England (1952) and with Cy Laurie in Denmark (1954), and worked mainly as a variety artist. After extensive tours in Asia and Australia, where he recorded with Tom Pickering (1956) and again as leader (1957), he settled in Japan.

based on *ChiltonW*

Banks, Don(ald Oscar) (*b* Melbourne, Australia, 25 Oct 1923; *d* Sydney, 5 Sept 1980). Australian composer, pianist, and educator. He grew up in a musical family, and from the late 1930s worked as a pianist with various jazz bands and also played boogie-woogie. During the 1940s he increasingly incorporated elements of the bop style into his work; from 1948 to 1950 he led a group, the Boptet, which performed and recorded his own compositions (and also *Cherokee*, 1950, Jazzart 48). Thereafter he moved to England, where he became influential as a composer, writing both third-stream and avant-garde classical works. Among his important pieces in the former style are *Meeting Place* (1970) for chamber ensemble, jazz group, and electronics, and *Nexus* (1971) for jazz quintet and orchestra. He returned to Australia in 1973, and the following year became the head of the composition department at the Canberra School of Music. In 1978 he was appointed head of the composition department at the Sydney Conservatorium, where he played a vital role in the development of jazz studies. His scholarly approach to the subject is exemplified by his paper "Third Stream Music," in *Proceedings of the Royal Musical Association*, xcvii (1970–71), 59.

BIBLIOGRAPHY

F. Callaway and D. Tunley: *Australian Composition in the Twentieth Century* (Oxford, England, 1978)
B. Johnson: "Banks, Donald Oscar," *The Oxford Companion to Australian Jazz* (Melbourne, Australia, 1987)

JEFF PRESSING (with JOHN WHITEOAK)

Banner. Record company and label. The label was owned by the Plaza Music Co., New York, and its first issues were made in January 1922. At first its catalogue was drawn from those of Paramount and Emerson; the company opened its own recording studios late in 1922. The catalogue was firmly oriented towards popular styles, and most items of jazz interest are in fact hot dance music, but the company also issued important material by such artists as Clarence Williams and Fletcher Henderson, as well as recordings by vaudeville blues singers. The Banner label survived Plaza's merger with Cameo and Pathé, and was continued under later owners, eventually becoming one of the five "dime-store" labels of the AMERICAN RECORD COMPANY in the 1930s, sharing with the others important jazz and race catalogues. Like the others, it was discontinued after ARC–BRC was taken over by CBS in 1938.

BIBLIOGRAPHY

J. Godrich and R. M. W. Dixon: *Blues & Gospel Records, 1902–1942* (Hatch End, nr London, 1964, rev. 2/1969, rev. and enlarged 3/1982 as R. M. W. Dixon and J. Godrich: *Blues & Gospel Records, 1902–1943*), 22
R. M. W. Dixon and J. Godrich: *Recording the Blues* (London, 1970)
B. Rust: *The American Record Label Book* (New Rochelle, NY, 1978), 23

Baquet, Achille (Joseph) [Joe] (*b* New Orleans, 15 Nov 1885; *d* Hollywood, CA, 20 Nov 1956). Clarinetist and saxophonist, brother of George Baquet. He worked in New Orleans with Papa Jack Laine's first Reliance Brass Band, then in 1915 he went to New York, where he played with Jimmy Durante's Original New Orleans Jazz Band. This group later made some recordings, including *Ole Miss/Ja Da* (1918, OK 1156) and *He's had no lovin for a long long time/Ja Da* (1919, Gen. 4508). Baquet recorded a further title, *Why Cry Blues* (1920, Gen. 9045), with an almost identical band under the leadership of Durante. He settled in Los Angeles in 1920. (A. Barrell: "B is for . . . Baquet," *Fn*, xvii/3 (1986), 4; contd as "Back to Baquet," xvii/4 (1986), 10; contd as "The Baquets: Some Concluding Notes," xviii/2 (1986–7), 4)

ALAN BARRELL

Baquet, George (F.) (*b* New Orleans, 1883; *d* New Orleans, 14 Jan 1949). Clarinetist, brother of Achille Baquet. At the age of 14 he played E♭ clarinet in the Lyre Club Symphony Orchestra, an amateur group conducted by his father, Theogene V. Baquet (*b* New Orleans, *c*1858; *d* New Orleans, *c*1920), a clarinetist who in 1880 founded the Excelsior Brass Band and led the group until 1904. Later he played with the first Onward Brass Band (1900) and Manuel Perez's Imperial Orchestra (1901–2), and he is believed to have worked with Buddy Bolden and the trombonist Frankie Dusen. From 1902 to 1904 he toured with P. T. Wright's Georgia Minstrels, after which he returned to New Orleans and performed with John Robichaux, the Magnolia Orchestra, and the Olympia Orchestra. With Freddie Keppard, Baquet went to Los Angeles in 1914 to play with the Original Creole Orchestra. In 1917 he settled in Philadelphia, where he remained for most of the rest of his life, leading his own groups. He recorded with Jelly Roll Morton's Red Hot Peppers in 1929.

SELECTED RECORDINGS

As sideman with J. R. Morton: Burnin' the Iceberg/Tank Town Bump (1929, Vic. 38075); Courthouse Bump/Sweet Aneta Mine (1929, Vic. 38093); New Orleans Bump (1929, Vic. 38078)

BIBLIOGRAPHY

ChartersJ; *ChiltonW*
W. J. Schafer: "Breaking into 'High Society : Musical Metamorphoses in Early Jazz," *JJS*, ii/2 (1975), 53
A. Barrell: "B is for . . . Baquet," *Fn*, xvii/3 (1986), 4; contd as "Back to Baquet," xvii/4 (1986), 10; contd as "The Baquets: Some Concluding Notes," xviii/2 (1986–7), 4

ALAN BARRELL

Baraka, Amiri [Jones, (Everett) LeRoi] (*b* Newark, NJ, 7 Oct 1934). Writer. He studied piano, drums, and trumpet privately and attended Howard University (BA 1954). In the early 1960s he achieved wide recognition for his poetry and plays and for his writings about jazz, which included articles for *Down Beat*, *Jazz*, and *Jazz Review*; a selection of his writings, many from *Down Beat*, was published in 1967 as *Black Music*. His book *Blues People* (1963), the first full-length study of jazz by a black writer, is both a sociological enquiry, using blues and jazz as a means of understanding how Blacks became assimilated into American culture, and a superb discussion of the cultural context of the music in the USA. Besides his activities as a writer, Baraka has been involved in many black cultural and community projects. He was a founder of the Black Arts Repertory Theater–School, which was in existence from 1964 to 1965, and has also taught African studies at SUNY, Stony Brook, from 1980.

Baraka has had a profound influence on jazz criticism, ranging beyond its conventional boundaries to examine such topics as the relationship to jazz and the blues of black nationalism and Marxism. In addition to his works on jazz his published writings include more than 20 plays (of which the best-known is *Dutchman*, New York and Toronto, 1964) and 12 volumes of poetry. Among his works in progress in the late 1980s were a book on John Coltrane and a collaboration with Max Roach entitled *Bumpy: a Bopera*.

WRITINGS
(selective list)

"Introducing Wayne Shorter," *JR*, ii/10 (1959), 22
Blues People: Negro Music in White America (New York, 1963)
Black Music (New York, 1967/*R*1980)
The Autobiography of Leroi Jones (New York, 1984)
with Amina Baraka: *The Music: Reflections on Jazz and Blues* (New York, 1987)

BIBLIOGRAPHY

K. W. Benston: *Baraka: the Renegade and the Mask* (New Haven, CT, and London, 1976)
——, ed.: *Imamu Amiri Baraka (LeRoi Jones): a Collection of Critical Essays* (Englewood Cliffs, NJ, 1978)
L. W. Brown: *Amiri Baraka* (Boston, 1980)

DANIEL ZAGER

Baranco, Wilbert (*b* ?USA, *c*1912). Pianist, leader, and singer. After working with the drummer Curtis Mosby from around 1933 to 1934 he ceased full-time performing, but he played in a band during his military service. On recordings made in Los Angeles in late 1945 he accompanied the singer Ernie Andrews with his own trio (which included Charles Mingus) and Dinah Washington as a member of Lucky Thompson's All Stars. He also formed the Rhythm Bombardiers with a number of fellow servicemen; this group recorded with such well-known musicians as Vic Dickenson, Willie Smith, and Dizzy Gillespie, who played for reduced fees. Baranco's playing and singing may be heard on *Everytime I think of you/Baranco's Boogie* (1946, Black & White 42). In 1946 he recorded with Mingus and by 1947 he was leading a trio, in which Ulysses Livingston was a sideman. He later worked as a music teacher in California. (D. Saleman: Liner notes, *Small Label Gems of the Forties*, Solid Sender SOL513, *c*1980)

HOWARD RYE

Barbarin. Family of musicians active in New Orleans.

(1) Isidore Barbarin (*b* New Orleans, 24 Sept 1872; *d* New Orleans, 12 June 1960). Alto horn player. He started playing cornet at the age of 14, then took up alto horn and became a member of the first Onward Brass Band (for illustration *see* BRASS BAND, fig.1). He also played with other groups, notably the Excelsior and the Tuxedo brass bands, for concerts, parades, funerals, and parties. In 1945 he made some recordings with Bunk Johnson, including *Didn't he ramble/Tell me your dreams* (AM 103). Isidore had four sons who were musicians: (2) Paul and (3) Louis (see below), and also Lucien (*b* New Orleans, *c* 1905; *d* New Orleans, before 1960), a drummer, and William (*b* New Orleans, *c*1907; *d* New Orleans, 18 Dec 1973), who played cornet. He was the grandfather of Danny Barker. (D. Barker: *A Life in Jazz*, ed. A. Shipton, London, 1986)

Oral history material in *LNT*.

(2) (Adolphe) Paul Barbarin (*b* New Orleans, 5 May 1899; *d* New Orleans, 17 Feb 1969). Drummer, son of (1) Isidore Barbarin. He first acquired a drum set and played professionally in 1915, and soon afterwards was a member of Buddy Petit's Young Olympia Band. In 1917 he went to Chicago to work in the stockyards, and a year later played at the Royal Garden with King Oliver and Jimmie Noone. After returning home (1920) he performed at Tom Anderson's with Albert Nicholas; he then resumed playing with Oliver in Chicago (1924) and worked with him at the Plantation (1925). In 1928 Barbarin joined Luis Russell in New York, and he recorded with the band between 1929 and 1935, sometimes under the leadership of Jelly Roll Morton or Louis Armstrong; in 1935 Armstrong took over the group for touring and recording purposes. Barbarin returned to New Orleans in 1939, though he spent a further period in Chicago, where he led a band, played as a member of Henry "Red" Allen's sextet (1942–3), and worked with Sidney Bechet (1944). For the rest of his life he performed mostly in New Orleans with small groups and brass bands, in which he played snare drum or, less frequently, bass drum. In 1960 he formed the second Onward Brass Band (*see* ONWARD BRASS BAND (ii)), which he was leading in a carnival parade at the time of his death.

Barbarin's playing was simple and unspectacular – his drum set usually consisted only of snare drum, large bass drum, one cymbal, tom-tom, and woodblock – and he rarely took solos; following the style of Mack Lacey and other early drummers, he used the cymbal only for the last chorus of a piece. He derived his swinging beat from the driving rhythms of parade bands, and at times he adopted the older, two-beat rhythms, which he thought dancers preferred. A number of his compositions have become jazz standards, including *Bourbon Street Parade* and *The Second Line*.

Oral history material in *LNT*.

SELECTED RECORDINGS

As leader: *Barbarin's Best at Dixieland Hall* (1964, Nobility 707)

As sideman: K. Oliver: Too Bad/Snag it (1926, Voc. 1007); L. Armstrong: Mahogany Hall Stomp (1929, OK 8680); L. Russell: The New Call of the Freaks/Jersey Lightning (1929, OK 8734); L. Armstrong: Dallas Blues (1929, OK 8774); E. Barrett: *Sweet Emma Barrett and her New Orleans Music* (1963, Slnd 241)

BIBLIOGRAPHY

ChiltonW

J. Norris: "Paul Barbarin: his Story," *Eureka*, i/1 (1960), 23

C. Bolton: "All Gone Now," *New Orleans Magazine*, v/8 (1971), 32; repr. in *SL*, xxiv (1972), win., p.19; spr., p.19 [extract from unpubd autobiography]

(3) Louis Barbarin (*b* New Orleans, 24 Oct 1902). Drummer, son of (1) Isidore Barbarin. He was taught by Louis Cottrell, Sr., and joined the first Onward Brass Band around 1918, when Manuel Perez was the leader. He played at dances with Kid Rena, the trombonist Jack Carey, and Punch Miller, and on excursion boats with Sidney Desvigne. In 1937 he began a long association with Papa Celestin's band, which continued when, after Celestin's death, the band was taken over by the banjoist Albert French. Among the many recordings he made was an album with French, *A Night at Dixieland Hall* (1963, Nobility 702B). Barbarin also taught drums. He toured widely during the 1970s, and continued to play until 1982.

Oral history material in *LNT*.

BILL RUSSELL

Barber, Bill [John William] (*b* Hornell, NY, 21 May 1920). Tuba player. He studied at the Institute of Musical Art in New York and first played with the Kansas City PO; after army service (1942–5) he performed with Claude Thornhill (1947–8). In 1949 he was a founding member of Miles Davis's nonet, and took part in the famous "Birth of the Cool" recording sessions (for illustration *see* JAZZ (i), fig.6); he then recorded with the Sauter–Finegan Orchestra (1952–4), Pete Rugolo (1954), and the orchestra led by Davis and Gil Evans (1957–62). From 1960 he taught music at public schools on Long Island, and performed only sporadically. Barber may have been the first tuba player to take solos in a modern-jazz style and to participate in intricate ensemble passages. His technique allowed him to play both slow, legato melodies and rapid lines, and he generally employed the entire range of the instrument. His solo in a blues chorus on *Woofer*, from Dick Hyman's album *The Hi-fi Suite*, is a good example of his playing.

SELECTED RECORDINGS

As sideman: M. Davis: Move (1949, Cap. 15404); on D. Hyman: *The Hi-fi Suite* (1956, MGM 3494), Woofer; M. Davis: *Miles Ahead* (1957, Col. CL1041), incl. The Duke; G. Evans: *Out of the Cool* (1960, Imp. 4); J. Coltrane: *Africa/Brass* (1961, Imp. 6)

BIBLIOGRAPHY

FeatherE; *Feather–Gitler '70s*

LEROY OSTRANSKY

Barber, (Donald) Chris(topher) (*b* Welwyn Garden City, England, 17 April 1930). English trombonist and bandleader. He studied trombone and double bass at the Guildhall School of Music in London, and formed his first traditional jazz band in 1949. In 1953 he helped to organize a band that was led by Ken Colyer, at that time the most ardent British propagandist for traditional New Orleans music. The following year Barber took over the band; Colyer was replaced by Pat Halcox, and the ensemble soon became one of the most popular and technically accomplished groups of its kind. Renewed interest in traditional jazz in the early 1960s brought wide success to Barber and his group, which included as its singer his wife, Ottilie Patterson; among his other sidemen was Monty Sunshine. Barber also expanded his interests, recording classic rags (scored for his band) long before the popular rediscovery of Scott Joplin, and working with musicians from other areas of jazz (notably Bertie King and Joe Harriott). From the mid-1950s he helped foster British interest in rhythm-and-blues by bringing over such American blues musicians as the guitarist and singer Muddy Waters, the harmonica player Sonny Terry, and the guitarist and singer Brownie McGhee. He made several tours of the USA beginning in 1959, and also recorded two albums with his American Jazz Band, which included Sidney De Paris, Edmond Hall, and Hank Duncan. After rhythm-and-blues achieved general popularity in the early 1960s, he re-

Chris Barber's band, 1959: (left to right) Barber (trombone, leader), Pat Halcox (trumpet), Monty Sunshine (clarinet), Dick Smith (double bass), Eddie Smith (banjo), Graham Burbidge (drums), and Ottilie Patterson (voice)

formed his group as Chris Barber's Jazz and Blues Band, and, while retaining his roots in New Orleans jazz, regularly engaged such rock and blues musicians as the guitarist John Slaughter and the drummer Pete York. During the 1970s the band toured frequently in Europe; at various times its sidemen included Sammy Rimington and the clarinetist John Crocker. In 1976 Barber made a tour of Britain entitled "Echoes of Ellington" with Russell Procope and Wild Bill Davis, and in 1981–2 he collaborated with the rock singer and keyboard player Dr. John in the show *Take me Back to New Orleans*, which was performed widely in Britain, Europe, and the USA.

Barber is a skillful trombonist and a highly original arranger, and the identity he has achieved for his band has been imitated throughout Europe.

For further illustration *see* FILMS, fig.6.

SELECTED RECORDINGS

As leader: When Erastus plays his old kazoo (1951, Tempo A102); Bobby Shaftoe/The Martinique (1954, Decca F10492); Chimes Blues (1954, Decca F10417); Stevedore Stomp (1954, Decca DFE6463); I'd love it (1954, Decca DFE6238); Whistlin' Rufus (1956, Nixa 2011); There'll be a hot time (1959, Col. DB4333); *Ragtime* (1960, Col. 33SX1245), incl. Elite Syncopation; *Chris Barber's American Jazz Band* (1960, Col. 33SX1321); *Chris Barber at the London Palladium* (1961, Col. 33SX1346); Trad Tavern (1961, Col. SCD2167); *Battersea Rain Dance* (1967–8, Marmalade 608009), incl. Battersea Rain Dance, Dancy dancy, Mercy, mercy, mercy; *Get Rolling!* (1969–71, Pol. 2683001); *Echoes of Ellington* (1976, BL 001), incl. Slappin' 7th Avenue with the sole of my shoe; with Dr. John: *Take me Back to New Orleans* (1980, BL 157007), incl. Big Bass Drum

BIBLIOGRAPHY

FeatherE; *Feather '60s*

B. Harvey: "Chris Barber: the Man, his Band, its Success," *JB*, ii/7 (1958), 6

B. Gladwell: "Barber Approved," *JJ*, xii/8 (1959), 25

E. Souchon: "Chris Barber's Band in New Orleans," *JJ*, xiii/2 (1960), 1

G. Bielderman: *Chris Barber Discography, 1949–1975* (Zwolle, Netherlands, 1976; looseleaf suppl. *c*1978)

D. Fairweather: "Barber, Chris," in I. Carr, D. Fairweather, and B. Priestley: *Jazz: the Essential Companion* (London, 1987), 25

CHARLES FOX/DIGBY FAIRWEATHER

Barbieri, Gato [Leandro J.] (*b* Rosario, Argentina, 28 Nov 1934). Argentine tenor saxophonist and composer. Several members of his family were musicians, and he studied clarinet as a child. He moved in 1947 to Buenos Aires, where he learned alto saxophone and became first alto saxophonist in Lalo Schifrin's band; his early influences were Charlie Parker and John Coltrane. Later he formed his own quartet and changed to the tenor instrument. In 1962 he moved to Rome, and the following year he joined Don Cherry's group in Paris. Thereafter he began to develop his own approach, moving away from Cherry's free-jazz style towards Latin American music; he became known internationally through his performances at festivals in Bologna (1965, 1974), and Montreux (1971, 1973), and at the Newport Jazz Festival New York (1973, 1974). His playing on the soundtrack to the film *Last Tango in Paris* (1972), for which he also composed the music, brought him to the attention of a larger audience. Barbieri then returned to Buenos Aires, and in 1973 assembled a large group of South American musicians; he continued to play a fusion of Latin American and folk music, political cabaret songs, and jazz. In the mid-1970s he began to work in popular and more commercial styles, while still maintaining his unique and instantly recognizable tone. Barbieri's fundamental timbre is much like that of Coltrane, but it is modified by a wide, romantic vibrato. At frequent climactic points in his music he brings an exciting, distorted edge to the sound, which he achieves either by humming and blowing at the same time or by producing a high-pitched wailing tone. Among his many compositions are *La padrida* and *Viva Emiliano Zapata*.

SELECTED RECORDINGS

Duos with D. Brand: *Hamba kahle* (1968, Togetherness 004)
As leader: *In Search of the Mystery* (1967, ESP 1049); *The Third World* (1969, FD 10117); *Under Fire* (c1971, FD 10156); *Last Tango in Paris* (c1972, UA LA045-F); *Chapter One: Latin America* (1973, Imp. 9248); *Chapter Three: Viva Emiliano Zapata* (1974, Imp. 9279), incl. La padrida, Viva Emiliano Zapata; *Chapter Four: Alive in New York* (1975, Imp. 9303); *Caliente* (1976, A&M 4597); *Para los amigos* (1983, Doctor Jazz 39204)
As sideman with D. Cherry: *Complete Communion* (1965, BN 84226)

BIBLIOGRAPHY

Feather '60s; *Feather–Gitler '70s*
P. Carles: "Gato Barbieri: l'autre Amérique," *Jm*, no.197 (1972), 26
E. Jost: *Free Jazz* (Graz, Austria, 1974), 140
R. Palmer: "Gato: I Need a Lot of Rest," *DB*, xli/12 (1974), 14 [interview]
M. Garztecki: "The Cat that Walks by Himself," *JF* [intl. edn], no.36 (1975), 34 [incl. discography]
B. McRae: "Avant courier: el Gato," *JJ*, xxix/10 (1976), 22
L. Birnbaum: "Gato Barbieri: the Argentine Eclectic," *DB*, xliv/8 (1977), 15 [incl. discography]

CATHERINE COLLINS

Barbour, Dave [David Michael] (*b* Long Island, NY, 28 May 1912; *d* Malibu, nr Los Angeles, 11 Dec 1965). Acoustic guitarist. After first playing banjo he changed to guitar and worked with Wingy Manone (1934) and Red Norvo (1934–5). During the 1930s he was in great demand as a studio musician, and he recorded prolifically with Teddy Wilson (1935), Bunny Berigan (1936), and Louis Armstrong (1936, 1938). He was a member of Benny Goodman's orchestra in 1942–3, and in the mid-1940s he briefly led his own band; he also made recordings with such musicians as Jack Teagarden (1943), Charlie Barnet (1945), and Boyd Raeburn (1946). From 1943 to 1951 Barbour was married to the singer Peggy Lee and worked as her music director; together they composed several songs that became hits. After a short-lived career as an actor (he appeared in the film *The Secret Fury* in 1950) he became ill, and he retired in the mid-1950s, although he recorded with Benny Carter in 1962. The majority of Barbour's work was as a section member of swing bands, but in his rare solos he displayed a tasteful and fluent style influenced by Charlie Christian.

SELECTED RECORDINGS

As sideman: T. Wilson: You let me down/Spreadin' Rhythm Around (1935, Bruns. 7581); B. Goodman: Six Flats Unfurnished (1942, Col. 36652); Mission to Moscow (1942, Col. 36680); B. Carter: *BBB & Co.* (1962, Swingville 2032)

BIBLIOGRAPHY

ChiltonW; *FeatherE*; *Feather '60s*

NORMAN MONGAN

Barcelona, Danny [Daniel] (*b* Honolulu, 23 Aug 1929). Drummer. At 18 he played in the Hawaii Dixie All-Stars led by Trummy Young. When Young left to work with Louis Armstrong in 1952 Barcelona took over the leadership of the group, which toured the Far East until 1953. He joined Armstrong in New York in early 1958 and remained until the trumpeter's death in 1971; as well as making many recordings, he appeared with the band in films and on television. He returned to Honolulu and played locally until 1979, when he moved to Monterey Park, California. During Barcelona's tenure with Armstrong, the band played a commercialized form of jazz. Consequently, Barcelona's technique is based less on traditional dixieland revival styles than on those of the 1960s; his playing is characterized by extensive use of the ride cymbal, crisp, clean fills and breaks, and solos that exploit asymmetrical phrasing and demonstrate his accuracy of hand and foot at speed.

SELECTED RECORDINGS

As sideman with L. Armstrong: *Louis Armstrong with Duke Ellington* (1961, Roul. 52074); *Great Reunion* (1961, Roul. 52103); *The Essential Louis Armstrong* (1965–7, Van. 91–2), incl. Stompin' at the Savoy, Ole Miss

BIBLIOGRAPHY

FeatherE

T. DENNIS BROWN

Barefield, Eddie (Emmanuel) [Edward Emanuel] (*b* Scandia, nr Madrid, IA, 12 Dec 1909). Alto and tenor saxophonist and clarinetist. He studied piano from the age of ten and alto saxophone from the age of 13. After working in 1930 with the cornetist Bernie Young he played with Bennie Moten (1932), Zack Whyte (1933), McKinney's Cotton Pickers (1933), Cab Calloway (1933–6, and at intervals to 1958), Les Hite (1937), Fletcher Henderson (1938, 1950), and Don Redman (1938). In the 1940s he was a staff musician for ABC and for WOR radio, and also worked with Benny Carter (1941), in Ella Fitzgerald's band (1942), and with Duke Ellington (1947). While conducting pit orchestras on Broadway (1948–70), for which he also wrote arrangements, he played with Sammy Price (1958), Wilbur De Paris (1964), and the group Saints and Sinners (1969). He belonged to the orchestra of the Ringling Brothers and Barnum & Bailey Circus from 1971 to 1982 and worked as a freelance into the late 1980s with the clarinetist Stan Rubin, Dick Vance, the Harlem Blues and Jazz Band, and Illinois Jacquet. Barefield composed (with Buster Moten) the exciting, frenetic riff tune *Toby*, and wrote the arrangement for Bennie Moten's well-known recording of this tune, made in 1932 (on which Barefield may be heard as a clarinet soloist); he also wrote other arrangements for Moten, as well as for Calloway, Glenn Miller, Benny Goodman, Paul Whiteman, and Jimmy Dorsey. He appeared in the films *The Swinging Kid* with Al Jolson (1935), *Every Day's a Holiday* with Louis Armstrong (1937), and *The Night they Raided Minsky's* (1968).

Oral history material in *MoKmh*, *NjR*, *NjR* (JOHP).

SELECTED RECORDINGS

As leader: What's mine is yours/That ain't Right (1946, Son. 102); Clarinet Blues/If tain't One Thing it's Another (1946, Son. 112); *The Indestructible Eddie Barefield* (1977, FaD 113)
As sideman: B. Moten: Toby (1932, Vic. 23384); C. Calloway: Moon Glow/Hotcha Razz-ma-tazz (1934, Vic. 24690); F. Henderson: Moten Stomp (1938, Voc. 4180); D. Redman: Down Home Rag/Margie (1938, Bb 10061); Pete Johnson: 627 Stomp (1940, Decca 18121); H. L. Page: Lafayette/South (1940, Decca 18124); B. Holiday: Let's Do it/Georgia on my Mind (1941, OK 6134); B. Carter: Midnight/My Favorite Blues (1941, Bb 11288); S. Oliver: A Slow Burn/My Daddy-o (1947, MGM 10004); R. Eldridge: *Swing Goes Dixie* (1956, Verve 1010); C. Calloway: *Cab Calloway Accompanied by Eddie Barefield's Orchestra* (1958, Gone 101)

BIBLIOGRAPHY

ChiltonW
A. J. McCarthy: "The Eddie Barefield Story," *JM*, v/3 (1959), 11
H. Panassié: "Quelques notes sur la musique d'Eddie Barefield," *BHcF*, no.201 (1970), 6
L. Verdeaux: "Eddie Barefield," *BHcF*, no.201 (1970), 3 [interview]
J. Chilton: *McKinney's Music: a Bio-discography of McKinney's Cotton Pickers* (London, 1978), 50
E. Townley: "Hitting the Road," *Storyville*, no.76 (1978), 141
S. Dance: *The World of Count Basie* (New York and London, 1980), 312
L. D. Holmes and J. W. Thompson: *Jazz Greats: Getting Better with Age* (New York, 1986) [colln of interviews]

ALBERT VOLLMER

Barelli, Aimé (*b* Loda, nr Lantosque, France, 1 March 1917). French trumpeter, singer, and bandleader. He was largely self-taught as a musician. He went to Paris in January 1940 and played with the bandleader and saxophonist Raymond Legrand (1940), Fred Adison's band, the pianist Raymond Wraskoff (1940–41), Hubert Rostaing (1940–41), Alix Combelle's group the Jazz de Paris (1940–41), the banjoist and guitarist Maceo Jefferson, and André Ekyan (1941). In 1943–5 he performed and recorded as the leader of a successful group consisting of a trumpet, five saxophones, and a rhythm section. He recorded in jam sessions with Dizzy Gillespie (1948), Charlie Parker (1949), Sidney Bechet (1949), and Django Reinhardt (1952), and from 1966 worked as a bandleader in Monte Carlo. Barelli was the most technically proficient French trumpeter; his performance on *Verlaine* (Swing 105), recorded by Combelle and the Jazz de Paris in 1941, well illustrates his style. (M. Laplace: "Aimé Barelli," *Brass Bulletin*, no.50 (1985), 22)

MICHEL LAPLACE

Baritone. In general musical terminology the vocal part or range lying below the tenor and above the bass; the word is also used as a qualifying adjective to distinguish those members of certain families of instruments (especially wind) that play in that range (e.g., baritone horn; *see* SAXHORN). In jazz argot "baritone" (also shortened to "bari" or "bary") is used alone to mean the baritone saxophone (*see* SAXOPHONE), and sometimes to mean the player of that instrument.

Baritone horn. The baritone instrument of the SAXHORN family, pitched in B♭. The name is also used for the euphonium (tenor TUBA), especially in the USA, where the two instruments are structurally less dissimilar than in Europe and are often used interchangeably.

Baritone saxophone. The baritone instrument of the saxophone family, pitched in E♭; the compass of the standard instrument is *D♭–a♭′*, though many baritone saxophones have a key for concert *C*. *See* SAXOPHONE, §5.

Barker, Blue Lu [Lu Blue; née Dupont, Louise] (*b* New Orleans, 13 Nov 1913). Singer. She began her career as a singer and dancer, but after her marriage in 1930 to DANNY BARKER and their move to New York she concentrated from 1938 on singing. She generally eschewed public performance in favor of the recording studio, and the majority of the items she recorded were with bands led by her husband; the best of these were issued under her name by Decca (1938–9), Apollo (1946), and Capitol (1948–9). Barker continued to perform sporadically in the 1960s and 1970s (she returned to New Orleans in 1965), and appeared at clubs and festivals in the early 1980s. The songs for which she is best known are *Don't you make me high* and *Here's a little girl*.

SELECTED RECORDINGS

He caught the B and O/Don't you make me high (1938, Decca 7506); That made him mad (1938, Decca 7538); A little bird told me (1948, Cap. 15308); Here's a little girl (1948, Cap. 15347)

BIBLIOGRAPHY

S. Harris: *Blues Who's Who: a Biographical Dictionary of Blues Singers* (New Rochelle, NY, 1979)
D. Barker: *A Life in Jazz*, ed. A. Shipton (London, 1986)
A. Shipton: "Blue Lu Barker," *Fn*, xvii/5 (1986), 15

ALYN SHIPTON

Barker, Danny [Daniel Moses] (*b* New Orleans, 13 Jan 1909). Guitarist, banjoist, singer, and composer, husband of BLUE LU BARKER. He spent his childhood in the home of his grandfather Isidore Barbarin, where he learned clarinet, ukulele, and finally banjo. He played with a spasm band, the Boozan Kings, and in the early 1920s toured Mississippi with Little Brother Montgomery and the trumpeter Willie Pajeaud. In 1928 he joined Lee Collins and David Jones and made a tour of Florida. Barker moved in 1930 to New York, where the following year he worked with Dave Nelson and Harry White, soon abandoning the banjo in favor of the guitar. His principal associations in the early 1930s were with Sidney Bechet, Fess Williams, Albert Nicholas, and James P. Johnson; he also recorded prolifically, particularly with his wife and with Henry "Red" Allen. From 1937 his main work was in the big bands of Lucky Millinder (1937–8), Benny Carter (1938), and Cab Calloway (1939–46; for illustration *see* CALLOWAY, CAB). Thereafter he played mainly with small groups. In 1947 he took part in the dixieland revival through the series of radio broadcasts "This is Jazz" and recordings with Mutt Carey and Bunk Johnson, at the same time taking up six-string banjo. He recorded in Los Angeles (1948–9) and New Orleans (1949) before returning to New York, where he performed at Ryan's with the trombonists Conrad Janis and Wilbur De Paris and with his own band. Barker returned to New Orleans in 1965 and served as assistant curator of the New Orleans Jazz Museum (1965–75), while also continuing to work as a bandleader, guitarist, and grand marshal of the Onward Brass Band (1965–72). He has written and lectured on jazz history (a notable publication being "A Memory of King Bolden," *Evergreen Review*, no.37 (1965), 66) and contributed to the education of young musicians through the formation of the Fairview Baptist Church Brass Band.

Barker's most distinguished work is as a rhythm guitarist, though his occasional solos on recordings with Blue Lu Barker (particularly *He's so good*) and his duets with Pops Foster on the "This is Jazz" broadcasts reveal an accomplished chordal and single-string technique. His compositions (notably *Don't you make me high*, *Here's a little girl*, and *Save the bones for Henry Jones*) have been widely recorded by artists as diverse as Joe Turner (ii) and Nat "King" Cole.

Oral history material in *LNT*, *NjR* (JOHP).

See also BANJO.

SELECTED RECORDINGS

As leader: Chocko ma fendo hey/My Indian Red (*c*1948, King Zulu 0001)
As sideman: H. Allen: Smooth Sailing/Whose honey are you? (1935, Ban. 33355); Mills Blue Rhythm Band: Prelude to a Stomp/Rhythm Jam (1937, Var. 546); C. Berry: Sittin' in/Forty-six West Fifty-two (1938, Com. 516); B. L. Barker: He's so good (1939, Decca 7695); M. Mezzrow: House Party (1945, King Jazz 143); C. Thompson: 20th Century Blues/The Street Beat (1945, Apollo 759); M. Carey: Shim-me-sha-wobble/Cake Walking Babies (1947, Cen. 4017); B. Johnson: *The Last Testament of a Great Jazzman* (1947, Col. GL520); Journey into Jazz: *Journey into Jazz* (1967, GHB 65), incl. Save the bones for Henry Jones

BIBLIOGRAPHY

N. Shapiro and N. Hentoff, eds.: *Hear me Talkin' to ya: the Story of Jazz by the Men who Made it* (New York and London, 1955/*R*1966)
J. R. Failows: "Danny Barker, de la Nouvelle-Orléans," *BHcF*, no.99 (1960), 6
"Danny Barker Comes Home," *SL*, xiii (1967), 3
J. V. Buerkle and D. Barker: *Bourbon Street Black: the New Orleans Black Jazzman* (New York, 1973)
D. Barker: *A Life in Jazz*, ed. A. Shipton (London, 1986)

ALYN SHIPTON

Barker, Thurman (*b* Chicago, 8 Jan 1948). Drummer and percussionist. He attended Roosevelt University in Chicago, and was an early member of the Association for the Advancement of Creative Musicians; he played with Anthony Braxton, and performed and recorded with Joseph Jarman (1966–8), Muhal Richard Abrams (1967, 1970), and Kalaparusha Maurice McIntyre (1969). From 1968 to 1980 he played in theater orchestras. He toured and recorded with Braxton (1978–80) and Sam Rivers (1979–80), and played in sessions with Roscoe Mitchell (1978), Abrams (1978, 1980), John Lindberg (1981), and Amina Claudine Myers and Pheeroan Ak Laff (both 1983). He performed in trios with Jarman and Rivers (both 1985) and played marimba in a quintet led by Cecil Taylor with Freddie Waits and Leroy Jenkins (1987).

SELECTED RECORDINGS

As sideman: J. Jarman: *Song for* (1966, Del. 410); A. Braxton: *Seven Compositions 1978* (1979, Moers 01066); S. Rivers: *Contrasts* (1979, ECM 1162); P. Ak Laff: *Fits Like a Glove* (1983, Gram. 8207)

BIBLIOGRAPHY

V. Wilmer: *As Serious as your Life: the Story of the New Jazz* (London, 1977, rev. 1980)

H. Mandel: "Thurman Barker: Drummer for All Seasons," *DB*, liii/3 (1986), 26 [incl. discography]

E. Hazell: "Portraits: Thurman Barker," *MD*, xi/11 (1987), 36

Barksdale, Everett (*b* Detroit, 28 April 1910; *d* Inglewood, CA, 29 Jan 1986). Guitarist. He first worked with Erskine Tate's band in Chicago (1930), then toured and recorded with Eddie South (1932–9). After playing with Benny Carter's orchestra in New York in 1940 he worked with Herman "Ivory" Chittison's trio (1942), then led his own quartet intermittently (1942–5); around this time he was also a staff musician for CBS. He came to prominence as a member of Art Tatum's trio (1949–56), with which he did some of his most characteristic work; his playing is well represented on the album *The Art Tatum Trio* (1955–6, Jazz Anthology 5138). He played electric bass guitar with Buddy Tate in the late 1950s. During the 1960s he was a staff musician for ABC television in New York, and worked as a freelance, playing both electric guitar and electric bass guitar. Having returned to California, he continued to work into the 1970s. Although he was a contemporary of Charlie Christian, Barksdale played in a style closer to that of Al Casey. He was far from being a virtuoso, but played engagingly simple yet swinging lines, tinged with blues inflections. Like other players of his generation he never completely mastered the art of legato playing on the electric guitar; his hard, percussive attack originated in his technique on the acoustic instrument. (*ChiltonW*; *FeatherE*)

NORMAN MONGAN

Barnard, Bob [Robert Graeme] (*b* Melbourne, Australia, 24 Nov 1933). Australian trumpeter, brother of Len Barnard. He gained early experience in brass bands, and first played jazz in 1947 with a group consisting of members of his family. From 1947 to 1955 he belonged to his brother Len's traditional-jazz ensemble; he continued to make recordings with this group (among them *The Naked Dance*, 1961, Swaggie S1287 [incl. previously released tracks]) at intervals until 1968, and also recorded as a leader in 1952, 1957, and 1962. In 1957 he moved to Sydney, where he played with a number of bands, including the Graeme Bell All-Stars (with which he recorded, 1962–4). He formed his own band in 1974, and toured Australia, North America, Europe, India, and South-East Asia; he toured the USA as a soloist in 1985. As a sideman Barnard has worked in Australia and overseas with, among others, Bud Freeman, Ralph Sutton, Wild Bill Davison, Milt Hinton, Don Burrows, and Peanuts Hucko. His warm, fluid playing has its origins in the styles of Louis Armstrong, Bunny Berigan, and Bobby Hackett, and may be heard to advantage on *Stars Fell on Alabama*, from Kenny Powell's album *Music to Midnight* (1981, ABC L38208).

BIBLIOGRAPHY

A. Bisset: *Black Roots, White Flowers: a History of Jazz in Australia* (Sydney, 1979)

D. Hughes: "Bob Barnard," *Jazz: the Australasian Contemporary Music Magazine*, i/6 (1981), 13

M. Williams: *The Australian Jazz Explosion* (London and elsewhere, 1981), 23

B. Johnson and others: *The Oxford Companion to Australian Jazz* (Melbourne, Australia, 1987)

TONY GOULD

Barnard, Len [Leonard Arthur] (*b* Melbourne, Australia, 23 April 1929). Australian drummer, brother of Bob Barnard. He first played jazz in his family's band, then in 1947 formed his own traditional-jazz ensemble, which recorded from 1949 and made one of the first Australian jazz albums. The group continued to record until 1968, often under the name Len Barnard's Famous Jazz Band; its albums include *The Naked Dance* (1961, Swaggie S1287 [incl. previously released tracks]). Barnard also played with the orchestra of the Palais de Danse in Melbourne (1956–60), and was later a member of the trio led by the pianist Les Patching (1961–70); during this period he recorded with Roger Bell, Frank Johnson, Ade Monsbourgh, and Dave Dallwitz. After moving to Sydney in 1974 he performed and recorded with Judy Bailey, Errol Buddle, and John Sangster. In 1976 he joined the group Galapagos Duck, led by the saxophonist and flutist Tom Hare, with which he toured abroad in 1978–9; he also toured with the group led by his brother Bob (1980, 1983). Barnard's playing is sympathetic, at times witty, and always highly rhythmic; besides drums, he also plays other percussion and keyboards.

BIBLIOGRAPHY

A. Bisset: *Black Roots, White Flowers: a History of Jazz in Australia* (Sydney, 1979)

L. Barnard: "The Len Barnard Story," *Jazz: the Australasian Contemporary Music Magazine*, i (1981), no.1, p.48; no.2, p.48; no.3, p.48; no.4, p.48; no.5, p.6; no.6, p.48; ii/1 (1982), 48

M. Williams: *The Australian Jazz Explosion* (London and elsewhere, 1981), 15

B. Johnson and others: *The Oxford Companion to Australian Jazz* (Melbourne, Australia, 1987)

TONY GOULD

Barnes, Emile [Milé] (*b* New Orleans, 18 Feb 1892; *d* New Orleans, 2 March 1970). Clarinetist, brother of Polo Barnes. He was taught by Lorenzo Tio, Jr., Alphonse Picou, George Baquet, and Big Eye Nelson, and first worked with Buddy Petit. In 1919 he began an association with Chris Kelly that lasted throughout the 1920s. Barnes then joined Wooden Joe Nicholas's Camellia Band, but during the Depression years returned to his trade as a mattress maker. He played with Kid Howard during the late 1940s and from 1951 made a number of recordings as a leader, including an album (untitled) for the American Music label (1951, 641). His style was exciting, rough, bluesy, and full of feeling.

Oral history material in *LNT*.

BIBLIOGRAPHY

A. Ashforth: Liner notes, *Dauphine Street Jam Session* (FW 2857, 1951)

B. Martyn: Liner notes, [untitled album] (Mono 4, 1962)

B. Colyer: Liner notes, *Emile Barnes's New Orleans Band* (Sto. 164, *c*1963)

MARCEL JOLY

Barnes, George (*b* South Chicago Heights, IL, 17 July 1921; *d* Concord, CA, 5 Sept 1977). Electric guitarist. He made his first recordings with the blues singers Big Bill Broonzy, Blind John Davis, and Washboard Sam. He toured the Midwest with his own quartet (1935–7), worked as a staff musician at NBC in Chicago (1937–42), and played with Bud Freeman's band. After serving in the army he was a staff musician at ABC in Chicago (1946–51), then had an extended contract as a guitarist, composer, and arranger with Decca Records in New York. In 1961 he and Carl Kress formed a guitar duo, which toured nationally; Kress died in 1965 and Barnes later played in a duo with Bucky Pizzarelli (1969–72). The following year he formed a quartet with Ruby Braff, which lasted until 1975; during this period he also worked with Joe Venuti and again with Freeman.

Barnes was early influenced by blues musicians (notably Lonnie Johnson), later by Louis Armstrong, Jimmie Noone, and Benny Goodman. He was one of the few guitarists in the 1930s to develop an individual single-string style, and was among the first jazz musicians to play electric guitar (1931) and to record on it (1937). His light-hearted, melodic swing style reflected the influence of Chicago wind players, and his tone had a distinctive edge, which suited his vital, extrovert, and well-articulated improvisations; the sound he produced was partly the result of the instrument he played, which was built to his own design.

SELECTED RECORDINGS

Duos with C. Kress: *Something Tender* (1963, UA 6335)

As leader: with R. Braff: *The Ruby Braff/George Barnes Quartet Plays Gershwin* (1974, Conc. 5); with J. Venuti: *Live at the Concord Summer Festival* (1976, Conc. 30)

BIBLIOGRAPHY

FeatherE; *Feather '60s*; *Feather–Gitler '70s*

B. Yelin: "Jazz Guitar Wouldn't be the Same Without George Barnes," *GP*, ix/2 (1975), 26

E. Townley: "Everything's George," *Sv*, no.80 (1978–9), 60 [incl. discography]

NORMAN MONGAN

Barnes, John [Johnny] (*b* Manchester, England, 15 May 1932). English reed player. He first played flugelhorn and then clarinet, which became his principal instrument. In 1955 he performed and recorded with a traditional jazz band, the Zenith Six, then moved to London. While working part-time with the Delta Jazzmen, a group led by the trumpeter Mike Daniels, he began playing alto saxophone. Later he worked full-time with the trumpeter Alan Elsdon's band (1961–4) and took up baritone saxophone, which thereafter became his main instrument (though he continued to play clarinet and other saxophones). From 1964 to 1978 he performed and made recordings (including the album *Strike One!*, 1966, Strike One 102) with Alex Welsh. During this period he also played flute and soprano saxophone. After leaving Welsh in 1978 he worked as a freelance with the trombonist Roy Williams and others and played in Keith Nichols's Midnite Follies Orchestra; around this time he also took up bass saxophone. He joined Humphrey Lyttelton's band in 1979 and continued to perform with it through the 1980s, making many recordings.

CLARRIE HENLEY

Barnes, Polo [Paul D.] (*b* New Orleans, 22 Nov 1901; *d* New Orleans, 13 April 1981). Clarinetist and soprano and alto saxophonist, brother of Emile Barnes. In 1919, with Lawrence Marrero, he formed the Original Diamond Band. He played with Kid Rena in 1922 and the following year joined Papa Celestin's Tuxedo Jazz Orchestra, with which he made a number of recordings (1925–7), including his own composition *My Josephine*. In 1927 he went to St. Louis to work with King Oliver. After Oliver's band broke up, Barnes performed and recorded with Jelly Roll Morton; his soprano saxophone solo on *Deep Creek Blues* (1928) is particularly splendid. He spent further periods with Oliver (1931, 1934–5) and also led his own band in Lake Charles, Louisiana (1932), before returning to New Orleans. He played in various bands, notably those of Chester Zardis and Kid Howard, and from 1942 to 1945 served in navy bands at Algiers. After five years with Celestin he moved to California and virtually retired from music, but resumed playing with Paul Barbarin's band in New Orleans in 1959. He worked at Disneyland, Anaheim, California, from 1961 to 1964 with the Young Men from New Orleans, and thereafter performed in his home town at Preservation and Dixieland halls. He toured Europe in 1973 and 1974, but illness forced him to retire in 1977. Barnes's playing was never loud or spectacular, but always full of elegance and impeccable taste.

SELECTED RECORDINGS

As leader: *The Viol, the Violet and the Vine* (1960, Icon 5); *Quartets* (1969, 1974, Camelia 12-2); *Portrait of a New Orleans Clarinet Player* (1973, CSA 1010)

As sideman: P. Celestin: Careless Love/Black Rag (1925, OK 8198); My Josephine/Station Calls (1926, Col. 636D); J. R. Morton: Deep Creek (1928, Vic. 38055); Charlie Love: [untitled album] (1959, Sounds of New Orleans 1); K. Thomas: *Sonnets from Algiers* (1960, Icon 3); on P. Bocage and Love–Jiles Ragtime Orchestra: *Peter Bocage* (1961, Riv. 9379), West Indies Blues; Kid Sheik Colar: *Far Across the River* (1966, Dixie 3)

BIBLIOGRAPHY

ChiltonW

G. Mills: Liner notes, *The Viol, the Violet and the Vine* (Icon 5, 1960)

B. Demeusy: "A Jazz Giant is Born," *Fn*, vi/3 (1975), 4

M. MacMurray: "Paul D. 'Polo' Barnes," *SL*, xxxiii/3 (1981), 11

M. Jones: "Giving Some More," *MM*, lvi (9 May 1981), 29

MARCEL JOLY

Barnes, Walter (*b* Vicksburg, MS, 8 July 1905; *d* Natchez, MS, 23 April 1940). Bandleader, clarinetist, and saxophonist. After studying music in Chicago, he formed his own quartet (1926); he later led the Royal Creolians, which held many engagements in Chicago (to 1930) and was also resident at the Savoy Ballroom, New York (1929). In 1928–9 he made several recordings with the band, among them *If you're thinking of me* (1929, Bruns. 4480). It toured the South and Midwest (1930s), where it became very popular, and by 1938 it comprised 16 musicians. In 1939 Barnes re-formed the band for a residency at the Savoy Ballroom, Chicago. While on tour in 1940 he and a number of his sidemen were killed in a fire.

BIBLIOGRAPHY

Obituary, L. Hill, *Pittsburgh Courier* (4 May 1940)

A. McCarthy: "Life and Death of Walter Barnes," *JM*, no.179 (1970), 7

A. McCarthy: *Big Band Jazz* (New York and London, 1974), 29

based on *ChiltonW*

Barnet, Charlie [Charles Daly] (*b* New York, 26 Oct 1913). Saxophonist and bandleader. He was born into a wealthy family, but rebelled in his teens to become a musician. Although he was never a major jazz improviser, he led a very popular dance band during the swing period which was also admired for its jazz playing. Barnet was one of the first white bandleaders to employ Blacks, usually as solo stars, among them Roy Eldridge, Charlie Shavers, Benny Carter, and Frankie Newton (who joined the band as early as 1937). Barnet was especially influenced by the Duke Ellington Orchestra, and played many arrangements which frankly imitated Ellington's. In 1939 his hit recording of Billy May's arrangement of *Cherokee* made him one of the most popular swing bandleaders (*see also* IMPROVISATION, §3). However, with the decline of the big bands in the late 1940s, he was forced to disband his orchestra, which thereafter regrouped only for special occasions. Although at various times he dabbled in music publishing and the restaurant business, Barnet continued to play occasionally into the 1970s.

Oral history material in *NjR* (JOHP).

For further illustration *see* PETTIFORD, OSCAR.

SELECTED RECORDINGS

(recorded for Bluebird unless otherwise indicated)

The Gal from Joe's (1939, 10153); Cherokee (1939, 10373); The Duke's Idea/The Count's Idea (1939, 10453); The Wrong Idea (1939, 10804); The Right Idea (1939, 10530); Shake, Rattle and Roll (Afternoon of a Moax) (1940, 10721); Pompton Turnpike (1940, 10825); The sergeant was shy (1940,

Charlie Barnet's band at the Park Central Hotel, New York, 1944: (front row, left to right) Buddy DeFranco (alto saxophone), Kurt Bloom and Barnet (tenor saxophones), Eddie Bert and Ed Fromm (trombones); (back row) Harold Hahn (drums), Al Killian, Jimmy Pupa, and Lyman Vunk (trumpets)

10862); Redskin Rhumba (1940, 10944); Good-for-nothin' Joe (1941, 11037); Harlem Speaks (1941, 11281); Drop me off at Harlem (1944, Decca 18810); Skyliner (1944, Decca 18659); Portrait of Edward Kennedy Ellington (1949, Cap. 57-60010)

BIBLIOGRAPHY

E. Edwards, Jr., G. Hall, and B. Korst: *Charlie Barnet and his Orchestra* (Whittier, CA, 1965, rev. 2/1970)
J. Burns: "Charlie Barnet," *JM*, no.183 (1970), 9
I. Crosbie: "Clap Hands, Here Comes Charlie," *JJ*, xxvi (1973), no.5, p.10; no.7, p.25
C. Garrod: *Charlie Barnet and his Orchestra* (Spotswood, NJ, and Zephyrhills, FL, 1973, rev. 2/1984) [discography]
C. Barnet and S. Dance: *Those Swinging Years: the Autobiography of Charlie Barnet* (Baton Rouge, LA, and London, 1984) [incl. discography]

JAMES LINCOLN COLLIER

Barnyard effects. A range of instrumental effects current in early jazz in which woodwind or brass instruments emulated animal noises. These are epitomized by the Original Dixieland Jazz Band's recordings of *Barnyard Blues* (*Livery Stable Blues*) (1917).

Barone, Gary (*b* Detroit, 12 Dec 1941). Trumpeter and flugelhorn player, brother of Mike Barone. After graduating from Michigan State University he moved to southern California (1965), where he studied at San Fernando Valley State College (1965–7). He recorded (1965) and performed (1966) with Stan Kenton's Los Angeles Neophonic Orchestra, and worked with Gerald Wilson (1967–9), his brother's band (1967–70), Bud Shank (1968–9), and Shelly Manne (1969–73). Later he worked as a freelance in and around Los Angeles, playing for television, and on film soundtracks with Lalo Schifrin, Dave Grusin, and Tom Scott; he also worked with Frank Zappa (1972), Willie Bobo (1974), and Frank Strazzeri (*c*1975). He led a band with his brother that recorded in 1979.

SELECTED RECORDINGS

As sideman with S. Manne: *Outside* (1969, Cont. 7624); *Alive in London* (1970, Cont. 7629); *Mannekind* (1972, Mstr. 375)

BIBLIOGRAPHY

Feather–Gitler '70s
L. Tomkins: "In Depth: the Shelly Manne Sextet," *CI*, ix/2 (1970), 8 [interviews]

ROBERT DICKOW

Barone, Mike [Michael] (*b* Detroit, 27 Dec 1936). Trombonist, composer, and arranger, brother of Gary Barone. He grew up in Cleveland, and first studied trombone with his father. He also learned guitar and the Schillinger method of composition. After military service, during which he played in army bands, he moved to Los Angeles in 1959. He worked with Si Zentner, Louie Bellson, and Gerald Wilson, and played sessions with Dave Grusin, Tom Scott, and Lalo Schifrin. He led the first big band at Donte's in 1967. Although after the turn of the decade Barone continued to record occasionally, he largely ceased performing and concentrated on composing and arranging. In these capacities he has become extremely well known; he has written and orchestrated music for several television shows and commercials, and composed scores for the Grammy and Academy Award ceremonies. His large-scale orchestral piece Themes and Variations won the first annual Shelly Manne award in 1985.

RECORDED COMPOSITIONS
(selective list)

Recorded by others: Just Messin' Around, on T. Scott: *Rural Still Life* (1967, Imp. 9171); L. Bellson: *Breakthrough* (1968, Project 5029); Spirit of 1976, on E. Richards: *Spirit of 1976* (1969, Imp. 9182)

SELECTED RECORDINGS

As leader of Barone Brothers Band (with G. Barone): *Blues and Other Happy Moments* (1979, PAlt 8004)
As sideman with Victor Burghardt: *Maiden Switzerland* (1976, Dis. 790)

BIBLIOGRAPHY

Feather–Gitler '70s

ROBERT DICKOW

Barrelhouse. A style of piano playing that originated among black American blues musicians in the early 20th century. It was probably first practiced in the makeshift saloons of lumber camps in the South and is related to BOOGIE-WOOGIE, which it may have preceded as a blues piano style (*see* BLUES, §4). Whereas boogie-woogie developed as fast music largely of eight beats to the bar, barrelhouse was played in regular 4/4 meter. Ragtime bass figures or the heavy left-hand vamp known as stomping were often employed with occasional walking bass variations. Elements of barrelhouse were adopted by jazz musicians (*Kentucky Stomp* (Para.12661), recorded in 1928 by Jimmy Blythe's Dixie Four, offers a good example of this) and blended with the New Orleans style to form the hybrid known as BARRELHOUSE JAZZ. Many barrelhouse themes became standards, and were played by blues pianists after other styles had superseded the form. The term "barrelhouse" was also used to mean "rough" or "crude." (E. Kriss: *Barrelhouse and Boogie Piano*, New York, 1974)

PAUL OLIVER

Barrelhouse jazz. An informal, loosely organized style of jazz played by small groups. It developed in cabarets and cafés on the South Side of Chicago during the mid-1920s, and was a blend of New Orleans jazz and barrelhouse piano blues. It is characterized by a free, exuberant atmosphere; the frequent presence of such ad hoc musical instruments as the kazoo and washboard heightens the sense of informality.

The musician most prominent in the development of the style was Jimmy Blythe, who, after making several successful recordings with Jimmy O'Bryant's Washboard Band, led a series of small barrelhouse-jazz groups that were chiefly active in studios; the most important of these was the State Street Ramblers (1927–31). Other bands that adopted the style in the mid- and late 1920s included Junie Cobb's Grains of Corn, King Mutt and his Tennessee Thumpers, the Beale Street Washboard Band, and the Memphis Night Hawks. These ensembles recorded mainly for Gennett, Paramount, and Vocalion.

As the Depression took hold in the early 1930s many record companies rejected the style in favor of a safe, smooth, commercially oriented music. By the time the musicians of the South Side recorded again in the late 1930s their music had changed fundamentally. The influence of country blues on barrelhouse jazz produced a new hybrid, the Chicago blues style of the late 1930s. Many of the best bands of this period (including the State Street Swingers and the Harlem Hamfats) retained much of the barrelhouse-jazz style, but by the end of the decade its importance had declined. Nevertheless elements of the genre survived to be incorporated into Louis Jordan's rhythm-and-blues style of the 1940s.

BIBLIOGRAPHY

C. Hillman: "Paramount Serenaders 1923–1926," *Sv*, no.67 (1976), 8; no.68 (1976), 52; no.69 (1977), 91; no.70 (1977), 149; no.72 (1977), 226; no.73 (1977), 29; no.74 (1977), 67; no.75 (1978), 84 [incl. discography]

J. O'Neal: Liner notes, *Okeh Chicago Blues* (Epic EG37318, 1982)

J. Buzelin and D. Waterhouse: Liner notes, *Chicago Blues* (RCA NL89588, 1985)

C. Hillman and M. Tovey: "Chicago South Side 1927–1932," *Sv*, no.124 (1986), 124; no.125 (1986), 203 [incl. discography]

MICHAEL TOVEY

Barrelhouse Jazzband. German band, formed in 1953 in Frankfurt am Main by the cornetist Horst Dubuque. Its instrumentation was at first typical of a New Orleans band, consisting of a cornet, clarinet, trombone, piano, banjo, tuba, and drums; the band developed a more distinctive sound when its trombone was replaced by an alto saxophone (by 1963) and its tuba by a double bass (in the early 1970s). The band has toured more than 40 countries and performed with such American guest soloists as Albert Nicholas, Sam Wooding, Jimmy McPartland, Dick Cary, Carrie Smith, Buddy Tate, Adelaide Hall, Al Grey, and Sammy Price. After Reimer von Essen assumed leadership of the band in 1962 Dubuque remained a member until 1971. The Barrelhouse Jazzband is the oldest traditional-jazz group in Germany. Its playing displays the influence of all types of New Orleans music (including classic blues, a style that is re-created by the band's singer, Angie Domdey) and of swing; this is well represented by its albums *You're Driving me Crazy* (1976, Bellaphon 19247) and *Barrelhouse Plays Early Swing* (1983, L+R 40020). The band should not be confused with others of the same name from Austria and the Netherlands.

BIBLIOGRAPHY

G. Conrad: "Let's Play Happy Music: Traditional Jazz in Germany Today," *SL*, xxvi (aut. 1974), 5

D. Nentwig: "The Barrelhouse Jazzband," *JF* [intl edn], no.38 (1975), 52

GERHARD CONRAD

Barrett, Sweet Emma (*b* New Orleans, 25 March 1897; *d* New Orleans, 28 Jan 1983). Pianist and singer. She became active musically in the early 1920s, and acquired, probably in the 1950s, the epithet "the bell gal" by wearing red garters with bells that jingled in performance. She played in the Original Tuxedo Orchestra under the leadership of Papa Celestin and the trombonist William "Baba" Ridgley until 1925, then under Ridgley until 1936, and also worked with Sidney Desvigne, John Robichaux, and A. J. Piron. During the 1950s she performed at Happy Landing and after 1961 appeared regularly at Preservation Hall (for illustration *see* HUMPHREY); she also toured abroad leading her Preservation Hall band, and worked in Memphis, in Minneapolis, and at Disneyland. Among her recordings as a leader is the album *Sweet Emma Barrett and her New Orleans Music* (1963, Slnd 241); a good example of her playing may be heard on the track *Breeze*. In 1967 a stroke caused paralysis on her left side, but Barrett continued to perform, using only her right hand, until her death.

BIBLIOGRAPHY

Feather '60s

P. McCauley: "Sweet Emma," *SL*, xiii/3–4 (1962), 13

A. Rose and E. Souchon: *New Orleans Jazz: a Family Album* (Baton Rouge, LA, 1967, rev. 2/1978, rev. and enlarged 3/1984), 11

L. Borenstein and B. Russell: *Preservation Hall Portraits* (Baton Rouge, LA, 1968) [pictures by N. Rockmore]

ALDEN ASHFORTH

Barretto, Ray(mond) (*b* New York, 29 April 1929). Bandleader and conga player of Puerto Rican descent. He first played in jam sessions while serving with the US Army in Germany, and worked with several important jazz musicians on his return to New York. Before forming his own group in 1961 he was a member of Tito Puente's band; he also worked with Herbie Mann and recorded with Cannonball Adderley, Gene Ammons, Red Garland, and Dizzy Gillespie. He issued the Latin-jazz album *Acid* in 1967, and from then on was recognized as a major leader of salsa bands. In the late 1970s he signed a contract with Atlantic Records, for which he recorded the jazz-influenced albums *Eye of the Beholder* (1977) and *Can you Feel it?* (1978). During the 1980s Barretto continued to play salsa concerts in the USA and abroad, and to appear at jazz clubs in New York. Like many older jazz and salsa bandleaders he is notable for his frequent recruitment of young musicians to revitalize the sound of his ensemble.

SELECTED RECORDINGS

As leader: *Acid* (1967, Fania 346); *Eye of the Beholder* (1977, Atl. 19140); *Can you Feel it?* (1978, Atl. 19198); *Aqui se puede* (1987, Fania JM642)

As sideman: R. Garland: *Manteca* (1958, Prst. 7139); G. Ammons: *Blue Gene* (1958, Prst. 7146); D. Gillespie: *Carnegie Hall Concert* (1961, Verve 68423); O. Nelson: *Afro-American Sketches* (1961, Prst. 7225); Jimmy Smith and W. Montgomery: *The Dynamic Duo* (1966, Verve 68678); J. Steig and E. Gomez: *Rain Forest* (1980, CMP 12)

BIBLIOGRAPHY

J. S. Roberts: *The Latin Tinge: the Impact of Latin American Music on the United States* (New York, and Oxford, England, 1979)
S. Id-Deen: "Barretto's Back," *Jazz Spotlite News*, i/5 (1980), 33
J. Brody: "Ray Barretto, King of Salsa," *International Herald Tribune* (11 July 1981), §W, p.8 [interview]

JOHN STORM ROBERTS/R

Barriteau, Carl (*b* Trinidad, 7 Feb 1914). Trinidadian clarinetist. He was brought up in Maracaibo, Venezuela. After learning tenor horn in Trinidad (1926–32) he played clarinet with a police band (1933–6). He moved to London, where he was a principal soloist in Ken "Snake Hips" Johnson's West Indian Swing Band (1937–41), with which he recorded *Tuxedo Junction* (1940, HMV BD5576). He was named "best clarinetist" in *Melody Maker* for seven consecutive years. After Johnson's death in 1941 Barriteau performed as a soloist with several bands before forming his own recording group in 1942; his recordings as a leader include *Ol' man Mose/A Sultan Goes to Harlem* (1944, Decca 8457). He entertained American troops in Europe and North Africa (1958–66) and South-east Asia. In 1970 he moved to Australia and settled in Sydney, where he retired. (C. Hayes: "Carl Barriteau," *Memory Lane*, no.66 (1985), 12)

RAINER E. LOTZ

Barron, Bill [William, Jr.] (*b* Philadelphia, 27 March 1927). Tenor and soprano saxophonist, composer, and teacher, brother of Kenny Barron. He played tenor saxophone in Philadelphia with Red Garland and Jimmy Heath; Dexter Gordon influenced his early style. He moved to New York in 1958, played and in 1959 recorded with Cecil Taylor, recorded with Philly Joe Jones in 1959–60, and formed a group with Ted Curson. While continuing to play in bop groups he directed the Muse Jazz Workshop of the Children's Museum in Brooklyn (1968–74) and taught at City College of New York, CUNY (1974), and at Wesleyan University, where he became chairman of the music department in 1984. Barron's best-known compositions include *Motivation* and *Hold Back Tomorrow*; he received a grant for composition from the NEA.

SELECTED RECORDINGS

As leader: *The Tenor Stylings of Bill Barron* (1961, Savoy 12160); with T. Curson: *The Leopard* (1963, Audiophile 6123); *Variations in Blue* (1984, Muse 5306)

BIBLIOGRAPHY

Feather '60s; *Feather–Gitler '70s*
B. Staples: "Bill Barron and Ted Curson," *DB*, xlvi/18 (1979), 40
B. Rusch: "Bill Barron," *Cadence*, xiii/10 (1987), 11

PAUL RINZLER

Barron, Ed. *See* BERNHARDT, CLYDE

Barron, Kenny [Kenneth] (*b* Philadelphia, 9 June 1943). Pianist, composer, and teacher, brother of Bill Barron. He played piano from the age of 12 and with the help of his brother secured an engagement when he was 15 with a rhythm-and-blues orchestra led by Mel Melvin. He played with Philly Joe Jones (1959) and Jimmy Heath, and in Detroit with Yusef Lateef (1960). In 1961 he moved to New York and began appearing regularly at the Five Spot with James Moody, on whose recommendation he was engaged by Dizzy Gillespie; he toured Europe and North America with Gillespie in 1962–6. He played briefly with Stanley Turrentine and belonged to several groups led by Freddie Hubbard (1967–9); by 1970 his compositions had been recorded by Gillespie, Hubbard, and Moody. He played again with Lateef from 1971 to 1975, except for a period in 1974 during which he belonged to Buddy Rich's sextet. From 1976 into the 1980s he played in a group led by Ron Carter and in the early 1980s was one of the founders of the group SPHERE. He was appointed to the faculty of Rutgers in 1973. Barron is a reliable mainstream pianist, whose style has been influenced chiefly by Tommy Flanagan and Wynton Kelly.

SELECTED RECORDINGS

As unaccompanied soloist: *At the Piano* (1981, Xan. 188)
As leader: *Peruvian Blue* (1974, Muse 5044); *Lucifer* (1975, Muse 5070); *Golden Lotus* (1980, Muse 5220)
As sideman: B. Barron: *The Tenor Stylings of Bill Barron* (1961, Savoy 12160); D. Gillespie: *Charlie Parker Memorial Concert* (1965, Lml. 86017); J. Henderson: *The Kicker* (1967, Mlst. 9008); F. Hubbard: *High Blues Pressure* (1967–8, Atl. 1501); Y. Lateef: *The Gentle Giant* (1971, Atl. 1602); *Ten Years Hence* (1974, Atl. 2-1001); R. Carter: *Piccolo* (1977, Mlst. 55004); S. Fortune: *Serengeti Minstrel* (1977, Atl. 18225)

BIBLIOGRAPHY

N. Tesser: "Kenny Barron: Communicating with his Keys," *DB*, xlii/18 (1975), 17 [incl. discography]
S. Bloom: "Kenny Barron: Pianist's Progress," *DB*, xlvii/6 (1980), 26 [incl. discography]
D. Green: "Spotlight on Kenny Barron," *JSN*, ii/1 (1980), 12

PAUL RINZLER

Barth, Benny (*b* 1929). Drummer, member of the MASTERSOUNDS.

Bartkowski, Czesław [Maly] (*b* Łódź, Poland, 19 April 1943). Polish drummer. He received his first piano lessons at the age of seven, then studied at the Wrocław School of Music (from 1955), where he took up drumming at the age of 15; in 1960 he joined Jerzy Parulski's Far Quartet in Wrocław. After moving to Warsaw in 1963 to play with Zbigniew Namysłowski, he recorded with Krzysztof Komeda (1963, 1964, 1966) and worked briefly with Michal Urbaniak. His career was interrupted by three years' army service but in 1969 he toured New Zealand, Australia, and India with Namysłowski. On his return to Poland Bartkowski became active in jazz-rock, touring with the rock singer Czesław Nieman and in the USA with Urbaniak's group Fusion (1974). He played with Jan Wróblewski and Wojciech Karolak's group Mainstream (1973), with Unit led by Tomasz Stańko and Adam Makowicz (1975), and throughout the 1970s with the orchestra of the Polish Radio Jazz Studio under Wróblewski. In 1981 he was a member of Slawomir Kulpowicz's group In/formation. Bartkowski is one of the busiest and most versatile drummers in Poland. He has performed with the leading Polish jazz musicians and is able to adapt his technique to play in many different styles. He names Elvin Jones and Tony Williams as the principal influences on his playing, which is heard to advantage on *Drums Dream* (1976–7).

SELECTED RECORDINGS

As leader: *Drums Dream* (1976–7, Muza 1419)
As sideman: Z. Namysłowski: *Lola* (1964, Decca SLK4644); R. Kühn: *Solarius* (1964, Amiga 850046); M. Urbaniak: *Super Constellation* (*c*1973, CBS 65744); Z. Namysłowski: *Kujawiak Goes Funky* (1975, Muza 1230)

BIBLIOGRAPHY

Feather–Gitler '70s
J. Byrczek: "Eurojazz Personalities: Poland," *JF* [intl edn], no.17 (1972), 85
P. Brodowski: "Czesław Bartkowski: Drumming a Dream," *JF* [intl edn], no.47 (1977), 54 [incl. discography]

WOLFRAM KNAUER

Barton, Billy [William] (*b* USA, *c*1890; *d* ? USA, after 1933). Alto and tenor saxophonist, clarinetist, and singer. His first known engagements were in China (1920) and Australia. After moving to England in 1925 he played in Bert Ralton's Savoy Havana Band and recorded with Bert Firman (1925–6). He toured South Africa with Ralton (1926) and led the band after Ralton's death in 1927. He returned to England and recorded again with Firman before moving to Germany in 1928 where he played and made recordings as a leader (including *Trumbology*, 1929, Orchestrola 2250), with his own studio dance band (1930–31), and with the bands of Ben Berlin, Julian Fuhs, Harry Jackson, Marek Weber, and Theo Mackeben; on his numerous recordings he is occasionally heard playing hot solos. He toured Germany and Switzerland (1932–3) and probably then returned to the USA.

RAINER E. LOTZ

Bartz, Gary (Lee) (*b* Baltimore, MD, 26 Sept 1940). Alto and soprano saxophonist. He learned soprano saxophone from the age of 11, and played as a teenager at his father's jazz club in Baltimore, the North End Lounge. While attending the Juilliard School in New York for two years, he was influenced by such players as Grachan Moncur III and Lee Morgan. After further study in Baltimore, he began his professional career with Max Roach and Abbey Lincoln in 1964, and then played in Art Blakey's Jazz Messengers (1965–6). He formed his own group, the Ntu Troop, in 1967; in the following years he also worked with Blue Mitchell, recorded with both Roach and Charles Tolliver (1968), and played with McCoy Tyner (recording with him intermittently, 1968–76). He joined Miles Davis in August 1970 and remained with him until the end of 1971, while also making albums as a leader (1970) and with Woody Shaw (1970). Thereafter he recorded primarily under his own name. In 1973 he toured Europe, recording in Copenhagen with Lee Konitz and with Jackie McLean, and made a children's album, *Singerella*. He also composed scores for television. Bartz's early work was marked by a full, raw sound, together with advanced ideas and political consciousness. From the late 1970s onwards his style tended to be blander and more oriented towards popular taste, although in 1981 he recorded fine bop solos as a guest artist with Shaw's group on the album *United*.

SELECTED RECORDINGS

As leader: *Harlem Bush Music: Taifa* (1970, Mlst. 9031); *Singerella: a Ghetto Fairy Tale* (1973, Prst. 10083); with J. McLean: *Ode to Super* (1973, Ste. 1009); *Music is my Sanctuary* (1975, Cap. ST11647)

As sideman: C. Tolliver: *Paper Man* (1968, Ari. 1002); M. Davis: *Live–Evil* (1970, Col. G30954); W. Shaw: *Blackstone Legacy* (1970, Cont. 7627–8); on Shaw: *United* (1981, Col. FC37390), What is this thing called Love?, Blues for Wood

BIBLIOGRAPHY

Feather–Gitler '70s

H. Nolan: "Music is my Religion!," *DB*, xl/12 (1973), 14

D. C. Hunt: "Gary Bartz," *Black Giants*, ed. P. Rivelli and R. Levin (New York and Cleveland, 1970/*R*1980 as *Giants of Black Music*) [colln of previously pubd articles], 80

R. Rusch: "Gary Bartz: Interview," *Cadence*, x/2 (1984), 5

DAVID WILD

Bary. Jazz argot for the baritone saxophone (*see* SAXOPHONE).

Barzizza, Pippo (*b* Genoa, Italy, 15 May 1902). Italian violinist, pianist, bandleader, arranger, and composer. In Genoa he studied violin and composition and played banjo for a brief period in an orchestra. He was the leader and an arranger for the group Blue Star (to 1931), of which Sid Phillips was a member, and the orchestra Cetra (from 1936), which from 1937 to 1943 performed on radio and made recordings. His leadership of the orchestra was interrupted by World War II, then resumed from 1946 to 1949. Barzizza was among the first musicians in Italy to play jazz; his work may be heard to advantage on his recording *Glad Rag Doll* (1929, Fonotecnica 2248). Among his compositions are *Sera* (1939) and *La canzone del Boscaiolo* (1945).

ADRIANO MAZZOLETTI

Bas, Vlady [Vladimiro] (*b* Bilbao, Spain, 2 Feb 1929). Spanish alto saxophonist, clarinetist, and flutist. He studied at the conservatory in Bilbao, then worked as a jazz critic for radio broadcasts. In 1952 he moved to Madrid, where he played with Joe Farreras. During the mid-1950s he toured Switzerland and the Middle East with a commercially oriented band until he was selected to play with Marshall Brown's International Youth Band at the Newport Jazz Festival (1958). Thereafter he played informally with Lee Konitz, Oscar Pettiford, and Paul Desmond, and began performing at clubs in Madrid in 1962. He has made three albums as a leader, including *Free jazz en la universidad* (1973, Accion 30022). Bas's work is influenced by that of Konitz, Desmond, Johnny Hodges, and Phil Woods.

ALFREDO PAPO

Bascomb, Dud [Wilbur Odell] (*b* Birmingham, AL, 16 May 1916; *d* New York, 25 Dec 1972). Trumpeter, brother of Paul Bascomb. While still in high school he joined the Alabama State Teachers College band, the 'Bama State Collegians, remaining a member after the group became known as the Erskine Hawkins Orchestra. From 1944 to 1947 he was leader, with his brother Paul, of a sextet and then a big band. He worked for Duke Ellington briefly in 1947, and thereafter led groups of his own, though from the 1960s he was also active as a studio and theater musician. He made three tours of Japan with Sam "the Man" Taylor and in 1968 visited Europe with Buddy Tate.

Although he was a great admirer of Louis Armstrong, Bascomb developed an original style that was based on sophisticated harmonic development. He was adept in the use of muting techniques and was widely admired by players of all schools for his improvisational abilities, heard to good effect on the recordings he made with Hawkins. He also composed *Country Boy*, recorded by Hawkins in 1942.

SELECTED RECORDINGS

As leader: Indiana (1946, Alert 201)

As sideman with E. Hawkins: Who's sorry now? (1938, Voc. 4072); Weary Blues (1938, Bb 7839); Swing Out (1939, Bb 10224); Gin Mill Special/ Tuxedo Junction (1939, Bb 10409); Country Boy (1942, Bb 300819); *Reunion!* (1971, Stang 1014), incl. Tuxedo Junction

BIBLIOGRAPHY

ChiltonW

S. Dance: *The World of Swing* (New York, 1974) [colln of previously pubd interviews], 192

FRANK DRIGGS

Bascomb, Paul (*b* Birmingham, AL, 12 Feb 1912; *d* Chicago, 2 Dec 1986). Tenor saxophonist, brother of Dud Bascomb. He won a scholarship to Alabama State Teachers College, where he helped to found the school's first dance orchestra, the 'Bama State Collegians; he also toured during the summer months with Jean Calloway, the Seals and Mitchell stock company, and C.S. Belton's Society Syncopators. The Collegians became known as the Erskine Hawkins Orchestra in the mid-1930s, and, apart from a few months in 1938–9, Bascomb remained a regular player in the group until 1944. After leading a sextet and then a big band with his brother Dud (1944–7), Bascomb headed his own groups, and during the 1950s and 1960s held long residencies in New York at Smalls' Paradise, in Detroit at the El Sino, and in Chicago at Robert's Show Lounge and the Esquire. He appeared at the Grande Parade du Jazz Nice in 1978, and continued playing into the mid-1980s.

SELECTED RECORDINGS

As leader: Nona (1946, Alert 205)

As sideman with E. Hawkins: Sweet Georgia Brown (1940, Bb 10854); Norfolk Ferry (1940, Bb 10932)

BIBLIOGRAPHY

ChiltonW

E. Townley: "The Man from Birmingham," *Sv*, no.84 (1979), 210

Obituary, J. Simmen, *BHcF*, no.351 (1987), 18

FRANK DRIGGS

Basie, Count [Bill; William] (*b* Red Bank, NJ, 21 Aug 1904; *d* Hollywood, CA, 26 April 1984). Bandleader and pianist. He was a leading figure of the swing era in jazz and, alongside Duke Ellington, an outstanding representative of big-band style.

1. Life. 2. Ensemble style. 3. Solo style.

1. Life. After studying piano with his mother, as a young man he went to New York, where he met James P. Johnson, Fats Waller (with whom he studied informally), and other pianists of the Harlem stride school. Before he was 20 he toured extensively on the Keith and TOBA vaudeville circuits as a solo pianist, accompanist, and music director for blues singers, dancers, and comedians, an early training that was to prove significant in his later career. Stranded in Kansas City in 1927 while accompanying a touring group, he remained there, playing in silent-film theaters. In July 1928 he joined Walter Page's Blue Devils which, in addition to Page, included Jimmy Rushing; both later figured prominently in Basie's own band. Basie left the Blue Devils early in 1929 to play with two lesser-known bands in the area; later that year he joined Bennie Moten's Kansas City Orchestra, as did the other key members of the Blue Devils shortly after. When Moten died suddenly in 1935 the band continued under Buster Moten, but Basie left soon thereafter. The same year, with Buster Smith and several other former members of Moten's orchestra, Basie organized a new, smaller group of nine musicians, which included Jo Jones and later Lester Young; as the Barons of Rhythm it began a long engagement at the Reno Club in Kansas City. The group's radio broadcasts led in 1936 to contracts with a national booking agency and the Decca Record Company; it expanded and within a year the Count Basie Orchestra, as it had become known, was one of the leading big bands of the swing era (see illustration). By the end of the 1930s the band had acquired international fame with such pieces as *One o'Clock Jump* (1937), *Jumpin' at the Woodside* (1938) and *Taxi War Dance* (1939), but gradual recourse to written arrangements began to lead it towards stylization and conformity, and to subdue its personality to the personalities of its arrangers.

In 1950 financial considerations forced Basie to disband, and for the next two years he led a six- to nine-piece group; among

Count Basie's orchestra at the Famous Door, New York, July 1938: (back row, left to right) Jo Jones (drums), Benny Morton and Dicky Wells (trombones); (middle row) Freddie Green (guitar), Buck Clayton, Ed Lewis, and Harry Edison (trumpets); (front row) Walter Page (double bass), Herschel Evans, Earle Warren, Jack Washington, and Lester Young (saxophones); (foreground) Basie (piano)

its sidemen were Clark Terry, Buddy DeFranco, Serge Chaloff, and Buddy Rich. After reorganizing a big band in 1952 he undertook a long series of tours and recording sessions that eventually led to his becoming an elder statesman of jazz, while his band was established as a permanent jazz institution and training ground for young musicians. He made the first of many tours of Europe in 1954, visited Japan in 1963, and issued a large number of recordings both under his own name and under the leadership of various singers, most notably Frank Sinatra. In the mid-1970s a serious illness hampered his career, and in the 1980s he sometimes had to perform from a wheelchair; he devoted time increasingly to his autobiography. After Basie's death the band continued under the direction of Thad Jones (1985–6) and Frank Foster (from 1986); as the COUNTSMEN, a number of his former sidemen have also reconvened occasionally for concerts and tours.

2. ENSEMBLE STYLE. Like all bands in the Kansas City tradition, the Count Basie Orchestra was organized about its rhythm section, which supported the interplay of brass and reeds and served as a backdrop for the unfolding of solos. Using an elliptical style of melodic leads and cues, Basie was able to control his band firmly from the keyboard while blending perfectly with his rhythm section. This celebrated group (for illustration *see* JONES, JO), consisting of Basie, Page, Jones, and, from 1937, Freddie Green, altered the ideal of jazz accompaniment, making it more supple and responsive to the wind instruments and helping to establish four-beat jazz (with four almost identically stressed beats to a bar) as the norm for jazz performance. Of particularly far-reaching significance was Jones's technique of placing the constant pulse in the hi-hat cymbal instead of the bass drum, thereby immeasurably lightening the timbre of jazz drumming. Another important factor was the accuracy and solidity of Page's walking bass technique, which obviated the need for left-hand patterns in the piano and imparted a buoyant swing to the ensemble. To attain its unique timbre and swing, Basie's rhythm section practiced for hours independently of the rest of the band. It was supreme in its day, and its innovations served as models for the even more spare and flexible rhythm sections of the bop school.

During the band's heyday in the late 1930s Basie preferred light, readily expandable arrangements which are particularly notable for their use of riffs, a legacy of the Moten band and of Southwest ensemble jazz generally. Ex.1 shows a typical riff pattern (another may be found in RIFF, ex.1), which might

Ex.1 Riff from *Shout and Feel It* (air-shot recording, first issued on *Shout and Feel It*, 1937, Alamac 2412); transcr. J. B. Robinson

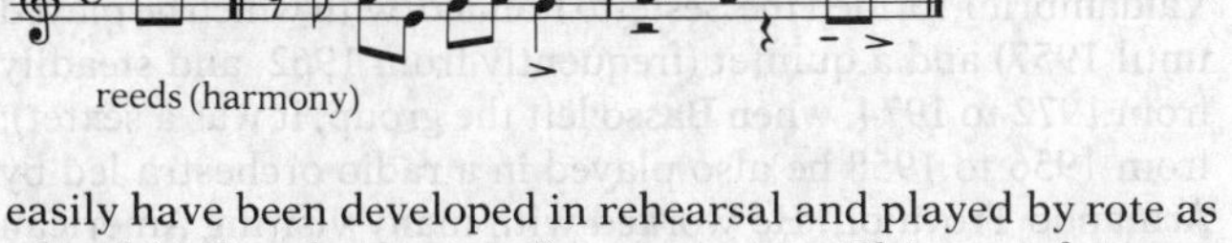

easily have been developed in rehearsal and played by rote as a head (rather than notated) arrangement. This sort of ensemble accompaniment, which contrasts with the more elaborate group writing of Duke Ellington, Don Redman, and Sy Oliver, gave full freedom to Basie's outstanding soloists. These included Harry Edison, Buck Clayton, Dicky Wells, Benny Morton, Helen Humes, Jimmy Rushing, and two excellent tenor saxophonists, Herschel Evans and Lester Young, whose widely differing styles and artistic personalities gave added breadth and tension to the group's performances. All of these soloists are prominently featured on the band's recordings between 1937 and 1941 for Decca and Vocalion, which represent some of the finest recorded jazz of the period (Evans, who died in 1939, plays only on the Decca sides). Basie also issued small-group recordings with his band's rhythm section and soloists (notably Young), which are masterpieces of their kind.

In his bands of the 1950s and 1960s Basie retained his swing-style rhythm section but chose soloists with more modern leanings, particularly Thad Jones, Eddie "Lockjaw" Davis, Frank Foster, Marshall Royal, and Frank Wess. Although the band's sound tended to change with its current arrangers (most notably Neal Hefti, Benny Carter, Quincy Jones, and Thad Jones), it was unequaled for its relaxed precision and control of dynamics. Basie's later bands, though musically less satisfying, never lost their large popular following. In the end, the Count Basie Orchestra proved the most long-lived and enduring in jazz.

3. SOLO STYLE. Basie's eminence as a bandleader tended to overshadow his considerable achievements as a jazz pianist. Early recordings with Moten, such as the introduction to *Moten Swing* (1932), reveal his mastery of the ragtime and stride idioms. By the mid-1930s, however, Basie had adopted a highly personal, laconic, blues-oriented style, compounded of short melodic phrases – often nothing more than jazz clichés – expertly placed and accented with wit and ingenuity. These seemingly fragmentary and disjoint solos, of which ex.2 is typical, were

Ex.2 Solo from *One o'Clock Jump* (air-shot recording, first issued on *Shout and Feel It*, 1937, Alamac 2412); transcr. J. B. Robinson

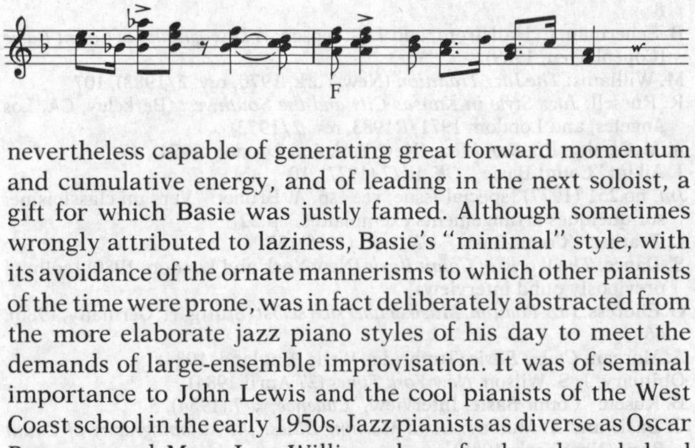

nevertheless capable of generating great forward momentum and cumulative energy, and of leading in the next soloist, a gift for which Basie was justly famed. Although sometimes wrongly attributed to laziness, Basie's "minimal" style, with its avoidance of the ornate mannerisms to which other pianists of the time were prone, was in fact deliberately abstracted from the more elaborate jazz piano styles of his day to meet the demands of large-ensemble improvisation. It was of seminal importance to John Lewis and the cool pianists of the West Coast school in the early 1950s. Jazz pianists as diverse as Oscar Peterson and Mary Lou Williams have freely acknowledged their debt to Basie. A volume of transcriptions of his performances has been published by B. Harding (*Count Basie's Boogie Woogie Styles*, New York, 1944).

Basie also worked as a theater organist in New York and made a few recordings on pipe organ (*see* ORGAN, §1).

Oral history material in *MoKmh* and *NjR* (JOHP).

See also ARRANGEMENT, §3 and Table 3; BLUES, §6; JAZZ (i), §IV, 3; and PIANO, §3; for further illustration *see* FILMS, fig.3.

SELECTED RECORDINGS

SWING PERIOD

(big band; recorded for Decca unless otherwise stated)

Swinging at the Daisy Chain (1937, 1121); One o'Clock Jump (1937, 1363); Good Morning Blues (1937, 1446); Sent for you yesterday and here you come today (1938, 1880); Every Tub (1938, 1728); Doggin' Around (1938, 1965); Jumpin' at the Woodside (1938, 2212); Shorty George (1938, 2325); Jive at Five (1939, 2922); Oh! Lady be Good (1939, 2631); Rock-a-bye Basie (1939, Voc. 4747)

Taxi War Dance (1939, Voc. 4748); Miss Thing (1939, Voc. 4860); Clap hands, here comes Charlie (1939, Voc. 5085); Ham 'n' Eggs (1939, Col. 35357); Tickle-toe (1940, Col. 35521); Gone with "What" Wind (1940, OK 5629); The World is Mad (1940, OK 5816); Stampede in G Minor (1940, OK 5987); Diggin' for Dex (1941, OK 6365); The King/Blue Skies (1945, Col. 37070)

(small group)

Shoe Shine Boy (1936, Voc. 3441); Oh! Lady Be Good (1936, Voc. 3459); Oh! Red/Fare thee, honey, fare thee well (1939, Decca 2780); Dickie's Dream/ Lester leaps in (1939, Voc. 5118)

LATER BANDS

Dance Session (1952-4, Clef 626, 647); *Count Basie Swings and Joe Williams Sings* (1955, Clef 678); *April in Paris* (1955–6, Verve 8012); *Basie Plays Hefti* (1958, Roul. 52011); *Chairman of the Board* (1959, Roul. 52032); *The Count Basie Story* (1960, Roul. RB1); *The Legend* (1961, Roul. 52086); *Basie at Birdland* (1961, Roul. 52065); *L'il Ol' Groovemaker* (1963, Verve 68549); *Basie Jam* (1973, Pablo 2310718); *On the Road* (1979, Pablo 2312112)

BIBLIOGRAPHY

W. Basie: *Blues by Basie* (New York, 1943)
H. Panassié: "Count Basie en Europe," *BHcF*, no.36 (1954), 3
J. Hammond: "Count Basie Marks 20th Anniversary," *DB*, xxii/22 (1955), 11; repr. in *Eddie Condon's Treasury of Jazz*, ed. E. Condon and R. Gehman (New York, 1956/*R*1975), 250
N. Shapiro and N. Hentoff, eds.: *Hear me Talkin' to ya: the Story of Jazz by the Men who Made it* (New York, 1955/*R*1966), 257
S. Dance: "The Conquering Count," *JJ*, x/12 (1957), 7
R. Horricks: *Count Basie and his Orchestra: its Music and its Musicians* (London and New York, 1957)
H. Panassié: "Reminiscing about the Count," *JJ*, x/4 (1957), 15
N. Shapiro: "William 'Count' Basie," *The Jazz Makers: Essays on the Greats of Jazz*, ed. N. Shapiro and N. Hentoff (New York, 1957/*R*1979), 232
E. Towler: "Vintage Basie," *JM*, iii/6 (1957), 2
A. Hodeir: "Du côté de chez Basie," *JR*, i/2 (1958), 6
N. Hentoff: *The Jazz Life* (New York and London, 1961/*R*1975) [incl. previously pubd articles], 143
B. Schiozzi: *Count Basie* (Milan, 1961)
A. Hodeir: *Toward Jazz* (New York, 1962/*R*1976), 97
D. Gelly: "The Count Basie Octet," *JM*, ix/5 (1963), 9
G. E. Lambert: "Count Basie: the Middle Years," *JM*, ix/7 (1963), 4
H. W. Shih: "Portrait of the Count," *DB*, xxxii/9 (1965), 23
A. Morgan: "Collector's Notes: Count Basie," *JM*, no.161 (1968), 15
J. Burns: "Lesser Known Bands of the '40s: Count Basie," *JM*, no.171 (1969), 8
B. Scherman, C. Hallstrom, and J. G. Jepsen: *A Discography of Count Basie* (Copenhagen, 1969)
M. Williams: *The Jazz Tradition* (New York, 1970, rev. 2/1983), 107
R. Russell: *Jazz Style in Kansas City and the Southwest* (Berkeley, CA, Los Angeles, and London, 1971/*R*1983, rev. 2/1973)
A. McCarthy: *Big Band Jazz* (New York and London, 1974), 47
J. Aikin: "Count Basie," *CK*, iii/7 (1977), 10
Jm, no.251 (1977) [special issue; see esp. A. Brunet: "Vers un classicisme: sur quelques arrangements exemplaires," p.22]
L. Feather: "Count Basie," *CK*, iv/3 (1978), 55
S. Dance: *The World of Count Basie* (New York and London, 1980) [colln of previously pubd interviews]
G. Endress: *Jazz Podium: Musiker über sich selbst* (Stuttgart, Germany, 1980), 46
A. Morgan: *Count Basie* (Tunbridge Wells, England, 1984)
Obituary, J. S. Wilson, *New York Times* (27 April 1984)
B. Rusch: "Count Basie: Interview," *Cadence*, x/7 (1984), 5
C. Basie and A. Murray: *Good Morning Blues: the Autobiography of Count Basie* (New York, 1985)
B. Clayton and N. M. Elliott: *Buck Clayton's Jazz World* (London, 1986)
C. Sheridan: *Count Basie: a Bio-discography* (Westport, CT, and London, 1986)

J. BRADFORD ROBINSON

Basin Street. A street in New Orleans, from which several nightclubs have derived their names; *see* NIGHTCLUBS AND OTHER VENUES.

Bass. The lowest part of the musical system (distinguished, specifically, from the treble); that part in a musical work executed by the performers playing the instruments of the lowest range, or having the lowest voices; the lowest pitch in a chord and hence the succession of lowest notes in a passage or composition ("bass line," *see* WALKING BASS); those notes that support the other parts and which are regarded as determining the harmonic identity of sonorities and thus of harmonic progressions, cadences, modulations, etc. (*see* HARMONY(i)); the instrument having the lowest range in a family of instruments (for example, bass saxophone, bass drum, bass clarinet; *see* SAXOPHONE, DRUM SET, CLARINET); the lowest segment of the range of an instrument ("bass register"). In jazz argot the word is used in particular for the DOUBLE BASS, or ELECTRIC BASS GUITAR (often also "electric bass"), or both (as when "bass player" denotes a musician who changes between the two instruments according to the style in which he is playing), and less often to mean the bass saxophone; the term "brass bass" is used of the TUBA, to distinguish it from the "string bass" (or double bass). "Bass" may also occasionally mean the player of one of these instruments. For the role of the bass player in marking the beat in jazz *see* BEAT, §4(ii).

Bass clarinet. The bass member of the clarinet family, normally pitched in B♭; *see* CLARINET, §§1 and 4.

Bass Clef. Nightclub in London; *see* NIGHTCLUBS AND OTHER VENUES.

Bass drum. The largest of the drums in the drum set; it is played with a foot pedal and often used to mark each beat of the bar (*see* DRUM SET, §§I, 2; II, 1, 4, 6, 8). In a BRASS BAND it is strapped to the player's chest and played with a beater held in the right hand.

Bass flute. The lowest member of the flute family, sounding an octave below the soprano instrument; *see* FLUTE, §§1 and 5.

Bass guitar. *See* ELECTRIC BASS GUITAR.

Basso, Gianni (*b* Asti, Italy, 24 May 1931). Italian clarinetist and soprano and tenor saxophonist. He studied clarinet at the conservatory in Asti, then accompanied American musicians in Belgium and Germany (1946–50). Having returned to Italy he played in dance orchestras led by Kramer Gorni, Beppe Mojetta, and Angelo Brigada. In 1955 he was a member of a quartet led by Gil Cuppini, and in the same year, with Oscar Valdambrini, formed the Sestetto Italiano (with which he played until 1957) and a quintet (frequently from 1962, and steadily from 1972 to 1974, when Basso left the group, it was a sextet); from 1956 to 1958 he also played in a radio orchestra led by Armando Trovajoli. He worked with many visiting American musicians and recorded with Chet Baker (1959), Buddy Collette (1961), Slide Hampton (1972), and Maynard Ferguson (1972). Later he belonged to the band Saxes Machine and in 1980 toured Denmark. Basso was influenced early in his career by Stan Getz and West Coast jazz, but after hearing Sonny Rollins he modeled his style on that of certain black-American saxophonists, and gradually developed the impetuosity and freshness for which he is known; his playing also displays some characteristics of free jazz.

SELECTED RECORDINGS

As leader: *Hit* (1975, Carosello 21016)
As leader with O. Valdambrini: *Basso–Valdambrini Quintet* (1959, Music 2079); *Bossa Nova!* (1962, Ricordi 8006); *Jazz* (1967, Cetra 5A)

BIBLIOGRAPHY

FeatherE; *Feather–Gitler '70s*

ADRIANO MAZZOLETTI

Bassoon. A double-reed woodwind instrument with a conical bore that doubles back on itself. It has a wide compass (usually *B♭'* to *e''*) and its tone-color ranges from richly sonorous at the bottom to expressively plaintive at the top. A larger version of the instrument, known as the double bassoon or contrabassoon, sounds an octave lower.

The bassoon is quite rare in jazz. It first appeared during the 1920s, largely through the influence of symphonic jazz; the arrangement of *Sweet Sue* recorded by Paul Whiteman's group in 1928 (Col. 50103D), for example, has a written bassoon part. The saxophonist Frankie Trumbauer played bassoon in Whiteman's band (though Red Mayer, also a saxophonist who doubled on bassoon, was probably the soloist) and on Joe Venuti's recording of *Runnin' Ragged (Bamboozlin' the Bassoon)* (1929, OK 41361). Garvin Bushell, primarily a clarinetist and saxophonist, has the remarkable distinction of having played bassoon on an unusual session with Fats Waller under the group name Louisiana Sugar Babes (1928, including *Sippi*, Vic. 21348) and more than 30 years later double bassoon with John Coltrane (on the track *India* from *The Other Village Vanguard Tapes*, 1961, Imp. 9325).

Use of the bassoon was still rarer between 1930 and the 1950s, when it was taken up again by members of the West Coast jazz and cool-jazz movements, for example, Errol Buddle in the Australian Jazz Quartet and Quintet (he may be heard on the quintet's album *At the Varsity Drag*, 1956, Beth. 6012) and Bob Cooper. One of the first musicians to open jazz to the influence of non-Western traditions, which led to the cultivation from the 1960s onwards of "world music," was Yusef Lateef, who often included in his ensemble ethnic instruments and others not normally associated with jazz, among them the bassoon; Josea Taylor is the bassoonist on Lateef's *The Centaur and the Phoenix* (1960, Riv. 9337) and Lateef himself played the instrument on the album *Jazz Round the World* (1963, Imp. 56). In the later 1960s notable jazz bassoon solos were recorded by Karl Porter (with Hubert Laws and Chick Corea on *Laws' Cause*, 1968, Atl. 1509) and Daniel Jones (with Roland Kirk on *Left and Right*, 1968, Atl. 1518). In the 1960s and 1970s the saxophonist Illinois Jacquet played bassoon in a blues idiom, with a rich, deep sound and fine dexterity, for example on the track *'Round Midnight* from *The Blues: that's me!* (1969, Prst. 7731). Another saxophonist, Frank Tiberi, who joined Woody Herman in 1969, has made a mark particularly as a bassoonist; he played with the band at the Monterey Jazz Festival in 1979 in a performance that was recorded and issued as *Woody and Friends* (Conc. 170). Among the few musicians to play bassoon exclusively is the free-jazz player Karen Borca, known primarily for her work with Jimmy Lyons, notably on *Wee Sneezawee* (1983, BS 0067).

For illustration *see* LATEEF, YUSEF.

BIBLIOGRAPHY

W. Jansen: *The Bassoon: its History, Construction, Makers, Players, and Music* (Buren, Netherlands, 1984)
W. Waterhouse: "Bassoon," *GroveI*

LEWIS PORTER

Bass saxophone. The bass instrument of the saxophone family, pitched in B♭, with a compass of *A♭'–e♭'*; *see* SAXOPHONE, §6.

Bass trumpet. The bass member of the trumpet family, usually pitched in B♭; *see* TRUMPET, §1.

Bates. Family of musicians.

(1) Bob [Robert] **Bates** (*b* Pocatello, ID, 1 Sept 1923; *d* San Francisco, 13 Sept 1981). Double bass player. He played tuba and other brass instruments during his school years before receiving classical training on double bass in New York and San Francisco (1944–8). Later he taught his brothers (2) Norman and (3) Jim Bates. His early commercial work included recordings in 1946 with Sonny Dunham. He began playing with Dave Brubeck's quartet in 1953 and first recorded with the group the following year; good examples of his playing are the walking-bass solos on *Why do I love you* and *Stompin' for Mili* and the ensemble passages on *A Fine Romance* and *Brother can you spare a dime*, all on the album *Brubeck Time* (1954, Col. CL622). Bates recorded with Dave Pell in 1956, then ceased to be active as a jazz musician. (*FeatherE*)

(2) Norman (Louis) Bates (*b* Boise, ID, 26 Aug 1927). Double bass player. He was taught by his brother (1) Bob Bates. After playing in the big bands of Jimmy Dorsey (1945–6) and Raymond Scott he worked in Dave Brubeck's early trio (1948). In 1950 he recorded with Jack Sheedy's Dixieland Jazz Band, with which he also occasionally played piano. He spent four years in the army, then performed and recorded with Wally Rose's Dixieland Band (1955) before succeeding his brother Bob in Brubeck's quartet. Some fine examples of his playing are his solos on *Bru's Blues* and *St. Louis Blues* and his walking-bass lines on *One Moment Worth Years*, all on the album *Jazz Goes to Junior College* (1957, Col. CL1034). Bates left Brubeck in 1958 and thereafter led his own trio in San Francisco. (*FeatherE*)

(3) Jim [James Bernard] **Bates** (*b* Boise, ID, 16 Nov 1930). Double bass player. He was taught by his brothers (1) Bob and (2) Norman Bates. He worked with jazz and commercial bands in San Francisco and Los Angeles and recorded with the vibraphone player Julius Wechter in 1957 (*Linear Sketches*, Jazz West 9).

LAWRENCE KOCH

Bates, Django (Leon) (*b* Beckenham, England, 2 Oct 1960). English pianist, electronic keyboard player, and composer. After studying at Kingsway College, London, he worked for a diploma as an external student at the London College of Music. He led a trio (1979–81) and then the band Humans (1981–4), from which he formed the duo Human Chain with the drummer Steve Arguelles in 1985; he expanded this to a trio, incorporating Stuart Hall (guitars, double bass, and violin), in 1987. Bates has also played as a sideman with Dudu Pukwana and Harry Beckett (1983–5) and the saxophonist Ken Stubbs (from 1984), and performed with LOOSE TUBES (from 1984) and Bill Bruford's jazz-rock group Earthworks (from 1986). His principal compositions include *Yellow Hill* (1982), *Eden Express* (1983), *Rowing Boat Delineation Egg* (1984), *Säd Afrika* (1985), *Delightful Precipice* (1985), and *Ikebana* (1986). The album *Delightful Precipice* (1986, Loose Tubes 003) provides a good example of his playing. Bates's contributions to Loose Tubes, as both composer and player, have been the most important and widely publicized part of his work. Besides his principal instruments he also plays the tenor horn. (R. Cook: "Django Bates: the Brilliant Spark," *The Wire*, no.32 (1986), 27)

DIGBY FAIRWEATHER

Batiste, Alvin (*b* New Orleans, *c*1937). Clarinetist. While in high school he played with Ed Blackwell, then, after army service, he began a lengthy association with Ornette Coleman, playing in jam sessions with him in Los Angeles (1956). He worked as a freelance musician in New Orleans and around 1958 toured in Ray Charles's band. From 1969 to the mid-1980s he directed a jazz course at Southern University, Baton Rouge, Louisiana. Towards the beginning of this period he started to record an album with Cannonball Adderley but his teaching commitments prevented him from completing it; he later took part in Adderley's final album, *Lovers* (1975, Fan. 9505). He appeared at the Montreux International Jazz Festival with Billy Cobham, with whom he also recorded, and played and recorded as a member of John Carter's quartet Clarinet Summit (from 1981). His work as a jazz composer, leader, and performer is well represented by *Musique d'Afrique Nouvelle Orléans* (1985, IndN 1064); he has also written music for the New Orleans Philharmonic SO.

BIBLIOGRAPHY

V. Wilmer: "Alvin Batiste and Ellis Marsalis," *Coda*, no.173 (1980), 8
L. Birnbaum: "Alvin Batiste," *DB*, xlix/10 (1982), 54
D. Fairweather: "Batiste, Alvin," in I. Carr, D. Fairweather, and B. Priestley: *Jazz: the Essential Companion* (London, 1987)

Batman. Nickname of TONY ORTEGA.

Battle, Puddinghead [Edgar William] (*b* Atlanta, 3 Oct 1907; *d* New York 6 Feb 1977). Trumpeter, arranger, and composer. He began playing trumpet at the age of eight. While studying at Morris Brown College he formed the Dixie Serenaders, and he later led the Dixie Ramblers in Atlanta, as well as playing with other leaders. He worked with Andy Kirk (1930), Blanche Calloway (1931), his own band (1933), Sam Wooding and Benny Carter (1934), and Alex Hill (1934); with Willie Bryant (1935–6) he played trumpet, valve trombone, and alto saxophone. In 1936 Battle performed on radio broadcasts of the revue *George White's Scandals*. He led his own band in 1937, but then stopped playing to devote himself to composition and writing arrangements. He wrote pieces for Cab Calloway, Paul Whiteman, Fats Waller, Earl Hines, Count Basie, Jack Teagarden, and Louis Prima, among others; his compositions include *Ratamacue* and *Topsy* (written with Eddie Durham, and recorded by Earl Hines as *Topsy-Turvy*), of which he made arrangements for Calloway and Hines respectively. He led big bands in the 1940s and again in the 1960s; in the 1950s he formed the Cosmopolitan Record Company.

SELECTED RECORDINGS

As sideman: A. Kirk: I lost my gal from Memphis (1930, Bruns. 4803); B. Calloway: Casey Jones Blues (1931, Vic. 22640); W. Bryant: Throwin' Stones at the Sun (1935, Vic. 24847)

RECORDED COMPOSITIONS

(selective list)

* – with Battle as singer

Recorded by A. Kirk: Puddin' Head Serenade (1936, Decca 1208)
Recorded by C. Calloway: Ratamacue (1939, Voc. 4700); *Crescendo in Drums (1939, Voc./OK 5062)
Recorded by E. Hines: Topsy-Turvy (1940, Bb 10870); Yellow Fire (1941, Bb 11308)

BIBLIOGRAPHY

ChiltonW
H. Panassié and M. Gautier: *Dictionnaire du jazz* (Paris, 1954, rev. and enlarged 2/1971, enlarged 3/1980)
A. J. McCarthy: "Notes on Two Neglected Jazzmen," *JM*, vi/11 (1961), 11
Obituary, *Variety*, cclxxxvi (2 March 1977), 79

FREDERICK A. BECK

Battle of bands [battle of music]. An event at which bands attempt to outplay one another in the manner of a CUTTING CONTEST. Such trials of skill originally occurred spontaneously when New Orleans bands, engaged in open-air advertising (or "ballyhoo"), encountered one another in the street; the wheels of the wagons on which the musicians rode were tied together to prevent either from escaping before the contest was decided. The attention these competitions attracted led promoters to set up similar events for financial gain. During the swing era, particularly in the mid-1930s, groups of three or four bands toured on the theater circuits, staging contests at a succession of venues; Irving Mills, for example, arranged such tours on the Keith-Orpheum circuit. Some of the contests that took place acquired legendary status, notably those between Chick Webb and Benny Goodman at the Savoy Ballroom in Harlem, New York, and Count Basie and Lucky Millinder in Baltimore.

ALYN SHIPTON

Bauduc, Ray(mond) (*b* New Orleans, 18 June 1909; *d* Houston, 8 Jan 1988). Drummer. A son of the cornetist Jules Bauduc, Sr., he was taught drums by his brother Jules Bauduc, Jr. (*b c*1904), a successful New Orleans bandleader; his sister was a pianist. He first played professionally in a band accompanying films, and while still at school he performed in a five-piece band with the cornetist Emmett Hardy and with the Six Nola Jazzers (which later became the Dixieland Roamers). After playing in a quartet in New Orleans he toured with the trumpeter Johnny Bayersdorffer (1924). He then worked with the Scranton Sirens, led by the violinist Billy Lustig (1925), with Joe Venuti and Eddie Lang (1926), and (as both drummer and tap dancer) with the vaudevillian Fred Rich (1926–8). From 1928 to 1934 he played in Ben Pollack's orchestra, and during the same period performed and recorded with Miff Mole (1927), Red Nichols (1930), Jack Teagarden (1930–31), Benny Goodman (1931), Wingy Manone (1934–6), and Louis Prima and Glenn Miller (both 1935). In 1935 Bauduc began a highly successful association with the Bob Crosby Orchestra which lasted until 1942 (for illustration *see* CROSBY, BOB). Among the works he recorded with the band were his own *South Rampart Street Parade* and a joint composition with Bob Haggart, *The Big Noise from Winnetka* (1938), in which he played with his drumsticks on the strings of Haggart's double bass. After military service Bauduc led a band with Gil Rodin and ensembles of his own. He made further recordings with Manone (1945–6), then worked with Crosby (1947), Jimmy Dorsey (1948–50), and Teagarden (1951–5); later he led a group with Nappy Lamare (1956–*c*1959). In the 1960s he worked as a freelance on the West Coast (he played with Pud Brown in 1967). Thereafter he occasionally performed with local musicians near his home in Bellaire, Texas.

Bauduc's syncopated fills (which show Gene Krupa's influence) and clean, technically precise accompaniment patterns set the standard for dixieland drumming. His playing epitomizes the evolution of New Orleans jazz drumming from the 1920s into the swing era; it is innovative, imaginative, and exciting. His *Dixieland Drumming* (Chicago, 1937) was one of the earliest jazz drumming methods.

SELECTED RECORDINGS

As leader: Li'l Liza Jane (1947, Cap. 15131); with N. Lamare: *Riverboat Dandies* (1957, Cap. T877), incl. Black and White Rag

As sideman: B. Pollack: My Kinda Love (1929, Vic. 21944); G. Gifford: New Orleans Twist (1935, Vic. 25041); B. Berigan: I'm Coming Virginia (1935, Decca 18116); B. Crosby: Between the Devil and the Deep Blue Sea (1937, Decca 1196); South Rampart Street Parade (1937, Decca 15038); The Big Noise from Winnetka (1938, Decca 2208); on. P. Fountain: *New Orleans to LA* (1954, 1956, Slnd 215), March of the Bob Cats (1956)

BIBLIOGRAPHY

G. Simon: "Dixieland Drums and Drummers," *Metronome*, lxviii/1 (1952), 12
J. Lucas: "Wild Drummers I Have Known," *JJ*, viii/3 (1955), 4
J. Chilton: *Stomp Off, Let's Go! The Story of Bob Crosby's Bob Cats & Big Band* (London, 1983), 181
M. L. Hester: *"Bobcat Tales from Ray Bauduc," MR*, xii/5 (1985), 1

T. DENNIS BROWN

Bauer, Billy [William Henry] (*b* New York, 14 Nov 1915). Guitarist. He played banjo as a child and changed to guitar in the early 1930s. He first worked in a band led by the clarinetist Jerry Wald, then in 1944 joined Woody Herman's First Herd (for illustration *see* HERMAN, WOODY, fig.1*a*); after the group disbanded in 1946 he played with Benny Goodman and Jack Teagarden. He enjoyed his most creative period between 1946 and 1949 as a member of Lennie Tristano's ensembles, where he ceased to be purely a rhythm guitarist and quickly became an advanced bop stylist; he was known particularly for his fleet improvisations and his remarkably precise playing of unison thematic statements. He also played on Tristano's recordings *Intuition* and *Digression* (1949), which are early explorations of free jazz. He received awards from *Down Beat* and *Metronome* magazines, and from 1947 to 1953 recorded in the Metronome All-Stars with such musicians as Charlie Parker, Dizzy Gillespie, Tristano, Miles Davis, and Fats Navarro. Bauer also played with the NBC staff orchestra and taught at the New York Conservatory of Modern Music (1950–53). He played in Europe with Goodman (1958) and performed frequently with Lee Konitz during the late 1950s and the 1960s. He continued to work as a freelance in New York during the 1970s and to teach privately in the early 1980s.

SELECTED RECORDINGS

As leader: *Plectrist* (1956, Norg. 1082)

As sideman with L. Tristano: Blue Boy (1947, Key. 861); Progression (1949, NewJ 832); Subconscious-Lee (1949, NewJ 80001); Wow/Crosscurrent (1949, Cap. 60003); Intuition (1949, Cap. 1224); Digression (1949, Cap. EAP1-491) [EP]

BIBLIOGRAPHY

P. Harris: "Think I'm Pioneering: Billy Bauer," *DB*, xvii/2 (1950), 6
R. Gogarty: "Billy Bauer," *GP*, vi/3 (1972), 18
M. J. Summerfield: *The Jazz Guitar: its Evolution and its Players* (Gateshead, England, 1978), 46

JIM FERGUSON

Bauer, Conrad (*b* Halle, Halle, Germany, 4 July 1943). German trombonist. He studied at the conservatory in Dresden and performed with Ernst-Ludwig Petrowsky's Manfred Ludwig Sextet (1968–70) and the Modern Soul Band (1970–73). He formed a free-jazz quartet, Exis, in 1971, then the group FEZ (1974–7), then various quartets, trios, and duos. In the 1970s he was a member of the Ulrich Gumpert Workshop Band and the quartet Synopsis (re-formed as the Zentral-Quartett in 1984); from 1976 he sometimes performed unaccompanied. In 1982 he formed a quartet with his younger brother Johannes, also a trombonist, and the guitarists Uwe Kropinski and Helmut "Joe" Sachse. He has also worked with Han Bennink, Derek Bailey, George Lewis (ii), and others. Bauer's playing can be heard to advantage on the album *Flüchtiges Glück* (1984, EfA 5817-08), which he recorded as an unaccompanied soloist.

BERT NOGLIK

Bauzá, Mario (*b* Havana, 28 April 1911). Cuban trumpeter. He was a bass clarinetist in the Havana SO before moving in 1930 to New York, where he worked with Noble Sissle (1932) and as trumpeter and music director for Chick Webb (1933–8; for illustration *see* WEBB, CHICK). After performing and recording with Don Redman (1938–9) he played with Cab Calloway (1939–41), and was responsible for bringing Dizzy Gillespie to Calloway's band. He joined Machito's Afro-Cubans in 1941, and later became the group's music director; he retained this post until 1976, and was responsible to a great extent for the band's success. Although principally a trumpeter, Bauzá has also performed on saxophones and clarinet; in the late 1970s he began playing salsa as well as jazz. He has continued to record as a leader and music director into the 1980s, and his work may be heard to advantage on the album *Afro-Cuban Jazz* (1986, Caimán 9017).

Oral history material in *NjR* (JOHP).

BIBLIOGRAPHY

ChiltonW
S. Woolley: "The Spanish Tinge," *JJI*, xxxviii/7 (1985), 9 [incl. discography]

CRISTÓBAL DÍAZ AYALA

Bavan, Yolande (Marie Wolffe) (*b* Colombo, Ceylon [now Sri Lanka], 1 June 1940). Ceylonese singer. She studied piano and cello as a child, and first heard jazz in broadcasts on Voice of America. She won a trip to Australia to sing with Graeme Bell in 1954, presented her own radio program in Ceylon, and toured Japan, Korea, and India with Toshiko Akiyoshi in 1955. The following year she moved to London, where she acted with the BBC Repertory Company and sang at jazz clubs. In 1959 she performed frequently at the Blue Note in Paris. She met Jon Hendricks and Dave Lambert in London in 1962 and moved to New York to join their vocal group as a replacement for Annie Ross, who had left because of illness; Bavan performed and recorded with the group until it disbanded in 1964. She stayed in New York, and acted with the New York Shakespeare Company and in Harold Arlen's play *House of Flowers*; she also performed in an early rock musical, *Salvation*, and in 1979 sang in an experimental production of *The Birds* by Aristophanes. In 1982 she performed at the Kool Jazz Festival, and in India.

For recording-list *see* LAMBERT, HENDRICKS, AND ROSS.

BIBLIOGRAPHY

"East Captures West – with One Note," *DB*, xxix/14 (1962), 13
L. Feather: "Vi presentiamo Yolande," *Musica jazz*, viii (1962), Sept, 14
J. S. Wilson: "Cabaret: Yolande Bavan," *New York Times* (10 Aug 1979), §C, p.6
——: "Bavan pour un trio défunt," *Jm*, no.307 (1982), 28

PHILIP GREENE

Bay, Francis [Bayetz, Frans] (*b* Rijkevorsel, Belgium, 1914). Belgian trombonist. In 1936 he formed an association with the violinist Paul Godwin in Germany, which was to continue intermittently until World War II. He worked in Belgium at Lionel's Club and played and recorded in the Netherlands with Dick Willebrandts (1943) and the Dutch group the Ramblers (1945–6). Bay was a founding member of the Skymasters in the mid-1940s and in 1948 formed a band with Boyd Bachmann, which worked in Switzerland, Sweden, and Belgium. His own big band, formed in Belgium in the 1950s, later became the dance orchestra of Belgian radio and television. Bay made numerous recordings as a leader (1958–61, 1971), many of them for the American market in connection with the Brussels World's Fair of 1958; he also recorded with David Bee (1956). He continued to lead the dance orchestra of the Belgian broadcasting service into the 1970s.

ROBERT PERNET

Bayeté [Cochran, Todd] (*b* San Francisco, 3 Sept 1951). Pianist and synthesizer player. He played with John Handy (*c*1969) and in a quintet led by Bobby Hutcherson and Harold Land (*c*1970–71). In 1972 he formed his own group, with which he recorded the album *Worlds Around the Sun* (1972, Prst. 10045). He also recorded with Hadley Caliman (1972), Julian Priester, John Klemmer (both 1973), and Stanley Clarke (1979). (*Feather–Gitler '70s*)

BD&M. *See* BRIDGEPORT DIE & MACHINE CO.

Beal, Charlie (*b* Los Angeles, 14 Sept 1908). Pianist, brother of Eddie Beal. In Los Angeles he played with Speed Webb (*c*1929) and Les Hite (*c*1930). He then moved to Chicago, where he worked as a soloist at the Grand Terrace and with Jimmie Noone, Erskine Tate, and Frankie Jaxon (all 1932). He performed and recorded with Louis Armstrong (1933), played with Carroll Dickerson, and toured with Noble Sissle before settling in New York, where he recorded with Buster Bailey (late 1934). Beal then concentrated on solo work before joining Eddie South (*c*1936). After army service he played in Los Angeles and appeared with Armstrong in the film *New Orleans* (1946); his playing is heard to advantage on the album *Original Motion Picture Soundtrack: New Orleans* (1946, Giants of Jazz 1025), particularly on the track *Mahogany Hall Stomp*. From October 1948 he worked regularly in Europe; he played in New York during the late 1950s. (B. Rusch: "Charlie Beal: Interview," *Cadence*, vii/5 (1981), 19)

based on *ChiltonW*

Beal, Eddie (*b* Redlands, CA, 13 June 1910; *d* Los Angeles, 15 Dec 1984). Pianist and songwriter. He played with the bandleaders Earl Dancer and Charlie Echols in the early 1930s. From 1934 to 1936 he performed with Buck Clayton in Shanghai, China, then returned to California, where he played in local groups and recorded with Maxine Sullivan (1939). After army service (1941–3) he briefly accompanied Billie Holiday and Ivie Anderson and took part in recording sessions with Jimmy Mundy, Herb Jeffries (both 1946), Helen Humes (1950), and Red Callender (1951–2, 1956). His solo on *Young Man's Blues*, recorded in 1946 with a group led by the singer Claude Trenier (Lamplighter 102), is a particularly good example of his style. Beal performed and recorded as a leader (1945, *c*1956), and from the mid-1950s worked mostly as a songwriter and music publisher. Later he led groups in Las Vegas (1973–4) and toured with the Tommy Dorsey Orchestra (1974–5). (*ChiltonW*; *FeatherE*; *Feather–Gitler '70s*)

Beamter, Jenő [Bubi] (*b* Budapest, 7 Aug 1912; *d* Budapest, 11 Jan 1984). Hungarian drummer and vibraphonist. He studied violin and piano, but later changed to drums and vibraphone; he was strongly influenced by Lionel Hampton. From 1932 until the end of his life he played in most of the big bands and small groups led by Lajos Martiny, making many recordings in the period 1940–42. After the war he played with the pianist Lulu Solymossy in Budapest and on tour in Hungary, Yugoslavia, and Austria (1953–7); he also recorded with Gábor Szabó (1956). He worked with the pianist József Szabó (1958–62), with whom he made several recordings (notably *Egy este a Duna Bárban* (A night at the Duna bar), 1962, Krém SLPX17725). He led a quartet with Martiny from 1981 to 1984. His life formed the basis of István Örkeny's novel *Bubi* (Budapest, 1946). (A. Csányi and G. G. Simon: Liner notes, *Jazz and Hot Dance in Hungary*, Harl. 2015, 1985)

GÉZA GÁBOR SIMON, RAINER E. LOTZ

Bean. Nickname of COLEMAN HAWKINS.

Bean, Billy [William Frederick] (*b* Philadelphia, 26 Dec 1933). Electric guitarist. He grew up in a musical family, and gained early experience playing with a minor group in and around Philadelphia. He worked with Charlie Ventura in 1956, then in 1958 moved to the West Coast and performed and recorded in Los Angeles with many leading groups, including those of Buddy Collette, Buddy DeFranco, Paul Horn, and Bud Shank. Two albums that he made as a leader with John Pisano in 1958 provide examples of his inventive improvisations and fluent virtuoso style; in contrast to the cool approach of Pisano, Bean showed a virile attack that revealed the influence of Tal Farlow. In 1961 he recorded an album with Walter Norris and the double bass player Harold Gaylor, but soon afterwards returned to Philadelphia and ceased to be active as a professional musician.

SELECTED RECORDINGS

As leader with J. Pisano: *Makin' it* (1958, Decca 9206); *Take your Pick* (1958, Decca 9212)
As leader with W. Norris and H. Gaylor: *The Trio* (1961, Riv. 9380)
As sideman: P. Horn: *Plenty of Horn* (1958, Dot 9002); F. Katz: *Folk Songs* (1958, WB 1277); B. Shank: *Slippery when Wet* (1959, WP 1265)

BIBLIOGRAPHY

FeatherE

NORMAN MONGAN

Bean, Floyd (R.) (*b* Grinnell, IA, 30 Aug 1904; *d* Cedar Rapids, IA, 9 March 1974). Pianist. After leading his own band (1919), he worked at the Linwood Inn in Davenport, Iowa (1923), where Bix Beiderbecke sometimes played informally with the band. He moved to Chicago in 1933, where he studied arranging and then played in a band led by the clarinetist Eddie Neibauer (1934–5). From around 1937 he worked with Jimmy McPartland, with whom he recorded a classic session of Chicago jazz for Decca (1939); he also played and recorded with Bob Crosby (1939). In the 1940s he joined Wingy Manone (1940), led his own trio, and worked in the big bands of Boyd Raeburn (1943), the singer Eddie Stone (1944–5), and Jess Stacy (1945), for whom he also wrote arrangements. He then returned to playing in small groups and worked with Paul Mares and Sidney Bechet (both 1948) and Miff Mole (1950). After 1950 he toured and recorded with Muggsy Spanier (1950–55), worked with Georg Brunis (1953–7, 1958–9) and Bob Scobey (1958), recorded again with McPartland (1959), and played with the clarinetist Bill Reinhardt (1960).

SELECTED RECORDINGS

As sideman: J. McPartland: Jazz me Blues (1939, Decca 18042); M. Spanier: Lazy Piano Man (1950, Mer. 5424); *Rare Custom 45's* (1956, IAJRC 42), incl. Tin Roof Blues

BIBLIOGRAPHY

ChiltonW; *FeatherE*
F. Bean: "Davenport Piano," *Selections from the Gutter: Jazz Portraits from "The Jazz Record"*, ed. A. Hodes and C. Hansen (Berkeley, CA, Los Angeles, and London, 1977), 156

MIKE HAZELDINE

Beason, Bill [William] (*b* Louisville, KY, 1908). Drummer. While studying at Wilberforce (Ohio) University he joined Horace Henderson's Collegians (1924), and he continued to work with Henderson throughout the 1920s. He then moved to New York and in 1930–31 played with Bingie Madison and recorded with Jelly Roll Morton, Clarence Williams, and King Oliver. He performed, toured Europe, and recorded with Teddy Hill (1935–7) and recorded with Dicky Wells in Paris (1937) and with Don Redman (1938–9). Wells's *Dicky Wells Blues* (1937, Swing 10) offers a good example of Beason's firm but unobtrusive small-group style; his playing with a larger ensemble is well represented by Hill's *King Porter Stomp* (1937, Bb 6988). He worked briefly with Roy Eldridge, then joined Chick Webb's orchestra, replacing Webb, who had left owing to illness; after Webb's death Beason remained with the band under Ella Fitzgerald's leadership until the end of 1941. He returned briefly to Henderson (1941), performed and recorded intermittently with John Kirby (from 1943), and worked with Eddie Heywood (1944), Ben Webster (1945), and Sy Oliver and Earl Bostic (both 1947). Nothing is known of his career after the 1940s.

based on *ChiltonW*

Beat. The basic pulse underlying measured music and thus the unit by which musical time is reckoned; the beat, though not always sounded, is always perceived as underpinning the temporal progress of the music, and it is only the presence of the beat that allows rhythm to be established. This article describes the ways in which the beat is expressed in jazz, and the relationship between the underlying pulse and the rhythms played by jazz musicians.

1. Meter. 2. Tempo. 3. The subdivision of the beat. 4. Accentuation: (i) Strong and weak beats (ii) Regular articulations (iii) Irregular articulations.

1. Meter. Meter is the grouping of beats in a regularly recurring pattern (the bar or measure) defined by accentuation (see §4 below). At a higher level than the beat and in more complex ways, meter (whether explicitly marked or only sensed) provides the temporal framework of the music within which rhythm is established and perceived. Meter is expressed in terms of the number of beats of a certain value that occur in the bar. In notated music it is indicated by a pair of numerals, one placed above the other, known as the time signature: the upper numeral indicates the number of beats in the bar, the lower the value accorded to each beat. Thus the time signature shown in ex.1 indicates that there are four beats to the bar and that each beat has the value of a quarter-note (so-called common time).

Ex.1

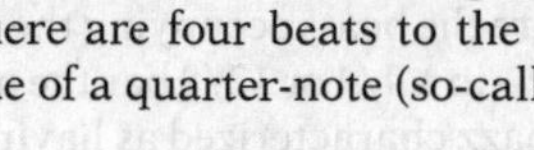

Because much jazz is never notated (and even notated pieces are not generally available) meter in jazz must usually be inferred by the listener and is consequently open to differences of interpretation. A fast piece, or one in which accents fall equally on every second beat might be interpreted by one listener as being in 2/4 and by another as being in 4/4; the typical boogie-woogie rhythm, described in jazz parlance as "eight to the bar," might be heard in 4/4 or 8/8.

In spite of such analytical difficulties (which often have more to do with the notation than the perception of the music) useful generalizations may be made about meter in jazz. Until the mid-1950s nearly all jazz was in duple meter (i.e., having two or four beats to the bar). Isolated examples of triple meter occur in the swing era, but only with the introduction of the "bop waltz" (early examples of which are Thelonious Monk's *Carolina Moon* (1952, BN 1603) and Sonny Rollins's composition *Valse hot* on the album *Sonny Rollins Plus 4* (1956, Prst. 7038)), did triple meter become well established in jazz. Two weeks after Rollins recorded *Valse hot* (in 3/4), Kenny Dorham recorded on the album *Kenny Dorham and the Jazz Prophets* (1956, ABC-Para. 122) his own composition *Tahitian Suite*, of which the opening theme and improvisation, and the closing statement of the theme, are in 6/8. Irregular meters made their appearance shortly afterwards and enjoyed a brief vogue; they are almost always found in composed pieces, the themes at least of which are notated. Examples include Dave Brubeck's *Take Five* (on the album *Time Out*, 1959, Col. CL1397), which is in 5/4, and *Blue Rondo a la Turk* (on the same album), which is alternately in 7/8 and 9/8; most of Don Ellis's compositions, including *33 222 1 222* and *New Nine* (on the album *Live at Monterey*, 1966, PJ 20112) and the pieces on the album *The Don Ellis Orchestra in* $3\frac{2}{3}$ *Time* (1966, PJ 20123); and the track *Ubava Zabava* on Chris Barber's album *Get Rolling!* (1969–71, Pol. 2683001), which has a succession of changing meters. At much the same time free jazz emerged, in which often there is neither an underlying beat nor a discernible meter. Yet throughout this period and later (most notably in the style known as jazz-rock), jazz continued to be dominated by pieces having four (less often two) beats to the bar.

2. Tempo. "Tempo" (the word derives from the Italian for "time") is generally used to mean the speed at which a performance proceeds: "up tempo" (sometimes "up") means, simply, "fast." In jazz parlance "tempo" and "beat" are sometimes used synonymously: a drummer or a bass player may be praised for his ability to maintain a steady tempo or a steady beat, when what is meant is that he plays the beat at a steady and unchanging speed. The player who has "a good beat" not only plays with rhythmic exactness but also imbues the rhythm with an indefinable energy and spirit, which makes the difference between a pedestrian and an exciting performance.

Steadiness of tempo is highly valued in jazz and is expected in all styles except free jazz, which in some (not all) instances proceeds at a free and varying tempo (as does, for example, Albert Ayler's *Holy Spirit* on his album *Ghosts*, 1964, Debut 144, and Cecil Taylor's *Steps* on his album *Unit Structures*, 1966, BN 84237). It is therefore not surprising that there are no terms in jazz parlance for the local easing and quickening of tempo familiar in Western classical music. "Rubato," the stretching or broadening of tempo, occurs often in performances by Art Tatum (as in the first and last choruses of *Time on my Hands*, 1949, Cap. 15712). It may also occur in the opening chorus of a Ballad, which is usually played at a slow tempo; examples may be heard on Miles Davis's *Stella by Starlight* and *My Funny Valentine* on the album *My Funny Valentine* (1964, Col. CS9106). "Accelerando" (acceleration of tempo) and "rallentando" (slowing down of tempo) are comparatively rare in jazz, but both occur in Charles Mingus's music; notable examples of accelerando may be heard in his suite *The Black Saint and the Sinner Lady* on the album of the same title (1963, Imp. 35).

The failure to adhere strictly to the beat and to play in a steady tempo is usually accidental, but a player will sometimes manipulate the beat for special effect; the degree to which he alters the rhythm will be infinitesimal and the irregularity may be momentary or prolonged (in the latter case the tempo of the entire ensemble may eventually be affected). To "lay back" or play "behind the beat" is deliberately to place notes slightly after the beat in a relaxed or hesitating manner; to "drag" may also mean to delay the beat intentionally but it is often used of an incompetent musician who cannot maintain a steady tempo. Conversely to play "ahead of the beat" is to place notes slightly before the beat, and to play "on top of the beat" is to place them slightly early or too precisely in time. Both terms may imply that the performer is anxious or not entirely in control of the music, but "on top of the beat" often carries more positive connotations: Art Blakey and Charles Mingus, for example, are both admired for their aggressive, driving style, which involves playing on top of the beat without rushing the tempo (*see also* BOOT and KICK).

3. THE SUBDIVISION OF THE BEAT. In the hierarchy of musical time, meter is a grouping of beats, each of which may in turn be subdivided into smaller values. Since the beat is normally thought of as a quarter-note, the subdivisions are usually referred to as eighth-notes, though the value accorded to the temporal unit and therefore to its subdivisions is a matter of individual interpretation in all jazz preserved only in recorded form. The way in which musicians articulate the beat and its subdivisions creates the rhythmic nuances that give jazz its character. In most ragtime, Latin jazz, and jazz-rock pieces, and in fusions of jazz with soul music, funk, and folk music the beat is subdivided into two equal parts, usually played strictly. But in much early jazz, music of the swing era, bop, and modal jazz the beat is divided unequally in a lilting fashion that implies three, rather than two subunits, though the subdivision is executed with such flexibility and variety as to give only an impression (and not an exact statement) of these values. The way in which the beat is subdivided in swing rhythms is exceedingly complex and may change constantly (for an attempt at a scientific measurement of such subtleties in the music of Charlie Parker *see* TRANSCRIPTION (i), §2); since they defy precise notation swing eighth-notes are variously represented as shown in ex.2. (*See also* NOTATION, §5(iv).)

Ex.2

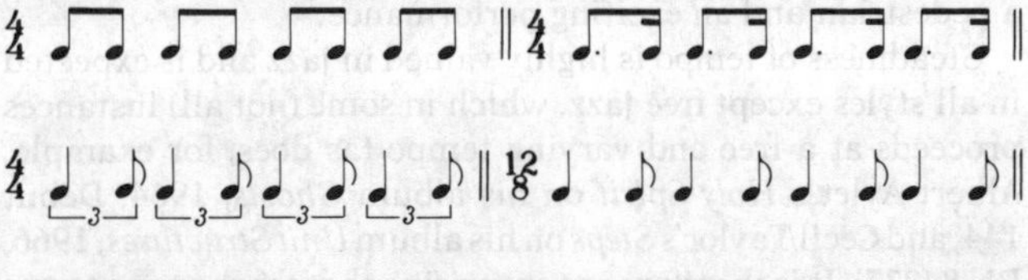

4. ACCENTUATION. The bar, the beat, and the subdivisions of the beat may be treated very regularly or with great rhythmic subtlety. Each element of the bar carries a different weight in relation to the others, these relative weights being determined not only by duration and stress but also by other factors such as the progress of the melodic line, changes of harmony, the instrumentation, etc. Much of the rhythmic interest of jazz lies in the manipulation or contradiction of the regular accentual pattern established by meter – the deliberate displacement of the expected accents, the slight precipitation or delay of articulations, the temporary cessation of a regularly marked beat, etc.

(i) Strong and weak beats. The grouping of beats into the metrical unit of the bar creates relatively stronger and weaker positions, which are reinforced by other elements of the music. In music that progresses regularly in 4/4 time, for example, the first beat of the bar is the strongest, the third is the next strongest, and the second and fourth less strong still; subdivisions of any of the beats are weaker than the main beats.

Several terms are used to describe the beats of the bar in terms of their metrical functions (ex.3). The "downbeat" is the first and strongest beat of the bar; it is followed by a succession of "afterbeats," that is, in 4/4 (or 12/8) the second, third, and fourth beats, all of which are weaker than the first (though not all of equal weight). Another term for any beat other than the first is "offbeat," but while "afterbeat" is essentially a neutral term, "offbeat" is often used in contexts where expected accentuation is overturned, especially where the downbeat is replaced by a rest or is tied over from the preceding bar; an offbeat rhythm is one in which beats that are metrically in weaker positions are emphasized and those in metrically stronger positions are understressed.

Ex.3

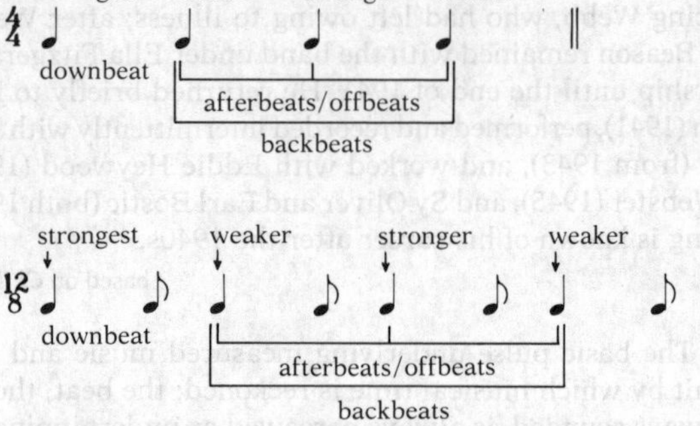

An "upbeat" is the impulse that immediately precedes a downbeat: in 4/4 (or 12/8) time the upbeat, metrically speaking, is the fourth beat of the bar, but the sensation of preparation for the following downbeat may be created by the last eighth-note, or even the last 16th-note, of the bar. Impulses that produce such an effect may occur at more than one level in a given rhythmic scheme: in ex.4 the metrical upbeat occurs at *b* but at a local level the 16th-note at *c* is also an upbeat and the 16th-note at *a* may be regarded as a lesser upbeat since it prepares for *b*, which at this level is a relatively important beat of the bar.

Ex.4

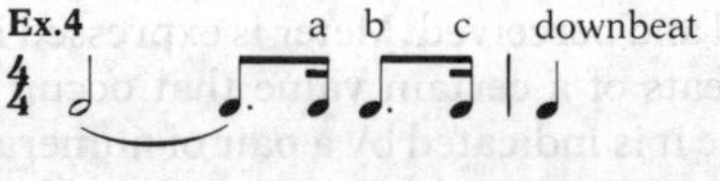

While all these terms are current in general musical theory "backbeat" is more specific to jazz and other forms of popular music. Backbeats are the beats occupying the weakest metrical positions in the bar – in a 4/4 or 12/8 bar the second and fourth beats (see ex.3). In jazz characterized as having a "heavy backbeat" these metrical impulses are consistently stressed, generally by strokes on the snare drum, or comping by the rhythm section, or both. An extended passage in which the backbeat is emphasized occurs in the tenth, 11th, 14th, and 15th (last) 12-bar blues choruses of Jack Teagarden's *Pitchin' a Bit Short* (1944, Comm. 1521), where the drummer George Wettling plays rim shots on the second and fourth beats of every bar throughout.

(ii) Regular articulations. In most styles of jazz the beat is expressed explicitly. In spite of the familiar notion of the drummer who "has a good beat," it is usually not the drums but the BASS instrument (most often the double bass, but in some contexts the tuba or electric bass guitar) that carries the responsibility for marking the beat. In music of the swing era the bass instrument is joined by the entire rhythm section (the bass drum and cymbal from the drum set, the piano, and the guitar) in striking every beat, but in other styles the members of the

rhythm section have considerably more rhythmic freedom than the bass player.

The way in which the bass player marks the beat varies in different styles of jazz. In the marches and rags on which early jazz drew, accents were placed on the first and third beats of the 4/4 bar, creating what is known as "two-beat" accentuation. As jazz became established as an independent form the two-beat pattern gradually gave way to a "four-beat" one, in which all four beats of the bar were firmly marked. (*See also* JAZZ, §II, 5.) A common form of bass line in many styles of jazz is the WALKING BASS, so called because the double bass player marks every beat, at the same time creating a coherent line moving mostly by step.

Although he may not be responsible for maintaining the beat, the drummer often plays patterns that reinforce it. Ex.5 shows a few simple, stereotypical rhythms that a drummer might play on certain components of the drum set to mark the beat

Ex.5

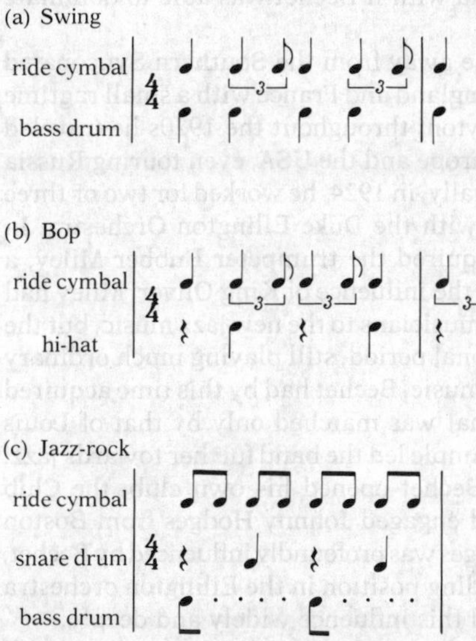

explicitly in different styles of jazz. In ex.5*b* the ride cymbal plays various combinations of the basic pattern of swing eighth-notes; in ex.5*c* the snare drum plays on the backbeats, against a steady stream of eighth-notes on the ride cymbal, and bass drum articulations of the first and third beats with varied patterns on other beats and upbeats.

Many styles of jazz use such rhythmic formulas, often repeated steadily in the rhythm section of the band beneath more varied lines in the melody instruments. Some formulas are related to dances (*see*, for example, CHARLESTON, SAMBA, and SHUFFLE); others derive from ethnic music, as is the case with the characteristic patterns of eighth-notes superimposed on 4/4 meter in BOSSA NOVA and LATIN JAZZ; and others are peculiar to a single piece or section of a piece (*see* OSTINATO and RIFF).

There are several performance conventions in which the explicit statement of the beat is suspended for a time, though they depend for their effect on the persistence of the beat by implication in the listener's mind. In a passage in double-time the prevailing note value is halved (in 4/4, for example, the basic quarter-note gives way to the eighth-note) so that an apparent doubling of the speed occurs, though the beat and harmonic rhythm do not change (ex.6). All members of an ensemble may go into double-time together (as in the first section of the theme of Mingus's *Fables of Faubus* on the album *Mingus Ah Um*, 1959, Col. CL1370), or the soloist may improvise in double-time while the rest of the ensemble continues in the original note values (as in Charlie Parker's break on his *Night in Tunisia*, 1946, Dial 1002). A reversal of this process, in effect "half-time," occurs in the second blues chorus of Armstrong's *Gully Low Blues* (1927, OK 8474). STOP-TIME is a device designed to highlight the playing of a soloist: typically the entire ensemble (or the rhythm section alone) plays, in rhythmic unison, a one- or two-bar formula consisting of sharp accents, interspersed with rests during which the soloist takes over. A similar interruption, though over a shorter period, occurs during a BREAK, in which the accompaniment ceases entirely for one or two bars while the soloist improvises. In both stop-time passages and breaks the underlying beat and harmony, though temporarily suspended in the accompaniment, are adhered to by the soloist in his improvisations.

Ex.6

(iii) Irregular articulations. The character and vitality of jazz derive to a considerable extent from the irregularity of its rhythms. While rhythmic tension can be created by the setting up of conflicting patterns (such as those discussed in §(ii) above) between the explicitly stated beat and the lines played against it, greater subtlety results from rhythmic articulations that shift and change in their relation to the beat.

Syncopation, which is fundamental to jazz rhythm and ubiquitous in both arranged and improvised pieces, involves the shifting of articulations from stronger beats to weaker ones or to metrical positions that do not fall on any of the main beats of the bar; the strong beats are silent, either because a rest occurs in those positions or because the articulation of a preceding weak beat is tied over (ex.7). Syncopation depends for its effect on a persisting sensation of the beat against which the articulated notes set up strong rhythmic contradictions; unless the beat is preserved in another voice in the ensemble or is swiftly reasserted, the listener loses his consciousness of the metrical framework, or even of the beat itself, and the syncopated pattern ceases to be perceived as such. Examples of syncopation are most obvious in (but by no means restricted to) performances in which a steady pattern of accents placed on the beat (for example, the two-beat formula of a ragtime

Ex.7 Syncopated rhythms

(a) From the stop-time section of *Spain*, on C. Corea: *Light as a Feather* (1973, Pol. 5525); transcr. B. Kernfeld

(b) From *Birdland*, on Weather Report: *Heavy Weather* (1976, Col. PC34418); transcr. B. Kernfeld

bass line or an unchanging jazz-rock drum ostinato) provides an accompaniment against which syncopated lines are created. Some fundamental rhythmic devices in jazz are based on syncopated patterns (see the discussion of backbeats and dance rhythms in §(ii) above; *see also* BOMB).

In the process known as "turning the rhythm (or beat or time) around" the meter is accidentally or deliberately redefined over a long period by the displacement of accents or the disturbance of phrase structures. The repositioning of strong and weak beats in the metrical unit of the bar, by means of dynamic accent, harmonic change, and the shaping of melodic lines, is at first perceived in conflict with the established meter, but gradually the ear is persuaded that the new positions are regular and a shift in the meter is thus achieved. Exciting, even disorienting, effects can be created if different members of the ensemble pursue their own independent definitions of the meter. A famous example is provided by Charlie Parker's quintet of 1947–8, whose playing was described by Miles Davis (one of the members) in an interview with Nat Hentoff ("Miles Davis: Last Trump," *Esquire*, li/3 (1959), 88). Parker was capable of improvising lines of extraordinary rhythmic complexity: always knowing exactly where he was in relation to the underlying beat, he could begin playing at bar 11 of a 12-bar blues as if he were playing the first bar of the progression, or he could accent the second and fourth beats of the bar as if they were the first and third; the other players, particularly those in the rhythm section, had to maintain the original metrical structure with great tenacity to prevent Parker from turning the rhythm around.

Few players have Parker's phenomenal ability to manipulate meter intentionally in this manner. Other examples of distinguished players' turning the rhythm around are due to error in performance (as on Bud Powell's recording of *Wail* (1949, BN 1567), in which after Roy Haynes's drum solo in the bridge Sonny Rollins and Fats Navarro re-enter at the wrong point as they begin the final statement of the theme) or to faulty editing of a recording (as on Charles Mingus's *Hora decubitus* from the album *Mingus, Mingus, Mingus, Mingus, Mingus* (1963, Imp. 54), where six beats are missing from the first 12-bar blues chorus of the tenor saxophone solo).

BARRY KERNFELD

Beatty, Josephine. *See* HUNTER, ALBERTA.

Bebop. *See* BOP.

Bebop Preservation Society. English group led by Bill Le Sage from 1970 to 1986.

Bechet, Sidney (Joseph) (*b* New Orleans, 14 May 1897; *d* Paris, 14 May 1959). Clarinetist and soprano saxophonist.

1. LIFE. He grew up in a musical family, and all of his four brothers played instruments; Leonard (Victor) Bechet (*b* New Orleans, 1886; *d* New Orleans, 17 Sept 1952) was briefly a professional trombonist before becoming a dentist, and his son, Leonard, Jr. (*b* New Orleans, 16 Aug 1927), played saxophone and was his uncle's manager for a while. Sidney Bechet took up clarinet as a young boy. He studied sporadically with the older clarinetists Lorenzo Tio, Jr., Big Eye Nelson, and George Baquet, but was principally self-taught. By about 1910 he was working with some of the incipient jazz bands in the city, but around 1916 he left New Orleans to wander (a habit which stayed with him into middle age), playing in touring shows and carnivals throughout the South and Midwest. He arrived in Chicago in 1917, and played with bands led by the New Orleans pioneers Freddie Keppard, King Oliver, and Lawrence Duhé.

In 1919 Bechet was discovered by Will Marion Cook, who was about to take his large concert band, the Southern Syncopated Orchestra, to Europe. The orchestra played mainly concert music in fixed arrangements with little improvising, but featured Bechet (who could not read music) in blues specialties. In London the Swiss conductor Ernest Ansermet heard the band, and in an article that has been widely reprinted referred to Bechet as "an extraordinary clarinet virtuoso" and an "artist of genius."

Bechet first discovered the curved soprano saxophone in Chicago; while in London he purchased a straight model and taught himself to play it. It became his primary instrument for the rest of his life, though he continued to play clarinet frequently. The soprano, although difficult to play in tune, has a powerful, commanding voice, and with it Bechet was able to dominate jazz ensembles.

In 1919 Bechet broke away from the Southern Syncopated Orchestra to work in England and France with a small ragtime band led by Benny Peyton; throughout the 1920s he traveled constantly between Europe and the USA, even touring Russia with a jazz band. Crucially, in 1924, he worked for two or three months in New York with the Duke Ellington Orchestra. In 1923 the band had acquired the trumpeter Bubber Miley, a growl specialist under the influence of King Oliver. Miley had awakened Ellington's musicians to the new jazz music, but the band was in a transitional period, still playing much ordinary jazz-flavored popular music. Bechet had by this time acquired a capacity to swing that was matched only by that of Louis Armstrong, and his example led the band further towards jazz. Not long afterwards Bechet opened his own club, the Club Basha, in Harlem, and engaged Johnny Hodges from Boston to play in his band. Hodges was profoundly influenced by Bechet, and from his commanding position in the Ellington orchestra from 1928 he extended this influence widely and deeply.

In 1924 and 1925 Bechet made a group of recordings with Armstrong which were variously issued under the names Clarence Williams's Blue Five and the Red Onion Jazz Babies. These constitute one of the most important bodies of New Orleans jazz, and were influential with musicians of the time. (On one of these numbers Bechet played SARRUSOPHONE – the only known example of this instrument on a jazz recording.) Through the next few years Bechet continued to wander, traveling in Europe and the USA. In the 1930s, as hot dance music lost its popularity to more sentimental styles, Bechet dropped into obscurity, playing when he could find work. He organized the NEW ORLEANS FEETWARMERS in 1932 with Tommy Ladnier, but largely owing to the group's musical style it was short-lived, and the following year the two men briefly managed a tailor's shop. However, with the New Orleans revival, from about 1939 Bechet was extolled by critics as one of the greatest jazz pioneers and his fortunes improved. He made several recordings, notably several fine titles with the BIG FOUR and a series with Mezz Mezzrow for King Jazz. In 1949 he returned to Europe for the first time in almost 20 years. He was received there with adulation and reverence, and in 1951 he settled permanently in France, where he lived out his final years as a show-business star.

2. MUSIC. Bechet was one of the second generation of New Orleans jazz pioneers who spread out from the city in the years

Sidney Bechet (left) with Clarence Williams (center) and Louis Armstrong at Decca's recording studios in New York, 27 May 1940

around World War I, giving the music its first national popularity. As one of the three or four best jazz musicians of the postwar period, he exerted a strong influence on northern musicians, and is regarded today as one of the consummate artists produced by this music. Because he traveled so much, especially abroad, he never developed the large popular following that he might have had if he had chosen to emulate Armstrong or Ellington in leading a large dance band. He was frequently bristly and difficult, with the *amour propre* of a star even in obscurity. His passions were free: he was expelled from both England and France for fighting, and spent almost a year in jail in Paris. He was certainly not temperamentally suited to the kinds of compromise that Armstrong and Ellington made to achieve popular success. But this same barely controlled passion is one of the hallmarks of his playing, which is everywhere filled with feeling, from the wild exuberance of *Sweetie Dear* (1932) to the brooding melancholy of *Blue Horizon* (1944). Bechet mastered the soprano saxophone to such a degree that few other jazz musicians were willing to challenge him, and until John Coltrane renewed the popularity of the instrument in the 1960s he had the field virtually to himself.

Like most of the New Orleans pioneers, Bechet tended to work out his figures in advance, and once he had arrived at a way of playing a tune he seldom changed it. But his playing was nonetheless passionate: his music was filled with movement, at fast tempos dashing headlong through the melody, at slow tempos swirling up and down the full range of the instrument in free-floating arpeggios. Because Bechet was such a solitary figure, his influence on jazz tended to be indirect, exercised through Ellington, Hodges, Buster Bailey (who managed a fair approximation of Bechet's style on soprano saxophone, which he adopted briefly), and a generation of younger players, including Bob Wilber, caught up in the New Orleans revival of the 1940s; but however indirect, it should not be undervalued. A considerable collection of material relating to his life and work is in the library of the Arkansas Arts Center at Little Rock; see LIBRARIES AND ARCHIVES, §2.

Oral history material in *LNT*.

See also BLUES, §§2, 8; for further illustration *see* FOSTER, POPS.

SELECTED RECORDINGS

As leader: Sweetie Dear/Maple Leaf Rag (1932, Vic. 23360); Lay your racket (1932, Vic. 23358); Summertime (1939, BN 6); Indian Summer (1940, Bb 10623); One o'Clock Jump (1940, Vic. 27204); Dear Old Southland (1940, BN 13); Saturday Night Blues (1940, BN 502); China Boy (1940, HRS 2001); Make me a pallet on the floor (1940, Bb 8509); Blue Horizon (1944, BN 43); with M. Mezzrow: Out of the Gallion (1945, King Jazz 142); Ce mossieu qui parle/Buddy Bolden Story (1949, Vogue 5013); *Deux heures du matin au Vieux Colombier* (1952, Vogue LD098)

As sideman: C. Williams: Wild Cat Blues (1923, OK 4925); E. Taylor: Jazzin' Babies Blues (1923, OK 8129); C. Williams: Texas Moaner Blues (1924, OK 8171); Mandy, make up your mind (1924, OK 40260); Red Onion Jazz Babies: Cake Walking Babies (1924, Gen. 5627); C. Williams: Cake-walking Babies from Home (1925, OK 40321); N. Sissle: Blackstick/When the sun sets down South (1938, Decca 2129); T. Ladnier: When you and I were young, Maggie (1938, Bb 10089); Port of Harlem Seven: Blues for Tommy (1939, BN 7); Pounding Heart Blues (1939, BN 6); J. R. Morton: Oh, didn't he ramble (1939, Bb 10429); L. Armstrong: Down in Honky Tonk Town/ Coal Cart Blues (1940, Decca 18091)

BIBLIOGRAPHY

E. Ansermet: "Bechet and Jazz Visit Europe, 1919," *Frontiers of Jazz*, ed. R. de Toledano (New York, 1947, rev. 2/1962)
H. Lyttelton: *I Play as I Please: the Memoirs of an Old Etonian Trumpeter* (London, 1954)
R. Mouly: *Sidney Bechet, notre ami* (Paris, 1959)
M. S.: "Le grand Sidney Bechet," *BHcF*, no.89 (1959), 7
S. Bechet: *Treat it Gentle: an Autobiography*, ed. D. Flower (New York and London, 1960/*R*1975; Ger. trans. as *Alle Kinder Gottes tragen eine Krone: eine Autobiographie*, Zurich, 1961)
G. E. Lambert: "Sidney Bechet and the Jazz Ensemble," *JJ*, xv/11 (1962), 5
M. Williams: *Jazz Masters of New Orleans* (New York and London, 1967/*R*1978)
G. Schuller: *Early Jazz: its Roots and Musical Development* (New York, 1968)
M. Williams: "Bechet the Prophet," *JJ*, xxi/4 (1968), 4
H. J. Mauerer: *A Discography of Sidney Bechet* (Copenhagen, 1969)
R. Blesh: *Combo, USA: Eight Lives in Jazz* (Philadelphia and London, 1971), 33

D. Hughes: "Treat him Gentle," *Music Maker* (1972), May
B. Martyn: "Bechet: all in the Family," *MM* (18 Aug 1973), 55
H. Lyttelton: *The Best of Jazz*, i: *Basin Street to Harlem: Jazz Masters and Masterpieces, 1917–1930* (London, 1978)
H. Rye: "How Come: Sidney Bechet's Brief Career as Chinese Laundryman/ Police Chief," *Sv*, no.76 (1978), 138
E. S. Walker: "The Red Devils and Sidney Bechet in England," *Sv*, no.76 (1978), 136
J.-R. Hippenmeyer: *Sidney Bechet* (Geneva, 1980)
W. Balliett: "Le grand Bechet," *Jelly Roll, Jabbo and Fats* (New York, and Oxford, England, 1983) [colln of previously pubd articles], 31
B. Priestley: "Blues to Bechet," *The Wire*, no.3 (1983), 14
M. Hazeldine: "Dear Wynne: a Review of the Events of 1945–6, concerning Bunk Johnson, Sidney Bechet, Boston and Beyond," *Fn*, xv/5 (1984), 4
R. Davies: "Sidney Bechet: A Grand Old Man of Jazz, Warts and all," *The Listener*, cxiv (28 June 1984), 11
J. Chilton: *Sidney Bechet: the Wizard of Jazz* (London and New York, 1987)
E. Lambert: "Bechet on Blue Note," *JJI*, xl/1 (1987), 10
B. Wilber and D. Webster: *Music was not Enough* (London and New York, 1987)

JAMES LINCOLN COLLIER

Bechet Legacy. Ensemble led by Bob Wilber. It was formed in 1981, and first performed at Bechet's Club in New York. At various times during its existence it had between four and seven members, one of whom was Wilber's wife, the singer Joanne "Pug" Horton. The group aimed not to copy Sidney Bechet's style, but to draw attention to his talents as a composer and performer. In so doing the Bechet Legacy quickly established its own musical identity. It toured the USA, Europe, and India, and won several popularity polls before disbanding in 1983; it may be heard to advantage on the album *Ode to Bechet* (1982, Bodeswell 104).

BIBLIOGRAPHY

E. Cook: "Keepers of the Flame," *JJI*, xxxiv/11 (1981), 16
M. Gabler: Liner notes, *Ode to Bechet* (Bodeswell 104, *c*1983)

DEREK WEBSTER

Beck, Gordon (James) (*b* London, 16 Sept 1936). English pianist. He learned classical piano between the ages of 12 and 15 and, after working for nine years as a draftsman, began a career as a jazz player in 1961. He quickly became known among musicians in London as a fluent, extremely creative pianist, and worked regularly with the bands of Tony Kinsey, Vic Ash and Harry Klein, Bobby Wellins, and Tony Crombie. In 1962 he joined Tubby Hayes's quintet, with which he recorded and gave his first performances outside the UK. Beck formed his own trio in 1965, and then spent several years as the house pianist at Ronnie Scott's. During his association with Phil Woods's European Rhythm Machine (1969–72) he toured extensively throughout Europe and visited the USA (1971). While a member of this group, Beck began to develop his talents as a composer and to attract wider appreciation for his writing. He has recorded a number of his own works, both with ensembles (notably on the albums *Gyroscope, Jazz Trio*, and *Seven Steps to Evans*) and as an unaccompanied soloist. In 1985 he toured the USA and Japan with Allan Holdsworth and Europe with Didier Lockwood.

SELECTED RECORDINGS

As unaccompanied soloist: *The French Connection 2* (1982, JMS 018); *Reasons* (1982, JMS 027)
As leader: *Gyroscope* (1968, Morgan 1); *Jazz Trio* (1972, Dire 341)
As sideman: P. Woods: *His European Rhythm Machine at the Frankfurt Jazz Festival* (1970, Embryo 530); [no leader]: *Seven Steps to Evans* (1979, MPS 68248)

BIBLIOGRAPHY

Feather–Gitler '70s
"Gordon Beck: Preparing for the Decline," *JF* [intl edn], no.41 (1976), 48 [incl. discography]
C. Bird: "Best of British, 4: Gordon Beck," *JJI*, xxxi/6 (1978), 10
P. Carles: "Gordon Beck: 'le plus sévère de mes critiques'," *Jm*, no.274 (1979), 44 [incl. discography]

STAN BRITT

Beck, Jeff (*b* Surrey, England, 24 June 1944). English electric guitarist. He first came to prominence in 1964 when he replaced the guitarist Eric Clapton in the Yardbirds, a rock group. He quickly forged a personal, virtuoso style, and was one of the first musicians to exploit the properties of the electric guitar, using controlled feedback and distortion as important elements of his sound. In 1967 he formed his own group, which played driving rock music; he continued to play in this style with various ensembles in the early 1970s. Thereafter, however, he recorded two jazz-rock albums: *Blow by Blow* (1975) and *Wired* (1976), the latter including a duo with Jan Hammer. On these recordings Beck combined the power of rock, jazz harmonies, and his own distinctive melodic sense. The results were acclaimed by rock and jazz audiences alike. He also played on albums by other jazz-rock musicians, including Stanley Clarke. Although in the late 1970s and early 1980s he returned to playing commercially-oriented music, he continues to employ a highly characteristic, instantly recognizable style.

SELECTED RECORDINGS

As leader: *Blow by Blow* (1975, Epic 33409); *Wired* (1976, Epic 33849); with J. Hammer: *Live* (1977, Epic 34433)

BIBLIOGRAPHY

L. Rohter: "Jeff Beck: the Progression of a True Progressive," *DB*, xliv/12 (1977), 13 [incl. discography]
J. Obrecht: "Jeff Beck," *GP*, xiv/10 (1980), 56 [incl. discography]

BILL MILKOWSKI

Beck, Joe (*b* Philadelphia, 29 July 1945). Guitarist. From 1964 to 1970 he established his career by playing with Paul Winter and Charles Lloyd (1964), Gary McFarland (1964–6), Chico Hamilton (1967), and Gil Evans (1967–70), and by recording with various leaders, including Kai Winding (1967), Bobby Timmons (*c*1968), and Brother Jack McDuff (1970). Although he then worked as a dairy farmer for several years (1971–3), he continued to record with Gato Barbieri (1971) and Gene Ammons (1972) among others. He resumed full-time performing in 1973, making recordings in that year with Woody Herman and Buddy Rich; he worked with Joe Farrell (1973–4) and Maynard Ferguson, and played on sessions with Idris Muhammad (1974), Larry Coryell (1976), Barbieri (1976), and Gerry Niewood (1985), among many others. He also recorded as a leader from 1975 and in duos with Attila Zoller and Red Mitchell. Through his associations with early exponents of jazz-rock, such as Farrell, Beck became one of the first jazz-rock guitarists; a versatile player, on the electric instrument he produces a sound colored by a slight distortion typical of rock music.

SELECTIVE RECORDINGS

As leader: *Beck!* (1975, Kudu 21)
Duos: with A. Zoller: *Happy Jam* (1979, Prog. 7048); with R. Mitchell: *Empathy* (1980, Gryphon 911)
As sideman: on K. Winding: *Penny Lane and Time* (1967, Verve 68691), Eleanor Rigby; G. Evans: *Big Stuff* (1969, Ampex 10102); J. Farrell: *Canned Funk* (1974, CTI 6053)

BIBLIOGRAPHY

Feather–Gitler '70s
A. Berle: "Joe Beck: New York's Hottest Sideman," *GP*, xi/9 (1977), 22 [incl. discography]

GARY CARNER

Beck, Pia [Pieternella] (*b* The Hague, 18 Sept 1925). Dutch pianist and singer. She is self-taught as a musician. She sang with a Hawaiian vocal group, the Samoa Girls (1939–42), sang and played piano with the Dutch group the Miller Sextet (1944–9), and appeared in shows sponsored by the USO. From 1949 she led a trio and worked as a soloist and between 1952 and 1967 made several visits to the USA (approximately at yearly intervals) during which she performed in Hollywood and at Birdland in New York. She operated a club in Torremolinos, Spain, from 1965. Beck's composition *Pia's Boogie*, which she recorded in 1950 (Phi. 34176H), became widely known. An autobiography, *De Pia Beck story*, was published in Amsterdam in 1978. (*FeatherE*)

WIM VAN EYLE

Beckenstein, Ray(mond) (*b* New York, 14 Aug 1923). Alto and soprano saxophonist. He studied violin, then learned saxophone, clarinet, and flute. As a member of big bands he performed and recorded with the trumpeter Bobby Sherwood (1943–5), recorded with Charlie Ventura (1949), and worked with Lee Castle and Benny Goodman. Thereafter he made recordings as a freelance in New York with George Handy (1955), Coleman Hawkins (1956), Gil Evans (1960), Stan Getz (1962), Kenny Burrell (1964), Wes Montgomery (1966), and Gary McFarland (1968). During the 1970s he made recordings with Louis Armstrong (1970) and Gap Mangione (1971–2). He continues to play in studios, but his most important work in the 1980s has been as the soprano saxophonist in the New York Saxophone Quartet with Dennis Anderson, Bill Kerr, and Wally Kane (respectively alto, tenor, and baritone saxophonists). The group's blend of classical music and several jazz styles may be heard on the album *An American Experience* (*c*1981, Stash 220).

Beckerhoff, Uli (*b* Münster, Germany, 6 Dec 1947). German trumpeter. After winning awards at several jazz competitions in Europe he was an original member in 1972 of the band Jazztrack, with which he toured. He made recordings for radio broadcast with Jasper van 't Hof (1974) and as a member of the group Riot, which toured Europe (1976–9); he also toured Africa with Volker Kriegel (1979). After performing and recording as a member of the band Changes he led a quintet from 1981. In 1986 and 1987 he played in a trio with van 't Hof and John Marshall. Beckerhoff's playing has been influenced chiefly by the early work of Miles Davis; in addition to his career as a performer he has written compositions and arrangements and led workshops.

SELECTED RECORDINGS

As leader: *Tomato Kiss* (1986, Nabel 8624); *Camporondo* (1987, Nabel 8729)
As sideman: Jazztrack: *First Call* (*c*1974, Happy Bird 5015); Riot: *Green and Blue* (1977, Nagara 1012); *Black Hill* (1978, Nagara 1017); Changes: *Some More Changes* (1980, Ego 4022)

BIBLIOGRAPHY

Feather–Gitler '70s
U. Vanek: "Uli Beckerhoff Group," *JP*, xxxii/7 (1983), 27
B. Ogan: "Uli Beckerhoff," *JP*, xxxiii/12 (1984), 37

HEIDI BOULTON

Beckett, Fred(erick Lee) (*b* Nellerton, MS, 23 Jan 1917; *d* St. Louis, 30 Jan 1946). Trombonist. During the 1930s he played in various bands in the Midwest, including those led by Buster Smith (1937, 1938), Tommy Douglas (1937, 1938–9), Andy Kirk (briefly, 1937), Nat Towles (1937–8), and Harlan Leonard (1939–40). In 1940 he was engaged by Lionel Hampton; this gave him his first chance of national prominence, but the prolonged recording ban which began in 1942 prevented him from receiving the exposure he might otherwise have had. He toured with Hampton until 1944, when he was drafted; during his military service he contracted tuberculosis, which led to his death at the age of 29. Although Beckett's playing was in the swing tradition it contained elements that in retrospect seemed prescient of modern jazz; his work was held in high esteem by J. J. Johnson. He left few recordings, but there are fine solos by him on Leonard's *My Gal Sal* and *A la Bridges*.

SELECTED RECORDINGS

As sideman: H. Leonard: My Gal Sal (1940, Bb 10625); A la Bridges (1940, Bb 10899); Skee (1940, Bb 10919); L. Hampton: Nola (1941, Decca 18285); Flying Home (1942, Decca 18394)

BIBLIOGRAPHY

ChiltonW

CHIP DEFFAA

Beckett, Harry [Harold Winston] (*b* St. Michael Parish, Barbados, 30 May 1935). Barbadian trumpeter and flugelhorn player. He moved to Britain in 1954 and in 1961 joined Graham Collier's group, with which he remained until about 1977. He appeared and played in the film *All Night Long* (1961) with Charles Mingus, and played with Mike Westbrook's orchestra and with the Brotherhood of Breath. He also performed with many English big bands, including those of Neil Ardley, Mike Gibbs, and John Warren, in the London Jazz Composers' Orchestra, and in the small groups of Tony Oxley, John Surman, and the guitarist Ray Russell. From 1975 he worked principally with the Stan Tracey Octet, various groups led by Elton Dean, and Dudu Pukwana's group Zila. Beckett has a distinctive sound on both his instruments and usually projects a lyrical amiability, but he is also capable of a fierceness that fits him well for the rapid fluxes of free jazz.

SELECTED RECORDINGS

As leader: *Flare Up* (1970, Phi. 6308026); *Warm Smiles* (1971, RCA SF8225); *Got it Made* (1977, Ogun 020); *Pictures of You* (1984, Paladin 2)
As sideman: G. Collier: *Deep Dark Blue Centre* (1967, Deram 1005); R. Russell: *Live at the ICA* (1971, RCA SR8214); G. Gaslini: *Gaslini Meets Jean-Luc Ponty* (1973, Produttori-Associati 622664); G. Collier: *Midnight Blue* (1975, Mosaic 751); Lysis: *Superimpositions* (1987, Soma 783)

BIBLIOGRAPHY

M. C. King: "British Jazzmen, no.11: Harry Beckett," *JJ*, xxiv/9 (1971), 13 [incl. discography]
I. Carr: *Music Outside: Contemporary Jazz in Britain* (London, 1973)
C. de Ledesma: "Got it Made," *The Wire*, no.14 (1985), 24

ROGER T. DEAN

Bedford, Ronnie [Ronald Hillier] (*b* Bridgeport, CT, 2 June 1931). Drummer. He toured and recorded with Louis Prima and Keely Smith (1950–51), then after military service he toured with Billy May (1954–6), performed and recorded with Sam Donahue (1956–7), and played in theater orchestras on Broadway. Later he worked as a studio musician, in clubs, and briefly with Eddie Condon before joining Rod Levitt's octet, with which he performed and recorded from 1963 to 1985. During this period he also worked sporadically with Chuck Wayne, recording in 1964 and 1976, and with Johnny Richards (1962–8), Bobby Hackett (1964), Pee Wee Russell (1965), and Lee Konitz (1966). After touring with Benny Goodman (1974–5) he worked with Buddy DeFranco (1977, 1979–80) and Benny Carter (intermittently, 1977–85), led a quartet (1979–80), and recorded frequently as a sideman with such leaders as Hank Jones (1976), Walter Norris and Harold Ashby (both 1978), Arnett Cobb (1980), and Bill Watrous (1982). His playing may be heard to advantage on DeFranco's album *Like Someone in Love* (1977, Prog. 7014). In the late 1970s he began performing as a freelance, and was a house drummer at the Newport and Kool jazz festivals (1980–85). He has also been active as a teacher; in 1986 he began teaching at Northwest Community College, Powell, Wyoming.

Bee, David [Sparks, Ernie; Travo, Manuel; Craps, Ernest] (*b* Brussels, 17 Oct 1903). Belgian arranger and composer. As a performer he played a number of instruments – saxophones, clarinet, piano, and harp. He was a member of the Bistrouille A. D. O. (1924–5) and in 1926 formed the Red Beans with the cornetist and trumpeter Peter Packay (with whom he also collaborated on compositions and arrangements); the group continued in existence until 1929, touring Italy, the Netherlands, Spain, and France. He wrote arrangements and made a number of recordings in Berlin and Italy (1930), before returning to Belgium, where he joined an orchestra led by Robert De Kers. During a visit to New York he met Benny Goodman, Stuff Smith, and others, and in Paris he played at Chez Florence with other American musicians, including Benny Carter and Willie Lewis. After World War II he performed with Chas Dolne. Bee recorded with the Red Beans (1928), Orchestra Jazz Columbia (1930), De Kers (1936), Gus Deloof (1940, 1941), Dolne (1940, 1942), the pianist Robert Bosmans (1942), and as leader of the Dixie Rag-a-Jazz Band (1965); he also led his own band on a number of sessions (1955–6, 1958). Many of his compositions and arrangements have been recorded; these include *High Tension* (Luis Russell, 1930, Decca 8849) and *Obsession* (Ted Heath, 1952, and the alto saxophonist Reg Owen, *c*1961).

ROBERT PERNET

Beecher, Johnny. Pseudonym of PLAS JOHNSON.

Bee Hive. Record company and label. The company was established by Jim Neumann late in 1977 in Chicago; issue began – with albums by Nick Brignola and Dizzy Reece – in 1978. Bee Hive (called after the city's club of the same name) was devoted mainly to jazz in the bop tradition, and was especially keen to sponsor innovative playing. By 1987 it had issued nearly 20 albums, many of them by musicians whose careers began in Chicago, including Clifford Jordan and Junior Mance. Issue has been sporadic, but the albums are well conceived; the quality of the pressings is high, and the packaging attractive. The catalogue includes a collection of previously unreleased work by several artists. Although the company's recordings are available in many parts of the world it has not entered into leasing agreements with other companies, and is responsible for distributing its own material.

MARK GARDNER

Behind the beat. Expression used to describe the performance of a player or singer who deliberately places notes slightly after the beat, as articulated by the rhythm section or implied by the playing of the rest of the ensemble; *see* BEAT, §2.

Behounek, Kamil (*b* Blatny, nr Beroun, Bohemia [now in Czechoslovakia], 29 March 1916; *d* Bonn, 22 Nov 1983). Bohemian accordionist, tenor saxophonist, arranger, composer, and bandleader. He taught himself to play accordion by listening to British radio broadcasts and American recordings, performed as a soloist at the Gramoklub in Prague while studying law, and first recorded as a soloist in 1936. He played accordion with the Blue Music Orchestra, the pianist Rudolf Antonin Dvorsky (1939), and Karel Vlach, and tenor saxophone with Vlach, for whose ensemble he also wrote arrangements. He was forcibly sent to Germany in 1943 to make copies of recordings by English and American bands to be used in propaganda broadcasts; in 1945 these copies formed the basis of a repertory for his own band, which was the first in Czechoslovakia to use five saxophones. He moved to Germany in 1946, wrote arrangements for radio big bands, and played occasionally in and around Bonn with his own group. Behounek was the first European to play jazz on the accordion, and his arrangements influenced such musicians as Ferdinand Havlík. His playing can be heard to advantage on the album *Kamil Behounek Memorial* (1936–46, Black Jack 3015); among his best-known compositions are *Hot and Simple*, *Utržený knoflík* (Torn-off button), *Hudba s Marsu* (Music from Mars), and *Red Circle Jump*.

BIBLIOGRAPHY

K. Behounek: "Ein Musiker erzählt," *Der Jazzfreund*, no.67 (1972), 4
G. Conrad: Liner notes, *Kamil Behounek Memorial* (Black Jack 3015, 1984)

GERHARD CONRAD

Beiderbecke, (Leon) Bix (*b* Davenport, IA, 10 March 1903; *d* New York, 6 Aug 1931). Cornetist. As a boy he had a few piano lessons, but he was self-taught on cornet and developed an unorthodox technique by playing along with recordings. His family disapproved of his interest in jazz, and sent him in 1921 to Lake Forest Academy, but the opportunity to play and hear jazz in nearby Chicago caused frequent truancy and eventually his expulsion. After several months working for his father in Davenport he turned to a career in music. Based in Chicago, he became known through his playing and recordings with the Wolverines in 1924. In the same year he began a long association with Frankie Trumbauer, recording with him in New York; after working with Jean Goldkette's dance band (1924), he played with Trumbauer's group in St. Louis (1925–6). His association with Trumbauer broadened his musical experience and improved his music reading, in which, however, he was never to become adept. In late 1926 he and Trumbauer joined Goldkette (see illustration), and were prominent members of his group in New York until it disbanded in September 1927. They then joined Paul Whiteman's band, with which, and with various groups under their own names, they made a series of influential recordings. Beiderbecke's alcoholism caused his health to deteriorate and he was frequently unable to perform. He left Whiteman in September 1929; his hopes of rejoining the group after recuperation were not realized. Until his death he worked in New York, in a radio series, with the Dorsey brothers a few times, with the Casa Loma Orchestra, and with Benny Goodman.

From relatively undistinguished influences Beiderbecke developed a beautiful and original style. His distinctive, bell-like tone (his friend Hoagy Carmichael described it as resembling a chime struck by a mallet) achieved additional intensity through his unorthodox fingering, which often led him to play certain notes as higher partials in lower overtone series, imparting a slightly different timbre and intonation to successive pitches. With his basically unchanging tone as a foil, Beiderbecke relied for expressiveness on pitch choice, pacing, and rhythmic placement (as opposed to Louis Armstrong, who systematically used variety of timbre). Beiderbecke played and composed at the piano throughout his working life; *In a Mist*, *Flashes*, *Candlelights*, and *In the Dark* (his published piano compositions), in their use of pandiatonicism, whole-tone scales, and parallel 7th and 9th chords, reflect his interest in impressionist harmonic language (*see also* PIANO, §4). However, his cornet playing, nearly always in settings over which he had no control, had to conform to the harmonic usages of contemporary jazz and popular music. His playing was largely diatonic and made sparing use of nondiatonic 9ths and 13ths as

Jean Goldkette's band at the Bronx Zoo, New York, in October 1926: (back row, left to right) Ray Lodwig (trumpet), Itzy Riskin (piano), Don Murray (clarinet), Steve Brown (double bass), Spiegel Wilcox (trombone), and Frankie Trumbauer (C-melody saxophone); (front row) Charlie Horvath (manager), Howdy Quicksell (banjo), Bix Beiderbecke (cornet), Fred "Fuzzy" Farrar (trumpet), and zookeeper with snake

well as the lowered 3rds and 7ths common in jazz. By avoiding harmonically functional chromatic pitches his improvisations often seemed to transcend the ordinary harmonic progressions of their accompaniment without contradicting them, as his solo on *Royal Garden Blues* of 1927 (ex.1) shows. This characteristic, together with his unique timbre, gave his work a restrained, introspective manner and often set his playing apart from its surroundings.

Ex.1 Solo from *Royal Garden Blues* (1927, OK 8544); transcr. J. Dapogny

Beiderbecke's originality made him one of the first white jazz musicians to be admired by black performers; Louis Armstrong recognized in him a kindred spirit, and Rex Stewart exactly reproduced some of his solos on recordings. Beiderbecke's influence on such white players as Red Nichols and Bunny Berigan was decisive. Although he was largely unknown to the general public at the time of his death, he acquired an almost legendary aura among jazz musicians and enthusiasts; on account of such popularized accounts as Dorothy Baker's novel *Young Man with a Horn* (Boston, 1938), based very loosely on his life and career, he soon came to symbolize the "Roaring Twenties" in the popular imagination. Only in recent years have legend and fact become clearly separated and Beiderbecke's career and achievement been seen in a true perspective.

See also JAZZ (i), §III, 3; and TRUMPET, §3; for further illustrations *see* RECORDING, fig.3, and WOLVERINES.

SELECTED RECORDINGS

As unaccompanied piano soloist: Bixology (In a Mist) (1927, OK 40916)

As leader: Davenport Blues (1925, Gen. 5654); At the Jazz Band Ball/Jazz me Blues (1927, OK 40923); Royal Garden Blues/Goose Pimples (1927, OK 8544); Sorry/Since my best gal turned me down (1927, OK 41001)

As sideman with Wolverines (all recorded in 1924): Jazz me Blues (Gen. 5408); Riverboat Shuffle (Gen. 5454); Tiger Rag (Bruns. 02205); Tia Juana (Gen. 5565)

As sideman with F. Trumbauer (all recorded in 1927): Singin' the Blues (OK 40772); Riverboat Shuffle (OK 40822); I'm coming, Virginia/' Way down yonder in New Orleans (OK 40843); Humpty Dumpty (OK 40926); Krazy Kat (OK 40903); Borneo (OK 41039)

As sideman with P. Whiteman (all recorded in 1928): Lonely Melody (Vic. 25366); Dardanella (Vic. 25238); From Monday on (Vic. 25368); Sweet Sue (Col. 50103D)

BIBLIOGRAPHY

E. Nichols: "Bix Beiderbecke," *Jazzmen*, ed. F. Ramsey, Jr., and C. E. Smith (New York, 1939/*R*1977), 143

G. Johnson: "The Wolverines and Bix," *Frontiers of Jazz*, ed. R. de Toledano (New York, 1947, rev. 2/1962)

N. Shapiro and N. Hentoff, eds.: *Hear me Talkin' to ya: the Story of Jazz by the Men who Made it* (New York and London, 1955/*R*1966), 132

C. Wareing and G. Garlick: *Bugles for Beiderbecke* (London, 1958) [incl. discography]

B. James: *Bix Beiderbecke* (London, 1959); repr. in *Kings of Jazz*, ed. S. Green (South Brunswick, NJ, and New York, 1978)

——: *Essays on Jazz* (London, 1961/*R*1985), 96

B. Green: *The Reluctant Art: Five Studies in the Growth of Jazz* (London, 1962), 18

R. Hadlock: *Jazz Masters of the Twenties* (New York, 1965/*R*1985)

"A Letter from Bix," *Sv*, no. 9 (1967), 29

G. Schuller: *Early Jazz: its Roots and Musical Development* (New York, 1968), 187

P. Tanner: "Did Bix Record with Sunny Clapp?," *Sv*, no.29 (1970), 185

M. Williams: *The Jazz Tradition* (New York, 1970, rev. 2/1983)

V. Castelli and others: *The Bix Bands: a Bix Beiderbecke Disco-biography* (Milan, 1972)

R. Berton: *Remembering Bix: a Memoir of the Jazz Age* (New York and elsewhere, 1974)

A. McCarthy: *Big Band Jazz* (New York and London, 1974), 72

R. M. Sudhalter, P. R. Evans, and W. Dean-Myatt: *Bix: Man & Legend* (New Rochelle, NY, and London, 1974)

J. P. Perhonis: *The Bix Beiderbecke Story: the Jazz Musician in Legend, Fiction, and Fact* (diss., U. of Minnesota, 1978)

JAMES DAPOGNY/J. BRADFORD ROBINSON

Beirach, Richard [Richie] (*b* New York, 23 May 1947). Pianist and composer. As a youth he was trained in both the classical and jazz traditions; he studied at the Berklee College of Music and the Manhattan School of Music (BA 1972). His first major engagement was with Stan Getz (1972), but his most important association has been with Dave Liebman. In the mid-1970s he was a member of Liebman's innovative group Lookout Farm, whose music drew on the influences of jazz, rock, and ethnic music; although he mainly plays piano Beirach also used electronic keyboards with this group. After Lookout Farm disbanded in 1976 Beirach formed his own trio, Eon. He was also one of the original members of John Abercrombie's quartet (formed 1978). In 1981 Beirach and Liebman established the group Quest, which performed and recorded into the mid-1980s. The influence of classical composers upon Beirach's work has often been noted; he has attempted to combine jazz with the Romantic music of Chopin and Liszt and the densely chromatic style of Schoenberg, Webern, and Berg.

SELECTED RECORDINGS

As unaccompanied soloist: *Hubris* (1977, ECM 1104); *Breathing of Statues* (1982, CMP 17)

As leader: *Eon* (1974, ECM 1054); with D. Liebman: *Forgotten Fantasies* (1975, A&M Hor. 709)

As sideman: D. Liebman: *Lookout Farm* (1973, ECM 1309); J. Abercrombie: *Arcade* (1978, ECM 1133)

BIBLIOGRAPHY

C. Berg: "Profile: Richie Beirach," *DB*, xlii/16 (1975), 34

D. Liebman and others: *Lookout Farm: a Case Study of Improvisation for Small Jazz Group* (n.p., 1978)

R. Henschen: "Richard Beirach: from Classical Piano to Jazz Keyboards (and Back Again)," *Music Journal*, xxxvii/4 (1979), 9 [incl. discography]

J. Aikin: "Richard Beirach: Defining the New Jazz Piano," *CK*, vii/4 (1981), 6 [incl. discography]

"Richard Beirach," *SJ*, xxxvi/7 (1982), 252 [discography]

L. Gourse: "Richie Beirach & Dave Liebman's 'Quest': What's in a Name?," *JT* (1985), Feb, 5

PAUL RINZLER

Bell, (Samuel) Aaron (*b* Muskogee, OK, 24 April 1922). Double bass and tuba player. He studied at Xavier University and worked with several bands in New Orleans. After navy service (1942–6) he joined Andy Kirk in 1947, then returned to Oklahoma and taught music before resuming his own education at New York University. In the early 1950s he played and recorded with Lucky Millinder, Teddy Wilson, and Lester Young, and led his own trio, with which he recorded in 1955 and 1958. He also worked with various singers and small groups and in the Broadway show *Compulsion* before joining Duke Ellington in April 1960. With Sam Woodyard, Bell formed one of Ellington's finest rhythm sections, contributing bass lines of great strength and richness. After leaving Ellington in October 1962 he played as a freelance and worked in the theater; he was resident composer at La Mama, an experimental theater in New York (1969–72), taught music in Newark, New Jersey, and studied at Columbia University (MEd 1975).

Oral history material in *CtY, NjR*.

SELECTED RECORDINGS

(all as sideman with D. Ellington)

Swinging Suites by Edward E. & Edward G. (1960, Col. CS8397), incl. Lay-by; *Piano in the Foreground* (1961, Col. CS8829), incl. Blues for Jerry; *Goodyear Jazz Concert*, i (1962, Goodyear 106657), incl. Satin Doll; *Duke Ellington Meets Coleman Hawkins* (1962, Imp. 26), incl. Wanderlust

BIBLIOGRAPHY

S. Dance: *The World of Duke Ellington* (London and New York, 1970/*R*1981) [colln of previously pubd articles and interviews]

C. Carrère: "Pitter Panther Patter: les bassistes de Duke Ellington," *Jh*, no.316 (1975), 10

EDDIE LAMBERT

Bell, Graeme (Emerson) [Gay] (*b* Melbourne, Australia, 7 Sept 1914). Australian bandleader, composer, and pianist, brother of Roger Bell. He led a pioneering jazz residency at Leonard's Café, Melbourne (1941), then, after working briefly in Queensland (1943), returned to Melbourne, where he took over the group led by his brother at Heidelberg Town Hall. In 1946 he started the Uptown Club and helped to inaugurate the Australian Jazz Convention. Having established his reputation in Australia with recordings in dixieland style made in 1947, he toured Europe with his band (1947–8) under the sponsorship of the Eureka Youth League. In England his "jazz for dancing" policy was influential in promoting the acceptance of jazz as a major form of youth entertainment. In 1949 he founded the label SWAGGIE and arranged an Australian tour for Rex Stewart, with whom he also recorded. Following a second European tour (1950–52), with Ade Monsbourgh and John Sangster among his sidemen, he visited Korea and Japan (1954–5), then settled in Sydney (1957). He led groups known as the All Stars (1962–6, 1972–), which played residencies in Sydney, toured nationally and overseas, and made recordings. Bell was awarded the Queen's Jubilee Medal (1977) and made an MBE (1978).

SELECTED RECORDINGS

Alma Street Requiem (1945, Ampersand 3); Smokey Mokes (1947, Regal-Zonophone 25116); Czechoslovak Journey (1947, Sup. C8162); *Top of the Town* (1950, Swaggie 4515); *Cakewalkin' Babies Back Home* (1951, Parl. R3455); *Hernando's Hideaway* (1962, Festival FK305)

BIBLIOGRAPHY

A. Van Starrex: "Graeme Bell," *Coda*, xii/6 (1975), 9 [interview]

A. Bisset: *Black Roots, White Flowers: a History of Jazz in Australia* (Sydney, 1976), 114

M. Williams: *The Australian Jazz Explosion* (London and elsewhere, 1981)

B. Johnson: "Bell, Graeme Emerson (Gay)," *The Oxford Companion to Australian Jazz* (Melbourne, Australia, 1987)

BRUCE JOHNSON

Bell, Roger (Emerson) (*b* Melbourne, Australia, 4 Jan 1919). Australian trumpeter, washboard player, composer, and bandleader, brother of Graeme Bell. He first worked as a drummer, then began to play cornet in 1938. He played in Melbourne with his brother at Leonard's Café and briefly led the band at Heidelberg Town Hall (1943) until Graeme Bell returned from Queensland to take over its leadership. He remained in Graeme's dixieland groups during their European tours (1947–8, 1950–52), then worked with Max Collie (1953) and in the house band at the Melbourne Jazz Club (from 1958). He was active as a freelance musician and led a band called the Pagan Pipers, which with various personnel (among them Len Barnard and Ade Monsbourgh) performed and recorded for many years; its recordings include a number of Bell's own compositions. Bell's playing is heard to advantage on *Roger Bell and his Pagan Pipers* (1968, Swaggie 1244). He continued to perform in the 1980s, notably at the Australian Jazz Convention.

BIBLIOGRAPHY

A. Bisset: *Black Roots, White Flowers: a History of Jazz in Australia* (Sydney, 1976), 114

B. Johnson: "Bell, Roger Emerson," *The Oxford Companion to Australian Jazz* (Melbourne, Australia, 1987)

BRUCE JOHNSON

Bellest, Christian (*b* Paris, 8 April 1922). French trumpeter and arranger. He appeared at the Moulin Rouge in Paris (1939) and played with the banjoist and guitarist Maceo Jefferson (1939–41), Alix Combelle's group the Jazz de Paris (1940–41), Fred Adison's band, the pianist Raymond Wraskoff (1940–41), the drummer Jerry Mengo (1941–2), the violinist Claude Laurence (1942), and again with Combelle (1943). In 1945 he led a big band that made several recordings (including *Rockin' the Blues/Two o' Clock Jump*, BStar 9). He also worked with the bandleader and saxophonist Raymond Legrand (1953), the pianist Christian Chevallier (1955, 1957), Lucky Thompson (1956), and Jacques Hélian's band (1956). He collaborated frequently with André Hodeir in the 1960s and continued to appear with him in the 1970s; also during the 1970s he played with the trumpeter Sonny Grey (1970) and Roger Guérin (1973). He retired in 1985. (F. Ténot: "Les quatre générations du jazz français," *Jh*, no. 23 (1948), 9)

MICHEL LAPLACE

Bellson, Louie [Louis; Balassoni, Louis Paul; Balassoni, Luigi Paulino Alfredo Francesco Antonio] (*b* Rock Falls, IL, 26 July 1924). Drummer, bandleader, and composer. He won a nationwide drumming contest sponsored by Gene Krupa in 1940, and played professionally with Benny Goodman when he was only 17. From 1946, after military service, he quickly became a leading big-band drummer, working with Goodman, Tommy Dorsey, Harry James, Count Basie, and especially Duke Ellington (1951–3), who performed some of Bellson's early arrangements. He returned to Ellington occasionally for special performances (for example, to record *A Drum is a Woman* in 1956, and to take part in the first sacred concert in 1965), but otherwise worked variously as music director for his wife, Pearl Bailey, and as the leader of his own highly successful big bands; his sidemen have included Cat Anderson, Conte Candoli, Bobby Shew, Don Menza, Joe Romano, John Heard, and George Duvivier. During the late 1970s and the 1980s Bellson has been active in jazz workshops at many universities; he has also recorded frequently for the Pablo and Concord labels with his big band and in smaller groups with Basie, Oscar Peterson, and others.

Bellson's excellent, precise technique and flamboyant solo style have placed him, with Buddy Rich, among the foremost big-band drummers of the post-swing period. He is known particularly for his tight ensemble playing and his virtuoso control of two pedal-operated bass drums, an ability he ascribes to his childhood training as a tap-dancer. Besides contributing many of the scores for his bands, he has composed a jazz ballet, *The Marriage Vows* (1962), and other pieces for jazz groups and symphony orchestra.

SELECTED RECORDINGS

As leader of big bands: *Big Band Jazz from the Summit* (1962, Roul. 52087); *Sunshine Rock* (1977, Pablo 2310813); *Dynamite!* (1979, Conc. 105); *The London Gig* (1982, Pablo 2310880)

As leader of small groups: *Louis Bellson Quintet* (1954, Norg. EPN 70-3); *Louie Bellson Jam* (1978, Pablo 2310838); *Side Track* (1979, Conc. 141); *Cool Cool Blue* (1982, Pablo 2310899)

As sideman with D. Ellington: *Duke Ellington's Coronets* (1951, Mercer 1005); *Ellington Uptown* (1952, Col. ML4639); *A Drum is a Woman* (1956, Col. CL951); *Duke's Big 4* (1973, Pablo 2310703)

BIBLIOGRAPHY

L. Feather: "Back to Duke," *DB*, xxxii/21 (1965), 15

L. Bellson: "Working with the Ellington Band was the Highlight of my Career," *Crescendo*, v/6 (1967), 5

R. Kettle: "The Artistry of Bellson: an Analysis," *DB*, xxxiv/6 (1967), 22

L. Tomkins: "Louie in London," *Crescendo*, viii/12 (1970), 20

P. Willard: "Louis Bellson," *DB*, xliii/11 (1976), 12

Z. Knauss: "Conversations with Jazz Musicians (Detroit, 1977), 2

L. Tomkins: "On Names, Clinics, Concerts," *CI*, xv/6 (1977), 20

——: "At Last: the Big Band of Louie Bellson Plays in Britain," *CI*, xviii/5 (1979), 20

——: "Louie Bellson Talking," *CI*, xviii/8 (1980), 6; xix/2 (1980), 5

R. Flans: "Louie Bellson," *MD*, iv/5 (1980), 12

L. Birnbaum: "The Perpetual Motion of Louie Bellson," *DB*, l/9 (1983), 20

G. Copley: "Louie Bellson," *JJI*, xxxvi/2 (1983), 22 [interview]

R. Flans: "Louie Bellson," *MD*, x/1 (1986), 21

J. BRADFORD ROBINSON

Benavent, Carles (*b* Barcelona, 1 March 1954). Spanish electric bass guitarist. He studied double bass for two years at the conservatory in Barcelona; at the age of 14 he began playing with local blues groups. After dedicating himself for two years to the study of Brazilian music he joined Música urbana, one of Spain's foremost jazz-rock groups, in 1975. In 1980 he began playing in the group Jazz Fusion with the saxophonist Tito Duarte and the pianist Josep Mas. He has also worked with the pianist Jordi Sabatés, and made many recordings, both as a leader (including the album *Carles Benavent*, 1983, Nuevos Medios 13051) and as a sideman. Benavent has toured extensively and played with many groups, both in Spain and abroad. He is considered one of the finest young Spanish jazz musicians.

ALFREDO PAPO

Bend. A variation in pitch (often microtonal) upwards or downwards during the course of a note; to execute such a variation. Typically the player or singer attacks the note at "true" pitch, bends the intonation, then returns it to true pitch. (For the various symbols used for microtonal inflections of pitch, *see* NOTATION, §2 (1).) A bend may be introduced into any note, but it often occurs on blue notes, which are already of "impure" intonation (*see* BLUE NOTE (i)). On wind instruments bends are produced without changes of fingering by means of embouchure, though on some brass instruments the player may also use half-valving (*see* HALF-VALVE). On fretless string instruments small variations in pitch may be achieved by pivoting the hand over the finger as if executing a single cycle of a vibrato in slow motion. On fretted strings a bend of a 3rd or more may be produced by simultaneously stopping the string against a fret and pushing or pulling the string across the fingerboard; this technique is most effective on electric guitar (because the notes are sustained for longer than on the acoustic instrument). The bend may also be achieved on electric guitar by means of the tremolo arm, which, according to whether it is pushed towards or pulled away from the body of the instrument, lengthens or shortens the vibrating length of the strings, producing an upward or downward bend. The pitch bend is a standard feature of most synthesizers, on which the control may be a slider, a joystick, or a wheel. (*See also* SMEAR; for related instrumental effects *see* GLISS.) (*GoldJL*)

ROBERT WITMER

Beneke, Tex [Gordon] (*b* Fort Worth, 12 Feb 1914). Tenor saxophonist, singer, and bandleader. As a child he played soprano saxophone, and in his teens he worked with territory bands in Texas and Oklahoma. In 1938 he joined Glenn Miller (for illustration *see* MUTE, fig.3), to whom he had been recommended by Gene Krupa. Miller gave him a highly prominent role; his playing may be heard on *In the Mood* and other pieces. Beneke also became one of the band's principal singers. He often took duets with Marion Hutton, and sang with the Modernaires on such recordings as *Chattanooga Choo Choo*. He also appeared with the band in the film *Sun Valley Serenade* (1941), and became extremely popular, winning several polls. When the ensemble disbanded in 1942 Beneke toured with the Modernaires. During World War II he directed a navy dance band in Oklahoma, and after being discharged he was selected by the administrators of Miller's estate to assume leadership of the latter's band (1946). After ceasing to direct this in 1950 he established a similar ensemble that emulated Miller's style. He has remained active as a bandleader into the 1980s, and also continues to perform with groups of Miller's former sidemen, including the Big Band Academy of America (1987).

SELECTED RECORDINGS

As sideman with G. Miller (all recorded for Bluebird unless otherwise indicated): King Porter Stomp (1938, 7853); In the Mood (1939, 10416); My Melancholy Baby (1940, 10665); Alice Blue Gown (1940, 10701); Chattanooga Choo Choo (1941, 11230); Serenade in Blue (1942, Vic. 27935); Sleepy Town Train (1942, Vic. 201509); *Soundtracks of Sun Valley Serenade and Orchestra Wives* (1941–2, 20C 904)

As sideman with others: Metronome All Stars: Bugle Call Rag (1941, Vic. 27314); Royal Flush (1941, Col. 36499); first issued on Metronome All Stars: *Swing Era; Modern Era* (1940–50, Har. 7044), Dear Old Southland (1941); Glenn Miller Singers [re-formed]: *Reunion in Hi Fi* (*c*1958, MCA 1512)

BIBLIOGRAPHY

T. Beneke: "Swing was Never King!," *Metronome*, lxiii/2 (1947), 20
"Beneke Book, Properties Grabbed by Ex-manager," *DB*, xviii/4 (1951), 1
C. Garrod: *Tex Beneke and his Orchestra* (Spotswood, NJ, 1973, rev. 2/1986) [discography]
J. Burns: "Tex Beneke," *Mainstream*, no.1 (1974), 10
G. T. Simon: *Glenn Miller and his Orchestra* (New York, 1974), 123, 437

BRIAN PEERLESS

Benford, Bill [William] (*b* Charleston, WV, 1902). Tuba player and bandleader, brother of Tommy Benford. He was educated at Jenkins' Orphanage then moved to New York in the early 1920s. He played with various groups and recorded with Jelly Roll Morton (1928–30); his playing is well represented on Morton's *Kansas City Stomps* (1928), *Shoe Shiners Drag* (1928), and *Little Lawrence* (1930). In the mid- to late 1920s he led his own band. (For recording details and bibliography *see* BENFORD, TOMMY.)

BRIAN PEERLESS

Benford, Tommy [Thomas P.] (*b* Charleston, WV, 19 April 1905). Drummer, brother of Bill Benford. The brothers received their musical education at Jenkins' Orphanage and toured with one of its bands, visiting England in 1914. To escape from the orphanage they joined the Green River Minstrels (*c*1920), then, around 1922, played together in New York, where they worked for a number of bandleaders including Marie Lucas and Elmer Snowden. Tommy played (for two or three years) and recorded (1926) with the pianist Charlie Skeete, and worked with Jelly Roll Morton, contributing to Morton's classic recordings *Kansas City Stomps* and *Shreveport* (both 1928). From around 1928 he played in his brother's band. After working with Edgar Hayes for several years he went to Europe in 1932 with a quintet led by the clarinetist and alto saxophonist Sy Devereaux; he played and recorded there with Coleman Hawkins (1937), Eddie Brunner, Bill Coleman, and Eddie South (all 1938), and Willie Lewis (1938, 1941), and in a duo with Joe Turner (i) (1939). After his return to the USA he played with Noble Sissle (1943) and Snub Mosley (1946–8), and in a band led initially by Bob Wilber (1948–9) and later by Jimmy Archey (1950–52). During the 1950s he worked as a freelance musician with numerous leaders, including Rex Stewart (1953), then toured Europe in the revue *Jazz Train* directed by Eddie Barefield (1960–61). In the 1960s he worked in New York, then played and toured with Clyde Bernhardt's Harlem Blues and Jazz Band (1973–9, 1981) and with Bob Greene's World of Jelly Roll Morton (1973–4, 1982).

SELECTED RECORDINGS

Duos with D. Wellstood: *The Stride Piano of Dick Wellstood* (1954, Riv. 2506)

As sideman: J. R. Morton: Kansas City Stomps (1928, Vic. 38010); Shoe Shiners Drag/Shreveport (1928, Vic. 21658); Little Lawrence (1930, Vic. 38135); C. Hawkins: Crazy Rhythm (1937, Swing 1); Out of Nowhere (1937, HMV K8511); E. Brunner: I Double Dare you/Montmartre Blues (1938, Swing 30); B. Wilber: Limehouse Blues (1949, Cir. [USA] 1064); S. Bechet: I'm Through, Goodbye (1949, Cir. [USA] 1059); R. Stewart: *Dixieland Free-for-all* (1953, Jzt. 1202); C. Bernhardt: *Sittin' on Top of the World!* (1975, Barron 401); B. Wilber and K. Davern: *Soprano Summit*, (1977, World Jazz 13); D. Hyman: *Music of Jelly Roll Morton* (1978, Smithsonian 006)

BIBLIOGRAPHY

ChiltonW
J. Chilton: *A Jazz Nursery; the Story of the Jenkins' Orphanage Bands of Charleston, South Carolina* (London, 1980)
P. Carr, A. Vollmer, and L. Wright: "Have Drum, Will Travel," *Sv*, no.100 (1982), 124; no.111 (1984), 105 [interview]
W. Balliett: *Jelly Roll, Jabbo and Fats* (New York, and Oxford, England, 1983) [colln of previously pubd articles], 45

BRIAN PEERLESS

Benjamin, Joe [Joseph Rupert] (*b* Atlantic City, NJ, 4 Nov 1919; *d* Livingston, nr Morristown, NJ, 26 Jan 1974). Double bass player. He studied violin with Hall Johnson, took up the double bass, and worked as a music copyist for Jimmie Lunceford. After playing double bass with Mercer Ellington in 1946 he recorded with Ellington (1947) and Sy Oliver (1949, 1950, on the latter session accompanying Louis Armstrong and Billie Holiday) and played with Fletcher Henderson, Billy Taylor (i), and Artie Shaw. For a brief period in 1951 he belonged to Duke Ellington's band (recording in January); he later worked as a copyist for Ellington, made occasional recordings with him until 1971 (including *Edward the Second* (1971), which he recorded as a member of a trio), and worked with him regularly from 1970. He performed and recorded in Paris with Dizzy Gillespie (1952) and from May 1953 to June 1955 played with Sarah Vaughan (for illustration *see* VAUGHAN, SARAH), with whom he made several recordings, including one celebrated session on which Clifford Brown also performed. In 1957 he recorded with Gerry Mulligan and Bob Brookmeyer, in the following year recorded with Dave Brubeck, and in the 1960s worked in studios; he also played with Paul Desmond. Benjamin had a warm tone and a strong sense of swing; he was equally adept at working in big bands and at playing cool jazz in small groups with such musicians as Desmond and Brookmeyer.

SELECTED RECORDINGS

As sideman: S. Vaughan: *Sarah Vaughan* (1954, EmA 36004); G. Mulligan and P. Desmond: *The Gerry Mulligan–Paul Desmond Quartet* (1957, Verve 8246); D. Brubeck: *Newport 1958* (1958, Col. CL1249); on D. Ellington: *The Intimate Ellington* (1969–71, Pablo 2310787), Edward the Second (1971)

BIBLIOGRAPHY

M. Jones: "I don't Know why she Called me 'Crazy Joe'," *MM*, xxxii (25 May 1957), 9

——: "Joe, the Ducal Bassman," *MM* (20 Nov 1971), 34; repr. with addns in *Talking Jazz* (London, 1987), 225

Obituaries: H. P.[anassié], *BHcF*, no. 235 (1974), 5; [unsigned], *DB*, xli/5 (1974), 11

L. Tomkins: "The Long Build-up of Experience: Ellington Bassist Joe Benjamin Tells his Story," *CI*, xii/6 (1974), 24

C. Carrère: "Pitter panther patter: les bassistes de Duke Ellington," *Jh*, no. 316 (1975), 10

MICHAEL ULLMAN

Benkó, Sandor (*b* Budapest, 25 Aug 1940). Hungarian bandleader, clarinetist, and alto saxophonist. He learned violin (1947–52) and clarinet (1950–58) and in 1957 he formed the Benkó Dixieland Band. Although it originally also played dance music, from 1962 the group performed only in the dixieland style. It made a large number of recordings, often performing with such soloists as Wild Bill Davison and George Probert (*Jubileum*, 1977, Pepita SLPX17545) and Al Grey, Buddy Tate, Joe Newman, and the banjoist Eddie Davis (*Live at Budapest Sportcsarnok*, 1982, Krém SLPX17764). Benkó won several prizes and his group received awards at various jazz festivals. He performed as a leader in Germany (1966), the USA (1982, 1983, 1986), Mexico (1984), and Indonesia (1985), and at the Oude Stijl Jazz Festival Breda (1976), the Sacramento Dixieland Jubilee (1983, 1986), and the Singapore Jazz Festival (1985). His group is the best known Hungarian jazz ensemble and its *Benkó Dixieland Band* (1972, Pepita SLPX17440) is the only jazz recording to have become a golden disc in Hungary.

BIBLIOGRAPHY

G. Koltay: *Benkó Dixieland Band Story* (Budapest, 1982)

A. Kő, ed.: *Benkó Dixieland Band* (Budapest, 1983, 3/1987)

G. Riskó: *Bingó, Benkó!* (Budapest, 1985)

G. G. Simon: *Benkó Dixieland Band: Bibliográfia és cikkgyűjtemény* [The Benkó Dixieland Band: bibliography and selected articles] (Budapest, 1988)

GÉZA GÁBOR SIMON, RAINER E. LOTZ

Bennett, Betty (*b* Lincoln, NE, 23 Oct 1921). Singer. She studied piano and singing, continuing with singing lessons while studying at Drake University. She sang with Georgie Auld in 1943, and after serving in the Navy in 1945 she performed and recorded in the bands of Claude Thornhill, Alvino Rey (both 1946), and Charlie Ventura (1949,1951); she also worked with Stan Kenton (1949), Woody Herman (1950), and Charlie Barnet (1952). In 1953 and 1955 she made recordings (including *Nobody Else but me*, 1955, Atl. 1226) under the direction of André Previn, who was her husband at that time. She later married Mundell Lowe, with whom she made occasional appearances. In 1987 she performed on the opening night of Wolsey's club in London and at the Pizza Express, and accompanied her husband on a European tour.

BIBLIOGRAPHY

FeatherE

L. Tomkins: "The Return of Betty Bennett," *CI*, xxiv/7 (1987), 10

Bennett, Lou [Benoit, Louis] (*b* Philadelphia, 18 May 1926). Organist and leader. He started his career as a pianist in Baltimore (1947), but by 1956, under the influence of Jimmy Smith, he had begun to play organ instead. From 1957 to 1959 he toured the Midwest and the East Coast with his own bop organ trio. The following year he moved to Paris, where he performed at the Blue Note with Jimmy Gourley and Kenny Clarke and made recordings as a leader (from 1960, including *The Lou Bennett Quartet*, 1960, RCA 430050) and with Clarke; Clarke and René Thomas were among his regular sidemen during the 1960s. Since then Bennett has performed at many European jazz festivals and in films, but has made only one appearance in the USA – at the Newport Jazz Festival in 1964. In the 1980s he led his own quintet, among the members of which was Gerard Badini.

BIBLIOGRAPHY

Feather '60s

J.-L. Ginibre: "Lou et les hommes d'Hammond," *Jm*, no.113 (1964), 69

A. Gildo: "Lou Bennet [*sic*] & Kenny Clarke," *Jazz Blues and Co.*, nos.52–4 (1982), 4 [interview]

Bennett, Max (Ramon) (*b* Des Moines, IA, 24 May 1928). Bass player and composer. In his teens he played trombone, then guitar. He played double bass with Herbie Fields (1949) and Georgie Auld (1951), then served in the US Army (1951–3). After playing with Stan Kenton from 1954 to 1955 he settled in Los Angeles and in 1957 accompanied Ella Fitzgerald, with whom he toured as part of the Jazz at the Philharmonic series the following year. From 1958 to 1972 he chiefly worked in Los Angeles as a studio musician except for a period during which he worked as the conductor of Peggy Lee's backup orchestra (1961–3). In the early 1960s he took up electric bass guitar, which became his principal instrument. He first played with Quincy Jones in 1968 and continued to be associated with him until 1980. He was a member of Tom Scott's group L. A. Express (1972–7), which accompanied the popular singer Joni Mitchell on tours in 1973–4 and 1976. He continued to be active as a studio musician and played with the Crusaders (1972–3, 1975), the soul singer Aretha Franklin (1977), and Victor Feldman (1984), among many others. In 1984 he formed his own group, Freeway. Bennett plays both double bass and electric bass guitar with a warm, even tone; he composed much of the material played by the L. A. Express and Freeway.

SELECTED RECORDINGS

As leader: *Max Bennett Plays* (1955, Beth. 50); *The Drifter* (*c*1985, TBA 216)

As sideman: C. Mariano: *Johnny One Note* (1954, Beth. 25); S. Kenton: *Contemporary Concepts* (1955, Cap. T666); L. Levy: *A Most Musical Fella* (1956–7, RCA LPM1491); T. Scott: *Tom Scott and the L. A. Express* (1973, Ode 77021); J. Mitchell: *Court and Spark* (1974, Asy. 1001)

BIBLIOGRAPHY

FeatherE; *Feather '60s*; *Feather–Gitler '70s*

S. Buckingham: "Max Bennett: from LA Studios to the LA Express," *GP*, x/12 (1976), 12 [incl. discography]

L. Feather: "Freeway on Express Trip to Fusion," *Los Angeles Times* (8 Aug 1985), § vi, p. 3

JOHN VOIGT

Bennett, Tony [Bari, Joe; Benedetto, Anthony Dominick] (*b* New York, 3 Aug 1926). Singer. He sang with military bands during World War II and then studied singing at the American Theatre Wing school. In 1950, while performing with Pearl Bailey in a nightclub in New York, he was discovered by Bob Hope, who suggested he change his stage name from Joe Bari to Tony Bennett. The same year Bennett signed a recording contract with Columbia, and during the 1950s he had a series of popular hit singles. In the 1960s he went on to perform with swing bands, such as those led by Count Basie, Duke Ellington, and Woody Herman. Later he recorded two albums with Bill Evans (ii), *The Tony Bennett–Bill Evans Album* (1975, Fan. 9489) and *Together Again* (1977, Improvisation 7117). Bennett's voice is a lyric baritone with a distinctively husky edge. An admirer of classic jazz, he claims to have modeled his breathing and phrasing on the playing of Art Tatum and his relaxed delivery on that of Mildred Bailey.

BIBLIOGRAPHY

"Tony Bennett Talks to Crescendo," *Crescendo*, v/5 (1966), 16
W. Conover and others: "20 Years with Tony," *Billboard*, lxxx (30 Nov 1968), 1–40 [incl. discography]
W. Balliett: "A Quality that Lets you in," *New Yorker*, xlix (7 Jan 1974), 33
——: *Alec Wilder and his Friends* (Boston, 1974) [colln of previously pubd articles]
L. Gourse: *Louis' Children: American Jazz Singers* (New York, 1984), 293
G. Giddins: *Rhythm-a-ning: Jazz Tradition and Improvisation in the '80s* (New York, and Oxford, England, 1985) [colln of previously pubd articles], 65

STEPHEN HOLDEN/R

Bennink, Han (*b* Zaandam, nr Zaanstad, Netherlands, 17 April 1942). Dutch drummer and percussionist. His early musical development was strongly influenced by his father, a classical percussionist. He began playing drums while in his teens, studied clarinet for a brief period, and played with local groups (1960–61). Between 1962 and 1969 he worked with several American musicians during their visits to the Netherlands, including Johnny Griffin, Eric Dolphy, Dexter Gordon, Hank Mobley, Sonny Rollins, and Ben Webster; in 1962–3 he also belonged to Pim Jacobs's trio. With Misha Mengelberg, Piet Noordijk, and the double bass player Rob Langreis he formed a quartet in 1963, which performed at the Newport Jazz Festival in 1966. He played free jazz with Mengelberg, and with Mengelberg and Willem Breuker formed the Instant Composers Pool (1967), a nonprofit organization that sponsors performances and recordings by members of the Dutch avant garde. From around 1969 he played in a trio with Peter Brötzmann and Fred van Hove; after van Hove's departure around 1976 Bennink continued to work in a duo with Brötzmann, with which Mengelberg also played occasionally, until 1979. He also performed and recorded as a soloist (from 1971), worked in duos with Mengelberg (from 1966), Derek Bailey (1969–77), the pianist Cees Hazvoet (1978), and Conrad Bauer (1983), performed with Bailey's group Company (1976–77; for illustration *see* JAZZ (i), fig. 9), and performed and recorded with Breuker (1966–70, 1973), Alex Schlippenbach's octet (1969), the Globe Unity Orchestra (1970, 1974), Don Cherry (1970–71), Paul Bley (1971), Michel Portal (1977, 1982), large groups affiliated with the Instant Composers Pool (1977–83), and the pianist Leo Cuypers (1981). Bennink is a versatile musician whose playing incorporates elements of African drumming, gamelan music, and tap-dance rhythms; his performances often include comic theatrical episodes. In addition to the standard trap set he plays exotic percussion instruments, piano, clarinets, banjo, violin, trombone, accordion, and instruments of his own construction.

SELECTED RECORDINGS

As unaccompanied soloist: *Tempo comodo* (1982, Data 823)
Duos with M. Mengelberg: *Einepartietischtennis* (1974, FMP SAJ03)
As leader with P. Brötzmann and F. van Hove: *The End* (1971, FMP 0050); *Outspan nr.2* (1974, FMP 0200)
As sideman: D. Gordon: *Live at the Amsterdam Paradiso* (1969, Catfish 336–7); I. C. P. Tentet: *Tetterettet* (1977, ICP 020); L. Cuypers: *Heavy Days are here Again* (1981, BVHaast 037)

BIBLIOGRAPHY

M. Thiem: "The Bizarre World of Han Bennink," *JF* [intl edn], no.47 (1977), 50 [incl. discography]
F. Lagerwerff: "Han Bennink," *Jazz nu*, iii/8 (1981), 340
R. Cook: "Turning Lots of Buttons: Han Bennink," *The Wire*, no.29 (1986), 31
B. Shoemaker: "Hal Bennink/Peter Brotzmann: First Entrances and Last Exits," *DB*, liv/1 (1987), 24 [incl. discography]

ROBERT J. IANNAPOLLO

Benskin, Sammy [Samuel] (*b* New York, 27 Sept 1922). Pianist and leader. He first played at Café Society and Nick's in New York with Bob Burnet's sextet (1941), then worked with Stuff Smith (1942) and Gene Sedric (1943), recorded with Freddie Green and Billie Holiday (both 1945), and performed and recorded with Don Redman (1943) and Benny Morton (1945). In 1945 he appeared as a soloist and as the leader of a trio, with which he recorded four titles, including *Cherry/When all the world is waiting for the sunrise* (BN 522). The following year he made some recordings with John Hardee's Swingtet, and his playing may be heard to advantage on *Idaho* (BN 514). During the 1950s Benskin accompanied many singers, notably Al Hibbler (1958–9), but thereafter he worked mainly as a singing teacher and occasionally as an arranger and record producer. In the mid-1980s he performed in New York with the Harlem Jazz and Blues Band. (*FeatherE*)

Benson, George (*b* Pittsburgh, 22 March 1943). Electric guitarist and singer. He sang in nightclubs at the age of eight and formed a rock-and-roll group when he was 17. During the early

George Benson, New York, mid- to late 1970s

part of his career in jazz he worked exclusively as an electric guitarist; as a member of Brother Jack McDuff's quartet (for three and a half years, 1962–5) he played soul jazz at the Antibes–Juan-les-Pins Jazz Festival (1964) and in Stockholm, where he also took part in a television broadcast with Jean-Luc Ponty. After leading a trio with a double bass player and a drummer for three months in Pittsburgh he again played with McDuff, then performed and recorded as the leader of groups that included Ronnie Cuber and Jimmy Smith as sidemen. He was himself sought after as a sideman owing to his speed and agility on the electric guitar, and he recorded with Billy Cobham, Miles Davis, Herbie Hancock, Freddie Hubbard, Ron Carter, and Lee Morgan. From the early 1970s he made commercially oriented recordings on which he sang as well as played electric guitar; these reached a large popular audience. At the same time he continued to play more conventional jazz occasionally with Benny Goodman (on television) and others. A distinctive feature of Benson's style is his practice of playing a florid guitar melody while scat singing an identical vocal line.

SELECTED RECORDINGS

As leader: *Benson Burner* (1966–7, Col. CG33569); *Giblet Gravy* (1968, Verve 68749); *Shape of Things* (1968, A&M 3014); *Beyond the Blue Horizon* (1971, CTI 6009); *White Rabbit* (1971, CTI 6015); *Breezin'* (1976, WB 3111); *Weekend in L.A.* (1977, WB 3139); *Give me the Night* (1980, WB 3453); *20/20* (?1984, WB 125178); *While the City Sleeps* (?1986, WB 125475)

As sideman: M. Davis: *Miles in the Sky* (1968, Col. CS9628)

BIBLIOGRAPHY

S. Dance: "George Benson: Guitar in Ascendancy," *DB*, xxxiv/13 (1967), 20

J.-J. Poinsot and L. Verdeaux: "George Benson," *BHcF*, no.175 (1968), 12 [interview]

J. De Muth and B. Rusch: "George Benson Double Interview," *Cadence*, i/11–12 (1976), 5

C. Mitchell: "Breezin' along with a Bullet," *DB*, xliii/15 (1976), 16

L. Feather: "George Benson: Superstar Update," *DB*, xlv/7 (1978), 13

L. Tomkins: "The Jazz Success Story of George Benson," *CI*, xvi/12 (1978), 20; contd as "How to Make the Most of yourself," xvii/1 (1978), 6 [interview]

J. Sievert: "George Benson: Platinum Jazz," *GP*, xiii/7 (1979), 86

G. T. Simon and others: *The Best of the Music Makers* (Garden City, NY, 1979)

L. Gilbert: "George Benson Puts on his Dancing Shoes," *DB*, xlvii/11 (1980), 19

G. Giddins: "Bensonality," *Riding on a Blue Note: Jazz and American Pop* (New York, and Oxford, England, 1981) [colln of previously pubd articles], 266

LEE JESKE/R

Bent note. A note into which a BEND is introduced.

Benton, Walter (Barney) (*b* Los Angeles, 9 Sept 1930). Tenor saxophonist. He began playing saxophone in high school. After performing in army bands (1950–53) he recorded in Los Angeles with Kenny Clarke (*The Kenny Clarke Sextet*, 1954, Savoy 15051) and in a jam session with Clifford Brown and Max Roach. He then worked with the pianist Perez Prado (1954–7), making an extensive tour of Asia in 1956. Later he recorded as a soloist in Victor Feldman's orchestra (1959) and with his own group in New York (1960–61). Benton performed and recorded bop and free jazz with the adventurous groups led by Roach, Julian Priester, and Abbey Lincoln before returning in 1961 to Los Angeles, where he worked with Gerald Wilson and later recorded with John Anderson (1966).

BIBLIOGRAPHY

FeatherE

R. Gordon: *Jazz West Coast: the Los Angeles Jazz Scene of the 1950s* (London and New York, 1986)

Berendt, Joachim-Ernst (*b* Berlin, 20 July 1922). German writer and record producer. After studies in Berlin and at the University of Karlsruhe (1940–42) he was a founder in 1945 of the Südwestfunk Baden-Baden, where he led the jazz department until 1987, and of the Deutsche Jazz Föderation (1951). During the following decades he organized and directed many festivals and concert series (including Jazztime Baden-Baden, from 1947, the American Folk Blues Festival, 1962–8, the Berliner Jazztage, later known as the Jazzfest Berlin, 1964–72, the New Jazz Meeting Baden-Baden, which he founded in 1966, and the Olympic Games Jazz Festival in Munich, 1972) and was the producer and host of broadcasts both on radio (from the Baden-Baden festival) and television ("Jazz, gehört und gesehen," 1954–72); he also organized an annual jazz concert at the Donaueschingen Festival for Contemporary Music (from 1954). A champion from the early 1960s of non-Western folk music and of its fusion with jazz, he founded the World Music Festival in 1965 and the German-Japanese Jazz Meeting in 1971. He has produced more than 250 recordings and in 1970 was voted "leading European jazz producer" by *Jazz & Pop*. Among his published writings are more than 20 books, most of which are about jazz; they include *Das Jazzbuch* (1953), which has been translated into 16 languages and is believed to be the only book about jazz to have sold more than one million copies. He has also edited the *Calendar Jazz and Rock* (from 1954), a yearbook in English and German. His collection of photographs of jazz subjects, and important parts of his library of recordings, books, and periodicals are now held by the Internationales Jazz Zentrum at the Internationales Musikinstitut in Darmstadt, Germany; *see* LIBRARIES AND ARCHIVES, §2.

WRITINGS
(selective list)

Der Jazz: eine zeitkritische Studie (Stuttgart, Germany, 1950)

Das Jazzbuch: Entwicklung und Bedeutung der Jazzmusik (Frankfurt am Main, Germany, 1953, rev. 2/1959 as *Das neue Jazzbuch: Entwicklung und Bedeutung der Jazzmusik*, It. trans., Florence, Italy, 1959, Eng. trans., New York, 1962, Sp. trans., Mexico City, *c*1962; rev. and enlarged 5/1981 as *Das grosse Jazzbuch: von New Orleans bis Jazz Rock*, Eng. trans. as *The Jazz Book: from New Orleans to Fusion and Beyond*, Westport, CT, 1982)

Variationen über Jazz (Munich, 1956)

Ein Fenster aus Jazz: Essays, Portraits, Reflexionen (Frankfurt am Main, Germany, 1977)

Photo-Story des Jazz (Frankfurt am Main, Germany, 1978; Eng. trans., New York and London, 1979)

Nada Brahma: die Welt ist Klang (Frankfurt am Main, Germany, 1983)

H. L. LINDENMAIER

Berg, Bob [Robert] (*b* New York, 7 April 1951). Tenor saxophonist. He studied in New York at the High School of Performing Arts and the Juilliard School, then toured the USA with Brother Jack McDuff in 1969. His enthusiasm for the hard-bop style found expression in the bands of Horace Silver (1973–6) and Cedar Walton (1977–83). From 1984, when he joined Miles Davis, Berg played in a band made up mainly of electric and electronic instruments that draws upon the idioms of rock, soul, and funk as well as jazz.

With Michael Brecker and Bob Mintzer, Berg is one of the most prominent members of the New York school of white tenor saxophonists that emerged in the 1970s and which blended and elaborated upon the styles of John Coltrane, Wayne Shorter, Sonny Rollins, and Joe Henderson. Although he does not have a prodigious technique like Brecker's, Berg possesses a secure command of the contemporary saxophone vocabulary. His brief but dramatic solo on the title track of Sam Jones's album *Visitation* (1978) best exemplifies his sound, which is bright and robust, but suffused with warmth and poignancy.

SELECTED RECORDINGS

As sideman: H. Silver: *Silver 'n' Brass* (1975, BN LA406G); T. Harrell: *Aurora* (1976, Adamo 9502); S. Jones: *Visitation* (1978, Ste. 1097), incl. Visitation;

C. Walton: *Eastern Rebellion 4* (1983, Tim. 184); M. Davis: *You're Under Arrest* (c1985, Col. FC40028); M. Stern: *Upside Downside* (1986, Atl. 81656–1)

BIBLIOGRAPHY

M. Gilbert: "Bob Berg," *JJI*, xxxviii/10 (1985), 8 [incl. discography]

MARK GILBERT

Berger, Karl(hanns) (*b* Heidelberg, Germany, 30 March 1935). German vibraphonist and teacher. He studied classical piano from the age of ten. As the house pianist for jam sessions at the Club 54 in Heidelberg, he learned to play bop in the company of such visiting American servicemen as Leo Wright, Cedar Walton, Lex Humphries, and Don Ellis; he also took up vibraphone and became interested in free jazz. After studying musicology and philosophy in Heidelberg and Berlin (PhD 1963) he joined Don Cherry's free-jazz quintet, then based in Paris (1965). When the group recorded in New York in September 1966 Berger remained in the USA, playing in schools for Young Audiences, Inc., with Horacee Arnold's group (1967–71) and periodically touring with his own bands. In autumn 1972, with Ornette Coleman, he founded the Creative Music Studio in Woodstock, New York. As its director he has created a program that concentrates on bringing out students' own ideas rather than directing them towards established jazz styles. Sam Rivers, Jack DeJohnette, Anthony Braxton, and Lee Konitz are among the musicians who have assisted Berger in workshops and concerts in Woodstock and New York. In 1982 he led a 28-piece orchestra at the "Jazz and World Music" section of the Kool Jazz Festival. He reduced his teaching activities in 1985–6 to make an international tour, during which he served as guest conductor and composer for the Westdeutscher Rundfunk in Cologne, Germany, performed at percussion festivals in New Delhi and Bombay as a pianist in a duo with the African percussionist Michael Babaunde Olatunji, and recorded in Tokyo with the *shakuhachi* player Hozan Yahamoto.

SELECTED RECORDINGS

As unaccompanied soloist: *Interludes* (1977, FMP 0460)
Duos: with D. Holland: *All Kinds of Time* (1976, Sack. 3010); with L. Konitz: *Seasons Change* (1979, Cir. [G] 19)
As leader: *Karl Berger Quartet* (1966, ESP 1041); *Tune in* (1970, Mlst. 9026); *We are You* (1971, Calig 30607); *With Silence* (1972, Enja 2022); *Live at the Donaueschingen Music Festival* (1979, MPS 68250)
As sideman: D. Cherry: *Symphony for Improvisers* (1966, BN 84247); *Eternal Rhythm* (1968, Saba 15204); Musica Elettronica Viva: *United Patchwork* (1977, Horo 15–16)

BIBLIOGRAPHY

R. DiNardo: "Karl Berger," *Coda*, xi/12 (1974), 2 [interview]
E. Jost: *Free Jazz* (Graz, Austria, 1974)
P. Occhiogrosso: "Karl Berger: Music Universe c/o Woodstock, N.Y.," *DB*, xliii/11 (1976), 18
"Karl Berger: l'école de Woodstock," *Jm*, no.280 (1979), 28
M. Ullman: *Jazz Lives: Portraits in Words and Pictures* (Washington, 1980), 163
E. Jost: *Jazzmusiker: Materialen zur Soziologie der afro-amerikanischen Musik* (Frankfurt am Main, Germany, Berlin, and Vienna, 1981), 168
J. Blum: "Karl Berger: Beyond the Creative Music Studio," *JT* (1986), June, 13

BARRY KERNFELD

Bergh, Øivind (*b* Hamar, Norway, 3 Dec 1909; *d* Oslo, 25 Jan 1987). Norwegian violinist and bandleader. He studied music in Dresden, Germany, and played jazz from the early 1930s. He belonged to the Funny Boys, the Scala-orkesteret, and Røde Mølle's Melody Boys and from 1939 to 1946 led the Bristolorkesteret, a swing group in Oslo comprising ten to eleven instrumentalists and a singer that made many recordings (including *Swing it herr lektor/Swing ling lei*, 1941, Col. GN806). From 1946 he led the dance orchestra of Norsk Rikskringkasting, which consisted principally of musicians who had belonged to the Bristolorkesteret. Later he was a guest conductor in Scandinavia and New York and of several European radio orchestras, and became increasingly involved in popular orchestral music; he retired from work as a professional musician in 1976. In addition to his principal instrument he played tenor saxophone and double bass.

Oral history material in *NOnj*.

BIBLIOGRAPHY

O. Angell, J. E. Vold, and E. Økland: *Jazz i Norge* (Oslo, 1975)
K. Michelsen, ed.: *Cappelens musikkleksikon* (Oslo, 1978)

VIDAR VANBERG

Bergheim, Kristian (*b* Asker, Norway, 6 June 1926). Norwegian tenor saxophonist. He began his career as a clarinetist and in 1948 moved to Göteborg, Sweden, to play in an orchestra led by the trumpeter Sven Sjøholm. He played swing and bop with the drummer Stein Lorentzen, Thorleif Østreng, Rowland Greenberg, the group Ny Norsk Jazz, and his own small groups; he remained active in the 1980s, principally in Oslo. An example of his work is his recording *Tupsi* (1954, RCA YNJL1 – 801).

BIBLIOGRAPHY

K. Sandegren and others: *Boken om jazz* (Oslo, 1954)
O. Angell, J. E. Vold, and E. Økland: *Jazz i Norge* (Oslo, 1975)
K. Michelsen, ed.: *Cappelens musikkleksikon* (Oslo, 1978)

VIDAR VANBERG

Berghofer, Chuck [Charles Curtis] (*b* Denver, 19 June 1937). Double bass player. He played with Skinnay Ennis, Pete Jolly, and the pianist Bobby Troup in Los Angeles. In the early 1960s he performed and made recordings with Shelly Manne's quintet (including *Shelly Manne and his Men at the Manne-hole*, 1961, Cont. 7593–4), then played in recording sessions under Herb Ellis (1960), Barney Kessel (1962), Jolly (1963–5, c1969), Howard Roberts (1963-7), and Gil Fuller (1965–6). Thereafter he recorded with Sarah Vaughan (1972), Ray Charles (1976), the Capp–Pierce Orchestra (1977–8), Ellis (1983), and Zoot Sims and Jimmie Rowles (both 1984). (*Feather '60s*)

Berigan, Bunny [Rowland Bernart] (*b* Hilbert, WI, 2 Nov 1908; *d* New York, 2 June 1942). Trumpeter and bandleader. He began playing in local groups while a teenager, and in the early 1930s moved to New York as a freelance musician and sometime member of such important bands as those led by Hal Kemp, Paul Whiteman, the Dorsey Brothers, Benny Goodman, and Tommy Dorsey. In 1933 he made a number of recordings under his own name, and from 1937 led his own successful big band. He rejoined Dorsey for a few months in 1940, then briefly led his own group until his death. Berigan and Bix Beiderbecke are often compared for the similarities of their lives and musical conceptions. As did many white trumpeters of his generation, Berigan showed the influence of Louis Armstrong in the variety of his timbre and attack, his wide range, and use of chromatic pitches. He showed too the influence of Beiderbecke in his use of "ghost" notes, lengthy concentrations of eighth-notes played with bell-like attack, and melodic lines that encompass more than one contrapuntal part. Berigan integrated these elements and a fine harmonic sense into a distinctive, uninhibited style, heard to advantage on Tommy Dorsey's recording of *Marie* (1937).

SELECTED RECORDINGS

As leader: I can't get started (1936, Voc. 3225); I nearly let love go slipping through my fingers (1936, Voc. 3254); I can't get started (1937, Vic. 36208)

As sideman: B. Goodman: King Porter Stomp (1935, Vic. 25090); B. Holiday: Billie's Blues (1936, Voc. 3288); T. Dorsey: Marie (1937, Vic. 25523)

BIBLIOGRAPHY

G. Frazier: "Bunny Berigan," *Jam Session: an Anthology of Jazz*, ed. R. Gleason (New York and London, 1958), 42

W. Mellers: *Music in a New Found Land: Themes and Developments in the History of American Music* (London, 1964/*R*1975), 380

I. Crosbie: "Bunny Berigan," *JJ*, xxvii/9 (1974), 8

A. McCarthy: *Big Band Jazz* (New York and London, 1974), 187

O. Coyle: "He Gave the Kid a Break: the Discovery of Bunny Berigan," *MR*, ii/11 (1975), 10

V. Danca: *Bunny: a Bio-discography of Jazz Trumpeter Bunny Berigan* (Rockford, IL, 1978)

E. Jenkins and J. Kline: "Touring with Bunny," *MR*, x/4 (1983), 1

JAMES DAPOGNY/R

Berimbau [berimbau de barriga, urucungu]. A Brazilian musical bow of African origin. It consists of a flexible, curved stave of berimba wood, between the ends of which is stretched a single wire string; an open-ended gourd resonator, attached to both stave and string by a tie, projects behind the stave. The tie attaching the gourd to the bow may act as a movable bridge, changing the relative lengths of the two portions of the string and thus the notes that may be produced by playing either portion. The player holds the bow with the string on the side further from him and the gourd towards him; with one hand he supports the instrument and stops the string, and with the other he plucks the string with the fingers or taps it with a stick. The gourd amplifies the vibrations of the instrument and thus its sound; by manipulating the open end of the gourd against his body the player may alter the timbre, producing muted or wa-wa effects, for example. The renowned exponents of the berimbau in jazz are Airto Moreira and Nana Vasconcelos; Vasconcelos plays the instrument unaccompanied on *O berimbau* from his album *Saudades* (1979, ECM 1147).

BIBLIOGRAPHY

L. Underwood: "Airto and his Incredible Gong Show," *DB*, xlv/8 (1978), 15

J. M. Schechter: "Berimbau," *GroveI*

BARRY KERNFELD

Berk, Dick [Richard Alan] (*b* San Francisco, 22 May 1939). Drummer. He attended the Berklee College of Music from 1959 to 1960 and played with local bands in Boston. After moving to New York he performed with Charles Mingus, Mose Allison, and Freddie Hubbard, and recorded with the quintet led by Ted Curson and Bill Barron (1962–4) and with Don Friedman (1963–4). In 1964 he performed and recorded with Walter Bishop, Jr., and took part in a recording session with Curson and Barron in Paris. The following year he recorded in the Netherlands with Rita Reys. He then moved to Los Angeles, where he performed and recorded with Milt Jackson (1969), George Duke (1969–71), and Cal Tjader (1970–73); he also played in sessions for Jean-Luc Ponty (1969), Groove Holmes (*c*1971), Frank Strazzeri (1973), Blue Mitchell (1977), and Ray Linn (1980). Later he recorded as a leader the album *Big Jake* (1982, Dis. 890); this includes the track *If I were a Bell*, which offers a particularly good example of his style. (*Feather–Gitler '70s*)

Berking, Willy (*b* Düsseldorf, Germany, 22 June 1910; *d* Frankfurt am Main, Germany, 21 May 1979). German bandleader, trombonist, and arranger. He moved to Berlin in 1934, when he began to study trombone; he played with Heinz Wehner from 1934 and the GOLDENE SIEBEN from 1936, and in 1938 formed his own big band, with which he made numerous recordings (1939–43; including *Syncope/Tonleiter*, 1940, Imperial 17314). From the late 1930s Berking was one of the most sought-after studio musicians in German dance music influenced by jazz: he recorded with Wehner (1935–9), the Goldene Sieben (1936–9), the violinist and bandleader Hans Rehmstedt (1938), the clarinetist Franz Thon (1939), and Lutz Templin (1941–2), among others. He founded the dance orchestra of the Hessischer Rundfunk in Frankfurt am Main in 1946. (*Reclams J*)

GÜNTHER HUESMANN

Berlin, Ben [Bick, Herman] (*b* Reval [now Tallinn], Estonia, *c*1900; *d* ?Hollywood, CA). Estonian bandleader, pianist, and arranger. He toured Europe in the early 1920s as a concert pianist and conductor, then settled in Berlin as music director of the Vox company. Between 1928 and 1930 he recorded several titles as a novelty pianist and as leader of his own studio dance bands; these include *You're the cream in my coffee* (1929, Grammophon 22401) and *Piccolo Pete* (1929, Grammophon 22899). Among the hot soloists he engaged were Danny Polo, Billy Barton, Louis de Vries, and René Weiss. Berlin left Germany after the Nazis came to power in 1933, toured in Europe, and then emigrated to the USA, where he worked in Hollywood in the film industry. (R. E. Lotz: *Hot Dance Bands in Germany: a Photo Album*, ii: *The 1920s*, Menden, Germany, 1982)

RAINER E. LOTZ

Berliner Jazztage. Name by which the JAZZFEST BERLIN was known until 1982.

Berlin Jazz Festival. *See* JAZZFEST BERLIN.

Berman, Sonny [Saul] (*b* New Haven, CT, 21 April 1925; *d* New York, 16 Jan 1947). Trumpeter. After joining Louis Prima's band at the age of 15 he worked from 1940 to 1945 as a section player in various orchestras, including those of Sonny Dunham, Tommy Dorsey, Georgie Auld, Harry James, and Benny Goodman. He joined Woody Herman's first Herd in February 1945, and became an important part of the band, sharing the trumpet solos with Pete Candoli; he remained with Herman until the group disbanded in December 1946, and died shortly afterwards of a heart attack while participating in an all-night jam session.

Berman's playing was influenced by the styles of Roy Eldridge and Dizzy Gillespie. He did much of his best work with Herman: he takes an excellent solo on *Sidewalks of Cuba*, and a brief but poignant one on *Let it Snow! Let it Snow! Let it Snow!*; there is also a humorous bitonal outburst on *Your Father's Mustache*. His lengthiest improvisations may be heard in four harmonically adventurous solos included on the album *Jazz Immortal*, and on the very haunting recording *Nocturne*.

SELECTED RECORDINGS

As leader: *Jazz Immortal* (1946, Eso. 322); Curbstone Scuffle (1946, Dial 1006); Nocturne (1946, Dial 1020)

As sideman with W. Herman: Your Father's Mustache (1945, Col. 36870); Let it Snow! Let it Snow! Let it Snow! (1945, Col. 36909); *One Night Stand with Woody Herman* (1945–6, Joyce 1021); Sidewalks of Cuba (1946, Col. 37197)

BIBLIOGRAPHY

I. Gitler: *Jazz Masters of the Forties* (New York, 1966/*R*1983 with discography)

H. S. Kaye: "A Birthdate for Sonny," *IAJRCJ*, xix/4 (1986), 9

SCOTT YANOW

Bernhardt, Clyde (Edric Barron) [Barron, Ed] (*b* Gold Hill, NC, 11 July 1905; *d* Newark, NJ, 20 May 1986). Trombonist and singer. Brought up in Harrisburg, Pennsylvania, he first played professionally in 1923 before moving to New York in

1928. He toured with King Oliver (1931, who first encouraged him to sing) and played with the Alabamians (led by the clarinetist and saxophonist Marion Hardy, 1931–2), the baritone saxophonist Billy Fowler (1932–3), the guitarist and banjoist Vernon Andrade (1934–7), Edgar Hayes (1937–42), with whom he toured Europe (1938), and Horace Henderson (1941). He toured with Fats Waller (1942) and Luis Russell, and worked with Jay McShann (1942–3), Cecil Scott (1943–4), Claude Hopkins (1944), and the Bascomb brothers, Dud and Paul (1945). After leading his own group, the Blue Blazers (1946–8), he worked again with Russell (1948–51), then played with Joe Garland's Society Orchestra (1952–70). He recorded as a leader under his own name and under the pseudonym Ed Barron. From 1972 to 1979 he led the HARLEM BLUES AND JAZZ BAND; having relinquished the leadership of that group owing to ill health, he joined the LEGENDS OF JAZZ, with which he played until 1986.

Oral history material in *NjR*.

SELECTED RECORDINGS

As leader: Blues in the Red/Scandalmonger Mama (1945, Musi. 348); Cracklin' Bread (1951, Derby 780); *Sittin' on Top of the World!* (1975, Barron 401)

As sideman: Alex Hill: Ain't it Nice? (1934, Voc. 2826); E. Hayes: Without you (1938, Decca 2193)

BIBLIOGRAPHY

D. Stewart-Baxter: "The Clyde Bernhardt Story," *JJ*, xx/9 (1967), 15; xx/10 (1967), 11; xxi/1 (1968), 31; xxi/2 (1968), 11

——: "Blues & Views," *JJ*, xxi/12 (1968), 13

——: Liner notes, *Blowing my Top: the All Star Bands of Clyde E. B. Bernhardt* (Matchbox SDR216, 1971)

G. Gaster: "Clyde Bernhardt," *Sv*, no.44 (1972–3), 54

C. Bernhardt, B. Demeusy, and D. Griffiths: "Clyde Bernhardt: a Nostalgic Tribute to Musical Americana, Reminiscences of a Musical Artist," *Record Research*, nos.173–202 (1980–83) [incl. discography]

C. Bernhardt and S. Harris: *I Remember: Eighty Years of Black Entertainment, Big Bands, and the Blues* (Philadelphia, 1986) [autobiography; incl. discography]

BRIAN PEERLESS

Bernhardt, Warren (*b* Wausau, WI, Nov 1938). Pianist and keyboard player. He studied classical piano and gave his first concert at the age of nine. While attending college he played jazz as a soloist in Chicago, then played in Paul Winter's sextet (1961–4), with which he toured South America (1962). After moving to New York in 1963 he played with Gerry Mulligan (1966), Clark Terry (1967), George Benson, and Jeremy Steig, and worked as a studio musician with the popular singers Tim Hardin, Richie Havens, Liza Minnelli, and Carly Simon. A turning-point in his career came through his association with Jack DeJohnette, with whose group Directions he toured and recorded in 1976. He played in a duo with Mike Mainieri (1975–80), in a trio with Peter Erskine and Eddie Gomez (1983), and in another trio with Jimmy Cobb and Dave Holland (1985–6). From 1984 to 1985 he led STEPS AHEAD with Mike Brecker, Erskine, Gomez, and Mainieri. He has also recorded as a solo pianist, taught jazz piano, and composed music for films. He plays in an eclectic, modal style and is noted for his adaptability to various styles and instrumental groupings.

SELECTED RECORDINGS

As unaccompanied soloist: *Solo Piano* (1977, AN 3001)

As leader: with M. Mainieri: *Free Smiles* (1978, AN 3009); *Trio '83* (1983, Digital Music 441)

As sideman: M. Mainieri: *Journey through an Electric Tube* (1969, SolS 18049); J. DeJohnette: *Directions* (1976, ECM 1074); C. Ogerman and M. Brecker: *Cityscape* (1982, WB 23698); Steps Ahead: *Modern Times* (1984, Elek. Mus. 60351)

BIBLIOGRAPHY

C. Berg: "Warren Bernhardt: Finding Himself at 40," *DB*, xlvi/5 (1979), 18

PATRICK T. WILL

Bernhart, Milt (*b* Valparaiso, IN, 25 May 1926). Trombonist. He studied tuba from the age of ten but took up trombone instead when he was 12. At 16 he belonged briefly to Boyd Raeburn's orchestra in Chicago, then moved to Hollywood in 1943. He was one of Stan Kenton's trombone soloists from 1946 to late 1951 and also played again with Raeburn in 1947 and with Benny Goodman in 1948–9. In the 1950s he recorded West Coast jazz on many occasions with such musicians as Maynard Ferguson (1950–55), Howard Rumsey (1952-3), and Shorty Rogers (1952–4). He was a member of the staff orchestra at Columbia Pictures from 1955 to 1958; later he worked as a freelance in clubs, television, films, and recording studios. Bernhart was in large measure responsible for the rounded tone of Kenton's trombone section; his numerous solos, many of which he played on ballads, are characterized by powerful playing, a full sound and harmonics typical of early bop. His style prefigured those of J. J. Johnson and Kai Winding.

SELECTED RECORDINGS

(recorded for Capitol unless otherwise indicated)

As leader: *Modern Brass* (1955, RCA LPM1123)

As sideman with S. Kenton: Somnambulism (1947, F527); Solitaire (1950, 28001); Evening in Pakistan (1950, 1043); Theme for Alto (1951, EAP1-508) [EP]

BIBLIOGRAPHY

FeatherE

C. Easton: *Straight Ahead: the Story of Stan Kenton* (New York, 1973)

WILLIAM F. LEE III

Bernstein, Artie [Arthur; Bernie] (*b* New York, 4 Feb 1909; *d* Los Angeles, 4 Jan 1964). Double bass player. He learned to play cello as a child, but later changed to double bass and, while studying law at New York University, decided to become a professional musician. He performed with Red Nichols in 1931, with whom he also recorded, and then worked with the Dorsey brothers' studio band (1932–4). He made recordings with the singer Cliff Edwards (1933), Putney Dandridge (1935), Teddy Wilson and Billie Holiday (1936), and Claude Thornhill and Larry Clinton (both 1937). He played in Benny Goodman's big band and sextet from 1939 to 1941 (for illustrations *see* BANDS, fig.4, and GOODMAN, BENNY), when he moved to California to work in film studios. He was named "best double bass player" by *Down Beat* in 1943. After serving in the air force during World War II, he again worked as a studio musician until he became seriously ill. Bernstein's superb timing and technique and his rhythmic drive are clearly demonstrated on the recordings he made with small groups, particularly *Night Owl*, *In a Mist*, and *Dance of the Octopus*.

SELECTED RECORDINGS

As sideman: C. Edwards: Night Owl (1933, Voc. 2587); R. Norvo: In a Mist/Dance of the Octopus (1933, Bruns. 6906); B. Goodman: Soft Winds (1939, Col. 35320); Seven Come Eleven (1939, Col. 35349); Metronome All-star Band: Bugle Call Rag/One o'Clock Jump (1941, Vic. 27314)

BIBLIOGRAPHY

ChiltonW; *FeatherE*; *Feather '60s*

LAWRENCE KOCH

Berry, Bill [William R.] (*b* Benton Harbor, MI, 14 Sept 1930). Trumpeter and bandleader. After traveling with Midwestern territory bands (1947-50) and serving in the air force (1951–5) he studied at the Cincinnati College of Music (1955) and the Berklee College of Music. While in Boston he played with Herb Pomeroy, then in 1957 he joined Woody Herman. In the early 1960s he settled in New York, where he worked mainly with Maynard Ferguson; he also toured with Duke Ellington (1961–

4), and became known for the obbligato he played for the tap dancer Bunny Briggs on Ellington's album *My People* (1963). Thereafter Berry took up regular television and studio work, recording with such bands as the Thad Jones–Mel Lewis Orchestra (1966–8). In 1964 he formed the New York Big Band, which performed locally to critical acclaim. He moved to Los Angeles in 1971 and reorganized the group as the L. A. Big Band; this ensemble, which takes its inspiration from the music of Ellington, has performed and recorded extensively and appeared at the Concord and Monterey jazz festivals. Its sidemen have included Blue Mitchell, Cat Anderson, Britt Woodman, Marshall Royal, and Richie Kamuca. Berry later toured England with Louie Bellson's big band (1980) and Japan with Benny Carter.

Oral history material in *CtY*.

SELECTED RECORDINGS

As leader: *Hot and Happy* (1974, Beez 1); *Hello Rev* (1976, Conc. 27); *For Duke* (1977, RT 101); *Shortcake* (1978, Conc. 75)

As sideman with D. Ellington: *All American* (1962, Col. CS8590); *My People* (1963, Contact 1), incl. David Danced before the Lord with all his Might

BIBLIOGRAPHY

P. Willard: "Territorial Imperatives: Genus Californica," *DB*, xliv/11 (1977), 16

B. Crowther: "The Bill Berry Story," *JJI*, xxxiii/2 (1980), 12

L. Tomkins: "My Pleasurable Jazz Life," *CI*, xxii/5 (1984), 6 [interview]

——: "Bill Berry: the Pros and Cons of a Part-time Band," *CI*, xxiv/10 (1987), 16 [interview]

STEVEN STRUNK

Berry, Chu [Leon Brown] (*b* Wheeling, WV, 13 Sept 1908; *d* Conneaut, OH, 30 Oct 1941). Tenor saxophonist. He grew up in a musical family, and was inspired by Coleman Hawkins to take up saxophone. He played the alto instrument in high school and during his three years at West Virginia State College, then in 1929 received his first important professional engagement on tenor saxophone in Sammy Stewart's Chicago-based big band. The following year he settled in New York, where he worked in many leading bands, including those of Benny Carter (1932) and Charlie Johnson. He also took part in Spike Hughes's famous recording sessions in New York in 1933. After periods with Teddy Hill (1933–5) and Fletcher Henderson (1935–6), which established his reputation, he joined Cab Calloway's band in 1937, remaining as its star soloist until his death in an automobile accident. From 1935 he was also a prolific freelance recording artist.

Berry was strongly influenced by Coleman Hawkins, but soon developed his own distinctive style, and even became influential in his own right during Hawkins's long absence from the American jazz scene (1934–9). His sound was less voluptuous than Hawkins's and his melodic imagination not as fertile, but he was the older man's equal in harmonic sophistication and his superior when it came to swing and drive. Berry excelled at performing in fast tempos, where his remarkable breath control, unerring sense of time, and even, strong tone-production stood him in good stead. His early ballad playing was sometimes too florid, but in recordings such as *A Ghost of a Chance* and *Lonesome Nights* (both made with Calloway's band in 1940) a new maturity became evident. Had he lived, Berry might well have offset the overwhelming influence of Lester Young on later tenor saxophonists.

See also IMPROVISATION, §4 (i); for illustrations *see* CALLOWAY, CAB, and CARTER, BENNY.

SELECTED RECORDINGS

As leader: Indiana (1937, Var. 587); Sittin' in/Forty-six West Fifty-two (1938, Com. 516); Blowin' up a breeze (1941, Com. 541)

As sideman: R. Norvo: Blues in E Flat (1935, Col. 3079D); H. Allen: Rosetta (1935, Voc. 2965); L. Hampton: Sweethearts on Parade (1939, Vic. 26209); Shufflin' at the Hollywood (1939, Vic. 26254); Ain't cha comin' home? (1939, Vic. 26362); Hot Mallets (1939, Vic. 26371); C. Basie: Oh! Lady be good (1939, Decca 2631); C. Calloway: A Ghost of a Chance (1940, OK 5687); Bye Bye Blues (1940, OK 6084); Lonesome Nights (1940, OK 5827)

BIBLIOGRAPHY

D. Ioakimidis: "Chu Berry," *JM*, x/1 (1964), 13

D. Morgenstern: "Three Forgotten Giants," *DBY 1965* (Chicago, 1964)

A. J. Bishop: "Chu Berry: an Appreciation," *JJI*, xxix/8 (1976), 18

J. Evensmo: *The Tenor Saxophone of Leon Chu Berry* (n.p. [Oslo], n.d. [?1976]) [discography]

D. Chamberlain and R. Wilson, eds.: *The Otis Ferguson Reader* (Highland Park, IL, 1982)

M. Hinton and D. Berger: *Bass Lines: the Stories and Photographs of Milt Hinton* (Philadelphia, 1988)

DAN MORGENSTERN

Berry, Emmett (*b* Macon, GA, 23 July 1915). Trumpeter. He was brought up in Cleveland and first worked in Toledo, Ohio, with the Chicago Nightingales (1932). In 1933 he moved to New York, where he played with numerous large and small groups. From November 1936 until June 1939 he worked with Fletcher Henderson, and then became a member of Horace Henderson's band. Thereafter he worked with Earl Hines, Teddy Wilson (1941–2, 1943–4; for illustration *see* WILSON, TEDDY), Raymond Scott (at CBS, 1942–3), Lionel Hampton, Don Redman, and Benny Carter (all 1943), John Kirby (1944), and Eddie Heywood (1945). Berry was a member of Count Basie's band from 1945 to 1950. After a brief period with Jimmy Rushing at the Savoy Ballroom he worked with Johnny Hodges (1951–4) and Earl Hines and Cootie Williams (both 1955). He made a tour of France with Sammy Price (1955–6) and visited Europe with Buck Clayton (1959, 1961). In the early 1960s he worked mainly in Los Angeles, but later in the decade he performed regularly in New York with such musicians as Peanuts Hucko, Wilbur De Paris, and Buddy Tate. In 1970 he retired owing to ill-health and moved back to Cleveland.

Berry had a broad tone and an excellent technique that allowed him to play complex phrases with ease; his style was influenced by that of Louis Armstrong, Roy Eldridge, and his close friend Buck Clayton. He made a large number of recordings, and his most successful solos are played on open trumpet; his recorded performances on the muted instrument are often marred by saturation and distortion of tone.

SELECTED RECORDINGS

As sideman: H. Henderson: Ain't Misbehavin' (1940, OK 5900); C. Cole: Stompin' at the Savoy (1944, Savoy 518); A. Sears: Now Ride the "D" Train (1951, King 4489); Berry Well (1951, King 4520); Nell don't wear no button-up shoes (1951, King 4540); J. Hodges: Globe Trotter (1951, Clef 8958); A Pound of Blues (1952, Clef 8961); What's I'm Gotchere (1952, Clef 89000); Jappa (1952, Clef 89086); J. Rushing: *Listen to the Blues* (1955, Van. 8505); B. Donaldson: *Bobby Donaldson and his 7th Avenue Stompers* (1958, World Wide 20005); on A. Gibson: *Mainstream Jazz* (1959, Camden, 554), Blue Print

BIBLIOGRAPHY

ChiltonW; *Feather E*; *Feather '60s*; *Feather–Gitler '70s*

R. Horricks: *Count Basie and his Orchestra: its Music and its Musicians* (London and New York, 1957)

P. Vacher: "The Forgotten Ones: Emmett Berry," *JJI*, xxxvi/1 (1983), 10

JOHNNY SIMMEN

Berry's. Swiss swing, show, and dance band. In 1935 Berry Peritz (drums), Ernst Berner (piano), and Johnny Ruckstuhl (saxophones) formed a trio called the Berry's in Lucerne, Switzerland. It was gradually enlarged by the addition of the singer and guitarist Billy Toffel, the double bass player Fred Jacquillard, and the tenor saxophonist Omer de Cock. On recordings made by the group in 1936 (including *Tiger Rag*, Parl. B35513) it was led by Coleman Hawkins, and the principal soloists were Hawkins, the clarinetist Ernst Höllerhagen, and Peritz's brother Hugo, who played tenor saxophone and clarinet. The Berry's performed in and around Zurich, mainly as a septet, until 1938, when it disbanded. For a while Peritz worked with Fred Böhler and Eddie Brunner, and also with Walter Baumgartner, with whose group the Magnolians he had already recorded in 1934; then in 1941 he reorganized the Berry's with the English trumpeter and singer Len Baker as the principal soloist. It made a large number of recordings for HMV in Switzerland (among them *The Berry's Stomp*, 1941, HMV HE555), but ceased performing in 1943. Peritz then formed a third group, a sextet, which performed in and around Lausanne, Switzerland, from 1945 to 1955; it did not record until 1985, when the musicians met at a reunion in Zurich.

BIBLIOGRAPHY

J.-R. Hippenmeyer: *Le jazz en Suisse, 1930-1970* (Yverdon, Switzerland, 1971)

E. W. Buser: "Swing Made in Switzerland: die grosse Zeit der Schweizer Big-Bands, 1938-1950," *Neue Zürcher Zeitung* (31 March 1984), 84

U. Staub: "The Berry's: Comeback für einen Sonntag," *Tages-Anzeiger Zürich* (24 May 1985)

RAINER E. LOTZ

Bert, Eddie (*b* Yonkers, NY, 16 May 1922). Trombonist. In his teens he studied with Benny Morton and he later learned from the playing of his friend Trummy Young. At the age of 18 he joined Sam Donahue's band; he recorded his first solo, on *Jersey Bounce*, in 1942 as a member of Red Norvo's orchestra. He played with Charlie Barnet (1943) and Woody Herman (1943–4), then, after army service, performed and recorded with the bands of Herbie Fields (1946), Stan Kenton (1947–8, 1950–51), Benny Goodman (1948–9), Herman (1950), Ray McKinley (1952), and Les Elgart (1954). He also began to work in small groups, joining the three-trombone ensemble led by Bill Harris (i) (1952), recording as a leader (1952–5), and leading groups regularly on Monday nights at Birdland, New York (from 1955); he belonged briefly to Charles Mingus's Jazz Workshop (1955–6). While continuing his career in jazz Bert played in Broadway theaters with Elliot Lawrence from 1954 to 1968, and gained a degree in music education from the Manhattan School of Music (1957). He played again with Goodman (1957–8) and Mingus (1962) and with the saxophonist Gil Melle (1962) and Thelonious Monk (1963–4). From 1968 to 1972 he worked on Dick Cavett's television show, during which time he also toured Europe with the Thad Jones–Mel Lewis Orchestra (for illustration *see* JONES, fig.1*b*). In 1978 he recorded with Sal Salvador's sextet, and he also made recordings in big bands led by Lionel Hampton (1978) and Teo Macero (1983). Bert's trombone playing is noted for its strength and adaptability.

SELECTED RECORDINGS

As leader: *Eddie Bert Quintet* (1953, Dis. 3020); Eddie Bert (1953, Dis. EP20); *Encore* (1955, Savoy 12019); *Eddie Bert's All Stars* (1955, Jzt. 1223); *Let's Dig Bert* (1955, Trans-World 208)

As sideman: R. Norvo: Jersey Bounce/Arthur Murray taught me dancing in a hurry (1942, Col. 36557); B. Goodman: Undercurrent Blues (1949, Cap. 15409); T. Monk: *The Thelonious Monk Orchestra at Town Hall* (1959, Riv. 1138)

BIBLIOGRAPHY

FeatherE; *Feather '60s*; *Feather–Gitler '70s*

Liner notes, *Like Cool* (Somerset 5200, 1955)

L. Tomkins: "Eddie Bert Talking," *CI*, ix/8 (1971), 26 [interview]

LAWRENCE KOCH

Berton [Cohen], **Vic(tor)** (*b* Chicago, 5 July 1896; *d* Hollywood, CA, 26 Dec 1951). Drummer and percussionist. He began playing professionally at an early age in his father's dance orchestra and later toured with a regional tent show. He played in clubs and theaters in the Chicago area before joining Sousa's US Navy band in World War I; after the war he returned to Chicago and studied timpani with Joseph Zettleman of the Chicago SO. He recorded frequently with the commercial bands of Sam Lanin, Paul Whiteman, Vincent Lopez, Roger Wolfe Kahn, and Don Vorhees, and with the dixieland musicians Red Nichols, Miff Mole, and Bix Beiderbecke, as well as leading his own groups; he also played with symphony orchestras, including the New York PO and Los Angeles PO. His last 20 years were spent in Hollywood as a music director and percussionist for Paramount and 20th Century-Fox.

Berton's playing epitomized the northern drumming style heard on recordings made in the early 1920s by Ben Pollack and Frank Snyder. Berton's recordings of 1926–9 with Nichols are remarkable for the choppy, syncopated figures played on a choked, suspended cymbal and for his improvised bass lines and solos on two pedal-operated timpani. An inveterate inventor, in 1926 Berton patented a precursor of the modern hi-hat cymbal.

SELECTED RECORDINGS

As leader: Devil's Kitchen/I've been waiting all winter (1935, Col. 3074D)

As sideman: Red Heads: Poor Papa (1926, PAct 36387); R. Nichols: That's no Bargain (1926, Bruns. 3407); Boneyard Shuffle (1926, Bruns. 3477); Davenport Blues (1927, Vic. 20778); Oh! Peter (1931, Bruns. 6198)

BIBLIOGRAPHY

ChiltonW

R. Berton: *Remembering Bix* (New York, 1974)

T. D. Brown: *A History of Jazz Drumming to 1942* (diss., U. of Michigan, 1976)

——: "Vic Berton: a Forgotten Giant of the Drums," *ARJS*, ii (1983), 181

T. DENNIS BROWN

Bertoncini, Gene (*b* New York, 6 April 1937). Guitarist. He played electric guitar from the age of seven and performed on television when he was 16. After studying architecture at the University of Notre Dame he returned to New York, where he belonged to a small group led by Buddy Rich in which Mike Mainieri and Sam Most also were sidemen (1961). He worked in studios with Clark Terry (1963), Paul Winter (1968), Nancy Wilson (1969), Wayne Shorter (1970), and Charles McPherson (1971) and from 1965 made frequent appearances on the "Tonight Show." In the late 1970s he formed a bop duo with the double bass player Michael Moore; he also recorded in a trio with Moore and Michal Urbaniak (1981). In addition to his work as a performer he has led workshops and taught at the Eastman School.

SELECTED RECORDINGS

Duos with M. Moore: *Bridges* (*c*1977, MPS 68176)

As leader with M. Moore: *Close Ties* (1984, Omni. 3334); *O grande amor* (1986, Stash 258)

BIBLIOGRAPHY

J. E. Siegel: "Gene Bertoncini," *Radio Free Jazz*, xxi (1980), March, 10

G. Lees: Liner notes, *Close Ties* (Omni. 3334, 1984)

J. S. Wilson: Review of *O grande amor* (1986), *New York Times* (28 March 1986), §C, p.27

FRANK A. DIBUSSOLO

Bertrand, Jimmy [James] (*b* Biloxi, MS, 24 Feb 1900; *d* Chicago, Aug 1960). Drummer, percussionist, and leader. He was a cousin of Andrew Hilaire. From 1918 to 1928 he worked mainly with Erskine Tate, performing at the Vendome Theater in Chicago and recording in 1923 and 1926. He also played in sessions with Tiny Parham (1926), Jimmy Blythe (1927), and the blues singer Blind Blake (1928), and made recordings as leader of the Washboard Wizards (1926–7, 1929); these last include *Easy Come Easy Go Blues/The Blues Stampede* (1927,

Voc. 1100), on which Johnny Dodds and Louis Armstrong play as sidemen. During the 1920s Bertrand was active as a teacher, and his pupils included Lionel Hampton and Sid Catlett. He joined Dave Peyton in 1928, then worked with Parham, Lee Collins, and Junie Cobb, and played and recorded with Eddie South (1931–3). He continued to perform, principally as leader of his own band, until 1945. (*ChiltonW*)

Oral history material in *LNT*.

Best, Clifton. *See* BEST, SKEETER.

Best, Denzil (de Costa) (*b* New York, 27 April 1917; *d* New York, 24 May 1965). Drummer and composer. He began piano lessons at the age of six, then later took up trumpet, and by 1940 was performing professionally with Chris Columbus and Joe Gordon. After a lung disorder was discovered he was advised to cease playing, and he began working as a pianist; he also played double bass and drums, which by 1943 had become his main instrument. An engagement with Ben Webster in 1943–4 established his reputation as a drummer, and he was immediately employed by Coleman Hawkins, with whom he worked from 1944 to 1945. Best then played with Illinois Jacquet and toured Sweden with Chubby Jackson (1947–8). His membership of George Shearing's quintet (1949–52; for illustration *see* SHEARING, GEORGE) ended when an automobile accident forced him into temporary retirement. In 1953, however, he resumed working, and toured with Artie Shaw's Gramercy Five and with Erroll Garner (1955–6). In the late 1950s he worked in New York with Tyree Glenn and the singer Nina Simone. Best's subtle, pulsing brushwork made his style readily identifiable, and is best heard on his recordings with Shearing. His melodic, effervescent compositions include *Move*, *Bemsha Swing* (which he wrote with Thelonious Monk), *Dee Dee's Dance*, *Nothing but D. Best*, and *Wee* (originally known as *Allen's Alley*).

SELECTED RECORDINGS

As leader: All Alone (1947, Wax 104)

As sideman: B. Holiday: Girls were made to take care of boys (1948, Decca 24551); L. Konitz: Marshmallow (1949, NewJ 807); G. Shearing: I Hear Music (1951, MGM 30624); E. Garner: *Concert by the Sea* (1955, Col. CL883); P. Newborn: *Fabulous Phineas* (1958, RCA LPM1873); S. Smith: *Sweet Swingin' Stuff* (1959, 20CF 3008)

RECORDED COMPOSITIONS
(selective list)
* – with Best as sideman

Recorded by others: C. Hart: *Dee Dee's Dance (1944, Savoy 998); C. Hawkins: Allen's Alley (1946, Vic. 400133); M. Davis: Move (1949, Cap. 15404); G. Shearing: *Nothing but D. Best (1949, MGM 10596); Bemsha Swing, on T. Monk: *Thelonious Monk Trio* (1952, Prst. 142)

BIBLIOGRAPHY

"Amerikanskt stjärnalbum [Album of American stars]: Denzil Best," *Orkester journalen*, xix/11 (1951), 5
P. Harris: "None Better than Best with a Brush," *DB*, xviii/8 (1951), 18
Obituary, *MM*, xl (12 June 1965), 6
I. Gitler: *Jazz Masters of the Forties* (New York, 1966/*R*1983 with discography), 190
D. Stewart: "The Forgotten Ones: Denzil Best," *JJI*, xxxix/11 (1986), 18

JEFF POTTER

Best, Johnny [John McClanian, Jr.] (*b* Shelby, NC, 20 Oct 1913). Trumpeter. He learned piano as a child; after changing to trumpet at the age of 13 he quickly began playing at dances. He was briefly a member of the bands of Les Brown and Charlie Barnet before working with Artie Shaw (1937–9). His playing, inspired by that of Louis Armstrong, was given great prominence. Best was later employed to good effect by Glenn Miller (1939–42; for illustration *see* MUTE, fig.3). A period with Bob Crosby preceded military service, during which he played in bands led by Shaw (1942–3) and Sam Donahue (1944–5). After leaving the navy he worked with Benny Goodman (1945–6), then moved to Hollywood, where he played on radio broadcasts with Crosby (1946–51) and worked again with Goodman (1947). He combined this with prolific activity as a freelance in studio big bands from the late 1940s. In 1953 he toured with Billy May, and from the late 1950s he performed at clubs in San Diego. He toured Japan with Crosby in 1964, and traveled to South America and Europe with Ray Conniff in the 1970s. Although serious injury in an accident caused him to be confined to a wheelchair, he continued to play into the mid-1980s, working with former members of Miller's band (in Australia, 1984) and of Crosby's (1985).

SELECTED RECORDINGS

As sideman: A. Shaw: The Chant (1937, Bruns. 7952); S. Donahue: I've found a new baby/Deep Night (1945, V-disc 583); B. Goodman: Oh, Baby! (1946, Col. 55039); B. Crosby: *Greatest Hits* (1960, Dot 25278); B. May: *The Swing Era: Curtain Call* (*c*1971, TL 352), incl. Struttin' with some Barbecue; San Diego Jazz Club: *Sound of Jazz* (1977, SDJC 22477)

BIBLIOGRAPHY

ChiltonW; *FeatherE*
G. T. Simon: *Glenn Miller and his Orchestra* (New York, 1974), 180
J. McVicar: "Fall from a Tree didn't Hurt his Lip," *San Diego Union* (15 May 1982), §D, p.1

BRIAN PEERLESS

Best, Skeeter [Clifton] (*b* Kinston, NC, 20 Nov 1914; *d* New York, 27 May 1985). Electric guitarist. He worked in Philadelphia in the late 1930s, then played with Earl Hines from 1941 until he joined the navy in 1942. After being discharged in 1945 he spent most of his career working as a freelance with various small groups, including one led by Milt Jackson and Ray Charles. He also recorded with Mercer Ellington in 1958. During his last years he was active as a teacher in New York. Although Best worked mainly as a rhythm guitarist his playing on *Soul Brothers* by Charles and Jackson includes several extended solos which show his style to have been influenced by that of Charlie Christian.

SELECTED RECORDINGS

As sideman: E. Hines: Stormy Monday Blues (1942, Bb 11567); Modern Jazz Sextet: *Modern Jazz Sextet* (1956, Norg. 1076); R. Charles and M. Jackson: *Soul Brothers* (1957, Atl. 1279); E. Hines: *Jazz is his Old Lady and my Old Man* (1977, Cat. 7622)

BIBLIOGRAPHY

FeatherE
M. J. Summerfield: *The Jazz Guitar: its Evolution and its Players* (Gateshead, England, 1978)
Obituary, *DB*, lii/10 (1985), 13

SCOTT DEVEAUX

Bet-Car. Record company and label established by BETTY CARTER in 1971.

Bethlehem. Record company and label. The company was founded in 1953, and quickly established offices in New York and Hollywood. More than 40 albums (the first of which was by Chris Connor) were issued on a series of 10-inch discs before Bethlehem changed to a 12-inch format in 1955. Thereafter the company was consistently successful for several years, creating a large catalogue (of variable quality) that included the work of such leaders as Dexter Gordon, Frank Rosolino, Charlie Mariano, Duke Ellington, Oscar Pettiford, Art Blakey, Booker Ervin, Zoot Sims, Herbie Nichols, Charles Mingus, Conte Candoli, and Claude Williamson. Contracts were also signed with several singers, among them Connor, Johnny Hartman, Carmen McRae (who made her first recording for the company), and Mel Tormé.

Howard McGhee made three LPs for the label; also included in the catalogue were albums by Stu Williamson, Booker Little, and Ruby Braff. At its peak in the late 1950s Bethlehem offered a representative cross-section of the styles then contemporary on both the East and West coasts, as well as more mainstream material by Jack Teagarden, Charlie Shavers, and Pete Brown.

While the quality of the company's 10-inch records was good, that of the 12-inch discs was frequently poor. Sessions were produced variously by Creed Taylor and Teddy Charles, among others, and several during the early 1960s were engineered by Peter Ind at his own studio in New York. Around this time, however, Bethlehem was bought by King, and jazz recording all but ceased. Much of the catalogue has nevertheless remained available into the 1980s, and is frequently reissued under arrangements with other companies, notably (in the 1980s) Affinity in England. (M. Ruppli and B. Daniels: *The King Labels: a Discography* (Westport, CT, and London, 1985) [incl. complete listing of Bethlehem recordings])

MARK GARDNER

Betts, Keter [William Thomas] (*b* Port Chester, NY, 22 July 1928). Double bass player. He played drums as a youth and by 1946 had taken up double bass, which he was playing professionally within a year. He accompanied Earl Bostic (1949–51) and Dinah Washington (1951–6) in rhythm sections that at times included Wynton Kelly and Jimmy Cobb. He worked briefly with Cannonball Adderley (1956) before moving to Washington, where he played with Charlie Byrd (1957–64); he and Byrd toured with Woody Herman in 1959. In 1964 he played with Bobby Timmons and in 1965 he began a long association with Tommy Flanagan, which lasted until 1978; they performed in trios and accompanied Ella Fitzgerald, with whom Betts continued to work independently into the 1980s. Betts plays with a full, rich tone, in a style reminiscent of that of Ray Brown.

SELECTED RECORDINGS

As sideman: C. Byrd: *Blues for Night People* (1957, Savoy 12116); *Bossa nova pellos passaros* (1962, Riv. 9436); T. Flanagan: *The Tommy Flanagan Tokyo Recital* (1975, Pablo 2310724); E. Fitzgerald: *Montreux '77* (1977, PL 2308206); T. Flanagan: *Something Borrowed, Something Blue* (1978, Gal. 5110)

BIBLIOGRAPHY

FeatherE

L. Tomkins: "Keter Betts," *CI*, xiii (1975), no.11, p.22; no.12, p.14

JOHN VOIGT

Bey, Andy [Andrew W., Jr.] (*b* Newark, NJ, 28 Oct 1939). Singer. He began playing piano when he was very young and later studied both piano and singing in Newark. He performed with Louis Jordan at the Apollo Theatre in New York (1953) and for more than ten years he led a group with his sisters Salome and Geraldine, Andy and the Bey Sisters, which made a number of recordings and toured in Europe (1958–9). He recorded with Max Roach (1968), Duke Pearson (1969), Horace Silver, Gary Bartz, and Stanley Clarke. In the early 1970s he spent nine months with the Thad Jones–Mel Lewis Orchestra and in 1979 he worked with Bobby Vidal in New York. He toured with Horace Silver in 1987. Bey is able to adapt his vocal style to suit the demands of the music he performs: he sings standard ballads and blues songs in a soft, lyrical voice, and yet can bring intensity and rhythmic drive to hard-bop and modal-jazz improvisations.

SELECTED RECORDINGS

As leader: *Andy and the Bey Sisters* (1959, Fon. 464451); *Experience and Judgment* (1973, Atl. 1654)

As sideman: H. Silver: *That Healin' Feelin'* (1970, BN 84352); G. Bartz: *Harlem Bush Music: Uhuru* (1970, Mlst. 9032); S. Clarke: *Children of Forever* (1972, Pol. 5531)

BIBLIOGRAPHY

Feather–Gitler '70s

L. Gourse: *Louis' Children: American Jazz Singers* (New York, 1984), 337

SCOTT FREDRICKSON

Bhumibol Adulyadej [Rama IX Bhumibol; Phoemipol Aduldej] (*b* Cambridge, MA, 5 Dec 1927). Thai clarinetist and reed player. He was brought up in the USA and in Switzerland, where he learned to play clarinet; he later mastered the whole family of reed instruments, favoring soprano saxophone. Although he is interested in early jazz he was influenced predominantly by Benny Goodman, and has participated in jam sessions with Goodman and other jazz musicians who have visited Thailand, notably Jack Teagarden and Lionel Hampton. He occasionally plays with his court orchestra in a swing style of the 1940s that is modified by the strong influence of traditional Thai music, but, on account of his official status as the King of Thailand, no recordings by him have been authorized for distribution. (H. Esman and V. Bronsgeest: "Een jazz king: Koning Phoemipol," *Doctor jazz*, no.84 (1978), 5)

RAINER E. LOTZ

Bickert, Ed(ward Isaac) (*b* Hochfeld, Manitoba, Canada, 29 Nov 1932). Canadian guitarist. He first played in Toronto with Ron Collier (from 1956), Moe Koffman (from 1957), and Rob McConnell (from the early 1960s), and continued to work with them intermittently during the 1960s and 1970s. In 1974–5 he performed and made recordings in the USA and Canada with Paul Desmond (including *Pure Desmond*, 1974, CTI 6059). He then worked in Canada, both as the leader of small groups with Don Thompson (1975–80), and as a sideman with visiting American musicians. In 1979 he toured Japan with Milt Jackson. Bickert has recorded with Oscar Peterson (1980), Rosemary Clooney (1983–4), and Benny Carter (1985), and has made several albums as a leader (including *Bye Bye Baby*, 1983, Conc. 232).

BIBLIOGRAPHY

FeatherE; *Feather–Gitler '70s*

M. Miller: "Profile: Ed Bickert," *DB*, xliii/10 (1976), 36

——: "Ed Bickert: Toronto's Premiere Session Guitarist and Jazz Performer," *GP*, xii/9 (1978), 35 [incl. discography]

"Ed Bickert: Quiet Man of Music," *CI*, xix/4 (1980), 14

M. Miller: "Ed Bickert in a Mellow Tone," *DB*, li/11 (1984), 20 [incl. discography]

——: "Ed Bickert," *Boogie, Pete & the Senator: Canadian Musicians in Jazz: the Eighties* (Toronto, 1987), 48

Biddell, Kerrie (*b* Sydney, 8 Feb 1947). Australian singer. She first studied piano. From 1968 to 1971 she sang with a cooperative group, the Affair, touring Australia and England. She then joined the Daly–Wilson Big Band, and worked as a studio musician and in cabaret. In 1973–4 she toured North America, appearing on television, and performing with her ensemble Compared to What. After her return to Australia she presented her own radio program, "Kerrie Biddell and Friends," for the Australian Broadcasting Company. During the 1970s she recorded three albums as a leader. In 1982 she formed a duo with the pianist Julian Lee and joined the faculty of the New South Wales Conservatorium in Sydney to teach jazz. Biddell possesses a powerful voice with a wide range. She is a gifted improviser, and may be heard to particular advantage on the track *Superwoman*, from her album *Compared to What, Featuring Kerrie Biddell* (1979, EMI SS301).

BIBLIOGRAPHY

A. Bisset: *Black Roots, White Flowers: a History of Jazz in Australia* (Sydney, 1979)

J. Jensen: "The Jazz Ladies," *Jazz: the Australasian Contemporary Music Magazine*, i/4 (1981), 5

M. Williams: *The Australian Jazz Explosion* (London and elsewhere, 1981), 131

B. Johnson and others: *The Oxford Companion to Australian Jazz* (Melbourne, Australia, 1987)

TONY GOULD

Bigard. Family of musicians.

(1) Emile (L.) Bigard (*b* New Orleans, ?1892; *d* New Orleans, ?1935). Violinist. He was a pupil of A. J. Piron, and in the years before and during World War I played lead violin in the Magnolia Orchestra (which included King Oliver) and in Kid Ory's Creole Ragtime Band. In 1919 he joined the Maple Leaf Orchestra, but left in the early 1920s to work with the cornetist Hypolite Charles. He ceased to perform around 1935. Bigard taught the fundamentals of music to his nephew (the son of his half-brother) (3) Barney Bigard. (B. Bigard: *With Louis and the Duke*, ed. B. Martyn, London, 1985)

(2) Alex(ander Louis) Bigard(, Jr.) (*b* New Orleans, 25 Sept 1899; *d* New Orleans, 27 June 1978). Drummer, brother of (3) Barney Bigard. He grew up in a musical family (among his cousins were Natty Dominique and A. J. Piron), and from the age of 18 studied drumming, including strict rudiments, with Louis Cottrell, Sr.; he occasionally played as a substitute for Cottrell in A. J. Piron's orchestra. He first worked professionally with Peter DuConge at Tom Anderson's, and about 1919 he became a member of the Excelsior Brass Band and the Maple Leaf Orchestra. He also performed with Buddy Petit and Chris Kelly, then in 1925 joined Sidney Desvigne's orchestra. Later he played with the trumpeter Kid Shots Madison and, possibly as early as 1926, with John Robichaux; he worked regularly with Robichaux from 1934 to 1939. Between 1944 and 1947 he was with Kid Rena, then in the 1950s he led his own group, the Mighty Four. He made his first recording in 1952 with the trumpeter Kid Clayton (*The First Kid Clayton Session*, FW 2859); *Shake it and break it* is an example of his classic New Orleans drumming style. During the 1960s Bigard performed frequently at Preservation Hall with De De and Billie Pierce, among others, but he was forced to retire in 1967 on account of deafness.

Oral history material in *LNT*.

BIBLIOGRAPHY

B. Martyn: "The Story of Alex Bigard," *Eureka*, ii/1 (1962), 5 [incl. discography]; repr. (without discography) in *Sv*, no.8 (1966–7), 3

B. Bigard: *With Louis and the Duke*, ed. B. Martyn (London, 1985)

(3) Barney [Albany Leon] **Bigard** (*b* New Orleans, 3 March 1906; *d* Culver City, CA, 27 June 1980). Clarinetist, brother of (2) Alex Bigard. He first learned to play E♭ clarinet, studying with Lorenzo Tio, Jr., and using an Albert system instrument. Discouraged on the clarinet, he adopted the tenor saxophone and joined Albert Nicholas's band late in 1922. After working briefly with the double bass player Oke Gaspard and with Amos White, he returned to Nicholas, with whom he traveled to Chicago late in 1924. There they joined King Oliver for an important engagement at the Plantation Café from February 1925 to March 1927. On four titles recorded on 10 March 1926 with a contingent from Oliver's band (under the leadership of Luis

Louis Armstrong's All Stars at the Barn, Wilmington, NC, 7 June 1949: (left to right) Jack Teagarden (trombone), Cozy Cole (drums), Velma Middleton (voice), Armstrong (trumpet), and Barney Bigard (clarinet)

Russell), Bigard displayed a cleanly executed saxophone style in the slap-tongue manner characteristic of that era. On the following day he made the first of a long series of recordings with Oliver for the Vocalion label.

As Oliver altered his band's personnel, Bigard was occasionally called upon to play clarinet, which soon became his principal instrument. He also recorded with Jelly Roll Morton and, in April 1927, with Johnny Dodds and Louis Armstrong. At the end of April, Bigard went with Oliver's band to New York, where they played for a fortnight at the Savoy Ballroom. The band broke up later while on tour, and Bigard joined Charlie Elgar's group in Milwaukee for the summer. He then returned to New York, playing with Russell for two months before joining Duke Ellington at the end of 1927 or the beginning of 1928.

Except for a brief absence in summer 1935, Bigard remained with Ellington until June 1942 (for illustration *see* BANDS, fig.3). This was the high-water mark of his career. During this period he perfected a highly individual clarinet style characterized by a warm tone in all registers, sweeping chromatic runs, and long, continuous glissandos. His quickly became a distinctive voice in the Ellington orchestra, and he was prominently featured on hundreds of recordings, most notably on *Clarinet Lament (Barney's Concerto)*, which he wrote with Ellington in 1936 (Bigard also collaborated on *Mood Indigo*, *Ducky Wucky*, and *Saturday Night Function*, among others). In addition he made many recordings with contingents from the Ellington band, and found time to record again with Oliver in 1928 and to produce four outstanding titles with Morton in 1929.

After leaving Ellington, Bigard continued to play and record with his own groups in Los Angeles and New York. His work during the autumn of 1946 with Louis Armstrong in the film *New Orleans* led to his next important association, as clarinetist with Armstrong's All Stars (see illustration). During his long tenure with this group (1947–52, 1953–5, 1960–61) he toured the world and took part in many outstanding recording sessions. Bigard went into semiretirement in 1962, but continued to play occasionally at concerts, for recording dates and television appearances, and at numerous jazz festivals both in the USA and overseas.

Oral history material in *LNT*, *NjR* (JOHP).

SELECTED RECORDINGS

As leader: Barney goin' easy (1939, Voc. 5378); Step steps up/Step steps down (1944, Sig. 28114); Rose Room/Coquette (1945, Key. 617); *Clarinet Gumbo* (1973, RCA APL1-1744)

As sideman with D. Ellington: Sweet Mama (1928, Har. 577H); Saturday Night Function (1929, Vic. 38036); Mood Indigo (1930, Bruns. 4952); Ducky Wucky (1932, Bruns. 6432); Clarinet Lament (Barney's Concerto) (1936, Bruns. 7650); Across the Track Blues (1940, Vic. 27235)

As sideman with others: L. Russell: 29th and Dearborn/Sweet Mumtaz (1926, Voc. 1010); K. Oliver: Too Bad (1926, Voc. 1007); A. Wynn: That Creole Band (1926, OK 8350); J. Dodds: Weary Blues (1927, Voc. 15632); K. Oliver: Showboat Shuffle (1927, Voc. 1114); J. R. Morton: That's like it ought to be (1929, Vic. 38601); L. Armstrong: Tea for Two (1947, Decca 9-28099–9-28100); C Jam Blues (1947, Decca 9-28102); Just you, just me (1951, Decca 9-28175)

BIBLIOGRAPHY

B. McRae: "Barney Bigard," *JJ*, xviii/4 (1965), 14
A. Judd: "Barney Goin' Easy," *JJ*, xx/9 (1967), 4 [interview]
L. Feather: "Barney Bigard: Blindfold Test," *DB*, xxxvi/12 (1969), 30
B. Bigard: "Me and Brother Satch," *Jh*, no.263 (1970), 16
S. Dance: *The World of Duke Ellington* (London and New York, 1970/*R*1981) [colln of previously pubd articles and interviews], 81
R. Stewart: "Illustrious Barney Bigard," *Jazz Masters of the Thirties* (New York and London, n.d. [?1972]), 113
D. Ellington: *Music is my Mistress* (Garden City, NY, 1973), 114
C. Battestini and J.-P. Battestini: "Barney Bigard," *BHcF*, no.273 (1979), 6 [interview]
D. Koechlin: *50 ans de jazz avec Barney Bigard* (n.p. [Darnetal, France], n.d. [1979])
A. Barrell: "Last of the Line: an Appreciation of Barney Bigard," *Fn*, xi/6 (1980), 4
B. Russell: "Jelly Roll Morton: an Interview with Barney Bigard," *Fn*, xi/6 (1980), 15
B. Bigard: *With Louis and the Duke*, ed. B. Martyn (London, 1985)

ALDEN ASHFORTH (1, 2)
LEWIS PORTER (3)

Big band. A term used principally to describe the swing bands of the 1930s and 1940s, which consisted of ten to 15 instruments, although it may be applied to any large ensemble; *see* BANDS, esp. §§4(ii), (iii).

Big Bands International. Organization of jazz enthusiasts formed in 1977 by Roy Belcher, who remained its president into the late 1980s. The group encourages the exchange of information on big bands among its members, who in 1987 numbered more than 4000; it also issues a quarterly journal, *Big Bands International* (first published in July 1977). Several prominent bandleaders have been involved in the organization, including John Dankworth, Maynard Ferguson, Woody Herman, Mel Lewis, Buddy Rich, and Artie Shaw. Big Bands International has its headquarters in Reading, England, and representatives in Australia, Belgium, and the USA.

Big Black [Ray, Danny] (*b* Georgia, 1934). Conga player. During the 1950s he played in groups at clubs and hotels in Miami and in calypso bands in the Bahamas. In the early 1960s he moved to New York, where he worked mostly with Randy Weston, though he also performed with Junior Cook. In 1965 he played with Dizzy Gillespie and Ray Bryant, and performed and recorded with Freddie Hubbard. He has also recorded with Charles Tolliver (1975) and Pharoah Sanders, and made several albums under his own name, including two of duos (*Message to our Ancestors* (*c*1969, Universal City 73012) with the flutist Black Harold, and *Ethnic Fusion* (1981–2, 1750 Arch 1790) with the guitarist Arthur Wheaton). (*Feather '60s*)

Big Chief Jazzband. Norwegian traditional-jazz group. Formed in 1951, its original members were the trombonist Gerhard Aspheim, the trumpeter Eivind Solberg, the banjoist and double bass player Bjørn Pedersen, the pianist Egil Fjelldahl, the clarinetist Svein Sundby, and the drummer Øistein Lund. The group first recorded in 1953 (*Tishomingo Blues/When the saints go marching in*, HMV AL3307) and performed in several European countries; it remained active in the 1980s. (O. Angell, J. E. Vold, and E. Økland: *Jazz i Norge*, Oslo, 1975)

VIDAR VANBERG

Big Daddy. Nickname of ERIC DIXON.

Big Four. Recording group. Formed in New York in 1940, it was led by Sidney Bechet (clarinet and soprano saxophone) and Muggsy Spanier (cornet) and also included Carmen Mastren (guitar) and Wellman Braud (double bass). The group recorded eight tracks for the Hot Record Society on 28 March and 6 April of 1940 that well illustrate the virtuosity of its members. The name Big Four was also used by quartets led by Buddy Rich and Charlie Ventura in 1951 and by Louis Nelson and George Lewis (i) in 1963.

SELECTED RECORDINGS
(all recorded in 1940 for Hot Record Society)

Sweet Lorraine/Lazy River (2000); Four or Five Times/China Boy (2001); That's a Plenty (2002); Sweet Sue (2003)

BIBLIOGRAPHY

E. Lambert: Liner notes, *Bechet–Spanier Big Four 1940* (Swaggie 1392, 1980)

MIKE HAZELDINE

Big Jim. Nickname of JIM ROBINSON.

Big Sid. Nickname of SID CATLETT.

Big T. Nickname of JACK TEAGARDEN.

Bilk, (Mr.) Acker [Bernard Stanley] (*b* Pensford, England, 29 Jan 1929). English clarinetist. He learned clarinet while in the army, and after being discharged (1950) he began playing with Ken Colyer's band (1954). After forming his own group in 1956 he performed in London and toured Germany. He was highly influenced by early traditional jazz; his Paramount Jazz Band, formed in 1958, played in a New Orleans style and enjoyed great popularity during the trad craze in the late 1950s and early 1960s. In 1962 he gave a royal command performance and toured the USA, and his recording of his own composition, *Stranger on the Shore* (1961), reached the top of the pop charts in Britain and the USA. He has recorded prolifically as a leader into the 1980s, and has continued to perform frequently all over the world.

SELECTED RECORDINGS

(recorded for Columbia unless otherwise indicated)

As leader: Snake Rag, Fancy Pants/Original Dixieland One Step, Goodnight, sweet prince (1960, SEG8089) [EP]; *Mr. Acker Bilk and his Paramount Jazz Band* (1962, SEG8178) [EP]

As sideman: B. Wallis: *Storyville Revisited* (1957, 77 LA12), incl. Dippermouth Blues, St. Louis Blues; *Clarinet Jamboree* (1959, 33SX1204)

BIBLIOGRAPHY

Feather '60s

T. Brown: "Anatomy of a Jazzman," *MM*, xxxvi (16 Dec 1961), 2

I. Berg, I. Yeomans, and N. Brittan: *Trad: an A to Z Who's Who of the British Traditional Jazz Scene* (London and elsewhere, 1962), 18

B. Matthew: *Trad Mad* (London, ?1962)

D. Fairweather: "Bilk, Acker," in I. Carr, D. Fairweather, and B. Priestley: *Jazz: the Essential Companion* (London, 1987)

RAYMOND J. GARIGLIO

Billberg, Rolf (*b* Lund, Sweden, 22 Aug 1930; *d* Uddevalla, Sweden, 17 Aug 1966). Swedish alto saxophonist. He played clarinet in a military band and worked in jazz from the 1950s as a tenor saxophonist in local groups and as a member of Sven Sjöholm's orchestra in Göteborg. He then moved to Stockholm, where he changed from tenor to alto saxophone; he performed with Simon Brehm (1954) and Carl-Henrik Norin (1957–8), and, most successfully, with Lars Gullin and Jan Allan. Towards the end of his career he played with Danish bands in Copenhagen. A good example of Billberg's playing is his recording *We'll be Together Again* (1965, Odeon 054-34830).

BIBLIOGRAPHY

S. Foerster: "Fulltonad folktonsimpressionist" [Sonorous, folklike impressionist], *Orkester journalen*, xxxii (1964), July–Aug, 12

ERIK KJELLBERG

Billings, Josh [Frank R.] (*b* Chicago, 1904; *d* New York, 13 March 1957). Drummer. He was inspired to play jazz after hearing the Austin High School Gang in Chicago. After moving to New York he performed and made recordings with Jack Teagarden, Eddie Condon, and Red McKenzie in the Mound City Blue Blowers (1929–31, including *Tailspin Blues*, 1929, Vic. 38087), drumming on a suitcase wrapped in paper. He also played, with Benny Goodman and Bud Freeman, in a session led by McKenzie (1930). From the mid-1930s he performed only intermittently.

BIBLIOGRAPHY

FeatherE

E. Condon and T. Sugrue: *We Called it Music: a Generation of Jazz* (New York, 1947/*R*1985)

Billy Berg's Swing Club. Nightclub in Hollywood; *see* NIGHTCLUBS AND OTHER VENUES.

Binyon, Larry (*b* Cicero, IL, 5 July 1908). Tenor saxophonist, clarinetist, and flutist. His association with Ben Pollack began in 1927 when he worked and recorded for him in Chicago; he recorded in New York regularly with Pollack from 1928, and also with his sidemen under Irving Mills (1928–30). He is heard to advantage on *Whoopee Stomp* (1928, Cameo 9030) recorded by Mills' Musical Clowns. In 1930 he left Pollack to play in the Broadway show *Girl Crazy* with Red Nichols and to work in the studio band of Victor Young. He also recorded with Nichols (1929–32), Fats Waller (1929), Benny Goodman (1930–31), the Boswell Sisters (1932–3), and Mildred Bailey (1933). Throughout the early 1930s Binyon recorded and worked for radio as a member of the Dorsey Brothers' band; he continued to play for New York radio stations until 1946. After moving to California he became a recording contractor for the AFM. During the early 1950s he led his own 20-piece band on a tour of the Far East, and he continued to perform regularly until 1955.

based on *ChiltonW*

Biondi, Ray [Remo] (*b* Cicero, IL, 5 July 1905; *d* Chicago, 28 Jan 1981). Guitarist, violinist, trumpeter, and mandolin player. He studied violin as a child and mandolin from the age of 12; during his early career the violin was his principal instrument. From 1927 to 1935 he worked chiefly in Chicago, where he recorded with Wingy Manone and Danny Altier. He played trumpet and violin in Earl Burtnett's band (1935) and after moving to New York in 1936 in that of Joe Marsala, with whom he performed and recorded; with Marsala he also played guitar occasionally in place of Eddie Condon. After playing guitar (1938–45) and violin (1944) with Gene Krupa (for illustration *see* O'DAY, ANITA) he returned to Chicago in 1945, then played again with Krupa (1950–51) and settled permanently in Chicago. Later he played guitar and mandolin as a freelance, recorded with Louis Armstrong (1953) and Woody Herman (1956), taught from 1961, and worked with Art Hodes and others from 1966. Biondi may be heard playing amplified violin on *Remo Blues* and *Biondi Bounce*, recorded in 1952 with Johnny Wicks and the Swinging Ozarks, and first issued in 1986 on the album *Jockey Jack Boogie* (1952, Pearl 13).

based on *ChiltonW*

Bird. Nickname of CHARLIE PARKER.

Birdland. Nightclub in New York; *see* NIGHTCLUBS AND OTHER VENUES.

Birth. Record company and label established in 1969 by GUNTER HAMPEL.

Biscoe, Chris(topher Dennis) (*b* East Barnet, England, 5 Feb 1947). English alto, soprano, and baritone saxophonist and alto clarinetist. A self-taught musician, he began to play alto saxophone in 1963. After a period in the National Youth Jazz Orchestra (1970–73) he became a professional musician and worked with such groups as Broken Biscuits (1973–6) and Red Brass (1975–8, recording in 1976). From 1979 he has been a member of Mike Westbrook's bands, recording with them from

1980; a good example of his playing may be heard on the album *Love for Sale* (1985, HA 2031). In 1980 Biscoe formed his own quintet, which he has occasionally augmented to a sextet (notably for an album recorded in 1986). He composes most of the group's material. He has also worked as a sideman with Brotherhood of Breath (from 1983), in a quintet led by the double bass player Didier Levallet and with Grand Union (both from 1985), performed on Working Week's first album (1985), and toured with George Russell in Europe (1986, 1987). A fluent, quick-witted player, he concentrates on modern mainstream jazz styles. (R. Cotterrell, ed.: *Jazz Now: the Jazz Centre Society Guide*, London, 1976)

SIMON ADAMS

Bishop, Joe (*b* Monticello, AR, 27 Nov 1907; *d* Houston, 12 May 1976). Flugelhorn player and arranger. His first professional work was as a tuba player. He then took up flugelhorn and toured and recorded with Isham Jones (*c*1930–1935). From 1936 to 1940 he was a member of the new Woody Herman Orchestra, and he returned to Herman as a staff arranger in 1942; his arrangements include versions of *Woodchopper's Ball* (1939, Decca 2440) and his own composition *Blue Flame* (1941, Decca 3634). He also played in studio sessions with the pianist Cow Cow Davenport and the singer Jimmy Gordon (both 1938). From 1942 Bishop worked as a freelance arranger, but ill health forced him to retire from music in 1951.

BIBLIOGRAPHY

ChiltonW
A. McCarthy: *Big Band Jazz* (New York and London, 1974)

Bishop, Wallace (Henry) [Bish] (*b* Chicago, 17 Feb 1906; *d* Hilversum, Netherlands, 2 May 1986). Drummer. He studied drumming with Jimmy Bertrand, worked with the blues pianist Thomas Dorsey (from 1923) and Richard M. Jones (1927), and toured with Jelly Roll Morton; he also played with Bernie Young, Les Hite, Erskine Tate (1929–30), and the pianist Jerome Carrington (1931). He first achieved prominence as Earl Hines's drummer (1931–6; for illustration *see* HINES, EARL), and in the 1940s performed and recorded with Jimmie Noone (1941), Coleman Hawkins (1943), the pianist Phil Moore (1944–5), Sammy Price (1946), and John Kirby and Sy Oliver (both 1947). After recording in New York with Louis Armstrong and Billie Holiday (both 1949) he traveled to Europe with Buck Clayton, worked in Switzerland (1950), and toured with George Johnson (1951). From 1951 he lived in the Netherlands, where he played occasionally with the pianists Rob Pronk (1951), Pia Beck (1952), and Frans Elsen (1956). In 1967–8 he made recordings with Buddy Tate, Milt Buckner, Johnny Letman, and Tiny Grimes, and he continued to work sporadically into the 1980s. Bishop's playing may be heard to advantage on Buddy Tate's recording *Crazy Rhythm* (1967–8, BB 33018).

BIBLIOGRAPHY

R. Richard: "A Jazzman in Europe: Wallace Bishop," *Storyville*, no.26 (1969), 44
J. Simmen: "Wallace Henry Bishop," *BHcF*, no.185 (1969), 3; no.186 (1969), 6
S. Dance: *The World of Earl Hines* (New York, 1977) [interviews]
H. Kleinhout and W. van Eyle: *The Wallace Bishop Story* (Alphen aan de Rijn, Netherlands, 1981)

WIM VAN EYLE

Bishop, Walter, Jr. [Bish] (*b* New York, 4 Oct 1927). Pianist. In the late 1940s he played with Art Blakey, and in the 1950s with Charlie Parker and Miles Davis (1951–3), Oscar Pettiford, and Kai Winding. During this period he became addicted to drugs, but had overcome his habit by the end of the decade. After playing with Curtis Fuller (1960) he formed his own trio with Jimmy Garrison and G. T. Hogan (1961). Bishop toured with Terry Gibbs's quartet in 1964, and in the late 1960s studied at the Juilliard School with Hall Overton. After moving to Los Angeles in 1969 he continued his studies and played and recorded with many groups and musicians, including Supersax and Blue Mitchell. He taught jazz theory both privately and at local colleges from 1972 to 1975, when he returned to New York. Later he played with Clark Terry's big band and quintet (1977), led his own groups, and made a tour of Switzerland (1979). In the early 1980s he began teaching at the University of Hartford, and in 1983 he gave a solo concert at Carnegie Hall, New York.

Bishop is the son of the songwriter Walter Bishop, who was a close friend of Art Tatum, and he cites Tatum, Bud Powell and Nat "King" Cole as important influences on his style. He is the author of a book of jazz theory, *A Study in Fourths* (New York, 1976).

SELECTED RECORDINGS

As unaccompanied soloist: *Soliloquy* (1975, Sea Breeze 1002)
As leader: *Walter Bishop Trio: 1965* (1962–3, Prst. 7730); *Coral Keys* (1971, Black Jazz 2); *Keeper of my Soul* (1973, Black Jazz 14); *Cubicle* (1978, Muse 5151)
As sideman: C. Parker: Au privave/Star Eyes (1951, Mer./Clef 11087); on M. Davis: *Collector's Items* (1953–6, Prst. 7044), Compulsion

BIBLIOGRAPHY

R. G. Reisner: *Bird: the Legend of Charlie Parker* (New York, 1962/*R*1975)
M. Gardner and F. Gibson: "Walter Bishop Jr.: Discography," *JJ*, xvii (1964), no.9, p.29; no.10, p.24
D. Nelsen: "Resurgent Piano: Walter Bishop Jr.," *DB*, xxxiii/18 (1966), 24
I. Gitler: "Walter Bishop Trio," *DB*, xxxv/20 (1968), 33
B. Primack: "Jazz Warrior Marches On," *DB*, xliv/6 (1977), 16
——: "Walter Bishop: New Directions for a Bebop Legend," *CK*, iv/12 (1978), 24 [incl. discography]

PHILIP GREENE

Bistrouille A(mateurs) D(ance) O(rchestra). Belgian big band. It was established by the drummer René Vinche and his brother in Brussels in 1920 after they had heard the Jazz Kings led by Louis Mitchell. The orchestra originated as an amateur group and, although it very quickly became professional, it recorded only two sides (for Columbia, 1930). Most of Belgium's best-known jazz musicians performed with the ensemble at different times.

ROBERT PERNET

Bivona, Gus (*b* New London, CT, 25 Nov 1915). Clarinetist. He grew up in a musical family and played the violin at the age of ten, and alto saxophone and clarinet when he was 16. After performing with lesser-known bands in Connecticut he moved to New York in the early 1930s. He worked with Bunny Berigan and Will Hudson (both 1938) and Teddy Powell (1939–40), then played with Benny Goodman (1940–41) and Jan Savitt and Les Brown (both 1942). After leading his own band during military service he worked with Tommy Dorsey (1945, 1947) and Bob Crosby (1946). In 1947 Bivona joined the studio orchestra at MGM in Hollywood, and during the 1950s he was associated with Steve Allen, performing on television, recording albums, and working at the Roundtable in New York. He continued to lead bands and work as a session musician into the 1970s. Bivona was highly influenced by Allen, and his playing is reminiscent of Goodman's.

SELECTED RECORDINGS

As sideman: B. Berigan: Flashes/Davenport Blues (1938, Vic. 26121); G. Gray: *Sounds of the Great Casa Loma Band* (1957, Cap. T1588); S. Allen:

Allen's All Stars (1958, EmA 36138); *Steve Allen at the Roundtable* (1959, Roul. 25053), incl. Even Stephen, I got rhythm

BIBLIOGRAPHY

ChiltonW; *FeatherE*

RAYMOND J. GARIGLIO

Björksten, Hacke [Gunnar] (*b* Helsinki, 17 Feb 1934). Swedish tenor saxophonist and bandleader of Finnish birth. He moved to Sweden in 1945 and gained recognition in the early 1950s in Göteborg, where he worked with the drummer Kenneth Fagerlund (1952–4). From 1954 to 1959 he led a group at the Nalen in Stockholm that included Åke Persson and for which Jan Johansson wrote arrangements; the recording *On the Alamo* (1955, Met. 167 [EP]), which he made as the leader of a quintet that included Persson, shows to advantage his fluent technique and large tone. After several years of inactivity he recorded again as a leader (1972, 1979) and remained active into the 1980s. ("På omslaget" [On the cover], *Orkester journalen*, xxii/4 (1955), 4)

ERIK KJELLBERG

Black, Dave [David John] (*b* Philadelphia, 23 Jan 1928). Drummer. From 1948 he worked as house drummer at the Blue Note club in Philadelphia, where he accompanied Charlie Parker, Buddy DeFranco, Georgie Auld, and others. He then toured and recorded with Duke Ellington (1953–5); a good example of his playing may be heard on *Gonna tan your hide* (1954) on *Ellington Showcase* (1953–5, Cap. T679). He also performed and recorded traditional jazz with Bob Scobey (1957–60). *(FeatherE)*

Black, Lou(is Thomas) (*b* Rock Island, IL, 8 June 1901; *d* Rock Island, 18 Nov 1965). Banjoist. He took up banjo as a young child and played professionally from 1917. He played in the band of the pianist Carlisle Evans on the SS *Capitol* (1919–21) but left Evans to join the Friars Society Orchestra (later the New Orleans Rhythm Kings), which was playing regularly at the Friar's Inn in Chicago; he took part in the group's first recordings (including *Bugle Rag*, 1922, Gen. 4967) but left it in 1923 to perform and record with the Original Memphis Melody Boys and then to record with the Elmer Schoebel Midway Dance Orchestra. He played again with Evans for a brief period and then worked as a staff musician in radio (1925–31); he ceased to be active as a musician in the 1930s and resumed playing only in 1961.

For illustration *see* NEW ORLEANS RHYTHM KINGS.

BIBLIOGRAPHY

W. Balliett: "Lou Black: a Burning Desire," *Such Sweet Thunder* (Indianapolis, 1966) [colln of previously pubd articles and reviews], 90

Obituary, B. Mantler, *SL*, xvii (1966), 11

based on *ChiltonW*

Black and Blue. Record company and label. The company was established in France in 1968, and was devoted to hot jazz and blues. At first most of the records were reissues of material originally put out on small American labels; later the company began recording its own repertory. As well as sponsoring sessions in the USA it recorded the work of black musicians when they visited France. Within a few years Black and Blue's rapidly expanding catalogue of material by such musicians as Buddy Tate, Jo Jones, Milt Buckner, Sammy Price, Jay McShann, Illinois Jacquet, Ray Bryant, and Panama Francis had made the company one of the most important sources of swing and mainstream jazz in the world; it has continued to make recordings, and has retained its position, into the 1980s. (E. Townley: "The Black and Blue Label," *Jazz Circle News*, no.11 (1978), 14)

Black & White. Record company and label. The company was established in 1944 by Paul and Lillian Reiner; the recording director was Ralph Bass. The jazz catalogue included contributions from Barney Bigard, Lil Armstrong, and Willie "the Lion" Smith, and from younger musicians, such as Erroll Garner, Jack McVea, and Wilbert Baranco. Although it existed only for a few years, Black & White was one of the first companies to issue 12-inch 78 r.p.m. discs in unbreakable material. Paul Reiner was also associated with the label Comet, and some material appears in both catalogues.

BIBLIOGRAPHY

A. Shaw: *Honkers and Shouters: the Golden Years of Rhythm and Blues* (New York, 1978), 226

D. Salemann: Liner notes, *Small Label Gems of the Forties*, ii (Solid Sender SOL513, ?1980)

Black Arthur. Nickname of ARTHUR BLYTHE.

Black Artists Group [BAG]. Artists' collective. It was formed in St. Louis in 1968 and modeled after the Association for the Advancement of Creative Musicians. The group sponsored performances by its members, which ranged from solo recitals to big-band concerts. Among those who performed were Hamiet Bluiett, Joseph Bowie, Baikida Carroll, Julius Hemphill, Charles "Bobo" Shaw, Oliver Lake, the trumpeter Floyd LeFlore, and the reed player J. D. Parran; actors, poets, and visual artists also took part in mixed-media presentations. The Human Arts Ensemble had a particularly close association with the collective; this was a band of as many as 13 members of which Shaw was a leader. The BAG also maintained a building that included a performance space, living quarters, and teaching studios. It disbanded in 1972 when grants from the NEA and the Missouri Arts Council were discontinued.

BIBLIOGRAPHY

V. Wilmer: "Politics, the Media and Collectivism," *As Serious as your Life: the Story of the New Jazz* (London, 1977, rev. 1980), 215

J. Litweiler: *The Freedom Principle: Jazz after 1958* (New York, 1984), 187

ED HAZELL

Black bottom. A quick-tempo social dance performed in the 1920s. It is thought to have originated in the early 1900s in the "juke" (black) bawdy houses of the "Bottoms," the black quarter of Nashville. The popularity of the black bottom and other related dances, such as the CHARLESTON, developed from the success of Eubie Blake and Noble Sissle's revue *Shuffle Along* (1921), which introduced dancing to jazz. Among the finest of Jelly Roll Morton's recordings with the Red Hot Peppers was his composition *Black Bottom Stomp* (1926, Vic. 20221).

BIBLIOGRAPHY

M. Stearns and J. Stearns: *Jazz Dance: the Story of American Vernacular Dance* (New York and London, 1968)

L. F. Emery: *Black Dance in the United States from 1619 to 1970* (Palo Alto, CA, 1972)

P. Oliver: *The Meaning of the Blues* (New York, 1972)

PAULINE NORTON

Black Bottom Stompers. Septet. Formed in Chicago in 1927 to record for Brunswick and Vocalion, it was led by Johnny Dodds (clarinet) and included as its other members Louis Armstrong (cornet), Roy Palmer (trombone), Barney Bigard (tenor saxophone), Earl Hines (piano), Bud Scott (banjo), and Baby Dodds (drums); Johnny Dodds and Armstrong had earlier recorded for Okeh as members of the Hot Five (1925–6) and of Jimmy Bertrand's Washboard Wizards (21 April 1927). The Black Bottom Stompers recorded four tracks on 22 April 1927, of which *Wild Man Blues* (Bruns. 3567) and *New Orleans Stomp* (Voc. 15632) are particularly outstanding. On October 8 of the same year Dodds recorded four more tracks for Vocalion (including *Come On and Stomp Stomp Stomp*, Bruns. 3568) as the leader of a group that included the cornetists George Mitchell and Natty Dominique, a trombonist (possibly John Thomas), the pianist Charlie Alexander, the banjoist Bud Scott, and the drummer Baby Dodds. (B. Rust: Liner notes, J. Dodds: *Clarinet King*, Ace of Hearts 169, 1968)

MIKE HAZELDINE

Blackburn, Lou (*b* Rankin, nr Pittsburgh, 12 Nov 1922). Trombonist. He studied at Roosevelt University, and formed his own group while serving in the army; during this period he was transferred to Europe, where he was a member of the 7th Army SO (1955–6). Thereafter he worked with Charlie Ventura (1956), toured Europe and North Africa and recorded with Lionel Hampton (1958–9), and joined Cat Anderson's group (1960). After playing with Duke Ellington for eight months in 1961 he settled in Los Angeles, where he undertook work in film studios and accompanied many singers. From 1970 Blackburn has lived in Europe, first in Berlin and then in Switzerland. He has played with big bands and led his own groups, one of which, Mombasa, includes African musicians, and performs in a style strongly influenced by African music. Blackburn's playing is characterized by an expressive tone and a strong rhythmic attack.

SELECTED RECORDINGS

As leader: *Mombasa: African Rhythm & Blues* (1975, Intercord 160020); *Mombasa 2: African Rhythm & Blues* (1976, Intercord 160049); *Ode to Kalahari* (1979, Intercord 145601); *Mombasa: Tathagata* (1980, Wind 002); *Peacemaker* (1981, Pläne 88268)

As sideman with Charles Mingus: *Mingus at Monterey* (1964, Charles Mingus 001–2)

BIBLIOGRAPHY

Feather '60s; *Feather–Gitler '70s*

G. Endress: "Afrika spricht aus Mombasa," *JP*, xxiv/4 (1975), 4

ROLAND BAGGENAES

Black Jazz. Record company and label. The company was established in Glenview, Illinois, in 1971, by Gene Russell, who produced sessions in both New York and Los Angeles. Black Jazz was distributed by Ovation, Inc., of Glenview.

MARK GARDNER

Black Lion. Record company and label. The company was established by Alan Bates in London around 1968; from that time, apart from a period of inactivity in the early 1980s, it has issued material in two series. The International Series contains new recordings by such musicians as Stephane Grappelli, Barney Kessel, Dexter Gordon, Hampton Hawes, Earl Hines, Teddy Wilson, Philly Joe Jones, Sun Ra, Paul Gonsalves, Ray Nance, and Thelonious Monk. In addition it is used to reissue much very diverse material: swing and bop first put out on Sunset; recordings of broadcasts made by Art Tatum and Jay McShann; V-discs by Tatum; items recorded in Europe in the 1960s by Ben Webster, Hines, Bud Freeman, Bud Powell, Don Byas, and Coleman Hawkins; and lesser-known items by Duke Ellington. The British Series consists mainly of newly-made recordings by Chris Barber, Freddy Randall, Humphrey Lyttelton, and Alex Welsh among others. The company also had a subsidiary, Freedom, which was used for free jazz, though some exchange of material took place between the two labels; as a result, when Arista bought Freedom in 1975 it also acquired the rights to several recordings on Black Lion. The company has relied for the distribution of its discs on larger organizations, including Polydor; thus many albums which were issued in Europe, the USA, and Japan on Black Lion have also been put out on Polydor. (G. Murphy: "Black Lion Roars Back," *The Wire*, no.16 (1985), 24)

Black Patti. Record label. It was owned by the Chicago Record Company, and was founded around March 1927 by J. Mayo Williams, who had previously been responsible for artists and repertory for Paramount's race series. The label was named after the opera singer Sissieretta Jones, who was known as "Black Patti." The first 20 of the label's 55 issues were advertised in May 1927; trading appears to have ceased around four months later. The recordings were made at Gennett's studios, and many of them were also put out on Gennett and associated labels.

BIBLIOGRAPHY

M. Wyler: "The Black Patti Story," *Sv*, i/1 (1965), 11 [incl. discography]

"More about Black Patti," *Sv*, i/4 (1966), 11

R. M. W. Dixon and J. Godrich: *Recording the Blues* (London, 1970), 44

D. Jones: "The Black Patti Project," *Matrix*, nos.102–3 (1974), 27

H. Henriksen: "Black Patti Numerical," *Record Research*, nos.189–90 (1982), 8; nos.191–2 (1982), 8; nos.193–4 (1982), 9; nos.195–6 (1983), 13; nos.197–8 (1983), 9; nos.201–2 (1983), 11

——: "Black Patti Records Artists Panorama," *Record Research*, nos.205–6 (1984), 1; nos.207–8 (1984), 1

H. Henriksen and L. Kunstadt: "Black Patti Records," *Record Research*, nos.209–10 (1984), 10

Black Saint. Italian record company and label. The company was established in 1975 in Milan by Giacomo Pellicciotti, then taken over and greatly expanded from 1978 by Giovanni Bonandrini. Concentrating on free jazz, it has issued many significant recordings by such individuals and groups as David Murray, Old and New Dreams, the World Saxophone Quartet, Roscoe Mitchell, and Anthony Braxton. (F. Davis: *In the Moment: Jazz in the 1980s* (New York, and Oxford, England, 1986) [colln of previously pubd articles], 206)

Black Swan. Record company and label. The company was established in New York in January 1921 as a subsidiary of the Pace Phonograph Corp. Its president and general manager was Harry H. Pace, who had formerly been W. C. Handy's partner in the music publishing firm Pace & Handy. The operation was named after the opera singer Elizabeth Taylor Greenfield, whose nickname was "the Black Swan"; it was the first record label owned and run by black businessmen, and issued exclusively to the race market material recorded entirely by black musicians. The first discs were issued in May 1921, and the catalogue contained all kinds of material, including European classical and light music as well as jazz and blues. Fletcher Henderson was the house accompanist, and may be heard not only with such singers as Ethel Waters and Trixie Smith, and with his own band, but also playing for classical musicians.

In April 1922 Pace purchased the Olympic Disc Record Corp. (the producer of the label Olympic, which had failed in December of the previous year) in partnership with one of its former executives, John Fletcher. Olympic was reorganized as the Fletcher Record Corp., and its plant in Brooklyn was turned over to the production of Black Swan's records. Though the latter's owners continued to claim in advertisements that the enterprise was run solely by Blacks and that they put out only recordings by race musicians, and despite their continued release of items by Henderson, they began to use the label to issue material from Olympic's catalogue (often under the misleading pseudonym Henderson's Dance Orchestra) that included both undistinguished dance music of the era and work by such white ensembles as the Original Memphis Five. This continued after the Fletcher Record Corp. revived the label Olympic later in 1922.

In March 1923 the Pace Phonograph Corp. was renamed the Black Swan Phonograph Co.; after July that year no new records were announced. In May the following year Pace entered into an arrangement with Paramount whereby recordings made by Black Swan were reissued (bearing Black Swan's logo) in a special section (12100–189) of Paramount's race series. Paramount also took over Black Swan's artist contracts, and in return made a fixed monthly payment to Black Swan. This transaction was successful only for a short period, for a letter from Pace to *The Afro-American* (a newspaper based in Baltimore) of 16 January 1926 stated that the leasing agreement had been terminated. Though the masters were then returned to Black Swan, the company issued no further records. In January 1987 Jazzology announced its intention to revive the name Black Swan for a series of reissues of material taken mainly from Paramount.

BIBLIOGRAPHY

"The Black Swan Story," *Record Research*, i (1955), no.4, p.3; no.5, p.5
"Black Swan Catalogue," *Record Research*, i (1955), no.5, p.7; no.6, p.21; ii (1956–7), no.1, p.10; no.2, p.13; no.3, p.23; no.5, p.10; iii (1957–8), no.1, p.12; no.2, p.20; no.3, p.24; no.4, p.11
J. Godrich and R. M. W. Dixon: *Blues & Gospel Records, 1902–1942* (Hatch End, nr London, 1964, rev. 2/1969, rev. and enlarged 3/1982 as R. M. W. Dixon and J. Godrich: *Blues & Gospel Records, 1902–1943*), 24
M. Wyler: "A Glimpse into the Past, 3: Black Swan," *Sv*, i/4 (1966), 12
R. Ottley and W. J. Weatherby, eds.: *The Negro in New York: an Informal Social History* (New York, 1967), 232
R. M. W. Dixon and J. Godrich: *Recording the Blues* (London, 1970), 13
M. E. Vreede: *Paramount 12/13000 Series* (London, 1971) [discography]
W. C. Allen: *Hendersonia: the Music of Fletcher Henderson and his Musicians: a Bio-discography* (Highland Park, NJ, 1973) [incl. discography], 10, 24, 491
B. Rust: *The American Record Label Book* (New Rochelle, NY, 1978), 35, 218
C. Kendziora, Jr., and P. Armagnac: "The Labels Behind Black Swan," *Record Research*, nos.221–2 (1986), 1
G. H. Buck, Jr.: "Up and Coming Projects . . .," *CRC Newsletter*, xiii/1–2 (1987), 5
L. Kunstadt: "The Labels Behind Black Swan: the Black Swan–Olympic Connection," *Record Research*, nos.229–30 (1987), 1

HOWARD RYE

Blackwell, Ed(ward Joseph) (*b* New Orleans, 10 Oct 1929). Drummer. He was influenced at an early age by the drumming of Paul Barbarin; in the late 1940s he played in a rhythm-and-blues band led by Plas Johnson and Raymond Johnson. He moved in 1951 to Los Angeles, where he first worked with Ornette Coleman, and two years later to Texas before returning in 1956 to New Orleans. In 1960 he settled in New York, where he replaced Billy Higgins in Coleman's quartet; as a member of this group during the following decade he became well-known for his skillful adaptation of New Orleans rhythms to free jazz. He also made a series of important recordings with Don Cherry, worked with Mal Waldron and Richard Davis in a quintet led by Booker Little and Eric Dolphy (recording in 1961), played with Randy Weston from 1965 (touring Africa in 1967), and recorded with Archie Shepp (1965, 1967). He became an artist-in-residence at Wesleyan University in 1975 and from the following year toured and recorded as a member of Old and New Dreams. Later he belonged to several groups led by Cherry and to quartets led by Anthony Braxton (recording in 1981), Dewey Redman (recording in 1982), and David Murray (recording in 1983). In 1987 he toured England and Scotland with the group Nu, which was led by Cherry. One of the most melodic of drummers, Blackwell often emphasizes the sonorities of his tom-toms and bass drum, and sometimes produces rhythms that have a quality approaching that of singsong.

SELECTED RECORDINGS

As leader of Old and New Dreams (with D. Cherry, C. Haden, and D. Redman): *Old and New Dreams* (1979, ECM 1154)

As sideman: O. Coleman: *This is our Music* (1960, Atl. 1353); *Twins* (1960, Atl. 1588); *Free Jazz* (1960, Atl. 1364); *Ornette on Tenor* (1961, Atl. 1394); E. Dolphy: *Eric Dolphy at the Five Spot* (1961, NewJ 8260); D. Cherry: *Complete Communion* (1965, BN 84226); *Symphony for Improvisers* (1966, BN 84247); *Where is Brooklyn?* (1966, BN 84311); *Mu* (1969, BYG 529301, 529331); O. Coleman: *Science Fiction* (1971, Col. KC31061); D. Cherry: *Old and New Dreams* (1976, BS 0013); *El Corazon* (1982, ECM 1230)

BIBLIOGRAPHY

V. Wilmer: "Ed Blackwell: Well-tempered Drummer," *DB*, xxxv/20 (1968), 18
B. Mintz: *Different Drummers* (New York and London, 1975)
R. Palmer: "Ed Blackwell: Crescent City Thumper," *DB*, xliv/12 (1977), 17
S. Fish: "Ed Blackwell: Singin' on the Set," *MD*, v/8 (1981), 14

MICHAEL ULLMAN

Blair, Lee (L.) (*b* Savannah, GA, 10 Oct 1903; *d* New York, 15 Oct 1966). Banjoist and guitarist. He taught himself to play the banjo and guitar left-handed, and he later received a little tuition from Paul Whiteman's banjoist, Mike Pingitore. In 1926 he joined an orchestra in New York that included Tommy and Bill Benford and was led by the pianist Charlie Skeete; in the following year the band (now led by Bill Benford) became resident at the Rose Danceland and in May 1928 the management engaged Jelly Roll Morton as leader. With Morton, Blair recorded (1928 and 1930) and toured from December 1928 until April 1929. At this time he also worked with a band led by Morton's former trombonist Billy Kato (1928, 1930–31) and worked as a freelance musician in and around New York. In 1934 he joined the orchestra led by Luis Russell, and after Louis Armstrong took over in October 1935 remained and recorded with the band until May 1940. During the 1940s he worked as a part-time musician before joining Wilbur De Paris (*c*1955), with whom he recorded (1955–6, 1958) and toured Africa (1957). He also recorded with Dick Cary and Pee Wee Erwin (both 1959). In the 1960s he continued to play part-time in New York; he recorded with Leonard Gaskin (1962), briefly re-joined De Paris (1964), and played at the New York World's Fair in a banjo trio that included Danny Barker (summer 1964).

SELECTED RECORDINGS

As sideman: J. R. Morton: Kansas City Stomps (1928, Vic. 38010); W. De Paris: *Wilbur De Paris and his "New" New Orleans Jazz* (1955, Atl. 1219), incl. March of the Charcoal Greys

BIBLIOGRAPHY

ChiltonW
L. Wright: *Mr. Jelly Lord* (Chigwell, England, 1980), 55

MIKE HAZELDINE

Blake, Cyril (Macdonald) [Midnight] (*b* Trinidad, 7 Nov–3 Dec 1900; *d* London, 3 Dec 1951). Trinidadian trumpeter. He moved to Great Britain around 1918, and in 1921 he played guitar in the Southern Syncopated Orchestra. In the 1920s he performed in clubs in London and Paris and changed to trumpet. After returning to London in 1930 Blake worked with Leon Abbey, his brother Happy Blake (who played drums) and the clarinetist Rudolph Dunbar (both 1933), Leslie Thompson's Emperors of Jazz (1936), and Joe Appleton (1937). He led his own bands from 1938 and was resident at various clubs; the raw energy of his group's playing is evident from the recordings of one of its performances at Jig's Club (including *Cyril's Blues*/

Frolic Sam, 1941, Regal-Zonophone MR3597). His later recordings show that he was becoming more closely associated with Afro-Caribbean music. Blake continued working as a leader until his final illness. (Obituary, *MM*, xxvii (8 Dec 1951), 7)

JOHN COWLEY, HOWARD RYE

Blake, Eubie [James Hubert] (*b* Baltimore, 7 Feb 1883; *d* New York, 12 Feb 1983). Pianist and composer. When he was six years old his parents, who had been slaves, purchased a home organ and arranged for him to have lessons. Later he studied music theory with a local musician, Llewelyn Wilson. Blake began to play professionally in a nightclub in Baltimore at the age of 15, and in 1899 wrote his first piano rag, *Sounds of Africa* (later titled *Charleston Rag*). In 1915 he formed a songwriting partnership with Noble Sissle, and the two men had an immediate success with *It's all your fault*, performed by Sophie Tucker. Blake and Sissle then went to New York and joined James Reese Europe's Society Orchestra, and after World War I they formed the Dixie Duo, a vaudeville act. In 1921 they produced an extremely successful musical, *Shuffle Along*, which ran for more than 14 months on Broadway and subsequently went on tour. Blake continued to collaborate with Sissle (see illustration) and other lyricists in the 1920s and 1930s, writing for several Broadway and London shows; many of his more than 300 songs are infused with the syncopated ragtime rhythms that swept Tin Pan Alley between 1900 and 1920. During World War II he toured as music director for USO productions, but in 1946 he retired and returned to the study of composition, completing the Schillinger system of courses at New York University three years later. Thereafter he spent much time notating many of his works.

Blake made his first recordings in 1917, and continued to record as a soloist (making piano rolls as well as phonograph records) and with his orchestra into the 1930s. A ragtime revival in the 1950s focused attention on him as the foremost rag pianist in the USA and launched him on a new career as a touring artist and lecturer, and he resumed recording in 1969 with the album *The Eighty-six Years of Eubie Blake*. His playing demonstrates strikingly the interconnections among brass-band music, ragtime, and jazz; his own ragtime piano pieces have prominent "oom-pah" rhythms in the left hand and a syncopated interpretation of the melody in the right, but he also introduces a compelling sense of swing and virtuoso improvised breaks into his performances, reflecting the influence of jazz. His works, along with others written in the 1920s by such composers as Fats Waller and James P. Johnson, had a direct influence on the development of the Harlem stride-piano school.

In 1972 Blake established his own publishing and record company, Eubie Blake Music, and the following year he cut some piano rolls, this time for the QRS company. He became a legendary figure, performing constantly on television and at jazz festivals in the USA and elsewhere. He received many awards from the music and theater industries and from civic and professional organizations, notably the Presidential Medal of Freedom (1981), and honorary degrees from Brooklyn College (1973), Dartmouth College, Rutgers, and the New England Conservatory (all 1974), and the University of Maryland (1979). His life was celebrated in documentary films and on Broadway in the show *Eubie* (1978). The Eubie Blake Cultural Center in Baltimore and the Maryland Historical Society hold collections of his music, papers, and memorabilia.

Oral history material in *CtY, TNF.*

SELECTED RECORDINGS

* – composed by Blake

As unaccompanied soloist: *Sounds of Africa (Charleston Rag) (1921, Emerson 10434); *The Eighty-six Years of Eubie Blake* (1969, Col. C2S847)

As leader: *The Wizard of Ragtime Piano* (1958, 20CF 3003), incl. *Eubie's Boogie Rag, *I'm just wild about Harry

Eubie Blake (seated at piano) and Noble Sissle, St. Louis, 1925

BIBLIOGRAPHY

R. Blesh and H. Janis: *They all Played Ragtime* (New York, 1950, rev. 4/1971)
J. R. T. Davies: "Eubie Blake: his Life and Times," *Sv*, i/6 (1966), 19; contd as "Blake and Noble Sissle," ii/7 (1966), 12
R. Blesh: "Little Hubie," *Combo, USA: Eight Lives in Jazz* (Philadelphia and London, 1971), 187
E. Southern: *The Music of Black Americans: a History* (New York and London, 1971, rev. 2/1983)
P. Bailey: "A Love Song to Eubie," *Ebony*, xxviii/9 (1973), 94
W. Bolcom and R. Kimball: *Reminiscing with Sissle and Blake* (New York, 1973) [incl. work-list, discography]
E. Southern and B. King: "Conversation with Eubie Blake," *Black Perspective in Music*, i (1973), 50, 151
L. T. Carter: *Eubie Blake: Keys of Memory* (Detroit, 1979)
A. Rose: *Eubie Blake* (New York, 1979)
E. A. Berlin: *Ragtime: a Musical and Cultural History* (Berkeley, CA, Los Angeles, and London, 1980/*R*1984 with addns)
B. Doerschuk: "The Eubie Blake Story: a Century of American Music," *Keyboard*, viii/12 (1982), 52
E. Southern: *Biographical Dictionary of Afro-American and African Musicians* (Westport, CT, 1982)
M. Jones: "Britain Salutes: Eubie Blake, 100," *Jazz Express*, no.39 (1983), 1
L. Norment: "Farewell to Ragtime's Apostle of Happiness," *Ebony*, xxxviii/7 (1983), 27

EILEEN SOUTHERN

Blake, Jerry [Chabania, Jacinto] (*b* Gary, IN, 23 Jan 1908; *d* *c*1961). Saxophonist, clarinetist, arranger, and singer. He studied violin, then alto saxophone and clarinet. After playing briefly with Charlie Turner's Arcadians he took ship for Europe with Sam Wooding (1928), with whom he recorded in Barcelona and Paris (1929). He then moved to New York, played with Chick Webb, and toured with Zack Whyte's Chocolate Beau Brummels. He performed and recorded with Don Redman (1933–4) and Willie Lewis (in Europe, 1935), played with Claude Hopkins in New York, and in 1936 joined Fletcher Henderson's group, with which he made several recordings the following year (including *Stealin' Apples*, first issued on *The Sound of Jazz Genius*, 1927–39, Columbia Record Club D77). In 1938 he left the group to become Cab Calloway's music director (for illustration *see* CALLOWAY, CAB); later he recorded with Count Basie (1942) and after leaving Calloway's employ played briefly with Basie and Earl Hines (1942) and Lionel Hampton and Redman (1943). His career was ended by a mental breakdown.

based on *ChiltonW*

Blake, Ran (*b* Springfield, MA, 20 April 1935). Pianist, composer, and teacher. He studied piano with Ray Cassarino while in his teens and developed an interest in gospel music and the music of Béla Bartók and Claude Debussy. He attended Bard College (1956–60), where his major subject was jazz and where he met the singer Jeanne Lee, with whom he played for many years; at the same time he studied in Lenox, Massachusetts, with Oscar Peterson, John Lewis, and Gunther Schuller. In 1963 he toured Europe with Lee. In 1967 he became music director of the community services department of the New England Conservatory, in which capacity he gave concerts in prisons and old people's homes (1969–72), and in 1973 he was appointed chairman of the conservatory's third stream department. He teaches and frequently performs, usually as a soloist, in Boston and Europe. He received a Guggenheim Fellowship and a grant from the NEA, both for composition, in 1982. Blake is one of the foremost theorists and performers of third stream improvisation.

See also THIRD STREAM.

SELECTED RECORDINGS

As unaccompanied soloist: *Ran Blake Plays Solo Piano* (1965, ESP 1011); *Breakthru* (1975, ImA 373842); *Third Stream Recompositions* (1977, Owl 017); *Duke Dreams: the Strayhorn/Ellington Legacy* (1982, SN 1027)
Duos with J. Lee: *The Newest Sound Around* (1961, RCA LSP2500)
As leader: *Rapport* (1978, AN 3006); *Film noir* (1980, AN 3019)

BIBLIOGRAPHY

M. Ullman: *Jazz Lives: Portraits in Words and Pictures* (Washington, 1979), 175
A. Lange: "Ran Blake's Third Stream," *DB*, xlvii/2 (1980), 24 [incl. discography]
B. McRae: "Ran Blake," *The Wire*, no.1 (1982), 10 [incl. discography]
L. Lyons: "Ran Blake," *The Great Jazz Pianists, Speaking of their Lives and Music* (New York, 1983), 194
B. Rusch: "Ran Blake," *Cadence*, xiii/1 (1987), 5

ED HAZELL

Blakeney, Andy [Andrew] (*b* Quitman, MS, 10 June 1898). Trumpeter and bandleader. He worked in Chicago with King Oliver, Doc Cook, and others, then in 1926 moved to Los Angeles, where he played and toured with a number of lesser-known groups and recorded with the pianist Sonny Clay (1926) and the bass saxophonist Reb Spikes (*c*1926). In 1935 he joined Lionel Hampton. He led his own band in Hawaii (1936–41), then performed and recorded with Ceele Burke's big band (1942–6), and worked briefly with Horace Henderson (1946) and Kid Ory (1947); among the recordings he made with Ory is *Savoy Blues* (1947, Cir. [USA] 12001). For the next 20 years Blakeney led his own groups. He toured Europe in 1974 with the LEGENDS OF JAZZ and continued to play into the 1980s, recording with the Eagle Brass Band in 1984.

Oral history material in *NjR* (JOHP).

BIBLIOGRAPHY

ChiltonW
P. Vacher: "Andrew Blakeney: a Lifetime in Music," *Sv*, no.58 (1975), 124
A. Ashforth: "The Eagle Brass Band in Los Angeles," *Fn*, xv/2 (1983–4), 4
B. Mitchell: "A Talk with Andrew Blakeney," *MR*, xii/9 (1985), 1

FRANK DRIGGS

Blakey, Art [Buhaina, Abdullah ibn] (*b* Pittsburgh, 11 Oct 1919). Drummer and bandleader. He received some piano lessons at school and by seventh grade was playing music full-time, leading a commercial band. Shortly afterwards he changed to drums, on which he taught himself to play in the aggressive swing style of Chick Webb, Sid Catlett, and Ray Bauduc. In autumn 1942 he joined Mary Lou Williams for an engagement at Kelly's Stable in New York. He then played with the Fletcher Henderson Orchestra (1943–4), with which he made a long tour of the South. On leaving Henderson, Blakey briefly led a big band in Boston before joining Billy Eckstine's new band in St. Louis. During his years with Eckstine (1944–7) Blakey became associated with the modern-jazz movement along with his fellow band members Miles Davis, Dexter Gordon, Fats Navarro, and others.

When Eckstine disbanded his group in 1947 Blakey organized the Seventeen Messengers, a rehearsal band, and recorded with an octet called the Jazz Messengers, the first of his many groups bearing this name. He then traveled in Africa, probably for more than a year, to learn about Islamic culture. In the early 1950s he performed and broadcast with such musicians as Charlie Parker, Davis, and Clifford Brown, and particularly with Horace Silver, his kindred musical spirit of this time. After recording together several times, in 1955 Blakey and Silver formed a cooperative group with Hank Mobley and Kenny Dorham, retaining the name Jazz Messengers. When Silver left the following year the leadership of this important band passed to Blakey (for illustration *see* BANDS, fig.5), and he has been associated with it from then into the late 1980s. It was the archetypal hard-bop group of the late 1950s, playing a driving, aggressive extension of bop with pronounced blues

Art Blakey

roots. Over the years the Jazz Messengers have served as a springboard for young jazz musicians such as Donald Byrd, Johnny Griffin, Lee Morgan, Wayne Shorter, Freddie Hubbard, Keith Jarrett, Chuck Mangione, Woody Shaw, JoAnne Brackeen, and Wynton Marsalis. In addition to his numerous tours and recordings with the Messengers, Blakey also made a world tour in 1971–2 with the Giants of Jazz (with Dizzy Gillespie, Kai Winding, Sonny Stitt, Thelonious Monk, and Al McKibbon) and frequently appeared as a soloist at the Newport Jazz Festival in New York, most memorably in a drum battle with Max Roach, Buddy Rich, and Elvin Jones (1974). He continued to maintain a busy performing schedule into the 1980s. Among his sidemen from 1982 were Terence Blanchard and Donald Harrison, and in 1987 he was leading a septet of young musicians that included the trombonist Delfayo Marsalis and the pianist Benny Green.

Blakey is a major figure in modern jazz and an important stylist on his instrument. From his earliest recording sessions with Eckstine, and particularly in his historic sessions with Monk in 1947, he exudes power and originality, creating a dark cymbal sound punctuated by frequent loud snare- and bass-drum accents in triplets or cross-rhythms. Although Blakey discourages comparison of his own music with African drumming, he adopted several African devices after his visit in 1948–9, including rapping on the side of the drum and using his elbow on the tom-tom to alter the pitch. Later he organized recording sessions with multiple drummers, including some African musicians and pieces. His much-imitated trademark, the forceful closing of the hi-hat on every second and fourth beat, has been part of his style since 1950–51. A loud and domineering drummer, Blakey also listens and responds to his soloists. His contribution to jazz as a discoverer and molder of young talent over three decades is no less significant than his very considerable innovations on his instrument.

SELECTED RECORDINGS

As leader: Message from Kenya/Nothing but Soul (1953, BN 1626); *A Night at Birdland* (1954, BN 5037–9); *Drum Suite* (1956–7, Col. CL1002); *A Message from Blakey: Holiday for Skins* (1958, BN 4004); *Des femmes disparaissent* (1958, Fon. 660224); *The Freedom Rider* (1961, BN 84156); *Buttercorn Lady* (1966, Lml. 86034); *Jazz Messengers '70* (1970, Cat. 7902); *Anthenagin* (1973, Prst. 10076); *Recorded Live at Bubba's* (1980, Who's Who in Jazz 21019); *Album of the Year* (1981, Tim. 155)

As sideman: B. Eckstine: Blowin' the Blues Away (1944, De Luxe 2001); *Together!* (1945, Spot. 100), incl. Mister Chips; I love the rhythm in a riff (1945, Nat. 9014); T. Monk: Who Knows (1947, BN 1565); M. Davis: Weirdo (1954, BN 45-1650); H. Silver: *Horace Silver and the Jazz Messengers* (1954, BN 5058), incl. Doodlin'

BIBLIOGRAPHY

H. Frost: "Art Blakey in St. Louis," *Metronome*, lxiii/2 (1947), 26
H. Lovett: "Art Blakey," *Metronome*, lxxii/6 (1956), 17
J. Tynan: "The Jazz Message," *DB*, xxiv/21 (1957), 15
R. Horricks and others: *These Jazzmen of our Time* (London, 1959), 131
Z. Carno: "Art Blakey," *JR*, iii/1 (1960), 6
J. Cooke: "Art Blakey and the Jazz Messengers," *JM*, vi (1960), no.3, p.4; no.8, p.4
J. Goldberg: *Jazz Masters of the Fifties* (New York and London, 1965/*R*1980), 45
T. Humphrey: "The Art of Blakey Considered," *JB*, iii/7 (1966), 7
J. Litweiler: "Bu's Delights and Laments," *DB*, xliii/6 (1976), 15
A. Taylor: *Notes and Tones: Musician-to-Musician Interviews* (Liège, Belgium, 1977/*R*1982), 251
M. Hennessey: "The Enduring Jazz Message of Abdullah ibn Buhaina," *JJI*, xxx/9 (1977), 6
I. Gitler: "Art Blakey Speaks his Mind," *Jazz Magazine*, iv/1 (1979), 40
H. Nolan: "New Message from Art Blakey," *DB*, xlvi/17 (1979), 19
"Art Blakey and the Jazz Messengers," *SJ*, xxxiii/2 (1979), 224 [discography]
P. Danson: "Art Blakey," *Coda*, no.173 (1980), 14
G. Endress: *Jazz Podium: Musiker über sich selbst* (Stuttgart, Germany, 1980)
F. Paudras: "Art Blakey: le message," *Jh*, nos. 374–5 (1980), 16
B. Rusch: "Art Blakey: Interview," *Cadence*, vii (1981), no.7, p.8; no.9, p.12
C. Stern: "Art Blakey," *MD*, viii/9 (1984), 8
Z. Stewart: "Art Blakey in his Prime," *DB*, lii/7 (1985), 20
D. H. Rosenthal: "Conversation with Art Blakey: the Big Beat!," *Black Perspective in Music*, xiv (1986), 267

LEWIS PORTER

Blanchard, Terence (*b* New Orleans, 13 March 1962). Trumpeter. At the age of 16 he enrolled at the New Orleans Center for the Creative Arts, where he played with Donald Harrison. He went on to study at Rutgers, during which time he spent two years performing in Lionel Hampton's big band. In 1982 he renewed his association with Harrison, and the two replaced Wynton and Branford Marsalis in Art Blakey's Jazz Messengers. As leaders they recorded the album *New York Second Line* (1983), which was later awarded the Grand prix du disque; they were principal soloists on the Jazz Messengers' recording *New York Scene* (1984), which includes their compositions and earned a Grammy Award. In 1984 they left Blakey to form their own quintet, a group that has gained considerable public and critical acclaim. While continuing to work as leaders, in 1986 they began playing with Blakey once more. Miles Davis has described Blanchard as one of the most promising trumpet players of his generation; his playing is technically accomplished and distinguished by its emotional poignancy, and it displays the influence of ethnic music and earlier jazz styles.

SELECTED RECORDINGS

As leader with D. Harrison: *New York Second Line* (1983, Conc. 3002); *Discernment* (1986, Conc. 3008); *Nascence* (1986, Col. BFC40335)

As sideman with A. Blakey: *New York Scene* (1984, Conc. 256); *Live at Kimball's* (1986, Conc. 307)

BIBLIOGRAPHY

L. Jeske: "Profile: Terence Blanchard," *DB*, l/8 (1983), 44
G. Giddins: *Rhythm-a-ning: Jazz Tradition and Innovation in the '80s* (New York, and Oxford, England, 1985) [colln of previously pubd articles], 262

R. Cook: "Terence Blanchard: Mouthpiece of Integrity," *The Wire*, no.28 (1986), 20
H. Mandel: "Terence Blanchard, Donald Harrison: Young, Gifted & Straight Ahead," *DB*, liii/12 (1986), 22 [incl. discography]

ROBERT DICKOW

Bland, Jack (*b* Sedalia, MO, 8 May 1899). Guitarist and banjoist. He played banjo in and around St. Louis in the early 1920s before joining Red McKenzie's MOUND CITY BLUE BLOWERS (1924; for illustration *see* LANG, EDDIE). He recorded with the group (1924–5, 1929–31) and appeared with it in the short film *The Opry House* (1929). During the 1930s he worked as a freelance musician in New York and recorded with a band known variously as Billy Banks and his Orchestra, the RHYTHMAKERS, and Jack Bland and his Rhythmakers (1932). He recorded with George Wettling (1940), led his own group (1940–41, 1944), worked with Marty Marsala (1942) and Art Hodes (1943–4), and recorded with Muggsy Spanier in Chicago (1943) and with Hodes (1944). When he retired from full-time playing he moved to Los Angeles.

SELECTED RECORDINGS

As leader: It's gonna be you (1932, Mlt. 12510); Someone Stole Gabriel's Horn (1932, Ban. 32605)
As sideman: Mound City Blue Blowers: Arkansaw Blues (1924, Bruns. 2581); R. McKenzie: Hot Honey (1925, Voc. 15166); B. Banks: Take it Slow and Easy (1932, HRS 17)

BIBLIOGRAPHY

ChiltonW
J. Bland: "The Kazoo Comes On," *Selections From the Gutter: Jazz Portraits from "The Jazz Record"*, ed. A. Hodes and C. Hansen (Berkeley, CA, Los Angeles, and London, 1977), 143

MIKE HAZELDINE

Blanton, Jimmy [James] (*b* Chattanooga, TN, Oct 1918; *d* Los Angeles, 30 July 1942). Double bass player. He played locally in groups led by his mother, a pianist, and attended Tennessee State College briefly before moving in the late 1930s to St. Louis, where he performed in the Jeter–Pillars Orchestra and in Fate Marable's riverboat bands. There he was discovered in late 1939 by Duke Ellington, who engaged him immediately for his orchestra (for illustration *see* BANDS, fig.3). Blanton's playing subtly altered the Ellington sound, stabilizing the band's rhythm and greatly enhancing its swing; it also ushered in Ellington's most creative period as a composer, particularly in masterpieces such as *Ko-Ko* and *Concerto for Cootie*, where Blanton's bass part is especially prominent. Blanton also took part in a few of the informal jam sessions at Minton's Playhouse in New York that contributed to the genesis of the bop style. From 1941 his playing became somewhat erratic, and late that year he was obliged by ill-health (diagnosed as congenital tuberculosis) to take up residence in a California sanatorium, where he died shortly afterwards.

In his tragically brief career Blanton revolutionized jazz bass playing, and until the advent of the styles of Scott LaFaro and Charlie Haden in the 1960s all modern bass players drew on his innovations. He possessed great dexterity and range, roundness of tone, accurate intonation, and above all an unprecedented sense of swing. His strong feeling for harmony led him to incorporate many nonharmonic passing notes in his accompaniment lines, giving them a contrapuntal flavor and stimulating soloists to their own harmonic explorations. Blanton also contributed the earliest fully satisfying jazz solos on this instrument, which depart in their inventive melody and flexible rhythms from the walking bass style that was then prevalent. Despite his short career Blanton left a large recorded legacy, not only in his 130-odd recordings with Ellington's orchestra, but also in many small-group performances with some of Ellington's sidemen, and especially in a remarkable series of duos with Ellington himself. As adapted by his followers Oscar Pettiford, Ray Brown, and Charles Mingus, Blanton's innovations also led indirectly to the creation of the bop rhythm section.

SELECTED RECORDINGS

Duos with D. Ellington: Plucked Again/Blues (1939, Col. 35322); Pitter Panther Patter/Sophisticated Lady (1940, Vic. 27221); Body and Soul/Mr. J. B. Blues (1940, Vic. 27406)
As sideman with D. Ellington: Jack the Bear (1940, Vic. 26536); Conga Brava/Ko-Ko (1940, Vic. 26577); Concerto for Cootie (1940, Vic. 26598); Sepia Panorama/Harlem Air Shaft (1940, Vic. 26731); In a Mellotone (1940, Vic. 26788)
As sideman with others: B. Bigard: Lost in Two Flats (1939, OK 5422); Cootie Williams: Black Butterfly (1940, OK 5618); J. Hodges: Squatty Roo (1941, Bb 11447)

BIBLIOGRAPHY

R. G. Reisner: *The Jazz Titans* (Garden City, NY, 1960/*R*1977)
I. Kanth: *A Discography of Jimmy Blanton* (Stockholm, 1970)
D. Ellington: *Music is my Mistress* (Garden City, NY, 1973)
C. Carrère: "Pitter Panther Patter: les bassistes de Duke Ellington," *Jh*, no.316 (1975), 10

J. BRADFORD ROBINSON

Blesh, Rudi [Rudolph Pickett] (*b* Guthrie, OK, 21 Jan 1899; *d* Gilmanton, NH, 25 Aug 1985). Writer, record producer, and broadcaster. He became interested in jazz while at Dartmouth College. In the 1940s he served as jazz critic for the *San Francisco Chronicle* and promoted concerts with such veteran New Orleans musicians as Bunk Johnson and Kid Ory, and in 1944 he moved to New York and became jazz critic for the *New York Herald Tribune*. Blesh wrote a history of jazz, *Shining Trumpets* (1946), and, with Harriet Janis, the first history of ragtime, *They all Played Ragtime* (1950). This latter work established him as the leading authority in the ragtime field and eventually prompted a revival of the music. Also with Janis, Blesh founded Circle (*see* CIRCLE (i)), a small but significant jazz record company which became the first to issue the recordings made by Jelly Roll Morton for the Library of Congress; later they sold the enterprise and its catalogue – apart from the Morton recordings – to Jazzology. From 1947 to 1950, and again in 1964, Blesh wrote and narrated radio programs on jazz and American folk music, notably the series "This is Jazz." Beginning in 1956 he taught jazz history at Queens College, CUNY, and New York University, and in the 1970s he provided liner notes for numerous ragtime recordings. He also compiled collections of ragtime piano music and wrote books on modern art and the cinema. Throughout his career, Blesh was a strong advocate of jazz and other American art forms. A pioneer writer of serious jazz history, he rescued ragtime from historical neglect and rediscovered such musicians as Eubie Blake and Joseph Lamb.

WRITINGS

(selective list)

This is Jazz: a Series of Lectures Given at the San Francisco Museum of Art (San Francisco, 1943)
Shining Trumpets: a History of Jazz (New York, 1946, rev. and enlarged 2/1958/*R*1975)
with H. Janis: *They all Played Ragtime* (New York, 1950, rev. 4/1971)
Combo, USA: Eight Lives in Jazz (Philadelphia and London, 1971)
"Scott Joplin: Black-American Classicist," *The Collected Works of Scott Joplin*, ed. V. B. Lawrence (New York, 1971)

BIBLIOGRAPHY

J. E. Hasse: "Rudi Blesh and the Ragtime Revivalists," *Ragtime: its History, Composers, and Music* (London, 1985), 178
Obituary, S. Holden, *New York Times* (28 Aug 1985)
P. Elwood: "Remembering Rudi," *San Francisco Examiner* (6 Sept 1985)

JOHN EDWARD HASSE

Bley [neé Borg], **Carla** (*b* Oakland, CA, 11 May 1938). Composer, bandleader, and keyboard player. She learned the fundamentals of music from her father, a church musician, but is otherwise self-taught. At the age of 17 she moved to New York, where she worked intermittently as a pianist and cigarette girl, writing jazz tunes for musicians such as George Russell, Jimmy Giuffre, and her husband at the time, Paul Bley. In 1964, with her second husband, Mike Mantler, she formed the Jazz Composers Guild Orchestra, known from 1965 as the Jazz Composer's Orchestra. In 1966 she helped found the JAZZ COMPOSER'S ORCHESTRA ASSOCIATION, a novel nonprofit organization which commissions, produces, and distributes commercially unviable jazz. Although already highly regarded by this time among critics, she first came to public notice with *A Genuine Tong Funeral* (1967), a cycle of pieces recorded with the Gary Burton Quartet, and with her compositions and arrangements for Charlie Haden's *Liberation Music Orchestra* (1969, Imp. 9183). In 1971 she completed her most substantial work, the eclectic "jazz opera" *Escalator over the Hill.* This work was extraordinarily well received by the international jazz press, and led to several composing grants. During the 1970s and 1980s Bley has continued to compose, expand the activities of the Jazz Composer's Orchestra Association, and lead her own ten-piece touring band; her sidemen have included Mantler, Roswell Rudd, and Steve Swallow. An indifferent keyboard player, Bley is an outstanding jazz composer with a wide range of styles at her command. Much of her best work is infused with a spirit of parody and sardonic humor. Among her compositions are *3/4* for piano and orchestra, which has been performed by musicians as varied as Keith Jarrett, Ursula Oppens, and Frederic Rzewski, and the soundtrack for the film *Mortelle randonnée* (1985).

Carla Bley, London, 1983

RECORDED COMPOSITIONS

(selective list)

* – with Bley as sideman

As leader: *Escalator over the Hill* (1968–71, JCOA EOTH); *Tropic Appetites* (1973–4, Watt 1); with M. Mantler: 3/4, on *13-3/4* (1975, Watt 3); Dreams so Real, Ida Lupino, Sing me softly of the blues, on *Dinner Music* (1976, Watt 6); Drinking Alone, Wrong Key Donkey, on *European Tour 1977* (1977, Watt 8); 440, Musique mécanique, on *Musique mécanique* (1978, Watt 9); Copyright Royalties, Reactionary Tango, Valse sinistre, on *Social Studies* (1980, Watt 11); *Night-glo* (1985, Watt 16)

Recorded by P. Bley: King Korn, Vashkar (both 1963), on *Footloose* (1962–3, Savoy 12182); Around Again, Ida Lupino, King Korn, Syndrome, on *Turning Point* (1964, ImA 373841); And now, the queen, Around Again, Batterie, Walking Woman, on *Barrage* (1964, ESP 1008); And now, the queen, Batterie, Closer, Ida Lupino, on *Closer* (1965, ESP 1021)

Recorded by G. Burton: **A Genuine Tong Funeral* (1967, RCA LSP3988); Olhos de gato, on *The New Quartet* (1973, ECM 1030)

BIBLIOGRAPHY

M. Cuscuna: "Carla Bley's New Opera: Worth the Toil and Trouble," *DB*, xxxix/6 (1972), 16

G. Buhles: "Die Jazzkomponistin Carla Bley: Kurzbiographie, Werkanalyse, Würdigung," *Jf*, viii (1976), 11

H. Mandel: "Carla Bley: Independent Ringleader," *DB*, xlv/11 (1978), 18

B. Primack: "Carla Bley: First Lady of the Avant-garde," *CK*, v/2 (1979), 9

R. Zabor: "Carla Bley: the Toast of the Continent," *Musician*, no.35 (1981), 64

L. Dahl: *Stormy Weather: the Music and Lives of a Century of Jazzwomen* (London, Melbourne, Australia, and New York, 1984)

D. Palmer: "My Dinner with Carla," *DB*, li/8 (1984), 24

——: "Carla Bley Returns to Form," *New York Times* (10 Feb 1985)

J. BRADFORD ROBINSON

Bley, Paul (*b* Montreal, 10 Nov 1932). Canadian pianist. He studied violin as a child and took up the piano at the age of eight. His first professional engagements were in New York in the early 1950s; among these were performances as a member of Jackie McLean's quintet with Donald Byrd, Doug Watkins, and Art Taylor. After 1955 he moved to the Los Angeles area and from 1956 to 1958 led a small group that included Ornette Coleman and Don Cherry as sidemen; from around 1957 to around 1966 he was married to Carla Bley. He returned to the East Coast, where he led a trio that included Steve Swallow and Pete La Roca, and performed with Charles Mingus, Jimmy Giuffre, and Don Ellis; he also recorded with Ellis on the West Coast (1962). Between 1962 and 1969 he worked principally as a leader of trios in New York; at the same time he played with Sonny Rollins (1963), took part in the "October Revolution in Jazz" in New York, and was a founding member of the Jazz Composers Guild (both 1964). From 1969 to 1971 he gave performances and made recordings as an electronic keyboard player, sometimes in collaboration with his second wife, the singer and electronic keyboard player Annette Peacock; later he abandoned electronic instruments, and performed and recorded as an unaccompanied soloist and as a leader into the 1980s. In 1974, with the artist Carol Goss, he established the record company and label Improvising Artists. Bley's playing is notable for its strong linearity, unpredictable pulse, and subtle harmonic progressions.

Oral history material in *CaQMG*.

SELECTED RECORDINGS

As unaccompanied soloist: *Alone Again* (1974, ImA 373840); *Open for Love* (1972, ECM 1023); *Tango Palace* (1983, SN 1090)

As leader: *Introducing Paul Bley* (1953, Debut 7); *Footloose* (1962–3, Savoy 12182); *Closer* (1965, ESP 1021)

As sideman: O. Coleman: *Coleman Classics* (1958, ImA 373852); D. Ellis: *Essence* (1962, PJ 55); S. Rollins: *Sonny Meets Hawk* (1963, RCA LSP2712)

BIBLIOGRAPHY

K. Knox: "Paul Bley," *JM*, xii/10 (1966), 6 [incl. discography]
M. Cuscuna: "Paul Bley: being Together," *DB*, xxxv/21 (1968), 20
I. S. Peterson and L. Goddet: "Discographie de Paul Bley," *Jh*, no.332 (1976), 26; repr. in *Coda*, no.166 (1979), 9; no.168 (1979), 38
L. Lyons: "IAI: Paul Bley's Bold Experiment," *DB*, xliv/10 (1977), 50
G. Endress: *Jazz Podium: Musiker über sich selbst* (Stuttgart, Germany, 1980), 190
M. Miller: "Bley, Paul," *Encyclopedia of Music in Canada*, ed. H. Kallmann, G. Potvin, and K. Winters (Toronto, Buffalo, and London, 1981) [incl. discography]
L. Lyons: *The Great Jazz Pianists: Speaking of their Lives and Music* (New York, 1983), 158 [incl. interview, discography]
M. Miller: "Paul Bley," *Boogie, Pete & the Senator: Canadian Musicians in Jazz: the Eighties* (Toronto, 1987), 56

RAN BLAKE

Bliziński, Marek (*b* Warsaw, 22 March 1947). Polish electric guitarist. A self-taught musician, he began his career playing in the Polish pop groups the Pessimists (1965), the Four (from 1966), which played rock transcriptions of classical music, and the Generation (from 1971). In the early 1970s he began to play in a style nearer to jazz and in his work for Mainstream, led by Jan Wróblewski and Wojciech Karolak, the influence of the guitarists Barney Kessel and George Benson is clearly audible. His playing is heard to advantage on the album *Mainstream* (1973, Muza 1139). He then became a busy studio musician, working for the Polish Radio Jazz Studio and with the best Polish players, such as Michal Urbaniak, Zbigniew Namysłowski, Tomasz Stańko, Andrzej Kurylewicz, and the Novi Singers. (J. Byrczek and H. Matuszewska: "Eurojazz Personalities: Poland," *JF* [intl edn], no.33 (1975), 65)

WOLFRAM KNAUER

Block [Bloch], **Sandy** [Sid] [Block, Sidney Sanford] (*b* Cleveland, 16 Jan 1917). Double bass player. He worked as a sideman in the big bands of Alvino Rey (1940–41), Tommy Dorsey (1943–7, 1950), and Jerry Wald (1944), and recorded as a member of the Charlie Shavers Quintet (1945). He also recorded with Sy Oliver (1951, 1958), Louis Armstrong (1951, 1953, 1957), Ella Fitzgerald (1951–3, 1955), Jimmy McPartland (1955–7), and Joe Williams (1965), and appeared in a television broadcast with Charlie Parker (1952). According to Feather, Block's favorite recording of his own work is *Then I'll be happy* (1946, Vic. 20–1938), made when he was with Dorsey. (*FeatherE*)

Block chords. A series of unadorned chords, usually rich in dissonance, arranged in widely spaced voicings, and moving in parallel motion; they occur in accompaniments played on piano or by the wind sections of a big band. *See* HARMONY (i), §1 (iv).

Blood, Sweat and Tears. Jazz-rock group. It was formed in New York in 1968 by Al Kooper (*b* New York, 5 Feb 1944), a singer, songwriter, keyboard player, and record producer, with seven other musicians, and became popular after Kooper was replaced as lead singer later that year by David Clayton-Thomas (*b* Surrey, England, 13 Sept 1941). From its inception, Blood, Sweat and Tears made considerable use of brass instruments and elements drawn from jazz; notwithstanding its attempt to create a jazz-rock fusion, however, the group seldom engaged in improvisation. Its first album, *Child is Father to the Man* (1968, Col. 9619), included folk music, blues, and pop songs (among them Billie Holiday's *God Bless the Child*), arranged in a style influenced by Maynard Ferguson and Stan Kenton; the most successful of its recordings was *Blood, Sweat and Tears* (1968, Col. 9720). The group disbanded in 1977.

For illustration *see* BANDS, fig.6.

STEPHEN HOLDEN/R

Bloom, Rube (*b* New York, 24 April 1902; *d* New York, 30 March 1976). Pianist and composer. Although self-taught, he became an excellent pianist at an early age and in 1919 began working as an accompanist for vaudeville shows. He recorded in the Sioux City Six with Bix Beiderbecke and Frankie Trumbauer (1924) and performed in studio groups with Red Nichols, Miff Mole, Eddie Lang, Joe Venuti, and the Dorsey brothers (1924–31). He arranged songs for numerous publishing companies (1920s) and made several recordings as a soloist (1927–8, including versions of his own rags *Soliloquy*, OK 40867, and *Silhouette*, OK 40901, both 1927); he also led a recording group called the Bayou Boys that included Tommy Dorsey, Benny Goodman, and Adrian Rollini (1930). Although Bloom is perhaps best remembered for his popular songs, he made important contributions to the novelty piano idiom with such jazz-influenced pieces as *Spring Fever* (1926). A collection of his personal papers and song lyrics is in the library of the American Heritage Center at the University of Wyoming in Laramie; *see* LIBRARIES AND ARCHIVES, §2.

BIBLIOGRAPHY

D. A. Jasen: *Recorded Ragtime, 1897–1958* (Hamden, CT, 1973)
D. A. Jasen and T. J. Tichenor: *Rags and Ragtime: a Musical History* (New York, 1978)

DAVID THOMAS ROBERTS

Blount, Herman ("Sonny"). *See* SUN RA.

Blow. Originally to play a wind instrument; by extension (from the mid-1940s) to play any instrument, and especially to play it well. When a musician is given the opportunity to improvise at length and fully to explore a theme or musical idea he is said to be allowed "blowing room" (*see also* STRETCH OUT). A "blowing session" is a musical performance, usually in an organized context such as a concert or recording, in which improvisation predominates (*see also* JAM SESSION). (*GoldJL*)

ROBERT WITMER

Blowers, Johnny [John] (*b* Spartanburg, SC, 21 April 1911). Drummer and percussionist. He moved to New York with Lou McGarity in 1937 and began playing at Nick's in December. In 1938 he performed and recorded with Bobby Hackett and Bunny Berigan and from 1940 he worked regularly as a studio musician. He made recordings as a freelance with Billie Holiday (1944), Yank Lawson (1944–5), Eddie Condon (1944–7), Louis Armstrong (1945–50, including *Jodie Man*, 1945, Decca 18652), and Georg Brunis (1946). In the 1960s he continued to work as a studio musician; he also appeared at Eddie Condon's (1967) and played often with Johnny Mince (late 1960s). He visited Europe in 1981, and in the mid-1980s played regularly in New York with the Harlem Jazz and Blues Band.

BIBLIOGRAPHY

W. Vaché, Sr.: "Looking Back," *MR*, viii/12 (1981), 1
C. Deffaa: "Portraits: Johnny Blowers," *MD*, ix/7 (1985), 38

based on *ChiltonW*

Blu-disc. Record label. It was apparently used for just nine issues, which were made in December 1924. Among these were three items that included Duke Ellington and were the first recordings of his work to be released; a fourth was put out on the Up-to-date label, which was evidently related. After 1979 the names Blu-disc and Up-to-date were used by the Meritt Record Society to reissue on LPs obscure recordings of early jazz, concentrating on Ellington's work. (B. Rust: *The American Record Label Book*, New Rochelle, NY, 1978)

Bluebird. Record label. It was a subsidiary of RCA Victor, and was first used (from summer 1932) to issue eight-inch discs; these were sold in Woolworths stores. From March 1933 until March 1950 conventional ten-inch discs were issued for general distribution. Bluebird was used as Victor's race label during the 1930s; race discs were numbered in a series separate from the general sequence. Bluebird's catalogue included material by such important musicians as Earl Hines (1939–1942), Artie Shaw (1938–9), Fats Waller, and Jelly Roll Morton. The label was also used for reissues of early jazz classics, and some first releases of similar material not originally issued; these included items by Morton, and by the Jones and Collins Astoria Hot Eight. The label name was revived in 1976 for a series of reissues on album of early jazz and swing; it was also used in the 1970s by French RCA.

BIBLIOGRAPHY

H. Panassié: *144 hot jazz Bluebird and Victor Records* (Camden, NJ, 1939)
J. Godrich and R. M. W. Dixon: *Blues & Gospel Records, 1902–1942* (Hatch End, nr London, 1964, rev. 2/1969, rev. and enlarged 3/1982 as R. M. W. Dixon and J. Godrich: *Blues & Gospel Records, 1902–1943*), 16
R. M. W. Dixon and J. Godrich: *Recording the Blues* (London, 1970)
R. D. Kinkle: "Bluebird Numerical List," *The Complete Encyclopedia of Popular Music and Jazz, 1900–1950* (New Rochelle, NY, and Westport, CT, 1974), iv, 2090
B. Rust: *The American Record Label Book* (New Rochelle, NY, 1978), 38

Blue-blowing. The playing of dixieland jazz on non-standard and homemade wind instruments, such as the kazoo, jug, and comb-and-paper. The term derives from the name of Red McKenzie's group the Mound City Blue Blowers, in which McKenzie himself played comb-and-paper and Dick Slevin kazoo and tin can; it has subsequently been applied to European jazz in the dixieland style (for example, Sydney Sterling's playing of kazoo on recordings with Eduardo Andreozzi's band in Berlin in 1926). (*ReclamsJ*)

Blue Devils. Band formed in Oklahoma City in 1925 by WALTER PAGE.

Blue Five. Name of several recording groups organized between 1923 and 1927 by CLARENCE WILLIAMS.

Blue note (i). A microtonally lowered third, seventh, or (less commonly) fifth degree of the diatonic scale, common in blues, jazz, and related musics. The pitch or intonation of blue notes is not fixed precisely but varies according to the performer's instinct and expression. Together with other, non-inflected, pitches they make up the blues scale.

The origin of blue notes has been the subject of much speculation, and will probably never be clarified. Traditionally they were attributed to the difficulty in adapting West African pentatonicism to European diatonicism experienced by the American slaves, who were caused thereby to invent two new scale degrees of indistinct pitch. However, the proponents of this view overlook the fact that some West African scales are diatonic, and that pitch inflection occurs in West African music and may thus form part of the African heritage of the blues. Further, they misrepresent the early blues scale as diatonic, whereas in practice it is a pentatonic scale (ex.1, blue notes

Ex.1

marked by asterisks) in which the diatonic second and sixth degrees occur occasionally as extrascalar passing notes and all scale degrees may be inflected to some extent. Whatever their origins, blue notes are universally associated with black-American music in North America, and are unaccountably absent from other Afro-American musics of the western hemisphere.

The blues scale in jazz differs from that shown in ex.1, being in essence merely the diatonic scale to which inflected third, fifth, and seventh degrees may be added to impart a blues flavor (ex.2). The inflected fifth degree is rare in blues performances

Ex.2

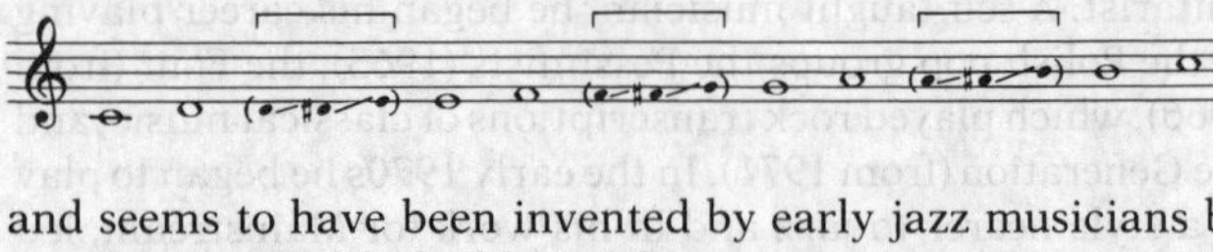

and seems to have been invented by early jazz musicians by aural analogy with the blues. Blue notes were common in jazz from the earliest times, and have long been used as a criterion for separating authentic early jazz from jazz-related commercial music of the day. At first they were apparently associated with particular pitches (notably C♯–D in the key of B♭) and were not transposable, which probably indicates their dependence on certain characteristic instrumental fingerings; later, as jazz musicians gained greater fluency in remote keys, blue notes could be heard on other pitches as well. Eventually blues-like inflections were applied to other degrees of the scale, as may be heard in *Saeta* from Miles Davis's *Sketches of Spain* (1959–60, CS8271) and above all in the work of Ornette Coleman, who from the early 1960s applied blue-note inflections to all degrees of the chromatic scale. The characteristic sound of blue notes has also left an imprint on jazz harmony, examples being the familiar augmented 9th and augmented 11th chords whose semitone clashes may represent an attempt to "verticalize" the ambiguous pitch level of the third- and fifth-degree blue notes (ex.3). Blue notes have also influenced jazz

Ex.3

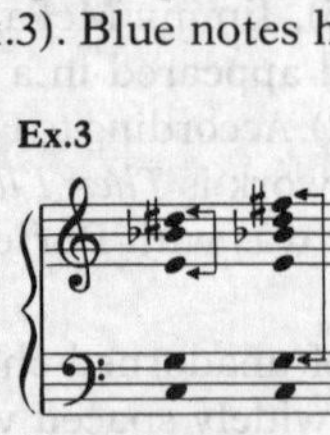

Ex.4

pianism (where microtonal inflections are physically impossible), whether in the "crushed" notes familiar from the blues and boogie-woogie styles or in more complex figurations such as those shown in ex.4, a pianistic equivalent of the "whinnying" vibrato of blues guitarists.

BIBLIOGRAPHY

W. Sargeant: "The Scalar Structure of Jazz," "The Derivations of the Blues," *Jazz, Hot & Hybrid* (New York, 1938, rev. and enlarged 3/1964/R1975 as *Jazz: a History*)

E. Bornemann: "The Roots of Jazz," *Jazz: New Perspectives on the History of Jazz*, ed. N. Hentoff and A. J. McCarthy (New York, 1959/*R*1974)
L. A. Pyke: *Jazz, 1920 to 1927: an Analytical Study* (diss., U. of Iowa, 1962), 78
G. Schuller: *Early Jazz: its Roots and Musical Development* (New York, 1968), 43
J. Fahey: *Charley Patton* (London, 1970), 38
J. Shepherd and others: *Whose Music? A Sociology of Musical Languages* (London, 1977), 166

J. BRADFORD ROBINSON

Blue Note (ii). Record company and label. The company was established in New York in 1939 by Alfred Lion, and was one of the first to use 12-inch 78 r.p.m. discs to accommodate longer pieces. Blue Note's earliest sessions produced records now acknowledged as classics, by such musicians as Sidney Bechet, Earl Hines, Albert Ammons, and Meade "Lux" Lewis. Lion was soon joined by another executive, Francis Wolff, and during the 1940s the company established an important catalogue of traditional jazz and swing; James P. Johnson, Art Hodes, Edmond Hall, Sidney Bechet, Ike Quebec, and Tiny Grimes were among the musicians who recorded for the label. Artists and repertory were directed by Quebec, who was responsible for Blue Note's being among the earliest to record the work of bop musicians; items by Thelonious Monk are particularly notable (see illustration).

The company expanded its operations in the LP era, and began to concentrate on styles that were then contemporary, though it also reissued some earlier material on album. From 1953 the recording engineer Rudy van Gelder supervised most of Blue Note's sessions, and he is particularly associated with the company's close involvement in the late 1950s and early 1960s with soul jazz and hard bop. This is represented on numerous albums by, among others, Jimmy Smith, Grant Green, Stanley Turrentine, Horace Silver, Art Blakey, Donald Byrd, Johnny Griffin, Hank Mobley, Lee Morgan, Jackie McLean, Freddie Hubbard, and Quebec.

After Quebec's death in January 1963 his position was taken by Duke Pearson: later that year Blue Note was purchased by the company Liberty. The policy continued much as before; musicians who began recording for the company at this time include Herbie Hancock, Wayne Shorter, Andrew Hill, McCoy Tyner, and Bobby Hutcherson. Lion retired in 1967; Wolff and

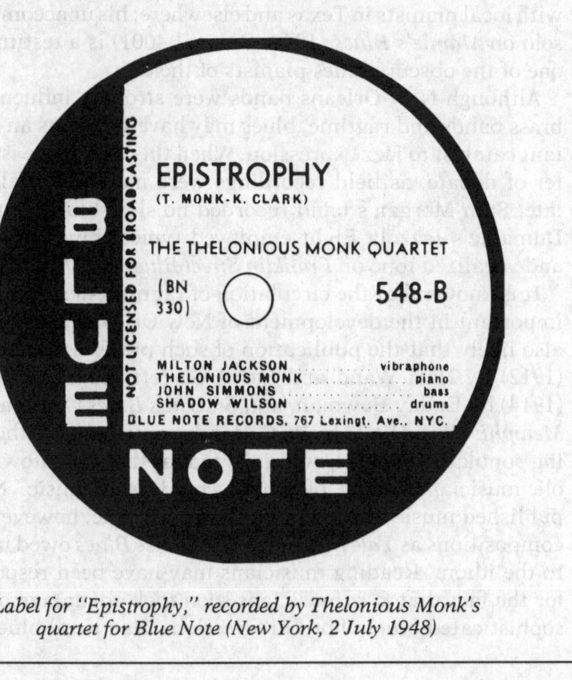

Label for "Epistrophy," recorded by Thelonious Monk's quartet for Blue Note (New York, 2 July 1948)

Pearson continued to direct the company until Wolff's death in 1971. After this Blue Note began recording a considerable amount of jazz-rock and more commercially-oriented music; Byrd's album *Black Byrd* (*c*1972) became the company's best-selling album to that date. In 1975, under the direction of Michael Cuscuna and Charlie Lourie, systematic reissue of the back catalogue began; in the 1980s reissues (including much previously unreleased material) appeared on MOSAIC.

The connection with Liberty meant that Blue Note records were distributed throughout the world by EMI. Independent reissue programs were instituted in various countries, including France and Japan. In 1980 EMI purchased Liberty, thus also acquiring Blue Note; control of the label passed in 1985 to Manhattan, a subsidiary of Capitol. A new publicity campaign and revival of promotion began in 1985, under the direction of Cuscuna and Bruce Lundwall. In addition to an internationally coordinated reissue scheme, the company began making new recordings again. These included items by such younger musicians as Stanley Jordan, Bobby McFerrin, and Michel Petrucciani, as well as albums by established musicians, among them Tyner, McLean, Hubbard, Woody Shaw, Don Pullen, and George Adams.

See also RECORDING, §II, 6.

BIBLIOGRAPHY

"International Record Scene," *J&B*, i (1971), no.7, p.27; no.8, p.34
M. Doyle: "Blue Note 12″ 78s Label Listing," *Journal of Jazz Discography*, no.1 (1976), 16
B. Rust: *The American Record Label Book* (New Rochelle, NY, 1978), 41
C. Sheridan: "The Lion and the Wolff Revisited," *JJI*, xxxii/11 (1979), 22
P. Elwood: "'New' Blue Notes," *San Francisco Examiner* (8 March 1985), §E, p.6
M. Hennessey: "Blue Note," *JJI*, xxxviii/6 (1985), 10
F. Wolff: "L'émouvante aventure d'Alfred et Francis: Blue Note, vingt-cinq ans de jazz," *Jm*, no.338 (1985), 33
M. Cuscuna: "The Blue Note Swingtets," *The Benny Morton and Jimmy Hamilton Blue Note Swingtets* (Mosaic MR1–115, 1986) [liner notes]

Blue Note (iii). The name of several nightclubs, notably ones in New York and Paris; *see* NIGHTCLUBS AND OTHER VENUES.

Blue Note Jazzmen. Name used by various small groups that recorded traditional jazz and swing for Blue Note under the leadership of Sidney Bechet (1940, 1944–5, 1949), Edmond Hall (1943), Art Hodes, James P. Johnson, and Sidney De Paris (all 1944).

Blue Notes. South African group formed by CHRIS MCGREGOR in 1963.

Blue Rhythm Band. Big band formed in 1930 by the drummer Willie Lynch, which the following year became known as the MILLS BLUE RHYTHM BAND.

Blues. There is no single definition of the term "blues." It may indicate a state of mind, describe a music that expresses that state of mind, define a form or structure for performing the music, or identify a manner of performance; it is frequently applied to performances and song types that have a number, if not all, of these characteristics. An ability to "play the blues" has been a requisite of all jazz musicians, who, on first meeting one another or when taking part in a jam session, will often use the blues framework for improvising.

1. Origins. 2. Blues and New Orleans jazz. 3. Blues accompanists. 4. Blues and white jazz. 5. Arranged and big-band jazz. 6. Territory and Kansas City bands. 7. White swing bands. 8. The New Orleans revival. 9. Blues shouters.

10. Rhythm-and-blues. 11. Blues in bop and derivative styles. 12. Blues in free jazz. 13. Blues in jazz-rock and fusions of jazz with other forms of popular music.

1. ORIGINS. It is evident that the term "blues" has a number of interrelated meanings. In the 16th century the "Blue Devils" referred to a fit of melancholy, an interpretation that persisted and came into popular usage in the mid-19th century. Although its use by black Americans to describe a state of mind has been recorded from the 1860s, it is not known to have been applied to a song form until the 20th century, when it emerged through the conflation of hollers and ballads. Hollers were freely extemporized songs performed by individual workers in the South as accompaniment to field labor, and they largely replaced group-labor work songs after the decline of the plantation system. Black ballads, which flourished from approximately 1870 to 1915, sometimes took the conventional Anglo-American pattern of four or eight lines, but a form of couplet and refrain line sung over eight or 12 bars was favored (for example, *Railroad Bill* and *Stack o' Lee*). In the 1900s a three-line stanza, consisting of one line repeated and a third, rhyming, line, became widely standardized, and is considered the most familiar blues form. It is performed over 12 bars in common time, though frequent liberties may be taken with stanza length, and usually follows the harmonic progression of tonic, subdominant, and dominant chords: I, I, I, I; IV, IV, I, I; V, V, I, I (*see* BLUES PROGRESSION). A number of variants are known.

Qualities of timbre and tone particular to the blues include the so-called blue notes achieved by microtonal flattening of the third and seventh (and, less often, other degrees) of the scale (*see* BLUE NOTE (i)). Bending of the notes, both in vocal and instrumental blues, is common (*see* BEND), and unconventional techniques of sliding on guitar strings and striking adjacent notes on the piano not quite simultaneously to convey a passing note in imitation of the voice are used extensively by folk blues singers and instrumentalists.

Blues, stemming from rural areas of the deep South, has a history largely independent of jazz. Exponents of blues usually accompanied themselves on guitar, piano, or harmonica, or were supported by small groups who often played unconventional or homemade instruments. The older work-song tradition, with its call-and-response pattern (in which a lead singer received a choral reply, sometimes antiphonally), was reflected in the use of instrumental responses to vocal lines. Other earlier black traditions, including ragtime, minstrel, and coon songs, and rural dance music performed by string groups, also contributed to the content of vocal blues and the instrumental skills of the performers. The earliest of these were probably the songsters (born from the 1870s to the 1890s), who possessed a mixed repertory and often worked in traveling shows. They were followed by the first blues singers (born 1890–1900), whose repertories frequently consisted wholly of blues. Some of the latter became semiprofessional, joining the songsters in minstrel shows and circuses.

Rural blues traditions often remained extremely localized, and a number of styles have been identified. The use of the guitar to provide a complementary response to a singer, poetic lyrics, and "rolling" piano accompaniments have been associated with Texas, while greater emphasis on repeated rhythms and the use of rasp in vocal parts with nonsequential stanzas have been linked with the Mississippi Delta. Instrumental facility and melodic inventiveness have been noted in the approach of singers from Georgia and the eastern coastal states. A number of urban styles also arose, that of Memphis being characterized by strong rhythms and the use of jug bands and string groups as accompanists. Others have been identified in Dallas, Shreveport, Atlanta, and Durham, and later in St. Louis, Indianapolis, and Chicago. It is notable, however, that there were no significant and identifiable traditions in New Orleans and Kansas City, and it is possible that instrumental jazz offered an alternative route for blues expression in these cities.

Tonally, all blues derive ultimately from the voice, and the use of "vocalized" tone by jazz musicians in all periods is marked. Bent notes and blue notes are transferred to wind and brass instruments; vocal timbre and rasp are mimicked on trumpet and trombone, frequently by the use of mutes; and call-and-response patterns, typical of black church music (which may have been the source), are reinterpreted in instrumental jazz.

2. BLUES AND NEW ORLEANS JAZZ. The early influence of blues on jazz has been widely assumed, but there is insufficient research to document it. Many jazz musicians have shown little interest in or awareness of blues singers from rural areas, regarding them as a lower caste of musician. Some (for example, the Keppard family) may have been influenced by the blues through participation in string bands, others through working with traveling shows, circuses, and fairs in which blues singers also worked. Some "uptown" New Orleans musicians, who were born on the Magnolia and other plantations, may have received an influence directly from the rural traditions. Buddy Bolden and Chris Kelly are reported to have played blues, though Bunk Johnson's alleged and probably imagined recollections of Bolden's style on the album *This is "Bunk" Johnson Talking* (1943, AM 643) suggest a "ragged time" approach.

Whereas blues guitarists may not have had a great influence on early jazz (the blues in B♭, as most commonly played by jazz bands, presented difficulties for guitarists, who preferred E or A), some of the pianists who worked in turpentine camps and logging towns in northern Louisiana are known to have visited New Orleans. But the majority of the "professors" and brothel or band pianists in the city were formally trained and did not accommodate themselves well to the genre: little recorded as blues by Clarence Williams, Spencer Williams, or Richard M. Jones is of merit. An exception was Jelly Roll Morton, who left New Orleans early in his career and competed with local pianists in Texas and elsewhere; his unaccompanied solo on *Mamie's Blues* (1939, General 4001) is a testimony to one of the obscure blues pianists of the city.

Although New Orleans bands were strongly influenced by brass bands and ragtime, blues may have served as an important catalyst to jazz expression. When this took place is a matter of debate, as field recordings were made only relatively late. Sam Morgan's band recorded no slow blues, but Louis Dumaine's Jazzola Eight employed typical blues inflections and vocalized tone on *Franklin Street Blues* (1927, Vic. 20580).

It is known that the circulation of ragtime sheet music was important in the development of New Orleans jazz, and it is also likely that the publication of such pieces as *Dallas Blues* (1912) by Hart Wand and Lloyd Garrett, *Kansas City Blues* (1914) by Euday Bowman, and *St. Louis Blues* (1914) and *The Memphis Blues* (1915) by W. C. Handy contributed to the growing popularity of blues, especially among the "downtown" Creole musicians, many of whom could read music. Not all published music labeled "blues" was genuine, however: such compositions as *Yale Blues* and *Limehouse Blues* owed nothing to the idiom. Reading musicians may have been responsible for the fact that jazz musicians soon took advantage of more sophisticated blues chord progressions than rural blues singers; they made regular use of chordal substitutions, and, as in King Oliver's *Riverside Blues* (1923, Para. 20292), sometimes employed more than one 12-bar sequence in a single tune.

Oliver's reputation as a blues player rested on his subtle use of the mute, as in his solo on *Dippermouth Blues* (1923, OK 4918), which rapidly became a standard. Other of Oliver's recordings highlight the blues playing of members of his band, for example *Camp Meeting Blues* (1923, Col. 14003D), on which Jimmie Noone's fluid "downtown" Creole approach may be heard. The harder, agile "uptown" style of Johnny Dodds is brilliantly displayed on many titles recorded by Louis Armstrong's Hot Five: his use of piercing blue notes is evident on *Lonesome Blues* (1926, OK 8396), on which Armstrong sings a typically gritty vocal line, though his habit of filling in the "response" phrases illustrates a jazz rather than a blues technique.

New Orleans jazz in Chicago was probably represented at its purest by Freddie Keppard's Jazz Cardinals, whose slow and impressive *Salty Dog* (1926, Para. 12399) is sung by Papa Charlie Jackson, one of the very few songsters or self-accompanied blues singers to work in a jazz band. Another was Lonnie Johnson, an inventive guitarist who recorded many blues but who also worked with Charlie Creath in St. Louis and made recordings with Armstrong, Oliver, Eddie Lang, and even Duke Ellington. Richard M. Jones led several small bands in Chicago; his sidemen Shirley Clay (cornet) and Artie Starks (clarinet) employ blues form and timbre on *Boar Hog Blues* (1927, Vic. 21203). Conversely, some jazz musicians worked with blues singers or instrumentalists; Johnny Dodds, for example, recorded with the Dixieland Jug Blowers (from Louisville, Kentucky) and the barrelhouse pianist Jimmy Blythe.

While King Oliver was in Chicago, Clarence Williams was recording with his Blue Five in New York; this group featured Thomas Morris and later Louis Armstrong on cornet and exceptional blues playing by Sidney Bechet on, for example, *Kansas City Man Blues* (1923, OK 4925). Bechet, one of the most individual and inventive soloists within the New Orleans idiom, continued to be a fluent and creative soprano saxophonist for several decades.

3. Blues accompanists. A close relationship between blues and jazz was evident in the accompaniments provided for recordings by the so-called classic blues singers. Most of these were female and experienced in working on the professional stage, and also, in many cases, in performing in a more "legitimate" style. Among the earliest accompanists was Johnny Dunn, who played on the first race record hit, Mamie Smith's *Crazy Blues* (1920, OK/Phonola 4169); his use of the mute is evident on Edith Wilson's *What do you care* (1922, Col. A3674), but the singer is of little blues interest. Born in Memphis, Dunn may have had direct contact with blues singers in that city. Another important center for the blues was St. Louis, where Charlie Creath and Dewey Jackson had riverboat bands. They and a number of other significant early blues trumpeters were not from New Orleans but, like Joe Smith (from Ohio), Jabbo Smith (from Georgia), and Bubber Miley (from South Carolina), were from distant states and worked with road shows, playing, and in many cases recording, with the female singers. Notable accompaniments were recorded by the trumpeters Louis Metcalf, Lee Collins, and Henry Mason, who gave sympathetic backing to Cleo Gibson on *Nothing But Blues* (1929, OK 8700). Other fine accompanists were Freddie Jenkins and J. C. Higginbotham (with Clara Smith), Tommy Ladnier (with Lovie Austin's group backing Ida Cox), and, exceptionally, Henry "Red" Allen, with members of Luis Russell's orchestra, fiercely complementing Victoria Spivey on *Telephonin' the Blues* (1929, Vic. 38546). But for many the epitome of blues accompaniment is the work of Louis Armstrong with Ma Rainey, Chippie Hill, and the "Empress of the Blues," Bessie Smith. Armstrong's call-and-response exchange with Smith on *Careless Love Blues* (1925, Col. 14083D) is a model of this aspect of blues performance in jazz. Smith's singing was powerful, deeply felt and

1. Ma Rainey with her Georgia Jazz Band, Chicago, 1925: (left to right) Gabriel Washington (drums), Al Wynn (trombone), Dave Nelson (trumpet), Edward Pollack (alto saxophone), and Thomas A. Dorsey (piano)

expressive. Although she had a limited vocal range, she had an intuitive sense of timing and a use of blue intonation which inspired a generation of jazz singers and instrumentalists.

4. BLUES AND WHITE JAZZ. Blues is in essence a black music, with its roots in black culture and its most profound expression arising from the condition of Blacks within a dominant white society. Very few white singers have felt comfortable in the idiom. "Talking blues" was developed by such white singers as Chris Bouchillon and, later, Woody Guthrie. One popular country singer, Jimmy Rodgers, invented the "blue yodel," and was even accompanied by Louis Armstrong on *Blue Yodel no.9* (1930, Vic. 23580) and Clifford Hayes's Louisville Jug Band on *My Good Gal's Gone Blues* (1931, Bb 5942). Very few white jazz singers were confident with blues – a significant exception being Jack Teagarden, who was part native American; his warm-toned voice had a distinctive quality, evident on *Beale Street Blues* (1931, Voc. 15864) recorded with Joe Venuti and Eddie Lang.

Blues were among the first jazz titles recorded, several being made by the Original Dixieland Jazz Band. Although many were marred by "hokum" routines and animal imitations, *Todd-lin' Blues* (1922, OK 4738) shows some awareness of blues expression. A strong lead was given by the cornetist Johnny De Droit on *Number Two Blues* (1924, OK 40150), with his New Orleans Jazz Orchestra showing some feeling for blues, while the New Orleans Rhythm Kings (with the addition of Jelly Roll Morton) exhibit a more mellow, relaxed approach on *Sobbin' Blues* (1923, Gen. 5219), which was modeled substantially on the recording made by King Oliver's Creole Jazz Band. Eddie Lang recorded a number of titles with the blues singer and guitarist Lonnie Johnson; although they made an effective team, Lang on his own (or accompanied by Frank Signorelli) plays immaculately but reveals little blues quality on *Church Street Sobbin' Blues* (1928, OK 8633). Lang and Johnson took part in one of the most idiosyncratic recording sessions of the 1920s, made under the name of Blind Willie Dunn's Gin Bottle Four, in which King Oliver played muted cornet and Hoagy Carmichael contributed scat vocal and improvised percussion on *Blue Blood Blues* (1929, OK 8689).

Most white bands had no direct contact with blues, and instrumentalists tended either to copy blues performances or to eschew them altogether. The jazz of the Austin High School Gang and the Chicagoans was too agitated and nervous for the blues. Bix Beiderbecke brought a more relaxed style of playing to white jazz, but his pure tone and dancing phrasing lacked blues timbre or expression. Many groups in Chicago and New York commenced their recording careers with blues standards – compositions by W. C. Handy or Spencer Williams were common – but they soon dispensed with them to play popular tunes of the day. Mezz Mezzrow had a genuine feeling for blues, but had neither the ideas nor the technique to give adequate performances. Art Hodes, though not an exceptional player, also had a sympathetic ear for blues, which figured prominently among the solo and small-group recordings he made in 1939–40. By that time, however, the first phase of the "revival" period was under way (see §8 below). In much of the white jazz of the 1930s – whether by Red Nichols, Glen Gray and the Casa Loma Orchestra, Miff Mole, or any of the much recorded New York bands – the inclusion in the repertory of blues was at best infrequent, and was then generally incorporated as a token gesture.

5. ARRANGED AND BIG-BAND JAZZ. When played by jazz musicians, blues has manifested predominantly as a solo instrumental voice with rhythmic support. While blues is not unsuited to collective improvisation (which is in fact facilitated by its familiar chord sequence and structure), its expressive nature is given greater freedom in solos. This would suggest that arranged and big-band jazz, in which soloists are featured against scored settings, would be ideal for the blues, and even inspired by it. However, just as rags were replaced by popular songs, so sentimental tunes and ballads were substituted for blues. In the earliest recordings of many large bands, blues standards, particularly the compositions of W. C. Handy, were frequently heard, but as recordings grew in number, blues became proportionately fewer. Most of the arrangers who came to prominence in the 1930s were formally trained, were ambitious as music directors, and had little or no experience of, or often interest in, the blues. As more complex arrangements were introduced, blues further diminished in importance, while the appeal of swing bands to white audiences lay largely in their repertory of dance music. Between the wars blues probably accounted for fewer than 5% of recordings. Similarly, blues techniques were largely discarded: qualities of tone and timbre were progressively modified and blue thirds and sevenths little used.

Against this general tendency, however, was the arranged jazz of the 1920s by New Orleans musicians. Jelly Roll Morton's recordings with the Red Hot Peppers include many blues featuring Omer Simeon, Kid Ory, and George Mitchell, who takes a fine blues solo on *Cannon Ball Blues* (1926, Bb 10254). While he recorded fewer blues after 1927, Morton produced a particularly beautiful example in *Deep Creek* (1928, Vic. 38055). King Oliver also continued to record blues, though less frequently after Carroll Dickerson became his music director.

New trends in arrangement were evident in the early recordings made by Fletcher Henderson. Even Coleman Hawkins's brief but forceful solo could not overcome the band's turgid arrangement of *12th Street Blues* (1925, Pathé 036214), but as it developed a greater feeling for blues – which it had to "learn" – the orchestra's playing became more adventurous; there are strong performances by Hawkins and Rex Stewart on *The House of David Blues* (1931, Ban. 32733), including a call-and-response chorus.

Don Redman seems to have had little interest in blues: there are hardly any examples in the 60 recordings made by McKinney's Cotton Pickers. However, he did arrange some "hokum" items that had previously been recorded by the blues musicians Georgia Tom (Thomas A. Dorsey) and Tampa Red (Hudson Whittaker), *Sellin' that Stuff* (1929, Vic. 38052) having generally hot solos by John Nesbitt – albeit with some split notes – and a vocal part by George Thomas devoid of blues expression. Duke Ellington based many of his compositions on the blues, and some of his recordings from the 1920s make extensive use of blues color and vocalized tone. Ellington's sidemen Bubber Miley and Tricky Sam Nanton were masterly in their use of mutes, which, however, they often employed more for "jungle" effects than for blues associations. On *Creole Love Call* (1927, Vic. 21137) Miley's growl technique is heard to excellent effect, providing a fine contrast with Adelaide Hall's vocal line (which owes nothing to blues). *The Blues with a Feelin'* (1928, OK 8662) is one of several important recordings made by Miley and Nanton. After Miley's departure from the band his place was taken by Cootie Williams, who played muted trumpet on many later recordings.

6. TERRITORY AND KANSAS CITY BANDS. The so-called territory bands had closer contact with the blues. The bands led by Nat

Towles and Milt Larkin were popular in Houston, while groups based in Dallas included those of Terrence Holder, Troy Floyd, and Alphonso Trent. The Dallas bands worked in the Central Tracks area of the city, where blues singers were also to be heard; a number did not record, and those that did may not have left their best work to posterity. Floyd's two-part *Dreamland Blues* (1929, OK 8719) features Herschel Evans and a good solo by Don Albert. Although born in New Orleans, the latter played extensively in Texas, and, with the soprano saxophonist Siki Collins, accompanied the blues singer Hattie Burleson on an excellent version of *Superstitious Blues* (1928, Bruns. 7042). Among the many good blues musicians native to the region were Snub Mosley, Buster Smith, Budd Johnson, Buddy Tate, and Lloyd Glenn.

The wide-open environment of Kansas City acted as a stimulus to big-band blues. George E. Lee's Novelty Singing Orchestra provided a stumbling beginning with *Down Home Syncopated Blues* (1927, Merritt 2206); Lee's sister Julia, who has been overrated as a blues singer and pianist, takes the vocal part. A more substantial recording is *Squabblin'* by Walter Page's Blue Devils (1929, Voc. 1463), on which the singer is Jimmy Rushing; it also introduced one of the best blues trumpeters, Hot Lips Page, who later recorded many blues with Bennie Moten's impressive Kansas City Orchestra. *Kansas City Breakdown* (1926, Vic. 21693) is a 16-bar blues based on the chord sequence of *Careless Love*, the sonorous brass contrasting with the wind instruments.

Count Basie's orchestra, more than any other, based its work on the blues, making extensive use of riffs to offset solos by its many talented musicians. Eddie Durham's arrangement of *Swinging the Blues* (1938, Decca 1180) is typical, with a short passage by Basie followed by solos from Buck Clayton (muted) and Bennie Morton, a supple offering by Lester Young, a lush contribution by Herschel Evans, and a derby mute chorus from Clayton. Basie recorded a score of other examples, including many on which Rushing and, later, Helen Humes provided vocal parts. Billie Holiday sang frequently with Basie's sidemen, but, while she claimed a debt to Bessie Smith and invested popular songs with blues feeling, she hardly ever performed blues and was essentially a jazz singer.

Andy Kirk's Clouds of Joy sustained the Kansas City approach in a somewhat less extrovert form; Mary Lou Williams made an important contribution as pianist and arranger to *Dallas Blues* (1930, Bruns. 6129) (which is marred by Billy Massey's vocal part) and many other recordings by the band. Jay McShann carried the Kansas City sound into the 1940s and provided a testing ground for Charlie Parker's blues on such recordings as *Hootie Blues* (1941, Decca 8559), on which Walter Brown is the singer.

Most of the big bands either toured or held residencies in dance halls, particularly in New York, where new arrangements of popular songs were required as each established its identity. Among the most important orchestras was that led by Jimmie Lunceford, though Sy Oliver was not noted for his interest in blues arrangements; the band shows what it can do with only a head arrangement on a splendid version of *Uptown Blues* (1939, Voc./OK 5362). In their arrangements for Lunceford, Eddie Durham and Billy Moore placed greater emphasis on blues, a notable example being the latter's *Barefoot Blues* (1940, Col. 35860). Earl Hines, who from 1928 to 1948 led bands principally in Chicago, plays blues solos in his inimitable style on a number of recordings; he had a hit with *Boogie Woogie on St. Louis Blues* (1940, Bb 10674). Billy Eckstine became Hines's principal vocalist in 1939 and, in spite of a somewhat insinuating voice, made a success of *Stormy Monday Blues* (1942, Bb 11567).

Many other bands that were in many respects very different from one another, such as those led by Teddy Hill, Claude Hopkins, Tiny Bradshaw, Chick Webb, and Cab Calloway, had excellent sidemen. A number of these had considerable experience playing blues, though this is often detectable only after determined listening. While it is not entirely lacking in blues influence, the recorded evidence yields a preponderance of popular and novelty songs, a certain amount of instrumental and personality showmanship, boogie-woogie orchestrations, and an extensive use of riffs; the competitive nature of much big-band jazz tended to suppress pure blues performance.

7. White swing bands. As noted above, blues is a manner of performance and a structure for improvisation. White musicians who may not have shared the black experience could still simulate black blues techniques and tone color and could improvise within the blues form. Woody Herman's first orchestra was billed as "the Band that Plays the Blues." For about four years following *Dupree Blues* (1937, Decca 1288) the band recorded a fair number of blues items, *Dallas Blues* (1939, Decca 2629) being notable for a solo by the leader, but by 1941 (during the craze for boogie-woogie) Herman was performing novelty songs, and blues was thereafter of less importance.

Rather more feeling for blues was evident in some recordings by Artie Shaw, particularly on the two-part *The Blues* (1937, Bruns. 7947). Hot Lips Page joined the orchestra to sing *St. James Infirmary* (1941, Vic. 27895), with Max Kaminsky playing muted trumpet in support. Harry James was clearly influenced at times by Count Basie's orchestra, several of whose titles he recorded in alternation with more sentimental or commercial numbers. *Jeffries' Blues* (1941, Col. 36190) is one of the small number of recordings that feature his blues playing, which is efficient but soulless.

Of the other white leaders, Benny Goodman had technical ability and a number of skillful sidemen, yet, except for a few standards, blues was almost unrepresented in the several hundred recordings by his orchestra. Among the exceptions were the rare forays, such as *The Blues in Your Flat* (1938, Vic. 26044), made with the black vibraphonist Lionel Hampton. A brief flirtation with boogie-woogie by Tommy Dorsey's big band resulted in such titles as *Boogie Woogie* (1938, Vic. 26054), a rather mechanical piece with Charlie Spivak and Howard Smith as sidemen; but the "Sentimental Gentleman of Swing" was not well disposed towards blues. In general, white swing bands appear to have regarded blues as another novelty, and, at best, went through the motions of performing it competently, but had little feeling for or understanding of the meaning of the idiom.

8. The New Orleans revival. The revival of interest in earlier forms of jazz, but almost exclusively that of New Orleans, had many aspects: the return to older styles by the musicians themselves; the initiation of recording sessions with pioneer musicians by critics and historians of jazz; the continuation of the New Orleans tradition within the city; and the simulation of the music by white (including European) enthusiasts. All these aspects produced blues, which was perceived, if sometimes self-consciously, as a formative element in jazz, and the revival served to underline the essential role of blues in jazz as an expressive music (*see also* Traditional jazz).

An early event in the revival was the re-formation by Wingy Manone of the New Orleans Rhythm Kings. An uneven musician, he played well with Georg Brunis and Sidney Arodin on

Tin Roof Blues (1934, Decca 161). The first phases of dixieland may also be considered as part of the revival, in particular the activities of Bob Crosby, whose recording sessions with large and small groups sometimes included blues. *Milk Cow Blues* (1938, Decca 1962), with a vocal contribution by Nappy Lamare, is based on the original recording made by the blues singer James "Kokomo" Arnold; the title was popular with a number of groups, including those, such as the band led by Johnny Lee Wills, who played in the Western swing idiom. New versions by the Original Dixieland Jazz Band of their early recordings were inclined to be raucous, but *Bluin' the Blues* (1936, Vic. 25525) has some incisive clarinet playing by Larry Shields. Far more convincing were the recordings made by Muggsy Spanier and his Ragtime Band: there is fine blues playing on muted trumpet by Spanier on *Relaxin' at the Touro* (1939, Bb 10532), with excellent support from Brunis and Rod Cless. Mention should also be made of *Magnolia Blues* (1937, Col. 36159) by Santo Pecora and his Back Room Boys, with Shorty Sherock playing trumpet and Riley Scott singing in the manner of Jack Teagarden.

An important stage in the renewed recognition of blues in jazz was initiated by John Hammond when he rediscovered Meade "Lux" Lewis late in 1935. This led to the revival of the careers of Albert Ammons (see fig.2), Jimmy Yancey, and other pianists (*see* BOOGIE-WOOGIE and PIANO, §3); it also stimulated a temporary craze for boogie-woogie among jazz musicians and made them aware of blues roots. The recording sessions arranged by Hugues Panassié were a landmark in the revival. *Really the Blues* (1938, Bb 10089) by Tommy Ladnier was notable for the rapport among Ladnier, Sidney Bechet, and Mezz Mezzrow. Bechet made many blues with his New Orleans Feetwarmers, the band often being overridden by his powerful playing on soprano saxophone; perhaps the most remarkable title is *Blues of Bechet* (1941, Vic. 27485), on which, by overdubbing, he played clarinet, tenor and soprano saxophone, and piano. A more modest performance is the accompaniment to the New Orleans singer Cousin Joe on *Layin' my Rules in Blues* (on the album *The Mezzrow-Bechet Quintet: the King Jazz Story*, 1945, Sto. SLP153), with Hot Lips Page playing sympathetic muted trumpet.

For many, the essence of the revival was the discovery, or rediscovery, and recording of New Orleans veterans in their own city. Kid Rena's *Lowdown Blues* (1940, Delta 803) was disappointing, but the finding of Bunk Johnson led to a succession of important documentary recordings. A long, slow example of the 24-bar *Blues* (on the album *Blues & Spirituals*, 1944–5, AM 638), recorded in 1944 with Kid Shots Madison, George Lewis (i), and Jim Robinson at San Jacinto Hall, is exceptional, and *Tishomingo Blues* (1945, Decca 25131) is a tight performance; Lewis is heard at his best with his own band on *Deep Bayou Blues* (1943, Climax 101). Other New Orleans groups laid a greater emphasis on blues that had characterized the later phases of music in the city. The blues swing generated by playing fractionally behind the beat is evident on Wooden Joe Nicholas's *Original Blues (Artesan Hall Blues)* (1945; on the album *Wooden Joe's New Orleans Band, 1945–1949*, Sto. 204), which incorporates expressive performances by the leader and Albert Burbank. Kid Ory's Creole Jazz Band (which was recorded in Hollywood) was one of the most dynamic of the revival bands; it gained much impetus from the presence of Mutt Carey, who plays both open and muted trumpet on *Blues for Jimmie* (1944, Crescent 2), dedicated to Jimmie Noone.

Significant recordings of blues in the New Orleans tradition were made by other veterans, including Billie and De De Pierce, Kid Howard and Capt. John Handy, Kid Sheik Colar, and Kid Thomas, though as this generation of musicians grew older they produced few recordings of value after the 1960s. A great many white bands – American, European, and Australian – sought to imitate the pioneer New Orleans groups; some were successful in re-creating the sounds of such ensembles playing marching and dance music, though they made only a small contribution to the blues in jazz. Mention should be made, however, of the occasional blues recorded with older black musicians taking the lead, notably Bunk Johnson with the Yerba Buena Jazz Band, George Lewis (i) with Ken Colyer, and Kid Thomas with Barry Martyn.

9. BLUES SHOUTERS. The bands of Kansas City and the Southwest included a number of blues singers whose strength of voice and extrovert delivery caused them to be termed "blues shouters." One of the most important was Jimmy Rushing (see fig.3), who recorded with Bennie Moten's Kansas City Orchestra in 1930, though at this stage his voice was still relatively high. It had filled out and gained its crackling texture by the time he made *Sent for you yesterday and here you come today* (1938, Decca 1880) with Count Basie's orchestra. Rushing's capacity to swing a band and his excellent sense of timing are evident on many of Basie's recordings (his replacement in the band, Joe Williams, had a warm voice but lacked Rushing's drive). Although he was not lucky with some of his accompanists in later years, Rushing made some fine titles with Emmett Berry and, in 1955–6, with Buck Clayton. *Piney Brown Blues* (on his own album *Jazz Odyssey*, 1956, Col. CL963) features Buddy Tate and Vic Dickenson and has some excellent blues playing by Cliff Jackson. The title is usually associated with Joe Turner (ii), a Kansas City blues shouter who rose rapidly to fame during the boogie-woogie revival as the singer with Pete Johnson and the Boogie Woogie Trio; under Johnson's

2. Meade "Lux" Lewis (right) and Albert Ammons at Café Society, New York, 1939

3. Jimmy Rushing with Count Basie's orchestra at the Apollo Theatre, New York, January 1939

leadership he recorded a memorable, rich-toned version of *Cherry Red* (1939, Voc./OK 4997), with Hot Lips Page (also a fine blues shouter) and Buster Smith. In the 1940s Turner recorded several numbers for the emerging rhythm-and-blues market, and on some he is accompanied by such jazz musicians as Frankie Newton and Don Byas. He made a number of exceptional titles in the mid-1950s on which he was again accompanied by Johnson, together with several members of Count Basie's orchestra. Given shape by Ernie Wilkins's inspired scoring, a traditional blues such as *How Long Blues* (on the album *Boss of the Blues*, 1956, Atl. 1234) receives a supremely relaxed yet firm treatment, with good solos by Joe Newman and Pete Brown.

Both Rushing and Turner, who were primarily blues singers, were able to bring blues expression and intonation to a wide range of ballads and popular songs, and in so doing drew their accompanists back to the blues. Jimmy Witherspoon's best performances had the same qualities, though his voice did not have their timbre. Witherspoon joined Jay McShann's band as a replacement for Walter Brown, whose performance on *Confessin' the Blues* (1941, Decca 8559) is also notable. Witherspoon's recordings with McShann include a movingly sung slow blues, *Ain't nobody's business* (1947, Supreme 1506), which dates back to the first decade of the century. *C. C. Rider* (on the album *Witherspoon, Mulligan, Webster at the Renaissance*, 1959, Hifijazz 426), recorded at the Renaissance Club, Hollywood, reveals good backing by Ben Webster and an excellent solo by Gerry Mulligan. Although Witherspoon later sang a higher proportion of popular ballads, he retained a strong element of blues in his performances.

Apart from their intrinsic merits, the blues shouters succeeded in relating to the mainstream of jazz and skillfully reintroduced the essential blues at a time when it was in danger of being forgotten. Turner, and to a lesser extent Witherspoon, also established an important bridge between the blues tradition and rhythm-and-blues.

10. Rhythm-and-blues. In the 1930s there were repeated attempts to match jazz musicians with blues singers, the most successful being the combination of New Orleans musicians and Mississippi guitarists in the Harlem Hamfats: *Black gal, you better use your head* (1937, Decca 7439) is a relaxed blues sung by Joe McCoy with Odell Rand playing clarinet. Other groups brought together Lee Collins and Lil Johnson, Chu Berry and Ollie Shepard, Tommy Ladnier and Rosetta Howard, and even Charlie Christian and Edmond Hall accompanying Ida Cox. These associations were mainly the ideas of record promoters, but the singer and guitarist Big Bill Broonzy included Punch Miller in a number of his later groups, notably the Chicago Five (1942).

A stronger influence of jazz on the blues emerged in the 1940s with the early stages of rhythm-and-blues. An extremely popular small group was Louis Jordan's Tympany Five, which performed jive and jump music (*see* Jump). Jordan had previously worked as a singer with Chick Webb. His witty lyrics and spirited saxophone playing are evident on a number of his wartime recordings, and *Saturday Night Fish Fry* (1949, Decca 24725) was a major hit. He also made several titles with a 16-piece band that included Oliver Nelson and Bill Doggett. Doggett played on Lucky Millinder's early recordings, accompanying Sister Rosetta Tharpe on such titles as *I want a tall skinny papa* (1942, Decca 18386). Millinder later employed Wynonie Harris as blues singer. The latter possessed a strong, shouting voice, and although many of his rhythm-and-blues hits were comedy numbers his witty delivery may also be heard on such straight blues as *I want my Fanny Brown* (1948, King 4304), where he is accompanied by Cat Anderson and Hal Singer.

Another powerful blues singer with his roots well established in jazz was the alto saxophonist Eddie "Cleanhead" Vinson. His recording of *My big brass bed is gone* (1950, King 4381) is typical of his ironic blues and hard-edged playing. Vinson grew up in Houston, which emerged as an important center of the blues in the 1940s. So, belatedly, did New Orleans, largely on account of the rhythm-and-blues singer and pianist Fats Domino and his arranger Dave Bartholomew. Domino had a plaintive voice and a mellow boogie-woogie style on piano; his typically hammered beat and light swing may be heard on *La la* (1955, Imperial 5348).

The most influential blues instrumentalist and singer to adopt jazz accompaniments was T-Bone Walker, who was based in Los Angeles and worked with Ida Cox, Les Hite, and, in 1944, Fletcher Henderson. His clear, arpeggiated style of playing on electric guitar compensated for a somewhat colorless voice, while large bands filled out the general sound; the orchestra for *Call it Stormy Monday* (1947, Black & White 122) included Bumps Myers, Teddy Buckner, and Lloyd Glenn. Another of the many rhythm-and-blues singers on the West Coast who employed jazz musicians was Pee Wee Crayton, a considerable guitarist in whose band Ornette Coleman played for some years. Although from the late 1940s the rising cost of maintaining big bands caused their number to decline, B. B. King, who owes much to T-Bone Walker, has continued to employ jazz musicians for more than 35 years.

11. BLUES IN BOP AND DERIVATIVE STYLES. Blues progressions and popular-song forms form the basis of all styles related to bop. The occurrence of blues in bop is therefore not remarkable: the style emphasized improvisation, for which the blues provided a strong and familiar foundation. Nonetheless it may be noted that bop musicians contributed numerous blues themes of such distinctive character that they became standards. Examples include Charlie Parker's *Billie's Bounce* (1945, Savoy 573), *Au privave* (1951, Mer./Clef 11087), and *Blues for Alice* (1951; on the EP *Charlie Parker*, 1951–3, Clef 287; *see* BLUES PROGRESSION); Thelonious Monk's *Misterioso* (1948, BN 560), *Straight no Chaser* (1951, BN 1589), and *Blue Monk* (on the album *Thelonious Monk Trio*, 1954, Prst. 189); Johnny Carisi's *Israel* (1949, Cap. 60011), recorded by Miles Davis; Milt Jackson's *Bags' Groove* (1952, BN 1593); Davis's *Walkin'* (1954, Prst. 45-157); and Horace Silver's *Señor Blues* (on the album *Six Pieces of Silver*, 1956, BN 1539).

Parker's playing on alto saxophone exhibits two important elements that were absorbed to differing degrees in the styles derived from bop. One was his extraordinary facility and harmonic imagination in the treatment of fast-moving chord progressions, while the other was his wonderfully relaxed approach to the blues, rooted in the tradition of Kansas City blues shouters and heard to advantage on *Parker's Mood* (1948, Savoy 936). Generally, cool-jazz musicians, and especially those of the West-Coast school, concentrated on the harmonic implications of Parker's playing, while hard bop and soul jazz developed from the perceived need to restore to jazz some elements of its roots in black-American blues and gospel music. The claim should be treated with caution, however, since there were accomplished blues players associated with the cool-jazz and West-Coast jazz movements; Gerry Mulligan's fine solo on the blues *Mulligan's Stew* (on the album *Gerry Mulligan Blows*, 1951, Prst. 141), recorded well before he became a leading figure on the West Coast, provides an example. Nonetheless it is largely true that the blues feeling, if not the blues form, became lost. It later re-emerged, its most important exponent being Silver, whose hard-bop blues recordings include *Opus de Funk* (1953, BN 1625) and *The Preacher* (on the album *Horace Silver and the Jazz Messengers*, 1955, BN 5062). Other leading interpreters were Cannonball Adderley, Art Blakey, Davis, and Charles Mingus.

Tenor saxophonists have been involved in some special aspects of blues playing in bop, hard bop, and soul jazz. Firstly, several well-known recordings were made that were built on blues cutting contests between two prominent players, and subsequently a number of groups were formed on the same basis. Examples include the encounters between Gene Ammons and Dexter Gordon on Billy Eckstine's *Blowin' the blues away* (1944, De Luxe 2001) and Gordon and Wardell Gray on *The Chase* (1947, Dial 1017), and the quintets led by Ammons and Sonny Stitt (whose playing may be heard on *Blues Up and Down*, 1950, Birdland 6005) and by Johnny Griffin and Eddie "Lockjaw" Davis. Secondly, some informal terms have arisen to describe saxophonists who play in an aggressive blues-oriented manner: "tough tenors" and, for those who were active in Texas, "Texas tenors." Among the members of one or both of these bodies are Ammons, Arnett Cobb, Davis, Wilton Felder, Gordon, Griffin, Harold Ousley, Houston Person, and Stitt. (The alto saxophonist Eddie "Cleanhead" Vinson, a "tough" blues player from Texas, may also be considered an honorary member of either group.)

12. BLUES IN FREE JAZZ. In many ways some substyles of free jazz may be considered as closely related to the blues. The musical expression of blues emotions is, if anything, carried further in free jazz than ever before: there are frequent and extreme instances of instrumental squeals, cries, shouts, moans, and whispers; instrumentalists trade riffs back and forth and play blues formulas; and blue notes abound on all degrees of the scale – not only on thirds, fifths, and sevenths. Significant differences are that there may be no steady beat (in this respect free jazz recalls the playing of early downhome blues singers and guitarists) and, for the first time, blue notes and blues formulas are independent of functional harmony.

It is usual for musicians who grew up after 1940 to have played in rhythm-and-blues bands before taking up jazz, and it is noteworthy that the three greatest free-jazz saxophonists – Ornette Coleman, John Coltrane, and Albert Ayler – began their careers in this manner; all three musicians transferred to the free-jazz idiom a command of blues formulas and, particularly, the honks and squeals introduced into rhythm-and-blues by Illinois Jacquet and others. The cross-fertilization ran both ways in some instances: Ayler later led a rhythm-and-blues group, and in his last years made recordings in that vein, while Archie Shepp, after establishing his reputation in free jazz, turned to rhythm-and-blues and made the fine album *Attica Blues* (1972, Imp. 9222).

The blues helped greatly in bridging the otherwise abrupt transition from bop to free jazz, and a number of fine performances straddle the boundary between the two genres. The title track of Oliver Nelson's *Screamin' the Blues* (1960, NewJ 8243) juxtaposes the 12-bar form and Nelson's growling rhythm-and-blues playing on tenor saxophone with Eric Dolphy's pantonal improvising. Mingus describes *Folk Forms no.1* (on the album *Charles Mingus Presents Charles Mingus*, 1960, Can. 9005) as based on a "traditional folk form" – the 12-bar blues – but it is a collective improvisation for trumpet, alto saxophone (Dolphy), double bass, and drums, in which an explicit, steady beat is rarely present and in which no chordal instrument participates. *Pursuance*, the third part of John Coltrane's suite *A Love Supreme* (1964, Imp. 77), is a 12-bar bop blues which Coltrane (like Dolphy) treats in a harmonically free manner. *Dancing in the Sun* (on the album *The Heliocentric Worlds of Sun Ra*, 1965, ESP 1014) combines bop rhythms, a bluesy walking bass line, and the suggestion of blues form in the opening theme with a piano ostinato which obscures that suggestion and free collective improvisation among the wind instruments.

The most important figure in free jazz is Ornette Coleman. Jost points out that six tracks among Coleman's first recordings for Contemporary (in a style that pits his new mode of playing against a bop accompaniment – as in the aforementioned pieces) use blues form. An example is *Tears Inside* (on the album *Tomorrow is the Question*, 1959, Cont. 3569), based on the 12-bar blues progression, but with pauses between each four-bar phrase rather than a continuous beat. Although Coleman soon discarded conventional structures, his improvising has always shown a heavy reliance on blue notes and blues formulas, as may be heard on *Lonely Woman* (on the album *The Shape of Jazz to Come*, 1959, Atl. 1317) and *Broadway Blues* (on the album *New York is Now!*, 1968, BN 84287).

13. Blues in jazz-rock and fusions of jazz with other forms of popular music. The blues form is rare in jazz-rock and related styles, but an abundance of blue notes and blue formulas may be heard in such pieces as *Put it where you want it*, recorded by the Crusaders on *Crusaders 1* (1971, Blue Thumb 6001), the title track of Jean-Luc Ponty's album *Imaginary Voyage* (1976, Atl. 19136), and the title track of David Sanborn's album *Backstreet* (*c*1982, WB 23906).

More important is the introduction into jazz of a "dirty" blues timbre by musicians playing electric guitar. Apart from the performance by Floyd Smith on an early recording with Andy Kirk's band, *Floyd's Guitar Blues* (1939, Decca 2483), jazz electric guitarists remained for several decades devoted to a smooth, round, clean sound, wholly independent of the approach taken by such players as T-Bone Walker, B. B. King, and Muddy Waters. From the mid-1960s rock musicians, notably Jimi Hendrix and Eric Clapton, absorbed the lessons of the Chicago blues guitarists, and in turn influenced younger jazz players. Examples of the latter who began to make a connection between blues formulas (which had always been an element of jazz guitar) and blues timbres are John McLaughlin (as may be heard on *Vital Transformation* on the Mahavishnu Orchestra's album *The Inner Mounting Flame*, 1971, Col. KC31067) and Mike Stern; Stern plays a notable solo on the title track of Miles Davis's *Star People* (1982–3, Col. FC38657), a piece that provides an uncommon instance in jazz-rock of a conventional 12-bar blues form.

See also Singing, §§2, 3, 4, and 5.

BIBLIOGRAPHY

F. Ramsey, Jr.: *Been Here and Gone* (New Brunswick, NJ, and London, 1960)
S. B. Charters and L. Kunstadt: *Jazz: a History of the New York Scene* (Garden City, NY, 1962/*R*1981)
L. Jones: *Blues People: Negro Music in White America* (New York, 1963)
H. Courlander: *Negro Folk Music U.S.A.* (New York and London, 1964)
P. Oliver: *Conversation with the Blues* (London, 1965)
G. Schuller: *Early Jazz: its Roots and Musical Development* (New York, 1968)
P. Oliver: *The Story of the Blues* (London, 1969/*R*1982)
R. M. W. Dixon and J. Godrich: *Recording the Blues* (London, 1970)
C. Gillett: *The Sound of the City: the Rise of Rock and Roll* (New York, 1970, rev. 2/1983)
D. Stewart-Baxter: *Ma Rainey and the Classic Blues Singers* (New York and London, 1970)
J. Broven: *Walking to New Orleans: the Story of New Orleans Rhythm and Blues* (Bexhill-on-Sea, England, 1974; Gretna, LA, 1983, as *Rhythm & Blues in New Orleans*) [incl. discography]
E. Jost: *Free Jazz* (Graz, Austria, 1974)
A. Murray: *Stomping the Blues* (London and New York, 1976)
Arnold Shaw: *Honkers and Shouters: the Golden Years of Rhythm and Blues* (New York, 1978)
P. Oliver: *Songsters and Saints: Vocal Traditions on Race Records* (Cambridge, England, and elsewhere, 1984)
D. D. Harrison: *Black Pearls: Blues Queens of the 1920s* (New Brunswick, NJ, 1988)

PAUL OLIVER (1–10)
BARRY KERNFELD (11–13)

Blues Alley. Nightclub in Washington; *see* Nightclubs and other venues.

Blues progression. The underlying harmonic structure of the blues. In the broad sense, the term can refer to the harmonic basis of any piece called a Blues (an exhaustive survey of these progressions can be found in Dauer). In the narrow sense, it refers to a flexible, cyclic 12-bar structure, consisting of three four-bar phrases with the chord pattern shown in ex.1 (*see* Forms, esp. §1(b)). Many variants of this pattern are possible: frequently IV is used in place of I in bar 2, or in place of V in bar 10. The chord shape most commonly chosen for this pattern by blues musicians is a major triad with an added flatted seventh, though the functional implications that such chords carry in 18th-century classical music are not necessarily present in blues. Country or "downhome" blues guitarists characteristically vary the rhythms and harmonies of the basic progression, and sometimes discard harmonic function altogether by maintaining a tonic drone on the bass strings; in this case a blues harmonic progression may be intimated by the vocal and treble-string melodies.

Ex.1 Basic harmonic structure of the 12-bar blues progression

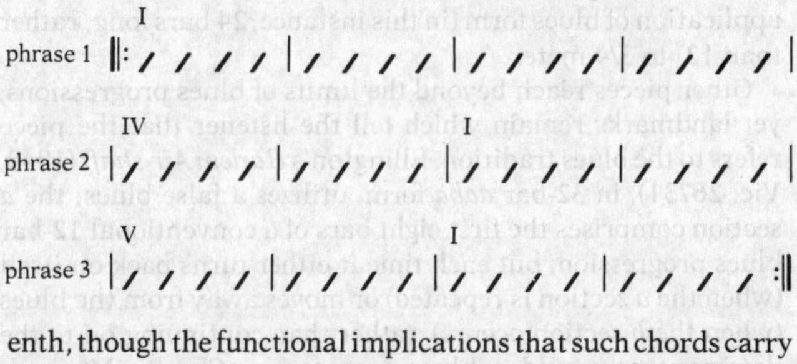

There is evidence to suggest that the blues progression originated as early as the 1890s among blues guitarists of the Mississippi delta and itinerant southern boogie-woogie pianists, though recordings of this music did not appear until the mid-1920s. By that time the blues progression had already been adapted to serve in other styles. Themes based on 12-bar blues progressions appeared in ragtime compositions from 1904; later, composer–collectors of the blues published multithematic "blues," combining 12-bar blues progressions with 16-bar ragtime themes and popular songs (e.g., W.C. Handy's *Memphis Blues*, 1912). These hybrid pieces were popularized by "classic" blues singers such as Mamie Smith and Bessie Smith from 1920. A few years later, in 1923, recordings by innovative black jazz ensembles from New Orleans revealed that there were several established variants from the standard blues pattern. Only later were field recordings made of rural blues musicians. Because of this confusion in the sources it is impossible to establish an original form of the blues progression.

Jazz musicians took advantage of the flexibility inherent in the blues progression, presenting it in new guises. It might be placed in a new harmonic or rhythmic context, played in a deceptive manner, or transferred to a percussion instrument, yet the reference to blues form and harmony would remain clear. The simple 12-bar scheme of ex.1 has been subjected to a wide variety of substitute and passing harmonies. An extreme example is provided by Charlie Parker's *Blues for Alice* (1951), on the EP *Charlie Parker* (1951–3, Clef 287), with its sequences of interpolated secondary-dominant progressions (ex.2). A minor-mode form of the blues progression also exists, a notable early example occurring in Duke Ellington's *Ko-Ko* (1940, Vic. 26577; for illustration *see* Ellington, duke, ex.1); later it became a common characteristic in soul jazz. Wayne Shorter's bop waltz, *Footprints*, on Miles Davis's album *Miles Smiles* (1966,

Ex.2 Harmonic structure of C. Parker: *Blues for Alice* (1951), on the EP *Charlie Parker* (1951–3, Clef 287)

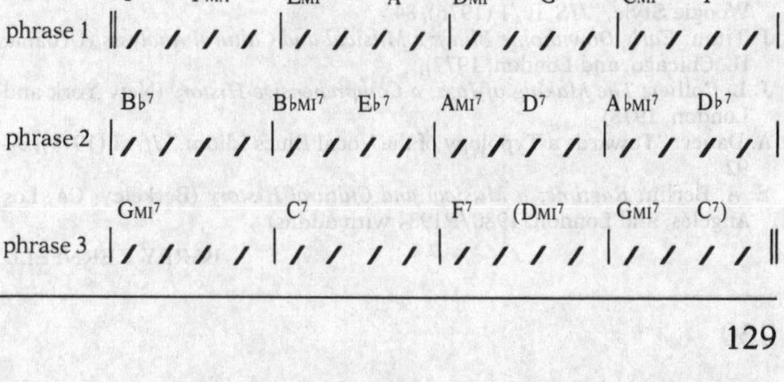

Col. CS9401), provides an unusual example of a convincing application of blues form (in this instance, 24 bars long, rather than 12) to 3/4 meter.

Other pieces reach beyond the limits of blues progressions, yet landmarks remain which tell the listener that the piece refers to the blues tradition. Ellington's *Harlem Air-shaft* (1940, Vic. 26731), in 32-bar *aaba* form, utilizes a false blues: the *a* section comprises the first eight bars of a conventional 12-bar blues progression, but each time it either turns back on itself (when the *a* section is repeated) or moves away from the blues (when the *b* section occurs), rather than continuing on to the dominant as would a blues progression. Charles Mingus's *Goodbye Pork Pie Hat*, on the album *Mingus Ah Um* (1959, Col. CL1370), may be heard as a special type of blues because of its subject (a lament for Lester Young), its 12-bar form, and its move to the subdominant at bar five (ex.3). Apart from being permeated with the blues formulas that are basic to his style, Horace Silver's *Sister Sadie*, from the album *Blowin' the Blues Away* (1959, BN 4017), utilizes a 32-bar form in which the harmony remains on I for 16 bars, moving to IV at bar 17; if this is not a proper blues, it at least evokes a strong impression of one.

Ex.3 Harmonic structure of C. Mingus: *Goodbye Pork Pie Hat*, from the album *Mingus Ah Um* (1959, Col. CL1370)

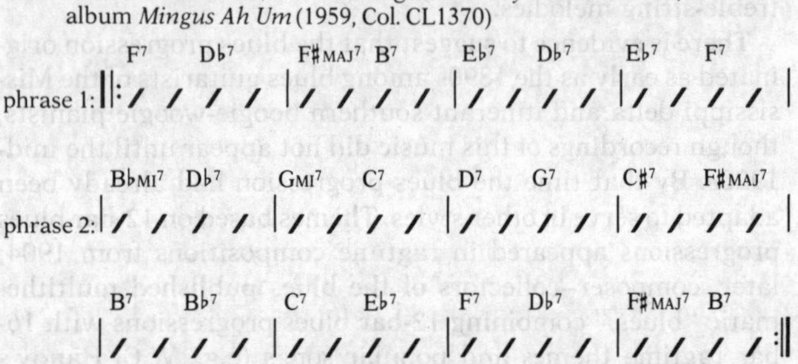

Drummers, most notably Max Roach, have adapted the blues progression and poetic form to unaccompanied solos, translating the 12-bar blues into percussive terms. That is, a drummer may convey the sense of the phrases and harmonies of ex.1, as well as the feeling of the couplet and response poetry of the blues, by playing a four-bar phrase on one drum or cymbal, repeating half of the phrase on another drum or cymbal and half on the first one, then ending with a new phrase, half on still another drum or cymbal, half again on the first one. The components of the drum set need not be tuned to pitches that correspond to I, IV, and V in order to capture the impression of a 12-bar blues. Fine examples of this occur in Roach's solo in the middle of *Blue Seven*, from Sonny Rollins's album *Saxophone Colossus* (1956, Prst. 7079), and Dannie Richmond's solo on *Folk Forms no.1*, from the album *Charles Mingus Presents Charles Mingus* (1960, Can. 9005).

BIBLIOGRAPHY

C. Keil: *Urban Blues* (Chicago and London, 1966)
G. Schuller: *Early Jazz: its Roots and Musical Development* (New York, 1968)
L. Koch: "Structural Aspects of King Oliver's 1923 Okeh Recordings," *JJS*, iii/2 (1976), 36
E. Newberger: "Archetypes and Antecedents of Piano Blues and Boogie Woogie Style," *JJS*, iv/1 (1976), 84
J. Titon: *Early Downhome Blues: a Musical and Cultural Analysis* (Urbana, IL, Chicago, and London, 1977)
J. L. Collier: *The Making of Jazz: a Comprehensive History* (New York and London, 1978)
A. Dauer: "Towards a Typology of the Vocal Blues Idiom," *Jf*, xi (1979), 9–92
E. A. Berlin: *Ragtime: a Musical and Cultural History* (Berkeley, CA, Los Angeles, and London, 1980/*R*1984 with addns)

BARRY KERNFELD

Blues Serenaders (i). Recording band led in 1924–5 by LOVIE AUSTIN.

Blues Serenaders (ii). Southwest dance band. It was formed by Jesse Stone around 1920 and its varying personnel included Jack Washington, Budd Johnson, and Eddie Thompkins. It played in Kansas City and the Southwest, recorded for Okeh (1927), and disbanded in 1928.

For bibliography *see* STONE, JESSE.

Blue Star. Record company and label. The company was established in Paris in 1945 by the pianist and bandleader Eddie Barclay, who directed a ten-piece band for the label's first release. Between 1947 and 1954 Blue Star recorded sessions by Don Byas, Django Reinhardt, Hubert Rostaing, Howard McGhee, Sidney Bechet, James Moody, Henri Renaud, and Bernard Peiffer. Some of these recordings were also issued in the USA on Atlantic, and some were reissued after the owner founded a new company and label, Barclay, around 1954. Blue Star's own catalogue remained relatively small, but the company issued several recordings that had originally appeared on Norman Granz's Clef and Norgran labels; thus in France many reissues, and releases of new material from Granz's later company, Verve, also carried Blue Star's name.

Blue Stars. Vocal group led in the mid-1950s by BLOSSOM DEARIE.

Bluiett, Hamiet (*b* Lovejoy, nr East St. Louis, IL, 1940). Baritone saxophonist. His aunt, a choral director, taught him music when he was a child, and from the age of nine he learned clarinet. He attended Southern Illinois University and studied flute and, later, baritone saxophone, but left school before graduating. After several years in the navy, he moved to St. Louis in the mid-1960s, where he played with Lester Bowie, Joseph Bowie, Charles "Bobo" Shaw, Julius Hemphill, Oliver Lake, and others, and was associated with the Black Artists Group. In 1969 he moved to New York, and joined Sam Rivers's large ensemble. After playing as a freelance with a variety of musicians, in 1972 he became a member of Charles Mingus's quintet, which also included Don Pullen (with whom Bluiett later recorded as a sideman); he remained with the group until mid-1975. Concerts that he gave in 1976 (as a leader) and 1977 (as a soloist) resulted in the albums *Endangered Species* and *Birthright*. In December 1976 he formed a quartet with Hemphill, Lake, and David Murray for a concert in New Orleans; the group continued to perform as the WORLD SAXOPHONE QUARTET into the 1980s. At the same time he played with his own ensembles and made further recordings as a sideman. Bluiett is one of very few avant-garde musicians to concentrate on the baritone saxophone. His large sound, wide range, developed technique, and command of tone-color did much to establish the identity of the World Saxophone Quartet.

SELECTED RECORDINGS

As unaccompanied soloist: *Birthright* (1977, IndN 1030)
As leader: *Endangered Species* (1976, IndN 1025); *Orchestra, Duo and Septet* (1977, Chi. 182); of World Saxophone Quartet (with J. Hemphill, O. Lake, and D. Murray): *Steppin' with the World Saxophone Quartet* (1978, BS 0027); *Dangerously Suite* (1981, SN 1018); *Ebu* (1984, SN 1088)
As sideman: J. Hemphill: *'Coon Bid'ness* (1972–5, Ari. 4012); S. Murray: *Applecores* (1978, Philly Jazz 1004); D. Pullen: *A Well Kept Secret* (1980, Shemp 2701)

BIBLIOGRAPHY

C. Stern: "Stars on the Rise: Hamiet Bluiett," *DB*, xlv/15 (1978), 24
V. Alexandre: "Hamiet Bluiett: 'aucune école ne peut vous apprendre à être noir'," *Jm*, no.291 (1980), 14 [incl. discography]

B. Case: "De-subdued Baritone," *MM*, lvi/4 (1981), 26
B. McRae: "Avant courier: Hamiet Bluiett," *JJI*, xxxvi/11 (1983), 10 [incl. discography]

For further recordings and bibliography *see* WORLD SAXOPHONE QUARTET.

DAVID WILD

Blythe, Arthur (Murray) [Black Arthur] (*b* Los Angeles, 5 July 1940). Alto saxophonist and leader. He grew up in San Diego, and played in school bands from the age of nine; as a teenager he studied with Kirtland Bradford, a former lead alto saxophonist with Jimmie Lunceford's orchestra. After returning to Los Angeles in 1960, he began to work with Horace Tapscott, with whom he appeared regularly until 1974; the two men were also founding members of the Union of God's Musicians and Artists Ascension in 1961. Blythe then moved to New York, where he played with Chico Hamilton (1974–7) and Gil Evans (1976–80) and performed in lofts with his own groups. From 1978 to 1980 he frequently appeared with Lester Bowie and in Jack DeJohnette's Special Edition.

Blythe rose to prominence as the leader of two very different groups. The earlier of these, In the Tradition, based its repertory on swing and bop and included Fred Hopkins, Steve McCall, and either Stanley Cowell or John Hicks; the other, which played in less traditional styles, was a quintet with Abdul Wadud, Bob Stewart, the drummer Bobby Battle, and at various times the guitarists James "Blood" Ulmer and Kelvyn Bell. After a brief experiment with pop music, Blythe returned to jazz in 1984 with an all-star free-jazz sextet, the LEADERS; he also led jazz groups, playing again with Stewart, Bell, and Battle. Blythe's work is notable for its exploration of harmony, group counterpoint, and unusual instrumentation; these features, coupled with his rapid, wide vibrato, his swinging style, and his interest in the standard jazz repertory, have won him praise from an unusually wide audience, which includes listeners to both bop and avant-garde music.

SELECTED RECORDINGS

As leader: *The Grip* (1977, IndN 1029); *Bush Baby* (1977, Adelphi 5008); *In the Tradition* (1979, Col. JC36300); *Illusions* (1980, Col. JC36583)

As sideman: H. Tapscott: *The Giant is Awakened* (1969, FD 10107); L. Bowie: *The 5th Power* (1978, BS 0020); G. Evans: *Parabola* (1978, Horo 31–32); J. DeJohnette: *Special Edition* (1979, ECM 1152); Leaders: *Mudfoot* (1986, Black Hawk 52001)

BIBLIOGRAPHY

H. Rock: "Arthur Blythe: Interview," *Cadence*, iii/11–12 (1978), 7
C. Stern: "Arthur Blythe," *Musician*, no.19 (1979), 44
B. Blumenthal: "Arthur Blythe: Refreshing Traditions," *DB*, xlvii/4 (1980), 25 [incl. discography]
"Arthur Blythe Discography," *SJ*, xxxvii/2 (1983), 206
B. McRae: "Avant courier: the Work of Altoist Arthur Blythe," *JJI*, xxxvi/1 (1983), 16 [incl. discography]
F. Davis: "Apples, Oranges, and Arthur Blythe," *In the Moment: Jazz in the 1980s* (New York, and Oxford, England, 1986) [colln of previously pubd articles], 186
J. Levenson: "Arthur Blythe's Creative Challenges," *DB*, liv/10 (1987), 23 [incl. discography]

ED HAZELL

Blythe, Jimmy [James Louis] (*b* Louisville, KY, *c*1901; *d* Chicago, 21 June 1931). Pianist. He moved to Chicago as a teenager and was taught by the pianist Clarence Jones. By the time he made his first recordings in 1924 (*Chicago Stomp/Armour Ave. Struggle*), he had fully developed his own style as a jazz soloist. From the mid-1920s until three months before his death he led studio bands in Chicago for such companies as Paramount, Gennett, and Okeh: these included the STATE STREET RAMBLERS, the Washboard Wizards, the Dixieland Thumpers, and the Chicago Footwarmers. Because of his frequent recordings for Paramount with jazz musicians of the stature of Johnny Dodds, Jimmy Bertrand, Natty Dominique, Jimmy O'Bryant, Freddie Keppard, John Lindsay, Roy Palmer, and Bill Johnson (i) as his sidemen, it has been assumed that Blythe had the status of house pianist for the company; if this was so, he may have organized many of the important sessions of that period. Besides his work as a leader he also recorded with solo singers and again as an unaccompanied soloist. Blythe's style varied according to context: he was equally adept at delicate blues, barrelhouse, and basic comping to accompany a soloist.

SELECTED RECORDINGS

As unaccompanied soloist: Chicago Stomp/Armour Ave. Struggle (1924, Para. 12207); Sweet Papa (1928, Voc. 1181)

Duo with Charlie Clark: Bow to your Papa (1931, Champion 16451)

As leader: Ape Man/Your Folks (1926, Para. 12428); Hot Stuff/Have Mercy! (1927, Voc. 1136)

BIBLIOGRAPHY

ChiltonW; *FeatherE*
C. Hillman: "Paramount Serenaders, 1923–1926," *Sv*, no.67 (1976), 8; no.68 (1976–7), 52; no.69 (1977), 91; no.70 (1977), 149; no.72 (1977), 266; no.73 (1977), 29; no.74 (1977–8), 67; no.75 (1978), 84 [incl. discography]

JOHN COLLINSON

Bob Cats. Dixieland octet. It was formed by Bob Crosby around 1936 from the members of his big band, and before recording it had already gained a wide following as a result of the vitality and sincerity of its performances. It made its first recording in 1937; the members of the group on this occasion were Yank Lawson, Warren Smith (i), Matty Matlock, Eddie Miller, Bob Zurke, Nappy Lamare, Bob Haggart, Ray Bauduc, and Crosby; though the personnel of the group changed occasionally its robust and spontaneous musical style was always consistent. The Bob Cats played sets during performances by Crosby's big band and broke up at the same time as the latter, in 1942. From that time Crosby formed various ensembles under the name the Bob Cats for engagements that included a tour of the Far East (1964) and a performance at the Grande Parade du Jazz Nice (1981).

SELECTED RECORDINGS

You're Driving me Crazy/Can't we be Friends (1937, Decca 1680); Five Point Blues (1938, Decca 2108); Mournin' Blues (1939, Decca 2482); *Live! at the Rainbow Grill* (1966, MonE 6815)

BIBLIOGRAPHY

"Swing: Frenzied Cats Churn as Hot Bands go to Town to Mark the Swing Age," *Life*, iv (6 June 1938), 60
J. Chilton: *Stomp Off, Let's Go! The Story of Bob Crosby's Bob Cats & Big Band* (London, 1983), 44

BRIAN PEERLESS

Bobo, Willie [Correa, William] (*b* New York, 28 Feb 1934; *d* Los Angeles, 15 Sept 1983). Percussionist and bandleader. The son of a Puerto Rican immigrant, he grew up in Spanish Harlem. He taught himself to play bongos when he was 14, worked as a "band boy" for Machito, and played in Latin bands in New York and then with Perez Prado. He recorded with Mary Lou Williams (who gave him the nickname Bobo) in 1951, then worked with the percussionist Tito Puente (1954–8), Cal Tjader (1957–61), and Herbie Mann (1961–3). In 1963 he made his first recording as a leader, on which Clark Terry and Joe Farrell performed as sidemen. After settling in California in 1969 he played jazz and Latin music throughout the 1970s, sometimes adding his own vocal part to his band's performances in order to broaden its appeal; he also recorded as a freelance sideman with Miles Davis, Chico Hamilton, Les McCann, Cannonball Adderley, and Terry Gibbs. Bobo's importance as a bandleader lay in his ability to combine elements of jazz, Latin music, and rhythm-and-blues to create exuberant and entertaining performances.

SELECTED RECORDINGS

As leader: *Bobo's Beat* (1963, Roul. 52097); *Spanish Grease* (1965, Verve 68631); *Feelin' so Good* (1966, Verve 68669); *Bobo Motion* (1966, Verve 68699); *New Dimension* (1968, Verve 68772); with P. Humphrey, S. Manne, and L. Bellson: *The Drum Session* (1974, IC 6051)

As sideman: C. Tjader: *Concert by the Sea* (1959, Fan. 3295); *Soul Sauce* (1964, Verve 68614); C. Hamilton: *El Chico* (1965, Imp. 9102)

BIBLIOGRAPHY

L. Feather: "Blindfold Test: Willie Bobo," *DB*, xxxvi/26 (1969), 38
H. Siders: "Drum Schticks," *DB*, xl (1973), no.5, p.15; no.6, p.18
L. Feather: "Blindfold Test: Willie Bobo," *DB*, xliv/14 (1977), 35
W. Bobo: "Foundations of a Fusion," *CI*, xx/9 (1982), 22

JEFF POTTER

Bob Shots. Modern-jazz group. Formed in Liège, Belgium, by the guitarist Pierre Robert (1944), it served as a training ground for many Belgian jazz musicians. It was commended by *Down Beat* magazine in 1947 and included, at various times, Bobby Jaspar, Fats Sadi, Jacques Pelzer, Toots Thielemans, Francy Boland, and the double bass player Jean Warland. The group recorded in Brussels (1947) and later in Paris (1949).

ROBERT PERNET

Bocage, Peter (Edwin) (*b* New Orleans, 31 July 1887; *d* New Orleans, 3 Dec 1967). Cornetist and violinist. In about 1900 he began to study guitar and violin; he played violin in Tom Albert's band (1904), the Eagle Band (*c*1905–6), the Superior Orchestra (*c*1907), and Gilbert "Bab" Frank's Peerless Orchestra. He worked in dance halls in Storyville with Papa Celestin (1910–13) and King Oliver (1915). From 1910 he also played cornet and baritone horn with the Onward, Tuxedo, and Excelsior brass bands and the band of Henry Allen, Sr.; he led the Excelsior from 1920. Except for a brief period with Fate Marable on the SS *Capitol* in 1918, he was a member of A. J. Piron's orchestra from 1915 to 1928 playing various instruments but most often cornet; the band made recordings in New York in 1923 and 1924. Together with several other members of Piron's orchestra, he formed the Creole Serenaders; when it disbanded in 1939 he stopped working as a full-time musician. He performed briefly with Sidney Bechet in 1945 in Boston and continued to play regularly in New Orleans, recording with Emile Barnes in 1954 and as a leader in the early 1960s; from 1960 he was a member of the Eureka Brass Band. Besides his principal instruments Bocage played trumpet, trombone, banjo, and xylophone. His light, swinging style and fine musicianship made him one of the most respected New Orleans players of his time.

Peter's brothers, Henry (Clay) Bocage (*b* New Orleans, March 1894; *d* ?New Orleans, after 1939), a tuba and double bass player, and Charles (Leopold) Bocage (*b* New Orleans, 14 Jan 1900; *d* New Orleans, 4 Nov 1963), a banjoist, guitarist, and singer, also joined Piron's orchestra, in about 1918; Charles went with the band to New York in 1923–4. Both men belonged to the Creole Serenaders, in which Henry occasionally played trumpet. Charles continued to play in New Orleans into the 1950s.

Oral history material in *LNT*.

For illustrations *see* BANDS, fig.1, and BRASS BAND, fig.1.

SELECTED RECORDINGS

As leader: with E. Barnes: *Barnes–Bocage Big Five* (1954, New Orleans Jazz Society 0002); *Peter Bocage* (1961, Riv. 9379); *Peter Bocage* (1962, Mono 3)

As sideman: A. Piron: Bouncing Around/Kiss me Sweet (1923, OK 40021); New Orleans Wiggle/Mamma's Gone, Good-bye (1923, Vic. 19233)

BIBLIOGRAPHY

ChartersJ
J. De Donder: "Peter Bocage: a Musician's Musician," *Fn*, xiii/4 (1981), 4

MIKE HAZELDINE

Bodner, Phil(ip L.) (*b* Waterbury, CT, 13 June 1919). Woodwind player. He worked as a sideman in studio bands in New York, playing flute, saxophone, clarinet, oboe, and english horn. He recorded with Benny Goodman (1955), the Miles Davis–Gil Evans Orchestra (1958), Oliver Nelson (1962), J. J. Johnson (1965–6, 1968), Bill Evans (ii) (1974), and many other prominent musicians, including Oscar Peterson, Peanuts Hucko, Wild Bill Davison, and Ralph Sutton. In 1981 he performed and recorded as a clarinetist, leading a swing quartet with Marty Napoleon and a quintet with George Duvivier and Mel Lewis (both heard on the album *Fine and Dandy*, Stash 214). (*FeatherE*)

Boeuf sur le Toit, le. Nightclub in Paris; *see* NIGHTCLUBS AND OTHER VENUES.

Bohanon, George (Roland, Jr.) (*b* Detroit, 7 Aug 1937). Trombonist. He played in Chico Hamilton's quintet, making recordings in 1962–3 (including *Passin' Thru*, 1962, Imp. 29); he also recorded as leader of his own quintet (1962) and in a sextet with Roy Brooks (1963). From 1969 he was active as a studio musician in big bands, accompanying Sarah Vaughan (1971), Gene Ammons (1973–4), Sonny Rollins (1976), and Lionel Hampton (1980–81); he also belonged to Benny Carter's big band, with which he toured Japan, and played with the blues singer Bobby "Blue" Bland. (*Feather '60s*; *Feather–Gitler '70s*)

Böhler, Fred [Alfred] (*b* Zurich, 26 July 1912). Swiss pianist and bandleader. He played violin when he was young, began working professionally in 1933, and in 1936 he formed his own band, which included Eddie Brunner. It first came to prominence as one of the main attractions at the national fair in Zurich (1939) and it toured Switzerland throughout the 1940s. For a short spell in 1943 he led a show band that experimented with the instrumentations used in symphonic jazz. He made almost 50 recordings as a leader for Columbia (1940–44, including *Board Meeting*, 1941, Col. ZZ1047), employing such soloists as Hazy Osterwald; he also recorded piano solos (among them *China Boy*, 1941, Col. ZZ1020) and as a sideman with Eddie Brunner (1940). His recordings on Hammond organ, which he was the first to use in jazz in Switzerland, include *Boogie-woogie* (1944, Col. ZZ1163). Although Böhler was strongly influenced by Fats Waller, he performed mainly in a driving swing style. (J.-R. Hippenmeyer: *Le jazz en Suisse, 1930–1970*, Yverdon, Switzerland, 1971)

RAINER E. LOTZ

Boiarsky, Andrés (*b* Buenos Aires, 9 Oct 1957). Argentine tenor saxophonist. After recording with Jorge López Ruiz (1978) he moved to London, where he made his first recording as a leader (1980) and attended the Royal College of Music (graduated 1981). He returned to Argentina, where he made recordings as a leader (including *Ballottage*, 1982, CBS 80228), and with Jorge Navarro (1982) and Carlos Franzetti (1984). From 1984 he lived alternately in Buenos Aires, where he taught music, and New York, where he performed with Paquito D'Rivera and Mike Wolff. He toured Peru in 1985 with the Trío Argentina and in the following year recorded with Jamaaladeen Tacuma and performed in Poland.

LAUREANO FERNÁNDEZ, OMAR GARCÍA BRUNELLI

Bojangles. Nickname of BILL ROBINSON.

Boland, Francy [Francis, François] (*b* Namur, Belgium, 6 Nov 1929). Belgian composer, arranger, pianist, and bandleader. After conservatory training he wrote arrangements for Bobby Jaspar, Bernard Peiffer, Henri Renaud, and Fats Sadi. Later he worked in Paris as a pianist and arranger for Aimé Barelli (1954), toured Europe with Chet Baker (1955), lived in the USA (1957–8), and wrote arrangements for Kurt Edelhagen's big band in Frankfurt, Germany (1958). From 1959 he was associated with Kenny Clarke, with whom he formed the CLARKE–BOLAND BIG BAND. Boland wrote all the ensemble's scores, among them masterful arrangements of American popular songs (*All Smiles*, 1968) and his own compositions *Sabbath Message*, *Sax no End*, and *Griff's Groove*. His larger works include the suites *All Blues*, *Fellini 712*, *Off Limits* (which sketches the development of jazz during the 1960s), and the challenging *Change of Scenes* (which was described by Stan Getz, who played the principal solo part, as "the greatest advance in big band music in twenty or thirty years."). Like Duke Ellington, Boland wrote to exploit each instrumentalist's musical personality; *Faces* features the playing of every member of the band in turn.

After the Clarke–Boland Big Band broke up in 1973, Boland moved to Geneva, where he worked as a composer and arranger for European jazz orchestras. In 1976 he wrote scores for albums he made as a leader which featured the work of former members of the big band, and in 1984 he arranged Sarah Vaughan's album of songs to poems by Pope John Paul II, *The Planet is Alive . . . Let it Live* (1984, Jazzletter 1). He has also recorded several albums as the leader of small groups, on which his abilities as a pianist may be heard to particular advantage. Boland's compositions display a swinging style, highly integrated formal structures, and his ability to transcend standard jazz idioms and explore innovative ideas.

SELECTED RECORDINGS

(all arranged by Boland)

* – composed by Boland

As leader with K. Clarke: *Now Hear our Meanin'* (1963, Col. CS9114), incl. *Sabbath Message; *All Smiles* (1968, MPS 15214); **Faces* (1968, MPS 15218); **Fellini 712* (1968, MPS 15220); *Volcano* (1969, Pol. 583054), incl. *Griff's Groove; *Rue Chaptal* (1969, Pol. 583055), incl. *Sax no End; *All Blues* (1969, MPS 15288), incl. *All Blues; *Off Limits* (1970, Pol. 2310147), incl. *Off Limits; **Change of Scenes* (1971, Verve 2304034)

As leader of other groups: *Papillon noir* (1967, Freedom 40167); *White Heat* (1976, MPS 68189)

BIBLIOGRAPHY

L. Tomkins: "Stan Getz: on Leaving the States, his LP Dates, the Jazz Fates," *CI*, x/4 (1971), 6

R. Waschko: "Francy Boland Orchestra: Old Spirit and New Sound," *JF* [intl edn], no.42 (1976), 47

G. Lees: "A Journey to Cologne," *Gene Lees Jazzletter*, iv (1985), no.8, p.1; no.9, p.1; no.10, p.1; no.11, p.1

YVES GAGNON, ANDREW HOMZY

Bolar, Abe (*b* Oklahoma City, OK, 26 March 1908). Double bass player. He played in many bands in and around Oklahoma City, and regularly with Walter Page's Blue Devils from 1932. He moved to New York in 1936 and performed and recorded with Claude Hopkins (1937), Hot Lips Page (1938–40), and Lucky Millinder (1940–41); he also substituted for Walter Page in Count Basie's orchestra. In 1939–40 he made recordings as a freelance with Pete Johnson (including *Kansas City Farewell*, 1939, BN 10) and Joe Turner (ii), and from 1942 to 1963 he recorded with Ed Allen, Floyd Casey, and the pianist Benton Heath in New York. His wife is the pianist Juanita Bolar.

based on *ChiltonW*

Bolden, Buddy [Charles Joseph] (*b* New Orleans, 6 Sept 1877; *d* Jackson, LA, 4 Nov 1931). Cornetist and bandleader. The first of the New Orleans cornet "kings," he was highly regarded by contemporary black musicians in the city, who in their reminiscences embroidered his life with a great many legends and spurious anecdotes. A careful sifting of such data and contemporary records reveals that Bolden, unlike many of his peers, came late to music, adopting the cornet around 1894 after completing his schooling, and that he emerged not from the brass marching-band tradition but rather from the string bands which played for private dances and parties. By 1895 he was leading his own semiprofessional group with Frank Lewis (clarinet) and, later, Willie Cornish (valve trombone) (for illustration *see* JAZZ (i), fig.1), though city records continued to refer to him as a plasterer. By 1901, when his name first appears in city directories as a professional musician, his group had stabilized into a six-piece unit with cornet, clarinet, valve trombone, guitar, double bass, and drums. Bolden's rise to fame coincided with the emergence of a black pleasure district – Black Storyville – at South Rampart and Perdido streets, where he soon became a local celebrity playing in the dives and tonks (but not the brothels). By 1905, when his fame was at its peak, his group performed regularly in the city's dance halls and parks, and undertook excursions to outlying towns. In the following year Bolden showed distinct signs of violent mental derangement, and his band rapidly disintegrated, eventually passing to the leadership of the trombonist Frank Dusen. In 1907, in a state of hopeless indigence and alcoholism, Bolden was admitted to a mental institution in Jackson, where he spent his remaining years. His life formed the basis of M. Ondaatje's novel *Coming through Slaughter* (New York, 1976).

Contemporary musicians universally praised the power of Bolden's tone, his rhythmic drive, and the emotional content of his slow blues playing, often contrasting his performances with those of the more genteel Creole bands of John Robichaux and others. Bolden apparently did not improvise melodies freely in the manner of later jazz musicians, but found ingenious ways of ornamenting existing melodies, often incorporating a distinctive lick which functioned as a signature. Although he left no known recordings (a cylinder allegedly recorded in the late 1890s has never been located), Bolden undoubtedly had a formative influence on Freddie Keppard, Bunk Johnson, and other New Orleans cornetists and, by his example, helped to standardize the New Orleans jazz ensemble and repertory.

BIBLIOGRAPHY

M. Berger: "Early New Orleans Jazz Bands," *Jazz Record* (April 1944), 6

D. Barker: "A Memory of King Bolden," *Evergreen Review*, ix/37 (1965), 66

D. M. Marquis: "The Bolden–Peyton Legend: a Revaluation," *JJ*, xxx/2 (1977), 24

——: *Finding Buddy Bolden, First Man of Jazz: the Journal of a Search* (Goshen, IN, 1978)

——: *In Search of Buddy Bolden, First Man of Jazz* (Baton Rouge, LA, and London, 1978)

J. BRADFORD ROBINSON

Bolling, Claude (*b* Cannes, France, 10 April 1930). French pianist, composer, and leader. He was a child prodigy as a pianist and in 1944 won an amateur jazz contest in Paris; the following year he formed a small group that played in a style that was both reminiscent of the small groups of Duke Ellington and also influenced by New Orleans jazz. After accompanying Chippie Hill at a jazz festival in 1948 he played swing with such American musicians as Roy Eldridge, Lionel Hampton, Rex Stewart (recording in 1948), Cat Anderson, and Paul Gonsalves, and, from 1955, with his own orchestra. He continued

Claude Bolling in the 1970s, France

to lead orchestras, which were known by the name Show Bizz Band, into the 1980s; among those who have performed with him as sidemen are Roger Guérin and Gérard Badini. He has also written music for films (including Jacques Deray's *Borsalino*, 1970) and become particularly well-known for his semiclassical compositions, which he has recorded with such performers as the flutist Jean-Pierre Rampal (*Suite for Flute and Jazz Piano*, 1975) and the trumpeter Maurice André (*Toot Suite*, 1981). His piano style displays the influence of Ellington, Earl Hines, Teddy Wilson, and Art Tatum; he is considered the leading ragtime pianist in France.

SELECTED RECORDINGS

As unaccompanied soloist: *Original Ragtime* (1966, Phi. 70341)
Duo with R. Eldridge: Wild Man Blues (1951, Vogue 5092)
As leader: *Claude Bolling joue Duke Ellington* (1956, Club français du disque 69); *Les succès de Django Reinhardt* (1956, Club français du disque 90); *Claude Bolling Plays Duke Ellington* (1959, Fon. 680204); with C. Anderson: *Cat Anderson, Claude Bolling and Co* (1965, Phi. 77731); *Swing Session* (1973, CY 3003); *Suite for Flute and Jazz Piano* (1975, CBS 73900); *Jazz Gala 79* (1979, Amer. 015–16); *Toot Suite* (1981, CBS 73999); *Claude Bolling Live at the Méridien* (1984, CBS 39245); *Jazz à la française* (1984, CBS 39244)
As sideman: L. Hampton: *Free press oui* (1953, Vogue 166); *Real Crazy* (1953, Vogue 167); *More Crazy* (1953, Vogue 168)

BIBLIOGRAPHY

"Claude Bolling vous présente son grand orchestre," *Jm*, no.27 (1957), 15
S. Dance: "The Best European Big Band Yet!," *JJ*, x/7 (1957), 5
"Claude Bolling," *Jh*, no.256 (1969), 30

ANDRÉ CLERGEAT

Bolton, (Bewis) Dupree (*b* Oklahoma City, OK, 1920s). Trumpeter. He ran away from home at the age of 14 and first emerged as a musician in 1944, playing in Buddy Johnson's orchestra in New York. In late 1945 he joined Benny Carter's big band, but after two recording dates he disappeared in 1946, suffering from the effects of drug abuse. In 1959 he re-emerged and, as a sideman with Harold Land, recorded *The Fox*, the album on which his reputation rests. Almost immediately, however, he again committed drug offenses, and he did not play again until 1962–3, when he worked with Curtis Amy. Before and after a brief tenure with Bobby Hutcherson (1967) he served further prison sentences, culminating in an absence of 15 years; he continued to play while in prison and in 1980 performed on a recording produced by the Joseph Harp Correctional Center in Tulsa, Oklahoma. After his release in 1982 he played in his home town with Dexter Gordon, among others, but he then moved to the West and again sank into obscurity. His few recordings reveal Bolton to have been a brilliant and stylish player; a mysterious figure, his reputation has, if anything, been enhanced by his tormented private life and obsessive personal secrecy.

SELECTED RECORDINGS

As sideman: B. Johnson: *Buddy Johnson at the Savoy Ballroom, 1945–1946* (1945–6, Jazz Archives 25), incl. Jodi, Opus Two; H. Land: *The Fox* (1959, Hi-fi 612); C. Amy: *Katanga* (1963, PJ 70)

BIBLIOGRAPHY

B. Weir: *Dupree Bolton Discography* (Cardiff, 1986, rev. and enlarged 2/1986)

CHRIS SHERIDAN

Bomb. A loud, unexpected, heavily accented note, played on the bass drum. With the emergence of bop the bass drum's function changed from time-keeping (steadily marking a quarter-note pulse in rhythmic unison with the double bass) to supplying accents. By placing accents irregularly and unpredictably, for example on upbeats or eighth-note offbeats, the drummer is said to be "dropping bombs."

ROBERT WITMER

Bonano, Sharkey [Joseph Gustaf; Sharkey] (*b* New Orleans, 9 April 1902; *d* New Orleans, 27 March 1972). Trumpeter and singer. He played with bands in and around New Orleans in the early 1920s, including those of Chink Martin (1921) and the pianist Freddy Newman. In New York he auditioned for a place with the Wolverines, but joined a band led by the pianist Jimmy Durante (1924), then returned to the South and led his own band (1925) and recorded with Norman Brownlee. Thereafter he worked with Jean Goldkette (1927) and led a band, the Melody Masters, with Leon Prima (*c*1928–1930). He played with Larry Shields in California, then returned to New Orleans, where he played a six-year residency (1930–36). After working with Ben Pollack (1936) he led his own band in New York, the Sharks of Rhythm, with which he made his best-known recordings. During this period he also played occasionally with the Original Dixieland Jazz Band. After military service he played in and around New Orleans, forming a band in 1949 which enjoyed great popularity, largely because of Bonano's potent trumpet playing and lively singing. He continued to play into the 1960s, working in Chicago, New York, and New Orleans, before illness caused him to retire.

Oral history material in *LNT*.

SELECTED RECORDINGS

As leader: Swingin' on the Swanee Shore (1937, Voc. 3470); She's crying for me (1950, Cap. 15704); *Midnight on Bourbon Street* (1951–2, Cap. T367); *Dixieland at the Roundtable* (1960, Roul. 25112)
As sideman: Brownlee's Orchestra of New Orleans: Peculiar/Dirty Rag (1925, OK 40337); Johnnie Miller: Panama/Dippermouth Blues (1928, Col. 1546D); M. Hazel: High Society (1928, Bruns. 4181)

BIBLIOGRAPHY

G. Hoefer: "Sharkey Brings Dixie to Austere Palmer House," *DB*, xviii/4 (1951), 11

——: "The Saga of Nick's," *DBY 1964*, 55

P. Haby: "Sharkey Bonano, 1902–1972," *Fn*, ix (1978), no.5, p.4; no.6, p.4 [incl. discography]

BRIAN PEERLESS

Bond, Jimmy [James Edward, Jr.] (*b* Philadelphia, 27 Jan 1933). Double bass player and composer. He studied double bass and tuba, and took private lessons in composition and orchestration. From 1950 to 1955 he attended the Juilliard School while living and working in Philadelphia, where, as the resident double bass player at the Blue Note club, he played with Thelonious Monk and Charlie Parker. After graduating from Juilliard he played with Chet Baker (1955–6), Ella Fitzgerald (1956–7), Sonny Rollins and Buddy DeFranco (both 1957), Don Shirley (1957–8), and Carmen McRae (1958). He toured with George Shearing from 1958 to 1959, then settled in Los Angeles, where he played with Ben Webster, Art Pepper, Jim Hall, and Jimmy Giuffre while in residence at the Renaissance club (1959–63), and performed and recorded with Paul Horn's quintet (1960–61). He worked in studios in Los Angeles frequently from 1962 to 1970, then occasionally into the 1980s. Bond's style as a double bass player is inspired by that of Oscar Pettiford; he plays economically constructed bass lines with a rich, deep, percussive tone and displays a strong sense of rhythm. As a composer he is best known for his film score *Persia 2500* (1971).

SELECTED RECORDINGS

As leader: *The James Bond Songbook!* (*c*1966, Mirwood 7001)

As sideman: Nina Simone: *Little Girl Blues* (1957, Beth. 6028); Red Mitchell: *Rejoice!* (1960, PJ 22); Jazz Crusaders: *Lookin' Ahead* (1961, PJ 43); Gerald Wilson: *Moment of Truth* (1962, PJ 61)

BIBLIOGRAPHY

FeatherE; *Feather '60s*

K. Mohr: "The Musical Career of Jimmy Bond," *Jazz Statistics*, no.8 (1959), 6

J. L. Ginibre and P. Carles: "Dictionnaire de la contrebasse," *Jm*, no.166 (1969), 30

JOHN VOIGT

Bone. Shortened form of TROMBONE.

Bonfils, Kjeld (*b* Copenhagen, 23 Aug 1918; *d* Copenhagen, 13 Oct 1984). Danish pianist and vibraphonist. He played and recorded with Svend Asmussen (1940–43) and Peter Rasmussen (1943–5), performed with the Harlem Kiddies in Sweden (1945), and led groups in Sweden and Norway (1945–6). He also made a series of remarkable recordings as a soloist and as the leader of a trio with the clarinetist Poul Hindberg, including *Morrocco* (D900) and *Sara O'Hara* (D942), both made for Odeon in 1943. From 1946 he was principally a composer of popular tunes.

ERIK WIEDEMANN

Bongos [bongo drums]. A pair of Afro-Cuban drums with conical or cylindrical hardwood shells. They are generally played with the bare hands; an experienced player may obtain from them subtle differences of timbre, as well as such unusual effects as glissandos, by varying the amount of pressure applied to a drumhead, and the part of the hand that is used to strike it (e.g., the tips of the fingers, the flat fingers, or the butt of the hand). Bongos have played a less important role in jazz than the conga, to which they are related, perhaps because the thinner tone and higher pitch of the bongos tend to intrude on melodic instruments rather than support them. There have nonetheless been some important bongo players in Afro-Cuban jazz. The conga player Chano Pozo played bongos occasionally in Dizzy Gillespie's orchestra (1947–8), and around the same time Jack Costanzo figured prominently as a soloist in Stan Kenton's orchestra, as a member of which he recorded such pretentious compositions by Pete Rugolo as *Chorale for Brass, Piano and Bongo* (1947, Cap. 10183) and *Fugue for Rhythm Section* (1947, Cap. 10127). In the 1950s and 1960s Fats Sadi often used bongos on recordings. The bandleaders Machito and Mongo Santamaria regularly included them in their rhythm sections, and Santamaria also sometimes played them himself. Other jazz bongo players of note have included Cal Tjader in his early career and Armando Peraza. A later example of the prominent use of bongos may be heard on *Little Linda* from Spyro Gyra's album *Morning Dance* (1979, Infinity 9004).

BARRY KERNFELD

Bonner, Joe [Joseph Leonard] (*b* Rocky Mount, NC, 20 April 1948). Pianist. He played piano from an early age and studied music at Virginia State College. He performed with Roy Haynes's Hip Ensemble in New York (1970–71) and with Freddie Hubbard (1971–2), Pharoah Sanders (1972–4), and Billy Harper; in 1978–9 he toured Europe with Harper while based in Copenhagen. In 1980 he returned to the USA and later worked in New York and Denver. He has recorded as a soloist (1974, 1983), as the leader of a trio with Johnny Dyani and Billy Higgins (1979), and as a leader with Dyani (1983). Bonner's chordal, at times dissonant, style has to some degree been influenced by the work of McCoy Tyner.

SELECTED RECORDINGS

As unaccompanied soloist: *The Lifesaver* (1974, Muse 5065); *Devotion* (1983, Ste. 1182)

As leader: *Angel Eyes* (1974–6, Muse 5114); *Parade* (1979, Ste. 1116); *Impressions of Copenhagen* (1981, The. 114); with J. Dyani: *Suburban Fantasies* (1983, Ste. 1176)

As sideman: P. Sanders: *Elevation* (1973, Imp. 9261)

BIBLIOGRAPHY

Feather–Gitler '70s

A. Heineman: Review of *The Lifesaver*, *DB*, xlii/20 (1975), 29

M. Shera: Review of *Parade*, *JJI*, xxxii/11 (1979), 29

A. Axelrod: Review of *Devotion* (1983), *DB*, li/6 (1984), 50

PAUL RINZLER

Boogie-woogie. A percussive style of piano blues favored, for its volume and momentum, by bar-room, honky-tonk, and rent-party pianists. The term appears to have been applied originally to a dance performed to piano accompaniment, and its widespread use stems from the instructions for performing the dance on the recording *Pine Top's Boogie Woogie* (1928, Voc. 1245) by Pine Top Smith. The boogie style is characterized by the use of blues chord progressions combined with a forceful, repetitive left-hand bass figure; many bass patterns exist, but the most familiar are the "doubling" of the simple blues bass (ex.1) and the walking bass in broken octaves (ex.2).

Walking basses are reported to have been developed by ragtime pianists in the 19th century, and the first published example appears to be in Blind Boone's *Rag Medley no.2* (1909).

Ex.1 Doubling of the blues bass

Ex.2 Walking bass in broken octaves

Similar bass figures are used by Artie Matthews in his *Pastime Rag no.1* (published 1913), and are applied to a blues in his *Weary Blues* (1915). George Thomas used the same device in his *New Orleans Hop Scop Blues* (1911, published 1916) and on his recording *The Rocks* (1923, OK 4809), which he made under the pseudonym Clay Custer and which appears to be the first recorded example of a walking bass. Such figures consisted of even eighth-notes, dotted eighth- and 16th-notes, and triplets, and were loosely identified by musicians, sometimes by names such as the "Rocks," the "Chains," the "Fives." The right-hand configurations played against the bass patterns were both rhythmic and melodic, with sharp ostinato passages and sequences in 3rds and 6ths. Some performances, such as Meade "Lux" Lewis's *Bass on Top* (1940, BN 16), display subtly shifting patterns, while Wesley Wallace's train imitation *No.29* (1930, Para. 12958) employs 6/4 time in the bass and 4/4 in the treble. Such a feat is possible through the independence of the right-hand improvisations from the steady, rolling rhythm maintained by the left hand. Startling dissonances occur through the juxtaposition of the two strands, and cross-rhythms are also frequently created. Deliberate discords and rapid "crushed" or "press" notes, obtained by the striking of adjacent notes in rapid succession, are evident on Lewis's *Honky Tonk Train Blues* (1927, Para. 12896).

The first generation of boogie-woogie pianists – blues pianists who prominently featured walking bass and "eight-to-the-bar" rhythms – recorded some notable examples, among them Romeo Nelson (*Head Rag Hop*, 1929, Voc. 1447), Arthur Montana Taylor (*Indiana Avenue Stomp*, 1929, Voc. 1419), and Charles Avery (*Dearborn Street Breakdown*, 1929, Para. 12896); these were rent-party pianists who were forgotten in the Depression years. In 1938 a revival was initiated by John Hammond, who sought out Albert Ammons and Meade "Lux" Lewis, then working in Chicago as taxi-drivers. With Pete Johnson from Kansas City and Joe Turner (ii), the Boogie Woogie Trio became popular at Café Society, New York (for illustration *see* BLUES, fig.2), and, linked with the swing craze, boogie-woogie enjoyed a brief vogue. These authentic boogie pianists made a number of outstanding recordings, including Johnson (*Goin' Away Blues*, 1938, Voc. 4607) with Turner, and Ammons (*Chicago in Mind*, 1939, BN 4). The brief but widespread popularity of boogie-woogie also led to the discovery of Jimmy Yancey and Cripple Clarence Lofton, who brought singular rhythmic conceptions to their playing. The connection with swing is exemplified in such recordings as *Boogie Woogie* by Tommy Dorsey and his orchestra (1938, Vic. 26054) and Count Basie's *Basie Boogie* (1941, OK 6330); some recordings, such as Will Bradley's *Boogie Woogie Conga* (1941, Col. 35994), Charlie Barnet's *Scrub me, mama, with a boogie beat* (1940, Bb 10975), and the Andrews Sisters' *Boogie Woogie Bugle Boy* (1941, Decca 3598), despite their titles, bear little relation to the original idiom.

By the 1950s boogie-woogie had reverted to the blues, becoming a standard element in the performances of every blues pianist; although its relevance to jazz declined, it proved to be one of the most enduring aspects of blues, and the foundation of much of the Chicago blues idiom.

See also PIANO, §3.

BIBLIOGRAPHY

W. Russell: "Boogie Woogie," *Jazzmen*, ed. F. Ramsey, Jr., and C. E. Smith (New York, 1939/*R*1977)

E. Borneman: "Boogie Woogie," *Just Jazz*, i, ed. S. Traill and G. Lascelles (London, 1957)

M. Harrison: "Boogie Woogie," *Jazz: New Perspectives on the History of Jazz*, ed. N. Hentoff and A. J. McCarthy (New York, 1959/*R*1974)

P. Oliver: "Piano Blues and Boogie Woogie," *Jazz on Record: a Critical Guide to the First 50 Years: 1917–1967*, ed. A. McCarthy and others (London, 1968)

P. Oliver: *The Story of the Blues* (London, 1969/*R*1982), 73, 114

E. Kriss: *Barrelhouse and Boogie Piano* (New York and London, 1974) [incl. transcrs. and discography]

PAUL OLIVER

Book. In jazz argot the collection of written arrangements and compositions constituting a group's (particularly a big band's) repertory. Each musician's parts, which may take the form of a manuscript book or a set of loose leaves, may also be referred to as the "book."

ROBERT WITMER

Booker, Beryl (*b* Philadelphia, 7 June 1922; *d* Berkeley, CA, 30 Sept 1978). Pianist and leader. In the early 1940s she worked in clubs in Philadelphia as a leader and a sideman. A jam session with Slam Stewart led to her joining his trio, and this association continued for several years, though it was interrupted by periods during which Booker accompanied Dinah Washington and led an all-female trio. In 1952–4 she again led a series of trios, playing a long-term engagement at the Embers, New York (1953), and touring Europe (early 1954). In the late 1950s she performed with various small groups, including Stewart's (1955–7), and in 1959 she returned to Europe with Washington. *Low Ceiling/Don't blame me* (1946, Vic. 40-0147) is typical of the lightly swinging style of her trios, while a more intense approach is revealed in her piano solo on *Billie's Blues* (from the album *Lady Love*, 1954, UA 5014), which she recorded with Billie Holiday at a concert in Cologne.

BIBLIOGRAPHY

FeatherE

L. Feather: "Girls in Jazz: Beryl Best since Mary Lou?," *DB*, xix/7 (1952), 8

L. Perrin: "They don't Play like Girls," *New Musical Express*, no.360 (4 Dec 1953), 4

Obituary, *MM*, liii (28 Oct 1978), 46

HOWARD RYE

Booker, Walter (M., Jr.) (*b* Prairie View, nr Hempstead, TX, 17 Dec 1933). Double bass player. While at college he played clarinet and alto saxophone with the concert band. During military service he changed to double bass, and after being discharged he played in Washington with Andrew White in the JFK Quintet (1960–63). After moving to New York he worked with Donald Byrd (1964), Sonny Rollins and Ray Bryant (both 1965), Art Farmer (1966–7), and Milt Jackson and Chick Corea (both 1967). He began playing with Cannonball Adderley in 1968, and toured and recorded extensively with him until 1975. Thereafter he recorded with Betty Carter (1976), Nick Brignola and Billy Higgins (both 1979), Richie Cole and Phil Woods (both 1980), John Hicks (1981–3), Pharoah Sanders and Nat Adderley (both 1982), and Clifford Jordan (1984); he also performed with Arnett Cobb (1983).

Everything happens to me, recorded with Rollins in 1965, shows that Booker was early influenced by Charles Mingus in his use of such techniques as tremolo, double-stopping, and playing in an extremely high register. A dark tone, voice-like inflections, and glissandos form a style of accompaniment that expands on the work of Mingus, Wellman Braud, and Wilbur Ware. His work with the bow may be heard to advantage on Adderley's *To Wisdom the Prize* (1982). Booker's exceptional technique enables him to bring a wholly modern approach to the traditional role of the double bass player.

SELECTED RECORDINGS

As sideman: S. Rollins: *Sonny Rollins on Impulse* (1965, Imp. 91), incl. Everything happens to me; A. Farmer: *The Time and the Place* (1967, Col. CS9449); C. Adderley: *Inside Straight* (1973, Fan. 9435); *Phenix* (1975, Fan. 9004); R. Cole and P. Woods: *Side by Side* (1980, Muse 5237); J. Hicks: *Some other Time* (c1981, The. 115); P. Sanders: *Live* (1982, The. 116); N. Adderley: *On the Move* (1982, The. 117), incl. To Wisdom the Prize; C. Jordan: *Repetition* (1984, SN 1084)

BIBLIOGRAPHY

Feather '60s; Feather–Gitler '70s

JOHN CURRY

Boone, Harvey (G.) (*b* Newport News, VA, *c*1898; *d* 1939). Alto saxophonist and clarinetist. After recording in New York and touring with Lucille Hegamin and the Blue Flame Syncopators (*c*1921) he studied at the New Haven Conservatory in Connecticut. He played with Duke Ellington (1926) and performed and recorded with Fletcher Henderson (1929–31), Noble Sissle (*c*1933–5), and Don Redman (1936–7); later he taught music in Atlanta. Boone seldom took solos, but he is believed to be the alto saxophonist on Sissle's *Loveless Love* (1934, Decca 154).

based on *ChiltonW*

Boone, Lester (*b* Tuskegee, AL, 12 Aug 1904). Alto saxophonist, clarinetist, and baritone saxophonist. In Chicago he played with Charlie Elgar (1927) and performed and recorded with Earl Hines (1928–9) and Louis Armstrong (1931–2); in New York he played with Kaiser Marshall, then joined the Mills Blue Rhythm Band (1933). After working with Eubie Blake's orchestra and Willie Bryant in 1934 he rejoined Marshall the following year and played with Jelly Roll Morton (1936) and Cliff Jackson (1937); he also worked with Hot Lips Page and Eddie South (in New York and Chicago in the late 1930s) and performed as a leader (1940). Later he recorded with Billie Holiday (1941), played with Leon Abbey, and worked again as a leader in the New York area. A good example of Boone's playing is his solo on Armstrong's recording of *I got rhythm* (1931, OK 41534), to which Armstrong gives a spoken introduction.

based on *ChiltonW*

Boone, Richard (*b* Little Rock, AR, 23 Feb 1930). Singer and trombonist. He sang in the local Baptist church as a child. At the age of 16, through winning second prize in a talent contest, he spent a month on tour with Lucky Millinder. He played trombone in an army band from 1948 to 1953 and after studying music at Philander Smith College he moved to Los Angeles (1958), where he performed first as a singer and then as a trombonist. He worked in studios and clubs with Gerald Wilson, Dolo Coker, and Sonny Criss and recorded on trombone with Dexter Gordon and Teddy Edwards (1960). He toured with the singer Della Reese (1962–6) and with Count Basie (1966–9); during his time with Basie he became known for the humorous way in which he combined blues scat singing with a straightforward vocal style. From 1970 he traveled widely in Europe and spent much of his time in Copenhagen. In the 1980s he performed and recorded with Clark Terry and Jesper Thilo and with Ernie Wilkins's big band.

SELECTED RECORDINGS

As leader: *I've Got a Right to Sing the Blues* (1969, Nocturne 703)

As sideman: D. Gordon: *The Resurgence of Dexter Gordon* (1960, Jlnd 929); C. Basie: *Basie's Beat* (1967, Verve 68687), incl. Boone's Blues, I got rhythm; C. Terry and J. Thilo: *Tribute to Frog* (1980, Sto. 4072); E. Wilkins: *Montreux* (1983, Ste. 1190)

BIBLIOGRAPHY

Feather–Gitler '70s

S. Dance: *The World of Count Basie* (New York and London, 1980) [colln of previously pubd interviews], 228

SCOTT FREDRICKSON

Boot. To play an instrument, particularly a wind instrument or drums, in a loud, vigorous, propulsive manner so as to create momentum in a performance; such a player is said to "boot along" his fellow musicians or the piece they are performing. A booting style requires an incisive, even urgent, sense of rhythm and a powerful tone; musicians whose playing combines these attributes have often acquired the nickname Boots or Booty.

Bop [bebop, rebop]. One of the main styles of jazz. It was first developed in the early and mid-1940s by such musicians as Dizzy Gillespie, Charlie Parker, Bud Powell, Thelonious Monk, Kenny Clarke, and Max Roach. During the 1950s and 1960s the term "bop" was used more generally to encompass also the various substyles that grew out of the original genre: cool jazz, West Coast jazz, hard bop, soul jazz, and funk.

The word "bop" is a shortened form of the vocables (nonsense syllables) "bebop" or "rebop," which were commonly used in scat singing to accompany the distinctive two-note rhythm shown in ex.1. Although bop was solidly grounded in

Ex.1 L. Armstrong: *Hotter than that* (1927, OK 8535); transcr. T. Owens

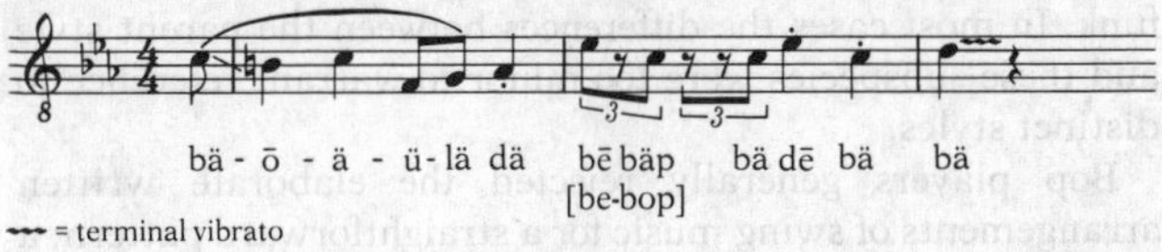

earlier jazz styles (New Orleans jazz and swing), it represented a marked increase in complexity, and was considered revolutionary at the time of its development. Perhaps its most significant characteristic was the highly diversified texture created by the rhythm section – a considerable contrast to the insistent four-beat approach that was taken by swing musicians. In the newer style, the basic beat was stated by the double bass player and elaborated by the drummer on ride cymbal and hi-hat, while a variety of on- and off-beat punctuations were added on the piano, bass drum (*see* Bomb), and snare drum (ex.2). These punctuations sometimes reinforced and sometimes complemented the melody, causing much rhythmic interplay during improvised solos; spurred on by an active rhythm section, the best bop soloists were adept at extemporizing rapid melodies filled with asymmetrical phrases and accent patterns.

Ex.2

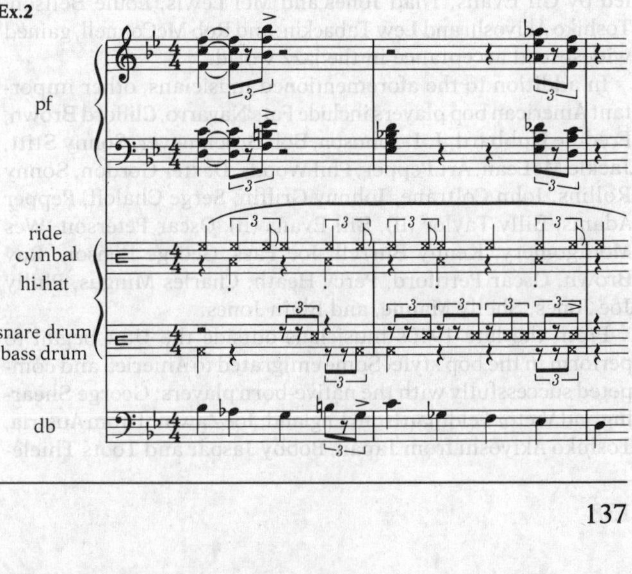

Ex.2 also illustrates the enriched harmonic vocabulary of the bop style, which made far more frequent use of altered 9th, 11th, and 13th chords than earlier jazz. Moreover, since many bop themes and improvisations were based largely on such chords, the melodies of bop were also more complex (i.e., more chromatic) than those of swing.

Many early bop themes, such as *Ornithology* (Parker and Little Benny Harris), *Anthropology* (Parker and Gillespie), *Groovin' High* (Gillespie), *Donna Lee* (Parker), and *Hot House* (Gillespie), were intricate melodies based on the harmonic structures of earlier popular songs. However, by the late 1940s the most common themes had become simpler, and some were even based on the overworked swing-era device known as the riff (e.g., Milt Jackson's *Bag's Groove* and Clifford Brown's *Blues Walk*). The shift from complex to simple themes had no effect on the procedures followed by the rhythm section or the style of the improvised solos. Other developments did cause slight alterations in the character of the music. In the late 1940s and 1950s, for example, a number of bop musicians (Miles Davis, Lee Konitz, Paul Desmond, Stan Getz, Gerry Mulligan, Milt Jackson, and John Lewis, among others) began playing in a soft, subtle manner later called COOL JAZZ. From the mid-1950s other bop players (including Cannonball Adderley, Horace Silver, Jimmy Smith, and Art Blakey) began incorporating folk elements from the blues and black gospel traditions into their playing, attracting such labels as HARD BOP, SOUL JAZZ, and funk. In most cases the differences between the parent style and these subspecies were too minor to warrant reference to distinct styles.

Bop players generally rejected the elaborate written arrangements of swing music for a straightforward pattern: a unison statement of the theme followed by a string of improvised solos, then a concluding unison statement (*see* FORMS, §5). They also preferred to work in small groups, a typical instrumentation being that of the quintet led by Charlie Parker (trumpet, saxophone, piano, double bass, and drums). (For further discussion of bop ensembles *see* BANDS, §4(v).) Nonetheless, some big bands that were formed in the 1940s (notably those led by Billy Eckstine and Dizzy Gillespie), played in the bop style, but these were short lived. Permanent inroads into the big-band style were made in the late 1940s and early 1950s, when swing bandleaders such as Woody Herman, Stan Kenton, and Count Basie began employing younger bop musicians. Arrangers and players, finding that bop rhythm sections could support large brass and reed sections, and that the harmonies of swing-style riffs could be modernized, developed ways of fusing the two styles. Later bop bands, among others those led by Gil Evans, Thad Jones and Mel Lewis, Louie Bellson, Toshiko Akiyoshi and Lew Tabackin, and Rob McConnell, gained widespread acceptance in the jazz world.

In addition to the aforementioned musicians, other important American bop players include Fats Navarro, Clifford Brown, Freddie Hubbard, J. J. Johnson, Bob Brookmeyer, Sonny Stitt, Jackie McLean, Art Pepper, Phil Woods, Dexter Gordon, Sonny Rollins, John Coltrane, Johnny Griffin, Serge Chaloff, Pepper Adams, Billy Taylor (ii), Bill Evans (ii), Oscar Peterson, Wes Montgomery, Kenny Burrell, Joe Pass, George Benson, Ray Brown, Oscar Pettiford, Percy Heath, Charles Mingus, Philly Joe Jones, Shelly Manne, and Elvin Jones.

From the late 1940s musicians outside the USA began to perform in the bop style. Some emigrated to America and competed successfully with the native-born players: George Shearing and Victor Feldman from England, Joe Zawinul from Austria, Toshiko Akiyoshi from Japan, Bobby Jaspar and Toots Thielemans from Belgium, Valery Ponomarev from the USSR, and George Mraz from Czechoslovakia. Others earned a position of respect while working principally outside the USA: the British players Tubby Hayes, Ronnie Scott, and John Dankworth, the Swedes Lars Gullin and Arne Domnérus, the Dane Niels-Henning Ørsted Pedersen, the Germans Joki Freund and Albert Mangelsdorff, the Spaniard Tete Montoliu, the Algerian Martial Solal, the Canadian Rob McConnell, and the Japanese Sleepy Matsumoto and Sadao Watanabe, among others. The Canadian Oscar Peterson, who has performed internationally throughout his career, has become one of the best known of all jazz musicians.

Bop was overshadowed from around the late 1950s to the mid-1970s by other new styles: modal jazz, free jazz, jazz-rock, Latin jazz, and fusions of jazz and soul music. While some players, including Gillespie, Monk, the members of the Modern Jazz Quartet, Silver, Smith, Mulligan, Griffin, Gordon, and, most fervently, Blakey, remained faithful to bop, other major figures turned to the new genres, among them Davis, Coltrane, Pepper, Woods, Rollins, Benson, Mingus, and Elvin Jones. A new generation of innovative musicians, many of whom were not skilled at playing bop, had also appeared. From the late 1970s, however, there has been frequent mention in jazz literature of a bop revival. It has been marked by specific events: for example, the expatriates Gordon and Griffin returned to the USA and took part in performances that were highly acclaimed; Woods formed a quartet (later a quintet) that proved long lived; free-jazz musicians such as Anthony Braxton, Archie Shepp, and Pharoah Sanders began to perform and record bop; a formidable new player, Wynton Marsalis, became an articulate spokesman for the style. More generally, the bop revival is distinguished by the perception that the once revolutionary bop style has become – together with New Orleans jazz and swing, and in contrast to the newer styles – a "classic" jazz genre.

See also JAZZ (i), §V.

BIBLIOGRAPHY

Feather '60s

L. Feather: *Inside Bebop* (New York, 1949/*R*1977 as *Inside Jazz*)

A. Hodeir: *Hommes et problèmes du jazz, suivi de la religion du jazz* (Paris, 1954; Eng. trans., rev. Hodeir, as *Jazz: its Evolution and Essence*, New York, 1956/*R*1975)

A. Morgan and R. Horricks: *Modern Jazz: a Survey of Developments since 1939* (London, 1956/*R*1977)

M. W. Stearns: *The Story of Jazz* (New York, 1956, rev. and enlarged 2/1958/*R*1970), 155

L. Feather: *Modern Jazz: an Exciting Story of the Past 20 Years* (Los Angeles, 1958)

R. Horricks and others: *These Jazzmen of our Time* (London, 1959)

R. Russell: "Bebop," *The Art of Jazz: Essays on the Nature and Development of Jazz*, ed. M. Williams (New York, 1959/*R*1979), 187

J. Goldberg: *Jazz Masters of the Fifties* (New York and London, 1965/*R*1980)

I. Gitler: *Jazz Masters of the Forties* (New York, 1966/*R*1983 with discography)

J. S. Wilson: *Jazz: the Transition Years, 1940–1960* (New York, 1966) [listeners' guide]

L. Feather: *From Satchmo to Miles* (New York, 1972), 129

R. Russell: *Bird Lives: the High Life and Hard Times of Charlie (Yardbird) Parker* (New York, 1973; Ger. trans., Vienna, 1985)

T. Owens: *Charlie Parker: Techniques of Improvisation* (diss., UCLA, 1974)

M. Harrison and others: *Modern Jazz: the Essential Records: a Critical Selection* (London, 1975)

J. L. Collier: *The Making of Jazz: a Comprehensive History* (New York and London, 1978), 336

D. Gillespie and A. Fraser: *To be, or not . . . to Bop: Memoirs* (Garden City, NY, 1979; Ger. trans., Vienna, 1984)

S. Strunk: "The Harmony of Early Bop: a Layered Approach," *JJS*, vi/1 (1979), 4–53

B. D. Kernfeld: *Adderley, Coltrane, and Davis at the Twilight of Bebop: the Search for Melodic Coherence (1958–59)* (diss., Cornell U., 1981)

J. K. Williams: *Themes Composed by Jazz Musicians of the Bebop Era: a Study of Harmony, Rhythm, and Melody* (diss., Indiana U., 1982)

R. Horricks: *Dizzy Gillespie and the Be-bop Revolution* (Tunbridge Wells, England, and New York, 1984) [incl. discography by T. Middleton]
I. Gitler: *Swing to Bop: an Oral History of the Transition in Jazz in the 1940s* (New York, and Oxford, England, 1985)

THOMAS OWENS

Bop City. The name of nightclubs in New York and San Francisco; *see* NIGHTCLUBS AND OTHER VENUES.

Borchard, Eric(h) (*b* Berlin, 7 Feb 1886; *d* Amsterdam, 30 July 1934). German bandleader, alto saxophonist, and clarinetist. He played first clarinet with the Dresden PO before World War I. After hearing jazz in the USA in 1918–19, he organized a band modeled on the Louisiana Five. He accompanied silent films and also appeared as a jazz bandleader in two films (1921–2). From 1920 to 1925 he made more than 150 recordings of jazz and hot dance music for Grammophon (including *Hula Lou*, 20115, and *Aggravatin' Papa*, 20116, both 1924). He often worked with visiting American musicians, among them Emile Christian, the drummer Creighton Thompson, and the trumpeter Wilbur Kurz. After 1925 Borchard ceased to be active as a musician, though he made one further recording in 1932. (H. J. Bergmeier and R. E. Lotz: *Eric Borchard Bio-discography*, Menden, Germany, in preparation)

RAINER E. LOTZ

Bosco. Record company and label established by PETE CHRISTLIEB in 1981.

Bose, Sterling (Belmont) [Boze, Bozo] (*b* Florence, AL, 23 Feb 1906; *d* St. Petersburg, FL, June 1958). Trumpeter and cornetist. After working in the early 1920s with several bands in New Orleans he moved to St. Louis. He played with the Arcadian Serenaders at the Arcadia Ballroom, where Frankie Trumbauer's band also performed, and Bose became familiar with the work of Bix Beiderbecke. As a member of a band led by Jean Goldkette in Kansas City (1927–8) he gained attention for his solos, which were strongly reminiscent of Beiderbecke's; his contributions to Goldkette's recordings of *Just Imagine* and *My Blackbirds are Bluebirds Now* are particularly representative. From 1930 to 1933 he played with Ben Pollack; for the rest of the decade he worked as a freelance, achieving great popularity. He performed and recorded with the bands of Joe Haymes (1934), Tommy Dorsey (1935), Ray Noble and Benny Goodman (both 1936), Glenn Miller (1937), Bob Crosby (1938–9), Bobby Hackett (1939), and others. After joining Bob Zurke's short-lived big band Bose played with Jack Teagarden, then worked as a freelance in Chicago. He returned in 1943 to New York, where he performed at Nick's in small groups led by Miff Mole and Art Hodes. After another brief period in Chicago he settled in Florida, and continued to perform at clubs until shortly before his death.

SELECTED RECORDINGS

As sideman: Arcadian Serenaders: You gotta know how/Angry (1925, OK 40517); J. Goldkette: Just Imagine (1928, Vic. 21565); My Blackbirds are Bluebirds Now/Don't be like that (1928, Vic. 21805); J. Teagarden: Rockin' Chair/Loveless Love (1931, Crown 3051); You rascal, you (1931, Col. 2588D); B. Pollack: Two Tickets to Georgia (1933, Vic. 24284); J. Mercer: Lord, I give you my children/The bathtub ran over again (1934, Decca 142); R. Noble: Big Chief De Sota (1936, Vic. 25346); B. Crosby: I'm Prayin' Humble (1938, Decca 2210); B. Zurke: Between the Devil and the Deep Blue Sea/I've found a new baby (1939, Vic. 26355)

BIBLIOGRAPHY

ChiltonW; *FeatherE*
Obituary, *SL*, ix/7–8 (1958), 21
B. Koester: "Sterling Belmont Bose," *JJ*, xii/2 (1959), 2
P. W. Russell: "Sterling Bose," *Sv*, no.27 (1970), 108
H. Wood: "Words for a Friend," *SL*, xxvii (sum. 1975), 29
M. Peart: "Talking about Boze," *Selections from the Gutter: Jazz Portraits from "The Jazz Record,"* ed. A. Hodes and C. Hansen (Berkeley, CA, Los Angeles, and London, 1977), 186

RICHARD SUDHALTER

Bossa nova. A musical style of Brazilian origin blending elements of the samba and cool jazz; it was popular in the USA in the 1960s, but many bossa nova tunes have become staple to the jazz repertory. Bossa nova music is subdued, and its challenging harmonies have elicited fine improvisations. In a typical song, a drummer and an acoustic guitarist superimpose soft, precise ternary figures on a duple meter (ex.1). Characteristically, light syncopations delivered by a saxophonist or singer with a vibrato-free, breathy, quiet tone permeate the melody. 7th and 9th chords, rapid modulations, and major-minor alternations are common; lyrics, if present, are generally sung in Portuguese or English and convey bittersweet sentiments.

Ex.1 A typical bossa nova rhythm

Bossa nova probably began in Brazil with João Gilberto's recording of Antonio Carlos Jobim's composition *Chega da saudade* (1958). The guitarist Charlie Byrd, having visited Brazil, initiated the bossa nova craze in the USA through his recording with Stan Getz, *Jazz Samba* (1962), which included Jobim's *Desafinado*. Jazz recording companies, in attempting to cash in on Getz's Grammy award-winning success, produced a disastrous concert at Carnegie Hall in November 1962 and numerous mediocre recordings, but neither failures in jazz nor distortions in pop (e.g., Eydie Gorme's 1963 hit *Blame it on the Bossa Nova*) destroyed the original style. João and Astrud Gilberto's rendition of Jobim's *The Girl from Ipanema* was the milestone among a number of other excellent recordings in the bossa nova style in the mid-1960s, including those of Herbie Mann, Paul Winter, and Sergio Mendes.

BIBLIOGRAPHY

J. Tynan: "The Real Story of the Bossa Nova," *DB*, xxix/28 (1962), 21
G. Behague: "Bossa and Bossas: Recent Changes in Brazilian Urban Popular Music," *Ethnomusicology*, xvii (1973), 209
M. J. Budds: *Jazz in the Sixties: the Expansion of Musical Resources and Techniques* (Iowa City, IA, 1978)
J. S. Roberts: *The Latin Tinge: the Impact of Latin American Music on the United States* (New York, and Oxford, England, 1979)

BARRY KERNFELD

Bostic, Earl (*b* Tulsa, OK, 25 April 1913; *d* Rochester, NY, 28 Oct 1965). Alto saxophonist. During the early 1930s he worked in several bands in the Midwest before studying at Xavier University of Louisiana. He left New Orleans to tour with various groups, including one led by Charlie Creath and Fate Marable (1935–6), then moved to New York, where he was a soloist in the big bands of Don Redman (1938), Edgar Hayes, and Lionel Hampton (1943–4). He also played with Hot Lips Page (1941). He was better known, however, for his work as the leader of his own small groups; among his sidemen were Jimmy Cobb, John Coltrane, Blue Mitchell, Stanley Turrentine, and Benny Golson. From the early 1950s he toured extensively and later settled in Los Angeles. Heart ailments curtailed his activities during the last decade of his life.

Bostic was recognized as an accomplished saxophonist and a skillful arranger in the 1930s and 1940s, but was not considered to be a major soloist. After recording *Flamingo* (1951), however, he gained widespread fame, and his records sold in vast quantities. He often emphasized glissandos and deliberately exaggerated his vibrato, but despite these inelegant effects, Bostic regularly showed that he retained considerable technical prowess, particularly in producing high harmonics – a skill he taught Coltrane.

SELECTED RECORDINGS
(all recorded for King)

Flamingo (1951, 4475); Cherokee (1952, 4623); Indiana (1956, 4954); Exercise (1957, 5056); Answer me (1957, 5081); Twilight Time (1958, 5136)

BIBLIOGRAPHY

R. Cage: "Rhythm & Blues Notes," *DB*, xxi/26 (1954), 8
H. Friedrich: "Earl Bostic Discography," *Jazz Statistics*, no.4 (1956), 3; no.14 (1960), 2; no.17 (1960), 8
Obituary, *DB*, xxxii/25 (1965), 10
Obituary, H. Panassié, *BHcF*, no.154 (1966), 4
V. Schonfield: "The Forgotten Ones: Earl Bostic," *JJI*, xxxvii/11 (1984), 14

JOHN CHILTON

Boswell, Connee [Connie] (*b* New Orleans, 3 Dec 1907; *d* New York, 11 Oct 1976). Singer. She was a member of the Boswell Sisters (Connee, Martha, and Helvetia), a vocal trio which specialized in intricately arranged close-harmony singing, and with which she also performed occasionally on saxophone, trombone, and piano. The group achieved international fame during the early 1930s, its recordings with the Dorsey Brothers' band being notably successful. Connee's voice, which was heavily featured, was rich in feeling, and her sense of timing and rhythmic phrasing made her a favorite with jazz enthusiasts. Despite having to spend most of her life in a wheelchair (as a result of poliomyelitis), she embarked on a successful career as a soloist in 1935. She was able to interpret a wide range of material with warmth and subtlety, and her work influenced many other singers, including Ella Fitzgerald. Boswell continued touring and appearing in films (including *Artists and Models*, 1937, *Kiss the Boys Goodbye*, 1941, and *Syncopation*, 1942) until the 1950s; thereafter she made occasional public appearances, and an admirable album (1956) with a re-formed version of the Original Memphis Five, including Miff Mole and Tony Sbarbaro.

SELECTED RECORDINGS

As leader: I'm all dressed up with a broken heart (1931, Bruns. 6162); Me Minus You (1932, Bruns. 6405); *Connie Boswell and the Original Memphis Five* (1956, RCA LPM1426), incl. Japanese Sandman
As leader of the Boswell Sisters (with Helvetia and Martha Boswell): You oughta be in pictures (1934, Bruns. 6798)
As sideman with Bing Crosby: Yes Indeed (1940, Decca 3689)

BIBLIOGRAPHY

"Boswell would Refuse Cure for Paralyzed Legs to Help Economic Cripples!," *DB*, v/8 (1938), 8
J. Lucas: "Connee Boswell," *JJ*, xxvii/1 (1974), 5
C. Ellis: "Connee Boswell," *Sv*, no.71 (1977), 166

JOHN CHILTON

Bothwell, Johnny (*b* Gary, IN, 23 May 1919). Alto saxophonist and bandleader. After playing in Chicago (1940) he moved to New York, where he recorded with Woody Herman (1943) and Sonny Dunham (1944–6), and was a soloist with Boyd Raeburn (1944–5) and Gene Krupa (1945). He then led his own big bands (1945–7), also recording with a small group in 1946 (*Dear Max/Chelsea Bridge*, Sig. 15085). He led another small group in Chicago (1948), worked in New England, and again led a band in New York (1949), after which he left music and moved to Miami.

BIBLIOGRAPHY

ChiltonW; *FeatherE*
J. Burns: "Lesser Known Bands of the Forties, no.11: Buddy Rich and Johnny Bothwell," *JM*, no.175 (1969), 6
C. Garrod and B. Korst: *Boyd Raeburn and his Orchestra plus Johnny Bothwell and George Handy* (Zephyrhills, FL, 1985) [discography]

Botschinsky, Allan (*b* Copenhagen, 29 March 1940). Danish trumpeter and flugelhorn player. While studying music he belonged to Ib Glindemann's big band (1956–9). He played in the group Jazz Quintet '60 (1959–63), the Danish Radiojazzgruppen (1961–5), and the Radioens Big Band (1964–82) and worked as a leader from 1966. He also worked with several American musicians on their visits to Denmark, including Kenny Dorham, in whose quintet he played flugelhorn on an album recorded in concert (1963). Botschinsky's style, which displays the influence of the work of Miles Davis, is well represented by his album *Allan Botschinsky Quintet* (1982, Stunt 8301), which includes the track *Autumn in New York*.

ERIK WIEDEMANN

Bourke, Sonny. *See* SUN RA.

Boutté, Lillian (Theresa) (*b* New Orleans, 6 Aug 1949). Singer. She was a member of the Golden Voices Choir at an early age and studied music therapy at Xavier University of Louisiana. She began her professional career in 1973 performing with such local rhythm-and-blues artists as Allen Toussaint, and later became a star of the show *One Mo' Time*. She made a lengthy tour of Europe in 1981–2. In 1983 she formed an international group, the Music Friends, led by the reed player Thomas l'Etienne, whom she married the following year; she has made a number of recordings with the group, including *Music is my Life* (1984, Turning Point 30007). She continued to tour frequently in the USA and Europe, appearing at international festivals, including the Festa New Orleans Music in Ascona (1985–8), and in 1988 performing with Humphrey Lyttelton at the Barbican Arts Centre, London. Boutté is one of the most versatile traditional jazz singers, who excels in the performance of gospel, blues, ballads, and rhythm-and-blues.

BIBLIOGRAPHY

M. G. Larsen: Liner notes, *New Orleans Gospel* (Herman 1004, 1981)
M. Joly: Liner notes, *I Sing because I'm Happy* (Tim. 11003, 1985)

MARCEL JOLY

Bowie, Joseph [Joe] (*b* St. Louis, ?1953). Trombonist, brother of Lester Bowie. Inspired by his brother's work in Chicago, he pursued a similar career in St. Louis, joining the Black Artists Group at the age of 17 to play with free-jazz musicians such as Oliver Lake and Julius Hemphill. He recorded with Lake's group in 1971, and later, in Toronto, they recorded the duo album *In Concert* (1976, Sack. 2010). He toured as a member of Charles "Bobo" Shaw's Human Arts Ensemble, recording in St. Louis, New York, and Germany (1972–8), and played with Shaw in the St. Louis Creative Ensemble led by the alto saxophonist Luther Thomas (1977–9). Around 1980 he formed the group Defunkt, with Kelvyn Bell and Martin Aubert (electric guitars), another brother, Byron Bowie (saxophone and flute), Ronnie Burrage (drums), and Melvin Gibbs (electric bass guitar). The group worked with the rock singer and saxophonist James White (Chance), then played in New York clubs. It played a fusion of free jazz, funk, and punk rock, and in 1981 recorded the album *Defunkt* (Hannibal 1301).

BIBLIOGRAPHY

S. Bloom: "Jazz-Punk-Funk: Defunkt," *DB*, xlviii/6 (1981), 25
P. Hewitt: "Defunking the Bunk," *MM*, lvi (13 June 1981), 18

Bowie, Lester (*b* Frederick, MD, 11 Oct 1941). Trumpeter, brother of Joseph Bowie. He grew up in St. Louis and gained early musical experience in blues and rhythm-and-blues bands, including those of Albert King and Little Milton Campbell. In

1965 he moved to Chicago to become the music director for the rhythm-and-blues singer Fontella Bass, to whom he was married. He was a founder of the Association for the Advancement of Creative Musicians, a musicians' cooperative of which he became the second president, and in 1969 he was a founding member of the ART ENSEMBLE OF CHICAGO, with which he has performed and recorded into the 1980s. In addition to his work with the Art Ensemble he has led the groups From the Root to the Source, which developed an unusual fusion of jazz, rock, and gospel, and Brass Fantasy; he has also played in the LEADERS (from 1986) and recorded as a sideman with Amina Claudine Myers, Archie Shepp, Jack DeJohnette, and David Murray.

Lester Bowie, New York, 1986

Bowie is among the most original trumpeters in jazz. He commands an exceptionally large stock of effects, including half-valving, growls, bent notes, and a wide vibrato. His witty, irreverent style is well represented by the track *Jazz Death?* (from Roscoe Mitchell's album *Congliptious*, 1968) and by his playfully distorted version of the rock-and-roll song *The Great Pretender* (from his own album of the same name, 1981).

SELECTED RECORDINGS

As unaccompanied soloist: on R. Mitchell: *Congliptious* (1968, Nessa 2), Jazz Death?

As leader: *Gittin' to Know y'all* (1969, MPS 2120728); *Fast Last!* (1974, Muse 5055); *Rope-a-dope* (1975, Muse 5081); *The 5th Power* (1978, BS 0020); *The Great Pretender* (1981, ECM 1209), incl. The Great Pretender; *All The Magic* (1982, ECM 1246–7)

RECORDED COMPOSITIONS

(selective list)

Recorded by Art Ensemble of Chicago: on *Fanfare for the Warriors* (1973, Atl. 1651), Barnyard Scuffel Shuffel

As leader: on *All the Magic* (1982, ECM 1246–7), Donald Duck Meets Miles Davis

BIBLIOGRAPHY

Feather–Gitler '70s
V. Wilmer: "Extending the Tradition," *DB*, xxxviii/9 (1971), 13
R. Townley: "Lester . . . Who?," *DB*, xli/2 (1974), 11
B. Rusch: "Lester Bowie: Interview," *Cadence*, v/12 (1979), 3
M. Luzzi: *Uomini e avanguardie jazz* (Milan, 1980)
B. McRae: "Avant Courier: Lester Bowie," *JJI*, xxxiii/11 (1980), 12
J. Rockwell: "Jazz, Group Improvisation, Race & Racism: the Art Ensemble of Chicago," *All American Music: Composition in the Late Twentieth Century* (New York, 1983), 164
H. Mandel: "Lester Bowie M.D.: Magic Dimensions," *DB*, li/3 (1984), 14

LEE JESKE/R

Bowles, Russell (*b* Glasgow, KY, 17 April 1909). Trombonist. He played with Ferman Tapp's Melody Lads (1926–8), with Horace Henderson's group (December 1928 to 1929), and in a theater orchestra in Buffalo (1929–30). He belonged to Jimmie Lunceford's orchestra from January 1931 until Lunceford's death in 1947 (for illustration *see* LUNCEFORD, JIMMIE), and played on virtually all the band's recordings during this period (including *Peace and Love for All*, 1941, Decca 3892). He then played for several years with Eddie Wilcox and occasionally with Cab Calloway in the early 1950s before abandoning his musical career.

based on *ChiltonW*

Bowman, Dave [David Walter] (*b* Buffalo, 8 Sept 1914; *d* Miami, 28 Dec 1964). Pianist. Born to Canadian parents, he was brought up in Hamilton, Canada. He played piano from an early age and later studied music in Hamilton and Pittsburgh. He worked with Jack Hylton's orchestra in London (1936–7) and then moved to New York, where he first recorded in 1938, with Bobby Hackett and Sidney Bechet. He was a member of Bud Freeman's Summa Cum Laude Orchestra, which played at Nick's in New York (1939–40). After leaving Freeman he performed with Jack Teagarden (1940), Joe Marsala (1941), and Muggsy Spanier (1941–2), and recorded with Lee Wiley in a group led by Eddie Condon (1943). From 1943 Bowman worked on radio and in studios in New York; as a staff pianist at ABC and NBC he accompanied the popular singer Perry Como. He performed in a trio led by Freeman (1954–5), as a freelance in Florida (late 1950s), and with Phil Napoleon's dixieland band (1964). Bowman was an accomplished player, both as a soloist and accompanist, though he mainly exercised these skills as a sideman, and did little work as a leader.

SELECTED RECORDINGS

As leader: Cow Cow Boogie/Stars Fell on Alabama (1946, Sig. 28126)

As sideman: S. Bechet: Hold Tight/Jungle Drums (1938, Voc. 4537); B. Freeman: As Long as I Live/Sunday (1939, Decca 2849)

BIBLIOGRAPHY

ChiltonW
E. Condon and H. O'Neal: *The Eddie Condon Scrapbook of Jazz* (New York, 1973)
M. Miller: "Bowman, Dave," *Encyclopedia of Music in Canada*, ed. H. Kallmann, G. Potvin, and K. Winters (Toronto, Buffalo, and London, 1981)

JAMES M. DORAN

Bown, Patti [Patricia Anne] (*b* Seattle, 26 July 1931). Pianist. She studied music in Seattle and then moved to New York. She toured Europe (1959–60) and recorded (1959–63) with Quincy Jones, played in bop sessions with Gene Ammons (1961–2), James Moody (1964), Oliver Nelson (1964–7), Illinois Jacquet (1965), and the Joe Newman Jazz Interactions Orchestra (1967) and was also associated with Dinah Washington (1962–4) and Sarah Vaughan (1964–5). She recorded as a leader in 1959 (*Patti Bown Plays Big Piano*, Col. CL1379), and continued to play in clubs and shows in New York into the 1980s. In 1987 she performed at Cornell University with Marian McPartland and JoAnne Brackeen. As well as working as a pianist she also sings, and writes much of her own material; her compositions have been performed by Duke Ellington, Count Basie, and Kenny Burrell. In addition to her activities as a performer, Bown has lectured and taught at several colleges and universities.

BIBLIOGRAPHY

FeatherE; *Feather–Gitler '70s*
H. Dance: "Down Patti: a Profile of Patti Bown," *DB*, xxxiv/21 (1967), 23
S. Placksin: *American Women in Jazz, 1900 to the Present: their Words, Lives, and Music* (New York, 1982), 260

Boyd, Nelson (*b* Camden, NJ, 6 Feb 1928). Double bass player. He began playing professionally in Philadelphia during World War II and in 1947 moved to New York, where he performed in clubs on 52nd Street with Coleman Hawkins, Tadd Dameron, and Dexter Gordon. The following year he briefly replaced Al McKibbon in Dizzy Gillespie's big band, which he rejoined in 1956 for a tour of the Middle East and Asia. He played on numerous bop recordings in the late 1940s and early 1950s; these include *Half Nelson* (1947, with Miles Davis and Charlie Parker) and one of Davis's "Birth of the Cool" sessions (1949). After 1960, however, he performed infrequently. Boyd's playing was characterized by a full, rich tone and considerable agility in the handling of difficult harmonic progressions.

SELECTED RECORDINGS

As sideman: T. Dameron: The Squirrel/Our Delight (1947, BN 540); M. Davis: Half Nelson (1947, Savoy 951); Boplicity (1949, Cap. 60011); T. Monk: Let's cool one (1952, BN 1602); D. Gillespie: *World Statesman* (1956, Norg. 1084); on M. Roach: *Max Plays Charlie Parker* (1958, EmA 36127), Billie's Bounce, Ko-ko, Parker's Mood

BIBLIOGRAPHY

FeatherE
"Annuaire biographique de la contrebasse," *Jm*, no.94 (1963), 22
L. Feather: *Inside Be-bop* (New York, 1949/*R*1977 as *Inside Jazz*)

SCOTT DeVEAUX

Boykins, Ronnie (*b* Chicago, *c*1935; *d* New York, 20 April 1980). Double bass player. He studied in Chicago with Walter Dyett and Ernie Shepard. From 1958 to 1966, and intermittently afterwards, he was an important member of the Sun Ra Arkestra; among the solos he recorded with Sun Ra was *Rocket Number Nine* on *Interstellar Low Ways* (1959, Saturn 203). During the same period he recorded with Bill Barron (1962), Elmo Hope (1963), and Archie Shepp and the New York Contemporary Five (1964). In the late 1960s he formed his own group, the Free Jazz Society. He also played and made recordings with Roland Kirk (1967) and Charles Tyler (*Voyage from Jericho*, 1974–5, Akba 1000), performed with Sarah Vaughan and Mary Lou Williams, and recorded with Joe Lee Wilson (1975) and Steve Lacy (1979).

BIBLIOGRAPHY

J. Caux and D. Caux: "Ronnie Boykins," *Jm*, no.223 (1974), 14
V. Wilmer: *As Serious as your Life*: *the Story of the New Jazz* (London, 1977, rev. 1980)
R. Welburn: "Ronnie Boykins: Interview," *JSN*, i/6 (1980), 6

Boze [Bozo]. Nickname of STERLING BOSE.

Brackeen [née Grogan], **JoAnne** (*b* Ventura, CA, 26 July 1938). Pianist and composer. She attended the Los Angeles Conservatory of Music, but taught herself jazz piano by listening to recordings by Frankie Carle and imitating his solos. During the late 1950s she worked in Los Angeles with Teddy Edwards, Harold Land, Dexter Gordon, and Charles Lloyd. She married the saxophonist Charles Brackeen in the early 1960s and moved with him to New York in 1965. There she began to attract attention as a pianist with Art Blakey's Jazz Messengers (1969–72) and with Joe Henderson's group (1972–5). From 1975 to 1977 she spent an eventful period as a member of Stan Getz's quartet, which brought a wider audience for her playing, much critical acclaim, and offers to record as a leader. Thereafter Brackeen has performed, toured, and recorded with her own groups, working principally in a trio format with such sidemen as Eddie Gomez, Cecil McBee, Sam Jones, Clint Houston, Billy Hart, Jack DeJohnette, and Freddie Waits.

Brackeen has become a major figure among contemporary jazz pianists. Although clearly influenced by McCoy Tyner and Chick Corea, she was also inspired by the music of Ornette Coleman. Her approach to playing is unique, particularly in regard to rhythmic development, and she has increasingly recorded her own compositions. Her compositions on the album *Special Identity* are typical of her writing, which makes use of complex harmonies and a variety of moods.

SELECTED RECORDINGS

As leader: *Snooze* (1975, Choice 1009); *Tring-a-ling* (1977, Choice 1016); *Special Identity* (1981, Ant. 1001), incl. Enchance, Friday the Thirteenth, Special Identity
As sideman: A. Blakey: *Jazz Messengers '70* (1970, Cat. 7902); S. Getz: *Live at Montmartre* (1977, Ste. 1073–4)

BIBLIOGRAPHY

A. J. Smith: "Profile: JoAnne Brackeen," *DB*, xliv/5 (1977), 30
C. J. Safane: "JoAnne Brackeen: Profile of an Emerging Jazz Piano Headliner," *CK*, v/11 (1979), 18
L. Feather: *The Passion for Jazz* (New York, 1980), 144
N. George: "JoAnne Brackeen: Pianist for a New Era," *DB*, xlvii/7 (1980), 22
B. Blumenthal: "JoAnne Brackeen: First Comes the Sound," *DB*, xlix/8 (1982), 26

BILL DOBBINS/R

Bradford, Bobby (Lee) (*b* Cleveland, MS, 19 July 1934). Cornetist, trumpeter, and composer. He took up cornet in 1949 and played with Leo Wright, Buster Smith, and John Hardee (1952), with Ornette Coleman and Eric Dolphy in Los Angeles (1953), and in air force bands. After belonging to the Ornette Coleman Quartet in New York (1961) he attended Huston-Tillotson College (BM 1963) and moved to Los Angeles (1964), where he formed the New Art Jazz Ensemble with John Carter. He taught elementary school (1966–71), lived and worked in England (1971), then rejoined Coleman's group for a brief period in New York. From 1974 he taught at Pasadena City College and Pomona College, and from 1976 to 1978 belonged to the Little Big Horn workshop with Carter, Arthur Blythe, James Newton, and other free-jazz musicians. Bradford has performed most often with Carter; he has also appeared with the David Murray Octet (1982–4), Charlie Haden's Liberation Music Orchestra (from 1982), John Stevens's Freebop (1986), and his own group, Mo'tet. As a composer he has been influenced by the blues and the music of Coleman. Bradford's son, the drummer Dennis Bradford, was a founding member in 1979 of the Jeff Lorber Fusion.

SELECTED RECORDINGS

As leader: *Bobby Bradford with the S. M. E.* (1971, Fre. 40111); *Love's Dream* (1973, Emanem 302); *Lost in L. A.* (1983, SN 1068)
As leader or sideman with J. Carter: *Flight for Four* (1969, FD 108); *Secrets* (1971–2, Rev. 018); *Dauwhe* (1982, BS 0057)
As sideman with O. Coleman: *Science Fiction* (1971, Col. KC31061)

BIBLIOGRAPHY

L. Jones: "1962: Introducing Bobby Bradford," *Black Music* (New York, 1967), 99
F. Kofsky: "John Carter and Bobby Bradford," *Black Giants*, ed. P. Rivelli and R. Levin (New York and Cleveland, 1970/*R*1980 as *Giants of Black Music*), 41
D. Wild and M. Cuscuna: *Ornette Coleman 1958–1979: a Discography* (Ann Arbor, MI, 1980)
M. James: "Order and Feeling, Discipline and Fire: an Introduction to the John Carter and Bobby Bradford Quartet," *J&B*, iii/1 (1973), 6

ED HAZELL

Bradford, (John Henry) Perry [Mule] (*b* Montgomery, AL, 14 Feb 1893; *d* New York, 20 April 1970). Music director, composer, and pianist. He worked in minstrel shows and as a solo pianist before concentrating on song writing and music direction. In 1920 he was responsible for Mamie Smith's recording début, the first recording session to feature a black blues singer. Smith's version of Bradford's composition *Crazy Blues* sold more than a million copies and initiated a craze for blues singing. During the 1920s Bradford organized recording groups that included Louis Armstrong, Buster Bailey, James P. Johnson, and other important early jazz musicians. In the same decade he achieved considerable success with various compositions, such as *You can't keep a good man down*, *Evil Blues*, and *That thing called Love*, but thereafter his songs were never again in vogue.

RECORDED COMPOSITIONS
(selective list)

Recorded by Mamie Smith: That thing called love/You can't keep a good man down (1920, OK 4113); Crazy Blues (1920, OK 4169)
Recorded by Edith Wilson: Evil Blues (1922, Col. A3746)

BIBLIOGRAPHY

S. B. Charters and L. Kunstadt: "The 'Crazy Blues'," *Jazz: a History of the New York Scene* (Garden City, NY, 1962/*R*1981), 83
P. Bradford: *Born with the Blues: . . . the True Story of the Pioneering Blues Singers and Musicians in the Early Days of Jazz* (New York, 1963)
M. Stearns and J. Stearns: *Jazz Dance: the Story of American Vernacular Dance* (New York and London, 1968), chaps. 14, 15

JOHN CHILTON

Bradley, Will [Schwichtenberg, Wilbur] (*b* Newton, NJ, 12 July 1912). Trombonist and bandleader. He played in New York with the bandleader Milt Shaw (from 1928), then performed and recorded with Red Nichols (1931–2) and Ray Noble (1935–6) and also worked in the studios of CBS and other companies. In 1939 he formed a band with Ray McKinley that achieved considerable success. Many of its songs were based on commercialized versions of boogie-woogie patterns, and *Beat me, daddy, eight to the bar* and *Scrub me, mama, with a boogie beat* (both 1940) became hits. After the band broke up in 1942 Bradley returned to studio work and performed and recorded as a freelance. A widely respected trombonist, Bradley seemed most comfortable playing ballads rather than boogie-woogie. His style, reminiscent of Tommy Dorsey's, was highly polished. His interest in classical music (particularly the work of the composer Alban Berg) was reflected by his numerous compositions for symphony orchestras and chamber ensembles.

His son, Bill (William Ackerson) Bradley (*b* New York, 15 Feb 1938) was a drummer. From 1954 he played in bop groups with Johnny Smith, Tony Scott, Kai Winding, and George Wallington. He recorded with Woody Herman's big band in 1956.

SELECTED RECORDINGS

Strange Cargo (1940, Col. 35545); Beat me, daddy, eight to the bar (1940, Col. 35530); Scrub me, mama, with a boogie beat (1940, Col. 35743)

BIBLIOGRAPHY

FeatherE
G. T. Simon: *The Big Bands* (New York, 1967, rev. and enlarged 2/1971, rev. 3/1974, 4/1981), 92
I. Crosbie: "The Will Bradley–Ray McKinley Orchestra," *JJ*, xxvi/2 (1973), 14 [incl. discography]
J. Woelfer: *Will Bradley & his Orchestra: a Discography* (Langenhagen, Germany, 1984)
C. Garrod and B. Korst: *Will Bradley, Freddie Slack* (Zephyrhills, FL, 1986)

WAYNE SCHNEIDER

Bradshaw, Tiny [Myron] (*b* Youngstown, OH, 23 Sept 1905; *d* Cincinnati, 26 Nov 1958). Bandleader, singer, and drummer. He attended Wilberforce University, where he sang with Horace Henderson's Collegians. He then moved to New York and played drums with Marion Hardy's Alabamians, the Savoy Bearcats, and the Mills Blue Rhythm Band (all 1932), and sang with Luis Russell. In 1934 he formed his own big band, which included Shad Collins, Russell Procope, and Happy Caldwell; among the titles he recorded are *The Darktown Strutters' Ball* and *The Sheik of Araby* (1934, Decca 194). He continued to lead big bands into the 1950s, toured Japan in 1945, and recorded regularly from 1944; in the late 1940s and early 1950s several of his recordings became hits on the rhythm-and-blues chart.

BIBLIOGRAPHY

ChiltonW
A. McCarthy: *Big Band Jazz* (New York and London, 1974), 274
W. Maxie: "Kings of Rhythm and Blues," *Girl Illustrated*, ix/4 (1977), 27
D. Penny and M. Harris: "Boogie in the Dark," *Pickin' the Blues*, no.19 (1983), 10

Brady, Stumpy [Floyd Maurice] (*b* Brownsville, PA, 4 Aug 1910). Trombonist. He performed and recorded with Zack Whyte's Chocolate Beau Brummels (1928–9), toured with Al Sears (to 1930), and played with Andy Kirk in New York (1930–4, recording with Blanche Calloway in 1931). He replaced Ed Cuffee in McKinney's Cotton Pickers, then performed and recorded with Claude Hopkins (1936–8) and Teddy Wilson (1939–40). He also worked with Lucky Millinder, Al Sears, and Count Basie, toured with Joe Guy's big band, which accompanied Billie Holiday (1945), and played briefly with Jay McShann, Fletcher Henderson, Roy Eldridge, and Cat Anderson. After a period of inactivity in the 1950s he resumed playing during the following decade with Slide Hampton's band, Luckey Roberts's orchestra, and Edgar Battle's big band. Brady's playing is shown to advantage on *Boogie Woogie Moan* (Decca 8575), recorded with Sam Price and his Texas Blusicians in 1941.

based on *ChiltonW*

Braff, Ruby [Reuben] (*b* Boston, 16 March 1927). Cornetist. He worked in and around Boston from the 1940s, recording in 1949 with Edmond Hall and performing at Storyville with Pee Wee Russell in the early 1950s. In 1953 he moved to New York, where his mainstream style flavored with modern influences won him instant recognition and engagements with a variety of groups playing everything from dixieland to bop. Later that year he recorded with Vic Dickenson; this was one of a series of important recordings Braff made for Vanguard, with other leaders, including Buck Clayton and Urbie Green (both 1954), and under his own name (1955). His collaboration with Clayton for Columbia under Mel Powell (1954) and Clayton (1955) was also particularly fruitful. In 1955 he recorded with Bud Freeman and Benny Goodman (with whom he also performed), and the following year he appeared on television in a play about a jazz group called *The Magic Horn*.

Although he was much admired for his musical ability, Braff's high standards, uncompromisingly maintained, and his strongly held and frankly expressed opinions sometimes impeded his career. For a time his popularity waned and he was less in demand, but this changed in the 1960s as a result of his affiliation with George Wein's Newport All Stars; he began to work steadily, touring as a guest soloist in the USA and Europe and making a number of successful recordings. In 1973, with George Barnes, he formed a quartet with Barnes as its lead guitarist, Wayne Wright as its rhythm guitarist, and John Giuffrida as its double bass player (Giuffrida was later replaced by Michael Moore); the group performed at the Newport Jazz Festival later that year, made several recordings, and toured widely. Disagreement between the leaders caused it to disband, but by then Braff had established an international reputation and was much in demand as a soloist.

Braff's style is characterized by a strong melodic sense, a full, warm tone, and a raspy vibrato. His playing is particularly effective in the cornet's lower register. A particular feature of his playing is the embellishment of a melody with flurries of notes in a manner developed directly from swing.

SELECTED RECORDINGS

Duos: with E. Larkins: *Grand Reunion* (1972, Chi. 117); with D. Hyman: *America the Beautiful* (1984, Conc. 3003)

As leader: with P. W. Russell: *Jazz at Storyville*, i, ii (1952, Savoy 15014, 15016); *Holiday in Braff* (1954–5, Beth. 1034); *Ruby Braff Special* (1955, Van. 8504); *Braff!* (1956, Epic 3377); *The Music of Ruby Braff and his International Jazz Quartet* (1972, Chi. 115); with G. Barnes: *The Ruby Braff/George Barnes Quartet Plays Gershwin* (1974, Conc. 5), *To Fred Astaire with Love* (1975, RCA APL1-1008); with D. Hyman: *Fats Waller's Heavenly Jive* (1977, Chi. 162); *Very Sinatra* (1981, Finesse 37988); with S. Hamilton: *A Sailboat in the Moonlight* (1986, Conc. 296)

As sideman: V. Dickenson: *The Vic Dickenson Septet*, i (1953, Van. 8001); M. Powell: *Mel Powell and his All Stars at Carnegie Hall* (1954, Col. CL557); B. Clayton: *Buck Meets Ruby* (1954, Van. 8008)

BIBLIOGRAPHY

FeatherE; *Feather '60s*; *Feather–Gitler '70s*
H. Panassié: "Ruby Braff," *BHcF*, no.60 (1956), 4
A. J. McCarthy: "Ruby Braff and the American Scene," *JM*, iii/3 (1957), 28
——: "Ruby Braff Discography," *JM*, iii/12 (1958), 24; iv/1 (1958), 26
G. Hall: *The Ruby Braff Discography* (Laurel, MD, 1965)
G. E. Lambert: "Ruby Braff in England," *JM*, xi/7 (1965), 16
P. J. Sullivan: "Ruby Braff: Jazz Enigma," *JJ*, xx/10 (1967), 15
A. McCarthy: Liner notes, *Ruby Braff Special* (Van. 8504, 1973)
W. Balliett: "Aesthetic Vitamins," *Alec Wilder and his Friends* (Boston, 1974) [colln of previously pubd articles], 111
K. Hazan: "That Braff is Back!," *MR*, i/5 (1974), 10
J. McDonough: "Ruby Braff: Salty Dog with a Hot Lip," *DB*, xliv/2 (1977), 17
G. Endress: "Ruby Braff," *Jazz Podium: Musiker über sich selbst* (Stuttgart, Germany, 1980), 34
B. Rusch: "Ruby Braff," *Cadence*, ix/6 (1983), 13 [interview]
M. Jones: *Talking Jazz* (London, 1987)
S. Voce: "Ruby Braff," *JJI*, xl/10 (1987), 8

WARREN VACHÉ, SR.

Brand, Dollar. *See* IBRAHIM, ABDULLAH.

Brandt, Helmut (*b* Berlin, 1 Jan 1931). German baritone saxophonist. He played tenor saxophone and clarinet as the leader of an amateur dixieland group, which entertained American troops after World War II; it recorded *Dixieland-Jazzfantasie* (Metrophon 6004) in 1949. In 1953 he joined Kutte Widmann and after changing to baritone saxophone (1954) he led his own small swing and bop groups (1955–9); he made several recordings as a leader, including *Sum* (1955, Met. 1039 [EP]), one of his own compositions. He worked with the dance orchestra of RIAS in Berlin from 1959 and became its chief arranger. In the 1960s he recorded again as a leader (1960, 1963) and with the singer Inge Brandenburg (1960), Emil Mangelsdorff's German All Stars, Hans Koller, and Klaus Doldinger (all 1963), the Blue Sounds, again with Doldinger, and with others (1964). He recorded numerous commercials with the Mainstream Orchestra, which he formed in 1975. Brandt has written a number of works for orchestra, among them *Concert for Jazzcombo* (1958).

BIBLIOGRAPHY

ReclamsJ
Liner notes, *Deutscher Jazz-Salon Berlin 1959* (Ariola 66162C, 1959)

RAINER E. LOTZ

Branscombe, Alan (*b* Wallasey, England, 4 June 1936; *d* London, 27 Oct 1986). English pianist, vibraphonist, and alto saxophonist. He was involved in music from an early age and as a child prodigy broadcast on a talent show playing a drum duet with Victor Feldman. After performing in an army band with Jeff Clyne (1954–6) he recorded with Vic Ash (1958) and Tony Kinsey (1959), and made tours of the USA with Ash (1959) and Japan with the pianist Stanley Black (*c*1960). A long association with John Dankworth included several recording sessions (1961, 1963–4, 1967, 1972) and an appearance in the film *The Servant* (1963). Branscombe was also active as a studio musician and recorded with Tubby Hayes (1964), Stan Tracey (1966, 1968), Paul Gonsalves (1969), Ben Webster (1970), the orchestra led by the trombonists Bobby Lamb and Ray Premru (1971), and Albert Nicholas (1973). As a leader, with Tony Coe and Kinsey as sidemen, he recorded six of his own blues compositions on the album *The Day I Met the Blues* (1977, EMI 3197).

BIBLIOGRAPHY

Feather '60s
B. Dawbarn: "Branscombe comes back to jazz," *MM* (14 March 1970), 12
R. Cotterell, ed.: *Jazz Now: the Jazz Center Society Guide* (London, 1976)

NEVIL SKRIMSHIRE

Brashear, Oscar (*b* Chicago, 18 Aug 1944). Trumpeter. He played piano from the age of seven and trumpet from the age of 11. He studied privately with Charlie Allen, learning both classical and jazz trumpet techniques. He attended Wright College and Roosevelt University, where he studied with Renold Schilke. In 1967 he toured with Woody Herman, and the following year he joined Count Basie. He was house trumpeter at The Apartment, a jazz club in Chicago, in 1970, and played with several leading bop artists, among them Dexter Gordon, Gene Ammons, Sonny Stitt, and James Moody. Later that year he moved to Los Angeles, where he became a respected session musician and freelance player, recording with Bobby Hutcherson (1971), Hampton Hawes (1972–3), Joe Henderson (1973–5), Harold Land (*c*1973, 1981), Horace Silver (*c*1975), Dizzy Gillespie (1977), Hubert Laws (*c*1978), J. J. Johnson (1979), Jimmy Smith (1980), and Gerald Wilson (1981–2). Brashear's jazz playing has been influenced by Clifford Brown, Miles Davis, and Freddie Hubbard; although he has taken part in numerous sessions, his playing is consistently good and is characterized by a fresh and enthusiastic approach.

SELECTED RECORDINGS

As sideman: H. Hawes: *Universe* (1972, Prst. 10046); H. Laws: *A Hero ain't Nothing but a Sandwich* (*c*1978, Col. JC35046); J. J. Johnson: *Pinnacles* (1979, Mlst. 9093); J. Smith: *The Cat Strikes Again* (1980, IC 1121); H. Land: *Xocia's Dance* (1981, Muse 5272); G. Wilson: *Jessica* (1982, Trend 531)

BIBLIOGRAPHY

L. Underwood: "Profile: Oscar Brashear," *DB*, xlii/21 (1975), 42
B. Hood: "Ten Outstanding Trumpet Players in the Los Angeles Area," *Brass Bulletin*, no.41 (1983), 43

FREDERICK A. BECK

Brass band. Term applied to a marching band made up of wind (at first brass, later brass and woodwind) and percussion players. It came into use in this sense after the American Civil War, when such groups became particularly important in black-American communities; distinctive ensembles evolved, consisting of between eight and 14 pieces and generally including one or more cornets (or trumpets), one or more trombones, alto or baritone horn or both, sousaphone or tuba, and a battery of snare drum and bass drum (with cymbal attached). From the early 20th century, in emulation of military-band instrumentation, at first clarinets and then alto or tenor saxophones were also adopted.

The principal center of brass-band activity has been New Orleans, where bands were most often associated with funeral processions: slow, solemn hymns or dirges were played on the way to a burial, and hot jazz and lively marches on the return journey, while followers (known as the "second line") marched and danced on the streets with the musicians. The bands also played for parades, picnics, dances, and other social occasions, where their repertory consisted of standard military-band marches and light concert music (which the players read from band-card scores), though they also improvised or created head arrangements of standard hymns, popular dance music, and jazz standards. The music included such multithematic compositions as *Panama*, *High Society*, and *My Maryland*.

The first brass band to be recorded was Bunk's Brass Band (led by Bunk Johnson) in May 1945, and earlier styles and repertories are undocumented. Recordings from the 1940s show that the bands tended to play in a jazz-oriented style. The music of the New Orleans bands is characterized by a dense musical texture and loose polyphony. The musicians played loudly and made use of harsh timbres and wide vibrato in order to project their music to maximum effect in outdoor settings; as a result their intonation was often poor. The early bandsmen were, however, regarded as skilled readers and musical virtuosos, and their music served important functions in the community.

After World War II showmanship and crowd-pleasing elements came to the fore as the purposes the music had once served became less significant in community life. But the performance style of brass bands has remained essentially unchanged. The tempo for the marching band is set by the drummers; the bass drum marks the first and third beat of each bar, while the second and fourth are often marked by the cymbal attached to the top of the drum, which is beaten with a wire hoop. For slow dirges, the snare drummer produces a muffled roll by releasing the instrument's snares, preventing them from resonating. The lead trumpet sounds the key note, and frequently the first phrase of the tune to be played. Although the melody is carried predominantly by the trumpets (doubled by reeds or with clarinet obbligato), the texture of the ensemble changes during each repetition of the chord sequence of a tune, so that the melody passes from trumpets to reeds to trombones. On final or "out" choruses, one trumpeter will generally improvise a solo in the high register, which soars above the sound of the whole band. From the 1950s the formal adherence to written arrangements declined, and head arrangements preserved through aural tradition have tended to prevail.

The brass-band tradition fostered many early jazz musicians. In New Orleans musicians associated with formal bands were Manuel Perez, Peter Bocage, the trumpeter Willie Pajeaud, and members of the Baquet and Barbarin families; major jazz musicians who received their early training in brass bands included King Oliver, Louis Armstrong, Johnny and Baby Dodds, Kid Ory, and Papa Celestin. After World War II Kid Howard, George Lewis (i), Jim Robinson, Percy Humphrey, Joseph "Red" Clark, Albert Warner, and Charles "Sunny" Henry were active bandsmen.

Among the most important and enduring groups in New Orleans were the Excelsior Brass Band (1880–1931), the Onward Brass Band (i) (1885–1930; see fig.1), the Reliance Brass Band (*c*1892–1918), the Tuxedo Brass Band (1917–25), and the Eureka Brass Band (1920–75; see fig.2, p.146). Later ensembles that have played in the traditional style include the Young Tuxedo Brass Band (1938–63; revived 1972), a new Onward Brass Band (1970s), the Olympia Brass Band, Doc Paulin's Brass Band, and the Eagle Brass Band. During the 1970s the Fairview Baptist Church Brass Band was founded under the auspices of Danny Barker for young players; in the late 1970s, led by the trumpeter Leroy Jones, this became the Hurricane Brass Band. The Dirty Dozen Brass Band (established in the 1980s) has branched out from orthodox practices to encompass in its performances ensemble and solo passages in the bop style.

Elsewhere in Louisiana there were successful groups in such towns as New Iberia (the Banner Band), Parks (Hypolite

1. The first Onward Brass Band, New Orleans, 1913: (left to right) Manuel Perez, Andrew Kimball, and Peter Bocage (cornets), Lorenzo Tio, Jr. (clarinet), Adolphe Alexander (alto horn), Baby Mathews (snare drum), Dandy Lewis (bass drum), Isidore Barbarin (alto horn), Buddy Johnson and Vic Gaspard (trombones), Eddie Atkins (baritone horn and trombone), and Eddie Jackson (tuba)

2. The Eureka Brass Band during the Odd Fellows Day parade in New Orleans, 1951: (from back, left to right) Percy Humphrey, Willie Pajeaud, and Eddie Richardson (trumpets); Edmond "Son" Washington (snare drum) and Robert Lewis (bass drum); Emanuel Paul (tenor saxophone) and Ruben Roddy (alto saxophone); Albert Warner, Charles "Sunny" Henry (trombones), and Joseph "Red" Clark (sousaphone)

Charles's Parade Band), Crowley (the Black Eagle Band), Laplace (the Duhé Brothers' Band), and Opelousas (the Martel Family Band). The Jenkins Orphanage in Charleston, South Carolina, which organized bands from among its pupils, became noted for the number of jazz musicians who emerged from its ranks; these included Cat Anderson, Peanuts Holland, Jabbo Smith, and Tommy Benford.

New Orleans musicians have been active on the West Coast, where the Eagle Brass Band toured and recorded under the leadership of Barry Martyn from the mid-1970s to the mid-1980s. The early recordings by New Orleans brass bands stimulated the formation of groups in Europe after World War II, notably such ensembles as Ken Colyer's Omega Brass Band (1953–61), Mike Casimir's Paragon Brass Band (1961–82), and Mike Brown's Excelsior Brass Band (from 1976) in Britain, the Inter City Brass Band in the Netherlands, and the Red Roses Brass Band in Belgium. In Japan, a band was organized in 1968 by the trumpeter Yoshio Toyama, who spent some time in New Orleans in the early 1960s.

See also BANDS, and entries on individual brass bands.

BIBLIOGRAPHY

ChartersJ
A. Lomax: *Mister Jelly Roll: the Fortunes of Jelly Roll Morton, New Orleans Creole and "Inventor of Jazz"* (New York, 1950, 2/1973)
F. Ramsey, Jr.: "Country Brass Bands," *JM*, i/11 (1956), 2
C. E. Smith: "New Orleans and Traditions in Jazz," *Jazz: New Perspectives on the History of Jazz*, ed. N. Hentoff and A. J. McCarthy (New York, 1959/*R*1974)
M. T. Zander: *The Brass-band Funeral and Related Negro Burial Customs* (diss., U. of North Carolina, 1962)
A. Rose and E. Souchon: *New Orleans Jazz: a Family Album* (Baton Rouge, LA, 1967, rev. 2/1978, rev. and enlarged 3/1984)
W. J. Schafer and R. B. Allen: *Brass Bands and New Orleans Jazz* (Baton Rouge, LA, and London, 1977)
A. M. Sonnier, Jr.: *Willie Geary "Bunk" Johnson: the New Iberia Years* (New York, 1977)
J. Darensbourg: *Telling it Like it is*, ed. P. Vacher (London, 1987)

WILLIAM J. SCHAFER

Brass bass. *See* TUBA.

Brass Company. Ensemble led by BILL HARDMAN, Billy Higgins, and Bill Lee from 1972.

Brass section. A term applied to the brass instruments (i.e., trumpets and trombones) within a big band; *see* BANDS, §§2, 4.

Braud [Breaux], **Wellman** (*b* St. James Parish, LA, 25 Jan 1891; *d* Los Angeles, 27 Oct 1966). Double bass player. He began performing on various string instruments in New Orleans around 1910 or 1911, played guitar with A. J. Piron, and was a drummer in brass bands. After touring he settled in 1917 in Chicago, where he took up double bass and played with Charlie Elgar (1920–22). He went to Europe with Will Vodery's Plantation Revue (1923), then worked in New York before joining Duke Ellington (1927). Braud remained with Ellington until 1935, and the strong rhythmic foundation he provided for the band was an important element in its success. His composition *Double Check Stomp* was recorded by the group in 1930. Braud played with and managed the Spirits of Rhythm from late 1935 and formed his own trio in 1937. Around 1940 he opened a poolroom in New York, but continued to play and record with Jelly Roll Morton (1939–40), Sidney Bechet (1940–41), Bunk Johnson (1947), and others. He toured Europe with Kid Ory in 1956, then in 1958 moved to California.

The main characteristic of Braud's playing was his swinging beat, but he also thought of his instrument in harmonic terms, and he claimed to have developed the concept of the walking bass. He stressed the importance of creating a big and pure tone, though he admitted to "overplaying" (producing too much noise from slapping the strings against the fingerboard) on some of the early recordings he made with Ellington, notably *Saturday Night Function*.

Oral history material in *LNT*.

SELECTED RECORDINGS

(all as sideman)

D. Ellington: Saturday Night Function (1929, Vic. 38036); Misty Mornin'/ Saratoga Swing (1929, Vic. 38058); S. Greer: Saturday Night Function (1929, Col. 1868D); D. Ellington: Double Check Stomp (1930, Vic. 38129); J. R. Morton: Sweet Substitute/Panama (1940, General 1703); Bechet–Spanier Big Four: Sweet Lorraine/Lazy River (1940, HRS 2000); B. Johnson: *Last Testament of a Great Jazzman* (1947, Col. GL520), incl. Maria Elena, Some of these days, That Teasin' Rag; K. Ory: *The Legendary Kid* (1955, GTJ 12016), incl. Mahogany Hall Stomp, Make me a pallet on the floor, Snag it

BIBLIOGRAPHY

ChiltonW

G. Schuller: *Early Jazz: its Roots and Musical Development* (New York, 1968)

C. Carrère: "Pitter panther patter: les bassistes de Duke Ellington," *Jh*, no.316 (1975), 10

BILL RUSSELL

Braxton, Anthony (*b* Chicago, 4 June 1945). Alto saxophonist, contrabass clarinetist, and composer. In his teens he pursued the study of jazz and European art music, eventually reading philosophy and composition at Roosevelt University. After army service he returned to Chicago, where in 1966 he joined the Association for the Advancement of Creative Musicians, and the following year, with Leroy Jenkins and Leo Smith, he formed the Creative Construction Company. Along with other AACM members, they journeyed to Paris in 1969 in an attempt to find steady work, but Braxton himself was not well received. He left Paris for New York in 1970 and joined the Italian improvisation ensemble Musica Elettronica Viva, then played with Chick Corea's free-jazz quartet Circle (1970–71). From 1972, following the delayed success of *For Alto*, the first album for unaccompanied saxophone ever recorded, he was invited to present numerous solo concerts. He also appeared frequently from 1971 to 1976 as the leader of his own quartets, which included his fellow sidemen from Corea's group, Dave Holland (see illustration) and Barry Altschul, and a brass player – either Kenny Wheeler or George Lewis (ii); at times Phillip Wilson or Jerome Cooper replaced Altschul. Braxton performed and recorded with Derek Bailey and Company in London (1974–7; for illustration *see* JAZZ (i), fig.9) and with the Globe Unity Orchestra in Germany (1975). He has continued to record regularly as a soloist, composer, and leader into the mid-1980s. In 1985 he secured a three-year appointment as a professor of music at Mills College.

Anthony Braxton (alto saxophone) and Dave Holland (double bass), Woodstock, NY, 1976

As a wind player, Braxton stands solidly within jazz traditions. He is among the finest free-jazz alto saxophonists, and his contrabass clarinet playing deserves particular mention for its novelty. He is also a fluent performer on all members of the saxophone and clarinet family and on percussion instruments – reflecting his interest in exploring timbral contrasts. He expanded his repertory in the 1970s to include bop improvisation. As a composer, he is justifiably irritated by the attempts to categorize his music as either free jazz or contemporary art music (surprisingly, it has not been termed "third stream," though it offers perhaps the finest examples of this concept). He makes use of geometrical designs, poetic arrangements of numbers and letters, and human and animal figures as titles of individual pieces on his albums. As well as works for small groups, Braxton has written humorous pieces for parade band and ambitious compositions for large orchestra, some of which have incorporated theatrical elements.

SELECTED RECORDINGS

* comprising or including compositions by Braxton

As unaccompanied soloist: **For Alto* (1968, Del. 420–21); **Saxophone Improvisations Series F* (1972, America 30AM011–2); **Composition 113* (1983, Sound Aspects 003)

Duos: with J. Jarman: **Together Alone* (1971, Del. 428); with G. Lewis: **Elements of Surprise* (1976, Moers 01036); with M. Roach: *Birth and Rebirth* (1978, BS 0024); with J. Lindberg: **Six Duets (1982)* (1982, Cecma 1005)

As leader of small groups: **Three Compositions of New Jazz* (1968, Del. 415); *In the Tradition* (1974, Ste. 1015, 1045); **Anthony Braxton Quartet Live at Moers New Jazz Festival* (1974, Ring 01010–11); **New York Fall 1974* (1974, Ari. 4032); **Five Pieces 1975* (1975, Ari. 4064); **The Montreux–Berlin Concerts* (1975–6, Ari. 5002); **For Trio* (1977, Ari. 4181); **Seven Compositions 1978* (1979, Moers 01066); **Six Compositions: Quartet* (1981, Ant. 1005); **Performance 9/1/79* (1979, HH 19); **Four Compositions (Quartet) 1983* (1983, BS 0066); **Four Compositions (Quartet) 1984* (1984, BS 0086)

As leader of large ensembles: **Creative Orchestra Music 1976* (1976, Ari. 4080); **For Four Orchestras* (1978, Ari. 8900)

As sideman: Creative Construction Company: *Creative Construction Company* (1970, Muse 5071, 5097); Circle: **The Paris Concert* (1971, ECM 1018–9); D. Holland: *Conference of the Birds* (1972, ECM 1027)

BIBLIOGRAPHY

V. Wilmer: "Anthony Braxton," *J&B*, i/2 (1971), 27 [interview]

B. Smith and others: "Anthony Braxton," *Coda*, xi/8 (1974), 2 [incl. discography]

R. Townley: "Anthony Braxton," *DB*, xli/3 (1974), 12

J. De Muth: "Anthony Braxton – George Lewis," *Cadence*, ii/2 (1976), 3

P. Occhiogrosso: "Anthony Braxton Explains Himself," *DB*, xliii/14 (1976), 15 [incl. discography]

B. Tepperman: "Perspectives on: Anthony Braxton," *JF* [intl edn], no.45 (1977), 34

L. Goddet and A. Dutilh: "Anthony Braxton, ou l'art de la surprise," *Jh*, no.349 (1978), 7; no.350 (1978), 15
G. Gazzoli: "Anthony Braxton: an Alternative Approach," *JF* [intl edn], no.62 (1979), 32
M. Ullman: *Jazz Lives: Portraits in Words and Pictures* (Washington, 1980), 199
H. de Craen and E. Janssens: *Anthony Braxton Discography* (Brussels, 1982)
H. Wachtmeister: *A Discography & Bibliography of Anthony Braxton* (Stocksund, Sweden, 1982)
J. Carey: "Anthony Braxton: Interview," *Cadence*, x/3 (1984), 5
J. Litweiler: *The Freedom Principle: Jazz after 1958* (New York, 1984), 265
C. Ahlgren: "Anthony Braxton: He Puts an Analytic Mind to his Musical Matters," *San Francisco Examiner* (13 Oct 1985)
G. Lock: "Let 100 Orchestras Blow," *The Wire*, no.16 (1985), 19
R. Radano: *Anthony Braxton and his Two Musical traditions: the Meeting of Concert Music and Jazz* (diss., U. of Michigan, 1985)
G. Lock: *Anthony Braxton: Interviews, Notes and Tours* (in preparation)

BARRY KERNFELD

Break. A brief solo passage occurring during an interruption in the accompaniment, usually lasting one or two bars and maintaining the underlying rhythm and harmony of the piece. Breaks appear most frequently at the ends of phrases, particularly the last phrase in a structural unit (e.g., a 12-bar blues or a 32-bar song), or at the end of a 16-bar unit of a multithematic piece (e.g., a march or rag). The break probably formed an evolutionary link between brass-band music and improvised jazz, at a stage when soloists were capable of creating short stretches of new material but not complete choruses; the first coherent, extended solos may have evolved from chains of breaks. The break may also have developed by analogy with the cadenza of art music.

Jelly Roll Morton stressed the importance of the break to early jazz in his Library of Congress recordings of 1938 (AAFS 1651). His performances of the 1920s, as well as the legendary duet breaks by King Oliver and Louis Armstrong in 1923 and Don Redman's arrangements for Fletcher Henderson's band, illustrate the compositional function of the break as a source of textural contrast. An improvisatory function is apparent in recordings of the same period by Armstrong and Sidney Bechet, who took advantage of the break for moments of unrestrained melodic spontaneity. Although the break fell out of fashion as a compositional device in the 1930s (except for the drum breaks at the end of many big-band recordings), it remains common as an improvisatory device, being often used to introduce a solo chorus. Transcriptions of 125 solo breaks by Armstrong were published in 1927 for study purposes, and a particularly spectacular break by Charlie Parker on an otherwise abortive take of *A Night in Tunisia* in 1946 (Dial matrix D1013-1) has been issued separately as *The Famous Alto Break*.

BIBLIOGRAPHY

G. Schuller: *Early Jazz: its Roots and Musical Development* (New York, 1968)

BARRY KERNFELD

Breau, Lenny [Leonard] (*b* Auburn, ME, 5 Aug 1941; *d* Los Angeles, 12 Aug 1984). Guitarist. His parents were the country-music performers Hal "Lone Pine" Breau and Betty Cody. He began playing country music, working mostly in Canada. In 1968–9, however, he recorded two albums with his own trio that established him as one of the most innovative guitarists in jazz. Later he played with the guitarists Chet Atkins and George Benson (1977) and made an acclaimed recording with Don Thompson and Claude Ranger (1979). Breau was an impressive solo artist: he could weave extended improvisations, often in two or three independent parts, that were sprinkled with elements of bop, swing, and rock as well as classical, flamenco, and East Indian music, but he was perhaps best known for his dazzling skill in the execution of octave harmonics. In the early 1980s he began using a seven-string guitar; unlike most players of this instrument, who prefer the addition of a low A string, Breau made use of a high A. He also wrote a monthly instructional column, "Fingerstyle Jazz," for the magazine *Guitar Player* (1981–4).

SELECTED RECORDINGS

As unaccompanied soloist: *Five O'Clock Bells* (1978–9, Adelphi 5006)
As leader: *The Guitar Sounds of Lenny Breau* (1968, RCA LSP4076); *The Velvet Touch of Lenny Breau* (1969, RCA LSP4199); *Lenny Breau* (1979, Direct Disk Labs 112)
As sideman with C. Atkins: *Standard Brands* (1979–81, RCA AYL1-4191)

BIBLIOGRAPHY

M. K. Webb: "Lenny Breau: Atkins-style Jazz on a 6-string 12!," *GP*, viii/9 (1974), 14
M. Miller: "Breau, Lenny," *Encyclopedia of Music in Canada*, ed. H. Kallmann, G. Potvin, and K. Winters (Toronto, Buffalo, and London, 1981)
B. Smoot: "Lenny Breau: Fingerstyle Jazz Impressionist," *GP*, xv/10 (1981), 22 [incl. discography]
J. Ferguson: "Lenny Breau Remembered," *GP*, xviii/11 (1984), 77 [incl. discography]

JIM FERGUSON

Brecker, Mike [Michael] (*b* Philadelphia, 29 March 1949). Tenor saxophonist, brother of Randy Brecker. He played clarinet and alto saxophone as a youth, then took up tenor saxophone in high school; bop and the music of John Coltrane were formative influences. While attending Indiana University he worked mainly in rock groups, then in 1969 he moved to New York, where he played rhythm-and-blues; the same year he formed the jazz-rock band Dreams with his brother and Billy Cobham. After working with Horace Silver (1973–4) and briefly with Cobham again (1974) he led the Brecker Brothers with Randy; when this disbanded in 1979 he established the group Steps (known from 1982 as STEPS AHEAD) with Mike Mainieri. From 1970 Brecker has also worked frequently as a session musician in New York. In 1987 he toured the USA and Japan as a member of Herbie Hancock's quartet and recorded his first album as a sole leader, on which he may be heard playing a synthesizer controller, the Electronic Wind Instrument. His stylistic versatility and ability to transmit emotion have brought him considerable popularity.

SELECTED RECORDINGS

As leader: of Dreams (with R. Brecker and B. Cobham): *Dreams* (*c*1970, Col. C30225); of Brecker Brothers (with R. Brecker): *Don't Stop the Music* (*c*1976, Ari. 4122), *Straphangin'* (*c*1979, Ari. 9550); *Michael Brecker* (1987, MCA/Imp. 5980)
As sideman: H. Galper: *The Guerrilla Band* (*c*1970, Mstr. 337); B. Cobham: *Total Eclipse* (1974, Atl. 18121); F. Zappa: *Zappa in New York* (*c*1977, Discreet 2D-2290); H. Galper: *Speak with a Single Voice* (1978, Enja 4006); C. Mingus: *Me, Myself an Eye* (1978, Atl. 8803); C. Corea: *Three Quartets* (1981, WB 3552); Steps Ahead: *Steps Ahead* (1983, Elek. Mus. 60168); K. Wheeler: *Double, Double you* (1983, ECM 1262)

BIBLIOGRAPHY

H. Nolan: "Mike Brecker: Music is what I Do!," *DB*, xl/12 (1973), 14
R. Palmer: "Sneakin' up the Charts with the Brecker Brothers," *DB*, xlii/16 (1975), 12
S. Bloom: "Brecker Brothers: the Studio and its Discontents," *DB*, xlvi/12 (1979), 24
L. Tomkins: "The Field is Wide Open for Development," *CI*, xix/2 (1980), 22 [interview]
H. Mandel: "Steps Ahead," *DB*, l/8 (1983), 18
D. Demsey: "Michael Brecker," *Saxophone Journal*, xi/4 (1987), 22 [incl. discography]
B. Milkowski: "Michael Brecker: On Impulse," *DB*, liv/6 (1987), 16 [incl. discography]

BRENDA PENNELL

Brecker, Randy (*b* Philadelphia, 27 Nov 1945). Trumpeter and flugelhorn player, brother of Mike Brecker. He learned classical trumpet in Philadelphia before attending Indiana University, where he studied jazz theory with Dave Baker and played in the big band that won first prize at the collegiate jazz festival at Notre Dame. During a tour of Europe with this band he decided to leave university and remained abroad for some months before moving to New York, where he joined Blood, Sweat and Tears (1967). Preferring a stronger jazz orientation than this group provided, he played with Horace Silver's quintet (1968–9), and worked with several big bands, including those led by Clark Terry, Duke Pearson, Thad Jones and Mel Lewis, Joe Henderson, and Frank Foster. In 1969 Brecker and his brother formed the jazz-rock band Dreams with Billy Cobham. The band was not commercially successful, but the brothers were in constant demand as studio musicians, and after it disbanded Brecker played with Larry Coryell's Eleventh House (1973–4) and Cobham (1974). From 1974 to 1979 he and Mike led the Brecker Brothers. *Some Skunk Funk*, from the group's first album, typifies the Brecker Brothers' approach: it includes a complex, angular melody that is played rapidly and precisely over staccato funk rhythms. Thereafter Brecker led a group with his wife, Eliane Elias, and continued to work as a studio musician. He is a versatile musician who has played bop, rock, and jazz-rock; he has expressed a preference for the last named because it offers him the greatest scope for inventive composition and performance.

SELECTED RECORDINGS

As leader: *Score* (c1968, SolS 18051); of Dreams (with M. Brecker and B. Cobham): *Imagine my Surprise* (c1971, Col. C30960); of Brecker Brothers (with M. Brecker): *The Brecker Brothers* (1975, Ari. 4037), incl. Some Skunk Funk, *Heavy Metal Be-bop* (c1978, Ari. 4185), *Detente* (c1979, Ari. 4272)

As sideman: H. Silver: *You Gotta Take a Little Love* (1969, BN 84309); L. Coryell: *The Eleventh House* (1972, Van. 79342); B. Cobham: *Crosswinds* (1974, Atl. 7300); *Blue Montreux* (1978, Ari. 4245); C. Mingus: *Me, Myself an Eye* (1978, Atl. 8803); D. Liebman: *Pendulum* (1978, AH 8); L. Tabackin: *Lew Tabackin Quartet* (1983, Ewd 90025)

BIBLIOGRAPHY

M.Cuscuna: "Young Man with Two Horns," *DB*, xxxvi/10 (1969), 15
J. Schaffer: "Randy Brecker," *DB*, xli/2 (1974), 16
R. Palmer: "Sneakin' up the Charts with the Brecker Brothers," *DB*, xlii/16 (1975), 12
S. Bloom: "Brecker Brothers: the Studio and its Discontents," *DB*, xlvi/12 (1979), 24
L. Tomkins: "We're Putting it all Together," *CI*, xix/2 (1980), 20
J. Levenson: "Brecker on Brass," *DB*, li/5 (1984), 20 [incl. discography]
D. Ancrum: "Randy Brecker: a Short Talk," *Cadence*, xii/10 (1986), 12

BRENDA PENNELL

Brehm, Simon (*b* Stockholm, 31 Dec 1921; *d* Stockholm, 11 Feb 1967). Swedish double bass player and bandleader. After taking part in an amateur contest in 1941 he played professionally with Arne Hülphers and in 1946 formed a quintet. He made recordings as the leader of a quintet, the Royal Swingers, that included Stan Hasselgård and Thore Swanerud (notably *Somebody loves me*, 1947, Musica 9200), and in 1946–7 of a sextet (*All the things you are*, 1947, Musica 9201); the latter included Hasselgård, Swanerud, and (from 1947–8) Arne Domnérus and Gösta Theselius. One of the best Swedish double bass players in the bop idiom during the 1940s and 1950s, Brehm recorded with many visiting Americans and Europeans, such as Tyree Glenn (1947), Zoot Sims, Toots Thielemans, and Rolf Ericson (all 1950), and Lars Gullin, George Wallington, and Quincy Jones (all 1953). From 1951 to 1958 he led a group in Stockholm that had a somewhat commercial orientation, and in 1952 he founded the record label Karusell; he was also well known as a music critic and radio producer. In his later years Brehm became increasingly involved in the popular-music business.

BIBLIOGRAPHY

"Svenskt stjärnalbum" [Swedish star-album], *Orkester journalen*, xii/9 (1945), 5
"På omslaget" [On the cover], *Orkester journalen*, xxiv/11 (1956), 4
Obituary, R. Dahlgren, *Orkester journalen*, xxxv/3 (1967), 8

ERIK KJELLBERG

Brenders, Stan [Constant] (*b* Brussels, 31 May 1904; *d* Brussels, 1 June 1969). Belgian pianist and bandleader. He worked in Brussels and London with Chas Remue (1925–6, 1927). In 1926 he performed as a soloist in one of the world's earliest jazz festivals, staged in Brussels, and in 1932, for Belgian radio, he gave the first performance of George Gershwin's Concerto in F outside the USA. Brenders established in 1936 Belgian radio's first jazz orchestra, which included some of the best musicians working in the country. He recorded extensively between 1938 and 1943, and in 1942 his band accompanied Django Reinhardt.

ROBERT PERNET

Breuker, Willem (*b* Amsterdam, 4 Nov 1944). Dutch saxophonist, clarinetist, and composer. He was a founder of the Instant Composers Pool, a nonprofit organization that sponsors performances and recordings of music by members of the Dutch avant garde. He played with the Globe Unity Orchestra under Alex Schlippenbach (1965–8), Gunter Hampel (1966–73), Peter Brötzmann, Misha Mengelberg, Han Bennink (1967–70), various groups associated with the Instant Composers Pool (1968–73), and his own quartet (1969–73) and recorded with Schlippenbach (1966), Brötzmann (1968, 1970), Hampel (1969–70), and in a duo with Bennink (1970). In 1974 he formed the Willem Breuker Kollektief, which toured Europe and in 1983 and 1985 visited the USA and Canada; the group's performances combine theatrical episodes and music of various genres (including free jazz, avant-garde classical music, and burlesque versions of Latin dances, film music, and marches), and are informed with a broad sense of humor and an irreverence towards the musical and political establishments. Breuker's compositions include the operas *The Life of Wolfgang A. Mozart*, *The Message*, and *Kain and Abel*, incidental music to Georg Büchner's *Woyzeck* and Bertolt Brecht's *Baal*, works for orchestra, pieces for barrel organ, and film scores. He was awarded the Dutch National Jazz Prize in 1970 and the Jazz Prize of the West German Music Critics in 1976.

SELECTED RECORDINGS

The European Scene (1975, MPS 68168); *On Tour* (1977, BVHaast 020); *Summer Music* (1978, Marge 05); *In Holland* (1981, BVHaast 041–2); *Driebergen–Zeist* (1983, BVHaast 050); *Willem Breuker Collective* (1983, About Time 1006)

BIBLIOGRAPHY

D. Lee: "Willem Breuker Kollektief," *Coda*, no.159 (1978), 33
W. F. van Eyle: "Het BVHaast verhaal" [The BVHaast story], *Jazz press*, no. 52 (1978), 4
G. Giddins: "Willem Breuker Battles the Bourgeoisie," *VV*, xxiv (2 July 1979), 69
B. Noglik: "Willem Breuker," *Jazzwerkstatt international* (Berlin, 1981), 226 [incl. interview, discography]
J. Pareles: "Willem Breuker Band Delivers a European Jazz," *New York Times* (28 Oct 1983), §C, p.26

WIM VAN EYLE

Brewer, Teresa [Theresa] (*b* Toledo, OH, 7 May 1931). Singer. She sang in public and on broadcasts frequently from the age of two, and began recording in the late 1940s, performing popular songs in a vigorous, crisp style with a biting tone that owed more to country music than jazz or blues. Between 1950 and 1956 she had six gold records. At the same time she achieved great success singing in nightclubs (particularly in Las Vegas), in stage shows, and on television. In 1972, shortly after her marriage to the jazz record producer Bob Thiele, she began to include more jazz in her repertory, often working with swing musicians. Although her characteristic vocal timbre has become somewhat smoother, especially in such ballads as *It had to be you*, she continues to sing as exuberantly as she did in the 1950s; she has transferred many of her nuances from this period to her later work, as may be heard, for example, on *I'm beginning to see the light*. Brewer brings a sense of swing to song texts, but preserves an accurate emphasis on key words. Generally she adheres closely to a melody during its first statement and in subsequent choruses; rather than being improvised, many of her variations of a tune are precomposed or based on formulas.

SELECTED RECORDINGS

As leader: with C. Basie: *The Songs of Bessie Smith* (1973, FD 10161); with D. Ellington: *It Don't Mean a Thing: Duke & Teresa* (1973, FD 10166), incl. I'm beginning to see the light; with E. Hines: *We Love you Fats* (1978, Doctor Jazz 60008); *Teresa Brewer: Live at Carnegie Hall & Montreux, Switzerland* (1978, Doctor Jazz 39521), incl. It don't mean a thing; *A Sophisticated Lady* (c1980, Col. PC37363); with S. Grappelli: *On the Road Again* (1981, Doctor Jazz 38448), incl. It had to be you

BIBLIOGRAPHY

Feather–Gitler '70s
L. Feather: "Lucky Number up again: Teresa Brews 4/4 'Waltz'," *DB*, xx/5 (1953), 2
——: "Blindfold Test: Bob Thiele & Teresa Brewer," *DB*, xliv/7 (1977), 34
——: Liner notes, *Teresa Brewer: Live at Carnegie Hall & Montreux, Switzerland* (Doctor Jazz 39521, 1984)

MARTY HATCH

Breyre, Jos [Joseph] (*b* Malmédy, Belgium, 10 Sept 1912). Belgian trombonist. He began his career as a member of the Bistrouille A. D. O. and, in 1929, played with the Famous Midnight Serenaders. He worked for two years in Brussels and Knokke-Heist with the Broadway Melodians, then performed with a band led by Louis de Vries in the Netherlands, Switzerland, and Belgium. In 1935 he played with Fud Candrix and the following year joined an orchestra newly formed for Belgian radio by Stan Brenders. From 1937 until the outbreak of World War II Breyre played in a French band led by Ray Ventura; he also worked with Willie Lewis. In the late 1940s he led his own band in Brussels and became active as a studio musician and arranger. Breyre recorded with the Racketeers (1931), the Radiolians, led by Gus Deloof (1932), Louis de Vries and his brother Jack de Vries (1933–4), Philippe Brun (1937), Ventura (1939), the bandleader Adolf Steimel (1940), Ernst van 't Hoff (1941), Freddie Brocksieper (1942), Lutz Templin (1942), the drummer Harry van Dyk (1942), the pianist Primo Angeli (1942–3), the Peter Sisters (1952), Candrix (1954), the trumpeter Janot Morales (1956), and the Decca Studio Orchestra (1958). He was one of the best-known European trombonists of the 1930s.

ROBERT PERNET

Brice, Percy (*b* New York, 25 March 1923). Drummer. After working with Luis Russell (1944–5), Benny Carter, and Mercer Ellington (1947), he played with Tab Smith, Cootie Williams, Tiny Grimes, Lucky Thompson, and Oscar Pettiford. In early 1954 he led his own groups at Minton's Playhouse, New York, and then joined a trio led by Billy Taylor (ii), with which he stayed for two years. As a member of George Shearing's quintet (1956–8) he appeared in the film *The Big Beat* (1957), and in 1958 he returned to Minton's Playhouse to work with Kenny Burrell for a year. He worked as an accompanist to Sarah Vaughan (1959–61) and the popular singer Harry Belafonte (1961 to late 1960s), during which time he also performed with Carmen McRae and Ahmad Jamal. He then led his own group for five years, before beginning in 1978 to work in Broadway musicals; from 1983 he both played in and conducted the revue *Bubbling Brown Sugar*. Between tours he has worked with Illinois Jacquet.

SELECTED RECORDINGS

As sideman: first issued on B. Carter: *Benny Carter in Hollywood, 1943–1946* (1943–6, Jazz Society 502), Jump Call, Oofdah (both 1946); O. Pettiford: *The New Oscar Pettiford Sextet* (1953, Debut 8); B. Taylor: *The Billy Taylor Trio with Candido* (1954, Prst. 7051); G. Shearing: *Black Satin* (1956, Cap. T858); S. Vaughan: *Dreamy* (1960, Roul. 52046)

BIBLIOGRAPHY

FeatherE

RICK MATTINGLY

Bricktop's. The name of nightclubs established in Paris, Biarritz, Rome, and Mexico City by the singer Ada Smith (Bricktop); *see* NIGHTCLUBS AND OTHER VENUES.

Bridge. A term applied generally in music to a passage in which a formal transition is made. In popular music it is used of the penultimate section in the refrain of a popular song, leading to the final repeat of the opening section (section *b* in the form *aaba*); the bridge provides a contrast, often tonal as well as harmonic and melodic, with the opening section. In ragtime and early jazz the bridge is a short section (normally of four or eight bars) that links the separate strains of multithematic compositions; it often incorporates a change of key. *See* FORMS, esp. §1(i)(a) and (d).

Bridgeport Die & Machine Co. [BD&M]. Record company. It was based in Bridgeport, Connecticut, and from about 1922 issued records on the labels Broadway, Puritan (later Puretone), and Triangle. BD&M also produced discs for other labels, all owned by various small companies (such as phonograph manufacturers): Baldwin, Carnival, Chautauqua, Embassy, Hudson, Lyratone, Mitchell, Music Box, National, Pennington, Resona, and Ross Stores. All of these drew on the same repertory, mostly derived from that of the New York Recording Laboratories, and including a large amount of important jazz from Paramount. Material was also taken at various times from Emerson and Plaza, and from such very small labels as Bludisc. One side of Duke Ellington's first recording – issued first on Blu-disc – was also issued on several of BD&M's small satellites. Although many of these labels used the same catalogue numbers, it is unlikely that all the repertory was put out on all of them. BD&M went bankrupt in 1925, and most of the satellites ceased trading around the same time; Broadway and Puritan, however, were continued by the New York Recording Laboratories. The labels Mitchell and Resona were later revived, but neither was used to issue material of any jazz significance.

BIBLIOGRAPHY

B. Rust: *The American Record Label Book* (New Rochelle, NY, 1978)
M. E. Vreede: "Puritan-ism in Discography," *Sv*, no.89 (1980), 178

Bridges, Henry (*b* Oklahoma City, OK, *c*1908). Tenor saxophonist. He played in local bands with Charlie Christian, then in bands of which Christian was the leader. He toured with Alphonso Trent (1938), played in Leslie Sheffield's band (1939), and from September 1939 was a soloist in Harlan Leonard's group, with which he recorded (*A la Bridges*, 1940, Bb 10899). After leading a military band in the USA and Europe he moved to Los Angeles, where he played through the 1950s. (J. Evensmo: *The Tenor Saxophones of Henry Bridges, Robert Carroll,*

Herschal [*sic*] *Evans, Johnny Russell* (n.p. [Oslo], n.d. [?1976] [discography])

based on *ChiltonW*

Bridgewater, Cecil (Vernon) (*b* Urbana, IL, 10 Oct 1942). Trumpeter, arranger, and composer. He studied music at the University of Illinois (1960–64, 1968–9), where he performed with and wrote arrangements for the college jazz band; while touring with the group in Europe (1968) and the USSR (1969) he met Dee Dee Garrett, whom he married in 1970. Bridgewater gained critical acclaim early in his career both for his sensitive trumpet and flugelhorn playing and for his ability as a composer. In 1969 he formed the Bridgewater Brothers Band with his brother Ron, a saxophonist, but the following year he moved to New York to join Horace Silver's quintet. He then worked with the Thad Jones–Mel Lewis Orchestra (1970–76), touring the USA, Europe, the USSR, and Japan; he was the principal soloist on the band's recording of his own composition, *Love and Harmony*. He also performed frequently with Max Roach, as well as with Art Blakey, Randy Weston, Harold Vick, Jimmy Heath, Joe Henderson, Sam Rivers, Roy Brooks, and Dizzy Gillespie, and recorded with Abdullah Ibrahim (1973), Charles McPherson (*c*1973), and Frank Foster and Klaus Weiss (both 1974). Bridgewater has also been active as a teacher. He has continued to tour and record with Roach's quartet into the mid-1980s.

SELECTED RECORDINGS

As sideman: M. Roach: *Lift Every Voice and Sing* (1971, Atl. 1587); H. Person: *Houston Person* (1971, Prst. 10017); T. Jones and M. Lewis: *Suite for Pops* (1972, 1975, A&M Hor. 701); *Potpourri* (1974, Philadelphia International 598); *New Life* (1975, A&M Hor. 707), incl. Love and Harmony; M. Roach: *In the Light* (1982, SN 1053)

BIBLIOGRAPHY

Feather–Gitler '70s
C. Sheridan: "Greetings and Salutations," *JJI*, xxxi/6 (1978), 6

FREDERICK A. BECK

Bridgewater [née Garrett], **Dee Dee** [Denise] (*b* Memphis, 27 May 1950). Singer. She began performing in Michigan in the 1960s and in 1969 she toured the USSR with the big band of the University of Illinois. She married Cecil Bridgewater in 1970 and moved to New York; they were divorced in the mid-1970s. From 1972 to 1974 she was a principal soloist with the Thad Jones–Mel Lewis Orchestra; she then appeared in the Broadway musical *The Wiz* (1974–6), for her role in which she won a Tony Award (1975). In 1976 she sang at Hopper's in New York and studied with Roland Hanna, before moving to Los Angeles to work as a pop singer. Thereafter she lived abroad for some years; in 1986–7 she appeared in Paris and London in the principal role of *Lady Day*, a play by Stephen Stahl about the life of Billie Holiday. She performed in New York in December 1987, and later toured the Far East, with an all-star band that included Clark Terry, James Moody, Jimmy McGriff, and Grady Tate. Bridgewater is best known in jazz for her sometimes mournful, sometimes jubilant wordless improvisations in the style of gospel music; *The Great One* on *Suite for Pops* (A&M Hor. 701), recorded by the Thad Jones–Mel Lewis Orchestra in 1972, is a good example of her work in this manner.

BIBLIOGRAPHY

Feather–Gitler '70s
L. Underwood: "Profile: Dee Dee Bridgewater," *DB*, xliii/17 (1976), 38
C. Flicker and C. Carrière: "Dee Dee Bridgewater," *Jm*, no.235 (1975), 14 [incl. discography]

SCOTT FREDRICKSON

Briggs, Arthur (*b* Charleston, SC, 9 April 1899). Trumpeter, cousin of Pete Briggs. He was trained at Jenkins' Orphanage in Charleston, and traveled to England in 1919 with the bandleader Will Marion Cook. He studied in London with John Solomon, a professor at the Royal Academy of Music, and was one of the first black-American jazz musicians to settle in Europe, where he was held in high esteem. From 1928 to 1931 he worked intermittently as a sideman with Noble Sissle; he also played in Louis Armstrong's European groups. Briggs led his own bands, mainly in France, during the mid-1930s, and continued to lead groups into the 1960s; in 1964 he began teaching. As a founder member of the Hot Club de France he recorded with Django Reinhardt and Stephane Grappelli (to 1935). He also made recordings as a leader, and his playing may be heard to advantage on *Braggin' the Briggs* (1940, Swing 205).

Oral history material in *NjR* (JOHP).

BIBLIOGRAPHY

ChiltonW
A. McCarthy: *Big Band Jazz* (New York and London, 1974), 309
C. Goddard: *Jazz away from Home* (London and New York, 1979), 281
R. Lotz: Liner notes, *Arthur Briggs in Berlin, 1927* (Black Jack 3006, 1979)
R. Pernet: "Some Notes on Arthur Briggs," *Sv*, no.84 (1979), 204
A. Möller: *Arthur Briggs* (Menden, Germany, 1981)

JEFFREY P. GREEN

Briggs, Bunny (*b* ?New York, 1923). Dancer. As a child he was influenced by Bill Robinson. By 1931 he was working in private houses in New York with Luckey Roberts and his Society Entertainers. Later he sang with Lucky Millinder's band, was the featured dancer with Erskine Hawkins, and performed with Baby Laurence, who was another influence on his dancing. Around 1943 Briggs spent three weeks dancing for Earl Hines, whose sidemen Dizzy Gillespie and Charlie Parker helped him to adapt his style to bop. He also developed his own version of the paddle and roll dancing technique, to which he added elements of pantomime. Briggs left Hines to work with Count Basie, then sang and danced for Charlie Barnet, with whom he recorded in 1947–9 and 1958. Between 1963 and 1965 he danced for Duke Ellington; especially famous was his solo tap-dancing to *David Danced before the Lord with all his Might*, which was recorded on Ellington's album *Concert of Sacred Music* (1965, RCA LSP3582) and filmed by Ralph J. Gleason. He later recorded with Oliver Jackson (1977) and appeared in the documentary film *No Maps on my Taps* (1978). He has performed and toured internationally into the late 1980s.

BIBLIOGRAPHY

H. McNamara: "Bunny Briggs: Jazz Dancer," *DB*, xxxiii/4 (1966), 15
M. Stearns and J. Stearns: *Jazz Dance: the Story of American Vernacular Dance* (New York and London, 1968)
J. Hamlin: "Bunny Briggs Danced before the Lord: Legendary Master Featured at First-ever S.F. Jazz Tap Festival," *San Francisco Chronicle Datebook* (5 July 1987), 19

Briggs, Pete (*b* Charleston, SC, *c*1904). Tuba and double bass player, cousin of Arthur Briggs. He started his career as a tuba player. In Chicago he performed with Carroll Dickerson's orchestra (*c*1926), remaining with the band in 1927 when it was reorganized as Louis Armstrong's Stompers; in the same year he also played with Jimmie Noone. He made recordings as a member of Armstrong's Hot Seven (1927, including *Weary Blues*, OK 8519) and worked again with Dickerson and Armstrong in Chicago (1928) and New York (1929); also in New York he played with Edgar Hayes (1929–30) and recorded with Jelly Roll Morton (1930). Briggs worked frequently with the guitarist and banjoist Vernon Andrade during the mid-1930s, playing double bass, and with Herman Autrey in 1943–4, but then retired from music. (*ChiltonW*)

Bright, Ronnell (Lovelace) (*b* Chicago, 3 July 1930). Pianist and composer. He displayed talent from an early age, won a piano competition at the age of nine, and played with the Chicago Youth Piano SO in 1944. Later he attended the Juilliard School (summer 1946) and graduated from the University of Illinois (BM 1952). He first played jazz in a navy band (1953), then worked in Chicago with the double bass player Johnny Tate and as an accompanist to Carmen McRae (1954–5). After moving to New York (1955) he performed and recorded with Rolf Kühn (1956) and formed his own trio (1957). He was a member of Dizzy Gillespie's big band (1957–8) and served as accompanist and conductor for the singers Sarah Vaughan (1958–60, 1963), Lena Horne (1961), and Gloria Lynne (1963), and as pianist, music director, conductor, and arranger for Nancy Wilson (1964–7). While with Wilson, Bright moved in 1965 to Los Angeles, where he worked in television. He was a member of Supersax from 1972 to 1974, and taught high school in 1974–5. Many of Bright's compositions have been recorded by other musicians, among them Vaughan, Cal Tjader, Horace Silver, and Blue Mitchell. Bright has also collaborated with the lyricist Johnny Mercer.

SELECTED RECORDINGS

As leader: *Bright's Spot* (1956, Reg. 6041); *Bright Flight* (1957, Van. 8512)
As sideman: S. Vaughan: *Dreamy* (1960, Roul. 52046); C. Hawkins: *The Hawk Relaxes* (1961, Mdsv. 15); Supersax: *Supersax Plays Bird* (1972, Cap. ST11177)

RECORDED COMPOSITIONS
(*selective list*)

Recorded by others: Sweet Pumpkin, on B. Mitchell: *Blue's Moods* (1960, Riv. 9336); Cherry Blossom, on H. Silver: *The Tokyo Blues* (1962, BN 84110)

BIBLIOGRAPHY

FeatherE; *Feather '60s*; *Feather–Gitler '70s*
L. Feather: "Ronnell Bright: the Compleat Accompanist," *DB*, xxxvii/3 (1970), 17

PAUL RINZLER

Brignola, Nick [Nicholas Thomas] (*b* Troy, NY, 17 July 1936). Baritone saxophonist and flutist. He was mainly self-taught, though he studied music theory at Ithaca (New York) College and the Berklee College of Music. In 1957 he played and recorded with the pianist Reese Markewich and the following year he recorded under Herb Pomeroy in Boston and worked with Cal Tjader and the Mastersounds in San Francisco; he returned to the Albany area to form his own group in 1959. He played and recorded with Sal Salvador and Woody Herman in 1963, and toured Europe with Ted Curson in 1967; on his return he performed in and around Troy and recorded his first album as a leader (on his own label, Priam). For several years he abandoned the bop style in favor of electronic jazz-rock, which he explored with his own group formed in 1969. He renewed his association with Curson in 1974 and continued to perform and record with him into the 1980s; he was also active as a leader, regularly recording albums from 1977, on two of which, *Baritone Madness* and *Burn Brigade*, he was joined by other baritone saxophonists (respectively Pepper Adams, and Ronnie Cuber and Cecil Payne). Brignola is best known as an exciting player of the baritone saxophone, on which he produces a sound that is both husky and biting; as a leader, however, he has also played soprano, alto, and tenor saxophones, clarinets, and flutes.

SELECTED RECORDINGS

As leader: *This is it!* (1967, Priam 101); *Baritone Madness* (1977, Beehive 7000); *Burn Brigade* (1979, Beehive 7010); *Signals . . . in from Somewhere* (1983, Dis. 893)
As sideman with T. Curson: *Jubilant Power* (1976, IC 1017)

BIBLIOGRAPHY

"Dictionnaire du baryton," *Jm*, no.143 (1967), 30 [incl. discography]
C. Berg: "Nick Brignola: the Upstate Burner," *DB*, xlv/10 (1978), 21 [incl. discography]
J. L. Atkins: "Nick Brignola: Interview," *Cadence*, viii/5 (1982), 5

GARY CARNER

Bril, Igor (Mikhaylovich) (*b* Moscow, 9 June 1944). Russian pianist, teacher, and composer. At the Vserossiyskoye Gastrol'no-kontsertnoye Ob'yedinenie (All-Russian society for guest performances) he led a trio in which he also played piano. From 1966 to 1969 he belonged to VIO-66 (the Vocal-instrumental Orchestra, directed by the bandleader Yuri Saulsky) and played with Aleksey Kozlov; he then worked with German Luk'yanov (1969–70) and led a septet (1972–81) and a quintet (from 1982) that performed throughout the USSR, in Europe, and in Cuba and made several recordings, including *Pered zakhodom solntsa* (Twilight; 1985, Mel. C6021873003). He was the head of the creative department at the Eksperimental'naya studiya estradnoy i dzhazovoy muzïki (Experimental studio of improvised music) from 1969 to 1974 and in 1971 he graduated as a pianist from the Gnessins State Musical and Pedagogical Institute, Moscow, where he led the department of jazz and light music from 1984. Bril has recorded several of his own compositions, including *Pered zakhodom solntsa*, *Orkestr priyekhal* (An orchestra came), *Nasha samba* (Our samba), and *V puti* (On the way). (S. F. Starr: *Red and Hot: the Fate of Jazz in the Soviet Union, 1917–1980* (New York, and Oxford, England, 1983), 279, 313)

WALTER OJAKÄÄR

British Institute of Jazz Studies. Library formed in Crowthorne, Berkshire, as a resource for the study of jazz; *see* LIBRARIES AND ARCHIVES, §2 (Great Britain).

British Rhythm Society. Record label. It was established in 1948 as part of Dante Bolletino's Globe Industries of New York. The catalogue contained reissues of early jazz drawn without authorization from all the major labels of the 1920s, and was the first such series to be openly offered for sale. From about June 1951, similar issues appeared on the labels Wax Shop and Jolly Roger; the latter was principally an LP series with a coverage that extended into the swing era. In January 1952 Bolletino was sued by Columbia and Louis Armstrong for illegal use and publication of their material. No defense was entered and the operations of the labels ceased the following month. Most of the smaller companies that operated in this manner stopped trading at the same time. (D. Mahony, B. Whyatt, and others: "The Dante Bolletino Labels," *Matrix*, no.58 (1965), 3)

Broadbent, Alan (*b* Auckland, New Zealand, 23 April 1947). Composer, arranger, and pianist. He studied at the Royal Trinity College of Music in Auckland (1954–60) and then at the Berklee College of Music (1966–9); he also took private lessons with Lennie Tristano. In 1969 he became pianist and arranger for Woody Herman, and contributed several compositions, including *Bebop and Roses*, to the band's repertory; *Variations on a Scene*, an extended work for chamber and big-band jazz ensembles and orchestra, was given its première by Herman's band and the Houston SO in 1975. The same year Broadbent joined John Klemmer's group. Later he recorded with Bill Berry's septet (1978), Bud Shanks's trio (1979), and a quintet led by Warne Marsh and Gary Foster (1982). In 1987 he performed in San Francisco as a member of Charlie Haden's Quartet West.

He has also written chamber music, notably a sonata for cello and piano.

SELECTED RECORDINGS

Duo with I. Kral: *Where is Love?* (1974, Choice 1012)

As sideman: B. Shank: *Crystal Moments* (1979, Conc. 126); W. Marsh and G. Foster: *Warne Marsh Meets Gary Foster* (1982, Ewd 90024)

RECORDED COMPOSITIONS

(selective list: recorded by W. Herman with Broadbent as sideman)

on *Giant Steps* (1973, Fan. 9432), Bebop and Roses; on *Children of Lima* (1975, Fan. 9477), Variations on a Scene

BIBLIOGRAPHY

Feather–Gitler '70s

ANDREW JAFFE

Broadcast transcription. *See* TRANSCRIPTION (iii).

Broadway. Record label. It was established by the Bridgeport Die & Machine Co. in the early 1920s, and drew on recordings made by the New York Recording Laboratories, who took over the label after its first owner went bankrupt in 1925. Most of the repertory also appeared on other labels owned by these groups. In the late 1920s Broadway's catalogue also included material recorded by the Plaza group. The New York Recording Laboratories also issued the Broadway 5000 race series, which consisted of items from Paramount's race catalogue issued under pseudonyms. Broadway ceased to operate in 1931.

BIBLIOGRAPHY

R. M. W. Dixon and J. Godrich: *Recording the Blues* (London, 1970), 58

B. Rust: *The American Record Label Book* (New Rochelle, NY, 1978), 44

Broadway Rastus. Pseudonym of FRANK MELROSE.

Brocksieper, Freddie [Fritz, Friedrich; Brocksi] (*b* Constantinople [now Istanbul], 24 Aug 1912). German drummer and bandleader. He first played professionally in Nuremberg in 1930 and later moved to Berlin (1939). He recorded with the GOLDENE SIEBEN (1939), Benny De Weille (1940), and Willy Berking (1940–41), and as a soloist with Lutz Templin's orchestra (1941–3), with which he also played on a radio station that broadcast propaganda outside Germany. In the 1940s he led his own quartets, quintets, and big bands, making several recordings; his composition *Die Trommel und ihr Rhythmus* (1942, Bruns. 82238) gives an impressive display of his rhythmic playing, which is strongly influenced by Gene Krupa, and *Cymbal Promenade* (1943, Bruns. 82314) is considered a milestone in European big-band jazz. After World War II he led various groups, entertaining American troops in Stuttgart and Munich, where he had a long engagement at Studio 15, and also performing in Berlin and Spain. From 1964 he played mainly in trios and often accompanied visiting American soloists. He received the Deutscher Schallplattenpreis in 1980.

BIBLIOGRAPHY

ReclamsJ

K. Ude, ed.: *25 Jahre schwabinger Kunstpreis: Katalog zur Ausstellung "Ausserdem"* (Munich, 1986) [exhibition catalogue]

GÜNTHER HUESMANN, RAINER E. LOTZ

Brokensha, Jack [John Joseph, John Jazza] (*b* Adelaide, Australia, 5 Jan 1926). Australian vibraphonist, drummer, arranger, composer, and bandleader. He became interested in jazz while serving in an RAAF entertainment unit (1944–6). After the war he led groups in Adelaide and played in coffee lounges and at concerts in Melbourne (1947–8). Among his sidemen at this period was Errol Buddle; Brokensha's playing is well represented by the recording *Buddle's Bebop Boogie* (1948, Jazzart 3–4). Extensive touring established his reputation in Australia and he worked in Sydney (1949–50), Brisbane (1950), where his group disbanded, and Adelaide (1951). With Bryce Rohde he traveled in 1953 to Canada, where he became a founder member of the Australian Jazz Quartet (December 1954, with Rohde, Buddle, and Dick Healey); later expanded to a quintet and occasionally a sextet, the group disbanded in 1958 after a tour of Australia and Brokensha moved to Detroit, where he established a music production company. He recorded again in 1963, as the leader (playing vibraphone) of a bop quartet that included Art Mardigan, and in 1980.

BIBLIOGRAPHY

FeatherE

A. Bisset: *Black Roots, White Flowers: a History of Jazz in Australia* (Sydney, 1976), 101

B. Johnson: "Brokensha, John Joseph," *The Oxford Companion to Australian Jazz* (Melbourne, Australia, 1987)

BRUCE JOHNSON

Brom, Gustav (*b* Velke Levary, nr Malacky, Czechoslovakia, 22 May 1921). Czechoslovak clarinetist and bandleader. He studied violin and clarinet and in 1940 formed a student big band, which in 1945 toured Eastern Europe and made the first of several recordings. With the band he played for several months in Switzerland (1947), then returned to Czechoslovakia to record and play regularly for radio stations in Bratislava and (from 1948) Brno. In 1955 he formed a new ensemble that played swing, dixieland, and West Coast jazz, and chamber jazz in the manner of the Modern Jazz Quartet; his concerts, during which he discoursed on the history of jazz, helped to gain acceptance and popularity for the music in Czechoslovakia. In 1960 his band recorded in Czechoslovakia with Edmond Hall; during the following decade, when it began to play in a bop style, it performed at festivals in Manchester, England (1963), Warsaw (1964), Munich (1965), Antibes–Juan-les-Pins, France (1965), and Prague (regularly), and worked with such musicians as Ted Curson, the vibraphonist Jerzy Milian, Maynard Ferguson, the trumpeter Ack van Rooyen, and Peter Herbolzheimer.

SELECTED RECORDINGS

Gustav Brom se svým orchestrem (1965, Sup. 9009); *Kyrie eleison* (1966, Sup. 55849); *Swinging the Jazz* (1967, Saba 15122); *Maynard & Gustav* (1969, Sup. 1150716)

BIBLIOGRAPHY

Feather–Gitler '70s

J. Fukač: "Brom 1963: nové otazníky, nové jistoty" [Brom 1963: new questions, new confidence], *Taneční hudba a jazz, 1964–1965* [Dance music and jazz, 1964–1965], ed. L. Dorůžka, J. Hořec, and J. Kotek (Prague, 1965), 107

M. Juranek: "Two Interviews from Czechoslovakia: Jan Konopasek and Gustav Brom," *JM*, xi/9 (1965), 17

GERHARD CONRAD

Bronx, Pat. Name by which PETER SCHILPEROORT is sometimes known.

Brookmeyer, Bob [Robert] (*b* Kansas City, MO, 19 Dec 1929). Valve trombonist, arranger, and pianist. He studied at the Kansas City Conservatory and began his career as a pianist in various dance bands. In 1952 he took up valve trombone and immediately became an important figure among performers of the West Coast style of jazz, particularly after replacing Chet Baker in Gerry Mulligan's "pianoless" quartet, with which he played from 1953 to 1954. At the same time he continued to work as a pianist, and in 1959 recorded a revealing album in a quartet with Bill Evans (ii). He led a group with Clark Terry in the early 1960s that achieved some popularity, and in 1965 he was a founding member of the Thad Jones–Mel Lewis Orchestra, to which he contributed several outstanding arrangements. From 1968 Brookmeyer worked as a studio musician on the West Coast and frequently played as a sideman with well-known mainstream jazz musicians. By 1980 he was music director of Lewis's reorganized big band, for which he has also performed as a soloist and written arrangements. Scores by him are in the Georges P. Vanier Library of Concordia University, Montreal; *see* LIBRARIES AND ARCHIVES, §2.

Brookmeyer is the first noteworthy jazz musician since Juan Tizol to have specialized on valve trombone, but unlike Tizol he is an excellent soloist, playing in a good-humored linear style with, at times, pronounced overtones of blues and swing. As a pianist he has developed a distinctive percussive and dissonant manner entirely outside the main traditions of jazz pianism.

SELECTED RECORDINGS

As leader: *Kansas City Revisited* (1958, UA 5008); with B. Evans: *The Ivory Hunters* (1959, UA 6044); *Jazz is a Kick* (1960, Mer. 60600); *The Blues Hot and Cool* (1960, Verve 68385); with S. Getz: *Stan Getz/Bob Brookmeyer* (1961, Verve 68418); *Gloomy Sunday* (1961, Verve 68455); *Bob Brookmeyer and Friends* (1964, Col. CS9037); with C. Terry: *Tonight* (1964, Mstr. 6043), *The Power of Positive Swinging* (1964, Mstr. 6054), *Gingerbread Men* (1966, Mstr. 6086); *The Bob Brookmeyer Small Band* (1978, Gryphon 785); with M. Lewis: *Live at the Village Vanguard* (1980, Gryphon 912)

As sideman: G. Mulligan: [*Paris Concert*] (1954, Vogue 7381, 7383)

SELECTED ARRANGEMENTS

(all recorded by T. Jones and M. Lewis)

ABC Blues, Willow weep for me, on *Presenting Thad Jones–Mel Lewis and the Jazz Orchestra* (1966, SolS 18003); Samba con getcha, on *Live at the Village Vanguard* (1967, SolS 18016)

BIBLIOGRAPHY

L. Feather: "Brookmeyer's Tale of Three Cities," *DB*, xxii/18 (1955), 9

B. Coss: "Bob Brookmeyer: Strength and Simplicity," *DB*, xxviii/2 (1961), 19

D. Morgenstern: "Bob Brookmeyer: Master of the Brass Stepchild," *DB*, xxxiv/2 (1967), 14

M. Williams: "Giuffre, Brookmeyer Reunion," *DB*, xxxv/2 (1968), 15

"A Gallery of BMI Jazz Composers," *BMI: the Many Worlds of Music* (1981), no.3, p.25

J. BRADFORD ROBINSON

Brooks, Harvey (Oliver) (*b* Philadelphia, 17 Feb 1899; *d* Los Angeles, 17 June 1968). Pianist and composer. He toured and recorded with Mamie Smith in the early 1920s, settled in California, and with Paul Howard led the Quality Four from 1923, with which he recorded; he also made recordings with Howard's Quality Serenaders (including *Stuff*, 1930, Vic. 38122), of which he was a member until 1930. From 1931 to 1935 his most important association was with Les Hite's orchestra, for which he was the music director; in this capacity he worked frequently in film studios in Hollywood and wrote music for soundtracks (including the songs *That Dallas Man* and *They Call me Sister Honky Tonk* for Wesley Ruggles's film *I'm no Angel*, 1933). Later he worked as a leader, continued to write songs into the 1950s, played in Kid Ory's band (from 1952), performed and recorded with Teddy Buckner (1955–6) and Joe Darensbourg (1957–60), and belonged to the Young Men of New Orleans (from 1961), which he led in the last year of his life. (J. Darensbourg: *Telling it Like it is*, ed. P. Vacher (London, 1987; Baton Rouge, LA, 1987, as *Jazz Odyssey: the Autobiography of Joe Darensbourg*)

based on *ChiltonW*

Brooks, Roy (*b* Detroit, 3 Sept 1938). Drummer, percussionist, and jazz educator. He cites Elvin Jones as his first important influence. He first worked with Yusef Lateef; with three colleagues from Detroit, Louis Hayes, Gene Taylor, and Doug Watkins, he joined the Horace Silver Quintet, to which he belonged from 1959 to 1964. Later he performed with Lateef, Pharoah Sanders, James Moody, Wes Montgomery, Sonny Stitt, Jackie McLean, Dexter Gordon, Dollar Brand, Randy Weston, Milt Jackson, and Charles Mingus. In 1970 he became a founding member, with other post-bop percussionists, of Max Roach's group M'BOOM RE: PERCUSSION. He returned to Detroit in 1976 and founded a center for teaching jazz to young people; his Aboriginal Percussion Choir performed at the Music Hall in Detroit during the Montreux–Detroit International Jazz Festival in 1980. Under the aegis of his educational program, Musicians United to Save Indigenous Culture (MUSIC), he has performed and recorded with the Artistic Truth, an ensemble dedicated to "redeveloping the dying arts of African-American music, dance, and poetry."

SELECTED RECORDINGS

As leader: *Roy Brooks' Beat* (1963, Jazz Workshop 220); *The Free Slave* (1970, Muse 5003); *The Smart Set* (1979, Bay. 15)

As sideman: H. Silver: *Horace-Scope* (1960, BN 84042); *At the Village Gate* (1961, BN 84076); S. Scott: *Blue Seven* (1961, Prst. 7376); C. Baker: *Groovin'* (1965, Prst. 7460); Y. Lateef: *The Golden Flute* (1966, Imp. 9125); D. Brand: *African Space Program* (1973, Enja 2032); M. Roach: *M'Boom Re: Percussion* (1979, Col. JC36247); *Collage* (1984, SN 1059)

BIBLIOGRAPHY

B. McLarney: "Roy Brooks: Unsung Hero," *DB*, xxxiv/16 (1967), 15

J. Dulzo: "Exquisite Thunder," *Detroit News* (6 Feb 1981), §F. p.4

J. KENT WILLIAMS

Brooks, Tina [Harold Floyd] (*b* Fayetteville, NC, 7 June 1932; *d* New York, 13 Aug 1974). Tenor saxophonist and composer. He first studied C-melody saxophone, beginning soon after his family moved to New York in 1944. He was nicknamed "Tina" (a corruption of "teeny") because of his small stature as a teenager. He first played professionally with a rhythm-and-blues band led by the pianist Sonny Thompson (recording in 1951), then performed with Lionel Hampton (1955) before working as a freelance musician in New York, where he was befriended by Little Benny Harris and Elmo Hope; Harris was instrumental in gaining for him a recording contract with Blue Note in 1958. In 1959–60 Brooks was Jackie McLean's understudy in the leading role of Jack Gelber's play *The Connection*. Brooks recorded 12 sessions for Blue Note (four as a leader) with such musicians as Art Blakey, Kenny Burrell, Johnny Coles, Kenny Drew, Freddie Hubbard, McLean, Blue Mitchell, Jimmy Smith, and Bobby Timmons; they reveal a soloist capable of creating shapely statements and developing them with exceptional clarity and an urgent, infectious sense of swing. An intriguing and original performer, highly rated by his contemporaries, Brooks was influenced by Lester Young, Sonny Rollins, and above all the blues. He died after years of illness caused by drug abuse.

SELECTED RECORDINGS

(all recorded for Blue Note)

As leader: *True Blue* (1960, 4041)

As sideman: K. Burrell: *On View at the Five Spot Cafe* (1959, 4021); F. Hubbard: *Open Sesame* (1960, 4040); J. McLean: *Street Singer* (1960, GXF3067)

CHRIS SHERIDAN

Brother Cornbread. Nickname of JOE THOMAS (i).

Brotherhood of Breath. Big band formed in London in 1970 by CHRIS McGREGOR.

Brother Matthew. Name adopted by BOYCE BROWN in 1953.

Brötzmann, Peter (*b* Remscheid, Germany, 6 March 1941). German tenor saxophonist. He attended the Art Academy of Wuppertal and taught himself to play saxophone. He worked with local dixieland bands from 1959, was associated with the Fluxus movement in Germany in the early 1960s, and by 1964 was playing free jazz. In 1965 he formed a group with Peter Kowald and the drummer Sven-Åke Johansson (*b* Mariestad, Sweden, 1943); the following year he toured Europe in a quintet led by Mike Mantler and Carla Bley and began an association with the Globe Unity Orchestra that lasted until 1981. He was a founder in 1969 of FMP, which sponsors performances and issues recordings of free jazz; around the same year, with Fred van Hove and Han Bennink, he formed a trio that incorporated into its performances elements of European folk music, African rhythms, and an anarchic brand of theater, and which influenced strongly the shape and direction of free jazz in Europe; among those who performed with the trio as guest soloists were Don Cherry and Albert Mangelsdorff. Around 1976 van Hove left the group; Brötzmann began to make recordings as an unaccompanied soloist and continued to work in a duo with Bennink, with which Misha Mengelberg also played occasionally, until 1979. Brötzmann later played in a trio with Harry Miller and Louis Moholo (1979–81), in duos with the drummer and vibraphonist Willi Kellers (1980) and Andrew Cyrille (1982), in a trio with Cyrille and Kowald (1984–5), and in such large ensembles as the Alarm Orchestra (1984). In 1986 he performed with Cecil Taylor in Berlin and was a member of Last Exit, a cooperative quartet with Sonny Sharrock, Bill Laswell, and Ronald Shannon Jackson. Brötzmann uses the entire range of his instrument, including its harmonics, to play long solos of great intensity. His playing shows the influence of such American jazzmen as Albert Ayler and Pharoah Sanders, but unlike these musicians his style does not have its roots in the blues.

SELECTED RECORDINGS

As unaccompanied soloist: *Solo* (1976, FMP 0360)

As leader: *Machine Gun* (1968, FMP 0090); with F. van Hove and H. Bennink: *The End* (1971, FMP 0050), *Brötzmann, van Hove, Bennink* (1973, FMP 0130); of Last Exit (with S. Sharrock, B. Laswell, and R. S. Jackson): *Last Exit* (1986, Enemy 101)

As sideman: Globe Unity Orchestra: *Globe Unity* (1966, Saba 15109); D. Cherry and Krzysztof Penderecki: *Actions* (1971, Phi. 6305153); Globe Unity Orchestra: *Evidence*, i (1975, FMP 0220)

BIBLIOGRAPHY

K. Knox: "Peter Brotzmann," *JM*, no.155 (1968), 15

W. Panke: "A Portrait of Peter Brotzmann," *JF* [intl edn], no.38 (1975), 47

H. L. Lindenmaier: "Peter Brötzmann: Interview," *Cadence*, iv/10 (1978), 3

B. Noglik: "Peter Brötzmann," *Jazzwerkstatt international* (Berlin, 1981), 190 [incl. interview, discography]

S. Lake: "Great Recordings: the Peter Brötzmann Octet," *The Wire*, no.13 (1985), 45 [review of *Machine Gun* (1968)]

B. Shoemaker: "Hal Bennink/Peter Brotzmann: First Entrances and Last Exits," *DB*, liv/1 (1987), 24 [incl. discography]

ROBERT J. IANNAPOLLO

Brown, Andrew (*b* 2 Feb 1900; *d* New York, Aug 1960). Bass saxophonist and reed player. He worked in the orchestra at the Cotton Club in New York from 1925 and remained with the band when it became the Missourians and came under the leadership of Cab Calloway in the late 1920s; he is probably the tenor saxophonist on its recording *Vine Street Drag* (1929, Vic. 38103). He traveled with the orchestra to Europe in 1934 and played under Calloway until 1945, when he opened a teaching studio in New York.

For illustration *see* CALLOWAY, CAB.

based on *ChiltonW*

Brown, Boyce [Brother Matthew] (*b* Chicago, 16 April 1910; *d* Hillsdale, nr Rock Island, IL, 30 Jan 1959). Alto saxophonist and clarinetist. He began his career at the age of 17 playing with a band led by the drummer Don Carter in Chicago. After working in New York in the early 1930s with the alto saxophonist Benny Meroff, he returned to Chicago to join Wingy Manone (1933), then played and recorded with the Friars Society Orchestra led by Paul Mares (1934–5). From 1936 until the mid-1940s he led his own small group at the Liberty Inn, Chicago, and at the same time recorded with the bands of Charlie LaVere (1935), Jimmy McPartland (1939), and Wild Bill Davison (1940). After working in a trio led by the pianist Chet Roble (1947–8) and with Danny Alvin (1949), he returned with his group to the Liberty Inn. In 1953 he entered a monastery and adopted the name Brother Matthew. He took his vows in February 1956 and, following the related publicity, returned briefly to jazz, recorded a fund-raising album with Eddie Condon (April 1956), and appeared in a jam session on television (May 1956).

SELECTED RECORDINGS

As leader: *Brother Matthew with Eddie Condon's Jazz Band* (1956, ABC–Para. 121)

As sideman: J. McPartland: The World is Waiting for the Sunrise (1939, Decca 18043)

BIBLIOGRAPHY

ChiltonW; *FeatherE*

C. M. Jacobsen: "The Saga of Boyce Brown," *Jazz Session*, [no.13] (July 1946), 14

B. Esposito: "Do you Remember Boyce Brown?" *JJ*, xxiv/5 (1971), 10

MIKE HAZELDINE

Brown, Brian (*b* Melbourne, Australia, 29 Dec 1933). Australian composer, tenor and soprano saxophonist, and bandleader. He was self-taught as a musician. He formed his first group, a quintet, in 1956, and this quickly became prominent in Australian experimental jazz. Later he led and composed for a number of ensembles, making eight albums between 1958 and 1986. He toured Europe with his Australian Jazz Ensemble (1978) and with various groups that performed experimental and newly composed classical works (1980–86). In 1981 Brown established a course in jazz at the Victorian College of the Arts, which he has continued to direct into the late 1980s. After playing both tenor and soprano saxophones he began to concentrate on soprano in the mid-1970s; he has also played flute. His phrasing and intensely lyrical tone are highly individual; these qualities may be heard to particular advantage on *In the Clouds*, from his album *Winged Messenger* (1986, AIJA 004), which also includes several pieces representative of his compositional style. Brown is an important figure in Australian jazz, committed to developing a national identity in improvised music.

BIBLIOGRAPHY

A. Bisset: *Black Roots, White Flowers: a History of Australian Jazz* (Sydney, 1979)

M. Williams: *The Australian Jazz Explosion* (London and elsewhere, 1981), 105

A. Jackson: "Brian Brown, still a Force," *Jazz: the Australasian Contemporary Music Magazine*, iii/2 (1983), 4

B. Johnson: "Brown, Brian," *The Oxford Companion to Australian Jazz* (Melbourne, Australia, 1987)

TONY GOULD

Brown, Cameron (Langdon) (*b* Detroit, 21 Dec 1945). Double bass player. After studying piano for six years he began playing double bass in his high school band. He attended Columbia University, where he belonged to a jazz quartet that won awards in intercollegiate competitions. He then performed and recorded in Europe with George Russell (1965), and while living in Stockholm for a year, played there with Don Cherry, Bill Barron, and Donald Byrd (all 1965-6). He taught at elementary level in New York (1969–72) before joining Beaver Harris and the pianist Hod O'Brien in the house band at St. James Infirmary, a New York club; the band accompanied, among others, Al Cohn, Zoot Sims, Charlie Rouse, and Chet Baker (all 1975). He recorded with Sheila Jordan (1975), toured Europe and recorded with Archie Shepp (1975–6, 1977), toured Europe and Japan with Art Blakey (1976), and toured and recorded with Harris (1979). He was a founder member of a quartet led by George Adams and Don Pullen (from 1979), played and recorded with Dannie Richmond's quintet (from 1980), and played again with Cherry (1986–7) and Shepp (1987).

Influenced by Paul Chambers, Jimmy Garrison, Charles Mingus, and Gary Peacock, Brown has developed an individual style in a small-group context. His full tone and impelling swing provide a solid underpinning for the often complex rhythmic interplay of Pullen and Richmond in the Adams–Pullen quartet; his facility and inventiveness as a soloist are heard to good effect on *Intentions* (1983, SN 1094), recorded by the quartet.

SELECTED RECORDINGS

As sideman with G. Adams and D. Pullen: *Live at the Village Vanguard* (1983, SN 1094, 1144), incl. Intentions; *Decisions* (1984, Tim. 205); *Breakthrough* (1986, BN 85122)

As sideman with others: G. Russell: *George Russell Sextet at Beethoven Hall* (1965, Saba 15059–60); S. Jordan: *Confirmation* (1975, EW 8024); B. Harris: *Beautiful Africa* (1979, Cadence 1002); D. Richmond: *Dionysius* (1984, Red 161)

BIBLIOGRAPHY

J. L. Ginibre and P. Carles: "Dictionnaire de la contrebasse," *Jm*, no.166 (1969), 27

C. L. Brown: "Puttin' it All Together Except a Place to Play it," *J&P*, ix/12 (1970), 36

C. Carriere and A. Terchinet: "De Archie Shepp à Art Blakey: Cameron Brown," *Jh*, no.337 (1977), 14

G. Rouy: "24 heures basse en main," *Jm*, no.327 (1984), 32

JOHN CURRY

Brown, Cleo(patra) (*b* Meridian, MS, 8 Dec 1909). Pianist and singer. She moved to Chicago with her family in 1919, and first played professionally at the age of 14 for a touring show. In the late 1920s she worked in and around Chicago, and later played regularly on radio (she had her own series on WABC). She led a group at the Three Deuces intermittently from the 1930s to the 1950s and also played regularly in New York and Hollywood. Her career was interrupted by illness from 1940 to 1942. She is perhaps best known for her recordings as the leader of a quartet (1935–6) that sometimes included Gene Krupa; *Boogie Woogie* (1935, Decca 477) helped to popularize the boogie-woogie style, which she is said to have learned from her brother, the pianist Everett Brown, who was a friend of Pine Top Smith. (*ChiltonW*; *FeatherE*)

Brown, Clifford [Brownie] (*b* Wilmington, DE, 30 Oct 1930; *d* Pennsylvania, 26 June 1956). Trumpeter. He took up trumpet at the age of 13, and under the tutelage of his band director at high school, Harry Andrews, developed an extraordinary technical facility. While studying mathematics at Delaware State College and music at Maryland State College he attracted attention through his exceptional performances with the college jazz bands and his brief appearances in Philadelphia with

Clifford Brown, early 1950s

such leading jazz musicians as Fats Navarro, Dizzy Gillespie, and Charlie Parker, all of whom praised and encouraged him. Navarro's style was particularly important as a model for Brown, and the two men formed a close friendship. Brown spent a year in the hospital after an automobile accident in June 1950, but thereafter resumed his career in Philadelphia, and in March 1952 made his first recordings, with Chris Powell's Blue Flames. He joined Tadd Dameron's band for a recording session (the results of which were later issued as *The Clifford Brown Memorial Album*) and for appearances in summer 1953 at Atlantic City, New Jersey. In September of that year Brown toured Europe with Lionel Hampton's big band and made a number of recordings with American and European jazz musicians; Hampton's trumpet section at the time consisted of Art Farmer, Quincy Jones, Walter Williams, and Brown, all of whom were superb players. On his return to the USA Brown performed with several East Coast groups, including a newly formed ensemble led by Art Blakey. In 1954, with Max Roach, he formed the Brown–Roach Quintet, with which he was associated until he was killed two years later in an automobile accident. The quintet, whose other members were Harold Land (replaced in December 1955 by Sonny Rollins), George Morrow, and Richie Powell, was one of the most significant groups of the 1950s, and had a major influence on the establishment of the style later known as hard bop.

Brown was one of the outstanding jazz trumpeters of the 1950s, and his reputation as an extraordinary improviser endures. His playing reflected a synthesis of certain stylistic aspects of Gillespie, Miles Davis, and Navarro; it was characterized by a rich, broad tone and a percussive attack, unusually long yet carefully shaped phrases, exceptional virtuosity, and a seemingly unending flow of logically developed musical ideas. The brilliantly impeccable technique he displayed in solos at fast tempos, which were projected with equal fluidity from the highest to the lowest register of his instrument, was complemented by the haunting, introspective lyricism that distinguished his performances of ballads. His most mature work was with the Brown–Roach Quintet, as reflected in the albums *Study in Brown* and *At Basin Street*. Brown's style exerted a pervasive influence on jazz improvisation in the 1960s and 1970s, and represented an alternative approach to the subdued manner of Davis. This influence may be seen most directly in the work of Lee Morgan and Freddie Hubbard.

See also TRUMPET, §5.

SELECTED RECORDINGS

As leader: with A. Farmer: *Swedish All-stars* (1953, Prst. 167); with M. Roach: *Study in Brown* (1955, EmA 36037), *At Basin Street* (1956, EmA 36070)

As sideman: C. Powell: Ida Red (1952, OK 6875); T. Dameron: *A Study in Dameronia* (1953, Prst. 159); A. Blakey: *A Night at Birdland* (1954, BN 5037–9); S. Rollins: *Sonny Rollins Plus Four* (1956, Prst. 7038)

BIBLIOGRAPHY

A. Hodeir: *Hommes et problèmes du jazz, suivi de La religion du jazz* (Paris, 1954; Eng. trans., rev. Hodeir, as *Jazz: its Evolution and Essence*, New York, 1956/R1975)
R. Atkins: "Clifford Brown," *JR*, ii/11 (1959), 24
——: "Clifford Brown," *JM*, vi/6 (1960), 4
M. Crawford: "Benny Remembers Clifford," *DB*, xxviii/21 (1961), 22
B. Gardner: "The Legacy of Clifford Brown," *DB*, xxviii/21 (1961), 17
A. Morgan: "Clifford Brown," *Jazz on Record: a Critical Guide to the First 50 Years: 1917–1967*, ed. A. McCarthy and others (London, 1968), 29
R. Bolton: "Clifford Brown," *JJ*, xxii/5 (1969), 6
J. G. Jepsen: "Clifford Brown: a Complete Discography," *Down Beat Music: 15th Yearbook* (1970), 109
M. L. Stewart: *Structural Development in the Jazz Improvisational Technique of Clifford Brown* (diss., U. of Michigan, 1973); pubd in *Jf*, vi–vii (1974–5), 141–273
C. Sheridan: "A Study in Brown," *JJ*, xxix/6 (1976), 4
M. L. Stewart: "Some Characteristics of Clifford Brown's Improvisational Style," *Jf*, xi (1979), 135
H. West: "Clifford Brown: Trumpeter's Training," *DB*, xlvii/7 (1980), 30
B. Weir: *Clifford Brown Discography* (Cardiff, 1982, rev. and enlarged 2/1983, rev. and enlarged 3/1984, rev. and enlarged 3[*recte* 4]/1986)

OLLY WILSON

Brown, Garnett(, Jr.) (*b* Memphis, 31 Jan 1936). Trombonist. After a year at college he played with Charles Lloyd, but his first major association was with Chico Hamilton, whom he joined in 1962. During the 1960s he taught at public schools in New York and worked with groups that played Latin music. He toured Sweden with George Russell (1964), and performed and recorded with the Thad Jones–Mel Lewis Orchestra (1966–8), Duke Pearson (1967–8), and Herbie Hancock (1970–72); he also performed at the Newport Jazz Festival with Billy Taylor (ii), Benny Carter, and others. In 1975 he moved to Los Angeles where he worked in theater orchestras and as a studio musician; he played on albums by the Capp–Pierce Juggernaut (1978) and Lionel Hampton (1981). Brown's playing is influenced by the work of Frank Rosolino, Jimmy Cleveland, J. J. Johnson, and Slide Hampton; he is a remarkably flexible player in many styles, including swing, bop, modal jazz, and jazz-rock; he has also composed and written arrangements for a variety of bands.

SELECTED RECORDINGS

As sideman: G. Russell: *The Outer View* (1962, Riv. 9440), incl. Au privave, You are my sunshine; C. Hamilton: *Drumfusion* (1962, Col. CS8607); H. Laws: *Flute By-Laws* (1965, Atl. 1452); B. Ervin: *Heavy!!* (1966, Prst. 7499); H. Hancock: *Fat Albert Rotunda* (*c*1970, WB 1834); B. Cobham: *Crosswinds* (1974, Atl. 7300)

BIBLIOGRAPHY

Feather '60s; *Feather–Gitler '70s*
A. J. Smith: "Garnett Brown's Slide down the Middle of the Road," *DB*, xlii/10 (1975), 19 [incl. discography]

LEROY OSTRANSKY

Brown, Gerry (*b c*1951). Drummer and leader. After conservatory training in Philadelphia in the early 1970s he traveled to Holland with John Lee in 1972. Together they toured Europe and recorded with Chris Hinze (1972–4) and Joachim Kühn (1974, 1976), recorded with Toots Thielemans and Charlie Mariano (both 1974) and Philip Catherine (1974, 1975), and led a jazz-rock group. Brown performed and recorded in New York with Stanley Clarke (1976) and Chick Corea (*Return to Forever Live*, 1977, Col. C4X35350). After recording again with Clarke in 1979 he returned to Europe, where he performed and recorded at the Montreux International Jazz Festival with Didier Lockwood, and toured France and Germany as a leader (both 1980). He also toured Japan with the trumpeter Terry Masson (1980) and recorded with Arthur Blythe (1984). He should not be confused with Gerald Brown (*b* Cincinnati, 20 April 1936), the drummer who worked with Roland Kirk from the late 1950s.

BIBLIOGRAPHY

M. Rosenstiehl and J.-F. Zermati: "Gerry Brown: un batteur, du bop . . . au funk," *Jh*, no.337 (1980), 17
R. Tolleson: "Portraits: Gerry Brown," *MD*, viii/6 (1984), 86

Brown, Jewel (Hazel) (*b* Houston, 30 Aug 1937). Singer. She studied piano from the age of seven. In 1957–8 she worked as a singer with the organist Earl Grant, then in 1961 joined Louis Armstrong, remaining with his band until 1968. She toured extensively and appeared at the Newport (1961) and Monterey (1965) jazz festivals and on television; she also appeared in the film *Louis Armstrong and the All Stars* (1961), and sings *My Man* with Armstrong in the film *Solo* (1965), directed by Jorn Winter. Her recordings with Armstrong include *The Best Live Concert* (1965, Festival 200). (*Feather '60s*)

Brown, John (Benjamin Peabody) (*b* Dayton, OH, 13 March 1906; *d* New York, 12 Aug 1987). Double bass player. He moved to New York in 1928, played violin and banjo in Herbert Cowens's Royal Garden Orchestra, and worked with Sam Wooding from 1932. In 1935 he took up double bass, then played with Snub Mosley (from 1936) and performed and recorded with Stuff Smith (1938–41) and Mosley (1941–2); at the same time he played with Wilbur De Paris and Cowens in the musical *The Pirate* in New York (1941–2). From 1945 to 1950 he worked principally with Claude Hopkins, first in his big band, then in a quartet that recorded. He took part in Fletcher Henderson's last recording sessions (1950), toured Europe with Mosley under the auspices of the USO (1952), rejoined Hopkins (1953), and played with Herman Chittison (1954). From 1955 and throughout the 1960s he belonged to Jonah Jones's quartet, with which he performed and made many recordings (including *Muted Jazz*, 1957, Cap. ST839).

based on *ChiltonW*

Brown, Lawrence (*b* Lawrence, KS, 3 Aug 1907). Trombonist. He grew up in California, and learned piano, violin, and tuba before concentrating on trombone, an instrument that attracted him because it could sound like a cello. He played with various bands on the West Coast, recording with Paul Howard's Quality Serenaders (1929–30) and Les Hite's band under the direction of Louis Armstrong (1930). Irving Mills recruited him for Duke Ellington's orchestra in 1932, and he was featured with that band for most of his career (for illustrations *see* BANDS, fig.3; TROMBONE; and TRUMPET); his solos in ballads, blues, and fast pieces were authoritative, and he was also a superb section leader. His work was marked by a beautiful and distinctive tone and he had a profound understanding of the needs of Ellington's highly idiosyncratic music. Brown was one of those who left Ellington in 1951 to work in a small band led by

Johnny Hodges. After leaving Hodges in 1955 Brown worked as a freelance in New York and as a studio musician for CBS. He rejoined Ellington in 1960 and again became one of the chief personalities in the band; during this period he added an adaptation of Tricky Sam Nanton's plunger-mute technique to his repertory of effects. Brown retired from music in 1970 and worked briefly for the government before retiring fully and settling in California in 1974.

Oral history material in *NjR* (JOHP).

SELECTED RECORDINGS

As sideman: D. Ellington: The Sheik of Araby (1932, Bruns. 6336); Ducky Wucky (1932, Bruns. 6432); Slippery Horn (1933, Bruns. 6527); Stompy Jones (1934, Vic. 24521); Rose of the Rio Grande (1938, Bruns. 8186); Across the Track Blues (1940, Vic. 27235); Golden Cress (1947, Col. 38236); On a Turquoise Cloud (1947, Col. 38254); J. Hodges: Used to be Duke (1954, Norg. 145); D. Ellington: *Hits of the '60s* (1964, Rep. 6122), incl. Never on Sunday

BIBLIOGRAPHY

V. Wilmer: "Lawrence Brown Talks to Valerie Wilmer," *JM*, xi/2 (1965), 18
S. Dance: *The World of Duke Ellington* (London and New York, 1970/*R*1981) [colln of previously pubd articles and interviews]
D. Ellington: *Music is my Mistress* (Garden City, NY, 1973), 122
G. Colombe: "How Do They Age so Well?, no.4: 'Lawrence, Dicky and Vic'," *JJ*, xxix/8 (1976), 4
L. D. Holmes and J. W. Thompson: *Jazz Greats: Getting Better with Age* (New York, 1986) [colln of interviews]

EDDIE LAMBERT

Brown, Les(ter Raymond) (*b* Reinerton, PA, 14 March 1912). Bandleader, arranger, and composer. He received his musical training at Ithaca College (1926–9), at the New York Military Academy (1929–32), and at Duke University (1932–6), where he also led his first dance band, the Duke Blue Devils (1935–6). After this band split up he worked as an arranger in New York, then in 1938 he formed a 12-piece dance orchestra. During the 1940s the group made many radio broadcasts, toured extensively, appeared in leading hotels, and had hit recordings with *Sentimental Journey* (1944, Col. 36769, with Doris Day) and *I've got my love to keep me warm* (1946, Col. 38324). Despite the band's orientation towards subdued dance music, Brown included several able jazz soloists within its ranks, including Abe Most (1939–42, *c*1949–1950), Ted Nash (1944–6), and Warren Covington (1945–6). 1947 marked the beginning of Brown's long association with Bob Hope, when he became music director for the entertainer's radio and television shows; with Hope he went on 16 Christmas tours around the world to entertain American troops. From the 1950s Brown's activities were centered on work for television in Hollywood, where with his "Band of Renown" he took part in such programs as "The Steve Allen Show" (1959–61) and "The Dean Martin Show" (1963–72). Dave Pell led an octet within the orchestra from 1953 to 1955. A collection of Brown's scores and other materials is held in the American Heritage Center of the University of Wyoming in Laramie; *see* LIBRARIES AND ARCHIVES, §2.

BIBLIOGRAPHY

G. T. Simon: *The Big Bands* (New York, 1967, rev. and enlarged 2/1971, rev. 3/1974, 4/1981), 99
C. Garrod: *Les Brown and his Orchestra, 1936–1952* (Spotswood, NJ, 1974, rev. and enlarged 2/1986 as *Les Brown and his Orchestra, 1936–1960* [discography]

MARK TUCKER/R

Brown, Marion(, Jr.) (*b* Atlanta, 8 Sept 1935). Alto saxophonist. He played reed instruments in high school and in army bands. He attended Clark College until 1965, then moved to New York and recorded with Archie Shepp and John Coltrane. In 1967 he formed the first of his own groups, and from 1968 to 1970 toured and recorded in Europe with Steve McCall, Ambrose Jackson, and Gunter Hampel. In 1970 he returned to the USA and began teaching African and Afro-American music at Bowdoin College; he also toured with Leo Smith. He studied ethnomusicology at Wesleyan University in the mid-1970s, and recorded as a leader (regularly from 1973) and with Hampel in Europe (1983). Brown was a major figure in the avant-garde movement of the mid- to late 1960s.

SELECTED RECORDINGS

Duos: *Duets: with Elliott Schwartz and Leo Smith* (1970, 1973 Ari. 1904)
As leader: *Afternoon of a Georgia Faun* (1970, ECM 1004); *Geechee Recollections* (1973, Imp. 9252); *Sweet Earth Flying* (1974, Imp. 9275)
As sideman: A. Shepp: *Fire Music* (1965, Imp. 86); J. Coltrane: *Ascension* (1965, Imp. 95)

BIBLIOGRAPHY

B. Quinn: "Marion Brown: Topside Underground," *DB*, xxxiv/3 (1967), 14
B. Palmer: "Marion Brown: Geechee Recollections in New England," *DB*, xli/4 (1974), 12
"Marion Brown," *SJ*, xxxii/13 (1978), 322 [discography]
M. Brown: *Recollections: Essays, Drawings, Miscellanea* (Frankfurt am Main, Germany, 1984)
H. de Craen and E. Janssens: *Marion Brown Discography* (Brussels, 1985)

DAVID G. SUCH

Brown, Marshall (Richard) (*b* Framingham, MA, 21 Dec 1920; *d* New York, 13 Dec 1983). Teacher, bandleader, and trombonist. He taught himself to play various instruments at an early age. After gaining a BS degree in music from New York University (1949) he directed high-school bands in the New York area (1949–57). His dance band from Farmingdale, the Dalers, played at the Newport Jazz Festival in 1957 to unprecedented acclaim, winning Brown international fame and an appointment to the Newport Festival board. He then toured Europe with George Wein to select members for the International Youth Band, which performed at the Brussels World's Fair and at Newport in 1958. In New York Brown organized the Newport Youth Band, which played at Newport and other festivals (1959–60). Many members of Brown's groups, such as Dusko Goykovic, Albert Mangelsdorff, George Gruntz, Gábor Szabó, Gil Cuppini, Eddie Gomez, and Jimmy Owens, have become well-known jazz artists. After the dissolution of the Newport Festival Corporation (1960) Brown played and recorded with Ruby Braff (1960–61), Pee Wee Russell (1961–2, 1965), Bobby Hackett (1964), and Lee Konitz (1966–7, 1971–4), and performed with the house bands at Eddie Condon's and Jimmy Ryan's clubs. He also continued to teach.

SELECTED RECORDINGS

As leader: of International Youth Band: *Newport 1958* (1958, Col. CL1246); of Newport Youth Band: *At the Newport Festival* (1959, Coral 57306); with R. Braff: *Ruby Braff–Marshall Brown Sextet* (1961, UA 4093)
As sideman: P. W. Russell: *New Groove* (1962, Col. CS8785); *Ask me Now!* (1965, Imp. 96)

BIBLIOGRAPHY

FeatherE; *Feather '60s*; *Feather–Gitler '70s*
G. Hoefer: "Newport Youth Band: Marshall Brown's Talent Incubator," *DB*, xxxiv/19 (1967), 19

STEVEN STRUNK

Brown, Olive (*b* St. Louis, 30 Aug 1922). Singer. She was brought up in Detroit, where in 1941 she sang in a revue with Todd Rhodes's orchestra. She performed in clubs with Earl Bostic and Cecil Scott (New York, 1943), Tiny Bradshaw (Chicago, 1943), and Ted Buckner (Detroit, 1944–7), among others, and she first recorded in 1949. After singing in Buffalo in the 1950s she worked in Texas (1958–60) and later in Toronto (1963–8), where she made another recording around 1964. From 1970 to 1973 she performed on riverboats based in St. Louis, after which she returned to Detroit and recorded her highly regarded album *The New Empress of the Blues* (1973, Jim Taylor Presents JTP103) with Buckner and J. C. Heard. She also worked with the New McKinney's Cotton Pickers and recorded with Don Ewell (1976). (S. Harris: *Blues Who's Who: a Biographical Dictionary of Blues Singers*, New Rochelle, NY, 1979)

HOWARD RYE

Brown, Oscar, Jr. (*b* Chicago, 10 Oct 1926). Singer and songwriter. He worked in a variety of jobs and became a professional singer and songwriter only in 1956. He collaborated with Max Roach on the album *We Insist! Freedom Now Suite* (1960, Can. 9002) and the same year recorded his own first album, *Sin and Soul* (Col. CS8377). He acted as host for the television series "Jazz Scene USA" (1962), performed in London with Annie Ross in the revue *Wham! Bam! Thank you Ma'am* (1963), and worked in clubs in New York, Los Angeles, and London with Jonah Jones, Dizzy Gillespie, and others. Brown is well known for adding lyrics to soul-jazz and modal-jazz themes, such as Nat Adderley's *Work Song* and Miles Davis's *All Blues*.

BIBLIOGRAPHY

Feather '60s
M. Aldred: "Oscar Brown," *Crescendo*, ii/1 (1963), 14
L. Barrett: "Oscar Brown, Junior," *JM*, ix/8 (1963), 12
A. Barnett: "Oscar Brown, Jr.," *JB*, ii/8 (1965), 16
P. Brand: "The Many Faces of Oscar Brown Jr.," *Crescendo*, iv/1 (1965), 29

Brown, Pete [James Ostend] (*b* Baltimore, 9 Nov 1906; *d* New York, 20 Sept 1963). Alto saxophonist. He worked in a variety of musical settings in Baltimore before moving to New York in 1927. After playing as a freelance in many New York bands he became, in 1937, an original member of John Kirby's group. A year later he left Kirby to lead his own bands, and subsequently held residencies at several clubs in New York, including Kelly's Stable and the Onyx; he also led a group with Frankie Newton (1940). Although ill-health curtailed his activities in the 1950s, he appeared at the Newport Jazz Festival in 1957 and continued to play into the 1960s.

Brown was a highly original musician whose terse, intensely rhythmic phrasing made him a central figure in the "jump band" movement that flourished in Harlem during the 1930s. His wheezy tone, and the seemingly inexhaustible flow of his cryptic improvisations, made his alto saxophone style instantly recognizable; he also recorded on trumpet and tenor saxophone. Brown might have been more famous had he accepted offers to play in big swing bands instead of preferring to work and record in small groups. Echoes of his saxophone phrasing were later heard in the work of many rhythm-and-blues players; his harsh, reedy sound was also much copied.

SELECTED RECORDINGS

As leader: It all depends on you (1944, Key. 1312)
As sideman: F. Newton: Please don't talk about me when I'm gone (1937, Var. 518); Willie "the Lion" Smith: The Old Stamping Ground (1937, Decca 1380); J. Noone: Four or Five Times (1937, Decca 1621); J. Marsala: Three o'Clock Jump (1940, General 3001)

BIBLIOGRAPHY

L. Feather: "Forgotten Man of Jazz," *MM*, xvi (28 Dec 1940), 3
G. Hoefer: "The Hot Box," *DB*, x/20 (1943), 16
W. H. Miller: "Jumpin' Pete," *Jazz*, i/7 (New York, 1943), 8
J. Postgate: "Pete Brown: a Casualty of Be-bop," *JJ*, xxix/4 (1976), 4

JOHN CHILTON

Brown, Pud [Albert] (*b* Wilmington, DE, 22 Jan 1917). Reed player and trumpeter. A member of a musical family, he toured with the family band from 1927 and played in theater orchestras in the early 1930s. He then moved to Chicago, where he worked with Bud Freeman, Jimmy Dorsey, the clarinetist Bud Jacobson, and the cornetist Pete Daily. After four years in Shreveport, Louisiana (1945–9), he moved to Los Angeles; he remained in California until 1973. As well as recording with Nappy Lamare (*c*1949, 1950), Jack Teagarden (1951–2), Kid Ory (1953), and Teddy Buckner (1958), he made broadcasts with Ory and also led his own band. His playing on both clarinet and tenor saxophone may be heard on the album *Lee Collins–Ralph Sutton's Jazzola Six*, i (1953, Rarities 31), taken from broadcasts made by a group at the Club Hangover, San Francisco. Brown began to double on cornet and trumpet in the early 1960s. From 1973, when he returned to Shreveport, he frequently played in New Orleans, notably with the guitarist and banjoist Les Muscutt at the Blue Angel in Bourbon Street. He recorded with his own all-star band, which included Dick Cary, Eddie Miller, Shelly Manne, and Lamare, in 1977. Besides his principal instruments, he has occasionally played double bass. In the 1980s he played clarinet regularly with Clive Wilson's Original Camellia Jazz Band in New Orleans, and in 1984–5 worked for six months in Singapore under the leadership of the drummer Trevor Richards.

based on *ChiltonW*

Brown, Ray(mond Matthews) (*b* Pittsburgh, 13 Oct 1926). Double bass player. He moved to New York around 1945 and immediately became part of the musical establishment. He took part in a number of early bop recording sessions with Charlie Parker, Dizzy Gillespie, Bud Powell, and others, and played in Gillespie's big band (1946–7). Thereafter he toured for several years as the music director for Ella Fitzgerald, who was at that time his wife. In 1951 he performed and recorded with the Milt Jackson Quartet (the forerunner of the Modern Jazz Quartet) and began a long affiliation with Oscar Peterson's trio (for illustration *see* PETERSON, OSCAR), which brought him international recognition and a popular following; for more than a decade he dominated jazz popularity polls for the double bass. Following the example of Oscar Pettiford, he took up the cello, and in 1960 he had made for him a hybrid instrument combining features of the cello and double bass, which was a forerunner of the PICCOLO BASS. After leaving Peterson's trio in 1966 Brown settled on the West Coast, where he became active as a freelance and studio musician, recording frequently for the Concord label; he made two albums of duos with Jimmie Rowles and at least nine albums with the L. A. FOUR. In 1972 he recorded an album with Duke Ellington, in which the two men re-created the latter's well-known performances of 1939–40 with Jimmy Blanton. In 1987 he toured in a trio with Gene Harris and Mickey Roker. Along with Pettiford and Charles Mingus, Brown has established himself as a leading bassist in the bop style; he is noted for the precision of his playing, the beauty of his tone, and the tastefulness of his solos.

SELECTED RECORDINGS

Duos: with D. Ellington: *This One's for Blanton* (1972, Pablo 2310721); with J. Rowles: *As Good as it Gets* (*c*1978, Conc. 66); *Tasty!* (1979, Conc. 122)
As leader: *Jazz Cello* (1960, Verve 68390); *Brown's Bag* (*c*1976, Conc. 19); of L. A. Four (with L. Almeida, B. Shank, and S. Manne): *Montage* (1981, Conc. 156); *Soular Energy* (1984, Conc. 268); *Don't Forget the Blues* (1985, Conc. 293)
As sideman: D. Gillespie: One Bass Hit (1946, Musi. 404); Two Bass Hit (1947, Vic. 20-2603); O. Peterson: *The Oscar Peterson Trio at the Stratford Shakespearean Festival* (1956, Verve 8024), incl. How High the Moon; *Porgy and Bess* (1959, Verve 8304), incl. I got plenty of nothin'

BIBLIOGRAPHY

M. Gaudry and M. Peynet: "This is Ray Brown," *Jh*, no.167 (1961), 28; no.168 (1961), 10
G. Lees: "In Walked Ray," *DB*, xxviii/18 (1961), 18
L. Feather: "The New Life of Ray Brown," *DB*, xxxiv/5 (1967), 24

J. Tracy: "Rhythm + Rosin = Royalty: Ray Brown," *DB*, xliii/2 (1976), 12
L. Lyons: "The L. A. Four: Journeymen United," *DB*, xliv/15 (1977), 18
M. Hennessey: "First Bass," *JJI*, xxxv (1982), no.7, p.8; no.8, p.10

J. BRADFORD ROBINSON

Brown, Sam(uel T.) (*b* St. Louis, 19 Jan 1939; *d* Bloomington, IN, 28 Dec 1977). Electric guitarist. He studied classical guitar before achieving prominence as a jazz session musician during the late 1960s and early 1970s. After touring with Astrud Gilberto (1965) and Ella Fitzgerald (1965–6) he recorded with Charlie Haden (1969), Richard Davis, Gary Burton, Ron Carter (1973), and, most notably, Keith Jarrett. From 1974 he played with Dave Matthews. Brown's approach to jazz was colored by his classical training, and his fertile harmonic imagination lent variety and sensitivity to his accompaniments. He was an excellent sight reader, and was therefore often in demand for pit orchestras and hastily organized recording sessions. Unfortunately his solos were often marred by his lack of familiarity with the relevant style, especially in his recordings with Jarrett of music that was inspired by gospel and rock, but in other contexts his simple melodic approach is heard to good effect.

SELECTED RECORDINGS

As sideman: G. Burton and K. Jarrett: *Gary Burton and Keith Jarrett* (1970, Atl. 1577); R. Davis: *The Philosophy of the Spiritual* (*c*1971, Cob. 9003); K. Jarrett: *Expectations* (1972, Col. KG31580); M. Murphy: *Bridging a Gap* (1972, Muse 5009); *Mark II* (1973, Muse 5041)

BIBLIOGRAPHY

Feather–Gitler '70s
Obituary, *DB*, xlv/4 (1978), 15

ANDREW WAGGONER

Brown, Sandy [Alexander] (*b* Izatnagar, nr Bareilly, India, 25 Feb 1929; *d* London, 15 March 1975). Scottish clarinetist and bandleader. He was self-taught, and from 1946 led his own band in Scotland, playing traditional jazz and swing. In 1954 he moved to London, where he played occasionally with Humphrey Lyttelton, Ken Colyer, and Chris Barber. He recorded frequently as a leader (1949–73) as well as under the name of his trumpeter Al Fairweather (1955–6, 1959–62), and with Sammy Price (1969), Brian Lemon (1970), and Phil Seamen (1971). In 1974 he recorded in the USA with Earle Warren. Brown's playing, notably on *Everybody Loves Saturday Night* (1955, Tempo EXA13), was strongly influenced by Johnny Dodds; his aggressive attack may be heard on *Fifty-fifty Blues* (1956, Tempo EXA49). Later, however, his work veered away from the traditional towards mainstream and jazz-rock (*Hair at its Hairiest*, 1968, Fon. 921). Brown was also author of *The McJazz Manuscripts* (London, 1979), a collection of essays and autobiographical notes.

BIBLIOGRAPHY

FeatherE
A. Morgan: "Sandy Brown: a Personal Tribute," *JJ*, xxviii/5 (1975), 10
G. Bielderman: *Sandy Brown Discography* (Zwolle, Netherlands, 1985)

Brown, Sonny [Gerald] (*b* Cincinnati, 20 April 1936). Drummer. He studied at the Cincinnati Conservatory, and first worked with Eddie "Cleanhead" Vinson and Dinah Washington. During the early 1950s he played with several gospel groups in the Midwest. After moving to New York in 1961 he performed with Frank Foster, Randy Weston, Ray Bryant, and Kenny Burrell; he worked with Jon Hendricks in 1963–4, and also played with Curtis Fuller, Coleman Hawkins, Sonny Rollins, and Charles Mingus. He was also a vital force in the later groups of Roland Kirk (with whom he had recorded in 1960). From 1968 Brown has performed with the New York Bass Violin Choir, and he has written an opera with its director, Bill Lee. In 1969 he recorded with Attila Zoller in a band that included Herbie Hancock, and the following year he toured Scandinavia with Joe Henderson and Ron Carter; he recorded with Zoller again in Munich in 1976. He has also devoted much of his time to teaching. Brown's drumming is characterized by a subtle attack that is more atmospheric than hard-driving. He prefers delicate timbres and communicates a strong sense of rhythm by ignoring the fixed pulse, a quality that made his playing particularly attractive to Kirk.

SELECTED RECORDINGS

As sideman: R. Kirk: *Introducing Roland Kirk* (1960, Argo 669); *Boogie-woogie String Along for Real* (1977, WB 3085); B. Lee: *New York Bass Violin Choir* (1980, SE 8003)

BIBLIOGRAPHY

Feather–Gitler '70s

ANDREW WAGGONER

Brown, Steve [Theodore] (*b* New Orleans, 13 Jan 1890; *d* Detroit, 15 Sept 1965). Double bass player, brother of Tom Brown. He played tuba, then double bass, in his brother's band and moved with it to Chicago in May 1915. There he joined the New Orleans Rhythm Kings, with whom he recorded in 1922. With Murphy Steinberg he played in the Original Memphis Melody Boys and the Midway Dance Orchestra (also known as the Midway Garden Orchestra) in 1923. He was a member of Jean Goldkette's orchestra from 1924 to 1927 and rejoined it in 1928 to make recordings, one of which (*That's just my way of forgetting you*, Vic. 21590) provides a fine example of Brown's ability to drive the playing of a big band. He also played in Paul Whiteman's band (1927–8) and for one season in Kansas City. In the 1930s and 1940s he worked in Detroit as a freelance player and bandleader. In 1950 he recorded as an additional member of the Frank Gillis Dixie Five.

For illustrations *see* BEIDERBECKE, BIX, and NEW ORLEANS RHYTHM KINGS.

BIBLIOGRAPHY

F. Gillis: "From Ragtime to Jazz: an Exclusive Interview of Steve Brown," *MR*, i/9 (1974), 1
R. M. Sudhalter, P. R. Evans, and W. Dean-Myatt: *Bix: Man & Legend* (New Rochelle, NY, and London, 1974), 172

based on *ChiltonW*

Brown, Ted [Theodore G.] (*b* Rochester, NY, 1 Dec 1927). Tenor saxophonist. He learned banjo and violin from his father, and an uncle taught him clarinet and tenor saxophone. After performing in army bands (1945–7) and undertaking various engagements in Hollywood (1947–8) he moved to New York to study with Lennie Tristano. He worked with Tristano and his associates Lee Konitz and Warne Marsh from 1955 to 1957, during which time he recorded as a leader (*Free Wheeling*, 1956, Van. 8515) and also with Ronnie Ball and in Hollywood with Marsh (*Jazz of Two Cities*, 1956, Imperial 9027). Brown then returned to New York, where he played in clubs. He recorded with Konitz in 1959 and again in 1976, when the two musicians led a quintet. Brown also led his own quartet during the late 1970s. (*FeatherE*)

Brown, Tom [Red] (*b* New Orleans, 3 June 1888; *d* New Orleans, 25 March 1958). Trombonist, brother of Steve Brown. He first played violin, then took up the trombone. After playing in Papa Jack Laine's Reliance Band he worked as a leader (from *c*1910); his group held an engagement in Chicago as Brown's Ragtime Band in 1915 and was said to be one of the first ensembles to play New Orleans jazz there. Later that year he formed a vaudeville group, the Five Rubes, in New York. It disbanded after a short time and he returned to Chicago; he again led his own groups and made recordings as a freelance in Chicago and New York. He worked with the bandleader Ray Miller in Chicago (*c*1922–3) and then moved back to New Orleans, where he performed and recorded with the cornetist Johnny Bayersdorffer (1924) and the pianist Norman Brownlee (1925), among others. In the 1930s he often played double bass and in the 1940s he worked as a freelance on double bass and trombone. He made recordings with Johnny Wiggs (1950, 1953) and as a leader with Wiggs and Harry Shields among his sidemen (1954, 1958, including *Tom Brown's Band from Dixie Land*, 1954, GHB 3).

Oral history material in *LNT*.

BIBLIOGRAPHY

ChiltonW; *FeatherE*
Obituary, *SL*, ix/3–4 (1958), 11

KARL KOENIG

Brown, Vernon [Brownie] (*b* Venice, IL, 6 Jan 1907; *d* Los Angeles, 18 May 1979). Trombonist. He was brought up in St. Louis and played there with Frankie Trumbauer (1925–6) before working as a freelance musician in Chicago. He played with Jean Goldkette (1928) and the violinist and bandleader Benny Meroff (1935), then moved to New York where he worked with Mezz Mezzrow (1937) and Benny Goodman (1937–40); although Goodman's band seldom gave the opportunity for a trombone solo, Brown's vigorous playing reached a wide audience on recordings such as *One o'Clock Jump* (1938). He left Goodman to join Artie Shaw in 1940, then played with Jan Savitt (1941), as a principal soloist in Muggsy Spanier's band (1941–2), and with the Casa Loma Orchestra (1943). Because of his prodigious technique he was in demand as a studio musician in New York, but his love of improvisation ensured that he also frequently took part in jazz sessions throughout the 1940s. After leading a band in Seattle (1950) he returned to studio work but occasionally undertook engagements with such musicians as Goodman (in Brussels and at the Newport Jazz Festival, 1958) and Tony Parenti (1963). After retiring from music he settled in Florida.

SELECTED RECORDINGS

As sideman: B. Goodman: *Carnegie Hall Concert* (1938, Col. SL160), incl. One o'Clock Jump; H. James: Lullaby in Rhythm (1938, Bruns. 8136); M. Spanier: Little David, play on your harp/Hesitating Blues (1942, Decca 4271); Billy Taylor (i): Carney-Val in Rhythm (1944, Key. 615); B. Freeman: Inside on the Southside/Town Hall Blues (1945, Key. 638); S. Bechet and M. Mezzrow: *Feetwarmers* (1947, Wax Shop 201); M. Powell: *Jam Session at Carnegie Hall* (1954, Col. CL557)

BIBLIOGRAPHY

ChiltonW; *FeatherE*

BRIAN PEERLESS

Browne, (Scoville) Toby (*b* Atlanta, 13 Oct 1915). Clarinetist and saxophonist. He first played with Junie Cobb in Chicago (*c*1929), then performed in a band led by the drummer Fred Avendorph (1931–2), and with Louis Armstrong (1933, 1935), Jesse Stone (1934), Jack Butler, Claude Hopkins (1936), Blanche Calloway (1937), Don Redman, Fats Waller, and Hot Lips Page (1939–41). He attended Chicago Musical College in 1938–9, and in 1943–4 studied with the classical clarinetist Simeon Bellison. Having worked with Lucky Millinder in 1942, he then formed his own quartet. After military service (1943–5) Browne played alto saxophone with Hopkins, joined Teddy Wilson's band at CBS, and later performed and recorded with Buck Clayton (1946–7). He then led his own band (1948–52, 1958–60), toured with Lionel Hampton (1956–7), and performed with Muggsy Spanier (1959–60); he continued playing into the 1980s. Browne is noted for his fluent technique and mellow tone, and his playing is influenced by the styles of Benny Goodman, Artie Shaw, Buddy DeFranco, and the classical clarinetist Reginald Kell.

Oral history material in *NNC*.

SELECTED RECORDINGS

As sideman: L. Armstrong: Basin Street Blues (1933, Vic. 24351); Snowball (1933, Vic. 24369); St. Louis Blues (1933, Vic. 24320); D. Redman: You ain't nowhere/About Rip Van Winkle (1940, Bb 10615); B. Clayton: Dawn Dance/It's Dizzy (1946, HRS 1024); L. Hampton: *Jazz Flamenco* (1956, RCA LPM1422)

BIBLIOGRAPHY

ChiltonW; *FeatherE*

RAYMOND J. GARIGLIO

Brownie (i). Nickname of VERNON BROWN.

Brownie (ii). Nickname of CLIFFORD BROWN.

Brubeck, Dave [David Warren] (*b* Concord, CA, 6 Dec 1920). Pianist, composer, and bandleader. He received early training in classical music from his mother, a pianist, and by the age of 13 he was performing professionally with local jazz groups. In 1941–2, while a music major at the College of the Pacific in Stockton, California, he led a 12-piece band; he also studied classical composition with Darius Milhaud at Mills College. During World War II he was sent to Europe to lead a service band (1944). After his discharge in 1946 he resumed his studies with Milhaud, and, with fellow students, founded the experimental Jazz Workshop Ensemble, which recorded in 1949 as the Dave Brubeck Octet. Also in 1949, with Cal Tjader and Norman Bates (whose place was later taken by Ron Crotty), he organized the Dave Brubeck Trio. This group existed until 1951, when, with the addition of Paul Desmond, Brubeck formed his first quartet. The "classic" Brubeck quartet was created when Brubeck and Desmond were joined by Joe Morello (1956) and Gene Wright (1958); this group remained together until 1967, when Brubeck disbanded it to concentrate on composing.

Brubeck's quartet was immensely popular on college campuses in the 1950s; the album *Jazz at Oberlin*, recorded in concert at that college in 1953, contains some of Brubeck's and especially Desmond's finest improvisations. In 1954, as a sign of his growing popularity, Brubeck's picture appeared on the cover of *Time* and he left Fantasy for Columbia Records. During the 1950s and 1960s he began experimenting with time signatures unusual in jazz, such as 5/4, 9/8, and 11/4. By 1959 he had recorded the first jazz instrumental piece to sell a million copies – Desmond's *Take Five* (in 5/4 meter), which was released with his own *Blue Rondo à la Turk* (in 9/8, grouped 2+2+2+3). Only Max Roach had preceded Brubeck in the successful integration of irregular meters and jazz forms.

Brubeck, who considers himself in essence "a composer who plays the piano," has written and, in some instances, recorded several large-scale compositions since the 1960s, including two ballets, a musical, an oratorio, four cantatas, a mass, and works for jazz group and orchestra, as well as many pieces for solo piano. In the 1970s he organized several new quartets which at various times included one or more of his sons: the keyboard player (David) Darius Brubeck (*b* San Francisco, 14 June 1947); the trombonist and electric bass guitarist Chris Brubeck (*b* Los Angeles, 19 March 1952); and the drummer and percussionist Danny (Daniel) Brubeck (*b* Oakland, CA, 4 May 1955). Brubeck has appeared at the Newport (1958, 1972, 1981), Monterey (1962, 1980), Concord (1982), and Kool jazz festivals, and performed at the White House (1964, 1981). During the 1950s and 1960s he was a frequent winner of popularity polls in *Down*

Dave Brubeck (piano) and Paul Desmond (alto saxophone) at Columbia's recording studios in New York, October 1954

Beat, *Metronome*, and other magazines. In 1976 Brubeck performed and recorded again with Desmond, Morello, and Wright to celebrate the 25th anniversary of the formation of his first quartet.

Oral history material in *CtY*.

SELECTED RECORDINGS

* – composed by Brubeck

AS LEADER

Dave Brubeck Octet (1949, Fan. 4019–20); Squeeze me/How High the Moon (1950, Fan. 515); *Jazz at College of the Pacific* (1953, Fan. 4054–5); *Jazz at Oberlin* (1953, Fan. 3245); *Jazz Goes to College* (1954, Col. B1940, B1943); *Jazz: Red Hot and Cool* (1954–5, Col. CL699), incl. *The Duke; *Brubeck Plays Brubeck* (1956, Col. CL878); *Jazz Impressions of Eurasia* (1958, Col. CL1251); *Time Out* (1959, Col. CL1397), incl. *Blue Rondo à la Turk, Take Five; **Dialogues for Jazz-combo and Orchestra* (1959, Col. CL1466)

Time Further Out (1961, Col. CS8490), incl. *It's a Raggy Waltz; *Jazz Impressions of Japan* (1964, Col. CS9012); *Jazz Impressions of New York* (1964, Col. CS9075); **Elementals for Jazzcombo, Orchestra and Baritone-solo* (1970, Decca 71081); *Adventures in Time* (1972, Col. CG30625); *Two Generations of Brubeck* (1973, Atl. 1645); *All the Things we are* (1973–4, Atl. 1684), incl. *In your own Sweet Way; *The Dave Brubeck Quartet 25th Anniversary Reunion* (1976, Hor. 714); *Concord on a Summer Night* (1982, Conc. 198)

OTHER

As unaccompanied soloist: *Solo Piano* (1957, Fan. 3259)

Duos with P. Desmond: *Brubeck and Desmond: Duets* (1975, Hor. 703)

BIBLIOGRAPHY

D. Brubeck: "Jazz Evolvement as Art Form," *DB*, xvii (1950), no.1, p.12; no.2, p.13

"Brubeck, Dave (W.)," *CBY 1956*

R. Gleason: "Dave Brubeck Remembers: 'They Said I was too Far out'," *DB*, xxiv/16 (1957), 17

I. Brubeck and D. Brubeck: "Jazz Perspective," *Jam Session: an Anthology of Jazz*, ed. R. Gleason (New York and London, 1958)

H. Brubeck: *Dave Brubeck* (New York, 1961) [BMI pubn; incl. discography]

L. Tomkins: "It's not Easy to Take Criticism – or Praise," *Crescendo*, i/6 (1963), 6 [interview]

L. Feather: "Dave Brubeck, Composer," *DB*, xxxiii/13 (1966), 18

D. Locke: "Early Dave," *JM*, xii/6 (1966), 2

Biography of Dave Brubeck (New York, 1972)

D. Morgenstern: "Two Generations of Brubecks: a Talk with Dave, Darius, and Chris," *DB*, xxxix/10 (1972), 12

L. Tomkins: "Dave Brubeck Today," *CI*, xi/5 (1972), 20 [interview]

A. J. Smith: "The Dave Brubeck Quartet: a Quarter of a Century Young," *DB*, xliii/6 (1976), 18 [interview]

C. J. Stuessy: *The Confluence of Jazz and Classical Music from 1950 to 1970* (diss., Eastman School, 1978), 296–320, 396ff

L. Tomkins: "The Diversified World of Dave Brubeck," *CI*, xviii/3 (1979), 20 [interview]

"Dave Brubeck," *SJ*, xxxiv/2 (1980), 164 [discography]

I. Storb: "Dave Brubeck, Komponist und Pianist," *Jf*, xiii (1981), 9–43 [incl. list of works]

L. Lyons: *The Great Jazz Pianists: Speaking of their Lives and Music* (New York, 1983), 102

RICHARD WANG

Bruce, Jack [John Symon Asher] (*b* Glasgow, 14 May 1943). Scottish bass player. After studying at the Royal Scottish Academy of Music and Drama in Glasgow he moved to London, where he played with Alexis Korner (1962–3) and the blues musicians Graham Bond (mid-1960s) and John Mayall (1965). Bruce is best known as the bass guitarist with the highly influential blues and rock group Cream, which was formed in 1966, but he also pursued a parallel career as a jazz musician, and early in the decade he worked with Dick Heckstall-Smith and Henry Lowther. After Cream disbanded in 1968 Bruce recorded his first album as a leader, *Things we Like*, which was oriented towards jazz; among his sidemen was John McLaughlin. Later in the 1960s he worked with Neil Ardley, Larry Coryell, Carla Bley, Michael Gibbs, and others, and in 1970 he joined McLaughlin in Tony Williams's group Lifetime. Thereafter he led his own bands, though he also worked with Charlie Mariano (1976), recorded with Soft Machine (1980), and played with Joachim Kühn (1986).

SELECTED RECORDINGS

As leader: *Things we Like* (1968, Pol. 2343033); *Harmony Row* (1971, Pol. 2310107)

As sideman: C. Bley: *Escalator over the Hill* (1968–71, JCOA EOTH); T. Williams: *Turn it Over* (1970, Pol. 244021); Kip Hanrahan: *Desire Develops an Edge* (1983, American Clave 1009)

BIBLIOGRAPHY

R. Williams: "Bruce: Just the World's Best Bass Guitarist," *MM* (17 Oct 1970), 9

M. C. King: "British Jazzmen, 10: Jack Bruce," *JJ*, xxiv/8 (1971), 26

A. Jones: "Bruce: a Journey Through the Past," *MM*, l (12 April 1975), 8

G. Roy: "Bruits & cris de Bruce," *Jm*, no.343 (1985), 29

G. Twigg: "Out of the Storm," *Guitarist*, iii/7 (1986), 60

MARK GILBERT

Bruder, Rudy [René] (*b* Brussels, 15 June 1914). Belgian pianist. In 1935 he played as a member of a band led by his father, Pierre Bruder. He performed and recorded from 1937 in an orchestra led by Jean Omer, with which he appeared at le Boeuf sur le Toit, Brussels, alongside Coleman Hawkins, Benny Carter, Bill Coleman, and Bobby Martin. Later he worked in Switzerland with Jean Robert (1941–2) and again with Omer, and from 1942 led his own group. Bruder made several recordings with Gus Deloof (1939–40, 1945–6) and as a leader (1941–2, 1946); his playing may be heard to advantage on *Rudy's Boogie* (1946, Victory 9009).

ROBERT PERNET

Bruford, Bill [William Scott] (*b* Sevenoaks, England, 17 May 1949). English drummer. He listened extensively to American jazz as a youth, and was later influenced by the English organist Graham Bond. In 1968 he formed the rock group Yes with the singer John Anderson and the electric bass guitarist Chris Squire; the ensemble's use of unusual and rapidly changing meters (suggesting the influence of Don Ellis) became highly popular. Thereafter Bruford worked with other rock groups, including King Crimson (1972–5), Gong, and Genesis. From 1978 to 1980 he led a jazz-rock band, Bruford, with the electric guitarist Allan Holdsworth, the electric bass guitarist Jeff Berlin, and the keyboard player Dave Stewart; the ensemble toured internationally and recorded three highly acclaimed albums. Later Bruford worked again with King Crimson (1980–84) and in a duo with the keyboard player Patrick Moraz. He is also a member of the jazz-rock group led by the electric guitarist David Torn, and has worked as a studio musician with Kazumi Watanabe, Jamaaladeen Tacuma (1983), and Al Di Meola (1983). From 1986 he has led his own quartet, Earthworks, with Django Bates, Iain Ballamy, and the bass player Mick Hutton.

SELECTED RECORDINGS

Feels Good to me (1978, Pol. 6149); *One of a Kind* (1979, Pol. 6205); *Gradually going Tornado* (c1980, Editions EG 44); *Music for Piano and Drums* (c1983, Editions EG 33); *Flags* (c1984, Editions EG 63); *Earthworks* (1986, Editions EG 48)

BIBLIOGRAPHY

M. Shore: "Bill Bruford," *MD*, iii/1 (1979), 9
S. K. Fish: "Bill Bruford," *MD*, vii/6 (1983), 8
A. Lange and C. Doherty: "Bill Bruford: a Drummer's Discipline," *DB*, li/2 (1984), 16 [incl. discography]
N. Coleman: "Bill Bruford: Don't Blame the Drummer," *The Wire*, no.37 (1987), 10

BILL MILKOWSKI

Brun, Philippe (*b* Paris, 29 April 1908). French trumpeter. He studied violin and taught himself to play trumpet. He performed with Gregor and with Danny Polo (intermittently from 1929), recorded with Ray Ventura's Collegians (1929), and played in London with the bands of Jack Hylton (1930–35), Bert Ambrose, and Fred Waring; in Paris he played with the group Jazz du Poste Parisien (1936), Ventura (1937–40), Django Reinhardt (1937), and Alix Combelle (1938), and between 1937 and 1940 made recordings as a leader (including *College Stomp/Harlem Swing*, 1937, Swing 15). In 1941–4 he worked in Switzerland with André Ekyan, Edmond Cohanier, Teddy Stauffer, and Eddie Brunner; later he played most often with his own bands. Brun is considered the first French trumpeter to merit comparison with players of international importance.

BIBLIOGRAPHY

"Les grandes figures du jazz," *Jazz tango*, no.6 (1931), 12
H. Panassié: "Cinq grandes figures du jazz français," *BHcF*, 1st ser., no.1 (1945), 4
[P. Brun]: "Philippe Brun," *Jh*, no.4 (1946), 6
M. Laplace: *Portraits of French Jazz Musicians* (Menden, Germany, 1985), 4

MICHEL LAPLACE

Brunies. Family of musicians, active principally in New Orleans. Henry Brunies, a baker who played violin, and his wife, Elizabeth, a pianist, had six sons and a daughter, all of whom were musical. The daughter, Ada, played guitar, and the oldest son, Rudy (1884–1955), played double bass, although he earned his living as a brewer. The second son, Richie (Richard) Brunies (*b* New Orleans, 29 Nov 1889; *d* New Orleans, 28 March 1961), played cornet in Fischer's Brass Band (1907–8) and also in Papa Jack Laine's Reliance Brass Band, where he was noted for his powerful tone.

(1) Henny [Henry] **Brunies** (*b* New Orleans, 1891; *d* New Orleans, 1932). Trombonist. He played in brass bands in New Orleans but also toured in California and performed and recorded in Chicago (1923–6) with a group led by his brother (2) Merritt Brunies. He was billed there as "the world's greatest jazz trombonist," and his youngest brother (4) Georg Brunis considered him the best musician in the family.

For selected recordings *see* (2) Merritt Brunies.

(2) Merritt Brunies (*b* New Orleans, 25 Dec 1895; *d* Biloxi, MS, 5 Feb 1973). Cornetist and trombonist. He led a band in New Orleans and Chicago from around 1916 to 1918 (*see* ORIGINAL NEW ORLEANS JAZZ BAND (i)), then in Chicago played cornet and led a band that succeeded the New Orleans Rhythm Kings at Friar's Inn. Around 1930 he returned to New Orleans and played trombone in various clubs, then settled in Biloxi, Mississippi, where from 1946 he played in the Brunies Brothers Dixieland Jazz Band. With his brother (1) Henny Brunies and Jules Cassard, he wrote the jazz standard *Angry*.

Oral history material in *LNT*.

SELECTED RECORDINGS

As leader: Angry/I weep over you (1924, Aut. 610); Flamin' Mamie/Hangin' Around (1926, OK 40579); with A. Brunies: *Brunies Brothers Dixieland Band* (1957, AM 651)

(3) Abbie [Albert] **Brunies** (*b* New Orleans, 19 Jan 1900; *d* Biloxi, MS, 2 Oct 1978). Cornetist. He was best known as the leader of the Halfway House Orchestra (1919–27), whose recording personnel in 1925 included Leon Roppolo. He also played in other clubs in New Orleans before moving around 1944 to Biloxi, where he led the Brunies Brothers Dixieland Jazz Band.

SELECTED RECORDINGS

As leader: Pussy Cat Rag/Barataria (1925, OK 40318); Maple Leaf Rag/Let me call you sweetheart (1925, Col. 476D); with M. Brunies: *Brunies Brothers Dixieland Band* (1957, AM 651)

(4) George(e Clarence) Brunis [Brunies] (*b* New Orleans, 6 Feb 1902; *d* Chicago, 19 Nov 1974). Trombonist. He shortened his name on the advice of a numerologist. By the age of eight he was playing alto horn in a family trio and with Papa Jack Laine's Reliance Brass Band; he changed to trombone when he was ten or eleven. About 1920 he went to Chicago, where he played in a band led by Paul Mares. After working on a Mississippi riverboat he joined Mares's Friars Society Orchestra, remaining with the band when it became known as the NEW ORLEANS RHYTHM KINGS. In 1924 Brunis began a long association with Ted Lewis, touring extensively and making a number of recordings. He became active in New York around 1935, playing at several clubs – in particular Nick's. He also joined Muggsy Spanier's Ragtime Band (1939; for illustration *see* SPANIER, MUGGSY) and played frequently with Art Hodes and Lewis, as well as with Eddie Condon. In late 1949 he returned to Chicago, where he led his own band and, from 1951 to 1959, held a residency at Club 1111. He also led groups in Madison, Wisconsin, and Cincinnati, and continued to play until the early 1970s.

Brunis was entirely self-taught and never learned to read music; he apparently did not practice and was known for his ability to play without warming up. His solo on *Tin Roof Blues* (a piece he wrote in collaboration with Mares and Leon Roppolo) demonstrates his lyrical style and the broad tone he produced over a wide range of the instrument.

SELECTED RECORDINGS

As leader: Ugly Chile/That Da Da Strain (1943, Com. 546)
As sideman: New Orleans Rhythm Kings: That's a Plenty/Tin Roof Blues (1923, Gen. 5105); M. Spanier: I wish I could shimmy like my sister Kate/Dipper Mouth Blues (1939, Bb 10506); Dinah/Black and Blue (1939, Bb 10682); W. B. Davison: That's a Plenty/Panama (1943, Com. 1511); All Star Stompers: *This is Jazz* (1947, Rarities 33), incl. Baby, won't you please come home

(5) Little Abbie [Albert] **Brunies** (*b* New Orleans, 1914; *d* New York, 12 Feb 1955). Drummer. He was a cousin of the Brunies brothers. He worked principally in New Orleans, but at the time of his death was playing with Sharkey Bonano's band in New York. In 1946 he made recordings with Irving Fazola, including *Bluin' the Blues/Original Dixieland One Step* (Vic. 40-0140).

Oral history material in *LNT*.

BIBLIOGRAPHY

ChiltonW

A. Lee: "Brunies Faked Magnificently," *Metronome*, lvii/2 (1941), 19

G. M. Erskine: "Last of the New Orleans Rhythm Kings," *DB*, xxix/10 (1962), 22

P. Van Vorst: "The Chicago Jazz Scene Saved," *MR*, i/3 (1974), 11

G. W. Kay: "George Brunies Comes Home," *SL*, xxvii (win. 1975), 3

M. Tovey: "Biloxi Clarinet: the Jules Galle Story," *Fn*, xv/1 (1983), 4

BILL RUSSELL

Brunner, Eddie [Eduard] (*b* Zurich, 19 July 1912; *d* Zurich, 18 July 1960). Swiss tenor saxophonist and clarinetist. After performing locally on piano, clarinet, and alto saxophone, he worked with the saxophonist René Dumont's orchestra in Berlin (1931) and recorded with the brothers Jack and Louis de Vries (1933), the violinist Marek Weber (1933), the GOLDENE SIEBEN (1936–7), and Louis Bacon (1939); he also made recordings as a leader, mainly on clarinet (including *Bagatelle*, 1938, Swing 41, one of his own compositions). He lived in Paris from 1936 to 1939 but on the outbreak of World War II he returned to Switzerland, where he joined Teddy Stauffer's Original Teddies as a tenor saxophone soloist. Stauffer left in 1941 and Brunner then led the group until it disbanded in 1947. He recorded prolifically in the 1940s, both with the Original Teddies and under his own name, and he also made a recording with Philippe Brun (1944). In 1948 he formed his own sextet. He continued to record through the 1950s and worked in radio and television. Brunner was the most important Swiss hot-jazz soloist of his time; his playing was influenced by Coleman Hawkins and Eddie Miller.

SELECTED RECORDINGS

As leader: Smoke-house Rhythm (1940, Col. ZZ1001); Old and New (1940, Col. ZZ1003); of the Original Teddies: Möni Stomp (1941, ES 4075); Swingin' with Benny Carter (1942, ES 4140)

BIBLIOGRAPHY

J.-R. Hippenmeyer: *Le jazz en Suisse, 1930–1970* (Yverdon, Switzerland, 1971)

J. Schütte and A. Stöcklin: *Teddy Stauffer: Discographie der Original Teddies (Teddy Stauffer und Eddie Brunner) und der kleinen Formationen mit Musikern der Teddies* (Menden, Germany, 1983)

RAINER E. LOTZ

Brunswick. Record company and label. The company was owned by a firm of piano manufacturers, Brunswick–Balke–Collender of Dubuque, Iowa. Records were first issued in 1916; four years later the company released its first discs manufactured using lateral cutting methods. Among the jazz musicians who recorded early for the company were the Original Memphis Five (under the pseudonym the Cotton Pickers) and Fletcher Henderson. Around November 1924 the company acquired VOCALION from the Aeolian Co.; it operated the two labels separately, but with considerable interchange of material and cataloguing. The resulting confusion of issues and matrix numbers continues to perplex discographers. Although it recorded such vaudeville blues singers as Rosa Henderson and Lena Wilson in 1923–4, Brunswick did not have a race series as such until the launch of its 7000s in March 1927. Like Vocalion's race catalogue, it was directed by Jack Capp; issue was particularly prolific towards the end of the decade under the supervision of J. Mayo Williams.

In Britain, issue of Brunswick's recordings began in 1923; the discs, manufactured by Cliftophone, Ltd., and bearing American issue numbers, were marketed by the Chappell Piano Co., Ltd. In 1927 the operation was transferred to the British Brunswick Company, formed by Count Anthony de Bosdari, then taken over by the Duophone and Unbreakable Record Co., Ltd., in August 1928. Trading ceased within a year, but the company released on the Duophone label a number of recordings made for, but never issued by, American Brunswick. These included items by Red Nichols. Among those who recorded material specifically for British Brunswick at this time was Fred Elizalde.

In April 1930 Warner Bros. bought Brunswick–Balke–Collender and moved the company headquarters from Chicago to New York, but in December the following year they sold it to Consolidated Film Industries, which already owned the AMERICAN RECORD COMPANY. Brunswick and ARC remained formally independent, but were effectively run as one organization (and have often been referred to collectively as ARC–BRC). The 7000 series was discontinued in July 1932. During the 1930s Brunswick's catalogue included work by some of the most important jazz musicians, including Duke Ellington (from 1932), Red Norvo and Mildred Bailey (both from 1933), and Teddy Wilson and Billie Holiday (both from 1935). In February 1938 ARC–BRC was bought by CBS, which in 1940 discontinued the label name Brunswick in favor of Columbia. In 1942 the Brunswick trademark was sold to Decca, which had already acquired the rights to Brunswick's pre-1932 catalogue and was using the name for its own issues in territories other than the USA. The Brunswick label was used in the USA by American Decca from 1944 for the 80000 series of reissues of early jazz, but otherwise was little used there until 1957, when it was revived, mainly for popular music. Brunswick's significance as a jazz label ended in 1967 when MCA, which by that date owned American Decca, adopted a policy of using its own name for issues outside the USA.

Warner Bros. revived the British label Brunswick in December 1930; in April 1932 the rights to use the trademark in Britain, and to issue there material recorded by American Brunswick, were purchased by British Decca. Companies using the Brunswick name also operated in several European countries, including France, where many sessions involving American expatriates were organized. In Germany the Deutsche Grammophon Gesellschaft established a Brunswick label in 1926; issues in the A100 series (1926–9) and the A7500 series (from 1928) included alternative takes of recordings made for Vocalion in the USA by King Oliver and others. In the late 1920s American Brunswick began pressing, specifically for issue in Germany, versions of recordings without the vocal part; of particular jazz interest are items by Red Nichols and King Oliver. After 1934, however, most of the European Brunswick companies began drawing their material from American Decca after its foundation. Many of these, especially those in Britain and Germany, remained active for many years; there were many important reissues of early jazz on German Brunswick in the 1950s and 1960s.

BIBLIOGRAPHY

E. Jackson and L. Hibbs: *Decca, Brunswick, Vocalion Encyclopedia of Swing* (London, 1941)

F. Dutton: "Brunswick Modern Rhythm Series," *Matrix*, no.50 (1963), 3

J. Godrich and R. M. W. Dixon: *Blues & Gospel Records, 1902–1942* (Hatch End, nr London, 1964, rev. 2/1969, rev. and enlarged 3/1982 as R. M. W. Dixon and J. Godrich: *Blues and Gospel Records, 1902–1943*), 20

P. Burgis: "Discs from Down Under," *Sv*, no.11 (1967), 4
J. Hayes: "Brunswick Special Series (Golden Era Jazz Series/Sepia Series)," *Matrix*, no.74 (1967), 3
R. M. W. Dixon and J. Godrich: *Recording the Blues* (London, 1970)
H. Sagawe: "A Glimpse of the Past: the Green Label German Brunswick A100 to A499 Series," *Sv*, no.42 (1972), 230
R. D. Kinkle: "Brunswick Numerical Listing," *The Complete Encyclopedia of Popular Music and Jazz, 1900–1950* (New Rochelle, NY, and Westport, CT, 1974), iv, 2199
F. Dutton: "Numbers Runners Blues," *Sv*, no.79 (1978), 8
B. Rust: *The American Record Label Book* (New Rochelle, NY, 1978), 47
F. Dutton: "Numbers Runners Blues, 2," *Sv*, no.106 (1983), 125
P. Pelletier: "The Brunswick Label," *Record Information*, no.3 (1984), 13
J. Hayes, B. Luxton, and D. Luxton: *English Brunswick 78/45 r.p.m. (0)1000 Series*, i: *Issues 1001 to 02000 (Dec 1930 to May 1935)*, Numerical Catalogue Listings, no.E1 (n.p., n.d.)

Brush. A fan of wire or plastic strands with a hollow or stick handle, used as an alternative to the drumstick; *see* DRUM SET, §§I, 8; II, 4, 6.

Bryan, Mike [Michael Neely] (*b* Byhalia, MS, 1916; *d* Los Angeles, 20 Aug 1972). Acoustic guitarist. He was self-taught. He played in the area around Memphis (1934) before joining Red Nichols in Chicago (1935). He led his own band in Mississippi (1938–9), then worked with Benny Goodman (1940–41), and played briefly in the big bands of Bob Chester, Artie Shaw, and Jan Savitt. After military service (1942–4) he performed and recorded (1945) with Slam Stewart and (with Dizzy Gillespie, Charlie Parker, and Don Byas) in Clyde Hart's octet; although Bryan was principally a rhythm guitarist, he occasionally played solos, one of which may be heard on Hart's *4-F Blues* (1945, Contl 6020). From 1945 to late 1946 he was again with Goodman, recording with both the orchestra and the sextet. He worked as a studio musician in California for several years, and later ran a music store in Los Angeles. He toured Vietnam with the singer Martha Raye shortly before his death. (*ChiltonW*; *FeatherE*; *Feather–Gitler '70s*)

Bryant, Bobby [Robert, Sr.] (*b* Hattiesburg, MS, 19 May 1934). Trumpeter. He played trumpet and tenor saxophone in school bands, then moved in 1952 to Chicago, where he studied classical trumpet at the Cosmopolitan School of Music. After graduating in 1957 he played in small groups and with Red Saunders, and led a band that accompanied the singer Billy Williams on tour. In 1960 he recorded in New York as a member of big bands accompanying Johnny Griffin and Eddie "Lockjaw" Davis. He moved to Los Angeles in 1961, then toured internationally until 1965 as a lead trumpeter with the singer Vic Damone. He also recorded with Charles Mingus (at the Monterey Jazz Festival, 1964) and Oliver Nelson (1966–*c*1969). In the late 1960s he led his own sextet and big band, and from that time he has made several recordings with Gerald Wilson (1967–8, 1970, 1981). In the 1980s he has worked as a freelance with the Capp–Pierce Juggernaut and other groups. Bryant is a versatile musician who has been said to blend elements of the styles of Maynard Ferguson, Cat Anderson, and Don Ellis. He is an accomplished high-note player, and his tone resembles that of Fats Navarro, although it is not quite as full. His son, Robert Bryant, Jr., is a tenor saxophonist.

SELECTED RECORDINGS

As leader: *Swahili Strut* (1967, Cadet 50011); *Ain't Doing too B-A-D, Bad* (1967, Cadet 795); *The Jazz Excursion into Hair* (1968, PJ 20159)
As sideman: Z. Sims: *Passion Flower* (1979, PT 2312120); G. Wilson: *Lomelin* (1981, Dis. 833)

BIBLIOGRAPHY

Feather–Gitler '70s
H. Siders: "Jazz from 9 till 2 only," *DB*, xxxiv/2 (1967), 20
S. Jones: "Bobby Bryant's Hattiesburg Happenings," *DB*, xxxvii/18 (1970), 16

ROBERT DICKOW

Bryant, Ray [Raphael] (*b* Philadelphia, 24 Dec 1931). Pianist and composer, brother of Tommy Bryant. He began playing jazz piano at the age of 14. As house pianist at the Blue Note, Philadelphia (from 1953), he accompanied Charlie Parker, Miles Davis, Lester Young, Sonny Rollins, and others. He toured with Carmen McRae (1956–7) and Jo Jones (1958) and performed and recorded with Coleman Hawkins at the Newport Jazz Festival (1957). In 1959 he settled in New York, where he played with Rollins, Charlie Shavers, and Curtis Fuller. In the 1960s Bryant worked with his own trio and as an unaccompanied soloist. He has recorded with a large number of musicians, including Ella Fitzgerald, Davis (1955), and Dizzy Gillespie (1957). He traveled regularly to Europe during the 1970s and he has continued to perform and record with such musicians as Zoot Sims (1976) and Benny Carter (1977).

Bryant made a very successful recording of his composition *Little Susie* (1959). Among his other compositions are *Blues Changes* and *Cubano Chant*, which was also recorded by several other musicians, including Oscar Peterson and Art Taylor. In his solo playing, which is well represented by his two recorded versions of *Take the "A" Train* (1976, 1977), he often plays blues figures in the right hand against stride or boogie-woogie patterns in the left. On his recordings as an accompanist the influence of blues and boogie-woogie is less strong and he plays in a variety of styles.

SELECTED RECORDINGS

As unaccompanied soloist: *Alone with the Blues* (1958, NewJ 8213); *Alone at Montreux* (1972, Atl. 1626); *Solo Flight* (1976, Pablo 2310798), incl. Take the "A" Train; *Montreux '77* (1977, PL 2308201), incl. Take the "A" Train
As leader: *Ray Bryant Trio* (1957, Prst. 7098)
As sideman: S. Rollins: *Worktime* (1955, Prst. 7020); D. Gillespie: *The Greatest Trumpet of them All* (1957, Verve 8352); D. Gillespie, S. Rollins, and S. Stitt: *Sonny Side Up* (1957, Verve 8262)

RECORDED COMPOSITIONS
(*selective list*)

As leader: on *Ray Bryant Trio* (1956, Epic 3279), Cubano Chant; Little Susie (1959, Sig. 12026)
As sideman: on M. Davis: *Milt and Miles* (1955, Prst. 7034), Blues Changes

BIBLIOGRAPHY

FeatherE; *Feather '60s*
N. Hentoff: "Introducing Ray Bryant," *JR*, iii/3 (1960), 18
O. Keller: "Encore un jeune jazzman . . . Ray Bryant," *BHcF*, no.95 (1960), 3
"Ray Bryant," *SJ*, xxvii/14 (1973), 280 [discography]
S. Klett: "Ray Bryant: Interview," *Cadence*, v/8 (1979), 13
R. Palmer: "Pianos in the Background," *JJI*, xxxvii/6 (1984), 12 [incl. discography]

STEVE LARSON

Bryant, Tommy [Thomas] (*b* Philadelphia, 21 May 1930; *d* Philadelphia, 3 Jan 1982). Double bass player, brother of Ray Bryant. He began learning double bass at the age of 12 and later performed in Philadelphia with local groups and visiting jazz musicians. From 1949 to 1952 he worked with Elmer Snowden, with whom he later recorded (1960). He performed and made recordings with Jo Jones (1958–9) and Charlie Shavers (1959–63) and during the 1960s he played intermittently in his brother's trio. From 1972 until his death he worked with the popular vocal group the Ink Spots as a double bass player and singer. Bryant's playing may be heard on *Sonny Side Up*

(1957, Verve 8262), a recording led by Dizzy Gillespie, Sonny Rollins, and Sonny Stitt. (*FeatherE*)

STEVE LARSON

Bryant, Willie [William Steven] (*b* New Orleans, 30 Aug 1908; *d* Los Angeles, 9 Feb 1964). Bandleader and singer. He began his career as a soft-shoe dancer in 1926 and toured extensively as a dancer and singer until 1933. From 1934 to 1938 and again from 1945 to 1948 he led his own big band, which at times included Benny Carter, Teddy Wilson, Ben Webster, Cozy Cole, and Taft Jordan. The band's compelling swing may be heard on *A Viper's Moan* and Bryant's sentimental style of singing on his own composition *It's over because we're through* (both 1935, Vic. 24858). Bryant later worked as master of ceremonies for radio broadcasts from the Apollo Theater in New York, and as a disc jockey, an actor, and a radio announcer.

BIBLIOGRAPHY

ChiltonW
A. McCarthy: *Big Band Jazz* (New York and London, 1974), 275

Bryden, Beryl (Audrey) (*b* Norwich, England, 11 May 1926). English singer. Soon after leaving school she organized jazz clubs in Cambridge and Norwich, then moved to London in 1945. She began singing part-time, working with the bands of George Webb, Freddy Randall, Cy Laurie, Chris Barber, Monty Sunshine, Alex Welsh, and others. In 1952 she met Maxim Saury, and with his assistance she began a career as a full-time musician. She worked at clubs in Paris during the summer of 1953. In the mid-1950s she sang in the Netherlands with the Dixieland Pipers and in Germany with Fatty George, then returned to England towards the end of the decade. Thereafter she performed, recorded, made frequent radio broadcasts, and toured the Far East (1963) and Africa (1972). Bryden has continued to record prolifically with many different ensembles in several countries; the album *Down Yonder in New Orleans* (1975, ES 514) offers good examples of her work. She is also an experienced photographer of jazz subjects.

BIBLIOGRAPHY

Feather–Gitler '70s
G. Bielderman: *Beryl Bryden: Discography, Biography* (Zwolle, Netherlands, 1979, rev. and enlarged 4/1985)
D. Fairweather: "Bryden, Beryl," in I. Carr, D. Fairweather, and B. Priestley: *Jazz: the Essential Companion* (London, 1987)

CLARRIE HENLEY

Bubbles, John (W.) [Sublett, John "Bubber"] (*b* Louisville, KY, 1902; *d* Baldwin Hills, CA, 1984). Singer and tap-dancer. Around 1912 he formed a vaudeville duo, Buck and Bubbles, with Buck Washington, which remained active until 1953. In the early 1920s he created a new dance style which later became known as "rhythm tap"; this brought him considerable success at the Hoofers Club in Harlem. Although in the early part of his career he used his given name, he later became known as John Bubbles. His most important appearance in a Broadway show was with the *Ziegfeld Follies of 1931*, and in 1935 he took the role of Sportin' Life in Gershwin's *Porgy and Bess*. Buck and Bubbles recorded for Columbia between 1927 and 1933; later they made recordings for the same company in London, including *Breakfast in Harlem* (1936, Col. FB1524). Bubbles appeared in several films (including *Cabin in the Sky*, 1942) during the 1940s, and in the following decade he performed frequently on television. Some of his routines are recorded on the LP *Bubbles, John W. that is* (1964, VJ 1109). He remained active until shortly before his death; he appeared in the film *No Maps on my Taps* (1978), and recorded in a duo with the pianist Frank Owens (1980).

Oral history material in *NjR* (JOHP).

BIBLIOGRAPHY

M. Stearns and J. Stearns: *Jazz Dance: the Story of American Vernacular Dance* (London, 1968)
H. T. Sampson: *Blacks in Black and White: a Source Book on Black Films* (Metuchen, NJ, 1977)
F. Driggs and H. Lewine: *Black Beauty, White Heat: a Pictorial History of Classic Jazz, 1920–1950* (New York, 1982)

RAINER E. LOTZ

Buck and Bubbles. Duo formed around 1912 by John Sublett (who took the name JOHN BUBBLES) and BUCK WASHINGTON.

Bucket mute. *See* MUTE, §2(g).

Bucking contest. *See* CUTTING CONTEST.

Buckner, Milt(on Brent) (*b* St. Louis, 10 July 1915; *d* Chicago, 27 July 1977). Pianist and organist, brother of Ted Buckner. He grew up in Detroit and while in his early teens gained experience playing with local groups. In 1932 he joined the band led by the drummer Don Cox and began to experiment with patterned parallel chords; Buckner was the first pianist to employ this technique, which later became known as the "locked hands" style. He served briefly as staff arranger for McKinney's Cotton Pickers in 1934 and continued to work in and around Detroit, often with Cox or the saxophonist Jimmy Raschel, until joining Lionel Hampton's band as pianist and arranger in November 1941. His association with Hampton brought him considerable prominence and many recording opportunities. Buckner formed his own short-lived big band in 1948, then from 1950 to 1952 spent a further period with Hampton; during this period he changed to organ, the instrument he played for the remainder of his career. Thereafter he led his own small groups, with which he toured extensively and recorded regularly. He began to work in Europe from the late 1960s, often with Jo Jones or in trios led by Illinois Jacquet, and continued to record frequently, occasionally with Hampton. Buckner's originality was most evident in his performances on piano, but as an organist he invariably lent a group drive and swing. He also played valve trombone and vibraphone. His work as an arranger was highly regarded.

SELECTED RECORDINGS

As leader: M. B. Blues (1949, MGM 10504); *Rockin' with Milt* (1955, Cap. T642); with B. Tate: *Milt Buckner* (1967, BB 33013), *Crazy Rhythm* (1967–8, BB 33018); *More Chords* (1969, MPS 15237)
As sideman: L. Hampton: Three Minutes on 52nd Street (1947, Decca 24429); I. Jacquet: *Genius at Work* (1971, BL 146); *Jacquet's Street* (1976, BB 33112); L. Hampton: *Blues in Toulouse* (1977, BB 33130)

SELECTED ARRANGEMENTS
(all recorded by L. Hampton)

Nola (1941, Decca 18285); The Lamplighter (1944, Decca 18910); Hawk's Nest (1947, Decca 24505)

BIBLIOGRAPHY

B. Fulford: "Milt Buckner," *DB*, xxii/12 (1955), 13
M. Jones: "The Spirit of St. Louis Swings on," *MM*, xliv (24 May 1969), 8
A. Persiany: "Milt Buckner," *BHcF*, no.190 (1969), 3
P. Vacher: "The Milt Buckner Story," *J&B*, ii/9 (1972), 15
L. Tomkins: "Milt Buckner," *CI*, xi/9 (1973), 8
A. Balalas: "Milton Buckner (1915–1977)," *BHcF*, no.261 (1977), 3
A. Offstein: "The Milt Buckner Interview," *Coda*, no.154 (1977), 2
G. Endress: *Jazz Podium: Musiker über sich selbst* (Stuttgart, Germany, 1980)

PETER VACHER

Buckner, Ted [Theodore Guy] (*b* St. Louis, 14 Dec 1913; *d* Detroit, 12 April 1976). Alto and soprano saxophonist, brother of Milt Buckner. His formative years were spent in Detroit, where he performed with local bands and played with McKinney's Cotton Pickers. He enjoyed his greatest renown during the period he spent with Jimmie Lunceford's orchestra (1937–43; for illustration *see* LUNCEFORD, JIMMIE), where he was considered an excellent section player (on alto saxophone) and an able soloist. Thereafter he worked with small groups in and around Detroit, though he made tours of Europe in 1975 and 1976. He took part in a number of commercial recording sessions for the Motown label, directed his own groups, and, with the trombonist Jimmy Wilkins (brother of Ernie Wilkins), led a big band. He continued to perform, appearing with the New McKinney's Cotton Pickers, until his death.

SELECTED RECORDINGS

As sideman with J. Lunceford: Margie (1938, Decca 1617); 'Tain't what you do (1939, Voc./OK 4582); Ain't she sweet? (1939, Voc./OK 4875); Well, all right then (1939, Voc./OK 4887)

BIBLIOGRAPHY

ChiltonW
J. Chilton: *McKinney's Music: A Bio-discography of McKinney's Cotton Pickers* (London, 1978)

PETER VACHER

Buckner, Teddy [John Edward] (*b* Sherman, TX, 16 July 1909). Trumpeter and singer. In the early 1920s he settled on the West Coast, where he worked with a number of leaders, including Speed Webb. He then performed in Shanghai, China, as a member of Buck Clayton's orchestra (1934). After returning to Los Angeles he joined Lionel Hampton's band, of which he became leader when Hampton left (1936), and worked with Benny Carter (1943–*c*1945, 1948), Hampton (1947–8), and Kid Ory (1949–54). From 1955 Buckner performed and recorded with his own group, choosing musicians who were able to perform New Orleans jazz; his sideman included Sammy Price, Trummy Young, J. C. Heard, Albert Nicholas, and Edmond Hall. He also played with Sidney Bechet in Europe in 1958. He may be heard on the soundtracks to many films, in some of which he also appeared; he was Louis Armstrong's stand-in during the making of *Pennies from Heaven* (1936) and *Louis Armstrong: Chicago Style* (1975). Buckner's forceful and enthusiastic trumpet style was influenced by Armstrong. He has continued to perform as a leader into the early 1980s, and his many recordings provide particularly fine examples of the work of a New Orleans revival group.

SELECTED RECORDINGS

As leader: *An Evening with Teddy Buckner* (1978, Real Jazz 2521)
As sideman with K. Ory: Milenberg Joys/Creole Love Call/Bucket's got a hole in it (1953, GTJ 1041) [EP]; *Kid Ory Plays W. C. Handy* (1959, Verve 6061)

BIBLIOGRAPHY

ChiltonW; *FeatherE*; *Feather '60s*; *Feather–Gitler '70s*
J. Darensbourg: *Telling it Like it is*, ed. P. Vacher (London, 1987; Baton Rouge, LA, 1987, as *Jazz Odyssey: the Autobiography of Joe Darensbourg*)

JOHNNY SIMMEN

Buddle, Errol (Leslie) (*b* Adelaide, Australia, 29 April 1928). Australian reed player. He played in Adelaide (1945–7), then worked with Jack Brokensha's group in Melbourne (until 1949). After moving to Canada in 1952 he became the first Australian to play often with major American jazz musicians; he worked with Elvin Jones, Pepper Adams, Tommy Flanagan, and others. In 1954 with Brokensha and Bryce Rohde he founded the Australian Jazz Quartet, which recorded prolifically and played frequently in the USA. Buddle was the first musician to use the bassoon extensively in jazz. He returned to Australia in 1958 and has continued to perform and record with a variety of musicians. His fluent tenor saxophone style and facility for doubling on several instruments may be heard to advantage on *Buddle's Doubles* (1977, M7 216).

BIBLIOGRAPHY

A. Bisset: *Black Boots, White Flowers: a History of Jazz in Australia* (Sydney, 1979)
E. Myers: "Errol Buddle and the A.J.Q.," *Jazz: the Australasian Contemporary Music Magazine*, iii/1 (1983), 22
——: "Errol Buddle: Back Home in Australia," *Jazz: the Australasian Contemporary Music Magazine*, iii/3 (1983), 24
B. Johnson: "Buddle, Errol," *The Oxford Companion to Australian Jazz* (Melbourne, Australia, 1987)

JEFF PRESSING (with JOHN WHITEOAK)

Buddy. Record label. It was established by the Buddy Phonograph Company in about 1923 and existed for some three years. On it were issued recordings produced by Gennett and derived from that company's catalogue; these included titles by the New Orleans Rhythm Kings, Jelly Roll Morton, and Duke Ellington. It is believed that the recordings were not actually offered for sale, but distributed free to purchasers of Buddy phonographs. (J. Godrich: "A Glimpse of the Past, 10: Buddy," *Sv*, no.18 (1968), 10)

Budimir, Dennis (Matthew) (*b* Los Angeles, 20 June 1938). Electric guitarist. After first studying piano he took up guitar in 1948, and worked professionally in Los Angeles from 1952. He played with big bands led by Ken Hanna (1955), Keith Williams (1957–8), and Harry James (1958). By 1959 he had joined Chico Hamilton's quintet, in which Eric Dolphy was also a sideman; he then worked with Bud Shank and as an accompanist for Peggy Lee (both 1960–61). After serving in the army (1961–3) he returned to Los Angeles, where he was much in demand as a studio guitarist. He worked with the singer Julie London, and toured Japan with the pianist Bobby Troup (1963), then performed in and around Los Angeles with Shank and Emil Richards. Highly respected as a session musician, he played with Quincy Jones (1972), Lalo Schifrin, Don Ellis, and Marty Paich, among others. He also recorded with Milt Jackson (1976, 1978, 1981). Budimir produces an authoritative pulse on rhythm guitar, and acknowledges the influence of Jimmy Raney and Tal Farlow, although he favors a harder tone. Several of his own recordings demonstrate his spare, lean, yet highly inventive style of improvisation.

SELECTED RECORDINGS

As unaccompanied soloist: *Alone Together* (1964, Rev. 1) [incl. 2 duos with G. Foster]
As leader: *A Second Coming* (1964, Rev. 4); *Sprung Free* (1964, Rev. 8); *The Session with Albert* (1964, Rev. 14)
As sideman: H. James: *The New James* (1958, Cap. T1037); C. Hamilton: *Gongs East* (1958, WP 1271); B. Shank: *New Groove* (1961, PJ 21)

BIBLIOGRAPHY

FeatherE; *Feather '60s*; *Feather–Gitler '70s*

NORMAN MONGAN

Budwig, Monty (Rex) (*b* Pender, NE, 26 Dec 1929). Double bass player. He began studying double bass in high school and in 1951 worked with Vido Musso. He spent three years in an air force band, then moved to Los Angeles, where he played with Barney Kessel, Zoot Sims, and Red Norvo's trio (1954–5). In autumn 1955 Budwig performed with Woody Herman's group in Las Vegas and later joined Herman's big band; he recorded with both ensembles (1955–6). In 1957 he began an association with Shelly Manne that continued intermittently into the late 1970s. From the 1960s, however, Budwig worked mainly as a freelance at studios and nightclubs in California. He also made international tours with Benny Goodman (1964, 1973) and Carmen McRae (1974). In 1975 he became a house musician for the Concord record company, and by the mid-1980s had recorded more than 30 albums. He is a strong player whose solid timekeeping has made him much in demand.

SELECTED RECORDINGS

As leader: *Dig* (1978, Conc. 79)

As sideman: W. Herman: *Jackpot* (1955, Cap. T748), incl. Bass Face; S. Rogers: *Portrait of Shorty* (1957, RCA LPM1561); S. Manne: *At the Blackhawk* (1959, Cont. 3577); *Perk Up* (1976, Conc. 21); B. Kessel: *Soaring* (1976, Conc. 33); S. Getz: *The Dolphin* (1981, Conc. 158)

BIBLIOGRAPHY

FeatherE; *Feather '60s*; *Feather–Gitler '70s*

"Annuaire biographique de la contrebasse," *Jm*, no.94 (1963), 24

BRENDA PENNELL

Bullock, Chick [Charles] (*b* Butte, MT, 16 Sept 1908; *d* California, 15 Sept 1981). Singer. He began singing in a vaudeville theater to accompany the projection of series of photographs and also took small acting roles in silent films. Success with his first recording coupled with a disfiguring eye ailment caused him to concentrate on radio and recording work. Between 1930 and 1941 he made over 4000 recordings, many as leader of his studio band, the Levee Loungers. Among the sidemen in this group at various times were several major jazz musicians, including Bunny Berigan, Bill Coleman, Jack Teagarden, the Dorsey brothers, Joe Venuti, and Eddie Lang; *Back Home Again in Indiana* (1940, OK 6261) is a particularly good example of a fine ensemble. Bullock also recorded as a sideman with others, notably Duke Ellington (1931). In the mid-1940s, he retired from music and moved to the West Coast.

BIBLIOGRAPHY

N. Skrimshire: "Junkshoppers' Three Bs," *Sv*, no.13 (1967), 16

P. Tanner: "Chick Bullock: Leader of the Levee Loungers," *JJ*, xxvii/6 (1974), 4

P. Murphy: *Chick Bullock: a Discography of his Recordings* (Melbourne, Australia, 1983)

Bull's Head. Pub in Barnes, London; *see* NIGHTCLUBS AND OTHER VENUES.

Bunch, John (L., Jr.) (*b* Tipton, IN, 1 Dec 1921). Pianist. He studied piano and harmony from the age of 11 and had his first engagements, playing in local clubs, when he was 12. He was influenced first by Fats Waller and later by Bud Powell and Teddy Wilson. His career did not begin in earnest until the late 1950s, when he belonged to big bands led by Woody Herman (1956–7), Benny Goodman (1957–8), and Maynard Ferguson (1958); he then played bop and swing in small groups led by Buddy Rich (1959), Al Cohn and Zoot Sims (1961–2), and Gene Krupa (1961–4). He also performed and recorded with Rich's orchestra (1966) and toured Europe with his septet (1974). From 1966 to 1972 he worked with Tony Bennett as a pianist, conductor, and music director. He played with Goodman through the 1960s and 1970s and accompanied him on his tours of the USSR (1962), Mexico (1963), and Europe (1973). In 1982–3 he performed and recorded with Scott Hamilton's quintet.

SELECTED RECORDINGS

As unaccompanied soloist: *John Bunch Plays Kurt Weill* (1975, Chi. 144)

As leader: *John's Bunch* (1975, FaD 107); *John's Other Bunch* (1977, FaD 114); *Slick Funk* (1977, FaD 118)

As sideman: M. Ferguson: *Message from Newport* (1958, Roul. 52012); B. Rich: *Swingin' New Big Band* (1966, PJ 20113); J. Venuti and Z. Sims: *Joe Venuti and Zoot Sims* (1975, Chi. 142); B. Goodman: *The King* (1978, Cen. 1150)

BIBLIOGRAPHY

FeatherE; *Feather '60s*; *Feather–Gitler '70s*

L. Tomkins: "John Bunch," *CI*, x (1971–2), no.7, p.26; no.8, p.14

J. Balleras: "John Bunch," *DB*, xlii/1 (1975), 35

M. Richards: "John Bunch," *JJI*, xl/7 (1987), 14

PAUL RINZLER

Bunink, Nico (*b* Amsterdam, 22 April 1936). Dutch pianist. He moved in 1956 to Paris, where he led a quartet with the tenor saxophonist Barney Wilen from 1957 (when the group recorded) to 1958. After moving to the USA the following year he played with Charles Mingus (1959–60), Zoot Sims (1960), and Dinah Washington (1960) and worked in California with the Montgomery Brothers, Chet Baker, Bobby Hutcherson, Harold Land, and Charles McPherson (1961–8). He recorded with Mingus (1960), Washington, John Handy, and McPherson (in New York, 1971) and led a trio in New York from 1968 until his return in 1972 to the Netherlands, where he worked into the 1980s with small groups and as an unaccompanied soloist. Bunink's playing can be heard to advantage on Jimmy Knepper's album *Tell me* (Daybreak 001), recorded in the Netherlands in 1979.

WIM VAN EYLE

Bunker, Larry [Lawrence Benjamin] (*b* Long Beach, CA, 4 Nov 1928). Drummer, vibraphonist, and percussionist. He worked regularly in television, film, and recording studios with such arranger-composers as Henry Mancini, Quincy Jones, Dave Grusin, Neal Hefti, Nelson Riddle, Lalo Schifrin, and Oliver Nelson. At the same time he was active in West Coast jazz from the 1950s and played with Gerry Mulligan, Stan Getz, Warne Marsh, and Clare Fischer. He also played with Bill Evans (ii) (1963–5), Jim Hall, Gary Burton, and Dizzy Gillespie. Bunker is a versatile performer, equally adept with a trap set, keyed percussion instruments (especially vibraphone), and timpani; he is highly regarded for his sensitivity and his wide-ranging interest in music. Besides working as a jazzman he has played with a number of symphony orchestras.

SELECTED RECORDINGS

(all as sideman)

As drummer: G. Mulligan: Lady be Good/Loverman (1953, PJ 609); B. Evans: *At Shelly's Manne-Hole* (1963, Riv. 9487); C. Fischer: *Extension* (1963, PJ 77); B. Evans: *Trio '65* (1965, Verve 68613); G. Burton: *The Time Machine* (1966, RCA LSP3642); C. Fischer: *T'Da-a-a!* (1972, Rev. 23); L. Tabackin and W. Marsh: *Tenor Gladness* (1976, IC 6048)

As vibraphonist: D. Grusin: *Discovered Again!* (1976, Sheffield Lab 5)

As percussionist: Pat Williams: *Threshold* (1973, Cap. ST11242)

BIBLIOGRAPHY

B. Dawbarn: "Everybody Digs Bill Evans," *MM*, xxxix (22 Aug 1964), 16

J. Tynan: "Natural Flow: the Bill Evans Trio," *DB*, xxxii/13 (1965), 20

H. Siders: "Drum Shticks," *DB*, xl (1973), no.5, p.15; no.6, p.18

J. KENT WILLIAMS

Bunn, Teddy [Theodore Leroy] (*b* Freeport, NY, 1909; *d* Lancaster, CA, 20 July 1978). Guitarist and singer. He was born to a musical family and was largely self-taught as a musician. After beginning his career in the backup group of a calypso singer he became acquainted with Leo Watson and in the late 1920s joined the Washboard Serenaders. He recorded in 1929 as a member of Duke Ellington's orchestra, with which he also toured as a substitute for Fred Guy. In the 1930s he worked as a freelance and at Watson's suggestion joined the Sepia Nephews in Washington (1932); this group, later known as the SPIRITS OF RHYTHM, held long engagements at the Onyx Club and Nick's and achieved great popularity. He left the band to lead his own small groups (1937–8) and record with Jimmie Noone

(1937), Johnny Dodds, Trixie Smith, and Mezz Mezzrow and Tommy Ladnier (all 1938), J. C. Higginbotham (1939), and Sidney Bechet (1939–40). In 1939 he rejoined the Spirits of Rhythm, with whom he moved in 1940 to California and recorded during the following decade, while at the same time continuing to make recordings as a freelance. He also recorded in 1940 with Lionel Hampton, and at this time abandoned the acoustic guitar in favor of the electric guitar, which he played with his thumb and forefinger (without using a plectrum) in a style that was predominantly melodic rather than chordal. Later he worked with Edgar Hayes (in the 1940s and 1950s), visited Hawaii with Jack McVea (1954), and played with Louis Jordan (1959); he also toured with a rock-and-roll show in the late 1950s and in spite of failing health continued to perform occasionally in the following decades.

SELECTED RECORDINGS

As sideman: J. Noone: Four or Five Times (1937, Decca 1621); J. Dodds: Wild Man Blues (1938, Decca 2111); Melancholy (1938, Decca 1676); T. Smith: Trixie Blues (1938, Decca 7469); M. Mezzrow: Comin' On with the Come On (1938, Bb 10085); M. Mezzrow and T. Ladnier: If you See me Comin' (1938, Bb 10087); E. Hayes: Century Room (1947, Exclusive 78); Sunday Morning Blues (1947, Exclusive 106)

BIBLIOGRAPHY

R. G. Craik: "Teddy Bunn on Record," *JJ*, xxiv/6 (1971), 2
P. Tanner: "A Discography of Teddy Bunn," *JJ*, xxiv (1971), no.11, p.8; no.12, p.28; xxv/1 (1972), 11
——: "Teddy Bunn Today," *JJ*, xxix/10 (1976), 12
——: Obituary, *Sv*, no.79 (1978), 3

JOHNNY SIMMEN

Burbank, Albert (*b* New Orleans, 25 March 1902; *d* New Orleans, 15 Aug 1976). Clarinetist and singer. He began playing clarinet at the age of 17 and in the 1920s worked regularly with the band led by the drummer Arnold DePass; he also performed with Buddy Petit, the double bass player Bob Lyons, Chris Kelly, Punch Miller, and the trumpeter Leonard Parker. He played mainly in taxi dance halls during the 1930s, and by the end of the decade had his own quartet. After navy service Burbank recorded with Wooden Joe Nicholas (1945, 1949) and worked with the drummer Albert Jiles (1946), De De Pierce (1947), Herb Morand (1949–50), Paul Barbarin (1950–52), and the trumpeter Kid Clayton (1952–3). In 1954 he went to Los Angeles to join Kid Ory, but later the same year returned to his home town, where he worked regularly at the Paddock Lounge (until 1966) and then at Dixieland Hall with the banjoist Albert French. Burbank recorded with Kid Thomas in 1961, and from 1969 to 1973 played at Preservation Hall with Thomas's band, also making an international tour in 1971. He joined Percy Humphrey's group in 1973, but a series of strokes curtailed his playing career.

Burbank was one of the greatest New Orleans clarinetists. His tone in the chalumeau register of the instrument was full and rounded; a fine example of his playing may be heard on Nicholas's recording of *Shake it and break it* (1945). In the upper register, his urgent vibrato and distinctive tone, at once plaintive and sinewy, gave his work an intensity that was fiercely emotional; he would swoop and soar like a bird in flight, playing across and around the beat, alternating long, looping, baroque phrases with rushing, stabbing passages in double time to create an overall effect of great beauty.

Oral history material in *LNT*.

SELECTED RECORDINGS

As leader: *Albert Burbank* (1969, Smoky Mary 1969)
As sideman: first issued on J. Nicholas: *Wooden Joe Nicholas* (1945–9, AM 640), Shake it and break it (1945); K. Thomas: *Kid Thomas and his Algiers Stompers* (1961, Riv. 9365); K. Howard: *Kid Howard's Olympia Band ... Featuring Albert Burbank, "the Clarinet Wizard"* (1962, Icon 8); K. Thomas: *Kid Thomas' Jazzband* (1972, CSA 1007)

BIBLIOGRAPHY

J. C. Hillman: "Albert Burbank: the Clarinet Wizard," *JJ*, xxi/5 (1968), 26 [incl. discography]
M. Jones: "Albert Memorial," *MM* (27 Nov 1971), 18
A. Barrell: "Albert Burbank: some Significant Recordings," *Fn*, vii/5 (1976), 4
P. Van Vorst: "Albert Burbank," *MR*, iii/12 (1976), 1
K. Davern: "Memories of Albert Burbank," *Fn*, ix/1 (1977), 16

MICHAEL TOVEY

Burch(ell), John (Alexander) (*b* London, 6 Jan 1932). English pianist. He learned piano as a child, and worked with Allan Ganley's Jazzmakers in 1960. The following year he joined Don Rendell's group, with which he recorded the album *Roarin'* (1961, Jlnd 951). From 1964 to 1966 he led an octet which included at various times Ray Warleigh, Peter King, and Hank Shaw. Thereafter he worked with many important American musicians, including Roland Kirk (1966) and Freddie Hubbard (1967). Later he was a member of the quartet led by Warleigh and the drummer Tommy Chase, with which he recorded in 1978, accompanying Jon Eardley. From 1978 he has been associated with Kathy Stobart, and in 1980–81 he toured and recorded with Eddie "Cleanhead" Vinson. He re-formed his octet in 1984; Shaw and Dick Morrissey were among its members. Burch has also been active as a composer; his most famous piece, *Preach and Teach*, was a hit for the rhythm-and-blues singer Georgie Fame in 1966, and was later recorded by Buddy Rich and issued on the album *Mercy, Mercy* (1968, PJ 20133).

BIBLIOGRAPHY

Feather '60s
R. Cotterrell, ed.: *Jazz Now: the Jazz Centre Society Guide* (London, 1976)

SALLY-ANN WORSFOLD

Burke, Ed(ward) (*b* Fulton, MO, 13 Jan 1909). Trombonist. He worked in the bands of Walter Barnes (1928–30), Cassino Simpson (1931), and others, occasionally also performing on violin, before playing with Erskine Tate (1934–5) and Horace Henderson (1937). From 1938 to 1940 he performed and made recordings (including *Gator Swing*, 1939, Bb 10763) with Earl Hines. After working with Walter Fuller (1940) and in Chicago with Coleman Hawkins (1941) he moved to New York, where from 1942 he spent long periods with Cootie Williams's big band. He then toured with Cab Calloway (1950–51) and recorded with Buddy Johnson (1955–6). Although he began to work less frequently in the 1960s, he continued to perform into the 1980s.

based on *ChiltonW*

Burke, Ray(mond) [Barrois, Raymond (N.)] (*b* New Orleans, 6 June 1904; *d* New Orleans, 21 March 1986). Clarinetist. In 1913 he began playing instruments he had made himself, including kazoo and a primitive clarinet; at the age of 16 he adopted the conventional instrument, but he retained a lifelong fascination for unusual or homemade ones. He also played saxophone during the big-band era. His career was almost entirely confined to New Orleans, where he led several small groups that included such musicians as Wooden Joe Nicholas (1949) and Johnny Wiggs (1952); early examples of his work were first issued on *Ray Burke's Speakeasy Boys* (1937, 1945, New Orleans Jazz 7202). As a sideman he played with Sharkey Bonano (1949), Wiggs (from 1954), Johnny St. Cyr (1954), and others. From its inauguration around 1960 Burke became associated with Preservation Hall and the musicians who played there, working with Punch Miller (*c*1960) and intermittently over a period of 20 years with Kid Thomas. Burke's understated, sweet-toned playing graced many recordings and his powers did not diminish with age; a late example of his ensemble and solo style may be heard on Wendell Eugene's *West India Blues* (1978, Nola 20). The Raymond Barrois Collection of jazz recordings is held in New Orleans (*see* LIBRARIES AND ARCHIVES, §2).

Oral history material in *LNT*.

BIBLIOGRAPHY

ChiltonW

A. Rose: "The Rabais of Raymond Burke," *SL*, ix/9–10 (1958), 1
J. Steiner: "The Emergence of Raymond Burke," *SL*, ix/9–10 (1958), 7
J. Trussell: "A Tribute to Raymond Burke," *SL*, ix/9–10 (1958), 5
P. Van Vorst: "The Original Ray Burke," *MR*, ii/10 (1975), 10
G. Kay: "Ray Burke: New Orleans Living Legend," *SL*, xxxiv (win. 1982), 29

Burke, Sonny [Joseph Francis] (*b* Scranton, PA, 22 March 1914; *d* Santa Monica, CA, 31 May 1980). Arranger and bandleader. He studied violin and piano from the age of five and while studying music at Duke University (to 1937) played in various bands. After moving to New York he assumed leadership in 1938 of Sam Donahue's band, with which he made several recordings; his arrangement of *Jimmie Meets the Count* (1940, OK 5813) demonstrates his admiration for the bands of Jimmie Lunceford and Count Basie. Burke then wrote arrangements for Charlie Spivak (1940–42) and Jimmy Dorsey (1942–*c*1945); among his pieces for the latter band is *Sunset Strip* (1944, V-disc 326A). From the late 1940s into the 1970s he directed recording sessions for Decca, Reprise, Warner Bros., and his own company, Daybreak. For Decca he recorded an album of mambos (1951); his orchestra accompanied such musicians as Ella Fitzgerald (1949) and Louis Armstrong (1955), and he remained active as an arranger. He should not be confused with the pianist and keyboard player Reginald "Sonny" Burke, who recorded with Stanley Turrentine (1974) and Dizzy Gillespie and John Handy (both 1977).

BIBLIOGRAPHY

FeatherE

G. T. Simon: *The Big Bands* (New York, 1967, rev. and enlarged 2/1971, rev. 3/1974, 4/1981), 459

Burke, Vinnie [Bucci, Vincent J., Jr.] (*b* Newark, NJ, 15 March 1921). Double bass player and bandleader. He taught himself violin and guitar as a child, but he took up the double bass instead after having lost the use of a finger during World War II. He worked with Joe Mooney and Tony Scott, then spent three years in a trio led by the pianist Cy Coleman. After working briefly with the Sauter–Finegan Orchestra he played with Marian McPartland, and recorded with her in 1953. From the mid-1950s into the 1980s Burke led his own swing and bop groups (mostly trios and quartets), which performed with numerous prominent jazzmen; his playing may be heard to advantage on *Vinnie Burke's String Jazz Quartet* (1957, ABC-Para. 170). He made recordings alone and with the pianist John Mehegan (1952, 1955), Chris Connor (1954, 1957), Eddie Costa, Tal Farlow, Don Elliott, and the saxophonist Gil Melle (all 1956). In 1959 he worked with Vic Dickenson, and he later recorded in a duo with Bucky Pizzarelli (1961), and with Mat Mathews (*c*1961) and Bobby Hackett (1963). (*FeatherE*)

Burnet, Bob [Robert W.] (*b* Chicago, 1912; *d* Guadalajara, Mexico, 3 Aug 1984). Trumpeter. He played drums, piano, and banjo before taking up trumpet. After moving to New York he worked with Charlie Barnet (1938–40) and made a number of recordings with the band (including *The Right Idea*, 1939, Bb 10530). He then led his own sextet, which played at Café Society and Nick's, and when it disbanded in 1941 rejoined Barnet. He ceased full-time playing shortly after leaving Barnet the following year, but later recorded with Freddie Wacker's Windy City Seven (*c*1957). He moved to Mexico in 1958.

based on *ChiltonW*

Burns, Billy [Henry William] (*b* Cleveland, *c*1904; *d* New York, Dec 1963). Trombonist. He played in Buffalo with Sam Wooding (1928), then performed and recorded in Europe with him (1929) and with Noble Sissle (1930). He recorded again with Sissle in New York in 1931, after which he spent a long period in Europe working mainly with Willie Lewis; he may be heard to advantage on Lewis's *Stomping at the Savoy* (1936, PAct. 898). He also played with Fud Candrix in Belgium and recorded with Freddy Johnson in Paris (1933). In December 1938 Burns went to Egypt to join Bill Coleman and the Harlem Rhythmakers. After working with Lewis in the Netherlands, Switzerland, and Portugal he returned in 1941 to the USA, where he continued to play occasionally.

based on *ChiltonW*

Burns, Dave [David] (*b* Perth Amboy, NJ, 5 March 1924). Trumpeter, flugelhorn player, pianist, and teacher. He studied trumpet from the age of nine; he was influenced by Louis Armstrong and Roy Eldridge, and by Dizzy Gillespie, whom he heard at Minton's Playhouse in New York when he was 16. He played with Al Cooper's Savoy Sultans (1941–3), then led an air force band that included James Moody (1943–5). He played in Gillespie's big band (1946–9) and was at times asked to reproduce Gillespie's solos (as, for example, on the recording of the second part of *One Bass Hit*, 1946). He played with Duke Ellington (1950–52) and Moody (1952–7), and then worked for three years in New York as a freelance. He was a member of the sextet led by Billy Mitchell and Al Grey in 1962–3 and played with Willie Bobo from 1964 to 1966; in the late 1960s he played with several groups, including those of Moody and Mitchell. From 1970 he was active in jazz education.

SELECTED RECORDINGS

As leader: *Dave Burns* (1962, Van. 9111); *Warming up* (1964, Van. 9143)

As sideman: D. Gillespie: One Bass Hit, pt ii (1946, Musi. 404); Things to Come (1946, Musi. 447); J. Moody: *Modern Jazz* (1948, BN 5006), incl. Cuba, Moodamorphosis; G. Wallington: *George Wallington Showcase* (1954, BN 5045); J. Moody: *James Moody* (1954–5, Prst. 192); A. Taylor: *A. T.'s Delight* (1960, BN 4047); on M. Jackson: *Big Bags* (1962, Riv. 9429), Round Midnight; E. Jefferson: *Body and Soul* (1968, Prst. 7619)

BIBLIOGRAPHY

Feather–Gitler '70s

J. Burns: "Trumpeter, where are you Sounding now?," *JJI*, xvi/7 (1963), 23
D. Gillespie and A. Fraser: *To be, or not . . . to Bop: Memoirs* (Garden City, NY, 1979)

ANDRÉ BARBERA

Burns, Ralph (*b* Newton, MA, 29 June 1922). Arranger, composer, and pianist. He studied at the New England Conservatory in 1938–9 and worked in the band of Charlie Barnet, who recorded his piece *The Moose* in 1943. Burns then joined Woody Herman, playing an important role in the band's rhythm section during 1944–5. He withdrew in order to work as a freelance, but continued writing for Herman and also made recordings under his own name until the late 1950s (including the album *Very Warm for Jazz*, 1958, Decca 9207). A period of concentration on orchestrating for the Broadway stage led to considerable film work in the 1970s.

Burns's early arrangements for Herman's band, however, are his most important contribution. As well as intelligent versions of contemporary popular songs, his original pieces *Apple Honey* and *Bijou* effectively harnessed the ensemble's power and that of its soloists. More ambitious works such as *Lady McGowan's Dream* and *Summer Sequence* (the last part of which became a song with lyrics by Johnny Mercer under the title *Early Autumn*) betray the rewarding but not predominant inspiration of Ellington. Many of Burns's arrangements of the 1960s and 1970s have not required the creation of original material, but he has been associated with some significant film directors, and has arranged the film scores of Woody Allen's *Bananas* (1971), Bob Fosse's *Sweet Charity* (1969), *Cabaret* (1972), and *Lenny* (1974), and Martin Scorsese's *New York, New York* (1977). The two last-named projects, by calling on Burns's jazz experience, lent authenticity to an area too often bowdlerized in the film industry.

For illustration *see* HERMAN, WOODY, fig.1*a*.

RECORDED COMPOSITIONS

(selective list)

* – with Burns as sideman

As leader: Places Please (1951, Clef 8971); Someday, Somewhere/Spring Is (1951, Clef 8974)

Recorded by C. Barnet: The Moose (1943), on *Hop on the Skyliner* (1942–5, Decca 8098)

Recorded by W. Herman: *Apple Honey (1945, Col. 36803); *Bijou (1945, Col. 36861); *Lady McGowan's Dream (1946, Col. 38365-6); *Summer Sequence (1946–7, Col. 38365-7)

BIBLIOGRAPHY

FeatherE; *Feather '60s*

I. Gitler: *Jazz Masters of the Forties* (New York, 1966/*R*1983 with discography), 279

BRIAN PRIESTLEY

Burrell, Dave [Herman Davis, II] (*b* Middletown, OH, 10 Sept 1940). Pianist and composer. He was introduced to jazz at an early age by his mother, a singer. He attended the University of Hawaii (1958–60) and graduated from the Berklee College of Music in 1965. He played with Tony Williams and Sam Rivers in Boston, then moved to New York (1965), where he played with Grachan Moncur III and Marion Brown. He formed the Untraditional Jazz Improvisational Team with Byard Lancaster, Bobby Kapp, and Sirone in 1965, and the cooperative group 360 Degree Music Experience with Moncur and Beaver Harris in 1968. In 1969 he attended the Pan African Festival in Algiers and taught music for the Community Thing Organization in Harlem. He played and recorded with Pharoah Sanders, Harris, Alan Silva, and Sunny Murray, and (from 1969) most often with Archie Shepp. In the late 1970s he wrote a jazz opera, *Windward Passages*, parts of which he has performed in solo and trio settings. Burrell has been influenced by ethnic music and has played with African and West Indian musicians on his many international tours; also evident in his eclectic, Romantic style of composing and solo playing is the influence of opera composers such as Giacomo Puccini.

SELECTED RECORDINGS

As unaccompanied soloist: *Lush Life* (1978, Denon 7533); *Windward Passages* (1979, HH 5)

As leader: *Dave Burrell* (1965, Douglas 798); *La vie de Bohème* (1969, BYG 529330); of 360 Degree Music Experience (with B. Harris): *In: Sanity* (1976, BS 0006-7)

As sideman: P. Sanders: *Tauhid* (1966, Imp. 9138); M. Brown: *Three for Shepp* (1966, Imp. 9139); G. Moncur III: *New Africa* (1969, BYG 529321); A. Shepp: *Montreux Two* (1975, Ari. 1034)

BIBLIOGRAPHY

R. Riggins: "Dave Burrell," *Coda*, no.175 (1980), 16 [incl. discography]

L. Jeske: "Dave Burrell: Candy Girl's Son Makes Good," *DB*, xlviii/2 (1981), 26 [incl. discography]

B. Primack: "Dave Burrell: a Jazz Odyssey from Hawaii to Harlem," *Keyboard*, vii/9 (1981), 22

ED HAZELL

Burrell, Duke [Alexander] (*b* New Orleans, 9 July 1920). Pianist. He began his career in New Orleans as a member of Alexander "Battleaxe" Purnell's band. From 1946 to 1949 he led his own group, the French Quarter Trio, in New Orleans at the nightclubs El Morocco, the Famous Door, and the Paddock Lounge. In 1950 after a brief tour of the USA Burrell moved to Hawaii and performed at the Brown Derby and the Trade Winds clubs in Honolulu. He returned to New Orleans, where he remained for several years before moving to Los Angeles in 1963. In 1974 he formed the Louisiana Shakers Band, which gave its first performances in Los Angeles and San Francisco with a show called *A Night in New Orleans* and received critical acclaim for its appearance at the RFK Theater in New York; the band recorded in 1974 (*Louisiana Shakers Band*, Crescent Jazz 3), and in 1975 toured Europe and the USA. During the 1970s Burrell also recorded with Louis Jordan's group the Tympany Five (1973) and Barney Bigard's Pelican Trio (1978). (D. Griffiths: "World Shakers," *MR*, ii/6 (1975), 13)

FLOYD LEVIN

Burrell, Kenny [Kenneth Earl] (*b* Detroit, 31 July 1931). Guitarist. A member of a musical family, he began playing guitar at the age of 12. In 1951, while studying music at Wayne State University, he worked for a month with Dizzy Gillespie's sextet, making his recording début. After graduating (BM 1955) he toured with Oscar Peterson, and then moved to New York in 1956. He soon began performing and recording with many famous players, and established his reputation as an outstanding guitarist. As well as making between 30 and 40 LPs as a leader, he has played as a sideman on about 200 albums, recording in many styles under such leaders as John Coltrane, Gil Evans, Stan Getz, Billie Holiday, Milt Jackson, Quincy Jones, Thad Jones, Yusef Lateef, Hubert Laws, Herbie Mann, Sonny Rollins, Lalo Schifrin, Jimmy Smith, and Stanley Turrentine. Burrell performs most frequently in a trio with a double bass player and a drummer. However he has also worked as an unaccompanied soloist, and in larger groups, such as the nine-piece Philip Morris Superband, with which he toured internationally in 1985–6. He has also made recordings on banjo, including *Hot and Bothered* as a sideman with Mercer Ellington. In addition to performing and recording he has been active as a teacher; he began leading seminars at colleges in 1971, and has taught courses in the music of Duke Ellington at universities around Los Angeles, where he settled in 1972.

Burrell's playing is in the bop style, but is more conservative than that of some of his colleagues, for he favors simple, often singable, melodic lines rather than flights of virtuosity. His tone is particularly mellow.

SELECTED RECORDINGS

As leader: with J. Coltrane: *Kenny Burrell and John Coltrane* (1958, NewJ 8276); *A Night at the Village Vanguard* (1959, Argo 655); *Midnight Blue* (1963, BN 84123); *Guitar Forms* (1964–5, Verve 68612); *Asphalt Canyon Suite* (1969, Verve 68773); *Ellington is Forever* (1975, Fan. 79005); *Generation* (1986, BN 46756)

As sideman: D. Gillespie: Birk's Works (1951, Dee Gee 3601); J. Smith: *Midnight Special* (1960, BN 84078); M. Ellington: *Hot and Bothered* (1984, Doctor Jazz 40029)

BIBLIOGRAPHY
FeatherE; Feather '60s; Feather–Gitler '70s
I. Gitler: "Kenny Burrell," DB, xxx/17 (1963), 22
D. Morgenstern: "In his own Right," DB, xxxiii/14 (1966), 26
L. K. McMillan, Jr.: "Kenny Burrell: Man with a Mission," DB, xxxviii/12 (1971), 12
H. Siders: "The Plectrum Spectrum," DB, xxxix/11 (1972), 12
K. Aoki: "Kenny Burrell Discography," SJ, xxix/4 (1975), 234
K. Harris: "Rediscovering Kenny Burrell," JJI, xxxi/11 (1978), 6
M. J. Summerfield: *The Jazz Guitar: its Evolution and its Players* (Gateshead, England, 1978), 62
F. Bouchard: "Kenny Burrell," *Radio Free Jazz* (Oct 1979), 16
A. Berle: "Kenny Burrell: a Pillar of Mainstream Jazz," GP, xv/4 (1981), 59 [incl. discography]
J. Sallis, ed.: *Jazz Guitars: an Anthology* (New York, 1984), 201
Z. Stewart: "Kenny Burrell: Boppin' the Blues," DB, liii/7 (1986), 20 [incl. discography]

THOMAS OWENS

Burroughs, Alvin [Mouse] (*b* Mobile, AL, 21 Nov 1911; *d* Chicago, 1 Aug 1950). Drummer. He performed and recorded with Walter Page's Blue Devils (1928–9) and with Alphonso Trent (1930). After settling in Chicago he worked with Horace Henderson (1937–8) and Earl Hines (1938–40); his recordings with Hines include *G. T. Stomp* (1939, Bb 10391). He then played with Milt Larkin (1941), Benny Carter (1942), his own band, and Henry "Red" Allen (1944–6). After leading his own band again he joined George Dixon's quartet, of which he was a member until his death. (D. Ioakimidis: "Alvin Burroughs," *Pj*, no.4 (1971), 28)

based on *ChiltonW*

Burrows, Don(ald Vernon) (*b* Sydney, 8 Aug 1928). Australian reed player and flutist. He began playing in clubs regularly at the age of 14, and later worked in studios, radio, and television and performed at festivals in Australia and elsewhere. From the late 1950s he has been associated with George Golla, playing in his septet in the mid-1960s and touring North America, Asia, Europe, and Australia. In 1972 Burrows's group played at the Montreux and Newport jazz festivals, and he was made an MBE; in 1977 he toured Australia and recorded with Stephane Grappelli. He became the director of jazz studies at the New South Wales Conservatorium of Music in 1980, and from 1981 he has introduced a series of television programs about jazz, "The Burrows Collection." A tireless promoter of jazz, he was one of the first musicians to take a jazz group to China (1983). Burrows is a versatile player who performs in a number of styles – traditional, swing, bop, and cool jazz; a debt to Benny Goodman is apparent in his clarinet work.

SELECTED RECORDINGS
(all recorded for Cherry Pie)

Duos with G. Golla: *This Time Tassie* (1979, 70201–2)
As leader: *Just the Beginning* (1970, 1009); *Live at Montreux* (1972, 1010); *The Don Burrows Quartet at the Sydney Opera House* (1974, 1017); *Don Burrows and the Brazilian Connection* (1977, 1035)
As sideman with S. Grappelli: *Steph 'n' us* (1977, 1032)

BIBLIOGRAPHY
Feather–Gitler '70s
A. Bisset: *Black Roots, White Flowers: a History of Jazz in Australia* (Sydney, 1979)
M. Williams: *The Australian Jazz Explosion* (London and elsewhere, 1981), 59
B. Johnson: "Burrows, Donald Vernon," *The Oxford Companion to Australian Jazz* (Melbourne, Australia, 1987)

JEFF PRESSING (with JOHN WHITEOAK)

Burton, Ann (*b* Amsterdam, 4 March 1933). Dutch singer. She is self-taught as a musician. She began her career in 1955, having been encouraged to do so by Eddie de Haas, and toured Germany with the double bass player Ted Powder. She played with Pia Beck (1958) and Piet Noordijk (in Morocco and Spain, 1960) and in the early 1960s worked regularly in The Hague. In 1965 she played with the pianist Frans Elsen and made the first of several fine recordings; she sang at the festival in Sopot, Poland, the following year and also made several tours of Japan. Burton's singing is well represented by her albums *Am I Blue* (1981, Kt. 711) and *It might as Well be Love* (1984, Turning Point 30002).

WIM VAN EYLE

Burton, Gary (*b* Anderson, IN, 23 Jan 1943). Vibraphonist and leader. He taught himself to play vibraphone, and made his first recordings, for RCA with the country guitarist Hank Garland, when he was 17. After studying for two years at Berklee College of Music, during which time he recorded as a leader for RCA, he joined George Shearing's quintet (1963), then rose to prominence as a member of Stan Getz's quartet (1964–6). In 1967 Burton formed his own quartet with Larry Coryell, Steve Swallow, and Bob Moses (later Roy Haynes), a group whose style was influenced by rock music. He recorded with Stephane Grappelli in Paris in 1969, and in the early 1970s made tours of Europe, Japan, and Australia. Burton has continued to lead small ensembles with such musicians as Sam Brown, Mick Goodrick, Pat Metheny, John Scofield, Abe Laboriel, Eberhard Weber, Bill Goodwin, and Dick Hyman; by the late 1970s he was using different instrumentation, and his sidemen included the trumpeter Tiger Ogashi and the alto saxophonist Jim Odgren. He has also performed and recorded in duos, notably with Chick Corea, Ralph Towner, and Swallow, and as a soloist; he has occasionally played marimba. Burton's activities as a teacher form a major part of his career. In 1971 he became a member of the faculty at Berklee; he has published method books and has toured the USA with his groups presenting lecture-concert programs.

A virtuoso vibraphonist, Burton developed an original style of improvisation quite distinct from those of his influential predecessors on the instrument, Lionel Hampton and Milt Jackson. In the early 1960s he promoted a playing style that made use of four mallets at once, and in many ways he created a compromise between contemporary jazz piano and wind styles (he cites Bill Evans (ii) and Thelonious Monk as inspirations). He has employed electronic attachments that produce fuzz tone and reverberation, and has performed on a vibraphone that has no pulsator. Burton is one of the few modern jazz improvisers not to have drawn substantially on the melodic conceptions of the bop pioneers Charlie Parker and Dizzy Gillespie. He replaced their vocabulary with a fresh one that emphasizes 20th-century classical music as well as country music. He frequently employs accompanying devices rich in vamps and pedal points, reminiscent of country music, as well as the flavor of Latin American styles.

Oral history material in *NjR*.

SELECTED RECORDINGS
(all recorded for ECM unless otherwise indicated)

As unaccompanied soloist: *Alone at Last* (1971, Atl. 1598)
Duos: with C. Corea: *Crystal Silence* (1972, 1024); with S. Swallow: *Hotel Hello* (1974, 1055); with R. Towner: *Matchbook* (1974, 1056); with C. Corea: *Duet* (1978, 1140); *In Concert, Zürich* (1979, 1182–3)
As leader: *Duster* (1967, RCA LSP3835); *Country Roads and other Places* (1968, RCA LSP4098); with S. Grappelli: *Paris Encounter* (1969, Atl. 1597); with K. Jarrett: *Gary Burton and Keith Jarrett* (1970, Atl. 1577); *In the Public Interest* (1973, Pol. 6503); *The New Quartet* (1973, 1030); *Seven Songs for Quartet and Chamber Orchestra* (1973, 1040); *Ring* (1974, 1051); *Easy as Pie* (1980, 1184); *Picture This* (1982, 1226); *Real Life Hits* (1984, 1293)

BIBLIOGRAPHY
D. DeMicheal: "Gary Burton: Portrait of the Artist as a Young Vibraharpist," DB, xxxii/16 (1965), 20

G. Burton: "My Approach to the Vibes," *CI*, vi/1 (1967), 23
D. Morgenstern: "Gary Burton: Upward Bound," *DB*, xxxv/16 (1968), 14
L. Tomkins: "Gary Burton," *CI*, x/2 (1971), 26 [interview]
C. Suber: "Gary Burton's Back-home Bag," *DB*, xxxix/3 (1972), 12
L. Tomkins: "You Don't Have to Follow the Crowd," *CI*, xi/6 (1973), 6 [interview]
C. Mitchell: "Gary Burton: Four Mallet Candor," *DB*, xlii/19 (1975), 10
M. Ruppli and E. Raben: "Discographie de Gary Burton," *Jh*, no.342 (1977), 26
R. Stringer: "Gary Burton: a Love Affair with Music," *JJI*, xxx/8 (1977), 6 [interview]
C. Stern: "Vibist Gary Burton," *DB*, xlv/21 (1978), 16; xlvi/1 (1979), 17
L. Tomkins: "Gary Burton Today," *CI*, xvi (1978), no.11, p.20; no.12, p.23 [interview]
N. Tesser: "Many Facets of Burton," *Jazz Magazine*, iii/3 (1979), 44
M. Bateson: "Gary Burton: 4 Mallet Master," *JJI*, xxxiii/8 (1980), 27
A. Stevens: "Gary Burton," *CI*, xix/7 (1981), 22 [interview]
——: "Gary Burton: How my Vibes Identity Developed," *CI*, xxiv/11 (1987), 12 [interview]

Burton, Rahn [Ron; Burton, William; Jabulani] (*b* Louisville, KY, 10 Feb 1934). Pianist. He learned piano from the age of 13 and first performed professionally in and around Louisville in the early 1950s. In 1953 he began playing with Roland Kirk, and toured the Midwest with him for six years. His composition *Jack the Ripper* was included on Kirk's album *Introducing Roland Kirk* (1960, Argo 669). After working as a freelance in New York (1960), Syracuse (1960–61), and Louisville he toured with George Adams as an organist (1964–5), then played in Atlanta with Sirone. From 1967 to 1973 he was again a member of Kirk's band; he appeared with the group at the Newport Jazz Festival in 1968 and made a number of recordings, including *Bright Moments* (1973, Atl. 2-907). In 1972 he formed his own group, African American Connection, with which he has continued to work at intervals. Burton played with Michael Carvin from 1974 and recorded with him the following year. He has also worked with Stanley Turrentine, Leone Thomas, Carlos Garnett, Hannibal Peterson (from 1983), Charlie Rouse (1984), and others, and recorded with Adams (1978, 1984) and Beaver Harris (1979). (*Feather–Gitler '70s*)

Bush, Lennie [Leonard Walter] (*b* London, 6 June 1927). English double bass player. He made his professional début in 1944, and from that time has performed and recorded with many of the principal modern-jazz players in the UK, including Ronnie Scott (1949–64), Victor Feldman (1952–7), Jimmy Deuchar (1954–6), Dizzy Reece (1955–7), Tony Crombie (1955–8), Alan Clare (1956–8), George Chisholm (1956–73), and Tony Kinsey (1957–74). Always much in demand for studio and broadcasting work, he has accompanied many visiting American and European musicians (including Stephane Grappelli, Clark Terry, Zoot Sims, Joe Pass, Ben Webster, and Carmen McRae) both at Scott's club and on recordings. He worked with the European bands led by Benny Goodman, recording in London (1969) and Stockholm (1970), and also recorded with Eddie "Cleanhead" Vinson (1980). His flexible rhythmic approach and contribution to an ensemble may be heard to advantage on Sandy Brown's album *Hair at its Hairiest* (1968, Fon. 921). (*FeatherE; Feather–Gitler '70s*)

Bushell, Garvin (Payne) (*b* Springfield, OH, 25 Sept 1902). Clarinetist and saxophonist. He grew up in a musical family and was playing piano by the age of six and clarinet by 13; later he also learned bassoon, oboe, and flute. After moving to New York in 1919 he worked in vaudeville. In 1921 he joined Mamie Smith's Jazz Hounds and made his earliest recordings with that group and with the singer Daisy Martin. He then played and recorded with Ethel Waters (1921–2) and toured Europe, the eastern USA, and South America with Sam Wooding (1925–7). The four sides he recorded in 1928 with James P. Johnson, Fats Waller, and Jabbo Smith as the Louisiana Sugar Babes include improvised bassoon solos by him, which are among the earliest examples of jazz bassoon on record. During the 1930s Bushell worked with Bessie Smith, Fletcher Henderson (1934–6), Cab Calloway (1936–7), Chick Webb (1937–9; for illustration *see* WEBB, CHICK), and Ella Fitzgerald (1939–40), then in the 1940s and 1950s he led his own groups. He toured internationally with Wilbur De Paris's band from 1959 until 1964, when he went to Africa with Paul Taubman's orchestra; he also recorded, on double bassoon, with John Coltrane in 1961. After playing again with Calloway (1966) he moved to Puerto Rico, then settled in Las Vegas, where he worked as a music teacher.

Oral history material in *NjR* (JOHP).

SELECTED RECORDINGS

As sideman: M. Smith: Royal Garden Blues/Shim-me-king's Blues (1921, OK 4254); S. Wooding: By the waters of the Minnetonka/Dreaming of a castle in the air (1926, Deutsche Grammophon/Pol. 20690); J. Dunn: Sergeant Dunn's Bugle Call Blues/Buffalo Blues (1928, Col. 14306D); Louisiana Sugar Babes: Willow Tree/'Sippi (1928, Vic. 21348); B. Smith: Keep it to yourself/New Orleans Hop Scop Blues (1930, Col. 14516D); E. Waters: Baby, what else can I do?/I just got a letter (1939, Bb 10517); on J. Coltrane: *The Other Village Vanguard Tapes* (1961, Imp. 9325), India

BIBLIOGRAPHY

ChiltonW
N. Hentoff: "Garvin Bushell and New York Jazz in the 1920s," *JR*, ii (1959), no.1, p.11; no.2, p.9; no.3, p.16; repr. as "Jazz in the Twenties: Garvin Bushell," in *Jazz Panorama*, ed. M. Williams (New York and London, 1962/*R*1979), 71
S. B. Charters and L. Kunstadt: *Jazz: a History of the New York Scene* (Garden City, NY, 1962/*R*1981)
P. Gaffey: "Garvin Bushell: Jazz Roots from the Beginning," *Arts Alive*, iii/3 (Las Vegas, NV, 1983), 18; contd as "A Life in Jazz," iii (1983), no.4, p.20; no.5, p.26; no.6, p.28
G. Bushell and M. Tucker: "On the Road with the Chocolate Kiddies in Europe and South America, 1925–1927," *Sv*, no.131 (1987), 182; no.132 (1987), 213

RAYMOND J. GARIGLIO

Bushkin, Joe [Joseph] (*b* New York, 7 Nov 1916). Pianist and trumpeter. He began playing professionally in New York at the Roseland Ballroom, Brooklyn, with Frank LaMarr in 1932. He worked at the Famous Door (1935), and recorded with Billie Holiday (1936) and as a member of Bunny Berigan's band (1935–6, 1938). He also performed regularly with Eddie Condon (1936–7), Louis Prima and Muggsy Spanier (both 1939), and intermittently with Joe Marsala (1936–40). From 1940 to 1942 he was a member of Tommy Dorsey's orchestra (for illustration *see* DORSEY, TOMMY), with which he recorded his well-known song *Oh! Look at me Now* (1941). After military service he replaced Mel Powell as the pianist in Benny Goodman's band and in 1949–50 he acted and played in Garson Kanin's *The Rat Race* on Broadway. In the early 1950s he was house pianist at the Embers in New York and toured and recorded with Louis Armstrong (1953). Bushkin led his own groups in the 1950s and 1960s and then stopped playing for about five years. He accompanied the popular singer Bing Crosby on tour (1976–7) and resumed performing in New York in the 1980s.

SELECTED RECORDINGS

As unaccompanied soloist: Serenade in Thirds/I can't get started with you (1940, Com. 532)
As leader: Every Day is Christmas/The Lady is a Tramp (1950, Col. 39172)
As sideman: B. Holiday: No Regrets (1936, Voc./OK 3276); Summertime (1936, Voc./OK 3288); T. Dorsey: Oh! Look at me Now (1941, Vic. 27274)

BIBLIOGRAPHY

ChiltonW
J. Bushkin: "Joe Bushkin's Tapeology," *JJ*, xxiii/3 (1970), 4

L. Tomkins: "Joe Bushkin," *CI*, xv (1976–7), no.3, p.6; no.4, p.14
W. Balliett: "Jazz: Joe Bushkin," *New Yorker*, lix (21 Feb 1983), 98
M. Jones: *Talking Jazz* (London, 1987) [colln of previously pubd interviews], 208

JAMES M. DORAN

Bushler, Herb (*b* New York, 7 March 1939). Bass player. After learning piano for two years he changed to tuba, but later took up double bass, which he played as a soloist with several major symphony orchestras. He performed and recorded on double bass and electric bass guitar in many jazz styles with Ted Curson (1964–5), Gil Evans (intermittently, 1967–81), Blossom Dearie, Paul Winter, and Tony Williams (all 1971–3), and David Sanborn (1979–81). From 1970 Bushler worked at intervals with David Amram, and he recorded with him around 1977; he also recorded with Enrico Rava (1973), Joe Farrell (1973–4), Harold Vick (1975), and Ryo Kawasaki (in Japan, 1975–6). Between 1966 and 1980 he collaborated with the composer Coleridge-Taylor Perkinson on ballet and film scores and concerts. (*Feather–Gitler '70s*)

Butch. Nickname of IRVING FAZOLA.

Butler, Billy (*b* Philadelphia, 15 Dec 1924). Guitarist. After touring with the Harlemaires, a vocal group (1947–9), he worked as a leader until 1952 and then joined the trio led by the organist Doc Bagby (1953). While he was a member of Bill Doggett's band (1954–61) he co-wrote *Honky Tonk*, which became one of the group's best-known recordings (1956, King 4950). As a studio musician Butler recorded with King Curtis (1961–2), Dinah Washington and Panama Francis (both 1963), Johnny Hodges (1965, 1967), Jimmy Smith (1966), and David "Fathead" Newman (1968). He was employed in show bands on Broadway from 1968, but he continued to make recordings, playing with such musicians as Houston Person (1969–71) and Norris Turney (1975); he also recorded soul jazz with his own group for Prestige (1968–70) and a particularly fine album with Al Casey and the drummer Jackie Williams (*Guitar Odyssey*, 1974, Jazz Odyssey JO012). From 1976 Butler has visited Europe regularly and has continued to record there and in the USA.

BIBLIOGRAPHY

H. Panassié and M. Gautier: *Dictionnaire du jazz* (Paris, 1954, rev. and enlarged 2/1971, enlarged 3/1980; Eng. trans., London, 1956, rev. A. A. Gurwitch as *Guide to Jazz*, Boston, 1956)
C. Battestini and J.-P. Battestini: "Billy Butler," *BHcF*, no.318 (1984), 3 [interview]

HOWARD RYE

Butler, Frank (*b* Kansas City, MO, 18 Feb 1928; *d* Ventura, CA, 24 July 1984). Drummer. He took part in a school-band program in Omaha, Nebraska, played in shows sponsored by the USO, then moved to Kansas City, where he worked with local groups and studied with Jo Jones. In San Francisco he worked with Dave Brubeck (1950) and accompanied Billie Holiday and others at the clubs Blackhawk and Bop City. After touring briefly with Duke Ellington (1954) he moved to Los Angeles, where he recorded with Curtis Counce from 1956; in the late 1950s he worked as a freelance around Los Angeles. Apart from recordings with Art Pepper (1960), Miles Davis (1963), and John Coltrane (1965) he was largely inactive from the 1960s to the mid-1970s; his only recordings as a leader were made in 1977 and 1978. Butler was a superb timekeeper, a sympathetic accompanist, and an imaginative soloist; he was perhaps the only drummer on the West Coast in the 1950s who played in the hard-bop tradition of Max Roach, Philly Joe Jones, and Art Blakey.

SELECTED RECORDINGS

As leader: *Wheelin' and Dealin'* (1978, Xan. 169), incl. Mr. October
As sideman: C. Counce: *Landslide* (1956, Cont. 3526), incl. A Fifth for Frank; H. Land: *The Fox* (1959, Hi-Fi 612); J. Coltrane: *Kulu se Mama* (1965, Imp. 9106); D. Coker: *Dolo!* (1977, Xan. 139); Xanadu All Stars: *Xanadu at Montreux* (1978, Xan. 162–5); A. Pepper: *Among Friends* (1978, Inter. 7718)

BIBLIOGRAPHY

A. Gerber: "Butler, à l'ouest le meilleur," *Jm*, no.131 (1966), 48
V. Wilmer: "What the Butler Plays," *MM*, li (4 Sept 1976), 35
B. Blumenthal: "Neglected Jazz Figures of the 1950s and Early 1960s," *Introspection* (New World 275, 1977) [liner notes]
P. Willard: Obituary, *JT* (1984), Sept, 10

J. KENT WILLIAMS

Butler, Jacques [Jack] (*b* 29 April 1909). Trumpeter and singer. He grew up in Washington, and began playing trumpet at the age of 17. After moving to New York in the late 1920s he worked with Cliff Jackson and with Horace Henderson (1930–31); he also led his own band (1934–5) and performed and recorded with Willie Bryant (1936). He then moved to Europe, where he worked mainly with Willie Lewis (1936–9); his recordings with Lewis include *Swingin' for a Swiss Miss* (1937, PAct 1296). In 1939 he recorded in Paris with a septet led by Frank "Big Boy" Goudie and toured Scandinavia. After his return to New York (1940) Butler led his own band and played with Mezz Mezzrow (1943), Art Hodes (1943–4), and Bingie Madison (1945). In 1948 he worked in Toronto, and in 1950 went once more to Europe, where he led his own band on tour and in a long residency at La Cigale, Paris. He returned to New York in 1968 and continued to play frequently. (P. Vacher: "Montmartre Mainstream," *JJ*, xvi/2 (1963), 15)

Oral history material in *NjR* (JOHP).

based on *ChiltonW*

Butler, Joe [Kid Twat; Joseph] (*b* New Orleans, 25 Dec 1907; *d* New Orleans, 19 June 1982). Double bass player. As a boy in New Orleans he followed parades in the company of Henry "Red" Allen. He began playing double bass in 1923 and spent most of his career working with Kid Thomas, though he also played with Sidney Desvigne and A. J. Piron. He was well known for his renditions of *Big Lunch Blues*, in which he performed the vocal part in a distinctive "talking" style. He recorded this piece with Thomas's band a number of times, and a version is included on the album *Kid Thomas and his Algiers Stompers with the Hall Brothers Jazz Band* (1964, GHB 24). (P. Van Vorst: "The Annotated Joe Butler," *MR*, ix/5 (1982), 1)

Oral history material in *LNT*.

BILL RUSSELL

Butterfield, Billy [Charles William] (*b* Middletown, OH, 14 Jan 1917; *d* North Palm Beach, FL, 18 March 1988). Trumpeter and flugelhorn player. After working with the bandleaders Andy Anderson and Austin Wylie (both 1935) he was a member of Bob Crosby's band (1937–40). His powerful playing was used to good effect on many of Crosby's recordings, including *What's New?* (*I'm Free*) by the big band, and *Spain* by the Bob Cats. Butterfield then played for radio broadcasts in Chicago and later worked with Artie Shaw (1940–41). He was originally engaged to play on the soundtrack to the film *Second Chorus*, but he reached a wider audience when *Star Dust*, to which he contributed a lyrical solo, became a hit; he also participated in recordings by the Gramercy Five. Thereafter he worked with Benny Goodman (1941–2) and Les Brown (1942). Butterfield's versatility and skill as a sight reader brought him many offers of studio work, and he played regularly for NBC and CBS before military service (1944–5). After leading a financially unsuccessful big band (1945–7) he assumed leadership of the house band at Nick's, New York (1947). He then returned to studio work, and recorded with many important musicians, including Louis Armstrong; his playing is particularly prominent on *Blueberry Hill*. During the 1950s Butterfield led small groups on tours of colleges. He settled in the mid-1960s in Florida, where he worked as a freelance. From 1968 to 1972 he was a member of the World's Greatest Jazz Band; his playing was an essential part of the ensemble's sound. He continued to perform and record, both as a leader and a freelance in other groups, into the 1980s.

SELECTED RECORDINGS

As leader: *Billy Butterfield at NYU* (1955, Essex 402), incl. West End Blues

As sideman: B. Crosby: What's New? (1938, Decca 2205); Spain (1940, Decca 3248); A. Shaw: Star Dust (1940, Vic. 27230); B. Goodman: Something New (1941, Col. 36209); B. Gowans: *New York Nine* (1946, RCA LJM3000); L. Armstrong: Blueberry Hill (1949, Decca 24752); E. Condon: *Jammin' at Condon's* (1954, Col. CL616); All Stars: *Session at Riverside* (1956, Cap. T761); B. Crosby: *Porgy and Bess* (1958, Dot 25193); World's Greatest Jazz Band: *Extra* (1969, Project 5039); *Live at the Roosevelt Grill* (1970, Atl. 1570)

BIBLIOGRAPHY

ChiltonW

D. L. Wolff: "The Ten Most Underrated Jazzmen Picked by Critic," *DB*, x/3 (1943), 17

L. Tomkins: "The Billy Butterfield Story," *CI*, xiii/5 (1974), 6

S. Voce: "Billy Butterfield: I can Hit as High as I ever did," *MM*, xlix (2 Nov 1974), 60

B. Korall: Liner notes, A. Shaw: *The Complete Artie Shaw*, iv: *1940–41* (RCA AXM2-5572, 1980)

J. Chilton: "Billy Butterfield," *Stomp Off, Let's Go! The Story of Bob Crosby's Bob Cats & Big Band* (London, 1983), 209

A. Littlejohn: "Billy Butterfield," *JJI*, xxxviii/2 (1985), 16 [interview]

BRIAN PEERLESS

Butterfield, Don (*b* Centralia, WA, 1 April 1923). Tuba player. After army service (1942–6) he studied at the Juilliard School, then undertook studio work for CBS and NBC. He performed with symphony orchestras and local big bands until he became a full-time member of the resident orchestra at Radio City Music Hall. From 1955 to 1956 he participated in concerts of the Jazz Composers' Workshop with Charles Mingus, Teo Macero, and Teddy Charles; during this period he also led his own sextet. He performed again and recorded with Mingus in 1962–3, and in 1983 he played on an album by Macero that was devoted to Mingus's music. He also recorded with Bill Evans (ii) (1974) and the Thad Jones–Mel Lewis Orchestra (1976). Butterfield's technique is uncommonly florid, a skill that has made him of value as a jazz musician. He was one of the first players who, rather than simply marking out the bass line, brought to the instrument a facility akin to that of a trumpeter.

SELECTED RECORDINGS

As sideman: T. Macero: *What's New?* (1955, Col. CL842); G. Melle: *Gil's Guests* (1956, Prst. 7063), incl. Ghengis, Sixpence, Still Life; S. Rollins: *Brass/Trio* (1958, Metro. 1002); C. Adderley: *African Waltz* (1961, Riv. 9377); C. Mingus: *The Black Saint and the Sinner Lady* (1963, Imp. 35); L. Schifrin: *Dissection* (1966, Verve 68654); on T. Jones and M. Lewis: *New Life* (1976, A&M Hor. 707), Little Rascal on a Rock

BIBLIOGRAPHY

FeatherE; *Feather '60s*

LEROY OSTRANSKY

Buttola, Ede [Buttler, Eddy] (*b* Budapest, 1902; *d* Budapest, *c*1981). Hungarian alto saxophonist, singer, and bandleader. He learned to play piano at the age of seven and led his first band when he was 14. At 16 he began to study singing at the National Conservatory in Budapest. He performed on alto saxophone and sang as the leader of the Jolly Boys (also known as Buttola Ede jazz-zenekara), who toured Denmark, Norway, Germany, and Austria (1927–34) and first recorded in Copenhagen in 1929. From 1936 to 1943 he made many recordings with his own big band in Budapest (including *Caravan*, 1937, Radiola 70, and *Bei mir bist du schön*, 1938, Radiola 116). Besides his principal activities he also played clarinet, baritone saxophone, piano, and accordion. (A. Csányi and G. G. Simon: Liner notes, *Jazz and Hot Dance in Hungary*, Harl. 2015, 1985)

GÉZA GÁBOR SIMON, RAINER E. LOTZ

Butts, Jimmy [James H.] (*b* New York, 24 Sept 1917). Double bass player. He worked with Art Hodes (1940), Les Hite (1941), Chris Columbus (1942), and Don Redman (1943), and recorded with Hodes and Redman. As a member of Tiny Grimes's band he played on Charlie Parker's first commercial recordings with a small group (1944) and participated in a session with Trummy Young (1946); he also recorded with Lem Johnson (1944), and Sir Charles Thompson (1945). His strong, rhythmic playing may be clearly heard on Helen Humes's *Jumpin' on Sugar Hill/Today I Sing the Blues* (1947, Mer. 8077). From the late 1940s to the 1960s Butts led his own bands; in 1968 he began working in a duo with his wife, the drummer and singer Eydie Byrd. He continues to play in and around New York. (*ChiltonW*; *Feather–Gitler '70s*)

Buzz-wow mute. *See* MUTE, §2(e).

Byard, Jaki [John A., Jr.] (*b* Worcester, MA, 15 June 1922). Pianist, tenor saxophonist, and composer. He grew up in a musical family and learned trumpet and piano as a child. During army service (1941–6) he played trombone. After touring and recording as a pianist with Earl Bostic (1949–50) he worked in Boston as a solo pianist and then as tenor saxophone soloist in Herb Pomeroy's big band (1955–7). From 1959 to 1961 he was the pianist in Maynard Ferguson's band. Byard recorded with some of the most innovative musicians of the 1960s, including Eric Dolphy and Don Ellis (both 1960), Charles Mingus (1962–4), Booker Ervin and Charlie Mariano (both 1963), and Roland Kirk (1965). He began teaching at several schools, notably the New England Conservatory, from the late 1960s; he also performed and recorded as a soloist and with his own groups. From the late 1970s he led two big bands, both called the Apollo Stompers, in Boston and New York. Byard's compositions, such as *Aluminum Baby*, are characterized by their humor, and frequently embrace a number of disparate styles; his method of improvisation is similarly eclectic, a quality that made him especially effective as a sideman with Mingus.

Oral history material in *CtY*, *NjR*.

SELECTED RECORDINGS

As unaccompanied soloist: *There'll Be Some Changes Made* (1972, Muse 5007); *To them – to us* (1981, SN 1025)

As leader: *Here's Jaki* (1961, NewJ 8256); *Jaki Byard with Strings!* (1968, Prst. 7573); *The Jaki Byard Experience* (1968, Prst. 7615); of Apollo Stompers: *Phantasies* (1984, SN 1075)

As sideman: H. Pomeroy: *Life is a Many Splendored Gig* (1957, Roul. 52001), incl. Aluminum Baby; E. Dolphy: *Outward Bound* (1960, NewJ 8236); C. Mingus: *The Black Saint and the Sinner Lady* (1963, Imp. 35); *Mingus, Mingus, Mingus, Mingus, Mingus* (1963, Imp. 54); *Town Hall Concert* (1964, Charles Mingus 005); *The Great Concert of Charles Mingus* (1964, America 003–5)

BIBLIOGRAPHY

D. Morgenstern: "Ready, Willing, and Able: Jaki Byard," *DB*, xxxii/22 (1965), 18

M. Walker: "Jaki Byard," *JM*, [no.159] (1968), p.29; no.160 (1968), p.30; no.161 (1968), p.30 [discography]

R. Brown: "Jaki Byard: Romping, Stomping, and Waiting for the Break," *DB*, xlvi/5 (1979), 15 [incl. discography]
L. Lyons: *The Great Pianists: Speaking of their Lives and Music* (New York, 1983), 185
G. Giddins: *Rhythm-a-ning: Jazz Tradition and Innovation in the '80s* (New York, and Oxford, England, 1985) [colln of previously pubd articles], 3, 122
S. Vandermark: "Jaki Byard: Interview," *Cadence*, xi (1985), no.3, p.5; no.4, p.12

ANDREW JAFFE

Byas, Don [Carlos Wesley] (*b* Muskogee, OK, 21 Oct 1912; *d* Amsterdam, 24 Aug 1972). Tenor saxophonist. During the 1930s he played with a variety of bands, including those of Lionel Hampton (1935), Eddie Barefield, Buck Clayton (1936), Don Redman, Lucky Millinder, and Andy Kirk (1939–40); he first recorded with Timme Rosenkrantz (1938). In 1941 he joined Count Basie's orchestra, occupying the chair formerly held by Lester Young (for illustration *see* FILMS, fig.3), then from 1943 to 1946 played in small groups led by Coleman Hawkins, Dizzy Gillespie, and others, as well as leading his own bands. Byas traveled to Europe in autumn 1946 with Redman's band and soon took up permanent residence there – first in France, and later in the Netherlands and Denmark. Thereafter he worked most frequently as a soloist, performing at a number of festivals; he also played with Duke Ellington (1950), toured with Jazz at the Philharmonic, and recorded with Ben Webster (1968). During the last years of his life he undertook jazz and dance-band engagements intermittently throughout Europe. He returned to the USA only once, in 1970, when he appeared at the Newport Jazz Festival.

Ex.1 Byas's solo from the second chorus of *I got rhythm* (1945, Jazz Star 47102); transcr. T. Owens

∪ = dip

Byas began his playing career as one of the many imitators of Coleman Hawkins, but by the mid-1940s he had become an important transitional figure who combined the tone quality and vibrato of Hawkins with some of the rhythmic and melodic ideas of Charlie Parker and other bop musicians. In a remarkable duet performance with Slam Stewart of *I got rhythm*, for example, he plays long strings of eighth-notes in the bop style, and even produces some of the melodic formulas used regularly by Parker; these are marked by brackets in ex.1.

SELECTED RECORDINGS

Duos with S. Stewart: Indiana (1945, Jazz Star 47101); I got rhythm (1945, Jazz Star 47102)
As leader: Riffin' and Jivin' (1944, Savoy 582); Laura (1945, American 1001–4); How High the Moon (1945, Savoy 597); Laura (1947, Blue Star 27); on *Americans in Europe* (1963, Imp. 37), I remember Clifford; with B. Webster: *Don Byas Meets Ben Webster* (1968, Saba 15159)

Don Byas, New York, c1944

As sideman: T. Rosenkrantz: A Wee Bit of Swing (1938, Vic. 25876); H. L. Page: Lafayette (1940, Decca 18124); on *The Harlem Jazz Scene* (1941, Eso. 4), D. Gillespie: Stardust, pt i; C. Basie: Harvard Blues (1941, OK 6564); Royal Garden Blues (1942, Col. 36710); C. Hawkins: Battle of the Saxes (1944, Key. 1316); D. Gillespie: Bebop (1945, Manor 5000); S. Stewart: Slamboree (1945, Ari. 5001)

BIBLIOGRAPHY

R. Horricks: *Count Basie and his Orchestra: its Music and its Musicians* (London and New York, 1957), 177
D. Byas: "In my Opinion," *JJ*, xiv/3 (1961), 5
A. Barnett: "Don Byas: Tenor Saxophonist," *JM*, xi/7 (1965), 13
J. Burns: "Don Byas," *JJ*, xviii/9 (1965), 5
V. Wilmer: "The Big Noise from Muskogee," *JB*, ii/10 (1965), 4 [interview]
M. Hennessey: "Don Byas: Emphatic Expatriate," *DB*, xxxiv/15 (1967), 23
W. F. van Eyle: *Don Byas Discography* (Zaandam, Netherlands, 1967)
H. Panassié: "Don Byas," *BHcF*, no.221 (1972), 3
D. Morgenstern: Liner notes, *Savoy Jazz Party* (Savoy 2213, 1976)
D. B. Wilke: "A Don Byas Discography, 1938–1972 (Part 1: 1938–1943)," *Micrography*, no.46 (1978), 17

THOMAS OWENS

Byers, Billy [William Mitchell] (*b* Los Angeles, 1 May 1927). Arranger and trombonist. He learned piano and studied composition as a child. The onset of arthritis when he was 14 forced him to give up keyboard performance, so he changed to trombone and shortly afterwards played with Karl Kiffe's Hollywood Canteen Kids, for whom he also provided some arrangements. After army service (1944–5) he worked as trombonist and arranger for Georgie Auld, Buddy Rich, and Benny Goodman (all 1949) and Charlie Ventura and Teddy Powell (*c*1950). He then joined the staff of WMGM in New York to write music for radio and television, and did similar work for Ray Ventura in Paris, where he also recorded an album as the leader of a small group (*Jazz on the Left Bank*, 1956, Phi. B081124). He later returned to Europe as a member of Quincy Jones's orchestra and played for Harold Arlen's blues opera *Free and Easy* (1959–60). From 1960 to 1965 he was Jones's assistant at Mercury Records and arranged the music for a series of albums by Count Basie; he also recorded some arrangements of pieces by Duke Ellington under his own name. Thereafter he worked as an arranger and orchestrator, predominantly of film scores. In 1974 he toured Europe and Japan with Frank Sinatra.

SELECTED ARRANGEMENTS

As leader: *Impressions of Duke Ellington* (1962, Mer. 6028)
Recorded by C. Basie: *More Hits of the 50's and 60's* (1963, Verve 68563); *Basie Land* (1963, Verve 68597); *Basie Picks the Winners* (1965, Verve 68616)

BIBLIOGRAPHY

FeatherE; *Feather '60s*; *Feather–Gitler '70s*
B. Byers and W. L. Fowler: "How to Design your Basie-type Chart," *DB*, xlii/17 (1975), 44
W. L. Fowler: "Billy Byers: Everybody's Expert," *DB*, xlii/19 (1975), 14 [incl. discography]

DAVID FLANAGAN

Byrd, Charlie [Charles L.] (*b* Chuckatuck, VA, 16 Sept 1925). Guitarist. He grew up in a musical family and began learning guitar as a child. In France during World War II he had a chance to play with his idol, Django Reinhardt. After the war he played with Sol Yaged (1947), Joe Marsala (1948), and Freddie Slack (1949), but he became dissatisfied with the lack of professional opportunities open to jazz musicians and decided to pursue a career as a concert guitarist; he studied classical guitar with Sophocles Papas (1950) and Andrés Segovia (1954). Although Byrd has performed the concert repertory, he has concentrated on applying the techniques of playing classical guitar to the performance of jazz and popular music. From the 1950s he played regularly in and around Washington; he also performed and recorded with Woody Herman (1958–9). His interest in Latin music was intensified by a tour of South America sponsored by the US State Department (1961), and in 1962 he recorded the album *Jazz Samba* with Stan Getz, which first popularized bossa nova in the USA. In 1973 he formed the group Great Guitars with Barney Kessel and Herb Ellis. Byrd has considerable technical ability; although he admires the playing of Reinhardt, Les Paul, and Antonio Carlos Jobim, his own style remains distinctive. He has written an instruction manual, *Charlie Byrd's Melodic Method for Guitar* (New York, 1973).

Byrd's brother, Joe (Gene) Byrd (*b* Chuckatuck, VA, 21 May 1933), studied at the Peabody Conservatory and first played guitar and double bass on recordings led by his brother in 1962. From about 1964 he has been a regular member of the latter's groups, playing double bass and electric bass guitar.

Donald Byrd (left) and Hank Mobley, 1956

SELECTED RECORDINGS

As leader: *Jazz Recital* (1957, Savoy 12099); *Blues for Night People* (1957, Savoy 12116); *Brazilian Byrd* (1965, Col. CS9137); *Hit Trip* (1968, Col. CS9627); *Blue Byrd* (1978, Conc. 82); of Great Guitars (with H. Ellis and B. Kessel): *Great Guitars at the Winery* (1980, Conc. 131)
As sideman with S. Getz: *Jazz Samba* (1962, Verve 68432)

BIBLIOGRAPHY

Feather '60s; *Feather–Gitler '70s*
T. Scanlan: "Chuckatuck's Gift to Guitar," *DB*, xxvii/15 (1960), 26
M. Joyce: "Charlie Byrd: Interview," *Cadence*, iv/5–6 (1978), 14
L. Tomkins: "The Charlie Byrd Story," *CI*, xvii/6 (1979), 12
J. Hatlo: "Charlie Byrd," *Jazz Guitars: an Anthology*, ed. J. Sallis (New York, 1984), 217

DAVID FLANAGAN

Byrd, Donald(son Toussaint L'Ouverture, II) (*b* Detroit, 9 Dec 1932). Trumpeter, flugelhorn player, and teacher. His studies at Wayne State University (BM 1954) were interrupted by military service, during which he played in an air force band. He then attended the Manhattan School of Music (MA in music education). At the same time he was the favorite studio trumpeter of the bop label Prestige (1956–8), though he also recorded frequently for Riverside and Blue Note. He gave performances with George Wallington (1955), Art Blakey, Max Roach, Sonny Rollins, John Coltrane, and others, before settling into a partnership with Pepper Adams (1958–61). After studying composition in Europe (1962–3) Byrd began a career in black music education, teaching at Rutgers, the Hampton Institute, Howard University, and (after receiving a law degree, 1976) North Carolina Central University; in 1982 he was awarded a doctorate by Columbia Teachers College.

Following the death of Clifford Brown in 1956, Byrd was for a few years arguably the finest hard-bop trumpeter. He had not only a masterful technique, displayed on all his albums from this period, but also a beautiful tone, heard to best advantage on a rendition of *They can't take that away from me* with Red Garland (1957). He resumed playing in the 1970s and made several pleasant recordings in a jazz-rock style, but his music became increasingly tasteless and shallow. His best-selling album *Black Byrd* led to the formation of his students into the Blackbyrds, a hit group of the mid-1970s.

Oral history material in *NjR*.

SELECTED RECORDINGS

As leader: with A. Farmer: *Two Trumpets* (1956, Prst. 7062); with P. Woods: *The Young Bloods* (1956, Prst. 7080); *Byrd in Flight* (1960, BN 4048); *Royal Flush* (1961, BN 84101); *Free Form* (1961, BN 84118); *A New Perspective* (1963, BN 84124); *Electric Byrd* (1970, BN 84349); *Black Byrd* (c1972, BN LA047); *Street Lady* (1973, BN LA140)

As sideman: J. McLean: *Lights Out* (1956, Prst. 7035); A. Blakey: *The Jazz Messengers* (1956, Col. CL897); H. Silver: *Six Pieces of Silver* (1956, BN 1539); S. Rollins: *Sonny Rollins* (1956, BN 1542); R. Garland: *All Mornin' Long* (1957, Prst. 7130), incl. They can't take that away from me; J. Coltrane: *Lush Life* (1958, Prst. 7188); P. Adams: *10 to 4 at the 5 Spot* (1958, Riv. 265); D. Gordon: *One Flight Up* (1964, BN 84176)

BIBLIOGRAPHY

M. James: "Donald Byrd," *JM*, ix/1 (1963), 6
N. Hentoff: "Donald Byrd," *BMI: the Many Worlds of Music* (1967), June, 17
B. Quinn: "Donald Byrd: Campus Catalyst," *DB*, xxxviii/17 (1971), 19
H. Nolan: "Donald Byrd: 'Infinite Variations'," *DB*, xl/13 (1973), 18
B. Palmer: "Black Byrd's Jazz Flies High," *RS*, no.184 (10 April 1975), 22
U. B. Davis: *The Afro-American Musician and Writer in Paris during the 1950s and 1960s: a Study of Kenny Clarke, Donald Byrd, Chester Himes and James Baldwin* (diss., U. of Pittsburgh, 1983) [incl. oral histories]

BARRY KERNFELD

Byrd, Joe (*b* 1933). Bass player, brother of CHARLIE BYRD.

Byrne, Bill [William E., Jr.] (*b* Stamford, CT, 26 April 1942). Baritone saxophonist. He studied music at San Francisco State College (BA 1965), where he played clarinet, and first worked professionally around Oakland, California. After army service he joined Harry James's orchestra, with which he performed in the USA and Europe. From 1970 he worked as a studio musician in Los Angeles, and recorded with the big bands of Bill Berry (1974), Louie Bellson (1974–5), Terry Gibbs, Chuck Mangione, and Neal Hefti. Byrne also played and recorded intermittently from 1976 into the mid-1980s with the Toshiko Akiyoshi–Lew Tabackin Big Band; he takes a fine solo on *Henpecked Old Man*, on the album *Roadtime* (1976, RCA CPL2-2242). He should not be confused with the trumpeter Bill Byrne who played and worked as road manager for Woody Herman's band from 1965 to the mid-1980s. (*Feather–Gitler '70s*)

Byrne, Bobby [Robert] (*b* Columbus, OH, 10 Oct 1918). Trombonist. At the age of 16 he joined the Dorsey Brothers' Orchestra; after the brothers separated in 1935 he continued to perform and record as the trombone soloist in Jimmy Dorsey's band. In 1940 he formed his own big band, engaging Don Redman as his arranger in 1941; after army service he organized another band (1946), then worked as a freelance in New York. His dixieland group appeared on Steve Allen's television show and recorded in 1953 and 1954 (*Dixieland Jazz*, Grand Award 313). As a member of studio orchestras Byrne played for such musicians as Pearl Bailey (1952–3, 1958), Cannonball Adderley (1956), Cootie Williams and Charlie Barnet (both 1958), and Urbie Green and Lionel Hampton (both 1960); he also recorded as the leader of his own big band (1958). He ceased playing professionally in the late 1960s and became an executive for Command Records.

BIBLIOGRAPHY

FeatherE
G. T. Simon: *The Big Bands* (New York, 1967, rev. and enlarged 2/1971, rev. 3/1974, 4/1981), 107

C

Cab Jivers. Small group, made up of members of Cab Calloway's big band. It was organized in 1938 around the tenor saxophonist Chu Berry, and included at various times the trumpeters Irving "Mouse" Randolph and Jonah Jones; Tyree Glenn, who played vibraphone and trombone; the clarinetist Jerry Blake; and the rhythm section of the big band. When Berry died in 1941 the group disbanded, but it was re-formed after World War II with Jones, Glenn, Ike Quebec, and the clarinetist Al Gibson. Neither ensemble recorded, but new versions of the group, still including Jones, made recordings in the late 1940s.

FRANK DRIGGS

Cables, George (Andrew) (*b* New York, 14 Nov 1944). Pianist, keyboard player, and composer. He studied at the Mannes College and formed the Jazz Samaritans with Steve Grossman and Billy Cobham when he was 18; he was strongly influenced by Thelonious Monk and Herbie Hancock. He played with Art Blakey (1969), Sonny Rollins (1969), Joe Henderson (1969–71), and Freddie Hubbard (1971–6). In Los Angeles he formed a trio, Cable Car, and performed at local clubs, sometimes on electric piano. In the mid- to late 1970s he played with Gábor Szabó, Art Pepper, and Bobby Hutcherson. He performed at the Keystone Korner in San Francisco with Dexter Gordon in December 1976, then played regularly with Gordon from 1977 to 1978; during this period the acoustic piano again became his principal instrument. In 1984 he recorded with the group Bebop and Beyond. Cables's recorded work has been well received, but he has been described as an accomplished sideman rather than an assertive leader. *Morning Song* is among his best-known compositions.

SELECTED RECORDINGS

As leader: *Cables Vision* (1979, Cont. 14001), incl. Morning Song; *By George* (1987, Cont. 14030)

As sideman: J. Henderson: *In Pursuit of Blackness* (1970–71, Mlst. 9034); F. Hubbard: *Liquid Love* (1975, Col. PC33556); B. Hutcherson: *Waiting* (1976, BN LA615G); D. Gordon: *Sophisticated Giant* (1977, Col. JC34989); R. Haynes: *Thank you, Thank you* (1977, Gal. 5103); A. Pepper: *Saturday Night at the Village Vanguard* (1977, Cont. 7644); D. Gordon: *Manhattan Symphonie* (1978, Col. JC35608); B. Hutcherson: *Un poco loco* (*c*1980, Col. FC36402); Bebop and Beyond: *Bebop and Beyond* (1984, Conc. 244)

BIBLIOGRAPHY

L. Feather: "Profile: George Cables," *DB*, xlv/5 (1978), 34

L. Lyons: "George Cables: Rising Young Jazz Pianist," *CK*, v/5 (1979), 14

S. Freedman: "George Cables: *Cables Vision*," *DB*, xlviii/2 (1981), 36 [review]

G. Cables: "Jazz with Art, and the Art of Jazz," *CI*, xx/3 (1981), 22

L. Underwood: "George Cables," *DB*, xlviii/8 (1981), 27 [incl. discography]

J. Aikin: "George Cables Takes a Phantom Solo," *Keyboard*, xii/2 (1986), 42

PAUL RINZLER

Caceres, Ernie [Ernesto] (*b* Rockport, TX, 22 Nov 1911; *d* San Antonio, 10 Jan 1971). Clarinetist and saxophonist. In his youth, and at the end of his life, he also played guitar. In the 1930s he played clarinet and baritone saxophone in San Antonio and, later, New York, in groups organized by his brother the violinist Emilio Caceres (1897–1980). In 1937 the Emilio Caceres Trio played on Benny Goodman's "Camel Caravan" radio show and recorded six titles. Ernie then performed with Bobby Hackett (1938–9, 1944–5), Jack Teagarden (1939–40), Bob Zurke (1940), Glenn Miller (1940–42; for illustration *see* MUTE, fig.3), Tommy Dorsey (1943), Goodman (1943, 1944), Woody Herman (1944), and Billy Butterfield (1944–5), playing mainly alto or baritone saxophone but sometimes solo clarinet. He also recorded with Sidney Bechet, Muggsy Spanier, and (in 1947) Louis Armstrong. From 1942 to 1948 he appeared often with Eddie Condon (for illustration *see* NIGHTCLUBS AND OTHER VENUES, fig.5) and he also served briefly in an army band (1945–?1946). Caceres had his own quartet in New York (1949) and then joined a television studio orchestra. In the 1950s he recorded with various artists, particularly Hackett, for whom he played baritone saxophone at the Henry Hudson Hotel (1956–7). Following a short reunion with Butterfield, in and around Newport News, Virginia, in the early 1960s, he returned about 1962 to San Antonio, where he played with Jim Cullum's Happy Jazz Band and Chuck Reilly's Alamo City Jazz Band. He and Emilio made a final recording in 1969.

Caceres's clarinet sound, sometimes reedy or even raspy but always full-bodied, suited his hard-driving, ebullient style; his solos with Miller, mostly in the upper register of the instrument, are succinct and well-shaped. As a baritone saxophonist he was admired for his big sound, agility, and ability to improvise in a group.

SELECTED RECORDINGS

As leader with Emilio Caceres: *Ernie and Emilio Caceres* (1969, Audiophile 101)

As sideman: J. Teagarden: Persian Rug (1939, Bruns. 8370); Muddy River Blues/Wolverine Blues (1939, Col. 35297); G. Miller: Anvil Chorus (1940, Bb 10982); *Glenn Miller Concert*, iii (1940, RCA LPT3001), incl. Dipper Mouth Blues; Long Tall Mama (1941, Vic. 27943); B. Hackett: *Gotham Jazz Scene* (1957, Cap. T857); *Jazz Ultimate* (1957, Cap. T933)

BIBLIOGRAPHY

ChiltonW; *FeatherE*
C. Roscoe: "Virtuoso: A Guy Named Ernie Caceres," *SL*, xxiv (1970), 417; repr. in *Jazz Report*, vii/5 (1971), 1
Obituary, *DB*, xxxviii/4 (1971), 8

JEFFREY COOPER

Cadet. Name taken in 1965 by the record label formerly known as ARGO.

Cadillac (i). Nickname of NELSON WILLIAMS.

Cadillac (ii). English record company and label. The company was founded by John Jack and Mike Westbrook in London in 1973. By 1987 it had issued 16 albums, which included recordings by Westbrook, Mike Osborne, Stan Tracey, Harry Beckett, Trevor Watts, David Murray, and the Jazz Doctors.

SIMON ADAMS

Café Bohemia. Nightclub in New York; *see* NIGHTCLUBS AND OTHER VENUES.

Café Society. The name of two nightclubs in New York, one downtown and the other uptown, both under the same management; *see* NIGHTCLUBS AND OTHER VENUES.

Cagnolatti, Cag [Ernie J.] (*b* Madisonville, LA, 2 April 1911; *d* New Orleans, 7 April 1983). Trumpeter. In about 1929 he began trumpet studies with Arnold Metoyer, and from 1933 to 1942 he played in a big band led by the trumpeter Herbert Leary; he also worked occasionally with Sidney Desvigne and Papa Celestin. In the 1940s and 1950s he was a regular member of the brass band led by the bass drummer George Williams. He played with Alphonse Picou in the early 1950s and recorded frequently with Paul Barbarin (1950–51, 1954, 1962, 1964–5). In the early 1960s Cagnolatti was associated principally with Jim Robinson, and his playing may be heard to advantage on *Lily of the Valley* on Robinson's album *Spirituals & Blues* (1961, Riv. 9393). From 1974 to 1980, when he suffered a stroke, Cagnolatti appeared regularly at Preservation Hall.

Oral history material in *LNT*.

BIBLIOGRAPHY

L. Borenstein and B. Russell: *Preservation Hall Portraits* (Baton Rouge, LA, 1968) [pictures by N. Rockmore]
M. MacMurray and S. Hall: "Ernest Cagnolatti," *SL*, xxxiv (1982), win., 27

ALDEN ASHFORTH

Caiazza, Nick (*b* New Castle, PA, 20 March 1914). Tenor saxophonist and clarinetist. His first important engagements were with Joe Haymes (1936–7) and Muggsy Spanier (1939). Later he played with Woody Herman, the band led by Will Bradley and Ray McKinley, and Bobby Hackett (all 1940), and worked with Spanier's big band (1941–2), Teddy Powell, Alvino Rey, and the pianist Chico Marx (1943). During the mid-1940s Caiazza made many V-discs with Louis Armstrong, Jack Teagarden, Hot Lips Page, and others. He may be heard to advantage on *Tea for Two* by Bill Stegmeyer and his Hot Eight (1945, V-disc 603). Later he worked as a staff musician for CBS and NBC, then with Paul Whiteman at ABC (1950–59). During this period he also performed and recorded with Tommy Dorsey, McKinley, Benny Goodman, and Billy Butterfield. He also played with the New York PO, and studied with the classical composer Paul Creston; several of Caiazza's compositions have been performed in public. In 1960 he moved to Boston and later in the decade he taught at the Berklee College of Music.

based on *ChiltonW*

Cain, Jackie (*b* 1928). Singer who formed a duo with ROY KRAL in the late 1940s.

Caldwell, Happy [Albert W.] (*b* Chicago, 25 July 1903; *d* New York, 29 Dec 1978). Tenor saxophonist and clarinetist. He began playing clarinet in 1919 and studied with his cousin Buster Bailey. His first professional performances and recordings were with Bernie Young's Creole Jazz Band (1922–3), after which a tour with Mamie Smith (1923) took him to New York. Around this time he began playing tenor saxophone, and throughout the 1920s and 1930s he worked with many bands, including those of Elmer Snowden (1925), Fletcher Henderson, Vernon Andrade (1929–33), and Tiny Bradshaw and Louis Metcalf (both *c*1935). He recorded with Louis Armstrong and Eddie Condon in 1929 and with Jelly Roll Morton in 1939; the recordings with Condon are the result of a significant early interracial session. From 1941 to 1944 Caldwell worked in Philadelphia with his own group, the Happy Pals, which he continued to lead after returning to New York in 1945; during the 1950s and 1960s he also played with Metcalf and Jimmy Rushing. Later he recorded with Clyde Bernhardt (1972–3) and toured Scandinavia (1975). Caldwell was an extremely sensitive musician – highly influenced by the playing of Coleman Hawkins – whose best work was evident during passages of group improvisation. His name has frequently been misspelled Cauldwell.

Oral history material in *NjR* (JOHP), *NjR*.

SELECTED RECORDINGS

As sideman: E. Condon: I'm gonna stomp, Mr. Henry Lee/That's a serious thing (1929, Vic. 38046); L. Armstrong: Knockin' a Jug (1929, OK 8703); B. Miley: I lost my gal from Memphis/Without you, Emaline (1930, Vic. 38138); J. R. Morton: Oh, didn't he ramble/Winin' Boy Blues (1939, Bb 10429)

BIBLIOGRAPHY

ChiltonW
H. Cauldwell [sic]: "Albert 'Happy' Cauldwell," *BHcF*, no.35 (1953), 3
L. Feather: *The Book of Jazz: a Guide to the Entire Field* (New York, 1957, rev. 2/1965)
R. Stewart: "My Good Friend Happy Cauldwell [sic]," *JJ*, xv/5 (1962), 11
L. Wright and A. Vollmer: "Happy Horn: an Interview with Happy Caldwell," *Sv*, no.99 (1982), 84

RAYMOND J. GARIGLIO

Calhoun, Eddie (*b* Clarksdale, MS, 13 Nov 1921). Double bass player. He grew up in Chicago and, after army service, performed and recorded with the tenor saxophonist Dick Davis (1947–9) and Ahmad Jamal (1949–52). He played with Horace Henderson (1952–4) and Johnny Griffin (1954), and worked as a freelance with Roy Eldridge, Billie Holiday, and Miles Davis (all 1954–5). From 1955 to 1966 he toured and recorded with Erroll Garner in the USA and Europe; his playing is well represented on the album *Erroll Garner in England* (1963, Jazz Groove 008). Later Calhoun played with the pianist and singer Norvel Reed (1967–8). He then ran his own nightclub, Cal's Place, in Chicago (1972–4) and led a six-piece group at the Fantasy Club (1975–80); he also worked as an accompanist to the pianist Lennie Capp (1980–86). In 1986 Calhoun toured Europe with the pianist Irwin Hoffer and the Chicago All-Stars.

BIBLIOGRAPHY

Feather '60s
J. M. Doran: *Erroll Garner: the Most Happy Piano* (Metuchen, NJ, 1985), 88

JAMES M. DORAN

California Ramblers. Recording group. The name was used for a constantly changing group of studio players led by the singer Ed (Wallace T.) Kirkeby, who assembled between nine and 14 musicians at a time to record under this name from 1921 to 1937. The violinist Arthur Hand was music director to the group in 1922–5 and Kirkeby sang on the group's recordings from 1926 to 1935. Regular members were the pianist Irving Brodsky, the banjoist Tommy Fellini, and the saxophonist Adrian Rollini, and at different times it included the best contemporary jazz musicians, among them the Dorsey brothers, Stan King, Miff Mole, Bill Moore, Red Nichols, and Chelsea Quealey. The band was also known as the Golden Gate Orchestra, and recording groups such as the Five Birmingham Babies, the Goofus Five, the Vagabonds, the Varsity Eight, and Ted Wallace's orchestra often consisted of substantially the same personnel.

The California Ramblers recorded prolifically on numerous labels and were among the pioneers of the big-band style of jazz. Their material was culled predominantly from popular dance hits of the decade, presented in tight, deft arrangements influenced by classic ragtime; in performance the players realized these pieces with agile accuracy, adding fluent melodic improvisations, though the vocal lines were sometimes banal and hackneyed. Besides recording, the group appeared for some years at its own roadhouse, the Ramblers Inn, near New York.

SELECTED RECORDINGS

(all recorded for Edison)

Charleston (1925, 51542); Collegiate (1925, 51580); Clap Hands! Here Comes Charley/Five Foot Two, Eyes of Blue (1925, 51661); Up and at 'em (1926, 51820)

BIBLIOGRAPHY

B. Ulanov: *A History of Jazz in America* (New York, 1952/R1972)
G. Lascelles: "Makin' Whoopee (New York White Jazz)," *The Decca Book of Jazz*, ed. P. Gammond (London, 1958), 102
O. Keepnews: Liner notes, California Ramblers: *Jazz of the Roaring Twenties* (Riv. 1008, 1957)
W. J. Schafer: "'Rhythm King': California Ramblers, Coon–Sanders, Isham Jones," *MR*, v/9 (1978), 7
A. Rollini: *Thirty Years with the Big Bands* (London, Urbana, IL, and Chicago, 1987)

KEN RATTENBURY

Caliman, Hadley (Harold) (*b* Idabel, OK, 1 Dec 1932). Tenor saxophonist. He began playing clarinet at the age of 14, but disliked the instrument; he changed to alto saxophone and then to the tenor instrument in high school. At the age of 16 he toured with various groups, and from 1949 to 1951 he worked with Roy Porter's big band. After studying music at Pomona College and the San Francisco Conservatory of Music he performed and recorded on the West Coast. He led his own group, and was a sideman with Gerald Wilson (1967), Don Ellis, and the English saxophonist Johnny Almond (both 1969), Luis Gasca (1971), Hampton Hawes (1973), Azar Lawrence (1974), Eddie Henderson and Jon Hendricks (both 1975), Bobby Hutcherson (1976–7), and Freddie Hubbard (1979). Caliman was first influenced by Dexter Gordon and later inspired by Lester Young, John Coltrane, and Joe Henderson; his energetic and searching playing has been likened to that of Sonny Rollins.

SELECTED RECORDINGS

As leader: *Iapetus* (1972, Mstr. 342), incl. Dee's Glee, Green Eyes, Iapetus; *Projecting* (1975, Cat. 7604)
As sideman: G. Wilson: *Live and Swinging* (1967, PJ 20118); J. Almond: *Hollywood Blues* (1969, Deram 1057); H. Hawes: *Blues for Walls* (1973, Prst. 10060)

BIBLIOGRAPHY

Feather–Gitler '70s
J. Tynan: "Take Five," *DB*, xxx/13 (1963), 36
M. Bourne: "Hadley Caliman," *DB*, xxxix/9 (1972), 16 [record review]

DIANNA RHYAN

Call and response. The performance of musical phrases or longer passages in alternation by different voices or distinct groups, used in opposition in such a way as to suggest that they answer one another; it may involve spatial separation of the groups, and contrasts of volume, pitch, timbre, etc. The term (the equivalent of which in more formal analytical language is "antiphony") originates in descriptions of the singing of Afro-American work-songs, in which a leader and a chorus respectively sang verse and refrain or successive phrases in alternation. In jazz it is used of exchanges between instrumentalists, two sections of a big band, and even a singer and his own instrumental accompaniment; the most characteristic forms of call and response in jazz occur when musicians trade fours (*see* FORMS, §1(ii)) and take part in a CHASE.

BARRY KERNFELD

Callender, Red [George Sylvester] (*b* Haynesville, VA, 6 March 1916). Double bass and tuba player. He worked in New York until a tour with Blanche Thompson and the Brownskin Models led him to settle in Los Angeles in 1936. He made his recording début the following year with Louis Armstrong, and thereafter played with various small groups in Hollywood. He spent three years in the band led by Lester and Lee Young before forming his own trio, which toured extensively. He also played in Erroll Garner's trio (1946) and took part in many important bop recording sessions with Charlie Parker, Wardell Gray, and Dexter Gordon (1947). From the 1950s Callender became heavily involved in commercial recording and work for television and films, which occupied him almost to the exclusion of jazz performance. An association with Art Tatum, however, resulted in some outstanding studio recordings, reaffirming Callender's remarkable sensitivity as a jazz musician and his capability to drive a group with his sense of swing. He has continued to perform regularly in the mid-1980s with James Newton's quintet (in which he plays tuba), in a duo with Gerry Wiggins, and in Jeannie and Jimmy Cheatham's Sweet Baby Blues Band, with which he appeared in Europe in 1987. Callender plays the tuba with unusual fluency and mobility, and is credited with reviving interest in the instrument's use in jazz. He is also an exceptional performer on double bass and a skilled arranger and composer; among his compositions are *Pastel*, *Skyline*, and *Red Light*.

Oral history material in *NjR* (JOHP).

SELECTED RECORDINGS

Duos with G. Wiggins: *Night Mist Blues* (1983, Hemisphere 1002)
As leader: Get Happy (1945, Sunset 10056); *Swingin' Suite* (1956, Crown 5025); *Red Callender Speaks Low* (1957, Crown 5012)
As sideman: L. Young: D. B. Blues (1945, Ala. 123); L. Armstrong: Where the blues were born in New Orleans/Mahogany Hall Stomp (1946, Vic. 202088); C. Parker: Cool Blues (1947, Dial 1015); D. Gordon: The Chase (1947, Dial 1017); The Duel (1947, Dial 1028); T. Edwards: Blues in Teddy's Flat (1947, Dial 1033); H. Humes: Airplane Blues (1950, Dis. 535); A. Tatum: *Art Tatum Trio* (1956, Verve 8118); *Art Tatum–Ben Webster Quartet* (1956, Verve 8220); Danny Turner: *First Time Out* (1983, Hemisphere 0001), incl. Flight of the Bird, The Blues and Me; Jeannie and Jimmy Cheatham: *Sweet Baby Blues* (1984, Conc. 258); *Homeward Bound* (1987, Conc. 321)

BIBLIOGRAPHY

S. Dance: "Red Callender," *Coda*, no.167 (1979), 9 [interview]
R. Callender and E. Cohen: *Unfinished Dream: the Musical World of Red Callender* (London, 1985)

J. M. Doran: *Erroll Garner: the Most Happy Piano* (Metuchen, NJ, 1985), 69
R. Gordon: *Jazz West Coast: the Los Angeles Jazz Scene of the 1950s* (London and New York, 1986)

PETER VACHER

Calloway, Blanche (*b* Baltimore, 1902; *d* Baltimore, 16 Dec 1978). Singer and bandleader, sister of Cab Calloway. In the mid-1920s she worked as a soloist at the Ciro Club, New York, then toured extensively in revues. She held residencies in Chicago and in 1931 performed with Andy Kirk's band at the Pearl Theatre, Philadelphia. She then led her own orchestra, which included such sidemen as Puddinghead Battle, Vic Dickenson, Clyde Hart, and Ben Webster; it toured and made recordings (including *Catch on*, 1934, Per. 16054) until 1938, when bankruptcy forced Calloway to disband. Apart from a short period in 1940 when she again led a band, she worked as a soloist for several years. In the early 1960s she became the director of a radio station in Florida. (A. J. McCarthy: *Big Band Jazz* (New York and London, 1974), 32)

based on *ChiltonW*

Calloway, Cab(ell) (*b* Rochester, NY, 25 Dec 1907). Singer and bandleader, brother of Blanche Calloway. He spent his childhood in Baltimore and began his professional career in Chicago as a singer and dancer. In 1928–9 he led such groups as the Alabamians in Chicago and New York and the Missourians in New York, where in 1929 he appeared in the revue *Hot Chocolates*. In 1930 the Missourians played and recorded under Calloway's name; they appeared with great success at the Cotton Club in 1931–2, and soon replaced Duke Ellington's band there as house orchestra. The group toured Europe in 1934, appeared in several films (including *The Big Broadcast*, 1932, *The Singing Kid*, 1936, and *Stormy Weather*, 1943), and made a large number of recordings until 1948, when it was disbanded. Calloway then performed mainly in musical theater, taking the role of Sportin' Life in Gershwin's *Porgy and Bess* and performing in *Hello, Dolly!*, but he occasionally assembled bands for specific occasions. He continued to perform and tour into the 1980s, appearing on television, in the film *The Blues Brothers* (1980), and with his daughter Chris in the show *His Royal Highness of Hi-de-ho: the Legendary Cab Calloway* (1987).

Calloway was one of the most successful bandleaders of the 1930s and 1940s, and was famous for his extroverted singing and flamboyant appearance (Gershwin modeled the role of Sportin' Life on him), as well as for his scat singing, from which his sobriquet "the Hi-de-ho Man" derived. He also composed a large number of songs for his group. The band's most important contribution, however, was to promote the careers of a great many jazz musicians, among them Chu Berry, Ben Webster, Milt Hinton, Cozy Cole, Jonah Jones, and Dizzy Gillespie, and with these soloists Calloway made a number of excellent recordings. He donated his private collection to Boston University in 1976; *see* LIBRARIES AND ARCHIVES, §2.

SELECTED RECORDINGS

The Viper's Drag (1930, Domino 4686); St. James' Infirmary (1930, Bruns. 6105); Minnie the Moocher (1931, Bruns. 6074); Bugle Call Rag (1931, Bruns. 6196); The Scat Song (1932, Bruns. 6272); Reefer Man (1932, Ban. 32944); I gotta right to sing the blues (1932, Bruns. 6460); Congo (1937, Var. 593); At the Clambake Carnival (1938, Voc. 4437); Ratamacue (1939, Voc. 4700); Pluckin' the Bass (1939, Voc./OK 5406); Pickin' the Cabbage (1940, Voc./OK 5467); Come on with the "come on"/A Ghost of a Chance (1940, OK 5687); Jonah joins the Cab (1941, OK 6109); Special Delivery (1941, OK 6147); Hey Doc (1941, OK 6354)

BIBLIOGRAPHY

B. Edwards: "The Callow Ways of Cab: a Revealing Close-up of the Man of the Moment," *MM*, x (10 March 1934), 13
S. Voce: "The Marquis of Harlem," *JJ*, xi/6 (1958), 9
O. Flückiger: *Discography and Solography of Cab Calloway* (Reinach, Switzerland, 1960); repr. in *JJ*, xiv (1961), no.5, p.1; no.6, p.13; no.7, p.11
A. J. McCarthy: "Cab Calloway," *JM*, v/12 (1960), 7
G. T. Simon: *The Big Bands* (New York, 1967, rev. and enlarged 2/1971, rev. 3/1974, 4/1981)
S. Dance: *The World of Swing* (New York, 1974) [colln of previously pubd interviews]
C. Calloway and B. Rollins: *Of Minnie the Moocher and me* (New York, 1976)
J. Popa: *Cab Calloway and His Orchestra* (Zephyrhills, FL, 1976) [discography]
D. Gillespie and A. Fraser: *To be, or not . . . to Bop: Memoirs* (Garden City, NY, 1979)
H. Rye: Visiting Firemen, 3: Cab Calloway and his Cotton Club Orchestra," *Sv*, no.91 (1980), 30
D. J. Travis: *An Autobiography of Black Jazz* (Chicago, 1983) [incl. interviews], 219

Cab Calloway's orchestra at the Panther Room, Sherman Hotel, Chicago, 1941: (back row, left to right) Cozy Cole (drums), Dizzy Gillespie, Lammar Wright (i), and Jonah Jones (trumpets); (middle row) Bennie Payne (piano), Milt Hinton (double bass), Danny Barker (guitar), Keg Johnson (trombone), Tyree Glenn (trombone, vibraphone), and Quentin Jackson (trombone); (front row) Calloway (voice, leader), Chu Berry (tenor saxophone), Jerry Blake (clarinet, baritone saxophone), Hilton Jefferson and Andrew Brown (alto saxophones), and Foots Thomas (tenor saxophone)

B. Fong-Torres: "Cab Calloway is no 'Moocher' off Life," *San Francisco Chronicle Datebook* (24 Nov 1985), 39
D. Barker: *A Life in Jazz*, ed. A. Shipton (London and New York, 1986) [incl. discography]
M. Hinton and D. Berger: *Bass Lines: the Stories and Photographs of Milt Hinton* (Philadelphia, 1988)

JOSÉ HOSIASSON

Calypso. A style of music, dance, and song of the southern and eastern Caribbean that evolved from African and West Indian folk music. Calypso songs generally have four short verses that alternate with four-line refrains; they are in duple meter and the accompaniments are usually highly syncopated and based on simple tonal progressions. Early recordings of pieces in the style include Artie Shaw's *The Calypso* (1940, Vic. 27315).

The impact of calypso upon jazz has been slight compared with that of Afro-Cuban and Brazilian music, and some recordings (such as Nat "King" Cole's *Calypso Blues*, 1949, Cap. 915) are connected to the style by name only. Nevertheless some successful fusions of calypso and jazz have occurred. These include Dizzy Gillespie's *Poor Joe* and *Don't try to keep up with the Joneses* (from the album *Jambo Caribe*, 1964, Lml. 86007); Sonny Rollins's *St. Thomas* (from *Saxophone Colossus*, 1956, Prst. 7079) and *The Everywhere Calypso* (from *Sonny Rollins's Next Album*, 1972, Mlst. 9042); and Monty Alexander's *Jamento* (1978, Pablo 2310826).

BIBLIOGRAPHY

T. VanDam: "The Influence of the West African Songs of Derision in the New World," *Record Changer*, xiii (1954), April, 7; May, 4
G. Holder: "That Fad from Trinidad," *New York Times Magazine* (21 April 1957), 14
D. J. Crowley: "Toward a Definition of Calypso," *Ethnomusicology*, iii (1959), 57, 117
E. Hill: "On the Origin of the Term Calypso," *Ethnomusicology*, xi (1967), 359
J. S. Roberts: *Black Music of Two Worlds* (New York, Washington, and London, 1972)
——: *The Latin Tinge: the Impact of Latin American Music on the United States* (New York, and Oxford, England, 1979)

THOMAS OWENS

Camelia Brass Band [Camelia Dance Orchestra]. New Orleans group, led by Wooden Joe Nicholas, which performed from 1917 to 1925. As a brass band it had about ten members and a typical instrumentation of trumpets, trombones, clarinet, tuba, snare drum, and bass drum. When the group worked as a dance orchestra there were generally six players: trumpet, trombone, clarinet, banjo, double bass, and drums. Among the musicians who were members of the ensemble at various times were Buddy and Joseph Petit, Alphonse Picou, the double bass player Billy Marrero, and Marrero's son Lawrence.

WILLIAM J. SCHAFER

Cameo. Record label. It was the most important label of the Cameo Record Corp. The records were mainly sold in Macy's stores. The parent company engaged Lucille Hegamin on an exclusive contract in October 1921, and issued a disc by her on Cameo every two months until 1926. The label was also used to put out recordings by the Original Memphis Five (under the pseudonym Jazz-Bo's Carolina Serenaders) and a group made up of members of the California Ramblers (as the Varsity Eight). The corporation later established the labels Lincoln (January 1924) and Romeo (1926), before merging with Pathé early in 1928. The combined company then joined Plaza in August 1929, forming the AMERICAN RECORD COMPANY, which dropped the Cameo label name in the early 1930s.

BIBLIOGRAPHY

J. Godrich and R. M. W. Dixon: *Blues & Gospel Records, 1902–1942* (Hatch End, nr London, 1964, rev. and enlarged 3/1982 as R. M. W. Dixon and J. Godrich: *Blues & Gospel Records, 1902–1943*), 22
R. M. W. Dixon and J. Godrich: *Recording the Blues* (London, 1970)
B. Rust: *The American Record Label Book* (New Rochelle, NY, 1978), 55

Camero (de Guerra), Candido (*b* Havana, 22 April 1921). Cuban bongo and conga player. He first played double bass and guitar, and took up drums at the age of 14. Entirely self-taught, he learned by listening to native drummers and to recordings by Kenny Clarke and Max Roach; the main influences upon his style, however, were Spanish folk melody and the rhythms of Yoruba music. He recorded in Cuba with the Latin bands of Machito and others, performed with the house band at the radio station CMQ, and was a member of the resident group at the Tropicana Club in Havana for six years. His playing was heard by Dizzy Gillespie, who encouraged him to move to New York and introduced him to important musicians there in 1952. Camero first performed with Gillespie that year, and recorded with him in 1954; he also worked with the trio led by Billy Taylor (ii) (1953–4) and toured and recorded with Stan Kenton (1954). Around this time he began leading his own groups, which played in Miami and New York and included such sidemen as Al Cohn (1956) and Phil Woods (1959). As a freelance he recorded with Erroll Garner (1954), Gene Ammons, Kenny Burrell (both 1956), Art Blakey (1957), Sonny Rollins (1962), Wynton Kelly (1964), Illinois Jacquet, Wes Montgomery (both 1965), Elvin Jones (1969, 1973), and Lionel Hampton (1977). By the mid-1980s he concentrated exclusively on studio work. Camero has helped to extend the influences of Afro-Cuban drumming styles in American jazz.

SELECTED RECORDINGS

Candido, Featuring Al Cohn (1965, ABC-Para. 125); *Candido in Indigo* (1958, ABC-Para. 236); *Latin Fire* (1959, ABC-Para. 286); *Conga Soul* (1962, Roul. 52078); *Candido's Comparsa* (1963, ABC-Para. 453); *Thousand Finger Man* (1970, SolS 18066); *Candido the Beautiful* (1970, BN 84357); *Drum Fever* (1973, Pol. 5063)

BIBLIOGRAPHY

FeatherE; *Feather '60s*; *Feather–Gitler '70s*
"Top Bongo Drummer," *Ebony*, ix/6 (1954), 87
"Swinging News: Candido the Volcanic," *JF* [intl edn], no.21 (1973), 22

CATHERINE COLLINS

Cameron, Jay (*b* New York, 14 Sept 1928). Baritone saxophonist. He played with Ike Carpenter in 1946–7, and, after moving to Europe, played in France and Italy with Rex Stewart (1949), in Germany, Belgium, and Scandinavia (1950–54), and in Paris with Fats Sadi and Henri Renaud; he also recorded in Paris with Bill Coleman (1951) and Roy Haynes (1954) and as the leader of a bop septet. He returned to the USA in 1955 and thereafter worked with Dizzy Gillespie (1957–8), Maynard Ferguson (1957–8), and Paul Winter (1963); he played and recorded with Woody Herman (1956) and Slide Hampton (1960–62), and recorded with Ted Curson (1961). In 1966 he opened a music store in Pennsylvania.

SELECTED RECORDINGS

As leader: *International Onal Sax Band* (1955, Swing 33341)
As sideman: M. Ferguson: *A Message from Newport* (1958, Roul. 52012); P. Winter: *The Winter Consort* (1963, Col. CS8955)

BIBLIOGRAPHY

FeatherE; *Feather '60s*

PAUL RINZLER

Campbell, Jimmy [James L.] (*b* Wilkes-Barre, PA, 24 Dec 1928). Drummer. After working in dance bands (from 1950) he spent six months as a member of the quartet led by Don Elliott, whom he re-joined at intervals during the 1950s, and with whom he recorded in 1954, 1956, and 1957; he had a similarly sporadic association with Sal Salvador, recording in 1953, 1954, 1956, and 1958. Among the other leaders with whom he played in the 1950s were Claude Thornhill, Matt Dennis (1955), Tex Beneke, and Maynard Ferguson (in the group Birdland Dreamband). From 1957 to 1962, except for a year with Stan Kenton (1959), he belonged to Woody Herman's band. After leaving Herman he worked in Broadway musicals, including the original production of *Hello Dolly* (1964), until 1966, when he played with the pianist Page Cavanaugh. He led his own group in Phoenix, Arizona, for two years from 1967 and then worked as a freelance in Las Vegas. He retired from professional playing in 1973 owing to ill health, but returned to his freelance activities in Las Vegas in 1983.

SELECTED RECORDINGS

As sideman: S. Salvador: *Sal Salvador Quartet* (1954, Cap. H6505); M. Ferguson: *Maynard Ferguson Conducts the Birdland Dreamband* (1956, Vik 1070); T. Farlow: *This is Tal Farlow* (1958, Verve 8289); S. Kenton: *Standards in Silhouette* (1959, Cap. ST1394); W. Herman: *The New Swingin' Herman Herd* (1960, Crown 205)

BIBLIOGRAPHY

FeatherE

RICK MATTINGLY

Candid. Record label. It was owned and managed by Nat Hentoff in the early 1960s. The catalogue contained around 12 albums, including notable recordings by Charles Mingus, Cecil Taylor, Abbey Lincoln, and the Newport Rebels. Candid was later purchased by the popular singer Andy Williams; reissue began in the early 1970s on his label Barnaby. The name was later revived for reissues in Japan and Europe. (R. Williams: "Candid Story," *MM* (16 Dec 1972), 46)

Candido. *See* CAMERO, CANDIDO.

Candoli, Conte [Secondo] (*b* Mishawaka, IN, 12 July 1927). Trumpeter, brother of Pete Candoli. His early associations were with Woody Herman (1943, 1945, 1950), Chubby Jackson (with whom he toured Scandinavia, 1947–8), Stan Kenton (intermittently, 1948, 1950–53; for illustrations *see* KENTON, STAN, and PEPPER, ART), Charlie Ventura (1949), and Charlie Barnet (1951). He led his own group in Chicago in 1954, and later that year moved to California, where until 1960 he played with Howard Rumsey's Lighthouse All Stars; during this period he also led a band with his brother and recorded with Stan Levey (1954–7). As a freelance he played and recorded with Terry Gibbs (1959–62), performed with Woody Herman at the Monterey Jazz Festival (1960), recorded and toured Europe with Gerry Mulligan (1960–61), played in Kenton's Los Angeles Neophonic Orchestra (1965–9), and recorded with Sonny Criss (1968), Frank Strazzeri (1973), and Teddy Edwards (1974). He also worked regularly with Shelly Manne (1961–*c*1969) and in film and television studios; he was a member of the band led by Doc Severinsen that played for the "Tonight Show" (from 1968). As a member of Supersax (from 1972) he emulated the style of Dizzy Gillespie (whose work has been a major influence upon his playing) in the group's re-creations of Charlie Parker's music. In 1973 Candoli led a band with his brother at Monterey, and has continued to perform with this group into the 1980s. He has also been active as a teacher, and is highly respected by other musicians as a versatile, strong, and sensitive player.

SELECTED RECORDINGS

As leader: *Sincerely, Conte: Conte Candoli* (1954, Beth. 1016); with L. Levy: *West Coast Wailers* (1955, Atl. 1268); *Mucho Calor* (1957, Andex 3002); with P. Candoli: *The Brothers Candoli Sextet* (1959, Mer. 20515); *Conte Candoli All-Stars* (1960, Crown 5162)

As sideman: W. Herman: Bijou (1945, Col. 36861); H. Rumsey: *Music for Lighthousekeeping* (1956, Cont. 3528); S. Manne: *Boss Sounds* (1967, Atl. 1469); Supersax: *Supersax Plays Bird* (1972, Cap. ST11177)

BIBLIOGRAPHY

FeatherE; *Feather '60s*; *Feather–Gitler '70s*
I. Gitler: *Jazz Masters of the Forties* (New York, 1966/*R*1983 with discography), 94
A. McCarthy and others: *Jazz on Record: a Critical Guide to the First 50 Years: 1917–1967* (London, 1968), 341
P. Willard: "Pulse: Candoli," *DB*, xli/9 (1974), 44
B. Crowther: "Brothers in Brass," *JJI*, xxxviii/10 (1985), 16

FREDERICK A. BECK

Candoli, Pete [Walter Joseph] (*b* Mishawaka, IN, 28 June 1923). Trumpeter, brother of Conte Candoli. He worked as a lead trumpeter in many big bands, including those of Sonny Dunham (1940–41), Will Bradley (1941–2), Ray McKinley (1942), Tommy Dorsey (1943–44), Teddy Powell, Woody Herman (1944–6), Boyd Raeburn (1947; for illustration *see* RAEBURN, BOYD), Tex Beneke (1947–9), and Jerry Gray (1950–51). After moving to the West Coast in the early 1950s he played with Les Brown and Stan Kenton (1952, 1954–6), and established a reputation as a good studio musician and a high-note player. From 1957 to 1962 he led a group with his brother; later he led his own band, and in 1972 he established a nightclub act with his wife, the singer Edie Adams, in which he sang, danced, played, and directed the orchestra. He appeared with the Candoli Brothers band at the Monterey Jazz Festival in 1973, and performed and recorded at the Aurex Jazz Festival (Tokyo) with Lionel Hampton in 1981. He has continued to work with his brother into the 1980s.

SELECTED RECORDINGS

As leader with C. Candoli: *Bell, Book, and Candoli* (1958, Dot 3168); *The Brothers Candoli Sextet* (1959, Mer. 20515); *Blues, when your Lover has Gone* (1961, Somerset 17200)

As sideman with W. Herman: Apple Honey (1945, Col. 36803)

BIBLIOGRAPHY

FeatherE; *Feather '60s*; *Feather–Gitler '70s*
B. Crowther: "Brothers in Brass," *JJI*, xxxviii/10 (1985), 16

FREDERICK A. BECK

Candrix, Fud [Alfons] (*b* Tongeren, Belgium, 17 July 1908; *d* Brussels, 11 April 1974). Belgian tenor saxophonist and violinist. He began his career in the mid-1920s playing in an orchestra led by his brother Jeff Candrix in the Netherlands, Germany, France, Morocco, and Italy. While working in Belgian nightclubs he met Gus Deloof and Jules Testaert. In 1929 he formed the Carolina Stomp Chasers, which performed in Paris and Italy. In 1931 he played and recorded in Germany with Bernard Etté and performed in France with Robert De Kers, in Spain, and in Belgium with Jean Omer and the Hot Melodians led by Chas Remue. He resumed his association with Deloof, and together they composed jazz numbers. In the mid-1930s he played all over Belgium, then formed an orchestra, which became the basis of his big band (1937). He recorded prolifically as a leader from 1937 to 1954 and also took part in sessions with Django Reinhardt (1942, 1943), Hubert Rostaing (1943), and Aimé Barelli (1943). He continued to lead groups of various sizes after the war.

ROBERT PERNET

Capitol. Record company and label. The company was established in Los Angeles in April 1942 by Johnny Mercer, the record store executive Glenn Wallichs, and Buddy de Sylva of Paramount Pictures. At first it was called Liberty, but in June 1942 the name was changed to Capitol; the label was launched the following month. Jazz formed a large part of the catalogue from the start. At first lighter, more commercially-oriented styles were emphasized, but soon coverage broadened; under the supervision of Dave Dexter (who directed artists and repertory) Capitol became an important label for jazz. Among the best-remembered recordings of this period are items by many small bands of the late swing era, as well as material by Nat "King" Cole's trio (1943–7), Stan Kenton (1943–68), Benny Goodman (1947–9), Duke Ellington (1953–5), Marian McPartland (1954–7), George Shearing (1955–68), and Jonah Jones (1957–63); the company also sponsored the sessions by Miles Davis of 1949 that were later issued as *The Birth of the Cool.* A separate race series, the 57-70000s, ran from March 1949 to January 1950, and included recordings by Julia Lee and Blue Lu Barker.

In Britain a Capitol label was launched by British Decca in December 1948 to issue selections from Capitol's American catalogue. This operation ceased when in 1955 the British company EMI purchased a controlling interest in Capitol, and shortly thereafter established Capitol labels in Britain and elsewhere to provide outlets for the recordings it now controlled. The American management continued to operate the company autonomously, and to organize many new recordings; Cannonball Adderley was one of the company's most important musicians from 1962 to 1970. Thereafter new jazz recordings decreased in number, and their quality declined. Major reissue programs were instigated in the 1970s by several of the company's European subsidiaries; a large-scale operation of this nature in France has continued into the 1980s. Capitol became a wholly-owned subsidiary of EMI in 1979.

BIBLIOGRAPHY

A. Morgan: "Classics on Capitol," *J&B*, ii (1972), no.3, p.7; no.5, p.22

"The Record Scene: Capitol Turn Back the Clock," *Jazz Circle News* (Jan–Feb 1979), 8

B. Bennett: "Capitol Research," *Record Research*, nos.183–4 (1981), 11; nos.185–6 (1981), 12; nos.187–8 (1981), 12; nos.189–90 (1982), 11; nos.191–2 (1982), 12; nos.193–4 (1982), 10; nos.197–8 (1983), 11; nos.199–200 (1983), 13

P. Pelletier: *British Capitol 45 r.p.m. Singles Catalogue: 1954–1981* (Chessington, England, 1982) [Record Information Services pubn]

B. Daniels and G. Gart: "Capitol," *Whiskey, Women, and . . .*, no.14 (1984), 37

D. Dexter, Jr.: Liner notes, *The Capitol Jazzmen 1943–47* (Swaggie S1406, 1984)

B. Bennett: "Capitol 15000 Series," *Record Research*, nos.227–8 (1987), 2; nos.229–30 (1987), 10

——: *Capitol Record Listing 101–3031* (Zephyrhills, FL, 1987)

Capon, Jean-Charles (*b* Vichy, France, 29 July 1936). French cellist. After beginning his career as a double bass player with Albert Nicholas and Bill Coleman (around 1960) he moved in 1962 to Paris and from around 1965 worked exclusively as a cellist. He performed with Jean-Luc Ponty (1965), recorded with Jef Gilson (*Tears for Billy*, 1968, Palm 2), Coleman (1968), and Philly Joe Jones (accompanied by Gilson's band, 1969), and performed as a leader; he also performed as a sideman with Chet Baker and Billy Cobham (1977) and Didier Lockwood (1979). He is considered the leading jazz cellist in France.

BIBLIOGRAPHY

P. Cressant: "Jean-Charles Capon," *Jh*, no.264 (1970), 32

A. Dutilh: "Jean-Charles Capon, le violoncelle à coeur ouvert," *Jh*, no.362 (1979), 14

MICHEL LAPLACE

Capp, Frank [Frankie; Cappuccio, Frank] (*b* Worcester, MA, 20 Aug 1931). Drummer. He worked with Stan Kenton (1951) and Neal Hefti, and in 1953 settled in Los Angeles, where he performed with the singers Peggy Lee (1953–4), and Dorothy Dandridge, Betty Hutton, and Ella Fitzgerald (all 1955–6), as well as with Billy May, Harry James, and Charlie Barnet. From 1953 to 1956 he played West Coast jazz with Stan Getz, Red Mitchell, Marty Paich, Art Pepper, and Dave Pell (with whom he also recorded in 1959–61). In 1957 he joined a trio led by André Previn, with whom he made several recordings (1957–64), and through his association with Previn he was engaged to play in the film studios of Warner Bros. He recorded with a number of musicians at this time, among them Benny Goodman (1958), Terry Gibbs (1960), Turk Murphy (1961, in his dixieland band), and Barney Kessel (1965). He performed in many television shows in the 1960s, and in the 1970s he worked with such musicians as Ernestine Anderson, Bill Berry, and Joe Williams. He came to prominence as the leader with Nat Pierce of a big band; formed in 1975 as the Capp–Pierce Orchestra, it was soon renamed the Capp–Pierce Juggernaut. It played and recorded on the West Coast, and its sideman have included Marshall Royal, Blue Mitchell, Herb Ellis, Richie Kamuca, Britt Woodman, Benny Powell, and Plas Johnson.

SELECTED RECORDINGS

As leader with N. Pierce: *Juggernaut Strikes Again* (1981, Conc. 183)

As sideman: A. Previn: *Like Previn!* (1960, Cont. 7575); *Previn Plays "My Fair Lady"* (1964, Col. CS8995); B. Berry: *Hello Rev.* (1976, Conc. 27); on *Jazz Monterey, 1958–80* (1958–80, PAlt 8080-2), J. Williams: You can depend on me (1979)

BIBLIOGRAPHY

FeatherE

H. Siders: "Frankie Capp: Studio Swinger," *DB*, xxxv/6 (1968), 22

S. Voce: "The Jazz Odyssey of Frankie Capp," *JJI*, xxxv (1982), no.3, p.6; no. 4, p.12

RICK MATTINGLY

Capp–Pierce Juggernaut. Big band formed by FRANK CAPP and NAT PIERCE in 1975 and originally called the Capp–Pierce Orchestra.

Captain Fingers. Nickname of LEE RITENOUR.

Cara, Mancy. Name by which MANCY CARR has often (and incorrectly) been identified.

Cardinal. Record label. It was established in December 1920 by the Cardinal Phonograph Co. of New York, and is noteworthy for having issued Ethel Waters's first recording, which was made in March 1921. By mid-1922 the label was being used to issue material from Gennett's catalogue. (B. Rust: *The American Record Label Book* (New Rochelle, NY, 1978), 58)

Carey, (Papa) Mutt [Thomas] (*b* Hahnville, LA, 1891; *d* Elsinore, CA, 3 Sept 1948). Trumpeter. He first played drums, then guitar and alto horn, and changed to cornet about 1912. His early work was with brass bands in the New Orleans area (1913–17). He joined Kid Ory in 1914, then in 1917 toured on the vaudeville circuit and played in Chicago; he returned to New Orleans in 1918. The following year he went to California to work with Ory, and took over leadership of the group when Ory left (1925). He played with Louis Armstrong's group on some of the sessions prerecorded for (but not used in) the film *New Orleans* (1946). Carey rejoined Ory's band in 1944; on leaving Ory in 1947 he made recordings as a leader in New York (his New Yorkers was one of the most influential recording bands in the revival of traditional jazz in the late 1940s). He worked for other leaders before returning to California, where he again led a group of his own.

On his early recordings Carey produced a sound similar to that of Nick LaRocca, though his tone was more uniform and the clipped staccato attack employed by most trumpeters at that time was replaced by a short sustain and a quick decay, which created a less declarative effect; he introduced melodic embellishment to vary repetition and a soft flutter on long notes. In the 1940s he played with notable drive, his tone was bright in the upper range, and he employed an anachronistically wide vibrato; in his solos he clung closely to the melody.

SELECTED RECORDINGS

Duos with Hociel Thomas: Nobody knows you when you're down and out, first issued on *Mutt Carey Plays the Blues* (1946, Riv. 1042)
As leader: Slow Drivin' (1947, Cen. 4018)
As sideman: Spikes' Seven Pods of Pepper [K. Ory]: Ory's Creole Trombone/Society Blues (1922, Nordskog 3009); K. Ory: Eh la bas (1946, Col. 37275)

BIBLIOGRAPHY

ChiltonW
G. Williams and M. Stuart: "Papa Mutt Carey," *Jazz*, i/7 (New York, 1943), 5
M. Carey: "New Orleans Trumpet Players," *Jazz Music*, iii/4 (1946), 10
Obituary, *JJ*, i/11 (1948), 10
W. Russell: "Mutt Carey," *Record Changer*, vii (1948), Nov, 7
N. Shapiro and N. Hentoff, eds.: *Hear me Talkin' to ya: the Story of Jazz by the Men who Made it* (New York and London, 1955/R1966)
M. Webb: "Papa Mutt Carey: Forgotten New Orleans Trumpet Man," *Fn*, iii/5 (1972), 21
M. Harrison, C. Fox, and E. Thacker: *The Essential Jazz Records*, i: *Ragtime to Swing* (London, and Westport, CT, 1984), 58
J. Darensbourg: *Telling it Like it is*, ed. P. Vacher (London, 1987; Baton Rouge, LA, 1987 as *Jazz Odyssey: the Autobiography of Joe Darensbourg*)

BOB ZIEFF

Carey, Scoops. Name by which SCOOPS CARRY has occasionally (and incorrectly) been identified.

Carisi, Johnny [John E.] (*b* Hasbrouck Heights, NJ, 23 Feb 1922). Composer, arranger, and trumpeter. Mainly self-taught, he first worked as a trumpeter and arranger with Babe Russin in New York (1940) and with Glenn Miller's orchestra (from late 1942). From 1945 he wrote arrangements for various big bands, including those of Ray McKinley, Charlie Barnet, and Claude Thornhill, with whom he recorded on trumpet (1949, 1950). While he was studying with the composer Stefan Wolpe (1948–50) he wrote *Israel*, a polyphonic piece based on the 12-bar blues progression; it was composed for Miles Davis's band of that period (Carisi and Davis were both among a group of experimental musicians associated with Thornhill) and Davis's recording of it (1949) was one of the items later issued on the album *The Birth of the Cool*. In 1959 Carisi wrote arrangements for and conducted a recording by the Guitar Choir (organized by Barry Galbraith). An eclectic and ingenious composer, Carisi continued to write fine works for small ensembles (including the National Jazz Ensemble), for solo performers, and for television and radio, though few of these have been strictly in the jazz idiom; his compositions and arrangements recorded by Marvin Stamm in 1968 are early examples of the influence of rock music on jazz. In 1969 Carisi became a member of the faculties at the Manhattan School of Music and Queens College, CUNY. He performed briefly with Brew Moore in 1969–70 and again in 1984, at a party given in New York to honor jazz pioneers.

RECORDED COMPOSITIONS

Recorded by others: M. Davis: Israel (1949, Cap. 60011); B. Moore: Lestorian Mode (1949, Savoy 953); on G. Evans: *Into the Hot* (1961, Imp. 9), Ankor Wat, Barry's Tune, Moon Taj

SELECTED ARRANGEMENTS

* – with Carisi as conductor

Recorded by Guitar Choir: **The New Jazz Sound of "Show Boat"* (1959, Col. CL1419), incl. Make Believe, Why do I love you?
Recorded by M. Stamm: *Machinations* (1968, Verve 68759)

BIBLIOGRAPHY

FeatherE; *Feather '60s*; *Feather–Gitler '70s*
Liner notes, *The New Jazz Sound of "Show Boat"* (Col. CL1419, 1960)

LAWRENCE KOCH

Carlisle, Una Mae (*b* Xenia, OH, 26 Dec 1915; *d* New York, 7 Nov 1956). Pianist, singer, and composer. She was heard by Fats Waller while she was working as a radio musician in Cincinnati in 1932, and went on to work with him; in 1939 she sang on his recording *I can't give you anything but love* (Bb 10573). She also gave solo performances, and in 1937–9 worked and recorded in Europe; for a time she held a residency in Paris. After her return to the USA she worked in New York night clubs and recorded *Walkin' by the River* and *I See a Million People*, which became the most popular of her compositions. In other recordings for Bluebird she led groups which included Lester Young, Benny Carter, and John Kirby (1940–41). She toured throughout the 1940s, and presented her own radio and television series late in the decade. She continued to record as a leader and in 1950 she also recorded with Don Redman and with the tenor saxophonist Bob Chester. Illness forced her to retire in 1954. Carlisle's voice was expressive, accurately pitched, and well suited to the tender, tuneful ballads that she composed. Her piano playing was modeled on Waller's and incorporated many of his stylistic devices.

SELECTED RECORDINGS

Mean to me (1938, Voc. 198); Walkin' by the River (1940, Bb 11033); Blitzkrieg Baby (1941, Bb 11120); I See a Million People (1941, Bb 11181); 'Tain't Yours (1944, Beacon 7170); You and your Heart of Stone (1944, Beacon 7174); If it ain't Mine (1946, Savoy 617); Long/Gone (1950, Col. 38881)

BIBLIOGRAPHY

ChiltonW; *FeatherE*
H. Smith: "Una Mae Carlisle Takes Final Bow," *Record Research*, ii/5 (1957), 24

JOHNNY SIMMEN

Carlson, Frank (L.) (*b* New York, 5 May 1914). Drummer and percussionist. He studied drums in New York and from 1936 to 1943 was a member of Woody Herman's original big band, with which he made a number of recordings, including *Dallas Blues* (1939, Decca 2629). He also recorded with Glenn Miller in 1939 (Carlson's brother Tony (Anthony G.) Carlson played double bass in Miller's band). After settling in Los Angeles he played with Benny Goodman (1942) and recorded with Red Nichols (1944), Georgie Auld (1952), and June Christy (1953). Later he recorded as a percussionist with Stan Kenton (1963–5), played in Kenton's Neophonic Orchestra (1965–6), performed and recorded with the Los Angeles PO, then moved to Hawaii. (*FeatherE*; *Feather '60s*)

Carlton, Larry (Eugene) (*b* Torrance, CA, 2 March 1948). Guitarist. He worked as a session musician on the West Coast in the early 1970s, and played on albums by such pop singers as Vicki Carr and Andy Williams, as well as recording for films and television. He joined the Crusaders in 1971, adding a hint of the aggression of rock music to the group's smooth, comfortable style. His tastefully funky, economical playing, steeped in the blues tradition, became a hallmark of the Crusaders' work on six albums. He also played with Tom Scott's L. A. Express in the mid-1970s, and worked with such musicians as the singer Joni Mitchell and the rock group Steely Dan. Later he left the Crusaders to pursue a career as a soloist, and in 1978 his first recordings as a leader were issued by Warner Bros. His album *Friends*, released in 1983, included a performance by the blues guitarist B. B. King, who has been one of Carlton's greatest sources of inspiration. In 1985 he began recording for MCA, playing acoustic guitar on the album *Alone but Never Alone*. He continues to blend pop, rock, and jazz to form a style that is sharp, concise, and full of feeling.

SELECTED RECORDINGS

(all recorded for Blue Thumb unless otherwise indicated)

As leader: *Larry Carlton* (c1977, WB 3221); *Larry Carlton Strikes Twice* (c1979, WB 3380); *Sleepwalk* (c1981, WB 3635); *Friends* (c1982, WB 23834); *Alone but Never Alone* (c1985, MCA 5689); *Discovery* (1987, MCA 42003)

As sideman with the Crusaders: *Crusaders I* (1971, 6001); *The 2nd Crusade* (1972, 7000); *Unsung Heroes* (c1973, 6007); *Scratch* (c1974, 6010); *Southern Comfort* (c1975, 9002); *Chain Reaction* (1975, 6022); *Those Southern Knights* (1976, 6024)

BIBLIOGRAPHY

Feather–Gitler '70s

L. Underwood: "The Crusaders: Knights without Jazz" *DB*, xliii/12 (1976), 12 [incl. discography]

M. Small: "Larry Carlton: in Search of the Emotional Response," *GP*, x/9 (1986), 16 [incl. discography]

L. Hildebrand: "Ace Guitarist Loves Doing It his Own Way: Session Jazz Man Scores Big with Three Albums," *San Francisco Chronicle Datebook* (23 Aug 1987), 45

BILL MILKOWSKI

Carmichael, Hoagy [Hoagland Howard] (*b* Bloomington, IN, 22 Nov 1899; *d* Rancho Mirage, CA, 27 Dec 1981). Songwriter, singer, pianist, and bandleader. He studied piano with his mother, a professional pianist, and also learned the rudiments of jazz piano from Reginald DuValle of Indianapolis. He began playing for dances while at high school, and later attended Indiana University in Bloomington, where he organized a college band. He formed a friendship with Bix Beiderbecke in 1924, and the same year the Wolverines recorded one of his earliest compositions, *Riverboat Shuffle* (Gen. 5454). Carmichael made his first recordings in 1925 with Hitch's Happy Harmonists. In 1927 he played piano with Jean Goldkette's orchestra and recorded his *Washboard Blues* with Paul Whiteman, then in 1929 he moved to New York to pursue a career as a songwriter. There he performed and recorded with Louis Armstrong, Mildred Bailey, the Dorsey Brothers, Benny Goodman, Eddie Lang, Bubber Miley, Red Norvo, Jack Teagarden, and others.

Many leading musicians recorded Carmichael's compositions, the earliest of which, including *Boneyard Shuffle*, *Manhattan Rag*, and *March of the Hoodlums*, were multistrain instrumental works. *Stardust*, first recorded in 1927, was originally a fast, rather raggy, piece; in a later slower version it became one of the most-recorded tunes in the jazz and popular repertories. In about 1935 Carmichael moved to Hollywood and found work in the film industry, though a number of his later songs, including *The Nearness of You* (recorded by Connee Boswell, 1940, Decca 3366) and *Skylark* (performed by Billy Eckstine with Earl Hines's orchestra, 1942, Bb 11512), also became jazz standards. Between 1937 and 1954 he took musical or dramatic roles in 14 films, most notably *To Have and Have Not* (1944), *The Best Years of our Lives* (1946), and *Young Man with a Horn* (1950); he usually portrayed an easy-going pianist with an unpretentious singing style. In the 1940s and 1950s he worked for radio and television. His two autobiographies, *The Stardust Road* (1946) and *Sometimes I Wonder* (1965), illuminate his life and the worlds of early white jazz, popular song, and film. His collection of recordings and scores is in the Indiana Archives of Traditional Music in Bloomington; *see* LIBRARIES AND ARCHIVES, §2.

SELECTED RECORDINGS

* – composed by Carmichael

As unaccompanied soloist: *Stardust/*Cosmics (1933, Vic. 24484); on *The Stardust Road* (1960, RCA LSP2246), *Stardust

As leader: *Stardust (1927, Gen. 6311); *March of the Hoodlums/Walkin' the Dog (1928, Gen. 6474); *Lazy River (1930, Vic. 23034) [collab. S. Arodin]; *New Orleans (1938, Bruns. 8250); **Hoagy Sings Carmichael* (1956, PJ 1223)

As sideman: Hitch's Happy Harmonists: *Boneyard Shuffle (1925, Gen. 3066); P. Whiteman: *Washboard Blues (1927, Vic. 35877); L. Armstrong: *Rockin' Chair (1929, OK 8756); Blind Willie Dunn's Gin Bottle Four: Blue Blood Blues (1929, OK 8689); F. Trumbauer: *Manhattan Rag (1929, OK 41330)

BIBLIOGRAPHY

H. Carmichael: *The Stardust Road* (New York and Toronto, 1946/*R*1983)

H. Carmichael and S. Longstreet: *Sometimes I Wonder: the Story of Hoagy Carmichael* (New York, 1965/*R*1976)

A. Wilder: *American Popular Song: the Great Innovators, 1900–1950* (London and New York, 1972), 371

An Exhibition Honoring the 75th Birthday of Hoagland Howard Carmichael, Ll.B., 1926, D.M., 1972, Indiana University (Bloomington, IN, 1972) [catalogue]

D. Schiedt: *The Jazz State of Indiana* (Pittsboro, nr Lebanon, IN, 1977)

T. Buckley: "Profile and Interview with Songwriter Hoagy Carmichael," *New York Times* (27 June 1979)

J. Lucas: "The Unknown Hoagy," *SL*, xxxii (aut. 1980), 20

J. E. Hasse: *The Works of Hoagy Carmichael* (Cincinnati, 1983)

——: "LP Recordings Devoted to Hoagy Carmichael," *Jazz Notes* (1983), Oct, 5

JOHN EDWARD HASSE

Carney, Harry (Howell) (*b* Boston, 1 April 1910; *d* New York, 8 Oct 1974). Baritone saxophonist. He first played piano and later turned to clarinet and alto saxophone. He was active professionally in Boston from the age of 13, and in 1927 moved to New York, where he began a lifelong association with Duke Ellington's orchestra (for illustrations *see* BANDS, fig.3, and ELLINGTON, DUKE, fig.2), first playing several reed instruments, especially alto saxophone, and occasionally bass clarinet. The baritone saxophone was Carney's preferred instrument, however, and he was the first (for many years the only) important jazz soloist on that instrument. In later years he made use of the technique of CIRCULAR BREATHING, which allowed him to sustain the flow of sound indefinitely. His distinctive, rich tone was an essential element of the Ellington sound, and his deep and precise voice anchored the reed section and added an unmistakable touch to the orchestra's performances.

SELECTED RECORDINGS

(all as sideman with D. Ellington)

East St. Louis Toodle-oo (1927, Vic. 21703); Doin' the voom voom (1929, Vic. 38035); Harlem Speaks (1933, Decca 800); Jive Stomp (1933, Bruns. 6638); Saddest Tale (1934, Bruns. 7310); Slap Happy (1938, Bruns. 8297); Cotton Club Stomp (1939, Bruns. 8405); Jumpin' Punkins (1941, Vic. 27356); Perdido (1942, Vic. 27880); Prelude to a Kiss (1945, Vic. 270054); *Ellington Showcase* (1953–5, Cap. T679), incl. Serious Serenade (1955); *All American in Jazz* (1962, Col. CS8590), incl. We speak the same language; *Far East Suite* (1966, RCA LSP3782), incl. Agra; *The Greatest Jazz Concert in the World* (1967, Pablo 2625704), incl. Chromatic Love Affair; *Duke Ellington's 70th Birthday Concert* (1969, SolS 19000), incl. Sophisticated Lady

BIBLIOGRAPHY

J. Staples: "Harry Carney," *Crescendo*, ii/12 (1964), 28

V. Wilmer: "Harry Carney," *JM*, x/2 (1964), 8

G. Schuller: *Early Jazz: its Roots and Musical Development* (New York, 1968), 336

S. Dance: *The World of Duke Ellington* (London and New York, 1970/*R*1981) [colln of previously pubd articles and interviews]

B. McRae: "Harry Carney," *JJ*, xxiv/6 (1971), 30

R. Stewart: *Jazz Masters of the Thirties* (New York and London, n.d. [?1972]), 129

N. Nielsen: "Before Baritone Madness," *JJI*, xxxv/7 (1982), 16

J. L. Collier: *Duke Ellington* (New York and London, 1987)

JOSÉ HOSIASSON

Carolina Cotton Pickers. Band formed in Florida in 1933; its members had previously played together in the JENKINS' ORPHANAGE BANDS.

Carpenter, Ike [Isaac M.] (*b* Durham, NC, 11 March 1920). Pianist and bandleader. He studied piano from 1929 and during his time at Duke University played with college and territory bands. He was a soloist with Boyd Raeburn (1944–5) and then led his own octet on the East Coast (1945–6). In 1947 he formed a big band in Hollywood, which at times included Shorty Rogers, Gerald Wilson, Lucky Thompson, and Maynard Ferguson among its sidemen; it was at first known for its innovative arrangements and adventurous harmonic vocabulary, but it later played a more commercialized form of jazz; Carpenter's playing may be heard to advantage on *Sleepy Time Gal/Sleepy Time Down South* (1952, Intro 7504). The band worked in television, radio, and films, and from 1952 played long engagements in Las Vegas, Hollywood, and Lake Tahoe, Nevada. After it broke up in 1956 Carpenter performed as a soloist; he played only occasionally after 1967, when he joined a publishing and recording company. (*FeatherE*)

Carr, Ian (*b* Dumfries, Scotland, 21 April 1933). Scottish trumpeter, flugelhorn player, bandleader, composer, writer, and teacher, brother of Mike Carr. He grew up in northeast England, and taught himself trumpet. After studying English literature at university he served in the army (1956–8), then played with his brother in a band, the Emcee Five (1960–62). With Don Rendell he led a quintet from 1962 to 1969; during this period he also worked with Joe Harriott, Don Byas, and John McLaughlin. In 1969 he formed his own band, Nucleus, which rapidly became recognized internationally for its experiments with jazz-rock. As a result of its performance at the Montreux International Jazz Festival in 1970 the group was invited to play at the Newport Jazz Festival later that year. By the mid-1980s Nucleus had toured extensively throughout the world, recorded 13 albums, and made many radio and television broadcasts. Carr has also been associated with other ensembles, recording with Neil Ardley's New Jazz Orchestra (1965, 1968) and the Spontaneous Music Ensemble and Keith Tippett's Centipede (both 1971), and working with Michael Garrick (1965–7). In 1975 he helped to establish the United Jazz and Rock Ensemble, with which he has continued to perform and record into the mid-1980s.

From 1970 Carr has been active as a composer, and has been commissioned to write several pieces, including *Will's Birthday Suite* (1974) for the celebrations of William Shakespeare's birthday at the Globe Theatre, London. His other works include *Conversations with the Blues* (1979) and *Spirit of Place* (1986). He has also written three books: *Music Outside: Contemporary Jazz in Britain* (London, 1973), *Miles Davis: a Critical Biography* (London and New York, 1982; Ger. trans., Baden-Baden, Germany, 1985), and, with Digby Fairweather and Brian Priestley, *Jazz: the Essential Companion* (London, 1987). In 1982 he became an associate professor at the Guildhall School of Music and Drama, London; he was made a member of the Royal Society of Musicians of Great Britain, and given the Calabria (Italy) Award for his contribution to jazz, the same year.

SELECTED RECORDINGS

As leader: with D. Rendell: *Shades of Blue* (1964, Col. 33SX1733); of Nucleus: *Elastic Rock* (1970, Vertigo 6360008), *Belladonna* (1972, Vertigo 6360076), *In flagranti delicto* (1978, Cap. ST11771), *Awakening* (1980, Mood 24400)

As sideman: Emcee Five: Let's Take Five (1961, Col. SEG8153) [EP]; M. Garrick: *The Heart is a Lotus* (1970, Argo 135); N. Ardley: *Kaleidoscope of Rainbows* (1976, Gull 1018)

BIBLIOGRAPHY

B. Priestley: "Ian Carr," *JM*, xii/8 (1966), 2 [incl. discography]
P. J. Sullivan: "Rendell/Carr," *JJ*, xxi/6 (1968), 21
J. Fordham: "Nucleus," *Time Out*, no.39 (30 May 1970), 54
R. Brown: "Ian Carr," *Into Jazz*, i/1 (1974), 7
G. Smith: "Carr in Top Gear," *MM*, lii (30 April 1977), 40
L. Underwood: "Profile: Ian Carr," *DB*, xlvi/17 (1979), 66
C. Fox: "Learning the Midnight Oil," *Radio Times* (22 Nov 1980), 18
P. Brodowski: "Ian Carr: Nuclear Fusion," *JF* [intl edn], no.76 (1982), 30

STAN BRITT

Carr, Mancy [Peck] (*b* Charleston, WV, *c*1900; ?*d*). Banjoist and guitarist. He worked with Carroll Dickerson in Chicago during the mid- and late 1920s, and is best remembered for his recordings with Louis Armstrong, then a member of Dickerson's band. His playing may be heard to advantage on *Too Busy* (1928, OK 8596), which he recorded as a member of Armstrong's Hot Four, accompanying the singer Lillie Delk Christian; here the absence of a drummer gives Carr's role a greater prominence. In 1929 he traveled with Dickerson's group to New York, where he made further recordings under Armstrong's leadership. After returning to Chicago Carr moved back to West Virginia, where he worked with his brother. His name is often misspelled Cara.

based on *ChiltonW*

Carr, Mike [Michael Anthony] (*b* South Shields, England, 7 Dec 1937). English organist, brother of Ian Carr. He first gained national recognition as a member of the Emcee Five (1960–62), a band based in Newcastle-upon-Tyne, in which he played piano and vibraphone. From 1963 to 1965 he worked in Africa, after which he played organ in the Nighttimers, a group led by the singer Herbie Goins. He performed frequently at Ronnie Scott's, principally as an organist (1966–7), and later toured extensively with Scott's trio (1971–5), making an appearance at Carnegie Hall, New York (1974). He also visited several European countries with his own quartet (1975–7). In the late 1970s and the 1980s Carr continued to work with his own ensembles, and also accompanied many distinguished soloists. After forming a jazz-rock group, Cargo, in 1980, he began to concentrate on producing and recording as well as performing and writing.

SELECTED RECORDINGS

As leader: *Live at Ronnie Scott's* (1979, Spot. 517)

As sideman: Emcee Five: Let's Take Five (1961, Col. SEG8153) [EP]; R. Scott: *Scott at Ronnie's* (1973, RCA LPL1-5056)

BIBLIOGRAPHY

"Mike Carr: the Man who has All Jazz Takes," *The Journal* (10 Nov 1962)
L. Henshaw: "Carr: on Top of the World!," *MM*, xlix (10 Aug 1974), 51
M. Jones: "Payne Joins Carr," *MM*, xlxi (27 Nov 1976), 20

STAN BRITT

Carroll, Baikida (E. J.) (*b* St. Louis, 15 Jan 1947). Trumpeter and flugelhorn player. After attending Southern Illinois University and the Armed Forces School of Music he directed the free-jazz big band of the Black Artists Group (BAG) in St. Louis. In 1973 he went to Europe with members of the group, and the following year recorded as a leader in Paris. He has taken part in sessions with Oliver Lake (1971, 1980–81), Michael Gregory Jackson (1979), Muhal Richard Abrams (1980–81, 1983), Jack DeJohnette (1982), and David Murray (1984), and has recorded one album as a soloist (1977–8) and another as a leader of a free-jazz quintet (*Shadows and Reflections*, 1982, SN 1023). He is also the composer of a number of film soundtracks and other scores. (V. Wilmer: *As Serious as your Life: the Story of the New Jazz* (London 1977, rev. 1980), 263)

Carroll, Barbara [Coppersmith, Barbara Carole] (*b* Worcester, MA, 25 Jan 1925). Pianist. After attending the New England Conservatory for a year she made a USO tour with a female trio. She then worked in New York as the leader of a bop trio, which recorded from 1949 and which included Chuck Wayne (1947–8), Charlie Byrd (1948), and, from 1949, Joe Shulman (her husband from 1954 until his death in 1957); Charlie Parker, Paul Desmond, and Stan Getz also sat in with the group in the late 1940s. From 1953 to 1957 Victor issued one album a year by the trio; Carroll's playing is heard to advantage on *Have you Met Miss Carroll?* (1955, RCA LPM1137), which includes her composition *Barbara's Carol*. After remarrying and bringing up a family Carroll resumed her career, recording as a leader (1976) and soloist (1980), and performing at the Newport Jazz Festival (1979) and in a concert given at Town Hall, New York, as a tribute to Mary Lou Williams (1981). Although jazz critics have often devalued Carroll's work as that of a supper-club pianist, her astute sense of harmony and her good musical taste have earned her the respect of musicians.

BIBLIOGRAPHY

FeatherE
L. Tomkins: "A Woman's Angle on Jazz Stated by Barbara Carroll," *CI*, xi (1973), no.10, p.26; no.11, p.12 [interview]
B. McRae: "Barbara Carroll: Playing the Words as Well as the Music," *JJI*, xxxi/7 (1978), 40
H. Siders: "Barbara Carroll: N.Y. Jazz Veteran back in the Spotlight," *CK*, v/8 (1979), 24
L. Dahl: *Stormy Weather: the Music and Lives of a Century of Jazzwomen* (London, Melbourne, Australia, and New York, 1984), 75

Carroll, Bob [Robert] (*b* Louisville, KY, *c*1905; *d* New York, 1952). Tenor saxophonist. He left Louisville when he joined Benny Carter's band in the late 1920s. After playing with Horace Henderson (1930) he worked in New York as a soloist in Don Redman's band (1931–6); his recordings with Redman include *Shakin' the African* (1931, Bruns. 6211). In 1937 he recorded with Willie "the Lion" Smith and Lil Armstrong, then joined Teddy Hill's band as a replacement for Cecil Scott. After working with Redman again in the late 1930s he played with Teddy Wilson's big band, Edgar Hayes (both 1940), Henderson again (1941), and Fats Waller (1941–2). He served in the army, and thereafter gradually ceased playing. (J. Evensmo: *The Tenor Saxophones of Henry Bridges, Robert Carroll, Herschal [sic] Evans, Johnny Russell* (n.p. [Oslo], n.d. [?1976]) [discography])

based on *ChiltonW*

Carroll, Joe "Bebop" (*b* Philadelphia, 25 Nov 1919; *d* New York, 1 Feb 1981). Singer. He worked with Dizzy Gillespie from 1949 to 1953, and performed and recorded with him again at the Monterey Jazz Festival in 1961; with Gillespie he wrote the song *Oo-shoo-be-do-be*. Carroll also made several recordings as a leader (1952–3, 1956, 1961–2), and toured and recorded with Woody Herman (1964–5). He was influenced by the scat singing of Leo Watson, and specialized in using fluid sequences of nonsense syllables as lyrics for entire choruses. Often categorized commercially as a comedy singer, he sometimes performed songs that contained light social satire or were ironic in tone, such as *Hey Pete! Let's eat mo' meat* (1949). His sense of swing and timing were solid, and his fluent phrasing and melodic lines were often reminiscent of Lester Young's playing, especially in scat choruses, and of the timbre of Jon Hendricks.

SELECTED RECORDINGS
(all as sideman with D. Gillespie)

Jump-did-le-ba (1949, Vic. 203481); first issued on *Dizzier and Dizzier* (1947–9, RCA LJM1009), Hey Pete! Let's eat mo' meat (1949); In the Land of Oo-bla-dee (1949, Vic. 203538); Honeysuckle Rose (1950, Cap. 57892); The Bluest Blues (1951, Dee Gee 3608); On the Sunny Side of the Street/Oo-shoo-be-do-be (1951–2, Dee Gee 3603)

BIBLIOGRAPHY

FeatherE; *Feather '60s*
D. Morgenstern: "Joe Carroll: Man with a Happy Sound," *Metronome*, lxxviii/7 (1961), 20

MARTY HATCH

Carruthers, Jock [Earl Malcolm] (*b* West Point, ?Bates Co., MO, 27 May 1910; *d* Kansas City, MO, 5 April 1971). Baritone saxophonist. He grew up in Kansas City and studied music at Fisk University. He joined Bennie Moten's orchestra in 1928, then moved to St. Louis, where he worked with such leaders as Dewey Jackson and Fate Marable. From 1932 he was a member of Jimmie Lunceford's orchestra (for illustration *see* LUNCEFORD, JIMMIE), in which after Lunceford's death (in 1947) he continued to play under the leadership of Joe Thomas (iii) and Eddie Wilcox. Later he returned to Kansas City, and played with local groups until the late 1960s. Carruthers was an accomplished section player (he also played alto saxophone and clarinet, and occasionally sang) and a soloist of considerable presence.

SELECTED RECORDINGS
(all as sideman with J. Lunceford)

Rose Room (1934, Decca 131); Harlem Shout (1936, Decca 980); Water Faucet (1947, Majestic 1122)

BIBLIOGRAPHY

ChiltonW; *FeatherE*

EDDIE LAMBERT

Carry, Scoops [George Dorman] (*b* Little Rock, AR, 23 Jan 1915; *d* Chicago, 4 Aug 1970). Alto saxophonist and clarinetist. He studied music with his mother when he was young and later at the Chicago Conservatory and the University of Iowa. In 1930 he began playing professionally in Chicago and toured with Boyd Atkins. He worked with various musicians in the 1930s, among them Lucky Millinder (1931), Zutty Singleton and Fletcher Henderson (both 1936), Roy Eldridge and Mildred Bailey (both 1937), Art Tatum (1938), and Horace Henderson (1939). He was a member of Earl Hines's band from 1940 to 1947; he became its deputy leader and first alto saxophonist, and occasionally played solos. After leaving Hines he ceased full-time playing in order to study law. Carry's solo style was assured and he used a wide variety of melodic patterns with notable dexterity and fluid phrasing. His name has been occasionally misspelled "Carey."

SELECTED RECORDINGS

As sideman: M. Bailey: You're laughin' at me (1937, Voc. 3456); E. Hines: Jelly, Jelly (1940, Bb 11065); Yellow Fire (1941, Bb 11308)

BIBLIOGRAPHY

ChiltonW
J. Steiner: "From the Inside," in S. Dance and others: *Jazz Era: the 'Forties* (London, 1961/*R*1985), 36 [interview]
Obituary, *JM*, no.190 (1970), 13
J. Simmen: Obituary, *BHcF*, no.205 (1971), 7
S. Dance: *The World of Earl Hines* (New York, 1977) [interviews]

EDDIE LAMBERT

Carter, Benny [Bennett Lester] (*b* New York, 8 Aug 1907). Alto saxophonist, trumpeter, arranger, composer, and bandleader.
1. Life. 2. Music.

1. LIFE. Carter received early musical training from his mother and several neighborhood teachers, but was primarily self-taught. He first played trumpet, then tried C-melody saxo-

Benny Carter at RCA Victor's recording studios in New York during a session for Lionel Hampton, 11 September 1939: (left to right) Ben Webster (tenor saxophone), Carter (arranger, alto saxophone), and Chu Berry and Coleman Hawkins (tenor saxophones)

phone, and shortly thereafter changed to alto saxophone, which became his principal instrument. From 1923 to 1928 he played in the bands of June Clark, Earl Hines, and others, but first attracted widespread attention during a year in Fletcher Henderson's orchestra (1930–31), to which he contributed many important arrangements. After leaving Henderson he succeeded Don Redman briefly as the music director of McKinney's Cotton Pickers in Detroit, then returned to New York, where he formed his own highly respected orchestra in 1932. This ensemble included at various times several major innovators in the early swing style: Bill Coleman, Dicky Wells, Ben Webster, Chu Berry, Teddy Wilson, and Sid Catlett. Carter disbanded his group late in 1934 and moved the following year to Europe; he settled in London, where he served as a staff arranger for the BBC dance orchestra (1936–8). During these years he met with resounding acclaim and did much to advance the cause of jazz, playing and recording with local musicians in England, France, and Scandinavia and leading his own interracial, multinational band in the Netherlands (1937); he regularly played alto and tenor saxophone, trumpet, and clarinet, and occasionally played piano and sang.

Carter returned to the USA in 1938 and formed a new orchestra which took up a residency at the Savoy Ballroom in Harlem through much of 1939 and 1940. After briefly leading a sextet he traveled with a new big band to the West Coast, and settled permanently in Los Angeles in 1942. There he continued to lead his orchestra (which in the mid-1940s included such modern-jazz musicians as Miles Davis, J. J. Johnson, and Max Roach), but otherwise turned increasingly to studio work. Beginning with *Stormy Weather* (1943), he composed and wrote arrangements for several major films and, later, television productions. One of the first black musicians to find acceptance in the Hollywood studios, Carter was instrumental in facilitating the entry of other talented Blacks, and was a leading force in the amalgamation of the black and white Musicians' Union locals.

From 1946 Carter no longer led a regular orchestra, though he continued to be active through tours with Jazz at the Philharmonic, occasional big-band engagements, and many recordings. In the 1950s and 1960s he also wrote arrangements for most of the leading singers, including Sarah Vaughan, Ella Fitzgerald, Ray Charles, Peggy Lee, and Louis Armstrong. Carter resumed a more active performing schedule in the 1970s; he appeared at major festivals and nightclubs, made annual tours of Europe and Japan, and, after a ten-year hiatus, resumed recording on a regular basis. He also began a new career as an educator, spending several periods in residence at universities. Princeton University, where he was a frequent lecturer, awarded him an honorary doctorate in 1974. He has remained active into the late-1980s.

2. Music. Carter is an extraordinarily versatile musician, and has made major contributions to jazz in several areas. As an instrumentalist he is recognized, along with Johnny Hodges, as the leading creator of an alto saxophone style before Charlie Parker. Even his early solos, such as *I'd love it* (1929), show the pure tone, facility, varied dynamics, and sophisticated harmonies that set his work apart from that of his contemporaries; later recordings, such as *Crazy Rhythm* (1937), with their long lines, legato phrasing, and understated attack, presaged future developments on this instrument (see ex.1). Carter's trumpet playing, if not as original as his alto saxophone style, is also distinctive, with a characteristic bright tone and delicate vibrato (*More than you know*, 1939), while his relatively few recordings on clarinet reveal him to be an accomplished player with a full, rich tone in the instrument's chalumeau register (*Shoe*

Ex.1 From *Crazy Rhythm* (1937, Swing 1); transcr. J. Mehegan

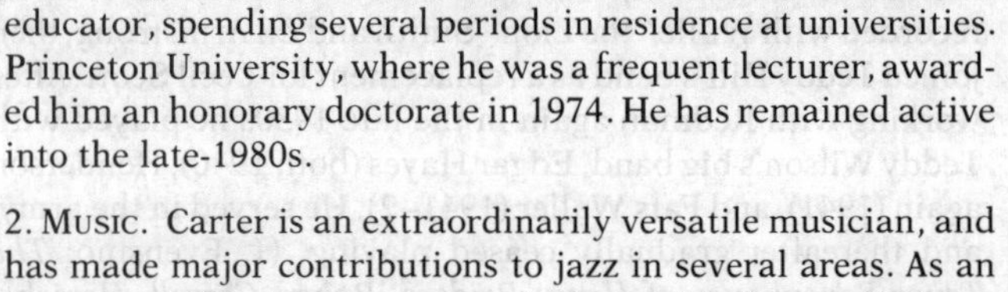

Shiner's Drag, 1938). Carter has also recorded competent solos on piano, tenor and soprano saxophone, and trombone. (*See also* IMPROVISATION, §4 (iv) and ex.4.)

As an arranger, Carter was a principal architect of the big-band swing style; his arrangement for Fletcher Henderson of *Keep a song in your soul* (1930) in particular is often cited as a landmark in the evolution of jazz arranging. *Lonesome Nights* and *Symphony in Riffs* (both 1933) display the innovative block-chord writing for reed instruments that marked his early scores and later became part of the stock in trade of most swing arrangers. His later work of the 1940s is more balanced, while still containing flowing choruses for the reed instruments. Carter also composed a wide range of works, from popular novelty items to extended pieces and dramatic scores; his best-known jazz standards are *Blues in my Heart* and *When lights are low*. His later recordings, such as *Further Definitions* (1961), continue to show his masterly writing for the reed section, as well as a new drive and momentum in his solo playing.

Oral history material in *NjR* (JOHP).

SELECTED RECORDINGS

* – arranged by Carter; † – composed and arranged by Carter

As leader: *Lonesome Nights (1933, OK 41567); *Symphony in Riffs (1933, Col. 2898D); *More than you know (1939, Voc./OK 5508) [tpt]; *Sleep (1940, Voc/OK 5399); †O.K. for Baby (1940, Decca 3294); *I surrender dear (1944, Cap. 200) [tpt]; †I can't escape from you (1944, Cap. 40048); †Malibu (1945, Cap. 200); **Further Definitions* (1961, Imp. 12); *Benny Carter 4: Montreux '77* (1977, PL 2308204) [a sax, tpt]; *Central City Sketches* (1987, Musicmasters CiJD-20126Z/27X), incl. †Blues in my Heart, †When lights are low

As sideman: McKinney's Cotton Pickers: I'd love it (1929, Vic. 38133) [a sax]; F. Henderson: *Keep a song in your soul (1930, Col. 2352D); Chocolate Dandies: Dee Blues (1930, Col. 2543D) [cl]; †Once upon a time (1933, OK 41568) [tpt]; C. Hawkins: *Honeysuckle Rose/*Crazy Rhythm (1937, Swing 1); L. Hampton: †I'm in the mood for swing [a sax]/*Shoe Shiner's Drag [cl] (1938, Vic. 26011); Chocolate Dandies: I can't believe that you're in love with me (1940, Com. 1506) [a sax]

BIBLIOGRAPHY

L. Feather: "Bennett L. Carter, Esquire," *MM*, xii (31 Oct 1936), 2

M. W.: "Benny 'King' Carter," *Musical News*, i/8 (1936), 25 [interview]

C. Emge: "'Jazz' Most Underrated Musician? Benny Carter," *DB*, xviii/10 (1951), 2

L. Feather: "The Enduring Benny Carter," *DB*, xxviii/11 (1961), 15

G. Schuller: *Early Jazz: its Roots and Musical Development* (New York, 1968), 272

J. Chilton: "No Trouble to Double," *Sv*, no.39 (1972), 94

R. Stewart: "The Benny Carter I Knew," *Jazz Masters of the Thirties* (New York and London, n.d. [?1972]), 168

S. Dance: *The World of Swing* (New York, 1974) [colln of previously pubd interviews], 135

J. Simmen: "Crystal Clear," *Coda*, xii/5 (1975), 25

C. Battestini and J.-P. Battestini: "Benny Carter (quelques précisions)," *BHcF*, no.281 (1980), 4

H. Lyttelton: *The Best of Jazz*, ii: *Enter the Giants, 1931–1944* (London, 1981), 132

H. Rye: "Visiting Firemen, 4: Benny Carter," *Sv*, no.93 (1981), 84

M. Berger, E. Berger, and J. Patrick: *Benny Carter: a Life in American Music* (Metuchen, NJ, and London, 1982)

J. Evensmo, P. Borthen, and I. S. Thomsen: *The Alto Saxophone, Trumpet and Clarinet of Benny Carter, 1927–1946* (n.p. [Oslo], n.d. [?1982]) [discography]

E. Okin: "Benny Carter: the Cat with Nine Lives," *The Wire*, no.9 (1984), 16

J. Armitage: "Benny Carter: le roi," *BHcF*, no.332 (1985), 1

EDWARD BERGER

Carter, Betty [Jones, Lillie Mae; Betty Bebop; Carter, Lorraine] (*b* Flint, MI, 16 May 1930). Singer. She grew up in Detroit, and as a teenager sang with Charlie Parker and other visiting bop musicians. By the time she joined Lionel Hampton's band in 1948 she was using the stage name Lorraine Carter; Hampton began calling her Betty Bebop, and hence she became known as Betty Carter. In 1951 she went with Hampton's band to New York, where she worked intermittently for the next two decades, appearing frequently at the Apollo Theatre. She also performed in Ray Charles's touring show (1960–63) and visited Japan (1963), London (1964), and France (1968). In the late 1950s and early 1960s Carter was associated with several recording companies, but refused to make the concessions to popular taste that they demanded of her; instead she preferred complex renditions of popular songs which, though often carefully planned, captured the spirit of bop improvisation. She began to work with her own trio in 1969, and in 1971 founded her own recording company, Bet-Car Productions. Her appearance in 1975 in Howard Moore's musical *Don't Call Me Man* prompted a number of club engagements, and she continued to perform with her trio into the mid-1980s, while also singing with string orchestras under David Amram in New York (1982) and Boston (1983).

SELECTED RECORDINGS

As leader: with R. Bryant: *Meet Betty Carter and Ray Bryant* (1955, Epic 3202); *Out There* (1958, Prog. 90); *The Modern Sound of Betty Carter* (1960, ABC-Para. 363); *'Round Midnight* (1962–3, Atco 33-152); *Finally Betty Carter* (1969, Roul. 5000); *Now it's My Turn* (1976, Roul. 5005); *The Audience with Betty Carter* (1979, Bet-Car 1003); *Whatever Happened to Love?* (1982, Bet-Car 1004)

As sideman with R. Charles: *Ray Charles and Betty Carter* (1961, ABC-Para. 385)

BIBLIOGRAPHY

B. McLarney: "Betty Carter: the 'In' Singer," *DB*, xxxiii/15 (1966), 18

M. Jacobson: "Betty Carter is Alive in Bed-Stuy," *VV*, xx (18 Aug 1975), 100

T. Joans: "Betty Carter," *Coda*, no.145 (1976), 10

H. Nolan: "Betty Carter's Declaration of Independence," *DB*, xliii/14 (1976), 23

D. Hollenberg: "Betty Carter," *DB*, xliv/8 (1977), 44

L. Prince: "Betty Carter: Bebopper Breathes Fire," *DB*, xlvi/9 (1979), 12

B. van Rooyen and P. Brodowski: "Betty's Groove," *JF* [intl edn], no.57 (1979), 28

M. Ullman: *Jazz Lives: Portraits in Words and Pictures* (Washington, 1980)

L. Gourse: *Louis' Children: American Jazz Singers* (New York, 1984), 324

C. Kuhl: "Betty Carter: Interview," *Cadence*, xi/2 (1985), 5

G. Locke: "Betty Carter: in her own Sweet Way," *The Wire*, no.24 (1986), 31

BARRY KERNFELD

Carter, Bob [Kahakalau, Robert] (*b* New Haven, CT, 11 Feb 1922). Double bass player. From 1945 he worked in New York, playing bop and swing with Tony Scott, Dizzy Gillespie, Charlie Parker, Dexter Gordon, Hank Jones, Ben Webster, Stuff Smith, Max Roach, and Charlie Shavers, and recording with Allen Eager (1946). He toured and recorded with Charlie Ventura (1947–8, 1953–4) and Benny Goodman (1949–50), and recorded with Buddy DeFranco (1949), Joe Mooney (1951), Marian McPartland (1951, 1953), and Johnny Smith (1952). A later recording made with Lou Stein, *Three, Four & Five* (1955, Epic 3148), well represents his solo playing. His first efforts at composition were recorded by a group led by the trombonist Bob Alexander, of which Carter was a member (*Progressive Jazz*, *c*1953, Grand Award 325). He then studied composition and arranging in California, where he played with and wrote for Red Norvo (1957). After working in Hawaii he returned to New York in 1958 and recorded with Bobby Hackett (1959). Later he performed and recorded in Europe with Bill Smith (1963) and Henri Chaix and Oscar Klein (both 1969). (*FeatherE*)

Carter, John (Wallace) (*b* Fort Worth, 24 Sept 1929). Clarinetist, alto saxophonist, composer, and teacher. He studied clarinet and alto saxophone, played with Ornette Coleman and Charles Moffett in the late 1940s, attended Lincoln University in Jefferson City, Missouri (BA 1949), and the University of Colorado (MA 1956), and taught in public schools in Fort Worth (1949–61) and Los Angeles (1961–82). In 1964 he formed the New Art Jazz Ensemble in Los Angeles with Bobby Bradford and the following year conducted orchestral music by Coleman at UCLA. From 1974 he played clarinet exclusively; he belonged to the Little Big Horn workshop with Bradford, James Newton, Arthur Blythe, and others (1976–8) and in 1983 formed the Wind College, a school for improvisation, with Newton, Red Callender, and Charles Owens. He has played at clubs and festivals in Europe and the USA, as a leader and as a sideman, with groups that have frequently included Bradford and Newton. In the 1980s he led the quartet Clarinet Summit (*see* CLARINET, §3). Carter is a virtuoso clarinetist with a command of the instrument's entire range. His early compositions show the influence of Coleman; his later ones are more personal and reflect his growing interest in varied instrumentation.

SELECTED RECORDINGS

As unaccompanied soloist: *A Suite of Early American Folk Pieces for Solo Clarinet* (1984, Moers 02014)

As leader: *Flight for Four* (1969, FD 108); with B. Bradford: *Secrets* (1971–2, Rev. 018); *Echoes from Rudolph's* (1977, Ibedon 1000); *Variations on Selected Themes for Jazz Quintet* (1979, Moers 01056); *Night Fire* (1980, BS 0047); *Dance of the Love Ghosts* (1986, Gram. 8704)

BIBLIOGRAPHY

F. Kofsky: "John Carter and Bobby Bradford," *Black Giants*, ed. P. Rivelli and R. Levin (New York and Cleveland, 1970/*R*1980 as *Giants of Black Music*), 41

M. James: "Order and Feeling, Discipline and Fire: an Introduction to the John Carter and Bobby Bradford Quartet," *JB*, iii/1 (1973), 6

M. Weber: "The John Carter Interview," *Coda*, no.157 (1977), 8

H. L. Lindenmaier: "John Carter: Interview," *Cadence*, vi/2 (1980), 11

L. Jeske: "John Carter, *DB*, xlix/11 (1982), 18 [incl. discography]

J. Green: "The Seeds are Set: Wind College," *Bebop and Beyond*, i/5 (1983), 8

ED HAZELL

Carter, Kent (*b* Hanover, NH, 12 June 1939). Double bass player. He studied at the Berklee College of Music from 1960 and played bop with Booker Ervin, Phil Woods, Lucky Thompson, and Sonny Stitt. He also worked in a trio with the pianist Lowell Davidson. In 1964 he joined the Jazz Composer's Orchestra. He continued his studies in Boston, but from 1965 traveled frequently to Europe, where he toured and recorded with Paul Bley (1965) and played free jazz with STEVE LACY; his playing is well represented on Bley's *Touching* (1965, Ari. 1901). In 1970 he settled in France and performed and recorded with Alan Silva (1970), Mal Waldron (1972), Bobby Bradford (1973), Trevor Watts (1975), Roswell Rudd (1982), and others. Carter also plays violin, viola, cello, keyboards, and percussion on his own recordings (1974–9).

BIBLIOGRAPHY

B. Case: "Kent Carter: Interview," *Into Jazz*, i/3 (1974), 15

S. Loupien: "Kent Carter: la beauté de la basse," *Jm*, no.262 (1978), 28 [incl. discography]

Carter, Lavaida (*b* 1914). Singer who toured and recorded with her sister VALAIDA SNOW.

Carter, Lorraine. *See* CARTER, BETTY.

Carter, Ron(ald Levin) (*b* Ferndale, MI, 4 May 1937). Double bass player. He began to play cello at the age of ten. Four years later his family moved to Detroit, where he encountered difficulties in his career as a cellist owing to his race, and in 1954 he changed to double bass. His interest in jazz developed only gradually. He played in the Philharmonia Orchestra of the Eastman School, where he gained the BM in 1959. After graduating he went to New York and joined Chico Hamilton's quintet (with Eric Dolphy) and enrolled at the Manhattan School of Music (MM 1961). In 1960, when Hamilton returned to the West Coast to form a new group, Carter chose to remain in New York, where he made important first recordings with Dolphy and Don Ellis. As a freelance, he played with Randy Weston, performed and recorded (1961–2) with Jaki Byard, and worked with Thelonious Monk's quartet. During the same period he toured and recorded with Bobby Timmons's trio (1961–2) and played with Cannonball Adderley, then in 1963 he joined Art Farmer's group; within a week, however, he had left to embark upon his most important association, as a member of Miles Davis's quintet.

Carter remained with Davis until 1968, participating in all his recording sessions and forming, with Herbie Hancock and Tony Williams, an essential part of Davis's innovative rhythm section. By this time he had become one of the most sought-after studio double bass players; he has recorded more than 1000 albums with scores of jazz and soul artists. Apart from periods as a member of the New York Jazz Sextet (from *c*1967) and then of the NEW YORK JAZZ QUARTET (*c*1971–1976), Carter has been active principally as a leader of his own small ensembles and as a freelance in internationally renowned all-star groups. The latter include V.S.O.P. (1976–7, 1980s; *see* V.S.O.P. (i)), the Milestone Jazzstars, a quartet with Sonny Rollins, McCoy Tyner, and Al Foster that toured the USA and recorded for its sponsor, Milestone (1978), and one of the groups in the film *Round Midnight* (1986). Carter has recorded regularly as a leader from 1972; his own groups have included a second double bass player whose role it is to mark the time and establish the harmony, so that Carter himself may act as the principal soloist, playing either double bass or PICCOLO BASS. In the 1980s he recorded in a duo with Cedar Walton and with Jim Hall, and performed in clubs in New York.

Carter possesses a flawless technique. Considerable tension exists, however, between his desire to express himself as a soloist and his natural great strength, to accompany others. Some of his work in duos and especially as a leader has been disappointing, the one overly cautious, the other both cautious and overly sweet. By contrast, his playing in rhythm sections represents the zenith of improvisation in the bop and modal-jazz styles. With Hancock and Williams in particular, he creates a foundation of rhythm and harmony that is fluid and propulsive; Carter himself contributes drones, ostinatos, walking bass lines, and snippets of melody in a wondrously quick, flexible interchange with his colleagues. Many examples of his best work may be found in his recordings with Davis and V.S.O.P., but none surpasses Hancock's album *Maiden Voyage*. A volume of transcriptions of Carter's solos has been published: *Ron Carter Bass Lines* (New Albany, IN, 1983).

SELECTED RECORDINGS

Duos: with C. Walton: *Heart and Soul* (1981, Tim. 158); with J. Hall: *Telephone* (1984, Conc. 270)

As leader: *All Blues* (1973, CTI 6037); *Piccolo* (1977, Mlst. 55004); *Peg Leg* (1977, Mlst. 9082)

As sideman with M. Davis: *Seven Steps to Heaven* (1963, Col. CS8851); *Miles Davis in Europe* (1963, Col. CS8983); *My Funny Valentine* (1964, Col. CS9106); *Four and More* (1964, Col. CS9253); *E.S.P.* (1965, Col. CS9150); *Miles Smiles* (1966, Col. CS9401); *Sorcerer* (1967, Col. CS9532); *Nefertiti* (1967, Col. CS9594); *Miles in the Sky* (1968, Col. CS9628); *Filles de Kilimanjaro* (1968, Col. CS9750)

As sideman with others: E. Dolphy: *Out There* (1960, NewJ 8252); D. Ellis: *How Time Passes* (1960, Can. 9004); E. Dolphy: *Far Cry* (1960, NewJ 8270); H. Hancock: *Maiden Voyage* (1965, BN 84195); W. Montgomery: *A Day in the Life* (1967–8, A&M 3001); Aretha Franklin: *Soul '69* (1969, Atl. 8212); New York Jazz Quartet: *The New York Jazz Quartet in Concert in Japan* (1975, Salvation 703); H. Hancock: *V.S.O.P.* (1976, Col. PG34688); Milestone Jazzstars: *Milestone Jazzstars in Concert* (1978, Mlst. 55006); W. Marsalis: *Wynton Marsalis* (1981, Col. FC37574)

BIBLIOGRAPHY

D. Heckman: "Ron Carter," *DB*, xxxi/9 (1964), 18
"Ron Carter," *SJ*, xxix/7 (1975), 42 [discography]
A. J. Smith: "The Acoustic Colors of Ron Carter," *DB*, xlii/6 (1975), 11
"Discography of Ron Carter and Tony Williams," *SJ*, xxxi/12 (1977), 290
A. Taylor: *Notes and Tones: Musician-to-Musician Interviews* (Liège, Belgium, 1977/*R*1982), 55
C. Albertson: "Ron Carter," *Stereo Review*, xl/6 (1978), 78
M. Hinton: "New Giant of the Bass," *Jazz Magazine*, ii/2 (1978), 46
E. Williams: "Ron Carter," *DB*, xlv (1978), no.2, p.12; no.3, p.20
L. Tomkins: "The Bass in the Foreground: Ron Carter," *CI*, xix/10 (1981), 6
L. Jeske: "Ron Carter: Covering all Basses," *DB*, 1/7 (1983), 22 [incl. discography]

BARRY KERNFELD

Carve. *See* Cut, (3).

Carver, Wayman (Alexander) (*b* Portsmouth, VA, 25 Dec 1905; *d* Atlanta, 6 May 1967). Flutist and saxophonist. He began playing flute at the age of 14 and later played with J. Neal Montgomery's Collegiate Ramblers. By 1931 he was in New York, where he recorded with Dave Nelson and the King's Men. He worked for Elmer Snowden (1931–2), then joined Benny Carter's orchestra; members of the orchestra formed the nucleus of an ensemble led by Spike Hughes for a session in 1933, on which Carver played some of the earliest recorded jazz flute solos. From 1934 he played both flute and saxophone for Chick Webb (for illustration *see* Webb, chick), remaining with the band under Ella Fitzgerald's leadership (1939–40) and returning briefly in 1941. After World War II he settled in Atlanta and became a professor of music at Clark College, where he directed the band program; he also played occasionally in local groups.

Carver's flute solos on *Devil's Holiday, Sweet Sue, just you*, and *I got rhythm* demonstrate that he was a fine executant, but also that the instrument does not lend itself to rhythmic swing. As a saxophonist he was a capable section player but seldom played solos.

SELECTED RECORDINGS

As sideman: D. Nelson: Loveless Love (1931, Timely Tunes 1577); S. Hughes: Sweet Sue, just you/How come you do me like you do? (1933, Decca F3972); B. Carter: Devil's Holiday (1933, Col. 2898D); C. Webb: Down Home Rag (1935, Decca 785); I got rhythm/Sweet Sue, just you (1937, Decca 1759)

BIBLIOGRAPHY

S. Hughes: *Second Movement* (London, 1951)
J. Evensmo: *The Flute of Wayman Carver, the Trombone of Dickie Wells, 1927–1942, the Tenor Saxophone of Illinois Jacquet* (n.p. [Oslo], n.d. [?1983]) [discography]

DAVID FLANAGAN

Carvin, Michael (*b* Houston, 12 Dec 1944). Drummer. He was taught by his father, a drummer, and gained early experience playing in a big band led by the organist Earl Grant (1965). After touring Vietnam (1966–8) he played with the blues guitarist B. B. King, then in the early and mid-1970s worked with Freddie Hubbard, Pharoah Sanders, Lonnie Liston Smith, McCoy Tyner, Jackie McLean, and the group Atmospheres, led by the saxophonist Clive Stevens. Later he recorded with the bass player Mickey Bass (1981) and with Charles Davis's quartet (1982). With Lenny White and Billy Cobham, Carvin defined a style of drumming appropriate to the more complex types of jazz and jazz-rock in the 1970s. His playing is clean and focused, and he achieves a sense of propulsiveness by attacking notes slightly before the beat. His formidable technique enables him to execute polyrhythmic fills with almost military precision. Unlike many drummers he is comfortable in freer styles, and projects a feeling of continuity without imposing too strict a beat; this skill may be heard in his work with Sanders, where in passages of metrical and durational ambiguity Carvin implies a pulse even when one is not present.

SELECTED RECORDINGS

Duos with J. McClean: *Antiquity* (1974, Ste. 1028)
As leader: *The Camel* (1975, Ste. 1038)
As sideman: P. Sanders: *Elevation* (1973, Imp. 9261); C. Stevens: *Voyage to Uranus* (1974, Cap. SM11676); M. Bass: *Sentimental Mood* (1981, Chi. 2031)

BIBLIOGRAPHY

Feather–Gitler '70s
A. J. Smith: "Michael Carvin," *DB*, xlv/7 (1978), 32
S. Silver: "Michael Carvin: Spreading the Word," *MD*, iii/6 (1979), 28

ANDREW WAGGONER

Carving contest. *See* Cutting contest.

Cary, Dick [Richard Durant] (*b* Hartford, CT, 10 July 1916). Pianist, alto horn player, trumpeter, and arranger. He first studied violin and appeared with the Hartford SO while still at high school. He then played piano, recording with Joe Marsala (1942) and working as an unaccompanied soloist at Nick's, New York (1942–3), wrote arrangements for Benny Goodman (1943), and played briefly with the Casa Loma Orchestra and Brad Gowans. He served in the army (1944–6), but continued to record – with Muggsy Spanier in 1944 and Wild Bill Davison in 1945. He joined Billy Butterfield, with whom he recorded on alto horn (1946), led his own band, and was the pianist in Louis Armstrong's original All Stars (1947–8). After playing piano with Jimmy Dorsey (1949–50), he appeared as an alto horn and mellophone player on Eddie Condon's television shows (for which he also wrote arrangements); he later worked as a trumpeter at Condon's club in Greenwich Village, New York (1954; for illustration *see* Nightclubs and other venues, fig.5). He arranged Pee Wee Russell's dixieland album *By Arrangement Only* (1953, Sto. 308) and recorded with Max Kaminsky (1953–4), Bud Freeman (1953, 1957–9), and Jimmy McPartland (1953, 1958–60). After playing with Bobby Hackett (1956–7) he worked again with Kaminsky, now also playing trombone and composing. In 1959 he moved to Los Angeles where he continued to work as a freelance musician, often with Red Nichols, Ben Pollack, and Bing Crosby. He toured the Far East with Condon (1964) and in the 1970s and 1980s continued to tour, playing trumpet, alto horn, and piano. He recorded in Europe with the Barrelhouse Jazzband (1975) and as a leader (1975, 1977), and in the USA as a leader (1980). He is a highly talented and versatile musician and has composed not only for jazz ensembles (small groups and swing bands) but also for the Rochester SO.

SELECTED RECORDINGS

As leader: *Dick Cary* (1957, Golden Crest 3024); *Hot and Cool* (1958, Stereocraft 106); *Dick Cary and his Dixieland Doodlers* (1959, Col. CS8222); *The Amazing Dick Cary* (1975, Riff 659014); *California Doings* (1980, FaD 140)
As sideman: L. Armstrong: Back o' Town Blues (1947, Vic. 40-4006); Rockin' Chair (1947, Vic. 40-4004); *Town Hall Concert 1947: the Unissued Part* (1947, RCA FXM17142); E. Condon: *Jammin' at Condon's* (1954, Col. CL616); *Bixieland* (1955, Col. CL719); on B. Hackett: *Live from the Voyager Room* (1956, Shoestring 108), Handle with Cary; E. Hall: *Rumpus on Rampart Street* (1959, Rae-Cox 1120)

BIBLIOGRAPHY

ChiltonW; *FeatherE*; *Feather '60s*; *Feather–Gitler '70s*
K. Gallacher: "Dick Cary," *JJ*, xvii/9 (1964), 8
A. Stevens: "A Mellow Man on the Alto Horn: Dick Cary," *CI*, xvi/3 (1977), 10

MIKE HAZELDINE

Casa Loma Orchestra. Big band. Formed in Detroit in 1927, it was originally known as the Orange Blossoms and consisted of members of Jean Goldkette's band. During the next three

The Casa Loma Orchestra at the Essex House Hotel, New York, 1933: (back row, left to right) Sonny Dunham (trumpet, trombone), Bobby Jones and Grady Watts (cornets), Tony Briglia (drums), and Howard "Joe Horse" Hall (piano); (middle row) Pee Wee Hunt (trombone, voice), Russell "Billy" Rauch (trombone), Gene Gifford (guitar), and Stanley Dennis (double bass); (front row) Pat Davis (tenor saxophone), Clarence Hutchenrider (alto saxophone, clarinet), Glen Gray (baritone saxophone), Kenny Sargent (baritone saxophone, voice), and Mel Jenssen (director)

years it came under the leadership of the clarinetist and saxophonist Glen Gray and acquired several new members; these included the trumpeter Sonny Dunham, the cornetist Grady Watts, the trombonist and singer Pee Wee Hunt, the clarinetist and alto saxophonist Kenny Sargent, and the guitarist Gene Gifford (see illustration). In 1929 the band appeared at the Roseland Ballroom in New York as the Casa Loma Orchestra and made its first recording for Okeh. It enjoyed its greatest success between 1930 and 1935, as it recorded for Brunswick, Victor, and Decca, fared well in popularity polls, and attracted a large following, particularly among college audiences; in 1933–4 it played on the first radio program to broadcast performances by a swing band. The orchestra's popularity diminished in the late 1930s as its original members left and new swing bands found favor with the public. The Casa Loma Orchestra was among the first white swing bands to adopt the sound of black orchestras and to introduce this sound to a wide audience. It became a model for many swing bands that followed, owing to the sophistication of its arrangements (which were written by Gifford) and the technical mastery that it showed in its ensemble playing. A collection of materials associated with the orchestra is in the Robert Gray Dodge Library of Northeastern University, Boston; *see* LIBRARIES AND ARCHIVES, §2.

SELECTED RECORDINGS

San Sue Strut (1930, OK 41403); White Jazz (1931, Bruns. 6092); Blue Jazz (1932, Bruns. 6358); Washboard Blues (1932, Bruns. 20108); Casa Loma Stomp (1933, Bruns. 7652); I Got Rhythm (1933, Bruns. 6800); Milenberg Joys (1934, Bruns. 6922); Moonglow (1934, Bruns. 6937); Who's Sorry Now? (1935, Decca 379); Bugle Call Rag (1936, Decca 869); Smoke Rings (1937, Decca 1473); Rockin' Chair (1939, Decca 2395)

BIBLIOGRAPHY

M. W. Stearns: *The Story of Jazz* (New York, 1956, rev. and enlarged 2/1958, enlarged 1970)
F. Littler: "Gray Jazz: a Study of the Casa Loma Band," *JM*, vii/3 (1961), 8
G. T. Simon: *The Big Bands* (New York, 1967, rev. and enlarged 2/1971, rev. 3/1974, 4/1981)
R. J. Hopf: "Casa Loma Swing," *JP*, xxii/9 (1973), 20
A. McCarthy: *Big Band Jazz* (New York and London, 1974)

RONALD M. RADANO

Casey, Al(bert Aloysius) (*b* Louisville, KY, 15 Sept 1915). Guitarist. He moved with his family to New York around 1930 and while still in his teens first worked with Fats Waller, with whom he made more than 230 recordings as a sideman in the 1930s and early 1940s (for illustration *see* WALLER, FATS); it is for this association that he is best known. He recorded with Frankie Newton (1939) in a session organized by Hugues Panassié, and several times with Billie Holiday between 1938 and 1944, notably under the leadership of Teddy Wilson, in whose big band he worked for brief periods (1939–40). He also played with Buster Harding (1940) and recorded with Chu Berry (1941). After Waller's death in 1943 Casey made several appearances with former members of Waller's Rhythm, under the direction of the pianist Pat Flowers. At the same time he led a trio of his own and in 1944 he worked as a sideman in a trio led by Clarence Profit. He also recorded under his own name for Capitol (1945) and as a freelance with Earl Hines (1944), Big Sid Catlett (1945), and others. Most of his work during his earlier years was on acoustic guitar, but by the mid-1940s he had changed to the electric instrument, and between 1957 and 1961 he performed and recorded rhythm-and-blues with King Curtis. He made recordings in 1973 in Paris with Helen Humes and Jay McShann and as a leader, and in 1980 with the Harlem Blues and Jazz Band; he has continued to work with this ensemble and perform as a soloist into the late 1980s.

Casey's early work on acoustic guitar was an accomplished

blend of chordal and single-string solo playing and propulsive rhythm playing. His best work is heard in extended blues improvisations, and the series of remarkable blues choruses on *Buck Jumpin'* (1941) is the zenith of his association with Waller. On the electric instrument, while retaining his ability to drive along the rhythm section, he developed an incisive solo style modeled on Charlie Christian's, which is typified by *How High the Moon*, recorded by his own sextet (1945).

Casey should not be confused with the electric guitarist Al Casey (*b* Phoenix, AZ, 26 Oct 1936), a rock-and-roll studio musician.

SELECTED RECORDINGS

As leader: How High the Moon/Sometimes I'm Happy (1945, Cap. 10034); *The Al Casey Quartet* (1960, Mdsv. 12); *Al Casey Remembers King Curtis* (1985, JSP 1095)

As sideman with F. Waller: Honeysuckle Rose/Blue Turning Grey Over you (1937, Vic. 36206); "Fats" Waller's Original E flat Blues (1940, Bb 10858); Buck Jumpin' (1941, Bb 11324)

As sideman with others: F. Newton: Who? (1939, Bb 10216); C. Berry: Blowing up a Breeze/Monday at Minton's (1941, Com. 541); S. Catlett: Love for Sale/Henderson Romp (1945, Cap. 15117); R. Stewart [as leader of Fletcher Henderson All Stars]: *The Big Reunion* (1957, Jzt. 1285), incl. Casey Stew

BIBLIOGRAPHY

E. Kirkeby, D. P. Schiedt, and S. Traill: *Ain't Misbehavin': the Story of Fats Waller* (London and New York, 1966)
S. Dance: *The World of Swing* (New York, 1974) [colln of previously pubd interviews], 356
J. Vance: *Fats Waller: his Life and Times* (Chicago, 1977)
P. Carr: "Buck Jumps Again," *JJI*, xxxiii/4 (1980), 5; contd as "Waller Days," xxxiii/5 (1980), 5 [interview]
L. Tomkins: "It All Happened After Fats, Says Guitar Great Al Casey," *CI*, xxiv/6 (1987), 26 [interview]

WARREN VACHÉ, SR.

Casey, Bob [Robert Hanley] (*b* Johnson County, IL, 11 Feb 1909; *d* Marion, IL, 9 April 1986). Double bass player. He first played guitar and worked with minor groups in Illinois and St. Louis. He took up double bass in 1929 and played both instruments for a while. After moving to Chicago he performed with Wingy Manone (1933) and worked as a staff musician for NBC. In 1939 he toured and made recordings (notably *At the Jazz Band Ball*, Bb 10518) with Muggsy Spanier (for illustration *see* SPANIER, MUGGSY); after the group disbanded he returned to Chicago, where he worked with Charlie Spivak and others. He joined Brad Gowans at Nick's, New York, in 1943, and spent several years playing there and at Eddie Condon's. During this period he recorded with several leaders, including Condon (1943–4), Wild Bill Davison (1943, 1945), Bobby Hackett (1943–4), and Spanier (1944–5); he also recorded in trios with Ralph Sutton (1951) and Joe Sullivan (1952). In 1957 he moved to Florida, where he performed and recorded with the Dukes of Dixieland (1962). In 1971, by which time he worked only occasionally, he undertook some engagements in New York.

based on *ChiltonW*

Casey, Floyd (*b* Poplar Bluff, MO, 1900; *d* New York, 7 Dec 1967). Drummer and washboard player. He played frequently on riverboats during the early 1920s, then worked in St. Louis with Dewey Jackson (*c*1921), Ed Allen's Whispering Gold Band (1922), and others. Later he moved to New York, where from 1927 he took part in many recording sessions with Clarence Williams (including *Cushion Foot Stomp*, 1927, OK 8462), and worked with the trombonist George Wilson at the Capitol Palace. During the 1930s he played in dance halls, and in 1941 he was a member of Jimmy Reynolds's band. He then worked with Allen again, as a member of Allen's band, and in a group led by the pianist Benton Heath which performed at the New Gardens for many years.

based on *ChiltonW*

Casimir, John (*b* New Orleans, 17 Dec 1898; *d* New Orleans, 12 Jan 1963). Clarinetist and bandleader. He began playing E♭ clarinet in a band led by Henry Allen, Sr. (1918–22), then joined the Eureka Brass Band (1922), and later worked with the Tuxedo Brass Band (1925–early 1930s) and the WPA Brass Band (1935–8). He also played B♭ clarinet in dance bands, and between 1922 and 1925 was leader of a group with Henry "Red" Allen. In 1938 he founded the Young Tuxedo Brass Band, which he led until his death and with which he recorded a fine album, *New Orleans Joys* (1958, Atl. 1297).

Oral history material in *LNT*.

BIBLIOGRAPHY

C. Hillman: "The Icons," *JJ*, xxiv/5 (1971), 12
M. Tovey: "On the Banquette: John Casimir," *Fn*, xii (1981), no.4, p.7; no.5, p.22; no.6, p.13; xv/2 (1983–4), 16

MICHAEL TOVEY

Castaldo, Lee. Name used by LEE CASTLE in the mid-1930s.

Castandet, Sam (*b* Ste. Marie, Martinique, 1906). Martinique clarinetist, bandleader, and double bass player. In 1936 he led a recording orchestra that included the trumpeter Bobby Jones as its principal soloist; among its recordings is *Sweet Georgia Brown* (1936, Col. DF2022). After World War II he was resident for many years at La Canne à Sucre in Paris. An exponent of French Creole music, Castandet succeeded in blending beguine and jazz. As a clarinet soloist he performed in the antillean style, while his double bass playing was influenced by John Kirby. (A. Boulanger: Liner notes, *Jazz and Hot Dance in Martinique*, Harl. 2018, 1985)

RAINER E. LOTZ

Castle [Castaldo], **Lee** [Castaldo, Aniello] (*b* New York, 28 Feb 1915). Trumpeter and bandleader. He began working professionally in the mid-1930s using the name Lee Castaldo, and was a featured soloist with many bands, including those of Joe Haymes (1936), Artie Shaw (1936, 1941, 1950), Tommy Dorsey (intermittently, 1937–41), Glenn Miller and Jack Teagarden (both 1939), Will Bradley (1941), and Benny Goodman (1943). From the late 1930s he also led his own bands with moderate success. Around 1942 he adopted the name Lee Castle. He joined the Dorsey Brothers Orchestra in 1953, and led it briefly. Shortly after Jimmy Dorsey's death in 1957 the band was divided into two memorial orchestras, one under each brother's name. Castle assumed leadership of the Jimmy Dorsey Orchestra, which he has continued to lead into the mid-1980s. A dedicated perfectionist, he remains committed to the big-band style. His trumpet playing ranges from a sweetness reminiscent of Harry James to a more driving approach in the manner of Louis Armstrong and Bunny Berigan.

SELECTED RECORDINGS

As leader: *The Lee Castle Jazztette* (*c*1952, Jay Dee 4)

As sideman: A. Shaw: Sugar Foot Stomp (1936, Bruns. 7735); T. Dorsey: I never knew (1938, Vic. 25813); W. Bradley: Basin Street Boogie (1941, Col. 36340); T. Dorsey: *Sentimental and Swinging* (1955, Col. CL1240); J. Dorsey: So Rare/Sophisticated Swing (1956, Fraternity 755)

BIBLIOGRAPHY

ChiltonW; *FeatherE*
G. T. Simon: *The Big Bands* (New York, 1967, rev. and enlarged 2/1971, rev. 3/1974, 4/1981)
C. Deffaa: "Lee Castle: a Trumpeter for St. Anthony," *MR*, xiv/3 (1987), 7; contd as "Lee Castle: the Third Dorsey," xiv/4 (1987), 8

WAYNE SCHNEIDER

Castleman, Jeff(ry Alan) (*b* Los Angeles, 27 Jan 1946). Bass player. He studied at the University of California, Riverside, and privately with Ralph Peña, then worked with Si Zentner (1964), Louie Bellson, and Joe Castro's trio. He also recorded in a septet with Johnny Hodges and Earl Hines (1967). From 1967 to 1968 he was a member of Duke Ellington's orchestra, in which he occasionally played electric bass guitar; among the recordings he made with Ellington is *Yale Concert* (1968, Fan. 9433). He married Ellington's singer, Trish Turner, and they settled in Los Angeles. Castleman toured with Sarah Vaughan and, briefly, with Tony Bennett, then performed and recorded with Shelly Manne (1971–3). From the mid-1970s he has played electric bass guitar and concentrated on commercial work.

BIBLIOGRAPHY

Feather–Gitler '70s
S. Dance: *The World of Duke Ellington* (London and New York, 1970/*R*1981) [colln of previously pubd interviews], 218

Castro, Joe [Joseph] (*b* Miami, AZ, 15 Aug 1927). Pianist. He grew up in Pittsburg, California, where he played professionally from the age of 15. After performing with an army band during his military service (1946–7) he formed his own trio, which worked mainly on the West Coast and in Hawaii. Later he accompanied Anita O'Day and June Christy (1958–9) before joining Teddy Edwards (1959), with whom he performed and made recordings both as a sideman (*Teddy's Ready*, 1960) and as a leader (*Groove Funk Soul*, 1959). Castro worked as the music director for the popular singer Tony Martin from 1961 to 1963. Thereafter he played commercially-oriented music, accompanied singers, and worked with bands for shows in Las Vegas. He has been active as a jazz musician only rarely in the 1980s. Castro is a fine bop pianist with a highly distinctive chordal style.

SELECTED RECORDINGS

As leader: *Mood Jazz* (1956–7, Atl. 1264); *Groove Funk Soul* (1959, Atl. 1324)
As sideman: J. Christy: *Ballads for Night People* (1959, Cap. ST1308); *Cool School* (1959, Cap. ST1398); T. Edwards: *Teddy's Ready* (1960, Cont. 7583)

BIBLIOGRAPHY

FeatherE; *Feather '60s*; *Feather–Gitler '70s*

SCOTT YANOW

Castro-Neves, (Carlos) Oscar (de) [Neves, Oscar] (*b* Rio de Janeiro, 15 May 1940). Brazilian guitarist. He grew up in a family of amateur musicians; his first instrument was the *cavaquinho*, a small plucked instrument that combines characteristics of the mandolin and the guitar. He studied composition in Los Angeles in the late 1950s, and during this period was among the musicians who, with Antonio Carlos Jobim, popularized the bossa nova style; in November 1962 he played at the first concert of bossa nova music to be given at Carnegie Hall. During the mid–1960s he played with Lalo Schifrin, Dizzy Gillespie, and Laurindo Almeida. He wrote arrangements for the Paul Winter Consort (from 1968) and also toured with the group (1969–70). From the 1970s he played with Quincy Jones, Lee Ritenour, and Dave Grusin, and recorded with Flora Purim (1974), Stan Getz (1975), John Klemmer (1977), and Ella Fitzgerald (1980); in 1981 he recorded in a quintet led by Milt Jackson (*Big Mouth*, Pablo 2310867). He wrote and produced the music for a television program, "Reflections through a Brazilian Eye," in 1984; later he recorded as a leader the album *Oscar* (*c*1986, Living Music 0010). Castro-Neves is a fine player, equally adept at lead and rhythm work. As well as performing he is active as an arranger and music director in Los Angeles. (*Feather–Gitler '70s*)

CATHERINE COLLINS

Catalogue [catalog] **number.** *See* ISSUE NUMBER.

Catalyst. Record company and label. The company was established in Los Angeles in May 1975. It recorded sessions by musicians as diverse as Gary Bartz, Hadley Caliman, Frank Foster, Terumasa Hino, Ahmad Jamal, Ron Jefferson, Irene Kral, Billy Mitchell, Sam Most, Sonny Stitt, and Frank Strazzeri. It also reissued albums by Paul Gonsalves, Charlie Mariano, and Michal Urbaniak that were made and originally issued in Brazil, Finland, and Poland respectively, and put out LPs by Hino, George Lewis (i), Carmen McRae, Mal Waldron, and Helen Merrill and Teddy Wilson that first appeared in Japan. Although recording ceased in 1977, the catalogue remained available into the mid-1980s.

Catherine, Philip (*b* London, 27 Oct 1942). Belgian guitarist of English birth. He first worked with Lou Bennett, and during the 1960s played for Belgian radio stations. In 1970 he began playing free jazz as a member of the Jean-Luc Ponty Experience. After leaving Ponty (1972) he traveled to the USA, enrolled at the Berklee College of Music (1973), then with Charlie Mariano and Jasper van 't Hof established the band Pork Pie, which recorded one album (1974). In the mid-1970s Catherine formed an association with Niels-Henning Ørsted Pedersen, and they continued to perform and record together into the mid-1980s.

Catherine's playing has such an uncanny affinity with the work of Django Reinhardt that Charles Mingus gave him the nickname Young Django; this was also the title of an album that Catherine recorded in 1979 with Reinhardt's former associate Stephane Grappelli. He has worked with Larry Coryell and Bireli Lagrene in a trio that has performed frequently all over the world, often at tributes to Reinhardt. Although Catherine is not well known in the USA, he is highly regarded in Europe.

SELECTED RECORDINGS

Duos: with L. Coryell: *Twin-house* (1976, Elek. 123); *Splendid* (1978, Elek. 153); with N.-H. Ørsted Pedersen: *The Viking* (1983, Pablo 2310894)
As sideman: N.-H. Ørsted Pedersen: *Jaywalkin'* (1975, Ste. 1041); *Live at Montmartre* (1978, Ste. 1083); S. Grappelli: *Young Django* (1979, MPS 68230)

BIBLIOGRAPHY

Feather–Gitler '70s
P. Thonnard: "Philip Catherine: Music that doesn't Lie," *JF* [intl edn], no.88 (1984), 40

BILL MILKOWSKI

Catlett, Buddy [George James] (*b* Long Beach, CA, 13 June 1933). Double bass player. He first studied clarinet, but he changed to saxophone, which he played in Seattle during the late 1940s and early 1950s. At this time he was also learning double bass, which became his principal instrument, and by 1958 he was performing with major jazz musicians as a member of the house band at the Melody Lounge, Denver. In 1959 he worked with Cal Tjader and toured Europe with Quincy Jones. He played with Chico Hamilton (1961), the quintet led by Eddie "Lockjaw" Davis and Johnny Griffin (1962), Count Basie (1962–4), Maynard Ferguson (1964), and Louis Armstrong (1965–8), recording with all but Ferguson; he also recorded with Benny Bailey (1960), Phil Woods (1961), Frank Foster (1963), and Coleman Hawkins (1965). A comparison of his recorded work with Basie and Hamilton shows that he can play in a light swing style that integrates well with a larger orchestra, but is also capable of a stronger, more individual attack when playing in a small group.

SELECTED RECORDINGS

As sideman: Q. Jones: *The Great Wide World of Quincy Jones* (1959, Mer. 20561); C. Fuller: *Boss of the Soul-stream Trombone* (1960, Warwick 2038), incl. Flutie, If I were a bell; on C. Hamilton: *Who's Who in the Swinging Sixties* (1961–2, Col. CS8565), Brazil (1961); E. Davis and J. Griffin: *Tough Tenor Favorites* (1962, Jlnd 976); E. Fitzgerald: *Ella and Basie!* (1963, Verve 64061), incl. Honeysuckle Rose

BIBLIOGRAPHY

FeatherE; *Feather '60s*

LAWRENCE KOCH

Catlett, Sid(ney) [Big Sid] (*b* Evansville, IN, 17 Jan 1910; *d* Chicago, 25 March 1951). Drummer. He played in several minor bands in Chicago before moving in 1930 to New York, where he began a career as a freelance; he made many recordings and appeared with Benny Carter (1932), McKinney's Cotton Pickers (1934–5), Fletcher Henderson (1936), and Don Redman (1936–8). From 1938 to 1942 he was prominently featured in the big band led by Louis Armstrong, whose preferred drummer he became. He also worked intermittently with Benny Goodman during 1941. After leading his own groups in various cities Catlett worked again with Armstrong in the latter's small group, the All Stars, playing New Orleans jazz (1947–9).

Catlett was among the outstanding drummers of the swing period, and many later jazz drummers were influenced by his work. He had a bright, firm touch and absolute metrical precision in his right-hand ride patterns, which allowed him to create unpredictable cross-accents with the left, including his famous, expertly timed rim-shots. By almost imperceptibly rushing the beat he could at times generate enormous intensity in a big-band performance. He was an expert accompanist in a small-group setting, carefully adjusting his timbres to suit the soloist and sometimes anticipating the course of the improvisation. He also provided some of the most satisfying extended solos in premodern jazz drumming, revealing a clear sense of logical development and drum "melody" which set him apart from contemporaries such as Gene Krupa. Perhaps most remarkable was his individual way of adapting to all the jazz styles then available, as reflected in his many recordings with leading musicians in the New Orleans, Chicago, swing, and even bop styles. His unrestrained manner is well captured in the film *Jammin' the Blues* (1944).

SELECTED RECORDINGS

As leader: Sleep/Linger Awhile (1944, Com. 546); Memories of You/Just a Riff (1944, Com. 1515); I never knew/Love for Sale (1945, Cap. 10032)

As sideman: F. Henderson: Jangled Nerves (1936, Vic. 25317); T. Wilson: Warmin' up (1936, Bruns. 7684); B. Goodman: Tuesday at Ten (1941, Col. 36254); D. Gillespie: Salt Peanuts (1945, Guild 1003); L. Armstrong: Boff-boff (1947, Decca 9-28102)

BIBLIOGRAPHY

H. Panassié: "Un grand musicien disparaît: Sidney Catlett," *BHcF*, no.8 (1951), 3

W. Balliett: *The Sound of Surprise* (New York, 1959/*R*1978) [colln of previously pubd articles and reviews], 143

G. Hoefer: "Big Sid," *DB*, xxxiii/6 (1966), 26

B. Esposito: "Big Sid Catlett," *JJ*, xxii/5 (1969), 10

R. Stewart: "My Man, Big Sid (Sidney Catlett)," *Jazz Masters of the Thirties* (New York and London, n. d. [?1972])

J. BRADFORD ROBINSON

Cauldwell, Happy. Name by which HAPPY CALDWELL has often (and incorrectly) been identified.

Caunedo, Jesús (*b* Havana, 24 Aug 1934). Cuban clarinetist, saxophonist, and flutist. He became a professional musician at the age of 19, and worked in several Cuban bands, including that of Chico O'Farrill. With Walfredo de los Reyes he founded the Cuban Jazz Club in the 1950s; they invited many important musicians to take part in jam sessions held every Sunday at the Tropicana nightclub in Havana. In 1960 Caunedo moved

Sid Catlett (drums) and Louis Armstrong (trumpet) at the Apollo Theatre, New York, 1938

to New York, where he played with Machito and the percussionist Tito Puente and for shows on Broadway. He settled in San Juan in 1976, and continues to be much in demand there as a studio musician, as well as in Cuba and New York. He may be heard to advantage on the album *Fire and Sugar* (Montilla 3976), which he recorded as a leader in 1973.

CRISTÓBAL DÍAZ AYALA

CBS [Columbia Broadcasting System]. Broadcasting and recording organization which owns the record company COLUMBIA (and that label in the USA) and the label EPIC. The acronym CBS has also been used by American Columbia as a record label, to issue its material in countries where it does not own the Columbia trademark.

Cecil, Malcolm (*b* London, 9 Jan 1937). English double bass player. From 1956 he played with Dizzy Reece, Don Rendell, Ronnie Scott, and Dill Jones, recording with the last named in 1957. After serving in the RAF (1958–61) he became an electronics consultant, but remained active in music, recording with Dick Morrissey and Tony Crombie (both 1961) and working with Vic Ash and Harry Klein (1962). Cecil performed with Jackie McLean and Freddie Redd in Jack Gelber's play *The Connection*. In 1963 he joined Stan Tracey's trio, which accompanied Stan Getz, Johnny Griffin, Roland Kirk, and others at Ronnie Scott's, and the following year he became a member of the BBC Radio Orchestra. From the mid-1960s Cecil suffered ill-health and ceased to play, working instead as a producer, recording engineer, and programmer for the Moog synthesizer, notably on a series of albums for the popular singer Stevie Wonder; he was also a founder of Tonto (the Original New Timbral Orchestra), an orchestra of synthesizers. He recorded with Jim Hall in New York in 1971.

BIBLIOGRAPHY

Feather '60s
J. Dilberto: "Synthesizer Pioneer: Malcolm Cecil," *Keyboard*, x/1 (1984), 34

Celesta [celeste]. A keyboard instrument in the form of a small upright piano, invented by the Frenchman Auguste Mustel in 1886. The sounding mechanism consists of a set of metal plates, equipped with dampers and suspended over box resonators; the plates are struck by hammers activated from the keyboard in the manner of the piano. There is a single sustaining pedal. The compass of the celesta is five octaves from *c*.

The celesta was first used in jazz in the 1930s, when Earl Hines and Fats Waller adopted it as a novelty instrument. Waller often played melody lines on the celesta with his right hand, accompanying himself on piano with his left, as on *Rhythm and Romance* (1935, Vic. 25131). The boogie-woogie pianist Meade "Lux" Lewis made recordings as an unaccompanied soloist in 1936, including *Celeste Blues* (Decca 819), and in 1941 made a remarkable series of recordings with Edmond Hall's Celeste Quartet, notably *Celestial Express* (BN 17), on which Charlie Christian's acoustic guitar playing may also be heard to advantage. Willie "the Lion" Smith, Art Tatum, and Duke Ellington all played the instrument occasionally in the late 1930s and early 1940s. In the 1950s Thelonious Monk played celesta in his own composition *Pannonica* (on the album *Brilliant Corners*, 1956, Riv. 226) and Spud Murphy made several recordings as a leader and celesta player, including *12-tone Jazz* (1955, Cont. 3506). Later the celesta was occasionally used by McCoy Tyner (*Trident*, 1975, Mlst. 9063), Keith Jarrett, and Roland Kirk. Its exotic, colorful quality found favor with several free-jazz players, among them Sun Ra, Fred van Hove, Carla Bley, and members of the Art Ensemble of Chicago.

ALYN SHIPTON

Celestin, Papa [Oscar Phillip] (*b* Napoleonville, LA, 1 Jan 1884; *d* New Orleans, 15 Dec 1954). Trumpeter and bandleader. In 1906 he moved to New Orleans, where he played in several brass bands before forming his own group in 1910. From 1917 to 1925, with the trombonist William "Baba" Ridgley, he led the ORIGINAL TUXEDO ORCHESTRA, but thereafter the two men led separate groups, Celestin's becoming known as the Tuxedo Jazz Orchestra. With its emphasis on popular songs and novelty pieces, the band enjoyed considerable success, and was always popular with dancers; it made several recordings during the late 1920s and toured (mostly in the South) until the early 1930s. Shortly afterwards Celestin left full-time music, but from 1946 began playing more regularly, and the Tuxedo Jazz Orchestra became nationally known during the early 1950s through its performances on radio and television. In 1953 Celestin played a command performance for President Eisenhower and took part in the film *Cinerama Holiday*.

Celestin's long-lasting popularity was due to his personality and to the way he presented his band's music rather than to his skills as a jazz trumpeter. He rarely promoted his own playing and was not a natural improviser, though he occasionally created muted solos that were full of feeling (as on *My Josephine*, 1926), and his singing was usually robust and cheerful. Some idea of the enthusiasm that the group engendered is apparent on *Li'l Liza Jane* (1950).

SELECTED RECORDINGS

Original Tuxedo Rag (1925, OK 8215); Black Rag (1925, OK 8198); My Josephine (1926, Col. 636D); When I'm with you (1927, Col. 14323D); Li'l Liza Jane (1950, New Orleans Bandwagon 6); At the Darktown Strutters Ball (1953, Col. 48009)

BIBLIOGRAPHY

J. G. Curren: "Oscar 'Papa' Celestin," *SL*, vi/1–2 (1955), 1
Obituary, G. Hoefer, *DB*, xxii/2 (1955), 2
G. Hulme: "Oscar 'Papa' Celestin," *Matrix*, no.47 (1963), 3; no.53 (1964), 18 [discography]
A. McCarthy: *Big Band Jazz* (New York and London, 1974), 97
P. R. Haby: "Oscar 'Papa' Celestin, 1884–1954," *Fn*, xii/5 (1981), 4
A. Ward and R. B. Allen: "Hot Tuxedoes: the Story of Oscar Celestin," *Fn*, xviii/5 (1987), 4

JOHN CHILTON

Cello. *See* VIOLONCELLO.

Ceroli, Nick (*b* Warren, OH, 22 Dec 1939; *d* Los Angeles, 11 Aug 1985). Drummer. In 1963 he toured South America and Mexico with Ray Anthony, recorded with Jack Teagarden, and played at the Monterey Jazz Festival with Gerald Wilson. He worked with Stan Kenton's Los Angeles Neophonic Orchestra (1965), then played with Herb Alpert's Tijuana Brass (1965–9). After settling in Hollywood he recorded with Pete Jolly (*c*1969), Zoot Sims (1976, 1984), Richie Kamuca (*c*1977), Warne Marsh and Ross Tompkins (both 1977), Bill Berry, Dave Frishberg, and Pete Christlieb and Marsh (all 1978), Bob Florence (1979, 1981), and Milt Jackson (1981). His playing may be heard to advantage on *Donna Lee* on Christlieb and Marsh's album *Apogee* (1978, WB 3236).

BIBLIOGRAPHY

Feather '60s; Feather–Gitler '70s
Obituary, *Variety*, no.320 (21 Aug 1985), 134

Cerri, Franco (*b* Milan, 29 Jan 1926). Italian guitarist and double bass player. He played guitar in Kramer Gorni's band from

1945 and worked regularly as a double bass player from the 1950s. He appeared at many festivals in Europe and the USA and played with Billie Holiday, Django Reinhardt, the Modern Jazz Quartet, Stephane Grappelli, Gerry Mulligan, Lars Gullin, Lee Konitz, Bud Shank, Phil Woods, Tony Scott, Dizzy Gillespie, Johnny Griffin, Lou Bennett, and Jean-Luc Ponty. He recorded as a guitarist with Flavio Ambrosetti (1955), Claude Williamson (1958), and the European Jazz Stars (1961), and as a double bass player with Chet Baker (1959) and Buddy Collette (1961). He also led his own groups, including one consisting of his son, the double bass player Stefano Cerri; the pianist Sante Palumbo; and the drummer Tullio De Piscopo. Cerri was influenced early in his career by Reinhardt and Barney Kessel and later chiefly by René Thomas. A good example of his style is his recording *Demoiselle* (1979, Dire 356).

ADRIANO MAZZOLETTI

Chair. A term applied to any individual musician's position within an ensemble; for example, a member of a band might be described as holding the "second trumpet chair."

Chaix, Henri (*b* Geneva, 1925). Swiss pianist and bandleader. He began playing professionally in 1943 when he became a member of Loys Choquart's Dixie Dandies. In 1951 he joined a band led by the soprano saxophonist Claude Aubert and in 1961 he assumed its leadership. He made recordings as an unaccompanied soloist (1954, 1959), as a leader (from the late 1950s), and with the Tremble Kids (1959, 1968, 1977, notably *25 Jahre: The Tremble Kids*, 1977, Intercord 180036), as well as with Buck Clayton and Rex Stewart (both 1966), and Oscar Klein (1969). He recorded frequently as a guest soloist with such musicians as Sidney Bechet (1950s), Milt Buckner (1967), Albert Nicholas (1969), the Dixie Dandies (1972), and Guy Lafitte (1975), and performed and recorded at jazz festivals in Zurich (1970) and Montreux (1971). Chaix' style was rooted in the traditions of swing and blues and he emerged as the leading exponent of mainstream jazz in Switzerland during the 1950s; his left-hand technique was particularly strong. He may be heard playing piano and also trombone on *It don't mean a thing* (1963, Ex Libris 340).

BIBLIOGRAPHY

J.-R. Hippenmeyer: *Le jazz en Suisse, 1930–1970* (Yverdon, Switzerland, 1971)
——: *Swiss Jazz Disco* (Yverdon, Switzerland, 1977)

RAINER E. LOTZ

Challis, Bill [William H.] (*b* Wilkes-Barre, PA, 8 July 1904). Arranger. He started on piano, then took up saxophone, and later led the student band at Bucknell University. In 1926 he joined Jean Goldkette's band as staff arranger, beginning a close association with Bix Beiderbecke which continued when both men joined Paul Whiteman's band the following year. Challis wrote some of Whiteman's most jazz-oriented arrangements, including *Lonely Melody*, *Changes*, and *Dardanella*, giving Beiderbecke ample solo space and sometimes scoring his cornet improvisations for the trumpet section. He also wrote excellent scores for smaller groups formed for recording sessions from Whiteman's band and led by Frankie Trumbauer. Challis's best work of this period reveals a tasteful synthesis of jazz and dance-band elements, a sure grasp of the new jazz style, and an awareness of the strengths of Whiteman's and Goldkette's musicians. After leaving Whiteman in 1930 Challis became a freelance arranger for, among others, Trumbauer, Fletcher Henderson, the Dorsey Brothers' Orchestra, the Casa Loma Orchestra, Lennie Hayton, Artie Shaw, and a number of radio orchestras. In later years he turned to popular music, remaining active into the 1960s. In 1974 he arranged Beiderbecke's piano compositions (which he had notated and edited for publication in 1930) for guitar quintet.

Oral history material in *NjR* (JOHP).

SELECTED ARRANGEMENTS

As leader: *Bill Challis and his Orchestra: 1936* (1936, Cir. [USA] 71–2)
Recorded by J. Goldkette: Sunday (1926, Vic. 20273); My Pretty Girl (1927, Vic. 20588); Slow River (1927, Vic. 20926)
Recorded by P. Whiteman: Changes (1927, Vic. 21103); Lonely Melody (1928, Vic. 21214); Dardanella (1928, Vic. 25238)
Recorded by others: F. Trumbauer: Ostrich Walk/Riverboat Shuffle (1927, OK 40822); F. Henderson: Singing the Blues (1931, Vic. 22721); Dorsey Brothers: The Blue Room (1933, Bruns. 6722); A. Shaw: Blues in the Night (1941, Vic. 27609); B. Pizzarelli: *The Bucky Pizzarelli Guitar Quintet Plays Beiderbecke/Challis* (1974, MonE 7066)

BIBLIOGRAPHY

R. M. Sudhalter, P. R. Evans, and W. Dean-Myatt: *Bix: Man & Legend* (New Rochelle, NY, and London, 1974)
J. H. Klee: "Bill Challis: Arranger," *MR*, ii/7 (1975), 8
B. Challis: Liner notes, *Bill Challis and his Orchestra: 1936* (Cir. [USA] 71, 1983)

DAN MORGENSTERN

Chaloff, Serge (*b* Boston, 24 Nov 1923; *d* Boston, 16 July 1957). Saxophonist. He studied piano and clarinet formally but was self-taught on baritone saxophone, being influenced by Harry Carney of Duke Ellington's band and Jack Washington of Count Basie's. He worked in various minor bands from 1939 to 1944; in 1945 he moved to Boyd Raeburn's group, then a progressive force in the definition of postwar jazz styles. In that year he also joined Georgie Auld's band and was decisively influenced by Charlie Parker, quickly absorbing the devices of melodic construction, harmonic vocabulary, and rhythmic variety needed to give his swing-based style a wider range of expression. His most important lengthy engagement was with Woody Herman (1947–9), when he was a member of the famous reed section known as the Four Brothers (for illustration *see* HERMAN, WOODY, fig.1*b*). Persistent ill-health made Chaloff less active in the 1950s, though he continued to record almost up to his death.

Chaloff was an important figure of the bop movement and one of the most significant improvisers on the baritone saxophone. Early performances such as *The Most* (1949) show him to have been a virtuoso, while others, for example *Gabardine and Serge* (1947), demonstrate the logic of his improvising and its often somber emotional content. Despite illness he continued to advance during the 1950s, adding to his style an integral use of dynamic and tonal shading and carefully varied degrees of intensity.

SELECTED RECORDINGS

Pumpernickel (1947, Savoy 956); Gabardine and Serge (1947, Savoy 978); Chickasaw/Bop Scotch (1949, Futurama 3003); The Most (1949, Futurama 3004); Fabel of Mabel (1954, Sto. 426); *Blue Serge* (1956, Cap. T742), incl. The Goof and I, Stairway to the Stars

BIBLIOGRAPHY

A. Morgan: "Serge Chaloff," *JM*, iii/8 (1957), 24
M. Harrison: "Serge Chaloff," *JM*, ix/3 (1963), 10
I. Gitler: *Jazz Masters of the Forties* (New York, 1966/*R*1983 with discography), 39
J. Burns: "Serge Chaloff," *JJ*, xxi/3 (1968), 14
A. McCarthy: *Big Band Jazz* (New York and London, 1974), 236
M. Harrison: *A Jazz Retrospect* (Newton Abbot, England, 1976, rev. 2/1977)
P. Moon: "Serge Chaloff Discography," *DF*, no.38 (1977), 3; no.39 (1977), 7; no.40 (1978), 7; no.41 (1978), 7
A. Groves: "Blue Serge Blues: the Recorded Evidence of the Great Serge Chaloff," *JJI*, xxxii/6 (1979), 8
G. von Jena: *Discografie [sic] of Serge Chaloff* (Berlin, 1986)

MAX HARRISON/R

Chambers, (Dallas) Elmer [Frog; Muffle Jaws] (*b* Bayonne, NJ, 1897; *d* Jersey City, NJ, *c*1952). Trumpeter. He met Sam Wooding while playing with an army band during World War I; after leaving the army he played with Wooding in Atlantic City, New Jersey, and then in Detroit and New York. In 1923 he left Wooding and worked as a soloist with Fletcher Henderson, recording with his small groups (1923–4) and with his orchestra (1924–5; for illustration *see* JAZZ (i), fig.2), often accompanying such blues singers as Rosa Henderson, Clara Smith, and Ida Cox; *Gulf Coast Blues* (1923, Para. 20235) is an excellent example of his playing. After leaving Henderson, Chambers played for the bandleader Billy Fowler (*c*1926–7), then toured with traveling shows before ceasing to play full-time.

based on *ChiltonW*

Chambers, Henderson (Charles) (*b* Alexandria, LA, 1 May 1908; *d* New York, 19 Oct 1967). Trombonist. He gained his first experience in the Morehouse College band, then in the 1930s played in territory bands led by Zack Whyte (1934), Al Sears (1935–6), and others. After playing with Tiny Bradshaw from 1937 to 1938, he moved to New York in 1939, where he worked at the Savoy Ballroom with Chris Columbus and then with Louis Armstrong (1941–3). During the rest of the 1940s he played intermittently with Edmond Hall, Don Redman, and Sy Oliver; he then spent three years with Lucky Millinder (1950–53). From 1953 he worked with Count Basie, Mel Powell, Duke Ellington, Cab Calloway, Doc Cheatham, and Mercer Ellington. He toured with Ray Charles (1961–3) and Basie (1964–6), and during this time also organized rehearsal bands with Puddinghead Battle. Chambers's powerful trombone style is best displayed on his recordings with small groups.

SELECTED RECORDINGS

As sideman: L. Armstrong: Cash for your Trash/I Never Knew (1942, Decca 4229); Edmond Hall's Swingtet: Besame Mucho/Opus 15 (1944, Bruns. 80125); Continental Blues/Face (1945, Contl 6018); Ellis Island/Lonely Moments (1945, Contl 6026); D. Redman: Midnight Moods/Mickey Finn (1946, Pick-Up 1002); M. Powell: *Mel Powell Septet* (1953, Van. 8004); R. Charles: *Ingredients in a Recipe for Soul* (1963, ABC-Para. 465)

BIBLIOGRAPHY

ChiltonW; *FeatherE*; *Feather '60s*; *Feather–Gitler '70s*
H. Panassié: "Henderson Chambers (1908–1967)," *BHcF*, no.172 (1967), 3

LAWRENCE KOCH

Chambers, Joe [Joseph Arthur] (*b* Stoneacre, VA, 25 June 1942). Drummer and composer. After working in Washington for three years he moved in 1963 to New York, where he played with Eric Dolphy, Freddie Hubbard, Jimmy Giuffre, and Andrew Hill. From 1965 to 1970 he performed and recorded with Bobby Hutcherson and was associated with Donald Byrd's quintet, Duke Pearson's big band, and Joe Henderson's sextet; he also recorded with Sam Rivers (1965), Chick Corea (1966), Wayne Shorter (1965–7), and Miroslav Vitous (1969). He was one of the original members of Max Roach's group M'BOOM RE: PERCUSSION, formed in 1970. During the 1970s he performed with Sonny Rollins and the group led by Tommy Flanagan and Art Farmer, performed and recorded with Charles Mingus (1972, 1978), and recorded as a percussionist with Joe Zawinul (1970). He played with Flanagan and Reggie Workman in the Super Jazz Trio (1978–9), and in the 1980s recorded with Chet Baker (1982) and worked with Ray Mantilla's Space Station. His compositions have been recorded on albums by Hubbard, Hutcherson, M'Boom Re: Percussion, and his own groups (including *The Almoravid*, 1971, 1973).

SELECTED RECORDINGS

As leader: *The Almoravid* (1971, 1973, Muse 5035); *New World* (1975, Finite 1976-2); *New York Concerto* (1981, Bay. 8018)
As sideman: B. Hutcherson: *Happenings* (1966, BN 84231); C. Mingus: *Me, Myself an Eye* (1978, Atl. 8803); M. Roach: *M'Boom Re: Percussion* (1979, Col. IC36247); R. Mantilla: *Hands of Fire* (1984, RR 174)

BIBLIOGRAPHY

Feather '60s; *Feather–Gitler '70s*
G. Giddins: Liner notes, *The Almoravid* (Muse 5035, 1974)

RICK MATTINGLY

Chambers, Paul (Laurence Dunbar, Jr.) (*b* Pittsburgh, 22 April 1935; *d* New York, 4 Jan 1969). Double bass player. From the age of 13 he lived in Detroit, and, after taking up double bass in 1949, was soon working with Kenny Burrell and other local jazzmen. A tour with Paul Quinichette took him in 1955 to New York, where he was immediately accepted by the bop elite. He made a tour of the South with Bennie Green, played at the Embers and at Birdland with Sonny Stitt and Joe Roland, performed with J. J. Johnson and with George Wallington, then in 1955 rejoined Johnson with Kai Winding in their group Jay and Kai. In October of the same year he became a member of Miles Davis's quintet. He spent eight years with the group, becoming Davis's longest serving sideman; initially he formed with Red Garland and Philly Joe Jones a rhythm section that, for the propulsive sense of swing it engendered, had no rivals. At the end of the 1950s Chambers played in Davis's acclaimed sextets, which also included Cannonball Adderley and John Coltrane. He took part in several recording sessions with Coltrane and also recorded with Kenny Clarke (1955), Adderley (1955, 1959), Donald Byrd (1955, 1960), Sonny Rollins (1956–7), Garland (1956–8), Lee Morgan (1956–7, 1960), Art Pepper, Gene Ammons, and Johnson (all 1957), Bud Powell (1957–8), Kenny Dorham (1959, 1961), and Freddie Hubbard and Jay and Kai (both 1960).

Chambers was a conservative musician who played in the tonal walking bass style and who faded unjustifiably into obscurity as jazz styles changed in the early 1960s. In 1963 he left Davis together with Wynton Kelly and Jimmy Cobb to form a trio that proved short-lived, but his subsequent activities were hampered by ill health. An edition of transcriptions of 20 of Chambers's solos, *The Music of Paul Chambers*, was published in 1984.

SELECTED RECORDINGS

As leader: *Bass on Top* (1957, BN 1569)
As sideman with M. Davis: *'Round about Midnight* (1955–6, Col. CL949); *Steamin'* (1956, Prst. 7200); *Cookin'* (1956, Prst. 7076); *Kind of Blue* (1959, Col. CL1355); *Someday my Prince will Come* (1961, Col. CS8456)
As sideman with J. Coltrane: *Black Pearls* (1958, Prst. 7316); *Stardust* (1958, Prst. 7268); *The Believer* (1958, Prst. 7292); *Bahia* (1958, Prst. 7353)
As sideman with others: C. Adderley: *Presenting Cannonball Adderley* (1955, Savoy MG12018); S. Rollins: *Tenor Madness* (1956, Prst. 7047); W. Kelly and W. Montgomery: *Smokin' at the Half Note* (1965, Verve 68633)

BIBLIOGRAPHY

N. Hentoff: "Detroit Producing Stars: Paul Chambers Big One," *DB*, xxiii/1 (1956), 12
B. Gardner: "Paul Chambers: Youngest Old Man in Jazz," *DB*, xxvii/15 (1960), 31
V. Wilmer: "Paul Chambers," *JJ*, xiv/3 (1961), 15 [interview]
"Dictionnaire de la contrebasse," *Jm*, no.166 (1969), 33
Obituary, M. Gardner, *JJ*, xxii/4 (1969), 5
J. Renaud: "Paul Chambers, 1935–69," *Jh*, no.248 (1969), 32

BARRY KERNFELD

Chamblee, Eddie [Edward Leon] (*b* Atlanta, 24 Feb 1920). Tenor saxophonist. He was brought up in Chicago, and after studying law at Chicago State University he led several army bands (1941–6). He worked as a leader of a small group in

Chicago from 1946 until the mid-1950s; its recordings include *Back Street/Lazy Mood* (1947, Miracle M133). During his association with Lionel Hampton (1955–7) Chamblee toured and recorded in Europe (1956). From 1957 he again worked as a leader of small groups and made a number of recordings with Dinah Washington (1957–8, 1963), to whom he was married for a short time. He returned to Europe with Milt Buckner (1976) and again with Hampton (1977, 1978) and recorded with both musicians; in 1976 he also made a number of recordings as a leader. He played briefly with Count Basie's orchestra as an alto saxophonist in late 1982.

BIBLIOGRAPHY

H. Panassié and M. Gautier: *Dictionnaire du jazz* (Paris, 1954, rev. and enlarged 2/1971, enlarged 3/1980; Eng. trans., London, 1956, rev. A. A. Gurwitch as *Guide to Jazz*, Boston, 1956)

J. Morgantini: "Eddie Chamblee," *BHcF*, no.58 (1956), 3

HOWARD RYE

Champion. Record label. It was established by the Starr Piano Co. of Richmond, Indiana, in September 1925 as a subsidiary of GENNETT. On it were issued cheap pressings (almost exclusively under pseudonyms) of items made available simultaneously on the parent label; these included many race records. Champion remained in operation after Gennett closed at the end of 1930, and was used to put out recordings by several important jazz groups, including the State Street Ramblers, at the height of the Depression. The label was finally discontinued in December 1934, and on 28 June 1935 the trademark was sold to Decca with the rights to certain parts of Gennett's catalogue. Later that year Decca revived the label for about twelve months, putting out both new recordings and reissues from Gennett and Paramount; the catalogue included a race series, the Champion 50000s.

BIBLIOGRAPHY

J. Godrich and R. M. W. Dixon: *Blues & Gospel Records, 1902–1942* (Hatch End, nr London, 1964, rev. 2/1969, rev. and enlarged 3/1982 as R. M. W. Dixon and J. Godrich: *Blues & Gospel Records, 1902–1943*)

M. Wyler: "A Glimpse of the Past, 11: Champion," *Sv*, no.20 (1968–9), 69

R. M. W. Dixon and J. Godrich: *Recording the Blues* (London, 1970)

B. Rust: *The American Record Label Book* (New Rochelle, NY, 1978), 60

Chan, Charlie. Nickname of CHARLIE PARKER.

Chancler, Ndugu Leon. *See* NDUGU.

Changes. The harmonic progression (that is, the series of harmonies) of an existing theme (often a popular song) on which a jazz performance is based; *see* HARMONY (i), §1(v)(b).

Channel. The penultimate section in the refrain of a popular song, leading to the final repeat of the opening section (section *b* in the form *aaba*); it provides a contrast, often tonal as well as harmonic and melodic, with the opening section. *See* FORMS, esp. §1(i)(a).

Chappy [Obendorfer [Orlay-Obendorfer], Jenő [Chappy]; Orlay, Jenő] (*b* Budapest, 31 Oct 1905; *d* nr Munich, 28 March 1973). Hungarian drummer and bandleader. He began his career as a dancer in Budapest. After teaching himself to play drums he toured Europe with Arthur Briggs's band (1926–8), with which he recorded in Berlin in 1927. He was active as a bandleader from around 1930 and performed in Java (1933–4) and Europe. He made recordings for various companies from 1942 to 1947 (including *Hooray for Hollywood*, 1943, Col. OH164). He often competed in drum battles, an example of which may be heard on *Dob-párbaj* (Drum battle) (1947, Mesterhang Super C40). Though principally an entertainer and dance-band leader, Chappy always employed the best Hungarian jazz musicians.

BIBLIOGRAPHY

J. Orlay: *Jazzdobbal a világ körül* [Around the world with jazz drums] (Budapest, 1943) [autobiography]

A. Csányi and G. G. Simon: Liner notes, *Jazz and Hot Dance in Hungary* (Harl. 2015, 1985)

GÉZA GÁBOR SIMON, RAINER E. LOTZ

Charig, Marc [Mark Bloomfield] (*b* London, 22 Feb 1944). English cornetist and alto horn player. After working with various rhythm-and-blues groups he began playing jazz regularly with Elton Dean (recording in 1971, 1976–7, and 1980) and Keith Tippett (1969–71). In 1970–71 he played briefly with Soft Machine and the rock group King Crimson before joining Chris McGregor, with whom he worked intermittently until 1981. In 1972 he began playing with the London Jazz Composers Orchestra; he has also performed with such free-jazz groups as the Alternative Music Orchestra (1977) and Musica Libera (1979), and recorded as a leader and with Harry Miller's quintet and sextet (both 1977, 1983). He played on Fred van Hove's album *Was macht ihr denn?* (1982, FMP SAJ42), and later was a member of his group Antwerpiae (1984). Having settled in Aachen, Germany, Charig has worked in the mid-1980s with Maarten Altena's octet, the cooperative free-jazz group King Übü Orchestrü of Berlin, the trombonist Radu Malfatti's group Ohr Kiste, and other ensembles. He has also continued to play occasionally with Dean, Tippett and the London Jazz Composers Orchestra. (R. Cotterrell, ed.: *Jazz Now: the Jazz Centre Society Guide* (London, 1976), 119)

SIMON ADAMS

Charles, Dennis (*b* St. Croix, VI, 4 Dec 1933). Drummer. He went to New York in 1945 and played with various calypso and mambo bands in Harlem before taking up jazz drumming. He played with Cecil Taylor in Jack Gelber's play *The Connection* and also made recordings intermittently with Taylor's free-jazz groups (1955–61, including the album *Looking Ahead!*, 1958, Cont. 3562). Charles also performed and recorded with Steve Lacy (1957, 1963–4, 1979, 1982), Gil Evans (1959), Archie Shepp (1967), and Billy Bang (1981–2).

BIBLIOGRAPHY

V. Wilmer: "Dennis Charles," *Jm*, no.223 (1974), 18 [incl. discography]

——: *As Serious as your Life: the Story of the New Jazz* (London, 1977, rev. 1980)

R. de Vries: "Het credo van Dennis Charles," *Jazz nu*, iv (1982), 273

L. van Trikt: "Dennis Charles," *Cadence*, xiii/10 (1987), 5

Charles, Ray [Robinson, Ray Charles] (*b* Albany, GA, 23 Sept 1930). Singer, pianist, arranger, and songwriter. He grew up in Greenville, Florida, in a very poor family, and at the age of five contracted glaucoma; it went untreated and within a year he was blind. When he was five he also began playing piano, and two years later he went to the St. Augustine School for the Deaf and the Blind, where he studied composition and learned to write music in Braille. In 1945 he left school to form a group, which toured Florida, and shortly afterwards he went to Seattle. There he played in a number of jazz trios and developed a style that was heavily influenced by Nat "King" Cole and Louis Jordan. It was about this time that he changed his name to Ray Charles, in order to avoid confusion with the prizefighter Sugar Ray Robinson. In 1954 Charles formed his own band, which had several rhythm-and-blues hits, including *I've got a woman* (1955). His piano and vocal style was heavily influenced by gospel music, and on the album he recorded at the Newport Jazz Festival in 1958 he established himself as a testifying rock-and-roll preacher, a smooth, sophisticated popular singer, a big-band leader, and a swinging bop pianist. Among the soloists in his bands were Hank Crawford (1958–63), Phil Guilbeau (1960–65), and Blue Mitchell (1969–71). In his arrangements Charles shows an appreciation of modern jazz (Quincy Jones received some tuition from him in Seattle), and his instrumental recordings with Milt Jackson (1957–8) and Count Basie's orchestra (1960, without Basie himself) have been particularly influential. He is best known, however, for his work in popular genres: a musician of fundamental importance and far-reaching influence, he was among the principal architects of the transformation of black popular music from the rhythm-and-blues style to soul.

SELECTED RECORDINGS

As leader: with M. Jackson: *Soul Brothers* (1957, Atl. 1279), *Soul Meeting* (1958, Atl. 1360); *Ray Charles at Newport* (1958, Atl. 1289); *Genius + Soul = Jazz* (1960, Imp. 2)

BIBLIOGRAPHY

A. Morrison: "Ray Charles," *JJ*, xiii/12 (1960), 3
M. Gautier: "Ray Charles," *BHcF*, no.201 (1970), 7
L. Goddet: "Ray Charles pas à pas . . .," *Jh*, no.329 (1976), 8
P. Welding: "Ray Charles: Senior Diplomat of Soul," *DB*, xliv/9 (1977), 12
R. Charles and D. Ritz: *Brother Ray: Ray Charles' own Story* (New York, 1978)
R. Palmer: "Soul Survivor Ray Charles," *RS*, no.258 (9 Feb 1978), 11
W. Balliett: *American Singers* (New York, 1979), 50
L. Feather: "Piano Giants of Jazz: Ray Charles," *CK*, vi/7 (1980), 62
B. Doerschuk: "Ray Charles! The Instrumental Side of a Legendary Singer," *Keyboard*, x/3 (1984), 19 [incl. discography]

DAVE MARSH/R

Charles [Cohen], **Teddy** [Cohen, Theodore Charles] (*b* Chicopee Falls, MA, 13 April 1928). Vibraphonist, composer, and arranger. He studied percussion at the Juilliard School in 1946, but taught himself to play vibraphone; later he studied composition with Hall Overton. After playing for a number of bandleaders from 1946 to 1952, he began leading various experimental jazz groups of his own, with which his career subsequently became associated; he was also an active participant in Charles Mingus's Jazz Composers' Workshop (1954–5). He was particularly concerned with the interaction of improvisation and composition in jazz, and both commissioned and recorded some unusually intelligent examples of jazz composition and arrangement, such as George Russell's *Lydian M-1*, Jimmy Giuffre's *The Quiet Time*, and Gil Evans's *You go to my head*. In his own compositions, too, Charles broke away from the conventional formal pattern of popular songs to write such works as his *Variations on a Theme by Bud* (1953), which has a 48-bar chorus made up of eight-bar sections in the form *abcded*. The written and improvised contrapuntal textures of his works of this period looked forward to the collective extemporization in the jazz of the 1960s; the modality of *Etudiez le cahier* and polytonal elements of *Further out* show a strong harmonic sense. Charles was throughout his career an outstanding vibraphonist, but is perhaps most important for his efforts to bring more diverse musical materials to jazz. *See also* WARWICK.

SELECTED RECORDINGS

Teddy Charles and his Trio (1951, Prst. 132); *New Directions* (1953, Prst. 164), incl. Etudiez le cahier, Further out, Variations on a Theme by Bud; *The Teddy Charles Tentet* (1956, Atl. 1229), incl. Lydian M-1, The Quiet Time, You go to my head; *A Word from Bird* (1956, Atl. 1274)

BIBLIOGRAPHY

I. Gitler: "Dialogue on Modern Jazz: an Interview with Teddy Charles," *Jazz: a Quarterly of American Music*, no.2 (1959), 161
M. Harrison: "Teddy Charles," *JM*, viii/9 (1962), 17
J. Burns: "Good Vibes," *J&B*, ii/5 (1972), 7
R. Atkins: "Teddy Charles," *Modern Jazz: the Essential Records: a Critical Selection*, ed. M. Harrison (London, 1975), 30
M. Harrison: *A Jazz Retrospect* (Newton Abbot, England, 1976, rev. 2/1977)

MAX HARRISON/R

Charleston. Lively, social dance of the 1920s, said to have originated in Charleston, South Carolina. It appeared for the first time in theatrical dance in the black musical comedy *Liza* (1922) and achieved enormous popularity in 1923 as a dance song, *The Charleston*, by James P. Johnson and Cecil Mack, in the musical *Runnin' Wild*. It became the symbol of the "Roaring Twenties," and was therefore much associated with the jazz age and the Black Renaissance. The music was fast, about 50–60 bars per minute, and the characteristic syncopated rhythm (ex.1) is used in other dances of black-American origin, notably the black bottom.

Ex.1 J. P. Johnson and C. Mack: *The Charleston* (1923)

BIBLIOGRAPHY

M. Stearns and J. Stearns: *Jazz Dance: the Story of American Vernacular Dance* (New York and London, 1968)
L. F. Emery: *Black Dance in the United States from 1619 to 1970* (Palo Alto, CA, 1972)

PAULINE NORTON

Charleston Chasers. Name of various groups that recorded for the Columbia label between 1925 and 1931. These were most often led by RED NICHOLS, though also by Dick Johnson, Phil Napoleon, and Benny Goodman.

Charleston cymbal. A cymbal of 25 cm diameter, often with a very large cup or bell, generally used as part of the hi-hat; *see* DRUM SET, §I, 5.

Charlie Parker Records. Record company and label founded by Doris Parker (Charlie Parker's widow) and Aubrey Mayhew in New York in 1961. Its original purpose was to make available previously unissued recordings by Parker, and two albums of such material were made. Three further albums, of recordings originally issued by Le Jazz Cool, were also released. In addition the company reissued the sides made by Red Norvo for Comet and made available for the first time commercially air checks of material by Lester Young and Billie Holiday. New albums were recorded by Cecil Payne, Duke Jordan, Jordan and Sadik Hakim, Joe "Bebop" Carroll, Barry Miles, Mundell Lowe, Teddy Wilson, and Slide Hampton. Many of the recordings made by the company were issued in the UK by Egmont Records of Lancashire.

Charlie Parker Records was active for only about two years. Its masters were eventually sold to Audiofidelity Enterprises of New York, which began in 1981 to reissue some of the Parker recordings together with further performances not previously available; this project, however, like its predecessor of 20 years before, was soon discontinued.

MARK GARDNER

Chart. Any printed or manuscript score or part from which a musician plays. Various kinds of chart are discussed in NOTATION, §2.

Charters, Samuel B(arclay) (*b* Pittsburgh, 1 Aug 1929). Writer. He grew up in a family of jazz musicians. After attending Sacramento City College and Tulane University he studied music at the University of California, Berkeley (BA 1956). His field recordings of blues performances in the New Orleans area, which he submitted to the Vanguard record company in 1954 at the suggestion of Frederic Ramsey, Jr., were the first of his many recordings to document the blues in the USA and the Caribbean; later he studied the background of the blues in West Africa, and in 1962 he produced the film *The Blues*. He has also written extensively on the genre, and in 1979 received an ASCAP–Deems Taylor award for his book *Roots of the Blues*. Among his other writings are studies of musical life in New Orleans, *Jazz: New Orleans, 1885–1957* (1958), and New York, *Jazz: a History of the New York Scene* (1962). From 1970 to 1984 Charters lived in Sweden, where he studied indigenous folk music, and in 1984 he combined his musical and literary interests in his book *Jelly Roll Morton's Last Night at the Jungle Inn: an Imaginary Memoir*.

WRITINGS

(*selective list*)

Jazz: New Orleans, 1885–1957: an Index to the Negro Musicians of New Orleans (Belleville, NJ, 1958, rev. 2/1963/*R*1983 as *Jazz: New Orleans, 1885–1963: an Index to the Negro Musicians of New Orleans*)
The Country Blues (New York and Toronto, 1959)
with L. Kunstadt: *Jazz: a History of the New York Scene* (Garden City, NY, 1962/*R*1981)
The Bluesmen: the Story and the Music of the Men who Made the Blues (New York, 1967)
The Roots of the Blues: an African Search (Boston and London, 1981)
Jelly Roll Morton's Last Night at the Jungle Inn: an Imaginary Memoir (New York, 1984)

KATHLEEN HAEFLIGER/R

Chase. A competition in improvisation between two (or occasionally more than two) soloists who play in turn, taking inspiration from and trying to outplay each other. The soloists normally take alternate choruses but the pace may quicken so that the players exchange half-choruses, then phrases, then half-phrases, and so on, creating the procedure called "trading" (*see* FORMS, §1(ii)). A "chase chorus" is a single chorus during which a chase occurs.

The most famous chases involved bop tenor saxophonists: Gene Ammons and Dexter Gordon on Billy Eckstine's *Blowin' the Blues Away* (1944, Deluxe 2001); Gordon and Wardell Gray on their recording *The Chase* (1947, Dial 1017); Ammons and Sonny Stitt on their recording *Blues Up and Down* (1950, Birdland 6005); and Johnny Griffin and Eddie "Lockjaw" Davis, who carried on the tradition a decade later on such albums as Davis's *Blues Up and Down* (1961, Jlnd 960).

BARRY KERNFELD

Chase, Bill [William] (*b* Boston, 1935; *d* nr Jackson, MN, 9 Aug 1974). Trumpeter and bandleader. He studied with Herb Pomeroy at the Berklee College of Music, and made his first recording there with a big band in 1957. The following year he made two albums as Maynard Ferguson's lead trumpeter, and in 1959 he recorded in New York with Stan Kenton and performed at the Monterey Jazz Festival with Woody Herman. He worked with Herman intermittently for ten years, and toured Europe with him in 1969; his playing may be heard to advantage on *Woody's Winners* (1965, Col. CS9236). He then organized Chase, a nine-piece jazz-rock group (four trumpets, a rhythm section, and a singer); its first album, *Chase* (1971, Epic 30472), was well received, but later recordings were less successful. He reorganized the group and took it on a tour in 1974 in an attempt to revive its popularity; he and three other members were killed in an airplane crash.

BIBLIOGRAPHY

Feather–Gitler '70s
J. Szantor: "Chase: Brass Roots Jazz Rock," *DB*, xxxviii/3 (1971), 12
——: "Focus on Bill Chase," *DB*, xxxix/2 (1972), 12
A. Scott: "Remembering Bill Chase," *Sabin's Radio Free Jazz!*, xiv/12 (1974), 8

Chat qui Pêche, le. Nightclub in Paris; *see* NIGHTCLUBS AND OTHER VENUES.

Chautemps, Jean-Louis (*b* Paris, 6 Aug 1931). French tenor saxophonist. He played with Jef Gilson (1950), Claude Bolling (1952–4), Albert Nicholas (1954), Chet Baker (1956), Jacques Hélian's band (1956–7), and Kurt Edelhagen (1959). During the next two decades he played with Nathan Davis (1965), the Paris Jazz All Stars (1967), Philly Joe Jones, André Hodeir (1969), John Lewis (1970), Lester Bowie (1974), the percussionist Bernard Lubat (1976–80), and Martial Solal; he joined the Quartette de Saxophones Français in 1979. He played with Lee Konitz (1980) and Michel Portal (1983), and from 1981 worked with such avant-garde composers as Paul Méfano and Vinko Globokar. Chautemps can be heard to advantage on the album *Mad Sax* (Cy 733613), recorded by the Quartette de Saxophones Français in 1982.

MICHEL LAPLACE

Cheatham, Doc [Adolphus Anthony] (*b* Nashville, 13 June 1905). Trumpeter. After moving to Chicago he played in Albert Wynn's band and led his own group (1926). He then worked in Philadelphia with Wilbur De Paris (1927–8) and, after a brief spell with Chick Webb, traveled to Europe with Sam Wooding (1928). Cheatham returned to the USA in 1930 and played in various big bands, including McKinney's Cotton Pickers (1931–2) and those led by Cab Calloway (1933–9), Teddy Wilson (1939), Benny Carter (1940), and Teddy Hill. The brief solos he played as a member of Eddie Heywood's sextet (1943–5), however, hinted at his jazz potential, and he belatedly gained a reputation as an interesting and consistent improviser. During the 1950s and 1960s Cheatham worked frequently with Latin-American bands; he also made tours with De Paris (Africa, 1957; Europe, 1960), Sammy Price (Europe, 1958), and Herbie Mann (Africa, 1960). He led his own band in New York (1960–65) and played with Benny Goodman (1966–7), but thereafter worked as a freelance, continuing to perform with enthusiasm well into the 1980s.

Cheatham always possessed an admirable technique, and his articulation and clarity of tone were striking (he was particularly expressive when using a cup mute); in later years he often added a rough burr to his sound which gave an invigorating edge to his solos. He occasionally played in big bands during the 1970s, but always returned to small-group settings, where he was best able to display his graceful improvisations, his flexibility, and his glorious high register. Unusually for a jazz musician, and particularly for a brass player, Cheatham's talents seemed to flower when he was in his 70s, and most of his best recordings date from this late stage of his career.

Oral history material in *NjR* (JOHP).

SELECTED RECORDINGS

As leader: *Adolphus "Doc" Cheatham* (1973, Jezebel 102), incl. Mandy, make up your mind; *Hey Doc!* (1975, BB 33090), incl. Rosetta; with J. Williams and H. Hall: *John, Doc & Herb* (1979, Metronome 627), incl. Little Happy

Caldwell; with S. Price: *Black Beauty* (1979, Sack. 3029), incl. Memphis Blues
As sideman: E. Heywood: I can't believe that you're in love with me (1944, Com. 577)

BIBLIOGRAPHY

A. J. McCarthy: "An Introduction to Doc Cheatham," *JM*, no.152 (1967), 8
R. Rains: "Conversations with Doc," *Sv*, no.14 (1967–8), 4
S. Dance: *The World of Swing* (New York, n.d. [?1974]) [colln of previously pubd interviews], 307
J. H. Klee: "Send for Doc Cheatham," *MR*, iii/12 (1976), 6
J. P. Battestini: "Doc Cheatham," *Coda*, no.161 (1978), 28
W. Balliett: "Jazz: a Burning Desire," *New Yorker* (5 Feb 1979), 118
W. Vaché: "Doc Cheatham," *JJI*, xxxii/12 (1979), 6
L. Ridley: "Profile, Subject: Doc Cheatham," *JSN*, i/5 (1980), 6
M. Ullman: *Jazz Lives: Portraits in Words and Pictures* (Washington, 1980), 17
L. Jeske: "Rx for the Blues," *DB*, xlviii/12 (1981), 25
W. Balliett: "Light Everywhere," *Jelly Roll, Jabbo and Fats* (New York, and Oxford, England, 1983) [colln of previously pubd articles], 74
E. Cook: "'Life has been very good to me; I can't complain'," *JJI*, xxxvii/6 (1984), 8
L. D. Holmes and J. W. Thomson: *Jazz Greats: Getting Better with Age* (New York, 1986) [colln of interviews]

JOHN CHILTON

Chekasin, Vladimir (Nikolayevich) (*b* Sverdlovsk, Russian SFSR, 24 Feb 1947). Russian reed and keyboard player. He studied violin from the age of six, took up clarinet and alto saxophone, and worked as a leader from 1967 to 1971; he graduated from the Urals M. P. Mussorgsky State Conservatory in Sverdlovsk as a clarinetist in 1970. In 1971 he moved to Vilnius, where he became an original member of the Ganelin Trio (later known as the G–T–Ch Trio); in Prague the same year he won first prize in a jazz competition and made his first recording. Later he taught at the Lithuanian State Conservatory in Vilnius (at which from 1982 he led a big band composed of his students) and led a quartet and several other groups. He has performed in many European countries and also in the USA (1986). Chekasin is a versatile instrumentalist who is particularly expert at playing two saxophones simultaneously; a good example of his work is his album *Prisiminimai* (The memoirs; 1985, Mel. C6023447000).

BIBLIOGRAPHY

B. Noglik: "Wjatsecheslaw Ganelin, Wladimir Tschekassin, Wladimir Tarassow," *Jazzwerkstatt international* (Berlin, 1981) [incl. interview, discography]
F. Maino: "Ganelin, Tarasov, and Chekasin: Interview," *Cadence*, ix/1 (1983), 18
A. Duncan: "Soviet Trio Takes Daring Liberties with Familiar Jazz Styles," *Christian Science Monitor* (30 June 1986), 29

WALTER OJAKÄÄR

Cherico, Gene [Eugene V.] (*b* Buffalo, 15 April 1935). Double bass player. He first played drums in an army band, but took up double bass as therapy for an injury to his right arm. While studying at the Berklee College of Music he met Toshiko Akiyoshi: he became a member of her first American trio and has worked with her intermittently into the mid-1980s. He has played as a sideman in swing and bop groups led by Herb Pomeroy (1957–9), Maynard Ferguson (1959–60), Red Norvo (1961), Benny Goodman (1962), George Shearing (1963), Stan Getz (1964–6), and the pianist Peter Nero (1966–70); he has also accompanied singers, notably Peggy Lee (1966), Carmen McRae (1970), Frank Sinatra (1973), and Nancy Wilson. In the 1970s he was a studio musician in Los Angeles, where he recorded with Frank Strazzeri (1973) and the big bands led by Louie Bellson and by Akiyoshi and Lew Tabackin (both 1974), and also performed with Gerry Mulligan (1974). He continued to record with Akiyoshi into the 1980s.

SELECTED RECORDINGS

As sideman: T. Akiyoshi: *The Many Sides of Toshiko* (1957, Verve 8273); G. Burton: *Something's Coming* (1961, RCA LSP2420); S. Getz: *Getz–Gilberto, no.2* (1964, Verve 68623); T. Akiyoshi and L. Tabackin: *Kogun* (1974, RCA JPL1-0236); L. Bellson: *150 MPH* (1974, Conc. 36); T. Akiyoshi: *Toshiko Akiyoshi* (1983, Ewd 90022)

BIBLIOGRAPHY

Feather '60s; *Feather–Gitler '70s*
J. L. Ginibre and P. Carles: "Dictionnaire de la contrebasse," *Jm*, no.166 (1969), 34
D. Matthews: "Gene Cherico," *CI*, xiv/2 (1975), 16

DIANNA RHYAN

Cherry, Don(ald Eugene) (*b* Oklahoma City, OK, 18 Nov 1936). Cornetist and bandleader. He first came to public notice as a regular member of Ornette Coleman's groups from 1957, playing a pocket cornet, which he called a pocket trumpet. He moved with Coleman to New York in 1959, and played on the leader's first seven albums, including *Something Else!!!!*, *Change of the Century*, and *Free Jazz*. After leaving Coleman in the early 1960s Cherry worked briefly with Steve Lacy and Sonny Rollins and then with Archie Shepp and Albert Ayler in Europe;

Don Cherry playing a pocket cornet (which he calls a pocket trumpet)

in 1963–4, with Shepp and John Tchicai, he was a leader of the New York Contemporary Five. From 1964 to 1966, with Gato Barbieri, he led a group based in Europe and recorded his most widely praised albums *Complete Communion* and *Symphony for Improvisers*. During this period his brass instrument was the full-sized cornet. He taught at Dartmouth College in 1970. Thereafter Cherry was based in Sweden for four years; he has visited much of Europe and the Middle East, where he has played informally, and studied other styles of music. In the late 1970s and early 1980s he worked with the rock singer and guitarist Lou Reed, the cooperative trio Codona (with Nana Vasconcelos and Collin Walcott), a group that performed a style of jazz incorporating characteristics of African, Indian, and other ethnic musics, and the band Old and New Dreams (with Charlie Haden, Dewey Redman, and Ed Blackwell, all of whom had formerly been sidemen with Coleman). By 1983 he had acquired another pocket cornet. Codona disbanded in 1984 and Cherry formed a new group, Nu, including Vasconcelos and Carlos Ward. He also played in the LEADERS (1984–6), appeared at the Berlin Jazzfest with Jabbo Smith (1986), and toured the UK with his quintet Nu (1987).

Cherry is a leading figure in free jazz. Although his improvisatory style derives considerably from that of Coleman, he has also cited the influence of Fats Navarro, Clifford Brown, Miles Davis, and Harry Edison, as well as Mexican trumpet styles and the sounds achieved by players of the french horn and the conch trumpet. His performances have a rough-hewn quality and he often unintentionally fluffs or splatters notes. On his recordings with Coleman his tone tends to be soft-textured and dry; however, in a few of his later recordings he achieved a fuller, brassier sound. Lacking the speed, agility, and range of the average modern jazz trumpeter, Cherry instead explores the varied tone qualities of his instrument, often changing tone dramatically within a single solo passage and using an uncommonly wide range of expressive devices. As an improviser he is unusually flexible in that he is able to construct intelligent solo lines as well as contribute appropriately to simultaneous collective improvisations; in this respect he resembles the earliest jazz improvisers, who prized both solo capability and skill in collective interplay. His improvisations are strikingly original, being filled with ideas that do not generally depend on the bop melodic vocabulary. His flexibility extends to an ability to switch back and forth between lines that swing and stay close to the beat and lines that go against the meter in a manner that suggests he is ignoring the beat and resisting swing feeling. Cherry's recorded improvisations usually dispense with preset song forms and accompanying chords, a characteristic they have in common with those of Coleman and also with the non-Western music he has explored. This so-called Third World music, or simply world music, has led Cherry to write for and play in groups using *tambūrā*, sitar, gamelan instruments, finger cymbals, conch horns, and other exotica. He also learned to play flute, bamboo flute, percussion instruments, and berimbau. Cherry's world music makes use of drones and extended vamps, as well as mantras chanted and played over and over again. While his earlier jazz tunes derived from Coleman's distinctive melodic style, his more recent compositions draw on a wide array of sources, including Indian and Arabic-Turkish music, South African urban folk music, hymns, rhythm-and-blues, riff themes, and what Jost has called "endless melodies" – tunes with a cyclic layout and little harmonic or rhythmic differentiation.

For further illustration *see* JAZZ (i), fig.7.

SELECTED RECORDINGS

As leader: of New York Contemporary Five (with A. Shepp and J. Tchicai): *Future I* (1963, Fon. 681013); *Complete Communion* (1965, BN 84226); *Symphony for Improvisers* (1966, BN 84247); *Where is Brooklyn* (1966, BN 84311); *Eternal Rhythm* (1968, Saba MPS 15204); *Mu* (1969, BYG 529301, 529331); *Human Music* (1969–70, FD 121); *The Creator Has a Master Plan* (1971, Caprice 44); *Eternal Now* (1973, Ant. 7034); *Brown Rice* (1975, A&M Hor. 717); *Hear and Now* (1976, Atl. 18217); *The Journey* (1977, Chi. 187); of Codona (with N. Vasconcelos and C. Walcott): *Codona*, ii (1980, ECM 1177), *Codona*, iii (1982, ECM 1243)

As sideman: O. Coleman: *Something Else!!!! The Music of Ornette Coleman* (1958, Cont. 3551); *Change of the Century* (1959, Atl. 1327); *Free Jazz* (1960, Atl. 1364); J. Coltrane: *The Avant Garde* (1960, Atl. 1451); S. Lacy: *Evidence* (1961, NewJ 8271); S. Rollins: *Our Man in Jazz* (1963, RCA LPM2612); A. Ayler: *New York Eye and Ear Control* (1964, ESP 1016); C. Haden: *Liberation Music Orchestra* (1969, Imp. 9183); Jazz Composer's Orchestra Association: *Relativity Suite* (1973, JCOA 1006); C. Walcott: *Codona* (1978, ECM 1132)

BIBLIOGRAPHY

L. Jones: "Don Cherry: Making it the Hard Way," *DB*, xxx/30 (1963), 16
M. Hennessey: "Cherry's Catholicity: the Kaleidoscopic View of Jazz," *DB*, xxxiii/15 (1966), 14
K. Knox: "Don Cherry's Symphony of the Improvisers," *JM*, xiii/6 (1967), 5 [interview]
E. Raben: *A Discography of Free Jazz* (Copenhagen, 1969)
K. Knox: "Whole Earth Jazz," *J&B*, ii/4 (1972), 6
"Don Cherry Discography," *SJ*, xxviii/4 (1974), 252
E. Jost: *Free Jazz* (Graz, Austria, 1974), 133
P. Occhiogrosso: "Emissary of the Global Muse: Don Cherry," *DB*, xlii/21 (1975), 14
A. Taylor: *Notes and Tones: Musician-to-Musician Interviews* (Liège, Belgium, 1977/*R*1982), 175
H. Mandel: "The World in his Pocket: Don Cherry," *DB*, xlv/13 (1978), 20
M. Hames and R. Wilbraham: *Don Cherry on Disc and Tape* (Ferndown, Dorset, England, 1980) [discography]
C. Silvert: "Old and New Dreams," *DB*, xlvii/6 (1980), 17
F. Davis: "Don Cherry: a Jazz Gypsy Comes Home," *Musician*, no.53 (1983), 53
L. Jeske: "Don: the Cherry Variations," *DB*, l/6 (1983), 18
F. Davis: *In the Moment: Jazz in the 1980s* (New York, and Oxford, England, 1986) [colln of previously pubd articles], 147

MARK C. GRIDLEY/R

Cherry Blossom. Nightclub in Kansas City; *see* NIGHTCLUBS AND OTHER VENUES.

Chiaroscuro. Record company and label. The company was established by Hank O'Neal in New York in 1970. Devoted to mainstream jazz, it issued about 100 albums of material recorded between 1969 and 1977 by such leading musicians as Earl Hines, Mary Lou Williams, Joe Venuti, Teddy Wilson, and Ruby Braff; in the last year it also recorded the work of free-jazz musicians, including Hamiet Bluiett, Abdullah Ibrahim, and Perry Robinson. O'Neal produced all the recordings himself, apart from the first in 1969, on which he collaborated with John Hammond, and two from 1977, which were supervised by his engineer Fred Miller. During this period the catalogue was distributed by Pye in England, Teichiku in Japan, and Microfon in Argentina. In 1978 O'Neal sold the company to Audiophile Enterprises, which continued to issue the original series of albums under the name Chiaroscuro, and also instituted a new series, mainly of reissues, that contained the work of players as diverse as Louis Armstrong, Ibrahim, and Elmo Hope. In 1987 O'Neal and Andrew Sordoni formed a new company, SOS Productions, in Forty Fort, Pennsylvania, and reacquired all rights to Chiaroscuro's catalogue, with the intention of reissuing the original series, and releasing new recordings and items produced by O'Neal after 1978.

Chiasson, Warren (*b* Cheticamp, Canada, 17 April 1934). Canadian vibraphone player. He played and recorded with George Shearing from 1958 to 1961 and again, intermittently, from 1972 to 1974. In New York he led his own groups (1962–3, 1968–70) and played at the World's Fair (1964–5). He has made recordings with Les McCann, Harold Vick (both 1966), Chuck Wayne (1976), and as a leader (*Quartessence*, 1973, Van Los 3608; and *Good Vibes for Kurt Weill*, 1977, MonE 7083). In 1974–5 he played with Chet Baker.

BIBLIOGRAPHY

FeatherE; *Feather–Gitler '70s*
M. Miller: "Chiasson, Warren," *Encyclopedia of Music in Canada*, ed. H. Kallmann, G. Potvin, and K. Winters (Toronto, Buffalo, and London, 1981)

Chiboust, Noël (*b* Thorigny-sur-Marne, France, 4 Oct 1909). French trumpeter, tenor saxophonist, and clarinetist. He was largely self-taught as a musician. He played violin with Ray Ventura's Collegians (1928–31), then changed to trumpet. After serving in the army he played with Freddy Johnson (1933), Michel Warlop (1934–5), Coleman Hawkins (1935), and Guy Paquinet (1934–6). He abandoned the trumpet for the tenor saxophone in 1937, then played with Bill Coleman (1938), Joe Keye's band, Serge Glykson (1939), Raymond Wraskoff (1940), and Fred Adison's band (1941). From 1941 to 1969 he was himself a noted bandleader, though he made one of his most characteristic recordings, *Sérénade d'hiver/Le sheik* (1940, Swing 86), earlier as the leader of a studio orchestra.

BIBLIOGRAPHY

A. Hodeir: "Panorama du jazz français," *BHcF*, 1st ser., no.1 (1945), 9
F. Ténot: "Les quatre générations du jazz français," *Jh*, no.23 (1948), 9
M. Laplace: *Portraits of French Jazz Musicians* (Menden, Germany, 1985), 22

MICHEL LAPLACE

Chicago Footwarmers. Recording group. Formed in Chicago in 1927, its members were the cornetist Natty Dominique, the clarinetist Johnny Dodds, the pianist Jimmy Blythe, and the washboard player Baby Dodds. The quartet had recorded as the Dixieland Thumpers for Paramount and as the STATE STREET RAMBLERS for Gennett before recording four tracks for Okeh as the Chicago Footwarmers on 3 and 15 December 1927 (including *Ballin' the Jack/Grandma's Ball*, 8533). With the trombonist Kid Ory and the double bass player Bill Johnson (i) the group recorded three tracks the following year on 2 July (including *Get 'em Again Blues/Brush Stomp*, 8599), and, with Honore Dutrey having replaced Ory, two more tracks in a session that took place two days later. (B. Rust: Liner notes, J. Dodds: *The Immortal Johnny Dodds*, VJM 48, 1981)

MIKE HAZELDINE

Chicago jazz. A subspecies of NEW ORLEANS JAZZ developed by young white musicians in the Chicago area during the early 1920s. A number of these musicians were associated with the so-called Austin High School Gang (Jimmy McPartland, Dave Tough, Frank Teschemacher, Joe Sullivan, and Bud Freeman); others such as Benny Goodman, Gene Krupa, and Muggsy Spanier were native to Chicago, while still others such as Eddie Condon, Pee Wee Russell, and Red McKenzie moved to Chicago early in their careers. Although only intermittently active in Chicago, Bix Beiderbecke and Frankie Trumbauer are also sometimes associated with this school. At first the "Chicagoans" merely copied the New Orleans style of King Oliver and the New Orleans Rhythm Kings, but brought to it in some cases a superior instrumental technique (Goodman) and a more hectic and extrovert rhythmic basis (Krupa), together with a greater emphasis on solo playing. In general, however, they varied the basic features of New Orleans jazz rather than developing an independent style. With the suppression of Chicago's speakeasy culture in the late 1920s most of these musicians moved to New York, where several of them became important figures in the swing style of the 1930s.
See also JAZZ (i), §III, 2.

BIBLIOGRAPHY

G. E. Lambert: "Reflections on Jazz History and the Chicagoans," *JM*, iv (1958), no.6, p.6; no.7, p.9
T. Standish: "Reflections in a Dusty Mirror," *JM*, iv/10 (1958), 25
J. Steiner: "Chicago," *Jazz: New Perspectives on the History of Jazz by Twelve of the Foremost Jazz Critics and Scholars*, ed. N. Hentoff and A. J. McCarthy (New York, 1959/*R*1974)

J. BRADFORD ROBINSON

Chicago Jazz Archive. Archive founded at the University of Chicago in 1976; *see* LIBRARIES AND ARCHIVES, §2.

Chicago Rhythm Kings. Name under which the recordings of several groups were issued. The most important of these was an octet that included Muggsy Spanier, Frank Teschemacher, Eddie Condon, Mezz Mezzrow, Joe Sullivan, and Gene Krupa. The group's recording *There'll be Some Changes Made/I Found a New Baby* (1928, Bruns. 4001) is regarded as a fine example of Chicago jazz; during the same week that it recorded these titles the group recorded others as the Jungle Kings. The name Chicago Rhythm Kings was also used in 1936 by a group that recorded several tracks (including *Shanghai Honeymoon*, Bb 6371), and of which Roy Palmer was a member. In addition, the name was used for an insignificant recording session by a dance band in 1936, by Art Hodes's group in 1940, and as a pseudonym for several other groups (including Billy Banks's Rhythmakers, 1932). (R. Hadlock: *Jazz Masters of the Twenties* (New York, 1965/*R*1985), 127)

PAIGE VAN VORST

Childers, Buddy [Marion] (*b* St. Louis, 12 Feb 1926). Trumpeter. He was largely self-taught. He played in a school band in Belleville, Illinois, and with several local bands. In December 1942 he became lead trumpeter for Stan Kenton, with whom he played at intervals until 1954. He also worked with Benny Carter (1944), Les Brown (1947), Woody Herman (1949), Tommy Dorsey (1951–2), Georgie Auld (1954), and Charlie Barnet (1954). After moving to Los Angeles he recorded with Oliver Nelson, Quincy Jones, and others, and performed in Las Vegas and throughout California. In 1981 he recorded with the Toshiko Akiyoshi–Lew Tabackin Big Band.
For illustrations *see* KENTON, STAN, and MULLIGAN, GERRY.

SELECTED RECORDINGS

As leader: *Buddy Childers Quintet* (1955, Liberty 6009)
As sideman: S. Kenton: *Portraits on Standards* (1953, Cap. H462), incl. April in Paris; *Music of Bill Holman* (1953–4, Cap. H526), incl. Solo for Buddy (1954); O. Nelson: *Live from Los Angeles* (1967, Imp. 9153); Pat Williams: *Threshold* (1973, Cap. ST11242); T. Akiyoshi and L. Tabackin: *Tanuki's Night Out* (1981, JAM 006)

BIBLIOGRAPHY

FeatherE
C. Easton: *Straight Ahead: the Story of Stan Kenton* (New York, 1973)
W. F. Lee: *Stan Kenton: Artistry in Rhythm* (Los Angeles, 1980)
L. Tomkins: "Buddy Childers," *CI*, xx (1981–2), no.6, p.20; no.7, p.16; no.8, p.23

WILLIAM F. LEE III

Chilton, John (James) (*b* London, 16 July 1932). English trumpeter, flugelhorn player, composer, and writer. After leading his own band (1954–7) he performed with and wrote arrangements for Bruce Turner's Jump Band (1958–63), Alex Welsh (1963), and the trumpeter Mike Daniels's Big Band (1963–5). In 1966 he formed the Swing Kings, with which he played until 1968. He led the Feetwarmers with Wally Fawkes from 1969 to 1973 and became sole leader in 1974. As George Melly's backup group it has toured Europe, Australia, the USA, and the Far East; its many recordings with Melly include *Makin' Whoopee* (1982, Pye PRTN147). Chilton has recorded a number of songs for and with Melly, and is the author of several definitive books on jazz.

WRITINGS

(selective list)

with M. Jones and L. Feather: *Salute to Satchmo* (London, 1970)
Who's Who of Jazz: Storyville to Swing Street (London, 1970, rev. and enlarged 4/1985)
with M. Jones: *Louis: the Louis Armstrong Story, 1900–1971* (London, 1971)
Billie's Blues: a Survey of Billie Holiday's Career, 1933–1959 (London, 1975)
McKinney's Music: a Bio-discography of McKinney's Cotton Pickers (London, 1978)
Jazz (Sevenoaks, England, 1979)
A Jazz Nursery: the Story of the Jenkins' Orphanage Bands of Charleston, South Carolina (London, 1980)
Stomp Off, Let's Go! The Story of Bob Crosby's Bob Cats & Big Band (London, 1983)
Sidney Bechet: the Wizard of Jazz (London and New York, 1987)

BIBLIOGRAPHY
P. Vacher: "The Compleat Jazzer," *MM* (7 July 1973), 48
J. Chilton: "A Bite at the Big Apple," *JJ*, xxvii/10 (1974), 4
E. Myers: Interview, *Jazz: the Australasian Journal of Contemporary Music*, iii/3 (1983), 18
D. Fairweather: "Chilton, John," in I. Carr, D. Fairweather, and B. Priestley: *Jazz: the Essential Companion* (London, 1987)

DIGBY FAIRWEATHER

Chinese cymbal. A large cymbal with upturned edges and a raised cup of distinctive profile; *see* DRUM SET, §I, 5.

Chisholm, George [Chis] (*b* Glasgow, 29 March 1915). Scottish trombonist. He took up trombone as a teenager after hearing Jack Teagarden. In 1936 he went to London with Teddy Joyce and played in clubs, notably the Nest Club, where the following year he took part in a jam session with Fats Waller, Coleman Hawkins, and Benny Carter. Carter took him to Holland with a band that recorded eight titles for Decca (1937), and he played and recorded with Bert Ambrose's orchestra in 1937–9. Chisholm was much in demand for session work: among his recordings was one with Waller for HMV in 1938. After joining the RAF he played in the all-star dance orchestra best known as the Squadronaires (1939–50). He was a member of the BBC Radio Show Band (1950–55) and played in Wally Stott's orchestra in the "Goon Show" radio series, then performed with Jack Parnell and in musical shows until 1965. He continued to play jazz into the 1980s, both as a soloist – notably with Keith Smith's Hefty Jazz – and with his own band, the Gentlemen of Jazz, in pubs, clubs, and festivals. He was awarded the OBE in 1984.

Chisholm has an individual style which was fully formed early in his career: stock phrases are interspersed with smooth, melodic improvisation. He is noted for his musicianship and for touches of humor in his playing.

Oral history material in *GBLnsa*.

SELECTED RECORDINGS

As leader: *George Chisholm and his Band* (1956, Decca 4147); *Stars Play Jazz* (1962, Embassy 6047); *In a Mellow Mood* (1973, Peerless Velvet 1002); *Trombone Showcase* (1976, Line 2030)

As sideman: B. Carter: Blues in my Heart/Somebody Loves me (1937, Decca F42128); F. Waller: Don't try your jive on me/Ain't Misbehavin' (1938, HMV 5415); Squadronaires: *There's Something in the Air* (1941–50, Eclipse 2112); K. Baker: *Kenny Baker's Dozen* (1955, Nixa 19003); *Kenny Baker Presents the Half Dozen* (1957, Nixa 10); T. Crombie: *Sweet, Wide, and Blue* (1960, Decca 4114); W. B. Davison: *Wild Bill Davison with the Freddie Randall Band* (1965, World Sound 552); S. Brown: *Hair at its Hairiest* (1968, Fon. 921)

BIBLIOGRAPHY
D. Ayres: "In Focus: George Chisholm," *Crescendo*, i/1 (1962), 6
L. Tomkins: "The George Chisholm Story," *CI*, xv (1976–7), no.4, p.6; no.5, p.14; no.6, p.14; no.7, p.23; no.8, p.23
M. N. Clutten: *A George Chisholm Discography* (Leicester, England, 1977; discographical suppl. i, 1980, discographical suppl. ii by S. R. Gallichan, 1984)
N. Skrimshire: "George Chisholm," *JJI*, xxxiii/12 (1980), 7

REG COOPER

Chittison, Herman "Ivory" (*b* Flemingsburg, KY, 15 Oct 1908; *d* Cleveland, 8 March 1967). Pianist. He studied at Waldron Boys School in Nashville and later at Kentucky State College (1927). He performed in the Chocolate Beau Brummels, led by Zack Whyte (1928–31), and recorded with Clarence Williams (1930, 1933). In New York in 1934 he joined Willie Lewis, with whom he traveled to Europe. Shortly after the band began playing at Chez Florence in Paris, Chittison signed a contract with Brunswick to make recordings as a soloist. Later the same year he made a concert tour with Louis Armstrong. He worked intermittently again with Lewis between 1935 and 1938, then he and some other members of Lewis's band, including Bill Coleman, left to form a group called the Harlem Rhythm Makers. It performed in Alexandria and Cairo, Egypt, from November 1938 until 1940, when the musicians returned to the USA. Chittison accompanied the actor and comedian Stepin Fetchit (1940) and Mildred Bailey in New York (1941) and performed on CBS radio as Ernie the Blue Note Pianist (1942–51). In the 1950s and early 1960s he was resident at several well-known clubs in New York and Boston, after which he worked in Akron, Columbus, and Cleveland until his death.

SELECTED RECORDINGS

As unaccompanied soloist: Honeysuckle Rose/Bugle Call Rag (1934, Bruns. 500438)

As leader: As Time Goes By/My Old Flame (1944, Audiophile 39); *Keyboard Capers* (1950, Col. CL6134), incl. Memories of you, Can't we be friends?

As sideman: Z. Whyte: Mandy/Hum All your Troubles Away (1929, Gen. 6781); W. Lewis: All of me (1936, PAct 817); Christopher Columbus (1936, PAct 898); G. Wettling: Home/Too Marvelous for Words (1944, Key. 1311)

BIBLIOGRAPHY
ChiltonW
G. W. Kay: "Herman Chittison: Sinbad of the Piano," *JJ*, xviii/8 (1965), 14
"Herman Chittison, 1913–1967," *Sv*, no.10 (1967), 24
M. Jones: "Chittison: Jazz Pianist in Alexandria," *MM* (25 March 1967), 12
A. McCarthy: *Big Band Jazz* (New York and London, 1974)
J. L. Collier: *Louis Armstrong: an American Genius* (New York, 1983, London, 1984, as *Louis Armstrong: a Biography*), 266

JAMES M. DORAN

Chizhik, Leonid (Arkadyevich) (*b* Kishinev, Moldavian SSR, 1 Jan 1947). Russian pianist and composer. He played in a trio led by German Luk'yanov (1965–7), in the orchestra of Moskontsert (1966–8), and in an orchestra led by Leonid Utyosov (1969–71), and studied piano at the Gorky M. I. Glinka State Conservatory (graduated 1970). Later he worked principally as a soloist and from 1973 to 1980 as the leader of a trio, performing in the USSR and Europe and at the Jazzyatra festival in India in 1986. Chizhik was the first pianist in the Soviet Union to give recitals of improvised music. His work can be heard to advantage on the album *Reministsentsii* (1980, Mel. C60161558); among his compositions are piano pieces, music for radio and television, and a ballet, *Nochnoy gorod* (City at night; 1979).

BIBLIOGRAPHY
S. F. Starr: *Red and Hot: the Fate of Jazz in the Soviet Union, 1917–1980* (New York, and Oxford, England, 1983), 310
B. Doerschuk: "Leonid Chizhik: Stride Piano Spoken Here," *Keyboard*, xiii/8 (1987), 21

WALTER OJAKÄÄR

Chocolate Dandies. Name used by various recording groups. It was taken from the title of the successful show in 1924 by Noble Sissle and Eubie Blake. The first ensembles to use it were directed by Don Redman and recorded for Okeh in 1928–9. Redman also supervised recordings made by McKinney's Cotton Pickers which were issued under the name Chocolate Dandies. Thereafter the appellation was used by a number of groups led by Benny Carter. Among the musicians in these ensembles in the early 1930s were Coleman Hawkins, Max Kaminsky, Floyd O'Brien, and members of his own and Fletcher Henderson's bands (1930, 1933, 1934); later sessions included Hawkins (for Commodore, 1940) and Buck Clayton (for the French label Swing, 1946). The collaborations between Carter and Hawkins produced some important recordings that serve as landmarks in the history of the swing style, notably *Bugle Call Rag/Dee Blues* (1930, Col. 2543D), and *I surrender, dear/I can't believe that you're in love with me* (1940, Com. 1506).

FRANK DRIGGS

Choice. Record company and label. The company was founded by Gerry Macdonald in Sea Cliff, New York, in 1972. It issued solo, duo, and small-group recordings by such swing and bop musicians as Eddie Daniels and Bucky Pizzarelli (1973), Roland Hanna (1973, 1977), JoAnne Brackeen (1975, 1977), Jimmie Rowles (1976), Lee Konitz (1977), and Adam Makowicz (1980). Later items from the catalogue were leased to Inner City; Choice itself, however, has become inactive.

Choke cymbal. Name applied to a thin cymbal of small diameter used to create staccato patterns (*see* DRUM SET, §I, 5); it derives from the choked cymbal crash, which is made by dampening a cymbal with the hand immediately after it is struck.

Chops. In general colloquial usage the mouth, jaw, or cheeks, thus in jazz argot originally the embouchure of a wind player (the lips and facial muscles, which control the flow of air into the instrument); by extension that part of any musician's body which is of prime importance in the playing of his instrument, and, more broadly still, a musician's technique. (*GoldJL*)

ROBERT WITMER

Choquart, Loys (*b* Geneva, 11 Oct 1920). Swiss clarinetist, saxophonist, and bandleader. He organized his own Jam Band at the age of 17 and in 1939 he made the first of more than 2000 half-hour broadcasts on Geneva radio. He made his first recording, with the New Rhythm Kings, in 1942, playing alto saxophone on *Arrêt facultatif* (Parl. B35544). In 1943 he formed the Dixie Dandies, which included Henri Chaix and, occasionally, Wallace Bishop. By 1945 he was considered the best Swiss saxophone and clarinet soloist; his clarinet playing may be heard on *Mississippi Moan* (1951, Col. DZ1008). After 1953 he performed mainly in the swing style, making a number of recordings with vibraphone and rhythm section for Philips, but he also worked with a dixieland ensemble called Creole Jazz; its recordings of 1952 (among them *Dippermouth Blues*, Col. ESDF1055 [EP]) were awarded the Prix Jazz Hot in 1955. Choquart ran his own club, La Tour, in Geneva, where he played with many visiting American soloists; he also occasionally took part in concert and recording tours in Switzerland, France, Denmark, and Germany. (J.-R. Hippenmeyer: *Le jazz en Suisse, 1930–1970*, Yverdon, Switzerland, 1971)

RAINER E. LOTZ

Chord progression. A succession of two or more chords that have a harmonic coherence, especially a pattern used repeatedly in the same form (such as cadential formulas or the 12-bar sequence known as the BLUES PROGRESSION). The series of harmonies underlying an existing theme (often a popular song) used as the basis of a jazz performance is called the set of "changes" or "chord changes." *See* HARMONY (i), §1(v).

Chord symbol. A sign used on a score or part to specify harmony. For a full explanation of the chord-symbol system and its use *see* NOTATION, §5(iii).

Chorus. (1) In general usage the refrain of a song or hymn, that section which is repeated, always with the same tune and text, after each verse; for the use of the harmonic and metric structures of song refrains as the basis of jazz pieces *see* FORMS, esp. §1(i)(a).

(2) In jazz any statement, or, more particularly, any restatement with variations, of a theme. The term is commonly applied to those clearcut forms that consist of a theme, followed by a series of variations on the theme, and then a repetition of the theme itself; it is not generally used in discussing those styles of jazz in which free improvisation takes the place of the series of variations on the theme. *See* FORMS; *see also* CHASE.

Chorus effect. An electronic treatment that transforms the sound of a single instrument or voice so that it approximates to the sound of many instruments or voices playing in unison.

Christensen, Bernhard (*b* Copenhagen, 9 March 1906). Danish composer and arranger. He was trained as an organist and spent his working life as a church musician while also playing an important role in Danish jazz from about 1930. Besides classical music, he wrote several jazz oratorios (including *De 24 timer* (The 24 hours), 1932) and instrumental pieces for Erik Tuxen's big band (including *Københavner-rhapsodie*, 1933, Polyphon XS50201); he made recordings as a leader (1932, 1935) and was the music director of two jazz vocal groups, the Fem Syncoper (1932–3) and the Kordt Sisters (1940–44). Christensen was also among the first to teach jazz in Denmark.

ERIK WIEDEMANN

Christensen, Jon (*b* Oslo, 20 March 1943). Norwegian drummer. He taught himself to play drums. From 1962 he worked with Bud Powell and other American musicians during their visits to Norway, and in 1964 he appeared with Karin Krog at the Antibes–Juan-les-Pins Festival. The following year he joined the big band and sextet of George Russell, with whom he recorded from 1966; he also played with Monica Zetterlund and Jan Garbarek, belonged to Steve Kuhn's trio, and performed at festivals in Scandinavia and Europe with Dexter Gordon, Sonny Stitt, Phil Woods, Gary Burton, Sonny Rollins, and Terje Rypdal. He toured Australia with the Novi Singers, performed with Zbigniew Namysłowski in Poland and at the festival in Molde, Norway (1967), and in 1971 worked for two months with Stan Getz in South Africa and at Antibes–Juan-les-Pins. In October 1973 Christensen joined a new quartet led by Garbarek, with which he appeared at the International Jazz Jamboree Festival in Warsaw; the same year he recorded with the quartet and joined a trio led by Rypdal, and later he played in Eberhard Weber's group Colours. In the 1980s he toured with John Surman, Miroslav Vitous, and John Taylor, and with Arild Andersen led a quintet, Masqualero, that included the pianist Jon Balke, the tenor saxophonist Tore Brunborg, and the trumpeter Nils Petter Molvaer as sidemen; with the group he toured England and the Continent, made recordings (1983, 1985), and performed at the Village Vanguard in New York (1986). Christensen is a versatile drummer who is equally adept at playing bop, free jazz, and jazz-rock; he received the Buddy Award from the Norwegian Jazz Federation in 1967.

SELECTED RECORDINGS

(recorded for ECM unless otherwise indicated)

As leader with A. Andersen: *Masqualero* (1983, Odin 08); *Bande à part* (1985, 1319)

As sideman: K. Krog: *Jazz Moments* (1966, Sonet 1404); S. Kuhn: *Watch What Happens* (1969, MPS 15193); J. Garbarek: *Afric Pepperbird* (1970, 1007); *Sart* (1971, 1015); B. Stenson: *Underwear* (1971, 1012); T. Rypdal: *Terje Rypdal* (1971, 1016)

BIBLIOGRAPHY

Feather–Gitler '70s

R. Hultin: "Jon Christensen," *JF* [intl edn], no.47 (1977), 43 [incl. discography]

S. Lake: "Song of Norway," *MM*, lii (12 Feb 1977), 48

C. Stormer: "Jon Christensen: European Jazz Master," *MD*, ix/9 (1985), 22

RANDI HULTIN

Christian. Family of musicians.

(1) Charles (Joseph) Christian (*b* New Orleans, 25 July 1885; *d* New Orleans, 11 June 1964). Trombonist. He gained early experience with his brothers in the bands of Papa Jack Laine and Alfred "Baby" Laine, and marched in Fischer's Brass Band (*c*1915). He never left New Orleans or made a recording, nor was he ever a full-time musician, but he worked regularly in the first group led by his brother (3) Frank Christian, then as a member of the Triangle Band (1917–25), and finally with the Domino Orchestra (until the early 1930s).

Oral history material in *LNT*.

(2) Emile (Joseph) Christian [Boot-mouth] (*b* New Orleans, 20 April 1895; *d* New Orleans, 3 Dec 1973). Trombonist, brother of (1) Charles Christian. Besides his principal instrument he also played soprano trombone (also known as slide cornet), double bass, and clarinet. He performed with his brothers in the bands led by the Laines and in Fischer's Brass Band (*c*1915), then played with his brother (3) Frank Christian. Around 1916 he played with Merritt Brunies in New Orleans and Chicago. Having declined an invitation to join Johnny Stein in Chicago in 1916, he went there in 1917 to play with Bert Kelly; later that year he re-joined Brunies, who was now leading the Original New Orleans Jazz Band in Chicago. Christian worked with Brunies until 1918, when he replaced Eddie Edwards in the Original Dixieland Jazz Band, with which he performed in London in 1919–20. He returned to New York and played briefly with the Original Memphis Five in 1921, then went back to London, where he joined the Broadway Sextet. From 1924 he played double bass and trombone in Germany, France, and Switzerland. He performed with Leon Abbey in Bombay from late 1936 and then undertook engagements in France and Denmark on his way back to New York (1939). In 1941 he returned to New Orleans, and he continued to play there until the late 1960s. Christian was the most widely traveled of the early jazz musicians.

Oral history material in *LNT*.

SELECTED RECORDINGS

As leader: *Emile Christian and his New Orleans Jazz Band* (1958, Slnd 223)
As sideman: Original Dixieland Jazz Band: Satanic Blues/'Lasses Candy (1919, Col. 759)

BIBLIOGRAPHY

"Informal Interview with Emile Christian," *SL*, vi/9–10 (1955), 16
H. O. Brunn: *The Story of the Original Dixieland Jazz Band* (Baton Rouge, LA, 1960/*R* 1977)
Obituary, J. Mares, *SL*, xxvi (1974), win., 29

(3) Frank (Joseph) Christian (*b* New Orleans, 3 Sept 1897; *d* New Orleans, 27 Nov 1973). Brass player, violinist, and bandleader, brother of (1) Charles Christian. The brass instruments he played were cornet, trumpet, tuba, and mellophone, though he was chiefly known as a cornetist. Like his brothers he played in bands in New Orleans, at the same time leading his own group, Frank Christian's Ragtime Band, from 1910 to 1918; his brothers both played as members of his group. He moved to Chicago, but by the winter of that year he was in New York, where he made recordings as a member of Jimmy Durante's Original New Orleans Jazz Band (1918–19) and with the same group, now under the name Jimmy Durante's Jazz Band, in 1920; his playing is well represented by *Ole Miss/Ja-da* (1918, OK 1156). Until 1919 he was the best-known of the brothers. He later returned to Chicago and continued his activities as a bandleader, and also joined Norman Brownlee as a tuba player.

Oral history material in *LNT*.

MIKE HAZELDINE

Christian, Buddy [Narcisse J.] (*b* New Orleans, *c*1895; *d* ?New York, *c*1958). Banjoist. From around 1910 he performed in New Orleans with various leaders, playing piano with King Oliver (*c*1915–16), then moved to New York (*c*1919), where he played both banjo and piano. He worked with Lucille Hegamin (*c*1921, 1926) and June Clark (*c*1923), and during the mid-1920s participated in many of Clarence Williams's recording sessions, notably in the Blue Five with Louis Armstrong and Sidney Bechet. In 1924 Christian recorded as a member of the Red Onion Jazz Babies, and in 1926 he made a few recordings with his own band, including *Sugar House Stomp* (OK 8342). He formed a banjo duo with Fred Jennings in 1929, but thereafter worked in obscurity. (A. Barrell: "Buddy Christian's Banjo," *Fn*, x/2 (1978), 4 [incl. discography])

based on *ChiltonW*

Christian, Charles (Joseph). *See* CHRISTIAN family, (1) Charles.

Christian, Charlie [Charles] (*b* Texas, 29 July 1916; *d* New York, 2 March 1942). Guitarist. He grew up in a slum in Oklahoma City. His father was a blind guitarist and singer, his brothers Edward and Clarence were musicians, and Charlie himself built and played cigar-box "guitars" during his elementary school days. When he grew up, he became a much-admired local musician in Oklahoma, playing an amplified acoustic guitar as early as 1937. Word of his skill reached John Hammond, who arranged for Christian to travel to Los Angeles in August 1939 for an audition with Benny Goodman. Goodman, deeply impressed by Christian's playing, engaged him and soon featured him on weekly radio broadcasts and in recordings; before the year was over he was a nationally prominent jazz soloist. Unfortunately his success was as brief as it was immediate: he contracted tuberculosis in mid-1941 and died a few months later.

Christian was among the first jazz guitarists to amplify his instrument in order to match the volume of wind instruments, and he was clearly the most brilliant soloist of his time on electric guitar. He was emulated by many swing-style players, and his posthumous impact on younger bop guitarists was enormous. Had he lived longer he doubtless would have become the first great bop guitarist, for he was a regular participant in the Harlem jam sessions at which Dizzy Gillespie, Kenny Clarke, Charlie Parker, and a few others played as they gradually developed the new idiom. Some of Christian's favorite melodic figures (especially the chromaticisms indicated by brackets in ex.1) became common property among bop musicians. Although his rhythmic and harmonic conceptions lagged somewhat behind those of the new leaders, Christian nevertheless remains among the most creative soloists of the swing

Ex.1 Extracts from Christian's solos on B. Goodman: *Breakfast Feud* (1941, Col. 36039); transcr. T. Owens

period and a seminal figure in the evolution of the jazz guitar. Two collections of transcriptions of Christian's performances have been published, *Charlie Christian: Harlem Jazz* (New York, 1958) and *Charlie Christian: Jazz Improvisation* (Tokyo, 1975).

See also GUITAR, §3; for illustrations *see* BANDS, fig.4, and GOODMAN, BENNY.

SELECTED RECORDINGS

As leader: Swing to Bop, first issued on *Jazz Immortal* (1941, Eso. 1); Up on Teddy's Hill, first issued on *The Harlem Jazz Scene* (1941, Eso. 4)

As sideman with B. Goodman: Flying Home (1939, Col. 35254); Stardust (1939, Col. 26134); Seven Come Eleven (1939, Col. 35349); Gone with "What" Wind (1940, Col. 35404); Breakfast Feud (1941, Col. 36039); Good Enough to Keep (Air Mail Special) (1941, Col. 36099)

As sideman with E. Hall: Profoundly Blue (1941, BN 17)

BIBLIOGRAPHY

L. Feather: *The Book of Jazz: a Guide to the Entire Field* (New York, 1957, rev. 2/1965 as *The Book of Jazz from Then till Now: a Guide to the Entire Field*)

R. Ellison: "The Charlie Christian Story," *Saturday Review*, xli (17 May 1958), 42; repr. in *JJ*, xii/5 (1959), 7

S. Dance, ed.: *Jazz Era: the 'Forties* (London, 1961/*R*1985), 74

G. Hoefer: "The Hot Box," *DB*, xxviii/29 (1961), 39 [incl. discography]

B. Green: *The Reluctant Art: Five Studies in the Growth of Jazz* (London, 1962)

J. Hammond: "The Advent of Charlie Christian," *DB*, xxxiii/17 (1966), 22

R. Blesh: "Flying Home," *Combo, USA: Eight Lives in Jazz* (Philadelphia and London, 1971/*R*1979), 161

J. Evensmo: *The Guitars of Charlie Christian, Robert Normann, Oscar Aleman (in Europe)* (n.p. [Oslo], n.d. [?1976]) [discography]

J. Hammond and I. Townsend: *John Hammond on Record: an Autobiography* (New York, 1977)

J. Callis: *Charlie Christian, 1939–1941: a Discography* (London, 1978)

J. L. Collier: *The Making of Jazz: a Comprehensive History* (New York and London, 1978), 342

R. Denyer, I. Guillory, and A. M. Crawford: *The Guitar Handbook* (London and Sydney, 1982), 9

THOMAS OWENS

Christian, Emile (Joseph). *See* CHRISTIAN family, (2) Emile.

Christian, Frank (Joseph). *See* CHRISTIAN family, (3) Frank.

Christie, Ian (*b* Blackpool, England, 24 June 1927). English clarinetist, brother of Keith Christie. He was mainly self-taught, and worked with local groups before moving to London in the mid-1940s. With his brother he joined Humphrey Lyttelton's band in 1949; two years later they left to form the Christie Brothers Stompers, which disbanded in 1953. Thereafter Christie worked with Alex Welsh in 1954–5, then played for Mick Mulligan's band from 1955 until it disbanded in 1962. Later he became the film critic for the *Daily Express*, and ceased working as a musician. After 10 years he began playing again on a part-time basis, recording the album *That's the Blues, Old Man* (Stomp Off 1060) with Wally Fawkes in 1982.

CLARRIE HENLEY

Christie, (Ronald) Keith (*b* Blackpool, England, 6 Jan 1931; *d* London, 16 Dec 1980). English trombonist, brother of Ian Christie. He began playing at the age of 14, and performed in local bands before moving to London to study at the Guildhall School of Music and Drama. In 1949 he joined Humphrey Lyttelton's band, with which he made many recordings. After leaving Lyttelton he formed the Christie Brothers Stompers with his brother. Ken Colyer was among its members. After this disbanded in 1953 he played modern jazz with John Dankworth's orchestra until 1955. Thereafter he was a member of the small group led by the tenor saxophonist Tommy Whittle (1955–6), worked as a freelance (1956), and returned to big bands. He toured the USA and recorded with Ted Heath (1956–8), and worked with the orchestra led by the trombonists Bobby Lamb and Ray Premru (1960). During the 1960s and 1970s he worked prolifically as a freelance; although most of his recordings were in modern styles, he also played traditional jazz with Humphrey Lyttelton (1969) and the pianist Max Harris.

SELECTED RECORDINGS

As leader with I. Christie: You always hurt the one you love/I'm so glad (1952, Melodisc 1220)

As sideman: H. Lyttelton: Careless Love Blues (1950, Parl. R3274); Panama (1951, Parl. R3346); on [various leaders]: *Retrospect through 21 Years of BBC Jazz Club* (1968, Phi. SBL7869), J. Dankworth: The Slider, H. South: Storm Warning; H. Lyttelton: *21 Years On* (1969, Pol. 2661001), incl. Tara's Theme

BIBLIOGRAPHY

FeatherE; *Feather–Gitler '70s*

Obituary, D. Knowles, *JJI*, xxxiv/2 (1981), 3

D. Fairweather: "Christie, Keith," in I. Carr, D. Fairweather, and B. Priestley: *Jazz: the Essential Companion* (London, 1987)

CLARRIE HENLEY

Christie, Lyn(don Van) (*b* Sydney, 3 Aug 1928). Australian double bass player. In Australia he led his own groups and recorded with Errol Buddle (1963) and Judy Bailey (1964). After moving to New York in 1965 he worked as a hospital doctor for two years, then attended the Juilliard School (1968–9). He played in symphony orchestras and also with Mike Mainieri (recording with him in 1967), Jaki Byard, Paul Winter, Chet Baker, Ahmad Jamal, and many others. In the 1970s he toured and recorded with Toshiko Akiyoshi (1971), toured Germany with Attila Zoller (1971, 1974), and appeared at the Colorado Jazz Party (1971–3), recording with Clark Terry and Flip Phillips in 1971; from that period he led his own groups, in which his sidemen at different times have included Randy Brecker, John Scofield, Walter Bishop, Jr., and Vic Juris. He became a member of the faculty at the Westchester (New York) Conservatory in 1973. He recorded with Tal Farlow (1976, 1981) and the harpist Daphne Hellman (*Hellman's Angels*, 1985, Plug 8); his playing is heard to advantage on the track *Moonlight in Vermont* on Hellman's album. Besides double bass Christie also plays electric bass guitar, drums, and several wind instruments; his compositions include a number of film scores.

BIBLIOGRAPHY

Feather–Gitler '70s

A. Bisset: *Black Roots, White Flowers: a History of Jazz in Australia* (Sydney, 1979)

Christlieb, Pete(r) (*b* Los Angeles, 16 Feb 1945). Tenor saxophonist. He was brought up in a musical family, studied violin from 1952 to 1957, and took up tenor saxophone at the age of 13. He worked with Si Zentner (1963), Jerry Gray (1963–4), Chet Baker (1964), and Woody Herman (1966) before starting an association with Louie Bellson (1967) that continued into the late 1980s. From the late 1960s he was also active in film and television studios, playing with numerous jazz groups including his own; he was a regular member of Doc Severinsen's orchestra on the "Tonight Show" and played in the back-up groups of singers such as Della Reese and Sarah Vaughan. His work in jazz has encompassed engagements with many leaders, notably Count Basie, Quincy Jones, Billy May, Eddie Sauter, Benny Goodman, Mel Lewis, Shelly Manne, Gene Ammons, Frank Rosolino, and Carl Fontana. In the 1980s he began to lead his own quartet, and in 1981 launched a record company, Bosco Records, which issued albums by Bellson and Bob Florence as well as by Christlieb himself. Influenced by Sonny Rollins and Zoot Sims, Christlieb plays with power even at the fastest tempos, yet his delivery of ballads invariably shows fine feeling; he is also a convincing interpreter of the blues. His proficiency on a number of reed and woodwind instruments and his strength as a tenor saxophone soloist explain his popularity with the leaders of studio bands.

SELECTED RECORDINGS

As leader: *Jazz City: a Quartet with Pete Christlieb* (1971, RAHMP 2); with W. Marsh: *Apogee* (1978, WB 3236); *Going my Way* (1982, Bosco 2); *The Pete Christlieb Quartet Live* (1983, Bosco 5)

As sideman: S. Vaughan: *Sarah Vaughan–Michel Legrand* (1972, Mstr. 361); B. Florence: *Soaring* (1983, Bosco 3); L. Bellson: *Don't Stop Now!* (1984, Bosco 7)

BIBLIOGRAPHY

Feather–Gitler '70s
L. Underwood: "Profile: Pete Christlieb," *DB*, xliii/13 (1976), 40
A. J. Liska: Liner notes, *Going my Way* (Bosco 2, 1982)
Z. Stewart: Liner notes, *The Pete Christlieb Quartet Live* (Bosco 5, 1983)

MARK GARDNER

Christmann, Günter (*b* Śrem, Poland, April 1942). German trombonist, double bass player, and cellist of Polish birth. He was inspired at an early age by the music of Kid Ory and George Lewis (i) and learned to play banjo, then trombone; he later became interested in free jazz through the recordings of John Coltrane and Ornette Coleman. He played with the tenor saxophonist Rudiger Carl (1969–72) and in Peter Kowald's quintet (1972–4) and from 1972 to 1981 worked in a duo with the percussionist Detlef Schönenberg, which collaborated on occasion with such dancers as Pina Bausch and Elisabeth Clarke and such musicians as the synthesizer player Harald Bojé. At the same time he played in the Globe Unity Orchestra (from 1973), for which he also wrote compositions; he performed as an unaccompanied soloist (from 1975), and worked in a duo with the cellist Tristan Honsiger (1978–81). From 1979 he worked in a loosely organized free-jazz group known as Vario, with, among others, Maarten Altena, Paul Lovens, Maggie Nicols, and a number of actors and mimes, and in a trio called Phon with Altena and Lovens. Later he developed a mixed-media presentation, Déjà vu (from 1982), in which he played solo trombone and cello against a background of film, *musique concrète*, and lighting effects, and belonged to a duo with the double bass player Torsten Müller (from 1984). Christmann employs a variety of mutes, plungers, and mouthpieces in his trombone playing, as well as such found objects as balloons.

SELECTED RECORDINGS

As unaccompanied soloist: *Solomusiken für Posaune und Kontrabass* (1976, Ring 01032)

Duos: with D. Schönenberg: *We Play* (1973, FMP 0120); *Remarks* (1975, FMP 0260); with T. Müller: *Carte blanche* (1985, FMP 1110)

As leader of Vario: *Vario II* (1980, Moers 01084)

As sideman with Globe Unity Orchestra: *Compositions* (1979, Japo 60027)

BIBLIOGRAPHY

W. Panke: "Christmann–Schönenberg Duo," *Coda*, no.154 (1977), 10
——: "Ohne Kompromiss: Weg mit den Jugendsunden des Jazz," *Fonoforum* (Oct 1979), 56
B. Noglik: "Günter Christmann," *Jazzwerkstatt international* (Berlin, 1981), 279 [incl. interview, discography]

ROBERT J. IANNAPOLLO

Christy, June [Leslie, Sharon; Luster, Shirley] (*b* Springfield, IL, 20 Nov 1925). Singer. She began her career in 1938 with local bands and later sang with Boyd Raeburn and others in and around Chicago. She replaced Anita O'Day in Stan Kenton's orchestra, and with it recorded *Tampico* (1945), which achieved great success; she was named "best female vocalist with a big band" by *Down Beat* in 1946, 1947, 1948, and 1950. In the late 1940s she appeared with Kenton's orchestra in several short films. She made recordings as a leader, and toured with Kenton (in the 1950s), Ted Heath (1957–8), and her husband, the tenor saxophonist Bob Cooper; she appeared with Kenton at the Newport Jazz Festival in New York in 1972. Christy was influenced by O'Day, Sarah Vaughan, and Dinah Washington; her breathy, husky sound and narrow vibrato were ideally suited to the cool jazz of the 1950s. Although she was criticized for faulty intonation and for a weak sense of swing, she achieved considerable popular success.

SELECTED RECORDINGS

(recorded for Capitol unless otherwise indicated)

As leader: I'll Remember April (1949, 57774); *This is June Christy* (1949–56, T1006), incl. Until the real thing comes along; *That Misty Miss Christy* (1955–6, T725); *Fair and Warmer* (1957, T833); *Gone for the Day* (1957, T902); *Those Kenton Days* (1959, T1202); *Cool School* (1959, T1398); *Impromptu* (1977, Inter. 7710)

As sideman: S. Kenton: Tampico (1945, 202); He's funny that way (1946, B98); Willow weep for me (1946, 287); S. Rogers: *Shorty Rogers plus Kenton and Christy* (1950–51, Pausa 9016), incl. Do it again

BIBLIOGRAPHY

R. J. Gleason: "I'd Like to do 'Recitals,' Says June," *DB*, xvi/5 (1949), 3
"Too Easy to Get Lost in Record Biz Jungle: June," *DB*, xxi/8 (1954), 7
J. Tynan: "That Misty Miss Christy," *DB*, xxiii/22 (1956), 13
G. Coulter: Review of *Gone for the Day* (1957), *JR*, ii/1 (1959), 39
L. Feather: "June Christy & Bob Cooper: the Blindfold Test," *DB*, xxvii/18 (1960), 39
M. Jones: "Misty Miss now Plays it Cool," *MM*, xl (23 Jan 1965), 6
W. F. Lee: *Stan Kenton: Artistry in Rhythm* (Los Angeles, 1980) [incl. discography]
S. Woolley: "The Misty Miss Christy," *JJI*, xl/10 (1987), 18 [incl. discography]

ANDRÉ BARBERA

Cicero [Ciceu], **Eugen** (*b* Cluj-Napoca, Romania, 26 June 1940). Romanian pianist. He studied piano at the National Conservatory in Bucharest. At the age of 18 he formed a quintet, with which he toured Austria and Switzerland, and in 1969 he traveled to South Africa as the leader of a trio with Charly Antolini and Hans Rettenbacher. In the 1970s he worked as a studio musician for radio stations in Germany and toured successfully in Japan. Cicero's recordings as an unaccompanied soloist and a leader include his improvisations on themes by classical composers (1965–7, 1970, 1983); examples of these and of his own jazz compositions may be heard on *My Lyrics: Eugen Cicero in Tokyo* (1977, Denon YX7510ND). He has also recorded as the leader with Toots Thielemans of a quintet and as a sideman with Leo Wright (1972). (*Reclams J*)

Cinélu, Mino [Dominique] (*b* St. Cloud, France, 10 March 1957). French percussionist of Martinique descent. He was brought up in Paris, where he accompanied singers and worked with Jef Gilson. From 1972 to 1977 he played with his brothers Patrice and Jean-Jacques in the trio Chute Libre, recording around 1976. In the late 1970s he worked in New York, where he recorded with Dizzy Gillespie and Gato Barbieri, and from 1980 to 1983 he was the leader of the Mino Cinélu Ensemble, whose sidemen were Bob Cunningham, Arnie Lawrence, Andy Bey, and Ricky Ford. During the early 1980s he worked, toured, and recorded with Miles Davis, whom he left in 1984 to join Weather Report. Later he was a member of the trio Drummers' Music with drummers Fabiano and Victor Jones (1984–5) and led a trio with John Scofield and the electric bass guitarist Darryl Jones (1985). In 1987 Cinélu led the quintet Who's Who, which included Kevin Eubanks, Onaje Allen Gumbs and the electric bass guitarist Victor Bailey. He continues to perform intermittently with Davis, and is featured prominently on the album *Decoy* (1983–4, Col. FC38991).

BIBLIOGRAPHY

H. Mandel: "Profile: Bill Evans, Mike Stern, and Mino Cinélu," *DB*, xlviii/11 (1981), 52
F. M. Coudert and R. Latxaque: "L' ascension de Mino," *Jm*, no.337 (1985), 32

Circle (i). Record company and label. The company was established by Rudi Blesh and Harriet Janis in 1946: its stated aim was to document fully the cultural continuity from African music to jazz. Between January 1946 and the end of 1952 nearly 550 masters by 138 different ensembles were recorded in six American cities. The label is best remembered for important items by Albert Nicholas, Baby Dodds, Chippie Hill, George Lewis (i), and many others, and also for recordings taken from "This is Jazz," a series of radio broadcasts promoted by Blesh during 1947. Circle also issued much material by Jelly Roll Morton: most of his sessions for the Library of Congress of 1938 were issued for the first time on 12 albums of 78 r.p.m. discs. LPs put out in 1951–2 contained both new and previously released items. During the 1950s Circle's catalogues were made available to Riverside, but in the mid-1960s the entire enterprise was sold to George H. Buck's company Jazzology. Reissues of a few recordings from Circle's catalogue have been made on GHB; the Circle label name itself was revived for an extensive series of rereleases of material by big bands and small swing groups originally put out on the World and Lang–Worth labels.

BIBLIOGRAPHY

R. Blesh: *Shining Trumpets: a History of Jazz* (New York, 1946, rev. and enlarged 2/1958/*R*1975)
F. J. Mitchell: "Circle & Blue Star in Australia," *Matrix*, no.53 (1964), 14
R. Blesh: "The Circle Story," *The Baby Dodds Trio: Jazz à la Creole* (GHB 50, 1969) [liner notes]
G. H. Buck, Jr.: "Rudi Blesh, 1899–1985," *C. R. C. Newsletter*, xi/4 (1985), 2 [obituary]

Circle (ii). Free-jazz group formed in 1970 by CHICK COREA.

Circle (iii). Record company and label. The company was established in Cologne, Germany, in 1976 by Rudolf Kreis. Dedicated mainly to free jazz and bop, it has issued albums by such musicians as Sam Rivers, David Murray, James Newton, Chet Baker, Archie Shepp, and Herb Geller.

Circular breathing. A technique used principally by wind players to enable them to produce a continuous stream of notes without breaking to draw breath. The player inhales through the nose, filling the lungs with air; simultaneously, using the diaphragm, he replenishes the reservoir of air in the mouth cavity, while continuing to expel air from the mouth into the instrument. A similar technique has been used by some singers. Circular breathing is thought to be the cause of lung ailments in some performers.

The first important exponent of circular breathing was Harry Carney; late examples of his use of the technique may be heard in his baritone saxophone solo on *La plus belle africaine* from Duke Ellington's album *Soul Call* (1966, Verve 68701) and his bass clarinet solo on *Intimate Interlude* (1971) from the album *The Intimate Ellington* (1969–71, Pablo 2310787). Inspired by Carney, Roland Kirk took up the technique in 1963; later practitioners include Anthony Braxton and Freddie Hubbard.

Circular breathing is often no more than a gimmick, used to impress an audience rather than because the music itself demands it, there being rarely any reason why a line should continue uninterrupted. But it has been used in good taste and for legitimate musical purposes by some players, notably Kirk. In some instances, playing three saxophones simultaneously, he breathed in this way in order to hold a drone on one instrument while playing moving lines on the others; elsewhere circular breathing enabled him to play long, sweeping, continuous phrases. An impressive example occurs in his tenor saxophone solo on the duo *Memories of you* recorded with Jaki Byard on the album *The Jaki Byard Experience* (1968, Prst. 7615).

BARRY KERNFELD

Cirillo, Wally [Wallace Joseph] (*b* Huntington, NY, 4 Feb 1927; *d* Boca Raton, FL, 5 May 1977). Pianist and composer. He was active in Chicago and New York during the 1950s, and in 1954 took part in a concert by the Jazz Composers' Workshop with Teo Macero and Charles Mingus. He then moved to southern Florida in 1961 and worked with a variety of musicians, including Flip Phillips, Phil Napoleon, and Ira Sullivan. He also composed many orchestral and electronic works, and taught university courses in jazz piano and improvisation. Cirillo played in a few obscure sessions as a sideman during his period in New York, but made only one important recording – in 1955 as leader of a quartet with Macero and Mingus. This album, which has frequently been reissued under Mingus's name, contains *Trans-season*, which was said to be the first jazz piece based on a 12-tone row. Elsewhere on the album Cirillo decorates standard sequences with lines reminiscent of Lennie Tristano. The duet albums he made with Joe Diorio in the 1970s show a similar approach, but have qualities that suggest that Cirillo is poorly represented by his few recordings.

SELECTED RECORDINGS

Duos with J. Diorio: *Rapport* (1973, Spitball); *Soloduo* (1975–6, Spitball 3)
As leader: *Wally Cirillo Quartet* (1955, Savoy 15055), incl. Trans-season

BIBLIOGRAPHY

FeatherE; *Feather '60s*; *Feather–Gitler '70s*
B. Coss: "And Two More," *Metronome*, lxxii/2 (1956), 19
W. Van Eyle: "Wie was Wally Cirillo," *Jazz press*, no.42 (1977), 8; no.44 (1977), 6 [incl. discography]

BRIAN PRIESTLEY

Claes, Johnny (*b* London, 1916; *d* Brussels, 3 Feb 1956). English trumpeter. He played in England with his own band, which included the writer Max Jones on reed instruments, and a group led by the pianist Billy Mason. He then worked in the Netherlands with Valaida Snow (recording in 1937), Coleman Hawkins, and the Dutch musician Johnny Fresco; he also recorded at this time with the pianist Gerry Moore (1937). He spent a considerable time in Belgium, where he played and recorded (1939) in the band of Jack Kluger. On his return to England he formed his own group, the Claepigeons, which recorded in 1941–2. In the late 1940s Claes settled permanently in Belgium and abandoned playing professionally for a career as a racing driver.

ROBERT PERNET

Clambake Seven. Dixieland octet. It was formed by Tommy Dorsey in 1935 as a group within his big band, and consisted of trumpet, trombone, clarinet, tenor saxophone, piano, guitar, double bass, and drums. The Clambake Seven grew out of Dorsey's enthusiasm for a rougher and more spontaneous jazz than that favored by the big bands of the 1930s; its style was good-humored and its songs (such as *Posin'* and *The Big Apple*) were often used in comic stage routines. These numbers, like most of the band's earlier recordings, feature the singer Edythe Wright. The Clambake Seven regularly provided interludes during performances by Dorsey's big band, as well as playing late-night jam sessions in a loose dixieland style. The group, whose performances were driven along by the drummer (a succession of great players in this role included Dave Tough, Cliff Leeman, and Alvin Stoller), provided a platform for strong solo work by such musicians as Yank Lawson, Bud Freeman, Pee Wee

Erwin, and Johnny Mince. An extra trumpet was occasionally added to the ensemble, as in *Don't be a Baby, Baby*, which is a good example of its less boisterous style. The group disbanded around 1952.

SELECTED RECORDINGS

Posin' (1937, Vic. 25605); The Big Apple (1937, Vic. 25652); Alla en el Rancho Grande (1939, Vic. 26370); Don't be a Baby, Baby (1946, Vic. 201842)

BIBLIOGRAPHY

G. T. Simon: Liner notes, *This is Tommy Dorsey and his Clambake Seven* (RCA VMP6087, 1973)

M. Goode: Liner notes, *The Complete Tommy Dorsey*, vi (RCA AXM2-5578, 1981)

BRIAN PEERLESS

Clare, Alan (George) (*b* London, 31 May 1921). English pianist. He learned piano from the age of three and when he was 16 he began working in London nightclubs, including the Nest Club, Le Suivi (with Stephane Grappelli, 1941), and the Coconut Grove. After World War II he again performed with Grappelli and played a residency at the Studio Club in London, where he worked with Lennie Bush. From 1951 he made recordings as a soloist and sideman, in duos, and as the leader of small groups (including *Jazz Around the Clock*, 1958, Decca LK4260); his sidemen included Tony Crombie, Bush, Tony Coe, and Kenny Napper. For most of his career he has continued to perform mainly in exclusive London nightclubs, though he has also appeared regularly on television; in the 1970s he recorded regularly with Grappelli. Clare is a stylish pianist with a controlled and delicate touch and a considered approach to harmony. Although his preference for small, intimate venues has meant that his talent is sometimes overlooked, he has long been recognized as a musician of international importance. (L. Tomkins: "Alan Clare Tells his Story," *CI*, xiv/12 (1976), 6)

DIGBY FAIRWEATHER

Clare, Kenny [Kenneth] (*b* London, 8 June 1929; *d* London, 11 Jan 1985). English drummer. After playing in a student band during his military service he worked in Oscar Rabin's dance orchestra (1949–54), then replaced Phil Seamen in Jack Parnell's band. From 1955 to 1960 he performed and recorded with the Johnny Dankworth Orchestra, taking over from Allan Ganley. In the 1960s Clare worked as a session musician in big bands led by Ted Heath, Johnny Spence, and others, and between 1967 and 1972 he was second drummer in the Clarke–Boland Big Band. He also made recordings as the joint leader of a big band with the drummer Ronnie Stephenson (1966), and as a sideman with Milt Buckner (1968–70), Joe Pass (1970), Stephane Grappelli (1971), the Bobby Lamb–Ray Premru Big Band (1971), Peter Herbolzheimer (1974), Michel Legrand (1975), Francy Boland (1976), and Shorty Rogers (1984). Clare made several world tours with Dankworth and Cleo Laine. A fine example of his work may be heard on *Sing, sing, sing* from the album *Big Swing Favourites*, recorded by Colin Busby (1984, Horatio Nelson YU100).

BIBLIOGRAPHY

R. Cotterrell, ed.: *Jazz Now: the Jazz Centre Society Guide* (London, 1976)

R. Mattingly: "Conservative Accompanist Kenny Clare," *MD*, vii/3 (1983), 18

J. Tagford: "In Memoriam: Kenny Clare," *MD*, ix/4 (1985), 64

NEVIL SKRIMSHIRE

Clarinet. A woodwind instrument of essentially cylindrical bore, played with a single reed; it is made in a number of sizes, pitched in different keys. The soprano instrument pitched in B♭, with the "Boehm system" of keywork and fingering, is by far the most widely used. The clarinet is found throughout the history of jazz, but was most prominent between the turn of the century and the 1940s.

1. The clarinet family. 2. The E♭ sopranino clarinet. 3. Soprano clarinets. 4. Bass clarinets. 5. Other clarinets.

1. THE CLARINET FAMILY. Clarinets have probably been made in a wider range of sizes and pitches than any other instrument. All members of the modern clarinet family have been used in jazz, except for the piccolo or octave clarinet (though see §5(a) below). The E♭ sopranino instrument was used in brass bands and early jazz (see §2). The soprano instrument pitched in B♭ is widely used, those pitched in A and C less commonly (see §3); the basset-horn in F and the E♭ alto clarinet (see §5) are very seldom found. The bass clarinet in B♭ was little used in jazz before World War II, but several notable exponents of the instrument emerged from the 1960s onwards (see §4).

The clarinet is generally made in five separate parts of wood or plastic: mouthpiece, barrel, upper or left-hand joint, lower or right-hand joint (the two joints constituting the body), and bell. (A less common structure, the so-called monocoque construction, used for metal instruments, has only three parts.) The reed is secured to the mouthpiece by a metal band adjusted by two screws (the ligature; see fig.2, p.215); covered toneholes, opened by the operation of keys, are positioned along the body of the instrument. The basic structure of the clarinet has barely changed during the period of its use in jazz, but various systems of keywork have been available: early players favored the simple systems (the Muller or Albert, the Oehler, and the Clinton), which are still current in parts of Europe; most clarinetists, however, play instruments that use the Boehm system, in "plain" or "full" form (the latter offering four modifications to the basic design). Different systems of fingering (which correspond to the different placing and size of the toneholes), together with minor differences in the bore between one instrument and another and the various possible configurations of mouthpiece, ligature, and reed, allow the jazz player to choose an instrument on which he can produce a distinctive timbre and tone-color.

The lowest pitch of the standard Boehm-system B♭ soprano clarinet is written *e*, sounding *d*; the upper limit is usually regarded as falling between *g'''* (*f'''*) and *e''''* (*d''''*). The compass of the clarinet is divided into four registers: the chalumeau (*e* to about *f'*), the clarinet (comprising the (overblown) 12ths above this series, *b'* to *c'''*), the throat (falling between the chalumeau and the clarinet), and the extreme (from *c♯'''* upwards). The sopranino clarinet is normally pitched in E♭, a 4th above the B♭ soprano, the basset-horn in F, a 4th below, and the alto in E♭, a 5th below. The bass clarinet is normally pitched in B♭, an octave below the soprano, and the contrabass in B♭ (also known as the pedal clarinet), two octaves below the soprano, or in E♭ (also sometimes referred to as the contra alto clarinet), an octave below the alto.

2. THE E♭ SOPRANINO CLARINET. The earliest use of the sopranino instrument in jazz was in brass bands, where it frequently carried the melody or played an obbligato to it in the final strains of multithematic marches. Its unreliability of pitch limited its use, however, and it became associated with a handful of virtuoso players from New Orleans, such as John Casimir, Polo Barnes, and George Lewis (i). Lewis recorded on the instrument in brass bands led by Bunk Johnson (1942, 1944) and with the Eureka Brass Band (1951). The sopranino clarinet has been used with some success by imitators of Lewis, notably the Englishman Sammy Rimington. Outside the context of the

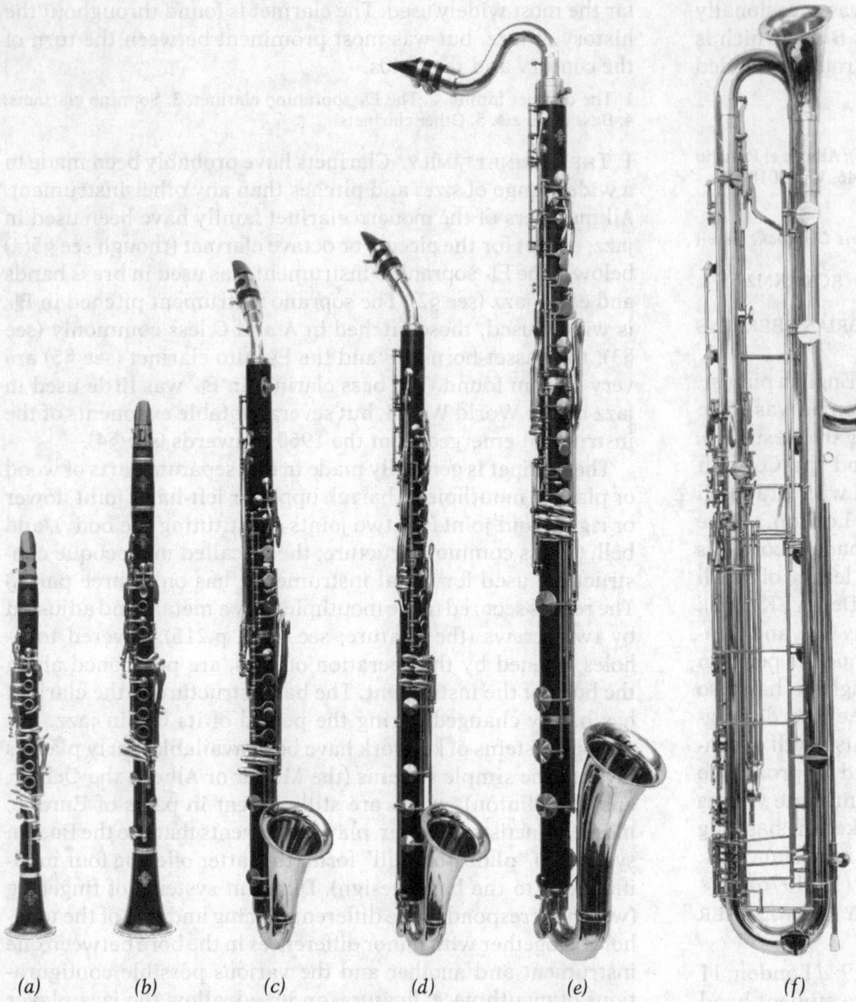

1. The modern clarinet family (Boehm system; all by G. Leblanc, Paris) (a) sopranino in E♭; (b) soprano in B♭; (c) alto in E♭; (d) basset-horn in F; (e) bass in B♭; (f) contrabass in B♭

brass band the sopranino's high, rather squeaky sound found little favor; one important exponent, however, was Odell Rand, in whose recordings with the Harlem Hamfats (1936–9) the unusual tone-color of the chalumeau register of the E♭ instrument may be heard.

3. SOPRANO CLARINETS. The principal soprano clarinet used in jazz, as in other forms of music, is that pitched in B♭. At the turn of the century the instruments pitched in A and C were more common than they are now, particularly in bands that played ragtime pieces, in which musicians were often required to double. Sidney Bechet began his career playing the C clarinet. The A instrument is now infrequently used and the C almost never, though the Englishman Tony Coe favors the latter for its unusual timbre.

The clarinet's role in early jazz bands was similar to its role in brass bands and in orchestrations of ragtime pieces – namely, to play florid obbligatos around the lead melodies. This required an understanding of chords and harmonic progression, and clarinetists evolved a method of improvisation based on arpeggios which later became the model for jazz saxophone playing. The clarinet remained the main woodwind instrument in jazz until the 1930s, when the saxophone began to be preferred. Its virtuoso role was apparent in what may broadly be regarded as two groups of players from New Orleans, the schooled creole players and the more expressive unschooled black players.

In the creole community the clarinet was taught privately by musicians such as the famous Tio family, who played in the French classical tradition long established in New Orleans. Creole clarinetists in early jazz bands were, with the pianists, usually the best readers of music and the members with the greatest degree of formal training; but while their musical education was in some ways an advantage it often meant that creole players, such as the Tios and Alphonse Picou, lacked skill as improvisers and fell back on the formulas of ragtime (which they knew from written scores) when called upon to improvise. In contrast to this tradition, an important influence on early jazz performance was vaudeville, which, with its dependence on jokes and funny sound effects and its emphasis on expressiveness, was the tradition from which Wilbur Sweatman, Ted Lewis, and Jimmy O'Bryant emerged.

Pupils of Lorenzo Tio, Jr., who combined virtuosity with improvisational ability included Sidney Bechet, Barney Bigard, and Albert Nicholas. Bigard was a very distinctive player, who achieved considerable technical facility and (particularly during his time with Ellington) specialized in long glissandos. Bechet's powerful virtuoso playing and unusually generous vibrato (exemplified by *Blue Horizon*, 1944, BN 43), provided an example for clarinetists who followed him, though his influence would have been greater had he not moved to Europe early in his career. Nicholas, who also lived in Paris and later in Switzerland, developed a facility throughout the clarinet's range, which he put to the service of a fertile musical imagi-

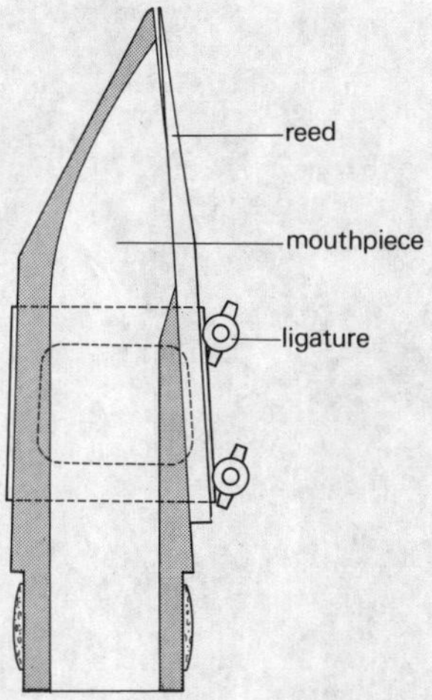

2. Clarinet mouthpiece with reed in position

nation. Bechet and Nicholas recorded duets with a rhythm section which display the similarities and differences between their styles; a good example is *Old Stack O'Lee Blues* (1946, BN 54). The playing of Bechet's pupil Jimmie Noone (see fig.3) had a far-reaching effect; his liquid sound, "legitimate" technique, and adoption of the eighth-note as the rhythmic unit established standards for the jazz clarinet throughout the 1930s. He influenced many white players, including Benny Goodman and Artie Shaw. Other white players who emulated the creole school and developed a well-rehearsed and technically proficient style included Larry Shields, Alcide "Yellow" Nuñez, and Leon Rappolo; the highest of technical standards was set by Jimmy Dorsey.

The non-creole black players developed a method of playing that derived more from black folk traditions and the blues than from classical antecedents. This school used a wide vibrato (a fast vibrato was particularly favored by the earliest of them) and incorporated distinctive glissandos and portamentos into their playing, which became the stock-in-trade of popular musicians and influenced many composers, including Gershwin (whose *Rhapsody in Blue*, 1924, opens with a long glissando). The principal players in this style were Johnny Dodds and George Lewis (i).

3. Jimmie Noone (clarinet) and Gideon Honore (piano) during a performance by Noone's trio at the Fox Head Tavern, Cedar Rapids, IA, 1942

From the mid-1920s clarinetists continued to search for an individual timbre. Lester Young (who was one of the players responsible for the move away from the clarinet to the saxophone) had a modest technique on clarinet but played with poetic sensitivity, which is exemplified by his recording with the Kansas City Six of *I want a little girl* (1938, Com. 509). Pee Wee Russell developed a unique, ironic vibrato and angular lines, which sounded equally at home with groups of the 1920s and of the 1960s. Benny Goodman's early playing was in the rough-hewn manner of Russell, Frank Teschemacher, and other players from Chicago; but around 1931 he adopted a more classical approach and developed the prodigious technique and spirited style for which he is known and which he employed in both big-band and small group settings. Edmond Hall created a biting, intense sound with vocal tone, which is often contrasted with Goodman's litheness.

At much the same time as clarinetists were developing an idiomatic solo style for their instrument, arrangers were using clarinets in groups in ensemble settings. Schuller presents examples and speculates on the origins of the trios of clarinets found in recordings from the mid-1920s, for example on Don Redman's arrangement of *Copenhagen* for Fletcher Henderson's orchestra (1924, Voc. 14926). Just as the clarinet as a solo instrument gave way to the saxophone, the clarinet section gave way to the saxophone section in big-band arrangements.

By the mid-1940s and the advent of bop, the saxophone was clearly the preferred instrument of the younger reed players, many of whom regarded mastering the clarinet simply as a stage in their development as saxophonists. The clarinet style in jazz had become increasingly classical and jazz musicians had begun to think the instrument relatively unexpressive, less capable than the saxophone of distinctive sounds in the hands of different players, thin in tone, lacking in continuity between the registers, and difficult to play at fast tempos. It was also associated with older styles from which musicians wanted to move on.

Despite its waning importance, the clarinet was adopted by a few younger players in the 1940s and 1950s. Some were overtly uninterested in bop and simply wished to continue the tradition of Benny Goodman; the most notable of these were Aaron Sachs, Sol Yaged, Peanuts Hucko, and Bob Wilber. The playing of Stan Hasselgård and Jimmy Hamilton developed from an initial approach modeled on that of Goodman into more modern directions. Among the more modern stylists to emerge were Buddy DeFranco, who was influenced by Charlie Parker's alto saxophone playing, Jimmy Giuffre, who at first made a specialty of the dark, warm sound of the chalumeau register, and Tony Scott, who created a highly individual style that combined elements of Parker's playing with the blues, ethnic music, and a consciousness of older forms of jazz. Other notable experimentalists included John LaPorta and Bill Smith. By contrast, in the 1980s Kenny Davern revived earlier styles of clarinet playing, though he continued to find new modes of expression within these contexts.

Since the 1950s most styles of jazz have been explored on the clarinet, but few innovations have taken place in the performance practice of the instrument. Perry Robinson, John Carter, and Anthony Braxton (the last named playing all the clarinets, including bass and contrabass) were the principal exponents of the clarinet in free jazz and set new standards of technical proficiency. The classical clarinetist Richard Stoltzman appeared as a jazz soloist frequently during the mid-1980s. It has continued to be the case that many saxophonists double on clarinet; among the most important have been Roland Kirk,

Bobby Jones, Rolf Kühn, and Eddie Daniels (from 1987 Daniels concentrated exclusively on clarinet). An ability to double is still demanded by many big-band arrangers. A few flutists have also played clarinet, including Sam Most and Paul Horn.

The clarinet is now used in many different styles and settings; amplification has meant that its lack of volume is no longer a problem and the classical connections of the instrument are not a disincentive to its use as they once were. In the 1980s John Carter introduced a new ensemble, the unaccompanied quartet Clarinet Summit, comprising three soprano instruments and one bass. The group's unique sound, together with its creative blend of swing, bop, and free jazz, are well represented on the album *Clarinet Summit in Concert at the Public Theatre* (1981, IndN 1062).

4. BASS CLARINETS. The most widely used instrument is the B♭ bass, though Anthony Braxton has often employed the contrabass in B♭. An interesting early use of the bass clarinet was by the assertive, Chicago-style player Omer Simeon on Jelly Roll Morton's *Someday Sweetheart* (1926, Vic. 20405). The instrument was also played in Duke Ellington's orchestra by Harry Carney, who produced a particularly rich tone, and Benny Goodman occasionally doubled on it, notably on recordings with Red Norvo in 1933. The bass clarinet was adopted by some bop players, among them Buddy DeFranco, who recorded on it in 1964. But it was John Coltrane's friend and colleague Eric Dolphy (see fig.4) who brought about the instrument's widespread use from the 1960s. His spectacular playing demonstrated a new flexibility and a wide range of tonal possibilities not previously exploited; while retaining the instrument's lush timbre in its lowest register, he took advantage of the ease with which the sound may be distorted in the middle and altissimo registers. His extraordinary playing is best represented by a series of unaccompanied solos on versions of *God Bless the Child* recorded in 1961 (on the albums *Here and There*, 1960–61, Prst. 7382; *Berlin Concerts*, 1961, Enja 3007, 3009; *Eric Dolphy in Europe*, 1961, Debut [Den.] 136; and *Stockholm Sessions*, 1961, Enja 3055). Dolphy inspired Coltrane and Pharoah Sanders to take up the instrument, and influenced many other players, including Anthony Braxton, Hamiet Bluiett, Willem Breuker, John Surman, and Gunter Hampel.

On the contrabass clarinet its main exponent, Braxton, produces sounds ranging from squawks and deep buzzing to pure, delicate, woody tones. An example of his unaccompanied playing may be heard in his solo on the track *4–16 CJF* from the album *The Complete Braxton, 1971* (1971, Fre. 40112–13).

5. OTHER CLARINETS. The piccolo or octave clarinet (usually pitched in A♭, a 7th above the soprano) is chiefly a military instrument and is not itself found in jazz, but the hot fountain pen resembles it in several respects. This is a miniature clarinet less than 30 cm long with keyless tone-holes; its peculiar tone is due in part to the use of a saxophone mouthpiece. Adrian Rollini played the instrument to create novelty effects in recordings led by him or Joe Venuti (1927, 1930) and used it during his two visits to England during the late 1920s, when he performed with Fred Elizalde. The Englishman Laurie Payne, influenced by hearing Rollini, is its only other notable exponent.

The alto clarinet in E♭, though virtually unknown as a solo instrument, has occasionally been used by jazz arrangers seeking its peculiar tone-color in ensembles. It is also used, along with soprano, bass, and contrabass clarinets, on Braxton's album *For Trio* (1977, Ari. 4181), where it is played by Joseph Jarman.

The basset-horn, normally pitched in F, has a compass that extends down to written *c* (sounding *F*). It is almost never used in jazz, though the Russian pianist and composer Vyacheslav Ganelin and his sideman Vladimir Chekasin have both played it on a number of their recordings made for the Leo label from 1978 onwards.

4. Eric Dolphy (bass clarinet) and Fred Katz (cello) during a performance by Chico Hamilton's quintet at the French Lick Jazz Festival, French Lick, IN, August 1959

For further illustrations *see* BAILEY, BUSTER; DODDS, JOHNNY; HALL; and MEZZROW, MEZZ.

BIBLIOGRAPHY

J.-E. Berendt: *Das Jazzbuch: Entwicklung und Bedeutung der Jazzmusik* (Frankfurt am Main, Germany, 1953, rev. 2/1959 as *Das neue Jazzbuch*, Eng. trans., New York, 1962; rev. and enlarged 5/1981 as *Das grosse Jazzbuch: von New Orleans bis Jazz Rock*, Eng. trans. as *The Jazz Book: from New Orleans to Fusion and Beyond*, Westport, CT, 1982), 181

L. Feather: *The Book of Jazz: a Guide to the Entire Field* (New York, 1957, 2/1965 as *The Book of Jazz from Then till Now: a Guide to the Entire Field*), 86

G. Schuller: *Early Jazz: its Roots and Musical Development* (New York, 1968), 260

J. Brymer: *Clarinet* (London, 1976)

N. Shackleton: "Clarinet," *GroveI*

R. Palmer: "Jazz Virtuosos Usher in a Second Golden Age of the Clarinet," *New York Times* (1 June 1986), §B, p.25

LEWIS PORTER

Clark, Bill [William E.] (*b* Jonesboro, AR, 31 July 1925; *d* Atlanta, 30 July 1986). Drummer. After working with Lester Young in 1950 he played with Mary Lou Williams, the popular singer Lena Horne, Hazel Scott, and Duke Ellington (February 1951). He recorded in Dizzy Gillespie's big band and small groups (1952) and with George Shearing (1953–5) and Toots Thielemans (1955). In 1956–7 he was a member of Rolf Kühn's group and he also recorded with Ronnell Bright. He again worked with Mary Lou Williams from 1957 to 1960. Nothing is known of his career after this date.

SELECTED RECORDINGS

As sideman: L. Young: The Little Words/Neenah (1950, Clef 8934); M. L. Williams: *Piano Panorama* (1951, Atl. 114); D. Gillespie: *At Home and Abroad* (1952, Atl. 138); G. Shearing: *The Shearing Spell* (1955, Cap. T648); R. Kühn: *Streamline* (1956, Van. 8510)

BIBLIOGRAPHY

FeatherE

RICK MATTINGLY

Clark, Buddy [Walter, Jr.] (*b* Kenosha, WI, 10 July 1929). Double bass player and arranger. He first learned piano and trombone, but changed to double bass in high school and later studied at the Chicago Musical College (1948–9). After working with Bud Freeman and Bill Russo he toured with Tex Beneke (1950–54) and Les Brown (1955–6), then settled in Los Angeles where, during the late 1950s, he played with Peggy Lee, Red Norvo, Dave Pell, and Jimmy Giuffre. In the 1960s he worked principally as a studio musician, though he also played with jazz groups, including that of Gerry Mulligan, on a freelance basis. Clark's playing is characterized by a round, singing tone and, in the higher register of the instrument, a light, airy quality. In 1972 he joined forces with Med Flory to transcribe and arrange Charlie Parker's solos for a saxophone section; Clark's arrangements are mostly of the "closed voicing" type, in which the lead alto and baritone saxophones double the melody in octaves and the other instruments move in parallel harmony. The two men then formed the group SUPERSAX and toured the USA, Canada, and Japan, but Clark left the group in 1975 and returned to his studio and freelance work.

SELECTED RECORDINGS

As leader of Supersax (with M. Flory): *Supersax Plays Bird* (1972, Cap. ST11177), incl. Hot House, Ko-ko, Night in Tunisia, Parker's Mood; *Supersax Plays Bird*, ii: *Salt Peanuts* (c1973, Cap. ST11271), incl. The Bird, Groovin' High, Loverman, Yardbird Suite; *Supersax Plays Bird with Strings* (1975, Cap. ST11371), incl. All the things you are, Kim, My Old Flame

As sideman: D. Pell: *Swingin' in the Old Corral* (1956, RCA LPM1394), incl. My Sombrero; G. Mulligan: *The Concert Jazz Band* (1960, Verve 68388)

BIBLIOGRAPHY

FeatherE; *Feather–Gitler '70s*

LAWRENCE KOCH

Clark, Charles (E.) (*b* Chicago, 11 March 1945; *d* Chicago, 15 April 1969). Double bass player. He studied double bass and jazz with Wilbur Ware and played professionally from 1963. He joined Muhal Richard Abrams's Experimental Band and was a founding member of the Association for the Advancement of Creative Musicians. From 1966 to 1968 he performed and recorded with Abrams, and played double bass, cello, koto, and percussion with Joseph Jarman in concert and on recordings, including *As if it were the Seasons* (1968, Del. 417). Clark's death was in part responsible for Jarman's decision to join the Art Ensemble of Chicago.

BIBLIOGRAPHY

Feather–Gitler '70s

V. Wilmer: *As Serious as your Life: the Story of the New Jazz* (London, 1977, rev. 1980)

Clark, Gus [De Clercq, Gustave] (*b* Antwerp, Belgium, 21 Oct 1913; *d* Antwerp, 10 April 1979). Belgian pianist. In 1929 he led his own band at a dance festival in Antwerp and then played in dance halls throughout the city. He was a member of bands led by the reed player Harry Pohl, the alto saxophonist Maurice Pinto, and Jack Hoedemaeker. After touring in the Netherlands and Luxembourg he returned to Antwerp and formed a band with which Coleman Hawkins performed. He appeared with Joe Smith at le Boeuf sur le Toit in Brussels and played in a dixieland band there. He also worked for a time with Jean Robert, before setting up a black group in Antwerp, the members of which included Buck Ram, Toni Morrow, Martin Sturman, and Lauderic Caton. Clark later formed a big band, whose recordings of the 1940s (including *Appel de la jungle/Parade nègre*, 1944, Hot 20) are among the best jazz sides issued in Belgium at this time. In the 1940s Clark also recorded with Jean Omer (1943) and played and recorded (1946) with Gus Deloof. He led another session of his own in 1951.

ROBERT PERNET

Clark, June [Algeria Junius] (*b* Long Branch, NJ, 24 March 1900; *d* New York, 23 Feb 1963). Cornetist. With James P. Johnson he toured in the revue *Black Sensations* and played in Toledo, Ohio, where the two met Jimmy Harrison and invited him to join them; the group accompanied the blues singer Alice Leslie Carter on recordings made in New York in 1921. Clark toured with Willie "the Lion" Smith and played again with Harrison before settling in New York, where he led a band that included the young Benny Carter (1924). In 1925 he made recordings with Smith as a member of the Gulf Coast Seven (including *Santa Claus Blues*, Col. 14107D) and with Harrison and Clarence Williams as an accompanist to Sara Martin. He worked as a leader and as a sideman with many bands until 1937, when ill health compelled him to retire.

BIBLIOGRAPHY

ChiltonW; *FeatherE*

H. Rosenberg and E. Williams: "June Clark: the Story of a Forgotten Giant," *Jazz Information*, ii/16 (1941), 11

B. McRae: "June Clark," *JJ*, xvi/5 (1963), 17

Clark, Sonny [Conrad Yeatis] (*b* Herminie, nr Elizabeth, PA, 21 July 1931; *d* New York, 13 Jan 1963). Pianist. He took up the piano at an early age, and apparently became interested in jazz around 1945 through the broadcasts of Count Basie's and Duke Ellington's orchestras and the recordings of Art Tatum and Fats Waller. He moved to California after 1951 and worked briefly in San Francisco with Vido Musso and Oscar Pettiford before settling in Los Angeles. After making his first recording (with Teddy Charles's West Coasters, 1953) he worked from 1953 to 1956 in Buddy DeFranco's quartet, with which he toured Europe in 1954; at the same time he performed and recorded in the quartets of Sonny Criss and Frank Rosolino, as a member of Howard Rumsey's Lighthouse All Stars, and with other groups in and around Los Angeles. In April 1957 he performed as a member of Dinah Washington's trio in New York, where during the following years (to 1962) he made many recordings as a leader, and as a sideman with Sonny Rollins, Hank Mobley, John Jenkins, Curtis Fuller, and Clifford Jordan (all 1957) and Bennie Green (1958, 1960). Although Clark's playing is often likened to that of Bud Powell, it is more crisp, relaxed, and flowing.

SELECTED RECORDINGS

As leader: *Dial S for Sonny* (1957, BN 1570); *Sonny Clark Trio* (1957, BN 1579); *Cool Struttin'* (1958, BN 1588); *Leapin' and Lopin'* (1961, BN 84091)

As sideman: T. Charles: *Teddy Charles with Wardell Gray* (1953, Prst. 1307); B. DeFranco: *Sweet and Lovely* (1955, Verve 8224); F. Rosolino: *I Play Trombone* (1956, Beth. 26); H. Rumsey: *Music for Lighthouse Keeping* (1956, Cont. 3528); S. Rollins: *The Sound of Sonny* (1957, Riv. 241); C. Fuller: *Bone and Bari* (1957, BN 1572); B. Green: *Bennie Green Quintet Swings the Blues* (1960, Enrica 2002)

BIBLIOGRAPHY

M. James: "Sonny Clark," *JM*, ix/3 (1963), 5

Obituary, *Jazz*, ii/2 (1963), 15

M. Gardner: "Sonny Clark," *JM*, xii/12 (1967), 21; xiii (1967), no.1, p.28; no.2, p.28 [discography]

——: Liner notes, *The Sonny Clark Memorial Album* (Xan. 121, 1975)
J. Simmen: "Sonny Clark," *Coda*, no.162 (1978), 16
I. Skovgaard and E. Traberg: *Some Clark Bars: Sonny Clark: a Discography* (Copenhagen and Madrid, 1984) [incl. biography]

GREGORY E. SMITH

Clarke, George (F.) (*b* Memphis, 28 Aug 1911). Tenor saxophonist. He studied at Manassas High School in Memphis with Jimmie Lunceford, in whose first band he played until 1933. He settled in Buffalo, where in 1935 he played with Lil Armstrong and Stuff Smith; he performed and recorded with Smith in New York (*c*1939–40). From 1942 to 1954 he led his own group at the Anchor Bar in Buffalo. He returned to New York, where he played and recorded with Cootie Williams, then toured Europe with Williams in 1959. He also made recordings with Jonah Jones (1954) and Wild Bill Davis (1959–60, including *Flyin' High*, 1959, Ev.1052), and toured Africa with Cozy Cole in 1962. (*ChiltonW*; *FeatherE*)

Clarke, Kenny [Kenneth Spearman; Klook; Klook-mop; Salaam, Liaquat Ali] (*b* Pittsburgh, 9 Jan 1914; *d* Montreuil-sous-Bois, nr Paris, 26 Jan 1985). Drummer and bandleader. A member of a musical family, he studied several instruments in high school and began performing as a professional drummer with Leroy Bradley's band in Pittsburgh when he was still a teenager. He later joined Roy Eldridge, and then played in the Midwest and the East in several major jazz groups, including, in St. Louis, the Jeter–Pillars Orchestra, and, in New York, the bands of the tenor saxophonist Lonnie Simmons, Edgar Hayes, Claude Hopkins, and Teddy Hill. While a member of Hill's group (1939–40) he and his fellow sideman Dizzy Gillespie began to experiment with new rhythmic conceptions. In the early 1940s he was in the house band at Minton's Playhouse, where his association with Gillespie, Thelonious Monk, Charlie Christian, Bud Powell, and others in an extraordinary series of jam sessions led to the development of the many innovative improvisational techniques that characterized the bop style. Clarke's nicknames Klook and Klook-mop were given to him at this time because he observed the then novel practice of interjecting off-beat accents ("klook" and "klook-mop") on the snare and bass drum against the steady pulse.

After military service in Europe (1943–6) Clarke returned to the USA and recorded with Gillespie, Tadd Dameron, Fats Navarro, and many others. In 1951 he became a founding member of the Milt Jackson Quartet, the forerunner of the MODERN JAZZ QUARTET; he played with the group until 1955. The following year he moved to Paris, where he worked with several groups, notably Powell's trio (1959–62). From 1960 to 1973, with Francy Boland, he led the Clarke–Boland Octet and the CLARKE–BOLAND BIG BAND; the members of these groups included the American expatriates Benny Bailey, Johnny Griffin, Sahib Shihab, Zoot Sims, and Idrees Sulieman, and such European performers as Derek Humble, Dusko Goykovich, Åke Persson, and Ronnie Scott. Clarke also played for the film *Ascenseur pour l'échafaud* (1957), appeared in *Les liaisons dangereuses 1960* (1959), and wrote music for *On n'enterre pas dimanche* (1959) and *La rivière du hibou* (1961). Although he made occasional concert tours of the USA, Clarke continued to perform, record, and teach in Europe until his death.

Clarke enjoyed a reputation as one of the most sensitive and innovative jazz musicians. During his years with Gillespie he revolutionized the drummer's technique by shifting the steady 4/4 pulse from the bass drum to the ride cymbal, thereby allowing the use of the bass and snare drum for independent coun-

Kenny Clarke at the Café Bohemia, New York, January 1956

terrhythms in support of the improvising musicians. This resulted in a polyrhythmic background that complemented the asymmetrical phrasing of the soloists, an ideal that became standard for modern jazz drumming. Among Clarke's compositions are the well-known *Salt Peanuts* (written with Gillespie) and *Epistrophy* (with Monk).

Oral history material in *NjR* (JOHP).

SELECTED RECORDINGS

As leader: Epistrophy/Oop-bop-sh'bam (1946, Swing 224); with E. Wilkins: *Kenny Clarke/Ernie Wilkins Septet* (1955, Savoy 12007), incl. Plenty for Kenny; *Bohemia after Dark* (1955, Savoy 12017); *The Trio* (1955, Savoy 12023); *Klook's Clique* (1956, Savoy 12065), incl. Volcano; with F. Boland: *Francy Boland Big Band* (1963, Atl. 1404)

As sideman: first issued on C. Christian: *Jazz Immortal* (1941, Eso. 1), Swing to Bop; D. Gillespie: Cubana Be/Cubana Bop (1947, Vic. 203145); Modern Jazz Quartet: La ronde (1952, Prst. 828)

BIBLIOGRAPHY

L. Feather: *Inside Be-bop* (New York, 1949/*R*1977 as *Inside Jazz*)
N. Shapiro and N. Hentoff, eds.: *Hear me Talkin' to ya: the History of Jazz by the Men who Made it* (New York and London, 1955/*R*1966), 299
R. Russell: "Bop Rhythm," *The Art of Jazz: Essays on the Nature and Development of Jazz*, ed. M. Williams (New York, 1959/*R*1979 as *The Art of Jazz: Ragtime to Bebop*), 187
M. Harrison: "Kenny Clarke," in S. Dance and others: *Jazz Era: the 'Forties* (London, 1961/*R*1985), 76
G. Hoefer: "Kenny Clarke's Early Recordings," *DB*, xxx/8 (1963), 23
B. Korall: "View from the Seine," *DB*, xxx/31 (1963), 17
W. F. Mellers: *Music in a New Found Land: Themes and Developments in the History of American Music* (London, 1964/*R*1975), 334
I. Gitler: *Jazz Masters of the Forties* (New York, 1966/*R*1983 with discography), 174
J. Shaw: "Kenny Clarke," *JJ*, xxii/10 (1969), 4
T. D. Brown: *A History and Analysis of Jazz Drumming to 1942* (diss., U. of Michigan, 1976), 476, 521
G. Endress: *Jazz Podium: Musiker über sich selbst* (Stuttgart, Germany, 1980), 80

B. Quinn: "Kenny Clarke: Rhythm Revolutionary," *JT* (1980), Nov, 12
U. B. Davis: *The Afro-American Musician and Writer in Paris during the 1950s and 1960s: a Study of Kenny Clarke, Donald Byrd, Chester Himes and James Baldwin* (diss., U. of Pittsburgh, 1983) [incl. oral histories]
E. Thigpen: "Kenny Clarke: Jazz Pioneer," *MD*, viii/2 (1984), 16
R. Mattingly: "In Memoriam: Kenny Clarke," *MD*, ix/4 (1985), 64

OLLY WILSON

Clarke, Pete [Frank] (*b* Birmingham, AL, 10 March 1911; *d* New York, 27 March 1975). Alto and baritone saxophonist, and clarinetist. He toured with J. Neal Montgomery's Collegiate Ramblers (1927) and played with Wayman Carver's Ramblers (1929), then from 1930 to 1936 performed and made recordings (including *Go Harlem*, 1936, Decca 995) with Chick Webb. After recording with Duke Ellington (1936) he worked with Louis Armstrong (1937–8) and Teddy Wilson's big band (1939–40). In 1946 he recorded with Rex Stewart, then went to Europe with Don Redman. For a brief time in 1947 Clarke played clarinet with John Kirby, and in the early 1950s he performed with Happy Caldwell at Smalls' Paradise in New York. He continued to work frequently during the 1960s, and was the clarinetist with Danny Barker's band in 1962; he played occasionally at Ryan's in the early 1970s.

Clarke had two brothers who were also musicians: Dick Clarke, a trumpeter, and Arthur "Babe" Clarke, who played saxophone.

based on *ChiltonW*

Clarke, Stanley (M.) (*b* Philadelphia, 30 June 1951). Electric bass guitarist. He first played accordion, but quickly changed to violin, then cello and double bass, before taking up electric bass guitar, which he played in rhythm-and-blues and rock bands in high school. Before graduating he went to New York in 1970 to find work in jazz, giving up his earlier plans to become a classical musician. He played double bass and electric bass guitar with Pharoah Sanders (1971), toured and recorded with Stan Getz (1972), recorded with Dexter Gordon and Art Blakey (both 1972), and also worked with Gil Evans, Mel Lewis, and Horace Silver. In 1971 he spent a year with Joe Henderson and met Chick Corea. Shortly afterwards he became a founding member of Corea's group RETURN TO FOREVER; from this time he concentrated on playing the electric instrument, and recorded eight albums with the band. After leaving in 1977 Clarke initiated several projects as a leader, playing with both jazz musicians and rock groups with equal success. His single *Sweet Baby*, made with George Duke, reached the Top 20 in 1981, and in 1983 he toured the USA with Return to Forever.

Clarke was early influenced by the playing of Charles Mingus, Paul Chambers, and Ron Carter, and also by the work of the rock guitarist Jimi Hendrix and the soul and funk singer James Brown. He plays rapid, precise, bass lines, and is well known for his manner of slapping the strings aggressively; this produces a stinging attack and a sound rich in treble frequencies which enlivens his syncopated phrases.

SELECTED RECORDINGS

As leader: with C. Corea: *Children of Forever* (1972, Pol. 5531); *Stanley Clarke* (1974, Nemperor 431); *Journey to Love* (1975, Nemperor 433); *School Days* (1976, Nemperor 900); *I Wanna Play for you* (1979, Nemperor 35680); *Rocks, Pebbles & Sand* (1980, Epic 36506); with G. Duke: *The Clarke/Duke Project* (1981, Epic 36918), incl. Sweet Baby; *Time Exposure* (1983, Epic 38688); with G. Duke: *The Clarke/Duke Project II* (1983, Epic 38934)
As sideman with C. Corea: *No Mystery* (1975, Pol. 6512)

BIBLIOGRAPHY

R. Baggenaes: "Stanley Clarke," *Coda*, xi/1 (1973), 8
C. Mitchell: "The Bass-ic Expansions of Stanley Clarke," *DB*, xlii/6 (1975), 14 [incl. discography]
C. Carman: "Stanley Clarke: Positively Modern Man," *DB*, xlv/13 (1978), 16
T. Mulhern: "Stanley Clarke," *GP*, xiv/5 (1980), 66 [incl. discography]
"Stanley Clarke," *SJ*, xxxv/7 (1981), 204 [discography]

CATHERINE COLLINS

Clarke, Terry [Terence Michael] (*b* Vancouver, Canada, 20 Aug 1944). Canadian drummer. While studying in Vancouver with the drummer Jim Blackley he worked in the bands of the pianist Chris Gage and the trombonist Dave Robbins. He toured the USA with John Handy's quintet (1965–7) and the pop group the 5th Dimension (1967–9), then settled in Toronto (1970), where he worked in clubs and studios. He toured and recorded with, among others, Frank Rosolino, Jay McShann, Jim Hall, Emily Remler, Ed Bickert, and Jim Galloway, and recorded with Ruby Braff and Sonny Greenwich; he also belonged to Rob McConnell's group Boss Brass and in 1981 to Oscar Peterson's trio. From 1985 he lived in New York while continuing to work with Canadian musicians.

SELECTED RECORDINGS

As sideman: J. Handy: *Live at the Monterey Jazz Festival* (1965, Col. CS9262); J. Hall: *Live!* (1975, A&M Hor. 705); Sackville All-Stars: *Saturday Night Function* (1981, Sack. 3028); O. Peterson: *Nigerian Marketplace* (1981, Pablo 2308231); M. Koffman: *One Moe Time* (1985, Duke Street 31023)

BIBLIOGRAPHY

H. Kallmann, G. Potvin, and K. Winters, eds.: *Encyclopedia of Music in Canada* (Toronto, Buffalo, and London, 1981)
T. O'Reilly: "Terry Clarke," *Coda*, no.186 (1982), 14 [incl. discography]
T. Wittet: "Terry Clarke: Playing in the Right Place," *MD*, vii/6 (1983), 18
M. Miller: "Terry Clarke," *Boogie, Pete & the Senator: Canadian Musicians in Jazz: the Eighties* (Toronto, 1987), 72

MARK MILLER

Clarke–Boland Big Band [CBBB]. Big band, active mainly in Europe. It was formed by the drummer Kenny Clarke and the Belgian composer, arranger, and pianist FRANCY BOLAND. The two musicians first played together in a quartet that also included Jimmy Woode (1959), and from the early 1960s made a few recordings as the leaders of smaller ensembles. Based in Cologne, Germany, the big band recorded its first album, *Jazz is Universal* (Atl. 1401), in 1961; thereafter it performed frequently and made many recordings (including *Volcano*, 1969, Pol. 583054) before disbanding in 1973. It received considerable critical acclaim, and included numerous excellent musicians of many nationalities, notably Benny Bailey, Dusko Goykovich, Idrees Sulieman, Åke Persson, Nat Peck, Johnny Griffin, Ronnie Scott, Karl Drewo, and Sahib Shihab.

BIBLIOGRAPHY

M. Hennessey: "Jazz Internationale: the Clarke–Boland Big Band," *DB*, xxxiv/8 (1967), 22
T. Brown: "The Kenny Clarke/Francy Boland Big Band," *CI*, vi/10 (1968), 20
P. J. Sullivan: "The Kenny Clarke–Francy Boland Big Band," *JM*, no.170 (1969), 2

ROLAND BAGGENAES

Clark Monroe's Uptown House. Nightclub in New York; *see* NIGHTCLUBS AND OTHER VENUES.

Classic Jazz. Record label, subsidiary of INNER CITY.

Clausen, Thomas (*b* Copenhagen, 5 Oct 1949). Danish pianist and composer. After studying piano and composition he belonged from 1970 to 1975 to the group V8, led by Palle Mikkelborg and Alex Riel, recorded with Jackie McLean (1973) and Dexter Gordon (1975), played in Mikkelborg's group Entrance (1975–

6), and recorded with Eddie "Lockjaw" Davis (1976); in the 1970s he was also a member of the Danish Radiojazzgruppen and the Crème Fraiche Big Band. He led a quartet, Mirror, with which he recorded in 1979, and a trio that included Niels-Henning Ørsted Pedersen (recording in 1980 and 1984), then belonged again to Entrance (1982–5) and to a trio with Ørsted Pedersen and Mikkelborg (1983–5). Clausen's playing may be heard to advantage on his album *The Shadow of Bill Evans* (1983, Bay. RJL8065). His compositions have a lyrical, impressionistic quality; good examples of his writing are *Rain* (1980) and *Sol* (1983).

ERIK WIEDEMANN

Clavichord. A keyboard instrument, usually rectangular, in which the sound is produced by tangents striking the strings. As on the piano, the force with which the keys are hit determines the loudness of the sound, but on the clavichord the tangent does not rebound (as does the hammer on the piano) but remains in contact with the string, so that by altering the pressure on the key after the initial attack the player may produce an alteration in the pitch of the note, a narrow gliss, a vibrato (known as the *Bebung*), or even the impression of a crescendo. The instrument's dynamic range is limited. Used throughout western Europe from the Renaissance to the 18th century, the clavichord fell into disuse in the 19th century but was revived in the 20th, when makers began to build instruments to new designs; the range of the modern clavichord is normally between four and five octaves with a lowest note around *C*.

The clavichord is seldom used in jazz, but Oscar Peterson plays it on the album *Porgy & Bess* (1976, Pablo 2310779), a duo with Joe Pass on acoustic guitar. To compensate for the low dynamic level of the sound produced by the clavichord, microphones were evidently placed close to the strings for the recording; the resulting timbre is biting, like that of the harpsichord. A feature of the performances is Peterson's playing of bends and blue notes by means of the kinds of alteration in key pressure described above. (*GroveI*)

BARRY KERNFELD

Claxton, Rozelle (*b* Memphis, 5 Feb 1913). Pianist and arranger. He played piano from an early age and made daily broadcasts on a Memphis radio station when he was only 15. After tuition from Jimmie Lunceford he joined the Rhythm Aces, led by the trumpeter Clarence Davis (1930), and later toured with them under the auspices of W. C. Handy (1932). From 1933 he lived in Kansas City, where he worked with Bennie Moten, Harlan Leonard, and the trombonist Ernie Fields (1939); a good example of his work as an arranger is Leonard's *Parade of the Stompers* (1940, Bb 10736). He moved to Chicago in 1940 to play with Eddie South, and then took other engagements there, including residencies with Walter Fuller and Roy Eldridge; he also played briefly with Lucky Millinder in New York, and, after his military service (1943–5), worked with George Dixon (1946–9). He studied music at the Chicago Conservatory (BM 1952, MM 1954) and was active as a teacher. From 1959 he played with Franz Jackson's Original Jass All Stars and later traveled widely as Pearl Bailey's accompanist (1978–83). In the 1980s he continued to work as a freelance musician in Chicago. Although he is an accomplished pianist in many styles, because he has spent most of his career in Chicago his achievements have been denied appropriate critical attention.

Oral history material in *ICU*.

SELECTED RECORDINGS

As sideman: E. Fields: T-Town Blues/Lard Stomp (1939, Voc. 5073); F. Jackson: *Jass, Jass, Jass* (1959, Phi. 600013); *A Nite at the Red Arrow* (1961, Pinnacle 104); *Chicago: the Living Legends* (1961, Riv. 9406); *Good Old Days* (1965, Pinnacle 109)

BIBLIOGRAPHY

ChiltonW; *FeatherE*

PETER VACHER

Claxtonola. Record label. It was established by the Brenard Manufacturing Company of Iowa City, Iowa, and began issuing records in 1918. Until 1924 its catalogue was derived from that of the New York Recording Laboratories, and included a number of race records which were put out in a 40000 series from spring 1920. Later items were drawn from Gennett's catalogue and issued under pseudonyms. The company appears to have ceased trading in March or April 1925. (M. Wyler: "A Glimpse of the Past, 4: Claxtonola," *Sv*, i/5 (1966), 15)

Clay, Shirley (*b* Charleston, MO, 1902; *d* New York, 7 Feb 1951). Trumpeter. He worked with bands in and around St. Louis from 1920, and after touring with the Synco Jazzers, led by John Williams (i) (*c*1923–4), settled in Chicago. In 1927 he played with Carroll Dickerson and briefly with Louis Armstrong; the following year he played in a big band led by the clarinetist Clifford King and took part in several recording sessions as a freelance. From 1929 to 1931 he performed and made recordings with Earl Hines (including *Have you ever felt that way*, 1929, Vic. 38048). He then worked with Don Redman until 1936, during which time he also recorded with other leaders, including Benny Goodman and Ben Pollack (both 1933). After a period with Claude Hopkins (1937–9) he worked with Hines (1940), Leon Abbey, Horace Henderson (1941), and Cootie Williams (1942). From 1944 until his death he led his own bands, though he also worked with Hopkins again and in Harry Dial's quartet; late in 1949 he joined Manzie Johnson's band.

BIBLIOGRAPHY

A. J. McCarthy: "Forgotten Men of Jazz, 1: Shirley Clay," *JM*, i/6 (1955), 27
H. Dial: *All that Jazz about Jazz: the Autobiography of Harry Dial* (Chigwell, England, 1984)

based on *ChiltonW*

Clayton, Buck [Wilbur Dorsey] (*b* Parsons, KS, 12 Nov 1911). Trumpeter and arranger. His early career was spent in California, where he organized a big band to play a residency in Shanghai, China, in 1934. After returning to Los Angeles he again led his own group and worked with various bandleaders. While Clayton was visiting Kansas City in 1936 he was persuaded to join Count Basie's band and soon became one of its leading soloists (for illustration *see* BASIE, COUNT). He was known for an attractive, burnished tone, a good technique, and a feeling for melodic improvisation; the sensitivity of his style made him an ideal accompanist for singers, notably Billie Holiday. He also wrote arrangements and compositions for the group. After leaving Basie, Clayton became one of the central figures of mainstream jazz. He made a tour of Europe in 1949–50, and during the 1950s he led his own sextet and worked frequently with Joe Bushkin, Tony Parenti, and Jimmy Rushing; he toured in Europe with Mezz Mezzrow (1953), appeared with Benny Goodman in the film *The Benny Goodman Story* (1955), and played in Brussels at the World's Fair with Sidney Bechet (1958). In 1959 he joined Eddie Condon's band and in 1964 toured Japan and Australia with the group. Clayton also made annual tours of Europe in the 1960s, playing frequently with Humphrey Lyttelton's band, and appeared at major jazz festivals throughout the USA. From 1967 illness interfered with his career, but he continued to provide arrangements for various groups. Later he recommenced playing and made a tour of Africa under the auspices of the State Department (1977). He taught at Hunter College, CUNY, in the early 1980s and led the Countsmen on a tour of Europe in 1983; in 1987 he led his own big band, which played his own compositions and arrangements.

Oral history material in *MoKmh*, *NjR* (JOHP), and *NjR*.

See also TRUMPET, §4; for further illustration *see* FILMS, fig.3.

SELECTED RECORDINGS

As leader: Robbin's Nest (1953, Col. B1836); Lazy River (1953, Vogue 5182)
As sideman: B. Holiday: He's funny that way (1937, Voc. 3748); C. Basie: Fiesta in Blue (1941, OK 6440); S. Bechet: *Brussels Fair '58* (1958, Col. CL1410), incl. All of me

BIBLIOGRAPHY

G. Hoefer: "Buck Clayton: a Brief Biography," *DB*, xxviii/2 (1961), 16
A. J. McCarthy: "Buck Clayton: the Post-Basie Period," *JM*, vii/2 (1961), 4
H. McNamara: "Travelin' Man," *DB*, xxxi/13 (1964), 13
B. McRae: "A B Basics, no.16: Buck Clayton," *JJ*, xxi/4 (1968), 20
V. Wilmer: "One for Buck," *Jazz People* (London, Indianapolis, and New York, 1970/*R*1985)
B. Rusch: "Buck Clayton: Interview," *Cadence*, iii/6 (1977), 11
S. Voce: "Buck Clayton: the Great Fight Back," *JJI*, xxxi/1–2 (1978), 24
"Buck Clayton: the Good Road Back," *CI*, xviii/2 (1979), 8
S. Dance: *The World of Count Basie* (New York and London, 1980) [colln of previously pubd interviews], 37
J.-P. Battestini: "Buck Clayton: l'arrangeur," *BHcF*, no.311 (1983), 5 [interview]
B. Clayton and N. M. Elliott: *Buck Clayton's Jazz World* (London, 1986) [incl. discography by B. Weir]
C. Deffaa: "A Tribute to Buck Clayton," *MR*, xiii/9 (1986), 5

JOHN CHILTON

Clear-tone mute. A name under which the double mute has been manufactured; *see* MUTE, §2(b).

Clef. Record label. It was established by NORMAN GRANZ in Los Angeles in 1946 as a subsidiary of Mercury. At first Granz used it mostly to issue recordings by groups associated with his organization Jazz at the Philharmonic; later it also recorded the work of many leading swing and bop musicians, including Charlie Parker. In 1953 Granz left Mercury in order to run Clef independently. Prior to 1956 some issues appeared in Australia under the Clef name, but in Europe many came out instead on other labels, including Columbia and His Master's Voice in England, Blue Star in France, and Karussel in Sweden; in 1956 Clef was absorbed with Granz's other labels into a new company, VERVE. (M. Ruppli and B. Porter: *The Clef/Verve Labels: a Discography*, New York, Westport, CT, and London, 1986)

Cless, (George) Rod(erick) (*b* Lenox, IA, 20 May 1907; *d* New York, 8 Dec 1944). Clarinetist. He grew up in a musical family and began learning clarinet in high school. In 1927 he moved to Chicago, where he played his first professional engagements with Frank Teschemacher and his brother-in-law Bud Freeman. After playing with several minor jazz and club bands he joined Muggsy Spanier's Ragtime Band in 1939 (for illustration *see* SPANIER, MUGGSY). He then worked for short periods with Art Hodes (intermittently, 1940–43), Marty Marsala (1941), Georg Brunis and Bobby Hackett (both 1942), Wild Bill Davison (1943), and Max Kaminsky (1944). His style was highly influenced by the playing of Teschemacher, Freeman, Johnny Dodds, and Jimmie Noone.

SELECTED RECORDINGS

As leader: Froggy Moore/Have you ever felt that way? (1944, Black and White 29); Make me a pallet on the floor/I know that you know (1944, Black and White 30)
As sideman: F. Teschemacher: Jazz me blues (1928, United Hot Clubs of America 61); M. Spanier: Big Butter and Egg Man/Eccentric (1939, Bb 10417); A. Hodes: Song of the Wanderer/There'll be some changes made (1940, Sig. 104); M. Kaminsky: Someday Sweetheart/Dippermouth Blues (1944, Bruns. 80137)

BIBLIOGRAPHY

B. Thiele: "Rod Cless," *Jazz*, i/8 (New York, 1943), 10
A. Hodes: "Remembering Rod Cless," *Jazz Report*, ix/1 (1975), 17
Ray Cless: "Rod Cless as I Knew him," *Selections from the Gutter: Jazz Portraits from "The Jazz Record"*, ed. A. Hodes and C. Hansen (Berkeley, CA, Los Angeles, and London, 1977), 171
D. Curan: "Hear that Ragtime Band," *Selections from the Gutter: Jazz Portraits from "The Jazz Record"*, ed. A. Hodes and C. Hansen (Berkeley, CA, Los Angeles, and London, 1977), 182 [interview]

RAYMOND J. GARIGLIO

Cleveland, Jimmy [James Milton] (*b* Wartrace, TN, 3 May 1926). Trombonist. He began to play trombone at the age of 16. He performed in his family's band, and with the Tennessee State University orchestra at Carnegie Hall before taking up his first important engagement, with Lionel Hampton (1950–53), with whom he toured Europe in 1953. He then worked with Oscar Pettiford (1954–7), Lucky Thompson (1956), James Moody, Eddie Heywood, Johnny Richards (1957–60), and Gerry Mulligan (1959). He formed a long-lasting association with Quincy Jones (a fellow member of Hampton's band) and recorded many film and television soundtracks with him, at first in New York and then, from the early 1970s, in California. He also worked in theater bands for a number of Broadway musicals. From the 1950s Cleveland was among the most frequently recorded of all jazz trombonists; his playing (predominantly in big bands) can be heard on hundreds of recordings with leaders as diverse as Dizzy Gillespie (1954–5), Donald Byrd (1957), Miles Davis (1957–9), Gil Evans (1957, 1959, 1963–4, 1969, 1971), Michel Legrand (1958), Oliver Nelson (1962–3, 1966–7), Jimmy Smith (1962–4, 1966, 1968), Wes Montgomery (1964, 1965), Lalo Schifrin (1964, 1965), Kenny Burrell (1964, 1967–9), Stanley Turrentine (1965, 1968), Bill Berry (1976), Hampton (1980–81), and Gerald Wilson (1981). A perfectionist with an astonishing technical mastery of his instrument, he maintains a warm, velvety, even tone no matter how fast the tempo. Some of his most accomplished jazz solos can be heard on albums he recorded in the 1950s.

SELECTED RECORDINGS

As leader: *Introducing Jimmy Cleveland and his All Stars* (1955, EmA 36066)
As sideman: A. Farmer: *Farmer Septet* (1953–4, Prst. 7031); G. Wallington: *George Wallington Showcase* (1954, BN 5045); D. Gillespie: Blue Mood/Rails (1954, Norg. 135); C. Terry: *Introducing Clark Terry* (1955, EmA 36007); L. Thompson: *Lucky Thompson Featuring Oscar Pettiford* (1956, ABC-Para. 111); O. Pettiford: *The Oscar Pettiford Orchestra in Hi-fi*, i (1956, ABC-Para. 135); *Oscar Pettiford and his Birdland Band* (1957, Spot. 153); G. Evans: *Gil Evans Plus Ten* (1957, Prst. 7120); Q. Jones: *The Great Wide World of Quincy Jones* (1959, Mer. 60221); A. Farmer: *The Aztec Suite* (1959, UA 5062); G. Evans: *The Individualism of Gil Evans* (1963–4, Verve 68555)

BIBLIOGRAPHY

FeatherE; *Feather '60s*; *Feather–Gitler '70s*
Liner notes, *Introducing Jimmy Cleveland and His All Stars* (EmA 36066, 1956)

MARK GARDNER

Climax. Record label. Its catalogue contained only five items, all by the band led by George Lewis (i). These were recorded and issued in 1943, and were among the earliest manifestations of the revival of the New Orleans style. The recordings were later acquired and reissued by Blue Note.

BIBLIOGRAPHY

T. Stagg and C. Crump: *New Orleans, the Revival: a Tape and Discography of Negro Traditional Jazz Recorded in New Orleans or by New Orleans Bands, 1937–1972* (n. p. [London], 1973), 138
B. Rust: *The American Record Label Book* (New Rochelle, NY, 1978), 67

Clinton, Larry (*b* New York, 17 Aug 1909; *d* Tucson, AZ, 2 May 1985). Arranger, composer, bandleader, and trumpeter. He played with or wrote arrangements for Ferde Grofé (1932), Isham Jones and Claude Hopkins (both 1933), the Dorsey brothers (1934), Jimmy Dorsey (1935–6), Glen Gray (1936–7), and Louis Armstrong, Tommy Dorsey, and Bunny Berigan (all 1937). He then led his own band (1937–41, 1948–50), and remained active in the music publishing and recording industries until he retired. More important as an arranger and composer than an instrumentalist or bandleader, Clinton became famous in the late 1930s for "swinging the classics," adding texts and light syncopation to tuneful pieces of art music, much as Paul Whiteman had done the previous decade. Among his best-known arrangements of this nature were *Martha* (1938, after Friedrich Flotow), *My Reverie* (1938, after Debussy), and *Our Love* (1939, after Tchaikovsky). A collection of his scores and other materials is held in the American Heritage Center of the University of Wyoming in Laramie; *see* LIBRARIES AND ARCHIVES, §2.

RECORDED COMPOSITIONS

(selective list; all recorded for Victor unless otherwise indicated)

As leader: Shades of Hades (1937, 25755); Strictly for the Persians (1938, 25863); A Study in Blue (1938, 25897); Zig Zag (1938, 26042); Dodgin' the Dean (1938, 26046); A Study in Green (1938, 26137); A Study in Surrealism (1940, 26481)

Recorded by J. Dorsey: Tap Dancer's Nightmare (1935, Decca 655); Dorsey Stomp (Dusk in Upper Sandusky) (1935, Decca 607); Dorsey Dervish (Waddlin' at the Waldorf) (1936, Decca 1040)

Recorded by others: Casa Loma Orchestra: A Study in Brown (1937, Decca 1159); T. Dorsey: Satan Takes a Holiday (1937, 25570); The Dipsy Doodle (1937, 25693)

BIBLIOGRAPHY

FeatherE

G. T. Simon: *The Big Bands* (New York, 1967, rev. and enlarged 2/1971, rev. 3/1974, 4/1981), 127

C. Garrod: *Larry Clinton and his Orchestra* (Spotswood, NJ, 1973) [discography]

WAYNE SCHNEIDER

Clooney, Rosemary (*b* Maysville, KY, 23 May 1928). Singer. She sang with her sister Betty in Tony Pastor's band in the late 1940s and then began working as a soloist. In 1950 she signed a contract with Columbia, for whom she recorded several popular songs which became hits. She appeared in a number of films during the 1950s, including *White Christmas* (1954). Her career declined for some time, but from 1977 to the mid-1980s she made a series of successful swing recordings for the Concord label. Clooney is most often accompanied by small groups, among them those led by Scott Hamilton and Warren Vaché. The distinctive quality of her voice and her skillful phrasing and timing are well represented on *Rosemary Clooney Sings the Lyrics of Ira Gershwin* (1979, Conc. 112).

BIBLIOGRAPHY

"Girl in the Groove," *Time*, lxi/8 (23 Feb 1953), 54

L. Gourse: *Louis' Children: American Jazz Singers* (New York, 1984), 301

WARREN VACHÉ, SR.

Clouds of Joy. The name by which the Dark Clouds of Joy, formed by TERRENCE HOLDER, were sometimes known; when the band was taken over by ANDY KIRK it regularly used this name, though it sometimes also appeared as the Twelve Clouds of Joy.

Club Alabam. The name of several nightclubs, notably ones in New York, Los Angeles, and Chicago; *see* NIGHTCLUBS AND OTHER VENUES.

Club Delisa [De Lisa]. Nightclub in Chicago; *see* NIGHTCLUBS AND OTHER VENUES.

Club Eleven. Nightclub in London; *see* NIGHTCLUBS AND OTHER VENUES.

Clubs. *See* NIGHTCLUBS AND OTHER VENUES.

Club Saint Germain. Nightclub in Paris; *see* NIGHTCLUBS AND OTHER VENUES.

Clyne, Jeff(rey Ovid) (*b* London, 29 Jan 1937). English bass player. After playing double bass with a military dance band during his national service (1955–7) he worked with Tony Crombie and many important British musicians in London. In 1958 he joined the Jazz Couriers, a group led by Tubby Hayes and Ronnie Scott; he continued to work with Hayes during the following decade, recording with him in 1959, 1961, and 1966. He also recorded with Stan Tracey (1964–6), Blossom Dearie (1966, 1970), Gordon Beck (1967–8), and Dudley Moore (1968). His versatility and eclectic tastes have enabled him to play comfortably in many contexts, ranging from bop groups to more adventurous bands such as the Spontaneous Music Ensemble (1966) and Trevor Watts's Amalgam (1969, 1973). Clyne has also played electric bass guitar with several jazz-rock groups, including Ian Carr's Nucleus (1969–71), Isotope (1973), and his own band Turning Point (1976–81). During the late 1970s and early 1980s he worked with such musicians as Kathy Stobart, Peter King, and the electric guitarist Phil Lee, and also performed and recorded with the quintet led by Beck and Allan Holdsworth (1977).

SELECTED RECORDINGS

As leader: *Creatures of the Night* (1977, Gull 1022)

As sideman: Jazz Couriers: *The Couriers of Jazz* (1958, London 15188); S. Tracey: *Under Milk Wood* (1965, Col. 33SX1774); G. Beck: *Gyroscope* (1968, Morgan 1); Nucleus: *Elastic Rock* (1970, Vertigo 6360008); J. Stevens: *Freebop* (1982, Affinity 101)

BIBLIOGRAPHY

Feather '60s

R. Cotterrell, ed.: *Jazz Now: the Jazz Centre Society Guide* (London, 1976), 121

B. Case: "Bassist Quits the Boiler Room," *New Musical Express* (22 Oct 1977), 48

STAN BRITT

C-melody saxophone. A saxophone pitched in C a tone above the tenor (*see* SAXOPHONE, §1). The only important exponent of the instrument in jazz is Frankie Trumbauer.

Coates, John (Francis, Jr.) (*b* Trenton, NJ, 17 Feb 1938). Pianist. He made his first recordings as the leader of a trio with Wendell Marshall and Kenny Clarke while he was still in high school (1955–6). In 1956 he joined Charlie Ventura's group, with which he recorded in 1957, and which he left after two years to attend Rutgers. He later became an editor, composer, and arranger for the Shawnee Press in Delaware Water Gap, Pennsylvania, where he also played frequently at the Deer Head Inn with such musicians as Al Cohn, Keith Jarrett, Zoot Sims, and (most often) Phil Woods. From 1974 to 1980 he recorded a number of albums, including one of a solo concert in Tokyo (1979, Omni. 1032). He left the Shawnee Press in 1977 to devote his time to playing and composing. In addition to the piano he has played vibraphone and, early in his career, clarinet.

BIBLIOGRAPHY

Feather–Gitler '70s

M. Camier: "The Jazz Piano of John Coates," *Jm*, no.278 (1979), 24

L.-V. Mialy: "John Coates, Jr.: le futur antérieur," *Jh*, no.386 (1981), 16 [interview]

D. Schaffer: "John Coates, Jr.: Interview," *Cadence*, vii/4 (1981), 5

Cobb(s), Arnett(e Cleophus) (*b* Houston, 10 Aug 1918). Tenor saxophonist. He studied piano, violin, then trumpet before taking up the saxophone. He worked with the drummer Frank Davis in Houston (1933), the trumpeter Chester Boone, and Milt Larkin (1936) before joining Lionel Hampton's orchestra in 1942 as Illinois Jacquet's replacement; he left the band in 1947 to form his own group and record for the Apollo label. After undergoing an operation on his spine in 1948 he resumed his career and continued to tour as a leader. An automobile accident in 1956 left him unable to walk without crutches, but he again resumed playing and from 1960 led a big band and managed the Ebony club in Houston. He worked in relative obscurity until 1973, when he performed at Town Hall in New York and made his first trip to Europe, where he was enthusiastically received. In the following years he recorded as a leader in France (1973, 1974, 1976), the USA (1978, 1980, 1984), and the Netherlands (1982), toured and recorded in Europe with Hampton (1978), and performed widely during annual tours of Europe, often as a member with Jacquet and Buddy Tate of the group Texas Tenors. Cobb's visceral, forthright, emotionally charged style and big sound have found particular favor with French audiences.

SELECTED RECORDINGS
(recorded for Apollo unless otherwise indicated)

Walkin' with Sid/Top Flight (1947, 770); Cobb's Idea (1947, 772); When I Grow Too Old to Dream (1947, 775); Dutch Kitten Bounce/Go, Red, Go (1947, 778); *Jumpin' at the Woodside* (1974, Bb 33175); *Funky Butt* (1980, Prog. 7054)

BIBLIOGRAPHY

ChiltonW

L. Tomkins: "Arnett Cobb Tells his Story," *CI*, xvii/7 (1979), 6

L. Birnbaum: "Arnett Cobb: Soul-wrenching Sax," *DB*, xlviii/4 (1981), 24 [incl. discography]

R. Horricks: "The Courage of Arnett Cobb," *CI*, xxi/10 (1983), 12

EDDIE COOK

Cobb, Jimmy [Wilbur James] (*b* Washington, 20 Jan 1929). Drummer. He is largely self-taught, though he studied briefly with Jack Dennett, a percussionist in the National SO. He played engagements with Charlie Rouse, Leo Parker, Frank Wess, Billie Holiday, and Pearl Bailey in Washington. After leaving the city in 1950 he played with Earl Bostic (with whom he made his first recordings), Dinah Washington (for three and a half years), Cannonball Adderley, Stan Getz, and Dizzy Gillespie. In 1958 he replaced Philly Joe Jones in Miles Davis's group, with which he remained until 1963. He then joined Paul Chambers in the Wynton Kelly Trio, which toured and recorded both on its own and with Wes Montgomery and J. J. Johnson. He accompanied Sarah Vaughan through the 1970s and later played with Richie Cole, Sonny Stitt, Nat Adderley, and Ricky Ford. Cobb's style of drumming is in the classic hard-bop tradition of Jones, Max Roach, and Art Blakey. As an accompanist he plays forcefully, aggressively, and slightly ahead of the beat; as a soloist he uses the entire drum set in a quasi-melodic fashion.

SELECTED RECORDINGS

As sideman: C. Adderley: *Jump for Joy* (1958, EmA 36146); M. Davis: *Kind of Blue* (1959, Col. CL1355); J. Coltrane: *Coltrane Jazz* (1959–60, Atl. 1354); M. Davis: *Someday my Prince will Come* (1961, Col. CS8456); *Miles Davis at Carnegie Hall* (1961, Col. CS8612); W. Kelly and W. Montgomery: *Smokin' at the Half Note* (1965, Verve 68633); S. Vaughan: *More from Japan Live* (1973, Mstr. 419); N. Adderley: *On the Move* (1982, The. 117); R. Ford: *Shorter Ideas* (1984, Muse 5314)

BIBLIOGRAPHY

V. Wilmer: "Jimmy Cobb: the Quiet Revolutionary," *MM*, l (20 Dec 1975), 33

L. Tomkins: "The Jimmy Cobb Story," *CI*, xvi/1 (1977), 14

R. Mattingly: "Jimmy Cobb: Seasoned Sideman," *MD*, iii/4 (1979), 28

R. Jackson: "Drum Soloist: Jimmy Cobb 'Four on Six'," *MD*, v/3 (1981), 44

J. KENT WILLIAMS

Cobb, Junie [Junius C.] (*b* Hot Springs, AR, *c*1896; *d c*1970). Clarinetist and alto and tenor saxophonist. He played piano in a small group with Johnny Dunn during his teens and later moved to Chicago, where he led his own band at the Club Alvadere (1920–21), performed on clarinet, and became known as a multi-instrumentalist. During the 1920s he worked with King Oliver (1924–5, 1926–7), mainly as a banjoist, and Jimmie Noone (1928–9). He also made several recordings as a leader (1926–9, including *Smoke Shop Drag*, 1929, Voc. 1269), playing mainly clarinet and alto and tenor saxophone; some of these employed the style known as barrelhouse jazz. After performing for about six months in Europe, Cobb worked in Chicago during the early 1930s as a leader in various clubs. He accompanied the singer Annabelle Calhoun until around 1946 and then held several long-term engagements as a solo pianist. Although he ceased full-time performing in 1955, he continued to play frequently. He wrote many compositions, among them *Once or Twice* (1929).

BIBLIOGRAPHY

B. Englund: "Introducing Junie Cobb," *JJ*, xiv/8 (1961), 7

J. R. T. Davies and L. Wright: "The Other Take," *Sv*, i/5 (1966), 22

C.-U. Dürr: "Junie C. Cobb," *Record Research*, no.75 (1966), 4 [discography]; no.82 (1967), 10, no.83 (1967), 5 [addns and corrections]

J. C. Hillman: "More Research on 'Junie Cobb'," *Record Research*, no.84 (1967), 5

C. Hillman and M. Tovey: "Chicago South Side, 1927–1932," *Sv*, no.124 (1986), 124; contd as "Junie Cobb's Corn Eaters and Grains of Corn, 1928–1929," *Sv*, no.126 (1986), 203 [incl. discography]

S. Lasker: "More on Junie Cobb," *Sv*, no.127 (1986), 5

based on *ChiltonW*

Cobblestone. Record label. It was established by Joe Fields in 1972 in New York as a subsidiary of the record company Buddah. Items in its catalogue were produced by Don Schlitten (*see* XANADU), who supervised important sessions by such musicians as Sonny Stitt, Jimmy Heath, and Pat Martino. Also released on Cobblestone were six albums containing highlights of the Newport Jazz Festival New York of 1972. The label was also used to issue a previously unreleased session by Grant Green with Big John Patton. After Schlitten left the company to join Muse, Cobblestone's importance as a jazz label quickly declined.

MARK GARDNER

Cobham, Billy [William C.] (*b* Panama, 16 May 1944). Drummer. When he was three he moved with his family to New York, where he later attended the High School of Music and Art. In the late 1960s he played in the New York Jazz Sextet and in groups with Billy Taylor (ii) and Horace Silver before helping to form an early jazz-rock band, Dreams, with which he played from 1969 to 1971. During these years he also played on Miles Davis's fusion recordings, and in 1971 he became a member of John McLaughlin's MAHAVISHNU ORCHESTRA. The power and precision of his playing with McLaughlin had an enormous impact on later jazz-rock drumming and placed him with Tony

Williams and Alphonse Mouzon among the leading drummers in this new style. From the mid-1970s he led his own fusion groups and played in a large number of studio bands with Stanley Turrentine, Ron Carter, and other jazz musicians. He is also active as a teacher in university and conservatory workshops. Cobham formed a new Mahavishnu Orchestra with McLaughlin in 1984.

For illustration *see* DRUM SET, fig.5.

SELECTED RECORDINGS

As leader: *Dreams* (1970, Col. C30225); *Spectrum* (1973, Atl. 7268); *Total Eclipse* (1974, Atl. 18121); *George Duke/Billy Cobham Band Live on Tour in Europe* (1976, Atl. 18194); *Stratus* (1981, INAK 813); *Observations &* (1982, Elek. 60123)

As sideman: H. Silver: *Serenade to a Soul Sister* (1968, BN 84277); M. Davis: *A Tribute to Jack Johnson* (1970, Col. KC30455); Mahavishnu Orchestra: *The Inner Mounting Flame* (1971, Col. KC31067)

BIBLIOGRAPHY

B. Priestley: "Alone . . . he's Cool," *DB*, xli/5 (1974), 14
A. J. Smith: "Billy Cobham: Percussive Ways, Commercial Means, Musical Ends," *DB*, xlii/20 (1975), 12
L. Underwood: "Cymbals: a Sonic Galaxy: Billy Cobham and Louis Bellson," *DB*, xliv/18 (1977), 13
C. Iero: "Billy Cobham," *MD*, iii/4 (1979), 10 [incl. discography]
J.-P. Patillot: "Billy's Bounce," *Jh*, no.361 (1979), 8
"Billy Cobham: Team Player," *JF* [intl edn], no.77 (1982), 34
B. Cleall: "Blues March," *MD*, vi/3 (1982), 54 [incl. transcr.]
B. Milkowski: "Billy Cobham: Have Drums, Will Travel," *DB*, li/4 (1984), 16
W. Miller: "Billy Cobham," *MD*, x/7 (1986), 16
B. Beuttler: "Billy Cobham on the Attack," *DB*, liv/4 (1987), 22 [incl. discography]

J. BRADFORD ROBINSON

Cochran, Todd. *See* BAYETÉ.

Cocoanut Grove Orchestra. Name used by the Blue Rhythm Band in 1930; *see* MILLS BLUE RHYTHM BAND.

Coda. In jazz, a phrase (usually a few bars, sometimes no more than a motif) added to the end of a theme, chorus, or entire piece; it may or may not be related thematically to the rest of the piece. *See* FORMS.

Codona. A cooperative trio formed in 1978 by DON CHERRY, NANA VASCONCELOS, and Collin Walcott.

Coe, Tony [Anthony George] (*b* Canterbury, England, 29 Nov 1934). English alto and tenor saxophonist and clarinetist. After studying clarinet formally he taught himself saxophone. He worked with the drummer Joe Daniels (1956–7) and Humphrey Lyttelton (1957–62, 1964–5), led his own quintet (1962–4), and was offered, but did not accept, a place with Count Basie (1965). Thereafter he performed with John Dankworth (1966–9), the Clarke–Boland Big Band (1967–73), John Picard, and Derek Bailey, and played and made recordings intermittently with Stan Tracey (1968–70, 1981, 1983); his playing in the late 1960s is well represented by the track *Lay by* on Tracey's *We Love you Madly*. Coe led several groups of his own, including Axel and (with Kenny Wheeler) Coe, Wheeler, and Co. He toured Europe with the United Jazz and Rock Ensemble (1978) and the UK with Mike Gibbs (1983), and recorded with Bob Moses (1983) and Norma Winstone (1986). From the 1970s he has collaborated with the arranger Henry Mancini as the soloist on soundtracks for the "Pink Panther" films. After his early success as an alto saxophonist, from 1962 Coe concentrated on tenor saxophone and clarinet. In 1987 he was music director during its run in London of Stephen Stahl's play *Lady Day*, starring Dee Dee Bridgewater. He is an internationally known musician of great versatility, with a profound understanding of both classic and avant-garde jazz. His saxophone playing is notable for its technical assurance; he produces a foggy tone and has a highly individual approach to phrasing, harmony, and timing. He has often been cited as a clarinetist of outstanding worth. Coe has also written a number of compositions, such as *Zeitgeist*.

SELECTED RECORDINGS

As leader: *Swingin' til the Girls Come Home* (1962, Phi. B10784L); *Tony Coe with the Brian Lemon Trio* (1971, 77 SEU41); *Zeitgeist* (1976, EMI 3207); with T. Oxley: *Nutty on Willisau* (1983, HA 2004), *Le chat se retourne* (1984, Nato 257)

As sideman: H. Lyttelton: *Triple Exposure* (1959, Parl. 1110); on S. Tracey: *We Love you Madly* (1968, Col. SCX6320), Lay by; H. Lyttelton: *Duke Ellington Classics* (1977, BL 127000)

BIBLIOGRAPHY

FeatherE; *Feather '60s*; *Feather–Gitler '70s*
H. Lyttelton: *Second Chorus* (London, 1958)
L. Tomkins: "A Fantastic Shock, says Tony Coe, Describing how he Felt when Basie Offered him a Job," *Crescendo*, iv/4 (1965), 21
P. Sullivan: "Best of British, no.8: Tony Coe: the Humility of Virtuosity," *JJI*, xxxi/10 (1978), 26
H. Charlton: "Tony Coe: existence pacifique," *Jm*, no.315 (1983), 32

DIGBY FAIRWEATHER

Coggins, Gil(bert Lloyd) (*b* New York, 23 Aug 1928). Pianist. In the early 1950s he played and recorded with Miles Davis and Lester Young and in 1957 played on the album *Ray Draper with John Coltrane* (NJ 8228) and made recordings with Jackie McLean and Sonny Rollins. He appeared at Minton's Playhouse and the West End in New York in the early 1970s and worked with Ed Lewis in 1974–5. By the early 1980s he was semiretired from music. (*FeatherE*)

Cohanier, Edmond (*b* Talloires, France, 28 Feb 1905). Swiss clarinetist and saxophonist. After studying music he played in France with the drummer George Marion (1925), Paul Gason's band (1926), Jack Purvis (1928), Gregor (1928–31), and the orchestra of the Paramount theater in Paris (1931–3); he also played under the bandleader Wal-Berg, and with Lud Gluskin (1932), the group Jazz du Poste Parisien (1933–5), the pianist Tom Waltham, the alto saxophonist Andy Foster (1933–4), Louis Armstrong (1934), the trumpeter Eddie Ritten, Herb Flemming (1935), and Bob Chrisler's band (1937). He moved to Switzerland and from late 1944 pursued a career outside jazz as a saxophone virtuoso; he also taught at the Zurich Conservatory. His playing is well represented on Gregor's recording *Gregorology* (1929, Edison Bell Radio 866).

BIBLIOGRAPHY

J. Hélian: *Les grands orchestres de music hall en France* (Paris, 1984), 190
M. Laplace: *Portraits of French Jazz Musicians* (Menden, Germany, 1985), 21

MICHEL LAPLACE

Cohen, Alan (Bernard) (*b* London, 25 Nov 1934). English arranger, composer, and soprano and tenor saxophonist. He studied composition at the Royal Academy of Music, London (1953–6), and first appeared with his own band at Ronnie Scott's in 1967. From the late 1960s he wrote compositions and arrangements for many musicians and groups, among them Humphrey Lyttelton, Chris Barber, Bing Crosby, and the orchestras of radio stations in Germany, Denmark (the Radioens Big Band), and England. In 1971 he formed a big band to play the music of Duke Ellington; its most celebrated reconstruction was recorded on the album *Duke Ellington's Black, Brown & Beige* (1972, Argo 159). The band broke up in 1973, and from

1978 Cohen and Keith Nichols led the Midnite Follies Orchestra, which toured, broadcast, and made recordings (including *Hotter than Hades*, 1978, EMI 1001). In 1985 Cohen wrote arrangements for the 31-piece band led by the drummer Charlie Watts, and the following year he formed his own quintet, in which he plays soprano saxophone. (C. Bird: "Cohen Versus the Blowers," *MM* (9 Jan 1971), 14)

DIGBY FAIRWEATHER

Cohen, Teddy. *See* CHARLES, TEDDY.

Cohn, Al(vin Gilbert) (*b* New York, 24 Nov 1925; *d* East Stroudsburg, PA, 15 Feb 1988). Tenor saxophonist and arranger. He studied piano from the age of six and clarinet from the age of 12, and took up tenor saxophone while in his teens. After working with Joe Marsala (1943) he played and wrote arrangements for Georgie Auld, then joined Boyd Raeburn (1946). In 1947 he worked with Alvino Rey and Buddy Rich, and the following year he replaced Herbie Steward in Woody Herman's band and became a member of the saxophone section that came to be called the Four Brothers; he also married Mary Ann McCall, the singer in Herman's band. After playing briefly with Artie Shaw (1949) he worked with Elliot Lawrence (1952–8) and then as a freelance, writing straightforward arrangements in the manner of Neal Hefti: his version of *Stardust* is a good example of his work in this field. From 1957 into the early 1980s Cohn led a quintet with Zoot Sims, also a former sideman of Herman's. The two players formed an interesting combination: they were both influenced by Lester Young, but Cohn's tone was slightly warmer than his partner's. They toured Scandinavia in 1974 and Japan in 1978. Cohn was principal arranger for the musicals *Raisin* (1973), *Music, Music, Music* (1974), and *Sophisticated Ladies* (1981), and he played solos on the soundtrack to the film *Lenny* (1974). In the 1980s he continued to perform in clubs in New York and appear at European festivals. Cohn had a broad, heavy tone; he played in an uncomplicated style, employing regular phrase lengths and idiomatic bop figures.

For illustrations *see* JACKSON, MILT, and SIMS, ZOOT.

Oral history material in *NjR*.

SELECTED RECORDINGS

Duos with J. Rowles: *Heavy Love* (1977, Xan. 145)

As leader: Let's get away from it all (1950, Triumph 812); *Al Cohn Quintet* (1953, Prog. 3004); *The Natural Seven* (1955, RCA LPM1116); *The Brothers!* (1955, RCA LPM1162); *From A to Z* (1956, RCA LPM1282); *Al and Zoot* (1957, Coral 57171); *Overtones* (1982, Conc. 194); *Standards of Excellence* (1983, Conc. 241)

As sideman: on W. Herman: *Jazz the Utmost* (1958, Verve 8014), Stardust; Xanadu All Stars: *Xanadu at Montreux*, ii (1978, Xan. 163); W. Herman: *Live at the Concord Jazz Festival* (1981, Conc. 191)

BIBLIOGRAPHY

L. Tomkins: "Al Cohn and Zoot Sims Duet," *Crescendo*, iii/11 (1965), 2 [interview]

L. Birnbaum: "Al Cohn Arranges to Make Longevity Count," *DB*, xlvii/4 (1980), 27 [incl. discography]

S. Woolley: "Al Cohn Now and Then," *JJI*, xxxiii/6 (1980), 21

L. Tomkins: "Al Cohn," *CI*, xx (1982), no.8, p.20; no.9, p.16

M. Isherwood: "Al Cohn," *JJI*, xxxvi/10 (1983), 8 [incl. discography]

K. D. Rusch: "Al Cohn: Interview," *Cadence*, xii/11 (1986), 5

LEROY OSTRANSKY

Cohn, Sonny [George Thomas] (*b* Chicago, 14 March 1925). Trumpeter. He gained considerable experience with local bands before becoming a professional musician in 1942, when he joined the group led by the saxophonist Richard Fox. He then played with Captain Walter Dyett's DuSable-ites and served as an army bandsman (1943–5). From 1945 to 1959 he was a member of Red Saunders's band, which during this period spent 11 years in residency at the Club DeLisa in Chicago. Cohn joined Count Basie in 1960, and soon became the mainstay of the band's trumpet section; from early 1974 he also took over as the group's road manager. He continued to be a key member of the band after Basie's death in 1984. Cohn's importance to Basie increased over the years as he established himself as a skilled and dependable section player with the versatility to undertake occasional lead and solo parts, mainly on ballads. He recorded notable solos on *Meetin' Time* and *Li'l Darlin'*.

SELECTED RECORDINGS

(all as sideman with C. Basie)

Kansas City Suite (1960, Roul. 52056), incl. Meetin' Time; *Standing Ovation* (1969, Dot 25938), incl. Li'l Darlin'; *Montreux '77* (1977, Pablo 2308207)

BIBLIOGRAPHY

P. Vacher: "The Sonny Cohn Story," *JJ*, xvi/9 (1963), 3

S. Traill: "Sonny Cohn: Trumpet Player," *JJ*, xxii/7 (1969), 6

——: "Sonny Cohn," *JJ*, xxx/2 (1977), 22 [interview]

S. Dance: *The World of Count Basie* (New York and London, 1980) [colln of previously pubd interviews], 209

BOB WEIR

Cohn, Zinky (Augustus) (*b* Oakland, CA, 18 Aug 1908; *d* Chicago, 26 April 1952). Pianist. His name is frequently spelled Cohen in early sources. From 1917 he lived in Chicago, where he studied music at the Conservatory. He played with Roy Palmer (*c*1928), Don Pasquall, and Jimmie Noone (1929–31), with whom he later recorded (1933–5). A good example of his playing can be heard on *Golden Lily Blues* (1930, Mlt. 12009), a recording made in Chicago with François Mosely's Louisianians. After touring Europe as an accompanist, he returned to Chicago and worked with Erskine Tate (1932), Eddie South (from 1933 in Chicago, and in 1934 and 1936 in New York), and Carroll Dickerson (1934–5); he left South in 1937 and led his own band at the Annex in Chicago. From 1938 he played only part-time; he accompanied Ethel Waters on a tour in 1944 and from 1950 organized weekly sessions at Jazz Ltd. in Chicago. (H. Rye: "Visiting Firemen, 8," *Sv*, no.108 (1983), 207, esp. 215)

based on *ChiltonW*

Coker, Dolo [Charles Mitchell] (*b* Hartford, CT, 16 Nov 1927; *d* Los Angeles, 13 April 1983). Pianist. He worked in Philadelphia with Ben Webster (1946), Kenny Dorham (1955), Sonny Stitt (1955–7), Gene Ammons, Lou Donaldson (both 1958), Philly Joe Jones (1959), and Dexter Gordon (1960–61), making his first recordings with Stitt. In 1961 he moved to Los Angeles, where he formed his own trio. During the 1970s he worked with such musicians as Herb Ellis, Blue Mitchell, Stitt, Red Rodney, and Lee Konitz; he also played with Supersax, and in 1973–4 was involved in a series of concerts at public schools with Sonny Criss. Coker made recordings under his own name in the late 1970s and with Harry Edison in 1977. His compositions and his approach to improvisation reveal his affiliations with the bop style and demonstrate his command of its idioms.

SELECTED RECORDINGS

As unaccompanied soloist: *All Alone* (1978, Xan. 178)

As leader: *Dolo!* (1976, Xan. 139)

As sideman: D. Gordon: *The Resurgence of Dexter Gordon* (1960, Jlnd 929); A. Pepper: *Intensity* (1960, Cont. 7607); R. Rodney: *Superbop* (1974, Muse 5046); S. Criss: *Out of Nowhere* (1975, Muse 5089)

BIBLIOGRAPHY

Feather '60s; *Feather–Gitler '70s*

C. Berg: "Dolo Coker: *Dolo!*," *DB*, xlv/4 (1978), 28 [record review]

PAUL RINZLER

Coker, Henry (L.) (*b* Dallas, 24 Dec 1919; *d* Los Angeles, 23 Nov 1979). Trombonist. After working with Benny Carter (*c*1944–8), Eddie Heywood (*c*1945–7), and Illinois Jacquet (1945, 1948–51) he became a member of Count Basie's band (1952), where he immediately registered his presence as a soloist on such pieces as *No Name*, *Redhead*, and *Peace Pipe*, and contributed to the strong, rich sound of the brass section. During his tenure with Basie, which lasted until 1963, he received many opportunities to take solos: he was the principal trombone soloist, for example, on the well-known retrospective album *The Count Basie Story*. After several years as a studio musician in New York he played with Ray Charles's orchestra (1966–71), though rarely as a soloist, then for most of the 1970s worked as a freelance in and around Los Angeles. In 1972 he played on the soundtrack for the film *Lady Sings the Blues*. He returned to Basie's band for four months in 1973, and played again with Charles in 1976.

SELECTED RECORDINGS

As sideman: I. Jacquet: Flyin' Home (1945, Philo 101); E. Heywood: It's Only a Paper Moon (1946, Decca 23812); C. Basie: *Count Basie Big Band* (1952, Clef 196) [EP], incl. No Name, Redhead; Peace Pipe (1953, Clef 89115); *The Count Basie Story* (1960, Roul. 1), incl. Out the Window

BIBLIOGRAPHY

R. Horricks: *Count Basie and his Orchestra: its Music and its Musicians* (London and New York, 1957), 207
V. Wilmer: "Texas Trombone: Henry Coker," *JJ*, xv/10 (1962), 11 [interview]
——: "Road Band Blues: a Three-way Rap with Henry Coker, Blue Mitchell, and Johnny Coles," *DB*, xxxviii/8 (1971), 16
B. Rusch: "Trombonist Henry Coker: a Short Talk," *Cadence*, i/8 (1976), 6

CHIP DEFFAA

Coker, Jerry (*b* South Bend, IN, 28 Nov 1932). Tenor saxophonist, composer, and teacher. He joined Woody Herman's orchestra in late 1953, interrupting his music studies at Indiana University, and toured with the group until summer 1954; his solo on *I Love Paris* (1953, Mars 1002) attracted considerable critical acclaim. He recorded in Paris for the Vogue label (1954), and in San Francisco as a leader and with Mel Lewis (both 1956), then worked as a freelance on the West Coast, playing for a brief period with Stan Kenton. His work with college bands led to his becoming a prominent teacher of jazz; from 1960 he has held several university posts. Coker has written a number of books about jazz, including *Improvising Jazz* (1964), and has composed for student bands. In the mid-1980s he was a professor of music at the University of Tennessee.

BIBLIOGRAPHY

FeatherE; *Feather '60s*
A. Morgan: "Woody's Tenors," *JM*, vi (1960–61), no.7, p.4; no.8, p.13; no.12, p.9

DAVE GELLY

Colar [Cola], **Kid Sheik** [George; George "Kid Sheik"; Sheik, Kid] (*b* New Orleans, 15 Sept 1908). Trumpeter and bandleader. After informal lessons from Wooden Joe Nicholas he formed his first band in 1925, and for 18 years played in and around the area of New Orleans formerly known as Storyville. From 1943 to 1945 he attended the US Air Force Music School, then formed another band before joining George Lewis (i) at Manny's Tavern in 1949. He was a member of the Eureka Brass Band from 1952 and of Harold Dejan's Olympia Brass Band. In 1961 Colar recorded with both his Swingsters and his Storyville Ramblers (the latter band, which included Capt. John Handy and Cié Frazier, also held a short residency in Cleveland), and in May 1963 he toured England with Barry Martyn's band. The album *Kid Martyn in New Orleans with Kid Sheik's Band* (1963, 77 LA20) is a fine example of his style as a lead player and as a soloist; on *Gloryland* he demonstrates aspects of his brass-band phrasing and attack. During the late 1960s he made several tours with Handy, recording with him in Europe (1966) and New York (1968). Colar played at Preservation Hall in New Orleans in the 1970s, his appearances becoming more frequent as the decade progressed. He visited England as a soloist in 1976, performing with local bands, and toured widely in the 1980s, generally with the Preservation Hall Band.

BIBLIOGRAPHY

"N. O. Jazz in Cleveland," *Eureka*, ii/1 (1962)
B. Martyn: Liner notes, *Kid Sheik and Capt John Handy in the Groove* (77 LEU15, 1966)
M. Hazeldine: "Kid Sheik in England," *Fn*, xix/2 (1987–8), 15

ALYN SHIPTON

Cole, Cozy [William Randolph] (*b* East Orange, NJ, 17 Oct 1906; *d* Columbus, OH, 29 Jan 1981). Drummer. He began his professional career working in New York with Wilbur Sweatman (*c*1928), and in the late 1920s led his own group. He recorded with Jelly Roll Morton (1930) and played in bands led by Blanche Calloway (1931–3), Benny Carter (1933–4), Willie Bryant (1935–6), and Stuff Smith (1936–8), gaining a wide range of experience which served as the basis of his later versatility. He achieved fame during his four years (1938–42) with Cab Calloway's orchestra (for illustration *see* CALLOWAY, CAB), with which he made several outstanding recordings. In the 1940s he studied at the Juilliard School and later worked as a percussionist in studio and theater ensembles; he also led his own quintet (1948) and septet (1949). He resumed touring as a member of Louis Armstrong's All Stars (1949–53; for illustration *see* BIGARD family, (3) Barney), but left the group to manage a drum school in New York in partnership with Gene Krupa. Cole appeared in several films, including *Make Mine Music* (1945) and *The Glenn Miller Story* (1953), and also played for the soundtrack of *The Strip* (1951). He achieved great success and large international sales in 1958 with his recording of *Topsy*; subsequently he led his own regular band, which remained popular in the 1960s. In 1969 Cole joined a quintet led by Jonah Jones, his former colleague in Cab Calloway's band. During the last decade of his life he continued to work as a freelance, touring Europe in 1976 with Benny Carter's quartet in Barry Martyn's show *A Night in New Orleans*.

Oral history material in *NjR* (JOHP), *NjR*.

SELECTED RECORDINGS

As leader: Thru' for the Night (1944, Key. 1301); Concerto for Cozy (1944, Savoy 575); Drum Fantasy (1954, MGM EP622); Topsy, pts i–ii (1957–8, Love 5004)

As sideman: C. Calloway: Crescendo in Drums (1939, Voc./OK 5062); Paradiddle (1940, Voc./OK 5467); R. Eldridge: St. Louis Blues (1944, Key. 607); L. Armstrong: Way down yonder in New Orleans (1951, Decca 928169)

BIBLIOGRAPHY

A. Gray: "Cozy Cole Still Takes Drum Lessons," *Rhythm*, no.143 (1939), 32
D. Morgenstern: "'Keep it Swinging': Cozy Cole," *DB*, xxxvi/6 (1969), 22
J.-P. Battestini: "Histoire de Cozy Cole," *BHcF*, no.241 (1974), 3
S. Dance: *The World of Swing* (New York, 1974) [colln of previously pubd interviews], 183
P. Vacher: "Cozy Conversing," *MR*, v/6 (1978), 10
S. Fish: "In Memoriam: Cozy Cole," *MD*, v/2 (1981), 62

JOHN CHILTON

Cole, June (Lawrence) (*b* Springfield, OH, 1903; *d* New York, 10 Oct 1960). Double bass and tuba player, and singer. He began his career in Springfield, Ohio, as the tuba player in the Synco Jazz Band (1923). In autumn 1926 he joined Fletcher Henderson in New York; he played tuba and sang on many of

Henderson's recordings (1926–8). He traveled to Europe in 1929 to tour with Benny Peyton and later that year joined Sam Wooding; during his time with Wooding (until late 1931) Cole changed to double bass. For the remainder of the 1930s he toured with Willie Lewis, though he was seriously ill from early 1936 to late 1938 and spent much time in the American Hospital in Paris. After returning to the USA in September 1941, Cole worked for the rest of his career in New York with his own groups and others; during the later years he also ran a record store in Harlem.

Cole was a workmanlike musician who was known principally for his ability to drive along the playing of a band; his style on both his instruments was characterized by great swing and energy.

SELECTED RECORDINGS

As sideman: F. Henderson: I need some lovin'/Sweet Thing (1926, Col. 854D); Bessie Smith: Dyin' by the Hour/Foolish Man Blues (1927, Col. 14273D); S. Wooding: Love for Sale/I have two loves (1931, Bruns. A500097); W. Lewis: Lady, be good/Chinatown (1941, ES 4072)

BIBLIOGRAPHY

ChiltonW

W. C. Allen: *Hendersonia: the Music of Fletcher Henderson and his Musicians: a Bio-discography* (Highland Park, NJ, 1973)

J. Chilton: *McKinney's Music: a Bio-discography of McKinney's Cotton Pickers* (London, 1978)

LAWRENCE KOCH

Cole, Nat "King" [Coles, Nathaniel Adams] (*b* Montgomery, AL, 17 March 1917; *d* Santa Monica, CA, 15 Feb 1965). Pianist and singer. His family moved to Chicago when he was four, and by the age of 12 he was playing organ and singing in the church where his father was pastor. At high school he came under the influence of the music educators N. Clark Smith and Walter Dyett. His three brothers (Eddie, Fred, and Isaac) were also jazz musicians, and he made his recording début for Decca in 1936 with Eddie Cole's band the Solid Swingers. The rhythmically vital playing of Earl Hines was a strong influence on Cole's piano style, and his own early groups, the Rogues of Rhythm and the Twelve Royal Dukes, often played Hines's arrangements. Cole left Chicago in 1936 to lead a band in a revival of Eubie Blake's revue *Shuffle Along*, and he set up permanent residence in Los Angeles after the show disbanded there the following year. He later formed a trio with Oscar Moore (guitar) and Wesley Prince (double bass), which performed at the Swanee Inn in Hollywood as King Cole and his Swingsters before becoming known as the King Cole Trio. The group's instrumentation proved musically stimulating and historically influential: Art Tatum adopted a similar trio format in 1943, as did Oscar Peterson and Ahmad Jamal during the early 1950s. Cole retained his trio (with some changes of personnel) until 1951, recording regularly for Decca and, from 1943, for Capitol.

Some of Cole's most influential jazz recordings date from the early 1940s. Among these were four masterpieces from a session in Los Angeles in 1942 with Lester Young and Red Callender – an event of seminal importance for both Cole and Young; *Indiana*, *Body and Soul*, *I can't get started*, and *Tea for Two* document Cole's impeccable jazz credentials as well as the continuing growth and mastery of Young. The King Cole Trio sometimes sang in unison on their early recordings, but in 1943 Cole had a national hit with his solo song *Straighten up and fly right*. His immaculate diction and liquid vocal style made this recording accessible to white audiences and launched his career as a popular singer. From this point he gradually appeared less often with his trio, though from 1944 to 1946 he gave concerts and recorded with Jazz at the Philharmonic. His hit recording *The Christmas Song* (1946) was the first of his solo vocal recordings to be accompanied by a studio orchestra.

Cole was one of the first black jazz artists to have his own weekly radio show (1948–9), and by the early 1950s was internationally known. Until 1965 he toured widely, performing in supper clubs, theaters, and concert halls, and appeared in several films, including *St. Louis Blues* (1958, in which he portrayed W. C. Handy). In the 1956–7 season he had a weekly show as a soloist on television.

Nat "King" Cole, Los Angeles, c1945–6

It is Cole's work as a pianist, however, that is of greatest musical significance. He developed the intricate right-hand style initiated by Hines and the sparse, rhythmic left-hand style of Count Basie, and his influence on other jazz pianists was enormous, as attested by artists as varied as Erroll Garner, Peterson, Red Garland, and Bill Evans (ii). Although in later years the piano was ancillary to his career as a popular singer, his place in the history of jazz piano is secure.

SELECTED RECORDINGS

As leader: Sweet Lorraine (1940, Decca 8520); with L. Young: Indiana/Body and Soul (1942, Philo 1000), I can't get started/Tea for Two (1942, Philo 1001); Straighten up and fly right (1943, Cap. 20009); It's only a paper moon/Easy Listening Blues (1943–4, Cap. 20012); The Christmas Song (1946, Cap. 311); When I take my sugar to tea (1947, Cap. 813); Nature Boy (1948, Cap. 15054); Mona Lisa (1950, Cap. 1010); *After Midnight* (1956, Cap. T782); *The Swinging Side of Nat King Cole* (1958, Cap. T1724)

As sideman: E. Cole: Thunder/Honey Hush (1936, Decca 7210); L. Hampton: Jack the Bellboy (1940, Vic. 26652); H. Haymer: Kicks (1945, Swing 370)

BIBLIOGRAPHY

B. Hoff: "Meet 'King' Cole of Hollywood," *Band Wagon*, no.6 (1940), 2

R. J. Gleason, ed.: *Jam Session: an Anthology of Jazz* (New York and London, 1958)

G. Hall: *Nat "King" Cole: a Jazz Discography* (Laurel, MD, 1965)

"Nat 'King' Cole, 1917–1965," *DB*, xxxii/7 (1965), 14

M. Cole and L. Robinson: *Nat King Cole: an Intimate Biography* (New York, 1971)

H. Pleasants: *The Great American Popular Singers* (New York, 1974), 213
L. Feather: "Piano Giants of Jazz: Nat King Cole," *CK*, iv/4 (1978), 57
D. Travis: *An Autobiography of Black Jazz* (Chicago, 1983) [incl. interviews], 179
J. Haskins and K. Benson: *Nat King Cole* (New York, 1984)
C. Garrod and B. Korst: *Nat "King" Cole: his Voice and his Piano* (Zephyrhills, FL, 1987) [discography]

BILL DOBBINS, RICHARD WANG

Cole, Richie [Richard] (*b* Trenton, NJ, 29 Feb 1948). Alto saxophonist. His father owned a jazz club, and he heard jazz at an early age. He began playing guitar when he was five, and took up alto saxophone at the age of ten. While in high school he studied with Phil Woods, and after graduating won a scholarship to the Berklee College of Music, where he studied for over two years; he left in 1969 and joined Buddy Rich's big band. In the early 1970s he played for Doc Severinsen, Lionel Hampton, and others, and also formed a group of his own, and in 1975 he began an association with Eddie Jefferson. This continued until Jefferson's death in 1979; from this date Cole has led his own small groups.

A saxophonist in the bop tradition, Cole is heavily indebted to his mentor Woods for his tone quality, phrasing, and many of his melodic ideas, though his intonation is less accurate. He possesses an impish sense of humor, and often interjects musical jokes into his solos and jests with the audience between pieces. Although his playing lacks the depth of expression found in the music of Charlie Parker, Cannonball Adderley, and other masters, Cole has enjoyed considerable popularity with jazz audiences; he is often named in readers' polls conducted by *Down Beat*, *Swing Journal*, and other magazines.

SELECTED RECORDINGS

As leader: *New York Afternoon* (1976, Muse 5119); *Alto Madness* (1977, Muse 5155); with P. Woods: *Side by Side* (1980, Muse 5237); *Richie Cole and . . .* (1982, PAlt 8023)

As sideman: B. Rich: *Keep the Customers Satisfied* (1970, Lib. 11006); E. Jefferson: *The Live-liest* (1976, Muse 5127); R. Rodney: *Red, White, and Blues* (1976, Muse 5111)

BIBLIOGRAPHY

C. Silvert: "Richie Cole's Alto Madness," *DB*, xlvii/10 (1980), 24 [incl. discography]
H. Wong: "Mr. Alto Madness: Richie Cole," *JT* (1980), Oct, 9
M. Bloom: "The Altology of Richie Cole," *DB*, li/9 (1984), 14 [incl. discography]
L. Darroch: "Richie Cole: the Music's for Real," *JT* (1984), Sept, 12
M. Richards: "Richie Cole," *JJI*, xl/9 (1987), 8

THOMAS OWENS

Cole, Rupert (*b* Trinidad, British West Indies, 8 Aug 1909). Trinidadian alto saxophonist and clarinetist. He was educated in Barbados, where he first studied clarinet. In 1924 he moved to New York and, after teaching himself to play alto saxophone, he began to perform professionally. He recorded with Bill Brown and his Brownies (1929), toured with Horace Henderson, and then played with Don Redman (1931–8), with whom he also made recordings (including *Bugle Call Rag*, 1937, Voc./OK 3354). He was a member of Louis Armstrong's orchestra (1938–44), then briefly re-joined Redman before playing in a big band led by Cootie Williams (1945–6). He worked with Lucky Millinder in the 1950s, and also occasionally with Wilbur De Paris. Although Cole gave up full-time performing, he continued to play as a freelance musician; he worked regularly in George Wettling's trio in New York (1964).

based on *ChiltonW*

Coleman, Bill [William Johnson] (*b* Centreville, nr Paris, KY, 4 Aug 1904; *d* Toulouse, France, 24 Aug 1981). Trumpeter. He began learning trumpet in 1916, and after performing with J. C. Higginbotham and Edgar Hayes he taught himself to read music. In 1927 he moved to New York, where he worked with Cecil and Lloyd Scott, Luis Russell (1929, 1931–2), Cecil Scott (1929–30), and Charlie Johnson (1930); in 1933 he performed in France with Lucky Millinder. His name first became known to jazz musicians and enthusiasts in the USA and Europe through the recordings he made with Fats Waller while he was a member of Teddy Hill's band (1934–5). He then worked in Paris with the dancer and bandleader Freddy "Snake Hips" Taylor (1935–6) and Willie Lewis (1936) and in Bombay with Leon Abbey's band (1936–7). After a second period with Lewis in Paris (1937–8) Coleman performed in Egypt in the Harlem Rhythm Makers (1938–40), which he formed with Herman "Ivory" Chittison and other members of Lewis's band. He then returned to New York and played with Benny Carter and Waller (both 1940), Teddy Wilson (1940–41), Andy Kirk (1941–2), Ellis Larkins (1943), Mary Lou Williams (1944), John Kirby (1945), Sy Oliver (1946–7), and Billy Kyle (1947–8). In 1945 he toured the Philippines and Japan with a group led by the drummer Herbie Cowens. Coleman moved to Paris in 1948 at the invitation of Charles Delaunay, and thereafter performed and recorded as a leader throughout Europe. By this time he was well known, and his lively singing and likable personality made him particularly popular. His autobiography was published in 1981.

Influenced mainly by Louis Armstrong, Coleman gradually developed an individual voice; his playing was noted for the elegance and fluidity of his phrasing and his highly musical melodic ideas. In the 1940s and 1950s he adopted some of the devices characteristic of bop, though during the last two decades of his life he returned to his former style.

Oral history material in *NjR* (JOHP).

SELECTED RECORDINGS

As leader: I'm in the mood for love/After you've gone (1936, HMV 7764); Joe Louis Stomp/Coquette (1936, HMV 7705); Bill Street Blues/After you've gone (1937, Swing 22); *Swingin' in Switzerland* (1957, BB 33182); *From Boogie to Funk* (1960, Bruns. 87905); *Bill Coleman Sings and Plays Spirituals* (1968, Concert Hall 1269); *Bill and the Boys* (1968, Concert Hall 1335); *Really I Do* (1980, BB 33162)

As sideman: F. Waller: Dream Man/I'm growing fonder of you (1934, Vic. 24801); Baby Brown (1935, Vic. 24846); Baby Brown (1935, Vic. 24847); D. Wells: Between the Devil and the Deep Blue Sea (1937, Swing 6); I got rhythm/I'm fer it too (1943, Sig. 90002)

BIBLIOGRAPHY

ChiltonW; *FeatherE*
D. Hague: "Reminiscing with Bill Coleman," *JJ*, xi/7 (1958), 1
W. Balliett: *Dinosaurs in the Morning* (Philadelphia, 1962) [colln of previously pubd articles], 128
A. McCarthy: "Bill Coleman," *JM*, xii/2 (1966), 3
C. Roby: "A Long Way from Kentucky: Bill Coleman," *JB*, iii/6 (1966), 20
V. Wilmer: "Bill Coleman: No Back Home Blues," *DB*, xxxiii/20 (1966), 19
J. Simmen: "Bill Coleman," *BHcF*, no.190 (1969), 10; no.191 (1969), 6; no.192 (1969), 13
——: "Crystal Clear," *Coda*, xii/3 (1975), 25
J. Postgate: "Young Bill Coleman," *JJ*, xxx/2 (1977), 16
J. Evensmo: *The Trumpets of Bill Coleman, 1929–1945, Frankie Newton* (n.p. [Oslo], n.d. [?1978]) [discography]
C. Battestini and J.-P. Battestini: "Bill Coleman," *BHcF*, no.275 (1979), 4; no.276 (1980), 6 [interview]
B. Coleman: *Trumpet Story: souvenirs d'un grand du jazz* (Paris, 1981; Eng. orig., London, in preparation)
M. G[autier] P[anassié]: "Bill Coleman nous a quittés," *BHcF*, no.291 (1981), 3
D. Waterhouse: Obituary, *JJI*, xxxiv/11 (1981), 22

JOHNNY SIMMEN

Coleman, Earl (*b* Port Huron, MI, 12 Sept 1925). Singer. He began his professional career with Jay McShann (1943) and Earl Hines (1944). In 1945 he traveled with McShann to the

West Coast, where his singing was heard by Charlie Parker; *This is Always*, which Coleman recorded with Parker in 1947, became a jazz hit. Thereafter Coleman performed only intermittently, working on his own and with various leaders, including Gene Ammons (mid-1950s), Gerald Wilson (1960), Don Byas (1962), and Frank Foster (mid-1960s). In 1968 he moved to Los Angeles to work as a freelance musician. He has recorded with such distinguished accompanists as Fats Navarro and Max Roach (both 1948), Art Farmer and Gigi Gryce (both 1956), and Hank Jones (1956, 1977). Coleman performs mainly ballads and blues songs; his rich baritone voice is imbued with echoes of Billy Eckstine's deep, romantic sound.

SELECTED RECORDINGS

As leader: Yardbird Suite/A Stranger in Town (1948, Dial 753); *Earl Coleman Returns* (1956, Prst. 7045); *Love Songs* (1966–7, Atl. 8172); *A Song for You* (1977, Xan. 147)

As sideman: C. Parker: This is Always (1947, Dial 1015); Dark Shadows (1947, Dial 1014); on S. Rollins: *Tour de force* (1956, Prst. 7126), My Ideal, Two Different Worlds

BIBLIOGRAPHY

FeatherE; *Feather '60s*; *Feather–Gitler '70s*

R. G. Reisner: *Bird: the Legend of Charlie Parker* (New York, 1962/*R*1975), 68

LAWRENCE KOCH

Coleman, George (*b* Memphis, 8 March 1935). Tenor saxophonist and bandleader. He taught himself to play alto saxophone while in his teens and was a colleague of Booker Little, Frank Strozier, and Harold Mabern. He toured with the blues singer and guitarist B. B. King from 1952 and took up the tenor saxophone in 1955; the following year he moved to Chicago, where he played with Walter Perkins's group MJT +3. He left Chicago to play with Max Roach's band from 1958 until 1959, when he settled in New York. After belonging to Slide Hampton's octet (1960–62) he toured California in the spring of 1963 with a sextet led by Miles Davis that included Strozier as a sideman; he also played in Davis's quintet, of which Herbie Hancock, Ron Carter, and Tony Williams were members, and took part in the recording of Hancock's album *Maiden Voyage* (1964). He left Davis's group in 1964 to work as a freelance with Elvin Jones and Charles McPherson. From 1974 into the 1980s he led an octet that included Strozier and Mabern as sidemen and that was critically acclaimed; at the same time he led a quartet and from 1975 to 1976 belonged to another quartet led by Cedar Walton. Despite his craftsmanship and his inventive approach to the saxophone, Coleman has achieved less commercial success than have Davis's other sidemen.

SELECTED RECORDINGS

Duos with T. Montoliu: *Meditation* (1977, Tim. 110)

As leader: *Revival* (1976, Cat. 73)

As sideman: M. Roach: *Deeds, not Words* (1958, Riv. 280); B. Little: *Victory and Sorrow* (1961, Beth. 6061); M. Davis: *Miles Davis in Europe* (1963, Col. CS8983); *My Funny Valentine* (1964, Col. CS9106); H. Hancock: *Maiden Voyage* (1964, BN 84195); E. Jones: *The Prime Element* (1969, BN LA506H2)

BIBLIOGRAPHY

L. Tomkins: "George Coleman Tells his Story," *CI*, xiv/7 (1976), 10

J. Howard: "Ein Begleiter wird zum Leiter," *JP*, xxix/7 (1980), 8

A. Sussman: "Survival of the Grittiest," *DB*, xlvii/3 (1980), 26 [incl. discography]

L. Tomkins: "George Coleman: Subtlety and the Octet," *CI*, xix/3 (1980), 20

B. Case: "Big George Straight Ahead," *MM*, lvi (21 Feb 1981), 27

B. Priestley: "George Coleman: from In to Out and Back Again," *The Wire*, no.25 (1986), 20

DAVID WILD

Coleman, Ornette (*b* Fort Worth, 9 March 1930). Saxophonist and composer.

1. Life. 2. Musical style.

1. Life. He began playing alto saxophone at the age of 14, and developed a style predominantly influenced by Charlie Parker. His early professional work with a variety of southwestern rhythm-and-blues and carnival bands, however, seems to have been in a more traditional idiom. In 1948 he moved to New Orleans and worked mostly at nonmusical jobs. By 1950 he had returned to Fort Worth, after which he went to Los Angeles with Pee Wee Crayton's rhythm-and-blues band. Wherever he tried to introduce some of his more personal and innovative ideas he met with hostility, both from audiences and musicians. While working as an elevator operator in Los Angeles he studied (on his own) harmony and theory textbooks, and gradually evolved a radically new concept and style, seemingly from a combination of musical intuition born of southwestern country blues and folk forms, and his misreadings – or highly personal interpretations – of the theoretical texts.

While working sporadically in some of the more obscure clubs in Los Angeles, Coleman eventually came to the attention of Red Mitchell and later Percy Heath of the Modern Jazz Quartet. Coleman's first studio recording (for Contemporary in 1958) reveals that his style and sound were, in essence, fully formed at that time. At the instigation of John Lewis, Coleman (and his trumpet-playing partner Don Cherry) attended the Lenox (Massachusetts) School of Jazz in 1959. There followed engagements at the Five Spot nightclub in New York, and a series of recordings for Atlantic entitled *The Shape of Jazz to Come* (which included his compositions *Lonely Woman* and *Congeniality*) and *Change of the Century* (with *Ramblin'* and *Free*). These recordings, which occasioned worldwide controversy, revealed Coleman performing in a style freed from most of the conventions of modern jazz. His recording *Free Jazz* (made on 21 December 1960) for double jazz quartet, a 37-minute sustained collective improvisation, was undoubtedly the single most important influence on avant-garde jazz in the ensuing decade. On another recording, *Jazz Abstractions* (made earlier the same week), Coleman is heard in a variety of more structured pieces, including Gunther Schuller's serial work *Abstraction* for alto saxophone, string quartet, two double basses, guitar, and percussion.

In 1962 Coleman retired temporarily from performing in public, primarily to teach himself trumpet and violin. His unorthodox treatment of these instruments on his return to public life in 1965 provoked even more controversy and led to numerous denunciations of his work by a number of influential American jazz musicians, including Miles Davis and Charles Mingus. However, Coleman was well received in Europe during his first tour there in 1965, giving a major impetus to the burgeoning European avant-garde jazz movement. In the mid- and late 1960s he also became interested in extended, through-composed works for larger ensembles, and produced among other pieces *Forms and Sounds for Wind Quintet* (1965, recorded in England by the Virtuoso Ensemble, 1965, Pol. 623246–7) and *Skies of America*, a 21-movement suite for symphony orchestra (1972).

By the early 1970s Coleman's influence had waned considerably, while John Coltrane's dominance of saxophone styles had correspondingly spread. As Coleman turned increasingly to more abstract and mechanical compositional techniques (as in *Skies of America*), his playing lost some of its earlier emotional intensity and rhythmic vitality. But a visit to Morocco in 1972 and the gradual influence (especially rhythmic) of certain popular rock, funk, and fusion styles seemed to have revitalized his ensemble performances, a direction clearly discernible in Coleman's powerful electric band Prime Time, founded in 1975. This group first recorded in France in the same year as a quintet, including two electric guitarists, an electric bass guitarist, and a drummer, but thereafter it usually worked as a sextet, with a second drummer; the double bass player Charlie Haden joined it for its performance at the Newport Jazz Festival New York in 1978, but not for its European tour later that year. In the 1980s the group has performed and recorded as a septet with two guitarists, two bass guitarists, and two drummers, all amplified. Prime Time's repertory draws on the various musical styles that have influenced Coleman (including Moroccan music, jazz-rock, and free-jazz improvisation). Coleman's own playing, however, a fascinating and basically inimitable amalgam of blues and modal, atonal, and microtonal music, remains unchanged.

From the 1960s Coleman was often joined by his son, the drummer Denardo Coleman (*b c*1956), in concerts and recordings. Although in the 1980s he performs in public only intermittently, the recording *Song X* (1985) and a tour (1986), both made with Pat Metheny, brought him and his music a degree of attention he had not enjoyed for some years. A film, *Ornette: Made in America*, directed by Shirley Clarke and compiled from footage made in the 1960s and the early 1980s, was released in 1984, and two concerts entitled "Ornette Coleman Celebration" took place at the Weill Recital Hall at Carnegie Hall in 1987; the works performed were *Notes Talking*, for solo mandolin (1986), *The Sacred Mind of Johnny Dolphin*, for chamber ensemble (1984), *Time Design*, for amplified string quartet and electric drum set (1983), *Trinity*, for solo violin (1986), and *In Honor of NASA and Planetary Soloist*, for oboe, english horn, *mukhavīṇā*, and string quartet (1986).

2. MUSICAL STYLE. Coleman's music cannot be understood solely in terms of the concept that has generally prevailed since the late 1920s – that jazz is primarily a form of expression for a virtuoso soloist. It is conceived essentially as an ensemble music; founded on traditional roots, it makes consistent use of spontaneous collective interplay at the most intimate and intricate levels. This accounts for its extraordinary unpredictability, freedom, and flexibility. Coleman's improvisations are highly mobile in tonality, rhythmic continuity, and form; they liberated the jazz solo both from an adherence to predetermined harmonic "changes" and a subservience to melodic variation.

Ex.1 Coleman's second "chorus" from *Congeniality* (1959, Atl. 1317); transcr. G. Schuller

Ornette Coleman (foreground) and Dewey Redman

They also abandon traditional chorus and phrase structure, reinterpreting jazz rhythm, beat, and swing along freer, nonsymmetrical lines. Although it appeared to many to be incoherent and atonal, Coleman's playing was (and remains) essentially modal in concept, rooted in older, simpler black folk idioms – in particular a raw blues feeling. His wailing saxophone sound (produced in his early years on a plastic instrument) is never far removed from the plaintive human voice of Afro-American musical folklore. This essentially lyric approach, best heard on *Lonely Woman* (1959) and *Sex Spy* (1977), is linked to his "horizontal" concept of improvisation, a tendency explored earlier by such players as Lester Young and Miles Davis (in his post-bop modal style). Released from a strict adherence to harmonic functions and conventional form and phrase patterns, Coleman's solos are intrinsically linear, evolving in a sometimes fragmented musical discourse (ex.1). His improvisations at fast tempos are marked by flurries of notes, or gliding, swooping, and at times bursting phrases, played with great intensity and conviction. Occasionally his work seems burdened by the overuse of sequential patterning. But it is the strength of conviction of his playing (especially when aided by like-minded colleagues such as Cherry, Charlie Haden, and Billy Higgins) that produces a sense of the inevitable in Coleman's art.

Technically Coleman plays as much "from his fingers" as by ear, an approach frequently resulting in nontempered intonation and unique tone-colors. These effects are even more noticeable in his less convincing performances on trumpet and violin, although even on these instruments Coleman can sometimes produce compelling improvisations by sheer instinct and musical energy.

Coleman's style has changed little since the early 1960s.

Whether he is working in Moroccan musical traditions, in atonal, classically oriented works or, indeed, in rock- or funk-influenced idioms, his playing seems, in both sound and substance, to be capable at once of dominating and being assimilated by its surroundings.

In recent years Coleman has espoused a theory which he calls "harmolodic." It is apparently based on the reiteration in varied clefs and "keys" of the same musical materials (lines, themes, melodies), thus producing a simplistic organum-like "polyphony," principally in unrelieved parallel motion. It is not clear, however, how this theory functions in Coleman's own improvisatory style (*see also* HARMOLODIC THEORY). He is also noted for his use of obscure, often contradictory, epigrams. Some observers see in these the "philosophical" analogues to his musical theories and concepts. Similarly, his notation of his own compositions – of which he has written several hundred – is imprecise, gestural, and in a sense graphic, leaving the performer free to give individual and differing interpretations.

While it may be impossible as yet to define specifically Coleman's influence in jazz (as one can do with Coleman Hawkins, Lester Young, Charlie Parker, or Coltrane), it is nonetheless clear that he opened up unprecedented musical vistas for jazz, the wider implications of which have not yet been fully explored – least of all by his many lesser imitators.

Oral history material in *NjR*.

See also BLUES, §12, and JAZZ (i), §VI, 1 and fig.7.

SELECTED RECORDINGS

* – composed by Coleman

Something Else!!!! The Music of Ornette Coleman (1958, Cont. 3551); *Tomorrow is the Question! The New Music of Ornette Coleman* (1959, Cont. 3569); *The Shape of Jazz to Come* (1959, Atl. 1317), incl. *Congeniality, *Lonely Woman; *Change of the Century* (1959, Atl. 1327), incl. *Free, *Ramblin'; *Twins* (1959–61, Atl. 1588), incl. First Take; *This is our Music* (1960, Atl. 1353); *Free Jazz* (1960, Atl. 1364); *Jazz Abstractions* (1960, Atl. 1365); *Ornette!* (1961, Atl. 1378); *Ornette on Tenor* (1961, Atl. 1394); *Town Hall, 1962* (1962, ESP 1006), incl. *A Dedication to Poets and Writers; *The Ornette Coleman Trio at the Golden Circle* (1965, BN 84224-5)

The Empty Foxhole (1966, BN 84246); *Saints and Soldiers* (1967, RCA LSC2982); *Ornette at 12* (1968, Imp. 9178); *Crisis* (1969, Imp. 9187); *Science Fiction* (1971, Col. KC31061); *Broken Shadows* (1971–2, Col. FC38029); **Skies of America* (1972, Col. KC31562); *Dancing in your Head* (1975, A&M Hor. 722); *Body Meta* (1975, AH 1); *Soapsuds* (1977, AH 6), incl. *Sex Spy; *Of Human Feelings* (1979, Ant. 2001); *Ornette and Prime Time: Opening the Caravan of Dreams* (1985, Caravan of Dreams 85001); with P. Metheny: *Song X* (1985, Geffen 24096); *In All Languages* (1987, Caravan of Dreams 85008)

BIBLIOGRAPHY

B. Abel: "The Man with the White Plastic Sax," *Hi-fi Stereo Review*, v/2 (1960), 40

G. Russell: "Ornette Coleman and Tonality," *JR*, iii/5 (1960), 7

N. Hentoff: "Biggest Noise in Jazz," *Esquire*, lv/3 (1961), 82

——: *The Jazz Life* (New York and London, 1961/*R*1975) [incl. previously pubd articles], 222

H. Pekar: "Tomorrow is the Question," *JJ*, xv/11 (1962), 8

T. Martin: "The Plastic Muse," *JM*, x (1964), no.3, p.13; no.4, p.14; no.6, p.20; xi/3 (1965), 21

J. Goldberg: *Jazz Masters of the Fifties* (New York and London, 1965/*R*1980), 228

D. Heckman: "Inside Ornette Coleman," *DB*, xxxii (1965), no.19, p.13; no.26, p.20

V. Wilmer: "Ornette Tells it Like it is," *JB*, ii/11 (1965), 16

J. Cooke: "Coleman Revisited," *JM*, xii/5 (1966), 9

M. Harrison: "Coleman and the Consequences," *JM*, xii/4 (1966), 10

A. B. Spellman: *Four Lives in the Bebop Business* (New York, 1966/*R*1970 as *Black Music: Four Lives*), 77

J. Cooke: "Ornette and Son," *JM*, xiii/5 (1967), 13

W. F. Mellers: *Caliban Reborn: Renewal in Twentieth-century Music* (London, 1968), 135

E. Raben: *A Discography of Free Jazz* (Copenhagen, 1969)

E. Jost: "Zur Musik Ornette Colemans," *Jf*, ii (1970), 105

M. Williams: *Jazz Masters in Transition, 1957–69* (New York and London, 1970/*R*1980) [colln of previously pubd reviews]

——: *The Jazz Tradition* (New York, 1970, rev. 2/1983), 207

M. Bourne: "Ornette's Innerview," *DB*, xl/19 (1973), 16

J. Pailhé: "Ornette Coleman, 1965," *Jh*, no.302 (1974), 21

E. Jost: "Ornette Coleman," *Free Jazz* (Graz, Austria, 1974)

M. Harrison: *A Jazz Retrospect* (Newton Abbot, England, 1976, rev. 2/1977)

A. Taylor: "Ornette Coleman," *Notes and Tones: Musician-to-Musician Interviews* (Liège, Belgium, 1977/*R*1982), 31

H. Mandel: "Ornette Coleman: the Creator as Harmolodic Magician," *DB*, xlv/16 (1978), 17 [incl. discography]

G. Endress: *Jazz Podium: Musiker über sich selbst* (Stuttgart, Germany, 1980), 182

D. Wild and M. Cuscuna: *Ornette Coleman, 1958–1979: a Discography* (Ann Arbor, MI, 1980)

C. Sheridan: "Ornette Coleman," *JJI*, xxxiii/11 (1980), 22; xxxiv/1 (1981), 16

A. Bresnick and R. Fine: "Ornette Coleman: Interview," *Cadence*, viii/9 (1982), 5

W. Balliett: "Ornette," *Jelly Roll, Jabbo and Fats* (New York, and Oxford, England, 1983) [colln of previously pubd articles], 187

J. Rockwell: "Free Jazz, Body Music and Symphonic Dreams," *All American Music: Composition in the Late Twentieth Century* (New York, 1983), 185

J. Litweiler: "Ornette Coleman: the Birth of Freedom," *The Freedom Principle: Jazz after 1958* (New York, 1984), 31

S. Lake: "Prime Time and Motion," *The Wire*, no.19 (1985), 31

F. Davis: *In the Moment: Jazz in the 1980s* (New York, and Oxford, England, 1986) [colln of previously pubd articles], 133

D. Richardson: "Playing it by Ear," *San Francisco Bay Guardian* (25 June 1986)

H. Mandel: "Ornette Coleman: The Color of Music," *DB*, liv/8 (1987), 16 [incl. discography]

GUNTHER SCHULLER

Coles, Johnny [John] (*b* Trenton, NJ, 3 July 1926). Trumpeter and flugelhorn player. A self-taught musician, he played first in a military band, then in a sextet called Slappy and his Swingsters (1945), then in Eddie "Cleanhead" Vinson's group with John Coltrane and Red Garland (1949). In the 1950s he played with Philly Joe Jones (1951), Bull Moose Jackson (1952), and James Moody (1956–8); he performed and recorded with the Gil Evans Orchestra from 1958 to 1964, and was featured on its album *Out of the Cool* (1960). He traveled to Europe with a sextet led by Charles Mingus (1964) and played at the Newport Jazz Festival (1966); also in the mid-1960s he made recordings with Duke Pearson and Astrud Gilberto. In 1968 Coles was a founding member of Herbie Hancock's sextet. He joined the Ray Charles Orchestra in 1969 but left two years later to play with Duke Ellington; he re-joined Charles on Ellington's death in 1974. In the mid-1980s he toured with Count Basie's orchestra (led by Thad Jones after Basie's death in 1984); he settled in the San Francisco Bay area in 1985 and left the orchestra the following year. Coles's trumpet style is warm, serene, and full of nuances. He has acknowledged the influence of Miles Davis and Dizzy Gillespie, and of Charles's vocal delivery. A versatile performer, he has played a variety of music besides jazz, including marches, rhythm-and-blues, and polkas.

SELECTED RECORDINGS

As leader: *Little Johnny C* (1963, BN 84144); *Katumbo (Dance)* (1971, Mstr. 346); *New Morning* (1982, Criss Cross 1005)

As sideman: G. Evans: *New Bottle Old Wine* (1958, WP 1246); *Out of the Cool* (1960, Imp. 4), incl. La Nevada; on C. Mingus: *The Great Concert of Charles Mingus* (1964, Amer. 003), So long Eric; D. Pearson: *Honeybuns* (1965, Atl. 3002); A. Gilberto: (1966, Verve 68643), incl. Look to the Rainbow; D. Pearson: *Prairie Dog* (1966, Atl. 3005); H. Hancock: *The Prisoner* (1969, BN 84321)

BIBLIOGRAPHY

M. James: "Johnny Coles," *JM*, xii/2 (1966), 7

G. Endress: "Johnny Coles: The Human Cry," *JP*, xix/2 (1970), 50

V. Wilmer: "Road Band Blues: a Three-way Rap with Henry Coker, Blue Mitchell, and Johnny Coles," *DB*, xxxviii/8 (1971), 16

S. Woolley: "Hot Coles," *MM*, li (23 Oct 1976), 49

ANDRÉ BARBERA

Colignon, Raymond "Coco" (*b* Liège, Belgium, 7 Feb 1907; *d* Wavre, Belgium, ?10 Feb 1987). Belgian pianist. After working in cinemas and music halls he performed in Switzerland (1928) and France (1929). In 1930 he toured Algeria and worked in Paris, and from 1931 to 1934 he was pianist, organist, and arranger at a nightclub in Liège. Colignon then played with Fud Candrix's orchestra, often as a principal soloist (1935–40), and led his own group in Brussels. After World War II he worked in Antwerp and later held residencies in Brussels (1947–53) and Charleroi. Thereafter he worked in Germany, mainly as an organist. He made recordings as an unaccompanied soloist (1937–8), as a leader (1939, 1941–2), and as a sideman with Candrix (1937–40), Kutte Widmann and the clarinetist and tenor saxophonist Jack Lowens (both 1942), and René Compère (1954).

ROBERT PERNET

Collective improvisation. Simultaneous improvisation by several or all members of a group, each contributing a line of equal importance to the others; *see* IMPROVISATION, esp. §2.

Collectors Items. Record label. It was established in the 1970s in Walton-on-Thames, England, by John A. Holley, who had previously been associated with various shortlived European reissue labels. The catalogue consists of high-quality pressings of early jazz and swing, including material by Richard M. Jones, Willie Hightower, Sippie Wallace, and Sara Martin. Issue has continued into the 1980s.

Collette, Buddy [William Marcell] (*b* Los Angeles, 6 Aug 1921). Saxophonist, clarinetist, flutist, and composer. He was taught piano as a child, then learned to play alto saxophone and other woodwind instruments; he later took up tenor and baritone saxophones. He gained early experience with various musicians, among them Les Hite (1942), and while serving in the navy during World War II he led a dance band. In the mid- to late 1940s he performed and recorded with a number of groups, including those led by Lucky Thompson (1946), Edgar Hayes (1947), Louis Jordan (1948), Benny Carter (1948–9), and Gerald Wilson (1949–50); in some he worked alongside Charles Mingus, whom he had known in high school. In the early 1950s he performed mainly on radio and television, but he came to prominence for his performances on flute as a member of Chico Hamilton's quintet (1955–6). He led various groups in and around Los Angeles at this time and began to record under his own name, making several albums that included his own compositions (*Santa Monica* (1956) and *Blue Sands* (1957), for example).

In the 1960s Collette concentrated on composing, scoring films (1964, 1966, 1967), and writing arrangements for Thelonious Monk, with whom he played (1964); he also appeared in a number of films from the 1960s onwards. He was a member of the resident band at the Monterey Jazz Festival (1964, 1965) and of Stan Kenton's Los Angeles Neophonic Orchestra (1965). He continued to compose and perform in the 1970s and in 1978 he traveled to Japan with Benny Carter. In 1973 he was a founder, with Al Aarons, of the record company Legend, of which he later became president (1975). A collection of his compositions was published as *The Buddy Collette Songbook* (Amsterdam and Los Angeles, 1985).

As a flutist, particularly during his association with Hamilton, Collette's fluent and unobtrusive playing of cool jazz helped to shape a basic style of jazz flute playing founded on the pioneering work of Sam Most and Herbie Mann. His virile approach to the saxophone is more closely related to the mainstream tradition.

SELECTED RECORDINGS

As leader: *Man of Many Parts* (1956, Cont. 3522), incl. Santa Monica; *Calm, Cool, and Collette* (1957, ABC-Para. 179); *Buddy's Best* (1957, Dooto 245), incl. Blue Sands; *Now and Then* (1973, Legend 1004)

As sideman: R. Norvo: *Red's Blue Room/Red's Rose Room* (1954, X 3034); C. Hamilton: *The Chico Hamilton Quintet with Buddy Collette* (1955, PJ 1209); *Chico Hamilton Quintet in Hi Fi* (1955–6, PJ 1216)

BIBLIOGRAPHY

FeatherE; *Feather '60s*; *Feather–Gitler '70s*

J. Tynan: "Buddy Collette," *DB*, xxiii/24 (1956), 18

B. Priestley: *Mingus: a Critical Biography* (London, Melbourne, Australia, and New York, 1982)

C. Hoffman: *Man of Many Parts: a Discography of Buddy Collette* (Amsterdam, 1985) [incl. interview and list of compositions]

LAWRENCE KOCH

Collie, (John) Max(well) (*b* Melbourne, Australia, 21 Feb 1931). Australian trombonist and bandleader. Originally a brass band musician, from 1948 he led his own semiprofessional jazz bands, the Jazz Bandits (1948–50) and the Jazz Kings (1950–62). He began playing professionally in 1962 as a member of the Melbourne New Orleans Jazz Band, which visited England in 1963. Collie remained in England and joined the London City Stompers (1963); when he became leader in 1966 the group was renamed the Rhythm Aces. It has performed at festivals, concerts, and in theaters throughout the world. During one of its three American tours (1973–5) it won the World Championship of Jazz in Indianapolis (August 1975). In 1984 Collie began touring with a show called *New Orleans Mardi Gras*, in which Ken Colyer and Cy Laurie appeared; from 1986, in addition, he presented *The High Society Show* with many of the same musicians. He has made a large number of recordings as a leader (from 1971), among them *World Champions of Jazz* (1976, BL 12137–8).

BIBLIOGRAPHY

A. Brewer: "Bearded Blower Max: the Jazzman who's Back," *Bromley Times* (16 June 1983), 5

G. Bielderman: *Max Collie Discography* (Zwolle, Netherlands, 1987)

DEREK COLLER

Collier, (James) Graham (*b* Tynemouth, England, 21 Feb 1937). English composer. After playing trumpet with an army band (1954–61) he won a scholarship to the Berklee College of Music, from which he was the first British student to graduate. He remained in the USA to tour briefly as a double bass player with Jimmy Dorsey's band (1963), then returned to England. He formed an ensemble, Graham Collier Music, to play his own compositions; it has included many of the finest English jazz musicians, among them Harry Beckett, John Surman, and Kenny Wheeler, and has varied considerably in size and instrumentation. In 1983 he established a big band, Hoarded Dreams, to perform his work of the same name, which received its première at the Bracknell Jazz Festival; the ensemble included Ted Curson, Eje Thelin, Conrad Bauer, Manfred Schoof, and Tomasz Stańko. The following year he formed a rehearsal ensemble that later became the nucleus of the band Loose Tubes. In the mid-1980s Collier has concentrated on conducting and directing his own work; he is also a professor, and the director of jazz studies, at the Royal Academy of Music, London. In 1987 he was awarded an OBE for his services to jazz. He has written music for plays, films, and television, and is the author of several books. From 1974 he owned and managed the record label Mosaic (*see* MOSAIC (i)).

Collier's many compositions combine written structures and improvisation, achieving a high level of integration between these two elements. The form of each piece is flexible enough to adapt to the individual player's solos, but sufficiently dictated to govern the shape of the entire work. His style has thus evolved beyond the established format of themes and solos to approach a synthesis of the controlled and the extemporized.

RECORDED COMPOSITIONS

(selective list; recorded for Mosaic unless otherwise indicated)

Down Another Road (1969, Fon. 922); *New Conditions* (1976, 761); *Symphony of Scorpions* (1976–7, 773); *Day of the Dead* (1978, 783-4); *Something British* (1985, 871)

WRITINGS

(selective list)

Inside Jazz (London, 1973)

Jazz: a Student's and Teacher's Guide (London, 1975; Ger. trans. as *Jazz: ein Führer für Lehrer und Schüler*, Wilhelmshaven, Germany, 1982)

BIBLIOGRAPHY

Feather–Gitler '70s
M. C. King: "British Jazzmen, 2: Graham Collier," *JJ*, xxiii/8 (1970), 10
R. Brown: "Spreading the Word: Graham Collier," *Into Jazz*, i/2 (1974), 12
R. Cotterrell, ed.: *Jazz Now: the Jazz Centre Society Guide* (London, 1976)
——: "Graham Collier: Composer," *The Wire*, no. 14 (1985), 43

SIMON ADAMS

Collier, Ron(ald William) (*b* Coleman, Canada, 3 July 1930). Canadian composer and trombonist. He studied with Gordon Delamont (in Toronto, 1951–4), George Russell, and Hall Overton (in New York, 1961–2) and collaborated with Duke Ellington on the ballet *The River* (1970) and the symphony *Celebration* (1972). He joined the faculty of Humber College in Toronto in 1974. Collier's compositions include *The City*, *Hear me Talkin' to ya*, *Aurora borealis*, and *Humber Suite*; his style is well represented by the album *Duke Ellington, North of the Border in Canada with the Ron Collier Orchestra* (1967, Decca 75069). With Delamont and the composer Norman Symonds (*b* near Nelson, Canada, 23 Dec 1920) he was a leader of the third-stream movement in Canada during the late 1950s. (M. Miller and H. McNamara: "Collier, Ron," *Encyclopedia of Music in Canada*, ed. H. Kallmann, G. Potvin, and K. Winters (Toronto, Buffalo, and London, 1981) [incl. discography])

MARK MILLER

Collins, Booker (*b* Roswell, NM, 21 June 1914). Double bass and tuba player. After studying music at the New Mexico Military Institute, he performed in Bat Brown's band and with the trombonist Bert Johnson. In 1934 he joined Andy Kirk, with whom he played and recorded until 1944 (for illustration *see* WILLIAMS, MARY LOU). A good example of his playing is Mary Lou Williams's *Corny Rhythm* (1936, Decca 1021), on which he takes a more prominent role than is typical of double bass players at that time. He was a regular member of Floyd Smith's trio from 1946 until the beginning of the 1950s; he then retired from full-time playing.

based on *ChiltonW*

Collins, Burt(on I.) (*b* New York, 27 March 1931). Trumpeter. He grew up in Philadelphia, and first played with Neal Hefti (1955), Woody Herman, Dizzy Gillespie, Claude Thornhill (all 1956), Johnny Richards (1957–9, 1964), Elliot Lawrence (1958), and Urbie Green (1959). By the early 1960s he was active as a freelance in New York; he worked in pit orchestras on Broadway, performed and recorded with Duke Pearson, and played with Cannonball Adderley at the New York Jazz Festival. Later he worked with Lee Konitz's nonet (1975–7) and Dave Matthews's big band (1975), recording with the latter, accompanying Green, in 1977. Collins has cited Harry James as an influence upon his work, but plays in the bop style.

SELECTED RECORDINGS

As sideman: W. Herman: *Blues Groove* (1956, Cap. T784); J. Richards: *Wide Range* (1957, Cap. T885), incl. Nippigon; E. Lawrence: *Big Band Sound* (1958, Fan. 3290); D. Matthews: *Live at the Five Spot* (1975, Muse 5073)

BIBLIOGRAPHY

FeatherE; *Feather–Gitler '70s*

FREDERICK A. BECK

Collins, Cal(vin) (*b* Cincinnati, 1933). Electric guitarist. He first played mandolin with local "bluegrass" groups, then took up the guitar, on which he is largely self-taught. He developed his skills during several years spent touring small clubs in the Midwest before his first major engagement, with Benny Goodman in the early 1970s. Thereafter he settled in Los Angeles, where he performed and recorded as a freelance. His most notable work has been with Warren Vaché and Scott Hamilton, with whom he has made recordings and played at concerts and festivals in the USA, Europe, and Japan. A technically well-equipped, fluid, and exciting soloist, Collins has forged a highly eclectic style. Although his early influences were Django Reinhardt and Charlie Christian, his admiration for Tal Farlow and George Van Eps is reflected by the way he plays soaring single lines over rich harmonic bases. With Vaché and Hamilton, he was part of the swing revival of the early 1970s.

SELECTED RECORDINGS

(all recorded for Concord)

As unaccompanied soloist: *By Myself* (1979, 119); *Cross Country* (1981, 166)
As leader: *Cincinnati to LA* (1978, 59); *Interplay* (1980, 137)
As sideman: W. Vaché: *Polished Brass* (1979, 98); S. Hamilton: *Scott's Buddy* (1980, 148)

BIBLIOGRAPHY

J. Schwartz: "Cal Collins: Benny Goodman's Sideman, Session and Solo Jazz Guitarist," *GP*, xiv/4 (1980), 28 [incl. discography]
L. Tomkins: "Cal Collins: Traveling on the Mainstream," *CI*, xix/3 (1980), 6

NORMAN MONGAN

Collins, Dick [Richard] (*b* Seattle, 19 July 1924). Trumpeter. While studying in Paris with the composer Darius Milhaud (1947–8) he recorded with Hubert Fol and the Be Bop Minstrels, and with Kenny Clarke. After returning to the USA he played with Dave Brubeck's octet in San Francisco (1948–50) and recorded on the West Coast with Charlie Barnet (1951), Charlie Mariano (1953), and Nat Pierce, Paul Desmond, and Cal Tjader (all 1954); also in 1954 he made recordings with his own groups in New York (including *Horn of Plenty*, RCA LJM 1019). He toured with Woody Herman (1954–6) and then worked with Les Brown (1957–62), with whom he toured Europe, Africa, and Asia. (*FeatherE*)

Collins, John (Elbert) (*b* Montgomery, AL, 20 Sept 1913). Guitarist. He gained valuable early experience playing for his mother, the pianist and bandleader Georgia Gorham, and began his professional career in 1935 accompanying Art Tatum. He then worked with Roy Eldridge (1936–40), Billie Holiday (1940–41), Lester Young (1941), Fletcher Henderson (1941), and Benny Carter. After army service he was a member of Slam Stewart's trio (1946–8) and played with Erroll Garner, Billy Taylor (ii), and Tatum. The longest association in Collins's career was that with Nat "King" Cole (1951–65), after which he spent a brief period with the singer Patti Page, then until 1971 worked with the pianist Bobby Troup. Thereafter he played with Carmen McRae, Snooky Young, and Ray Brown, and settled in the Los Angeles area as a teacher. Collins has worked principally as a rhythm guitarist, but he is also known for his sophisticated solo lines.

Oral history material in *NjR* (JOHP).

SELECTED RECORDINGS

As sideman: R. Eldridge: Wabash Stomp/Florida Stomp (1937, Voc. 3479); A. Tatum: Battery Bounce (1941, Decca 8526); S. Stewart: Blue Collins (1946, Musi. 396); S. Young: *Horn of Plenty* (1979, Conc. 91); C. McRae: *You're Lookin' at Me* (1984, Conc. 235)

BIBLIOGRAPHY

J. Ferguson: "John Collins: Sideman to Jazz Legends Art Tatum, Lester Young, & Roy Eldridge," *GP*, xix/1 (1985), 70 [incl. discography]

JIM FERGUSON

Collins, Lee (*b* New Orleans, 17 Oct 1901; *d* Chicago, 3 July 1960). Trumpeter. From the age of 12 he played in various bands in New Orleans, including the Young Eagles, the Columbia Band, and the Young Tuxedo Orchestra; he was also a sideman for Papa Celestin and Zutty Singleton. In 1924 he went to Chicago, where he joined King Oliver and also recorded with Jelly Roll Morton. During the late 1920s and the early 1930s he toured widely with his own bands and with others. He made some of his finest recordings in 1929 as the leader, with the saxophonist Davey Jones, of the JONES AND COLLINS ASTORIA HOT EIGHT; he also accompanied a number of blues singers during the 1930s and played with Lovie Austin's Blues Serenaders and Chippie Hill in 1946. Collins led his own trio at the Victory Club in Chicago from mid-1945, but he continued to work occasionally with other bands. He toured Europe with Mezz Mezzrow in 1951 and 1954, but was taken ill on the second trip and thereafter ceased to play.

Collins was a lyrical, exciting, and powerful player with a broad tone. His timing and phrasing, and the sheer verve of his playing on the Astoria Hot Eight recordings are reminiscent of Henry "Red" Allen, though the influence of Louis Armstrong is also apparent in his work, as are stylistic similarities with players active in the New Orleans revival – notably Kid Howard.

Oral history material in *LNT*.

SELECTED RECORDINGS

As leader of the Jones and Collins Astoria Hot Eight (with D. Jones): Astoria Strut/Duet Stomp (1929, Vic. 38576); Damp Weather/Tip Easy Blues (1929, Bb 10952)

As sideman: J. R. Morton: Fishtail Blues/High Society (1924, Aut. 606); C. Hill: Trouble in Mind/How Long Blues (1946, Cir. [USA] 1003); M. Mezzrow: Boogie Parisien/Clarinet Marmalade (1951, Vogue 5114)

BIBLIOGRAPHY

ChiltonW

H. Panassié: *The Real Jazz* (New York and Toronto, 1942, rev. and enlarged by Panassié 2/1960; Fr. orig. pubd as *La véritable musique de jazz*, Paris, 1945, rev. and enlarged 2/1952)

W. C. Allen: "Trumpet Giants, 2: Lee Collins," *Hot Notes*, ii/2 (1947), 2

E. Keartland: "Lee Collins Discography," *Hot Notes*, ii/2 (1947), 3

G. Beall: "Lee Collins," *BHcF*, no.49 (1955), 7

F. J. Gillis and J. W. Miner, eds.: *Oh, didn't he Ramble: the Life Story of Lee Collins* (Urbana, IL, Chicago, and London, 1974) [incl. discography]

P. Van Vorst: "Eight Years in a Barrelhouse," *MR*, i/11 (1974), 1

C. Hillman: "Lee Collins Plays the Blues," *Fn*, vii/6 (1976), 4

ALAN BARRELL

Collins, Rudy [Rudolph Alexander] (*b* New York, 24 July 1934). Drummer. He first studied trombone, then took up drums and in the early 1950s began playing professionally with such musicians as Hot Lips Page, Cootie Williams, and Johnny Smith at clubs in and around New York. In the late 1950s he provided a steady, discreet accompaniment for artists as disparate as Cecil Taylor and Herbie Mann. He performed and toured with Dizzy Gillespie from 1962 to 1966, playing in both large and small groups. From the late 1960s Collins has performed for Broadway shows and worked as a freelance in New York: his activities have included tours with Ray Bryant, Kenny Burrell, and Woody Herman (1967–8), and performances and recording sessions with Junior Mance (1968) and Randy Weston (1973–4). In 1974–5 he toured North America with Cleo Laine and John Dankworth.

SELECTED RECORDINGS

As sideman: J. J. Johnson: *Jay and Kai at Newport* (1956, Col. CL932); C. Taylor: *Love for Sale* (1959, UA 5046); H. Mann: *At the Village Gate* (1961, Atl. 1380); D. Gillespie: *Dizzy on the French Riviera* (1962, Phi. 600048); *In the Cool World* (1964, Phi. 600138); first issued on *25 Years of Prestige* (1949–70, Prst. 24046), G. Ammons: Night Lights (1970)

BIBLIOGRAPHY

FeatherE; *Feather '60s*; *Feather–Gitler '70s*

D. Gillespie and A. Fraser: *To be, or not . . . to Bop: Memoirs* (Garden City, NY, 1979), 449

SCOTT DeVEAUX

Collins, Shad [Lester Rallingston] (*b* Elizabeth, NJ, 27 June 1910; *d* New York, June 1978). Trumpeter. He grew up in Lockport, New York, and began his career with Charlie Dixon (1928), the pianist Eddie White (1929–30), Chick Webb (1931), Benny Carter (1933), and Tiny Bradshaw (1934). From 1936 he played with Teddy Hill, with whom he toured England and France the following year. He settled in Paris, where he recorded with Dicky Wells, and in 1939 he returned to the USA and joined the orchestra of Count Basie; *You can Depend on me* (1939), which Collins recorded with a small group (comprising Lester Young and a rhythm section that included Basie on piano), offers a good example of his style as a soloist. After working for brief periods in 1940 with Carter and Freddie Moore he played at Kelly's Stable in New York with Young's sextet; the same year he joined Cab Calloway's orchestra as Dizzy Gillespie's replacement, and he continued to work with Calloway at intervals until 1946. During the following years he played with Buster Harding (1948) and in the early 1950s worked with Al Sears and toured with Jimmy Rushing. In the mid-1950s he made recordings with rhythm-and-blues groups that do not show his playing to advantage, but he also made an album with Vic Dickenson in 1954 that represents his work more favorably; he ceased playing full-time in the 1960s. As a soloist Collins had a cutting, fiery tone and a percussive, staccato articulation; when accompanying and playing ballads he generally used a mute and showed great delicacy and subtlety. His lively, rhythmic playing is typical of the swing style of the mid-1930s to the mid-1940s.

SELECTED RECORDINGS

As sideman: T. Hill: San Anton'/King Porter Stomp (1937, Bb 6988); D. Wells: I got rhythm (1937, Swing 27); C. Basie: You can Depend on me (1939, Decca 2631); C. Calloway: I Want to Rock/Tain't No Good (1942, OK 6616); V. Dickenson: *Vic Dickenson Showcase* (1954, Van. 8012–13), incl. Everybody Loves my Baby, A New Kind of Love to me, Old Fashioned Blues, Running Wild

BIBLIOGRAPHY

ChiltonW

R. Horricks: *Count Basie and his Orchestra: its Music and its Musicians* (London and New York, 1957), 162

C. Basie and A. Murray: *Good Morning Blues: the Autobiography of Count Basie* (New York, 1985), 222

KEN RATTENBURY

Colorado Jazz Party [Dick and Maddie Gibson's Annual Jazz Party]. Private jazz festival held annually from 1963. It is organized by Dick Gibson, an investment banker from Denver, who became a full-time jazz promoter in the early 1980s, and who from 1986 has also selected and engaged musicians for 13 other jazz parties throughout the world. The festival takes place over three days in September and has been held successively in Vail (near Leadville), Aspen, and Colorado Springs, and (from 1982) at the Fairmount Hotel in Denver. The festival consists of a series of jam sessions, in which about 60 swing and bop musicians take part; Eddie "Lockjaw" Davis and Teddy Wilson appeared at the festival, as have George Chisholm, Scott Hamilton, Dick Hyman, and Ed Thigpen. Several musicians return to the festival every year. In the 1980s the festival was attended by about 600 guests each year. The Colorado Jazz Party was the first event of its kind to be held annually and has received wide recognition for its original programming. The 1976 festival was the subject of the film *The Great Rocky Mountain Jazz Party* (1977).

BIBLIOGRAPHY

L. Feather: "Solid, Gibson!," *Jazz Express*, no.57 (1984), 10
——: "Dick Gibson's 24th Jazz Party," *Jazz Express*, no.78 (1986), 8

PAUL R. LAIRD

Coltrane [née McLeod], **Alice** [Sagittinanda, Turiya] (*b* Detroit, 27 Aug 1937). Pianist, organist, and harpist, sister of Ernie Farrow. She studied classical music from the age of seven and jazz with Bud Powell, and gained early experience in church groups and in the jazz ensembles of Kenny Burrell, Johnny Griffin, Lucky Thompson, and Yusef Lateef. While touring and recording with Terry Gibbs (1962–3) she met John Coltrane, whom she married around 1965; in 1966 she joined his group as McCoy Tyner's replacement. After Coltrane's death (1967) she led many groups that at various times included the saxophonists Pharoah Sanders, Archie Shepp, Joe Henderson, Frank Lowe, and Carlos Ward, the double bass players Cecil McBee and Jimmy Garrison, and the drummers Rashied Ali, Ben Riley, and Roy Haynes. She moved to California in 1972 and in 1975 founded the Vedantic Center, a retreat for the study of Eastern religions. Although she seldom performed after this time she recorded the album *Transfiguration* with Haynes and Reggie Workman in 1978; she also published a book of inspirational, spiritual texts, *Endless Wisdom*. In 1987 she performed with a quartet that included her sons in a tribute to John Coltrane at the Cathedral of St. John the Divine in New York. Coltrane's piano and harp playing are characterized by rippling, rhythmically free arpeggios. Her organ playing is less flowing and makes greater use of dramatic pauses and trills.

SELECTED RECORDINGS

As leader: *Ptah the El Daoud* (1970, Imp. 9196); *Journey to Satchidananda* (1970, Imp. 9203); *Transfiguration* (1978, WB 3218)
As sideman: T. Gibbs: *Terry Gibbs Plays Jewish Melodies in Jazztime* (1963, Mer. 60812); J. Coltrane: *Concert in Japan* (1966, Imp. 9246); *Live at the Village Vanguard Again* (1966, Imp. 9124)

BIBLIOGRAPHY

P. Rivelli: "Alice Coltrane Interview," *J&P*, vii/9 (1968), 26; repr. in P. Rivelli and R. Levin, eds.: *Black Giants* (New York and Cleveland, 1970/*R*1980 as *Giants of Black Music*), 122
J. E. Berendt: "Alice Coltrane," *JF* [intl edn], no.17 (1972), 54
G. Endress: "Lady Trane," *JP*, xxii/2 (1973), 16
D. Lerner: "Alice Coltrane: Jazz Pianist, Inspirational Organist," *Keyboard*, viii/11 (1982), 22 [incl. discography]

ED HAZELL

Coltrane, John (William) (*b* Hamlet, NC, 23 Sept 1926; *d* New York, 17 July 1967). Tenor and soprano saxophonist, bandleader, and composer. He was, after Charlie Parker, the most revolutionary and widely imitated saxophonist in jazz.

1. Life. 2. Music. 3. Influence.

1. Life. Coltrane grew up in High Point, North Carolina, where he learned to play E♭ alto horn, clarinet, and (at about the age of 15) alto saxophone. After moving to Philadelphia he enrolled at the Ornstein School of Music and the Granoff Studios; service in a navy band in Hawaii (1945–6) interrupted these studies. He played alto saxophone in the bands led by Joe Webb and King Kolax, then changed to the tenor to work with Eddie "Cleanhead" Vinson (1947–8). He performed on either instrument as circumstances demanded while in groups led by Jimmy Heath, Howard McGhee, Dizzy Gillespie (with whom he made his first recording in 1949), Earl Bostic, and lesser-known rhythm-and-blues musicians, but by the time of his membership in Johnny Hodges's septet (1953–4) he was firmly committed to the tenor instrument. He performed infrequently for about a year, then leaped to fame in Miles Davis's quintet with Red Garland, Paul Chambers, and Philly Joe Jones (1955–7). Throughout the 1950s addiction to drugs and then alcoholism disrupted his career. Shortly after leaving Davis, however, he overcame these problems; his album *A Love Supreme* celebrated this victory and the profound religious experience associated with it.

Coltrane next played in Thelonious Monk's quartet (July–December 1957), but owing to contractual conflicts took part in only one early recording session of this legendary group. He rejoined Davis and worked in various quintets and sextets with Cannonball Adderley, Bill Evans (ii), Chambers, Jones, and others (1958–60). While with Davis he discovered the soprano saxophone, purchasing his own instrument in February 1960.

Having led numerous studio sessions, established a repu-

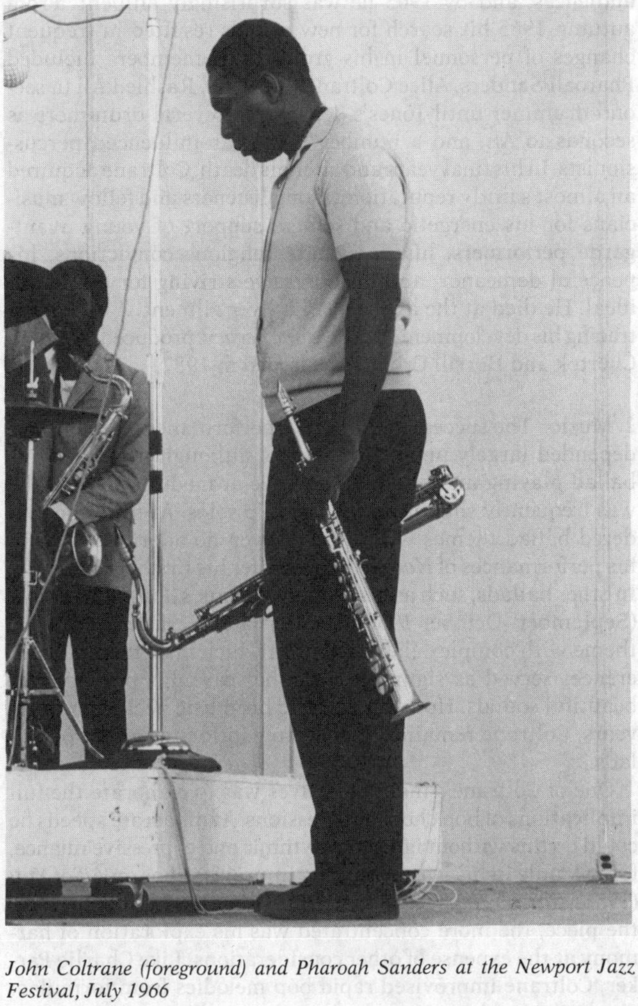

John Coltrane (foreground) and Pharoah Sanders at the Newport Jazz Festival, July 1966

Ex.1 Coltrane's improvisation (tenor saxophone) on *Ah-leu-cha*, from M. Davis: *Miles and Monk at Newport* (1958, Col. CL2178); transcr. A. White and B. Kernfeld

tation as a composer, and emerged as the leading tenor saxophonist in jazz, Coltrane was now prepared to form his own group; it made its début at New York's Jazz Gallery in early May 1960. After briefly trying Steve Kuhn, Pete La Roca, and Billy Higgins, Coltrane hired two musicians who became longstanding members of his quartet, McCoy Tyner (1960–65) and Elvin Jones (1960–66); the third, Jimmy Garrison, joined in 1961. With these sidemen the quartet soon acquired an international following. At times Art Davis added a second double bass to the group; Eric Dolphy also served as an intermittent fifth member on bass clarinet, alto saxophone, and flute from 1961 to 1963, and Roy Haynes was the most regular replacement for Elvin Jones during the latter's incarceration for drug addiction in 1963.

Coltrane turned to increasingly radical musical styles in the mid-1960s. These controversial experiments attracted large audiences, and by 1965 he was surprisingly affluent. From autumn 1965 his search for new sounds resulted in frequent changes of personnel in his group. New members included Pharoah Sanders, Alice Coltrane (his wife), Rashied Ali (a second drummer until Jones's departure), several drummers as seconds to Ali, and a number of African-influenced percussionists. In his final years and after his death, Coltrane acquired an almost saintly reputation among listeners and fellow musicians for his energetic and selfless support of young avant-garde performers, his passionate religious convictions, his peaceful demeanor, and his obsessive striving for a musical ideal. He died at the age of 40 of a liver ailment. A videotape tracing his development, *The Coltrane Legacy*, produced by David Chertok and Burrill Crohn, was issued in 1987.

2. Music. The success of Coltrane's performances in the 1950s depended largely upon their tempo: although mature in his ballad playing and often imaginative at medium tempos, he was frequently shallow in his fast bop solos. At times he rendered ballad themes with little or even no adornment, as in his performances of *Naima* (named after his first wife) in 1959. In other ballads, such as his version of Monk's *'Round Midnight* (September–October 1956), he alternated paraphrases of the theme with complex elaborations in which brief thematic references served as signposts. In either case, his priority was beautiful sounds. However esoteric his music became in later years, Coltrane remained a great romantic interpreter of ballads.

One of Coltrane's main objectives was to elaborate the full implications of bop chord progressions. At moderate speeds he could do this without ignoring rhythmic and expressive nuance, for example in his widely varying improvisations on *All of You* (1956), *Blues by Five* (1956), and *Blue Train* (1957). But the faster the piece, the more concentrated was his exploration of harmony at the expense of other considerations. Like Charlie Parker, Coltrane improvised rapid bop melodies from formulae: but unlike Parker he drew on a small collection of formulae, failed to juxtapose these in new combinations, and tended to place them in predictable relationships to the beat. Early solos on *Salt Peanuts* and *Tune-up* (both 1956) exemplify this practice, which culminated in a blistering performance in his composition *Giant Steps* (1959). This solo was impressive because of Coltrane's huge driving tone, his astonishing technical facility, and his complex harmonic ideas; but rigid, repetitious eighth-note formulae lay just beneath the surface (*see also* Harmony (i), §2, and Table 4).

Whereas Coltrane was far more important as an improviser than as a composer, he did write several pieces that have become jazz standards (including *Moment's Notice*, *Giant Steps*, *Naima*, *Equinox*, and *Impressions*), and from May 1959 to his death the vast majority of his recordings as a leader were of his own compositions.

By seeking to escape harmonic clichés in pieces such as *Giant Steps*, he had inadvertently created a confining, one-dimensional improvisatory style. In the late 1950s he pursued two alternative directions. First, his expanding technique enabled him to play what the critic Ira Gitler called "sheets of sound," as exemplified in his very fast 16th-note runs during a live performance of *Ah-leu-cha* recorded at Newport in 1958 (ex.1). Such flurries gradually replaced the clarity of his approach in *Giant Steps* and disguised his excessive reiteration of formulae. Second, when Miles Davis discarded bop chord progressions in favor of relaxed ostinatos, Coltrane abandoned formulae in favor of true motivic development. Davis's *So What* on the album *Kind of Blue* (1959) was the first recording on which Coltrane systematically varied motifs throughout a solo (ex.2). This process became increasingly prominent in his most famous recordings, including *My Favorite Things* and *Equinox* (1960), *Teo* and *Impressions* (1961), *Crescent* (1964), and the album *A Love Supreme* (1964). Initially he developed motifs only in performances when neither tempo nor harmonic rhythm was fast.

Ex.2 Motivic relationships in Coltrane's improvisation (tenor saxophone) on *So What*, from M. Davis: *Kind of Blue* (1959, Col. CL1355); transcr. A. White and B. Kernfeld

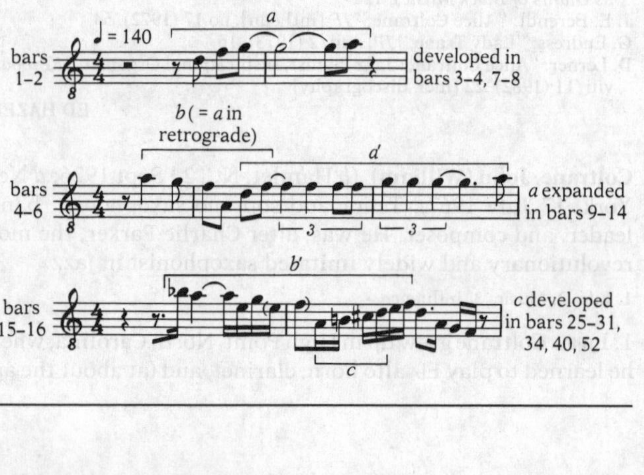

Eventually he was also able to avoid repetitive responses at high speeds; for example, large portions of *Impressions*, played at a metronome marking of 310, gained coherence by his continuous, inventive manipulation of distinctive eighth-note formulae. (These famous recordings of the early 1960s are often referred to as being "modal," or as exemplifying "modal improvisation" or "modal playing." The concept has less to do with Coltrane himself – whose complex, chromatic lines usually defy modal analysis – than with Tyner's accompaniments, some of which suggest modal scales; for example, in *My Favorite Things* the ostinato based on minor 9th chords on E and F♯ gives rise to a dorian scale starting from E: E–F♯–G–A–B–C♯–D (*see also* MODAL JAZZ and FORMS, §5).)

While consolidating his new manner of organizing melody, Coltrane embarked on a quest for new sonorities. Following Lester Young, Illinois Jacquet, and others, he used "false" fingerings to extend the tone-color and upper range of his instrument. The same quest led him to rescue from oblivion the soprano saxophone, which soon rivaled the tenor as his principal instrument. On both he learned to leap between extreme registers at seemingly impossible speed, and thus to convey the impression of an overlapping dialogue between two voices, as in the latter part of *My Favorite Things* (1963). Radical timbres akin to human cries dominate his late improvisations as his concern with tonality and pitch waned.

At this time Coltrane also developed a type of meditative, slow, rubato melody based upon black gospel preaching. In *Alabama* (1963), he interpreted a speech by Martin Luther King, Jr.; later, in *Psalm* from *A Love Supreme* (1964), he instrumentally "narrated" his own prayer (ex.3, with underlaid text from the album jacket). This technique also appears without obvious reference to a written source in several late recordings, including *Reverend King* (1966) and the album *Expression* (1967).

Ex.3 Opening of *Psalm*, on *A Love Supreme* (1964, Imp. 77); transcr. L. Porter

♩ = c60–70
tenor saxophone
[A Love Su-preme. I will do all I can
to be wor-thy of thee O Lord.]

Coltrane's expansion of individual sonority went hand-in-hand with an expansion of group texture. In the quartet, Tyner often kept time and established tonal centers with chordal oscillations, thus freeing Jones to create swirling masses of drum and cymbal accents. Jones (later, Ali) and Coltrane frequently engaged in extended coloristic duets. The addition of Davis's double bass, Dolphy's bird- and speech-like sounds on wind instruments, and Sanders's screaming tenor saxophone intensified the group's textures. Coltrane moved to the forefront of experimental jazz with *Ascension* (1965), which presented a sustained density of dissonant sound previously unknown to jazz. Two alto and three tenor saxophonists, two trumpeters, a pianist, two double bass players, and a drummer played through a scarcely tonal, loosely structured scheme; their collective improvisation and many of their "solos" stressed timbral and registral extremes rather than conventional melody. Thereafter, Coltrane's ensembles concentrated on maintaining extraordinary levels of intensity by filling a vast spectrum of frequencies, tone-colors, and (when he utilized extra percussionists) accents. The albums *Om* and *Meditations* (1965), the late versions of *My Favorite Things* and *Naima* (1966), and many other recordings exemplify this final stage of his musical evolution.

3. INFLUENCE. Coltrane's impact on his contemporaries was enormous. Countless players imitated his sound on the tenor saxophone, though few could approach his technical mastery. He alone was responsible for recognizing and demonstrating the potential of the soprano saxophone as a modern jazz instrument; by the 1970s most alto and tenor saxophonists doubled on this once archaic instrument (*see* SAXOPHONE, esp. §§2 and 4). Finally, by selling hundreds of thousands of albums in his final years, he achieved the rare feat of establishing avant-garde jazz, temporarily, as a popular music. A collection of transcriptions of Coltrane's solos, *The Works of John Coltrane*, was published in 1973 by Andrew White.

See also BLUES, §12; HARMONY (i), §1(v), and ex.16; IMPROVISATION, §§3, 4(iv), and ex.3; and JAZZ (i), §VI, 2, 4; for further illustrations *see* PARKER, CHARLIE, fig.2, and SAXOPHONE, fig.3.

SELECTED RECORDINGS

* – composed by Coltrane

AS LEADER

The First Trane (1957, Prst. 7105); *Lush Life* (1957–8, Prst. 7188); *Traneing In* (1957, Prst. 7123); *Blue Train* (1957, BN 1577), incl. *Blue Train, *Moment's Notice; *The Last Trane* (1957–8, Prst. 7378); *Soultrane* (1958, Prst. 7142); *Trane's Reign* (1958, Prst. 7213); *Black Pearls* (1958, Prst. 7316); *The Believer* (1958, Prst. 7292); *Standard Coltrane* (1958, Prst. 7243); *Stardust* (1958, Prst. 7268); *Bahia* (1958, Prst. 7353); *Giant Steps* (1959, Atl. 1311), incl. *Giant Steps, *Mr. P. C., *Naima; *Coltrane Jazz* (1959–60, Atl. 1354); *My Favorite Things* (1960, Atl. 1361)

Coltrane Plays the Blues (1960, Atl. 1382); *Coltrane's Sound* (1960, Atl. 1419), incl. *Equinox; *Africa/Brass* (1961, Imp. 6); *Olé Coltrane* (1961, Atl. 1373); *Live at the Village Vanguard* (1961, Imp. 10), incl. *Chasin' the Trane; *Impressions* (1961–3, Imp. 42), incl. *Impressions; *Coltrane* (1962, Imp. 21); *Selflessness* (1963, 1965, Imp. 9161), incl. My Favorite Things; *Live at Birdland* (1963, Imp. 50), incl. *Alabama; *Crescent* (1964, Imp. 66); **A Love Supreme* (1964, Imp. 77), incl. *Psalm; *Transition* (1965, Imp. 9195); *Ascension* (1965 Imp. 95); *Sun Ship* (1965, Imp. 9211); *Live in Seattle* (1965, Imp. 9202-2)

Om (1965, Imp. 9140); *Kulu se Mama* (1965, Imp. 9106); **Meditations* (1965, Imp. 9110); *Cosmic Music* (1966, Coast Recorders 4950), incl. *Reverend King; *Live at the Village Vanguard Again* (1966, Imp. 9124), incl. My Favorite Things, *Naima; *Interstellar Space* (1967, Imp. 9277); *Expression* (1967, Imp. 9120), incl. *Expression, *Offering

AS SIDEMAN

M. Davis: *Miles* (1955, Prst. 7014); *'Round about Midnight* (1955–6, Col. CL949), incl. All of You, 'Round Midnight; *Relaxin'* (1956, Prst. 7129); *Steamin'* (1956, Prst. 7200), incl. Salt Peanuts; *Workin'* (1956, Prst. 7166); S. Rollins: *Tenor Madness* (1956, Prst. 7047); M. Davis: *Cookin'* (1956, Prst. 7094), incl. Blues by Five, Tune up; 'Round Midnight (1956, Prst. 45–413); T. Monk: *Thelonious Monk with John Coltrane* (1957, Jlnd 946); R. Garland: *All Mornin' Long* (1957, Prst. 7130); *Soul Junction* (1957, Prst. 7181); M. Davis: *Milestones* (1958, Col. CL1193); *Jazz Track* (1958, Col. CL1268); *Miles and Monk at Newport* (1958, Col. CL2178), incl. Ah-leu-cha; *Jazz at the Plaza* (1958, Col. C32470); C. Adderley: *Cannonball Adderley Quintet in Chicago* (1959, Mer. 20449); M. Davis: *Kind of Blue* (1959, Col. CL1355), incl. So What; *Someday my Prince will Come* (1961, Col. CS8456), incl. Teo; D. Ellington: *Duke Ellington and John Coltrane* (1962, Imp. 30)

BIBLIOGRAPHY

I. Gitler: "Trane on the Track," *DB*, xxv/21 (1958), 16
A. Blume: "An Interview with John Coltrane," *JR*, ii/1 (1959), 25
Z. Carno: "The Style of John Coltrane," *JR*, ii (1959), no.9, p.17; no.10, p.13
J. Coltrane: "Coltrane on Coltrane," *DB*, xxvii/20 (1960), 26
J. Goldberg: *Jazz Masters of the Fifties* (New York and London, 1965/R1980)
A. Spellman: "Trane: A Wild Night at the Gate," *DB*, xxxii/26 (1965), 15
J. Cooke: "Late Trane," *JM*, no.179 (1970), 2
F. Kofsky: "Revolution, Coltrane, and the Avant-Garde," *Black Giants*, ed. P. Rivelli and R. Levin (New York and Cleveland, 1970/R1980 as *Giants of Black Music*) [colln of previously pubd articles]
M. Williams: *The Jazz Tradition* (New York, 1970, rev. 2/1983)
B. McRae: "John Coltrane: the Impulse Years," *JJ*, xxiv/7 (1971), 2
E. Jost: *Free Jazz* (Graz, Austria, 1974)
J. C. Thomas: *Chasin' the Trane: the Music and Mystique of John Coltrane* (Garden City, NY, 1975)
C. O. Simpkins: *Coltrane* (New York, 1975)
D. Wild: *The Recordings of John Coltrane* (Ann Arbor, MI, 1979)

D. Baker: *The Jazz Style of John Coltrane: a Musical and Historical Perspective* (Lebanon, IN, 1980) [incl. transcrs.]
B. Kernfeld: *Adderley, Coltrane, and Davis at the Twilight of Bebop: the Search for Melodic Coherence (1958–59)* (diss., Cornell U., 1981)
G. Filtgen and M. Ausserbauer: *John Coltrane: sein Leben, seine Musik, seine Schallplatten* (Gauting-Buchendorf, Germany, 1983)
B. Kernfeld: "Two Coltranes," *ARJS*, ii (1983), 7–66
L. Porter: *John Coltrane's Music of 1960 through 1967: Jazz Improvisation as Composition* (diss., Brandeis U., 1983)
L. Porter: "John Coltrane's *A Love Supreme*: Jazz Improvisation as Composition," *Journal of the American Musicological Society*, xxxviii (1985), 593
B. Priestley: *John Coltrane* (London, 1987) [incl. discography]

BARRY KERNFELD

Columbia. Record company and label. The company's activities began before the recorded history of jazz; the label's first items of jazz interest were made by the Original Dixieland Jazz Band in 1917, but were not issued until after the success of the group's discs on Victor. Later sessions, supervised by the drummer Harry A. Yerkes, produced important items by two black groups, Handy's Orchestra of Memphis (1917), and Wilbur Sweatman's Original Jazz Band (1918–20), as well as material by the Louisiana Five (1919) and many hot dance recordings. Several of these were led by Yerkes, who was also responsible for signing Ted Lewis to Columbia.

Following the example set by Okeh, Columbia began issuing race records in the early 1920s, putting out items by Bessie Smith, Clara Smith, and Johnny Dunn's Original Jazz Hounds; these were issued as part of the general numerical sequence. At the end of 1922 the company was placed in receivership, and the British branch, which was established before 1917 and managed by Louis Sterling, was sold to Sterling's Constructive Finance Co., Ltd. Financial problems notwithstanding, in November 1923 American Columbia launched its first race series, the 13000Ds; this ran to only eight issues, among them four by Bessie Smith and one by King Oliver's band. In December that year the series was restarted, out of deference to triskaidekaphobics, at 14000D; it is best remembered for its vaudeville blues recordings by Bessie Smith, Clara Smith, Ethel Waters, and others, a long series of discs by Clarence Williams, and important field recordings made in New Orleans of Oscar Celestin and Sam Morgan. Columbia continued to issue jazz in the general series; this included material by Paul Whiteman, and later by Jack Teagarden and Red Norvo, as well as a number of recordings made in Atlanta in the mid-1920s which form one of the few extensive documentations in existence of the work of white territory bands.

In March 1925 the Constructive Finance Co.'s subsidiary, the British-based Columbia Graphophone Co., bought the American parent company (which from February 1924 had been called the Columbia Phonograph Co.). In October the same year the whole group was reorganized, still under British ownership, as Columbia International, Ltd., which controlled both the British and American branches of Columbia, and the German group of companies formerly owned by Carl Lindström; throughout this period the company maintained a substantial catalogue of American jazz. Columbia International opened an Australian subsidiary in mid-1926, and in November that year it acquired Okeh; however, as the latter was maintained as a separate operation this barely affected the running of the Columbia label in the USA. In December 1928 Columbia International purchased Pathé Frères Pathéphone and Pathé Orient (though not Pathé USA), and in March 1931 it merged with the Gramophone Co., Ltd., to form EMI; the new company operated subsidiaries all over the world.

Because American Victor held shares in the Gramophone Co. it in effect became one of the owners of American Columbia, which had hitherto been one of its main competitors. Fears of anti-trust action in the USA against what would have amounted to a monopoly led EMI to transfer American Columbia and its subsidiaries to trustees, who sold it in May 1931 to Grigsby–Grunow, the manufacturers of Majestic Radios. The 14000D series was terminated at 14680D (by the Washboard Rhythm Kings) in April 1933. After Grigsby–Grunow went bankrupt in November 1933 the Columbia and Okeh labels were bought by ARC–BRC (*see* AMERICAN RECORD COMPANY and BRUNSWICK).

ARC discontinued the Columbia label in the USA, but it was maintained elsewhere by EMI; it became, and remains, one of the latter's most important labels. Jazz recordings were issued on Columbia in many countries; among the more unusual items by American expatriates are those by Midge Williams for Japanese Columbia (1934) and the long series by Teddy Weatherford for Indian Columbia (1941–44). The British company operated a swing series for several years. After 1934 American repertory from all the labels owned by ARC–BRC was made available to EMI for issue in countries other than the USA. From the 1950s, however, EMI's Columbia labels have been used mainly for the issue of material recorded by indigenous musicians. For example, British Columbia's Lansdowne series, under the direction of Denis Preston, was important in recording much material of the trad era of the 1960s.

Label for "Seven Come Eleven," recorded by Benny Goodman's sextet for Columbia (1939)

In February 1938 the Columbia Broadcasting System (CBS), a corporate derivative of Independent Broadcasters Inc. (which had itself been a subsidiary of the Columbia Phonograph Co.), bought ARC–BRC; the new American parent company revived the label Columbia in the USA the following year, and discontinued Brunswick in April 1940. Under the direction of Edward Wallerstein, who had previously been an executive with RCA, the label Columbia soon regained its importance in the USA. It was one of the first to be used for the reissue of early jazz; projects in this area were supervised first by George Avakian, later by John Hammond. Among the musicians who made new recordings for the label at this time were Benny Goodman (1939–46; see illustration), Count Basie (1942–6), Woody Herman (1945–7), and Duke Ellington (1945–51). In October 1945 the organization began to attend once more to what had formerly been the race market with a new series, the 30000s, which lasted into the 1950s.

In spring 1948 American Columbia issued the first LPs; EMI's slowness to do the same in other countries was a major factor in the Columbia Broadcasting System's decision to terminate its affiliation with the non-American Columbia labels in the mid-1950s. Thereafter recordings made by Columbia in the USA were sold in Europe and elsewhere through subsidiaries of the Dutch company Philips, and later through autonomous subsidiaries established within the Philips group. American Columbia became, and continues to be, one of the most important sources of jazz in the world; those who have recorded for the organization include Dave Brubeck (1953–68), Louis Armstrong (1955–6), Miles Davis (1955–86), Duke Ellington (1956–62), Charles Mingus (1959), Thelonious Monk (1962–8), the Mahavishnu Orchestra (1971–5, 1984), Weather Report (from 1971), Herbie Hancock (from 1972), Wynton Marsalis (from 1981), and Branford Marsalis (from 1983).

Beginning in 1964 the American company established subsidiaries in various European countries, both to issue material available in the USA on Columbia, and for reissue schemes; a particularly important example of the latter was the French series "Aimez-vous le jazz" of the 1970s, which was also issued in Italy as the series "Vi piace il jazz." All these discs bear the label CBS, as in most non-American territories the Columbia trademark remains the property of EMI (main exceptions are Japan, South America, and Spain).

BIBLIOGRAPHY

G. Avakian: *Jazz from Columbia: a Complete Jazz Catalog* (New York, 1956) [listeners' guide]
O. Read and W. L. Welch: *From Tin Foil to Stereo: Evolution of the Phonograph* (Indianapolis, 1959)
R. M. W. Dixon: "Columbia 30000 Series," *Matrix*, nos.35–6 (1961), 3; no.45 (1963), 9 [addns and corrections]
J. Godrich and R. M. W. Dixon: *Blues & Gospel Records, 1902–1942* (Hatch End, nr London, 1964, rev. 2/1969, rev. and enlarged 3/1982 as R. M. W. Dixon and J. Godrich: *Blues & Gospel Records, 1902–1943*), 18, 22
"Columbia 30000," *Blues Research*, no.14 (n.d. [?1965]), 2
D. Mahony: *The Columbia 13/14000-D Series: a Numerical Listing* (Stanhope, NJ, 1961, rev. 2/1966 with addns)
P. Burgis: "Discs from Down Under," *Sv*, no.11 (1967), 4
R. M. W. Dixon and J. Godrich: *Recording the Blues* (London, 1970)
R. D. Kinkle: "Columbia Numerical Listing," *The Complete Encyclopedia of Popular Music and Jazz, 1900–1950* (New Rochelle, NY, and Westport, CT, 1974), 2135
B. Rust: *The American Record Label Book* (New Rochelle, NY, 1978), 71
F. Andrews: *Columbia 10" Records 1904–30* (London, 1985) [pubn of City of London Phonograph and Gramophone Society]
P. Pelletier: "The Columbia and Parlophone Labels," *Record Information*, no.5 (1985), 6
[P. Pelletier]: *Complete British Directory of Popular 78/45 r.p.m. Singles, 1950–1980*, i: *Columbia, Decca, HMV* (London, 1986) [Record Information Services pubn]

Columbus, Chris(topher) [Morris, Joe; Morris, Joseph Christopher Columbus] (*b* Greenville, NC, 17 June 1902). Drummer and bandleader, father of Sonny Payne. He was active as a leader from the 1930s into the 1950s and his band was resident for a time at the Savoy Ballroom, New York. He played regularly with Louis Jordan's group (1946–52) and in the late 1950s and early 1960s worked mainly in Wild Bill Davis's trio; he then accompanied the singer Damita Jo and briefly worked with Duke Ellington (1967). In the 1970s Columbus again led his own band and toured Europe with Davis (1972); he recorded in France with Davis, Al Grey, and Floyd Smith (all 1972) and Milt Buckner (1973). His playing may be heard to advantage on the anthology *Wild Bill Davis at Birdland* (1951–4, Epic 3118), particularly on the track *Jumpin' at the Woodside* (1954, previously unissued). (M. Jones: "Discovering Columbus," *MM* (3 June 1972), 22)

based on *ChiltonW*

Columby, Bobby (*b* New York, 20 Dec 1944). Drummer. He was a founding member in 1968 of Blood, Sweat and Tears, with which he remained until 1976. His sophisticated jazz-rock drumming may be heard to advantage on the album *Blood, Sweat and Tears* (1968, Col. CS9720).

Colyer, Ken(neth) [the Guv'nor] (*b* Great Yarmouth, England, 18 April 1928; *d* South of France, 8 March 1988). English cornetist, trumpeter, and guitarist. A self-taught musician, in 1949 he was a founding member of the Crane River Jazz Band, which also included Monty Sunshine, John R. T. Davies, and later the pianist Pat Hawes; it made several recordings before disbanding in 1953. Colyer also worked with the Christie Brothers' Stompers (1951). While he was in the merchant navy he visited New Orleans (1952–3), where he played with George Lewis (i), among others, and recorded as the leader of a band that included Emile Barnes and the double bass player Albert Glenny (1953). In 1953 he returned to England and led the Jazzmen, which included Chris Barber and Sunshine (who had organized the band). When Barber assumed leadership of the Jazzmen in 1954 Colyer continued to lead his own bands, including a skiffle group, with which he sang and played guitar. Among his sidemen were Acker Bilk and Diz Disley. In the mid-1950s he led his most influential band, which included the clarinetist Ian Wheeler, the trombonist Mac Duncan, and the pianist Ray Foxley. It was the leading British revivalist band of the decade, and, although it did not achieve the popularity of Barber's, it was widely imitated; its style was based on the bands of George Lewis (i) and Bunk Johnson, but it developed its own distinctive sound through Colyer's sonorous, melodic lead. Colyer continued to lead his band during the 1960s and 1970s (though he was absent from time to time, owing to ill-health), with Sammy Rimington and, later, the pianist Ray Smith among his sidemen. He appeared regularly at his own club, Studio 51, in London and played on the soundtrack of the film *West 11* (1963), which was partly set there. During the 1960s he also briefly ran his own record company, KC Records. He performed in the early 1980s with his own All Star Jazzmen and in 1986–7 toured as a soloist with Max Collie's *New Orleans Mardi Gras* show.

Oral history material in *LNT*.

SELECTED RECORDINGS

Ken Colyer in New Orleans (1953, Vogue LDE 161); *New Orleans to London* (1953, Decca LF1152), incl. Goin' Home; *Club Session with Colyer* (1956, Decca LK4178); They All Played Ragtime (1958, Decca DFE6466) [EP]

BIBLIOGRAPHY

FeatherE; *Feather–Gitler '70s*
R. Flohil: "Pilgrim's Progress: the Story of Ken Colyer," *Music Mirror*, iii/7 (1956), 10
J. Reddihough: "Ken Colyer's Jazzmen," *JJ*, ix/7 (1956), 5
I. Berg, I. Yeomans, and N. Brittan: *Trad: an A to Z Who's Who of the British Traditional Jazz Scene* (London and elsewhere, 1962)
J. Cook: "Ken Colyer Today," *Sv*, no.26 (1969), 71
J. Guy: "Ken Colyer," *JJ*, xxiv/10 (1971), 23
J. Norris and B. Smith: "The Ken Colyer Interview," *Coda*, no.140 (1975), 2
T. Bethell: "Bunk-um!," *JJ*, xxix/3 (1976), 4
G. Bielderman: *Ken Colyer Discography, Incorporating the Crane River Jazz Band* (Zwolle, Netherlands, 1983)
J. Asman: Liner notes, *Ken Colyer's Jazzmen: the Decca Years*, ii (Lake 5004, 1986)
D. Fairweather: "Colyer, Ken," in I. Carr, D. Fairweather, and B. Priestley: *Jazz: the Essential Companion* (London, 1987)

NEVIL SKRIMSHIRE

Combe, Stuff [Etienne Stephen Jean Gustave] (*b* Berne, 12 March 1924). Swiss drummer. He recorded with a swing group led by Philippe Brun (1944), then joined a group led by Hazy Osterwald (1945), with which he recorded in 1946. He recorded with Eddie Brunner (1947) and Ernst Höllerhagen (1947–8), performed and recorded with Kurt Edelhagen (1957–65), and accompanied such swing and bop musicians as Buck Clayton, Benny Carter, Stan Getz, Kenny Clarke, and Oscar Pettiford. From 1967 he played with the jazz orchestra of Radio suisse romande. In the 1970s he made recordings as the leader of a quintet that included Benny Bailey and Francy Boland (*Stuff Combe Five with Percussion*, 1973, M Records 10205) and with the Swiss Dixieland group the Tremble Kids (1976). (*ReclamsJ*)

Combelle, Alix (*b* Paris, 15 June 1912; *d* Mantes, France, 27 Feb 1978). French clarinetist and tenor saxophonist. His father, François, was a classical saxophonist. He began his career as a drummer (1928–31), then played with Gregor (1932–3), Arthur Briggs (1934), and Coleman Hawkins (1935, 1937). With the Quintette du Hot Club de France he recorded as a leader (1935) and as a sideman (1940); he also led sessions in which his sidemen included Bill Coleman (1937) and Django Reinhardt (1940). He performed with Benny Carter (1938), Tommy Benford, Reinhardt, Philippe Brun (1937–8), Coleman, Ray Ventura (1938), and Freddy Johnson (1939), and led the group Jazz de Paris (1940–45) and various big bands (to the mid-1950s). He played again with Coleman (1949) and with Buck Clayton (1949–65), Lionel Hampton (1953), and Jonah Jones (1954). From 1963 he owned a nightclub. Combelle made many recordings, including *Avalon* (1937, Swing 24). He was the father of the drummer Philippe Combelle.

BIBLIOGRAPHY

P. Fouad and H. Panassié: "Alix Combelle," *Jh*, 1st ser., no.3 (1937), 8
B. Vian: "Alix Combelle," *Jh*, no.8 (1946), 4
J. Pescheux: "Alix Combelle et son orchestre," *BHcF*, no.79 (1958), 9
M. Perrin: "Alix Combelle (1912–1978)," *BHcF*, no.262 (1978), 6
R. Lobligeois: "Alix Combelle," *BHcF*, no.269 (1979), 3

MICHEL LAPLACE

Combo. A term, derived from the word "combination," used of a group of musicians and applied principally to small ensembles.

Comfort, Joe [Joseph George] (*b* Alcorn, MS, 18 July 1917). Double bass player. He first studied trombone with his father, and played other brass instruments in the army; he taught himself to play double bass. He recorded with Eddie Beal (1945) and played with Lionel Hampton (1946–7), Nat "King" Cole (1948–51), with whom he toured Europe in 1950, and Oscar Moore (1952). Among the numerous leaders with whom he recorded were Hampton, Cole, Harry "Sweets" Edison (1953, 1964), Moore (1953–4, 1965), Buddy Rich (1954), Red Norvo (1956), Buddy Collette (1956, 1958–60), Irving Ashby (*c*1957, 1976), Benny Carter (*c*1958), Stan Kenton (1961), and Earl Hines (1963). A good example of his playing may be heard on the album *Mood for Max* (1956, Motif 502), which he recorded with the drummer Max Albright.

BIBLIOGRAPHY

FeatherE
R. Gordon: *Jazz West Coast: the Los Angeles Jazz Scene of the 1950s* (London and New York, 1986), 71

Commodore. Record company and label. The label was established in 1938 by Milt Gabler, who operated the enterprise from his Commodore Music Shop in New York; at first its recordings were produced and manufactured by the American Record Company. Throughout the label's existence its catalogue contained much Chicago jazz, but recordings in swing styles also figured prominently. Among these were items by the Kansas City Five and Six, Coleman Hawkins, Hot Lips Page, and Edmond Hall, and a series by Billie Holiday that included the version of *Strange Fruit* that became famous. The label was also used to reissue some of Jelly Roll Morton's last recordings for General, and the company was one of the first to release 12-inch 78 r.p.m. discs. Although intensive activity ceased in the 1940s (Gabler joined the artists and repertory department at Decca) the label remained operational intermittently into the following decade.

Material from Commodore's back catalogue was reissued under a number of important schemes, including a series of ten-inch LPs (using the original label name), and items put out on Mainstream in the USA (1960s), and on London in the UK and Japan (1970s). After Gabler retired from Decca in the late 1970s he revived the label, issuing a series of LPs that contained much previously unreleased material. These were marketed by Columbia in the USA, and by Telefunken in Germany; the German Commodore series has continued into the late 1980s. In 1987 the American company Mosaic announced its intention to reissue the Commodore catalogue in its entirety.

BIBLIOGRAPHY

G. Millstein: "For Kicks," *New Yorker*, xxii (9 March 1946), 40; xxii (16 March 1946), 40; repr. as "The Commodore Shop and Milt Gabler," in *Eddie Condon's Treasury of Jazz*, ed. E. Condon and R. Gehman (New York, 1956/*R*1975), 98
F. Dutton: "Jazz Information, 211: Commodore 10-in 78 r.p.m. Series," *JJ*, xiii (1960), no.1, p.24; no.2, p.19; no.3, p.28; no.4, p.22; no.6, p.37; no.9, p.38; no.10, p.36; xiv/4 (1961), 25; xv/10 (1962), 37
——: "Jazz Information, 311: Commodore "Starmaker" Series," *JJ*, xv/11 (1962), 34; xvii/8 (1964), 23
A. Shaw: "Tape 18: Milt Gabler," *The Street that Never Slept: New York's Fabled 52nd Street* (New York, 1971/*R*1977 as *52nd Street: the Street of Jazz*)
B. Rust: *The American Record Label Book* (New Rochelle, NY, 1978), 85
G. Gold: "A Jazz Label Complete," *New York Times* (6 Dec 1987), 32

Comp. To provide a chordal accompaniment for a soloist; the word derives from "accompany" (or perhaps "complement"). Pianists, in particular, are said to comp when they improvise a rhythmically varied but essentially nonmelodic chordal backing.

ROBERT WITMER

Company. Ensemble formed in England in 1976 by Derek Bailey. Its personnel has fluctuated constantly, and by the mid-1980s more than 70 musicians had played with it at various times. At first it included only musicians with a background in jazz, among them Anthony Braxton, Steve Lacy, and Evan Parker. By 1980, however, improvising players with experience of folk and rock music, including the guitarist Fred Frith and the electric bass guitarist Bill Laswell, were working with the group. Later, in 1982, non-improvising musicians also became involved, and the ensemble began to incorporate elements of theater and dance into its performances. Company has played throughout Europe, and in North America and Japan, and may be heard to advantage on the album *Epiphany/Epiphanies* (1982, Incus 46–7). In 1977 the ensemble held the first of its Company Weeks, offering a week of improvised music at a single venue, with different guest musicians every night. From that time there have been several similar events; in 1987 the Company Week included a performance by Lee Konitz. (R. Bergerone:

Company, 1976–1983 (Radio Broadcasts, Records, Concerts), Sierre, Switzerland, 1983 [discography])

SIMON ADAMS

Compère, René (*b* Brussels, 28 Dec 1906; *d* Brussels, 24 April 1969). Belgian trumpeter. He first played in Brussels with the White Diamonds led by the drummer Billy Smith (1923), then worked throughout Belgium with his own band, the New Royal Dance Orchestra. In 1929 he recorded as the leader of a trio which included Fernand Coppieters. After touring in several countries with the singer Josephine Baker, in 1936 he became a member of a band aboard the SS *Normandie*, and made 18 voyages to New York. The following year he performed with Django Reinhardt at the Paris Exhibition and thereafter played for the French bandleader Joe Bouillon and worked mainly in Brussels in a group led by Joe Heyne. Compère also recorded with Eddie Tower (1942) and as the leader of a sextet (1954).

ROBERT PERNET

Conaway, Sterling (Bruce) (*b* Washington, 1898). Banjoist and mandolin player. He played with Duke Ellington in Washington (*c*1920), before moving to Chicago, where he played with Carroll Dickerson (*c*1923). During the late 1920s and the 1930s he worked mainly in Europe, with Noble Sissle (1931), Freddy Johnson (1933–4), with whom he also recorded, Freddy Taylor (1935), and Leon Abbey (1937), among others; he also led his own band. A good example of Conaway's secure and rhythmic playing can be heard on *My Baby's Gone* (1933, Bruns. 500277), a recording made by Johnson's band. His brother Lincoln (M.) Conaway (*d* Oct 1968) was a banjoist and guitarist.

based on *ChiltonW*

Concord. Record company and label. The company was founded in Concord, California, in 1973, by Carl Jefferson. From the mid-1970s, with Norman Granz's Pablo labels, it became the principal outlet for recordings made by older swing and bop musicians, as well as those by young players working in more traditional styles, such as Scott Hamilton and Warren Vaché. Linked with Jefferson's Concord Jazz Festival, the company has issued recordings of musicians performing at that event, mainly with their own groups, but occasionally in larger ensembles under such names as the Concord All Stars, Concord Jazz All Stars, and Concord Super Band. (M. Segrell: "Once More, Jazz is Big Business," *RS*, no.282 (1978–9), 78)

Condon, Eddie [Albert Edwin] (*b* Goodland, IN, 16 Nov 1905; *d* New York, 4 Aug 1973). Banjoist and guitarist. He first played ukulele and later took up banjo (both the G and tenor instruments) and four-string guitar. He served his apprenticeship in dance bands throughout the Midwest and performed in Chicago with members of the Austin High School Gang. From 1927, when he organized the McKenzie–Condon Chicagoans, he promoted and arranged several important recording sessions. He moved to New York in 1929, and continued to record into the 1970s. Among the accomplished instrumentalists who played for him intermittently were Joe Sullivan (1928–9, 1939, 1942), Gene Krupa (1928, 1944), Fats Waller (1940), Jack Teagarden (1928–61), Sid Catlett (1933–49), Max Kaminsky (1933–59), Pee Wee Russell and Bud Freeman (both 1933–64), George Wettling and Bobby Hackett (both 1938–62), Billy Butterfield (1944–58), and Wild Bill Davison (1946–71). Condon toured with Red Nichols (1929), worked in New York and Florida with Red McKenzie and the Mound City Blue Blowers (1930–31, 1933), recorded with the Rhythmakers (1932), and led a band with Joe Marsala (1936–7). From 1937 to 1944 he played frequently at Nick's, during which time he also performed with other bandleaders, notably Hackett, Freeman, Marsala, Brad Gowans, and Miff Mole. In 1945 he founded his own club, which he managed with Pete Pesci, on West 3rd Street in Greenwich Village. He continued his policy of organizing racially integrated bands when he presented one of the earliest jazz programs on television (1942) and promoted a series of concerts at Town Hall and Carnegie Hall (1942–6). From the 1950s he played only infrequently at Condon's (which moved in 1958 to East 56th Street), but made tours of Great Britain (1957) and Japan, Australia, and New Zealand (1964); he also appeared at many jazz festivals in the USA.

Condon earned a reputation as a jazz entrepreneur and media personality, and his music – hot jazz of the 1920s laced with elements of swing – played a prominent role in the traditional-jazz revival after World War II. He was also known for his dry wit, and his three books are a valuable source on dixieland jazz.

For illustration *see* NIGHTCLUBS AND OTHER VENUES, fig.5.

SELECTED RECORDINGS

I'm gonna stomp, Mr. Henry Lee (1929, Vic. 38046); Tennessee Twilight (1933, Bruns. 01690); Home Cooking (1933, Col. 35680); Love is just around the corner (1938, Com. 500); Meet me tonight in dreamland (1938, Com. 505); A good man is hard to find (1940, Com. 1504–5); *Jam Session Coast to Coast* (1953, Col. CL547), incl. Beale Street Blues; *Bixieland* (1955, Col. CL719), incl. Royal Garden Blues

WRITINGS

with T. Sugrue: *We Called it Music: a Generation of Jazz* (New York, 1947/*R*1985)

ed. with R. Gehman: *Eddie Condon's Treasury of Jazz* (New York, 1956/*R*1975)

with H. O'Neal: *The Eddie Condon Scrapbook of Jazz* (New York, 1973)

BIBLIOGRAPHY

E. Anderson, ed.: *Esquire's 1947 Jazz Book: Year Book of the Jazz Scene* (New York, 1947)

J. S. Wilson: "Eddie Condon: Jazz' Great Pitchman," *DB*, xix/7 (1952), 2

G. Frazier: "Eddie Condon," *Jam Session: an Anthology of Jazz*, ed. R. J. Gleason (New York and London, 1958)

D. Morgenstern: "Fond Reminiscence with Eddie Condon," *DB*, xxxii/3 (1965), 25

B. Esposito: "Condon + Green = Rhythm," *JJ*, xxiii/8 (1970), 16

———: "Remembering Eddie Condon," *JJ*, xxvi/10 (1973), 2

M. Jones: "The Father of Chicago Jazz," *MM* (11 Aug 1973), 20

W. H. Kenney III: "He Played Rhythm: Eddie Condon, the Musician," *JJS*, iv/2 (1977), 72

B. White: *The Eddie Condon "Town Hall Broadcasts" 1944–1945: a Discography* (Oakland, CA, 1980)

W. H. Kenney III: "Jazz and the Concert Halls: the Eddie Condon Concerts, 1942–48," *American Music*, i/2 (1983), 60

M. Jones: *Talking Jazz* (London, 1987) [colln of previously pubd interviews], 220

G. Lombardi: *Eddie Condon on Record, 1927–1971* (Milan, 1987) [discography]

WILLIAM H. KENNEY III

Condon, (Richard) Les(lie) (*b* London, 23 Feb 1930). English trumpeter. After playing in military and dance bands during his RAF service, he recorded with Vic Lewis (1954), Tony Crombie (1954–5, 1958, 1960), Ronnie Scott (1956), and Tony Kinsey (1957–9), and also wrote arrangements for and worked with Woody Herman's Anglo-American Herd (1959). Later he played with Joe Harriott and a ten-piece band led by Bill Le Sage and Ronnie Ross, and recorded with Kinsey (1963, 1974), Tubby Hayes (1964, 1966), Harry Smith (1966), Stan Tracey (1966, 1968), and John Dankworth (1967). He has also been active as a freelance musician and has worked in bands accompanying visiting American singers. He is heard to advantage on *Nutty* from the album *100% Proof* (1966, Fon. STL5410), recorded with Hayes's orchestra.

BIBLIOGRAPHY

FeatherE

J. Cotterrell, ed.: *Jazz Now: the Jazz Centre Society Guide* (London, 1976)

NEVIL SKRIMSHIRE

Condon's. Nightclub in New York, properly known as Eddie Condon's; *see* NIGHTCLUBS AND OTHER VENUES.

Conga [conga drum]. An Afro-Cuban drum with a tapered or barrel-shaped shell of as much as 90 cm in height and a single head of 25 to 30 cm in diameter. In jazz the conga is played with the fingers and the hollow palm of the hand and is generally used alone or in pairs; when more than one drum is used the instruments are of different pitches. Some alteration in pitch may be obtained on one instrument by varying the point at which pressure is applied to the drumhead, and the amount of pressure.

The conga has had a long history as a jazz instrument, which began with its uses in Afro-Cuban jazz. Chano Pozo, a member of Dizzy Gillespie's orchestra from 1947 to 1948, plays prominent conga solos on the second half of Gillespie's recording *Cubana Be/Cubana Bop* (1947, Vic. 203145). After Pozo's death the conga continued to be used in Gillespie's band, as well as in those of Mongo Santamaria, himself a renowned conga player, and Machito. Interest in the instrument was broadened by Gillespie's having included it in a big band, and by his having used it not only in Afro-Cuban jazz but also in bop. As a result it became common from the 1950s for one or more congas to be used in addition to a conventional drumset in such diverse styles as swing, bop, hard bop, soul jazz, and modal jazz, as well as in Latin jazz and jazz-rock based on Brazilian rhythms (such as some of the music of Return to Forever); the best-known conga players have included Ray Barretto, Big Black, Candido Camero, Sabu Martinez, Armando Peraza, and Carlos "Potato" Valdez. The conga has also been used occasionally in free jazz with an Africanist orientation, such as some of the work of the Art Ensemble of Chicago and of Sun Ra (for example, the tracks *Egypt Strut* and *Dawn* on the album *Sun Ra's Arkestra Meets Salah Ragab*, 1983, Praxis 106).

BARRY KERNFELD

Connie's Inn. Nightclub in New York; *see* NIGHTCLUBS AND OTHER VENUES.

Conniff, Ray (*b* Attleboro, MA, 6 Nov 1916). Trombonist and arranger. He toured and recorded with Bunny Berigan (1937–9), then worked in New York with Bob Crosby (1939–40), making a number of recordings. He performed and recorded with Artie Shaw (1940–41), led an octet (1941), and recorded again with Shaw (1941–5). He also recorded in dixieland groups led by Bobby Hackett (1943) and Art Hodes (1944). While serving in the army he provided arrangements for the Harry James Orchestra, with which he recorded after his discharge in 1946. Unable to accept the innovations of bop, he left music briefly around 1950. Around 1957 he formed a group of singers and instrumentalists that performed his arrangements of light popular music; as the Ray Conniff Singers it achieved great popular success and toured Europe, Japan, Mexico, and in 1974 the USSR.

BIBLIOGRAPHY

ChiltonW; *FeatherE*

S. Woolley: "Ray Conniff: Swing Era Musician," *Cadence*, ii/3–4 (1976–7), 6

Connor, Chris (*b* Kansas City, MO, 8 Nov 1927). Singer. She played clarinet as a child; although she had no formal training as a singer her first concert, which she gave in her late teens, was enthusiastically received. For a year and a half at the University of Missouri she sang with a large band that was modeled on Stan Kenton's orchestra; she then joined a group in Kansas City, and in 1949 moved to New York. She sang with Claude Thornhill, with Herbie Fields, again with Thornhill (1952–3), and then with Jerry Wald. On June Christy's recommendation she was engaged by Kenton in 1953; from the mid-1950s into the 1980s Connor has worked as a soloist with various accompanying groups, most of which have been trios.

Connor's vocal style, derived principally from that of Anita O'Day, and her presentation as a performer are among the most sensational in jazz. Her tone is husky and she uses little vibrato except for special effect. She employs a wide range of dynamics, often changing from one to another abruptly. She swings in fast pieces and alters rhythms in an unusual way in ballads. Her striking facial expressions, her postures, and her emotional intensity have perhaps been the most controversial aspects of her performances, and have been remarked on by critics.

SELECTED RECORDINGS

As leader: *Lullabys of Birdland* (1954, Beth. 1001); *Songs* (1956, Atl. 1228); *A Jazz Date* (1956, Atl. 1286); *Chris Craft* (1958, Atl. 1290); *Chris in Person* (1959, Atl. 8040), incl. Misty; *Witchcraft* (1959, Atl. 8032); *Portrait of Chris* (1960, Atl. 8046); *Double Exposure* (1960–61, Atl. 8049); *Sketches* (1972, Stanyan 10029); *Love being here with you* (1983, Stash 232)

As sideman: S. Kenton: Baia (1953, Cap. F2511); I get a kick out of you (1953, Cap. T20244); on C. Tjader, E. Anderson, and P. Togava: *Sessions, Live* (1956–8, Calliope 302), Love Walkin' in, 'S Wonderful

BIBLIOGRAPHY

"Chris Connors [*sic*] now a Nitery, Disc Singer," *DB*, xxi/18 (1954), 2

R. J. Gleason: "Perspectives," *DB*, xxiii/7 (1956), 8

G. Coulter: Review of *A Jazz Date* (1956), *JR*, ii/1 (1959), 39

G. Lees: "Caught in the Act: Chris Connor," *DB*, xxix/31 (1962), 39

R. Blake: "Caught in the Act: Chris Connor," *DB*, xxxvii/11 (1970), 28

L. Tomkins: "Chris Connor," *CI*, xx (1982), no.9, p.20; no.11, p.12; xxi/1 (1982), 13

ANDRÉ BARBERA

Connors, Bill [William A.] (*b* Los Angeles, 24 Sept 1949). Guitarist. He played electric guitar with Mike Nock and Steve Swallow in San Francisco, and recorded and toured Europe with RETURN TO FOREVER (1973–4). In 1974 he made his first solo album, as an acoustic guitarist, in Oslo (*Theme to the Guardian*, ECM 1057) and recorded with Stanley Clarke in New York. In 1977 he recorded free jazz with Lee Konitz, and on another recording led a group that included Gary Peacock, Jack DeJohnette, and Jan Garbarek. He later recorded with Garbarek's group (1977, 1978) and again as a soloist (1979); he resumed playing electric guitar on joining Garbarek's group in 1981, and recorded a rock-oriented album around 1984.

BIBLIOGRAPHY

F. Nemko: "Bill Connors: Before and After Chick Corea," *GP*, viii/10 (1974), 12

G. Santoro: "Bill Connors," *GP*, xix/5 (1985), 8 [incl. discography]

Connors, Chuck [Charles Raymond] (*b* Maysville, KY, 18 Aug 1930). Bass trombonist. He studied at the Boston Conservatory (MusB 1956). He worked for about nine months with Dizzy Gillespie in 1957, and in July 1961 joined the Duke Ellington Orchestra. After Ellington's death in 1974 he continued to play with the orchestra under Mercer Ellington. He recorded with Ellington and with a number of his sidemen: Johnny Hodges (1961), Ray Nance (1963), Cat Anderson (1965), Paul Gonsalves (1969), and Clark Terry (1974); a representative solo by Connors may be heard on *Perdido* from *The Popular Duke Ellington*

(1966, RCA LSP3576). With Terry he toured the USA in 1974 and Europe twice in the late 1970s. (*Feather '60s*)

Connors, Norman [Connor, Norman, Jr.] (*b* Philadelphia, 1 March 1947). Drummer and composer. He studied at Temple University, and in 1966 moved to New York, where he attended the Juilliard School and played with Marion Brown, Sun Ra, and Jackie McLean. In 1967 he recorded with Archie Shepp. He played and recorded with Sam Rivers (1971, 1973) and Pharoah Sanders (1971–2), then in 1972 formed his own group, with which he toured in the USA and abroad. Among the eminent players who recorded with him as sidemen (1972–5, 1978) were Eddie Henderson, Gary Bartz, Carlos Garnett, and Herbie Hancock. Besides his activities as a performer, Connors also composed several dance works and a film score. As both a drummer and composer he creates a blend of elements from modal jazz, bop, soul, free jazz, and Latin music. His album *Dark of Light* (1972–3, Cob. 9035) well illustrates his style.

BIBLIOGRAPHY

Feather–Gitler '70s
H. Nolan: "Norman Connors: a Brotherhood of Rhythm," *DB*, xlii/5 (1975), 18 [incl. discography]

Conqueror. Record label. Its records were sold through the Sears Roebuck mail-order catalogue. When issue began early in 1926 the material was drawn from the Plaza Music Co.; this association continued after Plaza became part of the American Record Company, and after the latter was acquired by CBS. A substantial race catalogue was maintained, and much jazz was issued. The label was discontinued in spring 1942.

BIBLIOGRAPHY

R. M. W. Dixon and J. Godrich: *Recording the Blues* (London, 1970), 80
B. Rust: *The American Record Label Book* (New Rochelle, NY, 1978), 87

Contact. Record company and label. The company was founded by Bob Thiele and Pauline Rivelli in New York in 1964. Archive material by Lester Young, Shelly Manne, and Coleman Hawkins was issued; in addition new sessions sponsored by the company resulted in two fine albums by Earl Hines and one by Steve Kuhn. LPs were packaged in substantial "gatefold" (that is, double-spread) liners and were decorated with fine photographs by Chuck Stewart.

MARK GARDNER

Contemporary. Record company and label. The company was established in Los Angeles in 1951. Under the impeccable artistic direction of its founder, Lester Koenig (*b* New York, 3 Dec 1918; *d* Los Angeles, 21 Nov 1977), it quickly acquired a large and varied catalogue. While the label became identified with a certain style of playing, as typified by Art Pepper, Chet Baker, Shelly Manne, Bob Cooper, Howard Rumsey, and André Previn, Contemporary also provided an outlet for the work of many black musicians. Hampton Hawes made some of his best recordings under Koenig's supervision, and Ornette Coleman played his first sessions for the label; Contemporary also issued material by Phineas Newborn, Harold Land, Teddy Edwards, Howard McGhee, Art Farmer, and Sonny Rollins. The company held longstanding contracts with Pepper, Hawes, Rumsey, Manne, Barney Kessel, and Lennie Niehaus. Koenig's catholicity of taste enabled him to direct with sensitivity sessions by such disparate leaders as Cecil Taylor, Benny Carter, and Benny Golson; ultimately he was responsible for the documentation of jazz activity on the West Coast for over 25 years. He also developed an excellent catalogue of traditional jazz on a subsidiary label, Good Time Jazz, which was used to issue the work of Lu Watters, Kid Ory, Bob Scobey, Bunk Johnson, Turk Murphy, the Firehouse Five Plus Two, and others. Other divisions of Contemporary produced and put out classical music.

Contemporary's imaginatively designed liners, with excellent notes, set a high standard and displayed concern for quality and presentation. After Koenig's death the company was managed by his son before it was acquired by Fantasy, which instituted an extensive reissue scheme, released much previously unavailable material, and recommenced recording, putting out new material by Bud Shank, Frank Morgan, Farmer, George Cables, Chris Connor, Terry Gibbs, Kessel, and others. Until his death in 1988 many sessions were supervised by Richard Bock, formerly the owner of Pacific Jazz.

MARK GARDNER

Continental. Record label. It was formed in late 1943 or early 1944 by Sascha Gabor, who had previously worked for Victor. Two series in its catalogue were of jazz importance; both contained mostly race records. The C6000 "Swing Classics" included items by Cozy Cole, Edmond Hall, Mary Lou Williams, and Sabby Lewis, and blues and gospel material (including famous recordings of Rubberlegs Williams with a band led by Clyde Hart that included Charlie Parker). The C10000 "Sepia Swing" series was devoted entirely to recordings by Slam Stewart and Ethel Waters. The enterprise existed for only a few years, after which its catalogues were made available to many small labels, such as Remington and Plymouth. The Continental label name was revived in the late 1960s for a short-lived series of LPs.

BIBLIOGRAPHY

H. Larsen: "A Listing of the Jazz Catalogue Series on the Continental Label," *Matrix*, no.98 (1972), 3
E. M. Bakker and C. Hofmann: "The Three Pleasures of Records, Musical, Sound, and Quality, are Always on Continental Records," *Names and Numbers*, no.4 (1986), 26; no.6 (1987), 4

Continuum. Cooperative quintet. It was established in the late 1970s to play the music of Tadd Dameron, and consists of the trombonist Slide Hampton, the saxophonist Jimmy Heath, the pianist Kenny Barron, the double bass player Ron Carter, and the drummer Art Taylor.

Contrabass. *See* DOUBLE BASS.

Contrabass clarinet. The lowest member of the clarinet family, pitched in B♭ (also known as the pedal clarinet) or E♭; *see* CLARINET, §§1 and 4.

Contrabassoon. A double-reed woodwind instrument pitched an octave below the BASSOON.

Contrabass saxophone. The lowest member of the saxophone family, normally pitched in E♭; *see* SAXOPHONE, §6(iv).

Cook, Doc [Cooke, Charles L.] (*b* Louisville, KY, 3 Sept 1891; *d* 25 Dec 1958). Pianist and arranger. After working as a composer and arranger in Detroit (1909), he moved to Chicago, where he led his own bands, became a music director, and studied at the Musical College (MusD 1926). His long residency as the leader of a 16-piece orchestra at the Dreamland Café (from 1922) was followed by engagements at several other clubs; among his sidemen were Freddie Keppard, Jimmie Noone, Joe Poston, Jerome Don Pasquall, George Mitchell, Johnny St. Cyr, and Andrew Hilaire. He worked as an arranger in New York from 1930 until he retired in the early 1940s. Cook was more important as a band director than as a player; his recordings as a leader are well represented by *Alligator Crawl/Brainstorm* (1927, Col. 1298D). (A. McCarthy: *Big Band Jazz* (New York and London, 1974), 22)

based on *ChiltonW*

Cook, Junior [Herman] (*b* Pensacola, FL, 22 July 1934). Tenor saxophonist. Both his father and older brother played trumpet. He played alto saxophone while he was in high school but soon took up the tenor instrument instead. He played with Dizzy Gillespie in early 1958 and joined the Horace Silver Quintet in May; also in that year he recorded with Kenny Burrell. After leaving Silver in 1964 he played until 1969 with Blue Mitchell, who had also been one of Silver's sidemen, and recorded with Barry Harris (1967) and the organists John Patton and Don Patterson (both 1968). He taught at the Berklee College of Music before working with Freddie Hubbard (1973–5). He played in a quintet with Louis Hayes (from 1975), for a short time as a leader with Hayes and then as a sideman; he and Hayes also recorded as joint leaders of another group in 1975–6. From 1977 Cook played with Danny Moore and Bill Hardman and recorded with Mickey Tucker (1977, 1979) and Eddie Jefferson (1977) and as a leader. Cook is an excellent saxophonist in the mainstream tradition; his timbre and the character of his improvisatory lines are reminiscent of those of Dexter Gordon.

SELECTED RECORDINGS

As leader: *Junior's Cookin'* (1961, Jlnd 958); with L. Hayes: *Ichi-ban* (1976, Tim. 102); *Somethin's Cookin'* (1981, Muse 5218)

As sideman: H. Silver: *Horace-scope* (1960, BN 4042); B. Mitchell: *Heads up!* (1967, BN 84272); F. Hubbard: *Keep your Soul Together* (1973, CTI 6036)

BIBLIOGRAPHY

Feather '60s; *Feather–Gitler '70s*

GARY CARNER

Cook, Willie [John] (*b* Tangipahoa, LA, 11 Nov 1923). Trumpeter. He grew up in East Chicago, Indiana, where he studied music in his teens. He began playing professionally in 1941 and performed with Jay McShann (1943), Earl Hines (1943–8), Jimmie Lunceford's orchestra (under the direction of Eddie Wilcox and Joe Thomas (iii), 1948), Dizzy Gillespie (1948–50), and Gerald Wilson. He also served as Billie Holiday's music director before ceasing to work as a musician in late 1950. In October 1951 he joined Duke Ellington, with whom he performed until 1958 and again in 1960–61. As a freelance player during the 1960s he worked with various musicians, including Mercer Ellington and Jimmy Jones. He performed again with Ellington (1968–70), but then moved to Houston and did not work again as a musician until 1977, when he played with Clark Terry and Count Basie. Thereafter he settled in Sweden and in the early 1980s he worked with several Scandinavian bands as well as with Ernie Wilkins. He appeared at the "Ellington '85" conference in England. Cook is an outstanding lead trumpeter and a notable soloist; his articulation is beautifully clean and precise.

SELECTED RECORDINGS

As sideman: D. Ellington: *Duke Ellington, Volume One* (1952, Stardust 201), incl. Tenderly; *Historically Speaking, the Duke* (1956, Beth. 60), incl. Unbooted Character; *All Star Road Band* (1957, Doctor Jazz 39137), incl. Mood Indigo; C. Basie: *Kansas City 6* (1981, Pablo 2310871)

BIBLIOGRAPHY

S. Dance: *The World of Duke Ellington* (London and New York, 1970/R1981) [colln of previously pubd articles and interviews], 174

L. Tomkins: "Willie Cook: Out on the Road Again," *CI*, xv/11 (1977), 21

P. Vacher: "Willie Cook," *JJ*, xxxvi/9 (1983), 6

EDDIE LAMBERT

Cook, Will Marion (*b* Washington, 27 Jan 1869; *d* New York, 19 July 1944). Composer and conductor. He studied the violin from an early age and after a few years as a concert violinist and conductor, began to work in musical comedy as a director and composer. In 1898 he collaborated with the poet Paul Lawrence Dunbar to produce on Broadway the pioneering revue *Clorindy, or The Origin of the Cakewalk*. From 1900 Cook continued to direct and compose works for the black musical theater; his writing consistently exploits themes and idioms derived from black folk traditions, and his basically neo-Romantic style is notable for its sophisticated melodies, bold, expressive harmonies, and vigorous rhythms. His songs, particularly *Swing Along*, *Exhortation*, and *Rain Song*, became extremely popular.

In 1918 Cook organized the New York Syncopated Orchestra (later renamed the Southern Syncopated Orchestra), which toured the USA and then traveled to London, where it played in major halls during the summer of 1919 and performed for George V; among the members were Sidney Bechet, Arthur Briggs, and Benny Peyton. Cook left the orchestra around 1920 and returned to New York, but some of the players remained to tour England and the Continent, thus extending Cook's influence in Europe. In the 1920s and 1930s Cook was active as a conductor, concert promoter, teacher, and music adviser. He was an important figure in the development of jazz in New York, both through his organization of "all-Negro-music" concerts, which included jazz performed by Bechet and James P. Johnson, among others, and through his role as the mentor of various jazz musicians, including Duke Ellington.

BIBLIOGRAPHY

M. Cuney-Hare: *Negro Musicians and their Music* (Washington, 1936/R1974)

W. M. Cook: "Clorindy, or The Origin of the Cakewalk," *Theatre Arts*, xxxi (1947), 61; repr. in *Readings in Black American Music*, ed. E. Southern (New York and Toronto, 1971, rev. 2/1983), 227

S. Bechet: *Treat it Gentle: an Autobiography*, ed. D. Flower (New York and London, 1960/R1975; Ger. trans. as *Alle Kinder Gottes tragen eine Krone: eine Autobiographie*, Zurich, 1961)

E. Southern: *The Music of Black Americans: a History* (New York and London, 1971, rev. 2/1983)

E. Walker: "The Southern Syncopated Orchestra," *Sv*, no.42 (1972), 204

A. Levy: "Cook, Will Marion," *Dictionary of American Biography*

E. Walker: "A New Look at the S.S.O.," *Sv*, no.51 (1974), 95

J. P. Green: *Edmund Thornton Jenkins: the Life and Times of an American Black Composer, 1894–1926* (Westport, CT, and London, 1982)

E. Southern: *Biographical Dictionary of Afro-American and African Musicians* (Westport, CT, 1982)

H. Rye: "The Southern Syncopated Orchestra," *Under the Imperial Carpet: Essays in Black History, 1780–1950*, ed. R. E. Lotz and I. Pegg (Crawley, England, 1986), 217

J. Chilton: *Sidney Bechet: the Wizard of Jazz* (London and New York, 1987)

M. Carter: *Will Marion Cook: Afro-American Violinist, Composer and Conductor* (diss., U. of Illinois, in preparation)

EILEEN SOUTHERN

Cool jazz. A term applied to diverse styles of modern jazz variously perceived as subdued, understated, or emotionally cool. There was some implication that performers in this style were emotionally detached from their creation; however, the players themselves often voiced distaste for the label because their music was as taxing to play as other styles of jazz and was by no means devoid of emotion.

Most saxophonists of the cool school were disciples of Lester Young. Young's emulators tried to match his relaxed rhythmic sense, his tuneful approach to improvisation, his soft, dry, lightweight tone, and his slow vibrato. Many cool saxophonists played in the big bands led by Woody Herman and Stan Kenton at some time during the late 1940s or early 1950s; among the most prominent were Lee Konitz, Stan Getz, Art Pepper, and Zoot Sims. A number of cool trumpeters, including Chet Baker and Shorty Rogers, drew on the style of Miles Davis, who used almost no vibrato, placed great emphasis on simplicity and lyricism, and avoided the upper register of the instrument. Cool drummers played more quietly and conservatively than other modern jazz drummers. Although there is no well-defined cool jazz piano style, George Shearing and John Lewis are sometimes classified as cool players because of their light, clean touch and their stress on economy and lyricism in improvisation. Sometimes the term is also applied to Lennie Tristano, whose style provided a modern alternative to bop, though this seems to contradict the high degree of intensity in Tristano's work.

The most influential arrangers in cool jazz were Claude Thornhill and Gil Evans, whose concepts supplied the foundations for Miles Davis's nonet recordings of 1949–50, later reissued collectively as *Birth of the Cool*. Five of the 11 arrangements in this series were contributed by Gerry Mulligan, who led several bands during the 1950s that used instrumentation similar to that of Davis's group. (Gil Evans revived this instrumentation for several albums with Davis between 1957 and 1962). Davis's nonet was originally seen as the smallest unit capable of reproducing the flavor of Thornhill's big band of the mid-1940s. It was unusual in that the tenor saxophone was frequently excluded and tuba (sometimes playing the melody line) and french horn were added. The musicians played without vibrato, using a dry tone. While many of the pieces for large ensemble had the floating, almost motionless, quality associated with Thornhill's *Snowfall* (1941), others gave way to the jumpier character of bop, though with soft tone-colors sometimes described as "pastel."

Prototypical cool groups of the 1950s and 1960s include the Modern Jazz Quartet, George Shearing's quintet, the quartets led by Dave Brubeck and Gerry Mulligan, and many ensembles led by Jimmy Giuffre. Some critics consider that the modern jazz produced on the West Coast during the 1950s (*see* WEST COAST JAZZ) constitutes a category of cool jazz. It is more accurate to designate as cool only a few communities of white jazz musicians playing at that time in Los Angeles, San Francisco, New York, and Boston, as well as the output of the Modern Jazz Quartet and some of the music made by Miles Davis's groups; these comprised black musicians who, though rooted in the bop style of the 1940s, often played in a smoother, less fiery manner than did most bop bands. Indeed, although much cool jazz of the 1950s owes a large stylistic debt to groups led by Count Basie and Lester Young in the late 1930s, cool musicians did not ignore the bop approaches that had emerged in the mid-1940s. Some cool saxophonists may have drawn almost exclusively on the work of Young, but most also incorporated the bop ideas of Charlie Parker. Furthermore, most used bop tunes rather than those associated with Basie.

In cool jazz, improvised counterpoint of the type practiced in the earliest days of ensemble jazz underwent a revival. In some performances by the Modern Jazz Quartet, John Lewis improvised lines simultaneously with Milt Jackson, as did Dave Brubeck with Paul Desmond, and Bob Brookmeyer with Gerry Mulligan and Jimmy Giuffre in other groups.

See also JAZZ (i), §V, 6.

BIBLIOGRAPHY

J.-E. Berendt: *Das Jazzbuch: Entwicklung und Bedeutung der Jazzmusik* (Frankfurt am Main, Germany, 1953, rev. 2/1959 as *Das neue Jazzbuch*, Eng. trans., New York, 1962; rev. and enlarged 5/1981 as *Das grosse Jazzbuch: von New Orleans bis Jazz Rock*, Eng. trans. as *The Jazz Book: from New Orleans to Fusion and Beyond*, Westport, CT, 1982)
M. Williams: "Bebop and After," *Jazz: New Perspectives on the History of Jazz*, ed. N. Hentoff and A. J. McCarthy (New York, 1959/*R*1974), 287
A. Hodeir: *Toward Jazz* (New York, 1962/*R*1976)
J. L. Collier: *The Making of Jazz: a Comprehensive History* (New York and London, 1978)
M. C. Gridley: *Jazz Styles* (Englewood Cliffs, NJ, 1978, rev. 2/1985 as *Jazz Styles: History and Analysis*, with suppl. *Instructor's Manual and Discography*)
H. Hellhund: *Cool Jazz: Grundzüge seiner Entstehung und Entwicklung* (Mainz, Germany, 1985)

MARK C. GRIDLEY

Coon, Carleton (A., Sr.) (1894–1932). Drummer, leader with JOE SANDERS of the Coon–Sanders Original Nighthawk Orchestra.

Cooper, (Lofton) Al(fonso) (*b* 1911; *d* 5 Oct 1981). Alto saxophonist, clarinetist, and bandleader. The half-brother of Grachan Moncur, he played early in his career at the 101 Club on Lenox Avenue in New York, for three months at Harlem-on-the Hudson, New Jersey, and at the White Towers in Pleasantville, New York. His most important contribution was as the leader of the Savoy Sultans from 1937 to around 1946 (*see* SAVOY SULTANS (i)).

Cooper, Bob (*b* Pittsburgh, 6 Dec 1925). Tenor saxophonist and oboist. He studied clarinet from 1940 and tenor saxophone from 1941. By 1945 he had joined Stan Kenton and in 1947 married Kenton's singer, June Christy, whom he began to accompany on recordings. He left Kenton in 1951 and worked as a freelance musician on the West Coast, his style evolving from swing to bop. From 1954 he played and recorded with Shorty Rogers and Pete Rugolo, and belonged to Howard Rumsey's Lighthouse All Stars, with which he remained into the 1960s; in the late 1950s he interrupted his career in the USA to tour Europe, South Africa, and Japan with his wife. From the 1960s he worked as a studio musician in Los Angeles. In 1966 the première of his *Solo for Orchestra* was given by Kenton's Los Angeles Neophonic Orchestra, which he joined in the same year. His continuing work in big bands has included recordings with Frank Capp and Nat Pierce (1978, 1981) and Bob Florence (1981); he has also played in small groups, recording with Terry Gibbs's sextet (1978), Harry Edison (1983), and Snooky Young (1985) and making occasional tours with Shorty Rogers.

For illustration *see* PEPPER, ART.

SELECTED RECORDINGS

As leader: *Tenor Sax Jazz Impressions* (1979, Trend 518); *Bob Cooper Plays the Music of Michel Legrand* (1980, Dis. 822); with S. Young: *In a Mellotone* (1985, Cont. 14017)

As sideman with S. Kenton: Abstraction (1947, Cap. 10184); *A Concert in Progressive Jazz* (1947–51, Cap. T172), incl. Introduction to a Latin Rhythm; on *The Kenton Era* (1940–54, Cap. WDX569), Coop's Solo; *Stan Kenton Presents Gabe Baltazar* (1977, CW 3005)

As sideman with H. Edison: *Blues for Lovers* (1983, Atlas-Japan 27-1027)

BIBLIOGRAPHY

FeatherE; *Feather–Gitler '70s*
C. Easton: *Straight Ahead: the Story of Stan Kenton* (New York, 1973)
W. F. Lee: *Stan Kenton: Artistry in Rhythm* (Los Angeles, 1980) [incl. discography]

WILLIAM F. LEE III

Cooper, Buster [George] (*b* St. Petersburg, FL, 4 April 1929). Trombonist. His first job, with his cousin's band, took him to Texas, where he joined Nat Towles. After studying harmony and counterpoint in New York he joined Lionel Hampton (1953), spent two years in the house band at the Apollo Theatre, then worked with Lucky Millinder and Benny Goodman. With his brother Steve Cooper, a double bass player, he formed the

Cooper Brothers band, and played in New York and Paris before joining Duke Ellington in June 1962. Cooper's specialty was the provision of blistering trombone solos, and sound musicianship and sensitivity, particularly in section work, were hallmarks of his playing. He left Ellington in 1969 and moved back to Florida, where he formed another band with his brother. In 1973 he went to Los Angeles and worked as a freelance, recording with the Capp–Pierce Orchestra (1976–81) and making regular appearances at jazz festivals.

SELECTED RECORDINGS

As sideman with D. Ellington: *Will the Big Bands Ever Come Back?* (1962–3, Rep. 6168), incl. One O'Clock Jump; *Afro Bossa* (1962–3, Rep. 6069), incl. Bonga; *The Popular Duke Ellington* (1966, RCA LSP3576), incl. The Twitch; *Ella and Duke at the Côte d'Azure* (1966, Verve 4072–2), incl. Trombonio–Bustoso-issimo; *Latin American Suite* (1968, Fan. 8419), incl. Chico cuadradino

As sideman with F. Capp and N. Pierce: *Juggernaut* (1977, Conc. 40), incl. Avenue C, Dickie's Dream; *Juggernaut Strikes Again* (1981, Conc. 183), incl. Things ain't what they used to be

BIBLIOGRAPHY

Feather–Gitler '70s
S. Dance: *The World of Duke Ellington* (London and New York, 1970) [colln of previously pubd articles and interviews], 210

EDDIE LAMBERT

Cooper, Harry (R.) (*b* Lake Charles, LA, 1903; *d* Paris, 1961). Trumpeter. During his teens he played with Bennie Moten and George E. Lee. In Baltimore he joined the band accompanying the singer Virginia Liston, with whom he made his first recordings in New York. The group expanded (among the players was Prince Robinson) and changed its name to the Seminole Syncopators; after playing with it in Atlanta, Cooper returned to New York, where he played with Billy Fowler (late 1924, 1926), Elmer Snowden, and the Cotton Club Orchestra under Andrew Peer (1925). His quartet, Harry's Happy Four, made recordings in 1925 and accompanied Sara Martin. He worked on occasions with Duke Ellington in 1926 and led his own group again before joining Leon Abbey, with whom he played in Europe from early 1928; he also performed with Sam Wooding (1929). He remained in Europe, playing with his own bands and with other leaders, among them Wooding (1929) and Hubert Rostaing; *Blues 1943/ Nuages* (1943, Swing 155) is a fine example of the recordings he made in Paris from 1942 to 1947.

based on *ChiltonW*

Cooper, Jerome (D.) (*b* Chicago, 14 Dec 1946). Drummer and percussionist. He studied drumming with Oliver Coleman (1958–63) and Walter Dyett (1963–5) and attended the American Conservatory and Loop College (1967–8). After playing in 1968 with Oscar Brown, Jr., and Kalaparusha Maurice McIntyre he moved in the following year to Europe, then worked with Steve Lacy (1969–71), toured Africa with Lou Bennett (1970), and played with the Art Ensemble of Chicago (1971), Alan Silva (1971–2), Frank Wright, and Noah Howard. On his return to the USA in 1971 he joined the REVOLUTIONARY ENSEMBLE, of which he remained a member until the group disbanded in 1977; as a member of the ensemble he sometimes played piano, bugle, and flute in addition to his principal instruments. At the same time he worked with Sam Rivers, George Adams, and Karl Berger (all 1973), Andrew Hill and Anthony Braxton (both 1974), and again with McIntyre (from 1974), and from 1976 into the 1980s worked as an unaccompanied soloist; in 1980 he played with Cecil Taylor. Cooper's solos reveal a remarkable sense of form and timbre; they often begin with short, repetitive phrases that become increasingly complex and powerful.

SELECTED RECORDINGS

As unaccompanied soloist: *The Unpredictability of Predictability* (1979, About Time 1002)

As leader: of Revolutionary Ensemble (with L. Jenkins and Sirone): *Vietnam* (1972, ESP 3007), *Manhattan Cycles* (1972, IndN 1023); *Positions 369* (1977, Karma 3–4)

As sideman: S. Lacy: *Wordless* (1971, Futura 22); A. Braxton: *New York, Fall 1974* (1974, Ari. 4032); on *Wildflowers 5: the New York Loft Jazz Sessions* (1976, Douglas 7049), Roscoe Mitchell: Chant; C. Taylor: *It is in the Brewing Luminous* (1980, HH 16)

BIBLIOGRAPHY

Feather–Gitler '70s
V. Wilmer: "The Drummer as Artist," *MM* (3 Feb 1973), 34
R. Riggins: "The Revolutionary Ensemble," *DB*, xl/19 (1973), 15
V. Wilmer: *As Serious as your Life: the Story of the New Jazz* (London, 1977, rev. 1980)
E. Hazell: "The Music of the Drums: Jerome Cooper," *MD*, x/4 (1986), 26

ED HAZELL

Copeland, Ray (M.) (*b* Norfolk, VA, 17 July 1926; *d* New York, 18 May 1984). Trumpeter, flugelhorn player, composer, and teacher. He studied classical trumpet and in his teens played with groups in Brooklyn. He toured with Mercer Ellington (1947–8) and Al Cooper's Savoy Sultans (?1948–9), but during the early 1950s worked only part-time as a trumpeter, for Andy Kirk, Sy Oliver, and others. He was featured in the film *Kiss her Goodbye* (1959), and in the late 1950s played bop and swing with Lionel Hampton, Randy Weston, Oscar Pettiford, and others. He was also a member of the Roxy Theater Orchestra in New York (1959–61), and played with Louie Bellson and Pearl Bailey (1962–4) and Ella Fitzgerald (1965). In 1966 he rejoined Weston, with whom he toured Africa (under the auspices of the US State Department) in 1967 and Morocco in 1970, performed at the Newport Jazz Festival (1973), and continued to play at intervals into the 1980s. He also toured Europe with Thelonious Monk (1968). During the 1970s Copeland led his own orchestras in the New York area and devoted time to composition; his *Classical Jazz Suite in Six Movements* was given its première at Lincoln Center in 1970. He also worked in Broadway shows, and in 1974 toured Europe with a revue, *The Musical Life of Charlie Parker*. Active as a teacher, Copeland gave many jazz workshops and courses on jazz history; he published *The Ray Copeland Method and Approach to the Creative Art of Jazz Improvisation* (St. Albans, NY, 1974). From 1979 he taught at Hampshire College.

SELECTED RECORDINGS

As sideman with R. Weston: on *The Modern Art of Jazz* (1956, Dawn DLP1116), In a Little Spanish Town, J and K Blues, Run Joe; *Little Niles* (1958, UA 5011); *African Cookbook* (1964, Bak. 1001); *Tanjah* (1973, Pol. 5055)

As sideman with others: T. Monk: *Thelonious Monk Quintet* (1954, Prst. 180); on E. Wilkins: *Top Brass* (1955, Savoy 12044), Taking a Chance on Love; A. Kirk: *A Mellow Bit of Rhythm* (1956, RCA LPM1302); A. Blakey: *Art Blakey's Big Band* (1957, Beth. 6027); C. Anderson: *Cat on a Hot Tin Horn* (1958, EmA 36142); J. Richards: *Kiss her Goodbye* (1959, WB 5078); G. Coleman: *Gloria Coleman Sings and Swings Organ* (1965, Mstr. 332)

BIBLIOGRAPHY

FeatherE; *Feather '60s*; *Feather–Gitler '70s*
Obituary, *Variety*, cccxv (6 June 1984), 95

ANDRÉ BARBERA

Coppieters, Fernand (*b* Brussels, 3 March 1905; *d* Brussels, 9 Sept 1981). Belgian pianist and organist. He began his career as a member of the Bistrouille A.D.O., with which he played in 1920–21. He worked at the Memling in Knokke-Heist, Belgium (1922), and then joined the Red Mills Ragtime Band (1924). After playing with the Rhythmic Novelty Dance Orchestra (1925–7), he worked in France with Fud Candrix and in the Netherlands (1927–8). He played at nightclubs in Brussels with René Compère and the Candrix brothers, and in 1929 he recorded in a trio with Compère. In 1930 and 1931 he played in Brussels and abroad, and toured Europe with Josephine Baker. He worked with the bandleader Roland Dorsay (1932), then with various groups, including those led by Candrix and Willie Lewis. He recorded for the Rythme and Victory labels with his own band (1943, 1951, 1958) and was the staff pianist of Radio Schaerbeek. Towards the end of his career he played organ at various venues throughout Belgium. He also played violin and saxophone.

ROBERT PERNET

Coppieters, Francis (*b* Brussels, 7 Sept 1930). Belgian pianist, son of Fernand Coppieters. He began his career playing in a quartet with Toots Thielemans (1947), with which he performed at the Salle Pleyel in Paris (1948) and later recorded (1949). He appeared at numerous concerts throughout Europe and toured with a Swiss band led by Hazy Osterwald. After working in Paris with Bobby Jaspar, he joined an orchestra led by Aimé Barelli (1955), in which he replaced Francy Boland. From 1957 he lived in Germany; until 1962 he played with Kurt Edelhagen in Cologne, where he also taught jazz at the conservatory. Although continuing to play occasionally he concentrated on teaching from that time. Besides the recordings he made with Thielemans in 1949 and Edelhagen in 1957–9, Coppieters played on sessions with Charly Antolini (1968) and the singer and trumpeter Taps Miller, and made two sides as an unaccompanied soloist.

ROBERT PERNET

Cor anglais (Fr.: english horn). The tenor member of the OBOE family, pitched in F, a 5th below the oboe.

Corb, Morty [Mortimer G.] (*b* San Antonio, 10 April 1917). Double bass player. He played with Jan Savitt and Louis Armstrong in Los Angeles in 1947, and recorded with Claude Thornhill (1950), Jess Stacy (1950–51), and Kid Ory (1950–51, 1953, 1959). He frequently performed the arco bass solo on *Blues for Jimmie* in recordings and concerts with Ory, a notable example being on the album *Henry "Red" Allen Meets Kid Ory* (1959, Verve 1018). In 1951 he joined Benny Goodman's band and later he worked frequently with two of its members, Nick Fatool and George Van Eps. He performed and recorded with Jack Teagarden (1952) and Bob Crosby (1956–8), then recorded regularly with Matty Matlock (1958–60), Red Nichols (1958–9), and Pete Fountain (1959–63). In 1957 he led his own group on the album *Strictly from Dixie* (Tops 1589). He also worked as a studio musician in films, radio, and television. (*FeatherE*; *Feather '60s*)

Corcoran, Corky [Gene Patrick] (*b* Tacoma, WA, 28 July 1924; *d* Tacoma, 3 Oct 1979). Tenor saxophonist. He began his professional career in 1940 with Sonny Dunham and the following year became a principal soloist in Harry James's band. When he left James in 1947 he worked briefly with Tommy Dorsey and worked as a freelance before leading his own group. He re-joined James in 1949 and played intermittently with the band in the 1950s and 1960s, during which time he also performed and recorded with his own groups on the West Coast; in the 1970s he again worked regularly in James's band. Corcoran's playing is characterized by swinging drive and a robust tone.

SELECTED RECORDINGS

As leader: The Sound of Love (*c*1960, Epic 3319)
As sideman: S. Dunham: Bar Babble (1941, Bb 11148); Mighty lak' a Rose (1941, Bb 11124); H. James: Skylark/The Clipper (1942, Col. 36533); Cherry/Jump Town (1942, Col. 36683)

BIBLIOGRAPHY

Feather E; *Feather '60s*; *Feather–Gitler '70s*
L. Tomkins: " 'If Something's Good – it's Timeless!' Says Corky Corcoran," *CI*, x/2 (1971), 20

WARREN VACHÉ, SR.

Corea, Chick [Armando Anthony] (*b* Chelsea, MA, 12 June 1941). Pianist and composer. He began playing piano at the age of four, learning the fundamentals of music from his father (a professional musician). By listening regularly to the recordings of Dizzy Gillespie, Charlie Parker, and Billy Eckstine, he developed an interest in jazz at an early age, and began to transcribe and memorize the tunes and improvised solos of Horace Silver; he also came under the influence of Bud Powell. His first important professional engagements were in the Latin bands of Mongo Santamaria and Willie Bobo (1962–3), and a love of Latin music has been evident throughout his career. He then worked extensively with Blue Mitchell (1964–6), recording his own compositions for the first time on Mitchell's sessions for Blue Note records. His interest, during this period, in the music of Joe Henderson, McCoy Tyner, Bill Evans (ii), and Herbie Hancock may clearly be heard in his first recordings as a leader, *Tones for Joan's Bones* (1966) and *Now He Sings, Now he Sobs* (1968).

In 1968 Corea joined Miles Davis's group, which was then involved in an abstract form of electronic jazz-rock that initiated the so-called fusion movement of the 1970s. Corea's involvement with Davis marked the beginning of his extensive exploration of free improvisation, but his desire to develop a more individual, nonelectronic approach to free jazz prompted him, along with Dave Holland, to leave the group in 1970. Inspired by the earlier work of Paul Bley and Gary Peacock, they formed a trio with Barry Altschul, later adding Anthony Braxton on reed instruments. This group, Circle, was very influential on the avant-garde jazz scene, but Corea soon felt a need to establish a more lyrical context for his music. The two solo albums *Piano Improvisations*, recorded in 1971 shortly before Circle disbanded, clearly reflect this urge. Corea also began the study of Scientology during this period, the dynamics of which greatly affected his subsequent work.

From late 1971 to 1973 Corea attracted a wider audience with the first of his groups called RETURN TO FOREVER, which made use of expansive melodies, romantic vocal lines, and infectious Latin rhythms. The second Return to Forever group was a powerful rock band in which Corea played the Fender-Rhodes electric piano, Hohner Clavinet, Yamaha organ, Minimoog and ARP Odyssey synthesizers, and various electronic gadgets and pedals; by the mid-1970s he had become very popular with rock audiences. He continued to develop as a composer throughout this period; several of his tunes, including *Windows*, *Spain*, and *Crystal Silence*, have become jazz standards. (For a fuller discussion of *Spain*, *see* FORMS, §7.) In the late 1970s he formed a third group under the name Return to Forever that included small string and brass ensembles, made less use of electronics, and drew on elements from the Latin, Spanish, and classical traditions. Unlike many "crossover" artists who left jazz for commercial rock, Corea has continued to perform and record regularly in a wide variety of acoustic jazz settings. These include solo performances, duos with Gary Burton or Hancock, a quartet with Mike Brecker, Eddie Gomez, and Steve Gadd, and the group Trio Music, formed in 1981 with Miroslav Vitous and Roy Haynes. In 1985 Corea established the Elektric Band, a trio with the double bass player John Patitucci and the drummer Dave Weckl.

See also PIANO, §6; and HARMONY (i), §2, and ex.24; for further illustration *see* JAZZ (i), fig.8.

Chick Corea playing at the Newport Jazz Saratoga Festival, 1985

SELECTED RECORDINGS

As unaccompanied soloist: *Piano Improvisations* (1971, ECM 1014, 1020)
Duos: with H. Hancock: *An Evening with Herbie Hancock and Chick Corea* (1978, Col. PC35664–5); with G. Burton: *In Concert, Zürich* (1979, ECM 1182–3)
As leader: *Is* (1969, SolS 18055); *The Song of Singing* (1970, BN 84353); *Return to Forever* (1973, ECM 1022); *Hymn of the Seventh Galaxy* (1973, Pol. 5536); *My Spanish Heart* (1976, Pol. 9003); *The Mad Hatter* (1979, Pol. 6130); *Three Quartets* (1980, WB 3552)
As sideman with M. Davis: *Miles Davis at Fillmore West* (1970, CBS Sony 39–40)

RECORDED COMPOSITIONS
(selective list)

Duo with G. Burton: Crystal Silence, on *Crystal Silence* (1972, ECM 1024)
As leader: Tones for Joan's Bones, on *Tones for Joan's Bones* (1966, Vortex 2004); Now he sings, now he sobs, on *Now He Sings, Now He Sobs* (1968, SolS 18039); Captain Marvel, 500 Miles High, Spain, on *Light as a Feather* (1972, Pol. 5525); *Three Quartets* (1980, WB 3552)
Recorded by S. Getz: Windows, on *Sweet Rain* (1967, Verve 68693)

BIBLIOGRAPHY

L. Kart: "The Chick Corea File," *DB*, xxxvi/7 (1969), 21
J. Toner: "Chick Corea," *DB*, xli/6 (1974), 14
T. Darter: "Chick Corea: Multi-keyboard Giant," *CK*, i/1 (1975), 20
L. Underwood: "Chick Corea: Soldering the Elements, Determining the Future," *DB*, xliii/17 (1976), 13
"Chick Corea," *SJ*, xxxii/7 (1978), 290 [discography]
L. Tomkins: "Chick Corea," *CI*, xvi (1978), no.10, p.20; no.11, p.4 [interview]
L. Underwood: "Armando in Wonderland," *DB*, xlvi/5 (1979), 14
L. Feather: "Piano Giants of Jazz: Chick Corea," *CK*, vi/6 (1980), 60
L. Jeske: "Chick Corea," *DB*, xlviii/6 (1981), 16
T. Darter and B. Doerschuk: "Chick Corea: Conversation with a Chameleon," *Keyboard*, ix/7 (1983), 54 [incl. discography]
L. Lyons: *The Great Jazz Pianists, Speaking of their Lives and Music* (New York, 1983), 257
J. Aikin: "Chick Corea's 'Now he Beats the Drum, Now he Stops'," *Keyboard*, x/4 (1984), 28
T. Darter and B. Doerschuk: "Chick Corea: State of the Artist," *Keyboard*, xi/10 (1985), 52 [incl. discography]
S. Adams: "Chick's Career," *JJI*, xxxix/1 (1986), 6 [incl. discography]
H. Mandel: "Chick Corea: Elektric Again," *DB*, liii/1 (1986), 16

BILL DOBBINS/R

Cornbread. Nickname of HAL SINGER.

Cornelius, Corky [Edward] (*b* Indiana, 3 Dec 1914; *d* New York, 3 Aug 1943). Trumpeter. He was taught music by his father. He played and recorded with Les Brown (1937), Benny Goodman (1939), and Gene Krupa (1939–40); his lively solo playing can be heard on *Hamtramck*, recorded with Krupa in 1940 (OK 6106). He also made several recordings as a member of the Casa Loma Orchestra, led by Glen Gray, with which he played from 1941.

based on *ChiltonW*

Cornet. A brass instrument pitched in B♭ (in France occasionally in C), having three valves and tubing that has a profile between the cylindrical shape of the trumpet and the conical shape of the orchestral horn; it is somewhat squatter than the trumpet, though the modern American "long" model has a more trumpet-like form. The tubing is "folded" through three reversals so that it lies parallel in a horizontal plane, with the bell of the instrument pointing forwards. The mouthpiece is deeper than that of a modern trumpet, the cup is more rounded, and the throat tends to be wider. The written compass of the cornet is *f♯–c'''* (sounding *e–b♭''*), though many players add a further octave to the upper limit of the range.

The cornet first appeared in France during the 1830s as a valved version of the small circular French posthorn. There were initially considerable differences in timbre between the trumpet and cornet, but the tonal characteristics of the two instruments have become increasingly alike as differences in the profile of their tubing have become less extreme. In the USA particularly trumpets are made with more conical tubing than European models.

Laplace has suggested that in New Orleans, with its pervasive French culture, the cornet – a fashionable solo instrument since the days of the great virtuoso J.-C. Arban (1825–89) – was used in early parade bands in imitation of the bands that provided music for higher social strata. Its respectable connections are confirmed by its use in early recordings of ragtime. The typical parade band of this period was relatively small, and could perform indoors as well as outdoors: it consisted of one or more cornets or trumpets, one or two clarinets, alto and baritone horns, one or more trombones, tuba, and snare and bass drums (*see also* BRASS BAND). Such bands were usually led by a cornet player or trumpeter, not only because he played the melody line but also because he was often the best musician in the group and had the most forceful playing style.

The use of the cornet (as of the other brass instruments) in jazz grew out of the New Orleans brass-band tradition. Alphonse Picou and Big Eye Nelson maintained that the first jazz cornetist was Manuel Perez, who played with the orchestra of John Robichaux around 1895; Perez later led the Imperial Orchestra and the first Onward Brass Band. Whether or not his jazz activities predated those of Perez, Buddy Bolden is regarded as the first of the New Orleans cornet "kings"; he was leading his own band by 1895 and was known for a robust and authoritative style of playing based on sheer power – attributes shared by many of the early New Orleans cornetists. (It was said that he could be heard two miles away on a quiet night; later King Oliver and Louis Armstrong had to be positioned 20 feet from the microphone when recording so that a correct balance could be achieved with the sound made by the rest of the band.) Bolden's "ragging" of popular melodies was a musical innovation that formed the basis for later developments in jazz.

Bufkin has observed that the word "cornet" was used in the USA in the 19th century to refer to any soprano brass instrument that played the melodic part. The interchangeable nature of the trumpet and cornet implied by this usage was carried over into jazz, and many players who began as cornetists later took up the trumpet as well as or instead of their original instrument. Moreover as the two instruments became physically increasingly similar the sounds they made became increasingly difficult to distinguish, so that it is not always possible to determine which is being played on recordings. For all these reasons the history of the soprano brass instrument in jazz is covered as a single tradition under the heading TRUMPET. The term "slide cornet" was used colloquially to refer to the soprano trombone (*see also* TROMBONE).

There were, however, a number of notable musicians who concentrated on the cornet, emphasizing and exploiting the differences between its timbre and that of the trumpet. The advantages of the cornet over the trumpet consist in its somewhat mellower tone (resulting from its wider bore), the comparative ease of muted playing, and the flexibility and readiness to "speak" of its middle range, which allow the successful articulation of complex and rapid figures. The most celebrated of the early cornetists to remain faithful to the instrument was Bix Beiderbecke, who produced the purest and most mellifluous of cornet tones. Another player who resisted the transition to trumpet was Rex Stewart; both in his work with Duke Ellington and later Stewart used the cornet to achieve a number of special effects, including glisses (as on *Rexercise,* 1945, Cap. 10035). Bobby Hackett, by contrast, having come to prominence in the mid-1930s as a cornetist, took up the trumpet and used both instruments regularly. Ray Nance, who also played with Ellington, adopted the cornet around 1960; in an interview with Stanley Dance he stated that besides the practical advantages of playing a shorter instrument, particularly when the mute is used, he wished to exploit the softer tone of the cornet, both in solo work and as the lowest voice of the trumpet section in ensemble arrangements, where he felt it blended well with both trumpets and trombones.

In traditional jazz the cornet continued to be favored by some players in the Chicago style, notably Jimmy McPartland, Wild Bill Davison, and Muggsy Spanier, all of whom took advantage of the strength of its middle range in playing the lead part. Ruby Braff adopted a similar role for the cornet in his work with Vic Dickenson's septet and in recordings for Vanguard in the 1950s; he later extended the instrument's expressive possibilities still further and continued to experiment into the 1980s both in small groups, such as "drumless" trios with piano and double bass and duos with Dick Hyman on Wurlitzer theater organ, and in conventional mainstream ensembles. The cornet has also been heard occasionally in bop (Nat Adderley, Thad Jones) and free jazz (Bobby Bradford and Lawrence "Butch" Morris). Don Cherry's principal instrument, which he terms a pocket trumpet, is a pocket cornet.

BIBLIOGRAPHY

L. Panico: *The Novelty Cornetist* (Chicago, 1923)
A. McCarthy: *The Trumpet in Jazz* (London, 1945)
R. Harris: *Jazz* (London, 1952, 5/1957)
J.–E. Berendt: *Das Jazzbuch: Entwicklung und Bedeutung der Jazzmusik* (Frankfurt am Main, Germany, 1953, rev. 2/1959 as *Das neue Jazzbuch,* Eng. trans., New York, 1962; rev. and enlarged 5/1981 as *Das grosse Jazzbuch: von New Orleans bis Jazz Rock,* Eng. trans. as *The Jazz Book: from New Orleans to Fusion and Beyond,* Westport, CT, 1982)
L. Feather: *The Book of Jazz: a Guide to the Entire Field* (New York, 1957, 2/1965 as *The Book of Jazz from Then till Now: a Guide to the Entire Field*)
H. W. Schwartz: *Bands of America* (Garden City, NY, 1957)
S. Dance: *The World of Duke Ellington* (London and New York, 1970/*R*1981) [colln of previously pubd articles and interviews]
A. Napoleon: "The Music Goes Down and Around: (A Case of Mistaken Identity)," *Sv,* no.37 (1971), 18
——: "Aw, Get a Piccolo: (Jazz Horns, Short & Long)," *Sv,* no.39 (1972), 100
W. A. Bufkin: *Union Bands of the Civil War (1862–1865)* (diss., U. of Louisiana, 1973)
M. Laplace: "La trompette et le cornet dans le jazz et la musique populaire," *Brass Bulletin,* no.42 (1983), 16; no.43 (1983), 44; no.44 (1983), 54; no.45 (1984), 38; no.46 (1984), 23; no.47 (1984), 39
A. C. Baines: "Cornet," *GroveI*

CLIFFORD BEVAN, ALYN SHIPTON

Correa, Mayuto [Mailto] (*b* Rio de Janeiro, 9 March 1943). Brazilian percussionist. He wrote tunes from the age of eight and appeared at a nightclub when he was 12; he played in several Brazilian samba bands. In 1970 he went to the USA to record with the pianist João Donato and settled in California, where he worked with Charles Lloyd (1971). After touring with Gábor Szabó (1971–2) he played with Hugh Masekela (1972) and Freddie Hubbard (1973–4), and in 1974 worked as a freelance with Hubbard, Szabó's octet, Kenny Burrell, Donald Byrd, Gato Barbieri, Cal Tjader, and Don Ellis. He ceased to be active as a studio musician after the mid-1970s. Besides his work as an instrumentalist Correa has written songs and other works, including incidental music to the play *Sortilegio* by Milton Nascimento (performed at the Black/Brazilian Festival in Los Angeles, 1975). He has sometimes been known by the name Mayuto alone.

SELECTED RECORDINGS

As sideman: H. Roberts: *Equinox Express Elevator* (1972, Imp. 9229); K. Burrell: *Up the Street, 'round the Corner, down the Block* (1974, Fan. 9458); D. Byrd: *Caricatures* (1976, BN LA711G)

BIBLIOGRAPHY

Feather–Gitler '70s ("Mayuto")
F. R. Nemko: "Profile: Mayuto Correa," *DB,* xlii/14 (1975), 32

JEFF POTTER

Correa Reis, Tania Maria. *See* MARIA, TANIA.

Coryell, Larry (*b* Galveston, TX, 2 April 1943). Electric guitarist and bandleader. He played in a band led by the pianist Mike Mandel when he was a teenager. In 1965 he moved to New York and worked with Chico Hamilton and with Free Spirits, an early jazz-rock band, and received wide exposure as a member of Gary Burton's quartet (1967–8), one of the first groups to combine jazz with rock and country music. From 1969 to 1973 Coryell performed in the group Foreplay with Steve Marcus and Mandel, and in 1973 he formed the jazz-rock band Eleventh House with Marcus, Mandel, the electric bass guitarist Danny Trifan, Alphonse Mouzon, and Randy Brecker (whose place was later taken by Mike Lawrence). He also worked sporadically with Miroslav Vitous and John McLaughlin, and with the latter recorded a series of outstanding duets, including *Rene's Theme* on Coryell's album *Spaces.* In the late 1970s Coryell was performing on hollow-bodied guitar and recording as a soloist as well as in small groups and duos, notably with John Scofield, Michal Urbaniak, Steve Khan, and Philip Catherine. During the same period he recorded with Charles Mingus, Stephane Grappelli, and Sonny Rollins. Coryell has an excellent technique and is versatile and imaginative; although he cannot be identified consistently with any particular jazz style, he is one of the most original improvisers on guitar to have emerged during the 1960s and 1970s. A collection of his own transcriptions of his playing was published as *Improvisations from Rock* *to Jazz* (n.d.), and a further volume, transcribed by D. Pritchard, as *Larry Coryell: Jazz Guitar Solos* (1980).

SELECTED RECORDINGS

As unaccompanied soloist: *European Impressions* (1978, AN 3005); *Bolero* (1981, String 33850)

Duos: with S. Khan: *Two for the Road* (1976, Arista 4156); with P. Catherine: *Twin House* (1976, Elek. 123)

As leader: *Lady Coryell* (1968, Van. 6509); *Spaces* (1970, Van. 6558), incl. Rene's Theme; *Fairyland* (1971, FD 515000); *Barefoot Boy* (1971, FD 10139); *The Eleventh House with Larry Coryell* (1974, Van. 79342); *Tributaries* (1979, AN 3017); *Return* (1979, Van. 79426)

As sideman: Free Spirits: *Free Spirits* (1966, ABC 593); C. Hamilton: *The Dealer* (1966, Imp. 9130); G. Burton: *Duster* (1967, RCA LSP3835); C. Mingus: *Me, Myself an Eye* (1978, Atl. 8803); S. Grappelli: *Young Django* (1979, MPS 68230); S. Rollins: *Don't Ask* (1979, Mlst. 61110)

BIBLIOGRAPHY

G. Hoefer: "Larry Coryell: Now!," *DB*, xxxiv/13 (1967), 17
H. Stamataky: "Larry Coryell: More to Come," *DB*, xxxix/18 (1972), 18
B. Ness: "Have you Dug . . . Larry Coryell," *DB*, xli/9 (1974), 16
——: "Larry Coryell and the Eleventh House," *Coda*, xi/9 (1974), 24
L. Coryell: "Modern Electric Eclecticism," *DB*, xlii/2 (1975), 18
N. Tesser: "Larry Coryell: Leveling Off," *DB*, xliii/4 (1976), 12
M. Brooks: "The Eleventh House," *The Guitar Player Book* (Saratoga, CA, and New York, 1978, 2/1979) [colln of previously pubd articles], 72
M. C. Gridley: *Jazz Styles* (Englewood Cliffs, NJ, 1978, rev. 2/1985 as *Jazz Styles: History and Analysis*, with suppl. *Instructor's Manual and Discography*)
S. Freedman: "Larry Coryell: Suburbanizing Flash Guitar," *DB*, xlvii/6 (1980), 20
"Larry Coryell," *SJ*, xxxiv/3 (1980), 172 [discography]

MARK C. GRIDLEY/R

Costa, Eddie [Edwin James] (*b* Atlas, PA, 14 Aug 1930; *d* New York, 28 July 1962). Pianist and vibraphonist. Although he studied classical piano, he taught himself to play vibraphone. His first important engagement was with Joe Venuti, whom he joined when he was 18. During the two years he spent in the army he performed in Japan and Korea. After his return to the USA he recorded with Sal Salvador (1954–7) and played with Tal Farlow, Kai Winding, and Don Elliott. He was named "new star" on both piano and vibraphone by *Down Beat* in 1957. From 1958 to 1959 he played with Woody Herman and also led his own trio with Henry Grimes and Paul Motian. He was an excellent reader and was much in demand for studio work. A player of great melodic inventiveness and with a strong sense of rhythm, Costa absorbed the intricacies of bop and played fluently in that idiom; at the time of his death, in an automobile accident, he was involved in exploring the developing styles of postbop and modal jazz.

SELECTED RECORDINGS

Eddie Costa with the Vinnie Burke Trio (1956, Jub. 1025); *Eddie Costa Quintet* (1957, Mode 118); *Guys and Dolls Like Vibes* (1958, Coral 57230)

BIBLIOGRAPHY

FeatherE
L. Feather: "Two Poll Winners: They're both Eddie Costa, who's much Surprised by it," *DB*, xxiv/21 (1957), 17
D. Nelsen: "Elegy for Eddie," *DB*, xxix/24 (1962), 13
D. Vincent: "Eddie Costa," *JJ*, xxv/7 (1972), 7

ANDREW JAFFE

Costanzo, Jack (James) (*b* Chicago, 24 Sept 1922). Bongo player. He taught himself to play bongos, studied congas from around 1940, and made three visits to Havana. He toured and recorded with Stan Kenton (1947–8) and performed and recorded with Nat "King" Cole (1949–53); he continued to play with both periodically, his association with Kenton lasting until 1957. He led his own groups on recordings made in 1954 and 1957 and while on tour in London in 1961. He also played with Peggy Lee, Perez Prado, and Harry James and recorded with Charlie Barnet (1954) and Pete Rugolo (1955, 1958). A good example of Costanzo's playing can be heard on Kenton's *Peanut Vendor* (1947, Cap. 904).

BIBLIOGRAPHY

FeatherE
R. Gordon: *Jazz West Coast: the Los Angeles Jazz Scene of the 1950s* (London and New York, 1986)

Cottiglieri, Piero (*b* Milan, 1911). Italian clarinetist and tenor saxophonist. He studied classical violin and was drawn to jazz after hearing the violinist Juice Wilson perform in Milan in the late 1920s. He took up saxophone and clarinet and in the early 1930s played with dance bands; at the same time he was associated with a group of musicians known as the Circolo jazz hot di Milano and in 1936 recorded with its orchestra. He also recorded as a soloist with I Maestri del ritmo during World War II, played with Aldo Rossi's Orchestra of the Moment in the late 1940s, and belonged to a trio led by the drummer Claudio Gambarelli; later he played dixieland in Milan. Cottiglieri's playing may be heard to advantage on his recording *Venutiana* (1936, Col. DQ2172).

ADRIANO MAZZOLETTI

Cotton, Mike [Michael Edward] (*b* London, 12 Aug 1939). English trumpeter. He first played professionally in 1960 with the drummer Pete Ridge's Jazzmen. From 1961 to 1971 he led his own band, which began as a traditional-jazz group; from 1963 its style took on elements of rhythm-and-blues and popular music and in 1964 it was re-formed as the Mike Cotton Sound. With the group Cotton played harmonica as well as trumpet and also sang. He worked with the Kinks, an English rock group, from 1971 until 1973, when he joined Acker Bilk's Paramount Jazz Band. He has made a number of recordings with Bilk, including *Mama told me so* (1980, Pye Piccadilly 128), on which his playing is heard to advantage. A strong and skillful trumpeter, Cotton also works as a freelance and has accompanied such touring American musicians as Bud Freeman, Peanuts Hucko, Kenny Davern, and Wild Bill Davison.

DIGBY FAIRWEATHER

Cotton City Jazz Band. Belgian New Orleans-style band. It was established in Ghent in 1961 and is Belgium's best-known New Orleans group. It has performed with such visiting musicians as George Lewis (i), Albert Nicholas, Louis Nelson, Percy Humphrey, Alvin Alcorn, Freddie Kohlman, Alton Purnell, Don Ewell, Kid Thomas, Emanuel Sayles, Capt. John Handy, Andrew Morgan, Polo Barnes, and Acker Bilk; the band has made a number of recordings, many of them with its guest soloists. It has also worked throughout Europe and in the USA and Africa. In the 1960s its leader was Rudy Balliu, and in the 1980s, the trumpeter Jacques Cruyt.

ROBERT PERNET

Cotton Club. Nightclub in New York; the name was subsequently adopted by a number of other clubs. *See* NIGHTCLUBS AND OTHER VENUES.

Cottrell, Louis (Albert), Jr. (*b* New Orleans, 7 March 1911; *d* New Orleans, 21 March 1978). Clarinetist and tenor saxophonist, son of Louis Cottrell, Sr. He studied clarinet with Lorenzo Tio, Jr., and Barney Bigard. In 1925 he played in the re-formed Golden Rule Orchestra, before joining Polo Barnes. He worked occasionally with the cornetist Chris Kelly and Kid Rena, and also with the Young Tuxedo Orchestra and Sidney Desvigne on the SS *Island Queen* in 1929. He accepted an offer to play tenor saxophone in Don Albert's orchestra, with which he toured the USA, Canada, and Mexico. He left Albert in 1939 and after returning to New Orleans joined Paul Barbarin in 1940 and A. J. Piron on the riverboats in 1941. He played again with Desvigne from 1942 to 1947 and in the 1950s with Barbarin, with whom he later recorded (1962–4). He performed and made recordings with Peter Bocage in the 1960s and led his own band until just before he died. Proud of his creole heritage, Cottrell did much from the late 1920s to organize the city's black branch of the AFM (Local 496); he became its president in the early 1940s.

Oral history material in *LNT*.

SELECTED RECORDINGS

As leader: *Bourbon Street Parade* (1961, Riv. 9385)

As sideman: D. Albert: Liza (1936, Voc. 3491); Rockin' and Swingin' (1936, Voc. 3401); P. Bocage: *Peter Bocage* (1962, Mono 3)

BIBLIOGRAPHY

ChiltonW

H. Wood: "Louis Cottrell: the Man, the Son," *SL*, xxviii (1976), spr., 3

W. Russell: "To Louis Cottrell: with Feeling," *SL*, xxx (1978), sum., 20

D. M. Marquis: "Louis Cottrell, Jr., 1911–1978," *Fn*, x/3 (1979), 18

P. Haby: "Louis Albert Cottrell, 1911–1978," *Fn*, xix/2 (1987–8), 4

MIKE HAZELDINE

Cottrell, Louis, Sr. (*b* New Orleans, 25 Dec 1878; *d* New Orleans, 17 Oct 1927). Drummer, father of Louis Cottrell, Jr. He played with John Robichaux's orchestra (until 1909) and the Olympia Orchestra (1900–14), before moving to Chicago with Manuel Perez (1915). After his return to New Orleans he performed, and also recorded, with A. J. Piron's orchestra until his death (for illustration *see* BANDS, fig.1). Cottrell is credited with introducing the press roll into jazz drumming; he influenced two generations of drummers in New Orleans, including Baby Dodds, Cié Frazier, and Alfred Williams.

BIBLIOGRAPHY

ChartersJ

T. D. Brown: *A History and Analysis of Jazz Drumming to 1942* (diss., U. of Michigan, 1976)

MIKE HAZELDINE

Couesnophone. *See* GOOFUS.

Coughlan, Frank [Francis James] (*b* Emmaville, Australia, 10 Sept 1904; *d* Sydney, 6 or 7 April 1979). Australian bandleader, trombonist, trumpeter, arranger, and singer. From 1922 he worked in Sydney and Melbourne with bands including those of Bill James (1923), Frank Ellis (1924), Walter Beban (1925), Carol Laughner (1926–7), and Linn Smith (1927–8). In England he worked with Jack Hylton, Fred Elizalde, Al Collins, and Al Starita (all 1928–9). After his return to Australia he played as a sideman and leader in Brisbane, Sydney, and Melbourne; during a residency at the Sydney Trocadero (1936–9) he established his reputation as a pre-eminent swing bandleader. He was an army bandleader in 1943–5, then played again at the Sydney Trocadero (1946–51, 1954–70), after which he gradually withdrew from musical activities. The finest dance-band and swing musicians in Australia passed through the ranks of Coughlan's band; its numerous recordings include *Darktown Strutter's Ball* (1957, Prestophone V1001).

BIBLIOGRAPHY

A. Bisset: *Black Roots, White Flowers: a History of Jazz in Australia* (Sydney, 1979), 17

B. Johnson: "Coughlan, Francis James (Frank)," *The Oxford Companion to Australian Jazz* (Melbourne, Australia, 1987)

BRUCE JOHNSON

Counce, Curtis (Lee) (*b* Kansas City, MO, 23 Jan 1926; *d* Los Angeles, 31 July 1963). Double bass player. He studied violin, double bass, and tuba while in his teens, played with Nat Towles's orchestra (1941–4), then settled in Los Angeles, where he worked with Edgar Hayes (1945–8), Billy Eckstine, Bud Powell, Buddy DeFranco, Wardell Gray, and Hampton Hawes, and in a group led by Benny Carter and Ben Webster; during this period he also studied arranging and composition with Spud Murphy and recorded with Lester Young (1946). His career developed rapidly in the 1950s. He recorded albums with Teddy Charles (1953), Shorty Rogers (1953–5), Buddy Collette, Claude Williamson, Herb Geller, Bob Cooper, and Clifford Brown (all 1954), and Milt Bernhart (1954–6). In 1956 he played with DeFranco, joined Stan Kenton's orchestra for a tour of Europe, then returned to Los Angeles, where he formed a quintet in which Jack Sheldon, Harold Land, Carl Perkins, and Frank Butler worked as sidemen; he continued to work as a leader until his death. Counce played with a full, virile sound and a strong sense of swing.

SELECTED RECORDINGS

The Curtis Counce Group (1956, Cont. 3526); *You Get more Bounce with Curtis Counce* (1957, Cont. 3539); *Carl's Blues* (1957–8, Cont. 3574); *Exploring the Future* (1958, Dooto 247)

BIBLIOGRAPHY

FeatherE; *Feather '60s*

JOHN VOIGT

Countsmen [Count's Men]. The name used by bands consisting of former sidemen of Count Basie. The first such group was established in 1973 by Earle Warren for occasional work in and around New York, notably at the West End. Its personnel up to the late 1970s has included Buddy Tate, Dicky Wells, Benny Morton, and Paul Quinichette, and among its recordings is the album *The Countsmen* (1973, RCA LFL1-5034). Nat Pierce also used the name Countsmen for the big bands he organized in the early 1980s for tours of Europe. Joe Williams was the star attraction of the tour in 1980, and Buck Clayton acted as leader, conductor, and arranger for the group in 1983. All the ensembles, often incorporating the original soloists, have performed the classic repertory of Basie's bands.

BIBLIOGRAPHY

L. Jeske: "The Return of Dicky Wells," *JJI*, xxxi/8 (1978), 6

M. Carrington: "The Count's Men: an Appreciation," *Red Bank Special*, ii/6 (1984), 13

BOB WEIR

Coupling [pairing]. A term applied to the numbers on the two sides of a 78 r.p.m. (or 45 r.p.m. single) disc.

Courbois, Pierre (*b* Nijmegen, Netherlands, 23 April 1940). Dutch drummer. He studied at the conservatory in Arnhem and first played jazz with a dixieland group (1954–8). He played with a quintet led by the pianist Ton Wijkamp (1960), the Original Dutch Free Jazz Group (1961–4), Gunter Hampel (1963–6), the Free Music Quartet (1966–9), Rein de Graaff (1966–70), and the Theo Loevendie Consort (1968) and led the group Association PC from 1970 to 1975; he also played with Mal Waldron (1972), the Waterland Ensemble, led by the pianist Loek Dikker (1975–8), and the European Jazz Quintet (1977–*c*1982). Later he worked as a soloist and led the group New Association. Courbois can be heard to advantage on his albums *Myria' Poda* (1975, Universe Hot 109) and *Independence* (1983, Tim. 188).

WIM VAN EYLE

Court, Raymond (*b* Lausanne, Switzerland, 2 Dec 1932). Swiss trumpeter. He taught himself to play trumpet from the age of 18 and from 1952 to 1955 belonged to the sextet of the trombonist Raymond Droz, with whom he recorded in 1956. After belonging for two years to Flavio Ambrosetti's quintet he toured France, Germany, and Belgium from 1958 in a sextet led by the vibraphonist Kurt Weil. He won a first prize at a jazz competition in Juan-les-Pins, France (1960), and worked in Paris with Martial Solal, Daniel Humair, and René Urtreger (1960, 1962); he also played with many visiting Americans in Switzerland. In 1964 he became less active in music to work as a cabinetmaker, but he resumed playing in 1975 and again worked full-time as a musician from 1982. He recorded the album *Standards for Paradise* (Jazz et rejazz 9201) with the Hot Mallets in 1984.

PETER SCHWALM

Covington, Warren (*b* Philadelphia, 7 Aug 1921). Trombonist, leader, and arranger. His first professional engagement was with Isham Jones in 1939. He worked with Les Brown (1945–6) and Gene Krupa (1946) and then joined the music staff of CBS in New York. He led the Commanders in 1946–7. In 1950 he recorded with Tommy Dorsey's band, and after Dorsey's death he became its leader (1958); from 1961 into the 1970s he toured with the band under his own name. He also recorded in studio big bands accompanying Charles Mingus (1971), Randy Weston (1972), Bobby Hackett (1973), and George Benson (1974). He continued to be active as a studio musician and in films. (*FeatherE*; *Feather '60s*; *Feather–Gitler '70s*)

Cowbell. A clapperless bell. Graduated sets of cowbells have been used in most periods of jazz history; *see* DRUM SET, §I, 6.

Cowell, Stanley (A.) (*b* Toledo, OH, 5 May 1941). Pianist and composer. He played piano from the age of four, and two years later heard Art Tatum. He studied at Oberlin College Conservatory (BM 1962) and the University of Michigan (MM 1966); he played with Roland Kirk while he was at Oberlin and later with Marion Brown (1966–7) and Max Roach (1967–70), and in a quintet led by Bobby Hutcherson and Harold Land (1968–71). From 1969 to 1973 and in the late 1970s he was a member of Music, Inc.; with the group's leader, Charles Tolliver, he founded Strata-East Records (1971), for which he recorded with, among others, Music, Inc., the Heath Brothers, Clifford Jordan, and the septet Piano Choir. He formed Collective Black Artists, Inc., with Reggie Workman, Jimmy Owens, and others, in 1970, and directed the CBA Ensemble in 1973–4. From 1974 to 1984 he worked principally with the Heath Brothers (for illustration *see* HEATH). He received a grant for composition from the NEA in 1978, and began teaching at Lehman College, CUNY, in 1981. Later he made international tours as a soloist and in duos and trios. Cowell acknowledges the influence of Tatum, Bud Powell, Barry Harris, and Tommy Flanagan; his playing combines disciplined forms and an eclectic approach to the entire range of jazz styles.

SELECTED RECORDINGS

As unaccompanied soloist: *Waiting for the Moment* (1977, Gal. 5104)
Duos with D. Burrell: *Questions and Answers* (1973, Trio 7089)
As leader: *Blues for the Viet Cong* (1969, Pol. 583740); *Brilliant Circles* (1969, Pol. 2383092); *Equipoise* (1978, Gal. 5125)
As sideman: M. Brown: *Why not* (1966, ESP 1040); M. Roach: *Members don't git Weary* (1968, Atl. 1510); C. Tolliver: *The Ringer* (1969, Pol. 583750); *Music, Inc.* (1970, Pol. 2383138); J. Heath: *Love and Understanding* (1973, Muse 5028); Heath Brothers: *In Motion* (*c*1979, Col. JC35816); *Brothers and Others* (1983, Ant. 1016)

BIBLIOGRAPHY

L. Lyons: "Stanley Cowell: Versatile Jazz Pianist and Multi-Keyboardist," *CK*, v/6 (1979), 30 [incl. discography]

ED HAZELL

Cox [née Prather], **Ida** (*b* Toccoa, GA, 25 Feb 1896; *d* Knoxville, TN, 10 Nov 1967). Singer. She joined a minstrel show as a child and was singing in theaters at the age of 14. Although her career paralleled that of other classic blues singers, she depended less on vaudeville songs, and most of her repertory consisted of blues in traditional form. The first of her many recordings, *Any Woman's Blues*, was a composition by her pianist Lovie Austin, and demonstrated the characteristic resonant, rather nasal quality of her singing. With appropriate material, particularly her own blues compositions, she was among the finest women singers. *Ida Cox's Lawdy Lawdy Blues* and *I've got the blues for Rampart Street*, both with excellent accompaniment by Tommy Ladnier on cornet and a trio including Austin, are strong yet relaxed. For several years Cox was accompanied professionally by Jesse Crump, who is heard playing a somber organ part in *Coffin Blues*. After 1929 Cox did not record for ten years, but *Four Day Creep*, recorded with a larger band than usual (including Hot Lips Page), showed that she was still in excellent form. Between 1940 and 1950 she worked intermittently as a singer, but made no recordings. In 1961, at the age of 65, she recorded a final session; her voice had lost its quality, however, and she retired from active performing thereafter.

SELECTED RECORDINGS

Duo with L. Austin: Any Woman's Blues (1923, Para. 12053)
As leader: Ida Cox's Lawdy Lawdy Blues (1923, Para. 12064); I've got the blues for Rampart Street (1923, Para. 12063); Coffin Blues (1925, Para. 12318); Jail House Blues (1929, Para. 12965); Four Day Creep (1939, Voc. 05298); *Blues for Rampart Street* (1961, Riv. 9374), incl. Wild women don't have the blues

BIBLIOGRAPHY

P. Oliver: *Conversation with the Blues* (London, 1965)
D. Stewart-Baxter: *Ma Rainey and the Classic Blues Singers* (New York and London, 1970)
——: Liner notes, *Ida Cox 1923 Recordings* (Fountain Vintage Blues 301, 1973)
S. Harris: *Blues Who's Who: a Biographical Dictionary of Blues Singers* (New Rochelle, NY, 1979)

PAUL OLIVER

Coxhill, Lol [Lowen] (*b* Portsmouth, England, 19 Sept 1932). English soprano and sopranino saxophonist. In the 1960s he played with such visiting American rhythm-and-blues musicians as Rufus Thomas, Lowell Fulson, and Champion Jack Dupree; during this period he began to develop the style of unaccompanied solo playing for which he is best known. He worked with the pianist Steve Miller's group Delivery (1969–70) and at the Berlin Free Music Festival (1969), but it was not until he recorded his first album, *Ear of the Beholder* (1971), that he began to attract attention as a distinctive free improviser. During the 1970s and 1980s he has been associated with many European bop and avant-garde musicians, including Chris McGregor, Trevor Watts, and Bobby Wellins, and with the group Company (for illustration *see* JAZZ (i), fig. 9). He has also been a member of several eclectic English groups, including the Recedents, Standard Conversions, and the Melody Four (with Tony Coe and Steve Beresford). Coxhill's early work is stylistically indebted to Charlie Parker, but his eccentricity and his often ironic approach have made him one of Europe's most immediately recognizable players.

SELECTED RECORDINGS

As unaccompanied soloist: *The Dunois Solos* (1981, Nato 95)
Duos with Daniel Deshays: *10.02* (1984, Nato 439)

As leader: *Ear of the Beholder* (1971, Dandelion 8008); with S. Miller: *The Story so Far . . . oh Really?* (1974, Car. 1507); with David Holland: *The Johnny Rondo Duo Plus Mike Cooper* (1980, FMP SAJ29); *Instant Replay* (1982, Nato 25, 32); with S. Miller: *The Steve Miller Trio Meets Lol Coxhill* (1985, Matchless 9)

BIBLIOGRAPHY

R. Cotterell, ed.: *Jazz Now: the Jazz Centre Society Guide* (London, 1976)
G. Rouy: "Lol Coxhill: 'avec un parfum très anglais'," *Jm*, no.274 (1979), 43
L. Coxhill: "Première apparence et au delà," *Jazz en suite*, no.1 (1983), 74
D. Ilic: "Just a Bald Headed Busker?," *The Wire*, no.5 (1983), 28

MARK GILBERT

Crabtree, Richie (*b* 1934). Pianist, member of the MASTERSOUNDS.

Craig, Al(fie) (*b* London, July 1907; *d* Nice, France, 25 Oct 1981). English drummer. He began learning drums at the age of 15 and, after playing in the orchestra for the show *Blackbirds of 1934*, led his own band at the Shim Sham Club, London. It performed with visiting American musicians, including Garland Wilson, Benny Carter (with whom he recorded in 1936–7), and Fats Waller. In 1938 Craig worked with the double bass player Jack Davis and then led the Rhythm Swingers, an all-black group which later became resident at the Hell Club. After World War II he moved to Paris, where he recorded with Django Reinhardt (1947). In 1949 he settled in Nice, and his work on the Côte d'Azur included a recording with the trio led by the pianist Jimmy Rena. From the 1960s Craig was based in Düsseldorf, Germany, and performed throughout Germany and Switzerland. He celebrated his career by recording the album *The Golden Jubilee Drummer* (1980, md 20060080).

BIBLIOGRAPHY

A. Doutart: "Le jubilé de Al Craig," *BHcF*, no.275 (1979), 7
"Echos et nouvelles," *BHcF*, no.292 (1981), 30

HOWARD RYE

Crane River Jazz Band. English traditional-jazz band formed in 1949 (*see* COLYER, KEN).

Cranshaw, Bob [Melbourne Robert] (*b* Evanston, IL, 10 Dec 1932). Bass player. He played piano and drums before taking up double bass and tuba in high school. He began to work professionally as a double bass player in the Chicago area, and in 1957 became a founding member of Walter Perkins's MJT + 3. Cranshaw went to New York with the group in 1960 and after it disbanded in 1962 joined Sonny Rollins, with whom he worked intermittently into the 1980s; his playing may be heard to advantage on *The Standard Sonny Rollins* (1964), which he recorded with Rollins's piano-less trio. He also played regularly with Duke Pearson's small groups and big bands (1962–73). From the 1960s Cranshaw has combined a career playing for television (notably such programs as "Sesame Street") and in theater orchestras with recording work for such leading swing and bop leaders as Lee Morgan, Wes Montgomery, Coleman Hawkins, Johnny Hodges, Horace Silver, James Moody, and Buddy Rich. He has also toured overseas with George Shearing, Joe Williams, Ella Fitzgerald, and Oscar Peterson. Cranshaw took up electric bass guitar in the early 1970s and is one of the few players of this instrument to be accepted by musicians in the mainstream of jazz – notably Rollins, Silver, and Milt Jackson. He has a light approach to the guitar and tends to imitate the sound of an amplified double bass.

SELECTED RECORDINGS

As sideman with MJT + 3: *Daddy-o Presents the MJT Plus 3* (1957, Argo 621); *Walter Perkins' MJT Plus 3* (1959, VJ 1013); *Make Everybody Happy* (1960, VJ 3008); *MJT Plus 3* (1960, VJ 3014)

As sideman with S. Rollins: *The Bridge* (1962, RCA LSP2527); *What's New* (1962, RCA LSP2572); *Our Man in Jazz* (1962, RCA LSP2612); *The Standard Sonny Rollins* (1964, RCA LSP3355), incl. Autumn Nocturne, I'll be seeing you, Love Letters, Night and Day, Three Little Words; *Reel Life* (*c*1982, Mlst. 9108)

As sideman with others: M. Tyner: *"Live" at Newport* (1963, Imp. 48), incl. All of you, Monk's Blues; D. Pearson: *Merry Old Soul* (1969, BN 84323), incl. Wassail Song; J. Heath: *Love and Understanding* (1973, Muse 5028)

BIBLIOGRAPHY

Feather '60s; *Feather–Gitler '70s*

LAWRENCE KOCH

Crash cymbal. A medium-sized cymbal used for accents; *see* DRUM SET, §I, 5.

Crawford, Hank [Bennie Ross, Jr.] (*b* Memphis, 21 Dec 1934). Alto saxophonist. He first played with the blues singer and guitarist B. B. King, and the rhythm-and-blues musicians Bobby Bland and Ike Turner, then moved to Nashville, where he studied music theory and composition at Tennessee State College. He led the college dance band and developed skills as an arranger, which were sharpened and refined by his work with Ray Charles, whom he joined as a baritone saxophonist in 1958; he changed to the alto instrument in 1959 and after becoming the music director of Charles's big band in 1960 he gained considerable experience and public exposure. In 1963 he left Charles to pursue an independent career. During the 1960s he recorded 12 albums as a leader for the Atlantic label; the tracks *Misty* and *Skunky Green* from two of these became hits. In the 1970s Crawford worked for the Kudu label, and was obliged to play commercially oriented arrangements by other composers. But a new contract which he signed with Milestone Records in 1983 allowed him to re-establish his original values and write his own arrangements once more.

Although Crawford's solos occasionally make reference to bop, his playing is essentially rooted in the rhythm-and-blues tradition represented by Earl Bostic and Louis Jordan. The hallmark of his style is an emotionally charged, keening tone on the alto saxophone, which has influenced the sound of such younger players as David Sanborn. Besides alto and baritone saxophones, Crawford also plays the tenor instrument and piano.

SELECTED RECORDINGS

As leader: *More Soul* (1960, Atl. 1356), incl. Misty; *From the Heart* (1961–2, Atl. 1387); *True Blues* (1963–4, Atl. 1423), incl. Skunky Green; *Dig these Blues* (1964–5, Atl. 1436); *Mister Blues Plays Lady Soul* (1969, Atl. 1523); *Wildflower* (1975, Kudu 15); *Midnight Ramble* (1982, Mlst. 9112); *Indigo Blue* (1983, Mlst. 9119); *Roadhouse Symphony* (1985, Mlst. 9140); *Soul Survivors* (1986, Mlst. 9142)

As sideman with R. Charles: *Ray Charles at Newport* (1958, Atl. 1289); *Modern Sounds in Country & Western Music* (1961, ABC-Para. 410, 415)

BIBLIOGRAPHY

Feather '60s; *Feather–Gitler '70s*
B. Niquet: "Hank Crawford," *Soul Bag*, no.68 (n.d. [?1968]), 26
L. Feather: "The Joy of Hank," *MM* (4 Dec 1971), 28
L. Underwood: "Hank Crawford: Fighting to Stay on the Scene," *Soul*, x (1 Sept 1975), 14
M. N. Varney: "Hank Crawford," *JJI*, xxxix/12 (1986), 12 [incl. discography]

MARK GILBERT

Crawford, Jimmy [Jimmie, James Strickland] (*b* Memphis, 14 Jan 1910; *d* New York, 28 Jan 1980). Drummer. He first recorded at the age of 17 with Jimmie Lunceford's Chickasaw Syncopators and he remained with Lunceford until 1943 (for illustration *see* LUNCEFORD, JIMMIE). Because of its stable personnel the band developed a precision in its ensemble work equaled by few others of the swing era. Crawford then worked and recorded with a large number of jazz musicians, including Ben Webster (1943), Billy Taylor (ii) (1944), Trummy Young

(1944–5), Edmond Hall (1945–9), Louis Armstrong, Benny Goodman, and Frank Sinatra (all in 1947), Billie Holiday (1949), Fletcher Henderson (1950, and with the reunited band under Rex Stewart, 1957), Ella Fitzgerald (1950–55), Dizzy Gillespie (1954), Count Basie (1960), and Tyree Glenn (1969). From 1952 he also played in many Broadway musicals. Although Crawford was a versatile musician, his style was always that of a big-band drummer. His playing, reminiscent of Chick Webb's, emphasized clean, crisp, well-controlled patterns in his accompaniments and meticulous solos.

SELECTED RECORDINGS

As sideman: J. Lunceford: Tain't what you do (1939, Voc./OK 4582); Well, all right then (1939, Voc./OK 4887); L. Armstrong: *Louis Armstrong with Edmond Hall* (1947, Palm Club 19), incl. Tiger Rag; E. Hall: *Jazz at the Savoy Cafe, Boston* (1949, Savoy 15028), incl. Limehouse Blues

BIBLIOGRAPHY

ChiltonW
B. Sapsford: "Jimmy Crawford: a Drummer Overlooked," *JJ*, xvii/4 (1964), 9
S. Dance: *The World of Swing* (New York, 1974) [colln of previously pubd interviews], 119

T. DENNIS BROWN

Crawford, (Holland) Ray (*b* Pittsburgh, 7 Feb 1924). Guitarist. He played clarinet and tenor saxophone with Fletcher Henderson (1942–3), then, after suffering from tuberculosis, took up guitar. He played and recorded with Ahmad Jamal's first trio in Pittsburgh and Chicago (1951–6); on many tracks of Jamal's album *Chamber Music of the New Jazz* (1955, Argo 602), in addition to playing guitar in a conventional bop style, Crawford produces a convincing electronic imitation of bongos by tapping on the strings. From 1956 to 1960 he performed and recorded in New York with Jamal (1956), Jimmy Smith (1958), and Gil Evans (1959–60), and may be heard to advantage on *Nevada* from Evans's album *Out of the Cool* (1960, Imp. 4). Crawford also worked with Tony Scott. He then settled in Los Angeles and recorded as the leader of a bop sextet that included Johnny Coles and Cecil Payne (1961), and as a sideman with Sonny Stitt (1963) and Sonny Criss (1975). In the mid-1960s and from 1971 into the 1980s he played frequently with Jimmy Smith.

BIBLIOGRAPHY

J. Tynan: "Focus on: Ray Crawford," *DB*, xxix/20 (1962), 26
R. Williams: "The Crawford Compendium," *MM*, liii (18 Feb 1978), 28
M. Weber: "Interview with Ray Crawford," *Coda*, no.184 (1982), 6

Crawley, Wilton (*b* Smithfield, VA, 18 July 1900; *d* ? after 1948). Clarinetist and singer. When his family moved to Philadelphia, he formed a band with his brother Jimmy, who played clarinet and saxophone. During the 1920s and 1930s he enjoyed much success with his own variety act. His best-known recordings are those he made in 1929 and 1930 as the leader of a group which included Jelly Roll Morton. These and his earlier recordings (1927–8), some of which included Eddie Lang, display a repetitive but striking improvisatory style on clarinet, characterized by conventional blues formulas (sometimes played with a timbre that resembles that of Bubber Miley's muted trumpet), extended passages of deliberately paced slap-tonguing, and an extraordinary cackling sound. Crawley may be heard both singing and playing on *I'm her papa, she's my mama* (1930, Vic. 23344). He performed in England in early 1930. (H. Rye: "Visiting Firemen, 8: Wilton Crawley," *Sv*, no.108 (1983), 212)

based on *ChiltonW*

Creath, Charlie [Charles Cyril] (*b* Ironton, MO, 30 Dec 1890; *d* Chicago, 23 Oct 1951). Trumpeter, bandleader, saxophonist, and accordionist. He spent his teens playing trumpet in circus and theater bands, and returned to the St. Louis area about 1919. He then led groups on the Streckfus fleet of riverboats, which traveled to and from New Orleans, and soon became so popular that he had several bands working under his name. He and Fate Marable were leaders of a group on the SS *Capitol* during 1927, but Creath's career was interrupted by a two-year illness. Thereafter he played mostly alto saxophone and accordion. Marable and he collaborated again during the mid-1930s, after which Creath opened a nightclub in Chicago. His last years were spent in illness. Although he was praised by his contemporaries for the rhythmic swing and brilliant tone of his trumpet playing, Creath is best remembered as a highly influential leader in St. Louis music circles. Among the members of his bands were Ed Allen, Pops Foster, Lonnie Johnson, and his brother-in-law Zutty Singleton.

SELECTED RECORDINGS

Pleasure Mad/Market Street Blues (1924, OK 8201); Way Down in Lover's Lane/Grandpa's Spell (1925, OK 8257); Butterfinger Blues/Crazy Quilt (1927, OK 8477)

BIBLIOGRAPHY

ChiltonW
M. Williams: "Zutty," *Jazz Masters of New Orleans* (New York and London, 1967/*R*1978), 185
G. Fernett: *Swing Out: Great Negro Jazz Bands* (Midland, MI, n.d. [?1970]), 146
A. McCarthy: *Big Band Jazz* (New York and London, 1974), 113

LAWRENCE KOCH

Creole. Record label. Its catalogue was issued in 1950–51 by the Creole Record Exchange of New York, and consisted of 28 reissues of early jazz classics. (B. Rothacker: "Creole Records," *Matrix*, no.55 (1964), 3)

Creole Band. Name used by several early jazz bands, including (on occasion) the ORIGINAL CREOLE BAND led by Bill Johnson (i). Similar names were used by a number of bands among the members of which were creole musicians from New Orleans: for example, Kid Ory's Creole Jazz Band, Peter Bocage's Creole Serenaders, and, pre-eminently, King Oliver's Creole Jazz Band.

Crescent. Record label. It was founded by Nesuhi Ertegun and used in 1944–5 by the owners of the Jazz Man Record Shop, Hollywood, to issue material by Kid Ory's Creole Jazz Band. The eight items in its catalogue were among the most important recordings in the revival of traditional jazz; the rights to these were later acquired by Good Time Jazz.

Crescent City Jazzers. Name by which the ARCADIAN SERENADERS were originally known.

Crimmins, Roy (*b* Perth, Scotland, 2 Aug 1929). Scottish trombonist. He grew up in London, and taught himself trumpet and later trombone. He played with the Galleon Jazz Band (1950), and performed and recorded with Mick Mulligan (1952, 1954) and Freddy Randall (1953). Thereafter he formed a band with Alex Welsh (1954) which proved to be highly successful. After leaving this ensemble in 1965 Crimmins took his own band to Germany, where he remained for 13 years. During this period he also worked in Switzerland and Austria, and for five years he had his own television show in Vienna. He also made several recordings, including three albums as a leader (1975–7) under the pseudonym Roy King. His playing may be heard to advantage on Fatty George's album *Chicagoan All Stars* (1973, MPS 2122098-2). After returning to England in 1978 he rejoined Welsh; after the latter's death he worked as a freelance, playing with Harry Gold and with Bob Wilber's British band. He has also led his own group.

BIBLIOGRAPHY

FeatherE
D. Fairweather: "Crimmins, Roy," in I. Carr, D. Fairweather, and B. Priestley: *Jazz: the Essential Companion* (London, 1987)

CLARRIE HENLEY

Criss, Sonny [William] (*b* Memphis, 23 Oct 1927; *d* Los Angeles, 19 Nov 1977). Alto saxophonist. He worked mostly in Los Angeles, where he lived from 1942; in 1946 he played in Howard McGhee's band with Charlie Parker and Teddy Edwards, then worked with the drummer Johnny Otis, Billy Eckstine, and Gerald Wilson. After touring in a band with Parker under the auspices of Norman Granz's Jazz at the Philharmonic (1948) he played during the 1950s with Eckstine (1950–51), Stan Kenton (1955), Howard Rumsey's Lighthouse All Stars, and Buddy Rich (1958); he also led groups of his own. From 1962 to 1965 he lived in Europe, recording, performing, and broadcasting. When he returned to Los Angeles, however, he had difficulty finding steady work; after recording several times in the late 1960s he spent much time in community service. In 1973–4 he toured Europe, and in 1975 he resumed recording. He took his own life.

Criss was a bop saxophonist, strongly influenced at first by Charlie Parker. But his mature style was more distinctive: he produced a warm, rich tone and a prominent vibrato that Parker lacked. He was capable of playing dazzling runs with such effortless grace that they never sounded ostentatious. An excellent jazz musician, through lack of opportunities Criss never gained the recognition he deserved.

Oral history material in *NjR*.

SELECTED RECORDINGS

As leader: *Up, Up and Away* (1967, Prst. 7530); *Sonny's Dream* (1968, Prst.7576); *Rockin' in Rhythm* (1968, Prst.7610); *Crisscraft* (1975, Muse 5068)

BIBLIOGRAPHY

H. Siders: "Sonny Criss: One-horn Man," *DB*, xxxiii/10 (1966), 27
B. Porter and M. Gardner: "The California Cats," *JM*, [no.158] (April 1968), 7; [no.159] (May 1968), 6
M. Gardner: "Sonny Criss Discography," *DF*, no.16 (1970), 9; no.17 (1970), 3; no.18 (1970), 3
H. Mandel: "Sonny Criss: Up from the Underground," *DB*, xliv/5 (1977), 20
D. Salemann, D. Hartmann, and M. Vogler: *Sonny Criss, 1943–1952: Solography, Discography, Band Routes, Engagements in Chronological Order* (Basle, Switzerland, 1987)

THOMAS OWENS

Criss Cross Jazz. Record company and label. The company was founded in 1981 in Enschede, Netherlands, by Gerry Teekens (*b* The Hague, 5 Dec 1935), who established the concern after arranging European tours for Jimmy Raney, Warne Marsh, and others. The first item released on the label was by Raney; later albums were issued by Stan Getz, Marsh, Clifford Jordan, Kirk Lightsey, Dave Pike, Cedar Walton, Tom Harrell, Chet Baker, and others. From the mid-1980s Criss Cross Jazz has recorded many albums in the USA, and has sponsored the first sessions by many promising young bop players, including the pianist Michael Weiss, the alto saxophonist Kenny Garrett, the guitarist Peter Leitch, and the tenor saxophonist Ralph Moore; it has also recorded the work of the Dutch tenor saxophonist Joe Van Enkhuizen. The company's albums are well produced, of high quality, and with well-designed jackets. The organization avoids reissues and releases around six new albums each year.

Criss Cross Jazz distributes its own recordings throughout the world, and has thus not entered into leasing arrangements. Late in 1987 the company issued its first compact disc, in response to demand from Japan and Germany. Teekens does not regard the enterprise as a commercial venture; his sole aim is to make enough money to fund further recording projects. The organization also has an associated publishing company, Criss Cross Music.

MARK GARDNER

Crombie, Tony [Anthony John] (*b* London, 27 Aug 1925). English drummer and composer. A self-taught musician, he played in London clubs from 1941 and performed with many visiting American bands, notably those of Glenn Miller and Sam Donahue. In the late 1940s he played on transatlantic liners with Ronnie Scott and toured Europe with Duke Ellington (1948); he also made weekly broadcasts as a member of Tito Burns's Accordian Club Sextet and played at the Club Eleven in London (1948–50). He later accompanied the singers Lena Horne, Carmen McRae, and Annie Ross (1954) on tour. Throughout the 1950s Crombie was a house drummer for Decca, but he also played with Scott (1951–4, 1956) and Victor Feldman's trio (1954–5), and formed a succession of groups, the first in 1954, the second (an early rock-and-roll band called the Rockets) in 1956, and Jazz Inc. in 1959; he occasionally doubled on piano and he recorded on that instrument with Dizzy Reece in 1955. After working as the resident drummer at Scott's club (1959–61), where he played with Coleman Hawkins and Ben Webster among others, he concentrated on composing, writing scores for films and television (notably the series "Man from Interpol"). Miles Davis included Crombie's *So Near so Far* on his album *Seven Steps to Heaven* (1963, CS8851); Blossom Dearie, Paul Gonsalves, Stephane Grappelli, and Ray Nance also recorded pieces by him. Having worked in a duo with Mike Carr, Crombie played in Carr's trio Pendulum in 1970–72; he then became a member of Scott's trio (1972–5) and of the Blue Flames, led by the singer Georgie Fame. In the 1980s he has accompanied such musicians as Peter King and Stan Tracey. A versatile and imaginative player and composer, Crombie was instrumental, with Ronnie Scott, in introducing bop to Britain.

SELECTED RECORDINGS

Duos with Alan Haven: *Thru Till Two* (1966, Fon. 5400)
As leader: *Man from Interpol* (1960, Top Rank 35-053); *Sweet, Wide and Blue* (1960, Decca SKL4114)
As sideman: R. Scott: *At the Royal Festival Hall with the Ronnie Scott Orchestra and Tony Crombie* (1956, Decca LF1261)

BIBLIOGRAPHY

FeatherE; *Feather '60s*; *Feather–Gitler '70s*
C. Winstone: "The Baron at Home: Tony Crombie," *CI*, vi/10 (1968), 24

SIMON ADAMS

Crosby, Bing [Harry Lillis] (*b* Tacoma, WA, 2 May 1904; *d* Madrid, 14 Oct 1977). Singer, brother of Bob Crosby. As a boy in Spokane, Washington, he played drums and sang with small jazz groups. With Al Rinker (Mildred Bailey's brother) and Harry Barris, he formed the Rhythm Boys, who appeared from 1926 to 1930 with Paul Whiteman's orchestra. Crosby began working independently about 1930, and the following year began a spectacularly successful career in radio and film (for illustration *see* FILMS, fig.2), notably in musical films such as *Holiday Inn* (1942, including the song *White Christmas*). He also made an appearance with Jack Teagarden in *The Birth of the*

Blues (1941, loosely based on the rise of the Original Dixieland Jazz Band), in which he played a clarinetist modeled on Larry Shields (the sound of the instrument was dubbed by Danny Polo). While he was never primarily a jazz singer, Crosby retained an interest in jazz and is best remembered in this context for his collaborations with Louis Armstrong, particularly in the film *High Society* (1956), and in recordings of songs arranged by Johnny Mercer, of which *Sugar* (on the album *Bing Crosby – Louis Armstrong*, 1960, MGM E3882) is an excellent example. In his later world tours he was accompanied by a quartet which included, for jazz sections of his concerts, Joe Bushkin and Milt Hinton.

Crosby was one of the first singers to master the use of the microphone and was important in introducing into the mainstream of popular singing an Afro-American concept of song as a lyrical extension of speech. As one of the first crooners, he used the microphone not so much for singing as for apparently talking (or even whispering) to a melody. His techniques – easing the weight of breath on the vocal chords, passing into a head voice at a low register, using forward production to aid distinct enunciation, singing on consonants (a practice of black singers), and making discreet use of appoggiaturas, mordents, and slurs to emphasize the text – were emulated by nearly all later popular singers.

BIBLIOGRAPHY

FeatherE
B. Crosby [and P. Martin]: *Call me Lucky* (New York, 1953)
H. Pleasants: *The Great American Popular Singers* (New York, 1974)
——: "Bing Crosby: a Bel Canto Baritone whose Art Disguises Art," *New York Times* (5 Dec 1976)
W. Balliett: *American Singers* (New York, 1979)
D. Shepherd and R. F. Slatzer: *Bing Crosby: the Hollow Man* (New York, 1981)
L. Gourse: *Louis' Children: American Jazz Singers* (New York, 1984)
S. O'Connell: *Bing: a Voice for All Seasons* (Tralee, Ireland, 1984) [incl. discography]

HENRY PLEASANTS/R

Crosby, Bob [George Robert] (*b* Spokane, WA, 25 Aug 1913). Singer and bandleader, brother of Bing Crosby. After performing with the bands led by Anson Weeks and the Dorsey Brothers (1934–5) he was appointed leader of a cooperative band made up of former members of Ben Pollack's band and newcomers recruited in New York. The Bob Crosby Orchestra's unique brand of big-band dixieland jazz achieved international popularity during the late 1930s; its star soloists Eddie Miller, Yank Lawson, Billy Butterfield, Irving Fazola, Matty Matlock, Nappy Lamare, Ray Bauduc, and Bob Haggart also played in Crosby's widely acclaimed small group, the BOB CATS (see illustration). An unpredictable vibrato marred much of Crosby's singing but his rhythmic phrasing did much to compensate. The original band broke up in 1942 and Crosby appeared in numerous films, including *Presenting Lily Mars* (1943), *Reveille with Beverly* (1943), and *The Singing Sheriff* (1944). During World War II he served with distinction in the US Marines, leading a service band in the Pacific area. After the war he was mainly active as a compère and singer on radio and television shows, occasionally organizing bands or reunions of the Bob Cats for specific engagements. He continued to lead these groups during the 1970s and 1980s. A collection of his scores and other materials is held in the American Heritage Center of the University of Wyoming in Laramie; *see* LIBRARIES AND ARCHIVES, §2.

SELECTED RECORDINGS

(all recorded for Decca)

South Rampart Street Parade/Dogtown Blues (1937, 15038); March of the Bob Cats (1938, 1865); The Big Noise from Winnetka (1938, 2208); Rose of Washington Square (1939, 2474); Spain (1940, 3248)

BIBLIOGRAPHY

C. Jones: *The Bob Crosby Band* (London, 1946)
F. Littler: "I just Blew in from Winnetka," *JM*, vi/4 (1960), 12
I. Crosbie: "That Dixieland Jazz," *JJ*, xxiii/3 (1970), 12

Bob Crosby's Bob Cats at the Blackhawk Restaurant, Chicago, 1938: (from back, left to right) Yank Lawson (trumpet), Nappy Lamare (guitar), and Bob Haggart (double bass); Ray Bauduc (drums), Warren Smith (i) (trombone), Irving Fazola (clarinet), Eddie Miller (tenor saxophone), Crosby (leader), and Gil Rodin (alto saxophone, seated)

G. Lombardi: "La storia dei 'Crosbiani'," *Musica jazz*, xxxiii (1977), 16
J. Chilton: *Stomp Off, Let's Go! The Story of Bob Crosby's Bob Cats & Big Band* (London, 1983)

JOHN CHILTON

Crosby, Israel (Clem) (*b* Chicago, 19 Jan 1919; *d* Chicago, 11 Aug 1962). Double bass player. He played trumpet from the age of five, took up trombone and tuba, then changed to double bass in 1934. Early in his career he recorded solos with Jess Stacy (1935), Gene Krupa (1935–6), and Teddy Wilson (1936). He performed and recorded with Albert Ammons (1935–6), and played with Fletcher Henderson's orchestra in 1936–9 and with Horace Henderson in Chicago (1940–41). As a studio sideman he made many recordings, with, among others, Edmond Hall (1941), Georgie Auld (1944), Roy Eldridge (1944), and Coleman Hawkins (1944). He belonged to Ahmad Jamal's trio between 1954 and 1962, except for a brief period when he toured with Benny Goodman's orchestra (1956–7), and also played and recorded with George Shearing (1962). Crosby was one of the earliest virtuoso jazz double bass players, capable of improvising melodic solos, rhythmically exciting accompaniment patterns, and scalar walking bass lines.

SELECTED RECORDINGS

As sideman: G. Krupa: Blues of Israel (1935, Parl. R2224); T. Wilson: Blues in C Sharp Minor (1936, Bruns. 7684); A. Jamal: *At the Pershing* (1958, Argo 628)

BIBLIOGRAPHY

ChiltonW
W. C. Allen: *Hendersonia: the Music of Fletcher Henderson and his Musicians: a Bio-discography* (Highland Park, NJ, 1973)

JOHN VOIGT

Crotty, Ron(ald O.) (*b* San Francisco, 1929). Double bass player. While in the US Army he spent some time in England, where he played with many British jazzmen. He then returned to the West Coast and joined Dave Brubeck, recording in the octet (1948–50), the trio, with Cal Tjader on drums (1950–51), and the early quartet (1952–3). He also worked with Wally Rose, Brew Moore, and Earl Hines, and recorded with his own trio (with Vince Guaraldi and Eddie Duran) in 1955 (*Modern Music from San Francisco*, Fan. 3213). Although Crotty was never really a soloist, his playing lent strong support to Brubeck's groups, particularly the quartet. (*FeatherE*)

Crouch, Stanley (*b* Los Angeles, 14 Dec 1945). Poet, writer, and drummer. He took up drumming in 1966 to play with the pianist Raymond King, and from 1967 worked with Arthur Blythe, Bobby Bradford, David Murray, and James Newton in the cooperative free-jazz groups Quartet and Black Music Infinity. During the 1970s he taught black cultural studies in California before moving to New York with Murray, where he became associated with the free-jazz community; he wrote for the *Soho Weekly News* and, into the late 1980s, the *Village Voice*, and has promoted the careers of such musicians as Leroy Jenkins and Leo Smith.

Crouch has established a reputation as a powerful performance poet. He recorded an album (1972, FaD 10105) based on his book *Ain't no Ambulances for no Nigguhs Tonight* (1972) and with Amiri Baraka and the Original Last Poets recorded *Pimp's Last Mack: a Death Request* on the album *Black Spirits: a Festival of New Black Poets in America* (1972, Motown Black Forum B456L). Besides his own collection, he has contributed to several important anthologies of black-American poetry. His poem *Albert Ayler: Eulogy for a Decomposed Saxophone Player* testifies to Ayler's influence on Crouch, whose percussion style attempts to reproduce the characteristic bent and sustained notes of the saxophone which were frequently used by Ayler. Crouch's work as a drummer is well represented by Murray's *Short Song* from the album *Wildflowers: the New York Loft Jazz Sessions*, iv (1976, Douglas 7048).

WRITINGS
(selective list)

Ain't no Ambulances for no Nigguhs Tonight (New York, 1972)
No New Music, Albert Ayler: Eulogy for a Decomposed Saxophone Player, in *The Poetry of Black America: Anthology of the 20th Century*, ed. A. Adoff (New York, 1973), 484

BIBLIOGRAPHY

Feather–Gitler '70s
P. Occhiogrosso: "Profile: Stanley Crouch, David Murray," *DB*, xliii/6 (1976), 38
E. Jost: *Jazzmusiker: Materialen zur Soziologie der afro-amerikanischen Musik* (Frankfurt am Main, Germany, 1982), 72

ANTHONY BARNETT

Crow, Bill [William Orval] (*b* Othello, WA, 27 Dec 1927). Double bass player. He played brass instruments and studied drums during his school years, and his early professional work, in the Seattle area, was as a drummer and trombonist. In 1952, only two years after taking up double bass, he performed with Stan Getz and Teddy Charles. He continued to play with leading jazz musicians, notably Terry Gibbs (1953–4), Marian McPartland (1954–5, 1957–8), and (in the early 1960s) the group led by Al Cohn and Zoot Sims, Quincy Jones, Mose Allison, and the Bob Brookmeyer–Clark Terry quintet. He also toured the USSR with Benny Goodman (1962). From 1956 to 1965 Crow played frequently in ensembles led by Gerry Mulligan (for illustration *see* RECORDING, fig.5), and his clean lines are heard to advantage on many of Mulligan's recordings, especially where the group does not include a piano. Crow treats the double bass in a percussive manner and, relying on physical power, accentuates the ringing power of the instrument. His solos are highly melodic. From the mid-1960s he has been more involved in commercial work, playing in the house band at the Playboy Club (1965–70) and in theater orchestras for Broadway shows (where he sometimes plays tuba). He has also been active as a record reviewer and writer on jazz.

SELECTED RECORDINGS

As sideman: S. Getz: Lullaby of Birdland/Autumn Leaves (1952, Roost 562); M. McPartland: *At the Hickory House* (1954, Cap. T574); *After Dark* (1955, Cap. T699); G. Mulligan: *Mulligan at Storyville* (1956, PJ 1228); *What is There to Say* (1958–9, Col. CL1307); *Concert Jazz Band at the Village Vanguard* (1960, Verve 68396); A. Cohn and Z. Sims: *Either Way* (1961, Fred Miles 1), incl. Morning Fun, P-Town; C. Terry and B. Brookmeyer: *Tonight* (1964, Mstr. 6043)

BIBLIOGRAPHY

FeatherE; *Feather '60s*

LAWRENCE KOCH

Crowder, Bob [Robert Henry; Little Sax] (*b* 1912). Tenor saxophonist. During the early 1930s he worked in Milwaukee; he played with François Mosely's Louisianians (1932) and Punch Miller at the Harlem Club in Chicago (1933). After touring with Mosely he joined Horace Henderson (July 1937), then played with Earl Hines (1938–40), with whom he made a number of recordings (1939–40), among them *Father Steps In* (1939, Bb 10377). He also performed with Walter Fuller (1940), the pianist Fletcher Butler (early 1941), and Coleman Hawkins (April 1941), and again with Hines (recording in 1941–2). He settled in Chicago and continued to play regularly during the 1960s.

based on *ChiltonW*

Crown. Record company and label. The company was established in 1930, and during the three years of its existence it organized several important recordings by the bands of Eubie Blake, Fletcher Henderson, and Gil Rodin. The label was also used to reissue race records previously put out by others. Crown's catalogue was later made available to the United States Record Corp. (*see* VARSITY). The label should not be confused with the short-lived subsidiary of Arto of the same name (1921), or with the English label Crown, which was used to issue recordings made by Crystalate for sale in Woolworth's stores in the mid-1930s. (B. Rust: *The American Record Label Book* (New Rochelle, NY, 1978), 89)

Crumbley, Elmer (E.) (*b* Kingfisher, OK, 1 Aug 1908). Trombonist. He played in the Midwest with the trumpeter Lloyd Hunter (1923–9, 1931–2), George E. Lee (1929–30), Tommy Douglas, Zack Whyte, Jabbo Smith, and Erskine Tate. In 1934 he led his own band in Omaha, Nebraska, before joining Jimmie Lunceford, with whom he made recordings from 1935 to 1942 (including *Well, all right then*, 1939, Voc. 4887); he performed with the band until Lunceford's death in 1947 (for illustration *see* LUNCEFORD, JIMMIE). After playing with Eddie Wilcox (recording *c*1949–1951) and Lucky Millinder (early 1950s), he joined Erskine Hawkins; in 1958 he played with Sammy Price in Europe. In the late 1950s and early 1960s he worked with Reuben Phillips's orchestra at the Apollo Theatre, New York. He went on to play in big bands re-formed by Cab Calloway and Earl Hines in the mid-1960s; in 1971 he recorded with another such band led by Hawkins.

based on *ChiltonW*

Crump, Jesse [Tiny] (*b* Paris, TX, 1906; *d* USA, 21 April 1974). Pianist and organist. He toured in vaudeville from about 1919 and during the 1920s led the first all-black band to play on the Pickwick Hotel's radio station in Kansas City. He also toured frequently with Ida Cox, whom he married, in the late 1920s and early 1930s, and is probably best known for the recordings he made with her in Chicago between 1923 and 1928; these include *Bear-mash Blues* (1923, Para. 12087) and *Coffin Blues/ Rambling Blues* (1925, Para. 12318), on which he plays reed organ. He also made solo recordings (not for commercial issue) in 1923. From 1937 to 1951 he worked mostly in the area around Muncie, Indiana, then moved to California, where he recorded five dixieland albums with Bob Scobey (1956), performed with Marty Marsala (1960), and played as a soloist.

BIBLIOGRAPHY

FeatherE
S. Harris: *Blues Who's Who: a Biographical Dictionary of Blues Singers* (New Rochelle, NY, 1979)
Obituary, *Orkester journalen*, xlii/9 (1974), 5

Crusaders. Hard-bop, later jazz-rock, group. It was formed in the early 1950s by three high-school students in Houston: the pianist Joe Sample, the saxophonist Wilton Felder, and the drummer Stix Hooper, who was the group's leader. Originally called the Swingsters, it was soon joined by the trombonist Wayne Henderson, the flutist Hubert Laws, and the double bass player Henry Wilson. As the Modern Jazz Sextet it played locally during the members' years in high school and college. In the late 1950s Sample, Felder, Hooper, and Henderson moved to California, and changed the group's name to the Night Hawks, and later the Jazz Crusaders (1961). In that year, augmented by the addition of a double bass player, the band made its first recordings, and soon became extremely successful. It played hard bop, performing and recording frequently, sometimes as a sextet with a guitarist.

By 1968 Sample, Hooper, and Felder had become active as studio musicians, and Henderson was working increasingly as a record producer. They ceased touring and concentrated instead on making recordings; in 1971 they shortened the group's name to the Crusaders and began playing music heavily influenced by rock, soul, and the popular style funk. Sample used electronic keyboards as well as piano and electric piano, and in the mid-1970s the ensemble included Larry Carlton (electric guitar) and Max Bennett (electric bass guitar). This change of approach brought considerable commercial success, and in 1979 the group's recording *Street Life* became a substantial hit. Henderson left in 1975, and Hooper in 1983; the latter was replaced by Ndugu. Sample and Felder continued to lead the group in the mid-1980s.

SELECTED RECORDINGS

Freedom Sound (1961, PJ 27); *Chile con soul* (1965, PJ 20092); *The Festival Album* (1966, PJ 20115); *Crusaders 1* (1971, Blue Thumb 6001); *Scratch* (*c*1974, Blue Thumb 6010); *Free as the Wind* (1976, Blue Thumb 6029); *Street Life* (1979, MCA 3094); *Royal Jam* (1981, MCA 8017); *Ongaku kai: Live in Japan* (1982, Crusaders 16002)

BIBLIOGRAPHY

J. Tynan: "Meet the Jazz Crusaders," *DB*, xxx/14 (1963), 18
H. Siders: "The Crusaders: Four of a Kind," *DB*, xl/13 (1973), 16
L. Underwood: "The Crusaders: Knights without Jazz," *DB*, xliii/12 (1976), 12 [incl. discography]
H. Nolan: "The Crusaders: the Sweet and Sour Smell of Success," *DB*, xlv/ 9 (1978), 12
A. J. Liska: "The Lone Crusaders," *DB*, l/11 (1983), 20 [incl. discography]

THOMAS OWENS

Cuber, Ronnie [Ronald Edward] (*b* New York, 25 Dec 1941). Baritone saxophonist. He played in Marshall Brown's Newport Youth Band at the Newport Jazz Festival (1959), recorded with Slide Hampton (1962), and performed and recorded with Maynard Ferguson (1963–5) and George Benson (1966–7). He worked with Lionel Hampton in 1968 and the following year joined Woody Herman, with whom he toured Europe. After playing in rock, soul, and Latin groups, he achieved some prominence as a bop soloist. He led his own groups in the USA and Europe, recording in 1976 (*Cuber libre*, Xan. 135), 1978, and 1982, and performed and recorded with Lee Konitz's nonet (1977, 1979) and with the Xanadu All Stars at the Montreux International Jazz Festival (1978). He also recorded with Mickey Tucker (1977) and Rein de Graaff and Nick Brignola (both 1979). In the 1980s he composed a number of jazz pieces for his own quartet, including *Roberta* (1982), *Passion Fruit* (1984), and *Afro Cuber* (1985). (*Feather–Gitler '70s*)

Cubop. *See* AFRO-CUBAN JAZZ.

Cuffee, Ed(ward Emerson) (*b* Norfolk, VA, 7 June 1902; *d* New York, 3 Jan 1959). Trombonist. In the mid-1920s he moved to New York, where he made numerous recordings with Clarence Williams (1927–8, 1929) and worked with Bingie Madison. He performed and recorded as a member of McKinney's Cotton Pickers (1929–34) and Fletcher Henderson's band (1935–8), then worked with Leon Abbey (1940), with whom he continued to play occasionally, Count Basie (1941), and Chris Columbus (1944). He performed and recorded with Bunk Johnson in 1947, after which he ceased to work as a full-time musician. Cuffee's thoughtful blues style may be heard on Williams's *Speakeasy* (1928, QRS R7004), while his livelier playing is well represented by *Zonky* (Vic. 38118), which he recorded with McKinney's Cotton Pickers in 1930. Owing to incorrect information in an early source Cuffee has often been referred to as Cuffee Davidson. (A. McCarthy: *Big Band Jazz*, New York and London, 1974)

based on *ChiltonW*

Cuíca [quíca, puíta]. Brazilian friction drum. It consists of a hollow chamber (an earthenware pot or a bucket with the bottom removed) that acts as the resonator, across the top of which is tightly stretched a membrane; a stick (or sometimes a pipe) passes through a hole in the membrane. The drum may be made to sound in two ways: either the player moves the stick up and down through the hole in the membrane, thus causing the membrane to vibrate, or, having wetted or rosined his fingers, or using a damp cloth, he rubs the stick or twirls it between his hands, in which case the vibrations from the stick are transmitted to the membrane. The cuíca has a remarkable range of pitches and timbres, which are produced by pressure on the stick; a characteristic sound is a curiously human cackle.

From the time of Airto Moreira's tour as a member of Miles Davis's group (1970), the cuíca has been among the arsenal of Brazilian instruments used in jazz-rock, free jazz, and Latin jazz. It may be heard clearly near the beginning of Gato Barbieri's *Encontros* (1973, first issued on *The Saxophone*, 1947–73, Imp. 9253); it enters after the tambourine, before the cowbell.

BARRY KERNFELD

Cullaz, Alby [Albert] (*b* Boulogne-Billancourt, nr Paris, 25 June 1941). French double bass player, brother of Pierre Cullaz. He has played bop and swing throughout Europe with Jean-Luc Ponty, Johnny Griffin, Stephane Grappelli, Philly Joe Jones, Dizzy Gillespie, and many others. He made recordings with Jef Gilson's big band (1965), Hank Mobley's sextet (*The Flip*, 1969, BN 84329), and Michel Graillier's trio (1970), and played and recorded in a duo with the guitarist Christian Escoudé (1979).

BIBLIOGRAPHY

Feather–Gitler '70s

J.-P. Leloir and D. Lemery: "7 noms, 7 têtes: voici les nouveau-nés du jazz français – Alby Cullaz: My Heart Belongs to Daddy," *Jm*, no.117 (1965), 35

Cullaz, Pierre (*b* Paris, 21 July 1935). French guitarist, brother of Alby Cullaz. He worked with Johnny Griffin, Hal Singer, and Dexter Gordon (all 1955), then played with such Parisian musicians as the vibraphonist Michel Hausser (1957) and the pianist Art Simmons (1958). He also recorded with Claude Bolling's big band, and in a group that included Hausser, Zoot Sims, Quincy Jones, and Kenny Clarke, accompanying Sarah Vaughan (both 1958). After his military service Cullaz concentrated on studio work, and played with Martial Solal (1962), Eddy Louiss (1964–5), the group Guitars Unlimited (1965–8), Elvin Jones and André Hodeir (both 1966), Guy Lafitte (1969–70), and the trumpeter Ivan Jullien (1970–72); Hodeir's recording *Anna Livia Plurabelle* (1966, Epic EPC64695) contains good examples of his playing. He recorded again with Bolling in 1973, and worked with Jef Gilson in 1978. Cullaz is the author of a two-volume tutor, *Technique pour guitaristes de tous styles* (1979, 1983). (*Feather–Gitler '70s*)

MICHEL LAPLACE

Culley, Wendell (Philips) (*b* Worcester, MA, 8 Jan 1906). Trumpeter. He played with bands around Boston before moving in 1930 to New York, where he performed with Horace Henderson and, until summer 1931, Cab Calloway. He spent 11 years with Noble Sissle, recording in 1934 and 1936–7, and then worked with Lionel Hampton (1944–9); he was principally a section trumpeter, but he occasionally played a solo, as on *Midnight Sun* (1947, Decca 24429). After another period with Sissle he played with Count Basie's orchestra from 1951 to late 1959. Culley then retired from music, moved to the West Coast, and entered the insurance business.

BIBLIOGRAPHY

Chilton W; FeatherE

R. Horricks: *Count Basie and his Orchestra: its Music and its Musicians* (London and New York, 1957), 265

M. Boujut: "Les trompettes de la famille," *Jm*, no.251 (1977), 42

Culver, Rollie [Rolland Pierce] (*b* Fond du Lac, WI, 29 Oct 1908; *d* Culver City, CA, 8 Dec 1984). Drummer. He took up drums in 1930 and played for almost a decade with Wally and Heinie Beau in Wisconsin. In 1941 he joined Red Nichols, with whom he worked regularly from 1945 until Nichols's death in 1965, making a number of recordings, among them *Blues and Old-time Rags* (1963, Cap. ST2065). He also recorded with Jack Delaney and Raymond Burke in the New Orleans All Stars (1954) and played on many film soundtracks.

BIBLIOGRAPHY

FeatherE; Feather '60s

Obituaries: *Coda*, no.200 (1985), 39; *Jazz Educators Journal*, xvii/3 (1985), 80

Cunningham, Bob (*b* Cleveland, 28 Dec 1934). Double bass player and composer. After working in Cleveland he moved to New York in 1960. The following year he performed and recorded with Dizzy Gillespie's quintet and big band, touring the Middle East and performing and recording at the Monterey Jazz Festival. During the 1960s he recorded with Bill Hardman and Eric Dolphy (both 1961), Ken McIntyre (1963), Walt Dickerson (*c*1965), Frank Foster (1965–6), and Junior Mance and Freddie Hubbard (both 1966); his playing may be heard to advantage on *Echoes of Blue* on Hubbard's album *Backlash* (1966, Atl. 1477). Cunningham also worked with Art Blakey, Betty Carter, Kenny Dorham, Sun Ra, Art Farmer, Max Roach, Joe Henderson, Pharoah Sanders, and Rashied Ali. After recording with the Jazz Composer's Orchestra (1968), Gary Bartz (1969), and Leone Thomas (*c*1970) he joined Yusef Lateef (1970), with whom he performed, recorded, and toured the USA, Europe, and Africa. He left Lateef in 1976, and later led his own trio, worked as a freelance, and recorded with the World Violin Ensemble (1982–3). Cunningham has collaborated with choreographers and writers on numerous occasions; he wrote the music to the dance-drama *Musical Safari in Living Color*, and has provided compositions and arrangements for other theatrical productions. (S. Chaka: "A Love Affair with the Bass," *JSN*, ii/3 (1981), 45)

Cup mute. *See* MUTE, §2(c).

Cupol. Record company and label. The company was founded in Sweden in 1947; artists and repertory were supervised by Helge Roundquist, who had previously worked as a recording director for Sonora. Until the mid-1950s the company made many recordings of Swedish jazz, and also of the work of visiting Americans. Thereafter activity was only intermittent; the company was absorbed by CBS in 1970. (B. Englund: *Jazz på Cupol*, Stockholm, 1982)

Cuppini, Gil(berto) (*b* Milan, 6 June 1924). Italian drummer and bandleader. He took up drums around 1945 and in 1947 performed and recorded with a swing sextet. In 1949 he joined a group led by Hazy Osterwald and during the first Paris Jazz Fair accompanied Armando Trovajoli and Kramer Gorni at the Salon du Jazz. He performed and recorded with Nunzio Rotondo (1952–4, 1958–60), joined a sextet led by Gianni Basso and Oscar Valdambrini, and led small groups and orchestras, for which he also wrote compositions and arrangements. In 1958 he visited the USA with the International Youth Band and performed with Teddy Wilson and Arvell Shaw in Brussels. During the 1960s he broadcast a series of concerts on RAI, and in the early 1970s made several albums with Joe Venuti. From the late 1970s he worked in a rhythm section with Franco D'Andrea and the double bass player Giorgio Azzolini that accompanied a number of American and European musicians. Cuppini's playing is well represented by his recording *No So Quiet Please* (1950, Col. CQ202). (*FeatherE*)

ADRIANO MAZZOLETTI

Curl, Langston (W.) (*b* Charles City, VA, 18 March 1899). Trumpeter. He learned to play trumpet at the age of six. He worked with bands in New York, before joining McKinney's Cotton Pickers in Detroit (*c*1928; for illustration see MCKINNEY'S COTTON PICKERS); led by Don Redman, the group made several recordings, including *It's a Precious Little Thing Called Love* (1929, Vic. 38061), on which the first trumpet solo is played by Curl. He remained with the group until 1931; after spending a further three years with Redman, he toured for some time and then stopped full-time playing in 1937.

based on *ChiltonW*

Curson, Ted [Theodore] (*b* Philadelphia, 3 July 1935). Trumpeter. He studied music in high school and with Albert, Percy, and Jimmy Heath, who were his neighbors; he was influenced at an early age by the music of the trumpeters Clifford Brown and Johnny Splawn. He worked with Charlie Ventura in the summer of 1953, and with the encouragement of Miles Davis moved in 1956 to New York, where he played with Red Garland and at Birdland with Vera Auer. After playing free jazz with Cecil Taylor in 1959 he belonged for two years to Charles Mingus's group with, among others, Eric Dolphy; in 1962 he left the group to work as a freelance and to lead a quartet with Bill Barron, with which he moved to Europe owing to a lack of opportunities to perform in the USA and with which he recorded *Tears for Dolphy* (1964) in Paris (the title track was used in Pier Paolo Pasolini's film *Teorama* in 1969). After the quartet disbanded Curson settled in Denmark and made regular appearances at the Pori International Jazz Festival; on his return to the USA in 1976 he formed a septet with Nick Brignola and Chris Woods that proved short-lived. In the 1980s he led open jam sessions at the Blue Note in New York.

SELECTED RECORDINGS

As leader: *Tears for Dolphy* (1964, Fon. 688310); *The New Thing and the Blue Thing* (1965, Atl. 1441); *Cattin' Curson* (1973, Marge 01); *Ted Curson & Co.* (1976, IndN 1054)

As sideman: C. Taylor: *Cecil Taylor Plays Cole Porter* (1959, UA 5046); C. Mingus: *Pre-Bird* (1960, Mer. 60627); *Charles Mingus Presents Charles Mingus* (1960, Can. 9005); A. Hill: *Spiral* (1974, Fre. 40156)

BIBLIOGRAPHY

L. Jones: "Trumpet on the Way up: Ted Curson," *DB*, xxix/23 (1962), 20
P. Lattes: "Tenace Ted Curson," *Jh*, no.222 (1966), 30
G. Giddins and R. Rusch: "Ted Curson Interview," *Cadence*, i/8 (1976), 3
C. Berg: "Ted Curson: Striving with Integrity," *DB*, xliv/1 (1977), 18 [incl. discography]
B. Priestley: "Ted Curson," *The Wire*, no.8 (1984), 38

DAVID WILD

Curtis, King [Ousley, Curtis] (*b* Fort Worth, 7 Feb 1934; *d* New York, 13 Aug 1971). Tenor saxophonist and bandleader. Inspired by Lester Young, he began playing saxophone at the age of 12. While he was in high school he performed in various bands in the Fort Worth area, playing a mixture of jazz, rhythm-and-blues, and popular music. He turned down several offers of college scholarships to accept a position in Lionel Hampton's band, where he polished his writing and arranging skills and learned to play guitar. In 1952 Curtis moved to New York and quickly found work as a session musician, eventually backing hundreds of performers on recordings and in concerts. With his own group, the King Pins (originally called the Noble Knights), he recorded extensively for the Prestige, Enjoy, Capitol, and Atco labels in the same hybrid style as that of his earlier bands; among his sidemen were Cornell Dupree, Chuck Rainey, and Richard Tee. He also recorded two albums with Nat Adderley and Wynton Kelly (1960), and between 1962 and 1971 recorded 15 singles which were successful on the pop chart. Owing to his syncopated, almost percussive style, Curtis became one of the best-known and most sought-after studio saxophone players of the 1950s and 1960s; his tone was deep and fruity, with a characteristic burr. In 1971, shortly after he was appointed music director to Aretha Franklin, he was stabbed to death in New York.

SELECTED RECORDINGS

The New Scene of King Curtis (1960, NewJ 8237); *Soul Meeting* (1960, Prst. 7222); *Soul Serenade* (1964, Cap. ST2095); *Live at Fillmore West* (1971, Atco 359)

BIBLIOGRAPHY

O. Keller: "King Curtis," *BHcF*, no.87 (1959), 3
J. Dufour: "King Curtis," *Soul Bag*, no.65 (1978), 13
R. Simonds: *King Curtis: a Discography* (Edgware, England, 1983, rev. 2/1984)
The Sound (1984–1985/6), from no.8 (1986) *Boss* [journal devoted to Curtis]

GARY THEROUX

Cut. (1) In jazz argot to record, or a recording. The usage derives from the recording technique in which the vibrations created by the sounds to be preserved are converted into analogous vertical or lateral deviations cut by a stylus in the spiral groove on a disc or cylinder (*see* RECORDING, §I). The word is used of a single TAKE at a recording session, one track on an LP or EP record, or any distinct and continuous segment of a recording.

(2) To edit out a section of a recording, originally literally by cutting and splicing the tape; *see* RECORDING, §§I, 3, and II, 7.

(3) [carve]. To outplay, as in a CUTTING CONTEST.

Cutshall, Cutty [Robert Dewees] (*b* Huntington Co., PA, 29 Dec 1911; *d* Toronto, 16 Aug 1968). Trombonist. After working with symphony orchestras and dance bands in Pittsburgh he played with the bandleader Jan Savitt (1938–40). He was then a member of Benny Goodman's band (1940–42), forming with Lou McGarity one of the best two-man trombone sections ever to work with the ensemble. After army service he returned to Goodman (1946), performed and recorded as a freelance (1947), and joined Billy Butterfield's band at Nick's, New York (1948). A long-lasting association with Eddie Condon began at this time; Cutshall performed frequently at Condon's club from 1949 until shortly before his death, and toured with Condon's band, visiting the UK in 1957. During the same period Cutshall undertook recording sessions, tours, and residencies with other leaders, including Yank Lawson, Peanuts Hucko, Max Kaminsky, and Bob Crosby. From the mid-1960s he performed and recorded with a band called at various times the Eight, Nine, or Ten Greats of Jazz; it first performed in Denver, and its earliest albums include fine duets by Cutshall and McGarity. Cutshall died shortly before he was due to take part in this ensemble's first performance as the World's Greatest Jazz Band.

Although Cutshall was often overshadowed by McGarity, particularly during his period with Goodman, the quality of his playing was highly consistent whether he was working as a section player or as a member of a small ensemble. His solo work, inspired by that of Jack Teagarden, ensured that he was always much in demand.

SELECTED RECORDINGS

As sideman: J. Savitt: Get Happy (1939, Decca 2583); B. Hackett and E. Condon: *Jam Session* (1948, Aircheck 28); on Condon: *Jam Session Coast to Coast* (1953, Col. CL547), Riverboat Shuffle; Condon: *Bixieland* (1955, Col. CL719); on D. Garroway: *Wide Wide World of Jazz* (1956, RCA LPM1325), D. Kincaide: Kansas City Stomp; W. B. Davison: *With Strings Attached* (1957, Col. CL983); E. Condon: *That Toddlin' Town* (1959, WB 1315); on L. Gaskin: *At the Jazz Band Ball* (1961, Swingville 2031), Tin Roof Blues; C. Hayes: *Happy Melodies* (1965, ABC-Para, 519); Nine Greats of Jazz: *Jazz in the Troc* (1966, WCS 1769); Ten Greats of Jazz: *Jazz in the Troc* (1968, WCS 3853)

BIBLIOGRAPHY

ChiltonW
Obituary, *DB*, xxxv/20 (1968), 13
P. H. Richter: "Robert D. ("Cutty") Cutshall: 1911–1968," *Jazzology*, xix/2 (1968–9), 1
H. Lyttelton: *Take it from the Top: an Autobiographical Scrapbook* (London, 1975), 134

BRIAN PEERLESS

Cutting [bucking, carving] **contest.** A competition between bands or soloists (often players of the same instrument) to determine which has superior skill, stamina, virtuosity, etc. The musicians play successive pieces or (especially in a contest between soloists) successive choruses in a single piece. Such a trial might take place spontaneously, during a performance or a JAM SESSION, or, in early New Orleans jazz, when two bands, each engaged in its own publicity, met by chance on the streets. *See also* BATTLE OF BANDS. (P. Clayton and P. Gammond: "Cut, also Carve," *Jazz A–Z*, Enfield, nr London, 1986)

Cymbal. A disc-shaped metal percussion instrument made in many sizes and grades of sound; a variety of cymbals are used in jazz (*see* DRUM SET, §I, 5).

Cyrille, Andrew (Charles) (*b* New York, 10 Nov 1939). Drummer. He played at the age of 11 in a drum and bugle corps and at 15 in a trio that included Eric Gale. After studying chemistry in his teens he enrolled in 1958 at the Juilliard School and in the late 1950s and early 1960s worked with Mary Lou Williams, Roland Hanna, Roland Kirk, Illinois Jacquet, Coleman Hawkins, Junior Mance, Walt Dickerson, and Howard McGhee's big band. In 1964 he replaced Sunny Murray in Cecil Taylor's group, as a member of which (to 1975) he became a leading free-jazz drummer. At the same time he performed with such musicians as Grachan Moncur III, Marion Brown, and Jimmy Giuffre, and recorded an album in Paris as an unaccompanied soloist (1969). With Rashied Ali and Milford Graves he took part in the mid-1970s in a series of concerts known as "Dialogue of the Drums," and from 1975 into the 1980s he led the group Maono, in which his sidemen included David Ware, the trumpeter Ted Daniel, the pianist Sonelius Smith, and the double bass players Lisle Atkinson and Nick DiGeronimo. In the 1980s he also belonged to the Group (with Brown, Billy Bang, Fred Hopkins, Sirone, and the trumpeter Ahmed Abdullah), and Pieces of Time (with Graves, Don Moye, and Kenny Clarke), worked as a sideman with John Carter and Muhal Richard Abrams, and led a quartet in New York. One of the most subtle free-jazz drummers of the 1960s, Cyrille is highly regarded for his tasteful, often restrained, melodic playing.

SELECTED RECORDINGS

As unaccompanied soloist: *What About?* (1969, BYG 529316)
Duos with M. Graves: *Dialogue of the Drums* (1974, IPS 001)
As leader: *The Loop* (1978, Ictus 0009); *Special People* (1980, SN 1012)
As sideman: C. Taylor: *Unit Structures* (1966, BN 84237); C. Haden: *Liberation Music Orchestra* (1969, Imp. 9183); C. Taylor: *Spring of Two Blue-J's* (1973, Unit Core 30551); L. Jenkins: *The Legend of Ai Glatson* (1978, BS 0022)

BIBLIOGRAPHY

E. Raben: "Diskofilsplaten," *Orkester journalen*, xxxvii/10 (1969), 19
J. Welch: "Different Drummers: a Composite Profile," *DB*, xxxvii/6 (1970), 18
V. Wilmer: "Dialogue of the Drummers," *Coda*, xi/6 (1974), 2
H. Howland: "Andrew Cyrille: an Aesthetic Endeavor," *MD*, v/9 (1981), 22
H. Mandel: "Andrew Cyrille: Passion for Percussion," *DB*, li/8 (1984), 28
V. Wilmer: "Andrew Cyrille," *The Wire*, no.9 (1984), 12
G. Giddins: "Note: Andrew Cyrille has a Band," *Rhythm-a-ning: Jazz Tradition and Innovation in the '80s* (New York, and Oxford, England, 1985) [colln of previously pubd articles], 75
F. Davis: "Other Musicians March to his Beat," *Philadelphia Inquirer* (27 Dec 1986), §C, p.3

MICHAEL ULLMAN

D

Da Costa, Paulinho (*b* Rio de Janeiro, 31 May 1948). Brazilian percussionist. He took up percussion at the age of seven, played and danced with samba troupes, and toured the world with several Brazilian ensembles. In 1973 he moved to the USA to play with Sergio Mendes (1973–7), then recorded with Dizzy Gillespie (1975–7), Milt Jackson (1976), and Freddie Hubbard (1977), as the leader with Joe Pass of a sextet (1978), and with Ella Fitzgerald (1981); he also made albums with Herbie Hancock, Ahmad Jamal, Nancy Wilson, and a number of pop and soul musicians. In the early 1980s he was active on the West Coast as a studio musician. Da Costa plays more than 200 percussion instruments and is noted for his energetic, exact playing and his ability to create diverse textures. He received Most Valuable Player awards from the National Academy of Recording Arts & Sciences in 1980, 1981, and 1982.

SELECTED RECORDINGS

As leader: *Agora* (1976, Pablo 2310785); *Happy People* (1979, PT 2312102); *Sunrise* (1984, PT 2312143)

As sideman with D. Gillespie: *Dizzy's Party* (1976, Pablo 2310784)

BIBLIOGRAPHY

D. Griffin: Liner notes, *Agora* (Pablo 2310785, 1977)

L. Feather: "Blindfold Test: Paulinho Da Costa," *DB*, xliv/8 (1977), 41

M. Rozek: "Portraits: Paulinho Da Costa," *MD*, vi/6 (1982), 42

JEFF POTTER

Dad. Nickname of HARRY GOLD.

Daffodil. Record label and company established by BLOSSOM DEARIE in 1974.

Dahlander, (Nils-)Bert(il) [Dale, Bert] (*b* Göteborg, Sweden, 13 May 1928). Swedish drummer. He studied violin and piano, led a quartet, and belonged to a radio band led by Thore Ehrling. After recording with Lars Gullin (1951, 1952) he moved to the USA (1954) and became a member of the house band at the Bee Hive in Chicago. He worked for one year with Terry Gibbs, toured Europe with Chet Baker (1955–6), then worked again with Gullin (with whom he recorded in 1956–7) and Gibbs. He toured and recorded with Teddy Wilson's trio (1957–60), played with Earl Hines (1965), and in 1966 settled in Aspen, Colorado, where he worked with Ralph Sutton and Peanuts Hucko and took part in several concerts in the Colorado Jazz Party series. Throughout the 1970s he performed regularly in Finland and Sweden and in 1973 recorded with Hines. Dahlander's style is firmly rooted in swing but has something of the complexity of bop.

SELECTED RECORDINGS

As leader: *Skal* (1958, Verve 8253); *Jazz with a Swedish Accent* (1976, Everyday 31309)

As sideman: T. Wilson: *Mr. Wilson and Mr. Gershwin* (1959, Col. CL1318); E. Hines: *An Evening with Earl Hines and his Quartet* (1973, Chi. 116)

BIBLIOGRAPHY

FeatherE; *Feather '60s*; *Feather–Gitler '70s*

J. Olsson: "Nils-Bertil Dahlander," *Orkester journalen*, xlii (1974), July–Aug, 10

JEFF POTTER

Dailey, Al(bert Preston) (*b* Baltimore, 16 June 1938; *d* Denver, 26 June 1984). Pianist and composer. He studied piano from an early age, belonged to the house band at the Royal Theater in Baltimore (1953–6), and attended Morgan State College (1955–6) and the Peabody Conservatory (1956–9). After touring with the singer Damita Jo (1960–63) he led a trio at the Bohemian Caverns in Washington (1963–4) and in 1964 moved to New York, where he worked with such well-known musicians as Dexter Gordon, Roy Haynes, Freddie Hubbard (recording in 1966), Sarah Vaughan, and Charles Mingus. He performed and recorded with Woody Herman at the Monterey Jazz Festival (1967), belonged to Art Blakey's Jazz Messengers (1968–9, 1975–6), and worked with Sonny Rollins (at intervals in the early 1970s) and Stan Getz (touring Europe in 1974 and recording in 1974–5); he also recorded with Elvin Jones (1976), Archie Shepp (1977), and the Upper Manhattan Jazz Society (1981), a quintet that included Charlie Rouse, Benny Bailey, and Buster Williams. In New York he performed at Carnegie Hall (1982) and at the Mobil Summerpier Concerts (1983). Dailey's compositions include *A Lady's Mistake*, which is included on his first album, *The Day after the Dawn* (1972), *Africa Suite* (1975), a work for voices and electronic instruments that he wrote after having received a grant from the NEA, and *Bittersweet Waltz*.

SELECTED RECORDINGS

Duos with S. Getz: *Poetry* (1983, Elek. 960370-1)

As leader: *The Day after the Dawn* (1972, Col. KC31278); *That Old Feeling* (1978, Ste. 1107); *Textures* (1981, Muse 5256)

As sideman: A Blakey: *Backgammon* (1976, Roul. 5003); B. DeFranco: *Mr. Lucky* (1980, Pablo 2310906)

BIBLIOGRAPHY
Feather '60s; *Feather–Gitler '70s*
S. Voce: "Albert Dailey: that Old Feeling," *JJI*, xxxii/7 (1979), 34
J. Pareles: Obituary, *New York Times* (3 July 1984), §B, p.8
R. Palmer: "Pianos in the Background: Albert Dailey," *JJI*, xxxviii/3 (1985), 17

GREGORY E. SMITH

Dale, Bert. *See* DAHLANDER, BERT.

Dallwitz, Dave [David Frederick] (*b* Freeling, nr Gawler, Australia, 25 Oct 1914). Australian composer, bandleader, pianist, arranger, and trombonist. He was first exposed to jazz through listening to recordings. He took over the leadership of the Southern Jazz Group, a dixieland band, in 1945 and appeared with it at the first Australian Jazz Convention in 1946; the band recorded several times between then and 1950 and Dallwitz remained its leader until 1951. He then withdrew from jazz, but continued to perform (on cello and bassoon) and compose in symphonic, chamber, and light-music contexts. He marked his return to jazz performance and composition with a recording in 1972. From that time he led several concert bands, including the Hot Six, a big band, and a ragtime ensemble, the last reflecting a change in his interests; these different groups have provided opportunities for the presentation of his prolific compositional output. His work is well represented by *Melbourne Suite* (1973, Swaggie 1342) and his most outstanding album is *Ern Malley Suite* (1975, Swaggie 1360).

BIBLIOGRAPHY
A. Bisset: *Black Roots, White Flowers: a History of Jazz in Australia* (Sydney, 1976), 120
B. Johnson: "Dallwitz, David Frederick (Dave)," *The Oxford Companion to Australian Jazz* (Melbourne, Australia, 1987)

BRUCE JOHNSON

Daly, Warren (James) (*b* Sydney, 22 Aug 1943). Australian bandleader, drummer, composer, and arranger. He first played in pop groups, then from 1959 worked in nightclubs and recording studios. After touring in the USA with the singer Kirby Stone, Si Zentner, and Buddy DeFranco (1967–8) he returned to Australia and, with Ed Wilson, formed the Daly–Wilson Big Band (1969). This group performed and recorded until 1971, then, after a period of inactivity, re-formed in 1973; its personnel included at different times the best Australian big-band and studio musicians of the period. Daly's work with the band is heard to advantage on *My Goodness* from *The Daly–Wilson Big Band on Tour* (1973, Rep. 4003). After this group disbanded in 1983 Daly formed his own big band in 1984; he has also worked as a music director in television.

BIBLIOGRAPHY
A. McCandless: "Music from Down Under: an Appreciation of the Daly–Wilson Big Band," *CI*, x/1 (1971), 27
——: "The Success of the Daly–Wilson Big Band," *CI*, xiii/5 (1974), 26
M. Williams: *The Australian Jazz Explosion* (London and elsewhere, 1981), 113
B. Johnson: "Daly, Warren James," *The Oxford Companion to Australian Jazz* (Melbourne, Australia, 1987)

BRUCE JOHNSON

Dameron, Tadd [Tadley Ewing Peake] (*b* Cleveland, 21 Feb 1917; *d* New York, 8 March 1965). Composer, arranger, bandleader, and pianist. After working with lesser-known groups he joined that of Harlan Leonard, scoring many of its arrangements, including *Dameron Stomp* and *A la Bridges*; he also wrote for Jimmie Lunceford, Coleman Hawkins (*Half step down, please*), and Sarah Vaughan (*If you could see me now*). In the late 1940s Dameron wrote arrangements for the big band of Dizzy Gillespie, who gave the première of his large-scale orchestral piece *Soulphony* at Carnegie Hall in 1948. Also in 1948 Dameron led his own group in New York, which included Fats Navarro; the following year he was at the Paris Jazz Fair with Miles Davis. After forming another group of his own with Clifford Brown in 1953, he became inactive owing to a problem with drugs, which led to his imprisonment in 1958. From 1961 he wrote scores for recordings by Milt Jackson, Sonny Stitt, and Blue Mitchell.

Dameron did not achieve full expression of his gifts as a composer because of his inability to maintain his own group for long. Navarro was the finest interpreter of his pieces, as their many joint recordings show. The best of these exhibit a pithy thematic invention uncommon in jazz: *Sid's Delight* and *Casbah* (both 1949) reveal Dameron's powers at their height. Like Thelonious Monk, Dameron was repeatedly linked with bop, though he rarely employed its stylistic devices. With other arrangers for Gillespie, he attempted to adapt bop to big bands, failing however to transfer the crucial rhythmic procedures of this essentially small-group style. In spite of this, his best pieces for Gillespie (e.g., *Good Bait* and *Our Delight*) show particular melodic and harmonic substance. Other notable compositions by Dameron include *Fontainebleau* (1956), an extended piece without improvisation; *Hot House* (1945), recorded by a group led by Gillespie with Charlie Parker; and *Lyonia* (1949), recorded by Ted Heath.

See also PIANO, §4; and HARMONY (i), §2, and ex.23.

SELECTED RECORDINGS

The Squirrel/Our Delight (1947, BN 540); The Chase/Dameronia (1947, BN 541); Symphonette (1948, BN 1564); Sid's Delight/Casbah (1949, Cap. 60006); *Fontainebleau* (1956, Prst. 7037); *The Magic Touch* (1962, Riv. 9419)

RECORDED COMPOSITIONS

(selective list)

Recorded by H. Leonard: A la Bridges (1940, Bb 10899); Dameron Stomp (1940), on *Harlan Leonard and his Rockets* (1939–40, RCA LPV531)
Recorded by D. Gillespie: Hot House (1945, Guild 1002); Good Bait (1947, Vic. 20-2878); Our Delight (1949, Musi. 399)
Recorded by others: C. Hawkins: Half step down, please (1947, Vic. 20-3143); S. Vaughan: If you could see me now (1946, Musi. 398); T. Heath: Lyonia (1949, Decca 9255)

BIBLIOGRAPHY
J. Cooke: "Tadd Dameron," *JM*, vi/1 (1960), 23
B. Coss: "Tadd Dameron," *DB*, xxix/4 (1962), 18
A. Morgan: "Tadd Dameron," *JM*, viii/2 (1962), 3
V. Wilmer: "The Magic Touch: a Swan-song for Tadd Dameron," *JB*, ii/5 (1965), 20
I. Gitler: *Jazz Masters of the Forties* (New York, 1966/*R*1983 with discography), 262
J. Burns: "Tadd Dameron," *JJ*, xx/8 (1967), 20
H. Woodfin: "The Complete Originality of Tadd Dameron," *J&B*, iii/1 (1973), 4
M. Harrison: *A Jazz Retrospect* (Newton Abbot, England, 1976, rev. 2/1977)

MAX HARRISON/R

Dameronia. Group dedicated to the performance of music by Tadd Dameron. It was active in the early 1980s and was led by the drummer Philly Joe Jones; its other members were the saxophonists Frank Wess, Charles Davis, and Cecil Payne, the trumpeters Don Sickler and Johnny Coles, the trombonist Britt Woodman, the pianist Walter Davis, Jr., and the double bass player Larry Ridley.

D'Amico, Hank [Henry] (*b* Rochester, NY, 21 March 1915; *d* New York, 3 Dec 1965). Clarinetist and saxophonist. He first played violin but later performed on clarinet in his high-school band. His first professional engagements were with the bandleader Paul Specht (1936) and Red Norvo (1936–8). In 1938 he broadcast on radio with his own octet, then the following year returned briefly to Norvo's band. From 1940 to summer 1941 he was with Bob Crosby, then led his own big band until 1942. After short periods with Les Brown, Norvo, and Benny Goodman (all 1942) D'Amico worked for CBS in New York, and played with Miff Mole in Toronto and with Tommy Dorsey (all 1943). From 1944 to 1954 he was a staff musician for ABC in New York, though he also played with Jack Teagarden in 1954. During the late 1950s and the 1960s he worked mainly with small groups, and occasionally led his own band. In 1964 he appeared at the New York World's Fair with Morey Feld's trio. D'Amico, whose playing was strongly influenced by Goodman, was considered to be one of the most fluent swing clarinetists.

SELECTED RECORDINGS

As leader: Hank's Pranks/Juke Box Judy (1944, Nat. 9047); *Holiday with Hank* (1954, Beth. 1006)

As sideman: R. Norvo: Remember/Jiving the Jeep (1937, Bruns. 7896); Liza/I would do anything for you (1937, Bruns. 7868); B. Crosby: Take me back again/I'll come back to you (1940, Decca 3576)

BIBLIOGRAPHY

ChiltonW; *FeatherE*; *Feather '60s*

RAYMOND J. GARIGLIO

Dance, Stanley (Frank) (*b* Braintree, England, 15 Sept 1910). English writer. After attending Framlingham College (1925–8) he first wrote about jazz in the French journal *Jazz hot* (from 1935) and in 1937 moved to the USA, where ten years later he settled in Connecticut. He wrote for such publications as *Down Beat*, *Metronome*, the *New York Herald Tribune*, *Saturday Review*, *Jazz Journal* (to which he contributed a monthly column, "Lightly and Politely," from 1948 to 1976), and *Jazz Times* (from 1980). His other writings, including *The World of Duke Ellington* (1970), *The World of Swing* (1974), *The World of Earl Hines* (1977), and *The World of Count Basie* (1980), consist largely of interviews with musicians. He had a particularly close association with Ellington, whom he accompanied on several international tours. He won a Grammy Award in 1963 for his liner notes to *The Ellington Era* (Col. C3L27, 1963), and the ASCAP–Deems Taylor Award in 1979 for the book *Duke Ellington in Person: an Intimate Memoir* (1978). In addition to his work as a writer Dance has been a record producer for Felsted, Columbia, Black Lion, and RCA Camden.

Dance's wife, Helen Oakley Dance, has collaborated with her husband and has also written a book on T-Bone Walker (*Stormy Monday: the T-Bone Walker Story*, Baton Rouge, LA, and London, 1987); her interviews with jazz musicians have been published in *Coda* and *Down Beat* magazines.

WRITINGS

(*selective list*)

ed. with J. Asman and B. Kinnell: *Jazz Notebook* (Chilwell, nr Newark-on-Trent, England, n.d. [?1945])

with others: *Jazz Era: the 'Forties* (London, 1961/*R*1985)

The World of Duke Ellington (New York, 1970/*R*1981) [colln of previously pubd articles and interviews]

with D. Wells: *The Night People: Reminiscences of a Jazzman* (Boston and London, 1971)

The World of Swing (New York, 1974) [colln of previously pubd interviews]

The World of Earl Hines (New York, 1977) [interviews]

with M. Ellington: *Duke Ellington in Person: an Intimate Memoir* (Boston and London, 1978)

The World of Count Basie (New York and London, 1980) [colln of previously pubd interviews]

with C. Barnet: *Those Swinging Years: the Autobiography of Charlie Barnet* (Baton Rouge, LA, 1984)

DANIEL ZAGER

Dance band. A term applied to the big bands that were active from about 1916 to the mid-1940s, and whose repertory consisted principally of dance music; *see* BANDS, §§4(ii), (iii).

D'Andrea, Franco [Francesco] (*b* Merano, Italy, 8 March 1941). Italian keyboard player. He first played piano and worked with Nunzio Rotondo (1963) and Gato Barbieri (1964–5). He recorded in Milan and Rome with Franco Ambrosetti (1965), with the double bass players Giorgio Azzolini (1966, 1968, 1975) and Giovanni Tommaso (1969–70), and with Gianni Basso (1973) and Enrico Rava (1974). From 1968 he led the Modern Art Trio, and from 1972 he performed with the rock and jazz group Perigeo, playing electric piano and synthesizer. He also performed with visiting American musicians, including Dexter Gordon, Slide Hampton, Max Roach, and Lucky Thompson, and recorded with Lee Konitz (1968), Conte Candoli (1973), and Johnny Griffin (1974). In 1979 he became a member of Rava's quartet, and in 1981 he formed his own quartet, with which he recorded the album *No Idea of Time* (1983, Red 202).

BIBLIOGRAPHY

Feather–Gitler '70s

D. Soutif: "L'enfance D'Andrea," *Jm*, no.306 (1982), 54 [incl. discography]

Dandridge, Putney [Louis] (*b* Richmond, VA, 13 Jan 1902; *d* Wall Township, NJ, 15 Feb 1946). Pianist and singer. From 1918 to 1926 he toured regularly with a traveling show, before playing in Buffalo for several years; during the early 1930s he accompanied the tap-dancer Bill "Bojangles" Robinson. After leading his own band in Cleveland (1932–4), he became solo pianist at Adrian's Taproom in New York (from 1935). He worked regularly in various clubs in New York and had a long engagement at the Hickory House. In 1935 and 1936 he recorded as a leader, accompanied by prominent players such as Roy Eldridge, Chu Berry, Henry "Red" Allen, Buster Bailey, Teddy Wilson, John Kirby, Cozy Cole, Eddie Condon, and Doc Cheatham; his pleasant singing and serviceable playing may be heard on *When I grow too old to dream* (1935, Voc. 2982), though typically the recording is chiefly remarkable for the accompaniment, which is dominated by Eldridge and Berry.

based on *ChiltonW*

Daniels, Eddie [Edward Kenneth] (*b* New York, 19 Oct 1941). Tenor saxophonist and clarinetist. He attended the High School of the Performing Arts in New York and in 1957 played alto saxophone in Marshall Brown's Youth Band at the Newport Jazz Festival. After graduating from Brooklyn College in 1963 he studied clarinet at the Juilliard School (MA 1966) and played at the Half Note with Tony Scott. In 1966 he joined the Thad Jones–Mel Lewis Orchestra (with which he remained for six years), won first prize as a saxophonist at the International Jazz Competition in Vienna, recorded with Friedrich Gulda, and made his first recording as a leader. He performed in 1969 on Freddie Hubbard's album *The Hub of Hubbard* in a style clearly influenced by Sonny Rollins, and on Richard Davis's *Muses for Richard Davis*. Later he recorded with Don Patterson (1972), in a duo with Bucky Pizzarelli (1973), with Airto Moreira (1974) and Morgana King (1977), and again as a leader (1977). With the New American Orchestra he gave the première in 1984 of Jorge Calandrelli's Concerto for Jazz Clarinet and Orchestra, which he recorded in the following year with other works for clarinet and orchestra on the album *Breakthrough*. He received a grant from the NEA in 1986. Daniels is a proficient, if not innovative, tenor saxophonist and one of the most technically gifted clarinetists in jazz.

SELECTED RECORDINGS

Duos with B. Pizzarelli: *A Flower for All Seasons* (1973, Choice 1002)

As leader: *First Prize!* (1966, Prst. 7506); *Brief Encounter* (1977, Muse 5154); *Breakthrough* (1985, GRP 91024)

As sideman: T. Jones and M. Lewis: *Monday Night* (1968, SolS 18048), incl. Mornin' Reverend; R. Davis: *Muses for Richard Davis* (1969, BASF 20725); F. Hubbard: *The Hub of Hubbard* (1969, BASF 20726)

BIBLIOGRAPHY

W. Conover: "Viennese Cookin'," *DB*, xxxiii/16 (1966), 23
G. Hoefer: "Newport Youth Band: Marshall Brown's Talent Incubator," *DB*, xxxiv/19 (1967), 19
R. Williams: "Junior of the Band," *MM* (6 Sept 1969), 8
M. Gardner: "Eddie Daniels: *A Flower for All Seasons*," *Coda*, no.148 (1976), 16 [review]
K. Tucker: "Eddie Daniels," *Billboard*, xc (30 Sept 1978), 38
Z. Stewart: "Clarinetist for All Seasons: Eddie Daniels," *DB*, liv/6 (1987), 23 [incl. discography]

MICHAEL ULLMAN

Danielsson, Palle (*b* Stockholm, 15 Oct 1946). Swedish double bass player. He studied at the Stockholm Conservatory and played with the pianist Staffan Abeleen (recording in 1965–6), Eje Thelin, and George Russell. With Bobo Stenson he formed the group RENA RAMA in 1971, with which he played at intervals until 1985; he also worked frequently with Jan Garbarek in Europe in the 1970s, and in 1979, as a member of a quartet led by Garbarek and Keith Jarrett, he toured Japan and recorded in New York. He played for a few years with Charles Lloyd in the early 1980s, and from the mid-1980s worked with Michel Petrucciani, with whom he toured the USA in 1984. Danielsson has become one of the best-known jazz double bass players in Europe, despite his having preferred to work as a sideman rather than as a leader.

SELECTED RECORDINGS

As sideman: J. Garbarek and K. Jarrett: *Belonging* (1974, ECM 1050); A. Mangelsdorff: *The Wide Point* (1975, BASF 2022569-0); C. Lloyd: *A Night in Copenhagen* (1983, BN 85104); M. Petrucciani: *Live at the Village Vanguard* (1984, Conc. 3005)

BIBLIOGRAPHY

L. O. Westin: "Palle Danielsson," *Orkester journalen*, xl/4 (1972), 10
M. Sandblad: "Palle Danielsson," *Dagens nyheter* (13 Aug 1984), 10
E. Kjellberg: *Svensk jazzhistoria: en översikt* [Swedish jazz history: an overview] (Stockholm, 1985), 249

PEKKA GRONOW

Danish Radio Big Band. *See* RADIOENS BIG BAND.

Danish Radio Jazz Group. *See* RADIOJAZZGRUPPEN (i).

Dankworth, John (Philip William) [Johnny] (*b* London, 20 Sept 1927). English alto saxophonist, bandleader, arranger, and composer. He began his career playing clarinet in a novelty traditional-style band, the Garbage Men, led by the drummer Freddy Mirfield. After studying at the Royal Academy of Music (1944–6) he performed on transatlantic liners in order to travel to the USA and hear jazz at first hand (1947–8). By this time Dankworth was playing alto saxophone (he was at first strongly influenced by Charlie Parker), and he quickly became a leading figure in postwar British jazz. He was a founding member in 1948 of the Club Eleven, and in 1950 he formed the Johnny Dankworth Seven, which included Jimmy Deuchar, Eddie Harvey, Bill Le Sage, and Don Rendell. From 1953 to 1964 Dankworth led his first large jazz orchestra (it departed from conventional big-band instrumentation by often employing a three-piece saxophone section), in which his wife, Cleo Laine, was the featured singer; among other sidemen in this band at various times were Dick Hawdon, Kenny Wheeler, Gus Galbraith, Harvey, Keith Christie, Rendell, Danny Moss, Peter King, Ronnie Ross, Vic Ash, Le Sage, Derek Smith, Dudley Moore, Alan Branscombe, Spike Heatley, Kenny Napper, Allan Ganley, and Kenny Clare. Dankworth became music director for Laine in 1971 and temporarily reduced the size of his band to ten musicians. In the early 1980s he was the leader of a touring quintet in which Le Sage and Clare were sidemen.

Dankworth is a composer of consummate skill. His many works (some written earlier in his career in collaboration with his staff arranger David Lindup) include several large-scale suites, such as *What the Dickens!* (1963), *The $1,000,000 Collection* (1969), and *Lifeline* (1973); he has also written an opera-ballet, pieces for jazz band with symphony orchestra (notably a third-stream work with the composer Mátyás Seiber, 1959),

John Dankworth and Cleo Laine, early 1980s

and a number of film scores. His early big-band arrangements, such as *Experiments with Mice* (1956, Parl. R4185) and *Take the "A" Train* (1956, Parl. R4213), were refreshing in their originality, and his later work, which has always reflected current musical trends, frequently achieves a sense of profundity without becoming ostentatious. In 1969, with Laine, Dankworth founded the Wavendon Allmusic Plan, a cultural organization based at his home near Milton Keynes. International artists from every musical sphere perform regularly in its 300-seat concert hall, and Dankworth also makes presentations to schools and holds various jazz courses, workshops, and masterclasses under its auspices. He was made a CBE in 1974.

Oral history material in *GBLnsa*.

SELECTED RECORDINGS
* – composed by Dankworth

Bremavin/Lover Man (1949, Esquire 10037); Strictly Confidential/Allen's Alley (1951, Esquire 10193); The Slider/It's the talk of the town (1953, Parl. R3820); Bugle Call Rag/You go to my head (1954, Parl. R3935); **What the Dickens!* (1963, Fon. TL5203), incl. Little Nell; **The $1,000,000 Collection* (1967, Fon. TL 5445); **Lifeline* (1973, Phi. 6308169), incl. Fighting the Flab; on *Concrete Cows* (1985, NYJ 1006), Lady Di

BIBLIOGRAPHY

FeatherE; *Feather '60s*; *Feather–Gitler '70s*
A. Morgan: "A Johnny Dankworth Discography," *JM*, ix/12 (1964), 3; x/1 (1965), 3
——: "A Vignette of John Dankworth, Esq., H.M.P.C.," *JM*, ix/12 (1964), 12

D. Grayson: "Johnny Dankworth Talking," *JB*, iii/4 (1966), 16
L. Tomkins: "The Way I see it," *CI*, vii/12 (1969), 16
M. C. King: "British Jazzmen, no.7: John Dankworth," *JJ*, xxiv/2 (1971), 10
L. Tomkins: "John Dankworth Explains the Operation of the Wavendon Allmusic Plan and Cleo Laine Adds her Opinions," *CI*, ix (1971), no.11, p.6; no.12, p.26
——: "The Wide Musical World of John Dankworth," *CI*, xi/8 (1973), 6
——: "John Dankworth Talks about Versatility and Broadmindedness," *CI*, xi/10 (1973), 8
——: "John Dankworth Today," *CI*, xix (1981), no.10, p.20; no.11, p.12; xx (1981), no.1, p.16; no.3, p.16

CHARLES FOX/DIGBY FAIRWEATHER

Danzi, Mike [Michael] (*b* New York, 1 Sept 1898; *d* New York, 13 Feb 1986). Banjoist. Having begun his career as a violinist, in 1918 he formed his own Red Devils Jazzband; he later changed to banjo (1921) and toured in vaudeville. He made his first recording in 1924 with Wilbur Sweatman's group, which also included Duke Ellington. In the same year he joined Alex Hyde's orchestra, which toured and recorded in Germany (1924–5); when it disbanded he remained in Europe. His playing may be heard on Hyde's *Counting the Hours* (1925, Grammophon 20223). He made a wide variety of recordings (ranging from jazz, ragtime, and dance music to film soundtracks and classical music) as a soloist, with his own orchestras, and as a sideman with most leading bands of the period. After returning to the USA (1939), he worked as a copyist and soloist at Radio City Music Hall, New York, until he retired in 1972.

BIBLIOGRAPHY

R. E. Lotz: "Michael 'Mike' Danzi," *Sv*, no.67 (1976), 24
——: "Mike Danzi: his own Recording Sessions," *Doctor Jazz*, no.79 (1977), 6
M. Danzi and R. E. Lotz: *American Musician in Germany, 1924–1939* (Schmitten, Germany, 1986) [autobiography]

RAINER E. LOTZ

Dapogny, James [Jim] (*b* Berwyn, IL, 3 Sept 1940). Editor, writer, teacher, and pianist. He studied composition at the University of Illinois (BMus 1962, MMus 1963, DMA 1971) and from 1966 taught jazz theory and history at the University of Michigan. In his work as an editor and writer he has devoted particular attention to the music of Jelly Roll Morton; his book *Ferdinand "Jelly Roll" Morton: the Collected Piano Music* (1982) remains the only virtually complete edition of transcriptions of a jazz musician's work, and also includes biographical material and analysis. He also wrote entries on major jazz musicians for *The New Grove Dictionary of Music and Musicians* (London, 1980) and contributed transcriptions of works by Morton, Fats Waller, Louis Armstrong and Earl Hines, Meade "Lux" Lewis, and Thelonious Monk to the collection *Smithsonian Classic Jazz Scores*, edited by Gunther Schuller (in preparation). As a pianist Dapogny has performed widely in concert and on radio and television, and recorded as a leader of the Chicago Jazz Band (*Back Home in Illinois*, 1984, Jlgy 140), and with the State Street Aces, the Mysterious Babies, and Sippie Wallace (*Sippie*, 1982, Atl. 19350).

WRITINGS
(selective list)

Ferdinand "Jelly Roll" Morton: the Collected Piano Music (Washington, 1982) [incl. transcrs.]
"Jelly Roll Morton and Ragtime," *Ragtime: its History, Composers, and Music*, ed. J. Hasse (New York and London, 1985), 257
"Ragtime," "New Orleans Jazz," "Jelly Roll Morton," "Blues," "Chicago Jazz," *The Smithsonian History of Jazz*, ed. M. Williams (in preparation)

BIBLIOGRAPHY

B. Byler: "Dapogny's Chicago Jazz Band Plays Ragtime, New Orleans, Chicago, Swing," *MR*, xi/6 (1984), 1

DANIEL ZAGER

Dara, Olu. *See* OLU DARA.

Darensbourg, Joe [Joseph Wilmer] (*b* Baton Rouge, LA, 9 July 1906; *d* Van Nuys, CA, 24 May 1985). Clarinetist and soprano saxophonist. After some tuition on clarinet from Alphonse Picou in New Orleans he gained early experience playing with local groups. He traveled with a medicine show and a circus band, then settled in Los Angeles to work with Mutt Carey's Liberty Syncopators, where he played alto saxophone alongside Pops Foster and Minor Hall. From 1929 to 1944 he was based in Seattle, working on cruise liners, playing in after-hours clubs and roadhouses, and appearing with many well-known entertainers. He achieved recognition as a jazz musician when in 1944, with the pianist Johnny Wittwer, he resumed playing clarinet in a traditional repertory. After returning to Los Angeles Darensbourg recorded with Kid Ory and toured briefly with the rhythm-and-blues pianist and singer Joe Liggins. He was a permanent member of Ory's band from 1947 to 1953, and for the rest of his career concentrated on music of the New Orleans style. He played with Gene Mayl and Teddy Buckner, then formed his own group, the Dixie Flyers, and had a national hit with his recording of *Yellow Dog Blues*. From 1961 to 1964 Darensbourg performed and made extensive overseas tours with Louis Armstrong's All Stars. Later he worked with his own and other revivalist bands and also toured with the LEGENDS OF JAZZ (1973–5). He recorded regularly and received belated appreciation for his musical versatility and for the quality of his warm-toned work on clarinet. Darensbourg composed several tunes, notably *Lou-easy-an-ia*.

Oral history material in *LNT*, *NjR* (JOHP).

SELECTED RECORDINGS

As leader: *On a Lark in Dixieland* (1957, Lark 331), incl. Yellow Dog Blues
As sideman: J. Wittwer: Joe's Blues (1944, Exner 1); K. Ory: *Kid Ory's Creole Jazz Band* (1945, Folk Lyric 9008); At a Georgia Camp Meeting (1950, Col. 38957); Mahogany Hall Stomp (1950, Col. 38956); T. Buckner: *Salute to Armstrong* (1956, Dixieland Jubilee 505)

BIBLIOGRAPHY

J. Wittwer: "A Tribute to Joe Darensbourg," *Jazz Record*, no.36 (1945); repr. in *Selections from the Gutter: Jazz Portraits from "The Jazz Record"*, ed. A Hodes and C. Hansen (Berkeley, CA, and London, 1977), 106
J. Bentley: "Joe Darensbourg," *Eureka*, i/5 (1960), 21
P. Vacher: "My Louisiana Story by Joe Darensbourg," *JM*, ix/8 (1963), 4
D. Melinsky: "Darensbourg Joys," *MR*, v/2 (1977), 10
A. Ashforth and L. Gushee: "An Interview with Joe Darensbourg," *Fn*, xv (1984), no.3, p.4; no.4, p.4
J. Darensbourg: *Telling it Like it is*, ed. P. Vacher (London, 1987; Baton Rouge, LA, 1987, as *Jazz Odyssey: the Autobiography of Joe Darensbourg*)

PETER VACHER

Dark Clouds of Joy. The name of two Kansas City jazz bands formed by TERRENCE HOLDER: the first, formed in 1926, was taken over by ANDY KIRK in 1929 (and became known as the Twelve Clouds of Joy, or simply the Clouds of Joy), at which time Holder formed a new band under the original name.

Darling, David (*b* Elkhart, IN, 4 March 1941). Cellist and composer. He learned piano and cello from an early age and while he was a high-school student played double bass and alto saxophone in the school dance band, which he also led. After studying cello and music education at Indiana University (to 1965) he taught for four years (1966–70). His first notable engagement as a jazz musician was with the Paul Winter Consort (1970–78), with which he toured the USA and recorded the album *Icarus* (*c*1971, Epic 31643). On his solo album *Journal October* (1979, ECM 1161) he played not only conventional cello, but a solid-bodied, eight-string electric cello of his own design, and a variety of percussion instruments. He recorded as a leader (1981) and was a founder member of the group Gallery, which recorded (1981) and toured the USA and Europe (1982). He has also made recordings with Glen Moore (1979), Ralph Towner (1979), the electric guitarist John Clark (1980), and Spyro Gyra (1980), and in a duo with Terje Rypdal (1983). From 1978 he has been active as a classical composer and his works have been performed by major American orchestras. (I. Carr: "Darling, David," in I. Carr, D. Fairweather, and B. Priestley: *Jazz: the Essential Companion*, London, 1987)

Dašek, Rudolf (*b* Prague, 27 Aug 1933). Czechoslovak guitarist. He formed a trio while attending the conservatory in Prague (1962–6) and became well-known as a guest soloist with Karel Velebný's group SHQ. In 1967–8 he played with Ladislav Déczi's quintet Jazz Cellula, and in 1968–70 belonged to the house band at the Blue Note club in Berlin and played with Lou Bennett's trio. During this period he also accompanied Benny Bailey, Carmell Jones, Tony Scott, Leo Wright, and many others. With Jiří Stivín he formed the duo Tandem (1971–5, re-formed 1985), which performed successfully at European festivals. He also performed with Philip Catherine and Christian Escoudé and toured repeatedly with Toto Blanke in an acoustic-guitar duo. A good example of Dašek's playing is his album *Dialogues* (1972–8, Sup. 11152533). (B. Noglik: "Rudolf Dašek," *Jazzwerkstatt international* (Berlin, 1981), 173 [incl. interview, discography])

BERT NOGLIK

Dash, (St.) Julian (Bennett) (*b* Charleston, SC, 9 April 1916; *d* New York, 25 Feb 1974). Tenor saxophonist. He began on alto saxophone in 1932 having been inspired by Lonnie Simmons, in whose band, the Charleston Nighthawks, he made his professional début in 1935. After playing tenor saxophone in the Revellers and the 'Bama State Collegians at Alabama State Teachers College (1935–6) he went to New York to study embalming. From 1936 to 1938 he led his own band at Monroe's Uptown House, then replaced Paul Bascomb in Erskine Hawkins's orchestra, remaining with the group until it disbanded in the mid-1950s. Thereafter he worked at a variety of jobs during the day, but continued to play at weekends. In the mid-1960s he performed at the Shalimar in Harlem with the Marlowe Morris Trio, and in 1970–71 he led his own quintet. He was co-composer of the jazz standard *Tuxedo Junction*.

SELECTED RECORDINGS

As leader: Zero (1955, VJ 144)

As sideman with E. Hawkins: No Soap (1939, Bb 10292); Tuxedo Junction (1939, Bb 10409); Norfolk Ferry (1940, Bb 10932); Bicycle Bounce (1942, Bb 11547); Holiday for Swing (1945, Vic. 201794)

BIBLIOGRAPHY

ChiltonW

O. Keller: "Julian Dash," *BHcF*, no.71 (1957), 3

B. Demeusy: "The Julian Dash Story," *JJ*, xvii/4 (1964), 12 [incl. discography]

FRANK DRIGGS

Date. In jazz parlance, from its common definition as an appointment for a set time, a recording session; more generally the term is used to refer to a club or concert engagement.

Dauner, Wolfgang (*b* Stuttgart, Germany, 30 Dec 1935). German pianist, composer, and bandleader. He studied trumpet, piano, and composition at the Musikhochschule in Stuttgart and in the early 1960s belonged to Joki Freund's sextet; he appeared at a number of festivals in Germany. His album *Dream Talk* (1964), which he recorded as the leader of a trio consisting of piano, double bass, and percussion, was one of the first European recordings of free jazz. In 1969 he became the leader of the Radio Jazz Group Stuttgart, for which he also wrote compositions, and in 1970 he formed the jazz-rock group Et Cetera. He led the Free Sound & Super Brass Big Band with Hans Koller in the mid-1970s, and in 1975 organized the UNITED JAZZ AND ROCK ENSEMBLE. Dauner's compositions often use synthesizers and *musique concrète*, incorporate elements of theater, opera, and dance, and reflect his social and political views; his works include *Vision 68* (performed at the Frankfurt festival, 1968), *Der Urschrei des Musikers* for symphony orchestra, five soloists, and quadraphonic tape (performed at the Berliner Jazztage, 1976), church music, a children's opera, and music for films, radio, and television.

SELECTED RECORDINGS

As unaccompanied soloist: *Solo Piano* (1981, Mood 28635)

As leader: *Dream Talk* (1964, CBS BPG62478); *Output* (1970, ECM 1006); *"Beobachtungen", Musica sacra nova* (1970, Schwann AMS Studio 602); of Et Cetera: *Knirsch* (1972, MPS 2121432); of United Jazz and Rock Ensemble: *Live in Berlin* (1981, Mood 28628); *United Live Opus Sechs* (1984, Mood 28642).

As sideman: J. Freund: *Yogi Jazz* (1963, CBS BPG62273); H. Koller: *Kunstkopfindianer* (1974, MPS 2122019-2); A. Mangelsdorff: *A Jazz Tune I Hope* (1978, MPS 68212)

BIBLIOGRAPHY

Feather '60s; *Feather–Gitler '70s*

G. Endress: "Weitgespanntes musikalisches Schaffen: Wolfgang Dauner," *JP*, xxii/9 (1973), 16 [incl. discography]

D. Zimmerle: "The Wide Musical World of Wolfgang Dauner," *JF* [intl edn], no.38 (1975), 44 [incl. discography]

J.-E. Berendt: "Wolfgang Dauner," *DB*, xlvii/3 (1980), 55

I. Carr: "Dauner, Wolfgang," in I. Carr, D. Fairweather, and B. Priestley: *Jazz: the Essential Companion* (London, 1987)

JOACHIM E. BERENDT/WOLFRAM KNAUER

Dauntless. Record label. It was established in the early 1960s as a subsidiary of Audio Fidelity, and was used to issue several jazz LPs, including items by Steve Kuhn and Toshiko Akiyoshi, and Babs Gonzales.

MARK GARDNER

Davenport, Wallace (Foster) (*b* New Orleans, 30 June 1925). Trumpeter and bandleader. He performed in New Orleans with the Young Tuxedo Brass Band (1938) and Papa Celestin (*c*1941), and returned there after serving in the navy. He played bop and swing with various local bands, and accompanied popular singers. Between 1953 and 1969 he toured the USA and Europe with Lionel Hampton, and while in Paris recorded with Mezz Mezzrow (*Mezz Mezzrow and his Orchestra*, 1955, Swing 30005). He played with Count Basie from 1964 to 1966 and around the same time also worked with the singers Ray Charles and Lloyd Price. In 1969 Davenport returned to New Orleans, where he played traditional jazz on recordings issued mainly on his own label, My Jazz (1971–6). By 1974 he had resumed touring; he recorded in Europe with George Wein (1974) and Panama Francis and Arnett Cobb (both 1976). He also led his own groups (1976–9), and the album *Jazz from New Orleans Dedicated to the Hot Club of France* (1977, Shalom 2214) is a good example of his playing during this period. From 1976 Davenport has intermittently renewed his association with Hampton while returning frequently to New Orleans. He has made numerous appearances and recordings with gospel singers, including the Zion Harmonizers and Aline White.

BIBLIOGRAPHY

M. Vernon: "Domino Men: Nat Perrilliat and Wallace Davenport," *JM*, xiii/6 (1967), 11

J.-P. Battestini: "Wallace Davenport," *BHcF*, no.242 (1974), 4 [interview]

V. Wilmer: "Davenport: Thinking in Dixie," *MM*, l (25 Jan 1975), 32
J. Shalom: Liner notes: *Jazz from New Orleans Dedicated to the Hot Club of France* (Shalom 2214, 1977)
E. Townley: "From Way Down Yonder," *Sv*, no.90 (1980), 207

Davern, Kenny [John Kenneth] (*b* Huntington, NY, 7 Jan 1935). Clarinetist and saxophonist. He became interested in jazz while in high school, and began to play professionally at the age of 16. In 1954 he joined Jack Teagarden and made his recording début. When Teagarden traveled to the West Coast, Davern remained in New York with Phil Napoleon's Memphis Five (1955), then played with Pee Wee Erwin (intermittently, 1956–61) as well as with Henry "Red" Allen, Buck Clayton, and Jo Jones. He led his own band at Nick's, New York (1961), before becoming a member of the Dukes of Dixieland (1962–3) and touring the USA. During the 1960s he worked with Eddie Condon, Herman Autrey, and Ruby Braff, and made several tours with leading mainstream musicians. His emergence as an important soloist was further consolidated in 1974 when Davern formed SOPRANO SUMMIT with Bob Wilber, which also allowed him to develop his uninhibited style on soprano saxophone. After the group disbanded in 1979 he toured widely. He again specialized on clarinet, preferring to work in quartets or trios, and in 1981 formed the Blue Three with Dick Wellstood and Bobby Rosengarden. He has performed at several European jazz festivals, appeared in films, and made numerous recordings. Davern is a player of outstanding technical skill whose style combines an eloquent distillation of classic jazz values with a wide-ranging harmonic awareness.

SELECTED RECORDINGS

As leader: with B. Wilber: *Soprano Summit* (1973, World Jazz 5), *Chalumeau Blue* (1976, Chi. 148); *The Hot Three* (1979, Monmouth 7091); of Blue Three (with D. Wellstood and B. Rosengarden): *The Blue Three at Hanratty's* (1981, Chaz Jazz 109); *The Very Thought of You* (1984, Milton Keynes Music 841); *Live Hot Jazz* (1984, Statiras 8077)

As sideman: on J. Teagarden: *Original Dixieland* (1954, Period 1110), King Porter Stomp, Milenberg Joys; D. Hyman: *Satchmo Remembered* (1974, Atl. 1671)

BIBLIOGRAPHY

D. Morgenstern: "Kenny Davern: Overdue," *DB*, xxxv/10 (1968), 23
S. Traill: "Two of a Kind," *JJI*, xxvii/10 (1974), 8
S. Klett: "Kenny Davern: Interview," *Cadence*, iv/3 (1978), 18
R. D. Johnson: "Goodbye, Soprano, Hello, Clarinet," *MR*, vi/6 (1979), 1
M. Jones: "Liquorice Sticking," *MM*, liv (22 Sept 1979), 53
L. Dirk and R. Cowie: "Kenny Davern Interviewed," *JJI*, xxxiii/9 (1980), 6

PETER VACHER

Davidson, Cuffee. Name by which ED CUFFEE has incorrectly been referred to in some sources.

Davidson, Trump [Jimmy, James Douglas] (*b* Sudbury, Canada, 26 Nov 1908; *d* Sudbury, 2 May 1978). Canadian cornetist, singer, and bandleader. He formed one of the first Canadian jazz bands, the Melody Five, in Sudbury around 1925 and then played in Toronto with the orchestra of the violinist Luigi Romanelli (1929–36). From 1937 to 1942 he led his own dance band, which made weekly broadcasts on NBC and in 1938–9 toured Britain with Ray Noble. After playing in the orchestra of the pianist Horace Lapp (from 1942), Davidson formed another dance band, which appeared regularly at the Palace Pier, Toronto, from 1944 until it broke up in 1962. Its performances usually included several numbers played by a dixieland jazz group, made up of members of the band. The smaller group also functioned independently and continued in existence after the demise of the band; it played on CBC radio from the 1940s to the 1960s and made a number of recordings (1961–71). Davidson later led a 16-piece band (1974–8), with which he sang and for which he wrote the arrangements. Davidson's brother Teddy (*b* Sudbury, 21 June 1914; *d* Toronto, 7 Aug 1983), a tenor saxophonist, played in dance bands in Toronto (including Davidson's) from the 1930s.

BIBLIOGRAPHY

M. Miller and H. McNamara: "Davidson, Jimmy," *Encyclopedia of Music in Canada*, ed. H. Kallmann, G. Potvin, and K. Winters (Toronto, Buffalo, and London, 1981)
M. Miller: "Trump and Teddy Davidson: Pretty Fancy Stuff," *Jazz in Canada: Fourteen Lives* (Toronto and elsewhere, 1982), 14

JACK LITCHFIELD

Davies, John R(oss) T(wiston) (*b* Wivelsfield, nr Haywards Heath, England, 20 March 1927). English alto saxophonist, trombonist, record producer, and discographer. He first worked in a trio (1948–9) and with Mick Mulligan (1949), then joined the Crane River Jazz Band. He remained with the group until 1951, recorded with it in 1953, and became a permanent member again in 1972, continuing to play into the 1980s. During the 1950s he played with the cornetist Steve Lane (1952), Cy Laurie (1953–4), Sandy Brown (1955–6), his own band, and Acker Bilk (1957). His principal later associations were with the Temperance Seven (1959–68) and the Anglo-American Alliance (1967–72, with which he recorded in 1967–8); he also played with the New Paul Whiteman Orchestra (1973–5) and is heard to advantage on *The New Paul Whiteman Orchestra Plays the Music of the Roaring 20s* (1975, Wave 27). In the 1980s he has led his own band, Gentle Jazz, and worked as a freelance musician.

Davies established the record label RISTIC in 1949 and issued around 50 recordings in limited editions up to 1972. He then became joint director of Retrieval Records, which produces reissues of specialist material, including hot dance music; he is well known among collectors for his expertise in remastering techniques. As a researcher he has worked for the magazine *Storyville* from its inception (1965) into the 1980s; his principal contributions are his discographies, notably that for Fats Waller (1965–7).

BIBLIOGRAPHY

FeatherE
R. Cotterrell, ed.: *Jazz Now: the Jazz Centre Society Guide* (London, 1976)

DIGBY FAIRWEATHER

Davis, Anthony (*b* Paterson, NJ, 20 Feb 1951). Pianist and composer. He grew up in New York and studied music at Yale University (BA 1975), where he became the leading young pianist within a circle of musicians whose philosophy derived from the principles of the Association for the Advancement of Creative Musicians. In New Haven in 1973 he was a co-founder of Advent, a free-jazz group which included George Lewis (ii), then from 1974 to 1977 he was a member of the New Dalta Ahkri band led by Leo Smith. After moving to New York he played with Leroy Jenkins's trio (1977–9), and from 1978 has led a duo and a quartet with James Newton. He has also worked with Lewis and Abdul Wadud in several ensembles, such as the octet Episteme (formed in 1981), that bridge jazz and European classical traditions. As a composer Davis endeavors to control improvisation by providing strict notation. His works are often constructed around complex, ever-changing atonal lines, but they also explore simplicity, as in meditative passages of repeated material inspired by gamelan music (for example, the *Wayang* series). His opera *X*, based on the life of Malcom X, was developed in a series of workshops at the American Music Theater Festival; it was performed in Philadelphia in 1985 and by the New York City Opera in 1986.

Oral history material in *CtY*.

SELECTED RECORDINGS
* – composed by Davis

As unaccompanied soloist: *Past Lives* (1978, Red 134), incl. Crepuscule: a Suite for Monk, Of Blues and Dreams, On a Azure Plane; **Lady of the Mirrors* (c1980, IndN 1047), incl. Beyond Reason, Five Moods from an English Garden, Man on a Turquoise Cloud, Under the Double Moon (Wayang no.IV)
Duos with J. Hoggard: **Under the Double Moon* (1980, MPS 68267)
As leader: **Of Blues and Dreams* (1978, Sack. 3020), incl. Graef, Lethe, Madame Xola; with J. Newton: *Hidden Voices* (1979, IndN 1041), incl. *Hocket in the Pocket, *Past Lives; *Episteme* (c1981, Gram. 8101), incl. *A Walk through the Shadows, *Wayang no.II (Shadowdance), *Wayang no.IV (Under the Double Moon); **Variations in Dream-time* (c1982, IndN 1056), incl. Enemy of Light; **Hemispheres* (1983, Gram. 8303)
As sideman: L. Smith: *Reflectativity* (1974, Kabell 2); O. Lake: *Life Dance of Is* (1978, AN 3003); L. Jenkins: *The Legend of Ai Glatson* (1978, BS 0022)

BIBLIOGRAPHY

C. J. Safane: "Profile: Anthony Davis," *DB*, xlvi/18 (1979), 64
R. Zabor: "Funny, You *Look* like a Jazz Musician," *VV*, xxiv (2 July 1979), 72
R. Palmer: "Anthony Davis' New Musical Language," *RS*, no.316 (1 May 1980), 26
B. Primack: "Anthony Davis: Pianist and Composer of the New Jazz," *CK*, vi/11 (1980), 48
F. Davis: "Anthony Davis," *DB*, xlix/1 (1982), 21 [incl. discography]
G. Giddins: *Rhythm-a-ning: Jazz Tradition and Innovation in the '80s* (New York, and Oxford, England, 1985) [colln of previously pubd articles], 59
F. Davis: *In the Moment: Jazz in the 1980s* (New York, and Oxford, England, 1986) [colln of previously pubd articles], 3
L. Van Trikt: "Anthony Davis: Interview," *Cadence*, xii/10 (1986), 15

BARRY KERNFELD

Davis, Art(hur D.) (*b* Harrisburg, PA, 5 Dec 1934). Double bass player. After studying piano, then tuba, he won a national competition as a tuba player; in 1951 he took up the double bass. He performed with Max Roach (from 1958 to February 1959), Dizzy Gillespie (1959–60, touring Europe), Gigi Gryce (1960), and the singer Lena Horne (1961) and recorded with Booker Little (1958, 1961), Quincy Jones, Roland Kirk, and Oliver Nelson (all 1961), Freddie Hubbard (1961–2), Clark Terry (1962), and Art Blakey (1963). He also played in John Coltrane's group (at intervals, 1961) and recorded with it in 1961 and 1965. He belonged successively to the orchestras of NBC (1962–3), Westinghouse television (1964–9), and CBS (1969–70) and from 1971 to 1973 taught at Manhattan Community College. After receiving a BA from Hunter College (1972), MA degrees in music and psychology from CUNY and New York University (1976), and the PhD in psychology (1981) he worked principally as a psychologist, while continuing to record (as a leader, 1984) and perform (in a duo with Hilton Ruiz, 1985–6). He is the author of *The Arthur Davis Method for Double Bass* (Crugers, NY, 1975).

Oral history material in *LNT*.

SELECTED RECORDINGS

As leader: *Live!* (1984, AKM 1)
As sideman: Leo Wright: *Blues Shout* (1960, Atl. 1358); J. Coltrane: *Olé Coltrane* (1961, Atl. 1373); *Africa/Brass* (1961, Imp. 6); *Ascension* (1965, Imp. 95)

BIBLIOGRAPHY

B. Coss: "The Emergence of Art Davis," *DB*, xxviii/20 (1961), 24
V. Wilmer: "Art Davis: a Struggle for Recognition," *JM*, vii/12 (1962), 6.
——: "Davis: a Martyr to his Art," *MM* (7 Oct 1972), 40
E. Bratton: "Art Davis," *Cadence*, xii/9 (1986), 12

MICHAEL ULLMAN

Davis, Charles (A.) (*b* Goodman, MI, 20 May 1933). Baritone saxophonist. He was educated at DuSable High School, Chicago, and at the Chicago School of Music (1948–50). He worked with Brother Jack McDuff (1954), Ben Webster (1955), Billie Holiday (1956), and Dinah Washington (1957–9), and established his reputation performing and recording with Kenny Dorham (1959–62). He began an association with Sun Ra in 1954, working regularly with his band until 1956 and then intermittently into the 1980s. In the 1960s he played with Illinois Jacquet, Lionel Hampton, and John Coltrane, and led his own group (1965–6). He performed with the Jazz Composer's Orchestra (1966–76), the cooperative group Artistry in Music (1972), the Louis Hayes Sextet (1972–4), Clark Terry's Big B-A-D Band (1973–9), and the Thad Jones–Mel Lewis Orchestra (1978). In 1974 he formed the Baritone Saxophone Retinue, an ensemble of six baritone saxophonists and a rhythm section. In the 1980s he appeared with Barry Harris (1980–82), Dameronia and the Philly Joe Jones Quartet (both 1981–4), and Abdullah Ibrahim (from 1983). He has also been prominent in New York jazz circles as a music director.

Davis is an able performer on tenor and soprano saxophones, but it is on the baritone instrument that he has chiefly made his mark. His tone is reminiscent of Leo Parker's, while his controlled technique recalls Serge Chaloff in its fine fluency. His bold solos and sensitive ensemble work, in both modern and mainstream contexts, make a significant contribution to any group in which he plays.

SELECTED RECORDINGS

As leader: *Ingia!* (1974, SE 7425); *Dedicated to Tadd* (1979, West 54 8006); *Super 80* (1982, Nilva 3410)
As sideman: K. Dorham: *The Arrival of Kenny Dorham* (1960, Jaro 5007); *Jazz Contemporary* (1960, Time 2004); S. Lacy: *The Straight Horn of Steve Lacy* (1960, Can. 9007); E. Jones and J. Garrison: *Illumination!* (1963, Imp. 49); D. Reece: *Manhattan Project* (1978, BH 7001); Dameronia: *To Tadd with Love* (1982, Upt. 2711); *Look, Stop, Listen* (1983, Upt. 2715)

BIBLIOGRAPHY

Feather '60s; *Feather–Gitler '70s*

MARK GARDNER

Davis, Eddie "Lockjaw" [Davis, Eddie [Edward]; Lockjaw] (*b* New York, 2 March 1922; *d* Culver City, CA, 3 Nov 1986). Tenor saxophonist. He was self-taught and in the late 1930s he began to perform at Monroe's Uptown House, New York. After working with various musicians, including Cootie Williams (1942–4), Lucky Millinder (1944), Andy Kirk (1945–6), and Louis Armstrong, he began to lead his own small group, with which he recorded from 1946. He was active as a leader for almost two decades except during periods when he performed and recorded with Count Basie (1952–3, 1957). From around 1955 to 1960 he led an organ trio which included Shirley Scott, and from 1960 to 1962 often led a quintet with Johnny Griffin, whose "tough" style well matched his own. In October 1964 he rejoined Basie, with whom he remained until 1973, when he settled in Las Vegas; during this time he occasionally performed in Europe, with Norman Granz and Ella Fitzgerald, among others. From 1974 he toured internationally as a leader and recorded regularly in the USA and Europe. Although Davis produced a funky sound, his rough-toned, driving playing is reminiscent of the styles of the 1940s.

For illustration *see* GRIFFIN, JOHNNY.

SELECTED RECORDINGS

As leader: Lockjaw/Afternoon in a Doghouse (1946, Haven 800); *Jazz with a Beat* (1956–7, King 566); *Trane Whistle* (1960, Prst. 7206); with J. Griffin: *Tough Tenor Favorites* (1962, JInd 976); *The Heavy Hitter* (1979, Muse 5202)
As sideman: C. Williams: Sweet Lorraine/Honeysuckle Rose (1944, Hit 8088); C. Basie: Bread (1952, Clef 89085); Paradise Squat (1952, Clef 89014); *Broadway Basie's Way* (1966, Command 905)

BIBLIOGRAPHY

FeatherE; *Feather '60s*; *Feather–Gitler '70s*
H. Panassié: "Eddie 'Lockjaw' Davis," *BHcF*, no.74 (1958), 3
J. Shaw: "Lockjaw Davis: a Musician who Matters," *JJ*, xxiii/9 (1970), 10
V. Wilmer: *Jazz People* (London, Indianapolis, and New York, 1970/*R*1985)

A. Taylor: *Notes and Tones: Musician-to-Musician Interviews* (Liège, Belgium, 1977/R1982), 83
V. Montgomery: "Jaws Unlocks," *JJI*, xxxvi/7 (1983), 14
T. Burke and D. Penny: "Eddie 'Lockjaw' Davis 'Hollerin' and Screamin',' 1945–1950," *Blues & Rhythm: the Gospel Truth*, no.7 (1985), 10; no.9 (1985), 7 [corrections]
B. Rusch: "Eddie Lockjaw Davis," *Cadence*, xiv (1988), no.1, p.5; no.2, p.5

LAWRENCE KOCH

Davis, Ham [Leonard] (*b* St. Louis, 4 July 1905; *d* New York, 1957). Trumpeter. In 1924–5 he played with Charlie Creath's bands in St. Louis. He then moved to New York, where he worked with Edgar Hayes (1927), the pianist Arthur Gibbs (1927–8), and Charlie Johnson (*c*1928–1929). In 1929 he recorded with Eddie Condon (*I'm gonna stomp, Mr. Henry Lee/ That's a serious thing*, Vic. 38046). During the 1930s he worked with Elmer Snowden (1930–31), Don Redman (1931), Russell Wooding (1932), Benny Carter (1933), and Luis Russell (1934–5), and from October 1935 to spring 1937 he was a member of Louis Armstrong's orchestra. During a further period with Hayes (1938–9) he made a tour of Europe; thereafter Davis worked as a freelance in New York, and in 1940 performed in a nine-piece band led by Sidney Bechet. In the 1940s he worked intermittently in a band led by Alberto Socarras before ceasing to work as a full-time musician.

based on *ChiltonW*

Davis, Kay [Wimp, Kathryn Elizabeth] (*b* Evanston, IL, 5 Dec 1920). Singer. She studied singing and piano at Northwestern University (1938–43), then taught and gave recitals for several years. Her singing with Duke Ellington (from the autumn of 1944), which was usually in the soprano range and wordless, inspired some of Ellington's most original works in the late 1940s; she also sang ballads occasionally as a contralto. In July 1950 she married and ceased working full-time in music.

SELECTED RECORDINGS

(all as sideman with D. Ellington)

Transblucency (1946, Vic. 202326); On a Turquoise Cloud (1947, Col. 38254); Creole Love Call (1949, Col. 38606)

BIBLIOGRAPHY

FeatherE
D. Ellington: *Music is my Mistress* (Garden City, NY, 1973), 219

EDDIE LAMBERT

Davis, Lem(uel Arthur) (*b* Tampa, FL, 22 June 1914; *d* New York, 16 Jan 1970). Alto saxophonist. He was a member of Charlie Brantley's Collegians in Tampa (1937–8) and, shortly after, recorded in New York with the Harlem Indians led by the pianist Harold Boyce (1941). He first came to prominence in the early to mid-1940s playing in the bands of Nat Jaffe, Coleman Hawkins, Eddie Heywood, and Rex Stewart. After performing with John Kirby in 1946 he rejoined Heywood; he made a number of recordings as a leader in 1945–6 and in 1951. During the 1950s and 1960s Davis worked in New York with Buck Clayton and the pianist Teacho Wiltshire as well as leading his own bands. He wrote several compositions, including *'Taint me*, which he recorded with Heywood in 1944.

SELECTED RECORDINGS

As sideman: E. Heywood: 'Taint me (1944, Com. 554); B. Clayton: *A Buck Clayton Jam Session* (1953, Col. CL546)

BIBLIOGRAPHY

ChiltonW

EDDIE LAMBERT

Davis, (Thomas) Maxwell (*b* Independence, KS, 14 Jan 1916; *d* Los Angeles, 18 Sept 1970). Tenor saxophonist, arranger, and bandleader. He played alto saxophone and violin as the leader of his own band in Wichita, Kansas, for four years, then in 1936 moved to the West Coast. After changing to tenor saxophone he played with the Woodman Brothers (1936–7) and in Seattle with the drummer Gene Coy (1939–41). He led his own bands in the 1940s and 1950s and worked as an artists and repertory agent and arranger. He played on a large number of race and rhythm-and-blues recordings with such musicians as Helen Humes, Lloyd Glenn, Pete Johnson, Jimmy Witherspoon, Red Callender, and the electric guitarist Gene Phillips, and wrote arrangements for Jimmie Lunceford (early 1940s) and for a series of big-band recordings for the Crown label (1958–60). Davis's style of Southwest jazz is well represented by his fiery performance on Jay McShann's *Soft Winds* (1949, Swing Time 205); he shows a more gentle approach on *Rainy Weather Blues* (1948, MGM 10397), which he recorded with Joe Turner (ii).

BIBLIOGRAPHY

A. J. McCarthy: "In Memoriam Maxwell Davis, 1916–1970," *JM*, no.190 (1970), 13 [obituary]
W. C. Allen: *Hendersonia: the Music of Fletcher Henderson and his Musicians: a Bio-discography* (Highland Park, NJ, 1973), 560
J. Simmen: "Maxwell Davis (14 janvier 1916–18 septembre 1970)," *BHcF*, no.323 (1985), 3
J. Wolffer: "Maxwell Davis Crown Records," *Names & Numbers*, no.1 (1985), 5

HOWARD RYE

Davis, Miles (Dewey, III) [Prince of Darkness] (*b* Alton, IL, 25 May 1926). Trumpeter and bandleader. An original, lyrical soloist and a demanding group leader, he was the most consistently innovative musician in jazz from the late 1940s through the 1960s.

1. Life. 2. Music.

1. Life. Davis grew up in East St. Louis, and took up trumpet at the age of 13; two years later he was already playing professionally. He moved to New York in September 1944, ostensibly to enter the Institute of Musical Art but actually to locate his idol, Charlie Parker. He joined Parker in live appearances and recording sessions (1945–8), at the same time playing in other groups and touring in the big bands led by Benny Carter and Billy Eckstine. In 1948 he began to lead his own bop groups, and he participated in an experimental workshop centered on the arranger Gil Evans. Their collaborations with Gerry Mulligan, John Lewis, and Johnny Carisi culminated in a series of nonet recordings for Capitol under Davis's name and later collected and reissued as *Birth of the Cool*. In 1949 Davis performed with Sonny Rollins and Art Blakey, and with Tadd Dameron, until heroin addiction interrupted his public career intermittently from mid-1949 to 1953. Although he continued to record with famous bop musicians, including Parker, Rollins, Blakey, J. J. Johnson, Horace Silver, and members of the Modern Jazz Quartet, he worked in clubs infrequently and with inferior accompanists until 1954.

In 1955 Davis appeared informally at the Newport Jazz Festival. His sensational improvisations there brought him widespread publicity and sufficient engagements to establish a quintet (1955–7) with Red Garland, Paul Chambers, Philly Joe Jones, and John Coltrane, who in 1956 was joined and later replaced by Rollins. In May 1957 Davis made the first of several remarkable solo recordings on trumpet and flugelhorn against unusual jazz orchestrations by Gil Evans. In the autumn he organized a quintet, later joined by Cannonball Adderley, that proved short-lived; in the same year he wrote and recorded music in Paris for Louis Malle's film *Ascenseur pour l'échafaud*.

Upon his return to the USA he re-formed his original quintet of 1955 with Adderley as a sixth member. For the next five years Davis drew the rhythm sections of his various sextets and quintets from a small pool of players: the pianists Garland, Bill Evans (ii) (1958–9), and Wynton Kelly; the drummers Jones and Jimmy Cobb; and the bass player Chambers. Personnel changes increased in early 1963, and finally Davis engaged a new rhythm section as the nucleus of another quintet: Herbie Hancock (1963–8), Ron Carter (1963–8), and Tony Williams (1963–9). To replace Coltrane, who had left in 1960, Davis tried a succession of saxophonists, including Sonny Stitt, Jimmy Heath, Hank Mobley (1961), George Coleman (1963–4), and Sam Rivers; ultimately he settled on Wayne Shorter (1964–70).

Because of his irascible temperament and his need for frequent periods of inactivity, these sidemen were by no means entirely faithful to Davis. Nevertheless, the groups of 1955–68 were more stable than his later ones of 1969–75. Often the instrumentation and style of his ever-changing recording ensembles (up to 14 players) diverged considerably from that of his working groups (generally sextets or septets). Influential new members joined him in the late 1960s and early 1970s: Chick Corea, Joe Zawinul, Keith Jarrett, John McLaughlin, Dave Holland, Jack DeJohnette, Bill Cobham, Al Foster, and Airto Moreira. As with Davis's previous colleagues, the excellence of these sidemen bore eloquent witness to his stature among jazz musicians.

For years Davis, who trained as a boxer, had always been physically equal to the exertions of playing jazz trumpet; however, in the mid-1970s serious ailments and the effects of an automobile accident obliged him to retire. He suffered for five years from pneumonia and other afflictions. But in 1980 he made new recordings, and in the summer of 1981 began to tour extensively with new quintets and sextets. Although he was incapacitated by a stroke in February 1982, he resumed an active career in the spring of that year. Only Foster remained with Davis, serving as a sideman to 1975 and again from 1980 to 1985. New young members of his groups have included Bill Evans (iii) (1980–84), Branford Marsalis (1984–5), Bob Berg (from 1985), John Scofield (1982–5), and the synthesizer player Robert (Bobby) Irving III (1980, from 1983).

In the 1980s Davis has been described as a "living legend," a title he detests because it goes against his continuing inclination to be associated with new popular music and energetic youthful activities, but one that is nonetheless accurate, reflecting his position as the former partner of both Parker and Coltrane. He received an honorary Doctorate of Music from the New England Conservatory in 1986 in honor of his longstanding achievements.

2. Music. Davis rejected the standards set for jazz trumpeters in the 1940s by Dizzy Gillespie's bop improvisations, partly because of his limited technique (some of his early recordings were marred by errors), but principally because his interests lay elsewhere. He created relaxed, tuneful melodies centered in the middle register. Not reluctant to repeat ideas, he drew from such a small collection of melodic formulae that many solos seemed as much composed as improvised. Harmonically he was also conservative, and tended to play in close accord with his accompanists. Beneath this apparent pervasive simplicity lay a subtle sense of rhythmic placement and expressive nuance.

These characteristics have remained central to Davis's playing throughout his career. Their mature expression first came on the nonet sessions (1949–50), which inspired the cool-jazz movement. Davis's liking for moderation meshed perfectly with his arrangers' concern for smooth instrumental textures, restrained dynamics and rhythms, and a balance between ensemble and solo passages. In the 1950s, as cool jazz became popular, Davis ignored this style, instead surrounding himself with fiery bop players.

Davis's fallow period in the early 1950s came to an end with his celebrated blues improvisation *Walkin'* in 1954. In a session with Sonny Rollins in the same year he introduced the stemless harmon mute to jazz; its intense sound led to delicate recordings by his first quintet (*Bye Bye Blackbird*, 1956; *'Round Mid-*

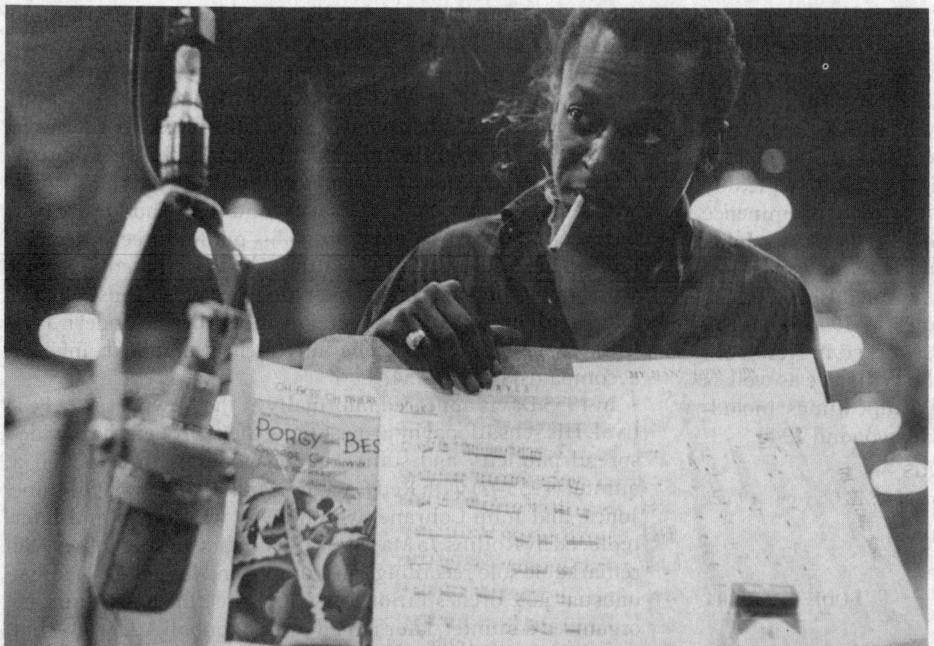

1. Miles Davis at Columbia's recording studios, 4 August 1958

2. *Miles Davis (trumpet) with Darryl Jones (electric bass guitar) at the JVC Grande Parade du Jazz Nice, France, 1985*

night, September–October 1956), which are even more memorable than the fierce swing of the Garland–Chambers–Jones rhythm section on fast bop tunes. Many jazz trumpeters turned to flugelhorn after Davis had demonstrated its potential in his collaborations with Gil Evans; these recordings offer rare examples in jazz of lush orchestral settings with sustained emotional substance, and present an ideal foil for the relaxed tunefulness, melodic and harmonic simplicity, and subtle swing of Davis's improvisations (ex.1).

By the late 1950s Davis had tired of bop structures, and turned to a new approach formulated at this time by Gil Evans and Bill Evans (ii) and later called "modal playing" (*see* MODAL JAZZ). However, the use of modes in Davis's recordings of 1958–9 (*Milestones*, *So What*, *Flamenco Sketches*) had less significance for the future than the slowing of harmonic rhythm. In place of fast-moving, functional chord progressions, Davis used diatonic ostinatos ('vamps'), drones, half-tone oscillations familiar from flamenco music, and tonic–dominant alternations in

Ex.1 Davis's improvisation on the first chorus of *Summertime*, from *Porgy and Bess* (1958, Col. CL1274); transcr. B. Kernfeld

the bass line. *Flamenco Sketches* is a composition in five segments: the first and third are in static major keys, which some analysts have preferred to call the ionian mode, and the second and the fifth suggest others of the ecclesiastical modes. The fourth section, which gives the piece its name, is based on a flamenco-like scale (D E♭ F♯ G A B♭ C/C♯), manifested most clearly in the oscillation of D and E♭ major chords in the piano; the soloists improvising against this background sometimes adhere strictly to the scale but at other points substitute F♮ for F♯, which clashes with the accompaniment and gives rise to the phrygian mode in the solo line. (*See also* FORMS, §5. It should be noted that the inadvertent exchange of the titles *Flamenco Sketches* and *All Blues* on Bill Evans's liner notes to the famous album *Kind of Blue* has caused great confusion; *Flamenco Sketches* has the form outlined here, *All Blues* is indeed, as Davis's later recordings of it prove, a 12-bar blues.)

Through 1964 on recordings, and later in public, Davis's groups performed a small repertory of bop, blues, popular songs, and ostinato tunes. During these years the technical and emotional compass of his playing expanded greatly. The addition of Wayne Shorter to the ensemble led to a change in repertory that began with *E.S.P.* in 1965. Discarding standard tunes, Davis's groups recorded improvisations in a chordless, tonally ambiguous bop style, as well as new ostinato pieces on which the Hancock–Carter–Williams rhythm section found extraordinarily flexible ways of expressing 4/4 rhythms.

In 1968–9 Davis popularized jazz-rock. *In a Silent Way* and *Bitches Brew* (both 1969) blended the sounds of acoustic and electronic instruments, and melodic jazz improvisations with open-ended rock accompaniment. (For further discussion of *Bitches Brew see* FORMS, §7.) From this point on Davis regularly edited his recordings from lengthy taped performances, both live and in the studio. Thus Teo Macero, his recording engineer, and producer from 1959 to 1983, became in a sense the most important "member" of Davis's ensembles. From 1969 to 1975 these various groups made use of electronically altered trumpet, Indian sitar and tablā, and African or Brazilian percussion instruments, as well as funky black-American dance rhythms, and their music is best described by the term "fusion," which embraces a blend of musical elements broader than "jazz-rock." At times, especially during Davis's efforts to resume his career in the 1980s, the results have been a rough juxtaposition of disparate sounds rather than a fusion, but the album *Decoy* offers fine examples of his style. Davis himself concentrates on trumpet, but he also plays synthesizer; his performance on both instruments may be heard to advantage on the title track of *Star People*, an unusual slow blues distinguished by the splashy sound of Foster's ostinato on a Chinese cymbal. Already the innovator of more distinct styles than any other jazz musician, Davis remains a stimulating leader and a masterful soloist.

Two volumes of transcriptions of Davis's solos have been published: *Miles Davis: Jazz Improvisation* by T. Hino (Tokyo, 1975) and *Miles Davis* by S. Isacoff (New York, 1978), the latter based entirely on Hino's edition.

Oral history material in *NjR*

See also JAZZ (i), §§V, 6; VI, 2, 4, and fig.6; HARMONY (i), §1(vi), Table 2, and §2; and TRUMPET, §§5 and 6.

SELECTED RECORDINGS

TO 1951

As leader (all recorded for Capitol): Move/Budo (1949, 15404); Jeru/Godchild (1949, 60005); Boplicity/Israel (1949, 60011)

As sideman with C. Parker: Billie's Bounce/Now's the time (1945, Savoy 573); A Night in Tunisia/Ornithology (1946, Dial 1002); Yardbird Suite (1946, Dial 1003); Half Nelson (1947, Savoy 951); Ah-leu cha (1948, Savoy 939); Au privave/Star Eyes (1951, Mer./Clef 11087)

FROM 1951

(recorded for Prestige)

Morpheus/Blue Room (1951, 734); Dig (1951, 777); *Collector's Items* (1953, 1956, 7044); Four (1954, 898); Walkin' (1954, 45-157); *Miles Davis Quintet* (1954,185); *Miles Davis Quintet* (1954, 187); *Miles Davis All Stars* (1954, 196); *Miles Davis All Stars* (1954, 200); *The Musings of Miles* (1955, 7007); *Milt and Miles* (1955, 7034); *Miles* (1955, 7014); *Relaxin'* (1956, 7129); *Steamin'* (1956, 7200); *Workin'* (1956, 7166); *Cookin'* (1956, 7094); 'Round Midnight (1956, 45-413)

(recorded for Columbia)

'Round about Midnight (1955–6, CL949), incl. Bye Bye Blackbird, 'Round Midnight; *Miles Ahead* (1957, CL1041); *Jazz Track* (1957–8, CL1268); *Milestones* (1958, CL1193); *Miles and Monk at Newport* (1958, CL2178); *Porgy and Bess* (1958, CL1274), incl. Summertime; *Jazz at the Plaza* (1958, C32470); *Kind of Blue* (1959, CL1355), incl. Flamenco Sketches, So What; *Sketches of Spain* (1959–60, CS8271)

Someday my Prince will Come (1961, CS8456); *In Person: Friday and Saturday Nights at the Blackhawk* (1961, C2S820); *Miles Davis at Carnegie Hall* (1961, CS8612); *Seven Steps to Heaven* (1963, CS8851); *Miles Davis in Europe* (1963, CS8983); *My Funny Valentine* (1964, CS9106); *Four and More* (1964, CS9253); *E.S.P.* (1965, CS9150); *Miles Smiles* (1966, CS9401)

Sorcerer (1962, 1967, CS9532); *Nefertiti* (1967, CS9594); *Miles in the Sky* (1968, CS9628); *Filles de Kilimanjaro* (1968, CS9750); *In a Silent Way* (1969, CS9875); *Bitches Brew* (1969, GP26); *Big Fun* (1969–72, PG32866); *A Tribute to Jack Johnson* (1970, KC30455); *Miles Davis at Fillmore* (1970, KG30038); *Live-Evil* (1970, G30954)

Get Up with It (1970–74, KG33236); *On the Corner* (1972, KC31906); *Agharta* (1975, PG33967); *Star People* (1982-3, FG38657); *Decoy* (1983–4, FC38991)

BIBLIOGRAPHY

P. Harris: "Nothing but Bop? 'Stupid,' Says Miles," *DB*, xvii/2 (1950), 18

A. Hodeir: *Hommes et problèmes du jazz, suivi de La religion du jazz* (Paris, 1954; Eng. trans., rev. Hodeir, as *Jazz: its Evolution and Essence*, New York, 1956/*R*1975)

N. Hentoff: "An Afternoon with Miles Davis," *JR*, i/2 (1958), 9

M. Davis: "Self-portrait," *The Jazz Word*, ed. D. Cerulli, B. Korall, and M. Nasatir (New York, 1960) [incl. previously pubd articles]

M. James: *Miles Davis* (London, 1961) [incl. discography]; repr. in *Kings of Jazz*, ed. S. Green (South Brunswick, NJ, and New York, 1978)

N. Hentoff: *The Jazz Life* (New York and London, 1961/*R*1975) [incl. previously pubd articles]

D. Heckman: "Miles Davis Times Three," *DB*, xxix/23 (1962), 16

J. Goldberg: *Jazz Masters of the Fifties* (New York and London, 1965/*R*1980)

G. Hoefer: "The Birth of the Cool," *DB*, xxxii/21 (1965), 24

——: "Early Miles," *DB*, xxxiv/7 (1967), 16

D. DeMicheal: "Miles Davis," *RS*, no.48 (13 Dec 1969), 22

D. Locke: "Many Miles," *JM*, no.178 (1969), 18

M. Williams: *The Jazz Tradition* (New York, 1970, rev. 2/1983)

L. Feather: *From Satchmo to Miles* (New York, 1972)

H. Pekar: "Miles Davis: 1964–69 Recordings," *Coda*, no.147 (1976), 8

T. Mortensen: *Miles Davis: den ny jazz* (Copenhagen, 1977)

M. C. Gridley: *Jazz Styles* (Englewood Cliffs, NJ, 1978, rev. 2/1985 as *Jazz Styles: History and Analysis*, with suppl. *Instructor's Manual and Discography)*

F. Kerschbaumer: *Miles Davis: stilkritische Unterschungen zur musikalischen Entwicklung seines Personalstils* (Graz, Austria, 1978) [incl. discography]

B. Goldberg: *WKCR-FM Miles Davis Festival Handbook* (New York, 1979) [discography]

D. Baker: *The Jazz Style of Miles Davis: a Musical and Historical Perspective* (Lebanon, IN, 1980) [incl. transcrs.]

B. D. Kernfeld: *Adderley, Coltrane, and Davis at the Twilight of Bebop: the Search for Melodic Coherence (1958–59)* (diss., Cornell U., 1981)

T. Naitho: *Miles* (Pyworthy, nr Holsworthy, England, 1981)

I. Carr: *Miles Davis: a Critical Biography* (London and New York, 1982; Ger. trans., Baden-Baden, Germany, 1985) [incl. discography by B. Priestley]

E. Nisenson: *'Round about Midnight: a Portrait of Miles Davis* (New York, 1982; Ger. trans., Vienna, 1985)

D. Breskin: "Searching for Miles: Theme and Variations on the Life of a Trumpeter," *RS*, no.405 (29 Sept 1983), 46

H. Brofsky: "Miles Davis and *My Funny Valentine*: the Evolution of a Solo," *Black Music Research Journal* (1983), 23

J. Chambers: *Milestones*, i: *The Music and Times of Miles Davis to 1960* (Toronto, Buffalo, and London, 1983)

H. Mandel: "Miles Davis," *DB*, li/12 (1984), 16 [incl. discography]

P. Wiessmüller: *Miles Davis: sein Leben, seine Musik, seine Schallplatten* (Gauting, Germany, 1984)

A. Baraka: "Miles Davis," *New York Times Magazine* (16 June 1985)

J. Chambers: *Milestones*, ii: *The Music and Times of Miles Davis since 1960* (Toronto, Buffalo, and London, 1985)

M. Gilbert: "Miles: Time after Time," *JJI*, xxxviii/9 (1985), 8

I. Skovgaard: "Miles Records in Denmark," *JJI*, xxxviii/3 (1985), 3

F. Davis: *In the Moment: Jazz in the 1980s* (New York, and Oxford, England, 1986) [colln of previously pubd articles], 248

K. Franckling: "Miles Davis: Shining a Light on the Prince of Darkness," *JT* (Aug 1986), 14

B. Doerschuk: "Miles Davis: the Picasso of Invisible Art," *Keyboard*, xiii/10 (1987), 64 [incl. discography]

B. McRae: *Miles Davis* (London, 1988) [incl. discography]

BARRY KERNFELD

Davis, Nathan (Tate) (*b* Kansas City, KS, 15 Feb 1937). Tenor saxophonist and educator. He grew up in a musical family, and while at high school briefly learned trombone before taking up clarinet and saxophone. At around the age of 18 he worked with Jay McShann. He won a scholarship to study at the University of Kansas, where he gained a BA in music education and led a hard-bop band that included Carmell Jones. During his military service he played in an army band in Berlin and began to work with Benny Bailey. After his discharge he remained in Europe and performed regularly in Paris with Kenny Clarke (whom he met through Bailey) and later worked there with Donald Byrd, Art Taylor, and Eric Dolphy; he also joined Art Blakey's Jazz Messengers for a European tour in 1965. Davis recorded a number of successful albums under his own name, playing in both hard-bop and free-jazz styles; his sidemen included Woody Shaw, Jones, Clarke, Taylor, Roland Hanna, and Richard Davis. In 1969 he returned to the USA to become director of jazz studies at the University of Pittsburgh; he later earned a doctorate in ethnomusicology at Wesleyan University and wrote a history of jazz, *Writings in Jazz* (Dubuque, IA, 2/1978, 3/1985). He has continued to perform and record into the 1980s, and in 1985 organized (partly as a tribute to Clarke) the Paris Reunion Band, an octet which toured Europe.

SELECTED RECORDINGS

As leader: *Hip Walk* (1965, Saba 15063); *Rules of Freedom* (1967, Hot House 1002); *The 6th Sense in the 11th House* (1972, Segue 1002); of Paris Reunion Band: *French Cooking* (1985, Sonet 945)

As sideman with B. Bailey and M. Waldron: *Soul Eyes* (1968, Saba 15158)

BIBLIOGRAPHY

Feather '60s; *Feather–Gitler '70s*

J. Elliott: "Letter from Paris: 'Introducing Nathan Davis'," *Crescendo*, iv/11 (1966), 11

P. Sullivan: "Nathan Davis," *Coda*, no.137 (1975), 10

I. Dittke: "Honoring Kenny Clarke," *JT* (April 1985), 11

G. Lock: "The Man who Never Wasn't," *The Wire*, no.22 (1985), 16

S. Woolley: "Nathan Davis: the Saxophonist who Blew in from the Cold," *JJI*, xl/6 (1987), 8

DAVID WILD

Davis, Quin(n Hall) (*b* Artesia, CA, 12 March 1944). Alto saxophonist and flutist. He toured and recorded with Buddy Rich in 1966–7 and performed with him again briefly in 1969–70 after his army service. From 1970 to 1973 he was solo alto saxophonist with Stan Kenton; among the recordings he made with the band is the album *Live at Redlands University* (1970, CW 1015). Davis began working with Harry James in 1973 and recorded with him in 1976. The following year he recorded with the Capp–Pierce Orchestra. Davis is a particularly fine section player whose abilities as a soloist are not reflected by his recordings.

BIBLIOGRAPHY

Feather–Gitler '70s

W. F. Lee: *Stan Kenton: Artistry in Rhythm* (Los Angeles, 1980) [incl. discography]

Davis, Richard (*b* Chicago, 15 April 1930). Double bass player. He studied privately from 1945 to 1954; at this time he played with a number of local orchestras in Chicago. His experience in dance bands led to engagements with Ahmad Jamal (1953–4) and the pianist Don Shirley (1954–5). In the late 1950s he worked mainly with Sarah Vaughan, with whom his precision of time and tone became evident. Davis's period of high productivity during the 1960s is well documented by his many recordings; at this time he also worked on a freelance basis with symphony orchestras, performing under Stravinsky and Leonard Bernstein. A highly sought-after player, he has recorded with musicians as varied as Eric Dolphy (1961, 1963, 1964), Booker Ervin (1963–4, 1966), Andrew Hill (1963–5; 1976, in Tokyo), Ben Webster and Stan Getz (both 1964), Earl Hines (1966), the Creative Construction Company (1970), Hank Jones (1976, 1978), and Billy Cobham. His work in the context of a large ensemble may be heard to advantage on recordings by the Thad Jones–Mel Lewis Orchestra. In 1977 Davis left New York to teach at the University of Wisconsin in Madison, where he has remained into the mid-1980s. He has continued to perform and record; in 1982 he appeared at the Aurex Jazz Festival, Tokyo, in a jam session led by J. J. Johnson and Kai Winding.

For illustration *see* Jones, fig.1*b*.

SELECTED RECORDINGS

Duos: with Jill McManus: *As One* (1975, Muse 5093); with W. Dickerson: *Divine Gemini* (1977, Ste. 1089)

As leader: *Muses for Richard Davis* (1969, MPS 2120725); *Epistrophy and Now's the Time* (1972, Muse 5002); *Fancy Free* (1977, Gal. 5102)

As sideman: E. Dolphy: *Out to Lunch* (1964, BN 84163); A. Hill: *Point of Departure* (1964, BN 84167); B. Ervin: *The Blues Book* (1964, Prst. 7340); B. Webster: *See You at the Fair* (1964, Imp. 65); T. Jones and M. Lewis: *Live at the Village Vanguard* (1967, SolS 18016); Jazz Composer's Orchestra: *The Jazz Composer's Orchestra* (1968, JCOA 1001–2); J. J. Johnson and K. Winding: *Aurex Jazz Festival '82: All Star Jam* (1982, Ewd 80238)

BIBLIOGRAPHY

D. Morgenstern: "Richard Davis: the Complete Musician," *DB*, xxxiii/11 (1966), 23

D. C. Hunt: "The Contemporary Approach to Jazz Bass," *J&P*, viii/8 (1969), 18

T. Tolnay: "Double Take: Ron Carter/Richard Davis," *DB*, xxxix/9 (1972), 14

B. Primack: "Profile: Richard Davis," *DB*, xliv/19 (1977), 32

A. Taylor: "Richard Davis," *Notes and Tones: Musician-to-Musician Interviews* (Liège, Belgium, 1977/*R*1982), 208

A. Berle: "Bassist Richard Davis: from Bo Diddley to Stravinsky," *GP*, xii/6 (1978), 30 [incl. discography]

BILL BENNETT/R

Davis, Steve [Stephen; Syeed, Luquman Abdul] (*b* Philadelphia, 1929; *d* Philadelphia, 21 Aug 1987). Double bass player. After working with various groups in Philadelphia he moved to New York, where he played with Lester Young, Jimmy Heath, and Sonny Stitt. He was a member of John Coltrane's first quartet (1960 to early 1961) and took part in several of its recordings, notably *My Favorite Things*. He played and recorded with James Moody (1961–2) and recorded with Dave Burns (1962), McCoy Tyner (1963), the vibraphonist Freddie McCoy (1965), and Eddie Jefferson (1968, with Burns and Moody). From the mid-1960s he worked as a freelance in New York. Davis made no recordings as a leader but he was known as a solid and reliable player in the mainstream tradition.

SELECTED RECORDINGS

As sideman: J. Coltrane: *My Favorite Things* (1960, Atl. 1361); J. Moody: *Cookin' the Blues* (1961, Argo 756); M. Tyner: *Nights of Ballads and Blues* (1963, Imp. 39)

BIBLIOGRAPHY

"Dictionnaire de la contrebasse," *Jm*, no.166 (1969), 36

GARY CARNER

Davis, Walter(, Jr.) (*b* Richmond, VA, 2 Sept 1932). Pianist. He played with Babs Gonzales's group Three Bips and a Bop while still in his teens, then moved to New York to play with Max Roach and Charlie Parker (1952); he remained in Roach's group and recorded with it in 1953. In 1956 he joined Dizzy Gillespie's group, with which he toured the Middle East and South America; he also played with Donald Byrd (in Paris, 1958) and the Jazz Messengers (1959). He gave up his musical career for a time to work as a tailor; later he joined a band in New Jersey, produced recordings, and wrote arrangements. He studied music in India in 1969. In the 1970s he played with Sonny Rollins (1973–4) and again with the Jazz Messengers (1975); he led his own group in New York and recorded as a leader in 1979.

SELECTED RECORDINGS

As leader: *Davis Cup* (1959, BN 4018); *Four Hundred Years Ago, Tomorrow* (1979, Owl 020)

As sideman: D. Gillespie: *World Statesman* (1956, Norg. 1084); J. McLean: *New Soil* (1959, BN 84013); D. Byrd: *Byrd in Hand* (1959, BN 4019); on A. Shepp: *Attica Blues* (1972, Imp. 9222), Attica Blues; S. Rollins: *Horn Culture* (1973, Mlst. 9051)

BIBLIOGRAPHY

FeatherE; *Feather–Gitler '70s*

B. Primack: "Profile: Walter Davis, Jr.," *DB*, xlv/11 (1978), 32

A. Axelrod: "Waxing on: Post-modern Piano," *DB*, li/6 (1984), 48 [incl. review of *Four Hundred Years Ago, Tomorrow* (1979)]

PAUL RINZLER

Davis, Wild Bill [William Strethen] (*b* Glasgow, MO, 24 Nov 1918). Organist, pianist, and arranger. He moved with his family to Parsons, Kansas, at an early age, and was taught music by his father, a professional singer. His early influences were Fats Waller and Art Tatum. After musical studies at Tuskegee Institute and Wiley College he moved to Chicago, where he played guitar and wrote arrangements for Milt Larkin (1939–42). He then provided arrangements for Earl Hines (1943) and Louis Jordan (1945–9), and also worked as pianist for the latter. After leaving Jordan, Davis took up Hammond organ and performed first as a soloist and, from 1951, as the leader of his own trio (which comprised either guitar or double bass with organ and drums). He continued to write arrangements, his most notable success being *April in Paris* recorded by Count Basie (1955, Verve 8012), which was adapted from a version he wrote for his own group. Davis also recorded with other musicians, including Johnny Hodges (1961, 1963–6) and Ella Fitzgerald (1963). From 1969 to 1971 he toured and recorded with Duke Ellington, serving the band as arranger, organist, and second pianist, and during the 1970s toured widely as a soloist. While in Paris he recorded with Buddy Tate, Al Grey, and Slam Stewart (all 1972), and Illinois Jacquet (1973). Later he worked with Lionel Hampton (1978–80) and led his own group in Europe; in the early 1980s he appeared at many festivals.

See also Organ, §2.

SELECTED RECORDINGS

As leader: *At Birdland* (1956, Epic 3118), incl. April in Paris; *One More Time* (1962, Coral 757417), incl. April in Paris; with J. Hodges: *Con Soul & Sax* (1965, RCA LSP3393); *Impulsions* (1972, BB 33037)

As sideman: E. Fitzgerald: *These are the Blues* (1963, Verve 64062); L. Hampton: *Live in Emmen, Holland* (1978, Tim. 120)

BIBLIOGRAPHY

ChiltonW; *Feather–Gitler '70s*

S. Dance: *The World of Duke Ellington* (London and New York, 1970/*R*1981) [colln of previously pubd articles and interviews], 234

C. Battestini and J.-P. Battestini: "Wild Bill Davis," *BHcF*, no.274 (1979), 3 [interview]

ANDREW JAFFE

Davis & Schwegler. Record label. It was owned by a music shop in Hollywood, and existed briefly in 1939. It was used to issue the first recordings made by Nat "King" Cole's trio. (B.

Rust: *The American Record Label Book* (New Rochelle, NY, 1978), 93)

Davison, Wild Bill [William Edward] (*b* Defiance, OH, 5 Jan 1906). Cornetist. After playing and touring with various local bands he went to Chicago, where he worked from 1927 to 1932. Late in 1931 he organized a big band with Frank Teschemacher, but after the latter's death moved to Milwaukee and led his own small groups. Davison's playing began to attract widespread attention after some of his recordings were issued in 1940, and the following year he settled in New York. He led his own group at Nick's, then, after army service, worked with Art Hodes and led a band in St. Louis. From 1945 he appeared regularly in Eddie Condon's club, New York, though he also led his own groups. He moved to the West Coast in 1960. Davison made several solo tours of Europe in the 1960s, and continued to undertake international tours in the 1970s and 1980s. He performed with the Jazz Giants in 1968 and in the 1970s and 1980s worked as a freelance, playing frequently in Europe.

Davison's early recordings (from the 1920s) reveal the clear influence of Bix Beiderbecke, but he soon developed a highly individual, robust style, exciting in fast numbers and warmly sentimental in ballads, that he maintained throughout his long career. He always preferred to play cornet rather than trumpet, though for one fascinating period (1933–41) he also performed on E♭ valve trombone. His driving lead, couched in a flamboyant, husky tone, usually imparted tremendous zest to dixieland-type ensembles. His solos were never intricate, and his improvisations generally embellished the melody rather than delving deeply into the underlying harmonies.

Oral history material in *ICU, LNT, NjR* (JOHP).

SELECTED RECORDINGS

As leader: Ghost of a Chance (1956, Col. CL871)

As sideman: A. Hodes: Shine (1945, BN 532); G. Wettling: *George Wettling's Jazz Band* (1951, Col. CL6189), incl. Collier's Clambake; E. Condon: *Jam Session Coast to Coast* (1953, Col. CL547), incl. I can't give you anything but love; *Bixieland* (1955, Col. CL719), incl. At the Jazzband Ball

BIBLIOGRAPHY

G. Hoefer: "The Hot Box," *DB*, xv/7 (1948), 12
H. McNamara: "The Irrepressible Wild Bill Davison," *DB*, xxxvi/4 (1969), 18
M. Jones: "Davison Goes Commercial," *MM*, 1 (15 Nov 1975), 52
——: "Wild Man of the Cornet," *MM*, liv (13 Jan 1979), 19
G. Endress: *Jazz Podium: Musiker über sich selbst* (Stuttgart, Germany, 1980), 18
E. Cook: "On the Right Track," *JJI*, xxxiv/4 (1981), 6
——: "Condon and Beyond," *JJI*, xxxiv/5 (1981), 24
B. Byler: "Call him Irrepressible," *MR*, xiv/1 (1986), 1

JOHN CHILTON

Dawson, Alan (*b* Marietta, PA, 14 July 1929). Drummer. He studied in Boston with Charles Alden in the early 1950s while working with many local jazz groups, including Sabby Lewis's band. After touring with Lionel Hampton in 1953 he spent another period with Lewis (1953–6), and in 1957 joined the faculty at the Berklee College of Music, beginning an association that lasted until 1975; among his pupils were Tony Williams, Clifford Jarvis, Harvey Mason, and Joe LaBarbera. He remained active in the Boston area, working as house drummer at a number of clubs, where he supported such visiting musicians as Roy Eldridge, Sonny Stitt, and Roland Kirk, playing in many different styles. His most frequent and productive collaboration during the early 1960s was with Jaki Byard and Booker Ervin, with whom he made an excellent series of albums for Prestige (1963–5). From 1968 to 1974 Dawson was a member of the Dave Brubeck Quartet, and recorded an outstanding solo on a new version of *Take Five* (1972). He has continued to teach privately, and has published several tutors, including *Blues and Odd Time Signatures* (1972) and, with Don DeMicheal, *A Manual for the Modern Drummer* (1964). A gifted and resourceful drummer, Dawson is also an accomplished vibraphonist.

SELECTED RECORDINGS

As sideman with D. Brubeck: *Blues Roots* (1968, Col. CS9749); *The Last Set at Newport* (1971, Atl. 1607); *We're All Together Again for the First Time* (1972, Atl. 1641), incl. Take Five

As sideman with others: B. Ervin: *The Freedom Book* (1963, Prst. 7295); *The Song Book* (1964, Prst. 7318); *The Space Book* (1964, Prst. 7386); J. Byard: *Live at Lennie's* (1965, Prst. 7419, 7477); T. Farlow: *Tal Farlow Returns* (1969, Prst. 7732); D. Gordon: *The Panther!* (1970, Prst. 7829); P. Woods: *Musique du bois* (1974, Muse 5037); W. Vaché: *Iridescence* (1981, Conc. 153)

BIBLIOGRAPHY

D. Morgenstern: "The Poll Winner as Teacher: Alan Dawson," *DB*, xxxiii/19 (1966), 27
A. Dawson: "The Book," *JJ*, xxiii/11 (1970), 25
M. Gardner: "Alan Dawson," *JJ*, xxiv (1971), no.4, p.2; no.5, p.18
F. Bouchard: "Alan Dawson: Teaching the Traps, Gigging with the Greatest," *DB*, xlvii/11 (1980), 22
S. Vandermark: "Alan Dawson: Interview," *Cadence*, ix/12 (1983), 5
J. Potter: "Alan Dawson," *MD*, ix/5 (1985), 8
S. Fish: "Alan Dawson," *MD*, x/1 (1986), 31

BILL BENNETT/R

Deacon. Nickname of LEM JOHNSON.

Dean, Demas (*b* Sag Harbor, NY, 6 Oct 1903). Trumpeter. He began playing cornet at the age of ten, and later studied violin. He first worked professionally while still in high school, and while studying at Howard University (1922–3) played with many bandleaders, including Elmer Snowden. In 1923–4 he toured and recorded with Lucille Hegamin. Later he worked in New York with Billy Butler and Leon Abbey and in Florida with an orchestra led by Ford Dabney. After touring South America with Abbey (1927) he returned to New York, where he made some recordings with Bessie Smith (including *Thinking Blues*, 1928, Col. 14292). Dean traveled to Europe with Noble Sissle in 1929, then worked with the bandleader Joe Jordan and others. He rejoined Sissle in 1934 and remained with him until 1944, when he ceased full-time playing and moved to Los Angeles. (P. Carr: "Travellin' Man: the Story of Demas Dean," *Sv*, no.72 (1977), 207)

based on *ChiltonW*

Dean, Donald (Wesley) (*b* Kansas City, MO, 21 June 1937). Drummer. He grew up in Kansas City, and by the early 1960s had established himself in Los Angeles, where he played with Kenny Dorham, Harold Land, Hampton Hawes, George Shearing, and others; he recorded with Carmell Jones in 1962. From 1968 to 1972 he was a regular member of Les McCann's popular soul-jazz group. Among the recordings he made with the band was the acclaimed album *Swiss Movement* (1969, Atl. 1547); Dean's playing may be heard at its best on the track *Compared to What?*, during which he builds a striking rhythm on the bass drum, placing the emphasis between (rather than on) the beat. In the mid-1970s Dean performed frequently with Jimmy Smith, making a notable contribution to the album *Bluesmith* (1972, Verve 68809). By the mid-1980s he was an important member of the innovative trio led by Horace Tapscott.

BIBLIOGRAPHY

Feather '60s
"Drum Talk Coast to Coast," *DB*, xxxi/8 (1964), 13

Dean, Elton (*b* Nottingham, England, 28 Oct 1945). English alto saxophonist and saxello player. After working in the mid-1960s in the group Bluesology with the pop singer Long John Baldry he began a long association with Keith Tippett, performing and recording in his sextet (1968–71) and groups Centipede (1970–71) and Ark (1978, 1980); he has worked with Tippett in a duo from 1976. His other activities include work with Soft Machine (1969–71), the London Jazz Composers Orchestra (from 1970), Alan Skidmore's El Skid (1976–8), Chris McGregor's Brotherhood of Breath (mid-1970s), and Carla Bley (1977). He has also led his own groups: Just Us (1972–4), a quartet (1974–80), Ninesense (which included Tippett and Skidmore, 1975–8), and a quintet (from 1981). Dean's skills as a composer and soloist may be heard on the first recording by Ninesense, *Oh! For the Edge* (1976, Ogun 900).

BIBLIOGRAPHY

S. Peacock: "Elton Dean: Two's Company," *Sounds* (26 June 1971), 7
K. Ansell: "Elton Dean," *Impetus*, no.3 (1976), 125
B. Case: "On the Road with the Dean," *New Musical Express* (2 Oct 1976), 22
R. Cotterrell, ed.: *Jazz Now: the Jazz Centre Society Guide* (London, 1976), 127
S. Loupien: "Elton Dean: 'beaucoup de musique dans mes tiroirs'," *Jm*, no.274 (1979), 47 [incl. discography]

MARK GILBERT

Dean, Vinnie [DiVittorio, Vincent] (*b* Mount Vernon, NY, 8 Aug 1929). Alto saxophonist. He played with Shorty Sherock and Johnny Bothwell in New York (1946), then performed and made recordings with the big bands of Charlie Spivak (1947–8, as Vincent DiVittorio, and 1949-50), Charlie Barnet (1948–9, including solos on *Overtime, O'Henry*, and *Really?*, all 1949, Cap. 15848, 57592, 71222), Elliot Lawrence (1951–2), and Stan Kenton (1952–3, including *Prologue: This is an Orchestra*, 1952, Cap. 15966–7). He also recorded with the Ralph Burns Orchestra (1952, 1954) and in a small group led by Eddie Bert (1953–5). Although in the late 1950s Dean began to devote less time to playing, he continued to perform occasionally, working with Benny Goodman, Lawrence, Hal McKusick, Ray McKinley, and Urbie Green; he also recorded with Barnet (1958) and Sal Salvador (1960). Besides alto saxophone he also played clarinet and flute. (*FeatherE*)

De Andrade, Djalma. *See* SETE, BOLA.

De Arango, Bill ("Buddy") [William] (*b* Cleveland, 20 Sept 1921). Guitarist. He played dixieland and Chicago jazz with bands in Chicago (1939–42) and in 1944 moved to New York and was engaged by Ben Webster. He recorded in 1945 with Charlie Parker and Dizzy Gillespie (under Sarah Vaughan's leadership) and with Ike Quebec, and in 1946 made a fine recording of *52nd Street Theme* with Gillespie. He also played with Ray Nance and led a group with Terry Gibbs. He retired from jazz in 1948, but later he played in Cleveland with the pianist Bill Dinasco and in 1954 recorded as a leader. He became the manager of the rock group Henry Tree and in 1970 recorded anonymously with it.

SELECTED RECORDINGS

As leader: I've got it bad (1946, Haven 802); *Bill De Arango* (1954, EmA 26020), incl. Alone Together

As sideman: S. Vaughan: Mean to me (1945, Contl 6024); I. Quebec: Jim Dawgs/I. Q. Blues (1945, Savoy 570); D. Gillespie: 52nd Street Theme (1946, Vic. 400130); E. Davis: Lockjaw (1946, Haven 800); B. Webster: Frog and Mule/Spang (1946, Haven 805)

BIBLIOGRAPHY

FeatherE
M. Gardner: "Bill Surfaces – in a Rock Band," *MM* (20 Feb 1971), 30
M. Gardner and H. Pekar: "Bill De Arango," *JJ*, xxiv/7 (1971), 24 [interview]
W. van Eyle: "Bill 'Buddy' DeArango [*sic*]," *Jazz Press*, no.36 (1977), 4 [discography]

PAUL RINZLER

Dearie, Blossom (*b* East Durham, NY, 28 April 1926). Singer and pianist. She began her career as a member of the Blue Flames, a vocal group within Woody Herman's orchestra, and the Blue Reys, a similar ensemble in Alvino Rey's band. In 1952 she recorded *Moody's Mood for Love* with King Pleasure, and the same year went to Paris, where she performed with Annie Ross. She also formed her own vocal group, the Blue Stars, whose members included such distinguished instrumentalists as Fats Sadi and Roger Guérin; its jazz rendition of *Lullaby of Birdland* (sung in French) was a big hit in the USA. Two other vocal groups, the Double Six and the Swingle Singers, developed from the Blue Stars. Dearie returned to the USA in 1956 and began to work in nightclubs in New York and Los Angeles, accompanying herself as the leader of her own trio; her sidemen on the album *Blossom Dearie* (1956) were Herb Ellis, Ray Brown, and Jo Jones. From 1974 she made recordings for her own company, Daffodil Records, and in 1985 she became the first recipient of the Mabel Mercer Foundation Award. She was married to Bobby Jaspar.

Dearie has a small, light voice and sometimes employs a thin, tight vibrato. She sings with intelligence, clarity and originality, and her performances are enhanced by the way she strokes and caresses certain words and pounces upon and attacks others; she also makes use of blues effects. Her repertory includes much original material. As a pianist, Dearie is a competent player in the bop style.

SELECTED RECORDINGS

As leader: of the Blue Stars: La légende du pays aux oiseaux (Lullaby of Birdland) (1954, Barclay 70004) [EP]; *Blossom Dearie* (1956, Verve 2037); *Blossom Dearie Sings* (1974, Daffodil 101)

As sideman with K. Pleasure: Moody's Mood for Love (1952, Prst. 924)

BIBLIOGRAPHY

J. S. Wilson: *The Collector's Jazz: Traditional and Swing* (Philadelphia, 1958) [listeners' guide]
W. Balliett: "Hanging out with Blossom Dearie," *Alec Wilder and his Friends* (Boston, 1974) [colln of previously pubd articles], 159
——"Absolutely Pure," *American Singers* (New York, 1979), 118
J. S. Wilson: "Cabaret: Blossom Dearie," *New York Times* (28 April 1983)

ED BEMIS

De Bie, Ivon (*b* Brussels, 13 Aug 1914). Belgian pianist and bandleader. He worked with the bandleader Jimmy Turner (*c*1936), then with the Blue Blythe Players. He formed his own band for an engagement in Brussels, after which Fud Candrix took over its leadership. Having led another band in the army, De Bie resumed his association with Candrix, playing with him from 1940 to 1943. At the end of the war he was engaged to entertain Allied troops stationed in Europe. He was appointed the artistic director of the Belgian division of RCA Records in 1957. De Bie made a number of recordings as a leader (1942–56), many of them with a band that played hot dance music; he also recorded with Candrix (1941–3), Hubert Rostaing (1942), Django Reinhardt (1942–3, including a duo session on which Reinhardt played violin), and Robert De Kers (1950), and as a member of various groups led by David Bee (1956–65).

ROBERT PERNET

De Boeck, Jeff [Joseph] (*b* Brussels, 2 Sept 1918). Belgian drummer. After working as an amateur musician with the group

Hot and Swing, De Boeck made his professional début with Robert De Kers (1937). He then formed a trio with Freddy Johnson and Jean Robert and worked with Fud Candrix (1940–43). With his own band he toured Belgium and Holland and performed for the Allied services in Europe. Later he was appointed head of the publishing department of the Belgian division of EMI. De Boeck recorded as a leader (1941–2) and with De Kers (1938–9, 1942, 1950), Gus Deloof (1940–41), Candrix (1940–43), Robert (1941), the pianist Leo Chauliac (1942), Ivon De Bie (1942), Ernst van 't Hoff (1943–4), the guitarist Jean Douchamps (1953), and David Bee (1958).

ROBERT PERNET

De Brest, Spanky [Jimmy, James] (*b* Philadelphia, 24 April 1937; *d* Philadelphia, 2 March 1973). Double bass player. He first worked with Lee Morgan and the drummer Jimmy DePreist, then left his home town to perform and record with Art Blakey's Jazz Messengers (1956–8; for illustration *see* BANDS, fig.5). After leaving Blakey he again played with several local groups in Philadelphia, then in 1958 joined J. J. Johnson's sextet, with which he recorded the following year. Owing to illness he remained inactive thereafter. De Brest had a large tone and his solid playing received critical acclaim.

RECORDINGS

As sideman: A. Blakey: *Hard Bop* (1956, Col. CL1040); *Jazz Messengers* (1957, Beth. 6023); R. Draper: *The Ray Draper Quintet Featuring John Coltrane* (1957, NewJ 8228); J. J. Johnson: *Really Livin'* (1959, Col. CL1383); C. Jordan: *Spellbound* (1960, Riv. 9340)

BIBLIOGRAPHY

FeatherE

BRENDA PENNELL

Dębski, Krzesimir (*b* Wałbrzych, Poland, 1954). Polish violinist. After taking piano and violin lessons at school in Lublin he studied composition at the High School of Music in Poznań and started to play jazz as a violinist. In the mid-1970s he was a member of the rock band Rhythm Machine and from 1975 to 1978 played in the pianist Danek Jarmolowicz's group Warsztat (Workshop), which won several prizes. After working briefly with the Eighth Day Orchestra he became a regular member of the orchestra of Polish Radio and Television in Poznań (1978). In 1979 he joined a quintet led by the drummer Kazimierz Jonkisz for concerts and tours. With String Summit he played at the New Jazz Meeting in Baden-Baden, Germany, and recorded *One World in Eight* (1980, MPS 68275). In 1981 he formed his own bop quartet, String Connection.

BIBLIOGRAPHY

M. Garztecki: "Krzesimir Dębski: String Connection," *JF* [intl edn], no.73 (1981), 46

WOLFRAM KNAUER

Decca. Record company. It was established in England by Edward Lewis in 1929; shortly thereafter it acquired the British rights to recordings made by the American Record Company (ARC), which it issued in the UK on a subsidiary label, Brunswick, which was only indirectly linked with the American company of the same name. Decca later obtained the rights to two British companies: Edison–Bell (1933) and Crystalate (1937); the latter company owned the Vocalion trademark in Britain.

In August 1934 an American branch of Decca was founded with the assistance of Jack Kapp, who had worked for the American company Brunswick before its absorption by ARC. The American branch soon began issuing race records, with J. Mayo Williams as a talent scout, and continued to do so in a 7000 series until 1944. In June 1935 this company purchased the rights to part of Gennett's catalogue and the Champion label. Expansion continued when in 1938 Decca bought from CBS the rights to the pre-1932 catalogues of Brunswick and Vocalion, which had been acquired by CBS as part of its purchase of ARC. The American organization quickly developed a substantial jazz catalogue, both of race records and items by musicians with broader appeal, including Louis Armstrong (1935–54), Woody Herman (1936–44), Andy Kirk (1936–46), Count Basie (1937–9), Louis Jordan (1938–54), Lionel Hampton (1941–50), and many others.

After 1934 British Decca derived most of its catalogue of Amerian recordings from its counterpart in the USA. It established subsidiary operations in several European countries; Dutch Decca was particularly active, recording American visitors and issuing very important work by Benny Carter and Coleman Hawkins. During World War II the British company had to dispose of its American interests; at this time American Decca became wholly independent. Nevertheless British Decca retained outright copyright on the pre-1932 Brunswick and Vocalion recordings, and maintained close connections with the American company into the mid-1970s. In 1947 British Decca established the LONDON label to issue recordings in the USA; London was later also used in Britain, initially (from October 1949) to issue the results of sessions organized by London's American management, and later (from 1951) to put out recordings made by independent American companies to which Decca had acquired British distribution rights. In June 1950 the company also put out the first LPs to be issued in Britain, and in 1954 it established the label FELSTED; this was used to put out in the UK some noteworthy jazz recordings made in the USA for British Decca in 1958–9. The company also instigated reissue programs, putting out items from Brunswick, American Decca, and Vocalion (on another subsidiary label, ACE OF HEARTS); from 1959 to 1971, when the company owned British rights to RCA, it also issued many RCA recordings. In 1980 the company was purchased by Polygram; from June 1983 it has traded under the name London.

After the split from the British company, American Decca, using also the labels Coral (from 1949) and Brunswick (extensively from 1957), remained independent until 1959, when it was acquired by the Music Corporation of America (MCA). At first MCA continued to issue items from American Decca's back catalogue on Decca. Later recordings were issued under the name MCA; these included major programs of reissues of early jazz and swing, made available in France, Germany, and Japan.

BIBLIOGRAPHY

E. Jackson and L. Hibbs: *Decca, Brunswick, Vocalion Encyclopedia of Swing* (London, 1941)
Jazz on 78s: a Guide to the Many Examples of Classic Jazz (London, 1954) [pubn of Decca Record Co.]
R. Fairchild: "Decca Matrix Letter System," *Matrix*, no.76, (1968), 7
R. M. W. Dixon and J. Godrich: *Recording the Blues* (London, 1970), 77
H. K. Zwartenkot: "Decca: label rood [red label]: M32000," *Doctor Jazz*, no.43 (1970), 22; no.44 (1970), 24; no.45 (1970-71), 29
R. D. Kinkle: *The Complete Encyclopedia of Popular Music and Jazz, 1900–1950* (New Rochelle, NY, and Westport, CT, 1974), iv, 2170-98 [numerical listing]
W. McGhie: "The Decca Record Company: a Postscript," *Sounds Vintage*, iii/3 (1981), 58
P. M. Pelletier: *Decca 78 rpm Ten-inch and 45 rpm Seven-inch Complete Singles Catalogue, 1954–1983* (Chessington, England, 1984) [Record Information Services pubn]
——: "The Brunswick Label," *Record Information*, no.3 (1984), 13

Déczi, Ladislav [Laco] (*b* Bernolákovo, nr Bratislava, Czechoslovakia, 29 March 1938). Czechoslovak trumpeter. He played

West Coast jazz with the Big Band Academia Club in Bratislava (1957), formed his own group (1959), and adopted a hard-bop style under the influence of Art Blakey and the Jazz Messengers. After serving in the army (1960–62) he moved to Prague; as a member of Karel Velebný's group SHQ he toured in Czechoslovakia and abroad and recorded in 1963–6. From 1968 he made recordings as the leader of the quintet Jazz Cellula, including *Pietoso* (1969, Sup. 1150596).

GERHARD CONRAD

Dedrick, Rusty [Lyle F.] (*b* Delevan, NY, 12 July 1918). Trumpeter, arranger, composer, and teacher. He trained to become a teacher at Fredonia (New York) College and studied with the composers Paul Creston and Stefan Wolpe. In 1938–9 he worked with the clarinetist and saxophonist Dick Stabile and then joined Red Norvo (1939), with whom his brother Arthur had previously played trombone. After leaving Norvo (1941) Dedrick performed and recorded with Claude Thornhill (1941–2, 1946–7) and played briefly with Ray McKinley (1946). He worked as a freelance trumpeter, arranger, and composer in studios in New York in the 1950s and 1960s, during which time he wrote music for Don Elliott, Maxine Sullivan, and Lee Wiley, among others; he performed with Urbie Green (1967) and Lionel Hampton (1970–71). In 1971 he joined the faculty of the Manhattan School of Music and later became its director of jazz studies. He has written on jazz education and has also been active as an arranger. Dedrick plays trumpet in a traditional swing style; in the 1930s and 1940s he was known for his solid technique and command of the instrument, rather than for his skills as an improviser.

SELECTED RECORDINGS

As leader: *Salute to Benny* (1957, Eso. 552); *Rusty Dedrick and his Orchestra* (1964, Four Corners 4207); *Harold Arlen in Hollywood* (1969, MonE 6918)

As sideman: C. Thornhill: Somebody else is taking my place (1942, Col. 36513); D. Elliott: *Counterpoint for Six Valves* (1955, Riv. 2517)

BIBLIOGRAPHY

FeatherE; *Feather–Gitler '70s*

R. D. Kinkle: *The Complete Encyclopedia of Popular Music and Jazz, 1900–1950* (New Rochelle, NY, and Westport, CT, 1974)

A. J. Smith: "Guardians of the Musical Future: Rusty Dedrick," *DB*, xliv/20 (1977), 17

FREDERICK A. BECK

Deems, Barrett (*b* Springfield, IL, 1 March 1914). Drummer. After touring with the violinist Paul Ash at the age of 15 he led his own groups during the early and mid-1930s. His first major association was with Joe Venuti (1937–44), after which he worked with Red Norvo (1948), Charlie Barnet (1951), and Muggsy Spanier (1951–4). From 1954 to 1958 he was a member of Louis Armstrong's All Stars; during these years the band traveled to Europe, Africa, and the Far East sponsored by the US State Department, and its tours were documented in the film *Satchmo the Great* (1956). Deems also appeared with Bing Crosby and Armstrong in the famous sequence that accompanied the song *Now you has jazz* in the film *High Society* (1956). From 1960 to 1964 he performed and recorded with Jack Teagarden, and from 1964 he played intermittently with the Dukes of Dixieland. Thereafter he worked mainly in Chicago, playing at clubs and accompanying such visiting musicians as Buck Clayton, Venuti, Roy Eldridge, Benny Carter, Teddy Wilson, Norvo, Dave McKenna, Peanuts Hucko, Urbie Green, Milt Hinton, and Jimmy McPartland. In 1976 he toured Eastern Europe with Benny Goodman's sextet, and in the early 1980s he went to South America with Wild Bill Davison and to Europe with Keith Smith. During the 1950s Deems was often publicized as the world's fastest drummer on account of his excellent technique; his true strength, however, was his ability to provide a firm, secure pulse to propel a band.

SELECTED RECORDINGS

As leader: *Deemus* (1979, Claremont 1001)

As sideman with L. Armstrong: 'T ain't what you do (1954, Phi. 321970); *Satchmo the Great* (1955–6, Col. CL1077), incl. When it's sleepy time down South (1955); *Ambassador Satch* (1955–6, Col. CL840), incl. Royal Garden Blues (1956); *Louis Armstrong at the Pasadena Civic Auditorium* (1956, GNP 11001); first issued on *I Love Jazz* (1957, Decca 74227), Frog-i-more Rag; *Louis and the Good Book* (1958, Decca 8741)

As sideman with Dukes of Dixieland: *World's Fair* (1964, Col. CS8994), incl. Caravan; *Sunrise, Sunset* (1966, Decca 74807)

BIBLIOGRAPHY

S. Voce: "Mr. Deems Comes to Town," *MM*, xxxi (9 June 1956), 3

"Deems Deemed Giant," *DB*, xlv/10 (1978), 46

J. McDonough: "Profile: Barrett Deems," *DB*, xlv/16 (1978), 46

——: "Barrett Deems: Deemus," *DB*, xlvii/2 (1980), 32 [review]

E. Cook: "The Wonderful World of Louis Armstrong," *JJI*, xxxiv/9 (1981), 7

D. J. Travis: *An Autobiography of Black Jazz* (Chicago, 1983) [incl. interviews], 275

T. Borst: "Portraits: Barrett Deems," *MD*, xi/2 (1987), 22

JEFF POTTER

De Faut, Volly [Voltaire] (*b* Little Rock, AR, 14 March 1904; *d* Chicago Heights, IL, 29 May 1973). Clarinetist. He grew up in Chicago, where he studied violin from the age of six. He changed to clarinet when he was 14, and in 1923 he replaced Leon Roppolo in the New Orleans Rhythm Kings. When this group disbanded De Faut worked with Mel Stitzel, then in 1924 he joined the band led by the tenor saxophonist Art Kassel, for whom he played both clarinet and saxophone. He performed and recorded with Merritt Brunies (1924–6), and also recorded with Muggsy Spanier in the Bucktown Five (1924) and the Stomp Six (1925), and with Jelly Roll Morton (1925). In Detroit he replaced Jimmy Dorsey in Ray Miller's band (1926) and joined Isham Jones; he then returned to Chicago, where he played with Jean Goldkette in 1928-9. From 1930 to 1940 De Faut worked in radio orchestras. For several years he pursued a career outside music, but later he played with the clarinetist Bud Jacobson (1945), Doc Evans (1950), and Art Hodes (1953). After another lengthy period of inactivity he performed and recorded again with Hodes. Although De Faut was one of the best jazz players in Chicago, he remained relatively unknown. He was so profoundly influenced by Roppolo that it is often difficult to distinguish his style from that of the older musician.

For illustration *see* NEW ORLEANS RHYTHM KINGS.

SELECTED RECORDINGS

As sideman: Bucktown Five: Steady Roll Blues/Really a Pain (1924, Gen. 5419); J. R. Morton: My Gal/Wolverine Blues (1925, Aut. 623); Stomp Six: Why can't it be poor little me?/Everybody loves my baby (1925, Aut. 626); M. Brunies: Sugar Foot Stomp/Want a little lovin' (1925, OK 40526); R. Miller: Spanish Shawl (1925, Bruns. 2989); J. Goldkette: Rosetta/For Old Times' Sake (1928, Vic. 21527); on A. Hodes: *The Trios* (1953, Para. 112), Copenhagen, Someday Sweetheart, Tishomingo, Washboard Stomp; Hodes: *Friar's Inn Revisited* (1968, Del. 215)

BIBLIOGRAPHY

ChiltonW

J. T. Schenk: "Life History of Voltaire De Faut," *Jazz Session*, no.8 (1945), 2

R. Venables: "The Story of Volly De Faut," *Jazz Notes* (1946), April, 13

J. Lukas: "Notes on Bunk and Jelly Roll," *Record Changer*, x/4 (1951), 5

A. Hodes: "Sittin' in: a Talk with Volly De Faut," *DB*, xxxiii/24 (1966), 22

P. Van Vorst: "Meeting De Faut," *MR*, iii/9 (1976), 10

RAYMOND J. GARIGLIO

DeFranco, Buddy [Boniface Ferdinand Leonardo] (*b* Camden, NJ, 17 Feb 1923). Clarinetist. At the age of 14 he won an amateur swing players' contest in Philadelphia that was sponsored by

Tommy Dorsey. After working in the big bands of Gene Krupa (1941–2) and Charlie Barnet (1943–4; for illustration *see* BARNET, CHARLIE) he was a principal soloist in Dorsey's orchestra (1944–8). Thereafter he twice attempted (unsuccessfully) to lead his own big band, but otherwise performed in smaller groups, including Count Basie's octet (1950) and a quartet with Art Blakey and Kenny Drew (1952–3). He toured Europe with Billie Holiday early in 1954. DeFranco gave the première of Nelson Riddle's *Cross-country Suite* in 1958, and from the same year conducted jazz workshops at schools in California. Between 1960 and 1963 he led an unusual quartet (clarinet, accordion, double bass, and drums) with Tommy Gumina, and the following year he made an acclaimed recording, *Blues Bag*, playing bass clarinet. Later he led the reconstituted Glenn Miller Orchestra (1966–74), but returned to teaching and playing intermittently in nightclubs. He made a tour of Sweden in 1975. With Terry Gibbs, DeFranco led a quintet that performed in London (1980) and New York (*c*1982); he also worked in New York in a duo with George Duvivier (1983). In the mid-1980s he made some fine recordings as the leader of a quintet with the clarinetist John Denman and a harpsichordist, and as a member of Oscar Peterson's quartet with Joe Pass and Niels-Henning Ørsted Pedersen. He has continued to lead a quintet with Gibbs.

DeFranco is a talented improviser with a liquid tone and a prodigious technique, but, because of the apparent incompatibility of his chosen instrument and his preferred musical style, bop (*see* CLARINET, §2), he has frequently been obliged to perform under circumstances that have failed to challenge his abilities.

SELECTED RECORDINGS

As leader: on L. Tristano: *Crosscurrents* (1949, Cap. 11060), A Bird in Igor's Yard; Gone with the Wind/Lover come back to me (1952, MGM 30679); Autumn in New York/Show Eyes (1953, Clef 89067); with A. Tatum: *Art Tatum-Buddy DeFranco Quartet* (1956, Verve 8229); *Buddy DeFranco Plays Benny Goodman* (1957, Verve 2089); *Cross-country Suite* (1958, Dot 9006); with T. Gumina: *Buddy DeFranco and Tommy Gumina* (1961, Mer. 60685); *Blues Bag* (1964, VJ 2506); *Free Sail* (1974, Choice 1008); with T. Gibbs, *Jazz Party: First Time Together* (1981, PAlt 8011), *On Tour: UK* (1983, Hep 2023); *Buddy DeFranco Presents John Denman* (*c*1984, Lud 101); *'Hark': Buddy DeFranco Meets the Oscar Peterson Quartet* (1985, Pablo 2310915)

As sideman with T. Dorsey: Opus no.1 (1944, Vic. 201608)

BIBLIOGRAPHY

L. Feather: "Dance Biz Needs Younger Leaders: DeFranco," *DB*, xviii/5 (1951), 1

"Buddy DeFranco's New Career," *DB*, xxvi/2 (1959), 22

G. Marne: "One Octave Down: One Career Up," *DB*, xxxii/11 (1965), 17

J. Burns: "The Forgotten Boppers," *J&B*, ii/3 (1972), 5

S. Voce: "Buddy DeFranco," *JJI*, xxxv (1982), no.1, p.8; no.2, p.24

BARRY KERNFELD

Defunkt. Fusion group formed by the trombonist JOSEPH BOWIE around 1980.

Degen, Bob [Robert William, Jr.] (*b* Scranton, PA, 24 Jan 1944). Pianist. He attended the Berklee College of Music (1961–4) and played at clubs in Boston. From 1965 he worked intermittently in Europe, performing with Art Farmer, Dexter Gordon, Carmell Jones, and Albert Mangelsdorff, and recording as a leader (1968). In the USA he led a trio with Paul Motian, made a tour of the East Coast with Gary Peacock, and toured with Buddy DeFranco (1969–71), then settled in Germany, where from 1974 he played and frequently recorded with the tenor saxophonist Heinz Sauer; they performed in a duo (1980) and as leaders of a quartet (1981–4), and worked together as sidemen with Makaya Ntshoko (1974), the Frankfurter Jazz Ensemble (1975), the group Voices (1981), and Adelhard Roidinger (1981). Degen also played with Gunter Lenz's group Springtime, led his own trios, and recorded with Joki Freund (1975), Leszek Zadlo (1977, 1980), Lenz (1979), and Uli Beckerhoff (1983). He may be heard to advantage on his album *Sequoia Song* (1976, Enja 2071), which consists largely of his own compositions. (G. Roberts: "Ein Amerikaner in Frankfurt: Bob Degen," *JP*, xxix/12 (1980), 13)

De Graaff, Rein (*b* Groningen, Netherlands, 24 Oct 1942). Dutch pianist. He is largely self-taught as a musician. He led a trio (1959–62), worked with the Jazzopaters (1962–3), led a quartet (1962–4), and played with the vibraphonist Erwin Somer (1963–4) and the baritone saxophonist Gijs Hendriks (1964–5). In 1964 he formed a quartet with the tenor saxophonist Dick Vennik that remained active into the 1980s; he also performed and toured with Hank Mobley, Lee Morgan, Johnny Griffin, Art Taylor, Clifford Jordan, Cecil Payne, Dexter Gordon, Clark Terry, Sonny Stitt, Philly Joe Jones, and Arnett Cobb, and played on several occasions in New York. He was awarded the Dutch National Jazz Prize in 1980. De Graaff's playing is exemplified by two recordings he made for Timeless, *Chasin' the Bird* (1981, 159) and *Cloud People* (1983, 191). (*Feather–Gitler '70s*)

WIM VAN EYLE

De Gregori, Rio (*b* Zurich, 22 Sept 1919; *d* Munich, 22 May 1987). Swiss pianist. He studied piano and from 1939 he worked as a professional musician with various leaders, including the drummer Willy Mac Allen (1939–40), the alto saxophonist James Boucher (1940–41), and René Weiss (1942–3, with whom he recorded *Bull Fiddle Blues*, 1943, Col. ZZ1086). He also made recordings as a sideman with the bandleader Bob Huber (1941), Philippe Brun (1942), and the Lanigiros (1942–3). In 1944 he joined Fred Böhler's quartet and, with Böhler playing Hammond organ, recorded *Boogie-woogie* (Col. ZZ1163). He formed his own band in Geneva in 1945, by which time he had already made several recordings as a leader of studio groups; among his sidemen were Stuff Combe and Flavio Ambrosetti. Shortly thereafter he settled in Munich. De Gregori's accomplished swing and boogie-woogie playing may be heard to advantage on his *At the Woodchoppers' Ball* (1942, Col. ZZ1108). (J.-R. Hippenmeyer: *Le jazz en Suisse, 1930–1970*, Yverdon, Switzerland, 1971)

RAINER E. LOTZ

Dejan, Harold [Duke] (*b* New Orleans, 4 Feb 1909). Alto saxophonist. He first became interested in music when he heard the bands in New Orleans in the cutting contests that took place on open wagons as they advertised their performances. He studied clarinet with Albert Nicholas and Lorenzo Tio, Jr., among others, and he began playing professionally around 1923. After working with such musicians as Kid Rena in various clubs in New Orleans he toured the USA and performed at jazz festivals overseas as a member of Sam Jefferson's band. Dejan served in the Algiers Navy Band in Louisiana (1942–6) and thereafter continued to work in New Orleans, concentrating on alto saxophone; he was a member of Alex Bigard's group the Mighty Four in the 1950s. In 1958 he formed the OLYMPIA BRASS BAND, with which he has performed at Preservation Hall and other local venues, and toured the USA and Europe. The band modernized the traditional BRASS BAND music of New Orleans, incorporating rhythm-and-blues, soul, and bop numbers into its repertory; its playing is well represented by the album *Harold Dejan's Olympia Brass Band* (1962, Mono 5). From the mid-1970s Dejan also led a small group, the Serenaders, at Preservation Hall. After a period of ill health in the mid-1980s he returned to an active career with both his ensembles. Dejan's brother, the trumpeter Leo Dejan (*b* New Orleans, 4 May 1911), is also active in traditional jazz, touring with the LEGENDS OF JAZZ and recording with the Eagle Brass Band (1983).

Oral history material in *LNT*.

BIBLIOGRAPHY

J. Roberts: "Talking to Harold Dejan," *JB*, ii/7 (1965), 19
B. Martyn: Liner notes, *Dejan's Olympia Brass Band in Europe* (77 LEU31, 1969)
G. Valentin: "Harold 'Duke' Dejan," *Fn*, vi/5 (1975), 4

KARL KOENIG

DeJohnette, Jack (*b* Chicago, 9 Aug 1942). Drummer and pianist. He began playing piano at the age of four, studying with a classical teacher for about ten years. By the time he reached high school he was playing blues and rock-and-roll on piano, but his interest soon turned to jazz and he started working in small groups, emulating Ahmad Jamal. At about the age of 18 he began to study drums, which quickly became his primary interest. While in junior college he became involved with the Association for the Advancement of Creative Musicians; he was also profoundly impressed by an opportunity to perform with John Coltrane in the early 1960s. In April 1966 DeJohnette moved to New York, where he again performed several times with Coltrane and often appeared with Jackie McLean (1966–9). He first came to nationwide attention as a member of the popular Charles Lloyd Quartet, with which he recorded and toured worldwide for more than two years (1966–8). He then joined Miles Davis's group, where he replaced Tony Williams in 1969 and took part in the pathbreaking recording sessions of that year for the album *Bitches Brew*. After leaving Davis in mid-1972 DeJohnette continued to be active in jazz-rock groups, including several under his own leadership, and worked with Dave Holland in John Abercrombie's trio Gateway (1975–7). From that time his own groups Directions and Special Edition, which have introduced such talents as David Murray and Arthur Blythe, have received high critical acclaim.

Jack DeJohnette playing with Miles Davis's group at Ronnie Scott's, London, c1970

DeJohnette is a powerful and widely admired drummer. Although his original inspiration was Vernel Fournier, his major influences were Max Roach, Philly Joe Jones, and, later, Elvin Jones. In New York he also came under the influence of Tony Williams, especially in regard to cymbal technique. In the 1980s he resumed playing piano, revealing a skill and creativity to rival his drumming. From 1975 he has been a director, with his wife, of the Creative Music Agency in Woodstock, New York, a nonprofit enterprise for the management, performing, and teaching of jazz, and in 1981 he published a manual, *The Art of Modern Jazz Drumming*.

SELECTED RECORDINGS

As leader: *Complex* (1968, Mlst. 9022); *Untitled* (1976, ECM 1074); *New Directions* (1978, ECM 1128); *Special Edition* (1979, ECM 1152); *New Directions in Europe* (1979, ECM 1157)

As sideman: C. Lloyd: *Dream Weaver* (1966, Atl. 1459); *Forest Flower* (1966, Atl. 1473); M. Davis: *Bitches Brew* (1969, Col. GP26); *Miles Davis at Fillmore* (1970, Col. KG30038)

BIBLIOGRAPHY

J. DeJohnette: "Jack DeJohnette Introduces his New Group, Compost," *DB*, xxxviii/16 (1971), 19
——: "DeJohnette on DeJohnette," *DB*, xlii/4 (1975), 16
B. Bennett: "Jack DeJohnette's 'Directions': Experimental Inheritors," *DB*, xliv/6 (1977), 12
C. Stern: "Jack DeJohnette: South Side to Woodstock," *DB*, xlv/18 (1978), 23
L. Jeske: "Jack DeJohnette: Naturally Multi-Directional," *DB*, xlviii/3 (1981), 17
P. Danson: "Jack DeJohnette," *Coda*, no.182 (1982), 12
R. Mattingly: "Jack DeJohnette," *MD*, vii/4 (1983), 8
B. Doerschuk: "Jack DeJohnette Trades Sticks for Keys in his Jazz Piano Debut," *Keyboard*, x/12 (1984), 10
H. Mandel: "Drummer, Drummer: Jack DeJohnette," *DB*, lii/2 (1985), 16 [incl. discography]
B. Beuttler: "The Jack DeJohnette Interview," *DB*, liv/9 (1987), 16 [incl. discography]

LEWIS PORTER

De Kers [De Keersmaeker], **Robert** (*b* Antwerp, Belgium, 10 Aug 1906; *d* Brussels, 16 Jan 1987). Belgian trumpeter and bandleader. From 1922 he played piano with amateur jazz groups in Brussels and, in 1924–5, worked as a pianist with the Bing Boys. After learning trumpet he went to Italy with the Original Berkeley's, led by Jeff Candrix. He was engaged by Carlo Benzi (1926) but left him shortly afterwards to replace Peter Packay in David Bee's group the Red Beans, which toured Europe. He worked with the entertainer Harry Fleming and also served as music director to the cabaret singer Josephine Baker. In 1932 he performed with Jean Robert and led his own band the Cabaret Kings in Belgium and throughout Europe. He later played with Jean Omer and after World War II spent some time entertaining American troops in Germany. He later became the director of the Belgian division of Wurlitzer. Throughout his career De Kers worked intermittently as a composer and arranger. He made many recordings as a leader (1936–56) for the Jazz Club, Decca, and Victory labels, and also recorded as a sideman with the Red Beans (1928) and Eddie Tower (1941–2).

ROBERT PERNET

Delamont, Gordon (Arthur) (*b* Moose Jaw, Canada, 27 Oct 1918; *d* Toronto, 16 Jan 1981). Canadian theorist, teacher, and composer. He led dance bands and played trumpet in Toronto (1939–49) before he ended his career as a performer for reasons of health and turned to teaching in 1950. He wrote texts on arranging, harmony, counterpoint, 12-tone music, and melody (New York, 1965–76) that became widely used, and he taught many leading jazz musicians in Canada in the 1950s and 1960s. He also composed several works in the third-stream idiom, of which he was an enthusiastic advocate; these include *Collage no.3* and *Song and Dance*, both of which are included on the album *Duke Ellington, North of the Border in Canada with the Ron Collier Orchestra* (1967, Decca 75069). His *Three Entertainments for Saxophone Quartet* (1969) was recorded by the New York Saxophone Quartet. (H. McNamara and M. Miller: "Delamont, Gordon," *Encyclopedia of Music in Canada*, ed. H. Kallmann, G. Potvin, and K. Winters, Toronto, Buffalo, and London, 1981)

MARK MILLER

Delaney, Jack (Michael) (*b* New Orleans, 27 Aug 1930; *d* New Orleans, 22 Sept 1975). Trombonist. He played with the alto saxophonist Johnny Reininger (1949–51), then performed and recorded with Sharkey Bonano (1951–6) and Tony Almerico (1953–8); between 1954 and 1956, with Almerico's Parisian Room Band, he made a number of recordings accompanying Lizzie Miles, including *Plain Ole Blues* (Cook 1182). Delaney also recorded, mostly in New Orleans, as the leader of his own bands, which included such sidemen as Lee Collins (1953) and Alvin Alcorn (1955), and as a sideman with Ken Colyer (1952), Pete Fountain (1956–7), and other revivalists. From 1958 he worked with the pianist Leon Kellner at the Roosevelt Hotel in New Orleans, and later played again with Fountain.

BIBLIOGRAPHY

FeatherE
Obituary, M. Menville, *SL*, xxviii (win. 1976), 8

De la Rosa, Frank [Francisco Estaban, Jr.] (*b* El Paso, TX, 26 Dec 1933). Double bass player. He studied at the Conservatory of Music and Fine Arts in Los Angeles from 1956 to 1958, then lived in Las Vegas, where he performed with local bands. After returning to Los Angeles (1965) he played with Don Ellis (1966–8); among his recordings with Ellis is the album *"Live" at Monterey* (1966, PJ 20112). In 1968–9 he worked with Harry Edison, and from 1969 to 1972 he toured internationally with Ella Fitzgerald; his recordings with the latter include the album *Sunshine of your Love* (1969, MPS 15250). Thereafter he played with Don Menza (1972–5) and Sarah Vaughan (1974–5), and recorded with Jay Migliori (1975). De la Rosa has a solid, dependable technique, and other musicians consider him to be both straightforward and reliable. While he is capable of playing in most styles he shows a particular interest in the rhythms of Latin jazz. (*Feather–Gitler '70s*)

LEROY OSTRANSKY

Delaunay, Charles (*b* Paris, 18 Jan 1911; *d* Vineuil St. Firmin, nr Paris, 16 Feb 1988). French writer. In 1933 he became a member of the Hot Club de France and in 1949 organized the Paris Jazz Festival. He established one of the earliest periodicals (*Jazz hot*, 1935) and one of the first record labels in France (Swing, 1937) devoted exclusively to jazz. From 1939 he was the host of various radio programs; he made weekly broadcasts (1945–55) and a series of live broadcasts of jazz performances ("Jazz Variétés," early 1950s) for French radio. Delaunay was particularly active in the promotion of the Quintette du Hot Club de France and Django Reinhardt. He also organized concerts, produced recordings, gave lectures, and produced several short films (including *Autour d'une trompette* and *Jam Session*, both 1950). John Lewis dedicated to him the composition *Delaunay's Dilemma* (1954). Delaunay's writings are characterized by a constant attention to detail and an openness towards widely differing styles. He is best known as a pioneer of jazz discography, as well as for having established the name of the discipline.

WRITINGS
(selective list)

Hot Discography (Paris, 1936, rev. 4/1943 as *Hot discographie*, rev. and enlarged by W. E. Schaap and G. Avakian as *New Hot Discography: the Standard Directory of Recorded Jazz*, New York, 5/1948/*R*1982)
De la vie et du jazz (Lausanne, Switzerland, 1939, 2/1941)
Hot Iconography (Lausanne, Switzerland, 1945)
Django Reinhardt: souvenirs (Paris, 1954; Eng. trans., London, 1961/*R*1981, 1982, rev. 2/1981) [incl. discography]
with K. Mohr: *Hot discographie encyclopédique* (Paris, 1951) [inc., A – Hefti, Neal only]
Souvenirs (Lausanne, Switzerland, 1954)
Sidney Bechet (Paris, 1963)
Django, mon frère (Paris, 1968)
Delaunay's Dilemma: de la peinture au jazz (Mâcon, France, 1985)
with P. du Peuty: *Noirs au blanc: images de jazzmen* (Paris, 1986) [portraits]

BIBLIOGRAPHY

L. Feather: "Meet the Critics," *The New Yearbook of Jazz* (New York, 1958), 85

ANDRÉ CLERGEAT

DeLisle, Louis Nelson. *See* NELSON, BIG EYE LOUIS.

Delmark [Delmar]. Record company and label. The company was established in the mid-1950s by Bob Koester in St. Louis. It was at first named Delmar, after the street on which it was situated; during the early part of its existence the label was used to issue a series of 10-inch albums of traditional jazz recorded by local musicians. In 1959 Koester transferred his premises to Chicago, where he changed the name to Delmark; catalogue numbers remained unchanged for re-pressings of Delmar originals on the new label.

The company became extremely important for its documentation of a wide variety of music in Chicago, issued in three series. One, Traditional Jazz, began with rereleases of material by George Lewis (i), but later put out the results of new sessions by such musicians as Albert Nicholas (1959), Art Hodes (1959, 1968), and Earl Hines (1969). A second sequence, Modern Jazz, offered music in styles that ranged from bop to free jazz, including items by Ira Sullivan and Jimmy Forrest (both 1959), and Sonny Stitt (1968); its catalogue also contained material originally recorded by Transition, including LPs by Sun Ra. Most notably, Modern Jazz issued work by the Association for the Advancement of Creative Musicians on albums made in the late 1960s and early 1970s by Roscoe Mitchell, Joseph Jarman, Muhal Richard Abrams, Anthony Braxton, Kalaparusha Maurice McIntyre, and the Art Ensemble of Chicago. A third series, Roots of Jazz, contained mainly blues. Recording apparently ceased after 1972, but the company has kept some items from the catalogue available into the 1980s. It also maintains a library, parts of which are available to the public; *see* LIBRARIES AND ARCHIVES, §2 (USA, Chicago).

Deloof, Gus [Auguste] (*b* Brussels, 26 Sept 1909; *d* Brussels, 8 May 1974). Belgian trumpeter. He made his professional début in Belgium in Ostend (1926) and then worked with the Michigans (1927), a group which also included several Cuban musicians. In 1928–9 he played in Monte Carlo with various members of a band previously led by Chas Remue. After performing in an orchestra with Fud Candrix in the Netherlands and Belgium he worked in the Netherlands with Spike Hughes, in Germany with Bernard Etté (1931), in Paris with the Carolina Stomp Chasers (1931), and with Willie Lewis. From 1934 to 1939 he was a member of Ray Ventura's band in France, and thereafter he played throughout Belgium and in Africa. Deloof recorded with Philippe Brun (1937), the Quintette du Hot Club de France (1937), Ventura, Candrix (1940–41), and as a leader (1931, 1939–46, 1950–53). He was also active as a composer and arranger; among his recorded compositions are *Easy Going'/Sweeping the Floor* (1940, Jazz Club 4206) and *Harlem Swing* (1941, Decca B8741).

ROBERT PERNET

Delta. Record label. It was used to issue only four discs, all by Kid Rena. These were made in New Orleans in 1940 by Heywood Hale Broun, Jr., and are widely regarded as the first recordings of the revival of the New Orleans style in the 1940s. The masters were acquired by the American company Circle, and the material was later reissued on LPs by Riverside and its successors.

BIBLIOGRAPHY

W. L. Grossman and J. W. Farrell: *The Heart of Jazz* (New York, 1956/R1976), 179

O. Keepnews: Liner notes, *New Orleans Legends* (Riv. RLP12-119, 1957)

De Luxe. Record company and label. The company was established early in 1944 by the four Braun brothers. Dud Bascomb, Benny Carter, and Billy Eckstine were the most prominent jazz musicians to record for the label during its earliest days. After a disastrous fire on 22 November 1947 at the company's headquarters in Linden, New Jersey, the organization was restructured and material by black musicians was transferred to a separate race series, the 3000s; this included recordings by Papa Celestin's Original Tuxedo Orchestra that were made on a field trip to New Orleans in October 1947. In August 1948 De Luxe was placed in receivership; the following month Syd Nathan's company King purchased a controlling interest in the enterprise. The Braun brothers continued to operate the label autonomously before leaving to form Regal in August 1949; the label name De Luxe was briefly revived by King in the 1950s.

BIBLIOGRAPHY

M. Leadbitter: "De Luxe," *Blues Unlimited*, no.104 (1973), 24

B. Daniels: "De Luxe Records 1944–1949," *Whiskey, Women, and . . .*, no.9 (1982), 28

DeMicheal, Don(ald Anthony) (*b* Louisville, KY, 12 May 1928; *d* Skokie, IL, 4 Feb 1982). Editor. After teaching percussion and leading his own band in Louisville (1951–60) he moved in 1960 to Chicago to become the managing editor of *Down Beat*, of which he was later the editor-in-chief (1961–7); at the same time he compiled and edited the *Jazz Record Review* (1961–4). During the following years he edited several periodicals devoted to nonmusical subjects. In 1975 he formed a group called the Swingtet, in which he played vibraphone successively with the clarinetists Jerry Fuller and Chuck Hedges; he also played drums in the Hot Three with Kenny Davern and Art Hodes. He was president of the Jazz Institute of Chicago from 1974 to 1978; later, as the institute's program chairman, he played an important role in planning the first Chicago Jazz Festival (1979).

DANIEL ZAGER

Dennis, Kenny [Kenneth Carl] (*b* Philadelphia, 27 May 1930). Drummer. He played with Earl Bostic (1953), the organist Jackie Davis (1954), and Erroll Garner (1955), then performed and recorded with Sonny Stitt (1956–7) and Billy Taylor (ii) (1957, 1959). As a freelance player in New York he worked occasionally with Thelonious Monk, and made recordings with Johnny Griffin, Sonny Rollins (both 1957), and Mal Waldron (*Mal 4*, 1958, NewJ 8208). He also recorded an album of jazz and poetry with Charles Mingus and Langston Hughes and took part in a session with Miles Davis and Michel Legrand (both 1958). In 1960 he moved to Los Angeles, where he accompanied Lena Horne, recorded with the pianist Marvin Jenkins and Roy Ayers (both 1963), and performed and recorded with his wife, Nancy Wilson (1963–4). By 1965 he had ceased to perform professionally. (*Feather '60s*)

Dennis, Matt(hew Loveland) (*b* Seattle, 11 Feb 1914). Songwriter, arranger, pianist, and singer. His parents were vaudeville artists, and he studied piano from an early age. He played piano in Horace Heidt's dance band in 1933, but for much of the 1930s worked in Hollywood as a nightclub singer and pianist and as a vocal coach for band singers. In the early 1940s he was composer and arranger for Tommy Dorsey, and wrote a number of hit songs for the band which were performed by Frank Sinatra. During World War II he played briefly in Glenn Miller's orchestra. Thereafter he worked principally as a nightclub entertainer, and issued some recordings under his own name, including *Matt Dennis Plays and Sings* (*c*1957, Kapp 1024). He also arranged music for radio programs (1946–8) and appeared in films and on television.

RECORDED COMPOSITIONS

(selective list; recorded by T. Dorsey unless otherwise indicated)

Everything happens to me (1941, Vic. 27359); Let's get away from it all (1941, Vic. 27377); Violets for your furs (1941, Vic. 27690); The night we called it a day (1942, Vic. 201553); D. Brubeck: *Angel Eyes* (1965, Col. CS9148)

BIBLIOGRAPHY

FeatherE

A. Wilder: *American Popular Song: the Great Innovators, 1900–1950* (London and New York, 1972), 505

DAVID FLANAGAN

Dennis, Willie [DeBerardinis, William] (*b* Philadelphia, 10 Jan 1926; *d* New York, 8 July 1965). Trombonist. He gained his early experience in big bands with leaders such as Elliot Lawrence (1946), Claude Thornhill, and Sam Donahue. In the 1950s he was associated intermittently with Charles Mingus, recording with him in 1953 and 1959 and making a tour of a few months as a member of his quintet in 1956–7. He played with Benny Goodman in Brussels and with Woody Herman in Latin America, both in 1958, and the following year he joined Buddy Rich's quintet. He performed frequently with the Gerry Mulligan Concert Jazz Band in the early 1960s and played in the band that Goodman took to the USSR in 1962. He was married to the singer Morgana King. Dennis's work was never widely appreciated except by other musicians. Some of his few recorded solos, including those on *Wednesday Night Prayer Meeting* (recorded with Mingus) and *Blueport* (recorded with Mulligan), have been attributed to other players. His playing is characterized by extreme agility and a legato style in which a combination of lip and slide movements is used to avoid conventional articulation by tonguing.

SELECTED RECORDINGS

As sideman: Jazz Workshop: *Trombone Rapport* (1953, Debut 5, 14); C. Mingus: *Blues and Roots* (1959, Atl. 1305), incl. Wednesday Night Prayer Meeting; G. Mulligan: *At the Village Vanguard* (1960, Verve 68396), incl. Blueport

BIBLIOGRAPHY

Feather E; *Feather '60s*
"Willie Dennis: trombone à suivre," *Jh*, no.161 (1961), 38

BRIAN PRIESTLEY

Deodato, Eumir (de Almeida) (*b* Rio de Janeiro, 22 June 1942). Brazilian arranger and pianist. He performed in Brazil with Astrud Gilberto and the guitarist Luis Bonfa. In 1967 he moved to New York, where he wrote arrangements for and recorded with Gilberto (1967–8, 1971), Stanley Turrentine (1971), the singer Aretha Franklin (1972), and Airto Moreira (1974). He also played guitar in a recording session with Antonio Carlos Jobim in 1970. After the commercial success of his recorded arrangement of Richard Strauss's *Also sprach Zarathustra* (on the album *Prelude*, 1972, CTI 6021) he toured the USA, Canada, Europe, and East Asia (1973–4). He then concentrated on popular music, and from 1979 to 1983 worked with the soul and funk group Kool and the Gang. (*Feather–Gitler '70s*)

De Paris, Sidney (*b* Crawfordsville, IN, 30 May 1905; *d* New York, 13 Sept 1967). Trumpeter and tuba player, brother of Wilbur De Paris. He studied music with his father, a bandleader, and worked as a sideman with Charlie Johnson (1926–31), Don Redman (1932–6, 1939), Zutty Singleton (1939–41), Benny Carter (1940–41), Art Hodes (1941), Roy Eldridge (1944), and Claude Hopkins (1946); he also recorded with Jelly Roll Morton (1939) and Sidney Bechet (1940). He is best known for his work with his brother Wilbur in traditional-jazz groups between 1943 and 1967. De Paris brought to his playing of traditional jazz several elements of swing, as well as growls and some unusual effects achieved with a cup mute. Although these features of his playing met with little favor from more conservative musicians (including Mezz Mezzrow, who dismissed De Paris from a recording session in 1938), they were consistent with the style of his brother's band.

SELECTED RECORDINGS

As leader of De Paris Brothers (with W. De Paris): I found a New Baby/Black and Blue (1944, Com. 552); Everybody Loves my Baby (1944, BN 40); *Blue Note Stompers* (1951, BN 7016)

As sideman: C. Johnson: The Boy in the Boat (1928, Vic. 21712); M. Mezzrow: Revolutionary Blues (1938, Bb 10088); Comin' On with the Come On (1938, Bb 10085); J. R. Morton: I Thought I Heard Buddy Bolden Say (1939, Bb 10434); Climax Rag (1939, Bb 10442); S. Bechet: Shake it and Break it/Wild Man Blues (1940, Vic. 26640); *The Fabulous Sidney Bechet and his Hot Six with Sidney de Paris* (1951, BN 7020), incl. There'll be Some Changes Made; W. De Paris: *Wilbur De Paris and his Rampart Street Ramblers* (1952, Atl. 141, 143); *Wilbur De Paris at Symphony Hall* (1956, Atl. 1253)

BIBLIOGRAPHY

ChiltonW; *FeatherE*; *Feather '60s*; *Feather–Gitler '70s*
M. Mezzrow and B. Wolfe: *Really the Blues* (New York, 1946/*R*1972), 322, 325
N. Shapiro and N. Hentoff, eds.: *Hear me Talkin' to ya: the Story of Jazz by the Men who Made it* (New York and London, 1955/*R*1966), 51, 172, 193
H. P[anassié]: "Sidney De Paris," *BHcF*, no.110 (1961), 3
Obituary, *DB*, xxxiv/22 (1967), 14
M. M. Mezzrow: "Mezz rend hommage à deux disparus," *BHcF*, no.177 (1968), 3

WILLIAM H. KENNEY III

De Paris, Wilbur (*b* Crawfordsville, IN, 11 Jan 1900; *d* New York, 3 Jan 1973). Bandleader and trombonist, brother of Sidney De Paris. He began his career as an alto horn player and performed on the TOBA circuit with his father's circus band. During a brief visit to New Orleans (1922) he played C-melody saxophone with Louis Armstrong and worked with A. J. Piron. He worked as a leader in Philadelphia from 1925 and in New York performed and recorded with the violinist LeRoy Smith (1928), Dave Nelson (1931), Noble Sissle (with whom he also toured Europe, 1931), and Edgar Hayes. After touring Europe with Teddy Hill's orchestra (1936–7) and recording with the Mills Blue Rhythm Band (1937) he played again with Armstrong (1937–40), led a group from 1943, and worked with Duke Ellington (1945–7); he also played with Ella Fitzgerald and belonged to Roy Eldridge's big band. He made recordings with Sidney Bechet in 1946 and 1949–50. From 1951 to 1962 he worked regularly at Ryan's in New York as the leader of a band that included his brother and Omer Simeon. The group had a varied repertory that included traditional-jazz standards, light classics, hymns, folksongs, spirituals, blues, and marches; its style evoked Jelly Roll Morton's Red Hot Peppers and at the same time had some of the rhythmic and harmonic characteristics of swing. De Paris made a tour of Africa sponsored by the US State Department in 1957 and continued to work as a leader until 1972.

Oral history material in *LNT*.

SELECTED RECORDINGS

As leader (all recorded for Atlantic): *Wilbur De Paris and his Rampart Street Ramblers* (1952, 141, 143); *Wilbur De Paris at Symphony Hall* (1956, 1253); *Wilbur De Paris Plays Cole Porter* (1957–8, 1288); *That's a'plenty* (1958–9, 1318); *The Wild Jazz Age* (1960, 1336); *Wilbur De Paris on the Riviera* (1960, 1363)

As sideman: Mills Blue Rhythm Band: Jammin' for the Jackpot (1937, Var. 634); L. Armstrong: I Double Dare you (1938, Decca 1636); R. Eldridge: Twilight Time (1944, Decca 23383); D. Ellington: Stomp, Look, and Listen (1947, Col. DB2504); Progressive Gavotte (1947, Col. 38237)

BIBLIOGRAPHY

ChiltonW; *FeatherE*; *Feather '60s*; *Feather–Gitler '70s*
G. W. Kay: "Wilbur De Paris and his Rampart Street Ramblers," *JJ*, viii/11 (1954), 1
N. Hentoff and A. J. McCarthy, eds.: *Jazz: New Perspectives on the History of Jazz* (New York, 1959/*R*1974), 319
G. W. Kay: "Wilbur De Paris and his New New Orleans Jazz," *JJ*, ix/7 (1956), 1
J. S. Wilson: Liner notes, *Marchin' and Swingin'* (Atl. 1233, 1956)
C. E. Smith: Liner notes, *Wilbur De Paris Plays Cole Porter* (Atl. 1288, 1958)
P. Bullis: "Wilbur deParis & his New New Orleans Band," *MR*, ii/12 (1975), 1
G. Kay and P. Bullis: "Voice from the Past," *MR*, iii (1976), no.11, p.10; no.12, p.10 [interview]

WILLIAM H. KENNEY III

Deppenschmidt, Buddy [William Henry, III; Depp] (*b* Philadelphia, 16 Feb 1936). Drummer and percussionist. After touring with Billy Butterfield (1959–60) he achieved fame as a member of Charlie Byrd's trio (1960–63); among the recordings he made with Byrd was the acclaimed album *Jazz Samba* (1962, Verve 68432), recorded under the leadership of Stan Getz. From 1964 to 1978 Deppenschmidt played in John Coates's trio, and during the same period he attended Trenton State College (1969) and studied privately with Joe Morello (1970–73). In 1974 he formed his own band, Jazz Renaissance, which at various times included Coates, Richie Cole, and Mike Melillo. The group disbanded in 1978, but Deppenschmidt re-formed it in 1981 as a quartet. In 1982 he performed in Philadelphia with Bob Dorough. He has also been active as a teacher. His father, Buddy Deppenschmidt II, performs as a dance-band leader in the Philadelphia area under the name Buddy Williams, and should not be confused with the drummer of that name. (*Feather '60s*)

Derby (mute) [hat] **(i).** *See* MUTE, §2(j).

Derby (ii). Record label. It was established in New York in 1949 by Larry Newton, and was devoted to race records. Derby is thought to have been one of the earliest independent labels used for the issue of 45 r.p.m. singles; this began late in 1949. At first the band led by the tenor saxophonist Freddie Mitchell was prominent in much of the label's catalogue. By late 1951 Eddie Wilcox had become music director, and by early 1953 the repertory was mainly pop music; in October the following year the label was bankrupt. With Lee Magid, formerly at Savoy, Newton founded a new label, Central, in October 1953. (V. Perlin: "Derby Records," *Whiskey, Women, and. . .*, no.14 (1983), 14)

Desmond [Breitenfeld], **Paul (Emil)** (*b* San Francisco, 25 Nov 1924; *d* New York, 30 May 1977). Alto saxophonist. He studied clarinet at San Francisco State University and played in various local groups before joining the Dave Brubeck Quartet in 1951. Because his career was almost solely with this group until its dissolution in 1967 he shared its success without receiving the recognition that was his due. Desmond continued to play occasionally with Brubeck in the 1970s, notably in 1975, when the two men recorded an album of duets. He also appeared at festivals and toured Europe, Australia, and Japan for George Wein. Later he worked in New York at the Half Note with his own group, which included Jim Hall (1974), and in Toronto as a soloist with a Canadian rhythm section (1974–5).

Desmond was one of the most capable representatives of the "cool" tendency in alto saxophone jazz, of which Lee Konitz was the chief exponent, and which Lester Young, Benny Carter, and others had foreshadowed in the late 1930s. His tone had a luminous quality, consistent over the instrument's whole range, that was particularly reminiscent of Carter, but his most notable gift as an improviser was his power of sustained melodic invention, which depended in part on an unusually imaginative use of sequence. Desmond's independent recordings, with the sidemen Gerry Mulligan (1962) and Hall (1959–65), for example, do him more justice than his numerous ones with Brubeck, for whom he composed the popular *Take Five* in 5/4 time.

See also BRUBECK, DAVE.

SELECTED RECORDINGS

Duos with D. Brubeck: *Brubeck and Desmond: Duets* (1975, A&M Hor. 703)

As leader: *Desmond* (1954, Fan. 321); *Paul Desmond and Friends* (1959, WB 1356); *Two of a Mind* (1962, RCA LSP2624); *Glad to be Unhappy* (1963–4, RCA LSP3407); *Skylark* (1973, CTI 6039); *The Paul Desmond Quartet Live* (1975, A&M Hor. 850)

As sideman: D. Brubeck: *Time Out* (1959, Col. CL1397), incl. Take Five

BIBLIOGRAPHY

M. McPartland: "Perils of Paul: a Portrait of Desperate Desmond," *DB*, xxvii/19 (1960), 15; repr. in *All in Good Time* (New York, and Oxford, England, 1987)
J. Goldberg: *Jazz Masters of the Fifties* (New York and London, 1965/*R*1980)
M. Williams: *Jazz Masters in Transition, 1957–69* (New York and London, 1970/*R*1980) [colln of previously pubd reviews], 99
L. Tomkins: "Giant Jazzman, Gentle Wit: Paul Desmond," *CI*, xii/12 (1974), 14; xiii/1 (1974), 9
A. J. Smith: "A Quarter of a Century Young: the Dave Brubeck Quartet," *DB*, xliii/6 (1976), 18
N. Hentoff: "The Solitary Floating Jazzman," *VV*, xxi (22 Aug 1977), 35

MAX HARRISON/R

De Souza, Raul [João José Pereira] (*b* Rio de Janeiro, 23 Aug 1934). Brazilian trombonist and bandleader. After serving in the Brazilian air force he toured Europe and recorded with Sergio Mendes (1963–4), and in Brazil led a session that included Airto Moreira (1965). While on a second visit to Europe in 1965 he played in Paris with Kenny Clarke; he then returned to Brazil, where he performed and recorded with his own group, Impacto 8. He worked in Mexico City from 1970 to 1973, then settled in the USA, where he played with the Crusaders, recorded with Milton Nascimento, and performed and recorded with Flora Purim (1974), Azar Lawrence and Sonny Rollins (both 1975), and Moreira (*c*1976). He also made several recordings during the 1970s as leader of his own bands; these include *Colors* (1974, Mlst. 9061).

BIBLIOGRAPHY

Feather–Gitler '70s
L. Underwood: "Profile: Raul De Souza," *DB*, xlv/2 (1978), 32

Desvigne, Sidney (*b* New Orleans, 11 Sept 1893, *d* Pacoima, CA, 2 Dec 1959). Trumpeter and bandleader. In the 1910s and early 1920s he played with the Silver Bell Band (led by the trombonist Leonard Bechet), the Excelsior Brass Band, and the Maple Leaf Orchestra. From about 1921 to 1925 he worked with Ed Allen and Fate Marable on the riverboat *Capitol*; he plays a stop-time solo on Marable's recording of *Frankie and Johnnie* (1924, OK 40113). In the late 1920s he led the Southern Syncopaters on the SS *Island Queen*, and in the 1930s directed the Sidney Desvigne Orchestra aboard the SS *Capitol*; he also led a big band that played for dances in New Orleans. Desvigne was not a hot jazz player and his bands played almost entirely from arrangements. However, he allowed for the occasional hot solo, especially when performing for black audiences, by hiring such players as the trumpeter Eugene Ware, the clarinetist Theodore Purnell, Emanuel Sayles, and Louis Nelson. His riverboat career extended to the end of 1945, when he moved to southern California and operated a nightclub. His name is often misspelled Desvignes.

Oral history material in *LNT*.

BIBLIOGRAPHY

ChartersJ
Obituary, *SL*, x/3–4 (1960), 18
A. Rose and E. Souchon: *New Orleans Jazz: a Family Album* (Baton Rouge, LA, 1967, rev. 2/1978, rev. and enlarged 3/1984), 35
F. Driggs and H. Lewine: *Black Beauty, White Heat: a Pictorial History of Classic Jazz, 1920–1950* (New York, 1982), 22

ALDEN ASHFORTH

Deuchar, Jimmy [Jimmie, James] (*b* Dundee, Scotland, 26 June 1930). Scottish trumpeter and flugelhorn player. While serving in the RAF he played at the Club Eleven in London. In 1950 he joined the Johnny Dankworth Seven, then played with the bandleaders Geraldo and Oscar Rabin and with Ronnie Scott's sextet in Paris (1951); he also recorded with Jack Parnell (1952, 1953) and Scott (1952–4). He worked with Tony Crombie (1955) and toured with Lionel Hampton (1956) and Scott (USA, 1957) before moving to Germany, where he played as a soloist with Kurt Edelhagen's band (1957–9). A further period with Scott (1960–62) was followed by work with Tubby Hayes's quintet, the Clarke–Boland Big Band (from 1963), and Edelhagen (from 1964). During the 1960s and 1970s he was active mainly as an arranger, but in 1979 he recorded an excellent album as a leader. Influenced by Fats Navarro and Howard McGhee, Deuchar became recognized as one of the leading bop trumpeters of his generation in Great Britain.

SELECTED RECORDINGS

As leader: *Pub Crawling* (1955, Tempo 15); *Pal Jimmy* (1958, Tempo TAP20); *The Scots Connection* (1979, Hep 2006)

As sideman: J. Dankworth: Get Happy (1950, Esquire 10103); R. Scott: *Presenting the Ronnie Scott Sextet* (1957, Phi. 7153); K. Edelhagen: *Kurt Edelhagen Presents* (1957, Pol. 46052); Z. Sims: *Zoot Sims at Ronnie Scott's* (1961, Fon. 5176); T. Hayes: *Late Spot at Scott's* (1962, Fon. 5200); K. Clarke and F. Boland: *Clarke-Boland Big Band* (1963, Atl. 1404); *Sax No End* (1967, Saba 15138)

BIBLIOGRAPHY
FeatherE; *Feather '60s*
M. Isherwood: "Jimmy Deuchar," *JJI*, xl/6 (1987), 10

CHRIS SHERIDAN

Deutsche Grammophon. Record company and label. The company was founded during World War I to take over the German interests of the Gramophone Co.; it also acquired the rights to use the latter's "dog and gramophone" trademark. Efforts by the Gramophone Co. to recover control of its German operations after the war proved unsuccessful; the English organization later established the label Electrola to issue its material in Germany, and Deutsche Grammophon remained independent. During the 1920s it established one of the most important catalogues of jazz recordings in Germany; this included material by such American expatriates as Arthur Briggs and Alex Hyde.

As Deutsche Grammophon owned its trademarks for use in Germany alone, most of its issues were also put out for export with Polydor labels. After World War II the company began to concentrate on classical music, and became one of the best-known organizations in that field. Little jazz of any consequence was recorded after that time.

DeVaughn, Ronald. *See* WADUD, ABDUL.

De Villers [De Montaugé], **Michel** (*b* Villeneuve-sur-Lot, nr Agen, France, 13 July 1926). French baritone and alto saxophonist and bandleader. He studied alto saxophone from the age of 14 and first played professionally (with a quartet) in 1944. He played and recorded with Django Reinhardt (1946–7) and toured with Don Byas (1947) and Bill Coleman (*c*1948). From 1946 to 1959 he recorded as a leader and played frequently on French radio with his band. Until 1950 he played mainly alto saxophone and occasionally clarinet, but the baritone saxophone later became his preferred instrument. He recorded in Paris under the French bandleaders Jean-Claude Fohrenbach (1948), André Persiany (1949, 1954–5, 1958), Geo Daly (1950, 1953), Gérard Pochonet (1953–4), and Jacques Dieval (1956–7, 1959), and the visiting American swing musicians Buck Clayton (1953), Jonah Jones (1954), Coleman (1955–6), and Lucky Thompson (1956). Besides playing in France and Germany he worked in Belgium, Austria, the Netherlands, the USSR, and Israel. Later he wrote scripts for radio and for a period largely ceased to be active as a musician. He led a workshop with Christian Garros in Mont-St.-Aignan, near Rouen (1980), and later was active playing in clubs and concerts, in a duo with the guitarist Marc Fosset, and as the leader of a quintet; he is heard to advantage on *Hershey Bar* (1981, Ahead 33759), recorded with Fosset.

BIBLIOGRAPHY
FeatherE
M. Laverdure: "Un pionnier: Michel De Villers," *Jm*, no.287 (1980), 36 [interview]

De Vries, Louis (*b* Groningen, Netherlands, 6 Jan 1905; *d* Zwolle, Netherlands, 5 Sept 1935). Dutch trumpeter. He began his career in the Tuschinsky Theatre Orchestra in Amsterdam (1920), then played with the Excellos Five (1925–6), with his brother, the bass player Jack de Vries (1926–9), with the violinist Marek Weber (1929) and Ben Berlin (1930), under the bandleader Juan Llossas (1931–2), and again with his brother (1932–5). He also toured Great Britain in 1935 and worked with Valaida Snow. Although Armstrong once called him the best trumpeter in Europe, none of de Vries's recordings, all of which he made as a sideman, shows his playing to advantage.

WIM VAN EYLE

De Weille, Benny (*b* Lübeck, Germany, 6 March 1915; *d* Westerland, nr Sylt, Germany, 17 Dec 1977). German clarinetist and bandleader. After studying clarinet with Hans Helmke, a member of the Concertgebouw Orchestra in Amsterdam, De Weille recorded with Teddy Stauffer (1937–9), Hans Rehmstedt's band (1938–9), and Willy Berking (1939–43). In 1940 he founded his Bar Trio, whose music was modeled on that of Benny Goodman's groups. It became successful and its recordings (including *Hallo, Benny*, 1940, Odeon O31655) are considered to be among the best examples of German swing. De Weille took an administrative post at Radio Frankfurt after World War II. Following a short period as conductor of the orchestra of Nordwestdeutscher Rundfunk in Hamburg, he made his last recordings with a dixieland band in 1951.

GÜNTHER HUESMANN

Dial. Record company and label. The company was founded in 1946 by Ross Russell in Hollywood, where he was the proprietor of the Tempo Music Shop; financial backing was provided by Marvin Freeman. Dial rapidly became one of the most important independent labels for bop; its first important musician was Charlie Parker, who later took part in seven sessions for the company. These produced some of his best studio work. Other leading players who recorded for the company were Dizzy Gillespie, Howard McGhee, Dodo Marmarosa, Dexter Gordon, James Moody, Erroll Garner, and Don Lanphere. Dial also issued recordings by sidemen from Woody Herman's Herd, and acquired from Comet an interesting item by Red Norvo (on which Parker and Gillespie figure prominently) and valuable material by Art Tatum.

In 1947 the company moved its premises to New York, where it resumed recording Parker, McGhee, and others. It enjoyed substantial and surprising success with Earl Coleman's *Dark Shadows* (1947, 1014), and with "tenor battles," which featured the work of Dexter Gordon and Wardell Gray (*The Chase*, 1947, 1017) and Gordon and Teddy Edwards (*The Duel*, 1947, 1028). The company also held a substantial catalogue of what it termed "historical jazz"; this included recordings by Sidney Bechet, Earl Hines, Roy Eldridge, and Willie "the Lion" Smith. Dial was innovative in releasing significant musical fragments (such as Charlie Parker's *The Famous Alto Break*, 1946, LP905) which would otherwise have been lost. In 1949, however, it ceased to record jazz, and concentrated instead on classical music.

All Dial's jazz sessions were recorded on 16-inch lacquer discs (which were then used to produce masters); a second set was kept for protection (tape recording began only after Dial discontinued its jazz operation). The company was among the first to use the $33\frac{1}{3}$ r.p.m. disc for jazz; in 1949 it released some of the earliest 12-inch jazz albums, though these were not welcomed by the industry, which took several years to accept them. Most Dial LPs were made from pure vinyl, but some later issues were manufactured from an unbreakable material, only partly vinyl, which created considerable background noise.

In 1955 Russell disposed of some of Dial's masters to the company Concert Hall, and the catalogue was dispersed; parts of it were reissued in chaotic disorder on various labels until the mid-1960s. In 1968, however, the material began to appear in coherent form, organized with Russell's cooperation on Tony

Williams's English label Spotlite. By 1981 all Dial's material that could be salvaged had been rereleased in Spotlite's Dial Master series, which made some of the finest jazz of the 1940s widely available once more. Many of Russell's original masters, and much of his correspondence relating to Dial, are now in the University of Texas at Austin; *see* LIBRARIES AND ARCHIVES, §2.

MARK GARDNER

Dial, Harry (*b* Birmingham, AL, 17 Feb 1907; *d* New York, 25 Jan 1987). Drummer and bandleader. He was brought up in St. Louis, where he led small groups and worked in clubs and on the riverboats with such leaders as Fate Marable, Dewey Jackson, the reed player Norman Mason, and the clarinetist Jimmy Powell (1927–8). He then moved to Chicago and performed with various musicians, among them the clarinetist Clifford King (1928–9). He also led his own studio band, which recorded a number of his compositions, including *Don't give it away/Funny Fumble* (1930, Voc. 1515). In 1933 Dial performed and recorded with Louis Armstrong, and from 1934 he worked in New York. He was a member of Wendell P. Talbert's relief band at the Cotton Club, recorded regularly and toured with Fats Waller's band (1934–5), and played with Ed Allen (1937–40). Later he led his own band at various clubs (1946–7), was resident at Smalls' Paradise (1948–55), and worked with Lester Boone's trio (1955–63). He made further recordings as a leader in 1946, 1947, 1961, and 1965.

BIBLIOGRAPHY

ChiltonW
F. S. Driggs: "The Story of Harry Dial," *JJ*, xi/12 (1958), 11; xii (1959), no.1, p.26; no.2, p.8
A. van Delden: "Harry Dial," *Doctor Jazz*, no.40 (1970), 3; no.41 (1970), 22; no.42 (1970), 24; no.43 (1970), 3
H. Dial: *All this Jazz about Jazz: the Autobiography of Harry Dial* (Chigwell, England, 1984) [incl. discography]
Obituary, J. Simmen, *BHcF*, no.351 (1987), 20

Di Ceglie, Cosimo (*b* Andria, Italy, 21 Oct 1913; *d* Milan, 1980). Italian guitarist. He studied guitar in Andria, performed with various groups, and recorded with Herb Flemming's dance orchestra. He performed and recorded with the clarinetist Piero Rizza (1936–7), the Orchestra del Circolo jazz hot di Milano (1936), and his own groups (from 1938). Among his best recordings are those made with the pianist Enzo Ceragioli and Kramer Gorni (1938–41). During World War II he performed on radio with a sextet; after the war he became progressively less active, but he made fine recordings as a leader in 1949, 1956, and 1959. Di Ceglie's playing may be heard to advantage on his recording *Star Dust* (1938, Odeon 19427).

ADRIANO MAZZOLETTI

Dickenson, Vic(tor) (*b* Xenia, OH, 6 Aug 1906; *d* New York, 16 Nov 1984). Trombonist. In the 1920s and early 1930s he worked with local bands in Columbus, Ohio; Madison, Wisconsin; and Kansas City, Missouri. He then played with Blanche Calloway (1933–6), Claude Hopkins (1936–9), Benny Carter (1939, 1941), Count Basie (1940), and Frankie Newton (1941, 1942–3). From 1943 to 1946 he was a member of Eddie Heywood's band, which performed in New York and California, and he continued to work on the West Coast as a freelance from 1947 to 1948. He was in Boston until the mid-1950s, mostly leading his own band, then settled in New York, where he played first with Henry "Red" Allen (1958). During the 1960s Dickenson was leader (with Red Richards) of the SAINTS AND SINNERS, made several tours with George Wein's All Stars, played with Wild Bill Davison (1961–2), and worked regularly at Eddie Condon's club; he also toured Asia and Australia with Condon (1964) and visited Europe as a soloist (1965). From 1968 to 1970 he was the leader, with Bobby Hackett, of a successful quintet, and in the 1970s he performed frequently with the World's Greatest Jazz Band. He continued to play as a freelance throughout the 1970s and the early 1980s.

Dickenson was first regarded as a section trombonist, and rarely took solos, but in the early 1940s he emerged as a highly individual stylist whose improvisations exhibited a rare blend of humor and relaxation. He was one of the most consistent mainstream jazz musicians, and seemed equally at home with such diverse stylists as Sidney Bechet and Lester Young; he was also a masterful accompanist of singers, plying them with soft asides that were invariably apt. His husky tone was always personal, and he was inventive at any tempo. The recordings he made for Vanguard with his own septet (including Ruby Braff and Edmond Hall) in 1953 rank among the finest examples of mainstream jazz.

Oral history material in *NjR* (JOHP).

SELECTED RECORDINGS

As leader: *The Vic Dickenson Septet*, i (1953, Van. 8001), incl. Jeepers Creepers; *The Vic Dickenson Septet*, iii (1954, Van. 8012), incl. When you and I were young Maggie

As sideman: S. Bechet: After you've gone (1943, V-disc 270); L. Young: D. B. Blues (1945, Ala. 123)

BIBLIOGRAPHY

J. Cosson: "Vic Dickenson," *BHcF*, no.37 (1954), 3 [interview]
J. G. Jepsen: "Vic Dickenson diskografi," *Orkester journalen*, xxvi (1958), Feb, 50
G. Hoefer: "The Many Moods of Vic Dickenson," *DB*, xxvi/9 (1959), 18
"Dickenson's Shaggy Dog Story," *JB*, ii/6 (1965), 21
D. Morgenstern: "Bouquets for the Living: the Eminent Vic Dickenson," *DB*, xxxix/2 (1972), 14
S. Dance: *The World of Swing* (New York, 1974) [colln of previously pubd interviews], 301
L. Jeske: "Vic Dickenson: Swing Master Escapes London Gang," *DB*, xlvii/3 (1980), 24
W. Balliett: "Three Tones," *Jelly Roll, Jabbo and Fats* (New York, and Oxford, England, 1983) [colln of previously pubd articles], 111

JOHN CHILTON

Dickerson, Carroll (*b* 1895; *d* Chicago, Oct 1957). Violinist and bandleader. He led bands, predominantly in Chicago, from 1920 until the 1940s. Among the musicians who worked for him were Johnny Dunn, Tommy Ladnier, Zutty Singleton, Buster Bailey, Earl Hines, and Jimmy Mundy. Louis Armstrong was in two of his bands (1926, 1927–8), and in 1929 took the second under his own leadership, with Dickerson as conductor, to New York; there, under Dickerson's name, the band (minus Armstrong) worked at Connie's Inn (1929–30). After playing briefly with the Mills Blue Rhythm Band and touring with King Oliver, Dickerson returned to Chicago.

Armstrong's second coterie of players for his Hot Five recordings was taken from Dickerson's membership, and recordings by Dickerson's band that feature Armstrong appear to have influenced the succession of orchestral textures in the latter's version of *Beau Koo Jack* (1928; its arranger, Alex Hill, also worked for Dickerson). The first series of recordings by Dickerson's group under Armstrong's name consist chiefly of dull arrangements serving as a backdrop to the leader's trumpet playing and singing in a manner that set the norm for Armstrong's recordings for the following 15 years. A good example is *Ain't Misbehavin'* (1929), on which the phrasing in Dickerson's brief solo shows his lack of jazz sense.

SELECTED RECORDINGS

As leader: Symphonic Raps/Savoyager's Stomp (1928, Argentine Odeon 193329)

As sideman with L. Armstrong: Ain't Misbehavin' (1929, OK 8714); That Rhythm Man (1929, OK 8717)

BIBLIOGRAPHY

ChiltonW

A. McCarthy: *Big Band Jazz* (New York and London, 1974), 26

J. R. Taylor: Liner notes, *Louis Armstrong/Earl Hines 1928* (Smithsonian R002, 1975)

J. L. Collier: *Louis Armstrong: an American Genius* (New York, 1983, London, 1984, as *Louis Armstrong: a Biography*)

BOB ZIEFF

Dickerson, (Lowell) Dwight (*b* Los Angeles, 26 Dec 1944). Pianist. He studied at the Berklee College of Music, Boston University, and California State University, Los Angeles (BA 1973). During his studies he played with Sergio Mendes (1969–70), Bola Sete (1970–71), James Moody and Bobby Bryant (both 1972), and Charles Lloyd (1973), and recorded with Gene Ammons (1971). From 1973 to 1976 he worked with Leroy Vinnegar and also performed with Bobby Hutcherson (1974), Sahib Shihab (1974–5), and Sonny Criss (1974–5). In 1977 he formed his own trio (with the drummer Carl Burnett and the double bass player Louie Spears), which in 1978 recorded the album *Sooner or Later* (Dis. 792); he also recorded with Charles Owens in 1978. After the trio disbanded (1980) he formed a quartet. He has also appeared as a soloist (sometimes singing as well as playing) in California, and in Japan, Korea, and New Zealand. (*Feather–Gitler '70s*)

Dickerson, R. Q. (*b* Paducah, KY, *c*1898; *d* Glens Falls, NY, 21 Jan 1951). Trumpeter. He grew up in St. Louis, where he played in local theaters (1918–20) before leaving to tour with Wilson Robinson's Bostonians (1923). After extensive traveling the band took up residency at the Cotton Club, New York; by this time it was led by the violinist Andrew Preer. When Preer died in 1927 the group worked as the Cotton Club Orchestra, then the Missourians, until in 1930 it became known as Cab Calloway's Orchestra; Dickerson may be heard to advantage on the Missourians' *Ozark Mountain Blues* (1929, Vic. 38071). He also took part in small-group sessions led by Harry Cooper (1925) and Jasper Taylor (1928); Johnny Dodds played on the latter recordings. Dickerson left Calloway in 1931 and ceased to work as a musician.

based on *ChiltonW*

Dickerson, Walt (*b* Philadelphia, 1931). Vibraphonist. He graduated from Morgan State College in 1953 and then served in the army (1953–5). He worked in California, in his spare time leading a group that included Andrew Hill and Andrew Cyrille; in 1962 he was named "new star" by *Down Beat* and began to perform full-time, playing in clubs in New York. He first worked with Sun Ra in 1965, when they recorded *Impressions of a Patch of Blue*, an arrangement by Dickerson of music written by Jerry Goldsmith for the film *A Patch of Blue*. Dickerson then ceased to perform until 1975, after which time he worked principally in northern Europe. He renewed his association with Sun Ra and also played with Pierre Dørge and Richard Davis. Dickerson's is one of few distinctive voices on the vibraphone; he prefigured the melodic clarity and harmonic diversity of such players as Bobby Hutcherson and Karl Berger. He generally uses only two sticks, but is capable nevertheless of playing complex harmonies.

SELECTED RECORDINGS

Duos: with Sun Ra: *Visions* (1978, Ste. 1126); with P. Dørge: *Open Door* (1978, Ste. 1115)

As leader: *To my Queen* (1963, NewJ 8283); *Impressions of a Patch of Blue* (1965, MGM 4358); *Peace* (1975, Ste. 1042); *To my Queen Revisited* (1978, Ste. 1112)

BIBLIOGRAPHY

R. Dean: "Jazz Vibes: Bebop and After," *JJ*, xxx/4 (1977), 4

J. Diliberto: "Profile: Walt Dickerson," *DB*, xlvii/7 (1980), 53

C. Sheridan: "Walt Dickerson," *JJI*, xxxiii/5 (1980), 29

ROGER T. DEAN

Didjeridu. A trumpet of the Australian aborigines that is made from a hollowed tree branch and blown from one end without a separate mouthpiece. It has been used as a jazz instrument by CRAIG HARRIS.

Dies, Werner (*b* Frankfurt am Main, Germany, 15 Jan 1928). German clarinetist, tenor and alto saxophonist, and guitarist. He played guitar and tenor saxophone with Willy Berking's big band from 1947 to 1956, and recorded with it from 1953. He also belonged to dixieland groups, playing tenor saxophone with the Hot Club Combo and clarinet with the Two Beat Stompers; his recordings include *Sweet Georgia Brown* with the Hot Club Combo (1949, first issued on *Trümmer Jazz: Jazz and Hot Dance after the Nazis, 1946–1949*, 1946–9, Harl. 2052) and *Panama* with the Two Beat Stompers (1954, Bruns. 10020 [EP]). After leaving Berking he joined Hazy Osterwald's small group, with which he made numerous recordings and gained a degree of popularity in his own right; during his time with Osterwald he also recorded with Joe Turner (i) (1958). He worked as a studio musician from 1965 and continued to record as a freelance; he played electric bass guitar on Charly Antolini's *Soul Beat* (1968, MPS 15195). From 1970 he was active as an arranger of popular music for several recording companies. (*ReclamsJ*)

RAINER E. LOTZ

Digital recording. A term applied to techniques of sound recording (and playback) that use digital technology either in combination with analogue methods or alone; it is also used of the recordings made by these means. *See* RECORDING, §§I, 4, and II, 7.

Dillard, Bill [William] (*b* Philadelphia, 20 July 1911). Trumpeter and singer. He moved to New York in 1929, then toured with Jelly Roll Morton, and played with Bingie Madison (1930) and Luis Russell (1931–2). In 1933 he performed and made recordings with Benny Carter (including *Symphony in Riffs*, Col. 2898D, and others under Spike Hughes's name), then traveled to Europe with Lucky Millinder. In the mid-1930s he was a member of Teddy Hill's orchestra in Europe and while in Paris with Hill in 1937 made recordings with Dicky Wells; he is heard to advantage on *Hot Club Blues* (1937, Swing 3), recorded with Wells. Later he worked with Coleman Hawkins (briefly, 1939), Louis Armstrong (1940), and Red Norvo (1942–3) before becoming an actor and singer in Broadway shows. He continued to perform and record (notably in 1974 with Earle Warren) and has played at intervals into the 1980s, occasionally organizing big bands for special events. In 1981 he returned to Europe to take part in the successful revue *One mo' Time*.

Oral history material in *GBLnsa*.

BIBLIOGRAPHY

ChiltonW

A. Jackson: "Bill Dillard," *Jazz: the Australasian Contemporary Music Magazine*, no.10 (1982), 24 [interview]

STAN BRITT

Di Meola, Al (*b* Jersey City, NJ, 22 July 1954). Guitarist. He enrolled at the Berklee College of Music in 1971, but left in the second semester to join a jazz-rock quartet led by Barry Miles. When this disbanded in 1974 he returned to Berklee to study arranging, but shortly afterwards he was invited by Chick Corea to join RETURN TO FOREVER; he made his début with the group at Carnegie Hall. After leaving Corea in 1976 Di Meola recorded several highly acclaimed albums for Columbia. These were in a vein very similar to the work of Return to Forever, but he also recorded two albums in a flamenco style as a member of a trio of acoustic guitarists with John McLaughlin and Paco de Lucia (1982, 1983). He also toured occasionally with this group in the early 1980s. His final album for Columbia, *Scenario*, included his first experiments with the Fairlight Computer Musical Instrument and was a collaboration with Jan Hammer. In 1985 he recorded two albums of melodic, ethereal music which blended acoustic guitar, advanced synthesizer technology, and the percussion playing of Airto Moreira. The effects were extremely effective and represented a new and radical approach.

SELECTED RECORDINGS

(all recorded for Columbia unless otherwise indicated)

As leader: *Land of the Midnight Sun* (1976, PC34074); *Elegant Gypsy* (1976, PC34461); *Casino* (1977, JC35277); *Splendido Hotel* (1979, C2X36270); with J. McLaughlin and P. de Lucia: *Friday Night in San Francisco* (1980, FC37152); *Electric Rendezvous* (1981, FC37654); *Tour de Force: Live* (1982, FC38373); with McLaughlin and de Lucia: *Passion, Grace, and Fire* (1983, FC38645); *Scenario* (1983, FC38944); *Cielo e terra* (1985, Manhattan 53002); *Soaring through a Dream* (1985, Manhattan 53011); *Tirami su* (1987, Manhattan 46995)

As sideman with Return to Forever: *Where have I Known you Before?* (1974, Pol. 6509); *No Mystery* (1975, Pol. 6512); *Romantic Warrior* (1976, PC34076)

BIBLIOGRAPHY

H. Nolan: "Score One for Elegance: Al Di Meola," *DB*, xlv/4 (1978), 16
V. Trigger: "Al Di Meola," *GP*, xii/2 (1978), 34 [incl. transcr.]
B. Milkowski: "Al Di Meola: a New Scenario," *DB*, l/9 (1983), 14 [incl. discography]
J. Ferguson: "Al Di Meola: Leaving Fusion Behind, Redefines Himself," *GP*, xx/2 (1986), 63 [incl. discography]
——: "John McLaughlin, Al Di Meola, Frank Zappa: Synclavier," *GP*, xx/6 (1986), 122
Z. Stewart: "The New, Improved Al Di Meola," *DB*, liii/2 (1986), 19 [incl. discography]

BILL MILKOWSKI

Dingbod. Nickname of BOB KESTERTON.

DiNovi, Gene [Eugene] (*b* New York, 26 May 1928). Pianist. He began playing professionally at the age of 14, and later worked with Boyd Raeburn, Benny Goodman, and Chubby Jackson. After recording with Brew Moore and Lester Young (both 1948) and Jackson and Buddy DeFranco (both 1949) he worked as an accompanist for such singers as Anita O'Day, Peggy Lee, Tony Bennett, and Lena Horne. During the 1960s he wrote film scores in Hollywood, and in the early 1970s he moved to Toronto. He recorded as a leader in 1960 (*Scandinavian Suite*, Roul. 25065) and as a soloist in 1977 (*Softly, as I Leave you*, Pedimega 1), and also made two albums of duets with Ruby Braff (including *My Funny Valentine*, 1985, Pedimega 2). DiNovi is highly accomplished technically; his playing is influenced by that of Bud Powell, and also reveals his respect for the work of Lennie Tristano.

BIBLIOGRAPHY

M. Gardner: "Musicians Talking: Gene DiNovi," pt i, *JM*, no.192 (1971), 19; pt ii, *J&B*, i/3 (1971), 31 [interview]
G. DiNovi: "Bebop Forever," *Coda*, no. 181 (1981), 20

MARK GARDNER

Diorio, Joe [Joseph Louis] (*b* Waterbury, CT, 6 Aug 1936). Guitarist. During the 1960s he played in Chicago with Sonny Stitt, Eddie Harris, and Bennie Green; he also appeared at the *Down Beat* Festival in New York (1964). From 1968 to 1977 he was in Miami, where he performed with Stan Getz, Ira Sullivan, Wally Cirillo, Stanley Turrentine, and Freddie Hubbard. Thereafter he became active in Los Angeles as a freelance musician and began teaching at the Guitar Institute of Technology in Hollywood. Although Diorio is a skilled mainstream performer, he is also adept at playing in free-form styles. He has a facility for creating scalar lines and a penchant for employing wide intervals, which add a kinetic, angular dimension to his improvisations. This approach to playing is discussed in his instruction book for the guitar, *21st Century Intervallic Designs* (1978).

SELECTED RECORDINGS

As unaccompanied soloist: *Solo Guitar* (1975, Spitball 2)
Duos with Steve Bagby: *Straight Ahead to the Light* (1976, Spitball 5)
As sideman with S. Stitt: *My Main Man* (1964, Argo 744)

BIBLIOGRAPHY

D. Spitzer: "Expanding the Horizons of the Jazz Guitar," *GP*, x/8 (1976), 10
M. J. Summerfield: *The Jazz Guitar: its Evolution and its Players* (Gateshead, England, 1978), 83
L. Underwood: "Joe Diorio," *DB*, xlvii/7 (1980), 54
J. Diorio: "Tapping the Right Side of the Brain," *GP*, xxi/7 (1987)

JIM FERGUSON

Dip. A rapid, wide vibrato applied to the beginning of a note and ceasing shortly after the attack; it is notated by a U-shaped symbol. (M. Laplace: "La trompette et le cornet dans le jazz et la musique populaire, pt vi," *Brass Bulletin*, no.47 (1984), 39)

Di Pasqua, Michael (*b* Orlando, FL, 4 May 1953). Drummer and percussionist. He was brought up in a musical family and started to play professionally at an early age. He worked with the quintet led by Zoot Sims and Al Cohn, and with Gerry Mulligan, Chet Baker, and Jackie and Roy; he also recorded with Don Elliott (1975) and Ralph Towner (1979). From 1977 to 1980 he was a member of Double Image, led by David Friedman and Dave Samuels, then in 1981 recorded with Gallery. He has also recorded with Adelhard Roidinger (1981), Eberhard Weber (1982), and Jan Garbarek (1983–4); he is heard to advantage on Garbarek's *Wayfarer* (1983, ECM 1259). (I. Carr: "Di Pasqua, Michael," in I. Carr, D. Fairweather, and B. Priestley: *Jazz: the Essential Companion*, London, 1987)

Dippermouth. Nickname of LOUIS ARMSTRONG.

Dire. Italian record company and label. Established around 1971 by Tito Fontana, the company was devoted almost exclusively to recordings of Italian jazz of the 1970s. It also issued a session recorded in Milan in 1967 by Flavio Ambrosetti's hard-bop group. (A. G.: "C'est à 'Dire'," *Jm*, no. 269 (1978), 6)

Direct-to-disc recording. A term applied to a sound-recording technique of the mid-1970s in which the recording is made immediately on to a disc – that is, without the use of magnetic tape as the initial medium; *see* RECORDING, §§I, 3(iv), and II, 7.

Dirty Dozen Brass Band. New Orleans marching band. It grew out of a band of drums and kazoos that followed parades in New Orleans, and reached its fully developed form around

1975. There have been few changes in the band's personnel, which from 1978 included Gregory "Blodie" Davis (trumpet), Efrem Towns (trumpet), Charles Joseph (trombone), Roger Lewis (soprano and baritone saxophones), Kevin Harris (tenor saxophone), Kirk Joseph (sousaphone), Jenell Marshall (snare drum and voice), and Lionel Batiste and Benny Jones (both on bass drum). Its style blends elements of traditional New Orleans music, modern jazz, rhythm-and-blues, and the street culture of the city, and members of the band write the arrangements it plays. It has performed at social events, parades, and nightclubs in New Orleans, and at festivals in Tokyo, New York, and Europe, and has made several recordings (including *My Feet Can't Fail me Now*, 1984, Conc. 3005).

BIBLIOGRAPHY

T. Dent: "The Dirty Dozen Brass Band," *My Feet Can't Fail me Now* (Conc. 3005, 1984) [liner notes]

L. Birnbaum: "The Dirty Dozen Brass Band: Funkifying the New Orleans Tradition," *DB*, lii/8 (1985), 26

E. Cook: "The Modern Sound of New Orleans, 8: The Dirty Dozen," *JJI*, xxxviii/11 (1985), 12

R. J. Spedale, Jr.: "Dirty Dozen Brass Band: Dancing in the Street," *JF* [intl edn], no.93 (1985), 23

MARCEL JOLY

Discography. The systematic cataloguing of sound recordings. Data for listings, in which aspects of the physical characteristics, provenance, and contents of sound recordings are described, are acquired from the recordings themselves (with their containers and any accompanying written and iconographic materials), as well as from logbooks, lists, and catalogues compiled by the record producer or manufacturer, journals and other printed materials, and oral sources.

Accurate information about recorded performances is essential in jazz, where recordings rather than scores or sheet music are the principal sources for study. The standard information contained in jazz discographies consists of the name of the leader or group, the date and place of recording, the players and their instruments, the titles of tunes, the Matrix number, Take number, Issue number, and sometimes other kinds of number (see, for example, Master (i)), and the Record label name. Before the development of long-playing (LP) recordings, a unique matrix number was etched, embossed, or stamped onto the surface of each disc near or under the label. Since it was a common practice for several versions of a performance to be made in case of mishap (such as the destruction of a master recording or the negative stampers made from it and used to produce commercial pressings), each of the versions (or "takes") was customarily assigned an additional number or letter, which often appeared immediately after the matrix number. Take numbers are particularly important to the study of jazz, since two versions of the same piece, recorded only minutes apart, may differ significantly. With the advent of the LP and tape mastering in the late 1940s, the discographically convenient use of matrix and take designations was lost; an LP may include many unrelated performances of diverse origins, the identification of which poses particular problems for the discographer. These difficulties are often compounded by insufficient or misleading information supplied by record manufacturers. (*See also* Recording.)

The term "discography" itself was introduced in the 1930s as growing numbers of jazz enthusiasts sought to establish accurate information about personnel and recording dates. Early researchers also had to contend with the pseudonymous issuing of numerous recordings by well-known jazz bands. The field of jazz discography has been dominated from the start by Europeans. Two pioneering discographical works were published in 1936, Charles Delaunay's *Hot Discography* (in France) and Hilton Schleman's *Rhythm on Record* (in England). Delaunay's work laid the foundation for discographical research, notably in its use of matrix numbers to identify recordings, which has become standard. In 1942 Charles Edward Smith, with Frederic Ramsey and others, issued an important critical survey of jazz recordings entitled *The Jazz Record Book*, but the first true discography of importance by an American was Orin Blackstone's *Index to Jazz* (1945–8).

The most prominent jazz discographer since the early 1960s has been Brian Rust, an English recording historian whose *Jazz Records, 1897–1942* (1961, rev. and enlarged 5/1983), though restricted to 78-r.p.m. issues, is the basic research tool for jazz recordings in the first half of the 20th century and the only general work with both artist and title indexes; it is complemented by two other works by him, published in 1973 and 1975, covering the popular and dance recordings of the period. The Danish discographer Jørgen Grunnet Jepsen extended coverage into the 1950s and 1960s with his 11-volume *Jazz Records, 1942–[1969]*. The most recent attempt at a comprehensive jazz discography was made by the Belgian researcher Walter Bruyninckx, whose *60 Years of Recorded Jazz* (1978–82) attempts to include all jazz recordings to approximately 1977; supplements extend coverage of the work into the 1980s.

As serious interest in jazz grew, discographers began to produce works that dealt with specific aspects of the music. Such specialized discographies may focus on a musical style (e.g., Eric Raben's *A Discography of Free Jazz*, 1969), a geographical area (lists of this sort deal with recordings made or issued in a particular region or country, or by performers of a certain nationality), a record label (e.g., the discographies compiled by Michel Ruppli), a recording format (e.g., piano rolls, phonograph cylinders, or radio transcription discs), or (most commonly) the work of an individual performer. Artist discographies trace not only the performer's recordings as both leader and sideman, but often his noncommercial recordings as well, including private tapes and airchecks (i.e., performances recorded off the air); some list solos by the performer and may even use incipits to distinguish between takes. Bio-discographies, such as W. C. Allen's *Hendersonia* (1973), a detailed chronicle of the career of Fletcher Henderson, integrate biographical and discographical information. A variant of the performer discography, the "solography," developed most notably by the Norwegian discographer Jan Evensmo, identifies all the recorded solos by an artist within a given period, listing lengths and tempos and offering critical commentary; the majority of the performers dealt with in solographies have been swing musicians. The Dutch discographer Dick Bakker, founder and editor of the important jazz periodical *Micrography* and author of discographies of Charlie Parker, Duke Ellington, Billie Holiday, and Teddy Wilson, has designed a system of abbreviations to identify the plethora of reissue LPs and to facilitate comparisons between them. In the 1980s Bruyninckx began to issue a series of discographies dealing with specific musical styles.

Jazz discographies are for the most part still being produced by dedicated amateurs, who usually work without the benefit of institutional affiliation or financial support. They are part of an informal, worldwide cooperative network, within which circulate drafts of discographic projects for review. Several organizations supplement the research efforts of these informal associations. The International Association of Jazz Record Collectors holds an annual convention and publishes the quarterly *IAJRC Journal* (1968–). Notable among other current periodical publications that regularly contain jazz discographies are *Down Beat* (founded in 1934), *Swing Journal* (1947), *Record Research* (1955), *Discographical Forum* (1960), *Storyville* (1965), *Jazzforschung* (1969), the *Annual Review of Jazz Studies* (founded in 1973 as the *Journal of Jazz Studies*), and *Cadence* (1976).

Although the *Bielefelder Katalog*, first published in 1959, is technically an annual sales catalogue rather than a discography, it is among the most useful sources of discographical information; it provides lists of personnel, tune titles, and dates of recording, and is indexed by performer and (in some years) by tune title. Similarly, *The New Schwann* (first issued in 1953 as *Long Playing Record Catalog*) in many instances proves the sole source of album titles.

BIBLIOGRAPHY

D. Morgenstern: "Discography: the Thankless Science," *DBY 1966*, 57
W. C. Allen, ed.: *Studies in Jazz Discography*, i (New Brunswick, NJ, 1971) [proceedings of *Discographical Research, i New Brunswick, NJ, 1968; Discographical Research, ii New Brunswick, NJ, 1969; Preservation and Extension of the Jazz Heritage: New Brunswick, NJ, 1969*]
J. S. Patrick: "Discography as a Tool for Musical Research and Vice Versa," *JJS*, i/1 (1973), 65
D. E. Cooper: *International Bibliography of Discographies: Classical Music and Jazz & Blues, 1962–1972* (Littleton, CO, 1975)
B. Rust: *The American Record Label Book* (New Rochelle, NY, 1978)
——: *Brian Rust's Guide to Discography* (Westport, CT, and London, 1980)
D. Allen: *Bibliography of Discographies*, ii: *Jazz* (New York and London, 1981)

EDWARD BERGER/R

Discovery. Record company and label. The company was established in New York at the end of 1948 by Albert Marx, who had been a record producer since the early 1930s and supervised Art Tatum's first sessions. It rapidly became one of the most important independent enterprises of its day, issuing the earliest recordings of George Shearing and Red Norvo, and organizing Art Pepper's first session as a leader (1952). The company also released material by Dizzy Gillespie (his first recordings with a string section), Hampton Hawes, Mary Ann McCall, Eddie Bert, and Georgie Auld, and many others. Several of the company's early masters were sold to Savoy, and reissued in various anthologies. Discovery's operations declined after the 1950s, as did those of its associate, Trend; in the 1980s, however, Marx revived both companies in Los Angeles, issuing new recordings by Cedar Walton, Leonard Feather, and others.

MARK GARDNER

Disley, Diz [William Charles] (*b* Winnipeg, Canada, 27 May 1931). English guitarist of Canadian birth. His family moved to England shortly after he was born, and he grew up in Yorkshire. He first played banjo, and recorded with the Yorkshire Jazz Band in 1949. After military service he studied at art college, then moved in 1953 to London. The recordings of Django Reinhardt inspired him to take up guitar, and he played with Mick Mulligan for eight months before performing and recording with Ken Colyer (1954) and Cy Laurie and Sandy Brown (both 1956–7). Disley played with skiffle groups during the craze for this style of the late 1950s. At the same time he led his own swing group, the Soho String Quintet. Thereafter he worked with Kenny Ball and Alex Welsh, then performed at folk clubs and worked in radio and television. In 1973 he formed an association with Stephane Grappelli, with whom he toured internationally and made recordings (including the album *I got Rhythm*, 1973, BL 30158-9) for ten years. He reformed the Soho String Quintet in 1983 and recorded with Bireli Lagrene in 1985.

BIBLIOGRAPHY

G. Melly: *Owning up* (London, 1965)
D. Fairweather: "Disley, Diz," in I. Carr, D. Fairweather, and B. Priestley: *Jazz: the Essential Companion* (London, 1987)

CLARRIE HENLEY

Distel, Sacha (*b* Paris, 29 Jan 1933). French guitarist and singer. He studied piano from the age of five and guitar from 1948. He played with Bernard Peiffer (1952) and Bobby Jaspar and Henri Renaud (both 1953), and recorded with the pianist Raymond Le Senechal (1953); around this time he also performed with René Urtreger, Kenny Clarke, and Martial Solal. After becoming a successful pop singer he rarely worked as a jazz musician, except for occasional performances on guitar. In the mid-1950s he took part in several recording sessions in Paris with Jaspar, Lionel Hampton, and John Lewis, and with his own swing and bop bands; he may be heard to advantage on the LP *Afternoon in Paris* (Atl. 1267), which he recorded as a leader with Lewis in 1957. He also sang on recordings he made as a leader with Slide Hampton in 1968. Distel is a nephew of Ray Ventura. (*FeatherE*)

Ditmas, Bruce (*b* Atlantic City, NJ, 12 Dec 1946). Drummer. He grew up in Miami, where he played in bop groups with Ira Sullivan (1962–4). After touring with Judy Garland for two years he accompanied other popular singers in New York (1966–70). He performed and recorded with the Gil Evans Orchestra from 1971 to 1975, and during this period began an association with Enrico Rava that has lasted into the 1980s; Rava was a member of Ditmas's trio for the album *Aeray Dust* (1977, Chi. 195), and Ditmas recorded as a sideman for Rava in 1979 and 1983. Ditmas also worked with Joe Newman, Chet Baker, and Lee Konitz in the early 1970s and recorded with Johnny Coles (1971), Steve Kuhn (1972), Paul Bley (1974), and with Mike Brecker in the group Stardrive. In 1982 he played with Konitz and Evans in sessions that were broadcast on Italian radio. (*Feather–Gitler '70s*)

Diva. Record label. It was established by Columbia, and was used to issue records that were sold through the chain of stores owned by G. T. Grant. At first the catalogue was the same as that of another subsidiary of Columbia, Harmony (*see* HARMONY (ii)), but in 1930 a separate race series, the 6000G sequence, was issued on Diva.

DiVittorio, Vincent. *See* DEAN, VINNIE.

Dixieland jazz. A term applied to the jazz played by white musicians of the early New Orleans school, but sometimes also to NEW ORLEANS JAZZ as a whole and often to the post-1940 revival of this music (also known as TRADITIONAL JAZZ). Owing to the absence of recorded evidence, it is impossible to assess the stylistic differences between early black jazz in New Orleans and its white counterpart played by groups such as Papa Jack Laine's and others. However, early commentators and observers are fairly unanimous in pointing out that white musicians were slower to grasp the rhythmic swing and blues inflections essential to jazz, though at the same time they made important contributions to its repertory and harmonic and melodic vocabulary. The name "dixieland" derives from the Original Dixieland Jazz Band, a white New Orleans group which became internationally successful through its tours and recordings from 1917; it played a bowdlerized form of jazz decorated with coloristic and novelty effects borrowed from black jazz. As later white jazz groups, such as the New Orleans Rhythm Kings, showed a fuller understanding of black jazz, it became less necessary to distinguish between the New Orleans and dixieland styles. From the 1950s, during the revival of New Orleans jazz, a number of older dixieland musicians were recorded, notably under the auspices of the New Orleans Jazz Club.

BIBLIOGRAPHY

G. Schuller: *Early Jazz: its Roots and Musical Development* (New York, 1968)

C. G. Herzog zu Mecklenburg: "Dixieland-Stil," *Stilformen des Jazz*, i: *Vom Ragtime zum Chicago-Stil* (Vienna, 1973) [incl. discography by M. Scheffner]

J. BRADFORD ROBINSON

Dixieland Thumpers. Name used by a quartet that later became known as the CHICAGO FOOTWARMERS.

Dixie Stompers. Traditional-jazz septet. It was formed in Mons, Belgium, by the pianist Jean Leclère, who was later replaced as leader by the trumpeter Albert Langue. Considered the finest Belgian ensemble of its kind, it performed at major jazz festivals and toured the Belgian Congo; it also recorded between 1944 and 1958, notably with Nelson Williams and Benny Waters (both 1956).

ROBERT PERNET

Dixie Syncopators. The name used in 1925–7 by the band of KING OLIVER. It was in existence by early 1925 and consisted of ten players, including Oliver, Albert Nicholas, Barney Bigard, Luis Russell, and Paul Barbarin, with Bud Scott and Kid Ory being added later. The band was resident at the Plantation Café, Chicago (February 1925 to March 1927), then played for two weeks at the Savoy Ballroom in New York. It made a number of recordings on Brunswick's Vocalion label (1926–7, including *Sugar Foot Stomp/Wa wa wa*, 1926, Voc. 1033), on some of which the group was called the Savannah Syncopators. By autumn 1927 the most important players had left, but, working with musicians from the bands of Clarence Williams and Luis Russell, Oliver continued to use the name Dixie Syncopators on recordings until late 1928. One further recording, which Oliver made in 1931 as the leader of Bingie Madison's band, was issued under the name Savannah Syncopators.

BIBLIOGRAPHY

W. C. Allen and B. A. L. Rust: *King Joe Oliver* (Belleville, NJ, 1955) [completely rev. version by L. Wright (Chigwell, England, 1987)]

B. Rust: Liner notes, *King Oliver and his Dixie Syncopators* (Swaggie, 821-3, 1984)

For recordings and further bibliography *see* OLIVER, KING.

MIKE HAZELDINE

Dixon, Bill [William Robert] (*b* Nantucket, MA, 5 Oct 1925). Trumpeter, composer, and teacher. He grew up in New York, where, after studying painting at Boston University, he worked as a trumpeter and arranger. In 1962–3, with Archie Shepp, he led a free-jazz quartet, and in 1964 he presented a series of six concerts at the Cellar Café entitled the "October Revolution in Jazz," in which the musicians – including Sun Ra, John Tchicai, Roswell Rudd, Paul Bley, Milford Graves, David Izenzon, and Dixon's own sextet – were little known. The concerts, all performed before capacity audiences, marked the emergence of free jazz as a mature movement. At the end of the same year Dixon organized the JAZZ COMPOSERS GUILD, an influential but short-lived collective that endeavored to support the playing of jazz independently of nightclubs and booking agents; among its charter members were Cecil Taylor, Shepp, Sun Ra, Paul and Carla Bley, Burton Greene, Mike Mantler, Rudd, and Tchicai. In 1965 he began a fruitful collaboration with the dancer Judith Dunn that lasted ten years; they presented concerts of free jazz and dance at such events as the Newport Jazz Festival (1966). From 1968 Dixon has taught at Bennington College, first assisting Dunn as a consultant in dance, and later founding a department of black music. In 1986 he published *L'Opéra: a Collection of Letters, Writings, Musical Scores, Drawings, and Photographs* (North Bennington, VT). As a trumpeter he has an unusual conception of melodic improvisation, and makes much use of squeezed notes, unconventional intonation, excessive vibrato, distorted tones, and other expressive devices. He has presented new compositions at the international jazz festivals in Paris (1976), Verona (1980), and Zurich (1981).

SELECTED RECORDINGS

As unaccompanied soloist: *Collection* (c1970–1976, Cadence 1024–5)

As leader: with A. Shepp: *Archie Shepp–Bill Dixon Quartet* (1962, Savoy 12178); *Intents and Purposes* (1967, RCA LSP3844); *Bill Dixon in Italy* (1980, SN 1008, 1011); *November 1981* (1981, SN 1037–8); *Thoughts* (1985, SN 1111)

RECORDED COMPOSITIONS

(selective list; all recorded as leader)

12th December, Winter Song, on *Bill Dixon Septet/Archie Shepp and the New York Contemporary Five* (1964, Savoy 12184); Metamorphoses 1962–1966, on *Intents and Purposes* (1967, RCA LSP3844); Summer Song, on *Bill Dixon in Italy* (1980, SN 1008, 1011)

BIBLIOGRAPHY

D. Morgenstern and M. Williams: "The October Revolution: Two Views of the Avant Garde in Action," *DB*, xxxi/30 (1964), 15

R. Levin: "The Jazz Composers Guild: an Assertion of Dignity," *DB*, xxxii/10 (1965), 17

J. Anderson: "Judith Dunn and the Endless Quest," *Dance Magazine*, xli/11 (1967), 48

E. Jost: *Free Jazz* (Graz, Austria, 1974)

V. Wilmer: *As Serious as your Life: the Story of the New Jazz* (London, 1977, rev. 1980), 213

R. Riggins: "Prof. Bill Dixon: Intents of an Innovator," *DB*, xlvii/8 (1980), 30

B. Rusch: "Bill Dixon: Interview," *Cadence*, viii (1982), no.3, p.5; no.4, p.20; no.5, p.14

BARRY KERNFELD

Dixon, Charlie [Charles Edward] (*b* Jersey City, NJ, *c*1898; *d* New York, 6 Dec 1940). Banjoist and arranger. He played in New York and Boston before joining Sam Wooding at the Nest Club, New York, in 1922; later he played with the violinist Ralph "Shrimp" Jones. He recorded with Fletcher Henderson in May 1923, and became a regular member of his band in January the following year (for illustration *see* JAZZ (i), fig.2); he continued to arrange pieces for Henderson after leaving the group around 1928. Dixon then led a band that accompanied the dancer Cora LaRedd. He was mainly active as an arranger and composer during the 1930s; his arrangement for Chick Webb of *Harlem Congo* (1937, Decca 1681) is a good example of his style. (W. C. Allen: *Hendersonia: the Music of Fletcher Henderson and his Musicians: a Bio-discography*, Highland Park, NJ, 1973)

based on *ChiltonW*

Dixon, Eric [Big Daddy] (*b* New York, 28 March 1930). Tenor saxophonist. He played bugle as a child and at the age of 12 took up the tenor saxophone, which he studied privately for five years. After acquiring further experience as a musician in the US Army (1951–3) he worked as a freelance in New York and played with Cootie Williams (1954) and Johnny Hodges (1955). In 1956 he played and recorded with Bennie Green and took up the flute in addition to his principal instrument; during the following years he worked again as a freelance, belonged to the house band at the Apollo Theatre in New York, and in

1959 toured Europe and recorded with the drummer Curly Hamner; in 1960 he joined the band of Quincy Jones, with whom in the following year he also toured Europe and recorded. From 1961 he was a tenor saxophone and flute soloist in Count Basie's orchestra. He retired from music in 1972, but resumed his career in 1975 when he rejoined Basie's orchestra, of which he became the principal tenor saxophone soloist in October 1977; he remained a member of the band after Basie's death in 1984.

SELECTED RECORDINGS

As leader: *Eric's Edge* (1974, MJR 8124)

As sideman: C. Basie: *Count Basie and the Kansas City 7* (1962, Imp. 15); *On my Way and Shoutin' Again* (1962, Verve 68511); *Lil' Ol' Groovemaker* (1963, Verve 68549); R. Eldridge: *The Nifty Cat Strikes West* (1966, MJR 8121)

BIBLIOGRAPHY

FeatherE; *Feather '60s*; *Feather–Gitler '70s*

S. Dance: *The World of Count Basie* (New York and London, 1980) [colln of previously pubd interviews], 216

D. J. Gibson: "Count Basie Saxophone Section Celebrates 50th Anniversary," *Saxophone Journal*, xi/3 (1986), 40; xi/4 (1987), 39 [interview]

EDDIE LAMBERT

Dixon, George (*b* New Orleans, 8 April 1909). Trumpeter, saxophonist, and arranger. He began playing violin as a youth in Natchez, Mississippi, and later took up alto saxophone. In 1926, after leading the band at Arkansas State College, he moved to Chicago, and played there and in Gary, Indiana. From 1928 to 1930 he was a member of Sammy Stewart's band. He then recorded with Alex Hill and joined Earl Hines in Chicago, remaining with the group until 1942 (for illustration *see* HINES, EARL); among his recordings during this period is *Hines Rhythm* (1937, first issued on *Oh, Father!*, 1933–8, Epic 3223), on which he may be heard playing both trumpet and saxophone. After leading a band at the Naval Air Station in Memphis (1942–5) he returned to Chicago, where he worked as a freelance and formed his own band, which from 1946 played a long residency at the Circle Inn. He ceased playing full-time in 1951, but continued to lead his own band into the 1980s.

BIBLIOGRAPHY

S. Dance: *The World of Earl Hines* (New York, 1977) [interviews], 160

D. J. Travis: *An Autobiography of Black Jazz* (Chicago, 1983) [incl. interviews], 284

based on *ChiltonW*

Dixon, Joe [Joseph] (*b* Lynn, MA, 21 April 1917). Clarinetist and saxophonist. He began learning clarinet at the age of eight, then had lessons in Boston and studied harmony at the New England Conservatory. He later took up saxophones and flute. In 1934 he moved to New York and joined the orchestra of the violinist Bill Staffon. He played with Tommy Dorsey from the summer of 1936 into 1947 and was a prominent member of his group the Clambake Seven. After a brief spell with the pianist Gus Arnheim and a year with Bunny Berigan (1937–8) he was for some time associated with Fred Waring's band (1939–43). He worked with Eddie Condon after leaving the navy (1946), and was a member of Miff Mole's group at Nick's, New York (1947–8). In the 1940s and 1950s he was active as a freelance, and in the early 1960s he led the Long Island Jazz Quartette (1960–63). His career as a performer was interrupted when he was injured in an automobile accident, but he worked as a disc jockey until 1970. From then for a decade he was leader of the Nassau County (New York) Jazz Festival Orchestra, and from 1973 to 1981 led his own Nassau Neophonic Jazz Ensemble. He formed the Swing Legacy Band in 1980. Dixon's playing is influenced by that of Don Murray, Irving Fazola, and Benny Goodman.

SELECTED RECORDINGS

As sideman: B. Staffon: Heartstrings (1935, Bb 6048); T. Dorsey: Rhythm Saved the World/At the Codfish Ball (1936, Vic. 25314); E. Condon: Oh! Lady be Good (1945, Decca 23431); B. Gowans: *New York Nine* (1946, RCA LPM3000), incl. Carolina in the Morning, I'm coming, Virginia

BIBLIOGRAPHY

ChiltonW; *FeatherE*

RAYMOND J. GARIGLIO

Dixon, Lawrence (*b* Chillicothe, OH, *c*1895; *d* Chicago, Jan 1970). Banjoist and guitarist. He grew up in a musical family. After playing with the pianist Sammy Stewart in Ohio and Chicago (1923–8) he joined Dave Peyton's band at the Regal Theatre in Chicago as a cellist. From 1931 to 1937 he was with Earl Hines (for illustration *see* HINES, EARL); his solid rhythm guitar playing may be heard on *I want a lot of love* (1933, Bruns. 6710; it is widely held that Dixon wrote the arrangement for this recording). He then worked as a freelance in Chicago, and from the early 1950s to the mid-1960s played frequently in Franz Jackson's Original Jass All Stars. Thereafter ill-health forced him to curtail his activities.

based on *ChiltonW*

Dobschinski [Dobrzynski], **Walter** (*b* Berlin, 29 Oct 1908). German trombonist, arranger, composer, and bandleader. He studied piano at the Berlin Conservatory and from 1930 played trombone in Teddy Stauffer's group, with which he toured Switzerland, Germany, and the Netherlands and played on the SS *Reliance* (1936). He heard Duke Ellington, the Casa Loma Orchestra, Adrian Rollini, and others in the USA. From 1936 to 1939 he recorded with Stauffer, for whom he also worked as a music director and arranger. He played with Kurt Hohenberger in 1939, various studio groups to the end of World War II, and the Deutsches Tanz- und Unterhaltungsorchester in 1942. In 1947 he formed a swing band for Radio Berlin with which he recorded about 70 tracks, including several with Rex Stewart (1948). He led a big band in the early 1950s and later worked exclusively as an arranger. Dobschinski's playing is well represented on the album *Walter Dobschinski und seine Swing Band* (1947–54, Odeon 1C134-32428–9); his best-known compositions, all of which were written after World War II, include *Dob's Boogie*, *Dob's Rag*, *Dob's Dixie*, and *Schade um die Zeit*. (G. Conrad: *Posaunen-Dob: kleine Biographie Walter Dobschinskis*, Menden, Germany, 1983)

GERHARD CONRAD

Dodds, Baby [Warren] (*b* New Orleans, 24 Dec 1898; *d* Chicago, 14 Feb 1959). Drummer, brother of Johnny Dodds. He played in New Orleans with Bunk Johnson, Papa Celestin, and others before working in Fate Marable's riverboat band (1918–21), where he acquired a commanding reputation among New Orleans jazz musicians. In 1922 he was invited to San Francisco to join King Oliver, with whom he made his first recordings the following year in Chicago. Dodds remained in Chicago for the next two decades, recording as a freelance in historic sessions with Jelly Roll Morton and Louis Armstrong (1927) and playing in small groups led by his brother. With the revival of New Orleans jazz around 1940, Dodds was much sought after for small traditional groups led by Jimmie Noone, Johnson, Sidney Bechet, and others. He played regularly for radio broadcasts in 1947 and toured Europe with Mezz Mezzrow in 1948. In the final decade of his life he was largely incapacitated by ill-health, but he continued playing until 1957.

Dodds was the leading jazz drummer in the New Orleans style, and his equipment and technique became standard. Many younger drummers learned directly from him in Chicago, among them Dave Tough and Gene Krupa, to whom he imparted his secrets of drum accompaniment and tuning. Dodds's basic style derived from the short roll or ruff, played with a drive and precision that set him apart from his contemporaries. By varying his patterns throughout a performance he developed some of the earliest idiomatic accompaniments to improvised jazz ensembles and solos. Late in life he set down his knowledge of jazz drumming in a remarkable series of recorded solos with explanatory commentary, which serve as unique documents of New Orleans drumming style.

Oral history material in *LNT*.

For illustrations *see* DRUM SET, fig.4, JOHNSON, BUNK, NIGHTCLUBS AND OTHER VENUES, fig.3, and OLIVER, KING.

SELECTED RECORDINGS

As leader: Careless Love (1945, BN 518); Drum Improvisation no.1 (1946, Cir. [USA] 1001); Drum Improvisation no.2 (1946, Cir. [USA] 1039); *Footnotes to Jazz* (1946–51, FW 30)

As sideman: K. Oliver: I'm going to wear you off my mind (1923, Gen. 5134); J. R. Morton: Billy Goat Stomp (1927, Vic. 20772); L. Armstrong: Wild Man Blues (1927, OK 8474); J. Dodds: Weary City (1928, Vic. 38004); B. Johnson: In Gloryland (1945, AM 101)

BIBLIOGRAPHY

G. Helliwell and P. Taylor: "Discography of Warren 'Baby' Dodds," *JJ*, iv (1951), no.3, p.3; no.4, p.19; no.5, p.17

N. Hentoff: "Warren 'Baby' Dodds," *The Jazz Makers: Essays on the Greats of Jazz*, ed. N. Shapiro and N. Hentoff (New York, 1957/*R*1979), 18

W. Dodds and L. Gara: *The Baby Dodds Story* (Los Angeles, 1959)

B. Russell: "Warren 'Baby' Dodds," *SL*, x/3–4 (1959), 7

B. King: "The Gigantic Baby Dodds," *JR*, iii/7 (1960), 12

G. Wettling: "A Tribute to Baby Dodds," *DB*, xxix/7 (1962), 21

M. Williams: *Jazz Masters of New Orleans* (New York and London, 1967/*R*1978)

E. Lambert: "William Russell's New Orleans Recordings," *JM*, no.183 (1970), 3

T. D. Brown: *A History and Analysis of Jazz Drumming to 1942* (diss., U. of Michigan, 1976), 204–45

W. Dodds: "'Oh, Play that Thing'," *Selections from the Gutter: Jazz Portraits from "The Jazz Record"*, ed. A. Hodes and C. Hansen (Berkeley, CA, Los Angeles, and London, 1977), 98

W. J. Schafer and R. B. Allen: *Brass Bands and New Orleans Jazz* (Baton Rouge, LA, and London, 1977), 75

L. Gara: "Baby Dodds Remembered," *MR*, x/2 (1982), 1

D. Read: "From the Past: Baby Dodds," *MD*, viii/8 (1984), 54

J. BRADFORD ROBINSON

Dodds, Johnny [John M.] (*b* New Orleans, 12 April 1892; *d* Chicago, 8 Aug 1940). Clarinetist, brother of Baby Dodds. He was brought up in a musical family, and may have played guitar before taking up clarinet at the relatively late age of 17; apart from some lessons from Lorenzo Tio, Jr., he was largely self-taught. Around 1912 he joined Kid Ory's band in New Orleans, where he played intermittently for the next six years. After touring in Fate Marable's riverboat band (1917) and with a road show he returned briefly to Ory's group in 1919, then left New Orleans permanently to join King Oliver in Chicago. During his years with Oliver he traveled to the West Coast, and, as a member of the Creole Jazz Band, took part in Oliver's historic recordings in Richmond, Indiana, and Chicago in 1923. A year later, also in Chicago, he assumed the leadership of Freddie Keppard's house band at Kelly's Stables. He directed this band for six years, during which time he also participated in studio recordings with Louis Armstrong (the Hot Fives and Hot Sevens), with Jelly Roll Morton, and with his brother in small groups (including the BLACK BOTTOM STOMPERS, the CHICAGO FOOTWARMERS, the Dixieland Thumpers, the STATE STREET RAMBLERS, and the Washboard Band). With the decline of the New Orleans style in the 1930s, Dodds continued to lead a band part-time at various locations in Chicago, often in conjunction with his brother.

Dodds was a leading clarinetist in the New Orleans style, which to many he represented in its purest form. Unlike his contemporaries Jimmie Noone and Sidney Bechet, he had an uneven command of technique, and his solos were sometimes marred by faulty execution; nevertheless his playing in ensembles was exemplary, as is attested by the several hundred small-band recordings he made with some of the leading jazz musicians of the day. Dodds's best work, played with a highly expressive vibrato centered slightly beneath true pitch, is permeated by a deep feeling for the blues, of which he was an outstanding early interpreter.

SELECTED RECORDINGS

As leader: After you've gone (1927, Bruns. 3568); Blue Clarinet Stomp (1928, Vic. 21554); Weary City (1928, Vic. 38004); Bull Fiddle Blues (1928, Vic. 21552)

As sideman: K. Oliver: High Society Rag (1923, OK 4933); L. Armstrong: Alligator Crawl (1927, OK 8482); S.O.L. Blues (1927, Col. 35661); J. R. Morton: Wild Man Blues (1927, Bb 10256)

BIBLIOGRAPHY

R. Leydi: "Johnny Dodds," *Musica jazz*, vi/2 (1950); repr. in *Jazz Reprints*, i/3 (1963), 44

A. Hodeir: *Hommes et problèmes du jazz, suivi de La religion du jazz* (Paris, 1954; Eng. trans., rev. Hodeir, as *Jazz: its Evolution and Essence*, New York, 1956/*R*1975)

G. E. Lambert: *Johnny Dodds* (New York, 1962); repr. in *Kings of Jazz*, ed. S. Green (New York, 1978)

S. Brown: "Johnny Dodds: a Clarinettist's View," *Sv*, no.3 (1966), 11

M. Williams: *Jazz Masters of New Orleans* (New York and London, 1967/*R*1978), 87

G. Schuller: *Early Jazz: its Roots and Musical Development* (New York, 1968)

J. Dodds II: Liner notes, *Chicago Mess Around* (Mlst. 2011, 1969)

J. F. Riesco: *El jazz clasico y Johnny Dodds, su rey sin corona* (Santiago, 1972), 193–273

L. Wright: "Dodds in Duo," *Sv*, no.41 (1972), 170; no.43 (1972), 11; no.45 (1973), 109

R. von Arx: "Johnny Dodds Discographically," *Sv*, no.49 (1973), 4

D. M. Bakker: "Johnny Dodds, 1923–1940," *Micrography*, no.44 (1977), 7 [discography]

H. Lyttelton: *The Best of Jazz*, i: *Basin Street to Harlem: Jazz Masters and Masterpieces, 1917–1930* (London, 1978)

J. BRADFORD ROBINSON

Dodge, Joe [Joseph George] (*b* Monroe, WI, 9 Feb 1922). Drummer. He moved with his family to San Francisco, where he played drums in school bands. During his military service (1942–6) he played in army bands and met Paul Desmond, with whom he played in 1947. He then toured and recorded with Nick Esposito (1948–9) and performed and recorded with Dave Brubeck (1953–6); he also recorded with Desmond. Good examples

Johnny Dodds, Chicago, 1938

of his playing may be heard on *I want to be happy* and *Le souk*, both on Brubeck's album *Jazz Goes to College* (1953–4, Col. CL566). (*FeatherE*)

Dodgion [née Giaimo], **Dottie** [Dorothy] (*b* Brea, nr Fullerton, CA, 23 Sept 1929). Drummer. She sang with Charles Mingus before taking up drumming in the early 1950s; she was greatly encouraged by Jerry Dodgion, whom she married in 1952. She worked in Las Vegas in the late 1950s with Carl Fontana, then settled in New York, where she immediately joined Benny Goodman (1961). Later she played with Marian McPartland, the septet led by Billy Mitchell and Al Grey, Wild Bill Davison, and the Al Cohn–Zoot Sims Quintet; she performed and recorded with Ruby Braff in 1972. In the mid-1970s she parted from her husband and moved to California, where she performed as a drummer and singer; she recorded the album *Now's the Time* (1977, Hal. 115) with McPartland's quintet in 1977. After serving as the music director of a jazz club in Washington she returned to New York in 1979; she played with Melba Liston's group the following year.

BIBLIOGRAPHY

Feather–Gitler '70s
C. Sloane: "A Drum is a Woman: the Swinging Dottie Dodgion," *DB*, xxxvi/6 (1969), 17
S. Placksin: *American Women in Jazz, 1900 to the Present: their Words, Lives, and Music* (New York, 1982), 235
K. Alleyne: "Portraits: Dottie Dodgion," *MD*, vii/9 (1983), 57
L. Dahl: *Stormy Weather: the Music and Lives of a Century of Jazzwomen* (London, Melbourne, Australia, and New York, 1984), 218

KIMBERLY McCORD

Dodgion, Jerry (*b* Richmond, CA, 29 Aug 1932). Alto and soprano saxophonist, and flutist. He played and recorded with Gerald Wilson (1953–5), then toured Europe and recorded with Red Norvo (1958–61); he also played in several of Benny Goodman's bands, touring South America (1961) and recording in Moscow (1962). As a freelance in New York during the 1960s he played occasionally in a quartet with his wife, Dottie Dodgion, and recorded regularly in Oliver Nelson's big bands (1961–7). He was one of the original members of the Thad Jones–Mel Lewis Orchestra (formed 1965) and remained with the band until 1979 (as the lead alto and soprano saxophonist from 1971; for illustration *see* JONES, fig.1*b*). He also performed and recorded with Duke Pearson's big band (1967–70), recorded with Count Basie (1966, 1970), and, while touring Europe with Jones and Lewis, recorded with George Gruntz and Klaus Weiss (both 1974). In 1983 he played with Astrud Gilberto.

Dodgion's saxophone playing, influenced by that of Charlie Parker, Art Pepper, and Jerome Richardson, is well represented by his inventive solo on *Tiptoe* (1970), which draws on blues formulas and demonstrates a relaxed rhythmic sense and an ability to develop motifs. His work for Jones and Lewis also includes the arrangement of Marian McPartland's *Ambiance* for the album *Potpourri* (1974, Philadelphia International 33152). As a studio musician he has played mostly with big bands, but he may also be heard as a soloist on recordings with small groups led by Charlie Mariano, Weiss, Tommy Flanagan, McPartland, and others.

SELECTED RECORDINGS

As sideman: C. Mariano: *Beauties of 1918* (1957, WP 1245); T. Jones and M. Lewis: *Live at the Village Vanguard* (1967, SolS 18016), incl. Little Pixie; H. Hancock: *Speak Like a Child* (1968, BN 84279); T. Jones and M. Lewis: *Consummation* (1970, BN 84346), incl. Tiptoe; M. McPartland: *Portrait of Marian McPartland* (1979, Conc. 101); T. Flanagan: *Communication* (1979, PW 3224)

BIBLIOGRAPHY

L. Henshaw: "Back when Swing was King," *MM* (6 Sept 1969), 9
J. Dodgion: "The Solution to Doubling Problems: just Do it," *CI*, x/7 (1972), 14

KIMBERLY McCORD

Doggett, Bill [William Ballard] (*b* Philadelphia, 16 Feb 1916). Pianist and organist. He led his own band in 1938 which toured accompanying Lucky Millinder. After performing and recording with Jimmy Mundy (1939) he played in Millinder's band (1940–42). Later he was the pianist and arranger for the popular group the Ink Spots (1942–4), then worked as a freelance in the mid-1940s. During this period he recorded with Jimmy Rushing and Lucky Thompson (both 1945), and most notably with Illinois Jacquet (1945–6). After working with Willie Bryant (1946) he joined Louis Jordan (1949). During this association he took up organ, influenced by the work of Wild Bill Davis, whom he had replaced in Jordan's group. Doggett left Jordan in 1951 and achieved considerable success as a rhythm-and-blues musician; several of his recordings (including *Honky Tonk*, 1956) became hits. He continued to lead his own groups into the 1980s, and from the 1970s toured Europe regularly. He also participated in occasional reunions with the Ink Spots. Doggett's early style as an organist did much to popularize the instrument. He is also a highly capable swing pianist.

For illustration *see* ORGAN, fig.2.

SELECTED RECORDINGS

As leader: Big Dog (1952, King 4530); *Everybody Dance to the Honky Tonk* (1956, King 531), incl. Honky Tonk; *Back Again with More Bill Doggett* (1959–60, King 723); *Bill Doggett* (1971, BB 33029); *Lionel Hampton Presents Bill Doggett* (1977, Who's who in Jazz 21002)

As sideman: I. Jacquet: Jacquet in the Box (1946, Savoy 910); Doggin' with Doggett (1946, Savoy 8069) [EP]; B. Tate: *Jumpin' on the West Coast* (1947, BL 172); E. Davis: Mountain Oysters/Huckle Boogie (1949, King 4321); L. Jordan: Blue Light Boogie (1950, Decca 27114); E. Fitzgerald: Smooth Sailing (1951, Decca 27693); P. Quinichette: Prevue/No Time (1952, EmA 6002) [EP]; V. Dickenson: Tenderly/Lion's Den (1952, BN 1600); Gettin' Sentimental/In a Mellotone (1952, BN 1601)

BIBLIOGRAPHY

ChiltonW; *FeatherE*; *Feather '60s*; *Feather–Gitler '70s*
A. Shaw: *Honkers and Shouters: the Golden Years of Rhythm and Blues* (New York, 1978)

SCOTT YANOW

Doit. A GLISS rising from the end of a note.

Doldinger, Klaus (*b* Berlin, 12 May 1936). German tenor and soprano saxophonist and leader. After studying classical piano and clarinet at the Robert Schumann-Institut der Musikhochschule Rheinland, Düsseldorf, he played traditional jazz as an amateur from 1952 and won several awards at jazz competitions as an alto saxophonist (1955–6). In 1960 he performed in New Orleans, Chicago, and New York (at Birdland) as the leader of the Feetwarmers, a traditional-jazz group, and of Oskar's Trio, which played hard bop. He formed a hard-bop quartet that included Ingfried Hoffman as a sideman, with which he toured Europe, Africa, South America (1965), and Asia (1969); at the same time he worked in Germany as a music director of a stage production. In 1970 he formed a group that became known as PASSPORT the following year; he led it in concerts and recordings into the 1980s. In addition to his work in jazz Doldinger has composed the scores to the films *Das Boot* and *The Eternal Story*.

SELECTED RECORDINGS

As leader: *Doldinger Live at the Blue Note, Berlin* (1963, Phi. 48067); *Doldinger Goes On* (1967, Phi. 843966); *Blues Happening* (1968, Lib. 83167); *Doldinger the Ambassador* (1969, Lib. 83317–8); of Passport: *Looking Thru* (1973, Atco 7042), *Cross-Colateral* (1974, Atco 36-107), *Infinity Machine* (1976, Atco 36-132), *Iguaçu* (*c*1977, Atco 36-149)

BIBLIOGRAPHY

Feather '60s; Feather–Gitler '70s
"Oskars Trio setzt sich durch," *JP*, x/3 (1961), 68
K.-U. Reinke: "Klaus Doldinger," *JP*, x/6 (1961), 156
"Doldinger unterschrieb Exklusiv-Vertrag," *JP*, xii/3 (1963), 51
"Doldinger mit Trunk," *JP*, xiii/5 (1964), 109
"Das Klaus Doldinger Quartett in Südamerika," *JP*, xiv/5 (1965), 112
H. Harig: "Klaus Doldinger und Passport," *Sounds*, v/7 (1973), 23
C. Mitchell: "Klaus Doldinger's Passport to the Sounds of Tomorrow," *DB*, xlii/14 (1975), 19 [incl. discography]
K. Doldinger: "Unser Jazz leidet an Vergangenheit," *Lui* (1978), no.11, p.74

HEIDI BOULTON

Dolphy, Eric (Allan) (*b* Los Angeles, 20 June 1928; *d* Berlin, 29 June 1964). Alto saxophonist, bass clarinetist, and flutist. He took up clarinet at about the age of six, and while in junior high school played alto saxophone professionally at dances. After studying music at Los Angeles City College he played lead alto saxophone in Roy Porter's band (1948–50). He then served in the US Army for two years, after which he transferred to the US Naval School of Music (1952). He returned to Los Angeles in 1953 and performed locally in various groups before joining Chico Hamilton's quintet early in 1958 (see illustration). Late the following year he settled in New York, where he joined Charles Mingus's group. During his time with Mingus (1959–60) he played a great deal as a freelance and recorded his first albums as a leader, but thereafter he ceased to work steadily, even as his fame grew. In mid-1961 he led a quintet with Booker Little. He played in Europe in August to September of that year, and again in November to December during a brief spell with John Coltrane (to March 1962). In March 1962 he formed a group which made few public appearances and proved short-lived, and in November he joined John Lewis's Orchestra U.S.A. He spent the rest of his short career working as a freelance with Mingus, Lewis, and Coltrane. He died after a heart attack occasioned by diabetes.

Dolphy was a highly versatile musician, playing jazz but also performing third-stream music by Gunther Schuller and pieces such as Edgard Varèse's *Density 21.5* at the Ojai (California) Music Festival in 1962. This close link to 20th-century art music influenced his fondness for dissonant harmonies in jazz. His startling intonation, especially on alto saxophone, reflected the acknowledged influence of Ornette Coleman, as well as his love of African and Indian music; he also imitated bird calls. As a jazz improviser Dolphy was unrivaled in his ability to leap fluently between traditional and avant-garde idioms. His lyrical interpretation on flute of *You don't know what love is* (1964) epitomizes the conventional side of his art, while his radicalism is most apparent in his bass clarinet improvisations on Coleman's revolutionary album *Free Jazz* (1960) and his bass clarinet or alto saxophone "conversations" with Mingus on *What Love* (1960) and *Epitaph* (1962). An intense, passionate improviser, Dolphy constantly surprised his listeners with his rapid flow of ideas and his unexpected phrasing and intervals. Perhaps his greatest contribution was his exploration of the bass clarinet as a medium for jazz improvisation. A volume of transcriptions of Dolphy's solos, *Dolphy Series Limited*, has been published by Andrew White.

See also CLARINET, §4.

SELECTED RECORDINGS

As leader: *Outward Bound* (1960, NewJ 8236); *Eric Dolphy at the Five Spot* (1961, NewJ 8260, Prst. 7294); *The Eric Dolphy Memorial Album* (1961, Prst. 7334); *Eric Dolphy in Europe* (1961, Debut [Den.] 136); *Conversations* (1963, FM 308); *Iron Man* (1963, Douglas 785); *Out to Lunch* (1964, BN 84163); *Last Date* (1964, Lml. 86013), incl. You don't know what love is

As sideman: C. Hamilton: *Gongs East* (1958, WB 1271); C. Mingus: *Charles Mingus Presents Charles Mingus* (1960, Can. 9005), incl. What Love; *Mingus!* (1960, Can. 9021); G. Schuller: *Jazz Abstractions* (1960, Atl. 1365); O. Coleman: *Free Jazz* (1960, Atl. 1364); on J. Coltrane: *Live at the Village Vanguard* (1961, Imp. 10), Spiritual; on J. Coltrane: *Impressions* (1961, Imp. 42), India; C. Mingus: *Town Hall Concert* (1962, UA 15024), incl. Epitaph; *The Great Concert of Charles Mingus* (1964, Amer. 003–5)

Members of Chico Hamilton's quintet at the French Lick Jazz Festival, French Lick, IN, August 1959: (left to right) Hamilton (drums), Wyatt Ruther (double bass), Fred Katz (cello), and Eric Dolphy (alto saxophone)

BIBLIOGRAPHY

D. DeMicheal: "John Coltrane and Eric Dolphy Answer the Critics," *DB*, xxix/8 (1962), 20

D. Heckman: "The Value of Eric Dolphy," *DB*, xxxi/27 (1964), 17

J. Cooke: "Eric Dolphy," *JM*, xi/11 (1966), 25

V. Simosko and B. Tepperman: *Eric Dolphy: a Musical Biography and Discography* (Washington, 1974)

R. Jannotta: "God Bless the Child: an Analysis of an Unaccompanied Bass Clarinet Solo," *Jf*, ix (1977), 37

U. Reichardt: *Like a Human Voice: the Eric Dolphy Discography* (Schmitten, Germany, 1986)

BARRY KERNFELD

Domanico, Chuck [Charles Louis] (*b* Chicago, 20 Jan 1944). Bass player. He first studied trumpet, and took up double bass in his last year at high school. After moving to Los Angeles in the mid-1960s, he performed and recorded with Don Ellis at the Monterey Jazz Festival (1966). He then worked with John Guerin and Tom Scott, recording in a quartet under the leadership of Roger Kellaway (1967), Scott (1969–70), and Victor Feldman (1973). Domanico also recorded in other ensembles under Scott (1968) and Feldman (1977), played in Kellaway's Cello Quartet (a group made up of double bass, piano, percussion and cello), and made several LPs with Shelly Manne (1977–80). Active as a studio musician in southern California, Domanico performs in both rock and jazz groups. He has played regularly on television shows, and has won several awards for studio players given by the National Academy of Recording Arts and Sciences.

SELECTED RECORDINGS

As sideman: C. McRae: *The Great American Songbook* (1971, Atl. 2–904); B. Kessel: *Barney Plays Kessel* (1975, Conc. 9); S. Manne: *Essence* (1977, Gal. 5101)

BIBLIOGRAPHY

J. L. Ginibre and P. Carles: "Dictionnaire de la contrebasse," *Jm*, no.166 (1969), 37, esp.39

S. Y. Bradley: "Profile: Chuck Domanico," *DB*, xlv/12 (1978), 42

WILLIAM S. BROCKMAN

Domicile. Nightclub in Frankfurt am Main, Germany, later known as Der Jazzkeller; *see* NIGHTCLUBS AND OTHER VENUES.

Dominique, Albert. *See* ALBERT, DON.

Dominique, Natty [Anatie] (*b* New Orleans, 2 Aug 1896; *d* Chicago, 30 Aug 1982). Trumpeter, uncle of Don Albert and cousin of Barney Bigard. As a youth he was coached by Manual Perez, and later played in parades with brass bands. Having left New Orleans in 1913, he spent almost a decade with brass bands, working in Chicago and Michigan. By the early 1920s he was an important figure in the musical life of Chicago. He performed with Jelly Roll Morton (recording in 1923), Carroll Dickerson, the violinist Al Simeon, Jimmie Noone, and Louis Armstrong. He also played and made recordings with Johnny Dodds (including, in 1928, his own composition *Brush Stomp*), with whom he remained for most of the 1930s. Early in the next decade, however, a heart condition forced Dominique to cease playing professionally, and he found employment as a porter at Chicago airport. He made an appearance at a jazz concert in 1949 and subsequently formed a group that worked on a part-time basis during the 1950s.

Dominique was an ensemble musician and section leader in the New Orleans tradition – a proficient but unspectacular player. His tone had a peculiar muffled quality and at times exhibited a certain shakiness; his solos were often muted and contained growl effects after the fashion of King Oliver.

Oral history material in *ICU*, *LNT*.

SELECTED RECORDINGS

As leader: *Natty Dominique and his New Orleans Hot Six* (1954, Windin' Ball 104), incl. Big Butter and Egg Man, Someday Sweetheart, Touching Blues, You rascal you

As sideman: J. R. Morton: Someday Sweetheart/London Blues (1923, OK 8105); J. Dodds: Bucktown Stomp/Weary City (1928, Vic. 38004); Chicago Footwarmers: Brush Stomp (1928, OK 8599); J. Dodds: Red Onion Blues/Gravier Street Blues (1940, Decca 18094)

BIBLIOGRAPHY

ChiltonW; *FeatherE*

W. C. Allen: "Trumpet Giants, 5: Natty Dominique," *Hot Notes*, ii/5 (1947), 3

B. Rusch: "Natty Dominique: Interview," *Cadence*, vii/7 (1981), 18

C. Hillman: "The Forgotten Ones: Natty Dominique," *JJI*, xxxvi/10 (1983), 16

LAWRENCE KOCH

Domino. Record label. It was a subsidiary of the Plaza Music Co., and was launched in 1924. Generally it was used to put out material also available on Plaza's other labels, but its early issues include some recordings by the New Orleans Jazz Band which were unique to Domino. The label was discontinued by the newly formed AMERICAN RECORD COMPANY in 1930, but was briefly revived in 1932–3. (B. Rust: *The American Record Label Book* (New Rochelle, NY, 1978), 102)

Domnérus, Arne (*b* Stockholm, 20 Dec 1924). Swedish alto saxophonist, clarinetist, and bandleader. He led his first small group in 1942 and appeared during the next few years with several Swedish dance and jazz orchestras. In 1949 he per-

Arne Domnérus, c1950s

formed at the Paris Jazz Fair, which brought international recognition to Swedish jazz, and made his first recordings as a leader. From 1951 to 1968 he led a group that over the years included many of the foremost Swedish musicians, including Lars Gullin and Jan Johansson. He was also a member of the Swedish Radio Big Band (1956–65) and the leader of its successor, the Radiojazzgruppen (1967–78). Later he led a Swedish group in New York, performed in a duo with Bengt Hallberg at the Monterey (California) Jazz Festival, and performed and recorded into the 1980s. He has also been active in the performance of jazz-oriented popular music.

Domnérus won international acclaim as a soloist in the early 1950s, mainly through a large number of recordings with Swedish and international all-star groups and others under his own name, and came to be regarded as a leading European alto saxophonist. His distinctive style blends elements from those of Charlie Parker, Lee Konitz, and Johnny Hodges.

Oral history material in *SSsv*.

SELECTED RECORDINGS

Duos with B. Hallberg: *Hypertoni* (1977, RCA PL40077); *Duets for Duke* (1978, Sonet 2618)

As leader: Conversation (1949, Met. 103); All the things you are (1950, Met. 150); You can count on me (1951, HMV X7757); Lady Estelle's Dream (1951, HMV X7759); I never knew (1952, HMV X7832); Walking Feet (1954, Phi. P50061); Rockin' Chair (1955, HMV X8548); Echoes of Harlem (1956, RCA S51) [EP]; The Topsy Theme (1958, Barben 10) [EP]; *Mobil* (1965, Megafon 8); *I Let a Song Go out* (1972, RCA LSA3128); *AD 1980* (1980, Phon. 7529)

BIBLIOGRAPHY

FeatherE

E. Kjellberg: "Domnérus, Arne," *Sohlmans musiklexikon* (Stockholm, rev. and enlarged 2/1975–9 ed. H. Åstrand)

——: *Svensk jazzhistoria: en översikt* [Swedish jazz history: an overview] (Stockholm, 1985)

ERIK KJELLBERG

Donahue, Sam (Koontz) (*b* Detroit, 18 March 1918; *d* Reno, NV, 22 March 1974). Tenor saxophonist and bandleader. He led his own band (1933–8), then played with Gene Krupa (1938–40), Harry James (1940), and Benny Goodman (1940), before working again with his own band (1940–42). After being drafted into the navy Donahue took over the leadership of Artie Shaw's navy band (1944–5), which he transformed into one of the most impressive in the armed services; he also recorded with it many times. After the war Donahue led another band intermittently and played with Tommy Dorsey (1952), Billy May (1954), and Stan Kenton (1960–61). He led the Tommy Dorsey Orchestra from 1961 until 1965, when the band stopped using Dorsey's name; in 1966 the group was reduced to an octet, and Donahue retired shortly afterwards. A dynamic, talented saxophonist, and a respected leader and teacher, Donahue was adept at creating big bands that were musically excellent, if rarely commercially successful.

SELECTED RECORDINGS

As leader: It counts a lot (1940, OK 6334); I found a new baby/Deep Night (1945, V-disc 583); *Young Moderns in Love* (1954, Cap. T613)

As sideman: G. Krupa: The madam swings it (1939, Bruns. 8335); B. May: Bill and Sam (1954, Cap. 2759); S. Kenton: *Adventures in Jazz* (1961, Cap. T1796)

BIBLIOGRAPHY

FeatherE; *Feather '60s*

M. Barker: "The Ghost Band," *Crescendo*, ii/6 (1964), 20

G. Brown and J. Dorsey: "They Only Buy the Name," *Crescendo*, ii/8 (1964), 11

G. T. Simon: *The Big Bands* (New York, 1967, rev. and enlarged 2/1971, rev. 3/1974, 4/1981)

A. McCarthy: *Big Band Jazz* (New York and London, 1974), 279

WAYNE SCHNEIDER

Donald, Barbara (Kay) (*b* Minneapolis, 9 Feb 1942). Trumpeter and leader. Her family moved to southern California around 1955. In the early 1960s she played rhythm-and-blues in New York and toured the South with a big band. She performed in Los Angeles with Dexter Gordon and Stanley Cowell, and from 1963 to 1972 played and recorded free jazz with Sonny Simmons, whom she married in 1964. She also worked with John Coltrane (1966), Richard Davis, Prince Lasha, Roland Kirk, and other bop and free-jazz players. She interrupted her career for five years, then left Simmons to perform with her own group; she appeared in Washington state and from 1978 made recordings as a leader, including *Olympia Live* (1981, Cadence 1011).

BIBLIOGRAPHY

Feather–Gitler '70s

S. Placksin: *American Women in Jazz, 1900 to the Present: their Words, Lives, and Music* (New York, 1982), 255 [incl. discography]

P. DeBarros: "Barbara Donald," *DB*, l/5 (1983), 47

B. Rusch: "Barbara Donald: Interview," *Cadence*, ix/6 (1983), 9

Donald, Peter (Alexander) (*b* San Francisco, 15 May 1945). Drummer. He grew up in Woodside, California, but at the age of 14 moved to Boston, where he studied drumming privately with Alan Dawson (1964–9) and composition at the Berklee College of Music (1968–70). He played with local bands in Boston before moving to Los Angeles in the early 1970s. He accompanied the pop singers Olivia Newton-John and Helen Reddy, and in 1972–3 he played in Carmen McRae's backup group; he also worked with Charlie Mariano and Herb Pomeroy. As a member of the Toshiko Akiyoshi–Lew Tabackin Big Band for five years, he played, recorded, and toured Japan (1974–8). The group's album *Road Time* (1976, RCA CPL2-2242) demonstrates his drumming in bop, rock, and Latin styles; the tracks *Warning: success may be hazardous to your health* and *Since Perry* are good examples of his work as a soloist. He later played and recorded with John Abercrombie (1978–82), worked in film and television studios (from 1975), and recorded as a member of a quintet led by Warne Marsh and Gary Foster (1982). In the mid-1980s he joined Denny Zeitlin's trio (1983) and Bob Florence's orchestra (1985), and in 1984 he was appointed to the faculty of the Grove School of Music, Los Angeles.

BIBLIOGRAPHY

R. Tolleson: "Peter Donald," *MD*, viii/6 (1984), 87

Donaldson, Bobby [Robert Stanley] (*b* Boston, 29 Nov 1922; *d* New York, 2 July 1971). Drummer. He was born into a musical family; his elder brother, Don, was music director for Fats Waller in the late 1930s. He played with local bands and, during army service, with Russell Procope in and around New York. After the war he toured (1946) and recorded (1947) with Cat Anderson, and studied composition and arranging (1947). He worked with Edmond Hall at the Café Society, New York (1950–52), and with the bandleaders Andy Kirk, Lucky Millinder, and Sy Oliver (recording under Louis Armstrong's leadership in 1952). From 1953 he played in New York with Buck Clayton at Basin Street and with Red Norvo's group at the Metropole bar. There followed a period during which he was particularly active in the recording studio: he recorded as a leader (1958, 1960), and as a sideman with Clayton (1953–4, 1956, 1957), Helen Merrill (1954), Mel Powell (1954, 1955), Ruby Braff and Benny Goodman (both 1955), Count Basie (1956), Bobby Jaspar, Herbie Mann, and André Hodeir (all 1957), Kenny Burrell (1957, 1960), Lonnie Johnson and Frank Wess (both

1960), Willis "Gator" Jackson (1962, 1968), and Johnny Hodges (1963). As a composer he is well represented by *Don-que-dee* on the album *Thingamagig* (1954), recorded by Powell's trio, on which his precise and sensitive drumming style is also heard to advantage.

For illustration *see* NIGHTCLUBS AND OTHER VENUES, fig.5.

SELECTED RECORDINGS

As leader: *Bobby Donaldson and his Seventh Avenue Stompers* (1958, World Wide 20005); *Dixieland Jazz Party* (1958, Savoy 12128)

As sideman: B. Clayton: *Buck Meets Ruby* (1954, Van. 8008), incl. I can't get started; M. Powell: *Thingamagig* (1954, Van. 8502), incl. Thingamagig, Don-que-dee; R. Braff: *Ruby Braff Quartet* (1954, Beth. 1005), incl. Blue and Sentimental, Mean to me; *Holiday in Braff* (1955, Beth. 1032), incl. Easy Livin'

BIBLIOGRAPHY

FeatherE
S. Dance: Liner notes, *Thingamagig* (Van. 8502, 1955)

KEN RATTENBURY

Donaldson, Lou (*b* Badin, NC, 1 Nov 1926). Alto saxophonist and singer. He began studying clarinet at the age of 15 and he continued to receive tuition when he joined the navy. After taking up the alto saxophone he performed in a navy band with Willie Smith, Clark Terry, and Ernie Wilkins. He first recorded with Milt Jackson and Thelonious Monk (both 1952) and as the leader of several small groups; among his sidemen were Blue Mitchell, Horace Silver, and Art Blakey (all 1952), and Clifford Brown and Philly Joe Jones (1953). In 1954 he and Brown joined Blakey's Jazz Messengers. He continued to lead small groups, mainly in the eastern USA; he performed in Stockholm (1965) and toured and recorded in Europe (1981, 1982). His early work for Blue Note (1952–62) showed his impressive mastery of the bop style, but when in 1963 he began to record for Argo (later renamed Cadet), which specialized in funk, some of his creative spark seemed to be sacrificed to the need for commercial success. After he returned to Blue Note (1967), however, he made a series of recordings (to 1975) in which he achieved a successful blend of elements of the two styles; in the early 1980s he once again concentrated on bop. Donaldson has a dazzling technique and at his best is a strong, inventive, expressive player.

SELECTED RECORDINGS

As leader: *New Faces, New Sounds* (1952, BN 5021); *Lou Donaldson with Clifford Brown* (1953, BN 5030); *Swing and Soul* (1957, BN 1566); *Sunny Side Up* (1960, BN 4036); *Cole Slaw* (1964, Argo 747); *Forgotten Man* (1981, Tim. 153)

As sideman: T. Monk: Skippy/Let's Cool One (1952, BN 1602); Hornin' in/Carolina Moon (1952, BN 1603); A. Blakey: *A Night at Birdland* (1954, BN 5037–9), incl. If I had you

BIBLIOGRAPHY

FeatherE; *Feather '60s*; *Feather–Gitler '70s*
J. Schafer: "Music is my Business," *DB*, xl/12 (1973), 16
L. Tomkins: "The Lou Donaldson Story," *CI*, xix (1981), no.11, p.20; no.12, p.16

LAWRENCE KOCH

Donato, Michel (André) (*b* Montreal, 25 Aug 1942). Canadian double bass player. He studied at the Quebec Conservatory in Montreal (1960–63) and performed with the Montreal SO (1964). From 1962 he worked with Michel Legrand, Carmen McRae, and Pierre Leduc, and performed and recorded with the tenor saxophonists Nick Ayoub (1964) and Lee Gagnon (1967–9), as well as with Sonny Greenwich and Don Thompson (1969–70). From 1970 he lived in Toronto, where he played with Benny Carter, Dave McKenna, Art Farmer, Milt Jackson, and local musicians. With Oscar Peterson's trio he made a world tour (1972–3), recording an album in Tokyo (*Live at Pales Hotel*, 1972, Nippon Col. NPC8501). He made recordings with Gerry Niewood (1976) and Buddy DeFranco (1977), and in 1977 returned to Montreal, where he worked with Bill Evans (ii) and became active as a studio musician. In 1982 he was leader of a quintet that won the first Concours de Jazz de Montréal at the Festival International de Jazz de Montréal; it subsequently recorded an album, *Le Quintette de Michel Donato* (1982, Spectra Scene 1707). The following year Donato began performing in a duo with the singer Karen Young, and from 1984 he has worked in a trio led by the pianist Lorraine Desmarais.

Oral history material in *CaQMG*.

BIBLIOGRAPHY

Feather–Gitler '70s
M. Miller: "Michel Donato," *Boogie, Pete & the Senator: Canadian Musicians in Jazz: the Eighties* (Toronto, 1987), 93

Donegan, Lonnie [Anthony James] (*b* Glasgow, 29 April 1931). Scottish singer, guitarist, and banjoist. He led his own band (1951–2) then worked very briefly with Chris Barber's quintet, which became Ken Colyer's band in 1953 and reverted to Barber's leadership in 1954. He also played and sang in Barber's skiffle group. Following the success of *Rock Island Line*, which featured Donegan (on Barber's *New Orleans Joy*, 1954, Decca 1198), Donegan left Barber and formed his own skiffle group. Although he then became well known as a popular singer and entertainer, he later renewed his jazz associations, recording with Barber in 1975 and working with Monty Sunshine in 1986.

BIBLIOGRAPHY

D. Boulton: *Jazz in Britain* (London, 1958)
G. Melly: *Owning up* (London, 1965)

DEREK COLLER

Donnelly, Ted [Theodore; Muttonleg] (*b* Oklahoma City, OK, 13 Nov 1912; *d* New York, 8 May 1958). Trombonist. He first learned violin, then took up trombone at the age of 20. After playing with George E. Lee and with Tommy Douglas (from 1934) he worked with Andy Kirk (1936–43; for illustration *see* WILLIAMS, MARY LOU); his playing may be heard to advantage on Kirk's *Big Jim Blues* (1939, Decca 2915). In the summer of 1943 he toured overseas with Al Sears, then from December 1943 to 1950 he played with Count Basie. Donnelly was briefly a member of Illinois Jacquet's band in 1950, and from 1951 to 1957 he worked mainly with Erskine Hawkins.

based on *ChiltonW*

Donner, (Henrik) Otto (*b* Tampere, Finland, 16 Nov 1939). Finnish composer and trumpeter. He studied composition with Joonas Kokkonen and György Ligeti, and in the 1960s the experimental composer Terry Riley. At the same time he studied jazz trumpet, and performed and made recordings with Christian Schwindt (1965), Lars Werner (1965–8), and the Otto Donner Treatment (*En soisi sen päättyvän* (I do not want it to end), 1970, Love 14). He was the head of light music for Oy Yleisradio Ab, the Finnish broadcasting company, in 1970–74. His compositions include jazz works, film and theater music, symphonic works, and political songs. (A. Granholm: *Finnish Jazz* (Helsinki, 1974, rev. and enlarged by M. Konttinen 2/1982, rev. and enlarged by J.-P. Vuorela 3/1986), 11)

PEKKA GRONOW

Dørge, Pierre (*b* Copenhagen, 28 Feb 1946). Danish electric guitarist, bandleader, and composer. He worked as a leader from 1960, played free jazz as a member of John Tchicai's big band (1969–71), then led or was a member of several groups that played a combination of free jazz and rock (1971–7). From 1978 he led a quartet, Thermænius, which played in a style influenced by Balkan folk music, and from 1980 he led the New Jungle Orchestra, which incorporated into its playing elements of African music and made several recordings (1982–5); at the same time he continued to collaborate with Tchicai, to lead other groups, and to write compositions that display a dadaistic sense of humor. Dørge's style of playing is expressive and draws on many influences, including rock and Japanese koto music.

SELECTED RECORDINGS

(all recorded for Steeplechase)

Duos: with W. Dickerson: *Landscape with Open Door* (1979, 1115); with J. Tchicai: *Ball at Louisiana Museum of Art* (1981, 1174)

As leader: *Ballad Round the Left Corner* (1979, 1132); *Very Hot: Even the Moon is Dancing* (1985, 1208)

As sideman with J. Tchicai: *Real Tchicai* (1977, 1075)

BIBLIOGRAPHY

M. Feldman: "Pierre Dørge & the New Jungle Orchestra," *DB*, liii/11 (1986), 26 [incl. discography]

ERIK WIEDEMANN

Dorham, Kenny [McKinley Howard] (*b* nr Fairfield, TX, 30 Aug 1924; *d* New York, 5 Dec 1972). Trumpeter. He played in swing orchestras and in the innovative bop big bands of Dizzy Gillespie and Billy Eckstine (1945); while with Gillespie he also appeared as a blues singer. In 1948 he began an important association with Charlie Parker's quintet, with which he remained until 1949. He was a founding member of the Jazz Messengers in 1954, and briefly led a similar group called the Jazz Prophets. From 1956 to 1958 he played in Max Roach's quintet, replacing Clifford Brown. Later he taught at the Lenox (Massachusetts) School of Jazz (1958–9), appeared in the films *Les liaisons dangereuses* and *Un témoin dans la ville* (both 1959), and in the mid-1960s led a quintet with Joe Henderson. In his best recordings of the mid- and late 1950s Dorham rivaled his greatest contemporaries in technical command, tunefulness, and beauty of timbre.

SELECTED RECORDINGS

As leader: *Kenny Dorham and the Jazz Prophets* (1956, ABC-Para. 122); *Jazz Contrasts* (1957, Riv. 239); *Blue Spring* (1959, Riv. 297); *Quiet Kenny* (1959, NewJ 8225); *Whistle Stop* (1961, BN 4063); *Trumpet Toccata* (1964, BN 84181)

As sideman: F. Navarro: Everything's Cool (1946, Savoy 586); J. J. Johnson: Opus V/Hilo (1949, NewJ 806); S. Rollins: *Sonny Rollins Quintet* (1954, Prst. 186); A. Blakey: *The Jazz Messengers at the Cafe Bohemia* (1955, BN 1507–8); M. Roach: *Jazz in 3/4 Time* (1957, EmA 36108); J. Henderson: *In 'n' Out* (1964, BN 84166)

BIBLIOGRAPHY

"Kenny Dorham's Three Careers," *DB*, xxvi/4 (1959), 20
G. Feehan: "Durable Dorham," *DB*, xxix/25 (1962), 16
J. Binchet: "Kenny Dorham: l'éternel second," *Jm*, no.147 (1967), 16
M. James: "Kenny Dorham: Soloist Extraordinary," *J&B*, i/9 (1972), 4
M. Gardner: "Farewell Kenny Dorham," *JJ*, xxvi/3 (1973), 7
Obituary, *DB*, xl/2 (1973), 10
B. Räftegård: *The Kenny Dorham Discography* (Karlstad, Sweden, 1982)

BARRY KERNFELD

Dorough, Bob [Robert Lrod] (*b* Cherry Hill, AR, 12 Dec 1923). Pianist, singer, and songwriter. After playing with various small groups in the army during World War II he studied composition and piano at North Texas State Teachers' College (1946–9). While attending Columbia University (1949–52) he began playing the piano professionally at clubs in New York; shortly thereafter he began singing. In the early 1950s he worked for two years as an accompanist for the boxer Sugar Ray Robinson, who was at that time performing as an entertainer. In 1954–5 he lived in Paris, where he worked as a pianist, accompanist, and music director, mostly for resident or touring American musicians. During this period he recorded with Blossom Dearie. After returning to the USA he pursued diverse musical activities from the late 1950s. He recorded with Miles Davis's sextet in 1962, and also performed at clubs and concerts. During the 1970s he wrote and directed the music for a series of instructional television programs, "Schoolhouse Rock." In 1980 he performed at Carnegie Hall. Dorough sings with a light, crisp timbre, and enunciates words clearly. He has composed several jazz ballads, including *Devil May Care*; his melodies are inventive and often highly rhythmic. He has also written lyrics and vocalese, including one to Charlie Parker's *Yardbird Suite*.

SELECTED RECORDINGS

As leader: *Devil May Care* (1956, Beth. 11), incl. Devil May Care, Yardbird Suite; *Master-singer Bob Dorough* (1966, Focus 336); *That's the Way I Feel Now* (c1984, A&M 6600), incl. Friday the Thirteenth

As sideman: on M. Davis: *Sorcerer* (1962, 1967, Col. CS9532), Nothing Like You (1962)

BIBLIOGRAPHY

FeatherE; *Feather–Gitler '70s*
S. Albin: "Bob Dorough: Bradley's, New York City," *DB*, xliv/6 (1977), 36
A. Levitt: "Le passé pas simple de Bob Dorough," *Jm*, no.322 (1983), 24; no.323 (1983), 30
L. Gourse: *Louis' Children: American Jazz Singers* (New York, 1984), 315
W. V. Hall: "Bob Dorough: Academic Hipster Mixes Math and Music," *Music Educators' Journal*, lxxii/3 (1985), 28

MARTY HATCH

Dorsey, Jimmy [James] (*b* Shenandoah, PA, 29 Feb 1904; *d* New York, 12 June 1957). Clarinetist, saxophonist, and dance-band leader, brother of Tommy Dorsey. He began playing slide trumpet and cornet at the age of seven, but changed to reed instruments in 1915. With his brother Tommy he led Dorsey's Novelty Six and Dorsey's Wild Canaries, then in the early 1920s performed with the Scranton Sirens. In September 1924 Jimmy joined the California Ramblers, a very popular dance band in New York. Between 1925 and 1934 he worked as a freelance with leading New York bands such as those of Paul Whiteman, Jean Goldkette, and Vincent Lopez. More importantly, from 1926 he began recording extensively with leading midwestern white jazz pioneers, including Bix Beiderbecke and Red Nichols. He played in Nichols's popular group the Five Pennies, a widely influential band not only in the USA but also in England; this established Dorsey as a leading jazz reed player.

In 1934 Dorsey founded with his brother the successful but short-lived Dorsey Brothers Orchestra. After a public argument in 1935 Jimmy took over the leadership of the group, building it into one of the leading dance bands of the late 1930s and early 1940s. He appeared with the group in several films, including *The Fabulous Dorseys* (1947), a fictionalized version of the brothers' careers. He continued to lead dance bands sporadically after World War II until his death, at one period joining Tommy to run a new Dorsey Brothers Orchestra (1953–6).

Because Dorsey led one of the most popular dance bands of the swing era and scored novelty hits such as *Oodles of Noodles* (1932), his importance as a jazz player has been neglected; yet in the 1920s he was a major model for other jazz musicians, both on clarinet and saxophone. Lester Young and Coleman Hawkins both acknowledged his influence. Like many of his contemporaries, Dorsey was attracted to jazz by the examples of the white musicians Larry Shields and Leon Roppolo, but by the late 1920s he came under the influence of the black player Jimmie Noone. Dorsey had an excellent technique and played in a fluid, polished style which could be strongly rhythmic. He can safely be placed among the finest jazz players of reed instruments during the period 1925 to 1935. (*See* SAXOPHONE, §3.)

For illustration *see* JAZZ (i), fig.3.

SELECTED RECORDINGS

As leader: St. Louis Blues (1930, Decca F6142); Oodles of Noodles (1932, Col. 36063); Amapola (1941, Decca 3629); Green Eyes (1941, Decca 3698)
As sideman: R. Nichols: Alabama Stomp/Hurricane (1927, Bruns. 3550)

BIBLIOGRAPHY

E. Edwards, Jr., G. Hall, and B. Korst: *Jimmy Dorsey and his Orchestra* (Whittier, CA, 1966) [discography]
G. T. Simon: *The Big Bands* (New York, 1967, rev. and enlarged 2/1971, rev. 3/1974, 4/1981)
H. Sanford: *Tommy and Jimmy: the Dorsey Years* (New Rochelle, NY, 1972)
C. Garrod: *Jimmy Dorsey and his Orchestra* (Zephyrhills, FL, 1980) [discography]

JAMES LINCOLN COLLIER

Dorsey, Tommy [Thomas] (*b* Shenandoah, PA, 19 Nov 1905; *d* Greenwich, CT, 26 Nov 1956). Trombonist and dance-band leader, brother of Jimmy Dorsey. He studied trumpet with his father, a part-time musician, and later changed to trombone. With his brother Jimmy he was leader of Dorsey's Novelty Six and Dorsey's Wild Canaries, then in the early 1920s played with the Scranton Sirens. Later in the decade Tommy worked with such prominent dance orchestras as those led by Jean Goldkette and Paul Whiteman. He then moved to New York, where he was in demand as a player in studio and pit orchestras. In 1934 he founded with Jimmy the successful but short-lived Dorsey Brothers Orchestra. After a public argument in 1935 the two separated, and Tommy organized a dance orchestra of his own which quickly became one of the most popular of the swing era (*see also* CLAMBAKE SEVEN). The band's music was characterized by smooth, well-crafted arrangements played with great precision and, at times, with excellent jazz solos by Bunny Berigan, Yank Lawson, Buddy Rich, and others. One of its most successful recordings was *Boogie Woogie* (1938), an orchestral adaptation of a piano piece by Pine Top Smith; other hits included lively swing versions of *Marie* and *Song of India* (1937), both with brilliant solos by Berigan. However, Dorsey's orchestra was known primarily for its renderings of ballads at dance tempos, frequently with singers such as Jack Leonard and Frank Sinatra. After the collapse of the swing-band movement in the late 1940s Dorsey struggled to keep his band intact. Eventually he brought in his brother Jimmy and the two ran another version of the Dorsey Brothers Orchestra (1953–6) which had some success, particularly in its television appearances.

Tommy Dorsey's orchestra, December 1940: (from bottom, first row, left to right) Paul Mason and Don Lodice (tenor saxophones), Fred Stulce (alto saxophone), Johnny Mince (clarinet, alto saxophone), and Heinie Beau (alto saxophone); (second row) Ray Linn, Ziggy Elman, Jimmy Blake, and Chuck Peterson (trumpets); (center, inset) Dorsey (trombone); (three left of center) Joe Bushkin (piano, top), Buddy Rich (drums, left), and Sid Weiss (double bass, bottom); (three right of center) Lowell Martin (trombone, top), George Arus (trombone, right), and Les Jenkins (trombone, bottom); (top row, center) Connie Haines and Frank Sinatra (voices) with the Pied Piper vocal group (left to right) John Huddleston, Clark Yocum (and guitar), Jo Stafford, and Chuck Lowry

Although Dorsey recorded, especially in the 1920s, with Bix Beiderbecke and other major jazz players, he was not a notable jazz soloist. He was vastly admired by other musicians, however, for his technical skill on his instrument. His tone was pure, his phrasing was elegant, and he was able to play an almost seamless legato line; as a player of ballads he has rarely been surpassed.

SELECTED RECORDINGS

As leader: I'm getting sentimental over you (1935, Vic. 25236); Marie/Song of India (1937, Vic. 25523); Boogie Woogie (1938, Vic. 26054); I'll never smile again (1940, Vic. 26628); Opus One (1944, Vic. 20-1608)
As sideman: J. Bland: Who stole the lock (1932, Ban. 32605); [no leader: Jam Session at Victor]: Honeysuckle Rose/Blues (1937, Vic. 25559)

BIBLIOGRAPHY

G. T. Simon: *The Big Bands* (New York, 1967, rev. and enlarged 2/1971, rev. 3/1974, 4/1981)
H. Sanford: *Tommy and Jimmy: the Dorsey Years* (New Rochelle, NY, 1972)
C. Garrod, W. Scott, and F. Green: *Tommy Dorsey and his Orchestra* (Zephyrhills, FL, n.d. [?1980–1982]) [discography]
S. Voce: "Talking of Tommy," *JJI*, xxxviii/2 (1985), 20

JAMES LINCOLN COLLIER

Double. In jazz argot, to be capable of playing a second (particularly a wind or brass) instrument; the term is also used to refer to the instrument concerned. (*GoldJL*)

Double bass [bass, string bass, contrabass]. The lowest-pitched instrument of the violin family. It has four (or, less often, five) strings, normally tuned *E'–A'–D–G* (the five-string instrument uses various tunings but normally has *B'* or *C'* as the lowest note), and is played with a bow (arco) or by plucking (pizzicato); on some four-string instruments a mechanical attachment allows the player to extend the length of the bottom string, thus lowering its pitch to *C'*. The instrument sounds an octave below written pitch.

The double bass was used in ragtime orchestras and string bands from the 1890s. It was present in many early New Orleans orchestras, and practitioners included Billy Marrero and Henry Kimball; early photographic evidence suggests that from the time of Buddy Bolden up to about 1920 the instrument was often bowed rather than plucked. In many ragtime pieces the double bass underpinned the texture by playing on the first and third beats of the bar and occasionally it doubled the trombone or cello part during melodic interludes or bridge passages

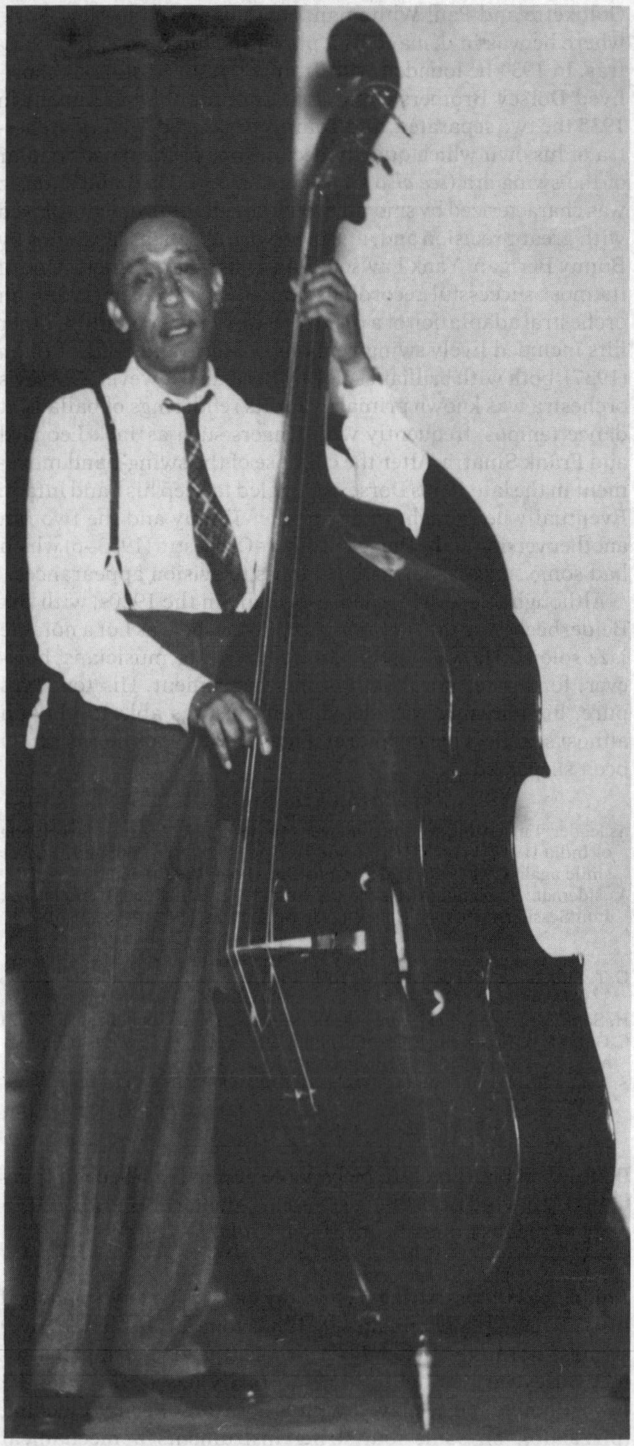

1. John Lindsay, Chicago, 12 June 1944

in multithematic compositions. These functions were transferred into early jazz, and they reached their highest development in the work of Bill Johnson (i) and John Lindsay during the classic-jazz era (1924–9). Lindsay's playing was particularly varied: Schuller has analyzed one performance (on Jelly Roll Morton's *Black Bottom Stomp*, 1926, Vic. 20221) on which Lindsay changes between two-beat rhythm (that is, playing on the first and third beats of the bar in 4/4 meter), hard-driving four-beat rhythm (playing on every beat), and stop-time rhythm (playing on the first beat only); he also employed occasional bowed notes and SLAP-BASS effects in most of his recorded oeuvre.

During the era of acoustic recording the double bass was often replaced by the tuba, probably (as Schuller suggests) because of its greater carrying power. This is not to say that the string bass was never used on acoustic recordings – for instance, the virtuoso Steve Brown recorded as early as 1922 with the New Orleans Rhythm Kings – but it was seldom clearly heard until electrical recording techniques were introduced around 1925. In the late 1920s, particularly in larger ensembles and embryonic big bands, the double bass came to be used as the basis for the rhythm section, and many tuba players (including John Kirby and Robert Ysaguirre) made the transition to the string bass. Among the notable exponents of the double bass at this period were Pops Foster (with Luis Russell and Louis Armstrong) and Al Morgan.

The double bass of the early 1930s was normally strung with gut strings (sometimes wound with steel), and the bridge was high, holding the strings well away from the fingerboard (as much as 2 cm away at the lower end) and resulting in what is known as "high action." In competition with the rest of the big band the sound of the double bass was difficult to hear, and the use of slap-bass technique to produce greater volume became prevalent; other solutions to this problem included the adoption by Foster of an aluminum-bodied instrument and by Wellman Braud (in Duke Ellington's band) of primitive electric amplification. In the course of the 1930s slap-bass became less popular and players sought a wider range of expressive possibilities.

The role of the double bass in establishing the FOUR-BEAT approach to meter in the swing period is epitomized by the work of Walter Page in Count Basie's band. Like most bass players at this time, Page's role was restricted to that of a member of the rhythm section and he took few solos. The development of the instrument as a solo voice was largely the work of Jimmy Blanton (with Ellington), whose arco and pizzicato playing in the orchestra (exemplified by *Jack the Bear*, 1940, Vic. 26536) and as Ellington's partner in a duo (exemplified by *Pitter Panther Patter/Sophisticated Lady*, 1940, Vic. 27221) displays a highly developed technique and a facility of articulation hitherto unknown. Blanton, and later Oscar Pettiford, still played instruments with a high action and used relatively little amplification.

The advent of bop in the early 1940s led to further advances in jazz double bass playing, though the instrument's role continued to be mainly that of keeping steady time by means of WALKING BASS lines, allowing the piano and drums to concentrate less on time keeping. Ray Brown came to prominence as a member of Dizzy Gillespie's band; using an instrument with a lower action and employing increasingly sophisticated amplification, he developed the expressive and melodic possibilities of the instrument further, both as an accompanist within the rhythm section and as a soloist on such pieces as *One Bass Hit* (1946, Musi. 404). On the West Coast Red Callender and Charles Mingus extended the application of bop style to the double bass. Mingus, in particular, synthesized characteristics from almost all preceding types of jazz into his own virtuoso style. Although he refined rather than developed double bass technique he began to break down the instrument's time-keeping role by placing notes before, on, or after the beat so as to vary the color and feel of the rhythmic accompaniment to soloists; his compositional gifts also enabled him to create highly original and beautiful solo lines of his own. Later in his career he frequently performed extended compositions and improvisations as an unaccompanied soloist. Another notable player of the bop period was Slam Stewart (who was a member of Gillespie's band and also performed with the entertainer Slim Gaillard); he combined complex solos using the bow with deft scat singing in unison with the solo line.

By the 1950s steel strings and improved amplification had largely eliminated the difficulty of producing sufficient volume on the double bass and the instrument could now perform its traditional function of time keeping with great efficiency. In search of new styles and modes of expression, players began to follow Mingus's lead in finding other accompanying roles for the bass and developing their technical skills as soloists. Until this time most players had used the four-string instrument tuned in the conventional way, but now some (notably Red Mitchell) adopted a tuning in 5ths, an octave below the cello, which involved extended left-hand positions, and others experimented with the five-string bass. A desire to achieve freer and more rapid melodic improvisation led to advances in left-hand technique and the abandoning of conventional symphonic fingering systems; this was accompanied by a revolution in pizzicato technique, and musicians began to use two or three right-hand fingers in quick succession to produce lines as fast and complex as those that can be executed on a wind or keyboard instrument. The players associated with Bill Evans (ii) (Scott LaFaro, Gary Peacock, and Eddie Gomez) became particularly accomplished exponents of such practices, and Ron Carter (who wrote the standard work on modern jazz double bass playing) extended his ideas to the cello and PICCOLO BASS. From the mid-1950s the double bass was liberated to a greater degree than ever before from its accompanying role in the rhythm section of the band; it assumed a major solo status in free and avant-garde styles of jazz.

2. Charles Mingus

Various avant-garde techniques have extended the expressive range of the double bass in directions other than mere dexterity and speed. Charlie Haden, Jimmy Garrison, Dave Holland, Barre Phillips, Barry Guy, and others have explored harmonics, double stopping, percussive methods of producing notes, the use of the instrument's body to make percussive sounds, the possibilities offered by the section of the string between the bridge and the tailpiece, and simultaneous independent improvisation on more than one string. Many of these techniques and effects are employed on Holland's and Phillips's *Music for Two Basses* (1971, ECM 1011). Technical developments to the instrument itself have included the use of a metal bridge and an adjustable bridge. Transducers built into the instrument or mounted on the bridge have assisted in more effective amplification.

In jazz-rock ensembles the ELECTRIC BASS GUITAR is normally preferred to the double bass, but in general the bass guitar has not supplanted the double bass in ensembles playing other styles of jazz (Gary Burton's quartet, in which Steve Swallow plays bass guitar, is a notable exception). It is, however, common for double bass players to be able also to play electric bass guitar (fretted or unfretted) and to change to that instrument for certain pieces as appropriate.

Some players, including Eberhard Weber, have experimented with solid-bodied electric double basses, which have small bodies and commensurately long necks; they are fitted with pickups and controls similar to those of the electric bass guitar. The sound they produce (whether played pizzicato or bowed) is an uneasy compromise between that of an amplified acoustic double bass and a fretless electric bass guitar. Their principal advantage is that they are more easily carried than the acoustic instrument.

For further illustrations *see* BAILEY, BUSTER; BRAXTON, ANTHONY; FOSTER, POPS; LACY, STEVE; MANGELSDORFF, ALBERT; PETTIFORD, OSCAR; and WEBER, EBERHARD.

BIBLIOGRAPHY

J.-E. Berendt: *Das Jazzbuch: Entwicklung und Bedeutung der Jazzmusik* (Frankfurt am Main, Germany, 1953, rev. 2/1959 as *Das neue Jazzbuch*, Eng. trans., New York, 1962; rev. and enlarged 5/1981 as *Das grosse Jazzbuch: von New Orleans bis Jazz Rock*, Eng. trans. as *The Jazz Book: from New Orleans to Fusion and Beyond*, Westport, CT, 1982)
M. W. Stearns: *The Story of Jazz* (New York, 1956, rev. and enlarged 2/1958, enlarged 1970)
L. Feather: *The Book of Jazz: a Guide to the Entire Field* (New York, 1957, 2/1965 as *The Book of Jazz from Then till Now: a Guide to the Entire Field*), 119
R. Carter: *Building a Jazz Bass Line* (New York, 1966, rev. and enlarged 2/1970)
G. Schuller: *Early Jazz: its Roots and Musical Development* (New York, 1968)
B. Turetzky: "The Bass as a Drum," *The Composer*, i (1969), 92
——: "Vocal and Speech Sounds: a Technique of Contemporary Writing for the Double Bass," *The Composer*, i (1969), 118
A. Shipton: "Styles of New Orleans Bass Playing," *Fn*, vii/1 (1976), 18
A. Roidinger: *Der Kontrabass im Jazz* (Vienna, 1980)
R. Brown: "Ray Brown and the Sound of a Bass," *CI*, xxiv/5 (1987), 5
T. Coolman: *The Bass Tradition: Past, Present, Future* (New Albany, IN, 1987)

ALYN SHIPTON

Double bassoon. A double-reed woodwind instrument, pitched an octave below the BASSOON.

Double mute. *See* MUTE, §2(b).

Double Six (of Paris). French vocal sextet. It was formed in 1959 by MIMI PERRIN, who also led the group and wrote arrangements for its repertory; these consisted of jazz themes to which she had added lyrics. The name Double Six derived from the group's practice of superimposing two separate recordings, which gave the impression that 12 voices were singing at once; on tours of the USA and Canada the group was known as the Double Six of Paris. The group underwent several changes in membership and at various times included Monique Aldebert-Guérin, Christiane Legrand, Louis Aldebert, Ward Swingle, Roger Guérin, and Eddy Louiss. It recorded music by Quincy Jones in 1959–60 and later made recordings with Dizzy Gillespie (*Dizzy Gillespie et les Double Six*, 1963, Phi. 200106) and Jerome Richardson's quartet (1964). After it disbanded in 1965 Perrin led a second group known by the same name from August of that year; this group was led by Jef Gilson for a brief period in 1966 (while Perrin was ill) before it too disbanded in the autumn.

MICHEL LAPLACE

Double-time. The apparent doubling of the tempo, generally in a recognizable four-, eight-, or 16-bar section of a piece, or in a BREAK, achieved by halving the prevailing note-value. The term may also be used to describe a great increase of tempo rather than an exact doubling. *See* BEAT, §4(ii).

Doucet, Clément (*b* Brussels, ?9 April 1894; *d* Brussels, 9 Sept 1950). Belgian pianist and composer. After studying music he worked in Paris for the organ builder Cavaillé-Coll (1912–14), then at Wannamakers in New York; during his two years in the USA he became a close friend of the composer George Gershwin. In 1923 he returned to Paris, where he met the French pianist Jean Wiener, with whom he was associated for more than 15 years. One of the pioneers of Belgian jazz, Doucet gave more than 2000 performances all over the world; he made many solo recordings (1924–35) and took part in a number of sessions with Wiener for French Columbia (1925–9, 1935, 1937).

ROBERT PERNET

Dougherty, Eddie [Edward] (*b* New York, 17 July 1915). Drummer. He began playing drums at the age of 13, and during the 1930s worked and recorded (1933) in a band at Dickie Wells's club in Harlem. He recorded extensively with such musicians as Taft Jordan and Frank Froeba (both 1935), Mildred Bailey (1935, 1939), and Harry James, Billie Holiday, Frankie Newton, Pete Johnson, and Meade "Lux" Lewis (all 1939). After deputizing for Dave Tough in Bud Freeman's orchestra (1940) he recorded with Art Tatum (1941) and worked with Newton, Joe Sullivan, Benny Carter (1941), Benny Morton (1944–5), and several others. Sessions with James P. Johnson's band in 1944 resulted in such recordings as *Hot Harlem* (Asch 5513); Dougherty also recorded a number of duos with Johnson. Thereafter he recorded with Cliff Jackson and Mary Lou Williams (both 1944), and Clyde Bernhardt (1946), and worked with Wilbur De Paris, Teddy Wilson, Albert Nicholas, and others. He then ceased to be a full-time musician, but continued to play occasionally as a freelance into the early 1980s.

based on *ChiltonW*

Douglas, Billy [William] (*b* New Haven, CT, 12 Aug 1912; *d* Springfield, MA, 14 April 1978). Trumpeter, singer, and arranger. He played in the big bands of Earle Howard (1932–3) and Percy Nelson (1933–4), then worked with Sidney Bechet, Jelly Roll Morton (mid-1930s), and the pianist Jimmie Gunn (1935). From 1935 to 1937 he was a soloist with Don Albert's band, and in 1936 recorded eight titles with the group, including his own arrangements of *True Blue Lou* (Voc. 3401), *On the Sunny Side of the Street* (Voc. 3423), and *Liza* (Voc. 3491). During the late 1930s and the 1940s Douglas played as a freelance in New York, Philadelphia, and Chicago, then from 1944 to 1945 worked with Earl Hines, recording again as a soloist on *Scoops Carry's Merry* (1945), first issued on *The Father Jumps* (1939–45, Bb AXM2-5508). His career was brought to an end by his dependence on alcohol. Douglas patterned his style after that of Henry "Red" Allen and, although his playing was less angular than Allen's, it had the same fire and expressiveness. (*ChiltonW*)

FRANK DRIGGS

Douglas, Louis (Winston) (*b* ?New York, 14 May ?1889; *d* ?New York, 19 May 1939). Dancer and singer. He performed in Europe with Belle Davis (1903–8), and his dancing during this period may be seen in the film *Die schöne Davis mit ihren drei Negern* (1906). He then worked with the singer Will Garland (1908–9), and continued to tour in Europe until 1915 as a solo act, in duos, and with his own troupes; in 1909 he appeared in the film *The Douglas Troupe*. Later he lived in the UK, where he starred in revues (1915–22) and formed an association with the dancer Sonny Jones. After moving to Paris he was employed extensively as a choreographer and was a co-director of *La revue nègre* (1925). Thereafter he worked in Berlin (1926) and New York (1927) and organized his own revues, with which he toured Europe and Egypt (1926–36). From 1936 to 1939 Douglas was the choreographer of annual revues at the Casino de Paris; shortly before his death he worked with James P. Johnson (1939). Although he was not an instrumentalist, he led his own bands, which included excellent jazz soloists such as Sidney Bechet. (R. E. Lotz: *German Ragtime and the Prehistory of Jazz*, i: *The Sound Documents*, Chigwell, England, 1985)

RAINER E. LOTZ

Douglas, Tommy [Thomas] (*b* Eskridge, KS, 9 Nov ?1906; *d* Sioux Falls, SD, 9 March 1965). Clarinetist, saxophonist, and arranger. He taught himself music while at school in Topeka, Kansas, and then attended the Boston Conservatory (1924–8); while in Boston he met Johnny Hodges, Otto Hardwick, and Harry Carney. At first he worked principally as an alto saxophonist and clarinetist in Kansas City: he played with George E. Lee (?1930–1931), Jelly Roll Morton (in Chicago, 1931), Clarence Love (1932–3), Bennie Moten (1934), and others. He also wrote arrangements for Love and for the Casa Loma Orchestra. In the 1930s and 1940s Douglas led many short-lived ten- or 12-piece bands that were active in the South and Midwest; later he played chiefly in smaller groups in and around Kansas City. During the 1940s he also recorded with Jay McShann's Kansas City Stompers (notably *On the Sunny Side of the Street*, 1944, Cap. 10039) and with Julia Lee, and in 1951 he spent three weeks in Duke Ellington's orchestra.

Douglas never achieved popular success, but he was considered a brilliant and innovative instrumentalist and arranger. He experimented with extended chords and double-time as early as 1935, and reputedly influenced the technique and harmonic thinking of Charlie Parker (who worked briefly in Douglas's septet in 1936). Jo Jones (who also played with him) favorably compared his instrumental skill with that of Benny Carter and Don Redman, and Driggs (1959) comments admiringly on his modern, "more flowing" arrangements of the 1930s. However, Douglas's few commercial recordings, which all date from the 1940s, are atypical, reflecting neither his considerable technique nor his advanced musical conceptions.

BIBLIOGRAPHY

F. Driggs: "Kansas City and the Southwest," *Jazz: New Perspectives on the History of Jazz by Twelve of the World's Foremost Jazz Critics and Scholars*, ed. N. Hentoff and A. J. McCarthy (New York and Toronto, 1959/*R*1974), 189

——: "Tommy Douglas," *JM*, vi/2 (1960), 4

R. Russell: *Jazz Style in Kansas City and the Southwest* (Berkeley, CA, Los Angeles, and London, 1971/*R*1983, rev. 2/1973)

A. McCarthy: *Big Band Jazz* (New York and London, 1974)

JEFFREY COOPER

Douglass, Bill [William] (*b* Los Angeles, 28 Feb 1923). Drummer. He performed and recorded with Benny Carter occasionally in and around Los Angeles during the early and mid-1950s, and recorded with Red Callender (intermittently 1954–*c*1958), Cal Tjader and Art Tatum (both 1956), Gerald Wiggins and Red Norvo (both 1956–7), and Harry Babasin (1957); his playing is well represented by the album *Art Tatum–Ben Webster Quartet* (1956, Verve 8220). During the 1960s he taught and worked as a freelance, and in 1978 he recorded with Earl Hines. He continued to be active in California in the 1980s, and in 1983 he played with Wild Bill Davis and the pianist Judy Carmichael at a festival in Colorado. He should not be confused with Bill Douglass, the double bass player and flutist who played with Art Lande's group in the mid-1970s. (*FeatherE*)

Dowdy, Bill (*b* Benton Harbor, MI, 15 Aug 1933). Drummer. He played with Johnny Griffin, J. J. Johnson, and local blues bands while attending Roosevelt University. In 1956 he formed the Four Sounds, which the following year became the THREE SOUNDS. He continued among its members until 1966, performing and making recordings, including the album *Feelin' Good* (1960, BN 84072). (*FeatherE; Feather '60s*)

Down Beat [Downbeat]. The name of several nightclubs, including ones in New York, Chicago, and Los Angeles; *see* NIGHTCLUBS AND OTHER VENUES. (Also the name of one of the foremost American jazz periodicals; see Appendix 1: Bibliography (Periodicals).)

Downbeat. The first and strongest beat of the bar; *see* BEAT, esp. §4(i).

Downes, Bob [Robert George] (*b* Plymouth, England, 22 July 1937). English flutist and saxophonist. He taught himself the saxophone from 1956; from 1968 he concentrated on the flute, playing alto and bass orchestral instruments and various ethnic flutes. From 1969 he worked with Mike Westbrook (until 1970) and led his own group, Open Music (until 1974). This ensemble, which fluctuated in size, played in styles ranging from rock and blues to free jazz; notable among its albums is *Diversions* (1973, Openian 001), recorded as a quintet with Barry Guy among the members. Downes also recorded with the London Jazz Composers Orchestra (1972). He worked from the mid-1970s mainly as an unaccompanied solo flutist, and from the late 1970s lived in Germany. He continued to be active intermittently as a leader, forming the Alternative Medicine Quartet in 1978 and the Flute Orchestra in 1984. His compositions include music for the Ballet Rambert and other contemporary dance companies.

BIBLIOGRAPHY

R. Cotterrell, ed.: *Jazz Now: the Jazz Centre Society Guide* (London, 1976)

I. Carr: "Downes, Bob," in I. Carr, D. Fairweather, and B. Priestley: *Jazz: the Essential Companion* (London, 1987)

DIGBY FAIRWEATHER

Drag. (1) Deliberately or unintentionally to play or sing slightly behind the beat, as articulated by the rhythm section or implied by the playing of the rest of the ensemble; *see* BEAT, §2.

(2) A synonym for SLOW DRAG.

(3) One of the drumstrokes collectively known as RUDIMENTS.

Drakes, Jesse (*b* New York, 22 Oct 1926). Trumpeter. As a youth he heard many jam sessions at Minton's Playhouse. From 1945 he played with Al Cooper's Savoy Sultans, J. C. Heard, Sid Catlett, Eddie Heywood, and the singer Deke Watson, and in 1947 he recorded with Sarah Vaughan. Between 1948 and 1956 he performed and made recordings at intervals with Lester Young, and a good example of his playing may be heard on *Jumpin' at the Woodside* (1953, on the EP *Lester Young*, 1953–4, Norg. 112); during the same period he also worked with a group led by Gene Ammons and Sonny Stitt (*c*1953), with Harry Belafonte and Louie Bellson (both 1955), and with Duke Ellington (1956). A tour with King Curtis led Drakes away from jazz and towards rhythm-and-blues; he worked with Motown artists in the 1960s, and from 1969 played dance music and sang in New York.

BIBLIOGRAPHY

FeatherE

B. Rusch: "Jesse Drakes: Interview," *Cadence*, x/3 (1984), 15

Draper, Ray(mond Allen) (*b* New York, 3 Aug 1940; *d* New York, 1 Nov 1982). Tuba player. He attended the High School of the Performing Arts and the Manhattan School of Music, performed hard bop with Jackie McLean (1956–7), with whom he also recorded, and Donald Byrd, and recorded with John Coltrane (1956–8). He belonged to Max Roach's quintet from 1958 to 1959, worked briefly with Don Cherry (1962), played with Big Black and Horace Tapscott, and from 1968 to 1969 led the jazz-rock band Red Beans and Rice. In 1969 he moved to England, where he worked with the saxophonists Kenneth Terroade and Archie Shepp and the rock singer and pianist Dr. John. After returning to the USA in 1971 he recorded with Brother Jack McDuff, taught briefly at Wesleyan University, and played with the group Gravity, led by Howard Johnson (ii). Although a musician of considerable talent, Draper led an irregular life (he spent three years in prison in California in the early 1960s and was killed in the course of a robbery), and he never fulfilled the promise he had shown early in his career.

SELECTED RECORDINGS

As leader: *Ray Draper with John Coltrane* (1957, NewJ 8228); *Red Beans and Rice Featuring Spareribs* (1969, Epic 26461)

As sideman: J. McLean: *Jackie McLean & Co.* (1957, Prst. 7087); M. Roach: *Deeds, not Words* (1958, Riv. 280); S. Criss: *Sonny's Dream* (1968, Prst. 7576)

BIBLIOGRAPHY

"Ray Draper: Just Call me a Musician," *MM* (27 June 1970), 24

"Ray Draper Talks to Mark Gardner," *JM*, no.187 (1970), 10

V. Wilmer: "Ray Draper: Problems, Promise & Poems," *DB*, xxxviii/3 (1971), 18

F. W. Bush: "Ray Draper Memorial," *Coda*, no.201 (1985), 11

DAVID WILD

Drasnin, Bob [Robert Jackson] (*b* Charleston, WV, 17 Nov 1927). Flutist and alto and tenor saxophonist. He studied music at UCLA as an undergraduate to 1949, and as a graduate student in composition from 1954 to 1957. He played in big bands under Les Brown (1950), Alvino Rey (1953), and Tommy Dorsey (1953), and recorded with Brown (from 1950), Ken Hanna (1953–4), and Frank Capp (1960). He also composed and conducted soundtracks for films and television. Drasnin is heard to advantage on his recordings with Red Norvo's quintet (1956–8), especially *Vibe-Rations* (1956, Lib. 6012). (*FeatherE*)

Dreamland Café. Nightclub (formerly the Dreamland Ballroom) in Chicago; *see* NIGHTCLUBS AND OTHER VENUES.

Dreams. Jazz-rock group formed in 1969 by Billy Cobham, Mike Brecker, and Randy Brecker; Cobham left in 1971 and the group disbanded in 1973.

Dreares, Al(fred, II) (*b* Key West, FL, 4 Jan 1929). Drummer. He studied drumming and vibraphone in New York (1949). After playing rhythm-and-blues in the mid-1950s he worked chiefly with bop musicians, including Teddy Charles (1955), Charles Mingus (1956), Kenny Burrell (1957), Gigi Gryce (1958), and Phineas Newborn (1959). He also performed and recorded with Randy Weston (*Jazz à la Bohemia*, 1956, Riv. 232) and Freddie Redd (1957), and recorded with Bennie Green (1959–60), Mal Waldron (1960–67), Frank Strozier (1962), the vibraphonist Freddie McCoy (1968), and Harold Ousley (1972). In the later 1970s he played with Paul Quinichette (1976) and Slide Hampton (1978), and from 1979 to 1983 led his own small group at a club in Brooklyn, New York. He moved to Miami in 1985. Besides playing, he has composed a number of jazz pieces and taught percussion. (*FeatherE*)

Drelinger, Art (*b* Gloucester, MA, 20 Aug 1916). Tenor saxophonist. He began playing locally and in 1935 he moved to New York, where he played with Adrian Rollini at Adrian's Tap Room (1936), Wingy Manone at the Famous Door, and Red McKenzie. He worked with Bunny Berigan (1936–7), Jack Jenney, and Artie Shaw, before joining Paul Whiteman (1938); he was a principal soloist in Whiteman's Swing Wing, with which he recorded in 1938–9. From the early 1940s Drelinger worked as a studio musician, notably for CBS; he made numerous recordings on tenor saxophone with such musicians as Louis Armstrong (1946, 1949, 1950), Billie Holiday (1947, 1949), Sy Oliver (1949–51), and Benny Carter (1952), but his style is better represented on an earlier session with Rollini (including *Tap Room Swing*, 1936, Decca 787). Besides his main instrument he also played clarinet and other saxophones.

based on *ChiltonW*

Dresser, Mark (*b* Los Angeles, 26 Nov 1952). Double bass player. He studied double bass privately with Bertram Turetzky in California and jazz with David Baker at Indiana University (1970–71); he played with the San Diego SO from 1973 to 1975. From 1972 he played free jazz with Stanley Crouch, Bobby Bradford, Arthur Blythe, James Newton, and David Murray on the West Coast. He moved east, and appeared with Murray at the Loft Jazz Festival at Studio Rivbea, New York (1975). He has recorded with Newton (*Binu*, 1977, Cir. [Ger.] 11), Ray Anderson (1980), and Bradford (1983). (*Feather–Gitler '70s*)

Drew, John (Derek) (*b* Sheffield, England, 23 Dec 1927). English double bass player. He learned piano as a child and began studying double bass in 1943. He became well known as a freelance musician in London from 1945, his engagements including work for the BBC. After emigrating to the USA in 1954, he joined the trumpeter Les Elgart and then played with Gene Krupa (1955–6), who was beginning to admit a bass player into his small groups to share the time-keeping role. While working with Krupa, he met the pianists Bobby Scott and Dave McKenna, with whom he later recorded. In the 1950s he performed with Stan Getz (1956), Barbara Carroll (1957), Marian McPartland (1958–9), and the Sauter–Finegan Orchestra (1958–9), and made recordings with Dick Garcia (1955), the pianist Joe Saye (1958), and Benny Carter (*c*1959); he was also a member of the Miami Beach SO (1957). He continued to work as a freelance, increasingly in areas outside jazz. Drew is known for the fine execution and rhythmic swing of his playing.

SELECTED RECORDINGS

As sideman: on D. Garcia: *Message from Garcia* (1955, Dawn 1106), Have you met Miss Jones?, I don't want to set the world on fire; D. McKenna: *Piano Scene* (1958, Epic 3558); J. Saye: *A Double Shot of Joe Saye* (1958, EmA 36147); B. Carter: *Can Can and Anything Goes* (*c*1959, UA 3055); B. Scott: *A Taste of Honey* (1960, Atl. 1355)

BIBLIOGRAPHY

FeatherE

LAWRENCE KOCH

Drew, Kenny [Kenneth Sidney] (*b* New York, 28 Aug 1928). Pianist. He studied piano from the age of five and gave his first recital when he was eight. He was influenced as a teenager by Fats Waller, Teddy Wilson, and Art Tatum, and later by Bud Powell. He attended the High School of Music and Art in New York. He made his first recordings in 1949 with Howard McGhee and in the 1950s played with many leading jazz musicians, including Coleman Hawkins, Lester Young, Charlie Parker, Milt Jackson, Art Blakey (in Buddy DeFranco's quartet), and Dinah Washington; in 1958 he joined Buddy Rich's band. He moved to Europe in 1961 and settled first in Paris, then in Copenhagen (1964). With Niels-Henning Ørsted Pedersen he formed a duo in 1966 that became resident at the Montmartre Jazzhus in Copenhagen and during the next two decades made several recordings; also in Copenhagen he formed a music publishing company, Shirew Publishing. From the late 1970s he devoted time to composition and orchestration. As a pianist Drew is noted for his ability to alternate seamlessly between a dense, chordal style and the single-note melodic lines that are identified with such bop pianists as Powell.

SELECTED RECORDINGS

As unaccompanied soloist: *It Might as well be Spring* (1981, SN 1040)
Duos with N.-H. Ørsted Pedersen: *Duo* (1973, Ste. 1002)
As leader: *Ruby my Dear* (1977, Ste. 1129); *Home is Where the Soul is* (1978, Xan. 166); *And Far Away* (1983, SN 1081)
As sideman: H. McGhee: Fluid Drive/Donello Square (1949, BN 1573); S. Stitt: Later/Ain't Misbehavin' (1950, Prst. 704); on S. Rollins: *Sonny Rollins Quartet* (1951, Prst. 137), Newk's Fadeaway; D. Gordon: Confirmation (1955, Beth. 11026); J. Coltrane: *Blue Train* (1957, BN 1577); J. Griffin: *Way out!* (1958, Riv. 274); D. Gillespie: *The Giant* (1973, Prst. 24047); G. Ammons: *Goodbye* (1974, Prst. 10093)

BIBLIOGRAPHY

M. Gardner: "Kenny Drew," *JM*, xiii/5 (1967), 2
M. Hennessey: "Caught in the Act: Kenny Drew–Jimmy Heath," *DB*, xxxvii/2 (1970), 30
J. Armstrong: "Kenny Drew," *JF* [intl edn], no.15 (1972), 64
"Kenny Drew Discography," *Disk in the World*, i (July 1980), 23
E. Southern: *Biographical Dictionary of Afro-American and African Musicians* (Westport, CT, 1982)
B. Taylor: *Jazz Piano: History and Development* (Dubuque, IA, 1982), 162

ANDRÉ BARBERA

Drew, Martin (*b* Northampton, England, 11 Feb 1944). English drummer. He studied for more than three years with George Fierstone, and played jazz in his spare time before becoming professional at the age of 29. His first engagement was with Frank Rosolino at Ronnie Scott's club in London, where he later became a house drummer. He also worked with Bill Le Sage, and performed and made recordings with the Bebop Preservation Society (including *Red Rodney with the Bebop*

Preservation Society, 1975, Spot. 7). In 1974 he began working with Scott's quartet and quintet, and the following year he began an association with Oscar Peterson which has continued, intermittently, into the mid-1980s; he recorded with Scott in 1977, and has recorded with Peterson on several occasions. Drew's flexibility and versatility have enabled him to perform with ease with many musicians, including Count Basie, Dizzy Gillespie, Michel Legrand, Anita O'Day, and Jimmy Witherspoon. He also recorded the album *Martin Drew and his Band* (Lee Lambert 003) as the leader of his own group in 1977.

For illustration *see* NIGHTCLUBS AND OTHER VENUES, fig.2.

BIBLIOGRAPHY

R. Cotterell, ed.: *Jazz Now: the Jazz Centre Society Guide* (London, 1976), 129

A. Morgan: "Oscar's Choice: Best of British, 7: Martin Drew," *JJI*, xxxi/9 (1978), 10

B. Case: "Martin Drew: Nailing it," *MM*, lv (12 Jan 1980), 21

S. Goodwin: "Martin Drew: British Jazz," *MD*, ix/6 (1985), 24

STAN BRITT

Drewo, Karl (*b* Vienna, 17 May 1929). Austrian saxophonist. From the age of ten he learned to play accordion and piano; he changed to tenor saxophone and worked in the orchestras of Charlie Gaudriot (1947) and Paul Reischmann (1948–51). He performed on the first Austrian bop recording as a member of Gert Steffens's orchestra in 1951. In the early 1950s Drewo worked in Horst Winter's orchestra and he then played and recorded with the Austrian All Stars (1954–6), Austria's leading modern-jazz group. After working with Fatty George from 1956 to 1958, he joined Kurt Edelhagen's orchestra in Germany, with which he remained until 1972. He made recordings as a member of the Golden Eight, together with Zoot Sims, Jimmy Woode, and Kenny Clarke (1961), and occasionally with the Clarke–Boland Big Band (including *Swing, Waltz, Swing*, 1966, Phi. 840246). From 1973 he played tenor and alto saxophones in the radio orchestra of Österreichischer Rundfunk. In 1981 he recorded with Peter Herbolzheimer and began to work as a freelance. He is a gifted player of bop and mainstream jazz and performs ballads in the style of Ben Webster.

KLAUS SCHULZ

Driscoll, Julie (Dawn). *See* TIPPETTS, JULIE.

D'Rivera, Paquito (*b* Havana, 4 June 1948). Cuban alto saxophonist. He was introduced to jazz by his father, who played tenor saxophone and gave him his first lessons; the styles of Benny Goodman, Charlie Parker, and Paul Desmond were early influences on his playing. He learned mainly from listening to recordings and the "Willis Conover Jazz Hour," a radio show broadcast on the Voice of America. From 1960 he studied at the conservatory in Havana, where he met Chucho Valdés, who became the main influence on his career. He played in musical theater from the age of 14 and during his army service (from 1965) was a member of an army band. He then joined the Orquesta Cubana de Música Moderna, the members of which formed the basis of the group IRAKERE (formed *c*1973). During a tour of Europe in 1980 D'Rivera defected while the band was in Spain; he moved to New York, where he played with David Amram, Dizzy Gillespie, and McCoy Tyner. He later formed his own group, which has toured the USA, Europe, and South America, and performed and worked as a studio musician in New York. D'Rivera is considered one of the foremost Latin American bop saxophonists; besides the alto instrument he also plays soprano saxophone, and flute and flugelhorn.

SELECTED RECORDINGS

(recorded for Columbia unless otherwise stated)

As leader: *Paquito Blowin'* (1981, FC37374); *Mariel* (1982, FC38177); *The New York/Montreux Connection* (1982, FC37652); *Live at Keystone Korner* (1983, FC38899); *Why not* (1984, FC39584)

As sideman: on D. Amram: *Havana/New York* (1977, Flying Fish 057), En memoria de Chano Pozo; Irakere: *Irakere* (1978, JC35655); *Irakere II* (1979, JC36107); M. Tyner: *La leyenda de la hora* (1981, FC37375); D. Amram: *David Amram's Latin Jazz Celebration* (1982, Elek. Mus. 60237)

BIBLIOGRAPHY

B. Lundvall: Liner notes, *Paquito Blowin'* (Col. FC37374, 1981)

L. Jeske: "Paquito D'Rivera: Alto in Exile," *DB*, l/11 (1983), 23 [incl. discography]

H. Mandel: "Paquito D'Rivera's Freedom Song," *JT* (May 1983), 10

B. Korall: "Paquito D'Rivera: Making his own Music, at Last," *IM*, lxxxiii/4 (1984), 5

S. Woolley: "Cuban Roots: a Profile of Paquito D'Rivera," *JJI*, xl/11 (1987), 9

CATHERINE COLLINS

Drootin, Al(bert M.) (*b* Boston, 24 Dec 1916). Clarinetist and bandleader, brother of Buzzy Drootin. He took part in dixieland jam sessions in Boston during the late 1930s. In New York he performed with Bud Freeman (1940), Muggsy Spanier (1941), and Boyd Raeburn (1942). After serving in the army he returned to Boston, where he played into the 1970s. He recorded with his brother in the Mahogany Hall All Stars (1953) and as a member of an octet that included Ruby Braff and Vic Dickenson (*Jazz at the Boston Arts Festival*, 1954, Sto. 311). He was a leader of the Drootin Brothers from 1973. (*Feather–Gitler '70s*)

Drootin, Buzzy [Benjamin] (*b* Russia, 22 April *c*1910). Drummer, brother of Al Drootin. When he was five his family emigrated to the USA and settled in Boston, where he began playing professionally with local groups in 1936; his father and two brothers (Al and Lewis) were also musicians. In the 1940s he toured with Ina Ray Hutton's All Boys Band (1940) and worked with traditional jazz players such as Jess Stacy, Wingy Manone, Buck Clayton, and Edmond Hall. He was the house drummer at Eddie Condon's club in 1947–51, and made recordings with Condon (1950, 1955, 1962) as well as with Tommy Dorsey (1950), Ruby Braff (1954–61), Bobby Hackett (1957, 1960), and the Dukes of Dixieland (1962–3). He also performed with many all-star groups, among them Jazz at Storyville (with Sidney Bechet, 1953), the Dixieland All-Stars (1958), Great Moments in Jazz (at the Newport Jazz Festival, 1964), and the Jazz Giants (including Wild Bill Davison, 1968–9). After leading a group in 1971–2 and working as a freelance in New York, he returned to Boston to lead the Drootin Brothers with his brother Al (1973). In the 1970s and 1980s he frequently appeared with other seasoned jazzmen at such events as the Los Angeles Classic Jazz Festival (1984); he also played occasionally with local musicians near his home outside Boston.

Drootin's playing is technically accomplished and reflects the trends in dixieland drumming from the 1950s onwards, emphasizing ride-cymbal accompanimental patterns complemented by snare-drum accents executed with the left hand. His recordings often include ostentatious, syncopated solos.

SELECTED RECORDINGS

As sideman: G. Wein: *Midnight Concert in Paris* (1961, Smash 67023); Jazz Giants: *The Jazz Giants* (1968, Sack. 3002)

BIBLIOGRAPHY

FeatherE; *Feather '60s*; *Feather–Gitler '70s*

D. Morgenstern: "Some Different Drummers," *DB*, xxxix/5 (1972), 20

T. DENNIS BROWN

Drop. A GLISS falling from the end of a note.

(a)

1. (a) Sonny Greer and his drum set, with Duke Ellington, Chicago, 1940: for key to components of the drum set see (b) opposite

Drum fill. A Fill played by the drummer.

Drum set [drum kit, trap set]. The term used to describe the basic equipment of the jazz drummer, usually a combination of percussion instruments including bass drum, snare drum, tom-toms, and cymbals.

I. Components. II. Use.

I. Components

1. General. 2. Bass drum. 3. Snare drum. 4. Tom-tom. 5. Cymbals. 6. Cowbell and other metal instruments. 7. Woodblock and temple block. 8. Drumsticks and brushes. 9. Timpani. 10. Washboard. 11. Electronic devices.

1. General. The drum set evolved during the last two decades of the 19th century when the invention of the bass-drum pedal with an attached cymbal striker allowed bass drum, snare drum, and cymbal to be played by only one performer. It was first adapted for use by drummers in theater orchestras and later by musicians in the ragtime, jazz, and society dance bands that were popular in the first 20 years of the 20th century. The drum set has at times included a large number of percussion instruments (see fig.1), and, although jazz styles have not in general been affected by the size of the set, they have been influenced by the instruments in regular use and the manner in which these have been played. Electronic drums and drum machines developed during the 1970s and 1980s have made dramatic and substantial changes to the drum set and to playing methods.

2. Bass drum. The bass drum in the earliest drum sets was an instrument in wide use in the USA during the 19th century. It was double headed and had a wooden shell ranging in size from 51 cm in diameter by 36 cm wide (that of the small military drum) to between 71 cm and 76 cm in diameter by 46 cm wide. The heads were of calfskin and were tensioned by ropes or, more generally, single or double tension rods. Later, holders for cymbals, woodblocks, cowbells, and tom-toms were clamped to the rims, or a trap rack or ring was placed on or over the bass drum to hold a variety of percussion instruments or accessories. Colorful paintings were executed on the front head and a light bulb was placed inside the drum. In the late 1920s drum shells were covered with laminated plastic in a variety of plain, pearl-textured, and glittering colors, and during the next decade the paintings were replaced by the initials of the drummer or bandleader.

(b)

1. (b) Components of the drum set: A – bass drum; B – snare drum; C – tom-tom; D – floor tom-tom; E – Chinese cymbal; F – Turkish cymbal; G – splash cymbal; H – hi-hat cymbals; I – cowbell; J – tam-tams; K – tubular bells; L – woodblock; M – set of five temple blocks; N – tray containing drumsticks (right), brushes (left), and timpani mallets (center); O – pair of timpani; P – vibraphone

From the 1930s the standard bass drum has been 56 cm by 36 cm (although there was a short-lived trend in the 1960s towards the use of smaller drums); major improvements have been the addition of external mufflers, tension lugs, telescoping spurs (supports), and plastic heads. Fiberglass, plastic, and metal shells were made in the 1970s, and by the following decade natural wood was also being used. While the demands made on the drum set by rock musicians have led to stronger construction of instruments, the size of the bass drum has changed little in the 1980s.

The first bass-drum pedal, a foot pedal designed to play the drum with a beater, was invented before 1850 by Cornelius Ward for use with a lithophone. There were three early types of pedal – the overhanging or swing pedal, the heel pedal, and the toe pedal – each of which was made of wood and had an attached cymbal striker. The three types were equally popular until 1909, when the Ludwig Drum Company patented an all-metal, double-posted, adjustable toe pedal (see fig.2, p.310); this was so successful that it was widely imitated by other companies and served as a model for nearly all subsequent pedals, improvements to which have mainly concerned the materials from which they are made.

A variety of bass-drum beaters have evolved. Originally a hard core was wrapped with string and cloth and covered with leather or burlap; later coverings were made of sheepskin, which some drummers either shaved or burned smooth in order to obtain a more percussive sound. Although from the 1960s solid-wood and half-wood, half-felt beaters have been used with varying degrees of success, the standard beater is of hard felt.

3. Snare drum. The only type of snare drum to be used in the drum set has been the shallow snare drum, popular in Europe and the USA from the mid-1800s. It had a shell and rims made of wood or metal, gut snares, and rod tensioning, and measured approximately 38 cm in diameter by 10 cm to 20 cm in width. Early drummers placed the instrument on a chair, but a more convenient position was found in 1898 with the invention by Ulysses Leedy of the adjustable snare-drum stand.

The structure of the snare drum has changed little since its first appearance in the drum set. However, internal mufflers were introduced in 1900, and in the second decade of the century all-metal instruments in a variety of sizes were being manufactured; by 1918 gut snares had been replaced by wire snares and a quick snare release was in use. In the 1920s drums

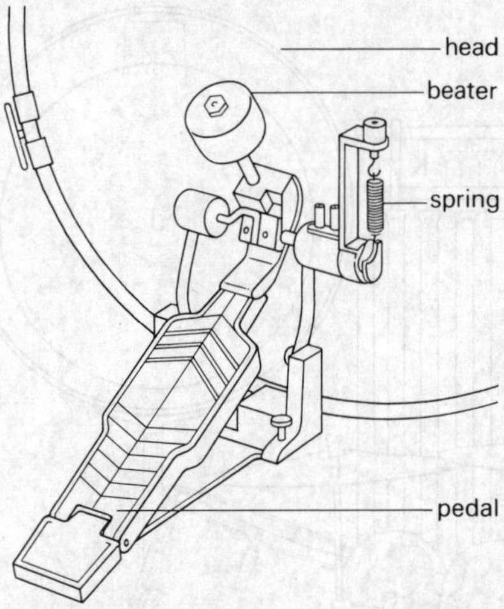

2. Bass-drum foot pedal; pressing the pedal causes the beater to hit the drum. When the foot is lifted, the beater returns to its original position by means of the spring on the right.

with individually tensioned snares and parallel snare release were available, as were wooden shells with metal rims and a wide variety of finishes, including wood tones, stipple gold or silver, and imitation pearl. Metal drums often had elaborately engraved shells or gold-plated rims. Later examples have incorporated such design modifications as flanged rims, spring tension lugs, plastic heads, and deeper shells. An individual contribution to the development of the drum set was made around 1932 by CHAUNCEY MOREHOUSE, who designed a set of 14 chromatically tuned snare drums.

4. TOM-TOM. Although single-headed tunable tom-toms were manufactured in the USA from the end of World War I, early drummers favored instruments imported from China. Chinese tom-toms were available in a variety of sizes, the smallest being some 13 cm in diameter and 8 cm deep, and had two thick pigskin heads attached to the shell by means of large brass tacks. Musicians tuned the drums either by heating the heads with a match or by piercing one or both heads. Traditionally, both heads were decorated with bright red and green Chinese drawings (usually one pictured a bird and the other a wide-eyed dragon), and authentic drums contained a wound strand of wire that rattled when the instrument was played. As a consequence of trade restrictions after World War I, American drum companies began to manufacture tom-toms in the Chinese style, but without the wire rattle and elaborate paintings.

Practically every jazz drummer of the 1920s attached a Chinese tom-tom to the set, and some drummers continued to do so until the end of the 1940s. By the 1930s, however, musicians began to use tunable tom-toms with adjustable tension rods, and in the middle of the decade both floor tom-toms and either one or two instruments mounted on the bass drum were commonplace. At first only the top head was tunable, the bottom head being tacked on in the Chinese fashion, but later both could be tuned by tension rods. In the bop era the drum set included two tom-toms – one on the floor and one mounted on the bass drum – and later drummers often added a further instrument mounted on the bass drum. From the 1960s graduated sets of multiple tom-toms (four, six, eight or more) have been popular with rock drummers, but jazz musicians have been slow to accept them as a regular part of the drum set.

A floor tom-tom with a timpani-like tuning pedal was first used in the 1960s, and by the end of the 1970s cable-operated pedal floor tom-toms were available. At the same time a number of instruments similar to the tom-toms were introduced. These included roto-toms (shallow, single-headed frame drums tuned by rotation on fixed, threaded spindles), usually used in sets of two or more, octobans (a set of eight single-headed drums 20 cm in diameter but of varying shell depth), and gong tom-toms (single-headed drums with deep shells).

5. CYMBALS. In the earliest drum sets, a Turkish cymbal (usually 36 cm or less in diameter) was clamped to the rim of the bass drum so that it was parallel to the drum head closest to the drummer. Known as a zinger cymbal, it was activated by a small striker attached to the bass-drum beater. Initially the cymbal was sounded each time the pedal was pressed, but later pedals had an adjustable striker that could be moved away from the cymbal to allow the bass drum to be played alone. Although the zinger cymbal was very popular among drummers during the first 20 years of the 20th century, early jazz recordings are void of its sound.

Shortly after the turn of the century two other cymbals were added to the drum set: a Chinese cymbal and either a second Turkish cymbal or an American-made brass cymbal. These were suspended from an adjustable T-shaped stand clamped to the rim of the bass drum, or placed, inverted or upright, on a heavy spring cymbal holder, 15 cm in length. Chinese cymbals found in early drum sets were some 41 cm to 56 cm in diameter and had a number of distinctive features, notably upturned edges and a raised cup in the center; they often had Chinese characters drawn in black ink on the upper surface. These cymbals sounded lower and more brittle than Turkish cymbals, and remained popular with jazz drummers until well into the 1940s. After a hiatus, in the 1970s the Chinese cymbal found favor once again as jazz and rock drummers sought new timbres.

During the 1930s musicians began to incorporate more cymbals in their drum sets. These were usually American-made Turkish cymbals, ranging in size from the small splash cymbal, about 10 cm in diameter, to instruments as large as 41 cm. Gene Krupa's drum set of 1938 was typical, with two splash cymbals (used for novelty effects), two crash cymbals (36 cm in diameter, and used for accents rather than steady timekeeping), two hi-hat cymbals (30 cm in diameter), and a Greeko cymbal – a small (5 cm) tuned cymbal which was generally clamped to the rim of the bass drum. Some drummers also made use of the choke cymbal, a small, thin cymbal 10 cm to 20 cm in diameter, to create staccato patterns.

The sizzle cymbal, popular in the 1920s, is created by placing rivets loosely in holes drilled around the edge of a Turkish or Chinese instrument; when the cymbal is struck, the rivets vibrate and produce a distinctive sustained sound. Although it is seldom heard on recordings from this period, it was favored by dixieland drummers in the 1930s and by some bop drummers in the 1960s.

The large Turkish cymbal (46 to 66 cm in diameter) known as the top or ride cymbal was made from the late 1930s to accommodate the particular needs of big-band and bop drummers. This instrument eventually became a standard part of the drum set, as did the crash and hi-hat cymbals.

Although the hi-hat (two cymbals brought together by means of a foot pedal) became popular during the 1930s, many similar devices existed previously. These included the low-boy, or low-sock cymbal, which was first used around 1926; it was identical to the hi-hat except that the cymbals were held 30 cm from the floor. The earliest hi-hats (which attracted such names as top hat, high boy, hi sock, sock cymbal, and off-beat cymbal) appeared in drum catalogues in 1927. In the 1920s most hi-hats used a pair of Charleston cymbals, brass instruments approximately 25 cm in diameter with a very large cup or bell, but in the 1930s these were replaced by Turkish cymbals 28 cm to 38 cm in diameter. In the 1980s drummers play matched hi-hat cymbals, the most common size being 36 to 38 cm in diameter.

With the exception of the cable-operated hi-hat introduced in the 1980s, the design of the hi-hat has remained unchanged since its inception. The cable-operated version allows the drummer to place the pedal to his left and the stand and cymbals to his right, and is usually used in conjunction with a traditional hi-hat.

Other types of cymbal in use in the 1980s include flat, cupless ride cymbals, large Chinese style cymbals, heavy unlathed (i.e., not machine-finished) cymbals, and colored cymbals.

6. Cowbell and other metal instruments. Cowbells of various sizes were first introduced into the drum set in the ragtime era. The most common arrangement consisted of two cowbells joined together at their closed ends and mounted on the rim of the bass drum. Sometimes four graduated cowbells were attached to the bass drum, either side by side or one inside the other. The instrument remained in the drum set throughout the swing era, and its sound became an important element during the dixieland revival period. Although it did not find a place in the bop drum set, it has maintained its popularity with rock and Latin-jazz musicians.

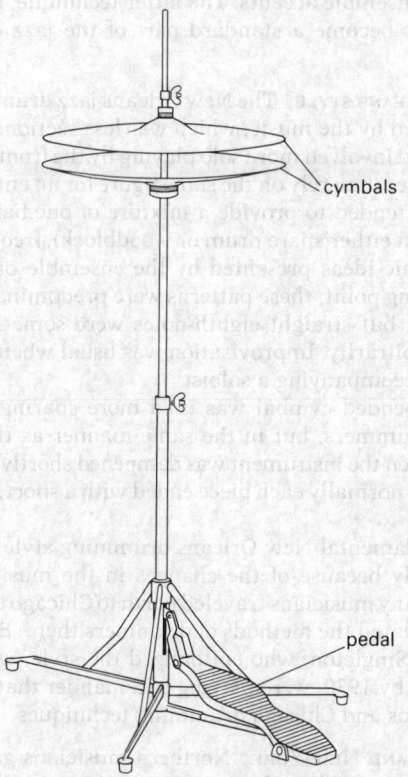

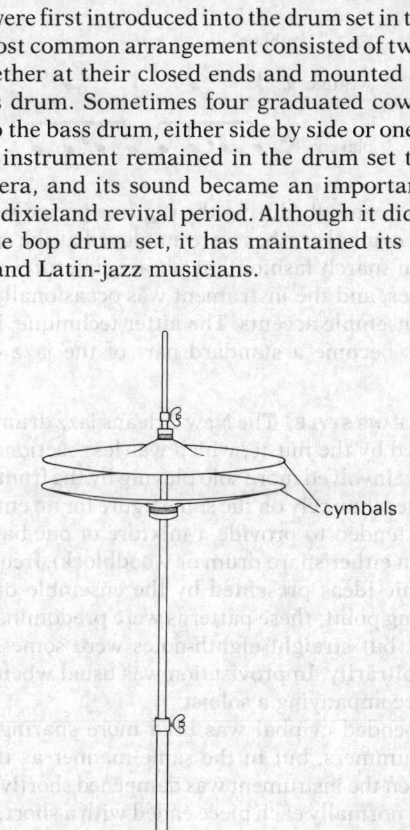

3. Hi-hat; pressing the pedal causes the top cymbal to be brought against the lower by a connecting rod. When the foot is lifted the cymbal returns to its original position by means of a spring

By the 1980s an assortment of metal instruments, such as windchimes, gongs, tam-tams, and bells, were included in the drum set.

7. Woodblock and temple block. Two types of slit-drum are commonly found in drum sets.

(i) The Chinese woodblock. The Chinese woodblock, which has been known in Europe and the USA from the 19th century by various names (clog box, slit-drum, tap box, tone block), is a small rectangular wooden box with slits cut into one or both sides. Cylindrical woodblocks in tuned pairs or groups of four were also available. The instrument was included in early drum sets for its unique sound capabilities: for example, it could be used when accompanying silent films to imitate tap-dancing or horses' hooves, and, when played by drummers in ragtime bands, it could be loud enough to penetrate the most blaring passage, yet soft enough to accompany a piano solo. Although the woodblock was used well into the 1930s, it remains associated principally with ragtime and dixieland jazz.

(ii) Temple block. The temple block is modeled on the hollow wooden temple block originally used in China. Roughly spherical in form, it has a slit carved in the top or front and is often painted bright red and gold to resemble an oriental fish. Temple blocks were included in the drum set from the 1920s, frequently in graduated sets of five, and were played by many big-band drummers, notably Sonny Greer, Chick Webb, Jo Jones, and Ray Bauduc.

8. Drumsticks and brushes. During the 1920s drum companies began to manufacture sticks specifically designed for the jazz or dance-band drummer. Most sticks were similar to those used by orchestral musicians, but, for example, thin, light Charleston drumsticks were made in the mid-1920s especially for "hot-cymbal" playing on Charleston cymbals. During the following decade some companies tried unsuccessfully to market drumsticks made of synthetic material such as fiberglass and plastic. Thereafter drumsticks became available in different lengths, weights, and woods, and with a variety of tip sizes and shapes. Nylon tips, designed to increase the longevity of wooden drumsticks, were introduced in the 1960s, and later a number of short-lived hybrid sticks, such as all-metal and metal-tipped models, appeared. In the 1980s technology has improved enough to make synthetic drumsticks viable contenders in a market that has come to include custom-made sticks.

Many drummers from the 1950s onwards – notably Sonny Greer, Chick Webb, Chico Hamilton, and Elvin Jones – have also employed timpani mallets (not those manufactured for use with xylophone or vibraphone). These have sturdy cylindrical drumstick-like handles of wood, rattan, or plastic and heads made of hard felt, wood, plastic, or (for playing tom-toms) soft cotton. A good example of a solo played with mallets is that performed by Vernel Fournier on *Poinciana* on Ahmad Jamal's album *Ahmad Jamal* (1958, Argo 636).

Brushes consist of a fan of wire strands, which may be telescoped into a hollow handle when not in use. They were first heard on jazz recordings during the late 1920s, when they were often substituted for drumsticks during slow numbers. Several variations of the original brushes (designed in 1912 as fly-swatters) have been marketed, including nonretractable brushes, brushes with drumstick handles, and brushes with thick strands of plastic instead of wire.

9. Timpani. A number of jazz ensembles during the 1920s and 1930s (the Scranton Sirens, 1921; the Moulin Rouge Synco-

pators, early 1920s; and the orchestras led by Chick Webb and Duke Ellington, both 1930s) included timpani in their instrumentation, although very few bands recorded with them. In 1926–7, however, Vic Berton made several memorable recordings (including *Mean Dog Blues*, 1927, Bruns. 3597) with Red Nichols and his Five Pennies on which he plays bass accompaniment figures and "hot-timpani" solos, a feat that has not been repeated.

10. Washboard. The washboard is a piece of corrugated metal, approximately 20 cm by 25 cm in size, played by placing thimbles on one or more fingers and scraping them across the surface. It has a restricted but curiously important history in jazz, since several well-known drummers – notably Jasper Taylor, Jimmy Bertrand, and Baby Dodds – made recordings with it. Dodds may be heard on *Piggly Wiggly* (1929, Bruns. 80076), recorded by the Beale Street Washboard Band.

11. Electronic devices. Several electronic drum-set devices appeared during the 1970s (although some electronic organs had percussion stops in the 1960s), all of which fall into one of two basic groups – the drum machine or the electronic drum pad. Only the latter, which is activated by drumsticks, has been freely incorporated into the drum set (and in some cases has actually replaced the drum set). Electronic drum pads are played by striking the drum-like pads to produce a series of preset analog or digital sounds; these are determined either by dials at the base of the pads or by a controlling unit (the "brain"). Acoustic drums may also be used to trigger the controlling unit, or, conversely, the brain can sample the sounds of acoustic drums, which can then be reproduced on the drum pads. The use of drum machines in jazz has been somewhat limited, although some well-known drummers (Harvey Mason, Peter Erskine, Danny Gottlieb, and Omar Hakim) have employed them on recordings made in the 1980s. (*See also* Synthesizer, §§1 and 2 (iii).)

II. Use

1. Early years. 2. Ragtime drummers. 3. New Orleans style. 4. Chicago and New York. 5. The swing era and big bands. 6. Bop drumming. 7. Free jazz. 8. Jazz-rock.

1. Early years. Early jazz drummers drew principally on European military percussion techniques of the 18th and 19th centuries, though they were also influenced by African and Caribbean drumming styles. The military or rudimental drumming elements comprise a series of single or double sticking patterns known by such mnemonic names as "ruff," "paradiddle," "ratamacue," and "drag," and the assimilation of rudimental drumming techniques has had a major impact upon drum-set performance – a point that has been somewhat belabored in jazz literature (*see* Rudiments). However, early set drummers made use of nonrudimentary terms to describe less familiar patterns; Baby Dodds, for example, used the "biff," "flim-flam," and "lick" in his playing. More importantly, Dodds recalled applying particular beats or rhythmic patterns to certain pieces, indicating that they required specific accompanying patterns in much the same way as some forms of Latin American music (the samba, cha-cha, and rumba).

Another frequently used technique was "double drumming," where the snare drum is placed at a sharp angle to the bass drum head, allowing the bass drum to be hit either with the butt or the tip of the drumstick, which is then quickly returned to the snare drum. Double drumming was common even after the adoption of the bass-drum pedal. An excellent (and probably the earliest) recorded example of this technique is played by Tony Sbarbaro with the Original Dixieland Jazz Band on *Dixie Jass Band One-step* (1917, Vic. 18255).

The first drum-set players performed parts originally written for two or three drummers; the music was relatively simple, however, and musicians frequently embellished the written part or (more often) improvised a new one.

2. Ragtime drummers. The first semblance of an original drum-set style was manifest during the ragtime era in the playing of William Reitz, James Lent, Buddy Gilmore, and Sbarbaro. This style combined simple, march-like figures with syncopation and improvisation. While single-stroke patterns were played for an entire chorus, open rolls, flams, and ruffs were used to follow or embellish the melodic rhythm on snare drum or woodblock; the pattern would then be changed for the next section. An important technique used by ragtime drummers was "doubling" (not to be confused with double drumming), in which the value of the written notes is halved (ex.1); this was probably done at the player's discretion in order to create excitement or simply to add interest to rather dull drum parts.

Ex.1 "Doubling"

The use of cymbals during the ragtime period was limited. Suspended cymbal crashes were employed at the end of introductions (in march fashion), at phrase junctures, and at the end of pieces, and the instrument was occasionally played to highlight ensemble accents. The latter technique, known as a "kick," has become a standard part of the jazz drummer's repertory.

3. New Orleans style. The New Orleans jazz drumming style was dictated by the music, which was less sectionalized than ragtime and involved more solo playing by the front-line musicians. Rather than rely on the same figure for an entire chorus, drummers tended to provide a mixture of one-bar rhythmic patterns (on either snare drum or woodblock), frequently taking rhythmic ideas presented by the ensemble or soloist as their starting point; these patterns were predominantly based on triplets, but straight eighth-notes were sometimes interspersed arbitrarily. Improvisation was usual when the drummer was accompanying a soloist.

The suspended cymbal was used more sparingly by New Orleans drummers, but in the same manner as their predecessors. Often the instrument was dampened shortly after being struck, and normally each piece ended with a short, crisp cymbal crash.

The fundamental New Orleans drumming style was short-lived, partly because of the changes in the music, but also because many musicians traveled north to Chicago in the 1920s and assimilated the methods of drummers there. Baby Dodds and Zutty Singleton, who epitomized the style, were among those who, by 1930, were playing in a manner that combined New Orleans and Chicago drumming techniques.

4. Chicago and New York. Northern musicians gained their experience in traveling shows, movie and vaudeville theaters, and territory bands. The music they performed therefore embraced a wide range of styles and was significantly different from that played by the New Orleans drummers. Furthermore, northern players were better trained than their New Orleans

4. Baby Dodds with Jimmie Noone, Chicago, 1941; Dodds's drum set includes two Chinese tom-toms, a ratchet, woodblock, and cowbells

colleagues, for many of them had studied with classical musicians.

There are obvious stylistic and conceptual differences in the drumming of New Orleans players and that of such musicians from Chicago as Frank Snyder (with the New Orleans Rhythm Kings, 1922) and Ben Pollack (1923). The Chicago drummers typically employed the suspended cymbal to play rhythmic accompaniment patterns, made integral use of the bass drum in combination with other instruments in fills (*see* FILL) and solos, and developed a standardized brush technique. One of the earliest jazz recordings on which brushes may be heard, Pollack's *Memphis Blues* (1927, Vic. 21184), suggests that northern musicians had developed their skills with brushes over a considerable length of time.

More substantial evidence of how the bass drum was likely to have been played was provided in 1926 with the advent of electrical recording techniques. The bass drum was often used to mark the second and fourth beats of the bar, and, occasionally, all four beats (especially during the out chorus); in any event, it was usually played to coincide with the double bass or tuba. The earliest jazz recordings demonstrate that drummers generally played on all four beats of the bar (sans bass drum) regardless of what the other musicians were doing. Consequently, the drummer might be playing in 4/4 meter on snare drum and cymbals, while the rest of the band was playing in 2/2 (or vice versa). The main function of the drummer was to improvise an accompaniment to or embellish the rhythmic activity of the front-line musicians; he did not take responsibility for maintaining a steady tempo within the rhythm section.

By the end of the 1920s several drumming styles had emerged in Chicago and New York. One, which may be traced back to the influence of the Original Dixieland Jazz Band, is typified by the hot-cymbal performances of Vic Berton (for example, *Boneyard Shuffle*, 1926, Bruns. 3477). Another is exemplified by such musicians as Dave Tough, Bob Conselman, Paul Kettler, and George Stafford, and culminated in the work of Gene Krupa; these drummers played repeated rhythmic patterns interspersed with rim shots on the snare drum and used the bass drum on all four beats of the bar. Krupa's influence on the role of the drummer in the jazz ensemble is immeasurable. Although some of his contemporaries commanded equal or greater skill (notably Buddy Rich and Cozy Cole) and musicianship (Tough, Jo Jones), and some possessed a more ostentatious style of performance (Sonny Greer, Chick Webb), none epitomized the swing era better than he.

There are few early recorded examples of lengthy drum solos, though drummers occasionally took short solo breaks. The main impetus for change came in the 1930s as a result of Krupa's drum feature on *Sing, sing, sing* (1937, Vic. 36205, played mostly on floor tom-tom), which was a staple in the repertory of Benny Goodman's band during its tour in 1936. With such players as Webb, George Wettling, and Ray Bauduc, Krupa advanced the role of the drummer so that it was comparable with that of a front-line soloist.

According to iconographical evidence, drummers in the 1930s had an assortment of instruments (including timpani) at their disposal, yet most solos of the period were played on snare drum (occasionally on tom-toms) accompanied by a constant four beats to the bar on the bass drum; solos also involved frequent cymbal crashes and sometimes patterns on cowbell and/or woodblock. Such solos were generally intended as a simple display of the musician's technical ability and, while this could create considerable excitement, the result was often suspiciously lacking in musical substance. A few drummers, however (Webb, Jones, Sid Catlett, Krupa, and Rich), combined technique with musicianship and sometimes broke away from the symmetrical phrasing, four-square bass accompaniment, and exhibitionism that were common at the time.

5. THE SWING ERA AND BIG BANDS. From the 1920s several drumming styles came to be associated particularly with large-ensemble playing. Initially the same techniques (ostinato patterns, choked-cymbal figures, and occasional one- or two-beat fills) were used in large and small groups, but drummers soon modified their playing to accommodate the more controlled approach of the big bands.

Commercial big-band arrangements from the swing period show that drummers still improvised their part (with probable suggestions from the bandleader), though arrangers often indicated which instruments should be used (for example, brushes, gong, triangle, tom-tom), and what technique employed (choked cymbal, double drumming). The score thus provided the player with an outline of events rather than a fully notated part (a practice that did little to encourage drummers to learn to read music).

The most significant developments in big-band drumming occurred after the introduction around 1927 of the hi-hat. Several recordings, notably by Kaiser Marshall (with Fletcher Henderson's orchestra) and Cuba Austin (with McKinney's Cotton Pickers), demonstrate the popularity of hot-cymbal playing. On *Whiteman Stomp* (1927, Col. 1059D) Marshall uses the hi-hat to accompany the ensemble and also in several solo breaks; Austin may be heard playing the hi-hat on the Chocolate Dandies' recording of *Four or Five Times* (1928, OK 8627).

Walter Johnson, Marshall's successor in Henderson's band, developed a smooth, legato hi-hat technique by striking the cymbals on all four beats of the bar, while opening them on the second and fourth beats and closing them on the first and third. This style of playing contrasted sharply with the choked-cymbal technique of the previous decade (a method which sounded old-fashioned in comparison), and is epitomized on such recordings by Jo Jones as *Boogie Woogie* (1936, Voc. 3459), with Jones–Smith Incorporated, and *Time Out* (1937, Decca 1538), with Count Basie's orchestra.

Approximately ten years after the introduction of the hi-hat, big-band drummers began to play the ride cymbal to accompany soloists (for example, Tough on Tommy Dorsey's *Keepin' out of mischief now*, 1936, Vic. 25482) and in ensemble work (Jones on Basie's *Honeysuckle Rose*, 1937, Decca 1141). The rhythm employed by these musicians and countless other drummers had been common from the early 1920s and became known as the ride-cymbal beat (ex.2). The use of the ride cymbal in the late 1930s had a lasting impact on the development of drum-set techniques well into the bop era.

Ex.2 Ride-cymbal beat

6. Bop drumming. Bop drummers drew on the styles of the 1930s, but their playing incorporated several significantly different characteristics: the use of the ride cymbal as the predominant accompanying instrument; the consistent employment of the hi-hat on the second and fourth beats of the bar; the execution of random punctuations ("bombs") on the bass drum rather than a regular four-beat accompaniment (*see* Bomb); and asymmetrical phrasing. Bop musicians also perfected the ability to play separate but coordinated rhythms with all four limbs. These techniques originated in the playing of a few important swing drummers (Tough, Jones, Cole, Tiny Kahn) and culminated in the mid-1940s in the work of Kenny Clarke (a notable recording being *Epistrophy*, 1946, Swing 224) and Max Roach (Dexter Gordon's *Dexter rides again*, 1946, Savoy 623). Clarke and Roach, and later Art Blakey, were the catalysts for the subsequent maturation of bop drumming in the 1950s and 1960s as exemplified by the styles of such musicians as Elvin Jones and Tony Williams.

In the playing of Jones, in particular, the gradual dissolution of any semblance of meter may be heard, though he retains a metric scheme. This is accomplished in two ways: first, the ride-cymbal pattern implies the meter rather than delineating each beat; secondly, the hi-hat is integrated with the other parts of the drum set to create a rhythmic wash of percussive sounds that interact with the phrasing and rhythmic motifs of the soloists. Jones's approach is well represented by his performance on John Coltrane's *India* (1961, on the album *Impressions*, 1961–3, Imp. 42) and *Out of this World* (on the album *Coltrane*, 1962, Imp. 21).

Another style of drumming during the 1950s was associated with the cool-jazz movement and is exemplified by the work of Shelly Manne, Joe Morello, and Paul Motian. These musicians made use of mainstream bop techniques but placed an emphasis on precision, subtlety, and melodically constructed solos. Motian's delicate playing – he frequently uses brushes – may be heard on *Israel* and *Nardis* on the album *Explorations* (1961, Riv. 9351) by Bill Evans (ii); later he carried the same approach into free jazz, as on his own trio album *Le voyage* (1979, ECM 1178). Cool-jazz players also experimented successfully with odd meters.

The main difference between drum solos of the bop era and those from earlier periods is that bop drummers imitated the phrasing and developed rhythmic motifs used by the other instrumentalists. For the first time the drum set was played as a cohesive unit rather than as several different percussion instruments (a good example being Roach's performance on Charlie Parker's *Ko-Ko*, 1945, Savoy 597). Although recorded solos in the 1940s were largely of four or eight bars in length, extended solos became more common as a number of drummers, including Clarke, Roach, Manne, and Elvin Jones, became leaders.

Other approaches to solo drumming were developed in the 1950s and remain basic to the repertory of players in the 1980s. Drummers frequently build their solos on one or more of the following: a display of technical ability; a melodic or rhythmic motif which may or may not be associated with the tune; the form of the composition. An outstanding example of the last named is Max Roach's solo on *Blue Seven* on Sonny Rollins's album *Saxophone Colossus* (1956, Prst. 7079); even though he is not actually sounding pitches corresponding to the blues harmonies I–IV–I–V–I, Roach creates a rhythmic analogue to the harmonic progression by playing four- and two-bar phrases on different drums and cymbals in such a way as clearly to delineate the 12-bar blues progression of the piece.

7. Free jazz. In the late 1950s, as more musicians moved away from traditional ideas and embraced the free-form jazz pioneered by Ornette Coleman, significant new concepts emerged in the role of the drummer. Ed Blackwell and Billy Higgins, both of whom worked with Coleman, had their roots in jazz and rhythm-and-blues drumming styles. While they played ostinato accompaniment patterns in much the same manner as earlier drummers, they made use of the entire drum set for this purpose instead of just the cymbals, and did not restrict themselves to the traditional cymbal rhythmic figures. They often employed figures derived from rhythmic ideas presented by the other musicians or played complementary patterns, changing them frequently to delineate each section of the piece. This style is well represented on Coleman's album *Free Jazz* (1960, Atl. 1364), where both Higgins and Blackwell accompany the leader's double quartet.

Considerably more freedom may be discerned in the playing of such drummers as Sunny Murray (on Cecil Taylor's *Trance*, 1962, Debut 138) and Andrew Cyrille (*Enter Evening*, on Taylor's album *Unit Structures*, 1966, BN 84237). These musicians avoid most ostinato patterns (except in straight-ahead sections) and complement the work of the ensemble with a constant rhythmic activity, making use of a wide variety of percussive textures and dynamic shadings.

Free jazz afforded the drummer the opportunity to experiment in ways never before realized. Drummers in the 1970s and 1980s combined the new ideas with traditional techniques, and such musicians as Omar Hakim, Rashied Ali, Beaver Harris, and Barry Altschul (notably on the album *Another Time/Another Place*, 1978, Muse 5176) have developed individual styles that display extraordinary virtuosity and a heightened musical sense.

8. Jazz-rock. With some notable exceptions, stylistic differences in jazz drumming have been less pronounced from the 1960s to the 1980s. Although such musicians as Roach, Blakey, and Jones continued to play in the established style, most drummers of the period have been strongly influenced by the fusion of jazz and rock techniques. Rock provided jazz drummers with a new pulse (based on straight eighth-note and later 16th-note patterns), allowing for experimentation on a broader level. Many established drummers embraced rock as a logical extension of their craft (Buddy Rich and Tony Williams, for example), while a corps of important new players emerged in

5. *Billy Cobham at the Montreux International Jazz Festival, Switzerland, 1975*

the jazz-rock groups of the 1960s and 1970s – notably Bobby Columby with Blood, Sweat and Tears, Billy Cobham with the Mahavishnu Orchestra (fig.5; a good example of his approach may be heard on the album *The Inner Mounting Flame*, 1971, Col. KC31067), and Alphonse Mouzon and Peter Erskine with Weather Report. Erskine's work with Steps Ahead on the album *Steps Ahead* (1983, Elek. Mus. 60168) demonstrates the versatility of the best young jazz and rock drummers: on *Pools* he plays in a jazz-rock style, emphasizing the syncopated rhythms of funky black-American dance music towards the end of the piece; on *Islands* and *Both Sides of the Coin* he makes use of Latin-jazz rhythms (the latter number is a samba), while on *Loxodrome* he draws on bop rhythms; on *Skyward Bound*, a jazz-rock ballad, he keeps a simple metronomic beat, playing with brushes.

The inclusion of two bass drums in the set, originally a gimmick introduced in vaudeville shows during the 1920s, was revived in the 1940s by Louie Bellson and again in the 1960s by a few drummers; Cobham is among the jazz-rock musicians who have used two bass drums. Other drummers who have successfully melded jazz and rock styles of drumming in the 1980s are Danny Gottlieb, Ronald Shannon Jackson, Marvin "Smitty" Smith, Harvey Mason, and Steve Gadd.

See also CONGA; NOTATION, §5(iv), and ex.16; and RUDIMENTS; for further illustrations *see* ALI, RASHIED; BLAKEY, ART; CATLETT, SID; DOLPHY, ERIC; JONES, fig.1*c*; ORIGINAL DIXIELAND JAZZ BAND; ROACH, MAX; SINGLETON, ZUTTY; WATTERS, LU; WILLIAMS, MARY LOU; and WILLIAMS, TONY.

BIBLIOGRAPHY

G. Hoefer: "The History of the Drum in Jazz," *Jazz*, iv/10 (1965), 11

J. Blades: *Percussion Instruments and their History* (London, 1970, rev. 3/1984)

T. D. Brown: *A History and Analysis of Jazz Drumming to 1942* (diss., U. of Michigan, 1976)

T. DENNIS BROWN

DSC. Dutch Swing College. The abbreviation is frequently used for the DUTCH SWING COLLEGE BAND, which grew out of the activities of the college; in the 1970s the label DSC Production was formed to record the band's music.

DuConge, Peter (*b* New Orleans, *c*1903; *d* Michigan, *c*1965). Saxophonist and clarinetist. Several members of his family were musicians: his father, Oscar, was a cornetist, and his brothers Adolphus, Albert, and Earl played piano, trumpet, and tenor saxophone respectively. He first worked professionally at the Elite Club in New Orleans. He played on riverboats before settling in New York, then in 1927 he toured in a revue with Vaughn's Lucky Sambo Orchestra and with Bill Brown and his Brownies. The following year he traveled to Europe with Leon Abbey. He remained in Europe until the outbreak of World War II, working with Abbey, Louis Armstrong (on his tours of 1932 and 1934), Coleman Hawkins (1935), and Benny Peyton. In 1933 DuConge made some recordings in Paris with a band led by Freddy Johnson and Arthur Briggs; *Foxy and Grapesy* (Bruns. A500278) displays his skill in transposing the New Orleans style into a swing context. (*ChartersJ*)

based on *ChiltonW*

Dudek, Gerd [Gerhard Rochus] (*b* Gross Döbern, nr Oppeln, Germany [now Opole, Poland], 23 Sept 1938). German tenor and soprano saxophonist. In Siegen he studied clarinet privately from 1954 and attended music school. He played in a big band led by his brother, the trumpeter Ossi Dudek (until 1958), in the Berliner Jazz Quintet (1960–64), and in Karl Blume's group; he also belonged to Kurt Edelhagen's orchestra (1960–65). Around 1965 he became interested in free jazz and joined Manfred Schoof's quintet; he took part in the first sessions of the Globe Unity Orchestra in 1966 and continued to be associated with the orchestra into the 1980s. He belonged to several groups led by Alex Schlippenbach (1968–70) and to Albert Mangelsdorff's quintet (1971–3), the Waterland Ensemble (1973–6), led by the pianist Loek Dikker, and the European Jazz Quintet (1977–82). In a trio with Buschi Niebergall and Edward Vesala he recorded at the Workshop Freie Musik in Berlin in 1977; he also took part in the workshop the following year. After playing in Mal Waldron's sextet (1979) Dudek formed a quartet in 1983 with Tony Oxley, the pianist Rob van den Broeck, and the double bass player Ali Haurand. Dudek is proficient both at improvising and at playing written music, and equally adept with the tenor and soprano saxophones. He also plays clarinet, flute, and śahnāī (an Indian oboe).

SELECTED RECORDINGS

As leader with B. Niebergall and E. Vesala: *Open* (1977, FMP 0570)

As sideman: M. Schoof: *Manfred Schoof Sextett* (1967, Wergo 80003); A. Mangelsdorff: *Birds of Underground* (1972, MPS 2121746); L. Dikker: *Tan Tango* (1975, Waterland 001); Globe Unity Orchestra: *Pearls* (1975, FMP 0380); [no leader]: *Relation* (1985, Konnex 5005)

BIBLIOGRAPHY

ReclamsJ

ROBERT J. IANNAPOLLO

Dudziak, Urszula (*b* Straconka [now Bielsko-Biała], Poland, 22 Oct 1943). Polish singer. She first studied piano, and, inspired by Ella Fitzgerald, took up singing in the late 1950s. Krzysztof Komeda heard her at a jam session and in 1962 invited her to join his group; she first met MICHAL URBANIAK when they were both members of this ensemble. In 1963 Dudziak began to study singing in Warsaw, and from late 1964 worked with Urbaniak; the two were married in 1967. They performed in Scandinavia (1965–9) and Poland, and by 1974 had settled in New York. From that time Dudziak has recorded prolifically with Urbaniak's band and as a leader. She has also worked with Archie Shepp, Lester Bowie (1984), and Bobby McFerrin, with whom she performed at the International Jazz Jamboree Festival in Warsaw (1985).

Dudziak has a wide vocal range that spans nearly five octaves, and is noted for her style of scat singing, in which she employs a large variety of extraordinary sounds; these are enhanced by the use of signal processors such as the ring modulator and echoplex. She may be heard as a soloist on some of the tracks on her album *Future Talk*. Her performance style has mirrored that of her husband, changing from bop to jazz-rock.

SELECTED RECORDINGS

Duos with A. Makowicz: *Newborn Light* (1972, Cameo 101)

As leader: *Urszula* (1975, Ari. 4065); *Future Talk* (1979, IC 1066); *Sorrow is not forever . . . but Love is* (1983, Kt. 726)

As sideman with M. Urbaniak: *Super Constellation* (*c*1973, CBS 65744); *Atma* (1974, Col. KC33184); *Fusion III* (*c*1975, Col. PC33542); *Urbaniak* (1977, IC 1036)

BIBLIOGRAPHY

Feather–Gitler '70s

J. Byrczek: "Urszula Dudziak," *JF* [intl edn], no.42 (1976), 37 [incl. discography]

H. Nolan: "Urszula Dudziak: Vocalese Vistas Unlimited," *DB*, xliii/1 (1976), 14 [incl. discography]

L. Feather: *The Passion for Jazz* (New York, 1980), 155

KIMBERLY McCORD

Duhé, Lawrence (*b* Laplace, LA, 30 April 1887; *d* Lafayette, LA, 1960). Clarinetist and bandleader. He first played in a band formed by his three older brothers. In 1913 he joined a local ensemble led by Kid Ory with which he traveled to New Orleans. Later he led his own band at various clubs before moving in April 1917 to Chicago. Until it was taken over by King Oliver he led the band that played nightly at the DeLuxe Café and the Royal Gardens. In 1923 Duhé returned to New Orleans and worked with the trumpeter Evan Thomas until 1932. During this period he also played with Bunk Johnson in a band led by the trombonist Gus Fortinet. Around 1932 he toured with the Rabbit Foot Minstrels. Thereafter he joined a band led by the trumpeter Frank Brown in Lafayette, and remained with it until he retired in 1945. Despite his prominence in the history of early jazz Duhé is not known to have made any recordings that were issued commercially. He is however reputed to have made some recordings privately, probably in 1953, for the Cinerama Song Company of Los Angeles.

Oral history material in *LNT*.

BIBLIOGRAPHY

ChartersJ

A. M. Sonnier, Jr.: *Willie Geary "Bunk" Johnson: the New Iberia Years* (New York, 1977), 68

——: "Lawrence Duhé, 1887-1960: Jazz Pioneer," *Fn*, xiii/5 (1982), 4

MICHAEL TOVEY

Duke, George (*b* San Rafael, CA, 12 Jan 1946). Keyboard player and record producer. He received extensive formal training in music, studying at San Francisco Conservatory (BA 1963) and San Francisco State College, now San Francisco State University (MA 1969). While still in high school he led a trio (which included John Heard) at the Half Note Club in San Francisco, then during his time at college became the leader of the resident rhythm section at the Both/And Club. After playing with Gerald Wilson and Bobby Hutcherson he spent six months with Don Ellis's orchestra (1968), then worked with Jean-Luc Ponty. Duke first played electronic keyboards while with Ellis, and used them more extensively during periods with Frank Zappa (1970–71, 1973–75) and Cannonball Adderley (1971–3); his best recordings date from this time. In 1975–6 he led a jazz-rock group with Billy Cobham and then played mostly rhythm-and-blues, soul, and funk until the late 1970s, when be began working as a record producer. While an early project was Raul De Souza's *Sweet Lucy* (1977, Cap. ST11648), he has concentrated on working with pop and soul singers such as Deniece Williams and Jeffrey Osborne. Despite the success of his new career, in 1984 Duke expressed the desire to play jazz again.

SELECTED RECORDINGS

As unaccompanied soloist: *The 1976 Solo Keyboard Album* (1976, Epic 32808)

As leader: *The Inner Source* (1971, MPS 68123); *Faces in Reflections* (1974, MPS 68022)

As sideman: J.-L. Ponty: *Jean-Luc Ponty Experience* (1969, PJ 20168); C. Adderley: *The Black Messiah* (1970, Cap. SWB0846); H. Ellis: *Soft Shoe* (1974, Conc. 3); Concord Festival All-Stars: *After you've Gone* (1974, Conc. 6); C. Adderley: *Phenix* (1975, Fan. 79004); S. Rollins: *Nucleus* (1975, Mlst. 9064)

BIBLIOGRAPHY

M. Bourne: "George Duke: the Whole Gamut," *DB*, xxxviii/18 (1971), 14

S. Metalitz: "Spotlight on George Duke: an Underexposed Mother," *DB*, xli/18 (1974), 14

T. Darter: "George Duke: Master of Many Keyboards," *CK*, iii/7 (1977), 32

L. Underwood: "George Duke: Plugged-in Prankster," *DB*, xliv/5 (1977), 14 [incl. discography]

T. Darter: "George Duke," *CK*, v/10 (1979), 36

S. Yanow: "George Duke: Dukin' out the Hits," *DB*, li/11 (1984), 16 [incl. discography]

SCOTT YANOW

Dukes of Dixieland. Dixieland group formed by Freddie and Frank Assunto in 1949; it grew out of an earlier group formed by them in 1946. In 1950 it began a long engagement at the Famous Door on Bourbon Street, New Orleans. Its original members were Frank Assunto (trumpet), Freddie Assunto (trombone), Stanley Mendelson (*b* New Orleans, 23 June 1923; piano), Henry Bartels (double bass), Tony Balderas (guitar), and Willie Perkins (drums); Papa Jac Assunto (trombone and banjo) joined the band in 1955 when it performed in Chicago and Las Vegas. From 1956 it was based in Las Vegas, but it also toured North America, Japan (1964), and South-east Asia (1967); its many recordings (1956–66), including some with Louis Armstrong (1958–60), were phenomenally successful and gained the group international popularity. With the death of Freddie Assunto (1966) the Dukes of Dixieland were based in New Orleans (from 1967). During Don Ewell's association with the group (1969) it tended to move away from its well-established and somewhat predictable performing style in favor of informal arrangements with extended solo passages. Frank Assunto died in 1974 but, with new members, the band continued to tour and perform in New Orleans, where, for some years in the late 1970s and early 1980s, it had its own club at the Monteleone Hotel.

SELECTED RECORDINGS

The Phenomenal Dukes of Dixieland (1956, Audio Fidelity 1823); *Marching Along* (c1957, Audio Fidelity 1851), incl. Bourbon Street Parade; *Breaking it up on Broadway* (1961, Col. CS8528); *Live at Bourbon Street* (1965, Decca 74653)

BIBLIOGRAPHY

D. Farrell: "How the Dukes Climbed to the Top," *New Orleans Times-Picayune* (18 Jan 1959)

KARL KOENIG

Dumas, Tony (*b* Los Angeles, 1 Oct 1955). Bass player and instrument maker. In 1974 he played soul jazz with Johnny Hammond, Freddie Hubbard, and Kenny Burrell, and recorded with Patrice Rushen. He worked as a studio musician (1975–7) and toured and recorded in Japan with a quintet led by J. J. Johnson and Nat Adderley (1977). He also recorded with Art Pepper (*No Limit*, 1977, Cont. 7639; 1979), with Joe Farrell, Billy Higgins, and Joe Henderson (all in 1979), with Pepper in a group led by Milcho Leviev (1980), and with Hubert Laws (1981). Dumas makes the Blitz electric double bass designed by John Dawson. (L. Underwood: "Tony Dumas," *DB*, xliv/15 (1977), 48)

Dunbar, Ted [Earl Theodore] (*b* Port Arthur, TX, 17 Jan 1937). Guitarist. He taught himself music, led a dance band while in high school, and played trumpet and guitar while studying pharmacy at Texas Southern University (1955–9). He worked with Arnett Cobb (in Houston, 1956–8), the tenor saxophonist Don Wilkerson (1957–9), and Joe Turner (ii) (1958). In Indiana he played and studied with Dave Baker (1961–3) and substituted on occasion for Wes Montgomery (1962–3). He moved to New York in 1966 and performed and recorded with Gil Evans (1970–73), Tony Williams's group Lifetime (1971–2), and Frank Foster (1973–9); he also played with Sonny Rollins, Ron Carter, Billy Harper, Roy Haynes, Billy Taylor (ii) (on the Jazzmobile), McCoy Tyner, the New Jazz Repertory Co., and the National Jazz Ensemble. He joined the faculty of music at Livingston College, Rutgers, in 1972. Dunbar has written a number of books on jazz harmony and guitar, including *A System of Tonal Convergence for Improvisors, Composers and Arrangers* (Kendall Park, nr Franklin Park, NJ, n.d. [?1975]) and *The Interrelationship of Chords, Scales and Fingerboard of Each One of the Twelve Tonalities of the Guitar* (Highland Park, NJ, 1977).

SELECTED RECORDINGS

As unaccompanied soloist: *Jazz Guitarist* (1982, Xan. 196)
Duos with K. Barron: *In Tandem* (1975, Muse 5140)
As leader: *Opening Remarks* (1978, Xan. 155)
As sideman: D. Newman: *House of David* (1967, Atl. 1489); M. Tyner: *Asante* (1970, BN LA223G); K. Barron: *Peruvian Blue* (1974, Muse 5044)

BIBLIOGRAPHY

Feather–Gitler '70s
"JF Reader's Profile: Ted Dunbar," *JF* [intl edn], no.56 (1978), 41

PAUL RINZLER

Duncan, Hank [Henry James] (*b* Bowling Green, KY, 26 Oct 1896; *d* Long Island, NY, 7 June 1968). Pianist. He studied piano in Louisville, Kentucky, and at Fisk University, Nashville; in 1919 he formed his own group in Louisville with Jimmy Harrison. After moving to New York in the early 1920s he played in the Royal Flush Orchestra under the leadership of Fess Williams (1925–30). He toured with King Oliver (1931) and performed and recorded with the NEW ORLEANS FEETWARMERS (1932–3). From around 1934 he worked in the Arcadians, which was led by the double bass player Charlie Turner until 1935, when members of the group joined Fats Waller's big band. He appeared with Waller on second piano, and the two men took part in nightly cutting contests as part of the band's performance. Duncan performed in Boston with Bunk Johnson and Sidney Bechet (1945) and in New York as a soloist at Nick's (1947–55) and with Zutty Singleton and Louis Metcalf at the Metropole (1955–6); he then returned to Nick's, where he worked until it closed in 1963. Illness later forced him to give up playing.

SELECTED RECORDINGS

As leader: Maple Leaf Rag/I Give you my Word (1944, Black & White 31)
As sideman: F. Waller: Functionizin'/I got rhythm (1935, HMV HE2902); T. Parenti: *Jazz, That's All* (1955, Jzt. 1215), incl. Bill Bailey, Frankie and Johnnie

BIBLIOGRAPHY

ChiltonW
F. Owens: "Hank Duncan, 1896–1968," *Sv*, no.25 (1969), 3
J. Simmen: "Henry James 'Hank' Duncan," *JJ*, xxii/6 (1969), 4; rev. Fr. version in *BHcF*, no.194 (1970), 7
A. McCarthy: *Big Band Jazz* (New York and London, 1974)

JAMES M. DORAN

Dunham, Sonny [Elmer Lewis] (*b* Brockton, MA, 16 Nov 1914). Trumpeter, trombonist, and bandleader. During the late 1920s he played trombone with Ben Bernie, and trumpet and trombone with Paul Tremaine. He played both instruments as a member of the Casa Loma Orchestra (1932–40; for illustration *see* CASA LOMA ORCHESTRA), but was known chiefly for his high-pitched trumpet solos, an example of which may be heard on the orchestra's recording of *Memories of you* (1937, Decca 1672). He worked for three months in Europe in 1937, and first led his own band in that year. He resumed his activities as a bandleader in 1940, and made a number of recordings between 1940 and 1949; Corky Corcoran and Pete Candoli were among his sidemen. He performed with Tommy Dorsey in 1951 and continued to lead bands into the 1960s.

BIBLIOGRAPHY

ChiltonW
G. T. Simon: *The Big Bands* (New York, 1967, rev. and enlarged 2/1971, rev. 3/1974, 4/1981)

Dunlop, Frankie [Francis] (*b* Buffalo, 6 Dec 1928). Drummer. He began studying drumming at the age of ten, and played his earliest professional engagement when he was 16. In 1950 he made his first recording, with Moe Koffman. After army service he led his own group in Buffalo and worked with the saxophonist Skippy Williams (1954). He then moved to New York, where he played at the Five Spot with John Coltrane in Thelonious Monk's quartet. This engagement was terminated after only three weeks because Dunlop did not have a local union card. After touring briefly with Charles Mingus he played with Sonny Rollins's trio for six months (1958) and toured with Maynard Ferguson's big band (1958–60). He then worked with the singer Lena Horne and toured with Duke Ellington's band (1960); Ellington was using two drummers at this time. During a further three years with Monk he traveled to Europe (October 1961) and Japan (April 1963) and made several recordings. After working with Rollins again (1966–7) he played in Broadway shows (1966–73), then worked with Earl Hines (1973–4) and Lionel Hampton (intermittently, 1975–81). Dunlop is a sensitive ensemble player, and asserts that his highly individual melodic style originated during his second year with Ferguson and matured during his association with Monk.

Oral history material in *NjR*.

SELECTED RECORDINGS

As sideman: T. Monk: *Two Hours with Thelonious* (1961, Riv. 9460–61); *Thelonious Monk in Stockholm* (1961, Duke 1020); *Criss-cross* (1963, Col. CS8838); *Thelonious Monk 1963: in Japan* (1963, Baybridge 2172); on *Miles and Monk at Newport* (1958, 1963, Col. CS8978), Blue Monk (1963); L. Hampton: *Live in Emmen/Holland* (1978, Tim. 120); *Outrageous* (1980–81, Tim. 163), incl. Tap Step; on [no leader]: *That's the Way I Feel Now: a Tribute to Thelonious Monk* (1984, A&M 6600), In Walked Bud

BIBLIOGRAPHY

I. Gitler: "Monk's Drummer, Frankie Dunlop," *DB*, xxxi/2 (1964), 16

S. K. Fish: "Frankie Dunlop: Making it Swing," *MD*, ix/8 (1985), 22

JEFF POTTER

Dunn, Blind Willie. Pseudonym of Eddie Lang.

Dunn, Johnny (*b* Memphis, 19 Feb 1897; *d* Paris, 20 Aug 1937). Trumpeter and bandleader. After attending Fisk University he began working as a solo act in a theater in Memphis (*c*1916). He then joined W. C. Handy's band, with which he worked in New York (1917–20), but left to play with Mamie Smith's Jazz Hounds, and recorded with her in 1920–21. He then formed his own Jazz Hounds, who accompanied the blues singer Edith Wilson (1921–2). After trips to Europe with Will Vodery (1923) and the show *Blackbirds of 1926* (1926) Dunn worked in the USA as a soloist and as the leader of his own big band in New York (November 1927); he toured and performed in Chicago (March 1928) and again led a band in New York (April 1928). He then rejoined the *Blackbirds* company for a short time, and worked in Paris with Noble Sissle's band (1928). He spent the last few years of his life based in the Netherlands.

Dunn was one of the most influential jazz trumpeters before Armstrong. His tone was strong and open, his articulation concise, and he often played staccato. Intricate passages, including triplet quarter-, eighth-, and/or 16th-notes and fills in double-time, were characteristic of his work, while other passages revealed a supple legato. His use of the mute to produce a wa-wa effect, exemplified on *Dunn's Cornet Blues*, influenced Bubber Miley (who replaced him in Mamie Smith's band); Miley employed similar techniques most notably in his important solos with Duke Ellington. Later Dunn stressed his relaxed legato, but his solos were marred by the interjection of stylized and outmoded staccato routines.

See also Blues, §3.

SELECTED RECORDINGS

As leader: Dunn's Cornet Blues (1924, Col. 124D); Sergeant Dunn's Bugle Call Blues (1928, Col. 14306D); You need some lovin' (1928, Col. 14358D)

As sideman: E. Wilson: What do you care (1922, Col. A3674)

BIBLIOGRAPHY

N. Hentoff: "Jazz in the Twenties: Garvin Bushell," *Jazz Panorama*, ed. M. Williams (New York and London, 1962/*R*1979) [colln of previously pubd articles], 88

G. Schuller: *Early Jazz: its Roots and Musical Development* (New York, 1968), 208

A. van Delden: "Dunn's Dutch Bugle Call Blues," *Doctor jazz*, no.37 (1969), 2; no.38 (1969), 2

H. Pekar: "Johnny Dunn," *JJ*, xxiv/3 (1971), 28

BOB ZIEFF

Duran, Eddie [Edward Lozano] (*b* San Francisco, 6 Sept 1925). Guitarist and leader. He studied piano, then guitar, and first played professionally at the age of 15. From the mid-1940s he performed with Stan Getz, Flip Phillips, Charlie Parker, George Shearing, Red Norvo, and other bop and swing musicians in San Francisco. He made recordings with Cal Tjader (1954), Ron Crotty (1955), Jerry Coker (1956), the baritone horn player Gus Mancuso (1956), his own group (1957), and a sextet led by Tjader and Getz (1958); he also worked with Earl Hines (1956) and Vince Guaraldi (1956, 1963–4). From 1960 to 1967 Duran led his own trio. Later he made recordings with Tjader (1973), Tania Maria (1980–82, whose *Come with me*, 1982, Conc. 200, provides a good example of Duran's playing), Eiji Kitamura (1981), and as a leader (1979). From 1976 to 1981 he was a member of Benny Goodman's band, and in the late 1980s he settled in New York and formed a quartet. Duran's brothers, Carlos (double bass) and Manuel (piano), recorded with Tjader in the 1950s.

BIBLIOGRAPHY

FeatherE

J. Ferguson: "Eddie Duran: San Francisco's Elder Statesman of Bebop," *GP*, xviii/4 (1984), 54 [incl. discography]

Durham, Eddie (*b* San Marcos, TX, 19 Aug 1906; *d* New York, 6 March 1987). Trombonist, guitarist, and arranger. He was taught music by an older brother and toured in minstrel shows with the Durham Brothers Band. He first played banjo, then took up guitar and trombone, performing on both instruments throughout his career. After touring in the Southwest with territory bands, including Walter Page's Blue Devils, he worked with Bennie Moten (1929–33; for illustration *see* Moten, Bennie) and provided several significant arrangements that were recorded by the band in 1932. He also experimented with guitar amplification, attracting the attention of Charlie Christian (upon whom he was a primary influence). Durham moved to New York in 1934 to work as an arranger for Willie Bryant, then played with Jimmie Lunceford and Count Basie (1937–8), making some early recordings on electric guitar with Basie and as a member of the Kansas City Six. During the late 1930s he prepared arrangements for such leaders as Glenn Miller and Artie Shaw, and in 1940 he formed a big band. He was music director for the International Sweethearts of Rhythm (1941–3) and later directed his own all-female orchestra as well as other small groups. Although he continued to work as a freelance arranger during the 1950s and 1960s, he performed less frequently, but resumed regular playing in 1969 when he joined Buddy Tate. He also appeared with the Countsmen and toured Europe in the 1980s with the Harlem Blues and Jazz Band. Durham was widely recognized as a valuable instrumentalist and an outstanding composer; among his best-known compositions is *Topsy*. He was a key figure in shaping popular Kansas City riff themes and encapsulating them in written arrangements.

Oral history material in *MoKmh*, *NjR* (JOHP), and *NjR*.

SELECTED RECORDINGS

As leader: *Eddie Durham* (1973-4, RCA LPL1-5029), incl. Blues for Mac, Good Morning Blues, Perdido; *Blue Bone* (1981, JSP 1030)

As sideman: Kansas City Five: Good Mornin' Blues (1938, Com. 511); Kansas City Six: Way down yonder in New Orleans (1938, Com. 512); Countless Blues (1938, Com. 509); E. Barefield: *Eddie Barefield* (1973, RCA LFL1-5035), incl. Sonny Boy, Warm up Blues

SELECTED ARRANGEMENTS

* – with Durham as sideman

Recorded by B. Moten: *Moten Swing (1932, Vic. 23384)

Recorded by J. Lunceford: *Avalon (1935, Decca 668); *Hittin' the Bottle (1935, Decca 765); *Harlem Shout (1936, Decca 980); *Lunceford Special (1939, Voc./OK 5326)

Recorded by C. Basie: *Time Out (1937, Decca 1538); *Topsy (1937, Decca 1770); *Swinging the Blues (1938, Decca 1880); Jumpin' at the Woodside (1938, Decca 2212)

BIBLIOGRAPHY

G. Hoefer: "Held Notes: Eddie Durham," *DB*, xxix/20 (1962), 54
A. McCarthy: Liner notes, *Eddie Durham* (RCA LPL1-5029, 1974)
V. Wilmer: "Eddie Durham," *Coda*, no. 158 (1977), 6
S. Dance: *The World of Count Basie* (New York and London, 1980) [colln of previously pubd interviews], 60
M. L. Hester: *Going to Kansas City* (Sherman, TX, 1980), 31
R. Russell: *Jazz Style in Kansas City and the Southwest* (Berkeley, CA, Los Angeles, and London, 1971/*R*1983, rev. 2/1973)
J. A. Siegel and J. Obrecht: "Eddie Durham: Charlie Christian's Mentor, Pioneer of the Amplified Guitar," *GP*, xiii/8 (1979), 55 [incl. discography]
S. Placksin: *American Women in Jazz, 1900 to the Present: their Words, Lives, and Music* (New York, 1982), 149

PETER VACHER

Dutch Swing College Band [DSC]. Dutch group. It was formed in 1945 by Peter Schilperoort and the pianist Frans Vink as an offshoot of the Dutch Swing College, a school of jazz which they had founded together in 1944. The band was led by Schilperoort from the summer of 1946 and later by the pianist Joop Schrier (1955–9); Schilperoort resumed the leadership in 1959. At various times the members included the trumpeters Joost van Os, Kees van Dorsser, Wybe Buma, Oscar Klein, Ray Kaart, and Bert de Kort; the trombonists Wim Kolstee and Dick Kaart; the reed players Dim Kesber, Jan Morks, and Bob Kaper; the banjoist Arie Ligthart; the double bass players Bob van Oven and Henk Bosch van Drakesteyn; and the drummers Arie Merkt, André Westendorp, Louis de Lussanet, and Huub Janssen. The band has made hundreds of recordings, including a number in the 1970s on the label DSC Production, which was formed specifically to promote its work. It recorded tracks with Sidney Bechet (1951) and albums with Jimmy Witherspoon (1970), Joe Venuti (1971), Teddy Wilson (1972–3), and Billy Butterfield (1973); its own albums include *Jubilee Concert* (1980, Phi. 6601003) and *40 Years* (1985, Phi. 8245851). The band has also toured internationally with, among others, Witherspoon, Venuti, Wilson, Butterfield, Hot Lips Page, and Albert Nicholas.

BIBLIOGRAPHY

Feather–Gitler '70s
R. Harris: *Enjoying Jazz* (London, 1961), 117, 120
G. Bielderman: *Dutch Swing College Band* (Zwolle, Netherlands, 1984) [discography]

WIM VAN EYLE

Dutrey, Honore (*b* New Orleans, *c*1887; *d* Chicago, IL, 21 July 1935). Trombonist. His brothers Sam and Peter (a violinist) were also highly proficient musicians. From 1910 to 1917 Honore worked in various New Orleans brass bands, including the Excelsior Brass Band, and in John Robichaux's orchestra. He left New Orleans to join the US Navy, and while in service suffered accidental damage to his lungs, but was eventually able to resume regular playing. He settled in Chicago and joined King Oliver's band, with which he worked from 1920 until 1924 (for illustration *see* OLIVER, KING), taking part in many recording sessions. He briefly led his own band in 1924, and subsequently worked for various leaders, including Carroll Dickerson, Louis Armstrong, and Johnny Dodds. He retired on account of ill-health in 1930. Although he was not an inventive improviser or the possessor of an exceptional sense of harmony, Dutrey had a sonorous tone and an effective way of playing long, legato phrases in the lower register. His main gift was probably his power of understatement, which served as an effective contrast to the volatile creativity of the musicians with whom he usually worked.

SELECTED RECORDINGS

(all recorded for Okeh as sideman with K. Oliver)

Snake Rag (1923, 4933); Jazzin' Babies' Blues (1923, 4975); Tears (1923, 40000); Riverside Blues (1923, 40034); Mabel's Dream (1923, 8235)

BIBLIOGRAPHY

Charters J
B. McRae: "A B Basics, no.43: Honore Dutrey," *JJ*, xxiii/7 (1970), 15
C. Hillman: "The Forgotten Ones: Roy Palmer & Honore Dutrey," *JJI*, xxxix/5 (1986), 12

JOHN CHILTON

Dutrey, Sam(, Jr.) (*b* New Orleans, 29 May 1909; *d* New Orleans, 27 Aug 1971). Clarinetist and saxophonist. He first played with Isaiah Morgan, then worked with Sidney Desvigne and Joseph Robichaux. In 1947 he toured with Freddie Kohlman, and in 1970 he visited Japan. Dutrey's uncle was Honore Dutrey, and his father, Sam Dutrey, Sr. (*b* ?New Roads, LA, before 1888; *d* New Orleans, 1941), was a clarinetist who played with various groups in New Orleans, including the Silver Leaf, Hypolite Charles, and Tulane brass bands; he also worked on excursion boats with Fate Marable (1918). (M. MacMurray: "Sam Dutrey, Jr.," *SL*, xxxiv (spr. 1982), 4)

Oral history material in *LNT*.

BILL RUSSELL

Duvivier, George (B.) (*b* New York, 17 Aug 1920; *d* New York, 11 July 1985). Double bass player, composer, and arranger. He studied violin at the Conservatory of Music and Art in New York and by the age of 16 was assistant concertmaster of the Central Manhattan SO, but his interest in jazz meant that he soon changed to double bass. Later he studied composition at New York University. He played with Coleman Hawkins (1940), Eddie Barefield, and Lucky Millinder (1942–3), and, after army service, worked as staff arranger for Jimmie Lunceford (1945–7). He then joined Sy Oliver's big band, where he continued to write many arrangements. From the 1950s Duvivier made extended tours of Europe with the singers Nellie Lutcher and Lena Horne. He was also much in demand for studio work, recording a number of film soundtracks and commercial jingles and appearing on television, though he continued to play in sessions with jazz musicians, most notably Bud Powell (1953–7). Duvivier was considered by his peers to be a supreme craftsman, and his ability to play in many styles led to his recording with leaders as diverse as Eric Dolphy, Benny Goodman, Chico Hamilton, Oliver Nelson, Clark Terry, Ben Webster, and Bob Wilber. From the late 1970s he toured extensively with Hank Jones and Benny Carter.

Duvivier made use of a strong attack and, in ensemble playing, laid considerable emphasis on low notes. When playing solos, however, he exhibited a fondness for rapid passages in the upper register of the instrument. His mature style is perhaps best illustrated by the album *2, 3, 4*, made with Shelly Manne in 1962. His compositions include *Autumn Landscape* and *Porch Light*.

Oral history material in *NjR* (JOHP).

SELECTED RECORDINGS

(all as sideman)

L. Millinder: Shipyard Social Function (1943, Decca 18674); S. Oliver: A Slow Burn/Hey daddy-o (1947, MGM 10004); Deep River/Siesta at the Fiesta (1950, Decca 24936); B. Powell: *The Amazing Bud Powell* (1953, BN 5041), incl. Collard Greens and Black-eye Peas, Glass Enclosure, Sure Thing; *Strictly Powell* (1956, RCA LPM1423); C. Hamilton: *The Chico Hamilton Trio* (1956, PJ 1220), incl. Autumn Landscape, Porch Light; S. Manne: *2, 3, 4* (1962, Imp. 20), incl. The Sicks of Us, Slowly, Take the "A" Train
A. Cohn and Z. Sims: *Body and Soul* (1973, Muse 5016), incl. Blue Hodge: J. Venuti and Z. Sims: *Joe and Zoot* (1974, Chi. 129); H. Jones: *Bop Redux* (1977, Muse 5123); W. Vaché: *Iridescence* (1981, Conc. 153)

BIBLIOGRAPHY

N. Hentoff: "The Bassist's Bassist: George Duvivier, though no Poll-winner, Finds Wide Favor among Fellow Artisans," *DB*, xxii/15 (1955), 10
L. Tomkins: "The George Duvivier Story," *CI*, xvii/8 (1979), 12

E. Townley: "First Generation American: an Interview with George Duvivier," *Sv*, no.87 (1980), 110

M. Seidel: "Abiding Bass by George Duvivier," *DB*, xlix/1 (1982), 27 [incl. discography]

C. Battestini and J.-P. Battestini: "George Duvivier: interview et notes," *BHcF*, no.306 (1983), 21

LAWRENCE KOCH

Du wah. The effect created on a brass instrument when the first of a pair of notes (usually of the same pitch) is muted and the second is played unmuted with a full tone; the term is onomatopoeic. On the first note of the pair the player covers the bell of the instrument with a plunger mute, which inhibits the vibrations of the air column and cuts out the higher frequencies, thus creating the "du"; on the second he removes the mute so that the air column vibrates freely in the normal way over the whole range of frequencies, creating the "wah." The du wah effect is often used to reinforce rhythmic articulation. A good example may be heard on Duke Ellington's *Ko-ko* (1940, Vic. 26577), where two trumpets and a trombone play the same chord for the duration of two 12-bar blues choruses (beginning at the second full chorus). The du wah effect is notated by means of the conventional signs for "closed" and "open" playing; *see* NOTATION, §5(v).

BARRY KERNFELD

Dvorak, Jim [James P.] (*b* New York, 16 Dec 1948). Trumpeter. After private tuition he attended the Eastman School of Music (1966–70) and gained a BMus degree. He then moved to London, where he worked with Keith Tippett (1970–72), Brotherhood of Breath (1970–75), and Louis Moholo (1975–6). From 1973 to 1979 he led the group Joy with the drummer Keith Bailey (recording in 1976), and from 1977 to 1979 he was the leader of Sun Sum, which included Elton Dean, Alan Skidmore, and the trombonist Nick Evans; he also led the group Dhyana (1980–82). In the 1980s he has worked with Dudu Pukwana's group Zila, District 6 led by Brian Abrahams, Evans's group Dreamtime, and again with Tippett (1985–6). Dvorak has taught privately and on Jazz Workshop tours. His playing may be heard to advantage on the album *Laws of Motion* (1982, View 022) recorded by the drummer Geoff Serle. (R. Cotterrell, ed.: *Jazz Now: the Jazz Centre Society Guide*, London, 1976)

NEVIL SKRIMSHIRE

Dyani, Johnny (Mbizo) (*b* East London, South Africa, 30 Nov 1945; *d* Berlin, 24 Oct 1986). South African double bass player and singer. He moved to London with Chris McGregor's group the Blue Notes in 1965; during the next few years he played with the newly formed Brotherhood of Breath, the Spontaneous Music Ensemble, Steve Lacy, and the Musicians Co-op. In the late 1960s he toured South America and recorded in a quartet with Steve Lacy, Enrico Rava, and Louis Moholo. He settled in Copenhagen in 1971 and made recordings throughout Europe; during this period he was associated with Don Cherry, John Tchicai, and others. After the death of Mongezi Feza, a fellow member of McGregor's groups, he returned to London to play on McGregor's album *Blue Notes for Mongezi* (1975). Later he led a number of bands of which most of the members were Danish, but his best recording, *Song for Biko* (1978), was made with Cherry, Dudu Pukwana, and Makaya Ntshoko. As well as leading his own groups Dyani worked with Joseph Jarman and David Murray. His commanding playing was at its most expressive in the setting of a small group, where his originality and quick responses were also exploited to best advantage.

SELECTED RECORDINGS

As leader: *Music for Xaba* (1972, Sonet 642); with C. Jarvis: *African Bass* (1977, RR 149); *Song for Biko* (1978, Ste. 1109); *Born under the Heat* (1983, Dra. 68)

As sideman: S. Lacy: *Forest and the Zoo* (1966, ESP 1060); C. McGregor: *Blue Notes for Mongezi* (1975, Ogun 001–2)

BIBLIOGRAPHY

J. Solothurnmann: "Johnny Dyani: 'Music is like Medicine'," *JF* [intl edn], no.87 (1984), 43

C. de Ledesma: "Afro Jazz: Evolution and Revolution," *The Wire*, no.12 (1985), 26, esp. 39

I. Carr: "Dyani, Johnny," in I. Carr, D. Fairweather, and B. Priestley: *Jazz: the Essential Companion* (London, 1987)

CHARLES DE LEDESMA

Dylag, Roman [Gucio] (*b* Kraków, Poland, 22 Feb 1938). Polish double bass player. He attended the Music Academy in Warsaw, recorded with several leaders, including Andrzej Kurylewicz (1958–62), and played and recorded with the group Melomani (*c*1957) and with Stan Getz (1960). In 1962 he appeared at festivals in Newport and Washington with the Polish bop group the Wreckers, and played and recorded with Don Ellis in Warsaw. He also played in Paris with Bud Powell and recorded in Warsaw with Krzysztof Komeda (1961–7). In 1963 he moved to Stockholm, where he recorded in 1964 with Brother Jack McDuff, Benny Golson, and Jimmy Witherspoon, and in 1967 with George Russell. He toured Asia and Australia with Zbigniew Namysłowski (1969), then recorded again in Stockholm with Jan Allan (1969), Nils Lindberg (1970), Rolf Ericson (1971), and Rune Gustafson (1977). He also played double bass and electric bass guitar with Michal Urbaniak (1972–3). (*Feather '60s*; *Reclams J*)

E

Eager, Allen (*b* New York, 10 Jan 1927). Tenor saxophonist. He began studying clarinet in his early teens and after changing to saxophone (1943) he worked with Bobby Sherwood, Sonny Dunham, Shorty Sherock, and Hal McIntyre (all 1943), Woody Herman (1943–4), and Tommy Dorsey and Johnny Bothwell (1945). He performed in clubs on 52nd Street, New York, with Shelly Manne (1945–6) and as a leader, and made a number of recordings with his own groups, mainly from 1946 to 1948. He won acclaim as a member of Tadd Dameron's small group, which performed at the Royal Roost on Broadway in 1948 and made a number of fine recordings. Eager recorded with Stan Getz in 1949. An erratic personality, he drifted away from jazz in the early 1950s, though he made occasional recordings (with Gerry Mulligan in 1951 and Terry Gibbs in 1952) and performed with Buddy Rich. From 1953 he led his own small group in New York and Boston, and played in sessions, notably at the Open Door in New York (1954–5); he also worked with Howard McGhee, Oscar Pettiford, and Tony Fruscella. In 1956–7 he lived in Paris, where he began to play alto saxophone. He recorded again with Mulligan in 1957 and then ceased full-time performing. He resumed his career in 1982, when he toured Europe and recorded with his own group. Eager is one of the most important early bop tenor saxophonists; his mature style reflects the influence of Lester Young and Charlie Parker, but he plays with a vibrant, singing tone of his own.

SELECTED RECORDINGS

As leader: Rampage/Booby Hatch (1946, Savoy 611); Vot's Dot (1946, Savoy 621); Symphony Sid's Idea (1946, Savoy 909); All Night, All Frantic/And That's for Sure (1947, Savoy 948); Donald Jay/Meeskite (1947, Savoy 908); Nightmare Allen/Church Mouse (1947, Savoy 958); *Renaissance* (1982, Upt. 2709)

As sideman: D. Lambert: Deedle (In the Merry Land of Bop) (1948, SiW 508); T. Dameron: Jahbero/Lady Bird (1948, BN 559); on Dameron: *Anthropology* (1948, Spot. 108), Hackensack, Just you, just me, Now's the Time; G. Mulligan: Funhouse/Mullenium (1951, Prst. 763); T. Fruscella: I'll be Seeing you (1955, Atl. 1220)

BIBLIOGRAPHY

FeatherE

I. Gitler: *Jazz Masters of the Forties* (New York, 1966/*R*1983 with discography), 217

J. Denis and H. Robberechts: "Discography," *Pj*, no.8 (1973), 110

B. Rusch: "Allen Eager: Interview," *Cadence*, i/6–7 (1976), 3

B. Rusch: "Allen Eager: Interview," *Cadence*, iv/10 (1978), 8

M. Isherwood: "Allen Eager," *JJI*, xxxv (1982), no.9, p.6; no.10, p.13

LAWRENCE KOCH

Eagle Band. New Orleans dance orchestra active from 1907 to 1917. It was led by the trombonist Frankie Dusen and formed, after Buddy Bolden was committed to an asylum, from Dusen's former associates in Bolden's band; it was named after the Eagle Saloon on South Rampart and Perdido streets, where its members met. The group's instrumentation consisted of cornet, trombone, clarinet, guitar, double bass, and drums, and the band followed the early ragtime traditions that it is assumed were those of Bolden. The Eagle Band played an important role in the musical development of many early bandleaders, and on occasion included among its personnel King Oliver, Freddie Keppard, Buddy Petit, Bunk Johnson, Mutt Carey, Sidney Bechet, Pops Foster, and Johnny and Baby Dodds.

For illustration *see* BANDS, fig.2.

WILLIAM J. SCHAFER

Eardley, Jon (*b* Altoona, PA, 30 Sept 1928). Trumpeter. He began playing trumpet when he was 11 years old. His father played in Paul Whiteman's band and from an early age Jon was familiar with the music of Louis Armstrong and Bix Beiderbecke; later he was influenced by Charlie Parker and Dizzy Gillespie. After playing in an air force band in Washington, DC (1946–9), he returned home to form a bop quartet (1950). In 1953 he moved to New York, where he recorded with Phil Woods in 1954. He joined Gerry Mulligan later that year, and after working with Hal McIntyre's orchestra re-joined Mulligan for a European tour in 1956. Eardley left the band the following year and again returned to Altoona. From 1963 he worked in studios and jazz clubs in Belgium and in 1969 he moved to Cologne, Germany, to play in a radio orchestra led by Harold Banter. He continued to make recordings in the 1970s and 1980s. Eardley is best known for his work with Mulligan's quartet and sextet; he is highly respected in Europe as a skilled player with a beautiful tone and a keen sense of melody.

SELECTED RECORDINGS

As leader: *The Jon Eardley Seven* (1956, Prst. 7033); *Namely Me* (1977, Spot. 17); with A. Haig: *Stablemates* (1977, Spot. 11)

As sideman: P. Woods: Pot Pie/Mad about the Girl (1954, Prst. 1364); G. Mulligan: *California Concerts* (1954, PJ 1201); C. Baker: *I Remember You* (1981, Cir. [Ger.] 28)

BIBLIOGRAPHY

A. McCarthy and others: *Jazz on Record: a Critical Guide to the First 50 Years: 1917–1967* (London, 1968), 342

P. Sullivan: "Jon Eardley," *J&B*, iii/9 (1973), 8 [interview]

L. Tomkins: "Jon Eardley," *CI*, xvi (1978), no.7, p.20; no.8, p.24

FREDERICK A. BECK

Earland, Charles (*b* Philadelphia, 24 May 1941). Organist and soprano saxophonist. He first learned alto saxophone in high school, where his fellow students included Pat Martino, Lew Tabackin, and Bobby Timmons, and played as a soloist on tenor saxophone with the Temple University band. He began working with Jimmy McGriff shortly afterwards. By the 1960s he was leading his own band, and in 1963 began to play organ after a number of organists had left his group in quick succession. His first major engagement as an organist was with Lou Donaldson (1968–9), after which he formed his own trio. His recording *Black Talk* (1969), consisting of his own compositions, was a great commercial success and won him a long-term contract with Prestige. From 1970 he toured with his own group, playing soprano saxophone, synthesizer, and electric piano as well as organ; he appeared at the Newport and Montreux jazz festivals, among others. In 1974 he played on the soundtrack to the film *The Dynamite Brothers*. He continued to work as a leader into the late 1970s.

SELECTED RECORDINGS

Black Talk (1969, Prst. 7758); *The Dynamite Brothers* (1973, Prst. 10082); *Leaving this Planet* (1973, Prst. 66002); *Smokin'* (1977, Muse 5126)

BIBLIOGRAPHY

Feather–Gitler '70s

ANDREW JAFFE

East Coast jazz. A term devised by writers on jazz in the mid-1950s to describe a style regarded as the antithesis of West Coast jazz and the related cool jazz – earthy, hard-driving, and influenced by the blues. The term was never commonly accepted, being more a literary conceit than a useful description, since music in that style was played in many places not on the East Coast; the more appropriate labels HARD BOP and SOUL JAZZ have had more lasting currency.

East: West. Record label. It was launched as a subsidiary of Atlantic in 1958, but was little used. However the catalogue is notable for having included recordings by George Wallington, Jackie Paris, Lars Gullin, and Tommy Potter; all sessions were supervised by Nesuhi Ertegun.

MARK GARDNER

East Wind (i). Japanese record label. It was founded in 1974 in Tokyo. Its catalogue contains recordings mostly of bop, both by native players and by visiting musicians of international renown.

East Wind (ii). Record label. It is owned by the East Wind Trade Associates company, founded in 1984 in Hartford, Connecticut, by Steve Boulay, Ted Everts, and David Barrick with the assistance of Gerald A. Friedman. Its catalogue is devoted to Russian jazz in styles ranging from bop to jazz-rock. (E. Schmitt: "3 in Hartford Importing Records of Russian Jazz," *New York Times* (12 Aug 1985), §B, p.2)

Eaves, Hubert (B.) (*b* St. Paul, MN, ?late 1940s). Pianist. A self-taught musician, he began playing professionally at the age of 16, mainly in a rhythm-and-blues style. During the late 1960s he played in nightclubs and was the leader of the house band at a jazz club in St. Paul. He went to California (*c*1970), where he led a quartet, then moved to New York (1971) and worked with local musicians. He performed, toured, and made recordings with Gary Bartz (1973–4, notably the album *I've Known Rivers and Other Bodies*, 1973, Prst. 66001), with whom he played electric as well as acoustic piano; from this period he recorded in Europe with various leaders, including Gerry Brown and John Lee (1973) and Zbigniew Seifert (1977). He also played and recorded with Carlos Garnett (1974–5) and recorded with Rene McLean and the guitarist Reggie Lucas (both 1975). (H. Nolan: "Profile: Hubert Eaves," *DB*, xli/6 (1974), 32)

Echo effect. An electronic treatment that produces a variety of delay effects, including a simulation of natural echo. Simpler devices (such as the Echoplex and Copicat) make use of a tape loop and several playback heads to achieve this; more advanced ones (such as Roland's Space Echo) employ digital technology, which permits a more extended range of transformations.

Eckinger, Isla (*b* Dornach, Switzerland, 6 May 1939). Swiss double bass player, trombonist, and vibraphonist. After studying classical cello in his youth he learned the trombone in his teens and worked with local groups in Basle. In the early 1960s he took up the double bass, which he played as a professional in the sextet of Mac Strittmatter. His familiarity with diverse styles, ranging from dixieland to a restrained form of free jazz, made him much sought after as a sideman, and he worked with many European and American musicians in Switzerland, Germany, Austria, and Italy. He recorded with Buck Clayton (1966), Albert Nicholas (1969), Mal Waldron (1969–70), Dusko Goykovich (at the Domicile in Munich in 1970, where he worked for many years as the house double bass player), Oscar Klein (1971, 1973–5), the big band of Slide Hampton and the pianist Joe Haider (at the Domicile, 1974), Stephane Grappelli (1975), Wild Bill Davison (1975), Hank Jones (*Have you Met this Jones*, 1977, MPS 68195), Horace Parlan (1980), and in 1985 with the singers Kim Parker (in Waldron's trio) and Lillian Terry (in Dizzy Gillespie's quartet); he also studied vibraphone and belonged to the Tremble Kids, with whom he recorded as a double bass player (1971–7). In the early 1980s he formed the group Hot Mallets, with which he played principally trombone and vibraphone, and in 1983 he recorded the album *Hot Mallets: Live!* (Jazzcharge 8302). He later moved to Los Angeles.

PETER SCHWALM

Eckstine, Billy [Eckstein, William Clarence; Mr. B] (*b* Pittsburgh, 8 July 1914). Singer and bandleader. As a singer he worked his way to Chicago in late 1937, where in 1939 he became the principal vocalist in Earl Hines's big band. He remained with Hines until 1943, learning to play trumpet while on the band's tours. From 1944 to 1947 he led an unsuccessful but now highly acclaimed bop big band. Thereafter he returned to a career as a solo singer, becoming the country's most popular vocalist in 1949–50 and gaining a lucrative five-year contract with MGM. Although his popularity waned from 1951, he and Bobby Tucker (his accompanist from June 1949) continued to fill major nightclubs in the USA and abroad for several decades.

Eckstine's achievements were inconsistent: on the one hand he supported young avant-garde jazz musicians, on the other he sang conservative popular ballads. He was instrumental in bringing Dizzy Gillespie, Charlie Parker, and Sarah Vaughan (among others) into Hines's band, and while with Hines he recorded a blues hit, *Jelly, Jelly* (1940); he also introduced new songs (such as *Skylark*) over network radio, being the first black singer allowed to do so because of his impeccable diction. For his own band he hired at different times Vaughan, Gillespie, Parker, Tadd Dameron, Fats Navarro, Miles Davis, Dexter Gor-

Billy Eckstine's band, 1946: (front row, left to right) Linton Garner (piano), Eckstine (leader), Gene Ammons (tenor saxophone), unidentified baritone saxophone player, Porter Kilbert and Robert "Junior" Williams (alto saxophones), and Frank Wess (tenor saxophone); (second row) Connie Wainwright (guitar), two unidentified trombone players, Alfred "Chippie" Outcalt and Howard Scott (trombones); (third row) Bill McMahon (double bass), unidentified trumpet player, Hibart Dotson, Leonard Hawkins, and King Kolax (trumpets); (back) Art Blakey (drums)

don, Sonny Stitt, Art Blakey (see illustration), and other young virtuosos. However, the band's experimental bop sounds are only hinted at in performances such as *Blowin' the Blues Away* and *Opus X* of 1944, the remainder of its recordings being largely romantic ballads featuring Eckstine's strong, vibrant baritone. Although he subsequently toured with all-star jazz groups, his recordings for MGM are sung to the accompaniment of a studio orchestra with strings. In the 1950s Eckstine developed his nightclub routine, in which he sang lovely ballads, undertook impersonations, performed soft-shoe dances, and also played trumpet.

SELECTED RECORDINGS

As leader: Blowin' the Blues Away (1944, De Luxe 2001); Opus X (1944, De Luxe 2002); *Billy Eckstine Orchestra 1945* (1945, Alamac 2415), incl. I wanna talk about you, Mean to me, Opus X; A Cottage for Sale (1945, Nat. 9014); Prisoner of Love (1945, Nat. 9017); Everything I have is yours (1947, MGM 10259); Caravan (1949, MGM 10368); I Apologize (1951, MGM 10903); *Billy Eckstine's Imagination* (1958, EmA 36129); *Basie/Eckstine Inc.* (1959, Roul. 52029); *Billy Eckstine and Quincy Jones at Basin Street East* (1961, Mer. 20674); *My Way* (c1966, Motown 646); *Feel the Warm* (c1971, Enterprise 1017)

As sideman with E. Hines: Jelly, Jelly (1940, Bb 11065); Skylark (1942, Bb 11512)

BIBLIOGRAPHY

B. Eckstine: "Crazy People like Me," *MM*, xxx (14 Aug 1954), 3; (21 Aug 1954), 5; (28 Aug 1954), 13; (4 Sept 1954), 5; (11 Sept 1954), 9
M. Shera: "The Billy Eckstine Band," *JJ*, xiii/11 (1960), 7
G. Hoefer: "The First Big Bop Band," *DB*, xxxii/16 (1965), 23
J. Burns: "The Billy Eckstine Band," *JM*, xiii/11 (1968), 6
F. Gibson: "The Billy Eckstine Band," *JJ*, xxiii/5 (1970), 2
S. Dance: *The World of Earl Hines* (New York, 1977) [interviews]
B. Niquet and K. Mohr: "Mister B. goes to Swing," *Pj*, no.13 (1977), 31
D. Salemann: "Billy Eckstine Orchestra 1944–1947," *Pj*, no.14 (1978), 57
E. Southern: "'Mr. B' of Ballad and Bop," *Black Perspective in Music*, vii (1979), 182; viii (1980), 54
D. J. Travis: *An Autobiography of Black Jazz* (Chicago, 1983) [incl. interviews], 311

BARRY KERNFELD

ECM. Record company and label. It was founded in Cologne, Germany, in 1969 by Manfred Eicher, who had formerly been a double bass player. By 1971 the label was recognized for its excellent recordings of free jazz, played by such artists as Paul Bley (issues of sessions recorded before the company was established), Jan Garbarek, and Marion Brown; by the late 1980s over 300 recordings had been issued on ECM, and around 15 on its affiliated label JAPO. Musicians who have recorded frequently for the company include Garbarek, Gary Burton, Chick Corea, Jack DeJohnette, Egberto Gismonti, Keith Jarrett, Pat Metheny, Terje Rypdal, Ralph Towner, and Eberhard Weber. In addition to directing the company Eicher remains active as a producer and engineer, often drawing praise from musicians for his sensitive approach in the studio.

ECM has issued several important recordings, and many of the leaders named above have contributed to what is now readily identifiable as a house style. Though this has occasionally been criticized by some as being too glossy and smooth, its exponents have nevertheless succeeded in uniting two genres – jazz-rock and free jazz – that have otherwise proved disparate. This is typically achieved by the combination of freely chromatic improvisations with simple bass and drum ostinatos.

BIBLIOGRAPHY

B. McRae: "ECM Music," *JJ*, xxiv/9 (1971), 26
K. Hyder: "ECM: Will it be Important Ten Years from Now?," *JJI*, xxxi/1–2 (1978), 22
G. Rava: "ECM: 'Juste après le silence'," *Jm*, no.274 (1979), 38
F. Billard: "Manfred est cher?," *Jm*, no.343 (1985), 32

Economy Hall. Dance hall in New Orleans; *see* NIGHTCLUBS AND OTHER VENUES.

Eddie Condon's. Nightclub in New York; *see* NIGHTCLUBS AND OTHER VENUES.

Edelhagen, Kurt (*b* Herne, Germany, 5 June 1920; *d* Cologne, Germany, 8 Feb 1982). German bandleader. In 1945, after studying piano and conducting in Essen, he led a trio in Herne, which played in British army clubs. He formed his first big band in 1946 and played for the radio station in Frankfurt am Main in 1948, before leading the big band of Bayerischer Rundfunk in Nuremberg (1949–52). He became well known as leader of the orchestra of Südwestfunk from 1952 to 1957; one of the leading postwar big bands in Germany, it was influenced by the music of Stan Kenton. Edelhagen took part as a bandleader in the première of Rolf Liebermann's Concerto for jazz band and orchestra under the direction of Hans Rosbaud at the Donaueschingen Musiktage für Zeitgenössische Tonkunst in 1954. After he joined Westdeutscher Rundfunk in Cologne in 1957, he built up an orchestra of musicians from several countries, including such soloists as the trombonist Jiggs Whigham and Dusko Goykovich; he also led a jazz class at the Hochschule für Musik in Cologne at this time (1958–60). He toured with the orchestra in the USSR and East Germany in 1964, performed in Prague in 1965 and 1968, and visited seven Arab states in 1968. When Westdeutscher Rundfunk decided to disband the orchestra in 1973, Edelhagen continued to play for the station, performing and arranging light dance music. His bands of the late 1950s and early 1960s were among the foremost in Europe; their unique combination of precision and power was particularly impressive.

SELECTED RECORDINGS

On a slow boat to China/Trumpet Blues (1949, Austroton 30018); My Funny Valentine/You go to my head (1955, Bruns. 10025) [EP]; *Live at Lucerna Hall* (1965, Sup. 15732)

BIBLIOGRAPHY

FeatherE; *ReclamsJ*

GÜNTHER HUESMANN

Edghill, Arthur (*b* New York, 21 July 1926). Drummer. He performed with Mercer Ellington (1949) and Ben Webster (1953), and then worked in hard-bop groups, playing with Horace Silver (1954) and Gigi Gryce (1956). In 1956 he recorded with Mal Waldron and played and recorded as a member of Kenny Dorham's Jazz Prophets. He toured with Dinah Washington (1957–8) and performed and recorded with Eddie "Lockjaw" Davis and Shirley Scott (1958–60); his playing is heard to advantage on a triple album recorded with Davis, *The Eddie "Lockjaw" Davis Cookbook* (1958, Prst. 7141, 7161, 7219). From 1976 he was a member of the Swing to Bop Quintet, with which he recorded. He was a founder of Jar-vard Publications, which produced jazz concerts in Brooklyn until 1984. His name has been consistently misspelled Edgehill. (*FeatherE*)

Edison. Recording company and record label. The company was established in Orange, New Jersey, by the inventor of sound recording, Thomas Alva Edison; issue of cylinders began in 1894. In 1913 the company began issuing recordings on vertically cut discs (given the trademark Edison Diamond Discs) which were about 7mm thick; production of cylinders, however, continued until 1929. The Blue Amberol cylinder series contained material mostly transferred from the Diamond Discs, but there are a few cylinders, including some jazz items, that have no equivalent on disc.

Edison himself kept close control of artists and repertory; as a result the label's jazz catalogue was never very extensive. It is recalled mainly for hot dance recordings made by such groups as the Georgia Melodians and the California Ramblers (who for Edison worked pseudonymously as the Golden Gate Orchestra). Items made for the race market are even more rare, but they include important sides by Fletcher Henderson and Clarence Williams. The label's only race series thus designated contained just three discs, all vaudeville blues recordings made in 1925.

The company did not adopt electrical recording techniques until June 1927, and was also late in issuing laterally cut discs. Edison ceased to make records in October 1929, thirteen days after its last session. The recording headquarters are now a historic site, run as a museum; the institution has revived the label occasionally for reissues, among them some of jazz recorded but not issued by the original company.

BIBLIOGRAPHY

D. D. Deakins: *Cylinder Records* (Bombay, 1956, 2/1958), 6

R. M. W. Dixon and J. Godrich: *Recording the Blues* (London, 1970), 29

E. S. Walker: "Jazz Research, 22: Ragtime and Jazz on Cylinder," *JM*, no.190 (1970), 30; no.191 (1971), 25

S. Hester: "Red Nichols Recordings on Edison, 1923–1928," *Micrography*, no.46 (1978), 4

R. R. Wile: *Edison Disc Recordings* (Philadelphia, 1977) [pubn of Eastern National Park and Monument Assn]

B. Rust: *The American Record Label Book* (New Rochelle, NY, 1978), 111

R. R. Wile: *Edison Disc Artists & Records, 1910–1929*, ed. R. Dethlefson (New York, 1985) [incl. dating guide]

——: "Edisonia: the Last Years of Edison Recording Activities Day by Day, January 1928 to October 1929," *Record Research*, nos.213–14 (1985), 1; nos.215–16 (1985), 8; nos.217–18 (1985), 12; nos.219–20 (1986), 13; nos.221–2 (1986), 11; nos.223–4 (1986), 11

J. Moore: "Edison Revisited," *Sv*, no.132 (1987), 228

Edison, Harry ("Sweets") [Sweets] (*b* Columbus, OH, 10 Oct 1915). Trumpeter. He spent his early childhood in Kentucky, where he was introduced to music by an uncle. At the age of 12 he moved back to Columbus and he began to play trumpet in local bands. In 1933 he became a member of the Jeter–Pillars Orchestra in Cleveland, and after a year moved with that group to St. Louis, where he spent the next two years. In 1937 he joined Lucky Millinder in New York, and six months later moved to the Count Basie Orchestra (for illustrations *see* BASIE, COUNT, and FILMS, fig.3). Edison became an important soloist with Basie, and occasionally composed and wrote arrangements for the group. In 1944 he played a prominent role in perhaps the finest jazz film ever made, *Jammin' the Blues*. Basie's orchestra disbanded temporarily in 1950, and thereafter Edison pursued a varied career, leading his own groups, traveling with Jazz at the Philharmonic, and working as a freelance with other orchestras. In the early 1950s he settled on the West Coast, where he became highly sought-after as a studio musician. He regularly led his own group in Los Angeles in the 1960s and rejoined Count Basie on several occasions. In the 1970s and early 1980s he traveled extensively, often with Eddie "Lockjaw" Davis. Edison's playing reflects the directness and full tone of his original inspiration, Louis Armstrong. A highly original soloist, he prefers the middle register, and has evolved a personal, spare, and often humorous style. He is noted for his perfect sense of timing and his manner of repeating a single note or phrase over several measures.

Oral history material in *NjR* (JOHP), *NjR*.

SELECTED RECORDINGS

Duos with O. Peterson: *Oscar Peterson & Harry Edison* (1974, Pablo 2310741)

As leader: Laura/I blowed and gone (1945, Ala. 119); Exit Virginia Blues/Ain'tcha gonna do it? (1945, Ala. 120); Pennies from Heaven (1953, PJ 612); *The Swinger* (1958, Verve MGV8295); *Edison's Lights* (1976, Pablo 2310780)

As sideman with C. Basie: Every Tub (1938, Decca 1728); Shorty George (1938, Decca 2325); Rock-a-Bye Basie (1939, Voc. 4747); Louisiana/Easy does it (1940, Col. 35448); Somebody stole my gal (1940, Col. 35500); 9:20 Special (1941, OK 6244)

BIBLIOGRAPHY
V. Wilmer: "Harry Edison: Sweet Talking," *JM*, xiii/9 (1967), 6
B. McRae: "A. B. Basics, 15: Harry Edison," *JJ*, xxi/3 (1968), 26
H. Edison: "I Play Better with Basie," ed. L. Tomkins, *CI*, viii/12 (1970), 8
D. Locke: "Harry 'Sweets' Edison," *J&B*, i/3 (1971), 4
L. Tomkins: "Harry Edison," *CI*, xvii/3 (1978), 20 [interview]
S. Dance: *The World of Count Basie* (New York and London, 1980) [colln of previously pubd interviews], 95
C. Battestini and J.-P. Battestini: "Harry 'Sweets' Edison," *BHcF*, no.288 (1981), 12 [interview]
D. Long: "Harry 'Sweets' Edison: Interview," *Cadence*, ix/3 (1983), 5

EDWARD BERGER

Edison–Bell. Record company. It was established in London in 1892, and began issuing cylinders in 1901. Under the ownership of J. E. Hough, Ltd., Edison–Bell Winner discs were introduced in 1912. In January 1922 the label began to issue recordings taken from Gennett, but the jazz repertory put out in this scheme was mostly of a commercial character, as was material taken from other American labels, such as Emerson, Plaza, and Paramount. Nevertheless Edison–Bell issued (from Paramount) a recording by Fletcher Henderson; this was the first disc involving Louis Armstrong to be issued in Britain. The company's other labels – Edison–Bell Radio, Velvet-Face, and Edison–Bell Electron – issued little more than hot dance music either, but items on Electron by the Belgian band of Chas Remue are highly regarded. The company's policy changed little after the death of J. E. Hough in February 1925. The operation was purchased in January 1933 by British Decca, which continued to issue Winner records, drawing on American Vocalion, until January 1935; these included some discs by Clarence Williams.

BIBLIOGRAPHY
A. Badrock and D. Spruce: "The Extent of the Gennett-Winner Link," *Matrix*, no.31 (1960), 23; no.32 (1961), 20
R. Jewson, D. Smith, and R. Webb: "Arthur Gainsbury's Guide to Junkshoppers: the Edison Family," *Sv*, no.20 (1968–9), 64
B. Rust: *The American Record Label Book* (New Rochelle, NY, 1978), 107
J. G. Hayes: *Edison Bell Winner: the W1 Series, 1933–1935* (Liverpool, England, 1984)

Edwards, Bass [Henry] (*b* Atlanta, 22 Feb 1898; *d* New York, 22 Aug 1965). Tuba and double bass player. During World War I he played in an army band, and from 1919 he worked in Philadelphia with various concert orchestras. In 1923 he played with Sam Wooding; later that year he became a member of Charlie Johnson's band, with which he remained until 1925, when he joined Duke Ellington. His warm tuba playing made an important contribution to the recordings of the Savoy Bearcats and may be heard to particular advantage on *Nightmare* (1926, Vic. 20182). He worked with Leon Abbey in New York and toured South America with him (1927), then joined Noble Sissle, with whom he performed and recorded in Europe (1929). After returning to New York he worked with Fats Waller, James P. Johnson, and Eubie Blake. From the 1930s he played mainly light and classical music on double bass in several orchestras.

based on *ChiltonW*

Edwards, Eddie [Edwin Branford; Daddy] (*b* New Orleans, 22 May 1891; *d* New York, 9 April 1963). Trombonist. He played violin from the age of ten, and took up trombone five years later. In his late teens he played with local brass bands, then worked briefly with Stein's Dixie Jass Band, led by Johnny Stein. After leaving this ensemble Edwards became a founding member of the ORIGINAL DIXIELAND JAZZ BAND; his strong, rhythmic ensemble playing was an important factor in the band's success. Edwards also composed with others several pieces which were later to become dixieland standards, such as *Tiger Rag*, *Fidgety Feet*, and *Original Dixieland One-step*. Except for a period during which he served briefly in the army (1918) and played in a band led by the pianist and comedian Jimmy Durante, Edwards remained with the Original Dixieland Jazz Band until 1925. Thereafter he left music, but in 1936 he returned to playing and worked with Larry Shields, Tony Sbarbaro, and various revivals of the Original Dixieland Jazz Band.

Oral history material in *LNT*.

SELECTED RECORDINGS

All recorded as a sideman with the Original Dixieland Jazz Band, for Victor unless otherwise indicated.
Livery Stable Blues/Dixie Jass Band One-step (1917, 18255); Skeleton Jangle/Tiger Rag (1918, 18472); Fidgety Feet/Lazy Daddy (1918, 18654); Skeleton Jangle/Tiger Rag (1936, 25524); Clarinet Marmalade/Bluin' the Blues (1936, 25525); Barnyard Blues/Original Dixieland One-step (1936, 25502); Clarinet Marmalade, Lazy Daddy, Original Dixieland One-step, Tiger Rag, first issued on *Original Dixieland Jazz Band* (1943, GHB 100)

BIBLIOGRAPHY
ChiltonW; *FeatherE*
E. Edwards: "Eddie Edwards Gives," *SL*, vi/9–10 (1955), 9
Obituary, *SL*, xiv/7–8 (1963), 1
For further bibliography *see* ORIGINAL DIXIELAND JAZZ BAND.

RICHARD SUDHALTER

Edwards, Teddy [Theodore Marcus] (*b* Jackson, MS, 26 April 1924). Tenor saxophonist. He grew up in a musical family and began playing alto saxophone when only a child. After working briefly in Detroit and Tampa, Florida, he toured widely with Ernie Fields's orchestra, then in 1945 settled in Los Angeles to work with the drummer and singer Roy Milton. He was invited to join Howard McGhee's group and changed to tenor saxophone, on which he built his reputation as a resourceful and fluent improviser. During the late 1940s Edwards participated fully in the after-hours club life of the city and became a key figure in the development of bop; he also took part in a number of significant recording sessions and played with the bands led by Benny Carter and Gerald Wilson. Thereafter he performed as a soloist and as leader of his own groups, although he also secured engagements with Howard Rumsey (1949–50), Max Roach (1954), and Carter (1955). In the early 1950s he spent a year at Bop City in San Francisco, returning to Los Angeles to join Wilson (with whom he appeared intermittently into the 1970s). He also worked with Benny Goodman in 1964. Edwards became known as a composer and arranger for television and radio during the 1970s, but continued to tour and record frequently in the 1980s, working with, among others, Tom Waits.

Oral history material in *NjR* (JOHP).

SELECTED RECORDINGS

As leader: Blues in Teddy's Flat (1947, Dial 1033); *Teddy's Ready* (1960, Cont. 7583); *Good Gravy* (1961, Cont. 7592)
As sideman: H. McGhee: Dialated Pupils/Midnite at Minton's (1946, Dial 1011); D. Gordon: The Duel (1947, Dial 1028); Hornin' in (1947), first issued on *The Duel* (Dial 204); F. Butler: *Wheelin' and Dealin'* (1978, Xan. 169)

BIBLIOGRAPHY
FeatherE; *Feather '60s*; *Feather–Gitler '70s*
I. Gitler: "Ever-ready Teddy Edwards," *DB*, xxxiv/15 (1967), 21
B. Case: "California, Here I Come," *MM*, lvi (4 April 1981), 28
S. Grove-Humphries and P. Hanson: "Teddy Edwards," *JJI*, xxxv/5 (1982), 12
P. Vacher: "Teddy's Ready," *Coda*, no.210 (1986), 7

PETER VACHER

Egan, Mark (McDanel) (*b* Brockton, MA, 14 Jan 1951). Electric bass guitarist and composer. He played trumpet from the age of ten, and took up the double bass at 15. He later studied at the University of Miami (BMus 1974) and took private lessons on electric bass guitar with Jaco Pastorius, double bass with

Dave Holland (1977), and piano with Andy LaVerne (1983). In 1972 he formed the group South Dade. After attending graduate school (to 1975) he worked with Ira Sullivan, toured with the Pointer Sisters and Eumir Deodato, and performed and recorded with David Sanborn. From 1977 he was active as a studio musician in New York. He performed with Pat Metheny and Danny Gottlieb (1977–80) and with Airto Moreira and Flora Purim (1981); with Gottlieb he formed a group in 1981, which recorded in 1982 and took the name Elements the following year. Among its members have been Bill Evans (iii) and the keyboard player Clifford Carter. Egan uses a variety of electronic devices and custom-made instruments, including an electric bass guitar with two necks, one of which carries eight strings in two sets of four, the sets tuned an octave apart. His work as a composer, which has ranged from film scores to commercials and videos, is well represented by the track *Valley Hymn* from his album *Mosaic* (1984). He has also been active as a teacher.

SELECTED RECORDINGS

As unaccompanied soloist: *Mosaic* (1984, Hip Pocket 104)

As leader of Elements (with D. Gottlieb): *Elements* (1982, Philo 9011); *Forward Motion* (1984, Ant. 1021)

As sideman: P. Metheny: *Pat Metheny Group* (1978, ECM 1114); *American Garage* (1979, ECM 1155); B. Evans: *Living in the Crest of a Wave* (1983, Elek. Mus. 60349)

BIBLIOGRAPHY

B. Milkowski: "The Elemental Music of Danny Gottlieb and Mark Egan," *DB*, li/2 (1984), 24 [incl. discography]

——: "Mark Egan: Studying with Jaco," *GP*, xviii/8 (1984), 61

T. Mulhern: "Mark Egan: Fretless Horizons," *GP*, xix/9 (1985), 40 [incl. discography]

G. Santoro: "Mark Egan: the Face of the Bass," *DB*, liii/3 (1986), 23 [incl. discography]

JOHN VOIGT

Ehrling, Thore (*b* Stockholm, 29 Dec 1912). Swedish bandleader, trumpeter, and arranger. He began his career in the band of the tenor saxophonist Frank Vernon (1930–34) and after attending the Royal Swedish Musical Academy in Stockholm (1931–5) worked with Håkan von Eichwald (1935–8); some of his many compositions and arrangements were recorded in 1936 by Benny Carter and Arne Hülphers. In 1938 he formed a seven-piece group, which later evolved into a big band and made several influential recordings; it disbanded in 1957. An excellent bandleader, Ehrling was also a founder in 1941 of the successful publishing house Ehrling & Löfwenholm (from 1952 Thore Ehrling Musik, from 1959 Ehrlingförlagen).

Oral history material in *SSsv*.

SELECTED RECORDINGS

Royal Strut (1939, Odeon D3037); Blues on Strings (1944, HMV X7067); Mississippi Mood (1944, HMV X7089); *Flash, Skansen 1947* (1947, Phon. 7655)

BIBLIOGRAPHY

"Svenskt stjärnalbum" [Swedish star-album], *Orkester journalen*, vi/5 (1938), 5

"Thore Ehrling orkester," *Estrad*, i/9 (1939), 13

"Mannen bakom orkestern" [The man behind the orchestra], *Estrad*, v/8 (1944), 11

B. Englund: "Ehrling, Thore," *Sohlmans musiklexikon*, (Stockholm, 1948–52, rev. and enlarged 2/1975–9 ed. H. Åstrand)

N. Hellström: "En 'institution' är borta" [An institution is gone], *Estrad*, xix/5 (1957), 3

E. Kjellberg: *Svensk jazzhistoria: en översikt* [Swedish jazz history: an overview] (Stockholm, 1985)

B. Westin: *Säg det med musik: Thore Ehrling och hans orkester* [Say it with music: Thore Ehrling and his orchestra] (Stockholm, 1987) [incl. discography]

ERIK KJELLBERG

Eiberg, Valdemar (Sophus Gerlach) (*b* Kolding, Denmark, 23 Aug 1892; *d* Copenhagen, 14 July 1965). Danish saxophonist and bandleader. He began his career as a banjoist and in 1923 became the first Danish jazz saxophonist, playing initially C-melody then alto saxophone. The same year he formed the first notable Danish jazz band, which during the 1920s included leading Danish jazz musicians such as Kai Ewans and Peter Rasmussen among its members; it made the earliest jazz recordings in Denmark (including *I've got a cross-eyed papa*, 1924, HMV X2122). In the 1930s he led a number of dance bands and in the 1940s made recordings of Hawaiian music.

ERIK WIEDEMANN

Eights. Eight-bar phrases, as in the expression "to trade eights"; *see* FORMS, §1(ii).

Ekyan [Echkyan], **André** (*b* Meudon, France, 24 Oct 1907; *d* nr Alicante, Spain, 9 Aug 1972). French clarinetist and saxophonist. He was self-taught as a musician. He led a band at Le Perroquet in Paris in the 1920s, then played with Jack Hylton (in London, 1930–31), Gregor (1932–3), and Tommy Dorsey (1936). He made a number of recordings as a leader between 1935 and 1946; on those from the period 1937–41 his alto saxophone and clarinet solos were accompanied by Django Reinhardt (they include *Margie/A pretty girl is like a melody*, 1940, Swing 194). He also played with Tommy Benford, Benny Carter, Coleman Hawkins (1937), Ray Ventura (1938), Joe Turner (i), Jack Butler, Frank "Big Boy" Goudie (1939), again with Ventura (in Switzerland, 1941), and with Bobby Nichols (1945) and Mezz Mezzrow. In 1950 he recorded again with Reinhardt as a member of the Quintette du Hot Club de France. Ekyan's playing influenced that of Michel De Villers.

BIBLIOGRAPHY

H. Panassié: "André Ekyan," *Jh*, 1st ser., no.13 (1936), 9

C. Delaunay: "Les débuts du jazz en France: souvenirs par André Ekyan," *Jh*, no.248 (1969), 38

MICHEL LAPLACE

Eldridge, Joe [Joseph] (*b* Pittsburgh, 1908; *d* 5 March 1952). Alto saxophonist, brother of Roy Eldridge. He began working in New York in 1927 and led the Elite Serenaders there and in Pittsburgh (late 1920s). In the early 1930s he played with various musicians, among them Speed Webb and Cecil Scott, and led a band with his brother (1933). He then performed with McKinney's Cotton Pickers (1934), Blanche Calloway (1935–6), his brother (1936–40), Buddy Johnson (1941), and in Zutty Singleton's quartet (1941–3). His own group was resident for a short time at Jimmy Ryan's, New York. In 1943 he moved to Los Angeles, where he re-joined Singleton, played tenor saxophone with his brother (1944), and performed with Hot Lips Page (1945). Eldridge worked in Canada in the late 1940s and after returning to New York (1950), he began to teach (1951). His playing may be heard to advantage on Roy Eldridge's *Mahogany Hall Stomp* (1939, first issued on *Roy Eldridge at the Arcadia Ballroom, 1939*, Jazz Archives 14). (A. McCarthy: *Big Band Jazz*, New York and London, 1974)

based on *ChiltonW*

Eldridge, (David) Roy [Little Jazz] (*b* Pittsburgh, 30 Jan 1911). Trumpeter, brother of Joe Eldridge.

1. Life. 2. Style.

1. LIFE. He played professionally from the age of 16, first with a touring carnival (where he imitated Coleman Hawkins's well-

known tenor saxophone solo in *Stampede*) and later with obscure midwestern bands. In 1930 he moved to New York and played in various dance bands in Harlem, including that of Teddy Hill; in 1932 he began a serious study of Louis Armstrong's style. From 1933 he worked in Pittsburgh and then in Baltimore before returning to New York, where his first recorded solos with Hill in 1935 immediately attracted attention; later that year he joined Fletcher Henderson's orchestra as lead trumpeter and occasional singer. In autumn 1936 he formed his own eight-piece band in Chicago with his older brother Joe Eldridge as saxophonist and arranger; the group broadcast nightly, and Eldridge took advantage of his position as leader to record several outstanding extended solos, including *After you've gone* and *Wabash Stomp*. After a brief period studying radio engineering in 1938 Eldridge formed a ten-piece band which the following year began a residency in New York at the Arcadia Ballroom and later at Kelly's Stable.

Roy Eldridge, 1941

By this time Eldridge was widely regarded as the outstanding jazz trumpet soloist of his time, and he began to receive liberal offers from white swing bands. In 1941 he joined Gene Krupa, becoming one of the first black jazz musicians to be accepted as a permanent member of the brass section of a white big band. While with Krupa he recorded his celebrated ballad performance of *Rockin' Chair* and became a nationwide celebrity, particularly in a novelty hit, *Let me off uptown*, with Anita O'Day. When Krupa's band broke up in 1943, Eldridge played as a freelance and led his own band in New York for a while before taking a position in Artie Shaw's band in 1944. A year later, after many racial incidents had occurred while the band was on tour, he left Shaw to organize a big band of his own. Like most large jazz ensembles at this time, his group was financially unsuccessful, and Eldridge soon reverted to small-group work. In 1948 he began a long association with Norman Granz's Jazz at the Philharmonic.

Although in the early 1940s Eldridge had taken a leading part in the jam sessions at Minton's Playhouse in New York, which later crystallized in bop, he was out of sympathy with that style, and by the late 1940s his music was considered old-fashioned. In a crisis of confidence he moved to Paris in 1950 while on tour with Benny Goodman. During his year in Paris he was lionized by the French jazz public, and made some of his finest recordings, including a version of *Fireworks* in a duo with Claude Bolling in which the two men reworked the ideas shared by Armstrong and Earl Hines in their recording of the same title (1928). After returning to the USA in April 1951 he joined the burgeoning mainstream jazz movement, performing in small groups with Benny Carter, Johnny Hodges, Ella Fitzgerald (1963–5), and, notably, Coleman Hawkins, with whom he made several outstanding albums for Verve. From 1970 until 1980, when he was incapacitated by a stroke, he led a traditional group at Ryan's in New York. Thereafter he performed occasionally as a singer, drummer, and surprisingly competent pianist.

2. Style. Eldridge was the leading trumpeter of the late swing period; his contemporaries saw in him a successor to Armstrong, who had turned increasingly to commercial music and the world of entertainment. Unlike other trumpeters of his generation, Eldridge took his main inspiration not from Armstrong but from the saxophonists Benny Carter and, especially, Coleman Hawkins, whose fleet arpeggio style and rich tone he adapted to his instrument. As a result, Eldridge early acquired a keen awareness of harmony, an unprecedented dexterity, particularly in the highest register, and a full, slightly overblown timbre, which crackled at moments of high tension. These features are fully apparent on his early solo performances with Teddy Hill (1935), and came even more to the fore in the next few years in his extended solos with his own band, as in his famous four-bar break in *After you've gone* (1937), with its high-register rips and easy mobility over a range of nearly three octaves (ex.1).

Perhaps equally important were Eldridge's exuberant personality and keen sense of competition (he thrived in a jam-session atmosphere, and even in later years challenged younger musicians to cutting contests), which kept his performances at a peak of emotional intensity and technical bravado. Most of all, his playing was infused with unusual rhythmic vigor, at times causing him to rush already breakneck tempos. In his big-band performances of the late 1930s and early 1940s he developed a unique facility for mounting and pacing high-note climaxes. This quality unfortunately marred many of his performances with small groups in the years that followed, but by then he often used a harmon mute, which concentrated and intensified his tone.

Ex.1 Eldridge's solo break from *After you've gone* (1937, Voc. 3458); transcr. J. B. Robinson

Eldridge had a formative impact on early bop musicians, and recordings such as *Heckler's Hop* (1937) may be seen as harbingers of the bop movement, just as *The Gasser* (1943) represents his closest approximation to the new style. However, he was never able fully to assimilate bop's rhythmic procedures, and his later style of the 1950s represents a broadening and deepening of the swing tradition. His influence is particularly apparent in the work of Dizzy Gillespie, whom he engaged in a long and mutually productive series of "trumpet battles" at Minton's in the early 1940s, and who freely admits his debt to the older musician. A later series of confrontations between Gillespie and Eldridge, recorded in the mid-1950s for Clef and Verve, offers a revealing comparison of the swing and bop trumpet styles in their most virtuoso manifestations.

Oral history material in *NjR* (JOHP), *NjR*.

See also Improvisation, §§4(i), 4(iii), and ex.1; and Trumpet, §4; for further illustrations *see* Nightclubs and other venues, fig.6; O'Day, anita; and Shaw, artie.

SELECTED RECORDINGS

Duos with C. Bolling: Wild Man Blues/Fireworks (1951, Vogue 5092)

As leader: Wabash Stomp (1937, Voc. 3479); Heckler's Hop (1937, Voc. 3577); After you've gone (1937, Voc. 3458); The Gasser (1943, Bruns. 80117); St. Louis Blues (1944, Key. 607); Dale's Wail (1953, Clef 89056); with D. Gillespie: *Roy and Diz* (1954, Clef MGC641, MGC671), incl. I found a new baby; with B. Carter: *The Urbane Jazz of Roy Eldridge and Benny Carter* (1955, Verve 8202); with C. Hawkins: *At the Opera House* (1957, Verve 8266); with D. Gillespie and H. Edison: *Tour de force* (1957, Verve 8212); *Montreux '77* (1977, PL 2308203)

As sideman: T. Hill: Here comes Cookie (1935, Ban. 33384); F. Henderson: Jangled Nerves (1936, Vic. 25317); G. Krupa: Let me off uptown (1941, OK 6210); Rockin' Chair (1941, OK 6352); A. Shaw: Little Jazz (1945, Vic. 201668)

BIBLIOGRAPHY

R. Eldridge: "Jim Crow is Killing Jazz," *Negro Digest*, viii/12 (1950), 44

L. Feather: *The Book of Jazz: a Guide to the Entire Field* (New York, 1957, rev. 2/1965 as *The Book of Jazz from Then till Now: a Guide to the Entire Field*)

N. Shapiro and N. Hentoff, eds.: *The Jazz Makers: Essays on the Greats of Jazz* (New York, 1957/R1979), 297

M. James: "Roy Eldridge: an Appreciation," *JM*, no.156 (1968), 5

R. Bolton: " 'Little Jazz' Roy Eldridge," *JJ*, xxiv/8 (1971), 7

D. Morgenstern: "Little Jazz: the Fire Still Burns," *DB*, xxxviii/3 (1971), 14

G. M. Colombé: "Roy's Progress," *JJ*, xxv/5 (1972), 22

——: "Rapping with Roy," *Into Jazz*, i/1 (1974), 4

——: "Roy Eldridge," *JJ*, xxvii/2 (1974), 10 [interview]

S. Dance: *The World of Swing* (New York, 1974) [colln of previously pubd interviews], 148

A. McCarthy: *Big Band Jazz* (New York and London, 1974), 43

J. McDonough: "Roy Eldridge: Legendary Lip in the Golden Years," *DB*, xliv/21 (1977), 24

J. Evensmo: *The Trumpet of Roy Eldridge, 1929–1944* (n.p. [Oslo], n.d. [?1979]) [discography]

G. Giddins: "The Excitable Roy Eldridge," *Rhythm-a-ning: Jazz Tradition and Innovation in the '80s* (New York, and Oxford, England, 1981) [colln of previously pubd articles], 68

J. BRADFORD ROBINSON

Electrical and Musical Industries. *See* Emi.

Electrical recording. A term applied to a technique of sound recording (and playback) that utilizes continuous variations in the electrical signal; it is also used of the discs produced by this process. *See* Recording, §1, 2.

Electric bass guitar [bass guitar]. A large electric guitar (*see* Guitar), usually with four heavy strings tuned *E'–A'–D–G*. The electric bass guitar was invented by Leo Fender and was first marketed as the Fender Precision Bass in 1951. The instrument was introduced to meet the needs of musicians playing the bass part in small dance bands in the USA: they wanted not only a more easily portable instrument than the double bass, but one that could match the volume of the increasingly popular solid-bodied electric guitar, and could be played with greater precision than their large, fretless, acoustic instruments. Fender's electric bass guitar answered all these requirements. It was based on his already successful Telecaster six-string electric guitar, with a similar body of ash and neck of maple. The four strings were tuned to the same notes as the double bass (an octave below the bottom four of the six-string electric guitar), and a single pickup fed controls for volume and tone. At first the instrument was manufactured only in models with a fretted fingerboard, which offered players the precision they wanted. Later, fretless models were also introduced; these enabled musicians to achieve greater agility and timbral variety than they could on fretted instruments.

For many years the name "Fender" was almost generic for electric bass guitars. The company introduced the Jazz Bass in 1960; this was a larger, heavier instrument than the Precision model and had two pickups. Both models have retained their popularity into the 1980s, and the designs remain practically unchallenged. The most notable attempt to change the construction of the electric bass has come in the 1980s from the American maker Ned Steinberger. The Steinberger Bass is constructed entirely from injection-molded plastics, lacks the conventional peghead at the upper end of the neck, and has a tiny body, barely wide enough to carry the pickups, control knobs, and machine heads.

The electric bass guitar was first used in jazz by sidemen with Lionel Hampton, who was highly influential in its acceptance among jazz musicians. Vernon Alley played a prototype of it as early as 1940, though the experiment was of little consequence. At the beginning of the following decade Hampton immediately adopted Fender's invention, allowing Monk Montgomery to join his orchestra only on the condition that he took up electric bass guitar. In 1953 Montgomery became the first jazz musician to record on the instrument; he may be heard to advantage on his brother Wes Montgomery's album *Montgomeryland* (1958, PJ 5).

Although bass players in most jazz styles have continued to prefer the acoustic instrument, in the 1960s and early 1970s many double bass players, including such notable musicians as Ron Carter, began to use the electric bass guitar when required to do so, particularly for concerts and for studio work in styles that were oriented towards rock; some, among them Steve Swallow, began playing the instrument exclusively. Its popularity increased after the rise of jazz-rock; from the mid-1970s many electric bass guitarists, often influenced by rock or rhythm-and-blues musicians (notably James Jamerson, a house musician for Motown), achieved prominence in jazz without first having played double bass. At this time several players developed new approaches to the instrument. Stanley Clarke established a virtuoso technique of highly melodic playing, which may be heard on the album *Stanley Clarke* (1974, Epic 36973); Jaco Pastorius, using a fretless model, achieved a panoply of unusual effects (including chords made up entirely of harmonics, and slow, chordal glissandos) and an extraordinarily full ringing tone on such recordings as his LP *Jaco Pastorius* (*c*1975, Epic 33949), and *Havona*, from Weather Report's *Heavy Weather* (1976, Col. PC34418). Other fine players include Anthony Jackson, a gifted improviser who has played with Al Di Meola and others, and uses an instrument with six strings. A few jazz musicians have taken up the Steinberger Bass; the most important of these is Jamaaladeen Tacuma, who praises the instrument's ability to produce a cutting tone without distortion and its suitability for his melodic playing. The title track of his album *Show Stopper* (1982–3, Gram. 8301) displays both the instrument's strengths and weaknesses. Although his solos are extremely crisp and penetrating, the walking bass lines with which he accompanies the solos of his sidemen often sound thin and high-pitched.

As the electric bass guitar has only a very brief performance tradition, there are no formalized approaches to its technique. Fingering follows either that method of double bass playing which involves stopping the strings with only the first, second, and fourth fingers of the left hand, or an approach derived from that of the guitar in which all four fingers are used. The strings are normally plucked with the first two fingers of the right hand, though some musicians, including Swallow, use a plectrum. A method of playing that has been adopted by some jazz players, notably Clarke, involves striking the lower two strings with the edge of the thumb of the right hand and rapidly flicking the higher ones with the tips or the knuckles of the fingers. This style, often known as slapping, is a variant of the slap-bass technique and produces a very percussive, stinging tone as the strings hit the fingerboard, and, on occasions, the pick-ups.

For illustrations *see* Davis, miles, fig.2; Jazz, fig.8; and Pastorius, jaco.

BIBLIOGRAPHY

J.-E. Berendt: *Das Jazzbuch: Entwicklung und Bedeutung der Jazzmusik* (Frankfurt am Main, Germany, 1953, rev. 2/1959 as *Das neue Jazzbuch*, Eng. trans., New York, 1962; rev. and enlarged 5/1981 as *Das grosse Jazzbuch: von New Orleans bis Jazz Rock*, Eng. trans. as *The Jazz Book: from New Orleans to Fusion and Beyond*, Westport, CT, 1982)

M. Newman: "Monk Montgomery: the First Man to Record on Bass Guitar," *GP*, xi/9 (1977), 26

T. Mulhern: "Stanley Clarke," *GP*, xiv/5 (1980), 66

A. Roidinger: *Der Elektrobass in Jazz* (Vienna, 1981)

J. Rosenbaum: "Steve Swallow: Renegade Jazz Bassist," *GP*, xv/12 (1981), 60

C. J. Gans: "Jamaaladeen Tacuma: 21st Century Electrical Bass Guitarist," *JF* [intl edn], no.80 (1983), 50

TONY BACON/JIM FERGUSON

Electric guitar. A type of guitar with integral electrical components, designed to be played through an electronic amplification system. *See* Guitar; *see also* Electric bass guitar.

Electric piano. An electronically amplified keyboard instrument capable of producing piano-like sounds; its sound-generating system may, but need not, include strings. *See* Piano, §6.

Electrola. Record label. It was the principal label of the subsidiary company set up in Germany during the 1920s by the Gramophone Co. (which later became EMI). From its foundation until the termination of EMI's affiliation with RCA Victor in May 1957 the label was used to issue in Germany items from Victor's catalogue. Thereafter little jazz was issued on the label, though its management has continued to run Odeon and other labels owned by EMI, and in the 1980s has made important reissues of material originally put out on Blue Note.

Electronic keyboards. Keyboard instruments in which the sound is wholly or partly produced by electronic means and is amplified electronically. The electric piano (*see* Piano, §6), electronic organ (*see* Organ, §2), and most synthesizers (*see* Synthesizer) fall into this group of instruments, as do instruments that combine attributes of these three kinds. Although originally designed to simulate the sound of the acoustic instruments, the electric piano and electronic organ now usually include tone-modifying devices that offer a range of sounds quite uncharacteristic of the conventional piano and organ; one of the principal attractions of the synthesizer from the start was its ability to create new timbres and effects. Electronic keyboards are found principally in jazz-rock, where, as in other forms of popular music, the player sometimes uses a group of instruments that may include an electric or acoustic piano (or both), an electronic organ, and one or more synthesizers.

Elektra Musician. Record label. It was established in New York in 1982 as a subsidiary of Elektra by Bruce Lundvall, who was at that time the organization's president. The label was first used to issue a recording made by the parent company of a concert (part of the Kool Jazz Festival of 1982) given by the Young Lions, an ad hoc group made up of leading free-jazz musicians. Thereafter, however, the catalogue developed very differently; it included the reissue of John McLaughlin's historic jazz-rock album *My Goal's Beyond*, and many fine new bop, modal-jazz, and jazz-rock recordings. These included work by such musicians and bands as Bill Evans (ii) (an issue of items made in 1979), Bill Evans (iii), Sphere, Woody Shaw, Steps Ahead, Joe Albany, Charles Lloyd, Dexter Gordon, McCoy Tyner, and Bobby McFerrin, and an all-star group that included Freddie Hubbard, Joe Henderson, and Chick Corea and recorded as Echoes of an Era and the Griffith Park Collection. Lundvall left the company in 1985; thereafter issue was only sporadic. (B. Lundvall: "Elektra Musician: from Monk to Punk to Funk," *Steps Ahead*, Elek. Mus. 60168-1, 1983 [liner notes])

Elements. Name by which a group formed in 1981 by Mark Egan and Danny Gottlieb was known from 1983.

Elgar, Charlie [Charles A.] (*b* New Orleans, 13 June 1885; *d* Chicago, Aug 1973). Bandleader. He learned violin from the age of 12 and later studied in Milwaukee and Chicago. He performed with string groups in New Orleans before moving to Chicago (*c*1913), where he held long-term engagements (notably at the Dreamland Cafe) with his own quintet and 15-piece band. After working in Europe with Will Marion Cook he led his own big band in Milwaukee (1925–8) and Chicago (1926–30). At different times his sidemen included Manuel Perez, Lorenzo Tio, Jr., Louis Cottrell, Sr., Barney Bigard, and Omer Simeon. He made only four recordings, as the leader of the Creole Orchestra (including *Cafe Capers*, 1926, Voc. 15477). In the 1930s he devoted most of his time to teaching.

Oral history material in *LNT*.

BIBLIOGRAPHY

A. McCarthy: *Big Band Jazz* (New York and London, 1974), 20

H. Sagawe: "Elgar's Creole Orchestra," *Sv*, no.52 (1974), 150 [incl. discography]

based on *ChiltonW*

Elias, Eliane (*b* São Paulo, 19 March 1960). Brazilian keyboard player. She began studying music at the age of ten. As the music director of the Centro Livre de Aprentysagem Musical in São Paolo she taught jazz. She performed and recorded with the big bands of Toquinho and Vinivius Moraes, and with the Brazilian guitarist Sebastão Tapajos. Eddie Gomez heard her play in Paris and on his advice she moved to New York in November 1981. Two years later she joined Steps Ahead; her playing may be heard to advantage on its album *Steps Ahead* (1983, Elek. Mus. 60168). From 1984, when she left the group, she performed and recorded with her husband, Randy Brecker; she has also recorded two albums as a leader (1985, 1987).

BIBLIOGRAPHY

H. Mandel: "Steps Ahead," *DB*, 1/8 (1983), 18 [incl. discography]

G. Kalbacher: "Eliane Elias," *JT*, (Feb 1988), 16

KIMBERLY McCORD

Elizalde, Fred [Federico] (*b* Manila, 12 Dec 1907; *d* Manila, 16 Jan 1979). Filipino bandleader, pianist, and composer. Although best known from around 1930 as a conductor of symphony orchestras, he was also influential as a jazz musician in Britain in the 1920s. At Cambridge University he formed a student band, the Quinquaginta Ramblers (1927), which he taught to perform in an American jazz style rather than a more derivative one that he termed "Viennese." Among his compositions is the suite *The Heart of a Nigger*, which was performed in June 1927 at the London Palladium by Bert Ambrose's orchestra; from autumn of the same year Elizalde led a band at the Savoy Hotel in which he also played piano, and which included as sidemen Chelsea Quealey, Harry Gold, and Adrian Rollini. He wrote many arrangements for the orchestra before it disbanded on Christmas Eve 1929. His most successful jazz compositions are probably his piano solos.

RECORDED COMPOSITIONS

(selective list; all recorded by Elizalde as unaccompanied soloist)

Siam Blues (1927, Bruns. 02327); Pianotrope (1927, Bruns. 02328); Vamp till Ready (1933, Decca M450)

BIBLIOGRAPHY

P. Tanner: "In Defence of Elizalde," *Sv*, no.36 (1971), 216
——: "Stompin' at the Savoy with Fred Elizalde," *JM*, no.191 (1971), 26
E. S. Walker: "Fred Elizalde," *Sv*, no.33 (1971), 92

WALTER STARKIE/CHARLES FOX/R

Ellboj, Lulle [Rune Fritiof] (*b* Stockholm, 3 Nov 1911; *d* Stockholm, 12 March 1960). Swedish bandleader and saxophonist. He played in the 1930s with Charles Redland and Helge Lindberg and worked as a leader from 1938; the following year he recorded with Valaida Snow. From 1943 to 1947 he performed as the leader of a big band that included Rolf Ericson, Arne Domnérus, Gösta Theselius, and Rolf Larsson among its sidemen; he also made recordings, including *Hot Gravy* (1945, Col. DS1600). Later he worked as the leader of small groups.

BIBLIOGRAPHY

M. Westin: "Lulle Ellboj ledde 40-talets sensationsband" [Lulle Ellboj leads 40-piece sensational band], *Orkester journalen*, li/4 (1983), 17
——: "Inspelningar med Lulle Ellbojs band" [Recordings by Lulle Ellboj's band], *Orkester journalen*, li/5 (1983), 17

ERIK KJELLBERG

Ellington, Duke [Edward Kennedy] (*b* Washington, 29 April 1899; *d* New York, 24 May 1974). Composer, bandleader, and pianist, father of Mercer Ellington. He was for decades a leading figure in big-band jazz, and remains the most significant composer of the genre.

1. Life. 2. Style and musical language. 3. Compositions.

1. LIFE. Ellington's father was a butler and intended him to become an artist. He began to study piano when he was seven, and was much influenced by the ragtime pianists; at the age of 17 he made his professional début. His first visit to New York, in early 1923, ended in financial failure, but on Fats Waller's advice he moved there later that year with Elmer Snowden's Washington band, the Washingtonians: Sonny Greer (drums), Otto Hardwick (saxophones), Snowden (banjo), and Artie Whetsol (trumpet). Between 1923 and 1927 this small group, which played at the Hollywood and Kentucky clubs on Broadway, was gradually enlarged to a ten-piece orchestra by the addition of Bubber Miley (trumpet), as well as another trumpeter, Tricky Sam Nanton (trombone), Harry Carney (baritone saxophone), Rudy Jackson (clarinet and tenor saxophone), and Wellman Braud (double bass); Fred Guy replaced Snowden on banjo. The band's early recordings (*East St. Louis Toodle-oo* and *Black and Tan Fantasy*) reveal growing originality.

1. Duke Ellington at the Columbia recording studios, New York, 1956

During the following period (1927–31), at the Cotton Club in Harlem, Ellington began to share with Louis Armstrong the leading position in the jazz world. The orchestra grew to 12 musicians, with Barney Bigard (clarinet) replacing Jackson, Johnny Hodges (saxophone), Freddie Jenkins (trumpet), and Cootie Williams (trumpet), the last replacing Miley. The group went to Hollywood to appear in the film *Check and Double Check* (1930), and in New York made about 200 recordings, many in the "jungle style" that was one of Ellington's and Miley's most individual creations (*see* JUNGLE MUSIC). The success of *Mood Indigo* (1930) brought Ellington worldwide fame, and in 1931 he began experiments in extended composition with *Creole Rhapsody* (*see* FORMS, §3, and Table 1), later to be followed by *Reminiscing in Tempo* and *Diminuendo in Blue/Crescendo in Blue*. The decade from 1932 to 1942 was Ellington's most creative. His band, consisting now of six brass instruments, four reeds, and a four-man rhythm section, performed in many American cities and made highly successful concert tours to Europe in 1933 and 1939. In 1939 there were several important additions to the band: Jimmy Blanton (double bass), Ben Webster (tenor saxophone), and most notably Billy Strayhorn, as arranger, composer, and second pianist. At this time Ellington created several outstanding short works, notably *Concerto for Cootie*, *Ko-Ko*, and *Cotton Tail*.

In the mid-1940s the orchestra was enlarged again: by 1946 it included 18 players. But the previous stability of personnel declined and Ellington's writing, based on his members' individual styles, began to suffer from the constant changes. Several excellent soloists, however, were added: Ray Nance (trumpet and violin), Shorty Baker (trumpet), and Jimmy Hamilton (clarinet). In January 1943 Ellington inaugurated a series of annual concerts at Carnegie Hall with his monumental work *Black, Brown and Beige*, a "tone parallel" originally conceived in five sections and intended to portray the history of the black people in the USA through their music. Other ambitious works followed (*Liberian Suite, Harlem, Night Creature, Such Sweet Thunder, Suite Thursday*). After Ellington abandoned these concerts in 1952, the development of the long-playing record allowed him to create other multimovement suites.

From 1950 Ellington continued to expand the scope of his compositions and his activities as a bandleader. His foreign tours became increasingly frequent and successful (including one of the USSR, in 1971); many of these stimulated him to write large-scale suites. He composed his first full-length film score, for Otto Preminger's *Anatomy of a Murder* (1959), and his first incidental music, for Alain René Le Sage's *Turcaret* (1960). He also made recordings with younger jazz musicians such as John Coltrane, Charles Mingus, and Max Roach (*Money Jungle*, 1962). In his last decade Ellington wrote mostly liturgical music: *In the Beginning God* (for orchestra, chorus, two soloists, and dancer) was performed in Grace Cathedral, San Francisco (1965). Other "sacred services" followed. Among his numerous awards and honors were doctorates from Howard University (1963) and Yale University (1967) and the Presidential Medal of Honor (1969); in 1970 he was made a member of the National Institute of Arts and Letters, and in 1971 he became the first jazz musician to be named a member of the Royal Academy of Music in Stockholm. A documentary film of Ellington and his orchestra, *On the Road with Duke Ellington*, was made in 1974. Ellington directed his band until his death, when it was taken over by his son Mercer Ellington.

2. STYLE AND MUSICAL LANGUAGE. Ellington taught himself harmony at the piano, and acquired the rudiments of orchestration by experimenting with his band; his orchestra was a workshop, in which he consulted his players and tried out alternative solutions. During the formative Cotton Club period, Ellington was obliged to work in a variety of musical categories: numbers for dancing, jungle-style and production numbers, popular songs, "blue" or "mood" pieces, as well as "pure" instrumental jazz compositions. During this period, too, Ellington developed an extraordinary symbiotic relationship with his orchestra – it was his "instrument" even more than the piano – enabling him to experiment with the timbral colorings, tonal effects, and unusual voicings that became the hallmark of his style; the "Ellington effect" (Strayhorn's term) was virtually inimitable because it depended in large part on the particular timbre and style of each player. Remarkably, though no two players in Ellington's orchestra sounded alike, they could, when called upon, produce the most ravishing blends and ensembles of sonority known to jazz.

An outstanding early example of the "Ellington effect" may be heard on *Mood Indigo* (1930), in which the traditional roles of the three front-line instruments in New Orleans collective improvisation – clarinet (high-register obbligato), trumpet (melody or theme), and trombone (bass or tenor counter-themes) – are inverted so that the muted trumpet plays on top; the plunger-muted trombone functions as a high-register second voice, and the clarinet sounds more than an octave below in its chalumeau register. Other innovations include Ellington's use of Harry Carney's special baritone saxophone timbre, not for root notes (a traditional role for the baritone) but for low-register sevenths or sixths of chords, which gives these harmonies a unique tone and feeling. Another is his use of Juan

2. Duke Ellington's orchestra at the Connecticut Jazz Festival, 28 July 1956: (back row, left to right) Cat Anderson and Ray Nance (trumpets); (middle row) Jimmy Woode (double bass), Quentin Jackson, unidentified player, and Britt Woodman (trombones); (front row) Paul Gonsalves, Jimmy Hamilton, Johnny Hodges, Russell Procope, and Harry Carney (saxophones); (front) Ellington

Tizol's valve trombone as a fourth voice added to an ensemble of three saxophones. A further Ellington innovation was the use, as early as 1927 (in *Creole Love Call*), of the voice (singing without text) as a jazz instrument.

In the early and mid-1920s orchestral jazz arrangements were rudimentary, serving only the simplest functions of dance music. But Ellington (along with Don Redman, Fletcher Henderson, and John Nesbitt) developed an elaborate, diversified concept of arranging, which incorporated the essence of the current "hot" style of solo improvisation. In this he was greatly aided and influenced by the extraordinary expressive and technical capabilities of his two principal brass players, Bubber Miley and Tricky Sam Nanton, who were both experts of the so-called growl and plunger style. These often pungent sonorities, when blended or juxtaposed with the smoother sounds of the saxophone, provided Ellington with an orchestral palette more colorful and varied than that of any other orchestra of the time (with the possible exception of Paul Whiteman's). Faced with the formal problem posed by jazz arrangement – how best to integrate solo improvisation – Ellington learned to exploit expertly the contrast produced by the soloist's entry, so as to project him into the music's movement and entrust him with its development. This partly explains why even Ellington's finest soloists seemed lusterless after leaving his orchestra. He also had a singular gift for devising orchestral accompaniments for improvisation; no arrangers, except perhaps Sy Oliver and Gil Evans, have imagined instrumental combinations as beautiful as those of *Mystery Song, Saddest Tale, Delta Serenade, Subtle Lament, Azure, Dusk, Ko-Ko* (ex.1), and *Moon Mist*.

Ellington's talents as a pianist are generally neglected or underrated. While he rarely featured himself as a soloist with his orchestra, he was nevertheless a remarkably individual contributor to the overall "Ellington effect." He saw himself primarily as a catalyst and accompanist, a feeder of ideas and rhythmic energy to the band as a whole or to its soloists. In this unobtrusive role, playing only when necessary, he was known for remaining silent during entire choruses or indeed pieces. His piano tone, produced deep in the keys, was the richest and most resonant imaginable; it had the ability to energize and inspire the entire orchestra. Although he was an erratic soloist in his early years, and sometimes relied on pianistic clichés – incessant downward-fluttering arpeggios, for instance – Ellington could on occasion vie with the best players. An outstanding example of his work as a pianist-composer is *Clothed Woman* (1947), remarkable for its virtually complete atonality (ex.2). He also wrote a *Piano Method for Blues* (1943).

3. Compositions. Ellington is generally recognized as the most important composer in jazz history. Most of the enormous number of works he recorded are his own; the exact number of his compositions is unknown, but is estimated at about 2000, including hundreds of three-minute instrumental pieces (for 78 r.p.m. recordings), popular songs (many consisting of instru-

Ex.1 From *Ko-Ko* (1940, Vic. 26577); transcr. G. Schuller (all parts notated at sounding pitch)

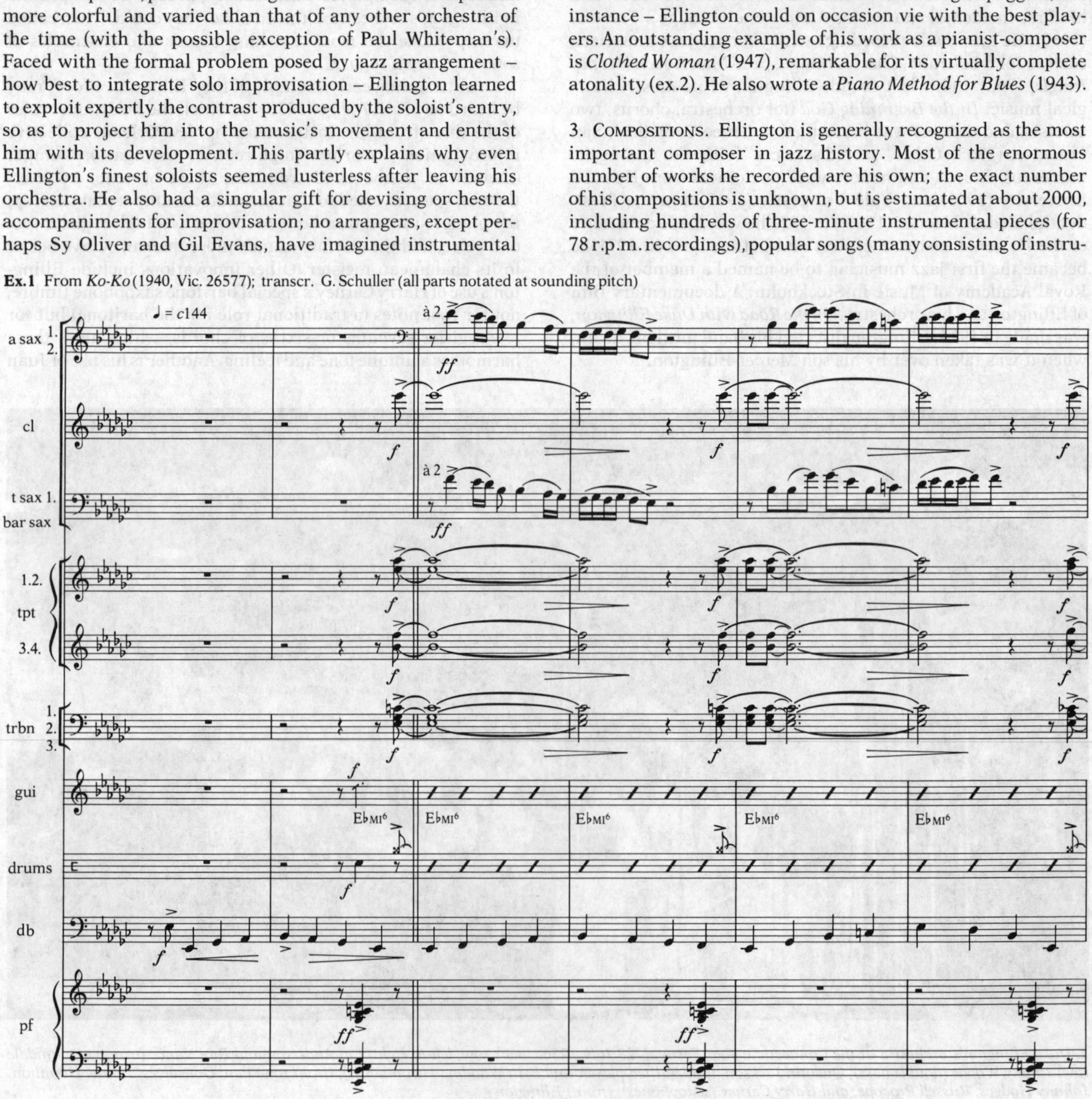

Ex.2 Introduction to *Clothed Woman* (1947, Col. 38236); transcr. G. Schuller

mental pieces to which lyrics by Irving Mills and others were added), large-scale suites, several musical comedies, many film scores, and an incomplete and unperformed opera, *Boola*. Ellington combined a flair for orchestration with extraordinary gifts as a bandleader; while other jazz composers had comparable talent, they lacked the organizational abilities necessary to create and maintain a permanent orchestral vehicle. The excerpt from *Ko-Ko* (ex.1), showing the orchestration of a passage from an ensemble section, is one of the most remarkable pieces in all of Ellington's writing. Scores by him are in the George P. Vanier Library of Concordia University, Montreal, and a large collection of recordings and other materials relating to his life and work is in the library of North Texas State University at Denton; *see* LIBRARIES AND ARCHIVES, §2.

Ellington was one of the first musicians to concern himself with composition and musical form in jazz – as distinct from improvisation, tune writing, and arranging. In *Concerto for Cootie*, ten-bar phrases are combined into a complex ternary form which abandons the chorus structure common to most jazz. In *Cotton Tail*, from the same period, Ellington made use of a call-and-response technique of writing in order to heighten the drama of the last climactic chorus (ex.3). *Black, Brown and Beige* uses symphonic devices (the fragmentation and development of motifs, thematic recall, and mottoes) as well as symphonic proportions in its several sections; it is thus perhaps unique among Ellington's earlier works, showing a preoccupation with form far in advance of his contemporaries. Only a few jazz musicians (among them Thelonious Monk, Charles Mingus, and Gil Evans) have followed Ellington in this respect.

Ex.3 From the fifth chorus of *Cotton Tail* (1940, Vic. 26610); transcr. G. Schuller (all parts notated at sounding pitch)

Ellington's relentless productivity makes an overview of his work virtually impossible. But it is generally agreed that he attained the zenith of his creativity in the late 1930s and early 1940s, and that he worked best in the miniature forms dictated by the three-minute ten-inch disc. Ellington's creativity declined substantially after the mid-1940s, many of the late-period extended compositions suffering from a diminished originality and hasty work, often occasioned by incessant touring. Serious study of Ellington's oeuvre has also been hampered by an almost total absence to date of his orchestral music in published form.

Oral history material in *CtY*.

See also ARRANGEMENT, §§2 and 3; FILMS; and JAZZ (i), §§IV, 1 and V, 9; for further illustrations *see* DRUM SET, fig.1*a*, and WASHINGTONIANS.

WORKS

(selective list; dates of composition are sometimes conjectural)

SUITES

(for jazz orchestra unless otherwise indicated)

Reminiscing in Tempo, 1935; Diminuendo in Blue/Crescendo in Blue, 1937; Black, Brown and Beige, 1943; Blue Belles of Harlem, 1943; Blutopia, 1944; New World a-Comin', 1945; Deep South Suite, 1946; Liberian Suite, 1947; The Tattooed Bride, 1948; Harlem (A Tone Parallel to Harlem), 1950; Night Creature, jazz orch, sym. orch; A Drum is a Woman, 1956; Such Sweet Thunder, 1957; Nutcracker Suite [after Tchaikovsky], 1960; Suite Thursday, 1960; Perfume Suite, 1963; Far East Suite, 1964

The Golden Broom and the Green Apple, 1965; Virgin Islands Suite, 1965; La plus belle africaine, 1967; Murder in the Cathedral, 1967; Latin American Suite, 1968; Afro-Eurasian Eclipse, 1971; The Goutelas Suite, 1971; New Orleans Suite, 1971; Togo Brava Suite, 1971

OTHER LARGE-SCALE WORKS

Stage: Jump for Joy (musical), 1941; Beggar's Holiday (musical), New York, 1946; Turcaret (incidental music, A. R. Le Sage), Paris, 1960; Timon of Athens (incidental music, Shakespeare), Stratford, Ontario, Canada, 1963; Sugar City (musical), Detroit, 1965; The River (ballet), New York, 1970; Boola (opera), inc.

Film scores: Symphony in Black, 1935; The Asphalt Jungle, 1950; Anatomy of a Murder, 1959; Paris Blues, 1960; Assault on a Queen, 1966; Change of Mind, 1968

Sacred, for solo vv, jazz orch: In the Beginning God, 1965; Second Sacred Concert, 1968; Third Sacred Concert, 1973

SHORT INSTRUMENTAL PIECES

Soda Fountain Rag, 1914; East St. Louis Toodle-oo, collab. B. Miley, 1926; Black and Tan Fantasy, collab. Miley, 1927; Creole Love Call, collab. Miley, 1927; Awful Sad, 1928; The Mooche, 1928; Mood Indigo (Dreamy Blues), collab. B. Bigard, 1930; Old Man Blues, 1930; Rockin' in Rhythm, 1930; Creole Rhapsody, 1931; Ducky Wucky, 1932; It Don't Mean a Thing, 1932; Sophisticated Lady, collab. O. Hardwick, 1932; Daybreak Express, 1933; Harlem Speaks, 1933; Delta Serenade, 1934; Saddest Tale, 1934; Solitude, 1934; Clarinet Lament (Barney's Concerto), collab. Bigard, 1935

Echoes of Harlem (Cootie's Concerto), 1935; In a Sentimental Mood, 1935; Uptown Downbeat (Blackout), 1936; Azure, 1937; Blue Light, 1938; Braggin' in Brass, 1938; Gypsy without a Song, 1938; Prelude to a Kiss, 1938; Prologue to Black and Tan Fantasy, 1938; Steppin' into Swing Society, 1938; Portrait of the Lion, 1939; Serenade to Sweden, 1939; Bojangles, 1940; Concerto for Cootie, 1940; Conga brava, 1940; Cotton Tail, 1940; Dusk, 1940; Harlem Air Shaft, 1940; In a Mellotone, 1940; Jack the Bear, 1940; Ko-Ko, 1940

A Portrait of Bert Williams, 1940; Sepia Panorama, 1940; Warm Valley, 1940; Chelsea Bridge, collab. B. Strayhorn, 1941; I Got it Bad, 1941; Main Stem, 1941; American Lullaby, 1942; C-jam Blues, 1942; Don't Get Around Much Anymore, 1942; Moon Mist, collab. M. Ellington, 1942; Don't You Know I Care, 1944; I'm Beginning to See the Light, collab. H. James, 1944; Air-conditioned Jungle, 1945; Carnegie Blues, 1945; Clothed Woman, 1947; Satin Doll, 1958

Principal publishers: Belwin-Mills, Robbins, Tempo

MSS in *DLC*

SELECTED RECORDINGS

EARLY PERIOD

Choo Choo (1924, Blu-disc 1002); Trombone Blues (1925, Pathé 36333); Animal Crackers (1926, Gen. 3342); East St. Louis Toodle-o (1926, Voc. 1064); Birmingham Breakdown (1927, Bruns. 3480); Black and Tan Fantasy (1927, Bruns. 3526); Creole Love Call (1927, Vic. 21137); Jubilee Stomp (1928, OK 41013); Yellow Dog Blues/Tishomingo Blues (1928, Bruns. 3987); The Mooche/Hot and Bothered (1928, OK 8623); Awful Sad (1928, Bruns. 4110); Stevedore Stomp (1929, Vic. 38053); Lazy Duke (1929, OK 8760); Double Check Stomp (1930, Vic. 38129); Old Man Blues (1930, Bb 6450); Ring dem Bells (1930, Vic. 22528)

Rocky Mountain Blues (1930, OK 8836); Mood Indigo (1930, Bruns. 4952); Rockin' in Rhythm (1930, OK 8869); Mood Indigo (1930, Vic. 22587); Creole Rhapsody (1931, Bruns. 6093); Limehouse Blues/Echoes of the Jungle (1931, Vic. 22743); The Mystery Song (1931, Vic. 22800); It Don't Mean a Thing (1932, Bruns. 6265); Ducky Wucky (1932, Bruns. 6432); Merry-go-round/Sophisticated Lady (1933, Col. 35837); Drop Me Off at Harlem (1933, Bruns. 6527); Daybreak Express (1933, Vic. 24501); Delta Serenade (1934, Vic. 24755); Symphony in Black (1934), first issued on *In Hollywood: on the Air* (1933–40, Max 1001)

Stompy Jones (1934, Vic. 24521); Solitude (1934, Vic. 24755); Saddest Tale (1934, Bruns. 7310); In a Sentimental Mood (1935, Bruns. 7461); Reminiscing in Tempo (1935, Bruns. 7546–7); Echoes of Harlem (1936, Bruns. 7650); The New East St. Louis Toodle-oo (1937, Master 101); Caravan/Azure (1937, Master 131); Diminuendo in Blue/Crescendo in Blue (1937, Bruns. 8004); I Let a Song Go out of my Heart (1938, Col. 36108); Braggin' in Brass (1938, Bruns. 8099); A Gypsy without a Song (1938, Bruns. 8186); Prelude to a Kiss (1938, Bruns. 8204)

Battle of Swing (1938, Bruns. 8293); Blue Light (1938, Bruns. 8297); Subtle Lament (1939, Bruns. 8344); Serenade to Sweden (1939, Col. 35214); Grievin' (1939, Col. 35310); Plucked Again (1939, Col. 35322); Jack the Bear (1940, Vic. 26536); Ko-Ko (1940, Vic. 26577); Concerto for Cootie (1940, Vic. 26598); Cotton Tail (1940, Vic. 26610); Dusk (1940, Vic. 26677); Harlem Air-shaft (1940, Vic. 26731); In a Mellotone (1940, Vic. 26788); Pitter Panther Patter (1940, Vic. 27221); Warm Valley (1940, Vic. 26796); Across the Track Blues (1940, Vic. 27235); Take the "A" Train (1941, Vic. 27380); Blue Serge (1941, Vic. 27356); Jump for Joy (1941, Vic. 27517); Chelsea Bridge (1941, Vic. 27740); The "C"-jam Blues/Moon Mist (1942, Vic. 27856); Main Stem (1942, Vic. 20-1556)

LATE PERIOD

I'm Beginning to See the Light/Don't you Know I Care (1944, Vic. 201618); Excerpts from Black, Brown and Beige (1944, Vic. 280400–01); Carnegie Blues (1945, Vic. 201644); Transblucency (1946, Vic. 202326); Magenta Haze (1946, Musi. 483); Happy-go-lucky Local (1946, Musi. 461); Jam-a-ditty (1946, Musi. 466); On a Turquoise Cloud (1947, Col. 38234); *Liberian Suite* (1947, Col. CL6073); Clothed Woman (1947, Col. 38236); *Masterpieces* (1950, Col. ML4418), incl. The Tattooed Bride; *Hi-Fi Ellington Uptown* (1951–2, Col. CL830), incl. Controversial Suite

Satin Doll (1953, Cap. 2458); *Ellington Plays Ellington* (1953, Cap. H477), incl. Retrospection; *A Drum is a Woman* (1956, Col. CL951); *Such Sweet Thunder* (1956–7, Col. CL1033); *Anatomy of a Murder* (1959, Col. CL1360); *Swinging Suites by Edward E. & Edward G.* (1960, Col. CS8397); *Money Jungle* (1962, UA 15017); *Duke Ellington with John Coltrane* (1962, Imp. 62), incl. Take the Coltrane; *Symphonic Ellington* (1963, Rep. 6097), incl. Night Creature; *Concert of Sacred Music* (1965, RCA LSP3582), incl. In the Beginning God; *Far East Suite* (1966, RCA LSP3872); *Second Sacred Concert* (1968, Prst. 24045)

BIBLIOGRAPHY

DISCOGRAPHIES

B. H. Aasland: *The "Wax Works" of Duke Ellington* (Stockholm, 1954); part rev. and enlarged as *The "Wax Works" of Duke Ellington*, i: *6 March 1940–30 July 1942: RCA Victor Period* (Järfälla, Sweden, 1978); ii: *31 July 1942–11 Nov 1944: the Recording Ban Period* (Järfälla, 1979) [contd in *D[uke] E[llington] M[usic] S[ociety] Bulletin*]
L. Sanfilippo: *General Catalogue of Duke Ellington's Recorded Music* (Palermo, Sicily, 1964)
L. Massagli, L. Pusateri, and G. M. Volonté: *Duke Ellington's Story on Records* (Milan, 1966–83)
D. M. Bakker: *Duke Ellington on Microgroove, 1923–February 1940* (Alphen aan de Rijn, Netherlands, 1972; rev. 2/1974 as *Duke Ellington on Microgroove, 1923–1942*; rev. 3/1977 as *Duke Ellington on Microgroove*, i: *1923–1936*)
A. Tercinet: "Hollywood Hangover: Filmographie de Duke Ellington," *Jh*, no.298 (1973), 24
J. Harper, H.-U. Hill, and D. M. Bakker: "Duke Ellington, 1943–1945," *Micrography*, no.41 (1976), 17; no.42 (1976), 12; no.43 (1977), 16; no.47 (1978), 17; no.50 (1979), 16; revs, addns, and corrections in no.47 (1978), 9; no.48 (1978), 19
"Duke Ellington's Capitol Transcriptions," *Micrography*, no.49 (1978), 19
J. Valburn: *The Directory of Duke Ellington's Recordings* (Hicksville, NY, 1986)

BIOGRAPHIES

D. Preston: *Mood Indigo* (Egham, England, 1946)
J. de Trazegnies: *Duke Ellington: Harlem Aristocrat of Jazz* (Brussels, 1946)
B. Ulanov: *Duke Ellington* (New York, 1946/*R*1975)
P. Gammond, ed.: *Duke Ellington: his Life and Music* (London and New York, 1958/*R*1977)
G. E. Lambert: *Duke Ellington* (London, 1959); repr. in *Kings of Jazz*, ed. S. Green (South Brunswick, NJ, and New York, 1978)
S. Dance: *The World of Duke Ellington* (London and New York, 1970/*R*1981) [colln of previously pubd articles and interviews]
D. Ellington: *Music is my Mistress* (Garden City, NY, 1973; index by H. F. Huon separately pubd, Melbourne, Australia, n.d. [?1977], rev. 2/1982)
D. Jewell: *Duke: a Portrait of Duke Ellington* (London and New York, 1977, 2/1978)
S. Dance and D. Morgenstern: "Duke Ellington," *Giants of Jazz* (TL J02, 1978)
M. Ellington and S. Dance: *Duke Ellington in Person: an Intimate Memoir* (Boston and London, 1978; Ger. trans., Stuttgart and Vienna, 1980)
D. George: *The Real Duke Ellington* (London, 1982)
H. Ruland: *Duke Ellington: sein Leben, seine Musik, seine Schallplatten* (Gauting, Germany, 1983)
P. Gammond: *Duke Ellington* (London, 1987) [incl. discography]
J. L. Collier: *Duke Ellington* (New York and London, 1987)

GENERAL STUDIES AND ESSAYS

R. D. Darrell: "Black Beauty," *Disques*, iii (1932), June, 152
H. Panassié: *Le jazz hot* (Paris, 1934; Eng. trans., rev. Panassié, London and New York, 1936/*R*1970; Sp. trans., Santiago, 1939)
F. Ramsey, Jr., and C. E. Smith, eds.: *Jazzmen: the Story of Hot Jazz Told in the Lives of the Men who Created it* (New York, 1939/*R*1977)
H. Panassié: *The Real Jazz* (New York and Toronto, 1942 [in Eng. trans.], rev. and enlarged by Panassié 2/1960; Fr. orig. pubd as *La véritable musique de jazz*, Paris, 1945, rev. and enlarged 2/1952)
R. Goffin: *Jazz: from the Congo to the Metropolitan* (Garden City, NY, 1944/*R*1975, rev. [2]/1946 as *Jazz: from Congo to Swing* [in Eng. trans.]; Fr. orig. pubd as *Histoire du jazz*, Montreal, 1945, rev. [2]/1948 as *Nouvelle histoire du jazz: Congo au bebop*)
D. Moulton: "The Ultimate in Ellington," *Hot Notes*, ii/1 (1947), 12
R. de Toledano: *Frontiers of Jazz* (New York, 1947, rev. 2/1962)
H. Panassié and M. Gautier: *Dictionnaire du jazz* (Paris, 1954, rev. and enlarged 2/1971, enlarged 3/1980; Eng. trans., London, 1956, rev. A. A. Gurwitch as *Guide to Jazz*, Boston, 1956)
V. Bellerby: "Duke Ellington," *JM*, i (1955), no.9, p.26; no.10, p.28; i/12 (1956), 9; ii/2 (1956), 28
R. Horricks: "Duke Ellington and the Harlem Suite," *JM*, ii/5 (1956), 8
L. Feather: *The Book of Jazz: a Guide to the Entire Field* (New York, 1957, 2/1965 as *The Book of Jazz from Then till Now: a Guide to the Entire Field*)
N. Shapiro and N. Hentoff, eds.: *The Jazz Makers: Essays of the Greats of Jazz* (New York, 1957/*R*1979)
P. Gammond, ed.: *The Decca Book of Jazz* (London, 1958)
D. Houlden and F. Dutton: "The Duke Steps Out – Once More," *JJ*, xi/11 (1958), 3
S. Voce: "And all the Duke's Men," *JJ*, xi/10 (1958), 2
B. Wood: "The Duke and Sidney Bechet," *JJ*, xi/7 (1958), 25
E. Lambert: "Duke Ellington, 1963," *JJ*, xvi/3 (1963), 1
——: "The Duke Steps Out," *JJ*, xvii/2 (1964), 2
——: "Ellingtonia '64," *JJ*, xvii/4 (1964), 2
——: "Duke Ellington and the Modernists," *JJ*, xviii/2 (1965), 24
M. Williams: "The Genesis of Duke," *JJ*, xviii/2 (1965), 6
R. Stewart: "On the Sidelines: a Duke Ellington Recording Session," *JJ*, xix/1 (1966), 15
H. Whiston: "Reminiscing in Tempo," *JJ*, xx/2 (1967), 4 [interview]
H. Dance: "God Has those Angels," *JJ*, xxi/8 (1968), 2
J. Lucas: "The Duchy of Ellington: Programmes & Annexations," *JJ*, xxii/11 (1969), 22
F. Levin: "The Duke in New Orleans," *JJ*, xxiii/8 (1970), 35
M. Williams: *The Jazz Tradition* (New York, 1970, rev. 2/1983)
W. Balliett: *Ecstasy at the Onion* (New York and Indianapolis, 1971) [colln of previously pubd articles and reviews]
L. Feather: *From Satchmo to Miles* (New York, 1972)
R. Stewart: *Jazz Masters of the Thirties* (New York and London, n.d. [?1972])
L. Verdeaux: "The Ellington Day," *BHcF*, no.222 (1972), 10
D. Ioakimidis: "Ellington: a Time of Transition," *JM*, viii/12 (1973), 5
JJ, xxvii/7 (1974) [special issue]
E. Lambert: "The Ellington Heritage," *Into Jazz*, i/6 (1974), 9
A. McCarthy: *Big Band Jazz* (New York and London, 1974)
G. Schuller: "Duke Ellington: Portrait of the Recording Artist at 75," *Schwann-1: Record & Tape Guide*, xxvi/4 (1974), 25
R. J. Gleason: *Celebrating the Duke: and Louis, Bessie, Billie, Bird, Carmen, Miles, Dizzy, and other Heroes* (Boston and Toronto, 1975), 154–266
M. Harrison: *A Jazz Retrospect* (Newton Abbot, England, 1976, rev. 2/1977)
F. Dutton: "Birth of a Band," *Sv*, no.80 (1978–9), 44; no.91 (1980), 7; no.98 (1981–2), 45
H. Rye: "Visiting Firemen, 1: Duke Ellington," *Sv*, no.88 (1980), 128

H. Ruland: *Duke Ellington: sein Leben, seine Musik, seine Schallplatten* (Gauting, Germany, 1983)
G. Giddins, S. Crouch, and W. Friedwald: "Ellington at 85," *VV*, xxix (28 Aug 1984)

MUSICAL ANALYSES

A. Hodeir: *Hommes et problèmes du jazz, suivi de La religion du jazz* (Paris, 1954; Eng. trans., rev. Hodeir, as *Jazz: its Evolution and Essence*, New York, 1956/*R*1975)
B. Jones: "The Impressionism of Duke Ellington," *JM*, iii/8 (1957), 5
N. Hentoff: "Duke Ellington: the Composer," *JJ*, xi/10 (1958), 7
M. Clar: "The Ellington Style," *JR*, ii/3 (1959), 6
R. Crowley: "*Black, Brown and Beige* after 16 Years," *Jazz: a Quarterly of American Music*, no.2 (1959), 98
M. Harrison: "The *Anatomy of a Murder* Music," *JR*, ii/10 (1959), 35
G. Schuller: "Early Duke," *JR*, ii/11 (1959), 6; iii (1960), no.1, p.18; no.2, p.18
——: "The Ellington Style: its Origins and Early Development," *Jazz: New Perspectives on the History of Jazz by Twelve of the World's Foremost Jazz Critics and Scholars*, ed. N. Hentoff and A. J. McCarthy (New York and Toronto, 1959/*R*1974), 231–74
M. Harrison: "Ellington's *Back to Back*," *JR*, iii/3 (1960), 24
——: "The Musicraft Recordings," *JM*, vii/9 (1961), 2
A. Bishop: "Duke's Creole Rhapsody," *JM*, ix/9 (1963), 12
——: "*Reminiscin' in Tempo*: an Analysis," *JJ*, xvii/2 (1964), 2
M. Harrison: "Duke Ellington: Reflections on Some of the Larger Works," *JM*, ix/11 (1964), 12
W. Mellers: *Music in a New Found Land: Themes and Developments in the History of American Music* (London, 1964/*R*1975)
W. W. Austin: *Music in the 20th Century: from Debussy through Stravinsky* (New York and London, 1966)
G. Schuller: *Early Jazz: its Roots and Musical Development* (New York, 1968)
E. Lambert: "Duke Ellington on Reprise," *JJ*, xxii/5 (1969), 2
——: "Quality Jazz, no.14: Duke Ellington's Nutcracker Suite," *JJ*, xxii/11 (1969), 11
B. Priestley: "The *Far East Suite*," *JM*, xv/1 (1969), 17
A. J. Bishop: "The Protean Imagination of Duke Ellington: the Early Years," *JJ*, xxiv (1971), no.10, p.2; no.12, p.12
M. Elliott: "Duke and the Blues," *JJ*, xxvii/11 (1974), 18
B. Priestley and A. Cohen: "*Black, Brown and Beige*," *Composer*, no.51 (1974), 33; no.52 (1974), 29; no.53 (1974–5), 29
C. Sheridan: "Piano in the Background," *Into Jazz*, i/6 (1974), 6
A. Murray and others: "Duke Ellington: an Explosion of Genius, 1938–1940," *Duke Ellington 1938–1940* (Smithsonian 2018, 1979) [liner notes]

ANDRÉ HODEIR/GUNTHER SCHULLER

Ellington, Mercer (Kennedy) (*b* Washington, 11 March 1919). Trumpeter, composer, and bandleader, son of Duke Ellington. He studied music in Washington and, after moving to New York in the mid-1920s, at the Institute of Musical Art, where he concentrated on saxophone, trumpet, and arranging. He worked in and around New York, and intermittently from the late 1930s led his own band, with such sidemen as Billy Strayhorn, Clark Terry, Cat Anderson, and Carmen McRae; he also contributed compositions, including *Things ain't what they used to be* and *Blue Serge*, to the repertory of the Duke Ellington Orchestra. During army service (1943–5) he played in a band under the leadership of Sy Oliver. Thereafter he continued to lead his own groups as well as to play occasionally with his father; he also worked as a salesman, disc jockey, and record company executive. In the mid-1950s he was manager and section trumpeter for Cootie Williams, and in 1965 he joined the Duke Ellington Orchestra in the same capacity. He took over the band on his father's death in May 1974 and later wrote a biography, *Duke Ellington in Person* (1978), in collaboration with Stanley Dance. He was director of the musical *Sophisticated Ladies* from 1981 to 1983.

Oral history material in *CtY*, *NjR*.

SELECTED RECORDINGS

Steppin' into Swing Society (1958, Coral 57225); *Colours in Rhythm* (1959, Coral 57293); *Continuum* (1974–5, Fan. 9481)

RECORDED COMPOSITIONS

Recorded by D. Ellington: Blue Serge (1941, Vic. 27356); Moon Mist (1942, Vic. 27856)
Recorded by J. Hodges: Things ain't what they used to be (1941, Bb 11447)

BIBLIOGRAPHY

M. Ellington: "Reminiscing in Tempo," *The Jazz Word*, ed. D. Cerulli, B. Korall, and M. Nasatir (New York, n.d. [?1960]) [incl. previously pubd articles], 54
"Mercer Ellington," *Crescendo*, iv (1966), no.9, p.20; no.10, p.32; no.11, p.29
S. Dance: *The World of Duke Ellington* (London and New York, 1970/*R*1981) [colln of previously pubd articles and interviews], 35
A. J. Smith: "Mercer Ellington: Extending a Tradition," *DB*, xliv/11 (1977), 14
C. Deffaa: "Keeping the Legend Alive," *MR*, xiv/12 (1987), 8

EDDIE LAMBERT

Ellington, Ray (*b* London, 1915; *d* London, 28 Feb 1985). English drummer and bandleader. He gained his first professional experience in Harry Roy's band (1937–42). After 1945 he became identified with the British bop movement, singing with Tito Burns's BBC Accordion Club Sextet (1947) and forming his own group (with Lauderic Caton, guitar, Dick Katz, piano, and Coleridge Goode, double bass) for engagements at the Downbeat Club, London, in 1948. In the same year the group began to record for Parlophone's Rhythm Style Series, and, using pseudonyms (Ellington's was Reggie Pitts), recorded with Ray Nance. Through his recordings and his weekly appearances (singing, playing, and also speaking) on BBC Radio's "Goon Show" (1951–60) Ellington became nationally and later internationally known; a representative example of his playing may be heard on *That's Nice!* (*c*1959, Pye 18032). Ellington's group played intricate bop arrangements on which he sometimes also sang in a style that borrowed rock-and-roll inflections; its repertory included novelty numbers. Although his popularity waned in the 1960s he continued to lead a quartet of changing personnel, which performed in London clubs. His son, Lance Ellington, is a trombonist. (Obituary, *Jazz Express*, no.61 (1985), 1)

DIGBY FAIRWEATHER

Elliott, Don [Helfman, Don Elliott] (*b* Somerville, NJ, 21 Oct 1926; *d* Weston, CT, 5 July 1984). Mellophonist, trumpeter, and vibraphonist. He first studied piano and accordion, then played baritone horn and mellophone in his high-school band. He changed to trumpet to play in local dance bands, and worked with Bill Evans (ii) when they were both teenagers. After studying harmony at the Institute of Musical Art in New York (1944–5) he played trumpet in an army band, then studied arranging and vibraphone at the University of Miami (1947). In New York he worked with George Shearing (1950–51), Teddy Wilson, and Benny Goodman (1952). After performing and recording with Terry Gibbs (1952–3) and spending a short period with Buddy Rich (1953) he formed his own group. For five years in succession he won the poll in *Down Beat* for "miscellaneous instrumentalist" (1953–7). In the 1960s and 1970s he performed in shows on Broadway, and composed film scores and music for radio and television commercials. He returned to playing jazz in 1975, when he was a guest soloist at Carnegie Hall with the New York Jazz Repertory Company. The principal influence upon his playing was the work of Harry James. His swinging, mainstream style brought him great popularity in the 1950s.

SELECTED RECORDINGS

As leader: Mighty like a Rose/Oh! Look at me now (1952, Savoy 882); *Counterpoint for Six Valves* (1955, Riv. 2517); *Jamaica Jazz* (1957, ABC-Para. 228); *Rejuvenation* (*c*1975, Col. PC33799)
As sideman: G. Shearing: Loose Leaf (1951, MGM 30419); P. Desmond: *Paul Desmond Quartet Featuring Don Elliott* (1956, Fan. 3235); M. Lowe: *Porgy and Bess* (1958, Camden 490)

BIBLIOGRAPHY

FeatherE; *Feather '60s*; *Feather–Gitler '70s*
D. Hague: "Don Elliott," *JJ*, xii/1 (1959), 5
J. Burns: "Good Vibes," *J&B*, ii/5 (1972), 7

LEROY OSTRANSKY

Elliott, Sticky [Ernest] (*b* Boonville, MO, Feb 1893). Saxophonist and clarinetist. After working in Detroit with Hank Duncan's band (1919) he moved to New York, where he worked with Johnny Dunn, Mamie Smith, Clara Smith, and many other blues singers. He made a large number of recordings, and played in three sessions with Bessie Smith (1927, 1928). *Good Looking Papa Blues* (1924, Col. 14026D), which he recorded with Clara Smith, is an excellent example of Elliott's sensitive approach; he may be heard playing solo and obbligato passages in a delicate, ethereal manner. Later he performed with Cliff Jackson's trio at the Astoria (1940) and with bands led by the pianists Sammy Stewart (1944) and Willie "the Lion" Smith (1947), but thereafter he retired from music.

based on *ChiltonW*

Ellis, Don(ald Johnson) (*b* Los Angeles, 25 July 1934; *d* Hollywood, CA, 17 Dec 1978). Trumpeter, composer, and bandleader. After studying composition at Boston University (BMus 1956) he worked as a trumpeter in bands led by Ray McKinley, Charlie Barnet (1958), Maynard Ferguson (1959), and George Russell (1961–2), among others. In 1961 he moved to New York and formed his own trio, and in 1963 he appeared as a soloist with the New York PO in Larry Austin's *Improvisations* and toured Poland and Scandinavia. Ellis then spent a year as a graduate student at UCLA, where he later taught. He also formed a large jazz orchestra, which, with the addition of a Latin percussionist, initially resembled an Afro-Cuban ensemble in its instrumentation, though the saxophonists also played flutes and clarinets; in about 1969 Ellis added a vocal group, and by the 1970s the ensemble made use of electric keyboards and incorporated an amplified string quartet. Ellis was the band's principal soloist, and among his distinguished sidemen were Sam Falzone, Ralph Humphrey, Milcho Leviev, and John Klemmer. The orchestra made regular tours of the West Coast, and recorded at the Monterey Jazz Festival and Shelly's Manne Hole (both 1966), Stanford University (1968), and the Fillmore Auditorium, San Francisco (1970); it also toured further afield, appearing at the Newport and Antibes–Juan-les-Pins festivals in 1969 and at Montreux in 1977.

Ellis worked as a "creative assistant" to the composer Lukas Foss at SUNY, Buffalo, in 1964–5, supported by a Rockefeller grant. Eventually he settled in Los Angeles, where he became active as a composer, performer, recording artist, and writer; he received a Grammy Award for his score for the film *The French Connection* in 1971. He suffered a heart attack in 1975, but resumed his performing career playing a "superbone" – a combination of valve and slide trombone.

Ellis is often associated with Ornette Coleman, John Coltrane, and Cecil Taylor as a proponent of the avant-garde jazz of the late 1950s and early 1960s. However, he generally avoided a radical free-form style, seeking instead to infuse traditional big-band styles with novel or exotic influences, particularly in his use from 1964 of Indian and Near Eastern rhythms. Because he sometimes employed serial and aleatory procedures in his earlier style he has also been identified with the third stream movement; later he renounced these approaches.

Ellis's significance to jazz composition lies in his pioneering use of various techniques and resources: complex meters, the electronic distortion of timbre, amplified trumpet, and the human voice used instrumentally. Perhaps his most important contribution was the use of quarter-tone melodic structures, particularly his invention of a 12-pitch quarter-tone scale for notating blues-type melodic variants. In 1975 Ellis consolidated his experience in this area in the textbook *Quarter Tones*, just as he had earlier brought together his rhythmic experiments in *The New Rhythm Book* (1972).

Don Ellis, Newport, RI, c1969

Like other avant-garde musicians, Ellis often weakened or deserted a firm tonal foundation. In *Tragedy*, for example, he uses clusters of four notes as incomplete tone rows within a formal framework which allows for a certain freedom in performance; *Improvisational Suite no.1* (1960) uses a 12-tone row as a point of departure for group improvisation. Ellis's interest in oriental music is illustrated by later compositions, such as *Indian Lady*, which begins in the manner of a raga. A number of Ellis's favorite devices appear in *Variations for Trumpet*, a large-scale work divided into six sections with meters such as 5/4, 9/4, 7/4, and 32/8, and employing exotic and whole-tone scales as well as quartal and quintal harmonies (see ex.1, where an E Mixolydian melodic structure is supported by a D in the bass). The work also uses synthesizer, amplified trumpet, and tape-delay echo effects.

Ex.1 From *Variations for Trumpet* on *Autumn* (1968, Col. CS9721); transcr. R. Dickow

As a trumpet player Ellis possessed an agile technique and a fine tone. Influenced by Dizzy Gillespie, Fats Navarro, and Clark Terry, he evolved a personal, innovative style, often applying electric amplification and ring-modulated modification to the timbre of the instrument. From 1965 he showed an interest in alternative tuning systems – partly as a result of his interest in the music of Harry Partch – and acquired a quarter-tone trumpet which allowed him to achieve a new subtlety of expression, particularly in traditional blues passagework.

See also TRUMPET, §§1 and 6.

SELECTED RECORDINGS

How Time Passes (1960, Can. 9004), incl. Improvisational Suite no.1; *New Ideas* (1961, NewJ 8257), incl. Tragedy; *Essence* (1962, PJ 55); *Live at Monterey* (1966, PJ 20112); *Electric Bath* (1967, Col. CS9585), incl. Indian Lady; *Shock Treatment* (1968, Col. CS9668); *Autumn* (1968, Col. CS9721), incl. Variations for Trumpet; *The New Don Ellis Band Goes Underground* (1969, Col. CS9889); *Tears of Joy* (1971, Col. G30927); *Soaring* (1974, MPS 2125123); *Music from Other Galaxies and Planets* (1977, Atl. 18227)

BIBLIOGRAPHY

G. Schuller: Liner notes, *How Time Passes* (Can. 8004, 1960)
D. Ellis and H. H. Rao: "An Introduction to Indian Music for the Jazz Musician," *Jazz*, iv/4 (1965), 20
D. Ellis: "The Avant-garde is not Avant-garde," *DB*, xxxiii/13 (1966), 21
P. Welding: "Times for Revolution," *DB*, xxxiv/8 (1967), 25 [interview]
A. Kooper: Liner notes, *Autumn* (Col. CS9721, 1968)
H. Siders: "Ellis through the Looking Glass," *DB*, xxxvii/8 (1970), 16
C. J. Stuessy, Jr.: *The Confluence of Jazz and Classical Music from 1950 to 1970* (diss., Eastman School, 1970), 321, 398
L. Feather: *From Satchmo to Miles* (New York, 1972), 211
H. Siders: "Don Ellis: Yet Another Phase," *DB*, xxxix/7 (1972), 12
P. Willard: "This is the Don Ellis Interview," *DB*, xli/2 (1974), 14
D. Heckman: "Don Ellis: Most Alive and Well," *DB*, xliv/2 (1977), 19
J. R. Killoch: "Don Who???," *JJ*, xxx/2 (1977), 4
——: "Don Ellis," *CI*, xv/12 (1977), 14 [interview]
A. J. Agostinelli: *Don Ellis: a Man for our Time (1934–1978)* (Providence, RI, 1986) [bio-discography]

ROBERT DICKOW/R

Ellis, (Mitchell) Herb(ert) (*b* Farmersville, TX, 4 Aug 1921). Guitarist. He attended North Texas State University (1941–3), where his classmates included Jimmy Giuffre, Gene Roland, and Harry Babasin. After playing with the Casa Loma Orchestra, Jimmy Dorsey (1945–7), and the trio Soft Winds he worked in Oscar Peterson's trio (1953–8; for illustration *see* PETERSON, OSCAR), during which time he established himself as one of the most technically accomplished of jazz guitarists. From 1958 to 1962 he accompanied Ella Fitzgerald, then until the early 1970s worked in Los Angeles as a studio musician. In 1973 he joined forces with Joe Pass, with whom he recorded a number of albums, and formed the group Great Guitars with Charlie Byrd and Barney Kessel. Ellis was strongly influenced by the playing of Charlie Christian, and the latter's swinging, bluesy style may be discerned as the basis of his own advanced harmonic and melodic thinking.

SELECTED RECORDINGS

As leader: *The Midnight Roll* (1962, Epic 17034); with J. Pass: *Jazz/Concord* (1973, Conc. 1); *Rhythm Willie* (1975, Conc. 10); of Great Guitars (with C. Byrd and B. Kessel): *Great Guitars at the Winery* (1980, Conc. 131)
As sideman: O. Peterson: *The Oscar Peterson Trio at the Stratford Shakespearean Festival* (1956, Verve 8024)

BIBLIOGRAPHY

A. Berle: "Herb Ellis on Guitars, Guitarists, and Technique," *GP*, xii/4 (1978), 38
M. Joyce: "Herb Ellis: Interview," *Cadence*, iii/11–12 (1978), 15
L. Tomkins: "Herb Ellis Talking," *CI*, xvii/5 (1978), 11
S. Voce: "Herb Ellis," *JJI*, xxxvi/1 (1983), 12

JIM FERGUSON

Elman, Ziggy [Finkelman, Harry] (*b* Philadelphia, 26 May 1914; *d* Los Angeles, 26 June 1968). Trumpeter. He grew up in New Jersey, where he played both reed and brass instruments. During the early 1930s he worked in a band led by Alex Bartha which recorded in 1932. After hearing the versatility of Elman's playing, in 1936 Benny Goodman recruited him and used his powerful tone to advantage on such recordings as *Bei mir bist du schön*, *Wrapping it up*, and two of Elman's compositions, *And the Angels Sing* and *Zaggin' with Zig*. He was also in demand for small-group sessions, notably those of Lionel Hampton. Later Elman worked with Joe Venuti (1940) and Tommy Dorsey (1940–43; for illustration *see* DORSEY, TOMMY; 1946–7); army service interrupted this association. Dorsey made a feature of his forceful style on such recordings as *Swing High* and *Swannee River*. Between periods spent leading his own bands (1947, 1948–9) Elman played again with Dorsey (1947–8). Towards the end of the decade he began working in film, radio, and television studios; he appeared, but did not play, in the film *The Benny Goodman Story* in 1955. The following year illness forced him into semiretirement, and thereafter he worked only sporadically.

SELECTED RECORDINGS

As leader: Fralich in Swing/Bublitchki (1938, Bb 10103); Bye 'n' Bye/Deep Night (1939, Bb 10855)
As sideman: B. Goodman: Bei mir bist du schön (1937, Vic. 25751); Wrapping it up (1938, Vic. 25880); And the Angels Sing (1939, Vic. 26170); L. Hampton: Ain't cha comin' home? (1939, Vic. 26362); Gin for Christmas (1939, Vic. 26423); B. Goodman: Zaggin' with Zig (1939, Col. 35356); T. Dorsey: Swing High (1940, Vic. 27249); Swannee River (1940, Vic. 27233); J. Stacy: *Tribute to Benny Goodman* (1954–5, Atl. 1225); [no leader]: *Escapade Reviews the Jazz Scene* (1957, Lib. 9005)

BIBLIOGRAPHY

ChiltonW; *FeatherE*
B. Goodman and I. Kolodin: *The Kingdom of Swing* (New York, 1939), 240
"Hall of Fame: Ziggy Elman," *Metronome*, lvii/4 (1941), 22
M. Goode: Liner notes, B. Goodman: *The Complete Benny Goodman*, iii: *1936* (RCA AXM2-5532, 1976); v: *1937–1938* (RCA AXM2-5557, 1978)
O. Ferguson: "The Boy from the Back Row," *The Otis Ferguson Reader*, ed. D. Chamberlain and R. Wilson (Highland Park, IL, 1982) [colln of previously pubd articles], 93

BRIAN PEERLESS

Elsdon, Alan (*b* London, 15 Oct 1934). English trumpeter, flugelhorn player, and bandleader. After studying the trumpet with Tommy McQuater and others, he played and recorded with Cy Laurie (1955–7), the trombonist Graham Stewart (1957–9), an RAF band (1957–9), and Terry Lightfoot (1959–61), under whose leadership he toured with Kid Ory and Henry "Red" Allen. In the 1960s he toured with Edmond Hall, Albert Nicholas, Wingy Manone, the blues singer Howlin' Wolf, and others, and from 1961 led his own band, which performed and recorded into the 1980s; the album *Jazz Journeymen* (1977, BL 12163) provides a good example of his playing. Elsdon was a principal soloist with Keith Nichols's Midnite Follies Orchestra from 1978 to 1985, and from 1980 played in Nichols's small groups. In the 1980s he has also performed at a number of international jazz festivals and worked as a teacher and writer. (R. Cotterell, ed.: *Jazz Now: the Jazz Centre Society Guide*, London, 1976)

DIGBY FAIRWEATHER

EmArcy. Record label founded in 1954 as a subsidiary of MERCURY.

Emborg, Jørgen (*b* Copenhagen, 29 March 1953). Danish pianist, leader, and composer. He worked with Danish groups from the mid-1970s and from 1978 to 1983 led a quartet that made two recordings (1979; *No.2*, 1983, Stunt 8302, which includes the track *Uranus*); these feature his compositions, which are written in a lyrical style, and his piano playing, which is reminiscent of the work of Keith Jarrett. At the same time he led a jazz-rock group, Alpha Centauri (recording in 1980), and in 1984 organized a commercially oriented quintet, Frontline (recording in 1985).

ERIK WIEDEMANN

Emerson. Record company and label. The company was established in 1916 by a former manager of Columbia's recording department, Victor H. Emerson; as early as 1918 it recorded a jazz band from New Orleans, the Louisiana Five. In 1921 Eubie Blake began recording for the company (as a soloist, with bands, and accompanying Noble Sissle), and a race series of material by vaudeville blues singers was inaugurated. Emerson organized a session by Bessie Smith in February that year, and the results of this would have been her first records; however the recordings were not issued and have never been found. In June 1922 the company (which had been placed in receivership as early as December 1920) was purchased by a syndicate organized by Benjamin Abrams and Rudolph Kamarek. In January 1924, however, the record company and label name were sold to the Scranton (Pennsylvania) Button Co. The latter organization's Consolidated Record Corp. continued to manufacture records and market them on the Emerson label until 1928, using both its own masters (some of which in turn appeared on other labels) and some leased from Plaza and Federal.

BIBLIOGRAPHY

B. Colton and L. Kunstadt: "The Emerson Diary," *Record Research*, ii (1956–7), no.4, p.3; no.5, p.13; iii (1957–8), no.1, p.7; no.2, p.11; no.3, p.13; no.5, p.2
R. M. W. Dixon and J. Godrich: *Recording the Blues* (London, 1970), 10
B. Rust: *The American Record Label Book* (New Rochelle, NY, 1978) 117

EMI [Electrical and Musical Industries]. Record company. It was formed in March 1931 by the merger of the GRAMOPHONE co. (which owned the labels His Master's Voice, Gramophone, Zonophone, and Electrola) and Columbia International Ltd. (which owned COLUMBIA, Parlophone, and Odeon throughout the world; Okeh, Harmony, Diva, and Velvet Tone in the USA only; and Regal and Pathé in territories other than the USA). Columbia's main American competitor, RCA Victor, was one of the owners of the Gramophone Co.; in order to avert antitrust action in the USA against the monopoly that would have resulted, EMI immediately disposed of those sections of its operation that had been Columbia International's American interests, putting the operations of the labels Columbia, Okeh, Harmony, Diva, and Velvet Tone in the hands of trustees.

As the main outlet in Europe and elsewhere for the catalogues of RCA Victor, Columbia, and, from 1934, Brunswick, Vocalion, and the other labels of the American Record Company, EMI was one of the most important sources of American recordings in Britain, Europe, India, Australia, and South America. In the early 1950s the company lost the rights in these territories to recordings made by American Columbia, and in 1957 it also relinquished RCA Victor's catalogues. In 1955, however, EMI acquired other American material when it took a controlling interest in CAPITOL; around this time the company also obtained the rights to several American independent labels with important catalogues. Among these were King, MGM, Verve, and Liberty (under the last arrangement EMI acquired the non-American rights to Blue Note).

From 1962 to 1974 EMI operated in the UK the label Stateside, which was used specifically to issue material first put out in the USA by American independents; jazz releases included important recordings from Prestige. Other subsidiaries have been used intermittently for reissue programs, particularly for recordings made by Okeh before 1931, the rights to which remained the property of EMI until the copyrights expired. Much of this material was released on LPs on Parlophone in the 1960s and 1970s. Some of these recordings were transferred to World Records, which established itself as the main reissue label for EMI's British back catalogue, and released, among other repertory, items recorded in the USA in the 1930s by John Hammond for Columbia and Parlophone. Reissue operations have also taken place in France (where items from Swing, and from the American independents Imperial and Aladdin, have been particularly notable). World Records was discontinued in the early 1980s, but much of the catalogue has reappeared on a new label, Retrospect. In 1980 Liberty and United Artists were taken over by EMI; as a result Blue Note, until that date owned by Liberty, became wholly owned by EMI.

BIBLIOGRAPHY

[P. Pelletier]: *British Top Rank, Stateside Long-play Listing* (London, 1975) [Record Information Services pubn]
——: *British Top Rank, Stateside, Triumph, Palette Singles/E.P. Listing* (London, 1975) [Record Information Services pubn]
J. Hammond: *John Hammond on Record: an Autobiography* (New York, 1977)
P. Pelletier: "The Columbia and Parlophone Labels," *Record Information*, no.5 (1985), 6
[P. Pelletier]: *Complete British Directory of Popular 78/45 r.p.m. Singles, 1950–1980*, i: *Columbia, Decca, H.M.V.* (London, 1986) [Record Information Services pubn]
P. Pelletier: "The HMV & MGM Labels," *Record Information*, no.6 (1986), 3

Emily. Record label established by ANITA O'DAY.

Enevoldsen, Bob [Robert Martin] (*b* Billings, MT, 11 Jan 1920). Trombonist, tenor saxophonist, and double bass player. His grandfather and both his parents were musicians. He studied music at the University of Montana (BM 1942) and after serving in the army (1942–6) he taught music in public schools in Salt Lake City; he also played clarinet in the Utah SO. In 1951 he moved to Los Angeles, where he played valve trombone and tenor saxophone with many West Coast jazz musicians, among them Gerry Mulligan, Shorty Rogers, Shelly Manne, and Marty Paich. He began to learn double bass, and in 1954–5 was the bass player in Bobby Troup's trio. His versatility and mastery of his three principal instruments are well demonstrated by the recordings he made as a leader in the mid-1950s, especially *Smorgasbord* (1954). He played in shows in Las Vegas (1959–62) and then worked as a staff arranger and studio musician for Steve Allen's television show (1962–4). From the mid-1960s he was active mainly as a session and freelance musician.

SELECTED RECORDINGS

As leader: *Bob Enevoldsen* (1954, Nocturne 6); *Smorgasbord* (1954, Lib. 6008), incl. Bob's Boy, Mr. Know-it-all, Oh! Look at me now; *Reflections in Jazz* (1955, Tampa 14)

As sideman: S. Manne: *Shelly Manne and his Men* (1953, Cont. 2503); M. Paich: *I Get a Boot out of you* (1959, WB 1349), incl. It don't mean a thing, Love for Sale

BIBLIOGRAPHY

FeatherE; *Feather '60s*
B. Troup: Liner notes, *Smorgasbord* (Lib. 6008, 1954)

LAWRENCE KOCH

Engels, John(, Jr.) (*b* Groningen, Netherlands, 13 May 1935). Dutch drummer. He first played professionally in 1953, belonged to groups led by the pianist Cees Slinger and Pia Beck (1957–8), and worked with the Diamond Five (from 1959) and Louis van Dijk's trio (from 1962). He played with many musicians visiting the Netherlands, including Dizzy Gillespie, Slide

Hampton, Johnny Griffin, Ben Webster (with whom he recorded in 1969–70), Zoot Sims, and Toots Thielemans. He appeared at many festivals and made numerous recordings as a sideman with van Dijk, Teddy Edwards (1981), and Arnett Cobb (1982).

WIM VAN EYLE

English, Bill (*b* New York, 27 Aug 1925). Drummer. He first played rhythm-and-blues, performing and recording in Chicago with the pianist Sonny Thompson (1951–2) and in Los Angeles with the singer Amos Milburn (1954). After working with Erskine Hawkins and Bennie Green (1956) he played in the house band at the Apollo Theatre, New York, and led his own quartet. In 1960 he performed and recorded with Earl Hines; he is heard to advantage on *Earl's Pearls* (1960, MGM 3832). Thereafter he worked as a freelance, recording as a leader in 1963. He also made recordings with the Prestige Blues Swingers, Joe Newman, Quincy Jones, and Gene Ammons (all 1961), Stanley Turrentine (1963), Kenny Burrell (1963–4), Eddie Jefferson (1968–9; including *Body and Soul*, 1968, Prst. 7619), and Eric Dixon (on *Eric's Edge*, 1974, MJR 8124). (S. Dance: "Lightly and Politely, 697: Earl's Four," *JJ*, xiii/7 (1960), 9)

English horn (Fr. *cor anglais*). The tenor member of the OBOE family, pitched in F, a 5th below the oboe.

Engstrøm, Kalle [Karl W.] (*b* Oslo, 5 Oct 1908; *d* Oslo, 17 Jan 1955). Norwegian clarinetist, alto saxophonist, and arranger. He played with local bands around Hamar, Norway, before returning to Oslo in the late 1920s; at that time he was one of the finest jazz soloists in Norway. He belonged to the Funny Boys (1933–9) and performed and recorded with the Bristolorkestret under Øivind Bergh (1939–46), for whom he also wrote arrangements (including *Midnattserenade/Kalles vuggevise*, 1943, Col. GN873). He was less active in music after 1945. A good example of his playing is his recording *Godnatt* (1943, Tel. 8363). (O. Angell, J. E. Vold, and E. Økland: *Jazz i Norge*, Oslo, 1975)

VIDAR VANBERG

Enja [European New Jazz Association]. German record company and label. The company was founded in 1971 in Munich by Horst Weber with the assistance of Matthias Winckelmann, and grew out of Weber's work as a producer for the Japanese RCA Victor company in Tokyo. Its catalogue includes albums made in West Germany by leading Japanese musicians; Yosuke Yamashita is especially well represented. Enja has become one of the major companies of its time, presenting new sessions by such varied and renowned musicians as Tommy Flanagan, the Ganelin Trio, Abdullah Ibrahim, Elvin Jones, Albert Mangelsdorff, John Scofield, Woody Shaw, Cecil Taylor, and Mal Waldron. The company has also issued for the first time important recordings of concerts given by Eric Dolphy both as a leader (1961) and as a sideman with Charles Mingus (1964). (G. Rouy: "Histoire d'Enja," *Jm*, no.252 (1977), 22)

EP. In popular-music usage the standard abbreviation for "extended-play disc" or "extended player"; *see* RECORDING, §I, 3(ii).

Epic. Record label. It was established in the 1950s as a subsidiary of Columbia, and was used to issue many jazz recordings. The catalogue included albums by Art Blakey, Horace Silver, Herb Ellis, Phil Woods, Dave Pike, Slide Hampton, Lionel Hampton, Illinois Jacquet, Ahmad Jamal, Wild Bill Davis, Johnny Dodds, Eddie Condon, Bobby Hackett, Dave Grusin, Dave Bailey, Mose Allison, Mike Wofford, Tubby Hayes, Lester Young, and Jack Teagarden. One of the principal producers was Mike Bernicker. Epic has remained in existence into the late 1980s, but its importance as a jazz label declined after the 1960s.

MARK GARDNER

Epstein, Melvin. *See* POWELL, MEL.

Ericson, Rolf (*b* Stockholm, 29 Aug 1922). Swedish trumpeter and flugelhorn player. He studied music from the age of eight, took an interest in jazz at the age of 11 when he heard Louis Armstrong perform in Stockholm, and worked professionally from 1938. He recorded with Alice Babs, Kjeld Bonfils, and Valaida Snow (1945–7), and, after moving to New York late in 1947, Charlie Barnet (1949) and Woody Herman (1950); he also worked occasionally with Benny Carter, Wardell Gray, Charlie Ventura, and Elliot Lawrence (1949–50). In 1950 he returned to Sweden, where he recorded as a leader and as a sideman with Arne Domnérus (1950–51) and Leonard Feather's Swinging Swedes (1951); he also toured with Charlie Parker (1950). Ericson moved again to the USA in 1952, where he worked with Charlie Spivak (1952–3), Harry James, and Jimmy and Tommy Dorsey, and on television with Les Brown; in 1956 he made a brief visit to Sweden to tour as a leader and record with Benny Bailey. He also toured with Art Taylor, Cecil Payne, Duke Jordan, Lars Gullin, and Ernestine Anderson. From 1956 to 1960 he worked in the USA with Dexter Gordon, Harold Land, and Stan Kenton, again with Herman, and with Maynard Ferguson; with the sponsorship of the US State Department he toured the Far East with Buddy Rich. He toured Scandinavia from 1961 to 1965 with Bud Powell, Brew Moore, Gullin, and Kenny Dorham, and at the same time played in the USA with Benny Goodman, Gerry Mulligan, Charles Mingus, and Duke Ellington, with whom he also toured Europe. After working from 1965 to 1970 as a freelance in radio, television, and film studios he settled in Germany (1971); there he also worked in studios, and performed with Ellington and the double bass player Hans Last. In 1974 he became a staff musician for Sender Freies Berlin; later he performed with Mercer Ellington in Europe and toured Belgium, Germany, and Portugal. Thoroughly professional and entirely eclectic in his approach, Ericson is a fluent and sensitive soloist whose style ranges over a wide spectrum.

Oral history material in *SSsv*.

SELECTED RECORDINGS

As leader: Miles Away/Perdido (1950, Artist 3041); with B. Bailey: Duo/Ohio (1956, Met. 242) [EP]; *Stockholm Sweetnin* (1984, Dra. 78)

As sideman: Expressen Elitorkester: Muskrat Ramble/If I could be with you One Hour Tonight (1946, Son. 658); D. Ellington: *The Seventieth Birthday Concert* (1969, So1S 19000), incl. Caravan, Perdido

BIBLIOGRAPHY

FeatherE; *Feather '60s*
L. Ostberg: "Rolf Ericson," *Orkester journalen*, xxiv (1956), Oct, 4
M. James: "Out of the Bag no.3: Rolf Ericson," *JM*, viii/9 (1962), 16
J. Lind: "Rolf Ericson: Still Waiting, Still Hoping," *DB*, xxix/28 (1962), 20
D. Hawdon: "Anglo-American Exchange," *Crescendo*, iii/1 (1964), 24

KEN RATTENBURY

Eriksberg [Eriksson], **Folke** (*b* Stockholm, 27 Oct 1910; *d* Stockholm, 11 June 1976). Swedish acoustic guitarist. He worked professionally from 1927 and belonged to Frank Vernon's band from 1928 to 1933. In 1934–6 he played with Benny Carter and

Django Reinhardt in Barcelona; after returning to Sweden he worked with Seymour Österwall (1936–8), Sam Samson (1938–40, recording in 1941), Thore Ehrling (recording in 1938–42, performing in 1941–2), the SVENSKA HOTKVINTETTEN (1939–42), and Gösta Törner (1943–5). He worked in theater orchestras for about ten years before retiring from music in the mid-1950s. Eriksberg was much sought after as an accompanist and recorded about 2000 tracks of jazz and popular music; the few recordings that he made as a soloist include *St. Louis Blues* (1937, Son. 3231) and *Dreaming Guitar* (1937, Son. 3397).

Oral history material in *SSsv*.

BIBLIOGRAPHY

A. von Konow: "En föregångsman: Folke Eriksberg" [A pioneer: Folke Eriksberg], *Orkester journalen*, xliii/7–8 (1975), 8
R. Dahlgren: Obituary, *Orkester journalen*, xliv/7–8 (1976), 7

ERIK KJELLBERG

Errisson, King [Johnson, Errisson Pallman] (*b* Nassau, Bahamas, 29 Oct 1941). Bahamian percussionist. He toured with the popular singer Diana Ross and recorded with the organist Freddie Roach (1966). By 1969 he had settled in Los Angeles, where he played conga on recordings with Blue Mitchell (1969), Groove Holmes (1971), Cannonball Adderley (*Inside Straight*, 1973, Fan. 9435), Donald Byrd (1973, 1975), Stanley Turrentine (1974), and Freddie Hubbard (1974), as well as with soul and blues groups. (*Feather–Gitler '70s*)

Erskine, Peter (*b* Somers Point, NJ, 5 June 1954). Drummer. He began drumming at the age of three, and participated in several of Stan Kenton's National Stage Band Camps from the age of six. He studied with Alan Dawson and Ed Soph, and attended Interlochen (Michigan) Arts Academy and Indiana University. From 1972 to 1975 he worked with Kenton; he then played with Maynard Ferguson (1976–8) and Weather Report (1978–82). From the late 1970s he was active as a session musician in New York and Los Angeles, and in 1979 joined the group Steps (later STEPS AHEAD). In 1985 Erskine began performing and recording with John Abercrombie's trio and the quartet Bass Desires; with these prominent groups he has produced some of his most distinctive work. Like many drummers who began their career during the 1970s, he is adept at playing both jazz and rock and his approach is influenced by that of Tony Williams. Although he tends to blend and adapt existing styles rather than create new ones, Erskine is a sophisticated, tasteful, and versatile player.

SELECTED RECORDINGS

As leader: *Peter Erskine* (1982, Cont. 14010); *Transition* (1986, Passport Jazz 88032)

As sideman: J. Farrell: *Sonic Text* (1979, Cont. 14002); Weather Report: *Night Passage* (*c*1980, Col. JC36793); *Weather Report* (*c*1981, Col. FC37616); Steps Ahead: *Steps Ahead* (1983, Elek. 601681); J. Abercrombie: *Current Events* (1985, ECM 1311)

BIBLIOGRAPHY

A. J. Smith: "Peter Erskine," *DB*, xliv/4 (1977), 34
A. J. Liska: "Peter Erskine, Weather Reporter's Sunny Outlook," *DB*, xlviii/8 (1981), 24 [incl. discography]
R. Mattingly: "Peter Erskine," *MD*, vii/1 (1983), 8
L. Jeske: "Blindfold Test: Peter Erskine," *DB*, l/6 (1983), 47
B. Beuttler: "Peter Erskine: Steppin' Out," *DB*, liii/12 (1986), 16 [incl. discography]
R. Mattingly: "Peter Erskine," *MD*, xi/6 (1987), 16

CHUCK BRAMAN

Ertegun, Ahmet (M.) [Nugetre] (*b* Constantinople [now Istanbul], 31 July 1923). Record producer, brother of Nesuhi Ertegun. He was educated in the USA (BA 1944). He first became involved with Herb Abramson in running two, small, short-lived record labels, Quality and Jubilee, then in late 1947 the two men founded the company and label ATLANTIC, with Ertegun as vice-president. It became one of the largest independent labels concerned with jazz and race recordings, retaining this position throughout the 1950s and 1960s. The company was purchased by Warner Bros. in 1967 but remained under its previous management. In the 1980s Ertegun continued to be an executive of great importance in popular music.

BIBLIOGRAPHY

M. Watts: "The Man with the Midas Touch," *MM* (16 Dec 1972), 44
C. Gillett: *Making Tracks: Atlantic Records and the Growth of a Multi-billion-dollar Industry* (London, 1975)
G. W. S. Trow, Jr.: "Profiles: Eclectic, Reminiscent, Amused, Fickle, Perverse," *New Yorker*, liv (29 May 1978), 37–83; (5 June 1978), 45–81
P. Grendysa: "Birth of a Legend: the Atlantic Label," *Record Collector's Monthly*, no.4 (1982), 1

Ertegun, Nesuhi (*b* Constantinople [now Istanbul], 27 Nov 1917). Record producer, brother of Ahmet Ertegun. He promoted jazz concerts in Washington (1941–4) then moved to Los Angeles, where he and his wife, Marili Morden, organized a band led by Kid Ory; they also established the record label Crescent in Hollywood to record the band. Later they operated the Jazzman label (1946–51), which again had a repertory of traditional jazz. In the mid-1940s Ertegun wrote for the journal *Clef* and was editor of *Record Changer*. From 1951 to 1954 he lectured in the history of American music at UCLA, and delivered the first courses on the history of jazz given for college credit in any American university; during this period he also worked for the Good Time Jazz and Contemporary labels. In 1955 he moved to New York to take charge of artists and repertory for his brother Ahmet's ATLANTIC record company and label, and under Nesuhi's direction the company became much more involved with contemporary jazz. He was vice-president of Atlantic until 1971, when he became president and chief executive officer of WEA (Warner Bros–Elektra–Atlantic); from 1985 he has been chairman and co-chief executive of the company. In 1976 he was responsible for the launch of Atlantic's "That's Jazz" reissue program.

BIBLIOGRAPHY

N. Ertegun: Liner notes, *Kid Ory's Creole Jazz Band 1944/45* (GTJ L10–11, 1953)
"Un homme du disque parle de ses problèmes," *Jm*, no.63 (1960), 28
P. Elwood: Liner notes, *Kid Ory's Creole Jazz Band* (Folklyric 9008, 1975)
C. Gillett: *Making Tracks: Atlantic Records and the Growth of a Multi-billion-dollar Industry* (London, 1975), 106
M. Jones: "That's Jazz – That's Nesuhi," *MM*, li (24 July 1976), 36

Ervin, Booker (Telleferro, II) (*b* Denison, TX, 31 Oct 1930; *d* New York, 31 Aug 1970). Tenor saxophonist. He was the son of a trombonist who worked for a time with Buddy Tate, and he inherited his father's instrument: between the ages of eight and 13 he played trombone. He taught himself to play saxophone while in the air force (1950–53), then studied music in Boston for two years. His first professional engagement was with Ernie Fields's rhythm-and-blues band, with which he made his earliest recordings (*c*1956). Ervin rose to prominence as a member of Charles Mingus's group (1958–62). He also worked frequently in a cooperative quartet, the Playhouse Four, with Horace Parlan, George Tucker, and Al Harewood, and with Randy Weston. His best work as a leader was on nine albums recorded for Prestige (1963–6).

Ervin was a powerful player whose hard tone and fondness for the blues marked him as a member of the Texas school in the tradition of Buddy Tate, Arnett Cobb, and Illinois Jacquet.

He never allowed his formidable technique to obscure the emotional intensity of his playing, and he was one of the very few tenor saxophonists of his generation to remain untouched by the influence of John Coltrane and develop a wholly personal style.

SELECTED RECORDINGS

As leader: *The Book Cooks* (1960, Beth. 6048); *That's it!* (1961, Candid 9014); *Exultation!* (1963, Prst. 7293); *The Freedom Book* (1963, Prst. 7295); *The Song Book* (1964, Prst. 7318); *The Blues Book* (1964, Prst. 7340); *The Space Book* (1964, Prst. 7386); *The Trance* (1965, Prst. 7462); *Lament for Booker Ervin* (1965, Enja 2054); *The In Between* (1967, BN 84283)

As sideman: C. Mingus: *Jazz Portraits* (1959, UA 5036); H. Parlan: *Up & Down* (1961, BN 84082); R. Weston: *Randy!* (1963, Bak. 1001)

BIBLIOGRAPHY

B. Coss: "Texas Tenor," *DB*, xxix/14 (1962), 19
P. Lattes: "Une voie de tenor," *Jh*, no.207 (1965), 42
I. Gitler: "The Good Book," *DB*, xxxv/5 (1968), 23
Obituary, M. Gardner, *JM*, no.188 (1970), 28
M. Cuscuna: Liner notes, *Back from the Gig* (BN LA488H2, 1977)
G. Wattiau: *Book's Book: a Discography of Booker Ervin* (Amsterdam, 1987)
E. P. Deckers: *Booker Ervin Discography* (in preparation)

MARK GARDNER

Erwin, Pee Wee [George] (*b* Falls City, NE, 30 May 1913; *d* Teaneck, NJ, 20 June 1981). Trumpeter. He grew up in a musical family, and began playing trumpet at the age of four; he made his first radio broadcast four years later. After traveling with territory bands he played with Joe Haymes (1931–3), Isham Jones (1933–4), and others, then settled in New York. His wide range and skills as a sight reader and improviser caused him to be much in demand for radio sessions, and he played on Benny Goodman's programs in 1934–5 and 1936. In 1935 he also worked with Ray Noble. Later he played with Tommy Dorsey (1937–9), who gave Erwin's powerful tone particular prominence on such pieces as *Who?*. After leaving Dorsey Erwin pursued a career as a studio musician, but interrupted this to run a big band (1941–2); he also rehearsed with another in 1946 without success. In 1949 he began leading an ensemble which became resident at Nick's, New York, for much of the 1950s. During the 1960s he ran a trumpet school with Chris Griffin and continued to perform. His playing retained its spirit and verve throughout the following decade, when he toured Europe with Warren Covington, the Kings of Jazz (his own band, 1974), and the New York Jazz Repertory Company. He gave his last performance in Holland in 1981.

SELECTED RECORDINGS

As leader: Eccentric Rag (1950, King 15073); *Oh Play that Thing!* (1958, UA 5010); *Pee Wee in New York* (1980, Qualtro 100); *Pee Wee in Hollywood* (1980, Qualtro 101); *Pee Wee Erwin Memorial* (1981, Jazz Crooner 2829581)

As sideman: H. Allen: It's written all over your face (1935, Ban. 33337); R. Noble: Dinah (1935, Vic. 25223); T. Dorsey: Stop, Look and Listen/Beale Street Blues (1937, Vic. 36207); Who? (1937, Vic. 25693); Shine on, Harvest Moon (1938, Vic. 25780); Chinatown, my Chinatown/The Sheik of Araby (1938, Vic. 26023); Sandy Williams: Sandy's Blues (1946, HRS 1022); S. Yaged: *Jazz at the Metropole* (1961, Phi. 600022); D. Hyman: *Some Rags, Some Stomps, and a Little Blues* (1973, Col. M32587)

BIBLIOGRAPHY

ChiltonW
P. Morris: "Pee Wee at Present," *MR*, i/3 (1974), 6
S. Traill: "Pee Wee Erwin," *JJ*, xxviii/10 (1975), 4 [interview]
E. Townley: "My Early Days: Pee Wee Erwin," *Sv*, no.63 (1976), 90 [interview]
Obituary, W. Vaché, Sr., *JJI*, xxxiv/10 (1981), 10
J. Coleman: "Pee Wee Erwin: Swing Era Genius," *Jazz: the Australasian Contemporary Music Magazine*, ii/6 (1982), 12
G. Giddins: *Rhythm-a-ning: Jazz Tradition and Innovation in the '80s* (New York, and Oxford, England, 1985) [colln of previously pubd articles], 88
W. W. Vaché, Sr.: *Pee Wee Erwin: this Horn for Hire* (Metuchen, NJ, 1987) [incl. discography]

BRIAN PEERLESS

Esbensen, Egon (*b* Næstved, Denmark, 4 July 1921; *d* Copenhagen, 26 March 1975). Danish tenor saxophonist. He played with Niels Foss (1941–2), Kai Ewans (1943–5), Peter Rasmussen (1945–53, 1956–9), and Bruno Henriksen, with whom he made recordings (including *Idaho*, 1952, Phi. 55002). In the 1940s and early 1950s he was considered the leading tenor saxophonist in Denmark; from 1960 he worked exclusively in dance bands.

ERIK WIEDEMANN

Eschete, Ron(ald P.) (*b* Houma, LA, *c*1949). Electric guitarist. He began to play guitar at the age of 14. After high school he went to New Orleans, where he played in clubs and with local jazz singers while studying classical guitar at Loyola University. In Las Vegas he worked with the popular singer Buddy Greco (1969–70), after which he moved to Los Angeles. He was appointed to the faculty of the Guitar Institute of Technology in Hollywood and continued to teach there into the 1980s; he has written several method books for guitar. Eschete has recorded with Dave Pike, both as a leader (1975) and as a sideman (1975, 1977), and with Milt Jackson (1980) and Ray Brown and Keely Smith (both 1985); his playing is well represented on the LP *Line-up* (1980, Muse 5246), which he recorded as the leader of a trio. He also performed with the Monterey Jazz Festival Guitar Ensemble (1983). Eschete plays a seven-string instrument, on which the extra string is tuned to *A'* (a fifth below the lowest string of a conventional electric guitar). (J. Ferguson: "The Artistry and Versatility of Ron Eschete," *GP*, xviii/5 (1984), 62 [incl. discography])

Escudero, Ralph [Rafael] (*b* Manati, nr Arecibo, Puerto Rico, 16 July 1898; *d* Puerto Rico, 10 April 1970). Double bass and tuba player. He began playing double bass at the age of 12 in a school band, and first worked professionally after moving to New York, where he played with the New Amsterdam Musical Association and recorded with Lucille Hegamin (1920–21) and Ethel Waters (1921). While working with Wilbur Sweatman at the Howard Theatre in Washington Escudero was heard and recruited by Fletcher Henderson, with whom he performed and made recordings (including *The Stampede*, 1926, Col. 654) until 1926 (for illustration *see* Jazz (i), fig.2). Thereafter he played with McKinney's Cotton Pickers (1926–31), Kaiser Marshall's Bostonians, and the Savoy Bearcats, and toured with W. C. Handy. After working in New York and California he returned to Puerto Rico, where he continued to play regularly throughout the 1960s.

For illustrations *see* JAZZ, fig.2, and MCKINNEY'S COTTON PICKERS.

based on *ChiltonW*

ESP–disk. Record company and label. The company was founded in New York by Bernard Stollman in 1963. Its earliest and most controversial albums were devoted to the work of Albert Ayler, Ornette Coleman, Pharoah Sanders, Sun Ra, Marion Brown, Paul Bley, Milford Graves, Burton Greene, Henry Grimes, Noah Howard, Sunny Murray, Charles Tyler, the New York Art Quartet, and other musicians and groups associated with avant-garde jazz. Later it began issuing swing and bop, releasing compilations of material taken from broadcasts by Billie Holiday, Charlie Parker, and Bud Powell. Many of the items planned, however, were never completed; only two of a projected series of 12 albums by Parker were released. The company also issued an album of recordings made by Powell in Paris in the early 1960s. It remained active into the 1970s, but appears to have ceased to operate thereafter.

The company's activities were always haphazard and rather eccentric; it often published messages in Esperanto on its liners, which sometimes carried hideously inappropriate designs. ESP–disk also issued one of the first albums with music on one side only (Albert Ayler's *Bells*, 1965, 1010).

MARK GARDNER

Esquire. Record company and label. The company was established in England in 1947 by Carlo Krahmer and Peter Newbrook. Issue commenced with Humphrey Lyttelton's first recordings, made at a concert given in Birmingham. Thereafter the company undertook large-scale documentation of British jazz, including the work of several bop musicians, such as John Dankworth and Ronnie Scott. Esquire soon obtained American repertory, at first by exchanging masters with small labels in the USA; from 1950 to 1964 the company was the British licensee for Prestige. Shortly thereafter the label was discontinued, and Krahmer became concerned mainly with the issue of jazz and blues material recorded in Chicago by Delmark. After Krahmer's death in 1976 the company was continued by his widow, Greta, then by Newbrook, who revived the Esquire label name for a series of reissues (including American material) that has continued into the 1980s.

BIBLIOGRAPHY

J. Martin: "Concerning Carlo," *Jazz News*, iv/28 (1960), 13
C. Krahmer: "The Esquire Label," *Matrix*, no.34 (1961), 6; nos.35–6 (1961), 25; no.37 (1961), 12
D. Dobell: "Krahmer: Post-war Pioneer," *MM*, li (8 May 1976), 49
G. Krahmer: "The Continuing Story of Esquire," *Jazz Circle News* (May 1978), 9
"Carlo: Pioneer British Jazzman," *Jazz at Ronnie Scott's* (Dec 1979–Jan 1980), 3

Essen, Reimer von (*b* Hamburg, Germany, 31 Oct 1940). German clarinetist and bandleader. He began his career with the Beale Street Seven (1957), formed the Blue Washboard Five (1958), then joined the Blue Note Jazzboys (1959). In 1962 he assumed leadership of the Barrelhouse Jazzband, with which he often recorded and accompanied American guest soloists, and the following year he was a founder of the Gesellschaft zür Förderung des New Orleans Jazz. From 1975 he belonged to the groups Ragtime Society Frankfurt and Jazz Classics, toured in Europe with a trio led by Art Hodes, and led a trio of his own; he has also written diverse essays about jazz. Essen was among the first leaders to evince from a small group a sound resembling that of a big band.

SELECTED RECORDINGS

As leader: *Barrelhouse Jazzband Plays Jelly Roll Morton* (1980, Intercord 145038)
As sideman: Ragtime Society Frankfurt: *Memories of you* (1981, Joke 217); A. Hodes: *Blues to Save the Trees* (1981, L+R 40015); Jazz Classics: *Yonder Comes the Blues* (1983, Stomp Off 1061)

GERHARD CONRAD

Etté, Bernard [Ette, Bernhard] (*b* Kassel, Germany, 13 Sept 1898; *d* Mühldorf, Germany, 26 Sept 1973). German bandleader and violinist. After playing piano, violin, and banjo in an orchestra directed by Carl Robrecht (whom he later employed as an arranger), he formed his first band in Bad Nauheim. In 1923 he led the house band at the Boston Club in Berlin and he also made radio broadcasts. He began to record in 1923, often employing white-American soloists; his recordings as a leader include *Sam, the Old Accordian Man* (1927, Vox 8528) and *Original Dixieland Onestep* (1929, Kristall 3042). He was a member of a small group, drawn from the larger band, which recorded as the Jazz Kings in 1927. He led orchestras until after World War II and recorded for many companies, his repertory gradually changing from hot dance music and jazz to light music. (R. E. Lotz: *Hot Dance Bands in Germany: a Photo Album*, ii: *The 1920s*, Menden, Germany, 1982)

RAINER E. LOTZ

Eubanks, Kevin (Tyrone) (*b* Philadelphia, 15 Nov 1957). Guitarist and leader. He led a jazz-rock band in Boston while attending the Berklee College of Music. In Europe he recorded with Chris Hinze (1978) and toured and recorded with Art Blakey (1980). After moving to New York he performed with Roy Haynes, Ronnie Mathews, and Slide Hampton in 1981. The following year he toured with Sam Rivers and recorded with Paquito D'Rivera, Chico Freeman, James Newton, Wynton Marsalis, and Bobby McFerrin; he also recorded an album as a leader, *Sundance* (1982, GRP 1008), on which he demonstrated his versatility by playing acoustic and electric guitars in bop, free-jazz, and jazz-rock styles. In 1987 Eubanks was a member of the quintet Who's Who, led by Mino Cinélu.

BIBLIOGRAPHY

B. Milkowski: "Profile: Kevin Eubanks," *DB*, 1/7 (1983), 48
J. Ferguson: "Don't Call Kevin Eubanks a Jazz Guitarist," *GP*, xx/5 (1986), 44
M. Bourne: "Kevin Eubanks: a New Breed of Guitarist," *DB*, liv/7 (1987), 20 [incl. discography]

Euell, Julian (Thomas) (*b* New York, 23 May 1929). Double bass player. He played bop with Little Benny Harris (?before 1953) and Joe Roland (1955) while attending New York and Columbia universities. He then worked with Freddie Redd (1956) and Phineas Newborn (1957), recorded with John Handy (1957) and Little Brother Montgomery (1960), and performed and recorded with Mal Waldron (1956–8, 1960) and Gigi Gryce (1956–7, 1960–61). His playing is heard to advantage on the album *Mal 2* (1957, Prst. 7111), recorded by Waldron's sextet, which also included John Coltrane. (*FeatherE*)

Euphonium. The tenor instrument of the TUBA family, pitched in B♭. The name is also used, chiefly by instrument makers in the USA, for some models of the baritone horn (*see* SAXHORN).

Eureka Brass Band. New Orleans group active from 1920 to 1975. Its first leader was its founder, the trumpeter Willie Wilson; after Wilson's death the leadership passed to the trumpeters Alcide Landry (1930s), Dominique "T-Boy" Remy (1940s), and Percy Humphrey (1950s and 1960s; for illustration *see* BRASS BAND, fig.2). Although the group varied in number from nine to 11 pieces, typically it comprised three trumpets, two trombones, two reed instruments, tuba, snare drum, and bass drum. The Eureka Brass Band was the most consistent of the late brass bands and was also the most frequently recorded; among notable recordings are *New Orleans Parade* (1951, Pax 9001), with Humphrey, the trombonists Charles "Sunny" Henry and Albert Warner, the tenor saxophonist Emanuel Paul, and the sousaphone player Joseph "Red" Clark, and *Jazz at Preservation Hall* (1962, Atl. 1408), on which the musicians include Percy and Willie Humphrey, Peter Bocage, Warner, Paul, and Cié Frazier.

BIBLIOGRAPHY

S. B. Charters: "A Footnote to Jazz: Recording the Eureka Brass Band," *JJ*, xiii (1960), no.4, p.10; no.5, p.16
J. De Donder: "'Red': some Words on Joseph 'Red' Clark," *Fn*, xviii/5 (1987), 12

WILLIAM J. SCHAFER

Europe, James Reese (*b* Mobile, AL, 22 Feb 1881; *d* Boston, 10 May 1919). Bandmaster and songwriter. He studied violin and piano as a child in Washington, then moved to New York (*c*1904), where he later became a director for musical comedies. In 1905 he participated in a pioneering public concert of syncopated music presented by the singer and entertainer Ernest Hogan, and in 1910 he organized the Clef Club, a black musicians' association. Europe's band was the first black group to make recordings (from 1913). During World War I he won respect with his superb military band, the 369th Infantry, and for his jazz concerts given in France. After returning to the USA in 1919 he embarked on a triumphant tour of the nation and was hailed everywhere for his "gorgeous racket of syncopation and jazzing," but he died during the course of the tour.

Although the few extant recordings of Europe's compositions reflect the ragtime style that was prevalent at the time, contemporary descriptions of his band's performance style indicate that he stood at least on the threshold of jazz; this is confirmed by his recording of *Memphis Blues* (1919, Pathé 22085). When asked about the unique sound of his music, he ascribed it not only to his wildly syncopated rhythms and use of black folk music materials, but also to a special way of producing tones on the wind instruments, particularly the "jazz spasms" of the trombones, the use of mutes, and his bandsmen's desire to "embroider their parts in order to produce new, peculiar sounds." Europe exerted considerable influence on the development of jazz in France and the USA, both through his performances and his role as the mentor of numerous jazz musicians.

BIBLIOGRAPHY

E. Scott: *Official History of the American Negro in the World War* (Washington, 1919)
J. W. Johnson: *Black Manhattan* (New York, 1930)
A. Little: *From Harlem to the Rhine* (New York, 1936)
S. B. Charters and L. Kunstadt: *Jazz: a History of the New York Scene* (Garden City, NY, 1962/*R*1981)
E. Southern: *The Music of Black Americans: a History* (New York and London, 1971, rev. 2/1983)
E. Southern, ed.: *Readings in Black American Music* (New York, 1971)
R. Kimball and W. Bolcom: *Reminiscing with Sissle and Blake* (New York, 1973)
J. Anderson: *This was Harlem: a Cultural Portrait, 1900–1950* (New York, 1982), 75, 118
E. Southern: *Biographical Dictionary of Afro-American and African Musicians* (Westport, CT, 1982)
G. Schuller: *Musings: the Musical Worlds of Gunther Schuller* (New York, and Oxford, England, 1986) [incl. previously pubd items]

EILEEN SOUTHERN

European Jazz Federation. Organization founded in the mid-1960s to promote cooperation between all European countries in the field of jazz. In 1977 it was renamed the INTERNATIONAL JAZZ FEDERATION.

European Jazz Quintet. European group. It was formed in 1977 by the tenor saxophonist Alan Skidmore, with two other tenor saxophonists, Gerd Dudek and Leszek Zadlo, the double bass player Ali Haurand, and the drummer Pierre Courbois. After giving its first public performance at the Moers festival in Germany in 1977 (a recording of which was issued as the album *Live at Moers Festival*, Ring 01018), it toured extensively, playing at numerous festivals and concerts throughout Europe. It released two further albums before disbanding in 1982. The quintet played a mixture of hard bop and freely improvised music; its unusual instrumentation made possible innovative combinations and the musicians often varied a full quintet format with trio groupings, each of the saxophonists playing in turn with the bass player and drummer.

SIMON ADAMS

European New Jazz Association. *See* ENJA.

European Rhythm Machine. Quartet formed in 1968 by PHIL WOODS.

Evans, Bill [William] **(i).** *See* LATEEF, YUSEF.

Evans, Bill [William John] **(ii)** (*b* Plainfield, NJ, 16 Aug 1929; *d* New York, 15 Sept 1980). Pianist. He attended Southeastern Louisiana University, worked occasionally with Mundell Lowe and Red Mitchell, and served in the army before beginning his jazz apprenticeship in earnest. He played with the clarinetist Jerry Wald, Tony Scott, and George Russell, among others, and met Paul Motian, a sensitive drummer who later became an important member of several of Evans's ensembles. Evans's first recording with a group of his own was made in 1956. Soon

Bill Evans (piano) with Shelly Manne (drums) and Eddie Gomez (double bass)

thereafter he recorded with Charles Mingus, and in 1958 joined Miles Davis. He played a significant role in the pivotal recording session the following year that produced Davis's album *Kind of Blue*, by which time his distinctive style had largely crystallized. His development from 1960 may be traced by examining the work of his various trios. Although his preferred format was piano, double bass, and drums, he occasionally made recordings in other contexts, such as playing against a prerecorded track of his own (*Conversations with Myself*, 1963) or as a member of a duo (e.g., with Bob Brookmeyer, Jim Hall, or Tony Bennett). Despite personal difficulties and health problems, Evans appeared in public and recorded with some regularity until shortly before his death.

Evans was one of the most influential jazz musicians of his generation, and the pianist who most successfully assimilated and developed a bop language based on the style of Bud Powell. He brought exceptional refinement and freshness to the jazz harmonic idiom, and this, together with his insistence on a more independent, quasipolyphonic role for his accompanists, his sensitive, well-modulated touch, and an often introspective, lyrical personality, had a lasting influence on many musicians, including Chick Corea, Herbie Hancock, Keith Jarrett, and Steve Kuhn.

Evans acknowledged a debt to most of the prominent figures of the bop era, and his early work bears the obvious stamp of Powell, Lennie Tristano, and – strikingly – Horace Silver. His relatively aggressive attack and strong links to the bop style in this period gradually receded in favor of a more lyrical approach including idiosyncratic melodic figures of irregular lengths and subtle voice-leading and harmony (ex.1). Still, his basic bop orientation never changed, and he showed little interest in the experiments of the 1960s and 1970s; even the use of the electric piano remained somewhat foreign to him.

Relationships with a few key double bass players (and, to a lesser extent, drummers) were important in Evans's career. Perhaps the most significant of these bass players was Scott LaFaro, who worked with Evans and Motian from 1959 to 1961. LaFaro's light sound, extraordinary facility, and melodic imagination were a fine foil for Evans, and the two evolved contrapuntal textures distinguished by rhythmic complexity and an elusive relationship to the pulse. This interplay was less in evidence in Evans's work with LaFaro's successor, Chuck Israels, though it re-emerged in his later recordings with Gary Peacock and Eddie Gomez. A similarly complex interaction may be heard in his recordings with Jim Hall, a performer whose capacities and temperament had much in common with Evans's. Here, too, Evans excels as an accompanist, combining discretion with rhythmic flair, an inexhaustible invention in the voicing of chords, and a wide variety of touch.

Evans chose his repertory of tunes carefully: over the years he increasingly emphasized his own compositions (*Waltz for Debby*, *Comrade Conrad*) and standard numbers unlikely to interest most other jazz musicians (*Beautiful Love, Some day my prince will come*). In his own tunes the progression of chords is often elaborately chromatic, though the tonality is always

Ex.1 First solo chorus of *Time Remembered*, on *Since We Met* (1974, Fan. 9501); transcr. J. Distler

in evidence. Evans also favored irregularities in phrase length (*Show-type Tune*) and metrical shifts (*Peri's Scope*). His recasting of familiar melodies was exceptionally resourceful: in *My Foolish Heart*, for example, by the careful placement of a few substitute bass notes and nonharmonic tones and a sensitive use of register, he produced a striking transformation of the original tune. Evans's last recording (1979) surveyed tunes from all phases of his career in what was for him an unusual instrumental grouping (trumpet, saxophone, and rhythm section), perhaps intimating a new stage in his development. A volume of transcriptions of Evans's performances has been published (*Bill Evans*, Fort Lauderdale, FL, 1965). A collection of material relating to his life and work is held at Southeastern Louisiana University; *see* LIBRARIES AND ARCHIVES, §2.

Oral history material in *NjR*.

See also HARMONY (i), §1(iv), and exx.2 and 10; JAZZ (i), §V, 8; and PIANO, §§5 and 6.

SELECTED RECORDINGS

As unaccompanied soloist: *Conversations with Myself* (1963, Verve 68526); *Further Conversations with Myself* (1967, Verve 68727)

Duos: with J. Hall: *Undercurrent* (1959, UA 14003); *Intermodulation* (1966, Verve 68655); with E. Gomez: *Intuition* (1974, Fan. 9475); with T. Bennett: *The Tony Bennett–Bill Evans Album* (1975, Fan. 9489)

As leader: *New Jazz Conceptions* (1956, Riv. 223), incl. Waltz for Debby; *Portrait in Jazz* (1959, Riv. 1162), incl. Peri's Scope, Some day my prince will come; *Explorations* (1961, Riv. 9351), incl. Beautiful Love; *Sunday at the Village Vanguard* (1961, Riv. 9376); *Moondreams* (1962, Riv. 9428); *Interplay* (1962, Riv. 9445); *How my Heart Sings* (1962, Riv. 9473), incl. Show-type Tune; *Trio '64* (1963, Verve 68578); *The Bill Evans Album* (1971, Col. C30855), incl. Comrade Conrad; *Since We Met* (1974, Fan. 9501); *We Will Meet Again* (1979, WB 3411)

As sideman: C. Mingus: *East Coasting* (1957, Beth. 6019); M. Davis: *Kind of Blue* (1959, Col. CL1355)

BIBLIOGRAPHY

N. Hentoff: "Introducing Bill Evans," *JR*, ii/9 (1959), 26

F. Manskleid: "Bill Evans Discusses the Jazz Scene," *JM*, vi/5 (1960), 10

J. F. Mehegan: *Jazz Improvisation*, iv: *Contemporary Piano Styles* (New York, 1965), 29

V. Wilmer: "Bill Evans," *JB*, ii/4 (1965), 4 [interview]

K. Knox: "Bill Evans," *JM*, xii/8 (1966), 5

M. Ruppli: "Discographie: Bill Evans," *Jh*, no.353 (1978), 45; no.354 (1978), 14

S. Britt: "The River Stops Flowing," *JJI*, xxxiii/11 (1980), 15

B. Taylor: *Jazz Piano: History and Development* (Dubuque, IA, 1982)

L. Lyons: *The Great Jazz Pianists, Speaking of their Lives and Music* (New York, 1983), 218

J. Mitchell: "Nardis: Bill Evans Remembered," *The Wire*, no.3 (1983), 22

G. E. Smith: *Homer, Gregory, and Bill Evans? The Theory of Formulaic Composition in the Context of Jazz Piano Improvisation* (diss., Harvard U., 1983)

P. H. Larsen: *Turn on the Stars: Bill Evans, the Complete Discography* (Holte, Denmark, 1984)

B. Hennessey: "Bill Evans: a Person I Knew," *JJI*, xxxviii/3 (1985), 8

C. Israels: "Bill Evans (1929–1980): a Musical Memoir," *Musical Quarterly*, lxxi (1985), 109

M. McPartland: "Bill Evans, Genius," *All in Good Time* (New York, and Oxford, England, 1987) [colln of previously pubd articles], 105

EDWARD MURRAY

Evans, Bill (iii) (*b* Clarendon Hills, nr Chicago, 9 Feb 1958). Tenor and soprano saxophonist. He learned piano as a child and later took up tenor saxophone. After university and conservatory training he studied privately in Chicago with Dave Liebman, then moved in 1978 to New York. Two years later, on Liebman's recommendation, he joined Miles Davis's group, and began receiving international acclaim. During this association he also recorded with the group led by Mark Egan and Danny Gottlieb, Elements (1982), and made his first album as a leader (1983). After leaving Davis in 1984 he pursued a career as a soloist, and also worked with John McLaughlin's re-formed Mahavishnu Orchestra and again with Elements. For his second album, *The Alternative Man* (1985), Evans employed contemporary technology – synthesizers, drum machines, and signal processors – to extend the jazz tradition and forge a style that represents a fine example of jazz-rock in the 1980s.

SELECTED RECORDINGS

As leader: *Living in the Crest of a Wave* (1983, Elek. Mus. 60349); *The Alternative Man* (1985, BN 85111)

As sideman: Elements: *Elements* (1982, Philo 9011); M. Davis: *Star People* (1982–3, Col. FC38657); *Decoy* (1983–4, Col. FC38991); Elements: *Forward Motion* (1984, Ant. 1021); Mahavishnu Orchestra: *Mahavishnu* (1984, WB 25190)

BIBLIOGRAPHY

H. Mandel: "Profile: Bill Evans, Mike Stern, and Mino Cinelu," *DB*, xlviii/11 (1981), 53

B. Milkowski: "Bill Evans: from Miles to Mahavishnu," *DB*, li/10 (1984), 29 [incl. discography]

BILL MILKOWSKI

Evans, Doc [Paul Wesley] (*b* Spring Valley, MN, 20 June 1907; *d* Minneapolis, 10 Jan 1977). Cornetist. He first worked as an amateur in and around Minneapolis and St. Paul (usually as a leader), and in the mid-1940s moved first to Chicago and then to New York, working successfully in both cities. He later returned to Minneapolis, where in 1947 he performed and recorded with Bunk Johnson. After playing in 1949 with Miff Mole he spent some time on the West Coast before returning again to Minneapolis. He made many successful recordings, including several in the 1950s for Audiophile. Evans was noted for his work as a lead cornetist in dixieland and traditional jazz bands; his lyrical solos were suggestive of the work of Bix Beiderbecke.

SELECTED RECORDINGS

As leader: Lulu's Back in Town/One Sweet Letter (1947, Dublin's 1); *Cornet Artistry* (*c*1956, Audiophile 31); *Traditional Jazz* (*c*1955–7, Audiophile 328–9, 33–4, 44–5)

As sideman with T. Murphy: *New Orleans Jazz Festival* (1955, Col. CL793)

BIBLIOGRAPHY

ChiltonW; *FeatherE*

J. Stanley: Liner notes, *Bunk Johnson and Don Ewell with Doc Evans and his Band* (Paragon PLE M102, 1972)

P. Evans: "Jazz & Swing in the Thirties," *MR*, vi/3 (1979), 11

WARREN VACHÉ, SR.

Evans, Gil [Green, Ian Ernest Gilmore] (*b* Toronto, 13 May 1912; *d* Cuernavaca, Mexico, 20 March 1988). Arranger, composer, pianist, and bandleader. A self-taught musician, he led his own band in Stockton, California, from 1933 to 1938. When the singer Skinnay Ennis then took over the band, Evans stayed on as arranger. In 1941 he joined Claude Thornhill's group in the same capacity, contributing in 1946–7 such outstanding arrangements as *Anthropology*, *Donna Lee*, *Yardbird Suite*, and *Robbins' Nest*. In these works and others of the period Evans used two french horns and a tuba (in addition to the standard swing era big-band instrumentation); this, along with a restrained vibrato in the saxophones and brass, produced a rich, dark-textured, "cool" orchestral sound, anticipated only by Duke Ellington and Eddie Sauter. Emphasizing ensemble over improvised solo, Evans's scores for Thornhill were far from being straightforward arrangements – they were in essence "recompositions" and "orchestral improvisations" on the original materials (for example, lines of Charlie Parker's, popular songs, and classical works such as Mussorgsky's *Pictures at an Exhibition*).

From 1948 to 1950 Evans contributed prominently to Miles Davis's nonet recordings for Capitol (later issued as the LP *Birth of the Cool*). In his memorable scores *Boplicity* and *Moon Dreams*, Evans captured the essential sound and texture of the Thornhill band with a smaller ensemble. Oddly, his work for both Davis and Thornhill was ignored by critics and jazz audiences alike. After a period of relative obscurity, during which he worked in radio and television, Evans returned to jazz with three notable albums, all written for and featuring Davis: *Miles Ahead* (1957), *Porgy and Bess* (1959), and *Sketches of Spain* (1960). In these, as well as *New Bottle, Old Wine* (1958), Evans extended his earlier orchestral concepts to larger instrumental forces (up to 20), often achieving a distinctive synthesis of varied timbral mixtures in which opaque, almost cluster-like voicings alternate with rich polyphonic textures, the whole being couched in an advanced harmonic language.

From the early 1960s Evans made several attempts to form permanent orchestras, but these were unable to establish

Gil Evans (right) with Miles Davis (center) and unidentified flutist and trombonist during a recording session for Columbia, c1960

themselves, although they occasionally produced such excellent recordings as *The Individualism of Gil Evans* (1963–4), *Blues in Orbit* (1969–71), and *Priestess* (1977). He also turned increasingly to composition, writing such notable works as *Flute Song*, *Las Vegas Tango*, *Proclamation*, *Variations on The Misery*, *Anita's Dance*, and (in collaboration with Miles Davis) *Hotel Me* and *General Assembly*. Later Evans incorporated electrified instruments (piano, bass guitar, synthesizer, etc.) into his ensembles, and tended to leave more space for solo improvisation in his arrangements and compositions. This led to a considerable loosening of his style in both form and texture, compared with the more compact structures and veiled sonorities of his earlier arrangements. Even so, the temper of his work remained moody, poignant, and introverted, as was reflected in his predilection for pieces in minor keys.

Although he was at first influenced by the middle-period works of Duke Ellington, Evans developed a style wholly his own, memorable especially for its richly chromatic, though always tonally oriented, harmonic language and its seemingly inexhaustible variety of timbral blendings; no mere coloristic effects, these are often the very substance of his art, providing imaginative frameworks for his soloists in ways equaled in the history of jazz only by Morton, Ellington, and Mingus. Even in his most elaborate scores Evans succeeded in preserving the essential spontaneity and improvisatory nature of jazz, achieving a rare symbiosis between composed and improvised elements.

Oral history material in *NjR* (JOHP).

See also ARRANGEMENT, §4 and ex.2; for further illustration *see* TRACEY, STAN.

SELECTED ARRANGEMENTS

* – composed by Evans

As leader: *Gil Evans and Ten* (1957, Prst. 7120); *New Bottle, Old Wine* (1958, WP 1246), incl. *Theme; *Great Jazz Standards* (1959, WP 1270); *Out of the Cool* (1960, Imp. 4), incl. *La Nevada, *Sunken Treasure; *Into the Hot* (1961, Imp. 9); *The Individualism of Gil Evans* (1963–4, Verve 8555), incl. *Flute Song, Hotel Me, *Las Vegas Tango; *Blues in Orbit* (1969, 1971, Ampex 10102), incl. General Assembly, *Proclamation, *Variations on The Misery; *Svengali* (1973, Atl. 1643), incl. *Zee Zee; *There Comes a Time* (1975, RCA APL1-10057), incl. *Anita's Dance; *Priestess* (1977, Ant. 1010); *Little Wing* (1978, Cir. [Ger.] 13)

Recorded by C. Thornhill: Early Autumn (1947, Col. 37593); Anthropology (1947, Col. 38224); Robbins' Nest (1947, Col. 38136); Donna Lee, first issued on *The Thornhill Sound* (1947, Har. 7088); Yardbird Suite (1947, Col. 39133)

Recorded by M. Davis with Evans as conductor: Boplicity (1949, Cap. 60011); Moon Dreams (1950), on *Classics in Jazz* (1949–50, Cap. H459); *Miles Ahead* (1957, Col. CL1041); *Porgy and Bess* (1958, Col. CL1274); *Sketches of Spain* (1959–60, Col. CS8271); *Quiet Nights* (1962, Col. CS8906)

BIBLIOGRAPHY

N. Hentoff: "The Birth of the Cool," *DB*, xxiv/9 (1957), 15; repr. in *The Jazz Word*, ed. D. Cerulli, B. Korall, and M. Nasatir (New York, 1960), 214
C. Fox: "Experiment with Texture," *These Jazzmen of our Time*, ed. R. Horricks and others (London, 1959), 93
D. Heckman: "Gil Evans on his Own," *JR*, iii/3 (1960), 14
——: *Gil Evans: a List of Compositions Licensed by B. M. I.* (New York, 1961)
A. Hodeir: *Toward Jazz* (New York, 1962/*R*1976), 151
L. Feather: "The Modulated World of Gil Evans," *DB*, xxxiv/4 (1967), 14
R. Palmer: "Refocus on Gil Evans," *DB*, xli/10 (1974), 12
M. Harrison: *A Jazz Retrospect* (Newton Abbot, England, 1976, rev. 2/1977)
A. J. Smith: "Gil Evans: 21st Century Synthesized Man," *DB*, xliii/10 (1976), 14
L. Tomkins: "Gil Evans," *CI*, xvi (1978), no.9, p.21; no.10, p.4; no.11, p.22 [interview]
T. Tajiri: *Gil Evans Discography, 1941–1982* (Tokyo, 1983)
L. Tomkins: "Gil Evans," *CI*, xxi (1983), no.9, p.20; no.10, p.6; no.11, p.12 [interview]
R. Horricks: *Svengali, or The Orchestra Called Gil Evans* (Tunbridge Wells, England, and New York, 1984) [incl. discography]
H. Mandel: "Gil Evans: the Lone Arranger," *DB*, li/4 (1984), 20
Obituary, I. Carr: *The Independent* (23 March 1988)

GUNTHER SCHULLER

Evans, Herschel (*b* Denton, TX, 1909; *d* New York, 9 Feb 1939). Tenor saxophonist. From 1926 he played professionally in southwestern territory bands, including those led by Troy Floyd (1929–31) and Bennie Moten (1933–5). A recording from these early years reveals that he had developed a personal style on his instrument somewhat before Coleman Hawkins, with whom he is often compared. In late 1936, after playing briefly with Lionel Hampton and Buck Clayton in Los Angeles, Evans began a permanent engagement with the Count Basie Orchestra (for illustration *see* BASIE, COUNT) which quickly brought him to national prominence. During these years he was a leading tenor saxophonist in the swing style, with a rich, powerful tone and forceful delivery. These attributes were diametrically opposed to the light, fluent manner of Basie's principal tenor saxophonist Lester Young, occasioning a rivalry between the two that became a hallmark of Basie's performances. Evans died of a heart ailment while still at the height of his powers. Among the arrangements he wrote for Basie was *Texas Shuffle* (*see* ARRANGEMENT, §3 and Table 3).

SELECTED RECORDINGS

As sideman with C. Basie: One o'Clock Jump/John's Idea (1937, Decca 1363); Georgianna (1938, Decca 1682); Blue and Sentimental/Doggin' Around (1938, Decca 1965); Texas Shuffle (1938, Decca 2030)

As sideman with others: T. Floyd: Dreamland Blues (1929, OK 8719); H. James: (I can dream) can't I? (1937, Bruns. 8038); L. Hampton: Shoe Shiner's Drag (1938, Vic. 26011)

BIBLIOGRAPHY

R. Horricks: *Count Basie and his Orchestra: its Music and its Musicians* (London and New York, 1957), 118
A. McCarthy: "Basie's other Tenor: the Herschel Evans Story," *J&B*, i/2 (1971), 10
J. Evensmo: *The Tenor Saxophones of Henry Bridges, Robert Carroll, Herschal [sic] Evans, Johnny Russell* (n.p. [Oslo], n.d. [?1976]) [discography]
S.-A. Worsfold: "The Forgotten Ones: Herschel Evans," *JJI*, xxxiv/10 (1981), 17
B. Clayton and N. M. Elliott: *Buck Clayton's Jazz World* (London, 1986)

J. BRADFORD ROBINSON

Evans, Stump [Paul Anderson] (*b* Lawrence, KS, 18 Oct 1904; *d* Douglas Co., KS, 29 Aug 1928). Saxophonist. He was taught music by his father. He first played alto horn, then changed to trombone, and took up alto saxophone before specializing on the baritone instrument during the early 1920s. After moving to Chicago he worked with the bandleader Oscar "Bernie" Young and played in King Oliver's Creole Jazz Band (1923) and Dixie Syncopators (1926). He made recordings (including *Wild Man Blues*, Bb 10256) as an alto saxophonist with Jelly Roll Morton's Red Hot Peppers in 1927, and also worked with Jimmy Wade and Erskine Tate, but had to leave Tate's band after contracting tuberculosis.

based on *ChiltonW*

Evans, Sue [Susan] (*b* New York, 7 July 1951). Percussionist. She studied privately with Warren Smith (ii) and Sonny Igoe, among others, and graduated from the High School of Music and Art in 1969. She then played drums on tours of Europe and the USA with the popular singer Judy Collins (1969–75) and toured and recorded as a percussionist with Gil Evans (1969–82). At the same time she worked with Steve Kuhn (1972–4) and the Jazz Composer's Orchestra under Roswell Rudd (1973), and recorded with Bobby Jones (*The Arrival of Bobby Jones*, 1972, Cob. 9022), George Benson (1975), Urbie Green (1976), and Art Farmer (1977). In the 1980s she has recorded with Morgana King (1981), again with Murphy (1982), and with Michael Franks (1985–6), and worked with the singers Suzanne Vega (1984–7) and Tony Bennett (from 1985).

BIBLIOGRAPHY

Feather–Gitler '70s

A. J. Smith: "Profile: Sue Evans," *DB*, xli/21 (1974), 32

R. Mattingly: "Susan Evans: Doin' it all," *MD*, v/5 (1981), 26

Evans, William. *See* LATEEF, YUSEF.

Everybody's. Record label. It was established in New York, and issue took place, in 1925 only, of material taken from several other companies, notably the New York Recording Laboratories and Consolidated. The catalogue included material by the Original Memphis Five, and also one of Duke Ellington's first two recordings as a leader, acquired from Blu-disc. In the 1970s and 1980s the label name was revived for reissues of early jazz, both in the USA (by the Meritt Record Society) and in Sweden (by Carl Hällstrom and Jonas Bernholm). (B. Rust: *The American Record Label Book* (New Rochelle, NY, 1978), 121)

Ewans, Kai [Nielsen, Kai (Peter Anthon)] (*b* Hørsholm, Denmark, 10 April 1906). Danish alto saxophonist, clarinetist, and bandleader. He began his career as a banjoist; in 1923 he acquired an alto saxophone and formed the pioneering Blues Jazz Band, which remained active until the following year. He then played with Valdemar Eiberg (1924–6), and after changing his surname from Nielsen to Ewans (1927) led the first Danish big band (1927–8). He led bands in Belgium and Germany (1928–31), worked with Bernard Etté in Germany, and played in Denmark with Kai Julian (1931–2) and Erik Tuxen (1932–6). In 1936 he formed a swing big band comprising the greater part of Tuxen's group; this recorded with Benny Carter in 1936 and made many recordings of its own, including *Murder in the Madhouse* (1941, Odeon D462) and *One Night Stand* (1944, Tono Z18009). After the group disbanded in 1947 Ewans worked principally as a businessman in the USA. In 1956 he moved to California, and after running a restaurant in Beverly Hills with Benny Carter (1960–64), resumed his musical career in Copenhagen before retiring to Connecticut. (M. Berger, E. Berger, and J. Patrick: *Benny Carter: a Life in American Music*, Metuchen, NJ, and London, 1982)

ERIK WIEDEMANN

Ewart, Douglas (Randolph) [Doug] (*b* Kingston, Jamaica, 13 Sept 1946). Alto saxophonist and wind player. In Jamaica he absorbed the native traditions of ska and calypso; in 1963 he moved to Chicago. He became interested in jazz through the recordings of Charles Mingus, Clifford Brown, Charlie Parker, and especially Eric Dolphy, whose mastery of several instruments inspired him to learn flute, bass clarinet, and bassoon. In 1967 he joined the Association for the Advancement of Creative Musicians and studied theory and performance with Roscoe Mitchell and Joseph Jarman. From that time he performed in groups with Fred Anderson and George Lewis (ii), in Muhal Richard Abrams's big band, and with Anthony Braxton and Chico Freeman. Ewart is a versatile musician whose playing displays considerable craftsmanship and discipline and who makes expert use of varied instrumental sonorities.

SELECTED RECORDINGS

As sideman: C. Freeman: *Morning Prayer* (1976, Whynot PA7155); G. Lewis: *George Lewis* (1977, BS 0016); A. Braxton: *For Trio* (1977, Ari. 4181); M. R. Abrams: *Lifea blinec* (1978, AN 3000)

BIBLIOGRAPHY

J. Litweiler: "Doug Ewart," *DB*, xliv/13 (1977), 22

V. Wilmer: *As Serious as your Life: the Story of the New Jazz* (London, 1977, rev. 1980)

H. L. Lindenmaier: "Doug Ewart: Interview," *Cadence*, v/11 (1979), 3

DAVID G. SUCH

Ewell, Don(ald Tyson) (*b* Baltimore, 14 Nov 1916; *d* Pompano Beach, FL, 9 Aug 1983). Pianist. He studied classical music at the Peabody Conservatory and led his own trios and performed with other groups in Baltimore. The influences on his early playing were Fats Waller and Earl Hines; his recordings of 1942 (which have never been commercially issued) show his awareness of Hines in particular. After military service he worked in New York with Bunk Johnson (1945–7), and around this time became fascinated with the music of Jelly Roll Morton; in 1949 he moved to Chicago, where he played with various musicians, among them Muggsy Spanier and Sidney Bechet, and made his first important recordings. As a result of his friendship and association with Jimmy Yancey (late 1940s), he absorbed many elements of Chicago blues into his style at this time. In 1951 he led a five-piece band in St. Louis, which included Dewey Jackson, and in 1953 he traveled to the West Coast to join Kid Ory. He worked as a leader and with Jack Teagarden (1957–64), after which he settled in New Orleans. He performed and recorded with his own groups, in a duo with Willie "the Lion" Smith, and as a sideman and soloist. He toured Europe (1971), Australia (1975), Japan (1975, 1981), and England (1980). Although Ewell created his own approach to traditional jazz, there are strong traces of Morton, Waller, and James P. Johnson in his style.

Oral history material in *LNT*.

SELECTED RECORDINGS

As unaccompanied soloist: *Ewell Plays King Oliver Creole Band Tunes* (1952–3, Windin' Ball 103), incl. Snake Rag, Weatherbird Rag; *Jazz on a Sunday Afternoon* (1969, Fat Cats Jazz 109), incl. Honey Hush; *Take it in Stride* (1974, Chi. 127), incl. Dr. Heckle and Mr. Jibe

Duos with W. Smith: *Grand Piano* (1967, Exclusive 501), incl. A Porter's Love Song to a Chambermaid

As leader: *Music to Listen to Don Ewell by* (1956, GTJ 12021), incl. Southside Strut

As sideman with B. Johnson: In the Gloaming (1946, AM 520)

BIBLIOGRAPHY

ChiltonW

S. A. Pease: "Don Ewell Goes 'Back' to New Orleans Rags," *DB*, xiii/23 (1946), 12

E. Kramer: "Don Ewell: an Appreciation," *Record Changer*, xiii (1954), May, 7

P. C. Bentley: "Don Ewell, Old-time Traditionalist, Bangs Hot Piano Contemporaneously," *SL*, x/9–10 (1960), 3

G. Hoefer: "Don Ewell: a Quiet Giant," *J&P*, vii/2 (1968), 22

E. Lambert: "Some Notes on Don Ewell," *JM*, no.167 (1969), 2 [incl. discography]

M. Jones: "Don Ewell: Piano Giant from New Orleans," *MM* (13 Feb 1971), 12

Obituaries, J. Lucas, F. Powers, and B. Thompson, *MR*, x/12 (1983), 7

A. Barrell: "The Last Testament: Letters from Bunk and Maude Johnson to Friend Don Ewell," *Fn*, xvi/3 (1985), 4

J. Collinson: "Don Ewell: a Discography," *Sv*, no.118 (1985), 130; no.119 (1985), 170; no.120 (1985), 206; no.121 (1985), 6; no.122 (1985–6), 66; no.123 (1986), 83

JOHN COLLINSON

Ewing, Streamline [John] (*b* Topeka, KS, 19 Jan 1917). Trombonist. He first played professionally at the age of 17 in local bands. After working with Horace Henderson (1938) he performed and recorded as a soloist with Earl Hines (1938–9, 1941–2), and his playing may be heard to advantage on *Swingin' on C* (1941, Bb 11465). He appeared briefly with Louis Armstrong's big band and with Lionel Hampton, then worked with Jimmie Lunceford (1943–5), Cab Calloway (1946), Jay McShann (1948), Cootie Williams (1950), Louis Jordan, and Earl Bostic. Thereafter Ewing moved to California, where he joined a band led by the drummer George Jenkins and also worked as a freelance studio musician. Although he played mostly blues, he also took part in sessions with Gerald Wilson's orchestra. From 1956 he worked with Teddy Buckner, and remained associated with him intermittently into the early 1980s; he also toured with Henderson in 1962 and performed with Rex Stewart in 1967. (S. Dance: *The World of Earl Hines* (New York, 1977) [interviews], 235)

based on *ChiltonW*

Excellos Five. Traditional-jazz band. Formed in Brussels in 1923, it made some highly regarded recordings in Berlin in 1925–6 under the leadership of the drummer Robert Kierberg; among the other members were the trumpeter Louis de Vries and the trombonist Henry Vandenbossche. The band later toured throughout Europe.

ROBERT PERNET

Excelsior Brass Band. New Orleans group active from 1880 to 1931. It was first led by its founder Theogene Baquet, and later by George Moret (1904–20) and Peter Bocage (1920–31). The group varied in size from ten to 12 pieces, but most frequently consisted of three cornets (trumpets), two trombones, two clarinets, alto horn, baritone horn, tuba, snare drum, and bass drum. It was one of the earliest and also one of the most versatile of the New Orleans brass bands, playing both complex scored music and head arrangements of marches, dance music, dirges, and hymns. At various times the personnel of the Excelsior Brass Band included John Robichaux, George Baquet, Alphonse Picou, Luis Tio, Lorenzo Tio, Sr., Honore Dutrey, Sam Dutrey, Sr., Isidore Barbarin, Louis Cottrell, Sr., and Willie Humphrey.

BIBLIOGRAPHY

A. Barrell: "B is for Baquet," *Fn*, xvii/3 (1986), 4
——: "The Baquets: Some Concluding Notes," *Fn*, xviii/2 (1986–7), 4

WILLIAM J. SCHAFER

Exclusive. Record label. It was established in Los Angeles in the mid-1940s by Leon René, brother of the songwriter Otis René (who also owned a label, Excelsior). Exclusive's musical director was Buddy Baker, and the label was used to issue many recordings made by Lucky Thompson, both as a leader and as a member of groups that accompanied singers.

BIBLIOGRAPHY

A. Shaw: "Groove 6: Leon René," *Honkers and Shouters: the Golden Years of Rhythm and Blues* (New York, 1978), 15
D. Salemann: Liner notes, *Small Label Gems of the Forties*, iii (Solid Sender SOL514, ?1980)

Experimental Band. Free-jazz ensemble, established in 1961 by Muhal Richard Abrams, which led to the development of the ASSOCIATION FOR THE ADVANCEMENT OF CREATIVE MUSICIANS.

Extended chord. A chord made up of the triad and one or more added 3rds above the fifth (generally the major seventh, ninth, 11th, and 13th); any of the notes between the root and the note defining the uppermost interval may be omitted. *See* HARMONY (i), §1(ii).

Extended-play disc [extended player, EP]. A vinyl microgroove disc, recorded and played back at 45 r.p.m. and normally having two tracks on each side; *see* RECORDING, §I, 3(ii).

F

Fabricius-Bjerre, Bent (*b* Copenhagen, 7 Dec 1924). Danish pianist, arranger, and bandleader. He led amateur bands from 1940, which made several recordings (including *The Jeep is Jumpin'*, 1942, Odeon D523). In 1942–3 he worked professionally with the alto saxophonist Kaj Møller and from 1943 to 1946 made recordings with his own studio big bands (including *Joy at Spring*, 1944, Parl. DP230). From 1950 he wrote film scores and worked in the film and recording industries. Under the pseudonym Bent Fabric he wrote and recorded the pop tune *Alley Cat* in 1962, which became a hit recording.

ERIK WIEDEMANN

Faddis, Jon(athan) (*b* Oakland, CA, 24 July 1953). Trumpeter. He gained early professional experience playing with rhythm-and-blues bands in and around San Francisco, then in 1971 moved to New York to play with Lionel Hampton; after six months he joined the Thad Jones–Mel Lewis Orchestra, with which he toured internationally and recorded until 1975. During this period he also studied at the Manhattan School of Music (1972–3), worked with Gil Evans, Charles Mingus (1972–4), Chuck Mangione, and Dizzy Gillespie, and began to receive critical acclaim for his playing. He toured Europe with Gillespie in 1977 (when he performed and recorded at the Montreux International Jazz Festival) and again in 1983. After making only a few recordings as a leader he began to concentrate on studio work, then in 1984 formed his own quintet; the following year he recorded in a quintet led by McCoy Tyner and Jackie McLean. Faddis is renowned as a powerful high-note player; his solo work has often been compared to that of Gillespie, but after returning to public performances and the recording studio in 1984 he began to develop a more individual style.

SELECTED RECORDINGS

Duos with O. Peterson: *Oscar Peterson and Jon Faddis* (1975, Pablo 2310743)
As leader: *Youngblood* (1976, Pablo 2310765); *Legacy* (1985, Conc. 291)
As sideman: C. Mingus: *Mingus at Carnegie Hall* (1974, Atl. 1667); E. Barefield: *The Indestructible Eddie Barefield* (1977, FaD 113); D. Gillespie: *Montreux '77* (1977, Pablo 2308211)

BIBLIOGRAPHY

Feather–Gitler '70s
G. Kalbacher: "The Return of Jon Faddis," *DB*, li/10 (1984), 18 [discography]
G. Giddins: *Rhythm-a-ning: Jazz Tradition and Innovation in the '80s* (New York, and Oxford, England, 1985) [colln of previously pubd articles], 192
M. Richards: "Jon Faddis," *JJI*, xxxix/3 (1986), 10 [interview]

ROBERT DICKOW

Fagerquist, Don(ald A.) (*b* Worcester, MA, 6 Feb 1927; *d* Los Angeles, 24 Jan 1974). Trumpeter. He began his career in 1943 with Mal Hallett and then became a principal soloist with Gene Krupa's orchestra, with which he made several recordings from 1944 to 1950. He played and recorded with Artie Shaw's orchestra and in the Gramercy Five (1949–50) and was a member of Woody Herman's Third Herd (1951–2); he also led a group that accompanied Anita O'Day. Fagerquist played as a soloist with Les Brown in 1953 and later that year joined Dave Pell's octet, which was drawn from the members of Brown's band; he remained with Pell's group until 1959, making numerous recordings. During this time he also recorded with Shelly Manne (1953) and John Graas (1954). In 1956 he began to work at the Paramount film studios in Los Angeles, but he continued to play jazz, working with Leonard Feather (1956), Pete Rugolo (1956–61), the singer Mel Tormé (1956–7), Art Pepper (1957), Louie Bellson (1959), and Laurindo Almeida (1962), among others; he also recorded as a leader. He was one of the first and best trumpeters in West Coast jazz.

SELECTED RECORDINGS

As leader: *8 by 8* (1957, Mode 124)
As sideman: D. Pell: *The Irving Berlin Gallery* (1953, Trend 1003); J. Graas: *Jazz Studio 2* (1954, Decca 8079); M. Tormé: *Tormé Sings Astaire* (1956, Beth. 52); A. Pepper: *Art Pepper Plays Shorty Rogers and Others* (1957, PJ 896)

BIBLIOGRAPHY

FeatherE

FREDERICK A. BECK

Faire du boeuf (Fr.). To "jam"; that is, to take part in a JAM SESSION.

Fairweather, Al(astair) (*b* Edinburgh, 12 June 1927). Scottish trumpeter and bandleader. In the mid-1940s he formed a band with Sandy Brown, with whom he played until he moved to London in mid-1953. He spent a year with Cy Laurie and in 1954 he re-joined Brown's band, becoming its leader in 1958. After working with Acker Bilk (1966–8) he ceased full-time performing and became a teacher, although in the early 1970s he also wrote arrangements and played in Stan Daly's band. He worked with Stan Greig's London Jazz Big Band from 1975 into the 1980s; also in the 1980s he played in the band of the trumpeter Alan Littlejohn. Fairweather made several recordings as a leader and sideman; his playing may be heard on Brown's *McJazz* (1957, Nixa 9).

BIBLIOGRAPHY
D. Boulton: *Jazz in Britain* (London, 1958)
J. Dawson: "Al's Easing Back," *MM*, xlix (6 April 1974), 20
D. Fairweather: "Fairweather, Al," in I. Carr, D. Fairweather, and B. Priestley: *Jazz: the Essential Companion* (London, 1987)

DEREK COLLER

Fairweather, Digby [Richard John Charles] (*b* Rochford, England, 25 April 1946). English cornetist. After working with local bands he formed his first group, Dig's Half Dozen, in 1971. Thereafter he worked with the soprano saxophonist Eggy Ley and others, and from 1973 recorded occasionally as Alex Welsh's deputy in the latter's band. After becoming a full-time musician in 1977 he worked with the Midnite Follies Orchestra, the quartet Velvet, and the Pizza Express All-Stars, then formed his own quartet and a touring band dedicated to the music of Nat Gonella. As well as continuing to lead his own groups and work frequently as a sideman with others, notably the Alex Welsh Reunion Band (1983–7), Fairweather has been active as an author and broadcaster, and is a dedicated teacher. In 1979, with the pianist Stan Barker, he formed the educational charity Jazz College, which teaches improvisation in schools and colleges. With Ian Carr and Brian Priestley, he wrote *Jazz: the Essential Companion* (London, 1987). A solid lead player and a versatile soloist, Fairweather has a warm tone, a wide range, and a capacity for playing with considerable tenderness. He may be heard to advantage on *Let's Duet* (1984, Essex 4KL311), an album of duos with Barker.

BIBLIOGRAPHY
B. Long: "Digby Fairweather: a Jazz Natural," *JJI*, xxxiii/7 (1980), 9
D. Fairweather: "Strictly Instrumental," *JJI*, xxxiv/5 (1981), 12

CLARRIE HENLEY

Fake book [fakebook]. An informal collection of scores used by performing musicians. A fake book presents (either in loose-leaf or bound form) the music to standards and popular tunes; the contents may range in number from a few dozen pieces to well over a thousand. Many books include transcriptions of items still protected by copyright, and are therefore illegal; as a result fake books are ephemeral and often difficult to obtain, and many are sold by dealers who depend largely on word of mouth for their trade. Bandleaders sometimes create their own fake books which are used by their members alone. Legal collections, where copyright has been cleared with the original publishers of the tunes, are also in existence.

Fake books exist both as manuscript (the pages of which are then photographically reproduced for publication) and in printed form. The notation typically follows that of the lead sheet (*see* NOTATION, §2), though some books present more detailed information about one or more of the following: important voicings, inner parts, comping figures, and bass parts. Scores giving this level of detail are often transcribed from recordings, and are intended to assist the user in replicating the original performance as closely as possible. Many fake books, however, are much less reliable than this; some are notoriously inaccurate. They present simplified (and often simply incorrect) versions of melodies, and chord symbols that bear little relation to those that would be played by a professional musician. Performers thus tend to use fake books as skeletal guides to performance, and learn by means of oral tradition how to interpret the notation in an authentic jazz manner. There are, however, a few exceptions; one of these is *The Real Book*, which was published in Boston in the early 1970s and distributed in the area of the Berklee College of Music, and has reappeared in several informal editions into the 1980s. The title refers to the book's unusually high level of accuracy, though it is by no means definitive. It includes about 400 swing, bop, free-jazz, and jazz-rock pieces. A second volume of *The Real Book* was published around 1985. A widely used legal fake book, made with the advice and authorization of the composers, is *The World's Greatest Fake Book* (San Francisco, 1983), edited by Chuck Sher.

ROBERT WITMER

Fake fingering. *See* FALSE FINGERING.

Falay, Maffy [Ahmed Muvaffak] (*b* Izmir, Turkey, 30 Aug 1930). Turkish trumpeter. He first played jazz at clubs and parties while attending Ankara University in the early 1950s. He lived in Germany (1956–9) and then in Sweden, where he performed and recorded with Nils Lindberg; he also played and in 1960 recorded with Harry Arnold, the singer Boris Lindquist, and Arne Domnérus. With Quincy Jones he recorded (1961), performed at the Swedish Jazz Festival (1963), and collaborated on film music. He recorded in Germany with Francy Boland (1963) and Kurt Edelhagen (1964) and later made recordings, principally in Stockholm, with Bernt Rosengren (1969, 1971, 1973), George Russell (1971), Gunnar Nilsson (1971–2), and Don Cherry (1971). His group Sveda developed a fusion of Turkish music and bop and recorded two albums in 1972–3, including *Sveda* (1972, Caprice 31), with Rosengren as a principal soloist. (*Feather '60s*)

Fall off. A GLISS falling from the end of a note.

Fallon, Jack (Patrick) (*b* London, Canada, 13 Oct 1915). Canadian double bass player. He went to England as a member of the Canadian Air Force and settled there in 1946. After working with Ted Heath and the trumpeter Jack Jackson that year, he performed and recorded with George Shearing (1948) and played with visiting musicians, including Duke Ellington and Ray Nance, Django Reinhardt, and Maxine Sullivan (all 1948) and Mary Lou Williams (1953). In the mid-1950s he led the sextet In Town Tonight (1954–5), which included Dizzy Reece and Kathy Stobart and with which he recorded *The In-town Jazz Group* (1955, Decca LF1217). From around 1950 Fallon was active as a freelance player, sometimes doubling on violin and electric bass guitar; he recorded jazz with many leaders, including Ralph Sharon (1950, 1952), Alan Clare (in a duo, 1952), Joe Harriott and Derek Smith (both 1954), Eddie Thompson (1956), Humphrey Lyttelton (1957), Kenny Baker (1957–8), Tony Crombie (1958), Lennie Felix, Tubby Hayes, and Tony Kinsey (all 1959), and Archie Semple, Little Brother Montgomery, and Alex Welsh (all 1960). He was also active in other styles, playing country music regularly and in 1968 recording (on violin) with the Beatles. Fallon's most important association in the 1970s was with Lennie Felix, but in the 1980s he began to work regularly with Stan Greig, Digby Fairweather (1983–5), Wally Fawkes, and many others.

DIGBY FAIRWEATHER

False [alternate, fake, substitute] **fingering.** On a wind instrument, a non-standard fingering. False fingerings were traditionally used to allow the rapid execution of passages that would have been difficult or impossible to play with conventional fingerings. They alter the timbre of the instrument (sometimes radically) and often produce notes that are slightly out of tune. In classical music these effects are tolerated and corrected as far as possible, but in jazz they are often the reason for a player's adopting false fingerings, since they add variety and nuance to a line.

False fingerings are used in jazz principally by saxophonists. A common practice is to close the tone-holes below those needed to produce a certain note (fig.1); because the third key in the upper hand is not employed, the pitch (determined by the length of the vibrating air column) is hardly affected, but the timbre becomes muffled with the closing of the lower three holes. The alternation of conventional and false fingering in the course of a note or on successive reiterations of a single pitch creates a wa-wa effect. The same effect may be achieved by producing the note alternately in the normal way and as an overtone of a lower fundamental. By the skillful use of embouchure the tenor saxophonist may, for example, produce a sequence of notes written *c″* (sounding *b♭*), but alternately fingered *c″* and *c′*; the sounds produced are respectively clear and muffled. Early examples of the wa-wa produced by means of false fingering occur in the playing of Jimmy Dorsey in the 1920s, but the technique is associated particularly with Lester Young and its effects may be heard in his solo on Count Basie's *Lester Leaps in* (1939, Voc. 5118) (see Porter).

False fingerings are used not only in alternation with conventional fingerings, but also as a substitute for them, in order to vary the timbre on certain notes in a melodic phrase. Stanley Turrentine, for example, employs false fingering for *f‴* on the tenor saxophone (sounding *e♭″*), which gives the note a unique hollow sound; he exploits this effect on the highest note of the melody in *Pieces of Dreams*, on the LP of the same name (1974, Fan. 9465).

By extension the term "false fingering" is applied to the obtaining of pitches that lie above the normal range of the instrument by a combination of fingering and embouchure (though this usage is somewhat misleading since there are no "conventional" fingerings for such notes). For example, the fingering shown in fig.2 produces a pitch lying a major 3rd

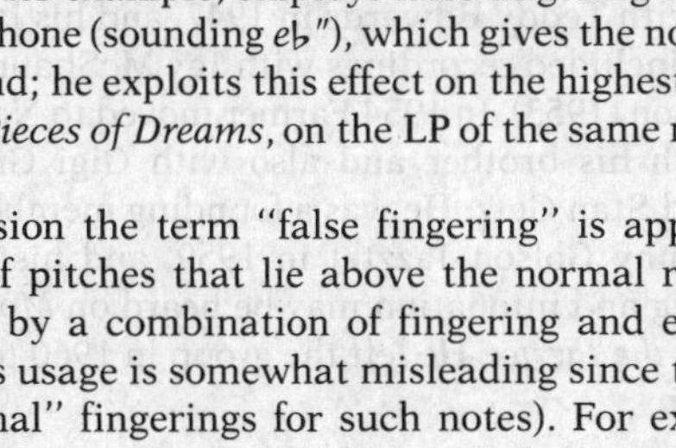

1. Fingerings for written A in the lower register of the saxophone: (a) conventional fingering, (b) false fingering

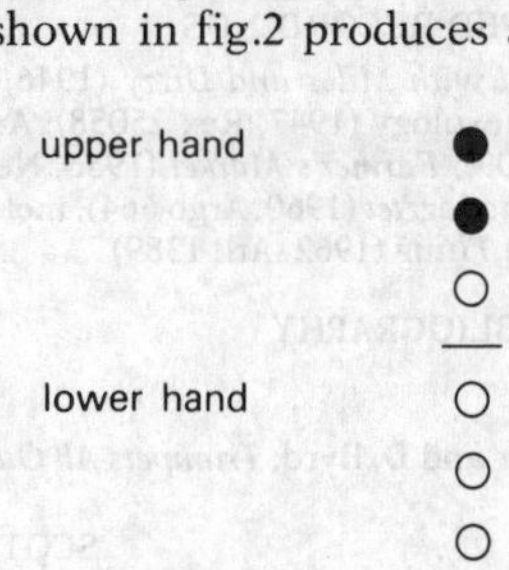

2. False fingering for written A in the highest register of the saxophone, which, in combination with a tight embouchure, produces a note a major 3rd above the "highest" note on the instrument

above the saxophone's "highest" note. Again Dorsey was a pioneer of this kind of false fingering in the 1920s, but a more notable example occurs near the end of Coleman Hawkins's famous improvisation on *Body and Soul* (1939, Bb 10523). From the time of John Coltrane the use of false fingerings to produce high notes has become common.

By comparison with woodwinds, valved brass instruments are far more dependent on the embouchure (especially in the high range) than on unusual fingerings to produce standard pitches, there being so few possible combinations of valves on a brass instrument compared with the combinations of keys available on a woodwind. Consequently uses of false fingerings are more conventional and far less significant for brass players than for saxophonists. There are nonetheless notable examples of the manipulation of timbre by means of unusual fingerings; for instance, the techniques used on the cornet by Bix Beiderbecke are explained in detail in Sudhalter, Evans, and Dean-Myatt.

BIBLIOGRAPHY

R. M. Sudhalter, P. R. Evans, and W. Dean-Myatt: *Bix: Man & Legend* (New Rochelle, NY, and London, 1974), appx C
L. Porter: *Lester Young* (Boston and London, 1985), 50

BARRY KERNFELD

Falzone, Sam [Salvatore Joseph] (*b* Buffalo, 20 Dec 1933). Tenor saxophonist, clarinetist, and flutist. He studied music at the SUNY campuses in Fredonia (BS 1960) and Buffalo. From 1964 to 1974 he played and recorded with Don Ellis; he also worked briefly with Buddy Rich (1968). From the mid-1970s he played and taught in Buffalo. His playing is exemplified by his performance on Ellis's album *Autumn* (1968, Col. CS9721). (*Feather–Gitler '70s*)

Famous. Record label. It was established in 1920 by the New York Recording Laboratories, who also owned Paramount. All known items in its catalogue were also issued (either previously or simultaneously) on Paramount or associated labels. It seems likely that records on Famous were for sale in a limited territory only, but details of such an arrangement have never been discovered. The label ceased to be used in 1924.

BIBLIOGRAPHY

M. Wyler: "A Glimpse of the Past, 8: Famous," *Sv*, no.13 (1967), 14
B. Rust: *The American Record Label Book* (New Rochelle, NY, 1978), 122

Famous Door (i). Nightclub in New York; the name was subsequently adopted by a club in New Orleans. *See* NIGHTCLUBS AND OTHER VENUES.

Famous Door (ii). Record company and label. The company was established by Harry Lim in 1972, and was named for the Famous Door nightclub. It issued recordings by such swing and bop musicians as George Barnes (1972–3), Bill Watrous (1972–3, 1980, 1982), Mundell Lowe (1972, 1974), Zoot Sims (1973), Red Norvo (1974–5, 1977), Eddie Barefield, Scott Hamilton, Dave McKenna, and Charlie Ventura (all 1977), Butch Miles (1977–82), and George Masso (1978, 1981).

Fantasy. Record company and label. The company was established in 1949 in Berkeley, California, by the brothers Max and Sol Weiss. The label has been of only modest importance to jazz; while it has been used to issue recordings by such musicians as Dave Brubeck (1948–54), Gerry Mulligan (1952–3),

Cal Tjader (1954–61), Vince Guaraldi (1955–66), Earl Hines (1956), Duke Ellington (intermittently, 1966–71), Cannonball Adderley, Kenny Burrell (both 1973–5), Flora Purim (1973–6), Bill Evans (ii) (1973–7), and Freddie Hubbard (1981), few of these albums represent the musicians' best work. The label is far better known for recordings of the comedian Lenny Bruce made in the late 1950s, and for albums in the late 1960s and early 1970s by the rock group Creedence Clearwater Revival.

Fantasy's significance as a jazz company lies instead in its acquisition or formation of other labels, and its programs of reissues. In 1955 Saul Zaentz joined the company, which as a result leased the catalogue of the label Debut, owned by Zaentz and his wife with Charles Mingus and Maz Roach. In 1964 Fantasy established a subsidiary label, GALAXY, and in 1967 Zaentz became president of the company when he led a group of investors who purchased it from the Weiss brothers. Shortly thereafter Fantasy began acquiring the catalogues of other labels. These included Prestige (1971), Riverside (1972), and MILESTONE (1973); the last-named remains active under Fantasy's ownership, recording new material. Orrin Keepnews, formerly the owner of Milestone and one of the joint owners of Riverside, was engaged in 1972 to supervise all jazz productions. He also instituted a highly regarded series of nearly 200 double (and sometimes triple) albums that drew principally upon material from Prestige and Riverside, but also from Milestone and Fantasy.

In the early 1980s Fantasy acquired CONTEMPORARY (which has also continued to make new recordings) and its subsidiary, Good Time Jazz. By this time the company had become one of the world's largest distributors of jazz recordings, and in 1985 its catalogues expanded yet further when it undertook distribution for Keepnews's label LANDMARK. In 1983 Fantasy established the subsidiary label Original Jazz Classics, which rendered the earlier reissue series obsolete by offering instead facsimile reproductions of albums from Contemporary, Debut, Fantasy, Jazz Workshop, and, most importantly, Prestige and Riverside. By 1987 the series contained over 300 albums; a companion series, Original Blues Classics, was also well under way.

Farlow, Tal(madge Holt) (*b* Greensboro, NC, 7 June 1921). Electric guitarist. He was self-taught on guitar and began playing professionally at the relatively late age of 22. In 1949 he joined Red Norvo's trio. Shortly afterwards Charles Mingus joined them; the combination proved extremely popular by jazz standards, and brought Farlow instant acclaim (for illustration *see* MINGUS, CHARLES). He left Norvo in 1953 to join Artie Shaw's reconstituted Gramercy Five for six months, and then to lead his own small groups. From 1958, when he married, he entered semiretirement. Thereafter he continued to study and perfect his art, but performed only occasionally in public, acquiring a legendary reputation among jazz guitarists. In the early 1980s Farlow began to appear more regularly in public. He was involved in the making of a documentary film, *Talmadge Farlow* (1981), performed once more with Norvo's trio, and toured widely in the USA and Europe; he played at the Grande Parade du Jazz Nice in 1984.

Farlow was a leading guitarist in the early bop style, with phenomenally fast execution (acquired, he claimed, to keep pace with Norvo's virtuoso vibraphone playing) and a rapid flow of ideas. He has been admired for the unusual intervals in his improvised lines, his original handling of artificial harmonics, and his gentle touch (even at exceedingly fast tempos), achieved partly by using his thumb instead of a plectrum.

Oral history material in *NjR*.

SELECTED RECORDINGS

As leader: *Tal Farlow Quartet* (1953, BN 5042); *The Artistry of Tal Farlow* (1954, Norg. 1014); *The Interpretations of Tal Farlow* (1955, Norg. 1027); *Tal Farlow Returns* (1969, Prst. 7732); *Trilogy* (1976, IC 1099); *Chromatic Palette* (1981, Conc. 154); *Cookin' on all Burners* (1982, Conc. 204); *The Legendary Tal Farlow* (1984, Conc. 266)

As sideman with R. Norvo: Move! (1950, Dis. 145)

BIBLIOGRAPHY

I. Gitler: "Whatever Happened to Tal Farlow?," *DB*, xxx/31 (1963), 18
B. Yelin: "Tal Farlow," *The Guitar Player Book* (Saratoga, nr Los Gatos, CA, and New York, 1978, 2/1979) [colln of previously pubd articles], 95
B. Korall: "Tal Farlow: Turning away from Fame," *DB*, xlvi/4 (1979), 21
A. Berle: "Tal Farlow: Return of a Jazz Legend," *GP*, xiv/7 (1980), 18
L. Tomkins: "Tal Farlow: My Approach to the Guitar," *CI*, xx/4 (1981), 20 [interview]
M. D. Watson: "Complete Control: a Survey of Tal Farlow's Work and Recordings," *JJI*, xxxiv (1981), no.4, p.12; no.5, p.20; no.6, p.22
L. Jeske: "Tal Farlow: Have Guitar, Won't Travel," *DB*, xlix/1 (1982), 24
L. Tomkins: "Signs of a Saner Scene: Tal Farlow," *CI*, xx/7 (1982), 12 [interview]
J. Ferguson: "Visualization: Building Melodies with Diminished Lines: a Private Lesson with Tal Farlow," *GP*, xviii/7 (1984), 68

J. BRADFORD ROBINSON

Farmer, Addison (Gerald) (*b* Council Bluffs, IA, 21 Aug 1928; *d* New York, 20 Feb 1963). Double bass player, twin brother of Art Farmer. He grew up in Phoenix, Arizona, and in 1945 moved to Los Angeles, where early the following year he played with Miles Davis and Charlie Parker. He made his first commercial recording with Teddy Edwards in 1947, and his later work as a freelance included recordings with Jay McShann (1948) and Gerald Wilson (1953). In 1954 Farmer moved to New York and worked with his brother and also with Gigi Gryce, Teddy Charles, and Stan Getz. He was a founding member of the Art Farmer–Benny Golson Jazztet in 1959, and his impeccable time-keeping and intonation may be heard on *Mox nix* on the album *Meet the Jazztet*. He left the group in 1960 to work with Mose Allison.

SELECTED RECORDINGS

As sideman: on C. Parker: *Bird with Miles and Dizzy* (1946, Queen 017), Anthropology; T. Edwards: Rexology (1947, Rex 25058); A. Farmer: *Art Farmer Quintet* (1955, Prst. 209); *Farmer's Market* (1956, NewJ 8203); A. Farmer and B. Golson: *Meet the Jazztet* (1960, Argo 664), incl. Mox nix; M. Allison: *I Don't Worry About a Thing* (1962, Atl. 1389)

BIBLIOGRAPHY

FeatherE
Obituary, *DB*, xxx/9 (1963), 11
I. Gitler: Liner notes, Art Farmer and D. Byrd: *Trumpets All Out* (Prst. 7344, 1965)

SCOTT DEVEAUX

Farmer, Art(hur Stewart) (*b* Council Bluffs, IA, 21 Aug 1928). Flugelhorn player and trumpeter. He studied piano and violin, then bass tuba, and first worked professionally in Los Angeles in 1945; during the early part of his career the trumpet was his principal instrument. On the West Coast he belonged to big bands led by Horace Henderson, Floyd Ray, Benny Carter, Gerald Wilson, and Lionel Hampton (for a year and a half from the autumn of 1952) and worked with the rhythm-and-blues drummer Johnny Otis, Joe Turner (ii), Wardell Gray, Hampton Hawes, Teddy Edwards, Sonny Criss, and Frank Morgan. After moving to New York in 1953 he worked in Teddy Charles's group New Directions (with Charles Mingus and Teo Macero) and in small groups led by Horace Silver and Gerry Mulligan (for illustration *see* RECORDING, fig.5), led a band with Gigi Gryce, and performed and recorded with George Russell; he also performed (in Paris) and recorded with Tony Ortega. In 1959 he formed a sextet with Benny Golson called the JAZZTET,

Art Farmer (flugelhorn) and Benny Golson (tenor saxophone)

and over the next few years he gradually turned from the trumpet to the flugelhorn, at the same time forging a gentle, lyrical style. After the Jazztet disbanded in 1962 he worked principally as a leader; he led a group with Jim Hall (to 1964) and in 1968 moved to Vienna, where during the late 1960s and 1970s he performed and recorded with the Clarke–Boland Big Band, Peter Herbolzheimer, and the big band of the Österreichischer Rundfunk (to 1977). Later he led a quartet (which toured the USA, Europe, and Japan) and a quintet (which toured Austria, Germany and Switzerland), re-formed the Jazztet (1982), with which he toured and recorded, and performed with Chico Freeman (1983). A collection of nine transcriptions of flugelhorn solos by Farmer has been published by D. Erjavec (*Art Farmer Solos*, Rottenburg, Baden-Württemberg, Germany, 1984).

SELECTED RECORDINGS

As leader: Evening in Paris/Elephant Walk (1954, Prst. 894); *Evening in Casablanca* (1955, Prst. 7017); with D. Byrd: *Two Trumpets* (1957, Prst. 7062); of Jazztet (with B. Golson): *Meet the Jazztet* (1960, Argo 664); *The Time and the Place* (1967, Col. CS9449); *Talk to me* (1974, Pye 18465); *On the Road* (1976, Cont. 7636); *Warm Valley* (1982, Conc. 212)

BIBLIOGRAPHY

G. Lees: "Farmer, Golson, and the Rise of the Jazztet," *DB*, xxvii/18 (1960), 20
L. Tomkins: "Personally Speaking: Art Farmer," *Crescendo*, iv/3 (1965), 16 [interview]
V. Wilmer: "Introspective Art," *JB*, ii/8 (1965), 20
D. Morgenstern: "Art Farmer and the Imperatives of the Small Group," *DB*, xxxiii/12 (1966), 22
L. Lystedt: "Art Farmer: Ambivalent Expatriate," *DB*, xxxvii/4 (1970), 18
V. Wilmer: *Jazz People* (London, Indianapolis, and New York, 1970/*R*1985)
B. Smith: "Art Farmer," *Coda*, no.144 (1976), 2 [interview]
"Art Farmer," *SJ*, xxxiii/4 (1979), 232 [discography]
L. Tomkins: "International Individualist of Jazz: Art Farmer," *CI*, xxi/10 (1983), 20; contd as "Art Farmer: Finding the Flugelhorn's Voice," xxi/11 (1983), 6
D. Erjavec: *Art Farmer Solos* (Rottenburg, Baden-Württemberg, Germany, 1984) [transcrs.]
D. Pagani: "Art Farmer: Interview," *Cadence*, x/5 (1984), 10
D. Waterhouse: "Gentleman Farmer," *JJI*, xxxvii (1984), no.2, p.8; no.3, p.14
J. Levenson: "The Understated Eloquence of Art Farmer," *DB*, lv/1 (1988), 22 [incl. discography]

LEE JESKE/R

Farras, Josep-María (*b* Tarrasa, Spain, 1942). Spanish trumpeter. He was one of the founders of a club, the Jazz cava, in Tarrasa, and played with most of the local groups there, including Swing Society (1959), the Modern Jazz Quintet (1966), and the Modern Jazz Sextet (1970s). He may be heard to advantage on *Israel*, by the Modern Jazz Sextet, on the album *Jam Session al natural* (1974, Nuria Feliu Productions 22893). In 1974 Farras was named "best soloist" at the San Sebastián jazz festival; he is considered one of the finest Spanish trumpeters of his generation. Although he prefers to play in the bop style, he is also comfortable with more traditional idioms and has performed in dixieland groups. Miles Davis, Lee Morgan, and Clifford Brown are the main influences upon his playing.

ALFREDO PAPO

Farrell, Joe [Firrantello, Joseph Carl] (*b* Chicago Heights, IL, 16 Dec 1937; *d* Los Angeles, 10 Jan 1986). Tenor saxophonist and flutist. Several members of his family were musicians, and he took up clarinet at the age of 11. In 1953 he began studying tenor saxophone in Chicago, and, although Charlie Parker, Sonny Rollins, and John Coltrane were major influences upon his playing, he was primarily interested in the cool-jazz style of Stan Getz. After graduating from the University of Illinois with a degree in music education (1959) he moved to New York, where he worked with Maynard Ferguson (1960–61) and Slide Hampton (1962); he also recorded with Charles Mingus (1960) and Dizzy Reece (1962). Later he performed with Jaki Byard (1965), the Thad Jones–Mel Lewis Orchestra (1966–9), and Elvin Jones (1967–70). As a freelance Farrell made several studio recordings accompanying jazz and popular musicians; he recorded his first album as a leader in 1970. Thereafter he moved to Los Angeles and performed with his own quartet and with an 18-piece band. His modal style, which incorporated inflections of Latin jazz, blended well with the approach of RETURN TO FOREVER, a group he joined in 1971. He played jazz-rock for much of the 1970s, but in 1979 he became a member of Mingus Dynasty, with which he toured the USA and Europe, and returned to a more lyrical jazz-oriented style. He recorded as a leader with Louis Hayes in 1983, and toured Europe with JoAnne Brackeen the following year.

SELECTED RECORDINGS

As leader: *Joe Farrell Quartet* (1970, CTI 6003); *Outback* (1972, CTI 6014); *Moon Germs* (1972, CTI 6023); *Penny Arcade* (1973, CTI 6034); with G. Benson: *Benson and Farrell* (1976, CTI 6069); *Skateboard Park* (1979, Xan. 174); *Sonic Text* (1979, Cont. 14002)

As sideman: C. Mingus: *Pre-Bird* (1960, Mer. 60627); J. Byard: *Live at Lennie's* (1965, Prst. 7419, 7477); E. Jones: *Puttin' it Together* (1968, BN 84282); *The Ultimate* (1969, BN 84305); C. Corea: *Return to Forever* (1973, ECM 1022); *Light as a Feather* (1973, Pol. 5525)

BIBLIOGRAPHY

I. Gitler: "Joe Farrell: Twice Blessed," *DB*, xxxv/10 (1968), 16
L. Hicock: "No Ordinary Joe: Joe Farrell," *DB*, xli/6 (1974), 13
H. Matuszewska: "What Joe Farrel [*sic*] Thinks About," *JF* [intl edn], no.30 (1974), 45
M. Zwerin: "Joe Farrell: up from under the Bridge," *The Wire*, no.18 (1985), 39

CATHERINE COLLINS

Farreras, Joe [Josep] (*b* Barcelona, 16 April 1916). Spanish drummer. He played guitar and mandolin as a youth, and became interested in jazz after hearing recordings in bars. He began playing drums in the mid-1930s; when the civil war broke out in 1936 he joined the crew of a cargo boat and traveled extensively, playing drums at ports whenever the opportunity arose. In the 1940s he began playing professionally with jazz groups in Barcelona, and during the 1950s he founded the Conjunto Jam Session del Hot Club de Barcelona, a group that included many of the best Catalan jazz musicians. He also played frequently with Don Byas and George Johnson when they visited the city. From 1965 to 1972 illness forced him to interrupt his career. Although he played again in the mid-1970s he finally retired in 1978. He was one of the most enthusiastic and influential Spanish jazz musicians.

ALFREDO PAPO

Farrow, Ernie [Ernest] (*b* Huntington, WV, 13 Nov 1928; *d* ?Detroit, 14 July 1969). Double bass player, brother of Alice Coltrane. He performed with Yusef Lateef from the early 1950s, and after playing with Terry Gibbs (1954) and Stan Getz (1955) he recorded several albums with Lateef (1957–64, including *Eastern Sounds*, 1961, Mdsv. 22). He also played with Barry Harris in Detroit (from the 1950s) and New York (from 1960) and with Red Garland (1960); he recorded with the pianist John Williams (1955), Harris (1960), and Gibbs (1963). He led bands in Detroit from 1964. (*FeatherE*; *Feather–Gitler '70s*)

Fat Man. Nickname of CHARLIE TURNER.

Fatool, Nick [Nicholas] (*b* Millbury, MA, 2 Jan 1915). Drummer. He studied and began his career in Providence, Rhode Island, then worked with Joe Haymes in New York (1937) and with the pianist Don Bestor in Dallas (1938). In 1939 he returned to New York to play briefly with Buddy Hackett before joining Benny Goodman in Cleveland (as Lionel Hampton's replacement); he made his first recordings with Goodman's band in August 1939, and also recorded in groups led by Goodman's sidemen Ziggy Elman and Toots Mondello (both 1939) and with Hampton (1940). In 1940–41 he toured extensively with Artie Shaw's band, then played with Claude Thornhill. Thereafter Fatool performed and recorded with many popular jazzmen, among them Les Brown and Jan Savitt (both 1942) and the guitarist Alvino Rey (1942–3). After moving in 1943 to Los Angeles, where he was a studio musician, he recorded with Billy Butterfield (1944), Harry James (1945, 1949, 1953), Erroll Garner (1946), Bob Crosby (1949–51), Louis Armstrong (1949, 1951), George Van Eps (1949, 1956), Jess Stacy (1950–51, 1954–5), Tommy Dorsey (1951), Matty Matlock (1951–8), Ray Anthony (1955), and Glen Gray (*c*1958–*c*1962); he also played on several film soundtracks, including *Pete Kelly's Blues* (1955) and *The Five Pennies* (1959). Later he toured the Orient with Crosby (1964) and played and recorded with Pete Fountain (1962–5), the Dukes of Dixieland (1964), and other well-known dixieland groups. He continued to work in and around Los Angeles into the 1980s, and in 1981 toured Europe with Crosby.

Fatool's early style reflects the gradual trend during the latter part of the swing era towards the use of well-disciplined accompaniment patterns (usually on the hi-hat) and a steady quadruple beat on the bass drum. Following the dixieland techniques of the 1950s onwards, his later work features ride-cymbal rhythms and syncopated fills and solos.

For illustration *see* BANDS, fig.4.

SELECTED RECORDINGS

As sideman: B. Goodman: There'll be some changes made/Jumpin' at the Woodside (1939, Col. 35210); The Sheik of Araby (1939, Polygon 6007); A. Shaw: This is Romance/Pyramid (1940, Vic. 27343); R. Anthony: *Big Band Dixieland* (1955, Cap. T678); G. Gray: *Sounds of the Great Bands* (*c*1958, Cap. W1022); P. Fountain: *Pete's Place* (1964, Coral 757453); B. Bigard: *Clarinet Gumbo* (1973, RCA APLI–1744); J. Lesberg: *Hollywood Swing* (1977, FaD 120)

BIBLIOGRAPHY

ChiltonW; *FeatherE*; *Feather '60s*; *Feather–Gitler '70s*
"Petite encyclopedia des drummers," *Jh*, no.291 (1973), 32

T. DENNIS BROWN

Favors, Malachi [Favors Magoustous, Brother Malachi] (*b* Chicago, 27 Aug 1937). Double bass player. He played double bass from the age of 15. As a bop musician he recorded with Andrew Hill (*c*1955) and performed with Dizzy Gillespie and Freddie Hubbard. He was a member of Muhal Richard Abrams's Experimental Band from 1961, and from 1966 he played in Roscoe Mitchell's quartets and trios, which evolved into the ART ENSEMBLE OF CHICAGO (AEC) when the musicians moved to Paris in 1969. Favors is associated principally with the AEC, with which he returned to the USA in 1971 and settled in Chicago, but he has also pursued independent activities; he recorded with Archie Shepp, Sunny Murray, and Dewey Redman in Paris (all in 1969), and led a quintet in Chicago in the early 1980s. By the mid-1970s he had added the prefix "Brother" and the surname "Magoustous" to his name. In addition to double bass, Favors plays zither, melodica, harmonica, banjo, and percussion, and contributes a range of vocal effects to the AEC's performances; the group's eclectic, theatrical repertory includes compositions by him.

SELECTED RECORDINGS

As unaccompanied soloist: *Natural and the Spiritual* (1977, AECO 003)
Duos with M. R. Abrams: *Sightsong* (1975, BS 0003)
As sideman: R. Mitchell: *Sound* (1966, Del. 408); L. Bowie: *Numbers 1 and 2* (1967, Nessa 1); R. Mitchell: *Congliptious* (1968, Nessa 2); S. Murray: *Live at Moers Festival* (1979, Moers 01054)
For further recordings *see* ART ENSEMBLE OF CHICAGO.

BIBLIOGRAPHY

V. Wilmer: *As Serious as Your Life: the Story of the New Jazz* (London, 1977, rev. 1980)
B. Case: "Favors: Bass Basic," *MM*, liv (19 May 1979), 52
R. Zabor: "Profile: the Art Ensemble," *Musician, Player, and Listener*, no.17 (1979), 39
E. Janssens and H. de Craen: *Art Ensemble of Chicago Discography: Unit and Members* (Brussels, 1983) [incl. list of compositions]

BARRY KERNFELD

Favre, Pierre (*b* Le Locle, Neuchâtel, Switzerland, 2 June 1937). Swiss drummer and percussionist. He taught himself to play drums and worked professionally from the age of 17; he played successively in bop and dixieland groups, from around 1955 with such American musicians as Albert Nicholas and Lil Armstrong, and from 1957 as a drummer and percussionist with the orchestra of Radio Basel. In the early 1960s he played with Bud Powell, Booker Ervin, and Benny Bailey and formed a trio with the pianist Joel Vandroogenbroeck and the double bass player Erich Peter; he then worked for Paiste & Sohn, a firm of cymbal and gong makers, in Nottwil, Switzerland. Around 1966 he became interested in free jazz; he formed a trio with Irène Schweizer and George Mraz (later replaced by Peter Kowald), which became a quartet when Evan Parker belonged to the group in 1968–9. Favre played with Peter Brötzmann, John Stevens, and Manfred Schoof in the late 1960s and performed and recorded as an unaccompanied soloist from 1969. Later he worked with the composers Urs-Peter Schneider and Rainer Boesch, the avant-garde performers Emmy Henz and Gertrud Schneider, the poet Pierre Imhasly, from 1978 with T. V. Gopalakrishnan, a player of the *mrdaṅga* (a set of tuned, double-headed Indian drums) with whom he gave a series of annual concerts, and from 1980 with the singer Tamia, with whom he toured the USA and Canada in 1985; he also led a percussion group, the Drum Orchestra, of which Paul Motian and Nana Vasconcelos were members. Favre's style of playing is melodic and reflects his interest in diverse folk traditions; his trap set is supplemented by a wide array of cymbals, gongs, and bells, and he often uses such unconventional beaters as bamboo sticks, pipes, rubber balls, and knitting needles.

SELECTED RECORDINGS

As unaccompanied soloist: *Mountain Wind* (1978, Gemini 1044)
As leader: *Santana* (1968, Favre 1); *Pierre Favre Quartett* (1969, Wergo 80004); *Arrivederci/Le Chouartse* (1980, HH 22); *Singing Drums* (1984, ECM 1274)
As sideman with M. Waldron: *Black Glory* (1971, Enja 2004)

BIBLIOGRAPHY

ReclamsJ
P. Carles: "Pierre Favre," *Jm*, no.216 (1973), 27

ROBERT J. IANNAPOLLO

Fawkes, Wally [Walter] (*b* Vancouver, Canada, 21 June 1924). English clarinetist of Canadian birth. He grew up in England, and was self-taught. In 1944 he joined George Webb's Dixielanders, with which he performed and recorded during the mid-1940s. He was one of the founding members of Humphrey Lyttelton's band in 1948. From this time Fawkes also worked as a cartoonist for the *Daily Mail* and various magazines, using the pseudonym Trog. During the next eight years he toured, recorded, and broadcast prolifically with Lyttelton; his own composition *Trog's Blues* (1951, Parl. R3379) offers a good example of his style. Fawkes also made recordings as the leader of a group with the alto saxophonist Bruce Turner, a colleague from Lyttelton's band (1954–6). Thereafter he formed his own ensemble, the Troglodytes, which included Lennie Felix, and performed and recorded frequently in the late 1950s. Fawkes was mainly active as a cartoonist in the 1960s, but he also worked with Lyttelton and others. In the early and mid-1970s he played with John Chilton's Feetwarmers. Thereafter he worked with several bands in London; he has continued to perform and record as a freelance into the mid-1980s.

BIBLIOGRAPHY

Feather '60s
H. Lyttelton: *I Play as I Please: the Memoirs of an Old Etonian Trumpeter* (London, 1954)
D. Fairweather: "Fawkes, Wally," in I. Carr, D. Fairweather, and B. Priestley: *Jazz: the Essential Companion* (London, 1987)

SALLY-ANN WORSFOLD

Fazola, Irving [Butch; Faz; Prestopnik, Irving Henry] (*b* New Orleans, 10 Dec 1912; *d* New Orleans, 20 March 1949). Clarinetist and saxophonist. His pseudonym may derive from the solfeggio notes "fa, sol, la." He studied C-melody saxophone and clarinet from the age of 13. In New Orleans he performed with the drummer Candy Candido, Louis Prima, Sharkey Bonano, Armand Hug, and, from 1935, Ben Pollack. In 1936 he went north with Pollack's orchestra. Thereafter he returned intermittently to New Orleans while playing in the big bands of Augie Schellang (1937), Gus Arnheim (1937), Glenn Miller (1937–8), Pollack (1938), Bob Crosby (1938–40), Jimmy McPartland (1940), Tony Almerico (1940–41), Claude Thornhill (1941), Muggsy Spanier (1942), Teddy Powell (1942–3), and Horace Heidt (1943). Owing to poor health he then resettled in New Orleans, where he appeared with Almerico and Louis and Leon Prima, and led various small groups.

An outstanding clarinetist, Fazola excelled not only in dixieland counterpoint and the blues but also in lyrical numbers, which displayed his pure, liquid sound and seemingly effortless execution. Ulanov wrote that he had "perhaps the most polished concept of the New Orleans reed tradition," and his presence in New Orleans during the 1940s influenced Pete Fountain. He is best known, however, for his work with Crosby's band the Bob Cats (for illustration *see* CROSBY, BOB). Fazola's shortcomings as a saxophonist apparently inspired Glenn Miller to revive the distinctive sound of the reed section led by clarinet, which he had developed when writing arrangements for Ray Noble.

SELECTED RECORDINGS

As leader: Sweet Lorraine (1945, Key. 624); Jazz me Blues (1945, Key. 658)
As sideman: B. Crosby: My Inspiration (1938, Decca 2209); My Inspiration (1939), first issued on *The Summer of '39: Bob Crosby's Camel Caravan* (1939, Legend 1037); Peruna (1939, Decca 2789); J. Stacy: Breeze (1939, Vars. 8121); B. Crosby: Jazz me Blues (1940, Decca 3040); M. Spanier: Hesitating Blues (1942, Decca 4271)

BIBLIOGRAPHY

ChiltonW
G. Hoefer: "Faz Greatest White Blues Man," *DB*, xvi/9 (1949) 12
B. Ulanov: *A History of Jazz in America* (New York, 1952/R1972)
A. Rose and E. Souchon: *New Orleans Jazz: a Family Album* (Baton Rouge, LA, 1967, rev. and enlarged 3/1984)
B. Esposito: "'Riding on a Blue Note' with Faz, Pete, and Eddie," *SL*, xxvi (win. 1974), 17
G. Simon: *Glenn Miller and his Orchestra* (New York, n.d. [1974])
J. Chilton: *Stomp off, Let's Go! The Story of Bob Crosby's Bob Cats & Big Band* (London, 1983), esp. chaps. 5, 21

JEFFREY COOPER

Feather, Leonard (Geoffrey) (*b* London, 13 Sept 1914). Writer, composer, and arranger. He attended St. Paul's School and University College in London (1920–32), studied piano and clarinet, and taught himself arranging. He produced recordings and wrote compositions for Benny Carter and George Chisholm in London, and after moving to the USA in the mid-1930s for Duke Ellington and Louis Armstrong. In the 1940s he organized jazz concerts at Carnegie Hall. He produced the first recordings of Dinah Washington, George Shearing, and Sarah Vaughan and wrote arrangements (for Count Basie), many blues songs (including *Evil Gal Blues* and *Salty Papa Blues*, recorded by Washington, *Blowtop Blues*, recorded by Washington and Lionel Hampton, and *Born on a Friday*, recorded by Cleo Laine), ballads (such as *Signing Off*, recorded by Vaughan, Ella Fitzgerald, and André Previn), and jazz compositions (including *I Remember Bird*, recorded by Cannonball Adderley, Phil Woods, and Sonny Stitt, and *Twelve Tone Blues*, recorded by Yusef Lateef). He also worked as a producer, commentator, and writer for radio and television programs on jazz. Feather has taught at Loyola Marymount University (1972–4), the University of California, Riverside (1973), California State University, Northridge, and UCLA (1987–8). He is perhaps best known as an author of scholarly works on jazz and as a columnist for the *Los Angeles Times*; because of his eminence as a writer his musical talent is often overlooked, yet it contributes much to his skillful reviews and articles, which have appeared in numerous jazz and popular periodicals, including *Metronome*, *Esquire*, *Down Beat*, *Playboy*, and *Jazz Times*.

RECORDED COMPOSITIONS
(selective list)

Recorded by D. Washington: Evil Gal Blues (1943, Key. 605)
Recorded by L. Hampton: Blowtop Blues (1945, Decca 23792)
Recorded by E. Fitzgerald: Signing Off, on *Clap Hands, Here Comes Charlie* (1961, Verve 64053)
Recorded by Y. Lateef: Twelve Tone Blues, on *Live at Pep's* (1964, Imp. 69)
Recorded by C. Adderley: I Remember Bird, on *Walk Tall* (1967, Cap. ST2822)

WRITINGS
(selective list)

Inside Be-bop (New York, 1949/*R*1977 as *Inside Jazz*)
The Encyclopedia of Jazz (New York, 1955, rev. and enlarged 2/1960/*R*1984) [*FeatherE*]
The Encyclopedia Yearbook of Jazz (New York, 1956)
The Book of Jazz: a Guide to the Entire Field (New York, 1957, 2/1965 as *The Book of Jazz from Then till Now: a Guide to the Entire Field*)
The New Yearbook of Jazz (New York, 1958)
with J. Tracy: *Laughter from the Hip: the Lighter Side of Jazz* (New York, 1963/*R*1979)
The Encyclopedia of Jazz in the Sixties (New York, 1966/*R*1986) [*Feather '60s*]
with J. Chilton and M. Jones: *Salute to Satchmo* (London, 1970)
From Satchmo to Miles (New York, 1972)
with I. Gitler: *The Encyclopedia of Jazz in the Seventies* (New York, 1976/*R*1987) [*Feather–Gitler '70s*]
The Passion for Jazz (New York, 1980)
The Jazz Years: Earwitness to an Era (London and New York, 1986)

BIBLIOGRAPHY

L. Feather: "Life with Feather," *DB*, xxxi (1964), no.21, p.18; no.30, p.22; xxxii (1965), no.5, p.25; no.8, p.25; no.15, p.19; no.19, p.20; xxxiii (1966), no.3, p.26; no.15, p.16
H. Lucraft: "The Leonard Feather Story," *Radio Free Jazz* (June 1979), 16

FRANKIE NEMKO

Featherstone, Benny [Geoffrey Benjamin] (*b* Brown's Creek, Tasmania, Australia, 30 July 1912; *d* Melbourne, Australia, 6 April 1977). Australian trumpeter and drummer. He grew up in Melbourne and at the age of 17 worked with Joe Watkins. The many instruments he played besides his principal ones included trombone, tuba, piano, and double bass; he also sang. He made recordings of hot dance music with the Beachcombers (among them *Beachcombers Blues*, 1930, Broadcast De Luxe) and played in bands in which he was billed as "Australia's Louis Armstrong." Following a visit to England (1933–4) he returned to Melbourne, where he joined Art Chapman, led groups at the Rex cabaret and the 40 Club, and played an important part in the Fawkner Park Kiosk jazz sessions (1937–40). He served in the merchant marines then led his own group, the Dixielanders (1943), and played at American service clubs in Mackay, Queensland (1944). In 1945, while visiting the USA, he played informally with Jimmie Lunceford. After the war he played less and later (1958–75) worked as a shipping clerk.

BIBLIOGRAPHY

A. Bisset: *Black Roots, White Flowers: a History of Jazz in Australia* (Sydney, 1976), 50
B. Johnson: "Featherstone, Geoffrey Benjamin (Benny)," *The Oxford Companion to Australian Jazz* (Melbourne, Australia, 1987)

BRUCE JOHNSON

Featherstonhaugh, Buddy [Rupert Edward Lee] (*b* Paris, 4 Oct 1909; *d* London, 12 July 1976). English tenor and baritone saxophonist. He was educated in England and first worked professionally in 1927 with the singer Pat O'Malley. He played with Spike Hughes (1930–32), recording two versions of *Buddy's Wednesday Outing*, a piece written for him by Hughes. In 1932 he toured Britain with the pianist Billy Mason in a back-up group for Louis Armstrong, and the following year he recorded with his own band the Cosmopolitans with Fletcher Allen as a sideman; later he recorded with Valaida Snow (1935) and Benny Carter (1936–7). While in the RAF he led a group that included Vic Lewis, the trombonist Don McAffer, and Jack Parnell; later it recorded as the BBC Radio Rhythm Club Sextet (1943–5). After the war Featherstonhaugh toured Iceland (1946), then, after a long period of inactivity, recorded as the leader of a bop quintet playing baritone saxophone (1956); his sidemen included the trumpeter Leon Calvert and the tenor saxophonist Roy Sidwell, later replaced by Kenny Wheeler and Bobby Wellins. He made a tour of the Middle East in 1957 and then retired from jazz.

SELECTED RECORDINGS

As leader: Jamboree Jive (1943, HMV B9358)
As sideman: S. Hughes: Buddy's Wednesday Outing (1932, Parl. R1172); Buddy's Wednesday Outing (1932, Decca F3089); B. Carter: Swingin' the Blues (1936, Voc. S5); Gin and Jive (1937, Voc. S57)

BIBLIOGRAPHY

FeatherE
P. Brand: "Buddy F.," *Crescendo*, iv/12 (1966), 16

NEVIL SKRIMSHIRE

Feed. In jazz argot, to provide a chordal accompaniment for a soloist. (*GoldJL*)

Feld, Morey (*b* Cleveland, OH, 15 Aug 1915; *d* Bow Mar, CO, 28 March 1971). Drummer. He began studying drums when he was 18, and later played with Ben Pollack (1936) and Joe Haymes (1938). His earliest recordings, made in 1940, were with the singer Buddy Clark and with Bud Freeman and his Summa cum Laude Orchestra. In 1943 he joined Benny Goodman, with whom he played and recorded regularly until 1945, and then occasionally until the 1960s. He was most active as a performer during the 1940s and 1950s, when he worked with Teddy Wilson and Slam Stewart (both 1945), Billy Butterfield (1946), Wild Bill Davison (1947), Peanuts Hucko (1947–57), Eddie Condon, and other well-known dixieland and swing musicians. Working as a staff musician for ABC in the mid-1950s he came into contact with a number of bop musicians, including Charlie Parker, with whom he recorded in 1955. He formed his own group, the Straight Ahead Six, in the same year, and recorded with it in 1956; in 1964 he led his own trio at the World's Fair in New York. Later he opened a drum school (1966) and was the first drummer with the World's Greatest Jazz Band.

Feld's career spanned dixieland jazz from the late 1930s through the 1960s, during which time he successfully accommodated several stylistic changes in his playing. He combined considerable technical skill with well-disciplined musicianship and his work in the 1960s was among the best in the dixieland style.

SELECTED RECORDINGS

As leader: *Jazz Goes to Broadway* (1956, Kapp 1007)
As sideman: B. Freeman: Oh! Baby/Sensation (1940, Decca 18065); B. Goodman: After you've Gone/Body and Soul (1945, Col. 36781); World's Greatest Jazz Band: *The World's Greatest Jazz Band* (1968, Project 5033)

BIBLIOGRAPHY

ChiltonW; *FeatherE*; *Feather '60s*; *Feather–Gitler '70s*

T. DENNIS BROWN

Felder, Wilton (Lewis) (*b* Houston, 31 Aug 1940). Tenor saxophonist and electric bass guitarist. He was a founding member in the early 1950s of the group that later became known as the CRUSADERS and for more than 30 years his career as a tenor saxophonist has been closely associated with it. His best work is as an aggressive, blues-based, hard-bop player on albums made in the early 1960s, when the group was called the Jazz Crusaders. As a composer he is well represented by *That's how I Feel* on the album *Crusaders 1* (1971, Blue Thumb 6001). As a saxophonist he only occasionally worked independently of the Crusaders, making two albums as a leader (1969, *c*1983), which were poorly received, and recording with the soul-jazz organist Charles Kynard (1969). Around 1968 he began to play electric bass guitar, both with the Crusaders and as a studio musician. He recorded with Archie Shepp (1968), Bobby Bryant, Jean-Luc Ponty, Blue Mitchell, and Milt Jackson (all 1969),

Groove Holmes (1969, *c*1971), Grant Green (1971, 1972), John Klemmer (1971, 1972, 1974), Stanley Turrentine (1974), Carmen McRae (1976), and Dizzy Gillespie (1977). The majority of these recordings involve fusions of jazz with rock, rhythm-and-blues, or soul; he also recorded regularly with popular groups in these genres. In the mid-1980s he and Joe Sample became co-leaders of the Crusaders (the other founding members having left) and the group became a septet. (*Feather '60s*; *Feather–Gitler '70s*)

For recordings and further bibliography *see* CRUSADERS.

Feldman, Victor (Stanley) [Vic] (*b* London, 7 April 1934; *d* Los Angeles, 12 May 1987). English pianist and vibraphonist. He began performing and recording at a very early age, and from 1941 to 1947 he played drums in a trio with his brothers. While still a teenager, he performed with Vic Lewis and Ted Heath, in Switzerland with Ralph Sharon (1949), and at a jazz festival in Paris (1952). By the time of his association with Ronnie Scott (1954), he was working mainly as a pianist and vibraphonist; his early playing shows the influence of Milt Jackson. In 1955 he emigrated to the USA. After touring with Woody Herman (1956–7) and briefly with Buddy DeFranco, Feldman moved to Los Angeles, where he played with Howard Rumsey's house band at the Lighthouse, Hermosa Beach (1957–9). He studied arranging with Marty Paich (1959) and subsequently wrote a number of successful arrangements and compositions. In 1960–61 he toured and recorded with Cannonball Adderley, and in 1962 he traveled to the USSR with Benny Goodman's band. He also performed with Miles Davis, who later made a recording of his composition *Seven Steps to Heaven* (1963, Col. CS8851), and with June Christy in London (1965). In the 1970s and 1980s Feldman worked with a number of rock groups and musicians, including Steely Dan and Joni Mitchell, and performed with John Guerin, Chuck Domanico, and Tom Scott, with whom he played jazz-rock.

SELECTED RECORDINGS

As leader: [untitled albums] (1955, Tempo LAP5–6); *Victor Feldman in London* (1956, Tempo TAP8); *The Arrival of Victor Feldman* (1958, Cont. C3549), incl. Waltz; *Merry Olde Soul* (1960–61, Riv. 9366); *Artful Dodger* (1977, Conc. 38); *To Chopin with Love* (1983, PAlt 8056); *High Visibility* (1985, TBA 208)

As sideman: S. Manne: *Shelly Manne & his Men at the Black Hawk* (1959, Cont. 7577–80); C. Adderley: *Cannonball Adderley and the Poll Winners* (1960, Riv. 9355); B. DeFranco: *Blues Bag* (1964, VJ 2506)

BIBLIOGRAPHY

FeatherE; *Feather '60s*; *Feather–Gitler '70s*
J. Tynan: "Victor Feldman: a Long Way from Piccadilly," *DB*, xxx/13 (1963), 13
L. Tomkins: "Victor Feldman Talking," *CI*, x/1 (1971), 6
D. Levine: "Victor Feldman: up-close," *MD*, iii/6 (1979), 42
B. Doerschuk: "Victor Feldman: the Double Life of a Jazz & Session Sensation," *Keyboard*, x/11 (1984), 53 [incl. discography]

STEVE LARSON

Felix, Lennie [Jacobus, Leonard] (*b* London, 16 Aug 1920; *d* London, 29 Dec 1980). English pianist. He began learning piano at the age of ten, and was influenced by Fats Waller, Art Tatum, and Earl Hines. He rapidly became an excellent soloist, and also worked in trios and larger ensembles. In 1950 he joined Freddy Randall's band, with which he also recorded. Shortly afterwards he traveled to New York, where he played with Henry "Red" Allen, Buster Bailey, and John Kirby, though he turned down the offer of a permanent post with Kirby because of commitments in England. After returning to London he joined Harry Gold's Pieces of Eight in 1953. Two years later he left to tour the Far East and Europe. He replaced Garland Wilson at le Boeuf sur le Toit, Paris, then played in England as a principal soloist with Wally Fawkes's Troglodytes (1957–8). After working in Vienna in 1959 he divided his time between England and the rest of Europe during the 1960s and 1970s. As well as making several recordings as a soloist and the leader of a trio (including the album *Lennie Felix Live at Nova Park, Zurich*, 1975, 88 Upright 003), he made frequent radio broadcasts.

BIBLIOGRAPHY

Feather '60s
G. Playfair: "A Case of Neglect," *JJ*, x/10 (1957), 27
E. Townley: "That Cat Felix," *Sv*, no.92 (1980–81), 61

CLARRIE HENLEY

Felsted. Record label. It was established by British Decca (*see* DECCA) in 1954, at first to reissue important American recordings, mostly of jazz. There was also a catalogue of popular material; this was also issued on a parallel label in the USA that was operated by London. However Felsted is chiefly remembered for an important series of recordings of mainstream jazz that were the result of sessions financed by British Decca and supervised by Stanley Dance in New York in 1958–9. These included highly acclaimed albums by Coleman Hawkins, Dicky Wells, Rex Stewart, Buster Bailey, Budd Johnson, and Buddy Tate; they were later reissued by Master Jazz in the USA and by Affinity in the UK. Some have also been re-released on a revived Felsted label by Polydor in Japan.

BIBLIOGRAPHY

D. Morgenstern: "The New York Scene," *JJ*, xii/6 (1959), 27
S. Dance: Liner notes, B. Tate: *Swinging like Tate* (MJR8127, 1975)
[P. M. Pelletier]: "The British Felsted Label," *British London Label Complete Listing, Part Four, plus Felsted & (Vogue-)Coral* (London, 1975) [Record Information Services pubn]

Felt mute. *See* MUTE, §2(k).

Ferguson, Maynard (*b* Verdun, Canada, 4 May 1928). Trumpeter and bandleader. He played in the big bands of Boyd Raeburn and Charlie Barnet during the late 1940s, and from 1950 to 1953 enjoyed an important association with Stan Kenton. He led a series of high-quality 13-piece bands, the earliest of which drew on the approaches of Kenton and Count Basie, while later groups assimilated the jazz-rock style. During the late 1960s Ferguson toured widely in Europe and the USA with a 16-piece band made up of English musicians. By 1974, when he achieved recognition in the popular field with a recording (1970) of Jim Webb's *MacArthur Park*, he was resident in California. He attained further success in 1978 with Jay Chattaway's arrangement of Bill Conti's *Gonna fly now*, which was the theme song of the film *Rocky*. Ferguson has continued to pursue an active career into the late 1980s, leading a combo instead of a big band.

Ferguson is noted for his exceptional command of the trumpet's highest register, and for his capacity for playing a number of different brass instruments – trumpet, french horn, trombone, euphonium – competently during a single performance. Although he is not a notable improviser, he has inspired many young trumpeters with his dazzling instrumental proficiency, heard to good effect in his renditions of Slide Hampton's composition *Frame for the Blues* and Don Sebesky's arrangement (1962) of Leonard Bernstein's *Maria*.

See also TROMBONE, §1, and TRUMPET, §§1, 4, and 6.

SELECTED RECORDINGS

As leader: *Message from Newport* (1958, Roul. 52012), incl. Frame for the Blues; *Maynard '62* (1962, Roul. 52083), incl. Maria; *M. F. Horn* (1970, Col.

C30466), incl. MacArthur Park; *Conquistador* (1978, CBS 81839), incl. Gonna fly now; *Storm* (1982, PAlt 8052N); *Live from San Francisco* (1983, PAlt 8077)

As sideman: S. Kenton: *New Concepts of Artistry in Rhythm* (1951, CW ST1002), incl. Invention for Guitar and Trumpet

BIBLIOGRAPHY

G. Hoefer and G. Lees: "The Man who Broke the Band Barrier," *DB*, xxvi/20 (1959), 20

I. Gitler: "Maynard Ferguson: a New Appraisal," *DB*, xxvii/20 (1960), 28

M. Ferguson: "Jazz Musicianship is an International Thing Now," *CI*, ix/7 (1971), 16

E. Berliner: "M. F.'s Back in Town," *DB*, xxxix/7 (1972), 16

H. Wong: "Maynard Ferguson: 'Out of the Exosphere and Back on the Scene'," *DB*, xl/18 (1973), 16

H. Nolan: "Maynard Ferguson's Rules of the Road," *DB*, xlii/11 (1975), 10

R. Belcher: *Maynard Ferguson File* (Caversham, England, 1975–6) [colln of articles and printed ephemera]

E. Harkins: *Maynard Ferguson: a Discography* (n.p. [Solana Beach, CA], 1976)

A. J. Smith: "Maynard Ferguson: Conquistador of Double High C," *DB*, xliv/16 (1977), 14

M. C. Gridley: *Jazz Styles* (Englewood Cliffs, NJ, 1978, rev. 2/1985 as *Jazz Styles: History and Analysis*, with suppl. *Instructor's Manual and Discography*)

L. Underwood: "Maynard Ferguson: Rocky Road to Fame and Fortune," *DB*, xlvii/7 (1980), 16

Z. Stewart: "Maynard's Changes," *DB*, lii/9 (1985), 20

MARK C. GRIDLEY/R

Ferris, Glenn (Arthur) (*b* Los Angeles, 27 June 1950). Trombonist. He learned classical trombone, and later studied theory and improvisation with Don Ellis (1964–6). At the age of 16 he joined Ellis's orchestra, with which he performed and toured until 1970. Later he worked as a freelance in and around Los Angeles with such musicians as Frank Zappa (1972), Harry James (1973–4), Billy Cobham (1974–6) and Bobby Bradford, and also played in a variety of classical, pop, rock, and soul ensembles. In 1977 he organized his own ten-piece band Celebration and formed a duo with Milcho Leviev. He recorded with Tony Scott in 1981 and toured Europe and recorded as a member of Jack Walrath's quintet in 1982–3. Although Ferris's work has earned him little commercial success, he is a versatile musician who is capable of playing in many styles.

SELECTED RECORDINGS

As sideman: D. Ellis: *The New Don Ellis Band Goes Underground* (1969, Col. CS9889), incl. Ferris Wheel: *Don Ellis at Fillmore* (1970, Col. G30243); B. Cobham: *Total Eclipse* (1974, Atl. 18121); *Shabazz* (1974, Atl. 18139); J. Walrath: *The Jack Walrath Quintet in Europe* (1982, Ste. 1172)

BIBLIOGRAPHY

Feather–Gitler '70s

L. Underwood: "Profile: Glenn Ferris," *DB*, xliv/21 (1977), 42

ROBERT DICKOW

Fess. Nickname of CHARLIE JOHNSON.

Festival International de Jazz de Montréal. Festival held annually from 1980 in Montreal. It was first organized by Alain Simard and André Menard and takes place over ten days in June and July, principally on outdoor stages and in clubs and theaters on the rue St.-Denis. The festival includes several series of concerts each year built around particular themes, such as "jazz dans la nuit," programs of contemporary jazz, or "hommage au jazz français." The programs cover a wide range of styles, including swing, bop, free jazz, and jazz-rock; among those who have appeared are Miles Davis, Wynton Marsalis, Bobby McFerrin, Steps Ahead, Steve Lacy, Ornette Coleman, Cecil Taylor, Art Blakey, and Stanley Jordan. The festival is among the world's largest; in 1986 1000 musicians from 20 countries performed before a combined audience of 425,000. Some of the performances are broadcast by the Canadian Broadcasting Company. The festival was preceded by the Montréal Jazz Festival at Loew's Theater (1961–?1963), which included performances by such musicians as Duke Ellington and Coleman Hawkins.

PAUL R. LAIRD

Festival International du Jazz Antibes–Juan-les-Pins. *See* ANTIBES–JUAN-LES-PINS JAZZ FESTIVAL.

Festival Mondial du Jazz Antibes–Juan-les-Pins. Name by which the ANTIBES–JUAN-LES-PINS JAZZ FESTIVAL was known until 1975.

Festivals. A music festival is a series of performances, of a generally celebratory nature, given by large numbers of individuals and groups over a limited period of time. The typical festival occurs annually over several days, at a fixed season of the year, and in a single city, sometimes at a single venue outdoors. Among festivals at which jazz is presented, most are devoted exclusively to this genre while in other cases jazz forms one component of a general music or arts event. Audiences number anything from hundreds to hundreds of thousands.

1. Introduction. 2. History and significance. 3. List.

1. INTRODUCTION. There are many exceptions to the "typical" jazz festival. A number of festivals take place at multiple or changing venues: examples include the Australian Jazz Convention, the Greenwich Village Jazz Festival, the touring Kool Jazz Festival and JVC Jazz Festival, and the festivals on Caribbean and other cruise ships. (A unique case – more a traveling concert series than a festival – is JAZZ AT THE PHILHARMONIC, which involved a loosely organized group of star performers annually making a worldwide tour.) Many festivals emphasize a particular theme; this may be based on style (e.g., the Sacramento Dixieland Jubilee), or musical instrument (as at the Free Music Antwerpen festival, where a different instrument is featured each year), or some other aspect of jazz (e.g., the Women's Jazz Festival in Kansas City). And some are private, open only to those who are invited – the most famous being the Colorado Jazz Party; typically such an event is named a "jazz party" rather than a "jazz festival," though it differs from a festival in no respect other than the means of admission.

Festivals present a wide spectrum of performers and events. Those described in the list below (§3) involve internationally renowned musicians, performing with their own groups or in all-star jam sessions; to this central focus may be attached auxiliary activities and attractions, such as jazz film series, photographic exhibitions, lectures, and symposia. Some portion of such a festival's events may be given over to performances by students, amateurs, and lesser-known professionals, and sometimes involve competitions. There are also hundreds of jazz festivals, not listed below, that focus on lesser-known players. These fall generally into two categories: provincial festivals and student festivals. In the USA the commonest kind of provincial festival is that devoted to dixieland jazz, at which bands known only within dixieland circles perform; these events are covered in the monthly newsletter *Mississippi Rag*. Alternatively the provincial emphasis may be defined not by style but by a nonmusical factor, such as cultural background, nationalism, or regionalism. Many American cities hold festivals for local performers who play in various styles, and this practice may extend to particular cultural groups, as, for example, in the Asian-American jazz festivals in New York and San

Francisco at which lesser-known players appear. Outside the USA many festivals aim to present the best jazz of a given nation or locality, and these often involve musicians who are not known internationally. The second category, the student festival, flourishes in the USA. Big bands, a white repertory, and white performers dominate these events, only small portions of which, if any, are given over to small groups and to the central black-American traditions of jazz; often the student bands accompany a famous guest soloist.

2. History and significance. Festivals were a late development in the history of jazz. They form a landmark in the shifting of the balance between jazz as a social event and jazz as a concert music. Throughout its early history jazz – the music itself – was in many respects secondary to the other activities pursued in the places where it was performed (*see* Nightclubs and other venues): the music provided a background for dancing, drinking, smoking, eating, and socializing, or for films, floor shows, or revues, all of which took precedence over listening. Certainly there were many people who came simply to listen to the music, but the conventional venues never catered to such a desire (hence the emergence in informal settings of the Jam session, in which the music was the foremost consideration). Occasionally formal concerts of jazz were presented, the most famous being John Hammond's "Spirituals to Swing" concerts at Carnegie Hall in 1938 and 1939, but these were isolated events that could not be repeated on a regular basis. The emergence of successful, informal festivals, maintained year by year, marked more than any other large-scale development a new attitude towards the music because at such events audiences were able to devote their whole attention to listening to performers on stage. Some festivals allowed dancing (at one's seat, in the aisles, or on outdoor grounds) and some provided opportunities for drinking, smoking, eating, and socializing, but above all those who attended sat and listened to the music.

Precursors of the jazz festival were the International Jazz Congress, held for six days in Chicago in the autumn of 1926 under the direction of the International Jazz Association, of which Paul Whiteman was the honorary chairman; and a series of outdoor concerts given by leading big bands at Randall's Island Stadium in New York in 1938, beginning with Martin Block's "Carnival of Swing" on 29 May. The first fully fledged jazz festival was probably the Australian Jazz Convention (1946), but at the time this now long-lived event had no influence outside Australia. The first festivals of international importance occurred in France: the Nice Jazz Festival (1948), generally credited in the literature as the first jazz festival, at which Louis Armstrong's All Stars performed; and the Festival International de Jazz (commonly known as the Paris Jazz Fair, 1949), which was as significant as the event in Nice since it offered acclaimed performances by such visiting American bop musicians as Charlie Parker, Miles Davis, and Tadd Dameron, and the traditional jazzman Sidney Bechet.

A number of important and long-lived festivals date from the 1950s. The most important one, at Newport, Rhode Island, began in 1954, to be followed by others in Monterey, California (1958), and Warsaw (1959). During the 1950s, too, the practice of making recordings and films at festivals became established, and again the Newport festival led the way. Yet by the mid-1960s festivals remained unusual events; perhaps one to two dozen were occurring in any one year in the USA at this time, and few lasted as long as several years. During this period the fact that a musician had performed at a festival was in itself a mark of distinction, certifying his stature within jazz.

The late 1960s witnessed new developments. Festivals of international importance proliferated and by the mid-1980s somewhere between 700 and 1000 such events were taking place annually. As the number of festivals multiplied, festival circuits developed informally, based on stylistic divisions; a successful player or group could work more or less regularly as a freelance simply by touring from festival to festival through the year. In one especially important instance this interrelationship among festivals was formalized. Around 1974, building on contacts and contracts established through his work in presenting the Newport Jazz Festival New York, George Wein set up an international organization to deal with all aspects of festival organization. His Festival Productions Inc. has coordinated the engagement of a distinguished body of groups and individuals (in this it resembles Norman Granz's Jazz at the Philharmonic) for the events that it runs in places as far apart as Boston, Tokyo, and Nice, as well as arranging national and international tours by performers working under the banner of the Newport (later the Kool, then the JVC) festival. It also works in association with independent festivals; for example, in 1987 the Concord Jazz Festival included two days of performances booked by the company, one as part of the JVC Jazz Festival international tour.

The reasons why festivals have flourished while other forums for the presentation of jazz have periodically fallen on lean times are unclear. One explanation is that they have not merely reflected but have reinforced an interest in jazz as a concert music, and in doing so have guaranteed their own future. Another is that they have revived the important tradition of the jam session in a more formal setting. With few exceptions, informal jam sessions died out in the 1950s, owing in part to the more careful enforcement by musicians' unions of the limits on the number of players allowed on stage at any one time. Only festivals (most notably the JVC Grande Parade du Jazz Nice and the Colorado Jazz Party) have provided opportunities for large numbers of prominent musicians to continue to play together in changing combinations. Finally the circumstances of many festivals – that the audience is large, that many of a performer's peers are present, that the performance is focused on a single hour or two – elicit a high frequency of memorable performances and therefore make the idea of a festival an attractive one.

Perhaps, too, the festival also has some economic advantage over the nightclub. Statistics are not readily available. In some instances the income from large audiences is offset by the cost of renting the location and engaging many distinguished players, as well as by the fact that a given festival is in operation for only a few days every year and not continually. (Wein himself was several times deeply in debt as the result of unsuccessful festivals and had to be encouraged by fellow musicians not to abandon his attempt to establish what eventually became a flourishing career as a promoter.) But it is clear that such considerations are more than balanced by other, more favorable, ones. Because a festival is a special event, lasting for only a short time, it generates a great deal of enthusiasm and interest (which are hard to maintain in the operation of a venue that opens nightly) and may attract extremely large audiences. Moreover, in many instances public bodies and industry supply funding for festivals, which of course is not the case with commercially run nightclubs. Lastly festivals have many secondary sources of revenue, from activities such as recording and filming, and from concessions for the sale of food, drink, and souvenirs.

BIBLIOGRAPHY

J. A. Byrczek: *World Jazz Calendar of Festivals and Events* (New York, 1982, rev. and enlarged 3/1984 as *Jazz Festivals International Directory, 1984–85*, rev. and enlarged 4/1985) [pubn of Jazz World Society]

K. Thomsen, B. Kabelmann, and A. Meyer: *Directory of Jazz Festivals and Related Major Jazz Events* (Rønnede, nr Fakse, Denmark, rev. and enlarged 2/1985)

3. List. The following is a selective list of jazz festivals that have achieved international signficance. The list focuses on festivals involving professional musicians of international renown. It excludes festivals presenting exclusively local or national artists (except in areas of geographical or political isolation, for which those festivals that present the best national professionals are included) and it excludes those devoted predominantly to amateurs or students.

The list is arranged alphabetically by country, city, and name of festival. Festivals that do not take place in the same city every year are entered alphabetically by title immediately after the name of the country; those that take place in a region are entered under the region, which stands in place of the name of a city. An asterisk indicates that the festival so marked has a separate entry in this dictionary. An index of festivals by name follows the list.

In each entry the current name of the festival (or the latest name if the festival is defunct) is used. (Parts of a name that are not always used are shown in parentheses, alternative names in brackets, and translated names in common use after a solidus.) Where a general arts festival has an important jazz component the latter's name is used and the details given are those of the jazz component; the affiliation is noted under a side-heading (see below). Cross-references for alternative and former names are included where necessary. The date of foundation (and of last occurrence where relevant) follows the name; a year standing alone indicates that the festival took place once. Former names and the years during which they were current are then shown in parentheses. Festivals take place annually unless otherwise indicated. Other details are given against appropriate side-headings, which use the abbreviations shown below. All information pertaining to affiliation, frequency, organizers, officers, duration and season, location, repertory, audiences, and sponsors is current (1987) for festivals still in existence. If not indicated, repertory is general.

aff.	–	affiliated to	freq.	–	frequency
aud.	–	audience(s)	incl.	–	include, included, including
contd	–	continued			
coord.	–	coordinator, coordinated by	loc(s).	–	location(s)
			orgr(s)	–	organizer(s)
dir(s).	–	directors, directed by	pr.	–	principal
			pres.	–	president
ds	–	duration and season	prod.	–	producer, produced by
fdr(s)	–	founder(s)	rep.	–	repertory
fl.	–	flourished			

ARGENTINA

Mardel Jazz 1981–
fdr and pres.: Walter Thiers
ds: five days in February–March
locs.: Mar del Plata (1981–2); Mar del Plata, and Teatro Colón, Buenos Aires (1983); Necochea (1985); Teatro Colón, Buenos Aires (1986–7)
pr. rep.: free jazz and jazz-rock, presented in association with other arts
aud.: 10,000
note: free admission

AUSTRALIA

Australian Jazz Convention 1946–
fdrs: Harry Stein and Graeme Bell
ds: 26 December–1 January
locs.: Melbourne (1946–9); one major city annually (1950–)
pr. rep.: traditional jazz and, occasionally in later years, other styles
bibliography: N. Lineham, ed.: *Bob Barnard, Graeme Bell, Bill Haesler, John Sangster, on the Australian Jazz Convention* (?Melbourne, Australia, 1981)

Sydney. **Music is . . . an Open Sky** 1975–7 [contd, from 1983, in New York, see USA, New York]
fdr: Horst Liepolt
ds: different durations and seasons each year
rep.: free jazz
note: the first festival was organized in association with the Australian Jazz Convention (see above)

——. **Qantas International Jazz Festival** 1977–81
aff.: Festival of Sydney
prod.: Horst Liepolt
ds: 11 days in January
loc.: Capitol Theatre
pr. rep.: swing and bop to free jazz and jazz-rock
note: the Festival of Sydney has continued to present some jazz

AUSTRIA

Bleiburg. **Ö 3 Jazzfestival Bleiburg** 1984–
fdr: Kulturinitiative Bleiburg
ds: two or three days in July
loc.: outdoor site
pr. rep.: bop and free jazz
note: sponsored and promoted by Österreichischer Rundfunk

Feldkirch. **Feldkircher (International) Jazztage** fl. 1980s
ds: four days in June

Hollabrunn. **Blue Danube Jazz Summit** [Jazzfest Hollabrunn] fl. early 1980s–1986 [contd in Vienna, see below]
fdr: Fritz Thom of Live Performance Service
ds: three days in July
loc.: Festgelände (outdoor site)
pr. rep.: hard bop, modal jazz, and jazz-rock; also blues
aud.: 10,000–12,000 per concert

Innsbruck. **Kunstdünger's Jazzfestival Innsbruck** fl. 1980s
ds: four days in April
loc.: Jazzclub Treibhaus

Saalfelden. **International Jazzfestival Saalfelden** 1978– (formerly Drei Tage Jazz)
fdr: Gerhard Eder
ds: three days in September
loc.: outdoor site
rep.: free jazz
aud.: 5000

Salzburg. **International Jazzfestival Salzburg** 1982– (formerly Jazz im Theater-Festival Salzburg)
fdr: Walter Struger
ds: three or four days in March–April
loc.: Elisabethbühne (theater)
pr. rep.: bop and free jazz
aud.: 1000 per concert

Vienna. **Blue Danube Jazz Summit** 1987– [contd from Hollabrunn, see above]
ds: two weeks in July
locs. incl.: Stadt Halle, Szene Wien, Fritz Music Hall
aud.: 10,000 per concert at main events

——. **Ö 3 Jazz Fest** 1987–
fdr: Fritz Thom of Live Performance Service
ds: two or three days in July
loc.: Stadt Halle
pr. rep.: bop and jazz-rock
aud.: 10,000
note: sponsored and promoted by Österreichischer Rundfunk

Wiesen. **Jazzfest Wiesen** 1976–
fdr: Franz Bogner
ds: three days in July
loc.: outdoor site
pr. rep.: bop to jazz-rock
aud.: 6000–8000

BELGIUM

Antwerp. **Free Music Antwerpen** 1974–
ds: four days in August
loc.: King-Kong (nightclub)
rep.: free jazz; a different instrument is featured each year
aud.: 600–1000 per concert

——. **Jazz(festival) Middelheim** 1969–
aff.: Flanders Festival
freq.: biennially in odd-numbered years
ds: five days in August
loc.: Den Brandt Park
pr. rep.: bop to free jazz and jazz-rock
note: Radiodiffusion-Télévision Belge broadcasts some performances

BRUSSELS. **Brosella** 1977–
fdr: Service Jeunesse of the City of Brussels
ds: two days in July (from 1981 one day devoted to jazz; see rep. below)
loc.: Théâtre de Verdure in the Parc d'Ossephem, near the Atomium
rep.: folk music (1977–80); folk music and jazz (swing and bop to free jazz and jazz-rock) (1981–)
aud.: 8000

COMBLAIN-LA-TOUR, nr Liège. **Comblain-la-Tour Jazz Festival** 1959–?1968
fdr and orgr: Joe Napoli
ds: two days in August
loc.: outdoor site
pr. rep.: dixieland, swing, and bop
aud.: 120,000 in 1967

DENDERMONDE. **Honky Tonk Jazz Festival Dendermonde** [Jazzfestival Dendermonde, International Jazz Festival van Dendermonde] 1971–
fdrs: Bert Heuvinck, Philemon Heuvinck, Piet Heuvinck, Alajos Van Petegem, and Stephan Van Wesemael
orgr: Jazzclub Honky Tonk
ds: two days in September (1971–85); two days in June (1986–)
loc.: VP-Plein, Gentsesteenweg (outdoor site)
pr. rep.: early jazz, swing, and bop; also blues
aud.: 3000–4000

GHENT. **International Jazzmeeting** 1969–
orgr: Lazy River Jazz Club
ds: three days in spring
aud.: 2000

BULGARIA

SOFIA. **Sofiakoncert / Sofia Jazz Festival** 1977–
ds: two days in December
loc.: Sofia University
pr. rep.: bop to free jazz
aud.: 3000 per concert

CANADA

EDMONTON. **Jazz City International Jazz Festival** 1980–
fdrs: Marc Vasey, Taras Ostachewsky, and Tevelee Goodwin
orgs: Edmonton Jazz Society and Jazz City Festival Society
ds: eight days in August (1980–85); eight days in June–July (1986–)
locs. incl.: Jubilee Auditorium, Shoctor Theatre, Château Lacombe Ballroom, Hawrelak Park, Sir Winston Churchill Square, and other indoor and outdoor venues
pr. rep.: swing and bop to free jazz, Latin jazz, and jazz-rock; also blues
aud.: 60,000–80,000

MONTREAL. ***Festival International de Jazz de Montréal** 1980–
fdrs: Alain Simard and André Menard
ds: ten days in June–July
locs. incl.: Théâtre St.-Denis, Spectrum (theater), nightclubs, and outdoor stages on the rue St.-Denis
pr. rep.: swing and bop to free jazz and jazz-rock
aud.: 425,000
notes: the CBC broadcasts some performances; preceded by the Montreal Jazz Festival at Loew's Theatre (1961–?1963), which presented such artists as Duke Ellington and Coleman Hawkins

OTTAWA. **Ottawa Jazz Festival** 1981–
ds: seven days in July
locs. incl.: Astrolabe (outdoor site)
pr. rep.: bop to free jazz and jazz-rock
aud.: 25,000

CARIBBEAN

Floating Jazz Festival [Norwegian Caribbean Lines Jazz Festivals] 1983–
fdrs: Hank O'Neal and Shelley Mae Shier in association with Norwegian Caribbean Lines
ds: two or more one-week cruises each year in October–November
locs.: SS *Norway* and other ships of Norwegian Caribbean Lines
pr. rep.: traditional jazz, swing, and bop
aud.: 1800 capacity per week on SS *Norway*; 750–1700 capacity per week on other ships
notes: cruises depart from Miami; concerts and jam sessions take place in three locations simultaneously; preceded by at least 12 jazz cruises on SS *Rotterdam* (Holland America Line) in the 1970s
bibliography: H. O'Neal: *Norwegian Caribbean Lines Floating Jazz Festival, 1985* (New York, n.d. [?1986])

CUBA

HAVANA. **Jazz Plaza** 1980–
ds: January
loc.: Teatro Karl Marx
pr. rep.: bop, especially Afro-Cuban jazz
note: the festival assumed international status in 1983, and in 1985 leading American musicians such as Dizzy Gillespie participated

CZECHOSLOVAKIA

BRATISLAVA. **Slavokoncert / Bratislava Jazz Days** fl. 1980s
ds: three days in October

PRAGUE. **Mezinárodní Jazzový Festival Praha / International Jazz Festival Prague** 1964–
freq.: usually biennially in even-numbered years
orgrs: Czechoslovak Music Instruments (1964–73); Pragokoncert, the Czechoslovak concert agency (1974–)
ds: four days in October
loc.: Lucerna Hall
aud.: 8000–10,000

DENMARK

COPENHAGEN. **Copenhagen Jazz Festival** 1979–
fdr: Copenhagen City Center
prod.: George Wein's Festival Productions Inc. (?1987–)
ds: ten days in July
locs.: outdoor sites and nightclubs in and around Copenhagen
note: preceded by the Tivoli Jazz Festival (1965)
bibliography: G. Turrell and D. Turrell: *And All that Jazz: Copenhagen Jazz Festival* (Copenhagen, 1983)

FEMØ. **Femø Jazz** fl. 1980s
ds: four days in August
pr. rep.: traditional jazz and swing
aud.: 2000

HOLSTEBRO. **Jassfestival** fl. 1980s
ds: two days in September
aud.: 2000 per concert

SORØ. **Sorø Jazzfestival** fl. 1980s
fdr: Jørgen Høy Hansen
ds: two or three days in August
loc.: Søskoven (outdoor site)
pr. rep.: traditional jazz, swing, and bop
aud.: 600 per concert

EAST GERMANY. See German Democratic Republic.

ENGLAND. See United Kingdom.

FEDERAL REPUBLIC OF GERMANY [BRD]

BADEN-BADEN. **New Jazz Meeting Baden-Baden** 1966–
fdr: Joachim-Ernst Berendt
ds: five days in November
locs.: venues in Baden-Baden and Mainz
rep.: free jazz; also non-Western music
aud.: 1000
note: Südwestfunk broadcasts some performances

BERLIN. ***Jazzfest Berlin / Berlin Jazz Festival** 1964– (1964–81, Berliner Jazztage / Berlin Jazz Days)
fdr: Joachim-Ernst Berendt
dirs.: George Gruntz (1973–) and Ralf Schulte-Bahrenberg (?1978–?1981)
ds: four or five days in October–November
locs. incl.: Philharmonie (concert hall), Delphi (cinema), and Musikinstrumenten-Museum
pr. rep.: swing and bop to free jazz and jazz-rock, with increasing emphasis from 1973 on mainstream jazz; also blues, gospel, and folk music; several countries, styles, or instruments are featured each year
notes: Westdeutscher Rundfunk broadcasts some performances; the festival runs concurrently with the Total Music Meeting (see below)

——. **Jazz in July** 1980– (except 1983) (1980–82, Summer Jazz Festival)
fdr: Klaus Achterberg
orgr: Major Minor Music
ds: 16 days in July
locs. incl.: Quartier Latin (outdoor sites), Metropol and Quasimodo (nightclubs), and Passionskirche

pr. rep.: bop to free jazz and jazz-rock
aud.: 500 per concert

——. **Total Music Meeting** 1968–
fdr: Jost Gebers
orgr: FMP
ds: five days in October–November
locs.: Quartier Latin (outdoor sites), FMP studio
rep.: free jazz
aud.: 500 per concert
note: runs concurrently with Jazzfest Berlin (see above)

——. **Workshop Freie Musik / Free Music Workshop** 1969–
fdr: Jost Gebers
orgr: FMP
ds: five days in March–April
loc.: Akademie der Künste
rep.: free jazz
aud.: 500 per concert

BURGHAUSEN. **Internationale Jazz-Woche Burghausen** 1970–
fdrs: Helmut Viertl and Joe Viera
orgs: Interessengemeinschaft Jazz Burghausen e.V. and City of Burghausen
ds: five days in March
locs. incl.: Wackerhalle, Stadtsaal, and Jazzkeller-Mautnerschloss (nightclub)
aud.: 7000
bibliography: H.-J. Dyck: *Eine Provinzstadt macht Jazzgeschichte* (Burghausen, 1979)

FRANKFURT AM MAIN. **Deutsches Jazz Festival Frankfurt** [Frankfurt Jazz Festival] 1953–
aff.: Musik Messe Frankfurt
fdrs: Horst Lippmann and Deutsche Jazz Föderation
ds: four days in February–March
loc.: Kongresshalle
pr. rep.: bop to free jazz and jazz-rock
aud.: 1800 per day
notes: Hessischer Rundfunk sponsors the festival and broadcasts some performances; the festival has received support from the city of Frankfurt am Main and the state of Hesse; emphasis is placed on introducing new West German musicians

FREIBURG. **Internationales Jazzfestival Freiburg** [Freiburger Jazztage] 1982–
fdr: Alexander Heisler
ds: three days in autumn
loc.: Stadthalle, the barn at the Jesuitenschloss, and the Audimax hall in the university
pr. rep.: swing and bop to free jazz
aud.: 800 per day

——. **Internationales Zelt-Musik-Festival Freiburg** 1982–
fdr: Alexander Heisler
ds: three weeks in June
locs.: outdoor sites at Mundenhof
pr. rep.: swing and bop to free jazz
aud.: 1000 per day
note: jazz is presented as a component in a general music festival

HOFHEIM. **Hofheimer Jazzfest** 1974–
fdr: Club der Jazzfreunde e.V.
ds: three days in January
loc.: Stadthalle
rep.: free jazz
aud.: 700 per concert
note: the festival often includes a photographic exhibition

LEVERKUSEN. **Leverkusener Jazztage** 1980–
fdrs: Erhard T. Schoofs and Wolfgang Orth
ds: nine days in October–November
pr. rep.: bop to free jazz and jazz-rock
aud.: 10,000

MAINZ. See Baden-Baden.

MOERS. ***International New Jazz Festival Moers** 1972–
orgr: Moers Music
ds: four days in May–June
locs.: indoor and outdoor venues
rep.: free jazz; also bop
aud.: 3500 per concert at main events
note: Westdeutscher Rundfunk helps to sponsor the festival and broadcasts some performances

MÜNSTER. **Internationales Jazzfestival Münster** 1979–
fdr: Asta der Universität Münster
ds: three days in June–July
loc.: Halle Münsterland
pr. rep.: swing and bop to free jazz
aud.: 1800 per day

NUREMBERG. **Jazz Ost-West** [International Jazzfestival Nürnberg] 1966–
freq.: biennially in even-numbered years
ds: four or five days in May–June
locs. incl.: Meistersingerhalle, Schauspielhaus, Jazz-Action-Center im Komm, and Dehnberger Hoftheater in Lauf-Dehnberg
pr. rep.: bop to free jazz and jazz-rock
aud.: 500–5000 per concert
notes: sponsored by Jazz-Studio Nürnberg; the festival aims to present eastern European, western European, and American musicians

FINLAND

HELSINKI. **Seajazz** 1984–
orgr: UMO Big Band
ds: four days in August (1984–6); four days in June (1987–)
locs.: indoor and outdoor venues
aud.: 2000–5000

PORI. ***Pori (International) Jazz (Festival)** 1966–
orgr: Pori Jazz 66 ry
ds: nine days in July
locs. incl.: outdoor sites beside River Kokemaenjoki, Concert Park on the island of Kirjurinluoto, and indoor venues including the Cotton Club
rep.: all styles of jazz; also blues and rock
aud.: 40,000–60,000

TAMPERE. **Tampere Jazz Happening** 1982–
orgr: Jazzkerho Break
ds: three days in October–November
pr. rep.: free jazz and jazz-rock
aud.: 2000–2500

TURKU. **Turun Jazztapahtuma** 1970–
orgr: Turku Jazz ry
ds: three days in March
pr. rep.: free jazz and jazz-rock
aud.: 1500–2000

FRANCE

ANGOULÊME. **Jazz en France** 1976–
ds: seven days in May
loc.: Théâtre Municipal
pr. rep.: bop to jazz-rock

ANTIBES. ***Festival International du Jazz Antibes–Juan-les-Pins/Antibes–Juan-les-Pins Jazz Festival** 1960– (to *c*1975, Festival Mondial du Jazz Antibes–Juan-les-Pins)
ds: ten days in July
loc.: La Pinède (outdoor site), Juan-les-Pins; indoor concerts at Palais des Congrès, Juan-les-Pins (mid-1970s)
pr. rep.: swing and bop to free jazz and jazz-rock
aud.: 4000 per concert at main events

COUTANCES. **Jazz sous les Pommiers** fl. 1980s
orgr: Centre d'Animation
ds: eight days in May
pr. rep.: bop to free jazz and jazz-rock
bibliography: *Jazz sous les pommiers, 83–84: festivals de Coutances* (Coutances, n.d. [?1985])

GRENOBLE. **Jazz: Musiques à Grenoble** fl. 1980s (to 1983, Cinq Jours de Jazz)
ds: seven or eight days in March
pr. rep.: bop to free jazz

JUAN-LES-PINS. See Antibes.

LE MANS. **Europa Jazz Festival** fl. 1980s
orgr: Le Mans Jazz Action
ds: four days in April
pr. rep.: free jazz
aud.: 2200

MONTAUBAN. **Festival de Jazz de Montauban / Montauban International Jazz Festival** 1982–
fdr and orgr: Hot Club de France
ds: six days in July
pr. rep.: dixieland, swing, and bop; also blues
aud.: 500–2000 per concert

NANCY. **Nancy Jazz Pulsations** 1973–
ds: 11 days in October
pr. rep.: bop to free jazz and fusion; also blues and rock
note: the festival includes jazz films and exhibitions

NICE. ***JVC Grande Parade du Jazz Nice** 1974– (to 1984, Grande Parade du Jazz)
fdrs: George Wein and Simone Ginibre
prod.: George Wein's Festival Productions Inc.
dir.: Simone Ginibre
ds: 11 or 12 days in July
loc.: Jardins des Arènes de Cimiez
pr. rep.: swing and bop to jazz-rock
aud.: 70,000
note: the principal sponsor is the Japanese Victor Corporation (1984–)

——. **Nice Jazz Festival** 1948
fdrs: Hugues Panassié and the Hot Club de France
rep.: traditional jazz
note: first international jazz festival

NÎMES. **Nîmes International Jazz Festival** fl. 1980s
orgr: Nîmes Jazz Club
ds: eight days in July
locs.: Arènes de Nîmes, Jardins de la Fontaine, and courtyard of the Musée du Vieux Nîmes
pr. rep.: bop to free jazz and jazz-rock

PARIS. **Festival de Jazz de Paris** 1980–
fdrs incl.: Michel Boutinard Rouelle, André Francis, and Martini Dewenger
ds: nine days in October–November
locs. incl.: Théâtre de la Ville, Théâtre Musical de Paris, Bercy sports stadium, and other indoor and outdoor venues
aud.: 14,000 per concert at main events
note: the radio service of ORTF broadcasts some performances

——. **Festival International de Jazz** [Paris Jazz Fair] 1949, 1952, 1954
fdr: Charles Delaunay
ds: seven to nine days in spring
loc.: Salle Pleyel
pr. rep.: dixieland to bop
aud.: 1500 per concert
notes: Charlie Parker, Miles Davis, Tadd Dameron, Dizzy Gillespie, Sidney Bechet, Thelonious Monk, Mary Lou Williams, Gerry Mulligan, and others participated; the festival included a jazz trade fair; Chaîne Parisien, Paris Inter, Poste Parisien, and BBC broadcast (or recorded for later broadcast) some performances at the festival of 1949; Jazz at the Philharmonic closed the festival in 1952

——. **Paris Jazz Festival** 1965–?1969
ds: two days in November
locs.: Palais de la Mutalité; Salle Pleyel (1966–)
pr. rep.: dixieland, swing, bop, and free jazz
note: partly sponsored by ORTF, which broadcast some performances

SAMOIS-SUR-SEINE. **Festival Django Reinhardt** 1968–
freq.: every five years (1968–81); annually (1981–)
fdrs and orgrs: Jean-Pierre Bechtold, Jean-François Robinet, Babik Reinhardt, Maurice Cullaz, Jean-Michel Lancery, and Yvon Roze
ds: two days in June
loc.: Ile du Berceau
pr. rep.: swing and bop, also other styles played on string instruments, especially guitar
aud.: 3000–5000
note: ORTF and BBC TV have broadcast some performances

SOUILLAC. **Festival de Jazz Sim Copans** 1976–
fdrs: Sim Copans and Jean Calvel
orgr: Bureau du Festival à Souillac
ds: three days in July
loc.: Palais des Congrès
pr. rep.: early jazz to bop
aud.: 1500

VIENNE. **Jazz à Vienne** fl. 1980s
orgr: Vienne Action Culturelle
prod.: Jean-Paul Boutelier (1987)
ds: 11 days in July
loc.: Théâtre Antique
pr. rep.: bop to free jazz and jazz-rock
aud.: 46,000

GERMAN DEMOCRATIC REPUBLIC [DDR]

BERLIN. **Jazzbühne Berlin** 1976–
ds: three days in June
loc.: Friedrichstadtpalast
pr. rep.: bop to free jazz and jazz-rock
note: Rundfunk der DDR broadcasts some performances

LEIPZIG. **Leipziger Jazztage** fl. 1980s
ds: four days in September–October
loc.: Kongresshalle
pr. rep.: bop to free jazz
aud.: 1800

GERMANY. See Federal Republic of Germany and German Democratic Republic.

GREAT BRITAIN. See United Kingdom.

GREECE

ATHENS. **Praxis Festival** 1978– (except 1981) (1978–9, Greek Jazz Festival)
fdr: Kostas Yannoulopoulos
ds: one week in November
locs. incl.: National Gallery of Art, Alambra Theater, Goethe Institute, and Orpheus Theater
rep.: free jazz
aud.: 1700 per concert at main events
note: sponsored by Praxis Records

HUNGARY

BUDAPEST. **Budapest Jazz Festival** fl. 1980s
aff.: Budapest Spring Festival
orgr: Magyar Rádió és Televizie
ds: four days in March
note: some performances are broadcast

——. **Szeged International Jazz Week** [Szeged Jazz Days], 1972–
orgr: Magyar Rádió és Televizie
ds: three days in ?November
note: some performances are broadcast

DEBRECEN. **Debreceni Dzsessznapok / Debrecen Jazz Days** 1972–
fdrs: Magyar Rádió és Televizie and Kölcsey Ferenc Müvelödési Központ (Kölcsey Ferenc Cultural Center)
ds: four or five days in November (1972); four or five days in September (1973–8); four or five days in July (1979–)
locs. incl.: ballroom of the Kölcsey Ferenc Müvelödési Központ, Bartók Hall at Arany Bika Szállóban (concert hall), and Sportscsarnok (sports center)
pr. rep.: bop to free jazz and jazz-rock, also one dixieland concert
aud.: 2000–4000
note: Magyar Rádió és Televizie and Organisation Internationale de Radio et Télévision (1981, 1983–) broadcast some performances

INDIA

BOMBAY. **Jazzyatra** 1978–
freq.: biennially in even-numbered years
fdr: Niranjan Jhaveri
ds: four days in February–March
locs. incl.: Brabourbe Stadium, Bombay; some events in New Delhi and Calcutta
pr. rep.: swing and bop to jazz-rock
aud.: 6000 per concert at main events

IRELAND

CORK. **Guinness Jazz Festival** 1978– (1978–81, John Player Jazz International Cork)
fdrs: James F. Mountjoy, Pearce Harvey, and Ray Fitzgerald
ds: four days in October
locs. incl.: Opera House and Metropole Hotel
pr. rep.: early jazz to bop
aud.: 30,000
note: sponsored by the brewer Guinness (1982–)

ISRAEL

Israel Jazz Festival 1981–
fdr and orgr: Israel Jazz Society
ds: seven to ten days in July–August
locs.: cities throughout Israel
aud.: 1000–5000 per concert

ITALY

BOLOGNA. **Rassegna Internazionale di Orchestre Jazz** fl. 1980s
ds: three days in July
pr. rep.: big-band music

CITTÀ DI CASTELLO. See Umbria.

FLORENCE. See Pisa.

FOLIGNO. See Umbria.

LIVORNO. See Pisa.

PALERMO. **Palermo Jazz Estate** fl. 1980s
ds: seven days in July
pr. rep.: jazz-rock

PERUGIA. See Umbria.

PESCARA. **Pescara Jazz** [Festival Internazionale del Jazz] 1969–
fdrs: Lucio Fumo and the Azienda di Soggiorno
ds: one week in July
locs.: Parco le Najadi and other outdoor sites; some events in nearby towns
pr. rep.: swing and bop
aud.: 4000–5000 per concert
note: from 1982 promoter has been Ente Manifestazioni Pescaresi with Lucio Fumo as art director
bibliography: *Quindici anni di jazz a Pescara* (Pescara, 1987) [pubn of Ente Manifestazioni Pescaresi]

PISA. **Rassegna Internazionale del Jazz di Pisa** 1976–
ds: five days in June–July
locs.: Pisa and Livorno (1976–7); Pisa and Florence (1978–9); Teatro Verdi, Pisa (1979–)
pr. rep.: free jazz

RAVENNA. **Ravenna Jazz** 1974–
fdr: Carlo Bubani
prod.: Filipo Bianchi (1987)
ds: five days in July
loc.: Rocca Brancaleone (ancient fortress)
pr. rep.: bop to free jazz and jazz-rock
aud.: 2500 per concert
bibliography: *Ravenna Jazz* (Ravenna, 1986) [pubn of Comune di Ravenna]

SAN REMO. **Festival Internazionale del Jazz** 1955–66
orgrs: Pino Maffei and Arrigo Polillo
ds: two or three days in spring
loc.: San Remo Casino
pr. rep.: swing and bop
note: Duke Ellington, Earl Hines, the Modern Jazz Quartet, Thelonious Monk, Martial Solal, and others participated

UMBRIA. **Umbria Jazz (Festival and Clinic)** 1973–6, 1982–
prod.: Carlo Pagnotta (1987)
ds: ten days in July
locs. incl.: Teatro Morlacchi, Studio R. Curi, Giardini del Frontone, and other indoor and outdoor venues in Perugia; venues in Terni, Foligno, Città di Castello, and other towns in the region
pr. rep.: swing and bop to jazz-rock
aud.: 7000–30,000 per concert at main outdoor events
notes: the festival began as a free outdoor event sponsored by the regional government; it was discontinued from 1977 owing to crowd disturbances

VERBANIA. **International Festival of Jazz** fl. 1980s
ds: one week
locs.: venues on the shores of Lake Maggiore
pr. rep.: big-band music

VERONA. **Verona International Jazz Festival** re-established in 1986
ds: three days in summer
loc.: Roman amphitheater
pr. rep.: bop to jazz-rock
aud.: 2000 per concert

JAPAN

International Jazz Festival of Japan 1977
ds: 15 days in February–March
locs.: eight Japanese cities, including Fukuako, Hiroshima, Osaka, Sapporo, Sendai, and Tokyo
pr. rep.: swing and bop
aud.: 4000 per concert in Osaka and Tokyo

World Jazz Festival 1964
orgrs: George Wein and the Japan Booking Corporation
ds: six days in July
locs.: indoor and outdoor venues in Kyoto, Nagoya, Osaka, Sapporo, and Tokyo
pr. rep.: dixieland, swing, and bop
note: Miles Davis, Gene Krupa, the Dukes of Dixieland, and other American and Japanese musicians participated

FUKUAKO. See International Jazz Festival of Japan.

HIROSHIMA. See International Jazz Festival of Japan.

KYOTO. See World Jazz Festival.

MADARAO, NR TOKYO. **Budweiser Newport Jazz Festival in Madarao** 1982–
prod.: George Wein's Festival Productions Inc.
ds: five days in August
loc.: mountaintop north of Tokyo
pr. rep.: bop
aud.: 7500 per day
note: sponsored by the brewer Budweiser

NAGOYA. See World Jazz Festival.

OSAKA. See International Jazz Festival of Japan; World Jazz Festival.

SAPPORO. See International Jazz Festival of Japan; World Jazz Festival.

SENDAI. See International Jazz Festival of Japan.

?TOKYO. **Aurex Jazz Festival** fl. early 1980s
note: recordings made of performances by all-star American swing and bop musicians, including Benny Goodman and Benny Carter (both 1980), Woody Herman (1982), and Art Blakey (1983)

TOKYO (Nemu-no Sato in the Mie prefecture). **Nemu Jazz Inn** 1969–
ds: one day in July
note: the festival consists of a single ten-hour concert

——. See also International Jazz Festival of Japan; World Jazz Festival; Toyohashi.

TOYOHASHI. **Toyohashi Black Heritage Festival** 1985–
prod.: George Wein's Festival Productions Inc.
ds: three or four days in July–August
locs.: venues in Toyohashi and Tokyo (1987–)
rep.: blues, folk, gospel, jazz, pop, reggae, and traditional African music
note: jazz musicians of international standing participate

NETHERLANDS

NOS Jazz Festival 1971– (1971–2 Loosdrecht Internationaal Jazz Festival; 1973–5, 1977–9, Laren Internationaal Jazz Festival; 1976, Rotterdam Internationaal Jazz Festival; 1980–85, Amsterdam Internationaal Jazz Festival)
fdr and orgr: Nederlandse Omroep Stichting
ds: three or four days in August–September
locs.: Loosdrecht (1971–2); Laren (1973–5, 1977–9); Rotterdam (1976); Amsterdam (1980–)
pr. rep.: bop to free jazz
aud.: 500 per concert

AMSTERDAM. See NOS Jazz Festival.

BREDA. **Oude Stijl Jazz Festival Breda** 1971–
ds: four days in May
locs. incl.: Congreszaal in the Turfschip arts center, and Graanpijp (concert hall)
pr. rep.: dixieland and swing
aud.: 100,000

THE HAGUE. ***North Sea Jazz Festival** 1976–
fdr: Paul Acket
coord.: George Wein's Festival Productions Inc. (responsible for sponsorship and booking)
ds: three days in July
locs.: 12 venues in the Congresgebouw
aud.: 40,000
notes: sponsored by the Japanese Victor Corporation (1986–); the festival includes jazz films and videos

LAREN. See NOS Jazz Festival.

LOOSDRECHT. See NOS Jazz Festival.

ROTTERDAM. See NOS Jazz Festival.

NORTHERN IRELAND. See United Kingdom.

NORWAY

BERGEN. **Natt Jazz / Night Jazz** 1973–
aff.: Bergen International Festival
ds: 15 days in May–June
locs. incl.: Studentsenteret, Grieghallen, and Haakonshallen
pr. rep.: bop to jazz-rock
aud.: 12,000

KONGSBERG. **Kongsberg Jazz Festival** 1963–
fdrs: Kjell Gunnar Hoff and Per Ottersen
ds: five days in June–July
locs.: indoor and outdoor venues
pr. rep.: bop to free jazz and jazz-rock
aud.: 6000–7000
notes: free admission to some outdoor events; the festival includes jazz films and exhibitions

MOLDE. ***Molde International Jazz Festival** 1961–
fdr and orgr: Storyville Jazz Club
ds: six days in July–August
locs.: indoor venues
aud.: 15,000
notes: supported by the Norwegian government; the festival includes jazz films and exhibitions

OSLO. **Oslo Jazzfestival** 1986–
dir.: Aage Teigen (1986)
ds: three days in August
locs. incl.: Oslo Konserthus (concert hall), and Oslo Jazzhus, New Orleans Workshop, and Hot House (nightclubs)
pr. rep.: traditional jazz and swing; also ragtime

VOSS. **Vossa Jazz / Voss Jazz Festival** 1974–
fdrs: Asle Haaland and Lars Mossefin of the Voss Jazz Club
ds: three days in March–April
locs. incl.: Voss Cinema Hall
aud.: 2000

POLAND

KRAKÓW. **All Souls' Day Jazz Festival** 1954–
fdr: Polskie Stowarzyszenie Jazzowe
ds: four days in October–November
aud.: 150–500 per concert

SOPOT. **Sopot Jazz Festival** 1956–7
rep.: dixieland (1956); dixieland and bop (1957)
notes: Albert Mangelsdorff and Albert Nicholas participated in 1957; the festival was banned after street disturbances in 1957; it led to the founding of the Warsaw International Jazz Jamboree Festival (see below)

WARSAW. ***International Jazz Jamboree Festival** 1959–
fdr: Polskie Stowarzyszenie Jazzowe
ds: four days in October
locs. incl.: Congress Hall of the Palace of Culture and Sciences
pr. rep.: swing and bop to free jazz and jazz-rock
aud.: 3500 per concert at main events
note: Polskie Radio i Telewizja records some performances for later broadcast

WROCŁAW. **Jazz on the Odra** 1964–
ds: four days in April–May
locs.: indoor venues
pr. rep.: bop to free jazz and jazz-rock
aud.: 600 per concert at each of eight concerts

PORTUGAL

CASCAIS. **Cascais International Jazz Festival** 1972–
fdr: Luiz Villas-Boas
ds: three days in November
pr. rep.: bop to jazz-rock
note: Emissora Nacional de Radiodifusão broadcasts some performances

ROMANIA

PLOIEŞTI. **Festivalul Naţional de Jazz** 1969–71 [contd in Sibiu, see below]
fdrs: Alexandru Comanescŭ, Puiu Mancaş, and Nelu Stan
ds: spring

SIBIU. **Festivalul Internaţional de Jazz Sibiu / Sibiu International Jazz Festival** 1974– (1974–9, Festivalul Naţional de Jazz) [contd from Ploieşti, see above]
aff.: Cîntarea României (from 1977)
fdrs: Nicolae Ionescu, Titi Stoiculescu, and Emil Stratulat
ds: four days in March
aud.: 1000 per concert
note: sponsors include Casa de Cultură a Tineretului Sibiu–Clubul de Jazz and (1980–) Radioteleviziunii Române

SCOTLAND. See United Kingdom.

SPAIN

MADRID. **Madrid Jazz Festival** 1981–
ds: ten days in November
locs. incl.: Palacio de los Deportes (sports center)
pr. rep.: bop
aud.: 15,000 per concert at main events

MURCIA. **Festival Internacional de Jazz en la Calle** 1981–
fdr: Ayuntamiento de Murcia
ds: three days in April
loc.: Plaza de Romea (outdoor site)
aud.: 4000–5000

SAN SEBASTIÁN. **Donostiako Jazzaldía** [Festival de Jazz de San Sebastián] 1966–
fdr: Centro de Atracción y Turismo
orgr: Patronato Municipal de Festivales y Teatros
ds: five or six days in July
loc.: Palacio Municipal de los Deportes (sports center) and Plaza de la Trinidad (outdoor site)
pr. rep.: bop to free jazz and jazz-rock
aud.: 32,000

SWEDEN

ÅHUS. **Åhus Jazzfestival** 1971–?1975, 1987– [contd, 1976–86, as Kristianstad Jazzfestival, see Kristianstad below]
ds: summer

GÖTEBORG. **Göteborgs Jazzdagar** 1969–
ds: five days in August
locs. incl.: Liseberg
rep.: jazz; also blues

KRISTIANSTAD. **Kristianstad Jazzfestival** 1976–86 [contd from Åhus Jazzfestival, see Åhus above]
ds: three days in July

STOCKHOLM. **Jazz & Blues All Star Festival** 1980–
ds: seven days in June–July
locs.: Skeppsholmen and other outdoor venues
aud.: 5000–8000 per concert

UMEÅ. **Umeå Jazzfestival** 1967–
ds: four days in October

SWITZERLAND

Festa New Orleans Music 1974–
fdr: Hannes Anrig
ds: ten days in June–July
locs.: Lugano (1974–84); Ascona (1985–)
pr. rep.: traditional jazz and swing; also blues (first three days)
aud.: 10,000 per night
note: free admission to outdoor events

Riverboat Jazz Festival 1981–
fdrs: Markus Rindermann and Flussfahrten Zentrale
ds: seven days in September–October
locs.: Rhine cruise ship *Rex Rheni* and cities on the Rhine
pr. rep.: dixieland and swing
aud.: 150
note: Société Suisse de la Radiodiffusion records some performances for later broadcast on television

ASCONA. See Festa New Orleans Music.

BERNE. **Internationales Jazzfestival Bern** 1976–
ds: five days in May–June
locs. incl.: Kursaal
pr. rep.: swing and bop
aud.: 2000 per concert
bibliography: J. Norris: "Anatomy of a Festival," *Coda*, no.203 (1985), 20

LUGANO. **Festa New Orleans Music.** See above.

——. **International Jazz Festival** 1962–9
ds: two days in autumn
loc.: Teatro Apollo
pr. rep.: bop to free jazz
note: Société Suisse de la Radiodiffusion broadcast all performances

——. **Lugano Estival Jazz** 1979–
fdrs: Andreas Wyden and Jacky Marti
ds: three days in July
locs. incl.: Piazza delle Riforma (outdoor site) and Arte-Casa (concert hall)
pr. rep.: bop to jazz-rock
aud.: 7000–8000
note: free admission

——. **New Orleans in Lugano: Traditional Jazz Festival** 1985–
fdrs: Marino Zimmermann, Elvio Gianni, Jacky Leuzinger, and Norman Hewitt
ds: three days in June
locs.: six outdoor sites
pr. rep.: ragtime to bop; also blues, rhythm-and-blues, and Cajun music
notes: sponsored by the City of Lugano, Ente Turistico Lugano, and Crédit Suisse; free admission; founded to replace the Festa New Orleans Music in Lugano

MONTREUX. ***Montreux International Jazz Festival** 1967– (mid-1970s, Montreux International Festival)

fdr and dir.: Claude Nobs
ds: 17 days in July
loc.: Montreux Casino
pr. rep.: swing, bop, and jazz-rock; also other styles of popular music
notes: many performances are recorded for commercial issue; the festival is associated with the Montreux–Detroit Kool Jazz Festival, where the winner of the Montreux band competition and other Swiss musicians perform (see USA, Detroit)

WILLISAU. **Jazz Festival Willisau** 1975–
fdr and dir.: Niklaus Troxler
ds: four days in August
loc.: Festhalle
pr. rep.: swing and bop to free jazz and jazz-rock
bibliography: A. Raggenbass and others: *Jazz in Willisau* (Lucerne, Switzerland, 1978)

ZURICH. **International Jazz Festival Zürich** ?1951–1973, 1975–?, 1978–
fdr: Präsidialabteilung der Stadt Zürich
ds: three to five days in October–November
locs. incl.: Schützenhaus Albisgütli, Tonhalle, and Volkshaus Zürich (1986–7)
pr. rep.: bop to free jazz; earlier festivals included traditional jazz
aud: 6000
note: in the late 1980s the sponsor was the Präsidialabteilung der Stadt Zürich; some events are broadcast on Swiss radio (DRS, RSR, RSI)

TURKEY

ISTANBUL. **Istanbul Jazz Festival** fl. 1980s
ds: ten days in May

UNION OF SOVIET SOCIALIST REPUBLICS [USSR]

DONETSK, UKRAINIAN SSR. **Donetsk-[100] / Donetsk Jazz Festival** 1969– (title changes to reflect the anniversary of the founding of Donetsk)
freq.: biennially in odd-numbered years (except festival of 1975 postponed to 1976)
fdr: Viktor Dubyljér, president of the Donetsk Jazz Club
orgrs: Donetsk Jazz Club, Donetsk Philharmonic Society, and (1979–) the Donetsk concert agency
ds: three days in February–March

KRASNOYARSK, RUSSIAN SFSR. **Jazz nad Yenisey-[80]** 1980– (title changes annually to reflect the date)
freq.: annually
fdr: J. Aisenberg, president of the Creative Jazz Union
orgrs: local Komsomol organizations
ds: three or four days in June, October, or December
notes: the festival usually consists of five or six concerts followed by a jam session; in 1982 it included the first jazz cruise to take place in Siberia; jazz musicians of international standing, such as Vladimir Chekasin, Sergey Kuryokhin, and Oleg Lundstrem, have participated

LENINGRAD. **Osennie Ritmï / Autumn Rhythms** [Leningrad Jazz Festival] 1965–78, 1986–
fdr: Vladimir Feyertag
orgr: Lenconcert, the Leningrad concert agency
ds: five days in November
loc.: Leningrad Palace of Culture (Kapranov Palace)
aud.: 1500 per concert
note: jazz musicians of international standing have participated from 1986

MOSCOW. **Jazz-[1962]** [Moscow Jazz Festival] 1962, 1965, 1966–8, 1978– (title changes to reflect the date)
freq.: biennially in even-numbered years (1978–)
fdr: Moscow branch of the Composers' Union
orgr: Rosconcert, the Moscow concert agency
ds: four or five days in May
loc.: Moscow Olympic Village
pr. rep.: swing and bop

ODESSA. **Odessa-['82]** 1982– (title changes annually to reflect the date)
fdr: Nikolay Goloshchapov, president of the Odessa Jazz Club
orgrs: Youth Clubs Unity of Odessa, Odessa Philharmonic Society, and Odessa Jazz Club
ds: four days in April
locs.: Odessa Polytechnic Institute Club and the concert hall of the Odessa Philharmonic Society

RIGA. **Ritmï Leta / Summer Rhythms** 1976–
fdr: Leonid Nojdbálski, president of the Riga Jazz Club
orgrs: Riga Jazz Club and the Riga (Latviga) concert agency
ds: four to six days in June
pr. rep.: free jazz
aud.: 10,000

TALLINN. **Tallinn Jazz Festival** 1949–50, 1959–67, 1985–
fdrs: Uno Naissoo and Walter Ojakäär
ds: April
notes: sponsored by the Estonian Ministry of Culture; jazz musicians of international standing performed in 1966–7

YAROSLAVL'. **Jazz nad Volgoy** fl. 1980s
freq.: irregular
fdr and orgr: Igor Gavrilov, president of the Yaroslavl' Jazz Club
ds: three or four days in March
aud.: 1000 per concert
note: sponsored by the Yaroslavl' Jazz Club

UNITED KINGDOM [UK]

BELFAST. **Belfast Festival at Queen's** 1964–
fdr: Michael Emmerson
ds: 18 days in November
loc.: Guinness Spot (temporary nightclub) and other venues at Queen's University
pr. rep.: dixieland to bop
aud.: 250 per concert
note: general arts festival, of which jazz forms a small part

BIRMINGHAM. **Birmingham International Jazz Festival** 1985–
fdr: Jim Simpson
ds: ten days in July
locs. incl.: more than 160 venues in Birmingham and the West Midlands
pr. rep.: dixieland to bop
aud.: 200,000
note: free admission to many events

BRACKNELL. **Bracknell Jazz Festival** 1975– (except 1985: see Tring)
fdr: South Hill Park Arts Centre, Bracknell
dir.: John Cumming (1975–)
ds: three days in July
loc.: South Hill Park Arts Centre
pr. rep.: free jazz and jazz-rock
aud.: 4000–5000

BRECON. **New Orleans Beneath the Beacons Festival** [Brecon Jazz] 1984–
ds: three days in August
locs.: indoor and outdoor venues
pr. rep.: dixieland, also bop and free jazz
aud.: 70,000

BRIGHTON. **Brighton Jazz Festival** 1983–
aff.: Brighton Festival
ds: 25 days in May
locs. incl.: the Dome (theater) and Concorde (nightclub)
aud.: 7500

CARDIFF. **Welsh Jazz Festival** 1974–
ds: one week in May
locs. incl.: Chapter Arts Centre, Sherman Theatre, St. David's Hall, and Great Western Hotel
pr. rep.: swing and bop
aud.: 2000 per concert at main events

CHICHESTER. **Chichester Jazz Festival** 1978– (1978, Sanyo Jazz Festival)
fdr: Paul Rogerson
ds: four to six days in October
loc.: Chichester Festival Theatre
pr. rep.: dixieland and swing
aud.: 8000

EDINBURGH. **Edinburgh International Jazz Festival** 1979–
aff.: Edinburgh International Festival
fdr: Michael Warner Hart
ds: eight days in August
locs.: 20 venues
pr. rep.: swing and bop
aud.: 20,000
note: sponsored by the brewer McEwan (1984–)

——. **Round Midnight** 1982–
ds: two weeks in August–September
loc.: Queen's Hall
pr. rep.: bop to free jazz
aud.: 700 per concert
note: runs concurrently with the Edinburgh International Jazz Festival (see above)

HAYFIELD. **Hayfield International Jazz Festival** 1983–
fdr: Sheila Collier
ds: two or three days in summer
aud.: 15,000

note: jazz musicians of international standing and local musicians participate, working together in jam sessions

KNEBWORTH, nr ST. ALBANS. **Capital Jazz Festival** 1981–2
orgrs: Capital Radio and George Wein's Festival Productions Inc.
ds: two days in July (1981); four days in July (1982)
loc.: outdoor site
rep.: jazz presented with other types of popular music
notes: temporary location for the festival normally held in London (see JVC–Capital Radio Jazz Parade); the festival of 1981 was scheduled for two weekends in July at Clapham Common, the first of which was canceled owing to riots in London, and the second of which took place at Knebworth

LLANGOLLEN. **Llangollen International Jazz Festival** 1986–
ds: three days in May
locs. incl.: ten venues in Llangollen
aud.: 8000
note: the Welsh Jazz Society serves as adviser on bookings

LONDON. **Actual Festival** 1980–84
fdr: Anthony Wood
ds: six days in August (1980–83); six days in October (1984)
locs.: Institute of Contemporary Arts Theatre (1980–83); Bloomsbury Theatre (1984)
rep.: free jazz
aud.: 1000
note: preceded by four concerts under the same name in Notre Dame Hall (February–April 1980)

——. **Ally Pally '79.** See JVC–Capital Radio Jazz Parade.

——. **Camden Jazz Week** 1973– (except 1982)
aff.: Camden Festival
ds: six days in March–April and six days in October (to *c*1980); six days in March–April (*c*1980–)
locs. incl.: Shaw Theatre and other venues in the London Borough of Camden; formerly at Logan Hall and the Roundhouse Arts Centre
pr. rep.: bop to free jazz; a different aspect of jazz is featured each year (e.g., composed jazz in 1987)
aud.: 2000–3000 per concert at main events
notes: from 1986 the festival included commissioned projects, involving British and foreign musicians, and associated workshops; the BBC broadcasts many performances

——. **Capital Jazz Festival.** See JVC–Capital Radio Jazz Parade.

——. **Company Week** 1977– (except 1979–80, 1985–6)
fdr and orgr: Derek Bailey
ds: five to seven days in May–July
locs.: Institute of Contemporary Arts Theatre (1977–84); Arts Theatre (1987–)
pr. rep.: free jazz
aud.: 1000–1200
note: similar two- and three-day events have been organized by Bailey in New York, Tokyo, Paris, Helsinki, Berlin, and Vienna

——. **JVC–Capital Radio Jazz Parade** 1979– (1979, Ally Pally '79; 1980–83, Capital Jazz Jestival)
aff.: Capital Radio Music Festival
ds: six days in July
locs.: Alexandra Palace (1979); Royal Festival Hall (1980, 1983–); the festival removed to Knebworth (see above) in 1981–2
rep.: jazz presented with other types of popular music
notes: associated with George Wein's Festival Productions Inc.; sponsored by Capital Radio (1979–) and the Japanese Victor Corporation (1984–); in the week preceding the festival Capital Radio and the Musicians' Union sponsor the promotion of British jazz at Ronnie Scott's club; Ally Pally '79 superseded the Cleveland International Jazz Festival (see Middlesbrough)

——. **London Expo ['67]** 1967–?1970 (title changed annually to reflect the date)
orgr: Jack Higgins of Harold Davison Organization
ds: seven or eight days in October–November
locs.: Royal Festival Hall and Hammersmith Odeon
pr. rep.: dixieland, swing, bop, and free jazz; also blues
aud.: 38,000
note: associated with George Wein

——. **Soho Jazz Festival** 1986–
fdr: Peter Boizot
ds: ten days in October
locs.: Ronnie Scott's, Pizza Express, Wag, 100 Club, Marquee Club, London Palladium, Astoria, Video Café, Limelight, and other restaurants and pubs in Soho
aud.: 12–1000 per concert

MIDDLESBROUGH. **Cleveland International Jazz Festival** 1978
orgr: Andy Hudson
ds: three days in July
loc.: Ayresome Park (sports stadium)
pr. rep.: swing and bop
aud.: 4000 per concert
note: sponsored by the Cleveland Council Leisure and Amenities Department; superseded by Ally Pally '79 (see London, JVC–Capital Radio Jazz Parade)

NEWCASTLE-UPON-TYNE. **Metro Radio Newcastle Jazz Festival** 1975–
orgr: Northern Arts
ds: seven days in May
locs. incl.: Playhouse and City Hall
aud.: 10,000
notes: sponsored by Metro Radio and Newcastle-upon-Tyne City Council; the festival includes commissioned projects, among which have been collaborations between jazz musicians and dancers and photographic exhibitions

TRING. **International Jazz Festival** 1985
orgr: John Cumming
ds: three days in July
loc.: Pendley Manor (outdoor site)
pr. rep.: free jazz and jazz-rock
note: organized in place of the Bracknell Jazz Festival (see above)

WIGAN. **Wigan International Jazz Festival** 1986–
orgr: Wigan Metropolitan Borough Council
ds: eight days in July
locs. incl.: Mill at the Pier
pr. rep.: dixieland, swing, bop, and jazz-rock
aud.: 12,000

UNITED STATES OF AMERICA [USA]

ANN ARBOR, MI. **Ann Arbor Jazz & Blues Festival** 1972–6
orgr: John Sinclair
ds: three days in autumn
loc.: University of Michigan (outdoor site)
pr. rep.: bop to free jazz; also blues
aud.: 12,000
notes: sponsored by Rainbow Multi-Media Corporation; National Educational Radio broadcast performances; preceded by the Ann Arbor Blues Festival (1969–70)

ASPEN, CO. See Denver.

ATLANTA. **Atlanta Free Jazz Festival** 1978–
ds: three days in August–September
locs. incl.: Piedmont Park
pr. rep.: swing and bop to free jazz and jazz-rock
aud.: 25,000
notes: free admission; partly sponsored by the Atlanta Department of Cultural Affairs

BERKELEY, CA. **U.C. Berkeley Jazz Festival** 1967–
ds: two days in May (1967–84); two days in August–September (1985–)
locs. incl.: Hearst Greek Theater and other venues on the Berkeley campus of the University of California
pr. rep.: swing and bop to free jazz and jazz-rock
aud.: 17,000

BOSTON. **Boston Globe Jazz & Heritage Festival** 1966– (1966–85, Boston Globe Jazz Festival)
fdr: George Wein
prod.: George Wein's Festival Productions Inc.
ds: two days in January (1966–71); 11 days in March (1972–)
locs. incl.: War Memorial Auditorium (1966–?1971); Opera House, Berklee Performance Center, Park Plaza Ballroom, Orpheum Theater, and Symphony Hall (?1972–)
pr. rep.: swing and bop to jazz-rock
notes: sponsored by Affiliated Communications; the events that constitute the "heritage" element of the festival include popular music connected with Boston

BUFFALO. See Lewiston, NY.

CHICAGO. **AACM Festival** 1966–
fdrs: Fred Anderson and Bill Brimfield
ds: three days in May
locs. incl.: Getz Theater
rep.: free jazz
notes: centers on the work of the Association for the Advancement of Creative Musicians; the festival of 1979 also included concerts in New York

——. **Big Horn Jazz Festival.** See Rosemont, IL.

——. **Chicago Jazz Festival** 1979– (1982–4, Chicago Kool Jazz Festival)
fdr and orgr: Jazz Institute of Chicago
ds: five to seven days in August–September

loc.: Grant Park
pr. rep.: swing, bop, and blues to free jazz and jazz-rock
aud.: 250,000
notes: the festival developed from an annual two-day event paying tribute to Duke Ellington, which was founded in 1974 and of which the JIC became a sponsor in 1977; the festival was sponsored in 1982–4 by the manufacturer of Kool cigarettes; it has become the largest free-admission jazz festival in the USA; PBS TV and National Public Radio broadcast some performances
bibliography: H. Mandel: "Chicago Jazz," *DB*, xlvi/12 (1979), 32

——. **Playboy Jazz Festival** 1959
orgr: Playboy Magazine
ds: three days in August
loc.: Chicago Stadium
pr. rep.: dixieland, swing, and bop
aud.: 68,000
note: one of the biggest jazz festivals of the 1950s; Count Basie, Dizzy Gillespie, Duke Ellington, and others participated; other festivals of the same name have been held in different locations (see Hollywood)

CLEARWATER, FL. **Clearwater Jazz Holiday** 1980–
ds: four days in October
loc.: Coachman Park
pr. rep.: bop

COLORADO SPRINGS, CO. See Denver.

CONCORD, CA. **Concord Jazz Festival** 1969–(1969–*c*1972, Concord Summer Music Festival)
fdr: Carl Jefferson
ds: four days in August
locs.: Boulevard Park (1969–74); Concord Pavilion (1975–)
pr. rep.: swing and bop
aud.: up to 8000 per concert
note: from 1985 the festival has included one concert produced by George Wein's Festival Productions Inc. and sponsored by the Japanese Victor Corporation
bibliography: P. Elwood: "Concord Jazz: the Festival and the Founder," *JT* (Aug 1985), 9

CONNEAUT LAKE PARK, nr MEADVILLE, PA. **Annual Conneaut Lake Jazz Party** 1982– (1982–6, Annual Conneaut Lake Jazz Festival)
fdrs: Allegheny Jazz Society and Joe Boughton (president of the society)
ds: three days in August
locs.: Hotel Conneaut and American Pie (nightclub)
pr. rep.: swing
aud.: 225

DAVENPORT, IA. **Bix Beiderbecke Memorial Jazz Festival** 1972–
fdr: Don O'Dette
ds: four days in July
locs. incl.: Le Claire Park and riverboats on the Mississippi
pr. rep.: dixieland
aud.: 25,000

DECATUR, IL. **Central Illinois Jazz Festival** 1976–
fdr: Pete George
ds: three days in January–February
loc.: Holiday Inn Conference Resort
pr. rep.: dixieland and swing
bibliography: E. Banjura: "The Unlikely Festival," *MR*, xii/5 (1985), 9

DENVER. ***Colorado Jazz Party** [Dick and Maddie Gibson's Annual Jazz Party] 1963–
fdrs and dirs.: Dick Gibson and Maddie Gibson
ds: three days in September
locs.: Fairmount Hotel (1982–); earlier parties held at Vail, Aspen, and Colorado Springs
pr. rep.: swing and bop
aud.: 600
notes: private festival partly funded through admission fees; the festival of 1976 was the subject of the film *The Great Rocky Mountain Jazz Party* (1977)

DETROIT. **Montreux–Detroit Kool Jazz Festival** 1980–
ds: six days in August–September
locs.: Music Hall, Hart Plaza, and other indoor and outdoor venues
pr. rep.: swing and bop to free jazz and jazz-rock
aud.: 100,000
notes: sponsors have included the Renaissance Foundation; the festival is associated with the Montreux International Jazz Festival from which the winner of the band competition and other Swiss artists go to perform in Detroit (see Switzerland, Montreux)

GREAT RIVER, NY. **Great South Bay Jazz Festival** 1957–9
orgr: Friends of American Jazz
ds: three days in July
loc.: Timber Grove Club
pr. rep.: dixieland to bop
note: Miles Davis, Coleman Hawkins, Charles Mingus, and others participated

GUERNEVILLE, nr HEALDSBURG, CA. **Russian River Jazz Festival** 1977–
fdr: Clive Hawthorne
ds: two days in September
locs.: Johnson's Beach (1977–85); Midway Beach (1986–)
pr. rep.: bop to free jazz and jazz-rock
aud.: 5000

HARTFORD, CT. **Real Art Ways [RAW] August Jazz Festival** 1979–
fdr: Joseph Celli
ds: two days in August
loc.: Bushnell Park
pr. rep.: free jazz
aud.: 2000

HERNDON, VA, nr WASHINGTON. **Manassas Jazz Festival** 1985– [contd from Manassas, VA, see below]
ds: three days in November–December
loc.: Ramada Renaissance Hotel, nr Dulles Airport
pr. rep.: dixieland and swing

HIGHLAND PARK, nr CHICAGO. **Jazz & Contemporary Music Series**
aff.: Ravinia Festival
prod.: Andy Cirzan
ds: July–September
notes: jazz is presented as a component in a general music festival; the Ravinia Festival of 1939 included a performance by Benny Goodman and the jazz component of the festival increased steadily from that time

HOLLYWOOD, CA. **Los Angeles Jazz Festival** 1959–60
orgrs: Hal Lederman and Pete Ekstein
ds: two days in October
loc.: Hollywood Bowl
pr. rep.: swing and bop
aud.: 9000–18,000 per concert

——. **Playboy Jazz Festival** 1979–
prod.: George Wein Festival Productions Inc.
ds: two days in June
loc.: Hollywood Bowl
pr. rep.: swing and bop to jazz-rock; also gospel music
aud.: 18,000 per concert
notes: sponsored by Playboy Enterprises; other festivals of the same name have been held in different locations (see Chicago)

JACKSONVILLE, FL. **Jacksonville Jazz Festival** 1983– (1983–4, Jacksonville and All that Jazz) [contd from Mayport and All that Jazz, see Mayport, FL]
co-prod.: George Wein's Festival Productions Inc. (1985–)
ds: three days in October
loc.: Florida National Pavilion in Metropolitan Park
aud.: 100,000
notes: sponsored by the Japanese Victor Corporation (1987–); free admission; the festival is the subject of an annual feature on PBS TV

KANSAS CITY, MO. **Women's Jazz Festival** 1978–85 (except 1984)
fdrs: Carol Comer and Dianne Gregg
ds: four days in May
locs.: hotels and theaters
pr. rep.: swing and bop to free jazz
aud.: 1500–2200 per concert at main events
note: the festival included educational activities such as workshops and free concerts in schools
bibliography: C. Wyman: "Women's Fest Returns," *DB*, iii/8 (1985), 12; ——: "The Women's Jazz Festival Returns . . . with a Different Look," *JT* (May 1985), 11

LEWISTON, NY. **Artpark Jazz Series** fl. 1980s
aff.: Artpark Summer Theater
ds: June–August
loc.: Artpark (outdoor site)
aud.: 3900 per concert

LOS ANGELES. **Dixieland Jubilee** 1948–60
ds: one day in autumn
loc.: Shrine Auditorium
pr. rep.: dixieland
aud.: 6700
note: renowned dixieland performers such as Bobby Hackett participated

——. **Los Angeles Classic Jazz Festival** 1984–
fdr: Chuck Conklin
ds: four days in September

loc.: Marriott Hotel
pr. rep.: dixieland

MANASSAS, VA. **Manassas Jazz Festival** 1966–84 [contd in Herndon, VA, see above]
fdr: Johnson "Fat Cat" McRee
ds: three days in November–December
locs.: nightclubs and hotels
pr. rep.: dixieland and swing

MAYPORT, nr JACKSONVILLE, FL. **Mayport and All that Jazz** 1980–82 [contd as Jacksonville and All that Jazz, see Jacksonville, FL]
fdr: Jake M. Godbold, mayor of Jacksonville
ds: one day in October
locs.: Mayport (1980–81); Florida National Pavilion in Metropolitan Park (1982)

MIAMI. See Caribbean.

MONTEREY, CA. ***Monterey Jazz Festival** 1958–
fdrs: Jimmy Lyons and Ralph J. Gleason
ds: three days in September
loc.: Monterey County Fairgrounds
pr. rep.: swing and bop
aud.: 7000 per concert
note: the festival includes extensive educational activities

NEW ORLEANS. ***New Orleans Jazz & Heritage Festival** 1968– (1968–9, New Orleans Jazz Festival)
fdr: City of New Orleans
dir.: Quint Davis (1970–)
ds: ten days in April–May
locs. incl.: Municipal Auditorium (1968–71), riverboat SS *President* (1968–), and Fairgrounds Race Track (1972–)
rep.: New Orleans jazz
aud.: 300,000
note: sponsored by Quint Davis and George Wein (1970–); the events that constitute the "heritage" element of the festival include blues, soul music, and Cajun music

NEWPORT, RI. **Cliff Walk Manor** 1960
fdrs: Charles Mingus and Max Roach
ds: three days in July
loc.: Cliff Walk Manor Hotel
pr. rep.: swing, hard bop, and free jazz
note: organized as a rival to the Newport Jazz Festival

——. **JVC Jazz Festival Newport** 1984–
fdr: George Wein's Festival Productions Inc.
ds: two days in August
loc.: Fort Adams State Park, nr Newport
pr. rep.: swing and bop to jazz-rock; also blues
aud.: 15,000
notes: sponsored by the Japanese Victor Corporation; offshoot of the Kool (later JVC) Jazz Festival, which originated as the Newport Jazz Festival, see below, see also New York

——. ***Newport Jazz Festival** 1954–71 (except 1961) [contd as Newport Jazz Festival New York, see New York]
fdrs: Louis Lorillard and Elaine Lorillard
dir.: George Wein
ds: three or four days in June
locs. incl.: Festival Field (1962–71)
pr. rep.: swing and bop to jazz-rock; also blues and at times rock
notes: the most important jazz festival in the world and the progenitor of events in other countries, which have used its name; the festival of 1958 was the subject of the film *Jazz on a Summer's Day* (1960); from the 1960s an annual tour was made by a group of musicians under the name Newport All-Stars; riots interrupted performances at Newport in 1960 and 1971, causing the cancellation of the festival in 1961 and its removal to New York

NEW YORK. **Greenwich Village Jazz Festival** 1982–
fdrs: Horst Liepolt and Mel Litoff
ds: 11 days in August–September
locs. incl.: nightclubs in Greenwich Village (Arthur's Tavern, Blue Note, Carlos 1, Discovery of Soho, Fat Tuesday's, 55 Bar, Sweet Basil, Village Corner, Village Gate, and Village Vanguard), the cruise ship *DeWitt Clinton*, and Bleecker Street Cinema
pr. rep.: bop to free jazz and jazz-rock
aud.: 50,000
note: the festival includes jazz films and a one-day event in association with Music is . . . an Open Sky (see below)
bibliography: I. Gitler: "New York Talk: the History of the Greenwich Jazz Festival," *Jazz Express*, no.77 (1986), 14

——. **Jazz in July (at the 92nd Street Y)** 1985–
fdrs: Hadassah B. Markson and Dick Hyman
ds: ten days in July
loc.: 92nd Street Y
pr. rep.: early jazz and swing; also blues and ragtime
aud.: 925 per concert

——. **JVC Jazz Festival New York** 1972– (1972–9, Newport Jazz Festival New York; 1980, Kool Newport Jazz Festival; 1981–5, Kool Jazz Festival) [contd from Newport Jazz Festival, see Newport, RI]
fdr: George Wein
prod.: George Wein's Festival Productions Inc.
ds: ten days in June
locs. incl.: Carnegie Hall, Avery Fisher Hall, Staten Island Ferry, and more than 50 other venues in the metropolitan area (see also notes)
notes: sponsored by the manufacturer of Kool cigarettes (1980–85), then by the Japanese Victor Corporation (1986–); associated activities took place from the mid-1970s in Waterloo, near Stanhope, NJ (1976–, see below), Saratoga Springs, NY (see below), and Purchase, near White Plains, NY; in addition musicians toured the USA under the festival's name from 1975 (e.g., as JVC Jazz Festival on Tour, 1985)
See *NEWPORT JAZZ FESTIVAL.

——. **Music is . . . an Open Sky** 1983– [contd from Sydney, see Australia, Sydney]
fdr: Horst Liepolt
ds: two weeks in January–February, and one day in September
loc.: Sweet Basil (nightclub)
rep.: free jazz
aud.: 500–1500
note: the event in September takes place as part of the Greenwich Village Jazz Festival (see above)
bibliography: M. Bourne: "Lester Bowie's Brass Fantasy," *DB*, lii/5 (1985), 53

——. **New York Jazz Festival** 1956–61, ?1966–70
orgrs: Don Friedman and Ken Joffe (1956–?1958); Frank Geltman (?1959–1961); Teddy Powell (?1966–70)
ds: two or three days in June (1956), two or three days in August (?1957–1961, ?1966–70)
loc.: Downing Stadium, Randall's Island
pr. rep.: swing, bop, free jazz, and jazz-rock; also gospel
aud.: 20,000–40,000
notes: the festival was revived around 1966 by Teddy Powell; Stan Getz, Carmen McRae, Oscar Peterson, and others participated

PHILADELPHIA. **Mellon Jazz Festival** fl. 1980s (to *c*1985, Kool Jazz Festival Philadelphia)
ds: ten days in June
locs. incl.: Academy of Music
pr. rep.: swing and bop to free jazz and jazz-rock

PITTSBURGH. **Pittsburgh Jazz Festival** [Mellon Jazz Festival Pittsburgh] 1984–
ds: ten days in August–September (1984–6); ten days in June (1987–)
locs. incl.: Heinz Hall, Hyatt Hotel Ballroom, Graffiti (nightclub), and Flagstaff Hill in Schenley Park; also McKeesport, near Pittsburgh (see notes)
pr. rep.: swing and bop to free jazz and jazz-rock
notes: sponsored solely by Mellon Bank (1987–); the festival includes a one-day event with free admission at McKeesport; in 1987 it included a photographic exhibition and jazz films

ROSEMONT, IL. **Big Horn Jazz Festival** fl. 1980s (to 1984, Festival of Traditional Jazz)
fdr: Buzz Snavely
ds: three days in November
locs.: O'Hare Airport (Holiday Inn, to 1984, Sheraton International, 1985–)
pr. rep.: dixieland and swing
aud.: 1000

SACRAMENTO, CA. ***Sacramento Dixieland Jubilee** 1974–
fdr: Bill Borcher
ds: four days in May
locs.: indoor and outdoor venues
pr. rep.: dixieland
aud.: 250,000
note: important dixieland bands from outside the USA have participated

ST. LOUIS. **Mid-America Jazz Festival** 1982–
fdr: Charles V. Wells
ds: three days in March
locs.: Chase-Park Plaza Hotel (1982–3); Sheraton St. Louis Hotel (1984–)
pr. rep.: traditional jazz and swing; also blues
aud.: 600–800

SARATOGA SPRINGS, NY. **Newport Jazz Saratoga** 1978–
fdr: George Wein and the Saratoga Performing Arts Center
ds: two days in June–July
loc.: Saratoga Performing Arts Center

pr. rep.: swing and bop to jazz-rock; also blues
aud.: 25,000
note: runs concurrently with the JVC Jazz Festival New York, of which it is an offshoot, see New York

SCOTTSDALE, AZ. **Paradise Valley Jazz Party** 1978–
fdr: Don Miller
ds: two days in March
loc.: Camelback Inn
pr. rep.: swing and bop; a different musician is featured each year
note: private festival

VAIL, CO. See Denver.

WATERLOO VILLAGE, nr STANHOPE, NJ. **JVC Jazz Festival–NJJS Waterloo Village Jazz Picnic** 1976– (1976–80, NJJS–Newport Jazz Festival; 1981–5, Kool Jazz Festival–NJJS Waterloo Village Jazz Picnic)
fdrs: New Jersey Jazz Society (NJJS) and George Wein's Festival Productions Inc.
ds: two days in June
pr. rep.: early jazz and swing
aud.: 5000–10,000
note: organized by the NJJS, one day in conjunction with the JVC Jazz Festival (formerly Newport Jazz Festival New York, then Kool Jazz Festival, see New York), the other in conjunction with the Waterloo Music Festival

UK. See United Kingdom.

USA. See United States of America.

USSR. See Union of Soviet Socialist Republics.

WALES. See United Kingdom.

WEST GERMANY. See Federal Republic of Germany.

YUGOSLAVIA

BELGRADE. **Belgrade Jazz Festival** 1970–
orgr: Dom Omladine Belgrade (Belgrade youth center)
ds: four days in November

LJUBLJANA. **International Jazz Festival Ljubljana** 1960–
ds: three to four days in June

NOVI SAD. **Novi Sad Jazz Days** fl. 1980s
ds: three days in September–October
pr. rep.: free jazz

ZAGREB. **Jazz Fair Zagreb** fl. 1980s
orgr: Center for Cultural Activities
ds: six days in October
pr. rep.: bop

INDEX

Entries are provided in this index for current and former festival names and for prominent sponsors, founders, etc. Each entry refers to the country and city or town in which the festival is held; standard abbreviations are used for country names, including the German abbreviations BRD for the Federal Republic of Germany and DDR for the German Democratic Republic. Where only the country is named, the festival takes place in different cities, and its entry will be found in the table immediately following the name of the country. An asterisk indicates that there is a separate entry on the festival in the dictionary, as well as an entry in the list.

Friends of American Jazz: USA, Great River
Gebers, Jost: BRD, Berlin (Total Music Meeting, Workshop Freie Musik)
Gibson, Dick: USA, Denver
Göteborgs Jazzdagar: Sweden, Göteborg
Grande Parade du Jazz: France, Nice
Great South Bay Jazz Festival: USA, Great River
Greek Jazz Festival: Greece, Athens
Greenwich Village Jazz Festival: USA, New York
Guinness Jazz Festival: Ireland, Cork
Hayfield International Jazz Festival: UK, Hayfield
Heisler, Alexander: BRD, Freiburg (Internationales Jazzfestival Freiburg, Internationales Zelt-Musik-Festival Freiburg)
Hessischer Rundfunk: BRD, Frankfurt am Main
Hofheimer Jazzfest: BRD, Hofheim
Honky Tonk Jazz Festival Dendermonde: Belgium, Dendermonde
Hot Club de France: France, Montauban, Nice (Nice Jazz Festival)
Interessengemeinschaft Jazz Burghausen e.V.: BRD, Burghausen
Internationale Jazz-Woche Burghausen: BRD, Burghausen
Internationales Jazzfestival Bern: Switzerland, Berne
Internationales Jazzfestival Freiburg: BRD, Freiburg
Internationales Jazzfestival Münster: BRD, Münster
Internationales Zelt-Musik-Festival Freiburg: BRD, Freiburg
International Festival of Jazz: Italy, Verbania
International Jazz Festival: Switzerland, Lugano
International Jazz Festival: UK, Tring
International Jazz Festival Ljubljana: Yugoslavia, Ljubljana
International Jazzfestival Nürnberg: BRD, Nuremberg
International Jazz Festival of Japan: Japan
International Jazz Festival Prague: Czechoslovakia, Prague
International Jazzfestival Saalfelden: Austria, Saalfelden
International Jazz Festival Salzburg: Austria, Salzburg
International Jazz Festival van Dendermonde: Belgium, Dendermonde
International Jazz Festival Zürich: Switzerland, Zurich
*International Jazz Jamboree Festival: Poland, Warsaw
International Jazzmeeting: Belgium, Ghent
*International New Jazz Festival Moers: BRD, Moers
Israel Jazz Festival: Israel
Istanbul Jazz Festival: Turkey, Istanbul
Jacksonville Jazz Festival: USA, Jacksonville
Japan Booking Corporation: Japan, World Jazz Festival
Japanese Victor Corporation (JVC): France, Nice (JVC Grande Parade du Jazz Nice); Netherlands, The Hague; UK, Knebworth, London (JVC–Capital Radio Jazz Parade); USA, Concord, Jacksonville, Newport (JVC Jazz Festival Newport), New York (JVC Jazz Festival New York), Saratoga Springs, Waterloo Village
Jassfestival: Denmark, Holstebro
Jazz & Blues All Star Festival: Sweden, Stockholm
Jazz & Contemporary Music Series: USA, Highland Park
Jazz à Vienne: France, Vienne
Jazzbühne Berlin: DDR, Berlin
Jazz City International Jazz Festival: Canada, Edmonton
Jazzclub Honky Tonk: Belgium, Dendermonde
Jazzclub Treibhaus: Austria, Innsbruck
Jazz en France: France, Angoulême
Jazz Fair Zagreb: Yugoslavia, Zagreb
*Jazzfest Berlin: BRD, Berlin
Jazzfest Hollabrunn: Austria, Hollabrunn
Jazzfestival Dendermonde: Belgium, Dendermonde
Jazz(festival) Middelheim: Belgium, Antwerp
Jazz Festival Willisau: Switzerland, Willisau
Jazzfest Wiesen: Austria, Wiesen
Jazz im Theater-Festival Salzburg: Austria, Salzburg
Jazz in July: BRD, Berlin
Jazz in July (at the 92nd Street Y): USA, New York
Jazz Institute of Chicago: USA, Chicago (Chicago Jazz Festival)
Jazzkerho Break: Finland, Tampere
Jazz Middelheim: Belgium, Antwerp
Jazz: Musiques à Grenoble: France, Grenoble
Jazz nad Volgoy: USSR, Yaroslavl'
Jazz nad Yenisey-[80]; USSR, Krasnoyarsk
Jazz-[1962]: USSR, Moscow
Jazz on the Odra: Poland, Wrocław
Jazz Ost-West: BRD, Nuremberg
Jazz Plaza: Cuba, Havana
Jazz sous les Pommiers: France, Coutances
Jazz-Studio Nürnberg: BRD, Nuremberg
Jazzyatra: India, Bombay
John Player Jazz International Cork: Ireland, Cork
JVC–Capital Radio Jazz Parade: UK, London
*JVC Grande Parade du Jazz Nice: France, Nice
JVC Jazz Festival Newport: USA, Newport
JVC Jazz Festival New York: USA, New York
JVC Jazz Festival–NJJS Waterloo Village Jazz Picnic: USA, Waterloo Village
Kölcsey Ferenc Müvelödési Központ: Hungary, Debrecen
Kongsberg Jazz Festival: Norway, Kongsberg
Kool Jazz Festival: USA, New York (JVC Jazz Festival New York)
Kool Jazz Festival–NJJS Waterloo Village Jazz Picnic: USA, Waterloo Village
Kool Jazz Festival Philadelphia: USA, Philadelphia
Kool Newport Jazz Festival: USA, New York (JVC Jazz Festival New York)
Kristianstad Jazzfestival: Sweden, Kristianstad
Kunstdünger's Jazzfestival Innsbruck: Austria, Innsbruck
Laren Internationaal Jazz Festival: Netherlands, NOS Jazz Festival
Lazy River Jazz Club: Belgium, Ghent
Leipziger Jazztage: DDR, Leipzig
Le Mans Jazz Action: France, Le Mans
Lenconcert: USSR, Leningrad
Leningrad Jazz Festival: USSR, Leningrad
Leverkusener Jazztage: BRD, Leverkusen
Liepolt, Horst: Australia, Sydney (Music is . . . an Open Sky, Qantas International Jazz Festival); USA, New York (Greenwich Village Jazz Festival, Music is . . . an Open Sky)
Llangollen International Jazz Festival: UK, Llangollen
London Expo ['67]: UK, London
Los Angeles Classic Jazz Festival: USA, Los Angeles
Los Angeles Jazz Festival: USA, Hollywood
Loosdrecht Internationaal Jazz Festival: Netherlands, NOS Jazz Festival
Lugano Estival Jazz: Switzerland, Lugano
Madrid Jazz Festival: Spain, Madrid
Magyar Rádió és Televizie: Hungary, Budapest (Budapest Jazz Festival, Szeged International Jazz Week), Debrecen
Major Minor Music: BRD, Berlin (Jazz in July)
Manassas Jazz Festival: USA, Herndon, Manassas
Mardel Jazz: Argentina
Mayport and All that Jazz: USA, Mayport
Mellon Jazz Festival: USA, Philadelphia
Mellon Jazz Festival Pittsburgh: USA, Pittsburgh
Metro Radio Newcastle Jazz Festival: UK, Newcastle-upon-Tyne
Mezinárodní Jazzový Festival Praha: Czechoslovakia, Prague
Mid-America Jazz Festival: USA, St. Louis
Moers Music: BRD, Moers
*Molde International Jazz Festival: Norway, Molde
Montauban International Jazz Festival: France, Montauban
*Monterey Jazz Festival: USA, Monterey
Montreal Jazz Festival: Canada, Montreal
Montreux–Detroit Kool Jazz Festival: USA, Detroit
*Montreux International Jazz Festival: Switzerland, Montreux
Moscow Jazz Festival: USSR, Moscow
Music is . . . an Open Sky: Australia, Sydney; USA, New York
Musik Messe Frankfurt: BRD, Frankfurt am Main
Nancy Jazz Pulsations: France, Nancy
National Educational Radio: USA, Ann Arbor
Natt Jazz: Norway, Bergen
Nederlandse Omroep Stichting: Netherlands, NOS Jazz Festival
Nemu Jazz Inn: Japan, Tokyo
New Jazz Meeting Baden-Baden: BRD, Baden-Baden
New Jersey Jazz Society: USA, Waterloo Village
New Orleans Beneath the Beacons Festival: UK, Brecon
New Orleans in Lugano: Traditional Jazz Festival: Switzerland, Lugano
*New Orleans Jazz & Heritage Festival: USA, New Orleans
*Newport Jazz Festival: USA, Newport
Newport Jazz Festival New York: USA, New York (JVC Jazz Festival New York)
Newport Jazz Saratoga: USA, Saratoga Springs
New York Jazz Festival: USA, New York
92nd Street Y: USA, New York (Jazz in July)
Nice Jazz Festival: France, Nice
Night Jazz: Norway, Bergen
Nîmes International Jazz Festival: France, Nîmes
NJJS–Newport Jazz Festival: USA, Waterloo Village
*North Sea Jazz Festival: Netherlands, The Hague
Norwegian Caribbean Lines Jazz Festivals: Caribbean
NOS Jazz Festival: Netherlands
Novi Sad Jazz Days: Yugoslavia, Novi Sad
Ö 3 Jazz Fest: Austria, Vienna
Ö 3 Jazzfestival Bleiburg: Austria, Bleiburg
Odessa-['82] USSR, Odessa
Organisation Internationale de Radio et Télévision: Hungary, Debrecen
ORTF: France, Paris (Festival de Jazz de Paris, Paris Jazz Festival), Samois-sur-Seine
Oslo Jazzfestival: Norway, Oslo
Osennie Ritmï: USSR, Leningrad
Österreichischer Rundfunk: Austria, Bleiburg, Vienna (Ö 3 Jazz Fest)
Ottawa Jazz Festival: Canada, Ottawa
Oude Stijl Jazz Festival Breda: Netherlands, Breda

Palermo Jazz Estate: Italy, Palermo
Paradise Valley Jazz Party: USA, Scottsdale
Paris Inter: France, Paris (Festival International de Jazz)
Paris Jazz Fair: France, Paris (Festival International de Jazz)
Paris Jazz Festival: France, Paris
PBS TV: USA, Jacksonville
Pescara Jazz: Italy, Pescara
Pittsburgh Jazz Festival: USA, Pittsburgh
Playboy Jazz Festival: USA, Chicago, Hollywood
Polskie Radio i Telewizja: Poland, Warsaw
Polskie Stowarzyszenie Jazzowe: Poland, Kraków, Warsaw
*Pori (International) Jazz (Festival): Finland, Pori
Poste Parisien: France, Paris (Festival International de Jazz)
Pragokoncert: Czechoslovakia, Prague
Praxis Festival: Greece, Athens
Qantas International Jazz Festival: Australia, Sydney
Radiodiffusion-Télévision Belge: Belgium, Antwerp (Jazz(festival) Middelheim)
Radioteleviziunii Române: Romania, Sibiu
Rassegna Internazionale del Jazz di Pisa: Italy, Pisa
Rassegna Internazionale di Orchestre Jazz: Italy, Bologna
Ravenna Jazz: Italy, Ravenna
Ravinia Festival: USA, Highland Park
Real Art Ways [RAW] August Jazz Festival: USA, Hartford
Riga Jazz Club: USSR, Riga
Riga (Latviga) concert agency: USSR, Riga
Ritmī Leta: USSR, Riga
Riverboat Jazz Festival: Switzerland
Rosconcert: USSR, Moscow
Rotterdam Internationaal Jazz Festival: Netherlands, NOS Jazz Festival
Round Midnight: UK, Edinburgh
Rundfunk der DDR: DDR, Berlin
Russian River Jazz Festival: USA, Guerneville
*Sacramento Dixieland Jubilee: USA, Sacramento
Sanyo Jazz Festival: UK, Chichester
Seajazz: Finland, Helsinki
Sibiu International Jazz Festival: Romania, Sibiu
Slavokoncert: Czechoslovakia, Bratislava
Société Suisse de la Radiodiffusion: Switzerland, Riverboat Jazz Festival, Lugano (International Jazz Festival)
Sofiakoncert / Sofia Jazz Festival: Bulgaria, Sofia
Soho Jazz Festival: UK, London
Sopot Jazz Festival: Poland, Sopot
Sorø Jazzfestival: Denmark, Sorø
Storyville Jazz Club: Norway, Molde
Südwestfunk: BRD, Baden-Baden
Summer Jazz Festival: BRD, Berlin (Jazz in July)
Summer Rhythms: USSR, Riga
Szeged International Jazz Week: Hungary, Budapest
Tallinn Jazz Festival: USSR, Tallinn
Tampere Jazz Happening: Finland, Tampere
Thom, Fritz: Austria, Hollabrunn, Vienna (Ö 3 Jazz Fest)
Tivoli Jazz Festival: Denmark, Copenhagen
Total Music Meeting: BRD, Berlin
Toyohashi Black Heritage Festival: Japan, Toyohashi
Turku Jazz ry: Finland, Turku
Turun Jazztapahtuma: Finland, Turku
U.C. Berkeley Jazz Festival: USA, Berkeley
Umbria Jazz (Festival and Clinic): Italy, Umbria
Umeå Jazzfestival: Sweden, Umeå
UMO Big Band: Finland, Helsinki
Verona International Jazz Festival: Italy, Verona
Vienne Action Culturelle: France, Vienne
Vossa Jazz / Voss Jazz Festival: Norway, Voss
Wein, George: Denmark, Copenhagen; France, Nice (JVC Grande Parade du Jazz Nice); Japan, World Jazz Festival, Madarao, Toyohashi; Netherlands, The Hague; UK, Knebworth, London (London Expo ['67]); USA, Boston, Concord, Hollywood (Playboy Jazz Festival), Jacksonville, New Orleans, Newport (JVC Jazz Festival Newport, Newport Jazz Festival), New York (JVC Jazz Festival New York), Saratoga Springs, Waterloo Village
Welsh Jazz Festival: UK, Cardiff
Welsh Jazz Society: UK, Llangollen
Westdeutscher Rundfunk: BRD, Berlin (Jazzfest Berlin), Moers
Wigan International Jazz Festival: UK, Wigan
Women's Jazz Festival: USA, Kansas City
Workshop Freie Musik: BRD, Berlin
World Jazz Festival: Japan
Yaroslavl' Jazz Club: USSR, Yaroslavl'

BARRY KERNFELD (1, 2)
PAUL R. LAIRD (3)

Fewclothes Cabaret. Nightclub in New Orleans; *see* NIGHTCLUBS AND OTHER VENUES.

Feza, Mongezi (*b* Queenstown, South Africa, 1945; *d* London, 14 Dec 1975). South African trumpeter. At the age of 16 he joined the Swinging City Six, led by the tenor saxophonist Ronnie Beer, in Cape Town. His playing attracted the attention of Chris McGregor and he was invited to join the Blue Notes; in 1965 he moved with the group to London, where he worked with McGregor's Brotherhood of Breath, playing an important role as a forceful soloist and ensemble leader. He moved to Denmark in 1972 and joined forces with Johnny Dyani (also formerly a member of McGregor's groups) and the percussionist Okay Temiz; they recorded Dyani's album *Music for Xaba* in Sweden for the Sonet label in the same year. Feza's playing was fiery and audacious, marked by passionate flourishes and spiky humor; a good example of his work is the recording *In the Townships* (1973, Car. 1504) by Dudu Pukwana's group Spear.

BIBLIOGRAPHY

R. Cotterrell, ed.: *Jazz Now: the Jazz Centre Society Guide* (London, 1976)
C. de Ledesma: "Afro Jazz: Evolution and Revolution," *The Wire*, no.12 (1985), 26, esp. 32

CHARLES DE LEDESMA

Fidelity. In sound-recording terminology the accuracy with which the original sound is reproduced by the recording and playback media; *see* RECORDING, esp. §I, 1(i).

Fields, Geechie [Julius] (*b* Georgia, *c*1903). Trombonist. He grew up in Jenkins' Orphanage, Charleston, South Carolina, and played regularly in the bands there. Around 1924 he moved to New York, where he worked with various leaders at John O'Connor's Club. Before he retired from music in the 1930s he played in bands led by Earle Howard (1926–7), Charlie Skeete (1929), and Bill Benford (1929–30). He also made recordings with Jelly Roll Morton in 1928 and 1930 (including *Mournful Serenade*, 1928, Vic. 38024), and with Clarence Williams in 1929. (J. Chilton: *A Jazz Nursery: the Story of the Jenkins' Orphanage Bands of Charleston, South Carolina*, London, 1980)

based on *ChiltonW*

Fields, Herbie [Herbert] (*b* Elizabeth, NJ, 24 May 1919; *d* Miami, 17 Sept 1958). Clarinetist and alto and tenor saxophonist. He attended the Juilliard School (1936–8), performed with Raymond Scott, Leonard Ware, and Hot Lips Page, and while serving in the army led a band at Fort Dix, New Jersey (1941–3). After his discharge he joined the band of Lionel Hampton, with which he remained until late in 1945 (recording at Carnegie Hall the same year); he also led small groups and big bands from 1944 (recording in 1944–7). In 1945 he was named a "new star" on the alto saxophone by *Esquire* and recorded with Miles Davis. His career in jazz declined in the 1950s and he recorded commercially oriented material for the rest of his life. Fields had a light, swinging approach to the clarinet and a raucous, undisciplined style on the alto saxophone influenced by swing.

SELECTED RECORDINGS

As leader: Jumpin' for Savoy/How Herbie Feels (1945, Savoy 560); Just Relaxin'/Four o'Clock Blues (1945, Savoy 592)
As sideman: on H. L. Page: *After Hours in Harlem* (1940–41, Onyx 207), Dinah (1940), I Got Rhythm (1940); L. Hampton: *All American Award Concert* (1945, Decca 8088)

BIBLIOGRAPHY

FeatherE
J. Tracy: "Caught in the Act," *DB*, xxii/25 (1955), 8
Obituary, *DB*, xxv/22 (1958), 10

MICHAEL ULLMAN

Fields, Kansas [Carl Donnell] (*b* Chapman, KS, 5 Dec 1915). Drummer. When he was 14 his family moved to Chicago, where he studied drums and, in 1933, began playing professionally with the trumpeter Eddie Mullens; later he worked with Jimmie Noone, Horace Henderson, and the trumpeters Johnny Long, King Kolax, Walter Fuller, and Roy Eldridge (1940–41). From 1939 to 1941 he sporadically led his own groups. He then moved to New York, where he joined Ella Fitzgerald's band (1941) and also played with Benny Carter, Edgar Hayes, and Charlie Barnet before joining the US Marines (1942). He made his first recordings in New York with Mel Powell's septet (which included Billy Butterfield and Benny Goodman) in 1942; in the same decade he performed at Minton's Playhouse with Eddie "Lockjaw" Davis and Clyde Hart, and worked with Cab Calloway (1945), Claude Hopkins (1946), Eddie Condon, Sidney Bechet (1947, 1949), and Dizzy Gillespie. After a European tour with Mezz Mezzrow in 1953, Fields remained in Europe, working frequently with visiting and expatriate American musicians; he toured and recorded with Bechet in 1958. In 1964 he returned to Chicago, and continued to perform with local musicians until the 1980s. His playing, which is based on a combination of traditional dixieland and swing drumming styles, demonstrates both excellent technique and musical sensitivity.

SELECTED RECORDINGS

As sideman: M. Powell: The world is waiting for the sunrise/Mood at Twilight (1942, Com. 544); D. Gillespie: *Tin Tin Deo* (1951, Dee Gee 1000); M. Mezzrow: *Jazz Time Paris* (1953, Vogue 3); on *Americans in Europe*, ii (1963, Imp. 37), A. Nicholas: My buddy run rabbits, Rose Room, Why daughter, how are you?

BIBLIOGRAPHY

ChiltonW; *FeatherE*
H. Panassié: "Kansas Fields," *BHcF*, no.26 (1953), 5
B. Rusch: "Kansas Fields: Interview," *Cadence*, xii/3 (1986), 18

T. DENNIS BROWN

Fields, Ted [Edward] (*b* Cleveland, *c*1905; *d* March 1959). Drummer. In 1927 he played with a band led by Paul Craig in Buffalo. The following year he traveled to Europe with Sam Wooding, and remained with the group until 1931; he then performed and made recordings (including *Christopher Columbus*, 1936, PAct 898) with Willie Lewis. Fields returned to New York in autumn 1938, and after playing with Benny Carter's big band at the Savoy (1939) ceased to work full-time, but continued to perform sporadically, notably in a sextet led by the pianist Sammy Stewart (1944).

based on *ChiltonW*

Fierstone, George (*b* London, 14 Nov 1916; *d* London, 13 April 1984). English drummer. After playing in a touring revue in 1931, he worked in London with many bandleaders, among them Bert Ambrose, Harry Roy, the clarinetist and alto saxophonist Sid Millward (recording in 1938), the clarinetist Frank Weir (recording in 1944), and Harry Hayes (recording in 1944–6); his playing may be heard to advantage on Hayes's *Keep Going – Don't Stop* (1945, HMV B9457). He also worked as a studio musician (1931–45) and was a member of the HERALDS OF SWING (1939). Also during World War II he played (as a civilian) in an RAF dance band, which made several recordings around 1943–4; taking the name the Skyrockets, it worked from 1946 to 1953 at the London Palladium, accompanying such prominent singers as Ella Fitzgerald and Frank Sinatra. Fierstone then returned to freelance work and formed bands of his own for specific occasions; he performed for the last time in 1983. He was also active as a booking agent for cabaret performers.

DIGBY FAIRWEATHER

52nd Street. Street in New York which was the center of jazz performance in the city for about a decade from the mid-1930s; many of the most famous nightclubs of the period were situated on the block between Fifth and Sixth avenues, including the Onyx, the Famous Door, the Three Deuces, Jimmy Ryan's, the Spotlite, and Kelly's Stable. *See* NIGHTCLUBS AND OTHER VENUES.

Fill [fill-in]. A short harmonic, rhythmic, or melodic figure played at points of inactivity or stasis (for example, between phrases, choruses, or solos, or during a sustained note) by a member or members of a group other than the soloist. Usually such a figure lasts no more than a beat or two and its rhythm and melody are independent of the theme. In written arrangements fills are typically played by the ensemble as a whole; for example, in the *a* sections that open Woody Herman's *Four Brothers* (1947, Col. 38304) the brass section plays fills between the phrases of the saxophone section's statement of the melody (ex.1). In improvised jazz, particularly that of small groups,

Ex.1 Brass fills in the opening chorus of Woody Herman's *Four Brothers* (1947, Col. 38304); transcr. B. Kernfeld

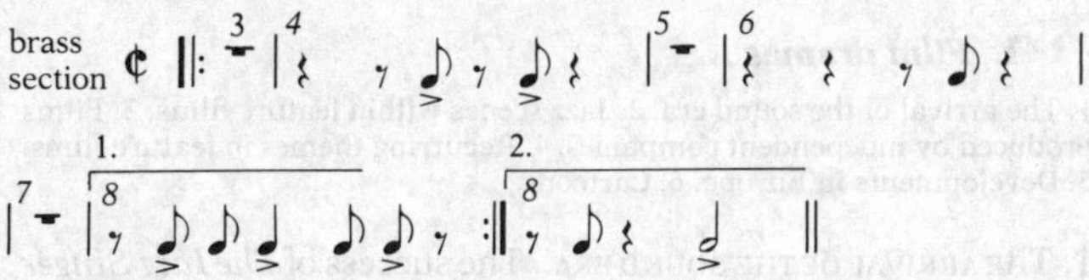

Ex.2 Drum fills played by Kenny Clarke on Charlie Christian's *Swing to Bop* first issued on *Jazz Immortal* (1941, Eso. 1); transcr. T. D. Brown

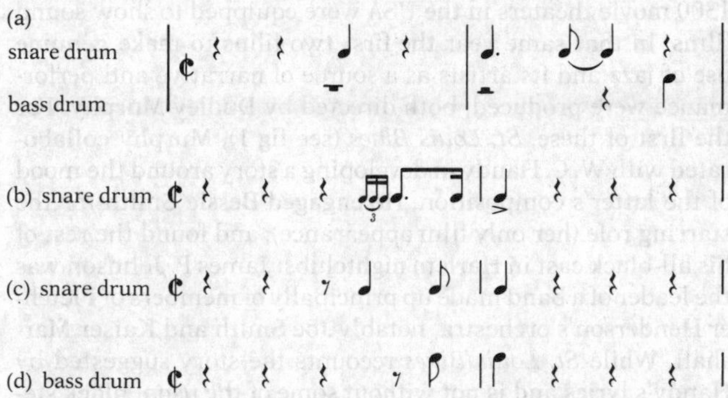

fills are usually played by a single member of the ensemble, most often the drummer, playing snare drum or snare and bass drums. Kenny Clarke was particularly adept and inventive in the playing of fills; ex.2 shows some of the varied fills he plays on Charlie Christian's *Swing to Bop* (1941).

ROBERT WITMER

Films. Motion pictures and jazz both evolved as art forms during the early years of the 20th century. Throughout the period between the end of World War I and the arrival of the sound era with *The Jazz Singer* (1927), jazz and other syncopated music played a persuasive and influential role in the social upheaval that shook American culture. Its home ground was speakeasies, nightclubs owned and frequented by gangsters, gambling dens, honky-tonks, bordellos, and cheap dance halls, and it was perceived as lowdown and erotic, vulgar and aggressive, cheap and unesthetic, new, freeing, and uninhibited. It was also seen as central to the new spirit, and became a perfect accompaniment to the 1920s, soon known as the "jazz age." It was therefore natural that the cinema should draw on jazz in order to appeal to the new public mood.

Hollywood immediately saw the commercial potential in producing "jazz spirit" motion pictures, and between 1917 and 1929 there appeared some 30 films with such titles as *The Jazbo Sheriff* (1918), *The Jazz Monkey* (1919), *Jazz and Jailbirds* (1919), *A Jazzed Honeymoon* (1919), *The Jazz Bandits* (1920), and *The Girl with the Jazz Heart* (1920), not only attesting to the popularity of the music but also proving that jazz was making enough of an impression to lend excitement and box-office allure to all kinds of subjects. By 1924, when speed, money, materialism, and fun dominated the American national appetite, *Sinners in Silk* was being advertised as a story of a new generation "whose hymn is jazz and whose slogan is speed." *Children of Jazz* (1923) and *The Fast Set* (1924) were also films whose stories showed aspects of the so-called jazz life in which the characters usually lived in a wild, reckless manner, their only goal seeming to be the pursuit of pleasure. These screen stereotypes became well established during the silent era.

I. Film dramas. II. Documentaries and other filmed performances. III. Jazz film scores.

I. *Film dramas*

1. The arrival of the sound era. 2. Jazz scenes within feature films. 3. Films produced by independent companies. 4. Recurring themes in feature films. 5. Developments in Europe. 6. Cartoons.

1. THE ARRIVAL OF THE SOUND ERA. The success of *The Jazz Singer* (1927, Warner Bros., dir. Alan Crosland), a film with synchronized musical accompaniment, proved the catalyst for Hollywood studios to convert to sound, and by 1929 more than 1300 movie theaters in the USA were equipped to show sound films. In that same year the first two films to make genuine use of jazz and its artists as a source of narrative and performance were produced, both directed by Dudley Murphy. For the first of these, *St. Louis Blues* (see fig.1), Murphy collaborated with W. C. Handy in developing a story around the mood of the latter's composition. He engaged Bessie Smith for the starring role (her only film appearance), and found the rest of his all-black cast in Harlem nightclubs: James P. Johnson was the leader of a band made up principally of members of Fletcher Henderson's orchestra, notably Joe Smith and Kaiser Marshall. While *St. Louis Blues* recounts the story suggested by Handy's lyrics and is not without some of the usual black stereotypes, Bessie Smith's majestic style and presence enhance the film immeasurably. Murphy's second film, *Black and Tan*, was built around Duke Ellington's orchestra, and also featured Fredi Washington, the Five Hotshots (a leading team of tapdancers), and a line of chorus girls from the Cotton Club. The plot is centered on Ellington's composition *Black and Tan Fantasy*, supposedly written for Washington to dance to; the début performance is cut short when the character she plays suffers a heart attack, and her deathbed scene becomes the setting for a superb rendition of the piece. Murphy fills the screen with rich shadow play combined with avant-garde prismatic lens effects.

An all-black cast was not unique to these films. Segregationist requirements were box-office reality, particularly in the South, and Hollywood did not wish to offend the sensitivities of white audiences. One option was to produce all-black motion pictures; the other was to structure films so that scenes with

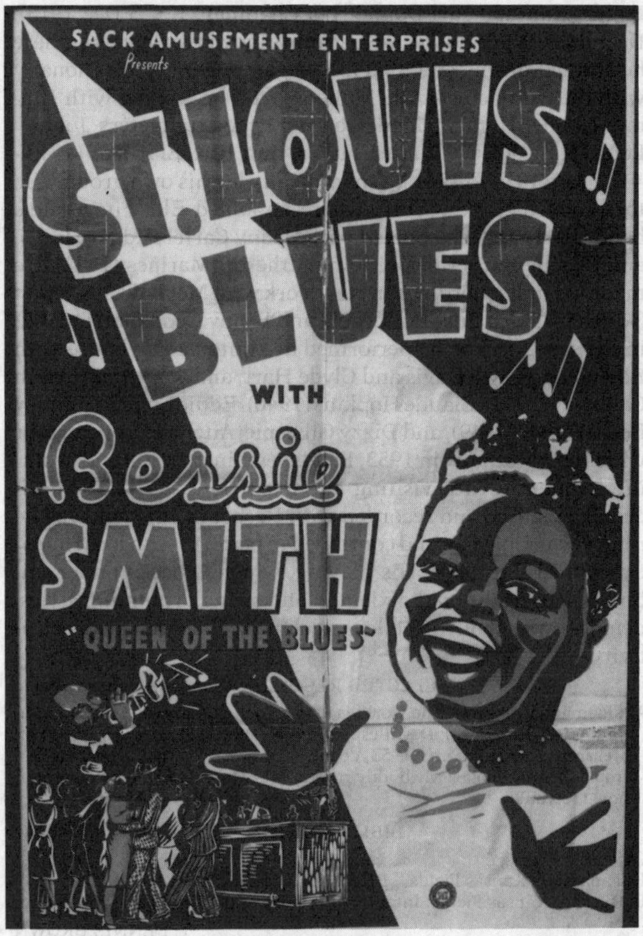

1. Poster advertising "St. Louis Blues," 1929

black performers could easily be excised. Thus, although they were frequently relegated to stereotyped roles, many Afro-Americans found employment in films, and most established jazz musicians, as a byproduct of other intentions of the industry, found their work immortalized.

2. JAZZ SCENES WITHIN FEATURE FILMS. Jazz was used frequently in early feature films, either to provide incidental music or to lend atmosphere to nightclub, dance-hall, and other "jazz life" scenes. Again, to satisfy audiences offended by seeing black entertainers or musicians on the screen, these portions could be neatly excised without harming the continuity of the plot. Musicals were also used to hang a series of jazz performances around a lightweight story. The orchestras led by Speed Webb, Mutt Carey, Les Hite, and the drummer Curtis Mosby, all based in California, were kept busy with casting calls. Webb's groups appeared in *His Captive Woman* (1929, First National-Warner Bros., dir. George Fitzmaurice), *Sins of the Fathers* (1928, Paramount, dir. Ludwig Berger), and *Riley the Cop* (1928, Fox, dir. John Ford). Mosby's band provided music for the performance by the singer Theresa Harris of *Daddy won't you please come home* in *Thunderbolt* (1929, Paramount, dir. Josef von Sternberg). Hite claimed his orchestra appeared in more than 60 films, which included *Taxi* (1932, Warner Bros., dir. Roy del Ruth), *Cabin in the Cotton* (1932, Warner Bros., dir. Michael Curtiz), *Sing, Sinner, Sing* (1933, Majestic, dir. Howard Christy), and *Girl Without a Room* (1933, Paramount, dir. Ralph Murphy).

Universal's *King of Jazz* (1930, dir. John Murray Anderson) capitalized on the enormous popularity of Paul Whiteman's orchestra and the attendant publicity that had enabled Whiteman to call himself the "King of Jazz." An extravagant technicolor revue, the film presents, among others, the Rhythm Boys (the singers Al Rinker, Harry Barris, and Bing Crosby) in one lavishly mounted production number after another. However, when it tackles a visual explanation of the creation of jazz in a finale entitled the "Melting Pot of Jazz," the Afro-Americans are the one group among the representatives of many different nationalities conspicuous by their absence.

Paramount's "Big Broadcast" series typifies the use of jazz to lend spice to a story. The aim of the first production, *The Big Broadcast* (1932, dir. Frank Tuttle), was to profit from the popularity of such contemporary radio personalities as Kate Smith, Arthur Tracy, the Boswell Sisters, George Burns and Gracie Allen, the Mills Brothers, and Vincent Lopez. It starred Bing Crosby, who in his brief rendition of *Please* is accompanied by Eddie Lang (see fig.2), and presented Cab Calloway and his orchestra (billed as "Cab Calloway and his Harlem-o-Maniacs in a heated Harlemania") performing *Minnie the Moocher* and Benny Carter's *Hot Toddy*. The second film in the series, *The Big Broadcast of 1936* (1935, dir. Norman Taurog), featured Ray Noble's orchestra, Ina Ray Hutton and her Melodears, and the Nicholas Brothers, who share the dancing with Bill Robinson. *The Big Broadcast of 1937* (1936, dir. Mitchell Leisen) marked the film début of Benny Goodman's orchestra; Goodman consolidated his growing reputation from the radio show "Camel Caravan" with a rousing swing version of *Bugle Call Rag*.

Meanwhile Republic Pictures produced a number of musical films, modeled on the "Big Broadcast" series, under the title "Hit Parade." The first, *Hit Parade of 1937* (1937, dir. Gus Meins),

2. Eddie Lang (guitar) and Bing Crosby in Paramount's "The Big Broadcast," 1932

includes a performance by Ellington's orchestra of *I've got to be a rugcutter*; Ivie Anderson is accompanied by Hayes Alvis, Rex Stewart, and Harry Carney. The bands led by Ray McKinley and Count Basie appeared in *Hit Parade of 1943* (1943, dir. Albert S. Rogell), Basie being central to an elaborate production number entitled *Harlem Sandman*, and *Hit Parade of 1947* (1947, dir. Frank McDonald) featured Woody Herman's First Herd.

Fats Waller gives a boisterous performance of *Gotta snap my fingers* in *Hooray for Love!* (1935, RKO, dir. Walter Lang), which also provides a cameo role for Bill Robinson (the two sing a delightful duet version of the piece). In the same year Waller was cast as a piano playing elevator operator in *King of Burlesque* (20th Century-Fox, dir. Sydney Lanfield), where, dressed in a white tail coat, he performs *I've got my fingers crossed* on a revolving stage.

Benny Goodman's orchestra made another appearance in *Hollywood Hotel* (1937, Warner Bros., dir. Busby Berkeley). There are prominent solos by Harry James and Gene Krupa on *Sing, sing, sing*. During the big-band numbers Johnny "Scat" Davis (who introduced the Hollywood anthem *Hooray for Hollywood*) appears to be a member of the trumpet section, but at Goodman's insistence he does not play. Despite the strict segregationist policy in force in the studios at the time, a swinging rendition of an interpretation of *I got rhythm* called *I've got a heartful of music* is given by the original – and racially integrated – Benny Goodman Quartet (Goodman, Krupa, Teddy Wilson, and Lionel Hampton).

Mae West starred in a number of films that make use of jazz as a musical backdrop: *Belle of the Nineties* (1934, Paramount, dir. Leo McCarey) provided Duke Ellington with some effective moments in *When a St. Louis woman goes down to New Orleans*, *My Old Flame*, and *Memphis Blues*; Louis Armstrong performed *Jubilee* as a trumpet-playing street cleaner leading a parade in a political rally in *Every Day's a Holiday* (1938, Paramount, dir. A. Edward Sutherland); and in *The Heat's On* (1943, Columbia, dir. Gregory Ratoff) Hazel Scott plays two pianos at once – one white and one black – as she sings *When the white keys join the black*.

In the decade from the mid-1930s to the mid-1940s, the heyday of the big band, bandleaders, singers, and star instrumentalists were idolized, and brief appearances by such artists in a major feature film, or even a modest "B" film, could ensure box-office success. A typical portrayal was that of Johnny "Scat" Davis in *Mr. Chump* (1938, Warner Bros., dir. William Clemons), where he is characterized as a kind of swing-hero trumpeter – a wholesome, optimistic, clean-living individual whom the public could admire and emulate.

Glenn Miller's orchestra, one of the most popular bands of the swing era, was featured in two films. In *Sun Valley Serenade* (1941, 20th Century-Fox, dir. H. Bruce Humberstone) it plays a number of the hits that brought it to fame, among them *I know why*, *The Kiss Polka*, and *In the Mood*; the most notable production number, *Chattanooga Choo Choo*, provided the music for a dance sequence by the Nicholas Brothers and Dorothy Dandridge. In *Orchestra Wives* (1942, 20th Century-Fox, dir. Archie Mayo) Miller plays *At Last*, *Serenade in Blue*, and *I've got a girl in Kalamazoo*.

Birth of the Blues (1941, Paramount, dir. Victor Schertzinger) was supposed to depict the authentic origins of the blues, "the musical idiom that paved the way for 'jazz' and 'swing'." The cast included Bing Crosby and Jack Teagarden's orchestra, but the plot of the film was riddled with errors and distortions; only Teagarden's solo on *Melancholy Baby* and *Memphis Blues* stand out as true jazz performances. *Syncopation* (1942, RKO, dir. William Dieterle) traced the rise of jazz from New Orleans, but, similarly, its plot bore little resemblance to reality. However, Rex Stewart and Bunny Berigan recorded the trumpet solos for Jackie Cooper and Todd Duncan, who played the characters based on Armstrong and Oliver, and much was made of a jam session by the All-American Dance Band composed of Goodman, Krupa, Harry James, Jack Jenney, Alvino Rey, Charlie Barnet, and Joe Venuti.

1943 was an excellent year for jazz in films. *Cabin in the Sky* (MGM, dir. Vincente Minnelli) was again full of stereotyped roles for the black musicians, but its score boasted such songs as *Happiness is a thing called Joe*, performed by Ethel Waters; Ellington's orchestra provided the soundtrack. In *Stormy Weather* (20th Century-Fox, dir. Andrew Stone) an all-black cast (including Fats Waller, Cab Calloway, the singer Ada Brown, the Nicholas Brothers and Katherine Dunham and her dancers) presented an endless stream of song and dance, the high point of which was Calloway's distinctive and characteristically exuberant rendition of *Jumpin' Jive*.

3. Films produced by independent companies. In the years between 1910 and 1950, owing to growing political awareness among Blacks and the realization that there was a waiting market in black communities throughout the USA, some 150 independent film companies, often with white management, were formed to produce films with all-black casts. Because of their inadequate financing and lack of experienced technicians, however, the quality of their films varied significantly, and many resorted to the use of musical interludes to prop up weak scripts and poor production.

Harlem is Heaven (1932, Lincoln, dir. Irwin C. Franklyn) starred Bill Robinson with Eubie Blake's orchestra, and *Bargain with Bullets* (1937, Million Dollar) featured Les Hite's band and a trio led by Eddie Barefield. Mamie Smith appeared in *Paradise in Harlem* (1940, Jubilee, dir. Joseph Seiden), in which she sang *Harlem Blues* accompanied by Lucky Millinder's orchestra, and in *Sunday Sinners* (1940, International Roadshow Release, dir. Arthur Dreifuss). The popularity of Louis Jordan and his Tympany Five was such that the group starred in a number of films, among them *Caldonia* (1945, Astor, dir. William Forest Crouch), *Beware* (1946, Astor, dir. Bud Pollard), and *Reet, Petite and Gone* (1947, Astor, dir. Crouch). The cast of *Killer Diller* (1947, All-American, dir. Josh Binney) included Andy Kirk's orchestra and Nat "King" Cole's trio.

Jivin' in Bebop (1946, Alexander, dir. Leonard Anderson) featured Dizzy Gillespie's big band playing arrangements of tunes closely associated with the bop idiom, notably *Things to Come*, *Ornithology*, *A Night in Tunisia*, and *Salt Peanuts*; Helen Humes performed *My Man Blues*. This film provides a rare visual record of Gillespie's contribution to the bop revolution.

Other jazz musicians who appeared in independent productions included Walter Fuller, John Kirby, Una Mae Carlisle, Sid Catlett, Andy Kirk, Noble Sissle, and the International Sweethearts of Rhythm.

4. Recurring themes in feature films.

(i) World War II. During the years of World War II film makers strove to devise escapist plots that were also laced with a strong dash of patriotic sentiment; many suggested that going to war was fun, and involved dancing and cavorting to big bands. Unsophisticated as they were, these plots allowed the same big bands with which audiences were familiar to be presented, and the films raised the morale of men in the services by reassuring them that everything at home – the way of life they were fighting to preserve – was just as they remembered it.

The war theme was best expressed by swing versions of such numbers as *When Johnny comes marching home*, *I'll be seeing you*, and *Don't sit under the apple tree (with anyone else but me)*. The last named is sung by the Andrews Sisters in *Private Buckaroo* (1942, Universal, dir. Edward F. Cline), which also featured Harry James and his Music Makers. *Ship Ahoy!* (1942,

3. Count Basie's band in "Stage Door Canteen," 1943: (back row, left to right) Lewis Taylor (trombone), Buck Clayton (trumpet), unidentified player, Eli Robinson (trombone), Jo Jones (drums), Walter Page (double bass), and Freddie Green (guitar); (middle row) Dicky Wells (trombone), Ed Lewis and Harry Edison (trumpets), and Buster Scott (trombone); (front row) Basie (piano), Ethel Waters (voice), Buddy Tate (tenor saxophone), Jimmie Powell and Earle Warren (alto saxophones), Jack Washington (baritone saxophone), and Don Byas (tenor saxophone)

MGM, dir. Edward Buzzell) incorporated appearances by Tommy Dorsey's orchestra (including Buddy Rich), and *Seven Days Leave* (1942, RKO, dir. Tim Whelan) placed Les Brown and his Band of Renown in the spotlight. In *Follow the Boys* (1944, Universal, dir. A. Edward Sutherland), Louis Jordan and his Tympany Five travel the USO circuit and play *Shoo Shoo Baby* in an impromptu performance on the back of an army truck. *Stage Door Canteen* (1943, United Artists, dir. Frank Borzage) brought together two powerful swing bands: Benny Goodman's orchestra, with Peggy Lee, played *Bugle Call Rag* and *Why don't you do right?*, and Count Basie's band, with Ethel Waters, performed *Quicksand* (see fig.3).

Another musical contribution to the war effort was *Thousands Cheer* (1943, MGM, dir. George Sidney), which featured Lena Horne singing *Honeysuckle Rose* and the orchestras of Kay Kyser, Bob Crosby, and Benny Carter. One of the highlights of *Top Man* (1943, Universal, dir. Charles Lamont) was the performance by Basie's orchestra of *Basie Boogie*. *Reveille with Beverly* (1943, Columbia, dir. Charles Barton) offers a plot set around a disc jockey (played by the dancer Ann Miller), who substitutes swing for classical music on her early morning program and dedicates the show to servicemen within the radio station's orbit. She is dismissed by the station manager, but rehired when fan mail from her devoted audience begins to pour in. Bands and artists are introduced with predictable regularity via camera dissolves through record labels on her turntable: Basie's orchestra plays *One o'Clock Jump*; Bob Crosby's performs *Big Noise from Winnetka*; Betty Roche, with Ellington's band, sings *Take the A Train*; and Ella Mae Morse sings *Cow Cow Boogie* accompanied by Freddie Slack's orchestra. There is also an appearance by Frank Sinatra performing *Night and Day*, and the final patriotic production number, *Thumbs up and V for Victory*, allows Miller's talents as a tap-dancer to be displayed.

(ii) Jazz music versus classical music. A favorite theme from the earliest days of sound films was the struggle to gain for syncopated music the kind of respect that classical music enjoyed. Although this became a rather overworked cliché, Hollywood capitalized on such successful concert performances as those in 1924 by Paul Whiteman at Aeolian Hall and Vincent Lopez at the Metropolitan Opera House, and the production in 1932 of James P. Johnson's *Harlem Symphony* at Carnegie Hall and the Brooklyn Academy of Music by resolving the conflict between the two genres in a concert hall finale.

In *Is Everybody Happy?* (1929, Warner Bros., dir. Archie L. Mayo) Ted Lewis portrays the son of a jazz-hating father whose lifelong hope that he has produced a concert violinist evaporates when he discovers that the boy has pawned his violin and is playing jazz clarinet in a Hungarian restaurant. After a chain of misunderstandings Lewis redeems himself with his father and furthers the cause of jazz by leading a band at Carnegie Hall. In *Jazz Preferred* (1930, Vitaphone, dir. Boris Petroff) Red Nichols and his Five Pennies are matched against an operatic opponent and win. However, in a lavish production number in *Murder at the Vanities* (1934, Paramount, dir. Mitchell Leisen) an outraged classical conductor takes a submachine gun and mows down the entire Duke Ellington Orchestra (dressed initially in 18th-century wigs and costumes) because it insisted on swinging Liszt's Second Hungarian Rhapsody in a hot version entitled *Ebony Rhapsody* (see fig.4).

Jazz history was the main source of the narrative for *New Orleans* (1947, United Artists, dir. Arthur Lubin), but the film also incorporates a concert hall finale. A generous amount of

4. Label for "Ebony Rhapsody" from "Murder at the Vanities," recorded by Duke Ellington and his orchestra for Victor, 12 April 1934

footage is devoted to some first-rate jazz musicians, including Louis Armstrong, Mutt Carey, Zutty Singleton, Barney Bigard, Budd Scott, Lucky Thompson, Meade "Lux" Lewis, Red Callender, Woody Herman, and Billie Holiday, who played the maid to an opera singer (Dorothy Patrick). The latter is fascinated with the new rhythmic music called jazz, and, with Holiday's help, visits a club in Storyville to experience it first hand – only to find her opera coach there listening to Armstrong. At first her newly acquired taste in music angers her shocked parents, who all but disown her, but there is a happy ending as she sings *Do you know what it means to miss New Orleans?* in a New York hall to everyone's approval.

Public acceptance of jazz is also achieved in the finale of *St. Louis Blues* (1958, Paramount, dir. Allen Reisner), when Eartha Kitt performs Handy's famous blues in a concert hall setting.

(iii) Swing as a theme. The word "swing," like the word "jazz," was also used by Hollywood to draw audiences, and between 1936 and 1949 more than 50 films with the word "swing" in the title were issued. Among these were *Swing it* (1936), *Swing Banditry* (1937), *Swing School* (1938), *Swing Hotel* (1939), *Swing Fever* (1943), *Synco-smooth Swing* (1945), and *Symphony in Swing* (1949). Towards the end of the 1940s the swing era was coming to an end, but it continued to inspire screenplays.

Sweet and Low-down (1944, 20th Century-Fox, dir. Archie Mayo) revolves loosely around the fortunes of Benny Goodman's orchestra on tour and includes one of Goodman's most exquisite and swinging solos when his quartet (Jess Stacy, Sid Weiss, and Morey Feld) performs *The World is waiting for the sunrise* during a jam session. Goodman also appeared in *A Song is Born* (1948, Samuel Goldwyn, dir. Howard Hawks), alongside such musicians as Tommy Dorsey, Louis Armstrong, Lionel Hampton, and Charlie Barnet.

(iv) Associations of jazz with crime and other sordid themes. Jazz has been identified from the silent era with film crime, murder, and mayhem. It was also used to suggest a close, mutual relationship with various forms of aberrant behavior, and associated with the mad, the deranged, the psychopathic, and the just plain eccentric. There was some truth in at least part of this screen image, since gangsters had played a dominant role in establishing the nightclubs, gambling rooms, and dance halls

in which jazz had flourished. Most gangster films set in the Prohibition or Depression era contained scenes that employed jazz bands for atmosphere.

Young Man with a Horn (1949, Warner Bros., dir. Michael Curtiz), inspired by Dorothy Baker's novel on the life of Bix Beiderbecke, casts Kirk Douglas as the trumpeter who slips down into alcoholism, only to be saved by his long-suffering and patient sweetheart (Doris Day). Harry James recorded the soundtrack for Douglas, whose loyal piano playing friend was portrayed by Hoagy Carmichael. *Pete Kelly's Blues* (1955, Warner Bros., dir. Jack Webb) depicts a trumpeter who comes into conflict with a group of gangsters. Webb assembled an exceptional group of musicians to appear as his band and enhance the narrative value of the story. In *The Man with the Golden Arm* (1955, United Artists, dir. Otto Preminger) Frank Sinatra gives an impressive performance as a professional card dealer and drummer with a drug problem. Original jazz-flavored music composed by Elmer Bernstein and some telling jazz arrangements by Shorty Rogers and Shelly Manne enhance the story of this dark melodrama.

In *The Crimson Canary* (1945, Universal, dir. John Hoffman) the singer of a jazz band is found murdered in a nightclub, and the bandleader becomes the prime suspect when he is seen leaving the scene of the crime with a dented trumpet, which turns out to have been the murder instrument. The detective on the case is a jazz fan, and his clue is a phonograph record that is a test pressing of the band's rendition of *China Boy*. The audience is treated to several numbers by the band (consisting of Coleman Hawkins, Howard McGhee, Sir Charles Thompson, Oscar Pettiford, and Denzil Best) before it is revealed that the club's owner is the murderer. *The Dark Corner* (1946, 20th Century-Fox, dir. Henry Hathaway) is a dark, moody mystery thriller that revolves around the efforts of a private detective to extricate himself from a false murder charge. It has some superb music by Eddie Heywood and his group, including *Heywood's Blues* and *Coquette*. *The Strip* (1951, MGM, dir. Leslie Kardos), in which a jazz drummer (Mickey Rooney, playing his own drums) gets involved with racketeers and murder, is laced with performances of such numbers as *Basin Street Blues*, *Shadrack*, *That's a Plenty*, and *A Kiss to Build a Dream on* by a band including Louis Armstrong, Jack Teagarden, Earl Hines, and Barney Bigard.

Nightmare (1956, United Artists, dir. Maxwell Shane) tells the story of a New Orleans jazz musician who is hypnotized into believing he has stabbed a man to death. The film is full of distorted visuals and jazz backgrounds to underscore the psychological state of the innocent musician; it incorporates performances by Billy May and Meade "Lux" Lewis. *The Wild Party* (1956, United Artists, dir. Harry Horner), a melodrama full of sex, violence, and jazz clubs, with Nehemiah Persoff portraying a homicidal jazz pianist, has appearances by Buddy DeFranco's quartet, including Pete Jolly, and also a group led by Teddy Buckner. Chico Hamilton's quintet is featured in a number of club scenes in *The Sweet Smell of Success* (1957, United Artists, dir. Alexander Mackendrick), and Red Norvo has a speaking role and leads a jazz quartet throughout the bizarre psychological thriller *Screaming Mimi* (1958, Columbia, dir. Gerd Oswald).

A new character was added to these various themes with films such as *The Beat Generation* (1959, MGM, dir. Charles Haas), a psychological melodrama about a vicious rapist and a group of beatniks, in which Louis Armstrong, rather out of place, leads a band that includes Peanuts Hucko, Trummy Young, and Billy Kyle; and *The Subterraneans* (1960, MGM, dir. Ranald McDougall), concerning the eccentric bohemian behavior of beatniks, where Carmen McRae, Gerry Mulligan, Art Pepper, Art Farmer, Shelly Manne, and Chico Hamilton are among those who provide the music.

(v) Fictional and semifictional biography. With the production of *The Fabulous Dorseys* (1947, United Artists, dir. Alfred E. Green) and *The Glenn Miller Story* (1953, Universal-International, dir. Anthony Mann), the studios acknowledged the importance of swing musicians as suitable subjects for film biographies. Steve Allen's portrayal of Goodman in *The Benny Goodman Story* (1955, Universal-International, dir. Valentine Davies) was sometimes inaccurate, but the film included some really fine re-creations of Goodman's famous hits and arrangements. Among the jazz personalities who appeared on the screen were Ben Pollack, Kid Ory, Buck Clayton, Teddy Wilson, Lionel Hampton, Gene Krupa, and Harry James.

Jazz-based biographies continued to be issued throughout the 1950s. Nat "King" Cole was cast as W. C. Handy in *St. Louis Blues* (1958); *The Five Pennies* (1959, Paramount, dir. Melville Shavelson) recounted the life of Red Nichols; and Krupa's career was chronicled in *The Gene Krupa Story* (1959, Columbia, dir. Don Weis). Later Billie Holiday's autobiography was transferred to the screen as a vehicle for the singer Diana Ross, but liberties taken with events and career details result in *Lady Sings the Blues* (1972, Motown/Weston/Furie/Paramount, dir. Sidney Furie) being more fiction than fact. The film offered many songs associated with Holiday, among them *Lover Man*, *God Bless the Child*, *Them There Eyes*, *Don't Explain*, and the wrenching *Strange Fruit*.

During the 1960s a number of studios made films about the lives of fictional jazz musicians. These included *The Rat Race* (1960, Paramount/Perlberg-Seaton, dir. Robert Mulligan), with music performed by Gerry Mulligan, Joe Bushkin, and Paul Horn; *Too Late Blues* (1961, Paramount, dir. John Cassavetes), with Slim Gaillard and a soundtrack played by Benny Carter, Jimmie Rowles, Red Mitchell, and Shelly Manne; and *Paris Blues* (1961, United Artists, dir. Martin Ritt). The score for the last named was written by Duke Ellington and provides a lively jam session sequence for Louis Armstrong and others; Murray McEachern and Paul Gonsalves dubbed trombone and tenor saxophone parts for the lead characters portrayed by Paul Newman and Sidney Poitier. *Sweet Love, Bitter* (1961, Film 2–Peppercorn Wormser–UM, dir. Herbert Danska) cast the comedian Dick Gregory in a role inspired by Charlie Parker; its score was by Mal Waldron.

Later fictional biographies are represented by *New York, New York* (1977, United Artists, dir. Martin Scorsese), for which Georgie Auld provided the saxophone solos and also coached the actor Robert DeNiro, who gave an unusually sharp and believable portrait of a swing musician, and *The Cotton Club* (1984, Orion, dir. Francis Coppola). The latter vividly recalls the jazz age and the Depression era with a mixture of real and created characters; with the Cotton Club in Harlem as a backdrop, there are marvelous moments of period music (arranged by Bob Wilber) and dance that do much to give the film an authentic jazz flavor.

5. Developments in Europe. European producers tended to favor documentary jazz films, though some were issued featuring jazz musicians in cameo appearances. The Soviet Film Season for 1934–5 advertised *Jazz Comedy* (dir. G. Alexandrov) as "Soviet Russia's first musical comedy featuring Leonid Utyosov, the Soviet Jazz King with his Band." *L'alibi* (1936, France, dir. Pierre Chenal), a murder melodrama, included a

sequence for the black expatriate Americans Bobby Martin and Valaida Snow. Sidney Bechet took roles in a number of European films, beginning with the comedy *Einbrecher* (1930, Germany, dir. Hanns Schwarz); near the end of his career he appeared with his protégé Claude Luter in the melodrama *L' inspecteur connaît la musique* (1955, France, dir. Jean Josipovici) and in the gangster film *Série noire* (1955, France, dir. Pierre Foucard). Hazel Scott was cast in *Le désordre et la nuit* (1958, France, dir. Gilles Grangier), a film about murder and nightclub life. Among the films produced by British studios were *Sing as you Swing* (1937, dir. Redd Davis), in which Nat Gonella and his Georgians shared the musical spotlight with the Mills Brothers, and the comedy *A Date with a Dream* (1948, dir. Dicky Leeman), featuring Vic Lewis and his band.

Virtually 50 years after *The Jazz Singer* a film was produced that drew upon jazz experience as a source of dramatic structure but avoided all the usual musical and narrative pitfalls. The plot of *Round Midnight* (1986, Warner's, dir. Bertrand Tavernier) is patterned after the relationship between Bud Powell and the Frenchman who worshiped him. Dexter Gordon – tall, majestic, mellow, and melancholic – plays the character of Dale Turner, a legendary alcoholic bop saxophonist who is attempting a comeback in Paris, with rare believability (Gordon was nominated for an Academy Award). The film offers other telling performances from Sandra Reaves-Phillips as the singer who is Gordon's guardian and companion and Lonette McKee in a role reminiscent of Billie Holiday. The camera rarely leaves the musicians when they are playing, and successfully captures the look and sound of jazz life in the late 1950s. Herbie Hancock composed and arranged the music and appears as the leader of bands that include Wayne Shorter, John McLaughlin, Pierre Michelot, and Billy Higgins, among others. *Round Midnight* is the first fiction feature film about jazz musicians that rings true and does not slight the music.

6. Cartoons. Sound had a profound impact on cartoon films, and jazz seemed particularly well suited to the art of animation. The early sound years yielded *Jungle Jazz* (1930), *Congo Jazz* (1930), *Blue Rhythm* (1931), *Ragtime Romeo* (1931), *Blues* (1931), and *The Birth of Jazz* (1932). Swing seemed especially appropriate for the soundtrack of cartoon films. Universal produced a "Swing Symphony" series around the boogie-woogie piano style: *Boogie Woogie Bugle Boy of Company B* (1941, dir. Walter Lantz), *Scrub me Mama with a Boogie Beat* (1941, dir. Walter Lantz), *Boogie Woogie Sioux* (1942, dir. Alex Lovy), and *Boogie Woogie Man* (1943, dir. James Culhane). "Puppetoons" utilized a combination of animated puppetry and live performance in *Date with Duke* (1947, Paramount), which featured Ellington at the piano playing selections from his *Perfume Suite*, and for *Rhapsody in Wood* (1947, Paramount), which tells the story of Woody Herman's clarinet from the time it was part of a tree until it becomes a fully fledged instrument.

Roy Eldridge may be heard on the soundtrack of *The Early Bird Dood It* (1942, MGM, dir. Ted Avery), while Bob Zurke plays on that for *Jungle Jive* (1944, Universal, dir. James Culhane) and Jack Teagarden on that for *Sliphorn King of Polaroo* (1945, Universal, dir. Dick Lundy). Walt Disney's feature-length musical pastiche *Make Mine Music* (1945, RKO) contains an animated sequence of hands, clarinets, and undulating piano keyboards to the accompaniment of *After you've gone* played by the Benny Goodman Quartet.

Some extremely imaginative avant-garde animations are evident in *Boogie Doodle* (1948, National Film Board of Canada, dir. Norman McLaren), in which the designs are scratched or painted directly onto each film frame; Albert Ammons provided the soundtrack. *The Oompahs* (1952, dir. John Hubley) employs the music of Ben Pollack's orchestra in telling a tale of a father (a tuba) who refuses to permit his son (a trumpet) to play jazz, but a jam session finale has them playing together. *Adventures of an Asterisk* (1957, dir. John Hubley) made use of abstract shapes animated to the music of Lionel Hampton and Benny Carter. But perhaps one of the funniest cartoons to draw on jazz imagery was *The Interview* (1960, dir. Ernest Pintoff), in which a fictitious and very hip jazz musician named Shorty Petterstein is questioned by a rather square interviewer against background music provided by Stan Getz's quartet.

II. Documentaries and other filmed performances

1. Short subjects. 2. Soundies. 3. Television. 4. Documentary films. 5. Videos.

1. Short subjects. The first short subjects incorporating popular music and jazz were well received, and during the period from 1928 to 1934 there was an explosion of such productions. In these experimental years, as sound and camera techniques improved, studios rushed to enlist talent from every available source – vaudeville, the Broadway stage, concert halls, nightclubs, and burlesque – at the same time competing for these entertainers with the rapidly developing radio industry. New York therefore became central in the production of such films as *Roger Wolfe Kahn and his Orchestra Assisted by the Mound City Blue Blowers* (1927, Vitaphone), *Carolynne Snowden and Company* (1927, Vitaphone), *Red Nichols and his Five Pennies* (1929, Vitaphone), and *Alice Boulden and her Orchestra* (1929, Paramount), which included Jimmy and Tommy Dorsey among the personnel. *Ben Pollack and his Park Central Orchestra* (1929, Vitaphone) gives a brief glimpse of early performances by Jimmy McPartland, Jack Teagarden, and Benny Goodman.

The musical short subject was also an ideal medium in which to present black talent, since if objections were raised, the short could be eliminated from the program. A wide range of black entertainers appeared in these films, but under the most trying of racial conditions. *After Seben* (1929, Paramount, dir. S. Jay Kaufman) used a racist plot about the adventures of a lazy janitor to present music and dance by Chick Webb's orchestra and some of the Savoy Ballroom's most famed lindy hoppers, including George "Shorty" Snowden. Louis Armstrong appeared in *Rhapsody in Black and Blue* (1932, Paramount, dir. Aubrey Scotto) dressed in leopard-skin robes and living in a dream-induced kingdom called "Jazzmania"; amid billowing soap bubbles passing for heavenly clouds he plays *Shine* and *I'll be glad when you're dead, you rascal you* in a superbly virile manner. Although *Symphony in Black* (1934, Paramount, dir. Fred Waller) presented the members of Duke Ellington's orchestra in stereotyped roles, the film was notable for the first screen appearance of Billie Holiday, singing *Saddest Tale*. The high-water mark for bizarre plot and setting was probably achieved by *Pie, Pie, Blackbird* (1932, Vitaphone, dir. Roy Mack), in which a freshly baked pie turns into an enormous pastry whose wedges open to reveal Eubie Blake's orchestra dressed in chef's outfits playing *Memories of You* and *I'll be glad when you're dead, you rascal you*; the film's finale has the heated dancing of the Nicholas Brothers to *China Boy* literally igniting the set and props in a flash of flame, and the band and dancers turn into smoking skeletons.

An outstanding short film was made by Warner Bros. in 1944. *Jammin' the Blues*, directed by Gjon Mili, had Norman Granz as musical adviser and some of the finest instrumentalists in jazz: Lester Young headed a list of personnel that included Harry Edison, Illinois Jacquet, Sid Catlett, Jo Jones, John Simmons, Red Callender, Marlowe Morris, and Barney Kessel. Mili's special talent with lighting created a marvelous mood around the combinations drawn from this superlative assembly, staging and framing each shot with an eye for dramatic composition. Although it is sometimes criticized as contrived and pretentious, *Jammin' the Blues* remains a landmark effort in jazz film making; it received a nomination for an Academy Award.

Louis de Rochemont's series *The March of Time* (Time/RKO Radio), which began in 1935, was a form of motion-picture journalism that combined archival film, fresh news footage, and reenacted scenes. *The Birth of Swing* (1937, Vol.3, Issue 7) touched on the making of a record by the Original Dixieland Jazz Band and showed performances in the Onyx Club, New York, by the orchestras of Glen Gray and Chick Webb and a group led by Stuff Smith. *Upbeat in Music* (1943, Vol.10, Issue 5), concerned with wartime music, contained performances by Glenn Miller's Army Band as well as by Tommy Dorsey, Duke Ellington, and Benny Goodman. *Music in America* (1944, Vol.10, Issue 12) surveyed the state of music across the country, the jazz segment concentrating on Goodman, the Original Dixieland Jazz Band, Eddie Condon's All Stars, and Art Tatum. Other issues of *The March of Time* devoted footage to Jimmy Dorsey and Paul Whiteman.

Whereas swing had captured the imagination of nearly the entire country, bop appealed to a much smaller audience and was therefore not a profitable prospect for film makers. By the 1950s there was also a marked decline in the production of short subjects as an added attraction to movie theater programming. Nevertheless, and despite the fact that bop was played principally by small groups, some big bands performing bop arrangements did appear in shorts. *Rhythm in a Riff* (1946, dir. Leonard Anderson) featured Billy Eckstine's orchestra with Gene Ammons and Frank Wess, and was followed by *Boyd Raeburn and his Orchestra* (1947), *Claude Thornhill and his Orchestra* (1947, 1950), and *Herman's Herd* (1949). Small bop ensembles also made short subjects. *Cool and Groovy* (1956, Universal-International, dir. Will Cowan) presented the Chico Hamilton Quintet and Buddy DeFranco's quartet with Anita O'Day, while *A Date with Dizzy* (1956, Storyboard, dir. John Hubley) introduced Dizzy Gillespie's quintet.

2. Soundies. Another reflection of the popularity and commercial potential of swing was the formation of the RCM Corporation, which produced short (three-minute) entertainment films known as soundies. Soundies were rear projected internally against a series of mirrors which reflected the image onto a small screen mounted on top of a coin-operated unit like a jukebox. These machines were found in bars, restaurants, and roadhouses across the USA, and offered a variety of selections of everything from bands and singers to star instrumentalists and dancers. An imposing catalogue of soundies was produced between 1940 and 1946, featuring most of the well-known musicians of the time.

Despite their poor production, inferior sets, bad synchronization, and, for the most part, unimaginative camera work, soundies provided not only an important source of work for a great many jazz artists but also an invaluable library of film documentaries. When the RCM Corporation went out of business around 1947 the films were sold to television interests; by the 1980s compilations were appearing on videocassette.

3. Television. In the late 1940s several new developments significantly affected the film industry in the USA, among them rising production costs, the US court rulings against block booking and studio-owned movie theater chains, the House Un-American Activities Committee hearings and the Hollywood blacklist, the postwar shift from urban to suburban living, the boom in the sales of high-fidelity and stereo music systems, and, the most important factor, television. This new medium immediately became very successful, with vaudeville and variety programs proving the most popular; whereas one million television sets were sold in 1949, the figure by 1952 had risen to ten million. As a result of this competition, film studios found it more difficult to realize profits, and by the mid-1950s film programming began to change. Short subjects, newsreels, and other types of short film were gradually dropped from the repertory; without the musical short subject a major film format was lost to jazz, for which television provided only a poor substitute.

"Eddie Condon's Floor Show," a pioneering 30-minute weekly jam session that was televised on NBC and CBS from January 1949 to June 1950, presented Condon as host and Wild Bill Davison, Cutty Cutshall, Sidney Bechet, Joe Bushkin, Billy Butterfield, and Pee Wee Russell as regular participants; among the guests were Armstrong, Woody Herman, Gene Krupa, and Ella Fitzgerald. Similar shows were "Chicago Jazz" (NBC, November–December 1949), "Adventures in Jazz" (CBS, January 1949), and "Cavalcade of Bands" (Dumont, January 1950–September 1951). Hazel Scott became the first black woman to have her own network series, "Hazel Scott" (Dumont, July–September 1950), a 15-minute show broadcast three times a week. The "Billy Daniels Show" (ABC, October–December 1952) featured Benny Payne as the leader of a group which accompanied such guests as the jazz tap-dancer Jimmy Slyde. Two short-lived shows that attempted to capture the sound of the 1940s were "America's Greatest Bands" (CBS, June–September 1955), in which Paul Whiteman introduced the bands of Ellington, Basie, Bob Crosby, and Les Brown, among others, and "Bandstand" (NBC, July–August, 1956), built around Tex Beneke's band.

In 1950 the Snader Telescriptions Corporation introduced their three-minute film musicals, each one consisting of a straight performance by a singer or group. These films differed both in style and purpose from the earlier shorts. They were offered to independent television stations across the USA as a way to create local jazz programming, since a number could be strung together (allowing space for inserting commercials) and given a catchy title. Among the artists listed in the Snader catalogue were Charlie Barnet, Count Basie's sextet, Cab Calloway, Nat "King" Cole, Pete Daily, Firehouse Five Plus Two, Red Nichols, Tony Pastor, George Shearing, Mel Tormé, Helen Humes, Les Brown, June Christy, Duke Ellington, Lionel Hampton, and Sarah Vaughan. As happened with the soundies, compilation films began to appear in later years under such titles as *Showtime at the Apollo* and *Rock and Roll Revue*.

A few of the performance programs made especially for television were outstanding. Unlike Hollywood films, which employed set backdrops and offered rehearsed and predictable camera work (including close-ups of riffing brass sections waving their instruments from side to side or the trumpeters fanning their instrument bells with derby mutes in unison), television programs brought a number of new dimensions to the presentation of jazz. One was informality: the musicians often dressed casually, as though they were at a jam session, and moved about freely – smoking, laughing, and obviously enjoying themselves. Another was immediacy, as the performances were presented in an unrehearsed and spontaneous manner. But probably the most significant factor was intimacy: cameras explored and poked about, picking out off-guard reactions and expressions, catching meaningful interplay between musicians, and moving in for extreme close-ups of facial expressions, hands, and instruments. This intimacy not only emphasized the spontaneous, improvisational aspect of jazz, it also permitted the personality of the artist to emerge. Hollywood films had never captured the extemporaneous, the physical effects, the obvious joy and excitement of jazz performance; television films very often allowed the viewer to feel a part of the musical event.

A landmark in the making of television programs was reached with Robert Herridge's *The Sound of Jazz* (1957, CBS, dir. Jack Smight), for which the musical advisers, Nat Hentoff and Whitney Balliett, put together an astonishing group of artists to create one of the most outstanding and memorable hours in television jazz history. Dressed in casual attire, they were assembled, with invited spectators, in an informal studio setting. The cameras seemed to have roamed freely among the participants, catching Billie Holiday smiling and nodding with satisfaction at a saxophone solo; Count Basie obviously enthused and delighted with a phrase played by Thelonious Monk; or Rex Stewart pleased with himself at a squeezed note he has produced. The skillful and sensitive direction set new standards for the visual presentation of jazz. Among the other musicians who took part were Henry "Red" Allen, Pee Wee Russell, Coleman Hawkins, Jo Jones, Milt Hinton, Vic Dickenson, Lester Young, Ben Webster, Danny Barker, Jimmy Giuffre, Doc Cheatham, Freddie Green, Jim Hall, Mal Waldron, and Jimmy Rushing.

Other exemplary television programs produced by Herridge were *The Sound of Miles Davis* (1959, dir. Jack Smight) and *Jazz from Studio 61* (1959, CBS, dir. Carl Genns). In the former John Coltrane appeared with Miles Davis's quintet playing *So What*, and Davis performed three numbers with Gil Evans's orchestra – *The Duke, Blues for Pablo*, and *New Rhumba*; the latter program featured Ahmad Jamal's trio and a group led by Ben Webster. *The Stars of Jazz* (1956, KABC-TV, dir. Norman Abbott), with Bobby Troup as host, won an Emmy Award as the best local television show of the year.

A number of jazz series were produced in the 1950s, including the excellent "The Subject is Jazz" (1958, USTV, 13 weeks), and "Art Ford's Jazz Party" (1958, WNTA-TV, 13 weeks; see fig.5), but it was during the 1960s that series flourished, with such programs as the "Goodyear Concert Series" (1961), "Frankly Jazz" (1962), "Jazz Scene – USA" (1962, Steve Allen's Meadowlane Productions, dir. Steve Binder), and Ralph J. Gleason's "Jazz Casual" (1963–4, KQED, National Educational Television).

British television also produced some notable series. The superlative "Jazz 625" (1964–6, BBC) presented such artists as Dizzy Gillespie, the Modern Jazz Quartet, Dicky Wells, Henry "Red" Allen, Ben Webster, Buck Clayton, Oscar Peterson, Bud Freeman, Erroll Garner, and Wingy Manone, and bands led by Maynard Ferguson, Woody Herman, Duke Ellington, Bruce Turner, Alex Welsh, Graeme Bell, and Kenny Baker. "Jazz Goes to College" (1966–7, BBC) presented the Horace Silver Quintet, the Dave Brubeck Quartet, and such instrumentalists as Darnell Howard, Earl Hines, Rex Stewart, Max Roach, and Stan Getz. "Jazz Scene at Ronnie Scott's" (1969–70, BBC) included performances by Thelonious Monk's quartet, Oscar Peterson's trio, Buddy Rich's orchestra, and Red Norvo's quartet.

Duke Ellington was the subject of a number of special films, among them *Duke Ellington Swings through Japan* (1964, CBS, dir. Peter Poor), with narration by Walter Cronkite; *Duke Ellington at the White House* (1969, prod. Sidney J. Stiber), in which President Nixon honors Ellington on his 70th birthday with the nation's Freedom Medal; *Duke Ellington – We Love you Madly* (1973), which was a celebration organized by Quincy Jones; and *On the Road with Duke Ellington* (1974), a first-rate film document of Ellington reminiscing, composing, receiving honors, and traveling with the band.

4. Documentary films. Between 1950 and 1960 documentary films using jazz-related subject matter were produced both in the USA and in Europe. One of the earliest was *Jazz Dance* (1954, Contemporary, dir. Roger Tilton), made at the Central Plaza Dance Hall in New York, which captured a spontaneous jazz session: Willie "the Lion" Smith, Pee Wee Russell, Jimmy McPartland, Jimmy Archey, Pops Foster, and George Wettling play such staples as *Royal Garden Blues* and *Ballin' the Jack*, and Leon James and Albert Minns perform a variety of period dance steps. *Satchmo the Great* (1957, United Artists, prod. Edward R. Murrow and Fred W. Friendly) follows Louis Armstrong and his All Stars (Edmond Hall, Trummy Young, Billy Kyle, Arvell Shaw, Jack Lesberg, Barrett Deems, and Velma Middleton) on a tour of Europe and Africa. A beautiful, straightforward tribute to Armstrong, the film has a number of moving

5. Maxine Sullivan and Stuff Smith (violin) performing on "Art Ford's Jazz Party," 1958

moments, among them the scene in which W. C. Handy, 80 years old and blind, is seen in the audience, smiling in response to Armstrong's performance of *St. Louis Blues* with the New York PO conducted by Leonard Bernstein. A controversial and outspoken semidocumentary that presents the idea that jazz is dead is Edward Bland's *Cry of Jazz* (1959), a visual essay on jazz and the Afro-American condition in the USA. Filmed mainly on Chicago's South Side, it is a passionate and angry film that emphasizes the black experience and the contribution it made to jazz.

Jazz on a Summer's Day (1960, Union Films, dir. Bert Stern) is a personal record of the 1958 Newport Jazz Festival. Although flawed, this rare and fascinating work was far ahead of the average effort to document jazz performance. It failed in the contrived excursions into beer parties, sailboat racing, and shots of Newport scenery, but it succeeded in the many intense close-ups of the artists, leaving an exciting first record, in color, of one of the most important and successful American jazz events. Armstrong is seen playing and singing *Lazy River* and performing a duet on *Rockin' Chair* with Jack Teagarden; Anita O'Day offers interpretations of *Sweet Georgia Brown* and *Tea for Two*; and Jimmy Giuffre's trio gives a rendition of *Train and the River*. Other musicians include Dinah Washington, Gerry Mulligan, Sonny Stitt, George Shearing, Chico Hamilton, and Thelonious Monk. Later the Monterey jazz festivals were captured on film in *Monterey Jazz Festival* (1967, dir. Lane Slate), *Monterey Jazz* (1968, prod. Ralph J. Gleason and Richard Moore), and *Monterey Jazz* (1973, dir. Norman Abbott).

Mingus (1968, dir. Thomas Reichman) is an extremely candid look at Charles Mingus during the period when he was being evicted from his apartment in New York; there is some fascinating footage of Mingus composing at the piano, philosophizing, reciting poetry, and playing with groups that included Dannie Richmond and Charles McPherson. *Journey Within* (1968, dir. Eric Sherman) is a sensitive documentary that traced the life of Charles Lloyd and presented concert performances that featured Jack DeJohnette and Keith Jarrett. *'Til the Butcher Cuts him Down* (1971, dir. Philip Spalding) shows the last days of Punch Miller, while *Salute to Louis Armstrong* (1972) is a 70th-birthday tribute to the trumpeter at the 1970 Newport Jazz Festival. A priceless treasure is *Jazz Hoofer: Baby Laurence* (1973, dir. Bill Hancock), including rare footage of Laurence in action.

A classic documentary which captures the spirit of the music that flourished in Kansas City during the 1920s and 1930s is *The Last of the Blue Devils* (1974–9, dir. Bruce Ricker). It shows a number of veterans along with some younger local musicians, reminiscing, joking, and performing, and celebrates the con tributions to Kansas City jazz made by Count Basie, Jay McShann, Joe Turner (ii), Jo Jones, Lester Young, Charlie Parker, Bennie Moten, and others.

Jazz in Exile (1978, dir. Chuck France) combines performance and interview to explore the lives and experiences of expatriate jazz musicians in Europe, notably Richard Davis, Phil Woods, Dexter Gordon, Carla Bley, and Steve Lacy. The life and music of modern jazz drummers is the focus of *Different Drummer: Elvin Jones* (1979, dir. Edward Gray) and *Max Roach: Drummer's Drummer* (1980, prod. Axis Video). Jackie McLean contributes a look at the stresses of his career as a teacher and performer in *Jackie McLean on Mars* (1980, dir. Ken Levis), and *Joe Albany: a Jazz Life* (1980, dir. Carole Langer) shows the pianist performing and being interviewed. *A Night in Tunisia* (1980, dir. Bryan Elson) preserves a rehearsal and performance of the title number by Dizzy Gillespie, along with interviews with Leonard Feather and Jon Faddis.

Europe was also an important source of jazz documentary and performance films. One of the first was *Momma Don't Allow* (1955, UK, dir. Tony Richardson and Karel Reisz), which showed Chris Barber's band playing in an English jazz club. *Tailgate Man from New Orleans* (1956, France, dir. Thomas L. Rowe) featured Kid Ory, *Django Reinhardt* (1958, France, dir. Paul Paviot) was a documentary on the life of the guitarist narrated by Yves Montand, and Ben Webster was the subject of the film *Big Ben* (1967, Netherlands, dir. Johann van der Keuken). *Max Roach* (1967, France, dir. Francis Leduc) also introduced Abbey Lincoln, Johnny Griffin, Maurice Vander, and Gilbert Rovère. *International Jazz Festival* (1962, Belgium, dir. Patrick Ledoux) recorded a jazz festival in the Ardennes which featured Cannonball Adderley's group.

The British director John Jeremy was responsible for two exceptional documentaries. *Jazz is our Religion* (1972) combined photographs by Valerie Wilmer and live performance footage with jazz poetry and a jazz soundtrack. *Born to Swing* (1973) took a loving look at some of the greatest jazz artists of the swing era through archival film interviews and contemporary performance sequences; among the musicians were Jo Jones, Earle Warren, Dicky Wells, Eddie Durham, Andy Kirk, and Buddy Tate.

Swingmen in Europe (1977, France, dir. Jean Mazeas) shows recording sessions by, among others, Jo Jones, J. C. Heard, Doc Cheatham, Teddy Buckner, Sammy Price, and Illinois Jacquet.

5. Videos. Music on video was developed in the late 1970s as a method of promoting popular and rock stars. MTV, founded in 1980, was devoted to rock, and BET, founded *c*1984, to soul music, though both offered occasional performances of jazz – mainly of a rather bland variety. Notable exceptions were videos by the rock singer and guitarist Sting, whose sidemen included Kenny Kersey and Branford Marsalis (1985–6) and Marsalis's own bop rendition of *Royal Garden Blues* (1987). As the production and distribution of prerecorded videotapes tailored to home consumption became a profitable business, many films that had originally been made for theatrical release or for television, as well as soundie and telescription compilations, became available. These included *The Last of the Blue Devils, Count Basie Live at the Hollywood Palladium, Born to Swing, After Hours, Playboy Jazz Festival*, and *The Sacred Music of Duke Ellington*. Videos would seem to provide a golden opportunity for jazz and jazz musicians.

III. Jazz film scores

1. Commercial recordings introduced into film soundtracks. 2. Original jazz scores.

1. Commercial recordings introduced into film soundtracks. At the beginning of the sound era Hollywood studios realized that a popular song could help promote a film, and a number of their early productions had such associations, notably *Ramona* (1928), *Coquette* (1929), *Glad Rag Doll* (1929), and *I Cover the Waterfront* (1933). W. C. Handy's *St. Louis Blues* was used in countless films and became a leitmotif for screen characters of questionable morality. Examples may be found in *Safe in Hell* (1931, First National-Warner Bros., dir. William Wellman), during a scene in which a brothel madam makes a telephone call to a prostitute, while the camera slowly travels up the length of her leg to the strains of the tune; *Dancers in the Dark* (1932, Paramount, dir. David Burton), where a gangster with an interest in a dance-hall hostess requests *St. Louis Blues* every time he visits her in a sleazy taxi-dance hall; and *The Way of All Flesh* (1940, Paramount, dir. Louis King), where the slide into disgrace and degradation of a respectable bank employee is emphasized in a scene in a speakeasy, as a black jazz band plays background blues to the popping of champagne corks.

The practice of using jazz in soundtracks to enhance screen drama and help establish the appropriate time period of the narrative came into its own in the 1950s. *Panic in the Streets* (1950, 20th Century-Fox, dir. Elia Kazan) was filmed on location in New Orleans and concerns the desperate search by a physician for a fleeing criminal who is suspected of being a carrier of bubonic plague. Much of the music was especially produced by such jazzmen as Ziggy Elman, Eddie Miller, Teddy Buckner, and Benny Carter, and each piece catches the flavor of the environment in which the action takes place; effective use is made of the blues, boogie-woogie, and dixieland as logical source music from jukeboxes, the radio, and a group playing in a restaurant.

Later films that make use of commercial jazz recordings as source music are *Carnal Knowledge* (1971, Avco Embassy/Icarus, dir. Mike Nichols), in which Glenn Miller's *Moonlight Serenade, Tuxedo Junction*, and *String of Pearls* evoke the college days of the two leading characters; *Save the Tiger* (1972, Paramount, dir. John G. Avildsen), with such period pieces as *Air Mail Special, Stompin' at the Savoy*, and *I can't get started*; and *Paper Moon* (1973, Paramount, dir. Peter Bogdanovich), where Nat Gonella's *The music goes 'round and around*, Paul Whiteman's *Mississippi Mud*, Hoagy Carmichael's *Georgia on my Mind*, and Tommy Dorsey's *After you've gone* do much to establish the era in which the story is set. *Raging Bull* (1980, Universal-International, dir. Martin Scorsese) employs an incredible array of nostalgic source music to give the film its flavor, including *Drumboogie* (Gene Krupa), *Jersey Bounce* (Benny Goodman), *Frenesi* (Artie Shaw), *Big Noise from Winnetka* (Bob Crosby), *I ain't got nobody* (Louis Prima), and *Stone Cold Dead in the Market* (Louis Jordan and Ella Fitzgerald). Woody Allen consistently drew on period recordings as a method of placing his stories in the proper time frame; such films as *Annie Hall* (1977), *Interiors* (1978), and *Stardust Memories* (1980) make generous and effective use of the hit recordings of big bands and such star instrumentalists as Tommy Dorsey, Isham Jones, Glenn Miller, Count Basie, Chick Webb, Sidney Bechet, Louis Armstrong, Django Reinhardt, and Lester Young.

2. Original jazz scores. From 1930 to World War II scoring of motion pictures was stylistically dominated by classical and operatic composers whose European backgrounds brought a romantic symphonic approach to the films of the period. When a film had to evoke imagery associated with crowded urban life or the sophistication of metropolitan living, nothing worked quite so well as a Gershwinesque concert piece with a soaring clarinet glissando. The closer the narrative came to street level and the pavements of crowded working-class tenements, the more jazz-oriented the music seemed to become; the bottom of the cinematic scale was generally reserved for the blues.

During the 1950s and 1960s the Hollywood studios tended to concentrate more and more on themes that had to do with crime, violence, loneliness, alienation, drug addiction, racial and generational conflict, juvenile delinquency, and the brittle antagonisms that were the result of a crowded and stressed existence. At the same time jazz-flavored scores and soundtracks became synonymous with these themes and with *film noir* productions, and a cadre of film composers, arrangers and orchestrators emerged to provide many of the original compositions and jazz-influenced music. Some found work in the studios and in television, and others began to write for television commercials as well. They were experimenting and making radical departures from traditional approaches to underscoring by moving away from jazz-tinged symphonic scores and utilizing the instrumentation of typical jazz groups – often relying on the improvisational aspect of jazz. The break up of the studio system and the emergence of independent producers encouraged the use of fresh ideas, not only in the selection of dramatic themes but also in the scoring of the films.

In the early 1950s, with the innovative work of Benny Carter, Leith Stevens, Alex North, Elmer Bernstein, David Raksin, Ray Heindorf, Buddy Bregman, Pete Rugolo, Duke Ellington, and Shorty Rogers, jazz-textured scores became dominant. *A Streetcar Named Desire* (1951, music North), *The Glass Wall* (1953, music Stevens), *On the Waterfront* (1954, music Leonard Bernstein), *The Wild One* (1954, music Stevens), and *The Man with the Golden Arm* (1955, music Elmer Bernstein) were social and psychological problem dramas; jazz-flavored underscoring seemed to suit best the mood of their dramatic content. The effectiveness of these film scores was influential in setting a pattern for the ensuing years. By the late 1950s the trend was further reflected in the music of such films as *The Wild Party* (1956, music Bregman), *Anatomy of a Murder* (1959, music Ellington), *Odds Against Tomorrow* (1959, music John Lewis), and *Shadows* (1959, music Charles Mingus). Lewis wrote the score for *Sait-on jamais* (1957, dir. Roger Vadim) and performed on the soundtrack with the other members of the Modern Jazz Quartet; Miles Davis improvised that for *Ascenseur pour l'échafaud* (1957, dir. Louis Malle).

In 1958 Mancini wrote the music for a highly successful television crime series produced by Blake Edwards, "Peter Gunn." A jazz club called Mothers served as the base of operations for the private detective who was the central character. The score, a seminal work, was entirely oriented towards jazz, with plenty of big-band sounds, lots of brass and saxophones, the blues, and cool jazz. Its background theme, which was nominated for an Emmy Award, created an overall mood for the series, which in turn became identified with a host of similar dramas that followed, and the commercial success of the soundtrack album prompted other producers to scout for jazz composers who would create comparable scores. Subsequent series, for which the musical hallmark became the sounds of screaming brass heard over the beat of drums (or bongos) and a steady walking bass, included "Richard Diamond, Private Detective" (1957–60, music Pete Rugolo), "Johnny Midnight" (1960, music Joe Bushkin), "Johnny Staccato" (1959–60, music Elmer Bernstein), and "Mr. Lucky" (1959, music Henry Mancini). The original musical theme for "M Squad" (1957–60) was discarded in the series' second season in favor of a jazz theme composed by Count Basie.

The "discovery" of jazz by the producers of motion pictures and television programs in the 1950s soon led to its overuse, and there were complaints from critics, fans, and even musicians about the increasing association of jazz with vice, violence and all things sordid. At the same time, making a living as a jazz performer was not easy, and musicians frequently set aside their personal objections for more practical considerations in order to accept assignments to work on soundtracks.

The trend thus continued in the late 1950s with such films as *I Want to Live* (1958, United Artists, dir. Robert Wise, music Johnny Mandel), a *film noir* melodrama based on the story of Barbara Graham, whose criminal way of life eventually led to her execution in San Quentin. Mandel's jazz score helped to establish a mood suitable for vice, drugs, and crime, and was performed by such prominent jazz musicians as Gerry Mulligan, Bud Shank, Art Farmer, Pete Jolly, Frank Rosolino, Red Mitchell, and Shelly Manne – who also appear in the nightclub scene which opens the film. Mancini's Afro-Cuban jazz-tinged score for *Touch of Evil* (1958, Universal-International, dir. Orson Welles) reinforces effectively the sleazy, decadent atmosphere of the drama.

Two British films of the period were *Look Back in Anger* (1959, ABP/Woodfall, dir. Tony Richardson, music Chris Barber; see fig.6, p.386), which starred Richard Burton as a trumpet playing malcontent (dubbed by Pat Halcox) with a dixieland band (played by Barber's group), and *Sapphire* (1959, Artna/Universal, dir. Basil Dearden, music Philip Green), for which the soundtrack was provided by John Dankworth.

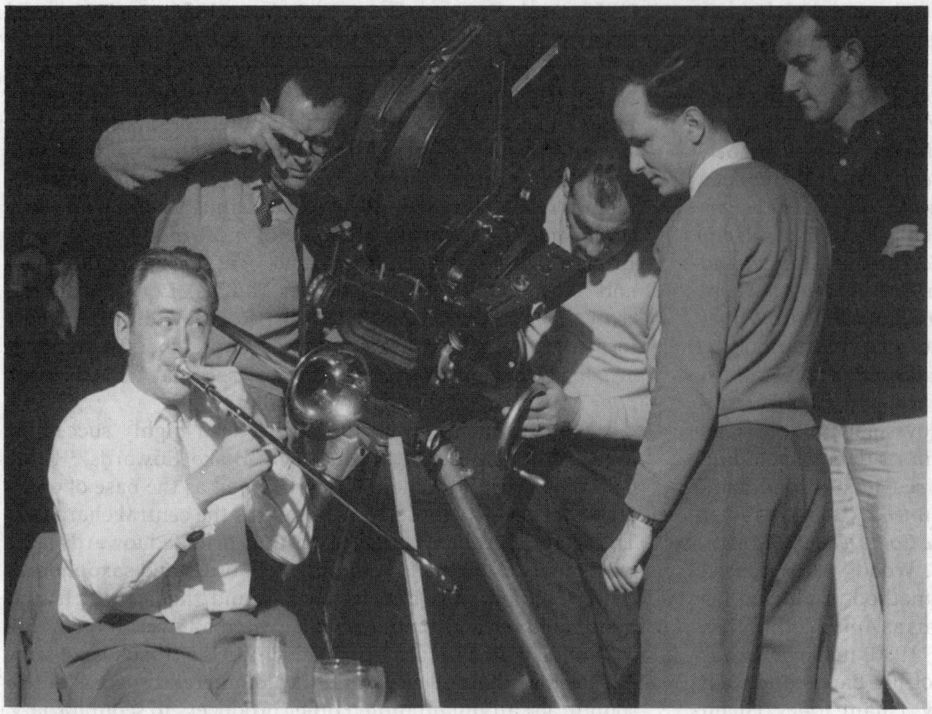

6. Chris Barber (trombone) being filmed in close up for "Look Back in Anger," 1959; the director, Tony Richardson, is on the extreme right

Violence, alienation, sex, drugs, and rebellion were strong components of films produced in the 1960s and 1970s. The jazz-filled score fit such themes rather well, and the list of composers and arrangers who wrote appropriate soundtracks grew to include Lalo Schifrin, Quincy Jones, Billy May, Frank DeVol, David Amram, Calvin Jackson, André Previn, Oliver Nelson, Nelson Riddle, Eddie Sauter, Gil Melle, Don Ellis, Jimmy Giuffre, Gerry Mulligan, Neal Hefti, Ralph Burns, Gary McFarland, Jerry Goldsmith, Chuck Mangione, Bob James, Fred Katz, and Herbie Hancock.

One of the most successful of these composers is Jones. From such early works as *Pojken i trädet* (*Boy in the tree*; 1961), *The Pawnbroker* (1965), and *The Slender Thread* (1966), he went on to create memorable scores for such films as *In the Heat of the Night* (1967), *In Cold Blood* (1967), for which he won an Oscar for Best Original Score, *Cactus Flower* (1969), *The Anderson Tapes* (1971), *The Getaway* (1972), and *The Wiz* (1978). His contributions to television include the theme music for NBC's "Ironside" (1967–75), "The Bill Cosby Show" (1969–71), and "Sanford and Son" (1972–7).

Schifrin has scored more than 70 successful films, some of the most notable being *The Cincinnati Kid* (1965), *The Fox* (1967), *Cool Hand Luke* (1967), and *Charley Varrick* (1973).

Among the composers in Europe who made important contributions to jazz-inspired motion-picture scores were John Dankworth, Allyn Ferguson, and Johnny Hawksworth in the UK; Claude Bolling, André Hodeir, and Hubert Rostaing in France; and Svend Asmussen in Denmark. Dankworth's work includes outstanding scores for *Saturday Night and Sunday Morning* (1960), *The Servant* (1963), *Darling* (1965), and *10 Rillington Place* (1970), while Bolling has scored dozens of films, notably *Pourvu qu'on ait l'ivresse* (1957), *L'homme à femmes* (1960), *Le solitaire* (1973), *Il faut vivre dangereusement* (1975), and *Le gitan* (1975).

Towards the 1980s the themes in many motion pictures began to reflect a number of changes. Although films concerning crime, sex, and violence were still popular, so were others with light, escapist plots – for example the many science-fiction adventures of the late 1970s; themes relating to social statements and the Vietnam War were also explored. The soundtracks for many of these films, made by performers who had established their reputations on television or in comedy clubs, were little more than commercially successful rock-and-roll or popular hit recordings.

BIBLIOGRAPHY

C. Emge: "Movie Music: Video Film Musicals Could Revolutionize Television," *DB*, xvii/21 (1950), 14
H. Gautier: *Jazz au cinéma* (Paris, 1961)
D. Morgenstern: "Jazz on Film," *DBY 1967*, suppl to *DB*, xxxiii (1966), 64
D. Meeker: *Jazz in the Movies: a Tentative Index to the Work of Jazz Musicians for the Cinema* (London, 1972)
H. Siders: "The Jazz Composers in Hollywood: a Symposium with Benny Carter, Quincy Jones, Henry Mancini, Lalo Schifrin, Pat Williams," *DB*, xxxix/4 (1972), 12
J. L. Limbacher: *Film Music: from Violins to Video* (Metuchen, NJ, 1974)
M. Evans: *Soundtrack: the Music of the Movies* (New York, 1975)
T. Cripps: *Slow Fade to Black: the Negro in American Films* (New York, 1977)
D. Meeker: *Jazz in the Movies: a Guide to Jazz Musicians, 1917–1977* (London, 1977, rev. 2/1981 as *Jazz in the Movies*)
R. M. Prendergast: *A Neglected Art: a Critical Study of Music in Films* (New York, 1977)
H. T. Sampson: *Blacks in Black and White: a Source Book on Black Films* (Metuchen, NJ, 1977)
P. R. Klotman: *Frame by Frame: a Black Filmography* (Bloomington, IN, and London, 1979)
L. Maltin: *Of Mice and Magic: a History of American Animated Cartoons* (New York, 1980)
J. Newsom: "A Sound Idea: Music for Animated Films," *Quarterly Journal of the Library of Congress*, xxxvii (1980), 279–309
J. L. Limbacher: *Keeping Score: Film Music, 1972–1979* (Metuchen, NJ, 1981)
M. Berger, E. Berger, and J. Patrick: *Benny Carter: a Life in American Music* (Metuchen, NJ, 1982)
U. Risak, ed.: *Drittes Jazz im Film Festival: Programmheft zur Veranstaltung* (Vienna, 1985)
J. Bany "Jazz Scene: Round Midnight," *International Society of Bassists*, xiii/2 (1987), 20

ERNIE SMITH

Filu [Schenkelbach, Fülöp] (*b* Stanislav [now Ivano-Frankovsk, Ukrainian SSR], 6 April 1902; *d* New York, Dec 1981). Hungarian reed player and bandleader. In 1914 he moved to Budapest, where he later studied violin; he played alto saxophone from 1926 and thereafter took up the tenor saxophone and clarinet. He toured Europe as a tenor saxophone soloist with Ede Buttola's group the Jolly Boys (1929–30) and worked at the Piccadilly club in Budapest (1931). He was a member of Chappy's orchestra in 1931–2, but he left to play in Vienna with the band of Harry Taffet (1932–4). After returning to Budapest (1934), he played in clubs and recorded with the trumpeter Len Hughes (1938–40) and the Bluebird Boys (1942). From 1946 to 1950 Filu performed and recorded as the leader of a big band and a swing group drawn from the larger ensemble; among his recordings is *Hey-ba-ba-re-bop* (1946, Durium Patria D47437). He visited Israel in 1950 and then emigrated to the USA, where he worked as a studio musician. (A. Csányi and G. G. Simon: Liner notes, *Jazz and Hot Dance in Hungary*, Harl. 2015, 1985)

GÉZA GÁBOR SIMON, RAINER E. LOTZ

Finch, Candy [Otis(, Jr.)] (*b* 1933 or 1934; *d* Seattle, 13 July 1982). Drummer. The tenor saxophonist Otis Finch, who recorded with the blues singers Joe Turner (ii) (1947) and John Lee Hooker (1951), may have been his father. During the 1950s Finch played in clubs in Detroit. He performed and made recordings with Shirley Scott (1961, 1964), Stanley Turrentine (1962, 1964), Milt Jackson (1965), and Dizzy Gillespie (1966–9, including *Swing Low, Sweet Cadillac*, 1967, Imp. 9149). He also recorded with Billy Mitchell (1962), Al Grey (1962–3), and Gene Ammons (1971). After working as a studio musician in Los Angeles he moved in 1978 to Seattle, where he led a bop group. (Obituary, *DB*, l/3 (1983), 14)

Finegan, Bill [William J.] (*b* Newark, NJ, 3 April 1917). Arranger, composer, and pianist. On the recommendation of Tommy Dorsey, who had bought his arrangement of *The Lonesome Road*, he was engaged in 1938 by Glenn Miller, and provided many of the orchestra's best-known arrangements as well as the music for the films *Sun Valley Serenade* (1941) and *Orchestra Wives* (1942). He then worked for Horace Heidt (1942–3) and Les Elgart (1946), but also wrote intermittently for Dorsey – notably for the film *The Fabulous Dorseys* (1947) – and provided him with a number of arrangements during the period 1950–52. From 1952 to 1957 Finegan was leader of a band with EDDIE SAUTER. Their group was never a commercial success, and its arrangements left little scope for improvisation, but it was noteworthy for its experimental approach to instrumentation: the six-man rhythm section made use of a variety of percussion, and the wind section included such instruments as piccolo, bass clarinet, and english horn. Finegan and Sauter worked together from 1959 composing advertising jingles for television, and Finegan continued to work in broadcasting through the 1960s. In the 1970s he wrote arrangements for the memorial Glenn Miller Orchestra and Mel Lewis's band.

RECORDED COMPOSITIONS

(selective list; all recorded by the Sauter–Finegan Orchestra)

New Directions in Music (1953–6, RCA LPM1227), incl. Doodletown Fifer; *The Sons of Sauter–Finegan* (1955, RCA LPM1104), incl. Procrastination; *Adventure in Time* (1956, RCA LPM1240)

SELECTED ARRANGEMENTS

Recorded by T. Dorsey: Lonesome Road (1939, Vic. 26508); Bingo, bango, boffo (1946, Vic. 202196); Pussy Willow (1949, Vic. 203492)

Recorded by G. Miller: Sunrise Serenade (1939, Bb 10214); Little Brown Jug (1939, Bb 10286); Song of the Volga Boatmen (1941, Bb 11029)

BIBLIOGRAPHY

FeatherE

G. Simon: "Inside Sauter–Finegan: the Nice Guys," *Metronome*, lxx/7 (1954), 17

J. Wilson: "Adventures in Sound: the Doodletown Fifers," *High Fidelity*, iv/4 (1954), 33

W. Balliett: "Jazz: New York Notes," *New Yorker*, lii (5 July 1976), 66

DAVID FLANAGAN

Finnish Jazz Federation. *See* SUOMEN JAZZLIITTO.

Firehouse Five Plus Two. Traditional jazz band. Formed in 1949 by the trombonist Ward Kimball, it drew its members from the staff of Walt Disney's animation studios in Hollywood, California; most of the sidemen were semiprofessional, though the clarinetists Tom Sharpsteen (1952) and George Probert (1954–69) achieved more widespread fame. The band's use of bass saxophone or tuba, and occasionally washboard (played by Kimball), gave its performances a distinctive and intentionally humorous sound. Its recorded legacy consists mainly of fast and furious dixieland tunes, some with a comic vocal part; notable are its LPs with thematic titles, such as *The Firehouse Five Plus Two at Disneyland* (1962, GTJ 10049) and *The Firehouse Five Plus Two Goes To a Fire* (1964, GTJ 10052).

ALYN SHIPTON

Fischer, Clare (*b* Durand, MI, 22 Oct 1928). Arranger, composer, and pianist. He studied at Michigan State University (BM 1951, MM 1955), where he developed an interest in Latin-American music. He wrote arrangements for the band at the United States Military Academy (1952–3), then became accompanist and arranger for the vocal group the Hi-Lo's. He won critical acclaim for his big-band arrangements for Dizzy Gillespie's album *A Portrait of Duke Ellington* (1960) and during the 1960s recorded a number of his works with his own studio band. From 1962 Fischer began to establish himself as a performer with a series of albums made as a solo pianist and others for small groups playing bop and Latin jazz; with Cal Tjader he made some of the first recordings in the USA of bossa nova (1962). He also recorded as an organist. Although Fischer achieved his reputation initially as an arranger, in the 1980s he is perhaps best known as a pianist; among his notable recordings is a duo album made with Gary Foster (1982). His compositions, a number of which are influenced by Latin-American rhythms, include *Elizete* and *Pensativa*.

SELECTED RECORDINGS

As unaccompanied soloist: *Jazz Song* (1973, Rev. 31)

Duos with G. Foster: *Starbright* (1982, Dis. 885)

As leader: *First Time Out* (1962, PJ 52); *The Reclamation Act of 1972* (1970, Rev. 15), incl. Pensativa; *Salsa Picante* (1978, Dis. 817); *Machaca* (1979, Dis. 835)

As sideman: C. Tjader: *Contemporary Music of Mexico and Brazil* (1962, Verve 68470), incl. Elizete

SELECTED ARRANGEMENTS

As leader: *Extensions* (1963, PJ 77); *Songs for Rainy Day Lovers* (1966–7, Col. CS9491); *Thesaurus* (1968, Atl. 1520)

Recorded by D. Gillespie: *A Portrait of Duke Ellington* (1960, Verve 68386)

BIBLIOGRAPHY

J. Tynan: "Star on the Rise," *DB*, xxviii/12 (1961), 18

R. F. Thompson: "Clare Fischer: the Pan-American Way," *Saturday Review*, xlvii (28 Nov 1964), 46

M. Gardner: "Clare Fischer: Piano Artistry," *JJ*, xx/10 (1967), 23

D. Zimmerle: "Voller neuer Pläne: Clare Fischer," *JP*, xxv/1 (1976), 12

L. Lyons: "The Multifaceted Careers of Two Top LA Jazz Pianists," *CK*, iv/4 (1978), 16

B. Irwin: "Clare Fischer: a Studio Master Fuses Jazz Chords & Latin Rhythms," *Keyboard*, xi/2 (1985), 44 [incl. discography]

STEVEN STRUNK

Fischer, John (*b* Brussels, *c*1931). Pianist. In the early 1940s he moved with his family to France, then briefly to Cuba, before settling in the USA in 1943. He studied piano as a youth and again from the age of 19. In the late 1960s he played free jazz in Boston and Syracuse, New York, with Perry Robinson. He recorded as a leader on *Poum!* (1974) and from around 1975 led the group Interface, which recorded in 1975, 1977, and 1978. In New York he became involved in the promotion of loft jazz, helping to found the venue Environ (*c*1975) and organize the Loft Jazz Celebration festival in 1976; he was responsible for introducing a number of European free-jazz musicians to audiences in New York. He recorded a series of duos with Lester Bowie, Charles Tyler, Arthur Blythe, Robinson, and others on *Duos for a New Decade* (1977–8, Re-entry 004), and also with Marion Brown. In 1981 he toured Europe, recording in Moscow with the clarinetist Hans Kumpf and performing as an unaccompanied soloist and with Interface. He recorded with the trumpeter Michael Sell in 1983.

BIBLIOGRAPHY

H. Kumpf: "John Fischer Interaktions-Musik," *JP*, xxvi/4 (1977), 16
C. Safane: "John Fischer: Face to Interface," *JF* [intl edn], no.71 (1981), 45 [incl. discography]

Fischer, Johnny (*b* Vienna, 3 May 1930). Austrian double bass player. He grew up in England, but later returned to Austria; he studied piano at the Vienna Conservatory (1947–50) and gained experience by playing in American clubs. After moving to Germany in 1952 he took up double bass and played with the bandleader Helmut Weglinski (1954–5), then performed and made recordings with Hans Koller (1955–6, including *Koller Plays Kovac*, 1955, Amadeo AVRS7013–14), and Kurt Edelhagen (1957–9). He also recorded with Lee Konitz (1956), Joe Zawinul (1957), the pianist Paul Kuhn (1958), and the saxophonist Heinz Kretschmar (1960), then in 1962 became a full-time studio musician and arranger in Cologne. Around 1970 he was appointed manager of the Kurt Edelhagen Orchestra at Westdeutscher Rundfunk and ceased to play double bass. He wrote an instruction manual, *Anleitung zur Improvisation für Bass* (1967). (*ReclamsJ*)

Fischer, William (S.) (*b* Shelby, MS, 5 March 1935). Arranger, composer, conductor, and keyboard player. After playing saxophone as a teenager with blues and rhythm-and-blues musicians he studied music at Xavier University of Louisiana, Colorado College (MA 1962), and the academy of music in Vienna (1965–6). He then became a freelance composer and arranger, and wrote material and directed studio sessions for Joe Zawinul (on whose album *The Rise and Fall of the Third Stream*, 1967, Vortex 2002, he also played tenor saxophone), Herbie Mann and Les McCann (both 1968–9), Gene Ammons (1970), Junior Mance (1973), and Pharoah Sanders (1982). He also recorded as a keyboard player with his own group (1970) and with Roland Kirk (1977). (*Feather–Gitler '70s*)

Fishkin(d), Arnold (*b* Bayonne, NJ, 20 July 1919). Double bass player. He played violin from the age of eight and double bass from the age of 14. He performed and recorded with Bunny Berigan (1937), Jack Teagarden (1939–41), and Les Brown (1942), and then served in the US Army. After recording with Chubby Jackson (1945), he worked with the clarinetist Jerry Wald (1945–6), Lennie Tristano (1946–7), and Charlie Barnet (1946–7), with whom he moved to the West Coast. In Los Angeles he recorded with the Mills Blue Rhythm Band and Freddie Slack (both 1947), among others. He resumed his association with Tristano in New York (1948–9), where he also performed and recorded with Lee Konitz (1949–51) and recorded with Ella Fitzgerald (1951). In the 1950s and 1960s he played in the staff orchestras of CBS and ABC; during this period he made recordings with numerous leaders, including Don Elliott (1952), Billy Bauer (*Let's Have a Session*, 1953, Ad Lib 5501), Mel Powell and Tony Aless (both 1955), Howard McGhee and Konitz (both 1956), Hank Jones (1958), and Toots Thielemans (1962). From 1966 he worked as a freelance musician in Los Angeles and Palm Springs, California. (*FeatherE*)

Fitzgerald, Ella (*b* Newport News, VA, 25 April 1918). Singer. She was orphaned in early childhood and moved to New York to attend an orphanage school in Yonkers. In 1934 she was discovered in an amateur contest sponsored by the Apollo Theatre, New York. This led to an engagement with Chick Webb's band, and she soon became a celebrity of the swing era with performances such as *A-tisket, A-tasket* (1938) and *Undecided* (1939). When Webb died in 1939 Fitzgerald took over the direction of the band, which she led for three years. She then embarked on a solo career, issuing commercial and jazz recordings, and in 1946 began an association with Norman Granz's Jazz at the Philharmonic which eventually brought her a large international following. She also sang in a jazz group led by her husband, Ray Brown (1948–52). Early in 1956 Fitzgerald severed her longstanding connection with Decca to join Granz's newly founded Verve label. Among their first projects was a series of "songbooks" dedicated to major American songwriters. The series made use of superior jazz-inflected arrangements by Nel-

Ella Fitzgerald, 1958

son Riddle and others and succeeded in attracting an extremely large nonjazz audience, establishing Fitzgerald among the supreme interpreters of the popular-song repertory. Thereafter her career was managed by Granz, and she became one of the best-known international jazz performers; she issued many recordings for Granz's labels and made frequent appearances at jazz festivals with Duke Ellington, Count Basie, Oscar Peterson, Tommy Flanagan, and Joe Pass. Among her many honors was a Grammy Award in 1980. Her collection of scores and photographs is now in the library of Boston University; *see* LIBRARIES AND ARCHIVES, §2.

For decades Fitzgerald has been considered the quintessential female jazz singer, and has drawn copious praise from admirers as diverse as Charlie Parker and the singer Dietrich Fischer-Dieskau. Her voice is small and somewhat girlish in timbre, but these disadvantages are offset by an extremely wide range (from *d* to *c'''*) which she commands with a remarkable agility and an unfailing sense of swing. This enables her to give performances that rival those of the best jazz instrumentalists in their virtuosity, particularly in her improvised scat solos, for which she is justly famous (for an example *see* SCAT SINGING). Unlike trained singers she shows strain about the break in her voice (*d''* and beyond) which, however, she uses to expressive purpose in the building of climaxes. Fitzgerald also has a gift for mimicry that allows her to imitate other well-known singers (from Louis Armstrong to Aretha Franklin) as well as jazz instruments. As an interpreter of popular songs she is limited by a certain innate cheerfulness from handling drama and pathos convincingly, but is unrivaled in her rendition of light material and for her ease in slipping in and out of the jazz idiom. She influenced countless American popular singers of the post-swing period and also international performers such as the singer Miriam Makeba.

For further illustration *see* WEBB, CHICK.

SELECTED RECORDINGS

Duos with J. Pass: *Take Love Easy* (1973, Pablo 2310702); *Speak Love* (1983, Pablo 2310888)

As leader: Flying Home (1945, Decca 23956); How High the Moon (1947, Decca 24387); *Ella & Ray* (1948, Jazz Live 8035); The Tender Trap (1955, Decca 29746); *Ella Fitzgerald at the Opera House* (1957, Verve 8264); *Ella Swings Brightly with Nelson* (1961, Verve 64054); *These are the Blues* (1963, Verve 64062); *Ella at Juan-les-Pins* (1964, Barclay 3716); *Ella in Hamburg '65* (1965, Verve 64069); *Fine and Mellow* (1974, Pablo 2310829); *Ella in London* (1974, Pablo 2310711); *Lady Time* (1978, Pablo 2310825)

Songbooks: *Ella Fitzgerald Sings the Cole Porter Song Book* (1956, Verve 4001); *Ella Fitzgerald Sings the Rodgers and Hart Song Book* (1956, Verve 4002); *Ella Fitzgerald Sings the Duke Ellington Song Book* (1956–7, Verve 4008–9); *Ella Fitzgerald Sings the George and Ira Gershwin Song Book* (1959, Verve 4024–8); *Ella Fitzgerald Sings the Harold Arlen Song Book* (1960–61, Verve 4046)

As sideman: C. Webb: Sing me a swing song (1936, Decca 830); B. Goodman: Did you mean it? (1936, Vic. 25469); T. Wilson: My Melancholy Baby (1936, Bruns. 7729); C. Webb: A-tisket, A-tasket (1938, Decca 1840); Undecided (1939, Decca 2323)

BIBLIOGRAPHY

J. Jungermann: *Ella Fitzgerald: ein Porträt* (Wetzlar, Germany, 1960)
R. Ambor: *Ella: ein Bildband* (Hamburg, Germany, 1961)
L. Feather: "Ella Today (and Yesterday too)," *DB*, xxxii/24 (1965), 20
L. Feather: *From Satchmo to Miles* (New York, 1972)
H. Pleasants: *The Great American Popular Singers* (New York, 1974)
S. Colin: *Ella: the Life and Times of Ella Fitzgerald* (London, 1986)
R. Nolden: *Ella Fitzgerald: ihr Leben, ihre Musik, ihre Schallplatten* (Gauting, Germany, 1986)

J. BRADFORD ROBINSON

Five Pennies. Recording group led in the late 1920s by RED NICHOLS.

Five Spot (Café). Nightclub in New York; *see* NIGHTCLUBS AND OTHER VENUES.

FJF [Finnish Jazz Federation]. *See* SUOMEN JAZZLIITTO.

Flagstad, Michael [Mikkel] (*b* Oslo, 23 April 1930). Norwegian tenor saxophonist and clarinetist. He studied clarinet from the age of nine with his father, Ole Flagstad, and later with Ragnar Birkedal and Richard Kjelstrup. His professional career began in 1946; later he played with Simon Brehm (1952–4), Einar Iversen, and the trumpeter Atle Hammer, and from 1957 worked as a leader of small groups, often in conjunction with Iversen and Hammer. From 1959 to 1964 he worked with the pianist Kjell Karlsen and led a quintet; he also made recordings with Brehm (1952–4) and Gösta Theselius's orchestra. He received the Buddy Award from the Norwegian Jazz Federation in 1960. Good examples of Flagstad's playing are the tracks *Easy to Love/Day by Day* (1952, Artist B3085), recorded as a member of an orchestra led by Rolf Ericson, and his recording as the leader of a quartet of *All the Things you are* (1959), first issued on *Norsk Jazz, 1960–1980* (1959–82, Odin LP09).

BIBLIOGRAPHY

K. Sandegren and others: *Boken om jazz* (Oslo, 1954)
O. Angell, J. E. Vold, and E. Økland, eds.: *Jazz i Norge* (Oslo, 1975)
K. Michelsen, ed.: *Cappelens musikkleksikon* (Oslo, 1978)

VIDAR VANBERG

Flag waver. A fast, energetic piece or part of a piece (typically the final chorus), designed to show off a band's technical prowess and excite the audience.

Flam. One of the drumstrokes collectively known as RUDIMENTS.

Flamingo. Nightclub in London; *see* NIGHTCLUBS AND OTHER VENUES.

Flanagan, Tommy (Lee) (*b* Detroit, 16 March 1930). Pianist. He began studying clarinet at the age of six, and took up piano when he was 11. In his early years he performed professionally in the Detroit area with Milt Jackson, Thad Jones, Elvin Jones, and others, playing in a style influenced by Art Tatum, Teddy Wilson, Hank Jones, and Bud Powell. After moving to New York in 1956 he occasionally substituted for Powell at Birdland, and was deeply affected by the music of Charlie Parker. In the late 1950s and early 1960s he worked as a freelance, and played with Oscar Pettiford, J. J. Johnson (1956–8), Miles Davis, Tyree Glenn, Harry Edison, and Coleman Hawkins. Flanagan is, perhaps, best known as pianist and music director for Ella Fitzgerald, with whom he worked for a number of years (1956, 1963–5, 1968–78). He also served as music director for Tony Bennett (1966). From 1978, however, having tired of accompanying singers, he began working with small instrumental ensembles. His tasteful skills as an accompanist have sometimes overshadowed his graceful but authoritative solo style. A master of bop, a poetic interpreter of popular tunes, and an eloquent spokesman for the music of Duke Ellington and Billy Strayhorn, Flanagan is one of the jazz world's most sought-after pianists.

SELECTED RECORDINGS

Duos with H. Jones: *Our Delights* (1978, Gal. 5113)

As leader: *The Tommy Flanagan Tokyo Recital* (1975, Pablo 2310724); *Confirmation* (1977–8, Enja 4014); *Something Borrowed, Something Blue* (1978, Gal. 5110); *Super-session* (1980, IC 3039)

As sideman with E. Fitzgerald: *Ella at Juan-les-Pins* (1964, Barclay 3716)

BIBLIOGRAPHY

S. Dance: "Tommy Flanagan: Out of the Background," *DB*, xxxiii/1 (1966), 20
E. Meadow: "The World of Tommy Flanagan," *DB*, xxxvii/20 (1970), 18
"Tommy Flanagan Discography," *SJ*, xxix/2 (1975), 240
L. Feather: "Piano Giants of Jazz: Tommy Flanagan," *CK*, v/11 (1979), 72
B. Primack and R. Dubin: "Detroit's Triple Gift to the Jazz Piano World," *CK*, v/12 (1979), 12
J. Réda: *L'improviste: une lecture de jazz* (Paris, 1980), 183
M. Ullman: *Jazz Lives: Portraits in Words and Pictures* (Washington, 1980), 111
L. Jeske: "Tommy Flanagan: on his own," *DB*, xlix/7 (1982), 25 [incl. discography]

BILL DOBBINS/R

Flanger. An electronic treatment that simulates the technique used in the recording studio of flanging, that is, playing two identical tape recordings simultaneously and varying slightly the speed of one by placing a hand on the flange of a tape-reel (or in some other manner). The resulting phase differences produce a modification of timbre. The electronic version of this process is more easily controllable, offers a greater variety of sound effects, and may be used in performance. It is particularly popular among electric guitarists, but it is frequently used to treat the sound of other electric and electronic instruments.

Flanigan, Phil (*b* Geneva, NY, 28 June *c*1960). Double bass player. He studied double bass at the Eastman School of Music for two years with Oscar Zimmerman and at the New England Conservatory. While visiting Providence, Rhode Island, at weekends, he played with various groups; he also met Scott Hamilton and the guitarist Chris Flory, and for a brief period was a member of the Widespread Depression Orchestra. After moving to New York to work as a freelance he appeared at Eddie Condon's club, performed in concerts with Benny Goodman, and recorded with Hamilton, Bob Wilber, and Warren Vaché, Jr. His playing is well represented by the album *Midtown Jazz* (1982, Conc. 203), recorded in a trio led by Vaché that also included John Bunch.

WARREN VACHÉ, SR.

Flare [flare-up]. A note or chord held at the end of the penultimate chorus of a piece, to prepare the band for the final climactic chorus (the out chorus or ride out); typically the note or chord is attacked vigorously and the final chorus is loud. The flare is characteristic of New Orleans jazz and related styles; an example may be heard on Louis Armstrong's *Willie the Weeper* (1927, OK 8482)

Flax, Marty [Flachsenhaar, Martin] (*b* New York, 7 Oct 1924; *d* Las Vegas, NV, 3 May 1972). Baritone and tenor saxophonist. He played baritone saxophone in the big bands of Lucky Millinder, Perez Prado, and Les Elgart (1956), recorded with Chubby Jackson (1949), Pete Rugolo (1954), and Sam Most (1957), and performed and recorded with Woody Herman (1950, 1958), Louis Jordan (1951), and Dizzy Gillespie (1956). He also made recordings in bop sextets under Most (1954–5, including *I'm Nuts about the Most*, 1955, Beth. 18) and Frank Rehak (1955–6). He toured the Middle East and South America with Gillespie (1956) and South America with Herman (1958) under the auspices of the State Department, then played tenor saxophone and recorded with Claude Thornhill (1959) and Buddy Rich (1966–7). From the late 1960s he performed in Las Vegas. (*FeatherE*; *Feather–Gitler '70s*)

For illustration *see* JACKSON, MILT.

Fleagle, Brick [Jacob Roger] (*b* Hanover, PA, 22 Aug 1906). Acoustic guitarist and arranger. In the late 1920s and early 1930s he played in dance bands under Orville Knapp, Roy Ingram, and Hal Kemp, then led his own orchestra (1934–5) and performed and recorded with Joe Haymes (1935–6). From 1936 he was associated with Rex Stewart: the two recorded together under Stewart's name (to 1945), under Fleagle's name (1947), and as sidemen with Jack Teagarden (1940). Fleagle also recorded with J. C. Higginbotham (1945) and Buck Clayton (1946). He wrote arrangements, chiefly for Chick Webb and Jimmie Lunceford but also for Duke Ellington (1939), Stewart (1939, including *San Juan Hill* (Voc. 5510), 1944), Fletcher Henderson (1941), Sonny Greer (1944), and his own big band (1945–6). In 1946 he became director of a music-copying business.

BIBLIOGRAPHY

ChiltonW; *FeatherE*
"Brick's Boys go Riding," *Time*, xlvi (30 July 1945), 54

Flemming, Herb [El-Michelle, Niccolaiih] (*b* Honolulu, 5 April 1900; *d* New York, 3 Oct 1976). Trombonist and singer of north African descent. He began learning brass instruments at the age of ten, playing first with a Jenkins' Orphanage band in Charleston, South Carolina. He was a member of James Reese Europe's 369th US Infantry Band (1917–19), accompanied Ethel Waters (1920), and then joined Will Vodery's band (1922). Between 1921 and 1924 he recorded with Johnny Dunn, Perry Bradford, and a number of female classic blues singers. He toured Europe and Argentina with Sam Wooding (1925–7) and after working as a freelance led his own group, the International Rhythm Aces, in 1929–30. He rejoined Wooding and also worked with the trumpeter Eddie Ritten and the bandleader Sesto Carlini before becoming co-leader of Josephine Baker's revue orchestra in Paris. He worked with Freddy Johnson (1933), toured extensively with his own bands, then returned to the USA in 1937. Thereafter he played with a large number of groups and individuals, including Earl Hines (1937), Duke Ellington (intermittently, 1938–40), Fats Waller (1940–42), Noble Sissle, Don Redman, Benny Carter, Lucky Millinder, Edgar Hayes, Louis Armstrong (1940s), Tommy Dorsey (1954), and Henry "Red" Allen (1953–8; for illustration *see* ALLEN, HENRY "RED"). From 1964 he worked in Spain at southern seaside resorts. One of the most widely traveled of jazz musicians, Flemming was a prolific recording artist, equally at home playing blues, swing, and mainstream and dixieland jazz.

SELECTED RECORDINGS

(all as sideman)

E. Wilson: Evil Blues (1922, Col. 3746); P. Bradford: Hoola Boola Dance (1924, Para. 20309); S. Wooding: Alabamy Bound (1925, Vox 1891); J. Dunn: You need some loving (1928, Col. 14358D); S. Carlini: At your Command (1932, Persic 0043); F. Johnson: Harlem Bound (1933, Bruns. 500340); I got rhythm (1933, Bruns. 500341); D. Ellington: Braggin' in Brass (1938, Bruns. 8099); H. Allen and C. Shavers: When the saints go marching in, on *Jazz at the Metropole* (1955, Beth. 21); H. Allen: *Red Allen Plays King Oliver* (1960, Verve 1025), incl. Balling the Jack
A. Grasso: Sweet Georgia Brown, on *40 anni di jazz in Italia* (1962, Ricordi 8008); Great Traditionalists in Europe: *The Great Traditionalists in Europe* (1969, MPS 15228), incl. Summertime; *For my Friends and me* (1969, Hage XFOE), incl. Sheik of Araby

BIBLIOGRAPHY

E. Biagioni: *Herb Flemming: a Jazz Pioneer around the World* (Alphen aan de Rijn, Netherlands, n.d. [?1977])
F. Driggs: "Herb Flemming," *Sv*, no.69 (1977), 84

RAINER E. LOTZ

Flip. A combination of two types of GLISS: a lift rising from the end of a note, followed by a fall off.

Flood, Bernard (*b* Montgomery, AL, 16 Dec 1907). Trumpeter. He studied music at Tuskegee Institute, and first worked professionally in New York with Bobby Neal (1930–31). Later he played with Fess Williams (1931–2), Teddy Hill (1933–5), Chick Webb, Luis Russell, and Charlie Johnson (1936–7). From 1937 to 1938 he was a member of the band led by Edgar Hayes, with which he toured Europe and made a number of recordings; he may be heard singing on *Laughing at Life* (1937, Bruns. 02520). Flood joined Hazel Scott's big band briefly in 1939. He then played with Louis Armstrong (1939–40, 1942–3), interrupted by a short period with Jimmy Reynolds (spring 1941). After military service he worked again with Russell (1946–7) and with Duke Ellington. From 1949 to 1953 he played regularly with Happy Caldwell; he also led his own band for several years, and continued to perform sporadically into the 1980s.

based on *ChiltonW*

Florence, Bob [Robert C.] (*b* Los Angeles, 20 May 1932). Arranger, pianist, and bandleader. From 1959 to 1964 he played piano and wrote arrangements for Si Zentner; his version of *Up a Lazy River* (1960, Lib. 55374) became a hit for Zentner in 1961. Recordings of his arrangements were also made by Jimmy Witherspoon (1959), the popular Brazilian pianist Sergio Mendes (1965), Joe Pass (1965–6), Frank Capp (1960), and Bud Shank (1966), on the last two of which he played piano. He led his own big bands in the Los Angeles area, and made recordings intermittently from 1958 to 1983 (including *Live at Concerts by the Sea*, 1979, Trend 523); among his sidemen were Herb Geller, Shank, Bill Perkins, and Bob Cooper. In 1984 he recorded as a member of Dave Pell's octet.

BIBLIOGRAPHY

Feather '60s
J. Wölfer: *Si Zentner and his Orchestra, also Including Bob Florence and his Orchestra: a Discography* (Langenhagen, Germany, 1981)

Flores, Chuck [Charles Walter] (*b* Orange, CA, 5 Jan 1935). Drummer and leader. He studied with Shelly Manne in 1953 and the same year joined Shorty Rogers and other West Coast musicians for a concert that was recorded and issued as *Superstars of Jazz* (1953, Jam Session 100). In 1954–5 he toured Europe and recorded with Woody Herman. After returning to Los Angeles he recorded with Al Cohn, Cy Touff (both 1955), Art Pepper (1956–8), and Conte Candoli (1957), and performed and recorded with Bud Shank (1956–9, 1963). Later he made recordings with Gil Fuller (1965–6) and Carmen McRae (1971). He was also active as the leader of a quartet (from 1972), a bop quintet (1974–7), which made several recordings, including *Drum Flower* (1977, Conc. 49), a ten-piece band (1975–84), and a 17-piece band (from 1985).

BIBLIOGRAPHY

FeatherE
R. Gordon: *Jazz West Coast: the Los Angeles Jazz Scene of the 1950s* (London and New York, 1986)
C. Deffaa: "The Drummers of Woody Herman," *MD*, xi/1 (1987), 26

Flory, Med [Meredith Irwin] (*b* Logansport, IN, 27 Aug 1926). Saxophonist, arranger, and bandleader. He played clarinet and later alto saxophone with Claude Thornhill, and was then a tenor saxophone soloist with Woody Herman (1953). In 1954 he formed his own group in New York; two years later he moved to California, where he organized a big band that performed at the first Monterey Jazz Festival in 1958. He performed with Terry Gibbs, recording as tenor saxophonist with both his nonet (1958) and orchestra (1959–60); he also recorded on the baritone instrument with Art Pepper and Herman (both 1959). During the 1960s Flory worked less frequently as a musician, and devoted more time to writing screenplays and acting in films and on television.

Flory's group SUPERSAX is devoted to the music of Charlie Parker. The concept for its formation developed out of his sessions with Pepper, during which the saxophone section played arrangements of Parker's improvisations. Flory later collaborated with Joe Maini on transcriptions of Parker's work; the project ceased with Maini's death in 1964, but was revived because of Buddy Clark's interest. Supersax was established in 1972, and won a Grammy Award for its first recording in 1973. After Clark's departure in 1975 Flory became the sole leader of the group; he continues to record with it, and sees its work as a tribute to Parker.

SELECTED RECORDINGS

As leader: *Jazz Wave* (1957, Jub. 1066); Shish-ka-bob/Nobody knows the trouble I've seen (1959, WP 45-816); of Supersax (with B. Clark): *Supersax Plays Bird* (1972, Cap. ST11177), *Supersax Plays Bird*, ii: *Salt Peanuts* (*c*1973, Cap. ST11271); of Supersax: *Chasin' the Bird* (1977, MPS 68160), *Supersax and L. A. Voices* (*c*1984, Col. FC39925)
As sideman: C. Thornhill: Mambo Nothing/Adios (1953, Trend 57)

BIBLIOGRAPHY

FeatherE; *Feather–Gitler '70s*
R. Townley and T. Hogan: "Supersax: the Genius of Bird × Five," *DB*, xli/19 (1974), 13
H. Lucraft: "Supersax," *JJI*, xxxiii/8 (1980), 12
J.-L. Ginibre: "Med Flory, Super Sax Maniac," *Jm*, no.326 (1984), 36

BRENDA PENNELL

Flugelhorn [fluegelhorn]. A trumpet-shaped valved brass instrument pitched in B♭. Related to the keyed bugle, it has that instrument's conical bore and wide bell; the mouthpiece is cup-shaped and is attached to a mouthpipe that serves as a tuning-slide. The flugelhorn has three valves and its compass is the same as that of the cornet (basically *f*♯–*c'''*, sounding *e*–*b*♭''); its timbre is mellow, smooth, and horn-like.

The flugelhorn was introduced into Woody Herman's band by Joe Bishop in 1936, but the more permanent adoption of the instrument in jazz dates from the 1950s: Shorty Rogers took it up early in the decade and it became established after Miles Davis used it on the album *Miles Ahead* (1957, Col. CL1041) arranged by Gil Evans. Its somewhat remote sound, straight and pure without vibrato, was ideally suited to cool jazz and other trumpeters were quick to adopt the flugelhorn as a doubling instrument. From the 1970s many jazz trumpeters have carried a case containing both trumpet and flugelhorn, and composers and arrangers have come to assume that both instruments are available to them. The flugelhorn has added a valuable new tone-color to the jazz orchestrator's palette, whether used as a solo voice or in a section of up to four instruments.

Among the players of the flugelhorn in jazz are Chet Baker, Bill Coleman, Art Farmer, Thad Jones, Clark Terry, Harry Beckett, and Kenny Wheeler. The jazz-rock musician Chuck Mangione gave up trumpet to play flugelhorn alone.

For illustration *see* ROGERS, SHORTY.

BIBLIOGRAPHY

J.-E. Berendt: *Das Jazzbuch: Entwicklung und Bedeutung der Jazzmusik* (Frankfurt am Main, Germany, 1953, rev. 2/1959 as *Das neue Jazzbuch*, Eng. trans., New York, 1962; rev. and enlarged 5/1981 as *Das grosse Jazzbuch: von New Orleans bis Jazz Rock*, Eng. trans. as *The Jazz Book: from New Orleans to Fusion and Beyond*, Westport, CT, 1982)
C. J. Bevan: *The Tuba Family* (London and New York, 1978)

CLIFFORD BEVAN

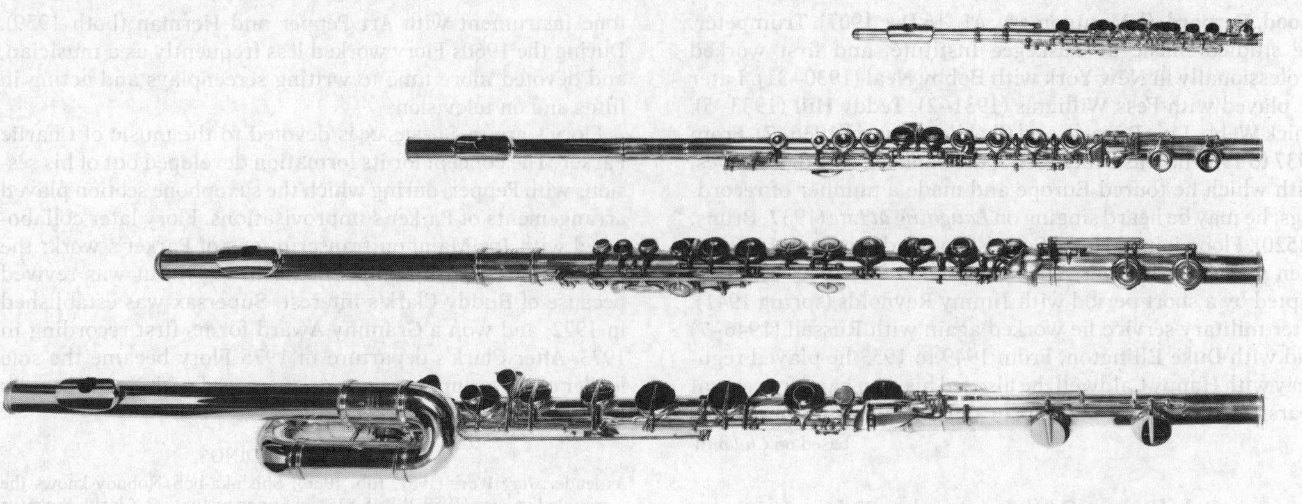

1. The modern flute family (Boehm system; all by Rudall, Carte & Co., London): (a) piccolo in C; (b) concert in C; (c) alto in G; (d) bass in C

Flute. A term applied generally to any wind instrument in which the air column is confined in a hollow body and activated by a stream of air from the player's lips striking against the sharp edge of an opening (producing what is known acoustically as an "edge tone"). The vast number of instruments covered by this definition may be subdivided according to various secondary characteristics: the shape of the body, the number and kind of tone-holes, the shape and position of the mouthhole, and so on. This article deals chiefly with the Western orchestral flute family and its use in jazz.

1. The flute family. 2. The flute. 3. The piccolo. 4. The alto flute. 5. The bass flute. 6. Ethnic flutes.

1. THE FLUTE FAMILY. The most commonly used design for the flute is that devised in the mid-19th century by Theobald Boehm. The instrument is made of metal (or wood), in three sections of mainly cylindrical bore; a system of keywork controls pads that close and open the tone-holes. The flute's basic scale begins on *d'* but tone-holes on the foot joint extend the compass to *c'* or sometimes *b*; the upper limit of its range is around *d''''*, though most players can exceed that by several notes. The other members of the flute family used in jazz are the piccolo, which is half the length of the flute, made in two sections, and pitched an octave higher; the alto flute (sometimes misleadingly called the bass flute), the lowest note on which is *g*; and the true bass flute, which sounds an octave below the soprano instrument (its lowest note being *c*). The bass flute is held differently from the others, resting on the seated player's thigh and having a mouthpiece connected to the body of the instrument by a U-shaped tube. All members of the family are usually built to Boehm's basic design.

2. THE FLUTE. Although some arrangements of ragtime pieces contain flute and piccolo parts, the flute was little used in jazz before the late 1920s. One of the earliest recordings of flute playing in a jazz context was made by the Cuban clarinetist Alberto Socarras, who played with a good classical technique but little jazz feeling on *You can't be mine* (1930, Col. 14557D) made by a group called Bennett's Swamplanders. The first true jazz flutist was the saxophonist Wayman Carver, who made a specialty of his second instrument from 1932. He recorded with Benny Carter (notably on *Devil's Holiday*, 1933, Col. 2898D) and for several years worked with Chick Webb's band; Carver's solo playing is well represented on Webb's *I got rhythm* (1937, Decca 1759). Another early jazz flute solo was played by Harry Klee on Ray Linn's recording *Caravan* (1944, Encore 510).

Before 1950, however, instances of the use of the flute in jazz are few and the instrument remained a novelty. It was generally thought that it was inherently unsuited to jazz: its comparatively low volume made it difficult to accommodate in ensemble work; its disembodied tone was insufficiently intense for solo work and too different from any of the timbres in the big band to blend successfully; and, perhaps because it was associated mainly with classical music, neither players nor arrangers believed it capable of conveying a convincing sense of swing. During the 1950s jazz took a number of directions that made the flute's sound more desirable. It was found to be possible to emulate on the flute some aspects of the enormously influential light, restrained saxophone style of Lester Young, and whereas the flute had formerly been regarded as inexpressive compared with the saxophone it was now seen as eminently controllable. Jazz composers, especially those on the West Coast, including Pete Rugolo, Shorty Rogers, and Marty Paich, began to be interested in the timbres and orchestral sonorities of classical chamber groups, and the flute found a place in their writing along with other instruments relatively unfamiliar in jazz. Finally the flute played an important role in some Latin groups and the 1950s saw the start of the powerful influence of Latin American music on jazz.

Beginning in 1953 Frank Wess started to specialize on flute in Count Basie's band. Although other players, notably Jerome Richardson, also played the instrument and recorded on it at this time, it was Wess who was chiefly responsible for its enhanced popularity, partly because of the huge following that Basie's band attracted and partly because his swinging improvisations demonstrated that the flute could be effective outside the limited context of West Coast jazz; a good example of his playing may be heard on *The Midgets* on Basie's album *April in Paris* (1955–6, Verve 8012). On the West Coast Bud Shank played the instrument with Howard Rumsey, as did Buddy Collette (followed by Paul Horn and then Eric Dolphy) with Chico Hamilton. Besides his activities as a sideman, Shank made an interesting recording with Bob Cooper of duets for flute or alto flute and oboe or english horn accompanied by piano, double bass, and drums (Howard Rumsey's Lighthouse All Stars' LP *Sunday Jazz*, iv, 1954, Cont. 2510). Collette was the first to record on all the instruments of the orchestral flute family, playing piccolo, flute, alto flute, and bass flute on the album *Buddy Collette's Swinging Shepherds* (1958, EmA 36133). In Canada Moe Koffman made several successful recordings, among them *The Swinging Shepherd Blues* on his album *Cool and Hot Sax* (1957, Jub. 1037). All these examples demonstrate the potential of the flute as a solo instrument, but it also found a new role as a member of the ensemble: Gil Evans began in the 1950s to explore the use of flutes in his orchestra (as for example in the accompanimental riffs in his arrangement of *Summertime* on Miles Davis's *Porgy and Bess*, 1958, Col. CL1274) and continued to include them.

In 1956 *Down Beat* established an award for the best flutist of the year. Soon many saxophonists learned to play the instrument and the ability to double has become commonplace and is required in most big bands. Among the foremost flutists of the 1950s were the Belgian Bobby Jaspar and Herbie Mann, who was probably the first jazz musician to base a career on playing flute (though he also played saxophone professionally). Mann developed a popular style based on the blending of jazz with a variety of ethnic musics, mostly from Latin America (where there is a thriving flute tradition) but also including elements from Middle Eastern music, black American soul, and Japanese gagaku. A fine example of his playing may be heard on his album *Standing Ovation at Newport* (1965, Atl. 1445).

Sam Most and Sahib Shihab were among the first to sing or hum into the flute while playing. Players using this technique sing (usually in octaves) with the instrumental line, and the resulting combination of differing timbres and intonations creates a low-pitched buzzing quality. This very African-sounding effect, which lends the flute's tone greater intensity, has been much favored by jazz flutists such as Herbie Mann from the 1960s onwards. A similar practice was adopted by Yusef Lateef, who spoke syllables into the instrument to achieve unusual

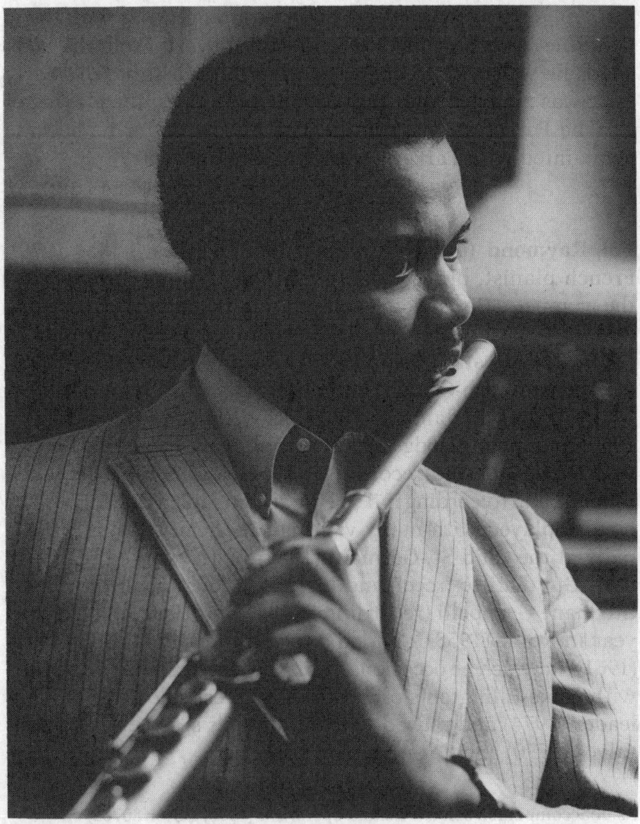

2. Hubert Laws

articulations; his work may be heard on *The Sounds of Yusef Lateef* (1957, Prst. 7122). Roland Kirk (who played a very wide range of reed and other woodwind instruments) took Lateef's idea further by speaking through the flute to create a rasping vocal timbre, as on *You did it, you did it* from the album *We Free Kings* (1961, Mer. 60679).

Many saxophonists have proved to be fine flutists, including James Moody, Charles Lloyd, and the brilliant and influential Eric Dolphy; even John Coltrane attempted the flute briefly. Paul Horn began by doubling on the two instruments but soon specialized on flute; he concentrated on the development of a beautiful sound, which he exploited in unusual acoustical settings, for example recording unaccompanied solos in the Taj Mahal and among the Egyptian pyramids. Jeremy Steig, by contrast, is an iconoclastic flutist, whose rough tone, incorporating many non-musical noises such as key clicking and air sounds, has enlivened jazz-rock, modal jazz, bop, and Latin jazz styles. Lew Tabackin, the principal soloist in Toshiko Akiyoshi's band, is also technically and expressively one of the finest jazz flutists.

Beginning in about 1966 Hubert Laws (see fig.2) demonstrated that an outstanding classical technique could be adapted to fine bop and modal-jazz playing. His background in classical music led him to record Chick Corea's Trio for flute, bassoon, and piano on his album *Laws' Cause* (1968, Atl. 1509), and to create jazz adaptations of works by Bach and Stravinsky, among others. He has also made recordings of jazz-rock and other fusion styles. Similarly, during the late 1970s the classically trained James Newton and Lloyd McNeil both became widely admired for their ability to develop a role in experimental improvisation; Newton's playing is well represented by his solo album *Axum* (1981, ECM 1214). Other fine flutists have included Ira Sullivan, Simeon Shterev, Bob Downes, and Chris Hinze.

3. The piccolo. The piccolo is comparatively rare in jazz, though it has found a place both as a solo and an ensemble instrument. The famous clarinet solo in *High Society*, regarded as a test-piece for New Orleans players, was adapted from a piccolo part. Many free-jazz wind players have used piccolo on occasion, notably those connected with the Association for the Advancement of Creative Musicians, including Joseph Jarman and Roscoe Mitchell (both of the Art Ensemble of Chicago), Anthony Braxton, and Douglas Ewart. Hubert Laws applied his fine technique to piccolo as well as flute, as on the album *The Laws of Jazz* (1964, Atl. 1432) recorded with his quartet. Marshall Allen plays piccolo with Sun Ra and has recorded notable solos, for example on *A House of Beauty* from *The Heliocentric Worlds of Sun Ra*, ii (1965, ESP 1017). Toshiko Akiyoshi often gives the instrument prominent written parts in her big band.

4. The alto flute. The haunting sound of the alto flute has been used in jazz from time to time since the 1950s. Herbie Mann and Bobby Jaspar both recorded on alto flute (a good example is Mann's *Tutti Fluttie* from the album *Flute Flight*, 1957, Prst. 7124) and Bud Shank plays an attractive solo on the instrument on *Lotus Bud* from his album *Shorty Rogers Compositions* (1954, Nocturne 2); Paul Horn continues to use it. As with the piccolo, the alto flute has been used by free-jazz instrumentalists such as Jarman, Mitchell, and Braxton in order to introduce another tone-color to their instrumental palette.

5. The bass flute. The bass flute requires a copious and powerfully directed supply of air and projects with difficulty, but

it has been used occasionally in jazz. Jimmy Giuffre, best known as a saxophonist and clarinetist, recorded beautiful solos on it in the 1970s (*Tibetan Sun* and *Om* on his album *River Chant*, 1975, Choice 1011) and Vinny Golia also plays the instrument. Like the other members of the family it is heard in free-jazz performances and recordings: Henry Threadgill plays it on the track *Air Song* from *X-75* (1979, AN 3013), the instrumentation of which also includes piccolo (Douglas Ewart), flute (Jarman), and alto flute (Wallace McMillan).

6. ETHNIC FLUTES. During the late 1950s jazz musicians, in search of new sonorities, began to adopt many hitherto unfamiliar instruments into jazz, including a great variety of non-Western and homemade flutes constructed of different materials (bamboo, wood, metal, ceramics, and plastics). Yusef Lateef recorded on various wood and bamboo instruments and Roland Kirk occasionally used a nose flute so that he could simultaneously play one or more saxophones. With the advent of influences from ethnic music and the folk aesthetic (fueled by Ornette Coleman), African, Asian, and ethnic European flutes were introduced into avant-garde groups as part of a new, broad approach to free improvisation. Don Cherry (better known as a trumpeter) plays several such flutes, as do Jarman, Mitchell, and Ewart. Cherry simultaneously plays a bamboo flute and a Bengali wooden flute in two-part harmony on *Baby's Breath*, the first part of his suite *Eternal Rhythm* (1968, Saba 15204). Ewart, a flute maker, plays his own bamboo flute as well as conventional bass flute and piccolo on Chico Freeman's album *Morning Prayer* (1976, Whynot 7155) on the title track and on *Pepe's Samba*.

BIBLIOGRAPHY

J.-E. Berendt: *Das Jazzbuch: Entwicklung und Bedeutung der Jazzmusik* (Frankfurt am Main, Germany, 1953, rev. 2/1959 as *Das neue Jazzbuch*, Eng. trans., New York, 1962; rev. and enlarged 5/1981 as *Das grosse Jazzbuch: von New Orleans bis Jazz Rock*, Eng. trans. as *The Jazz Book: from New Orleans to Fusion and Beyond*, Westport, CT, 1982), 261
P. Bate: *The Flute* (London, 1969, rev. 2/1979)
T. Howell: *The Avant-garde Flute: a Handbook for Composers and Flutists* (Berkeley, CA, Los Angeles, and London, 1974)
R. Dick: *The Other Flute: a Performance Manual of Contemporary Techniques* (London, 1975)
H. M. Brown: "Flute," *GroveI*

LEWIS PORTER

Flying Dutchman. Record label. It was established in New York by Bob Thiele in 1969. Its catalogue included recordings made between 1969 and 1975 by such diverse musicians as Gato Barbieri, Ornette Coleman, Bobby Hackett, Groove Holmes, Shelly Manne, Oliver Nelson, Lonnie Liston Smith, Horace Tapscott, Leone Thomas, the World's Greatest Jazz Band, and the duo of Bud Freeman and Bucky Pizzarelli. By 1971 Thiele's company, Flying Dutchman Productions, had been acquired by a division of Atlantic, Atco. Later (by 1976) manufacture and distribution was undertaken by RCA Victor, which continued to issue material from Flying Dutchman until 1984.

Flyright. Record label. It is owned by Interstate Music; although mainly devoted to blues, it has been used to issue jazz recorded by local English groups.

FMP [Free Music Production]. German promotional company, record company, and record label. The organization grew out of the New Artists Guild, a short-lived informal cooperative of the mid-1960s which involved such musicians as Manfred Schoof, Alex Schlippenbach, Peter Brötzmann, and Peter Kowald, all of whom later made recordings for FMP. In 1968 the New Artists Guild sponsored a jazz festival in Berlin which was intended to compete with the Berliner Jazztage and promoted a program of music stylistically different from that of the latter. The following year the organization took the name FMP, and began operating as a cooperative venture under the administrative guidance of a former double bass player, Jost Gebers. It made recordings solely of free jazz, particularly of the work of important German ensembles (including Schlippenbach's Globe Unity Orchestra), and has remained in operation into the late 1980s. The company's catalogue is divided into two series. One consists of recordings that are produced by the musicians themselves and remain their property. The other, in which issue numbers are preceded by the letters SAJ, includes items produced in collaboration with other labels, among them ICP (Instant Composers Pool), Bvhaast, and Claxon. For all sessions issued in this series the musicians are paid once only, as for a conventional session; the recording remains the property of the companies involved. FMP also sponsors concerts, workshops, and an art gallery and performance space, 360° Spielraum für Ideen.

See also FESTIVALS, §3.

BIBLIOGRAPHY

G. Rouy: "Berlin: Free Music Production," *Jm*, no.238 (1975), 12
J. Keefer and G. Rouy: "FMP Story," *Jm*, no.265 (1978), 22

Fol, Hubert (*b* Paris, 11 Nov 1925). French alto saxophonist and leader, brother of Raymond Fol. After learning to play piano from his mother he studied violin and, from 1942, clarinet. He played alto saxophone in the band of Claude Abadie (recording in 1945–7) and with his brother Raymond formed the Be Bop Minstrels (recording in 1947–8). He toured Europe with Coleman Hawkins (recording in 1949) and recorded as the leader of a quartet that included Kenny Clarke (*These Foolish Things*, 1950, Swing 339); he also toured Europe with Dizzy Gillespie (recording in 1952) and Rex Stewart. From the early 1960s he worked infrequently owing to ill health. Fol's early style was modeled after that of Johnny Hodges; the playing of Charlie Parker strongly influenced his own after he became acquainted with Parker's work in 1946. (*ReclamsJ*)

ANDRÉ CLERGEAT

Fol, Raymond (*b* Paris, 28 April 1928; *d* Paris, 1 May 1979). French pianist, brother of Hubert Fol. With his brother and the trumpeter Boris Vian he played traditional jazz with Claude Abadie (recording in 1945–7). He belonged with his brother to the Be Bop Minstrels (from 1946, recording in November 1948), worked with Jean-Claude Fohrenbach, Django Reinhardt (1949–51, recording in January 1952), Roy Eldridge (recording in 1950), and Johnny Hodges (recording in 1950), and toured Europe with Dizzy Gillespie (recording in 1952). As a member of Claude Luter's band (recording in 1952) he accompanied Sidney Bechet; he also played with many visiting American soloists, principally at the Club St.-Germain (1954–7). He worked regularly with Guy Lafitte (recording in 1954, 1960, and 1962–3) and Stephane Grappelli (recording in 1957 and 1969), played for a year in Rome (1958), and led a trio at the Mars Club in Paris (1961), in which he occasionally played celesta. Later he worked with Duke Ellington's orchestra as a guest soloist (1969) and leader (1974) and played with Ellington's sidemen Paul Gonsalves (1970) and Cat Anderson (1977).

SELECTED RECORDINGS

As unaccompanied soloist: *Echoes of Harlem* (1975, BStar 80702)
As leader: *Les quatre saisons "in jazz"* (1965, Phi. 70306); *The Sky was Blue* (1976, 1979, Chorus 33761)

BIBLIOGRAPHY

A. Rado: Liner notes, *Echoes of Harlem* (BStar 80702, 1975)
S. Simons: "Raymond Fol," *Swingtime*, no.40 (1979), 28 [discography]

ANDRÉ CLERGEAT

Fonsèque, Raymond (*b* Paris, 27 Nov 1930). French trombonist and tuba player. After studying piano and, at the Conservatoire in Bordeaux, cello he became a professional trombonist in 1950. He performed with Don Byas (1950, 1962–3), Peanuts Holland (1952, 1959–60), Nelson Williams (1952), Sidney Bechet (1953–4), Lil Armstrong (1953), and the blues singer and guitarist Big Bill Broonzy (1953), and led several groups, including Trombone Incorporated, the Pop Corn Brass Band, and from 1984 the Paris Big Band; he also performed with Bill Coleman (at intervals, 1967–76). In addition to his work as a performer in the New Orleans and swing styles he has taught jazz and harmony; he became the president of the Jazz club de France in 1966. Fonsèque's playing is well represented by his album *Fonsèque & Co Jazz Band* (1984, 1986, RFJB 86-1). (A. Clergeat: "Raymond Fonsèque," *Jh*, no.118 (1957), 28)

MICHEL LAPLACE

Fontana, Carl (Charles) (*b* Monroe, LA, 18 July 1928). Trombonist. He studied at an early age with his father, a saxophonist and bandleader, and played in his group from 1941 to 1945. He first distinguished himself as a soloist in Woody Herman's band, in which he played from 1952 to 1953; he then belonged to the big bands of Lionel Hampton (1954) and Hal McIntyre (1954–5). In 1955 he began to work with Stan Kenton, with whom he recorded such inspired solos as those on *Intermission Riff* and *Recuerdos*. During this period he also made two recordings in Paris with the Kentonians (a group drawn from Kenton's band), which demonstrate his style particularly well. After leaving Kenton in 1956, Fontana played and recorded in Kai Winding's group of four trombonists and rhythm section (1956–7). He then moved to Las Vegas, where he worked regularly in show bands, but he continued to play jazz occasionally: he joined Herman on a tour sponsored by the US State Department in 1966, led a group with Jake Hanna in 1975, and the same year toured and recorded with the World's Greatest Jazz Band. In the late 1970s he toured Japan with Georgie Auld. Fontana's solos quote with a wry humor from various sources and show an ability to develop themes inventively. He is highly respected and much liked by his fellow jazz musicians.

SELECTED RECORDINGS

As sideman: W. Herman: *The Third Herd* (1952, MGM 192); B. Perkins: *On Stage* (1956, PJ 1221); S. Kenton: *Stan Kenton in Hi Fi* (1956, Cap. W724), incl. Intermission Riff; M. Solal: *Martial Solal and the Kentonians* (1956, Swing LDM30044); Kentonians: *The Kentonians* (1956, Club des Amateurs de Disque 3003); S. Kenton: *Cuban Fire* (1956, Cap. T731), incl. Fuego cubana, Quien sabe, Recuerdos; K. Winding: *Trombone Panorama* (1957, Col. CL999); W. Herman: *Concerto for Herd* (1967, Verve V68764); Supersax: *Supersax Plays Bird*, ii: *Salt Peanuts* (c1973, Cap. ST11271), incl. Confirmation, Lover, Salt Peanuts, Yardbird Suite

BIBLIOGRAPHY

FeatherE; *Feather '60s*; *Feather–Gitler '70s*
J. Atkins: "Carl Fontana: Interview," *Cadence*, v/12 (1979), 7

LAWRENCE KOCH

Ford, Ricky [Richard Allen] (*b* Boston, 4 March 1954). Tenor saxophonist. He played drums before taking up the tenor saxophone at the age of 15, having been inspired by the example of Roland Kirk. With the encouragement of Ran Blake he enrolled when he was 17 at the New England Conservatory, where he studied saxophone with Bill Saxton; he left the conservatory in August 1974 to join the Duke Ellington Orchestra under the leadership of Mercer Ellington. In May 1976 he replaced George Adams in Charles Mingus's group and during the following years helped Mingus to transcribe music. At the same time he began working as a leader; his first album, *Loxodonta africana* (1977), consisted entirely of his own compositions. In 1979 he belonged to a group of Mingus's former sidemen led by Dannie Richmond and later played briefly with Mingus Dynasty. In the 1980s he continued to work as a leader and also worked with Lionel Hampton and Abdullah Ibrahim.

SELECTED RECORDINGS

As leader: *Loxodonta africana* (1977, New World 204); *Manhattan Plaza* (1978, Muse 5188); *Interpretations* (1982, Muse 5275)

As sideman: M. Ellington: *Continuum* (1974–5, Fan. 9481); C. Mingus: *Three or Four Shades of Blues* (1977, Atl. 1700); *Me, myself an Eye* (1978, Atl. 8803); D. Richmond: *Danny* [*sic*] *Richmond Plays Charles Mingus* (1980, Tim. 148); A. Ibrahim: *Ekaya* (1983, Ekapa 005)

BIBLIOGRAPHY

B. Primack: "Ricky Ford," *DB*, xlv/1 (1978), 40
L. Jeske: "Ricky Ford: Jazz Wolf," *DB*, xlix/3 (1982), 23 [incl. discography]
E. Davis: "Ricky Ford: a Natural," *JT* (1983), Feb, 10
C. Sheridan: "A Discography of Ricky Ford," *JJI*, xxxvi/6 (1983), 18
——: "Ricky Ford," *JJI*, xxxvi/5 (1983), 6
"Ricky Ford," *SJ*, xxxviii/2 (1984), 212 [discography]

DAVID WILD

Foreningen Norske Jazzmusikere [Association of Norwegian Jazz Musicians]. Association founded in 1979 to improve opportunities and working conditions for Norwegian jazz musicians. It works closely with the NORSK JAZZFORBUND in promoting concert tours throughout Norway.

Foresythe, Reginald (*b* London, 28 May 1907; *d* London, 23 Dec 1958). English pianist, composer, and bandleader. The son of a West African barrister and a German mother, he was educated in England. During the late 1920s he traveled to the USA, where he wrote arrangements for Earl Hines's orchestra and was commissioned by Paul Whiteman to compose new works. In 1933 he returned to Britain and formed a band made up of two clarinets, bassoon, three saxophones, piano, double bass and drums – an unconventional instrumentation for jazz and dance music at that time. For this and later ensembles he wrote many short pieces, including *Serenade for a Wealthy Widow/Angry Jungle* (1933, Col. CB675), *The Autocrat before Breakfast* (1934, Col. CB787), *Dodging a Divorcee* (1935, Col. 30120), and *Swing for Roundabout* (1936, Decca F6203). In 1934 Foresythe went again to the USA to perform with Whiteman, and the following year he recorded in New York with a band that included Benny Goodman, John Kirby, and Gene Krupa; apart from this occasion, however, he made little use of improvisation. After World War II he led another band, but his final years were spent in obscurity, playing piano in small drinking clubs in London around Soho and Kensington.

Foresythe's witty shorter compositions created a permanent impact on his prewar jazz contemporaries and anticipated by a couple of decades the use that American jazz arrangers were to make of woodwind and classical counterpoint; he also wrote longer works, such as *Southern Holiday: a Phantasy of Negro Moods* (1935, Col. DX638).

BIBLIOGRAPHY

FeatherE
A. McCarthy: "Reginald Foresythe Discography," *JM*, no.187 (1970), 26

CHARLES FOX/R

Forman, Bruce (*b* Springfield, MA, *c*1956). Guitarist and leader. He began as a pianist but, disliking classical studies, took up electric guitar. After moving to San Francisco in 1971 he played with local bands, and from 1978 to 1982 toured and recorded with Richie Cole. He left Cole to lead his own groups, and recorded albums in 1980, 1981 (including *20/20*, Muse 5273), and 1984. He also played with Bobby Hutcherson and George Cables, with whom he recorded an album of duos, *Dynamics* (1985, Conc. 279).

BIBLIOGRAPHY

J. Ferguson: "Bruce Forman: Rising Bebop Powerhouse," *GP*, xvii/2 (1983), 53 [incl. discography]

A. J. Liska: "Profile: Bruce Forman," *DB*, l/11 (1983), 53

Formanek, Michael (*b* San Francisco, 7 May 1958). Bass player. He studied double bass and later took up electric bass guitar, playing either instrument as occasion demanded. His first important engagements as a jazz musician were in the mid-1970s with Eddie Henderson, Joe Henderson, Tony Williams, and Dave Liebman, with whose quintet he recorded in 1976. After moving to New York in the late 1970s he performed with Chet Baker, Bill Connors, and Herbie Mann, among others. He then spent a period in Germany, playing and recording with the Media Band (1980–81). From 1982 he was a member of the group Gallery. His playing is well represented by the album *Memories of Pannonia* (1986, Enja 5027), which he recorded as a member of Attila Zoller's trio. (I. Carr: "Formanek, Michael," in I. Carr, D. Fairweather, and B. Priestley: *Jazz: the Essential Companion*, London, 1987)

Forms. Form is the constructive organizing element in music, governing the presentation, development, and interrelationship of ideas. The concept comprehends not only the basic structure of a work but also the techniques and procedures used to develop ideas within the structure. This article discusses the structures and procedures used in jazz and traces their application in different styles. For discussion of related aspects of jazz *see* ARRANGEMENT, HARMONY (i), and IMPROVISATION.

1. Structures, techniques, and procedures. 2. New Orleans jazz. 3. Swing. 4. Extended formal designs after the swing era. 5. Bop. 6. Free jazz. 7. Fusion forms.

1. STRUCTURES, TECHNIQUES, AND PROCEDURES. The principal forms in jazz are variation forms, in particular fixed-harmony variations. The commonest structure consists of a theme (that is, a harmonized melody, or in some cases (see §(i)(b) below) simply a series of harmonies, having its own internal formal design), followed without pause by a succession of improvised variations based on the harmonies of the theme, and then by a repetition of the theme itself. In many instances the chord progression is the single most significant formal element, and the one that defines and distinguishes the piece. Each statement of the theme and each variation on it is called a "chorus." The performance of a piece may begin with an introduction (or "intro") of a few bars, and end with a "tag" or "coda."

(i) Structural models. The themes used by jazz musicians as the basis for variations include popular songs, blues, religious songs, marches, rags, and ostinatos.

(a) Popular songs. Popular songs usually have two sections: a verse, which is often through-composed (i.e., having no repeated phrases) and ends on the dominant; and a refrain (also called a chorus). In jazz performances the verse is little used, if at all; in early jazz it was usually played only once, at the beginning of the piece, and after the 1920s it was generally discarded altogether and the refrain was taken as the sole material for the piece. Thus in jazz the term "song form" or "popular song form" refers to the structure of the refrain alone. The refrain is usually 16 or 32 bars long and made up of four- or eight-bar phrases grouped into designs such as *aaba* (or *aa'ba'*, or *aaa'a*), *abac* (or *abab'*), *aabc*, or *abcd*.

In *aaba* form the *b* section is called the "bridge," "channel," "release," "middle eight," or "inside"; the contrast it provides with the *a* section is not only melodic and harmonic but also tonal, for it often modulates to the subdominant, dominant, submediant, or mediant. Many themes used in jazz are in *aaba* form, including *Oh, Lady be good*, *I got rhythm* (34 bars, usually shortened to 32 by jazz musicians), and *The Man I Love*, all composed by George Gershwin, *Gee, Baby, ain't I good to you* by Don Redman (16 bars), *Blue Skies* by Irving Berlin, *Ain't Misbehavin'* and *Honeysuckle Rose* by Fats Waller, *Love for Sale* (64 bars) and *What is this thing called love?* by Cole Porter, *Cherokee* (64 bars) by Ray Noble, *Body and Soul* by Johnny Green, *Alone Together* (44 bars in phrases of 14, 14, 8, and 8 bars) by Arthur Schwartz, *Georgia on my mind* by Hoagy Carmichael, *Speak Low* (56 bars in phrases of 16, 16, 8, and 16 bars) by Kurt Weill, and *Mood Indigo* (16 bars), *Sophisticated Lady*, *Solitude*, and *In a Sentimental Mood* by Duke Ellington.

Of the remaining designs *abac* is the most common; examples include *Embraceable You* and *Summertime* by Gershwin, *Just Friends* by John Klenner, and *How High the Moon* by Morgan Lewis. Other designs are found in *What's New?* by Bob Haggart and *So What* by Miles Davis (*aaa'a*, where *a'* is a transposition of *a*), *Autumn Leaves* by Joseph Kosma (*aabc*), *Night and Day* by Porter (*ababcb*), and *Yesterdays* by Jerome Kern (*abcd*).

(b) The blues. The BLUES as a structure is a melody based on the 12-bar BLUES PROGRESSION or upon a compressed (eight-bar) or expanded (16- or 24-bar) version of it. The simplest form of jazz improvisation based on the blues consists of the repetition of the harmonic structure as the foundation for new melodies or variants of a single melody. In early jazz the choruses are sometimes paired: that is, each of a series of 12-bar melodies is repeated, with the same textures, arrangement, solos, passages of stop-time, breaks, and so on, over the unchanging chord sequence, giving rise to the form $A^1A^1\ A^2A^2\ A^3A^3\ A^4A^4$ . . . (superscript numerals indicate different melodies superimposed upon the fixed harmonic progression *A*). Other designs incorporate the blues progression: commonly found is a verse-and-refrain form in which the refrain, consisting of a 12-bar blues, is used as the basis for the improvisations, and the verse, having an independent harmonic structure, occurs only once, either at the beginning or after the first refrain.

(c) Religious songs. Religious songs, including hymns, gospel songs, and spirituals, account for a small percentage of jazz themes. Some consist of an eight- or 16-bar theme, divided into phrases of regular length (e.g., *Swing low, sweet chariot*). Others have the verse-and-refrain form of the popular song (*When the saints go marching in*).

(d) Marches and rags. Marches are multithematic pieces, each thematic unit of which is normally 16 bars long, except for modulating interludes and transitions, which, if they are present at all, are four or eight bars long. A typical example of a march might be represented diagrammatically as follows:

A	A	B	B	A	modulating interlude	C	transition (non-modulating)	C
16	16	16	16	16	4	16	4	16

Rags have a similar structure, but their melodies tend to be more syncopated than those of marches. The themes of a rag or a march may each be 16 bars long and in *abac* form, or there may be a mixture of themes in different forms ranging from eight to 40 bars in length.

(e) Ostinatos. Ostinatos are accompanimental patterns, usually of one, two, or four bars, repeated continuously beneath precomposed or improvised lines. The accompanimental pattern may be as simple as a pair of chords, such as Cmi–F or C–B♭, or it may be a distinctive bass melody, as in Herbie Hancock's *Chameleon* on *Headhunters* (1973, Col. KC32371). The structural boundaries in pieces based on ostinatos are less distinct than in pieces based on longer themes (see especially §7 below).

(ii) Other aspects of form. The structural divisions of variation form are typically reinforced in jazz by contrasts of timbre and texture; variation techniques common in classical music, such as contrasts of meter, tempo, and mode, are all but unknown in jazz. Timbral and textural contrasts are achieved by changes between ensemble and solo scoring, the juxtaposing of solos on different instruments or of ensemble passages played by different sections, the presence or absence of "riffs" (simple repeated background patterns) in big-band scoring, the shifting of accompanimental rhythms from one cymbal to another, the temporary silence of one or more members of the rhythm section, and so on.

In much small-group jazz (and occasionally in big-band jazz) musicians may take turns at playing four-bar solo phrases (less often eight-, two-, or one-bar phrases), a technique known as "trading fours (eights, twos, or ones)." This procedure usually occurs after the longer solos and before the return of the theme. The number of phrases is flexible but the end of the sequence of trades normally coincides with the end of a chorus. The procedure can involve as few as two or as many as all members of the group, who trade a series of solos of the same length; in a 12-bar blues, for example, the pattern might be as follows:

4 + 4 + 4	4 + 4 + 4
sax tpt sax	tpt sax tpt

Less common is a climactic shortening of the phrases traded from eights to fours to twos and so on, as in *The Blues Walk* (1955), recorded by the quintet led by Clifford Brown and Max Roach (on the album *Clifford Brown and Max Roach*, 1954–5, EmA 36036):

4 + 4 + 4	4 + 4 + 4	2 + 2 + 2 + 2 + 2 + 2
tpt sax tpt	sax tpt sax …	

1 + 1 + 1 + 1 + 1 + 1 + 1 + 1 + 1 + 1 + 1 + 1	$\frac{1}{2} + \frac{1}{2} + \frac{1}{2} + \frac{1}{2} + \frac{1}{2}$ …

All these techniques and procedures for creating contrast are used to articulate phrases, longer periods, and choruses. For example, the bridge of a 32-bar theme in *aaba* form might be marked out by a change in accompanimental style or figuration by members of the rhythm section, or by a change from ensemble to solo scoring. The beginning of a new chorus is usually the occasion for a change of scoring, or, for example, a move from collective improvisation to solo improvisation, a change from two-beat (2/2) to four-beat (4/4) rhythmic patterning, or a change from duple Latin rhythms to triplet (i.e., swing) eighth-note rhythms.

2. New orleans jazz. Most of the structures discussed above are found in the earliest recorded jazz. Blues, for example, are numerous. The 12-bar blues progression used as the foundation for paired choruses occurs in the Original Dixieland Jazz Band's *Livery Stable Blues* (1917, Vic. 18255) and King Oliver's *Chimes Blues* (1923, Gen. 5135). Some monothematic pieces named "blues" are based on chord sequences that bear no resemblance to the 12-bar blues progression: for example, Jelly Roll Morton's *Smoke-house Blues* (1926, Vic. 20296), which has a 16-bar theme in *abac* form, and Red Nichols's *Limehouse Blues* (1928, Bruns. 5081), on a 32-bar theme also in *abac* form. Other so-called blues have a verse-and-refrain design in which neither section follows the blues progression (King Oliver's *Krooked Blues*, 1923, Gen. 5274); still others have two or three main themes, only one of which is a 12-bar blues (the Original Dixieland Jazz Band's *Home Again Blues*, 1921, Vic. 18729).

Verse-and-refrain forms are common, the refrain usually consisting of the blues progression, or a 16- or 32-bar theme in *aaba* or *abac* form. Ordinarily the verse appears only once, before or after the first statement of the refrain, as in Louis Armstrong's *Heebie Jeebies* (1926, OK 8300). In other pieces two independent themes are used; commonly one or both of the themes is 16 bars long and in *abac* form, but themes of eight, ten, 12, 20, and 32 bars also occur. Variations on both themes result in formal designs such as $ABA^1B^1B^2$ (Oliver's *The Southern Stomps*, 1923, Para. 12088) and $ABB^1B^2B^3A^1A^2$ (Armstrong's *Muskrat Ramble*, 1926, OK 8300). Morton's *Sidewalk Blues* (1926, Vic. 20252) uses the 12-bar blues progression as its first theme and an independent 32-bar theme for the other, producing the following form:

intro	A^1	A^2	A^3	modulating interlude	B	B^1	tag
10	12	12	12	4	32	32	6

Pieces having three different themes, following the typical plan for a march or rag, also occur. All these themes may be 16-bar melodies in *abac* form, or there may be a mixture of melodies in *abac* (occasionally *aaba*) form, ranging in length from eight to 40 bars. Morton's *The Chant* (1926, Vic. 20221), for example, has themes of 40, 12, and 16 bars, the second of which is founded on the blues progression. In many works of this type collective improvisation is used throughout the performance, but in others collective improvisation gives way to solo improvisation, and here the final theme may be repeated several times to allow a number of players to take solos. The final chorus of a rag, march, or other lively piece, when played in a loud, spirited manner, is called a stomp chorus (*see* Stomp); an "all-in," Out chorus, "ride-out," or "sock chorus" is a collectively improvised final statement of the theme in a lively style. Morton's *Black Bottom Stomp* (1926, Vic. 20221) includes seven choruses on the final theme, with solos by the clarinetist, pianist, trumpeter, and banjoist, and ends with a rousing stomp chorus by the ensemble.

3. Swing. The great variety of formal schemes used in early jazz diminished sharply in the swing era. Few pieces with multiple themes appear in the books of swing bands; one of the most popular, Morton's *King Porter Stomp* (1923), is reduced from three themes to two in recordings by Fletcher Henderson, (1932, OK 41565), Benny Goodman (1935, Vic. 25090), and others. The differences in formal design between Morton's composition and Henderson's reworking of it are striking:

Morton (1923, Gen. 5289):

intro	A	A	B	B	modulating interlude	C	C	C	tag
4	16	16	16	16	4	16	16	16	2

Henderson (Goodman's recording, 1935, Vic. 25090):

intro	A	modulating interlude	C	C	C	C	C	C	C	tag
8	16	4	16	16	16	16	16	16	16	2
ens	tpt, ens	ens	ens	cl	cl	tpt	trbn	ens riffs	ens riffs	ens

Most performances by swing ensembles are variations on 12-bar blues, or 32-bar songs in *aaba* or *abac* form. If a song originally had a verse it seldom appears. Many of the themes, both borrowed and newly composed, have uncomplicated melodies: the popular song *I got rhythm* was a frequent choice for swing musicians and the main theme of Duke Ellington's *"C" Jam Blues* (1942, Vic. 27856) is a simple two-pitch riff repeated three times. Count Basie's *Lester Leaps in* (1939, Voc. 5118), in *aaba* form, has *a* sections made up of riffs and a *b* section based on a chord sequence with no precomposed melody.

But if themes and forms are simple in much swing, musical interest remains high, largely thanks to the improvisational talents of many gifted soloists and to ingenious arrangements that exploit the timbral and textural variety possible in the big band. Portions of a theme are often passed from one section of the band to another, and texture frequently changes dramatically between the *a* and *b* sections of themes in *aaba* form. Trading fours, either between a soloist and the ensemble or between soloists, occurs occasionally. Further, the interpolation of transitional passages and modulations (especially when a singer is involved in a performance) and the cutting of the final chorus to eight or 16 bars add variety to the standard forms.

The greatest structural variety in music of the swing era is found in the compositions of Duke Ellington; several of his works are extended explorations of the variation principle. In 1931 he recorded two versions of his *Creole Rhapsody* (Bruns. 6093 and Vic. 36049), both of which fill two sides of a 78 r.p.m. disc; the work includes changes of tempo, passages in free tempo, and a blues chorus of irregular length:

Part 1 (quarter-note = *c*114):

A				B		A			
E♭ minor				B♭ major	E♭ major	E♭ minor			
a	a	b	a′	blues	blues	a	a	b	a
8 +	8 +	8	+ 8	12	10 + 2	8 +	8 +	8	+ 8
brass with cl obbligato		unacc. pf solo		cl solo	tpt solo, saxs break	brass with sax obbligato		saxs, brass, solo tpt	brass with sax obbligato

Part 2 (quarter-note = *c*137):

interlude	B′			
G major	E♭ major		E♭ major	A♭ major
at first based on b	blues	tag (last part of blues)	irregular blues	blues
6	12	+ 4	5 + 5 + 6	12
unacc pf solo in free tempo	unacc. pf solo	sax, full band	trbns	muted tpts

A						tag
E♭ minor						
a	a	b			a	
8	+ 8 +	4	+ 3	+ 1	7	6
full band with sax obbligato	bar	tpt solo	cl solo	pf	full band	brushes on snare drum

Longer still was *Reminiscing in Tempo* (1935, Bruns. 7546–7). Extended single pieces gave way to works in several movements in the last 30 years of Ellington's career, beginning with *Black, Brown and Beige* (1943, first issued on *The Duke Ellington Carnegie Hall Concert, January 1943*, Prst. 34004). While most of Ellington's larger works are suites of variations on themes of straightforward design, *Black, Brown and Beige* is an extended tone-poem, in which the usual variation procedures found in jazz play only a part.

4. Extended formal designs after the swing era. These pieces by Ellington heralded a number of extended works in which elements of 20th-century classical music were combined with jazz. Ambitious pieces were written for Stan Kenton's bands (*see* Progressive jazz) and by composers whose prime purpose was to synthesize aspects of different styles of music (*see* Third stream). Many of these works employ variation form with changes of meter and tempo, while exploring the harmonic and melodic vocabularies of recent styles of Western composition. In others the standard use of variation form is avoided and structural patterns from much earlier styles of music are adapted to jazz. For example, Jimmy Giuffre's album *Tangents in Jazz* (1955, Cap. T634) is a jazz suite held together by four thematically connected pieces (*Scintilla One, Two, Three,* and *Four*); another of the movements, *Rhetoric*, is a well-crafted invention on a neo-Baroque theme, which undergoes various transformations. The compact forms and polyphonic interplay of Baroque music have also been exploited by other jazz composers. A few of John Lewis's works for the Modern Jazz Quartet (e.g., *Versailles* on the album *Fontessa*, 1956, Atl. 1231) utilize varied mixtures of fugal expositions and episodes.

Giuffre's works provide further examples of structural devices that are novel in jazz. His Piece for Clarinet and String Orchestra (on the album of the same name, 1960, Verve 68395) is a five-movement work in which most of the movements have an *ABA* form and one is based on a 15-note tone row. *Mobiles* (also on Verve 68395) is a series of 16 short, rhapsodic pieces; in three of them Giuffre improvises over a single chord repeated in various rhythms dictated spontaneously by the conductor, in another he improvises over a two-note motif played by the strings in various keys.

5. Bop. In the mid-1940s, during the early days of bop, players were preoccupied with the rhythmic, harmonic, and melodic complexities of the new idiom, and formal intricacies were a secondary concern. By far the commonest formal scheme in early bop consists of an introduction, the theme played in unison, a series of solo choruses improvised on the theme, a return to the theme played in unison, and a coda; the preferred themes are 12-bar blues and 32-bar themes in *aaba* or *abac* form (*I got rhythm* is again particularly favored). Even the textural variety found in much swing is largely missing from bop, since most bop groups were small combos, not big bands. But changes of timbre enliven bop recordings, especially the final improvised chorus or choruses, where players trade twos, fours, and eights: bop musicians often use this procedure, which typically involves exchanges between the drummer and other soloists (saxophone, drums, trumpet, drums, piano, drums, etc.). Sometimes bop players superimpose improvised phrases of irregular lengths on the four- or eight-bar phrases of symmetrical themes; Wynton and Branford Marsalis adopt this technique in *Hesitation* on *Wynton Marsalis* (1981, Col. FC37574).

Some bop pieces, which follow the standard format of two statements of the theme flanking a sequence of solo choruses improvised on it, have themes of unusual length. On Horace

Silver's album *Further Explorations* (1958, BN 1589) *The Outlaw* has a theme of 54 bars (13 + 13 + 10 + 18) and *Melancholy Mood* has one of 28 bars (7 + 7 + 7 + 7); the theme of *Nineteen Bars* on *Silver's Serenade* (1963, BN 84131) is divided into phrases of 7 + 8 + 4 bars; and *Helping Others* on *Guides to Growing Up* (1981, Silveto 101) has a 74-bar theme divided 16 + 16 + 16 + 16 + 10 in the form *aa'ba'b'*. Charles Mingus's *Fables of Faubus* on the album *Mingus Ah Um* (1959, Col. CL1370) has a complex 71-bar theme:

intro	theme			
	A	A'	B	A'
	19	18	16	18
a a	a a b c	a a b c'	d d e f	a a b c'
4 + 4	4 + 4 + 4 + 7	4 + 4 + 4 + 6	4 + 4 + 4 + 4	4 + 4 + 4 + 6

The announcement of the theme is followed by two choruses of improvisation, then a return to the second half of the theme (*BA'*).

Miles Davis's work in the bop style offers several examples of interesting formal procedures. On *Blue in Green* on *Kind of Blue* (1959, Col. CL1355), successive choruses shrink from ten bars to five bars and then to two and a half bars before the ten-bar structure is restored. *Flamenco Sketches*, from the same album, contains choruses of variable length in the form *abcde*; each section is identified by a different scale and tonality in which the soloist improvises for four or eight bars, at his own discretion. Because the improvisations are based loosely on a succession of modes (including the dorian and mixolydian) rather than on chord progressions, this piece and others following a similar pattern are examples of what is termed MODAL JAZZ. (*See also* DAVIS, MILES, §2.)

John Coltrane, inspired by the structure and improvising procedures in *Flamenco Sketches*, extended these concepts dramatically in his recordings of Richard Rodgers's song *My Favorite Things*. In the versions on the albums *My Favorite Things* (1960, Atl. 1361) and *Afro Blue Impressions* (1963, Pablo Live 2620101) 16-bar portions of the theme are separated by lengthy improvisations loosely based on the scales of E dorian and E major. The flexibility of the form Coltrane designed, which extends a piece of three choruses into a rondo that lasts 14 (1960) or 22 (1963) minutes, is clearly apparent from a comparison of the two performances:

	intro
1960	16
1963	44

Coltrane: solo chorus 1

	segment of theme	E dorian improvisation	segment of theme	E major improvisation	segment of theme
1960	16	8	16	24	16
1963	16	64	16	136	16

	segment of theme	E dorian improvisation
1960	16	16
1963	16	16

McCoy Tyner: solo chorus 2

	segment of theme	E dorian improvisation	segment of theme	E major improvisation	segment of theme
1960	16	32	16	148	16
1963	16	184	16	128	16

	E dorian improvisation	segment of theme
1960	32	16
1963	104	16

Coltrane: solo chorus 3

	E dorian improvisation	segment of theme	E dorian improvisation	segment of theme	E major improvisation
1960	8	16	136	16	136
1963	16	16	192	16	240

	segment of theme	segment of theme
1960	16	16
1963	16	16

	coda
1960	33
1963	33

6. FREE JAZZ. Although many of the works in free-jazz style begin and end with a theme played in unison, the improvisations are seldom obviously connected with either the harmonic structure or the length of the theme. Thus the form in these works is: the theme played in unison, improvisations, and a restatement of the theme played in unison. The middle section in this scheme can be quite lengthy; it is more than 30 minutes long in Archie Shepp's *Three for a Quarter, One for a Dime* on the album of the same name (1966, Imp. 9162). The subdivisions of the improvisation depend on the inspiration of the moment and are defined by such factors as texture (collective, solo, or unaccompanied improvisation), rhythmic activity, motivic development, and dynamics rather than by fixed variation form or techniques.

Other plans occur at times. In rondo form (e.g., Albert Ayler's *Prophet* on *Spirits Rejoice*, 1965, ESP 1020; and Anthony Braxton's *Z-42 0-500 NWK* on *Creative Orchestra Music, 1976*, 1976, Ari. 4080) a predetermined section recurs periodically between improvised sections. Cecil Taylor's *Enter Evening* (on *Unit Structures*, 1966, BN 84237) is in a compound three-section form, and his *Tales* (on the same album) is through-composed.

7. FUSION FORMS. Although fixed-harmony variations occur in jazz-rock and other contemporary fusion styles, more typical are improvisations over an ostinato bass pattern, a structural device borrowed from rock music. The accompanying ostinatos are normally one bar (as in Herbie Mann's *Memphis Underground* on the album of the same name, 1968, Atl. 1522), two bars (Miles Davis's *Bitches Brew* on the album of the same name, 1969, Col. GP26), or four bars long (Herbie Hancock's *Chameleon* on *Headhunters*, 1973, Col. KC32371; and Return to Forever's *The Romantic Warrior* on the album of the same

name, 1976, Col. PC34076). The concept of improvised choruses of fixed length is as inappropriate to jazz-rock as it is to free jazz: the middle section of a piece is built up from a succession of improvisations, but these have no predetermined length – one soloist simply plays until he or she feels it is time to end, and the next soloist may let two or three cycles of the ostinato go by before beginning to play.

In these pieces the theme, which serves as a beginning and ending, and sometimes as an interlude, usually falls into one of two main categories. In some pieces simple, repetitive melodies are superimposed on several statements of the ostinato; for example, a 16-bar theme in *aaaa* form frames the solos in *Memphis Underground*, while the one-bar ostinato drones on. In others the melodic material has a harmonic structure that differs markedly from and is far more inventive than that of the ostinato over which the improvisations are built (e.g., Grover Washington Jr.'s fusion of jazz and soul music, *Mr. Magic*, on the album of the same name, 1974, Kudu 20).

More elaborate forms than the standard theme–improvisations–theme also occur (though sometimes they may result from decisions made in editing rather than making recordings). Davis's *Bitches Brew* consists of two contrasting blocks of music which alternate: the first (making up sections 1, 3, and 5 of the work) is free-metered and rhapsodic, the second (making up sections 2 and 4) is based on an ostinato. Return to Forever's *Duel of the Jester and the Tyrant* (on *Romantic Warrior*, 1976, Col. PC34076) has several distinctively different sections, including two based on a five-bar ostinato, framed by thematically related introduction and coda. A complex example is offered by Chick Corea's *Spain* (on *Light as a Feather*, 1973, Pol. 5525), which incorporates elements of bop, rock, and Latin music; it consists of four distinct ideas that are ingeniously combined and recombined; the piece begins with unrelated material, a paraphrase of a fragment of Joachín Rodrigo's *Concierto de Aranjuez*.

intro:

*c*20 bars

theme:

group

a	b	b′	c	a	b	b′	c	d	b′	c
6	4	8	11 + 2	6	4	8	11	24	8	11

improvisations (several sections, each in the form):

soloist			group		
d	d	repeated . . . ad lib	d	b′	c
24	24		24	8	11

theme (replacing the group section at the end of the last improvisation):

group

d	b′	a	b	b′	c
24	8	6	4	8	10 + 1 + 1 + 1

BIBLIOGRAPHY

R. U. Nelson: *The Technique of Variation* (Berkeley, CA, 1948)
G. Schuller: "The Future of Form in Jazz," *Saturday Review*, xl (12 Jan 1957), 62; repr. in *The American Composer Speaks*, ed. G. Chase (n.p. [Baton Rouge, LA], 1966), 217
M. Kingston: "Form in Jazz, if Any," *JJ*, xx (1967), no.3, p.6; no.4, p.10
W. Russo: *Jazz Composition and Orchestration* (Chicago, 1968), 752
G. Schuller: *Early Jazz: its Roots and Musical Development* (New York, 1968), 26
G. Crane: *Jazz Elements and Formal Compositional Techniques in "Third Stream" Music* (diss., Indiana U., 1970)
L. O. Koch: "Structural Aspects of King Oliver's 1923 Okeh Recordings," *JJS*, iii/2 (1976), 36
T. Owens: "The Fugal Pieces of the Modern Jazz Quartet," *JJS*, iv/1 (1976), 25
M. C. Gridley: *Jazz Styles* (Englewood Cliffs, NJ, 1978, rev. 2/1985 as *Jazz Styles: History and Analysis*, with suppl. *Instructor's Manual and Discography*), 377
L. O. Koch: "The Jazz Composition/Arrangement," *ARJS*, iii (1985), 181

THOMAS OWENS

Forrest, Jimmy [James Robert, Jr.] (*b* St. Louis, 24 Jan 1920; *d* Grand Rapids, MI, 26 Aug 1980). Tenor saxophonist. As a child he played in the orchestra led by his mother, Eva Dowd, a noted bandleader in St. Louis, and while still in high school he worked with the pianist Eddie Johnson, Fate Marable, and the Jeter–Pillars Orchestra. He left home in 1938 with Don Albert's touring band, then joined Jay McShann's big band at the height of its fame, where he played alongside Charlie Parker (1940–42). In New York he commenced a fruitful association with Andy Kirk, remaining with his group for six years (1942–8). He performed briefly with Duke Ellington before returning to St. Louis in 1950. The following year he achieved great success with his recording of *Night Train* (based on Ellington's *Happy go Lucky Local*), with which he remained linked for the rest of his career. Forrest later returned to New York and from 1958 to 1963 was a member of Harry Edison's group. He recorded as a leader for Prestige (1960–62) and enjoyed a period of comparative prominence before touring with Count Basie (1972–7). He left Basie to form a partnership with Al Grey, with whom he worked until his death. Forrest had a big sound and an extrovert, hard-driving style influenced by Gene Ammons and Wardell Gray, although at times his playing was tinged with the mannerisms of rhythm-and-blues.

SELECTED RECORDINGS

As leader: Bolo Blues/Night Train (1951, United 110); *All the Gin is Gone* (1959, Del. 404); with A. Grey: *Out 'Dere* (1980, Greyforrest GF1001)
As sideman: Prestige Blues Swingers: *Outskirts of Town* (1958, Prst. 7145); H. Edison: *The Swinger* (1958, Verve 8295); S. Baker and A. Gibson: *Mainstream Jazz* (1959, Camden 554); C. Basie: *I Told you so* (1976, Pablo 2310767), incl. Plain Brown Wrapper; W. Reed: *46th and 8th* (1977, AH 410), incl. Blue Monk

BIBLIOGRAPHY

R. G. Reisner: *Bird: the Legend of Charlie Parker* (New York, 1962/*R*1975), 92
B. Porter: "Jimmy Forrest on Record," *JJ*, xxii/9 (1969), 18
S. Nepus: "Jimmy Forrest," *BHcF*, no.217 (1972), 3
B. Rusch: "Jimmy Forrest: Interview," *Cadence*, ii/8 (1977), 3
D. Tarrant: "Jimmy Forrest Discography," *Journal of Jazz Discography*, no.3 (1978), 8; no.4 (1979), 2
Obituary, *BHcF*, no.283 (1980), 31
P. Vacher: "The Last Night Train," *MM*, lv (13 Sept 1980), 30
——: "Jimmy Forrest," *JJI*, xxxiii/12 (1980), 13

PETER VACHER

Fortune, Sonny [Cornelius] (*b* Philadelphia, 19 May 1939). Alto saxophonist. He studied music from the age of 18 and worked with rhythm-and-blues groups in Philadelphia. He played jazz with the singer Carolyn Harris to 1967, then moved to New York, where he worked with Elvin Jones as Frank Foster's temporary replacement; he also played with Mongo Santamaria (1967–70) and McCoy Tyner (from 1971), worked as a leader for a brief period in 1973, and belonged to groups led by Buddy Rich and Miles Davis (August 1974 to May 1975). Later he worked again as a leader, favoring a more commercially oriented style in his recordings than in his performances. Although his albums have included his own compositions, Fortune is principally an instrumentalist; in addition to the alto saxophone he plays soprano saxophone and flute.

SELECTED RECORDINGS

As leader: *Long Before our Mothers Cried* (1974, SE 7423); *Awakening* (1975, A&M Hor. 704); *Serengeti Minstrel* (1977, Atl. 18225)

As sideman: M. Santamaria: *Stoned Soul* (1968, Col. CS9780); M. Tyner: *Sahara* (1973, Mlst. 9049); M. Davis: *Get up with it* (1974, Col. PG33236), *Agharta* (1975, Col. PG33967)

BIBLIOGRAPHY

A. J. Smith: "Sonny Fortune: Windfall on the Wind," *DB*, xliii/3 (1976), 16 [incl. discography]

W. A. Brower: "Sonny Fortune Splits the Difference," *DB*, xlvi/3 (1979), 20

DAVID WILD

45 (r.p.m. disc). A vinyl microgroove disc, recorded and played back at 45 r.p.m. *See* Recording, §I, 3(ii); *see also* Single (ii).

Foss, Niels (Hartvig) (*b* Copenhagen, 28 Jan 1916). Danish double bass player and bandleader. He began his career as a guitarist in Svend Asmussen's group (1933–4), then played double bass with Asmussen (1935–7) and others. From 1940 to 1948 he led and played trombone in his own bands, for which he composed much of the repertory; they made several recordings, including *Rain* (1942, Odeon D814). He also recorded a duo with Børge Roger Henrichsen in 1942 (*Prelude in C*, HMV DX6877). He played with Peter Rasmussen in 1949–51 and in 1957 moved to Switzerland, where he continued to play part-time.

ERIK WIEDEMANN

Foster, Al (*b* Richmond, VA, 18 Jan 1944). Drummer. He grew up in New York, was given a drum set when he was ten, and with the encouragement of his father, a double bass player, learned to play jazz by listening to recordings by Max Roach: while still in his teens he met Sonny Rollins, who exerted a strong influence. He worked with Hugh Masekela (1960), Ted Curson, Illinois Jacquet (1962–*c*1964), Blue Mitchell (with whom he made his first recording in 1964), Lou Donaldson (1966), and Kai Winding, played jazz-rock for three years as a member of Miles Davis's ensemble (from 1972), with which he toured widely, and toured the USA and recorded with the Milestone Jazzstars in the autumn of 1978. Later he resumed his association with Davis, recording from 1980 and touring from the following year. He has also performed and recorded as a leader, played bop and modal jazz with Steve Kuhn, Joe Henderson, and others in New York, and worked as a sideman in the group Quest, led by Dave Liebman and Richard Beirach. He is highly regarded for his ability to play in diverse styles.

SELECTED RECORDINGS

As sideman: B. Mitchell: *The Thing to Do* (1964, BN 84178); D. Jordan: *Duke's Delight* (1975, Ste. 1046); D. Gordon: *Biting the Apple* (1976, Ste. 1080); H. Silver: *Silver 'n' Percussion* (1978, BN LA853); M. Tyner: *Horizon* (1979, Mlst. 9094); S. Rollins: *Don't Ask* (1979, Mlst. 9090); F. Hubbard: *Outpost* (1981, Enja 3095); D. Liebman and R. Beirach: *Quest* (1981, PAlt 8061), incl. Dr. Jekyll; M. Davis: *Star People* (1982–3, Col. FG38657); J. Brackeen: *Havin' Fun* (1985, Conc. 280)

BIBLIOGRAPHY

E. Meadow: "Al Foster: a Journeyman Marks Time with Miles Davis," *DB*, xlii/13 (1975), 12

D. Clark: "Milestone Jazzstars on Tour," *DB*, xlv/19 (1978), 16

J. KENT WILLIAMS

Foster, Frank (Benjamin, III) (*b* Cincinnati, 23 Sept 1928). Tenor saxophonist, arranger, and composer. He played clarinet and alto saxophone as a youth, but changed to the tenor instrument in 1947, partly, he has said, because he needed to develop a musical personality independent of Charlie Parker's influence. From 1949 until he was drafted in 1951 he played in Detroit with Snooky Young, among others. After being discharged two years later he joined Count Basie's band and became one of its principal soloists. His fiery, bop-oriented improvisations and inventive arrangements (including *Down for the Count*, *Blues Backstage*, and his most famous composition, *Shiny Stockings*) were important factors in Basie's success during this period. Foster left Basie in summer 1964 and worked as a freelance in New York before joining Elvin Jones in the late 1960s. He also formed a large ensemble in 1964 (called from the early 1970s the Loud Minority), which he continues to lead occasionally. The band often consists of as many as 25 musicians and plays frequently on an informal basis, and with it Foster has experimented with combinations of spoken drama and jazz. In 1986 he assumed leadership of Basie's band (for illustration *see* Recording, fig.6). He has also continued to perform and record as the leader of small groups, and remains active as a composer. Among his works is *Lake Placid Suite*, a piece in several movements for jazz orchestra, which was commissioned for the Winter Olympics of 1980.

SELECTED RECORDINGS

As leader: *Basie is our Boss* (1963, Argo 717); *Fearless Frank Foster* (1965, Prst. 7461); *The Loud Minority* (1974, Mstr. 349); *Shiny Stockings* (1978, Denon 7545); with F. Wess: *Frankly Speaking* (1984, Conc. 276)

As sideman: C. Basie: *Blues Backstage* (1954, Clef MGC666), incl. Blues Backstage, Down for the Count, Two Franks; *Count Basie Swings, Joe Williams Sings* (1955, Clef 678), incl. The Comeback; *April in Paris* (1955–6, Verve 8012), incl. Shiny Stockings (1956); *Chairman of the Board* (1959, Roul. 52032); E. Jones: *Coalition* (1970, BN 84361)

BIBLIOGRAPHY

R. Horricks: *Count Basie and his Orchestra: its Music and its Musicians* (London and New York, 1957), 232

D. Morgenstern: "Fearless Frank Foster," *DB*, xxxii/24 (1965), 18

A. J. Smith: "Frank Foster: Seeking the Selective Minority," *DB*, xliv/17 (1977), 16

S. Dance: *The World of Count Basie* (New York and London, 1980) [colln of previously pubd interviews], 190

F. Foster: "I'll Never Make it Big in Music 'cause my Stuff is Just too Old Fashioned," *JSN*, i/5 (1980), 8

C. Kuhl: "Frank Foster: Interview," *Cadence*, viii/11 (1982), 5

S. Voce: "Frank Foster," *JJI*, xxxvi/2 (1983), 15

SCOTT DeVEAUX

Foster, (N.) Gary (*b* Leavenworth, KS, 25 May 1936). Alto, tenor and soprano saxophonist. After two years at Central College in Fayette, Missouri, he transferred to the University of Kansas, where his principal studies were clarinet and music education. He was active as a teacher while studying clarinet, saxophone, and music history for a year and after moving to Los Angeles (1961). In 1962 he began an association with the pianist and composer Clare Fischer, with whom he continued to work intermittently. Besides playing in the major film studios in Los Angeles, Foster belonged to the big bands of Fischer (1969–75), Louie Bellson (1968–9), Mike Barone (1969–70), Toshiko Akiyoshi and Lew Tabackin (1973–82), and Ed Shaughnessy (1974–6). In small groups he worked with Dennis Budimir (1963–4), Fischer (from 1965), Jimmie Rowles (1968), Warne Marsh (1968–73), and Laurindo Almeida (1974–7). Strongly influenced by Marsh and Lee Konitz, Foster is an assured improviser on both alto and tenor saxophones and a devoted adherent of Lennie Tristano's principle of pure improvisation; he has also been heard to good effect on the soprano saxophone. His ability as a flutist and clarinetist explains his presence on many studio sessions.

SELECTED RECORDINGS

Duos with D. Budimir: *Alone Together* (1964, Rev. 1), incl. No Cover, no Minimum, All the things you are

As leader: *Subconsciously* (1968, Rev. 5); *Grand cru classé* (1969, Rev. 19); with W. Marsh: *Report of the 1st Annual Symposium on Relaxed Improvisation* (1972, Rev. 17)

As sideman: C. Fischer: *One to Get Ready, Four to Go!* (1963–4, Rev. 6), incl. Lover Man, Freeways; D. Budimir: *The Session with Albert* (1964, Rev. 14); C. Fischer: *Thesaurus* (1968, Atl. 1520); W. Marsh: *Ne plus ultra* (1969, Rev. 12); C. Fischer: *T'da-a-a-a-a!* (1975, Rev. 23)

BIBLIOGRAPHY

Feather–Gitler '70s

J. W. Hardy: Liner notes, *Subconsciously* (Rev. 5, 1968)

G. Foster: Liner notes, *One to Get ready, Four to Go!* (Rev. 6, 1969)

C. Berg: "Gary Foster: a Kaleidoscope Kansan Thrives in L.A.," *DB*, xliii/19 (1976), 15 [incl. discography]

M. James: Liner notes, *Grand cru classé* (Rev. 19, 1976)

MARK GARDNER

Foster, Herman (*b* Philadelphia, 26 April 1928). Pianist. His principal association from 1953 to 1966 was with Lou Donaldson. He also played with Eric Dixon (1953) and Bill English and Seldon Powell (both 1956–7), and made recordings with King Curtis (1958–61), Al Casey (1960), and his own trio (1960–63, including *The Explosive Piano of Herman Foster*, 1961, Epic 17016). He recorded with Donaldson again in 1981, and continued to work with the latter's quartet in the early 1980s. Foster plays in a bop style characterized by a formidable attack and fluid and melodic passages of locked-hand work; in his energetic solo lines he draws on a large number of quotations from well-known popular songs.

BIBLIOGRAPHY

FeatherE

B. Niquet: "Herman Foster," *Pj*, no.15 (1979), 140

Foster, Pops [George Murphy] (*b* McCall, LA, 18 May 1892; *d* San Francisco, 30 Oct 1969). Double bass player, brother of Willie Foster. His first instrument was cello, but he soon changed to double bass and from around 1906 played with many bands in New Orleans. He later worked with Fate Marable's group, in which he also played tuba, on Mississippi riverboats (1918–21) and with Kid Ory's band in California. He spent some time in St. Louis, where he performed with Charlie Creath and Dewey Jackson, then in 1929 moved to New York to join Luis Russell. With his highly rhythmic pizzicato style, Foster continued to provide an emphatic pulse for the band under the leadership of Louis Armstrong (1935–40). Thereafter, with the revival of interest in traditional jazz, he worked in small groups, notably with Sidney Bechet (1945), Art Hodes (1945–6), Mezz Mezzrow, Bob Wilber, and Jimmy Archey (1950, 1952); the enormous sound and propulsive beat of his playing vitalized every ensemble with which he performed. He regularly took part in the radio series "This is Jazz" (1947) and also appeared in the film *Jazz Dance* (1954). After a tour of Europe with Sammy Price (1955–6) Foster moved to San Francisco, where in the late 1950s and early 1960s he played with Earl Hines. He also worked as a freelance (from 1962) and as a member of Elmer Snowden's trio (1963–4), and made a tour of Europe with the New Orleans All Stars (1966). Foster's autobiography, though not a model of chronological accuracy, is lively and vividly anecdotal.

Oral history material in *LNT*.

SELECTED RECORDINGS

As sideman: H. Allen: Feeling Drowsy (1929, Vic. 38080); L. Russell: Jersey Lightning (1929, OK 8734); Doctor Blues (1929, OK 8766); M. Mezzrow and S. Bechet: Bowin' the Blues (1945, King Jazz 141); E. Berry: Swingin' the Berry's (1956, Col. FP1076)

BIBLIOGRAPHY

P. Foster: "Forty-eight Years on the String Bass," *Jazz Record*, no.53 (1947), 18; repr. in *Selections from the Gutter: Jazz Portraits from 'The Jazz Record'*, ed. A. Hodes and C. Hansen (Berkeley, CA, Los Angeles, and London, 1977), 103

S. M. Peterson: "Reminiscing with Pops Foster," *SL*, xviii (1967), May–June, 108

Obituary, M. Mezzrow, *BHcF*, no.195 (1970), 7

K. Smith: "As I Remember Pops," *Sv*, no.27 (1970), 83

P. Foster, T. Stoddard, and R. Russell: *Pops Foster: the Autobiography of a New Orleans Jazzman* (Berkeley, CA, Los Angeles, and London, 1971) [incl. discography by B. Rust]

JOHN CHILTON

Foster, Willie (*b* McCall, LA, 27 Dec 1888; *d* after 1959). Violinist, banjoist, and guitarist, brother of Pops Foster. In New Orleans he played with, among others, King Oliver and Louis Armstrong, and during the 1920s he worked on Mississippi riverboats with Fate Marable, recording with the group in 1924. Foster also performed in New York with Oliver in 1927.

Oral history material in *LNT*.

MARCEL JOLY

Fountain, Pete(r Dewey, Jr.) (*b* New Orleans, 3 July 1930). Clarinetist. He began playing clarinet at the age of 12, and by 1948 was a member of the Junior Dixieland Band. In autumn 1949 he joined Phil Zito's International Dixieland Band, and made his first recordings, in 1950, with this group. Fountain was a founding member of the Basin Street Six (1950). After the group disbanded in 1954 he formed his own ensemble, Pete Fountain and his Three Coins, the following year. In 1955 he also played a seven-month engagement in Chicago with the Dukes of Dixieland. He then returned to New Orleans, where he worked with Tony Almerico and Al Hirt. From 1957 to 1959 Fountain gained great popularity through his appearances on the "Lawrence Welk Show." In 1959 he purchased a club in New Orleans where he continues to perform frequently, and he often plays at the New Orleans Jazz and Heritage Festival

Pops Foster (double bass) with Sidney Bechet (soprano saxophone) and James P. Johnson (piano), c1940

and on the "Tonight Show." He has been influenced in his playing by the large sound of Irving Fazola and the drive of Benny Goodman.

SELECTED RECORDINGS

As leader: *Music from Dixie* (1961, Coral 757401); *South Rampart Street Parade* (1963, Coral 757440)

As sideman: Basin Street Six: *Dixieland Jazz Concert* (1951, Mer. 25111); Dukes of Dixieland: *At the Jazz Band Ball* (1955, X 1025); L. Welk: *Lawrence Welk Presents Pete Fountain* (1957, Coral 57200)

BIBLIOGRAPHY

C. Suhor: "Pete Fountain," *DB*, xxviii/24 (1961), 20

P. Fountain and B. Neely: *A Closer Walk: the Pete Fountain Story* (Chicago, 1972)

H. Mandel: "Pete Fountain: Crescent City Clarinet," *DB*, lii/1 (1985), 23 [incl. discography]

RAYMOND J. GARIGLIO

Four-beat. A term applied to music in which all four main beats of a bar in 4/4 (or 12/8) meter are accented; it is pertinent to almost all jazz pieces cast in those meters. *See* BEAT, §4(ii).

Fournier, Vernel (Anthony) (*b* New Orleans, 30 July 1928). Drummer. He played rhythm-and-blues with King Kolax (1946–8) and Paul Bascomb, and in swing ensembles with Teddy Wilson (1949–53), then from 1953 to 1955 worked with Norman Simmons in the house band at the Bee Hive in Chicago, which accompanied J. J. Johnson, Kai Winding, Lester Young, Sonny Stitt, Ben Webster, and Bud Freeman, among others. He made recordings with Lorez Alexandria (1957, 1962), Gary Burton (1963), and others, but most frequently as a member of groups led by Ahmad Jamal (1958–61, 1965–6, including the album *Ahmad Jamal at the Pershing*, 1958, Argo 628) and George Shearing (1960–64). From 1966 Fournier was in the band that accompanied Nancy Wilson. He recorded with Clifford Jordan in 1984. (*FeatherE*; *Feather '60s*)

Fours. Four-bar phrases, as in the expression "to trade fours"; *see* FORMS, §1(ii).

Four Sounds. Group formed by Bill Dowdy in 1956 which the following year became the THREE SOUNDS.

Fourth Way. Quartet. Formed in 1968 in San Francisco by the electric pianist Mike Nock, its other members were the electric violinist Michael White (i), the electric bass guitarist Ron McClure, and the drummer Eddie Marshall. The group toured internationally and in 1970 recorded the album *Werwolf* (Harvest 666) at the Montreux International Jazz Festival before disbanding in the following year. The Fourth Way was one of the first important jazz-rock groups.

Fowlkes, Charlie [Charles Baker] (*b* New York, 16 Feb 1916; *d* Dallas, 9 Feb 1980). Baritone saxophonist. He learned violin, clarinet, and alto and tenor saxophones in his youth, but he chose the baritone saxophone when he began playing professionally. He worked with Tiny Bradshaw (1938–44) and Lionel Hampton (1944–8). In 1948, when Arnett Cobb, a fellow sideman in Hampton's band, formed his own small group, Fowlkes joined him; during his time with Cobb (to 1951) he also acted as manager for his wife, the singer Wini Brown. From 1951 Fowlkes was a member of Count Basie's band for 18 years, until a knee injury forced him to leave; he played with Basie again from 1975. Fowlkes was mainly a section musician, but he plays a notable solo on Basie's *Misty* (1959) and may also be heard to advantage on his recordings with the small groups led by Cobb, Buck Clayton, and J. C. Heard.

SELECTED RECORDINGS

As sideman: A. Cobb: That's all, Brother/Bee-bee (1950, Col. 39139); B. Clayton: *Buck Clayton Jam Session* (1953, Col. CL6325), incl. Moten Swing, Sentimental Journey; J. C. Heard: *This is me J. C.* (1958, Argo 633); C. Basie: *Dance Along with Basie* (1959, Roul. 52036), incl. Misty

BIBLIOGRAPHY

FeatherE; *Feather '60s*; *Feather–Gitler '70s*

LAWRENCE KOCH

Fox, Charles (Richard Jeremy) (*b* Weymouth, England, 1921). English writer. From the early 1960s he was the host in Britain of a weekly radio program, "Jazz Today." He became the jazz critic of the *New Statesman* and also contributed occasionally to *The Guardian*, the *Sunday Times*, and *The Gramophone*. In the USA he is best known for *The Essential Jazz Records*, i: *Ragtime to Swing* (1984), a guide to 250 jazz recordings written with Max Harrison and Eric Thacker. He has also written a brief, insightful book on Fats Waller (1960).

WRITINGS

(selective list)

Fats Waller (New York, 1960); repr. in *Kings of Jazz*, ed. S. Green (South Brunswick, NJ, and New York, 1978)

with P. Gammond and A. Morgan: *Jazz on Record: a Critical Guide* (London, 1960)

Jazz in Perspective (London, 1969)

with V. Wilmer: *The Jazz Scene* (London, 1972)

with M. Harrison and E. Thacker: *The Essential Jazz Records*, i: *Ragtime to Swing* (London and Westport, CT, 1984)

ROBERT GANNON

Francis, Panama [Dave, David Albert] (*b* Miami, 21 Dec 1918). Drummer. He began playing professionally in the 1930s, first with George Kelly (1934–8) and then with the Florida Collegians (1938). He moved to New York and worked briefly with Tab Smith, the trumpeter Billy Hicks, and Roy Eldridge (with whom he recorded in 1939), before joining Lucky Millinder in 1940, with whom he played at the Savoy Ballroom until 1946. He toured, recorded, and made several films with Cab Calloway (1947–52), after which he worked as a studio drummer in New York and California. During the 1950s he made several successful recordings with popular groups and singers, including Buddy Holly. Later, he toured and recorded with Ray Charles, Illinois Jacquet, the singer Mahalia Jackson, Lionel Hampton, Jimmy Witherspoon, and others. He appeared in the film *Lady Sings the Blues* (1972) and in 1979 he formed the Savoy Sultans, a jazz and dance band, which toured and recorded in Europe and in the 1980s played occasionally at the Rainbow Room, New York (*see* SAVOY SULTANS (ii)). He joined the re-formed Benny Goodman Quartet (with Teddy Wilson and Lionel Hampton) for numerous concert and festival appearances in 1982.

Francis's recordings demonstrate his excellent technique, accurate fills and kicks, imaginative solos, and complementary accompaniment figures. Of particular interest is an album recorded for the Smithsonian Institution in 1979, on which he plays in a traditional jazz style reminiscent of the finest New Orleans drummers (*The Music of Fats Waller and James P. Johnson*, Smithsonian 21).

Oral history material in *NjR* (JOHP).

SELECTED RECORDINGS

As leader: *The Battle of Jericho* (1962, Epic 3839); *Tough Talk* (1963, 20CF 5101); *Gettin' in the Groove* (1979, BB 33320–21)

BIBLIOGRAPHY

ChiltonW

J.-P. Battestini: "Panama Francis par lui-même," *BHcF*, no.239 (1974), 9; no.240 (1974), 5

S. Dance: *The World of Swing* (New York, n.d. [?1974]) [colln of previously pubd interviews], 375
A. Vasset: "Panama Francis et ses Savoy Sultans," *BHcF*, no.269 (1979), 20
L. Jeske: "Panama Francis," *DB*, xlvii/12 (1980), 22
H. Saunders: "Panama Francis at the Smithsonian Institute," *JSN*, i/5 (1980), 32
G. Giddins: *Rhythm-a-ning: Jazz Tradition and Innovation in the '80s* (New York, and Oxford, England, 1985) [colln of previously pubd articles]
C. Deffaa: "Portraits: Panama Francis," *MD*, xi/3 (1987), 38

T. DENNIS BROWN

Franco, Guilherme (*b* São Paulo, 25 Nov 1946). Brazilian percussionist and drummer. In Brazil he played bossa nova and jazz (1960–65), then worked as a studio musician and performed with the São Paulo SO. In 1968 he formed the Experimental Percussion Group of São Paulo City. After emigrating to the USA in 1971 he formed an association with Gato Barbieri that lasted into the mid-1980s; he also played and recorded (1974–5) with Keith Jarrett and performed as a percussionist with McCoy Tyner, recording in 1974–8. Other musicians with whom he recorded include Woody Shaw (1974) and Buster Williams and Terumasa Hino (both 1975). In 1980 he formed a samba group called Pe De Boi, which plays regularly in New York, and in 1981–2 he was a member of the Saheb Sarbeb Multi-National Big Band. As a percussionist he has recorded with a number of drummers, among them Elvin Jones (1975) and Louis Hayes (1976).

SELECTED RECORDINGS

As leader: *Made in New York* (1985, Pe De Boi Records GFMS 001)
As sideman: M. Tyner: *Atlantis* (1974, Mlst. 55002); K. Jarrett: *Treasure Island* (1974, Imp. 9274); W. Shaw: *Moontrain* (1974, Muse 5058); T. Hino: *Speak to Loneliness* (1975, EW 7008); M. Tyner: *The Greeting* (1978, Mlst. 9085)

RICK MATTINGLY

Franks, Michael (*b* La Jolla, CA, 1944). Singer and songwriter. He began playing guitar and singing at the age of 14. He had no formal musical training and his early style was influenced by blues and folk music; he wrote songs for such blues musicians as Sonny Terry and Brownie McGhee. He studied English literature at the University of California and was awarded an MA by the University of Oregon. In the early 1970s he taught a course on the history of American popular songs at UCLA and worked as a freelance songwriter. After writing the score for a film made by Warner Bros. (*Zandy's Bride*, 1974) he was granted a contract with the company's record division. He recorded with such distinguished sidemen as Joe Sample, Kenny Barron, Ron Carter, Bucky Pizzarelli, and Eddie Gomez. Recordings of his compositions have been made by a number of jazz musicians, including David Sanborn, Mike Brecker, Larry Carlton, Carmen McRae, Mark Murphy, and the group Manhattan Transfer. Franks sings in a relaxed but swinging style, with a soft, breathy tone. *Popsicle Toes* (1976) provides a typical example of his songs, the lyrics of which often rely partly for their effect on sexual innuendo.

SELECTED RECORDINGS

As leader: *The Art of Tea* (1976, Rep. 2230), incl. Popsicle Toes; *Sleeping Gypsy* (1977, WB 3004); *Objects of Desire* (1981, WB 3648)

BIBLIOGRAPHY

M. Shindler: "Michael Franks: Tea for One," *RS*, no.246 (25 Aug 1977), 21
D. Heckman: "Michael Franks is no Three-chord Composer," *High Fidelity and Musical America*, xxvii/3 (1977), 142
L. Feather: "Blindfold Test: Michael Franks," *DB*, xlvii/9 (1980), 50

SCOTT FREDRICKSON

Franzetti, Carlos (*b* Buenos Aires, 3 June 1948). Argentine pianist and composer. He studied piano from the age of six and composition in Mexico. After moving to New York he performed with Art Blakey, Ron Carter, Marvin Stamm, Paquito D'Rivera, and Joe Farrell, and recorded with D'Rivera and Farrell. He performed at the North Sea Jazz Festival in the Netherlands and at festivals in France, Boston, and California, and made several recordings (including *Galaxy Dust*, 1979–80, IC 1113) as a leader. His compositions include film scores, as well as classical works that have been performed by the symphony orchestras of Buffalo, Atlanta, and Buenos Aires. From 1984 he lived alternately in Buenos Aires and New York.

LAUREANO FERNÁNDEZ, OMAR GARCÍA BRUNELLI

Frazier, Cié [Josiah] (*b* New Orleans, 23 Feb 1904; *d* New Orleans, 10 Jan 1985). Drummer. A pupil of Louis Cottrell, Sr., his style was also influenced by Red Happy Bolton (who played with John Robichaux) and Face-O Woods (a member of Chris Kelly's band). About 1922 he joined the Golden Rule Band with his cousin Lawrence Marrero, and in the mid-1920s played with Marrero's Young Tuxedo Orchestra. He recorded with Oscar Celestin's Original Tuxedo Jazz Orchestra (1927), and also played with Celestin's Tuxedo Brass Band. About 1928 he became a member of A. J. Piron's orchestra, then worked with the Sunny South Band and the Sidney Desvigne Orchestra (from 1932). During the Depression years he played in WPA bands. While in the US Navy (1942–5) Frazier performed in a dance band and recorded with Wooden Joe Nicholas (1945). In the 1950s he worked with Celestin, Percy Humphrey, and the brass band led by the bass drummer George Williams, and occasionally with the Eureka Brass Band. From 1961 to 1983 he played regularly at Preservation Hall with various groups (for illustration *see* HUMPHREY) and recorded extensively; a good example of his playing may be heard on *In Gloryland* recorded with Kid Howard (on the album *Kid Howard's La Vida Band*, 1961, Icon 4). Frazier appeared in jazz sequences in two films: *The Cincinnati Kid* (1965) and *American Music: from Folk to Jazz and Pop* (1969), and made tours of England and Europe. His playing, combining a refined classical technique with an exhilarating rhythmic support that eschewed excessive showiness, is widely regarded as the quintessential embodiment of the New Orleans drumming style.

Oral history material in *LNT*.

BIBLIOGRAPHY

L. Borenstein and B. Russell: *Preservation Hall Portraits* (Baton Rouge, LA, 1968) [pictures by N. Rockmore]
M. Joly: "Talking to Josiah 'Cié' Frazier," *Fn*, x/3 (1979), 4
B. Martyn: "There's Nothing Like the Best," *Fn*, x/3 (1979), 12

ALDEN ASHFORTH

Freedom. Record label founded by Alan Bates as a subsidiary of BLACK LION; it was later acquired by ARISTA, and formed the basis for the catalogue of Arista–Freedom.

Free jazz. A term first applied to the avant-garde jazz of the 1960s, particularly the work of Ornette Coleman, Cecil Taylor, and Albert Ayler, and the late work of John Coltrane. The name derives from the title of Coleman's album *Free Jazz* (1960), an extended, free-form improvisation for two pianoless jazz quartets, which exercised an enormous influence on the jazz vanguard both in the USA and elsewhere. The music has also been described simply as "avant-garde" (*see* AVANT-GARDE JAZZ) or "the New Thing"; both terms emphasize its distance from the mainstream jazz movement. A further name, "action jazz," was suggested by the jazz critic Don Heckman, who considered that the essential quality of the new music was its energy. In

Europe (especially England) free jazz is also known simply as "improvised music."

"Free jazz" is a collective term applied to a very wide range of highly individual styles. The music is probably best defined by its negative features, though a performance need not be characterized by all these qualities: the absence of tonality and predetermined chord sequences; the abandonment of the jazz chorus structure and its replacement by loose designs in which collective improvisation takes place around predefined signals; an avoidance of "cool" instrumental timbres in favor of more "voice-like" sounds; and the suspension of standard timekeeping patterns for a free rubato.

New timbres have been sought either by distorting the sound of conventional jazz instruments (the method chosen by John Gilmore and Pharoah Sanders, who adopted a "shrieking" style on saxophone) or by taking up unusual or newly invented instruments (as did the members of the Art Ensemble of Chicago); electronic instruments and electronic manipulation of sound, on the other hand, are generally avoided. (For further observations on the instrumentation of free jazz *see* BANDS, §4(vii).) Free-jazz drummers have explored "multidirectional" rhythms implying various meters at once, and interact with other musicians by supplying percussion color and textures rather than a uniform pulse. The shape of a performance is often determined by the performers' powers of endurance, the piece coming to an end when their energy sags. Melody becomes much more varied and fragmented as long, sustained notes alternate with rapid flurries or timbral effects; many players concentrate on producing textures rather than melody, while others create internal "dialogues" or call-and-response patterns in different registers. Special emphasis is placed on collective improvisation, although at any given time one performer usually functions as a soloist. Some groups reveal a pronounced theatrical element, whether the naive exoticism of Sun Ra's Arkestra or the sophisticated parodistic skits of the Art Ensemble of Chicago and Carla Bley.

By casting aside most features of the bop style, the free-jazz players of the 1960s harked back in many respects to simpler forms of jazz and earlier music in which elements derived from African music predominated. This in turn encouraged an unusual influx into jazz of ethnic musics, examples being the "world music" of Don Cherry, the West African "talking drums" approach cultivated by Ed Blackwell, and the pygmy yodeling techniques adopted by Leone Thomas. Several free-jazz musicians, such as Roswell Rudd and Steve Lacy, bypassed bop entirely, entering the avant garde directly from New Orleans jazz; others, notably Albert Ayler, emerged from the gospel and folk traditions. The style was loosely linked to the Black Power movement in the USA, partly because of the radical political outlook of some of its practitioners and advocates (e.g., Archie Shepp and LeRoi Jones) and partly owing to the explosive, expressionistic nature of the music itself.

Although highly regarded by the critics, free jazz did not establish itself as a commercially viable form of music in the USA (although Coltrane was highly successful). This accounts for the number of artists' collectives that were formed for its promotion (e.g., the Association for the Advancement of Creative Musicians in Chicago, the Black Artists Group in St. Louis, and the Jazz Composer's Orchestra Association in New York), and for the fact that many of its important exponents resided, at least temporarily, in Europe. An indigenous school of free jazz grew up on the Continent, notably in West Germany, where it was linked with the development of the aleatory art music of such composers as Bernd Alois Zimmermann. Among the outstanding European free-jazz musicians of the time were the Germans Albert Mangelsdorff, Joachim Kühn, Manfred Schoof, and Alex Schlippenbach (who founded and led the Globe Unity Orchestra), and the Britons John Surman and Derek Bailey.

During the 1960s many performances of free jazz took place in lofts in New York, and annual festivals of loft jazz took place between 1972 and 1977. But the noncommercial nature of lofts and the radical artistic views of the audiences they attracted tended to perpetuate the opinion that free jazz was an avant-garde music. In the early 1970s, as jazz-rock became a more popular genre, the free-jazz movement seemed spent, but it underwent a resurgence later in the decade. Older groups, such as Old and New Dreams (consisting of former sidemen of Coleman), were able to re-form, while others, including Sun Ra's Arkestra and the Art Ensemble of Chicago, reached a wider public than before. Specialist labels, for example, FMP (in Germany), Black Saint (in Italy), and India Navigation (in the USA), were established to enable free-jazz musicians to record. New players added fresh dimensions to the style: for example, Anthony Braxton and Anthony Davis obliterated the boundaries between free jazz and contemporary European art music; the World Saxophone Quartet (especially its tenor saxophonist David Murray) created a successful blend of free jazz and the swing style; and the Ganelin Trio introduced a wild theatricality, as well as elements of its native Russian musical traditions, into the genre. Musicians not directly associated with free jazz, such as Pat Metheny (who performed and recorded with Ornette Coleman in 1985–6), made use of its stylistic devices; others experimented with new hybrids, an example being the "free funk" of James "Blood" Ulmer. In the mid-1980s free jazz was firmly established not only as a completed phase of jazz history but also as a continuing and developing style with a great many avenues still open for creative exploration.

See also FORMS, §6, and JAZZ (i), §VI, 1, 3, 5.

BIBLIOGRAPHY

L. Jones: *Black Music* (New York, 1967/*R*1980)
B. McRae: *The Jazz Cataclysm* (London, South Brunswick, NJ, and New York, 1967/*R*1985)
E. Raben: *A Discography of Free Jazz* (Copenhagen, 1969)
F. J. Kofksy: *Black Nationalism and the Revolution in Music* (New York, 1970; rev. and enlarged as *Black Nationalism and the Revolution in Music: Social Change and Stylistic Development in the Art of John Coltrane and Others, 1954–1967*, diss., U. of Pittsburgh, 1973)
P. Rivelli and R. Levin, eds.: *Black Giants* (New York and Cleveland, 1970/*R*1980 as *Giants of Black Music*) [colln of previously pubd articles]
P. Carles and J.-L. Comolli: *Free Jazz, Black Power* (Paris, 1971)
E. Jost: "Free Jazz und die Musik der Dritten Welt," *Jf*, ii–iv (1971–2), 141
——: *Free Jazz* (Graz, Austria, 1974)
J. Viera: *Der Free Jazz: Formen und Modelle* (Vienna, 1974)
H. Kumpf: *Postserielle Musik und Free Jazz: Wechselwirkungen und Parallelen* (Herrenburg, Germany, 1975, rev. 2/1981)
Liner notes: *Wildflowers: the New York Loft Jazz Sessions* (Douglas 7045–9, 1976)
S. Crouch: "Jazz Lofts: a Walk through the Wild Sounds," *New York Times Magazine* (17 April 1977), 40
D. J. Noll: *Zur Improvisation im deutschen Free Jazz: Untersuchungen zur Ästhetik frei improvisierter Klangflächen* (Hamburg, Germany, 1977)
R. Palmer: "A Jazz Festival in the Lofts," *New York Times* (3 June 1977), 18
"Qu'est-ce que la Loft Generation?," *Jm*, no.255 (1977), 13
V. Wilmer: *As Serious as your Life: the Story of the New Jazz* (London, 1977, rev. 1980)
B. Noglik: *Jazzwerkstatt international* (Berlin, 1981)
J. Litweiler: *The Freedom Principle: Jazz after 1958* (New York, 1984)
D. G. Such: *Music, Metaphor, and Values among Avant-garde Musicians Living in New York City* (diss., UCLA, 1985)

J. BRADFORD ROBINSON

Freeman, Bud [Lawrence] (*b* Chicago, 13 April 1906). Tenor saxophonist. He grew up in Chicago, and in the early 1920s was a member of the Austin High School Gang (for illustration see TESCHEMACHER, FRANK). In 1927 he moved to New York with Ben Pollack's band and in 1929 performed there with Red Nichols. By the following year he had formed an original, unmannered style, free of "novelty" effects and with a distinctive jazz timbre; as the first white saxophonist to do so he is often compared with his black contemporary Coleman Hawkins. In the 1930s Freeman performed and recorded frequently with well-known popular and jazz orchestras, including those of Paul Whiteman, Tommy Dorsey, and Benny Goodman. From the end of the decade he played, toured, and recorded with small jazz groups, at first with his own band, the Summa cum Laude Orchestra, which recorded for the Bluebird and Decca labels in a style that combined elements of swing and dixieland.

Freeman led his own groups during the 1950s and 1960s, while also sustaining a long-term association with the bands of Eddie Condon; he took part in numerous recording sessions under the aegis of many different leaders. From 1969 to 1971, and occasionally thereafter, he was a member of the World's Greatest Jazz Band. He lived in London in the late 1970s before returning to Chicago, and has continued to tour and record as a soloist. Although Freeman's approach to playing has remained essentially unchanged throughout his career, he has constantly refined his style.

Oral history material in *ICU*, *NjR* (JOHP).

SELECTED RECORDINGS

Duos with B. Pizzarelli: *Bucky and Bud* (*c*1975, FD BDL1-1378)
As leader: Crazeology (1928, OK 41168); China Boy/The Eel (1939, Bb 10368); Tia Juana (1940, Decca 18066)
As sideman: McKenzie–Condon Chicagoans: Nobody's Sweetheart/Liza (1927, OK 40971); R. Nichols: Rose of Washington Square (1929, Bruns. 4778); E. Condon: The Eel (1933, Bruns. 02006); Home Cookin' (1933, Col. 35680); T. Dorsey: At the Codfish Ball (1936, Vic. 25314)

BIBLIOGRAPHY

G. Hoefer: "Freeman Big Influence on Saxists," *DB*, xix/6 (1952), 2
B. Freeman: *You don't Look like a Musician* (Detroit, 1974)
——: *If you Know of a Better Life, Please Tell me* (Dublin, 1976)
J. Lucas: "Ya Hafta Hanid ta Bud: Half a Century of Freeman," *MR*, vi/1 (1978), 9
L. Tomkins: "I Love the Life in London," *CI*, xviii/7 (1980), 6 [interview]
D. Travis: *An Autobiography of Black Jazz* (Chicago, 1983), 321
M. Richards: "Bud Freeman," *JJI*, xxxvii (1984), no.9, p.8; no.10, p.14
C. Deffaa: "Bud Freeman: the Early Years," *MR*, xiv/2 (1986), 1

JAMES DAPOGNY/R

Freeman, Chico [Earl Lavon, Jr.] (*b* Chicago, 17 July 1949). Tenor saxophonist and leader, son of Von Freeman. He first played trumpet, having been inspired to do so by Miles Davis's recording *Kind of Blue* (1959), then took up the tenor saxophone in his third year at Northwestern University (1967–72), where he studied mathematics, then music education. He played with blues and rhythm-and-blues groups, studied with Muhal Richard Abrams, and joined the Association for the Advancement of Creative Musicians; he also played and studied with Fred Anderson, the pianist and tenor saxophonist Adegoke Steve Colson, and his uncle, the electric guitarist George Freeman. After enrolling in 1974 as a graduate student in composition and performance at Governors State University he performed as a soloist with the university's big band, with which he toured Brazil (1976). Later he moved to New York and worked with Elvin Jones (1977), Sun Ra, Sam Rivers's big band, Jack DeJohnette, and Don Pullen. He is best known for his work as a leader of quartets, which have usually included Cecil McBee; among his other sidemen have been the pianists Muhal Richard Abrams and John Hicks (the vibraphonist Jay Hoggard has sometimes taken the place of a pianist) and the drummers Don Moye and Steve McCall. He has also played in a quintet with his father and in 1984 joined the LEADERS. Freeman's style combines the energy and wide leaps of John Coltrane's later work with a classic conception of form and a strong sense of swing.

SELECTED RECORDINGS

As leader: *Morning Prayer* (1976, Whynot 7155); *Chico* (*c*1977, IndN 1031); *Kings of Mali* (1977, IndN 1035); *Spirit Sensitive* (1979, IndN 1045); *The Search* (*c*1982, IndN 1059); *Tangents* (*c*1984, Elek. Mus. 960361)
As sideman: C. McBee: *Music from the Source* (1977, Enja 3019); D. Pullen: *Warriors* (1978, BS 0019); J. DeJohnette: *Tin Can Alley* (1980, ECM 1189)

BIBLIOGRAPHY

V. Wilmer: "Chico the Free Man," *MM*, lii (24 Sept 1977), 42
P. Irwin: "Profile: Chico Freeman," *DB*, xlvi/5 (1979), 34
C. Sheridan: "Prometheus Observed: Chico Freeman," *JJI*, xxxii/11 (1979), 9
C. Gans: "Chico Freeman: New Music from the Source," *JF* [intl edn], no.68 (1980), 44
C. Sheridan: "Young Men Ascending: Some Notes on Chico Freeman and George Adams," *JJI*, xxxiii/10 (1980), 26 [incl. discography]
N. Tesser: "Von and Chico Freeman: Tenor Dynasty," *DB*, xlvii/7 (1980), 24 [incl. discography]

ED HAZELL

Freeman, Russ(ell Donald) (*b* Chicago, 28 May 1926). Pianist. He studied classical piano as a child, and during the late 1940s played with bop groups on the West Coast. He played with Howard McGhee and Dexter Gordon in 1947, with Art Pepper, Wardell Gray, and Shorty Rogers in the early 1950s, and with Chet Baker in 1954. His lasting association with Shelly Manne began in 1955, when Manne left Shorty Rogers's Giants; Freeman toured Europe with Benny Goodman (1959) and with Manne (1960). In 1962 he formed a publishing company, Encore Music, which issued a number of his own compositions. From the mid-1960s he was music director for nightclub acts, and worked in television and in Hollywood, where he played piano on numerous film soundtracks. Freeman's piano style is essentially bop with a strong sense of swing. He has indicated great respect for Bill Evans (ii) as a jazz pianist, although the latter's influence on Freeman's work has been limited; he has also said (see Tynan) that in the early 1960s his playing was influenced by bass players and drummers rather than pianists.

SELECTED RECORDINGS

As leader: *Russ Freeman Trio* (1953, PJ 8); with C. Baker: *Freeman/Baker Quartet* (1956, PJ 1232); with A. Previn: *Double Play* (1957, Cont. 3537); Invitation to the Blues (1959, Jazz West Coast 511)
As sideman: C. Baker: Russ Job (1953, PJ 610); on S. Manne: *New Works* (1954, Cont. 2511), Divertimento for Brass and Rhythm, Etude de Concerto, Lullaby; M. Ferguson: *Dimensions* (1954, EmA 26024); Clifford Brown: Joy Spring/Blueberry Hill (1954, PJ 4-27) [EP]; S. Manne: *With Russ Freeman* (1954, Cont. 2518); C. Touff: *Having a Ball* (1955, PJ 1211); S. Manne: *Boss Sounds!* (1966, Atl. 1469)

BIBLIOGRAPHY

FeatherE; *Feather–Gitler '70s*
T. Leyh: "Russ Freeman: Piano Perspektiven," *JP*, vii (1958), 123
J. Tynan: "Straight Talk from Russ Freeman," *DB*, xxx/7 (1963), 20

ANDRÉ BARBERA

Freeman, Von [Earl Lavon, Sr.] (*b* Chicago, 3 Oct 1922). Tenor saxophonist, father of Chico Freeman. He played clarinet and C-melody saxophone from the age of seven, took lessons from Walter Dyett, and played in Horace Henderson's group (1940–41) and in a navy band (1941–5); he worked briefly with Sun Ra (1948–9). As a member of the house band at the Pershing Hotel in Chicago with his brothers, the electric guitarist George Freeman and the drummer Bruz Freeman, he accompanied Charlie Parker, Roy Eldridge, and Lester Young (1946–50). In the 1950s he formed a quartet with his brothers and Ahmad Jamal (later replaced by Andrew Hill); he also worked with Malachi Favors, Muhal Richard Abrams, and Fred Anderson.

He toured in the early 1960s with the blues musicians Jimmy Reed, Gene Chandler, and Otis Rush and from 1966 to 1969 in a show band led by Milt Trenier. From 1969 he again worked exclusively in jazz, principally in Chicago; he has played most often as the leader of a quartet that includes as sidemen the double bass player Dave Shipp and the pianist John Young, and occasionally in a quintet with his son Chico. Freeman's style is well illustrated by his albums *Have No Fear* (1975, Nessa 6) and *Serenade and Blues* (1975, Nessa 11).

BIBLIOGRAPHY

J. Litweiler: "Von Freeman: Underrated but Undaunted," *DB*, xliii/18 (1976), 16 [incl. discography]
B. Rusch: "Von Freeman: Interview," *Cadence*, v/4 (1979), 3
E. Jost: *Jazzmusiker: Materialen zur Soziologie der afro-amerikanischen Musik* (Frankfurt am Main, Germany, Berlin, and Vienna, 1981), 213

ED HAZELL

Free Music Production. *See* FMP.

Freichel, Louis (*b* Frankfurt am Main, Germany, 21 Dec 1921). German pianist. After studying music in Frankfurt am Main, Germany (1938–41), he worked with the Hot Club Combo (1943–5), with which he made clandestine recordings as a guitarist; his piano playing may be heard on the group's *Sweet Georgia Brown* (1949, first issued on *Trümmer Jazz: Jazz and Hot Dance after the Nazis, 1946–1949*, 1987, Harl. 2052). He was a member of Benny de Weille's swing trio (1945–8) and from 1949 he performed on radio with Willy Berking's big band, recording with it in 1953–4 and 1956. He worked as a pianist, composer, and arranger with the big band of Hessischer Rundfunk (1956–83). Freichel has also made recordings with the dixieland band the Two Beat Stompers (including *The music goes 'round and 'round*, 1954, Bruns. 10020 [EP]), with Dusko Goykovich and Albert Mangelsdorff in the nine-piece group the Frankfurter All Stars (1955), and with the Main Stream Power Band, a German big band (1976–80).

BIBLIOGRAPHY

ReclamsJ
W. F. Lee: *People in Jazz: Jazz Keyboard Improvisers of the 19th and 20th Centuries* (Hialeah, FL, 1984)

RAINER E. LOTZ

French horn. A name frequently used for the orchestral horn; *see* HORN (2).

Fresh Sounds. Record company. It was founded in Barcelona, Spain, in the early 1980s. It aimed to reissue jazz albums which had to that date been unavailable for several years. These were issued as high-quality pressings in replicas of the original liners. Material was leased from numerous sources, both European and American; these included RCA–Victor, Pacific Jazz, Metrojazz, Jazz West, Bethlehem, Peacock, Hifijazz, Counterpoint, Roulette, Dawn, Columbia, Barclay, and French Brunswick. By 1987 the catalogue contained more than 300 albums, many of which were previously difficult to obtain. The company also issued at least one album of new material, a recording made by Pedro Iturralde with Hampton Hawes.

MARK GARDNER

Freund, Joki [Walter Jakob] (*b* Schwalbach, nr Frankfurt am Main, Germany, 5 Sept 1926). German saxophonist and arranger. After playing in the band of Joe Quitter (1947) he performed with Jutta Hipp from 1952 until 1955, when he formed a hard-bop quintet. He played tuba in a traditional-jazz group, Werner Rehm's Two Beat Stompers (1955–67), and performed at festivals in Europe with Donald Byrd, Art Taylor, and Doug Watkins. With Albert Mangelsdorff he belonged to a radio jazz group for which he also wrote arrangements, and from 1962 he played saxophone in the dance orchestra of the Süddeutscher Rundfunk under Erwin Lehn. Freund composed the music for the film *Praeludium in Jazz*.

SELECTED RECORDINGS

As leader: *Yogi Jazz* (1963, CBS BPG62273)
As sideman: E. Mangelsdorff: *Like a Drop of Oil* (1966, CBS S63058); E. Lehn: *Color in Jazz* (1973, MPS 2121963)

BIBLIOGRAPHY

FeatherE; *Feather–Gitler '70s*; *ReclamsJ*
P. Schmidt: "Joki, Albert & Co.," *JP*, vi/8 (1957), 11 [incl. interview]
J. Freund: "Mein Jazz-Koncept," *JP*, xiii/5 (1964), 122
H. Lippmann: "Jokis 'Yogi Jazz'," *JP*, xiii/5 (1964), 122

HEIDI BOULTON

Friars Society Orchestra. Name by which the band the NEW ORLEANS RHYTHM KINGS was originally known.

Friedman, David [Dave] (*b* New York, 10 March 1944). Vibraphonist and marimba player. The son of an amateur violinist, he studied drums from 1955 and marimba and xylophone from 1960. At the Juilliard School, where his major subject was percussion, he also took lessons from Teddy Charles and Hall Overton. In the early 1960s he performed with the New York PO and the Metropolitan Opera; during the following decades he worked with Wayne Shorter (recording in 1970), Horace Silver (recording in 1972), and Joe Chambers (recording in 1973). At the Newport Jazz Festival in New York (1973) he recorded with Hubert Laws and performed with Horacee Arnold. He toured widely, and often took part with Dave Samuels in workshops sponsored by the Ludwig Drum Co.; with Samuels he also formed the Mallet Duo in 1975 and led the quartet Double Image from 1977 to 1980. He recorded with Daniel Humair in 1979 and Chet Baker in 1982. Friedman taught in the mid-1970s at the Manhattan School of Music and the Institute for Advanced Musical Studies in Montreux, Switzerland.

SELECTED RECORDINGS

As leader: *Winter Love, April Joy* (1975, EW 8019); of Double Image (with D. Samuels): *Double Image* (1977, Enja 2096), *Dawn* (1978, ECM 1146); *Of the Wind's Eye* (1981, Enja 3089)
As sideman: W. Shorter: *Odyssey of Iska* (1970, BN 84363); H. Silver: *In Pursuit of the 27th Man* (1972, BN LA054F); Bob James: *One* (1974, CTI 6043); D. Humair: *Triple Hip Trip* (1979, Owl 014)

BIBLIOGRAPHY

Feather–Gitler '70s
H. Nolan: "Dave Friedman and Dave Samuels: Two Man Percussion Crusade," *DB*, xliii/20 (1976), 12

GARY THEROUX

Friedman, Don(ald Ernest) (*b* San Francisco, 4 May 1935). Pianist. He began learning piano at the age of five, and received a classical training. His first professional engagements were in 1956 with Dexter Gordon, Shorty Rogers, and Buddy Collette, with whom he also recorded. He then worked with Buddy DeFranco (1956–7) and Chet Baker and Ornette Coleman (both 1957). After moving to New York he played with Pepper Adams (1958) and led his own trio; he also recorded with Booker Little (1961). Friedman joined the Jimmy Giuffre Three in 1964, then led a quartet with Attila Zoller. He worked with Chuck Wayne's trio (1966–7), and became a member of Clark Terry's big band, with which he performed at Carnegie Hall (1970). From 1970 to 1975 he taught jazz piano at New York University, and in 1980 worked with the double bass player Bob Bodley. He has continued to work in New York into the late 1980s. Friedman uses the style of Bill Evans (ii) as a point of departure, but has also been influenced by classical music and avant-garde jazz. His lyricism and melodic sense are often compared to those of Evans, but Friedman has explored several types of music other than jazz, including 12-tone series and free-form styles.

SELECTED RECORDINGS

As unaccompanied soloist: *Avenue of the Americas* (1979, Owl 019)
As leader: *A Day in the City* (1961, Riv. 9384); *Hot Knepper and Pepper* (1978, Prog. 7036)
As sideman: E. Jones: *And Then Again* (1965, Atl. 1443); J. Henderson: *Tetragon* (1968, Mlst. MSP9017)

BIBLIOGRAPHY

D. Nelsen: "Don Friedman: a Pianist for All Seasons," *DB*, xxxi/28 (1964), 17
M. Williams: "Rehearsing with the Jimmy Giuffre 3," *DB*, xxxi/7 (1964), 18
T. Schnabel: "Don Friedman: Interview," *Cadence*, v/1 (1979), 7

PAUL RINZLER

Friedman, Izzy [Irving] (*b* Linton, IN, 25 Dec 1903). Clarinetist and saxophonist. He worked in a theater orchestra in Terre Haute, Indiana, and in 1923 moved to Chicago, where he studied with the principal clarinetist of the Chicago SO and played at the Moulin Rouge Café. The following year he went to New York and worked as a freelance musician, while also studying composition and conducting. He played with several bands, including that of Vincent Lopez (1925–6), then from 1928 to 1930 was a member of Paul Whiteman's orchestra. During this period he also made recordings with Bix Beiderbecke (including *Rhythm King/Louisiana*, 1928, OK 41173), Eddie Lang, Frankie Trumbauer, and Joe Venuti. After appearing with Whiteman in the film *King of Jazz* (1930) Friedman settled in Hollywood, where, until his retirement in 1963, he worked as a studio musician.

based on *ChiltonW*

Friesen, David (*b* Tacoma, WA, 6 May 1942). Double bass player. He first played during his military service in Germany in 1961, and is largely self-taught, though he took some private lessons and attended the University of Washington. In the 1960s he performed with John Handy in Vancouver and with Marian McPartland; he then worked with Joe Henderson in San Francisco for two years. While touring Europe with Billy Harper in 1975 he met Ted Curson in Copenhagen; it was with Curson's group that he attracted critical attention, at the Monterey Jazz Festival in 1977. Friesen's first recording under his own name, *Star Dance* (1976), featured the guitarist John Stowell, with whom he continued to work; he also recorded with Ricky Ford and Duke Jordan (both 1978). In the 1980s he has toured the USSR (with Paul Horn, 1983) and Europe (with Mal Waldron) and performed in duos with both Horn and Waldron at the Festival International de Jazz de Montréal (1985).

Friesen has frequently performed his own compositions; his experimentation with techniques may be heard on *Duet and Dialogue* (on *Star Dance*), where he plays with the bow and plucks the strings with both hands. He has occasionally played the Oregon bass, an electric solid-bodied instrument built to the length of a double bass and with a double bass fingerboard.

SELECTED RECORDINGS

As unaccompanied soloist: *Paths beyond Tracing* (1980, Ste. 1138)
Duos with P. Horn: *Heart to Heart* (1985, Golden Flute 2002)
As leader: *Star Dance* (1976, IC 1019); *Other Mansions* (1979, IC 1086); *Amber Skies* (1983, PAlt 8043); *Encounters* (1985, Muse 5305)

BIBLIOGRAPHY

T. Schnabel: "Profile: David Friesen," *DB*, xlv/7 (1978), 32
J. Howard: "Ein Virtuose par excellence: David Friesen," *JP*, xxviii/5 (1979), 10
H. Wong: "The Music of David Friesen: a Unification of Yin/Yang," *Radio Free Jazz*, xx/3 (1979), 13
L. Darroch: "David Friesen: Called to Play Music," *JT* (May 1987), 9

WILLIAM S. BROCKMAN

Friley, Vern(on) (*b* Marshall, MO, 5 July 1924). Trombonist. He performed and made recordings with Ray McKinley (1946–50), Woody Herman (1950, 1952–3, including *Four Others*, 1953, Mars 1003), the Sauter–Finegan Orchestra (1952–3), Les Brown (1954–5), and Terry Gibbs (1959, 1961–2). As a studio musician in New York he recorded with Jerry Gray (1951), Bill Harris (i) and Chico O'Farrill (both 1952), Chris Connor (1953), and Leo Anthony (1954). From 1955 he worked on the West Coast, where he played for radio and on a number of film soundtracks. He also recorded with Al Hibbler (1961) and Junior Mance and Benny Goodman (both 1964), and performed and recorded with Stan Kenton (1965–6). Friley is a well-respected session musician and section player, but he has recorded few solos. (*FeatherE*)

Frisco Jazz Band. Ensemble led in the 1950s by BOB SCOBEY.

Frisell, Bill [William Richard] (*b* Baltimore, 18 March 1951). Guitarist. He grew up in Colorado. He studied guitar with Jim Hall briefly in 1971 and composition with Mike Gibbs at the Berklee College of Music in the mid-1970s. In 1978 he toured England with Gibbs's big band and met Eberhard Weber, with whom he recorded the following year. Frisell soon became house guitarist at ECM, playing for recordings by Jan Garbarek and Paul Motian; he recorded his first album as a leader, *In Line*, for the company in 1982. He has maintained an association with Motian, and often plays in a duo with the alto saxophonist Tim Berne. He has also performed and recorded with various guitarists, including John Scofield.

Frisell's earliest influences were Jim Hall, Wes Montgomery, and Jimi Hendrix, and in his own playing he combines the various aspects of their styles to form an amalgam of jazz finesse, rock explosiveness, and avant-garde experimentation. He played clarinet before becoming a guitarist, and uses advanced technology (guitar synthesizers and effects units) to approximate the breathy sound of a wind instrument; in particular, he achieves an ethereal effect through his use of a volume pedal. In his attempts to explore sonorities more akin to those of a wind instrument or an organ, Frisell is redefining the function of the guitar.

SELECTED RECORDINGS

(all recorded for ECM unless otherwise indicated)

As leader: *In Line* (1982, 1241); *Rambler* (1984, 1287); *Lookout for Hope* (?1988, 1350)
As sideman: E. Weber: *Fluid Rustle* (1979, 1137); *Later that Evening* (1982, 1231); J. Garbarek: *Wayfarer* (1983, 1259); P. Motian: *The Story of Maryam* (1983, SN 1074); *It Should've Happened a Long Time Ago* (1984, 1283)

BIBLIOGRAPHY

R. Summers: "Profile: Bill Frisell," *DB*, li/2 (1984), 46
J. Woodard: "Bill Frisell: ECM's Lyrical 'House Guitarist'," *GP*, xix/4 (1985), 45 [incl. discography]
H. Mandel: "Bill Frisell: in Search of the Lost Chord and other Sound Effects," *DB*, liii/4 (1986), 19 [incl. discography]

BILL MILKOWSKI

Frishberg, Dave [David L.] (*b* St. Paul, MN, 23 March 1933). Pianist, singer, and songwriter. In 1957 he moved to New York, where he worked as an unaccompanied soloist and performed with Carmen McRae and Kai Winding (1958–9). He toured with Gene Krupa in 1960–61 and after returning to New York he played with Wild Bill Davison, Peanuts Hucko, Bud Freeman, Ben Webster (1963), the quintet led by Al Cohn and Zoot Sims (mid- to late 1960s), and Bobby Hackett and Charlie Shavers (both late 1960s). In the late 1960s he was the resident pianist at the Half Note in New York. After moving to Los Angeles in 1971 he performed and recorded with his own trio, with Jack Sheldon and Joe Pass (both 1972–3) and Bill Berry (1972–4), and in a duo with Richie Kamuca (1977). He continued working as an accompanist and soloist into the 1980s. His recordings of his own songs include *Van Lingle Mungo* (*c*1968) and *One Horse Town* (1984). His songs have also been recorded by Anita O'Day, Cleo Laine, Al Jarreau, and Jackie Cain and Roy Kral, and he wrote the lyrics to songs by Bob Dorough (notably *I'm Hip*, which he recorded himself) and Blossom Dearie (*Long Daddy Green*, recorded by her in 1970). Frishberg's broad experience is reflected in his eclectic musical style and the wry wit of his lyrics.

SELECTED RECORDINGS

As unaccompanied soloist: *Live at Vine Street* (1984, Fan. 9638), incl. One Horse Town

As leader: *Oklahoma Toad* (*c*1968, CTI 1004), incl. Van Lingle Mungo; *Getting some Fun out of Life* (1977, Conc. 37); *You're a Lucky Guy* (1978, Conc. 74); *The Dave Frishberg Songbook* (1981–2, Omni. 1040, 1051), incl. I'm Hip

As sideman: B. Berry: *Hot and Happy* (1974, Beez 1)

BIBLIOGRAPHY

Feather '60s; *Feather–Gitler '70s*

M. Pinfold: "Getting some Fun out of Life," *JJI*, xxxv/2 (1982) [interview, incl. discography]

STEVE LARSON

Froeba [Froba], **Frank(, Jr.)** (*b* New Orleans, Aug 1907; *d* Miami, 18 Feb 1981). Pianist and bandleader. He performed and recorded in New York with the cornetist Johnny de Droit (1924–5), led his own band in Atlantic City, New Jersey, and from 1927 worked in various dance orchestras. He recorded dixieland with Jack Purvis (1930) and Jack Bland's Rhythmakers (1932), performed and recorded with Benny Goodman (1933–5), and then led a band in New York (1935–44). From 1935 to 1952 he made a number of recordings as a leader (Bunny Berigan and Joe Marsala played with him in 1936), and also with others, notably Bob Howard (including *In my Mizz*, 1938, Decca 1869). As a house pianist for Decca he frequently accompanied singers, including Lil Armstrong (1938), and from 1941 he played regularly on radio station WNEW. In the 1950s he worked under the name Froba. He moved to Miami in 1955, where he was active mostly as a popular pianist. (*ChiltonW*)

Frog. Nickname of ELMER CHAMBERS.

Front. To act as the leader of a band; *see* BANDS, §3(a).

Front line. The melody instruments in an early jazz group; *see* BANDS, §2.

Fruit. Nickname of MORRIS WHITE.

Fruscella, Tony (*b* Orangeburg, NY, or New York, 4 Feb 1927; *d* New York, 14 Aug 1969). Trumpeter. After playing in an army band he worked with Lester Young and Gerry Mulligan (1954) and performed and recorded with Stan Getz (1955). He also made recordings with his own groups in 1955, including the album *I'll be Seeing you* (Atl. 1220). From the late 1950s Fruscella's career was impeded by his addiction to drugs, but he played occasionally with the trumpeter Don Joseph.

BIBLIOGRAPHY

FeatherE; *Feather–Gitler '70s*

D. Hague: "Cool and Hot," *JJ*, ix/2 (1956), 2

Obituary, *DB*, xxxvi/20 (1969), 7

R. Reisner: "Elegy for Tony Fruscella," *DB*, xxxvii/4 (1970), 17

Frye, Don(ald O.) (*b* Springfield, OH, 1903; *d* New York, 9 Feb 1981). Pianist. He traveled to New York with Lloyd and Cecil Scott (1924), where they recorded (1927, 1929) and performed through the early 1930s. He also recorded with King Oliver (1929–30). From 1933 to 1937 he played with Freddie Moore and in 1934 recorded with Clarence Williams. He worked with John Kirby (1937), with whose group he recorded under Buster Bailey's name. In the late 1930s he played with Lucky Millinder (*c*1938–9), and recorded and performed with Frankie Newton (1937, 1939). After appearing with Zutty Singleton in 1940 and on the West Coast in 1943, he was house pianist at Ryan's in New York, and recorded with Edmond Hall (1944), Danny Barker (1958), and Cecil Scott (1959). He also recorded four titles in 1945 as a soloist, including *Voulez-vous* (Disc 6009). (*ChiltonW*; *FeatherE*)

Fuhs, Julian (*b* Berlin, 20 Nov 1891; ? *d* USA, after 1933). German bandleader and pianist. He claimed to have been a member of one of Paul Whiteman's orchestras in the USA. He led the Follies Band in Berlin from around 1924, with which he made recordings (including *Copenhagen*, 1925, Homocord 1877, and *Ace in the Hole*, 1926, Elec. 386). By early 1925 the Homocord company was advertising the group as "the most successful jazz band in Berlin"; it was the house band at the Mercedes Palast for many years. Although he played piano for his band's regular performances, Fuhs was not a good jazz soloist and often employed white-American musicians for tours and recordings (1924–31). He emigrated to the USA in 1933. (R. E. Lotz: *Hot Dance Bands in Germany: a Photo Album*, ii: *The 1920s*, Menden, Germany, 1982)

RAINER E. LOTZ

Fukumura, Hiroshi (*b* Tokyo, 21 Feb 1949). Japanese trombonist and leader. After playing with Sadao Watanabe (1972–4), he attended the New England Conservatory and performed and recorded with its Jazz Repertory Orchestra (1974). He then returned to Japan, where he performed and recorded as the leader of a quintet that included two trombones (1973), with Watanabe (1977), and as the leader of a jazz-rock septet (*Hunt up Wind*, 1978, JVC 6015). (*Feather–Gitler '70s*)

Fulbright, Dick [Richard W.] (*b* Paris, TX, 1901; *d* New York, 17 Nov 1962). Double bass and tuba player. He toured with the Virginia Minstrels before working with the bandleader Alonzo Ross (1926–8), and played for a season in Florida with Luckey Roberts. He settled in New York, where he worked with Bingie Madison (1929, *c*1930) and Elmer Snowden (1931–2), and recorded with Clarence Williams (1930, 1934) and Frankie Newton (1937). He also joined Teddy Hill's band, with which he toured Europe in 1937. While in Paris he made a few recordings with Dicky Wells, and his playing on double bass may be heard to advantage on *Between the Devil and the Deep Blue Sea* (1937, Swing 6). After returning to New York Fulbright played in a band led by the pianist Dave Martin, and in December 1939 joined Zutty Singleton; he returned to Martin in 1941, then worked with Alberto Socarras from 1943 to 1947. He later worked as a freelance in New York, playing with Noble Sissle and Buck Washington among others, before retiring in 1958.

based on *ChiltonW*

Fulford, Tommy (*b* 1912; *d* New York, 16 Dec 1956). Pianist. In 1936 he played with Blanche Calloway in Indianapolis, then the same year moved to New York, where he performed with Snub Mosley and joined Chick Webb (for illustration *see* WEBB, CHICK). Apart from a brief absence in 1939 he remained with the band until 1942, working after Webb's death under the leadership of Ella Fitzgerald; his playing may be heard to advantage on Webb's *I ain't got nobody* (1937, Decca 1513). During the rest of the 1940s and the early 1950s Fulford worked as a solo pianist, then in 1955–6 played with Tony Parenti.

based on *ChiltonW*

Full, Romano. *See* MUSSOLINI, ROMANO.

Fuller, Bob [Robert] (*b* New York, *c*1898). Clarinetist and saxophonist. In the early 1920s he made a nationwide tour with Mamie Smith. He then became a freelance studio musician in New York and took part in sessions with numerous classic blues singers, including Bessie Smith. From 1925 to 1928 he made a large number of recordings as leader of a trio with Lou Hooper and Elmer Snowden; a good example of his clarinet playing may be heard on the group's *F Miner Blues* (1926, Voc. 1004), made under the pseudonym the Three Jolly Miners. Fuller also recorded with the Kansas City Five, which included Bubber Miley (1924) and Louis Metcalf (1925). After leading his own band in a long residency at the 125th Street Dance Hall Fuller retired from music and worked as a jailer.

based on *ChiltonW*

Fuller, Curtis (Dubois) (*b* Detroit, 15 Dec 1934). Trombonist and composer. His first important engagement was with an army band led by Cannonball Adderley (1953–5). He then played with Kenny Burrell and Yusef Lateef in Detroit and moved to New York, where he quickly became known for his powerful style. Later he performed and recorded as a leader, with the Jazztet (1959–60), and with Art Blakey's Jazz Messengers (1961–5). After touring Europe with Dizzy Gillespie's big band (1968) he worked as a freelance in New York. In the mid-1970s he engaged several young musicians, including Stanley Clarke and the electric guitarist Bill Washer, and recorded in a style that, though still rooted in bop, employed electric and electronic instruments. Fuller's work in this vein may be heard to advantage on the album *Crankin'* (*c*1973). Fuller toured with Count Basie from 1975 to 1977. In 1978 he recorded two albums as a leader, and in 1979–80 he led the hard-bop quintet Giant Bones with Kai Winding; he also recorded as a sideman with Blakey (1977–8), Cedar Walton (1979, 1983), and Benny Golson (1980–81). From the early 1980s he has toured Europe regularly with the Timeless All Stars and performed and recorded with the Jazztet.

Fuller reached maturity as a musician after he became acquainted with J. J. Johnson's use of the trombone as a solo instrument. While he associates his harmonic approach with that of Miles Davis, the life and work of John Coltrane have influenced his approach most profoundly. His technique allows him to overcome the innate clumsiness of his instrument, and he is able to execute rapid passages and wide leaps with ease. His solos are marked by effective contrasts and harmonic adventurousness; his rhapsodic sense of rhythm is inspired by the pulses of language, and derives in part from Coltrane's techniques in this area.

SELECTED RECORDINGS

As leader: *New Trombone* (1957, Prst. 7107); *Blues-ette* (1959, Savoy 12141); *Curtis Fuller's Jazztet* (1959, Savoy 12143); *Crankin'* (*c*1973, Mstr. 333); *Fire and Filigree* (1978, BH 7007); with K. Winding: *Giant Bones 80* (1979, Sonet 834)

As sideman: J. Coltrane: *Blue Train* (1957, BN 1577); A. Farmer and B. Golson: *Meet the Jazztet* (1960, Argo 664); A. Blakey: *Caravan* (1962, Riv. 9438); Timeless All Stars: *It's Timeless* (1982, Tim. 178)

BIBLIOGRAPHY

G. Lees: "Curtis Fuller," *DB*, xxix/5 (1962), 16
L. Tomkins: "The Curtis Fuller Story," *CI*, xiv/6 (1976), 6
B. Rusch: "Curtis Fuller: Interview," *Cadence*, ii/6–7 (1977), 5
A. Sussman: "Curtis Fuller's Great Depression," *DB*, xlviii/3 (1981), 24 [incl. discography]

ANDREW WAGGONER

Fuller, (Walter) Gil(bert) (*b* Los Angeles, 14 April 1920). Arranger. He began to transcribe big-band arrangements and tour with local bands while still in high school. After studying engineering at New York University, in the early 1940s he wrote for swing and Latin bandleaders, including Charlie Barnet and Tito Puente. He began to collaborate with Dizzy Gillespie in 1942, when both were associated with Les Hite, and the two continued to work together in Billy Eckstine's orchestra (1944). The first important recordings of Fuller's arrangements were made by Gillespie's sextet and big band in 1946 and include *Oop-bop-sh'bam*, on which Fuller may be heard scat singing; among other work he did for Gillespie was the orchestration of the latter's composition *Manteca* and the music for his concert in Carnegie Hall in 1948. Fuller recorded with his own big band in 1949 (*The Scene Changes*, Dis. 115) but thereafter pursued a career in engineering. He continued to write occasionally, most notably for Stan Kenton (1955), Ray Charles (1962), and Gillespie and Kenton (1966). He is regarded as one of the most influential arrangers in the bop style.

SELECTED ARRANGEMENTS

(all recorded by D. Gillespie)

* – with Fuller as sideman

*Oop-bop-sh'bam (1946, Musi. 383); Things to Come (1946, Musi. 447); Manteca (1947, Vic. 20-3023)

BIBLIOGRAPHY

G. Hoefer: "The Hot Box: Gil Fuller," *DB*, xxxi/9 (1964), 23
L. Feather: "Gil Fuller: Unrecognized Titan," *DB*, xxxiii/4 (1966), 20

ANDREW JAFFE

Fuller, Walter [Rosetta] (*b* Dyersburg, TN, 15 Feb 1910). Trumpeter and singer. He learned mellophone and trumpet at an early age, and made his professional début at the age of 14 with a medicine show. In 1925 he moved to Chicago, and from 1927 to 1930 played with the bandleader and pianist Sammy Stewart. In 1931 Fuller joined Earl Hines's orchestra, where he was a valuable sideman (for illustration *see* HINES, EARL). He played briefly with Horace Henderson in 1937–8, then left Hines in 1940 to form his own group, which from 1946 was based in San Diego. Although he then worked in obscurity for decades, Fuller was still active in the early 1980s. His early style (as heard on *Wolverine Blues*, 1934) was heavily indebted to that of Louis Armstrong, but he later came under the influence of Harry Edison, as may be heard on *G. T. Stomp* and *Lightly and Politely* (both 1939), and Roy Eldridge. Fuller is a talented trumpeter whose playing is often exciting; his solos contributed much to the sound of Hines's band. His exuberant singing on Hines's first recording of *Rosetta* (1934) earned him his nickname.

SELECTED RECORDINGS

As sideman with E. Hines: Rosetta (1934, Decca 337); Wolverine Blues (1934, Decca 577); G. T. Stomp (1939, Bb 10391); Lightly and Politely (1939, Bb 10727)

As sideman with L. Hampton: Down Home Jump/Rock Hill Special (1938, Vic. 26114); Fiddle Diddle (1938, Vic. 26173)

BIBLIOGRAPHY

ChiltonW
W. C. Fuller and H. Openeer, Jr.: "A Walter Fuller Story," *Doctor jazz*, no.39 (1969), 2
S. Dance: *The World of Earl Hines* (New York, 1977) [interviews], 166

SCOTT YANOW

Funk. (1) [funky jazz]. Synonym for SOUL JAZZ, used in the 1950s.

(2) A style of black American popular music which developed in the mid-1960s out of soul music. It is characterized above all else by complex, interlocking, syncopated rhythmic patterns in duple meter.

Funky Butt Hall. Venue in New Orleans; *see* NIGHTCLUBS AND OTHER VENUES.

Fusion. A term which came to be substituted for JAZZ-ROCK from the mid-1970s and which is applied predominantly to that style, but which has also been more generally applied after that period to closely related syntheses of jazz and soul music, jazz and pop, jazz and funk, jazz and light music, and jazz and folk music.

Fuzz. An electronic treatment that adds complex partials to a signal by means of a frequency multiplier. It imparts a harsh, unfocused timbre to the sound of an amplified instrument such as an electric guitar.

G

Gabriel, Percy (Julian) (*b* New Orleans, 11 July 1915). Double bass player. His father Manny (Martin Joseph) Gabriel (*b* New Orleans, 1876; *d* New Orleans, 25 Nov 1932) was a noted musician. Percy first played in a family band and in a trio led by his brother Clarence (*b* New Orleans, 3 June 1905; *d* New Orleans, *c*1982), a banjoist and pianist. Later he worked with Kid Rena and with Harold Dejan on boats sailing to New York. After spending some time in New York he traveled to Florida with the singer Jack Sneed (1938), then returned to New Orleans, where he played with Papa Celestin, Sidney Desvigne, A. J. Piron, and others. He went to Texas with Don Albert, led his own band in New Orleans (1939–42), and worked in Chicago with Lee Collins and Henry "Red" Allen. From 1944 to 1947 he toured with Jay McShann, but left the band in California to work with Jesse Price; he returned to New Orleans with Paul Barbarin, then toured with Lucky Millinder, Danny Barker, and Blue Lu Barker. Gabriel made few recordings, but his playing may be heard to advantage under the leadership of Blue Lu Barker on *Bow Legged Daddy* (1949, Cap. 807). In 1950 he moved to Detroit, where he played extensively and formed a band with his brother Martin Manuel (Manny) (*b* New Orleans, 9 Sept 1898), a clarinetist. He continued to perform into the 1970s. His nephew is the saxophonist Clarence Ford (*b* New Orleans, 1929).

BIBLIOGRAPHY

K. G. Zur Heide: "Percy and the Gabriel Family," *Fn*, vii/1 (1976), 4
B. Byler: "Percy and the Musical Gabriels," *MR*, iv/3 (1977), 8

based on *ChiltonW*

Gadd, Steve [Stephen K.] (*b* Rochester, NY, *c*1945). Drummer. He began playing drums at the age of three, and started formal lessons four years later. He attended both the Manhattan and Eastman schools of music, during which time he also performed with Gap Mangione (1971–2) and Sal Nistico (ii), and played in Europe with Chuck Mangione. After graduating he joined an army band, then formed a rock group and moved to New York. His work in studios there has included sessions with, among others, Chick Corea (1975–81), Roland Hanna, Bob James, and Quincy Jones; he has also performed with many popular groups and singers, such as James Brown, Aretha Franklin, Paul Simon, Stevie Wonder, and Steely Dan. In the early 1980s he toured with Al Di Meola, Tom Scott, Richard Tee, and Sadao Watanabe.

Ex.1 "Linear" drumming pattern on *Lenore*, from C. Corea: *The Leprechaun* (1975, Pol. 6062); transcr. C. Braman

Although Gadd is highly accomplished in the jazz drumming styles of the 1960s, his most notable innovations have been within the drumming styles of pop music and fusion. Some of his most intricate work has been with Corea: on *Lenore* he demonstrates his unique "linear" approach, in which the individual elements of the drum kit are rarely sounded simultaneously (ex.1).

SELECTED RECORDINGS

As sideman: on G. Washington, Jr.: *Feels so Good* (1975, Kudu 24), The Sea Lion; C. Corea: *The Leprechaun* (1975, Pol. 6062), incl. Lenore; *Friends* (1978, Pol. 6160); *Three Quartets* (1981, WB 9552); A. Di Meola: *Tour de force: Live* (1982, Col. FC38373)

BIBLIOGRAPHY

A. J. Smith: "Steve Gadd: Have Skins, Will Beat," *DB*, xliii/2 (1976), 14
A. Wald: "Steve Gadd: Playin' for the Music," *MD*, ii/4 (1978), 6
L. Tomkins: "Drummer of the Decade: Steve Gadd," *CI*, xix/7 (1981), 20
D. Pitt: "Gadd about Town," *DB*, xlix/7 (1982), 14 [incl. discography]
R. Mattingly: "Gadd," *MD*, vii/7 (1983), 8
R. Santelli: "Steve Gadd," *MD*, x/i (1986), 19
G. Kalbacher: "The Gadd Gang: Not Just the Same Old Stuff," *DB*, liv/10 (1987), 17 [incl. discography]

CHUCK BRAMAN

Gafa, Al(exander) (*b* New York, 9 April 1941). Guitarist. Between 1964 and 1969 he worked as a studio musician in New York and with Kai Winding (1966–7), Michel Legrand, Sam Donahue (1967–8), and Duke Pearson (1968–9). He was Carmen McRae's music director (*c*1969–71), then, after playing briefly with Dizzy Gillespie in 1971, recorded with Mike Longo (*c*1971–2); he played again with Gillespie in 1974–6, touring Europe and recording an album. From 1976 he led a series of small bop groups, among the members of which were Kenny Barron, Al Foster, and Andy LaVerne; he recorded the album *Leblon*

Beach (Pablo 2310782) with a quintet in 1976. While continuing to be active as a leader he was a member of Johnny Hartman's quartet (1978–82) and recorded with Joe Albany (1982). From 1980 he also worked in musical theater.

BIBLIOGRAPHY

Feather–Gitler '70s
M. J. Summerfield: *The Jazz Guitar* (Gateshead, England, 1978)

Gaillard, Slim [Bulee] (*b* Detroit, 1 Jan 1916). Singer, guitarist, and pianist. He first came to prominence in the late 1930s in a duo with Slam Stewart which toured and recorded with considerable success. When Stewart was drafted he was replaced by the double bass player Tiny "Bam" Brown. In 1941 Gaillard moved to Los Angeles, where he appeared in several films, most notably *Hellzapoppin'* (1941). During the 1940s he also performed and recorded with such musicians as Dizzy Gillespie, Dodo Marmarosa, Charlie Parker, and Leo Watson. With Brown he composed his masterpiece, *Opera in vout*, a performance of which was recorded in 1946. 'Vout' is a humorous language invented by Gaillard in which he inserts nonsense syllables into everyday words; the lyrics to many of his songs are in this style. Although later in the decade radio broadcasts sustained his career, during the 1950s his popularity faded. He concentrated on acting in the 1960s and 1970s, but in 1970 he reunited with Stewart for an appearance at the Monterey Jazz Festival. In the early 1980s he returned to prominence, performing at festivals in Europe and playing in London, where he recorded with Buddy Tate and others.

SELECTED RECORDINGS

As leader: The Flat Foot Floogie (1938, Voc. 4021); Tutti frutti (1938, Voc. 4225); Slim's Jam (1945, Bell Tone 761); *Opera in vout* (1946, Disc 6022-3) [album of 78 r.p.m. discs]; with B. Tate: *Anytime, Anyplace, Anywhere* (1982, Hep 2020)

BIBLIOGRAPHY

J. Burns: "Slim and Slam," *JJ*, xxi/9 (1968), 4
P. Budge: "A Matter of Taste," *The Wire*, no. 2 (1982), 8
S. Voce: "Slim Gaillard," *JJI*, xxxv/10 (1982), 20 [interview]
P. Bradshaw: "Voutie o roonie o scoodileroosimoe," *New Musical Express* (19 Jan 1985)
M. Doyle and P. Lowe: "Slim Gaillard Discography," *Discographical Forum*, no. 49 (1985), p. 4; no. 50 (1985), p. 3
M. Zwerin: "Vout's up, Doc?," *The Wire*, no. 19 (1985), 8
N. Darwen: "Slim Gaillard," *Blues & Rhythm: the Gospel Truth*, no. 21 (1986), 15 [interview]
S. Gaillard: *I was There* (London, 1986) [autobiography]

STAN BRITT

Gaines, Charlie [Charles] (*b* Philadelphia, 8 Aug 1900). Trumpeter and bandleader. He played with Charlie Taylor's dance band (1918–20) and in Atlantic City, New Jersey, with Charlie Johnson (1920). In 1921 he moved to New York, where he was based until 1930; he performed there with Johnson and Wilbur Sweatman, and recorded with the blues singer Mary Stafford. After touring with Earl Walton (1922–5) he played with the violinist LeRoy Smith (1925–9) and recorded with Smith (1928), the blues singers Elvira Johnson (1926) and Edith Wilson (1929), Fats Waller (1929), and Clarence Williams (1929–30). He played with Smith in Philadelphia (1930–31), then returned to New York to record with Louis Armstrong (1932) and Williams (1934). By 1930 he had formed the first of a series of bands in Philadelphia with which he performed steadily through the 1970s. Waller's recording *The Minor Drag* (1929, Vic. 38050) includes a solo by Gaines.

BIBLIOGRAPHY

ChiltonW
R. Shor: "Charlie Gaines," *Sv*, no. 68 (1976–7), 44

Galaxie Dream Band. Group formed in 1972 by GUNTER HAMPEL.

Galaxy. Record label. It was established by Max and Sol Weiss in Berkeley, California, in 1964. A subsidiary of Fantasy, it was used at first to issue only a few recordings. One of these was a collection of bop recordings made in the late 1940s in Detroit by Sonny Stitt and Milt Jackson for a small company, Sensation, that the Weiss brothers had acquired. Galaxy was sold with Fantasy to Saul Zaentz's corporation in 1967, but the label remained dormant for ten years. Thereafter it was revived, and a catalogue of more than 50 albums quickly accumulated; these included 12 by Art Pepper, and others by Hank Jones, Tommy Flanagan, Red Garland, Ira Sullivan, Philly Joe Jones, Roy Haynes, Johnny Griffin, Shelly Manne, Chet Baker, Stanley Cowell, and Nat Adderley. By the late 1980s, however, much of the catalogue had been deleted, although some sessions had been transferred to compact disc.

MARK GARDNER

Galbraith, (Joseph) Barry (*b* Pittsburgh, 18 Dec 1919; *d* Bennington, VT, 13 Jan 1983). Guitarist. In 1941 he moved to New York, where he performed with Babe Russin, Art Tatum, Red Norvo, Hal McIntyre, and the bandleader Teddy Powell. He was a member of Claude Thornhill's band from 1941 to 1942 and again, after army service, from 1946 to 1949. Thereafter he worked principally as a studio musician and recorded with numerous artists, including Benny Goodman, Ella Fitzgerald, Tony Bennett, Tal Farlow, and Gil Evans; he also toured with Stan Kenton in 1953. He played a prominent role in the film *After Hours* in 1961. From 1970 he devoted most of his time to teaching, and in 1982 published the *Barry Galbraith Guitar Study Series*. Galbraith was influenced by Eddie Lang, Carl Kress, Dick McDonough, George Van Eps, and Charlie Christian. He was highly respected for his sophisticated bop improvisations as well as his sight reading skills.

SELECTED RECORDINGS

As leader: *Guitar and the Wind* (1958, Decca 9200)
As sideman: T. Farlow: *The Tal Farlow Album* (1954, Norg. 35–6); on G. Evans: *Into the Hot* (1961, Imp. 9), Barry's Tune

BIBLIOGRAPHY

FeatherE
A. Berle: "Jazz Guitar: it's Nothing to Mess with unless you're Serious," *GP*, x/7 (1976), 24

JIM FERGUSON

Galbraith, Charlie [Charles Alfred] (*b* London, 13 Aug 1920). English trombonist and bandleader. He learned trombone in 1945 and later led his own band (1949). After working as a freelance, notably with Sidney Bechet in Paris (1950), he formed a second band (1951); its principal soloists included Kenny Ball. He also worked with the trumpeter Bobby Mickleburgh (1955–7) and recorded with Ball (1957). From the late 1950s he led a successful band which played in the style that came to be known as "trad." He recorded as a leader (1962) and played with Monty Sunshine (1968) and the drummer Joe Daniels. He formed a new band in 1969, and in the 1970s and 1980s worked regularly in England and (from 1978) Paris. His recordings include *Portrait* (*c*1979, Plant Life 006).

DIGBY FAIRWEATHER

Galbraith, Gus (*b* England, *c*1930). English trumpeter and flugelhorn player. He formed his own band, the Original Climax Jazz Band, in 1956, and re-formed it as a septet in the following year; this group, which played mainstream jazz, included Dick

Morrissey and (later) Peter King. From 1960 to 1964 Galbraith was a member of John Dankworth's orchestra, with which he recorded the album *What the Dickens!* (1963, Fon. 5203). After a period in South Africa (1965–*c*1966) he returned to England, where until 1971 he was active as a freelance musician; among the groups with which he played was the orchestra of Bobby Lamb and Ray Premru, which performed and recorded at Ronnie Scott's club in London in 1971. Galbraith then settled permanently in Johannesburg, and concentrated on composing for television.

DIGBY FAIRWEATHER

Gale, Eric (*b* New York, 20 Sept 1938). Guitarist. He worked briefly as a chemist before embarking on a career as a musician in the early 1960s. He taught himself to play guitar and toured with rhythm-and-blues musicians. He moved to New York where he worked as a session player with King Curtis (1963–70), Jimmy Smith (1967), David "Fathead" Newman (1968, 1970), Mongo Santamaria (1970), the soul singer Aretha Franklin (1970), Grover Washington, Jr. (1971–6), Stanley Turrentine (1971–7), and many others; around 1970 he became the permanent guitarist for the CTI record label. He also recorded with Johnny Hodges and Clark Terry (1966), Sonny Stitt (1968), and Carla Bley (1976). In 1973 he recorded *Forecast*, his first of several albums as a leader. After a brief retirement in Jamaica in 1975 he joined the rhythm-and-blues group Stuff and in 1982 he formed his own ensemble. Gale has a robust style that draws on his background as a rhythm-and-blues player.

SELECTED RECORDINGS

Forecast (1973, Kudu 11); *Ginseng Woman* (1976, Col. PC34421); *Part of you* (1979, Col. JC35715); *A Touch of Silk* (1980, Col. JC36570); *Blue Horizon* (1981, Elek. Mus. 60022); *Island Breeze* (1982, Elek. Mus. 60198)

BIBLIOGRAPHY

J. Obrecht and A. J. Smith: "Eric Gale: R & B–Funk Sideman, Soloist with Stuff," *GP*, xiii/9 (1979), 44 [incl. discography]

PATRICK T. WILL

Gales, Larry [Lawrence Bernard] (*b* New York, 25 March 1936). Double bass player. He studied double bass from the age of 11 with George Duvivier and later attended the Manhattan School of Music (1956). In 1960 he played with J. C. Heard and joined the quintet led by Eddie "Lockjaw" Davis and Johnny Griffin. He then played with Herbie Mann (1962) and the trio led by Junior Mance (1963–4), with whom he had already recorded (1961); while with Mance he also worked as an accompanist to Joe Williams. Gales played with Thelonious Monk from 1964 until 1969, when he moved to California and joined Erroll Garner. During the 1960s he made many recordings with the groups to which he belonged and with other leaders, among them Buddy Tate (1960), Bennie Green (1961), Charlie Rouse (1962), and Sonny Stitt and Mary Lou Williams (1963–4). After 1970 he played again with Joe Williams and with Willie Bobo, Red Rodney, Harold Land, Harry Edison, and Bill Berry. With Benny Carter he toured Japan (1973) and performed in California (1973–5, 1981). He recorded with Blue Mitchell (1971), Jimmy Smith (1974), Sonny Criss (1975), Clark Terry (1975–6), Dave Frishberg, Joe Turner (ii) (1977), and Kenny Burrell (1978). A fine player in the mainstream tradition, Gales combines a dependable technique with creativity and a deep, rich sound.

SELECTED RECORDINGS

As sideman: E. Davis and J. Griffin: *Tough Tenors* (1960, Jlnd 931); S. Stitt: *Sonny Stitt goes Latin* (1963, Roost 2253); T. Monk: *Underground* (1967–8, Col. CS9632); *Monk's Blues* (1968, Col. CS9806); C. Terry: *Clark Terry and his Jolly Giants* (1976, Van. 79365); K. Burrell: *When Lights are Low* (1978, Conc. 83)

BIBLIOGRAPHY

Feather '60s; *Feather–Gitler '70s*
"Dictionnaire de la contrebasse," *Jm*, no.166 (1969), 38

GARY CARNER

Gallery. Cooperative group formed in 1980 by David Darling, Michael Di Pasqua, Paul McCandless, and Dave Samuels. Other musicians who played with the group included Michael Formanek and the bass player Ratzo Harris.

Galli, Cesare (*b* Milan, 1908). Italian violinist, saxophonist, and bandleader. He studied violin as a youth and took up tenor saxophone around 1924, from which time he played in several bands that played an amalgam of jazz and dance music; these included the Mediolana Band (from 1926), the All Devils (to 1929), and the Ambassadors (from 1929), led by Carlo Benzi. He played in Sanremo, Italy, Milan, and Monte Carlo in the early 1930s, and in 1934 formed a band for an engagement at Mariánské Lázně, Czechoslovakia; he later led dance orchestras in northern Italy and recorded with a group led by Arturo Agazzi in 1932. In the 1940s he made recordings as a leader, including *Nobody's Sweetheart* (1940, Tel. A9074). As a violinist Galli was influenced chiefly by Joe Venuti.

ADRIANO MAZZOLETTI

Galloway, Jim [James Braidie] (*b* Kilwinning, Scotland, 28 July 1936). Canadian saxophonist of Scottish birth. In Glasgow he worked with Alex Dulgleish and led the Jazzmakers; after emigrating to Canada in 1964 he settled in Toronto. He assumed leadership of the Metro Stompers (1968), formed the swing group Wee Big Band (1978), and was the host of the weekly radio program "Toronto Alive!" (1981–7); he also performed at festivals in Europe and made recordings as a leader and as a sideman with Jay McShann (including *Thou Swell*, 1981, Sack. 4011), Buddy Tate, Dick Wellstood, and Ralph Sutton. Galloway plays soprano saxophone in a lyrical style reminiscent of that of Sidney Bechet and is also a capable swing player on the tenor and baritone saxophones.

BIBLIOGRAPHY

M. Jones: "Galloway's Heading the Soprano Invasion," *MM*, liii (8 April 1978), 44
L. Tomkins: "Keeping the Traditions Alive," *CI*, xviii/9 (1980), 16
M. Miller: "Galloway, Jim," *Encyclopedia of Music in Canada*, ed. H. Kallmann, G. Potvin, and K. Winters (Toronto, Buffalo, and London, 1981)
J. Norris: "Jim Galloway," *Coda*, no. 189 (1983), 8
M. Miller: "Jim Galloway," *Boogie, Pete & the Senator: Canadian Musicians in Jazz: the Eighties* (Toronto, 1987), 119

MARK MILLER

Galper, Hal [Harold] (*b* Salem, MA, 18 April 1938). Pianist. He received classical training (1945–8), and studied jazz at the Berklee College of Music (1955–8); his first important engagements were in Boston from 1959. He worked with a variety of performers and ensembles, including Herb Pomeroy's big band, Sam Rivers, Tony Williams, Chet Baker, Stan Getz, the Brecker brothers, Bobby Hutcherson, and Attila Zoller, and also accompanied several singers, among them Joe Williams and Anita O'Day. In 1973–5 he played electric piano in Cannonball Adderley's quintet, but he quickly became dissatisfied with the instrument. He received a grant from the NEA in the mid-1970s, which allowed him to give three concerts. In 1981 he joined Phil Woods's quintet. He has also contributed instructional articles to *Down Beat*. Galper's approach is firmly rooted in the bop tradition, but he shows inventiveness in all his work, from his harmonically sophisticated solos, notable for his fluid interaction with other musicians, to his ensemble playing in the context of the more formal arrangements of Woods's group.

SELECTED RECORDINGS

Duos with L. Konitz: *Windows* (1975, Ste. 1057)

As leader: *Inner Journey* (1973, Mstr. 398); *Reach Out* (1976, Ste. 1067); *Ivory Forest* (1979, Enja 3053)

As sideman: C. Baker: *Baby Breeze* (1965, Lml. 86003); S. Rivers: *A New Conception* (1966, BN 84249); P. Woods: *Birds of a Feather* (1981, Ant. 1006)

BIBLIOGRAPHY

A. J. Smith: "Profile: Hal Galper," *DB*, xliv/12 (1977), 46

J. Levenson: "Hal Galper: a Home in the Woods," *DB*, xlix/11 (1982), 24 [incl. discography]

PAUL RINZLER

Gandee, Al(bert) (*b* 1900; *d* Cincinnati, 3 June 1944). Trombonist. In 1924 he joined the Wolverines (for illustrations *see* RECORDING, fig.3, and WOLVERINES), with whom he toured briefly and recorded four titles, including *Jazz me Blues* (1924, Gen. 5408). He left the group to work in his own dairy business, but continued to play regularly in a theater orchestra in Cincinnati.

based on *ChiltonW*

Ganelin, Vyacheslav (Shevelevich) (*b* Kraskovo, nr Zhukovsky, Russian SFSR, 17 Dec 1944). Russian pianist and composer. He played in dance bands from 1961, formed a jazz trio in 1964, and attended the Lithuanian State Conservatory in Vilnius (graduated 1968). With Vladimir Tarasov he formed a duo in 1969; this became the Ganelin Trio (later known as the G–T–Ch Trio) when they were joined by Vladimir Chekasin in 1971. The group played free jazz in the USSR, Europe, Cuba, and in 1986 at the Jazzyatra festival in India and the JVC Festival in New York, and made many recordings, including *Con anima* (1977, Mel. C60073612), before disbanding in 1987; Ganelin and Tarasov also resumed their work as a duo for a recording in 1983. Ganelin's compositions include a ballet, *Pugachov* (1970), a rock opera, *Chortova nevesta* (The devil's bride; 1973), and an opera, *Rïzhaya lgun'ya i soldat* (The red-haired liar and the soldier; 1977). In addition to piano, on some recordings he may be heard playing synthesizer and various wind instruments. He emigrated to Israel in 1987.

BIBLIOGRAPHY

B. Noglik: "Wjatscheslaw Ganelin, Wladimir Tschekassin, Wladimir Tarassow," *Jazzwerkstatt international* (Berlin, 1981), 29 [incl. interview, discography]

F. Maino: "Ganelin, Tarasov, and Chekasin: Interview," *Cadence*, ix/1 (1983), 18

L. Feigin: "New Sound from behind the Iron Curtain," *The Wire*, no.7 (1984), 9

A. Duncan: "Soviet Trio Takes Daring Liberties with Familiar Jazz Styles," *Christian Science Monitor* (30 June 1986), 29

H. Mandel: "The Ganelin Trio: Jazz Detente," *DB*, liii/9 (1986), 26 [incl. discography]

WALTER OJAKÄÄR

Ganley, Allan (*b* Tolworth, England, 11 March 1931). English drummer. He played and recorded with John Dankworth (1953–5), Derek Smith (1955), and the New Jazz Group with Smith and Dizzy Reece (1956); he recorded with Mary Lou Williams (1953), Vic Ash (1954–8), Cleo Laine (1955), and Ronnie Scott (1956). After touring the USA with Scott (1957) and recording as the leader of a quartet (1957, 1958) he formed the Jazzmakers, which he led with Ronnie Ross from 1958 to 1960 and which performed at the Newport Jazz Festival in 1959. He recorded with Dave Brubeck (1961), belonged to Tubby Hayes's quintet (1962–4, recording in 1962 and 1964), and recorded with Dankworth and Laine (1964); as the resident drummer at Scott's club in London (1964–7) he accompanied Stan Getz, Freddie Hubbard, Roland Kirk, Jim Hall, and Art Farmer; he also recorded with Blossom Dearie (1966). After studying arranging at the Berklee College of Music (1970) he led a big band (1976–86), of which Ash, Kenny Wheeler, and Chris Pyne were members; at the same time he recorded with Hall, Tommy Flanagan, Ron Carter, and Art Farmer on Hall's album *Commitment* (1976, A&M Hor. 715, performing on the tracks *Indian Summer* and *Walk Soft*), with Al Haig (1977), and with Trombone Summit (1980). Later he worked as an arranger for Ross, Peter King, and others (from 1983), and as a composer (1986). (*FeatherE*; *Feather '60s*)

Garanyan, Georgy (Aramovich) (*b* Moscow, 15 Aug 1934). Russian alto saxophonist, composer, and bandleader of Armenian descent. He taught himself to play saxophone, worked as an amateur (1954–8), and played in Oleg Lundstrem's orchestra (1958–66). He belonged to the Kontsertny estradny orkestr Tsentral'novo TV i Vsesoyuznovo Radio (Concert variety orchestra of the central TV and all-union radio) from 1966 to 1970, and after studying conducting at the Moscow P. I. Tchaikovsky State Conservatory (until 1969) he led the orchestra from 1970 until it disbanded in 1973; he also led the Melodiya orchestra (1973–80) and the symphony orchestra of the ministry of cinematography (1973–6). As a saxophonist he has played at festivals in the USSR, Warsaw, Prague, Bombay, Havana, and Zagreb, Yugoslavia, and made many recordings, including *Labirint* (1974, Mel. C60052778). He was named a Merited Artist of the Russian SFSR in 1981. (S. F. Starr: *Red and Hot: the Fate of Jazz in the Soviet Union, 1917–1980* (New York, and Oxford, England, 1983), 247)

WALTER OJAKÄÄR

Garbarek, Jan (*b* Mysen, Norway, 4 March 1947). Norwegian tenor saxophonist. He was influenced at an early age by the music of John Coltrane and in 1965 came to the attention of Krzysztof Komeda and George Russell; the following year he appeared at festivals in Warsaw, where he made his first recording, and Prague. Later he performed and recorded with the sextet and big band of Russell, with whom he also studied music. In the late 1960s he formed a quartet with Terje Rypdal that often performed with Russell, and from 1973 he led a trio. He toured Europe and the USA as a member of Keith Jarrett's quartet in 1977, then formed a group with Eberhard Weber, the guitarist David Torn, and the drummer Michael Di Pasqua that performed in Warsaw in 1982 and later toured Europe, the USA, Japan, and Norway. Garbarek composed most of the music that he has recorded, and he has also written works for the theater, television, and films. As a saxophonist he combines elements of free jazz, jazz-rock, folk music, and the music of the European avant garde.

SELECTED RECORDINGS

(recorded for ECM unless otherwise indicated)

Duos with R. Towner: *Dis* (1976, 1093)

As leader: *The Esoteric Circle* (*c*1969, FD 10125); *Afric Pepperbird* (1970, 1007); *Triptykon* (1972, 1029); *Witchi-tai-to* (1973, 1041); with K. Jarrett: *Luminessence* (1974, 1049), *Belonging* (1974, 1050); with B. Stenson: *Dansere* (1975, 1075); with K. Jarrett: *My Song* (1977, 1115); *Wayfarer* (1983, 1259); with Z. Hussain and T. Gurtu: *Song for Everyone* (1985, 1286); *It's OK to Listen to the Gray Voice* (1985, 1294); *All those Born with Wings* (1987, 1324)

As sideman with C. Haden: *Magico* (1979, 1151); *Folk Songs* (1979, 1170)

BIBLIOGRAPHY

R. Hultin: "Jan Garbarek: a Remarkable Jazz Personality," *JF* [intl edn], no.40 (1976), 51

S. Lake: "Jan Garbarek: Saga of Fire and Ice," *DB*, xliv/19 (1977), 16 [incl. discography]

Jan Garbarek

M. Tucker: "Jan Garbarek: beyond the Nordic Ethos," *JJI*, xxx/10 (1977), 6 [incl. discography]
L. Tomkins: "From Norway to New Horizons: Jan Garbarek," *CI*, xix/12 (1981), 6
P. Brodowski and J. Szprot: "Jan Garbarek: Mysterious Wayfarer," *JF* [intl edn], no.86 (1984), 39 [incl. discography]
M. Tucker: "Jan Garbarek: the Poetics of Space," *The Wire*, no.7 (1984), 17
M. Bourne: "Jan Garbarek's Scandinavian Design," *DB*, liii/7 (1986), 26 [incl. discography]

RANDI HULTIN

Garcia, Dick [Richard Joseph] (*b* New York, 11 May 1931). Electric guitarist. He taught himself to play guitar at the age of nine and only later took lessons. He played with Tony Scott's quartet (1950) and performed and recorded with George Shearing (1952), Charlie Parker (1953), and Joe Roland (1955). In 1955 he played and recorded with Scott and recorded with Milt Buckner, Lenny Hambro, and his own groups; he also recorded with the trumpeter Johnny Glasel (1956) and the pianist Bobby Scott (1957). He toured and recorded with Shearing from 1959 to 1961 and recorded with Kai Winding in 1963. Garcia can be heard playing electric guitar on his album *Message from Garcia* (1955, Dawn 1106). (*FeatherE*)

Garcia, King [Louis K.] (*b* Juncos, PR, 25 Aug 1905; *d* Los Angeles, 9 April 1983). Trumpeter. He played in the Municipal Band of San Juan, then in the early 1920s moved to the USA. In New York he worked with the Original Dixieland Jazz Band (*c*1926), spent several years in the orchestra led by Emil Coleman, and recorded with the Dorsey brothers (1930–31) and Vic Berton (1935). He also recorded five titles, including *Swing, Mr. Charlie* (1936, Bb 6357), as leader of the Swing Band, an octet that included Joe Marsala. Thereafter he played in the big bands of Richard Himber (1936), Nat Brandwyne (1937–8), and Louis Prima (1939), and worked as a studio musician. From the late 1940s he led a Latin band. Shortly after moving to California in 1960 he was forced by ill-health to retire.

based on *ChiltonW*

Garcia, Russ(ell) (*b* Oakland, CA, 12 April 1916). Arranger, composer, and trumpeter. He studied with a number of composers, including Mario Castelnuovo-Tedesco and Ernst Krenek. After playing in the dance bands of Al Donahue and Horace Heidt he wrote studio arrangements, many of which employed strings, for Buddy DeFranco (1953–4), Charlie Barnet (1956), Roy Eldridge (1957), Johnny Hodges (in Stuttgart, Germany, 1958), Ray Brown (1960), and many others. He also wrote scores for television and films, and for Stan Kenton's Neophonic Orchestra (1965). His third-stream composition Variations, for flugelhorn, string quartet, bass, and drums, was recorded in 1979 (Trend 552). Garcia recorded as a leader in the West Coast style (1955–7), and his playing is well represented on the album *Rocky Road* (1955, Beth. 1040). (*FeatherE*; *Feather '60s*)

Gardner, Jack [Francis Henry; Jumbo Jack] (*b* Joliet, IL, 14 Aug 1903; *d* Dallas, 26 Nov 1957). Pianist and composer. In 1923 he moved to Chicago, where he played in Art Cope's band. He also toured and made recordings with his own group (1924–5) and recorded with Wingy Manone (1928) and Jimmy McPartland (1936). He spent a brief period in Detroit with Jean Goldkette (*c*1929). In 1937 he moved to New York, and from 1939 to 1940 was a member of Harry James's band. After returning to Chicago he led a trio at the Silver Palms and worked frequently as a soloist and an accompanist. Later he moved to Texas. Gardner composed a number of tunes, including *Bye, bye, pretty baby*; his solo piano version, recorded in 1944, was issued in conjunction with *Doll Rag*, a duet recording made with Baby Dodds (Steiner-Davis 508).

based on *ChiltonW*

Gare, Lou [Leslie Arthur] (*b* Rugby, England, 16 June 1939). English tenor saxophonist. After playing with Mike Westbrook for two years (1963–5) he became a founding member of the free-jazz group AMM with Eddie Prévost, the guitarist Keith Rowe, and the double bass player Laurence Sheaff. After the group disbanded in 1972 Gare and Prévost worked as a duo, AMM II, performing and making recordings, including the album *To Hear and Back Again* (1974, Matchless 3). Gare also played with other bands led by Prévost, and took part in sessions organized by the Musicians' Co-op at Ronnie Scott's, London. After moving to Exeter in 1977 he formed the Exeter Free Jazz Duo with the drummer Fred Burwood, which made several broadcasts. He has continued to work with Prévost and versions of AMM into the mid-1980s, and also performs with his own group and other free-jazz ensembles.

BIBLIOGRAPHY

Feather–Gitler '70s
R. Cotterell, ed.: *Jazz Now: the Jazz Centre Society Guide* (London, 1976)
K. Ansell: "AMM: the Sound as Music," *The Wire*, no.11 (1985), 21 [incl. discography]

SIMON ADAMS

Garland, Ed "Montudi(e)" [Tudi; Edward Bertram] (*b* New Orleans, 9 Jan ?1885; *d* Los Angeles, 22 Jan 1980). Double bass player. His first instrument was a washtub bass, which he played in a spasm band with Kid Ory. He performed on snare drum with the Onward and Excelsior brass bands, later taking up mellophone or tuba. By his own account he also worked with Buddy Bolden (1904) and Freddie Keppard (1908). Around 1910, when he was with Ory's Brownskin Babes, Garland played mainly with the bow, with some slapping or pizzicato. He moved to Chicago in 1914 and performed with Lawrence Duhé and Lil Hardin. Later he joined King Oliver, and in 1921 toured to the West Coast, where he elected to remain when Oliver returned to Chicago. He again worked with Ory, recording the following year. In 1927 Garland formed his own band in Los Angeles, then from 1944 to 1955 was once more a member of Ory's group. His many recordings with Ory demonstrate a light slapping and pizzicato style; his arco solo on the traditional theme from *Blues for Jimmy* became a set piece. After playing with Earl Hines (1955–6) Garland worked as a freelance on the West Coast. In 1971 he performed with Ory at the New Orleans Jazz & Heritage Festival, and during the 1970s he appeared regularly with Barry Martyn's LEGENDS OF JAZZ, with which he made several European tours.

Oral history material in *LNT*, *NjR* (JOHP).

SELECTED RECORDINGS

As sideman: Spikes' Seven Pods of Pepper [K. Ory]: Ory's Creole Trombone (1922, Nordskog 3009); Blues for Jimmy (1944, Crescent 2); K. Ory: *Live at the Club Hangover* (1953–4, Dawn Club 12013-14, 12016-17)

BIBLIOGRAPHY

ChiltonW

N. Shapiro and N. Hentoff, eds.: *Hear me Talkin' to ya: the Story of Jazz by the Men who Made it* (New York and London, 1955/R1966)

F. Levin: "Ed 'Montudie' Garland: Legend of Jazz," *JJI*, xxxii (1979), no. 6, p. 21; no. 7, p. 5; no. 8, p. 15; no. 9, p. 5

ALYN SHIPTON

Garland, Joe [Joseph Copeland] (*b* Norfolk, VA, 15 Aug 1903; *d* Teaneck, NJ, 21 April 1977). Arranger, composer, saxophonist, and clarinetist. He studied at Aeolian Conservatory, Baltimore, and Shaw University, and played in concert bands and orchestras before joining Graham Jackson's Seminole Syncopators in 1924. He then worked in dance bands led by Elmer Snowden (1925) and Leon Abbey (1927), and recorded with Jelly Roll Morton (1928). From 1932 to 1936 he was a member of the Mills Blue Rhythm Band (for illustration *see* MILLS BLUE RHYTHM BAND), to which he contributed many arrangements. After brief periods with Edgar Hayes (1937) and Don Redman (1938) he joined Louis Armstrong's big band (1939); Armstrong credited him with bringing a new discipline and precision to the ensemble, and in 1940 Garland replaced Luis Russell as its music director. Apart from some time working as a freelance in New York (1943–4), he remained in Armstrong's employ until 1947. During the late 1940s he was active in bands led by Herbie Fields, Claude Hopkins, and Earl Hines, but thereafter he played only occasionally. Garland's compositions include *In the Mood*, *Harlem after Midnight*, *There's Rhythm in Harlem*, *Congo Caravan*, and *Leap Frog*.

SELECTED RECORDINGS

As sideman: Seminole Syncopators: Sailing on Lake Pontchartrain (1924, OK 40228); J. R. Morton: Red Hot Pepper/Deep Creek (1928, Vic. 38055); Mills Blue Rhythm Band: Ridin' in Rhythm/Buddy's Wednesday Outing (1933, Col. CB734); D. Ellington: Happy as the day is long/Raisin' the Rent (1933, Bruns. 6571); Mills Blue Rhythm Band: Harlem after Midnight (1933, Voc. S6); Congo Caravan (1935, Col. 3087D); Harlem Heat/There's Rhythm in Harlem (1935, Col. 3071D); L. Armstrong: Leap Frog/I used to love you (1941, Decca 4106)

BIBLIOGRAPHY

ChiltonW

J. Simmen: "Crystal Clear: the Clarinet Player in Chick Webb's 'Jungle Mama'," *Coda*, no.143 (1975), 25

DAVID FLANAGAN

Garland, Red [William M.] (*b* Dallas, 13 May 1923; *d* Dallas, 23 April 1984). Pianist. He began musical studies on clarinet and alto saxophone in high school, changing to piano at the age of 18. His earliest influences were Count Basie and Nat "King" Cole; the music of Bud Powell and Art Tatum also made a strong impression on him when he first heard them play in New York during the late 1940s. Between 1946 and 1955 he worked in the New York and Philadelphia areas with noted jazz musicians such as Billy Eckstine, Charlie Parker, Coleman Hawkins, Lester Young, Ben Webster, Fats Navarro, and Roy Eldridge. It was as a member of Miles Davis's quintet, however, that Garland achieved international recognition (1955–8), particularly in the outstanding rhythm section with Paul Chambers and Philly Joe Jones. After leaving Davis's quintet Garland led his own trio for several years. When his mother died in 1968 he returned to Texas, where he remained in obscurity until his return to a brief but successful performing and recording career in the late 1970s.

SELECTED RECORDINGS

As leader: *All Mornin' Long* (1957, Prst. 7130); *Soul Junction* (1957, Prst. 7181); *High Pressure* (1957, Prst. 7209); *Red Alert* (1977, Gal. 5109)

As sideman with M. Davis: *Cookin'* (1956, Prst. 7094); *Milestones* (1958, Col. CL1193)

BIBLIOGRAPHY

"Red Garland," *SJ*, xxxiii/5 (1979), 220 [discography]

L. Lyons: "Red Garland: a Jazz Legend Returns," *CK*, v/2 (1979), 14

L. Feather: "Piano Giants of Jazz: Red Garland," *CK*, vi/2 (1980), 78

L. Lyons: *The Great Jazz Pianists, Speaking of their Lives and Music* (New York, 1983), 144

BILL DOBBINS

Garner, Erroll (Louis) (*b* Pittsburgh, 15 June 1921; *d* Los Angeles, 2 Jan 1977). Pianist, brother of Linton Garner. He played professionally in the Pittsburgh area from 1938 to 1941 with Leroy Brown's orchestra. By 1944 he had moved to New York, where he started to play in nightclubs; he served as a substitute for Art Tatum in Tatum's trio with Tiny Grimes and Slam Stewart, remaining when it became the Slam Stewart Trio (1945). He then formed his own trio with bass and drums, a format he retained for the whole of his career when not playing as a soloist, and quickly captured a large audience. In 1947, while working in the Los Angeles area, he recorded with Charlie Parker. In the 1950s and 1960s he was one of the most frequently seen jazz musicians on television, and in 1957–8 he undertook the first of many overseas tours. He remained active until February 1975, becoming one of the most familiar figures on the jazz scene and issuing a great many recordings.

A completely self-taught musician who never learned to read music, Garner developed an individual style that stands largely outside the main tradition of jazz pianism and, because of its virtuoso technique, has attracted few imitators. Although some of his early recordings show him using stride left-hand patterns, by the late 1940s he had developed a characteristic four-beat fixed pulse of block chords in the left hand, using wide-spaced voicings reminiscent of swing rhythm-guitar playing and often "kicking" the beat in the manner of a swing drummer. Against these patterns he embellished or varied a given melody with brilliant octave or chordal passages, sometimes lagging as much as an eighth-note behind the beat to generate enormous momentum and swing. Other trademarks of Garner's style were his sensitive manner of "strumming" right-hand chords at medium tempo and his witty passages of improvised two-part counterpoint. His interpretations of popular songs were orchestral in conception, exploiting the full range of the keyboard and employing contrasting textures and

Erroll Garner (piano) and Wyatt Ruther (double bass) at Basin Street East, New York, c1954

dynamics in the manner of big-band arrangements. In the 1950s he enriched his rhythmic basis by adopting Latin American dance rhythms.

Garner's recorded output is remarkably consistent in approach and level of invention. Of particular interest are his fanciful introductions, which function as small-scale, independent compositions, arresting the listener's attention with their dissonance or novelty without betraying the thematic material to follow. Garner also composed jazz piano pieces, such as *Erroll's Bounce* and *Blues garni*, part of the film score for *A New Kind of Love* (1963), and the well-known ballad *Misty*, which figured extensively in the film *Play Misty for Me* (1971) and exemplifies his rich, overly ornate manner at slow tempos. A collection of transcriptions of Garner's solos has been published by M. Feldman (*Erroll Garner Piano Solos*, Hollywood, CA, 1950–57).

See also PIANO, §4.

SELECTED RECORDINGS

As leader: Erroll's Bounce (1947, Vic. 20-3087); Play, piano, play/Fantasy on Frankie and Johnny (1947, Dial 1026); *Cocktail Time* (1947, Dial 205), incl. Blues garni; Laura (1951, Col. 39273); Easy to Love/Lullaby of Birdland (1953, Col. 39996); Misty (1954, Mer. 70442); *Afternoon of an Elf* (1955, Mer. 20090); *Concert by the Sea* (1955, Col. CL883); *That's my Kick* (1966–7, MGM 4463)

As sideman: S. Stewart: Hop, Skip and Jump (1945, Manor 1012); C. Parker: Cool Blues (1947, Dial 1015)

BIBLIOGRAPHY

W. Balliett: *The Sound of Surprise* (New York, 1959/*R*1978) [colln of previously pubd articles and reviews], 205

M. Clar: "Erroll Garner," *JR*, ii/1 (1959), 6

H. Siders: "The Natural," *DB*, xxxiv/21 (1967), 16

A. Shaw: *The Street that Never Slept: New York's Fabled 52nd Street* (New York, 1971/*R*1977 as *52nd Street: the Street of Jazz*)

A. Taylor: *Notes and Tones: Musician-to-Musician Interviews* (Liège, Belgium, 1977/*R*1982)

J. M. Doran: "Erroll Garner: a Discographical Update," *JJS*, vi/1 (1979), 64

W. Balliett: "Being a Genius," *Jelly Roll, Jabbo and Fats* (New York, and Oxford, England, 1983) [colln of previously pubd articles], 142

J. M. Doran: *Erroll Garner: the Most Happy Piano* (Metuchen, NJ, 1985)

B. Madson: "Erroll Garner," *JJI*, xl/8 (1987), 6

J. BRADFORD ROBINSON

Garner, Linton (S.) (*b* Greensboro, NC, 25 March 1915). Pianist and arranger, brother of Erroll Garner. From 1941 to 1943 he toured and recorded with a band of which Fletcher Henderson was leader by 1942. After serving in the US Army he wrote arrangements for and performed and recorded with Billy Eckstine (1946–7; for illustration *see* ECKSTINE, BILLY), and recorded with Earl Coleman (1948), Fats Navarro (1948), Babs Gonzales (1949), and Una Mae Carlisle (1950). In 1959 he recorded as the leader of a trio, the other members of which were Al Hall and Jimmie Crawford (*Garner Plays Garner*, Enrica 2001). From the mid-1970s he was the resident pianist at a hotel in Vancouver, Canada.

BIBLIOGRAPHY

FeatherE

J. M. Doran: *Erroll Garner: the Most Happy Piano* (Metuchen, NJ, 1985)

M. Miller: "Linton Garner," *Boogie, Pete & the Senator: Canadian Musicians in Jazz: the Eighties* (Toronto, 1987), 130

Garnett, Carlos (*b* Red Tank, Panama Canal Zone, 1 Dec 1938). Tenor saxophonist. During his childhood he absorbed the traditional and popular music of Panama, and as a teenager performed calypso and Latin music; his interest in jazz was stimulated by a film of a performance by Louis Jordan and by recordings of Clifford Brown and Max Roach. He played tenor saxophone with American musicians stationed in the Canal Zone, and in 1962 moved to New York, where he played in rock-and-roll groups and was influenced by leading free-jazz and bop saxophonists. He formed a group with the pianist Ronald Warrell (1968) and played and recorded with Freddie Hubbard (1968–9). He also played with the Jazz Messengers (1969–70), Charles Mingus (1970), Miles Davis (1972), Andrew Hill, Brother Jack McDuff, and Norman Connors. From 1970 he led a number of large ensembles that combined samba, Afro-Cuban, calypso, and rock rhythms; with these he played saxophones and flute, and sang.

SELECTED RECORDINGS

As leader: *Let this Melody Ring on* (1975, Muse 5079)

As sideman: A. Hill: *Lift Every Voice* (1969, BN 84330); N. Connors: *Dark of Light* (1972–3, Cob. 9035)

BIBLIOGRAPHY

Feather–Gitler '70s

M. Durham: "Carlos Garnett: up from Panama," *DB*, xxxviii/13 (1971), 14

DAVID G. SUCH

Garrett, Dee Dee. *See* BRIDGEWATER, DEE DEE.

Garrett, Donald (Rafael) [Garrett, Rafael] (*b* El Dorado, AR, 28 Feb 1932). Double bass player and bass clarinetist. He played hard bop in Chicago with Ira Sullivan (1960–62) and recorded with Roland Kirk (1960), Eddie Harris (1961), and Sullivan (1962). He was one of the original members of the Experimental Band formed by Muhal Richard Abrams in 1961. He made recordings in Seattle and California with Coltrane (including *Kulu se mama*, 1965, Imp. 9106) and Dewey Redman (1966), performed and recorded with Archie Shepp (1966, 1973), and performed in Paris with Frank Wright and Jean-Luc Ponty (both 1971). Besides his principal instruments he also plays flute, clarinet, and tenor saxophone, and from the late 1960s has designed and made bamboo flutes. With his wife, Zusaan

Fasteau, a singer, cellist, and player of non-Western instruments, he formed the Sea Ensemble, which toured and recorded in 1977. In 1981 he played a variety of instruments, including shell and bamboo winds, on a recording led by Joseph Jarman and Don Moye (*Earth Passage-Density*, BS 0052).

Oral history material in *ICJic*.

BIBLIOGRAPHY

P. Charles: "Rafael Garrett," *Jm*, no.216 (1973), 31
V. Wilmer: *As Serious as your Life: the Story of the New Jazz* (London, 1977, rev. 1980)

Garrick, Michael (*b* Enfield, England, 30 May 1933). English pianist, organist, and composer. He studied literature at London University and led a trio and a quartet in the late 1950s; from 1962 he combined these interests through more than 250 concerts with Poetry and Jazz in Concert, in which leading poets read their works in the context of a jazz accompaniment. In 1965 he formed his own sextet; he also played with and composed works for the Don Rendell/Ian Carr Quintet (1965–9) and with Neil Ardley's New Jazz Orchestra (1965–7). During the 1960s and early 1970s he made a series of popular recordings with his own groups, in configurations from trio to septet. He experimented with the use of the harpsichord in jazz on *Black Marigolds* (1966), and became increasingly interested in jazz settings of liturgical works, for soloist and for choir, through an association with the conductor Peter Mound; he found this a valid method of introducing schoolchildren to live jazz performance. He recorded an album of his choral compositions, *Jazz Praises at St. Paul's*, playing the organ at St. Paul's Cathedral, London, in 1968 (*see* ORGAN, §1). During the 1970s Garrick continued to play and compose; he also began teaching, and in 1979 founded the Travelling Jazz Faculty. From 1977 he has worked in a trio, Threesome, with Norma Winstone and the guitarist Phil Lee; he has also played with the saxophonist Chris Hunter (1982–84), and in a band led by the double bass player Dave Green (from 1983). He formed a sextet, Flybinite, in 1983, and began leading a big band in 1985.

SELECTED RECORDINGS

(all recorded for Argo unless otherwise indicated)

Black Marigolds (1966, DA88); *Jazz Praises at St. Paul's* (1968, Airborne 0021); *Poetry and Jazz in Concert 250* (1969, PR264-5); *Mr. Smith's Apocalypse* (1971, AGF1)

BIBLIOGRAPHY

R. Cotterrell, ed.: *Jazz Now: the Jazz Centre Society Guide* (London, 1976)
M. Garrick: "Portable Jazz," *Times Educational Supplement* (15 April 1983), 51

MARK GILBERT

Garrison, Arv(in Charles) (*b* Toledo, OH, 17 Aug 1922; *d* Toledo, 30 July 1960). Guitarist and leader. He led a trio from 1941. In 1946 he recorded bop and swing on the West coast with Dizzy Gillespie, Charlie Parker, Howard McGhee, Leo Watson, and Ralph Burns. From 1946 to 1948 he toured with his wife, the double bass player Vivien Garry. He performed in Toledo through the 1950s. Garrison plays fine bop solos on electric guitar on Parker's *A Night in Tunisia* (1946, Dial 1002) and *Yardbird Suite* (1946, Dial 1003).

BIBLIOGRAPHY

FeatherE
R. Gordon: *Jazz West Coast: the Los Angeles Jazz Scene of the 1950s* (London and New York, 1986)

Garrison, Jimmy [James Emory] (*b* Miami, 3 March 1934; *d* New York, 7 April 1976). Double bass player. He learned to play bass in Philadelphia, where he grew up. After moving to New York he worked for several bop leaders, including Philly Joe Jones, Curtis Fuller, Benny Golson, and Lennie Tristano, before distinguishing himself in the avant-garde quartets of Ornette Coleman (1961) and particularly John Coltrane (1961–7; for illustration *see* ALI, RASHIED). Garrison was an ideal accompanist for Coltrane, playing tonal walking bass lines for blues and standards, drone foundations (including bowed triple-stopped flamenco figures) for ostinato tunes, and esoteric rubato countermelodies during free improvisations. After leaving Coltrane he played in groups with Hampton Hawes (1966), Archie Shepp (1967–8, 1972), and Elvin Jones (1968–9, 1973–4), and periodically taught college students.

SELECTED RECORDINGS

As leader with E. Jones: *Illumination* (1963, Imp. 49)
As sideman with J. Coltrane: *Coltrane* (1962, Imp. 21); *Live at Birdland* (1963, Imp. 50); *A Love Supreme* (1964, Imp. 77); *Expression* (1967, Imp. 9120)
As sideman with others: P. J. Jones: *Blues for Dracula* (1958, Riv. 282); O. Coleman: *Ornette on Tenor* (1961, Atl. 1394); S. Rollins: *East Broadway Run Down* (1966, Imp. 9121); O. Coleman: *New York is Now!* (1968, BN 84287)

BIBLIOGRAPHY

D. Heckman: "Jimmy Garrison after Coltrane," *DB*, xxiv/5 (1967), 18
H. Nolan: "Jimmy Garrison," *DB*, xli/11 (1974), 18
C. Flicker: "Jimmy Garrison," *Jm*, no.234 (1975), 20

BARRY KERNFELD

Gary, Shelton (*b* Fairfield, AL, 13 Nov 1943). Drummer. He played in school bands and from 1955 worked at various local clubs around Fairfield and Birmingham, Alabama, often as a member of a band led by the guitarist James "Slick" Lawrence. After military service in Vietnam (1966–8) he returned to Fairfield, then moved to New York (1970). In 1971 he began work at the Professional Percussion Center, where he met and formed an association with Jo Jones; as Jones's protégé he later deputized for him in groups led by Illinois Jacquet, Tiny Grimes, and others. Late in 1975 Gary joined a band led by George Kelly at the West End, New York, and worked there until 1986 with such leaders as Franc Williams. He also performed and toured with the Harlem Blues and Jazz Band (1980–82); his varied and swinging drumming may be heard to advantage on *Bobby's Bounce* and *Six or Seven Times* from the album *Harlem Blues and Jazz: 1973–1980* (1980, Barron VLP403). Early in 1987 Gary toured France with Wild Bill Davis. (C. Battestini and J.-P. Battestini: "Shelton Gary (Drums)," *BHcF*, no.347 (1987), 1)

HOWARD RYE

Gasca, Luis [Louis Angel] (*b* Houston, 3 March 1940). Trumpeter and flugelhorn player. He played trumpet from the age of 13 and attended the Berklee College of Music (1959–60). After touring Japan with Perez Prado (1960) he recorded as a mellophone player with Stan Kenton (1962) and played trumpet with Maynard Ferguson and Lionel Hampton (1963–4). He performed and recorded with Woody Herman (1967, appearing at the Monterey Jazz Festival and touring Europe), Mongo Santamaria (1967–9), the rock singers Janis Joplin and Van Morrison, and Carlos Santana. From 1970 he performed with Count Basie and Cal Tjader, and played and recorded with George Duke (1971) and Joe Henderson (1973). As a leader he recorded *The Little Giant* (1968, Atl. 1527), with a group that included Lew Tabackin, Herbie Hancock, and Richard Davis, and two other albums (1971, *c*1975).

BIBLIOGRAPHY

Feather–Gitler '70s
L. Lyons: "Profile: Luis Gasca," *DB*, xxxii/10 (1975), 32

Gaskin, Leonard (*b* New York, 25 Aug 1920). Double bass player. He began his career in New York in 1943 as a member of the house band at Monroe's Uptown House, where he took part in numerous jam sessions that contributed to the formulation of the bop style. His skills as a timekeeper and his familiarity with the harmonic language of bop caused him to be much in demand in the 1940s: in 1944 he replaced Oscar Pettiford in the group led by Dizzy Gillespie and Budd Johnson at the Downbeat Club. For the remainder of the 1940s he worked as a freelance with groups led by Cootie Williams, Charlie Parker, Eddie South, Charlie Shavers, and Erroll Garner. In 1956 he joined Eddie Condon's dixieland group, with which he recorded several albums, but left Condon in 1960 to pursue a career as a studio musician, playing gospel music and pop. In the 1970s and 1980s he performed with Sy Oliver, Panama Francis, and the International Art of Jazz, an educational ensemble based in New York.

SELECTED RECORDINGS

As sideman: H. Allen and C. Shavers: *Trumpet Masters* (1944, Jazz Showcase 5009), incl. Amor, Deuce-a-rini; E. South: Eddie South's Blues/12 o'Clock at Night (1947, Contl 6044); K. Pleasure: Moody's Mood for Love (1952, Prst. 924); M. Davis: *Miles Davis Plays Al Cohn Compositions* (1953, Prst. 154), incl. Tasty Pudding, Willie the Wailer; E. Condon: *The Roaring 20s* (1957, Col. CL1089); O. Jackson: *Oliver Jackson Presents "Le Quartet"* (1982, BB 33180)

BIBLIOGRAPHY

FeatherE
G. Urban: "Leonard Gaskin Then and Now," *Radio Free Jazz*, xvii/6 (1976), 7
J. M. Doran: *Erroll Garner: the Most Happy Piano* (Metuchen, NJ, 1985)

SCOTT DEVEAUX

Gaskin, (Roderick) Vic(tor) (*b* New York, 23 Nov 1934). Double bass player. He learned guitar from his father, a flutist, and undertook conservatory study in New York. After playing with a rock-and-roll group in San Diego he moved in 1962 to Los Angeles, where he worked for a year with Paul Horn's quintet (recording in 1962). During this time he also played with Shelly Manne, Oscar Brown, Jr., Bud Shank, the Jazz Crusaders, and Harold Land; he joined Les McCann's trio in 1964. Gaskin played with Cannonball Adderley from 1966 to 1969, appearing with him at the Newport Jazz Festival in 1967. Thereafter he worked briefly with Thelonious Monk (1969), Duke Ellington (1969–70), the Harlem PO (1970), and Chico Hamilton (1971), and performed at the Montreux International Jazz Festival (1971, 1972) with such musicians as Oliver Nelson, Hamilton, and Leone Thomas. From 1971 he played in a group led by the English blues singer and harmonica player John Mayall, with whom he performed at the Newport Jazz Festival New York in 1973. In the 1980s he has recorded with Billy Taylor (ii) (1980), in Hank Jones's quartet (accompanying the vibraphonist Darji, 1982), and in a sextet with Doc Cheatham and George Kelly (1985); he has also worked as a commercial photographer.

Oral history material in *CtY*.

SELECTED RECORDINGS

As sideman: C. Adderley: *Mercy, Mercy, Mercy! Live at "the Club"* (1966, Cap. ST2663); J. Mayall: *Moving On* (1972, Pol. 5036); B. Taylor: *Where've You Been?* (1980, Conc. 145)

BIBLIOGRAPHY

Feather '60s; *Feather–Gitler '70s*

WILLIAM S. BROCKMAN

Gaslini, Giorgio (*b* Milan, 22 Oct 1929). Italian pianist and composer. He studied piano from the age of seven and gave his first performances at the age of 13. After leading his own orchestra and working in a duo with Achille Scotti, he formed a trio when he was 16 with Gil Cuppini and the clarinetist Gino Stefani; with this group he made his first recordings. In 1948 he appeared at the International Jazz Festival in Florence with a group that included among others Cuppini and Eraldo Volonté. He studied piano, composition, and conducting at the Conservatorio in Milan and in the late 1950s and early 1960s led several Italian symphony orchestras; he also composed film scores. At this time he also led his own quartet, with which he frequently performed at hospitals and factories as well as more conventional venues. During the following years he performed and recorded with Don Cherry and Gato Barbieri (1966), Steve Lacy (1966, 1968, 1973), Jean-Luc Ponty (1973), and Roswell Rudd (1978). Later he performed in the USA as an unaccompanied soloist (1980), as the leader of a quartet (1981), and again as a soloist (1986). He has taught jazz in Milan (1959) and Rome (1972). Gaslini's compositional language is essentially a fusion of jazz and serialism that also draws on such diverse sources as aleatory and electronic music and pop; the aim is a stylistic synthesis that Gaslini describes as "total music." In addition to works for jazz ensemble he has written operas, ballets, and orchestral, vocal, and instrumental works. He expounds his views on music in an article entitled "Jazz nuovo e musica nova" published in *Nuova rivista musicale italiana*, ii (1968), 473.

SELECTED RECORDINGS

(recorded for Dischi della querchia unless otherwise indicated)

As unaccompanied soloist: *Gaslini Plays Monk* (1981, SN 1020)
Duos: with R. Rudd: *Sharing* (1978, 28007); with E. Gomez: *Ecstacy* (1981, 28013); with A. Braxton: *Four Pieces* (1981, 28015)
As leader: Ow/Concerto Riff (1948, HMV HN2424); *Free Actions* (1977, 28003)

RECORDED COMPOSITIONS

(selective list; all recorded by Gaslini)

Tempo a relazione, opus 12 (1957, HMV 7EPQ581); *Oltre* (1963, HMV QELP8086); *Dall'alba all'alba* (1964, HMV QELP8139); *Nuovi sentimenti* (1966, HMV QELP8154); *La stagione incantata* (1968, HMV QELP8179); *Grido* (1968, Durium 77199); Jazz Makrokosmos, on *Newport in Milan* (1969, Off 302); Africa, Microkosmos, on *Africa!* (1969, Off 301); *Colloquio con Malcolm X* (1973–4, PDU 6004)

BIBLIOGRAPHY

Feather '60s; *Feather–Gitler '70s*
A. Bassi: *Giorgio Gaslini* (Milan, 1986) [incl. list of compositions and discography]
P. Elwood: "2 Jazz Pianists' Inspired Recital," *San Francisco Examiner* (17 April 1986) [review]

PIERO SANTI/ADRIANO MAZZOLETTI

Gate, Alan. Pseudonym of PIERRE GOSSEZ.

Gaudry, Michel (*b* Eu, France, 23 Sept 1928). French double bass player. He studied piano and clarinet before taking up double bass; he attended the conservatory in Geneva. In Paris from 1957 he accompanied Billie Holiday and Carmen McRae, recorded with Quentin Jackson (1959) and Billy Strayhorn (1961), and performed and recorded with the pianist Art Simmons (1959) and the Double Six (1960–62). He performed with Kenny Clarke and Bud Powell, and recorded with Elek Bacsik (1962), Sonny Criss (1962), Powell (1964), and a quintet led by Stuff Smith and Stephane Grappelli (1965). He worked principally as a studio musician from the late 1960s, but also played on sessions with Grappelli (1969), Barney Kessel (1969), the pianist Jacques Dieval (*c*1970), Sam Woodyard (*The Swing Machine*, 1975, BStar 80701), Lionel Hampton (1976), Raymond Fol (1976–7), Cat Anderson (1977), Jimmy Owens (1985), and Irvin Stokes (1986). (*Feather '60s*; *Feather–Gitler '70s*)

Gay, Al(bert) (*b* London, 25 Feb 1928). English tenor saxophonist and clarinetist. He studied at the Guildhall School of Music and Drama, London (1942), then played in a trio led by his brother Joshua Gay (1942–3), in various dance bands (1944–5), and with the Jive Bombers (1945–6). After a period during which he performed his military service and then trained as a nurse, he worked with Freddy Randall (1953–7), Harry Gold, the drummer Joe Daniels (1957–60), the trumpeter Bob Wallis (1961–2), and others. In 1963 he began to play with Alex Welsh, with whom he made a number of recordings, including *At Home – with Alex Welsh and his Band* (1967, Col. SCX6213); he was a full-time member of Welsh's group from 1963 to 1967 and again from 1977 to 1983. Gay also worked again with Randall (1965–7, and frequently from 1971), with the rhythm-and-blues singer Long John Baldry (1965), and with Stan Greig's quintet (from 1972), the London Jazz Big Band (1975–83), and the World's Greatest Jazz Band (in Stockholm, 1978). He then led his own quartet and worked as a freelance player from 1981. (R. Cotterrell, ed.: *Jazz Now: the Jazz Centre Society Guide*, London, 1976)

DIGBY FAIRWEATHER

Gaynair, Wilton "Bogey" (*b* Kingston, Jamaica, 11 Jan 1927). Jamaican tenor saxophonist. Early in his career he played with musicians such as Ossie Williams (who later led the reggae group Count Ossie and Mystic Revelation of Rastafari), then in 1955 went to Europe. After performing and recording in England he settled in Germany, where he studied arranging and composition; he worked there with George Maycock for eight years and with Kurt Edelhagen from 1964 until the latter's death in 1982. He also played in jam sessions with Randy Weston, Stan Getz, Johnny Griffin, Gerry Mulligan, and Nat Adderley, and with Alan Skidmore, Kenny Wheeler, and Ali Haurand formed the sextet Third Eye. He worked regularly with Peter Herbolzheimer until ill health curtailed his career in 1985. A confident player in the post-bop mold, Gaynair produced adventurous and driving solos; he seldom allowed his impressive technique to intrude upon his thoughtful approach to ballad playing. He was influenced principally by Coleman Hawkins, Don Byas, and Lucky Thompson.

SELECTED RECORDINGS

As leader: *Blue Bogey* (1959, Tempo TAP25); *One for Wilton* (1980, Ego 4018); with A. Haurand, A. Skidmore, and K. Wheeler (of Third Eye): *Third Eye Live!* (1982, View 0021)

As sideman: P. Herbolzheimer: *For Swinging Dancers Only* (*c*1984, Koala)

VALERIE WILMER

Gazell. Record label established in 1950 by Dag Haeggqvist; it became incorporated into SONET when its founder joined that company in 1960.

Gee, Matthew(, Jr.) (*b* Houston, 25 Nov 1925; *d* New York, 18 July 1979). Trombonist. He recorded with Dizzy Gillespie in 1949, then worked with the trumpeter Joe Morris, Gene Ammons, and Sonny Stitt. In 1951 he played with Count Basie, and from 1952 to 1954 he was with Illinois Jacquet; he recorded again with Gillespie in 1955. After touring Europe with Sarah Vaughan (1956) he joined the Duke Ellington Orchestra (1959), with which he worked intermittently until 1963; he often played as a soloist (a good example of his work may be heard on *C Jam Blues*), and also contributed some compositions to the band's repertory (including *The Swingers Get the Blues too,* which he wrote with Ellington). He then performed sporadically at clubs with small groups, often, in his later years, with Paul Quinichette and Brooks Kerr. Gee was considered an outstanding player in the mid- and late 1950s, but his career reached its peak early and quickly declined: his only important appearance during the 1970s was at a concert given in New York by former members of Ellington's orchestra in 1975.

SELECTED RECORDINGS

As leader: *Jazz by Gee!* (1956, Riv. 221); with J. Griffin: *Soul Groove* (1963, Atl. 1431)

As sideman with D. Ellington: *Blues in Orbit* (1959, Col. CL1445), incl. C. Jam Blues, The Swingers Get the Blues too

BIBLIOGRAPHY

FeatherE

Liner notes, *Jazz by Gee!* (Riv. 221, 1957)

J. Burns: "Bopping Bones," *J&B*, ii/7 (1972), 16

CHIP DEFFAA

Geller, Herb(ert) (*b* Los Angeles, 2 Nov 1928). Alto saxophonist. After playing with Joe Venuti in Los Angeles (1946) he traveled to New York (1949) and performed and recorded with Claude Thornhill. In 1951 he married Lorraine Walsh and they returned to Los Angeles, where Geller played with Billy May's big band (1952), then performed and recorded West Coast jazz with Maynard Ferguson (1954–6), Shorty Rogers, and Bill Holman (both 1954, 1957–9); he also led a quartet (1954–5) that included his wife. After his wife's death he played with Benny Goodman (intermittently, 1958–61) and Louie Bellson (1959); he went with Goodman to Brazil, where he remained for a period at the time that bossa nova was at the height of its popularity. He later toured Europe, and in 1962 moved to Berlin, where he played in the jazz orchestra of the radio station Sender Freies Berlin and ran a nightclub. Having settled in Hamburg (1965) he continued to work in radio, as a composer, performer, and arranger for Norddeutscher Rundfunk. He was a member of Friedrich Gulda's Euro-Jazz Orchestra (1965–6) and Peter Herbolzheimer's big band (1970–79). In 1984 he recorded as the leader of a bop quartet.

SELECTED RECORDINGS

As leader: *Herb Geller Sextette* (1954, EmA 36040); *The Gellers* (1955, EmA 36024); *Fire in the West* (1957, Jub. 1044); *An American in Hamburg* (1975, Nova 628332); *Hot House* (1984, Cir. [G] 30)

As sideman: C. Baker: *Compositions and Arrangements by Jack Montrose* (1953, PJ 9); B. Holman: *Stan Kenton Presents the Bill Holman Octet* (1954, Cap. H6500); S. Rogers: *Shorty Rogers Plays Richard Rodgers* (1957, RCA LPM1428); S. Manne: *Shelly Manne and his Men Play Peter Gunn* (1959, Cont. 3560)

BIBLIOGRAPHY

FeatherE; *Feather '60s*; *Feather–Gitler '70s*

J.-L. Ginibre and J. Wagner: "Entretien: un américain bien tranquille," *Jm*, no.84 (1962), 26

J. Lind: "Herb Geller's European Rebirth," *DB*, xxx/1 (1963), 23

H. Geller: "An American in Europe," *Crescendo*, v/3 (1966), 24

KIMBERLY McCORD

Geller [née Walsh], **Lorraine (Winifred)** (*b* Portland, OR, 11 Sept 1928; *d* Los Angeles, 13 Oct 1958). Pianist. She performed with the Sweethearts of Rhythm (1949–51), which was based in New York; in 1951 she married Herb Geller and moved to Los Angeles, where she performed with Shorty Rogers, Red Mitchell, Zoot Sims, Stan Getz, Dizzy Gillespie, and Charlie Parker. In 1954–5 she played and recorded West Coast jazz with her husband's quartet; the album *The Gellers* (1955, EmA 36034), on which she was joined in the rhythm section by Red Mitchell and Mel Lewis, well represents her playing. She also recorded as a leader (1956) and as a sideman with Mitchell on the album *Presenting Red Mitchell* (1957, Cont. 3538), and in 1957 accompanied the pop singer Kay Starr.

BIBLIOGRAPHY

FeatherE

L. Dahl: *Stormy Weather: the Music and Lives of a Century of Jazzwomen* (London, Melbourne, Australia, and New York, 1984), 76

KIMBERLY McCORD

Gene Norman Presents. *See* GNP.

General. Record label. It was owned by the General Records Division of Consolidated Records, Inc., of New York. It is chiefly remembered for having issued items made by Jelly Roll Morton in 1939–40; these were supervised by Gordon Mercer. Later in 1940 Leonard Feather directed some small-band recordings with Pete Brown, Bill Coleman, and Joe Marsala that were released on General. The label was later acquired by Commodore.

BIBLIOGRAPHY

C. E. Smith and others: *The Jazz Record Book* (New York, 1942/*R*1978) [listeners' guide and discography], 113

B. Rust: *The American Record Label Book* (New Rochelle, NY, 1978), 128

Gennett. Record company and label. The company was owned by the Starr Piano Co. of Richmond, Indiana, and was named after the latter's three most important managers, the brothers Harry, Fred, and Clarence Gennett. Issue began in 1917; the first discs were vertically cut. These included three items by the pianist Earl Fuller. Laterally cut discs were released from mid-1919; among these was a disc by the New Orleans Jazz Band. The company made its first forays into the race-record market with material by white bands, issuing a long series of discs recorded in 1921 by the Original Memphis Five (under the pseudonym Ladd's Black Aces), and a more important sequence made in 1922–3 by the New Orleans Rhythm Kings (as the Friars Society Orchestra). Sessions by a few vaudeville blues singers were organized, but extensive recording of race material did not begin until 1923, when King Oliver and Jelly Roll Morton both made discs for the label. These items were the start of a series of recordings now held to be classics. Gennett never had a designated race series: instead, from 1924, it printed the relevant labels with the legend "race record," and was the only company to adopt this policy. The discs were generally issued in batches as part of the general sequence, especially after December 1926, when the catalogue reached 6000; at this point the company started issuing electrically made recordings, the Electrobeams (see illustration).

As well as exchanging masters with other small labels, Gennett provided recording facilities for Black Patti in 1926 and Paramount in 1929. The company also undertook much custom recording, offering its services to individuals and ensembles who were prepared to pay to make their own discs. Important jazz from this scheme appears on unnumbered records either with Gennett or special labels; these included items by Jesse Crump. The label Gennett itself was discontinued in 1930, but the company continued to issue discs on its subsidiary labels CHAMPION and Superior before discontinuing its music labels at the end of 1934. The Champion trademark and the rights to some of Gennett's recordings were sold to Decca; as a consequence some of the company's more famous material was reissued on English Brunswick in the mid-1930s, but often with very poor sound quality. Gennett continued to make recordings (for sound effects and other purposes) throughout the 1930s, and as a result the company was given an allocation of shellac during World War II. Harry Gennett entered into an arrangement whereby this was made available to the promoter and producer Joe Davis, who put out a short race series, the Gennett

Label for "Mandy," recorded by Zack Whyte's Chocolate Beau Brummels for Gennett (1929)

5000s; this included reissues and new material. Davis soon discontinued the name Gennett in favor of his own labels Beacon and Joe Davis, though records were occasionally issued on Gennett in other series for a short period thereafter.

See also RECORDING, §II, 2, and fig.3.

BIBLIOGRAPHY

G. W. Kay: "The Gennett Discovery," *SL*, vi/5–6 (1955), 1

J. Godrich and R. M. W. Dixon: *Blues & Gospel Records, 1902–1942* (Hatch End, nr London, 1964, rev. 2/1969, rev. and enlarged 3/1982 as R. M. W. Dixon and J. Godrich: *Blues and Gospel Records, 1902–1943*), 23

R. M. W. Dixon and J. Godrich: *Recording the Blues* (London, 1970)

B. Rust: *The American Record Label Book* (New Rochelle, NY, 1978), 129

"Gennett Colored Artists Records," *Sv*, no.75 (1978), 94 [facsimile of race catalogue of 1924]

M. E. Vreede: "Can't we Talk it Over," *Sv*, no.110 (1983–4), 65

Gentry, Chuck [Charles T.] (*b* Belgrade, NE, 14 Dec 1911). Baritone saxophonist. He played swing in Los Angeles with Vido Musso (1939), and performed and recorded with Harry James (1940–41), Benny Goodman (1941–2), Glenn Miller (1943–4), and Artie Shaw (1944–6). After playing with Jan Savitt's band (1945–6) he worked again with Goodman (1946–7). Gentry took part in more than 100 studio sessions with Mel Powell (1947), Woody Herman (1947–57), Louis Armstrong (1951–6), June Christy (1952–9), Charlie Barnet (1954), Georgie Auld (1955–6), Benny Carter (1958), Shorty Rogers (1958–60), Nancy Wilson (1968), and others; a good example of his playing may be heard on *Collaboration* on the album *Reeds in Hi-fi* (1956, Mer. 20260), which he recorded with Pete Rugolo. In 1964–5 he recorded and performed with the Los Angeles Neophonic Orchestra under Stan Kenton. (*ChiltonW; FeatherE*)

George, Fatty [Pressler, Franz Georg] (*b* Vienna, 24 April 1927; *d* Vienna, 29 March 1982). Austrian clarinetist, alto saxophonist, and bandleader. He began to play saxophone in 1942 and then studied clarinet at the academy in Vienna. He formed his own bop group, the Hot Club Seven, in 1947. He spent some time in Germany (1949–52) and Innsbruck, Austria (1952–5), and after returning to Vienna in 1955 opened a club called the Jazz Casino. He became well known as leader of the Two Sounds Band, which included Oscar Klein, Karl Drewo, Bill Grah, and Joe Zawinul; it made many traditional and cool-jazz recordings in the mid-1950s. When the Jazz Casino closed in 1958

George opened Fatty's Saloon, which became an important center for the performance of jazz in Austria. He worked as a freelance player in Berlin (1963–7) and then moved back to Vienna, where he performed on radio with his own band; his recordings from this period include *Fatty 69* (1969, Preiser 3190). From 1974 he frequently appeared on television with his Chicago Jazz Band, and he continued to record as a leader into the 1980s. As an alto saxophonist George was influenced by Lee Konitz, and he played clarinet in a swing style. (*FeatherE*)

BIBLIOGRAPHY

FeatherE

D. H. Kraner and K. Schulz: *Jazz in Austria: historische Entwicklung und Diskographie des Jazz in Österreich* (Graz, Austria, 1972) [Eng., Ger. texts]

KLAUS SCHULZ

George, Karl (Curtis) (*b* St. Louis, 26 April 1913). Trumpeter. He worked in Detroit with McKinney's Cotton Pickers (*c*1933) and Cecil Lee's band, joined the Jeter–Pillars Orchestra, then played with Teddy Wilson (1939–40) and Lionel Hampton (1941–2). After army service he went to the West Coast, where he worked with Stan Kenton, Benny Carter, Count Basie (1945), and the trombonist Happy Johnson (1946), and recorded with a number of groups (1945–6), many of which included Charles Mingus and Lucky Thompson; *Why Not* (1945, Excelsior 145), made under Thompson's leadership, is a good example of his playing. George also led his own recording band, an octet in which J. J. Johnson and Buddy Tate were sidemen. Thereafter he suffered from ill-health and retired to St. Louis.

based on *ChiltonW*

Georgia Washboard Stompers. Name under which the personnel of the WASHBOARD RHYTHM KINGS also recorded.

Gerard, Fred [Monnin, Georges] (*b* Besançon, France, 18 March 1924). French trumpeter. After studying music he began his career performing hot jazz as a soloist in Lyons (1941–7). He then played with Alix Combelle (1948–9), Jacques Hélian's band (1949–51), Ernie Royal (1950–51), Aimé Barelli (*c*1951), the bandleader and saxophonist Raymond Legrand (1952), Gigi Gryce, Clifford Brown, Art Farmer, and Hubert Rostaing (1953). He also played with the pianists Christian Chevallier and (in 1955) André Persiany, and with Claude Bolling, Michel Legrand, Martial Solal (1956–8), the Paris Jazz All Stars (1966), the trumpeter Jean-Claude Naude (*c*1967), Slide Hampton, the trumpeter Sonny Grey, Dexter Gordon (1970), Roger Guérin (1973), and the double bass player Bob Quibel (1981–5); he has led various groups of his own. Gerard is known chiefly for his playing in the trumpet's upper register; his style is exemplified by his recording *Sonny Boy/Mon homme* (1953, Ducretet-Thomson 8720). (M. Laplace: *Portraits of French Jazz Musicians* (Menden, Germany, 1985), 8)

MICHEL LAPLACE

Gersh [Girsback], **Squire** [Girsback, William] (*b* San Francisco, 13 May 1913). Double bass and tuba player. In San Francisco he played traditional jazz with Lu Watters, Bob Scobey, Turk Murphy, and Mutt Carey, and recorded with Watters (1942) and Murphy (intermittently, 1950–66). He recorded and toured South America with Louis Armstrong (1956–8), and performed in Europe with Henry "Red" Allen and Kid Ory (1959). Gersh's agile double bass playing may be heard on *Some of these days* recorded by Darnell Howard's Frisco Footwarmers in San Francisco in 1950 (Jazz Man 33).

BIBLIOGRAPHY

FeatherE

J. Goggin: *Turk Murphy: Just for the Record* (San Leandro, CA, 1982)

Gershman, Nat(han) (*b* Philadelphia, 29 Nov 1917). Cellist. He attended the Curtis Institute (1936–40) and performed with the Cleveland Orchestra (1940–47). He then worked in studios in New York (1948–53) and (from 1954) Los Angeles; he was a member of Chico Hamilton's quintet (1957–61), with which he recorded the album *Gongs East* (1958, WB 1271). Later he played in ensembles that recorded with Nat Adderley (1974) and Ronnie Laws (1976–7). In the 1980s he continued to work as a freelance musician in Los Angeles and was also active as a teacher.

BIBLIOGRAPHY

FeatherE

R. Gordon: *Jazz West Coast: the Los Angeles Jazz Scene of the 1950s* (London and New York, 1986), 188

Getz, Stan(ley) (*b* Philadelphia, 2 Feb 1927). Tenor saxophonist and leader. He started playing professionally at the age of 15 in New York, and when he was only a year older made his first recording, as a sideman with Jack Teagarden. After playing in several important big bands, including those of Stan Kenton (1944–5) and Benny Goodman (1945–6), in 1947 he joined Woody Herman's Second Herd, where with his fellow saxophonists Zoot Sims, Serge Chaloff, and Herbie Steward he formed the famous reed section known as the Four Brothers. In 1948 his ballad improvisation on Ralph Burns's *Early Autumn* established him instantaneously as a major improviser in an advanced swing style. After leaving Herman the following year Getz began to lead his own small groups and immediately

Stan Getz playing at the Newport Jazz Festival, July 1965

started to dominate jazz popularity polls for his instrument, as he did for many of the next 25 years.

In the mid-1950s Getz's career was interrupted by difficulties associated with his addiction to drugs. He spent the latter part of the decade working from Scandinavia, where he performed and recorded with local musicians and with other American expatriates such as Oscar Pettiford and Kenny Clarke. After returning to the USA in 1961 he attempted a comeback with the album *Focus*, which included outstanding arrangements by Eddie Sauter. In the following year, with Charlie Byrd, he initiated a fusion of jazz and bossa nova which captured the public's fancy and brought Getz a considerable amount of popular acclaim. The movement, however, was short-lived; although Getz continued to lead jazz groups, and helped to launch the careers of Gary Burton, Steve Swallow, Chick Corea, Tony Williams, Airto Moreira, and other promising young musicians, he was out of sympathy with the free-jazz and rock movements, and he spent the years 1969 to 1972 in semiretirement in Europe. His album *Captain Marvel* (1972) marked his return to playing jazz on a regular basis. From that time he has led a number of small groups with such important young musicians as JoAnne Brackeen. In the mid-1980s he worked regularly in the San Francisco Bay area and taught at Stanford University.

Getz is an important exponent of his instrument and one of the supremely melodious improvisers in modern jazz, with a style deeply rooted in the swing period. Drawing his light, vibrato-less tone and basic approach from Lester Young, Getz developed a highly personal manner which, for its elegance and easy virtuosity, stood apart from the aggressive bop style of the late 1940s and 1950s. His justly celebrated performance on *Early Autumn* (1948), with its characteristically languorous melody and delayed rhythm, captured the imagination of many young white jazz musicians of the time and helped to precipitate the "cool" reaction to bop in the years that followed. Although ballad renditions of this sort were the basis of Getz's popularity, he was also among the few jazz musicians who could remain lyrical even at very fast tempos, thanks to a secure technical command of his instrument; performances such as *Crazy Chords* (1949), a breakneck rendering of the blues in all 12 keys, set new standards of virtuosity for jazz improvisation on the tenor saxophone. His fusion of jazz and bossa nova, though not as novel as was claimed at the time, was instrumental in restoring jazz to a large popular following, and paved the way for the later influx of Brazilian music and instruments into jazz in the early 1970s. A collection of transcriptions of Getz's solos, *Stan Getz: Improvised Saxophone Solos*, has been published by T. Kynaston (Hialeah, FL, 1982).

SELECTED RECORDINGS

As leader: Four and one Moore/Five Brothers (1949, NewJ 802); Crazy Chords (1949, NewJ 811); My Old Flame/The Lady in Red (1950, NewJ 829); 'Tis Autumn/Lover come back to me (1952, Clef 89042); *Stan Getz at the Shrine Auditorium* (1954, Norg 2000); *The Steamer* (1956, Verve 8294); *Stan Getz Meets Gerry Mulligan* (1957, Verve 8249); *Focus* (1961, Verve 68412); *Jazz Samba* (1962, Verve 68432); *Stan Getz–Bill Evans Quartet* (1964, Verve 68833); *Captain Marvel* (1972, Col. KC32706); with J. Rowles: *The Peacocks* (1975, Col. JC34873); *The Dolphin* (1981, Conc. 158); *Voyage* (1986, Blackhawk 51101)

As sideman with W. Herman: Four Brothers (1947, Col. 38304); Early Autumn (1948, Cap. 57-616)

BIBLIOGRAPHY

M. James: *Ten Modern Jazzmen: an Appraisal of the Recorded Work of Ten Modern Jazzmen* (London, 1960), 15
M. Williams, ed.: *Jazz Panorama* (New York and London, 1962/*R*1979) [colln of previously pubd articles], 154
L. Feather: "The Resurgence of Stan Getz," *DB*, xxx/5 (1963), 16
M. James: "The Cool Deviations," *JM*, x/2 (1964), 11
L. Tomkins: "It Feels Good to Flex your Muscles," *Crescendo*, ii/12 (1964), 24 [interview]
G. Hoefer: "Stan Getz: Always a Melodist," *DB*, xxxii/11 (1965), 14
D. DeMicheal: "A Long Look at Stan Getz," *DB*, xxxiii (1966), no.10, p.17; no.11, p.15
I. Gitler: *Jazz Masters of the Forties* (New York, 1966/*R*1983 with discography)
F. Tirro: "Constructive Elements in Jazz Improvisation," *Journal of the American Musicological Society*, xxvii (1974), 285–305
A. J. Smith: "Influentially Yours, Stan Getz," *DB*, xliii/14 (1976), 17
A. Astrup: *The Stan Getz Discography* (Texarkana, TX, 1978; rev. and enlarged 2/1984 as *The Revised Stan Getz Discography*)
R. Williams: "Stan Getz," *DB*, xlv/1 (1978), 17
L. Tomkins: "Stan Getz: the Enjoyable Endeavour," *CI*, xviii/2 (1979), 6
R. Palmer: "Stan Getz: an Appraisal," *JJI*, xxxvi/12 (1983), 8; xxxvii (1984), no.1, p.14; no.3, p.18
H. Hellhund: *Cool Jazz: Grundzüge seiner Entstehung und Entwicklung* (Mainz, Germany, 1985), 211
R. Palmer: "Stan Getz at Sixty," *JJI*, xl/7 (1987), 8 [incl. discography]

J. BRADFORD ROBINSON

GHB. Record label founded in 1954 as a subsidiary of JAZZOLOGY.

Ghost band. A band that performs under the name of a deceased leader. The repertory of such a group consists largely of the original band's arrangements, though it may also include items written in a similar style; some groups attempt to retain musicians who worked as sidemen for the leader concerned. Notable examples of ghost bands have been a number under the name of Glenn Miller and orchestras named after the Dorsey brothers; Duke Ellington's band was taken over in 1974 by his son Mercer Ellington, and Count Basie's orchestra has continued since the latter's death in 1984 under the leadership of Thad Jones (1985–6) and Frank Foster (from 1986).

Ghost(ed) note. A weak note, sometimes barely audible, or a note that is implied rather than sounded. Ghost notes may be produced intentionally as a subtle means of articulating a phrase, or they may occur accidentally when a player "fluffs" notes (that is, fails to produce them cleanly with a full tone). Numerous examples of intentional ghost notes occur on Miles Davis's solo on the fifth take of Charlie Parker's *Billie's Bounce* (1945,

Ex.1 From M. Davis's solo on C. Parker: *Billie's Bounce* (1945, Savoy 573) [5th take]; transcr. F. Kerschbaumer

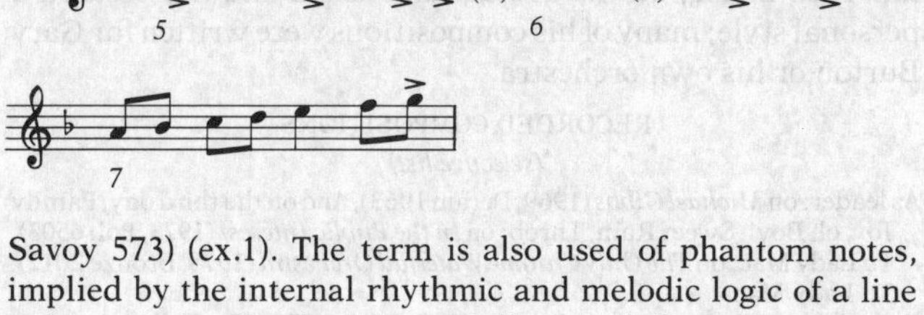

Savoy 573) (ex.1). The term is also used of phantom notes, implied by the internal rhythmic and melodic logic of a line or by voice leading but not actually sounded.

BARRY KERNFELD

Giaimo, Dottie. *See* DODGION, DOTTIE.

Giants of Jazz. All-star group active in 1971–2 whose members were Dizzy Gillespie, Kai Winding, Sonny Stitt, Thelonious Monk, Al McKibbon, and Art Blakey.

Gibbons, Irene. *See* TAYLOR, EVA.

Gibbs, Eddie [Edward Leroy] (*b* New Haven, CT, 25 Dec 1908). Acoustic guitarist, banjoist, and double bass player. From the late 1920s he played with Eubie Blake, Charlie Johnson, and Wilbur Sweatman; he recorded on banjo with Sweatman (1930, 1935), and on guitar with Alex Hill (1934). He then performed and recorded with Edgar Hayes (1937–8), and while touring Europe with Hayes's group, made recordings in Stockholm with Kenny Clarke (1938, including *Sweet Sue,* Odeon 2953). After working briefly with Teddy Wilson (1940) Gibbs performed and recorded with Eddie South and played in sessions with Chick Bullock (both 1940–41). From 1941 he worked mainly with the pianist Dave Martin, but also performed with Luis Russell, Claude Hopkins, and Cedric Wallace, and recorded with Eddie Barefield (1946). He then played and recorded (as banjoist) with Wilbur De Paris (1952–5). In 1959 he took up double bass, and later recorded with Claude Hopkins as a member of the backup group for Capt. John Handy (1966). (*ChiltonW*; *FeatherE*)

Gibbs, Mike [Michael Clement Irving] (*b* Salisbury, Rhodesia [now Harare, Zimbabwe], 25 Sept 1937). Rhodesian composer, bandleader, and trombonist. He learned piano from the age of seven, took up trombone when he was 17, and in 1959 went to the USA to study at the Berklee College of Music. After settling in Britain in 1965 he worked as a trombonist in Graham Collier's band (1965–*c*1967) and John Dankworth's orchestra. Gibbs swiftly established a reputation as a composer and arranger, and wrote music for radio, television, and films as well as for a number of his own bands (1968–74). He also worked as a studio musician and performed with radio big bands in Denmark, Sweden, and Germany. By the late 1960s he was receiving widespread critical acclaim (his album *In the Public Interest* was voted "best album of 1974" by readers of *Melody Maker*), and in 1974 he moved to the USA to take up a position as composer-in-residence at Berklee. Thereafter Gibbs toured Britain (1975–8), performed his music with radio orchestras in Finland, Sweden, and Germany (1978–81), and worked as a record producer, notably for Kevin Eubanks (1982). In 1983 he resigned from Berklee to become a freelance composer, arranger, and record producer; before moving back to London in 1985 he collaborated on works with Dankworth, Michael Mantler, Pat Metheny, and John McLaughlin.

Gibbs's music shows many influences, ranging from Charles Ives, Olivier Messiaen, and Gil Evans to Baroque composers and rock music, but he avoids eclecticism and has created a personal style; many of his compositions were written for Gary Burton or his own orchestra.

RECORDED COMPOSITIONS
(selective list)

As leader: on *Michael Gibbs* (1969, Deram 1063), And on the third day, Family Joy, oh Boy!, Sweet Rain, Throb; on *In the Public Interest* (1973, Pol. 6503), To Lady Mac; on *The Only Chrome Waterfall Orchestra* (1975, Bronze 2012), To Lady Mac

Recorded by G. Burton: on *Duster* (1967, RCA LSP3855), Ballet, Liturgy, Sweet Rain; on *Country Roads* (1968, RCA LSP4098), And on the third day, Family Joy, oh Boy!; on *Throb* (1969, Atl. 1531), Throb; on *The New Quartet* (1973, ECM 1030), Nonsequence

Recorded by S. Getz: on *Sweet Rain* (1967, Verve 68693), Sweet Rain

BIBLIOGRAPHY

Feather–Gitler '70s
L. Tomkins: "The Mike Gibbs Story," *CI*, ix/11 (1971), 14
R. Brown: "Mike Gibbs," *Into Jazz*, i/3 (1974), 11
L. Tomkins: "Mike Gibbs Today," *CI*, xvii/7 (1979), 12
F. Bouchard: "Profile: Michael Gibbs," *DB*, 1/9 (1983), 50

CHARLES FOX/DIGBY FAIRWEATHER

Gibbs, Terry [Gubenko, Julius] (*b* New York, 13 Oct 1924). Vibraphonist. Having been encouraged to study music by his father, a double bass player and violinist, he learned to play drums, timpani, and xylophone; as a xylophone player he won an amateur contest at the age of 12. During World War II he served for three years in the armed forces, during part of which he played drums in military bands. After his discharge he worked in New York with Bill De Arango (at clubs on 52nd Street) and Tommy Dorsey (for a brief period in 1946 and again in 1950), toured Scandinavia with Chubby Jackson (1947–8), and performed in the USA with Buddy Rich (1948), Woody Herman (1948–9), and Benny Goodman (1950–52). In 1950–51 he appeared regularly on the television series of the singer Mel Tormé and at the same time formed his own big band; after moving in 1957 to California he led his band at the Monterey Jazz Festival in 1961. He worked again in television (1964, 1968) and in 1965 became the music director of Steve Allen's band. Later he toured widely with Allen and with his own small groups; from 1980 he occasionally led a quintet with Buddy DeFranco. Gibbs's aggressive, swinging style may be described as the bop counterpart to the work of Lionel Hampton.

Oral history material in *NjR*.

SELECTED RECORDINGS

As leader: *Vibes on Velvet* (1955, EmA 36064); *Swingin' with Terry Gibbs* (1956, EmA 36103); *Launching a New Band* (1959, Mer. 60112); *The Exciting Big Band of Terry Gibbs* (1961, Verve 62151); *Take it from me* (1964, Imp. 58); with B. DeFranco: *Jazz Party: First Time Together* (1981, PAlt 8011)

As sideman with W. Herman: Early Autumn (1948, Cap. 57-616)

BIBLIOGRAPHY

J. Tynan: "Vamp Till Ready: Terry Gibbs' Big Band," *DB*, xxix/28 (1962), 18
A. Morgan: "Terry Gibbs," *JM*, xi/5 (1965), 14; xii (1966), no.2, p.27; no.6, p.17; no.153 (1967), 29 [incl. discography]
J. Burns: "Good Vibes," *J&B*, ii/5 (1972), 7
L. Tomkins: "Terry Gibbs," *CI*, xviii/12 (1980), 16; xix (1980–81), no.1, p.12; no.3, p.16; no.8, p.23
T. Gibbs: "Terry Gibbs on his Approach to the Vibes, and the Big Band," *CI*, xx/9 (1982), 12
L. Tomkins: "Terry Gibbs," *CI*, xxi (1982), no.1, p.20; no.2, p.12; no.4, p.16; xxii/8 (1983), 16

GARY THEROUX

Gibson, Andy [Albert Andrew] (*b* Zanesville, OH, 6 Nov 1913; *d* Cincinnati, 10 Feb 1961). Arranger, composer, and trumpeter. He played trumpet with Lew Redman's Bellhops (1931), Zack Whyte (1932–3), McKinney's Cotton Pickers (1934–5), Blanche Calloway (1936), and Willie Bryant and Lucky Millinder (both 1937). Thereafter he became a freelance arranger, working for such leaders as Count Basie, Charlie Barnet, Cab Calloway, and Harry James. He directed an army band from 1942 to 1945, in which he also played trumpet, then concentrated on writing arrangements for commercial musicians. In 1955 he joined King Records and in the late 1950s was appointed recording supervisor. Among his best-known compositions are *The Great Lie, Geechee Joe, I left my baby,* and *The Hucklebuck.*

RECORDED COMPOSITIONS
(selective list)

C. Basie: I left my baby (1939, Col. 35231); C. Calloway: Geechee Joe (1941, OK 6147); C. Barnet: on *Hop on the Skyliner* (1942–5, Decca 8098), The Great Lie; T. Dorsey: The Hucklebuck (1949, Vic. 203427)

SELECTED ARRANGEMENTS

Recorded by C. Basie: Shorty George (1938, Decca 2325); Tickletoe (1940, Col. 35521); Louisiana (1940, Col. 35448)

Recorded by others: C. Calloway: A Ghost of a Chance (1940, OK 5687); M. Ellington: on *Stepping into Swing Society* (1958, Coral 57255), Ruint

BIBLIOGRAPHY

ChiltonW
S. Dance: *The World of Swing* (New York, 1974), 224 [colln of previously pubd interviews]

FRANK DRIGGS

Giddins, Gary (Mitchell) (*b* New York, 21 March 1948). Writer. He studied at Grinnell College (BA 1972). After working as a freelance writer for a year he was appointed a contributing editor to *Down Beat*, and remained with the journal until 1974. A dedication to jazz has been apparent throughout his career, and in 1973 he took up the post of jazz critic for the *Village Voice;* the recurring themes in his essays include the underrated musician, the tensions between artistic integrity, fame, and financial reward, and the blurred interactions of jazz with white- and black-American popular music. Later Giddins held appointments as a Smithsonian fellow (1974–5), a disc jockey at radio station WBAI, New York (1975–80), and a regular contributor to *Hi-Fi Stereo Buyer's Guide* (1975–8) and *New York Magazine* (1975–80). He also works as a freelance writer and producer, and from 1977 he has taught at the School for Continuing Education at New York University and elsewhere. In 1985, with John Lewis and Roberta Swann, Giddins founded the AMERICAN JAZZ ORCHESTRA, and in 1987 a documentary film, *Celebrating Bird*, based on his book of the same name, was given its première at the North Sea Jazz Festival.

WRITINGS
(selective list)

Riding on a Blue Note: Jazz and American Pop (New York, and Oxford, England, 1981) [colln of previously pubd articles]
Rhythm-a-ning: Jazz Tradition and Innovation in the '80s (New York, and Oxford, England, 1985) [colln of previously pubd articles]
Celebrating Bird: the Triumph of Charlie Parker (New York, 1987)

BARRY KERNFELD

Gifford, Gene [Harold Eugene] (*b* Americus, GA, 31 May 1908; *d* Memphis, 12 Nov 1970). Arranger, banjoist, and guitarist. He started arranging for his high-school band in Memphis. After touring with his own bands (1925–6) and with Watson's Bellhops and Blue Steele, he joined Jean Goldkette's Orange Blossoms in 1929. Shortly afterwards this group became the cooperative ensemble called the CASA LOMA ORCHESTRA. As chief arranger, Gifford set the style for this influential band, which became a favorite with young dancers. Although somewhat repetitious and rhythmically stiff, his scores were expertly crafted and executed with a discipline and precision due, at least in part, to the stability of the band's personnel. Fast, showy instrumental pieces, for example the *Casa Loma Stomp* (1930), were based on riff patterns and call-and-response exchanges between brass and reed sections. Gifford also developed a contrasting, lush style for ballads, such as *Drifting Apart* (1937), making good use of the band's excellent trombone trio and exploring the reed section's capacity for playing various woodwind instruments. His ballad *Smoke Rings* (1932) was the orchestra's theme song. Although critics often slighted the Casa Loma for its metronomic approach to jazz and its unimpressive soloists, musicians found Gifford's arrangements stimulating, and most big bands before 1935 included pieces in his style in their repertory (Fletcher Henderson recorded *Casa Loma Stomp*). Gifford had a considerable influence on such prolific arrangers as Will Hudson, Nat Leslie, and Archie Bleyer, and stock editions of his works were widely circulated. After leaving the Casa Loma Orchestra in 1939 Gifford worked as a freelance for dance and radio bands. He rejoined the Casa Loma briefly (1948–9), then during the 1950s worked as a radio engineer and recording consultant. In 1969 he settled in Memphis as a music teacher. Arrangements made by him for the Casa Loma Orchestra are in the Robert Gray Dodge Library of Northeastern University, Boston; *see* LIBRARIES AND ARCHIVES, §2.

SELECTED ARRANGEMENTS
* – with Gifford as sideman

As leader: Nothin' but the Blues (1935, Vic. 25041); Dizzy Glide (1935, Vic. 25065)
Recorded by Casa Loma Orchestra: *Casa Loma Stomp (1930, OK 41492); *White Jazz (1931, Bruns. 6092); *Black Jazz (1931, Bruns. 6242); *Smoke Rings (1932, Bruns. 6289); *Blue Jazz (1932, Bruns. 6358); *Wild Goose Chase (1933, Bruns. 6588); Ol' Man River (1934, Bruns. 6800); Narcissus (1934, Bruns. 7321); Drifting Apart (1937, Decca 15042)

BIBLIOGRAPHY

M. W. Stearns: *The Story of Jazz* (New York, 1956, rev. and enlarged 2/1958/*R*1970)
A. McCarthy: *Big Band Jazz* (New York and London, 1974), 190

DAN MORGENSTERN

Gig. A term commonly applied to a musical engagement of one night's duration only; to undertake such an engagement. *(GoldJL)*

Gilberto, Astrud (*b* Bahia, Brazil, 1940). Brazilian singer. She came to prominence in the USA as the singer on *The Girl from Ipanema*, which she recorded in 1963 with João Gilberto (to whom she was married at the time), Antonio Carlos Jobim, and Stan Getz for the album *Getz/Gilberto*. A shortened version of the song was released as a single and became a substantial hit in 1964. Thereafter she recorded several albums in the bossa nova style, singing both in Portuguese and English. She has continued to perform and record in a similar idiom into the 1980s. In 1983 she performed in New York as the leader of a small group that included Jerry Dodgion, singing mainly bossa nova, but also the compositions of Michael Franks, whose understated songs are well suited to her approach.

Gilberto defined the style of bossa nova singing as it was adopted in the USA; she employed a smooth, cool, breathy timbre, and sang at a constant, moderate dynamic level with an even, flowing pulse. Her work often has an economy of melodic line and a steady momentum akin to that of Basie, but its rhythmic drive is often devoid of contours.

SELECTED RECORDINGS
(all recorded for Verve)

As leader: *The Astrud Gilberto Album* (1965, 68608); *Look to the Rainbow* (1965–6, 68643); with W. Wanderley: *A Certain Smile, a Certain Sadness* (1966, 68673)
As sideman: on S. Getz and J. Gilberto: *Getz/Gilberto* (1963, 68545), Corcovado, The Girl from Ipanema; S. Getz: *Getz a-gogo* (1964, 68600), incl. Only Trust your Heart, The Telephone Song

BIBLIOGRAPHY

Feather '60s
J. A. Tynan: "Caught in the Act: Stan Getz – Astrud Gilberto," *DB*, xxxi/24 (1964), 35
P. Welding: "Astrud Gilberto/Stanley Turrentine," *DB*, xxxviii/20 (1971), 19 [review]
G. Rava: "The Lady from Ipanema," *Jm*, no.323 (1983), 42
C. Groome: "The Girl from Ipanema's a Lady Now," *Ear: New Music News*, xi/5–xii/1 (1987), 13

MARTY HATCH

Gilberto, João (*b* Juazeiro, Brazil, June 1931). Brazilian singer, guitarist, and composer. He grew up in a musical family, cultivated an early interest in the samba, and as a teenager listened to American jazz, particularly the work of Gerry Mulligan. After moving to Rio de Janeiro in the early 1950s he collaborated with Antonio Carlos Jobim, developing a style of music based on the samba that became known as bossa nova. In 1958 they made their first recording, of Jobim's *Chega de saudade* and Gilberto's *Bim-bam;* it became extremely successful in Brazil, and set the standard for the genre for several years. In 1959 they released an album. Several pieces from this were later recorded on the album *Jazz Samba* (1962, Verve 68432) by Stan Getz and Charlie Byrd, who also arranged to bring Gilberto, Jobim, and other Brazilian musicians to perform in New York. Although the first concert was poorly received, Gilberto's later performances and recordings were more successful, and he recorded an album with Getz in 1963 which became a hit. With Astrud Gilberto, who was his wife at the time, he defined the bossa nova style of singing, using a light, slightly nasal timbre, and articulating Portuguese texts with great delicacy. His guitar playing is light, crisp, and moderate in volume. His songs possess a sense of swing that derives from the rhythmic impetus of the samba, though his vocal lines are strongly influenced by the speech rhythms of Portuguese, and the direction of his melodies is usually dictated by the intricate bossa nova harmonies.

SELECTED RECORDINGS

As leader: Chega de saudade/Bim-bam (1958, Odeon 3073); *Brazil's Brilliant João Gilberto* (1960, Cap. ST10280); with S. Getz: *Getz/Gilberto* (1963, Verve 68545), incl. Desafinado; *Getz/Gilberto no.2* (1964, Verve 68623)

BIBLIOGRAPHY

Feather '60s
G. Lees: "Bossa nova: Anatomy of a Travesty," *DB*, xxx/4 (1963), 22
G. Behague: "Bossa and Bossas: Recent Changes in Brazilian Urban Popular Music," *Ethnomusicology*, xvii (1973), 209 [incl. discography]

MARTY HATCH

Gillespie, Dizzy [John Birks] (*b* Cheraw, SC, 21 Oct 1917). Trumpeter, composer, and bandleader. He was one of the principal developers of bop in the early 1940s, and his styles of improvising and trumpet playing were imitated widely in the 1940s and 1950s. Indeed, he is one of the most influential players in the history of jazz.

1. Life. 2. Musical style.

1. Life. Gillespie was the youngest of nine children. His father, a bricklayer and weekend bandleader, died when he was ten; two years later he began to teach himself to play trombone and trumpet, and later took up cornet. His musical ability enabled him to attend Laurinburg Institute, North Carolina, in 1932, for the school needed a trumpet player for its band. During his years there he practiced the trumpet and piano intensively, still largely without formal guidance.

In 1935 he left school to join his family, who had moved to Philadelphia. Soon he joined a band led by Frankie Fairfax, which also included Charlie Shavers. Shavers knew many of the trumpet solos of Roy Eldridge, and Gillespie learned them by copying Shavers (he had previously known only a handful of phrases by Eldridge, the man who became his early role model). While he was in Fairfax's band Gillespie's clownish behavior earned him the nickname he has carried ever since.

Gillespie left Philadelphia in 1937 and moved to New York to try and become better known as a jazz player. After sitting in with many different bands and at many jam sessions he earned a job with Teddy Hill's big band, largely because he sounded much like Eldridge, who had been Hill's trumpet soloist. The band toured France and Great Britain for two months shortly after Gillespie joined. On returning to New York he again worked in several groups, including Al Cooper's Savoy Sultans and the Afro-Cuban band of Alberto Socarras, before returning to Hill's band. In 1939 he joined Cab Calloway's big band, one of the highest-paid black bands in New York at the time. While in this group he began to develop an interest in the fusion of jazz and Afro-Cuban music, largely because of his friendship with Mario Bauzá, who was also in Calloway's band. During the same period he was beginning to diverge from Eldridge's playing style both formally, in his solos with the band – such as *Pickin' the Cabbage* (1940) – and in an informal context, with the group's double bass player Milt Hinton.

While on tour in 1940 Gillespie met Charlie Parker in Kansas City. Soon he began participating in after-hours jam sessions in New York with Parker, Thelonious Monk, Kenny Clarke, and others. This group of young, experimenting players gradually developed the new, more complex style of jazz that was to be called bop. Recordings, such as *Kerouac* (1941), made at Minton's Playhouse, exemplify this emergent style.

A dispute with Calloway led to Gillespie's dismissal in 1941. He then worked briefly with many leaders, including Ella Fitzgerald, Coleman Hawkins, Benny Carter, Charlie Barnet, Les Hite, Lucky Millinder, Earl Hines (whose band also included Parker), and Duke Ellington. With Millinder he recorded a fully formed bop solo within a swing-band context on *Little John Special* (1942). After his solo, the band plays a riff which he developed into the composition *Salt Peanuts*. During the winter of 1943–4 Gillespie led a small group with Oscar Pettiford. In 1944 Billy Eckstine, singer with the Hines band, formed a bop band of his own and engaged Gillespie to play and to be music director. At about the same time Gillespie made some of the first small-group bop recordings, some with Hawkins's band, and others, including *Salt Peanuts* and *Hot House*, under his own name with Parker.

Early in 1945 Gillespie organized his own short-lived big band. Failing to achieve financial success with this group, he then formed a bop quintet with Parker in November. He later expanded the group to a sextet, but his desire to lead a big band inspired him to try once more, and this time he was able to keep its members together for four years. During this period

Dizzy Gillespie's band, 1948 including (left to right) James Moody (tenor saxophone), Chano Pozo (conga), and Gillespie (trumpet)

the band made some early attempts to fuse Afro-Cuban rhythms with Afro-American jazz (*see* AFRO-CUBAN JAZZ). Gillespie added Chano Pozo to the rhythm section, and the two men recorded *Cubana Be/Cubana Bop* (written by George Russell) and *Manteca* (by Gillespie and Pozo). By 1947 the band's rhythm section consisted of John Lewis, Milt Jackson, Kenny Clarke, and Ray Brown, who went on to form the Modern Jazz Quartet. At various times such prominent bop players as J. J. Johnson, Sonny Stitt, James Moody (see illustration), Jimmy Heath, Paul Gonsalves, and John Coltrane were also members of Gillespie's band. Financial pressures forced Gillespie to give up the big band in 1950. A short engagement as featured soloist with Stan Kenton's big band followed, and then he organized a sextet. In 1951 he formed his own record company, Dee Gee; it, too, was financially unrewarding and short-lived.

Early in 1953 someone accidentally fell on Gillespie's trumpet, which was sitting upright on a trumpet stand, and bent the bell back. Gillespie played it, discovered that he liked the sound, and ever since has had trumpets built for him with the bell pointing upwards at a 45° angle. The design is his visual trademark: even after more than three decades he is virtually the only major trumpeter in jazz playing such an instrument.

In 1956, after several years leading small groups, Gillespie formed another big band specifically to tour Iran, Lebanon, Syria, Pakistan, Turkey, Greece, and Yugoslavia on a cultural mission for the US State Department, and a few months later another sponsored tour, to South America, took place. He kept the band together for two years, but without government funding he was unable to keep such a large ensemble operational, and he returned to leading small groups.

Gillespie has continued to perform and record extensively with his various small groups into the late 1980s. In addition he appears occasionally in all-star groups such as the Giants of Jazz (1971–2), a sextet with Kai Winding, Sonny Stitt, Thelonious Monk, Al McKibbon, and Art Blakey, and he is a regular performer on Caribbean cruise ships that feature jazz artists. Although he was once viewed as a musical iconoclast, his music is no longer considered radical. He is viewed rather as an elder statesman of jazz, and his outgoing personality and impish sense of humor have endeared him to the general public through appearances on television.

2. MUSICAL STYLE. Gillespie's first recorded solos, especially that on *King Porter Stomp*, sound much like those of Roy Eldridge; he largely imitated the phrasing, tone quality, vibrato, and melodic ideas of his idol. But little by little his style changed during the years 1939 to 1944: he began using a lighter vibrato; his phrasing contained both swing eighth-notes (ex.1*a*) and even eighth-notes (ex.1*b*) instead of being dominated by the

Ex.1

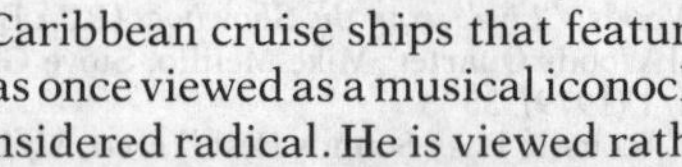

former; his melodies became more chromatic (sometimes self-consciously so), especially in his extensive use of the lowered second degree of the scale (used more sparingly by his swing-era elders Eldridge and Hawkins); and early versions of some of his characteristic melodic formulas (such as the phrase in triplets in ex.2) began to appear. By the middle 1940s his mature style was fully formed.

Gillespie's is a dramatic style, filled with startling contrasts. Simple, almost folklike phrases may suddenly give way to long, complex phrases filled with fast notes (ex.3). Similarly, soft,

Ex.2 From C. Parker: *Blue 'n Boogie,* (1951, Okiedoke [unnumbered]); transcr. T. Owens

• = lift
† = fall off

mid-register phrases may suddenly give way to high notes played fortissimo. And the drama is visual as well as aural, for he allows his cheeks to fill with air when he plays; over the years his cheek muscles have stretched, and the increase in the size of his face when he plays is striking. His tone is less full and rich than that of some of his predecessors and many of his followers, and sometimes he seems little concerned about accurate intonation. But his fertile melodic and rhythmic imagination, his technical facility, and his tireless dedication to bop have earned him a place among the great figures of jazz history.

Ex.3 From *Hot House* (1945, Guild 1003); transcr. T. Owens

Although his fame and his importance to jazz rest primarily on his trumpet playing, Gillespie has written a number of significant jazz compositions. During the 1940s and 1950s he wrote and collaborated with others on a variety of well-known pieces: the chromatic *Woody 'n' You* (filled with half-diminished seventh chords, one of his favorite harmonic sonorities); the simple, humorous, and riff-like *Salt Peanuts* (based on *I got rhythm*); the frantically fast *Bebop*; the Latin-tinged *A Night in Tunisia* and *Manteca*; the melodically complex *Groovin' High* (based on *Whispering*) and *Anthropology* (based on *I got rhythm* and written in collaboration with Charlie Parker); the harmonically ingenious *Con Alma*; and the basic blues theme *Birks Works*.

Oral history material in *NjR*.

See also JAZZ (i), §§V, 2, 3, and 5; and TRUMPET, §§1 and 5; for further illustrations see JAZZ (i), fig.5, and PARKER, CHARLIE, fig.2.

SELECTED RECORDINGS

Duos with O. Peterson: *Oscar Peterson and Dizzy Gillespie* (1974, Pablo 2310740)

As leader of small groups: Kerouac, first issued on *The Harlem Jazz Scene* (1941, Eso. 4); I can't get started (1945, Manor 1042); Salt Peanuts/Bebop (1945, Manor 5000); Groovin' High (1945, Guild 1001); Salt Peanuts/Hot House (1945, Guild 1003); Confirmation (1946, Dial 1004); Dynamo A/Dynamo B (1946, Dial 1001); A Night in Tunisia/Anthropology (1946, Vic. 400132); Birks Works (1951, Dee Gee 3601); *Duets with Sonny Rollins and Sonny Stitt* (1957, Verve 8260), incl. Con Alma; *Jazz for a Sunday Afternoon* (1967, SolS 18028); *Dizzy Gillespie's Big Four* (1974, Pablo 2310719)

As leader of big bands: *Live at the Spotlite* (1946, Hi-Fly 01); Oop-pop-a-dah (1947, Vic. 202480); Woody 'n' You (1947, Vic. 203186); Cubana Be/Cubana Bop (1947, Vic. 203145); Manteca (1947, Vic. 203023); *Reunion Big Band* (1968, Saba 15207)

As sideman: T. Hill: King Porter Stomp (1937, Bb 6988); Blue Rhythm Fantasy (1937, Bb 6989); L. Hampton: Hot Mallets (1939, Vic. 26371); C. Calloway: Pickin' the Cabbage (1940, Voc./OK 5467); L. Millinder: Little John Special (1942, Bruns. 03406); C. Hawkins: Woody 'n' You (1944, Apollo 751); C. Parker: Blue 'n Boogie (1951, Okiedoke [unnumbered]); Jazz at Massey Hall: *Quintet of the Year* (1953, Debut 2, 4), incl. Hot House, A Night in Tunisia, Wee

BIBLIOGRAPHY

L. Feather: *Inside Be-bop* (New York, 1949/*R*1977 as *Inside Jazz*), 19
R. Boyer: "Bop: a Profile of Dizzy," *Eddie Condon's Treasury of Jazz*, ed. E. Condon and R. Gehman (New York, 1956/*R*1975), 206
M. James: *Dizzy Gillespie* (London, 1959); repr. in *Kings of Jazz*, ed. S. Green (South Brunswick, NJ, and New York, 1978)
I. Gitler: *Jazz Masters of the Forties* (New York, 1966/*R*1983 with discography), 58
G. Hoefer: "The Big Bands: the Glorious Dizzy Gillespie Orchestra," *DB*, xxxiii/8 (1966), 27
J. Burns: "Dizzy Gillespie: the Early 1950s," *JJ*, xxii (1969), no.1, p.2; no.2, p.2
J. G. Jepsen: *A Discography of Dizzy Gillespie* (Copenhagen, 1969)
J. Burns: "Early Birks," *JJ*, xxiv/3 (1971), 18
——: "Dizzy Gillespie: 1945–50," *JJ*, xxv/1 (1972), 12
L. Feather: *From Satchmo to Miles* (New York, 1972), 147
R. Wang: "Jazz Circa 1945: a Confluence of Styles," *Musical Quarterly*, lix (1973), 531
R. J. Gleason: *Celebrating the Duke, and Louis, Bessie, Billie, Bird, Carmen, Miles, Dizzy, and other Heroes* (Boston and Toronto, 1975), 97
S. Dance: *The World of Earl Hines* (New York, 1977) [interviews]
J. L. Collier: *The Making of Jazz: a Comprehensive History* (New York and London, 1978), 346
C. Terry: "Dizzy Gillespie: Blowin' with Diz, via Mumbles," *DB*, xlv/8 (1978), 12
D. Gillespie and A. Fraser: *To be, or not . . . to Bop: Memoirs* (Garden City, NY, 1979)
J. Evensmo: *The Trumpets of Dizzy Gillespie, 1937–1943, Irving Randolph, Joe Thomas* (n.p. [Oslo], n.d. [?1982]) [discography]
J. R. Cook: "Re-doing Dizzy's Discography: 1942–1956 Sessions," *IAJRCJ*, xvi/2 (1983), 3
D. J. Travis: *An Autobiography of Black Jazz* (Chicago, 1983) [incl. interviews], 333
J. Blum: "Dizzy! The One and Only," *JT* (1984), Oct, 14
R. Horricks: *Dizzy Gillespie and the Be-bop Revolution* (Tunbridge Wells, England, and New York, 1984) [incl. discography by T. Middleton]
P. Koster and C. Sellers: *Dizzy Gillespie*, i: *1937–1953* (Amsterdam, 1985) [discography]
J. Woelfer: *Dizzy Gillespie: sein Leben, seine Musik, seine Schallplatten* (Waakirchen, nr Bad Tölz, Germany, 1987)
B. McRae: *Dizzy Gillespie* (Tunbridge Wells, England, in preparation) [incl. discography]

THOMAS OWENS

Gilmore, John (E.) (*b* Summit, MS, 28 Sept 1931). Tenor saxophonist. He studied clarinet in Chicago from the age of 14, and performed in bands while in the air force (1948–51). In 1952 he played tenor saxophone briefly with Earl Hines in a traveling show organized around the basketball team the Harlem Globetrotters, then the following year joined Sun Ra. Apart from a period with Art Blakey's Jazz Messengers (1964–5), Gilmore has remained a member of Sun Ra's band, often serving as a drummer. He has also recorded as a sideman with Freddie Hubbard (1962), Elmo Hope (1963), McCoy Tyner, Paul Bley, Andrew Hill, and Blakey (all 1964), Hill (1965), Chick Corea and Pete La Roca (both 1967), and as the leader of groups with Clifford Jordan (1957) and Dizzy Reece (1970). Members of the avant garde have credited Gilmore as the first to produce the sustained, screaming type of improvisation in the upper register of the tenor saxophone that became integral to the style of John Coltrane, Pharoah Sanders, and others in the mid-1960s.

SELECTED RECORDINGS

As leader: with C. Jordan: *Blowing in from Chicago* (1957, BN 1549); with D. Reece: *Dizzy Reece/John Gilmore* (1970, Futura 16)
As sideman: Sun Ra: *Jazz by Sun Ra* (1956, Tran. 10); *The Futuristic Sounds of Sun Ra* (1961, Savoy 12169); *The Heliocentric Worlds of Sun Ra* (1965, ESP 1017); A. Hill: *Compulsion* (1965, BN 84217); C. Corea: *Bliss* (1967, Muse 5011); Sun Ra: *Unity* (1977, Horo 19–20)

BIBLIOGRAPHY

V. Simosko: "John Gilmore," *Coda*, xii/7 (1975), 9 [incl. discography]
B. Rusch: "John Gilmore: Oral History/Interview," *Cadence*, iv/7 (1978), 18
V. Wilmer: "Gilmore and 'Trane: the Sun Ra Link," *MM*, lv (27 Dec 1980), 16
J. Diliberto: "John Gilmore: Three Decades in the Sun's Shadow," *DB*, li/5 (1984), 26 [incl. discography]
A. Sato: "John Gilmore," *Be-bop and Beyond*, iv/2 (1986), 15 [interview]

BARRY KERNFELD

Gilmore, Steve(n Dirk) (*b* Trenton, NJ, 21 Jan 1943). Double bass player. He played from the age of 12, and by 14 was working professionally in and around Philadelphia. In 1960 he attended Oscar Peterson's Advanced School of Contemporary Music. He played with Ira Sullivan, the Baker's Dozen Big Band, and Flip Phillips in Florida (1967–71), Al Cohn and Zoot Sims, and Mose Allison (1972–3), the Thad Jones–Mel Lewis Orchestra (1974–5), Phil Woods (from 1974), and Richie Cole (from 1975). He was later a member of the National Jazz Ensemble (from 1975) and played with John Coates, Dave Frishberg, and Toshiko Akiyoshi as well as continuing his association with Woods. Gilmore's walking bass lines create smooth melodic patterns rather than simply outlining the harmonies. He has described his approach as follows: "When I am playing well, I am not thinking of change, change, change. I am trying to map a melody to the song" (Wasserman). Two volumes of transcriptions of his bass lines have been published by F. Boaden (*Steve Gilmore Bass Lines, Exactly as Recorded*, New Albany, IN, 1984; and *Jam Session Bass Lines by Steve Gilmore*, New Albany, ?1986).

SELECTED RECORDINGS

Duos with H. Leahey: *Silver Threads* (1984, Omni. N1042A)
As sideman: P. Woods: *The New Phil Woods Album* (1975, RCA BGL1-1391); C. Marohnic: *Chuck Marohnic Quartet* (1978, Ste. 4002); P. Woods: *Birds of a Feather* (1981, Ant. 1006); *At the Vanguard* (1982, Ant. 1013)

BIBLIOGRAPHY

Liner notes, P. Woods: *"Live" from the Showboat* (RCA BLG2-2202, 1976)
J. DeMuth: "Phil Woods Quartet: Mike Melillo, Steve Gilmore, Bill Goodwin," *DB*, xlvi/1 (1979), 35
R. Wasserman: "Acoustic Bass Sounds Best," *Frets*, vi/11 (1984), 60

JOHN VOIGT

Gilson, Jef [Quiévreux, Jean-François] (*b* Guebwiller, France, 25 July 1926). French pianist and leader. After studying classical music he played clarinet at clubs in Paris (1944), then took up the piano and formed a small group, which he led for a brief period in 1950. In 1957 he formed a big band that included among its sidemen Jean-Louis Chautemps, Jean-Luc Ponty, Michel Portal, and the drummer Bernard Lubat. He took an interest in the early developments of free jazz. In 1965 he sang and toured as a member of the Double Six, which he left to teach music in Madagascar. He led many groups in the 1970s, including the band Europamerica, and also established a record label (Palm) and a jazz school in Paris; in the 1980s he ceased to perform while continuing to teach. Gilson has been more important for having helped the careers of other, younger musicians than for his own playing.

SELECTED RECORDINGS

As leader: *Oeil-vision* (1962, Club de l'échiquier 1); *Enfin* (1962–3, Club de l'échiquier 1002); *Jeff Gilson à Gaveau* (1965, Société française de Productions Phonographiques 10004); *Le massacre du printemps* (1971, Futura 33); *Europamerica* (1976, Palm 28)
As sideman: P. J. Jones: [untitled album] (1967, Vogue 357); S. Shihab: [untitled album] (1972, Futura 34)

BIBLIOGRAPHY

J.-R. Masson: "Enquêtes," *Jm*, no.78 (1962), 30
J.-L. Ginibre: "Entretien avec Jef Gilson," *Jm*, no.122 (1965), 59

D. Constant: "La manière Gilson," *Jm*, no.264 (1978), 29 [incl. discography]
A. Dutilh: "Jef Gilson: la sérénité," *Jh*, no.363 (1979), 16 [interview]
"Mes pages d'écriture," *Le jazzophone*, no.15 (1983)

ANDRÉ CLERGEAT

Gilt-edge. Record label. It was founded in Los Angeles in 1944, and was used for the issue of race records. The majority of these were by the blues singer and pianist Cecil Gant, but the catalogue also included recordings by Wingy Manone. By March 1946 the label had been discontinued, and the proprietor Richard Nelson transferred the remaining artists and repertory to his label 4-Star. (V. Pearlin: "Gilt-edge Discography," *Whiskey, Women, and . . .*, no.9 (1982), 24)

Girsback, Squire. *See* GERSH, SQUIRE.

Gismonti, Egberto (*b* Carmo, Brazil, 5 Dec 1947). Brazilian acoustic guitarist. He began studying piano at the age of six, and continued for many years before traveling to Paris to study orchestration and composition with Nadia Boulanger and Jean Barraqué. When he returned to Brazil in 1966 he became interested in choro, a popular Brazilian form of funk. He began to teach himself guitar, and was influenced by the Brazilian guitarists Baden Powell and Deno and the flutist Pixinguinha. At first he played a six-stringed instrument, but in 1973 he changed to an eight-stringed model; by 1981 he was using a guitar with ten strings on which the bass range was extended. Gismonti toured the USA in 1976 with Airto Moreira and Flora Purim, and again in 1978–9 with Nana Vasconcelos. In 1977 he spent some time studying the music of the Xingu Indians, which is reflected in two of his albums. He has recorded with Paul Horn, Charlie Haden's trio Magico, and with his own group, and is comfortable as a soloist or a member of an ensemble.

SELECTED RECORDINGS

(all recorded for ECM unless otherwise indicated)

As unaccompanied soloist: *Solo* (1978, 1136)
Duos with N. Vasconcelos: *Dança das cabeças* [Head dance] (1976, 1089); *Duas vozes* [Two voices] (1984, 1279)
As leader: *Sol do meio dia* [Sun of my day] (1977, 1116); *Sanfona* [Hurdy-gurdy] (1981, 1203–4)
As sideman: P. Horn: *Altura do sol* [Height of the sun] (1976, Epic 34231); C. Haden: *Magico* (1980, 1151)

BIBLIOGRAPHY

G. Medam: "Egberto Gismonti," *Jh*, no.342 (1977), 38 [interview]
C. Stern: "Egberto Gismonti: Finding the Avant-garde in the Jungles of Brazil with an 8-string Jazz Guitar," *GP*, xii/11 (1978), 45
J. Reese: "Egberto Gismonti," *Jh*, nos.379–80 (1980–81), 37
L. Tomkins: "Egberto Gismonti," *CI*, xix/11 (1981), 6

CATHERINE COLLINS

Gitler, Ira (*b* New York, 18 Dec 1928). Writer. After attending the University of Missouri (1946–50) and Columbia University (1950) he worked from 1950 to 1955 for Prestige Records. He collaborated with Leonard Feather on *The Encyclopedia of Jazz* (1955), for which he was an assistant writer and editor, and *The Encyclopedia of Jazz in the Sixties* (1966) and was an author with Feather of *The Encyclopedia of Jazz in the Seventies* (1976). Gitler wrote for such periodicals as *Metronome, Jazz Magazine, Down Beat* (of which he was an associate editor), and *Jazz Times*, produced film scripts on Louis Armstrong and Lionel Hampton for the US Information Service, and was a commentator for radio station WBAI, New York; he also taught at CUNY. Among his more notable writings is *Swing to Bop: an Oral History of the Transition in Jazz in the 1940s* (1985), a perceptive treatment of the big bands of the 1930s and bop groups of the 1940s.

WRITINGS

(selective list)

Jazz Masters of the Forties (New York, 1966/*R*1983 with discography)
with L. Feather: *The Encyclopedia of Jazz in the Seventies* (New York, 1976)
Swing to Bop: an Oral History of the Transition in Jazz in the 1940s (New York, and Oxford, England, 1985)

DANIEL ZAGER

Giuffre, Jimmy [James Peter] (*b* Dallas, 26 April 1921). Clarinetist, saxophonist, and composer. After graduating from North Texas State Teachers College (BMus 1942) he began his professional career with an army band. During the late 1940s he worked with Boyd Raeburn, Jimmy Dorsey, Buddy Rich, and Woody Herman. Thereafter he played with Howard Rumsey's Lighthouse All Stars (1951–3) and Shorty Rogers (1952–6), but left the latter's group to form his own trio with the guitarist Jim Hall and the double bass player Ralph Peña. In 1957 he formed a new ensemble, replacing Peña with the trombonist Bob Brookmeyer, and in the same year he taught at the Lenox (Massachusetts) School of Jazz. A reassessment of his musical philosophy preceded the formation in 1961 of a new trio with the pianist Paul Bley and the double bass player Steve Swallow, a group that was prominent in the emerging free-jazz movement, particularly in its recordings of 1961–2. In the 1960s Giuffre led various groups in this format, appearing at jazz

Jimmy Giuffre, August 1958

venues in the USA and touring in Europe. Later in the decade he resumed playing in a more conventional, blues-related style, but in the 1970s his trio with Kiyoshi Tokunaga (double bass) and Randy Kaye (drums) drew on Middle Eastern, African and oriental sounds and techniques. In 1978 he joined the faculty of the New England Conservatory of Music. By the early 1980s Giuffre had taken up soprano saxophone, flute, and bass flute and was performing in a bop-oriented style as the leader of a quartet with Peter Levin (keyboards), Bob Nieske (double bass), and Kaye.

Giuffre was an important figure in avant-garde jazz in the late 1950s and again in the early 1960s. He showed a preoccupation with the expressive potential of timbre as early as 1947 in his influential score *Four Brothers* for Herman, although he himself acknowledged that he had adopted the distinctive sound for Herman's saxophone section after hearing the instrumentation earlier the same year in Gene Roland's band. A concern with dulcet effects dominated his work of the 1950s, both in his solo performances and his compositions. By this time he was concentrating on clarinet, restricting himself to the chalumeau register of the instrument and achieving a dark, warm tone that suited his relaxed phrasing. Yet the simplistic surface of his work belied sophisticated sources, as is revealed by the atonality of *The Sidepipers* and the delicately contrapuntal *My Funny Valentine* (both 1956). In the early 1960s, however, Giuffre's playing became more assertive and expressionistic. His many compositions, written for his own and other jazz groups, include a clarinet quintet and several pieces for solo instruments and string orchestra; a number of them have been published by MJQ Music, New York. Giuffre has also written a manual, *Jazz Phrasing and Interpretation: Aspects of Jazz Performance, Analyzed for the Player . . . a Personal Approach* (New York, 1969).

See also ARRANGEMENT, §4; FORMS, §4; and HARMONY (i), §1 (iv), and ex.5.

SELECTED RECORDINGS

As leader: *The Giuffre Clarinet* (1956, Atl. 1238), incl. My Funny Valentine, The Sidepipers; *Jimmy Giuffre Three* (1956, Atl. 1254); *Fusion* (1961, Verve 68397); *Music for People, Birds, Butterflies and Mosquitos* (1972, Choice 1001); *River Chant* (1975, Choice 1011); *Quasar* (1985, SN 1108)
As sideman with S. Rogers: *The Swinging Mr. Rogers* (1955, Atl. 1212)

RECORDED COMPOSITIONS
(selective list)

As leader: on *Tangents in Jazz* (1955, Cap. T634), Rhetoric, Scintilla One, Scintilla Two, Scintilla Three, Scintilla Four; on *Piece for Clarinet and String Orchestra* (1960, Verve 68395), Mobiles, Piece for Clarinet and String Orchestra; on *Free Fall* (1962, Col. CS8764), Three Wee
Recorded by others: W. Herman: Four Brothers (1947, Col. 38304); Four Mothers, on S. Rogers: *Modern Sounds* (1951, Cap. H294); Four Others, on H. Rumsey: *Sunday Jazz à la Lighthouse* (1953, Cont. 3501)

BIBLIOGRAPHY

L. Gushee: "Jimmy Giuffre," *Jazz: a Quarterly of American Music*, no.1 (1958), 67
G. Russell: "Jimmy Giuffre," *JR*, i/1 (1958), 35
R. Horricks and others: *These Jazzmen of our Time* (London, 1959), 145
L. Stephens: "Jimmy Giuffre," *JR*, iii/2 (1960), 6
B. Korall: "The Musical Growth of Jimmy Giuffre: Search for Freedom," *DB*, xxviii/25 (1961), 16
D. Nelson: *Jimmy Giuffre: a List of Compositions Licensed by B.M.I.* (New York, 1961)
M. Williams: "Giuffre/Brookmeyer Reunion," *DB*, xxxv/2 (1968), 15
——: "What Ever Happened to the Clarinet?," *J&B*, ii/11 (1973), 9
B. Korall: "Jimmy Giuffre: Music for People, Birds, Butterflies and Mosquitos," *DB*, xli/6 (1974), 17
F. Bonchard: "Jimmy Giuffre: Four Brothers plus Three Decades," *DB*, xlviii/12 (1981), 28
L. Tomkins: "Jimmy Giuffre: My Journey Back to the Mainstream," *CI*, xxi (1983), no.7, p.20; no.8, p.6
——: "Jimmy Giuffre: Arrangers Must Regain their Originality," *CI*, xxii/1 (1983), 12

MICHAEL JAMES/R

Gladden, Eddie [Edward] (*b* Newark, NJ, 6 Dec 1937). Drummer. He played drums in a school band and orchestra and was influenced by Max Roach and Art Blakey, and by two drummers who worked in Newark, Bobby Thomas and Buddy Mack. He first worked full-time as a musician in Newark in 1962; his first important engagement was with James Moody from 1972. Later he worked with Eddie Jefferson, Richie Cole, Cecil Payne, Horace Silver, Shirley Scott, and Mickey Tucker. In 1977 he became a member of a quartet formed by Dexter Gordon after his return to the USA from Europe; with Gordon he toured widely and made several recordings. Gladden's use of varied, driving ride-cymbal patterns, intricate accompaniment, and drums made from natural materials, as well as his avoidance of muffling and dampening, place his style squarely within the hard-bop tradition.

SELECTED RECORDINGS

As sideman: J. Moody: *Never Again!* (1972, Muse 5001); R. Cole: *New York Afternoon* (1976, Muse 5119); M. Tucker: *Sojourn* (1977, Xan. 143); D. Gordon: *Manhattan Symphonie* (1978, Col. JC35608); *Nights at the Keystone* (1978–9, BN 85112); C. Baker: *Blues for a Reason* (1984, Criss Cross 1010)

BIBLIOGRAPHY

Feather–Gitler '70s
B. Rusch: "Eddie Gladden: a Short Talk," *Cadence*, vii/6 (1981), 8

J. KENT WILLIAMS

Gleason, Ralph J(oseph) (*b* New York, 1 March 1917; *d* Berkeley, CA, 3 June 1975). Writer. After studying at Columbia University (1934–8) he was a founder and (from 1939 to 1941) the editor of *Jazz Information*, one of the first jazz periodicals in the USA; from 1942 to 1944 he worked for the Office of War Information. He was associated from 1948 to 1961 with *Down Beat* and from 1950 until his death with the *San Francisco Chronicle*, to which he contributed columns and criticism on jazz and popular music. At the same time he wrote a syndicated weekly column on jazz (1957–70), contributed to many periodicals (including *Hi/Fi Stereo Review*, 1958–63), and was the editor and publisher of *Jazz: a Quarterly of American Music* (1958–60). Gleason was among the first writers on jazz to take an interest in popular music, and in 1967 was a founder of *Rolling Stone*, for which during the following years he also worked as an editor and columnist. In 1958, with Jimmy Lyons, he founded the MONTEREY JAZZ FESTIVAL. He was a host of jazz radio programs in San Francisco in the 1960s and of the television series "Jazz Casual" (for National Educational Television), which he also produced. In 1970 he became a vice president of the record company Fantasy. Gleason received an ASCAP–Deems Taylor Award for his article "Jazz: Black Art, American Art" in 1969 and for an article on Louis Armstrong in 1973.

WRITINGS
(selective list)

ed.: *Jam Session: an Anthology of Jazz* (New York and London, 1958)
"Jazz: Black Art, American Art," *Lithopinions* iv/3 (1969), 81
"God Bless Louis Armstrong," *RS*, no.88 (1971), 26
Celebrating the Duke, and Louis, Bessie, Billie, Bird, Carmen, Miles, Dizzy, and other Heroes (Boston and Toronto, 1975)

DANIEL ZAGER

Glenn, Lloyd (*b* San Antonio, 21 Nov 1909; *d* Los Angeles, 23 May 1985). Pianist and arranger. He first worked professionally at the age of 19 in San Antonio; a year later he moved to Dallas, where he played in a band led by the trombonist George Corley and other groups, then joined Terrence Holder. After Holder's ensemble disbanded in 1932 Glenn returned to San Antonio and worked with the drummer Clifford "Boots" Douglas. In 1934 he became a member of Don Albert's band, which was resident at Shadowland, San Antonio; his skill as an arranger and pianist is evident on his composition *Deep Blue Melody*, recorded by Albert in 1936 (Voc. 3423). From 1938 to 1942 Glenn played with various bands and did a little teaching; he then moved to California, and in 1944 joined Walter Johnson's trio. Thereafter he settled in Los Angeles, where he performed and recorded regularly with his own groups, played with Kid Ory (1949–53), and formed his own trio, with which he worked into the early 1960s. In the 1970s he toured several times with Joe Turner (i) and also with his own group in Europe.

BIBLIOGRAPHY

B. Demeusy: "Lloyd Glenn: Texas Pianist," *JJ*, xviii/10 (1965), 12
D. Stolper: "Old-time Shuffle," *Blues Unlimited*, no.107 (1974), 11
E. Townley: "San Antonio Piano Man: Lloyd Glenn," *Sv*, no.78 (1978), 220 [interview]
C. Battestini and J.-P. Battestini: "Lloyd Glenn: pas seulement le blues," *BHcF*, no.328 (1985), 4 [interview]
Obituaries: T. Burke, *Blues & Rhythm: the Gospel Truth*, no.10 (1985), 30; D. Shurman, *Living Blues*, no.68 (1986), 35

based on *ChiltonW*

Glenn, (Evans) Tyree (*b* Corsicana, TX, 23 Nov 1912; *d* Englewood, NJ, 18 May 1974). Trombonist and vibraphonist. He played in local bands during his teens and worked in Washington and Virginia, before moving to the West Coast, where he performed with the trumpeter Charlie Echols (1936) and Eddie Barefield. As a member of the group led by the trumpeter and saxophonist Eddie Mallory he accompanied Ethel Waters on tour. In 1939 he played briefly with Benny Carter and then joined Cab Calloway (for illustration *see* CALLOWAY, CAB), with whom he remained until 1946, when he toured Europe with Don Redman. He stayed in Europe to work as a freelance for a time. Shortly after returning to the USA he joined Duke Ellington's orchestra, with which he played (except on tour in 1950) from 1947 to 1951. In the 1950s and early 1960s Glenn combined studio work with occasional engagements and acting for television; he played with Louis Armstrong's All Stars from 1965 to 1968. He spent the last years of his life as a freelance musician in and around New York and again worked, for short periods, with Armstrong and Ellington. During his time with Ellington's band Glenn specialized in playing trombone with plunger mute, in the style developed by Tricky Sam Nanton though with a strongly individual sound. He also contributed fine solos on open trombone and occasionally on vibraphone.

SELECTED RECORDINGS

As sideman: C. Calloway: Bye Bye Blues (1940, OK 6084); D. Ellington: H'ya Sue (1947, Col. 38234); Sultry Serenade (1947, Col. 38363); *The Liberian Suite* (1947, Col. CL6073), incl. Dance no.2; *Masterpieces by Ellington* (1950, Col. ML4418), incl. Mood Indigo; L. Armstrong: *Louis* (1964–6, Mer. 61081)

BIBLIOGRAPHY

ChiltonW
M. Jones: "From TV Studios to Satch," *MM*, xl (12 June 1965), 6

EDDIE LAMBERT

Glindemann, Ib (*b* Copenhagen, 27 Sept 1934). Danish bandleader. While studying trumpet he led a big band from 1951 to 1959 that was modeled after the groups of Stan Kenton and included among its members Allan Botschinsky and Erik Moseholm. He conducted a regional symphony orchestra (1962–4) and from 1964 to 1968 led the Ny Radiodanseorkester, which later became known as the RADIOENS BIG BAND; he also wrote music for films, the ballet, and the theater (from 1956) and commercial music (from 1969). His work is well represented by the album *Presenting Ib Glindemann* (1963, Fon. TY887529), which includes the track *Two Bass Hit*.

ERIK WIEDEMANN

Gliss(ando) (Italianized, from Fr. *glisser*: "to slide"). A term used loosely to mean any slide in pitch up or down to or from a fixed note, or between two fixed notes; the range, speed, and duration of these effects vary greatly according to context.

1. Techniques. 2. Jazz glisses.

1. TECHNIQUES. The term "glissando" is properly applied to the effect obtained on keyboard instruments, fretted string instruments, and the harp, on which the slide is made up of a sequence of distinguishable pitches sounding like a very rapidly played scale. A continuous slide without distinguishable pitches (properly called a "portamento") can be executed on fretless string instruments, the slide trombone, some percussion instruments (notably the roto-toms and timpani) and many synthesizers, and with the voice. On some wind instruments it is possible to produce a true portamento over part of the range. In jazz the term "gliss" is used for both the glissando and the portamento, and this form of the word is preferred in both written and spoken usage; in general music theory the distinction between the two types of slide is more carefully observed and the form "glissando" is more common than "gliss."

On keyboard instruments, fretted strings (in jazz principally the guitar), and the harp the glissando is executed not by fingering in the normal way but by running the fingernail or fingertip rapidly over the keys or along a string; the skillful guitarist may sometimes obscure the individual pitches by lightness of touch. On fretless strings (in jazz principally the double bass, electric bass guitar, and violin) the portamento is executed by sliding the finger along a string, and on trombone by moving the slide continuously in or out while playing. On wind instruments the glissando with discrete steps may be achieved easily by playing rapid scales. The slide may be produced on reed instruments – most easily in the middle register of the clarinet and the high register of the saxophone and bass clarinet – by complex adjustments involving tightening and loosening of the embouchure in conjunction with swift movement through standard and false fingerings (*see* FALSE FINGERING); though these techniques in fact create discrete pitches a skilled player can effectively disguise them and produce a passable slide at speed. Similarly on a valved brass instrument a slide is created by depressing or partly depressing two or three valves while tightening or loosening the embouchure (*see* HALF-VALVE).

2. JAZZ GLISSES. In jazz different types of gliss (see (a) to (j) below) are distinguished from one another according to directions, speed, and in some cases method of production. The notational symbols used to indicate these effects are not standardized: straight, curved, wavy, or saw-toothed lines, or arrows may be used, or the scribe may simply write "gliss" or the name of a particular type of gliss (*see* NOTATION, §5(ii)).

(a) Doit. A gliss rising from the end of a note; it is the same as one of the forms of the lift (see (e) below). Examples may be heard on the track *Lester Leaps in* from Lester Young's *Pres in Europe* (1956, Onyx 218) and *Big Dipper* from *Central Park North* (1969, SolS 18058) by the Thad Jones–Mel Lewis Orchestra (ex.1).

Ex.1 Examples of the doit in the theme of *Big Dipper* from *Central Park North* (1969, SolS 18058) by the Thad Jones–Mel Lewis Orchestra; transcr. T. Owens

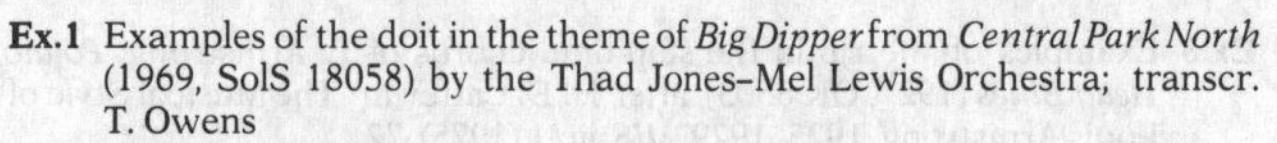

(b) Drop. See (c) Fall off.

(c) Fall off [drop, spill]. A gliss falling from the end of a note. Five consecutive examples occur in bars 13–15 of the final solo chorus of Louis Armstrong's *I gotta right to sing the blues* (1933, Vic. 24233) (ex.2). An example of a fall off followed by a lift is discussed in (e) below (*see also* GILLESPIE, DIZZY, ex.2).

Ex.2 Examples of the fall off (*a*) and lift (*b*) in the final solo chorus of L. Armstrong: *I gotta right to sing the blues* (1933, Vic. 24233); transcr. B. Kernfeld

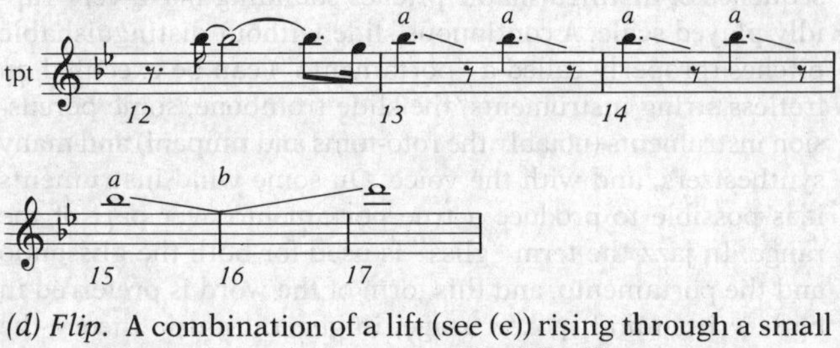

(d) Flip. A combination of a lift (see (e)) rising through a small interval from the end of a note and a fall off.

(e) Lift. A gliss rising to the beginning or from the end of a note. The latter kind of lift is the same as a doit (see (a) above). The Original Dixieland Jazz Band's *Tiger Rag* (1918, Vic. 18742) contains in the opening choruses many examples of lifts on the trombone (such raucous, deliberately placed slides from one note to another are an important element of the TAILGATE style of trombone playing); in the middle of the antepenultimate and final choruses of the same piece the clarinetist, Larry Shields, plays a fall off away from a note and a lift back to the same note. Similarly in bar 16 of ex.2 the direction of the gliss is reversed and the last of the fall offs leads without a break into a lift. The portamento effect at this point, achieved through half-valving, may be clearly heard on the recording.

(f) Lip. On wind instruments a gliss rising to the beginning or falling from the end of a note, achieved entirely with the embouchure (that is, without changes in fingering); it exploits in exaggerated form the technique of tuning notes by means of the embouchure (*see* LIP, (2)): on a reed instrument, for example, the gliss is executed by attacking the note with a slackened embouchure and lowered air pressure, then increasing the air pressure while raising the lower jaw until the lower lip makes normal contact with the reed; a slide of an interval up to a 4th can be produced in this way. The unchallenged master of the lip is the alto saxophonist Johnny Hodges; numerous examples occur in his solo on Duke Ellington's *Warm Valley* (1940, Vic. 26796). A lip up to a note is the same as a scoop (see (i) below).

(g) Plop. A rapid gliss falling to the beginning of a note; the gliss precedes the beat. The Original Dixieland Jazz Band's recording *Tiger Rag* (1918, Vic. 18472) provides some of the most famous examples of glisses in tailgate trombone playing: in the penultimate chorus Eddie Edwards plays a series of plops.

(h) Rip. A loud, violent gliss rising to the beginning of a note. Louis Armstrong used this effect frequently, as in bars 31 and 32 of his stop-time chorus on *Potato Head Blues* (1927, OK 8503) (ex.3).

Ex.3 Examples of the rip in the stop-time chorus of L. Armstrong: *Potato Head Blues* (1927, OK 8503), after H. D. Caffey in "The Musical Style of Louis Armstrong, 1925–1929", *JJS*, iii/1 (1975), 72

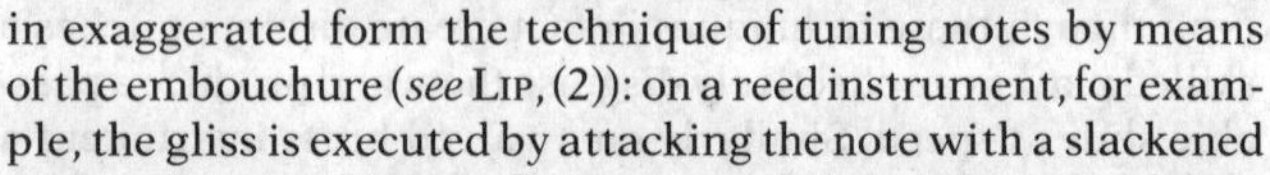

(i) Scoop. On wind instruments a gliss rising to the beginning of a note, achieved entirely with the embouchure (that is, without changes in fingering); it is the same as the lip up (see (f) above). Some reed players have taken the nickname Scoops from their use of this effect (for example, Scoops Carey).

(j) Spill. See (c) Fall off.

BIBLIOGRAPHY

G. Schuller: *Early Jazz: its Roots and Musical Development* (New York, 1968)
A. Napoleon: "The Music Goes Down and Around: (a Case of Mistaken Identity)," *Sv*, no.37 (1971), 18
A. Blatter: *Instrumentation/Orchestration* (New York and London, 1980)
M. Laplace: "La trompette et le cornet dans le jazz et la musique populaire," pt vi, *Brass Bulletin*, no.47 (1984), 39
L. Porter: *Lester Young* (Boston and London, 1985)

BARRY KERNFELD

Glissandi, Arpeggio. Pseudonym used by CASPER REARDON.

Globe Unity Orchestra. Big band. It was formed in Germany in 1966 by Alex Schlippenbach to perform *Globe Unity*, a work for 14 players that had been commissioned from him for the Berlin Jazztage; Schlippenbach continued to lead the orchestra into the 1980s. Among other free-jazz players the orchestra originally included members of Manfred Schoof's quintet and Peter Brötzmann's trio. During the following years the orchestra gave performances at the world's fair in Osaka, Japan (1970), at the Donaueschingen Music Festival in Germany (1971), where it performed a composition called *Actions* that had been written for the orchestra by the Polish composer Krzysztof Penderecki, with the chorus of the Norddeutscher Rundfunk (1974), at several festivals in Europe in the 1970s, and on tours of the Far East (1980) and North America (1983). The orchestra performs compositions by its members as well as standards (by jazzmen as diverse as Thelonious Monk and Jelly Roll Morton) and European folk melodies. It also engages in collective improvisations. The size and membership of the band vary; at times its members have included the trumpeters Schoof and Kenny Wheeler, the trombonists Günter Christmann, Albert Mangelsdorff, and Paul Rutherford, the reed players Brötzmann, Gerd Dudek, Steve Lacy, Evan Parker, and Michel Pilz, the tuba player Bob Stewart, the double bass players Peter Kowald, Buschi Niebergall, and Alan Silva, and the drummers and percussionists Han Bennink and Paul Lovens.

SELECTED RECORDINGS

Globe Unity (1966, Saba 15109) [issued under A. Schlippenbach's name]; *Live in Wuppertal* (1973, FMP 0160); *Hamburg '74* (1974, FMP 0650); *Evidence*, i (1975, FMP 0220); *Jahrmarkt/Local Fair* (1976, Po Torch 2); *Improvisations* (1977, Japo 60021); *Compositions* (1979, Japo 60027)

For further recordings *see* SCHLIPPENBACH, ALEX.

BIBLIOGRAPHY

L. Jeske: "Free Players from many Lands Form Globe Unity Orchestra," *DB*, xlvii/9 (1980), 28

ROBERT J. IANNAPOLLO

Glow, Bernie (*b* New York, 6 Feb 1926; *d* Manhasset, NY, 8 May 1982). Trumpeter. He worked as a sideman with Artie Shaw (1945–?1946), but did not take solos; he then played and recorded with Boyd Raeburn (1947) and Woody Herman (1947–9; for illustration *see* HERMAN, WOODY, fig.1*b*). After 1950 he worked frequently as a studio musician in New York, playing in more than 100 sessions with Herman (1953–9), Benny Goodman (1955–65), Bob Brookmeyer (1956–61), Manny Albam (1956–62), Miles Davis and Gil Evans (1957–62), Dizzy Gillespie (1961), J. J. Johnson (1968), and several others. He continued to work occasionally during the 1970s, recording with George

Benson (1970), Grover Washington, Jr. (1973), and Gato Barbieri (1976).

BIBLIOGRAPHY

FeatherE
Obituaries: *DB*, xlix/8 (1982), 17; *New York Times* (10 May 1982), §D, p.11

Gluskin, Lud [Grassnick, Ludwig] (*b* ?Russia, *c*1898). Bandleader and drummer. He played in dance bands in France in the mid-1920s. In 1927 he assumed leadership of the Playboys, a jazz band from Detroit that was stranded in Paris, for which he secured engagements in Venice (1927) and Paris (1928). This group formed the nucleus of Gluskin's own orchestra, which toured Europe between 1928 and 1933 and made more than 700 recordings in Paris and Berlin. The band played in the Chicago style and included such soloists as Arthur Briggs, Emile Christian, Léo Vauchant, and Danny Polo. Gluskin then returned to the USA, organized a sweet society band, and performed frequently on radio. He was appointed director of music at CBS in Hollywood in 1937.

BIBLIOGRAPHY

W. Plath: Liner notes, *Lud Gluskin et son jazz, Paris-Berlin, 1928–1932* (Wolverine 1–2, 1976–7)
——: Liner notes, *Black & White Jazz in Europe, 1929* (Wolverine 5, 1980)

RAINER E. LOTZ

GNP [Gene Norman Presents]. Record company and label. The company was founded by the impresario Gene Norman around 1947; at first the label was used to release recordings of concerts he had arranged on the West Coast. These were put out in a series, Just Jazz, for which GNP is chiefly remembered. The company became more active in the 1950s, issuing albums by Dizzy Gillespie, Charlie Ventura, Lionel Hampton, Gerry Mulligan, Paul Bley, Jack Sheldon, Frank Morgan, Teddy Buckner, Spud Murphy, and many others; it was also the first to record the important quintet led by Clifford Brown and Max Roach (1954).

MARK GARDNER

Godley, A. G. (*b* USA, *c*1900; *d* Seattle, Feb 1973). Drummer. He joined Alphonso Trent's band at Muskogee, Oklahoma, in 1924, and remained with it until 1933, apart from a period spent with Walter Page in 1929 and an engagement with Fate Marable in 1931. He was regarded by his contemporaries in the Southwest as one of the finest big-band drummers, and may be heard to advantage in this context on Trent's *Black and Blue Rhapsody* (1928, Gen. 6710). In 1940–41 he made a number of recordings in small groups led by Snub Mosley, Hot Lips Page, Joe Turner (ii), and Pete Johnson: Johnson's *627 Stomp* (1940, Decca 18121) displays his style in this setting. Godley's nickname in Trent's band was Ananias Garibaldi; this has sometimes mistakenly been cited as his given name.

BIBLOGRAPHY

H. Panassié and M. Gautier: *Dictionnaire du jazz* (Paris, 1954, rev. and enlarged 1971, enlarged 2/1980, rev. and enlarged by A. Vasset and J. Pescheux 3/1987; Eng. trans., London, 1956, rev. A. A. Gurwitch as *Guide to Jazz*, Boston, 1956), 122
A. McCarthy: *Big Band Jazz* (New York and London, 1974), 99, 118
F. Driggs and H. Lewine: *Black Beauty, White Heat: a Pictorial History of Classic Jazz, 1920–1950* (New York, 1982), 166

HOWARD RYE

Gojkovic, Dusan. *See* GOYKOVICH, DUSKO.

Gold, Harry [Dad] (*b* Dublin, 26 Feb 1907). English tenor and bass saxophonist and bandleader of Irish birth. He studied piano, reed instruments, harmony, and counterpoint at the London College of Music (1921), then played with a jazz band, the Metronomes (1925–8), before working with the bands of the clarinetist Jack Padbury and others in the late 1920s and early 1930s. After performing and recording with the bandleader Roy Fox and the violinist Oscar Rabin in the mid-1930s he formed his own band, the Pieces of Eight, in 1938. It has continued to perform regularly into the 1980s, and its recordings include Gold's compositions *Doubloon* (1946, Parl. R2993), *The Parade of the Pieces* (1949, Decca 9274), and *Long John Stomp* (1950, Decca 9456). Gold has continued to work as a freelance throughout this period, playing with the bandleaders Geraldo (1942), Bert Ambrose (1945), and Harry Roy (1970), and the cornetist Dick Sudhalter (1975). He has also taken part in many radio broadcasts and composed and arranged music for films.

Oral history material in *GBLnsa*.

BIBLIOGRAPHY

E. Cook: "The Midas Touch," *JJI*, xxxiv/6 (1981), 10 [interview]

CLARRIE HENLEY

Gold, Sanford (*b* Cleveland, 9 June 1911). Pianist. He played first with Babe Russin and then in dance bands led by Abe Lyman and Raymond Scott (both 1938–40). After army service he performed and recorded with Mary Osborne and recorded in swing and bop groups with Don Byas, Lem Davis, and Eddie Safranski, and also as leader (all 1946). From 1949 to 1954 he played in a studio orchestra for NBC, while also recording with Artie Shaw (1950), a quintet led by Stan Getz and Johnny Smith (1952), and Al Cohn (1954). He also recorded an album as soloist, *Piano d'or* (*c*1955, Prst. 7019). *(FeatherE)*

Goldberg, Stu(art W.) (*b* Massachusetts, *c*1955). Keyboard player. He grew up in Seattle, and while still a teenager performed in a bop quartet with Ray Brown and others at the Monterey Jazz Festival (1971). After graduating with a degree in jazz studies from the University of Utah in 1974 he moved to Los Angeles, and the following year he toured and recorded with the Mahavishnu Orchestra. He then worked with Miroslav Vitous, Al Di Meola, and Freddie Hubbard, and performed and recorded in Europe with Alphonse Mouzon (1976–7). In 1978 he toured Europe as a soloist. His own recordings embrace several styles, including modern jazz, jazz-rock, and a synthesis of jazz and Indian music. On the album *Solos-Duos-Trios* (1978, MPS 68202), for example, he plays electronic and acoustic instruments with L. Subramaniam and Larry Coryell; *Piru* (1980, MPS 68262) is a good example of his solo piano work. He has also recorded as a sideman with several musicians, including Charlie Mariano (1979), and as a leader (1979, 1981). (G. Wannamaker: "Profile: Stu Goldberg," *DB*, xlv/14 (1978), 44)

Goldene Sieben. German group. It was formed in Berlin in 1934, as the studio band for the Electrola company, by the guitarist and banjoist Harold Kirchstein (Henri René); its members, who were chosen from the leading bands in the city, included Kurt Hohenberger (trumpet), Erhard Krause and Willy Berking (trombone), Ernst Höllerhagen and Franz Thon (clarinet), Eddie Brunner and Kurt Wege (tenor saxophone), Willy Stech and Peter Igelhoff (piano), and Freddie Brocksieper (drums). From 1935 the group was led by the pianist and arranger Georg Haentzschel. It gained popularity through radio broadcasts and appeared in the film *Heimweh* (1937), but was prohibited, by its exclusive contract with Electrola, from performing in public. The band played in a wide range of light styles, which encompassed dance music and ballad accompaniments, and its repertory also included hot jazz. It made many recordings (including *Ach, verzeihen Sie meine Damen,* 1935, Elec. 3492, and *Swingin' the Jinx Away,* 1937, Elec. 3915). (D. Schulz-Köhn: "Die Goldene 7," *Tanzmusik der 20er Jahre* (Elec. 14830609–10, *c*1972) [liner notes])

RAINER E. LOTZ

Goldkette, Jean (*b* Valenciennes, France, 18 March 1899; *d* Santa Barbara, CA, 24 March 1962). Pianist, orchestra leader, and entrepreneur. He trained as a concert pianist in Greece and Russia before emigrating to the USA in 1911, but is remembered chiefly as a leader of dance orchestras and the employer of a number of outstanding jazz musicians during the 1920s. At its peak, his National Amusement Corporation, based in Detroit, controlled more than 20 bands throughout the Midwest. Goldkette's best-known ensemble was his Victor Recording Orchestra, which operated from the Graystone Ballroom in Detroit and included such notable jazz soloists as Bix Beiderbecke, Frankie Trumbauer, Joe Venuti, and Tommy and Jimmy Dorsey. Goldkette also helped organize and manage McKinney's Cotton Pickers, one of the leading black dance bands of the era. Another of Goldkette's groups, the Orange Blossoms, evolved into the Casa Loma Orchestra, a cooperative band which enjoyed immense national popularity during the 1930s.

Although sympathetic to and respected by jazz musicians, Goldkette never played their music and seldom appeared with his own orchestras. His own musical activities included performances as piano soloist with the Detroit SO. He gave up his band interests in the early 1930s and became a booking agent, while continuing to appear as a concert pianist. In later life he occasionally formed bands, chiefly for recording purposes.

For illustration *see* BEIDERBECKE, BIX.

BIBLIOGRAPHY

R. M. Sudhalter, P. R. Evans, and W. Dean-Myatt: *Bix: Man & Legend* (New Rochelle, NY, and London, 1974)

J. Chilton: *McKinney's Music: a Bio-discography of McKinney's Cotton Pickers* (London, 1978)

J. Kline: "Goldkette's Doc," *MR,* v/11 (1978), 1

RICHARD M. SUDHALTER

Golla, George (*b* Chorzów, Poland, 10 May 1935). Australian guitarist. He moved to Australia in the 1950s and began working steadily in Sydney in 1957. In 1959 he began a long-lasting association with Don Burrows which included appearances at the Montreux and Newport jazz festivals (both 1972), a performance with the Sydney SO in Don Banks's *Nexus* (1973), and tours of Asia, Australia, and Brazil. He has made more than a hundred recordings, including *The Don Burrows Quartet at the Sydney Opera House* (1974, Cherry Pie 1017). In 1977 he toured and recorded the album *Steph' n' us* (Cherry Pie 1032) as a sideman with Stephane Grappelli.

BIBLIOGRAPHY

A. Bisset: *Black Roots, White Flowers: a History of Jazz in Australia* (Sydney, 1979)

B. Johnson: "Golla, George," *The Oxford Companion to Australian Jazz* (Melbourne, Australia, 1987)

JEFF PRESSING (with JOHN WHITEOAK)

Goloshchokin, David (Semyonovich) (*b* Moscow, 10 June 1944). Russian flugelhorn player, violinist, saxophonist, pianist, drummer, double bass player, and composer. He studied violin at the secondary music school in Leningrad (graduated 1961) and attended a music school affiliated with the Leningrad N. A. Rimsky-Korsakov State Conservatory (1962–4). His first professional engagement was as a double bass player in a quartet led by the pianist Yuri Vikharev at a jazz festival in Tallinn, Estonian SSR (1961). In 1963–4 he led an ensemble and played piano in the jazz octet of the Leningrad Institute of Precision Engineering and Optics, and in 1965–7 he worked as a pianist under the bandleader Yosif Vainstein and belonged to a quintet led by Gennady Gol'shteyn and Konstantin Nosov. He toured with the orchestra of Ady Rosner (1967–8), conducted a variety orchestra in Odessa, Ukrainian SSR (1968–9), and formed a group in Leningrad (1969) that remained active, with several changes in membership, into the 1980s. Goloshchokin has performed throughout the USSR, in several European countries, and in Cuba; his versatility as an instrumentalist is well illustrated by his album *Dzhazovïe kompozitsii* (Jazz compositions; 1977, Mel. C600966970), on which he plays harpsichord, piano, flugelhorn, drums, electric bass guitar, double bass, violin, conga drums, and saxophone. He often plays his own compositions and features the singing of his wife, Elvira Trafova.

WALTER OJAKÄÄR

Golowin, Albert. Pseudonym used by FRIEDRICH GULDA.

Gol'shteyn, Gennady (L'vovich) (*b* Moscow, 25 Jan 1938). Russian reed player, composer, and teacher. He studied clarinet at a music school in Leningrad (graduated 1956) and taught himself to play saxophone and flute. From 1953 to 1959 he worked with the pianist Stanislav Pozhlakov, the violinist Arkady Liskovich, and the tenor saxophonist Valery Milevsky, and from 1959 to 1966 he played lead alto saxophone under the bandleader Yosif Vainstein, for whom he also wrote arrangements; at the same time he led a quintet with Konstantin Nosov consisting of members of Vainstein's orchestra. Later he toured with a big band led by Ady Rosner (1966–7), played in the orchestra of the Vsesoyuznoye radio (All-union radio) under the bandleader Vadim Ludvikovsky (1968–73), and belonged to Oleg Lundstrem's orchestra (1973–7). In 1978 he formed an early-music ensemble, Pro anima, took up the recorder, and became a saxophone teacher at the Mussorgsky Music School in Leningrad. Gol'shteyn has made recordings as a leader, and as a sideman with Ludvikovsky, Lundstrem, Nosov, and Vainstein; he can be heard leading a quartet with Nosov in a performance of his composition *Na zavalinke* on the album *Dzhaz-67,* ii (1967, Mel. D0209856). (S. F. Starr: *Red and Hot: the Fate of Jazz in the Soviet Union, 1917–1980* (New York, and Oxford, England, 1983), 254)

WALTER OJAKÄÄR

Golson, Benny (*b* Philadelphia, 26 Jan 1929). Tenor saxophonist, composer, and arranger. He studied piano, organ, tenor saxophone, and clarinet as a child, and later attended Howard University (1947–50). In 1951, in Bull Moose Jackson's band, he met Tadd Dameron, whose work was a great influence on Golson's compositional style; two years later he played in a band led by Dameron. He then performed with Lionel Hampton (1953) and Earl Bostic (1954–6), but began to make a name for himself as a member of Dizzy Gillespie's band (1956–7). By this time he had composed the first of many jazz standards – *Stablemates* and *I remember Clifford* – and had established a solo style that reflected the inspiration of Ben Webster and Coleman Hawkins. While with Art Blakey's Jazz Messengers (1958–9) Golson wrote *Whisper Not, Along came Betty, Blues March,* and *Are you real?.* He then worked as a freelance in New

York and studied with the composer Henry Brant. From 1959 to 1962, with Art Farmer, he was leader of the JAZZTET, a group with varying personnel that proved a successful vehicle for Golson's writing; the ensemble was revived (with one of its original members, Curtis Fuller) in 1982 for a tour of Europe and continues to perform and record in the late 1980s. From the late 1960s Golson worked in films and television, composing music for all the major studios, while continuing to write arrangements on a freelance basis. Manuscript scores of his works are in the holdings of the BMI Archives in New York.

For illustration *see* FARMER, ART.

SELECTED RECORDINGS

As leader: *Benny Golson's Philadelphians* (1958, UA 4020), incl. Stablemates; of Jazztet (with A. Farmer): *Meet the Jazztet* (1960, Argo 664), incl. I remember Clifford; *Stockholm Sojourn* (1964, Prst. 7361); *California Message* (1980, Tim. 177); *One More Mem'ry* (1981, Tim. 180); of Jazztet (with A. Farmer): *The Jazztet: Moment to Moment* (1983, SN 1066)

As sideman: A. Blakey: *Art Blakey with the Jazz Messengers* (1958, BN 4003), incl. Along came Betty, Are you real?, Blues March; *Paris Concert* (1959, Epic 16009), incl. Whisper Not; R. Kirk: *Roland Kirk Meets Benny Golson* (1963, Mer. 60844)

BIBLIOGRAPHY

H. Frost: "Benny Golson," *DB*, xxv/10 (1958), 19

"Benny Golson," *SJ*, xxxvi/5 (1982), 248 [discography]

L. Tomkins: "Benny Golson," *CI*, xxi (1982–3), no.3, p.20; no.9, p.16; no.12, p.12

S. Voce: "Benny Golson," *JJI*, xxxv/12 (1982), 8; xxxvi/1 (1983), 6

STEVEN STRUNK

Gomez, Eddie [Edgar] (*b* San Juan, 4 Nov 1944). Puerto Rican double bass player. He moved in his early childhood to New York and took up the double bass when he was 12. After attending the High School of Music and Art he studied with Fred Zimmerman at the Juilliard School and belonged to Marshall Brown's International Youth Band. In the early 1960s he played with Gary McFarland, Jim Hall, Giuseppi Logan, Rufus Jones, Marian McPartland, Paul Bley, Jeremy Steig, and Gerry Mulligan, and in 1966 he joined the trio of Bill Evans (ii), as a member of which he made many recordings and drew much critical attention (for illustration *see* EVANS, BILL (ii)). After leaving Evans's group in 1977 he belonged to the group STEPS AHEAD, and has performed and recorded in groups led by Bennie Wallace (from 1978), Jack DeJohnette (1978, 1979, 1985), Hank Jones (from 1980), and JoAnne Brackeen. Gomez is a virtuoso performer whose swift runs and agile mind make him an ideal accompanist in small groups.

SELECTED RECORDINGS

Duos: with L. Konitz on *Duets* (1973, Mlst. 9013), Variations on Alone Together, iv; with B. Evans: *Intuition* (1974, Fan. 9475)

As sideman with B. Evans: *A Simple Matter of Conviction* (1966, Verve 68675); *What's New* (1969, Verve 68777); *Live at Tokyo* (1973, Fan. 9457); *Crosscurrents* (1977, Fan. 9568)

As sideman with others: P. Bley: *Barrage* (1964, ESP 1008); J. DeJohnette: *New Directions* (1978, ECM 1128); J. Brackeen: *Special Identity* (1981, Ant. 1001)

BIBLIOGRAPHY

M. McPartland: "Looking to the Future: Ron McClure, Eddie Gomez: an Appreciation of Two Promising Young Bassists," *DB*, xxxiii/20 (1966), 20; repr. in *All in Good Time* (New York, and Oxford, England, 1987) [colln of previously pubd articles], 113

A. J. Smith: "Bass Lines," *DB*, xliv/2 (1977), 14

B. Robson: "Eddie Gomez," *Cadence*, vi/11 (1980), 14 [interview]

MICHAEL ULLMAN

Gonella, Nat(haniel Charles) (*b* London, 7 March 1908). English trumpeter, singer, and bandleader. He performed and recorded with the dance bands of Billy Cotton (1929–33), Roy Fox (1931–2), Ray Noble (1931, 1933–4), and Lew Stone (1932–5); *Georgia on my mind* (1932, Decca F2804), recorded with Fox, is a good example of his playing and singing and became extremely popular. From 1932 he worked as a leader in a style heavily influenced by that of Louis Armstrong; his band, the Georgians (1934–9), included his brother Bruts Gonella, who was also a trumpeter. During a visit to New York in 1939 Gonella recorded with John Kirby and performed at the Hickory House. After returning to London he led the New Georgians from 1940 to 1942, but worked less frequently in the late 1940s and early 1950s. In 1958 he formed the New Georgia Jazz Band, and in the 1960s and 1970s continued to perform and record in Holland and England. By the early 1980s he had ceased to play but still sang.

BIBLIOGRAPHY

ReclamsJ

B. Gladwell: "The Return of Nat Gonella," *JJ*, xiii/3 (1960), 13

R. Brown: "Two Hat Nat is Back," *Memory Lane*, no.53 (1981), 10

R. Brown and C. Brown: *Georgia on my Mind: the Nat Gonella Story* (Horndean, England, 1985)

Gonsalves, Paul [Mex] (*b* Boston, 12 July 1920; *d* London, 15 May 1974). Tenor saxophonist. After returning from US Army service in 1946 he joined Count Basie's band, where in three years he acquired a reputation as a leading saxophonist in the big-band style. He then played briefly in Dizzy Gillespie's bop-oriented big band of 1949–50 before joining the Duke Ellington Orchestra, where he filled the chair formerly held by Ben Webster. An electrifying 27-chorus improvisation on *Diminuendo and Crescendo in Blue* at the Newport Jazz Festival in 1956 marked his breakthrough to public fame and the beginning of a comeback for Ellington's band. Gonsalves remained with Ellington for the rest of his career, frequently taking prominent roles in Ellington's suites; he also recorded prolifically as a soloist with other groups, and as the leader of several ensembles consisting of important swing and bop musicians (including the Paul Gonsalves–Sonny Stitt Quintet). Gonsalves's playing represents a virtuoso extension of the swing tenor saxophone style of Coleman Hawkins and Ben Webster, whose rich tone and harmonically dense lines he mastered to perfection. Although famous for his driving solos at fast tempos, he is heard at his best in ballad performances, where he played with a unique breathy, barely focused tone.

For illustration *see* ELLINGTON, DUKE, fig.2.

SELECTED RECORDINGS

As leader: *Gettin' Together* (1960, Jlnd 936); with S. Stitt: *Salt and Pepper* (1963, Imp. 52); with R. Nance: *Just a-Sittin' and a-Rockin'* (1970, BL 191)

As sideman with D. Ellington: *Ellington at Newport* (1956, Col. CL934), incl. Diminuendo and Crescendo in Blue; *Such Sweet Thunder* (1957, Col. CL1033), incl. The Star-crossed Lovers; *Newport 1958* (1958, Col. CL1245), incl. Happy Reunion; *Concert in the Virgin Isles* (1965, Rep. 6185), incl. Chelsea Bridge; *The Far East Suite* (1966, RCA LSP3782), incl. Mount Harissa; *The New Orleans Suite* (1970, Atl. 1580), incl. Portrait of Sidney

BIBLIOGRAPHY

H. P[anassié]: "Un grand saxo ténor: Paul Gonsalves," *BHcF*, no.68 (1957), 3

B. McRae: "Paul Gonsalves," *JJ*, xvi/7 (1963), 25

P. Gonsalves: "Under the Influence of Ellington," *Crescendo*, ii/8 (1964), 22

S. Dance: *The World of Duke Ellington* (London and New York, 1970/*R*1981) [colln of previously pubd articles and interviews], 168

G. Colombé: "Time and the Tenor Postscript: Paul Gonsalves, 1920–1974," *Into Jazz*, i/5 (1974), 27

H. Panassié: "Paul Gonsalves," *BHcF*, no.283 (1974), 3

J. BRADFORD ROBINSON

Gonzales, Babs [Brown, Lee] (*b* Newark, NJ, 27 Oct 1919; *d* Newark, 23 Jan 1980). Singer. He worked briefly with Charlie Barnet and Lionel Hampton. In 1946 he and Tadd Dameron formed a vocal trio, Babs' Three Bips and a Bop, with the singer and guitarist Pee Wee Tinney; its purpose was to perform Dameron's arrangements. The group's first recording (1947) was of a song by Gonzales, *Oop-pop-a-da,* which became a hit in the version by Dizzy Gillespie (1947, Vic. 202480). A flamboyant personality, Gonzales ventured into jazz promotion, worked as a radio disc jockey, and managed several jazz musicians, including James Moody. He performed as a soloist in the late 1940s and with Moody from 1951 to 1954. He continued singing in the 1960s and 1970s, during which time he performed regularly in Europe. He published two volumes of autobiography (*I Paid my Dues: Good Times . . . No Bread,* 1967, and *Movin' on Down the Line,* n.d.). Gonzales was an accomplished singer and entertaining performer, though he sometimes allowed his slapstick humor to eclipse the music.

SELECTED RECORDINGS

As leader: Oop-pop-a-da/Stompin' at the Savoy (1947, BN 534); Capitolizing/Professor Bop (1949, Cap. 60000); *Voila!* (1958, Hope 001); *Cool Philosophy* (1959, Jaro 5000); *Sundays at Small's Paradise* (1963, Dauntless 6311)

As sideman: J. Moody: Hey Jim (1952, Mer. 8290); James Moody Story (1953, Mer. 70102)

BIBLIOGRAPHY

V. Wilmer: "Babs Gonzales," *JM,* ix/6 (1963), 7 [interview]
J. Cooke: "Babs Gonzales," *JM,* ix/7 (1963), 15
B. Niguet: "Babs Gonzales," *Jh,* no.274 (1971), 20 [incl. discography]
Obituary, M. Hennessey, *JJI,* xxxiii/4 (1980), 22

LAWRENCE KOCH

Goode, Coleridge (George Emerson) (*b* St. Andrew, Jamaica, 29 Nov 1914). Jamaican double bass player. He played violin in the 1930s while at university in Glasgow, then began his professional career as a double bass player at the Panama Club in London with the trumpeter Johnny Claes and his Claypigeons (1942). Goode was a founding member of the Caribbean Trio (1944) and performed and recorded with George Shearing and Stephane Grappelli (1945–6); he also recorded with Grappelli and Django Reinhardt (1946). He played with Ray Ellington's quartet from 1947 to 1951 and recorded with Ray Nance in 1948. Later he played with Joe Harriott's quintet (1958–62) and his group Indo-Jazz Fusions (1965–8); his work with the former ensemble may be heard to advantage on the album *Abstract* (1961–2, Col. 33SX1627). Having recorded intermittently with Michael Garrick (1963–6) Goode then worked as a regular member of Garrick's sextet (1968–71). In 1974 he joined the trio led by the pianist Iggy Quayle, and has continued to work with this ensemble into the late 1980s.

BIBLIOGRAPHY

Feather '60s
J. Massarik: "Coleridge Goode," *The Wire,* no.4 (1983), 17
I. Cruickshank: "Coleridge Goode: the veteran Jamaican bass player recounts his adventures with Joe Harriott, Django Reinhardt, George Shearing, and others," *JJI,* xl/8 (1987), 10

SIMON ADAMS

Goodman, Benny [Benjamin David] (*b* Chicago, 30 May 1909; *d* New York, 13 June 1986). Clarinetist, composer, and bandleader.

1. Early career. 2. Later years.

1. Early career. He received rudimentary musical training from 1919 at the Kehelah Jacob Synagogue and the next year joined the boys club band at Jane Addams's Hull House, where he received lessons from the director James Sylvester; more important during this period were two years of instruction from the classically trained clarinetist Franz Schoepp. Goodman made his professional début in 1921 at the Central Park Theater, Chicago, with an imitation of Ted Lewis. After entering Harrison High School in 1922 he played occasionally with the so-called Austin High School Gang (Bud Freeman, Jimmy McPartland, Frank Teschemacher, Dave Tough, and others), who modeled their music after the New Orleans Rhythm Kings; the clarinetist with the Rhythm Kings, Leon Roppolo, was an early influence on Goodman. During these formative years he also absorbed the music of New Orleans musicians such as King Oliver and Louis Armstrong, and especially the clarinetists Johnny Dodds, Jimmie Noone, Buster Bailey, Albert Nicholas, and Barney Bigard. In 1923 Goodman joined the musicians' union and played regularly with Murph Podalsky and Jules Herbevaux: that summer, on a lake excursion boat, he met Bix Beiderbecke for the first time. Beiderbecke's influence may be heard in Goodman's on-the-beat attacks, careful choice of notes, and across-the-bar phrasing on his recordings of *A Jazz Holiday* and *Blue* (1928) – especially on the latter, where Goodman played solos on both alto and baritone saxophone. In August 1925 Goodman left for Los Angeles to join Ben Pollack. In January 1926 Pollack returned to Chicago, where Goodman recorded his first solo, *He's the last word,* on 17 December 1926. Early in 1928 Pollack's band went to New York, which subsequently became Goodman's base. Goodman stayed with Pollack until September 1929 but also performed with Sam Lanin, Nat Shilkret, and Meyer Davis, and from 1929 to 1934 was a leading freelance musician. He worked for radio and in recording studios for Red Nichols, Ben Selvin, Ted Lewis, Johnny Green, and Paul Whiteman, and on Broadway in George Gershwin's *Strike up the Band* and *Girl Crazy* (both 1930), and Richard Whiting's *Free for all* (1931). His important associations with John Hammond and Teddy Wilson began during this period.

In spring 1934 Goodman organized his first big band, a 12-piece group (three saxophones, three trumpets, two trombones, and four rhythm instruments), auditioned successfully for Billy Rose's new Music Hall, and started recording for Columbia. His small repertory included a few distinctive arrangements by Deane Kincaide, Will Hudson, and especially Benny Carter. Carter's composition and arrangement of *Take my Word,* requiring four saxophones (Goodman played tenor) to play four-note chords in parallel motion in the style of improvised solos, set the standard for the treatment of saxophone sections during the swing period. In November 1934 Goodman auditioned successfully for "Let's Dance," an NBC radio series; since the program's budget included funds for new arrangements, with Hammond's encouragement he engaged Fletcher Henderson to write for him. Henderson's arrangements of traditional jazz instrumental numbers, for example, Jelly Roll Morton's *King Porter Stomp,* and such popular songs as *Sometimes I'm Happy* established the band's musical character. Under Goodman's exacting direction the playing of the members was a model of ensemble discipline; with his own impeccable musicianship he set a high standard for his sidemen, from whom he demanded accurate intonation, matched vibrato, uniform phrasing, and a careful balancing of parts – performance standards rare in the bands of that time. It was during these broadcasts that Gene Krupa joined Goodman.

In July 1935, after playing together in a jam session, Goodman asked Teddy Wilson to record with Krupa and himself; that summer, as the Benny Goodman Trio, they recorded four classic sides of jazz chamber music. Goodman's solo on *After you've gone* from that session (ex.1) is an example of his mature style: his flawless playing utilizes almost the complete range of the instrument, and his disciplined explorations of the harmony (bars 13–14, 20) and fondness for the blue 3rd (bars 9,

Ex.1 From *After you've gone* (1935, Vic. 25115); transcr. R. Wang

17, 19 – enharmonically B♮) reveal the technical mastery and controlled expression that formed the essence of his art.

After the conclusion of the "Let's Dance" series in May 1935 and a disappointing reception at an engagement at the Roosevelt Hotel in New York, Goodman's band embarked on its first tour, under the auspices of Willard Alexander and the Music Corporation of America. The trip culminated in the now historic performance on 21 August before a capacity crowd at the Palomar Ballroom, Los Angeles, which was broadcast nationwide to great critical and popular acclaim, and is often cited as the beginning of the swing era. Later that year, while appearing at the Congress Hotel, Chicago, Goodman began a series of important early jazz concerts in the USA; for the last of these (Easter Sunday 1936) he brought in Wilson from New York. In August 1936 the Benny Goodman Trio became a quartet with the addition of Lionel Hampton; the group made its first recording, *Moonglow*, on 21 August.

In 1936–9 Goodman's band reached the peak of its success. It began with a series of CBS broadcasts ("The Camel Caravan") that continued for more than three years, made its first films (*The Big Broadcast of 1937* and *Hollywood Hotel*), and (on 3 March 1937) began a three-week engagement at the Paramount Theater, New York. The success of these performances, attended by a large, predominantly teenage audience, and the resultant publicity clearly demonstrated that Goodman was the "King of Swing" and a popular idol. On 16 January 1938 Goodman brought a new level of recognition to jazz with a concert in Carnegie Hall, presenting Harry James, Ziggy Elman, Jess Stacy, Hampton, Krupa, and Wilson from his own entourage as well as guest soloists from the bands of Duke Ellington and Count Basie.

In the same period Goodman became the first famous jazz musician to achieve success performing the classical repertory. His early training with Schoepp had prepared him for this dual career by laying the foundation for a "legitimate" clarinet technique, which he continued to improve in later study with Reginald Kell. In 1935 he performed Mozart's Clarinet Quintet before an invited audience in the home of John Hammond, and three years later recorded the work with the Budapest String Quartet; he appeared in his first public recital at Town Hall, New York, in November 1938. That year he commissioned the work *Contrasts* from Bartók, and gave its première at Carnegie Hall in January 1939. He later commissioned clarinet concertos from Copland (1947) and Hindemith (1947). Goodman appeared with all the leading American orchestras, performing and recording works by Leonard Bernstein, Debussy, Morton Gould, Darius Milhaud, Carl Nielsen, Poulenc, Stravinsky, and Carl Maria von Weber.

2. Later years. In July 1940 illness forced Goodman to disband his group and, although he re-formed it in October, changes in personnel gave the new band a different sound. Krupa, James, Wilson, and Stacy had already moved on, and during the hiatus of 1940 Hampton and Elman also left. New members who had joined Goodman the previous year included Artie Bernstein, Fletcher Henderson, Johnny Guarnieri, Charlie Christian, and Eddie Sauter. Among the new soloists it was Christian, with his long melodic lines influenced by Lester Young, who contributed most to the band, but it was the compositions and arrangements of Sauter, who had been trained at the Juilliard School, that established the band's musical character. During World War II the recording ban by the musicians' union from August 1942 to November 1944 prevented Goodman from recording for Columbia, but he continued to make V-discs and transcriptions for the Armed Forces Radio Service.

In 1947 Goodman assembled his last and most controversial traveling band (his later groups were recruited for specific engagements) to play and record arrangements in the new bop style for Capitol Records. Although he had been critical of bop, he genuinely admired the playing of Wardell Gray, Fats Navarro, and Doug Mettome, whom he featured in the band and in his new sextet. As a soloist Goodman was more comfortable with the small group than the big band; even there, however, few of the harmonic or rhythmic novelties of bop penetrated his style. The recording *Stealin' Apples* (1948) is characteristic of this period; all the solos are in the new style except that of Goodman, who retained his classic manner. In October 1949 Goodman disbanded the group on completion of his recording contract with Capitol.

In the 1950s Goodman continued to record and tour occasionally with ad hoc small groups and big bands, visiting Europe (1950) and, under the auspices of the US Department of State, the Far East (1956–7). At the conclusion of another European tour in 1958 he made a triumphant appearance in the American Pavilion at the Brussels World's Fair. The original Benny Goodman Trio was reunited for a benefit recording for Fletcher Henderson (1951) and a television appearance on NBC (1953), and also appeared in a film based on Goodman's life, *The Benny Goodman Story* (1956). In the 1960s Goodman expanded his role as jazz ambassador with tours of South America (1961), the USSR (1962), and Japan (1964). During the 1960s and 1970s he toured about half of each year, dividing his time between appearances with small groups and increasingly frequent commitments to performing classical works. The 40th anniversary of his concert in Carnegie Hall was celebrated there on 17 January 1978; although he put together a big band for the occasion, he made no attempt to re-create the original program. A recording (released in 1982) with George Benson clearly demonstrated that Goodman had lost none of his creative energy or technical facility. He was one of the five recipients of the fifth annual Kennedy Center Honors awards (1982). Many of his recordings have been newly issued by Sunbeam, a label devoted largely to aspects of his work. His collection of scores,

Members of Benny Goodman's sextet during a performance at the Paramount Theater, New York, April 1941: (left to right) Georgie Auld (tenor saxophone), Goodman (clarinet), Charlie Christian (guitar), Artie Bernstein (double bass), and Cootie Williams (trumpet)

recordings, and other materials was bequeathed to Yale University; *see* LIBRARIES AND ARCHIVES, §2.

As a jazz clarinetist Goodman had no peer; his flawless solo improvisations set standards of excellence for jazz performance. He founded and directed the most important musical organization of the swing era and helped to open a new epoch in American popular music. He was the first white bandleader to adopt and popularize an uncompromising jazz style. He was also among the first to feature black jazz players, an action that might have compromised his own career at a time when racial integration was not a popular concept. His concerts brought a new audience and a new level of recognition to jazz.

Oral history material in *SSsv.*

See also ARRANGEMENT, §3; IMPROVISATION, §4 (i) and ex.1; and JAZZ (i), §IV, 3; for further illustration *see* WILLIAMS, COOTIE.

SELECTED RECORDINGS

Benny Goodman, i–x (RCA 730629, 730707, 731041, 731092, 741044, 741059, 741072, 741084, 741102, FXM17083) [collected reissue, incl. recordings with small groups (i–iv) and arrs. by F. Henderson (v–vi)]

AS LEADER

Of trio: Clarinetitis/That's a Plenty (1928, Voc. 15705); After you've gone (1935, Vic. 25115); Lady Be Good (1936, Vic. 25333)

Of quartet: Moonglow (1936, Vic. 25398); Exactly Like You (1936, Vic. 25406); Avalon (1937, Vic. 25644)

Of quintet: Liza (1945, V-disc 627B)

Of sextet/septet: Seven Come Eleven (1939, Col. 35349); Breakfast Feud (1941, Col. 36039); A Smo-o-o-oth One/Airmail Special (1941, Col. 36099); Just One of Those Things (1945, Col. 36924); Stealin' Apples (1948, Cap. 10173); *Seven Come Eleven* (1975, Col. FC38265)

Of big band: A Jazz Holiday/Wolverine Blues (1928, Voc. 15656); Jungle Blues/Room 1411 (1928, Bruns. 4013); Blue (1928, Bruns. 3975); Riffing the Scotch (1933, Col. 2867D); Take my Word (1934, Col. 2947D); Bugle Call Rag (1934, Col. 2958D); Sometimes I'm Happy/King Porter [Stomp] (1935, Vic. 25090); Stomping at the Savoy (1936, Vic. 25247); Sing, sing, sing (1937, Vic. 36205); *Carnegie Hall Concert* (1938, Col. SL160); Don't be that way (1938, Vic. 25792); Scarecrow (1941, Col. 36180); Solo Flight (1941, Col. 36684); Something New (1941, Col. 36209); Clarinet à la King (1941, OK 6544); Clarinade (1945, Col. 36823); Tattletale/Dizzy Fingers (1947, Cap. 439); Chicago (1947, Cap. 20125); *Benny Goodman in Moscow* (1962, RCA LSO6008); *Benny Goodman Today* (1970, Lon. 21); *Fortieth Anniversary Concert* (1978, Lon. 2PS918–19)

AS SIDEMAN

B. Pollack: He's the last word (1926, Vic. 20425); Waitin' for Katie (1927, Vic. 21184); R. Nichols: Indiana (1929, Bruns. 4373); China Boy (1930, Bruns. 4877); T. Lewis: Royal Garden Blues (1931, Col. 2527D); J. Venuti and E. Lang: Beale St. Blues (1931, Voc. 15864); Farewell Blues (1931, Voc. 15858); J. Venuti: Jazz me Blues/In de Ruff (1933, Col. CB686): A Rollini: Riverboat Shuffle (1934, Decca 265); G. Krupa: The Last Round-up (1935, Parl. 2268); M. Powell: Blue Skies (1942, Com. 543)

BIBLIOGRAPHY

B. Goodman and I. Kolodin: *The Kingdom of Swing* (New York, 1939; Ger. trans. as *Mein Weg zum Jazz: eine Autobiographie*, Zurich, 1961)

N. Shapiro and N. Hentoff, eds.: *Hear me Talkin' to ya: the Story of Jazz by the Men who Made it* (New York and London, 1955/*R*1966), 125, 313

B. Goodman: "That Old Gang of Mine," *Eddie Condon's Treasury of Jazz*, ed. E. Condon and R. Gehman (New York, 1956/*R*1975), 258

D. R. Connor: *BG off the Record: a Bio-discography of Benny Goodman* (Fairless Hills, PA, 1958, rev. and enlarged [2]/1969 as *BG on the Record: a Bio-discography of Benny Goodman*, rev. and enlarged [3]/1984 as *The Record of a Legend: a Bio-discography of Benny Goodman*)

B. Green: *The Reluctant Art: Five Studies in the Growth of Jazz* (London, 1962), 51–90

"La tournée Benny Goodman en URSS," *BHcF*, no.120 (1962), 12

I. Crosbie: "Benny Rides Again," *JJ*, xxiii/10 (1970), 2

L. Tomkins: "Benny Goodman's Story," *CI*, viii/8 (1970), 20 [interview]

A. McCarthy: "Early Benny Goodman," *J&B*, i/1 (1971), 8

F. Reidy: "Benny Goodman is Very Happy with his British Band," *CI*, ix/9 (1971), 20

G. G. Daniels, ed.: Liner notes, *The Swing Era: Benny Goodman into the '70s: the King in Person* (STA 354, 1972)

S. Dance: *The World of Swing* (New York, 1974) [colln of previously pubd interviews], 260, 271

A. McCarthy: *Big Band Jazz* (New York and London, 1974), 226

J. McDonough: "Benny Goodman: the King Swings on," *DB*, xliv/19 (1977), 14

[B. Goodman]: *Benny, King of Swing: a Pictorial Biography Based on Benny Goodman's Personal Archives* (London and New York, 1979; Ger. trans., Wilhelmshaven, Germany, 1984)

F. Kappler and G. Simon: Liner notes, *Giants of Jazz: Benny Goodman* (TL J05, 1979)

L. Jeske: "A Jazz Classic," *DB*, xlix/9 (1982), 21 [interview]

I. Crosbie: "Benny's Band," *JJI*, xxxix/10 (1986), 19 [incl. discography]

M. McPartland: "Benny Goodman: from the Inside – the Sideman's View," *All in Good Time* (New York, and Oxford, England, 1987)[colln of previously pubd articles], 91

A. Rollini: *Thirty Years with the Big Bands* (London, Urbana, IL and Chicago, 1987)

B. Crowther: *Benny Goodman* (London, 1988)
D. R. Connor: *Benny Goodman: Listen to his Legacy* (Metuchen, NJ, and London, 1988) [bio-discography]

RICHARD WANG (text)
ALYN SHIPTON (recordings list)

Goodman, Jerry (*b* Chicago, *c*1945). Violinist. His parents were professional violinists, and as a teenager he studied at seminars associated with the Juilliard School. From 1966 he was "band boy" and then violinist with a rock group, the Flock. His importance as a jazz musician lies in his associations with John McLaughlin; he played on McLaughlin's album *My Goal's Beyond* (1970, Douglas 9) and toured and made recordings as a member of the first MAHAVISHNU ORCHESTRA (1971–3). (J. P. Schaffer: "An Innermost Vision," *DB*, xl/8 (1973), 11)

Goodrick, Mick (*b* Sharon, PA, 9 June 1945). Electric guitarist. He began playing guitar at the age of 12 and later attended Stan Kenton's summer camps. After graduating from the Berklee School of Music (mid-1960s) he taught there for four years. He recorded with Woody Herman in 1970, and played at clubs in Boston in a trio with Alan Broadbent and Rick Laird, and in a duo with Pat Metheny. From 1973 to 1975 he performed, toured, and recorded with Gary Burton. During this period he played intermittently and made recordings with Jack DeJohnette (1974) and accompanied Joe Williams and Astrud Gilberto. In 1978 he recorded the album *In Pas(s)ing* (ECM 1139) as a leader, with sidemen Eddie Gomez, John Surman, and DeJohnette. He recorded with Charlie Haden in 1982.

BIBLIOGRAPHY

N. Tesser: "Profile: Mick Goodrick, Pat Metheny," *DB*, xlii/15 (1975), 36
M. A. Meltzer: "Pat Metheny, Mick Goodrick: Gary Burton's Star Guitarists," *GP*, x/3 (1976), 10 [incl. discography]
"Mick Goodrick," *Blues Notes*, no.37 (1979), 40

Good Time Jazz. Record label owned by the company CONTEMPORARY.

Goodwin, Bill [William Richard] (*b* Los Angeles, 8 Jan 1942). Drummer. He studied piano from the age of five, and took up tenor saxophone when he was 12; apart from some guidance from Stan Levey he is largely self-taught as a drummer. After his first professional engagement in Los Angeles with Charles Lloyd he worked with Mike Melvoin (intermittently, 1961–5), Bud Shank (1961–3), Frank Rosolino (1962), Howard Rumsey's Lighthouse All Stars (1964), Art Pepper (1964), Paul Horn (1965–6), Gábor Szabó (1967), George Shearing (1968), Mose Allison (intermittently, 1968–75), Gary Burton (1969–71), Toshiko Akiyoshi (1971), Stan Getz (1972), Gerry Mulligan (1973–4), Chuck Israels's National Jazz Ensemble (intermittently from 1973 to 1978), and the Al Cohn–Zoot Sims Quintet (1974). From 1974 Goodwin has been a member of Phil Woods's band, though he has also worked as a freelance for Michel Legrand, June Christy, Joe Williams, Bob Dorough, Tony Bennett, and Manhattan Transfer. In 1975 his playing reached a larger audience when he toured and recorded with Tom Waits.

Goodwin brings a modern approach to the conventions of swing and bop; the vigor and versatility of his playing are evident on Woods's album *"Live" from the Showboat.* But although he plays with considerable force, he achieves a graceful, flowing style that allows for interplay with the other members of an ensemble.

SELECTED RECORDINGS

As leader: *Solar Energy* (1979–80, Omni. 1029); *Network* (1982, Omni. 1050)
As sideman with P. Woods: *The New Phil Woods Album* (1975, RCA BGL1-1391); *"Live" from the Showboat* (1976, RCA BGL2-2202); *Birds of a Feather* (1982, Ant. 1006); *At the Vanguard* (1982, Ant. 1013); *Heaven* (1984, Black Hawk 50401)
As sideman with others: G. Burton and S. Grappelli: *Paris Encounter* (1969, Atl. 1597); G. Burton and K. Jarrett: *Gary Burton and Keith Jarrett* (1970, Atl. 1577); Jack Wilkins: *Windows* (*c*1973, Mstr. 396); T. Waits: *Nighthawks at the Diner* (1975, Asy. 7E2008)

BIBLIOGRAPHY

L. Feather: "Burton: surprises sans choc," *Jm*, no.166 (1969), 13
Liner notes, *"Live" from the Showboat* (RCA BGL2-2202, 1976)
B. Rusch: "Phil Woods Quartet: Interview," *Cadence*, v/10 (1979), 3
M. Rozek: "Ultimate Sideman Bill Goodwin," *MD*, iv/3 (1980), 22
L. Hollis and E. Ferguson: "Bill Goodwin: Interview," *Cadence*, xi/12 (1985), 5

JEFF POTTER

Goodwin, Henry (Clay) (*b* Columbia, SC, 2 Jan 1910; *d* New York, 2 July 1979). Trumpeter. He played drums, tuba, and trumpet at high school in Washington, and at the age of 15 he traveled to Europe in Claude Hopkins's band. From the late 1920s he worked in New York with Elmer Snowden and Cliff Jackson, with whom he recorded as a trumpeter and singer, and in 1933 he performed with Lucky Millinder in Europe. After returning to the USA he played with Willie Bryant, Charlie Johnson (1934–6), Cab Calloway (1936), Edgar Hayes (1937–40), Sidney Bechet (from 1940), and Cecil Scott (1942–4); he also recorded with Hayes in Kenny Clarke's Quintet in Stockholm (1938). From 1944 Goodwin concentrated on working in small groups with such musicians as Scott and Art Hodes (1946). In 1948, as a member of Mezz Mezzrow's band, he performed at the Nice Jazz Festival and toured Europe, after which he played with Bob Wilber (1948–9) and Jimmy Archey (1950–51, 1952), and on the West Coast with Earl Hines (1956). In the 1960s he worked as a freelance with dixieland groups in New York. Goodwin performed particularly well in small bands; as a soloist he often used a plunger mute and growl techniques.

SELECTED RECORDINGS

As sideman: C. Jackson: Torrid Rhythm (1930, Madison/Radiex 951); S. Bechet: Blues in the Air/The Mooche (1941, Vic. 201510); B. Wilber: Limehouse Blues/Zig zag (1949, Cir. [USA] 1064)

BIBLIOGRAPHY

ChiltonW; FeatherE
H. Goodwin: "Music is my Business," *Jazz Record*, no.43 (1946), 7; repr. in *Selections from the Gutter: Jazz Portraits from "The Jazz Record,"* ed. A. Hodes and C. Hansen (Berkeley, CA, Los Angeles, and London, 1977), 216
M. Pinfold: "The Forgotten Ones: Henry Goodwin," *JJI*, xxxvi/12 (1983), 13

EDDIE LAMBERT

Goofus [couesnophone]. A free-reed novelty instrument manufactured in the 1920s by Couesnon & Cie. of France. It is in effect a keyboard harmonica, which may be played by blowing either directly into a mouthpiece, or through a length of flexible tubing that allows the instrument to be laid flat on a surface in the manner of a conventional keyboard instrument. The only jazz musician of note to play the goofus was Adrian Rollini in the late 1920s.

Goofus Five. Recording band led in the 1920s by ADRIAN ROLLINI.

Gordon, Bob [Robert] (*b* St. Louis, 11 June 1928; *d* California, 28 Aug 1955). Baritone saxophonist. He played in the dance bands of Shorty Sherock (1946), Alvino Rey (1948–51), Billy May (1952), and Horace Heidt (1952–3). From 1952 to 1955 he also made recordings in the West Coast style with Shelly Manne (1952), Maynard Ferguson (1952–5), Chet Baker (1953), Stan Kenton, Clifford Brown, Shorty Rogers (all 1954), Pete Rugolo (1954–5), and Tal Farlow (1955). He recorded only one album as leader, *Meet Mr. Gordon* (1954, PJ 12).

BIBLIOGRAPHY

FeatherE

R. Gordon: *Jazz West Coast: the Los Angeles Jazz Scene of the 1950s* (London and New York, 1986)

G. J. Hoogeveen: *Bob Gordon Discography* (in preparation)

Gordon, Dexter (Keith) (*b* Los Angeles, 27 Feb 1923). Tenor saxophonist. He began to play clarinet at the age of 13 and studied music with Lloyd Reese, during which time he played in a rehearsal band with other pupils of Reese, including Charles Mingus and Buddy Collette. In 1940 he began a long engagement with Lionel Hampton's touring band, with which he took part in a recording session in 1942. After leaving Hampton in 1943 he made his first lengthy solo recordings, as the leader of a quintet session with Nat "King" Cole as a sideman. He

Dexter Gordon playing at the JVC Grande Parade du Jazz Nice, France, 1987

worked in the Los Angeles area with Lee Young, Jesse Price, and, for a few weeks in April and May 1944, with the Fletcher Henderson Orchestra (some of his performances with Henderson survive in recordings made from broadcasts). After playing briefly with Louis Armstrong he moved to New York by December 1944 to appear in Billy Eckstine's orchestra. His recordings with Eckstine, Dizzy Gillespie, Fats Navarro, and others soon made him a leading figure in the bop movement. Gordon returned to California in summer 1946 and played with the drummer Cee Pee Johnson in Honolulu for two months, then for the remainder of the decade continued to work alternately on the East and West coasts. He appeared with Tadd Dameron in New York early in 1949, and joined fellow tenor saxophonist Wardell Gray for a popular and sensational series of "saxophone duels" between 1947 and 1952. Difficulties associated with drug addiction curtailed his activities during the 1950s, but these problems had been resolved by 1960 when he served as composer, musician, and actor in the West Coast production of Jack Gelber's play *The Connection.* Thereafter he toured and recorded principally as a leader, moving back to New York early in 1962.

In September 1962 Gordon performed in London and then made a tour of the Continent that was so successful he remained in Europe for the next 15 years, taking infrequent trips to the USA. Based in Copenhagen, he appeared at all the major jazz festivals, taught, and recorded prolifically; he also toured Japan in autumn 1975. Encouraged by a visit to New York in 1976, however, he returned permanently to the USA the following year. He was elected to the Jazz Hall of Fame in 1980 and named "musician of the year" by readers of *Down Beat* magazine in 1978 and 1980. As the star of the feature film *Round Midnight* (1986), Gordon was the subject of renewed interest in the late 1980s (*see* FILMS, §I, 5); he received a nomination for an Academy Award for his role.

Gordon was a major force in the emergence of modern tenor saxophone styles. His main influence was Lester Young, but he also displays an extrovert intensity reminiscent of Herschel Evans and Illinois Jacquet. His rich, vibrant sound, harmonic awareness, behind-the-beat phrasing, and predilection for humorous quotations combine to create a unique style. Gordon's music strongly affected the two leading tenor saxophonists of the succeeding generation, Sonny Rollins and John Coltrane. Gordon was later influenced in turn by Coltrane, and even, following Coltrane's example, adopted the soprano saxophone during the late 1970s. A volume of transcriptions of his performances has been published by L. Niehaus (*Dexter Gordon Jazz Saxophone Solos: Transcriptions from the Original Recordings,* Hollywood, CA, 1979).

Oral history material in *NjR*.

SELECTED RECORDINGS

As leader: I found a new baby/Rosetta (1943, Mer./Clef 8900); Long Tall Dexter (1946, Savoy 603); with W. Gray: The Chase (1947, Dial 1017); *Doin' Allright* (1961, BN 84077); *Our Man in Paris* (1963, BN 84146); *Homecoming* (1976, Col. PG34650)

As sideman: B. Eckstine: Blowin' the Blues Away (1944, Deluxe 2001); D. Gillespie: Blue 'n' Boogie (1945, Guild 1001)

BIBLIOGRAPHY

I. Gitler: "Dexter Gordon: the Time for Recognition," *DB*, xxviii/29 (1961), 16

L. Tomkins: "The Dexter Gordon Story," *Crescendo*, i/4 (1962), 4 [interview]

I. Gitler: *Jazz Masters of the Forties* (New York, 1966/*R*1983 with discography), 201

R. Baggenaes: "Dexter Gordon: Interview," *Coda*, x/7 (1972), 2

J. Burns: "Dexter Gordon 1942–1952," *JJ*, xxv/4 (1972), 22

C. Berg: "Dexter Gordon: Making his Great Leap Forward," *DB*, xliv/3 (1977), 12

L. Tomkins: "Dexter Gordon," *CI*, xv (1977), no.8, p.6; no.9, p.14 [interview]

G. Endress: *Jazz Podium: Musiker über sich selbst* (Stuttgart, Germany, 1980), 128

B. Rusch: "Dexter Gordon: Interview," *Cadence*, vii/11 (1981), 5

R. Nieus: *A Discography of Dexter Gordon* (n.p. [Jambes, Belgium], n.d. [1986])

I. Gitler: "'Round Midnight': Starring Dexter Gordon," *JT* (1986), Oct, 14

T. Sjøgren: *Long Tall Dexter: the Discography of Dexter Gordon* (Copenhagen, 1986)

LEWIS PORTER

Gordon, Joe [Joseph Henry] (*b* Boston, 15 May 1928; *d* Santa Monica, CA, 4 Nov 1963). Trumpeter. He studied at the New

England Conservatory with Fred Berman and first worked professionally in 1947. After leading a group at the Savoy in Boston he played with Georgie Auld, Lionel Hampton, the alto saxophonist Jimmy Tyler, Charlie Parker (at intervals, 1953–5), Art Blakey (1954), and Don Redman (1955). With Dizzy Gillespie in 1956 he toured the Middle East and recorded; the same year he recorded as a member of Horace Silver's quintet. In 1957 he performed (at the Stables in Boston) and recorded as a member of Herb Pomeroy's band, with which he remained until May of the following year. After moving to Los Angeles he worked with Barney Kessel (recording in 1959), Benny Carter (recording in 1959), and Harold Land (recording in 1960), and while a member of Shelly Manne's quintet (1958–60) played with Dexter Gordon; in 1959 he appeared with Manne in the film *The Proper Time.* Towards the end of his life he worked as a freelance. Although Gordon's abilities exceeded the recognition that he was accorded, he achieved some renown for his hard bop trumpet playing with Blakey and Silver.

SELECTED RECORDINGS

As leader: *Introducing Joe Gordon* (1955, Mer. 36025); *Lookin' Good* (1961, Cont. 7597)

As sideman: A. Blakey: *The Jazz Messengers Featuring Art Blakey* (1954, EmA 26030); S. Manne: *The Proper Time* (1959–60, Cont. 7587); H. Land: *West Coast Blues* (1960, Jlnd 20)

BIBLIOGRAPHY

FeatherE; *Feather '60s*

V. Wilmer: "Joe Gordon," *JJ*, xiii/9 (1960), 4

GARY THEROUX

Görling, Miff [Uno] (*b* Stockholm, 21 March 1909). Swedish composer, arranger, and trombonist, brother of Zilas Görling. He played with the tenor saxophonist Frank Vernon (1928–32), the pianist Gösta Säfbom (1932–3), the singer Gösta Jonsson (1934–7), Arne Hülphers, and Seymour Österwall before forming his own band in 1938. He became particularly well known for his fine big-band compositions, such as *Miffologi*, recorded in 1935 by an all-star Swedish band (Sonora 3116), and *Ösregn* [Downpour] and *Hülphers Stomp*, written for Hülphers and recorded by him for Odeon (1936, 31234; 1938, 2979). Görling also wrote jazz arrangements and popular music (both arrangements and compositions), led bands in Stockholm until 1957, and played swing trombone in a style inspired by that of Miff Mole.

Oral history material in *SSsv.*

BIBLIOGRAPHY

"Svenskt stjärnalbum" [Swedish star-album], *Orkester journalen*, vi/10 (1938), 5

"Våra arrangörer" [Our arrangers], *Estrad*, iv/11 (1942), 7

"Mannen bakom orkestern" [The man behind the orchestra], *Estrad*, vi/11 (1944), 11

U. Söderholm: "Miffologi," *Musikern* (March 1979), 19

E. Kjellberg: *Svensk jazzhistoria: en översikt* [Swedish jazz history: an overview] (Stockholm, 1985)

ERIK KJELLBERG

Görling, Zilas (*b* Hudiksvall, Sweden, 21 April 1911; *d* Stockholm, 11 April 1960). Swedish tenor saxophonist, brother of Miff Görling. He played with the tenor saxophonist Frank Vernon (1929–32) and Arne Hülphers (1934–8) and under the bandleader Sune Lundwall (1939–44), and made several recordings as a member of a studio group, the Sonora Swingers; he also recorded with Benny Carter (1936), Thore Jederby, and Gösta Törner. Görling's recordings *Sleepy Time Gal* (1937, Son. 3257) and *Nagasaki* (1937, Son. 3364), both made with the Swing Swingers, are illustrative of his style of playing, which was strongly influenced by Coleman Hawkins.

BIBLIOGRAPHY

E. Kjellberg: *Svensk jazzhistoria: en översikt* [Swedish jazz history: an overview] (Stockholm, 1985)

ERIK KJELLBERG

Gorni, Kramer (*b* Rivarolo Mantovano, Mantova, 22 July 1913). Italian accordionist, double bass player, and bandleader. He studied accordion with his father, a professional folk musician, and double bass at the A. Boito Conservatory in Parma. He played double bass in symphony orchestras and accordion in dance groups, and from 1934 led a jazz-oriented quintet that at first included Romero Alvaro and made several recordings, including *After you've gone* (1938, Fonit 7890) and *Tiger Rag* (1940, Fonit 8357). He toured the UK with the accordionist Wolmer Beltrami (1948) and played double bass with Armando Trovajoli and Gil Cuppini at the Paris Jazz Fair (1949), the first international jazz festival to be held in Paris. In 1952 he ended his career in jazz to write show music and lead a television orchestra.

ADRIANO MAZZOLETTI

Gossez, Pierre [Gate, Alan] (*b* Valenciennes, France, 6 Aug 1928). French clarinetist and saxophonist. In the 1950s he played with Noël Chiboust and the accordionist Tony Murena, under the bandleader Jacques Hélian (1953–4), and with Claude Bolling, Michel Legrand (1956–8), and Martial Solal (1957); his association with Bolling lasted from 1956 until the late 1970s and he worked again with Solal from 1980. After 1960 he also played with Guy Lafitte, the vibraphonist Michel Hausser (1964), André Hodeir, the Paris Jazz All Stars (1966–7), the trumpeters Sonny Grey (1967) and Ivan Jullien, the bandleader and violinist Franck Pourcel (1960s), the vibraphonist Dany Doriz (1973), Gunther Schuller (1979), and the double bass player Bob Quibel (1980–88). A very talented and versatile reed player, Gossez has made many recordings, including *Struttin' with some Barbecue/ Sugar Blues* (Festival 2226), recorded around 1961 under the pseudonym Alan Gate.

MICHEL LAPLACE

Gottlieb, Danny [Dan, Daniel Richard] (*b* New York, 18 April 1953). Drummer and percussionist. He studied with Mel Lewis and Joe Morello and attended the University of Miami (BM 1975). After working as a sideman for a number of musicians, including the rock-and-roll singer Bobby Rydell, in 1976 he joined the Gary Burton Quartet, in which Pat Metheny also played; he achieved prominence as a member of Metheny's own group, to which he belonged from its formation in 1977 until 1983. In 1981 he formed a group with Mark Egan, which in 1983 took the name Elements, and with which Gottlieb mainly worked after leaving Metheny. He continued throughout this period to be active as a session musician. He joined John McLaughlin's group as a percussionist in 1984, and in 1985 began also to work with Al Di Meola. He collaborated with Egan in the composition of the soundtrack to the film *Blown Away* (1985). Gottlieb is noted for his light, supportive style as an accompanist and for his exceptional accuracy as a cymbal player.

SELECTED RECORDINGS

As leader with M. Egan: *Elements* (1982, Philo 9011); *Forward Motion* (1984, Ant. 1021)

As sideman: P. Metheny: *Watercolors* (1977, ECM 1097); *Offramp* (1981, ECM 1216); J. McLaughlin: *Mahavishnu* (1984, WB 25190); A. Di Meola: *Soaring through a Dream* (1985, Manhattan 53011)

BIBLIOGRAPHY

R. Mattingly: "Danny Gottlieb: In Pursuit of Excellence," *MD*, vi/2 (1982), 18

B. Milkowski: "The Elemental Music of Danny Gottlieb and Mark Egan," *DB*, li/2 (1984), 24 [incl. discography]
B. O'Donnell: "Danny Gottlieb: Sound Impressionist," *DB*, lii/9 (1985), 16 [incl. discography]
R. Mattingly: "Danny Gottlieb," *MD*, x/1 (1986), 25

PATRICK T. WILL

Goudie, Frank "Big Boy" (*b* Youngsville, LA, 13 Sept 1899; *d* San Francisco, 9 Jan 1964). Tenor saxophonist and clarinetist. He grew up in New Orleans, and first played cornet, performing with Papa Celestin's Original Tuxedo Band and other ensembles. In the early 1920s he worked in Texas, Louisiana, New Mexico, and California before moving to Europe; from 1925 he lived in France, where he began concentrating on tenor saxophone and clarinet, though he continued to play trumpet occasionally. He worked in many European countries with Benny Peyton, Louis Mitchell, Sam Wooding, Noble Sissle, and Freddy Johnson, and later played with Willie Lewis (1935–8); he may be heard to advantage on Lewis's *Christopher Columbus* (1936, PAct. 898). He also made recordings in Paris with Bill Coleman, including *Big Boy Blues* (1937, Swing 32). Goudie left Paris in 1940 and spent the rest of World War II in Brazil and Argentina, where he led his own small bands. In 1946 he returned to France and worked with Arthur Briggs and Harry Cooper. He played with Coleman from 1949 to 1951, when he began leading his own group in Berlin. This disbanded in 1956, and the following year Goudie returned to the USA, where he continued to play clarinet regularly with such musicians as Marty Marsala and Earl Hines.

For illustration *see* NIGHTCLUBS AND OTHER VENUES, fig.1.

BIBLIOGRAPHY

O. Stewart: "Brazil – a Country without Swing: 'Jive' would Start a Revolution, says Sax Player," *Baltimore Afro-American* (13 July 1940), 13
G. Mills: "Amos White and his New Orleans Ragtime Band," *Eureka*, i/5 (1960), 5

based on *ChiltonW*

Gould, Tony [Anthony James] (*b* Melbourne, Australia, 2 Feb 1940). Australian pianist. He began working professionally around 1960 in Melbourne, and in the early 1960s he performed regularly with Alan Lee's quartet; from 1964 to 1971 he played with Brian Brown. After a period of academic study and comparative inactivity he emerged in the mid-1970s as an important figure in Australian jazz; his albums *Gould Plays Gould* (1978, Move 3021) and *Best of Friends* (1984, Move 3046) show his mature, modern style. He also played with the trumpeter Keith Hounslow in a free-jazz duo, McJad. In the 1980s he has toured extensively, and worked with Clark Terry, Mark Murphy, Ernestine Anderson, and John Sangster.

BIBLIOGRAPHY

M. Williams: *The Australian Jazz Explosion* (London and elsewhere, 1981)
B. Johnson: "Gould, Anthony James," *The Oxford Companion to Australian Jazz* (Melbourne, Australia, 1987)

JEFF PRESSING (with JOHN WHITEOAK)

Gourley, Jimmy [James Pasco, Jr.] (*b* St. Louis, 9 June 1926). Electric guitarist. He replaced Jimmy Raney in Jay Burkhart's band in Chicago (1946–8). After working as a freelance with Sonny Stitt, Gene Ammons, and Anita O'Day he moved to Europe in 1951 and performed and recorded in Paris with Henri Renaud (1951–4). He also recorded with Lee Konitz, Clifford Brown, and Zoot Sims (all 1953). He moved back to Chicago briefly to play and record with Chubby Jackson (1956–7), but returned to Paris and from 1959 held long residencies at the Blue Note with Kenny Clarke and Lou Bennett. Although Gourley ran a club in the Canary Islands from 1970 to 1972, he returned again to Paris, and has performed throughout Europe with his trio. He plays and sings his own compositions.

In the 1950s, when guitar playing in Europe was dominated by Django Reinhardt, Gourley introduced to the Continent a style that was inspired by cool-jazz musicians, especially Lester Young. Influenced at first by Raney's subdued melodies, he gradually made greater use of the instrument's harmonic potential and played with increased rhythmic urgency, but his tone remained characteristic of cool jazz – smooth and free of vibrato.

SELECTED RECORDINGS

As leader: *Graffiti* (1977, Promophone 14); *The Jazz Trio* (1983, Bingow 3364)
As sideman: L. Bennett: *Lou Bennett Quartet* (1960, RCA 430050); on *Americans in Europe*, i (1963, Imp. 36), K. Clarke: Low Life, No Smokin'

BIBLIOGRAPHY

FeatherE; *Feather '60s*; *Feather–Gitler '70s*
"Jimmy Gourley," *Jh*, no.283 (1972), 39

NORMAN MONGAN

Gowans, (Arthur) Brad(ford) (*b* Billerica, MA, 3 Dec 1903; *d* Los Angeles, 8 Sept 1954). Valve trombonist, clarinetist, and cornetist. He made his professional début on clarinet, then briefly played slide trombone with the Rhapsody Makers Band, before replacing Sidney Arodin as the clarinetist in the New Orleans Jazz Band led by the drummer Tommy De Rosa in New York (1925). He played cornet with the bandleaders Joe Venuti and Jimmy Durante and recorded with the Red Heads led by Red Nichols (all in 1926). After ceasing to play for a short period in the early 1930s, he worked with Bobby Hackett (1936). He joined Wingy Manone in April 1938 as a valve trombonist, then returned to Hackett (summer 1938), now also playing saxophone. He worked with Joe Marsala and the Summa cum Laude Orchestra led by Bud Freeman, then played with Eddie Condon at Nick's in New York (1940); at this time he also wrote arrangements for Freeman and Lee Wiley (1939). In the 1940s he played with Ray McKinley (1942), Art Hodes (1942–3), Max Kaminsky (1945), and Condon (1946), before joining Jimmy Dorsey in 1948 and Nappy Lamare in 1949. Having left Lamare in 1950 he moved in 1951 to the West Coast, where he worked as a freelance musician; his last performance was in Las Vegas in January 1954, playing with a sextet led by the guitarist Eddie Skrivanek. In addition to his other instruments, Gowans also played valide; *see* TROMBONE, §1.

SELECTED RECORDINGS

As leader: I'm looking over a four-leaf clover (1927, Gen. 6039); Jazz me Blues/Singin' the Blues (1946, Vic. 20-3230)
As sideman: E. Condon: It's right here for you (1939, Com. 530); [no leader: Jam Session at Commodore, no.3]: A Good Man is Hard to Find (1940, Com. 1504–5)

BIBLIOGRAPHY

ChiltonW; *FeatherE*
E. Condon and T. Sugrue: *We Called it Music: a Generation of Jazz* (New York 1947/*R*1985)

MIKE HAZELDINE

Goyens, Al(phonse) (*b* Wetteren, Belgium, 1 Oct 1920). Belgian trumpeter, baritone saxophonist, and bandleader. He played with Jean Omer in 1940 and 1944 and with the pianist Vicky Thunus in 1945, and recorded with the tenor saxophonist Jean Tany in 1942. From 1946 to 1958 he led his own band, but it made no recordings; among its sidemen were Kenny Clarke, Lucky Thompson, Bobby Jaspar, and Francy Boland. (*ReclamsJ*)

Goykovich, Dusko [Gojkovic, Dusan] (*b* Jajce, Yugoslavia, 14 Oct 1931). Yugoslav trumpeter and flugelhorn player. After studying at the Academy of Music in Belgrade (1948–53) he played with the dance orchestra of the Belgrade radio. In 1955 he moved to Germany, where the same year he performed and recorded with the Frankfurt All Stars; he remained with this group until 1956, when he also played in Max Greger's orchestra. He belonged to Kurt Edelhagen's radio orchestra (1957–60) and to Marshall Brown's International Youth Band in 1958, when it appeared at the Newport Jazz Festival. From 1961 to 1963 he studied composition and arranging at the Berklee College of Music, and after playing in the orchestras of Maynard Ferguson (1963–4) and Woody Herman (1964–6) he returned to Germany, where he performed and recorded as the leader of the International Quintet at intervals into the 1970s; among the members of the quintet was Sal Nistico (ii). He was a principal soloist in the orchestra of Kenny Clarke and Francy Boland from 1968 to 1973 and in that of Peter Herbolzheimer in the early 1970s. From 1974 to 1975 he led a band with Slide Hampton, and in the 1980s he played with the drummer Alvin Queen (recording in 1981, and in 1983 as the leader with Queen of a quintet that included Nistico). He has also written arrangements for German radio orchestras and taught trumpet, improvisation, and arranging at the Swiss Jazz School in Berne and the Munich Jazz School. Goykovich's playing displays the influence of hard bop and of the work of Miles Davis in particular; his own compositions often use Yugoslav folk melodies and rhythms (this may be heard on, for example, his album *Swinging Macedonia*, 1966). He is the author of *Anleitung zur Improvisation für Trompete* (Mainz, Germany, 1968).

SELECTED RECORDINGS

As leader: *Swinging Macedonia* (1966, Phi. 843942); *After Hours* (1971, Enja 2020); with A. Queen: *A Day in Holland* (1983, Nilva 3407)

As sideman with K. Clarke and F. Boland: *The Golden Eight* (1961, BN 84092); *Felini 712* (1968, MPS 15220); *Rue Chaptal* (1969, Pol. 583055); *All Blues* (1969, MPS 15288)

As sideman with others: M. Brown: *Newport 1958* (1958, Col. CL1246); M. Ferguson: *The New Sound of Maynard Ferguson* (1964, Cameo 1040); W. Herman: *Woody's Winners* (1965, Col. CS9326); P. Herbolzheimer: *Soul Condor* (1970, MPS 2029035)

BIBLIOGRAPHY

FeatherE; *Feather '60s*; *Feather–Gitler '70s*

WOLFRAM KNAUER

Gozzo, Conrad (Joseph) (*b* New Britain, CT, 6 Feb 1922; *d* Burbank, CA, 8 Oct 1964). Trumpeter. He played with Isham Jones (1938) and Red Norvo (1940), then performed and recorded with Bob Chester (1941) and Claude Thornhill (1941–2). After working with Benny Goodman (1942) he joined the navy and played in a band led by Artie Shaw (1942–4). He rejoined Goodman in 1945, then toured and recorded with Woody Herman (he was featured as a soloist on *Stars fell on Alabama*, 1946, Col. 37197), and performed with Boyd Raeburn and Tex Beneke (1947). In Los Angeles he played on Bob Crosby's radio broadcasts (1947–51). Gozzo was highly acclaimed as a lead trumpeter and was much in demand as a studio musician; he also took part in sessions with Les Brown (1949), Jerry Gray (1949–53), Herman (1951–7), Ray Anthony (1951–8), Billy May (1951–64), Shorty Rogers (1953–7), Stan Kenton (1955), and Goodman (1955, 1958). He also recorded as a leader (1955).

BIBLIOGRAPHY

FeatherE; *Feather '60s*

R. Gordon: *Jazz West Coast: the Los Angeles Jazz Scene of the 1950s* (London and New York, 1986)

Graas, John (J.) (*b* Dubuque, IA, 14 Oct 1924; *d* Van Nuys, CA, 13 April 1962). French horn player, arranger, and composer. As a youth he won a national contest for solo instrumentalists and a scholarship to the Berkshire Music Center. In 1941 he became first horn player with the Indianapolis SO. He left the following year to play with Claude Thornhill, whose band, by Graas's own account, made the first "intelligent" use of the horn in jazz. After army service (1942–5) he was a member of the Cleveland Orchestra (1945–6) and Tex Beneke's band (1946–8) and toured with Stan Kenton's Innovations in Modern Music Orchestra (1950–51). Graas then settled in Hollywood, where he worked as a freelance studio musician, notably for Universal, and recorded West Coast jazz with his own small groups as well as with Shorty Rogers, Gerry Mulligan, and others. He also studied composition and wrote two large third-stream works, *Jazz Symphony no.1* and *Jazz Chaconne no.1* (commissioned by the Cincinnati SO), and music for television. A collection of his scores is in the possession of Ball State University at Muncie, Indiana (*see* LIBRARIES AND ARCHIVES, §2). Graas remained active as a soloist and teacher until his untimely death, and played an important role in securing a legitimate place for the french horn in jazz.

SELECTED RECORDINGS

As leader: *Jazz Studio 3* (1954–5, Decca 8104); *Coup de Graas* (1957, EmA 36117)

As sideman with S. Rogers: *Shorty Rogers and his Giants* (1953, RCA LPM3137); *Shorty Rogers Courts the Count* (1954, RCA LJM1004)

BIBLIOGRAPHY

FeatherE

B. Coss: "Horn of Plenty: John Graas," *Metronome*, lxxi (1955), Jan, 15

STEVEN STRUNK

Graettinger, Bob [Robert] (*b* Ontario, CA, 31 Oct 1923; *d* Los Angeles, 12 March 1957). Composer and arranger. After playing saxophone and arranging for Benny Carter, Johnny Richards, Alvino Rey, and Jan Savitt, he began to concentrate on composition. From 1947 he worked occasionally as an arranger for Stan Kenton and wrote studio arrangements for June Christy (1949). He composed a number of works that were performed and recorded by Kenton's band, the best-known of which are *Thermopolae* (1947, Cap. 908) and *City of Glass* (first performed in 1948, recorded 1951, Cap. 28062–3).

BIBLIOGRAPHY

FeatherE

R. B. Morgan: *The Music and Life of Robert Graettinger* (diss., U. of Illinois, 1974)

W. F. Lee: *Stan Kenton: Artistry in Rhythm* (Los Angeles, 1980) [incl. discography]

Grah, Bill [Wilhelm Josef] (*b* Bergisch Gladbach, Germany, 24 June 1928). Austrian vibraphonist and pianist. His father, Willi Grah, was a pianist and his brother Heinz a double bass player. He studied piano from the age of eight and in 1946 formed his first band with his brother; he took up the vibraphone in 1947. After leading a quintet (1949–53) he performed and recorded with Fatty George from 1954 to 1959, when he formed a bop quartet. In the 1960s he was the host of a radio program in Vienna. He became an Austrian citizen in 1970. During the next ten years he played with the Austrian Barrelhouse Jazz Band and led a quintet with the clarinetist and soprano saxophonist Alfons Würzl. He made many recordings both as a leader and a sideman, including *Bud's Birthday* (1975, Phi. 6322012) with Bud Freeman. Grah generally played vibraphone in a bop style and piano in the style of Chicago jazz.

KLAUS SCHULZ

Graham, Bill [William] (*b* Kansas City, MO, 18 Sept 1918). Alto and baritone saxophonist. He played with Count Basie, Lucky Millinder, Eddie Wilcox, and Erskine Hawkins (1945–

6), and toured and recorded intermittently with Dizzy Gillespie (1946–53). He also took part in sessions with Herbie Fields (1947), Eddie "Cleanhead" Vinson (1950), and Joe "Bebop" Carroll (1952–3). After leading a band in New York (*c*1953–1955) he toured and recorded with Basie (1955–7) and Duke Ellington (1958; he was featured as a soloist on *Black, Brown and Beige*, 1958, Col. CL1162). Graham also recorded with Paul Quinichette, and in Paris with Joe Newman (both 1956), then led his own group before joining Mercer Ellington (1959). From the late 1950s he taught music at public schools in New York. (*FeatherE*)

Graham, Kenny [Skingle, Kenneth Thomas] (*b* London, 19 July 1924). English saxophonist, composer, and arranger. He learned banjo at the age of six and played C-melody saxophone from 1935. After changing to the alto instrument he began to perform professionally in 1940 and after World War II he worked with Jiver Hutchinson, Nat Gonella, and Jack Parnell. In 1950 he formed his own band, the Afro-Cubists, in which he played tenor saxophone. It made several recordings for Esquire (1951–7, including *Mango Walk*, 1951, 308) and broadcast and toured until 1958, when Graham became ill; the group also recorded with Victor Feldman (1955). From 1959 Graham has written compositions and arrangements for Humphrey Lyttelton and Ted Heath as well as for films and radio programs. In the mid-1980s he concentrated on electronic keyboard instruments and alto saxophone. (*FeatherE*)

DIGBY FAIRWEATHER

Gramavision. Record company and label. Established in New York in 1979 by Jonathan F. P. Rose, the company issues mostly albums of free jazz, but its catalogue also includes recordings of fusions of that style with soul music (by Jamaaladeen Tacuma) and with reggae (by Oliver Lake). ("La marque rose," *Jm*, no.324 (1983), 9)

Gramercy Five. Small group. It was formed in 1940 by ARTIE SHAW as a unit within his big band, and named after the New York telephone exchange Gramercy; in comparison with other bandleaders Shaw was slow to form such an ensemble. The original recording band consisted of six members: Shaw (clarinet), Billy Butterfield (trumpet), Al Hendrickson (guitar), Nick Fatool (drums), Jud DeNaut (double bass), and Johnny Guarnieri (harpsichord). The combination of powerful solo work from Shaw and Butterfield with the sound of the harpsichord proved very popular and led to the highly successful recording *Summit Ridge Drive* (1940), of which a million copies were sold. In 1945 after his military service Shaw reorganized the band, including Roy Eldridge, Barney Kessel, and Dodo Marmarosa (for illustration *see* SHAW, ARTIE); this group recorded the tightly knit classics *The Sad Sack* and *Scuttlebutt* (1945). Although he continued to use the name Gramercy Five for small groups into the 1950s, none of Shaw's later ensembles had the impact of these earlier combinations.

SELECTED RECORDINGS

Special Delivery Stomp (1940, Vic. 26762); Summit Ridge Drive (1940, Vic. 26763); The Sad Sack (1945, Vic. 201647); Scuttlebutt (1945, Vic. 201929); *I Can't Get Started* (1953–4, Verve 2015)

BIBLIOGRAPHY

O. Peterson: "Artie Shaw," pt 2, *JJ*, xxii/10 (1969), 14

V. Simosko: "Artie Shaw and his Gramercy Fives," *JJS*, iv/1 (1973), 34 [incl. discography]

B. Korall: Liner notes, *The Complete Artie Shaw*, iii: 1939–40 (RCA AXM5556, 1978)

BRIAN PEERLESS

Gramophone Co. Record company. It was established in London in 1897 by William Barry Owen, who acted as agent for Emile Berliner, the inventor of the disc gramophone. Record manufacture took place mainly at Hanover, Germany; branches of the company were established all over the world, including India (1901), Russia (1902), Denmark, Sweden, Persia, and Spain. From its inception the Gramophone Co. was closely linked with the American holders of Berliner's patents, VICTOR. During World War I the Gramophone Co. lost control of its German interests to DEUTSCHE GRAMMOPHON, which became an autonomous organization. Thereafter the English company attempted to regain its outlet in Germany; it failed after protracted litigation, and was obliged instead to establish a new label, ELECTROLA, to fulfil this function. The Gramophone Co. however maintained subsidiaries in France, Italy, Spain, Australia, and Canada.

In 1899 the company acquired the "dog and gramophone" logo, which it first used in the USA on Victor and Monarch discs. In 1910, however, it began using the design in England, combining it with a new trademark, HIS MASTER'S VOICE. Because the label quickly became so successful its name superseded that of the Gramophone Co. The European subsidiaries at first issued discs bearing the label Gramophone; later they, too, adopted the name His Master's Voice, or translations of it, on a widespread basis. The label's operations were scarcely affected by the Gramophone Co.'s merger in 1931 with Columbia International, Ltd., to form EMI.

Grande Parade du Jazz. Name by which the JVC GRANDE PARADE DU JAZZ NICE was known until 1984.

Grand Terrace. Ballroom and nightclub in Chicago; *see* NIGHTCLUBS AND OTHER VENUES.

Granelli, Jerry [Gerald John] (*b* San Francisco, 30 Dec 1940). Drummer. He played drums from the age of five, and was later taught by Joe Morello. He performed and made recordings with Vince Guaraldi (1962–5), Jon Hendricks (1963), and Danny Zeitlin (1964–7, including the album *Carnival*, 1964, Col. CS9140). During the 1960s he also worked with John Handy and Earl Hines (1965), Jon Hendricks (1965–6), Ornette Coleman (1968), Martial Solal, Jimmy Witherspoon, and his own group, the Jazz Ensemble. He recorded with Mose Allison (1976) and the saxophonist Noel Jewkes (1977). He lived in San Francisco, then in Boulder, Colorado, where he formed the group Visions and taught music at the Naropa Institute, and then in Seattle. In 1982–3 he toured the USA and Europe with Ralph Towner and Gary Peacock. He recorded in a duo with the singer Jay Clayton in 1985 and as a sideman with the guitarist Nana Simopoulos the following year. (*Feather '60s*)

Granz, Norman (*b* Los Angeles, 6 Aug 1918). Impresario. In 1944 he supervised the production of an award-winning film, *Jammin' the Blues*, and in the same year began his concert series JAZZ AT THE PHILHARMONIC (JATP) with a concert at the Philharmonic Auditorium, Los Angeles. His concerts were in an informal jam-session format and toured most parts of the world, often being recorded live. Granz established two record labels, CLEF (1946) and NORGRAN (1953); later he bought all rights to his previous recordings, including the important series The Jazz Scene (1949), and formed a new company, VERVE, in 1956. From that time Granz has lived principally in Europe; he moved to Switzerland in 1960, and in his capacity as manager of JATP engaged many artists, notably Ella Fitzgerald, Oscar Peterson, and Duke Ellington. Although his concerts have frequently been criticized for their emphasis on unnecessary display they have been important in promoting the careers of Roy Eldridge, Art Tatum, Lester Young, Dizzy Gillespie, Charlie Parker, and many other outstanding jazz musicians, and brought modern jazz a much wider audience than it might otherwise have received. In 1973 Granz established in Los Angeles the record company PABLO, which, in addition to organizing concert tours, he has continued to manage into the 1980s.

BIBLIOGRAPHY

W. Balliett: "Pandemonium Pays Off," *The Sound of Surprise* (New York, 1959/*R*1978) [colln of previously pubd articles and reviews], 3
L. Tomkins: "Norman Granz," *Crescendo*, iv/9 (1966), 18
L. Feather: "The Granzwagon," *From Satchmo to Miles* (New York, 1972)
J. McDonough: "Norman Granz: JATP Pilot Driving Pablo Home," *DB*, xlvi (1979), no.16, p.30; no.17, p.35

J. BRADFORD ROBINSON

Grappelli [Grappelly], **Stephane** [Steph] (*b* Paris, 26 Jan 1908). French violinist. He is largely self-taught as a violinist and pianist, having studied formally only from 1924 to 1928. After playing both piano and violin in movie theaters and dance bands he worked in jazz professionally from around 1927. With Django Reinhardt he was the principal member of the QUINTETTE DU HOT CLUB DE FRANCE (formed 1934), the unusual instrumentation of which consisted of a violin, three guitars, and a double bass (for illustration *see* JAZZ (i), fig.4); through its many recordings the group became well-known in Europe and the USA. In 1939 he left the quintet and moved to England, where he was long associated with George Shearing; he worked again with Reinhardt in London (1946) and after returning to France in 1946 in Paris (1947–8) and Rome (1949). During the following years he became progressively less active as a leader, but in the 1960s his career was revived by a growing interest in the jazz violin, and in particular by the success of the album *Violin Summit* (1966), which he recorded as a member of a group of the same name. He made his first visit to the USA to perform at the Newport Jazz Festival (1969) and in 1973 received an unusual amount of attention for his first album with the classical violinist Yehudi Menuhin; others followed in 1975 and 1977. Around the same time he performed, recorded, and appeared at festivals with such diverse musicians as Joe Venuti (1969), Gary Burton (1969), Earl Hines (1974), Philip Catherine (1979), the mandolin player David Grisman (1979), and Martial Solal (1980).

Stephane Grappelli, c1980

With Venuti and Eddie South, Grappelli was a pioneer of the jazz violin. Although his playing in the Quintette du Hot Club de France tended to be overshadowed by that of Reinhardt, who was the greater innovator, he broadened his style throughout his long career and played with greater authority in his later years; still his playing remained rooted in the swing idiom and continued to be characterized by his sweet tone. He was important in furthering the careers of Jean-Luc Ponty and Didier Lockwood, and his recordings with Menuhin brought new recognition to the violin as a jazz instrument. He occasionally plays piano in a style indebted to that of Bix Beiderbecke.

SELECTED RECORDINGS

Duos: with E. Hines: *The Giants* (1974, BL 30193); with Marc Fossett: *Stephanova* (1983, Conc. 225)
As leader: of Quintette du Hot Club de France (with D. Reinhardt): Dinah (1934, Ultraphon 1422), Tiger Rag (1934, Ultraphon 1423), Minor Swing (1937, Swing 23); Stephane's Blues (1937, Swing 69); of Quintette du Hot Club de France (with Reinhardt): Them There Eyes (1938, Decca 6899); of Violin Summit (with S. Asmussen, J.-L. Ponty, and S. Smith): *Violin Summit* (1966, Saba 15099); *I Remember Django* (1969, BL 105); with G. Shearing: *The Reunion* (1976, MPS 68162); *Young Django* (1979, MPS 68230); *Tivoli Gardens, Copenhagen, Denmark* (1979, PL 2308220)

BIBLIOGRAPHY

FeatherE; *Feather '60s*; *Feather–Gitler '70s*
"'Django and I had the First Three-guitar Group – without Electricity!,' Says Jazz Violin Virtuoso Stephane Grappelli," *CI*, ix/4 (1970), 26
L. Tomkins: "Violon par excellence: Stephane Grappelli," *CI*, xii/6 (1974), 14
M. Ruppli: "Discographie: Stephane Grappelli," *Jh* (1978), no.349, p.30; no.350, p.19
G. Endress: "Stephane Grappelli," *Jazz Podium: Musiker über sich selbst* (Stuttgart, Germany, 1980), 26
D. Caldwell: "From the Heart," *JJI*, xxiv/4 (1981), 20 [interview; incl. discography]
M. Glaser and S. Grappelli: *Jazz Violin* (New York and elsewhere, 1981) [incl. interview, transcrs.]
L. Jeske: "Stephane Grappelli: Fiddler Fantastique," *DB*, xlviii (1981), no.4, p.15; no.5, p.18 [incl. discography]
R. Horricks: *Stephane Grappelli, or The Violin with Wings: a Profile* (Tunbridge Wells, England, and New York, 1983) [incl. discography]
G. Smith: *Stéphane Grappelli: a Biography* (London, 1987)

J. BRADFORD ROBINSON

Grasso, Alfio (*b* Lentini, Sicily, 8 Sept 1912; *d* Rome, after 1962). Sicilian violinist, guitarist, and alto saxophonist. He joined Sesto Carlini's dance orchestra in Rome around 1935 and in 1940 moved to Berlin, where he played and recorded with Benny de Weille, Tullio Mobiglia, Meg Tevelian, and the violinist Helmuth Zacharias. He made several tours of the Russian SFSR (1944–7) and worked in radio orchestras in Italy. In 1962 he played with Herb Flemming in Carlini's orchestra, which had been re-formed. As a soloist he performed on violin and guitar; a good example of his work is his recording of *Sweet Georgia Brown* (1962, Ricordi 8008).

ADRIANO MAZZOLETTI

Graves, Milford (Robert) (*b* New York, 20 Aug 1941). Drummer. He played conga drums as a child and began using sticks only at the age of 17; he later studied tablā with Wasantha Singh. He became known in the mid-1960s through his appearances with Giuseppi Logan and with the New York Art Quartet in the concert series known as the October Revolution in Jazz. In 1966 he recorded two albums of duos with Don Pullen at Yale University, and in the following year he performed at the Newport Jazz Festival with Albert Ayler. He took part in the mid-1970s in a series of concerts with Andrew Cyrille and Rashied Ali known as "Dialogue of the Drums," and established a practice of performing in black neighborhoods; in 1983 he recorded with Cyrille, Kenny Clarke, and Don Moye. One of the most flamboyant free-jazz drummers of the 1960s, Graves has been influenced by Indian approaches to percussion, and often appears in groups composed solely of drummers. In 1973 he joined the faculty of Bennington College.

SELECTED RECORDINGS

Duos: with S. Morgan: *Percussion Duo* (1964, ESP 1015); with D. Pullen: *Don Pullen and Milford Graves* (1966, SRP 286), incl. P. G. I, II; *Nommo* (1966, SRP 290), incl. P. G. III, IV; with A. Cyrille: *Dialogue of the Drums* (1974, IPS 001)

As sideman: R. Rudd and J. Tchicai: *The New York Art Quartet* (1964, ESP 1004); G. Logan: *Giuseppe Logan Quartet* (1965, ESP 1007)

BIBLIOGRAPHY

L. P. Neal: "Black Revolution in Music," *Liberator*, v/9 (1965), 14 [interview]
B. Mathieu: "Milford Graves Speaks Words," *DB*, xxxiii/22 (1966), 23 [interview]
J. Cooke: "Backwards, Forwards, Sideways: a Study of Milford Graves," *JM*, no.162 (1968), 4; no.163 (1968), 4 [incl. discography]
V. Wilmer: "Musicians Talking: Milford Graves," *JM*, no.173 (1969), 8
J. Welch: "Different Drummers: a Composite Profile," *DB*, xxxvii/6 (1970), 18
V. Wilmer: "Dialogue of the Drummers," *Coda*, xi/11 (1974), 2
——: "Milford Graves: Interview," *Coda*, no.150 (1976), 8
V. Gillis: "Milford Graves: Interview," *Cadence*, vi (1980), no.5, p.5; no.6, p.9
R. Riggins: "Milford Graves," *Coda*, no.183 (1982), 14

MICHAEL ULLMAN

Gray, Glen [Knoblaugh, Glen Gray; Spike] (*b* Roanoke, IL, 7 June 1906; *d* Plymouth, MA, 23 Aug 1963). Alto saxophonist and bandleader. In Detroit he played with Jean Goldkette (1924–8) and from 1927 led the Orange Blossoms, to which several of Goldkette's sidemen belonged; after other musicians joined this group it became known in 1929 as the Casa Loma Orchestra, which Gray led in performances and recordings until the late 1940s (from 1933 under the name Glen Gray and the Casa Loma Orchestra). After interrupting his career in music for several years Gray led studio orchestras from 1956 to 1962, which performed pieces from the Casa Loma Orchestra's repertory and other hits of the swing era. A collection of materials associated with Gray and the Casa Loma Orchestra is in the Robert Gray Dodge Library of Northeastern University, Boston; *see* LIBRARIES AND ARCHIVES, §2.

For recordings and further information *see* CASA LOMA ORCHESTRA.

BIBLIOGRAPHY

Obituary, *DB*, xxx/26 (1963), 13

RONALD M. RADANO

Gray, Jerry [Graziano, Generoso] (*b* East Boston, MA, 3 July 1915; *d* Dallas, 10 Aug 1976). Composer, arranger, and bandleader. He studied violin from the age of seven. From 1936 to 1939 he worked as a violinist and arranger for Artie Shaw, who made a highly successful recording of his version of *Begin the Beguine* (1938, Bb 7746). In 1939 he became chief arranger for Glenn Miller; he stayed with Miller's Army Air Force band during World War II, and from 1945 to 1946 conducted and kept together the Glenn Miller Orchestra after its founder's disappearance. Gray later moved to Hollywood, where he led a band on his own radio show (1946–52), did freelance work, directed the music for the "Bob Crosby Show," and eventually joined Warner Bros. as a staff arranger (1962). He scored the music for such films as *The Glenn Miller Story* (1954) and *What did you do in the war, Daddy?* (1966). In the 1970s he led ad hoc bands in nightclubs and studios in Texas.

Gray composed and arranged such standards as *Pennsylvania 6-5000* (1940), *Sun Valley Jump* (1941), and *A String of Pearls* (1941), and his distinctive scoring was one of the essential ingredients of the "Glenn Miller sound." He continued to write in the same manner for his own bands and studio ensembles.

RECORDED COMPOSITIONS

(selective list; all recorded by G. Miller for Bluebird)

Pennsylvania 6-5000 (1940, 10754); Sun Valley Jump (1941, 11110); A String of Pearls (1941, 11382)

BIBLIOGRAPHY

FeatherE
J. Flower: *Moonlight Serenade: a Bio-discography of the Glenn Miller Civilian Band* (New Rochelle, NY, 1972)
G. T. Simon: *Glenn Miller and his Orchestra* (New York, 1974)
C. Popa: *Jerry Gray and his Orchestra* (Zephyrhills, FL, 1984) [discography]

WAYNE SCHNEIDER

Gray, Wardell (*b* Oklahoma City, OK, 1921; *d* Las Vegas, NV, 25 May 1955). Tenor saxophonist. He spent his childhood in Detroit, where he learned clarinet and worked with local bands in his teens. In 1943 he joined Earl Hines, with whom he later recorded (1945). After moving to Los Angeles (1945) he came to prominence through his performances and recordings with the concert promoter Gene Norman and his playing in jam sessions with Dexter Gordon; his famous recording with Gordon, *The Chase* (1947), resulted from these sessions, as did an opportunity to record with Charlie Parker (1947). As a member of Benny Goodman's small group Gray was an important figure in Goodman's first experiments with bop (1948). He moved to New York with Goodman and in 1948 worked at the Royal Roost, first with Count Basie, then with the resident band led by Tadd Dameron; he made recordings with both leaders. After playing with Goodman's big band (1948–9) and recording in Basie's small group (1950–51), Gray returned to freelance work on the West Coast and in Las Vegas. He took part in many recorded jam sessions and also recorded with Louie Bellson in 1952 and 1953.

SELECTED RECORDINGS

As leader: with D. Gordon: The Chase (1947, Dial 1017); Stoned/Matter and Mind (1948, SiW 506); Twisted/Easy Living (1949, NewJ 817); Farmer's Market/Lover Man (1952, Prst. 770)

As sideman: C. Parker: Relaxin' at Camarillo (1947, Dial 1012); Cheers/Carvin' the Bird (1947, Dial 1013); B. Goodman: Stealin' Apples (1948, Cap. 10173); T. Dameron: Jahbero/Lady Bird (1948, BN 559); B. Goodman: Egg Head (1949, Cap. 57758); L. Bellson: *Just Jazz All Stars* (1952, Cap. H348), incl. The Jeep is Jumpin'

BIBLIOGRAPHY

FeatherE
A. Morgan: "Wardell Gray," *JM*, i/12 (1956), 7
M. James: "Wardell Gray," *Ten Modern Jazzmen: an Appraisal of the Recorded Work of Ten Modern Jazzmen* (London, 1960), 39
H. Butterfield: "Wardell Gray," *JJ*, xiv/10 (1961), 1
M. Harrison: "Backlog Ten: Wardell Gray," *JM*, viii/3 (1962), 19
I. Gitler: *Jazz Masters of the Forties* (New York, 1966/*R*1983 with discography), 209, 216
C. Schlouch: *In Memory of Wardell Gray: a Discography* (Marseille, France, 1983)

LAWRENCE KOCH

Graystone Ballroom. Ballroom in Detroit; *see* NIGHTCLUBS AND OTHER VENUES.

Great Guitars. Quintet formed in 1974 by BARNEY KESSEL, Charlie Byrd, and Herb Ellis.

Great Jazz Trio. Group formed in 1967 by Hank Jones; *see* JONES family, (1) Hank.

Greeko cymbal. A small tuned cymbal; *see* DRUM SET, §I, 5.

Green, Bennie (*b* Chicago, 16 April 1923; *d* San Diego, 23 March 1977). Trombonist. His family was musical and one of his brothers played tenor saxophone with Roy Eldridge's orchestra. Bennie Green studied trombone with the band director of the DuSable High School in Chicago and began his professional career playing in local groups. In 1942 he was recommended to Earl Hines by Budd Johnson and, except for two years' wartime service with the 343rd Army Band in Illinois, he remained a member of Hines's trombone section until January 1948. He worked briefly with Gene Ammons's small group, then played with Charlie Ventura (1948–50) and toured with Hines (1951–3). In the 1950s and 1960s he led his own combo, usually partnered by a tenor saxophonist, frequently either Charlie Rouse or Jimmy Forrest. He also employed important players such as Paul Chambers, Sonny Clark, and Elvin Jones. Early in 1968 he performed and recorded with Duke Ellington, playing in Ellington's second sacred service; he again worked with Ellington for four months in 1969 before leaving to settle in Las Vegas, where for the last years of his life he worked in hotel bands. He continued to record occasionally on jazz albums as a sideman, and his last recordings were made in 1972 at the Newport Jazz Festival New York.

Green had a flowing style and produced a large, round sound. Comfortable in both modern and mainstream contexts, his playing was stylistically closer to the swing of Trummy Young and Lawrence Brown than to the bop of his contemporaries such as J. J. Johnson and Kai Winding.

SELECTED RECORDINGS

As leader: La vie en rose/The Blues is Green (1950, Jub. 5032); *Bennie Green Blows his Horn* (1955, Prst. 210); *Soul Stirrin'* (1958, BN 1599); Minor Revelation (1958, BN 45-1732, 1733, 1734) [EP]; *Bennie Green Swings the Blues* (1960, Enrica 2002); *Bennie Green* (1960, Time 2021)

As sideman: S. Vaughan: Can't get out of this mood (1950, Col. 38898); Jazz Workshop: *Trombone Rapport* (1953, Debut 5); I. Quebec: *Congo Lament* (1962, BN 84103); B. Ervin: *Booker 'n' Brass* (1967, PJ 20127); Newport All Stars: *Newport in New York '72: the Jam Sessions*, i, ii (1972, Cob. 9025)

BIBLIOGRAPHY

FeatherE; *Feather–Gitler '70s*
I. Gitler: Liner notes, *Bennie Green Blows his Horn* (Prst. 210, 1955)
Liner notes, *Bennie Green* (Time 2021, 1961)
V. Wilmer: "Bennie Green," *JM*, xii/11 (1967), 7 [interview]
P. J. Sullivan: "Bennie Green: an Appreciation," *JJ*, xxi/4 (1968), 14
J. Burns: "Bopping Bones," *J&B*, ii/7 (1972), 16
S. Voce: "Duke of Bebop," *JJI*, xxx/7 (1977), 16
B. Porter: Liner notes, *Minor Revelation* (Jap. BN GXF3063, 1980)

MARK GARDNER

Green, Bill [William (Earnest)] (*b* Kansas City, KS, 25 Feb 1928). Alto saxophonist. He studied at the Los Angeles Conservatory of Music and Arts (1947–52), then taught there (1952–62). He recorded with big bands under Gerald Wilson (1953), Benny Carter (1959), and Louie Bellson (1959, 1961–2), and, as the leader of a quartet, recorded *Shades of Green* (*c*1962, Everest 1213). He worked in clubs, spending a period as a leader at Marty's in Los Angeles, accompanied popular artists such as Tony Bennett, Nat "King" Cole, Frank Sinatra, Dionne Warwick, and Nancy Wilson, played in the orchestras of Quincy Jones, Henry Mancini, and Buddy Rich, and made numerous appearances on television shows. He recorded with Gil Fuller (at the Monterey Jazz Festival, 1965), Oliver Nelson (1966), Blue Mitchell (1969), Sarah Vaughan (1971), Ella Fitzgerald (1972, 1978, 1982), Gene Ammons (1973–4), Sonny Rollins (1976), the Capp–Pierce Juggernaut (1977–8, 1981), and Lionel Hampton (1980–81). In the mid-1980s he worked with Bellson and Woody Herman on cruise ships (1985, 1986) and performed at the Hollywood Bowl with Fitzgerald and the Los Angeles PO (both 1987). He has also taught at California State University and the University of Southern California.

BIBLIOGRAPHY

Feather '60s
R. Gordon: *Jazz West Coast: the Los Angeles Jazz Scene of the 1950s* (London and New York, 1986), 42

Green, Charlie [Green, Big; Long Boy] (*b* Omaha, NE, *c*1900; *d* New York, Feb 1936). Trombonist. He played in brass bands and with Red Perkins in and around Omaha (1920–23), then worked with Fletcher Henderson in New York (July 1924–April 1926; autumn 1928–spring 1929; for illustration *see* JAZZ (i), fig.2). Thereafter he played intermittently with Henderson, and also with Benny Carter (1929–31, 1933) and Chick Webb (1930, 1932–3, 1934). He is best known as accompanist to Bessie Smith on many of her recordings (1924–5, 1927–30), though he also worked with Louis Armstrong and Fats Waller (both 1927), June Clark, and Waller and James P. Johnson (1928), Zutty Singleton (1929), Elmer Snowden, Jimmie Noone, McKinney's Cotton Pickers, and Charlie Johnson (all 1931), Sam Wooding and Don Redman (both 1932), Louis Metcalf (early 1935), and Kaiser Marshall.

Green played mostly in the middle range, less often in the lower register, and seldom in the upper; his tone was full, gruff, and sometimes husky, and he was one of the first to explore the more expressive resources of his instrument. Although he favored symmetrical, rather routine, songlike phrases, sometimes alternating with inventive fills, he could execute a supple, rhythmically easy legato and occasionally produced intricate phrasing, which in a rudimentary fashion foreshadowed the work of Jimmy Harrison and Jack Teagarden. Green's playing remained largely unchanged throughout his career, though some of his early work (around 1925–6) was more rangy and fleet, reflecting the style of Miff Mole. His skill as a melodist made him a noteworthy partner to many of the trumpet players with whom he recorded and he was perhaps the first to play riffs alone or in duet with a singer.

SELECTED RECORDINGS

As sideman: B. Smith: Work House Blues (1924, Col. 14032D); Salt Water Blues (1924, Col. 14037D); F. Henderson: The Gouge of Armour Avenue (1924, Voc. 14859); I. Cox: Misery Blues (1925, Para. 12258); F. Henderson: Sugar Foot Stomp (1925, Col. 395D); B. Smith: I've been mistreated (1925, Col. 14115D); M. Rainey: Chain Gang Blues (1926, Para. 12338); B. Smith: Empty Bed Blues, pt ii (1928, Col. 14312D); F. Henderson: Old Black Joe's Blues (1928, Cameo 9033)

BIBLIOGRAPHY

ChiltonW
"Charlie Green v. Jimmy Harrison," *JJ*, xix/3 (1966), 10
G. Schuller: *Early Jazz: its Roots and Musical Development* (New York, 1968), 235
W. C. Allen: *Hendersonia: the Music of Fletcher Henderson and his Musicians: a Bio-discography* (Highland Park, NJ, 1973)
G. Murphy: "The Forgotten Ones: Charlie Green," *JJI*, xxxix/3 (1986), 16

BOB ZIEFF

Green, Dave [David John] (*b* London, 5 March 1942). English double bass player. Self-taught, he began playing professionally in 1963, when he joined a quintet led by Don Rendell and Ian Carr, with whom he remained until 1969. He also worked with Stan Tracey at Ronnie Scott's, London, and Michael Garrick (both from 1964) and Humphrey Lyttelton (1965–83). As a member of Tracey's group he accompanied many American musicians, among them Coleman Hawkins, Sonny Rollins, Zoot Sims, Al Cohn, Benny Carter, and Lee Konitz. He recorded with such visiting leaders as Paul Gonsalves (1969), Ben Webster (1970), and Buddy Tate (1974). In 1979 Green formed his own quintet Fingers, which included Garrick, Bruce Turner, and Lol Coxhill, and also made a recording for Spotlite (*Fingers Remembers Mingus*, Spot. 521). In the 1980s he performed in Peter King's quintet (from 1982) and Didier Lockwood's quartet (1985–6). (T. Bannister: "Green Fingers," *JJI*, xl/3 (1987), 10)

NEVIL SKRIMSHIRE

Green, Freddie [Greene, Frederick William] (*b* Charleston, SC, 31 March 1911; *d* Las Vegas, NV, 1 March 1987). Guitarist. He moved to New York in 1930. A self-taught musician, he first performed as a banjoist, then in 1936 played guitar with Kenny Clarke. In 1937 John Hammond recommended him to Count Basie; he joined Basie's band as a replacement for Claude Williams and remained with the group, with minor interruptions, for nearly five decades. Green's light, propulsive style became an essential component of the band's rhythm section; his rhythmically precise and understated guitar accompaniment provided a perfect complement to the relaxed, driving pulse of Walter Page and Jo Jones. Although he seldom departed from the basic rhythm style of strumming chords on each beat of the bar (the single-string playing in his accompaniment to the folk singer Brother John Sellers is a rare occurrence), his playing was highly valued by other musicians, as is shown by the number of recordings on which he performed. In the 1980s he remained the principal exponent of the swing guitar style. Green was also active as a composer: his contributions to Basie's repertory include *Down for Double*, *Right on*, and *Corner Pocket*.

Oral history material in *NjR* (JOHP).

For illustrations *see* BASIE, COUNT, FILMS, fig.3, JONES, JO, and RECORDING, fig.6.

SELECTED RECORDINGS

As leader: *Mr. Rhythm* (1955, RCA LPM1210)

As sideman with C. Basie: Good Morning Blues (1937, Decca 1446); Topsy (1937, Decca 1770); Down for Double (1941, OK 6584); *Dance Session* (1952–4, Clef 626, 647), incl. Right on (1953); Two for the Blues (1954, Clef 89131); *April in Paris* (1955–6, Verve 8012), incl. Corner Pocket (1955); *Kansas City Shout* (1980, Pablo 2310859)

As sideman with others: Kansas City Six: Them there Eyes (1938, Com. 511); P. W. Russell: Dinah (1938, HRS 1000); L. Young: Blue Lester (1944, Savoy 581); B. J. Sellers: *Brother John Sellers Sings Blues and Folk Songs* (1954, Van. 8005); incl. Boll Weevil; J. Newman: *All I Wanna Do is Swing* (1955, RCA LPM1118)

BIBLIOGRAPHY

R. Horricks: *Count Basie and his Orchestra: its Music and its Musicians* (London and New York, 1957), 124

D. Cerulli: "Freddie Greene," *IM*, lx/7 (1962), 26

"Freddie Green Talking," *CI*, v/12 (1967), 17

D. Roberts: "A Jazz Guitar Pedigree," *JJ*, xxiii/5 (1970), 10

M. J. Summerfield: *The Jazz Guitar: its Evolution and its Players* (Gateshead, England, 1978)

SCOTT DeVEAUX

Green, Grant (*b* St. Louis, 6 June 1931; *d* New York, 31 Jan 1979). Electric guitarist. He gained important experience during the 1950s playing with Jimmy Forrest, Harry Edison, and Lou Donaldson. At the same time his collaborations with the organists Brother Jack McDuff, Baby Face Willette, Gloria Coleman, Larry Young, and Big John Patton helped to establish the trio of organist, guitarist, and drummer as a standard ensemble in the 1950s and early 1960s. Green's mature style manifested itself between 1961 and 1964, when he recorded both as a leader and a sideman for Blue Note; his reputation was somewhat overshadowed by that of Wes Montgomery, but he remained almost entirely free of the latter's influence. After a period of inactivity in the mid-1960s he resumed recording in the late 1960s and early 1970s. Apart from Charlie Christian, the main influences on Green's style were saxophonists, particularly Charlie Parker, and his approach was thus almost entirely linear rather than chordal. The simplicity and immediacy of his playing – he avoided chromaticism – derived from his early grounding in rhythm-and-blues; although at his best he achieved a curious but wholly successful melding of this style with bop, he was essentially a blues guitarist. Later in his career he returned almost exclusively to playing rhythm-and-blues.

SELECTED RECORDINGS

(all recorded for Blue Note unless otherwise indicated)

As leader: *Green Street* (1961, 4071); *Feelin' the Spirit* (1962, 84132); *Am I Blue* (1963, 84139); *Talkin' About!* (1964, 84183); *Iron City* (1967, Cob. 9002)

As sideman: H. Parlan: *Up and Down* (1961, 84082); I. Quebec: *Blue and Sentimental* (1961, 84098)

BIBLIOGRAPHY

Feather '60s; *Feather–Gitler '70s*

"Grant Green," *CI*, x/2 (1971), 16

Liner notes, *Iron City* (Cob. 9002, ?1973)

G. N. Bourland: "Grant Green," *GP*, ix/1 (1975), 10

Obituary, *DB*, xlvi/6 (1979), 9

ANDREW WAGGONER

Green, Urbie [Urban Clifford] (*b* Mobile, AL, 8 Aug 1926). Trombonist. He played with Gene Krupa (1947–50) and Woody Herman's Third Herd (from early 1951) and from 1953 worked as a freelance, principally in studios. He took part in important jam sessions with Buck Clayton in 1953–4, playing sweeping, often dramatic, solos on *The Hucklebuck* and *Robbins' Nest*. During the following years he worked occasionally with Benny Goodman (and appeared with him in the film *The Benny Goodman Story*), recorded a fine album as a leader (*Blues & Other Shades of Green*, 1955), and continued to work in studios; in 1963 he performed with Count Basie. He led Tommy Dorsey's orchestra in 1966–7 after Dorsey's death and recorded again as a leader in 1978. Green played with a robust, authoritative sound and an unusually full tone.

For illustration *see* NIGHTCLUBS AND OTHER VENUES, fig.5.

SELECTED RECORDINGS

As leader: *Blues & Other Shades of Green* (1955, ABC–Para. 101); *6-tet* (1961, Command 857); *Live at Rick's Cafe Americain* (1978, Flying Fish 079)

As sideman: W. Herman: Blue Flame (1951, MGM 11154); B. Clayton: *The Hucklebuck and Robbins' Nest* (1953, Col. CL546); *Buck Clayton Jams Benny Goodman* (1953–4, Col. CL614); B. Goodman: *Album of Swing Classics* (1955, Book of the Month Club SRL7673); *The Benny Goodman Story* (1955, Decca 8252–3)

BIBLIOGRAPHY

FeatherE; *Feather '60s*; *Feather–Gitler '70s*

H. Nolan: "Studio Slidemaster: Urbie Green," *DB*, xliii/16 (1976), 14 [incl. discography]

CHRIS SHERIDAN

Greenberg, Rowland (*b* Oslo, 28 Aug 1920). Norwegian trumpeter. He worked professionally from 1935 and in the late 1930s played in England with Vic Lewis, Eric Delaney, and George Shearing, then worked in Sweden with Thore Jederby, Simon Brehm, and Malte Johnson. He performed with Charlie Parker in Paris and Sweden in 1948–9 and recorded with him in 1950. Later he worked in radio and television, recorded swing as a leader (1970), and recorded with Bengt Hallberg (1977); he remained active in the 1980s. He received the Buddy Award from the Norwegian Jazz Federation in 1956. Greenberg's playing may be heard to advantage on his recording *Take Another Guess/After you've gone* (1953, Harmoni AAR).

Oral history material in *NOnj*.

BIBLIOGRAPHY

K. Sandegren and others: *Boken om jazz* (Oslo, 1954)
O. Angell, J. E. Vold, and E. Økland: *Jazz i Norge* (Oslo, 1975)
K. Michelsen, ed.: *Cappelens musikkleksikon* (Oslo, 1978)

VIDAR VANBERG

Greene, Bob (*b* New York, 4 Sept 1922). Pianist and bandleader. He played traditional jazz with Baby Dodds and recorded with the trombonist Conrad Janis (1950) and Sidney De Paris (1951). After working for several years as a writer of radio documentaries, he returned to music, playing and recording with Zutty Singleton (1967, 1969), his own band (1968), and Don Ewell (1970). In Copenhagen he recorded with Albert Nicholas (1970) and the Peruna Jazz Band (1972). In 1971 he began leading a re-creation of Jelly Roll Morton's Red Hot Peppers, which has included such sidemen as Danny Barker, Herb Hall, Milt Hinton, Johnny Williams, and Tommy Benford; as well as making recordings (including *The World of Jelly Roll Morton*, 1974, RCA ARL1-0504), the band toured extensively in the USA, South America, and Europe in the mid-1970s and early 1980s.

BIBLIOGRAPHY

Feather–Gitler '70s
E. Townley: "Bob Greene and Mister Jelly Lord," *Sv*, no.62 (1975), 67

Greene, Burton [Narada] (*b* Chicago, 14 June 1937). Pianist and composer. He studied classical music at the Fine Arts Academy in Chicago (1944–51) and jazz with Dick Marx (1956–8). In 1963 he formed the Free Form Improvisation Ensemble with Alan Silva in New York; this was one of the first jazz groups to play entirely improvised music. He was a member of the Jazz Composers Guild (1964–5) and led groups that included Marion Brown, Sam Rivers, Gato Barbieri, and others. He moved to Paris in 1969, studied music and culture for four months in India, then moved to Amsterdam. In Europe he performed with groups of unusual constitution, such as the East West Trio (formed 1973 and including sitar and percussion) and the vocal group New Age Jazz Chorale; he also took part in mixed-media events and performed as a soloist and in a quartet with the saxophonist Sean Bergin. Greene's early compositions show the influence of Cecil Taylor; later he wrote pieces based on Far Eastern scales and figures and vocal music (such as *Manifesto for Angels*, on the album *Light*, 1976).

SELECTED RECORDINGS

As unaccompanied soloist: *It's All One* (1978, Horo 27–8)
Duos with A. Silva: *The Ongoing Strings* (1980, HH 15)
As leader: *You Never Heard such Sounds in your Life!* (1965, ESP 1024); *Aquariana* (1969, BYG 529308); of New Age Jazz Chorale: *Light* (1976, Button-Nose 03); *Valencia Chocolate* (1985, Cat 57)

BIBLIOGRAPHY

M. Fine: "Burton Greene," *JF* [intl edn], no.49 (1977), 24
J. Ballaras: "Burton Greene: Jazzing the European Heritage," *DB*, xlvii/6 (1980), 28 [incl. discography]

ED HAZELL

Greenlee, Charles [Majeed, Harneefan] (*b* Detroit, 24 May 1927). Trombonist. After receiving early musical training at high school in Detroit he began playing professionally in the mid-1940s with Lucky Millinder and Benny Carter. He became associated with the bop movement, and was a member of Dizzy Gillespie's big band in 1946 and 1949. In the early 1950s he ceased playing, but returned to performing later in the decade, working with Yusef Lateef and Maynard Ferguson. From the 1960s he became increasingly involved with avant-garde jazz, and was associated with John Coltrane, Archie Shepp, Sam Rivers, and the Collective Black Artists Orchestra. His powerful and agile playing may be heard to advantage on his own composition, *El sino*, from Slide Hampton's album *Somethin' Sanctified*.

SELECTED RECORDINGS

As leader: *I Know about the Life* (1975, Bay. 6003)
As sideman: S. Hampton: *Somethin' Sanctified* (1960, Atl. 1362); R. Kirk: *Reeds and Deeds* (1963, Mer. 60800); S. Rivers: *Crystals* (1974, Imp. 9286); A. Shepp: *A Sea of Faces* (1975, BS 0002); The Detroit Four: *Cadillac and Mack* (1977, Ewd 98005)

BIBLIOGRAPHY

S. Rivers: Liner notes, *Crystals* (Imp. 9286, 1974)
G. Rouy: "Charles Greenlee," *Jm*, no.243 (1976), 12

SCOTT DeVEAUX

Greenwich, Sonny [Greenidge, Herbert Lawrence] (*b* Hamilton, Canada, 1 Jan 1936). Canadian electric guitarist. He played rhythm-and-blues in Toronto before touring with John Handy (1966–7) and recording with Hank Mobley (1967). In 1968 at the Village Vanguard in New York he led a group that included Jimmy Garrison and Jack DeJohnette. After performing briefly with Miles Davis (1969) and recording as co-leader of a quintet with the pianist Don Thompson (1969–71), he ceased to play regularly, though he gave occasional performances in Montreal and Toronto from 1974 and made two recordings as a leader (the first in 1974, the second – *Evol-ution: Love's Reverse*, PM 16 – in 1978). Although Greenwich does not consider himself principally a musician, and despite his interrupted career in jazz, some critics regard him as the most important Canadian jazzman.

BIBLIOGRAPHY

Feather–Gitler '70s
M. Miller: *Jazz in Canada: Fourteen Lives* (Toronto, Buffalo, and London, 1982), 188
——: "Sonny Greenwich," *Boogie, Pete & the Senator: Canadian Musicians in Jazz: the Eighties* (Toronto, 1987), 141

Greer, Sonny [William Alexander] (*b* Long Branch, NJ, 13 Dec *c*1895; *d* New York, 23 March 1982). Drummer. He first played in local bands in and around New Jersey and then worked as a member of the orchestra at the Howard Theatre in Washington, where in 1919 he met Duke Ellington. The following year he joined Ellington's band, and from 1927, during the group's residency at the Cotton Club in New York, the partnership between the two men began to flower. The exotic effects that Greer produced from a vast array of percussion equipment (including gongs, skulls, and chimes) added greatly to the "jungle" sounds which Ellington devised for the club's shows, and are prominently featured in many of his early arrangements. Greer was most effective rhythmically when working alongside Jimmy Blanton (who was with Ellington from 1939 to 1941); by this time he had developed an accomplished technique that enabled him to provide subtle shadings for Ellington's orchestrations rather than dominate them. After leaving Ellington in 1951 Greer joined Johnny Hodges and then worked as a freelance in other small groups, notably (in the 1950s) with Louis Metcalf, Henry "Red" Allen (1952–3), and Tyree Glenn (1959), and (in the 1960s) with Eddie Barefield and J. C. Higginbotham. In 1967 he led his own band at the Garden Cafe, New York, and took part in the film *The Night they Raided Minsky's*. Greer played regularly in Brooks Kerr's trio during the 1970s, and continued to work until shortly before his death.

Oral history material in *NjR* (JOHP), *NjR*.
For illustrations *see* BANDS, fig.3, DRUM SET, fig.1*a*, and WASHINGTONIANS.

SELECTED RECORDINGS

As leader: Ration Stomp (1944, Apollo 355)
As sideman: D. Ellington: Ko-Ko (1940, Vic. 26577); Cotton Tail (1940, Vic. 26610); Harlem Air Shaft (1940, Vic. 26731); J. Hodges: Squatty Roo (1941, Bb 11447)

BIBLIOGRAPHY

J. Cooke: "Credit Where Due: a Short Study of Sonny Greer," *JM*, vi/6 (1960), 7
B. Korall: "The Roots of the Duchy," *DB*, xxxiv/14 (1967), 21
S. Dance: *The World of Duke Ellington* (London and New York, 1970/R1981) [colln of previously pubd articles and interviews], 62
D. Ellington: *Music is my Mistress* (Garden City, NY, 1973), 69
T. D. Brown: *A History and Analysis of Jazz Drumming to 1942* (diss., U. of Michigan, 1976), 421, 530
D. Jewell: *Duke: a Portrait of Duke Ellington* (London and New York, 1977, 2/1978)
L. Jeske: "Sonny Greer, 83, Recalls the Time when the Aristocrats of Harlem Took London by Storm," *JJI*, xxxi/11 (1978), 22
S. Fish: "Sonny Greer: The Elder Statesman of Jazz," *MD*, v/8 (1981), 30
——: "In Memoriam: Sonny Greer," *MD*, vi/4 (1982), 72
J. McAfee, Jr.: Obituary, *JSN*, ii/4 (1982), 19
W. Balliett: "New York Drummers," *Jelly Roll, Jabbo and Fats* (New York, and Oxford, England, 1983) [colln of previously pubd articles], 42

JOHN CHILTON

Greger, Max (*b* Munich, 2 April 1926). German tenor saxophonist and bandleader. He studied classical piano and clarinet at the Konservatorium in Munich and from 1945 played in dance bands at American clubs. He played accordion, then clarinet and tenor saxophone, with the trumpeter Charly Tabor. From 1948 he led a sextet, which became in turn an octet and in 1955 a band with 13 members that played in the style of Glenn Miller; this group accompanied such singers as Ella Fitzgerald. He toured Germany with Lionel Hampton's orchestra and the USSR with his own band (1959). From 1963 into the 1980s he led an orchestra of 16 players that performed on television in Germany; among those who belonged to the orchestra for some time were Don Menza and Benny Bailey. Greger has made more than 150 recordings, including *European Jazz Sounds* (1963, Bruns. 87918) and *Maximum* (1965, Pol. 623203).

BIBLIOGRAPHY

ReclamsJ
C. O. Hess: "Max Greger und sein Keller-Orchester," *JP*, iii/1 (1954), 10
"Max Greger," *JP*, iii/9 (1954), 6
"Max Greger kommt," *JP*, v/1 (1956), 18
"Max Greger: heisse Musik für Russland," *JP*, viii/8 (1959), 180

HEIDI BOULTON

Gregor [Kélékian, Krikor] (*b* Turkey, 28 Feb 1898; *d c*1973). Armenian bandleader. He led a band called the Gregorians in France from 1928, among the members of which were Philippe Brun, Edmond Cohanier, and the pianist Lucien Moraweck; in May 1929 it made a number of recordings that are important in the history of French jazz. Gregor founded the first jazz journal in France, the *Revue du jazz*, in 1929 and was its editor until it ceased publication in 1930. He toured South America in 1930 with an orchestra that included such illustrious players as Léo Vauchant, Cohanier, and Stephane Grappelli, and returned the following year, when he recorded in Buenos Aires. He continued to lead orchestras of high quality, including such soloists as Alix Combelle, André Ekyan, and Michel Warlop, until 1934. Gregor initiated the French tradition of the show band, a versatile dance orchestra, the instrumentation of which was modeled on that of the big band; his work is well represented by *Le rugissement du tigre* (1930, Col. DF48). (J. Hélian: *Les grands orchestres de music hall en France* (Paris, 1984), 46)

MICHEL LAPLACE

Gregory, Michael. *See* JACKSON, MICHAEL GREGORY.

Greig, Stan(ley Mackay) (*b* Edinburgh, 12 Aug 1930). Scottish pianist, drummer, and bandleader. He played with Sandy Brown's first Jazz Band while at high school (1945), and later performed on piano and drums with Brown (1948–54). After moving to London he played drums with Ken Colyer (1954–5), Humphrey Lyttelton (1955–6), the Fairweather–Brown All Stars led by Brown and Al Fairweather (1956–60), and Acker Bilk's Paramount Jazz Band (1960–68). From 1969 he concentrated on piano and led his own trio and quintet, which played mainly swinging boogie-woogie and blues. In 1975 he formed the London Jazz Big Band, which performed a wide-ranging repertory of swing-based music but never recorded. After a spell with George Melly (1978–80) he worked as a freelance. He has played with the Harlem Blues and Jazz Band (from 1982) and, after the London Jazz Big Band broke up in 1985, he re-joined Lyttelton; though better known as a pianist he continues to perform occasionally on drums. His recordings as a leader include *Blues Every Time* (1985, Calligraph 004).

DIGBY FAIRWEATHER

Grey, Al(bert Thornton) (*b* Aldie, nr Middleburg, VA, 6 June 1925). Trombonist. He grew up in Pottstown, Pennsylvania, in a musical family. During World War II he played in a navy band. He then toured with Benny Carter (1945–6) and Jimmie Lunceford (1946–7), remaining with the band in New York after Lunceford's death. After playing with Lucky Millinder and touring with Lionel Hampton (1948–*c*1953) he worked with Dizzy Gillespie (1956). Late in 1957 he joined Count Basie, but he left in 1961 with Billy Mitchell to form a sextet and then led his own band. He had little success, however, and in 1964 returned to Basie's band, where he finally began to achieve widespread acclaim. His solos suited the style of the band, and his ability to improvise with humor – a tradition among trombone players – provided him with the impetus he needed, and he became a valued member of the group. In 1974 Grey toured with Jazz at the Philharmonic. After leaving Basie in 1977 he played frequently in small groups in the USA and Europe. In 1985 he participated in a jam session at the Village Vanguard which was part of the New York Kool Jazz Festival, and the following year, with Al Cohn, he led a quintet in New York.

SELECTED RECORDINGS

As leader: with B. Mitchell: *Al Grey with Billy Mitchell* (1961, Argo 689); *Struttin' and Shoutin'* (1976, Col. FC38505); with J. J. Johnson: *Things are Getting Better all the Time* (1983, PT 2312141)
As sideman: L. Hampton: Rag Mop (1949, Decca 24855); C. Basie: *Basie* (1957, Roul. 52003), incl. Teddy the Toad; *The Great Concert of Count Basie and his Orchestra* (1966, Festival 231), incl. Wee Baby Blues; *Basie Jam no.2* (1976, Pablo 2310786); *Prime Time* (1977, Pablo 2310797)

BIBLIOGRAPHY

R. Horricks: *Count Basie and his Orchestra: its Music and its Musicians* (London and New York, 1957)
H. Panassié: "Un grand trombone: Al Grey," *BHcF*, no.73 (1957), 3
P. Welding: "Difficulties Facing a New Group: the Al Grey–Billy Mitchell Sextet," *DB*, xxix/13 (1962), 16
B. Rusch: "Al Grey: Bandleader," *Cadence*, ii/2 (1976), 6 [interview]
L. Tomkins: "Al Grey," *CI*, xiv/6 (1976), 14
S. Dance: *The World of Count Basie* (New York and London, 1980) [colln of previously pubd interviews], 204

J. Reldy: "Al Grey," *BHcF*, no.280 (1980), 6 [interview]
E. Townley: "The Last of the Big Plungers," *Sv*, no.118 (1985), 124 [interview]
Karrah: "Al Grey," *Cadence*, xiii/5 (1987), 5

LEROY OSTRANSKY

Grey Gull. Record company and label. The company was founded in Boston before 1919. After initial experiments with a primitive type of extended-play record which ran for five and a half minutes, the company became a major purveyor of popular records, drawing its material in the early 1920s mainly from the catalogues of other companies. These included the New York Recording Laboratories, Emerson, and Plaza. After 1926 Grey Gull undertook more extensive original recording, much of it by a house band (with such musicians as the trumpeter Mike Mosiello and the reed player Andy Sannella), whose recordings were released under a wide range of colorful pseudonyms. More important were recordings by Clarence Williams and Cliff Jackson, and pickup groups such as the Wabash Trio. Much of Grey Gull's output also appeared on the company's other labels, including Madison (marketed by Woolworths), Radiex, Supreme, and Van Dyke. Grey Gull also supplied masters to the Globe label. This proliferation provided opportunity for further use of pseudonyms and alternative titles; the company's activities have proved fascinating for discographers. The Grey Gull label was discontinued in summer 1930, as were Radiex, Supreme, and Van Dyke; the company appears to have continued producing records on Madison into 1931. (B. Rust: *The American Record Label Book*, New Rochelle, NY, 1978)

Griffin, Chris [Gordon] (*b* Binghamton, NY, 31 Oct 1915). Trumpeter. He took up trumpet at the age of 12, played in local bands, and first worked professionally at a taxi-dance hall in New York three years later. After playing with Charlie Barnet (*c*1933–1934, 1935), the singer Rudy Vallee, and Joe Haymes he worked as a studio musician for CBS, then performed and recorded with Benny Goodman (1936–9). During the 1930s he also made recordings with Miff Mole, Mildred Bailey, Teddy Wilson (including *If I had rhythm in my nursery rhymes*, 1936, Bruns. 7612), and others. Although Griffin became a staff musician at CBS in 1939, he worked briefly with Jimmy Dorsey the following year, and played on several of Goodman's recordings in the 1940s and 1950s. He also ran a trumpet school with Pee Wee Erwin. In 1974 he toured Europe with Warren Covington.

BIBLIOGRAPHY

A. Stevens: "Chris Griffin: Swing Era Trumpetman," *CI*, xii/7 (1974), 18
S. Woolley: "Chris Griffin and the Swing Era," *Cadence*, i/11–12 (1976), 8
W. W. Vaché, Sr.: "Chris Griffin Remembers," *MR*, ix/8 (1982), 1

based on *ChiltonW*

Griffin, Johnny [John Arnold, III; Little Giant] (*b* Chicago, 24 April 1928). Tenor saxophonist. He began his career touring in Lionel Hampton's band (1945–7), then worked on the East Coast with the rhythm-and-blues trumpeter Joe Morris (1947–50) as well as with Philly Joe Jones, Percy Heath, Jo Jones, Gene Ramey, and Arnett Cobb. During the same period he also practiced regularly with Thelonious Monk and Bud Powell. After serving in an army band in Hawaii (1951–3) he played in Chicago for several years before beginning important engagements in New York with Art Blakey's Jazz Messengers (1957) and Monk's quartet (1958). From 1960 to 1962 he was the leader of a bop quintet with Eddie "Lockjaw" Davis, with whom he engaged in energetic improvisatory battles (see illus-

Johnny Griffin (left) with Eddie "Lockjaw" Davis

tration). Owing to tax and family problems Griffin emigrated to Europe in 1963 and settled in Paris. He played for several years at the Blue Note with such leading bop musicians as Powell, Kenny Clarke, Kenny Drew, and Art Taylor, and from 1967 to 1969 was the principal soloist in the Clarke–Boland Big Band; he also played regularly in groups led by Taylor. Around 1973 he moved to Bergambacht in the Netherlands. Griffin's greatest popularity stemmed from appearances that sparked renewed interest in the bop style, notably at Montreux (1975), in Tokyo (1976), and on tours of the USA (1978–9). He has continued to tour internationally, and appears annually in the USA, where his quartet includes Kenny Washington; the film *The Jazz Life Featuring Johnny Griffin* (*c*1985) documents one of their finest performances, at the Village Vanguard in New York.

SELECTED RECORDINGS

As leader: *Blowin' Sessions* (1957, BN 1559); *The Little Giant* (1959, Riv. 1149); *The Big Soul Band* (1960, Riv. 1179); with E. Davis: *Tough Tenors* (1960, Jlnd 931), *Blues Up and Down* (1961, Jlnd 960); *You Leave me Breathless* (1967, BL 30134); *Blues for Harvey* (1973, Ste. 1004); *Live in Tokyo* (1976, IC 6042); *Return of the Griffin* (1978, Gal. 5117); *Call it Whachawana* (1983, Gal. 5146)

As sideman: A. Blakey: *Jazz Messengers* (1957, Beth. 6023); T. Monk: *Thelonious in Action* (1958, Riv. 262); K. Clarke and F. Boland: *All Smiles* (1968, MPS 15214); D. Gillespie: *At the Montreux Jazz Festival 1975* (1975, Pablo 2310749)

BIBLIOGRAPHY

D. Gold: "Blowin' in from Chicago," *DB*, xxv/11 (1958), 17
D. DeMicheal: "Johnny Griffin," *DB*, xxviii/1 (1961), 20
P. Welding: "Jaws & Johnny," *DB*, xxviii/13 (1961), 20
"Johnny Griffin," *SJ*, xxx/3 (1976), 258 [discography]
G. Giddins: "Johnny Griffin: an American in New York," *VV*, xxiii (23 Oct 1978), 99
S. Woolley: "Johnny Griffin: Interview," *Cadence*, iv/2–3 (1978), 6

M. Hennessey: "Johnny Griffin and the Jazz Life Force," *JJI*, xxxii/5 (1979), 13
L. Lyons: "Johnny Griffin: Transatlantic Tenor," *DB*, xlvi/14 (1979), 14
H. Hill: "Johnny Griffin," *Coda*, no.191 (1983), 24
D. J. Travis: *An Autobiography of Black Jazz* (Chicago, 1983) [incl. interviews], 351
J. M. Green: "Johnny Griffin," *Be-bop and Beyond*, iv/2 (1986), 23 [interview]

BARRY KERNFELD

Griffiths, Malcolm (*b* Barnet, England, 29 Sept 1941). English trombonist. After studying economics (BS 1965) he attended the London College of Music (1965–7). From 1963 he was a member of Mike Westbrook's orchestra, with which he continued to play until 1984. He worked for six months with Buddy Rich's orchestra (1969–70) and was a founding member of the group Brotherhood of Breath (recording in 1971–2). Griffiths has performed and recorded as a member of various groups led by John Surman (1968, 1970, 1971, 1973) and as a sideman in Stan Tracey's octet and orchestra (1976, 1977, 1983). During the 1970s he led his own groups, which included Alan Skidmore, John Marshall, and the drummer Tony Levin. In the 1980s Griffiths has been associated with film and television music, working with the composers George Fenton and John Altman. His solo playing may be heard to advantage on *The Beginning* from Tracey's album *Genesis* (1987, Steam 114). (R. Cotterrell: *Jazz Now: the Jazz Centre Society Guide*, London, 1976).

NEVIL SKRIMSHIRE

Grimes, Henry (Alonzo) (*b* Philadelphia, 3 Nov 1935). Double bass player. He played violin, tuba, and double bass while in his teens and then attended the Juilliard School; he later toured with Arnett Cobb and Willis "Gator" Jackson. He played with Bobby Timmons, Lee Morgan, and Albert "Tootie" Heath in Philadelphia in the mid-1950s, and in 1957 with Anita O'Day and Sonny Rollins; he also toured and appeared on television with Gerry Mulligan (1957–8). At the Newport Jazz Festival in 1958 he performed with Benny Goodman's big band and with Lee Konitz, Rollins, Tony Scott, and Thelonious Monk; he appeared with Monk in the film *Jazz on a Summer's Day*, which was made at the festival. He then worked with Lennie Tristano (August 1958) and toured Europe with Rollins (1959). Over the next few years he became a leading free-jazz player, performing and recording with Cecil Taylor (1961–6), Perry Robinson (1962), Rollins (1962–3), Albert Ayler (1964–6), and Don Cherry (1965–6), but he abandoned his musical career in 1967. Grimes's early, bop, style was powerful, raw, and strongly percussive, with a rocking, rhythmic feeling; it owed something to the work of Paul Chambers and Charles Mingus. By contrast, in his free-jazz playing, conventional timekeeping usually gave way to drones and unmetered countermelodies, played both pizzicato and arco.

SELECTED RECORDINGS

As leader: *Henry Grimes Trio* (1965, ESP 1026)
As sideman: G. Mulligan: *Songbook*, i (1957, PJ 1237); S. Rollins: *Brass/Trio* (1958, Metro. 1002); Billy Taylor (ii): *Billy Uptown* (1960, Riv. 1168); M. Tyner: *Reaching Fourth* (1962, Imp. 33); R. Haynes: *Out of the Afternoon* (1962, Imp. 23); P. Robinson: *Funk Dumplin* (1962, Savoy 12177); D. Cherry: *Where is Brooklyn?* (1966, BN 84311); A. Ayler: *Albert Ayler in Greenwich Village* (1966–7, Imp. 9155)

BIBLIOGRAPHY

FeatherE; *Feather '60s*

JOHN VOIGT

Grimes, Tiny [Lloyd] (*b* Newport News, VA, 7 July 1916). Guitarist. He first played drums, and later worked as a pianist and dancer in Washington, and, in the late 1930s, in New York. Around 1938 he took up the amplified guitar, then little used in jazz; he adopted the rare four-string instrument, which he has preferred throughout his career. In 1940 he joined a jazz and novelty group called the Cats and the Fiddle; around this time he came under the pervasive influence of Charlie Christian. In 1943 Art Tatum, impressed by Grimes's fleet execution, engaged him for his first trio (with Slam Stewart), as a member of which he recorded several historic performances (for illustration *see* TATUM, ART). After leaving Tatum, Grimes led his own groups in New York; one of them in 1944 made a seminal bop recording (*Tiny's Tempo/I'll always love you just the same*) on which Charlie Parker played. Thereafter Grimes became less prominent; apart from a few years of inactivity in the 1960s, however, he has continued to perform and record into the 1980s.

Oral history material in *NjR* (JOHP), *NjR*.

SELECTED RECORDINGS

As leader: Tiny's Tempo/I'll always love you just the same (1944, Savoy 526); Romance without Finance (1944, Savoy 532)
As sideman: I. Quebec: Indiana (1944, BN 38); Hard Tack (1944, BN 510); A. Tatum: *The Art Tatum Trio* (1944, FW 2293)

BIBLIOGRAPHY

M. Chauvard and K. Mohr: "Discography of Tiny Grimes," *Jazz Statistics*, nos.26–7 (1962), 8
J. Morgantini: "Tiny Grimes," *BHcF*, no.181 (1968), 3; no.182 (1968), 16; no.183 (1968), 4
H. Panassié: "A Tribute to Tiny Grimes," *DB*, xxxvi/13 (1969), 17
S. Dance: "Tiny Grimes," *The World of Swing* (New York, 1974) [colln of previously pubd interviews], 360
A. Berle: "Tiny Grimes: the 4-string Guitarist of Swing Street," *GP*, xv/1 (1981), 58 [incl. discography]

EDWARD L. BONOFF

Grofé, Ferde [Ferdinand] **(Rudolf von)** (*b* New York, 27 March 1892; *d* Santa Monica, CA, 3 April 1972). Composer, arranger, and pianist. He grew up on the West Coast and studied piano and violin from an early age. When he was about 14 he traveled to the mining camps in northern California and worked as a pianist in dance halls. On his return to San Francisco he joined the Los Angeles SO as a violist; he also supported himself by playing piano in dance halls and gambling saloons, probably in the Barbary Coast area of San Francisco, where, after 1910, a number of New Orleans musicians were performing the new jazz music. Some time after 1914 Grofé joined forces with the drummer Art Hickman, who led a band in the St. Francis Hotel, and the two men developed the basic concept of the big jazz- or dance-band arrangement. Grofé was almost certainly the first arranger to provide different music for each chorus of a tune; the principle he established was to play off the saxophone section against other elements of the orchestra, mainly by setting countermelodies under the main theme. In 1919 he was engaged by Paul Whiteman as an arranger and pianist, and began combining jazz rhythms and sonorities with compositional concepts drawn from symphonic music. His arrangements of *Japanese Sandman*, *Whispering* (both 1920, Vic. 18690), and *Three o'Clock in the Morning* (1922, Vic. 18940) were all exceedingly popular and helped establish Whiteman as the leading figure in symphonic jazz. Grofé's own reputation was secured in 1924 with his orchestration of George Gershwin's *Rhapsody in Blue* for its première by Whiteman's band. He continued to provide Whiteman with arrangements until 1933, but became better known for his orchestral suites and other works, such as *Grand Canyon Suite* and *Metropolis*.

See also BANDS, §4(ii), and JAZZ (i), §III, 4.

BIBLIOGRAPHY
American Mercury, vii (1927), April, 385
Etude, lvi/7 (1938), 425
D. Ewen: *Men of Popular Music* (Chicago and New York, 1944), 105

JAMES LINCOLN COLLIER

Groove. Record label. It was established in 1953 as a subsidiary of RCA–Victor; from 1955 artists and repertory were directed by Bob Rolontz. The catalogue spanned the entire field of rhythm-and-blues, with a heavy commercial emphasis, but the label is noteworthy for having issued recordings by Jonah Jones's quartet (1956). Panama Francis and Kenny Burrell worked frequently for Groove as session musicians. The label was discontinued after a few years. (A. Shaw: "Groove 22: Bob Rolontz and Groove Records," *Honkers and Shouters: the Golden Years of Rhythm and Blues* (New York, 1978), 460)

Grossman, Steve(n) (*b* New York, 18 Jan 1951). Soprano and tenor saxophonist. He began studying alto saxophone in 1959, and in the mid-1960s moved to Pittsburgh. After returning to New York he took up soprano saxophone in 1967 and tenor saxophone in 1968. He led his own groups and played with the Jazz Samaritans, which included George Cables and Lenny White. In November 1969 he recorded with Miles Davis while studying at the Juilliard School, and in March 1970 replaced Wayne Shorter in Davis's group, with which he remained until September. He belonged in turn to Lonnie Liston Smith's quartet (May 1971 to December 1971), Elvin Jones's group (December 1971 to late 1973), and Gene Perla's Stone Alliance (1975). Grossman was among the first saxophonists to adapt to a jazz-rock setting a style of playing the soprano saxophone that was influenced by John Coltrane.

SELECTED RECORDINGS

As leader: *Some Shapes to Come* (1973, PM 002); *Steve Grossman* (1975, Horo 101-23); *Perspective* (1978, Atl. 19230)

As sideman: M. Davis: *A Tribute to Jack Johnson* (1970, Col. KC30455); *Miles Davis at Fillmore* (1970, Col. G30038); E. Jones: *Merry-go-round* (1971, BN 84414); *Live at the Lighthouse* (1972, BN LA015G)

BIBLIOGRAPHY
M. Garztecki: "Steve Grossman: the Rising Star," *JF* [intl edn], no.24 (1973), 43
G. Perla: "Steve Grossman–Azar Lawrence: a Session with Gene Perla," *DB*, xl/15 (1973), 18 [incl. discography]

DAVID WILD

Grosz, Marty [Martin Oliver] (*b* Berlin, 28 Feb 1930). Guitarist, banjoist, and singer. He emigrated to the USA with his family in 1933, settled in New York, and became a naturalized American. While attending Columbia University, he led a dixieland band with Dick Wellstood and Tommy Benford, which recorded in 1951. After army service he played in Chicago, recording on guitar with Dave Remington (1955–6), Art Hodes (1957), and Albert Nicholas (1959); he also recorded two albums as a leader in 1957 (*Hooray for Bix!*, Riv. 268) and 1959. He continued to work from Chicago until 1975, when he moved to New York. He toured and recorded with SOPRANO SUMMIT (*c*1975–1979), and recorded as a singer with Dick Meldonian, on guitar with Wayne Wright (1977–9), and as leader of a quintet with Wellstood (1978). Primarily an acoustic guitarist, he is known for his chordal solos in electric-guitar style.

BIBLIOGRAPHY
J. H. Klee: "Plenty Rhythm, Plenty Swing," *MR*, iii/11 (1976), 5
J. Onge: "Marty Grosz," *Coda*, no.153 (1977), 5
S. Klett: "Marty Grosz: Interview," *Cadence*, vi (1980), no.10, p.10; no.11, p.10

Grove, Dick [Richard Dean] (*b* Lakeville, IN, 18 Dec 1927). Arranger, composer, pianist, and teacher. After studying music at the University of Denver he played in concerts and sessions in Los Angeles with John Graas (1956). From 1962 he played with his own big band, and he recorded with it in 1963 (*Little Bird Suite*, PJ 74). He wrote scores for Paul Horn and Nancy Wilson, and made studio arrangements for Buddy Rich and Gerald Wilson. He also worked as a composer and arranger for television. From 1971 he devoted most of his time to teaching, leading workshops and publishing his own pedagogical texts.

BIBLIOGRAPHY
Feather '60s; *Feather–Gitler '70s*
L. Tomkins: "A Specific Approach for the Arranger – the Project of Hollywood Writer, Bandleader, and Jazz Educator, Dick Grove," *CI*, xi/3 (1972), 26
L. Underwood: "Dick Grove," *DB*, xliv/13 (1977), 29

Growl. A rough, "dirty" tone achieved in different ways by brass and woodwind players and singers. On wind instruments the growl may be produced by transmitting a guttural rasp from the throat through the lips to the mouthpiece of the instrument, or by flutter-tonguing (i.e., causing the tongue to oscillate rapidly by blowing, as if voicelessly rolling an R), or both. A comparable effect may be achieved by singing one note and playing another (*see* MULTIPHONICS). Singers, notably blues singers, create a growling tone by subtle manipulations of the throat, mouth cavity, and lips.

The growl is associated particularly with cornetists, trumpeters, and trombonists of the swing period, who often combined this tone with the use of the plunger mute (*see* MUTE, §§2(i) and 3). The outstanding exponents of the "growl and plunger" style of playing were members of Duke Ellington's brass section in the late 1920s and early 1930s, notably Bubber Miley and Tricky Sam Nanton, who may be heard using the technique on *Black and Tan Fantasy* (1927, Bruns. 3526) and *Creole Love Call* (1927, Vic. 21137). (*See also* JUNGLE MUSIC.) Another important exponent of the growl, also with Ellington, was Cootie Williams.

Numerous examples of the growl occur in recordings of female blues singers, notably Bessie Smith; her use of the technique is well represented on *Mean Old Bed Bug Blues/A Good Man is Hard to Find* (1927, Col. 142500) and on *Empty Bed Blues* (1928, Col. 14312D), where Smith and the growling trombonist Charlie Green engage in call-and-response exchanges. The tenor saxophonist Gato Barbieri frequently uses the growl; he plays in this manner, for example, throughout the last part of *Tupac Amaru* on his album *Fenix* (1971, FD 10144).

BIBLIOGRAPHY
A. Napoleon: "The Music Goes Down and Around: (a Case of Mistaken Identity)," *Sv*, no.37 (1971), 18
M. Laplace: "La trompette et le cornet dans le jazz et la musique populaire," pt vi, *Brass Bulletin*, no.47 (1984), 39
P. Clayton and P. Gammond: *Jazz: A-Z* (Enfield, nr London, 1986)

GRP [Grusin–Rosen Productions]. Record label established by DAVE GRUSIN that was taken over by ARISTA in the late 1970s.

Grunnet Jepsen, Jørgen. *See* JEPSEN, JØRGEN GRUNNET.

Gruntz, George (Paul) (*b* Basle, Switzerland, 24 June 1932). Swiss keyboard player, composer, and bandleader. After performing and recording at the Newport Jazz Festival in 1958 as a member of Marshall Brown's International Youth Band, he belonged in the 1960s to a bop trio that accompanied such American musicians as Dexter Gordon and Roland Kirk on their visits to Europe. He toured the Far East with Helen Merrill (1963), played in Phil Woods's European Rhythm Machine (1968–9), and was the principal music director of the Schauspielhaus in Zurich from 1970 to 1984. In 1973 he became the program director and producer of the Berliner Jazztage; the same year he was a founder with Flavio Ambrosetti, Franco Ambrosetti, and Daniel Humair of a big band, which Gruntz later led under the name Concert Jazz Band. Among those who have worked with the band as sidemen are Gordon, Woods, Benny Bailey, Woody Shaw, Dusko Goykovich, Jon Faddis, Tom Harrell, Palle Mikkelborg, Jimmy Knepper, Peter Herbolzheimer, Julian Priester, Charlie Mariano, Sahib Shihab, Eddie Daniels, and Niels-Henning Ørsted Pedersen. He also formed, in 1973, a group called the Piano Conclave, which consisted of a number of keyboard players from among whom Gruntz would make up a group of six for any one performance. Gruntz is a versatile musician: his principal instrument is piano, but he also plays harpsichord (on the album *Jazz Goes Baroque*, 1964–5), organ, electric and electronic keyboards, and several Middle Eastern instruments (on *Noon in Tunisia*, 1967). His compositions include a jazz opera, which was given its première in New York in 1982, and an oratorio, *The Holy Grail of Jazz and Joy*, which was first performed in Graz, Austria, the following year. In 1987 he toured the USA as the leader of a big band that included Joe Henderson, Lee Konitz, Enrico Rava, Manfred Schoof, and Kenny Wheeler.

SELECTED RECORDINGS

Jazz Goes Baroque (1964–5, Phi. 84076, 843727); *Noon in Tunisia* (1967, Saba 15132); *Theatre* (1983, ECM 1265)

BIBLIOGRAPHY

FeatherE; *Feather '60s*; *Feather–Gitler '70s*
I. Carr: "Gruntz, George Paul," in I. Carr, D. Fairweather, and B. Priestley: *Jazz: the Essential Companion* (London, 1987)

PETER SCHWALM

Grusin, Dave (*b* Denver, 26 June 1934). Pianist, electronic keyboard player, and composer. While studying at the University of Colorado he played with Terry Gibbs and Johnny Smith. He worked as a pianist and music director with the popular singer Andy Williams (1959–66) and began to compose for television and films; he also recorded with Benny Goodman's quintet (1960). He made recordings of hard bop as the leader of a trio comprising Milt Hinton and Don Lamond (1961–2) and a quintet that included Thad Jones and Frank Foster (1964). In the 1970s he wrote arrangements for and recorded with Sarah Vaughan (1972), Quincy Jones (1973–*c*1974), and Carmen McRae (1975), and played electronic keyboards with Gerry Mulligan (1973–4) and Lee Ritenour (from 1974). He produces recordings for various jazz-rock groups, including his own, on his record label GRP (Grusin–Rosen Productions).

SELECTED RECORDINGS

Kaleidoscope (1964, Col. CS9144); *Discovered Again* (1976, Sheffield Lab 5); *One of a Kind* (c1977, Pol. 6118); *Harlequin* (c1984, GRP 91015)

BIBLIOGRAPHY

Feather '60s; *Feather–Gitler '70s*
G. G. Vercelli: "Profile: Dave Grusin," *DB*, xliii/15 (1976), 38
L. Lyons: "Dave Grusin," *CK*, v/4 (1979), 24 [incl. discography]

STEVE LARSON

Gryce, Gigi [Quism, Basheer] (*b* Pensacola, FL, 28 Nov 1927; *d* Pensacola, 17 March 1983). Alto saxophonist, arranger, and composer. He grew up in Hartford, Connecticut, and began studies in composition with Daniel Pinkham and Alan Hovhaness at the Boston Conservatory in 1948; having won a Fulbright scholarship, he continued his studies in Paris with Nadia Boulanger and Arthur Honegger. After his return to the USA he became involved in jazz in New York, where he performed and recorded with Max Roach, Howard McGhee, Tadd Dameron, and Clifford Brown in 1953; later that year he toured Europe with Lionel Hampton's band. In 1954 he recorded with Donald Byrd, Lee Morgan, Thelonious Monk, and others, and the following year he began leading his own group, the Jazz Lab Quintet, which also included Byrd. In the 1960s he ceased playing jazz professionally and became a teacher.

Besides his principal instrument Gryce played clarinet and flute. His style was heavily influenced by Charlie Parker, though he had a thinner tone than Parker and lacked his melodic inventiveness. His skills as an arranger are represented by his recordings with Brown, Dizzy Gillespie, and Oscar Pettiford. His best-known jazz composition is *Minority*; among his classical compositions are three symphonies and various chamber works.

SELECTED RECORDINGS

As leader: *Gigi Gryce and his Orchestra* (1953, Vogue 173), incl. Brown Skins; with C. Brown: *Gigi Gryce–Clifford Brown Sextet* (1953, Vogue 175), incl. Minority; *Jordu* (1955, Savoy 12146), incl. Embraceable you, Jordu
As sideman: O. Pettiford: *Another one* (1955, Beth. 33), incl. Oscalypso; A. Farmer: *Evening in Casablanca* (1955, Prst. 7017); T. Charles: *Teddy Charles Tentet* (1956, Atl. 1229); D. Gillespie: *The Greatest Trumpet of them All* (1957, Verve 8352)

BIBLIOGRAPHY

M. Nevard: "A Guy Named Gigi," *MM*, xxix (28 Nov 1953), 7
N. Hentoff: "A New Jazz Corporation: Gryce, Farmer," *DB*, xxii/21 (1955), 10
R. Horricks: "Gigi Gryce: Smoke Signals," *These Jazzmen of our Time* (London, 1959), 187
M. Williams: "New Ears for Jazz: a Talk with Gigi Gryce," *Metronome*, lxxviii/6 (1961), 12
V. Pelote: "Fragments," *Jazz Magazine*, i/4 (1977), 78; ii/2 (1978), 82

THOMAS OWENS

Guaraldi, Vince(nt Anthony) (*b* San Francisco, 17 July 1928; *d* Menlo Park, CA, 6 Feb 1976). Pianist and composer. He performed and recorded with Cal Tjader (1950–51), then played in the sextet led by Bill Harris (i) and Chubby Jackson, and with Georgie Auld (1953) and Sonny Criss (1955). In between tours with Woody Herman (1956–7, 1959) he worked again with Tjader (1957–9). He also recorded with Frank Rosolino (1957) and Conte Candoli (1957, 1960), and played with Howard Rumsey's Lighthouse All Stars (1959). Guaraldi recorded a number of albums as a leader in the 1960s, and began to make a reputation as a composer; in 1962 he won a Grammy Award for *Cast your fate to the wind*, and in 1965 his jazz mass was performed in San Francisco. He was perhaps best known, however, for the jazz-oriented scores he wrote for the "Charlie Brown" television shows.

SELECTED RECORDINGS

Vince Guaraldi Trio (1956, Fan. 3225); *Black Orpheus* (1962, Fan. 8089), incl. Cast your fate to the wind; *Bola Sete and Friends* (1963, Fan. 8356); *A Boy Named Charlie Brown* (1964, Fan. 85017); *Vince Guaraldi at Grace Cathedral, San Francisco* (1965, Fan. 8367)

BIBLIOGRAPHY

FeatherE; *Feather '60s*; *Feather–Gitler '70s*
B. Doerschuk: "Vince Guaraldi," *Keyboard*, vii/7 (1981), 12

ANDREW JAFFE

Guardsman. Record label. It was established by Lugton and Co. in London in 1914; its records were pressed by British Vocalion, using material made available for release in the UK by various American companies, and distributed through cycle and hardware stores. Virtually all Guardsman's titles were issued under pseudonyms; its catalogue included a great deal of important hot dance music originally put out on the American Vocalion and Gennett labels. Also issued on Guardsman were early works by Fletcher Henderson and Fess Williams. The label is particularly noteworthy for its 7000 series (1926). This was the first non-American race series, and its 19 issues included 13 titles by Fletcher Henderson; of the remainder, 17 titles were in fact by white musicians. The label remained in existence until 1928.

BIBLIOGRAPHY

R. Jewson, D. Smith, and R. Webb: "Arthur Gainsbury's Guide to Junkshoppers," *Sv*, no.23 (1969), 170

Junkshop Three [R. Jewson, D. Smith, and R. Webb]: "A Glimpse of the Past, 13: Guardsman," *Sv*, no.23 (1969), 192

Guarente, Frank [Francesco Saverio] (*b* Montemiletto, Italy, 5 Oct 1893; *d* ?New York, 21 July 1942). Trumpeter. He emigrated to the USA in 1910. After playing in various groups he joined Paul Specht's orchestra (1921–4) and directed the Georgians, a group within the band that was modeled on the Original Dixieland Jazz Band, recording with them from 1922 to 1924. He toured Europe with his own New Georgians (1924–7), then worked with the Savoy Orpheans and others in England. He returned to the USA, rejoined Specht (1928–30), played first trumpet in the bands of Victor Young (1930–36), Jack Teagarden, the Dorsey Brothers, and others, and also accompanied popular singers in recording sessions.

SELECTED RECORDINGS

As leader: Georgians Blues (1926, Kalophon 401)

As sideman: P. Specht: You can have him, I don't want him (1922, Ban. 1090); Georgians: Old Fashioned Love (1923, Col. 30D); Someday, Sweetheart (1924, Col. 117D); Devonshire Restaurant Dance Band: Milenberg Joys (1927, Zonophone 2964); Savoy Orpheans: Vladivostock (1927, HMV B5373)

BIBLIOGRAPHY

ChiltonW

H. H. Lange: "Die Frank Guarente Story," *JP*, vi (1957), no.8, p.5; no.9, p.16; vii/1 (1958), 18

G. Barazzetta: "Frank Guarente: a Forgotten Pioneer," *JM*, xii/10 (1966), 2

RAINER E. LOTZ

Guarnieri, Johnny [John Albert] (*b* New York, 23 March 1917; *d* Livingston, NJ, 7 Jan 1985). Pianist, harpsichordist, and composer. He began classical studies on piano at the age of ten, and turned to jazz after coming into personal contact with Art Tatum and Willie "the Lion" Smith (although the latter counseled him against a career as a jazz pianist on account of his small hands). In 1939 Guarnieri succeeded Fletcher Henderson as pianist in Benny Goodman's band. The following year he joined Artie Shaw and made, with the GRAMERCY FIVE, what have been the only significant jazz harpsichord recordings. He played again with Goodman (1941) and Shaw (1941–2), then performed with Tommy Dorsey's orchestra (1942–3) and Cozy Cole's trio. Guarnieri made many recordings as a leader with Cole, Lester Young, and Slam Stewart (1944) and as a sideman with Young (1943), Roy Eldridge, Ben Webster, Cole, Coleman Hawkins, and Rex Stewart (all 1944), Don Byas and Slam Stewart (both 1945), and Louis Armstrong (1944, 1947). In the late 1940s he joined the staff of NBC in New York, then from 1963 worked as a solo pianist in California. He made a notable contribution to the film *After Hours* in 1961. Later he made tours of Europe with Slam Stewart (1974) and with an all-star group of pianists (1975); he also recorded in France with Stephane Grappelli and Vic Dickenson and as a leader. Guarnieri's mastery of the stride style was widely acknowledged. Later in his career he took to playing standards and his own compositions in 5/4 time.

For illustrations *see* BANDS, fig.4, and JAZZ (i), fig.3.

SELECTED RECORDINGS

As unaccompanied soloist: *Johnny Guarnieri Plays Harry Warren* (1973, Jim Taylor Presents 102); *Superstride* (1976, Taz-Jaz 1001)

As leader: These Foolish Things/Salute to Fats (1944, Savoy 511); Bowing Singing Slam/Gliss me again (1944, Savoy 530); *Songs of Hudson and DeLange* (1956, Coral 57085); *Walla Walla* (1975, BB 33078)

As sideman: B. Goodman: The Sheik/Poor Butterfly (1940, Col. 35466); A. Shaw: Special Delivery Stomp (1940, Vic. 26762); Summit Ridge Drive (1940, Vic. 26763)

BIBLIOGRAPHY

A. Lee: "Guarnieri Plays Greatest," *DB*, xvi/12 (1949), 2

L. Feather: "Johnny Guarnieri's New Bag," *DB*, xxxv/9 (1968), 24

Y. Fournier: "Many Faces of Johnny Guarnieri," *Pj*, no.4 (1971), 63

L. Feather: "Piano Giants of Jazz: Johnny Guarnieri," *CK*, iv/12 (1978), 58 [incl. transcr.]

B. Byler: "A Remembrance: Conversations with Johnny Guarnieri," *MR*, xii/4 (1985), 7

C. Deffaa: "Johnny Guarnieri's Last Performance," *MR*, xii/4 (1985), 9

L. D. Holmes and J. W. Thomson: *Jazz Greats: Getting Better with Age* (New York, 1986) [colln of interviews]

ANDREW JAFFE

Guerin, John (Payne) (*b* Hawaii, 31 Oct 1939). Drummer. He grew up in San Diego and taught himself to play drums. He performed and recorded with Buddy DeFranco (*c*1960–1961) then played with George Shearing (1965–6). From the late 1960s he performed and recorded with Roger Kellaway, Howard Roberts, Tom Scott, Victor Feldman, Ray Brown, and others, and worked as a studio musician for films and television. In 1973 he became a founding member of Scott's L. A. Express, which toured and recorded with the singer Joni Mitchell. Guerin later wrote with Mitchell the title track of her album *The Hissing of Summer Lawns* (1975). Later he recorded with Joe Farrell (1978), Milt Jackson (1981) and Bobby McFerrin (1982), but during the 1980s he has worked mainly as a producer and arranger.

SELECTED RECORDINGS

As sideman: F. Zappa: *Hot Rats* (1969, Bizarre–Rep. 6365); T. Scott: *Tom Scott and the L. A. Express* (1973, Ode 77021); J. Mitchell: *Court and Spark* (*c*1974, Asy. 1001); *Miles of Aisles* (1974, Asy. 202); *The Hissing of Summer Lawns* (1975, Asy. 1051)

BIBLIOGRAPHY

Feather–Gitler '70s

S. Bradley: "John Guerin," *DB*, xliv/13 (1977), 19

BILL MILKOWSKI

Guérin, Roger (*b* Sarrebrück, France [now Saarbrücken, Germany], 9 Jan 1926). French trumpeter. His first professional engagement was with Aimé Barelli (1947–8). He then played with Rex Stewart (1948), the saxophonist Tony Proteau, Kenny Clarke (1949), Charlie Parker (1950), Don Byas, James Moody (1951), Django Reinhardt (1951–3), Bobby Jaspar (from 1953), Peanuts Holland (1955), Claude Bolling, Michel Legrand (1956–7), and Louis Armstrong (1958). In 1956 he began two important associations, one with Martial Solal that lasted into the 1980s, and the other with André Hodeir, whose principal trumpet and flugelhorn soloist he was until 1972. He was the leader, with Benny Golson, of a recording session for Columbia in 1958. He continued to play principally as a sideman, with, among others, Quincy Jones, Duke Ellington (1960), Dizzy Gillespie (1962), Woody Shaw, the Clarke–Boland Big Band (1965), the Paris Jazz All Stars (1966), Slide Hampton (1969, 1970), John Lewis (1970), Cat Anderson, Gunther Schuller (1979), and Bill Coleman (1980), but from 1972 he also led his own big band. Influenced chiefly by Gillespie, Guérin became the most sought-after French sideman playing trumpet.

SELECTED RECORDINGS

As leader with B. Golson: *I Remember Clifford* (1958, Col. FP1117)
As sideman: K. Clarke: *Round Midnight* (1956, Phi. 77312); M. Solal: *Suite en ré bémol* (1959, Col. ESDF1278); A. Hodeir: *Bitter Ending* (1972, Epic 80544); M. Solal: *Coming on the Hudson* (1984, Carlyne 008)

BIBLIOGRAPHY

L. Malson: "Roger Guérin ou le culte de la relaxation," *Jm*, no.62 (1960), 22

MICHEL LAPLACE

Guilbeau, Phil(lip) (*b* Lafayette, LA, 16 Jan 1926). Trumpeter. He performed and recorded rhythm-and-blues and blues with Paul Williams (1948–9) and Joe Turner (ii) (1957). From 1960 to 1965 he toured and made recordings with Ray Charles (including the album *Genius plus Soul Equals Jazz* (1960, Imp. 2), on which he plays as a soloist) and recorded with Hank Crawford. In 1965–6 he performed and recorded in the USA and Europe with Count Basie.

BIBLIOGRAPHY

Feather '60s
V. Wilmer: "Phil the Gil," *JB*, ii/11 (1965), 14

Guild. Record company and label. The company was founded in New York in 1945, but by the end of that year it had ceased to operate. Nevertheless during its brief existence Guild proved extremely important to jazz history; it was the first company to record Charlie Parker and Dizzy Gillespie together, in a session held in February 1945 that yielded three of the first bop classics, *Groovin' High*, *All the Things you are*, and *Dizzy Atmosphere*. Three months later Parker and Gillespie made four more recordings – *Salt Peanuts*, *Hot House*, *Shaw Nuff*, and *Lover Man* – which Guild issued as two 78 r.p.m. discs. Gillespie was also a principal soloist on items by the bands of Georgie Auld and Boyd Raeburn, and participated in a sextet recording with Dexter Gordon which resulted in two discs, a version of *Groovin' High* (extremely rare until it was reissued by Phoenix in the 1970s) and *Blue 'n' Boogie*. After the company's demise Guild's masters were acquired by Musicraft, which later reissued parts of the catalogue, as did other companies, including Royal, Allegro, Savoy, Prestige, and Smithsonian. The company's material was later acquired by Pickwick.

MARK GARDNER

Guitar. A string instrument, plucked or strummed with the fingers or a plectrum, and normally having frets along the fingerboard.

1. Technical aspects. 2. Technical developments. 3. History.

1. Technical aspects. The standard classical (or Spanish) guitar has a hollow body and a flat table (or top) with a circular soundhole; its six strings, tuned *E–A–d–g–b–e'*, pass over a fixed bridge. The 12-string guitar, used mostly in blues and folk music, has the strings in six courses, some in unison, others an octave apart. Some jazz players, notably Tiny Grimes, have used an instrument with only four strings (for illustration *see* TATUM, ART), a practice that may be related to the use by blues musicians of the top four strings only of the six-string guitar. To differentiate it from the electric instrument, the standard classical guitar and all variants that do not have integral electrical components are known as "acoustic" guitars.

There are two main kinds of electric guitar: the hollow-bodied (also referred to as the "electric-acoustic" or "semi-acoustic"), and the solid-bodied, in which the body provides little resonance; a hybrid of the two, the "semisolid," has a hollow body the vibrations of which are reduced by a solid block of wood running the length of the instrument inside. Standard electric guitars have six strings, normally tuned like those of the acoustic guitar (the ELECTRIC BASS GUITAR usually has four); one or more pickups, placed on the body under the strings, convert the vibrations of the strings into an electrical signal, which is in turn converted into sound by means of an amplifier and loudspeakers. Controls on the instrument allow the player to alter the tone and volume and to select different pickups or combinations of pickups.

Amplifiers often incorporate sound-modifying devices, notably the kind that add reverberation. It is also common for players to connect such devices (usually in the form of pedals) between the instrument and the amplifier. They function by altering the electrical signal and thus enhancing, distorting, or otherwise changing the sound. The "wa-wa" (or "wah-wah") pedal produces a characteristic ululating effect. "Fuzz" or distortion is the electronic simulation of the sound of an overdriven amplifier. Echo, "phase shifting" (or "phasing"), "flanging," and the "chorus" effect, which are all time-delay effects originally produced by means of tape recorders in the studio, are now created electronically. Octave dividers supply parallel octaves above or below the notes played. Other devices include the compressor, limiter, harmonizer, and noise-gate.

The phenomenon of acoustic feedback can occur in any electronic amplification system. It is caused when a microphone or pickup is close enough to a loudspeaker to pick up its vibrations, which are then fed through the amplification system again; at a certain level of volume an obtrusive howl results, which, when carefully controlled, yields a range of clear pitches. This effect, normally carefully avoided, has been exploited by guitarists in rock music and jazz.

2. Technical developments. In the 20th century the desire for greater volume and penetration in the guitar's sound has led to the designing of instruments that differ to a greater or lesser degree from the traditional instrument. By the end of the 1920s steel-strung, flat-top guitars, altered structurally to bear the tension of heavier strings, were being manufactured. At much the same time the need for a guitar that could make itself heard in the large dance band gave rise to the arched-top (or "carved-top" or "cello-bodied") guitar. The first of these, the Gibson L5, issued in 1923 and 1924, had steel strings, a strong, thick top carved into an arched shape, two f-shaped holes (instead of a single circular soundhole) for greater projection, an adjustable bridge, and a tailpiece; it was designed for playing with a plectrum.

Other attempts made in the 1930s to increase the volume of the guitar included Mario Maccaferri's design (1932–3) for the French company Selmer of an instrument with an extra sound chamber inside the body; its clear, piercing tone became the hallmark of Django Reinhardt's playing (fig.1). A similar idea was exploited in the "ampliphonic" or "resophonic" guitar (commonly known by one of its trade names, Dobro).

The first experiments with electric amplification of guitars were carried out in the 1920s by Lloyd Loar, an employee of the Gibson company, and others, who had devised crude magnetic pickups for acoustic instruments. The earliest commercially produced electric guitars, made by the Rickenbacker company in 1931, had hollow circular bodies and long necks, but they were followed shortly by electric Spanish guitars. In 1935 or 1936 Gibson introduced the ES150, an electric arched-top guitar, which had a distinctive type of pickup later called the Charlie Christian pickup; it is this kind of electric guitar (known as the "electric-acoustic") that is used most often in jazz, except in those styles related to rock music.

1. The Quintette du Hot Club de France playing at the Big Apple Club, Paris, 1937: (seated, left to right) Django Reinhardt, Joseph Reinhardt, and Eugene Vees (Maccaferri Selmer guitars); (standing) Stephane Grappelli (violin) and Louis Vola (double bass)

The first commercially manufactured solid-bodied electric guitar was marketed by Fender in 1948; Gibson responded with the Les Paul guitar (1952; fig.2*a*, p.460) and Fender then (1954; fig.2*b*, p.460) produced an instrument with three (instead of the original two) pickups and a lever, or "tremolo arm," to create vibrato effects (*see* Bend). These three guitars formed the basis of solid-bodied electric guitar design. Later developments have included refinements in the design of pickups and increasing sophistication in amplification systems and sound-modification devices. Electric guitars with two necks (often one with six strings and one with 12, or one with standard tuning and one with bass tuning) have been made, and many players have adapted instruments to their own purposes or had instruments built specially for them.

Because the hollow-bodied electric guitar was found to be particularly susceptible to feedback, in the late 1950s Gibson introduced a range of guitars (known as "semisolid" or "thin-bodied" to distinguish them from the full-bodied, electric-acoustic guitar) designed to counteract this effect and to provide the long sustain of the solid-bodied electric combined with the warm, mellow sound of the acoustic instrument. The "300" series were hollow, thin-bodied guitars with arched table and back, f-shaped soundholes, and a solid block of wood running down the center of the body, which reduced the vibrations of the soundboard and thus helped to minimize feedback.

Digital technology has led to the development of the so-called guitar synthesizer, a Synthesizer which is controlled by an instrument that resembles an electric guitar.

3. History. Unlike brass and woodwind instruments, which have played important roles in jazz from its inception, the guitar did not become a principal voice in the genre until the rise of jazz-rock in the late 1960s and early 1970s. While the trumpet and saxophone were naturally suited from the outset to the requirements of jazz, guitarists had to struggle for decades to reconcile the characteristics of the music with their instrument's lack of volume and defiant technique. But although it was long before the guitar played a decisive role in the evolution of jazz, it has enjoyed a rich and eventful history, unlike that of any other instrument, as a presence in the music.

In the early days of jazz, when wind players were effectively combining elements of popular and classical styles to create vibrant, expressive solos, the guitar, like the banjo, was used only as a member of the rhythm section; the banjo, an instrument of limited scope but valued for its loud percussive sound, was often coupled with the tuba, while the guitar was matched with the double bass. In the big bands of the late 1920s and early 1930s the guitar superseded the banjo (just as the double bass ousted the tuba), gaining its first sure foothold as a jazz instrument. This was partly owing to the development of the arched-top guitar, which could compete with the volume of sound in a large ensemble: its bright tone had a cutting power that enabled the instrument to be sensed (it was often felt rather than heard) and thus to contribute effectively to the rhythm section. The other factor in the eclipse of the banjo by the guitar was the immense popularity of Eddie Lang, a brilliant and sophisticated player, who was a member of Paul Whiteman's orchestra and a busy session musician. His elaborate single-string work is well represented by *Eddie's Twister* (1927, OK 40807), which he recorded in a duo with Arthur Schutt. Under Lang's influence large numbers of banjoists changed to playing guitar; only a few years after Lang's emergence the banjo was all but obsolete, and the Gibson L5 arched-top guitar (the model favored by Lang) had become the standard

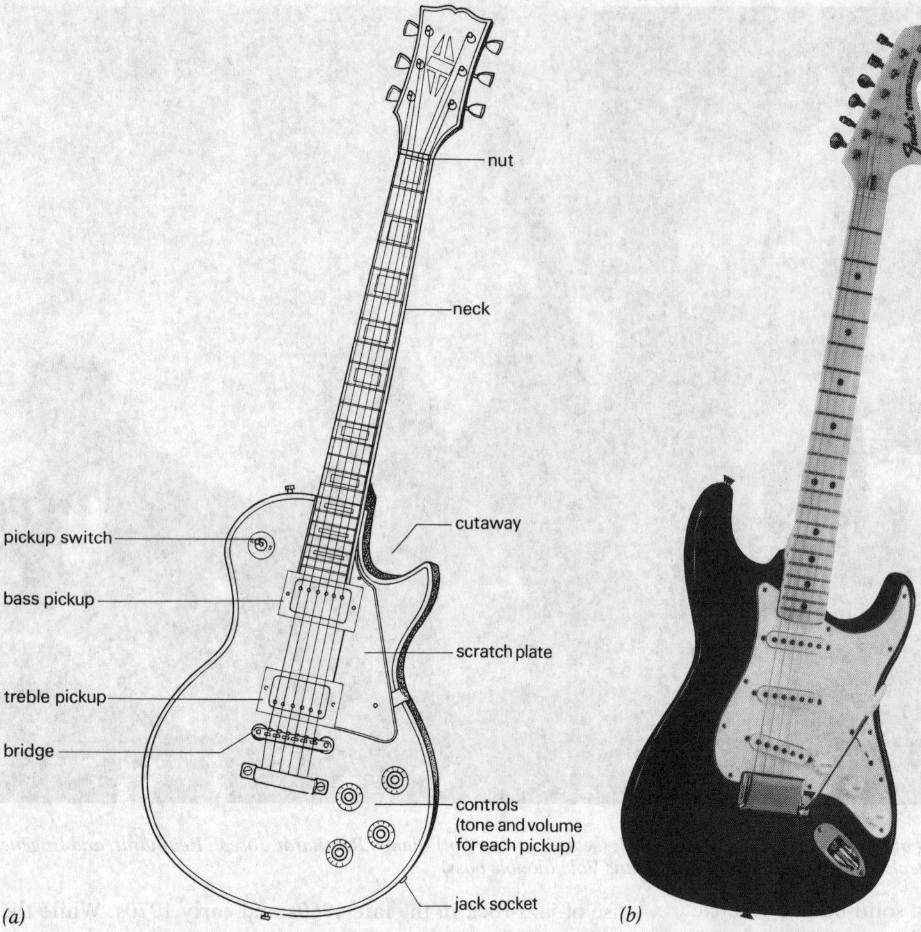

2. Solid-bodied electric guitars: (a) Gibson Les Paul (drawing showing features); (b) Fender Stratocaster (photograph showing the three pickups and "tremolo arm")

instrument for jazz players. Among the prominent rhythm guitarists of the 1930s was Freddie Green, whose playing was largely responsible for the unity of Count Basie's rhythm sections from 1937 onwards (for illustration *see* JONES, JO).

Although the guitar found relatively quick acceptance as a rhythm instrument it was slower to develop as a solo instrument. Lang and the blues guitarist Lonnie Johnson (whose exceptional musical ability and technique enabled him also to play jazz) proved that fluid, single-line solos, similar to those played on wind instruments, could be produced on guitar. The two men (Lang using the pseudonym Blind Willie Dunn) made a number of pioneering recordings as a duo (1928–9), including *Have to Change Keys to Play these Blues* (1928, OK 8637). In the context of ensembles Johnson's solos graced recordings by Louis Armstrong's Hot Five and Hot Seven (both 1927) and his Savoy Ballroom Five (1929) and by Duke Ellington's orchestra (1928–9), while Lang took choruses on recordings with Bix Beiderbecke (1930) and many others; however, the prominence of the guitar in these recordings was achieved through the strategic placement of the microphone and could not be replicated in performance. Until the late 1930s, when electric instruments became readily available, the guitar was used successfully as a solo instrument only in small groups and in ensembles the instrumentation of which was carefully selected to allow for the guitar's lack of volume. Important soloists to emerge in the mid-1930s were Django Reinhardt, a virtuoso player of single-line melodies, and George Van Eps, a brilliant guitarist who specialized in unaccompanied performances in which he supported his melodies with advanced harmonic concepts.

Early efforts to find a guitar that could be used in a solo capacity in a standard band included the adoption of resophonic instruments by Eddie Durham (in the bands of Jimmie Lunceford and Count Basie) and Oscar Alemán, and the experiments with amplification by Durham and George Barnes (playing with blues singers and with his own quartet); Barnes's recording of *I'm forever blowing bubbles* (1940, OK 05798), made with his quartet, displays his uncommonly refined single-string technique. It was soon recognized that amplification was the only practical solution to the instrument's lack of volume, and with the introduction in 1936 of Gibson's ES150 electric archedtop a viable electric guitar became generally available for the first time. Durham made some of the earliest recordings on the instrument in 1938, with the Kansas City Five and Kansas City Six. But he and his contemporaries, who continued to employ the technique they had used with the acoustic guitar, were unable to exploit the full potential of the new instrument. It was only when Charlie Christian attracted attention as a member of Benny Goodman's immensely popular groups in the late 1930s and early 1940s that the electric guitar made a significant impact. Christian was much before the public eye and this prominence allowed his swinging solo style to be heard by many other musicians; his formidable technique, his use of passing (instead of principal) harmonies as the basis for improvisation, and, more than anything else, his smooth, free-moving lines, in which the guitar attained the same expressive power as the saxophone, persuaded countless guitarists to take up the electric instrument. His style is epitomized by *Solo Flight* (Col. 36684), recorded by Goodman's big band in 1941.

Although it was the electric form of the guitar that was assimilated into the mainstream tradition of jazz, the acoustic instrument did not go completely neglected. Whether used with nylon or steel strings, the acoustic guitar brings a warmth and intimate immediacy to jazz that is lost through amplification. In the late 1940s, more than a decade before bossa nova achieved widespread popularity, the Brazilian player Laurindo Almeida, who favors a classical Spanish guitar with nylon strings, introduced South American elements to jazz. He first came to prominence as a soloist in Stan Kenton's orchestra and later led his own small groups. His example was followed by Charlie Byrd and by other South American guitarists, including Luiz Bonfa, Bola Sete, Baden Powell, and Egberto Gismonti.

The late 1940s, 1950s, and 1960s were a period of technological, technical, and musical refinement. Pickup and amplifier technology became more highly developed, facilitating playing at higher volume with cleaner tone. Influenced by the cool sounds of the styles that succeeded bop in the 1950s, guitarists adopted a warm, clear tone, which is still preferred by numerous mainstream players. Moreover the level of technique among guitarists was generally high enough to allow them to transfer to the guitar the ideas of innovative wind players such as Charlie Parker and Dizzy Gillespie, and, later, Miles Davis and John Coltrane.

A number of players who made important contributions to jazz guitar emerged during this period. In 1949 Billy Bauer, whose technique and musical concepts were uncommonly sophisticated for the time, joined Lennie Tristano's group in a brief but historic experiment in free jazz that produced the recordings *Intuition* (Cap. 1224) and *Digression* (Cap. EAP1-491). In the 1950s Tal Farlow's fluid bop-oriented single-note lines and advanced use of extended and altered harmonies (exemplified on his album *Tal*, 1956, Verve 8021) set a new standard for playing. On *Serenata Burlesca* (1956, from the album *Mr. Roberts Plays Guitar*, 1956–7, Verve 8192), Howard Roberts, supported by a string section, combined jazz techniques with a more classical approach. Other exceptional players included the swing stylist Oscar Moore; Barney Kessel and Herb Ellis, who drew on both swing and bop elements in their work; Kenny Burrell, whose playing combined blues and bop; Jim Hall, a classically trained guitarist whose improvisations often involved motivic development; Wes Montgomery, who used his thumb to execute rapid swinging octaves and chordal passages; and Pat Martino, who refined the advanced single-note work of players such as Bauer and Farlow.

By the 1960s jazz guitarists commonly commanded the same complex harmonic and melodic vocabulary as wind players. Although the guitar was no longer limited by a lack of volume, it continued to be less versatile than a wind instrument because of its staccato attack: while tones on a wind instrument can be sustained almost indefinitely (depending on the player's breath control), sounds generated on the guitar decay rapidly. However, with the advent of rock music in the late 1960s high-powered amplifiers, sound-modifying devices, and controlled feedback began to be exploited; the rock musician Jimi Hendrix was the first fully to explore these possibilities. It soon became clear that technological developments offered the guitarist a greater variety of sounds and effects than could be created on almost any other instrument.

Inspired by the innovations in jazz of John Coltrane and the experiments of Hendrix, guitarists such as John McLaughlin and Larry Coryell helped to create a new form, jazz-rock – the first in which the guitar played a leading role. In reaction to the styles of the 1950s and early 1960s, when the harmonic and melodic content of an improvisation were emphasized, jazz-rock musicians exploited high volume levels, sheets of sound, and long sustain, and experimented with complex time signatures, rhythms, and compositional approaches. To achieve their ends they took over the solid-bodied and semisolid instruments commonly used in rock, which afforded greater control at high volume than the electric-acoustic. Many of the most influential jazz-rock bands were led by guitarists, including McLaughlin's Mahavishnu Orchestra and Coryell's Eleventh House; McLaughlin and Coryell are heard to advantage on the album *Spaces* (Van. 6558), which they recorded together in 1970. Moreover guitarists played a central role in innovative groups such as Chick Corea's Return to Forever and units led by Miles Davis (from the late 1960s Davis's ensembles have included some of the most dynamic guitarists in jazz-rock, among them McLaughlin, Coryell, Sonny Sharrock, Mike Stern, and John Scofield).

At the same time a number of players remained faithful to the acoustic guitar, or, like McLaughlin, employed electric or acoustic instruments, depending on the style in which they were working. Among notable players of the acoustic guitar in the later period are Joe Pass, Kenny Burrell, Jim Hall, Coryell, Earl Klugh, Paco De Lucia, Al Di Meola, and Ralph Towner.

In the 1980s guitarists once more found a new range of possibilities – in the guitar synthesizer. Sophisticated systems not only make available an enormous variety of electronic and simulated instrumental timbres, they also, through digital sampling, offer the guitarist the opportunity to play back and modify the recorded sounds of brass and woodwind instruments. They thus make possible the fulfillment of the guitarist's desire to produce as versatile and varied a sound as a wind player. Just as banjoists changed to the acoustic arched-top in the late 1920s and early 1930s and rhythm guitarists adopted the hollow-bodied electric guitar in the late 1930s and early 1940s, players in the 1980s are taking up the guitar synthesizer. Among those who have used the instrument are Pat Metheny, Kazumi Watanabe, McLaughlin, Di Meola, Allan Holdsworth, and John Abercrombie.

The technical changes to the guitar that have taken place during the evolution of jazz have been accompanied by a continual development of players' techniques. The guitar has most commonly been played with a plectrum, which facilitates both rhythm work and the execution of single-line solos, especially at rapid tempos. However, many players have successfully employed the "finger-picking" technique (largely adopted from the classical tradition), which offers greater musical possibilities. Some guitarists, George Van Eps and Joe Pass, for example, employed a plectrum early in their careers only to abandon it as their approach became more sophisticated. While the plectrum is still preferred by many players, more and more are using the fingers alone, and most guitarists who customarily play with a plectrum sometimes vary their sound by employing finger-picking technique.

A number of players from the 1960s onwards have developed new and influential techniques. In the late 1960s Lenny Breau evolved a highly individual finger technique, based on conventional playing, which enabled him to create impressionistic tapestries of simultaneously improvised chords and melodies, as on his album *Five o'Clock Bells* (1978–9, Adelphi 5006). A gifted composer and bandleader, John McLaughlin developed a brilliant single-note technique (evident on the majority of his recordings) employing a plectrum, which enabled him to play complex passages at exceptionally fast speeds. On his album *Virtuoso* (1973, Pablo 2310708), recorded as an unaccompanied soloist, Joe Pass demonstrates a new and highly influential approach that combines intricate chordal work,

3. Stanley Jordan playing at the Newport Jazz Saratoga Festival, 1987

facile single-string improvisation and walking bass lines. Stanley Jordan, in the 1980s, treated the guitar somewhat like a keyboard, using the fingers of both hands to hammer contrapuntal lines on the fingerboard in a way unique in the history of guitar playing (fig.3); his first LP, *Magic Touch* (1985, BN 85101), prominently displays the results of this novel approach. Some guitarists, notably James "Blood" Ulmer, Sonny Sharrock, and Derek Bailey, have explored avant-garde forms; others, for example John Scofield, who makes extensive use of altered notes in his improvisations, have developed an advanced harmonic vocabulary.

For further illustrations *see* LANG, EDDIE; MCLAUGHLIN, JOHN; MINGUS, CHARLES; MONTGOMERY; PETERSON, OSCAR; REINHARDT, DJANGO; and SHEARING, GEORGE.

BIBLIOGRAPHY

J.-E. Berendt: *Das Jazzbuch: Entwicklung und Bedeutung der Jazzmusik* (Frankfurt am Main, Germany, 1953, rev. 2/1959 as *Das neue Jazzbuch*, Eng. trans., New York, 1962; rev. and enlarged 5/1981 as *Das grosse Jazzbuch: von New Orleans bis Jazz Rock*, Eng. trans. as *The Jazz Book: from New Orleans to Fusion and Beyond*, Westport, CT, 1982)

L. Feather: *The Book of Jazz: a Guide to the Entire Field* (New York, 1957, 2/1965 as *The Book of Jazz from Then till Now: a Guide to the Entire Field*)

R. Warner: "On Banjos and Guitars," *Sv*, no.73 (1977), 31

M. J. Summerfield: *The Jazz Guitar: its Evolution and its Players* (Gateshead, England, 1978)

R. Denyer: *The Guitar Handbook* (London, 1982)

N. Mongan: *The History of the Guitar in Jazz* (New York, London, and Sydney, 1983) [incl. transcrs. and discography]

S. Britt: *The Jazz Guitarists* (Poole, England, 1984)

TONY BACON/R (1, 2), JIM FERGUSON (3)

Gulda, Friedrich (*b* Vienna, 16 May 1930). Austrian pianist, flutist, baritone saxophonist, singer, and composer. He began his career as a classical pianist; after attending the Akademie in Vienna (from 1942) he made his début in 1944, won the Geneva Competition in 1946, and performed at Carnegie Hall in New York (1950). While continuing to play and record classical music he worked in jazz from the 1950s, performing from the spring of 1956 on Austrian radio with the Austrian All Stars (which included Karl Drewo and Joe Zawinul), in June of that year at Birdland in New York (with Idrees Sulieman, Phil Woods, and James Cleveland among his sidemen), and at the Newport Jazz Festival. He took up the wooden flute in the 1950s and the baritone saxophone around 1960. In September 1962 he formed a large orchestra, which included Benny Bailey, Nat Peck, and leading Austrian and Swedish musicians, and took part with it in the performance of two of his own compositions at the Berlin Festwochen (*Music for Three Soloists and Band*, in which he played baritone saxophone, and *Music for Piano and Band*). He recorded in São Paolo and Brasília with Jimmy Rowser and Albert Heath (April 1964) and in New York (January 1965), then formed the Eurojazz Orchestra, among the members of which were Zawinul, Art Farmer, J. J. Johnson, Herb Geller, Freddie Hubbard, Kenny Wheeler, Sahib Shihab, Ron Carter, Jimmy Woode, and Mel Lewis. He performed with the orchestra as its leader until 1966, when he founded a jazz competition in Vienna; he also founded the International Musikforum in Ossiach, Austria (1968).

In the late 1960s and early 1970s Gulda made many recordings (as a classical pianist, as a member of a jazz trio, and under the pseudonym Albert Golowin as a jazz singer) and he played free jazz with Jörg Fuchs and Limpe Fuchs in the trio Anima (1972). During the following years he helped to organize several festivals in which he also took part as a performer: the Tage freier Musik at Schloss Moosham, Salzburg, Austria, in August 1976, when he led a trio and played with Cecil Taylor, and in August 1977, when he played with Don Cherry and the Revolutionary Ensemble; the Friedrich Gulda Festival in Gmunden, Austria (September 1978); and the Weltmusiktage in Salzburg (1979), at which Dizzy Gillespie performed. Later he was the host of two Austrian television programs on music (1981), performed with Chick Corea and Gary Burton at the festival in Zeltweg, Austria (1983), and with Corea played a concerto by Mozart and jazz improvisations in Europe (1983–4). In the 1980s he has often worked with the drummer and singer Ursula Anders.

Gulda has consistently juxtaposed classical music and jazz in his programs, and confronted audiences with music with which they are unfamiliar. His own compositions, which include two piano concertos, a concerto for cello and brass band, vocal and orchestral pieces, and music for solo piano, are unimportant; the style is derivative, the influences ranging from the classics to impressionism, jazz, rock, and Viennese folksongs. His published writings include *Worte zur Musik* (Munich, 1971).

SELECTED RECORDINGS

As unaccompanied soloist: *The Master* (1983, Amadeo AVRS410078)

Duos: with K. Weiss: *It's All One* (1971, MPS 15271); with U. Anders: *Gegenwart* (1976, ERP 1)

As leader: *Friedrich Gulda at Birdland* (1956, RCA LPM1355); *Music for Three Soloists and Band* (1962, Col. STC83357); *Gulda Jazz* (1964, Amadeo AVRS9165); *From Vienna with Jazz* (1964, Col. CS9051); *Ineffable* (1965, Col. CS9146); *Music for Four Soloists and Band no.1* (1965, Saba 15097); *Internationaler Wettbewerb für Modernen Jazz* (1966, Amadeo 9213); *Friedrich Gulda und sein Eurojazz Orchester* (1966, Preiser 3141); *Vienna Revisited* (1969, Saba 15226); *The Long Road to Freedom* (1971, MPS CVC872); *Anima* (1972, MPS 2921655); *Musician of our Time* (1977, MPS 88034); *Concerto for Ursula* (1982, Amadeo AVRS6498)

BIBLIOGRAPHY

E. Jantsch: *Friedrich Gulda – die Verantwortung des Interpreten* (Vienna, 1953) [incl. discography]

G. Lees: "If Friedrich Gulda is Right: Jazz has had it!," *DB*, xxx/13 (1963), 18

J. Kaiser: "Glenn Gould und Friedrich Gulda," *Grosse Pianisten in unserer Zeit* (Munich, 1965; Eng. trans. as *Great Pianists of Our Time*, London, 1971)

W. Conover: "Viennese Cookin'," *DB*, xxxiii/16 (1966), 23

K. Geitel: *Fragen an Friedrich Gulda* (Berlin, 1973)

GERHARD BRUNNER/KLAUS SCHULZ

Gullin, Lars (Gunnar Victor) (*b* Visby, Sweden, 4 May 1928; *d* Vissefjärda, Sweden, 17 May 1976). Swedish baritone saxophonist, composer, and arranger. From the age of 13 he played bugle, then clarinet, in a military band; a few years later he began formal study of the piano. He became acquainted with Swedish folk music before turning to jazz in the late 1940s. He played with the orchestras of Charles Redland (as a pianist, 1947–8), Arthur Österwall (1948), and Seymour Österwall (1949–51), changing from alto to baritone saxophone; he next played with Arne Domnérus's orchestra (1951–3), then led his own small groups and worked as a freelance. Although at first influenced by the cool jazz of Miles Davis, Lee Konitz, and Stan Getz, he soon developed a highly personal, expressive style, both as a soloist and as a composer, and became one of the most highly regarded jazz musicians in Europe. In 1954 he became the first European performer to win a jazz poll in the USA (in *Down Beat*'s "new star" category); the same year he began a series of successful European tours. His last performance abroad was in Germany in 1976. From the mid-1960s Gullin devoted himself mainly to composition, showing a fine sense for scoring; his largest work is *Jazz amour affair* (1971) for symphony orchestra and jazz soloists.

SELECTED RECORDINGS

That's it (1951, Met. 180); Deep Purple (1951, Met. 191); Danny-o (1951, Gazell 2018); Alone (1951, Pol. 48600); First Walk (1952, Pol. 49580); on *Piano Holiday* (1953, Met. 34), Holiday for Piano, Night and Day; Dedicated to Lee (1953, Met. 646); Danny's Dream (1954, Met. 75) [EP]; Lars Meets Jeff (1955, Met. 105) [EP]; *The Great Lars Gullin*, i (1955–6, Dra. 36); Fedja (1956, Met. 196) [EP]; Summertime (1956, Met. 200) [EP]; *The Artistry of Lars Gullin* (1958, Sonet 1); *Portrait of my Pals* (1964, Col. SSX1010); *Jazz amour affair* (1970, Odeon 062-34289); *Aeros aromatica atomica Suite* (1976, Odeon 062-35282)

BIBLIOGRAPHY

K. Knox: "Lars Gullin," *JM*, no.161 (1968), 2
E. Kjellberg: "Gullin, Lars," *Sohlmans musiklexikon* (Stockholm, rev. and enlarged 2/1975–9 ed. H. Åstrand)
K. Knox: "Lament for Lars," *JJI*, xxx/10 (1977), 14 [incl. discography]
E. Kjellberg: *Svensk jazzhistoria: en översikt* [Swedish jazz history: an overview] (Stockholm, 1985)
K. Knox and G. Lindqvist: *Jazz amour affair: en bok om Lars Gullin* (Stockholm, 1986) [incl. discography]

ERIK KJELLBERG

Gumbs, Onaje Allen (*b* New York, 3 Sept 1949). Keyboard player, arranger, and composer. He studied piano from the age of seven and attended the High School of Music and Art in New York (graduated 1967) and SUNY, Fredonia (BM 1977). He began his career as a freelance studio musician and toured with Kenny Burrell (1971). In the mid-1970s he worked principally as a pianist and arranger for Norman Connors; he also performed and recorded with Betty Carter (1972), the group Natural Essence (1972–6), and Woody Shaw (1975, 1977–9), accompanied Dee Dee Bridgewater and Grady Tate, and was music director for the singer Phyllis Hyman. In 1987 he was a member of the quintet Who's Who, led by Mino Cinélu. As an arranger Gumbs is self-taught and has been influenced by Charles Stepney, the arranger for the rock group Earth, Wind and Fire, and Henry Mancini; his best-known arrangement is a version of *Betcha by golly wow*, which was sung by Hyman on Connors's album *You are my Starship* (*c*1975). He is the composer of *Dark of Light* and of works for woodwind quartet and chamber orchestra, and he has received a grant for orchestral composition from the NEA.

SELECTED RECORDINGS

As unaccompanied soloist: *Onaje* (1976, Ste. 1069)
As sideman: N. Connors: *Dark of Light* (1972–3, Cob. 9035); *Love from the Sun* (1973, Buddah 5142); *You are my Starship* (*c*1975, Buddah 5655); N. Adderley: *Hummin'* (1976, Little David 1012); W. Shaw: *Stepping Stones* (1978, Col. JC35560); E. Klugh: *Crazy for you* (1981, Lib. 51113)

BIBLIOGRAPHY

Feather–Gitler '70s
A. J. Smith: "Onaje Allen Gumbs," *DB*, xliv/7 (1977), 36
B. Primack: "Onaje Allen Gumbs," *Keyboard*, vii/11 (1981), 37 [incl. discography]

PAUL RINZLER

Gumina, Tommy [Thomas Joseph] (*b* Milwaukee, WI, 20 May 1931). Accordionist and bandleader. After studying in Milwaukee and Chicago he played with Harry James's band (1951–1953 or 1954). He later worked as a soloist and led his own groups, mainly in Las Vegas. From 1960 to 1963, he led a bop quartet with Buddy DeFranco; it made several recordings, including *Pacific Standard (Swingin') Time* (1960, Decca 74031). He recorded again, with Willie Smith, in 1965, and then retired from performing to concentrate on the design and promotion of musical instruments. (*Feather '60s*; *Feather–Gitler '70s*)

Gumpert, Ulrich (*b* Jena, Germany, 26 Jan 1945). German pianist and composer. He studied music in Weimar (1961–4) and Berlin and played in groups and big bands led by the trumpeter Klaus Lenz (1967–70). In 1969 he formed a quartet, some members of which later belonged to the experimental jazz-rock group SOK (1971–3). In 1972 he formed the Jazz-Werkstatt Orchester, which was active sporadically for a number of years (later under the name Ulrich Gumpert Workshop Band); it made several recordings, including *Echos von Karolinenhof* (1979, FMP 0710). He played with the quartet Synopsis (formed 1973, re-formed 1984 as the Zentral-Quartett), in a duo with Günter Sommer, in a trio with Sommer and the saxophonist Manfred Hering, and later in groups with the saxophonist Dietmar Diesner and the trombonist Johannes Bauer. He toured and recorded in the early 1980s with the trombonist Radu Malfatti and Tony Oxley, and in 1985 in a duo with Steve Lacy. He often performs as a soloist and has written music for films and the stage.

BERT NOGLIK

Gurtu, Trilok (*b* Bombay, 30 Oct 1951). Indian percussionist. He studied classical tablā from an early age, then, having heard recordings of Miles Davis and John Coltrane, he started to experiment with playing in jazz styles. After working in Europe (1973–5) he moved to New York (1976), where he played and recorded with Charlie Mariano (1977) and worked with Don Cherry and Barre Phillips; he is heard to advantage on *Three Day Moon* (1978, ECM 1264), recorded with Phillips. He played with Karl Berger at the Donaueschingen Musiktage (1979), with Lee Konitz at the New York Kool Jazz Festival, and at Woodstock (from 1982). He toured Europe in a duo with Nana Vasconcelos, and in a quartet with Vasconcelos, Jan Garbarek, and the violinist Lakshminarayana Shankar; he recorded *Song for Everyone* (1984, ECM 1286) with Garbarek, Shankar, and the tablā player Zakir Hussain. He has also worked with John Abercrombie, Philip Catherine, Archie Shepp, and Jasper van 't Hof, and in the group Oregon. (I. Carr: "Gurtu, Trilok," in I. Carr, D. Fairweather, and B. Priestley: *Jazz: the Essential Companion*, London, 1987)

Gushee, Lawrence (Arthur) [Larry] (*b* Ridley Park, PA, 25 Feb 1931). Writer. He was educated at Yale University (BA 1952, PhD 1963), where he taught from 1960 to 1967. He then joined the faculty of the University of Wisconsin, becoming associate professor in 1970, and in 1976 he was appointed to the faculty of the University of Illinois. Gushee's principal research interests are medieval music and jazz. His writings on jazz have included a number of contributions to the *Jazz Review* and a detailed review of albums by Charles Mingus (*Jazz: a Quarterly of American Music*, no.1 (1958), 55). In the 1980s, after extensive archival research in New Orleans and elsewhere, he published biographical articles on Jelly Roll Morton (*Sv*, no.95 (1981), 164; no.98 (1981–2), 56; no.127 (1986), 11). In these Gushee has brought to the subject the type of rigorous attention to detail that is expected in classical musicological studies but has not been apparent in jazz; his work should serve as a model to future scholars.

PAULA MORGAN/R

Gustafsson, Rune (Urban) (*b* Göteborg, Sweden, 25 Aug 1933). Swedish electric guitarist. After playing in Bert Dahlander's quartet in Göteborg (1952–4) and working with the clarinetist Putte Wickman (1954–6, 1957–9) he joined the orchestra of Arne Domnérus, with whom he made recordings from 1959 into the 1980s. He recorded in a duo with Jan Johansson (1961) and in groups led by Johansson (1964, 1968) and became much sought after as a studio musician for both jazz and popular music. Later he recorded as a leader (*Move*, 1977, Sonet 2601) and in Zoot Sims's trio (1984). He was among the first Swedish jazz guitarists to use modern instrumental techniques such as those of Jimmy Raney and Tal Farlow.

BIBLIOGRAPHY

FeatherE
E. Kjellberg: "Gustafsson, Rune," *Sohlmans musiklexikon* (Stockholm, 1948–52, rev. and enlarged 2/1975–9 ed. H. Åstrand)
A. Westin: "Blev gitarrist av en slump" [Became a guitarist by chance], *Orkester journalen*, xlvi (1978), Feb, 5

ERIK KJELLBERG

Gutbucket. In jazz argot, an unrestrained or earthy manner of playing. The term originated from the name of the bucket used in low-class saloons and barrelhouses to catch the drippings, or "gutterings," from the barrels.

Guy, Barry (John) (*b* London, 22 April 1947). English double bass player and composer. He studied composition with Graham Collier and attended the Guildhall School of Music in London. He became associated with a group of avant-garde musicians in London that included John Stevens, Evan Parker, Derek Bailey, and Tony Oxley, and was a member of the Spontaneous Music Ensemble (1967–70). In 1967 he formed the group Amalgam with Trevor Watts and Paul Rutherford to perform an eclectic music that mixes jazz, rock, folk, and improvisation. He played regularly in Howard Riley's trio (1969–79) and in Iskra 1903, a trio formed in 1970 with Bailey and Rutherford. In 1970 he formed the London Jazz Composers Orchestra; he later became director of this ensemble and continued to work with it into the late 1980s. He began an association with Oxley in 1971, and has also recorded as a member of Barre Phillips's group and in a duo with Peter Kowald, and worked in a duo, a trio, and quartets with Parker from 1981. He has written many compositions, some of which involve improvisation, such as *Ode* (1970–72) and a series of pieces called *Statement* (nos.V–IX of which (1976) are for solo double bass). He has also performed in contemporary-music ensembles, chamber orchestras, and groups specializing in Baroque music. Guy's innovative approach to improvised playing parallels to some degree the developments initiated by Fernando Grillo in Italy. He has, in particular, explored the use of electronic modification and amplification to create and project a great variety of timbres.

SELECTED RECORDINGS

As unaccompanied soloist: *Statements* (1976, Incus 22)
As leader: *Ode* (1972, Incus 6–7)
As sideman: H. Riley: *Discussions* (1967, Opportunity 2499); T. Oxley: *Ichnos* (1969–70, RCA SF8215); B. Phillips: *For All it Is* (1971, Japo 60003); H. Riley: *Flight* (1971, Turtle 301); London Jazz Composers Orchestra: *Stringer* (1980, FMP SAJ41)

BIBLIOGRAPHY

L. East: "Barry Guy," *Music and Musicians*, xx/15 (1971), 7
I. Carr: *Music Outside: Contemporary Jazz in Britain* (London, 1973)
K. Ansell: "Barry Guy: a Most Ingenious Paradox," *The Wire*, no.8 (1984), 20

ROGER T. DEAN

Guy, Fred (*b* Burkesville, GA, 23 May 1897; *d* Chicago, 22 Nov 1971). Banjoist and guitarist. He grew up in New York and played banjo in various bands, then in 1925 joined Duke Ellington, with whom he spent the remainder of his musical career (for illustration *see* Bands, fig.3). He changed to guitar in 1934, and received tuition from Eddie Lang. At first his playing was an integral part of Ellington's rhythm section, and his steady tempos were an asset in a section where more than one player tried to pull ahead in fast numbers. From the late 1930s, however, the importance of his role diminished, and from 1940, when Jimmy Blanton joined the band, Guy's contribution was rarely crucial. When he retired from music in 1949, to work as manager of a ballroom in Chicago, Ellington did not replace him.

SELECTED RECORDINGS

(all as sideman with D. Ellington)

Red Hot Band (1927, Voc. 1153); Echoes of the Jungle (1931, Vic. 22743); The sergeant was shy (1939, Col. 35214); Sentimental Lady, first issued on *Duke Ellington and his Orchestra*, ii (1943, Cir. [USA] 102)

BIBLIOGRAPHY

J. McDonough: "Reminiscing in Tempo: Guitarist Freddy Guy's Ellington Memories," *DB*, xxxvi/8 (1969), 16
D. Ellington: *Music is my Mistress* (Garden City, NY, 1973), 109

EDDIE LAMBERT

Guy, Joe [Joseph Luke] (*b* Birmingham, AL, 20 Sept 1920; *d* Birmingham, *c*1962). Trumpeter. He joined Teddy Hill's orchestra in the late 1930s, and from 1939 to 1940 was a principal soloist with Coleman Hawkins's big band. In 1941 he worked at Minton's Playhouse as leader of the house band, which included Thelonious Monk and Kenny Clarke; a number of private recordings of this group's performances were made. Guy joined Cootie Williams in 1942, and brought several tunes by Monk to the band's repertory, including *'Round about Midnight* and *Epistrophy* (composed with Clarke and recorded by Williams as *Fly Right*). From 1945 to 1947 he was Billie Holiday's lover and manager and performed on some of her recordings, but thereafter he ceased to be prominent in New York's musical life. Guy was an agile trumpeter whose full tone was influenced by the playing of Roy Eldridge; he is best remembered for his role in the creation of the bop style.

SELECTED RECORDINGS

As leader with H. L. Page: Rhythm-a-ning, Sweet Lorraine, first issued on *Trumpet Battle at Minton's* (1941, Xan. 107)
As sideman: C. Hawkins: Fine Dinner (1939, Bb 10523); Rocky Comfort (1940, OK 6284); C. Williams: Fly Right (Epistrophy), first issued on *Jazz Odyssey, iii: The Sound of Harlem* (1942, Col. C3L33); Jazz at the Philharmonic: Lady be Good (1945, Asch 4532–3); B. Holiday: Baby, I don't cry over you/I'll look around (1946, Decca 23957)

BIBLIOGRAPHY

FeatherE
B. Holiday and W. Dufty: *Lady Sings the Blues* (Garden City, NY, 1956/*R*1973) [incl. discography]

D. Morgenstern: Liner notes, *Trumpet Battle at Minton's* (Xan. 107, 1975)
D. Gillespie and A. Fraser: *To be, or not . . . to Bop: Memoirs* (Garden City, NY, 1979)

SCOTT DEVEAUX

Gwaltney, Tommy [Thomas O.] (*b* Norfolk, VA, 28 Feb 1921). Clarinetist and bandleader. He played clarinet in college jazz groups and, during his military service, in army bands; having suffered lung damage in the war he took up the vibraphone temporarily. In 1946–7 he played in New York with Charlie Byrd (a friend from his home town) in a group led by Sol Yaged. From 1951 to 1955 he lived in Norfolk, working for his family's business and playing infrequently. He joined Bobby Hackett in 1956, and played vibraphone, soprano saxophone, and clarinet on the album *Gotham Jazz Scene* (1957, Cap. T857). He later worked with Billy Butterfield (1958–9), again with Byrd (1962–3), and with his own groups (from 1959). In January 1965 he opened a jazz club, Blues Alley, in Washington; he worked there regularly with his own group, which included Steve Jordan. Gwaltney organized and promoted jazz festivals at Virginia Beach (1959–61, 1965), and performed and recorded under several leaders at the Manassas (Virginia) Jazz Festival (1966–73).

BIBLIOGRAPHY

Feather '60s
G. W. Kay: "Tommy Gwaltney: Musician with a Dream Come True," *IM*, lxv/3 (1966), 10

Gyllene Cirkeln. Nightclub in Stockholm; *see* NIGHTCLUBS AND OTHER VENUES.

H

Haas, Eddie [Edgar Otto] **de** (*b* Bandoeng, Dutch East Indies [now Bandung, Java, Indonesia], 21 Feb 1930). Dutch double bass player. He studied guitar from 1941, played Hawaiian music in Java during the Japanese occupation, and heard jazz on the radio of the Allied Forces. He moved in 1947 to the Netherlands and in 1949 took up the double bass, which he played professionally with Pia Beck by the following year. He toured Germany, Switzerland, and Denmark with Wallace Bishop (1952–3) and Bill Coleman (1952), recorded with Coleman in Paris (1953), and performed and recorded with Chet Baker (1955–6). In 1957 he emigrated to the USA and worked with Terry Gibbs, Blossom Dearie, Miles Davis, and Bernard Peiffer. Later he played with Benny Goodman, Kai Winding (with whom he recorded in 1958), Toshiko Akiyoshi, and Kenny Burrell and Roy Haynes (both 1959–61), toured with Gene Krupa (1964–5), and played with the Dukes of Dixieland (1966–7). From 1968 he worked as a freelance in Chicago with Sonny Stitt, Milt Jackson, Dexter Gordon, Lee Konitz, Al Cohn, Blue Mitchell, Billy Taylor (ii), Joe Venuti, and Teddy Wilson. He led a trio and a quintet from 1985. Haas plays with a boisterous yet precise sense of rhythm and produces a rich, even tone throughout the range of his instrument.

SELECTED RECORDINGS

As sideman: P. Beck: The Flight of the Bumble Bee/Beat me Pia! Eight to the Bar (1951, Phi. 17035); D. Amram: *Dave Amram Quintet* (1955, Swing 33355); C. Connor: *Chris in Person* (1959, Atl. 8040); R. Haynes: *Just us* (1960, NewJ 8245)

BIBLIOGRAPHY

FeatherE; *Feather '60s*

J. L. Ginibre and P. Carles: "Dictionnaire de la contrebasse," *Jm*, no.166 (1969), 36

JOHN VOIGT

Habart, Ladislav (*b* Svatonovice u Pisku, nr Trutnov, Bohemia, 26 June 1914). Bohemian clarinetist, tenor saxophonist, and bandleader. He studied violin from the age of six, formed a school band in Tabor, and accompanied silent films for 15 years. He formed another school band in Prague, then joined Jan Šima's Gramoklub Orchestra as an alto saxophonist and clarinetist. He recorded with the singer E. F. Burian from 1936, played in the Blue Music Orchestra with Kamil Behounek, and worked with Karel Vlach from 1938. He formed a big band in 1945 that played highly adventurous arrangements by Alex Fried. From 1949 he worked with various groups and from 1964 toured Finland, Poland, Austria, Germany, Canada, and Colombia. Habart's style is well represented by his recording of Irving Berlin's *Alexander's Ragtime Band* (1945, issued on *Česky Jazz, 1920–1960*, *c*1913–1959, Sup. DV101778H).

GERHARD CONRAD

Hackett, Bobby [Robert Leo] (*b* Providence, RI, 31 Jan 1915; *d* Chatham, MA, 7 June 1976). Cornetist and bandleader. He was originally a ukulele player, and graduated to guitar before specializing on cornet. After playing in local bands in Providence he worked in a trio in Boston with Pee Wee Russell and Teddy Roy (1933). He led his own band in 1936 and the following year moved to New York and played with Joe Marsala. Hackett led another group at Nick's (1938) and a big band at the Famous Door (1939), and also took part as a freelance in numerous recording sessions. He worked briefly in Glenn Miller's orchestra (1941–2), playing guitar and cornet, then took a job as a staff musician at NBC. From 1944 to 1946 he was a member of the Casa Loma Orchestra and thereafter worked on the staff of ABC, though during the 1950s he continued to play in clubs and lead his own groups, notably at the Henry Hudson Hotel (1956–7). Later he played with Benny Goodman (1962–3) and made tours of Europe with Tony Bennett (1965, 1966) and of Japan with George Wein (1971). He continued to perform regularly until shortly before his death.

Hackett was a supremely melodic jazz improviser whose cornet tone was glorious in all registers. Because much of his life was spent playing in clubs with small bands he was too readily described as a dixieland stylist; in fact, his sophisticated phrasing and subtle use of harmonies enabled him to fit into many types of jazz ensemble. He was an individualist whose inspiration came from the work of two dissimilar players, Louis Armstrong and Bix Beiderbecke. His skill at improvising attractive melodies is apparent in his solo on *String of Pearls*, recorded with Miller in 1941.

Hackett's son Ernie Hackett (*b* New York, *c*1952) played drums in New York with leading dixieland and swing musicians during the late 1970s.

For illustration *see* Teagarden.

SELECTED RECORDINGS

As leader: Embraceable You (1939, Voc./OK 4877); *Gotham Jazz Scene* (1957, Cap. T857)

As sideman: G. Miller: String of Pearls (1941, Bb 11382); M. Mole: I must have that man (1944, Com. 620); J. Teagarden: If I could be with you (1945, V-disc 587)

BIBLIOGRAPHY
P. Harris: "All Schools Dig Bobby Hackett," *DB*, xviii/3 (1951), 1
A. Napoleon: "A Conversation with Bobby Hackett," *JJ*, xxvi/1 (1973), 2
W. Balliett: "More Ingredients," *Alex Wilder and his Friends* (Boston, 1974) [colln of previously pubd articles], 67
R. D. Johnson: "Talking to Hackett," *MR*, iii/8 (1976), 6
M. Jones: "Hackett: Beauty in Brass," *MM*, li (19 June 1976), 33
W. W. Vaché, Sr.: "The Jazz Philosophy of Bobby Hackett," *MR*, xii/8 (1985), 1

JOHN CHILTON

Haden, Charlie [Charles Edward] (*b* Shenandoah, IA, 6 Aug 1937). Double bass player. He first played in Los Angeles with Art Pepper (1957), Paul Bley (1957–9), and Hampton Hawes (1958–9), then in 1959 traveled to New York with Ornette Coleman. He became a member of Denny Zeitlin's trio and worked with, among others, Archie Shepp. Haden recorded with Coleman in 1966 and the following year rejoined his group and also began an association with Keith Jarrett. Although he has performed principally as a sideman, he won critical attention in 1969 with his own album *Liberation Music Orchestra*, which consisted of a number of revolutionary and freedom songs, including Haden's own composition *Song for Chè*. Around the same time he also played with Carla Bley and the Jazz Composer's Orchestra. In 1976, with Don Cherry, Dewey Redman, and Ed Blackwell (all former sidemen with Coleman), Haden formed the group Old and New Dreams, and the same year he recorded an outstanding series of duets with various musicians, which were issued on two albums. Haden has continued to perform in the 1980s, and in 1982 recorded with a new Liberation Music Orchestra made up of members of Carla Bley's group and Old and New Dreams; the band toured the USA into the mid-1980s.

Haden has a large, warm tone, the subtle vibrato, richness, and manipulations of which are central elements in his improvisational vocabulary. In contrast to most jazz double bass players of his period, Haden is concerned with simplicity and traditional conceptions of accompaniment rather than weaving intricate underpinnings and producing horn-like solos. Haden was the perfect bass player for Coleman because he instantaneously aligned himself with the shifting directions and continuous modulations that typified Coleman's freely improvised lines; his accompaniments unified the improvisations of the saxophonist and helped the ensemble to swing, something that the horn lines could not always do by themselves.

For illustration *see* Jazz (i), fig.7.

SELECTED RECORDINGS

Duos: with A. Coltrane, K. Jarrett, O. Coleman, and P. Motian: *Closeness* (1976, A&M Hor. 710); with D. Cherry, H. Hawes, O. Coleman, and A. Shepp: *The Golden Number* (1976, A&M Hor. 727)

As leader: *Liberation Music Orchestra* (1969, Imp. 9183), incl. Song for Chè; *The Ballad of the Fallen* (1982, ECM 1248)

As sideman: O. Coleman: *The Shape of Jazz to Come* (1959, Atl. 1317); *Change of the Century* (1959, Atl. 1327); K. Jarrett: *The Mourning of a Star* (1971, Atl. 1596); *Backhand* (1974, Imp. 9305); O. Coleman: *Soapsuds* (1977, AH 6); Old and New Dreams: *Old and New Dreams* (1979, ECM 1154); *Playing* (1980, ECM 1205)

BIBLIOGRAPHY
D. Morgenstern: "Charlie Haden: From Hillbilly to Avant Garde: a Rocky Road," *DB*, xxxiv/5 (1967), 20
B. Palmer: "Charlie Haden's Creed," *DB*, xxxix/13 (1972), 16
M. Zipkin: "Charlie Haden: Struggling Idealist," *DB*, xlv/13 (1978), 27
J. Gicking: *Charlie Haden's Discography* (New York, 1979)
"Charlie Haden," *SJ*, xxxiv/7 (1980), 162 [discography]
B. McRae: "Avant Courier: Charlie Haden," *JJI*, xxxvii/8 (1984), 8
G. Lock: "Viva la humans!," *The Wire*, no.19 (1985), 36
H. Mandel: "Charlie Haden's Search for Freedom," *DB*, liv/9 (1987), 20 [incl. discography]

MARK C. GRIDLEY/R

Hadi, Shafi [Porter, Curtis] (*b* Philadelphia, 21 Sept 1929). Tenor and alto saxophonist. He played saxophone in rhythm-and-blues groups and studied composition at Howard University and the University of Detroit. From 1956 to 1958 and again in 1959 he played with Charles Mingus, with whom he recorded several albums (including *The Clown*, 1957, Atl. 1260) and around the spring of 1958 collaborated on the soundtrack to John Cassavetes's film *Shadows* (1961).

BIBLIOGRAPHY
FeatherE
B. Cross: "Shafi Hadi," *DB*, xxx/9 (1963), 15

Hafer, Dick [John Richard] (*b* Wyomissing, nr Reading, PA, 29 May 1927). Tenor saxophonist. He toured with Charlie Barnet, with whom he recorded his first solo, on *Overtime* (1949, Cap. F15848). After touring and recording with Claude Thornhill (1950–51) he joined Woody Herman (August 1951). He remained with the band until August 1955, recording regularly; his solo on *Wild Apple Honey* (from the album *The Woody Herman Band*, 1954, Cap. T560) is notable for its cool style, reminiscent of the playing of Herman's earlier saxophone section the Four Brothers. Hafer then worked as a freelance in and around New York, performing with Tex Beneke (1955), Bobby Hackett (1957–8), Nat Pierce, and Elliot Lawrence (1958–60), and recording with Ruby Braff (1957) and Urbie Green (1958). Later he worked with Benny Goodman (1962) and recorded with Johnny Hartman (1964); he may be heard playing various woodwind instruments on Charles Mingus's album *Town Hall Concert* (1962, UA 15024).

BIBLIOGRAPHY
FeatherE; *Feather '60s*
A. Morgan: "Woody's Tenors," *JM*, vi (1960–61), no.7, p.4; no.8, p.13; no.12, p.9

DAVE GELLY

Hagemann(-Larsen), Henry (*b* Copenhagen, 6 Sept 1910; *d* Copenhagen, 5 April 1964). Danish tenor saxophonist. He played in dance bands from 1931, then performed and recorded with Leo Mathisen (1936–44), Kai Ewans (1939–43), the musicians' collective Matadorerne (1940–42), and others. He led his own bands from 1944 to 1949 and made several recordings with these and with various studio groups (1941–4, including *Sweet Georgia Brown*, 1941, Odeon D472, and *Paintin'*, 1944, Imperial 1023). Later he worked again as a dance musician. Hagemann was the foremost Danish tenor saxophonist of the early 1940s.

ERIK WIEDEMANN

Haggart, Bob [Robert Sherwood] (*b* New York, 13 March 1914). Double bass player, composer, and arranger. As a teenager he played guitar, and changed to double bass at the age of 17. He was the only musician who had not formerly played with Ben Pollack to become a corporate member of Bob Crosby's band (1935), and his distinctive compositions and arrangements contributed greatly to the band's success. His duo for drums and double bass, *The Big Noise from Winnetka*, remains highly popular, and his playing earned him considerable success in polls organized by *Down Beat* and *Metronome* magazines. He also wrote a tutor for double bass which has become a standard text. After leaving Crosby in 1942 Haggart played for radio and television and in recording studios, and continued to work as an arranger. He took part in sessions led by Louis Armstrong, Billie Holiday, Duke Ellington, and others, and also led a band with Yank Lawson. Crosby used this ensemble as the core of many of his groups, including the band that recorded Haggart's arrangement of *Porgy and Bess* (1958). Crosby's reunions, and performances and recordings with the Greats of Jazz, eventually resulted in the formation in 1968 of the WORLD'S GREATEST JAZZ BAND (led by Haggart and Lawson). After this group disbanded in 1978 Haggart continued to work with Lawson; he also led his own groups and participated in reunions of Crosby's band.

For illustration *see* CROSBY, BOB.

SELECTED RECORDINGS

As leader: with Y. Lawson: *Jelly Roll's Jazz* (1951, Decca 5368); of World's Greatest Jazz Band (with Y. Lawson): *World's Greatest Jazz Band plays Rogers and Hart* (1975, World Jazz 7)

RECORDED COMPOSITIONS

Selective list; all recorded by Bob Crosby for Decca with Haggart as sideman.

South Rampart Street Parade/Dogtown Blues (1937, 15038); The Big Noise from Winnetka (1938, 2208); What's New? (1938, 2205); My Inspiration (1938, 2209)

SELECTED ARRANGEMENTS

(all recorded by Bob Crosby with Haggart as sideman)

Savoy Blues (1936, Decca 1094); I'm Prayin' Humble (1938, Decca 2210); *Porgy and Bess* (1958, Dot 25193)

BIBLIOGRAPHY

J. Roberts: "Leader of the Band," *MM* (18 Dec 1971), 38
B. Korall: *The World's Greatest Jazz Band of Yank Lawson and Bob Haggart* (n.p. [Phoenix, AZ], 1973)
C. Huisking: "Jazz Musician an Artist on Canvas as Well," *Sarasota Herald-Tribune* (14 May 1982)
J. Chilton: "Bob Haggart," *Stomp Off, Let's Go! The Story of Bob Crosby's Bob Cats & Big Band* (London, 1983), 191
M. L. Hester: "The Multi-talented Bob Haggart," *MR*, xi/2 (1983), 8

For further recordings and bibliography *see* WORLD'S GREATEST JAZZ BAND.

BRIAN PEERLESS

Hahn, Jerry (Donald) (*b* Alma, NE, 21 Sept 1940). Guitarist. He studied at Wichita State University and first played professionally in Kansas. He moved in 1962 to San Francisco, where he played in hotel and studio bands. From 1964 he played electric guitar in a group led by John Handy, with which he performed at the Monterey (California) Jazz Festival in 1965 and 1966; the earlier performance may be heard in part on the album *John Handy*, Col. CS9262. He recorded as the leader of a quintet that also included Jack DeJohnette and Michael White (i) (1967), toured with the popular vocal group the Fifth Dimension (1968), and joined Gary Burton's group, with which he toured Europe, Japan, Canada, and the USA (1968–9); he also toured the USA and the Bahamas with the Jerry Hahn Brotherhood, which he formed in 1970. He was appointed a lecturer at Wichita State University in 1972 and continued to perform, leading a quartet, which recorded in 1973 (*Moses*, Fan. 9426). He was a regular contributor to the magazine *Guitar Player* from 1974 to 1978.

BIBLIOGRAPHY

Feather '60s; *Feather–Gitler '70s*
J. Crockett: "Jerry Hahn," *GP*, v/2 (1971), 28

Al Haig, 1950

Haig, Al(lan Warren) (*b* Newark, NJ, 22 July 1924; *d* New York, 16 Nov 1982). Pianist. He served in Coast Guard bands during 1942–4 and played in several clubs around Boston before joining Dizzy Gillespie's band in 1945. He became unusually active in clubs on 52nd Street, New York, playing in numerous small groups under many different leaders during the late 1940s. Though he continued to work regularly all over North America from the 1950s to the early 1970s, he made ever fewer recordings, and lapsed into an obscurity that contrasted markedly with his former place at the center of jazz. With the bop revival in the mid-1970s he resumed an active performing and recording career, playing in a style that retained its former qualities whilst embodying further developments.

Haig was among the first jazz pianists to blend the postwar innovations of bop into a consistent, personal style. His exceptional technique, besides allowing him to relax even when improvising at very fast tempos, gave him a flexibility and quickness of response that made him a fine accompanist to soloists as stylistically diverse as Stan Getz and Fats Navarro, though his associations with Gillespie and Charlie Parker were musically the most significant of his career. His many brief solos on recordings led by other musicians during the 1940s show the ability he acquired for concise expression; while unflaggingly inventive, they are usually understated, with sensitive rhythmic and harmonic nuances. Haig's later work is richer in texture and of greater emotional depth.

See also PIANO, §4; for further illustration *see* JAZZ (i), fig.6.

SELECTED RECORDINGS

As unaccompanied soloist: *Solitaire* (1976, Spot. 14)
As leader: Liza/Stars fell on Alabama (1950, NewJ 822); *Trio* (1954, Eso. 7); *Invitation* (1974, Spot. 4); *Chelsea Bridge* (1975, EW 8023)
As sideman: D. Gillespie: Salt Peanuts (1945, Guild 1003); Shaw 'Nuff (1945, Guild 1002); A Night in Tunisia/Anthropology (1946, Vic. 40-0132); D. Lambert: Gussie G (1946, Key. 657); J. Hardee: Prelude to a Kiss (1948, SiW 503); D. Lanphere: Go (1949, NewJ 812); W. Gray: Sweet Lorraine (1949, NewJ 828)

BIBLIOGRAPHY

A. Morgan: "Al Haig," *JM*, ii/8 (1956), 26
M. Harrison: "Al Haig," *JR*, iii/5 (1960), 22
——: "Al Haig," *Jazz Era: the 'Forties*, ed. S. Dance and others (London, 1961/*R*1985), 119
E. Edwards, Jr., G. I. Hall, and B. Korst: *Modern Jazz Piano* (Whittier, CA, 1965) [discography]
G. Hoefer: "Al Haig," *DB*, xxxii/22 (1965), 17
I. Gitler: *Jazz Masters of the Forties* (New York, 1966/*R*1983 with discography), 132
M. Gardner: "Al Haig," *JM*, no.186 (1970), 4 [interview]

H. Renaud: "Bebop Highlights," *Jh*, no.305 (1974), 18
J. Shaw: "The Reminiscences of Al Haig," *JJI*, xxxii (1979), no.3, p.4; no.4, p.17 [incl. discography]
M. Harrison: "Al Haig Meets the Master Saxes," *JF* [intl edn], no.67 (1980), 53
R. Horricks: "Another Case of Haig," *JJI*, xxxiv (1981), no.5, p.16; no.6, p.18
B. Case: "Al Haig," *Music and Musicians* (1982), Oct, 10
"Al Haig," *SJ*, xxxvii/1 (1983), 200 [discography]

MAX HARRISON/R

Hakim, Omar (I.) (*b* New York, *c*1959). Drummer. A graduate of the High School of Music and Art in New York, he played with Roy Ayers, Mike Mainieri, David Sanborn, George Benson, Gil Evans, and various pop and soul-music artists, before joining WEATHER REPORT, with which he toured and recorded from 1982 for about three years. He has also recorded with Urszula Dudziak (*c*1982), Kazumi Watanabe (1983), and John Scofield (*Electric Outlet*, 1984, Gram. 8405). (A. J. Liska: "On the Road with Weather Report," *DB*, xlix/10 (1982), 21)

Hakim, Sadik [Thornton, Argonne (Dense)] (*b* Duluth, MN, 15 July 1919; *d* New York, 20 June 1983). Pianist. He studied music with his grandfather, played in Duluth, then moved to Chicago; there he was heard by Ben Webster, who invited him to join his group in New York. He played with Webster from 1944 to 1945 and performed on portions of Charlie Parker's recording session for Savoy with Dizzy Gillespie (1945); he lived with Parker for a time. With Lester Young he toured from 1946 to 1948 and recorded *Jumpin' with Symphony Sid* (1947). In the 1950s he toured with James Moody (1951–4) and played with Buddy Tate's orchestra (1956–60). Around 1966 he moved to Montreal, where he played in nightclubs. He toured Europe for a year before playing in a trio at a festival in Duluth (1976) and returning to New York; he toured Japan in 1979–80. He used his given name until the late 1940s, when he adopted the Muslim name Sadik Hakim.

SELECTED RECORDINGS

As soloist: *Memories* (1978, Prog. 83)
As leader: with D. Jordan: *East and West of Jazz* (1962, CP 805); *Sadik Hakim Plays Duke Ellington* (1974, Radio Canada International 379); *Witches, Goblins, etc.* (1977, Ste. 1091)
As sideman: D. Gordon: Dexter's Deck (1945, Savoy 576); C. Parker: Thriving on a Riff (1945, Savoy 903); L. Young: Jumpin' with Symphony Sid (1947, Ala. 163); J. Moody: A Hundred Years from Today (1954, Prst. 881)

BIBLIOGRAPHY

S. Hakim: "The Charlie Parker KoKo Date," *JR*, ii/2 (1959), 11
M. Gardner: "Sadik Hakim," *Coda*, x/4 (1971), 2
L. Barnes and G. Gallagher: "Sadik Hakim Made Jazz History but Lives for the Future," *Music Scene*, no.288 (1976), 5
S. Hakim: "My Experiences with Bird and Prez," *JSN*, ii/1 (1980), 32
"Profile of Sadik Hakim, Jazz Pianist," *JSN*, ii/2 (1980–81), 30
J. Levenson: "Sadik Hakim," *DB*, xlix/4 (1982), 27 [incl. discography]

PAUL RINZLER

Hála, Kamil (*b* Most, Czechoslovakia, 1 Aug 1931). Czechoslovak pianist, composer, arranger, and bandleader. He played with the pianist Zdenek Barták, then formed an octet that performed at the festival in Sopot, Poland (1956). He toured Eastern Europe, Belgium, Japan, Burma, and India and worked as an arranger and pianist for the jazz orchestra of Radio Praha under Karel Krautgartner, whom he eventually replaced as its leader. With the orchestra he made several recordings, including the album *Jazzovy orchestr Česko Slovensko Rozhlasu řidi Kamil Hála* (1978–9, Sup. 11152370). Hála's best-known compositions include *TU 104*, *Kult jazzu*, and Concertino for Alto Saxophone.

GERHARD CONRAD

Halcox, Pat(rick John) (*b* London, 18 March 1930). English trumpeter. As a part-time musician he led his own bands (1950–54) and performed with other leaders, including Chris Barber (January 1953). He became professional in 1954 when he was invited to replace Ken Colyer in Barber's band, with which he has continued to perform (for illustration *see* BARBER, CHRIS). Halcox played on the soundtracks to several films, among them *Look Back in Anger* (1959) and *The Loneliness of the Long-distance Runner* (1962), and has worked with such visiting American musicians as Don Ewell; his playing may be heard on Ewell's *Don Ewell Quintet* (1971, Jlgy J69). He led his own bands in the summers of 1980 to 1985.

BIBLIOGRAPHY

I. McLean: "Pat Halcox," *Jazz News*, v/28 (1961), 9
B. Matthew: *Trad Mad* (London, 1962)
B. Kinnell: "The Pat Halcox All Stars," *7th Avenue* (Plant Life 002, 1978) [liner notes]
D. Fairweather: "Halcox, Pat," in I. Carr, D. Fairweather, and B. Priestley: *Jazz: the Essential Companion* (London, 1987)

DEREK COLLER

Halcyon. Record company and label established in the 1970s by MARIAN MCPARTLAND.

Half-valve [cocked-valve]. A technique used by players of valved brass instruments, involving the opening of one or more valves to less than the full extent by depressing the controlling piston or key to half or two-thirds of its full depth. The partial opening of the valve allows a restricted column of air to pass through and produces a note of uncertain pitch, having a striking nasal timbre; complex adjustments to the embouchure combined with the gradual opening of the valve or valves to the full extent facilitate the production of various effects, including the GLISS, the SHAKE, other trills, and vibrato.

The principal exponent of half-valving is the cornetist Rex Stewart. Notable among many examples of his use of the technique are his solos on Duke Ellington's *Boy Meets Horn* (1938, Bruns. 8306) and *Low Cotton* (1939, Swing 203). (For examples of half-valving in Louis Armstrong's playing *see* GLISS, §2(e).) Among younger players Lester Bowie has employed the technique for humorous effect, as on the title track of his album *The Great Pretender* (1981, ECM 1209).

BIBLIOGRAPHY

A. Napoleon: "The Music Goes Down and Around: (a Case of Mistaken Identity)," *Sv*, no.37 (1971), 18
M. Laplace: "La trompette et le cornet dans le jazz et la musique populaire," pt vi, *Brass Bulletin*, no.47 (1984), 39

BARRY KERNFELD

Hall. Family of musicians.

(1) Edward Hall(, Sr.) (*b* Reserve, LA, *c*1875; *d* New Orleans). Clarinetist. He is known to have performed with the Onward Brass Band in Reserve (not to be confused with the New Orleans band of the same name), but he played only clarinet, not (as in some published accounts) cornet. He was the father of eight children, including five sons who became professional musicians. Apart from the four described below, Edward Hall, Jr. (*b* Reserve, 1905), a tuba player, was a member of a dance orchestra in Reserve led by Marshall Lawrence. Although Edward Hall, Sr., encouraged his family's music-making activities, there was not, as some records suggest, a family band.

(2) Robert Hall (*b* Reserve, LA, 29 Jan 1899). Clarinetist and saxophonist, son of (1) Edward Hall. He began on guitar, but soon took up E♭ clarinet and later learned alto, tenor, and baritone saxophone. Although early published accounts suggest a later birthdate, by 1920 Hall had joined the band led by the cornetist Hypolite Charles (replacing Sam Dutrey). He then worked with the cornetist and trumpeter Louis Dumaine and with Gus Metcalfe's orchestra before playing tenor saxophone in the Original Tuxedo Orchestra under the leadership first of the trombonist William "Baba" Ridgley and then Papa Celestin (with whom he recorded in 1927). After leaving Celestin (by 1928) Hall worked as a freelance in New Orleans. He retired from music in 1941.

(3) Edmond Hall (*b* New Orleans, 15 May 1901; *d* Boston, 11 Feb 1967). Clarinetist, son of (1) Edward Hall. He served his apprenticeship with various bands around New Orleans, including that of Buddy Petit (1921–3), before moving north in 1928 to play with big swing orchestras on both clarinet and baritone saxophone. From 1929 to 1935 he was with Claude Hopkins's band, but began in 1939 working in small groups, including Teddy Wilson's sextet (1941–4). Hall was regarded well enough by Duke Ellington in 1942 to be selected for his band as the replacement for Barney Bigard, but he turned down the opportunity, probably because of the uncertainties of wartime travel. He came to widespread attention in 1944 when he began a long engagement at both Café Society clubs in New York, and at about the same time he began recording with Eddie Condon. He became, after Pee Wee Russell, the most highly regarded of the dixieland clarinetists, although he always saw himself as more of a swing player in the mold of Benny Goodman than a disciple of such New Orleans musicians as Johnny Dodds. In 1950 he joined the house band at Condon's club, and in 1955 became a member of Louis Armstrong's All Stars. He played as a freelance musician from 1958 until his death.

Hall had an individual style, characterized by insistent drive and a broad, fast terminal vibrato, that was instantly recognizable. He made considerable use of vocal tone. He is heard to advantage in a series of recordings made in 1941 with Meade "Lux" Lewis on celeste, Charlie Christian (making an unusual contribution on acoustic guitar), and Israel Crosby; these show Hall playing in his preferred style, and the resemblance of the quartet to Goodman's small groups with Christian is not accidental. As a member of the All Stars, Hall supplied energy and drive to a band that was becoming increasingly a commercial backdrop for Armstrong's singing.

Oral history material in *LNT*.

For further illustration *see* WILSON, TEDDY.

SELECTED RECORDINGS

As leader: Profoundly Blue (1941, BN 17); Jammin' in Four (1941, BN 18)

As sideman: F. Newton: You showed me the way (1937, Var. 518); E. Condon: I'll build a stairway to paradise (1945, Decca 23433); *Bixieland* (1955, Col. CL719), incl. At the Jazz Band Ball

BIBLIOGRAPHY

M. Jones: "The Edmond Hall Story," *MM*, xxxi (14 April 1956), 8; (21 April 1956), 14; (28 April 1956), 14; repr. in *Talking Jazz* (London, 1987), 13

——: "Ghana Plans Didn't Work," *MM*, xxxv (2 Jan 1960), 11

J. Postgate: "The Happy Jazz of Edmond Hall," *JM*, x/5 (1964), 11

Obituary, *DB*, xxxiv/6 (1967), 13

B. McRae: "Edmond Hall," *JJ*, xxiii/12 (1970), 24

G. M. Erskine: "Four New Orleans Clarinetists: Sidney Arodin, Irving Fazola, Edmond Hall, Raymond Burke," *SL*, xxvii (1975), aut., 14

M. Selchow and K. Lohmann: *Edmond Hall: a Discography* (Westoverledingen and Göttingen, Germany, 1981)

(4) Clarence Hall (*b* Reserve, LA, 1903; *d* New Orleans, after 1961). Saxophonist, son of (1) Edward Hall. He is known to have played guitar, and then banjo, with Kid Thomas from 1915. Later he joined the nine-piece band in Baton Rouge,

Edmond Hall, 1950

Louisiana, led by the trumpeter Kid Augustin Victor, in which he performed on saxophone. After he moved to New Orleans in 1926 his place in the band was taken by his brother (5) Herb Hall, and by the following year he was a member of Papa Celestin's Original Tuxedo Orchestra. He was still with Celestin in 1931, and thereafter his career included a long association (as a tenor saxophonist) with the trumpeter Dave Bartholomew, with whom he made numerous rhythm-and-blues recordings (1947–61).

(5) Herb(ie) [Herbert L.] **Hall** (*b* Reserve, LA, 28 March 1907). Clarinetist, son of (1) Edward Hall. After playing banjo with the Niles Jazz Band in the early 1920s he took up clarinet and alto saxophone, and in 1926 replaced his brother (4) Clarence Hall in Kid Augustin Victor's band in Baton Rouge, Louisiana. The following year he moved to New Orleans and, after a period with Sidney Desvigne, joined Don Albert in 1929. He moved with Albert to San Antonio, and remained in the band until 1937, when he left to play in Pittsburgh, Cincinnati, and Cleveland; he was with Albert's group again between 1938 and 1940, and stayed in San Antonio until 1945 before going north. After playing in Philadelphia and New York with various bands Hall worked with Doc Cheatham in Boston (1955) and then toured Europe with Sammy Price (1955–6). He then returned to New York and became associated particularly with Jimmy Ryan's and Eddie Condon's clubs. He appeared in Toronto with Don Ewell in the 1960s, and during the 1970s and early 1980s toured widely with Bob Greene's World of Jelly Roll, as well as making two tours of Europe as a soloist.

Hall's clarinet tone is more pure and his style more lyrical than that of his brother (3) Edmond Hall; although he also lacks Edmond's fire, he displays a considerable command of dynamics and melodic invention. His work is heard to best effect in the context of a small group, notably on the album *In New Orleans* (1980, New Orleans 7209), which he recorded in a quartet with Ewell.

BIBLIOGRAPHY

F. S. Driggs: "A Biography of Herbert Hall," *JJ*, xi/1 (1958), 10 [incl. discography]
A. Barrell: "Four Brothers: Halls of Fame," *Fn*, x/6 (1979), 4
C. Wilson: "Herb Hall," *Fn*, xii/3 (1981), 4
P. Vacher: "Hallmarks," *JJI*, xxxiv/8 (1981), 9
L. Brown: "Herb Hall," *Sv*, no.113 (1984), 172

ALYN SHIPTON, CLIVE WILSON (1, 2, 4, 5)
JAMES LINCOLN COLLIER (3)

Hall, Adelaide (*b* New York, 20 Oct *c*1904). British singer of American birth. She began performing in shows and revues in the 1920s. She made recordings with Duke Ellington (1927, 1932) and as a leader (from 1928), and in the 1930s she was accompanied in the USA by various musicians, among them Art Tatum, Joe Turner (i), and Bernard Addison. She toured Europe and recorded with Turner in London (1931) and with Willie Lewis's orchestra in France (1936), where she also worked with Ray Ventura. She married and became a British citizen, settling in London in 1938; in the same year she made a number of recordings with Fats Waller. She sang in her own series on radio and again recorded as a leader (*c*1969); in 1974 she performed at the memorial service for Ellington at the church of St. Martin-in-the-Fields, London. She continued touring widely into the 1980s. Hall is best known for her expressive, wordless singing on *Creole Love Call*, which she recorded with Ellington in 1927.

Oral history material in *CtY*.

SELECTED RECORDINGS

As leader: I must have that man/Baby (1932, Bruns. 6518); *That Wonderful Adelaide Hall* (*c*1969, Col. SCX6422)
As sideman: D. Ellington: Creole Love Call (1927, Vic. 21137); The Blues I Love to Sing (1927, Vic. 21490)

BIBLIOGRAPHY

ChiltonW
C. Ellis: "Adelaide Hall: the Singing Blackbird," *Sv*, no.31 (1970), 8
D. Stewart-Baxter: "Blues and Views," *JJ*, xxiv/2 (1971), 12
H. Rye: "Visiting Firemen, 10(a): Adelaide Hall, Joe Turner, and Francis J. Carter," *Sv*, no.114 (1984), 211

SCOTT FREDRICKSON

Hall, Al(fred Wesley) (*b* Jacksonville, FL, 18 March 1915; *d* New York, 18 Jan 1988). Double bass player. Educated in Philadelphia, he first played cello and tuba, but concentrated on double bass from 1932. By 1937 he was in New York, where he performed and recorded with the trumpeter and singer Billy Hicks, both under Hicks's name and accompanying Midge Williams. He began recording with Teddy Wilson in 1938 and was later a member of his big band (1939–40) and sextet; Hall's playing at this time resembled that of Walter Page and Milt Hinton, both of whom had recorded with Wilson in the late 1930s. From 1942 to 1944 Hall performed in the trios of Ellis Larkins and Mary Lou Williams, and thereafter combined playing in clubs with work in Broadway theaters and as a studio musician. He made a number of recordings that combined elements of swing and bop, notably with Clyde Hart (1945) and Kenny Clarke (1946). At around the same time he established his own record label, Wax, for which he made several recordings as a leader; the label was later purchased by Atlantic. Hall's association with Erroll Garner began in 1945 and lasted intermittently until 1963. He also worked as a freelance from 1950, and appeared with such musicians as Benny Goodman (in Belgium, 1966), Tiny Grimes (1971), and Alberta Hunter (1977–8). In the mid-1980s Hall played regularly with Doc Cheatham at Sweet Basil in New York.

Oral history material in *NjR* (JOHP).

For illustration *see* NIGHTCLUBS AND OTHER VENUES, fig.5.

SELECTED RECORDINGS

As sideman: T. Wilson: Rosetta (1941, Col. 36632); K. Clarke: Oop-bop Sh-bam (1946, Swing 224); Rue Chaptal (Royal Roost) (1946, Swing 244)

BIBLIOGRAPHY

ChiltonW; *FeatherE*
J. Doran: *Erroll Garner: the Most Happy Piano* (Metuchen, NJ, and London, 1985), 79

ALYN SHIPTON

Hall, Jim [James Stanley] (*b* Buffalo, 4 Dec 1930). Guitarist. He began playing professionally in Cleveland while still in his teens. He attended the Cleveland Institute of Music (BM 1955) and then moved to Los Angeles, where he studied classical guitar with Vincente Gomez and joined Chico Hamilton's quintet. From 1956 to 1959 he played with the Jimmy Giuffre Three, an experience that led to his later preference for challenging arrangements and interactive improvisation in duos and trios. He also worked with Ben Webster (1959), Bill Evans (ii) (1959), Paul Desmond (1959–65), Lee Konitz (1960–61), Sonny Rollins (1961–2, 1964), and Art Farmer (1963–4). In 1965 he retired briefly to recover from alcoholism. After a secure but uncreative period performing in New York for "The Merv Griffin Show" on television, Hall returned to playing jazz full time and produced some memorable duo recordings with Evans (1966) and Ron Carter (1972). The album *Jim Hall Live!* (1975, with Don Thompson and Terry Clarke) is an example of his most fertile work: the individuality of his melodies and his great improvisational ability make him the rival of Django Reinhardt and Charlie Christian. His compositional approach to improvisation involves motivic development, which lends a strong characteristic to his passionate and often blues-laced playing. Hall has also recorded with George Shearing and the violinist Itzhak Perlman (both 1981), and has continued his association with Carter (1984–5). A volume of transcriptions of his performances has been published (*Jim Hall: Jazz Improvisation*, Tokyo, 1980).

SELECTED RECORDINGS

Duos: with B. Evans: *Intermodulation* (1966, Verve 68655); with R. Carter: *Alone Together* (1972, Mlst. 9045); with G. Shearing: *First Edition* (1981, Conc. 177)
As leader: *Concierto* (1975, CTI 6060); *Jim Hall Live!* (1975, A&M Hor. 705); *Circles* (1981, Conc. 161)
As sideman: J. Giuffre: *Seven Pieces* (1959, Verve 8307); S. Rollins: *The Bridge* (1962, RCA LSP2527); A. Farmer: *Live at the Half Note* (1963, Atl. 1421); P. Desmond: *Glad to be Unhappy* (1963–4, RCA LSP3407)

BIBLIOGRAPHY

B. Coss: "The Musical Philosophy of Jim Hall: Form, Function, Fulfillment," *DB*, xxix/20 (1962), 24
"Jim Hall," *SJ*, xxix/15 (1975), 264 [discography]
C. Berg: "Jim Hall: the Slow, Refined Triumph of Class," *DB*, xliii/21 (1976), 14 [incl. discography]
W. Balliett: "The Answer is Yes," *Improvising: Sixteen Jazz Musicians and their Art* (New York, 1977) [colln of previously pubd articles], 217
J. Hall and R. Mitchell: Liner notes, *Jim Hall/Red Mitchell* (AH 5, 1979) [incl. transcrs., discography]
J. Ferguson and A. Berle: "Jim Hall: Jazz Guitar Elegance," *GP*, xvii/5 (1983), 62
N. Mongan: *The History of the Guitar in Jazz* (New York, London, and Sydney, 1983) [incl. transcrs., discography], 173
B. Milkowski: "Jim Hall: New Notes from a Guitar Master," *DB*, liii/10 (1986), 23 [incl. discography]

JIM FERGUSON

Hall, Minor [Ram] (*b* Sellers, LA, 2 March 1897; *d* Sawtelle, CA, 16 Oct 1959). Drummer, brother of Tubby Hall. He began by deputizing for his brother in New Orleans groups, including those of Kid Ory and Sidney Bechet. He moved to Chicago in 1918 and replaced Tubby in Lawrence Duhé's band, which played in San Francisco in 1921, under King Oliver's leadership. Hall left Oliver after two months and returned to Chicago, where he later played with Jimmie Noone in 1926. Again on the West Coast, from 1927 to 1932 he worked with Mutt Carey's Jeffersonians who occasionally played in Hollywood films. He rejoined Kid Ory in 1945 and worked with him until 1956, appearing as a member of the band in the film *Tailgate Man from New Orleans* (1956). Hall made his first recordings in 1945, by which time he was using a mixture of traditional and swing drumming techniques. Although his solos were often marred by gimmickry, his accompaniments were subdued, methodical, and rhythmic; the most characteristic feature of his style is the strongly accented offbeat.

Oral history material in *LNT*.

SELECTED RECORDINGS

As sideman: K. Ory: Maryland my Maryland (1945, Crescent 3); L. Armstrong: Mahogany Hall Stomp (1946, Vic. 20-2088); K. Ory: 12th Street Rag (1949, Decca 9-11068); *Live at Club Hangover* (1953–4, Dawn Club 12013–14, 12016–17); *Kid Ory's Creole Jazz Band: 1955* (1954, Good Time Jazz 12008)

BIBLIOGRAPHY

ChiltonW

O. Keepnews: "Ory Rhythm," *Record Changer*, viii/1 (1949), 13

T. DENNIS BROWN

Hall, Skip [Archie] (*b* Portsmouth, VA, 27 Sept 1909; *d* Ottawa, Nov 1980). Arranger, pianist, and organist. He played in New York and in 1931–8 led a group in Cleveland. He worked as a freelance arranger from the late 1930s and between 1940 and 1944 wrote several arrangements for Jay McShann, including a version of *Cherokee* that was intended as a vehicle for Charlie Parker (then a member of McShann's orchestra) but never recorded, and *Sepian Bounce*, which was recorded in 1942 (Decca 4387); he also played piano on occasion with McShann's orchestra. He worked with Don Redman in 1941–2, and led a military band that was based in England. His long association with Buddy Tate began around 1948: he recorded as a sideman with Tate until 1968, was a member of his orchestra for five years from about 1950, and toured Europe with him in 1968. Over these two decades his principal instrument was organ and he is well represented as an organist and pianist on *Buddy Tate and his Celebrity Club Orchestra* (vol.i, 1954, BB 33006, incl. previously issued tracks). Besides his activities with Tate he recorded with Hot Lips Page (1949), as a leader (1949), and with Dicky Wells (1958–9) and Emmett Berry (1959), led his own trio (1955–6), and performed as a soloist (1958) and with George James (1963). He was a brother-in-law of Sy Oliver.

BIBLIOGRAPHY

ChiltonW; *FeatherE*

S. Dance: "Skip Hall and Eli Robinson," *JM*, iv/7 (1958), 27

I. Gitler: *Swing to Bop: an Oral History of the Transition in Jazz in the 1940s* (New York, and Oxford, England, 1985), 72

Hall, Tubby [Alfred] (*b* Sellers, LA, 12 Oct 1895; *d* Chicago, 13 May 1946). Drummer, brother of Minor Hall. He began his career in New Orleans with the Crescent Orchestra (1914), then played with the Eagle Band (1916), and the Silver Leaf Orchestra (1917). He moved to Chicago and joined Lawrence Duhé's band in 1918. After military service he rejoined the band, which was then led by King Oliver (1920). He played with Carroll Dickerson's orchestra, touring with it in 1924, and recording in 1927 (when Louis Armstrong was also a member). Hall played and recorded with Armstrong again in 1931–2 and with Jimmie Noone (1936, 1940). He led his own groups in 1935 and 1945–6. Hall's playing is barely audible on most of his recordings, but on the earliest he can be heard playing sparse choke-cymbal figures and occasional offbeat accents on the snare drum.

SELECTED RECORDINGS

As sideman with L. Armstrong: Chicago Breakdown (1927, Col. 36376); Alligator Crawl (1927, OK 8482); I'll be glad when you're dead, you rascal you (1931, OK 41504)

BIBLIOGRAPHY

ChiltonW

T. DENNIS BROWN

Hallberg, Bengt (*b* Göteborg, Sweden, 13 Sept 1932). Swedish pianist, composer, and arranger. He began to play piano professionally in his early teens and made his first trio recording at the age of 17. During the early 1950s he was the leading jazz pianist in Sweden; he played regularly with local orchestras in Göteborg and made numerous recordings with various international and Swedish all-star groups of which Lars Gullin, Arne Domnérus, Stan Getz, Quincy Jones, and Clifford Brown were members. His first long-playing recording with a trio was awarded a Gold Disc by *Orkester journalen* in 1957. After studying counterpoint and composition at the Royal Swedish Academy of Music (1954–7) his interests turned principally towards composing and arranging, especially for films, television, and stage productions. Nevertheless he continued to perform as a member of the Swedish Radio Big Band (1956–63) and the Radiojazzgruppen (from 1969). In the 1970s he was much sought after as a pianist, arranger, and composer; he performed as a soloist in George Russell's composition *Living Time* and worked with Domnérus and Ove Lind. He also made recordings with Domnérus and Karin Krog and in the early 1980s formed the Trio con Tromba with Jan Allan and Georg Riedel.

Oral history material in *SSsv*.

SELECTED RECORDINGS

Duos: with A. Domnérus: *Hypertoni* (1977, RCA PL40077), *Duets for Duke* (1978, Sonet 2618); with K. Krog: *A Song for you* (1977, Phon. 7512)

As leader: Lover Man (1950, Met. 134); Ablution (1952, Cupol 4654); Flying Saucer (1952, Met. 242); Zig-Zag (1952, Met. 247); On with the Dance (1953, Musica 9221); Whiskey Sour (1953, Met. 29) [EP]; Pink Lady (1953, Met. 34) [EP]; Red Head (1954, PJ 4-17) [EP]; *Dinah* (1957, Phi. B08201L); *At Gyllene Cirkeln* (1962, Met. 15122); *P som i piano* [P as in piano] (1965, Odeon 054-34570); *Vintage 77* (1977, Sveriges Radio 1303); *The Hallberg Touch* (1979, Phon. 7525); *Trio con Tromba* (1985, Four Leaf Clover 5079)

BIBLIOGRAPHY

FeatherE; *Feather–Gitler '70s*

E. Kjellberg: "Hallberg, Bengt," *Sohlmans musiklexikon* (Stockholm, rev. and enlarged 2/1975–9 ed. H. Åstrand)

——: *Svensk jazzhistoria: en översikt* [Swedish jazz history: an overview] (Stockholm, 1985)

ERIK KJELLBERG

Hambro, Lenny [Leonard William] (*b* New York, 16 Oct 1923). Alto saxophonist and leader. He played saxophone and clarinet with Gene Krupa from 1942, then after serving in the army (1943–6) worked with Billy Butterfield (with whom he recorded in 1946) and again with Krupa (1947–51). His association with Butterfield lasted intermittently into the 1980s, as did several that he formed early in his career (with Buddy Rich and Woody Herman, among others). He played with Ray McKinley and worked as his road manager (1951–2), toured and recorded with Machito (at intervals, 1951–6), and recorded with Chico O'Farrill (1951–2). He formed his own small group in 1950, which made its first recordings between 1953 and 1956 (including the EP *Lenny Hambro* (1953, Savoy 8109), on which Hank Jones played piano); with the group he joined the New Glenn Miller Orchestra under McKinley in 1956 and remained with the band, touring Europe in 1957 and 1958, until 1964. From 1966 into the 1980s he played in other ensembles led by McKinley, at the same time running a company that produced music for films and commercials. In 1984 he performed in New York at a party given by BMI in honor of many important jazz musicians.

BIBLIOGRAPHY

FeatherE
B. Coss: "Lenny Hambro: Latin from Manhattan," *Metronome*, lxxi/5 (1955), 24

Häme [Hämäläinen], **Olli** (*b* Helsinki, 19 May 1924; *d* Tampere, Finland, 11 June 1984). Finnish double bass player and bandleader. He formed a quintet in 1947, which was chiefly responsible for introducing bop in Finland; it made several recordings, including *I surrender, dear* (1948, Savel 9002) and *Lemon drop* (1950, Decca SD5110), and remained active until 1960. In the 1950s he turned to popular music and made a number of jazz-inspired hit recordings with the singer Brita Koivunen. He later became a record producer (1959–62) and television executive (1962–84). Häme wrote *Rytmin voittokulku* (The triumph of rhythm; Helsinki, 1949), the first history of jazz published in Finland.

PEKKA GRONOW

Hamfat. An expression used generally from around 1910 by older musicians to describe players who lacked musical knowledge and were not capable of playing the New Orleans jazz repertory, particularly the constantly changing flow of popular songs. The term derives from the use by trombonists of a piece of ham fat (which was very common in New Orleans kitchens) to grease the slides of their instruments; it was used jokingly but mostly with a note of contempt. There were many musicians who accepted jobs knowing they were poor readers and had a limited ability to play requests from the audience, as New Orleans bands often did; when the leader called tunes such as *Lady be good*, *Honeysuckle Rose*, *Someday Sweetheart*, or *The Heebie Jeebies*, they would fold their arms and look at him with a persecuted air. Some of the highest-paid players who went all over the world representing New Orleans jazz were "hamfat" musicians. In New York Willie "the Lion" Smith called such incompetent musicians "blisters."

DANNY BARKER

Hamilton, Chico [Foreststorn] (*b* Los Angeles, 21 Sept 1921). Drummer and bandleader. While in high school he played with Buddy Collette, Dexter Gordon, Illinois Jacquet, and Charles Mingus. Later he toured with Lionel Hampton, Lester Young, and others (1940–41), then served in the US Army. He regularly accompanied the singer Lena Horne from 1948 to 1955 and was a member of Gerry Mulligan's original "pianoless" quartet in 1952. In 1955 he founded the first of a series of quintets that introduced such emerging jazz musicians as Eric Dolphy (for illustration *see* DOLPHY, ERIC), Ron Carter, and Charles Lloyd. The group's innovative instrumentation (winds, cello, guitar, double bass, and drums) and soft, controlled sounds became, by jazz standards, extremely popular; performances were captured on film in *The Sweet Smell of Success* (1957) and *Jazz on a Summer's Day* (1958). From 1960 the quintet adopted a gutsy blues and swing style, and Hamilton ultimately replaced the cello with a trumpet. With the establishment of Chico Hamilton Productions in New York in 1966, Hamilton embarked on a second career composing music for advertisements. In the 1970s and 1980s he occasionally led jazz-rock and experimental groups.

SELECTED RECORDINGS

The Chico Hamilton Quintet with Buddy Collette (1955, PJ 1209); *The Chico Hamilton Quintet* (1956, PJ 1225); *The Sweet Smell of Success* (1957, Decca 8641); *Three Faces of Chico* (1959, WB 1344); *Chic Chic Chico* (1965, Imp. 82); *El Exigente* (*c*1970, FD 10135); *Nomad* (*c*1979, Elek. 257)

BIBLIOGRAPHY

J. Tynan: "Chico Hamilton," *DB*, xxiii/6 (1956), 12
D. Morgenstern: "Flexible Chico," *DB*, xxxiv/12 (1967), 18
J. Shaw: "Chico's Changes," *J&B*, ii/6 (1972), 6
H. Nolan: "Chico Hamilton: Pulsation Personified," *DB*, xlv/8 (1978), 19
J. Potter: "Uniquely, Chico Hamilton," *MD*, ix/4 (1985), 18

BARRY KERNFELD

Hamilton, Jeff (*b* Richmond, IN, 4 Aug 1953). Drummer. He studied snare drum for five years, learned to play the drum set, and while studying percussion for two years at Indiana University learned jazz drumming from John Von Ohlen in Indianapolis. He was a member of the New Tommy Dorsey Band under Murray McEachern, worked briefly with Lionel Hampton, and belonged for two years to Monty Alexander's trio; he then played in Woody Herman's orchestra until January 1978, when he succeeded Shelly Manne as the drummer in the L. A. FOUR. Hamilton is equally adept with sticks and brushes and works proficiently in several styles besides jazz, including rock, Caribbean music, and Latin music; some of his recordings include his own arrangements.

SELECTED RECORDINGS

(recorded for Concord unless otherwise indicated)

As leader: *Indiana* (1982, 187)

As sideman: M. Alexander: *Montreux Alexander* (1976, MPS 68170); W. Herman: *Chick, Donald, Walter, and Woodrow* (1978, Cen. 1110); L. A. Four: *Just Friends* (1978, 1001, 199); *Live at Montreux* (1979, 100), incl. Hammertones; M. Alexander: *Reunion in Europe* (1983, 231)

BIBLIOGRAPHY

L. Tomkins: "Jeff Hamilton and the Avoidance of Stereotyping," *CI*, xviii/4 (1979), 6
——: "Jeff Hamilton Speaks his Mind," *CI*, xviii/5 (1979), 25
R. Flans: "No Compromises: Jeff Hamilton," *MD*, x/7 (1986), 26

J. KENT WILLIAMS

Hamilton, Jimmy [James] (*b* Dillon, SC, 25 May 1917). Clarinetist. Originally a brass player, he changed to reed instruments and worked with Lucky Millinder, Jimmy Mundy, Teddy Wilson (1940–42), and Eddie Heywood. In 1943 he joined Duke Ellington's orchestra as principal clarinet soloist; he immediately established his own musical identity, and was much featured by Ellington until he left the band in 1968. He then moved to the Virgin Islands, where he continued to play and teach clarinet throughout the 1970s. In the 1980s he worked in the USA with Mercer Ellington, toured Europe as a soloist, and performed and recorded with John Carter's quartet Clarinet Summit.

Hamilton's clarinet technique was superb, and he was skillful at developing ideas within his improvised solos, but his exceedingly smooth execution and minimal vibrato often invested his solos with an inappropriate air of urbane detachment. By complete contrast, his occasional performances on tenor saxophone, on which he was not technically adept, have a guttural exuberance which transmits the joyful qualities so often lacking in his clarinet playing. Even though Hamilton occasionally led his own recording bands, he sounds much happier when working within Ellington's orchestra, particularly in the various suites.

SELECTED RECORDINGS

As leader: Slapstick (1945, BN 5027)

As sideman: D. Ellington: *Masterpieces* (1950, Col. ML4418), incl. The Tattooed Bride; J. Hodges: *Duke's in Bed* (1956, Verve 8203), incl. Take the "A" Train; *The Big Sound* (1957, Verve 8271), incl. Digits; D. Ellington: *The Nutcracker Suite* (1960, Col. CS8341); J. Carter: *Clarinet Summit*, i (1981, IndN 1062); *Clarinet Summit*, ii (1985, IndN 1067)

BIBLIOGRAPHY

A. Morgan: "Jimmy Hamilton: a Name Listing," *JM* (1967), no.152, p.27; no.154, p.29

"Quits Duke after 26 Years," *DB*, xxxv/17 (1968), 13

S. Dance: *The World of Duke Ellington* (London and New York, 1970/*R*1981) [colln of previously pubd articles and interviews], 140

D. Ellington: *Music is my Mistress* (Garden City, NY, 1973), 220

G. Giddins: *Rhythm-a-ning: Jazz Tradition and Innovation in the '80s* (New York, and Oxford, England, 1985) [colln of previously pubd articles], 119

JOHN CHILTON

Hamilton, John "Bugs" (*b* St. Louis, 8 March 1911; *d* St. Louis, 15 Aug 1947). Trumpeter. He played in New York in a band led by the trombonist Billy Kato (1930–31), and also worked briefly with Chick Webb. In 1935 he performed at the Ubangi Club with Kaiser Marshall's band, and later the same year joined Bobby Neal. From 1938 to 1942 he was a member of Fats Waller's band, and his playing may be heard to advantage on *The moon is low* (1940, Bb 10624). Later Hamilton worked with Eddie South (1943). He died of tuberculosis. (For illustration *see* WALLER, FATS.)

based on *ChiltonW*

Hamilton, Scott (*b* Providence, RI, 12 Sept 1954). Tenor saxophonist. He began playing at the age of 16, and in 1976 moved to New York, where he quickly gained public and critical acclaim. He has performed and recorded as the leader of a quintet with the guitarist Chris Flory, the drummer Chuck Riggs, the double bass player Phil Flanigan, and the pianist John Bunch; except Bunch, all these musicians worked with Hamilton in Providence. In 1976 he began an association with Warren Vaché which has continued into the 1980s. The two musicians have recorded many albums together and worked as sidemen with Benny Goodman (from 1977), Rosemary Clooney (periodically from 1978), and Woody Herman (at intervals in the 1980s). From 1982 Hamilton has worked with Ruby Braff. He has also performed with such touring bands as the Concord Jazz All-Stars, the Concord Superband, and the Newport Jazz Festival All-Stars, almost invariably with Vaché.

Hamilton's playing, although not derivative, is an extension of the tradition established by Coleman Hawkins, Ben Webster, and Illinois Jacquet. He is a gifted improviser, and is capable of transforming the most unlikely material into memorable music. His relaxed, elegantly constructed solo on *Nobody knows you when you're down and out* is a fine example of his playing.

SELECTED RECORDINGS

(all recorded for Concord unless otherwise indicated)

As leader: *Scott Hamilton is a Good Wind who is Blowing us no Ill* (1977, 42); *Grand Appearance* (1978, Prog. 7026); with W. Vaché: *Skyscrapers* (1979, 111), incl. You leave me breathless; with B. Tate: *Scott's Buddy* (1980, 148); *Close Up* (1982, 197); *The Second Set* (1983, 254), incl. For all we know; with R. Braff: *A First* (1985, 274)

As sideman: J. Bunch: *John's Other Bunch* (1977, FaD 114); R. Clooney: *Here's to my Lady* (1978, 81); W. Herman: *A Concord Jam*, i (1980, 142); Newport Jazz Festival All-Stars: *The Newport Jazz Festival All-Stars* (1984, 260), incl. Nobody knows you when you're down and out; M. Sullivan: *Uptown* (1985, 288)

BIBLIOGRAPHY

D. Morgenstern: "Doggin' Around: Great Scott!," *JJI*, xxx/8 (1977), 14

B. Blumenthal: "The Scott Hamilton Swing Revival," *RS*, no.298 (23 Aug 1979), 26

L. Jeske: "Scott Hamilton Grew up in the '70s but Swing's his Thing," *DB*, xlvi/18 (1979), 28 [incl. discography]

L. Feather: "Scott Hamilton: Sax Anachronism," *Los Angeles Times Calendar* (21 Sept 1980), 65

W. Vaché, Sr.: "Jazzman of the Month: Scott Hamilton," *Jersey Jazz*, xii/7 (1984), 12

C. Deffaa: "Scott Hamilton: Expanding the Tradition," *DB*, lii/3 (1985), 23 [incl. discography]

CHIP DEFFAA

Hammer, Jan(, Jr.) (*b* Prague, 17 April 1948). Czechoslovak keyboard player. He grew up in a musical family, and played jazz with Miroslav Vitous while still at high school. In 1966 he won an international competition in Vienna, and earned a scholarship to study at the Berklee College of Music, but remained in Prague to study composition and piano at the Academy of Musical Arts. In 1967 he performed with Stuff Smith at the Jazz Jamboree, Warsaw. He was playing in Munich in 1968 when the Russians invaded Czechoslovakia, and then emigrated to the USA and settled in Boston. Hammer toured Canada, the USA, and Japan with Sarah Vaughan (1970–71), and worked in New York with Jeremy Steig and Elvin Jones. In 1971 he joined the MAHAVISHNU ORCHESTRA, playing synthesizer, which became his preferred instrument. He also played drums with John McLaughlin and Carlos Santana (1972). From 1973 to 1975 he belonged to Billy Cobham's group Spectrum, after which he began to lead his own groups. He recorded the album *The First Seven Days* in 1975, and the following year led a group that toured the USA with Jeff Beck. In 1977 he formed a jazz-rock quartet. In the 1980s he has continued to work with Beck, and has toured and recorded with Al Di Meola; he has also reached a vast audience outside jazz with his music for the popular television series *Miami Vice* and his associations with various American rock musicians.

Hammer often uses polyrhythms and short, repeated figures which he builds into uneven phrases; complex, harmonically unstable chord progressions in such compositions as *Darkness/Earth in Search of a Sun* reveal the influence of his classical training.

SELECTED RECORDINGS

As leader: *The First Seven Days* (1975, Nemperor 432); *Oh, Yeah?* (1976, Nemperor 437); with J. Beck: *Jeff Beck with the Jan Hammer Group* (1976, Epic 34433), incl. Darkness/Earth in Search of a Sun

As sideman: Mahavishnu Orchestra: *The Inner Mounting Flame* (1971, Col. KC31067); J. McLaughlin and C. Santana: *Love, Devotion, Surrender* (1972, Col. KC32034); Mahavishnu Orchestra: *Birds of Fire* (1972, Col. KC31996); *Between Nothingness and Eternity* (1973, Col. KC32766); J. Goodman: *Like Children* (1974, Nemperor 430); E. Jones: *Elvin Jones is on the Mountain* (1975, PM 005); S. Grossman: *Terra Firma* (1976, PM 012); A. Di Meola: *Tour de Force – Live* (1982, Col. FC38373)

BIBLIOGRAPHY

H. Nolan: "Jan Hammer: Saved by the Synthesizer," *DB*, xliii/5 (1976), 17

C. Berg: "Caught!: Jan Hammer," *DB*, xlv/2 (1978), 36

D. Milano: "Jan Hammer," *CK*, iv/10 (1978), 20 [incl. discography]

K. Emerson: "Pop Music: Jan Hammer," *New York Times* (22 March 1979), 16

J. Hammer: "Why I've Switched to Rock," *CI*, xix/10 (1981), 23

PHILIP GREENE

Hammond, John (Henry, Jr.) (*b* New York, 15 Dec 1910; *d* New York, 10 July 1987). Record producer and critic. He was born into a wealthy family, and attended Yale University. As a teenager, he became fascinated by black music and was drawn to the clubs and theaters of Harlem. He produced his first records in the early 1930s, and in 1933 recorded an important series of sessions for English Columbia featuring Fletcher Henderson, Benny Carter, and Benny Goodman, whose orchestra he helped to form in 1934; from 1935 to 1937 he supervised many of Teddy Wilson's sessions for Brunswick with Billie Holiday as soloist. Hammond was also an early advocate of Count Basie, and was influential in bringing his orchestra to national prominence in 1936. In 1938 and 1939 he organized the two historic "Spirituals to Swing" concerts in Carnegie Hall. A tireless talent scout and champion of racial equality, he later furthered the careers of artists as varied as Charlie Christian (whom he teamed with Goodman in 1939), George Benson, the soul singer Aretha Franklin, the folk singer Bob Dylan, and the rock singer Bruce Springsteen. Although best known for his association with Columbia (1937, 1939–43, 1959–75), Hammond also served in executive positions with Brunswick/Vocalion, Keynote, Majestic, Mercury, and Vanguard. From 1931 he wrote widely on jazz and popular music for music periodicals and the general press; he also published an autobiography, *John Hammond on Record* (New York, 1977).

Oral history material in *Cty*, *NjR*.

BIBLIOGRAPHY

C. Graham: "Meet the A&R Man: John Hammond," *DB*, xxviii/21 (1961), 23
P. J. Sullivan: "John Hammond," *JJ*, xxi/9 (1968), 6
J. McDonough: "John Hammond: Man for all Seasons," *DB*, xxxviii/5 (1971), 13
——: Review of *John Hammond on Record*, *DB*, xlv/1 (1978), 58
"Hammond, John (Henry, Jr.)," *CBY 1979*
L. Feather: "John Hammond," *The Passion for Jazz* (New York, 1980), 176

EDWARD BERGER

Hammond, Johnny [Smith, Johnny Hammond; Smith, John Robert] (*b* Louisville, KY, 16 Dec 1933). Organist. He grew up in a musical family and studied piano as a child; his early influences were Bud Powell and Art Tatum. He first worked as a pianist in Cleveland (under the name Johnny Hammond Smith), but, after hearing Wild Bill Davis, soon changed permanently to the organ. In 1958 he worked as Nancy Wilson's accompanist. After moving to New York in the late 1950s he played with Chris Columbus and led his own groups, which recorded soul jazz for the Prestige label from 1959 to 1970. In 1971, shortly after taking the name Johnny Hammond, he signed a contract with Kudu Records, a company that specialized in soul music, and during the 1970s he began performing on other electronic keyboard instruments and on synthesizers. Hammond was one of a group of organists who helped popularize the use of the Hammond organ in the 1960s. He developed a basic approach and style early in his career and continued to refine it. One of his favorite devices is to build on a line of single notes to culminate in a shout chorus with large chords.

SELECTED RECORDINGS

As leader: with G. Ammons: *Angel Eyes* (1960, Prst. 7369); *Wild Horses Rock Steady* (1971, Kudu 04); *Gambler's Life* (1974, Salvation 702); *Gears* (1975, Mlst. 9062); *Forever Taurus* (1976, Mlst. 9068); *Storm Warning* (1977, Mlst. 9076)

BIBLIOGRAPHY

FeatherE ("Smith, Johnny Hammond"); *Feather '60s* ("Smith, Johnny Hammond"); *Feather–Gitler '70s*
"Johnny Hammond: Don't Let the System Get You," *DB*, xlv/17 (1978), 24

PAUL RINZLER

Hammond organ. An electronic organ developed in 1933–4 by the American engineers Laurens Hammond (1895–1973) and John M. Hanert (*b* 1909). For a discussion of its use in jazz *see* ORGAN, §2.

Hampel, Gunter (*b* Göttingen, Lower Saxony, Germany, 31 Aug 1937). German vibraphonist and composer. He studied music and architecture and formed his first group in 1958. In 1969 he established his own record company, Birth. His involvement in other forms of contemporary music, besides jazz, led to his working with the composer Krzysztof Penderecki, Don Cherry, and the New Eternal Rhythm Orchestra on the recording *Actions* (1971). In 1972 he formed the Galaxie Dream Band. After working mainly with European musicians, such as Manfred Schoof and Alex Schlippenbach, he formed lasting associations with several Americans, notably Perry Robinson and Jeanne Lee; Lee performs on many of his recordings and appears regularly with the Galaxie Dream Band. He has toured widely in Europe, the Middle East, Asia, Africa, and South America, often under the auspices of the Goethe Institute, and has also worked in New York. Hampel's playing tends to exploit the vibraphone's textural possibilities rather than his own virtuosity; he is also a proficient performer on piano, bass clarinet, and flute. As a composer he has written film music as well as compositions for his own ensembles, including *Transformation*.

SELECTED RECORDINGS

As leader: *Heartplants* (1965, Saba 15026); *Music from Europe* (1966, ESP 1042); *The 8th of July 1969* (1969, Birth 001); *Familie* (1972, Birth 008); [untitled album] (1969, ICP 007–8); *Out of New York* (1971, MPS 2120900–8); *Transformation* (1976, Birth 0026)
As sideman: K. Penderecki and D. Cherry: *Actions* (1971, Phi. 6305153)

BIBLIOGRAPHY

N. Hentoff: "Günter Hampel: an Introduction," *J&P*, ix/7 (1970), 25
B. Tepperman: "Birth," *Coda*, xi/3 (1973), 11
B. Noglik: "Gunter Hampel," *Jazzwerkstatt international* (Berlin, 1981), 383 [incl. interview, discography]

ROGER T. DEAN

Hampton, Lionel (*b* Louisville, KY, 20 April 1909). Vibraphonist, drummer, and bandleader. There is some confusion about the year of his birth, which has sometimes been given as 1908. Around 1916 he moved with his family to Chicago, where he began his career playing drums in various lesser bands. In the late 1920s he was based in Culver City, California, where he worked in clubs and took part in several recording sessions (1930) with Louis Armstrong, who encouraged him to take up vibraphone. Hampton soon became the leading jazz performer on this instrument, and achieved wide recognition through his many film appearances with Les Hite's band. After playing informally with Benny Goodman in 1936 he began to work in Goodman's small ensembles, with which he performed and recorded regularly until 1940; as a result he became one of the most celebrated figures of the swing period, and his resounding success allowed him to form his own big band in 1940. This group, which at times has included musicians of the stature of Cat Anderson, Illinois Jacquet, Clifford Brown, and Quincy Jones, has been one of the most long-lived and consistently popular large ensembles in jazz. From the 1950s Hampton undertook numerous foreign "goodwill" tours to Europe, Japan, Australia, Africa, the Middle East, and elsewhere, and made a large number of television appearances, attracting a huge and enthusiastic international following. He performed in the Royal Festival Hall, London, in 1957, and played at the White House for President Carter in 1978; during the same year he formed his own record label, Who's Who in Jazz, to issue mainstream recordings. In the mid-1980s his band continued to draw capacity crowds throughout the world. Hampton was honored as alumnus of the year by the University of Southern California in 1983.

Lionel Hampton, New York, 1960s

Hampton was not the first jazz musician to take up vibraphone (Red Norvo had preceded him in the late 1920s), but it was he who gave the instrument an identity in jazz, applying a wide range of attacks and generating remarkable swing on an instrument otherwise known for its bland, disembodied sound. Undoubtedly his best work was done with the Goodman Quartet from 1936 to 1940, when he revealed a fine ear for small-ensemble improvisation and an unrestrained, ebullient manner as a soloist. The big-band format was probably better suited to the display of his flamboyant personality and flair for showmanship, but after a few early successes, especially the riff tunes *Flying Home*, *Down Home Jump*, and *Hey Ba-ba-rebop*, the group was too often content to repeat former triumphs for its many admirers. Hampton has at times also appeared as a singer, played drums with enormous vitality, and performed with curious success as a pianist, using only two fingers in the manner of vibraphone mallets.

For further illustration *see* TURNER, JOE (ii).

SELECTED RECORDINGS

As leader: Drum Stomp (1937, Vic. 25658); Down Home Jump (1938, Vic. 26114); Hot Mallets (1939, Vic. 26371); Central Avenue Breakdown/Jack the Bellboy (1940, Vic. 26652); Flying Home (1942, Decca 18394); Hamp's Boogie Woogie (1944, Decca 18613); Hey Ba-ba-rebop (1945, Decca 18754); Air Mail Special (1946, Decca 18880); Midnight Sun (1947, Decca 24429); Real Crazy/I only have eyes for you (1953, Vogue 5176); *Lionel Hampton's Jazz Giants* (1955, Norg. 1080); *Newport Uproar* (1967, RCA LSP3891); *At Newport '78* (1978, Tim. 142); *Made in Japan* (1982, Tim. 175)

As sideman with B. Goodman: The Blues in your Flat/The Blues in my Flat (1938, Vic. 26044); Opus $\frac{1}{2}$ (1938, Vic. 26091); Gone with "What" Wind (1940, Col. 35404)

BIBLIOGRAPHY

Y. Bruynoghe: "'Hamp' nous revient," *BHcF*, no.43 (1954), 3
J. Aldam: "The Lionel Hampton Band," *JM*, iii/1 (1957), 5
——: "Footnote on Hampton," *JM*, iii/6 (1957), 28
F. Manskleid: "For Dancers Only," *JM*, vi/4 (1960), 29
B. Coss: "Lionel Hampton: Bothered and Bewildered," *DB*, xxix/10 (1962), 19
M. Harrison: "Lionel Hampton on Victor," *JM*, ix/1 (1963), 3
L. K. McMillan: "Good Vibes from Hamp," *DB*, xxxix/8 (1972), 12
S. Dance: *The World of Swing* (New York, 1974) [colln of previously pubd interviews], 265
J. H. Klee: "Good Vibes," *MR*, iv/3 (1977), 1
A. Balalas: "Lionel Hampton: jubilé musical (1928–1978)," *BHcF*, no.263 (1978), 3
B. Crowther and V. Schonfield: "Hamp the Champ," *JJI*, xxxi/7 (1978), 6
C. Jones: "The Illustrious Past and Present of Lionel Hampton," *CI*, xvi/7 (1978), 10
A. J. Smith: "Lionel Hampton: Half a Century Strong," *DB*, xlv/14 (1978), 20
O. Flückiger: *Lionel Hampton: Selected Discography, 1966–1978* (Reinach, Switzerland, 1978, rev. and enlarged 2/1980 as *Lionel Hampton: Porträt mit Discography, 1966–79*)
L. Tomkins: "Lionel Hampton Recalls when Swing Began," *CI*, xxi/11 (1983), 20
S. Woolley: "Flyin' Hamp," *JJI*, xxxvi/7 (1983), 6

J. BRADFORD ROBINSON

Hampton, Slide [Locksley Wellington] (*b* Jeannette, PA, 21 April 1932). Trombonist, composer, and arranger. He grew up in Indianapolis, and joined other members of his family in a band at the age of 14. During his association with Buddy Johnson's band (1955–6) he traveled to New York, and wrote his first compositions. After a year with Lionel Hampton he worked with Maynard Ferguson (1957–9), then formed his own octet, which he continued to lead during the 1960s; its members included Freddie Hubbard, Booker Little, Julian Priester, and George Coleman. At this time Hampton was also the music director of the big band that accompanied the rhythm-and-blues singer Lloyd Price. In 1968 he traveled with Woody Herman to Europe, where he remained for nearly a decade, working mostly as a soloist and leading bands, one with the German pianist Joe Haider. After returning to the USA in 1977 he played at clubs, and worked with several ensembles. He continues to lead World of Trombones, a band of nine trombonists and a rhythm section; he has also conducted the Collective Black Artists Orchestra, led the Manhattan Plaza Composers Orchestra, and worked with Continuum, a cooperative quintet dedicated to the music of Tadd Dameron comprising Hampton, Jimmy Heath, Kenny Barron, Ron Carter, and Art Taylor. Hampton is an outstanding, versatile trombonist, and a prolific composer and arranger. *Sister Salvation* and *The Fugue* are among his more notable pieces.

SELECTED RECORDINGS

As leader: *Sister Salvation* (1960, Atl. 1339), incl. Sister Salvation; *The Fabulous Slide Hampton Quartet* (1969, PAct CO6210156); *World of Trombones* (1978, West 8001); *Roots* (1985, Criss Cross 1015)

As sideman: M. Ferguson: *A Message from Newport* (1958, Roul. 52012), incl. The Fugue; P. J. Jones: *Advance* (1978, Gal. 5122); A. Blakey and G. Kawaguchi: *Killer Joe* (1981, Sto. 4100); Continuum: *Mad About Tadd* (1982, PAlt 8029)

BIBLIOGRAPHY

B. Gardner: "This is Slide Hampton," *DB*, xxviii/2 (1961), 14
S. Woolley: "Slide Hampton: Interview," *Cadence*, iv/8–9 (1978), 3
"Slide Brings Back 'Bones," *DB*, xlvi/12 (1979), 15
R. R. Verges: "Slide Hampton: Back at the Right Time," *JF* [intl edn], no.57 (1979), 34
W. A. Brower: "Slide Hampton: a Good Guy who's Winning," *JT* (Dec 1980), 8
M. Richards: "Slide Hampton," *JJI*, xl/1 (1987), 6
L. Tomkins: "Slide Hampton: Boning up on Band Sounds," *CI*, xxiv/10 (1987), 8

ROLAND BAGGENAES

Hancock, Herbie [Herbert Jeffrey] (*b* Chicago, 12 April 1940). Pianist and composer. Born into a musical family, he began

V.S.O.P. playing at the Grande Parade du Jazz, Nice, France, 1983: (left to right) Herbie Hancock (keyboards), Wynton Marsalis (trumpet), Ron Carter (double bass), and Tony Williams (drums)

studying the piano at the age of seven, and four years later performed the first movement of a Mozart concerto with the Chicago SO in a young people's concert. While attending Hyde Park High School he formed his own jazz ensemble. His knowledge of harmony was early influenced by Clare Fischer's arrangements for the Hi-Los and Robert Farnon's orchestral arrangements of standard popular songs. By the time he graduated from Grinnell College in 1960 he was already performing in Chicago jazz clubs with Coleman Hawkins and Donald Byrd. Byrd invited him to join his quintet and move to New York where, during Hancock's first recording session with the group, Blue Note was sufficiently impressed to offer him his first date as a leader in May 1962. The resulting album, *Takin' Off*, drew considerable public attention through an original tune with a strong gospel influence: *Watermelon Man*.

In May 1963 Hancock joined Miles Davis's quintet. His piano style had by that time evolved into a highly personal blend of blues and bop with colorful harmony and exquisite tone – a rich combination of elements heard in Davis's previous pianists Red Garland, Bill Evans (ii), Wynton Kelly, and Victor Feldman. Working with Ron Carter and Tony Williams, Hancock helped revolutionize traditional jazz concepts of the rhythm section and its relation to the soloists. He built on the earlier developments of such diverse groups as Bill Evans's trio and Ornette Coleman's quartet, and established a musical rapport with an extraordinary degree of freedom and interaction. During his five years with the quintet Hancock also composed several tunes which have become jazz standards, including *Maiden Voyage*, *Dolphin Dance*, *Cantaloupe Island*, *The Sorcerer*, and *Speak like a Child*.

From 1971 to 1973 Hancock led a sextet which combined elements of jazz, rock, and African and Indian music with electronic devices and instruments. Influenced by Davis's earlier fusion recordings, in which Hancock had participated, the sextet was notable for its colorful doubling of instruments, tasteful blend of acoustic and electronic sounds, and mastery of compound meters. Thereafter Hancock began to use electric and electronic instruments more extensively, playing the Fender-Rhodes piano through a variety of signal processors such as wa-wa and fuzz pedals. Later he turned to the Mellotron and the Hohner Clavinet, and, finally, various synthesizers, sequencers, and electronic percussion units. The album *Headhunters* (1973) marked the beginning of a commitment to more commercial types of music, particularly rock, funk, and disco, and contained the hit single *Chameleon*. Although Hancock returned occasionally to jazz projects from the late 1970s, particularly with his band V.S.O.P. (*see* V.S.O.P. (i)) and his piano duos with Chick Corea, some critics felt that his inventiveness and clarity of development had suffered as a result of his extended absence from the jazz scene. During this period he enjoyed considerable commercial success; in 1983 the single *Rockit* reached no.1 on the pop chart, and the promotional video for this recording received widespread critical acclaim. *Rockit* demonstrated Hancock's ability to use the most complex innovations in electronic technology to produce fascinating music. After this success he turned his attention almost exclusively to jazz for the next two years. He acted and played in the film *Round Midnight* (1986) and won an Oscar for his score. In 1987 he toured Europe in a trio with Buster Williams and Al Foster, and the USA and Japan leading a quartet that included Mike Brecker, Ron Carter, and Tony Williams.

Oral history material in *NjR*.

See also JAZZ-ROCK and PIANO, §6; for further illustration *see* JAZZ (i), fig.8.

SELECTED RECORDINGS

Duos with C. Corea: *An Evening with Herbie Hancock and Chick Corea* (1978, Col. PC35664–5)

As leader: *Takin' Off* (1962, BN 84109), incl. Watermelon Man; *My Point of View* (1963, BN 84126); *Empyrean Isles* (1964, BN 84175), incl. Cantaloupe Island; *Maiden Voyage* (1965, BN 84195), incl. Dolphin Dance; *Speak like a Child* (1968, BN 84279), incl. The Sorcerer; *Mwandishi* (1971, WB 1898);

Sextant (1973, Col. KC32212); *Headhunters* (1973, Col. KC32731); *Thrust* (1974, Col. PC32965); *V.S.O.P.* (1976, Col. PG34688); *V.S.O.P.: the Quintet* (1977, Col. C2-34976); *Feets, Don't Fail Me Now* (1978, Col. JC35764)
As sideman with M. Davis: *Miles Davis in Europe* (1963, Col. CS8983); *My Funny Valentine* (1964, Col. CS9106); *E.S.P.* (1965, Col. CS9150); *The Sorcerer* (1962, 1967, Col. CS9532); *Miles in the Sky* (1968, Col. CS9268)

BIBLIOGRAPHY

J. Mehegan: "Discussion: Herbie Hancock talks to John Mehegan," *Jazz*, iii/5 (1964), 23
B. Johnson: "Herbie Hancock: into his own Thing," *DB*, xxxviii/2 (1971), 14
R. Townley: "Hancock Plugs In," *DB*, xli/17 (1974), 13
L. Lyons: "Herbie Hancock: Keyboard Wizard," *CK*, i/2 (1975), 18
D. Milano and others: "Herbie Hancock," *CK*, iii/11 (1977), 26
C. Silvert: "Herbie Hancock: Revamping the Past, Creating the Future," *DB*, xliv/15 (1977), 16
D. N. Baker, L. M. Belt, and H. C. Hudson, eds.: *The Black Composer Speaks* (Metuchen, NJ, and London, 1978), chap. 5 [with list of compositions]
B. Primack: "Herbie Hancock: Chameleon in his Disco Phase," *DB*, xlvi/10 (1979), 12
L. Feather: "Piano Giants of Jazz: Herbie Hancock," *CK*, vi/3 (1980), 62
M. Ruppli: "Discographie: Herbie Hancock," *Jh*, no.371 (1980), 21; no.372 (1980), 29; no.373 (1980), 26
J. Balleras: "Herbie Hancock's Current Choice," *DB*, xlix/9 (1982), 15
L. Lyons: *The Great Jazz Pianists, Speaking of their Lives and Music* (New York, 1983), 269
H. Mandel: "Herbie Hancock: of Films, Fairlights, Funk . . . and All That Other Jazz," *DB*, liii/7 (1986), 16 [incl. discography]
L. Feather: "The Hancock Signature," *San Francisco Chronicle Datebook* (16 Aug 1987), 26

BILL DOBBINS

Handy, Capt. John [Cap, Cap'n] (*b* Pass Christian, MS, 24 June 1900; *d* Pass Christian, 12 Jan 1971). Alto saxophonist and clarinetist. He began on guitar, mandolin, and drums, and by the time he was 15 was performing in a family band with his father, John Handy, Sr. (violin), and his younger brothers Julius (guitar) and Sylvester (*b* Pass Christian, 8 Sept 1903; *d* New Orleans, 12 Oct 1973) (double bass). About a year later he taught himself clarinet and began to play informally with Punch Miller, Kid Rena, and Isaiah Morgan. He moved to New Orleans in 1918 and for six years was a member of the band led by the trumpeter Tom Albert, though he also worked with the trumpeter Charlie Love (1919–20). From 1924 to 1926 he was in Baton Rouge with the banjoist Toots Johnson, and the following year he returned to New Orleans to join Guy Kelly. Handy took up alto saxophone in 1928, and thereafter became principally identified with this instrument. In 1932, with his brother Sylvester, he formed the Louisiana Shakers, a highly successful group that toured Texas, Alabama, and Mississippi. During the mid-1930s he played with Kid Howard, Jim Robinson, and Lee Collins, and in 1938 he worked with Charlie Creath in St. Louis. After returning to New Orleans he was associated with the Young Tuxedo Brass Band (1940s) and the trumpeter Kid Clayton (1950s). In 1961 Handy joined the trumpeter Kid Sheik Colar, with whom he frequently played clarinet. It was about this time that he acquired the nickname "Captain," reportedly given to him, on account of his authoritative manner in rehearsal, by the banjoist Fred Minor. Thereafter he played frequently at Preservation Hall, made tours of England, Europe, Canada, and Japan (1967), and appeared at the Newport Jazz Festival (1970).

Although in the 1920s Handy was a pioneer saxophonist, his career was ironically impeded at the beginning of the New Orleans revival by an obdurate purist aversion to the inclusion of saxophones in traditional bands. His assertive, rhythmically busy, and frequently witty style is said to have influenced Earl Bostic and Louis Jordan.

Oral history material in *LNT*.

SELECTED RECORDINGS

As leader: *The December Band* (1965, Jazz Crusade 007–8); *Capt. John Handy with Geoff Bull and Barry Martyn's Band* (1966, Beautiful Dumaine 001); *Introducing Cap'n John Handy* (1967, RCA LSP3762)
As sideman with K. Howard: *Kid Howard's Band* (1962, MONO 2)

BIBLIOGRAPHY

M. Jones: "Handy: New Orleans Alto? I Played as if I was Playing Trumpet," *MM* (2 April 1966), 6
T. Stagg: "'Captain' John Handy," *Jazz Times*, iii/3 (1966), 7
——: "Captain John Handy: a Personal Appreciation," *Fn*, ii/4 (1971), 18
H. Herling: *Capt. John Handy: kleine Studie über Leben und Werk sowie seinen Einfluss auf die heutige "New Orleans Revival Jazz"-scene* (Menden, Germany, 1978) [incl. discography]

ALDEN ASHFORTH

Handy [Hendleman], **George (Joseph)** (*b* New York, 17 Jan 1920). Arranger, composer, and pianist. He was taught piano by his mother, and studied composition at the Juilliard School and New York University as well as privately with Aaron Copland. In 1941 he played with Raymond Scott, then from 1943 to 1946 worked sporadically for Boyd Raeburn; during this period he established his reputation as an arranger with such works as his compositions *Tonsillectomy* and *Dalvatore Sally*. He also wrote arrangements for the guitarist Alvino Rey, Ina Ray Hutton, and Herbie Fields, and went to Hollywood to work for Paramount Studios and the Armed Forces Radio Service. Handy became known in the 1940s and 1950s as an excellent composer whose advanced style drew on classical techniques; *Stocking Horse*, for example (written for Rey), makes use alternately of 4/4 and 5/4 time signatures. In 1946 he recorded his extended composition *The Bloos* (Jazz Scene [unnumbered]). He returned to New York the following year, but lived in relative obscurity until the mid-1950s, when he recorded two albums as a leader (including *By George!*, 1955, X 1032) and worked as pianist and arranger for Zoot Sims (1956–7). In the 1960s he composed works for the New York Saxophone Quartet, including *New York Suite* (1964).

Oral history material in *NjR* (JOHP).

SELECTED ARRANGEMENTS

(all recorded by B. Raeburn with Handy as sideman)

Starlight Avenue (1944, Grand 1004); Tonsillectomy (1945, Jewell 10000); Rip Van Winkle/Yerxa (1945, Jewell 10001); Dalvatore Sally (1946, Jewell 1-1)

BIBLIOGRAPHY

FeatherE
"George Handy Back in Music," *DB*, xxi/18 (1954), 1
"A Handy Man to Have Back," *Metronome*, lxx/10 (1954), 15
A. Jackson: "Boyd Raeburn: the 'Successful Failure'," *JM*, xii/9 (1966), 5
C. Garrod and B. Korst: *Boyd Raeburn and his Orchestra plus Johnny Bothwell and George Handy* (Zephyrhills, FL, 1985) [discography]

STEVEN STRUNK

Handy, John (Richard, III) (*b* Dallas, 3 Feb 1933). Alto saxophonist and teacher. He began learning clarinet at the age of 13. His first performances and recordings were as a tenor saxophonist with blues bands led by the guitarist Lowell Fulson and others in and around San Francisco. In 1958 he moved to New York, where he played alto saxophone with Charles Mingus and Randy Weston, and formed his own group. In the early 1960s he returned to the West Coast, where he studied at San Francisco State College (BA 1963) and formed a ten-piece group. He rejoined Mingus in 1964, but the following year he formed another group of his own, which gave a highly acclaimed performance at the Monterey Jazz Festival. In 1970 he performed his Concerto for Jazz Soloist and Orchestra with the San Francisco SO, and in 1971 he began giving concerts with the sarod player Ali Akbar Khan; they performed in a style that blended the improvisatory techniques of jazz and Indian music. Later in the 1970s Handy began playing jazz-rock, but he returned to the bop idiom in 1979 with the group Mingus Dynasty and played in the 1980s with a sextet called Bebop and Beyond.

By the 1960s Handy had become one of the finest saxophonists of his generation, possessing a clear tone, excellent technique and intonation, and great facility in the altissimo register. He also played flute and other wind instruments, and was one of the first players to master the rare saxello. He began his teaching career in 1968 at San Francisco State University and has also taught at the University of California, Berkeley, Stanford University, and other institutions.

Oral history material in *LNT*.

SELECTED RECORDINGS

As leader: *In the Vernacular* (1959, Roul. 52042); *Live at the Monterey Jazz Festival* (1965, Col. CS9262), incl. Spanish Lady; *Projections* (1968, Col. CS9689); with A. A. Khan: *Karuna Supreme* (1975, MPS 2022791)

As sideman: C. Mingus: *Jazz Portraits* (1959, UA 4036); *Mingus ah um* (1959, Col. CL1370); Bebop and Beyond: *Bebop and Beyond* (1984, Conc. 244)

BIBLIOGRAPHY

G. Hoefer: "Search for Self: John Handy," *DB*, xxviii/6 (1961), 15

J. Lind: "John Handy: Back up the Ladder," *DB*, xxxiii/10 (1966), 21

J. S. Wilson: "Handy: 'Just Playing the Sax was not Enough'," *New York Times* (12 Feb 1967), §II, p.28

B. Gallagher: "John Handy: Taking the Bible out of the Brothels," *DB*, xliii/3 (1976), 20 [incl. discography]

E. Kolb: "John Handy: Interview," *Cadence*, x/6 (1984), 15

THOMAS OWENS

Handy, Sylvester (1903–73). Double bass player who in 1932 formed a group with his brother CAPT. JOHN HANDY.

Handy, W(illiam) C(hristopher) (*b* Florence, AL, 16 Nov 1873; *d* New York, 28 March 1958). Composer, cornetist, and bandleader. He studied organ and music theory when he was young. From 1896 he was a soloist with Mahara's Minstrels and he later became its music director. He then toured with his own bands and in 1917 he moved with his Memphis Orchestra to New York; it made a number of recordings (1917–23), including *Livery Stable Blues* (1917, Col. A2419), which displays its blues-laden style while preserving the novelty aspects of other contemporary bands. From the early 1920s Handy acted only intermittently as a leader; he also toured with Jelly Roll Morton (*c*1926) and the trumpeter Clarence Davis (1932) and played in an orchestra led by the violinist Billy Butler at the Apollo Theatre, New York (1936). In 1939 he recorded with an all-star swing group, which included J. C. Higginbotham, Edmond Hall, Pops Foster and Sid Catlett. His musical activities were somewhat restricted after 1943 when he was blinded in an accident. Handy also owned a music publishing company and he is probably best known as a composer and collector of blues; many of his songs, such as *Memphis Blues* (1912), *St. Louis Blues* (1914, later used as the basis for several films; *see* FILMS, §§I, 1 and 4 (v)), and *Beale Street Blues* (1916), became part of the standard jazz repertory. He also founded the short-lived Handy Record Co. in 1922. His private collection was donated by his family to Fisk University and another collection of materials relating to his life and work is at the New York Public Library's Schomburg Center for Research in Black Culture; *see* LIBRARIES AND ARCHIVES, §2.

Oral history material in *NjR*.

BIBLIOGRAPHY

ChiltonW; *FeatherE*; *GroveAM*

W. C. Handy: *Father of the Blues: an Autobiography* (New York, 1941, 4/1970)

G. W. Kay: "William Christopher Handy: Father of the Blues," *JJ*, xxiv/3 (1971), 10

HOWARD RYE

Handy Record Co. Record company. It was established by W. C. Handy in September 1922. Although it organized sessions it issued no records. It has been deduced, however, that certain recordings (bearing matrix numbers in a 100 series) put out around this time on other labels (mostly Paramount and Black Swan) represent the company's recorded legacy. (W. C. Allen: "The Handy Record Company," *Sv*, i/4 (1966), 14)

Hanna, Jake [John] (*b* Boston, 4 April 1931). Drummer. He learned jazz drumming from Stanley Spector and by listening to the many touring bands that visited Boston. In 1957 he began a long, but intermittent, association with Woody Herman's band, of which he became a regular member from 1962 to 1964. He played in a trio with Toshiko Akiyoshi in 1957, with Maynard Ferguson in 1958, and in the late 1950s as the house drummer at the Storyville jazz club in Boston. Marian McPartland heard him at the Storyville and engaged him in 1959; he remained with her until 1961. He worked briefly with Duke Ellington, Bobby Hackett, Harry James, and Herb Pomeroy. From 1964 to 1975 he was the drummer for Merv Griffin's television program, moving with it to Los Angeles in 1970. He performed on the West Coast with Herman, Supersax, Herb Ellis, and others, and made numerous recordings for Concord. In 1975 he formed a group with Carl Fontana.

Although he began his career at the height of the bop era and is adept in a wide range of jazz styles, Hanna gradually came to prefer a style of playing reminiscent of the great swing drummers George Wettling, Jo Jones, and Gene Krupa. He is highly regarded for his unerring sense of time, his ability to control a band at any tempo, and his refined musical taste.

SELECTED RECORDINGS

As leader (all recorded for Concord): *Live at Concord* (1975, 11); *Kansas City Express* (1976, 22); *Jake Takes Manhattan* (1976, 35)

As sideman: W. Herman: *Encore: 1963* (1963, Phi. 600092); Supersax: *Supersax Plays Bird* (1972, Cap. ST11177); R. Clooney: *Everything's Coming up Rosie* (1977, Conc. 47); M. McPartland: *Portrait of Marian McPartland* (1979, Conc. 101); C. Basie: *Kansas City Seven* (1980, Pablo 2310908); A. Cohn: *Nonpareil* (1981, Conc. 155)

BIBLIOGRAPHY

M. McPartland: "Just Swinging: Jake Hanna," *DB*, xxx/27 (1963), 16; repr. in *All in Good Time* (New York, and Oxford, England, 1987), 81

C. Welch: "Dixieland or Modern – Jake's still at Home," *MM*, xlii (28 Oct 1967), 10

L. Tomkins: "Anglo-American Conversation: Kenny Clare and Jake Hanna," *CI*, xiii/6 (1975), 20

——: "Of Drummers and Others: Jake Hanna and Kenny Clare," *CI*, xiii/7 (1975), 8

——: "Talking about Jazz; Jake Hanna and Kenny Clare," *CI*, xiii/10 (1975), 14

S. Traill: "The Best Seat in the House," *JJI*, xxxiv/7 (1981), 16

D. Levine and P. Hulsey: "Jake Hanna," *MD*, vi/5 (1982), 82

J. KENT WILLIAMS

Hanna, Ken(neth L.) (*b* Baltimore, 8 July 1921; *d* ?El Cajon, CA, 10 or 11 Dec 1982). Trumpeter and arranger. While studying at the Peabody Conservatory he played trombone and wrote arrangements for local bands. Later his principal association was with Stan Kenton, for whom he worked during several periods: from 1942 until he began military service, as an arranger; from 1946 to 1948, as a trumpeter and arranger (a good example of his arrangements from this period is *Somnambulism*, 1948, Cap. F528); from 1950 to 1951; and in the 1970s, when he wrote arrangements, led workshops, and conducted the orchestra during Kenton's illness in 1972. Hanna also composed for Charlie Barnet (1949), worked as a freelance arranger in Los Angeles (in the early 1950s), and led a group that made recordings (1953–5, including the album *Jazz for Dancers*, 1955, Cap. T6512); later he became a record distributor.

BIBLIOGRAPHY

FeatherE
W. F. Lee: *Stan Kenton: Artistry in Rhythm* (Los Angeles, 1980) [incl. discography]

Hanna, Sir Roland (P.) (*b* Detroit, 10 Feb 1932). Pianist. His father began teaching him music in early childhood, and he studied classical piano from the age of 11. Later he was influenced by the jazz pianists Tommy Flanagan, Hank Jones, Art Tatum, and Teddy Wilson. After serving in the army during the early 1950s he studied music at both the Eastman and Juilliard schools. He played briefly with Charles Mingus, joined Sarah Vaughan (1960), and later worked as a freelance and led a trio at clubs such as the Five Spot in New York (1963–6). He was knighted by the Liberian government in 1970. Hanna's performances and recordings with the Thad Jones–Mel Lewis Orchestra from 1966 to 1974 brought him considerable critical acclaim but, unfortunately, scant public attention and few opportunities for further work; during that period he supported himself largely through teaching, though he also played with the New York Jazz Sextet, which he formed around 1967. Around 1971 he formed from this group the New York Jazz Quartet, the primary purpose of which is to publicize the work of its members. His improvisations and compositions show a rare grasp of piano history in all styles of music, giving Hanna an eloquence rarely matched by his peers.

See also Piano, §5.

SELECTED RECORDINGS

As unaccompanied soloist: *Live at Montreux* (1974, Fre. 40147); *Piano Soliloquy* (1979, L+R 40003)
As leader: *Child of Gemini* (1971, BASF 20875)
As sideman: C. Mingus: *Mingus Dynasty* (1959, Col. CS8236); T. Jones and M. Lewis: *Consummation* (1970, BN 84356); New York Jazz Quartet: *The New York Jazz Quartet in Concert in Japan* (1975, Salvation 703)

BIBLIOGRAPHY

R. Williams: "The Hanna Manner," *MM*, xliv (20 Dec 1969), 10
J. Hasse: "Roland Hanna: Inside Insight," *DB*, xxxvii/20 (1970), 16
R. Townley and E. Nemeyer: "The Two-fisted Rubato of Sir Roland Hanna," *DB*, xlii/7 (1975), 15
J. Stix: "Roland Hanna: Versatile Mainstream Pianist," *CK*, iv/5 (1978), 10
L. Tomkins: "The Magic of the Piano: Roland Hanna," *CI*, xviii/11 (1980), 20
——: "Roland Hanna on his Piano Preferences," *CI*, xviii/12 (1980), 23
R. Slater: "Roland Hanna," *JJI*, xxxix/4 (1986), 14 [incl. discography]

BILL DOBBINS

Hannibal. *See* Peterson, hannibal.

Hansen, Ole Kock (*b* Osager, nr Roskilde, Denmark, 4 April 1945). Danish pianist, arranger, and composer. In 1967–9 he played with the Danish Radiojazzgruppen and from 1968 he belonged to the Radioens Big Band (recording in 1978). He led groups (often with Niels-Henning Ørsted Pedersen), accompanied such visiting Americans as Ben Webster, Dexter Gordon, Roy Eldridge, and Dizzy Gillespie, and recorded as a sideman with Webster (1973), Warne Marsh (*Jazz Exchange*, 1975, Sto. 1017), Lee Konitz (1975), Ørsted Pedersen (1975, 1984), and Thad Jones's quartet (1984). He has also worked with the Swedish, Finnish, Belgian, and Yugoslav radio big bands. Hansen favors a bop style that is colored to some degree by Danish folk music.

PEKKA GRONOW

Hara [Tsukahara], **Nobuo** (*b* Toyama, Japan, 19 Nov 1926). Japanese tenor saxophonist and leader. He played in a navy band from 1943 and at an officers' club in Tokyo after World War II. In 1952 he became the leader of the Sharps and Flats, which in 1969 became the first Japanese big band to appear at the Newport Jazz Festival and which remained in existence into the 1980s. Hara has won several readers' polls conducted by *Swing Journal* (from 1956) and made about 100 recordings. His band's style recalls that of Woody Herman's First Herd; Hara's saxophone playing is in a more conservative swing style.

SELECTED RECORDINGS

3-2-1-0/Oliver Nelson (1969, Col. SW7060); *Double Exposure, Arranged by Akiyoshi Toshiko* (1970, TE 60008); *25th Anniversary Recital* (1976, Nadja 31112); *Giant Steps: Nobuo Hara Meets Elvin Jones, Frank Foster* (1978, King SKA3016); *Active Volcano* (1979, TBM PAP20020); *Big Band Big Boss* (1985, Atl. 32XL70); *The Jazz Crest* (1985, Atl. 32XL89)

BIBLIOGRAPHY

Feather–Gitler '70s

YOZO IWANAMI

Hardaway, Bob [Robert Benson] (*b* Milwaukee, 1 March 1928). Tenor saxophonist. He played clarinet in an air force band, then joined Ray Anthony's group, with which he recorded in 1952 and 1958. He worked with Hal McIntyre (1953) and Jerry Gray (1954), and recorded the album *Lou's Blues* with a quintet and a quartet (1955, Beth. 1026). He also played with Woody Herman (1956), recorded in the Los Angeles area with Ken Hanna (1953–5), Buddy DeFranco (1957), Benny Goodman (1964), Stan Kenton (1964), Bud Shank (1966), and Chuck Flores (*c*1975–1977), and performed and recorded with Bob Florence at intervals from 1959 to 1981.

BIBLIOGRAPHY

FeatherE
A. Morgan: "Woody's Tenors," *JM*, vi (1960–61), no.7, p.4; no.8, p.13; no.12, p.9

Hard bop. A term frequently applied to an intense, hard-driving style of jazz of the 1950s and 1960s, as represented by the work of Horace Silver, Art Blakey, Cannonball Adderley, and their colleagues; it is also sometimes extended to encompass the music made in this period by Miles Davis, J. J. Johnson, Sonny Rollins, the Art Farmer–Benny Golson Jazztet, and others. Hard bop is usually regarded as being characterized by dark, weighty, earthy timbres, soulful inflections of pitch, blues-like melodic figures, and, sometimes, harmonies and chord progressions reminiscent of the sanctified church; although less than half of the material played by the above-mentioned musicians has these characteristics, alternative labels such as "post-bop" have not found general acceptance. Musicians themselves often make no distinction between the bop styles that originated in the 1940s and later variants of these styles in the work of Clifford Brown, Silver, and Cannonball and Nat Adderley, referring to them all collectively as "bebop" or "bop." Nevertheless, the players of the 1950s took a different approach in that they adopted lighter, more flexible piano accompaniment, louder, more interactive drumming (as shown in the work of Blakey, Philly Joe Jones, and Louis Hayes), and more facile bass playing (notably that of Paul Chambers and Sam Jones). They also drew less frequently on the compositional form and chord sequences of popular songs.

Most players in the hard-bop idiom were black, and a large percentage of its most important exponents came from the metropolitan areas of Detroit (Chambers, Hayes, Thad Jones, Elvin Jones, Barry Harris, Tommy Flanagan, Kenny Burrell, Donald Byrd, Pepper Adams) and Philadelphia (Brown, Lee Morgan, McCoy Tyner, Philly Joe Jones, Jimmy Heath, John Coltrane, Bobby Timmons, Golson). The hard-bop recordings that gained widest circulation and became known to the general public usually contained the smallest amounts of improvisation, the simplest, most tuneful solos, the greatest number of straightforward, repetitive accompaniments, and the funkiest melodies. Among the better known were Silver's *Señor Blues* (1956) and *Song for my Father* (1964), Cannonball Adderley's *Sack o' Woe* (1960), Nat Adderley's *Work Song* (1960) and *Jive Samba* (1962), Timmons's *Moanin'* (1958), *Dis Here* (1959), and *Dat Dere* (1960), Joe Zawinul's *Mercy, mercy, mercy* (1966), Morgan's *The Sidewinder* (1963), Ben Tucker's *Comin' Home Baby* (1965), and Herbie Hancock's *Watermelon Man* (1962).

A number of players who introduced elements of black gospel music were also described as playing hard bop (or funky or SOUL JAZZ), though their contribution to the development of jazz was considerably slighter. These include Jimmy Smith, Richard "Groove" Holmes, Jack McDuff, Ramsey Lewis, Les McCann, Timmons, Stanley Turrentine, and occasionally, for their instrumental work, Ray Charles and his associates.

See also JAZZ (i), §V, 7.

BIBLIOGRAPHY

J.-E. Berendt: *Das Jazzbuch: Entwicklung und Bedeutung der Jazzmusik* (Frankfurt am Main, Germany, 1953, rev. 2/1959 as *Das neue Jazzbuch*, Eng. trans., New York, 1962; rev. and enlarged 5/1981 as *Das grosse Jazzbuch: von New Orleans bis Jazz Rock*, Eng. trans. as *The Jazz Book: from New Orleans to Fusion and Beyond*, Westport, CT, 1982)

M. Williams: "The Funky–Hard Bop Regression," *The Art of Jazz: Essays on the Nature and Development of Jazz* (New York, 1959/R1979 as *The Art of Jazz: Ragtime to Bebop*), 233

M. James: "Drum Roles," *JM*, vi/6 (1960), 9

J. Cooke: "Eight Years in Eight Minutes: an Outline of the Hard Bop Era," *JM*, xiii/2 (1967), 2

M. Harrison and others: *Modern Jazz: the Essential Records: a Critical Selection* (London, 1975)

M. C. Gridley: *Jazz Styles* (Englewood Cliffs, NJ, 1978, rev. 2/1985 as *Jazz Styles: History and Analysis*, with suppl. *Instructor's Manual and Discography*)

MARK C. GRIDLEY

Hardee, John (*b* Corsicana, TX, 20 Dec 1918; *d* Dallas, 18 May 1984). Tenor saxophonist. He played piano and mellophone, C-melody saxophone, then alto saxophone. He attended Bishop College, toured as a tenor saxophonist with Don Albert (1937–8), then returned to college, from which he graduated in 1941. Later he was a band director at a school in Texas and played clarinet in army bands. In New York he played with Tiny Grimes (1946) and from 1946 to 1948 recorded swing and bop tunes as a leader (including *Bad Man's Bounce/Baby, watch that stuff*, 1947, Reg. 121). He also recorded with Russell Procope, Earl Bostic, and Billy Kyle (all 1946), Helen Humes (1947), Billy Taylor (ii) (1949), and Lucky Millinder (1950). After moving to Dallas he played in clubs as a leader until the early 1960s and led school bands until around 1976. In 1975 he appeared at the festival in Nice, France.

BIBLIOGRAPHY

E. Townley: "A School Teacher from Dallas," *JJ*, xxix/5 (1976), 4

B. Rusch: "John Hardee: Interview," *Cadence*, iv/1 (1978), 16

Harden, Wilbur (*b* Birmingham, AL, 1925). Trumpeter and flugelhorn player. In the 1950s he worked as a rhythm-and-blues sideman in the bands of Roy Brown and Ivory Joe Hunter; he played in a navy band and then moved to Detroit. He first played jazz when he replaced Curtis Fuller in Yusef Lateef's group in the spring of 1957. In 1957 Harden recorded in New York with Lateef and the following year led four sessions for the Savoy label; three of these were made with John Coltrane and later reissued under Coltrane's name. Harden fell ill in 1959 and ceased full-time playing. He was one of the earliest trumpeters to take up flugelhorn, and he used that instrument on his recordings. His playing was noted for its melodic inventiveness and lyricism; he was strongly influenced by Miles Davis.

SELECTED RECORDINGS

As leader: *Mainstream 1958* (1958, Savoy 12127); *Tanganyika Strut* (1958, Savoy 12136); *Jazz Way Out* (1958, Savoy 12131); *The King and I* (1958, Savoy 12134)

As sideman: Y. Lateef: *Prayer to the East* (1957, Savoy 12117); J. Coltrane: *Standard Coltrane* (1958, Prst. 7243)

BIBLIOGRAPHY

FeatherE

M. Gardner: "Wilbur Harden and Louis Smith: Forgotten Faces of the Fifties," *JJ*, xxi/5 (1968), 19

FREDERICK A. BECK

Hardin, Lil(lian). *See* ARMSTRONG, LIL.

Harding, Buster [Lavere] (*b* Ontario, Canada, 19 March 1917; *d* New York, 14 Nov 1965). Arranger. He grew up in Cleveland, where at the age of 13 he played piano in the band of Marion Sears; after moving to New York in 1938 he worked as a pianist and arranger for Teddy Wilson's big band (1939–40). In the early 1940s he wrote many swing arrangements for such leaders as Cab Calloway (including *Jonah Joins the Cab*, often attributed, incorrectly, to Andy Gibson), Count Basie, Benny Goodman, Earl Hines, and Artie Shaw, and less frequently for Coleman Hawkins, Larry Clinton, Tommy Dorsey, Glenn Miller, and Lucky Millinder. After World War II he led a band that sometimes accompanied Billie Holiday, and played in the big band of Roy Eldridge during its brief existence. Harding's best arrangements are characterized by dense harmonies, a sense of drive, and strong blues influences; his work is far superior to the commercially oriented material that predominated during his career.

SELECTED ARRANGEMENTS

Recorded by C. Basie: Stampede in G minor (1940, OK 5987); Rockin' the Blues (1940, OK 6010); 9:20 Special (1941, OK 6244)

Recorded by C. Calloway: Jonah Joins the Cab (1941, OK 6109); Tappin' Off (1941, OK 6547); A Smo-o-oth One (1941, OK 6720)

Recorded by A. Shaw: The Sad Sack (1945, Vic. 201647); The Glider (1945, Musi. 378); The Hornet (1945, Musi. 409)

Recorded by others: B. Goodman: Scarecrow (1941, Col. 36180); E. Hines: Windy City Jive (1941, Bb 11329)

BIBLIOGRAPHY

ChiltonW; *FeatherE*; *Feather '60s*

P. Turley: "Three Forgotten Men," *JM*, iv/12 (1959), 29

CHRIS SHERIDAN

Hardman, Bill [William Franklin, Jr.] (*b* Cleveland, 6 April 1933). Trumpeter and flugelhorn player. He studied trombone and trumpet as a youth. Armstrong and Roy Eldridge were early influences, and at the age of 16 he heard Charlie Parker. While still in high school he played with Tadd Dameron, and after graduating he toured with Tiny Bradshaw (1953–5). He played with Jackie McLean (1955), Charles Mingus (1956, 1969–70), Art Blakey (1956–8, 1966–9, and in the 1970s), briefly with Horace Silver (1958), intermittently with Lou Donaldson (1959–66), and with Lloyd Price's big band (1963). From 1972, with Bill Lee and Billy Higgins, he led the Brass Company, a large ensemble including four or five trumpets, two flugelhorns, and a rhythm section, which sought to re-create the thick textures characteristic of the sound produced by Miles Davis's groups during the period of his collaboration with Gil Evans. In 1973 Hardman won the *Down Beat* Critics' Poll. In the late 1970s he led a group with Junior Cook. Hardman's trumpet playing was influenced chiefly by Benny Bailey, but also by Joe Gordon, Kenny Dorham, Fats Navarro, and Clifford Brown; his style is aggressive, straightforward bop.

For illustration *see* BANDS, fig.5.

SELECTED RECORDINGS

As leader: *Bill Hardman* (1961, Savoy 12170); of Brass Company (with B. Higgins and B. Lee): *Colors* (1975, SE 19752); *Home* (1978, Muse 5152); *Politely* (1981, Muse 5184)

As sideman: J. McLean: *Jackie's Pal* (1956, Prst. 7068); A. Blakey: *Hard Bop* (1956, Col. CL1040); *Art Blakey's Jazz Messengers with Thelonious Monk* (1957, Atl. 1278); *Buhaina: the Continuing Message* (1957, Beth. 6023); *Art Blakey's Big Band* (1957, Beth. 6027); L. Donaldson: *Fried Buzzard* (1967, Cadet 842); E. Jefferson: *Come Along with me* (1969, Prst. 7698)

BIBLIOGRAPHY

FeatherE; *Feather–Gitler '70s*

M. James: "Trumpet Trio: Bill Hardman, Freddie Hubbard, Lee Morgan," *JM*, vii/10 (1961), 4

J. B. Litweiler: "Profile: Bill Hardman," *DB*, xliii/7 (1976), 34

B. Case: "Hardman: Hard Bop Hero," *MM*, lv (26 Jan 1980), 30

ANDRÉ BARBERA

Hardwick(e), Otto [Toby] (*b* Washington, 31 May 1904; *d* Washington, 5 Aug 1970). Alto saxophonist. He began as a double bass player and changed to C-melody saxophone before specializing on the alto instrument. In Washington he was an early associate of Duke Ellington, with whom he spent much of his career, though he left the band in 1928 to visit Europe. He worked in Paris with several groups, including an orchestra of his own and that of Noble Sissle. The following year he returned to New York, played with Chick Webb, and then formed another group, which included Chu Berry and Fats Waller and had the rare distinction of defeating Ellington's orchestra in a "battle of the bands." After playing briefly with Elmer Snowden, Hardwick rejoined Ellington in 1932; during this second period he concentrated on section work, though he occasionally played sentimental solos in ballads. He left the band in 1946 and retired from music shortly afterwards.

During the 1920s Hardwick played clarinet and violin as well as members of the saxophone family, and he performed on bass saxophone until about 1939; but it was for his alto saxophone playing that he was particularly admired by other musicians. He also composed several pieces in collaboration with Ellington, of which the best-known is *Sophisticated Lady*.

For illustration *see* BANDS, fig.3, and WASHINGTONIANS.

SELECTED RECORDINGS

As leader: Come Sunday (1947, Wax 102)

As sideman: D. Ellington: Take it Easy (1928, OK 41013); Jubilee Stomp (1928, Vic. 21580); Got Everything but you (1928, Vic. 21703); Sophisticated Lady (1933, Col. CB591); In a Sentimental Mood (1945, Vic. 203291); S. Greer: The Mooche (1945, Cap. 10028)

BIBLIOGRAPHY

S. Dance: *The World of Duke Ellington* (London and New York, 1970/*R*1981) [colln of previously pubd articles and interviews], 55

D. Ellington: *Music is my Mistress* (Garden City, NY, 1973), 50

D. M. Bakker: *Duke Ellington on Microgroove*, i: *1923–1936* (Alphen aan de Rijn, Netherlands, rev. 3/1977), 7

EDDIE LAMBERT

Harewood, Al(phonse) (*b* New York, 3 June 1923). Drummer. He began his professional career in the 1950s, performing with J. J. Johnson and Kai Winding (1954–6), Gigi Gryce, Art Farmer, the tenor saxophonist George Barrow, and Lou Donaldson (1959–61); he also recorded with David Amram (1956), Curtis Fuller (1958), Benny Golson (1959), Horace Parlan (1960–61), and Grant Green (1961–3). In 1962, after playing briefly with Mary Lou Williams, he joined Stan Getz, with whom he remained until 1964, and in 1967–8 he was a member of Amram's quintet. In the 1970s he performed with Chuck Wayne and Joe Williams (1971), the Newport Jazz Festival All-Stars (1973–4), and the double bass player Lisle Atkinson, and again recorded with Fuller (*c*1975) and Parlan (1977). He also taught music at Livingston College, Rutgers (1973–5). From 1978 to 1981 he played with the Descendants of Mike and Phoebe and in 1983 he began working with Lee Konitz.

SELECTED RECORDINGS

As sideman: J. J. Johnson and K. Winding: *Jay and Kai, Dec. 3, 1954* (1954, Prst. 195); H. Parlan: *Speakin' my Piece* (1960, BN 4043); G. Green: *Idle Moments* (1963, BN 84154); B. Carter: *Betty Carter* (*c*1971, Bet-Car MK1001); L. Atkinson: *Bass Contra Bass* (1978, Jazzcraft 7)

BIBLIOGRAPHY

Feather '60s

RICK MATTINGLY

Harlem Blues and Jazz Band. Group formed in 1972 by Al Vollmer; its purpose was to give opportunities to several veteran musicians of the 1920s and 1930s who were then residing in New York and largely inactive as performers. Led by the trombonist Clyde Bernhardt, its other members were the trumpeter Franc Williams, the alto saxophonist George James, the pianist Reuben Jay Cole (replaced after his death in 1975 by Dill Jones and then Ram Ramirez), the tuba player Barbara Dreiwitz (later replaced by Johnny Williams), the drummer Tommy Benford, and the singer Miss Rhapsody (Viola Wells). In 1979 Bernhardt relinquished the leadership and from 1980 the group was led by the trumpeter Bobby Williams, who engaged a number of other musicians: the trombonist Eddie Durham, the saxophonist George Kelly (later replaced by Eddie Chamblee and Charlie Frazier), the drummer Shelton Gary (later replaced by Ronnie Cole, Belton Evans, and Johnny Blowers), the guitarist Al Casey, and, for occasional appearances, the singer Princess White. The group toured Europe annually from 1976 and remained in existence into the late 1980s; its playing may be heard to advantage on the albums *Harlem Blues & Jazz Band 1973–1980* (1973–80, Barron 403) and *Harlem Blues and Jazz Band* (*c*1980, Barron 404).

BIBLIOGRAPHY

D. Griffiths: "Harlem Blues," *MR*, ii/2 (1975), 7

C. Hillman: "Jazz in the 70s: a Profile of the Clyde Bernhardt Harlem Blues and Jazz Band," *JJI*, xxx/9 (1977), 14

C. Hillman: "The Bernhardt Band in Belgium," *JJI*, xxxi/8 (1978), 21

E. Townley: "The Clyde Bernhardt Harlem Jazz and Blues Band," *JJI*, xxxii/7 (1979), 16

C. Bernhardt and S. Harris: *I Remember: Eighty Years of Black Entertainment, Big Bands, and the Blues* (Philadelphia, 1986) [incl. discography]

MIKE HAZELDINE

Harlem Hamfats. Septet. It was formed by J. Mayo Williams, who gave the group its name, and led by the trumpeter Herb Morand and the guitarist Joe McCoy; the group's other instruments were mandolin (played by McCoy's brother, Charlie McCoy, who also sometimes played guitar), clarinet, piano, double bass, and drums. The Hamfats' unique sound, a fusion of the New Orleans jazz of Morand and the Mississippi blues of the McCoy brothers, and incorporating elements of the style known as barrelhouse jazz, was a precursor of rhythm-and-blues, and preceded by several years similar developments in the work of Louis Jordan (*see* BLUES, §10). The group's rollicking performances of such tunes as *Let's Get Drunk and Truck* (1936, Decca 7205) were heard often on jukeboxes in the late 1930s. (P. Van Vorst: "The Harlem Hamfats," *MR*, iv (1977), no.4, p.5; no.5, p.8)

PAIGE VAN VORST

Harlem Kiddies. Danish quintet. It was formed in 1940 by the black drummer Kaj Timmermann (*b* Copenhagen, 16 May 1912) and included two other Blacks, the alto saxophonist Jonny Campbell (*b* Copenhagen, 15 July 1917), and his brother, the guitarist Jimmy Campbell (*b* Oslo, 31 March 1916). Between 1941 and 1945 the group made a series of recordings (including *One o' Clock Jump*, 1941, Odeon D508) that reflected the influence of the Harlem jump style and of Cuban music. In 1947 Jonny Campbell assumed leadership of the group, which continued to perform under his name; from the mid-1950s it worked principally as a dance band.

ERIK WIEDEMANN

Harlequin. Record label. It was established by Bruce Bastin in Crawley, England, in 1981, as part of his company Interstate Music; the latter was formed to take over operation of the Flyright Record and Distributing Co. of Bexhill-on-Sea. (The organization's labels, Flyright and Magpie, continued to be devoted mainly to blues under Interstate's management, although both were used to issue some jazz.) The label Harlequin was launched in 1982; the catalogue has included reissues of material from the 1920s, swing (drawn from the labels Variety and Joe Davis), and various types of jazz from the 1950s and 1960s. The label is also notable for a special series, Jazz and Hot Dance; conceived and largely selected by Rainer Lotz, it consists of historical anthologies which document the development of jazz in various countries.

Harley, Rufus (*b* Raleigh, NC, 20 May 1936). Bagpiper. His family moved to Philadelphia when he was a child, and he played saxophone in high school. In the mid-1960s he took up bagpipes and formed his own group, with which he recorded four albums between 1965 and 1969 (including *Scotch and Soul*, 1966, Atl. 3006). He has also recorded single tracks as a guest musician with Sonny Stitt (1966), Herbie Mann (1967), and Sonny Rollins (at the Montreux International Jazz Festival, 1974). (*Feather–Gitler '70s*)

Harmograph. Record label. It was established in 1921 by the Harmograph Talking Machine Co., a subsidiary of the Shapleigh Hardware Co. of St. Louis. At first it issued recordings originally put out by Cameo; after about a year it began to draw material (often using alternate takes) from Paramount, including important jazz from the latter's race series. By mid-1924 Harmograph was being used to issue items from the catalogues of Pathé and Perfect; trading apparently ceased at the end of 1925.

BIBLIOGRAPHY

J. Randolph: "The St. Louis Labels: Harmograph and Herwin," *Playback*, ii/3–4 (1949), 6

M. Wyler: "A Glimpse of the Past, 7: Harmograph," *Sv*, no.10 (1967), 25

B. Whyatt: "Harmograph: a Numerical Listing," *Sv*, no.56 (1974–5), 50; no.57 (1975), 97; no.58 (1975), 135; no.59 (1975), 175; no.60 (1975), 208; no.61 (1975), 16; no.62 (1975–6), 53

——: "Harmograph Label: a Report," *Sv*, no.92 (1980–81), 54

Harmolodic theory [harmolodics]. A theory evolved by ORNETTE COLEMAN in the late 1970s relating to his improvisations with the electric band Prime Time. The nature and application in Coleman's music of harmolodic improvisation are unclear but, insofar as Coleman's explanation can be understood, it apparently involves the simultaneous sounding, in different tonalities and at different pitches (determined by, for example, a notional change of clef) but in otherwise unchanged form, of a single melodic or thematic line; the procedure produces a type of simple heterophony. (A table of typical pitch relationships between the lines that result is given in Loupias.) More generally the harmolodic theory espouses principles already well established in free jazz, namely equality among instruments (rather than the traditional separation between soloist and accompaniment) in harmonically free collective improvisation. According to Ronald Shannon Jackson, a member of Prime Time, the term derives from a conflation of the words "harmony," "movement," and "melody"; Jackson has also stated that, in his opinion, the term has no precise musical meaning (see Giddins). References to the harmolodic theory arise in discussions not only of Coleman's work but of the independent work of musicians who have been sidemen in his bands, notably James "Blood" Ulmer, Jamaaladeen Tacuma, and Don Cherry.

BIBLIOGRAPHY

H. Mandel: "Ornette Coleman: the Creator as Harmolodic Magician," *DB*, xlv/16 (1978), 17 [incl. discography]

C. J. Safane: "The Harmolodic Diatonic Funk of James "Blood" Ulmer," *DB*, xlvii/10 (1980), 22

D. Wild and M. Cuscuna: "A Note on the Harmolodic Theory," *Ornette Coleman, 1958–1979: a Discography* (Ann Arbor, MI, 1980), appx

B. Loupias: "James Blood Ulmer: un sang nouveau pour nos sillons?," *Jm*, no.294 (1981), 34

C. Tinder: "Jamaaladeen Tacuma: Electric Bass in the Harmolodic Pocket," *DB*, xlix/4 (1982), 19

A. Bresnick and R. Fine: "Ornette Coleman: Interview," *Cadence*, viii/9 (1982), 5

O. Coleman: "Prime Time for Harmolodics," *DB*, l/7 (1983), 54

G. Giddins: "Harmolodic Hoedown," *Village Voice*, xxix (27 March 1984), 38

——: *Rhythm-a-ning: Jazz Tradition and Innovation in the '80s* (New York, and Oxford, England, 1985) [colln of previously pubd articles], 95

BARRY KERNFELD

Harmonica [harp, mouth organ]. An instrument consisting of a small casing containing free reeds, which are housed in channels leading to holes on the side of the instrument. It is played by inhalation and exhalation, with the player's tongue used to block the channels of reeds that are not intended to sound. There are two main types of harmonica: the diatonic, upon which exhalation produces the notes of the tonic chord of the key in which the instrument is tuned and inhalation the other notes of the diatonic scale; and the chromatic, which consists of two sets of reeds tuned a semitone apart and a slide mechanism (operated by a small hand-lever) that enables the player to change from one set to the other. Both types of harmonica have a range of three octaves.

The harmonica would seem to have promise as a jazz instrument: it is a free-reed instrument capable of producing a wide range of voice-like timbres, and it is the most important reed instrument used in blues. In fact it has been of little importance in jazz, perhaps because of the inability of the diatonic instrument to play music that is harmonically complex, and the difficulty of achieving on the chromatic instrument a level of proficiency adequate to the technical demands of many jazz styles. There were no important harmonica players in early jazz, though the instrument was used occasionally in lesser-known jug bands and washboard bands that had repertories combining jazz and blues (such as the Dixie Jassers Washboard Band, which recorded in 1927). In later years there emerged two prominent jazz harmonica players: Larry Adler (whose work in jazz remains secondary to his work in classical and popular music) and Toots Thielemans; the latter's playing is well represented on his album *Man Bites Harmonica* (1957, Riv. 257). Other players of some importance have included Sonny Terry, who recorded with Chris Barber's band in 1958; Buddy Lucas, who toured and recorded as a guest soloist with the Thad Jones–Mel Lewis Orchestra in 1974; and Malachi Favors of the Art Ensemble of Chicago.

BARRY KERNFELD

Harmon [wa-wa, wah-wah] **mute.** *See* MUTE, §2(f).

Harmony (i). The combining of notes simultaneously to produce chords and the placing of chords in succession, whether or not to produce tonally functional progressions; the word is used also of the system of structural principles governing chords and progressions. For a discussion of harmony as the basis of formal organization *see* FORMS.

1. Terminology and theory: (i) Introduction (ii) Intervals and chords (iii) Dissonance (iv) Inversion and voicing (v) Chord progressions (vi) Extensions of tonality and modal harmony. 2. History.

1. TERMINOLOGY AND THEORY.

(i) Introduction. As interest in jazz has grown in institutions of higher learning, the discussion of jazz harmony has relied increasingly on the terms and concepts evolved by theorists to deal with Western classical music. This trend has had the beneficial effect of unifying what had been a rather disparate and uninformed usage, but it has brought with it certain problems. Because jazz differs in many ways from Western classical music, terms and concepts developed for the latter are not always applicable to jazz. Not all terms are neutrally descriptive, and the assumptions underlying some terms (such as "consonance" and "dissonance") need to be reconsidered in view of the realities of certain styles of jazz.

There has been nearly as great a range and variety of harmonic styles in the brief history of jazz as in all the centuries of Western classical music, and in many ways their developments have run the same course. In general the apparatus of harmonic analysis is best suited to music having a relatively simple harmonic basis, such as triadic early jazz or 18th-century classical music; bop and jazz of the 1960s and 1970s present harmonic complexities equivalent to (though in many ways different from) those of late Romanticism, Impressionism, and 20th-century tonal music. That traditional harmonic theory has been found to be inadequate by itself to explicate these classical styles is best illustrated by the development and application of alternative approaches to harmonic analysis, notably the theories of Heinrich Schenker. The difficulties posed by the harmonic analysis of jazz lie not only in applying inherited classical concepts to jazz but also in applying them to styles of jazz where they have differing degrees of relevance.

Western harmonic theory is based on two sets of relationships: that between the notes of a single chord and that between successive chords. In medieval and renaissance music vertical combinations are seen mainly as the result of contrapuntal movement, whereas, in later practice, voice-leading is seen to be governed principally by harmonic considerations. Although the contrapuntal origin of harmony has maintained its influence in the analysis of classical music, in jazz its importance has often been obscured by concentration on vertical structures in all but the most recent theory. The inability of jazz theory to deal with contrapuntal movement is but one indication that a complete understanding of jazz harmony has yet to be arrived at.

(ii) Intervals and chords. The commonly accepted definitions of intervals and chords are current in jazz theory, but the terminology and notation used in analyzing and describing jazz may differ somewhat from classical practice. Depending on context, minor or diminished intervals may be called "flat" or "lowered," and major or augmented ones "sharp" or "raised."

Triads retain their conventional names (major, minor, diminished, and augmented), except for one usage peculiar to jazz: a triad in which the third above the root is replaced by a fourth is called a "suspended triad" or a "triad sus 4"; in this case the fourth above the root is not necessarily suspended (in the classical sense) from the preceding chord. Names for types of seventh chords are conventional, with a few variations. Although classical theorists sometimes call a dominant seventh structure (major triad plus minor seventh) a "major-minor seventh chord," jazz musicians always call it a "dominant seventh chord," regardless of the scale degree on which it is built or its contextual function. Similarly, "augmented dominant seventh" is preferred in jazz usage to the classical term "augmented minor seventh." A dominant seventh structure built with a suspended triad is called a "suspended seventh" or "dominant seventh sus 4," or "suspended dominant seventh." The half-diminished seventh has been called "minor seventh flat 5" in jazz usage; however, the classical term has been gradually gaining favor. The names of other seventh chords agree with traditional usage: major seventh, minor seventh, diminished seventh, minor-major seventh (ex.1). (For notational conventions used in this article *see* NOTATION; see also §(v)(a) below).

Ex.1 Terms used in jazz for seventh chords

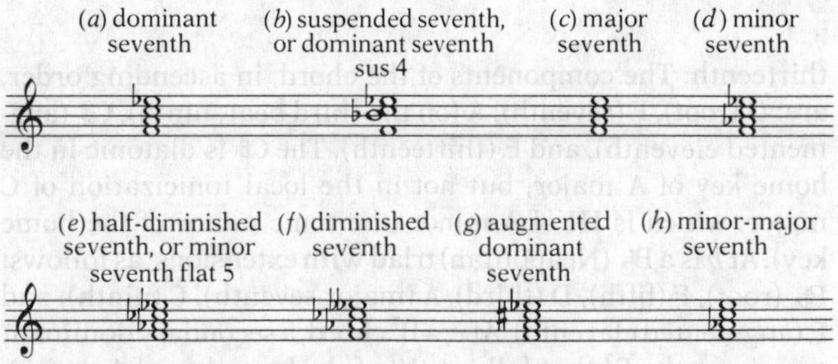

An extended chord is produced when 3rds beyond the seventh are added to the triad (i.e., the ninth, eleventh, thirteenth, etc.). The added notes are normally derived from the diatonic scale of the local key or tonicization (as, for example, in the first and last chords of ex. 2, which respectively include a major

Ex.2 Extensions in spread voicings at the opening of Benny Golson's *Starfire* from Maynard Ferguson's *A Message from Birdland* (1959, Roul. 52027); transcr. S. Strunk

ninth, and a major seventh and a major ninth, as the prevailing key dictates). Dominant sevenths are particularly subject to extension. An altered chord is one in which an element or elements of the chord other than the root, third, or seventh may be regarded as borrowings from the tonic minor key if the prevailing key is major, or the tonic major key if the prevailing key is minor, or from another scale altogether (such as the phrygian or lydian modes). Dominant chords and particularly extended dominants often contain such altered elements. In ex.3 at *a* is a G^7 chord, with ninth, augmented eleventh, and

Ex.3 Extended chords in the first chorus of *Waltz for Debby* from *The Bill Evans Album* (1971, Col. C30855); transcr. P. Dreyfuss

thirteenth. The components of the chord, in ascending order, are: G (root), F (seventh), A (on the third beat, ninth), C♯ (augmented eleventh), and E (thirteenth). The C♯ is diatonic in the home key of A major, but not in the local tonicization of C major, which is III of A minor (the tonic minor of the home key). At *b* is a B♭ (Neapolitan) triad with extensions, as follows: B♭ (root), F (fifth), D (third), A (major seventh), C (ninth), and E (augmented eleventh). At *c*, a B^7 chord, a secondary dominant tonicizing the E^7 that follows (V^7 of the home key of A major), might be expected to contain a G♯ as a thirteenth since the G♯ in the E^7 chord suggests a major mode for the B^7; however, the B^7 contains a G♮, which is a minor thirteenth borrowed from the parallel (E) minor mode. At *d*, an $F♯^7$ chord, dominant of B, is extended to include G♯ (ninth) and D♯ (thirteenth), which are members of the B major scale; on the third beat these extensions are altered to their minor counterparts, G♮ and D♮, members of the B minor scale. Similarly the second chord in ex.2 is an altered dominant in G containing a minor thirteenth (B♭) and a minor ninth (E♭).

(iii) Dissonance. The distinction between consonance and dissonance as they are regarded in the theory of tonal classical music has only residual relevance to jazz. In early jazz the two principal categories of dissonance (inessential dissonances being those that can be resolved within a single chord, and essential dissonances being those that can be resolved only upon a change of chord) continue to be operative. But the development of jazz harmony (like that of Western music generally) has resulted in a gradual erosion of these distinctions and a blurring of the concept of dissonance itself. For example, the notes added to the triad to form extended chords (discussed in §(ii) above) are, according to Western harmonic theory, nonessential diatonic (or, when altered, nondiatonic) dissonances; but they are often treated in jazz harmony as if they were essential – that is, their resolution is delayed until there is a change of harmony – and are thus incorporated into the chord. Furthermore, jazz harmony often contains "dissonant" notes the resolution of which is long delayed or never occurs at all; the commonest example of this kind is the added sixth. One view of such notes is that they are elements of "color" and therefore have to do with timbre rather than functional harmony; another is that the level of dissonance in jazz has simply risen to the point at which (as many texts on arrangement state) no chord "should" have fewer than four different notes.

(iv) Inversion and voicing. Perhaps because the bass lines of most jazz performances are improvised, and because bass players usually play the root of a chord at least once while that harmony lasts, jazz musicians tend to think of all chords as being in root position. Inversions appear in jazz in styles that make little use of extended chords (i.e., early jazz and jazz-rock) and in works with composed bass lines. Inversions are notated with letter chord symbols by placing the chord symbol before and the bass note after a slash (solidus) (ex.4). (Although

Ex.4 Introduction to and part of the first chorus of the duo *Weather Bird* (1928, OK 41454) by Louis Armstrong and Earl Hines

chord symbols are often placed above the staff in jazz notation, they are here placed below the staff, in the usual position for chord labels in analytical texts.) In classical theory a distinction is sometimes made between an inverted chord that can logically be replaced by its root-position form and one that cannot: the latter is considered an "apparent" inversion. This distinction holds for jazz. In ex.4 the first-inversion tonic triad at *a* represents tonic harmony and is a true inversion, as is the supertonic chord at *b*. However, the cadential 6–4 at *c* (an A♭ is implied on the third beat) acts as an embellishment of the root-position dominant seventh, which is the true harmony on the third and fourth beats. Similarly the triad with its fifth in the bass at *d* and the "apparent" third-inversion seventh chord that follows could not be replaced by their root-position forms, as they function as embellishments connecting a IV triad at *e* with a dominant seventh of B♭ (ii in A♭) at *f*. In ex.5 the descent

Ex.5 Inversions in Art Farmer's *Like Someone in Love* (original song by Johnny Burke and Jimmy Van Heusen), from *Modern Art* (1958, UA 4007); transcr. S. Strunk (all parts notated at sounding pitch)

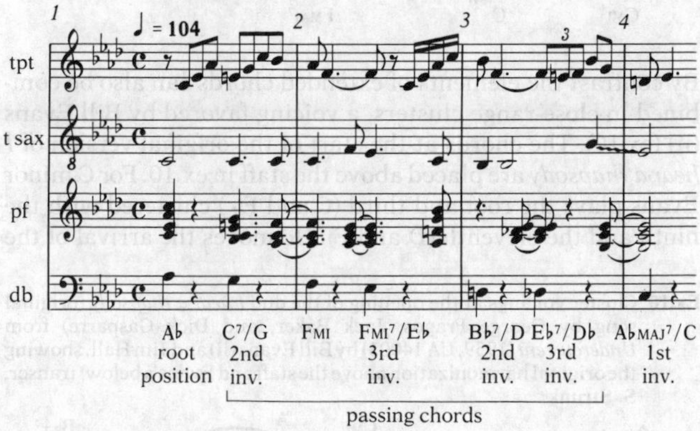

of the bass line from the tonic in bar 1 (supporting a root-position chord) to the mediant in bar 4 (supporting a first inversion of the same harmony) is filled in with stepwise passing-notes, harmonized with passing chords, some of which are in "apparent" inversion.

A further reason why the concept of inversion is less than helpful in the analysis of jazz is that most jazz is not notated. In such cases the identification of chords and progressions is made aurally, often for purposes other than analytical study (by musicians learning a piece from a recording, for instance), and the elements of the chords, not their precise distribution, are the important characteristic. (For further discussion of aural analysis *see* TRANSCRIPTION (i).)

The question of the relative prevalence of root-position and inverted chords in jazz is only one aspect of the difficulties posed by analyzing and notating an essentially improvised music; a basic harmony, as it is named by the analyst, may be realized in performance in many different ways. The particular sonority of a chord depends on the vertical ordering and spacing of its components – that is, its voicing. In a harmonic environment of triads and seventh chords, such as that of New Orleans jazz, the distribution of notes above the assumed root does not allow for much variety or for treatment different from that in any other kind of music. However, with the treatment of the ninth, eleventh, and thirteenth as if essential in the swing era and the subsequent deliberate emphasis on them in bop, musicians were able to use voicings as a means of jazz expression; in some cases particular voicings serve as hallmarks of styles, performers, or arrangers.

Some voicings common in stage-band arranging have been given names. In the voicing known as "four-way close" a melody is harmonized by three other voices grouped as closely as possible (ex.6*a*); "drop two" is a variant of four-way close in which the second voice from the top is pitched an octave lower (ex.6*b*); similarly in "drop two and four" the second voice from

Ex.6 Voicings based on the beginning of the first chorus from Jimmy Giuffre's *Four Brothers* recorded by Woody Herman (1947, Col. 38304)

(a) Four-way close (as performed); transcr. S. Strunk

(b) Drop two (hypothetical)

(c) Drop two and four (hypothetical)

the top of the four-way close arrangement and the bottom voice are both pitched an octave lower (ex.6*c*); "drop three" is a rare voicing, in which the third voice from the top of the four-way close arrangement is pitched an octave lower (ex.7*a*, p.488). In all of these an additional voice may double the melody at the lower octave. "Spread" is the voicing of an extended chord, usually in root position, over a relatively wide range (ex.7*b*, at the points marked with an asterisk, and ex.2; in ex.2 the range covered by the chords is more than two octaves). The playing of a series of chords rich in added dissonance in melodically unadorned voicings, often spread, and usually in parallel motion, is called playing "block chords"; this technique is associated particularly with pianists, but may also occur in scoring for winds (ex.7*c*), or in a climactic chorus of a big-band arrangement (ex.7*b*), or in saxophone voicings such as those shown in exx.6 and 7. A special kind of block chords is the pianistic voicing first popularized by George Shearing and known as "locked hands"; this is equivalent to four-way close in the right hand with the left hand doubling the melody at the lower octave (*see* SHEARING, GEORGE, ex.1, and PIANO, ex.9).

Most voicings in jazz do not make use of all possible extensions at once. Such lush, fully extended series of stacked thirds (root, third, fifth, seventh, ninth, eleventh, and thirteenth) are suitable only in limited contexts, and are normally used only when they are structured in such a way that the dissonant minor 9th interval is not created between one of the upper extensions and one of the triadic pitches in the lower part of the chord (with the exception of the minor ninth above the root of a dominant seventh chord). For example, a chord containing a major third does not usually include a perfect eleventh as an extension. Most voicings obtain their best effect and a desirable degree of dissonance by an economy of means: the minimal essential members of the chord are played (usually root, third, and seventh) with one, or at most two, extensions placed so as to form the interval of a 7th with one of the lower notes of the voicing. Such economy gives voicings character and clarity. For example, in a recording made in 1935 with Benny Goodman, Teddy Wilson voiced a series of dominant thirteenth chords

Ex.7 Voicings in Bill Mathieu's arrangement of Duke Ellington's *I'm beginning to see the light* on Ellington's *Piano in the Background* (1960, Col. CS 8346)

(a) Third chorus after the drum solo

(b) Second chorus

(c) First chorus

with the root in the bass, the third and seventh in inner voices, and the thirteenth placed in the soprano to obtain the "bite" of a major 7th interval between the seventh and the thirteenth (ex.8). Thelonious Monk was known for his stark voicings: for

Ex.8 Piano voicing of 13th chords by Teddy Wilson from the first chorus of Benny Goodman's *Body and Soul* (1935, Vic. 25115; original song by Johnny Green); transcr. S. Pease, *DB*, iv/8 (1937), 26

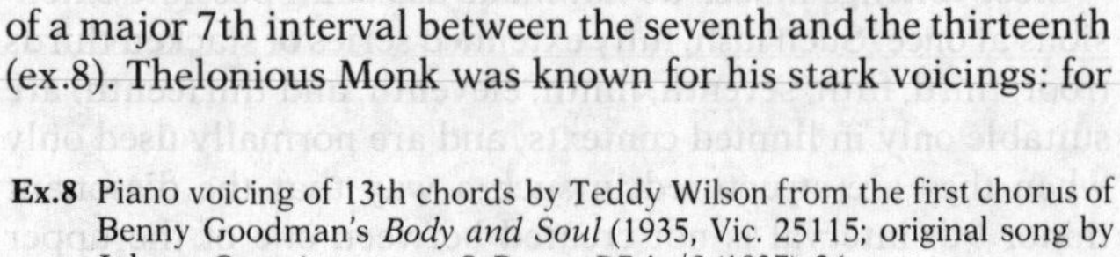

example, in the third chorus of his solo on *I Mean You* (1963) the first 15 bars consist of a series of 10ths each made up of two elements chosen from the succession of harmonies (ex.9).

Ex.9 Open voicing in the third chorus of Thelonious Monk's *I Mean You* from *Big Band and Quartet in Concert* (1963, Col. CS8964); transcr. B. Dobbins

By contrast the elements of extended chords can also be combined in close-range clusters, a voicing favored by Bill Evans (ii) (ex.10). The chords at the start of the original version of *I hear a rhapsody* are placed above the staff in ex.10. For C minor Evans plays the root and third (C and E♭) clustered with the ninth and the eleventh (D and F). He moves the arrival of the

Ex.10 Cluster voicings at the opening of the duo *I hear a rhapsody* (original song by George Fragos, Jack Baker, and Dick Gasparre) from *Undercurrent* (1959, UA 14003) by Bill Evans (ii) and Jim Hall, showing the original harmonization above the staff and Evans's below; transcr. S. Strunk

A♭ chord to the downbeat of the next bar, preceding it by an ambiguous voicing that could be interpreted either as the dominant seventh of A♭ (E♭7) or the substitute dominant (see §(v)(b) below) of A♭ (B𝄫7) (the notes of the chords in both interpretations are named in ex.10, with enharmonic changes shown in parentheses and using the notation described in §(v)(a) below). The A♭ chord has a major seventh (G) placed next to the root of the chord to form the lowest note. The B♭+7 chord of the original is replaced by another ambiguous voicing, which could represent either B♭7 or its substitute dominant (E7).

A characteristic voicing developed by bop musicians is the arrangement of harmonic elements to make stacks of 4ths – a sort of "quartal" harmony. However, few chords are arranged solely in 4ths. In ex.11, the four lower voices of the piano chords

Ex.11 Voicings in fourths in the first chorus of Paul Horn's *Mirage for Miles* from *The Sound of Paul Horn* (1961, Col. CS8477)

maintain constant 4ths, and there is one chord made up entirely of 4ths (marked with an asterisk). (Horn's reference to Miles Davis is musical as well as verbal: these voicings should be compared with those in ex.17, p.492.) The double bass arpeggiates stacked 5ths, inverting the 4ths of the upper parts. A further instance occurs in ex.3, where the chord in bar 5 is mainly constructed of 4ths. Because the sum of each pair of 4ths is a 7th, a voicing in 4ths produces the dissonant effect of a 7th interval between extension and chord tone in a manner similar to that achieved by the extended chord voicings described above.

(v) Chord progressions. The language of jazz harmony may be understood largely in terms of classical tonal analysis, but in certain respects the relationships that characterize tonal harmony do not govern jazz, any more than they govern much 20th-century music, experimental music, or other forms of popular music. The question of dissonance has already been discussed (see §(iii) above); similarly, parallel motion (regarded as undesirable in classical harmony) is standard in jazz, and seventh chords are the norm. Harmonic rhythm (the rate at which harmonies change) is less often attended to in traditional harmonic analysis than the constitution of the harmonies themselves; the case is the same with jazz but the importance of harmonic rhythm in different styles of jazz is decisive and easily identified (see §2).

The present thinking about harmonic progression is the result of the contributions over several centuries of many theorists, notably Jean-Philippe Rameau, Hugo Riemann, and Heinrich Schenker. Riemann's concept of functional harmony (according to which all progressions are seen to derive ultimately from the progression tonic–subdominant–dominant–tonic) has been adapted in jazz theory to classify chords that may be substituted for one another in improvisation, and to serve as a framework for the teaching of chord progressions. Schenker's theory of structural levels (which interprets long-term harmonic and tonal changes as elaborations on different levels of a fundamental tonic–dominant–tonic progression) has gained an important place in jazz analysis: it is particularly useful in the discussion of bop and other styles in which local complexities obscure simple underlying progressions; it has been applied fruitfully to the improvised melodies of Charlie Parker (by Thomas Owens) and Clifford Brown (by Milton Stewart), and to performances of *'Round Midnight* (by Steve Larson).

(a) Notation. The terminology and notation of chord symbols based on letter names is capable only of describing chords in isolation, not of expressing relations between chords (see, for instance, ex.4 above). Instead of using symbols of this kind alone, it is now common practice in the analysis of jazz to label chords in progressions by adapting a method of roman-numeral notation from that used in classical theory, which identifies chords in relationship to a given key. However, there are variations, both in the use of roman numerals in general, and in their use in jazz analysis in particular. In classical theory the roman numeral identifies the root of the chord as a scale degree. Thus in the key of C the roman numeral IV identifies the chord built on the fourth scale degree, F. The problem of expressing alterations or additions to the chord is dealt with in various ways. At times it may not be desirable to express the exact structure of the chord – certain analytical observations are most clearly shown by ignoring details of chord structure; in such a case one would write simply an upper-case roman numeral. Where alterations or additions must be shown the following practices are observed. It is assumed in classical usage that chords are built using the diatonic scale degrees of the key and that the context therefore suggests the chord structure: thus IV in C major would be an F major triad (F–A–C), and II a D minor triad (D–F–A). However, some theorists employ upper-case roman numerals for chords having major thirds, lower-case for chords having minor thirds (e.g., IV and ii in major keys), reinforcing the contextual clues for chord structure when that is desirable. For further reinforcement, special signs are sometimes added after roman numerals: ° for a diminished triad or diminished seventh chord (e.g., vii°), ᶿ for a half-diminished seventh chord (e.g., iiᶿ7 in minor keys), and + for augmented triads (e.g., III+ in minor keys). Nondiatonic roots of chords are indicated by an accidental preceding the roman numeral: thus ♭VII in C major is B♭–D–F. That a chord is a root-position seventh chord is indicated by the addition of the arabic numeral 7 after the roman numeral; ninths and other extensions may be similarly indicated. This usage is derived from Baroque figured-bass practice, the numerals representing diatonic intervals above the bass unless they are modified by flat or sharp signs. If need be, any note of a chord other than the root may be modified in this way: thus in C major, II♯3 is D–F♯–A, a major triad, which if it progressed to V might alternatively be labeled V of V (or V/V), the choice of roman numeral depending on the analytical purpose. Arabic numerals can also indicate the inversions of chords as well as nonharmonic effects such as suspensions and passing-notes.

Some jazz analysts use the classical system as described above. Others omit notation of inversions, believing the concept of inversion to be not generally relevant to jazz. In a popular system presented in *Down Beat*, roman numerals are simply substituted for the letter names in chord-symbol notation. Ex.12*a*

Ex.12 Roman-numeral notation

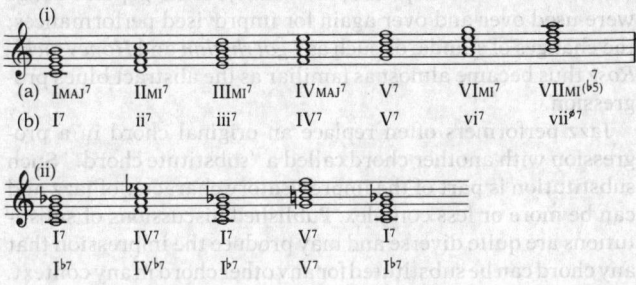

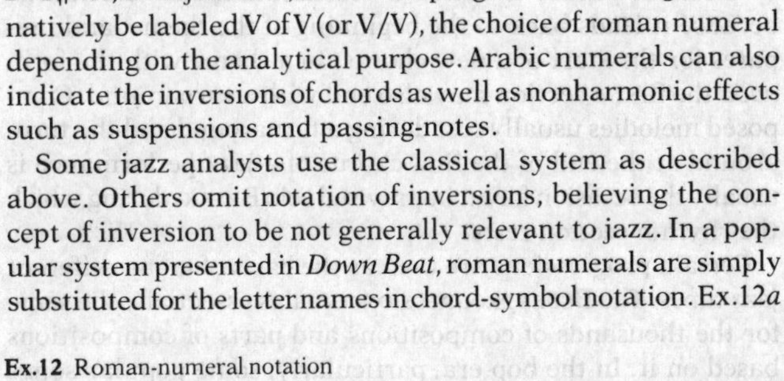

shows (i) the diatonic seventh chords of C major and (ii) a simple blues progression in this notation. Ex.12*b* shows the same in the form of classical notation with upper- and lower-case roman numerals and modified arabic numerals.

Roman-numeral notation is generally used to describe only the essential elements of a chord; the system breaks down if the analyst tries to account for every note, especially in later jazz styles in which extended harmony and altered chords are the norm. Lastly, because most jazz is not notated (or if it is, the notated version is often closely guarded by the musicians), much analysis of jazz harmony is carried out by ear and is therefore often approximate; the written description of a chord analyzed in this way may consequently lack some elements. *See also* NOTATION, §2(ii).

(b) Terms and definitions. Some concepts relating to chord progressions are more closely associated with jazz theory than with standard tonal theory. Among these are the repeated use of a progression for a whole composition, shorter chord patterns, and substitution.

The common practice in jazz of basing a performance on an existing work, most significantly through adopting its underlying harmonic structure, gives rise to a group of terms that describe how musicians treat the fundamental progression. Such a performance relies on the musicians' knowing the "set of changes" (i.e., the harmonic progression of the existing work, which is most often a 32-bar popular song) and being able fluently to perform them; to "run the changes" is to play the progression mechanically and without invention, while to "make the changes" is to play a difficult progression successfully and may further convey connotations of musical invention and ingenuity in its treatment. Similarly to play "inside" is to adhere strictly to the basic changes, while to play "outside" is to treat the changes with a degree of harmonic license.

A "chord pattern" is a progression of two bars which begins on and prepares for a return to the tonic (e.g., I–vi–ii–V). Such patterns occur often and in various locations in popular and jazz tunes, especially at the ends of phrases. One chorus (i.e., statement of or variation on the theme over the basic set of changes) is normally made up of eight-bar phrases, any of which may end with a chord pattern. The chord pattern at the end of the final phrase is called a "turnaround" or "turnback" because it leads back to the beginning of the theme, and prepares for the start of a new chorus. In a theme with the form *aaba* the first *a* section may also end with a turnaround. Composed melodies usually rest during a turnaround and the turnaround at the end of the first chorus of a jazz performance is usually the occasion for an improvised solo BREAK, during which the rhythm section rests.

Certain progressions are used as the basis of many different jazz tunes. The BLUES PROGRESSION remains essentially the same for the thousands of compositions and parts of compositions based on it. In the bop era, particularly, some popular songs were used over and over again for improvised performances; the changes of standards such as *I got rhythm* and *Honeysuckle Rose* thus became almost as familiar as the abstract blues progression.

Jazz performers often replace an original chord in a progression with another chord called a "substitute chord." Such substitution is part of the improvisatory character of jazz and can be more or less complex. Published discussions of substitutions are quite diverse and may produce the impression that any chord can be substituted for any other chord in any context. For most styles of jazz this impression is false. A distinction should be made between those substitutions that may be used freely by the rhythm section during an improvised solo, and those that disrupt the original harmonic plan to the extent that they constitute part of an arrangement, of which the improviser would expect to be informed in advance. The first may be called "improvisatory substitutions" and the second "arranged substitutions."

The main requirement for improvisatory substitutions is that the new chord preserve the essential lines of the original progression. The functional categories of tonic, subdominant, and dominant may each be taken as a set of chords closely enough

Ex.13

related to allow any one to be substituted for any other (ex.13). Within the dominant category the main substitute chord is the "substitute dominant," a dominant seventh structure built on the flatted second degree of the scale; the third and seventh degrees of the substitute dominant are equivalent respectively to the seventh and (enharmonically) the third of the true dominant, allowing the essential lines of progressions involving the dominant to be preserved. (The chords vii^{o7} and vii^{ø7}, although they represent V, are not much used as substitutes for it, as their pitches are already contained in the usual extended dominant ninth. They occur in early jazz, but not as improvisatory substitutes.) In the subdominant category chords IV and ii are substitutes for each other; if the chord on the fourth degree is minor, either a half-diminished seventh chord built on the second scale degree or a dominant seventh structure built on the subtonic (flatted seventh degree) may be substituted for it or for each other. Less frequently, ♭VI^7 and ♭II^7 (both major seventh structures) are substituted for iv. Substitutes for the tonic chord, in major keys only, are iii and vi; another common tonic substitute is the half-diminished seventh chord on the raised fourth degree of the scale, which often initiates a descending chromatic bass line as part of a coda to the final chorus of a performance.

The last substitution category is that of the common-tone diminished seventh. The main use of diminished seventh chords in jazz is as chromatic passing or neighbor chords connecting or embellishing diatonic chords. In each of the three most common configurations the diminished seventh has one or more tones in common with the diatonic chord it embellishes; hence it is usually called a "common-tone" diminished seventh to distinguish it from vii^{o7}, which has no tone in common with the tonic triad to which it usually resolves. Although in later styles of jazz, the common-tone diminished seventh is usually replaced by its substitutes (see ex.13 and below), it may be found in the New Orleans style. In ex.14*a* the tonic triad A♭ is embellished by neighbor-notes which form a common-tone diminished seventh chord. The added upper staff shows the voice-leading in its most logical spelling, which is in part enharmonically equivalent to that in the transcription (enharmonic spelling of diminished seventh chords is commonplace). The dominant ninth is embellished in a similar way in ex.14*b*. The F♯^{o7}/A acts as a lower neighbor to the E♭^{9}/B♭. The common tone, E♭, is not heard explicitly until the last beat of the example. The common-tone diminished seventh chord is a passing chord in ex.14*c* between the tonic chord in first inversion and ii^7, with A♭ as the common tone; again the upper staff shows the voice-leading. In its local context the common-tone diminished seventh chord always occurs as ♯ii^{o7} (F♯^{o7} in E♭ in ex.14*b*, B^{o7} in A♭ in exx.14*a* and *c*). Although in analysis embellishing chords seldom receive roman numerals, for purposes of identification the ♯ii^{o7} is listed in ex.13 along with those chords that are used as substitutes for it. Of these four dominant seventh structures spaced three semitones apart, by far

Ex.14 Common-tone diminished sevenths in the duo *Weather Bird* (1928, OK 41454) by Louis Armstrong and Earl Hines

(a) Embellishing the tonic triad (from the start of the coda)

(b) Embellishing the dominant ninth chord as a neighbor chord

(c) Passing between the tonic chord in first inversion and ii⁷

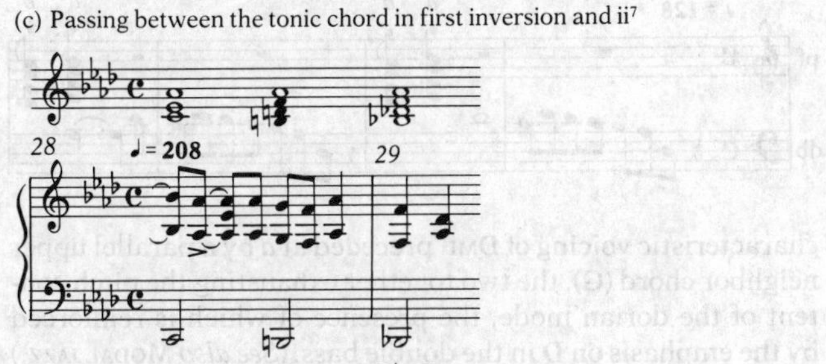

the most commonly used (especially in the bop style) is the one built on the leading note. The notes of the common-tone diminished seventh are (enharmonically) equivalent to the third, fifth, seventh, and minor ninth of each of its substitutes, enabling the essential lines of progressions to be maintained.

The progression ii–V, which is thought of as a unit, often substitutes for a single dominant seventh structure, regardless of whether that chord would be V^7 or one of those dominant seventh structures created by the substitutions described above. Such chromatic ii–V pairs should not be interpreted as suggesting a constant fluctuation of key, as they come into play as logical elaborations of basically simple diatonic progressions.

Arranged substitutions normally extend chromatically the style and syntax of their context. A well-known sequence of substitutions (essentially a reharmonization) is Dizzy Gillespie's series of chromatically falling ii–V pairings in bars 3–4 of *I can't get started*, which help to give his performance its bop character (ex.15) and became standard in later versions. (On

Ex.15 Opening of Dizzy Gillespie's *I can't get started* (1945, Manor 1042; original song by Vernon Duke), showing Duke's harmonization above the staff and Gillespie's below; transcr. S. Strunk

the recording cited – the earliest – Gillespie implies the ii chord melodically before each V.) In *Giant Steps* (1959, Atl. 1311) John Coltrane developed a system of progressions through symmetrically spaced tonal centers, which he then imposed on George Gershwin's *But not for me*, rearranging the melody as well as the harmony. In ex.16 on the first beat of each bar the

Ex.16 Opening of John Coltrane's *But not for me* (original song by George Gershwin) from *My Favorite Things* (1960, Atl. 1361), showing Gershwin's harmonization beneath the top staff and Coltrane's and McCoy Tyner's beneath the bottom staff

local tonality moves down four semitones (from E♭ to C♭ to G to E♭), creating three tonal levels which divide the octave symmetrically into three equal parts. Each local tonic is preceded by its own dominant, as shown by the roman numerals below the staff. The bass line carries the symmetrical division of the octave one step further by dividing each move of four semitones into two equal two-semitone steps, creating a descending whole-tone scale. In general this kind of arranged substitution lies more in the province of composition than of improvisation.

(vi) Extensions of tonality and modal harmony. Not all jazz harmony is based on simple tonal progressions. Successions of chords may have only a tenuous relationship to a diatonic

tonal structure, in an "extended tonality" similar to that which developed in art music at the turn of the 20th century. Structural chords may remain within a single key, but the chords that connect the structural points often follow another, usually contrapuntal, logic. ("Key" is used here in its broadest sense as including all the chromatic resources of a mixture of major and minor modes.)

TABLE 1: Extended tonality in the final chorus of Thelonious Monk's *Epistrophy* from *Monk's Music* (1957, Riv. 242)

a
| C♯^{7} D^7 | ⁒ | ⁒ | ⁒ | D♯^{7} E^7 | ⁒ | ⁒ | ⁒ |
F♯: V^7

a'
| D♯^{7} E^7 | ⁒ | ⁒ | ⁒ | C♯^{7} D^7 | ⁒ | ⁒ | ⁒ |
(under C♯^{7}: V^7)

b
| F♯MI | ⁒ | ⁒ | ⁒ | B^7 | ⁒ | C♯^{7} | D^7 |
(ii / i under F♯MI; V7) / IV$^{♭7}$ under B^7; V^7 under C♯^{7})

a'
| D♯^{7} E^7 | ⁒ | ⁒ | ⁒ | C♯^{7} D^7 | ⁒ | ⁒ | ⁒ | F♯^{7} ‖
(V^7 under C♯^{7}; I$^{♭7}$ under F♯^{7})

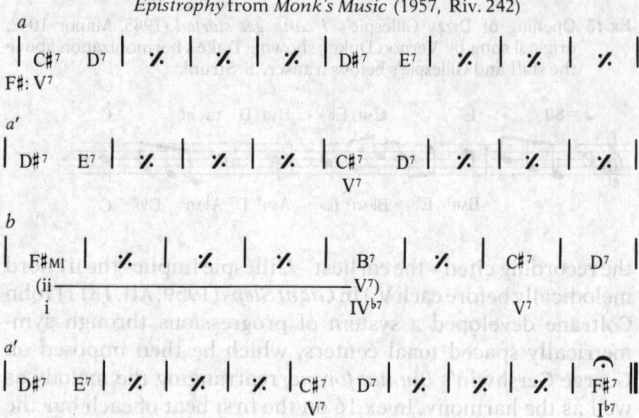

In Table 1 the key of F♯ is suggested by the chords labeled with roman numerals, but the many unlabeled chords have no harmonic explanation in the functional sense of the word. In the *b* section, the interpretation of the first two chords as a ii–V pair would suggest the relatively distant tonality of E, a key that is never realized. Even so, the piece begins on V and ends on I, which creates a solid tonal framework. A reduction to structural elements of the bass root motion in the second half of the piece might reveal the series F♯–C♯–E–C♯–F♯, an arpeggiation of vertical elements in the final tonic sonority.

TABLE 2: Extended tonality in Miles Davis's *Nefertiti* on the album of the same name (1967, Col. CS9594)

| A♭MAJ$^{7(♯11)}$ | D♭MAJ$^{7(♯11)}$ | G♯^{7} | C$^{7(♭9)}$ | C♭MAJ^7 | B♭MI^{11} | AMAJ$^{7(♯11)}$ | E♭$^{7(♯11,♭9)}$ |
(VI ii V) over vi (FMI)
A♭: I → vi (FMI) → ♭II V^7
circle of fifths — chromatic

| EMAJ$^{7(♯11)}$ | A$^{7}_{sus4}$ | D$^{7(♯9)}$/B♭ | E$^{7(♯11)}$ | E$^{7}_{sus4}$ | E♭$^{7(♯11)}$ | A$^{7(13,♭9)}$ | :‖
♭VI → (V^7) ♭II →
circle of fifths — chromatic

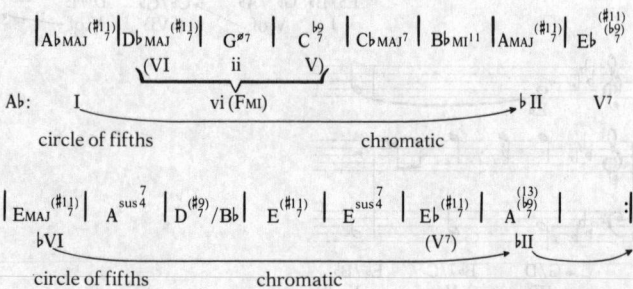

Table 2 reveals a further attenuation of tonality. The first phrase (bars 1–8) moves from I to V, the latter chord preceded by ♭II as a major seventh chord; the second phrase moves from ♭VI to ♭II as a substitute dominant for V. It is as if the second phrase makes use of substitute chords for the tonic and dominant of the first phrase. The two phrases both proceed by circle-of-fifths progressions (bars 1–4, 9–11) followed by chromatic descent (bars 4–7, 12–13). Although the underpinnings of tonality can still be seen here, the effect of the chord successions in bars 4–7 and 9–13 is one of strong tonal ambiguity. A special kind of tonal expansion, known in classical theory as "directional" or "progressive" tonality, in which a piece exhibits two or more apparently structurally equal keys, often beginning on one and ending on another, is shown in Table 3. Here two four-bar phrases present the key of E♭ then the key of C. Although the *b* section is in E♭, the piece ends in C, which again suggests that a single key may not govern this piece. Consideration of melodic and voice-leading aspects of these examples would be necessary for a better analytical understanding of their structure. The study of the expansion of tonality in jazz is one of the unfinished tasks facing jazz theorists.

Instead of harmonic progressions such as those discussed so far, a single chord (or, more rarely, a pair of chords) may be continued for a very long time (in classical analysis these might be termed a "drone" and a "chordal ostinato"), producing static harmony. For example, Eddie Harris's *Freedom Jazz Dance* (from *The In Sound*, 1965, Atl. 1448) has only one chord, B♭^{7}, with the root and fifth mostly treated as a drone. Static harmony is an important feature of modal jazz.

The term "mode" is used in jazz in its wider sense to mean not only scales that conform to the Western ecclesiastical modes (dorian, phrygian, lydian, mixolydian, and aeolian) but pentatonic scales and non-Western scales such as those borrowed from Arab, Indian, and African music. Such scales have been used in jazz in two ways: they have been taken as the source for melodic improvisations over chords in standard tonal progressions, and (of greater importance here) as the basis of chord successions and harmonic effects. In the 1950s musicians such as George Russell espoused the idea of associating modal scales with individual chords or groups of chords in tonal progressions: for example, chord ii in the progression ii–V might suggest a dorian mode, and the dominant seventh chord could be altered in such a way such as to correspond with a scale alternating in semitones and tones, known to jazz musicians as the "diminished" scale, to classical theorists as the "octatonic" scale. In a piece or section of a piece governed entirely by modal resources the chordal successions may be fixed, consisting, for example, of an ostinato that recurs throughout, or they may be improvised, and may include the use of chordally ambiguous combinations of pitches in a free pandiatonicism expressing the sound of the mode. In ex.17 at *b* the piano plays a characteristic voicing of DMI^7 preceded at *a* by a parallel upper neighbor chord (G), the two together exhausting the pitch content of the dorian mode, the presence of which is reinforced by the emphasis on D in the double bass. (*See also* MODAL JAZZ.)

Ex.17 The dorian mode in the opening chorus of Miles Davis's *So what* from *Kind of Blue* (1959, Col. CL1355); transcr. S. Strunk

2. HISTORY. The roots of jazz harmony lie in the merging of two traditions. The character of African melody, primarily pentatonic and having a tendency to circle round a central tone, informed the monophonic singing of the black slaves, but, when their songs and spirituals were first harmonized, white hymnody, with its simple progressions based on European harmonic language, was used as the model. Similarly ragtime borrowed its harmony from the European tradition, proceeding in a harmonic rhythm of one or two chords per bar and including such established classical effects as the cadential 6–4 chord. The harmonies of the blues, by contrast, changed only every two to four bars and incorporated certain unstable

TABLE 3: Directional (progressive) tonality in Dizzy Gillespie's *Con Alma* from *Duets with Sonny Rollins and Sonny Stitt* (1957, Verve 8260)

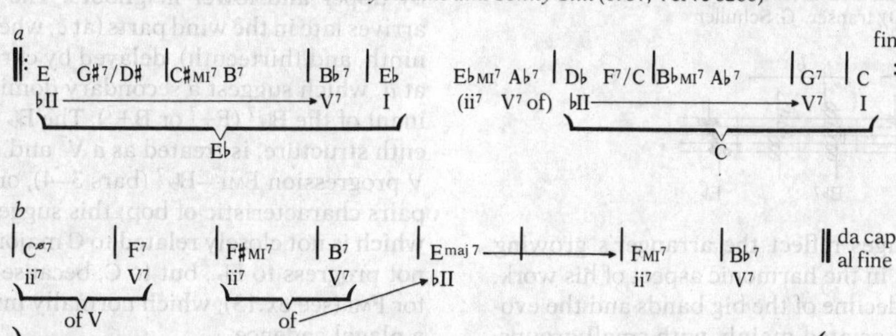

pitches found in black vocal music, the so-called blue notes (*see* BLUE NOTE (i)), as part of dominant seventh structures built on subdominant and tonic chords. Common melodic cadences in the blues involve movement from the blue or flatted third down to the tonic and from the sixth degree up to the tonic. Harmonization of these notes by an authentic cadence (V^7–I) produces extensions of the dominant seventh chord (the flatted third degree of the scale forms the minor thirteenth on the dominant chord), one of the continuing characteristics of jazz harmony (ex.18 *a* and *b*). Another common melodic motion from the flatted third to the second degree was easily harmonized on fretted string instruments by a chromatic semitone slide into V^7, producing an early instance of a progression from the substitute dominant of the dominant to the dominant (ex.18*c*).

Ex.18

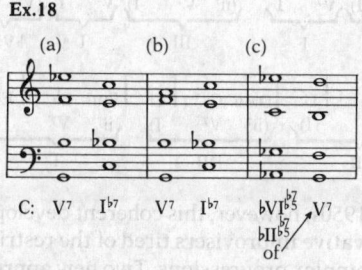

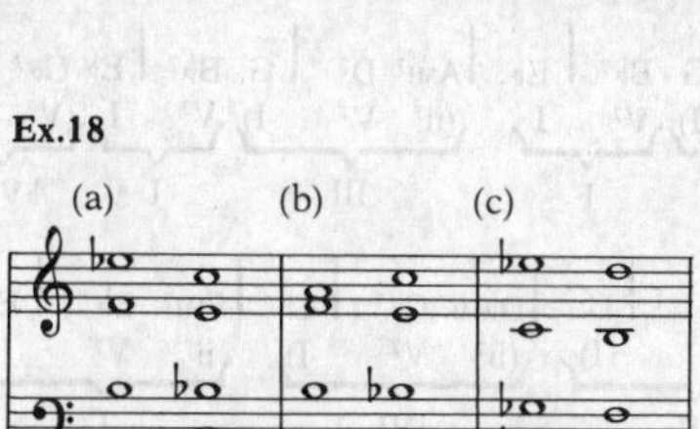

These features were incorporated into the harmony of New Orleans jazz, which otherwise was modeled after contemporary marching-band music and popular songs. Those styles were basically triadic, using diatonic chords and secondary dominants (resulting in local tonicizations of closely related keys). Fixed harmonies within the chorus form, proceeding at a relaxed rate of harmonic change (normally one chord per bar but often slower still), regulated collective improvisation by trumpet, clarinet, and trombone (ex.19). The polyphonic, horizontal nature of early jazz necessarily restricted the complexity and rate of change of the harmonies, which controlled the multiple lines.

In the late 1920s and 1930s big bands moved to the forefront of jazz performance; the music they played has a basically homophonic texture, which made possible harmonies of greater complexity than had been possible in early jazz. Arrangers such as Don Redman paid careful attention to voicings and progressions, at the same time increasing the rate of harmonic change to a norm of two chords per bar. During this period ninths, elevenths, and thirteenths began to be exploited in chord voicings and melodic improvisations. For instance, in ex.20 (p.494) a ninth (G) on F^7 treated conservatively as a suspension at *a* is followed by a less conservative unresolved thirteenth (G) on $B♭^7$ at *b*. On an early recording by Duke Ellington a voicing of $E♭^7$ contains a ninth (F) and a thirteenth (C), the latter placed (unusually) a semitone below the seventh (D♭) (ex.21, p.494). Chromatic embellishing chords and parallel ninth chords, which some writers claim were derived from the music of the French Impressionist composers, were introduced in this

Ex.19 Opening of the first chorus of *Dipper Mouth Blues* (1923, OK 4918) recorded by King Oliver's Creole Jazz Band; transcr. S. Strunk

* A second cornet part may be heard on other parts of the recording, but is inaudible during the bars transcribed here; no attempt at reconstruction has been made.

† A piano part is present on the recording, but the bass line is inaudible throughout most of it; no attempt at reconstruction has been made.

Ex.20 Accompaniment to the first trumpet solo on *Rocky Mountain Blues* arranged by Don Redman and recorded by Fletcher Henderson's orchestra (1927, Col. 970D); transcr. G. Schuller

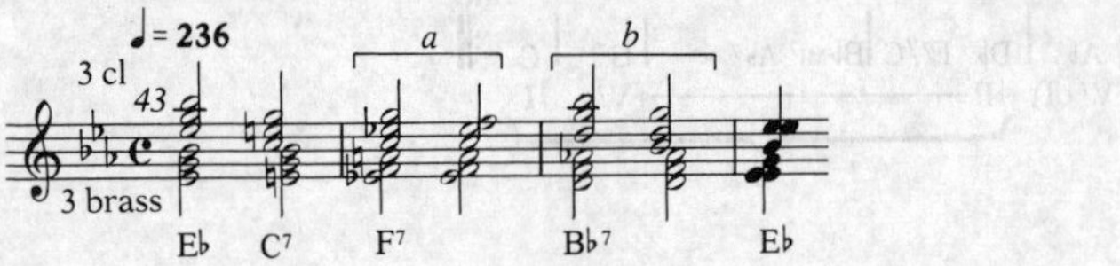

period (ex.22). Such changes reflect the arranger's growing knowledge of and interest in the harmonic aspect of his work.

The 1940s brought the decline of the big bands and the evolution of bop, which is associated mainly with small groups. Charlie Parker and his colleagues worked out numerous harmonic innovations, which to a great degree defined the new

Ex.21 Accompaniment to bar 12 of the trumpet solo on *Yellow Dog Blues* arranged by Duke Ellington and recorded by his orchestra (1928, Bruns. 3987); transcr. G. Schuller

style: they placed melodic emphasis on the upper pitches of extended chords, exploiting the dissonant leaps (especially augmented 4ths and major 7ths) that such extensions made available; they made much use of the progression ii⁷–V⁷ in transient tonalities (often with chromatic alterations that led far from the fundamental key); and they fully explored the possibilities offered by substitute chords, resorting particularly frequently to the dominant seventh structure on the flatted supertonic in place of chord V and the half-diminished

Ex.22 Parallel ninth chords in the accompaniment to the introduction of *Tishomingo Blues*, arranged by Duke Ellington and recorded by his orchestra (1928, Bruns. 3987); transcr. G. Schuller

seventh on the raised subdominant in place of the tonic. Harmonic rhythm and tempos both accelerated. The harmonic innovations of bop began a trend in the development of jazz harmony towards increased ambiguity, both of chord and key: chord substitutions fostered ambiguous voicings, which could fit various roots, and the chromatic progressions of chords ii and V weakened the fundamental sense of tonality. In ex.23

Ex.23 Opening theme of Tadd Dameron's *Lady Bird* (1948, BN 559); transcr. S. Strunk

the basic C sonority with added sixth at *a* and *b* is elaborated by upper and lower neighbors. The extended B♭⁷ harmony arrives late in the wind parts (at *c*, where they play the seventh, ninth, and thirteenth), delayed by chromatic upper neighbors at *d*, which suggest a secondary dominant or substitute dominant of the B♭⁷ (F+⁷ or B+⁷). The B♭⁷, being a dominant seventh structure, is treated as a V⁷ and is developed into the ii–V progression FMI⁷–B♭⁷ (bars 3–4), one of the chromatic ii–V pairs characteristic of bop; this suggests a tonicization of E♭, which is not closely related to C major. However, the B♭⁷ does not progress to E♭, but to C, because it arises as a substitute for FMI (see ex.13), which normally might move to C (bar 5) in a plagal cadence.

The development of jazz harmony from early styles through the 1950s may thus be characterized as a general movement from simple to complex chord progressions and from a relaxed to a rapid rate of harmonic change. No piece shows the culmination of this development better than John Coltrane's *Giant Steps* (1959, Atl. 1311). The tempo is 285 quarter-note beats to the minute and the rate of harmonic change is generally two chords per bar (i.e., more than 100 chords per minute); the difficult progression moves quickly through keys that are not closely related, involving local ii–V–I progressions in tonal centers that (like those in ex.16) divide the octave into three equal parts (Table 4).

TABLE 4: Rapid harmonic rhythm and tonicization of remote keys in John Coltrane's *Giant Steps* from the album of the same name (1959, Atl. 1311)

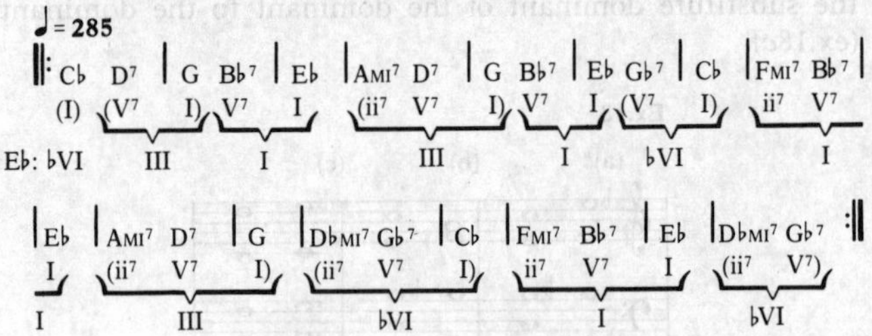

In the late 1950s, however, this coherent development ceased, as some innovative improvisers tired of the restrictions placed on them by complex progressions. Two new approaches to jazz harmony appeared simultaneously, each bound up with a new style of jazz – modal jazz and free jazz.

The concept of modes or other scales as the basis of harmony is discussed above (see §1(vi)). Although the pitch content of modal jazz represents an important development in the history of jazz harmony, perhaps more important still is the drastic slowing down of harmonic rhythm that characterizes the style. With a single mode dominating whole sections of a piece, harmonic rhythm comes to a near halt and the burden of providing interest is placed on the melodic line, which, having no chord progressions to express, has largely to be freely invented by the player within the new looser confines of the modes. The leading figure here was Miles Davis, who advocated (in interviews and by example) an emphasis on creating fine melodies in place of "running the changes."

Free jazz introduced an entirely new approach, in which themes and improvisations are no longer based on chord progressions or even nonfunctional successions; instead harmony emerges as a result of spontaneous improvisation. Except in so far as players carefully avoid conventional chord progressions, harmony is (perhaps more than any other element) incidental to free jazz. The principal innovators were Cecil Taylor, who plays in a dense, chromatic, atonal style, and Ornette

Ex.24 Excerpt from Chick Corea's *Space Circus*, pt ii from *Hymn of the Seventh Galaxy* (1973, Pol. 5536) by Return to Forever; transcr. S. Strunk

[1]Bar numbers pertain to the example, not to the performance.

Coleman, who at times uses drones to suggest tonal centers, as on his *Lonely Woman* (from *The Shape of Jazz to Come*, 1959, Atl. 1327), and who often uses bluesy harmonies without employing the blues progression.

During the 1960s jazz harmony consisted of an admixture of elements from bop, modal jazz, and free jazz. Coltrane, for example, improvised in a chromatically free manner over slow-moving chordal or modal ostinatos in many of his performances during the first half of the decade. The most extreme example of this is his *Ascension* (1965, Imp. 95), in which the four modes that underlie the piece are scarcely recognizable and hardly influence the chromatic improvisations. Beginning in 1965 (notably with Wayne Shorter's composition *E.S.P.* on Miles Davis's album of the same name, Col. CS9150) Davis's quintet explored an approach in which many of the conventions of bop (walking bass lines, fast tempos, complex chords, rapid harmonic rhythm, and fast-moving, carefully articulated melodies) are combined with a concept of harmony taken from free jazz: improvisers abandon chorus structures and functional progressions, basing both improvised harmony and melody on the "essence" of the tune rather than its specific form or harmony. In another synthesis of different elements some musicians assimilated the slowing of harmonic rhythm into bop. Chick Corea's *Windows* (recorded by Stan Getz with Corea as a sideman on *Sweet Rain*, 1967, Verve 68693) provides a good example: the first half features slow harmonic rhythms and the treatment of each sustained chord as a scale, suggesting a linear, pandiatonic approach to the harmonies; in the second half the harmonic rhythm accelerates and the progressions derive more directly from the bop vocabulary, suggesting a vertical orientation to voicings and melody.

In an independent development, after 1969 many jazz musicians consciously tried to meld jazz with other styles of contemporary popular music, notably rock, producing various kinds of "fusion" music. The most significant changes in sound and style in this music are in areas other than harmony. Rock harmony at that period was simple, modal, and triadic; jazz-rock incorporates modality or the suggestion or modality, but includes seventh chords, while reducing the use of extended chords characteristic of other jazz styles. Bars 3–9 of ex.24 illustrate simple triads and a major seventh chord within the D dorian mode (the C♯ and F♯ are momentarily borrowed from D major in bars 6–8). The pentatonic scale (seen at *a* and *b*) and the suspended dominant seventh chord became one identifying sound of the style (the pentatonic scale has the same interval content as a suspended dominant seventh with ninth). The same scale may be seen in ex.25 at *a*; and the suspended dominant seventh is the sole harmonic sonority of Herbie Hancock's *Maiden Voyage* (from the album of the same name, 1965, BN 84195), in which each of four chords of this structure, built on D, F, E♭, and D♭, suggests a different pentatonic scale. The suspended dominant seventh occurs at *b*, *c*, and *d* in ex.25, in

Ex.25 First statement of the closing theme of Joe Zawinul's *Birdland* recorded by Weather Report on *Heavy Weather* (1976, Col. PC34418); transcr. S. Strunk

the last instance replacing V^7 in the cadence of the phrase, a common usage in the style. The voicing at *d* represents a compromise between the harmonic complexity of the older jazz and the simplicity of rock; the upper elements of the chord (seventh, ninth, and eleventh) are here grouped in the upper register as a triad which clashes with the root in the bass, a

Ex.26 Jazz-rock voicings in the introduction to Wayne Shorter's *Harlequin* recorded by Weather Report on *Heavy Weather* (1976, Col. PC34418); transcr. S. Strunk

technique not limited to suspended dominants. All the chords of the nonfunctional progression in ex.26 are voiced in this manner. (The D♭/E♭ and B♭/C chords could have been symbolized as suspended dominant sevenths on E♭ and C respectively, but the notation as given conveys the voicing more accurately, and is commonly practiced in jazz of this style.) Owing to its triadic nature, jazz-rock also employs inversions more frequently than most other jazz styles (as in ex.25 at *e* and *f*).

BIBLIOGRAPHY

HISTORICAL AND ANALYTICAL

W. Sargeant: *Jazz, Hot & Hybrid* (New York, 1938, rev. and enlarged 3/1964/*R*1975 as *Jazz: a History*)

G. Schuller: *Early Jazz: its Roots and Musical Development* (New York, 1968)

M. L. Stewart: *Structural Development in the Jazz Improvisational Technique of Clifford Brown* (diss., U. of Michigan, 1973); pubd in *Jf*, vi–vii (1974–5), 141–273

E. Jost: *Free Jazz* (Graz, Austria, 1974)

T. Owens: *Charlie Parker: Techniques of Improvisation* (diss., UCLA, 1974)

P. Winkler: "Toward a Theory of Popular Harmony," *In Theory Only*, iv (1978), 3

S. Strunk: "The Harmony of Early Bop: a Layered Approach," *JJS*, vi (1979), 4–53

F. A. Howlett: *An Introduction to Art Tatum's Performance Approaches: Composition, Improvisation, and Melodic Variation* (diss., Cornell U., 1983)

B. Kernfeld: "Two Coltranes," *ARJS*, ii (1983), 7–66

L. Porter: "John Coltrane's *A Love Supreme*: Jazz Improvisation as Composition," *Journal of the American Musicological Society*, xxxviii (1985), 593

S. Strunk: "Bebop Melodic Lines: Tonal Characteristics," *ARJS*, iii (1985), 97

S. Larson: *Schenkerian Analysis of Modern Jazz* (diss., U. of Michigan, 1987)

PEDAGOGICAL TEXTS

J. Mehegan: *Jazz Improvisation*, i: *Tonal and Rhythmic Principles* (New York, 1959, rev. and enlarged 1984)

J. Coker: *Improvising Jazz* (Englewood Cliffs, NJ, 1964)

K. Stanton: *Jazz Theory: a Creative Approach* (New York, 1982)

A. Jaffe: *Jazz Theory* (Dubuque, IA, 1983)

STEVEN STRUNK

Harmony (ii). Record label. It was a subsidiary of COLUMBIA, and was operational from September 1925 to June 1932. Until summer 1929 all its issues were acoustically recorded, long after this process had largely been abandoned elsewhere. The material was recorded specially for the label, often by well-known bands using pseudonyms: items by Fletcher Henderson's band were issued under the name the Dixie Stompers. Most of Harmony's catalogue was also put out on Velvet Tone and Diva. From 1949 into the 1970s CBS used the Harmony label for cheap albums of reissues, and occasionally to release new material, including the results of a session in 1957 by George Wettling. (B. Rust: *The American Record Label Book* (New Rochelle, NY, 1978))

Harp (i). A plucked instrument consisting of a set of strings, a neck, to which the strings are attached, and a resonator. The modern, Western harp is a "double-action" instrument: it has a set of pedals that enables the player to sharpen each string by either one or two semitones. Because the harp's strings are not damped but rather allowed to vibrate freely, the sounds of the individual tones overlap; this and the instrument's quiet, velvety sound make the harp poorly suited to the loud dynamics and precise rhythms of much jazz, and its cumbersome system of strings and pedals makes the playing of rapid jazz chord progressions nearly impossible. Nevertheless a few players have surmounted these difficulties. Casper Reardon recorded as a harpist with Jack Teagarden in 1934, Adele Girard, the wife of Joe Marsala, played harp in his groups from 1937, and Corky Hale (Merrilyn Cecelia Hecht) (*b* Freeport, IL, 3 July 1931) recorded with the singer Kitty White (1954), as the leader of an all-star West Coast jazz group (1956), and with Anita O'Day (1956). Later Alice Coltrane used the instrument in bland, meditative modal jazz tunes. The finest exponent of the jazz harp is Dorothy Ashby, whose astounding facility enabled her to become an accomplished bop soloist. (S. Placksin: *American Women in Jazz, 1900 to the Present: their Words, Lives, and Music* (New York, 1982), 239, 243)

BARRY KERNFELD

Harp (ii). A term sometimes used to denote the HARMONICA.

Harper, Billy (R.) (*b* Houston, 17 Jan 1943). Tenor saxophonist. He studied tenor saxophone from the age of 11 and listened to the recordings of Sonny Rollins and Kenny Dorham; he also sang and played saxophone in church and while attending North Texas State College (BM 1965). After moving to New York in 1966 he toured California with Gil Evans, with whom he continued to work for many years, belonged to Art Blakey's Jazz Messengers, and played with Elvin Jones (briefly in 1970), Max Roach, the Thad Jones–Mel Lewis Orchestra, and Lee Morgan; from 1973 he led a sextet. Later he continued to work with Roach (to 1978) and made recordings as the leader of quintets that often included the trumpeter Everett Hollins, the double bass player Gregg Maker, and the drummer Malcolm Pinson. In addition to his work as a saxophonist Harper has been active as a composer; his compositions *Thoroughbred, Cry of Hunger*, and *Priestess* are often performed by Evans's orchestra.

SELECTED RECORDINGS

As leader: *Capra-black* (1973, SE 19739), incl. Cry of Hunger; *Soran-Bushi B. H.* (1977, Denon 7522); *Billy Harper Quintet in Europe* (1979, SN 1001), incl. Priestess

As sideman: G. Evans: *Gil Evans* (1969, Ampex 10102), incl. Thoroughbred; T. Jones and M. Lewis: *Consummation* (1969–70, BN 84346); M. Roach: *Live in Tokyo* (1977, Denon 134)

BIBLIOGRAPHY

E. Meadow: "Make Room for Billy Harper," *DB*, xxxviii/13 (1971), 16

P. Keepnews: "Billy Harper's Search for Truth," *DB*, xli/12 (1974), 13

B. Rusch: "Billy Harper: Interview," *Cadence*, v/8 (1979), 3

C. J. Gans: "Billy Harper: a Spiritual Messenger," *JF* [intl edn], no.70 (1981), 41

DAVID WILD

Harper, Herbie [Herbert] (*b* Salina, KS, 2 July 1920). Trombonist. After touring with Charlie Spivak from 1944 to 1947 he settled in Hollywood, where he played with Teddy Edwards's quintet, and in big bands led by Benny Goodman (1947), Charlie Barnet (1948), Stan Kenton (1950), and Jerry Gray (1950–52). He also performed as a member of Billie Holiday's band; he may be heard in this capacity on tracks recorded at a concert given by Holiday in 1949 and first issued on the album *Masters of Jazz*, iii (Sto. 4103). In the mid-1950s he led his own group, playing West Coast jazz and making several recordings. From 1955 Harper has been active mainly as a studio musician for NBC, but he has also recorded with June Christy (1952–7), Maynard Ferguson (1952, 1954), Barnet (1954), Kenton (1954–5), Ray Brown (1956), Benny Carter (1958), and Bob Florence (intermittently, 1959–81). (*FeatherE*)

Harpsichord. A keyboard instrument distinguished from the clavichord and piano by the fact that its strings are plucked by quills rather than struck by hammers or tangents. The instrument was in use from the Renaissance until the end of the 18th century when its place was taken by the piano. Its use was revived in the 20th century and many new instruments were built, usually with keyboards of between four and five octaves; while the harpsichord was taken up enthusiastically by many classical composers, in jazz the instrument has been used only infrequently, though with some success. Its most notable exponent was Johnny Guarnieri who, in his work with the Gramercy Five, attempted to create a valid chamber-jazz style for the instrument; his playing is well represented by *Special Delivery Stomp* (1940, Vic. 26762). In 1941 Meade "Lux" Lewis recorded four unaccompanied harpsichord solos, including *School of Rhythm/Feeling Tomorrow Like I Feel Today* (BN 20). The composer Alec Templeton (1910–1963), who worked with Jack Hylton, composed a parody of a two-part invention by Johann Sebastian Bach, *Bach Goes to Town*, which was frequently performed as a novelty piece by classically trained harpsichordists.

Many jazz pianists have used the harpsichord occasionally, including Erroll Garner on *Don't Look for me* and *Côte d'Azur* from his album *Paris Impressions* (1958, Col. C2L9). Michael Garrick played it in a series of influential poetry and jazz concerts and used it on the album *Black Marigolds* (1966, Argo 88). It has also been employed by free-jazz and avant-garde musicians; Cal Cobbs played harpsichord on some of Albert Ayler's later recordings (1967–8) and McCoy Tyner used it on his album *Trident* (1975, Milestone 9063).

ALYN SHIPTON

Harrell, Tom (*b* Urbana, IL, 16 June 1946). Trumpeter. He moved to San Francisco when he was five, and by the age of 13 was playing in small groups in and around Palo Alto; later he played bop on occasions at the Jazz Workshop in San Francisco. He toured with Stan Kenton (1969) and Woody Herman (1970–71), then joined Horace Silver (1973) and subsequently moved to New York. He played with Silver for four years, during which time he also performed and recorded with Chuck Israels's National Jazz Ensemble (1975) and Arnie Lawrence (from 1975). Thereafter he worked with Cecil Payne (1976), Bill Evans (ii) (1979), Lee Konitz's nonet (1979–81), and George Russell (1982), and joined a hard-bop group led by Phil Woods (1983). His album *Play of Light* (1984) was his first important work as a composer, arranger, and leader. Harrell is a remarkable improviser, and executes logical and highly expressive phrases with a beautiful tone. His playing is influenced by the styles of Blue Mitchell, John Coltrane, and, especially, Clifford Brown.

SELECTED RECORDINGS

As leader: *Aurora* (1976, Adamo 9502); *Play of Light* (1984, PAlt 8017)
As sideman: W. Herman: *Woody* (1970, Cadet 845); H. Silver: *Silver 'n' Brass* (1975, BN LA406G); P. Woods: *Live from New York* (1982, PAlt 8084); *Heaven* (1984, Black Hawk 50401)

BIBLIOGRAPHY

M. Rozek: "Tom Harrell," *DB*, xliii/8 (1976), 38
M. Bourne: "Tom Harrell: Quiet Volcano," *DB*, lii/4 (1985), 23 [discography]

ROBERT DICKOW

Harrington, John (David) (*b* Denver, 23 May 1910). Clarinetist and saxophonist. He first worked professionally in Denver with a band led by the violinist George Morrison (1927–8), then joined Terrence Holder's group. From 1929 to 1944 (except for a brief period in 1940 when he injured his jaw) he performed and recorded, mostly in New York, with Andy Kirk (for illustration *see* WILLIAMS, MARY LOU); *Christopher Columbus* (1936, Decca 729) provides a good example of his style. After working with the tenor saxophonist Skippy Williams (1945) and with Claude Hopkins (1946) Harrington returned to Denver, where he established a club with his brother Seaton "Jew" Harrington, an alto saxophonist.

based on *ChiltonW*

Harriott, Joe (Arthurlin) (*b* Kingston, Jamaica, 15 July 1928; *d* London, 2 Jan 1973). Jamaican alto saxophonist. After playing with Wilton "Bogey" Gaynair and Dizzy Reece he emigrated to Britain in 1951, where he worked as a freelance musician and soloist in London before joining the band of the trumpeter Pete Pitterson. He established a reputation playing in Tony Kinsey's quartet (from 1954) and in Ronnie Scott's short-lived big band (1955). At this time Harriott was growing away from the influence of Charlie Parker, a process that accelerated when he formed his first quintet in 1958, as the track *Señor Blues* (1959) from the album *Southern Horizons* demonstrates. During a period in hospital in 1960 he conceived a new approach to abstract improvisation which was to be his major contribution to jazz. Although reached independently, this coincided with the first release in the UK of free-jazz recordings by Ornette Coleman, and Harriott was initially dismissed as an imitator; his music, however, explored ensemble textures rather than soloists' freedom, and his programs in performance linked his new ideas with more straightforward bop styles. From 1965 Harriott moved into fusions of jazz with other elements and styles – poetry in his work with Michael Garrick and Indian music with the violinist John Mayer.

SELECTED RECORDINGS

As leader: *Southern Horizons* (1959–60, Jlnd 37), incl. Señor Blues; *Free Form* (1960, Jlnd 49); *Abstract* (1961–2, Col. 33SX1477), incl. Tonal Idioms; with J. Mayer: *Indo-Jazz Fusions*, ii (1967, Col. SCX6215)
As sideman: M. Garrick: *Black Marigolds* (1966, Argo 88)

BIBLIOGRAPHY

FeatherE; *Feather '60s*; *Feather–Gitler '70s*
J. Harriott: "The Truth about Free Form Jazz," *Jazz Scene*, ii/2 (1963), 23
V. Wilmer: "Joe Harriott: Jazz Abstractionist," *DB*, xxxi/25 (1964), 12
T. E. Martin: "Joe Harriott," *JM*, x/11 (1965), 2
M. Jones: "Joe Harriott: Ten Years After," *MM* (6 Feb 1971)

CHRIS SHERIDAN

Harris. Family of musicians.

(1) Le Roy (W.) Harris(, Sr.) (i) (*b c*1900; *d* 1969). Banjo player, guitarist, and flutist. He played with Fletcher Henderson's Rainbow Orchestra (1925), Clarence Williams (?1925–1930), the pianist Leroy Tibbs (1928), and others. His rhythm playing may be heard to advantage on Tibbs's *One o'Clock Blues/I got Worry (Love is on my Mind)* (Col. 14309D). During the 1930s he played with such musicians as Jesse Stone (1937); in the following decade he recorded with Horace Henderson (1940) and Willie Bryant (1946). Later he played rhythm-and-blues with the singers Wynonie Harris and Tiny Bradshaw (both 1949) and Red Miller (1950).

(2) Arville (S.) Harris (*b* St. Louis, 1904; *d* New York, 1954). Saxophonist and clarinetist, brother of (1) Le Roy Harris. From 1920 he worked on riverboats, and around the same time performed in a band led by the reed player Hershal Brassfield. Thereafter he played with Bill Brown and his Brownies (1925–8) and made several recordings for Clarence Williams (1927–30). In 1929 he recorded *The Minor Drag/Harlem Fuss* (Vic. 38050) with Fats Waller's quintet. Harris traveled to Europe while a member of Cab Calloway's orchestra (1931–5). Later he worked with Jacques Butler (1935), Claude Hopkins (1937, 1939), and the pianist Maurice Rocco (1938), then for the last ten years of his life led his own band at the Majestic Ballroom in New York.

(3) Le Roy (W.) Harris(, Jr.) (ii) (*b* St. Louis, 12 Feb 1916). Reed player and singer, son of (1) Le Roy Harris. After learning violin as a child he took up saxophone and clarinet in 1928. In 1929 he worked in a band led by the pianist Chick Finney; he then moved to Chicago where he played with Ray Nance (1931–6), Earl Hines (1937–43), and others. Although he was mainly a section player he may be heard taking a rare solo on alto saxophone on Hines's *Riff Medley* (1939, Bb 10531). After playing in a navy band (1943–4) he worked with Bill Doggett, Ben Thigpen, and others, then rejoined Hines again in the mid-1950s. From 1957 he played in St. Louis, where he later worked with the pianist Eddie Johnson (1960–71).

based on *ChiltonW*

Harris, Barry (Doyle) (*b* Detroit, 15 Dec 1929). Pianist. He began studying piano at the age of four, and was strongly influenced by Bud Powell, Thelonious Monk, and Charlie Parker. While still living in Detroit he worked frequently with Thad Jones, Miles Davis, Sonny Stitt, Wardell Gray, and Max Roach. By 1956 his reputation as a perfomer and articulate teacher of bop was such that visiting artists from New York and elsewhere frequently sought him out for his musical insights and camaraderie. He joined Cannonball Adderley's quintet in 1960 and soon afterwards moved to New York, where he performed and recorded with such musicians as Dexter Gordon, Illinois Jacquet, Yusef Lateef, and Hank Mobley. From 1965 to 1969 he had a productive association with Coleman Hawkins, and from time to time he also led his own groups. In 1982 he opened the Jazz Cultural Center, where he has been active as a teacher.

Harris is unquestionably the foremost exponent of the music of Powell, Tadd Dameron, and Monk, and is one of the few jazz musicians of the late 20th century who can teach and play the music with equal clarity. Among his compositions are *Luminescence, Like this!, Even Steven*, and *Nicaragua*.

SELECTED RECORDINGS

As leader: *The Barry Harris Trio: Breakin' it up* (1958, Argo 644); *Luminescence!* (1967, Prst. 7498), incl. Even Steven, Like this!, Luminescence, Nicaragua; *Barry Harris Plays Tadd Dameron* (1975, Xan. 113); *Live in Tokyo* (1976, Xan. 130)

As sideman: C. Adderley: *Them Dirty Blues* (1960, Riv. 1170); S. Stitt: *Constellation* (1972, Cob. 9021)

BIBLIOGRAPHY

M. Gardner: "Barry Harris," *JM*, no.151 (1967), 28; no.153 (1967), 31; no.154 (1967), 31; no.155 (1968), 31 [discography]
"Barry Harris," *SJ*, xxx/4 (1976), 80 [discography]
A. Lowe: "Barry Harris," *DB*, xliv/13 (1977), 18
B. Rusch: "Barry Harris: Interview," *Cadence*, iii/7–8 (1977), 18
B. Primack and R. Dubin: "Detroit's Triple Gift to the Jazz Piano World," *CK*, v/12 (1979), 12
C. Jennings: "Barry Harris: Autumn Vision," *JSN*, ii/2 (1980–81), 35
J. Saunders: "Barry Harris Ensemble: an Eloquent Be-bop Voice," *JSN*, ii/2 (1980–81), 36
L. Feather: "Piano Giants of Jazz: Barry Harris," *CK*, vii/1 (1981), 54
M. Bourne: "Barry Harris: Keeper of the Bebop Flame," *DB*, lii/9 (1985), 26 [incl. discography]

BILL DOBBINS/R

Harris, Beaver [William Godvin] (*b* Pittsburgh, PA, 20 April 1936). Drummer and bandleader. He played drums from the age of 20. After army service (from 1957), he returned to Pittsburgh, where he played informally with Benny Golson, Slide Hampton, Horace Silver, and others. In 1962 he moved to New York, and became associated with a group of progressive jazz musicians, working with such players as Sonny Rollins (1965), Marion Brown (1966), Albert Ayler (1966–7), Roswell Rudd (from 1966), Gato Barbieri (1969–70), Thelonious Monk (1970), and, most notably, Archie Shepp (from 1967). In 1968, with Grachan Moncur III and Dave Burrell, he formed the cooperative group 360 Degree Music Experience. This group became an important outlet for his playing and composition; it has undergone many changes in personnel, but in the late 1970s and 1980s frequently included the steel drummer Francis Haynes, Ken McIntyre, Hamiet Bluiett, Ricky Ford, Cameron Brown, Rahn Burton, and occasionally Don Pullen (as co-leader). Cecil Taylor was among the other musicians with whom Harris played in the 1970s; he also accompanied Chet Baker, Charlie Rouse, Al Cohn, and others at St. James Infirmary, a club in New York owned by Rudd and Hod O'Brien.

Although Harris made his name as a free-jazz player, his style is firmly based on swing rhythms. The full range of his abilities became apparent in the 1970s in his work with Shepp and 360 Degree Music Experience; in these contexts he uses a variety of rhythmic idioms and sometimes plays with a freer pulse. His splash-cymbal work is especially impressive.

SELECTED RECORDINGS

As leader of 360 Degree Music Experience: *From Ragtime to No Time* (1975, 360 Degree Music 2001); with D. Burrell: *In: Sanity* (1976, BS 0006–7); *Negcaumongus* (1979, Cad. 1003); with D. Pullen: *A Well Kept Secret* (1980, Shemp 2701)

As sideman: Marion Brown: *Three for Shepp* (1966, Imp. 9139); A. Ayler: *Albert Ayler Live in Greenwich Village* (1966–7, Imp. 9155); A. Shepp: *Archie Shepp Live at the Donaueschingen Music Festival* (1967, Saba 15148); G. Barbieri: *The Third World* (1969, FD 10117); R. Rudd: *Numatik Swing Band* (1973, JCOA 1007); A. Shepp: *U-jaama (unité)* (1975, Uniteledis 22975YX2); S. Lacy: *Trickles* (1976, BS 0008)

BIBLIOGRAPHY

B. Case: "Beaver's Base," *MM*, liv (6 Oct 1979), 57
L. S. Freeman: "The 360° of Beaver Harris," *JSN*, i/5 (1980), 8
K. Steiner: "The 360° Music Experience," *Coda*, no.175 (1980), 10
B. Rusch: "Beaver Harris: Stories," *Cadence*, ix (1983), no.2, p.5; no.3, p.12; no.4, p.19

ED HAZELL

Harris, Benny. *See* HARRIS, LITTLE BENNY.

Harris, Bill [Willard Palmer] **(i)** (*b* Philadelphia, 28 Oct 1916; *d* Hallandale, FL, 21 Aug 1973). Trombonist. He played piano, tenor saxophone, and trumpet before concentrating on trombone. During the 1930s he performed mainly in his home city, and began to work as a professional musician in 1938. After touring with big bands led by Gene Krupa and Ray McKinley he traveled to New York with Bob Chester. He gained widespread praise while a member of Benny Goodman's band (1943–4), particularly for his part on the soundtrack of the film *Sweet and Low-down* (1944). Harris performed briefly with Charlie Barnet in California, then led his own small group in New York. Most of his best work, however, was with Woody Herman's orchestra, in which he played intermittently from 1944 until 1959 (for illustration *see* HERMAN, WOODY, fig.1*a*). During this period he also led his own small groups, toured regularly with Jazz at the Philharmonic (from 1950), and worked with Charlie Ventura (1947), Oscar Pettiford (1952), and the Sauter–Finegan Orchestra (1953). After another spell with Goodman (1959) Harris settled in Florida, where in the 1960s he played with Red Norvo and Charlie Teagarden and continued to lead his own groups.

Harris was early influenced by J. C. Higginbotham, but he soon developed a totally original style full of dramatic contrasts. He often adopted a soft, purring tone that suggested sentimentality, only to give way suddenly to lusty phrases that seemed to be shouted out of the trombone's bell. The vigor of this spirited approach never affected his fluency or ingenuity, and much of his playing was marked by an inimitable good humor.

SELECTED RECORDINGS

As leader: Bill not Phil (1952, Clef 8969)

As sideman: W. Herman: Apple Honey (1945, Col. 36803); Goosey Gander (1945, Col. 36815); Bijou (1945, Col. 36861); Everywhere (1946, Col. 38369); B. Carter: *New Jazz Sounds* (1954, Norg. 1044), incl. That Old Black Magic

BIBLIOGRAPHY

L. Feather: "Bill Harasses his Horn," *Metronome*, lxi/12 (1945), 27
E. Edwards: *Bill Harris (Trombone): a Complete Discography* (n.p. [?Whittier, CA], 1966)
S. Voce: "The Herman Herds," *JJ*, xix/3 (1966), 4
——: "Willard Palmer not Phil," *JJI*, xxxiii/3 (1980), 17

JOHN CHILTON

Harris, Bill [Willie] **(ii)** (*b* Nashville, NC, 14 April 1925). Acoustic guitarist. He studied classical guitar at the Columbia School of Music in Washington, then played with the Clovers, a rhythm-and-blues group, from 1950 to 1958. Between 1956 and 1962 he made several recordings that proved he could play like Charlie Christian, Django Reinhardt, and Barney Kessel; they demonstrate a good technique, versatility, and the ability to play fine jazz on an unamplified guitar. He performed in and around Washington and began to teach (he has published several pedagogical texts). In 1972–3 he undertook a long tour of France, during which he made further recordings, and in 1977 he produced and distributed his own records. Though he is relatively unknown to jazz audiences, Harris's work as a jazz composer was recognized by the award of a fellowship from the NEA in 1972 (among his compositions is the *Wes Montgomery Suite*) and his mastery of the guitar by the invitation to give a concert at the Smithsonian Institution in 1977.

SELECTED RECORDINGS

As unaccompanied soloist: *Solo Guitar* (1956, EmA 36097); *Caught in the Act* (1962, Jazz Guitar 100); *Down in the Alley* (1973, BB 33042); *Bill Harris Rhythm* (1973, BB 33062)

As leader: *The Harris Touch* (1957, EmA 36113)

BIBLIOGRAPHY

FeatherE; *Feather '60s*; *Feather–Gitler '70s*
P. Welding: "Bill Harris," *DB*, xxviii/15 (1961), 22
B. McLarney: "Bill Harris: Acoustic Maverick," *DB*, xxxv/13 (1968), 21
J. Dallman: "From the Clovers to the Classics with Bill Harris," *GP*, ix/5 (1975), 10
B. Kirchner: "Bill Harris," *DB*, xliv/9 (1977), 39 [review]
M. J. Summerfield: *The Jazz Guitar: its Evolution and its Players* (Gateshead, England, 1978), 113

LEROY OSTRANSKY

Harris, Charlie [Charles Purvis] (*b* Alexandria, VA, 9 Jan 1916). Double bass player. He studied violin and double bass in Baltimore. From 1944 to 1948 he toured and recorded with Lionel Hampton; during this period he also worked with other musicians associated with Hampton, and played on recordings by the singer Wynonie Harris (including *In the Evenin' Blues*, 1945, Hamp-Tone 103), Herbie Fields, Milt Buckner (all 1945), and Arnett Cobb (1946). In 1951 he joined Nat "King" Cole, with whom he toured Europe and Australia; he recorded with Cole in 1952 and 1956, and again in 1960 under Stan Kenton's leadership. (*FeatherE*)

Harris, Craig (*b* Hempstead, NY, 10 Sept 1954). Trombonist. He played in rhythm-and-blues bands while in his teens and studied theory, arranging, and composition with Ken McIntyre at SUNY, Old Westbury (BA 1976). He worked with Sun Ra (1976–8), belonged to Abdullah Ibrahim's quintet (1979–81), and played in the pit orchestra of the Broadway show *The Lady and her Music*, which featured the popular singer Lena Horne. In the 1980s he worked with David Murray's octet and big band, Henry Threadgill's sextet, Olu Dara's Okra Orchestra, Charlie Haden's New Liberation Orchestra, Lester Bowie's Brass Fantasy, and Jaki Byard's Apollo Rhythm Stompers, and in big bands led by Muhal Richard Abrams, Cecil Taylor, and Sam Rivers. From 1981 he worked as the leader of several groups, including the Aqaustra (consisting in addition to his trombone of two reed instruments, violin, cello, horn, tuba, double bass, and percussion), Tailgater's Tales (consisting of trombone, clarinet, trumpet, tuba, and drums), and quartets and quintets of more conventional jazz instrumentation. In the summer of 1985 he collaborated with the Urban Bushwomen, a dance company, on a work entitled *Points*. Harris plays with a full-bodied, muscular sound and makes adept use of such techniques as multiphonics and circular breathing. Besides his principal instrument he plays the didjeridu, a wooden trumpet used by the aborigines of northern Australia.

SELECTED RECORDINGS

As leader: *Black Bone* (1983, SN 1055); *Aboriginal Affairs* (1983, IndN 1060); *Tributes* (1985, OTC 804)

As sideman: Sun Ra: *Cosmos* (1976, IC 1020); *Live at Montreux* (1976, IC 1039); A. Ibrahim: *Montreux '80* (1980, Enja 3079); M. R. Abrams: *Blues Forever* (1981, BS 0052); D. Murray: *Murray's Steps* (1982, BS 0065); *Live at Sweet Basil* (1984, BS 0085)

BIBLIOGRAPHY

J. Pareles: "Craig Harris's Horn Helps Keep Up Jazz Heritage," *New York Times* (22 July 1983), §C, p.4
F. Davis: "If it Sounds Good, it is Good," *HiFi/MusAm*, xxxv/10 (1985), 75 [incl. discography]; repr. in *In the Moment: Jazz in the 1980s* (New York, and Oxford, England, 1986)
M. Chenard: "The Many Slides of Craig Harris," *Coda*, no.211 (1986–7), 8

ROBERT J. IANNAPOLLO

Harris, Eddie (*b* Chicago, 20 Oct ?1934). Tenor saxophonist. He first played in the bop style, but his interest in employing novel methods and reaching larger audiences made itself apparent soon after he finished military service in 1961. His first recording, the theme from the film *Exodus*, sold more than two million copies and marked the start of a highly prolific and stylistically diverse career. Until 1965 he played mainly conventional, acoustic music; among his recordings was *Freedom Jazz Dance*, which became a standard after it was recorded by Miles Davis. In 1966 Harris adopted the electric tenor saxophone; this was a conventional instrument played through a signal processor, the Varitone. Thereafter he recorded on a variety of instruments which were modified by alterations to their structures and often played through amplifiers and signal processors. Harris has played the trumpet and trombone fitted with reed mouthpieces, and saxophones fitted with brass mouthpieces. From the late 1960s he has worked mostly as the leader of small groups, recording with many distinguished sidemen (including Cedar Walton, Ron Carter, Muhal Richard Abrams, and Tete Montoliu). In 1969 he joined Les McCann's soul-jazz group, with which he gave an acclaimed performance at the Montreux International Jazz Festival. He made his most dramatic and controversial departure from the jazz tradition when he recorded the album *Eddie Harris in the UK* with the rock musicians Steve Winwood and Jeff Beck. Though in the mid-1970s Harris returned temporarily to a purer bop style, he continued to experiment with unusual instruments into the 1980s.

SELECTED RECORDINGS

(all recorded for Atlantic unless otherwise indicated)

As leader: *Exodus to Jazz* (1961, VJ 3036); *The In Sound* (1965, 1448), incl. Freedom Jazz Dance; *The Tender Storm* (1966, 1478); *The Electrifying Eddie*

Harris (1967, 1495); *Silver Cycles* (1968, 1517); *Free Speech* (1969, 1573); *Eddie Harris in the UK* (1972, 1647); *Eddie Harris Sings the Blues* (1972, 1625); *That is Why you're Overweight* (1975, 1683); *Steps up* (1981, Ste. 1151)

As sideman with L. McCann: *Swiss Movement* (1969, 1537)

BIBLIOGRAPHY

G. Lees: "Have you Heard Eddie Harris?," *DB*, xxviii/6 (1961), 16
B. Quinn: "Eddie Harris: Groupless Leader," *DB*, xxxiv/12 (1967), 20
M. Durham: "Eddie Harris Speaks out," *DB*, xxxix/3 (1972), 16
S. Marks: "Eddie Harris: Plugged-in Pioneer Turns up his Lungs," *DB*, xliii/1 (1976), 16 [incl. discography]
H. Gray: "Eddie Harris: the Unheralded Genius," *JSN*, ii/3 (1981), 6
M. Zwerin: "Eddie Harris: a Freedom Jazz-funk Dance," *The Wire*, no.30 (1986), 17

MARK GILBERT

Harris, Gene [Eugene] (*b* Benton Harbor, MI, 1 Sept 1933). Keyboard player. As a child he taught himself to play piano in a boogie-woogie style inspired by the recordings of Pete Johnson and Albert Ammons; from 1951 to 1954 he belonged to a band while serving in the US Army. With Andy Simpkins and Bill Dowdy he formed a group in 1956 which the following year became the THREE SOUNDS. It performed around Michigan and Washington in a style oriented towards the blues before moving in 1958 to New York. There the group's style became more refined, and its repertory came to include show tunes and standards; during the following years it made several recordings. After the departure from the group of Dowdy (1966) and Simpkins (1968) Harris led larger ensembles known as the Three Sounds, which performed and recorded jazz-rock. Later he moved to Idaho and again played more conventional jazz: in 1980 he performed in a quartet at the Hacienda in Las Vegas and with Ernestine Anderson at Parnell's in Seattle, and in 1985 he appeared with Benny Carter at the Concord Jazz Festival and with Ray Brown's trio at the Half Note in New York.

SELECTED RECORDINGS

As leader: of Three Sounds (with B. Dowdy and A. Simpkins): *Introducing the Three Sounds* (1958, BN 1600); of Three Sounds (with Dowdy, A. O'Day, and Simpkins): *Anita O'Day and the Three Sounds* (1962, Verve 68514); *The Three Sounds* (1971, BN 84378); *Astral Signal* (1974, BN LA313G)

As sideman (all recorded for Concord): E. Anderson: *When the Sun Goes Down* (1984, 263); R. Brown: *Soular Energy* (1984, 268)

BIBLIOGRAPHY

FeatherE; *Feather '60s*; *Feather–Gitler '70s*
"Gene Harris: did you Higga-booms Today?," *Black Stars*, iv/1 (1974), 7
J. March: "Call and Response," *Cadence*, ii/3–4 (1977), 16
J. Sippel: "Concord Bash Offers Vintage Jazz," *Billboard*, xcvii (31 Aug 1985), 58 [review of Concord Jazz Festival (1985)]

GREGORY E. SMITH

Harris, Joe (i) (*b* Sedalia, MO, 1908; *d* Fresno, CA, sum. 1952). Trombonist and singer. He took up trombone at the age of 16, and played with local bands in Oklahoma, Texas, and Canada. After performing with Joe Haymes in Springfield, Missouri, he worked with Frankie Trumbauer in Chicago (1932), then took Jack Teagarden's place in Ben Pollack's band (1933). He worked in New York for a while as a freelance, then in 1935 joined Bob Crosby's band; later that year he became a member of Benny Goodman's orchestra, and is probably best remembered for his performance on Goodman's *Stompin' at the Savoy* (1936, Vic. 25247). In 1936 Harris moved to Hollywood, where he worked as a studio musician and performed with Spud Murphy (1938), Pollack (1940), Pee Wee Erwin (1942), and others. He rejoined Goodman in 1943, then played in Eddie Miller's big band. Later he resumed session work and played with obscure groups in California. He should not be confused with the New Orleans trombonist of the same name who led bands in the 1920s.

based on *ChiltonW*

Harris, Joe [Joseph Allison] **(ii)** (*b* Pittsburgh, 23 Dec 1926). Drummer and percussionist. He was introduced to the bop style as a teenager by Ray Brown and Art Blakey, who also grew up in Pittsburgh. In 1946 and 1948 he played with Dizzy Gillespie; he also performed in a quintet with Gillespie and Charlie Parker in a concert at Carnegie Hall in 1947. A versatile musician, proficient on congas, timbales, and timpani as well as the standard drum set, Harris was much in demand both for his bop drumming and his mastery of Latin rhythms. In the early 1950s he worked with Billy Eckstine, Erroll Garner, Lester Young, and James Moody, and played in the house band at the Apollo Theatre in Harlem. He moved to Europe in 1956, and spent nearly a decade performing in Sweden and Germany. In the late 1960s he returned to the USA, where his activities included a tour with Ella Fitzgerald in 1968. After a further stay in Germany (1972) he settled in Pittsburgh. Thereafter he taught at the University of Pittsburgh (1972–86) and also traveled extensively. In 1983 he received a grant to study traditional music in Japan; he has returned there several times to give jazz concerts.

SELECTED RECORDINGS

As sideman: C. Parker and D. Gillespie: *A Nite at Carnegie Hall* (1947, Birdland 425); J. Moody: *Moody's Moods* (1954, Prst. 192); on R. Charles: *The Genius After Hours* (1956, Atl. 1369), Music, Music, Music; H. Silver: *The Tokyo Blues* (1962, BN 84110); F. Boland: *Music for the Small Hours* (1967, Col. SMC74324); on P. Herbolzheimer: *My Kind of Sunshine* (1971, MPS 3321331), Timbales calientes

BIBLIOGRAPHY

FeatherE; *Feather–Gitler '70s*
I. Gitler: *Jazz Masters of the Forties* (New York, 1966/R1983 with discography), 58

SCOTT DeVEAUX

Harris, Little Benny [Benny, Benjamin Michel] (*b* New York, 23 April 1919; *d* San Francisco, 11 Feb 1975). Trumpeter and composer. He was a self-taught musician. In the mid-1930s he played with Thelonious Monk and later took part in early bop jam sessions with Dizzy Gillespie and Charlie Parker (it is said that he convinced Gillespie of Parker's ability by playing one of the latter's improvisations). Gillespie obtained work for Harris with Tiny Bradshaw (1939) and Earl Hines (1941, 1943), and he also played intermittently during the 1940s with Benny Carter, Pete Brown, John Kirby, Herbie Fields, Coleman Hawkins, and Monk, as well as with Boyd Raeburn (1944–5). His compositions include *Little Benny* (later recorded by Parker as *Craze-ology* and by Bud Powell as *Bud's Bubble*), *Lion's Den*, and the standard riff on *Perdido*; it is also probable that he wrote *Ornithology* in collaboration with Parker. Following brief periods in Gillespie's band, around 1952 Harris ceased to be active as a musician; he moved to California, first to Sacramento and then to San Francisco, where he was interviewed in 1961. As a performer he was not of the stature of his colleagues, but he played an important role in the development of bop and as a composer of a few tunes that have become jazz standards.

SELECTED RECORDINGS

As sideman: C. Hart: Little Benny (1944, Savoy 598); D. Byas: How High the Moon (1945, Savoy 597); C. Parker: La cucuracha (1952, Mer./Clef 11093)

BIBLIOGRAPHY

D. Hadlock: "Benny Harris and the Coming of Modern Jazz," *Metronome*, lxxviii/10 (1961), 18
G. Hoefer: "Little Benny Harris," *DB*, xxx/25 (1963), 38
J. Burns: "The Legendary Who?," *J&B*, ii/8 (1972), 12

STEVEN STRUNK

Harrison, Donald ("Duck") (*b* New Orleans, 23 June 1960). Alto saxophonist. While studying at the New Orleans Center for the Creative Arts with Ellis Marsalis he played with Terence Blanchard. He attended Southern University for a year and the Berklee College of Music (1979–80), led an organ trio in Boston that included Makoto Ozone, toured with Roy Haynes (1980–81), and worked with Brother Jack McDuff (1981). In 1982 he resumed his association with Blanchard: they replaced Branford and Wynton Marsalis in Art Blakey's Jazz Messengers in 1982, recorded the album *New York Second Line* (1983, Conc. 3002) as leaders, and left Blakey's group in 1984 to form a bop quintet, which they later continued to lead while playing occasionally with Blakey.

BIBLIOGRAPHY

S. Bloom: "Profile: Donald Harrison," *DB*, lii/1 (1985), 46
I. Gitler: Liner notes, A. Blakey: *Art Blakey Live at Sweet Basil* (1985, PW 6357)
H. Mandel: "Terence Blanchard, Donald Harrison: Young, Gifted & Straight Ahead," *DB*, liii/12 (1986), 22 [incl. discography]

Harrison, Jimmy [James Henry] (*b* Louisville, KY, 17 Oct 1900; *d* New York, 23 July 1931). Trombonist. He took up trombone at the age of 15 and was mostly self-taught. After touring with minstrel shows he played in Atlantic City, New Jersey, with Charlie Johnson and Sam Wooding; he also worked in Detroit and with June Clark and James P. Johnson in Toledo, Ohio. In 1922 he moved to New York with Fess Williams and subsequently played in Charlie Smith's band, remaining when Clark was appointed leader (1924). Later he worked with Duke Ellington and Elmer Snowden and joined Fletcher Henderson's orchestra, with which he recorded his best work (1927–30). An operation for stomach cancer incapacitated him in 1930 and, after attempts the following year to resume playing with Henderson and also with Chick Webb, he died at the height of his powers.

Harrison's sonorous tone, bold ideas, and flexible technique led to his being called "the father of swing trombone," and his influence on other jazz trombonists has been lasting. There is some controversy as to whether Harrison influenced the white trombonist Jack Teagarden or vice versa; certainly each was inspired by the other's playing. Harrison's outgoing personality enabled him to give successful imitations of the comedian Bert Williams, an example being his performance on Henderson's *Somebody loves me* (1930). At the time of his death he was developing a more advanced harmonic approach.

SELECTED RECORDINGS

As sideman: F. Henderson: I'm coming Virginia (1927, Col. 1059D); C. Johnson: Walk that thing (1928, Vic. 21712); F. Henderson: Somebody loves me (1930, Col. 2329D); Chocolate Dandies: Bugle Call Rag/Dee Blues (1930, Col. 2543D)

BIBLIOGRAPHY

H. Panassié: "Jimmie Harrison," *BHcF*, no.59 (1956), 3
D. Heckman: "Jazz Trombone: Five Views," *DB*, xxxii/2 (1965), 17 [incl. transcr.]
"Charlie Green v Jimmy Harrison," *JJ*, xix/3 (1966), 10
B. McRae: "A B Basics, no.42: Jimmy Harrison," *JJ*, xxiii/6 (1970), 4
R. Stewart: "The Father of Swing Trombone (Jimmy Harrison)," *Jazz Masters of the Thirties* (New York and London, 1972), 51
S.-A. Worsfold: "The Forgotten Ones: Jimmy Harrison," *JJI*, xxxvi/4 (1983), 12

JOHN CHILTON

Harrison, Lance (Easton) (*b* Vancouver, Canada, 23 June 1920). Canadian tenor saxophonist, clarinetist, and bandleader. After playing banjo and guitar as a youth he took up the saxophone. In the 1930s he played in several dance bands in Vancouver and he continued to perform while in the Canadian air force during World War II. He was a member of various theater and dance bands in Vancouver over the next 20 years but at the same time was active as a bandleader and arranger: his dixieland jazz band (formed in 1950) performed and recorded (1959–73) in Vancouver and played regularly on radio and television; on the CBC television program "Some of those Days" he led an orchestra that re-created in an authentic way the "hot" dance music of the 1920s and 1930s.

BIBLIOGRAPHY

M. Miller and B. Smith: "Harrison, Lance (Easton)," *Encyclopedia of Music in Canada*, ed. H. Kallmann, G. Potvin, and K. Winters (Toronto, Buffalo, and London, 1981)
M. Miller: "Lance Harrison," *Boogie, Pete, & the Senator: Canadian Musicians in Jazz: the Eighties* (Toronto, 1987), 146

JACK LITCHFIELD

Harrison, Max (*b* London). English writer. As a critic he has written on both jazz and classical music, providing articles for *The Times* and numerous jazz periodicals, and his wide knowledge in one field has often led to insights into the other. He contributed to Albert McCarthy's *Jazz on Record* (1968) and thereafter wrote two further critical guides to the recorded repertory; the second of these, *The Essential Jazz Records*, i: *Ragtime to Swing* (1984, written with Charles Fox and Eric Thacker), places each of 250 selected recordings in its musical context and offers a detailed critical review. Harrison is the author of the major article on jazz in *The New Grove Dictionary of Music and Musicians* (1980; revised and enlarged in *The New Grove Gospel, Blues and Jazz*, 1987). He is particularly interested in jazz of the 1930s, which he believes is a neglected area of research, and has also written about avant-garde movements in jazz and other forms of contemporary music in a series of articles in *The Wire* (1985–7).

WRITINGS
(selective list)

Charlie Parker (London, 1960); repr. in *Kings of Jazz*, ed. S. Green (South Brunswick, NJ, and New York, 1978)
with others: *Modern Jazz: the Essential Records: a Critical Selection* (London, 1975)
A Jazz Retrospect (Newton Abbot, England, 1976, rev. 2/1977)
"Jazz," *Grove6*; rev. and enlarged in P. Oliver, M. Harrison, and W. Bolcom: *The New Grove Gospel, Blues and Jazz* (London and New York, 1986 [*recte* 1987])
with C. Fox and E. Thacker: *The Essential Jazz Records*, i: *Ragtime to Swing* (London, and Westport, CT, 1984)

ROBERT GANNON

Hart, Billy [William W.; Jabali] (*b* Washington, 29 Nov 1940). Drummer. He taught himself to play drums. His first professional engagement was with the singer Shirley Horn, with whom he played for three years and later (1977–81) recorded. He played with Jimmy Smith (1964), Wes Montgomery, Eddie Harris, Pharoah Sanders, and Marian McPartland, and in 1970 joined Herbie Hancock's group, with which he remained for three years. He then played for a year with McCoy Tyner and, from 1974 into the 1980s, intermittently with Stan Getz. He also performed and recorded (often on the Steeplechase label) with many other leading figures in modern jazz, including Miles Davis (1972), Jimmie Rowles (1976), Niels-Henning Ørsted Pedersen (1977–9), Clark Terry (1979), Lee Konitz (1979), Chico Freeman (1980–82), and James Newton (1982–5). With the drummers Freddie Waits and Horacee Arnold he formed Colloquium III, a group that led percussion workshops at the New York Drummers' Collective. Hart is widely regarded as one of the most capable of modern-jazz drummers; he is equally at home in electronic and rock-influenced styles, in free jazz, and in bop.

SELECTED RECORDINGS

As leader: *Enhance* (1977, A&M Hor. 725)
As sideman: C. Fuller and T. Flanagan: *Jazz . . . it's Magic* (1957, Reg. 6055); H. Hancock: *Mwandishi* (1970, WB 1898); M. Davis: *On the Corner* (1972, Col. KC31906); S. Getz: *Live at Montmartre* (1977, Ste. 1073–4); Mingus Dynasty: *Live at Montreux* (1980, Atl. 16031); J. Newton: *Luella* (1983, Gram. 8304); L. Coryell: *Comim' Home* (1984, Muse 5303)

BIBLIOGRAPHY

B. Primack: "Drummers Colloquium III: Multiple Percussionists," *DB*, xlvi/17 (1979), 25
C. Iero: "Colloquium III: Freddie Waits, Horacee Arnold, Billy Hart," *MD*, iv/1 (1980), 12

J. KENT WILLIAMS

Hart, Clyde (*b* Baltimore, 1910; *d* New York, 19 March 1945). Pianist. He first gained recognition in New York during the late 1930s while working with Stuff Smith, Roy Eldridge, John Kirby, and Oscar Pettiford, and during the early 1940s, when the bop style was being formulated, played regularly at Minton's Playhouse and at clubs on 52nd Street. Hart was one of the first swing pianists to adapt his music to the new style of Charlie Parker and Dizzy Gillespie, both of whom he accompanied in several important early bop recording sessions. Abandoning the left-hand patterns of the stride style, he began to state the harmonic progressions in a spare, rhythmic manner, leaving the pulse to the bass player and drummer. Unfortunately, his early death from tuberculosis occurred before he had fully incorporated the new vocabulary into his solo style.
See also PIANO, §4.

SELECTED RECORDINGS

As leader: What's the matter now?/That's the Blues (1945, Contl 6013)
As sideman: T. Grimes: Tiny's Tempo (1944, Savoy 526); Red Cross (1944, Savoy 532); D. Gillespie: Dizzy Atmosphere/All the things you are (1945, Musi. 488)

BIBLIOGRAPHY

G. Hoefer: "Clyde Hart: Forgotten Pianist," *DB*, xxxi/3 (1964), 21
M. Pinfold and J. Burns: "Dead, but not . . . Remembered," *JJI*, xxx/12 (1977), 12

BILL DOBBINS

Hartman, Johnny [John Maurice] (*b* Chicago, 13 July 1923; *d* New York, 15 Sept 1983). Singer. He sang with his high-school jazz orchestra, studied at Chicago Musical College, and performed professionally before military service. After World War II he sang with Earl Hines (1947), Dizzy Gillespie (1948–9), and Erroll Garner (1949), then pursued a career as a soloist in nightclubs and on television. During the 1960s he worked with John Coltrane, recording a fine album of ballads, *John Coltrane and Johnny Hartman* (1963). He performed and recorded in Tokyo with Roland Hanna and George Mraz in 1977, and in 1981 his album *Once in Every Life* was nominated for a Grammy Award. Hartman's repertory encompassed country music (including *By the time I get to Phoenix*), jazz standards, popular songs, and easy listening (such as *Raindrops keep fallin' on my head*). In all these styles he enunciated clearly, rolling and caressing each syllable in a manner that imbued each word with power. This approach, the richness and depth of his full baritone voice, and his faithfulness to original melodies made his work appeal to a large audience. He was at his best on slower songs, such as *Lush Life*, but brought a sense of swing and inventive rhythmic phrasing to compositions of all tempos.

SELECTED RECORDINGS

As leader: *Songs from the Heart* (1955, Beth. 43); *I Just Dropped by to say Hello* (1963, Imp. 57); with J. Coltrane: *John Coltrane and Johnny Hartman* (1963, Imp. 40), incl. Lush Life; *Today* (1973, Perception 30), incl. By the time I get to Phoenix; *I've been there* (1975, Perception 41), incl. Raindrops keep fallin' on my head; *Live at Sometime* (1977, Trio 0096); *Once in Every Life* (1980, BH 7012)
As sideman: with D. Gillespie: That Old Black Magic (1949, Vic. 203481); E. Garner: September in the Rain (1949, Mer. 5378)

BIBLIOGRAPHY

Feather–Gitler '70s
D. Cerulli: "Johnny Hartman," *DB*, xxiv/10 (1957), 34
"Johnny Hartman," *Metronome*, lxxviii/8 (1961), 20
L. K. McMillan, Jr.: "Johnny Hartman," *Coda*, xi/11 (1974), 6

MARTY HATCH

Hartwell, Jimmy [James] (*b* c1900; *d* after 1942). Clarinetist and alto saxophonist. He played in Chicago with the Ten Foot Band and Russ Wilkins's Melody Boys (c1922), then became a founding member of the Wolverines (for illustrations *see* RECORDING, fig.3, and WOLVERINES). He remained with the group, making a number of recordings (including *Copenhagen*, 1924, Gen. 5453), until spring 1925, when he settled in Miami. During the late 1920s he led his own band in Florida, and during the 1930s, after suffering from asthma, changed to double bass.

based on *ChiltonW*

Harvey, Eddie [Edward Thomas] (*b* Blackpool, England, 15 Nov 1925). English trombonist, pianist, and arranger. A founding member of George Webb's Dixielanders in 1943, he played trombone with the band until 1946. After serving in the RAF he performed with Freddy Randall (1948–9, 1950) and Vic Lewis (1950). He was one of the founding members of the John Dankworth Seven (1950) and went on to work in Dankworth's big band (1953–5). He also studied at the Guildhall School of Music and Drama, London (1950–52). From the late 1950s he played both piano and trombone, and worked as a freelance musician with Don Rendell, Woody Herman, Kenny Baker, Ronnie Scott, Dankworth, and Maynard Ferguson. During the same period he wrote a number of arrangements, notably for his own television series (1960–64) and Humphrey Lyttelton, for whom he also worked as a pianist (1964–72). Later Harvey began to teach jazz; he wrote *Teach Yourself Jazz Piano* (1974) and studied education at Berklee College of Music (1983). From 1986 he worked as a member of various Arts Council panels.

BIBLIOGRAPHY

FeatherE
D. Boulton: *Jazz in Britain* (London, 1958)
I. Carr: "Harvey, Eddie," in I. Carr, D. Fairweather, and B. Priestley: *Jazz: the Essential Companion* (London, 1987)

NEVIL SKRIMSHIRE

Hasselgård, Stan [Åke] (*b* Sundsvall, Sweden, 4 Oct 1922; *d* nr Decatur, IL, 23 Nov 1948). Swedish clarinetist. In the early 1940s he belonged in Uppsala to the Royal Swingers, an amateur group; he played professionally with Arthur Österwall (1944–5) and Simon Brehm (1946–7) and recorded with Brehm, Bob Laine, and Gösta Törner (1942–7). In 1947 he received a master's degree from Uppsala University, then moved during the summer to the USA, where he worked with the vibraphonist Johnny White in Los Angeles and performed with Count Basie. He recorded four tracks as a leader for Capitol the same year, on which Barney Kessel and Red Norvo were among his sidemen, and it is on these recordings that his reputation largely rests. Towards the end of 1947 he joined Benny Goodman's septet, with which he remained until it disbanded the following summer. During the last months of his life he led a group that included Max Roach and Barbara Carroll. Hasselgård modeled his style after that of Goodman, though it was more lyrical and melodious; after he moved to the USA his playing displayed the influence of bop.

SELECTED RECORDINGS
As leader: My Melancholy Baby/On the Sunny Side of the Street (1947, Vecko-Revyn 4); Swedish Pastry/Who Sleeps? (1947, Cap. 15062); Sweet and Hot Mop/I'll never be the same (1947, Cap. 15302); with W. Gray of Benny Goodman Septet: *Swedish Pastry* (1948, Dra. 16)
As sideman: K. Bonfils: Blue Skies (1945, Odeon D5213); first issued on [no leader]: *Wardell Gray, Featuring Stan Hasselgård and his Orchestra* (1947–8, Spot. 134), C-Jam Blues, How High the Moon (1947)

BIBLIOGRAPHY
C.-E. Lindgren: "Vi glömmer honom aldrig" [We will never forget him], *Orkester journalen*, xxii (1954), Jan, 12 [incl. discography]
L. Westin: "Åke Hasselgård i USA," *Orkester journalen*, xxxviii (1970), Jan, 12; Feb, 10; March, 8; April, 10
J. Burns: "The Forgotten Boppers," *J&B*, ii/3 (1972), 4
H. Pekar: "Stan Hasselgård: an Unfulfilled Talent," *J&B*, iii/2 (1973), 20

ERIK KJELLBERG

Hastings, Lennie [Leonard] (*b* London, 5 Jan 1927; *d* London, 14 July 1978). English drummer. He first worked professionally entertaining servicemen during the last years of World War II. Later he performed and recorded with Freddy Randall (1949–54) before joining Alex Welsh's band (1955). One of the finest of the many recordings he made with Welsh is the album *Melody Maker Tribute to Louis Armstrong* (1970, Pol. 2460123-5). During this association, which lasted some 18 years, Hastings also recorded with several other musicians, including Earl Hines and Rex Stewart (both 1966) and Eddie "Lockjaw" Davis, Ben Webster, and Bill Coleman (all 1967). Illness forced him to leave Welsh in 1973, but he continued to perform and record; he played regularly at the Pizza Express, London, and shortly before his death commenced work with his own quartet. Hastings displayed a superb sense of timing and profound understanding of traditional jazz.

BIBLIOGRAPHY
B. Matthew: *Trad Mad* (London, 1962)
D. Fairweather: "Hastings, Lennie," in I. Carr, D. Fairweather, and B. Priestley: *Jazz: the Essential Companion* (London, 1987)

CLARRIE HENLEY

Hat. Name by which the derby mute is popularly known; *see* MUTE, §2(j).

Hat Hut. Swiss record company and label. The company was established in 1974 in Therwil, Switzerland, by Werner Uehlinger, and by the 1980s it had expanded to include the additional labels Hat Art and Hat Musics. It concentrates on free jazz; Joe McPhee and Steve Lacy are the musicians it has recorded most frequently. Its catalogue also includes important recordings by Anthony Braxton, Max Roach (in duos with Braxton and with Archie Shepp), Cecil Taylor, and the Vienna Art Orchestra.

BIBLIOGRAPHY
P. Carles and S. Loupien: "Hat Hut de A à Z," *Jm*, no.275 (1979), 24
P. Carles: "Deux faces du disque: Timeless, Hat Hut," *Jm*, no.338 (1985), 42

Hauger, Kristian (*b* Oslo, 24 Oct 1905; *d* Oslo, 18 Oct 1977). Norwegian pianist, bandleader, and composer. From 1928 to 1945 he led bands and from 1930 made hundreds of recordings, 12 to 15 of which may be classified as jazz (including *På toppen* (*On the top*)/*Karusell*, 1943, Tel. 8408); among those who played under him were the saxophonists Yngar Wang and Bjarne Hansen, the trumpeters Haakon Buntz and Kristian Sletmo, the trombonist Trygve Fjelddalen, the guitarist Guttorm Frölich, the violinist Øivind Bergh, and the drummer Harald Jaang. From 1937 until his death Hauger also took part in the leadership of music organizations in Norway. He is best known as a composer of popular tunes, of which he wrote more than a thousand.

Oral history material in *NOnj*.

BIBLIOGRAPHY
O. Angell, J. E. Vold, and E. Økland: *Jazz i Norge* (Oslo, 1975)
K. Michelsen, ed.: *Cappelens musikkleksikon* (Oslo, 1978)

VIDAR VANBERG

Haughton, Chauncey (*b* Chestertown, MD, 26 Feb 1909). Clarinetist, saxophonist, and pianist. He took up piano at the age of eight, and later played clarinet and saxophone in his college band. In the late 1920s and early 1930s he worked in various minor groups (including one led by Cab Calloway's brother Elmer) before traveling to New York in 1932 with a band led by Gene Kennedy. He performed with Blanche Calloway until 1935, then with Claude Hopkins, Noble Sissle, Fletcher Henderson, and Chick Webb, and his work on clarinet may be heard to advantage on Webb's *I got rhythm* (1937, Decca 1759). From 1937 to 1940 Haughton played with Cab Calloway. He then joined a band led by Ella Fitzgerald, and apart from a brief period with Benny Carter's big band in 1940 remained with Fitzgerald until 1942, when he joined Duke Ellington. After army service (1943–5) he toured Europe with Don Redman (1946), and after Redman's group disbanded played briefly in Scandinavia (1947). In the late 1940s Haughton worked again with Calloway before ceasing to be a full-time musician; he later resumed his association with Calloway, recording with him in 1958.

based on *ChiltonW*

Haurand, Ali [Alfred Antonius Josef] (*b* Viersen, Germany, 15 Nov 1943). German double bass player and percussionist. He played in an amateur dixieland band and then studied double bass at the Folkwangschule in Essen, Germany (1966–72). During this period he became a member of George Maycock's trio and also accompanied visiting American musicians such as Don Byas and Ben Webster. With the Dutch pianist Jan Huydts he organized the jazz-rock ensemble Third Eye (1970). He joined the European Jazz Quintet in 1977 and, in the following year, formed the trio SOH with Tony Oxley and Alan Skidmore; with this group he recorded the album *SOH* (1979, Ego 4011). He toured and recorded with the Hungarian clarinetist Lajos Dudas (1977–80), and from 1983 played with Oxley in a group called The Quartet. During the 1970s and 1980s Haurand was in great demand as a freelance musician; he formed Connexion, a group that aims to help musicians to manage their own careers. He has also taught double bass at several music schools.

BIBLIOGRAPHY
"On the Bandstand: Third Eye," *JF* [intl edn], no.38 (1975), 18
W. Panke: "Erfolg bei der Engagementsuche: Ali Haurand," *JP*, xxxi/7 (1982), 12
D. Speck: "Unermüdlicher Organisator und Integrator: Ali Haurand," *JP*, xxxv/6 (1986), 16
M. Wangler: "Ali Haurand," *JP*, xxxv/6 (1986), 17 [interview]

WOLFRAM KNAUER

Havens, Bob [Robert L.] (*b* Quincy, IL, 3 May 1930) Trombonist. He came from a musical family, learned violin, piano, and trombone as a child, and played in local jazz groups. He worked in New Orleans with the trumpeter George Girard (1956–7) and Al Hirt's band (1957–60), then in 1960 joined Lawrence Welk's orchestra, with which he remained into the 1980s. He also recorded with many important traditional-jazz musicians, including Sharkey Bonano, Emile Christian (both

1958), and Armand Hug (1958, 1959). He led his own dixieland group at Disneyland and also recorded two albums as a leader (including *Bob Havens and his New Orleans All Stars*, 1964, Slnd 243). Later he recorded with Ray Linn (1978, 1980).

BIBLIOGRAPHY

Feather '60s; *Feather–Gitler '70s*
E. Cook: "Bob Havens," *JJI*, xxxv/3 (1982), 10
"Bob Havens," *Fn*, xv/6 (1984), 15 [incl. discography]

Haverhoek, Henk [Hendrik] (*b* Schoorl, Netherlands, 11 Feb 1947). Dutch bass player. He studied clarinet and tenor saxophone, attended the Arnhem Conservatory, and took a correspondence course offered by the Berklee College of Music; in 1966 he took up the double bass. He worked with Pierre Courbois (1968–71) and belonged to a quartet led by Rein de Graaff and the tenor saxophonist Dick Vennik (1968–77); at the same time he played as a freelance with Dexter Gordon, Johnny Griffin (recording the album *The Jamfs are Coming*, 1975, 1977, Tim. 121), Art Taylor, Philly Joe Jones, Horace Parlan, Duke Jordan, Kenny Drew, Mal Waldron, Ben Webster (recording in 1973), Tete Montoliu, Slide Hampton, Carmell Jones, Don Byas (recording in 1972), Leo Wright, Sal Nistico (ii), Bobby Jones, Frank Rosolino, and Art Farmer. In 1978 he belonged to the group Just in Case and led a trio, and from the following year he played with Eddy Marron and worked again as a freelance. Later he recorded again with de Graaff in a quartet led by Teddy Edwards (*Good Gravy*, 1981, Tim. 139). (*Feather–Gitler '70s*)

WIM VAN EYLE

Havlik, Ferdinand (*b* Brno, Czechoslovakia, 18 June 1928). Czechoslovak clarinetist, alto saxophonist, and bandleader. He studied clarinet, then played under the bandleader J. Šubert (1945), with Arnošt Kavka, and with Zdenek Barták (1952). In 1954 he joined Jiří Prochazka's orchestra, with which he made his first recordings and began his career as an arranger, and in 1958 he formed a quartet that performed and recorded cool jazz. He made many recordings of dance music as a member of the band of the Semafor theater in Prague, joined the Swing kvartet Praha in 1974, and in 1979 formed a big band that performed in a style suggestive of Benny Goodman, Artie Shaw, and the Czech musicians Kamil Behounek and Jaroslav Ježek; the same year he made the first of several appearances at the Oude Stijl Jazz Festival in the Netherlands. In the 1980s Havlik was considered the most important leader of a swing group in Eastern Europe; his playing can be heard to advantage on his album *A ještě trochu swingu* (And even a little swing; 1981, Sup. 11152746H).

GERHARD CONRAD

Hawdon, Dickie [Dick, Richard] (*b* Leeds, England, 27 Aug 1927). English trumpeter and double bass player. He was first a trumpeter and led the Yorkshire Jazz Band (1948–50) and his own band (1950–51, which included Alexis Korner), and played with Chris Barber (1951–2), and the Christie Brothers Stompers (1952–3). He broadened his stylistic range by performing and recording with Don Rendell (1954–5), Tubby Hayes (1955–6, as both trumpeter and arranger), John Dankworth (1957–60, 1961–3, latterly as lead trumpeter), Sid Phillips, Harry Gold, and the bandleader Oscar Rabin (all 1960–61), and Terry Lightfoot (1961–4); he was also lead trumpeter in the house bands of London clubs. A good example of his playing may be heard in *Tribute to Chauncey* on Dankworth's *Jazz Routes* (1959, Col. 33SX1280). Hawdon also led his own quintets (1957–60, 1968–79). From 1980 his principal instrument was the double bass. As a lecturer at City of Leeds College of Music (from 1967), Hawdon instituted the first full-time jazz course in Europe; he became head of department there in 1972. (D. Fairweather: "Hawdon, Dick (Richard)," in I. Carr, D. Fairweather, and B. Priestley: *Jazz: the Essential Companion*, London, 1987)

DIGBY FAIRWEATHER

Hawes, Hampton [Hamp] (*b* Los Angeles, 13 Nov 1928; *d* Los Angeles, 22 May 1977). Pianist. He taught himself piano, and while still a teenager he played with Sonny Criss, Dexter Gordon, and Wardell Gray. As a member of Howard McGhee's band (1950–51) he worked with Charlie Parker, who had a strong influence on his music. He performed and recorded with Shorty Rogers and Howard Rumsey in the early 1950s, and after army service (1952–4), during which he played in Japan, he led a trio comprising Red Mitchell and Chuck Thompson (1955–6). In 1958 he was arrested for possessing heroin and spent five years in prison. Later he worked again with Mitchell (1965), led a group with Jimmy Garrison, and performed and recorded in Japan and Europe during a world tour (1967–9). Thereafter Hawes worked with Leroy Vinnegar (1969–70) and played in duos with the double bass players Carol Kaye (1974) and Mario Suraci (1975). His autobiography, which was published in 1974, won a Deems Taylor Award.

Hawes has been noted for his rhythmic playing at fast tempos; his early recordings in particular demonstrate his crisp articulation of rapid melodic lines and skillful playing with locked hands. When performing ballads he often used an extended unaccompanied rubato chorus as an introduction. From the early 1970s, as demonstrated by *High in the Sky* (*c*1971), he relied less on the cadence patterns typical of popular songs and adopted the technique of playing slow, rhythmic vamps. He experimented with electronic keyboard instruments and made recordings with strings (including *The Two Sides of Hampton Hawes*, *c*1970, Jas 4004), but towards the end of his career he again played piano.

SELECTED RECORDINGS

As unaccompanied soloist: *The Challenge* (1968, JVC SMJ7488); *Live at the Great American Music Hall* (1975, Conc. 222) [incl. duos with M. Suraci]
As leader: *Volume 1: the Trio* (1955, Cont. 3505); *All Night Session* (1956, Cont. 3545-7); *The Green Leaves of Summer* (1964, Cont. 7614); *I'm all Smiles* (1966, Cont. 7631), incl. Searchin'; *Spanish Steps* (1968, BL 122); with M. Solal: *Key for Two* (1968, BYG 529125); *High in the Sky* (*c*1971, Vault 9010); *Hampton Hawes at the Piano* (1976, Cont. 7637)
As sideman: S. Rogers: *Shorty Rogers and his Giants* (1953, RCA LPM3137), incl. Diablo's Dance; C. Mingus: *Mingus Three* (1957, Jub. 1054)

BIBLIOGRAPHY

FeatherE
J. Mehegan: "Jazz Pianists, 4: Hampton Hawes: an Analysis," *DB*, xxiv/15 (1957), 17
L. Feather: "Hampton Hawes Revisited," *DB*, xxxiii/21 (1966), 14
H. Siders: "Hamp's New Blues," *DB*, xxxv/21 (1968), 16 [interview]
M. Gardner: "Hampton Hawes: Japan Revisited," *JJ*, xxii/9 (1969), 22
H. Hawes and D. Asher: *Raise up off me: a Portrait of Hampton Hawes* (New York and Toronto, 1974; Ger. trans. as *Ganz tief Luft holen: Autobiographie eines Jazzmusikers*, Frankfurt am Main, Germany, 1983)
L. Lyons: "Hampton Hawes: Challenging the Charts, on Wood," *DB*, xliii/21 (1976), 23 [incl. discography]
L. Feather: "Piano Giants of Jazz: Hampton Hawes," *CK*, v/7 (1979), 84 [incl. partial transcr. of *Searchin'*]
R. Hunter and M. Davis: *Hampton Hawes Discography* (Manchester, England, 1986) [incl. biography and list of compositions]
A. Hamilton: "Hampton Hawes: Letting a Beat Go by," *The Wire*, no.37 (1987), 26

STEVE LARSON

Hawkins, Coleman (Randolph) [Bean, Hawk] (*b* St. Joseph, MO, 21 Nov 1904; *d* New York, 19 May 1969). Tenor saxophonist.

1. Life. 2. Musical style.

1. Life. He was taught piano from the age of five by his mother, a schoolteacher who played organ. He took up cello at about the age of seven, then requested a tenor saxophone, which he received on his ninth birthday. By the time he was 12 he was performing professionally at school dances. He went to high school in Chicago, then (by his own account) attended Washburn College in Topeka, Kansas, for about two years, during which time he studied harmony and composition.

Hawkins's first regular job, beginning in the spring of 1921, was playing in the orchestra of the 12th Street Theater in Kansas City. That summer Mamie Smith performed at the theater, and offered Hawkins a position touring with her group the Jazz Hounds. By March 1922 Hawkins was working with Smith at the Garden of Joy in New York. He made his first recordings with her shortly afterwards, but his contributions are frequently indiscernible, a notable exception being on *I'm gonna get you*. Early in 1923 he toured with the Jazz Hounds as far as California, where the group performed in the revue *Struttin' Along*, but he left after it returned to New York in June.

Hawkins then worked as a freelance player with various musicians, including Wilbur Sweatman, whose group opened the new club Connie's Inn in June 1923. Fletcher Henderson heard Hawkins with Sweatman and employed him to record with his band the following August. During this period Hawkins also joined the pianist Ginger Jones and the trumpeter Charlie Gaines at the Garden of Joy, and played with Cecil Smith and Lou Hooper at the Renaissance Casino. Both Hawkins and Henderson appear to have played under the violinist Ralph "Shrimp" Jones at the Bamville Club near the end of that year. The association with Henderson proved decisive for Hawkins, as Henderson engaged him when he formed a band to play at the Club Alabam in early January 1924. Hawkins remained with the group until March 1934, making numerous recordings and attracting worldwide notice. In his first substantial recorded solo, on *Dicty Blues* (1923), he reveals an authoritative style, big sound, and fast vibrato.

Until the end of 1930 Henderson's band spent most of each year at the Roseland Ballroom, although it played occasionally at other venues in the New York area, particularly the Savoy Ballroom. It also traveled widely, visiting New England, the East Coast, and the Midwest, and making a tour of the South during the first two weeks of 1933. Finally, when a tour of Great Britain fell through in 1934, Hawkins contacted the English bandleader and impresario Jack Hylton and arranged to tour the country on his own with local groups. He had clearly become the star of the Henderson group and felt it was time to move on.

Hawkins arrived in England on 30 March 1934 and toured as the guest of Jack Hylton's band and Mrs. Jack Hylton's band. His success was such that he decided to stay in Europe, performing with the Ramblers early in 1935 in The Hague, and then playing freelance in Paris, Laren, Zurich (with the Berry's), and elsewhere; he also made numerous recordings with the Ramblers, the Berry's, and other groups assembled for studio sessions. Perhaps the most famous of these sessions was one in Paris on 28 April 1937 that included Django Reinhardt and Benny Carter; Hawkins played with fervor and rhythmic drive, even beginning his solo on *Crazy Rhythm* with repeated riffs. Hawkins returned to England on 11 March 1939 and commenced a tour sponsored by the Selmer instrument company, where he was accompanied by local musicians at each performance. He finally returned to New York in July 1939.

Coleman Hawkins, 1939

American musicians, generally unaware of Hawkins's European recordings, anxiously awaited his return. He formed a nine-piece band and opened at Kelly's Stable on 5 October. At the end of a studio session a few days later he improvised two choruses on *Body and Soul*, a recording that was a commercial and musical success, and that reestablished his importance to musicians while introducing him for the first time to a mass audience. At the end of 1939 readers of *Down Beat* magazine voted Hawkins "best tenor saxophonist." He then formed a big band and played in New York at the Golden Gate Ballroom, the Savoy, and the Apollo Theatre, and also went on tour. In 1941 he resumed working with small groups, however, and for the next two years played mostly in Chicago and the Midwest before returning to New York.

Hawkins spent most of 1945 in California, performing and recording with a group that included the modernists Howard McGhee and Oscar Pettiford (this ensemble also appeared in the film *The Crimson Canary*). He returned to the East Coast, then joined a Jazz at the Philharmonic tour which took him back to California in April 1946. During the next five years Hawkins usually joined these tours for at least a few concerts, while spending most of the year with his own groups in New York. He returned to Europe in May 1948, in late 1949, in 1950, and again in 1954, the last as part of Illinois Jacquet's tour of American service bases. He continued to lead recording groups with such new talented players as Miles Davis, Fats Navarro, J. J. Johnson, and Milt Jackson. Around 1948 he recorded a fascinating unaccompanied improvisation, *Picasso*, a feat that was still beyond many of the younger generation.

During the late 1950s Hawkins continued to appear at all the major jazz festivals, often as leader of a group with Roy Eldridge. He joined the Jazz at the Philharmonic tour of 1957, the "Seven Ages of Jazz" tours in 1958 and 1959, traveled to Europe for brief engagements, and played on television in "The Tonight Show" (1955) and "The Sound of Jazz" (1957). He also recorded prolifically during this time, beginning with a series of albums for the subsidiaries of Prestige in 1958, and followed by several for Impulse, including his only collaboration with Duke Ellington (1962). During the 1960s he appeared in films and on television. He often recorded and performed at the Village Gate and the Village Vanguard with a quartet comprising Tommy Flanagan, Major Holley, and Eddie Locke.

Hawkins began to exhibit signs of emotional distress during the last two years of his life and was seriously affected by alcoholism. He collapsed while playing in Toronto in February 1967, and again in June while on the last tour of Jazz at the Philharmonic. He traveled to Europe with Oscar Peterson's trio and played for a month at the end of the year in Ronnie Scott's club in London with an English rhythm section, but a tour of Denmark at the beginning of 1968 was canceled owing to his ill-health. His last concert was on 20 April 1969 at the North Park Hotel, Chicago.

2. Musical style. Hawkins's powerful and original style was largely responsible for the popularity of the tenor saxophone as a jazz instrument (*see* Saxophone, §2). On his early recordings he made much use of the characteristic technique of the day – heavily articulated slap tonguing – but he later developed a more legato approach which eventually became the norm. During his years with Henderson he absorbed musical ideas from many nonsaxophonists, including his fellow band members. Most important among these was Louis Armstrong, whose smooth melodic lines and advanced sense of swing strongly influenced Hawkins, as may be heard on the recordings made from the end of September 1924 to November 1925. By 1926 Hawkins was also being impressed by the harmonic ideas of Art Tatum. On *The Stampede* (1926) he develops question-and-answer phrasing after the fashion of Armstrong along with his own trills and triplet ornaments. Highly technical patterns and chromatic sequences are introduced on the third take of *St. Louis Shuffle* (1927), which have achieved virtuoso complexity by *Wherever there's a will, baby* (1929). A comparison of the two issued versions of this piece shows that the patterns at crucial points, such as at the beginning and the middle, are memorized and repeated verbatim, but the rest is freely improvised. A week later Hawkins recorded a solo on *One Hour* that won acclaim among musicians for its richness of ideas, sensitive tone, and rhythmic flexibility; he also mingled speechlike rubato phrases with moments in double time. All of Hawkins's playing is characterized by intense emotional conviction.

Hawkins continued to experiment with a complex rubato approach for the next few years, creating highly elaborate structures even at fast tempos, as on *New King Porter Stomp* (1932). His solo on *Can you take it?* (1933), however, suggests a return to playing on the beat, and demonstrates his increasing ability to improvise memorable and logically constructed melodies. At the same session Henderson's band recorded a tune by Hawkins, *Queer Notions*, which explores the whole-tone scale. Hawkins's celebrated recording of *Body and Soul* (1939) is notable for its relaxed virtuosity, warmth of sound, harmonic ingenuity, consistent use of double time, and intricate development of motifs (ex.1; *see also* Improvisation, §§4(i), 4(iii), and ex.1).

Ex.1 From *Body and Soul* (1939, Bb 10523), bars 25–32; transcr. L. Porter

all notes at phrase endings have vibrato

Hawkins was a brilliant musical thinker who was remarkably open to new developments in jazz as well as classical music; this was reflected in both the personnel and the repertory of his groups. In February 1944 he led a band that featured Dizzy Gillespie, Max Roach, and others in what are generally considered to be the first bop recordings. Another session later the same year was the earliest to include Thelonious Monk.

By the late 1950s Hawkins's tone had hardened somewhat, and he developed a fierce approach to the blues. He still found new ideas during a sensitive, rhythmically complex treatment of *Body and Soul* (1959). He easily accepted the new bossa nova songs, recording some in 1962, but had more difficulty during a session the following year which paired him with Sonny Rollins and Paul Bley, both of whom were exploring ideas related to those of Ornette Coleman.

Young saxophonists continue to find inspiration in Hawkins's recordings. His influence has endured, even though it was somewhat eclipsed during the 1940s by that of Lester Young and after 1960 by that of John Coltrane – a testament to the intelligence and technical authority of his music. Hawkins recorded an interview for Riverside in 1956, *Coleman Hawkins: a Documentary* (Riv. 12117-18).

See also Blues, §5; for further illustration *see* Jazz (i), fig.2.

SELECTED RECORDINGS

As unaccompanied soloist: Picasso (*c*1948, Clef [unnumbered])

As leader: Honeysuckle Rose/Crazy Rhythm (1937, Swing 1); Body and Soul (1939, Bb 10523); Woody 'n' You (1944, Apollo 751); On the Bean (1944, Joe Davis 8251); *Coleman Hawkins and Roy Eldridge at the Opera House* (1957, Verve 8266), incl. The Walker; on [no leader]: *Playboy Jazz All-Stars Album* (1959, Playboy 1959A), Body and Soul; *Duke Ellington meets Coleman Hawkins* (1962, Imp. 26), incl. Self Portrait (of the Bean); *Desafinado* (1962, Imp. 28), incl. Desafinado, Samba para Bean; with S. Rollins: *Sonny Meets Hawk* (1963, RCA LSP2712), incl. Just Friends, Lover Man

As sideman: M. Smith: I'm gonna get you (1922, OK 4781); F. Henderson: Dicty Blues (1923, Voc. 14654); The Stampede (1926, Col. 654D); St. Louis Shuffle (1927, Vic. 20944); McKinney's Cotton Pickers: Wherever there's a will, baby (1929, Vic. 22736); Mound City Blue Blowers: Hello, Lola/One Hour (1929, Vic. 38100); F. Henderson: New King Porter Stomp (1932, OK 41565); Queer Notions/Can you take it? (1933, Voc. 2585)

BIBLIOGRAPHY

M. Levin: "Coleman Hawkins: One of Great Forces in Jazz," *DB*, xvii/21 (1950), 2

N. Hentoff: "The Hawk Talks," *DB*, xxiii/22 (1956), 13

L. Feather: "Coleman Hawkins," *The Jazz Makers: Essays on the Greats of Jazz*, ed. N. Shapiro and N. Hentoff (New York, 1957/*R*1979), 163

M. James: "Coleman Hawkins Today," *JM*, viii/1 (1962), 7

D. Heckman: "Pres and Hawk: Saxophone Fountainheads," *DB*, xxx/1 (1963), 20

A. McCarthy: *Coleman Hawkins* (London, 1963); repr. in *Kings of Jazz*, ed. S. Green (South Brunswick, NJ, and New York, 1978)
V. Wilmer: "Caught in the Act: Coleman Hawkins," *DB*, xxxv/3 (1968), 26
H. Panassié: "Coleman Hawkins," *BHcF*, no.189 (1969), 3
M. Williams: *The Jazz Tradition* (New York, 1970, rev. 2/1983)
R. Stewart: *Jazz Masters of the Thirties* (New York and London, n.d. [?1972]), 60
L. Keating: "Hawkins on Record," *J&B*, ii (1972), no.2, p.4; no.3, p. 12; no.4, p.25; no.5, p.25; no.6, p.23; no.7, p.23; no.8, p.34; no.9, p.33; ii/10 (1973), 7; iii (1973), no.3, p.10; no.4, p.8
W. C. Allen: *Hendersonia: the Music of Fletcher Henderson and his Musicians: a Bio-discography* (Highland Park, NJ, 1973)
D. Morgenstern: Liner notes, *The Hawk Flies* (Mlst. 47015, 1973)
G. Colombé: "Time and the Tenor: Coleman Hawkins in the Sixties," *Into Jazz*, i/4 (1974), 30
S. Dance: *The World of Swing* (New York, 1974) [colln of previously pubd interviews], 140
J. Simmen: "Coleman Hawkins in Switzerland, 1935/6/8: a Few Personal Souvenirs," *Sv*, no.55 (1974), 17
J. Evensmo: *The Tenor Saxophone of Coleman Hawkins, 1929–1942* (n.p. [Oslo], n.d. [?1976]) [discography]
J. McDonough: Liner notes, *Coleman Hawkins* (TL 06, 1979)
H. Rye: "Visiting Firemen, 5: Coleman Hawkins," *Sv*, no.97 (1981), 15; no.100 (1982), 147
Y. Delmarche and I. Fresart: *A Discography of Coleman Hawkins, 1922–1969* (n.p., n.d. [?1983])
B. James: *Coleman Hawkins* (Tunbridge Wells, England, 1984)
J. Godbolt: *A History of Jazz in Britain, 1919–50* (London, Melbourne, Australia, and New York, 1984), 250
J.-F. Villetard: *Coleman Hawkins*, i: *1922–1944* (Amsterdam, 1984) ii: *1945–1957* (Amsterdam, 1985) [discography]
S. Deveaux: *Jazz in Transition: Coleman Hawkins and Howard McGhee, 1935–1945* (diss., U. of California, Berkeley, 1985)

LEWIS PORTER

Hawkins, Erskine (Ramsey) (*b* Birmingham, AL, 26 July 1914). Trumpeter and bandleader. He started playing drums at the age of seven, and learned trombone before taking up trumpet when he was 13. While a student at Alabama State Teachers College, Montgomery, he was appointed leader of the college band, the 'Bama State Collegians. In 1934 he went with the band to New York, where at first it worked with limited success; from 1938 it became known as the Erskine Hawkins Orchestra, and its recording of *Tuxedo Junction* the following year brought it widespread popularity which continued into the early 1950s. Although Hawkins's orchestra was not known for its originality, it included musicians who had a fine sense of swing and who could play the blues extremely well; it also boasted such soloists as Paul Bascomb, Julian Dash, Haywood Henry, Avery Parrish, and Dud Bascomb. By 1953 Hawkins had reduced the band to a small group, although the larger ensemble came together occasionally for reunions. Hawkins continued to work sporadically into the 1980s. Earlier in his career he was billed as "The Twentieth Century Gabriel" and he sometimes made use of ostentatious displays in the upper register of his instrument; these aspects have caused him to be virtually ignored by jazz historians. He was, however, a talented and enthusiastic player in the swing style, who generously shared solo work with the equally gifted Dud Bascomb.
Oral history material in *NjR* (JOHP).

SELECTED RECORDINGS

Uproar Shout (1937, Voc. 3545); Swingin' on Lenox Avenue (1939, Bb 10292); Gin Mill Special/Tuxedo Junction (1939, Bb 10409); Uptown Shuffle (1939, Bb 10504); After Hours (1940, Bb 10879); Tippin' in (1945, Vic. 201639)

BIBLIOGRAPHY

"Hawkins, Erskine," *CBY 1941*
H. Panassié: "Erskine Hawkins et son orchestre," *BHcF*, no.94 (1960), 3
B. Niquet: "Erskine Hawkins: le parent pauvre du Savoy," *Pj*, no.5 (1971), 21 [incl. discography]
I. Crosbie: "Twentieth Century Gabriel," *JJ*, xxv (1972), no.7, p.12; no.8, p.14 [incl. discography]
C. Battestini and J.-P. Battestini: "Haywood Henry évoque ses riches années avec Erskine Hawkins," *BHcF*, no.272 (1979), 3 [interview]
I. Crosbie: "Erskine Hawkins and his Orchestra," *JM*, no.171 (1969), 15
T. Burke and D. Penny: "Erskine Hawkins Orchestra: 'The 20th Century Gabriel' 1942–1955," *Blues & Rhythm, the Gospel Truth*, no.8 (1985), 4 [incl. discography]

SCOTT YANOW

Hayes, Clancy [Clarence Leonard] (*b* Caney, KS, 14 Nov 1908; *d* San Francisco, 3 March 1972). Banjoist and singer. He learned drums as a child but later changed to guitar and then banjo. He worked with a vaudeville troupe in the Midwest (after 1923) and in 1927 he settled in San Francisco. His popularity as an entertainer grew during the 1930s, when he performed on radio and in clubs. In 1938 he joined Lu Watters's Yerba Buena Jazz Band and played an important part in the group's revival of New Orleans and Chicago jazz; his vaudeville style of singing added an appropriate element of comic play-acting to the band's performances. Hayes remained with Watters during the 1940s, though he also worked as a soloist and recorded as a drummer with Bunk Johnson (1944). In the 1950s he performed and recorded (1950–59) with Bob Scobey's revivalist band. He then worked with the Firehouse Five Plus Two, Turk Murphy, his own groups, as a soloist, and with the group led by Yank Lawson and Bob Haggart that in 1968 became known as the World's Greatest Jazz Band. Hayes was noted for his straightforward singing of ballads and his flamboyant delivery of livelier songs.

SELECTED RECORDINGS

As leader: *Clancy Hayes's Dixieland Band* (1960, Audio Fidelity 5937); *Swingin' Minstrel* (1963, GTJ 10050); *Live at Earthquake McGoon's* (1966, ABC-Para. 591)
As sideman: L. Watters: Muskrat Ramble/Smokey Mokes (1941, Jazz Man 3); B. Johnson: Careless Love (1944, Jay 5); B. Scobey: Ace in the Hole/Silver Dollar (1953, GTJ 78); Huggin' and a-chalkin' (1953, GTJ 86)

BIBLIOGRAPHY

ChiltonW; *FeatherE*
J. Goggin: *Turk Murphy: Just for the Record* (San Leandro, CA, 1982) [incl. discography], 136

LAWRENCE KOCH

Hayes, Edgar (Junius) (*b* Lexington, KY, 23 May 1904; *d* Riverside, CA, 28 June 1979). Pianist, arranger, and bandleader. He received a Bachelor of Music degree from Wilberforce University, and in 1922 toured the South with Fess Williams. From 1924 to 1931 he led his own groups, then joined the Mills Blue Rhythm Band, for which he played and wrote arrangements until 1936 (for illustration *see* MILLS BLUE RHYTHM BAND). His solo on *Blue Flame* (1931, Bruns. 6143) is a good example of his playing style. He then led a swing band (1937–41), whose members included Joe Garland and Kenny Clarke; in 1938 it toured Europe, and made a hit recording of Hayes's arrangement of *Star Dust* (Decca 1882). Hayes moved to California in 1942, and continued to play at clubs into the 1970s. He also recorded an album of piano solos (*c*1960).

BIBLIOGRAPHY

ChiltonW; *FeatherE*
L. Feather: "Edgar Steps Out," *MM*, xiv (26 Feb 1938), 2
B. Wood: "Three Pianists," *JJ*, ix/2 (1956), 3
A. McCarthy: *Big Band Jazz* (New York and London, 1974), 255, 282

Hayes, Harry [Henry Richard] (*b* London, 23 March 1909). English saxophonist. He was mainly self-taught. After performing for two years with Fred Elizalde at the Savoy Hotel in London (recording in 1928) he worked as a session musician, and in 1932 recorded with Spike Hughes. Thereafter he played with the pianist Billy Mason at the Café de Paris (during which time he accompanied Louis Armstrong on tour in Britain), the dance-band leader Sidney Lipton, the violinist Maurice Winnick (1934–6), Lipton again (1936–8), and the bandleader

Geraldo (1939–40). Following military service he led his own band at Churchill's club, which included George Shearing and Tommy Whittle (1945–7). From 1944 to 1947 he held a recording contract with HMV, using pickup bands, and a fine example of his playing may be heard on *Lucky Number* (1947, HMV B9566). Hayes led small groups and taught privately until 1965, when he retired. From 1946 he also ran several musical instrument outlets, but around 1959 he changed to record shops, which he maintained until 1986.

Oral history material in *GBLnsa*.

NEVIL SKRIMSHIRE

Hayes, Louis (Sedell) (*b* Detroit, 31 May 1937). Drummer. He led a group at clubs in Detroit before he was 16. He moved to New York in August 1956 to replace Art Taylor in the Horace Silver Quintet and in 1959 joined the Cannonball Adderley Quintet, with which he remained until mid-1965, when he succeeded Ed Thigpen in the Oscar Peterson Trio. He left Peterson in 1967 and formed a series of groups, which he led alone or with others; among his sidemen were Freddie Hubbard, Joe Henderson, Kenny Barron, and James Spaulding. He returned to Peterson in 1971. The Louis Hayes Sextet, which he formed in 1972, became in quick succession in 1975 the Louis Hayes–Junior Cook Quintet and the Woody Shaw–Louis Hayes Quintet (Cook remained as a sideman until Rene McLean joined); in its last form the quintet played successful engagements throughout Europe and (without McLean) acted as the host group when in 1976 Dexter Gordon visited the USA for the first time in many years. After Shaw left the group in 1977 Hayes continued to lead it as a hard-bop quintet. Hayes plays in a compelling, forceful style, marked by a tendency to push the beat and to goad the soloist with frequent fills.

SELECTED RECORDINGS

As leader: *Louis Hayes* (1960, VJ 3010); with J. Cook: *Ichi-ban* (1976, Tim. 102); *The Real Thing* (1977, Muse 5125); *Variety is the Spice* (*c*1979, Gryphon 787); with J. Farrell: *Vim 'n' Vigor* (1983, Tim. 197)

As sideman: C. Fuller: *New Trombone* (1957, Prst. 7107); H. Silver: *Finger Poppin'* (1959, BN 4008); C. Adderley: *The Cannonball Adderley Quintet at the Lighthouse* (1960, Riv. 9344); J. J. Johnson: *A Touch of Satin* (1960–61, Col. CS8537); O. Peterson: *Blues Etude* (1965–6, Lml. 86039); F. Hubbard: *The Hub of Hubbard* (1969, MPS 15267); C. Walton: *A Night at Boomer's* (1973, Muse 5010, 5022); D. Gordon: *Homecoming* (1976, Col. PG34650)

BIBLIOGRAPHY

P. Vacher: "The Louis Hayes Story," *JM*, vii/1 (1961), 13
L. Tomkins: "Keeping Jazz Alive our Way: Louis Hayes and Woody Shaw," *CI*, xv/3 (1976), 20
——: "Drummers Talking: on Practice, Rock, and Records," *CI*, xv/6 (1977), 21
L. Jeske: "Louis Hayes: Putting Things Together," *MD*, viii/7 (1984), 24

J. KENT WILLIAMS

Hayes, Tubby [Edward Brian] (*b* London, 30 Jan 1935; *d* London, 8 June 1973). English tenor saxophonist. He learned violin as a child, but changed to tenor saxophone at the age of 12 and soon became a virtuoso performer. At the age of 15 he became a professional musician and worked with the bands of Kenny Baker, Jack Parnell, Bert Ambrose, Vic Lewis, and others. In 1955–6 he led his own octet, and in 1957–9 he led a group, the Jazz Couriers, with Ronnie Scott. Thereafter he worked with his own small groups, led a big band (1961–3), and toured the USA (1961, 1962, 1964, 1965) and Europe as a soloist. In 1956 he took up vibraphone; he also played flute and soprano, alto, and baritone saxophones, and was an accomplished composer and arranger. The main influences upon his work were Charlie Parker, Zoot Sims, Sonny Rollins, and John Coltrane. Hayes was a resourceful hard-bop soloist who possessed a fluent technique. His solos, crowded with notes, were always logical, and earned him recognition as one of the most creative British musicians.

SELECTED RECORDINGS

As leader: *Tubby's Groove* (1959, Tempo TAP29); *Tubbs in N.Y.* (1961, Fon. 5183); *Late Spot at Scott's* (1962, Fon. 5200); *Return Visit* (1962, Fon. 5195); *A Tribute: Tubbs* (1963, Spot. 902); *100% Proof* (1966, Fon. 5410); *Mexican Green* (1967, Fon. 911)

As sideman with D. Reece: *Blues in Trinity* (1958, BN 4006)

BIBLIOGRAPHY

Feather '60s; *Feather–Gitler '70s*
J. Martin: "The Little Giant of the Tenor Sax," *Jazz News*, iv/30 (1960), 3
L. Tomkins: "The Tubby Hayes Story," *Crescendo*, i/11 (1963), 5
T. Hayes: Liner notes, *Mexican Green* (Fon. 911, ?1967)
Obituary, *MM* (16 June 1973), 29
R. Scott: Liner notes, *A Tribute: Tubbs* (Spot. 902, ?1973)
——: *Some of my Best Friends are the Blues* (London, 1979), 48
I. Carr: "Hayes, Tubby," in I. Carr, D. Fairweather, and B. Priestley: *Jazz: the Essential Companion* (London, 1987)

MARK GARDNER

Haymer, Herbie [Herbert] (*b* Jersey City, NJ, 24 July 1915; *d* Santa Monica, CA, 11 April 1949). Tenor saxophonist. He played with local groups in the early 1930s, and after moving to New York worked for brief periods with the singer Rudy Vallee and Charlie Barnet. In 1935 he joined Red Norvo's group, where he was featured as a soloist at concerts and on recordings, frequently performing arrangements by Eddie Sauter. From 1937 to 1941 he played swing with Jimmy Dorsey. After recording for Decca as a member of Woody Herman's band (1941–2) he played from early 1942 with the bandleader Kay Kyser, who adopted a swing style after several years of performing popular material; in the following year he worked with Benny Goodman and on the West Coast under the bandleader Dave Hudkins. Haymer served for a brief period in the armed forces, then played for about a year with Red Nichols, and worked frequently on the West Coast in studios and as a freelance. He recorded in 1945 as the leader of a quintet that included Charlie Shavers, Nat "King" Cole, and Buddy Rich, and in 1947 with Benny Goodman.

SELECTED RECORDINGS

As leader (all recorded in 1945 for Sun): Black Market Stuff/Laguna Leap (7561); I'll Never be the Same/Swinging on Central Avenue (10055)

As sideman: R. Norvo: Gramercy Square/Decca Stomp (1936, Decca 691); The Morning After/Do you Ever Think of me? (1937, Bruns. 7975); J. Dorsey: It's the Dreamer in me/Don't be That Way (1938, Decca 1733); The Darktown Strutter's Ball/Dusk in Upper Sandusky (1938, Decca 1939); K. Kyser: Can't Get Out of This Mood/Moonlight Mood (1942, Col. 36657)

BIBLIOGRAPHY

ChiltonW; *FeatherE*
Obituary, *DB*, xvi/9 (1949), 1
G. Hoefer: Obituary, *DB*, xvi/10 (1949), 1 [incl. discography]

WARREN VACHÉ, SR.

Haymes, Joe (*b* Marshfield, MO, 1908). Pianist and arranger. As a teenager he performed as a circus trapeze artist. He was a self-taught musician, and worked as a staff arranger for Ted Weems before forming his own band, which traveled to New York in the early 1930s and played residencies at the Roseland and Empire ballrooms. It made many recordings, some of which (including *He's the Life of the party*, 1932, Vic. 24052) were issued under Haymes's name, and others under pseudonyms. His sidemen included Pee Wee Erwin and Bud Freeman. In 1934 Haymes ceded leadership of this band to Buddy Rogers; later he organized another group, 12 members of which formed the nucleus of Tommy Dorsey's first band in 1935. Haymes continued to lead various groups and to record throughout the 1930s. During the 1940s he played in studios in Hollywood, then returned to New York and became a staff musician for CBS. (G. T. Simon: *The Big Bands* (New York, 1967, rev. and enlarged 2/1971, rev. 3/1974, 4/1981), 461)

based on *ChiltonW*

Haynes, Cyril (*b* Panama Canal Zone, *c*1915). Pianist and arranger. He grew up in New York, learned piano as a child, and played with local bands as a teenager. After studying music at Columbia University he toured with the revue "Dixie on Parade," then played with the trumpeter Billy Hicks, and in 1937 joined Al Cooper's Savoy Sultans. A fine solo by Haynes may be heard on Cooper's *Jumpin' at the Savoy* (1939, Decca 2526); he also arranged *Sophisticated Jump* (1940, Decca 3274) for the band. After leaving Cooper in 1943 Haynes performed with Frankie Newton, George James, and others, worked as the house pianist at various clubs, and led his own recording groups. In 1944 he recorded with Barney Bigard and played with Al Casey, and from 1948 to 1950 he worked as a soloist in California. In the 1950s he played with various bands, including those of Noble Sissle, Andy Kirk, and Cab Calloway; he continued to tour with Calloway into the 1960s, and played regularly in New York at Ryan's in 1978.

based on *ChiltonW*

Haynes, Roy (Owen) (*b* Roxbury, MA, 13 March 1926). Drummer. He began his professional career in Boston, where in 1944 he worked in swing groups with Frankie Newton and Pete Brown and also played with lesser-known big bands and dixieland groups. Two periods with Luis Russell's orchestra (1945–6, 1946–7) marked his only association with a significant big band. A natural and extremely flexible percussionist, he thereafter provided idiomatic accompaniments in many styles as a member of swing, bop, modal-jazz, free-jazz, and jazz-rock groups. Without ever achieving fame in his own right, he worked with such leading musicians as Lester Young (1947–9), Bud Powell and Miles Davis (both briefly, 1949), Charlie Parker (1949–52), Sarah Vaughan (1953–8; for illustration *see* VAUGHAN, SARAH), Thelonious Monk (1958), and Eric Dolphy (1960). From 1961 to 1965 he was the principal substitute for Elvin Jones in John Coltrane's group, and in 1960 he founded his own bop group, which later, under the name the Hip Ensemble, turned towards the jazz-rock idiom; among its distinguished sidemen were George Adams (1969–73) and Hannibal Peterson (*c*1972). Haynes has also appeared intermittently with Stan Getz and Gary Burton from the 1960s. He recorded with Duke Jordan in New York (1975) and while on tour in Japan (1976), and then spent a brief but intense period of activity in recording studios, taking part in sessions with Nick Brignola (1977–8), Burton, Hank Jones, and Art Pepper (all 1978), Ted Curson (1978–9), and Joe Albany and Horace Tapscott (both 1979). In 1979 he performed with Dizzy Gillespie at the Newport and Monterey jazz festivals, and in 1981, with Miroslav Vitous, he became a member of Chick Corea's group Trio Music. While continuing to tour internationally on an intermittent basis with Corea (playing timpani as well as a standard drum set), Haynes led bop quartets in New York in 1985–6.

SELECTED RECORDINGS

As leader: *We Three* (1958, NewJ 8210); *Out of the Afternoon* (1962, Imp. 23); *Hip Ensemble* (*c*1970, Mstr. 313); *Senyah* (*c*1972, Mstr. 351); *Vistalite* (1977, Gal. 5116)

As sideman: B. Powell: Dance of the Infidels/52nd Street Theme (1949, BN 1568); M. Davis: Morpheus (1951, Prst. 734); S. Vaughan: *In the Land of Hi-fi* (1955, EmA 36058); T. Monk: *Thelonious in Action* (1958, Riv. 262); E. Dolphy: *Outward Bound* (1960, NewJ 8236); S. Getz: *Focus* (1961, Verve 68412); J. Coltrane: *Selflessness* (1963, Imp. 9161); G. Burton: *Times Square* (1978, ECM 1111); C. Corea: *Trio Music* (1981, ECM 1232-3); F. Hubbard: *Sweet Return* (1983, Atl. 80108)

BIBLIOGRAPHY

P. Harris: "'Unknown' Haynes Sparks Bird's Strings," *DB*, xvii/24 (1950), 2

D. Ioakimidis: "Roy Haynes," *Jh*, no.175 (1962), 18 [incl. survey of recorded work]

L. Jones: "A Day with Roy Haynes," *DB*, xxix/7 (1962), 18

D. DeMicheal: "The Varied Peripteries of Drummer Roy Haynes, or They Called him Snap Crackle," *DB*, xxxiii/26 (1966), 18

"Boston Jazz Society Honors Roy Haynes," *JSN*, i/5 (1980), 24

S. Fish: "Roy Haynes: Jazz Legend Still Goin' Strong," *MD*, iv/5 (1980), 30

L. Jeske: "Royal of Haynes Swings sooo Good," *DB*, xlvii/2 (1980), 14 [incl. discography]

R. Horricks: "Roy Haynes: Drummer for all Seasons," *CI*, xxi/3 (1982), 12

S. Crouch: "Dark Horse of the Drums," *VV*, xxxi (24 June 1986), 72

J. Potter: "Roy Haynes," *MD*, x/2 (1986), 16

BARRY KERNFELD

Hayse, Al(vin Cooper) (*b* Detroit, 7 April 1921). Trombonist. He played with McKinney's Cotton Pickers (1939) and then Lionel Hampton's band (1943–6). In 1950 he performed and recorded with Milt Buckner and the following year returned to Hampton, with whom he remained until 1956; during this period he toured Europe twice with the band. His best work may be heard on *Walkin' at the Trocadero* and *Real Crazy*, which were recorded with Hampton in Paris in 1953 and issued on an untitled LP (Vogue LD167). (*FeatherE*)

Hayton, Lennie [Leonard George] (*b* New York, 13 Feb 1908; *d* Palm Springs, CA, 24 April 1971). Pianist, composer, and arranger. After formal piano tuition in New York he joined the Little Ramblers (1926) and Cass Hagen's orchestra (1927), then worked with Paul Whiteman as second pianist (1928–30). He participated as an arranger or pianist in numerous recording sessions during the late 1920s and the 1930s, performing with Red Nichols, Bix Beiderbecke, Frankie Trumbauer, Miff Mole, and Joe Venuti; he even played harmonium and timpani with Beiderbecke on one occasion in 1928. In the early 1930s Hayton led his own band, and after moving to Hollywood he became music director for Bing Crosby. He worked for MGM for about 12 years from 1941, first as an arranger and later as a music director, and was later music director for his wife, the singer Lena Horne.

SELECTED RECORDINGS

As sideman: R. Nichols: Feelin' no Pain (1927, Bruns. 3626); Charleston Chasers: Imagination (1927, Col. 1260D); Feelin' no Pain (1927, Col. 1229D)

BIBLIOGRAPHY

ChiltonW; *FeatherE*

R. M. Sudhalter, P. R. Evans, and W. Dean-Myatt: *Bix: Man & Legend* (New Rochelle, NY, and London, 1974)

MIKE HAZELDINE

Haywood, Cedric (*b* Houston, 1914; *d* Houston, 9 Sept 1969). Pianist. He played in a high-school band with Arnett Cobb, then worked with Milt Larkin (1935–40), the bandleader Floyd Ray (1940), Lionel Hampton (1941), and briefly with Larkin again before joining Sidney Bechet in Illinois (1944). After working with local bands in San Francisco and serving in the army during the mid-1940s he worked with the rhythm-and-blues singer Saunders King (1948), then performed and recorded with Illinois Jacquet (1948–51). He returned to San Francisco and joined Cal Tjader in 1952. The following year he recorded with Gerald Wilson in Los Angeles, and around this time he began working as a freelance pianist and arranger. From 1955 to 1959 he worked with Kid Ory, performing, recording, and touring Europe twice. His playing may be heard to advantage on the album *Kid Ory Plays W. C. Handy* (1958, Verve 6061). During the early 1960s Haywood played with Brew Moore. In 1963 he returned to Houston, where he led his own band at the Club Ebony.

BIBLIOGRAPHY

ChiltonW; *FeatherE*; *Feather–Gitler '70s*
V. Wilmer: "Cedric Haywood," *JJ*, xiii/7 (1960), 22

Hazel, Monk [Arthur] (*b* Harvey, LA [now in New Orleans], 15 Aug 1903; *d* New Orleans, 5 March 1968). Drummer and cornetist. He performed with many bandleaders in and around New Orleans in the 1920s, among them Abbie Brunies, Tony Parenti, Jules Bauduc, and Johnny Wiggs. In the late 1920s and early 1930s he led his own Bienville Roof Orchestra, with which he recorded in 1928. He toured with the singer Gene Austin and again worked in New Orleans until his military service in 1942–3. From the late 1940s he performed with several musicians, including Santo Pecora, and recorded with his own group (1954), Sharkey Bonano (1949–52), and many other leaders. Hazel worked mainly as a drummer, but doubled on cornet and mellophone; he may be heard playing cornet and drums on *China Boy/Bugle Call Rag* (1934, Voc. 2849), which he recorded in a group called Candy and Coco.

Oral history material in *LNT*.

BIBLIOGRAPHY

FeatherE; *Feather–Gitler '70s*
"Monk Hazel Honored: in Turn, Honors Museum," *SL*, xviii (1967), Nov–Dec, 161
Obituary, *SL*, xx (1968), March–April, 28

based on *ChiltonW*

Head. The theme on which a jazz performance is based (*see* FORMS, §1); the term is normally applied to a popular song used for this purpose. The repeat of the head at the end of the performance is sometimes referred to as the OUT CHORUS.

Head arrangement. An arrangement that is worked out in rehearsal and memorized by the musicians but generally not written down; *see* ARRANGEMENT, §1.

Heard, J(ames) C(harles) (*b* Dayton, OH, 8 Oct 1917). Drummer. He first performed as a dancer in vaudeville shows, and took up drums as a teenager. After playing with local groups in Detroit he went to New York in 1939 to join Teddy Wilson's big band. He slipped confidently into the city's testing musical environment, and later worked with Wilson's sextet, and with Benny Carter and Coleman Hawkins. From 1942 to 1945 he was a member of Cab Calloway's orchestra and also recorded frequently with small groups, some of which included pioneer bop musicians. The versatility he showed during this period was typical of Heard's attitude towards music; he has always refused to be confined artistically. After leaving Calloway he led his own band at Café Society (1946–7), played in Erroll Garner's trio (1948), and was associated with Jazz at the Philharmonic, traveling extensively and visiting Europe and Japan. He performed in Japan and Australia as a drummer, singer, and dancer from 1953 to 1957, then, after his return to New York, worked as a freelance with Wilson and Hawkins, among others, and toured Europe with Sammy Price. In 1966 Heard moved back to Detroit, where he has continued to lead a sextet and, occasionally, a big band, though he has also appeared at festivals in Europe. At its best, Heard's dynamic drumming may be favorably compared with that of his mentors, Sid Catlett and Jo Jones.

SELECTED RECORDINGS

As leader: The Walk (1946, Contl 6022); Bouncing for Barney (1946, Contl 6027)

As sideman: C. Hawkins: Chant of the Groove, I can't get Indiana off my mind (1940), first issued on *Coleman Hawkins at the Savoy* (Sunbeam 204); B. Holiday: Laughing at Life (1940, Voc./OK 5719); C. Calloway: 105 in the Shade (1943), We the cats (1944), Coastin' with JC (1946), first issued on *Jazz off the Air*, iv: *Cab Calloway and his Orchestra (1943–46)* (Spot. 148); C. Thompson: Takin' off (1945, Apollo 757); P. Johnson: Mr Drums meets Mr Piano/JC from KC (1946, Nat. 4006); H. McGhee: Dorothy (1947, Dial 1027); C. Hopkins: *Let's Jam* (1961, Swingville SVLP 2020), incl. Safari, The way you look tonight; I. Jacquet: *God Bless my Solo* (1978, BB 33167)

BIBLIOGRAPHY

ChiltonW
P. Hanson: "Catching up with J. C. Heard," *JM*, no. 157 (1968), 18
P. Vacher: "Heard about J. C.?," *MM*, liii (4 Nov 1978), 44
D. Gillespie and A. Fraser: *To be, or not . . . to Bop: Memoirs* (Garden City, NY, 1979), 130
M. Lipson: "Portraits: J. C. Heard," *MD*, vii/7 (1983), 48
J. M. Doran: *Erroll Garner: the Most Happy Piano* (Metuchen, NJ, 1985), 70
S. Dance: "J. C. Heard," *JJI*, xxxix/11 (1986), 10

PETER VACHER

Heard, John (William) (*b* Pittsburgh, 3 July 1938). Double bass player. He took up alto and baritone saxophones while in his teens and in 1958 joined the US Air Force. He played double bass with Tommy Turrentine, Booker Ervin, and J. C. Moses in Pittsburgh, with Al Jarreau at the Half Note in San Francisco (1966–8), and in 1967 with Wes Montgomery, Sonny Rollins, and Randy Weston. After moving to Los Angeles in 1969 he performed and recorded with Ahmad Jamal (1972–7), Count Basie (1974–80, until 1976 as a member of his orchestra), Toshiko Akiyoshi (1978–9), Louie Bellson (1977–82), and Oscar Peterson (from 1977 into the 1980s). He accompanied Nancy Wilson and Joe Williams from 1982 and in 1985 recorded with Bobby Hutcherson and worked with Tal Farlow, Barney Kessel, and Eddie "Lockjaw" Davis. A self-taught musician, Heard is noted for his rhythmically driving style.

SELECTED RECORDINGS

As sideman: C. Tjader: *Live at the Funky Quarters* (1972, Fan. 9409); G. Duke: *Feel* (1974, MPS 68023); *Faces in Reflections* (1974, MPS 68022); C. Basie and Z. Sims: *Basie & Zoot* (1975, Pablo 2310745); Z. Sims and H. Edison: *Just Friends* (1978, Pablo 2310841); O. Peterson: *The Silent Partner* (1979, PT 2312103); G. Cables: *Phantom of the City* (1985, Cont. 14014)

BIBLIOGRAPHY

L. Tomkins: "John Heard," *CI*, xviii (1979–80), no.7, p.16; no.8, p.12

JOHN VOIGT

Heath. Family of musicians.

(1) Percy Heath(, Jr.) (*b* Wilmington, NC, 30 April 1923). Double bass player. He grew up in Philadelphia in a musical family. After playing violin in junior high school he took up double bass in 1946 when he enrolled at the Granoff School of Music. Within months he was performing in local bands, and the following year he and his brother (2) Jimmy Heath moved to New York with Howard McGhee's sextet. During the next few years he played with many important bop musicians, including Miles Davis, Fats Navarro, J. J. Johnson, Dizzy Gillespie, Charlie Parker, Thelonious Monk, Clifford Brown, and Horace Silver. In 1951 he replaced Ray Brown in Milt Jackson's quartet, and remained with it when, in 1952, it was renamed the MODERN JAZZ QUARTET. In 1975, shortly after this group disbanded temporarily, he, Jimmy, and (3) Albert "Tootie" Heath formed a quartet, the Heath Brothers, with Stanley Cowell; at that time he began playing piccolo bass. He has contin-

Members of the Heath Brothers playing at the Newport Jazz Saratoga festival in the mid-1980s: (left to right) Stanley Cowell (piano), Percy Heath (double bass), and Jimmy Heath (tenor saxophone)

ued to work with the Modern Jazz Quartet and the Heath Brothers into the mid-1980s (see illustration), and has also participated in various short-term projects.

Heath is one of the finest ensemble players of his generation and produces well-crafted solos; some of the best of these may be heard on albums by the Heath Brothers and include *The Watergate Blues* on the album *Marchin' on* (1975, SE 19766) and *Yardbird Suite* on *Passing thru* (1978, Col. JC35573), both played on piccolo bass. His principal contributions in many contexts are the solid, flowing bass lines upon which others improvise.

SELECTED RECORDINGS

As sideman: D. Gillespie: [untitled EP] (1951, Dee Gee 3601), incl. Birk's Works, Tin tin deo; C. Parker: Chi chi (1953, Clef 89138); H. Silver: Opus de funk (1953, BN 1625); M. Davis: *Miles Davis Quintet* (1954, Prst. 185), incl. I'll Remember April; Walkin' (1954, Prst. 45-157); T. Monk: *Thelonious Monk Trio* (1954, Prst. 189), incl. Nutty, Work

BIBLIOGRAPHY

FeatherE; *Feather '60s*; *Feather–Gitler '70s*
V. Wilmer: "Percy Heath," *JJ*, xvii/6 (1964), 6
L. Tomkins: "The Heath Brothers," *CI*, xxi (1982–3), no.4, p.20; no.5, p.12 [interview]

For further recordings and bibliography see (2) Jimmy Heath; *see also* MODERN JAZZ QUARTET.

(2) Jimmy [James Edward] **Heath** (*b* Philadelphia, 25 Oct 1926). Saxophonist, flutist, composer, and arranger. He began playing alto saxophone at the age of 14. In 1947 he and his brother (1) Percy Heath went to New York as members of Howard McGhee's group, and in 1949–51 he played in Dizzy Gillespie's big band and sextet. His style was profoundly influenced by that of Charlie Parker, and he acquired the nickname "Little Bird," but the comparison ceased when he took up tenor saxophone. In 1955 he went to prison for drug offenses; after his parole in 1959 he replaced John Coltrane for two months in Miles Davis's quintet, then formed his own group. In 1965 he began leading groups with Art Farmer, and in 1975 he formed a quartet with his brothers and Stanley Cowell. As the leader of this group (which in 1978 became a quintet when the guitarist Tony Purrone joined) Heath played tenor and soprano saxophones and flute. From the early 1980s, however, the group has performed only intermittently, and Heath has worked mainly as the leader of his own quartet. Heath's saxophone style owes something to that of Coltrane, but his tone and vibrato are warmer and his melodic lines are usually less ornate.

In the late 1940s Heath began composing and arranging for his own groups and others; in 1975 he completed his most ambitious work, *Afro-American Suite of Evolution*, which was written for a 30-piece ensemble. Two of his best-known pieces were recorded by Davis: *CTA* was included on the album *Young Man with a Horn* (1953, BN 5022) and *Gingerbread Boy* on *Miles Smiles* (1966, Col. CS9401).

Oral history material in *NjR*.

SELECTED RECORDINGS

As leader of Heath Brothers: *Marchin' on* (1975, SE 19766); *Passin' thru* (1978, Col. JC35573), incl. Prince Albert; *In Motion* (1979, Col. JC35816); *Brothers and Others* (1983, Ant. 1016)

As leader of other groups: *The Thumper* (1959, Riv. 1160); *Really Big* (1960, Riv. 1188), incl. Big P.; *The Gap Sealer* (1972, Cob. 9012); *New Picture* (1985, Landmark 1506)

BIBLIOGRAPHY

P. Welding: "The Return of Jimmy Heath," *DB*, xxviii/5 (1961), 16
I. Gitler: "Jimmy Heath," *BMI: the Many Worlds of Music* (Dec 1971), 8
L. Feather: "The Heath Brothers: Together again for the First Time," *DB*, xlii/17 (1975), 18; repr. in *The Passion for Jazz* (New York, 1980), 87
B. Rosenblum: "Jimmy Heath," *Coda*, no. 148 (1976), 2 [interview]
B. Primack: "The Heath Brothers: Bebop Above and Beyond the Fads," *DB*, xlvi/6 (1979), 16 [interview]
W. A. Brower: "The Heath Brothers," *JT* (March 1981), 10
L. Tomkins: "The Heath Brothers," *CI*, xxi (1982–3), no.4, p.20; no.6, p.8 [interview]
D. Salemann: Jimmy Heath: *Solography, Discography, Band Routes, Engagements, in Chronological Order* (Basle, Switzerland, 1986)
D. Gross: "Jimmy Heath," *Windplayer*, iv/1 (1987), 28

(3) Albert "Tootie" [Al] **Heath** [Kuumba] (*b* Philadelphia, 31 May 1935). Drummer. In the late 1950s he followed his brothers (1) Percy and (2) Jimmy Heath to New York, where he became involved with the bop movement. He worked with J. J. Johnson (1958–60) and the Jazztet (1960–61), and during the same period recorded with Jimmy Heath, Nat Adderley, Johnny Griffin, Mal Waldron, Kenny Dorham, and others. In 1965 he moved to Scandinavia, where he remained for three years, often working with Dexter Gordon and Kenny Drew at the Montmartre Jazzhus in Copenhagen. After returning to the USA he performed with Cedar Walton and Yusef Lateef, and worked with Billy Taylor (ii) for Jazzmobile in New York. For several years from 1974 he divided his time between playing with the Heath Brothers in the USA and working in Europe. He left his brothers' group in the late 1970s, settled in Los Angeles, and ceased to work as a musician. By the mid-1980s, however, he was active again, playing on the West Coast as a sideman with the Jazztet (1982–3) and Tal Farlow (1984), and leading his own group. Heath's inventiveness, sensitivity to the needs of an ensemble, and propulsively rhythmic playing have made him one of the most respected bop drummers.

SELECTED RECORDINGS

As leader: *Kwanza (the First)* (1973, Muse 5031); *Kawaida* (1973, Trip 5032)
As sideman: J. Coltrane: *John Coltrane* (1957, Prst. 7105); J. J. Johnson: *J. J. in Person* (1958, Col. CL1161); J. Heath: *The Thumper* (1959, Riv. 1160); *Really Big* (1960, Riv. 1188); D. Gordon: *The Montmartre Connection* (1967, BL 108); J. Heath: *The Gap Sealer* (1972, Cob. 9012); T. Montoliu: *Catalonian Fire* (1974, Ste. 1017)

BIBLIOGRAPHY

FeatherE; *Feather '60s*; *Feather–Gitler '70s*
For further recordings and bibliography see (2) Jimmy Heath.

THOMAS OWENS

Heath, Ted [George Edward] (*b* London, 30 March 1900; *d* Virginia Water, nr Egham, England, 18 Nov 1969). English trombonist and bandleader. He studied tenor horn with his father before taking up trombone. After a period as a street musician (until 1922), he became a regular sideman with several prominent British dance bands, notably those of Bert Ambrose (1928–36), Sydney Lipton (1936–9), Geraldo (1939–44), and Jack Hylton. Though not a strong jazz soloist, Heath seized the chance in 1944 to form his own band, which made regular broadcasts, gave the "Swing Sessions" concerts at the London Palladium, and soon began to tour frequently. Employing the very best section players, Heath successfully emulated the precision and versatility of such American bandleaders as Tommy Dorsey and Woody Herman (American musicians were banned from performing in Britain from 1935 to 1956). The many jazzmen who worked with him included Kenny Baker, Jack Parnell, and (consecutively) Ronnie Scott, Tommy Whittle, Danny Moss, and Don Rendell; he also commissioned such enterprising arrangers as John Dankworth, Tadd Dameron (briefly in 1949), Kenny Graham, and Bill Russo. In the mid-1950s Heath's dance band was one of the most popular in Britain; through its recordings it also gained much admiration in the USA, and in 1956 it made the first of several visits there. As many critics and former sidemen noted, Heath preferred predictable excellence to unplanned excitement, and his contribution consisted of raising standards of musicianship rather than encouraging new developments in jazz. He also had some success as a songwriter.

SELECTED RECORDINGS
(all recorded for Decca)

Opus 1 (1944, F8512); Bakerloo Non-stop (1946, F8629); Turn on the Heath (1947, F8864); Lyonia (1949, F9255); Seven Eleven (1953, F10200); *100th Palladium Concert* (1954, LK4075); Kings Cross Climax (1955, F10713); *Our Kind of Jazz* (1957–8, LK4262)

BIBLIOGRAPHY

FeatherE; *Feather '60s*; *Feather–Gitler '70s*
"Listen to my Music," *Fanfare*, iv/5 (1946), 4
J. Dawson: "The Man they couldn't Keep Down: the Inside Story of Ted Heath's Rise to Fame," *MM*, xxx (4 Sept 1954), 3; (11 Sept 1954), 5; (18 Sept 1954), 7; (25 Sept 1954), 8
T. Heath: *Listen to my Music: an Autobiography* (London, 1957)
T. Brown: "A Tribute to Ted," *Crescendo*, iii/6 (1965), 2
S. Woolley: "Listen to my Music," *JJI*, xxxvii/3 (1984), 8

BRIAN PRIESTLEY

Heatley, Spike [Brian John] (*b* London, 17 Feb 1933). English double bass player. After studying privately, in 1958 he joined Vic Ash's sextet, with which he recorded during the same year. He then became a member of the Jazz Couriers led by Tubby Hayes and Ronnie Scott (1959), played with Eddie Thompson, and performed and recorded with John Dankworth's orchestra (1960–62), Tony Coe (1962), and various ensembles led by Ronnie Ross (1964–8). In the late 1960s he recorded with Bud Freeman (1966) and Ben Webster (1967). From 1972 to 1981 he worked with the Bebop Preservation Society led by Bill Le Sage, and his playing may be heard to advantage on *One Bass Hit* from the album *The Bebop Preservation Society* (1971, Dawn 3027). Heatley led his own quintet with the tenor saxophonists Jim Hastings and Dave Bishop, the pianist John Horler, and the drummer Kevin Harris from 1979 to 1981, and in the 1980s he was the leader of a quartet with Horler, the saxophonist Alan Barnes, and the drummer Malcom Mortimer. He has also worked extensively in Europe with leading American musicians. (*Feather '60s*)

NEVIL SKRIMSHIRE

Heckstall-Smith, Dick [Richard Malden] (*b* Ludlow, England, 26 Sept 1934). English tenor saxophonist. He was educated at Dartington, Devon (where he took up the soprano saxophone), and then studied at Cambridge University, where he led the Cambridge University Jazz Band in 1953–6. After freelance work in London, he joined Sandy Brown in 1958, and also played engagements with Ronnie Smith, the trumpeter Bert Courtley, the drummer Ginger Baker, and Ballets USA directed by the choreographer Jerome Robbins (1958–62). Later he played blues and blues-rock with groups led by Alexis Korner (1962–3), Graham Bond (1963–7), and John Mayall (1967–8), and with Jon Hiseman's Colosseum (1968–71), with which he recorded *Collector's Colosseum* (1968–71, Bronze 9173). He led the group DHS1, which was renamed Manchild, in 1972–3. While studying for a doctorate in sociology (completed in 1979) he curtailed his musical activities, though from 1976 he led another band, Big Chief; in 1981 he disbanded Big Chief to join the Main Squeeze Blues Band, which included the blues singer and electric guitarist Bo Diddley, and in 1985 he started to work as a freelance with various other blues and rock-influenced jazz musicians, including Jack Bruce and Julian Bahula. Influenced in his jazz playing by Sidney Bechet, Wardell Gray, Lester Young, and others, Heckstall-Smith was one of the first to commute successfully between jazz and blues-rock, at a time when such a move was less fashionable than it later became.

DIGBY FAIRWEATHER

Hedrenius, Gugge [Görjen] (*b* Sweden, 1938). Swedish bandleader and pianist. He played dixieland while in his teens and formed a septet in 1959. In the early 1960s this group acquired several new members (including Idrees Sulieman) and developed a rhythmic style that displayed the influence of Hank Crawford; it remained in existence until 1965. In 1971 Hedrenius re-formed the group as the Big Blues Band and during the following years made several recordings as its leader (including *Blues of Sweden*, 1972, Polar 240); among those who appeared with the band as guest soloists were Joe Newman and Willie Cook. (L. Westin: "Ömhet, kärlek och protest" [Tenderness, love and protest], *Orkester journalen*, xli (1973), April, 8)

ERIK KJELLBERG

Hefti, Neal (*b* Hastings, NE, 29 Oct 1922). Composer, arranger, and trumpeter. He began his career as a trumpeter with Charlie Barnet's band, and developed into a distinctive arranger during his stay with Woody Herman (1944–5). He gave up full-time playing to concentrate on composition, and recorded under his own name with studio bands from the late 1940s. The popularity of a number of these recordings, such as *Repetition*, featuring Charlie Parker, and *Coral Reef*, originally written for Count Basie under the title *Ours Alone*, led Hefti to form a touring band for a couple of years from 1952. Thereafter his writing diversified to include original music for a large number of films as well as for the television series "Batman" and compilations of Harold Lloyd. Although well regarded for his film work, he is likely to be best remembered for his earliest and most jazz-inflected writing. The unpretentiousness, firm sense of textural balance, and melodic architecture of his compositions often inspired dynamic renditions. His many pieces for Count Basie from 1950 display these qualities, although the pace-setting performances on the album *Basie* (1957, including *Li'l Darlin'* and *Whirly-bird*) exerted a stultifying influence on most big-band arranging thereafter.

RECORDED COMPOSITIONS

(selective list)

* – with Hefti as sideman

As leader: with C. Parker: Repetition (1948, Jazz Scene [unnumbered]); Coral Reef (1951, Coral 91022); *Pardon my Doo-wah* (1954, Epic 3481)

Recorded by W. Herman: *The Good Earth (1945, Col. 36985); *Wild Root (1945, Col. 36949)

Recorded by C. Basie: *Basie* (1957, Roul. 52003), incl. Li'l Darlin', Whirly-bird; *Basie Plays Hefti* (1958, Roul. 52011)

BIBLIOGRAPHY

R. Horricks: *Count Basie and his Orchestra: its Music and its Musicians* (London and New York, 1957), 239

M. Ullman: *Jazz Lives: Portraits in Words and Pictures* (Washington, 1980), 45

BRIAN PRIESTLEY

Hegamin [née Nelson], **Lucille** (*b* Macon, GA, 29 Nov 1894; *d* New York, 1 March 1970). Singer. After singing in a church choir and at local theaters she left home at the age of 15 to tour with a revue. In Chicago she married the pianist Bill Hegamin (*c*1914), and performed with him and others (Tony Jackson and Jelly Roll Morton were among her sidemen) before traveling to the West Coast with her own band. In 1919 she moved to New York, where she performed and recorded as the leader of the Blue Flame Syncopators; this group included Charlie Irvis. During the 1920s she also worked as a soloist, performed in several Broadway shows, and sang with the Southernaires, a band led by George "Doc" Hyder. After undertaking residencies at the Paradise, Atlantic City, New Jersey (1933, 1934) she retired from music, although she performed and recorded again briefly in the early 1960s.

Hegamin's earliest work (such as *Everybody's Blues*, 1920, Arto 9045) is representative of a transition between minstrelsy and early jazz. She later made recordings in a more authentic jazz style, the most interesting of which (including *Some Early Morning*, 1923, Cameo 407) were duos with her regular pianist Cyril J. Fullerton. In the 1960s she adopted a traditional blues style; a superb example of her work in this vein is *Number 12*, from the album *Basket of Blues* (1962, Spivey 1001).

BIBLIOGRAPHY

ChiltonW

L. Kunstadt: "The Lucille Hegamin Story," *Record Research*, no.39 (1961), 3; no.40 (1962), 3; no.41 (1962), 4; no.43 (1962), 6 [with introduction by V. Spivey]

D. Stewart-Baxter: "Blues," *JJ*, xx (1967), no.7, p.13; no.8, p.25

S. Harris: *Blues Who's Who: a Biographical Dictionary of Blues Singers* (New Rochelle, NY, 1979)

Helias, Mark (*b* Brunswick, NJ, 1 Oct 1950). Double bass player. He began to play double bass at the age of 20 and studied music at Yale University (MM 1976). He worked with Anthony Davis (from 1975), Leo Smith (1975–7), and Anthony Braxton (1977), and recorded with Davis and Dewey Redman (both 1978) and as a member of the trio Brahma with Barry Altschul and Ray Anderson (1979, 1980). He also played with Anderson in the cooperative groups Bass Drum Bone (from 1978) and the Slickaphonics, playing both double bass and electric bass guitar, (from 1980, recording in 1982 and 1983). In 1985 he formed Nu, another cooperative group, with Ed Blackwell, Don Cherry, Nana Vasconcelos, and Carlos Ward; it toured Britain in 1987. He has worked as a freelance musician with Muhal Richard Abrams, Karl Berger, Julius Hemphill, Oliver Lake, and George Lewis (ii), and recorded with Braxton (1981), Davis and Redman (both 1982), Altschul and Franco D'Andrea (both 1983), and Anderson (1984). From 1976 he was active as a composer, writing chamber ensemble and theater works in addition to jazz. As a leader he has worked with various sidemen and recorded his own compositions on the album *The Current Set* (1987, Enja 5041).

BIBLIOGRAPHY

P. Carles and C. Gauffre: "Les harmonies d'Helias," *Jm*, no.320 (1983), 30

D. Soutif: "Le free funk de Slickaphonics," *Jm*, no.314 (1983), 36

Helicon. A type of bass TUBA distinguished from other members of the tuba family by its circular shape.

Helm, Bob [Robert] (*b* Fairmead, CA, 18 July 1914). Clarinetist. In 1935 he met Lu Watters and Turk Murphy in San Francisco. He played in Watters's Yerba Buena Jazz Band intermittently from 1940 to 1950 (for illustration *see* WATTERS, LU), and with Murphy's band, with occasional absences, from 1947 to 1981. His style is well represented by a solo on *Wolverine Blues*, on Murphy's album *Turk no.4* (1952, GTJ 18).

BIBLIOGRAPHY

FeatherE

J. Goggin: *Turk Murphy: Just for the Record* (San Leandro, CA, 1982) [incl. discography]

Hemphill, Julius (*b* Fort Worth, *c*1940). Alto saxophonist. He learned clarinet in Fort Worth with John Carter and later studied music at North Texas State College. He performed in an army band and with various bands in Texas, including that of the rhythm-and-blues guitarist and pianist Ike Turner, before moving in 1968 to St. Louis, where he joined the Black Artists Group. In 1972 he formed his own recording company, Mbari. From the mid-1970s he was based in New York, where he recorded as a sideman with Anthony Braxton and Lester Bowie (1974) and took part in loft sessions. With Oliver Lake, David Murray, and Hamiet Bluiett he formed the WORLD SAXOPHONE QUARTET in 1976, and he has led several groups of his own, including one, with Olu Dara, Abdul Wadud, and Warren Smith, that toured Europe. Besides his principal instrument Hemphill plays soprano saxophone and flute.

SELECTED RECORDINGS

Duos with O. Lake: *Buster Bee* (1978, Sack. 3018)

As leader: *Dogon, A.D.* (1972, Mbari 5001); *'Coon Bid'ness* (1972–5, Ari. 1012); *Blue Boye* (1977, Mbari 1000); of World Saxophone Quartet (with H. Bluiett, O. Lake, and D. Murray): *Steppin' with the World Saxophone Quartet* (1978, BS 0027)

BIBLIOGRAPHY

Feather–Gitler '70s

D. Jackson: "Profile: Julius Hemphill, Oliver Lake," *DB*, xlii/12 (1975), 32

B. Smith and D. Lee: "Julius Hemphill Interviews," *Coda*, no.161 (1978), 4

C. Ware: "Julius Hemphill × Two," *JSN*, ii/2 (1980–81), 54

P. Giacomo: "Spirit of Saint Louis," *Jm*, no.309 (1982), 50

B. Shoemaker: "Julius Hemphill and the Theater of Sound," *DB*, liii/2 (1986), 20 [incl. discography]

DAVID G. SUCH

Hemphill, Shelton [Scad] (*b* Birmingham, AL, 16 March 1906; *d* New York, Dec 1959). Trumpeter. He first worked with the pianist Fred Longshaw accompanying Bessie Smith (1924–5), and made his recording début on Smith's *Lonesome Desert Blues* (1925, Col. 14123D). In 1924 he enrolled at Wilberforce (Ohio) College and became a member of Horace Henderson's Collegians. After working in New York with Benny Carter (1928–9) and Chick Webb (1930–31) he was a member of the Mills Blue Rhythm Band (1931–7; for illustration *see* MILLS BLUE RHYTHM BAND). Thereafter Hemphill played with Louis Armstrong (1937–44) and Duke Ellington (1944–9), then worked as a freelance in New York before ill-health forced him to retire.

based on *ChiltonW*

Henderson, Bill [William Randall] (*b* Chicago, 19 March 1930). Singer. He performed in local shows from the age of four and worked professionally from 1952. After working sporadically in Chicago with Ramsey Lewis he moved to New York, and from 1958 made recordings as a leader on which his sidemen included Horace Silver and Jimmy Smith; one of these, *Señor Blues* (1958), was commercially successful. He won a poll conducted by *Down Beat* in 1960, then moved to Chicago, where he again worked at intervals with Lewis; later he performed with Oscar Peterson (1963–4) and Count Basie (1965–6). After settling in Los Angeles he worked principally as an actor, while continuing to sing frequently on television and occasionally on recordings.

SELECTED RECORDINGS

As leader: Tippin'/Señor Blues (1958, BN 45-1710); *Bill Henderson Sings* (1959, VJ 1015); *Bill Henderson with the Oscar Peterson Trio* (1963, MGM 959); *Street of Dreams* (1979, Dis. 802)

As sideman with J. Smith: Ain't that Love/Willow Weep for me (1958, BN 45-1728)

BIBLIOGRAPHY

FeatherE; *Feather '60s*; *Feather–Gitler '70s*

M. Gardner: "Señor Blues," *JJ*, xviii/11 (1965), 12

CHRIS SHERIDAN

Henderson, Eddie [Edward Jackson] (*b* New York, 26 Oct 1940). Trumpeter. His family moved to San Francisco when he was 14, and he learned trumpet at the San Francisco Conservatory of Music. He then studied medicine, and qualified as a doctor in 1968; from 1964 he also played during the summer with John Handy. Encouraged by Miles Davis, he gave up medicine to pursue a career as a musician, and worked with Handy, the tenor saxophonist Tyrone Washington, and Joe Henderson, then led his own quintet. From 1970 to 1973 he played with Herbie Hancock's sextet, and during the same period made his first recordings as a leader. Thereafter Henderson toured with Art Blakey, worked with Mike Nock, and recorded with Charles Earland (all 1973), and continued to play with Hancock's former sidemen Julian Priester and the synthesizer player Patrick Gleeson. Into the late 1970s he led a rock-oriented septet; his first album for Capitol, *Comin' Through*, included the tune *Prance on*, which was a hit on the pop chart in 1977. Henderson also recorded with Richard Davis (1977), Stanley Cowell (1977, 1978), and Pharoah Sanders (*c*1981).

SELECTED RECORDINGS

Realization (1973, Capricorn 0118); *Inside Out* (1973, Capricorn 0122); *Sunburst* (1975, BN LA464G); *Heritage* (1976, BN LA636G); *Comin' Through* (1977, Cap. ST11671), incl. Prance on

BIBLIOGRAPHY

Feather–Gitler '70s

E. Meadow: "Eddie Henderson: Hancock's Horn," *DB*, xl/4 (1973), 20

L. Means: "How the Other Half Lives: Profile: Julian Priester, Eddie Henderson, Patrick Gleeson," *DB*, xli/12 (1974), 34

L. Lyons: "Profile: Eddie Henderson," *DB*, lii/10 (1975), 32

FREDERICK A. BECK

Henderson, Fletcher (Hamilton, Jr.) [Smack] (*b* Cuthbert, GA, 18 Dec 1897; *d* New York, 29 Dec 1952). Bandleader, arranger, and pianist, brother of Horace Henderson. He led the most important of the pioneering big bands, which helped to set the pattern for most later big jazz bands playing arranged music.

1. Early years. 2. 1925–52.

1. EARLY YEARS. Henderson was born into a middle-class black family, and studied European art music with his mother, a piano teacher. He grew up to be a good-looking, well-mannered youth, and (atypically for someone of his race at that time) went on to take a degree in chemistry and mathematics at Atlanta University. Despite his advantages of means and station, Henderson was almost painfully diffident. In 1920 he moved to New York, ostensibly to find a career as a chemist, but this was then well-nigh impossible for a Black, and especially so for a young man of Henderson's passive temperament. He picked up work as a song demonstrator with the Pace-Handy Music Company, an early black publishing firm, and when Harry Pace founded Black Swan, the first black recording company, Henderson joined it as musical factotum. He began to put together groups to back the company's singers, and in this way drifted into a career as a bandleader. He occasionally obtained work for these little bands at clubs and dances, and probably in January 1924 began to perform in the Club Alabam on Broadway. The same year he was offered a position at the Roseland Ballroom, later to become the best-known dance hall in New York. (These clubs were restricted to white customers.) Henderson's band remained there for a decade, using the Roseland as a springboard to national fame.

At the outset Henderson's group was an ordinary dance band, not a jazz band, though its music was inflected with the "raggy" rhythms that had been popular for some time. Northern Blacks of the time had little first-hand experience of spirituals, work songs, and the blues, and only slowly came to grips with the new jazz that was emerging from the South. Henderson, although he had been brought up in Georgia, had been insulated from black folk forms by his middle-class parents who, like many Blacks of their position, frowned on "low" music. Henderson had to learn to play jazz in his 20s, and never became more than an adequate jazz pianist.

Henderson's band was no different from the thousands of dance bands that were springing up across the USA in response to the vogue for social dancing. But musicians everywhere were drawn to the new jazz music, and in 1924 Henderson brought Louis Armstrong, whom he had heard briefly in New Orleans three years earlier, into his band as a jazz specialist. Armstrong's style was rapidly maturing, and his playing entranced not only Henderson's men, but other New York musicians, with its propulsive swing and melodic invention. Although Armstrong was not the only jazz influence on New York musicians, he was the most important one, and Henderson's band members began to emulate his solo style.

At about the same time the band's music director, Don Redman, was working out what was to become the basic pattern of big-band arrangements for decades: the interplay of brass and reed sections, sometimes in call-and-response fashion, at other times with one section playing supporting riffs behind the other. Many solos were interspersed between the arranged

Fletcher Henderson's band, Atlantic City, NJ, July 1932: (left to right) Russell Procope (clarinet and alto saxophone), Coleman Hawkins (tenor saxophone), Edgar Sampson (alto saxophone and violin), Clarence Holiday (guitar), Walter Johnson (drums), John Kirby (double bass), Henderson (piano), Russell Smith and Bobby Stark (trumpets), Rex Stewart (cornet), and J. C. Higginbotham and Sandy Williams (trombones)

passages. Redman and Henderson were not alone in developing this formula: the Paul Whiteman Orchestra was employing the technique in rudimentary form in 1920, but Redman and Henderson developed it fully. However, in 1924 and 1925 the band was still learning to play with a jazz feeling, and the recordings made then are notable mainly for solos by Armstrong; among these are *Copenhagen*, *Go 'long mule*, *Shanghai Shuffle*, and *Sugar Foot Stomp*, a reworking of King Oliver's *Dippermouth Blues*. The last piece became the band's first hit, and pressings of it remained available for a decade.

2. 1925–52. Armstrong left Henderson's band in the fall of 1925; but the seed sown by him and others took root, and by 1926 the band was playing excellent jazz, with first-rate soloists and an ability to make the arranged passages swing. From this time until the mid-1930s the Fletcher Henderson Orchestra was one of the principal models for big jazz bands.

Until 1927 Redman wrote virtually all of the band's arrangements, and it is difficult to estimate Henderson's particular contribution to the development of the big-band format. However, in 1927 Redman left Henderson to become music director of McKinney's Cotton Pickers, and Henderson was forced to take on much of the band's arranging (though he continued to buy arrangements from freelance musicians, and in 1930–31 his sideman Benny Carter supplied a number of important scores). He proved to have a remarkable talent for it: his arrangements were spare, clean, and delicate, with an easy and natural manner that made them comfortable for his musicians to play and yet generated an infectious swing. Among his best works from this period are *King Porter Stomp*, *Down South Camp Meeting*, and *Wrappin' it up*.

Henderson also had a remarkable gift for discovering new talent; in steady succession he engaged virtually all of the major black jazz players of the time, many of whom, like Armstrong and Lester Young, he raised from obscurity. As a consequence few bands ever matched his in the quality of their soloists. Unfortunately Henderson lacked the traits that make a successful leader: he had little understanding of salesmanship and promotion, and could not control his frequently unruly players, who were often lured away by other bandleaders; several times his bands broke up owing to his poor management. In 1934 financial problems forced him to sell some of his best arrangements to Benny Goodman, who was then in the process of starting his own band. Henderson's arrangements were an important element in Goodman's rapid rise to popularity, which in turn triggered the enormous success of swing bands from 1935 to 1945. Henderson led bands until 1939, when he joined Goodman as a full-time staff arranger. From 1941 he returned to bandleading, writing arrangements for a living, left behind by the swing-band boom which he had played so large a part in bringing about. He suffered a severe stroke in December 1950 and was partially paralyzed until his death.

Despite his lack of personal force, Henderson's musical intelligence and taste were important factors in creating the character of big-band jazz. Although he was not alone in shaping the big-band style, his group was the principal model for this music, and its influence at second hand, through the bands of Goodman and others, was profound. His personal papers are in the holdings of the Amistad Research Center at Tulane University in New Orleans; *see* LIBRARIES AND ARCHIVES, §2.

See also FORMS, §3; HAWKINS, COLEMAN, §1; and JAZZ (i), §IV, 1, and fig.2.

SELECTED RECORDINGS

Go 'long mule (1924, Col. 228D); Copenhagen (1924, Voc. 14926); Shanghai Shuffle (1924, Pathé 036157); Sugar Foot Stomp (1925, Col. 395D); The Stampede (1926, Col. 654D); Hop off (1928, Bruns. 4119); Just Blues (1931, Mlt. 12239); Hocus Pocus (1934, Bb 5682)

SELECTED ARRANGEMENTS

As leader: Down South Camp Meeting (1934, Decca 213); Wrappin' it up (1934, Decca 157)

Recorded by B. Goodman: King Porter Stomp (1935, Vic. 25090)

BIBLIOGRAPHY

H. Panassié: "Fletcher Henderson et son orchestre," *BHcF*, no.25 (1953), 3; no.26 (1953), 6; no.27 (1953), 6

N. Shapiro and N. Hentoff, eds.: *Hear me Talkin' to ya: the Story of Jazz by the Men who Made it* (New York and London, 1955/R1966), 184

F. Manskleid: "Henderson Notes," *JM*, iii/10 (1957), 27

E. Hersey: "Henderson on Record," *JR*, ii/9 (1959), 48

R. Hadlock: *Jazz Masters of the Twenties* (New York, 1965/R1985), 194

G. Schuller: *Early Jazz: its Roots and Musical Development* (New York, 1968), 252

W. C. Allen: *Hendersonia: the Music of Fletcher Henderson and his Musicians: a Bio-discography* (Highland Park, NJ, 1973)
J. R. Taylor: Liner notes, *Fletcher Henderson: Developing an American Orchestra* (Smithsonian R006, 1977)
J. L. Collier: *The Making of Jazz: a Comprehensive History* (New York and London, 1978)
M. Audibert: *Fletcher Henderson et son orchestre 1924–1951: sa place dans l'histoire du jazz* (Bayonne, France, 1983)

JAMES LINCOLN COLLIER

Henderson, Horace (W.) (*b* Cuthbert, GA, 22 Nov 1904). Arranger, pianist, and bandleader, brother of Fletcher Henderson. While he was still a student at Wilberforce University he performed in New York (1924) and on tour with his band, the Collegians (which later included Rex Stewart and Benny Carter). He formed other bands during the 1920s, 1930s, and 1940s, but also worked as a sideman for such leaders as Don Redman (1931–3), Vernon Andrade (1935), and, most importantly, his brother, for whom he played and wrote arrangements intermittently from 1931 to 1947; he was also a freelance arranger for Benny Goodman, Charlie Barnet, Jimmie Lunceford, Earl Hines, and many others. He continued his activities as a bandleader into the 1970s.

At least 30 arrangements written for Fletcher Henderson's ensembles have been identified as Horace's work, and the small group taken from the band of 1933 (led on such recordings as *Jamaica Shout* by Coleman Hawkins) gained much from his mobile but unflamboyant writing. Most of his other arrangements were recorded by big bands; the first of these, *Hot and Anxious/Comin' and Goin'* (1931), convey the impression of spontaneous sequences of solos hung loosely around simple themes. *Hot and Anxious* is based on the traditional riff that later became known as the basis for Glenn Miller's *In the Mood*; *Comin' and Goin'* draws upon the melody from *Doin' the Voom Voom* by Duke Ellington and Bubber Miley. The majority of Henderson's output is more conventional, but all his arrangements are impressively rhythmic; *Christopher Columbus* may be regarded as a definitive example of his style. Although he was not known primarily as a pianist, Henderson was a potent soloist. His style was rhythmically more dynamic and melodically more modern than that of his brother.

Oral history material in *NjR* (JOHP)

SELECTED ARRANGEMENTS
* – with Henderson as sideman

As leader: Happy Feet (1933, Parl. R1792); Ol' Man River (1933, Parl. R1766); Oh boy, I'm in the groove/Kitty on Toast (1940, Voc. 5433)
Recorded by F. Henderson: *Hot and Anxious/*Comin' and Goin' (1931, Col. 2449D); Yeah Man! (1933, Voc. 2527); Queer Notions (1933, Voc. 2583); *Big John's Special (1934, Decca 214); Rug Cutter's Swing (1934, Decca 342); *Christopher Columbus/*Blue Lou (1936, Voc./OK 3211)
Recorded by others: D. Redman: *I Heard (1931, Bruns. 6233); *Hot and Anxious (1932, Bruns. 6368); C. Hawkins: *Jamaica Shout (1933, OK 41566); B. Goodman: Japanese Sandman/Always (1935, Vic. 25024); C. Berry: *Too Marvelous for Words (1937, Var. 532); *Indiana (1937, Var. 587); C. Barnet: Charleston Alley (1941, Bb 11037)

BIBLIOGRAPHY

S. A. Pease: "Swing Piano Styles: Horace Henderson's College Band Started him to the Top," *DB*, vii/17 (1940), 16 [incl. transcr.]
W. C. Allen: *Hendersonia: the Music of Fletcher Henderson and his Musicians: a Bio-discography* (Highland Park, NJ, 1973), 206, 499

BRIAN PRIESTLEY

Henderson, Joe [Joseph A.] (*b* Lima, OH, 24 April 1937). Tenor saxophonist. He studied music at Kentucky State College and Wayne University (1956–60), where his fellow students included Curtis Fuller and Yusef Lateef. In Detroit he played with local musicians, worked briefly with Sonny Stitt (1959), and led his own band (1960). After touring with an army band (1960–62) he joined Brother Jack McDuff and led a group with Kenny Dorham, then rose quickly to fame in the bands of Horace Silver (1964–6) and Herbie Hancock (1969–70). Thereafter Henderson has led his own groups and worked as a freelance. In the mid-1970s he moved to San Francisco, where in the 1980s he has appeared regularly with Freddie Hubbard and others in a group known variously as Echoes of an Era, the Griffith Park Band, and the Griffith Park Collection, and has also been active as a teacher.

Henderson developed an influential style of modern jazz improvisation, which made far less direct use of John Coltrane's approach than did the majority of young saxophonists during the 1960s and 1970s; he seemed to amalgamate the style of Sonny Rollins with soul music and with free jazz as typified by Ornette Coleman. Demonstrating a high level of instrumental proficiency and a tone with a razor-sharp edge, he delivered solos with searing intensity. Brief bursts of notes, shakes, trills, and sporadic double-time figures characterized his improvisations at this period. A similar freshness in his tune writing (exemplified by *Recordame*, *Tetragon*, and *Isotope*) was so appealing to players in the 1970s that many compositions by saxophonists, otherwise drawing primarily from Coltrane, displayed the marked influence of Henderson. He has cited Charlie Parker, Sonny Stitt, and the classical composers Bartók, Hindemith, and Stravinsky as favorites.

SELECTED RECORDINGS

As leader: *Page One* (1963, BN 84140), incl. Recordame; *Inner Urge* (1964, BN 84189); *Tetragon* (1967–8, Mlst. 9017); *Power to the People* (1969, Mlst. 9024), incl. Isotope; *Barcelona* (1977, Enja 3037); *Relaxin' at Camarillo* (1979, Cont. 14006)
As sideman: Lee Morgan: *The Sidewinder* (1963, BN 84157); Andrew Hill: *Point of Departure* (1964, BN 84167); H. Silver: *Song for my Father* (1964, BN 84185); *Cape Verdean Blues* (1965, BN 84220); H. Hancock: *The Prisoner* (1969, BN 84321); Griffith Park Collection: *In Concert* (1982, Elek. Mus. 960262-1)

BIBLIOGRAPHY

B. McRae: Joe Henderson," *JJ*, xxii/1 (1969), 9
A. Tercinet: "Joe Henderson," *Jh*, no.292 (1973), 18
R. Townley and E. Nemeyer: "The Herculean Tenor of Joe Henderson," *DB*, xlii/1 (1975), 18
M. Gilbert: "Joe's Mode," *JJI*, xxxviii/8 (1985), 8

MARK C. GRIDLEY/R

Henderson, Michael (*b* Yazoo City, MS, 7 July 1951). Electric bass guitarist. He studied cello while in high school, and later took up bass guitar, on which he was largely self-taught. He began working professionally in Detroit in 1966, playing with several soul groups and singers associated with the Motown label; he then toured with Aretha Franklin (1968) and Stevie Wonder (1969–70). In 1970 he joined Miles Davis, with whom he performed and recorded until 1975. Playing persistent, biting, syncopated ostinatos – heard, for example, on the album *Live–Evil* (1970, Col. KC30954) – Henderson provided the tonal and rhythmic underpinning to Davis's music of this period. He also made tours of Europe and Japan with the group. From 1976 Henderson recorded with Norman Connors, for whom he also wrote material; later he recorded as a leader.

BIBLIOGRAPHY

Feather–Gitler '70s
J. Chambers: *Milestones, ii: The Music and Times of Miles Davis since 1960* (Toronto, Buffalo, and London, 1985), 202

Henderson, Rick [Richard Andrew] (*b* Washington, 25 April 1928). Alto and tenor saxophonist. From 1946 to 1949 he led bands in local clubs, and in 1953, after military service, he joined Duke Ellington's orchestra. He played regularly with Ellington until 1955, and continued to work with him intermittently until late 1957. He also recorded with Michel Legrand (1962). He played in clubs in New York into the 1980s and worked with the alto saxophonist Jimmy Tyler; he performed at the Copacetics' annual concert in 1979. His ability to reconcile the technical innovations of Charlie Parker with the swing tradition may be heard to particular advantage on *I let a song go out of my heart* on Dinah Washington's album *After Hours with Miss D.* (1954, EmA 26032). (*FeatherE*)

Oral history material in *CtY*.

Henderson [née Deschamps], **Rosa** (*b* Henderson, KY, 24 Nov 1896; *d* New York, 6 April 1968). Singer. From 1913 to 1918 she toured, mainly in Texas, with her uncle's carnival troupe, after which she married Slim Henderson and toured for several years in the Mason–Henderson Show. She then settled in New York, and during the 1920s appeared in several musicals. Beginning in 1923 she made a large number of recordings, some of which were issued under the pseudonyms Flora Dale, Rosa Green, Mae Harris, Mamie Harris, Sara Johnson, Sally Ritz, Josephine Thomas, Gladys White, or Bessie Williams. She was frequently accompanied by Fletcher Henderson (or by Henderson's small group), and also recorded six titles, including *Can't be bothered with no sheik* (1931, Col. 14627D), with James P. Johnson. One of her finest recordings, *Strut yo' Puddy* (1924, Ajax 17055), was made with the Choo Choo Jazzers. From the 1930s Henderson worked in a department store in New York, and performed only occasionally.

BIBLIOGRAPHY

L. Kunstadt: "Rosa Henderson Yesterday and Today," *Record Research*, no.75 (1966), 3

D. Stewart-Baxter: "Blues and Views: Farewell Rosa Henderson," *JJ*, xxi/7 (1968), 15

S. Harris: *Blues Who's Who: a Biographical Dictionary of Blues Singers* (New Rochelle, NY, 1979)

based on *ChiltonW*

Henderson, Wayne (Maurice) (*b* Houston, 24 Sept 1939). Trombonist. From the mid-1950s he was a member of the group which took the name the Jazz Crusaders in 1961 and ten years later became known as the CRUSADERS. Among his compositions for the band was *Young Rabbits*, which became a hit. After leaving the group in 1975 Henderson pursued a career as a soloist, recording as a leader in 1977 and 1978. He has also worked as a record producer for Ronnie Laws and other musicians.

SELECTED RECORDINGS

As leader: *Big Daddy's Place* (1977, ABC 1020); *Living on a Dream* (1978, Pol. 6145)

As sideman with the Jazz Crusaders: *Freedom Sound* (1961, PJ 27); *Lookin' Ahead* (1961, PJ 43); *Tough Talk* (1963, PJ 68); *Young Rabbits* (1962–8, BN LA530HZ), incl. Young Rabbits

BIBLIOGRAPHY

Feather '60s; *Feather–Gitler '70s*

For further recordings and bibliography *see* CRUSADERS.

ROBERT DICKOW

Hendricks, Jon [John Carl] (*b* Newark, OH, 16 Sept 1921). Singer and lyricist. At the age of 14 he often sang with Art Tatum. He continued to sing and also played drums while attending college in Toledo, Ohio, where he studied literature and, later, law. On one occasion during this period he worked with Charlie Parker, who advised him to take up music professionally. After moving to New York Hendricks recorded *Four Brothers* (1955) with Dave Lambert and *Sing a Song of Basie* (1957) with Lambert and Annie Ross. The vocal trio LAMBERT, HENDRICKS, AND ROSS soon became popular for its settings of lyrics to jazz arrangements; it continued until 1964 (Yolande Bavan replaced Ross in 1962). In 1960 Hendricks wrote and directed *Evolution of the Blues Song* for the Modern Jazz Festival at Monterey, California. After the trio disbanded he continued to sing with various ensembles. In 1968 he moved to London and performed in Europe and Africa for five years, then moved to California, where he was a jazz critic for the *San Francisco Chronicle* (1973–4) and taught classes in jazz. He continues to record, and from the 1960s he has often performed with his wife Judith and children Michelle and Eric, and with Bobby McFerrin.

Hendricks excels both at setting lyrics to complex melodies and at performing those lyrics in an articulate manner, with the finesse of a virtuoso saxophonist. He is a fine scat singer, and is so adept at imitating instrumental sounds that his improvisations often surpass the solos played by his accompanists.

SELECTED RECORDINGS

Cloudburst/Four Brothers (1955, Decca 29572); *A Good Git-together* (1959, WP 1283); *Evolution of the Blues Song* (1960, Col. CS8383); *Tell me the Truth* (1975, Ari. 4043); *September Songs* (c1976, Stanyan 10132)

BIBLIOGRAPHY

FeatherE; *Feather '60s*; *Feather–Gitler '70s*

L. Feather: "Jon Hendricks, Blindfold Test," *DB*, xxvii/4 (1960), 39

J. Hendricks: "Jazz and its Critics," *Liberator*, ix/11 (1969), 14

L. Tomkins: "Here and There, According to Jon Hendricks," *CI*, xi/7 (1973), 15

M. Joyce and K. Joyce: "Jon Hendricks: Interview," *Cadence*, ix/1 (1983), 5

J. S. Wilson: "Jazz: 'Tempo,' Reminiscence by Hendricks," *New York Times* (4 July 1983), 13

For further recordings and bibliography *see* LAMBERT, HENDRICKS, AND ROSS.

PHILIP GREENE

Hendrickson, Al(ton Reynolds) (*b* Eastland, TX, 10 May 1920). Guitarist. He moved to California in 1925, and his first important engagements were with Artie Shaw's band and the Gramercy Five in 1940. He worked with Benny Goodman's big band and sextet (1947), then toured and recorded with Ray Noble, Boyd Raeburn, Woody Herman (intermittently, 1947–59), Billy May (1954–7), Johnny Mandel (1958), Neal Hefti, and Bill Holman. In 1955 he made a recording with Barney Kessel on which his playing is particularly prominent. He performed with Dizzy Gillespie and Louis Bellson at the Monterey Jazz Festival in 1962. Hendrickson has accompanied many popular singers and has worked with such arrangers as Quincy Jones, Lalo Schifrin, and Nelson Riddle. He has also taken part in many sessions for films and television, and has been a long-standing member of two studio recording groups, Guitars Inc. and Guitars Unlimited; his playing was an important component of many recordings in the bossa-nova style during the early 1960s. Hendrickson's metronomic, full-bodied rhythmic pulse has brought cohesion to many rhythm sections; his light, buoyant beat is reminiscent of the Chicago jazz style.

SELECTED RECORDINGS

As sideman: B. Kessel: *To Swing or Not to Swing* (1955, Cont. 3513); All Stars: *Session at Midnight* (1955, Cap. T707); Guitars Inc.: *Invitation* (1959, WB 1206); D. Gillespie: *New Continent* (1962, Lml. 86022); Capp–Pierce Orchestra: *Juggernaut* (1977, Conc. 40)

BIBLIOGRAPHY

FeatherE; *Feather '60s*; *Feather–Gitler '70s*

NORMAN MONGAN

Henkels, Kurt (*b* Solingen, Germany, 17 Dec 1910; *d* Hamburg, Germany, 12 July 1986). German bandleader. He learned classical violin in his youth and led various ensembles which played in cafés throughout Germany. In 1935 he organized an orchestra and began to perform in dance halls and nightclubs.

After World War II he became familiar with American jazz and in 1948 in Berlin formed a swing big band modeled on Count Basie's; its principal soloists included Rolf Kühn, the trumpeter Horst Fischer, and the tenor saxophonist Werner Baumgart. It quickly became the leading jazz orchestra in East Germany and made many recordings; it received particular acclaim for *Cherokee* (1950, Regina 70124). Henkels was appointed leader of the Staatlicher Rundfunk-Tanzorchester Leipzig, but in 1959 he was reprimanded by the authorities for playing jazz and he fled to West Germany. He organized a new band which performed dance music and worked in radio, television, and film studios until the early 1970s, when he retired to Hamburg. Henkels made more than 250 recordings, of which those from the period 1948–59 are of jazz interest.

BIBLIOGRAPHY

J. Schütte: *Kurt Henkels Discographie* (Menden, Germany, 1971)
H. H. Lange: Liner notes, *Die grossen Tanzorchester, 1930–1950: Kurt Henkels* (Pol. 2437776, ?1978)
A. Weber: "Vom 'Stehgeiger' zum Orchesterchef: Erinnerungen an swingenden Henkels-Sound," *Solinger Tageblatt* (14 Dec 1985)

RAINER E. LOTZ

Henrichsen, Børge Roger. *See* ROGER HENRICHSEN, BØRGE.

Henriksen, Bruno (*b* Copenhagen, 6 Jan 1910; *d* Copenhagen, 27 Feb 1984). Danish pianist and bandleader. He played with dance bands (1935–40) and with the Harlem Kiddies (1941), then led big bands from 1941 to 1953. These were to some degree inspired by the dance music of Glenn Miller, but they also played in a more authentic jazz style, as may be heard on their recordings of *Darktown Strutters Ball* (1943, Odeon D902) and *Idaho* (1952, Phi. 55002H). From 1952 Henriksen worked as a record producer.

ERIK WIEDEMANN

Henry, Ernie [Ernest Albert] (*b* New York, 3 Sept 1926; *d* New York, 29 Dec 1957). Alto saxophonist. He learned violin as a child but changed to saxophone at the age of 12. In 1947 Tadd Dameron began to show an interest in his playing and made him known to musicians who worked in the clubs on 52nd Street; as a result he performed with Dameron, Fats Navarro, Charlie Ventura, Max Roach, Georgie Auld, and Kenny Dorham. After working with Dizzy Gillespie's big band (1948–9) Henry joined Illinois Jacquet (1950), with whom he recorded in 1952. He played only occasionally from 1952 until 1956, but then became a member of Thelonious Monk's group, with which he made some particularly fine recordings (1956, 1957). He also recorded with Matthew Gee (1956) and Dorham (1957), and as a leader. In 1957 he performed and recorded with Gillespie's re-formed big band. Although Henry's playing in the late 1940s and early 1950s was influenced by Charlie Parker, his later recordings show that he was beginning to develop a strongly individual style.

SELECTED RECORDINGS

As leader: *Presenting Ernie Henry* (1956, Riv. 222); *Seven Standards and a Blues* (1957, Riv. 248); *Last Chorus* (1957, Riv. 266)

As sideman: H. McGhee: The Skunk/Boperation (1948, BN 558); D. Gillespie: Swedish Suite (1949, Vic. 203457); T. Monk: *Brilliant Corners* (1956, Riv. 226), incl. Ba-lu Bolivar Ba-lues-are, Brilliant Corners; K. Dorham: *Two Horns, Two Rhythm* (1957, Riv. 255), incl. Is it true what they say about Dixie?, S'posin'

BIBLIOGRAPHY

FeatherE
J. Cooke: "Fading Flowers: a Note on Ernie Henry," *JM*, vii/5 (1961), 9
I. Gitler: *Jazz Masters of the Forties* (New York, 1966/*R*1983 with discography), 41
D. Ansell: "The Forgotten Ones: Ernie Henry," *JJI*, xl/9 (1987), 21

LAWRENCE KOCH

Henry, (Frank) Haywood (*b* Birmingham, AL, 7 or 10 Jan 1913). Baritone saxophonist and clarinetist. He played clarinet in high school, where Dud Bascomb was among his classmates. At Alabama State Teachers College in Montgomery he played in the 'Bama State Collegians with Bascomb and Erskine Hawkins (1931–2). After playing in New York he rejoined the Collegians, who were on tour. The group soon became known as Hawkins's band, and Henry remained a member from 1935 until the mid-1950s; a good example of his clarinet playing may be heard on *Junction Blues* (1940, Bb 10790). He also recorded with Julian Dash (1951), played with Tiny Grimes, and performed and recorded with Rex Stewart (1957–8), then became active as a freelance with rhythm-and-blues groups. In the early 1960s he worked with Wilbur De Paris, and from 1969 to 1971 he toured and recorded with Earl Hines. He recorded again with Hawkins (1971), with Ella Fitzgerald and Sy Oliver (both 1973), and as a leader with Oliver Jackson (1977), and has continued to play into the 1980s, with Panama Francis, among others.

BIBLIOGRAPHY

ChiltonW; *FeatherE*
J. Armitage: "Haywood Henry," *BHcF*, no.207 (1971), 7
S. Dance: *The World of Swing* (New York, 1974) [colln of previously pubd interviews], 203
E. Townley: "'Bama State Collegian," *Sv*, no.77 (1978), 180 [interview]
C. Battestini and J.-P. Battestini: "Haywood Henry évoque ses riches années avec Erskine Hawkins," *BHcF*, no.272 (1979), 3 [interview]
K. Mohr: "Haywood Henry: le requin aimable," *Soul Bag*, no.109 (1987), 5

Hentoff, Nat(han Irving) (*b* Boston, 10 June 1925). Writer. He studied at Northeastern University (BA 1945) and Harvard University (1946) while working for radio station WMEX in Boston (1944–53). For *Down Beat* (in the 1950s) and for his book *The Jazz Life*, he wrote biographical profiles and social commentaries that were models of thoughtful, accurate inquiry; during his years as associate editor of *Down Beat* (1953–7), he drew attention to the black-American musicians who created jazz and, with Nat Shapiro, published *Hear me Talkin' to ya*, the first history of jazz to be related by the musicians themselves. He was co-editor of the *Jazz Review* (1958–61) and the anthology *Jazz*. From 1960 he has concentrated on writing about general social and political issues, especially civil liberties, but he continues to contribute articles on music regularly to several periodicals.

WRITINGS
(selective list)

ed. with N. Shapiro: *Hear me Talkin' to ya: the Story of Jazz by the Men who Made it* (New York and London, 1955/*R*1966; Ger. trans. as *Jazz erzählt*, Munich, 1959/*R*1984)
——: *The Jazz Makers* (New York, 1957/*R*1979 as *The Jazz Makers: Essays on the Greats of Jazz*)
ed. with A. J. McCarthy: *Jazz: New Perspectives on the History of Jazz by Twelve of the World's Foremost Jazz Critics and Scholars* (New York and Toronto, 1959/*R*1974)
with D. Stock: *Jazz Street* (Garden City, NY, and London, 1960)
The Jazz Life (New York and London, 1961/*R*1975) [incl. previously pubd articles]

BARRY KERNFELD

Hep. Record company and label. The company was established in Edinburgh in 1974 by Alastair Robertson (*b* Aberdeen, Scotland, 3 March 1941). The first release on the label was a reissue of material recorded in the 1940s by Boyd Raeburn. In its early years the company concentrated on putting out on album items originally pressed for broadcasting purposes on transcription discs, but later it began recording its own sessions, working with such musicians as Eddie Thompson, Don Lanphere, and Buddy DeFranco. By the end of 1987 Hep's catalogue contained more than 90 LPs, including 36 collections of mainstream jazz and bop and 21 compilations of material from the 1930s by Don Redman, Andy Kirk, Fletcher Henderson, Jimmie Lunceford, and others. Among the most popular releases were sets by Slim Gaillard and Slam Stewart, and the 1000 series of big-band music, with its informative liner notes and photographs, has been particularly well received.

Robertson maintains the company as a single-person, self-financing operation, and has established Hep – with its distinctive trademark, a drawing of Lester Young – as the most important jazz label in Scotland. Assistance from the engineer John R. T. Davies has enabled the company to issue records on which surface noise and interference from the original discs are eliminated. Hep has good distribution arrangements in most European countries and in North America. Plans were announced in 1987 to issue the catalogue on compact disc as well as on record; some of the company's material is also put out on cassette tape.

MARK GARDNER

Heralds of Swing. English swing band. It was formed in London in February 1939 by five of Bert Ambrose's principal sidemen: Tommy McQuater and Archie Craig (trumpets), George Chisholm (trombone), Bert Barnes (piano), and Tiny Winters (double bass); the other members were Dave Shand and Norman Maloney (alto saxophones), Benny Winestone (tenor saxophone), Sid Colin (guitar, voice), and George Fierstone (drums). While resident at the Paradise Club, London (February–March) the band appeared at two major jazz concerts. When the management at the Paradise asked that it reduce its numbers it disbanded. It re-formed in summer 1939 for a concert at the First Avenue Hotel, London, and for two BBC broadcasts; the latter, the only performances by the group that were recorded (it made no commercially issued recordings), took place in a studio with poor acoustics and received unfavorable reviews. The outbreak of World War II in September 1939 and more work from Ambrose ended the band's brief existence, but many of the members, as a result of their army service, found themselves playing together again in the Squadronaires. (A. McCarthy: "The Heralds of Swing," *J&B*, i/1 (1971), 47)

DIGBY FAIRWEATHER

Herbert, Arthur (*b* New York, 28 May 1907). Drummer. He first played on Long Island in 1930, and the following year worked in Brooklyn and at Dickie Wells's club in Harlem. During the 1930s he performed with various bandleaders before his first professional engagement with Eddie Williams's band at the Savoy in 1935. After leading his own group, the Rhythm Masters, he worked with Edgar Hayes (1938) and Pete Brown (1939), then performed and made recordings (including *Fine Dinner*, 1939, Bb 10523) with Coleman Hawkins (1939–40). During the 1940s Herbert worked with Eddie Durham (late 1940), Hot Lips Page and Sidney Bechet (both 1941), George James (1942–3), Mezz Mezzrow (1943), Brown (1946), and others. He then ceased to work as a full-time musician, but continued to play regularly, performing frequently with Lem Johnson in the 1960s. He is the uncle of Herbie Lovelle.

based on *ChiltonW*

Herbert, Gregory (Delano) (*b* Philadelphia, 19 May 1947; *d* Amsterdam, 31 Jan 1978). Alto and tenor saxophonist, and flutist. Encouraged by his father, he began playing saxophone at the age of 12; four years later he played informally with Miles Davis, and in summer 1964 he worked in the Duke Ellington Orchestra. Although he studied music at Temple University (1965–71), he did not graduate, but left to devote more time to practicing and performing. His first recording was with Pat Martino on the album *Baiyina* (1968). He took up tenor saxophone when he joined Woody Herman's Thundering Herd in 1971, and during his time with the band was frequently a principal soloist. From 1975 to 1977 Herbert worked as a soloist with the Thad Jones–Mel Lewis Orchestra, with Chuck Israels's National Jazz Ensemble, and with a quartet in New York, after which he joined Blood, Sweat and Tears. He was a fine player, noted for his expressive renditions of ballads.

SELECTED RECORDINGS

As sideman: P. Martino: *Baiyina* (1968, Prst. 7589); J. Coles: *Katumbo* (1971, Mstr. 346); W. Herman: *The Raven Speaks* (1972, Fan. 9416); *Giant Steps* (1973, Fan. 9432); *Children of Lima* (1974–5, Fan. 9477); C. Israels: *National Jazz Ensemble* (1975, Chi. 140); T. Lewis and M. Jones: *Live in Munich* (1976, A&M Hor. 724)

BIBLIOGRAPHY

Feather–Gitler '70s
B. Kirchner: "Profile: Gregory Herbert," *DB*, xliv/11 (1977), 34
Obituary, *DB*, xlv/6 (1978), 10

DIANNA RHYAN

Herbert, Mort [Pelovitz, Morton Herbert] (*b* Somerville, NJ, 30 June 1925; *d* Los Angeles, 5 June 1983). Double bass player. He was self-taught and first worked in minor swing bands in the 1940s. He attended Rutgers (1949–52), then worked with Marian McPartland, Don Elliott (with whom he made his first recording), and the Sauter–Finegan Orchestra. In 1956 he made the album *Night People* (Savoy 12073) with his own sextet, which included Bobby Jaspar, Sahib Shihab, and Kenny Clarke. He played frequently with Sol Yaged in New York (1955–8) and he also recorded with Gene Krupa (1957). From 1958 to 1961 he was a member of Louis Armstrong's band, with which he toured and recorded; while he was with Armstrong he appeared in the films *The Beat Generation* and *Die Nacht vor der Premiere* (both 1959). While pursuing a distinguished legal career in Los Angeles he continued to play as a freelance, notably with Herb Ellis. (*FeatherE*; *Feather '60s*)

Herbolzheimer, Peter (*b* Bucharest, 31 Dec 1935). German bandleader, trombonist, composer, and arranger of Romanian birth. After living for two years in Germany he moved in 1953 to Detroit, where he played guitar in clubs; he returned to Germany in 1957, took up the trombone, and for one year attended the Konservatorium in Nuremberg. In the 1960s he played in the dance orchestra of the Nuremberg radio under Josef Nissen and in 1968 had his first important engagement as a member of the pit orchestra at the Deutsches Schauspielhaus, of which Hans Koller was the music director. He belonged in the late 1960s to Wolfgang Dauner's Radio Jazz Group Stuttgart and in 1969 formed a big band, Rhythm Combination and Brass, that included leading musicians from European radio orchestras, and for which he also wrote arrangements; among those who were at various times associated with the band were Dusko Goykovich, Herb Geller, Art Farmer, Palle Mikkelborg, Ack van Rooyen, Karl Drewo, Bo Stief, Ferdinand Povel, Niels-Henning Ørsted Pedersen, Alex Riel, and Allan Botschinsky. He wrote music for the Olympic Games in Munich in 1972 and the same year won the International Jazz Composers Competition in Monaco. Later he worked in television in Germany as a leader and arranger, and accompanied such visiting American musicians as Al Jarreau and Dizzy Gillespie. Herbolzheimer's arrangements are a distinctive amalgam of swing and rhythmic rock. He contributed to a chapter on arranging and composition included in *Jazzrock* (Reinbek, Germany, 1983), edited by Burghard König.

SELECTED RECORDINGS

My Kind of Sunshine (1971, MPS 3321331); *Wide Open* (1973, MPS 2121948); *Jazz Gala Concert* (1976, Atl. 1693); *Jazz Gala '77 All Star Big Band* (1977, Tel. 628438); *Bandfire* (1981, Panda 1)

BIBLIOGRAPHY

"Zwischen Rock und Free Jazz," *JP*, xxi (1972), 192 [interview]
M. Henkels: "Peter Herbolzheimer and the Rhythm Combination & Brass," *JF* [intl edn], no.38 (1975), 49
D. Sollner: "Peter Herbolzheimer: weil es uns Spass macht," *JP*, xxiv/9 (1975), 13 [incl. discography]
B. König: *Jazzrock: Tendenzen einer modernen Musik* (Reinbek, Germany, 1983)

WOLFRAM KNAUER

Herfurt, Skeets [Arthur] (*b* Cincinnati, 28 May 1911). Alto and tenor saxophonist, clarinetist, and singer. He grew up in Denver, and began playing in bands while at the University of Colorado. During the 1930s he performed with Smith Ballew (1934), the Dorsey Brothers (1934–5), Jimmy Dorsey (1935–6), Ray Noble, and Tommy Dorsey (1937–9); his playing may be heard to advantage on *Honeysuckle Rose* by the Dorsey Brothers Orchestra (1934, Decca 296). He then settled on the West Coast and worked in Alvino Rey's band. After army service (1944–5) Herfurt undertook studio work in Hollywood, played with Benny Goodman (1946–7), and led his own band. Thereafter he worked as a session musician, recording with Billy May (early 1950s), Louis Armstrong (1955), and Georgie Auld, Jack Teagarden, and Stan Kenton (all 1956). Later he recorded with Benny Goodman (1961, 1964).

based on *ChiltonW*

Herman, Woody [Woodrow Charles] (*b* Milwaukee, 16 May 1913; *d* Los Angeles, 29 Oct 1987). Bandleader, clarinetist, alto saxophonist, and singer. After early experience in Chicago with the bands led by Tom Gerun and Harry Sosnik he toured with Gus Arnheim. In 1934 he joined Isham Jones, and when Jones's group disbanded in 1936 Herman used its leading sidemen as the nucleus for his own orchestra (*see* BLUES, §7). This band went through a number of changes of personnel, such as the inclusion in 1943 of Chubby Jackson and in 1944 of Neal Hefti, Ralph Burns, Flip Phillips, and Bill Harris (i); by the mid-1940s, under the name Herman's Herd, it was internationally famous for the force and originality of its music. Herman re-formed the band in 1947, and the distinctive feature of the Second Herd was the group of saxophonists (three tenor and one baritone) who came to be known as the Four Brothers; among the musicians who played in the section were Serge Chaloff, Stan Getz, Zoot Sims, Al Cohn, and Gene Ammons.

After the demise of the Second Herd in 1949, Herman continued to lead bands; these were perhaps less creative, but their consistently high level of musicianship assured his continuing reputation. The Anglo-American Herd, which he organized in 1959, was significant in the history of English Jazz; another of the more distinctive later bands, the Swinging Herd, was formed in 1962 and featured such excellent soloists as Bill Chase, Phil Wilson, and Sal Nistico (ii). Herman broadened his scope in the late 1960s, when he took up soprano saxophone and included young jazz-rock players in his groups. He toured widely in the 1970s, and in the early 1980s held a residency in a club in New Orleans. Thereafter he worked principally on the West Coast, before taking up another residency in the St. Regis Hotel, New York, in 1985. He celebrated his 50th anniversary as a bandleader with the formation of a new orchestra in 1986.

Although Herman's instrumental expertise was considerable, his essential importance was as an organizer. His rare ability to assemble and sustain bands notable for the quality of their musicians grew especially clear in the late years of World War II, when his group consisted of brilliant improvisers whose ensemble playing was exuberant and incisive; Igor Stravinsky was so impressed by its sound that in 1945 he composed his *Ebony Concerto* for the band. The harmonic procedures of bop influenced Herman's next orchestra even more deeply, confirming his freedom from the contemporary sectarianism in jazz. The ebullient *Lemon Drop* (1948), with its succession of exciting improvisations, illustrates Herman's shrewd open-mindedness as a bandleader, as do more overtly ambitious recordings like the two-part *Lady McGowan's Dream* (1946) and the four-part *Summer Sequence* (1946–7), both composed by Burns.

Oral history material in *NjR* (JOHP).

SELECTED RECORDINGS

Woodchopper's Ball (1939, Decca 2440); Blue Flame (1941, Decca 3643); Apple Honey (1945, Col. 36803); Caldonia (1945, Col. 36789); *At Carnegie Hall* (1946, MGM 30601–8); Ebony Concerto (1946, Col. 7479M); Lady McGowan's Dream (1946, Col. 38365-6); Summer Sequence (1946–7, Col. 38365-7); Four Brothers (1947, Col. 38304); Lemon Drop (1948, Cap. 15365); Early Autumn (1948, Cap. 57-616); Blues in Advance/Terrissita (1952, Mars 100); *Woody Herman's New Big Band at the Monterey Jazz Festival* (1959, Atl. 1328); *Encore: 1963* (1963, Phi. 600092); *Light my Fire* (1968, Cadet 819); *Woody and Friends at the Monterey Jazz Festival* (1979, Conc. 170)

BIBLIOGRAPHY

A. Lee: "Will Keep Progressing: Woody," *DB*, xvii/22 (1950), 1
R. J. Gleason: "A Quarter-century-plus of Woody Herman," *Hi Fi/Stereo Review*, v/4 (1960), 50
S. Dance and others: *Jazz Era: the 'Forties* (London, 1961/R1985), 134
E. Edwards, Jr.: *Woody Herman and his Orchestra: a Discography*, i, ii (Brande, Denmark, 1961); iii: *1959–1965* (Whittier, CA, 1965)
G. Lees: "Herman's Swinging New Herd," *DB*, xxx/10 (1963), 22
D. Ioakimidis: "Woody," *Jh*, no.204 (1964), 30; no.205 (1965), 26; no.206 (1965), 16; no.208 (1965), 16
J. Szantor: "Right on! Woody Herman, 1970," *DB*, xxxvii/8 (1970), 13
H. Nolan: "Woody Herman: 40 Years of the Nomadic Herd," *DB*, xliii/18 (1976), 12
R. Palmer: "Woody's Winners," *JJI*, xxxi/10 (1978), 6
J. A. Treichel: *Keeper of the Flame: Woody Herman and the Second Herd, 1947–1949* (n.p. [Zephyrhills, FL], 1978) [bio-discography]
S. Crouch: "Woody Herman's Black and White Concerto," *VV*, xxx (9 April 1985)
C. Garrod: *Woody Herman and his Orchestra*, i: *1936–1947* (Zephyrhills, FL, 1985); ii: *1948–1957* (Zephyrhills, 1986) [discography]
G. Giddins: *Rhythm-a-ning: Jazz Tradition and Innovation in the '80s* (New York, and Oxford, England, 1985) [colln of previously pubd articles], 111
J. McDonough: "Woody Herman: 50 Years in the Big Band Business," *DB*, liii/11 (1986), 18 [incl. discography]
S. Voce: *Woody Herman* (London, 1986) [incl. discography by T. Shoppee]

MICHAEL JAMES/R

Herwin (i). Record label. It was established in 1925 by Herbert and Edwin Schiele of the St. Louis Music Co., and issued race records; these were sold almost exclusively by mail order in the southern and mid-western states by means of advertisements in farming journals. Its catalogue included many important jazz recordings (often issued under pseudonyms) that had previously been put out on Paramount and Gennett. The label was bought in 1930 by the Wisconsin Chair Co., Paramount's parent organization.

BIBLIOGRAPHY

J. Randolph: "The St. Louis Labels: Harmograph and Herwin," *Playback*, ii/3–4 (1949), 6

(a)

(b)

1. (a) Herman's Herd at the Columbia recording studios, New York, 19 February 1945: (back row, left to right) Sonny Berman, Charlie Frankhauser, Ray Wetzel, Pete Candoli, and Carl Warwick (trumpets); (middle row) Chubby Jackson (double bass), Billy Bauer (guitar), Dave Tough (drums), Bill Harris (i), Ralph Pfeffner, and Ed Keifer (trombones); (front row) Ralph Burns (piano), Herman (leader), Flip Phillips, John LaPorta, Sam Marowitz, Pete Mondello, and Skippy DeSair (saxophones); (b) Herman's Second Herd at the Commodore Hotel, New York, May 1948: (back row, left to right) Ernie Royal, Bernie Glow, and Marky Markowitz (trumpets); (middle row) Harry Babasin (double bass), Ollie Wilson and Bob Swift (trombones); (front row) Fred Otis (piano), Mary Ann McCall (voice), Stan Getz and Zoot Sims (saxophones); (standing, foreground) Herman (leader), Serge Chaloff (saxophone), Shorty Rogers (trumpet)

J. Godrich: "Herwin 92000 & 93000," *Matrix*, no.52 (1964), 3
M. Wyler: "A Glimpse into the Past, 2: Herwin," *Sv*, i/2 (1965), 9
R. M. W. Dixon and J. Godrich: *Recording the Blues* (London, 1970), 54

Herwin (ii). Record label. It was established by Bernard Klatzko in 1971 to reissue with improved sound quality rare items of early jazz. The catalogue included many masterpieces of small-group jazz made available for the first time since their original issue. The label was later taken over by new management which ceased new reissue projects but maintained the back catalogue. (R. D. Laing and C. Sheridan: *Jazz Records: the Specialist Labels* (Copenhagen, 1981) [discography], 273)

Heymans, Phyllis (*b* Beijing, 1919). Dutch singer. She spent her youth in Batavia (now Jakarta) and performed as a cabaret singer in Holland at the age of 15. When war broke out in 1939 she emigrated to Switzerland, where she joined the Lanigiros; among the several recordings she made with the group was *Ride, Tenderfoot, Ride* (1941, Col. ZZ1013). As a member of the Original Teddies (under Eddie Brunner) from 1941 she became the most important jazz singer in Switzerland; her solo singing may be heard on *That Solid Old Man* (1942, ES 4176). Heymans also made recordings in the vocal quartet the Four Cacadoes (1943) and a sextet led by the pianist Achille Christen (1945); she then seems to have ceased performing. (J.-R. Hippenmeyer: *Le jazz en Suisse, 1930–1970*, Yverdon, Switzerland, 1971)

RAINER E. LOTZ

Heywood, Eddie [Edward, Jr.] (*b* Atlanta, 4 Dec 1915). Pianist, arranger, and bandleader. He was taught piano by his father, a pianist and bandleader, and was playing professionally by the age of 14. After performing with Wayman Carver (1932) and the bandleader Clarence Love (1934–7) he spent a period working as a freelance in New York. He then played with Benny Carter (1939–40), Zutty Singleton, and Don Redman, but thereafter led his own groups. Billie Holiday recorded with Heywood's octet in 1941. His first important engagement as a bandleader came in 1943 when his sextet (which included Vic Dickenson and Doc Cheatham) held a residency at the Village Vanguard in New York. The following year he achieved popular success with his arrangement of *Begin the Beguine*, which led to steady work in New York and California; his group appeared in two films, *The Dark Corner* and *Junior Prom* (both 1946; *see* FILMS, §I, 4(iv)). From 1947 to 1950 Heywood was afflicted by partial paralysis of the hands and was unable to perform; when he resumed playing his work became more commercial in character, and in 1956 he had a great success with his composition *Canadian Sunset*. During the late 1960s he suffered a second attack of paralysis, but after recovering continued to work in New York and New England. He held a long engagement at the Cookery, New York, in 1984.

SELECTED RECORDINGS

As leader: T'ain't me/Save your sorrow (1944, Com. 554); Begin the Beguine/I cover the waterfront (1944, Com. 1514)
As sideman: B. Holiday: Let's do it (1941, OK 6134); C. Hawkins: Crazy Rhythm/Get Happy (1943, Sig. 28104); The Man I Love/Sweet Lorraine (1943, Sig. 9001)

BIBLIOGRAPHY

ChiltonW
S. A. Pease: "Foundation in Classics: Eddie Thanks his Dad," *DB*, xv/21 (1948), 12
D. Gold: "Comeback of Year: They all Want Eddie Heywood," *DB*, xxiii/24 (1956), 56
S. Dance: *The World of Swing* (New York, 1974) [colln of previously pubd interviews], 318
"Back from the Vineyard," *New York Times* (22 July 1980), §C, p.19

ANDREW JAFFE

Hibbler, Al(bert) (*b* Little Rock, AR, 16 Aug 1915). Singer. He began singing professionally in the early 1930s and in 1942 he performed and recorded with Jay McShann. He is best known for his work with Duke Ellington, with whom he was associated from 1943 to 1951. He recorded as a leader with groups directed by Harry Carney (1945), Mercer Ellington (1947), Billy Kyle and Billy Taylor (ii) (both 1950), Jimmy Mundy (1951), and Gerald Wilson (1961). He also made recordings with the Ellingtonians (1950), Count Basie (1952), and Roland Kirk (1972). In 1971 he performed at Louis Armstrong's funeral. *It shouldn't happen to a dream* (1946, Musi. 484), which Hibbler recorded with Ellington's orchestra, well represents his appealing baritone voice; he sings with a full, round tone, and his sharp attack and clear enunciation impart rhythmic momentum to his delivery.

Oral history material in *CtY*.

BIBLIOGRAPHY

FeatherE
D. Ellington: *Music is my Mistress* (Garden City, NY, 1973)

SCOTT FREDRICKSON

Hickory House. Nightclub in New York; *see* NIGHTCLUBS AND OTHER VENUES.

Hicks, John (*b* Atlanta, 1941). Pianist. He learned piano from the age of six and studied music at Lincoln University, Missouri. He later attended the Berklee School of Music in Boston, where he also performed as a freelance musician. In 1963 he moved to New York and gained recognition through his work with Art Blakey (1964–6). After playing with Betty Carter (1966–8) and Woody Herman (1968–70) Hicks recorded with Oliver Lake (1970) and performed and recorded in the Netherlands with Charles Tolliver (1972). He worked again with Blakey (1973) and Carter (1975–80) and recorded with Lester Bowie (1974) and Chico Freeman (1978–9); he also taught music at Southern Illinois University (early 1970s). During the 1980s Hicks played with his own trio and as a sideman in numerous groups, including those led by Arthur Blythe, David Murray, Harriet Bluiett, Art Davis, and Pharoah Sanders. He is a well-respected and versatile musician, whose style has become more personal throughout his career.

SELECTED RECORDINGS

As leader: *Hell's Bells* (1978, SE 8002); *After the Morning* (1979, West 54 8004); *Some Other Time* (1981, The. 115); *John Hicks* (1984, The. 119)
As sideman: A Blakey: *'S Make it* (1964, Lml. 86001); H. Mobley: *High Voltage* (1967, BN 84273); L. Bowie: *Fast Last!* (1974, Muse 5055); C. Freeman: *Spirit Sensitive* (1979, IndN 1045); B. Carter: *The Audience with Betty Carter* (1979, Bet-Car 1003); A. Blythe: *Illusions* (1980, Col. JC36583); P. Sanders: *Journey to the One* (1980, The. 108–9); *Rejoice* (1981, The. 112–3); *Pharoah Sanders Live* (1982, The. 116); D. Murray: *Morning Song* (1983, BS 0075)

BIBLIOGRAPHY

J. Herson: "Profile: John Hicks," *DB*, xlvi/11 (1978), 32
G. Kalbacher: "John Hicks: First Call Piano," *DB*, liii/6 (1986), 26 [incl. discography]

SCOTT YANOW

Hides. Slang term for drums; *see* DRUM SET.

Hifijazz. Record company and label. The company was founded in Hollywood in 1958 by David Axelrod, who directed artists and repertory. Over several years an interesting catalogue was assembled that included distinguished albums by Elmo Hope and Harold Land, and some fine recordings by Gerry Wiggins, King Pleasure, Jimmy Witherspoon, and Paul Horn. By the end of the 1960s, however, Hifijazz was no longer active. The material by Hope and Land was bought and reissued by Contemporary; Hope's album reappeared as late as 1986, reissued by the Spanish company Fresh Sounds.

MARK GARDNER

Higginbotham, J. C. [Jay C.] (*b* Social Circle, GA, 11 May 1906; *d* New York, 26 May 1973). Trombonist. In his youth he played with obscure bands in the South and Midwest. He went to New York in the late 1920s, joining Luis Russell in 1928. In the early 1930s he worked with other leading black bands, including those of Fletcher Henderson, Chick Webb, and Benny Carter. He achieved his widest acclaim for his many solos with Russell's band, which he rejoined during the period it was providing the backing for Louis Armstrong (1937–40). He also recorded with numerous small groups, especially ones whose music had a New Orleans flavor, including those led by Sidney Bechet and Henry "Red" Allen, and a group of his own. During these years Higginbotham was considered one of the best of the swing trombonists; he played essentially in the legato style pioneered by Jimmy Harrison, but employed many smears and rips to create a rougher and more raucous sound that seemed closer to the older New Orleans approach. With the decline of the swing style in the late 1940s he performed as a freelance, mainly around New York.

For illustrations *see* HENDERSON, FLETCHER, and MILLS BLUE RHYTHM BAND.
Oral history material in *NjR* (JOHP).

SELECTED RECORDINGS

As leader: Higginbotham Blues (1930, OK 8772)
As sideman: L. Armstrong: Mahogany Hall Stomp (1929, OK 8680); H. Allen: It should be you (1929, Vic. 38073); L. Armstrong: Save it pretty mama (1939, Decca 2363); Port of Harlem Six: Mighty Blues (1939, BN 3); Metronome All-Stars: One o'Clock Jump (1941, Vic. 27314)

BIBLIOGRAPHY

"Jay C. Higginbotham," *DB*, viii/6 (1941), 10
C. Jones: *J. C. Higginbotham* (London, 1944)
B. Houghton: "Higginbotham Blues," *JJ*, xxi/1 (1968), 4
F. Hoffman: *Henry "Red" Allen (Jan. 7th 1908 – Apr. 17th 1967)/J. C. Higginbotham (May 11th 1906 – May 26th 1973): Discography, 1927–1968; Excerpt out a Future "Red Allen Bio-Disco"* (MS, Berlin, 1982) [unpubd typescript]
——: *Henry "Red" Allen (Jan. 7th 1908 – Apr. 17th 1967)/J. C. Higginbotham (May 11th 1906 – May 26th 1973): Compiled Negro-press Material about Bands with Henry Red Allen, 1927–1940* (MS, Berlin, 1979, rev. 1982) [unpubd typescript]

JAMES LINCOLN COLLIER

Higgins, Billy (*b* Los Angeles, 11 Oct 1936). Drummer. He began his career playing rhythm-and-blues and rock-and-roll with such musicians as Amos Milburn and Bo Diddley in the Los Angeles area, then played jazz with the Jazz Messiahs (led by Don Cherry and the saxophonist James Clay) and Dexter Gordon, and from the mid-1950s took part in rehearsals with Ornette Coleman; in 1958 he recorded with Coleman and with Red Mitchell. He performed with Coleman's quartet in New York (1959) and with Thelonious Monk in San Francisco (recording in 1959–60). During the following decades he became one of the most widely recorded drummers in jazz; he made albums with the quintets of Steve Lacy (1961), Sonny Clark (1961), and Lee Morgan (1963, 1966), as well as with Donald Byrd (1961), Gordon (1962, 1975), Jackie McLean (1966, 1967), Hank Mobley (1967), Mal Waldron (1973), Clifford Jordan (1975), and Niels-Henning Ørsted Pedersen (1975, 1976), and was a leader with Bill Lee and Bill Hardman of the Brass Company (1972–3). He performed and recorded with Cedar Walton (1975–85), led a quartet (recording in 1979 and 1980), and made recordings as a sideman with Milt Jackson (1976, 1978), Art Pepper (1979), J. J. Johnson (1979), Joe Henderson's quartet (1980), Pat Metheny (1982), David Murray's big band (1984), and Slide Hampton's quintet (1985). He also performed and recorded as a member of the Timeless All-Stars (*see* TIMELESS) and played occasionally with Coleman in New York (1977, 1987). Higgins has been influenced by Ed Blackwell, Roy Haynes, and Kenny Clarke and is highly regarded for his restrained, loosely swinging manner. He plays and briefly acts in the film *'Round Midnight* (1986).

SELECTED RECORDINGS

As leader: *The Soldier* (1979, Tim. 145)
As sideman with O. Coleman: *Something Else!!!! The Music of Ornette Coleman* (1958, Cont. 7551); *The Shape of Jazz to Come* (1959, Atl. 1317); *Change of the Century* (1959, Atl. 1327); *Free Jazz* (1960, Atl. 1364)
As sideman with others: S. Rollins: *Our Man in Jazz* (1962, RCA LSP2612); D. Gordon: *Go!* (1962, BN 84112); J. McLean: *Action* (1964, BN 84218); H. Mobley: *Dippin'* (1965, BN 84209)

BIBLIOGRAPHY

V. Wilmer: "Billy Higgins: Drum Love," *DB*, xxxv/6 (1968), 27; repr. as "A Lesson in Lovemaking," *Jazz People* (London, Indianapolis, and New York, 1970/*R*1985), 55
C. M. Bernstein: "The Traditional Roots of Billy Higgins," *MD*, vii/2 (1983), 20
L. Hildebrand: "Jazzman Billy Higgins: He's had Time for Everyone but Himself," *San Francisco Chronicle Datebook* (5 Oct 1986)

MICHAEL ULLMAN

Hightower, Willie (*b* Nashville, Oct 1889; *d* Chicago, Dec 1959). Cornetist and trumpeter. He first worked in New Orleans, leading a band, the American Stars (*c*1908–*c*1917). While touring as a member of the band that accompanied the revue *The Smart Set* he met the pianist Lottie Frost, whom he later married. After performing together at the Strand Theater, Jacksonville, Florida (*c*1916–1917), they toured Mississippi in a trio with a drummer (1917), then moved to Chicago. Hightower played with lesser-known bands in the early 1920s, then worked with Carroll Dickerson in 1925. Thereafter he joined his wife's band, Lottie E. Hightower's Nighthawks, with which in 1927 he made the recording *Boar Hog Blues/Squeeze me* (Black Patti 8045) with Richard M. Jones on piano. He worked with Dickerson again and played with theater orchestras in the 1930s. In 1933 he was a member of Andrew Hilaire's band; later in the decade he ceased to work as a full-time musician.

Oral history material in *LNT*.

BIBLIOGRAPHY

ChiltonW

MICHAEL TOVEY

Hi-hat [sock cymbal]. Apparatus consisting of two cymbals on a stand, which may be brought together by means of a foot pedal; *see* DRUM SET, §§I, 5; II, 5, 6.

Hilaire, Andrew (H.) (*b* New Orleans, *c*1900; *d* Chicago, *c*1936). Drummer. He played with Lil Hardin in Chicago around 1921, and in 1924 joined Doc Cook's band, with which he recorded from 1926 to 1928. He is best known for his playing in a single recording session with Jelly Roll Morton which included *Black Bottom Stomp* (1926, Vic. 20221) (for illustration *see* MORTON, JELLY ROLL). After working in theaters in the late 1920s he performed with Don Pasquall (1930) and briefly with Eddie South (1931), then led his own groups (1933, 1935).

BIBLIOGRAPHY

ChiltonW
G. Schuller: *Early Jazz: its Roots and Musical Development* (New York, 1968), 155

Hill, (William) Alex(ander) (*b* North Little Rock, AR, 19 April 1906; *d* North Little Rock, 1 Feb 1937). Arranger, pianist, and singer. He studied piano with his mother. After working with

Alphonso Trent he organized his own group (1924) and played in studios in Hollywood. He moved to Chicago, where he arranged *Beau Koo Jack* for Louis Armstrong's recording with his Savoy Ballroom Five (1928); he also performed with and wrote arrangements for Jimmy Wade (1928), played with Jimmie Noone (1928–9), and worked as an arranger for Earl Hines and Paul Howard (both 1929). He then joined the bandleader Sammy Stewart (1929), with whom he traveled to New York in 1930. In the early 1930s Hill became known as one of the best arrangers in Harlem, working with Benny Carter, Claude Hopkins, Andy Kirk (all 1930), Eddie Condon (1933), Mezz Mezzrow (1934), the Mills Blue Rhythm Band (1934–5), and Fats Waller and Willie Bryant (both 1935). He began leading his own orchestra in 1935, but was forced to retire through illness.

SELECTED RECORDINGS

Duos with J. Wells: Stompin' 'em Down/Tack Head Blues (1929, Voc. 1270)
As sideman: J. Noone: Chicago Rhythm/I Got a Misery (1929, Voc. 1267); E. Condon: Tennessee Twilight/Madame Dynamite (1933, Col. 36009)

SELECTED ARRANGEMENTS

As leader: Ain't it Nice?/Functionizin' (1934, Voc. 2826)
Recorded by others: E. Condon: Tennessee Twilight (1933, Bruns. 01690); M. Mezzrow: Old Fashioned Love (1934, Vic. 25202); Mills Blue Rhythm Band: Back Beats (1935, Col. 3020D)

BIBLIOGRAPHY

ChiltonW
R. Gulliver: "No Jubilees for Alex: the Tragedy of Alex Hill," *Sv*, no.38 (1971–2), 60 [incl. discography]
C. Morgan: "Piano Jazz in Sheet Music, 1: a Look at Alex Hill," *Sv*, no.41 (1972), 192

JAMES M. DORAN

Hill, Andrew (*b* Chicago, 30 June 1937). Pianist and composer. His place of birth has often been given incorrectly as Port-au-Prince. He played piano from 1950 and studied with the composer Paul Hindemith (1950–52). As a teenager he played with Charlie Parker, Miles Davis, and Johnny Griffin at clubs in Chicago, and in 1961 moved to New York to work as Dinah Washington's accompanist. He played with Roland Kirk in Los Angeles in 1962, then returned to New York, where he recorded for Blue Note with Joe Henderson, Eric Dolphy, Freddie Hubbard, Woody Shaw, and many other bop and free-jazz musicians (1963–9). He was music coordinator for LeRoi Jones's Black Arts Repertory Theatre (1965) and composer-in-residence (1970–72) at Colgate University, from which he received the doctorate. He toured with the Smithsonian Heritage Program (1972–5) and received a Smithsonian Fellowship from 1975. He taught in public schools and prisons in California, toured worldwide, and recorded for several labels. Hill composes well-proportioned melodies that often have shifting meters and tempos; his solos, influenced by Art Tatum, Bud Powell, and Thelonious Monk, are dense and sensual, marked by skillfully developed melodic phrases of irregular length and sudden changes of tempo.

SELECTED RECORDINGS

As unaccompanied soloist: *Live at Montreux* (1975, Ari. 1023); *From California with Love* (1978, AH 9)
As leader: *So in Love with the Sound of Andrew Hill* (1955, Warwick 2002); *Black Fire* (1963, BN 84151); *Point of Departure* (1964, BN 84167); *Compulsion* (1965, BN 84217); *Divine Revelation* (1975, Ste. 1044)
As sideman: Dave Shipp: Romping/Let's Live (1954, VJ 145); R. Kirk: *Domino* (1962, Mer. 60748); B. Hutcherson: *Dialogue* (1965, BN 84198); S. Rivers: *Involution* (1966, BN LA453)

BIBLIOGRAPHY

D. Heckman: "Roots, Culture, and Economics," *DB*, xxxiii/9 (1966), 19
B. Rusch: "Andrew Hill: Interview," *Cadence*, i/10 (1976), 3
C. Berg: "Andrew Hill: Innovative Enigma," *DB*, xliv/5 (1977), 16 [incl. discography]
——: Liner notes, *From California with Love* (AH9, 1980) [incl. discography]
K. Raether: "Obscurity? It's in the Eye of the Beholder," *Albuquerque Tribune* (4 Jan 1985), 3

ED HAZELL

Hill, Buck [Roger] (*b* Washington, 1928). Tenor saxophonist and leader. He started playing soprano saxophone at the age of 13, and began playing professionally in 1943. After working at various clubs in Washington he recorded with Charlie Byrd (1958–9). In the 1960s he was active only intermittently, but he regained prominence in Washington in the early 1970s. In 1973 he recorded with a local trumpeter, Allan Houser, and between 1978 and 1981 made four albums, including *This is Buck Hill* (1978, Ste. 1095), as leader of his own quartet. He appeared at the North Sea Jazz Festival in 1981.

BIBLIOGRAPHY

FeatherE
B. Shoemaker: "Buck Hill," *DB*, xlviii/9 (1981), 54

Hill, Chippie [Bertha] (*b* Charleston, SC, 15 March 1905; *d* New York, 7 May 1950). Singer. She left home at an early age and worked as a dancer in New York in a show led by Ethel Waters. Later she toured as a singer and dancer with Ma Rainey's Rabbit Foot Minstrels (early 1920s) and worked on the Theater Owners' Booking Association circuit as a solo blues singer before settling in Chicago. She worked with many important musicians, including King Oliver, Louis Armstrong, Richard M. Jones, and Lovie Austin (with whom she toured in 1929) and the blues singers Thomas A. Dorsey and Tampa Red. Throughout the 1930s she worked, often on a part-time basis, at clubs around Chicago, including the Cabin Inn (with Jimmie Noone, 1937) and the Club DeLisa (1939–40). After leaving music for some six years to raise her family she recorded with Austin (1946) and worked again at the Club DeLisa (1946–7). She moved to New York in 1947 and participated in the radio series "This is Jazz." In 1947–8 she undertook residencies at the Village Vanguard and Jimmy Ryan's. During this period she also performed at Carnegie Hall with Kid Ory (1948) and at a jazz festival in Paris (1948). After working at the Riviera Club (1949–50) she was resident with Art Hodes's quintet at the Blue Note, Chicago, before working again in New York at Ryan's and the Stuyvesant Casino. At the peak of her renewed popularity she was killed in a traffic accident.

SELECTED RECORDINGS

Trouble in Mind (1926, OK 8312); Pleadin' for the Blues/Pratt City Blues (1926, OK 8240); Weary Money Blues/Christmas Man Blues (1928, Voc. 1224); Trouble in Mind (1928, Voc. 1248); I ain't gonna do it no more (1929, Voc. 1406); Mistreatin' Mr Dupree (1946, Cir. [USA] 1067)

BIBLIOGRAPHY

R. Blesh: *Shining Trumpets: a History of Jazz* (New York, 1946, rev. and enlarged 2/1958/*R*1975), 137
B. Klatzko: Liner notes, *The Jazz Wizards*, ii (Herwin 103, *c*1972)
S. Harris: *Blues Who's Who: a Biographical Dictionary of Blues Singers* (New Rochelle, NY, 1979)

MICHAEL TOVEY

Hill, Ernest ("Bass") (*b* Pittsburgh, 14 March 1900; *d* New York, 16 Sept 1964). Double bass player. From 1924 to 1928 he worked with Claude Hopkins, touring Europe with the group in 1925. He played tuba in a recording session with Henry "Red" Allen in 1930 and recorded on double bass with Benny Carter, Spike Hughes, and the Chocolate Dandies; his powerful sense of swing may be heard on Hughes's *Firebird* (1933, Decca F3717). He worked sporadically with Carter (1931–4), and performed and recorded with Willie Bryant (1935–6), Putney Dandridge (1936), and Bobby Martin (in Europe, 1937). Later he recorded with Eddie South and Hot Lips Page (both 1940) and with Sammy Price (1941). Thereafter Hill played with Hopkins (intermittently, 1941–4), Zutty Singleton and Louis Armstrong (both 1943), and Cliff Jackson (1944), and recorded with Punch Miller (1947). After visiting Europe again (1949), where he worked with Bill Coleman and Frank "Big Boy" Goudie, he became a member of Happy Caldwell's band.

BIBLIOGRAPHY

ChiltonW
J. Simmen: "Ernest 'Bass' Hill: tel que je l'ai connu," *Pj*, no.6 (1972), 20–54

Hill, Freddy [Frederick Roosevelt] (*b* Jacksonville, FL, 18 April 1932). Trumpeter. He attended Florida Agricultural and Mechanical College, and played in the college band with Cannonball and Nat Adderley. After serving in the army (1953) he taught music at public schools in Florida (1955–7), then settled in Los Angeles, where he worked intermittently with Gerald Wilson (1957–66) and with Earl Bostic (1959–60). He made recordings in small groups led by Leroy Vinnegar (*Leroy Walks Again!*, 1962, Cont. 7608), Lou Blackburn (1963), and Buddy DeFranco (1964), and in big bands under Wilson (1962–6), Louie Bellson (1964), Gil Fuller and Dizzy Gillespie (1965), Oliver Nelson (1967), and Bobby Bryant (1969, 1971). (*Feather '60s*)

Hill, Teddy [Theodore] (*b* Birmingham, AL, 7 Dec 1909; *d* Cleveland, 19 May 1978). Tenor saxophonist and bandleader. After moving to New York in 1927 he joined the drummer George Howe, whose band was taken over that year by Luis Russell; Hill later recorded as a soloist with the group under the nominal leadership of Henry "Red" Allen. He worked with James P. Johnson in 1932, and then organized his own successful big band. Among his sidemen in 1935 were Roy Eldridge, Bill Coleman, Chu Berry, Dicky Wells, and Russell Procope; Frankie Newton, Shad Collins and Cecil Scott replaced Eldridge, Coleman, and Berry the following year, and Dizzy Gillespie (who recorded his first solos with the band) joined in 1937. The group played regularly at the Savoy Ballroom, broadcast over station WJZ, and toured in England and France (1937). Hill ceased to work as a bandleader in 1940 in order to manage Minton's Playhouse (for illustration *see* NIGHTCLUBS AND OTHER VENUES, fig.6) and, through his selection of talent and his encouragement of jam sessions during the early 1940s, earned the club its reputation as the birthplace of bop. From 1969, when Minton's no longer offered live music, Hill was manager of the Baron Lounge.

SELECTED RECORDINGS

As leader: Uptown Rhapsody/Passionette (1936, Voc. 3294); At the Rug Cutter's Ball/Blue Rhythm Fantasy (1936, Voc. 3247); The Harlem Twister (1937, Bb 6908); San Anton'/King Porter Stomp (1937, Bb 6988)
As sideman with H. Allen: Feelin' Drowsy/Swing Out (1929, Vic. 38080)

BIBLIOGRAPHY

ChiltonW
A. McCarthy: *Big Band Jazz* (New York and London, 1974), 286
H. Rye: "Visiting Firemen, 6: Teddy Hill and the Cotton Club Revue," *Sv*, no.100 (1982), 144

STEVEN STRUNK

Hill-and-dale [vertical cut] **recording.** A term applied to a sound-recording technique in which, in both recording and playback, the stylus moves up and down in the spiral groove on a cylinder or disc; *see* RECORDING, esp. §I, 1(i).

Hillyer, Lonnie (*b* Monroe, GA, 25 March 1940; *d* New York, 1 July 1985). Trumpeter. He grew up in Detroit, where he studied with Barry Harris, performed and recorded with Yusef Lateef (1959), and worked with Joe Henderson at the Bluebird (1960). After moving to New York (1960) he became known through his association with Charles Mingus's groups (1960–61, 1964–7). He joined Mingus at the same time as Charles McPherson, with whom he worked closely for several years; they played together in Harris's band (1961–3) and led a hard-bop quintet (1966). Hillyer also played with Slide Hampton (1960) and Charles Davis. He continued to work in the 1970s, recording with McPherson in 1971, and performing with Mingus again from 1971 to 1973.

SELECTED RECORDINGS

As sideman: Y. Lateef: *Cry! Tender* (1959, NewJ 8234); C. Mingus: *Mingus!* (1960, Can. 9021), incl. Lock 'em up; B. Harris: *Newer than New* (1961, Riv. 9413); C. Mingus: *Charles Mingus* (1965, Charles Mingus 0013–14); C. McPherson: *The Quintet: Live!* (1966, Prst. 7480); *Charles McPherson* (1971, Mstr. 329)

BIBLIOGRAPHY

Feather '60s; *Feather–Gitler '70s*
B. Priestley: *Mingus: a Critical Biography* (London, Melbourne, Australia, and New York, 1982)
Obituary, *Variety*, cccxix (24 July 1985), 133

FREDERICK A. BECK

Hines, Earl (Kenneth) [Earl "Fatha," Fatha] (*b* Duquesne, PA, 28 Dec 1903; *d* Oakland, CA, 22 April 1983). Pianist and bandleader. He studied trumpet briefly with his father, and took his first piano lessons with his mother, later studying with other teachers in Pittsburgh. He first played professionally in 1918, accompanying the singer Lois Deppe, with whom he later made his first recordings; his earnings allowed him to study with two local jazz pianists.

Hines moved to Chicago in 1923 and during the next few years played with several important Chicago bands: Sammy Stewart's (at the Sunset Cafe), Erskine Tate's Vendome Theater Orchestra, and Carroll Dickerson's (on a 42-week tour). In 1926 Dickerson's band returned to the Sunset Cafe and, with Hines, Louis Armstrong, and other important musicians, soon became well known, influencing a generation of musicians. Hines became its director in 1927 under Armstrong's nominal leadership. After an unsuccessful attempt to manage their own club in 1927, Armstrong and Hines separated, Armstrong returning to Dickerson, and Hines joining Jimmie Noone's band at the Apex Club. In 1928 Hines recorded several titles with Noone, including *Apex Blues*, and made a series of influential recordings with Armstrong, among them the highly original trumpet and piano duet *Weather Bird* (for excerpts *see* HARMONY (i), exx.3 and 14); he also recorded a group of solos for QRS.

On his 25th birthday Hines inaugurated his own band at the Grand Terrace in Chicago, where he played for ten years; the band became known through nationwide tours and, from 1934, radio broadcasts. Until 1948 he continued to lead big bands, featuring such important figures as Billy Eckstine, Sarah Vaughan, Charlie Parker, Dizzy Gillespie, and many others. From 1948 to 1951 Hines played with Armstrong's All Stars and afterwards worked with small groups led by himself and others, attracting critical notice in the mid-1960s for his solo, trio, and quartet playing. Hines led his own small band into the 1980s, and continued to perform regularly in the USA and abroad until the weekend before his death.

One of a small number of pianists whose playing shaped the history of jazz, Hines was an ensemble pianist from the beginning of his career (unlike many earlier pianists, primarily soloists who adapted to ensemble playing). Many pianists of the time, particularly in the Midwest, had largely eliminated rag-

Earl Hines's band at the Pearl Theater, Philadelphia, 1932: (back row, left to right) Charlie Allen, Wallace Bishop, Cecil Irwin; (front row) Lawrence Dixon, George Dixon, Billy Franklin, Omer Simeon, Hines, Darnell Howard, Quinn Wilson, Lewis Taylor, Walter Fuller

time influence from their right-hand techniques, preferring a sparse linear approach to the thicker texture of ragtime and integrating the piano with the ensemble. Hines's version of this, present in nascent form in his earliest recordings, is often called "trumpet style": clearly articulated melody without ragtime figuration, often played in octaves, and tremolo approximating wind vibrato. The left-hand technique of the period was similar among pianists of otherwise widely divergent styles – a single note, octave, or 10th on the strong beats of the bar, with a chord, usually centered about *c′*, on the weak beats; the result was an explicit statement of the pulse. Hines, using 10ths a great deal, took this common technique as a point of departure, interrupting its regularity to play off-beat accents and to contradict or all but dissolve the meter. These qualities were already apparent in his early performances with Armstrong, as shown by his famous break in *Skip the Gutter*. Into the 1930s he extended this device to produce solos of great textural variety; his playing was also characterized by the use of arpeggios through several octaves, intermittent silences, and constant attention to line – features impersonal enough, taken in isolation, to point out new directions to a generation of pianists.

Hines's ability to change his style but retain his identity as a pianist undoubtedly conditioned his attitudes as a bandleader. Over two decades he led innovative jazz groups, and he was among the few musicians of his generation to appreciate the new features of bop, which he introduced into his band through the presence of bop musicians.

Oral history material in *GBLnsa*, *NjR*, and *NNC*.

See also Blues, §6, and Piano, §§1, 5, and 6.

SELECTED RECORDINGS

As unaccompanied soloist: Blues in Thirds/Off Time Blues (1928, QRS 7036); Chicago High Life/A Monday Date (1928, QRS 7037); Caution Blues (1928, OK 8832); Fifty-seven Varieties (1928, OK 8653); Child of a Disordered Brain (1940, Bb 10642); *Spontaneous Explorations* (1964, Contact 2); *Paris Session* (1965, Ducretet-Thomson 300V140); *Earl Hines Plays Duke Ellington* (1971, MJR 8114)

Duo with L. Armstrong: Weather Bird (1928, OK 41454)

As leader: Beau Koo Jack (1929, Vic. 38043); Cavernism/Rosetta (1933, Bruns. 6541); Angry (1934, Decca 183); Pianology (1937, Voc. 3501); Father steps in (1939, Bb 10377); Boogie Woogie on St. Louis Blues (1940, Bb 10674); Deep Forest (1940, Bb 10727); Tantalizing a Cuban (1940, Bb 10792); Second Balcony Jump (1941, Bb 11567); Spooks Ball (1945, Jazz Selection 611); Throwing the Switch/Bamby (1946, Jazz Selection 618)

As sideman with L. Armstrong: Fireworks (1928, OK 8597); Skip the Gutter (1928, OK 8631); A Monday Date/Sugar Foot Strut (1928, OK 8609); Two Deuces/Squeeze me (1928, OK 8641); Save it pretty mama (1928, OK 8657)

As sideman with others: J. Dodds: Wild Man Blues (1927, Bruns. 3567); J. Noone: Apex Blues (1928, Voc. 1207); S. Bechet: Blues in Thirds (1940, Vic. 27204)

BIBLIOGRAPHY

S. Dance: "Earl 'Fatha' Hines in San Francisco," *JM*, iii/6 (1957), 2

R. Wilson: "Bringing up 'Fatha'," *DB*, xxx/13 (1963), 18

W. F. Mellers: *Music in a New Found Land: Themes and Developments in the History of American Music* (London, 1964/*R*1975), 375

R. Hadlock: *Jazz Masters of the Twenties* (New York, 1965/*R*1985)

D. Morgenstern: "Today's Life with Fatha Hines," *DB*, xxxii/18 (1965), 25

H. P[anassié]: "La carrière d'Earl 'Fatha' Hines," *BHcF*, no.146 (1965), 5

M. Mezzrow: "Earl 'Fatha' Hines," *BHcF*, no.157 (1966), 3

S. Traill: "Earl Hines and Marva Josie," *JJ*, xxiv/3 (1971), 2

J. R. T. Davies: "The Alternate Earl Hines," *Sv*, no.40 (1972), 127

A. McCarthy: *Big Band Jazz* (New York and London, 1974), 20

L. Wright: "Earl Hines: Genius at Work and Play," *Sv*, no.63 (1976), 84

W. Balliett: "Sunshine always Opens out," *Improvising: Sixteen Jazz Musicians and their Art* (New York, 1977) [colln of previously pubd articles], 33

S. Dance: *The World of Earl Hines* (New York, 1977) [interviews]
K. Hazen: "A Talk with 'Fatha'," *MR*, iv/7 (1977), 10 [interview]
L. Moxhet: *A Discography of Earl Hines, 1923–1977* (Paris, 1978)
D. Keller: "Earl Hines: Fatha on down the Road," *DB*, xlvi/10 (1979), 14

JAMES DAPOGNY/R

Hino, Motohiko (*b* Tokyo, 3 Jan 1946). Japanese drummer, brother of Terumasa Hino. He worked professionally as a tap dancer from the age of eight and as a drummer from 1963. He played with a quartet led by the tenor saxophonist Konosuke Saijo, with the Stardusters, and with quintets led by the guitarist Shungo Sawada and by his brother, then formed a trio. He moved to New York in 1978 to join a trio led by JoAnne Brackeen, then returned to Japan in 1980, where he played with the pianist Aki Takase and the double bass player Nobuyoshi Ino. Hino has been acclaimed for his sharp, dynamic drumming.

SELECTED RECORDINGS

As leader: *First Album* (1970, Col.–Tact XMS10029); *Toko: Motohiko Hino Quartet at Nemu Jazz* (1975, Bellwood OFL3004); *Ryūhyo: Hino Motohiko Quartet + 1* (1976, TBM 61); *Flash* (1977, Apollon BY305061)
As leader with G. Kawaguchi: *The Drum Battle: George Kawaguchi vs Hino Motohiko* (1975, Tei. GM5005)

BIBLIOGRAPHY

Feather–Gitler '70s

YOZO IWANAMI

Hino, Terumasa (*b* Tokyo, 25 Oct 1942). Japanese trumpeter and flugelhorn player, brother of Motohiko Hino. He made his professional début in 1955, in 1964 joined a quintet led by the drummer Hideo Shiraki (with which he appeared at the Berliner Jazztage the following year), and in 1967 formed a quintet with Masabumi Kikuchi. After his album *Hi-nology* (1969) achieved great success he performed at the Berliner Jazztage in 1971 and at many other festivals. From the mid-1970s he recorded regularly in Japan, Europe, and the USA (he settled in New York in June 1975), both as a leader and as a sideman with Kikuchi (1974, 1976), Joachim Kühn (1975), Ken McIntyre (1976), Hal Galper (1977), Carlos Garnett (1977), Sam Jones (1978), Dave Liebman (1980), and Elvin Jones (1982). Hino has a large, brilliant tone that he exploited effectively on many albums of jazz-rock in the 1970s and early 1980s. He is the editor of *Miles Davis: Jazz Improvisation* (Tokyo, 1975), a two-volume set of transcriptions of Davis's solos.

SELECTED RECORDINGS

As leader: *Alone, Alone and Alone* (1967, Col.–Tact 7692); *Hi-nology* (1969, Col.–Tact 7691); *Love Nature* (1971, Tei. Overseas ULS1854); *Speak to Loneliness* (1975, EW 7008); *City Connection* (1979, FDisk V1J4006); *New York Times* (1983, CBS–Sony 28AH1588); *Trans Blue* (1985, CBS–Sony 32DH180); *Retour* (?1987, Toshiba–EMI RT28-5149)
As leader with M. Kikuchi: *Hino–Kikuchi Quintet* (1968, Col.–Tact 32C387873)
As sideman with H. Shiraki: *Japan Meets Jazz* (1965, Saba MPS15065)

BIBLIOGRAPHY

Feather–Gitler '70s

YOZO IWANAMI

Hinton, Milt(on John) [the Judge] (*b* Vicksburg, MS, 23 June 1910). Double bass player. He grew up in Chicago, where his first professional work was with Boyd Atkins, Tiny Parham, and Jabbo Smith in the early 1930s. He also played with Eddie South, Erskine Tate, Zutty Singleton, and Fate Marable. From 1936 to 1951 he was a member of Cab Calloway's band (for illustration *see* CALLOWAY, CAB), where with his full tone and tremendous drive he became a mainstay of the band's rhythm section. After leaving Calloway he worked as a freelance in New York, and was soon one of the most sought-after jazz musicians; he played with, among others, Count Basie and Louis Armstrong's All Stars, and took part in innumerable recording sessions. In the 1970s Hinton undertook a few overseas tours (he was a member of the band that accompanied Bing Crosby on his final trip to Europe), and he has continued to perform regularly in the 1980s. He taught at Hunter College, CUNY, in the mid-1970s, and has also held occasional exhibitions of his work as a jazz photographer.

Hinton's impressive sound and his sense of time were linked with a consummate feeling for harmony. These attributes gained him a strong reputation for playing many styles of music, including work with popular singers. His harmonic experiments in the 1940s with Dizzy Gillespie made him a forerunner of modern jazz bass players.

Oral history material in *CtY*, *NjR* (JOHP), and *NNC*.

SELECTED RECORDINGS

As leader: *The Trio* (1977, Chi. 188)
As sideman: C. Calloway: I beeped when I shoulda bopped (1949, Bb 30-0012); on B. Clayton: *Buck Clayton Jams Benny Goodman* (1954, Col. CL614), Don't be that way; J. Newman: *All I Wanna Do is Swing* (1955, RCA LPM1118), incl. Topsy; All Stars: *Session at Riverside* (1956, Cap. T761), incl. Undecided

BIBLIOGRAPHY

N. Shapiro and N. Hentoff, eds.: *Hear me Talkin' to ya: the Story of Jazz by the Men who Made it* (New York and London, 1955/R1966)
M. Jones: "Milt Hinton," *JJ*, xxi/4 (1968), 16
S. Dance: *The World of Swing* (New York, 1974) [colln of previously pubd interviews]
——: *The World of Earl Hines* (New York, 1977) [interviews], 187
B. Rusch: "Milt Hinton," *Cadence*, iv/12 (1978), 14, 24
S. Woolley: "Milt Hinton," *Coda*, no.159 (1978), 10
L. Birnbaum: "Milt Hinton: the Judge Holds Court," *DB*, xlvi/2 (1979), 14
E. Townley: "The Judge," *Sv*, no.89 (1980), 164
C. Battestini and J.-P. Battestini: "Milt Hinton raconte quelques souvenirs sur son passage dans l'orchestre Cab Calloway," *BHcF*, no.292 (1981), 26
R. D. Johnson: "Meet Milt," *MR*, viii/4 (1981), 6
S. Voce: "A Bass for all Seasons," *JJI*, xxxiv (1981), no.11, p.8; no.12, p.10
D. Travis: *An Autobiography of Black Jazz* (Chicago, 1983) [incl. interviews], 365
J. Armitage: "Jugeons le Juge," *BHcF*, no.330 (1985), 8
L. D. Holmes and J. W. Thomson: *Jazz Greats: Getting Better with Age* (New York, 1986) [interviews]
M. Hinton and D. Berger: *Bass Lines: the Stories and Photographs of Milt Hinton* (Philadelphia, 1988)

JOHN CHILTON

Hinze, Chris(tiaan Herbert) (*b* Hilversum, Netherlands, 30 June 1938). Dutch flutist. He played piano (1960–64), studied flute at the Royal Conservatory in The Hague, and played under the bandleader Boy Edgar (1966) and with the double bass player Dick van der Capellen (1967). He attended the Berklee College of Music and recorded under his own name from 1969; the following year he won the award for best soloist at the Montreux International Jazz Festival and formed the Chris Hinze Combination, with which he toured widely in Europe. He founded a record company, Keytone, in the Netherlands, before moving to the USA in 1976. In 1980 he formed a duo with Sigi Schwab, who later also toured with Combination. Hinze has achieved some success with his jazz versions of Baroque compositions; among his representative recordings are *Variations on Bach* (1976, CBS 80745) and *Backstage* (1983, Kt. 730).

BIBLIOGRAPHY

B. Czajkowska: "Chris Hinze," *JF* [intl edn], no.21 (1973), 39 [incl. discography]
L. Tomkins: "Chris Hinze," *CI*, xiii/11 (1975), 6
I. Carr: "Hinze, Chris," in I. Carr, D. Fairweather, and B. Priestley: *Jazz: the Essential Companion* (London, 1987)

WIM VAN EYLE

Hipp, Jutta (*b* Leipzig, Germany, 4 Feb 1925). German pianist and leader. She studied piano from the age of nine, and later studied painting at the Academy of Arts in Leipzig. She became interested in jazz around 1940, and after World War II, having moved to Munich, she formed a small group. She performed and recorded with Hans Koller (*c*1950–1953) and led her own bop quintet (1953–5), with which she toured Europe. Late in 1955 she moved to the USA and formed a trio with Peter Ind and Ed Thigpen, which played in and around New York; the track *After Hours* from the trio's album *Jutta Hipp at the Hickory House* (1956, BN 1515–16) well represents her playing. Besides her work with this group, she recorded with Zoot Sims (1956). By 1958, however, she had ceased to play in public and was active as an artist.

BIBLIOGRAPHY

FeatherE
F. Manskleid: "I Remember Jutta," *JM*, ix/2 (1963), 12

Hirst, George F(rederick) (*b* Tonyrefail, Wales, 7 June 1906). Trumpeter. He emigrated in 1921 to the USA, where, around 1925, he joined Al Mitchell's orchestra, playing alongside Phil Napoleon. In 1928–9 he made recordings with Enoch Light's orchestra in France (including *What do you say?*, 1929, Odeon 166081). After moving to Germany, he played under Julian Fuhs, Oscar Joost, Marek Weber, and many others, and made numerous recordings as a session musician on the Ultraphon label (1929–31). In France (1931–50) he played and recorded with Fred Adison, Django Reinhardt, Stephane Grappelli, Lud Gluskin, Hubert Rostaing, and others. Having returned to the USA in 1950, he became personnel manager of the Rhode Island PO in 1963; he retired to Florida in 1975.

BIBLIOGRAPHY

R. E. Lotz: *George F. Hirst* (Menden, Germany, 1982) [incl. discography]
M. Danzi: "Trumpeters in Berlin during the 1920s," *The Trumpet of George Hirst* (Black Jack 3013, 1983) [liner notes]

RAINER E. LOTZ

Hirt, Al(ois Maxwell) (*b* New Orleans, 7 Nov 1922). Trumpeter, bandleader, and singer, brother of Gerald Hirt. He studied classical trumpet at the Cincinnati Conservatory (1940–43), learning jazz styles from the recordings of Harry James and Roy Eldridge. After playing in swing bands, including those of Tommy and Jimmy Dorsey, he returned in the late 1940s to New Orleans, where he immersed himself in the dixieland idiom. From 1955 he led a group that included Pete Fountain, which by 1960 had gained a national following; a good example of Hirt's playing may be heard on the album *Our Man in New Orleans* (1962, RCA LPM2607). At the peak of his popularity in the mid-1960s, when he recorded his country-music hits *Java* (1963) and *Cotton Candy* (1964), Hirt was the best-known trumpeter in the USA, admired by musicians and public alike for his technique and showmanship. Later he resumed playing in a more jazz-oriented style and ran his own club in New Orleans. In 1984 he appeared in New York as the leader of a quartet.

BIBLIOGRAPHY

Feather '60s
"Hirt, Al(ois Maxwell)," *CBY 1967*
J. S. Wilson: "Al Hirt Quits Bourbon St. for the Road, Drops in on Fat Tuesday's," *New York Times* (13 July 1984), §C, 17

MICHAEL J. BUDDS/R

Hirt, Gerald (P.) [Slick] (*b* New Orleans, 29 July 1924). Trombonist, brother of Al Hirt. After playing with the New Orleans Philharmonic SO (1941–2) and in army bands (1942–6), he worked with Louis Prima (1947) and several groups in New Orleans (1948–50). He then ceased full-time performing, but in the 1960s he joined his brother's dixieland band, with which he recorded in 1965. (*Feather '60s*)

Hiseman, Jon [Philip John] (*b* London, 21 June 1944). English drummer and bandleader. He played locally while still in high school, and from the age of 18 worked semiprofessionally. His early experience was with pop and rhythm-and-blues musicians – including Graham Bond (1966), Georgie Fame, and John Mayall (1968, 1971) – but his resourcefulness enabled him to play jazz with ease. Hiseman's reputation as a jazz musician was enhanced during this period by associations with Mike Taylor, John Dankworth, Neil Ardley (including recordings with the New Jazz Orchestra, 1965 and 1968), and Howard Riley. In 1968 he established his own group, Colosseum, which became one of the seminal British jazz-rock groups. After this disbanded in 1971 Hiseman led two other ensembles, Tempest (1973–4) and Colosseum II (1975–8); he was also a founding member of the United Jazz and Rock Ensemble (1975). He then played with Paraphernalia, the band led by his wife Barbara Thompson. The album *About Time, Too!*, which he recorded as a leader in 1986, offers an excellent example of his skill and versatility.

SELECTED RECORDINGS

As leader: *About Time, Too!* (1986, TM 8)
As sideman: M. Taylor: *Pendulum* (1966, Col. 33SX6042); H. Riley: *Discussions* (1967, Opportunity 2499); Paraphernalia: *Live in Concert* (1980, MCA 309); United Jazz and Rock Ensemble: *United Live Opus Sechs* (1984, Mood 28642)

BIBLIOGRAPHY

M. C. King: "British Jazzmen, 5: Jon Hiseman," *JJ*, xxxiii/11 (1970), 39 [incl. discography]
S. Clarke: "What we Have Here, I Think, is Quite Extraordinary," *New Musical Express* (9 Aug 1975), 12
R. Cotterell, ed.: *Jazz Now: the Jazz Centre Society Guide* (London, 1976), 138
S. Goodwin: "Jon Hiseman: Interaction," *MD*, viii/4 (1984), 22

STAN BRITT

His Master's Voice [HMV]. Record label. The picture of the dog Nipper sitting by a gramophone has become one of the world's best-known trademarks; painted by Francis Barraud, it was bought by the GRAMOPHONE CO. in 1899, and first used on Victor and Monarch records in the USA. In 1910 the company began using the design on a new label, His Master's Voice, for issue in England. This rapidly became the company's most important outlet, and the name of the label superseded that of the organization, so that at an early point in its history the company became popularly known as His Master's Voice, rather than the Gramophone Co.

Some of the earliest records arguably identifiable as jazz, those made by James Reese Europe's Society Orchestra for Victor in 1913, were issued in territories other than the USA on HMV. This began a tradition that lasted until the 1950s whereby much of Victor's material was put out on various HMV labels throughout the world. An exception was Germany, where the Gramophone Co.'s subsidiary Electrola did not have the rights to the HMV trademark. Elsewhere in Europe the logo was sometimes used in conjunction with the label Gramophone; later the company began to use translations of the HMV label name – La voix de son maître (France), La voce del padrone (Italy), and La voz de su amo (Spain). Discographers have traditionally listed all non-American records bearing the dog and gramophone as HMV, irrespective of whether His Master's Voice or Gramophone (or translations thereof) appears on the label. Outside Europe important jazz was put out on

HMV in Canada in the early 1920s, and in Australia. In the 1950s the label was used for reissues of material from RCA Victor's catalogue, but this ceased when the licensing agreement between RCA and EMI was terminated in 1957. Little jazz was released on HMV in the 1960s; thereafter the label became almost exclusively devoted to classical music.

BIBLIOGRAPHY

O. Read and W. L. Welch: *From Tin Foil to Stereo: the Evolution of the Phonograph* (Indianapolis, 1959), 405, 506

L. Petts: *The Story of "Nipper" and the "His Master's Voice" Picture* (London, 1973, 2/1983)

B. Rust: *The H. M. V. Studio House Bands, 1912–1939* (Chigwell, England, 1976)

——: *The American Record Label Book* (New Rochelle, NY, 1978), 150

[P. Pelletier]: *Complete British Directory of Popular 78/45 r.p.m. Singles, 1950–1980*, i: *Columbia, Decca, H.M.V.* (London, 1986) [Record Information Services pubn]

P. Pelletier: "The HMV & MGM Labels," *Record Information*, no.6 (1986), 3

Hite, Les (*b* DuQuoin, IL, 13 Feb 1903; *d* Santa Monica, CA, 6 Feb 1962). Alto saxophonist and bandleader. He played with many bands in Los Angeles in the 1920s, including those of Mutt Carey and the drummer Curtis Mosby. In 1930 he assumed leadership of Paul Howard's Quality Serenaders. Louis Armstrong later performed with this group (1930–32), calling it his New Sebastian Cotton Club Orchestra. Although it was based on the West Coast the band occasionally held residencies in the East (1937, 1940–42) before disbanding in 1945, when Hite retired from bandleading. Later he became a partner with an important booking agency on the West Coast. Hite never became famous as an instrumentalist and his band never enjoyed popular acclaim, but he did foster many important players. His sidemen included Louis Armstrong, Lionel Hampton, Marshall Royal, Lawrence Brown, and Fats Waller (all 1930s) and Dizzy Gillespie, Britt Woodman, and Joe Wilder (all 1940s).

SELECTED RECORDINGS

As leader: T-Bone Blues (1940, Var. 8391)

As sideman: L. Armstrong: Body and Soul (1930, OK 41468); You're drivin' me crazy/The Peanut Vendor (1930, OK 41478); Just a Gigolo/Shine (1931, OK 41486)

BIBLIOGRAPHY

ChiltonW; *FeatherE*

A. McCarthy: *Big Band Jazz* (London and New York, 1974), 178

K. Stratemann: *Negro Bands on Film*, i: *Big Bands, 1928–50: an Exploratory Filmo-discography* (Lübbecke, Germany, 1981)

T. Burke and D. Penny: "Les Hite's Orchestra 'T-Bone Blues,' 1935–42," *Blues & Rhythm: the Gospel Truth*, no.9 (1985), 8

WAYNE SCHNEIDER

Hit of the Week. Record label. It was established by the Durium Products Corp. of New York in February 1930, and was used to issue records that were pressed on only one side. The discs were made of Durium, a heat-resistant synthetic resin, on a base of fiber, and were sold at low prices from newsstands. Most of the catalogue consisted of dance music, but jazz enthusiasts value recordings by Duke Ellington that were issued under the pseudonym the Harlem Hot Chocolates. After early success, the label's popularity faded rapidly, possibly because the records warped easily and, though unbreakable, were readily damaged by poor equipment or careless use. The operation was put into receivership in March 1931, and in May was sold to the Irvin–Wasey Advertising Agency, which continued to make weekly issues until June 1932.

BIBLIOGRAPHY

H. J. Waters: "The Hit-of-the-Week Record: a History and Discography," *Record Research*, no.26 (1960), 2

B. Rust: *The American Record Label Book* (New Rochelle, NY, 1978), 159

HJCA. *See* HOT JAZZ CLUB OF AMERICA.

HMV. *See* HIS MASTER'S VOICE.

Hnilička, Jaromír (*b* Bratislava, Czechoslovakia, 11 Feb 1932). Czechoslovak trumpeter, arranger, and composer. He studied trumpet at the conservatories of Brno and Bratislava and played with the Slovak Philharmonic Society. From 1956 he was a member of Gustav Brom's orchestra, with which he took part in festivals in Karlovy Vary and Prague, performed, and recorded, and for which he wrote many compositions (including *Egyptian Suite*, 1957) and arrangements. In 1965 he recorded with the trumpeter Richard Kubernat in the ČSSR All Stars. Hnilička introduced the quarter-tone trumpet in Czechoslovakia; his playing can be heard on the album *Jazz workshop ost-west* (Col. SMC83875), recorded by a group of the same name in 1965.

GERHARD CONRAD

Hodeir, André (*b* Paris, 22 Jan 1921). French composer, arranger, and writer. After studying at the Paris Conservatoire, where he received three *premiers prix*, he performed as a violinist under the pseudonym Claude Laurence with Django Reinhardt and Kenny Clarke, recording for the Swing label. After ceasing to play, in 1954 he formed the Jazz Groupe de Paris with Bobby Jaspar, the repertory of which consisted entirely of Hodeir's music; the group appeared at many festivals and remained in existence until 1969. He also taught in Paris and in 1976 at Harvard University. Hodeir's compositions include third stream works (such as *Anna Livia Plurabelle*, a setting of a passage from Joyce's *Finnegans Wake* for two singers and 23 instrumentalists) and more than 30 film scores; his work as an arranger is well represented by the album *The Kenny Clarke Sextet Plays André Hodeir* (1956, Phi. 77312). His classical training gave him a mastery of counterpoint, which he has attempted to apply in new ways to the writing of jazz works, creating intricate textures and subtle structures, within which space is left for passages of improvisation.

Hodeir was one of the pioneers of jazz criticism and from 1947 to 1950 the chief editor of the influential journal *Jazz hot*. He has written many penetrating analytical articles and a number of books, which have achieved international renown. From the 1980s he increasingly turned away from composition in order to concentrate on writing.

RECORDED COMPOSITIONS

(selective list)

As leader: *Autour d'un récif, St-Tropez* (1949, 1952, Swing 33343); *Essais* (1954, Swing 33353); *Le jazz groupe de Paris joue André Hodeir* (1956, Vega 752); *Jazz et jazz* (1963, Fon. 680208); *Anna Livia Plurabelle* (1966, Epic 64695); *Bitter Ending* (1972, Epic 80544)

WRITINGS

(selective list)

Le jazz, cet inconnu (Paris, 1945)

Introduction à la musique de jazz (Paris, 1948)

Hommes et problèmes du jazz, suivi de La religion du jazz (Paris, 1954; Eng. trans., rev. Hodeir, as *Jazz: its Evolution and Essence*, New York, 1956/*R*1975)

Toward Jazz (New York, 1962/*R*1976)

Les mondes du jazz (Paris, 1970; Eng. trans., New York, 1972)

BIBLIOGRAPHY

W. Otey: "Hodeir through his Own Glass," *Jazz: a Quarterly of American Music*, no.2 (1959), 105

L. Malson: "Le jazz en France: André Hodeir ou la recherche d'une esthétique," *Jm*, no.64 (1960), 30

H. Woodfin: "The Exercises of André Hodeir," *JM*, x/12 (1965), 26

C. Bellest: "Anna Livia Plurabelle," *Jh*, no.280 (1972), 26

ANDRÉ CLERGEAT

Hodes, Art(hur W.) (*b* Nikoliev, Ukraine [now Nikolayev, Ukrainian SSR], 14 Nov 1904). Pianist, broadcaster, and writer. His family moved to Chicago when he was six months old. He began his career there as a soloist at the Rainbow Café, then toured with the Wolverines (1926). After returning to Chicago he joined Wingy Manone, with whom he made his first recording (1928); he continued to work mainly in Chicago in the 1930s, then in 1938 moved to New York, where he played with Joe Marsala (1939) and Mezz Mezzrow (1940), and formed his own band (1941). He did much to encourage a new public awareness of earlier jazz styles and musicians: he presented a weekly radio program for WNYC, founded his own record label, Jazz Record, and edited an excellent magazine of the same title (1943–7), extracts from which, edited by Hodes and Chadwick Hansen, were published as *Selections from the Gutter: Jazz Portraits from "The Jazz Record"* (Berkeley, CA, Los Angeles, and London, 1977). During this period he recorded with Sidney Bechet (1945–9) and led various small groups in and around New York. In 1950 he moved back to Chicago and throughout the next decade toured the Midwest from there. He was the host of a television series "Jazz Alley," contributed to *Down Beat* (mid-1960s), and taught at the Park Forest (Illinois) Conservatory. Later he toured Denmark (1970), the USA (with Eddie Condon, 1971), and Europe (1977, 1980), but from the 1970s he worked mainly as a leader and unaccompanied soloist. His individual style is based on a deep love and understanding of the music of earlier stride and blues players.

Oral history material in *NjR* (JOHP).

Johnny Hodges playing with Duke Ellington's orchestra, New York, 1940

SELECTED RECORDINGS

As unaccompanied soloist: *Art Hodes: South Side Memories* (1983, Sack. 3032)
Duos: with Truck Parham: *Plain Old Blues* (1962, EmA 26005); with M. Yancey: *Mama Yancey Sings, Art Hodes Plays Blues* (1965, Verve 9015)
As leader: KMH Drag (1945, BN 51)

BIBLIOGRAPHY

FeatherE; *Feather '60s*; *Feather–Gitler '70s*
D. Curran: "Art Hodes," *Jazz*, new ser., i/2 (New York, 1945), 3
A. Hodes: "From Twenty Years Ago," *Sv*, no.3 (1966), 2 [autobiography]
G. Endress: "Art Hodes," *Jazz Podium: Musiker über sich selbst* (Stuttgart, Germany, 1980), 8
S. Freedman: "Hodes' Blues: Still Art after All these Years," *DB*, xlix/6 (1982), 23 [incl. discography]
D. J. Travis: *An Autobiography of Black Jazz* (Chicago, 1983), 381 [incl. interviews]
Liner notes, *Art Hodes: South Side Memories* (Sack. 3032, 1984)
R. Morris: "Feeling the Blues," *MR*, xi/8 (1984), 8
R. Horricks: "Custodian of the Blues," *JJI*, xxxviii/12 (1985), 14

MIKE HAZELDINE

Hodges, Johnny [Hodge, John(ny); Hodge, Cornelius; Jeep; Rabbit] (*b* Cambridge, MA, 25 July 1907; *d* New York, 11 May 1970). Alto and soprano saxophonist. He played drums and piano before taking up saxophone at about the age of 14, beginning on the soprano and later specializing on the alto instrument. Originally self-taught, he later received some instruction from Sidney Bechet. During the 1920s Boston served as his base, but on weekends he traveled to New York, where he played with Bobby Sawyer, the drummer Lloyd Scott, Chick Webb, and Luckey Roberts, succeeded Bechet in Willie "the Lion" Smith's quartet at the Rhythm Club (around 1924), and performed with Bechet at the Club Basha in Harlem (1925).

In May 1928 Hodges joined Duke Ellington's orchestra, and he remained a mainstay of this group for the next 40 years. From his first recording session with Ellington in 1928 he revealed considerable authority and technical mastery, playing with a broad, sweeping tone and producing impressive florid runs; in the opinion of many, he soon became Ellington's most valuable soloist. Besides making hundreds of recordings with Ellington's orchestra, from 1937 he also led a small studio group drawn from the band, usually consisting of seven pieces, which made its own commercially successful series of recordings; these included such masterpieces as *Jeep's Blues*, *Hodge Podge*, *The Jeep is Jumpin'*, and *Wanderlust*, all of which were written by Hodges in collaboration with Ellington. During this time he was much in demand by other musicians, taking part in classic sessions led by Lionel Hampton and by Teddy Wilson, and performing on alto and soprano saxophone at Benny Goodman's concert at Carnegie Hall in 1938.

By 1941 Hodges was becoming best known for his earthy blues playing and for his sensuous ballad interpretations, opposing sides of his art exemplified by two recordings made in that year, *Things ain't what they used to be* and *Passion Flower*. From this time on he concentrated exclusively on alto saxophone, on which instrument he regularly won the popularity polls in *Down Beat*, *Metronome*, and *Esquire* magazines. He also collaborated on Ellington's best-selling song *I'm beginning to see the light* (1944).

In March 1951 Hodges left Ellington to form his own small band, along with his fellow sidemen Lawrence Brown and Sonny Greer. The group's first recording session in that year produced a hit record, *Castle Rock*. Hodges disbanded his group in spring 1955 and rejoined Ellington's orchestra in August of that year; apart from a few brief periods he stayed with Ellington for the remainder of his life. He worked with Ellington's close associate Billy Strayhorn in spring 1958, and in 1961 toured Europe with other band members as the Ellington Giants.

He continued to record in a variety of contexts under his own name, issuing a series of albums with Wild Bill Davis, two with Earl Hines, and even one with the dance-band leader Lawrence Welk. Ellington and Strayhorn continued to write arrangements, such as the lush *Isfahan* movement from the *Far East Suite*, to display Hodges's unique talents. A collection of Hodges's own compositions was published as *Sax Originals* (New York, 1945, 2/1972).

Hodges won the admiration of generations of saxophonists for his exceptional command of the sound and expressive nuances possible on his instrument. Ben Webster learned much from Hodges when he played in Ellington's saxophone section around 1940, and even John Coltrane, who appeared in Hodges's small group in 1953–4, listed Hodges among his favorite players. In his later years Hodges used fewer and fewer notes, remaining close to the melody in ballad performances and improvising relatively simple riffs on a blues. The power of his playing derived from the majesty of his sound, his endless vocabulary of expressive ornaments, and the soulfulness of his melodic ideas. He generated a great deal of swing in these numbers, and built effectively from one chorus to the next. He is usually ranked with Benny Carter and Willie Smith among the outstanding alto saxophonists of the swing period (*see* SAXOPHONE, §3).

SELECTED RECORDINGS

As leader: Jeep's Blues (1938, Voc./OK 4115); The Jeep is Jumpin' (1938, Voc./OK 4386); Hodge Podge/Wanderlust (1938, Voc./OK 4573); Passion Flower (1941, Bb 300817); Things ain't what they used to be (1941, Bb 11447); Castle Rock (1951, Clef 8944); *Back to Back* (1959, Verve 8317); *Side by Side* (1959, Verve 8345)

As sideman with D. Ellington: Yellow Dog Blues/Tishomingo Blues (1928, Bruns. 3987); Ring dem bells (1930, Vic. 23022); It don't mean a thing (1932, Bruns. 6265); The Gal from Joe's/I let a song go out of my heart (1938, Bruns. 8108); Warm Valley (1940, Vic. 26796); Come Sunday (1944, Vic. 280401); I'm beginning to see the light (1944, Vic. 201618); *Ella and Duke on the Cote d'Azur* (1966, Verve 64072), incl. The Old Circus Train Turn-around Blues; *Far East Suite* (1966, RCA LSP3782), incl. Isfahan

As sideman with others: L. Hampton: On the Sunny Side of the Street (1937, Vic. 25592); B. Goodman: on *Carnegie Hall Concert* (1938, Col. SL160), Blue Reverie

BIBLIOGRAPHY

B. James: "Johnny Hodges," *JM*, v/1 (1959), 7

——: *Essays on Jazz* (London, 1961/R1985), 144

M. Jones: "The Time I Played with King Oliver," *MM*, xxxix (29 Feb 1964), 6

L. Tomkins: "Too Late for me to Change," *Crescendo*, ii/8 (1964), 16 [interview]

H. Whiston: "Johnny Hodges," *JJ*, xix/1 (1966), 8 [interview]

S. Dance: *The World of Duke Ellington* (London and New York, 1970/R1981) [colln of previously pubd articles and interviews], 91

D. Ioakimidis: "Johnny Hodges," *Jh*, no.263 (1970), 32; no.264 (1970), 20

B. James: "Johnny Hodges on Record," *JJ*, xxiii/12 (1970), 18

D. Ellington: *Music is my Mistress* (Garden City, NY, 1973), 116

D. Jewell: *Duke: a Portrait of Duke Ellington* (London and New York, 1977, 2/1978)

S. Dance: Liner notes, *Johnny Hodges* (TL J19, 1981)

——: "Layin' on Mellow à propos de Johnny Hodges," *BHcF*, no.318 (1984), 1

LEWIS PORTER

Hoefer, George (*b* Laramie, WY, 1909; *d* Brielle, nr Spring Lake, NJ, 19 Nov 1967). Writer. He graduated from the University of North Carolina, Chapel Hill, with a degree in engineering (1930), moved to Illinois, and from 1935 until the end of World War II worked as an engineer in Chicago. He took a great interest in jazz recordings and from 1935 to the 1960s contributed a column entitled "The Hot Box" to *Down Beat*; this contained important discographical and biographical material on jazz musicians. In the mid-1940s he also wrote for *Esquire's Jazz Book*. Hoefer moved in 1951 to New York, where he wrote for the periodicals *Metronome*, *Jazz*, and *Melody Maker*, and from 1958 to 1961 was an editor of *Down Beat*. His writings are notable for their accuracy and unusual attention to detail.

WRITINGS

(selective list)

"Bix Beiderbecke," "Bessie Smith," *The Jazz Makers*, ed. N. Shapiro and N. Hentoff (New York, 1957/R1979 as *The Jazz Makers: Essays on the Greats of Jazz*), 90, 127

with W. Smith: *Music on my Mind: the Memoirs of an American Pianist* (Garden City, NY, 1964/R1975)

DANIEL ZAGER

Hoffman, Ingfried (*b* Stettin, Germany [now Szczecin, Poland], 30 Jan 1935). German pianist and organist. His principal association was with Klaus Doldinger, with whom he toured and recorded from 1963 to 1969. He also made recordings as a leader (*From Twen with Love*, 1966, Phi. 843779) and with Karin Krog (1967), Lucky Thompson (1969), and Rolf Kühn (*Sextet*, 1971, Intercord 71208), and participated in several German jazz festivals and workshops. (*Feather '60s*)

Hogan, G(ranville) T(heodore, Jr.) (*b* Galveston, TX, 16 Jan 1929). Drummer. After playing tenor saxophone in high school he took up drumming, and gained early experience with rhythm-and-blues bands, most notably that of Earl Bostic (1953–5). He moved in 1955 to New York, where he worked with Randy Weston; he also recorded with Kenny Drew and Kenny Dorham. Thereafter he was briefly associated with Charles Mingus, and in 1959 he visited Paris, where he played with Bud Powell. In the early 1960s he worked with Walter Bishop, Jr., and Elmo Hope (1963), and recorded again with Weston. He later returned to Texas, where he became relatively inactive as a musician. Hogan's style was unobtrusive and unelaborate. A dependable timekeeper, he was equally adept with sticks or brushes. His playing was modeled on that of Kenny Clarke, Max Roach, and Philly Joe Jones. His recorded work with Weston, Hope, Drew, and Bishop is especially noteworthy. Hogan should not be confused with the drummer Wilbur (Wilbert) Hogan (*d* New York, 1967), who also worked with Weston and toured with Lionel Hampton in 1956–8.

SELECTED RECORDINGS

As sideman: E. Bostic: *Altotude* (1955–6, King 515); K. Drew: *This is New* (1957, Riv. 236); K. Dorham: *Two Horns/Two Rhythm* (1957, Riv. 255); R. Weston: *New Faces at Newport* (1958, Metro. 1005); *Uhuru Afrika* (1960, Roul. 65001); W. Bishop, Jr.: *Speak Low* (1961, Jazztime 002); *Walter Bishop Trio* (1962, Opus 3001); E. Hope: *High Hope!* (1963, Beacon 401)

BIBLIOGRAPHY

FeatherE

L. Feather: Liner notes, *New Faces at Newport* (Metro. 1005, ?1959)

MARK GARDNER

Hogg, Derek (*b* Oldham, England, 8 April 1928). English drummer. After training in show bands he worked with various musicians, among them Freddy Randall (1953), Don Rendell (1954), and Sandy Brown and Kenny Baker (1958); he also played with the Fairweather–Brown All Stars led by Brown and Al Fairweather (1959) and with the Squadronaires (1960). In 1960 he toured the USA with Vic Lewis's orchestra and in 1961 he performed in the revue *Beyond the Fringe* as a member of Dudley Moore's trio. From 1962 to 1987 Hogg played in a quartet led by Danny Moss; he also toured Great Britain with Rosemary Clooney (1963), Budd Johnson (1966), and Teddy Wilson (1974). In 1977 he performed at the Pizza Express, London, with Dave McKenna, Sir Charles Thompson, and Joe Albany. From 1979 he played frequently and made recordings with Moss's quartet (including *Straighten Up and Fly Right*,

1979, Flyright 209); he also worked as a teacher and freelance musician before retiring in 1987.

DIGBY FAIRWEATHER

Hoggard, Jay (*b* New York, 24 Sept 1954). Vibraphonist. He first studied piano and saxophone, but in the late 1960s abandoned these in favor of the vibraphone, which he studied with Lynn Oliver. He entered Wesleyan University as a philosophy student, transferred to the ethnomusicology department, and toured Europe in 1973 with Jimmy Garrison and Clifford Thornton, who were members of the faculty at Wesleyan. He joined a group at Yale that included Anthony Davis, Leo Smith, and Pheeroan Ak Laff, and during a summer of study in Tanzania learned to play the balo, a West African xylophone. After graduating from Wesleyan he taught at the Educational Center for the Arts in New Haven. He moved to New York in mid-1977 and in the autumn recorded with Chico Freeman. *A Solo Vibes Concert* was recorded at the Public Theater in 1978 and a more commercially oriented album, *Days like these*, made with his group in 1979. He has continued to lead his own groups and has played with Davis, Sam Rivers, Cecil Taylor, James Newton, and others. Hoggard has added an ethnomusicological perspective to the groups with which he has worked.

SELECTED RECORDINGS

As unaccompanied soloist: *A Solo Vibes Concert* (1978, IndN 1040)

As leader: *Days like these* (1979, Ari. 5004); *Rain Forest* (1980, Cont. 14007); *Mystic Winds, Tropic Breezes* (1981, IndN 1049)

As sideman: C. Freeman: *Kings of Mali* (1977, IndN 1035); A. Davis: *Under the Double Moon* (1980, Pausa 7120); J. Newton: *Luella* (1983, Gram. 8304)

BIBLIOGRAPHY

L. Jeske: "Jay Hoggard: Banking on the Vibes," *DB*, xlix/12 (1982), 26 [incl. discography]

DAVID WILD

Hohenberger, Kurt (*b* nr Stuttgart, Germany, *c*1908; *d* Kernen-Stetten, nr Stuttgart, 15 July 1979). German trumpeter. In Berlin he played in broadcasts and recorded with the Goldene Sieben (1934–9), and performed regularly with Oscar Joost. As a freelance player, his concert, club, dance, and studio work included recordings with Peter Kreuder (1936–9), Peter Igelhoff (1936–42), Teddy Stauffer (1937), Willy Berking (1939–41), and Bimbo Weiland (1939–43). His own group was resident at the Quartier Latin from 1937 to 1943; a good example of its recordings is *Jammin'* (1937, Tel. A2416). After military service he organized a new swing band with which he made recordings from 1947 to 1949 (including *String of Pearls*, 1947, Amiga 1118). Having spent some time in Brazil (1949–51), he returned to Germany and again made recordings as a leader (1953–5). He retired from music in the late 1950s. (Obituary, *JP*, no.9 (1979), 28)

RAINER E. LOTZ

Hokum. A term used in the world of entertainment for any kind of stage trick, routine, or "business" intended to deceive or amuse the audience. From the theater it passed to minstrel and medicine shows, circuses, and other traveling entertainments, and to black music and jazz. In musical contexts the word was used of faking or improvisation that gave the illusion of reading music, and to effects that appeared difficult, or which pleased the crowd, such as performing on a trumpet mouthpiece alone or adopting comic or absurd playing techniques; humorous spoken routines and songs were also described as hokum. Jazz entertainers such as Ted Lewis and Boyd Senter, who cultivated comic instrumental effects and exaggerated styles of presentation, may be regarded as hokum performers; much of the appeal of the Original Dixieland Jazz Band when it first played in New York was attributable to the element of hokum in its performances.

PAUL OLIVER

Holder, Terrence (*b c*1898). Trumpeter and bandleader. He first came to prominence as a principal soloist with Alphonso

Billie Holiday with Lester Young (right) and Sonny White at the Golden Gate Ballroom in Harlem, New York, 1940

Trent (1922–5). In 1926 he formed the Dark Clouds of Joy, which included Andy Kirk and Don Byas. Although it made no recordings, it was a successful territory band. When Holder left the group suddenly in 1929 owing to domestic and financial troubles, Kirk assumed leadership and Holder began leading another band, also called the Dark Clouds of Joy. It was very well known in the early 1930s; among its sidemen were the brothers Keg and Budd Johnson, Jesse Stone, and Herschel Evans (all 1929), Earl Bostic (1930–32), Carl Smith (1931), Lloyd Glenn (1931–2), and Buddy Tate (1930–33). It disbanded during the Depression and in the late 1930s Holder led a small group. He later worked as a freelance musician in Montana (1940s) and performed with Nat Towles (early 1950s).

BIBLIOGRAPHY

F. S. Driggs: "Kansas City and the Southwest," *Jazz: New Perspectives on the History of Jazz by Twelve of the World's Foremost Jazz Critics and Scholars*, ed. N. Hentoff and A. J. McCarthy (New York and Toronto, 1959/*R*1974), 189

R. Russell: *Jazz Style in Kansas City and the Southwest* (Berkeley, CA, Los Angeles, and London, 1971/*R*1983, rev. 2/1973)

A. McCarthy: *Big Band Jazz* (New York and London, 1974), 102

EDDIE LAMBERT

Holdsworth, Allan (*b* Bradford, England, 6 Aug 1948). English electric guitarist. He first came to prominence in the early 1970s with the group Soft Machine. After leaving in 1975 he joined Tony Williams's Lifetime, with which he recorded two albums. In the late 1970s he worked with the avant-garde rock bands Gong and UK, and also performed and recorded with the Spontaneous Music Ensemble (1977) and Jean-Luc Ponty. Much of Holdsworth's most memorable work dates from the early 1980s, when he performed and recorded as the leader of his own group, IOU. In the mid-1980s he began using a guitar synthesizer, the SynthAxe. Although a good deal of Holdsworth's playing is oriented towards rock his sophisticated approach to melody and harmony and his formidable technique are essentially rooted in jazz. His single-line improvisations are often reminiscent of John Coltrane's sheets of sound.

SELECTED RECORDINGS

As leader: *Velvet Darkness* (1977, CTI 6068); of IOU: *Road Games* (1983, WB 23959), *Metal Fatigue* (1984, Enigma 74002); *Atavchron* (1985, Enigma 72064)

As sideman: Soft Machine: *Bundles* (1974, Harvest 4044); T. Williams: *Million Dollar Legs* (1976, Col. PC34263); J.-L. Ponty: *Enigmatic Ocean* (1977, Atl. 19110)

BIBLIOGRAPHY

B. Milkowski: "Allan Holdsworth's New Horizons," *DB*, lii/11 (1985), 19 [incl. discography]

T. Mulhern: "Allan Holdsworth, Lee Ritenour: SynthAxe," *GP*, xx/6 (1986), 109

JIM FERGUSON

Holiday, Billie [Fagan, Eleanora; Lady Day] (*b* Baltimore, 7 April 1915; *d* New York, 17 July 1959). Singer, daughter of Clarence Holiday. Her early life is obscure, as the account given in her autobiography, *Lady Sings the Blues*, is self-serving and inaccurate. Her father abandoned the family early, and refused to acknowledge his daughter until after her first success. At some point in her childhood her mother moved to New York, leaving her in the care of her relatives who, according to Holiday, mistreated her. She did menial work, had little schooling, and in 1928 went to New York to join her mother. Again according to her own story she was recruited for a brothel, and was eventually jailed briefly for prostitution. At some point after 1930 she began singing at a small club in Brooklyn, and in a year or so moved to Pods' and Jerry's, a Harlem club well known to jazz enthusiasts. In 1933 she was working in another Harlem club, Monette's, where she was discovered by the producer and talent scout John Hammond. Hammond immediately arranged three recording sessions for her with Benny Goodman and found engagements for her in New York clubs. In 1935 he began recording her regularly, usually under the direction of Teddy Wilson, with studio bands that included many of the finest jazz musicians of the day. These recordings, made between 1935 and 1942, constitute a major body of jazz music; many include work by Lester Young, with whom Holiday had particular empathy. Though aimed mainly at the black jukebox audience, the recordings caught the attention of musicians throughout the USA, and soon other singers were working in Holiday's light, rhythmic manner.

Popularity with a wider audience came more slowly. Holiday joined Count Basie in 1937 and Artie Shaw in 1938, becoming one of the first black singers to be featured with a white orchestra. Then, in 1939, she began an engagement at Café Society (Downtown), an interracial nightclub in Greenwich Village which quickly became fashionable with intellectuals and the *haut monde*, especially those on the political left. At about the same time she recorded for Commodore a song about the lynching of Blacks called *Strange Fruit*; it was admired by intellectuals, and very quickly Holiday began to acquire a popular following. She started to have success with slow, melancholy songs of unrequited love, particularly *Gloomy Sunday* (1941), a suicide song, and *Lover Man* (1944). By the end of the 1940s she was a popular star, and in 1946 took part in the film *New Orleans* with Louis Armstrong and Kid Ory (*see* FILMS, §I, 4(ii)).

At the same time Holiday's private life was deteriorating. She started using hard drugs in the early 1940s and was jailed on drug charges in 1947 after a highly publicized trial. She compulsively attached herself to men who mistreated her, and she began drinking heavily. Her health suffered; she lost most of her by then substantial earnings, and her voice coarsened through age and mistreatment. Although she continued to sing and record, and to tour frequently until the mid-1950s, it was no longer with her former spirit and skill.

Holiday is often considered the foremost female singer in jazz history, a view substantiated by her influence on later singers. Her important work is found in the group recordings made, mostly for Hammond, between 1936 and 1944. Her vehicles were mainly popular love songs, some of them long forgotten, others among the best of the time. Her voice was light and untrained, but she had a fine natural ear to compensate for her lack of musical education. She always acknowledged her debt to Armstrong for her singing style, and it is certainly in emulation of him that she detached her melody line from the ground beat, stretching or condensing the figures of the melody, as on the opening of *Did I remember?* (1936). More than nearly any other singer, Holiday phrased her performances in the manner of a jazz instrumental soloist, and accordingly she has to be seen as a complete jazz musician and not merely a singer. Nevertheless her voice, even in the light and lively numbers she often sang during her early period, carried a wounded poignancy which was part of her attraction for general audiences. Although Holiday claimed also to have taken Bessie Smith as her model, she sang few blues, and none in the powerful, weighted manner of Smith. She was, however, a master of blues singing, as for example on *Fine and Mellow* (1939), which she built around blue thirds descending to seconds to create an endless tension perfectly suited to the forlorn text.

SELECTED RECORDINGS

Did I remember?/No Regrets (1936, Voc./OK 3276); Billie's Blues (1936, Voc./OK 3288); Strange Fruit/Fine and Mellow (1939, Com. 526); Loveless Love (1940, OK 6064); God bless the child (1941, OK 6270); Gloomy Sunday (1941, OK 6451); Lover Man (1944, Decca 23391)

BIBLIOGRAPHY

B. Holiday and W. Dufty: *Lady Sings the Blues* (Garden City, NY, 1956/ *R*1973, 1984; Ger. trans., Hamburg, Germany, 1983) [incl. discography]
B. James: "Billie Holiday and the Art of Communication," *JM*, v/6 (1959), 9
——: *Essays on Jazz* (London, 1961/*R*1985), 45
B. Green: *The Reluctant Art: Five Studies in the Growth of Jazz* (London, 1962), 119
A. Hodeir: *Toward Jazz* (New York, 1962/*R*1976), 191
M. Williams: "Billie Holiday: Actress without an Act," *JJ*, xxi/10 (1968), 22
——: *The Jazz Tradition* (New York, 1970, rev. 2/1983)
R. Blesh: "Lady Day," *Combo, USA: Eight Lives in Jazz* (Philadelphia and London, 1971)
L. Kuehl and E. Schokert: *Billie Holiday Remembered* (New York, 1973)
S. Dance: *The World of Swing* (New York, 1974) [colln of previously pubd interviews]
D. M. Bakker: *Billie & Teddy on Microgroove, 1932–1944* (Alphen aan de Rijn, Netherlands, 1975)
J. Chilton: *Billie's Blues: a Survey of Billie Holiday's Career, 1933–1959* (London, 1975) [incl. discography]
J. L. Collier: *The Making of Jazz: a Comprehensive History* (New York and London, 1978)
J. Millar: *Born to Sing: a Discography of Billie Holiday* (Copenhagen, n.d. [?1979])
B. James: *Billie Holiday* (Tunbridge Wells, England, 1984)
M. Jones: "The Trouble with Billie," *The Wire*, no.7 (1984), 6
D. Widgery: "Billie Holiday: the Woman who Moved the World," *The Wire*, no.7 (1984), 2
A. Yamato: "Billie Holiday: the Verve Years, 1946–1959," "A Discography of Billie Holiday," *Billie Holiday on Verve, 1946–1959* (Verve 00MJ3480–89, 1985) [liner notes]
J. White: *Billie Holiday* (Tunbridge Wells, England, and New York, 1987) [incl. discography]

JAMES LINCOLN COLLIER

Holiday, Clarence (E.) (*b* Baltimore, *c*1900; *d* Dallas, 1 March 1937). Guitarist, father of Billie Holiday. From 1928 to 1933 he was a member of Fletcher Henderson's orchestra (for illustration *see* HENDERSON, FLETCHER). He then recorded with Benny Carter (1934) and Bob Howard (1935), and his fine rhythm guitar playing may be heard to advantage on Howard's *Whisper Sweet* (1935, Decca 347). After working with Charlie Turner (1935) and Louis Metcalf (1935–6) Holiday performed and recorded with Don Redman (1936–7). (W. C. Allen: *Hendersonia: the Music of Fletcher Henderson and his Musicians: a Bio-discography*, Highland Park, NJ, 1973)

Holland, Dave [David] (*b* Wolverhampton, England, 1 Oct 1946). English double bass player. He began playing double bass in 1963, and in 1964–8 attended the Guildhall School of Music and Drama, London; during this period he performed with John Surman, Chris McGregor, Humphrey Lyttelton, Evan Parker, Tubby Hayes, Ronnie Scott, Kenny Wheeler (recording in 1968), and the Spontaneous Music Ensemble. He then went to the USA with Miles Davis and worked with him until 1970. In 1970–71 he was a member of Chick Corea's free-jazz group Circle with Barry Altschul and Anthony Braxton; while continuing to work with Braxton (until 1976; for illustration *see* BRAXTON, ANTHONY), he also performed with Stan Getz (1973–5) and in John Abercrombie's trio Gateway with Jack DeJohnette (1975–7). He played regularly with Sam Rivers in 1976–80. After a brief illness he formed his own group in 1982; its members have included Wheeler, the saxophonist Steve Coleman, the drummer Marvin "Smitty" Smith, and the trombonists Robin Eubanks and Julian Priester. Holland also performed and recorded with Karl Berger (1970–76), Joe Henderson (1972), Paul Bley (1972–3), and Lee Konitz (1974), again with Wheeler (1975, 1977, 1983) and Altschul (1977), and with Kenny Barron (1985). As an unaccompanied soloist he has performed and recorded on double bass and cello (from 1977). He also plays bass guitar. In the 1980s he was increasingly active as a teacher; from 1982 he taught on the summer program at the Banff Centre School of Fine Arts, Canada, and in 1987 he joined the faculty of the New England Conservatory.

In whatever setting he performs, Holland can play with lightning speed, rhythmic precision, and perfect intonation. His solos are marked by a clear, clean, rounded tone and by thoughtful control and development of ideas. His style and dexterity put him on a level with Scott LaFaro and Gary Peacock.

SELECTED RECORDINGS

As unaccompanied soloist: *Emerald Tears* (1977, ECM 1109)
Duos with S. Rivers: *Dave Holland, Sam Rivers* (1976, ImA 373843)
As leader: *Conference of the Birds* (1972, ECM 1027); *Seeds of Time* (1984, ECM 1292)
As sideman: Spontaneous Music Ensemble: *Karyöbin* (1968, Isl. 9079); M. Davis: *Filles de Kilimanjaro* (1968, Col. CS9750); *Bitches Brew* (1969, Col. GP26); A. Braxton: *The Complete Braxton* (1971, Fre. 40112–13); Circle: *Paris Concert* (1971, ECM 1018–19); A. Braxton: *The Montreux–Berlin Concerts* (1975–6, Ari. 5002); S. Rivers: *Contrasts* (1979, ECM 1162)

BIBLIOGRAPHY

B. Primack: "Dave Holland: Diverse and Dedicated," *DB*, xlv/10 (1978), 18 [incl. discography]
E. Jost: *Jazzmusiker: Materialen zur Soziologie der afro-amerikanischen Musik* (Frankfurt am Main, Germany, Berlin, and Vienna, 1981), 134
C. Wright and M. Gilbert: "Dave Holland," *JJI*, xxxix/1 (1986), 16 [incl. discography]

ED HAZELL

Holland, Peanuts [Herbert Lee] (*b* Norfolk, VA, 9 Feb 1910; *d* Stockholm, 7 Feb 1979). Trumpeter and singer. He learned trumpet while at the Jenkins' Orphanage in Charleston, South Carolina. From 1928 to 1933 he played mainly with Alphonso Trent, though he also worked with Al Sears (1932). He then led his own bands (1933–8) and made brief appearances with Willie Bryant, Jimmie Lunceford, and Lil Armstrong. After playing with Coleman Hawkins (1941), Fletcher Henderson (1941–2), and Charlie Barnet (1942–6; for illustration *see* PETTIFORD, OSCAR) he again led his own band (1946). Late in 1946 he went with Don Redman's orchestra to Europe, where he led his own groups and made concert appearances until his health failed in the early 1970s. Holland became highly regarded as a member of Trent's band. Although he was initially influenced by Louis Armstrong, he developed from a player with a slippery, rough-edged technique into a musician with an original voice; his later work with Barnet, however, was more conservative. A good example of his solo style may be heard on Trent's *I found a new baby*.

SELECTED RECORDINGS

As sideman: A. Trent: Clementine/I found a new baby (1933, Champion 6587); C. Barnet: I like to riff (1942, Decca 18378); Oh! Miss Jaxon/Washington Whirligig (1942, Decca 18547)

BIBLIOGRAPHY

ChiltonW
G. Schuller: *Early Jazz: its Roots and Musical Development* (New York, 1968), 302
R. Russell: *Jazz Style in Kansas City and the Southwest* (Berkeley, CA, Los Angeles, and London, 1971/*R*1983, rev. 2/1973)
J. Chilton: *A Jazz Nursery: the Story of the Jenkins' Orphanage Bands of Charleston, South Carolina* (London, 1980), 28

FRANK DRIGGS

Höllerhagen, Ernst (*b* Barmen [now Wuppertal], Germany, 5 Oct 1912; *d* Interlaken, Switzerland, 11 July 1956). German clarinetist and alto saxophonist. He studied violin as a youth and made his professional début at the age of 18 on alto saxophone with Sam Wooding's band (1930). He played and recorded with the violinist Juan Llossas (1933), Jack Hylton, Coleman Hawkins and the Berry's (1936), the vibraphonist Kurt Engel (1936), Kurt Hohenberger (1937), the GOLDENE SIEBEN (1936–9), Teddy Stauffer (1936–41), Eddie Brunner (1940–48), Willie Lewis (1941), and Philippe Brun (1942–4). He led his own groups from 1942 to 1948, and in 1947 joined Hazy Osterwald and toured Europe and the Middle East. Höllerhagen was influenced by Benny Goodman and later by Tony Scott and Buddy DeFranco.

SELECTED RECORDINGS

As leader: Get Happy/Louis XV (1947, ES 4651)

As sideman: K. Hohenberger: Jammin' (1937, Tel. A2416); Goldene Sieben: Crazy Jacob (1937, Elec. EG6186); T. Stauffer: Big Apple (1938, Tel. A2566); Original Teddies Saxophone Quartet: Möni Stomp (1941, ES 4075); W. Lewis: Lover come back to me (1941, ES 4070); P. Brun: Blue Party (1942, ES 4149)

BIBLIOGRAPHY

W. Muth: *Ernst Höllerhagen: ein deutscher Jazzmusiker* (Magdeburg, Germany, n.d. [1964])

J. Schütte and A. Stöcklin: *Teddy Stauffer: Discographie der Original Teddies (Teddy Stauffer und Eddie Brunner) und der kleinen Formationen mit Musikern der Teddies* (Menden, Germany, 1983)

RAINER E. LOTZ

Holley, Major (Quincy, Jr.) [Mule] (*b* Detroit, 10 July 1924). Double bass player. He first played violin and tuba, and took up double bass while playing in navy bands, where he also acquired his nickname (Clark Terry referred to him, when he was carrying both his instruments, as a pack mule). After he was discharged Holley played with Dexter Gordon, Charlie Parker, and Ella Fitzgerald, and in 1950 made his first recordings, in a duo with Oscar Peterson. In the mid-1950s he went to London to work as a studio musician for BBC television. He joined Woody Herman's orchestra for a tour of South America (1958), then returned to the USA and played with the group led by Al Cohn and Zoot Sims (1959–60). He became well known during the early 1960s for his studio work, but also performed with such jazz musicians as Kenny Burrell, Coleman Hawkins, and Duke Ellington. After teaching at the Berklee College of Music (1967–70) Holley continued to work as a freelance in clubs in New York. He made several tours of Europe with Helen Humes and with the Kings of Jazz, and recorded with Roy Eldridge, Lee Konitz (1975), and Roland Hanna (1979). He has also appeared at numerous European festivals in the 1980s. When playing a solo with the bow, Holley often sings in octave unison (in the manner of Slam Stewart); although such vocal excursions are usually rough-toned and wordless, he uses lyrics to great humorous effect on *Razzle Dazzle*, recorded with Konitz in 1975.

SELECTED RECORDINGS

Duos with O. Peterson: Robbins Nest/Exactly like you (1950, Clef 8930)

As leader: *Mule!* (1974, BB 33074)

As sideman: W. Herman: *Woody Herman* (1958, Ev. 5010); T. Wilson: *And Then They Wrote* (1959, Col. CS8238); A. Cohn and Z. Sims: *You 'n Me* (1960, Mer. 60606); C. Hawkins: *Today and Now* (1962, Imp. 34); L. Konitz: *Chicago 'n all that Jazz* (1975, GM 3306), incl. Me an' my baby, Razzle Dazzle

BIBLIOGRAPHY

FeatherE; *Feather '60s*; *Feather–Gitler '70s*

J.-P. Battestini: "Major Holley," *BHcF*, no.244 (1975), 6 [interview]

"Major Holley," *CI*, xviii (1980), no.7, p.18; no.9, p.12

M. Richards: "Major Holley," *JJI*, xl/4 (1987), 6

LAWRENCE KOCH

Hollywood. Record label. It was established in California in the mid-1920s, and is best remembered for having been used to issue material by Harvey Brooks and the saxophonist Reb Spikes (1924) and the first recordings by Fred Elizalde (1926). Issues seem to have ceased around 1927. (B. Rust: *The American Record Label Book* (New Rochelle, NY, 1978), 161)

Holman, Bill [Willis Leonard] (*b* Olive, nr Orange, CA, 21 May 1927). Composer, arranger, and tenor saxophonist. He studied music at Westlake College (1948–51), and played with Charlie Barnet (1950–51), Stan Kenton (1952–6; for illustration *see* KENTON, STAN), and Shorty Rogers (from 1956); he also wrote compositions for Maynard Ferguson's big band and led a hard-bop quintet with Mel Lewis in 1958. He wrote arrangements for the Gerry Mulligan Concert Jazz Band (1960), Kenton (from 1961), and Woody Herman (from 1963). In 1966 he ceased playing saxophone to devote his time wholly to composing and arranging; as a freelance he wrote arrangements for a number of television series and for Kenton, Buddy Rich, Peggy Lee, Ed Shaughnessy, and Sarah Vaughan. From the mid-1970s he led a big band in the Los Angeles area and worked as a producer for Westdeutscher Rundfunk, Cologne, Germany, with Mel Lewis, Mark Murphy, and Phil Woods. His saxophone playing can be heard on two albums he recorded as a leader, *Big Band in a Jazz Orbit* (1958, Andex 3004) and *Bill Holman's Great Big Band* (1960, Cap. T1464).

RECORDED COMPOSITIONS

(selective list; recorded by S. Kenton)

on *The Kenton Era* (1940–54, Cap. WDX569), Zoot (1953); on *Kenton '76* (1975, CW 1076), Tiburon

SELECTED ARRANGEMENTS

on C. Barnet: *Charlie Barnet Big Band 1967* (1966, Vault 9004), 'Deed I do; on B. Rich: *Big Swing Face* (1967, PJ 20117), Norwegian Wood; on S. Kenton: *Birthday in Britain* (1973, CW 1065), Happy birthday to you

BIBLIOGRAPHY

FeatherE; *Feather '60s*; *Feather–Gitler '70s*

C. Easton: *Straight Ahead: the Story of Stan Kenton* (New York, 1973)

W. F. Lee: *Stan Kenton: Artistry in Rhythm* (Los Angeles, 1980) [incl. discography]

L. Tomkins: "Big Band Arranger *par excellence*: Bill Holman," *CI*, xxiv/2 (1987), 6; contd as "Have Band, will Travel," xxiv/3 (1987), 12 [interview]

WILLIAM F. LEE III

Holmes, Charlie [Charles William] (*b* Boston, 27 Jan 1910; *d* nr Boston, 12 Sept 1985). Alto saxophonist. He was a childhood friend of Johnny Hodges, and later emulated his style. After moving to New York in 1927 he played briefly with Chick Webb and others before joining a band led by the drummer George Howe, which was soon taken over by Luis Russell. Apart from a period with the Mills Blue Rhythm Band (1931–2), Holmes worked with Russell at intervals until 1940, recording under him with King Oliver (1928–9), Henry "Red" Allen (1929–30), J. C. Higginbotham (1930), and Louis Armstrong (1935–40); he may be heard to advantage on Allen's *It should be you* (1929, Vic. 38073). After leaving Russell, Holmes worked with Cootie Williams (1942–5), toured the Far East with Jesse Stone, played with John Kirby (1947) and Billy Kyle, and recorded with Al Sears (1951). After a period of retirement he recorded with Clyde Bernhardt (1972–5) and in Sweden with the group Kustbandet (1975).

Oral history material in *NjR* (JOHP).

BIBLIOGRAPHY

S. Dance: *The World of Swing* (New York, 1974) [colln of previously pubd interviews], 249

S. Klett and A. Vollmer: "Charlie Holmes: Interview," *Cadence*, v (1979), no.6, p.19; no.7, p.3; no.8, p.8

Holmes, Groove [Richard Arnold] (*b* Camden, NJ, 2 May 1931). Organist. He taught himself to play organ and worked in local clubs for a number of years. In 1960 Les McCann heard him in Pittsburgh and persuaded Pacific Jazz to issue him with a contract; his first recording was as the leader of a sextet that included McCann and Ben Webster (1961). Thereafter Holmes recorded a series of albums with his own trio, using guitar and drums; his greatest commercial success was his spirited version of *Misty* (1965). He also recorded with big bands and with other artists, notably McCann, Joe Pass, and Jimmy McGriff. Holmes's style is characterized by his use of powerful bass lines (he also plays double bass) and harmonically oriented melodies in the bop idiom that suggest the influence of saxophonists; his playing always maintains a strong sense of swing. He has occasionally experimented with the addition of piano to his trio format, and in 1976 he led a trio in New York with the keyboard player Khalid Moss and the drummer Mel Roach as his sidemen.

SELECTED RECORDINGS

Groove! (1961, PJ 23); *Soul Message* (1965, Prst. 7435), incl. Misty; *Living Soul* (1966, Prst. 7468); *Super Soul* (1967, Prst. 7497); *Soul Power* (1967, Prst. 7543)

BIBLIOGRAPHY

Feather '60s; *Feather–Gitler '70s*
M. Hennessey: "Organic Groove," *DB*, xxxvii/3 (1970), 16, 39
H. Nolan: "Groove Holmes," *Different Drummer*, i/12 (1974), 11
J. S. Wilson: "Jazz Combination of Organ and Piano is Used by Holmes," *New York Times* (25 May 1976), 42
J. Dulzo: "In the 'Groove'," *Detroit News* (20 Feb 1981), §F, p.5

ANDREW JAFFE

Holmes, Johnny [John] (*b* Montreal, 8 June 1916). Canadian bandleader, trumpeter, arranger, and composer. He played in Montreal in a dance band called the Escorts (1940–41), the leadership of which he took over in 1941; under his name the band played regularly in and around Montreal for the next ten years and became very popular. From 1959 Holmes led a big band with which he performed regularly on CBC radio (to 1969) and made a number of recordings that included notable jazz solos (1966–73). Always skilled at detecting talent in young musicians, Holmes engaged many players who later became well known in jazz, including Oscar Peterson and Maynard Ferguson. Besides performing with his band, Holmes has written a large number of arrangements for it and has composed songs and several more extended works. His collection of arrangements, recordings, and photographs is now in the archives of Concordia University, Montreal; *see* LIBRARIES AND ARCHIVES, §2.

Oral history material in *CaQMG*.

BIBLIOGRAPHY

C. Gauthier, H. McNamara, and M. Miller: "Holmes, Johnny," *Encyclopedia of Music in Canada*, ed. H. Kallmann, G. Potvin, and K. Winter (Toronto, Buffalo, and London, 1981)

JACK LITCHFIELD

Holt, Redd [Red; Isaac] (*b* Rosedale, MS, 16 May 1932). Drummer. He took up drums in high school in Chicago, and played in a band with Ramsey Lewis and Eldee Young. During his military service in 1955 he played with an army band in Germany, then from the following year to 1966 he was a member of Lewis's trio. *Fantasia for Drums*, from Lewis's album *Gentlemen of Swing* (1958, Argo 611) offers a good example of his style. He also recorded with James Moody and Earl Bostic (both 1958). After leaving Lewis in 1966 Holt and Young led a soul group, Young–Holt Unlimited, which recorded several albums until 1974; Holt later led a similar ensemble, Redd Holt Unlimited. From 1976 he was involved with an educational organization, Urban Gateways, which presented performances and lectures on jazz at schools in Illinois. Thereafter he led his own community-oriented project, the Gumption (1980–85). (*FeatherE*; *Feather '60s*)

Honda, Toshiyuki (*b* Tokyo, 9 April 1957). Japanese alto and soprano saxophonist and flutist. His father was the jazz critic Toshiyuki Honda. He taught himself to play saxophone and flute, in 1976 joined a sextet led by the drummer George Otsuka, and the following year formed the group Burning Wave; he also played with Kazumi Watanabe and wrote arrangements for Tatsuya Takahashi's album *Beauties* (1985, TDK T28P1007). Honda began his career as a jazz-rock player but from 1985 worked in a more conventional jazz idiom.

SELECTED RECORDINGS

As leader: *Burning Wave* (1978, King–EB SKS8002); *Spanish Tears and Burning Wave* (1981, King–EB K28P6051); *Shangrira* (1982, Toshiba–EMI–Ewd 90013); with C. Corea: *Dream* (1983, Toshiba–EMI–Ewd 90027); *Modern* (1983, Toshiba–EMI–Ewd 90029); *Super Quartet* (1986, Toshiba–EMI EWJ90047)

YOZO IWANAMI

Honey Bear. Nickname of GENE SEDRIC.

Honk. A loud blaring note in the middle or lower range of the saxophone, unenlivened by vibrato or other pitch fluctuations; the effect is achieved by attacking the note sharply and with full air pressure, which makes the upper partials more prominent than in notes attacked with less force. (It contrasts with SUBTONE, a soft, breathy tone produced on low notes by the suppression of the upper partials). An excellent example of the honk occurs on the title track of the album *Two for the Blues* (1983, Pablo 2310905) by Frank Foster and Frank Wess: during the two 12-bar blues choruses (immediately preceding the final chorus of the piece) a riff is heard 14 times, each ending with a honk played in unison (ex.1). A saxophonist who plays in a "honking" style uses this effect frequently; its overuse by some players has led to the word's carrying derogatory connotations. It is particularly characteristic of some rhythm-and-blues musicians. (For a symbol used to denote the honk *see* NOTATION, ex.18.)

Ex.1 Riff from the title track of F. Foster and F. Wess: *Two for the Blues* (1983, Pablo 2310905); transcr. B. Kernfeld (written at sounding pitch)

ROBERT WITMER

Hood, Bill [William Harrison] (*b* Portland, OR, 13 Dec 1924). Baritone saxophonist, brother of Ernie Hood. He studied piano as a child, and taught himself to play saxophones, flutes, and clarinets. He played with Freddie Slack (1946–7), and later moved to California, where from 1954 to 1981 he worked in Hollywood studios. As a freelance he made recordings with Chet Baker (1956), Bill Holman (1958), Shorty Rogers (1958–62), Marty Paich (1959), Dizzy Gillespie (1962, 1965), Sarah Vaughan (1962, 1972), and Zoot Sims (1976); his playing is well represented on Paich's *I Get a Boot out of you* (1959, WB 1349), especially the track *Warm Valley*. He also performed with Benny Carter (intermittently from the 1950s to the 1970s, recording in 1966), Benny Goodman (1961, 1965), and Terry Gibbs (1965), played at the Monterey Jazz Festival (1958, 1962, 1965), and toured Japan with Quincy Jones (1975). In the mid-1960s he led a quintet with Jack Nimitz, the other members of which included Jack Wilson and Nick Ceroli, and in 1974 he formed the Love Brothers, which continued to be active into the 1980s. He has composed and written arrangements for a number of jazz musicians, including Med Flory, Terry Gibbs, Goodman, and Mike Barone. (*Feather '60s*; *Feather–Gitler '70s*)

Hood, Ernie (*b* Charlotte, NC, 2 June 1923). Guitarist and zither player, brother of Bill Hood. He recorded as a guitarist with Charlie Barnet (1945) and played with Wingy Manone and Lucky Thompson. For many years he was active as a studio musician in Portland, Oregon. His zither playing may be heard on Flora Purim's album *Butterfly Dreams* (Mlst. 9052), which was recorded in New York in 1973. (*Feather–Gitler '70s*)

Hooper, Les (*b* Baton Rouge, LA, 27 Feb 1940). Composer, arranger, and pianist. He taught himself to play piano as a child, and first composed and wrote arrangements for groups he organized in high school and at Louisiana State University, where his major subject was composition (1958–60). After moving to Chicago (1964) he began writing advertising jingles, an enterprise that throughout his career has provided an economic base for his artistic activities. He also wrote material for various jazz groups and recorded an album with a big band, *Look What They've Done* (1974), which received three Grammy nominations. His *Rock-jazz Symphony no.1* (1977), for which he received an NEA grant, was given its première at the University of Colorado, Denver. In 1978 Hooper settled in Los Angeles, where he composed music for television and continued to record as a leader. The American Orchestra has commissioned two works from him. Hooper's work is characterized by wide electicism and a basic feeling of blues and swing.

SELECTED ARRANGEMENTS

Look What They've Done (1974, CW 3002); *Dorian Blue* (1975, Churchill 67234); *Hoopla* (1975, Churchill 67235); *Raisin' the Roof* (1982, Jazz Hounds 0004), incl. I want a little girl; *Hoopla* (1984, Pausa 7185)

STEVEN STRUNK

Hooper, Lou(is Stanley) (*b* North Buxton, nr Windsor, Ontario, Canada, 18 May 1894; *d* Charlottetown, Prince Edward Island, Canada, 17 Sept 1977). Canadian pianist. He studied music at the Detroit Conservatory and played in dance bands in the city before moving to New York, where he worked with Elmer Snowden and Bob Fuller in Harlem. Between 1924 and 1928 he made numerous recordings, mostly with Snowden and Fuller; they included instrumental trios and accompaniments to female singers, notably Rosa Henderson, Lizzie Miles, Monette Moore, and Ethel Waters. In 1928 he toured with the revue *Blackbirds of 1928*, then in 1932 returned to Canada; he joined Mynie Sutton's black dance band, the Canadian Ambassadors, in Montreal, where he continued to play in jazz and dance bands and as a soloist for the next 40 years. In the 1970s he was a member of the Montreal Vintage Music Society, which sought to promote early jazz styles. In 1973 he recorded an album of ragtime pieces (*Lou Hooper, Piano*, RCI 380), which included a number of his own compositions. He moved in 1975 to Charlottetown, where he taught at the University of Prince Edward Island. Shortly before his death he appeared several times on CBC television.

BIBLIOGRAPHY

ChiltonW
J. Kidd: "Louis Hooper," *Record Research*, no.77 (1966), 2
E. B. Moogk: *Roll Back the Years: History of Canadian Recorded Sound and its Legacy: Genesis to 1930* (Ottawa, 1975)
——: "Hooper, Lou," *Encyclopedia of Music in Canada*, ed. H. Kallmann, G. Potvin, and K. Winter (Toronto, Buffalo, and London, 1981)

JACK LITCHFIELD

Hooper, Stix [Nesbert] (*b* Houston, 15 Aug 1938). Drummer. He began playing drums as a child and during his teens he formed and led a group called first the Swingsters, later the Modern Jazz Sextet and the Night Hawks. In the late 1950s the group moved to California and in 1961 changed its name to the Jazz Crusaders. It made a number of recordings of its own, and others as a studio band with various musicians, including Grant Green and George Shearing. Its music became increasingly influenced by soul music and funk; in 1971 the word "jazz" was dropped from the group's name and it became the CRUSADERS. Hooper made his first album independently of this group in 1979 and in 1983 he left to work in television. In the 1980s he became the vice-president of the Los Angeles chapter of the National Academy of Recording Arts and Sciences.

SELECTED RECORDINGS

As leader: of Jazz Crusaders: *Lookin' Ahead* (1961, PJ 43), *Live at the Lighthouse, 1966* (1966, PJ 20098); of Crusaders: *Street Life* (1979, MCA 3094); *The World Within* (1979, MCA 3180)

As sideman: G. Green: *Shades of Green* (1971, BN 84413); G. Shearing: *Light, Airy, and Swinging* (1974, MPS 2121960-7)

BIBLIOGRAPHY

Feather '60s; *Feather–Gitler '70s*
H. Siders: "The Crusaders, Four of a Kind," *DB*, xl/13 (1973), 16 [incl. interview]
L. Underwood: "The Crusaders: Knights without Jazz," *DB*, xliii/12 (1976), 12 [incl. interview]
H. Nolan: "The Crusaders: the Sweet and Sour Smell of Success," *DB*, xlv/9 (1978), 12 [incl. interview]
C. Iero: "Stix Hooper: Finding the Groove," *MD*, vi/1 (1982), 15

RICK MATTINGLY

Hootie. Nickname of JAY MCSHANN.

Hope, (St.) Elmo (Sylvester) (*b* New York, 27 June 1923; *d* New York, 19 May 1967). Pianist. He studied classical piano from an early age and from 1948 to 1951 toured with the rhythm-and-blues trumpeter Joe Morris (recording in 1948). In New York he made recordings as a leader and as a sideman with Sonny Rollins (1954), Lou Donaldson, and Jackie McLean (1956); he also performed at clubs with Rollins and Clifford Brown. He was no longer able to perform in New York after his cabaret card was revoked owing to his addiction to drugs, and from 1957 he toured with Chet Baker. Later he settled in Los Angeles, where in 1959 he recorded an album with Harold Land that was critically acclaimed; the same year he performed with Lionel Hampton at the Moulin Rouge in Hollywood. He made several recordings as a leader after returning to New York in 1961 but worked infrequently during the last years of his life.

SELECTED RECORDINGS

As leader: with F. Foster: *Hope Meets Foster* (1955, Prst. 7021); *Informal Jazz* (1956, Prst. 7043); *Homecoming* (1961, Riv. 9381); *Last Sessions* (1966, IC 1018, 1037)

As sideman: L. Donaldson: *Lou Donaldson and Clifford Brown* (1953, BN 5030); H. Land: *The Fox* (1959, Hi Fi 612)

BIBLIOGRAPHY

FeatherE; *Feather–Gitler '70s*
J. Tynan: "Bitter Hope," *DB*, xxviii/1 (1961), 16

M. Gardner: Obituary, *JJ*, xx/7 (1967), 7
L. Kart: "Harold Land: *The Fox*," *DB*, xxxvii/2 (1970), 21 [review]
A. Groves: "The Forgotten Ones: Elmo Hope," *JJI*, xxxvi/6 (1983), 10 [incl. discography]

GREGORY E. SMITH

Hopkins, Claude (Driskett) (*b* Alexandria, VA, 24 Aug 1903; *d* New York, 19 Feb 1984). Pianist and bandleader. He studied music and medicine at Howard University, where his parents were members of the faculty. He led his own bands and played briefly in New York with Wilbur Sweatman, then toured Europe as music director for the singer Josephine Baker, leading a band that included Sidney Bechet (1925). After returning to the USA in 1926 he continued to work with his own groups, and in 1930 took over Charlie Skeete's band at the Cocoanut Grove in Harlem; under his leadership the band enjoyed successful extended engagements between 1930 and 1936 at the Savoy Ballroom, the Roseland Ballroom, and the Cotton Club. These appearances led to a number of radio broadcasts, which helped to establish Hopkins's group as one of the most popular black bands of the decade. Among his sidemen were such notable soloists as Vic Dickenson, Jabbo Smith, and Edmond Hall. Hopkins's first recording as a leader was his own composition *I would do anything for you* (1932); the band also appeared in the films *Dance Team* (1931), *Wayward* (1932), and *Barbershop Blues* (1933). After the group disbanded in 1940 Hopkins performed in ensembles of various sizes; he led a big band (1944–7) and played with a quintet (1947–9) and a sextet (1950–51). From 1954 he appeared regularly with Henry "Red" Allen's group, and in the late 1950s he worked in Herman Autrey's trio. He led his own small group from 1960 to 1966, then from 1968 was a member of the Jazz Giants under Wild Bill Davison. Hopkins continued to perform during the 1970s, appearing at several jazz festivals.

SELECTED RECORDINGS

As unaccompanied soloist: *Crazy fingers* (1972, Chi. 114); *Soliloquy* (1972, Sack. 3004)

As leader: I would do anything for you (1932, Col. 2665D); *Claude Hopkins and his Orchestra* (1935, Jazz Panorama 13), incl. Chasin' my blues away, Hodge Podge; Church Street Sobbin' Blues (1937, Decca 1286)

BIBLIOGRAPHY

S. Dance: *The World of Swing* (New York, 1974) [colln of previously pubd interviews], 31
J.-P. Battestini: "Souvenirs de Claude Hopkins," *BHcF*, no.263 (1978), 26
W. Vaché, Sr.: "'I would do anything for you': the Story of Claude Hopkins," *MR*, xiii (1986), no.4, p.1; no.5, p.8; no.6, p.10

BILL DOBBINS/R

Hopkins, Fred(erick J.) (*b* Chicago, 11 Oct 1947). Double bass player. He began playing while a student at DuSable High School in Chicago. During the late 1960s he became involved with the Association for the Advancement of Creative Musicians, and later played and recorded free jazz with Kalaparusha Maurice McIntyre (1970). He worked in the trio Reflection with Henry Threadgill and Steve McCall (1971–2), then studied with the classical double bass player Joseph Guastafeste of the Chicago SO (*c*1972–1975) and played in clubs. After moving to New York in 1975 he commenced his longest and most significant association, rejoining Threadgill and McCall to form the trio Air; he may be heard to advantage with this group on the album *Open Air Suite* (1978, Ari. 3002). Hopkins also recorded with Anthony Braxton and Marion Brown (both 1976), Oliver Lake (1976, 1984), David Murray (1976, 1977, 1979, 1984), Hamiet Bluiett (1977, 1984), Don Pullen (1978, 1985), Bobby McFerrin (1982), the World Bass Violin Ensemble (1982–3), and Craig Harris (1983). (T. Trombert: "Fred Hopkins," *Jm*, no.255 (1977), 20)

Horizon [A&M Horizon]. Record label. A subsidiary of the record company A&M, it was established in Los Angeles in 1975 by the producer John Snyder. Over a period of about two years it was used to issue around two dozen items, all notable for the quality of the music, the fidelity, and the packaging. Recorded variously in studios and at concerts, the albums offered important material by Thad Jones and Mel Lewis, Dave Brubeck and Paul Desmond, Jim Hall, Ornette Coleman and Charlie Haden, and Coleman's quintet. These were pressed on excellent vinyl (despite the shortage then current), and the liners were elaborate; decorated with sophisticated artwork and photographs, they gave details of the recording, selected discographies, facsimiles of compositional sketches, structural diagrams of performances, transcriptions of solos, or excerpts from arrangements. After leaving A&M Snyder started a similar but independent venture, Artists House, in 1977. Although no further recordings were issued on Horizon after this, much of the catalogue has remained available into the late 1980s. (M. Ullman: *Jazz Lives: Portraits in Words and Pictures* (Washington, 1980), 141)

Horn. (1) In jazz argot originally any wind instrument, though especially a saxophone, played by a soloist; by extension any instrument that is not part of the rhythm section.

(2) The orchestral horn (also commonly called the french horn). The horn is a brass instrument having a long, gradually tapering, coiled tube that terminates in a widely flared bell, a relatively small, funnel-shaped mouthpiece, and three to five (occasionally six) rotary valves, which are used alone and in combination to alter the length of the tube and thus the pitch of the instrument. The single horn is usually pitched in F, but players more commonly use one of the double horns (in which a fourth valve closes off a section of the tube, thus altering the fundamental pitch of the instrument), usually that in F/B♭; jazz players often use the triple horn in F/B♭/F alto, and sometimes the single horn in F alto (known as the descant horn). The valves are operated by the player's left hand and the right is inserted into the bell, where it is manipulated to produce exact tuning of certain pitches and to affect the instrument's tone.

Despite the existence of pictorial evidence for the use of the orchestral horn in early jazz groups (e.g., Doc Cook's band of the mid-1920s) there is no proof that it was played in jazz before the early 1940s; as in marching bands, the technically less demanding Mellophone (or tenor cor) was used in early jazz bands to provide a horn-like sound.

Curtiss Blake's discography ("Jazz Discography by Player," *Horn Call*, 1982) lists more than 250 recordings of jazz in which the horn is used and includes about 100 players. Julius Watkins played on more than 150 recordings, with Pete Rugolo, Oscar Pettiford, Charles Mingus, and Quincy Jones, and also with his own soft bop quintet, the Jazz Modes (1956–9). John Graas, another pioneer of the horn's use in jazz, advocated that players should not follow the jazz convention of distorting traditional sounds; he worked with Claude Thornhill (who by 1946 was regularly using a horn in his band), and played with Gerry Mulligan's tentet, Stan Kenton, and Shorty Rogers. From the mid-1950s Willie Ruff made many recordings on horn, notably in a duo with the pianist Dwike Mitchell, but also with Gil Evans and Lionel Hampton and as an unaccompanied soloist. Other bandleaders who have occasionally used the horn include

Miles Davis (nonet, 1948–50), Dizzy Gillespie, Stanley Turrentine, Maynard Ferguson, Carla Bley, and Sun Ra; four horns were included in the band assembled for Benny Golson in London in 1964. In the 1980s more horn players, especially in New York, have been attracted to jazz, particularly in the setting of the small group; they include Tom Varner and Peter Gordon.

(3) A term applied to some members of the SAXHORN family.

For illustration *see* RAEBURN, BOYD.

BIBLIOGRAPHY

O. Keepnews and B. Grauer, Jr.: *A Pictorial History of Jazz: People and Places from New Orleans to Modern Jazz* (New York, 1956, rev. 2/1966)

J. Agrell: "Jazz and the Horn," *Brass Bulletin*, no.40 (1982), 41; no.41 (1983), 20; no.42 (1983), 36; no.45 (1984), 34; no.47 (1984), 55; no.50 (1985), 31

CLIFFORD BEVAN

Horn, Paul (*b* New York, 17 March 1930). Flutist, clarinetist, and saxophonist. He learned piano from the age of four and took up saxophone when he was 12. He studied flute at Oberlin College Conservatory (BM 1952) and received the master's degree from the Manhattan School of Music (1953). He then joined the Sauter–Finegan Orchestra as tenor saxophone soloist. From 1956 to early 1958 he played in Chico Hamilton's quintet, and later worked in film studios in Hollywood. In 1965 he was the principal soloist in Lalo Schifrin's *Jazz Suite on the Mass Texts*, a role that brought him national publicity, and shortly afterwards he performed with Tony Bennett (1966). In 1967, after studying in India, Horn became a teacher of transcendental meditation. The following year he recorded unaccompanied flute solos in the Taj Mahal at Agra, India, using to full advantage the acoustic properties of the building, where the reverberation time is nearly half a minute; he also played in the Great Pyramid of Cheops, near Cairo. A collection of transcriptions of Horn's solos on the album *Inside* was published as P. Horn: *Inside* (New York, 1972). He moved in 1970 to an island near Victoria, British Columbia, where he formed his own quintet; he also had his own weekly television show and wrote film scores for the Canadian National Film Board, from whom he received an award for his music to *Island Eden*. Horn toured China in 1979 and the USSR in 1983, and from 1981 he has managed his own record company, Golden Flute. His experiments have included recording the sounds made by killer whales as an accompaniment to his playing, but, although such innovations have earned him many admirers, critics have generally not been enthusiastic. Horn's style is cool and restrained, and he refers to his work as "universal" music.

SELECTED RECORDINGS

As unaccompanied soloist: *Inside* (1968, Epic 26466)

As leader: *Jazz Suite on the Mass Texts* (1965, RCA LSP3414); *Paul Horn and the Concert Ensemble* (1970, Ovation 1405); *A Special Edition* (1975, Isl. 6); *Live at Palm Beach Casino, Cannes 1980* (1980, Rare Bid 155505); *The Magic of Findhorn* (1981, Golden Flute 2003); *Jupiter 8* (1983, Golden Flute 2004)

As sideman: C. Tjader: *Concerts by the Sea* (1959, Fan. 3295)

BIBLIOGRAPHY

FeatherE; *Feather '60s*; *Feather–Gitler '70s*

"Paul Horn Quits US: Seeks 'Gentler Life'," *DB*, xxxvii/19 (1970), 11

R. Palmer: "Paul Horn's Orient Expression," *RS*, no.293 (14 June 1979), 38

L. Feather: *The Passion for Jazz* (New York, 1980), 56

LEROY OSTRANSKY

Horn, Shirley (*b* Washington, 1 May 1934). Singer, pianist, and leader. She learned piano from the age of four and later studied music at Howard University. She led her own trio from 1954, and gained recognition in the early 1960s when her career was aided by Miles Davis, Quincy Jones, and others. Her piano playing is well represented by *Softly as a Morning Sunrise* on the album *Embers and Ashes* (1961, Hi-Life 55). In 1963 she recorded two albums, one with Jones's orchestra, and the other with a band of important swing and bop musicians, including Hank Jones and Kenny Burrell; Joe Newman and Frank Wess were among her sidemen for a third album (1965). She later recorded for the Steeplechase label as the leader of a trio with Billy Hart and Buster Williams (who was replaced in 1981 by Charles Ables). In 1987 she made a highly acclaimed album, *I Thought About You* (Verve 833235-2), recorded during a performance at the Vine Street Bar and Grill in Hollywood.

BIBLIOGRAPHY

Feather '60s

J. S. Wilson: "Shirley Horn, after a Gap of 20 Years, Sings Again," *New York Times* (28 May 1982), §3C, p.6

Horowitz, David (Joel) (*b* New York, 29 July 1942). Keyboard player. From 1968 he was active in New York as a studio musician, playing mostly jazz-rock. He joined Gil Evans's orchestra in 1970, recording with him from 1973 to 1975; his playing on synthesizers is a major contribution to the sound of the ensemble on *Blues in Orbit* on the album *Svengali* (1973, Atl. 1643). He recorded with Joe Henderson (1972) and Enrico Rava (1973), and performed and recorded with Tony Williams's group Lifetime (1972–4). He also worked as a record producer and arranger (1968–75), and has composed numerous film scores and music for televison and radio commercials. His brother Marc Horowitz, a guitarist and banjoist, is a studio musician. (*Feather–Gitler '70s*)

Horrox [Horrocks], **Frank** (*b* Bolton, England, 15 Feb 1924). English pianist. He studied at Trinity College of Music (where he won three exhibitions), recorded with Vic Lewis in 1947, and from 1950 to 1958 played in Ted Heath's group (recording at Carnegie Hall, 1958), for which he also wrote arrangements; he is heard to advantage playing bop solos on *Lullaby of Birdland* (1953, Decca F10200) and *Our Waltz*, from the album *Ted Heath's 100th London Palladium Sunday Concert* (1954, London LL1000). After leaving this ensemble he led his own small groups (including a quartet with which he recorded in 1960–61), played organ as a sideman with Shake Keane (1962), and continued to write arrangements for Heath. In 1970 he recorded with Louie Bellson. (*FeatherE*)

Hot. In jazz parlance, the term is used to suggest the qualities of excitement, passion, and intensity; it has been applied to tune titles, bands, individual musicians, and aspects of performance. It was used in the USA in the 1920s in order to distinguish jazz from other genres, and later to differentiate "real" jazz from the "sweet" music played by the more commercial dance bands.

Tune titles making use of the adjective first occurred in the ragtime era, well-known examples being Theodore Metz's *A Hot Time in the Old Town Tonight* (1886) and Paul Pratt's *Hot House Rag* (1914); several in the early jazz period included the word, notably *Hot and Anxious*, *Hotter than that*, and *Hot Lips*. The last named denotes hot trumpet or trombone playing (the style of the trumpeter Oran Page led to his being nicknamed "Hot Lips"), and similar titles referring to the playing of other instruments may be found, such as *Hot Piano*, *Hot Mallets*, and *Hot Sax*.

The term was used relatively vaguely to describe all types of band – from dixieland sextets to large dance orchestras whose repertories occasionally included jazz-oriented pieces or solos. Notable groups that referred to themselves as "hot" were Louis

Armstrong's Hot Five and Hot Seven, Jelly Roll Morton's Red Hot Peppers, and the Quintette du Hot club de France, an ensemble that was supported by the growing movement in France of clubs of enthusiasts devoted to "hot jazz."

The term "hot jazz" was used by such pioneer promoters of early jazz as Hugues Panassié (in *Le jazz hot*, 1934) and Charles Delaunay (in *Hot Discography*, 1936), and is generally confined to music of the early and swing periods and the continuation of styles emanating from that time. From the late 1940s it has sometimes been used to distinguish traditional jazz from more modern styles. (The concept has remained current, however, and found its antithesis in the schools of "cool" jazz in the late 1940s and the 1950s). Hot solos were generally performed at considerable speed and were characterized by a frenetic quality, an urgent sense of rhythm, agitated syncopation, eager anticipations of the beat, and an earthy or "dirty" tone. Such solos were played in some instances over whole or successive choruses, but orchestrated jazz frequently gained impetus from hot breaks or licks of as little as one or two bars. Examples of these may be found in Louis Armstrong's *50 Hot Choruses for Cornet* and *125 Jazz Breaks for Cornet* (both Chicago in 1927).

ERIC THACKER

Hot Club de France. French organization of jazz enthusiasts, dedicated to the promotion of traditional jazz and swing and of other aspects of black American culture. It was established in Paris in 1932 by Hugues Panassié and Jack Auxenfans and in 1934 the QUINTETTE DU HOT CLUB DE FRANCE was formed as a result of its activities. The club's presidents later included Madeleine Gautier (1975–83) and Jacques Pescheux; Louis Armstrong was honorary president from 1936 until his death in 1971.

With the assistance of Charles Delaunay the Hot Club de France sponsored recording sessions on the Swing label by, among others, Coleman Hawkins and Dicky Wells (both 1937), Bill Coleman (1937–8), and Benny Carter (1938). Throughout its history the club has adopted a fiercely partisan stance, rejecting all developments in jazz from the emergence of bop; Delaunay's interest in bop in the 1940s alienated other members, especially Panassié, and he was forced to resign in 1947. The club organized the first international jazz festival in Nice in 1948 and a festival in Montauban (from 1982) (*see* FESTIVALS), and in the 1960s arranged tours by Bill Harris (i), Earl Hines, the blues pianist Memphis Slim, and Rosetta Tharpe. Its publications include the journals *Jazz hot* (1935–9) and *Bulletin du Hot Club de France* (1950–), among the principal contributors to which have been Panassié, Gautier, Michel Perrin, Alix Combelle, Claude and Jean-Pierre Battestini, Pescheux, Stanley Dance, Johnny Simmen, Alain Balalas, and André Vasset.

The headquarters of the Hot Club de France moved from Paris to Montauban in 1948 and then to St.-Vrain (near Corbeil-Essonnes) in 1977; it has about 25 local chapters in France. It also maintains a library in Villefranche-de-Rouergue containing 16,000 records and other materials (*see* LIBRARIES AND ARCHIVES).

Hot Five. Recording group led by LOUIS ARMSTRONG in Chicago from 1925. The original members were Armstrong (cornet), Kid Ory (trombone), Johnny Dodds (clarinet), Johnny St. Cyr (banjo), and Lil Armstrong (piano); Lonnie Johnson (guitar) joined the group for one session. Between 1925 and 1927 it made many recordings for the Okeh label, including *Gut Bucket Blues* (1925), *Cornet Chop Suey*, *You're next*, and *Jazz Lips* (1926), and *Savoy Blues* (1927); it also recorded for Vocalion as Lil's Hot Shots. With the addition of Pete Briggs (tuba) and Baby Dodds (drums), and sometimes of Johnson as an eighth member, the group recorded 11 titles in May 1927 as the Hot Seven; among the finest were *Wild Man Blues*, *Key Hole Blues*, and *Potato Head Blues*. In 1928–9 Armstrong worked with a varying group of players, the most important of whom were Earl Hines and Zutty Singleton; it also included Jimmy Strong (clarinet), Fred Robinson (trombone), and Mancy Carr (banjo). Leaving behind the ensemble style of New Orleans jazz, this group allowed Armstrong to attain new heights of solo virtuosity in *West End Blues* (1928).

BIBLIOGRAPHY

M. Jones and J. Chilton: *Louis: the Louis Armstrong Story, 1900–1971* (London, 1971), 95

B. Rust: Liner notes, *The Louis Armstrong Legend* (World 421–4, 1978)

J. L. Collier: "Hot Fives," *Louis Armstrong: an American Genius* (New York, 1983, London, 1984, as *Louis Armstrong: a Biography*)

For recordings and further bibliography *see* ARMSTRONG, LOUIS.

MIKE HAZELDINE

Hot fountain pen. A small, keyless woodwind instrument, resembling the high A♭ piccolo or octave clarinet; *see* CLARINET, §35.

Hot jazz. A term used to describe jazz, particularly early jazz and swing, of an exciting and energetic nature; *see* HOT.

Hot Jazz Club of America [HJCA]. Record label. It was founded late in 1947, and was dedicated to the unauthorized reissue of jazz of the 1920s; the identities of the proprietors have never been satisfactorily established. As well as some 125 conventional 10-inch 78 r.p.m. discs the label issued a series of 12-inch 78s (ostensibly made of unbreakable material) that each contained four tracks. Recordings were also issued on a French label HJCA, run apparently by SOFRADI (Société Française du Disque) of Paris; these discs bore the same catalogue numbers as the American issues, and gave an American address thought to be fictitious. HJCA records were also issued in Sweden, but their catalogue numbers are unrelated to the American series. ("HJCA," *Matrix*, no.87 (1970), 3; no.88 (1970), 3; no.93 (1971), 14; no.94, (n.d. [1971]), 12; no.96 (1972), 16)

Hot Mallets. Group formed in the early 1980s by ISLA ECKINGER.

Hot Record Society [HRS]. Record company and label. The label was established in New York in 1937, and was at first used for a series of reissues of early jazz which continued until 1940. The company began making its own recordings in August 1938; the most famous of these are the sessions by the Muggsy Spanier–Sidney Bechet Big Four (1940). Extensive recording of small groups of the late swing era took place in 1946; shortly thereafter the company ceased to operate, although its catalogue was reissued by Riverside in the early 1960s.

BIBLIOGRAPHY

O. Keepnews: Liner notes, *Giants of Small Band Swing* (Riv. RLP43–4, 1960)

B. Rust: *The American Record Label Book* (New Rochelle, NY, 1978), 165

Hot Seven. Recording group led by Louis Armstrong in 1927; *see* HOT FIVE.

House band. A group established to perform permanently at a specific venue; in many clubs, a house band is engaged in order to support visiting soloists.

Houston, Clint(on Joseph) (*b* New Orleans, 24 June 1946). Double bass player. After working in the house band at Slugs in New York with George Cables and Lenny White he played with the singer Nina Simone (1969) and with Roy Haynes (1969–70). In 1970, with Dave Liebman and others, he formed Free Life Communications, an organization dedicated to performing and promoting free jazz. He played in small groups led by Roy Ayers (1971–3), Charles Tolliver (1973–5), Stan Getz (1975–7), Woody Shaw (1977–9), and Pepper Adams (1983), in large ensembles with Tolliver (1975), Slide Hampton (World of Trombones, 1981), and Frank Foster (1984–6), in duos and trios with JoAnne Brackeen (1978–86), and in duos with Roland Hanna (1986); his association with Brackeen (which began when they were both members of Getz's rhythm section) resulted in several recordings and a European tour (1985). Houston acts as a driving force in a rhythm section and he plays solos with virtuoso agility and lyricism, as *What was*, recorded with Brackeen, demonstrates. The albums he recorded with Shaw and as a leader contain examples of his compositions.

SELECTED RECORDINGS

Duos with J. Brackeen: *New True Illusion* (1976, Tim. 103), incl. What was
As leader: *Inside the Plane of the Elliptic* (1979, Tim. 132)
As sideman: C. Tolliver: *Live in Tokyo* (1973, SE 19745); on S. Getz: *The Best of Two Worlds* (1975, Col. PC33703), Double Rainbow; W. Shaw: *Stepping Stones* (1978, Col. PC35560); on W. Shaw: *Woody III* (1978–9, Col. JC35977), Escape Velocity (1978); P. Adams: *Live* (1983, Upt. 2716)

Oral history material in *GBLnsa*.

BIBLIOGRAPHY

Feather–Gitler '70s
H. Mandel: "Building a Bass Career: Clint Houston," *DB*, xlvi/2 (1979), 17

JOHN CURRY

Houston, John (Charles) (*b* Philadelphia, 22 March 1933). Pianist. He played with various local groups before working with Gene Ammons and Sonny Stitt, recording on the East Coast and in Chicago with both musicians (1952, 1961), and with Ammons alone (1952–5). In the early 1960s he moved to Los Angeles, where he performed and recorded with Curtis Amy (1962) and Harold Land (1963). Good examples of his work may be heard on the track *In your own sweet way* on Amy's album *Tippin' on Through* (1962, PJ 62), and on Land's album *Jazz Impressions of Folk Music* (1963, Imperial 12247). (*Feather '60s*)

Howard, Bob [Joyner, Howard] (*b* Newton, MA, 20 June 1906; *d* Mount Kisco, NY, 3 Dec 1986). Singer and pianist. In 1926 he moved to New York, where he performed as a solo act and held long residencies at various clubs, including the Famous Door and the Hickory House. He began his recording career in 1931, and during the mid-1930s made a number of recordings with such notable musicians as Benny Carter, Teddy Wilson, Cozy Cole, Ben Webster, Rex Stewart, and Barney Bigard; *Pardon my Love* (1935, Decca 400) provides a good example of his whimsical singing. He had his own radio series from 1935 and his own television show during the 1950s. He also made successful tours of Europe as a solo artist, and while in London in 1936 recorded a medley of piano pieces (*Swing it Bob*, Bruns. 02230, 02239), which includes a particularly lively version of *Tiger Rag*. (P. Carr: "Bob's Back in Town: the Story of Bob Howard," *Sv*, no.91 (1980), 14)

based on *ChiltonW*

Howard, Darnell (*b* Chicago, 25 July *c*1900; *d* San Francisco, 2 Sept 1966). Clarinetist and saxophonist. He began as a violinist while still in his teens and made his first recordings on violin with W. C. Handy in 1917 (his style was a strong influence on Eddie South). He led his own group in Chicago for a period (1918–21) and then toured in the USA and Europe with Charlie Elgar, James P. Johnson, and the Singing Synocopators. In the mid-1920s he distinguished himself as a fluent woodwind player with Carroll Dickerson, Dave Peyton, and, especially, King Oliver (1925, 1926); influenced by Jimmie Noone, he developed a warm-toned style on clarinet for which he became famous. He played with many of the most important leaders in Chicago, including Erskine Tate (1926–7), Dickerson (1927), Elgar (1928), and Peyton (1929–30), and led various groups of his own. From 1931 to 1937 he was with Earl Hines's big band (for illustration *see* HINES, EARL), then resumed working with his own groups in Chicago while playing under other bandleaders, including Fletcher Henderson (1938–9), Coleman Hawkins (1941), Kid Ory (1945, in California), and Doc Evans. In 1948 he returned to California to join Muggsy Spanier, then worked with Bob Scobey (1953) and Jimmy Archey (1954). His last long association was with Earl Hines's small group (1955–62); he also recorded some fine solos under Don Ewell (1956–7).

Oral history material in *LNT*.

SELECTED RECORDINGS

As sideman: W. C. Handy: Fuzzy Wuzzy Rag/The Snaky Blues (1917, Col. A2421); K. Oliver: Tack Annie/New Wang-wang Blues (1926, Voc. 1049); C. Elgar: When Jenny does her low down dance/Cafe Capers (1926, Voc. 15477); E. Hines: Take it easy/Harlem Lament (1933, Bruns. 6771); Bubbling Over/Blue (1935, Decca 714); K. Ory: Maryland, my Maryland/Didn't he ramble (1945, GTJ 65); M. Spanier: Home/It's a long way to Tipperary (1950, Mer. 5494); D. Ewell: *Music to Listen to Don Ewell by* (1956, GTJ 12021); E. Hines: *A Monday Date* (1961, Riv. 9398), incl. Bill Bailey, Lonesome Road

BIBLIOGRAPHY

ChiltonW; *FeatherE*
J. T. Schenk: "The Colorful Saga of Darnell Howard," *Jazz Session*, no.6 (1945), 2
——: "Darnell Howard Joins Kid Ory's Band," *Jazz Session*, no.9 (1945), 22
A. J. McCarthy: "Darnell Howard," *JM*, vi/5 (1960), 7
W. C. Allen: *Hendersonia: the Music of Fletcher Henderson and his Musicians: a Bio-discography* (Highland Park, NJ, 1973)

LAWRENCE KOCH

Howard, Kid [Avery] (*b* New Orleans, 22 April 1908; *d* New Orleans, 28 March 1966). Trumpeter. He began his career as a self-taught drummer in 1924, playing with Isaiah Morgan, Andrew Morgan, and Chris Kelly, who gave him his first cornet lessons and initially shaped his style. In the late 1920s he led his own band in New Orleans, though he also toured Louisiana and Mississippi and made excursions to Chicago in 1928. Thereafter he played with the Tuxedo Brass Band, then organized his own brass band, which was active in the early 1930s. During the mid-1930s he worked with Jim Robinson and Capt. John Handy at the Fern and La Vida dance halls, and from 1938 to 1943 he played in the pit band at the Palace Theater. Amateur recordings made in the late 1930s attest to the strong influence of Louis Armstrong on his style. Howard first recorded commercially in a landmark session with George Lewis (i) in 1943 and later as the leader of the Original Zenith Brass Band in 1946. His playing was at its finest during this period, exhibiting a crisp, incisive attack and a propulsive rhythmic flair. During the 1950s Howard worked intermittently with Lewis, and made tours of the USA, England, and Europe; by this time his lip had become unreliable and the quality of his playing was frequently uneven. He made a strong recovery after an illness in 1960 and continued to perform close to his best, principally at Preservation Hall.

Oral history material in *LNT*.

SELECTED RECORDINGS

As leader: (of Original Zenith Brass Band): Fidgety Feet/Shake it and break it (1946, Cir. [USA] 1007); *Kid Howard's Band* (1962, MONO 2); *Kid Howard's New Orleans Band* (1962, Icon 10); *Kid Howard's Olympia Band* (1962, Icon 8)

As sideman with G. Lewis: Climax Rag/Deep Bayou Blues (1943, Climax 101)

BIBLIOGRAPHY

ChartersJ
M. Jones: "New Orleans Brassmen," *MM*, xxxiv (10 Jan 1959), 11
J. C. Hillman: "Avery 'Kid' Howard over in Gloryland," *JJ*, xx/3 (1967), 21
C. Jordan: "A Kid from New Orleans," *Fn*, iii/4 (1972), 8
G. Russell: "That's Where the Waa Waa Came in at," *Sv*, no.52 (1974), 124 [interview]
T. Bethell: *George Lewis: a Jazzman from New Orleans* (Berkeley, CA, and London, 1977) [incl. discography]
D. Donahoe: "Some New Facts on Kid Howard," *Fn*, xv/3 (1984), 22

ALDEN ASHFORTH

Howard, Noah (*b* New Orleans, 6 April 1943). Alto saxophonist. As a child he sang in church choirs. In the early 1960s he moved to California and performed with Dewey Redman, the alto saxophonist Byron Allen, and Sonny Simmons; this experience stimulated his interest in free jazz and led him to study formally alto saxophone and trumpet. In 1965 he moved to New York, where he played with Archie Shepp, Marion Brown, Pharoah Sanders, Sun Ra, Bill Dixon, Donald Ayler, and Sonny Sharrock. He formed a quartet, recorded two albums for ESP (1965, 1966), and in 1969 joined Frank Wright's group with the pianist Bobby Few and the drummer Muhammad Ali and toured Europe. Through the 1970s he performed in the USA and in Europe, where he recorded regularly as a leader. Howard claims to have been influenced not only by Ornette Coleman, but also by Charlie Parker, Johnny Hodges, and other swing and bop alto saxophonists.

SELECTED RECORDINGS

As leader: *The Black Ark* (1969, Pol. 2383093); *Schizophrenic Blues: the Noah Howard Quartet Live in Berlin* (1977, FMP 13)

As sideman: A. Shepp: *Black Gypsy* (1969, Amer. 6099); F. Wright: *One for John* (1969, BYG 529336)

BIBLIOGRAPHY

R. Williams: "Noah: a Child of the Avant-Garde," *MM*, xlvi (28 Aug 1971), 14
R. Terlizzi: "Noah Howard Interview," *Coda*, no.146 (1976), 10 [incl. discography]
H. Rock: "Noah Howard Interview," *Cadence*, ii/12 (1977), 3
V. Wilmer: *As Serious as your Life: the Story of the New Jazz* (London, 1977, rev. 1980), 270

DAVID G. SUCH

Howard, Paul (Leroy) [Ox Blood] (*b* Steubenville, OH, 20 Sept 1895; *d* Los Angeles, 18 Feb 1980). Saxophonist and clarinetist. After moving to Los Angeles in 1911 he worked with a number of local bands. He played with King Oliver and Jelly Roll Morton (early 1920s), then performed and recorded with Harvey Brooks's Quality Four (1922–3) and worked with the pianist Sonny Clay (1925). From 1925 to 1930 he led his own band, the Quality Serenaders; with such sidemen as Lawrence Brown and Lionel Hampton this was one of the finest bands on the West Coast, and in 1929–30 Howard made a number of recordings with it, including *Quality Shout/Stuff* (1929, Vic. 38122). After the Quality Serenaders disbanded Howard worked for Ed "Montudi" Garland and Freddie Washington (1931–4), Lionel Hampton (1935), Eddie Barefield (1936–7), and the trumpeter Charlie Echols (1937–8). From 1939 to 1953 he again led his own band, and he continued to play throughout the 1950s.

Oral history material in *NjR* (JOHP).

BIBLIOGRAPHY

ChiltonW
B. Wood: "George Orendorff: Quality Serenader," *JJ*, x (1957), no.1, p.4; no.2, p.4
——: "Paul Leroy Howard," *JJ*, x (1957), no.11, p.6; no.12, p.13
A. McCarthy: *Big Band Jazz* (New York and London, 1974), 169

FRANK DRIGGS

Howard, Rosetta (*b* Chicago, *c* 1914; *d* Chicago, 1974). Singer. She began singing professionally in 1932 and worked in Chicago for Herb Morand, with whom she visited New York in 1937 and 1938. After returning to Chicago she sang in various bands, then during the 1940s performed as a soloist. She made a number of recordings with Morand's group, the Harlem Hamfats, as well as with other musicians, including *Plain Lenox Avenue* (1939, Decca 7627). (P. Van Vorst: "The Harlem Hamfats," *MR*, iv/5 (1977), 9)

based on *ChiltonW*

HRS. *See* HOT RECORD SOCIETY.

Hubbard, Freddie [Frederick Dewayne] (*b* Indianapolis, 7 April 1938). Trumpeter. He played and first recorded in Indianapolis with the Montgomery brothers. After moving in 1958 to New York he began a series of brief associations with established jazz musicians, including Philly Joe Jones (1958–9, 1961),

Freddie Hubbard, New York, 1968

Sonny Rollins (1959), Slide Hampton (1959–60), J. J. Johnson (1960), and Quincy Jones, with whom he toured Europe (1960–61). In 1961 he joined Art Blakey's Jazz Messengers, but left in 1964 to lead his own group; he also played as a sideman with Max Roach (1965–6). From 1966 Hubbard worked principally with his own quintets and quartets, though he made a tour of the USA with Herbie Hancock's group V.S.O.P. in 1977 (*see* V.S.O.P. (i)). His most constant sideman was Kenny Barron, who played in his groups of the late 1960s (with Louis Hayes), early 1970s (with Hayes and Junior Cook), and early 1980s (with Buster Williams and Al Foster). In the mid-1980s Hubbard made a number of international tours and recorded with all-star groups, often in the company of Joe Henderson, playing a repertory of hard-bop and modal-jazz pieces. He continues to perform and record as a leader, and in 1985 made an album with Woody Shaw.

Hubbard has recorded scores of bop, modal-jazz and jazz-rock albums, both as a sideman and as a leader. In the early 1960s he also participated in such radically experimental sessions as those for Ornette Coleman's *Free Jazz* and John Coltrane's *Ascension* albums, but was subsequently criticized for his overly conventional playing. His recordings of the mid-1960s with Hancock placed him among the foremost hard-bop trumpeters, his improvisations combining imaginative melody with a glossy tone, rapid and clean technique, a brilliant high register, a subtle vibrato, and bluesy, squeezed half-valve notes. In the early 1970s he issued several commercially successful albums with musicians who had formerly played with Miles Davis (*Straight Life* won a Grammy Award), but for the remainder of the decade he unsuccessfully sought widespread recognition and financial security. He tried funk, all-electronic rock, disco, and overarranged pop music, and concentrated on ostentatious virtuoso displays; his trademark, a climactic trill between nonadjacent pitches (a shake), became a cliché. During the 1980s, however, he reverted to his former style, improvising on lyrical ballads and complex bop tunes; unfortunately the histrionic elements did not entirely disappear from his playing.

Oral history material in *NjR*.

SELECTED RECORDINGS

As leader: *Hub-tones* (1962, BN 84115); *Breaking Point* (1964, BN 84172); *Backlash* (1966, Atl., 1477); *Red Clay* (1970, CTI 6001); *Straight Life* (1970, CTI 6007); *First Light* (1971, CTI 6013); *Live at the Northsea Jazz Festival* (1980, PT 2620113); *Outpost* (1981, Enja 3095); *Born to be Blue* (1981, PT 2312134); *Sweet Return* (1983, Atl. 80108); with W. Shaw: *Double Take* (1985, BN 85121)

As sideman: E. Dolphy: *Outward Bound* (1960, NewJ 8236); O. Coleman: *Free Jazz* (1960, Atl. 1364); A. Blakey: *Buhaina's Delight* (1961, BN 84104); E. Dolphy: *Out to Lunch* (1964, BN 84163); H. Hancock: *Maiden Voyage* (1965, BN 84195); J. Coltrane: *Ascension* (1965, Imp. 95); H. Hancock: *V.S.O.P.* (1976, Col. PG34688)

BIBLIOGRAPHY

I. Gitler: "Focus on Freddie Hubbard," *DB*, xxix/2 (1962), 22
R. Bower: "Freddie Hubbard Discography," *JM*, xi (1965), no.8, p.28; no.9, p.29; no.10, p.25; xi/2 (1966), 27 [addns and corrections]
B. Priestley: "Freddie Hubbard," *JM*, xi/8 (1965), 18
D. Morgenstern: "Toward Completeness: an Interview with Freddie Hubbard," *DB*, xxxiii/24 (1966), 19
P. Griffith: "Freddie Hubbard: 'Music is my Purpose'," *DB*, xxxix/20 (1972), 15
N. Tesser: "Freddie Hubbard," *DB*, xli/2 (1974), 12
A. Taylor: *Notes and Tones: Musician-to-Musician Interviews* (Liège, Belgium, 1977/*R*1982), 197
H. Mandel: "Freddie Hubbard: New Direction, Fresh Perspective," *DB*, xlv/12 (1978), 17
S. Bloom: "Freddie Hubbard: Money Talks, Bebop Walks," *DB*, xlviii/11 (1981), 17
"Freddie Hubbard," *SJ*, xxxv/3 (1981), 198 [discography]

BARRY KERNFELD

Hubble, Ed(die) [John Edgar] (*b* Santa Barbara, CA, 6 April 1928). Trombonist. At the age of 13 he worked with the Los Angeles County Band, and in 1944 his family moved to New York, where he played with Bob Wilber. The following year he toured with the guitarist Alvino Rey, after which he spent short periods with Buddy Rich, Shorty Sherock, and McKenzie's Candy Kids, led by Red McKenzie (1947). From 1948 to 1959 Hubble played with Johnny Windhurst; later he was a member of bands led by Billy Maxted (1959–61) and Phil Napoleon (1962–4). He worked with the entertainer Jackie Gleason (1964–5) and led his own group, then joined the Dukes of Dixieland (1966) and played with the trumpeter George Mauro (1967–8). Thereafter he worked as a freelance, and achieved recognition as a member of the World's Greatest Jazz Band (1970–73). He then worked in Florida with Flip Phillips (1973–4) and toured Europe with Pee Wee Erwin (1974), and others. His playing, which drew on the styles of Jack Teagarden and Miff Mole, continued to be much in demand during the 1970s. He was seriously injured in an automobile accident in 1979, but soon resumed work, performing both in Europe and the USA. After moving to Texas, Hubble played as a member of a band led by the cornetist Jim Cullum(, Jr.) (1986–7) and then continued his career as a freelance musician.

SELECTED RECORDINGS

As sideman: D. Evans: Original Dixieland One Step (1947, Disc 6070); Wild B. Davison: *Jazz at Storyville* (1951, Savoy 15025); Walt Gifford: *New Yorkers* (1952–4, Delmar 206); E. Condon: *Jam Session* (*c*1970, Jlgy J100); World's Greatest Jazz Band: *Century Plaza* (1972, World Jazz 1), incl. Heavy Hearted Blues; Chicago Jazz Giants: *Live* (1976, MPS 68172); P. W. Erwin: *Pee Wee Erwin Memorial* (1981, Jazz Crooner 2829581)

BIBLIOGRAPHY

FeatherE
P. Hart: "Introducing Wilber's Wildcats," *American Jazz Review*, iii/2 (1946), 3
W. Balliett: "The Westchester Kids," *Improvising: Sixteen Jazz Musicians and their Art* (New York, 1977) [colln of previously pubd articles], 237
E. Townley: "Slippery Horn: Ed Hubble," *JJ*, xxx/3 (1977), 8 [interview]

BRIAN PEERLESS

Hübner, Ralf(-Rainer) (*b* Berlin, 3 May 1939). German drummer. From 1958 to 1962 he studied percussion and double bass at the Hochschule für Musik in Berlin. His first professional engagements were with Benny Bailey and Nathan Davis, then in 1962 he played with the Hessian Radio Jazz Band and joined a quintet led by Albert Mangelsdorff; he continued to perform and made recordings with Mangelsdorff until 1971, and his style is well represented by the album *Now Jazz Ramwong* (1964, CBS 62398). Later he took part in recording sessions with Eberhard Weber (1973, 1984), the Frankfurt Jazz Ensemble, Joki Freund, and the group From (all 1975), and Manfred Schoof (1976–9). In 1978 he recorded in a trio with Michael Pilz and the trumpeter Itaru Oki, and with Volker Kriegel. (*ReclamsJ*)

Hucko, Peanuts [Michael Andrew] (*b* Syracuse, NY, 7 April 1918). Clarinetist and tenor saxophonist. He worked in the bands of Will Bradley (1939, 1940–41), Joe Marsala (1940), Charlie Spivak (1941–2), and the tenor saxophonist Bob Chester (1942). He joined Glenn Miller's Army Air Force band, with which he often performed as a clarinet soloist. From the mid-1940s he played with Benny Goodman (1945–6), Ray McKinley (1946–7), and Eddie Condon (1947–50). In 1956 Hucko toured Japan with Goodman and in 1957 he toured Europe in an all-star group led by Jack Teagarden and Earl Hines. He played with Louis Armstrong's All Stars (1958–60) and at the Newport Jazz Festival (1963, 1964), and then led his own band at Eddie

Condon's, New York (1964–6). In 1967 he toured the UK as a soloist and he then settled in Denver, where he worked with Yank Lawson and Bob Haggart in a group that later became known as the World's Greatest Jazz Band. He was resident at various clubs and performed on television (1970–72), then led and played as a soloist in the Glenn Miller Orchestra. He also led a band in which his wife, the singer Louise Tobin (formerly a sideman of Goodman's), was the principal soloist. Hucko performed and made several recordings in Europe and the Far East and in 1981 he toured with his own Pied Piper Quintet.

SELECTED RECORDINGS

As leader: *Stealin' Apples* (n.d., Showtime 113); *Peanuts Hucko with his Pied Piper Quintet* (1978, World Jazz 15)

As sideman: G. Miller: *Rare Performances 1943–1944*, ii (1943–4, Rarities 68), incl. Moonlight Serenade; E. Condon: *Midnight in Moscow* (1962, Epic 16024)

BIBLIOGRAPHY

ChiltonW

S. Traill: "Peanuts Hucko," *JJI*, xxxii/12 (1979), 20

E. Cook: "The Miller Years," *JJI*, xxxv/2 (1982), 12

B. Rusch: "Peanuts Hucko: Interview," *Cadence*, xi (1985), no.5, p.13; no.6, p.5

EDDIE COOK

Hudson, Will (*b* Barstow, CA, 8 March 1908; *d* South Carolina, 1981). Arranger, composer, and bandleader. He first wrote arrangements for McKinney's Cotton Pickers, Erskine Tate (both *c*1930), and Cab Calloway (1932), then became a staff arranger for Irving Mills. His scores were used by Calloway, Joe Venuti (1933), Fletcher Henderson and Jimmie Lunceford (both 1933–4), Benny Goodman (1934), the Mills Blue Rhythm Band (1935), and other prominent bandleaders; his arrangement of *Hocus Pocus*, which was recorded by Henderson (1934, Bb 5682), is a good example of his style. In 1935 he began leading a big band with the singer and lyricist Eddie De Lange; from 1938 to 1941 he assumed sole leadership of the group, and also continued to provide arrangements for other bands. During his military service (1943–5) he wrote scores for Glenn Miller; he then worked as a freelance until 1948, when he enrolled at the Juilliard School. After this he abandoned jazz to work in other genres. His best-remembered composition is *Moonglow*, which he wrote with De Lange.

BIBLIOGRAPHY

ChiltonW; *FeatherE*

G. T. Simon: *The Big Bands* (New York, 1967, rev. and enlarged 2/1971, rev. 3/1974, 4/1981), 258

A. McCarthy: *Big Band Jazz* (New York and London, 1974), 289

Hug, Armand (*b* New Orleans, 6 Dec 1910; *d* New Orleans, 19 March 1977). Pianist. At the age of 14 he played for silent films, then in 1926 joined Harry Shields's band at the Fern dance hall. He continued to work with a number of groups in New Orleans, making his first recordings with Sharkey Bonano in 1936. After 1941 Hug pursued a career as a solo pianist, appearing at most of the city's better hotels and clubs; he soon became highly sought after, and in 1967 signed a life-time contract to play at the Royal Orleans Hotel. He worked extensively on radio, had his own television series, and made more than 250 recordings. Good examples of his playing are *Bouncin' Around*, *Purple Rose of Cairo*, and *Sister Kate*, on the album *Armand Hug Plays Armand Piron* (1953, Para. 114).

Oral history material in *LNT*.

BIBLIOGRAPHY

"Libretto: Armand Hug," *SL*, iv/11–12 (1953), 1

M. Askenaizer: "New Orleans' Hug," *MR*, ii/1 (1974), 10

G. Kay: "There will Never be a Farewell," *SL*, xxix (sum. 1977), 8

S. Lord: "Armand Hug: the Man," *SL*, xxix (sum. 1977), 10

Obituary, *SL*, xxix (sum. 1977), 7

P. Smith: "It's Never Easy to Say Goodbye," *SL*, xxix (sum. 1977), 15

BILL RUSSELL

Hughart, Jim [James David] (*b* Minneapolis, 28 July 1936). Double bass player. He studied double bass with his father, a professional orchestral musician, and music theory at the University of Minneapolis in 1959. He played in the 7th US Army Symphony Orchestra in Europe from 1960 to 1961; after his discharge from the army he toured with Ella Fitzgerald for three years. Thereafter Hughart has worked as a studio musician in southern California, and has performed and recorded with Joe Williams, Oscar Peterson, Zoot Sims, Johnny Griffin, Cannonball Adderley, Joe Pass, Barney Kessel, Dave Frishberg, and Tom Scott. He has three times won the award given by the National Academy of Recording Arts and Sciences for the most valuable player on his instrument, and in 1987 won the academy's MVP Emeritus Award. He also plays electric bass guitar.

SELECTED RECORDINGS

As sideman: E. Fitzgerald: *Ella & Duke at the Côte d'Azur* (1966, Verve 64072); J. Pass: *The Joe Pass Trio Live at Donte's* (1974, PL 2620114); D. Frishberg: *You're a Lucky Guy* (1978, Conc. 74); T. Waits: *Heartattack and Vine* (1980, Asy. 6E-295)

WILLIAM S. BROCKMAN

Hughes, Bill [William Henry] (*b* Dallas, 28 March 1930). Trombonist. During his years at high school in Washington he studied violin, but through the influence of his father, a trombonist, he concentrated instead on trombone. While studying pharmacy at Howard University (1948–52), he played with Andy Kirk (1949) and intermittently with Frank Wess (1950–52). Hughes is best known for his association with Count Basie, which lasted from 1954 until mid-1957; his solo on *Magic* (1956) shows to advantage his characteristic use of short, riff-like phrases punctuated by staccato notes, his rough tone, and strong blues feeling. In 1955 he recorded with his fellow sidemen Thad Jones and Wess in a band led by Osie Johnson; these albums provide rare examples of Hughes's style when playing in small groups. Hughes stopped performing between 1957 and 1963, when he re-joined Basie; he changed to bass trombone in 1964 and remained with the band into the 1980s.

SELECTED RECORDINGS

As sideman: C. Basie: *Basie* (1954, Clef 666); on O. Johnson: *Osie's Oasis* (1955, Period 1108), Jumpin' at the Waterhole; on Johnson: *Johnson's Whacks* (1955, Period 1112), Cat Walk; C. Basie: *April in Paris* (1955–6, Verve 8012), incl. Magic; *Basie Picks the Winners* (1965, Verve 68616)

BIBLIOGRAPHY

Feather '60s

E. Meadow: "The Road to Success," *JJI*, xxxiv/2 (1981), 12 [interview]

LAWRENCE KOCH

Hughes, Spike [Patrick Cairns] (*b* London, 19 Oct 1908; *d* London, 2 Feb 1987). English double bass player, composer, and writer. He was a self-taught double bass player and first worked with the Night Watchmen (1929–30). In the early 1930s he performed and wrote arrangements for the impresario C. B. Cochrane (1931), toured with Jack Hylton (1931–2), and recorded in New York with his All American Orchestra (originally known as the Negro Orchestra, 1933), which included Henry "Red" Allen and Coleman Hawkins. He contributed material for, and appeared in, several films, and from 1931 to 1944 wrote for *Melody Maker* under the pseudonym Mike. Hughes later abandoned playing professionally to concentrate on writing criticism, and was of enormous importance in establishing a place for American bands and their recordings in England. Although he was seriously involved with jazz for only four years, he made numerous delightful recordings in England, with such groups as the Decca-dents and the Three Blind Mice. His American recordings, which include his compositions *Arabesque*, *Pastorale*, *Nocturne*, and the popular *Donegal Cradle Song*, are undeservedly neglected by critics. Among Hughes's larger works are *A Harlem Symphony* and the jazz ballet *High Yellow*.

RECORDED COMPOSITIONS

(selective list; all recorded for Decca)

A Harlem Symphony (1931, F2711); *Six Bells Stampede* (1932, F2844); *Nocturne* (1933, F3563); *Pastorale* (1933, F3606); *Arabesque* (1933, F3639); *Donegal Cradle Song* (1933, F3717)

BIBLIOGRAPHY

FeatherE; *Grove6*
S. Hughes: *Opening Bars* (London, 1946) [autobiography]
——: *Second Movement* (London, 1951) [autobiography]
M. Harrison: "Backlog 19: Spike Hughes," *JM*, xii/9 (1966), 9
P. Tanner: " 'Spike': an Analytical Study of Spike Hughes's British Recordings, 1930–33," *J&B*, i (1971), no.3, p.8; no.4, p.13

DIGBY FAIRWEATHER

Hulan, Ludek (*b* Prague, 11 Oct 1929; *d* Prague, 22 Feb 1979). Czechoslovak double bass player. He played as an amateur for 17 years at the Hootie Club, and professionally with Arnošt Kavka (1948), at the Favorit Club (1949), and with Ladislav Habart (1950). He belonged to Gustav Brom's orchestra from 1953 to 1957; he also performed and recorded with Karel Krautgartner, with the group Studio 5 (from 1958), and in a trio led by the pianist Rudolf Rokl. He appeared at festivals in Warsaw, Munich, and Bled, Yugoslavia, and at the Olympia theater in Paris. In the 1970s he worked with the singing group Hot Aunts. Hulan was the best-known double bass player in Czechoslovakia; he also played a prominent role in Prague's musical life as an organizer of concerts and jam sessions. His playing can be heard to advantage on the album *Ludek Hulan* (1965, Sup. 10165).

GERHARD CONRAD

Hülphers, Arne (*b* Trollhättan, Sweden, 4 April 1904; *d* Stockholm, 24 July 1978). Swedish bandleader and pianist. He played piano at the Felix-Kronprinsen, a dance hall in Stockholm (1924–7), and belonged to various dance orchestras. From 1934 to 1940 he led a big band that toured Europe and made several recordings, including *Swinging in the Promised Land* (1939, Son. 3576). He led dance bands in the 1940s that had little jazz in their repertory. Scores used by his band are in the Svenskt Visarkiv, Stockholm; *see* LIBRARIES AND ARCHIVES, §2.

BIBLIOGRAPHY

R. Dahlgren: Obituary, *Orkester journalen*, xlvi (1978), Sept, 6
E. Kjellberg: *Svensk jazzhistoria: en översikt* [Swedish jazz history: an overview] (Stockholm, 1985)

ERIK KJELLBERG

Hultcrantz, (Johan) Torbjörn (*b* Stockholm, 2 May 1937). Swedish double bass player. He began piano lessons at the age of seven, and took up the double bass when he was 18. In 1956 he joined Lars Gullin's group; he recorded with Gullin in 1957 and 1958 and with Leonard Feather in 1959. He was then a longstanding member of Bernt Rosengren's group, with which he made a number of recordings (1959–74). His performances with Bud Powell at the Gyllene Cirkeln in Stockholm in April 1962 were recorded and later issued on a series of five albums. Also in 1962 he played on Albert Ayler's first album, but his bop playing was not compatible with Ayler's new free-jazz style. He recorded with several Swedish musicians in Stockholm from the late 1960s, including the tenor saxophonist Stefan Isaksson (1983). (*FeatherE*)

Humair, Daniel (*b* Geneva, 23 May 1938). Swiss drummer. After playing dixieland while in his teens he moved in 1958 to Paris. He belonged to a quartet led by the vibraphonist Michel Hausser (1958), the Swingle Singers, Martial Solal's trio (1960–5), and Phil Woods's European Rhythm Machine (1968–72), and recorded with many leading soloists, including Lucky Thompson (1960), Stephane Grappelli (1962, 1973–6), George Gruntz (1964–77), Jim Hall (1969), Ray Nance (1971), Bill Coleman (at the Montreux International Jazz Festival, 1973), Lee Konitz (at the Antibes–Juan-les-Pins Jazz Festival, 1974), Joe Henderson (1974), Franco Ambrosetti (1974, 1983, 1985), Jimmy Gourley (1977), and Kenny Barron (1985). He has also worked as a music director for the Musée d'Art Moderne in Paris (from 1967; *see* NIGHTCLUBS AND OTHER VENUES) and played in trios with François Jeanneau and the double bass player Henri Texier (1978–81) and with Joachim Kühn and Jean-François Jenny-Clark (with which Michel Portal often plays as well). Humair was influenced early in his career by Sid Catlett and Kenny Clarke and later by Elvin Jones and Tony Williams. His playing is always relaxed and inventive, and his adaptability allows him to provide a tasteful accompaniment in many styles.

SELECTED RECORDINGS

As leader: with P. Michelot and R. Urtreger: *HUM* (1960, Vega 837); with E. Louiss and J.-L. Ponty: *Trio HLP* (1968, CBS BPG63140); with F. Jeanneau and H. Texier: *Akagera* (1980, JMS 2473934)

As sideman: M. Solal: *Suite en ré bémol* (1961, Col, ESDF1278); *Suite pour une frise* (1962, Col. ESDF1430); J.-L. Ponty: *Jazz Long Playing* (1964, Phi. 77810); P. Woods: *Alive and Well in Paris* (1968, Pathé-Marconi 340844); M. Solal: *Suite for Trio* (1978, MPS 68021)

BIBLIOGRAPHY

L. Malson: "Daniel Humair ou les certitudes de la jeunesse," *Jm*, no.71 (1961), 30
A. Gerber: "Daniel Humair ou Le défi européen," *Jm*, no.182 (1970), 26
L. Goddet: "Daniel Humair," *Jh*, no.289 (1972), 5
B. Gauthier: "Aimer Humair," *Jm*, no.271 (1979), 20; no.273 (1979), 44
J.-P. Moussaron: "Humair à découvert," *Jm*, no.346 (1986), p.18; no.347 (1986), p.34; no.348 (1986), 12 [interview]

ANDRÉ CLERGEAT

Humble, Derek (*b* Livingston, nr Durham, England, 1931; *d* Easington, England, 22 Feb 1971). English alto saxophonist. He began to play professionally at an early age, and by 1951 was well enough established to be engaged for tours and recordings by Vic Lewis and Kathy Stobart. He then became a member of Ronnie Scott's band, with which he played from 1952 to 1956. He recorded with Victor Feldman (1952, 1955, 1956), Jimmy Deuchar (1953–8), Tony Crombie (1955), and Kenny Clarke and Francy Boland (from 1961). He played in Cologne with Kurt Edelhagen's orchestra (1957–67) then worked as a freelance musician and with Phil Seamen's quartet (1970–71). He was an excellent lead alto saxophonist with clear articulation and a timbre that was penetrating but never thin. He was also an accomplished improviser and may be heard to advantage on the bop blues *New Box* (on which he plays the third solo) from the album *Sax No End* (1967, Saba 15136) and on the ballad *November Girl* from *More Smiles* (1968, MPS 746), both recorded with the Clarke–Boland Big Band. (B. Priestley: "Humble, Derek," in I. Carr, D. Fairweather, and B. Priestley: *Jazz: the Essential Companion*, London, 1987)

Humes, Helen (*b* Louisville, KY, 23 June 1913; *d* Santa Monica, CA, 13 Sept 1981). Singer. She recorded several blues for Okeh when she was only 13. In 1938 she replaced Billie Holiday in Count Basie's orchestra, and before she left the band in 1941 achieved fame as a singer of ballads and popular songs. By 1945 she had moved to Los Angeles, where she recorded her highly successful jump blues *Be-ba-ba-le-ba*. This assured her entry in the burgeoning rhythm-and-blues market, and several hit recordings followed, notably *Million Dollar Secret* (1950). After her performances with Red Norvo and a tour of Australia in the mid-1950s her career declined for some years, but she appeared in New York at the Newport Jazz Festival in 1973 and the following year drew high acclaim from jazz critics during a residency at the Cookery in New York. Humes had a very strong, high voice which she handled like a brass instrument with superb intonation, drawing her phrasing and coloration from the black swing and blues styles. She was an excellent ballad singer with jazz inflections, and yet could be an electrifying blues shouter.

Oral history material in *NjR* (JOHP).

SELECTED RECORDINGS

As leader: Black Cat Blues/A Worried Woman's Blues (1927, OK 8467); Be-ba-ba-le-ba (1945, Philo 106); Million Dollar Secret (1950, Modern 20–779); *Swingin' with Humes* (1961, Cont. 7598)

As sideman with C. Basie: Blues with Helen (1938, Van. 1523); My heart belongs to Daddy (1939, Decca 2249); Between the Devil and the Deep Blue Sea (1939, Col. 35357)

As sideman with others: Pete Brown: Gonna buy me a telephone (1942, Decca 8625); R. Norvo: *Red Norvo in Hi-fi* (1958, RCA LPM1711)

BIBLIOGRAPHY

J.-P. Battestini: "Helen Humes," *BHcF*, no. 238 (1974), 5 [interview]
W. Balliett: "Just a Singer," *New Yorker*, li (24 Feb 1975), 98; repr. in W. Balliett: *American Singers* (New York, 1979), 42
J. McDonough: "Still the Talk of the Town," *DB*, xliii/10 (1976), 17
E. Townley: "Million Dollar Singer," *Sv*, no.64 (1976), 126 [interview]
S. Dance: *The World of Count Basie* (New York and London, 1980) [colln of previously pubd interviews]
M. Pinfold: "Beyond the Blues," *JJI*, xxxiv/2 (1981), 16
J. Barlow: "A Tribute to Helen Humes, 1913–1981," *JSN*, ii/4 (1982), 22
G. A. Moonoogian: "The Artistry of Helen Humes," *Whiskey, Women, and* ..., no.9 (1982)
J. O'Neal: "Helen Humes," *Living Blues*, no.52 (1982), 24
L. Dahl: *Stormy Weather: the Music and Lives of a Century of Jazzwomen* (London, Melbourne, Australia, and New York, 1984), 225

J. BRADFORD ROBINSON

Humphrey. Family of musicians, active primarily in New Orleans. The oldest member was Professor Jim (James B.) Humphrey (*b* New Orleans, 25 Nov 1859; *d* New Orleans, 1937), who was a noted trumpeter and music teacher and led the Eclipse Brass Band. His son, Willie (Eli) Humphrey(, Sr.) (*b* New Orleans, June 1880; *d* New Orleans, 8 Jan 1964), a clarinetist who worked with the Eclipse Brass Band, was active as a teacher; he was also the father of the three Humphrey brothers (see 1–3 below).

(1) Willie [William James] **Humphrey(, Jr.)** (*b* New Orleans, 29 Dec 1900). Clarinetist. He was taught by his grandfather, Professor Jim Humphrey; after beginning on violin he took up clarinet at the age of 14 and worked with his father. Later he performed on riverboats before traveling in 1919 to Chicago, where he played with Freddie Keppard and King Oliver. In 1920 he returned to New Orleans and worked with several important leaders, including Kid Rena. After moving in 1925 to St. Louis, Humphrey played in the bands of Fate Marable and Dewey Jackson. In 1932 he moved back to New Orleans, where he continued the family tradition of music teaching, but he left again to play with Lucky Millinder (1935–6). After he settled in New Orleans his vigorous, melodic playing was heard in many local ensembles until World War II, during which he joined a navy band. In the late 1940s he worked with the Eureka Brass Band and other ensembles, and performed with his brother (3) Percy Humphrey. Thereafter he played with Paul Barbarin (including a period in New York, 1955), led his own group, and worked with Sweet Emma Barrett at Preservation Hall (see

A Preservation Hall Jazz Band outside Preservation Hall, New Orleans, in the mid-1960s: (left to right) Alcide "Slow Drag" Pavageau (double bass), Jim Robinson (trombone), Emanuel Sayles (banjo), Willie Humphrey (clarinet), Cié Frazier (drums), Percy Humphrey (trumpet), and Sweet Emma Barrett (piano)

illustration). In 1967 he toured Europe with Billie and De De Pierce. From 1969 he has played regularly with Percy Humphrey, performing on tours and at festivals with the Preservation Hall Jazz Band.

Oral history material in *LNT*.

SELECTED RECORDINGS

As leader: *New Orleans Clarinet* (1974, Smokey Mary 1974W)

As sideman: D. Jackson: Capitol Blues (1926, Voc. 1040); P. Barbarin: *New Orleans Jazz* (1955, Atl. 1215); E. Barrett: *Sweet Emma "the Bell Gal" and her Dixieland Boys* (1961, Riv. 9364); B. Pierce and D. Pierce: *Billie and Dee Dee Pierce in Scandinavia* (1967, Rarities 15); Preservation Hall Jazz Band: *New Orleans*, i (1977, Col. M34549), iii (1983, Col. FM38650)

BIBLIOGRAPHY

ChartersJ; *ChiltonW*

A. Rose and E. Souchon: *New Orleans Jazz: a Family Album* (Baton Rouge LA, 1967, rev. 2/1978, rev. and enlarged 3/1984), 58

B. Carter: Liner notes, *New Orleans Clarinet* (Smokey Mary 1974W, ?1974)

C. DeVore: "Talking with Willie," *MR*, ix/8 (1982), 1

(2) Earl Humphrey (*b* New Orleans, 9 Sept 1902; *d* New Orleans, 26 June 1971). Trombonist. He took trombone lessons from his grandfather, and in 1919 joined a circus band with his father. Although he frequently returned to New Orleans he spent most of the 1920s traveling. In 1927 he made recordings with the cornetist Louis Dumaine, including *To-wa-bac-a-wa*, Vic. 20723). He continued to play during the 1930s, but by 1940 he had retired and settled in Virginia. After moving back to New Orleans in 1963 he made something of a return to prominence, helped by his brother (3) Percy Humphrey. In 1966 he made the album *Igor's Imperial Orchestra* (Center 6) as the leader of his own band.

Oral history material in *LNT*.

BIBLIOGRAPHY

ChartersJ

A. Rose and E. Souchon: *New Orleans Jazz: a Family Album* (Baton Rouge, LA, 1967, rev. 2/1978, rev. and enlarged 3/1984), 58

A. T. Wiatt: "Earl Humphrey," *Jazz Report*, v/1–6 (1967) [interview]

Obituary, *SL*, xxiii (sum. 1971), 30

(3) Percy Humphrey (*b* New Orleans, 13 Jan 1905). Trumpeter and singer. He played drums before changing to trumpet, and performed at dance halls, but achieved a reputation playing with brass bands. He was a member of the Eureka Brass Band and eventually became its first trumpeter, and by the 1950s was the leader of the group. In the late 1940s and early 1950s he also led his own group and worked with George Lewis (i) (1951–3). Thereafter he worked in dance bands until 1961, when Preservation Hall opened. He performed there regularly, both with his own group and with Sweet Emma Barrett (see illustration). After the Eureka Brass Band disbanded he played with the New Orleans Joymakers (1972) and the Preservation Hall Jazz Band, with which he has continued to perform, record, and tour into the 1980s.

Oral history material in *LNT*.

SELECTED RECORDINGS

As leader: of Eureka Brass Band: *New Orleans Parade* (1951, Pax 9001); *At Manny's Tavern* (1953, Center 13); *Percy Humphrey's Crescent City Joymakers* (1961, Riv. 9378); *Living New Orleans Jazz* (1974, Smokey Mary 1974P); of Preservation Hall Jazz Band: *New Orleans* (1977, 1981, 1983, Col. M34549, FM37780, FM38650)

As sideman: P. Barbarin: *Paul Barbarin and his Jazz Band* (1954, Slnd 203)

BIBLIOGRAPHY

A. Rose and E. Souchon: *New Orleans Jazz: a Family Album* (Baton Rouge, LA, 1967, rev. 2/1978, rev. and enlarged 3/1984)

BRIAN PEERLESS

Humphrey, Paul (Nelson) (*b* Detroit, 10 Oct 1935). Drummer. He studied piano as a child, and after playing drums with local groups he made his first professional recording in 1961 with the Montgomery Brothers. In 1960–61 he led his own small group, which played in the production of Jack Gelber's play *The Connection* in San Francisco. He performed with Gene Ammons (1962), Lee Konitz (1962), and Les McCann (1963–5), and recorded with Monty Alexander (1965). After periods with Harry James (1966) and a quartet led by Harry Edison (1967) he worked mostly as a session player with pop, blues, and rock musicians until 1972, though he continued to play jazz, recording with Jean-Luc Ponty in 1969. In the 1970s he recorded with McCann (1974, 1976) and Eddie Harris (1975, 1977), among others; from the mid-1970s into the 1980s he was active in television, then performed and toured with leaders who included Gerald Wilson, Buddy Collette, and Jimmie Rowles. He led his own sextet in 1981–3, which included Oscar Brashear; it recorded in 1981. Humphrey should not be confused with the trumpeter from New Orleans of the same name who has remained active into the 1980s. (*Feather '60s*; *Feather–Gitler '70s*)

Humphrey, Ralph (S.) (*b* Berkeley, CA, 11 May 1944). Drummer. After receiving a master's degree in percussion performance from California State College, Northridge, he toured with Don Ellis's orchestra (1969–73); he had already recorded with Ellis in 1968. He was able effortlessly to execute unusual rhythms, such as those on *Bulgarian Bulge*, from the album *Tears of Joy* (1971, Col. G30927); and he also contributed a chapter to Ellis's publication *The New Rhythm Book* (1972). After playing on the soundtracks for the films *The French Connection* (1971) and *Kansas City Bomber* (1972) Humphrey toured with Frank Zappa (1973–4), then worked as a freelance in Los Angeles, accompanying Tony Bennett, Joe Williams, Carmen McRae, Clare Fischer, and John Klemmer. In 1979 he recorded with L. Subramaniam and Ray Pizzi, and in 1982 he joined Free Flight, a group that specializes in the performance of insipid jazz versions of classical music.

BIBLIOGRAPHY

Feather–Gitler '70s

T. Lackner: "Ralph Humphrey: Session Drumming," *Musician, Player, and Listener*, no.12 (1978), 43 [interview]

BARRY KERNFELD

Humphries, Lex (P., III) (*b* Rockaway, NJ, 22 Aug 1936). Drummer. In 1956 he worked with Chet Baker and Lester Young, with whom he recorded in Germany. He joined Dizzy Gillespie's group in 1958 and in that year also performed with Lee Morgan and Bud Powell; from 1959 to 1960 he was a member of the Jazztet led by Benny Golson and Art Farmer. He made recordings with John Coltrane and Junior Mance (both 1959), Donald Byrd and Duke Pearson (both 1959–60), Paul Chambers and Doug Watkins (both 1960), Wes Montgomery (1961), and McCoy Tyner (1963). He also played with Chris Connor (1959, 1962) and Yusef Lateef (1960–63). In 1965 he joined Sun Ra, with whom he played an assortment of African drums and exotic percussion instruments, then in 1981 he left to begin working as a freelance musician in Philadelphia.

SELECTED RECORDINGS

As sideman: D. Byrd: *Fuego* (1959, BN 84026); D. Gillespie: *The Ebullient Mr. Gillespie* (1959, Verve 6068); Jazztet: *Meet the Jazztet* (1960, Argo 664); Y. Lateef: *Eastern Sounds* (1961, Mdsv. 22); M. Tyner: *Nights of Ballads and Blues* (1963, Imp. 39); Sun Ra: *The Solar Myth Approach* (1970–71, BYG 529340–41)

BIBLIOGRAPHY

FeatherE

RICK MATTINGLY

Humphries, Roger (*b* Pittsburgh, 30 Jan 1944). Drummer. He studied music from an early age, and led his own band at Carnegie Music Hall, Pittsburgh, in 1960. From 1964 to 1966 he toured with Horace Silver, and played on three of his highly acclaimed albums, including *Song for my Father* (1964, BN 84185). He also recorded with Silver's trumpeter Carmell Jones (1965), performed at the Newport Jazz Festival with Ray Charles (1968), and recorded with Nathan Davis (1971). (*Feather '60s*)

Hunt, (Herbert) Fred(erick) (*b* London, 21 Sept 1923; *d* Weybridge, England, 25 April 1986). English pianist. He was self-taught, and his love of light classical music gave his jazz style a degree of individuality from the outset. He worked in London with groups led by the trumpeter Mike Daniels and Cy Laurie (1951), but it was not until he joined Alex Welsh's dixieland band (1954) that his reputation spread. He became a principal soloist with this ensemble and performed and recorded with it for more than 20 years. During this period he also recorded with Eddie "Lockjaw" Davis, Bud Freeman, Eddie Miller, and Ben Webster in the group Tenor of Jazz (1967), and made the album *Pearls on Velvet* (1968, 77 LEU27) as the leader of a trio. After leaving Welsh in 1975 he worked as a soloist in South Africa before moving to Denmark. He played frequently in several European countries, often working with Wild Bill Davison. Hunt recorded as a leader in Germany (1979), then returned to England, where he undertook a residency at the Pizza Express, London, and worked again with Welsh (1980) before illness forced him to retire. (Obituaries: D. Coller, *MR*, xiii/8 (1986), 6; C. Henley, *Jazz Express*, no.72 (1986), 20)

Oral history material in *GBLnsa*.

CLARRIE HENLEY

Hunt, George [Rabbit] (*b* Kansas City, MO, *c*1906; *d* Chicago, *c*1946). Trombonist. He worked with Bennie Moten from about 1932 to 1935, then in 1936 joined Count Basie's band, with which he traveled to New York. After leaving the group he played with Fletcher Henderson (1937–8, 1939) and Earl Hines (1938, 1940–42), and worked in Chicago with Erskine Tate (1940). Although he made a number of recordings with Basie and Hines, Hunt was principally a section musician; he may be heard playing a solo, however, on Basie's *One O'Clock Jump* (1937, Decca 1363).

Hunt, Pee Wee [Walter] (*b* Mount Healthy, OH, 10 May 1907; *d* Plymouth, MA, 22 June 1979). Trombonist, singer, and bandleader. After completing his studies at Ohio State University and the Cincinnati Conservatory, he played with Jean Goldkette's band (1927–9). He was one of the original members of the Casa Loma Orchestra (formed in 1929) and remained with it until 1943 (for illustration see CASA LOMA ORCHESTRA); his playing may be heard to advantage on *Casa Loma Stomp* (1930, OK 41492). He then worked briefly as a disc jockey in Hollywood. In 1946 he formed his own sextet, with which he recorded until 1955, combining dixieland jazz with comic parodies of the traditional style. (*ChiltonW; FeatherE*)

Hunter, Alberta [Beatty, Josephine] (*b* Memphis, 1 April 1895; *d* New York, 17 Oct 1984). Singer. From 1914 she sang in nightclubs and cabarets in Chicago, and in 1921 she moved to New York, where she appeared in theaters and made many recordings; because she was under contract to Gennett she sometimes recorded for other labels under the pseudonym May Alix and the name of her half-sister Josephine Beatty. She was accompanied most often by Fletcher Henderson, as well as by Louis Armstrong, Fats Waller, and Sidney Bechet, and in 1922 composed *Downhearted Blues*, which was recorded in the following year by Bessie Smith and became a popular classic. Between 1927 and 1937 she worked chiefly in Europe, and in 1934 appeared in the film *Radio Parade*; at the same time she continued to sing occasionally in the USA. She took part from 1944 to 1953 in several tours sponsored by the USO, including one of Europe and Korea with Snub Mosley (1952–3). After beginning a career as a nurse in 1954 she worked infrequently in music, apart from recording with Lovie Austin (1961) and Jimmy Archey (1962). She again worked full-time as a musician from 1977; during the following years she made recordings and until the summer of 1984 sang regularly at the Cookery in New York.

Oral history material in *NjR* (JOHP).

SELECTED RECORDINGS

Downhearted Blues (1922, Para. 12005); Jazzin' Baby Blues (1922, Para. 12006); Stingaree Blues (1923, Para. 12049); Texas Moaner Blues (1924, Gen. 5594); Your jelly roll is good (1925, OK 8268); Sugar (1927, Vic. 20771); *Alberta Hunter with Lovie Austin and her Blues Serenaders* (1961, Riv. 9418)

BIBLIOGRAPHY

N. Shapiro and N. Hentoff, eds.: *Hear me Talkin' to ya: the Story of Jazz by the Men who Made it* (New York and London, 1955/*R*1966), 85, 246
R. M. W. Dixon and J. Godrich: *Recording the Blues* (London, 1970)
F. Driggs: "Alberta Hunter," *Sv*, no.60 (1975), 223
C. Albertson: "Roots of Jazz," *Stereo Review*, xxxix/6 (1977), 76
N. J. Darden: "No Tea for the Fever: Alberta Hunter is Back and Happy to Sing the Blues," *Essence*, ix/6 (1978), 82
"Home is the Hunter – and her Castle's Still Rockin'," *JJI*, xxxi/6 (1978), 28
J. Reynolds: "Alberta Hunter with Jimmy Daniels," *Interview*, viii/6 (1978), 36
W. Balliett: *American Singers* (New York, 1979), 21
"Hunter, Alberta," *CBY 1979*
L. Jeske: "Alberta Hunter: Singer of Songs," *DB*, xlvii/1 (1980), 22
S. Placksin: "Alberta Hunter," *American Women in Jazz, 1900 to the Present: their Words, Lives, and Music* (New York, 1982), 36
Obituary, J. S. Wilson, *New York Times* (19 Oct 1984)
F. C. Taylor and G. Cook: *Alberta Hunter: a Celebration in Blues* (New York and elsewhere, 1987)

RONALD M. RADANO

Hunter, Chris (topher Lionel Robert) (*b* London, 21 Feb 1957). English alto saxophonist and flutist. He learned saxophone from the age of 12, and later studied improvisation with Don Rendell and in various jazz workshops. In 1976–8 he was a member of the National Youth Jazz Orchestra, with which he recorded in 1977 and also toured Europe and the USSR. He then played in Changing Face, led by John Williams (iii) (1978), and in the Mike Westbrook Brass Band (1978–9, recording in 1979 and again in 1982). Thereafter he led his own quintet (1981–3) and worked extensively as a studio session player; he was also a featured soloist with Gil Evans's British orchestra (1983) and toured with Evans in Japan (1983, 1984). After moving to New York in 1983, he played regularly with Evans's Monday Night Orchestra at the club Sweet Basil. Hunter has also performed and recorded with, among others, a sextet led by the pianist Michel Camilo (from 1984) and Mike Gibbs (1984, 1987). An example of his playing may be heard on the album *Early Days* (Original 104), which he recorded as a leader in 1980.

SIMON ADAMS

Hurley, Clyde (L., Jr.) (*b* Fort Worth, 3 Sept 1916; *d* Texas, September 1963). Trumpeter. He taught himself trumpet by playing to recordings by Louis Armstrong. After working with local bands he was discovered by Ben Pollack, who was touring in Texas. He joined Pollack in 1937, but left the band when it was in Los Angeles the following year to become a studio musician. Glenn Miller engaged him as a principal soloist shortly afterwards, and he contributed a now famous solo to the recording of *In the Mood* (1939). After periods with Tommy Dorsey (1940–41) and Artie Shaw (1941), Hurley worked as a freelance musician in studios, notably MGM (1944–9) and NBC (1950–55). He was an excellent dixieland player, and often performed with such groups as Matty Matlock's Rampart Street Paraders. Much of his finest work was with Miller, however: a version of *One O'clock Jump*, recorded at Carnegie Hall, New York, in 1939, includes a solo that is a fine example of his playing; he can also be heard at his best on recordings of his broadcasts with Ralph Sutton.

SELECTED RECORDINGS

As sideman: G. Miller: In the Mood (1939, Bb 10416); *Carnegie Hall Concert* (1939, RCA LPM1506), incl. Bugle Call Rag, One O'Clock Jump; R. Sutton: *Ralph Sutton and the All Stars Live at Club Hangover* (1954, Jazz Archives 45)

BIBLIOGRAPHY

ChiltonW; *FeatherE*

SCOTT YANOW

Hutchenrider, Clarence (Behrens) (*b* Waco, TX, 13 June 1908). Clarinetist and saxophonist. His name is often misspelled Hutchinrider. He took up the clarinet and saxophone in his early teens, leading his own group in high school. After playing in dance bands he established his reputation as a jazz clarinetist with the Casa Loma Orchestra (1931–43; for illustration *see* CASA LOMA ORCHESTRA); he was probably their best soloist. He spent three years with Jimmy Lytell's band on ABC radio before a lung ailment led to his temporary retirement. Thereafter Hutchenrider stayed close to New York, playing as a freelance, appearing with Walter Davidson (?1952–?1958), and then leading his own trio, most frequently at the Gaslight Club (from 1958) and Bill's Gay Nineties. He also performed with Vince Giordano's dixieland band the New California Ramblers (1976, 1979) and with the New Orleans Nighthawks (1978).

Hutchenrider's clarinet playing was best in his many fast, driving solos in the upper register. His thin, sometimes wispy, tone was offset by shapely phrasing and, as early as 1931, a well-developed sense of swing.

SELECTED RECORDINGS

(all as sideman with the Casa Loma Orchestra)

Black Jazz/Maniac's Ball (1931, Bruns. 6242); Smoke Rings (1932, Bruns. 6289); Casa Loma Stomp (1933, Vic. 24256); Smoke Rings (1937, Decca 1473); Casa Loma Stomp (1937, Decca 1412); No Name Jive (1940, Decca 3089)

BIBLIOGRAPHY

ChiltonW
D. Hague: "Interview with Clarence Hutchenrider," *JJ*, xiv/11 (1961), 9
B. Hutchenrider: "Clarence Hutchenrider," *IM*, lxxiv/6 (1975), 6

JEFFREY COOPER

Hutcherson, Bobby [Robert] (*b* Los Angeles, 27 Jan 1941). Vibraphonist. He studied piano as a child and while in his teens was inspired by a recording of Milt Jackson to take up the vibraphone, which he studied briefly with Dave Pike. After working on the West Coast with Curtis Amy, Charles Lloyd, and a group led by Al Grey and Billy Mitchell he moved in 1961 to New York, where he was acclaimed for his full, fresh sound on an instrument that was still a rarity in jazz. From the 1960s he played with Jackie McLean, Grachan Moncur III, Charles Tolliver, Archie Shepp, Eric Dolphy, Hank Mobley, and Herbie Hancock and recorded with Andrew Hill, Tony Williams, McCoy Tyner, and Grant Green; in 1965 he played with Gil Fuller's big band at the Monterey Jazz Festival. He led a quintet with Harold Land from 1967 to 1971; among those who belonged to the group as sidemen were the pianists Chick Corea, Stanley Cowell, and Joe Sample, the double bass players Reggie Johnson and Albert Stinson, and the drummers Donald Bailey and Billy Higgins. From the 1970s he lived in San Francisco, and he continued to perform and record as a leader on both vibraphone and marimba into the 1980s, often with Eddie Marshall as one of his sidemen. From around 1981 he also toured internationally and made recordings as a member of the Timeless All-Stars (*see* TIMELESS).

SELECTED RECORDINGS

(recorded for Blue Note unless otherwise indicated)

Dialogue (1965, 84198); *Components* (1966, 84213); *Happenings* (1966, 84231); *Stick up!* (1966, 84244); *Montara* (1975, LA551); *Knucklebean* (1977, LA789); *Waiting* (1976, LA615); *Highway One* (1978, Col. 35550); *Un poco loco* (1979, Col. FC36402); *Solo/Quartet* (1982, Cont. 14009)

BIBLIOGRAPHY

A. Z. Kronzek: "Back to the Woodshed: Bobby Hutcherson," *DB*, xxxiii/5 (1966), 16
B. McLarney: "Urge to Merge: the Harold Land–Bobby Hutcherson Quintet," *DB*, xxxvii/3 (1970), 14
B. Hutcherson: "About the Vibes," *CI*, ix/9 (1971), 24
M. Bourne: "A Natural Player," *DB*, xli/5 (1974), 18
"Bobby Hutcherson Discography," *SJ*, xxviii/13 (1974), 244
L. Underwood: "Bobby Hutcherson: Cruisin' down Highway One," *DB*, xlvi/8 (1979), 14 [interview; incl. discography]

LEE JESKE/R

Hutchinson, Jiver [Leslie George] (*b* Jamaica, 1907; *d* Weeting, England, 22 Nov 1959). Jamaican trumpeter and bandleader. After working with Bertie King's band in Jamaica (1934) he moved to Great Britain, where he joined the Cuba Club Band led by the drummer Happy Blake. He performed with Leslie Thompson's Emperors of Jazz (1936), recorded with Ken "Snake Hips" Johnson (1938), and worked as the principal jazz soloist with the dance-band leader Geraldo. In March 1944 he formed his own band, which in its original form included many of the former members of the Emperors of Jazz. It toured Great Britain, India (1945), and Europe; Hutchinson's playing may be heard to advantage on *I can't get started* (1947, Sup. C18167), which the group recorded in Czechoslovakia. After it disbanded (1950) Hutchinson worked both with Geraldo and as a leader, and also performed with Mary Lou Williams (1952). He was killed in an automobile accident while traveling with his band.

BIBLIOGRAPHY

M. Burman: "'Jiver': an Early Star of Jazz in Britain," *MM*, xxxiv (28 Nov 1959), 4 [obituary]
"Jiver Hutchinson Fund is Opened," *MM*, xxxiv (28 Nov 1959), 1

HOWARD RYE, JOHN COWLEY

Hutton, Ina Ray [Cowan, Odessa] (*b* Chicago, 13 March 1916; *d* Ventura, CA, 19 Feb 1984). Bandleader and singer. She worked as a singer and dancer in New York until Irving Mills engaged her to lead a female swing band in 1934. Hutton and her Melodears became one of the most popular groups of the decade. Although it seems that Hutton's role was mainly that of a glamorous figurehead, the band included several excellent musicians and may be heard to advantage on *Truckin'* (1936, issued on *Jazz Highlights*, i: *1927–1938*, Bandstand 7127), which it performed in the short film *Accent on Girls* (1936). Hutton led a male band in the 1940s and organized other bands for sporadic engagements during the 1950s, but she never regained the fame she had earlier enjoyed.

BIBLIOGRAPHY

ChiltonW; *FeatherE*

S. Placksin: *American Women in Jazz, 1900 to the Present: their Words, Lives, and Music* (New York, 1982), 95

Hyams, Margie [Marjorie] (*b* New York, 1923). Vibraphonist. She recorded with Flip Phillips (1944) and was a soloist with Woody Herman's First Herd (1944–5) before leading her own trio (1945–8). In 1946 she also made recordings with Mary Lou Williams (including *Boogie Misterioso*, Vic. 400145) and Charlie Ventura; the following year she performed at a concert with Williams and Ventura at Carnegie Hall. In February 1949 she began working with George Shearing (for illustration *see* SHEARING, GEORGE), and performed and recorded with him until she married and retired from music in 1950. (L. Dahl: *Stormy Weather: the Music and Lives of a Century of Jazzwomen* (London, Melbourne, Australia, and New York, 1984), 79, 87)

Hyde, Alex (*b* ?Hamburg, Germany, 17 Feb 1898; *d* Santa Monica, CA, 7 July 1956). Bandleader and violinist. His family emigrated to the USA when he was two years old. He performed in New York (1919–22) and toured the northern states and Canada with his dance band, the Romance of Rhythm Orchestra (1922–3), which began recording in 1923. While touring Germany in 1924 the band made several recordings (including *I'm going south*, Vox 01625, and *Mama Goes where Papa Goes*, Vox 01627); among Hyde's soloists at this period were the saxophonist Eddie Grosso, the pianist Walker O'Neill, and Howard McFarlane. He again toured and recorded as a leader in Germany in 1924–5, but with a different band, which was occasionally joined by such other visiting American musicians as Gene Sedric. After returning to the USA he formed a talent agency, then joined the air force as a composer and bandleader; he later worked in Hollywood. Hyde was not himself a jazz musician, but his bands contained excellent jazz soloists.

BIBLIOGRAPHY

R. E. Lotz: "Alex Hyde's Hot Dance Recordings for Deutsche Grammophon Gesellschaft," *Sv*, no. 74 (1977–8), 50

R. E. Lotz: Liner notes, *Jazz and Hot Dance from Germany, 1925: Alex Hyde*, ii (Harl. 2034, 1985)

H. J. P. Bergmeier and R. E. Lotz: *The Alex Hyde Bio-discography* (Menden, Germany, 1985)

RAINER E. LOTZ

Hylton, Jack (*b* Great Lever, nr Bolton, England, 2 July 1892; *d* London, 29 Jan 1965). English bandleader and pianist. He worked as the director of a touring pantomime company (1909), as a cinema organist in London (1913), and as a freelance musician in various clubs. After military service he was appointed relief pianist for the dance band of the Queen's Hall Roof; later he became this group's arranger and director. Hylton made a number of recordings for HMV (from 1921), of which the early example *Wang-wang Blues* (1921, Zonophone 2167) is representative. He performed at various venues, including the Grafton Galleries, Piccadilly Hotel (1922–3), before enlarging his band to full orchestra size for a highly successful residency at the Alhambra Theatre (1924). In 1925 he set up a booking agency. During the late 1920s his orchestra became the English equivalent of Paul Whiteman's show band and achieved huge commercial success. Between 1927 and 1938 it completed 16 European tours and numerous substantial engagements in the UK; it was also the earliest British band to broadcast direct to the USA (1931). In 1935–6 Hylton led a band briefly in the USA. He was responsible for the negotiation of the first British visits of Duke Ellington (1933) and Coleman Hawkins (1934)

Jack Hylton and his orchestra, London, c1933

and made two recordings with Hawkins, including *The Darktown Strutters Ball* (1939, HMV BD5550). After his orchestra disbanded in 1940, he became involved in the production of various London stage shows, including *Camelot* (1964).

From 1933 to 1937 Mrs. Jack Hylton led a variety band which toured in the UK and Europe.

BIBLIOGRAPHY

FeatherE
A. Fenton: "Jazz Research," *JM*, no.173 (1969), 13
A. McCarthy: *The Dance Band Era: the Dancing Decades from Ragtime to Swing, 1910–1950* (London, 1971/*R*1982)

DIGBY FAIRWEATHER

Hyman, Dick [Richard Roven] (*b* New York, 8 March 1927). Keyboard player and composer. He studied classical music at an early age, and while studying at Columbia University (BA 1948) he won 12 lessons from Teddy Wilson in a contest sponsored by a radio station. He played swing and bop with Charlie Parker, Dizzy Gillespie, and Lester Young, and for longer periods with Red Norvo (1949–50) and Benny Goodman (in Europe in 1950 and from that time intermittently into the 1980s). From the early 1950s he worked principally as a studio musician, and was a staff pianist and organist for NBC from 1952 to 1957; he was also music director for the entertainer Arthur Godfrey (1959–62). In the 1950s and 1960s he made a number of recordings as the leader of a trio. An enthusiast for early styles of jazz piano, he recorded novelty and honky-tonk tunes (in the 1950s under several pseudonyms) and the complete piano music of Scott Joplin, and made transcriptions of works by Jelly Roll Morton, James P. Johnson, Fats Waller, and Louis Armstrong, some of which he performed on a tour of the USSR with the NEW YORK JAZZ REPERTORY COMPANY in 1975. In 1976 he formed the Perfect Jazz Repertory Quintet, which has included among its sidemen Pee Wee Erwin, Milt Hinton, and Panama Francis. He has written compositions and arrangements for Count Basie, the Mills Brothers, Cozy Cole, J. J. Johnson, Bobby Hackett, Al Hirt, and Doc Severinsen; pieces for synthesizer (his album *The Electric Eclectics*, *c*1969, was one of the first recordings of popular music for the instrument) and other keyboards (*The Happy Breed* for solo organ, 1972; Etudes for Jazz Piano, 1982); orchestral music (including *Event*, given its première by André Kostelanetz in Winnipeg, Canada, in 1971); and film music (including the score to *Scott Joplin*, 1976). He has also given lectures on the history of jazz. In 1985 he was a founder in New York of the festival Jazz in July (at the 92nd Street Y).

See also ORGAN, §1.

SELECTED RECORDINGS

As unaccompanied soloist: *Genius at Play* (1973, MonE 7065); *Themes and Variations on "A Child is Born"* (1977, Chi. 198)

As leader: *The Electric Eclectics* (*c*1969, Command 938); *The Sensuous Piano of "D"* (*c*1971, Project 3 5054); *Some Rags, Some Stomps, and a Little Blues* (1973, Col. M32587); *Satchmo Remembered* (1974, Atl. 1671); *Traditional Jazz Piano* (*c*1975, Project 3 5080); *Charleston* (*c*1977, Col. M33706); *Come and Trip it* (*c*1978, New World 293); with R. Braff: *Fireworks* (1983, IC 1153)

BIBLIOGRAPHY

FeatherE; *Feather '60s*; *Feather–Gitler '70s*
J. S. Wilson: "Hyman and the Studio Men," *High Fidelity/Musical America*, xix/5 (1969), 50
B. Primack: "Dick Hyman: Jazz Chameleon in the NY Studios," *CK*, v/5 (1979), 10 [incl. discography]

PAUL RINZLER

Hyman, John. *See* WIGGS, JOHNNY.

I

IAJRC (i). Record label. It was established in the early 1970s by the International Association of Jazz Record Collectors as a nonprofit venture; the organization aimed to make rare and historic recordings more widely available so that they could be enjoyed by a larger audience. By 1987 50 albums had been released. Among the most valuable are a recording of a Christmas concert given in 1949 at Carnegie Hall, New York, by Bud Powell, Stan Getz, Sarah Vaughan, Lennie Tristano, and Miles Davis; a collection of bop trumpet tracks by Red Rodney, Conte Candoli, Dizzy Gillespie, and Howard McGhee; and a compilation of Tubby Hayes's broadcast performances.

MARK GARDNER

IAJRC (ii). *See* INTERNATIONAL ASSOCIATION OF JAZZ RECORD COLLECTORS.

Ibrahim, Abdullah [Brand, Dollar; Brand, Adolph Johannes] (*b* Cape Town, 9 Oct 1934). South African pianist and composer. He played piano from the age of seven. As Dollar Brand he belonged to the Jazz Epistles with Hugh Masekela, the drummer Makaya Ntshoko, the alto saxophonist Kippie Moeketsi, and the trombonist Jonas Gwanga from 1959; they recorded the first South African jazz album, *Jazz Epistles: Verse I*, in 1960. Owing to the political climate in South Africa and the lack of opportunities in jazz, Brand and his wife, the singer Sathima Bea Benjamin, moved in 1962 to Zurich, where Duke Ellington heard a performance by Brand's trio and furthered his career by arranging a recording session for him (1963) and sponsoring an appearance by him at the Newport Jazz Festival (1965); later Brand substituted for Ellington on a tour. He played with Elvin Jones (1966) and toured Europe as a soloist and in groups that included, among others, Don Cherry, Gato Barbieri, Ntshoko, and the double bass player Johnny Gertze (1966–9). His music reflected his growing involvement in religion and politics after his conversion to Islam in 1968 and the riots in Soweto, South Africa, in 1976; from the mid-1970s he was known by his Muslim name. He returned to South Africa for a brief period in 1976 and recorded several albums, then moved to New York. From that time he performed frequently as a soloist and in a duo with Carlos Ward; in 1982 he led a performance of the mixed-media opera *Kalahari Liberation* in Europe, and the following year formed a septet, Ekaya.

Ibrahim's music draws on many sources: South African popular music, African traditional music, and the piano styles of Ellington and Thelonious Monk. His melodic gifts as a soloist are complemented by a strong left-hand technique, a percussive attack, and an African sense of rhythm; he is also a fine player of ballads. Besides piano, he plays soprano saxophone, flute, and cello.

Oral history material in *CtY*.

SELECTED RECORDINGS

As unaccompanied soloist: *Ode to Duke Ellington* (1973, IC 6049); *Autobiography* (1978, Planisphare 1267-6, 1267-7)

Duos: with M. Roach: *Streams of Consciousness* (1977, Bay. 6016); with J. Dyani: *Echoes from Africa* (1979, IC 3019); with C. Ward: *Live at Sweet Basil*, i (1983, Ekapa 004)

As leader: with H. Masekela and K. Moeketsi: *Jazz Epistles: Verse I* (1960, Gallo Continental 14); *Duke Ellington Presents the Dollar Brand Trio* (1963, Rep. 6111); *African Marketplace* (1979, Elek. 6E252); *Ekaya* (1983, Ekapa 005); *Zimbabwe* (1983, Enja 4056)

As sideman with Elvin Jones: *Midnight Walk* (1966, Atl. 1485)

BIBLIOGRAPHY

V. Wilmer: "Two in Harmony," *JB*, ii/6 (1965), 22

I. S. Petersen: "Dollar Brand: Universal Silence," *Coda*, xi/6 (1974), 2

B. Primack: "Dollar Brand (Abdullah Ibrahim): Serving Allah through Jazz Piano," *CK*, vi/5 (1980), 28 [incl. discography]

M. Zwerin: "Abdullah Ibrahim," *International Herald Tribune* (27 Oct 1982), 18

G. Lock: "In Struggle, in Grace: Abdullah Ibrahim: Music, Revolution, and Prayer," *The Wire*, no.8 (1984), 12 [incl. discography]

D. Palmer: "Abdullah Ibrahim: Capetown Crusader," *DB*, lii/1 (1985), 20 [incl. discography]

ED HAZELL

IGJ. *See* INTERNATIONALE GESELLSCHAFT FÜR JAZZFORSCHUNG.

Igoe, Sonny [Owen Joseph] (*b* Jersey City, NJ, 8 Oct 1923). Drummer. He first gained prominence working for Benny Goodman (1948–9). From 1950 to 1952 he was a member of Woody Herman's Third Herd, and was principal soloist on Herman's recording of *New Golden Wedding* (1951, MGM 1010). He performed and recorded with Charlie Ventura (1953–5), then worked as a studio musician in New York. From the late 1960s his principal activity has been as a teacher, but he has continued to perform with small groups and, with Dick Meldonian, as the leader of a big band, with which he recorded in 1982 and 1983. Igoe's playing was initially influenced by that of Gene Krupa, but he soon incorporated elements of the work of Max Roach and others, and eventually developed an exuberant and individual style.

BIBLIOGRAPHY

FeatherE
C. Deffaa: "Sonny Igoe," *MD*, viii/11 (1984), 20

CHIP DEFFAA

IJF. *See* INTERNATIONAL JAZZ FEDERATION.

IJS. *See* INSTITUTE OF JAZZ STUDIES.

Ilcken, Wessel (*b* Hilversum, Netherlands, 1 Dec 1923; *d* Loosdrecht, nr Hilversum, 13 July 1957). Dutch drummer. In Paris he learned to play drums, belonged to an orchestra led by Piet van Dijk (from 1942), and met Rita Reys, whom he married (1945). He formed a quintet in 1950, toured Germany, lived in Sweden (1953), and returned to the Netherlands, where he achieved prominence as a drummer. He played on most of the tracks included on *Jazz behind the Dikes* (1955–6, Phi. 10077, 08000, 08004), a series of three LPs that were the first important albums of Dutch jazz; he also performed with Lars Gullin, Dizzy Gillespie, Joe Carroll, Herbie Mann, Bob Cooper, and Stan Kenton. In 1963 a jazz prize bearing his name was inaugurated in his honor; this later became known as the Boy Edgar Prize, then as the Dutch National Jazz Prize.

WIM VAN EYLE

Imperial. Record company and label. The company was established in Hollywood in the 1940s, and recorded jazz only intermittently. In the 1950s it produced three important LPs by Sonny Criss, and two by Charlie Mariano; a fine album by Harold Land appeared on Imperial in 1963. Nevertheless the company's involvement with jazz remained sporadic; Imperial was taken over by Liberty in the early 1960s.

MARK GARDNER

Imperial Orchestra. New Orleans dance band active from 1901 to 1908. The group, which comprised five to seven musicians, was led by Manuel Perez and played from written arrangements; it was widely admired by early jazz musicians for its polished performances. Among its sidemen were George Baquet, Big Eye Nelson, the trombonist George Filhe, the violinist James A. Palao, the double bass player Billy Marrero, the baritone horn player Adolphe Alexander, Sr., and the drummer Jean Vigne.

WILLIAM J. SCHAFER

Improvisation. The spontaneous creation of music as it is performed. It may involve the immediate composition of an entire work by its performers, or the elaboration or other variation of an existing framework, or anything in between. All the performers in a group, or a soloist, or any intermediate combination of players may improvise.

1. Introduction. 2. Solo and collective improvisation. 3. Improvisation and form. 4. Techniques and procedures: (i) Paraphrase improvisation (ii) Use of motifs (iii) Formulaic improvisation (iv) Motivic improvisation (v) Interrelated techniques (vi) Modal improvisation. 5. Intangible elements: (i) Extramusical meaning (ii) Risk and repetition.

1. INTRODUCTION. Improvisation is generally regarded as the principal element of jazz since it offers the possibilities of spontaneity, surprise, experiment, and discovery, without which most jazz would be devoid of interest. Almost all styles of jazz leave some room for improvisation – whether a single chorus or other short passage during which a soloist may improvise over an accompaniment, a sequence of choruses for different soloists, or the entire piece after the statement of a theme – and some jazz is spontaneously created without the use of a predetermined framework (see §3 below). Improvisation is the defining characteristic of much of New Orleans jazz and its related styles, some big-band music, nearly all small-group swing, most bop, modal jazz, and free jazz, and some jazz-rock.

It is, however, demonstrably untrue that all jazz must involve improvisation. Many pieces that are unquestionably classifiable as jazz are entirely composed before a performance, and take the form of an ARRANGEMENT, either fixed in notation or thoroughly memorized by the players; this approach to jazz is characteristic of much music for big band, notably that of Duke Ellington, extended works that combine elements of jazz and Western art music (*see* PROGRESSIVE JAZZ and THIRD STREAM), and much jazz-rock.

Since improvisation is by nature evanescent, its study poses certain obvious difficulties. The principal medium for the preservation of jazz is the recording, and most of the observations made about jazz improvisation result from repeated listening to recorded performances. In many cases, however, scholars and musicians have made transcriptions from recordings in order the better to be able to examine or reproduce jazz works; for a discussion of the purposes and difficulties of notating improvised jazz *see* TRANSCRIPTION (i).

2. SOLO AND COLLECTIVE IMPROVISATION. The element of improvisation in jazz is sometimes described in terms of the relationship between the members of the ensemble. Generally speaking, attention is concentrated on individual musicians, who, in the succession of choruses (statements of and variations on a theme) that make up the most common form of jazz performance, play (or "take") solos; a solo normally consists of a single chorus or a continuous succession of choruses during which the player improvises on the harmonies (maybe also to a greater or lesser degree the melody) of the theme, while some or all of the other musicians provide an accompaniment. The terms "solo," "to play a solo," and "soloist" are therefore often used as synonyms for "improvisation," "to improvise," and "improviser." This conflation of meanings can, however, be misleading: not all solos are improvised and not all improvisations are played by soloists. For example, the accompaniment played by some or all of the ensemble while a soloist improvises may itself to some extent be improvised: in jazz that contains no element of written arrangement the musicians are restricted, if at all, only by the fixed chord sequence and metric structure of the theme, and each may elaborate the harmonies and rhythms at will, as is appropriate to his role within the ensemble. In such a context it is the nature of the improvisation – the freedom of invention, virtuosity, and ornamental elaboration allowed by his function – and not the mere fact of improvising that distinguishes the soloist from the accompanists.

The degree to which an accompaniment is improvised increases as the framework on which a piece is based becomes less and less rigidly fixed. In a performance by a big band, for example, the accompanists often play from written arrangements and only the soloist is free to improvise; in a bop quartet, playing without music but working on an existing theme, the members of the ensemble have considerable freedom in the choice of harmonies and rhythms; in modal jazz the confines are those of a scale or a general tonal area; in free jazz the restrictions are fewer still, the style being characterized chiefly by the lack of fixed elements such as tonality, chord sequences, and meter.

The use of the term "collective improvisation" is related to the concepts of soloist and accompanists. Where these functions are sharply differentiated the term is not normally used, even though all or most of the players may be improvising more or less freely. It is commonly applied in contexts where some or all members of a group participate in simultaneous improvisation of equal or comparable "weight," for example New Orleans jazz (in which it is used chiefly of reeds and brass) and its related styles, and free jazz; it does not preclude the presence of a soloist but it implies a degree of equality among all the players in the ensemble.

3. Improvisation and form. The interaction of fixed and free elements in jazz may be examined not only in terms of the functions of different players but also in terms of structures or Forms. Almost all jazz consists of a combination of predetermined and improvised elements, though the proportion of one to the other differs markedly.

In all periods of jazz history there may be found examples of pieces in which improvisation is allowed only a minor role; commonly a soloist improvises a brief interlude or a single chorus in an otherwise rigidly fixed context. The majority of instances are found among performances by those big bands of the swing era that had few or no distinguished improvisers and which therefore favored a repertory of written arrangements; the improvisations allowed in these scores are short passages, which are not the main attraction of the performance. For example, in the second chorus of Charlie Barnet's *Cherokee* (1939, Bb 10373) the pianist Bill Miller improvises softly beneath the ensemble, but the only principal soloist in the piece is Barnet himself, playing tenor saxophone. After presenting, in the first chorus, a slightly ornamented version of the first half of the 64-bar theme in *aaba* form, he improvises during the second *a* section of the second chorus a rhythmically stiff melody, which consists of a simple blues riff, slightly altered in the repetitions, a quotation of the military call "reveille" and a variation on it, and a brief variation on a riff familiar from Count Basie's *One o'Clock Jump*. Barnet's improvisation here is much less interesting than the complex melody composed by Billy May for the trumpet section at the end of the first chorus of the piece, which has more of the character of an improvised swing melody; nor does it rival the main attraction of the performance – the delicate riffs traded among sections of the band. The reason why Barnet takes a solo is partly because he is the bandleader but more importantly because, as a result of Coleman Hawkins's overwhelming influence, big bands of the swing era mostly included an improvising tenor saxophone soloist, who imitated Hawkins's sound (as Barnet did).

By far the majority of pieces of jazz involve variations on an existing theme, such as a popular song or the blues progression, or a newly composed piece. Two statements of the theme in a more or less fixed form customarily frame a series of variations, several or all of which involve improvisation by a soloist or soloists over an accompaniment supplied by the ensemble. The freedom with which the theme is treated varies from piece to piece and according to the style of the players; indeed, the main reason for the popularity of this form is that it offers so adaptable a scheme within which improvisatory skills can be explored.

The fertility of invention of the greatest improvisers may be gauged by the variety of possibilities they find in a single theme chosen again and again as the basis for a performance. For example, the popular song *What is this thing called love?*, a 32-bar theme in *aaba* form, has served as the basis for numerous improvisations by distinguished players. A version for solo piano by James P. Johnson (1930, Bruns. 4712) in the stride style includes sharp contrasts between thundering bass notes and tinkling treble melodies, and incorporates passages of boogie-woogie playing. Norman Granz's *Jam Session no.2* (1952, Clef 4002) presents a performance that consists of an informal succession of 26 choruses of individual swing and bop improvisations by Oscar Peterson, Flip Phillips, Charlie Shavers, Johnny Hodges, Barney Kessel, Benny Carter, Ben Webster, Charlie Parker, Peterson again, and Ray Brown, followed by three choruses during which the soloists trade fours. The rendering by the trio of Bill Evans (ii) on the album *Portraits in Jazz* (1959, Riv. 1162) is devoted primarily to Evans's bop piano playing, but also includes improvisations by the double bass player Scott LaFaro (one and a half choruses) and the drummer Paul Motian (half a chorus). A lengthy, radically altered version, retitled *What Love*, on the album *Charles Mingus Presents Charles Mingus* (1960, Candid 9005) includes improvisations by Ted Curson and Eric Dolphy (who both combine characteristics of bop and free-jazz playing), an unaccompanied solo by Mingus, and a hilarious, improvised, "conversation" between Mingus's double bass and Dolphy's bass clarinet. A much later performance is recorded by the singer Bobby McFerrin accompanied on piano by Herbie Hancock on the album *The Other Side of Round Midnight* (1985, BN 85135).

The completely spontaneous creation of new forms by means of free improvisation, independent of an existing framework, is rarer in jazz than it might seem, not least because where two or more musicians play together, no matter how intimately they know one another's work, some agreed decisions about the progress of a piece are normally necessary. Free jazz often gives the impression that musicians follow their inspiration and invention, reacting to and interacting with one another from moment to moment; but, as Eberhard Jost has demonstrated by means of detailed analyses of recordings, free-jazz performances may be as dependent on themes as other styles of jazz, though the themes and the way they are treated are often of unusual character. Even where no theme is used, certain prearranged schemes, such as the sequence in which soloists should play and the signals by which players will communicate decisions, are usually followed.

Two of Jost's analyses provide good examples of the kinds of formal determinant present in free-jazz performances. In discussing Cecil Taylor's difficult and largely spontaneously created piece *Unit Structures* on the album of the same name (1966, BN 84237) Jost supplies a running commentary, detailing textural contrasts, delineating whenever possible the roles of the instruments (e.g., "one double bass player plays pizzicato in the low register, the other arco in the high register"), transcribing brief themes and motifs, and noting the "soloists" who in turn come to the fore during the collective improvisation that is central to the piece. On the two takes of John Coltrane's *Ascension* (1965, both issued, at different times, as Imp. 95) Jost identifies the succession of soloists whose improvisations alternate with passages of collective improvisation; he describes several recurring modal areas, which provide a loose underpinning for each solo, and exposes Coltrane's technique of holding pitches to signal a movement from one modal area to another. Such factors do not compromise the extraordinary originality and creativity of free-jazz performances; rather they call attention to the necessary limits of spontaneity. An entirely spontaneous improvisation might well be incoherent.

4. Techniques and procedures. Although no two jazz improvisations ever evolve in exactly the same way, certain techniques and procedures may be identified as common or even standard. For the purposes of description they may be regarded

Ex. 1 *Body and Soul*
(a) Section *a*: (i) Opening of the original theme (ii) Opening of Benny Goodman's solo (1935, Vic. 25115), transcr. B. Kernfeld (iii) Opening of Coleman Hawkins's solo in the first chorus (1939, Bb 10523), transcr. H. Jones, *DB*, vii/17 (1940), 16 (iv) Second *a* section from Hawkins's solo (v) Opening of Roy Eldridge's solo, beginning at the second chorus, on the version by Chu Berry (1944, Com. 1502), transcr. B. Russo and L. Lifton, *DB*, xvii/11 (1950), 12 (all written at sounding pitch)

as falling roughly into three categories, though in practice a player may use several or even all in the course of a single improvisation, often overlaying one with another. Paraphrase improvisation is the ornamental variation of a theme or some part of it, which remains recognizable. Formulaic improvisation is the building of new material from a diverse body of fragmentary ideas (either in response to a theme or independently). And motivic improvisation is the building of new material through the development of a single fragmentary idea (again either in response to a theme or independently).

(i) Paraphrase improvisation. Melodic paraphrase – the ornamentation of the melody of the theme or some part of it – is a crucial procedure in jazz. It is heard in any piece based on a tuneful theme, especially in early jazz, swing, jazz-rock, and performances in any style based on ballads, but regularly in

(b) Section *b*: (i) From the original theme (ii) From Teddy Wilson's solo in the first chorus, on the version by Benny Goodman, transcr. S. Pease, *DB*, iv/8 (1937), 26 (iii) From Coleman Hawkins's solo in the first chorus (iv) From Roy Eldridge's solo in the second chorus, on the version by Chu Berry (all written at sounding pitch)

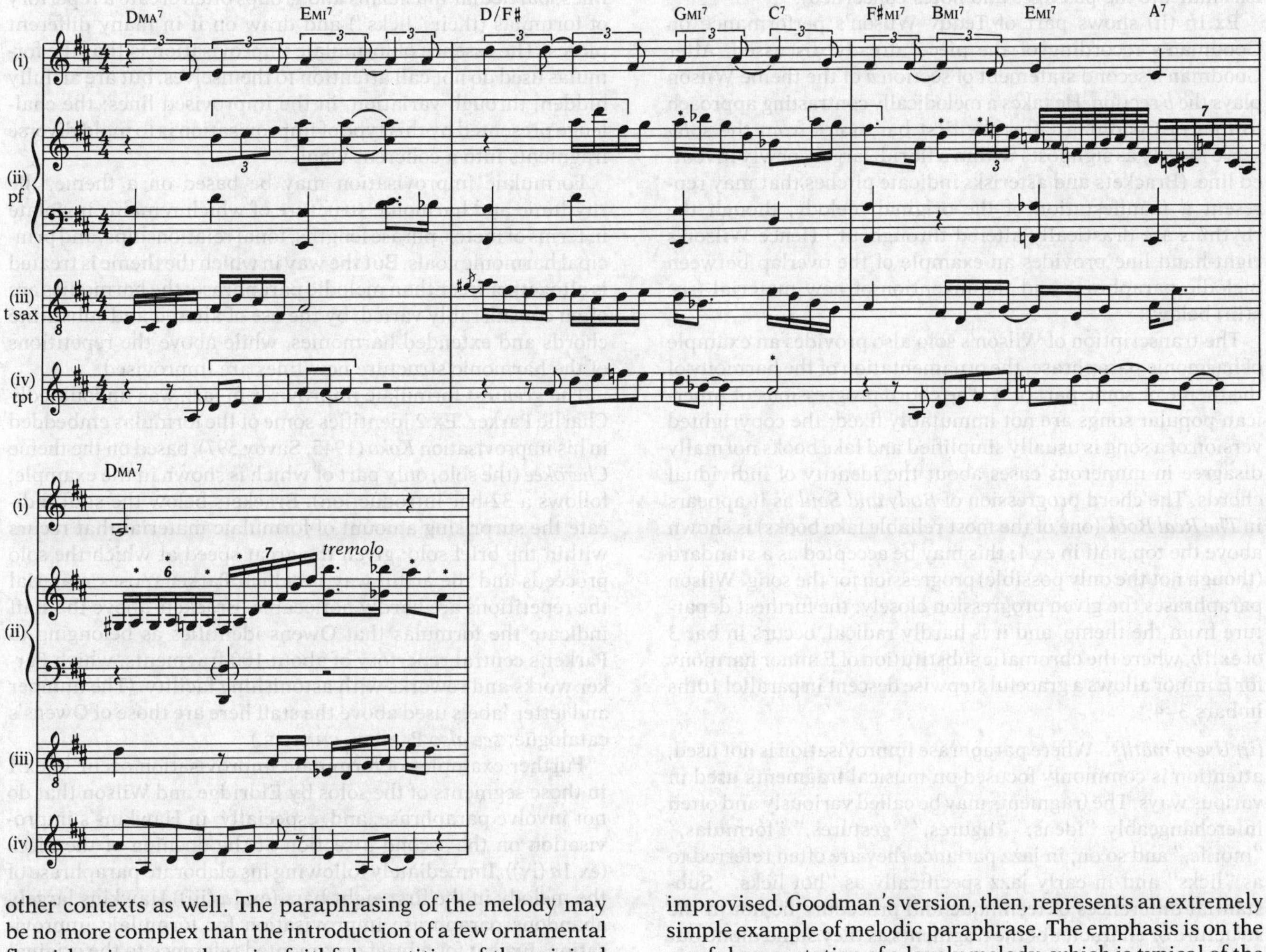

other contexts as well. The paraphrasing of the melody may be no more complex than the introduction of a few ornamental flourishes into an otherwise faithful repetition of the original tune. But at its most inventive it may involve a highly imaginative reworking of the melody, which remains recognizable only by its outline or the preservation of certain distinctive turns of phrase or figure. The underlying harmonic structure, which in jazz is the element that chiefly identifies a theme, remains essentially unchanged, though that too may be subjected to local alteration and embellishment.

Several famous improvisations on the theme of *Body and Soul* (a 32-bar melody in *aaba* form) are presented in ex.1, showing a range of possibilities for paraphrase improvisation. The top staff shows the melody of the eight-bar *a* section of the theme (ex.1*a*) and the first four bars of the *b* section (ex.1*b*) (notated in triplet groupings of quarter- and eighth-notes, which approximate to the subtle lilt of a performance characterized by a sense of swing). It may be seen that Benny Goodman's version of the melody (ex.1*a* (ii)) scarcely alters the theme. Goodman slightly enhances the feeling of swing by placing several notes ahead of the beat and repeating several others; in bar 2 his use of vibrato and a subtle "push" of breath suggest the presence of the second *b*♭′ found in the original melody; and he extends the descending line in bar 5. His nearly literal repetition of this rendition of the *a* section twice more in the opening chorus, and again when the theme recurs at the end of the performance shows that his paraphrase is scarcely improvised. Goodman's version, then, represents an extremely simple example of melodic paraphrase. The emphasis is on the careful presentation of a lovely melody, which is typical of the way in which Goodman states a melodic theme (though it is by no means characteristic of his procedure in the middle stages of a piece, where he often creates highly inventive formulaic improvisations).

Ex.1*a* (iii) shows Coleman Hawkins's melodic paraphrase at the beginning of his renowned version of the piece (1939, Bb 10523). To a far greater extent than Goodman, Hawkins ornaments the melody by repeating notes, adding neighbor notes and passing notes, placing notes ahead of or behind the beat, and interpolating brief, nonthematic flourishes into the phrases. (*See also* HAWKINS, COLEMAN, ex.1.)

Excerpts from the solo played by Roy Eldridge in a performance of *Body and Soul* by Chu Berry's group (1944, Com. 1502) constitute exx.1*a* (v) and 1*b* (iv). (The rhythms represented here by even eighth-notes have the same lilt and swing as those notated by triplet groupings of quarter- and eighth-notes above.) In jazz performances based on standards such as *Body and Soul* melodic paraphrase tends to occur at the beginning and end of the piece rather than in the middle; by the time Eldridge begins his solo Berry himself has already stated the theme in the first chorus so that Eldridge is not obliged to. Moreover Eldridge's solo is taken in "double-time" (the apparent tempo, in fact, nearly trebles, while the harmonic rhythm remains constant), and one might therefore expect to hear fast running phrases rather than the deliberately paced, plaintive melody. Thus the extent to which Eldridge's paraphrase follows the melody of the theme is perhaps unexpected (brackets and asterisks indicate the passages and notes concerned).

Ex.1*b* (ii) shows part of Teddy Wilson's performance on Goodman's recording of the piece already discussed. After Goodman's second statement of section *a* of the theme Wilson plays the *b* section. He takes a melodically contrasting approach to that of Goodman: after the first bar, notes from the song serve merely as signposts within a florid, largely newly invented line. (Brackets and asterisks indicate pitches that may represent a manifestation of the original melody, though the rhythms are drastically altered throughout.) Hence Wilson's right-hand line provides an example of the overlap between melodic paraphrase and the invention of new material (see §(iii) below).

The transcription of Wilson's solo also provides an example of harmonic paraphrase, the ornamentation of the harmony of the theme or some part of it. The chord progressions of American popular songs are not immutably fixed: the copyrighted version of a song is usually simplified and fake books normally disagree in numerous cases about the identity of individual chords. The chord progression of *Body and Soul* as it appears in *The Real Book* (one of the most reliable fake books) is shown above the top staff in ex.1; this may be accepted as a standard (though not the only possible) progression for the song. Wilson paraphrases the given progression closely: the furthest departure from the theme, and it is hardly radical, occurs in bar 3 of ex.1*b*, where the chromatic substitution of F minor harmony for E minor allows a graceful stepwise descent in parallel 10ths in bars 3–4.

(ii) Use of motifs. Where paraphrase improvisation is not used, attention is commonly focused on musical fragments used in various ways. The fragments may be called variously and often interchangeably "ideas," "figures," "gestures," "formulas," "motifs," and so on; in jazz parlance they are often referred to as "licks" and in early jazz specifically as "hot licks." Substantial differences of technique and procedure lie not in the structure or character of the fragments as they stand alone but rather in the ways in which they are combined and manipulated in improvisation. For the sake of clarity the word "motif" is used here in the discussion of motivic improvisation, and "formula" in the discussion of formulaic improvisation.

The fragmentary ideas used in jazz are usually distinguished by rhythmic and intervallic shape and can seldom be described as melodic in the tuneful sense, though they provide the material on which most of the players in the ensemble improvise; their tempo, outline, tonal implications, and so on are determined by stylistic conventions, so that an idea used in free jazz will be different in nature from one used in jazz-rock. The introduction of a new fragment or new stages in its development occur in response to a particular context (a certain tempo or key change, for example), determined by the players in advance or enshrined in the conventions of the style. In some types of jazz in which the form of the piece is built up from fragments, most notably jazz-rock, a foundation is often supplied by an ostinato, a short phrase strongly stating (on chordal instruments) or implying (on melodic ones) a sequence of harmonies, which is repeated virtually unchanged by the bass instrument.

(iii) Formulaic improvisation. The principal manifestation of the fragmentary idea in jazz is in formulaic improvisation. This is the most common kind of improvisation in jazz, spanning all styles. In formulaic improvisation (a concept borrowed from studies of epic poetry and Western ecclesiastical chant) many diverse formulas intertwine and combine within continuous lines; particular musicians and groups often create a repertory of formulas (their "licks") and draw on it in many different pieces. The essence of formulaic improvisation is that the formulas used do not call attention to themselves, but are artfully hidden, through variation, in the improvised lines; the challenge presented by this type of improvisation is to mold diverse fragments into a coherent whole.

Formulaic improvisation may be based on a theme, the rhythmic and harmonic structure of which remains inviolate in terms of meter, phrase lengths, tonal relationships, and principal harmonic goals. But the way in which the theme is treated is altogether freer than melodic paraphrase; the harmonies are often considerably varied, by the use of altered and substitute chords and extended harmonies, while above the repetitions of the harmonic structure new lines are improvised.

The greatest formulaic improviser in jazz was undoubtedly Charlie Parker. Ex.2 identifies some of the formulas embedded in his improvisation *Koko* (1945, Savoy 597), based on the theme *Cherokee* (the solo, only part of which is shown in the example, follows a 32-bar introduction). Brackets below the staff indicate the surprising amount of formulaic material that recurs within the brief solo; given the great speed at which the solo proceeds and the artful way in which Parker reuses material the repetitions are hardly noticeable. Brackets above the staff indicate the formulas that Owens identifies as belonging to Parker's central repertory of about 100 fragments, which Parker works and reworks with astonishing facility. (The number and letter labels used above the staff here are those of Owens's catalogue; *see also* PARKER, CHARLIE.)

Further examples of formulaic improvisation occur in ex.1 in those segments of the solos by Eldridge and Wilson that do not involve paraphrase, and, especially, in Hawkins's improvisation on the second *a* section at the opening of the piece (ex.1*a* (iv)). Immediately following his elaborate paraphrase of the melody in the first eight bars (ex.1*a* (iii)) Hawkins largely abandons paraphrase improvisation for formulaic improvisation. Except for a brief ornamented reference to the original melody, centered on bar 4 (as the brackets indicate), Hawkins invents a new melody, fitting the rhythmic and harmonic structure of *Body and Soul*. Another example occurs in ex.6 (see p.562), an improvisation by Jean-Luc Ponty, which includes some of the formulaic pentatonic runs characteristic of jazz-rock. In none of these cases are the characteristic formulas for the musicians concerned indicated: such identification would require for these soloists the same careful and detailed analysis that Owens has carried out for Parker.

Where formulaic improvisation is not linked to a theme it may be founded on the imitation of established performers, on the collective invention of members of a group working together, or on the individual's own explorations. The procedure may be detected in music as difficult as Albert Ayler's free-jazz improvisations from 1964, in which recurring formulas – leaps over wide intervals, rapid, unmeasured, sweeping lines of undistinguished pitches, freely placed, vocalistic exclamations in extreme high or low registers – provide a basis for improvised lines. By comparison with the types of formula that are normally played in response to a familiar theme, such gestures as Ayler's may seem highly distinctive and hardly in accord with the idea that the essence of formulaic improvisation is to disguise the presence of the formulas: however, in the context of a free-jazz performance such sounds are characteristic rath-

Ex.2 Opening of Charlie Parker's solo on *Koko* (1945, Savoy 597); transcr. J. Mehegan (written at sounding pitch)

er than distinctive, and the formulas are both difficult to hear precisely and sometimes impossible to transcribe. Hence in formulaic improvisation, regardless of the style, sustained accomplishment may be measured in terms of the improviser's ability to avoid turning formulas into clichés.

(iv) Motivic improvisation. In motivic improvisation one or more motifs (but never more than a few) form the basis for a section of a piece, an entire piece, or a group of related pieces. The motif is developed or varied through such processes as ornamentation, transposition, rhythmic displacement, diminution, augmentation, and inversion. Unlike those used in formulaic improvisation, musical ideas in this type of improvisation call attention to themselves by the way in which they are treated, and indeed they must be recognized and followed through a piece or section if the music is to be properly appreciated; the difficulty here lies not in disguising the motif but in avoiding both trivial restatement and variations that effectively obscure its character. The most commonly occurring form of motivic improvisation is that in which a single motif forms the basis of a piece or section, but sometimes two or three motifs are used simultaneously, and elsewhere one motif follows another by a process of chain reaction, each being varied until it is transformed into the next.

Motivic improvisation in jazz rarely involves the kind of systematic repetition and transposition heard in classical music. An unusual example may be heard in *Acknowledgement*, the first movement of John Coltrane's suite *A Love Supreme* (1964, Imp. 77). As ex.3 demonstrates, Coltrane repeats a motif more than 30 times, eventually transposing it into all 12 keys. Far more characteristically in jazz, the rhythmic and intervallic

Ex.3 Motivic work at the end of John Coltrane's solo on *Acknowledgement* from *A Love Supreme* (1964, Imp. 77); transcr. A. White (written at sounding pitch)

Ex.4 Benny Carter's solo (final section of the first chorus and part of the second) on the Chocolate Dandies' *I can't believe that you're in love with me* (1940, Com. 1506); transcr. B. Kernfeld (written at sounding pitch)

shape of a motif is not repeated literally, but is subjected to the processes of variation described above. Fine examples occur in Coltrane's solo on *So What* from Miles Davis's album *Kind of Blue* (1959, Col. CL1355; for a transcription and analysis of this solo *see* COLTRANE, JOHN) and on the title track (1961) of Coltrane's album *Impressions* (1961–3, Imp. 42), especially in choruses 5, 6, 9, 14, 16, 21, 22, 23, 26, 27, 29, and 30 of his solo.

In some pieces motivic procedures are applied not to freely invented material but to a motif or series of motifs drawn from a theme stated at the outset; this subcategory of motivic improvisation may be termed thematic improvisation, though the derivation of a motif from the theme is generally incidental and merely convenient rather than structurally significant. Thematic improvisation is regularly mentioned in jazz literature in connection with the music of Sonny Rollins, but it has scarcely any meaning for Rollins's work (for further discussion *see* ROLLINS, SONNY). It is a more appropriate concept in some free jazz, where musicians develop fragments of thematic material in ways that cannot be construed as melodic paraphrase. Examples include Albert Ayler's deconstruction of the theme in early versions of *Ghosts* recorded in 1964 (on the albums *Spiritual Unity*, ESP 1002, and *Ghosts*, Debut 144) and Don Cherry's and Gato Barbieri's improvisations on Cherry's album *Complete Communion* (1965, BN 84226).

Before the late 1950s motivic improvisation occurred in jazz far less often than either paraphrase or formulaic improvisation. The reasons are clear: until that time a jazz improvisation was expected to accord with an underlying theme; the given theme usually involves a functional progression, which moves at the rate of one, two, or four chords per bar; the improvisation itself often moves along quickly. Given these conditions it is extremely difficult to develop a motif systematically without stumbling. Hence among the greatest improvisers in early, swing, and bop styles, perhaps only three players consistently utilized motivic techniques: Benny Carter, Count Basie, and Thelonious Monk (*see also* LEWIS, JOHN).

Carter stands apart from his peers in his deliberate, elegant, intellectualized approach to improvising on standard tunes. One manifestation of this is his tendency to develop a motif, transposing it as necessary to fit the underlying chord progression. Ex.4 presents an excerpt from his solo on *I can't believe that you're in love with me* (1940, Com. 1506) by the Chocolate Dandies (beginning at the last *a* section of the 32-bar *aaba* theme). Brackets indicate the recurring motifs, repeated literally, transposed, or slightly ornamented: there is a close relationship between motif *a* (step down, leap up), *a′* (step up, leap up), and *a″* (step down, leap down, step down), the leaps being predominantly of a 6th, less often a 5th or 7th; the octave leap in motif *b* and the stepwise descent in motif *c* may also be interpreted as deriving from *a*.

Basie sometimes (though not when playing in the stride style) and Monk often incorporate motivic work into their improvisations because they prefer subtle variations on simple, repeated material to fast-moving, ever-changing formulaic lines. The beginning of Monk's solo on *In Walked Bud* (1968) from the album *Underground* (1967–8, Col. CS9632) is shown in ex.5. The monophonic line consists of a motif (bracketed in the example) that descends through two octaves; Monk plays it eight times, varying the pitches somewhat, but more importantly varying the rhythm by compressing the idea as he repeats it and by displacing individual notes. A second example occurs later in the same solo: beginning at the end of bar 32 and continuing through bar 46 he repeats a single pitch, the tonic, against a chromatically descending line in the left hand; the motivic variation consists entirely of manipulations of rhythm and accentuation, in his placement of the single note in strong and weak rhythmic positions and in his strong and weak attacks.

From the late 1950s new styles have provided a more suitable framework within which motivic improvisation can occur, and

Ex.5 Opening of Thelonious Monk's solo, beginning at the third chorus, on *In Walked Bud* (1968) from *Underground* (1967–8, Col. CS9632); transcr. B. Kernfeld

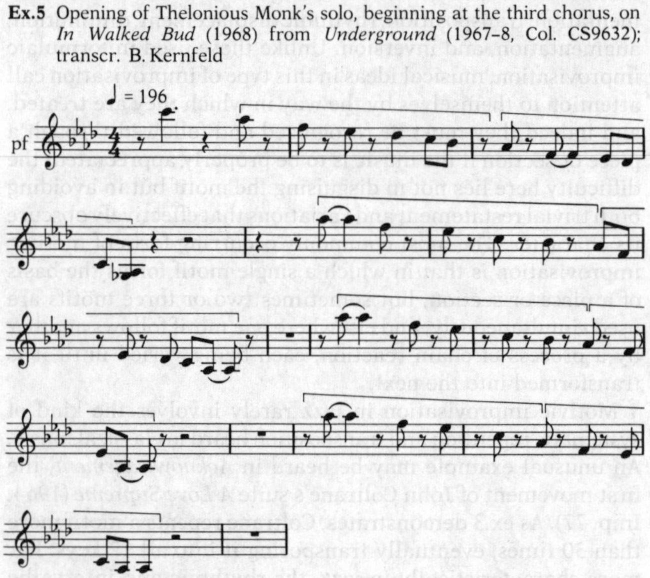

it has become more regularly used, rivaling paraphrase and formulaic improvisation in importance. On the one hand free jazz has discarded the characteristic themes of previous styles in favor of ad hoc structures, and on the other modal jazz, jazz-rock, and other fusions of jazz and popular music have discarded them in favor of simple drones or ostinatos. In all cases improvisers, freed from the need to follow a fast-moving chord progression, have been able to give greater attention to motivic improvisation. Furthermore the repetition and development of motifs provides an element of coherence and stability, which in a sense fill the same role as a conventional theme.

(v) Interrelated techniques. The three categories of improvisatory technique described here are not mutually exclusive in performance: two or more may be in operation within a single improvisation, often simultaneously. Their complex interrelationships may be summarized as follows: paraphrase involves the strict, bar-by-bar embellishment of pre-existing material in such a way that it remains recognizable; formulaic and motivic improvisation create new ideas. Paraphrase and motivic improvisation involve the constant development respectively of a specific theme and fragment, which give a piece a particular identity; formulaic improvisation proceeds by means of the ingenious weaving together of fragments from a general repertory that is common to many diverse pieces. In paraphrase and motivic improvisation theme and motif must remain recognizable if the improvisation is to achieve its intended effect, but at the same time the player must be inventive enough to create ever new variations; in formulaic improvisation formulas must be disguised and the player's skill in this case must be directed towards the creation of interesting and coherent new lines built round a succession of small elements.

The ways in which the different procedures of improvisation are combined can be complex and constantly changing. Different members of an ensemble may simultaneously employ several improvisatory techniques, or a keyboard player may employ one in the right hand and another in the left (as Wilson does). In a bop quartet's performance of a popular song, for example, the saxophonist might paraphrase the theme and then invent a new, fast-moving formulaic melody, while the pianist maintains the harmonic structure, though with his own local variations, the double bass player creates a formulaic walking bass line from the given harmony, moving in quarter-notes from chordal root to chordal root, and the drummer plays strings of rhythmic patterns, including variations on swinging cymbal rhythms and irregularly placed bass-drum beats (or bombs). At a higher level an improvisation that was originally generated by motivic or formulaic procedures may be adopted as a pre-existing theme and subjected to melodic paraphrase in its turn; among the great improvisers such an approach is characteristic of Louis Armstrong (see §5(ii) below) and of Miles Davis's blues playing.

(vi) Modal improvisation. Performances may also be analyzed in terms that cut across the categories already drawn and which may employ variously the techniques of paraphrase, formulaic improvisation, or motivic improvisation. For example, an improvisation may be described in terms of pitch – not so much how the pitches are put together as what pitches are selected – and indeed much of the conceptual discussion of improvisation in the realm of jazz education has been directed towards this issue. The use of tonal or atonal vocabulary, though it deeply affects the character of the music, has no bearing on the improvisatory techniques used, each of which applies to all or many styles of jazz. However, in one important case, improvisation based on modal scales, the controlled, systematic approach to pitch selection gives the music a sufficiently distinct identity to warrant separate discussion.

The defining characteristic of modal improvisation is that it explores the melodic and harmonic possibilities of a collection of pitches, often corresponding to one of the ecclesiastical modes or to a nondiatonic scale from traditional or ethnic music. The mode is expressed harmonically through drones or through two or more chords that oscillate beneath melodic lines using the same pitches; a typical feature of modal improvisation is therefore harmonic stasis and consequently an absence of incident and progression in the short term. Modal improvisation is not coterminous with MODAL JAZZ, a style in which improvisers regularly select pitches in a loose, perhaps free, perhaps chromatically complex relation to underlying modes. It is much more likely to be found in jazz-rock and other fusions, which not only involve a simple, static harmonic underpinning, but in which the soloist is expected to improvise in close accord with such an underpinning.

A fine example of modal improvisation is shown in ex.6 (p.562), an excerpt from Jean-Luc Ponty's *Gardens of Babylon* (beginning in the last bar of an interlude following an acoustic guitar solo) from his album *Imaginary Voyage* (1976, Atl. 19136). He plays for the most part within a six-note scale (F♯–G♯–A–B–C♯–E); his occasional use of D and its recurrence as an element in the ostinato bass line identify the mode as aeolian (the ecclesiastical mode with a minor third, sixth, and seventh above the final) on F♯. It should not be presumed that such a single-minded procedure as modal improvisation necessarily yields a boring result. In this example the aeolian scale on F♯ unquestionably provides the basis for Ponty's improvised melody, but Ponty enriches this limited collection of pitches with an abundance of blue notes, bends, and glisses; he achieves these effects not only by exploiting the possibilities for pitch variation inherent in the violin but also by using a wa-wa pedal. In the transcription grace notes linked by slurs to the principal melodic notes and straight lines indicating glisses from one principal note to another indicate only approximately the variety of Ponty's use of these microtonal effects.

5. INTANGIBLE ELEMENTS.

(i) Extramusical meaning. As with any improvised music, jazz gives the player an opportunity for self-expression which is to a large degree absent when he reproduces composed or arranged works. The extent to which he attempts to communicate, succeeds in communicating, or unwittingly communicates ideas or images through his music depends not only on his own approach but also on that of the listener. Indeed, the listener may make his own subjective interpretations of the music, whether representational or abstract, which the player would entirely repudiate; such responses are not peculiar to improvised jazz, nor even to jazz in general, but are common among listeners to all kinds of music.

A straightforward extramusical meaning, of course, attaches to pieces that have lyrics; purely instrumental improvisation may form part of this connection, especially where the singer engages in an exchange with an improvising player (as in the call-and-response passages of pieces in which Billie Holiday is accompanied by Lester Young, the two having an extraordinary rapport and quickness of reaction to each other's music). A similar conversational impression, often with humorous overtones, is created by the dialogues between the double bass player Charles Mingus and the bass clarinetist Eric Dolphy (an

Ex.6 Jean-Luc Ponty's solo on *Gardens of Babylon* from *Imaginary Voyage* (1976, Atl. 19136); transcr. B. Kernfeld

example of which is discussed in §3 above), the unison singing and double bass playing in improvisations by Slam Stewart, and the hilarious mumbling discussions with himself that color Clark Terry's playing. Soul-jazz musicians may convey the effect of black gospel preaching, seeming to translate the preacher's typical formulaic phrases into formulaic melody. The instrumental howls and exclamatory noises of free-jazz players have been interpreted by some as protests against racism in the USA. But for the most part such interpretations of improvisation are of little importance except to those who feel the need to make them.

(ii) Risk and repetition. The essence of improvisation in jazz is the delicate balance between spontaneous invention, carrying with it both the danger of loss of control and the opportunity for creativity of a high order, and reference to the familiar, without which, paradoxically, creativity cannot be truly valued. Improvisation allows a musician to experiment, and, in the process of exploring timbres and techniques, to redefine conventional standards of virtuosity. Musicians learn to transform accidents, instantaneously adjusting the direction of a line to accommodate an unintended, but perhaps refreshing, "mistake." The element of risk in improvisation is the source of great vitality in jazz, but many improvisers do not take risks constantly. Repetition may permeate not only general improvisatory procedures to a greater or lesser degree but also specific solos, which are essentially the same in performance after performance, changing only gradually if at all.

Widely recognized as the two greatest jazz improvisers, Charlie Parker and Louis Armstrong best illustrate the extremes of risk and repetition. Parker never repeated an entire solo, and successive performances based on the same tune are sometimes startlingly different (as, for example, in the two takes of *Embraceable you*, recorded on 28 October 1947 and issued on Dial 1024). By contrast, Armstrong, once having arrived at a successful approach, might repeat the contour and many details of a solo in different performances (as on two recordings of the same tune made on 13 and 14 May 1927 and released as *S.O.L. Blues*, Col. 35661, and *Gully Low Blues*, OK 8474). In inventing his ideas Armstrong was no less creative or original an improviser than Parker; moreover, his well-rehèarsed reiterations of many of his solos convey, if not surprise, at least all other qualities of great improvisation.

BIBLIOGRAPHY

THEORY AND ANALYSIS

J.-E. Berendt: *Das Jazzbuch: Entwicklung und Bedeutung der Jazzmusik* (Frankfurt am Main, Germany, 1953, rev. 2/1959 as *Das neue Jazzbuch*, Eng. trans., New York, 1962; rev. and enlarged 5/1981 as *Das grosse Jazzbuch: von New Orleans bis Jazz Rock*, Eng. trans. as *The Jazz Book: from New Orleans to Fusion and Beyond*, Westport, CT, 1982)

A. Hodeir: *Hommes et problèmes du jazz, suivi de La religion du jazz* (Paris, 1954; Eng. trans., rev. Hodeir, as *Jazz: its Evolution and Essence*, New York, 1956/*R*1975)

G. Schuller: *Early Jazz: its Roots and Musical Development* (New York, 1968)

A. M. Dauer: "Improvisation: zur Technik der spontanen Gestaltung im Jazz," *Jf*, i (1969), 113

F. Waidacher: "Freiheit in der Beschränkung: zur schöpferischen Arbeit am Grazer Jazz-Institut," *Jf*, i (1969), 140

M. L. Stewart: *Structural Development in the Jazz Improvisational Technique of Clifford Brown* (diss., U. of Michigan, 1973); pubd in *Jf*, vi–vii (1974–5), 141–273

E. Jost: *Free Jazz* (Graz, Austria, 1974)

T. Owens: *Charlie Parker: Techniques of Improvisation* (diss., UCLA, 1974)

L. O. Koch: "Ornithology: a Study of Charlie Parker's Music," *JJS*, ii (1974–5), no.1, p.61; no.2, p.61

J. Patrick: "Charlie Parker and Harmonic Sources of Bebop Composition," *JJS*, ii/2 (1974–5), 3

R. Byrnside: "The Performer as Creator: Jazz Improvisation," *Contemporary Music and Music Cultures*, ed. C. Hamm, B. Nettl, and R. Byrnside (Englewood Cliffs, NJ, 1975), 223

T. D. Brown: *A History and Analysis of Jazz Drumming to 1942* (diss., U. of Michigan, 1976)

D. J. Noll: *Zur Improvisation im deutschen Free Jazz: Untersuchungen zur Ästhetik frei improvisierter Klangflächen* (Hamburg, Germany, 1977)

D. Bailey: *Improvisation: its Nature and Practice in Music* (Ashbourne, England, 1980; Ger. trans., Hofheim, Germany, 1986)

L. Gushee: "Lester Young's 'Shoeshine Boy'," *IMSCR*, xii *Berkeley 1977*, ed. D. Heartz and B. Wade (Basle, 1981), 151

B. D. Kernfeld: *Adderley, Coltrane, and Davis at the Twilight of Bebop: the Search for Melodic Coherence (1958–59)* (diss., Cornell U., 1981)

D. B. Zinn: *The Structure and Analysis of the Modern Improvised Line*, i: *Theory* (New York, and Bryn Mawr, PA, 1981)

M. Berger, E. Berger, and J. Patrick: *Benny Carter: a Life in American Music* (Metuchen, NJ, and London, 1982), i, 91

J. Pressing: "Pitch Class Set Structures in Contemporary Jazz," *Jf*, xiv (1982), 133–72

W. A. Fraser: *Jazzology: a Study of the Tradition in which Jazz Musicians Learn to Improvise* (diss., U. of Pennsylvania, 1983)

B. Kernfeld: "Two Coltranes," *ARJS*, ii (1983), 7–61

L. Porter: *John Coltrane's Music of 1960 through 1967: Jazz Improvisation as Composition* (diss., Brandeis U., 1983)

P. Rinzler: "McCoy Tyner: Style and Syntax," *ARJS*, ii (1983), 109–49
D. L. Moorman: *An Analytic Study of Jazz Improvisation, with Suggestions for Performance* (diss., New York U., 1984)
L. Porter: *Lester Young* (Boston, 1985)

PEDAGOGICAL TEXTS

J. Mehegan: *Jazz Improvisation* (New York, 1959–65)
J. Coker: *Improvising Jazz* (Englewood Cliffs, NJ, 1964)
J. LaPorta: *A Guide to Improvisation* (Boston, 1968)
D. Baker: *Jazz Improvisation: a Comprehensive Method of Study for all Players* (Chicago, 1969, rev. 2/1983)
D. Baker: *Advanced Improvisation* (Chicago, 1971, rev. 1979)
A. Jaffe: *Jazz Theory* (Dubuque, IA, 1983)
B. Benward and J. Wildman: *Jazz Improvisation in Theory and Practice* (Dubuque, IA, 1984)

BARRY KERNFELD

Improvised music. Term used in Europe (especially England) for FREE JAZZ.

Improvising Artists. Record company and label founded in 1974 by PAUL BLEY and the artist Carol Goss.

Impulse! Record company and label. The company was established in New York in 1960 as a subsidiary of ABC-Paramount; issue began in 1961 with a recording by Kai Winding and J. J. Johnson. Impulse! rapidly became the most important jazz label of its time. After the producer of the company's earliest sessions, Creed Taylor, left to join Verve, recordings were supervised by Bob Thiele. The organization lived up to its slogan – "the new wave of jazz is on Impulse!" – by recording the work of John Coltrane, Archie Shepp, and Cecil Taylor, but it also built up a valuable catalogue of bop and mainstream jazz by Gil Evans, Coleman Hawkins, Art Blakey, Freddie Hubbard, Curtis Fuller, Terry Gibbs, Yusef Lateef, Benny Carter, Max Roach, Duke Ellington, Oliver Nelson, Gary McFarland, Paul Gonsalves, and McCoy Tyner. Issue was prolific: over a hundred albums were released in five years.

During his final years Coltrane made studio recordings exclusively for Impulse!; with his death in 1967 the company lost its most important and successful musician, and from that time its fortunes declined. It remained active into the 1970s, and issued posthumously much of Coltrane's unreleased material, but otherwise the catalogue grew more commercially-oriented and gradually lost impetus. When replica reissues became popular in the 1980s Impulse! put out much of its early material in the distinctive "gatefold" (double-spread) jackets that became the company's hallmark in the 1960s; a large amount of the catalogue was also rereleased on MCA, Affinity, and Jasmine.

MARK GARDNER

Incus. English record company and label. The company was founded in London in 1970 by Derek Bailey, Evan Parker, and Tony Oxley. It is devoted to English free jazz and dominated by the activities of Bailey and Parker, who, after Oxley's departure from the venture, have continued to produce recordings into the mid-1980s. (G. Rouy: "Incus ou la force tranquille," *Jm*, no.254 (1977), 20)

Ind, Peter (Vincent) (*b* Uxbridge, England, 20 July 1928). English double bass player. He played on the ship the *Queen Mary* (1949–51) before settling in New York (1951), where he taught, and performed and recorded with Lennie Tristano (1951), Lee Konitz (1954–7), and Buddy Rich (1957). He established a recording studio in 1957, and in 1961 started his own record company, WAVE. His album *Looking Out* (1958–61, Wave 1) includes solos, duos with Joe Puma and the drummer Dick Scott, and tracks recorded with a trio and with a quartet. While living in Big Sur, California (1963–6), he became the first double bass player to give concerts and broadcasts as an unaccompanied soloist. In 1965 he played with Konitz and Warne Marsh. Thereafter he returned to England and continued to perform, teach, and manage Wave. He toured with Konitz and Marsh in 1975–6. In 1984 he opened the Bass Clef in London, which became one of the city's most popular clubs.

BIBLIOGRAPHY

FeatherE; *Feather '60s*; *Feather–Gitler '70s*
F. A. Kirk: "Ind Imp," *JB*, iii/8 (1966), 7
M. Gardner: "Peter Ind," *JM*, 180 (1970), 8; no.181 (1970), 15; no.182 (1970), 15
A. MacIntosh: "Peter Ind: Jazzman who's Brought the Message Home," *JF* [intl edn], no.35 (1975), 40
L. Tomkins: "Peter Ind: 'Coping Alone Helps Combining with Others'," *CI*, xvii/2 (1978), 14 [interview]; contd as "Peter Ind Speaks his Mind," *CI*, xviii/7 (1980), 20

SIMON ADAMS

Inge, Edward (Frederick) (*b* Kansas City, MO, 7 May 1906). Clarinetist, saxophonist, and arranger. He began learning clarinet at the age of 12 and studied at conservatories in St. Louis and in Madison, Wisconsin. His first professional engagements were with George Reynolds's orchestra in 1924; he then played with Dewey Jackson before making his first recording in 1926 with the bandleader Art Simms. After Simms's death Inge worked with the bandleader Bernie Young until late 1928. An engagement with McKinney's Cotton Pickers was followed by a long association as a composer, arranger, and performer with Don Redman (1931–9); Inge also worked with Andy Kirk (1940–43), Jimmie Lunceford, and Louis Armstrong. From 1945 into the 1970s he played with his own groups in Cleveland and Buffalo. Inge's work as an arranger was influenced by Don Redman, Victor Young, and Sy Oliver and may be heard to advantage on *You're Driving me Crazy* (1930); his playing was reminiscent of the styles of Buster Bailey and Benny Goodman.

SELECTED RECORDINGS

As sideman: A. Simms: How do you Like it Blues/Soapstick Blues (1926, OK 8373); McKinney's Cotton Pickers: You're Driving me Crazy (1930, Vic. 23031); D. Redman: Chant of the Weed/Shakin' the African (1931, Bruns. 6211); I got rhythm (1932, Bruns. 6354); That Blue-eyed Baby from Memphis (1933, Bruns. 6560)

BIBLIOGRAPHY

H. Panassié: *Le jazz hot* (Paris, 1934; Eng. trans., rev. Panassié, London and New York, 1936/*R*1970)
J. Chilton: *McKinney's Music: a Bio-discography of McKinney's Cotton Pickers* (London, 1978)

RAYMOND J. GARIGLIO

Ingham, Keith (Christopher) (*b* London, 5 Feb 1942). English pianist. He was mainly self-taught and first played professionally in 1964. During the next ten years he worked with Sandy Brown, Bruce Turner, and Wally Fawkes, and often performed with visiting American musicians. He recorded in London with Bob Wilber and Bud Freeman (1974) and made two albums as a soloist for EMI. In 1978 he settled in New York, where he played with, among many others, Benny Goodman and the World's Greatest Jazz Band. As a music director and producer he accompanied the singer Susannah McCorkle on four recordings and made three albums with Maxine Sullivan (including *The Great Songs from the Cotton Club by Harold Arlen and Ted Koehler*, 1984, Milan 270). From 1984 Ingham has played at the Kool Jazz Festival and Sarasota Jazz Festival, Florida, and has continued to work as a freelance in New York. (R. Cotterell, ed.: *Jazz Now: the Jazz Centre Society Guide*, London, 1976)

DIGBY FAIRWEATHER

Inner City. Record company and label. The company was founded in New York in 1976 by Irv (Irving) Kratka. A subsidiary of the MMO (Music Minus One) Music Group, Inc., it owns three labels, two of which are devoted to jazz. These are Classic Jazz (which should not be confused with the Swedish label Classic Jazz Masters) and Inner City. Although the company is largely concerned with reissuing material first made available by other companies in the USA, Japan (East Wind), and Europe (principally Enja), it also puts out new recordings. New albums in early swing and bop styles are issued on Classic Jazz; Inner City's catalogue includes material ranging in style from bop to free jazz and jazz-rock. (M. Segell: "Once More, Jazz is Big Business," *RS*, no.282 (1978–9), 78)

Inside [in] **(i).** To play "inside" or "in" is to improvise within the confines of the harmonic structure of a theme. The term came into use in the early 1960s in conjunction with its antonym OUTSIDE.

Inside (ii). The penultimate section in the refrain of a popular song, leading to the final repeat of the opening section (section *b* in the form *aaba*); it provides a contrast, often tonal as well as harmonic and melodic, with the opening section. *See* FORMS, esp. §1(i)(a).

Institute of Jazz Studies [IJS]. A research center and archival collection at Rutgers, the State University of New Jersey, Newark. It was founded in New York in 1952 by Marshall W. Stearns and was transferred to the campus at Newark in 1966, shortly before Stearns's death. The first director was Chris White, who was succeeded in 1976 by Dan Morgenstern. The institute's collection has been greatly expanded through donations and acquisitions and now constitutes the foremost archive of jazz and jazz-related materials under university auspices; it includes phonograph records, books, periodicals, record catalogues, research files, photographs, films, and jazz memorabilia (*see also* LIBRARIES AND ARCHIVES). IJS conducts a major program in jazz oral history. From 1973 to 1981 it issued the only scholarly publication in the English language devoted to jazz, the biannual *Journal of Jazz Studies*, which was superseded in 1982 by the *Annual Review of Jazz Studies*, and in 1979 it produced the first number of the *IJS Jazz Register*, a general discography on microfiche. In 1982, in collaboration with Scarecrow Press, it published the first of a series of monographs entitled Studies in Jazz. The institute also sponsors and organizes occasional concerts and seminars, and produces a radio program, "Jazz from the Archives," in collaboration with station WBGO in Newark.

BIBLIOGRAPHY

S. Harris: "The Institute of Jazz Studies," *JJ*, xvi/6 (1963), 23
M. P. Griffin: "The Institute of Jazz Studies: a Unique Resource," *ARJS*, i (1982), 110

EDWARD BERGER/R

Institut für Jazzforschung. Research institute. It was formed in 1969 in Graz, Austria, when the Institut für Jazz (formed 1964), a branch of the Akademie in Graz, was reorganized. The institute sponsors research in jazz and in such related disciplines as bibliography, ethnology, transcription, pedagogy, and aesthetics. Through its affiliate the INTERNATIONALE GESELLSCHAFT FÜR JAZZFORSCHUNG the institute organizes meetings and conferences; the institute and this affiliate issue jointly the annual publication *Jazzforschung/Jazz Research* and a series of occasional papers under the heading *Beiträge zur Jazzforschung/Studies in Jazz Research*.
See also LIBRARIES AND ARCHIVES, §2.

ELISABETH KOLLERITSCH

International Association of Jazz Record Collectors [IAJRC]. Association of record, tape, and film collectors. Formed in Pittsburgh in 1964 by William C. Love, the group encourages the exchange among its members of recordings and information about jazz. It has also issued more than 50 recordings (mostly of concerts and live broadcasts) by such musicians as Duke Ellington, Louis Armstrong, Benny Goodman, Lionel Hampton, and Pee Wee Russell, and sponsored the publication of important books such as Walter C. Allen's *Hendersonia: the Music of Fletcher Henderson and his Musicians: a Bio-discography* (Highland Park, NJ, 1973). In 1967 it began issuing a quarterly newsletter, *IAJRC Record* (from 1969 *IAJRC Journal*), and in the early 1970s it established its own record label (*see* IAJRC (i)). The association has more than 1200 members in the USA, Canada, Britain, Japan, Germany, and 15 other countries and holds an annual convention in August. Bruce D. Davidson of Nashville became the association's president in 1985.

Internationale Gesellschaft für Jazzforschung [IGJ, International Society for Jazz Research]. Organization formed in 1969 by Friedrich Körner (who remained its president into the late 1980s) and Dieter Glawischnig. The organization seeks to apply musicological methods to the study of jazz, and it pursues this aim in 18 specialized areas such as bibliography, discography, historiography, ethnology, and sociology; besides musicologists and scholars of jazz its 300 members include anthropologists, teachers, and performers. The society is an affiliate of the INSTITUT FÜR JAZZFORSCHUNG, with which it has organized meetings and conferences (including international congresses at Graz, 1969, Strobl, 1972, and Schielleiten am Stubenbergsee, near Hartberg, 1977 (all in Austria), and Hamburg, Germany, 1980) and published the yearbook *Jazzforschung/Jazz Research*, as well as a series of occasional papers and books under the heading *Beiträge zur Jazzforschung/Studies in Jazz Research*. The IGJ has its headquarters in Graz, Austria.

BIBLIOGRAPHY

L. Putz: "Erste jazzwissenschaftliche Tagung in Graz," *Jf*, i (1969), 191
E. Brixel and F. Kerschbaumer: "Zweite internationale jazzwissenschaftliche Tagung in Strobl am Wolfgangsee, 17.–22. April 1972," *Jf*, iii–iv (1971–2), 240
F. Kerschbaumer: "Dritte internationale jazzwissenschaftliche Tagung in Schielleiten am Stubenbergsee," *Jf*, x (1978), 177
——: "4. internationale jazzwissenschaftliche Tagung der IGJ in Hamburg 1980," *Jf*, xii (1980), 9

Internationales Jazz Zentrum. Library formed in Darmstadt, Germany, in 1983; *see* LIBRARIES AND ARCHIVES, §2.

International Jazz Federation [IJF]. International organization dedicated to the promotion of jazz. It was founded as the European Jazz Federation in Venice, Italy, in the mid-1960s, and in 1973 became a member of the International Music Council of UNESCO; it took its present name at its conference in Nancy, France, in 1977. Administered from a secretariat at the Internationales Musikinstitut, Darmstadt, Germany, the federation also has offices in Stockholm, London, and Warsaw; a branch which opened in New York in 1977 became an independent organization, the JAZZ WORLD SOCIETY. The IJF comprises jazz associations and institutions in more than 20 countries; those in 1987 included the Danish Jazz Center of

Ronnede, the Israel Jazz Society, Paris Jazz Action, the Polish Jazz Society, and the Swedish Jazz Federation. Individuals are granted membership in recognition of outstanding service to jazz, particularly if their own countries have no national jazz organizations. The federation sponsors the annual European Jazz Competition (founded in 1982) at the Leverkusener Jazztage at Leverkusen, Germany; the record label International Jazz Junction; and jazz camps and seminars. In addition to a bimonthly journal, *Jazz Forum*, it publishes the *Directory of Jazz Festivals and Related Major Jazz Events* and the *Directory of Jazz Schools*, both of which are periodically revised. (B. A. Witherden: "The European Jazz Federation," *Jazz Studies*, ii/1 (1968), 17)

International Jazz Jamboree Festival. Festival held annually from 1959 in Warsaw, following the initial important Polish jazz festivals held in Sopot (1956–7). It is organized by the concert agency of the Polska Federacja Jazzowa with the cooperation of the Polskie Radio i Telewizja (which tapes some of the events for later broadcast), the city of Warsaw, and other sponsors, and takes place over four days in October at venues including Congress Hall at the Palace of Culture and Sciences. The festival offers six concerts in which about 25 internationally known musicians and groups take part (these have included Duke Ellington, Dizzy Gillespie, Woody Herman, Albert Mangelsdorff, Thelonious Monk, Sarah Vaughan, and Eastern European groups such as the Dixieland Band of Leningrad, USSR), and others that feature Polish performers. Nightly jam sessions are presented in Warsaw jazz clubs. The International Jazz Jamboree Festival is the most important jazz festival in Eastern Europe, from which it draws most of its audience; it has also received much critical attention in the West.

PAUL R. LAIRD

International New Jazz Festival Moers. Festival of free jazz held annually from 1972 in Moers, Germany. It is organized by Moers Music and takes place over four days in May and June. The festival is sponsored by the city of Moers, which in 1980 expended three-quarters of its budget for cultural events on the festival, and the Westdeutscher Rundfunk. In addition to public concerts held at indoor and outdoor venues, the festival offers performances and demonstrations in schools. The festival is among the most important events of its kind dedicated to free jazz but also includes some bop. Among prominent musicians who have appeared at Moers in the 1980s are Betty Carter and Paquito D'Rivera. In 1985 300 musicians from 14 countries took part in concerts attended by as many as 3500 listeners. Several important free-jazz albums issued on the Moers label have been recorded at the festival, including those by Anthony Braxton as an unaccompanied soloist (1974), Phillip Wilson's quartet (1978), and Sunny Murray's quartet (1979).

PAUL R. LAIRD

International Society for Jazz Research. *See* INTERNATIONALE GESELLSCHAFT FÜR JAZZFORSCHUNG.

International Sweethearts of Rhythm. Big band. It was formed in 1939 from a swing band that started at the Piney Woods (Mississippi) Country Life School. Its 18 members were all women, and the word "International" was used in its name because they were of a variety of ethnic origins. Its leader was the singer Anna Mae (Darden) Winburn, and it included such excellent musicians as Pauline Braddy (drums), Roz Cron (alto saxophone), Vi (Viola) Burnside (tenor saxophone), Willie Mae Wong (baritone saxophone), Tiny (Ernestine) Davis (trumpet), Helen Jones (trombone), and Carline Ray (double bass). The band's arrangers included Eddie Durham and Jesse Stone. After a successful début in 1940 at the Howard Theater, Washington, the band gradually gained popularity; it performed at the Apollo Theatre, New York, and made tours of the USA and Europe (1945). It became widely recognized as the foremost female band of the time; among its recordings were *Don't get it twisted/Vi Vigor* (1946, Vic. 400146). In the late 1940s it disbanded, but Winburn continued to lead bands called the Sweethearts of Rhythm into the 1950s. A documentary film about the band, *The International Sweethearts of Rhythm: America's Hottest All-girl Band*, was made by Greta Schiller and Andrea Weiss in the mid-1980s.

BIBLIOGRAPHY

S. Placksin: *American Women in Jazz, 1900 to the Present: their Words, Lives, and Music* (New York, 1982), 132

D. A. Handy: *The International Sweethearts of Rhythm* (Metuchen, NJ, and London, 1983)

L. Dahl: *Stormy Weather: the Music and Lives of a Century of Jazzwomen* (London, Melbourne, Australia, and New York, 1984), 53

M. McPartland: "The Untold Story of the International Sweethearts of Rhythm," *All in Good Time* (New York, and Oxford, England, 1987) [colln of previously pubd articles], 137

KIMBERLY McCORD

International Teddies. *See* ORIGINAL TEDDIES.

International Youth Band. Group organized in 1958 by MARSHALL BROWN.

Interstate Music. Company owned by Bruce Bastin that issues the labels HARLEQUIN, Flyright, Magpie, and Krazy Kat.

Intro(duction). A passage at the beginning of a piece; it may or may not be related thematically to the rest of the piece. The length of an introduction is generally between a few bars and one or two phrases, though much longer examples exist. *See* FORMS.

Inzalaco, Tony [Anthony Frank, Jr.] (*b* Passaic, NJ, 14 Jan 1938). Drummer. He studied at the Manhattan School of Music (BA, MMEd 1960). He played with many musicians, including Billy Taylor (ii), Johnny Smith, Buddy Rich, Vinnie Burke, Maynard Ferguson (with whom he recorded in 1964–5), Jim Hall, Chris Connor, Ben Webster, Jaki Byard, and Lee Konitz, before moving to Europe in 1968. Until 1974 he worked in Germany as a staff musician in radio, television, and record companies. He also played percussion with the Clarke–Boland Big Band, recording in 1968 and 1971. As a drummer he made recordings with Peter Herbolzheimer (1970–73), Ben Webster (1972), Art Farmer (1972, 1974), Horace Parlan (1975), Dexter Gordon (*Stable Mable*, 1975, Ste. 1040), and Fritz Pauer (1978). He led a group that made broadcasts and recordings in the Netherlands and Germany in 1976. He returned to the USA in 1978 and worked as a freelance in and around Boston. (*Feather–Gitler '70s*)

Irakere. Cuban group. It was founded in Havana around 1973 by musicians who had formerly played in the Orquesta Cubana de Música Moderna and other smaller groups: these were the pianist Chucho Valdés, the trumpeters Arturo Sandoval and Jorge Varona, the saxophonists Carlos Averoff and Paquito D'Rivera, the guitarist Carlos Emilio, the singer and percussionist Oscar Valdés, and others. It recorded in Havana (*c*1975) before visiting the USA (1978–9); the albums *Irakere* (1978, Col. JC35655) and *Irakere II* (1979, Col. JC36107), recorded live at concerts, document the success of the tour. The group also recorded with visiting American musicians in Havana (1979), and in Japan (1980). D'Rivera left in 1980, as did Sandoval the following year, but Irakere has continued to tour extensively into the mid-1980s, blending Afro-Cuban rhythms, the harmonic language of bop, and elements of classical music in a highly effective manner.

BIBLIOGRAPHY

R. Palmer: "The Cubans are Coming! The Cubans are Coming," *RS*, no.282 (1978–9), 48
C. J. Gans: "Irakere," *JF* [intl edn], no.60 (1979), 36
P. Zervigón: "Irakere: en la percusión está la diferencia," *El reportero* (San Juan, 25 Nov 1982), 23
S. Steward: "Cubana be, cubana bop," *The Wire*, no.21 (1985), 26

CRISTÓBAL DÍAZ AYALA

Irvis, Charlie [Charles] (*b* ?New York, *c*1899; *d* ?New York, *c*1939). Trombonist. He first played in a boys' band with Bubber Miley and then worked in New York with Lucille Hegamin and Willie "the Lion" Smith. In 1924 he joined the Washingtonians, then under the direction of Elmer Snowden, and remained with the band after Duke Ellington took over its leadership (for illustration *see* WASHINGTONIANS). From 1923 to 1927 he also recorded regularly as a member of Clarence Williams's ensembles, accompanying classic blues singers. After leaving Ellington in 1926 he played with Charlie Johnson (1927–8), Jelly Roll Morton (1929–30), and Miley (1931).

Irvis was the first of Ellington's trombonists to make use of the growl and plunger-mute technique. His few recordings with the group do not include work in this style, however, and those he made with Fats Waller and Thomas Morris in 1927 probably give a better impression of his contribution to Ellington's band.

SELECTED RECORDINGS

As sideman: D. Ellington: Rainy Nights (1924, Blu Disc 1002); Trombone Blues (1925, PAct 36333); F. Waller: Fats Waller Stomp (1927, Vic. 20890); Savannah Blues/Won't you take me home? (1927, Vic. 20776); C. Williams: Close Fit Blues (1927, OK 8510); F. Waller: The Minor Drag/Harlem Fuss (1929, Vic. 38050)

BIBLIOGRAPHY

ChiltonW
N. Shapiro and N. Hentoff, eds.: *Hear me Talkin' to ya: the Story of Jazz by the Men who Made it* (New York and London, 1955/*R*1966), 228
S. Dance: *The World of Duke Ellington* (London and New York, 1970) [colln of previously pubd articles and interviews]

EDDIE LAMBERT

Irwin, Cecil (*b* Evanston, IL, 7 Dec 1902; *d* nr Des Moines, IA, 3 May 1935). Saxophonist, clarinetist, and arranger. After working with Carroll Dickerson, Erskine Tate, and Junie Cobb in the mid-1920s he joined Earl Hines in 1928 as a tenor saxophonist and arranger (for illustration *see* HINES, EARL). His work in both capacities may be heard on Hines's *Swingin' Down* (1934, Voc. 3392). Irwin was killed in a traffic accident while touring.

based on *ChiltonW*

Irwin, Dennis (Wayne) (*b* Birmingham, AL, 28 Nov 1951). Double bass player. He played clarinet from the age of nine, and changed to double bass ten years later while studying music at North Texas State University (1969–74). After playing bop with Red Garland (1973–4) he moved to New York, where he worked with Ted Curson (1975), Jackie Paris (1975–6), Albert Dailey (1975–84), Mose Allison (from 1975), and Betty Carter (1976). He recorded in Italy in 1977 in a duo with James Williams. From late 1977 to 1980 he worked with Art Blakey's Jazz Messengers. Among his several recordings with Blakey are the two albums *In my Prime* (1977–8, Tim. 114, 118). The first of these includes Irwin's composition *Kamal*. Irwin also recorded with Curtis Fuller (1978) and Williams (1979), and worked with Al Haig (1978–82), Chet Baker (from 1980), Horace Silver (1981), Mel Lewis (from 1981), and Bennie Wallace.

Isaacs, Ike [Charles Edward] **(i)** (b Akron, OH, 28 March 1923; *d* Atlanta, 27 Feb 1981). Double bass player. He first played trumpet, then tuba, and took up double bass while in the army in 1941. After he was discharged he worked with Tiny Grimes (1948–50), Earl Bostic (1951–3), Paul Quinichette (1953), Bennie Green (1954), and his own group (in Ohio, 1955). In 1956 he married Carmen McRae, and for the next two years toured as the leader of her accompanying trio; in the late 1950s and early 1960s he led the trio that backed Lambert, Hendricks, and Ross. Later he toured Sweden with Count Basie (1962), accompanied and served as manager for the singer Gloria Lynne (1962–4), and led a trio at the Pied Piper in Los Angeles. From 1966 to 1970 he toured the USA with Erroll Garner, and in 1969 he appeared in the film *They Shoot Horses, Don't They?*.

SELECTED RECORDINGS

As leader: *Ike Isaacs at Freddie Jett's Pied Piper* (1967, RGB 2000)
As sideman: R. Bryant: *Django* (1957, Prst. 7098); C. McRae: *After Glow* (1957, Decca 8583); Lambert, Hendricks, and Ross: *The Hottest New Group in Jazz* (1959, Col. CL1403); H. Edison and E. Davis: *Jawbreakers* (1962, Riv. 9430); C. Basie: *Basie in Sweden* (1962, Roul. 52099); E. Garner: *Up in Erroll's Room* (1967, MGM 4520)

BIBLIOGRAPHY

FeatherE; *Feather–Gitler '70s*
J. L. Ginibre and P. Carles: "Dictionnaire de la contrebasse," *Jm*, no.166 (1969), 42
Obituary, *DB*, xlviii/6 (1981), 13

DIANNA RHYAN

Isaacs, Ike (ii) (*b* Rangoon, Burma, 1 Dec 1919). British guitarist. He was self-taught. While studying chemistry at Rangoon University he played regularly with Cedric West. In November 1946 he moved to England, where he worked as a freelance musician, played with Billy Munn on the BBC radio program "Jazz Club," and became a founding member of the BBC Show Band, led by Cyril Stapleton. Isaacs recorded with Ralph Sharon (1952), George Chisholm and Alan Clare (both 1956), Barney Kessel (1968), and Stephane Grappelli (1975), and as a leader (1966). He worked with Diz Disley and Grappelli in association with the Hot Club of London, which was modeled on the Hot Club de France. In the 1970s he also belonged to the cooperative quartet Velvet, other members of which were Digby Fairweather and the guitarist Denny Wright. His preferred instrument as a performer is the acoustic guitar, but he has also established himself as an authority on the electric instrument; for many years he contributed to periodicals including *Crescendo International*. In the 1980s he moved to Australia and took up a position at the Sydney Guitar School. (I. Isaacs: "The Guitar," *CI*, ix (1970–71), no.4, p.35; no.5, p.34)

Ishikawa, Hisao (*b* Tokyo, 9 Oct 1931). Japanese tenor and soprano saxophonist and flutist. He attended the Tokyo University of Economics, studied tenor saxophone with the trumpeter Saburo Okada, and played at American military bases; the tenor saxophonist School Boy Porter influenced his early style. He played with Junior Cook, Blue Mitchell, and Stanley Turrentine in Japan and belonged to a group led by the drummer Ricky Nakayama and to the Seven Fukuzin. In 1981 he recorded as a leader (*A Song for you*, Col.–Denon YX7300) and as a sideman with the guitarist Takaaki Miyanoue and Jimmy Smith (*Touch of Love*, VAP 30016-28). Ishikawa is sometimes known by the nickname Q.

YOZO IWANAMI

Isola, Frank (*b* Detroit, 20 Feb 1925). Drummer. He was inspired to play after hearing Gene Krupa, and took up drums in 1936. He played in the Army Air Force Band (1943–5), studied in California, then moved to New York (1947), where he worked with Johnny Bothwell and Elliot Lawrence. After recording with Eddie Bert (1952) he performed and recorded with Stan Getz (intermittently, 1952–5), with whom he also recorded under Jimmy Raney's leadership (1953). Isola began working with Gerry Mulligan in 1953; the following year he recorded with Mulligan in Paris (*Paris Concert*, Vogue 7381, 7383) and with Bob Brookmeyer and John Williams (ii) in the USA. After recording with Mose Allison in 1957 he returned to Detroit. In the mid-1970s he moved back to New York, where he played at the West End with the tenor saxophonist Victor Lesser and others.

BIBLIOGRAPHY

FeatherE
R. Gordon: *Jazz West Coast: the Los Angeles Jazz Scene of the 1950s* (London and New York, 1986)

Israels, Chuck [Charles H.] (*b* New York, 10 Aug 1936). Double bass player. After a formal musical education in the USA and France he became interested in jazz. He made his first recording in 1958 with Cecil Taylor, joined George Russell's sextet the following year, and later recorded both with Russell (1960–61) and as a member of a group led by Eric Dolphy (1961). Israels came to prominence in 1961, when he replaced Scott LaFaro in the trio led by Bill Evans (ii). His thoughtful and sensitive playing proved more sympathetic to his leader's stylistic concepts than LaFaro's had been, and resulted in a highly successful association that was to last for five years. During his period with Evans he also played and recorded with J. J. Johnson, Herbie Hancock, and Gary Burton (all 1963), Stan Getz (1964), and Hampton Hawes (1965). Thereafter he worked mainly in larger groups and formed a rehearsal band to play his own compositions, many of which have since been performed by a number of European orchestras. In 1973 Israels formed the National Jazz Ensemble, which concentrated on the re-creation of arrangements and improvisations originally recorded by Jelly Roll Morton, Louis Armstrong, Duke Ellington, Thelonious Monk, and others. Its sidemen included Tom Harrell, Jimmy Maxwell, Jimmy Knepper, Sal Nistico (ii), and Bill Goodwin. This group was in existence for only five years, and after it disbanded Israels became less active as a performer; however, he recorded with Rosemary Clooney in the San Francisco area in 1985.

SELECTED RECORDINGS

As leader: *National Jazz Ensemble* (1975–6, Chi. 140, 151)
As sideman with B. Evans: *How my Heart Sings!* (1962, Riv. 9473); *Trio '64* (1963, Verve 68578); *Trio '65* (1965, Verve 68613)

BIBLIOGRAPHY

Feather '60s; *Feather–Gitler '70s*
J. L. Ginibre: "Il parle, le trio dont on parle," *Jm*, no.116 (1965), 34

STAN WOOLLEY

Issue [catalog(ue)] **number.** A number assigned by a record company to a recording when it is issued commercially; the recording is identified by that number in the company's catalogue and in other published listings. The catalogue number distinguishes the recording in its marketed form, as a 78 r.p.m. disc, a 45 r.p.m. single, an extended player, a long-playing disc (in mono or stereo form), a cassette, or a compact disc, carrying items in particular versions and arranged in a certain order. If the recording is reissued at a later date a new number is normally assigned to it, whether or not any aspect of its contents or presentation has been changed. Exceptions to this general rule have sometimes occurred, particularly on 78 r.p.m. discs: occasionally a single disc was issued with a different number for each side; conversely different takes of the same title were sometimes issued at different times with the same number. Because of practices of this kind, throughout the era of the 78 the only sure means of identifying a particular TAKE of a title is the MATRIX NUMBER. With the advent of mastering on magnetic tape (which allowed performances to be edited in the studio) and of the long-playing disc (which might present a number of distinct performances on one side), the direct, one-to-one relationship between a single distinct performance and a single distinct number was for the most part lost. Consequently, the matrix number gave way to the issue number in supplying the most useful means of identifying a disc uniquely.

Iturralde, Pedro (*b* Falces, Spain, 13 July 1929). Spanish saxophonist, clarinetist, composer, and arranger. He began playing saxophone and clarinet at the age of nine, and undertook his first professional engagements two years later. In the late 1940s he lived in Madrid, where he played with several groups and studied saxophone at the conservatory. After touring the Middle East and Germany he returned to Madrid as the leader of a group of German jazz musicians. His experiments with fusions of flamenco and jazz led him to record several albums in this vein, including *Flamenco Jazz* (1967, Saba 15143), on which the guitarist Paco de Lucia was among his sidemen. In 1972 he went to the Berklee College of Music, and his composition *Like Coltrane* was awarded a prize at the composers' competition in Monaco. Thereafter he served as professor of saxophone at the conservatory in Madrid and has continued to perform and record.

ALFREDO PAPO

Iversen, Einar (Pastorn) (*b* Mandal, Norway, 27 July 1930). Norwegian pianist and flutist. He studied piano with Inge Rolf Ruignes and flute with Ørnulf Gulbrandsen, and worked professionally from the late 1940s. He played with Rowland Greenberg (recording in 1953 and the late 1950s), Kristian Bergheim, Michael Flagstad, Arild Andersen, and Jon Christensen, and with the trumpeter Atle Hammer he led a trio, and a quartet. In addition to touring Norway and Europe he has often accompanied musicians who have visited Norway. As a pianist Iversen favors a swing style that displays the influence of Teddy Wilson and Oscar Peterson; it is well represented by his album *Me and my Piano* (1967, Nor-Disc LPS17). He received the Buddy Award from the Norwegian Jazz Federation in 1958.

BIBLIOGRAPHY

O. Angell, J. E. Vold, and E. Økland: *Jazz i Norge* (Oslo, 1975)
K. Michelsen: *Cappelens musikkleksikon* (Oslo, 1978)

VIDAR VANBERG

Izenzon, David (*b* Pittsburgh, 17 May 1932; *d* New York, 8 Oct 1979). Double bass player. He studied double bass from 1956 and soon began playing with jazz musicians in Pittsburgh, including the pianist Dodo Marmarosa (1958). In 1961 he moved to New York, where he played free jazz with Paul Bley, Archie

Shepp, Sonny Rollins, and Bill Dixon; he joined Ornette Coleman's trio in October 1961 and recorded with it at Town Hall in December 1962. He worked as a freelance in jazz and classical music, played again with Coleman in the USA, in England and on the Continent (1965–8), and then returned to New York, where he played with Perry Robinson, the pianist Lowell Davidson, Paul Motian, and the New York PO. He received the PhD in psychotherapy in 1973 and began a private practice. In 1977 he performed with Coleman and recorded with Motian. Although he began playing late in his life, Izenzon was a virtuoso player, especially proficient in his use of the bow.

SELECTED RECORDINGS

As sideman: on B. Dixon: *New Music, Second Wave* (1964, Savoy 12184), 12th December, Winter Song; O. Coleman: *Chappaqua Suite* (1965, Col. 62896–7); *The Ornette Coleman Trio at the Golden Circle* (1965, BN 84224–5); J. Byard: *The Sunshine of my Soul* (1967, Prst. 7550); P. Motian: *Dance* (1977, ECM 1108)

BIBLIOGRAPHY

V. Wilmer: "David Izenzon and the Hazards of Virtuosity," *DB*, xxxiii/11 (1966), 18

D. Wild and M. Cuscuna: *Ornette Coleman, 1958–1979: a Discography* (Ann Arbor, MI, 1980)

J. Litweiler: *The Freedom Principle: Jazz after 1958* (New York, 1984), 48

JOHN VOIGT

J

Jabulani. Name sometimes used by RAHN BURTON.

Jackel, Conny [Conrad] (*b* Offenbach am Main, Germany, 30 Aug 1931). German trumpeter. After playing at American servicemen's clubs around Europe (1952) he performed and made recordings with Helmut Brandt (intermittently, 1955–63); good examples of his playing may be heard on Brandt's *Berlin Calling* (1955, Met. 1039) and *Manhattan* (1957, Met. 1729) (both EPs). He worked with Erwin Lehn (1961) and recorded with Horst Jankowski (1961, 1963) and Charly Antolini (1966). From 1967 he played with Willy Berking, the jazz ensemble of Hessischer Rundfunk (Frankfurt am Main), and his own group, as well as with Rudi Sehring and Joki Freund. Jackel also recorded with Hans Koller (1975), Brandt (1978), and as a member of the Main Stream Power Band, a swing group led by the clarinetist Heinz Schoenberger (1976–80). (*ReclamsJ*)

Jackie and Roy. Duo formed in the late 1940s by Jackie Cain and ROY KRAL.

Jackson, Butter. *See* JACKSON, QUENTIN.

Jackson, Calvin (*b* Philadelphia, 26 May 1919; *d* Encinitas, CA, 9 Dec 1985). Pianist, composer, and leader. He studied at the Juilliard School (to 1941) and then worked as assistant music director at MGM in Hollywood (1943–7). He wrote arrangements for Harry James's orchestra (1943) and recorded with the band of the pianist Phil Moore (1947). The following year he moved to New York, where he played with Mildred Bailey at the Café Society and made his first recording as a leader; from that time until 1961 he recorded frequently, usually with his own trio or quartet. After touring the Americas he settled in Toronto in 1950; he played regularly with his quartet at the Park Plaza Hotel and presented a weekly television program for CBC. By 1957 he had returned to the USA and after 1961 he lived in Los Angeles, where he played with small groups. His compositions include music for films and television. (*FeatherE*)

JACK LITCHFIELD

Jackson, Chubby [Greig Stewart] (*b* New York, 25 Oct 1918). Double bass player and songwriter. He started playing double bass in 1935, and from 1937 worked in various dance bands. He played in Charlie Barnet's orchestra (1942–3), then as a member of Woody Herman's First Herd (1943–6; for illustration *see* HERMAN, WOODY, fig.1*a*), and continued to work with Herman intermittently into the 1950s. He provided the band with several compositions (including *Northwest Passage*, written in collaboration with Herman and Ralph Burns), and contributed a sense of humor and showmanship; he also persuaded Herman to engage Burns and Neal Hefti. From the late 1940s Jackson played a five-string instrument of his own design. He performed and recorded with Charlie Ventura (1947), then toured Scandinavia as the leader of a bop septet with, among others, Conte Candoli, Terry Gibbs, and Billy Bauer. He also led a bop big band (1949) and an all-star recording group that included J. J. Johnson, Zoot Sims, and Gerry Mulligan (1950). In 1951 he rejoined Ventura and in 1953, with Bill Harris (i), led a sextet. Jackson then settled in Chicago, where he worked as a freelance musician and acted as host for a children's television program. During the 1960s he again led his own bands, working mostly in the Miami area, and in the 1970s he played as a freelance in Los Angeles and Las Vegas.

SELECTED RECORDINGS

As leader: Bass Face/Don't get wild child (1944, Queen 4103); Tiny's Blues/All Wrong (1949, Col. 38623); Flying the Coop/I may be wrong (1950, NewJ 825); *Chubby's Back!* (1957, Argo 614)

As sideman: C. Barnet: Bunny/Atlantic Jump (1946, Apollo 1065); W. Herman: Lemon Drop/I ain't gonna wait too long (1948, Cap. 15365)

RECORDED COMPOSITIONS

(*selective list*)

As leader: Follow the Leader/Mom Jackson (1947, MGM 10354)

Recorded by W. Herman with Jackson as sideman: Northwest Passage (1945, Col. 36835); Four Men on a Horse (1946, MGM 30603)

BIBLIOGRAPHY

ChiltonW

R. J. Gleason: "We're Just Trying to be Natural: Jackson–Harris," *DB*, xx/11 (1953), 6

J. Burns: "Charlie Ventura and Chubby Jackson," *JM*, no.163 (1968), 14

E. Edwards, Jr.: Liner notes, *Chubby Jackson Sextet and Big Band* (Prst. 7641, 1969)

L. Tomkins: "Chubby Jackson Talking," *CI*, xvii/3 (1978), 6; contd as "Leave us to Create our Own Sound," xvii/11 (1979), 12 [interview]

J. Sohmer: "Chubby Jackson Speaks Out," *JT* (1984), Aug, 5

DAVID FLANAGAN

Jackson, Cliff [Clifton Luther] (*b* Culpeper, VA, 19 July 1902; *d* New York, 24 May 1970). Pianist. He studied classical music as a child. After working briefly at the Tent in Atlantic City, New Jersey, he moved in 1923 to New York, where he played in Harlem with Lionel Howard and his Musical Aces (1924) and worked as a solo pianist and vocal accompanist. In the early 1920s he led an orchestra at the Apollo Theatre and in the 1920s and 1930s played at the Lenox Club. He made his first recording in 1927 with Bob Fuller and Elmer Snowden, and in the same year formed a big band, the Krazy Kats (also known as the Crazy Cats), which included Henry Goodwin and Rudy Powell and with which he recorded in 1930. After recording in 1940 and 1941 with Sidney Bechet he worked principally as a house pianist at several clubs in New York, including Nick's, the downtown branch of Café Society (1943–51), Ryan's (1964–7), and the RX Room (from 1968 until his death). He occasionally performed with his wife, Maxine Sullivan. Jackson's playing combined elements of ragtime and stride.

SELECTED RECORDINGS

As unaccompanied soloist: *Carolina Shout!* (1961–2, BL 121)
As leader: Waiting thru' the Night (1930, Grey Gull 1880); The Terror (1930, Grey Gull 1879); Quiet Please/Squeeze me (1944, Black & White 3)
As sideman with B. Berigan: I'm Coming Virginia/Blues (1935, Decca 18116)

BIBLIOGRAPHY

ChiltonW; *FeatherE*; *Feather '60s*; *Feather–Gitler '70s*
J. Simmen: "Cliff Jackson: ce qui se passait au 818 Ritter Place," *BHcF*, no.182 (1968), 5; no.183 (1968), 9
Obituary, A. McCarthy, *JM*, no.186 (1970), 21
J. Simmen: "Crystal Clear," *Coda*, xi/12 (1974), 25
B. Rusch: "Cliff Jackson: Interview," *Cadence*, ix/1 (1983), 12

JAMES M. DORAN

Jackson, Dewey (*b* St. Louis, 21 June 1900). Trumpeter and bandleader. He worked mainly on riverboats with Charlie Creath (from 1919), his own bands (from 1920), and Fate Marable (from 1924); apart from an engagement in 1926 with a band led by the violinist Andrew Preer at the Cotton Club in New York, he continued to play on riverboats until 1941. He made recordings as a leader in 1926 (including *She's cryin' for me/ Capital Blues*, Voc. 1040, on which he may be heard playing muted trumpet) and with Creath the following year. Among the sidemen in his bands were John Lindsay, Pops Foster, Willie Humphrey (all 1925–6), Don Stovall and Jock Carruthers (early 1930s), Singleton Palmer (intermittently, 1932–41), and Clark Terry (1937). He continued to lead bands in St. Louis during the 1940s, and after a brief interruption returned to playing regularly in the 1950s with Palmer (with whom he recorded in 1950), Don Ewell's trio (1951), and his own band. From the 1960s he played only occasionally.

BIBLIOGRAPHY

ChiltonW
A. McCarthy: *Big Band Jazz* (New York and London, 1974), 114
E. Crowther and A. F. Niemoeller: "St. Louis Jazzman," *Selections from the Gutter: Jazz Portraits from "The Jazz Record"*, ed. A. Hodes and C. Hansen (Berkeley, CA, Los Angeles, and London, 1977), 208

Jackson, Franz (R.) (*b* Rock Island, IL, 1 Nov 1912). Tenor saxophonist and clarinetist. He studied at the Chicago Musical College, played with various bands (from 1926), then worked with Albert Ammons, Cassino Simpson (1931), Carroll Dickerson (1932, 1934–6), Jimmie Noone (1934), Roy Eldridge (1937), and Fletcher Henderson (1937–8). He re-joined Eldridge in 1938 and went with him to New York; in both the Henderson and Eldridge bands he had the distinction of replacing Ben Webster. He recorded (1939), toured California with Earl Hines (1940–41), then returned to New York and worked with Fats Waller (1941) and Cootie Williams (1942). He played in Boston with Frankie Newton (1942–3), toured with Eldridge (1944), and worked with Wilbur De Paris (1944–5). He visited the Pacific with Jesse Stone (1946) in the first of a series of USO

Milt Jackson during a performance by Woody Herman's band at Bop City, New York, June 1950: visible behind are (left to right) Bob Graf, Al Cohn, Phil Urso (tenor saxophones), and Marty Flax (baritone saxophone)

tours in which he took part in the late 1940s and early 1950s. After returning to Chicago Jackson formed his own band, the Original Jass All Stars (1957), which included Bob Shoffner and Al Wynn; the band was a huge success and played a long residency at the Red Arrow, near Chicago. During this period he also recorded with Lil Armstrong (1961) and formed his own record company, Pinnacle. After playing in New York (late 1968), the Original Jass All Stars undertook several USO tours, visiting Vietnam (1969) and the Far East, among other places. In 1974 Jackson recorded with Art Hodes. He formed another group, the Jazz Entertainers, in Chicago in 1980 and toured Europe as a soloist in 1981.

SELECTED RECORDINGS

As leader: *No Saints* (1957, Replica 1006); *A Night at The Red Arrow* (1961, Pinnacle 104); *Let's Have a Party* (1981, Pinnacle 101)

BIBLIOGRAPHY

ChiltonW; *FeatherE*; *Feather '60s*
D. R. Parks: "Franz Jackson and his Original Jass All-Stars," *SL*, ix/5–6 (1958), 1
S. Dance: *The World of Earl Hines* (New York, 1977) [interviews], 246
Liner notes, *Let's Have a Party* (Pinnacle 101, 1981)
D. J. Travis: *An Autobiography of Black Jazz* (Chicago, 1983) [incl. interviews], 389

MIKE HAZELDINE

Jackson, Michael Gregory [Gregory, Michael] (*b* New Haven, CT, 28 Aug 1953). Guitarist. He studied drums as a child but changed to guitar at the age of seven. He later learned various other instruments including cello, flute, marimba, and vibraphone. In 1973 he became associated with Leo Smith, who encouraged him to pursue his own musical ideas. He played free jazz in the mid-1970s with Smith, David Murray, Anthony Braxton, and Oliver Lake; during this period he formed the trio Clarity with Anthony Davis and Pheeroan Ak Laff. Gregory's style gradually became more commercialized, combining free-jazz techniques with pop rhythms and song forms. Eventually he abandoned jazz altogether to pursue a career in pop music; he then changed his name to Michael Gregory in order to avoid being mistaken for the singer Michael Jackson.

SELECTED RECORDINGS

As unaccompanied soloist: *Cowboys, Cartoons, & Assorted Candy* (1982, Enja 4026)
Duos with O. Lake: *Karmonic Suite* (1978, ImA 373857)
As leader: *Clarity* (1976, Bija 1000); *Heart and Center* (1979, AN 3051)
As sideman: O. Lake: *Holding Together* (1976, BS 0009); on *Wildflowers: the New York Loft Sessions*, ii (1976, Douglas 7046), A. Braxton: 73°-S Kelvin; O. Lake: *Life Dance of Is* (1978, AN 3003)

BIBLIOGRAPHY

B. Rusch: "Michael G. Jackson: Interview," *Cadence*, ii/10–11 (1977), 6
T. Mulhern: "Michael Gregory Jackson: a Jazz-rock Career with an Avant-garde Foundation," *GP*, xiv/10 (1980), 30 [incl. discography]
C. Safane: "Michael Gregory Jackson: Avant Heads for the Center," *DB*, xlvii/3 (1980), 29 [incl. discography]
T. Lozaw: "Michael Gregory on the Rocks," *Creem*, xv/11 (1984), 15

PAUL RINZLER

Jackson, Milt(on) [Bags] (*b* Detroit, 1 Jan 1923). Vibraphonist. He began playing guitar at the age of seven and piano at the age of 11 before taking up xylophone and vibraphone in his teens. He first performed in public as a member of a touring gospel quartet, in which he sang tenor. In 1945 he was part of a local jazz group that played with Dizzy Gillespie in a concert in Detroit. Shortly afterwards Gillespie engaged Jackson for his New York sextet and later for his big band of 1946. In 1948–9 Jackson worked with Howard McGhee, Thelonious Monk, Charlie Parker, Woody Herman, and others. He returned to Gillespie from 1950 to 1952, at the same time issuing some recordings under the name of the Milt Jackson Quartet. By the end of 1952 this group was renamed the MODERN JAZZ QUARTET. Jackson's career was centered around the MJQ for more than 20 years; only in the summer months when the MJQ did not perform did he regularly take on other jazz engagements as a leader or sideman. In 1974, frustrated over his economic position after his many years with the MJQ, Jackson triggered the dissolution of the group. He then toured alone, performing with local bands in various cities. Thereafter he has organized and performed with a number of small combos, but has rejoined his colleagues in the MJQ for annual concert tours.

Jackson was one of the first vibraphonists to master the bop style, and is generally regarded as one of the finest performers on his instrument in the history of jazz. His improvisations exhibit great rhythmic variety, with sudden outbursts of short notes often adjoining languid, sustained phrases. He also utilizes a wide range of dynamics to highly expressive ends. His great control of rhythm and dynamics is clearest in his masterly improvisations at slow tempos, but he also has an affinity for the 12-bar blues, and has recorded many excellent blues solos. He was one of the first vibraphonists to slow the speed of the instrument's oscillator to about 3.3 revolutions per second (as opposed to Lionel Hampton's vibrato speed of about 10 per second), thus warming his long notes with a subtle vibrato and avoiding the nervous shimmy on shorter notes that is heard in the work of earlier vibraphonists. Jackson has also written a number of well-known jazz tunes, such as *Bluesology*, *Bags' Groove*, *The Cylinder*, and *Ralph's New Blues*, whose simple pentatonicism and formal design often contrast sharply with the complexity of his improvisations.

Oral history material in *NjR*.

See also PIANO, §4.

SELECTED RECORDINGS

As leader: Bluesology (1951, Dee Gee 3702); Bags' Groove (1952, BN 1593); What's New? (1952, BN 1592); with R. Charles: *Soul Brothers* (1957, Atl. 1279); *Ballad Artistry* (1959, Atl. 1342), incl. The Cylinder; with J. Coltrane: *Bags and Trane* (1959, Atl. 1368); *Sunflower* (1973, CTI 6024); with C. Basie: *Milt Jackson + Count Basie + the Big Band* (1978, Pablo 2310822-3); with R. Brown: *It Don't Mean a Thing if You Can't Tap Your Foot to it* (1984, Pablo 2310909)
As sideman: D. Gillespie: Anthropology (1946, Vic. 40-0132); A Night in Tunisia (1946, Vic. 40-0132); T. Monk: Misterioso (1948, BN 560); O. Peterson: *Very Tall* (1962, Verve 68429); Benny Carter: *The King* (1976, Pablo 2310768)

For further recordings *see* MODERN JAZZ QUARTET.

BIBLIOGRAPHY

B. Randle: Liner notes, *Soul Brothers* (Atl. 1279, 1957)
D. Morgenstern: "Bags' Groove," *DB*, xxv/24 (1958), 17
D. DeMicheal: "Jackson of the MJQ," *DB*, xxviii/14 (1961), 18
——: "Jazz Vibes: Three Eras," *DB*, xxix/1 (1962), 15
A. Hodeir: *Toward Jazz* (New York, 1962/*R*1976), 135
T. Owens: *Improvisation Technique of the Modern Jazz Quartet* (thesis, UCLA, 1965)
R. J. Wilbraham: *Milt Jackson: a Discography and Bibliography* (London, 1968) [addns in *DF*, no.12 (1969), 2; no.18 (1970), 17; *JJ*, xxii/5 (1969), 22]
B. S. Page: "Open Bags," *DB*, xxxvii/9 (1970), 18
J. Burns: "Good Vibes," *J&B*, ii/5 (1972), 7
L. Lyons: "Milt Jackson: Dollars and Sense," *DB*, xlii/9 (1975), 14
J. Blum: "Milt Jackson: Vibes Original," *JT* (1984), July, 13
L. Feather: "The Evolution of Milt Jackson," *Los Angeles Times Calendar* (2 Sept 1984), 55
R. Palmer: "Milt Jackson Revisited," *JJI*, xxxix (1986), no.5, p.8; no.7, p.14 [incl. discography]

THOMAS OWENS

Jackson, Oliver(, Jr.) [Bops Junior] (*b* Detroit, 28 April 1933). Drummer. He began performing locally with various musicians, including Thad Jones, Paul Chambers, and Tommy Flanagan. Around 1948 he formed a variety act with Eddie Locke called Bop and Locke and they continued performing together until 1953. After spending two years with Yusef Lateef (1954–6) he moved to New York, where he worked as a freelance; he substituted for Zutty Singleton at the Metropole (1957–8) and played at the Embers with Teddy Wilson. He toured with Charlie Shavers's quartet (1959–61), Buck Clayton (Europe, 1961), Benny Goodman's big band and small groups (1962), and Lionel Hampton's big band (1962–4); he then worked with Kenny Burrell. He was a member of a quartet led by Earl Hines (1964–70) and he also played with larger groups that Hines occasionally assembled during that period; in 1969 he formed the JPJ Quartet with Budd Johnson, Bill Pemberton, and Dill Jones. From 1975 to 1980 he played in Sy Oliver's nine-piece band, and in the late 1970s and early 1980s he performed as a freelance with Hampton (1977, 1978) and Oscar Peterson, among others; he also belonged to George Wein's Newport Jazz Festival All-Stars, with which he recorded in 1984.

SELECTED RECORDINGS

As sideman: Y. Lateef: *The Sounds of Yusef* (1957, Prst. 7122); K. Burrell: *The Tender Gender* (1966, Cadet 772); E. Hines: *Blues and Things* (1967, MJR 8101); Newport Jazz Festival All-Stars: *The Newport Jazz Festival All-Stars* (1984, Conc. 260)

BIBLIOGRAPHY

O. Keller: "Oliver Jackson et Eddie Locke," *BHcF*, no.99 (1960), 3
V. Wilmer: "Oliver Jackson: the Versatile Swinger," *DB*, xxxiv/25 (1967), 26
H. Panassié: "Une tournée qui promet: Charlie Shavers et Budd Johnson avec Oliver Jackson, 'Pépé,' et Lobligeois," *BHcF*, no.194 (1970), 3
S. Dance: *The World of Earl Hines* (New York, 1977) [interviews]
S. Traill: "On the Beat," *JJI*, xxxiv/1 (1981), 8
B. Rusch: "Oliver Jackson: Interview," *Cadence*, ix/11 (1983), 17
A. Vasset: "Oliver Jackson Quintet (octobre–novembre 1984)," *BHcF*, no.323 (1985), 25
C. Deffaa: "Portraits: Oliver Jackson," *MD*, x/8 (1986), 54

RICK MATTINGLY

Jackson, Preston [McDonald, James Preston] (*b* New Orleans, ? 3 Jan 1902; *d* Blytheville, AR, 12 Nov 1983). Trombonist. He moved in 1917 to Chicago, where he studied with Roy Palmer and Honore Dutrey. There and in Milwaukee he worked as a sideman (first recording in 1923), and as a leader (recording in 1926). Thereafter he was associated with Jimmie Noone (recording in 1936 and 1940), Roy Eldridge (recording around 1938), and Johnny Dodds (recording in 1940); he also recorded and in 1931–2 toured with Louis Armstrong. Later he worked with Lil Armstrong (performing in 1959, recording in 1961), toured and recorded in Europe with Kid Thomas as a member of the New Orleans Joymakers (1973–4), and played regularly at Preservation Hall in New Orleans and with its touring bands. He contributed articles to several jazz periodicals in the 1930s and wrote an autobiography published in 1974. Jackson's playing evolved during his career from a tailgate style to a fiercely expressive brand of swing before becoming more mellow and subdued in his later years.

Oral history material in *LNT*.

SELECTED RECORDINGS

As leader: Yearning for Mandalay/Trombone Man (1926, Para. 12411)
As sideman: Young's Creole Jazz Band: Tin Roof Blues (1923, Para. 20272); R. M. Jones: Dusty Bottom Blues/Scagmore Green (1926, OK 8431); J. Noone: He's a Different Type of Guy/The Blues Jumped a Rabbit (1936, Parl. R2303); New Orleans Hop Scop Blues/Keystone Blues (1940, Decca 18095); New Orleans Joymakers: *New Orleans Joymakers*, i (1973, Paragon 104)

BIBLIOGRAPHY

ChiltonW
P. Jackson: "Recapturing Yesterday," *MR*, i/7 (1974), 1; contd as "Reminisce is the Word," i/10 (1974), 6
P. Van Vorst: "Preston Jackson," *MR*, xi/3 (1984), 1

RICHARD B. ALLEN

Jackson, Quentin (Leonard) [Butter] (*b* Springfield, OH, 13 Jan 1909; *d* New York, 2 Oct 1976). Trombonist. He learned piano and violin when he was young and was taught trombone by his brother-in-law Claude Jones, who was a member of McKinney's Cotton Pickers. In 1930 he worked with Zack Whyte and on Jones's recommendation he was then engaged by the Cotton Pickers as a trombonist and singer. He played regularly with Don Redman from 1932 until the end of the 1930s. He was a member of Cab Calloway's orchestra from 1940 to 1948 (for illustration *see* CALLOWAY, CAB), except for a period of several months in 1946, when he toured Europe with Redman. In 1948 he worked briefly with Lucky Millinder before joining Duke Ellington, with whom he remained for 11 years. In the 1960s he toured Europe with Quincy Jones (1960) and performed with Count Basie (1961–2), Charles Mingus (1962), Ellington (1963), Louie Bellson (1964), and Gerald Wilson (1966). He played in theater bands and worked with Al Cohn and the Thad Jones–Mel Lewis Orchestra (1971–5); in the last year of his life he performed only occasionally. Jackson was a soulful, fervent soloist, known, particularly during his time with Ellington, for his use of the plunger mute, which is well represented by his solo on *Deep Night*; he was also an adept section player.

Oral history material in *NjR* (JOHP).

SELECTED RECORDINGS

As sideman: McKinney's Cotton Pickers: Do you believe in love at first sight?/Wrap your Troubles in Dreams (1931, Vic. 22811); D. Ellington: Fancy Dan (1951, Col. 39428); Jam with Sam (1951, Col. 39670); Deep Night (1951, Col. 39545); *Ellington '55* (1953–4, Cap. W521), incl. Black and Tan Fantasy; on C. Mingus: *Mingus, Mingus, Mingus, Mingus, Mingus* (1963, Imp. 54), Celia; T. Jones and M. Lewis: *Suite for Pops* (1972, 1975, A&M Hor. 701), incl. The Great One

BIBLIOGRAPHY

ChiltonW; *FeatherE*; *Feather–Gitler '70s*
"Interviews with the Men Besides [*sic*] Duke Ellington: Quentin "Butter" Jackson," *Jazz Statistics*, no.8 (1959), 9
Q. Jackson and V. Wilmer: "A Lifetime of Big Bands," *JM*, viii/4 (1962), 3
S. Dance: *The World of Swing* (New York, 1974) [colln of previously pubd interviews], 293

LAWRENCE KOCH

Jackson, Ronald Shannon (*b* Fort Worth, TX, 12 Jan 1940). Drummer. He began learning drums as a boy, and played professionally with the tenor saxophonist James Clay at the age of 15. Around 1966 he moved to New York, where he played with Charles Mingus (1966), Betty Carter, Stanley Turrentine, Jackie McLean, McCoy Tyner, Kenny Dorham, and Joe Henderson's big band. His first association with a leading free-jazz musician was in 1966–7, when he worked with Albert Ayler. After a period of retirement (*c*1970–1975), during which he practiced extensively, he returned to free jazz, working with Ornette Coleman and Prime Time (1975–9) and with Cecil Taylor (1978–9). He also played with James "Blood" Ulmer (1979–80), and in 1979 formed his own band, the Decoding Society, the members of which have included Vernon Reid (electric guitar), Zane Massay (saxophone), Henry Scott (trumpet), Akbar Ali (violin), Billy Bang, and Byard Lancaster. Jackson recorded as a member of Albert Mangelsdorff's trio at the Montreux International Jazz Festival (1980) and played with the A-1 Band, led by the trombonist Garrett List (1982), Craig Harris (1986), and Last Exit, a group that includes Peter Brötzmann, Sonny Sharrock, and Bill Laswell (from 1986).

Jackson has created an eclectic style, characterized by strong influences from rock and funk and by dense textures made up of lines in contrasting rhythms. He commands an impressive technique and the power and drive to propel an ensemble's performance.

SELECTED RECORDINGS

As leader of Decoding Society: *Eye on you* (1980, About Time 1003); *Mandance* (1982, Ant. 1008); *Decode yourself* (1985, Isl. 90247-1)
As sideman: A. Ayler: *Albert Ayler Quintet Live at Slug's Saloon* (1966, Base 3031–2); O. Coleman: *Dancing in your Head* (1975, A&M Hor. 722); C. Taylor: *Three Phasis* (1978, New World 303)

BIBLIOGRAPHY

R. Zabor: "Ronald Shannon Jackson: the Future of Jazz Drumming," *Musician*, no.33 (1981), 60
C. Doherty: "Decoding the Society," *DB*, xlix/8 (1982), 24
J. Solothurnmann: "Ronald Shannon Jackson: Jazz from Ten Worlds," *JF* [intl edn], no.75 (1982), 40
V. Wilmer: "Ronald Shannon Jackson: a Shaman for the 80's," *DB*, xlix/8 (1982), 22 [incl. discography]
J. Macnie: "Ronald Shannon Jackson," *Coda*, no.196 (1984), 10
C. Stern: "Ronald Shannon Jackson's Rhythms of Life," *MD*, viii/3 (1984), 14
G. Giddins: *Rhythm-a-ning: Jazz Tradition and Innovation in the '80s* (New York, and Oxford, England, 1985) [colln of previously pubd articles], 95

ED HAZELL

Jackson, Rudy [Rudolph] (*b* Fort Wayne, IN, 1901; *d* Chicago, *c*1968). Clarinetist and alto and tenor saxophonist. He grew up in Chicago. His parents were musical, and he studied clarinet in high school. In 1918 he began playing in local bands. He then worked with Carroll Dickerson (early 1920s) and King Oliver (1923–4) and toured with lesser-known musicians. He rejoined Oliver in 1927 and later that year became a member of Duke Ellington's orchestra, but in December was replaced by Barney Bigard. From 1929 to 1933 Jackson worked with Noble Sissle in Europe and New York, and during the mid-1930s performed in India with Leon Abbey and Teddy Weatherford. After another tour of Europe he went to Colombo, Ceylon (now Sri Lanka), with Weatherford. He remained in India throughout World War II before returning to Chicago. Jackson played in a classical, restrained style: he had a thin sound and used almost no vibrato.

SELECTED RECORDINGS

As sideman: S. Wallace: Being down don't worry me/Advice Blues (1925, OK 8276); D. Ellington: East St. Louis Toodle-oo (1927, Vic. 21703); N. Sissle: Camp Meeting Day/Miranda (1929, HMV 5709)

BIBLIOGRAPHY

ChiltonW
A. McCarthy: *Big Band Jazz* (New York and London, 1974), 296
F. Driggs and H. Lewine: *Black Beauty, White Heat: a Pictorial History of Classic Jazz, 1920–1950* (New York, 1982)

RAYMOND J. GARIGLIO

Jackson, Tony [Anthony] (*b* New Orleans, 5 June 1876; *d* Chicago, 20 April 1921). Pianist. He was the archetypal "Storyville professor," playing piano and singing in the high-class "sporting houses" of New Orleans during the early years of the 20th century. Although he never recorded, his extraordinary talents were praised by several New Orleans veterans, including Jelly Roll Morton, who particularly admired his qualities as an entertainer and the breadth of his repertory. Jackson's popularity apparently rested on his remarkable piano technique and his ability to play a wide variety of music, from operatic melodies to blues. He specialized in ragtime, and is also said to have been a highly original improviser; his high, clear voice was reputed to have been particularly expressive in ballads and blues. He was a skillful accompanist of other singers, and also a successful composer; one of his works, *Pretty Baby*, has achieved lasting popularity. During the last decade of his life he worked mainly in Chicago.

BIBLIOGRAPHY

M. Jones: "Tony Jackson," *Jazz Music*, ii/3 (1943), 48
R. Blesh and H. Janis: *They all Played Ragtime* (New York, 1950, rev. 4/1971), 159
G. W. Kay: "Basin Street Stroller: New Orleans and Tony Jackson," *JJ*, iv (1951), no.6, p.2; no.7, p.1
R. J. Carew: "He Knew a Thousand Songs: a Recollection of Tony Jackson," *JJ*, v/3 (1952), 1
G. W. Kay: "Remembering Tony Jackson," *SL*, xv/11–12 (1964), 5; xvi/1–2 (1965), 5
H. Holmquist: "Tony Jackson," *MR*, iv/8 (1977), 12

JOHN CHILTON

Jackson, Willis "Gator" [Gator Tail] (*b* Miami, 25 April 1928; *d* New York, 25 Oct 1987). Tenor saxophonist and bandleader. He played in local bands from 1946, alongside Blue Mitchell and Cannonball Adderley, among others. Later he studied theory and harmony at Florida Agricultural and Mechanical University, and played with Cootie Williams's octet, sextet, and septet (1948–55); the septet's recording of Jackson's composition *Gator Tail* (1948, Mer. 8131) earned him his nickname. He led his own band from 1950, making recordings (including *Thunderbird*, 1962, Prst. 7232) and touring the USA. He was married for eight years to the rhythm-and-blues singer Ruth Brown, with whom he recorded (1951) and performed; he also worked with Charlie Parker and Dizzy Gillespie. He played regularly at Club Harlem in Atlantic City, New Jersey, from 1963, and recorded frequently into the 1980s, often accompanied by all-star groups of sidemen. In 1979–80 he toured France; the following year he played in New York with Sammy Price. Jackson designed a modified saxophone, called the Gator horn, for playing ballads.

BIBLIOGRAPHY

Feather–Gitler '70s
"Discographie de Willis Jackson," *Soul Bag*, no.65 (1978), 11

Jacobs, Pete [Edward] (*b* Asbury Park, NJ, 7 May 1899; *d c*1952). Drummer. He first played in the Musical Aces, then from 1926 to 1928 worked with Claude Hopkins. After performing with the bandleader Charlie Skeete in 1928 he rejoined Hopkins, remaining with the group until 1937, when illness caused him to retire prematurely. His playing is well represented by Hopkins's *Everybody Shuffle* (1934, Bruns. 6916).

based on *ChiltonW*

Jacobs, Pim [Willem Bernard] (*b* Hilversum, Netherlands, 29 Oct 1934). Dutch pianist. In 1954 he formed a trio with his brother Ruud (Rudolf, Rudy) Jacobs (*b* Hilversum, 3 May 1938) on double bass and Wessel Ilcken on drums; later Rita Reys, who was then married to Ilcken, and the guitarist Wim Overgaauw joined the group. After Ilcken's death Pim Jacobs and Reys were married and embarked on a career as a duo; they made many recordings and appeared at festivals in Antibes–Juan-les-Pins (France), Warsaw, Prague, Budapest, Berlin, Lugano (Switzerland), Palermo (Sicily), Zagreb (Yugoslavia), New Orleans, and The Hague. Jacobs also worked as a producer of radio and television programs from 1964, operated the Go Go Club in Loosdrecht, near Hilversum, from 1967, and recorded with Herbie Mann and Bob Cooper. His playing can be heard to advantage on his album *Come Fly with me* (1982, Phi. 6423529). (*FeatherE*)

WIM VAN EYLE

Jacobson, Pete(r Paul George) (*b* Newcastle upon Tyne, England, 16 May 1950). English pianist. Jacobson, who is blind, began playing the piano at the age of four and learned jazz from the age of six. He studied organ in 1968–72 (from 1969 at the Royal Academy, London), then enrolled at Durham University as an external music student. After playing in Newcastle he worked as a freelance musician in London from 1969; he joined Barbara Thompson in 1974. He also played in Don Weller's Major Surgery (1974–5), with the guitarist Gary Boyle (1975), and in Bobby Wellins's quartet (from 1976), with which he recorded *Jubilation* (1978, Vortex 1). Jacobson has played at festivals at Nice (1980) and elsewhere, and has toured with Jimmy Knepper (1982); he has given solo concerts at the Bracknell Festival and at the Purcell Room, London, as well as appearing regularly in a duo with the alto saxophonist Chris Biscoe.

DIGBY FAIRWEATHER

Jacquet, (Jean Baptiste) Illinois (*b* Broussard, nr Lafayette, LA, 31 Oct 1922). Tenor saxophonist, brother of Russell Jacquet. He was brought up in Houston and began playing drums at high school, before learning soprano and alto saxophones. He performed in various bands in the late 1930s and in 1941 he moved to the West Coast with the bandleader Floyd Ray. He joined Lionel Hampton as a tenor saxophonist and became well known through his solo on Hampton's *Flying Home* (1942). After leaving Hampton he played with Cab Calloway (1943–4), performed and recorded with Jazz at the Philharmonic (JATP) and appeared in the film *Jammin' the Blues* (both 1944), and worked with Count Basie (1945–6). From 1950 he toured as a principal soloist with JATP and occasionally led his own groups; he began playing bassoon in 1965. Jacquet has performed at the Monterey, Nice, and North Sea jazz festivals, and although he settled in New York he has continued to tour Europe with the Texas Tenors, the group which includes Arnett Cobb and Buddy Tate.

Jacquet's wild, full-toned solo on *Flying Home* started a new approach to tenor saxophone playing, which became known as the "Texas tenor style"; it was marked by the use of notes at the extremes of the instrument's upper range, obtained as harmonics by means of false fingerings. His playing later mellowed and became less extrovert and aggressive; it shows the influence of Herschel Evans, Coleman Hawkins, and Lester Young but remains thoroughly individual. He performs ballads with particular mastery in a slow rhapsodic style.

SELECTED RECORDINGS

As leader: Memories of You/Merle's Mood (1945, Apollo 760); Jumpin' Jacquet/Blues Mood (1947, Savoy 593); Minor Romp/Berry's Blues (1947, Savoy 594); Illinois Blows the Blues (1947, Ala. 3001); *Swing's the Thing* (1957, Verve 8023); *Genius at Work* (1971, BL 118); *On Jacquet's Street* (1976, BB 33112); *God Bless my Solo* (1978, BB 33167)

As sideman with L. Hampton: Flying Home (1942, Decca 18394)

BIBLIOGRAPHY

FeatherE; *Feather '60s*; *Feather–Gitler '70s*

A. Morgan: "Illinois Jacquet," *JM*, ix/7 (1963), 8

J. Burns: "The Two Jacquets," *JJ*, xix/8 (1966), 25

——: "Lesser Known Bands of the Forties, 6: Illinois Jacquet, Roy Porter, Machito," *JM*, no.164 (1968), 7

G. Endress: *Jazz Podium: Musiker über sich selbst* (Stuttgart, Germany, 1980), 114

C. Battestini and J.-P. Battestini: "Jean-Baptiste Illinois Jacquet," *BHcF*, no.292 (1981), 4

J. Evensmo: *The Flute of Wayman Carver, the Trombone of Dickie Wells, 1927–1942, the Tenor Saxophone of Illinois Jacquet* (n.p. [Oslo], n.d. [?1983]) [discography]

T. Burke and D. Penny: "Big Band Blues: Illinois and Russell Jacquet," *Blues & Rhythm: the Gospel Truth*, no.4 (1984), 7 [incl. discography]

G. Giddins: *Rhythm-a-ning: Jazz Tradition and Innovation in the '80s* (New York, and Oxford, England, 1985) [colln of previously pubd articles], 178

EDDIE COOK

Jacquet, (Robert) Russell (*b* St. Martinville, LA, 4 Dec 1917). Trumpeter and singer, brother of Illinois Jacquet. He toured with Illinois and a second brother, Linton, who played drums, in the California Playboy Band (1934–7) and performed in an orchestra led by Floyd Ray (1939–40). After studying at Wiley College (1940–42) and Texas Southern University (1942–4), where he led a big band, he moved with Illinois Jacquet's group to California and took part in two recording sessions. His own group held an engagement at the Cotton Club, Hollywood, and he made a number of recordings as a leader (*c*1945–1949). In 1946 he rejoined Illinois, with whom he performed and recorded regularly until 1954, when the band toured Europe. Thereafter he worked only intermittently with his brother, but recorded with the group in New York on two further occasions (1965, 1969). He played in Oakland, California, in 1959, and performed in Houston in a band that included Arnett Cobb in 1966. In 1985 he again worked with Illinois in New York. Jacquet's solo playing may be heard on *Merle's Mood* (1945, Jazz Selection 518).

BIBLIOGRAPHY

J. Burns: "The Two Jacquets," *JJ*, xix/8 (1966), 25

B. Rusch: "Russell Jacquet: Interview," *Cadence*, v/11 (1979), 5

T. Burke and D. Penny: "Big Band Blues: Illinois and Russell Jacquet," *Blues & Rhythm: the Gospel Truth*, no.4 (1984), 7 [incl. discography]

EDDIE COOK

Jædig, Bent (*b* Copenhagen, 18 Oct 1935). Danish tenor saxophonist. His first professional associations were in Germany with Attila Zoller, Albert Mangelsdorff, and others; these he interrupted briefly to play with Jazz Quintet '60 (1959), and the Danish Radiojazzgruppen and Radioens Big Band (1965–6). He took part in performances of Gunther Schuller's opera *The Visitation* (Hamburg, Germany, 1966, Montreal and New York, 1967) and from the early 1970s worked in Denmark as the leader of a quintet with Richard Boone, again as a member of the Radioens Big Band, and with Thad Jones's group Eclipse (1979–80) and Ernie Wilkins's Almost Big Band (from 1980). His playing may be heard to advantage on *Danish Jazzman 1967* (1967, Debut 1149), notably on the track *Atlicity*. (*ReclamsJ*)

ERIK WIEDEMANN

Jaffe, Nat(haniel) (*b* New York, 1918; *d* New York, 5 Aug 1945). Pianist. He moved with his family to Europe at the age of two, lived in Berlin from 1921 to 1932, and undertook classical training. After returning to the USA at the age of 14 he took an interest in jazz. In New York he accompanied the actress Noel Francis at Central Park Casino, played under the bandleader Emery Deutsch at the New Yorker, and performed as an unaccompanied soloist at Mammy's Chicken Coop on 52nd Street; he also led a band at the Clover Club, played with Charlie Barnet (at the Famous Door, 1938) and Jack Teagarden (1939–40), and at Kelly's Stable worked as a soloist, in a trio, and in a sextet. Among others he recorded with Louis Armstrong (1938) and Sarah Vaughan (1945).

SELECTED RECORDINGS

As leader: How can you Face me?/Keepin' Out of Mischief Now (1944, Sig. 28112); A Hundred Years from Today/If I Had you (1944, Black & White 1209)

As sideman: L. Armstrong: I can't give you anything but love/Ain't misbehavin' (1938, Decca 2042); C. Barnet: Tin Roof Blues/Knockin' at the Famous Door (1939, Bb 10131); J. Teagarden: You, you Darling/The Moon and the Willow (1940, Vars. 8196)

BIBLIOGRAPHY

ChiltonW; *FeatherE*

A. Shaw: *The Street that Never Slept: New York's Fabled 52nd Street* (New York, 1971/R1977 as *52nd Street: The Street of Jazz*), 213

J. Burns: "Dead, but Not . . . Remembered," *JJI*, xxx/12 (1977), 13
W. van Eyle: "Nat Jaffe: een onbekende pianist" [Nat Jaffe: an unknown pianist], *Jazz Press*, no.34 (1977), 6 [incl. discography]

JAMES M. DORAN

Jam. To improvise, usually in a group, whence to take part in a JAM SESSION.

Jamal, Ahmad [Jones, Fritz] (*b* Pittsburgh, 2 July 1930). Pianist. He studied with the singer Mary Caldwell Dawson and the pianist James Miller in Pittsburgh where he began playing professionally at the age of 11. He left Westinghouse High School in the late 1940s to join an orchestra led by the trumpeter George Hudson. In 1951 he formed his first trio, the Three Strings, which, after an extended engagement at the Blue Note in Chicago, attracted the critical support of John Hammond while appearing at the Embers in New York. On his conversion to Islam in the early 1950s, he changed his name. In 1958, with Israel Crosby and Vernel Fournier, Jamal recorded his most popular and influential album, *Ahmad Jamal at the Pershing*. Miles Davis admired Jamal's lean style, use of space, and simple embellishments in this album, which are stylistic features of Davis's own later recordings. Jamal's trio disbanded in 1962 but, with new personnel (among them Jamil Nasser and the drummer Frank Gant), he has continued to tour and to record for Argo/Cadet and Impulse. On later recordings for 20th Century Jamal sometimes played electric piano and made use of backup orchestras including string and wind instruments.

SELECTED RECORDINGS

Ahmad Jamal at the Pershing (1958, Argo 628); *Ahmad Jamal at the Blackhawk* (1961, Argo 703); *At the Top – Poinciana Revisited* (1968, Imp. 9176); *Jamal Plays Jamal* (1974, 20C 459); *Ahmad Jamal Live at Bubba's* (1981, Who's Who in Jazz 21021)

BIBLIOGRAPHY

N. Tesser: "'Cut out the Jass': Ahmad Jamal," *DB*, xli/1 (1974), 14
L. Lyons: "Ahmad Jamal, Mainstream Jazz Pianist," *CK*, iii/6 (1977), 8
L. Goddet: "Ahmad Jamal: une musique du désir," *Jh*, no.359 (1979), 4; no.360 (1979), 6
L. Tomkins: "A Quality Product Can Succeed," *CI*, xviii/1 (1979), 16 [interview]
L. Birnbaum: "Ahmad Jamal," *DB*, xlviii/3 (1981), 14
E. Southern: *Biographical Dictionary of Afro-American and African Musicians* (Westport, CT, 1982)
L. Lyons: *The Great Jazz Pianists, Speaking of their Lives and Music* (New York, 1983), 113

RICHARD WANG

Jamal, Khan [Cheeseboro, Warren Robert] (*b* Jacksonville, FL, 23 July 1946). Vibraphonist. His mother, Willa Mae McGhee, was a stride pianist. He took up the vibraphone in 1964, belonged in the late 1960s to the Cosmic Forces, which included several of Sun Ra's former sidemen, and in the early 1970s formed the Sounds of Liberation with Byard Lancaster. After studying vibraphone with Bill Lewis and percussion at the Combs College of Music he performed and recorded in the late 1970s with Sunny Murray's Untouchable Factor. From 1980 he worked in Ronald Shannon Jackson's Decoding Society and in groups led by the pianist Joe Bonner and Billy Bang; he also performed as a leader in Europe and Philadelphia. A versatile musician, Jamal is equally adept at playing smooth, flowing lines and rapid, brittle, percussive ones, and at working with such diverse material as the jazz-rock of Jackson, the free jazz of Murray, and the elaborately arranged compositions of Bang. In addition to his principal instrument he is an accomplished player of the marimba, on which he recorded a series of duets with Lewis in 1977.

SELECTED RECORDINGS

Duos with B. Lewis: *The River* (1977, Philly Jazz 2)
As leader (recorded for Steeplechase): *Dark Warrior* (1984, 1196); *Three* (1984, 1201)
As sideman: R. S. Jackson: *Nasty* (1981, Moers 01086); B. Bang: *Outline no.12* (1982, OAO 5004)

BIBLIOGRAPHY

D. Hollenberg: "Khan Jamal," *DB*, xlvi/12 (1979), 50
G. Futrick: "Khan Jamal," *Coda*, no.196 (1984), 27
R. Iannapollo: "Khan Jamal," *Option*, issue J (1986), 23
L. van Trikt: "Khan Jamal," *Cadence*, xi/3 (1987), 5

ROBERT J. IANNAPOLLO

James, Billy [William] (*b* Pittsburgh, 20 April 1936). Drummer. He first played with Lionel Hampton (1954), then with Booker Ervin (1956–7), James Moody (1960–61), and Candido Camero (1961). Together with Don Patterson, he performed and recorded with Gene Ammons and Sonny Stitt (1961–2) and Eddie "Lockjaw" Davis (1962–3); James later worked with Patterson in a duo and in small groups, recording under his leadership (1964–9) and that of Stitt (1964–8) and Eric Kloss (1965–6). He recorded with Eddie Harris in 1971 (*Instant Death*, Atl. 1611) and Houston Person in 1982. (*Feather '60s*)

James, Bob [Robert] (*b* Marshall, MO, 25 Dec 1939). Pianist, keyboard player, arranger, composer, and record producer. After studying composition at the University of Michigan (MA 1962) he recorded as the leader of a bop trio (1962) and a free-jazz group (1965), then worked as music director for Sarah Vaughan (1965–8). As a session musician in New York from 1968 to 1972 he played with Quincy Jones and Morgana King, and the soul singers Roberta Flack and Dionne Warwicke. In 1973 he became an arranger for CTI, and also composed and acted as a producer for nearly every musician signed to the label. These included Grover Washington, Jr., Freddie Hubbard, Stanley Turrentine, Hubert Laws, Ron Carter, and Eric Gale. He made his first album as a leader in 1974; the following year he joined CBS and began working with such pop singers as Neil Diamond and Paul Simon. In 1977 he formed his own recording company, Tappan Zee, to help promote the work of other musicians, including Richard Tee and Mongo Santamaria. He has continued to record prolifically as a leader into the mid-1980s, and has also composed music for films and television, including the theme for the television series "Taxi."

James is adept at blending pop and jazz, and, although his music is often formulaic, his use of technology and distinguished soloists has enabled him to remain innovative and commercially successful.

See also PIANO, §6.

SELECTED RECORDINGS

(all recorded for Tappan Zee unless otherwise indicated)

As leader: *Bold Conceptions* (1962, Mer. 69768); *One* (1974, CTI 6043); *Heads* (1977, JC34896); *Touchdown* (1978, JC35594); with E. Klugh: *One on One* (1979, FC36241); *Hands Down* (1982, FC38067); *12* (1984, FC39580)

BIBLIOGRAPHY

Feather '60s; *Feather–Gitler '70s*
J. Levenson: "Bob James: Hybrid Harmonies," *DB*, li/7 (1984), 28 [incl. discography]

BILL MILKOWSKI

James, Elmer (Taylor) (*b* Yonkers, NY, 1910; *d* New York, 25 July 1954). Double bass and tuba player. He played tuba with Gene Rodgers (1928), June Clark (1929), and Chick Webb (1929–33, making a recording with Louis Armstrong, 1932). After changing to double bass he played briefly with Benny Carter, and again with Webb, then joined Fletcher Henderson in March

1934; later that year he recorded with Henderson and with Henry "Red" Allen (on whose *Rug Cutter Swing* (1934, Ban. 33178) his forceful, almost ferocious, bass playing may be heard). While he was a member of the Mills Blue Rhythm Band (1934–6; for illustration *see* MILLS BLUE RHYTHM BAND) he also recorded with Carter and Buster Bailey (both 1934), Bob Howard (1935), and Allen (1935–6). He performed and recorded with Edgar Hayes (intermittently, 1937–9), Mezz Mezzrow (1937–8), and Claude Hopkins (1940), and recorded with Jabbo Smith and Tommy Ladnier (both 1938). He retired from music in the early 1940s.

BIBLIOGRAPHY

ChiltonW; *FeatherE*

W. C. Allen: *Hendersonia: the Music of Fletcher Henderson and his Musicians: a Bio-discography* (Highland Park, NJ, 1973), 565

James, George (*b* Beggs, OK, 7 Dec 1906). Reed player. After playing with one of Charlie Creath's bands in the mid-1920s he moved in 1928 to Chicago, where he worked with many bandleaders, including Jimmie Noone, and led his own groups. In 1931 he toured with Louis Armstrong, and the following year he played with the Savoy Bearcats. In the mid-1930s he was a member of Fats Waller's orchestra, after which he played for the *Blackbirds Revue* (1938–9) and worked with James P. Johnson and Benny Carter (both 1940), Teddy Wilson, and Lucky Millinder (1941–2). Thereafter James led bands in New York (holding residencies at the Famous Door and Café Society), Pittsburgh, and Detroit, and rejoined Johnson (1944). He performed with Claude Hopkins in 1945, then spent two years with Noble Sissle and formed his own band, which he continued to lead into the 1960s. From 1973 into the early 1980s he toured internationally with Clyde Bernhardt and the Harlem Blues and Jazz Band; his playing may be heard to advantage on the album *Harlem Blues & Jazz Band 1973–1980* (1973–80, Barron 403).

BIBLIOGRAPHY

B. Demeusy: "George James," *JM*, xi/12 (1966), 25 [interview]

L. Wright: "George James, no Relation to Harry . . .," *Sv*, no.86 (1979–80), 43

based on *ChiltonW*

James, Harry (Hagg) (*b* Albany, GA, 15 March 1916; *d* Las Vegas, NV, 5 July 1983). Trumpeter and bandleader. He began playing professionally at an early age, working with his father's circus band. He performed with various bands in Texas and worked for a year with Ben Pollack (1935–6) before becoming a leading member of Benny Goodman's band (1937). James's exciting playing was given great prominence by Goodman, and is shown at its most typical on his recording of *Ridin' High*. After leaving Goodman in late 1938 James formed his own big band, which by the early 1940s had an enormous following. Among his principal soloists were Sam Donahue (1940), Vido Musso (1940–41), and Corky Corcoran (intermittently, 1941–1970s). He appeared in several films, including *Syncopation* (1942), *Best Foot Forward* (1943), *Mr. Co-ed* (1944), *Kitten on the Keys* (1946), *Carnegie Hall* (1947), and *The Benny Goodman Story* (1955), and in the 1950s made regular tours with the band, traveling to Europe in 1957. During the 1960s, though he spent long periods in Nevada, James performed frequently in New York. He made further tours of Europe in 1970 and 1971, visited Argentina in 1981, and continued to lead the band until a few days before his death.

James's admiration for the playing of Louis Armstrong never overwhelmed his individuality; he was noted for the boldness of his style, the richness of his tone, his range, and his stamina. The popularity that he gained with his bravura performances of such test pieces as *Carnival of Venice* and *Flight of the Bumble Bee* has tended to obscure the fact that he was a very fine jazz improviser, possessing a verve that enhanced many small-group and big-band recordings. A collection of his scores and other materials is held in the American Heritage Center of the University of Wyoming in Laramie; *see* LIBRARIES AND ARCHIVES, §2.

For illustration *see* WILLIAMS, COOTIE.

SELECTED RECORDINGS

As leader: Texas Chatter (1938, Bruns. 8067); Boo woo (1939, Bruns. 8318); Carnival of Venice (1940, Var. 8231); Flight of the Bumble Bee (1940, Var. 8298); I'm confessin' (1944, Col. 36773)

As sideman: B. Pollack: Spreading Knowledge Around (1936, Voc. 3342); T. Wilson: Just a Mood (1937, Bruns. 7973); B. Goodman: *Jazz Concert, no.2* (1937–8, Col. ML4590), incl. Ridin' High

BIBLIOGRAPHY

C. Emge: "The History of Harry James," *DB*, xviii/4 (1951), 3

J. Tynan: "The Horn Still Blows," *DB*, xxv/2 (1958), 17

L. Tomkins: "The Harry James Story," *CI*, ix/4 (1970), 20

G. Hall: *Harry James and his Orchestra* (Laurel, MD, 1971) [discography]

C. Garrod and P. Johnston: *Harry James and his Orchestra*, i: *1937–1946*, ii: *1947–1954* (Zephyrhills, FL, 1975); iii: *1955–1982* (Zephyrhills, 1985)

L. Tomkins: "The Classic Interview: Harry James," *CI*, xxiv/7 (1987), 12

JOHN CHILTON

James, (Sydney) Michael (*b* Reading, England, 13 Sept 1932). English writer. His career began in earnest in 1957, when he first wrote articles for *Jazz Monthly*, to which he continued to contribute until the magazine ceased publication in 1971. He also wrote many articles for the *Jazz Review* (1959–61) and *Melody Maker* (1978–80), and occasionally for *Coda* and *Jazz Forum*. His brief monographs on Miles Davis and Dizzy Gillespie include not only biographies of their subjects and assessments of their influence, but also detailed analyses of their recordings, which illustrate how the musicians departed from conventional harmony, rhythm, and phrasing to establish their own distinctive styles.

WRITINGS

(selective list)

Dizzy Gillespie (London, 1959)

Ten Modern Jazzmen: an Appraisal of the Recorded Work of Ten Modern Jazzmen (London, 1960)

Miles Davis (London, 1961); repr. in *Kings of Jazz*, ed. S. Green (South Brunswick, NJ, and New York, 1978)

ROBERT GANNON

James, Pinocchio [Cornelius] (*b* Macon, GA, 23 Dec 1927). Singer. Both his parents were musicians, and he studied piano and singing at the Cosmopolitan School of Music in Cincinnati. He made recordings under his own name in New York in 1951, and with Todd Rhodes in Cincinnati in 1953, including *Your mouth got a hole in it* (King 4648); he then worked as a solo performer before joining Lionel Hampton's band in 1957. He remained with Hampton into the mid-1960s, making a number of international tours with the group and taking part in several recordings. (*Feather '60s*)

James, Stafford (Louis) (*b* Evanston, IL, 24 April 1946). Double bass player. He studied at the Chicago Conservatory (1967–8) and the Mannes College (1972–4). After moving to New York in late 1968 he worked with Monty Alexander and recorded (on electric bass guitar) with Sun Ra. In the 1970s he played with Melba Moore (1971), Roy Ayers (1972–3), Gary Bartz (1972–3, with whom he appeared at the Montreux International Jazz Festival), Betty Carter (from 1973), Art Blakey (1973–4), Al Haig and Barry Harris (both 1974–5), Andrew Hill, Robin Kenyatta, Andrew Cyrille, and Chico Hamilton (all 1975), Dexter Gordon and Woody Shaw (both 1976), and John Scofield (1978); he played with Shaw again in 1980–83. After leaving Shaw he played with Philly Joe Jones and Dameronia, Slide Hampton, Cecil Payne, and Jimmy Heath. James has also led and made recordings with small groups of his own; these have included a quartet (from the mid-1970s), a quintet (from 1977), a trio with the pianist Marc Cohen and drummer Mike Smith (from 1983), and (from 1985) a string and percussion ensemble that included Buster Williams, the drummer Victor Lewis, and the percussionist Guilherme Franco.

SELECTED RECORDINGS

As leader: *Stafford James Quartet* (1975, Horo 101-26); *Stafford James Ensemble* (1979, RR 142)

As sideman: A. Ayler: *Music is the Healing Force of the Universe* (1969, Imp. 9191); R. Ali: *New Directions in Modern Music* (1973, Survival 104); on A. Hill: *Invitation* (1974–5, Fre. 40156), Spiral; W. Shaw: *Little Red's Fantasy* (1976, Muse 5103); *Lotus Flower* (1982, Enja 4018)

BIBLIOGRAPHY

Feather–Gitler '70s

JOHN VOIGT

Jam session. An informal gathering of jazz musicians playing for their own pleasure. Jam sessions originated as spontaneous diversions when musicians were free from the constraints of professional engagements; they also served the function of training young players in a musical tradition that was not formally taught and accepted in music schools and academic institutions until the 1960s. In the late 1930s jam sessions came to be organized by entrepreneurs for audiences; this undermined their original purpose, and by the 1950s true jam sessions were becoming increasingly rare. However, in the 1970s and 1980s the concept of "sessions" has made a comeback among younger jazz musicians, especially those trained in conservatories. An "open" session is one in which anyone who is more or less competent may take part. The so-called loft scene of the late 1970s in New York may also be seen as a quasi-commercial offshoot of the jam session. (B. Cameron: "Sociological Notes on the Jam Session," *Social Forces*, xxxiii (1954), 177)

GUNTHER SCHULLER

Jankowski, Horst (*b* Berlin, 30 Jan 1936). German pianist and bandleader. From 1949 to 1953 he studied piano, double bass, and trumpet at the Hochschule für Musik in Berlin. He then played with Kurt Hohenberger (1953–4) and accompanied the singer Caterina Valente (1954–5). From 1955 to 1960 he worked with Erwin Lehn's jazz orchestra at Süddeutscher Rundfunk, Stuttgart; during the same period he toured Yugoslavia with Tony Scott (1957), performed as a soloist with Benny Goodman at the Brussels World's Fair (1958), and played with many visiting American jazz musicians. He was the leader of the RIAS dance band in Berlin. Jankowski has made recordings as the leader of his own groups (1956–70) and as a soloist (*Jankowskeyboard*, 1971, MPS 3320880), and has taken part in sessions with Rolf Kühn (*c*1956, 1959), and Lehn and Helmut Brandt (both 1978); he played again with Brandt in the mid-1980s. (*FeatherE*)

Janssen, Guus (*b* Heiloo, Netherlands, 13 May 1951). Dutch pianist and composer. He studied at the Sweelinck Conservatory in Amsterdam (1970–77) and belonged to a group with his brother, the drummer Wim Janssen (1972–5). He played in the Netherlands with the Boventoon (a workshop orchestra led by the tenor saxophonist Herman de Wit), the violinist Maurice Horsthuis, the alto saxophonist Paul Termos, Theo Loevendie, and Maarten Altena, and in Great Britain and Germany with Evan Parker, Günter Christmann, the guitarist Peter Cusack, John Tchicai, and Paul Lovens. Janssen's playing is well represented by two albums he recorded for Claxon, *On the Line* (1979, 4) and *Septet* (1984, 14). As a composer he combines material that is written out with improvisation; his work *Toonen* was given its première at the Donaueschingen (Germany) Musiktage in 1980. The following year he was awarded the Dutch National Jazz Prize.

WIM VAN EYLE

Jaremko, Zbigniew (*b* Skarżysko-Kamienna, Poland, 27 May 1946). Polish tenor saxophonist. He studied musicology at the Academy of Catholic Theology in Warsaw and then attended the High School of Music there. He made his début as a jazz musician with the dixieland group Old Timers (1967) and in 1971 played and recorded with the big band of the Stodola student club. He led the Jazz Carriers, a quintet that won a prize at the Jazz on the Odra festival in 1972 and recorded *Carry On* (1973, Muza 0962). In the 1970s he occasionally played with the Polish Radio Jazz Studio and in Krzysztof Sadowski's Organ Group. He is active as a bop musician within Poland but is not well known outside his own country. (J. Byrczek and H. Matuszewska: "Eurojazz Personalities: Poland," *JF* [intl edn], no.33 (1975), 65)

WOLFRAM KNAUER

Jarman, Joseph (*b* Pine Bluff, AR, 14 Sept 1937). Reed player and composer. He played drums in high school in Chicago (1952–5) and saxophone and clarinet in army bands. Having returned to Chicago in 1958, he played in Muhal Richard Abrams's Experimental Band (formed 1961) and a hard-bop sextet led by Roscoe Mitchell, and became one of the founding members (in 1965) of the Association for the Advancement of Creative Musicians. He gave solo concerts from around 1967 and in 1966–8 led a free-jazz group; after the deaths of his pianist, Christopher Gaddy, and double bass player, Charles Clark, he joined the ART ENSEMBLE OF CHICAGO (formed in Paris in 1969), with the other members of which – Mitchell, Lester Bowie, and Malachi Favors – he had already recorded under Bowie's leadership in 1967. Besides working with this group in Paris and, from 1971, the USA, Jarman has performed and recorded as a soloist, and in duos and small groups with Anthony Braxton, Oliver Lake, Don Moye, and Don Pullen.

Jarman plays saxophones, flutes, homemade wind instruments, and many percussion instruments; the most theatrical member of the Art Ensemble of Chicago, he also dances, recites poetry, and employs a wide range of vocal effects. Although his compositions and improvisations grew out of free jazz and show the influence of Eric Dolphy, they are eclectic and inventive and defy stylistic classification.

Oral history material in *ICU*.

SELECTED RECORDINGS

As unaccompanied soloist: *Sunbound* (1976, AECO 002)

Duos: with A. Braxton: *Together Alone* (1971, Del. 428); with D. Moye: *Egwu-anwu* (1978, IndN 1033)

As leader: *Song for* (1966, Del. 410); *As if it were the Seasons* (1968, Del. 417); with D. Pullen and D. Moye: *The Magic Triangle* (1979, BS 0038); with D. Moye: *Earth Passage-Density* (1981, BS 0052)

As sideman: L. Bowie: *Numbers 1 and 2* (1967, Nessa 1)

For further recordings *see* ART ENSEMBLE OF CHICAGO.

BIBLIOGRAPHY

B. Case: "Jarman: Dreaming of the Masters," *MM*, liv (28 April 1979), 44
B. Rusch: "Joseph Jarman: Interview," *Cadence*, v/5 (1979), 3

J. Litweiler: "The Art Ensemble of Chicago: Adventures in the Urban Bush," *DB*, xlix/6 (1982), 19 [incl. discography]
E. Janssens and H. de Craen: *Art Ensemble of Chicago Discography: Unit and Members* (Brussels, 1983) [incl. list of compositions]

BARRY KERNFELD

Jaro. Record label. It was established New York in 1959 by the J. Arthur Rank Organization, as a subsidiary of the record company Top Rank. In the USA Jaro existed only for about two years; during that time Manny Albam was a talent scout, and the label was used to issue albums by Babs Gonzales, Georgie Auld, Kenny Dorham, J. R. Monterose, and Cootie Williams. Although the parent organization was based in London, no records were released on Jaro in the UK. After the label was discontinued in 1961 the material ceased to be available; from the late 1970s, however, much of the catalogue has been reissued by Xanadu.

MARK GARDNER

Jarreau, Al (*b* Milwaukee, 12 March 1940). Singer. He earned an MA in psychology at the University of Iowa and worked as a counselor in San Francisco in the late 1960s. After achieving success singing in local clubs he took up music full-time, releasing his first album in 1975. The following year he toured Europe, where he has acquired a large following. Jarreau developed his style from the bop school of Jon Hendricks and Dave Lambert, which he extended with great refinement and virtuosity and adapted to a fusion of jazz and soul music. Using a nasal, vibratoless voice with superb intonation, he commands a wide range and a large repertory of ancillary expressive sounds such as groans, tongue-clicks, and gasps; in scat singing he makes use of nonsense syllables that range from those conventionally associated with bop to mock-oriental and mock-Arabic sounds. Although his recordings sometimes reveal a commercial bent, particularly in his own compositions, his live performances, such as *Take Five* on the album *Look to the Rainbow*, place him with Bobby McFerrin among the foremost jazz and scat singers of his generation.

For illustration *see* SINGING, fig.3.

SELECTED RECORDINGS
(all recorded for Warner Bros.)

We Got By (1975, 2224); *Glow* (1976, 2248); *Look to the Rainbow* (1977, 3052), incl. Take Five; *All Fly Home* (1978, 3329); *Breakin' Away* (1981, 3576); *Jarreau* (1983, 23801)

BIBLIOGRAPHY

J.-E. Berendt: "Al Jarreau: a Ritual from the Throat," *JF* [intl edn], no.49 (1977), 35
L. Goddet: "Le chanteur de jazz: Al Jarreau," *Jh*, nos.345–6 (1978), 47
L. Underwood: "Al Jarreau: the Amazing Acrobat of Scat," *DB*, xlv/6 (1978), 15
S. Bloom: "Al Jarreau: Breaking Away," *DB*, xlix/2 (1982), 25
J. Reese: "Les voix multiples d'Al Jarreau," *Jh*, nos.391–2 (1982), 23

J. BRADFORD ROBINSON

Jarrett, Keith (*b* Allentown, PA, 8 May 1945). Pianist and composer. He began studying the piano at the age of three, and by the time he was seven had presented a full recital and was composing and improvising. He played professionally throughout his elementary school years, and during his teens toured for one season as piano soloist with Fred Waring's Pennsylvanians. In 1962 he moved to Boston, where he spent one year, on a scholarship, studying at the Berklee College of Music. He then began working in the Boston area with his own trio and also with such visiting artists as Tony Scott and Roland Kirk. He moved to New York in 1965 but, having decided to avoid commercial work, was scarcely noticed until Art Blakey heard him during a jam session at the Village Vanguard. He joined Blakey's Jazz Messengers in December of that year and stayed with them for four months, gaining critical notice and making his first recording with an established group.

Jarrett rose to international acclaim as a member of the quartet led by Charles Lloyd (1966–9). One of the first groups to explore a broad range of improvisational styles, Lloyd's quartet attracted a large youthful following extending as far as the USSR, where it toured in 1967; Jarrett's flawless technique, intense lyricism, and total physical involvement with the piano were among its strongest assets. Jarrett also played soprano saxophone and percussion for Lloyd, a practice he has continued throughout his career. From 1969 to 1971 he worked with Miles Davis, first on electric organ while Chick Corea was playing electric piano, then playing both instruments after Corea left the group. Jarrett made good use of Davis's frequent periods of inactivity to work and record with his own band, which included Charlie Haden, Paul Motian, and later Dewey Redman, and had a fruitful performing and recording career until 1976. Although encompassing a much broader stylistic range, their music revealed a strong kinship with the earlier work of Bill Evans (ii), Paul Bley, and Ornette Coleman.

Keith Jarrett (piano) with Cecil McBee (double bass) at the Newport Jazz Festival, July 1966

In 1972 Jarrett began performing solo concerts which consisted simply of two extended improvisations, each usually 30 to 45 minutes in length. The music spanned a rich variety of traditions, but was developed in a manner that seemed holistic rather than merely eclectic, illuminating Jarrett's reference to his work as universal folk music. Through the international success of these concerts he became the only jazz artist of the 1970s to capture a mass audience without conforming to commercial trends. Furthermore he has spearheaded a revival of interest in acoustic music, having refused to play electronic instruments since he left Davis's band. Avoiding easy categorization, his projects remain extremely varied. He has played in a highly acclaimed quartet with Jan Garbarek and in a trio with Gary Peacock and Jack DeJohnette, recorded solo improvisations on the pipe organ, and performed works from the classical piano repertory, such as Barber's Piano Concerto. His own compositions include pieces for classical chamber groups, symphony orchestra, and orchestra with improvising soloists.

Oral history material in *NjR*.

See also JAZZ (i), §VI, 7.

SELECTED RECORDINGS

(all recorded for ECM unless otherwise indicated)

An unaccompanied soloist: *Facing You* (1971, 1017); *Solo Concerts* (1973, 1035–7); *The Köln Concert* (1975, 1064–5); *Sun Bear Concerts* (1976, 1100); *Invocations* (1979–80, 1201–2)

As leader: *Somewhere Before* (1968, Vortex 2012); *Expectations* (1972, Col. KG31580); *Fort Yawuh* (1973, Imp. 9240); *In the Light* (1973, 1033–4); *Belonging* (1974, 1050); *Arbour Zena* (1975, 1070); *My Song* (1977, 1115); *Nude Ants* (1979, 1171–2); *Standards*, i (1983, 1255); *Changes* (1983, 1276); *Standards*, ii (1983, 1289)

As sideman: A. Blakey: *Buttercorn Lady* (1966, Lml. 86034); C. Lloyd: *Dream Weaver* (1966, Atl. 1459); *Forest Flower* (1966, Atl. 1473); *Charles Lloyd in the Soviet Union* (1967, Atl. 1571)

BIBLIOGRAPHY

J. Klee: "Keith Jarrett: Spontaneous Composer," *DB*, xxxix/1 (1972), 12
B. Palmer: "The Inner Octaves of Keith Jarrett," *DB*, xli/17 (1974), 16
L. Lyons: "Keith Jarrett: Pianist and Composer," *CK*, ii/3 (1976), 22
J.-E. Berendt: *Ein Fenster aus Jazz: Essays, Portraits, Reflexionen* (Frankfurt am Main, Germany, 1977), 83
M. Ruppli: "Discographie de Keith Jarrett," *Jh*, no.348 (1978), 22
J. Aikin: "Keith Jarrett," *CK*, v/9 (1979), 38
T. Darter: "Piano Giants of Jazz: Keith Jarrett," *CK*, vii/4 (1981), 56
L. Lyons: *The Great Jazz Pianists, Speaking of their Lives and Music* (New York, 1983), 294
J. Rockwell: "Mystical Romanticism, Popularity and the Varied Forms of Fusion," *All American Music: Composition in the Late Twentieth Century* (New York, 1983), 176
A. Lange: "Keith Jarrett," *DB*, li/6 (1984), 16 [interview]
U. Andresen: *Keith Jarrett: sein Leben, seine Musik, seine Schallplatten* (Gauting, Germany, n.d. [1985])
B. Doerschuk: "Keith Jarrett," *Keyboard*, xii/9 (1986), 80 [incl. discography]

BILL DOBBINS

Jarvis, Clifford (Osbourne) (*b* Boston, 26 Aug 1941). Drummer. After studying with Alan Dawson at the Berklee College of Music (1953–8) he moved to New York, where he recorded with Chet Baker and Randy Weston (both 1959), Yusef Lateef (1960), Freddie Hubbard (1960, 1962, 1965), Barry Harris (1961–2), Jackie McLean (1965), and Elmo Hope (1966), and played with Grant Green and Roland Kirk. He may be heard to advantage on Hubbard's album *Hub-tones* (1962, BN 84115). Intermittently from 1962 to 1976 he played free jazz with Sun Ra, making several recordings with his group; during this period he also worked with Pharoah Sanders (including a performance at the Newport Jazz Festival in New York, 1972) and recorded with Sonny Simmons (1970) and Alice Coltrane (1971). Later Jarvis recorded bop albums with Kenny Drew (1977), Walter Davis (1979), and Archie Shepp (1985). (*Feather–Gitler '70s*)

Jarzebski, Pawel (*b* Poznán, Poland, 21 April 1948). Polish double bass player. He performed and recorded with Michal Urbaniak, also playing electric bass guitar, from 1970 to 1972. After working with Zbigniew Namysłowski (1973) he rejoined Urbaniak, with whom he toured Europe and the USA and recorded (both 1973–4) and performed at the Newport Jazz Festival New York (1974). After returning to Poland Jarzebski again worked with Namysłowski, performing with him at the Cascais (Portugal) jazz festival (1974), and recording (1975, 1978). He is heard to advantage on *Loaded* (1979, Leo 010), recorded with the Quartet, a Polish group that included Janusz Stefanski. (*Feather–Gitler '70s*)

Jaspar, Bobby [Robert B.] (*b* Liège, Belgium, 20 Feb 1926; *d* New York, 4 March 1963). Belgian tenor saxophonist and flutist. He learned piano and clarinet at an early age, but soon took up alto and tenor saxophones, and at the age of 19 played the tenor instrument in a dixieland group with Toots Thielemans. In 1954 he started playing flute, and after studying chemistry at university he turned to music as a profession. He worked with his own groups, and with Henri Renaud (recording in 1951 and 1953) and Sacha Distel; he also performed with visiting Americans, including Jimmy Raney (1954), Chet Baker (1955), and Blossom Dearie (1956), whom he married. Shortly after his arrival in New York in 1956 he became a member of J. J. Johnson's quintet (for illustration *see* JOHNSON, J. J.), which also included Elvin Jones. Jaspar left Johnson in 1957 and played briefly with Miles Davis; the following year he joined Donald Byrd's quintet, and from 1959 he worked as a freelance, mainly in New York, with Bill Evans (ii), Raney, Chris Connor, the International Jazz Quartet, and others. During a stay in Europe in 1961–2 he worked with European players and recorded with Baker in Rome.

Jaspar was considered one of the most talented European jazz musicians. His playing was influenced by Don Byas, Lester Young, and Sonny Rollins, but, as his recordings demonstrate, he developed his own expressive style, which led to his being highly respected by American musicians and critics alike.

SELECTED RECORDINGS

As leader: *Bobby Jaspar Quartet* (1956, Col. FPX123); *Bobby Jaspar with George Wallington* (1957, Riv. 240); *Bobby Jaspar All Stars* (1958, Barclay 84063)

As sideman: H. Jones: *Hank Jones Quartet* (1956, Savoy 12087); J. J. Johnson: *Mr. Jay Jay Johnson: Live* (1957, Queen-Disc 046); C. Baker: *Chet is Back* (1962, RCA LPM10307)

BIBLIOGRAPHY

FeatherE; *Feather '60s*
D. Hague: "Bobby Jaspar," *JJ*, ix/6 (1956), 9
F. Manskleid: "Jaspar's Jump," *Metronome* (1960), Aug, 26
——: "The Foreign-born Jazz Musician in the USA," *JM*, x/1 (1964), 8
E. De Voghelaere: *Bobby Jaspar: a Biography, Appreciation, Record Survey and Complete Discography* (Antwerp, Belgium, 1967); addns and corrections in *Swingtime*, no.24 (1977), 10
D. Morgenstern: Liner notes, *Bobby Jaspar in Paris* (Swing 8413, 1986)

ROLAND BAGGENAES

JATP. *See* JAZZ AT THE PHILHARMONIC.

Jaume, André (*b* Marseilles, France, 7 Oct 1940). French clarinetist and saxophonist. He studied clarinet (1956) and played with dixieland groups (to 1958). He then played with the pianist Fred Ramamonjiarisoa (1965), Edmond Tober's big band (1970–71), Barre Phillips, the trumpeter Ambrose Jackson (1972–3), the electric bass guitarist Sylvain Marc (1974), the group Sartan (1975), Jef Gilson (1975–9), Steve McCall, Gunter Hampel, Lawrence "Butch" Morris, Frank Lowe, Byard Lancaster, the flutist and trumpeter Itaru Oki, and the keyboard player François Couturier (1979); he made a solo album, playing tenor saxophone and bass clarinet, in 1978 (*Saxanimalier*, HH R). In 1979 he began an association with Joe McPhee, with whom in 1980 he recorded as a duo. Besides McPhee, in the 1980s Jaume played with the double bass player Didier Levallet (1980–81), Irène Schweizer (1980), the group Module (1980–81), and Jimmy Giuffre (1985); he led and recorded with his own groups, including an octet, and his playing can be heard to advantage on his album *Cinoche* (*c*1984, CE 1).

MICHEL LAPLACE

Jaxon [Jackson], **Frankie "Half Pint"** (*b* Montgomery, AL, 3 Feb 1895). Singer and composer. He gained his nickname on account of his short stature. He grew up in Kansas City, where at the age of 15 he began singing in local clubs and cinemas.

After touring from 1912 to 1914 he worked at the Paradise Cafe in Atlantic City, New Jersey, and at the Sunset Cafe in Chicago, alternating between the two venues until 1926. He was based in Chicago from 1927 to 1941 and, though he occasionally made tours and performed elsewhere – notably in 1930 with Bennie Moten in Kansas City – worked mostly with his own group. He made a number of recordings during this period, including *You got to wet it* (1929, Voc. 1472); among the musicians who accompanied him were Bob Shoffner and George Mitchell (1933), the Harlem Hamfats (1937–8), Barney Bigard (1939), and Henry "Red" Allen (1940). From 1931 he also sang regularly on radio, and used his own composition *Fan it* as his signature tune. He ceased to be active in music in 1941, when he became a government employee.

BIBLIOGRAPHY

W. H. Miller: "Great Little Guy: the Life and Times of Frankie 'Half Pint' Jaxon," *Australian Jazz Quarterly*, no.3 (1946), 3

H. Rye: Liner notes, *Can't you Wait till you Get Home* (Collectors Items 014, n.d. [1984])

based on *ChiltonW*

Jazz (i). A music created mainly by black Americans in the early 20th century through an amalgamation of elements drawn from European-American and tribal African musics. A unique type, it cannot safely be categorized as folk, popular, or art music, though it shares aspects of all three. It has had a profound effect on international culture, not only through its considerable popularity, but through the important role it has played in shaping the many forms of popular music that developed around and out of it.

I. Introduction. The attraction of jazz, as with any music, lies in its particular combination of rhythm, melody, harmony, instrumental sound, and the like. But three distinctive characteristics of jazz have given it a special appeal. One is the phenomenon of swing (see §§II, 5, and IV, 1–2, below; *see also* SWING (i)). The second is what may be called "individual code" – those subtle factors that make a jazz player instantly recognizable to knowledgeable listeners. Although some players can be identified by their ways of shaping melody, with most the individual code is expressed in more subtle qualities such as timbre, sharpness of attack, length of decay, vibrato, pitch variations, and various distortions produced by throat tones, mutes, and other techniques and devices. The individual code is an important part of the communication between player and listener, and has to be taken into account in any discussion of a jazz musician's work. The third important characteristic of jazz is its ecstatic function. Jazz usually takes place in the context of an actual or simulated JAM SESSION, which has some aspects of a ritual. The players do not merely reproduce prescribed sequences of notes, they participate in a sort of ceremony in which they interact with the audience and one another, somewhat as a preacher interacts with the congregation at a "sanctified" church. As in any ritual there are certain forms of behavior to be observed: players are expected not to push themselves forward at one another's expense; audiences are permitted, indeed encouraged, to become part of the ceremony by dancing, stamping their feet, or offering cries of encouragement or bursts of applause. The relationship to West African dance ceremonies, and the practices of the black-American churches, which descended from them, is obvious. These three elements are probably present to some degree in all musical performances, but in jazz they are central, almost indispensable. A jazz performance that lacked any of them would not be rated highly by most jazz enthusiasts.

It has been said that jazz, in a half-century, recapitulated the history of four centuries of European music, moving from the heterophonic polyphony of the early New Orleans style, through the big-band romanticism of the 1930s, to the chromaticism of bop and the free-form experiments after 1960. While this analysis is simplistic, it is nevertheless true that jazz has shown a penchant for rapid change, often rooted in youthful rebellion and accompanied by tensions between players of different generations. Two patterns emerge clearly within this development. One is the gradual emergence of jazz from the bohemian, even underground, environment in which it was originally played, through various levels of the entertainment business into the concert hall as a new form of art. The rise of jazz to respectability was part of a large shift in American culture as a whole, and is still by no means complete: although a great deal of jazz is now played in concert settings, it is still firmly rooted in the popular entertainment business through its continuing connection with commercial clubs, films, television, and radio. The second pattern is traced by the shifting balance between the free, improvisatory, and spontaneous aspects of the music, often seen as African or "black," and the more formal, arranged elements, sometimes viewed as European or "white." Jazz has continually crossed and recrossed an imaginary line between these opposites, always being drawn back when it strayed far in either direction.

II. Origins and early history. The genesis of jazz was a three-stage process: first, the development, in the 18th and 19th centuries, of an indigenous black folk music out of African and European-American elements; second, the rise out of this music of subforms, notably plantation and minstrel songs, ragtime, and blues; third, the appearance of jazz itself, from an imperfectly understood merging of blues, ragtime, and mainstream popular music.

1. AFRICAN BACKGROUND. Black slaves, the bulk of them from West Africa, were imported into the New World by the hundreds of thousands from the 16th century. The music of these people varied from one cultural group to another, but all of it shared certain characteristics. It was in the main functional, intended to accompany religious ceremonies and ecstatic dancing, to inspire hunters, to make work easier, and even to celebrate minor events such as the appearance of a child's first tooth; and it was woven into the culture, forming a part of ordinary living almost as ubiquitous as speech.

Although the slaves' musical heritage was chiefly vocal, there was also a great deal of instrumental music, in which the drum was the principal instrument and rhythm the dominant element. The foundation of West African instrumental music was the piling up of layers of rhythm, which might vary in character, meter, and tempo; the different layers frequently resulted in meters of three against two, but the relationships were often much more complicated, one rhythm being delivered fractionally faster than another so that thick textures were created. These contrasting rhythms, however, were not usually improvised spontaneously, but were set in advance or called out by a master drummer as the music progressed. The locking and unlocking of the rhythmic layers as they passed across each other was the chief characteristic of the music. Melodically it was comparatively simple, though melismas were common. It used scales roughly similar to European ones, but they tended to be pentatonic and seem to have avoided half-steps, either by skipping over them or by the raising or lowering of one of the pitches to widen the interval; pitches were frequently inexact by the standards of European music. A great deal of vocal music was in call-and-response form, and singers often used falsetto; heterophony was common. Instruments were fitted with rattles or shakes of metal, shell, or bone to enliven the sound.

When Africans were brought to the Americas they carried their music with them. In part this reflected a deliberate policy of the slave traders, who encouraged or even forced slaves on board ship to sing and dance in order to help maintain their physical condition and keep them from despair and suicide; once settled in the New World the slaves were still permitted or encouraged to keep their music alive, again on the theory that it kept them happy and docile. (However, at some times and in some places large drums, which slave owners feared could be used to signal revolt, were banned.) Even in New York and New England, as late as the 18th century Blacks gathered at certain times for ceremonial ecstatic dancing to music that was still essentially African. Because there was a continuous flow of new arrivals from Africa until well into the 19th century, the African influence remained fresh; as late as the period after the Civil War the old dances were still being performed to the old music (though probably in modified form) in Place Congo in New Orleans.

About three-quarters of the Blacks in the USA before Emancipation were plantation slaves. Living in communities often rigorously controlled, they found it difficult to preserve the old culture, and inevitably they adopted North American religions, language, rites of passage, and other folkways. However, such a process of acculturation is seldom total: characteristically, a form from the new culture is imbued with emotional or functional significance from the old. Thus the black slaves adopted European instruments, musical devices such as the diatonic scale, standard meters, and popular song forms, but they used them to reproduce African effects. For example, just as some African tribal musicians seem to have avoided half-steps, so the slaves tended to adjust the diatonic scale to similar effect by lowering the third, seventh, and sometimes fifth scale degrees microtonally, thereby creating the so-called blue note (*see* Blue note (i)). And just as African musicians used falsetto and enlivened the sound of their instruments with rattles, so the slaves coarsened their voices with falsetto or throat tones at points of emotion and drama in the music. Again, like African music, this black-American folk music was often functional, intended to accompany work, dancing or religious ceremonies, and was thus far more ubiquitous than comparable music of white Americans.

From the point of view of jazz the most important aspect of the music of the slaves was the re-creation, by different means, of the counterrhythms of West African music. (Although counterrhythms are found in European-American concert music, they have never been an essential characteristic, and are largely absent from white-American vernacular music.) To reproduce the old effect, Blacks began to undergird most of their music with an explicitly stated ground beat, which could be made by handclaps, dancers' footfalls, drums, or the blows of axes and sledgehammers. (Most European music, military marches aside, does not use an explicit ground beat; rather the beat arises out of the music itself.) Given such a continuous beat, they were then able to vary the rhythm of a melody by holding back and pressing on, stretching and condensing it, to create a semblance of the elaborate counterrhythms of Africa. This technique differed significantly from the ethnic original in that, far from being carefully worked out, the rhythmic effect was achieved by improvised, free performance. It is difficult to say how much of the slaves' music displayed these rhythmic characteristics: Whites who left descriptions of early black music probably often missed subtle variations in time which their training had not equipped them to notice; but they remarked on rhythmic complexities often enough to suggest that playing with time was a common practice among black musicians.

19th-century black music fell into several categories, including work songs, spirituals, and field hollers. These types, however, were probably all based on a single musical practice employing the aforementioned rhythmic devices: black church and dance music, for example, were not different in essentials.

2. Plantation songs, ragtime, the blues. The second stage in the evolution of jazz began as the black folk music of the 19th century generated other forms, which worked their way into the mainstream of popular music, not only in the USA but also elsewhere in the world. White Americans have always been interested in, indeed fascinated by, the black subculture in their midst, and one manifestation of this fascination has been an interest in black music. Early in the 19th century Whites began producing songs supposedly in the manner of the Blacks' plantation music. Many such "plantation songs" were incorporated in the minstrel shows that were vastly popular during much of the century; they were heavily "Europeanized" – imbued with the harmonic and other stylistic elements of European-American music – and suggested true black folk music only through the use of plagal cadences, frequently implied by extensive use of the sixth degree of the scale, and occasional syncopations, especially the prototypical rhythm shown in ex.1.

Ex.1

The best-known composer of plantation songs was Stephen Foster, but there were hundreds of others, some of them black. A similarly modified version of black folk music was the so-called spiritual, as brought to national consciousness by such concert groups as the Fisk Jubilee Singers. By the end of the 19th century both plantation songs and spirituals were the common property of all Americans.

A further offspring of 19th-century black music was Ragtime, which apparently came into being after Emancipation, when Blacks were freer to travel and began to find employment as musicians in saloons, dance halls, and brothels. Ragtime may have developed from the transfer of a black banjo style to the piano. By comparison with European-American music it was highly syncopated, undoubtedly in an effort to capture a sense of African cross-rhythms. By the end of the 19th century it had broken out of the saloons where it developed and had become astonishingly popular throughout the USA.

A fourth subform to arise from black folk music was the Blues. Although some writers have speculated that the blues date well back into the 19th century, there is no first-hand reference to this music before the 20th century. The blues are known to have existed in New Orleans and the Mississippi Delta region just after 1900, but none was formally published until 1912; the vogue for the blues in white mainstream culture increased markedly in the 1920s.

3. The creation of jazz. Jazz itself evolved from the fusion of black folk forms such as ragtime and blues with various popular musics. The earliest is generally known as New orleans jazz, since New Orleans has been traditionally regarded as the birthplace of jazz. Writers of a later period revised this view, insisting that jazz evolved more generally throughout the South and pointing particularly to the Southwest; however, the pioneer jazz musicians, both those from New Orleans and those from elsewhere, invariably said that jazz came from that city. Why jazz crystallized in New Orleans is obscure, but several factors seem to have made the city unique. New Orleans was a center for music of all kinds (it was considered by some to be the most musical of American cities), and as a consequence its black population was generally more musically sophisticated than Blacks elsewhere. Further, it had an established brass-band tradition, which intensified during the Civil War, when military bands were quartered there; in the Reconstruction period following the war Blacks were able to take advantage of the availability both of teachers and of band instruments (which became the basis of jazz instrumentation) in New Orleans, whereas their counterparts in other areas had to depend to a greater extent on homemade instruments such as cigar-box guitars.

The presence in New Orleans and its environs of the black Creole subculture peculiar to this area also contributed to the musical sophistication of the black population. Descendants of mixed blood of the original French settlers, the black Creoles were, for political purposes, regarded as Blacks and were so treated under the segregation laws of the 1880s and 1890s. But they clung to as much as possible of their distinctive culture and maintained a tradition of music wholly European in manner; they also had a strong tradition of dancing, and may have brought a special rhythmic concept to jazz. Their musical training influenced the laboring Blacks around them.

A final element in the evolution of jazz in New Orleans was the existence there of blues at a very early period. This music may have found its way to the city from the Mississippi Delta region around the turn of the century, when a substantial migration of rural Blacks into New Orleans took place.

4. Prototypes of the jazz band. By 1900 there existed in New Orleans a large number of black and Creole bands playing many kinds of music. At least four general types of band are evident (*see also* Bands, §4(i)). A few of the more skilled groups, such as those led by John Robichaux and A. J. Piron, were playing arrangements of waltzes, quadrilles, and sentimental ballads, and, inevitably, ragtime in places such as Lincoln Park (patronized by Blacks) and in elegant restaurants and clubs frequented by wealthy Whites. Then there were street bands, made up of various combinations of brass instruments, clarinets, and drums, which played marches, hymns, popular songs, and old favorites such as Henry Bishop's *Home, Sweet Home* and Septimus Winner's *Listen to the mockingbird*. This music was not played in what came to be the classic New Orleans polyphonic style, with trombone or clarinet answering the cornet or playing countermelodies to it; it was instead in a style that lay somewhere between true polyphony and heterophony, in which perhaps as many as a dozen winds played roughly parallel lines that at times doubled the lead, harmonized it, or answered it, usually in a fairly ragged manner. The effect was often cacophonous, though rhythmically stirring. Parade bands have often been considered the spawning ground for jazz, and it is true that many of the pioneer jazz musicians, including Buddy Bolden, Bunk Johnson, and Louis Armstrong, played in them. But two other types of band are closer to the true jazz bands that emerged in the second decade of the 20th century.

In the black area of Storyville, the pleasure district of New Orleans, was the famous Funky Butt Hall, and there were honky-tonks on nearly every corner; these were rough, dangerous bars with small dance floors, gambling rooms, and rooms upstairs where prostitutes took their customers. The characteristic dance in the honky-tonks was the slow drag, for which the blues were the most suitable music; the bands that played blues and a limited repertory of other tunes were informal groups of two to four pieces, and among the musicians who belonged to them were such seminal jazz players as Louis Armstrong, Jelly Roll Morton, and Sidney Bechet.

The principal model for the early jazz bands, however, was the New Orleans dance band, which consisted usually of violin, cornet, clarinet, trombone, drums, double bass, and guitar, though variants also existed. Contrary to a widely held belief, these bands rarely included tubas or banjos: the tuba was used primarily in parades, and the banjo, which became fashionable in jazz between about 1918 and 1931, was used by Blacks mainly as a solo instrument or in string bands. Nor did the dance bands normally use two cornets: the lead was taken by cornet and violin. Black dance bands evolved into the classic New Orleans jazz band in the years between 1900 and 1915. They played not only for dances but at picnics and funerals, and on street wagons to advertise sporting events, store openings, and their own performances. As a consequence they needed a broader repertory than either the parade bands or the "stink" bands in the honky-tonks; they played all types of dance music (the blues for the slow drag, quadrilles, polkas, and other social dances), rags, marches, hymns, popular songs, and even themes from concert pieces. Although the functions and sometimes even the personnel of the different types of New Orleans band inevitably overlapped, it was the dance bands more than any others that combined ragtime, the blues, and other popular forms to produce the first rough jazz.

5. The emergence of hot music. The black bands in New Orleans played a highly varied body of music, much of it inflected with elements drawn from 19th-century black music. Probably shortly after the turn of the century, the ingredients combined in a novel way to produce a new kind of music. Even at the time few people grasped the exact nature or cause of this change, but throughout the first decade of the century there was a growing recognition that a new type of music had been born. It was not at first called jazz: the musicians referred to their music as ragtime, and spoke of "playing hot" (*see* Hot).

At least two processes were at work. The first was the inflecting of other forms of music, especially ragtime, with the blues; it was inevitable that musicians such as Armstrong and Bechet, who so frequently played in the honky-tonks, would carry blues devices into the other music that they played. Features such as blue notes, slurring, bent notes, growls, and most particularly a loosening of the melody line from the ground beat were carried over into rags, marches, and ordinary popular melodies of the time.

The second process was the undergirding of the two-beat marches, and especially rags, with a 4/4 ground beat. Virtually all rags were written in two-beat time; in fact most were based on march forms, which necessarily require a duple meter. At some point early in the century musicians began to play ragtime in 4/4. Morton claimed to have done this in 1902 by stomping his foot in four while playing ragtime, and on this basis maintained that he invented jazz. Whatever Morton's role, musicians were quite conscious of the process taking place. Steve Brown, a white New Orleans double bass player, said: "The type of music played in the red light district was slow drags, barrel house, and a little plantation music, along with what we referred to as 'bumpy' music; for instance, *St. Louis Blues* . . . would be played in 4/4 time, while in ragtime it would be played in 2/4 time." Brown dates the "jazz craze" from 1905 (letter to Rufus C. Harris, *LNT*). William Ridgely, a black trombonist of the period, said that Buddy Bolden played ragtime in a two-beat style: "It would sound a little different from today's bands with the double beat which is fast 4/4 time." Other musicians have said the same.

Thus, there was a well-defined and clearly recognized difference between ragtime and the new hot music. At the same time the practice of setting the rhythms of the melody at variance with the ground beat, drawn from 19th-century black music, was beginning to enter ragtime. The most important effect of this was that players began to divide the new 4/4 beat unevenly, a technique that has become a definitive characteristic of jazz. Jazz musicians almost invariably play eighth-notes unevenly, in terms both of accent and duration, though there is considerable variation in style among players and at different times in the history of jazz. This manner of phrasing is an important element in producing the swing crucial to jazz, and it is present in at least rough form in the earliest jazz recordings. It can be assumed to have made its appearance by about 1910, and possibly earlier. How it relates either to blues rhythms or to the new 4/4 approach to ragtime is difficult to say.

Jazz, then, seems to have resulted from three developments: the addition of blues rhythms and pitch inflections to rags and other popular song and dance forms; the undergirding of rags and other two-beat forms with a 4/4 ground beat; and the uneven playing of eighth-notes. The new music was not forged instantaneously: recordings made as late as the early 1920s by New Orleans players show a close connection with ragtime, and stiff, somewhat cumbersome rhythms. But during and beyond that decade jazz continued to evolve steadily, from the even rocking motion of ragtime to the supple, flowing line of 1930s swing players.

6. New Orleans jazz musicians. The man generally credited with being the first jazz musician is Buddy Bolden (fig.1); it is almost certain, however, that he played not jazz but ragtime and the blues, though perhaps with traces of the new jazz feeling. After Bolden came a cadre of players eager to try their hands at the new music, though little is known of many of them except their names, a few dates, the names of their bands, and a number of anecdotes. Perhaps the most highly regarded of this first generation of jazz musicians were the trombonist Willie Cornish; the drummer Dee Dee Chandler; John Robichaux, a leader much admired for his smooth and well-schooled "polite" orchestra; the clarinetist Frank Lewis; and the Tio family, who were formally trained musicians and taught many of the others. Following them was a group born in the 1880s and 1890s, some of whom, notably Armstrong, Bechet, Johnny Dodds, Kid Ory, and King Oliver, went on to become famous names in jazz history; others, such as Buddy Petit, the trombonist Frankie Dusen, and the drummer Benny Williams, never recorded and are known about only through those who heard them play.

Although it is clear that jazz was created by New Orleans Blacks from musics also created by Blacks, white musicians played a role, although a subordinate one, almost from the beginning. They were familiar with ragtime, and they had ample opportunity to hear the new hot music in the streets, at Lincoln Park, and in the honky-tonks of black Storyville, which drew many Whites. By about 1910 young white musicians such as Nick LaRocca, Paul Mares, Larry Shields, Leon Roppolo, Papa Jack Laine, and the Brunies brothers were playing creditable

1. Buddy Bolden's band, New Orleans, c1900: (standing, left to right) Frank Lewis (clarinet), Willie Cornish (valve trombone), Bolden (cornet), Jimmy Johnson (double bass); (seated) William Warner (clarinet) and Jeff "Brock" Mumford (guitar)

jazz. Although the claim that these Whites invented jazz is untrue, their influence was not negligible. Coming from the European-American musical tradition, from which they were familiar with polyphony but not heterophony, they tended to give their music a formal shape that was closer to concert music than that of black jazzmen. The polyphony they knew best was that of the band music of John Philip Sousa and others, and it was probably these Whites who firmly pushed jazz towards the classic New Orleans style in which the cornet states the melody, the clarinet provides a countermelody above or around the lead, and the trombone supplies connecting links and harmonic support emphasizing dominant and tonic.

This should not be taken to mean that the Whites were ahead of the Blacks in developing jazz: black bands were rhythmically looser, closer to the blues, and played with more characteristic jazz feeling. And it was certainly the Blacks who brought to the music its ecstatic nature, transferred from their church rituals, dance ceremonies, and, in some places, voodoo rites, which in turn were indebted to African trance ceremonies. It was almost inevitable that they would use jazz as a way of achieving states of heightened emotion. Blacks were also more influential in developing individual code in jazz performances. White musical practice was based on the accurate reproduction of a set composition, whether written or memorized. Blacks had no such tradition but tended to see music as a means of personal expression.

It is precisely because black elements were less apparent in their playing that white musicians were able to make jazz accessible to white audiences. Although early black jazz musicians frequently played for Whites at fraternity dances, at exclusive New Orleans restaurants, on the riverboats, and at private parties and dances, most early jazz was intended for black listeners and dancers. However, jazz could not have achieved its present significance if it had depended solely on the support of Blacks, an impoverished minority constituting roughly 10% of the American population. It needed a white audience, and fortunately there was one waiting for it. By 1915 American Whites had been prepared for the new jazz music by decades of plantation songs, spirituals, and, most important, more than a decade of ragtime. Many visitors to New Orleans heard the music, and interest in it began to grow during the second decade of the century.

III. The spread of jazz

1. Jazz enters the cultural mainstream. 2. The dissemination from New Orleans. 3. Armstrong and Beiderbecke. 4. The rise of symphonic jazz. 5. Stride and blues piano. 6. Jazz in the entertainment industry and the press.

1. Jazz enters the cultural mainstream. Jazz did not spread over the USA solely on the strength of its own merits, but as part of a profound social upheaval that shook American culture in the years between 1890 and 1920. In the 1890s an old American ethic of hard work and emotional constraint began to shatter before a new ideal that emphasized pleasure and self-expression as acceptable routes to personal well-being. This shift in the American ethic led to the development of new institutions: dance halls, cabarets, opulent restaurants, and theaters. Although such institutions had long existed in less elegant form in underworld districts such as New York's Tenderloin, in bohemian areas such as San Francisco's Barbary Coast, and in black ghettoes, around the turn of the century middle-class Whites adopted them, made them respectable, and integrated them into the mainstream of American culture. This process whereby art forms spawned in the subculture are gradually expurgated and accepted into the mainstream has repeated itself many times in 20th-century American life: it occurred in the case of ragtime, developed in the black brothels and saloons especially around St. Louis, and with such dances as the turkey trot and the charleston, which evolved in low bars; the cabaret and cinema achieved respectability in the second decade of the century, and jazz became respectable in the 1920s.

By the end of World War I white Americans had discovered a new life-style, and it is no accident that the cinema, the Broadway theater, the dance hall, Tin Pan Alley, and the jazz band all arose around this time and crystallized in the professional entertainment industry, which has become one of the dominant institutions of American life. Jazz was seen as central to the new spirit, even lending its name to the 1920s, which were commonly called "the jazz age."

These new cultural and social trends were accompanied by a rapidly rising interest in Blacks, and especially in black entertainment. American Blacks were seen – by both white and black intellectuals – as liberated, expressive people who typified the new ideal, and whose arts, music, and folkways could be looked to as guideposts to a better future. Inevitably, this focused attention on black music, and there was an upsurge of interest in black show business. Plantation songs, spirituals, and minstrelsy in general had been popular with white Americans for decades, but to a considerable extent this music had been adapted and presented by Whites. By the 1920s there was a current of interest in more authentic black forms. Eubie Blake's and Noble Sissle's Broadway hit *Shuffle Along* (1921) triggered a demand for black musical theater that reached a peak by the end of the decade.

Another element that contributed to the spread of jazz was the Prohibition law of 1920, which made the sale of alcohol illegal. A great many Americans opposed Prohibition simply because they wanted to drink, but intellectuals, and young people in general, saw it as a residue of the old Victorian repressiveness, directly opposed to their new ideals. The illegal speakeasies and cabarets of the Prohibition era were regarded as romantic, and jazz as the appropriate musical backdrop for their activities.

Particularly important to the spread of jazz was the beginning, about 1910, of a craze for social dancing. Unlike the relatively complex reels and quadrilles of the 19th century, the new trots, tangos, and one- and two-steps were simple couple dances which, because the partners were in close physical contact, had distinct sexual implications. This dance boom in turn produced two institutions important to jazz: the dance hall and the cabaret. Furthermore all of this dancing needed music. It is not clear what kind of music was played in the earliest part of the dance boom, but there is evidence that in New York and probably elsewhere there was a vogue for black bands (with banjos and drums figuring prominently in them) which almost certainly played raggy versions of popular tunes. The trots also called for music with uneven rhythms (it has been noted that such rhythms increased sharply in ragtime after 1910), and since jazz was to a considerable extent based on uneven rhythms the dance bands adopted it as ideal for the new dances. Moreover, it fitted the new social mood: to many young people after World War I, jazz was a symbol of the rebellion against the old morality.

The popularization of jazz was also aided by the development of sound recordings, which from 1910 became increasingly common in American homes. Record producers turned out thousands of new discs to enable people to dance at home, and much jazz, or jazz-oriented, music reached the public through this means.

Thus jazz was swept along by a wide array of currents –

technological, intellectual, artistic, cultural, and social – all moving in parallel.

2. The dissemination from New Orleans. Jazz began to spread out from New Orleans almost simultaneously with the rise of the dance boom. Undoubtedly the first jazz musicians to leave were those who joined black vaudeville minstrel shows as they passed through the city. The first authentic black jazz band known to have made a mark outside New Orleans was organized by Bill Johnson (i), who left for California in 1908. His group, the Original Creole Band, toured on the vaudeville circuits, and in 1915 played in a Broadway revue called *Town Topics*; although it made no great impression, it helped to encourage other jazz musicians to leave New Orleans. Jelly Roll Morton went to California, and in 1917 brought Buddy Petit and a group to play there. King Oliver went to Chicago in 1918 and formed his own band there in 1920; Kid Ory went to Los Angeles in 1919 and shortly afterwards organized a band with musicians he brought from New Orleans. Evidently a fair amount of jazz was played on the West Coast at an early stage – possibly as early as 1910. Oliver's group was in Los Angeles and San Francisco in 1921–2, and the first jazz recordings to be made by a black band, Ory's "Sunshine" sides, were made in Los Angeles in 1922.

However, the greatest impact was made in Chicago in 1915–16 by two white groups from New Orleans, led by Tom Brown and Johnny Stein. Working in cafés and cabarets frequented by white entertainers and the sporting crowd, they attracted a good deal of attention. After some shifts of personnel, in 1917 Stein's group, renamed the Original Dixieland Jazz Band and now led by Nick LaRocca, went to New York to play at Reisenweber's, an elegant Broadway "lobster palace" catering to a mixture of entertainers, the wealthy, and large crowds of tourists. The move of the Original Dixieland Jazz Band from the somewhat disreputable cabarets of Chicago to Reisenweber's was part of the aforementioned general movement from the Tenderloin into the entertainment mainstream. The band was an enormous success, and in February 1917 it made the first jazz recordings, for Victor. These became hits and by the end of 1917 jazz was becoming a nationwide phenomenon with a large, primarily white, audience.

As jazz became popular, musicians everywhere in the USA were drawn to it both for its own qualities and because it was in vogue. They began to assemble bands on the model of the Original Dixieland Jazz Band, and started playing the new music with greater or lesser success. In New York a group formed around Phil Napoleon, Miff Mole, and Frank Signorelli; it became popular and from 1922 made dozens of recordings under various names, the best-known of which was the Original Memphis Five. In the Midwest a group centered on Bix Beiderbecke, who had begun copying LaRocca's cornet phrases from recordings by the Original Dixieland Jazz Band, began working as the Wolverines. Another group, informally called the Austin High School Gang after the school in Chicago that some of its members attended, included Benny Goodman and Jimmy McPartland. Among the most influential of these early groups was one that included Red Nichols, Mole, and Jimmy Dorsey; recording mainly as Red Nichols and his Five Pennies, it attracted followers and imitators from the mid-1920s. Nichols was especially influential in Europe, where his recordings were available by the late 1920s. The musicians in these groups were all white, but Blacks, such as Al Wynn in Chicago and Buster Bailey in Memphis, were also attempting to learn the new music. By about 1923 groups modeled on the Original Dixieland Jazz Band were working in cabarets and dance halls all over the USA. The vogue for jazz inevitably drew other bands and individual musicians from New Orleans, among them the white Arcadian Serenaders and New Orleans Rhythm Kings, much admired by young musicians in the Midwest, and individual Blacks such as Oliver and Morton.

During the same period many New Orleans musicians moved to Chicago. They were drawn there in part by the fact that Chicago, dominated by criminal gangs, was a city that suffered from few restrictions and where the many cabarets and dance halls required the hot music of the jazzmen. Also important was the mass migration of Blacks to northern cities, and Chicago in particular, which created there a large audience for black music, especially the blues. These immigrants clustered in an area of the South Side called the Black Belt. The South Side was the home of a substantial proportion of the vice that gave Chicago its tone, and here, through much of the 1920s, the seminal New Orleans jazz figures worked: Oliver at Lincoln Gardens, the Pekin, and the Plantation; Jimmie Noone, Earl Hines, and others at the Nest and the Apex; Armstrong at the Sunset and the Savoy; and Morton at various locations. Clustered in an area of a few blocks, these clubs and dance halls were mostly "black and tans," attracting audiences that were largely black on week nights but perhaps 75% white on weekends. Here the young white musicians Beiderbecke, Goodman, Freeman, Krupa, and many others came with their fans, and here they heard at first hand the music of the New Orleans style. Through much of the 1920s the "western" bands of Chicago were seen as more advanced than those in New York and elsewhere.

The music of the Chicago bands was, in the main, the classic New Orleans polyphonic jazz, though touches of heterophony remained. It was primarily an ensemble music with few solos, and depended on a thick texture and a rocking swing for its effects. It was not essentially improvised: performers generally worked from set parts, memorized rather than written, which they embellished or varied within narrow limits. Even solos tended to be played more or less the same, night after night.

The most important of these bands was King Oliver's Creole Jazz Band. A descendant of the Original Creole Band formed by Bill Johnson (i), by 1920 it was playing in the chief black and black-and-tan clubs in Chicago and elsewhere. More significantly, in 1923 it made a series of seminal recordings which constitute the first substantial body of black recorded jazz. Although Oliver eventually developed a reasonably wide following, the audience for these early recordings was made up mainly of Blacks and some white musicians. In fact white musicians were so much drawn to the group that the managers of Lincoln Gardens (which was a black dance hall) put on "midnight rambles" on Wednesdays especially for them.

The heyday of Chicago as the center of jazz was brief: in 1928 a reformist government swept away the illegal cabarets and dance halls there, and by the following year the musicians were beginning to look towards New York. The movement out of Chicago robbed the old New Orleans style of what little viability it still had. The nightlife of Chicago had resounded to the music for a decade, but it had been little played in other cities, especially New York, and to dancers there it sounded unfamiliar and somewhat dated. After 1930 very little New Orleans jazz was recorded until the revival of the style in the 1940s.

3. Armstrong and Beiderbecke. Another service Oliver performed for the development of jazz was his sponsorship of

2. Fletcher Henderson's orchestra, New York, 1924: (back row, left to right) Charlie Green (trombone), Howard Scott (trumpet), Louis Armstrong (cornet), Elmer Chambers (trumpet), Ralph Escudero (tuba); (front row) Kaiser Marshall (drums), Coleman Hawkins (tenor saxophone), Buster Bailey (clarinet, alto saxophone), Don Redman (alto saxophone), Charlie Dixon (banjo), Henderson (piano)

Louis Armstrong, who had grown up in New Orleans and served a rough apprenticeship there in the honky-tonks. In 1922 Oliver brought Armstrong to Chicago to join his Creole Jazz Band. Here he was seen only as a member of the band, but in 1924 he joined Fletcher Henderson's orchestra in New York as a jazz specialist (fig.2); he was given ample solo space, both on recordings and in performances at the segregated Roseland Ballroom, the band's principal venue. Armstrong was immediately recognized as something extraordinary by musicians and a burgeoning group of jazz fans. The most striking qualities of his playing were a beautiful tone, a virtuoso technique that placed him far ahead of most other jazz musicians, an astonishing capacity for melodic invention, a virtually unmatched ability to "swing," and a "presence" or sense of exposed personality that permeated his music. The men in Henderson's band in particular were awed by his music and attempted to capture its essence, as did many other musicians, both black and white.

On his return to Chicago in 1925 Armstrong began to make the 60 or so recordings of the so-called Hot Five series. These brought him even greater exposure, and by 1928, when the series was completed, his name was becoming increasingly familiar to the general public and he was recognized in the jazz world as its leading figure. The earliest of the recordings by the Hot Five were essentially in the old New Orleans style, but Armstrong was increasingly pushed forward, both as a trumpeter and a singer, by record producers who recognized his commercial appeal to the public. By the end of the series the recordings had become vehicles for Armstrong, the other players merely supplying backing and solo relief. Jazz musicians, overwhelmed by Armstrong's genius, began to emulate him, copying his solos not merely on trumpet but on other instruments as well. What they now wanted was to play solos like Armstrong, not just share in carefully organized ensembles like those of Oliver and Morton. From this point on, although jazz continued to include improvised ensemble playing, it was essentially a soloist's music. As a soloist Armstrong was important in bringing forward the concept of improvising against chord sequences, and it was his example that made this the principal solo method in jazz. In his early period he tended to stay close to or paraphrase the original melodic line, but as he gained confidence in his powers he increasingly abandoned the melody altogether and ventured into flights of original invention, built on the harmonies of the song rather than developed around its melody.

Although Armstrong was by far the most influential jazz player of the day, there was a secondary line of development. Many young white players outside New Orleans had learned about jazz from the Original Dixieland Jazz Band and the New Orleans Rhythm Kings. They began to form their styles before they had heard Armstrong, or even Oliver. Inevitably they tended to play a somewhat more polished type of jazz with fewer of the blues inflections characteristic of black playing but with more harmonic diversity. Foremost among them were several musicians from the Midwest, the most important of whom was Bix Beiderbecke. He had formed his style on that of Nick LaRocca, and while he later absorbed influences from Armstrong and the blues singers, his playing remained rooted in the earlier tradition. Beiderbecke exercised an influence on both black and white jazz musicians of the 1920s second only to that of Armstrong, and through him and his confreres an unbroken line can be traced from the Original Dixieland Jazz Band to the traditional jazz and allied musics of today. (Writers have applied the term "Chicago style" to this music, but in fact it was simply a variant of the New Orleans style; *see* CHICAGO JAZZ.)

4. THE RISE OF SYMPHONIC JAZZ. Even as the New Orleans style was becoming widely popular, others, principally FERDE GROFÉ, were developing a new approach to jazz. Grofé received a thorough education in classical music and began playing piano in dance halls, theaters, and brothels at an early age. In about 1914 he formed an alliance with the drummer Art Hickman, who led a dance band at the St. Francis Hotel in San Francisco. At this time virtually all dance music was played by relatively anonymous groups that generally consisted of violin, piano, drums, and perhaps one or two wind instruments. Such ensembles did not play from written arrangements; they simply repeated the melody of a song, with little variation, as many times as necessary.

It occurred to Grofé that a band using written arrangements incorporating devices drawn from symphonic music, such as counterpoint and harmonized choirs of instruments, could play a more interesting kind of dance music. He began working out dance-band arrangements, probably for Hickman, employing two principles that later became central to jazz writing: the use of a choir of instruments, in this case two saxophones, as the main means of exposing the melody, and the playing off of different instruments against one another in a rudimentary contrapuntal manner. By 1919 Hickman's orchestra, consisting of trumpet, trombone, two saxophones, and a rhythm section, had become well known on the West Coast and was beginning to develop a national reputation – unique for a dance band at that time – through its recordings for Columbia.

Around 1918 Paul Whiteman, another musician with a classical training and an interest in jazz, became aware of Grofé's work with Hickman; he engaged Grofé as pianist and arranger for his own dance orchestra and set out to emulate Hickman's success. Whiteman never learned to play jazz himself, but he had a discerning ear. More importantly, he had a talent for self-promotion: he managed to obtain a booking for his orchestra in a prestigious location in Atlantic City, New Jersey, where his immediate success led to a recording contract with Victor. Grofé's arrangements added to the popularity of Whiteman's band; in particular, the orchestra's recording of *Three o'Clock in the Morning* (1922, Vic. 18940) sold 3,500,000 copies, one for every other phonograph in the country. Whiteman named his new music "symphonic jazz" and proclaimed himself "King of Jazz." He became one of the most influential figures in 20th-century popular music, and, inevitably, other bandleaders around the world began to imitate him; by about 1923 the word jazz, in the popular mind, meant the symphonic jazz of Whiteman and his followers.

The New Orleans style did not die out, however. In fact it reached an apogee during the years 1925–7, when Armstrong (with the Hot Five) and Morton (with the Red Hot Peppers) made some of the finest recordings in the genre. Nonetheless the flood of symphonic jazz overwhelmed the older style, and by the latter years of the 1920s New Orleans jazz was moribund; the emerging bands led by such musicians as Jean Goldkette, Duke Ellington, Ben Pollack, and Fletcher Henderson worked from written and memorized head arrangements modeled after those of Grofé. Even King Oliver, whose New Orleans band had been highly influential among musicians in the North, added saxophones to his lineup and began to play in the new style.

5. STRIDE AND BLUES PIANO. Because the piano can function without accompaniment, it has evolved as a jazz instrument to some degree independently of the rest of the jazz band. Early on there were two lines of development. One was the evolution out of ragtime of the stride style (*see* PIANO, §2). Stride involves the alternation of chords and single notes (or octaves) in the left hand and the rapid, pianistic figures typical of ragtime in the right. Early stride was, in fact, ragtime imbued with a more improvisatory feel and the new, looser rhythms of jazz; it was sophisticated and thick-textured music. The second tradition of piano playing, essentially a transfer to the piano of the blues, was created by untutored Blacks working in rough bars in the rural South and black urban areas. It used a simple, repetitive bass, usually composed of single notes, and single-note figures in the right hand, also often repeated. The form was usually the 12-bar blues, though the more accomplished of the unschooled pianists might have a small repertory of tunes as well. This tradition of playing encompassed the styles known as BARRELHOUSE and BOOGIE-WOOGIE; in direct contrast to stride it was primarily rhythmic and harmonically unsophisticated.

There was very little contact between the two traditions at first. The stride style was brought to its peak in the mid-1920s in northeastern cities by such well-trained players as James P. Johnson, Willie "the Lion" Smith, Luckey Roberts, and Johnson's protégé Fats Waller, while the barrelhouse and boogie-woogie styles were played mainly in the South and Midwest. The two traditions merged in the work of such pianists as Morton and, most notably, Earl Hines, who had had contact with both styles. Hines developed a technique that employed a great many octaves and single notes in the right hand, and stride patterns interrupted by jagged patches of chords and single-note figures in the left. He received a good deal of attention in the second half of the 1920s as a result of his recordings with Armstrong and Noone, and became extremely influential. In the 1930s Teddy Wilson worked out a somewhat smoother, more refined version of Hines's style. Wilson tended to use single-note lines in the right hand rather than the repetitive pianistic figures typical of ragtime and stride; with his left hand he would sometimes stride and sometimes comp – punctuate his playing irregularly with brief chords that were more rhythmic than harmonic in function. After 1935 Wilson worked with the highly popular trio and quartet of Benny Goodman, and through him Hines's manner of playing pushed aside the older stride style based on ragtime to become the standard approach to jazz piano.

6. JAZZ IN THE ENTERTAINMENT INDUSTRY AND THE PRESS. By the second half of the 1920s jazz was no longer a specialty music confined to honky-tonks, parties, and low cabarets but a popular music tightly enmeshed in a thoroughly commercial entertainment business that was to a considerable extent dominated by organized crime. The musicians who made the classic New Orleans jazz recordings earned their livelihood in dance and show bands in cabarets, theaters, and dance halls, and also on vaudeville stages; their music mostly fulfilled the function of an accompaniment to dancing or films or the backing for an act. During the 1920s the main audience for jazz became white. By 1924 the bands led by Ellington and Henderson were playing mainly in segregated clubs, and those directed by Armstrong, Noone, Oliver, and others were doing the same after

1926 or so; although they continued to play frequently for black audiences in theaters and dance halls, it was more remunerative for these bands to perform for Whites. They were also broadcasting regularly, in some cases every night, from clubs, again mainly for white audiences. By the end of the 1920s, then, jazz had taken a large step on its way to respectability. It had become part of the mainstream of American show business; its leading figures were known to increasingly large audiences and were making in some cases considerable incomes. It is thus not true, as is almost universally believed, that jazz was despised or ignored at this time by the American public.

The American press began writing about jazz in 1917, when it first became known outside New Orleans, and during the 1920s hundreds of newspaper and magazine articles appeared on the subject. These were by no means all approving: both older and younger generations saw jazz as being related to the changing morality, and inevitably the older generation decried it for corrupting the morals of youth. Nonetheless, probably the larger part of this press attention was, if not favorable, at least neutral. Jazz was popular, and the press could hardly ignore it.

Much of the coverage of jazz was ill-informed and tended to focus on the symphonic style of Whiteman and others. But there were also signs of a deeper understanding. As early as 1920 jazz fans and record collectors on college campuses were attempting to develop an aesthetic, however rough, for the music, and to distinguish between the authentic and the spurious. Throughout the 1920s many artists and intellectuals made a point of listening to jazz as part of their response to the new American spirit, and by the later years of the decade knowledgable, thoughtful articles on jazz had begun to appear occasionally in magazines such as *The Bookman*, *New Republic*, and *Literary Digest*. From about 1925 *Orchestra World*, a magazine aimed at the general musical public, gave jazz some attention. And, most notably, by 1927 Robert Donaldson Darrell, writing in the *Phonograph Monthly Review* and *Disques*, was giving perceptive reviews of the music of Armstrong, Ellington, and other major jazz figures. Darrell was the first writer on jazz to make judgments in print that generally hold up today; he was, for example, the first writer to single out Ellington's *Black and Tan Fantasy* for extended comment, and, through his writings in *Disques*, it was he who drew the attention of Europeans to Ellington. Darrell may thus be considered the first true jazz critic.

Not everybody was happy to see jazz elevated to show-business respectability. Some musicians, like some fans, saw the new, acceptable style as a bastardization of the pure New Orleans form, and they spoke out against it, or tried to play in the old manner for whatever audiences they could find. But they were, for the moment at least, a tiny minority. From the current vantage point jazz is often viewed as an art and the musicians as artists. In the 1920s, however, few jazz musicians, least of all the Blacks, saw themselves as anything but show-business professionals attempting to make a living in a tough, highly competitive trade, and the accusation that they had "sold out" meant little to them.

IV. The big-band era

1. The rise of the big bands. 2. Swing as a musical phenomenon. 3. The big-band boom. 4. Small-group jazz. 5. Jazz spreads abroad. 6. The growth of jazz criticism in the USA. 7. The New Orleans revival.

1. THE RISE OF THE BIG BANDS. During the years between about 1921 and 1926 symphonic jazz and New Orleans jazz were poised against each other. Although initially symphonic jazz seemed to be more popular, by 1924 or 1925 it was becoming clear that a substantial number of Americans preferred a "hotter" type of arranged music than Whiteman and his imitators were providing. Several bandleaders responded to the demand for hot music, motivated not only by a concern for popularity but also by a preference for playing in what later came to be seen as the "true" style of jazz, rather than the "polite" style of Whiteman.

Of particular importance in the development of hot symphonic jazz were Fletcher Henderson and his music director Don Redman (fig.2). Henderson was an educated middle-class Black, and when he formed his band in 1923 neither he nor his musicians (most of whom were not from the Deep South) had any better idea of how jazz was played than did the Whites in bands such as Whiteman's. The following year, when his orchestra was booked into the Roseland Ballroom in New York, Henderson recognized that he had to offer his audiences a hotter style of music. He therefore engaged Louis Armstrong specifically to play hot solos, and, with Redman, set about learning how to write and play jazz arrangements. Henderson and Redman have usually been credited with developing the principle, sketched out by Grofé, by which the brass and reed sections of the orchestra were played off against one another, though such arrangers as Bill Challis and Gene Gifford also made notable contributions. Under the influence of Armstrong, the members of Henderson's band rapidly became skilled at mixing solos and arranged passages and making whole pieces swing, and by 1926 the orchestra was considered the best of the hot jazz bands.

In the late 1920s there emerged a number of orchestras playing the hot version of arranged jazz, and gradually this style became dominant. In 1927 Whiteman himself saw what was happening and engaged a group of the best white jazz musicians in the USA, including Beiderbecke, Frankie Trumbauer, and Jack Teagarden, to increase the jazz content of his music. Yet despite the presence of such fine soloists, Whiteman's was never a first-rate jazz orchestra, and by the end of the decade it had been overtaken by the hot bands; in 1931 it was beaten in a popularity poll by Ellington's orchestra, and the following year the press was speaking of Whiteman's "come-back" attempts.

An important factor in the development of big-band jazz was the new popularity of the saxophone. Although the instrument was invented in 1840, it played no significant role in American music until after the turn of the century, when it began to appear as a novelty in vaudeville shows, singly and in groups made up of instruments of various sizes and ranges. The saxophone proved to work well in such choirs, and by the early 1920s the instrument was an essential part of the dance band.

The creation of the big band was thus the result of a number of trends; when popular music emerged from the economic collapse of 1929, which had a far-reaching effect on entertainment as on all areas of American life, it was clear that the big band, on the Henderson model, was the shape of jazz for the new decade. The twin streams of symphonic and New Orleans jazz had finally merged: the new music used arrangements and choirs of instruments, but it also featured hot jazz solos and, most important, it swung.

Precisely when the term "swing" – used to describe the rhythmic "lilt" central to jazz – was coined is difficult to pinpoint, but it was current by the early 1930s. It was then particularized and applied to the big bands which supposedly produced this rhythmic effect, though many of them did not swing very much; in the end, therefore, there were "swing" bands that did not swing, and small jazz bands, not categorized as swing bands, that did. (It is best, in general, to refer to the ten- to 15-piece dance bands as "big bands," or "big jazz bands" when appropriate.)

By 1930 there existed many big dance bands working out styles of their own based on ideas drawn from Henderson, Goldkette, and Whiteman, among them the black groups of Duke Ellington, Bennie Moten, and Luis Russell, as well as McKinney's Cotton Pickers, and the white bands led by Ben Pollack and Red Nichols, and the Casa Loma Orchestra. Ellington's band was particularly important in the evolution of the new style, though it was never widely used as a model for other bands; its influence, rather, was the result of Ellington's composing style. The group, originally a standard dance band, had been drawn towards New Orleans jazz by the playing of Sidney Bechet, who was a member briefly during the 1920s, and Bubber Miley, a disciple of King Oliver. From 1927 to 1931 the band held an engagement in New York at the Cotton Club in Harlem, the country's most famous cabaret, from which it broadcast regularly. Ellington – following the example of Whiteman, though with far greater success – attempted in his compositions to combine jazz and symphonic forms, and drew heavily on members of his orchestra for his musical ideas. His recording of *Black and Tan Fantasy* (1927) was regarded by many intellectuals as an indication that jazz was to be taken seriously, and throughout his long career his music was adduced as evidence that jazz was an art. Ellington had little formal training in music, but a fine musical intelligence and sound judgment allowed him to create scores of popular hits and hundreds of brilliant compositions, large and small. He was aided immensely in achieving this success by his talent for surrounding himself with such fine jazz musicians as Johnny Hodges, Cootie Williams, and Ben Webster, and drawing the best out of them.

The role of New Orleans musicians in bringing a jazz spirit to these early dance bands was critical. Bechet and others in Ellington's band, Armstrong in Henderson's, Pops Foster, Henry "Red" Allen, and Luis Russell in Russell's, and others elsewhere inspired the musicians around them to attempt to capture the swing feeling. This was not, however, the rocking swing of the New Orleans band. The nature of jazz rhythm had subtly changed.

2. Swing as a musical phenomenon. Because the sense of rhythm is so subjective, and because differences in timing of a 20th of a second can be critical, it is very difficult to analyze exactly the change that occurred in jazz rhythm in the big-band era. Jazz rhythms had grown out of the black musical practices of shading the melody away from the ground beat at some points, splitting the beat into two uneven parts, and undergirding two-beat ragtime with 4/4 time. The pioneer jazz musicians of New Orleans by no means applied these principles uniformly, nor understood them completely – into the 1920s many of them were playing the relatively stiff rhythms of ragtime. But by 1924, when a substantial number of recordings by New Orleans musicians were being released, it was clear that at least three among them had moved beyond ragtime. Bechet, Morton, and Armstrong – all of whom had, significantly, spent time playing the blues in New Orleans honky-tonks – were playing with a light rhythmic spring, which is easy to feel but almost impossible to analyze or describe. However, certain common practices can be detected: the addition of a terminal vibrato, especially on longer notes, which seems to make them suddenly come to life; the spicing of the melodic line with accents and dynamic changes, so that it seems to take on the characteristics of speech; the placing of the notes to either side of the beat, which imparts lightness to the line; and the division of the beat into the uneven eighth-notes so characteristic of jazz. Armstrong, Bechet, Morton, and other New Orleans pioneers used some or all of these techniques, which were absorbed by the players they influenced. By the late 1920s such practices had been so widely adopted as to become characteristic of jazz, and any players who failed to grasp them were seen as not "swinging." Furthermore, new and even more subtle devices were being employed, such as the "secondary pulse" (the accenting of a note after it has been struck) and sudden pitch sags, both of which create the impression that the note has changed its nature or been struck again.

These techniques for creating swing spread through jazz during the 1920s, and by 1930 or so the swing style had become the accepted way of playing; anything else was old-fashioned. Whether as a result or simply as a parallel development, there came at the same time a marked change in the way the ground beat was played. In two-beat ragtime and the early jazz that followed it, odd- and even-numbered beats were distinctly different. Double bass players played on only the first and third quarters of a four-quarter measure. The stride piano bass produced a similar "boom-chick, boom-chick" effect. Drummers alternated quarter-notes and pairs of eighths. The effect was a back-and-forth rocking motion in the ground beat. After 1931 the guitar and double bass were reintroduced in place of the banjo and tuba; this sharpened and lightened the beat. Guitarists began to stroke downwards, instead of up and down, to even the beat. Double bass players began to play on all four quarters in the bar. Pianists tended more and more to comp rather than rely on the rocking stride-bass style. Drummers began to furnish the basic beat on the ride cymbal instead of the snare drum, which not only lightened the sound but made the pulse more subtle. Ragtime drummers had played accurate, precise rhythms, such as that shown in ex.2*a*. In the transition to jazz the drum figure took on a less rigid character

Ex.2

(a) (b) (c)

(ex.2*b*), and in the swing style drummers played something freer still (ex.2*c*). Taken as a whole, the pulse became lighter, drier, and more flowing, tending to rush on ceaselessly from one bar to the next instead of proceeding in a rocking motion with rhythmic hitches.

One effect of all of these changes was that musicians began – or perhaps were forced – to deal with smaller fractions of time, and by 1930 or so jazz was being played with a perceptibly different rhythmic quality. Few musicians attempted to analyze it, but they (and their fans) recognized that a new element had entered the music. The New Orleans two-beat style was outdated; it had been replaced by four-beat swing. Indeed, so different did the new swing seem at the time that some musicians felt it necessary to insist that it was nevertheless jazz.

3. The big-band boom. The big-band era, which extended roughly from 1929 to the mid-1940s, was characterized by two features: the distinctive ensemble that played written arrangements, and the modification of the jazz beat. But social factors also exercised an influence. One such was the economic depression following the crash of the stock market in 1929; this badly hurt

the entertainment business in general and nearly destroyed the record industry, which was faced with free competition from the newly popular medium of radio. Cabarets, dependent on an affluent clientele, were forced to close, and the arrival of sound films meant that thousands of musicians who had been playing in theaters for silent films were thrown out of work. There was, furthermore, a sense among desperate entrepreneurs that the American public no longer wanted hot jazz, but preferred dreamy, escapist music that would help it forget its troubles; a feeling grew that jazz was dead, a craze of the 1920s that had had its day.

In retrospect it is clear that, although cabarets, dance halls, and the record business were suffering from the financial crisis, interest in hot music was still strong, and perhaps even growing. Hot dance bands continued to work steadily, and during the early years of the 1930s hundreds of jazz recordings, many of which later became recognized as classic, were issued.

The ground was thus prepared for what became the big-band boom of 1935–45. The immediate cause was the enormous success of Benny Goodman's band, which had been formed in 1934 very much on the model of the bands led by Pollack and Henderson and the Casa Loma Orchestra. The rise to fame of Goodman's band began when it obtained a radio contract for a late-night show, during which it played a great many hot "swing" numbers. Despite some setbacks, within months the band became an enormous success, and very quickly musicians formed dozens, and then hundreds, of similar groups to capitalize on the big-band boom. Goodman filled a vacuum. In the 20th century there appears to be a need in young people for a strongly rhythmic, relatively simple music to which they can dance as well as listen. The Depression and allied conditions had stifled the peppy jazz music of the preceding generation, and there was nothing to replace it until the appearance of Goodman's band.

Goodman's success was not the only factor in the revival of the dance bands. Somewhat improved economic conditions, and the repeal of Prohibition in 1933, which allowed clubs and dance halls to sell liquor legally once again, created a considerable appetite for dance music. Goodman simply indicated the direction that this dance music would take. Like the early jazz bands of the preceding decade, the big bands were basically dance and show bands, an important part of the entertainment business. Well-known leaders such as Goodman, Tommy and Jimmy Dorsey (fig.3), Glenn Miller, and others became celebrities whose private and social lives were chronicled in the gossip columns. The repertory of these bands was by no means exclusively jazz: many of them, denigrated by jazz fans as "mickey mouse" bands, played sweet music with little jazz feel, and even the best of them had to play a good deal of ordinary popular music of little lasting interest. But the music as a whole was rooted in jazz. All the big dance bands used rhythm sections to set a ground beat, employed a jazz feel at least occasionally in the section work, and made room for jazz solos. A few of them frequently produced excellent jazz: hard-swinging ensemble riffs interspersed with superior solos over driving rhythms. The best white orchestras were led by Goodman, Charlie Barnet, Woody Herman, and Bob Crosby; the best of the black orchestras were those of Jimmie Lunceford, Chick Webb, Ellington, and Count Basie.

Basie's orchestra represented a special strain in the big-band movement. Although Basie came from New Jersey, he had spent much of his time as a young musician in Kansas City. This crime-ridden city had many rough cabarets where jazz was played, and these provided the context for the development of

3. Jimmy Dorsey's orchestra, 1943: (back row, left to right) Jack Ryan (double bass), Nate Kazebier, unknown (trumpets), Andy Russo (trombone); (middle row) Buddy Schutz (drums), Nick Dimaio, unknown, Sonny Lee (trombones); (front row) Johnny Guarnieri (piano), Tommy Kay (guitar), Frank Lagone (alto saxophone), Dorsey, Babe Russin (tenor saxophone), Milt Yaner (alto saxophone), Charlie Frazier (tenor saxophone), unknown (baritone saxophone)

a style of playing known as Kansas city jazz; this relied heavily on the blues and on simple riffs, frequently invented on the club bandstands in the lengthy competitive jam sessions that were a feature of the musical life of the area. The bands that played in this style depended more on simple head arrangements (worked up by the musicians themselves) and strong solo work than on the type of complex arrangement favored by Henderson, Ellington, and other eastern bandleaders. Besides Basie's band, those of Andy Kirk and Jay McShann came out of Kansas City, and by the late 1930s their approach had become influential. Important to Basie's place in jazz history were soloists such as Dicky Wells, Buck Clayton, and (especially) Lester Young. Young was not widely known to the general public, but he was highly regarded by many musicians, who saw him as the chief rival to Coleman Hawkins. Whereas Hawkins's style was harmonically thick, busy, and powerful, Young employed an extremely light tone and constructed simple, spare, but highly imaginative statements. In time a whole group of followers, including Stan Getz, Wardell Gray, and Zoot Sims, adopted his style and technique.

4. Small-group jazz. By far the largest part of the big-band jazz of the period from 1935 to 1945 was essentially commercial dance music, in which the jazz elements were considerably diluted. During the same period a much more serious-minded interpretation of swing was developed by small, informal jazz bands, often put together for a brief club engagement or single recording session. The center of this activity was 52nd Street in New York, though small-group jazz was also played in other cities and elsewhere in New York. During the period of Prohibition, midtown Manhattan had been dotted with speakeasies, many of them operating in the basements of the narrow brownstone houses typical of New York. The Onyx club on 52nd Street had long been popular with jazz musicians, and after the repeal of Prohibition it continued to present their music; very quickly its neighboring competitors also began to engage musicians to play jazz. These small clubs could accommodate big bands only with difficulty; they tended instead to use small groups, and it was quickly discovered that in order to attract an audience it was necessary only to hire one well-known jazz musician and back him with a rhythm section. From 1935 until the 1950s (when it was found to be more profitable to offer striptease acts) the clubs along 52nd Street, particularly in the block between Fifth and Sixth avenues, engaged virtually every important jazz musician born between 1900 and 1925. Particularly associated with "the Street" (as musicians called it) were Billie Holiday, Art Tatum, Roy Eldridge, Coleman Hawkins, Lester Young, and various dixieland players, who usually appeared at Jimmy Ryan's.

The popularity of the new form encouraged big-band leaders to organize small groups from the personnel of their bands to perform special jazz "spots" during the course of an evening. Goodman's trio and quartet, the first important racially integrated groups to perform publicly in the USA, led the way, but very quickly Bob Crosby, Woody Herman, Tommy Dorsey, and others followed suit; small groups were also formed for recording purposes out of Ellington's and Basie's bands. Goodman's groups were particularly successful, both musically and commercially, and helped to build a following for small-band jazz. Such ensembles usually consisted of one or two wind instruments and a rhythm section that invariably included piano and drums and sometimes double bass or guitar. The size of these groups was in part dictated by economics, but it was also encouraged by the desire of the best jazz musicians to have a greater scope for improvising than the big bands allowed. Small-group jazz was a development of the form that had been worked out for Armstrong in the later Hot Five recordings: the soloist stated the melody with considerable freedom, stepped back to allow one or two other members of the band to play solos, then took over again for one or more solo choruses as it suited him. (This formula was to remain the basic pattern of jazz playing for decades.) The main differences in the groups of the 1930s were the lighter, more flowing playing of the rhythm sections and the generally enhanced feeling of swing.

Along with the small swing bands there arose a number of small, independent recording companies specializing in jazz and often run for little or no profit. The principal bandleaders were under contract to the "big three" – Columbia, Victor, and Decca – but their star soloists and other jazz musicians outside the big bands were not. John Hammond took advantage of this fact to make for Brunswick during the second half of the 1930s a series of recordings led by Teddy Wilson and frequently featuring Billie Holiday and other important jazz musicians. In the main, however, the biggest companies were not interested in recording small-group jazz, and small ones moved in to fill the gap. The first of them, Commodore, was founded in 1938 specifically to record the work of a number of white dixieland players under the leadership of Eddie Condon, but it also issued excellent recordings by important black figures, such as Coleman Hawkins, Chu Berry, and Roy Eldridge. The success of Commodore encouraged the establishment of other independent recording companies, and by the end of the 1940s there were dozens, though most of them were short-lived. In time the major companies recognized that there was a market for small-band jazz, and from about 1940 sporadically recorded some of their stars, such as Armstrong, Basie, and various members of Ellington's orchestra, in such contexts. But the small labels played a critical role (as they had in the 1920s, and have ever since) in preserving the important jazz of the time.

5. Jazz spreads abroad. As early as 1919 the Original Dixieland Jazz Band made a tour of England, and during the 1920s a few other jazz musicians, most notably Sidney Bechet, spent time in Europe, either individually or with such touring show bands as that led by Sam Wooding. None of these musicians had much impact, however: the Original Dixieland Jazz Band's music perplexed listeners in London and received uniformly bad reviews, while Bechet and others aroused little interest. More successful were tours made by those belonging to the symphonic-jazz contingent, among them Hickman, Whiteman, and Irving Aaronson, though their bands did not achieve the popularity abroad that they had at home. Nonetheless, throughout the early 1920s there was a growing interest in American dance music in Europe. But as the interest increased, so did a demand for American musicians, and eventually there were so many Americans in Europe that indigenous players demanded they be barred from performing.

There was little understanding of true jazz in Europe in the early 1920s, but by 1927 Spike Hughes in England and Hugues Panassié in France were writing criticism of good jazz recordings. In 1929 some editors from *Melody Maker* visited New York to hear the music at first hand, and Parlophone began to issue its New Rhythm Style Series, which included some of the best American jazz recordings.

One of the most important influences on early European players was Red Nichols and his various groups, especially those that included Miff Mole. Beiderbecke replaced Nichols as model when his recordings became available in the late 1920s, and at about the same time the partnership between Eddie Lang and Joe Venuti was becoming known. Ellington was also a major force, though Europeans, whose musical traditions were centered largely on composition, saw him predominantly as a composer. After the swing-band boom Benny Goodman also set an important example.

By the end of the 1920s a handful of European musicians were emulating the Americans. The French were probably the first to produce a cadre of good jazz players: Ray Ventura, for example, was performing a passable version of big-band jazz with his group the Collegians in 1928 (although it was heavily dependent on such visiting Americans as Danny Polo), as were Gregor and his Gregoriens, with such soloists as Alix Combelle, by 1930. Perhaps the best French jazz musician of the period was Philippe Brun, who in 1930 was working in England with Jack Hylton's orchestra. By the early 1930s Brun, Combelle, Michel Warlop, André Ekyan, Noël Chiboust, and a few others were performing at the general level of American players.

The English were not far behind. As early as 1927 Bert Firman was organizing recording sessions with a floating group of musicians; under the name the Rhythmic Eight, they produced occasional moments of acceptable jazz, although much of it was provided by visiting Americans. In the same year Fred Elizalde formed a student jazz band at Cambridge University, which later included a number of American players, most notably Adrian Rollini. The first English jazz musician of importance, however, was Nat Gonella: he began, as did many Europeans, as a disciple of Beiderbecke, but soon fell under the influence of Armstrong, and by 1932 was producing an excellent imitation of the work of his idol.

In Belgium, as early as 1927 Chas Remue and his New Stompers were playing in a rather stiff worked-out dixieland style patterned after the groups led by Nichols. In the Netherlands, the Ramblers, formed in 1926 by Theo Uden Masman, acquired an international following after making recordings with Coleman Hawkins (1935, 1937) and Benny Carter (1937). Teddy Stauffer's Original Teddies, a Swiss group with strong German connections, was popular in both Switzerland and Germany in the mid-1930s, when it performed a competent if unforceful imitation of American swing.

The position in Germany and Italy was complicated by the political situation. Jazz was never actually banned by Hitler's regime, but it was severely frowned upon, and by and large musicians had to be cautious in its performance. (During the 1940s, however, the German authorities broadcast arrangements by Lutz Templin of American jazz recordings for propaganda purposes.) The most important jazz band in Germany between 1927 and 1933 was the Weintraub Syncopators; the majority of its members were Jewish, however, and after 1933 the group worked elsewhere in Europe. Ernst Landl in Austria and Ernst van 't Hoff in the Netherlands were among the musicians who remained at home during the German occupation, defying the Nazis by playing jazz clandestinely. By the mid-1930s there were a few bands in Germany playing competently in the American swing style; one of the best was James Kok's Jazz Virtuosen, which included some good jazz soloists. Jazz was virtually nonexistent in Italy until after World War II, although there was a Hot Club in Rome by 1938. Ironically, Romano Mussolini, the son of the dictator Benito Mussolini, led a successful career as a professional bop pianist in the 1950s.

There was little jazz played in countries further east, such as Poland and Czechoslovakia, until around the 1950s. In the USSR, however, a few bands were attempting to play American dance music in the early 1930s, but even later in the decade their efforts to achieve a sense of swing were stiff and they lacked musicians who could produce good jazz solos. Aleksandr Tsfasman, who formed a band in 1926, is generally considered the first virtuoso jazz musician in the USSR. The first well-known player in Eastern Europe was Ady Rosner, a German who was popular in Poland and Czechoslovakia in the 1930s before fleeing to the USSR in 1939.

Jazz developed even later in the Far East. There were a few isolated appearances by Westerners: Teddy Weatherford worked in various Asian countries, including India, Singapore, and the Philippines, for most of the period between 1926 and 1945; Buck Clayton took a band in 1934 to China, where it played for a lengthy engagement in Shanghai; bands led by Herb Flemming (1933–4) and Leon Abbey (1935–6, 1936–7) held residencies in India; and from the late 1930s Reuben Solomon and Cedric West performed in Burma; but the presence of all these musicians reflected little jazz interest.

There were similarly few players of international interest in South America during the 1930s. Sam Wooding toured the continent in 1927 with a group that included Tommy Ladnier, Garvin Bushell, and Gene Sedric, and Hernán Oliva led a band in Argentina from 1935. Of greater importance was Oscar Alemán, who worked in Europe from the late 1920s until 1941, and who later became recognized as one of the finest swing guitarists.

Jazz in Australia developed much in parallel with jazz in England. The first significant Australian musician was Frank Coughlan, who led his own swing bands from 1936 into the 1970s, after having spent a period working in English dance orchestras.

The most important of all the early jazz players was unquestionably Django Reinhardt, who was almost the only European to have a major influence on the Americans. He made some of his finest recordings with the Quintette du Hot Club de France in 1934, when he formed his partnership with Stephane Grappelli (fig.4). The two men were inspired particularly by the earlier partnership of Lang and Venuti, which was highly popular in the USA and also well known to jazz fans in Europe. Reinhardt and Grappelli very quickly developed individual styles and established themselves as the leading European jazz musicians of the 1930s. Recordings by Reinhardt with the quintet and with visiting Americans were made available in the USA during the late 1930s, and he became the model for many young American guitarists, including, in the latter stages of his brief career, Charlie Christian.

By the mid-1930s both Armstrong and Ellington had appeared in London to high acclaim; Benny Carter and Coleman Hawkins, along with such lesser-known of their compatriots as Freddy Johnson and Arthur Briggs, were resident in Europe; and American recordings were readily available. European musicians by now understood the music and there were a few excellent players among them, notably Svend Asmussen in Denmark, Tommy McQuater and George Chisholm in England, those associated with the Hot Club in France, the Ramblers and the Dutch Swing College in the Netherlands, and the members of Kok's and Stauffer's bands in Germany.

The main problem for European players was that the audience for jazz was small, and in places almost nonexistent. There were no clubs such as those in the USA which presented jazz on a full-time basis and paid musicians steady salaries, and there was little jazz broadcast on radio. As late as 1939 concerts given by Reinhardt in Paris might draw an audience of only

4. *The Quintette du Hot Club de France at the Casanova club, Paris, c1937: (left to right) Stephane Grappelli (violin), Joseph Reinhardt, Django Reinhardt, and Eugene Vees (guitars), Louis Vola (double bass)*

400 people, and until after World War II jazz remained a genre enjoyed by a small coterie.

The early 1930s saw the beginning of jazz criticism in Europe. Contrary to what is widely believed, it was Americans such as Carl Van Vechten, Robert Donaldson Darrell, Charles Edward Smith, and Abbe Niles rather than Europeans who were the first to write seriously about jazz. Europeans were in fact influenced particularly by Darrell and also by John Hammond, the most powerful critic of the time, who began writing for *Melody Maker* in 1932. Nonetheless the first books – Robert Goffin's *Aux frontières du jazz* (1932) and Panassié's *Le jazz hot* (1934) – were produced by Europeans; although both volumes were full of errors, Panassié's in particular was influential (if taken less seriously by fans in the USA). Panassié was also contributing articles regularly to the dance-band magazine *Jazz Tango*, and in 1935 he founded *Jazz hot*, the most important of the early jazz periodicals, which inevitably depended on Americans for much of its material. Through these writings, and his endless proselytizing, Panassié became regarded by Europeans, if not Americans, as the first important jazz critic.

6. THE GROWTH OF JAZZ CRITICISM IN THE USA. In the 1930s, largely for reasons having to do with attitudes towards Blacks, the American left-wing press took up jazz as a subject, and from 1936 there began to appear in the *New Republic*, the *New Masses*, *The Nation*, and similar publications frequent reviews and discussions of jazz by such writers as Otis Ferguson, John Hammond, Charles Edward Smith, Bernard Haggin, and others. *Down Beat*, founded in 1934, was essentially a trade paper for dance-band musicians, but it carried reviews of jazz recordings and frequent articles on jazz history. In 1938 there appeared the first of a spate of American books on jazz, many of them written by people associated with the political left. The most influential of them was *Jazzmen* (1939), edited by Frederic Ramsey, Jr., and Charles Edward Smith. Journals devoted to jazz, among them *Jazz Information*, *Society Rag*, and *Record Changer*, emerged at about the same time. In some measure this flurry of critical activity was intended to be a corrective to Panassié's *Le jazz hot*, which was published in the USA in translation in 1936.

This early criticism was not without its flaws. Students of the subject lacked many of the tools developed later, such as reliable discographies and biographical dictionaries. Few of them had much, if any, formal musical training and could not make useful musicological analyses of jazz styles. Moreover, because so much of the writing was done by people from the political left, there was a pervasive tendency to picture the music as neglected and despised by a materialistic American bourgeois society. Some players, such as Armstrong, who had become commercially successful, were anathematized for having "sold out" to the capitalist entertainment business. The early American critics were also responsible for helping to promote the myth that jazz was appreciated more in Europe than at home, though European jazz writers also contributed to it. Yet despite the problems of this early jazz writing, much of it was sensitive and intelligent, and it opened the way for later students.

The burgeoning of jazz criticism had another important effect: it advanced the concept of jazz as an art, and the jazz musician as an artist. The idea was hardly new: jazz had been termed one of the "lively arts" as early as 1921 (by Gilbert Seldes), and before long at least some were agreed that it was a "serious" art as well, even if the musicians continued to function as entertainers. The rise of a body of formal criticism in the 1930s presupposed that jazz was an art form, and throughout the big-band period there was an increasing tendency for both critics and musicians themselves, in however confused a way, to think of it as such. The general acceptance of this concept had several implications: that jazz was a proper subject for academic study and could be taught in schools as painting or writing was; that the musicians must be treated with respect; and that it was appropriate to play the music in the concert hall. The only one of these ideas to have an immediate effect was the last. In 1938 Benny Goodman, with some players from Ellington's and Basie's bands, gave a concert in Carnegie Hall, New York, and later the same year John Hammond, with the sponsorship of the *New Masses*, presented a group of jazz and blues musicians there. These concerts were successful, and henceforward jazz was heard increasingly in the concert hall.

7. THE NEW ORLEANS REVIVAL. Many early jazz critics, in part for political reasons, disdained the new swing music, which they saw as "commercial," and took the position that the only true jazz was that of the early black pioneers and their white followers, especially those from the Midwest. The effect was to create an appetite among many jazz fans, especially younger ones, for the older music, and this in turn made it economically feasible for recording companies to reissue earlier recordings. From the late 1930s recordings made in the 1920s by Oliver, Morton, Armstrong, Noone, Beiderbecke, Nichols, Goodman, and others became increasingly available, and a market for secondhand copies of the original records, desirable to collectors, opened up. Jazz fans who had been unfamiliar with the music began to understand it, and in the late 1930s a movement to revive the New Orleans style, or DIXIELAND JAZZ as it had come to be called, was set in motion.

The revival movement developed in several different ways. On the one hand there was a group of younger men, such as Lu Watters and Turk Murphy in San Francisco, who wanted to re-create the music of Oliver, Morton, and the Armstrong of the Hot Fives as faithfully as possible. They used the instrumentation current in the 1920s, including tubas and banjos, held fast to the old repertory, and attempted to recapture the rolling two-beat rhythm of the earlier bands. The second school was built by a cadre of somewhat older men, centered on Eddie Condon in New York, and included Wild Bill Davison, Georg Brunis, Pee Wee Russell, Max Kaminsky, and Edmond Hall; these were musicians who had known New Orleans jazz at first hand and wanted to play it in the newer swing style, using the swing beat and subordinating ensemble playing to solo work. Eventually the interest in the New Orleans style focused attention on the New Orleans pioneers themselves. Sidney Bechet, who had fallen into obscurity, found himself in demand. Players such as Bunk Johnson and George Lewis (i), who had remained unnoticed in New Orleans, came to prominence in the early 1940s and began to work regularly. Armstrong and other New Orleans musicians were asked occasionally to record in the old style. (*See also* TRADITIONAL JAZZ.)

The revived New Orleans style achieved considerable popularity by jazz standards. The dixielanders in Condon's circle were especially influential, and they created a substantial body of followers, especially on college campuses, who formed bands of their own. Although there exist dixieland jazz clubs in most major American and European cities, the style is now cultivated largely by part-time players; it continues to show strength, however, constantly attracting young audiences and young players.

V. Bop and modern jazz

1. The climate for change. 2. Harmonic and rhythmic experiments. 3. Further developments in the musical language. 4. Bop piano. 5. The commercial growth of bop. 6. The cool school. 7. Hard bop. 8. Jazz piano in the 1950s. 9. General trends, from the late 1940s to the early 1960s. 10. Developments outside the USA.

1. THE CLIMATE FOR CHANGE. By 1941, when the USA was drawn into World War II, big-band jazz was the dominant popular music of the country: there were hundreds of big bands, some 50 of which were nationally known, had large followings,

5. Charlie Parker and Dizzy Gillespie's quintet at Town Hall, New York, 1945: (left to right) Doc West (drums), Curly Russell (double bass), Parker (alto saxophone), and Gillespie (trumpet)

recorded regularly, and worked in dance halls and theaters all the year round. A few, such as those of Barnet, Ellington, Basie, and Goodman, played a considerable amount of jazz, while others, such as the orchestras led by Guy Lombardo, Kay Kyser, and Sammy Kaye, performed little or none; most played a mixture. Although musicians and a growing body of jazz fans scorned the commercial dance bands, American taste in general was indiscriminate. Yet there was enough enthusiasm for good jazz to make Goodman and Ellington wealthy, and to keep such musicians as Coleman Hawkins, Billie Holiday, and Roy Eldridge steadily employed at good fees.

Among some younger musicians, however, there was a sense that the possibilities of swing had been exhausted. The causes were not all musical. A generation of black musicians born around 1920 had come to maturity in a social climate quite different from the one in which the jazz pioneers had grown up. Armstrong, for example, had been raised in the deep South, where to have spoken out against racial oppression would have been to end his career as an entertainer; later, working in a gang-dominated entertainment industry, he was again at risk of injury or death if he behaved too intractably. Throughout the 1930s, however, there was a growing consciousness among Whites, especially on the political left, that in a democracy Blacks could not be treated as second-class citizens. Blacks were encouraged to believe that at least some Whites would support their demands for equality. The migration north during the first decade of the century had produced a large population of Blacks who had grown up in this more liberal atmosphere. A new militant spirit began to be felt by Blacks, particularly jazz musicians, who by 1940 were hearing from critics that they were artists worthy of respect; they also realized that white players in big bands usually commanded higher salaries than they could, for playing what Blacks were beginning to conceive of as their music. Furthermore, black musicians constantly suffered the indignity of having their families and friends refused entry into white clubs and dance halls where they were playing. Many became bitter as well as militant.

These attitudes had two effects on black jazz musicians. The first was the development of a strong distaste for the show-business antics of Fats Waller, Cab Calloway, and Armstrong, whose routines suggested the stereotype of the grinning, carefree Black with a natural gift for song and dance; Armstrong in particular was castigated on this account. The second was their turning away from the seemingly impenetrable white culture in favor of black culture, which was at least their own, and would welcome them; musically, this meant a turning away from the swing style of the big bands, whose very popularity among Whites made it suspect.

The two men chiefly responsible for finding an alternative to big-band swing that would also effectively exclude white elements were Charlie Parker and Dizzy Gillespie (fig.5). They were opposite personalities: Gillespie, a fractious, obstreperous, but intelligent and ultimately balanced personality, complementing Parker, a pathological, childlike genius. Disentangling the contributions of these men to the evolution of Bop (or bebop) is difficult; certainly others contributed as well. In the main, it appears that Gillespie was the theorist of the movement, analyzing and pointing out to others how the parts fitted together. Parker, on the other hand, was simply an instinctive musician who could play the new music before he could theorize about it. Both men grew up musically in the swing period, and came to be outstanding improvisers in that style, Gillespie under the influence first of Harry James and then of Eldridge, Parker following various saxophonists, particularly Lester Young, whose light, dry style made him seem antithetical to most other swing musicians and therefore more in tune with the bop philosophy.

2. Harmonic and rhythmic experiments. Gillespie seems to have been mainly responsible for introducing many of the harmonic devices that characterize bop. By 1939, and probably before, he was occasionally jumping into distant keys for brief moments in his solos; he also began to "alter" chords, especially by lowering one or more notes in various combinations to produce a highly chromatic line which listeners and musicians found very discordant. Gillespie was probably also responsible for introducing a third harmonic innovation – the use of substitute chords, a simple procedure that involved the improviser's replacing standard chords with certain related ones; Art Tatum and Coleman Hawkins also employed this technique at an early stage.

Parker's first contribution was characteristically intuitive. Perhaps as soon as late 1939 or early 1940 he had begun, by means of heavy accents and an original mixture of legato and detached notes, to construct phrases that suggest the technique of "turning the beat around" or more generally creating patches of conflicting meters. It is probable that he was influenced to a degree in this by the work of Charlie Christian, who at that time was rising to jazz stardom with the Benny Goodman Sextet. It has been claimed that Parker was also responsible for at least some of the harmonic innovations of bop. The story of how he "invented" bop has been told often. In December 1939, while playing *Cherokee* during an engagement in Harlem, he discovered that he could form melodies by using the notes of extended tertiary chord structures – ninths, 11ths, and 13ths. These chords were not unknown in jazz (the 13th, with its topmost note a 6th above the chord root, was a cliché of the swing period), but their upper notes had earlier been used mainly as passing tones, for color, or to fill out a melodic conception; in the main, jazz musicians had built their melodies from triads and 7th chords. Parker now began to fill his line with these higher chord notes, to create harmonic effects that jazz musicians and listeners found novel and startling.

3. Further developments in the musical language. In 1940, just as Parker and Gillespie were making their first tentative experiments, a former musician named Henry Minton took over a small club in Harlem and asked the bandleader Teddy Hill to manage it. Hill brought in a house band of young men, mainly unknown, who could be hired for small wages. The group included Kenny Clarke and Thelonious Monk. Minton's club quickly became established as a place where musicians could sit in after hours. Gillespie became a regular visitor, and so did Christian. At first the musicians simply played in the swing style, using standard tunes. But Clarke had worked out a system of playing a very even 4/4 on the ride cymbal instead of placing the ride beat on the hi-hat, which was the practice of virtually all drummers of the time; Christian was shaping his phrases at odd angles to the original phrase structures of tunes; Monk was beginning to develop a spare, angular, eccentric piano style; and Gillespie was working on harmonic experiments of his own. In 1941 these musicians invited Parker to play with them at Minton's and the novelties they had introduced began to settle into a style.

The harmonic devices introduced into jazz by the boppers were not new; they had been in use in art music for nearly a century. But few of the black jazz musicians had much experience of concert music, and what little acquaintance they had was with the musical vocabulary of the Baroque and Classical eras, not the highly chromatic harmony of the late 19th century. It was all new and fresh to them. Important though the harmonic innovations of bop were, its changes in the rhythm of jazz were probably more significant. Several processes seem to have been at work here. First, there was a strong tendency for the bop musicians, following Parker, to phrase so regularly around the second and fourth beats of the bar (rather than the first and third) that they "turned the beat around," making the second beat of the bar "feel like" the downbeat. In general bop musicians apparently heard the beat in its correct place, while improvising a melodic line that contradicted that perception. But the effect of turning the beat around was sometimes so pronounced that the musicians themselves lost track of the meter; according to Miles Davis (*Down Beat*, xxii/22, 1955, p.14), when Parker began to introduce the technique, the drummer, Max Roach, "would scream at Duke [Jordan, the pianist] not to follow Bird, but to stay where he was. Then eventually, it came around as Bird had planned and we were together again." This practice of turning the beat around was not employed constantly, and some of the boppers, including Bud Powell, used it less frequently than others, such as Gillespie and Parker. But it was nonetheless an important characteristic of bop.

Another even more subtle effect, commensurately difficult to analyze, was created by shifting the melody line not a beat away from the meter, but a half-beat away. Analysis of Parker's compositions is instructive in this respect, for a substantial number of them begin with what sounds like an eighth-note upbeat, but it is placed directly on the downbeat instead of ahead of it, as would be usual. The boppers also had a tendency to place the final eighth-note of a fast figure on the second half of the fourth beat, instead of on the first beat of the succeeding bar, a practice particularly evident in the work of Christian.

Bop musicians tended to cut their phrases irregularly against the form of the underlying tune, phrasing in odd lengths (such as one and a quarter or three and a half bars) instead of the more regular two- and four-bar segments of the basic tune and its harmonies. Jazz musicians had of course always phrased in irregular lengths: Armstrong, in his work after 1930, habitually used abbreviated figures to suggest longer ones. But the boppers employed irregular phrasing more frequently than earlier players had done.

Finally, in bop, strings of eighth-notes were played more evenly than had been common in earlier jazz. There had always been some variation in the method of executing eighth-notes: Coleman Hawkins divided the beat far more unevenly than did Benny Carter, for example. But the boppers played eighth-notes quite evenly – though not exactly so, for it is impossible to achieve swing unless there is at least some distortion of the rhythmic flow.

The new rhythmic features of bop were created largely instinctively by the musicians and are more evident in the playing of some than of others. They not only made the music less approachable for uninitiated listeners, they even troubled some musicians. Many of the older ones, including Hawkins, Eldridge, and Goodman, attempted to adopt them, but one of the few swing players who had much success with bop was Don Byas.

4. Bop piano. Once again the piano followed a somewhat independent line of development in the bop period. During the big-band era Art Tatum had come to be seen as the pre-eminent pianist in jazz. He had begun as a stride player, taking as his model Fats Waller, but he possessed an extraordinary technique and he quickly developed a style that depended on much interrupted movement in both hands, sudden leaps into different keys, and extremely sophisticated and varied harmonies, involving frequent use of substitute chords. Tatum's harmonic innovations affected musicians as different as Hawkins and Parker, and the bop pianists were very conscious of his work.

However, bop piano was rooted primarily in the styles of Earl Hines and Teddy Wilson. The principal figure, Bud Powell, had begun as a swing pianist, modeling himself on Kenny Kersey, a follower of Wilson. Like Wilson, Powell and other boppers tended to use strings of single notes in the right hand, though these were based on the new bop harmonies. In the left hand they abandoned the stride system in favor of spare, irregular comping, especially when accompanying soloists; bop harmonies had become sufficiently thick to make it necessary for the pianist to stay out of the way of the soloist so as to avoid too much dissonance. The double bass now performed the piano's former function of outlining the chord changes as well as helping to carry the pulse. All the pianist needed to do was suggest the harmonic skeleton of the tune.

5. The commercial growth of bop. The evolution of bop and its acceptance by fans was a rapid process. In 1942 some of the experimentalists, including Parker and Gillespie, joined the big band led by Earl Hines, and according to Gillespie, it was here, in 1943, that the bop movement took shape. When Hines's band collapsed in that year, several of his musicians went on to work in Billy Eckstine's band. In the winter of 1943–4 Gillespie took a small group with Max Roach and George Wallington, who both became influential bop musicians, to the Onyx club in New York. It is unfortunate that a dispute between the American Federation of Musicians and the recording companies forced a recording ban from 1942 into 1944, so that only a few private recordings of the developing music were made. In 1944 a group that included Parker and Roach played at the Three Deuces, giving the style further publicity, and in the same year some of the bop players, under the leadership of Hawkins (who was not a bopper), made the first bop recordings, including *Woody 'n' you* and *Disorder at the Border*. Also in that year Gillespie was chosen by a panel of critics as the "new star" on trumpet, and finally, in February 1945, Gillespie and Parker began to make the first of a series of classic bop recordings which eventually included *Groovin' High*, *Salt Peanuts*, *Hot House*, *Billie's Bounce*, *Now's the Time*, and *Koko*. These recordings established bop as the jazz movement of the future, though it was still highly controversial. Younger musicians were drawn in, and very quickly bop swept everything before it. One factor that contributed to the success of bop was the collapse of the big bands. At the end of 1946 a half-dozen of the most famous ones broke up. The causes were several, but the main ones were the increasing cost of maintaining a big band and a shift in public taste in favor of vocalists. Their demise left a sudden vacuum, which the boppers partly filled.

Despite the inherent difficulty of the style, by the late 1940s bop was in the ascendant. Gillespie had an excellent bop big band, which also introduced Latin rhythms to jazz through the conga drummer Chano Pozo (*see* Afro-cuban jazz). Ultimately Gillespie's band was not economically successful, but both he and Parker were in demand and were making good incomes, and many of their followers were working regularly and recording frequently. Among the best of them were Fats

Navarro, Clifford Brown, Sonny Stitt, Sonny Rollins, and J. J. Johnson.

6. THE COOL SCHOOL. Running parallel to bop from about the mid-1940s there was a movement, mainly among white musicians, to adopt more advanced harmonies and musical procedures suggested by European art music, especially that of Stravinsky and Debussy. Enlarged bands, employing instruments such as french horns and oboes, hitherto rare in jazz, began to appear. Foremost among them were the orchestras of Stan Kenton, Woody Herman, Boyd Raeburn, and Claude Thornhill, which consisted mainly of white musicians (*see* PROGRESSIVE JAZZ). These groups were essentially dance bands that had evolved out of the old big bands, but they used advanced harmonies and other elements drawn from bop (Gillespie arranged music for some of them, and played in Raeburn's band briefly), and occasionally performed "tone poems" and longer concert pieces in several movements. Although the musicians were thoroughly conscious of bop, and many of them in fact played in the bop style, the majority, including Stan Getz and Bill Harris (i) in Herman's band, were at heart swing players. They saw jazz moving towards a merger with European classical music, or at least increasingly adopting devices from symphonic music. This new manifestation of the tension in jazz between African and European-American elements was expressed directly in racial terms: on the one hand were the predominantly black boppers, working in a forceful, spontaneous, improvised mode, and on the other were the Whites, who cultivated a more thoughtful and carefully constructed manner. For a time it seemed that the balance would shift in the direction of the white, European-American style. The most advanced of the dance orchestras, Herman's and Kenton's, continued to do well, which suggested that the symphonic approach might prevail, though economics dictated that the future of the music lay in small groups rather than large ensembles.

The first important small group was one organized principally by members of Thornhill's band, notably Gil Evans and Gerry Mulligan. They began rehearsing to play advanced arrangements employing the new harmonies and novel structures. Eventually Miles Davis, who had worked with Parker, was brought in to front the band; it played a brief engagement at the Royal Roost in New York in 1948, and in 1949 and 1950 made some recordings, now collectively known as the "Birth of the Cool" (fig.6). The group failed entirely with the public, but the recordings interested musicians (*see* COOL JAZZ). At the same time an even more advanced group, led by Lennie Tristano and including Lee Konitz and Warne Marsh, was making recordings and occasionally playing in clubs. Its esoteric music employed shifting tonalities and meters and frequently ignored bar-lines altogether. The group was even less successful than that of Davis and Mulligan, puzzling musicians and audiences alike.

These two were New York groups. On the West Coast similar but less extreme experiments were being made by a number of musicians, of whom the most influential proved to be Dave Brubeck, a former student of the composer Darius Milhaud. Brubeck and his quartet, which included Paul Desmond, attempted to apply to jazz ideas drawn from European music; they were among the first to experiment with improvisation in meters other than 4/4 – *Take Five* (1959), in 5/4, was a landmark. Brubeck's music was strongly rhythmic and greatly appealed to the young, especially those on college campuses. Also on the West Coast, Gerry Mulligan and Chet Baker formed a quartet without a piano, which produced a light, dry music that depended for its effect on color and counterpoint. It too became extremely popular. These and other groups came to

6. "The Birth of the Cool": Miles Davis's group at the Capitol recording studios, New York, 21 January 1949: Bill Barber (tuba), Junior Collins (french horn), Kai Winding (trombone), Gerry Mulligan (baritone saxophone), Lee Konitz (alto saxophone), Davis (trumpet), Al Haig (piano), and Joe Shulman (double bass)

be regarded as members of a "West Coast school" of light, cool jazz (*see* WEST COAST JAZZ), which, for a jazz style, was very successful with the public.

The most important adherents of the cool school, however, with its European, classical orientation, were not Whites, but two Blacks, John Lewis and Miles Davis. Lewis was the music director of and driving force behind the Modern Jazz Quartet, which also included Milt Jackson. He was interested in many art-music forms, especially those of Baroque and Renaissance music, and he deliberately introduced elements of them into his compositions. The quartet was widely popular and continued to be active into the 1980s. Davis was even more influential. After something of a false start as a bopper, he developed a spare, dry style, based in part on modal scales, which were also being exploited at the time by John Coltrane and others. Unlike the Modern Jazz Quartet, which maintained a light, shimmering surface to its music, Davis's groups usually included a forceful drummer, such as Philly Joe Jones, and strong saxophonists, among them Rollins and Coltrane. More successfully than any other member of the cool school, Davis preserved the balance between African and European-American elements – the heavy, powerful drums and saxophones contrasting with his own spare, even minimalist, style.

7. HARD BOP. During the late 1940s and early 1950s it seemed, from the success of the groups led by Herman, Kenton, Brubeck, and Mulligan, and a little later those of Davis and Lewis, that jazz would follow the "classical" road. Indeed, an attempt to create a fusion of jazz and art music, which was called THIRD STREAM, was made by some classically trained musicians, notably Gunther Schuller; the movement failed, but it was regarded as significant. As has always been the case in jazz, however, the music had been forced too far in one direction, and such tension had been created that a backlash was inevitable. Blacks, particularly, felt that the music had become too "white" and lacked the earthy, black elements they believed were essential to jazz. They were supported in this opinion by adherents of the civil-rights movement that had grown up during the 1950s, who insisted that the black subculture was not only legitimate but central to their experience, and called upon Blacks to stop emulating Whites and devote themselves to their own folkways.

Black jazz musicians, however, had been brought up in cities, and saw their musical roots not in the blues and work songs of the rural South but in the gospel songs of the "sanctified" church. This music was very close to the black folk music of the 19th century: it used plagal cadences and blue notes, handclaps to establish a ground beat, and call-and-response patterns between preacher and congregation, and it was sometimes accompanied by ecstatic confession and trances. From the mid-1950s black bop groups began to introduce elements from gospel music, usually reinterpreted, into their jazz: blue notes, for example, were presented as ordinary minor thirds and sevenths. They developed a hard-swinging, coarse-toned, simplified form of bop. Instrumentation was confined to piano, double bass, drums, and two wind instruments, usually trumpet and tenor saxophone. Form became standardized as a melodic chorus played in unison to open and close the piece, with a series of solos sandwiched between. This HARD BOP (and its related genres, funky or SOUL JAZZ) attracted substantial jazz audiences in the second half of the 1950s and beyond, and was commercially successful. Leaders of the movement were Art Blakey, who led his Jazz Messengers for decades, and Charles Mingus, who played more complex and wide-ranging music and is known especially for his strikingly original compositions. Both Blakey and Mingus were quite overt in their attempts to return jazz to what they considered its roots, and often lectured audiences on the subject.

8. JAZZ PIANO IN THE 1950S. While the stylistic upheavals of the late 1940s and 1950s were going on, the piano again developed somewhat independently of the main currents. The boppers continued to follow the method developed by Bud Powell, but the most influential pianist of the day was Bill Evans (ii). In Evans's playing the left hand lost most of its rhythmic function and was used primarily to supply supporting harmonies; the right hand tended to employ fewer of the strings of single notes typical of the boppers, focusing instead on chords. Evans's playing was essentially more harmonic than melodic, meditative on the whole, and less rhythmic than had been customary in jazz piano; he frequently played in 3/4. He was able to adopt such a style because he usually worked with a rhythm section that stated the beat. Evans was also interested in modes and varied tone-colors. He influenced many later musicians, including Herbie Hancock and Chick Corea, the dominant jazz pianists of the 1970s and early 1980s.

9. GENERAL TRENDS, FROM THE LATE 1940S TO THE EARLY 1960S. Despite the consolidation of bop and the proliferation of styles growing out of it, what has come to be called MAINSTREAM JAZZ continued to attract substantial audiences. The term "mainstream" has been variously defined, but in general it is used of the 1930s swing style tempered by bop and cool influences. Among its leading proponents were Roy Eldridge, Ben Webster, Stan Getz, Zoot Sims, and Buddy Tate, and the orchestras of Ellington, Goodman, Herman, and Basie. All of these remained active into the 1970s, and some into the 1980s. The Duke Ellington Orchestra, whose reputation had suffered in the early 1950s, found its fortunes revived in 1956 after an astonishing performance of *Diminuendo and Crescendo in Blue* at the Newport Jazz Festival, during which the audience was transfixed by a long, fiery tenor saxophone solo by Paul Gonsalves. Although Ellington grew increasingly preoccupied with his extended compositions, especially the three Sacred Concerts, the orchestra continued to present much of the band's music of the 1930s and 1940s. Basie's band continued to perform successfully even after the leader's death in 1984, playing a hard-driving, if not always imaginative, swing with bop inflections. Thus, although the innovations of the 1940s and 1950s pushed the older music from the center of attention among critics and younger fans, it continued to attract strong support from audiences.

As a whole the period from the late 1940s into the early 1960s was a good one for jazz. In earlier eras many jazz musicians had been able to make a living from music, and a few, like Armstrong, Waller, and Goodman, had grown wealthy; but they had all done so by tempering their jazz with ordinary popular music and plain entertainment. In the 1950s a considerable number of jazz musicians lived comfortably from performing, and a few became wealthy playing jazz unalloyed with commercial elements. Nor was it only the boppers who achieved such success: the Ellington and Basie bands, maintaining their swing style only slightly modified by bop, continued to be profitable despite their high costs (Ellington's band was helped to an extent by royalties from his songs). There were dixieland clubs in most major cities, and several in New York. Brubeck, Desmond, Mulligan, and others of the cool school were in considerable demand, and the Modern Jazz Quartet and Miles Davis's groups gained what verged on wide popularity. For the first time since the 1920s true jazz attracted a broad audience and was able to stand financially on its own feet.

As a concomitant, the music took a further step away from the entertainment business towards the status of art. It was increasingly presented in concert settings, especially on college campuses, where Brubeck's group in particular had a large following. The Newport Jazz Festival, founded in 1954 by the impresario George Wein and his wealthy patrons the Lorillard family in imitation of classical music festivals, further promoted the idea that jazz was art and therefore to be taken seriously.

Jazz criticism, too, was becoming more sophisticated. Bibliographies, improved discographies, and more accurate histories began to appear. Especially highly regarded were Marshall Stearns's *The Story of Jazz* (1956), generally considered the best of the histories to that date, and Nat Shapiro and Nat Hentoff's *Hear me Talkin' to ya* (1955), an anthology of interviews with jazz musicians. Although most of the authors of such writing were jazz enthusiasts rather than musicologists or professional historians, the best of it attempted to meet standards of good scholarship, suggesting again that jazz was to be treated not as mere entertainment but with the serious consideration usually accorded to art.

In spite of all this activity jazz did not become in the broad sense "popular": indeed, at no point in its history has it ever been the dominant popular music in America, although at times, as in the big-band era, simplified versions of it have attracted mass audiences. Nonetheless, in the 1950s pure jazz had an audience that probably numbered millions.

10. Developments outside the USA. The period from the 1940s to the 1960s saw a rapid increase in jazz activity outside the USA. One contributing factor was that Hitler's Germany had condemned jazz as pertaining to Blacks and Jews and therefore non-Aryan, which predisposed other Western Europeans in its favor; attending jazz concerts became for many a patriotic act. Also, from about 1943 Europe was swept by the dixieland revival that had taken place a few years earlier in the USA. Precisely what triggered this interest in New Orleans jazz is not clear, though the American book *Jazzmen* had discussed the style in some detail, and many recordings by the American revivalists had become widely available. Perhaps most important, however, was the influence of Panassié, who was a strong supporter of early jazz.

As had been the case in the USA, traditional jazz (or trad, as it came to be called) received support from the political left, who considered it the "authentic" music of the downtrodden black proletariat. Only a few specialists understood the New Orleans tradition, however, and to most Europeans the music was quite new. Trad rapidly became very popular, particularly among students, and dozens of dixieland bands were formed, mostly by young amateurs. Although many of these musicians were inexperienced, the bands produced such excellent players as Humphrey Lyttelton in England and Claude Luter in France.

Europeans were to a considerable extent cut off from jazz developments in the USA during the war years, and as a consequence many were stunned by the introduction of bop in the late 1940s. Panassié in particular attacked the new music, which led to a schism in the jazz world in France and, to some extent, elsewhere. Although trad continued to remain the most popular style, bop slowly made headway, especially after concerts given in Paris by Gillespie (1948) and Parker (1949). The European bop contingent therefore remained relatively small, but by 1960 it included such players as Ronnie Scott in England, Arne Domnérus, Rolf Ericson, and Lars Gullin in Sweden, Hans Koller and Friedrich Gulda in Austria, Bobby Jaspar in Belgium, Tete Montoliu in Spain, Roger Guérin and Pierre Michelot in France, Gil Cuppini in Italy, George Gruntz in Switzerland, and Dusko Goykovich in Yugoslavia.

The increased interest in jazz, particularly in its early forms, quickened the pace of European jazz scholarship, most notably in the field of discography. In the early 1930s Charles Delaunay began listing personnels and other information concerning recordings for the benefit of local jazz enthusiasts; his research was later published as *Hot Discography* (1936, rev. and enlarged 5/1948). There followed such works as Brian Rust's *Jazz Records* (1961, rev. and enlarged 5/1983), the standard work for the period 1897 to 1942, Jørgen Grunnet Jepsen's *Jazz Records, 1942–[1969]* (1963–70), and Walter Bruyninckx's *50 Years of Recorded Jazz, 1917–1967* ([1968–?1975], rev. and enlarged 2/[1978–80]). Small magazines devoted to jazz, many of them short-lived, proliferated in Europe after World War II. There was also a steady stream of books on the subject, the best and best-known being André Hodeir's *Hommes et problèmes du jazz* (1954), which was translated as *Jazz: its Evolution and Essence* (1956).

Jazz remained a phenomenon primarily of the USA and Western Europe until the 1950s. During the Cold War Stalin forbade its performance and the music went underground, not only in the USSR, but also in other eastern countries under Soviet dominance; a few groups, however, such as Oleg Lundstrem's big band (originally modeled on Ellington's orchestra), maintained a legal existence. The jazz programs broadcast by Willis Conover on Voice of America, which the Soviet authorities failed to suppress, also contributed to the growing interest in the genre in the East.

After the death of Stalin in 1953 there was a cultural thaw, and jazz was again tolerated. The bands that were formed during this period ranged in style from dixieland to bop. In Poland, Andrzej Trzaskowski founded an important early group, Melomani, in 1951, and the first Sopot Jazz Festival in 1956 marked the emergence of a strong jazz community in that country, led by Krzysztof Komeda and Jan Wróblewski. The principal figure in Czechoslovakia was Gustav Brom, who formed a versatile jazz ensemble in 1955, and among the most highly regarded players in the USSR was Gennady Gol'shteyn, a bop musician who experimented with other forms in the 1960s and 1970s.

The swing and bop styles predominated in Japan when jazz began to take hold there after World War II. The Hot Club of Japan was founded in 1946 with an initial membership of 100, and *Swing Journal* began publication in the same year. Sleepy Matsumoto emerged as an important soloist in the first bop group in 1949, and Nobuo Hara established his big band the Sharps and Flats in 1952; Eiji Kitamura became a leading swing clarinetist in the mold of Benny Goodman, with whom he played in Tokyo in 1957. Among other visiting Americans were Oscar Pettiford (1951), Gene Krupa and Hampton Hawes (both 1952), a Jazz at the Philharmonic group and Louis Armstrong (both 1953), Jack Teagarden (1959), Art Blakey (1961, 1963), Horace Silver (1962), and George Lewis (i) (1963, 1964). By far the most important figure in Japan was Toshiko Akiyoshi, who moved to the USA in 1956 after having been discovered by Peterson.

The American influence even penetrated as far as Thailand, where the king, Bhumibol Adulyadej, participated in jam sessions with Goodman and other touring jazz musicians.

A strong interest in traditional jazz developed in Australia in the 1940s; its principal exponent was Graeme Bell, who helped to inaugurate the Australian Jazz Convention in 1946. Other styles also flourished on the continent: Don Burrows was fluent in swing and bop as well as early jazz, while Jack Brokensha, Errol Buddle, and Bryce Rohde all played bop from the late 1940s.

VI. After 1960

1. The rise of free jazz. 2. The modal alternative: Davis and Coltrane. 3. Further developments in free jazz. 4. Jazz-rock. 5. Explorations of new forms outside the USA. 6. The resurgence of jazz in the USA. 7. Conclusions.

1. THE RISE OF FREE JAZZ. By 1960 the bop movement was declining. One extra-musical factor was the appetite for heroin shown by this generation of musicians and their close followers. Although jazz had always been associated with such drugs as alcohol and marijuana, the use of heroin by the musicians of the 1940s to the 1960s reached epidemic proportions. It destroyed the careers, and in some cases the lives, of important players such as Parker, Red Rodney, Fats Navarro, Chet Baker, and Wardell Gray; and it damaged the careers of Sonny Rollins, Miles Davis, John Coltrane, Stan Getz, and many others. Had such men not suffered from heroin addiction it is entirely possible that the music would have developed quite differently.

The main musical reason for the decline of bop was the failure of the boppers to develop the form. 15 years after Gillespie and Parker made the classic early bop recordings, players were still using the same limited instrumentation and still sandwiching strings of solos between unison themes built on the chord sequences of a standard repertory of tunes. Audiences were losing interest, and the players themselves were bored with simply "running the changes." One response to the sameness was to build ever more complicated sets of chord substitutions, a method adopted from the mid-1950s by Coltrane, who began thickening the harmonic texture to the point where the harmony was sometimes changing on every beat. A different approach, taken by Davis and Coltrane, was to base improvisation on modal harmonies rather than chord progressions; this had the effect of reducing chordal sequences to two or three elements. Modal jazz proved successful and such harmonies became a permanent part of the jazz language. But by the late 1950s a few musicians were taking a far more dramatic way out of the chordal straitjacket of bop. As early as 1949 Tristano and his group made a recording, *Intuition*, that was harmonically quite free. It puzzled listeners and was quickly forgotten. Then in 1956 Mingus included in his work *Pithecanthropus erectus* a good deal of exceedingly free nonharmonic playing, though the music was essentially in the standard tonal system. Mingus's experiment received much attention, but it did not inspire imitators – free jazz was to be built by younger men.

The first of these was Cecil Taylor, a classically trained pianist. Taylor, like many jazz musicians of the time, was interested in the music of Stravinsky and the French impressionists, as well as in the experiments of Dave Brubeck, who was attempting to introduce something from the same composers into jazz. He developed a highly percussive piano style, in which chords, bars, and formal structures were ignored and passages of sound were strung together, acting as patches of color rather than related parts of a whole. By the late 1950s Taylor was working with a quartet that included a white musician, Steve Lacy (who had begun as a dixielander), playing in a manner that many jazz fans found incomprehensible. In 1956 Taylor made some recordings and the following year he began, with Lacy and others, to play casually at the Five Spot, a nightclub in New York frequented by artists, writers, and others sympathetic to Taylor's innovations. The raffish atmosphere and the strange music attracted the attention of the press: very quickly Taylor became a prominent, though highly controversial, figure in jazz, and in the summer of 1957 he was invited to play at the Newport Jazz Festival.

At the same time, in Los Angeles, Ornette Coleman (who had come to maturity playing in rhythm-and-blues bands in Texas) was developing an equally difficult music, which also ignored chords and bar-lines, and frequently employed sounds not in the equal-tempered chromatic scale. Unlike Taylor, Coleman arrived at his method by instinct rather than study and theory. He was accused by other musicians of not understanding what he was doing, and was often driven from bandstands by the boppers he tried to play with. However, he eventually gathered some younger musicians around him, among them Don Cherry, who began rehearsing under Coleman's tutelage (fig.7). In 1958 Coleman's group was recorded by the small Contemporary label. The recording, *Something Else!!!! The Music of Ornette Coleman*, did not at first sell well (though it remained available for decades), but it gave Coleman some legitimacy and impressed a few established musicians, notably John Lewis and Gunther Schuller. With their support more recordings were issued, and in autumn 1959 Coleman's group began an engagement at the Five Spot. It caused a furor in the jazz world and attracted the attention of formidable musical figures, such as Leonard Bernstein, and inevitably that of the press as well.

The majority of jazz musicians disliked, even detested, the music of Taylor and Coleman, and many jazz critics agreed with them. However, some younger musicians, especially Blacks, were excited by it. Again, sociological forces contributed to the interest. By the late 1950s civil rights for Blacks had become an important national concern; Blacks were vociferously and explicitly demanding "freedom." It occurred to young black jazz musicians that they should seek freedom in their playing as well – freedom from the tyranny of bar-lines, chords, and formal structures. Their main aim was to express themselves unfettered by outmoded conventions: this meant not only throwing off the shackles of the conventional rules of music, but also, because no instrument should be subordinate to another, bringing forward rhythm instruments from their traditional supporting role to a place in the front line. These ideas were pursued to some extent by Coleman in his recording *Free Jazz* (1960). While one duo of double bass and drums maintained a steady beat, providing walking bass lines and swinging ride-cymbal patterns, a second duo engaged in collective improvisation with the wind instruments; the latter either played solos of variable length and indeterminate harmonic content, or supported one another by performing wildly changing short accompanying motifs that served the same function as did riffs in the swing style.

By the mid-1960s there were a number of young players at home in the new music – by then variously called "the New Thing," "avant-garde jazz," or FREE JAZZ – among them Archie Shepp, Albert Ayler, John Tchicai, Donald Ayler, Sunny Murray, Milford Graves, and Roswell Rudd, as well as the musicians around Coleman and Taylor. It is difficult to describe their music, since, by its nature, it was built on few musical principles that were common to all. At its most free, as on Coltrane's album *Ascension* (1965), it may appear to some listeners a cacophonous jumble of musical sounds; others, surmounting the common first impression of the piece as noise, discover an orderly progression of solos and collective pas-

7. *Ornette Coleman (right, saxophone), Don Cherry (pocket cornet), and Charlie Haden (double bass) playing at the Newport Jazz Festival New York, 1979*

sages, a variety of imaginative timbres, a loose (but extant) harmonic underpinning. Other performances of free jazz are quite simple and draw largely on the more standard jazz modes of bop or even swing, as does much of Shepp's work on the album *Four for Trane* (1964). Indeed, some of Coleman's themes, such as *Peace* or *Lonely Woman*, could easily have been transformed into popular tunes. However, certain principles run through much of free jazz. One is the employment, to some extent, of shouts, cries, or simple noise – sounds that are not musical in the ordinary sense; a second is the complete freedom of the improviser (apart from the requirement, at times, to work from a given theme or idea); and a third is the avoidance of order: if the music seems to be falling into a pattern, some means are usually found to break it.

The free-jazz movement did not find easy acceptance. Older jazz fans, who were at ease with the New Orleans style or the big bands, had had considerable trouble in coming to terms with bop, and many were not prepared to make the effort to learn yet another musical language; they tended to dismiss free jazz as the ranting of angry men. Even younger fans, accustomed to the relatively uncomplicated cool and hard-bop styles, found avant-garde jazz difficult. But the new music was not easily dismissed. It appeared to be saying something, and many musicians and critics who basically disliked it acknowledged that they had to come to terms with it.

2. The modal alternative: Davis and Coltrane. Alongside free jazz, alternative approaches continued to be explored, among them Davis's modally based music. A landmark in the development of Modal jazz was Davis's album *Kind of Blue* (1959), to which Coltrane also contributed. This album was extremely influential with jazz musicians for two decades. The pieces were sketched out only very roughly in advance (it is likely that the pianist, Bill Evans (ii), was as responsible for them as Davis) and were fleshed out by the musicians in the studio. To achieve spontaneity, only one take was made of each. The music, largely modal, consisted mainly of solos played fairly independently of harmonies. Nonetheless, probably because of its modality, it was quite accessible and attracted many musicians; nor was it incidental to the success of the recording that the liner notes by Evans gave hints of how the music had been put together, so that the album as a whole acted as a kind of tutor for other musicians.

Davis was outspoken in his contempt for free jazz; nevertheless, in the early 1960s he continued to look for new forms and new ways to play. He began working with younger men in touch with avant-garde musicians, in particular Wayne Shorter and Tony Williams, and conducting avant-garde experiments of his own; these included his recordings *Sketches of Spain* (1959–60), which is hard to classify as jazz, and *Nefertiti* (1967), which incorporates pieces that are largely free of fixed forms. Coltrane likewise responded to the challenge of free jazz. Having established himself in 1959 as perhaps the foremost saxophonist in jazz of the time with *Giant Steps*, a racing bop number built on novel and swiftly shifting chord changes, he familiarized himself not only with modal theory but also with polytonality and nontonal scales drawn from outside jazz. He began during the 1960s to experiment with all of these musical materials, making forays into free jazz with *Impressions* (1961–3) and *Expression* (1967) but achieving his greatest popular success with such modal pieces as *My Favorite Things* (1960) and *A Love Supreme* (1964), both of which drew buyers from beyond the jazz market. Coltrane was impelled to play free music in part by his sporadic association with Eric

Dolphy, who played a number of woodwind instruments but specialized in bass clarinet. Dolphy began as a bop musician, but increasingly worked in the free-jazz idiom; a likable personality, he was very influential with the free-jazz players of the 1960s. In the end, however, it was the eclectics Davis and Coltrane, rather than Taylor, Coleman, and their followers, who were the most influential in fostering the experimental spirit among younger musicians. Indeed only Armstrong and Parker had a greater impact on jazz than these two.

3. FURTHER DEVELOPMENTS IN FREE JAZZ. Free music never became the dominant mode in jazz in the same manner as did swing and bop, but it continued to develop alongside the mainstream. In the late 1960s a second generation of free-jazz players arose, the most important of whom were drawn from a loose group called the Association for the Advancement of Creative Musicians (AACM), founded by Muhal Richard Abrams in 1965. Associated with this organization at various times were Anthony Braxton, Roscoe Mitchell, Lester Bowie, and Leroy Jenkins, among others. Out of the AACM grew a number of performing ensembles, the best known of which was the Art Ensemble of Chicago.

The music of this second generation was extremely varied and therefore less relentlessly inaccessible than some of the work of Coleman, Taylor, and Shepp; at times it sounded like ordinary bop, at others it was almost completely unstructured. Much of it used principles derived from the work of John Cage and other composers: in such cases the musicians worked to an outline, perhaps with predetermined emotional connotations, which allowed the improviser much freedom; randomness was deliberately sought, and there was considerable emphasis on variety of tone-color, produced by a huge array of conventional and unconventional instruments.

Even harder to categorize is the music of Sun Ra, one of the most highly regarded figures in the jazz avant garde. Sun Ra began his career as a stride pianist, under the influence of Earl Hines, and continued to play occasionally in this style into the 1970s. But generally his music is more advanced, ranging from fairly approachable pieces in a bop style with inflections borrowed from Coltrane (in which the saxophonist John Gilmore figures prominently) to extraordinary cacophonies played by two dozen musicians on a wide variety of standard and exotic instruments and sound makers. Sun Ra's music is supported by a simplistic mystic philosophy and is often presented theatrically, with outlandish costumes and unusual lighting effects.

Despite the fact that free jazz never took precedence over other forms, it has continued to show strength and attract followers into the 1980s. Furthermore, almost all the players who came into jazz after 1960 occasionally used passages of free playing in their work; by the 1970s this practice, called playing "outside" the conventional scale, chord changes, and rhythmic structure, was common in many performances.

There is some question as to whether all these forms of free music can be defined as jazz. Free jazz frequently lacks a fixed ground beat or pulse – an indispensable characteristic of earlier jazz – and such usual hallmarks of jazz as blue notes, the conventional scale, tonal harmonies, and the like; however, it utilizes such standard features of jazz as improvisation, jazz instrumentation, bent pitches, distinctive tone-colors, and polyrhythms. Sun Ra's *Saturn* and Coleman's *Lonely Woman* are certainly jazz, and the Art Ensemble of Chicago's *Ninth Room* is at least jazz-like. But it is hard to see how a definition of jazz could be formulated that would encompass Sun Ra's *Somewhere There* and Braxton's *Composition 69N*.

4. JAZZ-ROCK. Possibly the most important impact on jazz of the 1960s and 1970s was that produced not by the avant garde, or any jazz musician at all, but by rock musicians. The rock-and-roll of the 1950s and the rock music that followed it in the 1960s captured the devotion of millions of young fans who might otherwise have become followers of jazz. In part the fault lay with jazz itself: the music had become abstract, thick-textured, and frequently arrhythmic. Although accessible styles continued to be played (for example, by the dixielanders around Condon, swing musicians such as Goodman and Eldridge, and boppers such as Gillespie and Stitt), young people born after World War II regarded such music as old-fashioned, and they were not interested in it. With the collapse of the big bands in the late 1940s and the rise of singers such as Eddie Fisher and Perry Como, who performed smooth, romantic songs, a whole generation of adolescents was left without the simple, direct, strongly rhythmic music that modern American youth seems to need. Earlier generations had found it in ragtime, the jazzy dance music of the 1920s, and the big swing bands of the next two decades. In the 1950s young people found what they wanted outside jazz, first in black rhythm-and-blues, and then in the forms that evolved out of it.

As a result, the jazz audience contracted. New York, which had had as many as 20 jazz clubs open at one time, had only half a dozen in the 1960s. The recordings even of successful players such as Davis and Brubeck did not sell well. Perhaps more painful still to these and other established performers was the attention paid by the press, even such longtime supporters of jazz as the magazine *Down Beat*, to rock musicians who were growing wealthy on a music of which jazz musicians were bluntly contemptuous. By the end of the 1960s many jazz fans were in despair: some announced the death of the music, and others predicted that it was flowing into forms so disparate that it might as well be dead.

Yet it was the rock fans, among them even those who had disparaged jazz at first, who were to revive the music. By the end of the 1960s many of those involved with rock, especially those who were playing it, found it limited; they wanted something more challenging and many of them found it in jazz, to which they were drawn, in part, by Coltrane. Towards the last years of his life Coltrane came to be regarded not merely as a great musician but as something of a prophet or "guru"; he seemed to exemplify a spirit of brotherhood and love for his fellow humans which was particularly attractive to young people who had found a creed and culture in the "flower-power" movement of the period. Although Coltrane hardly had a following equal to that of the Beatles or Jefferson Airplane, he was known to many, especially those who had bought his album *A Love Supreme*, as much for spiritual as musical reasons. Through Coltrane a considerable number of young rock musicians became interested in jazz, first in Coltrane's experiments in free form, then in the bop from which he had developed his style. Coltrane was not the only jazz figure to attract these young people (a surprisingly large number came from families that had an enthusiasm for earlier forms of jazz), but he was an important influence. Inevitably it occurred to them that some fusion of rock and jazz might be possible. Various claims have been made for the invention of JAZZ-ROCK or "fusion": some of the earliest musicians to attempt to create a new form were Randy and Mike Brecker in the group Dreams, which included Billy Cobham; others were Larry Coryell and John McLaughlin.

Another route into jazz-rock was taken in the late 1960s by a few jazz musicians who were looking for a way to capture part of the enormous rock audience. The most important of these was Miles Davis, who throughout the 1960s had continued to associate with young players and experiment with new forms. On *Filles de Kilimanjaro* (1968) he made use of loose constructions, much arhythmic playing in the winds, and at times a heavier beat suggestive of rock; Chick Corea played electric piano on the album. *Filles de Kilimanjaro* did not sell very well. In 1969 Davis made *In a Silent Way*, which explicitly attempted a rapprochement with rock. Many electronic instruments and three keyboards were used on the recording, and for the most part the music was free and formless; more significantly, it had also something approaching the rock beat. *In a Silent Way* was not a great success, but it did well enough to encourage Davis to take a further step in the same direction. The album that followed, *Bitches Brew* (1969), was a true jazz-rock fusion, combining a good deal of jazz solo work with electronic instruments and a rock beat; it was an enormous commercial success for a jazz recording, and once again put Davis in the forefront of modern jazz. At much the same time the group Weather Report, which had as its guiding spirits Joe Zawinul and Wayne Shorter (an earlier collaborator with Davis), began to make headway with the fans. The popularity of these musicians encouraged others to emulate them, and by the mid-1970s there existed a strong fusion movement, which included among its leaders Corea and Herbie Hancock (fig.8).

As had been the case with free jazz, many musicians and fans thought that fusion could not properly be defined as jazz. Jazz enthusiasts disliked the emphasis on electronic instruments, but their chief reservation concerned the beat. Rock had evolved from rhythm-and-blues, a style performed principally by Blacks, which had grown out of the blues and blues-related styles and incorporated some aspects of the music of black swing bands; its beat, and much else about it, swung in the jazz manner. However, particularly after the Beatles became the dominating influence in rock, the nature of the rock beat changed. In part this resulted from a misperception of the execution by some jazz drummers, such as Sid Catlett, of rim shots on the even-numbered beats of the bar; apparently some

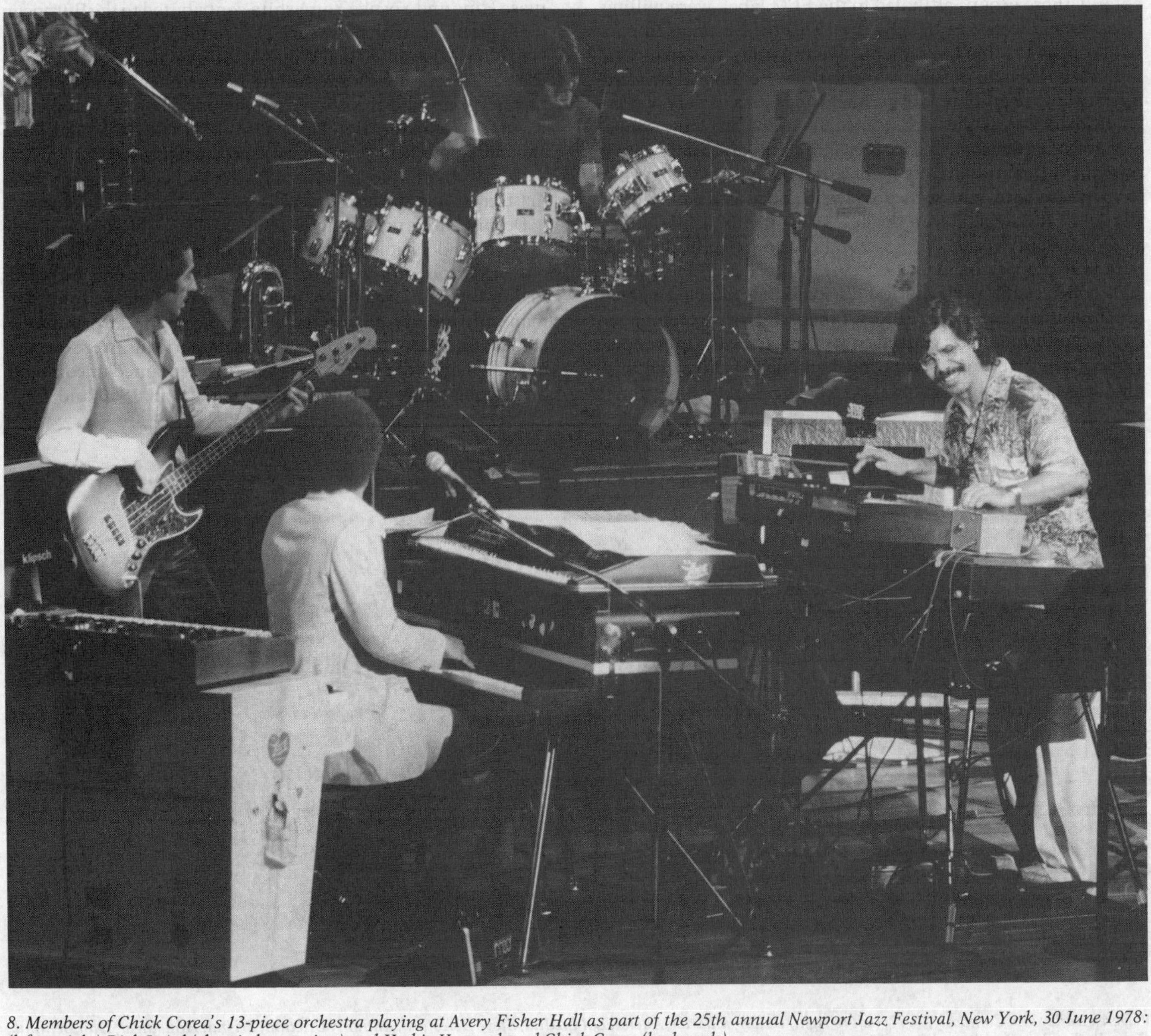

8. Members of Chick Corea's 13-piece orchestra playing at Avery Fisher Hall as part of the 25th annual Newport Jazz Festival, New York, 30 June 1978: (left to right) Rick Laird (electric bass guitar) and Herbie Hancock and Chick Corea (keyboards)

rock musicians took this rhythm to be the basic beat and in imitating it produced a ground beat for rock half as fast as that of jazz. Another characteristic of the beat in rock of the 1960s was created by the tendency of rhythm sections to play strings of eighth-notes precisely in time and without differentiation, a practice totally antithetical to jazz. Either of these rhythmic attributes would have made it difficult for rock players to produce the swing essential to jazz; together they eliminated swing altogether. And if jazz-rock failed to swing in the accepted jazz sense, could it be considered jazz? It is probably most appropriate to think of jazz-rock as another of those popular musics derived from jazz, like the symphonic jazz of Whiteman and the "polite" dance music of some of the big bands, rather than as part of the main line of development of jazz itself.

5. Explorations of new forms outside the USA. The majority of jazz musicians in the USA had initially been hostile towards avant-garde jazz, and most felt that jazz-rock was too commercial, and not really jazz at all. European fans, however, more readily accepted both, and European musicians, most notably those groups affiliated to the ECM label, were willing to combine the two genres. By the 1970s the Germans in particular believed that the center of avant-garde jazz had moved to Europe. German musicians such as Alex Schlippenbach and Albert Mangelsdorff were experimenting with a variety of non-traditional forms; the technical innovations and new sound resources employed by the English guitarist Derek Bailey were proving influential (fig.9); and Steve Lacy, Cecil Taylor's former associate, had settled in Paris and was developing a European following. From the late 1970s the French violinist Jean-Luc Ponty reached a large audience touring in the USA with his jazz-rock bands.

Although avant-garde music of various kinds received a great deal of critical attention in Europe, other forms of jazz remained strong: traditional jazz continued perhaps to be the most popular of these, while a number of big bands were active, notably the Clarke–Boland Big Band.

There was a different line of development in Eastern Europe in the 1970s and 1980s. Although from the late 1950s jazz had become more politically acceptable in these countries, it remained subject to changing official attitudes. In general Eastern governments disliked the adoption of Western modes, and held that their musicians should develop their own form of jazz, and draw for substance on national folk styles. A large number of players began to introduce folk elements into their work, partly in a cynical attempt to make their music acceptable to the authorities, but also from a quite genuine interest in folk songs and modes. Among the musicians who incorporated folk-based jazz in their repertories were Vyacheslav Ganelin in the USSR, Urszula Dudziak and Zbigniew Namysłowski in Poland, and György Szabados in Hungary. During the same period players in other countries also drew on folk music, notably Seppo Paakkunainen in Finland, Jan Garbarek in Norway, Bengt-Arne Wallin in Sweden, Maffy Falay in Turkey, and Gato Barbieri in Argentina.

Free jazz was of little importance in Japan, where interest in new styles was focused on jazz-rock (the expatriates Terumasa Hino and Yosuke Yamashita contributed to the European free-jazz movement, however). The leading Japanese bop musician after Akiyoshi, Sadao Watanabe, began incorporating jazz-rock in his repertory from the late 1960s; other notable players to emerge around the same time included Ryo Kawasaki and Kazumi Watanabe. Bop also continued to flourish, and three Japanese double bass players – Isao Suzuki (1969), Mikio Masuda (1974), and Yoshio Suzuki (1976) – became members of Art Blakey's Jazz Messengers.

Despite its crucial importance as a central source of the musical and sociological elements of jazz, Africa has played only a peripheral role in the music's development. Although Arthur Briggs toured Egypt in 1937 and Bill Coleman and Herman Chittison led a band there that played in Cairo and Alexandria in 1938–40, such visits by Americans were almost unknown until the 1960s, and even then remained uncommon. Armstrong made tours with the All Stars in 1960 and 1961;

9. Derek Bailey and Company, 1977: (left to right) Bailey, Maarten Altena, Lol Coxhill, Steve Beresford, Anthony Braxton, Tristan Honsinger, Han Bennink, Evan Parker, Leo Smith, and Steve Lacy

Randy Weston ran a nightclub in Tangiers from 1968 to 1972 after having toured in 1961, 1963, and 1967; and Oliver Nelson took his septet in 1969. Similarly, the continent did not produce any important jazz performers until the 1960s; significantly, these all emerged from the most European of the African countries, South Africa, and were primarily free-jazz musicians, such as Abdullah Ibrahim and the group of players associated with Chris McGregor. Sun Ra visited Cairo in 1971 and 1983, when he recorded with the Egyptian conga player Salah Ragab.

The audience for jazz outside the USA continued to be relatively small throughout the 1960s and 1970s, and to some extent musicians depended on grants of various kinds from governments, radio stations, and similar organizations rather than on direct support from the public through the sale of records and admissions to concerts and nightclubs. Nonetheless, by the 1980s jazz had become a truly international music, with a variety of national styles surrounding its general traditions.

6. THE RESURGENCE OF JAZZ IN THE USA. The 1970s saw a substantial improvement in the fortunes of jazz in the USA. By the end of the decade there were as many jazz clubs operating as there had been in the good times of the 1920s and the 1950s. It was, however, a period dominated by no single jazz style or aesthetic. Perhaps the most important movement was the bop revival. Younger players, many of them initially rock musicians who were inspired by John Coltrane to take up jazz, began to explore the work of Charlie Parker and the other boppers; by the mid-1970s they were playing such famous lines of Parker's as *Cool Blues* and *Ornithology* all over the country. Even though they frequently inflected their playing with "outside" elements drawn from Coltrane and Coleman and employed electronic instruments, their music was essentially bop. The Brecker brothers, Sonny Fortune, and Jon Faddis were among the best-known members of this school. The renewed interest in bop was related to the revival of the careers of some early bop musicians: Dexter Gordon returned from a long stay in Europe to make successful tours; Art Pepper, whose career had been blighted by drug addiction, published a well-received autobiography and began to tour; and others, such as Johnny Griffin and Sonny Stitt, attracted new followings.

The bop revival, however, was only part of a larger movement that included jazz-rock and free jazz, and the continuing cultivation of dixieland, swing, and even the original New Orleans jazz. Each of these styles had its adherents and venues, and good samples of all of them were available on recordings. In the 1970s the jazz audience was not merely split between two or three contending schools, as it had been in the 1950s, but fragmented among many.

The precise cause of the rising interest in jazz is difficult to pinpoint. In part it was the result of the natural cycle of life in any society: by 1970 people who had become jazz fans as youths in the 1920s and 1930s had risen to positions of authority in government, educational institutions, and the media, and were able to establish jazz grants from public and private foundations, encourage reviews of jazz performances in the press, institute courses in jazz in universities, and the like. In part the revival was fueled by younger listeners reaching beyond the rock music they had grown up with. In part it was related to the more widespread acceptance of Blacks in white society. In part it had to do with the respectability jazz had achieved. And, of course, in part the virtues of the music itself were responsible for its new popularity.

Both a cause and an effect of the attention attracted by jazz from the 1970s was a further advance in jazz criticism. In 1968 Gunther Schuller published his seminal *Early Jazz*, a thoroughgoing stylistic analysis of the most important works of jazz to the early 1930s. There had been earlier analytic studies of jazz, notably Winthrop Sargeant's *Jazz, Hot & Hybrid* (1938) and Hodeir's *Hommes et problèmes du jazz* (1954); but Sargeant was not essentially a jazz enthusiast and his book was at points superficial and contained many errors, while Hodeir's account was idiosyncratic and dealt with the American scene from a distance. Schuller's book was the first systematic study of jazz using sophisticated techniques of musical analysis. Other books based on sound scholarship followed, including Chris Albertson's *Bessie: Empress of the Blues* (1972), Ekkehard Jost's *Free Jazz* (1974), *Bix: Man & Legend* (1974), by Richard Sudhalter, Philip Evans, and William Dean-Myatt, James Lincoln Collier's *The Making of Jazz* (1978), Don Marquis's *In Search of Buddy Bolden* (1978), Ian Carr's *Miles Davis* (1982), Brian Priestley's *Mingus* (1982), and John Chilton's monographs on Bob Crosby's band, McKinney's Cotton Pickers, and other groups. However, this growing tendency to analyze jazz with the tools of academic musicology, though useful, had its drawbacks. Jazz has certain elements, such as blue notes, pitch variations, timbral modifications, rhythmically free melody, individual code, and ecstatic function, that are not susceptible to analysis using the standard musicological techniques evolved to deal with European art music. An analytic method for jazz, employing what is relevant from academic musicology, is only in the process of being devised, as is a comprehensive formulation of a jazz aesthetic.

The new enthusiasm for jazz was also responsible for an extraordinary increase in the number of reissues of early jazz recordings. Sets of recordings of the work of older players such as Fats Waller, Bessie Smith, and Charlie Parker (in some cases the entire recorded output of a musician) poured into record stores, many of them from Europe and Japan. By 1980 the amount of historical material available was beyond the resources of most private collectors to amass.

Especially important to jazz scholarship was the establishing of specialist libraries and archives such as the Institute of Jazz Studies at Rutgers, the State University of New Jersey, and the William Ransom Hogan Jazz Archive at Tulane University in New Orleans. Both institutions house important research tools for the jazz scholar: extensive record collections, files of clippings, jazz publications, and oral history material.

Schools and colleges also began to institute courses in jazz studies; in fact such courses became so numerous that, according to *Down Beat*, in the late 1970s a quarter of a million people were studying jazz formally. The US government and state and local governments began to offer grants totaling millions of dollars to jazz musicians and students.

7. CONCLUSIONS. Interest in jazz remains strong in the 1980s, though it has become extremely diffuse. In the past a single mode usually dominated the music – for instance, big-band swing prevailed in the 1930s, hard bop in the 1950s; in the 1980s it seems uncertain what path the music will take. There is, for example, a strong tendency for players, both young and old, to draw into their performances elements from extremely disparate sources. From the 1960s, following the lead of the Beatles, many jazz musicians, among them John McLaughlin and a number of free-jazz players, have attempted to incorporate effects from Indian music into their work. Others, such as Airto Moreira, have brought in elements from various South American forms, and Abdullah Ibrahim has introduced char-

acteristic features of African music. This eclecticism is perhaps best seen in the work of Keith Jarrett, a pianist who was trained in the European-American concert tradition and came relatively late to jazz. Jarrett has developed a style in which he improvises without interruption for an hour at a time, borrowing freely from extremely diverse sources – 19th-century piano pieces, bop, the blues, traditional songs – and performing with a passionate energy that may involve standing at the keyboard and even attacking it with some physical force. Jarrett's popularity in the late 1970s and early 1980s was phenomenal, though to some critics his music seemed superficial.

As ever, all of the older styles continue to show strength. An annual dixieland festival in Sacramento, California, draws hundreds of bands and thousands of listeners. Big bands, such as those of Lew Tabackin and Toshiko Akiyoshi, and Louie Bellson on the West Coast, have found audiences. Boppers such as Gillespie, Johnny Griffin, and Al Cohn were still active at the beginning of the decade, and even some swing players, such as Doc Cheatham and Max Kaminsky, continued to play well into the 1980s. In 1975 Ornette Coleman attempted to revive his fortunes with a group called Prime Time, which combined free playing with electronic instruments and a jazz-rock beat; out of this ensemble came the guitarist James "Blood" Ulmer, who mixes a blues style with elements of free jazz.

If jazz in the 1980s shows a predominant trait, it is this general interest in older styles. Once the energy had gone out of the old conflicts between the generations, younger players began to regard swing, dixieland, and bop simply as elements in a common past. Many of them have chosen to perform in one or more of these idioms, as it suits them personally: Warren Vaché and Scott Hamilton have worked in the swing style; Jon Faddis, a protégé of Gillespie, and Wynton Marsalis, who gained a lot of attention as a result of his Grammy awards in 1984, play bop. There have been revivalist movements before, such as the return to New Orleans jazz in the 1940s and 1950s and the formation in the 1970s of (generally short-lived) repertory companies to re-create the music of Armstrong, Morton, and others. But the 1980s have seen a somewhat different type of revival, in that young players have chosen, individually, to express themselves in one or another of the older styles.

It is not clear whether this eclecticism will fuse into a more unified form, as happened in the first decade of the century when jazz itself evolved from diverse sources. It is apparent, however, that jazz has traveled a long way on its journey from the disreputable subculture to social and artistic respectability. It is widely considered an art; indeed, some writers insist that it is the most significant musical form of the century. Although it is heard increasingly in concert settings, jazz also continues to function as entertainment both in clubs and, by means of recordings and radio, at home. Even in the concert hall it is generally treated with less reverence than is usual with art music, the audiences perpetuating the accepted tradition of response to and interaction with the players. This suggests that jazz continues to attract a following that is genuinely involved with it and will help to keep the music alive and developing in the future.

For bibliography *see* Appendix 1.

JAMES LINCOLN COLLIER

Jazz (ii). Record label. It was established in 1946 by James Asman and Bill "Foo" Kinnell, who ran the Jazz Appreciation Society of Newark, England. It was the first privately owned jazz specialist label in Britain; on it were issued some of the earliest recordings of the traditional-jazz revival in England.

BIBLIOGRAPHY

B. Kinnell and J. Asman: "Stocktaking," *American Jazz*, no.2 (Newark, England, 1946), 1

J. Asman: "Bill Kinnell," *Jazz Express*, no.86 (1987), 21

Jazz and People's Movement. An organization, led by ROLAND KIRK, that was active in the early 1970s; its aim was to obtain recognition for jazz and to promote black music and performers on radio and television. ("Grass Roots Jazz Protest Hits TV," *DB*, xxxvii/20 (1970), 12)

Jazz Artists Guild. Organization formed in Newport, Rhode Island, in 1960 by Max Roach, Charles Mingus, and Jo Jones; its formation took place at the conclusion of a jazz festival that had been held to protest the commercial orientation of the Newport Jazz Festival. Among the purposes of the guild was to negotiate on behalf of its members with record companies and promoters. Several musicians who were associated with the guild took part in the recording of the album *Newport Rebels* (1960, Can. 9022), including Roach, Mingus, Jones, Roy Eldridge, and Kenny Dorham. Although the Jazz Artists Guild remained in existence only for a few months its example may have inspired the formation of other groups such as the Jazz Composers Guild and the Association for the Advancement of Creative Musicians.

BIBLIOGRAPHY

N. Hentoff: Liner notes, *Newport Rebels* (Can. 9022, 1961)

B. Priestley: *Mingus: a Critical Biography* (London, Melbourne, Australia, and New York, 1982), 116.

BRIAN PRIESTLEY

Jazz at the Philharmonic [JATP]. Name used by a series of concerts, and by a loosely organized ensemble that took part in these concerts. The series began in 1944 when Norman Granz organized performances of jazz, blues, and popular music at Philharmonic Auditorium in Los Angeles. In the following year Granz applied the name Jazz at the Philharmonic to concerts that took place in various cities; by the 1950s the series lasted seven months each year and included about 150 performances in the USA, Canada, Europe, Japan, and Australia. From 1957 the tours were limited to Europe, and after a final tour of the USA in 1967 were discontinued altogether; the series was resumed for a few years in the 1970s. Among those who were associated with Jazz at the Philharmonic were the trumpeters Dizzy Gillespie and Roy Eldridge, the trombonists J. J. Johnson and Bill Harris, the clarinetist Buddy DeFranco, the alto saxophonists Willie Smith, Charlie Parker, Benny Carter, and Cannonball Adderley, the tenor saxophonists Illinois Jacquet, Lester Young, Coleman Hawkins, Flip Phillips, Ben Webster, Don Byas, and Stan Getz, the pianists Nat "King" Cole, Hank Jones, and Oscar Peterson, the guitarists Barney Kessel and Herb Ellis, the drummers Gene Krupa, Buddy Rich, Jo Jones, and Louie Bellson, the vibraphonist Lionel Hampton, the singers Billie Holiday and Ella Fitzgerald, and the big bands of Duke Ellington and Count Basie.

SELECTED RECORDINGS

Blues (1944, Disc 6024–5); Lester Leaps In (1944, Disc 6025–6); Rosetta (1944, Disc 6027); Blues for Norman (1946, Disc 2001); JATP Blues (1946, Clef 101–2); The Closer (1949, Mer. 35013); *JATP in Tokyo* (1953, Verve 9061–3); *JATP at the Montreux Jazz Festival* (1975, Pablo 2310748)

BIBLIOGRAPHY

W. Balliett: "Pandemonium Pays Off," *Saturday Review*, xxxvii (25 Sept 1954), 45

C. Emge: "How Norman Granz' Flourishing Jazz Empire Started, Expanded," *DB*, xxi/25 (1954), 3

B. Harvey: "Jazz at the Philharmonic," *Beat*, ii/5 (1958), 8

M. James: "A Survey of Jazz at the Philharmonic Recordings," *JM*, v/6 (1959), 4
L. Feather: "The Granzwagon," *From Satchmo to Miles* (New York, 1972), 173
L. Keating: "On Stage: Jazz at the Philharmonic," *J&B*, ii/10 (1973), 22

THOMAS OWENS

Jazz Brothers. Hard-bop group formed in 1960 by Chuck and GAP MANGIONE.

Jazz Cardinals. Recording group. Formed in 1926 in Chicago and led by the cornetist Freddie Keppard, its other members were Eddie Vincent (Venson) (trombone), Johnny Dodds (clarinet), Arthur Campbell (piano), and Jasper Taylor (washboard). The quintet recorded four tracks for Paramount in September 1926: *Stock Yards Strut/Salty Dog* (12399), a second take of *Salty Dog*, and *Messin' Around*, which was never issued. The issued titles by the Jazz Cardinals are considered by many to be the finest examples on record of the early New Orleans style of brass playing.

MIKE HAZELDINE

Jazz Cellar. Nightclub in San Francisco; *see* NIGHTCLUBS AND OTHER VENUES.

Jazz Centre Society. British society for the promotion of jazz. It was established in London in 1968 by a group of musicians and enthusiasts concerned about the lack of opportunities for jazz musicians in the UK. It first organized a series of concerts in London, and soon extended its activities to other major cities; it also provided management and programming support for jazz festivals. Regional offices were opened in Manchester in 1976 and Birmingham in 1978. That year the society began to establish a national jazz center, using as its premises a converted warehouse in London; a limited company was formed in 1982 to raise funds for the project. The following year the Jazz Centre Society was re-formed as JAZZ SERVICES, a national educational and managerial organization which has remained active into the late 1980s. Preparations for the national center, however, were suspended in 1986 when the company went into liquidation.

SIMON ADAMS

Jazz Composers Guild. Organization formed in 1964 by BILL DIXON; operating on a cooperative basis, it aimed to promote the performance of free jazz independently of nightclubs and booking agents. Founder members of the guild included Sun Ra, Archie Shepp, John Tchicai, Cecil Taylor, Dixon, Paul Bley, Carla Bley, and Mike Mantler. An associated ensemble, the Jazz Composers Guild Orchestra, was established under the leadership of Mantler and Carla Bley. After the guild dissolved in 1965 the two musicians continued to direct the group, which became known as the Jazz Composer's Orchestra. The following year, Bley and Mantler formed another musicians' collective, the JAZZ COMPOSER'S ORCHESTRA ASSOCIATION.

Jazz Composer's Orchestra Association [JCOA]. Musicians' collective. It was formed in New York in 1966 by Carla Bley and Mike Mantler, who had previously been members of the Jazz Composers Guild and leaders of its orchestra. After the guild's demise they continued to lead the ensemble, which in 1965 became known as the Jazz Composer's Orchestra and appeared at the Newport Jazz Festival and the Museum of Modern Art, New York. The Jazz Composer's Orchestra Association was established as an affiliated supporting organization. It commissioned, from such musicians as Mantler, Bley, Don Cherry, Roswell Rudd, Clifford Thornton, Grachan Moncur III, and Leroy Jenkins, free-jazz works, which were usually scored for large forces and intended in particular for the Jazz Composer's Orchestra; it also sponsored performances and issued recordings of these works. In 1968 the JCOA formed the New Music Distribution Service, which distributed all of the association's recordings, as well as others of free jazz and 20th-century classical music issued by small, independent companies. The Jazz Composer's Orchestra performed at the Electric Circus in New York (1969) and in the early 1970s appeared at the Public Theater in New York and held rehearsals that were open to the public; it gave its last performance in 1975. In the late 1980s the operation of the New Music Distribution Service was the JCOA's only activity.

BIBLIOGRAPHY

"The Jazz Composer's Orchestra," *JM*, no.161 (1968), 7
E. Van Der Mei: "The Jazz Composer's Orchestra," *Jh*, no.245 (1968), 36
A. Dister: "The Jazz Composer's Orchestra," *Jh*, no.281 (1972), 4
L. Goddet: "Carla Bley and Mike Mantler," *Jh*, no.281 (1972), 4

ED HAZELL

Jazz Composers' Workshop. Group of musicians organized in 1953 by CHARLES MINGUS and others to perform experimental music.

Jazz Crusaders. Name used from 1961 to 1971 by the CRUSADERS.

Jazzfest Berlin [Berlin Jazz Festival]. Festival held annually from 1964; it was known until 1981 as the Berliner Jazztage and directed successively by its founder, Joachim-Ernst Berendt (1964–72), and George Gruntz (from 1973); Rolf Schulte-Bahrenberg co-directed the festival for a period in the late 1970s and early 1980s. The festival receives funds from the Senate of Arts and Letters in Berlin and the sale of broadcasting rights to the Westdeutscher Rundfunk, and is among the most lavishly subsidized jazz events in the world. The concerts, which are given primarily at the Philharmonie in Berlin, take place over four days in late October and early November and consist not only of jazz but also of blues, gospel, and folk music; the Total Music Meeting, a series of free-jazz concerts sponsored by FMP, takes place concurrently. Among the festival's important jazz performances have been the première of Don Cherry's first work for large jazz orchestra and the first concerts by Ornette Coleman and Charles Mingus after their brief retirements in the mid-1960s. Performers at recent festivals have included Lester Bowie, the Globe Unity Orchestra, the Steve Lacy Sextet, Mel Lewis, and Kenny Wheeler. In its early years the festival drew recognition for its diversity and adventurousness; it was later criticized by some writers, notably Berendt himself, for having become more predictable in its programming.

BIBLIOGRAPHY

B. Priestley: "The Enduring Vitality of the Berliner Jazztage," *JJI*, xxxii/1 (1979), 17
J.-E. Berendt: "The 1979 Berlin Jazz Festival," *DB*, xlvii/2 (1980), 60

PAUL R. LAIRD

Jazz Institute of Chicago [JIC]. Organization dedicated to the fostering and preservation of all forms of jazz, particularly those associated with Chicago. It was founded in 1969 by a group of Chicago jazz enthusiasts, including Don DeMicheal, who served for a time as president; other presidents have included Penny Tyler, Richard Wang and Edward Crilly. In the mid-1980s it had about 1300 members. Although it is primarily funded through membership fees, the institute has received grants from various government and corporate agencies.

The original goals of the JIC were to sponsor performances and to establish an archive. The many events it promotes have included premières of works by Chicago composers, concerts that take as their themes certain aspects of jazz in Chicago, and the fourth annual outdoor tribute to Duke Ellington (1977). The rapid growth of its concert-promoting activities led the institute to found in 1979 the annual Chicago Jazz Festival, a five-night free concert series at Grant Park, which attracts audiences of 250,000 (*see* FESTIVALS). In addition the JIC holds a one-day event, the Jazz Fair, every January, at which jazz performances and films are presented and records, books, and other merchandise are on sale.

The JIC's library (named the Don DeMicheal Archives after DeMicheal's death in 1982) contains recordings, photographs, oral history material, and scores of Chicago jazz; a catalogue is in preparation. Much of the collection was lodged with the University of Chicago in 1982 (*see* LIBRARIES AND ARCHIVES, §2). The institute publishes a monthly newsletter, *JazzGram*.

Jazz Interactions, Inc. An educational organization formed in the early 1960s by JOE NEWMAN and others.

Jazzkeller, der. Nightclub in Frankfurt am Main, Germany; *see* NIGHTCLUBS AND OTHER VENUES.

Jazzkerho Break [Jazz Society Break]. Finnish jazz society. Formed in 1968 by Matti Poijärvi and Juhani Lehto, it has its headquarters in Tampere and is the largest jazz organization in Finland. It sponsors and organizes concerts and festivals (such as the Finnish National Jazz Days from 1978 to 1981 and the Tampere Jazz Happening from 1982), produces radio programs, and presents lectures; in addition the society's staff manages Hieronymus Oy, the largest importer of jazz records in Finland. The society issued the quarterly periodical *Break Bulletin* from 1978 to 1981, and in 1982 established an informal relationship with the magazine *Rytmi*, through which it disseminates information about its activities. In the late 1980s Jazzkerho Break was led by Jari-Pekka Vuorela (chairman) and Aila Manninen (managing director) and had about 700 members.

Jazzland. Record label established as a subsidiary of RIVERSIDE in 1960.

Jazzline. Record company and label. The company was founded in 1961 by Fred Norsworthy, Duke Pearson, and Dave Bailey; at first it was called Jazztime, and the offices were based in Pekin, Illinois. Early issues included albums by Walter Bishop, Jr., and the tenor saxophonist Rocky Boyd. Thereafter the headquarters were moved to New York, where the company's name was changed to Jazzline, and LPs were released by Bailey and Pearson. Although it was only operational until around 1963, the company created a small catalogue of mainstream jazz that proved very durable, even if the sound quality was sometimes inferior. Issue and reissue alike were both sporadic and idiosyncratic. Some items recorded by the company were never released; others were issued on Jazzline but later put out under other names on other labels, often overseas. An LP by the trombonist Willie Wilson later appeared under Freddie Hubbard's name on Fontana in the UK, and under Pearson's on Prestige in the USA; a trio recording led by Pearson was only issued in Europe, by Polydor; an album by Pearson's quintet was repackaged as a recording by Donald Byrd; and the recording by Bailey was reissued on Muse in 1973, credited to Grant Green.

MARK GARDNER

Jazz Messengers. Name used by ART BLAKEY for a number of groups, including a cooperative formed by Blakey and HORACE SILVER in 1953.

Jazzmobile. Organization dedicated to jazz performance and education in New York. In 1964, after leading his big band in a street concert, Billy Taylor (ii) helped to found the Harlem Cultural Council, which aimed to foster arts programs in the deprived area of Harlem. The council oversaw the early activities of Jazzmobile, which Taylor and other jazz musicians set up in 1965 and of which Taylor has been the only president; the drummer Dave Bailey has served as executive director from the late 1960s. The organization's principal activity is to give summer concerts in Harlem, the Bronx, Brooklyn, and other parts of the city, using a mobile stage. Among the performers at various times have been George Benson, Art Blakey, Duke Ellington, Dizzy Gillespie, Lionel Hampton, Herbie Hancock, Jimmy Heath, Thad Jones, and Mel Lewis. The Jazzmobile's performance schedule is determined by invitations from community associations, which request the type of jazz to be presented.

As an outgrowth of its performance programs, the Jazzmobile has organized extensive educational activities. As early as 1974 Taylor gave lectures and concerts in New York public schools, and in the mid-1970s this work became part of an arts education program funded by the Department of Health, Education, and Welfare and the United States Office of Education. A grant awarded in 1977–8 allowed Jazzmobile to support ten full-time instructors in music, dance, drama, poetry, and the visual arts. The organization has also maintained a Saturday jazz school in New York; in the late 1970s this had 20 faculty members, teaching an integrated curriculum of harmony and theory, music reading, instrumental playing, and ensemble work to about 400 students (children and adults). Heath and Lewis are among the musicians who have taught there.

The activities of the Jazzmobile are restricted mostly to the New York area, but similar, unrelated organizations have used its name elsewhere.

BIBLIOGRAPHY

A. J. Smith: "Jazzmobile: Billy Taylor and Dave Bailey, Magnetizing the Arts," *DB*, xliv/20 (1977), 14 [interview]

V. Wilmer: *As Serious as your Life: the Story of the New Jazz* (London, 1977, rev. 1980), 218

Jazz Modes. Bop quintet formed, as Les Modes, in 1956 by Charlie Rouse and JULIUS WATKINS.

Jazzology. Record company and label. Owned by George H. Buck, the label was first used in 1949 to issue the results of sessions by Tony Parenti. No further recording was undertaken until 1954, when a second label, GHB, was launched. In the following decade the company expanded considerably and moved its headquarters to Columbia, South Carolina; it became known for its new recordings of traditional jazz. At first music in the Chicago style was issued on Jazzology, and material in the New Orleans style on GHB. From the mid-1960s the company began purchasing the back catalogues of other labels that specialized in traditional jazz, among them Icon, MONO (Music of New Orleans), the American label Circle, Southland, and Jazz Crusade. Circle was revived for reissues of big-band recordings and other material from the swing era first put out on the World label; it was later used to rerelease items from Lang–Worth's catalogue.

In 1970 the company took over John Steiner's revived Paramount label, but from 1973 to 1975 it was largely inactive; during this period its premises were transferred to Atlanta. Thereafter trading resumed, but it was discovered that RCA, which had previously undertaken pressing and production, had discontinued its custom pressing facilities and destroyed Jazzology's masters. While recovering from this setback the company purchased Audiophile, thereby acquiring another important catalogue of dixieland jazz; the Audiophile label name, however, was used mainly for popular music rather than jazz. Jazzology acquired the catalogues of Jazz Record around 1980 and Lang–Worth in 1981. Two labels specializing in mainstream jazz, Bodeswell (established by Bob Wilber) and Monmouth–Evergreen, were taken over in 1983 and 1985 respectively, and in 1984 the company obtained its first material in later styles when it purchased Gus Statiras's label Progressive. The company also runs the Collector's Record Club, which from 1978 has published the journal *CRC Newsletter*.

BIBLIOGRAPHY

"The Jazzology, Progressive & G.H.B. Labels," *Matrix*, no.65 (1966), 3

G. H. Buck, Jr.: "Jazzology: 1949–1979," *Jazzology Newsletter*, v/2 (1979), 2

Jazz Record. Record label. It was established in 1946 by Art Hodes, under the auspices of his magazine of the same name. On it were issued a small number of recordings by various groups led by Hodes; some of the items had been recorded for other purposes in 1940. The label ceased to operate in 1947, but the rights to its material were acquired by George H. Buck's company Jazzology around 1980.

BIBLIOGRAPHY

G. H. Buck, Jr.: "Buck Box," *CRC Newsletter*, vi/3 (1980), 3

A. Hodes: Liner notes, *The Jazz Record Story* (Jlgy J82–3, 1980)

Jazz-rock. A style of music, developed in the late 1960s and early 1970s, that combines the techniques of modern jazz improvisation with the instrumentation and approach to rhythmic accompaniment of soul and rock music of the 1960s. It became the most common and popular style of jazz during the 1970s and 1980s, and was almost the only one heard frequently on radio during the 1970s; it was often described as Fusion in this period, though that term is commonly used more generally of syntheses of jazz with any other style of popular music. Jazz-rock was adopted not only by emerging young musicians but also by many older, established jazz players.

Until the 1970s jazz musicians had generally shunned electric instruments except for the guitar and organ. During the 1970s, however, most instruments, including trumpets and saxophones, were highly amplified, and their sounds were often modified electronically, using devices such as Echoplex, ring modulator, and Octavoice. The range of tone-colors was expanded by frequent use of the Fender-Rhodes electric piano and the ARP, Clavinet, Oberheim, Prophet, Moog, and Minimoog synthesizers. Conventional or "acoustic" piano was avoided in most jazz-rock groups, and the traditional double bass gave way to the electric bass guitar. In many groups, electronically altered sounds completely replaced the amplified and unamplified acoustic sounds of the instruments. (*See also* Bands, §4 (vi).)

The nature of jazz swing feeling underwent marked changes during the 1960s with the development of new approaches to jazz: players began to project less bounce and lilt and less regular alternation of tension and relaxation in their performances. With the incorporation of rock, this trend was complete: the use of traditional jazz swing feeling by new bands came to a halt. By the 1970s most newly formed groups employed repeated and highly syncopated bass figures instead of the traditional walking bass, and used piano and rhythm-guitar riffs in place of the more flexible and spontaneous comping that had previously characterized the accompaniment in modern jazz. Improvising soloists drew far more heavily on the work of John Coltrane, Freddie Hubbard, Chick Corea, and Herbie Hancock than on that of their bop predecessors Charlie Parker, Dizzy Gillespie, and Bud Powell. In particular, the rhythmic properties of Coltrane's lines were found far more compatible with rock accompaniment than were bop lines. Jazz-rock drummers were more indebted to the work of Tony Williams, Billy Cobham, and Steve Gadd than to Art Blakey or Max Roach, and many adopted Williams's practice of closing the hi-hat on every beat of the measure instead of only the second and fourth beats as in earlier jazz. The rhythm section was more inclined to "sit on the beat," as in rock, rather than to "pull" or "lead" the beat as in modern jazz.

The jazz-rock style was foreshadowed in the late 1960s by bands such as Fourth Way and Free Spirits, and several groups that emphasized a commercial vocal style (Ten Wheel Drive; Blood, Sweat and Tears; and Chicago). But the largest single source of high-quality groups to fuse jazz and rock, and consequently succeed in crossing over from the small following of jazz to the larger market for popular music, was the pool of musicians associated with Miles Davis between 1968 and 1971: John McLaughlin formed the Mahavishnu Orchestra, Herbie Hancock organized a sextet, Chick Corea led various ensembles called Return to Forever, and Tony Williams formed Lifetime. Many members of these ensembles in turn organized bands of their own, among them Jean-Luc Ponty (formerly in McLaughlin's band), whose group became very popular with the record-buying public. Davis recognized the influence of such rock groups as those led by Billy Preston and Jimi Hendrix on his music of the 1970s and, for the first half of that decade, indirectly acknowledged an entire pop music style by using the electric bass guitarist Michael Henderson, who had formerly been associated with Motown groups. By incorporating elements of soul music and rock, several established jazz figures achieved peaks of recognition rivaling that accorded to jazz musicians in the swing era, when jazz-oriented band music achieved relatively wide appreciation. For example, despite his formidable composing talent and prolific jazz recording activity during the 1960s, Hancock achieved great financial success when, on his album *Headhunters* (1973, Col. KC32731), he used accompaniment rhythms like those of the rock and soul group Sly and the Family Stone (whose album *There's a Riot Going On* had at one time in 1971 occupied the top position on the pop album chart); *Headhunters* reached no.13 on the album chart, earned a gold record, and proved more popular than Davis's *Bitches Brew*.

Much of the most popular instrumental music identified as jazz-rock during the 1970s and 1980s consisted of little more than funky rhythm vamps and elementary chord progressions (or no progressions at all) set beneath an improvised saxophone, guitar, or piano solo. This applies, for example, to much of the music of Grover Washington, Jr., Earl Klugh, and the bands Jeff Lorber Fusion and Spyro Gyra. A greater amount of jazz improvisation is apparent in the work of the Mahavishnu Orchestra and, especially, Weather Report, whose members (most formerly sidemen with Davis) are fresh and original composers and also expert in creating exotic tone-colors and rhythmic textures.

See also FORMS, §7, and JAZZ (i), §VI, 4, 5.

BIBLIOGRAPHY

E. Jost: "Zur Ökonomie und Ideologie der sogenannten Fusion Music," *Jf*, ix (1977), 9

J. Coryell and L. Friedman: *Jazz-rock Fusion* (New York and London, 1978)

M. C. Gridley: *Jazz Styles* (Englewood Cliffs, NJ, 1978, rev. 2/1985 as *Jazz Styles: History and Analysis*, with suppl. *Instructor's Manual and Discography*)

MARK C. GRIDLEY

Jazz Services. British society for the promotion of jazz. It was formed in April 1983 as a result of the reorganization of the JAZZ CENTRE SOCIETY. Dedicated to the development of jazz and related music, and funded largely by the Arts Council of Great Britain, it operates principally in five areas: national touring (the sponsorship and administration of tours and performances throughout the UK); education (monitoring and encouraging the teaching of jazz in schools and colleges); information services (the maintenance of registers of musicians and venues); marketing (the promotion of jazz to venues); and media (representing jazz to the press). Jazz Services has organized Young Band of the Year, a national competition, and the Jazz in Education Forum (both 1986), and National Jazz Month (a period of extensive promotion of jazz) and the National Jazz in Education Convention (both 1987). The executive board of Jazz Services includes members from the autonomous jazz societies funded by regional arts associations, and from the Musicians' Union.

Jazz Society (i). Record label. It was established in Paris around 1950 by SOFRADI (Société Française du Disque). Its catalogue consisted of reissues of jazz classics from the 1920s and 1930s. At first these were put out on 10- and 12-inch 78 r.p.m. discs; from 1952 to 1955, however, 10-inch LPs of similar material were issued. (F. Dutton and J. Godrich: "Jazz Society: a Label Discography," *Matrix*, no.39 (1962), 3)

Jazz Society (ii). Record label established in Stockholm in 1970 by Carl Hällstrom. It was devoted to swing of the late 1930s and 1940s, and was used to reissue the work of Don Byas, Duke Ellington, Count Basie, Benny Goodman, and others. Hällstrom also issued similar material on another label, Tax. Both labels were acquired by the company Mr R&B Records in the mid-1980s.

Jazz Society Break. *See* JAZZKERHO BREAK.

Jazztet. Bop sextet. It was formed in 1959 by Art Farmer and Benny Golson and was made up of trumpet (Farmer), tenor saxophone (Golson), trombone, and a rhythm section. Farmer and Golson were members throughout the group's existence but the other personnel changed frequently, especially up to the middle of 1960; among the members were Curtis Fuller and Grachan Moncur III (trombone), McCoy Tyner, Cedar Walton, and Harold Mabern (piano), and Albert Heath and Roy McCurdy (drums). The group made six albums, most of which included compositions and arrangements by Golson and one of which consisted of music by John Lewis. Although the arranged sections of the music were important to the group's style, there was ample opportunity for solo improvisation, and this dichotomy resulted in balanced, interesting performances. The Jazztet disbanded in 1962 but in 1982 Farmer and Golson re-formed it (with Curtis Fuller from among the other original members) to make a tour of Europe; it has remained active into the late 1980s.

SELECTED RECORDINGS

Meet the Jazztet (1960, Argo 664), incl. Blues March, I remember Clifford, Killer Joe, Park Avenue Petite; *The Jazztet and John Lewis* (1960–61, Argo 684); *Here and Now* (1962, Mer. 20698), incl. Whisper not; *Voices All* (1982, Ewd 90016); *Back to the City* (1986, Cont. 14020)

BIBLIOGRAPHY

R. Gleason: Liner notes, *Meet the Jazztet* (Argo 664, 1960)

G. Lees: "Farmer, Golson, and the Rise of the Jazztet," *DB*, xxvii/18 (1960), 20

R. W. Lewis: Liner notes, *Here and Now* (Mer. 20698, 1962)

LAWRENCE KOCH

Jazztime. Name by which the company JAZZLINE was at first known.

Jazztone. Record company and label. The label was established in February 1955 by the Concert Hall Society, a mail-order company that specialized in classical records. Items in its catalogue were offered as monthly selections to members of the Jazztone Society, though many later became available in retail outlets. A substantial catalogue of original recordings in a wide range of jazz styles was created under the supervision of George T. Simon, who was director of artists and repertory; availability of the recordings, however, tended to be unusually erratic. Much of Jazztone's material later became available in Germany on a label of the same name, and in France on Guilde du Jazz. The last recordings known to have been undertaken by the company were made in 1957; the company ceased to operate shortly thereafter. Much of the catalogue was reissued in a comprehensive series on the Hall of Fame label in the 1970s. (P. Russell: "The Jazztone Originals," *JJ*, xii (1959), no.5, p.27; no.6, p.9)

Jazz West. Record company and label. The company was founded by Herbert Kimmel in Los Angeles in 1954, and was associated with the labels Score and Intro. The small catalogue included the first two albums made as a leader by Jack Sheldon, and outstanding LPs by Kenny Drew, and by Larry Marable and the tenor saxophonist James Clay. Records on Jazz West rapidly became extremely rare, and prized by collectors; in the 1980s, however, some of them were reissued by King in Japan, and by Fresh Sounds in Spain.

MARK GARDNER

Jazz World Society [JWS]. Organization based in New York, dedicated to the compilation and dissemination of information concerning the jazz industry. Founded by Jan A. Byrczek, it evolved as a result of his efforts to establish a New York branch of the INTERNATIONAL JAZZ FEDERATION in 1977. It was originally called the International Jazz Federation, Inc., but adopted the title Jazz World Society in 1983, by which time it had established itself as an independent body. Its membership includes jazz musicians and composers, booking agents, promoters, journalists, and other jazz professionals. It publishes the bimonthly journal *Jazz World*, the annual *Jazz World Directory*, *European Jazz Directory*, and *Jazz Festivals*, *International Direc-*

tory, and other works in its Jazz Reference Series. The JWS also publishes mailing lists covering specific areas of jazz, such as booking agents and nightclubs.

JCOA. *See* JAZZ COMPOSER'S ORCHESTRA ASSOCIATION.

Jeanneau, François (*b* Paris, 1935). French saxophonist and flutist. He achieved recognition as a member of the quintet of Georges Arvanitas (1960–61, recording in 1961) and recorded with Jef Gilson (1962–3, 1966, 1976). After interrupting his career in jazz (1966–75) he worked as a leader, performed as a sideman with Ran Blake (1977), Michel Portal (1980), and Martial Solal (1980–84), and with Daniel Humair performed and recorded as a leader of a trio that included the double bass player Henri Texier (1978–83). From 1985 to 1986 he was the first formal leader of the Orchestre national de jazz, with which he recorded (*Orchestre national de jazz 1986*, 1986, MFA 6503–4). His work has been strongly influenced by that of John Coltrane, and shows a particular inclination towards unusual sonorities and instrumental groupings. ("Dico Disco & Co.," *Jm*, no.298 (1981), 33)

MICHEL LAPLACE

Jederby, Thore (*b* Stockholm, 15 Oct 1913; *d* Stockholm, 10 Jan 1984). Swedish double bass player and record and radio producer. He attended the Royal Swedish Academy of Music in Stockholm and belonged to big bands led by Arne Hülphers (1934–8) and Thore Ehrling (1938–46); he led the Swing Swingers, a studio band, from 1936 and performed as a leader of small groups, with which he also made recordings (including *Busters idé*, 1941, Scala 395). After World War II he led a bop group and in 1950 managed Charlie Parker's tour of Sweden; later he produced radio programs and records and from 1977 belonged to a commission on Swedish jazz history.

Oral history material in *SSsv*.

BIBLIOGRAPHY

B. Englund: "Jederby, Thore," *Sohlmans musiklexikon* (Stockholm, rev. and enlarged 2/1975–9 ed. H. Åstrand)
J. Bruér: "Thore Jederby berättar" [Thore Jederby tells], *Svensk jazzhistoria*, ii (Caprice 2010, 1982) [liner notes]
L. Collin: "Thore Jederby: en jazzklassiker," *Orkester journalen*, li (1983), Oct, 15

ERIK KJELLBERG

Jeep. Nickname of JOHNNY HODGES.

Jefferson, Eddie [Edgar] (*b* Pittsburgh, 3 Aug 1918; *d* Detroit, 9 May 1979). Singer, lyricist, and dancer. For many years he worked principally as a tap dancer. In the late 1940s he created what came to be called (misleadingly) jazz vocalese by setting lyrics to the famous improvisation on *Body and Soul* by Coleman Hawkins; a decade later this type of piece became an important element in the success of Lambert, Hendricks, and Ross. From 1952, following King Pleasure's popular recording of Jefferson's *Moody's Mood for Love* (based on a saxophone solo by James Moody), Jefferson was able to record his own gritty-voiced vocalese. For two decades he sang with and managed Moody's bop group (1953–73). Later he worked with Roy Brooks (1974–5) and Richie Cole (1975–9), and had just begun to receive critical recognition for his work when he was murdered in Detroit. A film of Jefferson performing with Cole's group, *Eddie Jefferson: Live at the Showcase*, was made two days before his death.

SELECTED RECORDINGS

As leader: Body and Soul/I got the blues (1952, Hi-Lo 1413); *Body and Soul* (1968, Prst.7619); *Come Along with Me* (1969, Prst.7698); *Things are Getting Better* (1974, Muse 5043); *Still on the Planet* (1976, Muse 5063); *The Liveliest* (1976, Muse 5127); *The Main Man* (1977, IC 1033)

As sideman with R. Cole: *New York Afteroon* (1976, Muse 5119); *Alto Madness* (1977, Muse, 5155), incl. Moody's Mood '78; *Keeper of the Flame* (1978, Muse 5192)

BIBLIOGRAPHY

C. Crawford: "Woodshed: Eddie Jefferson, Vocalese Giant," *JM*, iii/1 (1978), 46
Obituary, *DB*, xlvi/12 (1979), 15
K. Silsbee: "An Interview with Eddie Jefferson," *Coda*, no.174 (1980), 10
G. V. Johnson, Jr.: "Eddie Jefferson the Innovator," *JSN*, ii/3 (1981), 46

BARRY KERNFELD

Jefferson, Hilton (W.) [Jeff] (*b* Danbury, CT, 30 July 1903; *d* New York, 14 Nov 1968). Alto saxophonist. He began playing banjo professionally in 1925, but later changed to alto saxophone. At the end of 1925 he moved to New York, where he worked with Claude Hopkins (1926–8, 1932, 1934–6, 1939), Chick Webb (1929–30, 1930–31, 1936, 1938; for illustration *see* WEBB, CHICK), King Oliver (1930), McKinney's Cotton Pickers (1931–2), Benny Carter (1932, 1933), Fletcher Henderson (1932–4, 1936–8), and Henry "Red" Allen (1934). In 1938–9 he made a number of recordings with Ella Fitzgerald. Jefferson joined Cab Calloway's big band in 1940 (for illustration *see* CALLOWAY, CAB) and later played in his small groups, but left in 1949 and performed in several clubs in New York. After another short spell with Calloway (1951) he worked with Duke Ellington (1952–3), then accompanied Pearl Bailey as a member of Don Redman's orchestra (1953). He played only part-time in the 1950s and 1960s, though he recorded with various musicians, among them Rex Stewart and Buster Bailey. A particularly fine lead alto saxophonist, Jefferson was also an excellent soloist. He performed in a melodic style and displayed a keen sense of structure and a distinctive, forceful attack.

SELECTED RECORDINGS

As sideman: H. Allen: Rug Cutter Swing (1934, Ban. 33178); F. Henderson: Wrappin' it up (1934, Decca 157); C. Calloway: Willow, weep for me (1940, OK 6109); R. Stewart: *The Big Reunion* (1957, Jzt. 1285); on B. Bailey: *All About Memphis* (1958, Fel. 7003), Bear Wallow

BIBLIOGRAPHY

ChiltonW
B. McRae: "A B Basics, no.25: Hilton Jefferson," *JJ*, xxii/1 (1969), 21
W. C. Allen: *Hendersonia: the Music of Fletcher Henderson and his Musicians: a Bio-discography* (Highland Park, NJ, 1973)
G. Murphy: "The Forgotten Ones: Hilton Jefferson," *JJI*, xxxv/5 (1982), 21

EDDIE LAMBERT

Jefferson, Ron [Roland Parris] (*b* New York, 13 Feb 1926). Drummer. A swing and bop musician, he played with Roy Eldridge (1950) and Coleman Hawkins (1951), then worked with Joe Roland (1954–6). After recording with Oscar Pettiford (1954) and Freddie Redd (1955) he played briefly with Pettiford (1956), and with Lester Young (1956–7), Randy Weston, Horace Silver, Lou Donaldson, and Charles Mingus. From 1957 to 1959 he was a member of the Jazz Modes with two of his former colleagues in Pettiford's group, Julius Watkins and Charlie Rouse. Jefferson then moved to California, where he recorded with Teddy Edwards (1959), Groove Holmes (1961–2), and Leroy Vinnegar, Carmell Jones, Tricky Lofton, and Victor Feldman (all 1962); during this period he also toured and recorded as a member of Les McCann's groups. In the early 1970s he was involved with the Jazz and People's Movement, an organization led by Roland Kirk. Jefferson has recorded two albums as the leader of his own groups, in 1961 (*Love Lifted Me*, PJ 36), and around 1976.

BIBLIOGRAPHY

FeatherE

V. Wilmer: *As Serious as your Life: the Story of the New Jazz* (London, 1977, rev. 1980), 215

Jeffrey, Paul (H.) (*b* New York, 8 April 1933). Tenor saxophonist, arranger, and bandleader. After studying music at Ithaca College he worked with Illinois Jacquet (1958), Sadik Hakim (1961), and Howard McGhee (1966). In 1968 he joined Dizzy Gillespie for a tour of Europe and also led a recording session in which he played electronically enhanced saxophone (*Electrifying Sounds*, Savoy 12192). He recorded with Charles Moffett (1969), joined Count Basie briefly (1970), then played with Thelonious Monk (intermittently, 1970–75); he also led his own groups, with which he recorded three albums (1972–*c*1975). In 1977–8 he played, conducted, and wrote arrangements for Charles Mingus. Later he recorded with Lionel Hampton (1979, 1982). Jeffrey has also been active as a teacher; during his time at Rutgers he led the university's jazz ensemble. (*Feather–Gitler '70s*)

Jeffries, Herb (*b* Detroit, 24 Sept 1916). Singer. He worked with Erskine Tate (early 1930s), Earl Hines (1931–4), and Blanche Calloway. After acting in films he returned to singing; as a member of Duke Ellington's band (1940–42) he enjoyed considerable success with *Flamingo* (1940, Vic. 27326) and other ballads; he also recorded with Sidney Bechet (1940). Later he sang at clubs in Hollywood and between 1945 and 1956 recorded several times under his own name, accompanied by, among others, Lionel Hampton's orchestra (without Hampton), Eddie Beal, Lucky Thompson, Bobby Hackett, and Russ Garcia's orchestra. He was active into the 1970s, both as a musician and an actor; in 1978 he formed his own record company, United National Records.

BIBLIOGRAPHY

R. D. Kinkle: *The Complete Encyclopedia of Popular Music and Jazz, 1900–1950* (New Rochelle, NY, and Westport, CT, 1974) [incl. discography]

S. Dance: *The World of Earl Hines* (New York, 1977) [interviews], 93

"Head and Christian Shops: Unusual Distribution for Herb Jeffries' New Label," *Billboard*, xc (2 Dec 1978), 86

Jenkins, Edmund Thornton (*b* Charleston, SC, 9 April 1894; *d* Paris, 12 Sept 1926). Composer, reed player, and bandleader. He played in bands at Jenkins' Orphanage, which was established in Charleston by his father, Reverend Daniel Jenkins. From 1914 to 1921 he studied at the Royal Academy of Music in London, and in 1921 he made some recordings (including *Come Along*, HMV B1299) on which he played clarinet and saxophone. Since Jenkins had few contacts with his homeland during his period in London, these recordings may be taken to represent a style current in the USA before 1914; their advanced nature indicates that the jazz idiom was already well established at that time. Whilst in England he worked with James P. Johnson (1923), and Will Marion Cook's Southern Syncopated Orchestra; he also played with bands in France, Italy, and Belgium, and wrote some compositions in which he attempted to fuse Afro-American and European music. (J. P. Green: *Edmund Thornton Jenkins: the Life and Times of an American Black Composer, 1894–1926*, Westport, CT, and London, 1982)

JEFFREY P. GREEN

Jenkins, Freddie [Posey; Frederic] (*b* New York, 10 Oct 1906; *d* Texas, 1978). Trumpeter. He was a left-handed player. He first performed in a boys' military band, then, while a student at Wilberforce University, worked with Edgar Hayes and Horace Henderson's Collegians (1924–8). In 1928 he joined Duke Ellington, and his jaunty, extrovert solos grace many of the band's recordings of the late 1920s and early 1930s; his sense of showmanship also added flair to the group's stage appearances (for illustration *see* TRUMPET). A serious lung ailment compelled him to leave Ellington in 1934, but he resumed playing the following year, recording as a leader in New York. He worked with Luis Russell briefly in 1936 and rejoined Ellington in March 1937, but after a year of playing intermittently left to form his own band with Hayes Alvis. He was forced to retire from music after a further bout of illness in 1938.

SELECTED RECORDINGS

(all as sideman with D. Ellington)

Tiger Rag (1929, Bruns. 4238); High Life (1929, Vic. 38036); Harlemania (1929, Vic. 38045); Harlem Speaks/In the shade of the old apple tree (1933, Bruns. 6646); Sump'n 'bout Rhythm (1934, Bruns. 7310)

BIBLIOGRAPHY

ChiltonW

D. Ellington: *Music is my Mistress* (Garden City, NY, 1973), 121

R. Ringo: "Reminiscing in Tempo with Freddie Jenkins," *Sv*, no.46 (1973), 124

EDDIE LAMBERT

Jenkins, John(, Jr.) (*b* Chicago, 3 Jan 1931). Alto saxophonist and bandleader. He played clarinet in high school, but changed to alto saxophone; in 1955 he worked briefly with Art Farmer and also led his own quartet. After moving to New York in 1957 he played with Charles Mingus for a short time, then worked as a freelance, making two albums as leader of a bop quintet (including *John Jenkins*, 1957, BN 1573); the other members were Sonny Clark, Kenny Burrell, Paul Chambers, and Dannie Richmond. He also recorded as a leader with Jackie McLean and Donald Byrd, and as a sideman with Hank Mobley, Paul Quinichette, Clifford Jordan, Sahib Shihab, and Wilbur Ware (all 1957). By 1965 he had ceased to work as a musician. (*FeatherE*)

Jenkins, Karl (William Pamp) (*b* Swansea, Wales, 17 Feb 1944). Welsh baritone and soprano saxophonist, oboist, and keyboard player. He studied music at Cardiff University (1963–6), where he first played jazz, and then at the Royal Academy of Music, London (1966–7). Having recorded with Graham Collier in 1967, he played in his band in 1968–9. He was a founding member of Ian Carr's Nucleus, with which he worked from 1969 to 1972, recording *Elastic Rock* in 1970 (Vertigo 6360008). He also worked with Julie Tippetts in 1969 and with Keith Tippett's Centipede, the Spontaneous Music Ensemble, and the London Jazz Composers Orchestra in the early 1970s, before joining SOFT MACHINE in 1972; from 1977 he was this group's joint leader with John Marshall. From 1981, when Soft Machine disbanded, he worked with Mike Ratledge (another former member of the group), composing and recording music, some of it orchestral, for films, television, and the theater. (R. Cotterell, ed.: *Jazz Now: the Jazz Centre Society Guide*, London, 1976)

For further recordings and bibliography *see* SOFT MACHINE.

SIMON ADAMS

Jenkins, Leroy (*b* Chicago, 11 March 1932). Violinist, composer, and bandleader. He was influenced by the violinists Jascha Heifetz, Eddie South, and Bruce Hayden, and also by Charlie Parker, Ornette Coleman, and John Coltrane. After working with various bands he taught high school in Mobile, Alabama, for four years. He then returned to Chicago, where from 1965 to 1969 he played with the Association for the Advancement of Creative Musicians, and in 1967, with Anthony Braxton and Leo Smith, he founded the Creative Construction Company; he soon became established as the leading violinist in the free-jazz style. In 1971 he was a founding member of the REVOLUTIONARY ENSEMBLE, a trio whose members performed on a wide variety of instruments, though during the early 1970s he also played as a sidemen with others. Thereafter Jenkins has toured extensively in Europe and led his own groups, including a trio with Anthony Davis and Andrew Cyrille (1978–9), for which he wrote a number of compositions, and a quintet (1982–3). In the mid-1980s he was a member of the board of directors of the Composer's Forum, an organization based in New York and dedicated to the presentation of concerts of new music. In 1987 he played in a quintet led by Cecil Taylor.

Jenkins is known for expanding the vocabulary of sounds associated with the violin in jazz, and for integrating free-form and composed approaches in music for small groups. He has presented numerous performances of collective improvisation, and has written works for soloist (such as *Why am I here?*, *Opus/Supo*, *Keep on trucking, brother*), small group (*The Legend of Ai Glatson*), and large ensemble (*For Players Only*).

SELECTED RECORDINGS

As unaccompanied soloist: *Solo Concert* (1977, IndN 1028), incl. Why am I here?, Opus/Supo, Keep on trucking, brother

Duos with A. Wadud: *Straight Ahead/Free at Last* (1979, Red 147)

As leader: *For Players Only* (1975, JCOA 1010); *The Legend of Ai Glatson* (1978, BS 0022); *Space Minds, New Worlds, Survival of America* (1978, Tomato 8001); *Mixed Quintet* (1979, BS 0060); *Urban Blues* (1984, BS 0083)

As sideman: M. R. Abrams: *Levels and Degrees of Light* (1967, Del. 413); A. Braxton: *Three Compositions of New Jazz* (1968, Del. 415); Creative Construction Company: *Creative Construction Company* (1970, Muse 5071, 5097), incl. Muhal; R. Kirk: *Rahsaan, Rahsaan* (1970, Atl. 1575); D. Cherry: *Relativity Suite* (1973, JCOA 1006); M. R. Abrams: *Mama and Daddy* (1980, BS 0041)

For further recordings *see* REVOLUTIONARY ENSEMBLE.

BIBLIOGRAPHY

B. Primack: "Leroy Jenkins: Gut-plucking Revolutionary," *DB*, xlv/19 (1978), 23

Ms. Ayobami: "Leroy Jenkins," *JSN*, i/5 (1980), 7

B. McRae: "Beyond the Mainstream: Leroy Jenkins," *JJI*, xxxiii/7 (1980), 28

B. Blumenthal: "Leroy Jenkins: For the Record," *DB*, xlix/3 (1982), 20

Jenkins, Pat [Sidney] (*b* Norfolk, VA, 25 Dec 1914). Trumpeter. In 1934 he moved to New York, where he worked regularly with Al Cooper's Savoy Sultans (1937–44); his playing is well represented by *Jeep's Blues* (Decca 7502) recorded with Cooper in 1938. After serving in the army he played with Tab Smith for about three years, then briefly led his own group. In 1951 he joined Buddy Tate with whom he played in New York and recorded intermittently from 1954 to 1973; the group also recorded with Jimmy Rushing (1954). (*ChiltonW*; *FeatherE*)

Jenkins, Posey. *See* JENKINS, FREDDIE.

Jenkins' Orphanage bands. Brass bands. Daniel Joseph Jenkins established his orphanage in Charleston, South Carolina, around 1890. The children, who were taught to play instruments that members of the public had donated, performed on the streets to gain publicity and raise money for the institution. In time the bands grew in number and proficiency until up to six, each with 20–30 members, were active at once; they toured the USA, Britain (from 1895), and Canada (*c*1922), playing a repertory that consisted of military-band music, ragtime favorites, and popular songs. Many of the orphans later became professional musicians; they included the trumpeter Gus Aitken, Cat Anderson, Bill and Tommy Benford, Geechie Fields, Peanuts Holland, and Jabbo Smith. Other players associated with the Jenkins bands were Freddie Green, Rufus Jones, Cliff Smalls, and Willie Smith. The Carolina Cotton Pickers, which toured (from 1933) and recorded (1937), was made up of musicians who had first performed together in the orphanage bands. Since some children came to the orphanage through the police courts, it was sometimes regarded (mistakenly) as a penal institution; this led some players to refuse to acknowledge their musical instruction there. By the early 1950s there were only enough children at the orphanage to form one band, and widespread touring ceased.

BIBLIOGRAPHY

J. Chilton: *A Jazz Nursery: the Story of the Jenkins' Orphanage Bands of Charleston, South Carolina* (London, 1980)

B. Bastin: "A Note on the Carolina Cotton Pickers," *Sv*, no.95 (1981), 177 [incl. discography]

J. P. Green: *Edmund Thornton Jenkins: the Life and Times of an American Black Composer, 1894–1926* (Westport, CT, and London, 1982)

H. Rye: "Visiting Fireboys: the Jenkins' Orphanage Bands in Britain," *Sv*, no.130 (1987), 137

JEFFREY P. GREEN

Jenney, Jack [Truman Elliot] (*b* Mason City, IA, 12 May 1910; *d* Los Angeles, 16 Dec 1945). Trombonist. As a child he learned trumpet then played trombone in his father's band. In the early 1930s he played and recorded with Isham Jones, and from 1934 to 1938 he worked in studios in New York, recording with Red Norvo (1934–5), Glenn Miller (1935), and Johnny Williams and Dick McDonough (both 1937), among others; he also recorded with his wife, the singer Kay Thompson (1937). In 1938 he led his own studio band, and the following year a big band, but this soon failed financially. After playing with Artie Shaw (1940 to early 1942), he returned to studio and film work (he made two films with Benny Goodman in 1942–3, the first of which was *Syncopation*). He led Bobby Byrne's band for a short time after Byrne joined the navy (1943), then again led his own band until he also enlisted in the navy (1943); he resumed his activities as a studio musician in California in 1944. A representative example of his playing may be heard on Shaw's *Stardust* (1940, Vic. 27230).

Jenny-Clark, Jean-François (*b* Toulouse, France, 12 July 1944). French double bass player. He taught himself to play double bass, worked with Aldo Romano, and played in Paris at Le Chat qui Pêche with Jackie McLean (1961). In the early 1960s he undertook conservatory training, winning a *premier prix* in 1968, and at the same time played bop with Johnny Griffin, Bud Powell, and Kenny Drew and free jazz with the trumpeter Bernard Vitet (1965); he also worked with Don Cherry (in Europe and in 1967 in New York) and Gato Barbieri. In France he has played with Slide Hampton, Charles Tolliver, and Michel Portal and in a trio with Joachim Kühn and Daniel Humair (with which Portal also plays frequently); during the mid-1980s he led the German–French Jazz Ensemble with Albert Mangelsdorff. He has also worked with the contemporary composers Luciano Berio and Karlheinz Stockhausen, and the conductor Diego Masson. Jenny-Clark received the Prix Django Reinhardt from the Académie du jazz in 1974.

SELECTED RECORDINGS

As leader with J. Kühn and D. Humair: *Easy to Read* (1985, Owl 043)

As sideman: M. Solal: *Sans tambour ni trompette* (1970, RCA 730105); E. Gismonti: *Orfeo novo* (1970, MPS 15048); G. Beck: *Sunbird* (1979, JMS 07); M. Petrucciani: *Michel Petrucciani* (1981, Owl 025)

BIBLIOGRAPHY

J.-P. Leloir and D. Lémery: "J.-F. Jenny-Clark: Portrait of Jenny," *Jm*, no.117 (1965), 31
P. Carles and A. Gerber: "Pièges pour Jenny-Clark," *Jm*, no.174 (1970), 30
A. Dutilh and P. Cardat: "Portrait of Jenny-Clark," *Jh*, no.301 (1974), 6

ANDRÉ CLERGEAT

Jensen, Arne Bue. *See* PAPA BUE.

Jepsen, Jørgen Grunnet (*b* Aug 1927; *d* Copenhagen, 24 Aug 1981). Danish discographer. As a member of the staff of *Orkester journalen* from 1953 to 1965 he wrote a regular column and compiled discographies of such musicians as Clifford Brown, Gerry Mulligan, Sonny Rollins, Art Pepper, Benny Carter, and Cecil Taylor; in all he contributed more than 100 discographies to this journal and to English, American, French, and Belgian periodicals. From the late 1950s he also compiled discographies that were published separately; these cover the careers of Thelonious Monk, Bud Powell, Fats Navarro, Clifford Brown, and others. His most important work, *Jazz Records, 1942–[1969]* (1963–70), was the first widely available general jazz discography to give information on recordings of the postwar era.

WRITINGS
(selective list)

A Discography of Fats Navarro, Clifford Brown (Brande, Denmark, 1960)
Jazz Records, 1942–[1969]: a Discography, v, vi (Copenhagen, 1963); vii, viii, i-iv*a* (Holte, Denmark, 1964–8); iv*b–d* (Copenhagen, 1969–70)
with B. Scherman and C. Hallstrom: *A Discography of Count Basie* (Copenhagen, 1969)
A Discography of Thelonious Monk & Bud Powell (Copenhagen, 1969)

BIBLIOGRAPHY

Obituary, B. Englund, *Orkester journalen*, l/1 (1982), 2

Jerome, Jerry (*b* New York, 19 June 1912). Tenor saxophonist. He played in dance bands to pay his fees as a medical student. After accepting Harry Reser's invitation to play in the Clicquot Club Eskimos (1935) he gave up studying to become a full-time musician, and made his first recording with Reser in 1936. He played clarinet and tenor saxophone with Glenn Miller (1936–7), with whom he also recorded, before working as a tenor saxophonist with Red Norvo (1937–8). He was a member of the house band of the New York radio station WNEW until 1938, when he replaced Bud Freeman in Benny Goodman's band. Jerome made several recordings with Lionel Hampton (1939–40) and performed with Artie Shaw (1940–41), appearing with his band in the film *Second Chorus* (1940). He then worked in radio and television as a music director and conductor (NBC, 1942–6; ABC TV, 1949; WPIX TV, 1950–54) and in the artists and repertory department of Apollo Records (1946–8); he also established a successful business as a writer of advertising jingles. After retiring to Florida he continued to play at jazz concerts and festivals into the 1980s. A collection of his scores and other materials is held in the American Heritage Center at the University of Wyoming in Laramie; *see* LIBRARIES AND ARCHIVES, §2.

SELECTED RECORDINGS

As sideman: H. Reser: Top of the Town (1936, Var. 510); G. Miller: Doin' the Jive (1937, Bruns. 8062); R. Norvo: Please Be Kind (1938, Bruns. 8088); B. Goodman: Undecided (1938, Vic. 26134); The Siren's Song (1939, Vic. 26230); L. Hampton: The Munson Street Breakdown (1939, Vic. 26453); Gin for Christmas (1939, Vic. 26423); Flying Home (1940, Vic. 26595); A. Shaw: Concerto for Clarinet (1940, Vic. 36383)

BIBLIOGRAPHY

ChiltonW; *FeatherE*
D. Pomus: "The World of Doc Pomus," *Whiskey, Women, and . . .*, no.14 (1984) [incl. discography], 11

WARREN VACHÉ, SR.

Jeru. Nickname of GERRY MULLIGAN.

Jeter–Pillars Orchestra. Big band. It grew out of a sextet formed by the alto saxophonist James (L.) Jeter and the tenor saxophonist Hayes Pillars (*b* North Little Rock, AR, 30 April 1906), both of whom had played with Alphonso Trent's orchestra before it disbanded in 1933. The band was engaged in 1934 to play for the opening of the Club Plantation, St. Louis, and remained there as the house band into the mid-1940s. Its sidemen included Jimmy Blanton, Harry "Sweets" Edison, Walter Page, Sid Catlett, Floyd Smith, Jimmy Forrest, Kenny Clarke, and Jo Jones. It made four recordings for Vocalion in 1937, but none of these represented the band well. After a successful tour of the Far East and brief engagements in Chicago and New York the ensemble disbanded in the early 1950s.

BIBLIOGRAPHY

FeatherE
G. Fernett: *Swing Out: Great Negro Jazz Bands* (Midland, MI, 1970)
A. McCarthy: *Big Band Jazz* (New York and London, 1974), 120
B. Rusch: "Hayes Pillars," *Cadence*, xii/12 (1986), 17

FRANK DRIGGS

Jewel. Record label. It was owned by the Plaza Music Co., and issue began around April 1927. Most of its catalogue was also put out on Plaza's other labels, though unusual takes were sometimes released on Jewel. Its repertory contained several items of hot dance music, including material by the Original Indiana Five and the Whoopee Makers. The label was maintained after Plaza became part of the AMERICAN RECORD COMPANY, but was discontinued in 1932. It should not be confused with the label of the same name of the early 1920s which was used to issue items first put out on Grey Gull.

BIBLIOGRAPHY

J. Godrich and R. M. W. Dixon: *Blues & Gospel Records, 1902–1942* (Hatch End, nr London, 1964, rev. 2/1969, rev. and enlarged 3/1982 as R. M. W. Dixon and J. Godrich: *Blues & Gospel Records, 1902–1943*), 22
B. Rust: *The American Record Label Book* (New Rochelle, NY, 1978), 171

Ježek, Jaroslav (*b* Prague, 25 Sept 1906; *d* New York, 1 Jan 1942). Bohemian pianist, composer, arranger, and bandleader. He spent his childhood at a home for the blind and studied piano at the Prague Conservatory (1924–7). From 1927 he led an orchestra at the Osvobozené divadlo (Unbound theater) in Prague with which he recorded from 1930 to 1938; his work from this period can be heard to advantage on the album *Echoes of Prague Music Hall* (1930–38, Sup. 10132887). He emigrated to the USA in 1939. Ježek was influenced first by Jack Hylton and other English bandleaders, then by Duke Ellington. He wrote prolifically for the musical stage and was known as the "Czech Gershwin." (J. Kota: Liner notes, *Echoes of Prague Music Hall*, Sup. 10132887, 1982)

GERHARD CONRAD

JIC. *See* JAZZ INSTITUTE OF CHICAGO.

Jimbo's Bop City. Nightclub in San Francisco; *see* NIGHTCLUBS AND OTHER VENUES.

Jim Crow. Nickname of JIM ROBINSON.

Jimmy Ryan's. Nightclub in New York; *see* NIGHTCLUBS AND OTHER VENUES.

Jobim, Antonio Carlos [Tom, Ton] (*b* Rio de Janeiro, 25 Jan 1927). Brazilian songwriter, guitarist, and pianist. In 1958, as music director of Odeon Records, he persuaded the company to record João Gilberto performing one of his compositions, *Chega de saudade*. The recording was a great commercial success and launched a modification of the Brazilian samba style which became known as the bossa nova ("new wrinkle" or "new wave"). The bossa nova was popularized in the USA by Stan Getz and Charlie Byrd with their album *Jazz Samba* (1962), which included one of Jobim's best-known songs, *Desafinado*; later the same year Jobim and Gilberto appeared with them and Dizzy Gillespie at a concert in Carnegie Hall. A number of bossa nova recordings by other jazz musicians followed, many making use of Jobim's compositions, others embracing the new rhythmic idiom. Jobim acknowledges the songs of Cole Porter and the playing of Gerry Mulligan as decisive influences on his style, which avoids the use of any jarring effects, and which integrates simple but poetic lyrics with syncopated melodic figures and sophisticated cool-jazz chord progressions.

RECORDED COMPOSITIONS
(selective list)
* – with Jobim as sideman

As leader: *The Composer of "Desafinado" Plays* (1963, Verve 68547), incl. Chega de saudade; *Wave* (1967, A&M 3002); *Tide* (1967, A&M 3031); *Stone Flower* (1970, CTI 6002); *Terra Brasilis* (1980, WB 3409)

Recorded by S. Getz: *Jazz Samba* (1962, Verve 68432), incl. Desafinado, Samba de una note so; *Jazz Samba Encore* (1963, Verve 68523); **Getz/Gilberto* (1963, Verve 68545), incl. Corcovado, The Girl from Ipanema; F. Sinatra: *Francis Albert Sinatra, Antonio Carlos Jobim* (1967, Rep. 1021)

BIBLIOGRAPHY

G. Lees: "Bossa Nova: Anatomy of a Travesty," *DB*, xxx/4 (1963), 22
——: "Contrast," *DB*, xxxi/7 (1964), 14
G. Behague: "Bossa and Bossas: Recent Changes in Brazilian Urban Popular Music," *Ethnomusicology*, xvii (1973), 209 [incl. discography]
S. Rosen: "Antonio Carlos Jobim: 'Black Orpheus' was only part of the story," *GP*, xiii/5 (1974), 14
A vida de Tom Jobim: depoimento (Rio de Janeiro, n.d. [1982])

DAVID FLANAGAN

Johansen, Bjørn (John) (*b* Fredrikstad, Norway, 23 May 1940). Norwegian saxophonist. He studied in Switzerland with George Gruntz and in Copenhagen, played with Kjell Karlsen's orchestra (1958–64), and led a quartet in Oslo; among those who played under his leadership were Egil Kapstad and the drummers Sven Erik Gaardvik and Svein Christiansen. He also made recordings with Kapstad and Verden Rundt and as a leader (including *T'rubyait*, 1963, Harmoni 505–6). He received the Buddy Award from the Norwegian Jazz Federation in 1962.

BIBLIOGRAPHY

O. Angell, J. E. Vold, and E. Økland: *Jazz i Norge* (Oslo, 1975)
K. Michelsen, ed.: *Cappelens musikkleksikon* (Oslo, 1978)

VIDAR VANBERG

Johansen, Egil (*b* Oslo, 11 Jan 1934). Norwegian drummer. He was self-taught and first played piano before taking up the drums in 1950. Active chiefly as a studio musician in Stockholm, from 1954 he made numerous recordings as a sideman, often playing alongside or under the leadership of Georg Riedel or Arne Domnérus in bop groups, small swing groups, or big bands; other European musicians with whom he recorded include Harry Arnold (1957–9), Alice Babs (1957, 1959), Bengt Hallberg (1958, 1971, 1977), Jan Johansson (1960–68), and Svend Asmussen (1966, 1968–9). He also played with visiting Americans, among them Dizzy Gillespie, Eric Dolphy, Stan Getz, Lucky Thompson, and Teddy Wilson, and recorded with Herbie Mann and Ernestine Anderson (both 1956), Tony Scott (1957), Jimmy Witherspoon (1964), Thad Jones (1975, 1977), and Lee Konitz (1983). He led quintets for recordings in 1957 and 1976 and played and recorded with the Swedish Radiojazzgruppen (from 1966). He also composed and recorded for television and films.

Oral history material in *SSsv*.

BIBLIOGRAPHY

Feather–Gitler '70s
G. Holmberg: "Visst tackar Egil ja till guldet!" [Of course Egil gratefully accepts the gold!], *Orkester journalen*, xlix/2 (1981), 5

Johansson, Jan (*b* Söderhamn, Sweden, 16 Sept 1931; *d* Stockholm, 9 Nov 1968). Swedish pianist, composer, and arranger. He abandoned his engineering studies at Chalmers University of Technology, Göteborg, and played professionally from about 1955. He was a member of Gunnar Johnson's quintet (1956–9) and from 1959 of Stan Getz's quartet, with which he toured Europe the following year. From 1961 he was a pianist and arranger for Arne Domnérus's orchestra; he was also a member of the Radiojazzgruppen from its formation in 1967.

An inventive, individual jazz pianist, Johansson won an international reputation about 1960. He gained a particularly large audience through his recordings of folk music from Sweden, Russia, Hungary, and other countries, which he interpreted with a unique sensibility. He was also a highly original composer and arranger: he contributed several works to the Swedish Radiojazzgruppen, including the large-scale *Musik i Norrköping* (1967) for symphony orchestra and jazz musicians, and frequently wrote arrangements for films, ballets, and television.

SELECTED RECORDINGS

As leader (all recorded for Megafon): *8 bitar Johansson* [Johansson in 8 pieces] (1961, 1); *Innertrio* (1962, 2); *M* (1965–7, 24–5); *300.000* (1967–8, 18)

As sideman with A. Domnérus (all recorded for Sveriges Radio): *Höstspelor* [Autumn games] (1966–8, 1058); *Vårdkasar* [Beacons], (1967–8, 1071)

BIBLIOGRAPHY

E. Kjellberg: "Johansson, Jan," *Svenskt biografiskt lexikon* (Stockholm, 1918–) [incl. complete discography, list of works]
——: "Johansson, Jan," *Sohlmans musiklexikon* (Stockholm, rev. and enlarged 2/1975–9 ed. H. Åstrand)
——: "Jan Johansson och bluesen," *Orkester journalen*, xlvi/12 (1978), 12
——: *Svensk jazzhistoria: en översikt* [Swedish jazz history: an overview] (Stockholm, 1985)

ERIK KJELLBERG

Johnson, Alphonso (*b* Philadelphia, *c*1951). Electric bass guitarist. After playing double bass and trombone he took up the electric bass guitar around 1968. He worked with Horace Silver, and recorded with Woody Herman (1972), Chuck Mangione (1973), and Chet Baker (1973). As a member of Weather Report from 1974 he played on three of the group's recordings and toured with it until 1976; typical examples of his syncopated ostinatos may be heard on *Cucumber Slumber* from the album *Mysterious Traveler* (*c*1974, Col. KC32494). He also recorded with Cannonball Adderley and Eddie Henderson (both 1975), Billy Cobham (1976–7, with whom he toured Europe), Flora Purim (1976), the Crusaders (*c*1979), an all-star group led by Freddie Hubbard and Joe Henderson (1980), and Arthur Blythe (1984). (A. J. Smith: "Alphonso Johnson: Barometric Bump in Weather Report Grind," *DB*, xliii/2 (1976), 14 [incl. discography])

Johnson, Bill [William Manuel] **(i)** (*b* ?Talladega, AL, 10 Aug 1872 or 1874; *d* New Braunfels, TX, 3 Dec 1972). Double bass player. He began as a guitarist, but by 1900 was active in New Orleans as a double bass player at Tom Anderson's Annex and with the Peerless and Eagle bands; he also performed on tuba with brass bands. In 1908, with a small group of musicians, he toured across the Southwest to Los Angeles, thus becoming the first New Orleans jazzman to carry the emerging style of music to the West Coast; the band was known under several names, including the ORIGINAL CREOLE BAND. The group toured widely, and finally disbanded in 1918. In 1922 Johnson worked with King Oliver in Chicago at the Lincoln Gardens (where he also played banjo; for illustration *see* OLIVER, KING); he left Oliver the following year, but continued to be active in Chicago throughout the 1930s, performing there with Bunk Johnson as late as 1947. He ceased to play in the 1950s, and retired to Texas. Johnson's classic style is heard to advantage in *Bull Fiddle Blues/Blue Washboard Stomp* (Vic. 21552), which he recorded with Johnny Dodds's Washboard Band in 1928. Anecdote credits him with having been the first to employ the plucked-string style of playing; an alternation of bowed notes and pizzicato can be heard on his recordings of the late 1920s. He played with propulsive rhythmic power, and in moderate tempos used triplet figures and lively syncopation. His historical importance rests upon his role as a pioneer in disseminating the distinctive style of New Orleans double bass players.

BIBLIOGRAPHY

ChiltonW

F. Ramsey, Jr., and C. E. Smith, eds.: *Jazzmen: the Story of Hot Jazz Told in the Lives of the Men who Created it* (New York, 1939/*R*1977), 20

ALDEN ASHFORTH

Johnson, Bill [William K.] **(ii)** (*b* Lexington, KY, *c*1905; *d* Lexington, sum. 1955). Banjoist, guitarist, and singer. He performed with local bands in and around Louisville, Kentucky, then late in 1926 traveled to New York with the Dixie Ramblers. After playing the following year in a band led by the drummer George Howe he worked with Luis Russell from 1927 to 1932. During this period he also made recordings with King Oliver, including *Slow and Steady* (1928, Bruns. 4469), on which he may be heard playing both guitar and banjo. Occasionally he also recorded as a singer, as on Henry "Red" Allen's *You might get better, but you'll never get well* (1930, Vic. 38140). After working with Fess Williams in 1933–4 and as a freelance in the late 1930s Johnson ceased to work as a full-time musician, and returned to Lexington.

based on *ChiltonW*

Johnson, Bill [William] **(iii)** (*b* Jacksonville, FL, 30 Sept 1912; *d* New York, 5 July 1960). Alto saxophonist, clarinetist, and arranger. He first played piano, then took up alto saxophone at the age of 16. After working with lesser-known bands he studied in conservatories in Wisconsin and Illinois, then attended Marquette University; while in Milwaukee he played with Jabbo Smith and others. He worked with Baron Lee and Tiny Bradshaw before joining Erskine Hawkins in 1936, with whom he performed and made recordings (including *Bear Mash Blues*, 1942, Bb 300813) into the early 1940s. He also wrote several arrangements for the band, and composed *Tuxedo Junction* with Hawkins.

based on *ChiltonW*

Johnson, Budd [Albert J.] (*b* Dallas, 14 Dec 1910; *d* Kansas City, MO, 20 Oct 1984). Tenor saxophonist and arranger, brother of Keg Johnson. In 1929 he toured with Terrence Holder, after which he performed with Jesse Stone and George E. Lee. He moved to Chicago, where he played with Louis Armstrong (1932–3) and Earl Hines (1934–6, 1937, 1938–42), the bandleader Gus Arnheim (1937), and Fletcher and Horace Henderson (both 1938); he also worked as an arranger for Hines (from 1938), Billy Eckstine, Buddy Rich, and Woody Herman, among others. In the 1940s he was associated with several leaders, including Don Redman (1943), Dizzy Gillespie (mid–1940s), J. C. Heard (1946), and Sy Oliver (1947). He led his own groups during the 1950s and performed in Europe with Snub Mosley (1952) and in Asia with Benny Goodman (1957). He played with Quincy Jones (1960) and Count Basie (1961–2) and again worked with Hines (1964–9), with whom he toured the USA, Europe, the USSR, and South America. In 1969 he formed the JPJ Quartet with Oliver Jackson, Dill Jones, and Bill Pemberton; it made several recordings before it disbanded in 1975. He toured Europe with Charlie Shavers (1970) and played intermittently with Sy Oliver. In 1974 he was the music director for the New York Jazz Repertory Company's *Musical Life of Charlie Parker*, with which he traveled to Europe. He appeared in the documentary film on Kansas City jazz *Last of the Blue Devils*, made over the course of five years (1974–9). During the 1970s and 1980s he played at many international jazz festivals and taught music at several universities.

Johnson was one of the most important musicians in the emergence of bop, writing arrangements for the big bands of Hines, Eckstine, Herman, and Gillespie, which had a seminal influence on the new style, and playing with Gillespie in the first small bop group (1944). Although principally a tenor saxophonist Johnson also played and recorded on soprano, alto, and baritone saxophones.

Oral history material in *NjR* (JOHP).

SELECTED RECORDINGS

* arranged by Johnson

As leader: *Ya! Ya!* (1964, Argo S736)

As sideman: E. Hines: *Grand Terrace Shuffle (1939, Bb 10351); *Father Steps In (1939, Bb 10377); *Riff Medley/*XYZ (1939, Bb 10531); L. Hampton: Till Tom Special (1940, Vic. 26604); E. Hines: Call me Happy (1940, Bb 10835); B. Eckstine: Blowin' the Blues Away (1944, DeLuxe 2001); E. Hines: *Blues and Things* (1967, Master Jazz 8101); on *L'aventure du jazz: musique du film* (1970, Jazz Odyssey 0005-6), Panassié Stompers: Montauban Blues; JPJ Quartet: *JPJ Quartet* (1973, RCA LPL1-5033)

BIBLIOGRAPHY

ChiltonW; *FeatherE*

H. Panassié: "Budd Johnson," *BHcF*, no.29 (1953), 3

F. Driggs: "Budd Johnson: Ageless Jazzman," *JR*, iii/9 (1960), 4; iv/1 (1961), 14 [incl. discography]

H. Panassié: "Charlie Shavers et Budd Johnson," *BHcF*, no.194 (1970), 3

Y. Fournier: "Budd Johnson," *Blues et Jazz*, no.5 (n.d. [?1971]), 38

S. Dance: *The World of Earl Hines* (New York, 1977) [interviews], 202

J. Evensmo: *The Tenor Saxophones of Budd Johnson, Cecil Scott, Elmer Williams, Dick Wilson, 1927–1942* (n.p. [Oslo], n.d. [?1977]) [discography]

G. Colombé: "Budd Johnson Backstage," *JJI*, xxxiv/1 (1981), 12

——: "An Appreciation of Budd Johnson," *JJI*, xxxviii/1 (1985), 14

EDDIE COOK

Johnson, Buddy [Woodrow Wilson] (*b* Darlington, SC, 10 Jan 1915; *d* New York, 9 Feb 1977). Pianist and bandleader. He toured Europe as a pianist in the Tramp Band with the *Cotton Club Revue* and in 1939 he returned to New York, where he recorded with his own group (1939–42). He then formed a big band, which held long-term engagements at the Savoy Ballroom, toured, and became popular with rhythm-and-blues enthusiasts. He again made recordings as a leader from the mid-1940s until the late 1950s (including *Shufflin' and Rollin'*, 1952, Decca 28293) and in the 1960s he led a small group. Among his sidemen at different times were Don Stovall, Shad Collins, Dan Minor, Geezil Minerve, and Slide Hampton. (D. Penny and T. Burke: "Buddy Johnson: the Decca Years (1939–1952)," *Blues & Rhythm: the Gospel Truth*, no.1 (1984), 12)

based on *ChiltonW*

Johnson, Bunk [Willie, William Geary] (*b* New Orleans, ?27 Dec 1889; *d* New Iberia, LA, 7 July 1949). Trumpeter. Until recently he was thought to have been born in 1879. Marquis (1978) argues convincingly that he was far younger than he claimed, thus casting doubt on Johnson's assertions that he performed with the orchestras of the cornetists Adam Olivier and Buddy Bolden during the 1890s and made many tours with circuses, minstrel shows, and ocean-liner bands in the early 1900s. He was active in New Orleans from 1910 to 1914, working with the Eagle Band, led by the trumpeter Frankie Dusen, and other groups, then traveled widely. By 1934 dental problems had largely forced his retirement from music, and he settled in New Iberia as a field laborer. There he was rediscovered by Bill Russell and Fred Ramsey, who had been directed to him by Louis Armstrong and Clarence Williams as a

Bunk Johnson's band at the Stuyvesant Casino, New York, 1945: (left to right) Jim Robinson (trombone), Alcide "Slow Drag" Pavageau (double bass), Johnson (trumpet), Baby Dodds (drums), and George Lewis (i) (clarinet)

source for research. The resulting information on Johnson in the book *Jazzmen* (1939) stimulated interest in his music and he resumed playing. He was first recorded in 1942 in New Orleans, where he mainly worked, though by late 1947 he had spent four periods performing in New York. Apart from a brief engagement with Sidney Bechet in 1945 he led his own groups, and produced a substantial corpus of recordings.

Johnson's "second career" of the 1940s caused stereotyped notions of the prehistory of New Orleans jazz to be reconsidered. His insistence on performing rags and current popular songs (instead of blues and the simpler early New Orleans standards) and his clear preference for playing with schooled musicians challenged the concept of early jazz as an unspoiled folk art. But conclusions about the earliest jazz trumpet styles must be drawn cautiously from his recorded work, for his best solos and ensemble lead parts resemble those of Louis Armstrong, by whom they may have been influenced.

Oral history material in *LNT*.

See also BLUES, §8.

SELECTED RECORDINGS

Weary Blues (1942, Jazz Man 9); Pallet on the Floor (1942, Jazz Man 16); Tiger Rag/See See Rider (1944, AM 251); Careless Love/Down by the Riverside (1944, GTJ 63); Milenberg Joys/Days Beyond Recall (1945, BN 564); Maryland, my Maryland (1945, Decca 25132); *Bunk Johnson: the Last Testament* (1947, Col. GL520)

BIBLIOGRAPHY

ChartersJ
W. Russell and S. W. Smith: "New Orleans Music," *Jazzmen: the Story of Hot Jazz Told in the Lives of the Men who Created it*, ed. F. Ramsey, Jr., and C. E. Smith (New York, 1939/*R*1977), 23
B. Johnson: "Bunk Johnson's Talking Records," *Record Changer* (1943), June [unpaginated]; July, 5 [interview]
V. Thompson: *The Musical Scene* (New York, 1945), 28
I. L. Jacobs: "Bunk at the Stuyvesant Casino," *American Jazz*, no.2 (1946), 2
M. Berger: "Bunk Johnson and Jazz Pre-history," *Frontiers of Jazz*, ed. R. de Toledano (New York, 1947, rev. 2/1962) [colln of previously pubd articles], 91
H. Drob: "Bunk Johnson: an Appreciation," *Record Changer*, xi/10 (1952), 3; contd as "Bunk Johnson: his Last Date," xi/11 (1952), 3
E. Souchon: "Weeks Hall and Bunk Johnson," *SL*, xv/9–10 (1964), 16
M. Harrison: "Bunk Johnson: Notes Towards a Reassessment," *JM*, xiii/1 (1967), 8
M. Williams: *Jazz Masters of New Orleans* (New York and London, 1967/*R*1978), 222
E. Lambert: "William Russell's New Orleans Recordings," *JM*, no.183 (1970), 3
P. A. Larsen: "Bunk is History: Bunk Johnson's First Recorded Words," *Sv*, no.43 (1972), 4
T. Bethell: "The Revival of Bunk Johnson," *MR*, ii/9 (1975), 1
L. C. Johnson: "Bunk in Brief," *MR*, ii/9 (1975), 3
T. Bethell: *George Lewis: a Jazzman from New Orleans* (Berkeley, CA, and London, 1977)
A. M. Sonnier, Jr.: *Willie Geary "Bunk" Johnson: the New Iberia Years* (New York, 1977) [incl. discography]
D. M. Marquis: *In Search of Buddy Bolden, First Man of Jazz* (Baton Rouge, LA, and London, 1978), 4
M. Hazeldine: "Dear Wynne: a Review of the Events of 1945–6 Concerning Bunk Johnson, Sidney Bechet, Boston and Beyond," *Fn*, xv/5 (1984), 4
A. Barrell: "The Last Testament: Letters from Bunk and Maude Johnson to Friend Don Ewell," *Fn*, xvi/3 (1985), 4
E. Kraut: *The Revival: Documents of the American Music Sessions, 1940–45* (Arcegno, nr Ascona, Switzerland, 1986)[exhibition catalogue, Festa New Orleans Music, Ascona; text in Ger. and It.]
L. Gushee: "When was Bunk Johnson Born and why should we Care?," *Jazz Archivist*, ii/2 (1987), 4
C. Hillman: *Bunk Johnson* (Tunbridge Wells, England, in preparation) [incl. discography]

J. R. TAYLOR/R

Johnson, Candy. *See* JOHNSON, FLOYD "CANDY."

Johnson, Charlie [Charles Wright; Fess] (*b* Philadelphia, 21 Nov 1891; *d* New York, 13 Dec 1959). Pianist and bandleader. In October 1925 he began playing at Smalls' Paradise, New York (which remained his base for the next ten years), leading an orchestra that he had formed in Atlantic City, New Jersey; Sidney De Paris was its principal trumpeter. In the late 1920s Johnson's was one of the very best bands, and its few recordings (particularly the superb *The Boy in the Boat*) show that it was comparable with the orchestra of Duke Ellington and Fletcher Henderson. However, Johnson was poorly promoted, and he did not record after the onset of the Depression in 1929; in 1938 he ceased full-time work as a bandleader, and poor health restricted his activities in the 1950s. Sam Wooding, who heard him perform in Atlantic City around 1917, described Johnson as the first pianist to play in a modern style, as opposed to ragtime. His sidemen included such important players as Jabbo Smith, Jimmy Harrison, Benny Carter, and Roy Eldridge. He should not be confused with the trumpeter Charlie Johnson (*d* 1937) who played with Ellington.

SELECTED RECORDINGS

(all recorded for Victor)

Birmingham Black Bottom (1927, 20551); Charleston is the Best Dance after All (1928, 21491); The Boy in the Boat/Walk that Thing (1928, 21712); Harlem Drag (1929, 38059)

BIBLIOGRAPHY

J. R. T. Davies and L. Wright: "Charlie Johnson," *Sv*, no.35 (1971), 184 [discography]
A. McCarthy: *Big Band Jazz* (New York and London, 1974), 41
L. Wright: "Charlie Johnson," *Sv*, (1978), no.75, p.99; no.77, p.190

CHIP DEFFAA

Johnson, Dick [Richard Brown] (*b* Brockton, MA, 1 Dec 1925). Alto saxophonist, clarinetist, and flutist. He played piano in his childhood, clarinet from the age of 16, and alto saxophone from 19. He studied for two years at the New England Conservatory and after the war worked in and around Boston for a time. He played with Charlie Spivak (1952–4) and then performed and made recordings with his own bop quartets (1956–7, including *Most Likely* (1957, Riv. 253), on which Johnson played alto saxophone); Dave McKenna was one of his sidemen in 1957, and the two men recorded together again in a trio and a quartet under McKenna's leadership (1973, 1980), in another quartet under Johnson's leadership (1979), as a duo (1980), and as sidemen in Woody Herman's group (1980). Johnson also appeared at the Newport Jazz Festival with Eddie Costa (1957) and recorded with the big band of the Berklee College of Music under Herb Pomeroy (1959–60). (*FeatherE*)

Johnson, Dink [Ollie, Oliver] (*b* Biloxi, MS, 28 Oct 1892; *d* Portland, OR, 29 Nov 1954). Pianist, clarinetist, and drummer. He began his career as a pianist in the Storyville district of New Orleans, then in 1913 joined the Original Creole Band in California as a drummer. He left the band after a year but stayed in Los Angeles, where he played drums briefly with Jelly Roll Morton and recorded on clarinet with Kid Ory's band Spikes' Seven Pods of Pepper (*Ory's Creole Trombone/Society Blues*, 1922, Nordskog 3009). In the early 1920s he led the Five Hounds of Jazz, renamed the Los Angeles Six for a residency in Chicago in 1924. He then worked in clubs throughout California and played piano in his sister's bar in Las Vegas. He ceased full-time performing in the 1940s but continued to make recordings as a pianist (1946–50), including a number of duos with the drummer John Joseph (1948, first issued on B. Campbell and D. Johnson: *The Professors*, 1964, Euphonic 1201–2). (*ChiltonW*; *FeatherE*)

Oral history material in *LNT*.

KARL KOENIG

Johnson, Floyd "Candy" (*b* Madison Co., IL, 1 May 1922; *d* June 1981). Tenor and baritone saxophonist. He began playing drums around 1935, but changed to alto and then tenor saxophone. While studying at Wilberforce College he performed with the student band, then joined Ernie Fields and Tiny Bradshaw before working as a ballad soloist with Andy Kirk (1942–7). Later he led his own group in Detroit, where he returned after working with Count Basie (1951–3). He made a number of recordings on tenor and baritone saxophone as a member of Bill Doggett's band (1958–64, including *High and Wide*, 1958–9, King 633). Johnson then ceased full-time performing until 1971, when he worked with Milt Buckner in France (1971) and Europe (1973); his playing may be heard to advantage on *Midnight Slows*, iii (1973, BB 333055), which he recorded as a member of a cooperative band with Buckner, Arnett Cobb, and others. He also led a small group at Bowling Green (Ohio) State University, and in 1974 he briefly replaced Paul Gonsalves in Duke Ellington's orchestra.

BIBLIOGRAPHY

H. Panassié: "'Candy' Johnson," *BHcF*, no.237 (1974), 3
C. Battestini and J.-P. Battestini: "Floyd 'Candy' Johnson (st, sb)," *BHcF*, no.319 (1984), 4

HOWARD RYE

Johnson, Frank [Francis Walter] (*b* Melbourne, Australia, 22 May 1927). Australian trumpeter and bandleader. In 1945 he was one of the founders of a traditional-jazz band that became known as Frank Johnson's Fabulous Dixielanders. Its style was initially influenced by that of Graeme Bell's band, and Johnson promoted it tirelessly: it began to work regularly in 1947, and recorded extensively in 1949–50. *Swing it out there* (1950, Parl. A7751) is representative of the distinctive, exuberant, and "larrikin" sound that brought the group remarkable success. It made numerous radio broadcasts and concert appearances before disbanding around 1956. Johnson continued to lead groups in Melbourne until the late 1970s, when he began working as an occasional freelance in Brisbane.

BIBLIOGRAPHY

A. Bissett: *Black Roots, White Flowers: a History of Jazz in Australia* (Sydney, 1979)
M. Williams: *The Australian Jazz Explosion* (London and elsewhere, 1981), 8
B. Johnson: "Johnson, Francis Walter," *The Oxford Companion to Australian Jazz* (Melbourne, Australia, 1987)

JEFF PRESSING (with JOHN WHITEOAK)

Johnson, Freddy (*b* New York, 12 March 1904; *d* New York, 24 March 1961). Pianist. He formed his own band in 1924, then the following year worked with Elmer Snowden. After playing with Noble Sissle he joined Sam Wooding, with whom he toured Europe in 1928. The following year he went to Paris, where he worked as a soloist and led his own band, assisted by Arthur Briggs. With this ensemble Johnson made several recordings, including his own composition *Harlem Bound* (1933, Bruns. A500340). Thereafter he played in Belgium and in Amsterdam, where he was associated with Coleman Hawkins and Willie Lewis; he also opened his own club, La Cubana. He was arrested by the Nazis in 1941 and after being imprisoned in Germany was repatriated in 1944. On his return he worked with George James, then played with Garvin Bushell's band at Tony Pastor's club. During the late 1940s and the 1950s he was active mainly as a piano teacher and vocal coach, but also held a number of residencies. (A. McCarthy: *Big Band Jazz* (New York and London, 1974), 311)

based on *ChiltonW*

Johnson, Gene [Eugene McClane] (*b* Hartford, CT, 1902; *d* New York, Feb 1958). Alto saxophonist and clarinetist. He worked in New York from the mid-1920s with several bands, including Charlie Skeete's and Bill Brown's Brownies. From 1930 to 1937 he performed and made recordings with Claude Hopkins (including *Mush Mouth*, 1932, Col. 2674D), and during this period he occasionally played baritone saxophone. Later he played with Chick Webb and Erskine Hawkins; he also worked as a drummer. During the 1950s Johnson was a member of Machito's band.

based on *ChiltonW*

Johnson, George (*b* Grand Rapids, MI, 25 April 1913). Alto saxophonist and clarinetist. After working with Zack Whyte and Benny Carter in the early 1930s he sailed to Europe with the entertainer Freddy Taylor in 1935. Later that year he went to Paris, where he joined Willie Lewis's band and made recordings with the pianist Garnet Clark; *Rosetta* (Gramophone K7618), offers a fine example of Johnson's beautiful tone in the lower register of the clarinet. In 1937 he formed his own band, with which he played residencies in several Parisian clubs. He then returned to the USA (1939) and worked with Frankie Newton (1940–41), Raymond Scott at CBS (1942), John Kirby's sextet (1943–5), and Rex Stewart (1946). In late 1946 he led his own band in Spain, and remained in Europe (other than a visit to New York in the mid-1950s), leading groups in France, Spain, Switzerland, and Holland, where he eventually settled. Johnson should not be confused with the white tenor saxophonist who was a member of the Wolverines.

based on *ChiltonW*

Johnson, Gus (, Jr.) (*b* Tyler, TX, 15 Nov 1913). Drummer. After graduating from high school he moved to Kansas City, where he formed a semiprofessional vocal quartet, the Four Rhythm Aces, and also played double bass. He first worked as a full-time musician in 1935, playing drums with Jo Jones's sextet in Omaha, but left Jones for the trumpeter Lloyd Hunter. He joined the pianist Ernest "Speck" Redd in Iowa in 1937, then returned to Kansas City to play with Jay McShann (1938–43) in a band that included Charlie Parker. After World War II he worked in Chicago with the trumpeter Jesse Miller and Eddie "Cleanhead" Vinson, and in New York with Earl Hines (1947) and Cootie Williams. Johnson first played with Count Basie for two weeks in 1948, and re-joined him in 1950, first to play in his small group, then in the big band. He played on the important *Dance Session* recordings (1952–4) before having to leave the band because of illness; his aggressive but fluid and dance-like style made him the best drummer Basie had after Jo Jones. From early 1955 he worked in backup groups for singers, including Lena Horne and (for nine years) Ella Fitzgerald, but continued to play with a wide variety of mainstream bands, notably Buck Clayton's. He recorded with Zoot Sims (1956), Al Cohn (1961), Woody Herman and Gerry Mulligan (both 1962), Ralph Sutton (1969), Jay McShann (1972, 1977), Eddie "Lockjaw" Davis (1974), Basie (1979), and Peanuts Hucko (1983). He also worked with Stan Getz and the World's Greatest Jazz Band. He settled in Denver in 1973.

Oral history material in *NjR* (JOHP).

SELECTED RECORDINGS

As sideman: J. McShann: 'Fore Day Rider/Hootie's Ignorant Oil (1941, Decca 8635); C. Basie: *Dance Session* (1952–4, Clef 626, 647); R. Stewart and C. Williams: *The Big Challenge* (1957, Jzt. 1268); B. Clayton: *Buck and Buddy Blow the Blues* (1961, Swingville 2030); E. Fitzgerald: *Ella in Hollywood* (1961, Verve 4052); G. Mulligan: *The Gerry Mulligan Quartet* (1962, Verve 68466); L. Brown: *Inspired Abandon* (1965, Imp. 89); World's Greatest Jazz Band: ***World's Greatest Jazz Band of Yank Lawson and Bob Haggart in Concert at Massey Hall*** (1972, World Jazz 3)

BIBLIOGRAPHY

ChiltonW; *FeatherE*; *Feather '60s*; *Feather–Gitler '70s*
"Gus Johnson talks to Valerie Wilmer," *JM*, vii/10 (1961), 12
S. Dance: *The World of Count Basie* (New York and London, 1980) [colln of previously pubd interviews], 284
C. Sheridan: *Count Basie: a Bio-discography* (Westport, CT, and London, 1986)

CHRIS SHERIDAN

Johnson, Howard (William) [Swan] **(i)** (*b* Boston, 1 Jan 1908). Alto saxophonist. He played with bands in Boston before moving to New York, where he worked with Fess Williams, James P. Johnson, and others. In the early 1930s he played with Elmer Snowden before joining Benny Carter (1932). Thereafter he played with Teddy Hill for several years, visiting Europe in 1937. While in Paris he made recordings (including *Nobody's Blues but my Own*, Swing 39) with Dicky Wells. In the early 1940s Johnson played with Claude Hopkins, toured the South in Carter's band, accompanying Maxine Sullivan, and worked as an arranger. From 1946 to 1948 he was a member of Dizzy Gillespie's big band. He remained active through the 1950s and 1960s, playing regularly with Lem Johnson. During the 1970s he performed with the Harlem Blues and Jazz Band, recorded with Panama Francis's Savoy Sultans (1979), and worked as a freelance. In 1972 he took part in a reunion of former members of Carter's orchestra at the Newport Jazz Festival New York. (S. Dance: *The World of Swing* (New York, 1974) [colln of previously pubd interviews], 241)

based on *ChiltonW*

Johnson, Howard (Lewis) (ii) (*b* Montgomery, AL, 7 Aug 1941). Tuba player and baritone saxophonist. He was brought up in Ohio, and taught himself music, playing baritone saxophone from the age of 13 and tuba from the age of 14. He first worked as a merchant seaman, and in England met John Surman, who was influenced by his saxophone playing. After settling in New York in 1963, he worked with Charles Mingus (1964, 1965–6), Hank Crawford (1965), and Archie Shepp (1966), and in 1966 began an association with Gil Evans which has extended to the mid-1980s. Also in 1966 he formed Substructure, a group which included four tubas and performed with the folksinger Taj Mahal. Johnson wrote arrangements for Maria Muldaur and for the blues musicians Paul Butterfield and B. B. King around this time. In the late 1970s he led the house band for the NBC television show "Saturday Night Live" and formed a new all-tuba group, Gravity, with which he performed in New York and toured Europe (1977). Later he recorded with Crawford (1983–4), Jack DeJohnette's Special Edition (1984) and Jimmy Heath (1985).

Although he has worked frequently as a saxophonist and has recorded on flugelhorn with Evans and Gato Barbieri, it is as a tuba player that Johnson has made most impact. In demonstrating that his invention and range are not limited by its cumbersome nature, he has given it a new role as a solo instrument and pointed the way for other important exponents such as Bob Stewart.

SELECTED RECORDINGS

As sideman: C. Mingus: *Charles Mingus* (1965, Charles Mingus 0013–14); A. Shepp: *Mama too Tight* (1966, Imp. 9134); G. Evans: *Svengali* (1973, Atl. 1643); J. DeJohnette: *Album Album* (1984, ECM 1280)

BIBLIOGRAPHY

Feather–Gitler '70s
D. Kastin: "Howard Johnson: Substructural Master," *DB*, xlv/9 (1978), 17
B. Priestley: *Mingus: a Critical Biography* (London, Melbourne, Australia, and New York, 1982), 166, 196
L. Jeske: "Howard Johnson: Center of Gravity," *DB*, l/1 (1983), 29 [incl. discography]

BRIAN PRIESTLEY

Johnson, James P(rice) (*b* New Brunswick, NJ, 1 Feb 1894; *d* New York, 17 Nov 1955). Pianist and composer. He first learned music from his mother, singing songs at the piano. In 1908 the family settled in New York, where Johnson was exposed to ragtime, blues, show music, and the classical piano virtuosos of the day. He took lessons with Bruto Giannini, and also learned from such contemporary ragtime pianists as Abba Labba (Richard McLean) and Eubie Blake, who stimulated him to develop an orchestral approach to the keyboard. By 1913 he had begun to work at clubs in the black section of Hell's Kitchen in New York known as "The Jungles," where laborers from the South danced most of the night to the accompaniment of solo piano. It was in these dance halls that Johnson developed many of the rhythmically driving shout pieces for which he later became famous. In 1917 he published the first of some 200 songs, *Mama's Blues* and *Stop it, Joe*, and recorded his earliest piano rolls.

In the 1920s Johnson's career flourished. He recorded a series of inspired solo performances of his own compositions, beginning in 1921 with *The Harlem Strut*, *Carolina Shout* (his best-known work for piano), and *Keep off the Grass*, and culminating in 1930 with *Jingles* and *You've Got to be Modernistic*. It was virtuoso pieces of this sort that he played in competitive cutting contests with his contemporaries, and he soon came to be regarded as the best of the Harlem pianists. He recorded with many blues singers of the day, notably Bessie Smith and Ethel Waters. In 1923 Johnson wrote his first Broadway musical, *Runnin' Wild*, which ran for 213 performances; its score included the successful songs *Old Fashioned Love* and *The Charleston*. He continued, with mixed success, to write for the Broadway stage throughout his career, producing more than a dozen scores. At the same time he began composing large-scale orchestral works based loosely on classical models and incorporating elements of jazz. The first of these, *Yamekraw*, a piano rhapsody, was orchestrated by William Grant Still and was performed in Carnegie Hall in 1927 with Fats Waller as soloist. The following year Waller and Johnson collaborated on the revue *Keep Shufflin'*, each man composing different songs. They also performed on two pianos for the show and during its intervals, and subsequently recorded as the Louisiana Sugar Babes (with Jabbo Smith and Garvin Bushell from the pit band), Waller playing organ in contrast to Johnson's piano.

During the Depression Johnson turned his attention increasingly to the composition of large-scale works. He wrote his *Harlem Symphony* in 1932, followed by a piano concerto, *Jassamine*, in 1934 and *Symphony in Brown* in 1935; *De Organizer*, a one-act "blues opera" with a libretto by Langston Hughes, received one performance at Carnegie Hall in 1940. A true assessment of this music is hampered by the loss of many of the scores, but some commentators have questioned the success of Johnson's orchestral compositions.

With the revival of traditional jazz in the late 1930s and 1940s, Johnson began again to appear frequently in clubs and concerts, and to take part in recording sessions. He led a recording band for the Blue Note label, and in 1947 performed in the radio series "This is Jazz." Details of his final years are sketchy. He suffered several minor strokes in the 1940s, and a major one in 1951 which left him incapacitated until his death.

Despite his great versatility, Johnson's main contribution was as a jazz pianist. He perfected the style known as stride piano, which infused the midwestern ragtime of Scott Joplin and his contemporaries with elements of jazz, blues, and popular song, as well as greatly increasing the demands on the pianist. Johnson's stride pieces share with ragtime a more or less composed, multistrain format and an oom-pah bass figure. However, he often makes use of broken 10ths and other deviations in the left hand, while his right-hand patterns depart from the stereotyped syncopations and broken chord melodies of ragtime (both of these features are evident in *Carolina Shout*, ex.1). Furthermore, he never repeats strains without varying them. Perhaps most importantly, the rhythmic feel of his style is more relaxed and closer to the swing of jazz than to the even eighth-notes of ragtime. At the same time he generates more

Ex.1 *Carolina Shout* (1921, OK 4495); transcr. W. Rouder

rhythmic intensity by using shifts of register, riffs, and blues-like clusters in the treble to imitate the call-and-response patterns of black church music. It is this rhythmicization of his musical ideas that, by allowing for variation and improvisation, lies at the heart of the new freedom of his style. Thus, like his New Orleans contemporary Jelly Roll Morton, Johnson developed a viable jazz piano style by fusing the diverse musical influences of his youth. He exercised a major influence on succeeding generations of jazz pianists, from his friend and pupil Fats Waller through Count Basie, Duke Ellington, Art Tatum, and Teddy Wilson to modern players such as Erroll Garner, Jaki Byard, and Thelonious Monk. Johnson's private collection was donated by his family to Fisk University; *see* LIBRARIES AND ARCHIVES, §2.

For illustrations *see* FOSTER, POPS, and MEZZROW, MEZZ.

WORKS

(selective list; complete listing in Brown, 1982, 1986)

STAGE

(unless otherwise stated, dates are those of first New York performance)

Runnin' Wild (C. Mack), Washington, 25 Aug 1923 [incl. Old Fashioned Love, The Charleston]; Mooching Along (J. Schipp, C. Mack, J. Johnson), 1925; Keep Shufflin' (H. Creamer, A. Razaf), addl music F. Waller, C. Todd, 27 Feb 1928; Messin' Around (P. Bradford), 22 April 1929; Shuffle Along of 1930 (A. Razaf, H. Creamer), addl music F. Waller, April 1930; Kitchen Mechanics Revue (A. Razaf), 1930; Sugar Hill (J. Trent), 25 Dec 1931; Harlem Hotcha (A. Razaf), 1932; Policy Kings (L. Douglass), 30 Dec 1939; De Organizer (blues opera, 1, L. Hughes), 31 May 1940; Dreamy Kid (opera, 1, after E. O'Neill), *c*1942; Meet Miss Jones (F. Miller), 1947

INSTRUMENTAL

Orch: Yamekraw, rhapsody, pf, orch, 1927; Harlem Sym., 1932; Jassamine Conc., A♭, pf, orch, 1934; Sym. in Brown, 1935; Old Time Suite, 1942; American Sym. Suite (Sym. Suite on the St. Louis Blues), ?1942; Ode to Dorie Miller, *c*1945; Two Tone Poems (Love, Reflections), *c*1945; Improvisations on Deep River, 1946; City of Steel (Etude); Fantasia, c; Manhattan Street Scene, ballet; Mississippi Moon, sym. poem

Pf: Gut Stomp, *c*1914–17; Mule Walk, *c*1914–17; Caprice Rag, 1917; Daintiness Rag, 1917; Over the Bars (Steeplechase Rag), 1917; Carolina Shout, *c*1917; Eccentricity Waltz, 1918; The Harlem Strut, 1921; Keep off the Grass, 1921; Scoutin' Around, 1923; Toddlin' Home, 1923; Weeping Blues, 1923; Worried and Lonesome Blues, 1923; Jingles, 1926; Snowy Morning Blues, 1927; Feelin' Blue, 1929; Riffs, 1929; You've Got to be Modernistic, 1929–30; A-flat Dream, 1939; Blueberry Rhyme, 1939; Lonesome Reverie, 1939; Carolina Balmoral, 1943; J. P. Boogie, 1943; Jersey Sweet, 1944; Just Before Daybreak, ?1945

SONGS

Mama's Blues, 1917; Stop it, Joe, 1917; It takes love to cure the heart's disease, 1921; Ivy, 1922; Ukulele Blues, 1922; The Charleston, 1923; Don't never tell nobody what your good man can do, 1923; Ginger Brown, 1923; Love Bug, 1923; Old Fashioned Love, 1923; Open your Heart, 1923; Alabama Stomp, 1926; If I could be with you one hour tonight, 1926

Give me the sunshine, 1928; 'Sippi, 1928; Skiddle de skow, 1929; Sorry that I strayed away from you, 1929; You don't understand, 1929; Go Harlem, 1930; A Porter's Love Song to a Chambermaid, 1930; Ain'tcha got music, 1932; Harlem Woogie, 1938; You, you, you, 1938; You can't lose a broken heart, 1947

Principal publishers: Bradford, Harms, MCA, Mills, Williams

SELECTED RECORDINGS

Collections: *James P. Johnson* (1921–39, Col. CL1780)[JPJ]
Original James P. Johnson (1943–5, FW 2850)[OJPJ]

As unaccompanied soloist: The Harlem Strut (1921, Black Swan 2026); Keep off the Grass/Carolina Shout (1921, OK 4495); Mule Walk, Blueberry Rhyme (1939), first issued on JPJ; Worried and Lonesome Blues (1923, Col. A3950); Scouting Around (1923, OK 4937); Snowy Morning Blues (1927, Col. 14204D); You've Got to be Modernistic/Jingles (1930, Bruns. 4762); Caprice Rag (1943, BN 26); Liza (1945), first issued on OJPJ; Daintiness Rag/Ain'tcha got music (1947, Cir.[USA] 3005)

As leader [some as "Jimmy" or "Jimmie" Johnson]: Chicago Blues/Mournful Tho'ts (1928, Col. 14334D); You Don't Understand/You've Got to be Modernistic (1929, Vic. 38099); Go Harlem/Just a Crazy Song (1931, Col. 2448D); Old Fashioned Love (1939, Col. DZ545); Harlem Woogie/After Tonight (1939, Voc. 4768); After You've Gone (1944, BN 33)

As sideman: P. Bradford: Lucy Long/ I ain't gonna play no second fiddle (1925, Voc. 15165); B. Smith: Preachin' the Blues/Backwater Blues (1927, Col. 14195D); Louisiana Sugar Babes: 'Sippi/Thou Swell (1928, Bb 10260); E. Waters: Guess Who's in Town (1928, Col. 14353D); B. Smith: Blue Spirit Blues (1929, Col. 14527D); M. Mezzrow: Comin' on with the Come On (1938, Bb 10085); E. Hall: Night Shift Blues/Royal Garden Blues (1943, BN 29); S. De Paris: Ballin' the Jack/Who's Sorry Now (1944, BN 41); S. Bechet: September Song/Who? (1949, Cir.[USA] 1057)

BIBLIOGRAPHY

R. Russell: "Grandfather of Hot Piano," *Jazz Information* (Nov 1941), 21; repr. in *The Art of Jazz: Essays on the Nature and Development of Jazz*, ed. M. Williams (New York, 1959/*R*1979), 49

R. Blesh and H. Janis: *They All Played Ragtime* (New York, 1950, rev. 4/1971), 202

T. Davin: "Conversations with James P. Johnson," *JR*, ii (1959), no.5, p.14; no.6, p.10; no.7, p.13; no.8, p.26; iii/3 (1960), 11; repr. in *Ragtime: its History, Composers, and Music*, ed. J. E. Hasse (London, 1985), 166

M. Harrison: "James P. Johnson," *JM*, v/7 (1959), 4

P. Bradford and N. Sissle: Liner notes, *Yamekraw: Negro Rhapsody* (FW FJ2842, 1961)

R. Hadlock: *Jazz Masters of the Twenties* (New York, 1965/*R*1985), 145

G. Schuller: *Early Jazz: its Roots and Musical Development* (New York, 1968), 214

M. Montgomery: Liner notes, *James P. Johnson, 1917–21* (Biograph 10030, 10090, 1973)

H. Lyttelton: *The Best of Jazz*, i: *Basin Street to Harlem: Jazz Masters and Masterpieces, 1917–1930* (London, 1978)

J. J. Johnson (trombone) and Bobby Jaspar (tenor saxophone) at the Club Continental in Brooklyn, New York, 1956

F. Kappler, D. Wellstood, and W. Rouder: Liner notes, *Giants of Jazz: James P. Johnson* (TL 18, 1981)

F. H. Trolle: *James P. Johnson: Father of the Stride Piano* (Alphen aan de Rijn, Netherlands, 1981) [discography; incl. rollography by M. Montgomery]

S. E. Brown: *A Case of Mistaken Identity: the Life and Music of James P. Johnson* (diss., Yale U., 1982); rev. and enlarged as *James P. Johnson: a Case of Mistaken Identity* (Metuchen, NJ, and London, 1986)[incl. R. Hilbert, Jr.: *A James P. Johnson Discography, 1917–1950*]

D. Hyman: "Thinking about James P. Johnson (1891–1955)," *Keyboard*, viii/8 (1982), 59 [incl. transcr.]

W. Rouder: Liner notes, *The Symphonic Jazz of James P. Johnson* (Musicmasters 20066, 1983)

WILLA ROUDER

Johnson, Jimmie [James Leroy, Jr.] (*b* Philadelphia, 20 Jan 1930). Drummer. He first worked in Philadelphia in a band led by his father, then in March 1959 replaced Sam Woodyard in Duke Ellington's orchestra. He remained with the group until March 1960, working briefly in a two-drummer team with Woodyard on his return. Among the recordings Johnson made during this period were *Dual Fuel* (on the album *Festival Session*, 1959, Col. CL1400) and *Skin Deep* (on the album *Duke Ellington Live*, 1959, Affinity 28).

EDDIE LAMBERT

Johnson, J. J. [James Louis] (*b* Indianapolis, 22 Jan 1924). Trombonist and composer. He studied piano with a church organist between the ages of nine and 11, and took up trombone when he was 14. In 1941–2 he toured with bands led by Clarence Love and Isaac "Snookum" Russell, whose trumpeter Fats Navarro had a strong impact on Johnson's playing. He then began an important engagement with Benny Carter's orchestra (1942–5), touring the country, writing a few arrangements, and making numerous radio broadcasts and transcriptions. He took his earliest recorded solo on *Love for Sale* (1943) and appeared at the first Jazz at the Philharmonic concert (1944).

By May 1945 Johnson was playing with the Count Basie Orchestra, mostly in New York. He moved permanently to New York in mid-1946, and for the next few years played small-group jazz at various clubs with Bud Powell, Max Roach, Miles Davis, Navarro, Charlie Parker, Dizzy Gillespie, and others, becoming increasingly absorbed in the new bop style. In 1951 he toured Korea, Japan, and the South Pacific for the USO in a band under Oscar Pettiford, and during 1952 he toured with an all-star group that included Davis. His worsening financial situation forced him to retire from music in August 1952; he worked as a blueprint inspector at the Sperry Gyroscope Company, and performed only sporadically.

Then, in August 1954, Johnson formed a highly successful trombone duo with Kai Winding. Their group, called Jay and Kai, remained intact until 1956, bringing Johnson's work to a larger audience and establishing his reputation as the leading jazz trombonist. His *Poem for Brass* (also known as *Jazz Suite for Brass*), recorded in 1956, drew attention to his talents as a composer: many of his skillfully orchestrated works, several of which have been published by MJQ in New York, employ fugal passages and out-of-tempo chorales as well as more conventional jazz swing sections.

After disbanding Jay and Kai, Johnson led his own quintet until summer 1960, touring Europe and composing large-scale works such as *El camino real* and *Sketch for Trombone and Band*, which were first performed at the Monterey Jazz Festival in 1959. He taught at the Lenox (Massachusetts) School of Jazz in summer 1960, and in the following year wrote a new major work, *Perceptions*, for Gillespie.

Johnson continued to combine careers as a performer and composer throughout the 1960s. He played with Davis's group (1961–2), formed a new quartet of his own (1963), and led a sextet, which included Clark Terry and Sonny Stitt, on a tour of Japan (1964). By 1967 he was staff composer and conductor for MBA Music in New York. From 1970, when he moved to Los Angeles, he primarily wrote scores for television and films; his infrequent recordings and performances, however, invariably re-established his pre-eminence among jazz trombonists. In 1987 he returned to Indianapolis and became more active as a player.

Johnson is the most important postwar jazz trombonist and a major influence on all players of the instrument. His earliest recorded solos up to 1945 reveal a thick tone, aggressive manner, and impressive mobility. They are not yet far removed, though, from the solos of his early influences – Lester Young, Roy Eldridge, and the trombonist Fred Beckett, who emphasized the linear qualities of the instrument rather than the effects of the slide.

During the 1940s Johnson developed such an astounding technical facility that some record reviewers insisted, erroneously, that he played a valve trombone; the speed of his playing and the clarity and accuracy he achieves at fast tempos have never been surpassed. In 1947 he began to play with a lighter tone (occasionally enhanced by a felt mute) and reserved vibrato for special effects. The result was a rather dry but attractive sound resembling that of a french horn. Johnson also worked diligently at this period to adapt bop patterns to the trombone, and his solos suffer from an emphasis on speed and an overreliance on memorized formulas incorporating such bop trademarks as the flatted 5th. His performances on both versions of *Crazeology* with Charlie Parker (1947) begin with the same phrase and contain other whole phrases in common. The same is true of the two renditions of Johnson's celebrated solo on *Blue Mode* (1949), despite their very different tempos.

During the late 1950s Johnson's playing matured: he relied less on formulas and speed, and more on a scalar approach and motivic development. Recordings of live performances dating from this time provide examples of brilliant developmental sequences that were delivered with powerful emotion. The features of Johnson's mature style are well illustrated in ex.1 (from *Mack the Knife*), where the opening phrase is a rhythmicized version of Kurt Weill's theme and the rest of the chorus is built in the modal manner from a single scale, connecting without a break to the next chorus.

Ex.1 *Moritat*, on *Mack the Knife* (1961, Col. CS8541); transcr. L. Porter

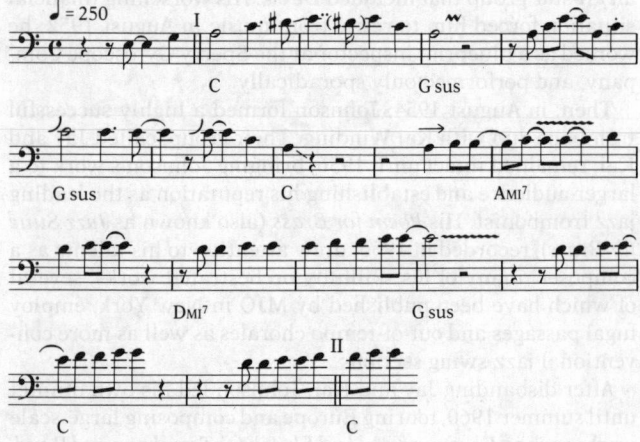

SELECTED RECORDINGS

* – composed by Johnson

As leader: *Mad Bebop (1946, Savoy 930); *Boneology (1947, Savoy 942); Blue Mode (1949, NewJ 814); *Turnpike (1953, BN 1621); with K. Winding: Jay and Kai (1954, Savoy 8140-42)[EPs], incl. *Blues for Trombones, *Lament; **Poem for Brass* (1956, Col. CL941); with S. Getz: *At the Opera House* (1957, Verve 8265); with A. Previn: *Mack the Knife* (1961, Col. CS8541); *J. J.!* (1964, RCA LPM3350), incl. *El camino real; *The Total J. J. Johnson* (1966, RCA LSP3833), incl. *Ballade, *Blue, *Euro, *In walked Horace, *Little Dave, *Say When, *Short Cake, *Space Walk; *Concepts in Blue* (1980, PT 2312123), incl. *Azure, *Blue Nun, *Concepts in Blue, *Mohawk, *Nermus

As sideman: B. Carter: Love for Sale (1943, Cap. 10038); Jazz at the Philharmonic: Blues (1944, Disc 6024-5); Body and Soul (1944, Disc 6028-9); K. George: Grand Slam (1945, Melodisc 111); C. Parker: Crazeology (1947, Dial 1034); D. Gillespie: The Champ (1951, DeeGee 3604); M. Davis: *Enigma (1953, BN 1618); *Kelo (1953, BN 1620); Jazz at the Philharmonic: *In Europe* (1960, Verve 68539-42); D. Gillespie: *Perceptions* (1961, Verve 68411); on F. Gulda: *Friedrich Gulda und sein Euro-Jazz Orchester* (1966, Preiser 3141), *Euro-suite

BIBLIOGRAPHY

M. Harrison: "Some Early J. J. Johnson Recordings," *JJ*, xii/10 (1959), 6
R. Horricks and others: *These Jazzmen of our Time* (London, 1959), 52
I. Gitler: "The Remarkable J. J. Johnson," *DB*, xxviii/10 (1961), 17
M. Harrison: "J. J. Johnson," *Jazz News* (18 Feb 1961), 9
G. Schuller: *J. J. Johnson: a List of Compositions Licensed by B.M.I.* (New York, 1961)
M. Harrison: "'Perceptions' and a Question of Unity," *JM*, viii/5 (1962), 25
L. Feather: "Blindfold Test," *DB*, xxxi/3 (1964), 30
G. Hoefer: "Early J. J.," *DB*, xxxii/2 (1965), 16
I. Gitler: *Jazz Masters of the Forties* (New York, 1966/R1983 with discography), 137
D. Baker: *Jazz Styles & Analysis: Trombone: a History of the Jazz Trombone via Recorded Solos, Transcribed and Annotated* (Chicago, 1973), 73
J. Burns: "J. J. Johnson: the Formative Years," *JJ*, xxviii/8 (1975), 4
L. Feather: Liner notes, *Mad Bebop* (Savoy SJL2232, 1978)
D. Baker: *J. J. Johnson, Trombone* (New York, 1979) [transcrs.; incl. discography and list of works]
M. Hennessey: "The Return of J. J. Johnson," *JJI*, xxxiii/5 (1980), 6
L. G. Bourgois III: *Jazz Trombonist J. J. Johnson: a Comprehensive Discography and Study of the Early Evolution of his Style* (diss., Ohio State U., 1986)
G. Kalbacher: "J. J. Johnson: Bringing it all back Home," *DB*, lv/3 (1988), 16 [incl. discography]

LEWIS PORTER

Johnson, Keg [Frederic H.] (*b* Dallas, 19 Nov 1908; *d* Chicago, 8 Nov 1967). Trombonist, brother of Budd Johnson. He began to study music with his father and continued with the noted teacher Portia Pittman; he concentrated on trombone from 1927. During the late 1920s he and his brother worked in various bands in Dallas; after traveling to Kansas City with Jesse Stone's group in 1929, they (and Stone) joined George E. Lee. In 1930 the brothers settled in Chicago, where they often played with Louis Armstrong. Keg moved to New York in 1933; he performed and recorded there with Benny Carter (1933-4) and Fletcher Henderson (1934) and in 1935 began his long association with Cab Calloway (for illustration *see* CALLOWAY, CAB), which lasted until 1949. During the 1950s he moved to California, where he worked part-time as a musician, sometimes playing guitar as well as trombone. After returning to New York, he recorded with Gil Evans in 1960 and toured with Ray Charles from 1961 until his death. Johnson usually exploited his command of the high register in his solos; his fluency and inventiveness were reminiscent of Jack Teagarden's but his tone was less opulent. His playing is heard to particular advantage on *St. Louis Blues* (1933).

SELECTED RECORDINGS

As sideman: L. Armstrong: High Society/Mahogany Hall Stomp (1933, Vic. 24232); Dusky Stevedore/St. Louis Blues (1933, Vic. 24320); C. Calloway: Baby it's cold outside/ The Huckle-buck (1949, Hi-Tone 135); I've got the world on a string/Why can't you behave? (1949, Sig. 15243); R. Charles: *Modern Sounds in Country and Western Music* (1962, ABC-Para. 410)

BIBLIOGRAPHY

ChiltonW
J. Simmen: "Keg Johnson," *BHcF*, no.174 (1968), 7

LAWRENCE KOCH

Johnson, Ken "Snake Hips" [Kendrick Reginald Huymans] (*b* Georgetown, British Guiana [now Guyana], 22 June 1917; *d* London, 8 March 1941). British Guiana bandleader and dancer. He had no musical training, and traveled in 1929 to London. His interest in dancing developed from his contact with the black-American choreographer Clarence "Buddy" Bradley. It is alleged that he danced for Fletcher Henderson in the USA; he certainly visited the USA and the West Indies in 1935. With Johnson's encouragement Leslie Thompson formed a band, the Emperors of Jazz, with which he danced in 1936; however the two men disagreed, and in 1937 Johnson assumed leadership of the group and recruited to it Dave Wilkins and three other musicians from Trinidad. The band was known by various names, including the West Indian Orchestra; it toured, made recordings (among them *Snakehips Swing*, 1938, Decca F6854), and broadcast on radio until 1941, making English audiences more aware of the contributions of black musicians to jazz. Johnson was killed when a bomb struck the Café de Paris in London.

BIBLIOGRAPHY

A. Gray: "Getting the Real Low-down on London's After-dark Swing Spots," *MM*, xiii (29 May 1937), 2
A. McCarthy: *Big Band Jazz* (New York and London, 1974), 321

JOHN COWLEY, JEFFREY P. GREEN

Johnson, Lem(uel Charles) [Deacon] (*b* Oklahoma City, OK, 6 Aug 1909). Tenor saxophonist, clarinetist, and singer. After playing clarinet with local bands in the mid-1920s he took up saxophone in 1928 and received tuition from Walter Page, while playing with Page's Blue Devils. The following year he undertook regular radio work with Sammy Price. Thereafter he performed with various bands in Milwaukee and spent three years with the bandleader Eli Rice, mainly in Minneapolis. He made a short tour with Earl Hines before moving in 1937 to New York, where he worked with Fess Williams, Luis Russell, and Louis Jordan (1938–9) before leading his own groups in the early 1940s. During this period he also played briefly with Buster Harding and Eddie Durham (both 1940), Edgar Hayes and Sidney Bechet (both 1941), and Claude Hopkins (1942–3); his saxophone playing may be heard to advantage on Durham's *I want a little girl* (1940, Decca 18126). Johnson held several residencies in and around New York and in New Jersey with his own group. He ceased to work full-time as a musician in the late 1940s, but continued to lead bands into the 1960s. (J. Simmen: "The Lem Johnson Story," *JJ*, xx/12 (1967), 16)

based on *ChiltonW*

Johnson, Lonnie [Alonzo] (*b* New Orleans, 8 Feb 1889; *d* Toronto, 16 June 1970). Guitarist and singer. The son of a musician and a member of a large musical family, he started playing guitar and violin professionally in Storyville, New Orleans, while in his teens. By 1920 he was working on the riverboat *St. Paul* with Charlie Creath's Jazz-o-Maniacs; he recorded with the band in 1925. He made many of his early recordings as a blues singer under his own name, accompanying himself on violin, but it was as a guitarist that he became famous; he plays brilliantly on such solos as *Stompin' 'em along slow* (1928) and in the many duets he recorded with Eddie Lang. Johnson was unique among blues performers in working with jazz musicians, recording with Duke Ellington, Louis Armstrong, and, as a member of Blind Willie Dunn's Gin Bottle Four, King Oliver. He was also a sensitive accompanist and provided sympathetic support for blues singers such as Alger "Texas" Alexander. Johnson's own voice was reedy and rather insinuating. His lyrics were generally interesting and, although he had a liking for sentimental themes, he was particularly effective when singing serious blues. Johnson made some 500 recordings over a span of 40 years. Greatly respected for his accomplished playing, he was not a profound artist, but a very professional one.

See also BLUES, §4.

SELECTED RECORDINGS

As unaccompanied soloist: Stompin' 'em along slow (1928, OK 8558)
Duo with E. Lang: A Handful of Riffs (1929, OK 8695)
As sideman: D. Ellington: Move Over (1928, OK 8638); L. Armstrong: Mahogany Hall Stomp (1929, OK 8680); Blind Willie Dunn's Gin Bottle Four: Jet Black Blues (1929, OK 8689)

BIBLIOGRAPHY

V. Wilmer: "Lonnie Johnson," *JM*, ix/10 (1963), 5 [interview]
P. Oliver: *Conversation with the Blues* (London, 1965)
"Lonnie Johnson: a Name Listing for the Period from 1943," *Matrix*, no.79 (1968), 3
P. Garon: "Remembering Lonnie Johnson," *Living Blues*, i/2 (1970), 20
R. Groom: "Lonnie Johnson," *Blues World*, no.35 (1970), 3
V. Clapp: "I Remember Lonnie," *JJ*, xxv/1 (1972), 22
S. Harris: *Blues Who's Who: a Biographical Dictionary of Blues Singers* (New Rochelle, NY, 1979)

PAUL OLIVER

Johnson, Manzie (Isham) (*b* Putnam, CT, 19 Aug 1906; *d* New York, 9 April 1971). Drummer. Brought up in New York, he played in Harlem in the 1920s with Fats Waller, James P. Johnson, and other stride pianists, and later worked with the pianist Willie Gant (1926), Elmer Snowden (*c*1927), and Horace Henderson (1930). After making his first recordings with Jelly Roll Morton in 1928, he performed and recorded for a considerable period with Don Redman (1931–7); he also recorded with Henry "Red" Allen (1933), Benny Morton, (1934), Lil Armstrong (1937, 1940), and Mezz Mezzrow (1938). In the 1940s he briefly worked again with Redman (1940, *c*1944) and continued to play with well-known traditional and swing musicians, including James P. Johnson (1940), Ovie Alston (1940–44, late 1940s), Fletcher Henderson and Frankie Newton (both 1941), and Horace Henderson; in the late 1940s he led his own group for a short time. Although he retired from full-time work in the 1950s, he played regularly throughout the 1960s.

Johnson based his early style on traditional jazz drumming, using hot-cymbal licks and tight press-roll accompaniments. Later he incorporated swing techniques into his drumming, but he always maintained a restrained role within the ensemble.

SELECTED RECORDINGS

As sideman: D. Redman: Doin' What I Please (1932, Bruns. 6429); L. Armstrong: Sixth Street (1940, Decca 7739); S. Bechet: Jazz me Blues (1944, BN 44); *The Fabulous Sidney Bechet* (1951, BN 7020), incl. Original Dixieland One-step

BIBLIOGRAPHY

ChiltonW; *FeatherE*; *Feather–Gitler '70s*
J. Simmen: "Manzie Isham Johnson, 19 août 1906 / 9 avril 1971," *BHcF*, no.210 (1971), 11; no.211 (1971), 3

T. DENNIS BROWN

Johnson, Money [Harold] (*b* Tyler, TX, 23 Feb 1918; *d* New York, 28 March 1978). Trumpeter. He began playing at the age of 15; in 1936 he moved to Oklahoma City, where he took part in jam sessions with Charlie Christian and Henry Bridges. The following year he joined Nat Towles's band; after leaving Towles he played with Horace Henderson and the saxophonist Bob Dorsey, but he rejoined Towles in Chicago in 1944. He worked with Count Basie (1944), Cootie Williams and Lucky Millinder (mid-1940s), Lucky Thompson, Sy Oliver, and Herbie Fields. In 1953 he played in South America with Panama Francis. Johnson performed regularly in a band led by Reuben Phillips at the Apollo Theatre, New York, in the 1960s; he was also active as a studio musician. In 1966 he went with Earl Hines to the USSR on a tour sponsored by the US State Department. He played with Duke Ellington in 1968 and replaced Cat Anderson in the band the following year. In 1970 he played with Oliver again before re-joining Duke Ellington. After Ellington's death in 1974 Johnson continued to perform in New York; he made a recording with Buck Clayton in 1975.

SELECTED RECORDINGS

As sideman: H. Henderson: You Don't Mean me no Good (1940, OK 5953); C. Williams: Cherry Red Blues (1944, Hit 7084); R. Phillips: *Reuben Phillips and his Orchestra* (1961, Ascot 13004); D. Ellington: *Second Sacred Concert* (1968, Prst. 24045); H. Person: *Houston Express* (1971, Prst. 10017); on B. Clayton: *Jam Session*, ii (1975, Chi. 163), Glassboro Blues

BIBLIOGRAPHY

S. Dance: "Money Johnson: Duke's New Trumpet," *DB*, xxxvi/18 (1969), 18
A. McCarthy: *Big Band Jazz* (New York and London, 1974), 133
Obituary, *DB*, xlv/11 (1978), 10

FREDERICK A. BECK

Johnson, Ollie [Oliver]. *See* JOHNSON, DINK.

Johnson, (James) Osie (*b* Washington, 11 Jan 1923; *d* New York, 10 Feb 1966). Drummer and arranger. He left high school in 1941 to begin playing professionally. After working with Sabby Lewis in Boston for six months (1942–3) he was a member of a navy band that included Clark Terry (1944–5). He then worked as a freelance in Chicago, and from 1951 to 1953 played for Earl Hines; during this period he also performed at Minton's Playhouse with Tony Scott's quartet. In 1954 he joined a trio led by the pianist Dorothy Donegan and also toured Europe with Illinois Jacquet. From the mid-1950s Johnson worked principally as a session musician in television and recording studios in New York, while continuing to perform occasionally with groups led by Clark Terry and Bob Brookmeyer, Al Cohn and Zoot Sims, and others. He participated in hundreds of sessions, working with such musicians as Joe Newman (1954, 1956–7), Frank Wess (1954, 1962), Johnny Hodges (1954, 1962–4), Coleman Hawkins (1955–6, 1958–60, 1963, *c*1965), Dinah Washington (1956), Jimmy Raney (1956, *c*1964), Wes Montgomery (1963), Sonny Stitt (1963, *c*1965), and Ben Webster (1964). Johnson wrote a number of arrangements for Washington, notably *Fool that I am* (1947, Mer. 8050) and *It's too soon to know* (1947, Mer. 8107).

SELECTED RECORDINGS

As leader: *Osie's Oasis* (1955, Period 1108); *Johnson's Whacks* (1955, Period 1112); *A Bit of the Blues* (1956, RCA LPM1369); *The Happy Osie Johnson* (1957, Beth. 66)
As sideman: C. Hawkins: *At Ease with Coleman Hawkins* (1960, Mdsv. 7), incl. While we're young; P. Gonsalves: *Tell it the Way it is* (1963, Imp. 55)

BIBLIOGRAPHY

"Osie Johnson Sought as Drummer, Arranger," *DB*, xxii/6 (1955), 22
Obituaries: R. Dahlgren, *Orkester journalen*, xxxiv/3 (1966), 7; *DB*, xxxiii/6 (1966), 14

JEFF POTTER

Johnson, Otis (*b* New York, 13 Jan 1910). Trumpeter. He first worked in New York with bands led by Gene Rodgers (1928), Charlie Skeete and Eugene Kennedy (both 1929), and Luis Russell (1929–30). He then played with Kennedy in New England, and with Russell (1932) and Benny Carter (1934), and performed and made recordings with Willie Bryant (1935, including *Long Gone from Bowling Green*, Vic. 25129). After playing briefly in a group led by Eddie Condon and Joe Marsala (1936) Johnson worked with Don Redman (1936–7, 1940) and Louis Armstrong (1938–9). He ceased to be a professional musician at the outbreak of World War II.

based on *ChiltonW*

Johnson, Pete(r) (*b* Kansas City, MO, 25 March 1904; *d* Buffalo, 23 March 1967). Pianist. He played drums while in his teens and piano from 1922. In Kansas City he accompanied the singer Edna Taylor at the Hole in the Wall Club and Jazzland, and Joe Turner (ii) at the Sunset Cafe; there he was heard by John Hammond, at whose invitation he moved in 1936 to New York to perform at the Famous Door. At Carnegie Hall in 1938 he took part in the concert "From Spirituals to Swing," which Hammond organized, and in December performed as a member of the Boogie-Woogie Trio with Meade "Lux" Lewis and Albert Ammons; the trio also appeared in 1939 at Café Society. During the next decade he worked regularly in a duo with Ammons and occasionally in a duo with Lewis, and also performed as an unaccompanied soloist. He moved to Buffalo (1950), toured with Lewis, Art Tatum, and Erroll Garner (1952), and toured Europe and performed at the Newport Jazz Festival (1958). He ceased playing after suffering a stroke in 1958 that left him partly paralyzed.

See also PIANO, §3; for illustration *see* TURNER, JOE (ii).

SELECTED RECORDINGS

As unaccompanied soloist: Pete's Blues/Let 'em Jump (1939, Solo Art 12005)
Duos with J. Turner: Goin' Away Blues/Roll 'em Pete (1938, Voc. 4607)
As leader: Vine Street Bustle/Some Day Blues (1939, BN 11)

BIBLIOGRAPHY

S. Pease: "Swing Piano Styles: Pete Johnson Got his Start Shining Shoes in Kaycee," *DB*, vi/15 (1939), 22 [incl. transcr.]
J. Simmen: "My Life, my Music," *JJ*, xii/8 (1959), 8 [interview]; Fr. trans. as "Ma vie, ma musique," *BHcF*, no.89 (1959), 3; no.90 (1959), 8
H. A. Woodfin: "Pete Johnson: Jazz Pianist," *JM*, viii/7 (1962), 2
H. J. Mauerer: *The Pete Johnson Story* (New York, and Frankfurt am Main, Germany, 1965) [incl. discography]
Obituary, *DB*, xxxiv/9 (1967), 12

JAMES M. DORAN

Johnson, Plas (John, Jr.) (*b* Donaldsonville, LA, 21 July 1931). Tenor saxophonist. His father taught him soprano saxophone and his brother the pianist Ray Johnson recorded with him as a leader and a sideman in the 1950s. He was active mainly in studios on the West Coast, recording with Irving Ashby (1957–8), Benny Carter (1959), and many popular, rhythm-and-blues, and rock-and-roll artists. He is best known as the soloist with Henry Mancini's orchestra on the soundtrack of the film *The Pink Panther* (1963). During the 1960s he did other work in television and films and recorded as a sideman in many big bands, most notably as a soloist with Glen Gray; around 1962 he made recordings with his own quintet under the pseudonym Johnny Beecher (including *Sax Fifth Avenue*, 1962, Charter 102). He joined the band of Merv Griffin's television program in 1970, performed and recorded with Herb Ellis (1974–5) and his own group (1974–6), and also recorded with the Capp–Pierce Orchestra (1977).

BIBLIOGRAPHY

FeatherE; *Feather '60s*; *Feather–Gitler '70s*
V. Wilmer: "Plas: Rhythm of the Tenor," *MM*, li (11 Sept 1976), 42
B. Greensmith: "Plas Johnson," *Blues Unlimited*, no.133 (1979), 12 [incl. discography]

Johnson, Reggie [Reginald Volney] (*b* Owensboro, KY, 13 Dec 1940). Double bass player. He played trombone as a youth and in army bands, and after 1961 began working as a double bass player. He played in Bill Dixon's avant-garde concert series known as the "October Revolution in Jazz" in New York (1964). In the mid-1960s he was active as a sideman with Archie Shepp and Bill Barron (1964–5), Burton Greene, Roland Kirk, and Sun Ra (1965), and Art Blakey (1965–6); he recorded with the Jazz Composer's Orchestra (1968) and Stanley Cowell (1969). In 1970 he played with a quintet led by Bobby Hutcherson and Harold Land, and in 1971 he recorded with Walter Bishop, Jr., and John Klemmer. He worked occasionally with Kenny Burrell (1973–8), recorded with Horace Parlan's trio (1981) and with Parlan and Johnny Coles (1982), and played with Mingus Dynasty (1982) and with Coles and Frank Wess (1983). He recorded an album as a leader in 1985.

SELECTED RECORDINGS

As leader: *First Edition* (1985, Jeremiah Robinson 19000)
As sideman: M. Brown: *Marion Brown Quartet* (1965, ESP 1022); A. Blakey: *Hold on, I'm Coming* (1966, Lml. 86032); on [no leader]: *Live at the Festival* (1970, Enja 2030), B. Hutcherson and H. Land: The Creators; K. Burrell: *Tin tin deo* (1977, Conc. 45); Mingus Dynasty: *Reincarnation* (1982, SN 1042); F. Wess and J. Coles: *Two at the Top* (1983, Upt. 2714)

BIBLIOGRAPHY

Feather '60s
D. Morgenstern: Liner notes, *First Edition* (1985, Jeremiah Robinson 19000)

JOHN VOIGT

Johnson, Walter (*b* New York, 18 Feb 1904; *d* New York, 26 April 1977). Drummer. His career, which was based mainly in New York, began in the bands of Freddy Johnson (1924), Elmer Snowden (1925, 1927–8), and Te Roy Williams (1927). He played in the Fletcher Henderson Orchestra (1929–34, for illustration *see* HENDERSON, FLETCHER; 1936–7, 1941–2) and also with Putney Dandridge, Lucky Millinder (1938–9), Claude Hopkins (1939), and Edgar Hayes (1940). From 1944 to 1954 he played and recorded with Tab Smith. In the 1960s he worked as a freelance drummer. An unobtrusive drummer, who rarely played solos, Johnson is sometimes credited with having been the first to use the hi-hat effectively. His earliest big-band recordings certainly provide rich examples of his simple, metrically accurate, legato hi-hat accompaniments, which bridged the gap between the choke-cymbal style of the 1920s and the swing style of the 1930s.

SELECTED RECORDINGS

As sideman with F. Henderson: Sweet and Hot (1931, Col. 2414D); Clarinet Marmalade (1931, Col. 2513D); New King Porter Stomp (1932, OK 41565); Yeah Man!/King Porter's Stomp (1933, Voc. 2527)

BIBLIOGRAPHY

ChiltonW
J. Simmen: "Walter Johnson, le drummer qui fait que cette cymbale danse," *BHcF*, no.215 (1972), 3
W. C. Allen: *Hendersonia: the Music of Fletcher Henderson and his Musicians: a Bio-discography* (Highland Park, NJ, 1973)

T. DENNIS BROWN

Johnson, Willie. *See* JOHNSON, BUNK.

Jolly, Pete [Ceragioli, Peter A.] (*b* New Haven, CT, 5 June 1932). Pianist and accordionist. He studied accordion from the age of three and piano from about the age of eight. After moving to Los Angeles he played with Georgie Auld (1952), Shorty Rogers (1954–6), Buddy DeFranco (1956), and Terry Gibbs, and also led his own groups. He recorded with Red Norvo (1954), Rogers (1954–5, 1957–62), Richie Kamuca and Chet Baker (both 1956), Buddy Collette (1957), DeFranco (1957, 1959), Gibbs (1957–9), Art Pepper (1960), and his own ensembles (intermittently, 1955–*c*1969). From the 1960s he concentrated on studio work in films and television, though he continued to play with his own small groups; he recorded in 1980 as the leader of a quartet which included Pepper. Jolly wrote a number of compositions, and achieved popular success with *Little Bird*. Although a good pianist, he is more important as a jazz accordionist in the single-line style.

SELECTED RECORDINGS

As leader: *Jolly Jumps In* (1955, RCA LPM1105); *Little Bird* (1962–3, Ava 22); *The Sensational Pete Jolly Gases Everybody* (1963, CP 825); *Strike up the Band* (1980, Atlas 1003)
As sideman: B. DeFranco: *Live Date!: Buddy DeFranco Septette* (1957, Verve 8383)

BIBLIOGRAPHY

FeatherE; *Feather '60s*; *Feather–Gitler '70s*
S. A. Pease: "Jolly Jumps into Scene," *DB*, xxii/25 (1955), 24
J. Tynan: "Pete Jolly: He Wants to Help Make Accordion Part of Jazz," *DB*, xxiv/23 (1957), 21
E. Barr: "Pete Jolly: from M*A*S*H to Dallas: Journey of a Jazz Piano Survivor," *Keyboard*, xiii/8 (1987), 21

ANDREW JAFFE

Jones. Family of jazz musicians.

(1) Hank [Henry] **Jones** (*b* Vicksburg, MS, 31 July 1918). Pianist. He grew up in Pontiac, Michigan, where he studied piano at an early age and came under the influence of Earl Hines, Fats Waller, Teddy Wilson, and Art Tatum. By the age of 13 Jones was performing locally in Michigan and Ohio. While playing with territory bands in Grand Rapids and Lansing he met Lucky Thompson, who invited him to New York in 1944 to work at the Onyx Club with Hot Lips Page.

In New York Jones regularly listened to leading bop musicians, and was inspired to master the new style. While practicing and studying the music he worked with John Kirby, Howard McGhee, Coleman Hawkins, Andy Kirk, and Billy Eckstine. In autumn 1947 he began touring in Norman Granz's Jazz at the Philharmonic concerts, and from 1948 to 1953 he was accompanist for Ella Fitzgerald, developing a harmonic facility of extraordinary taste and sophistication. During this period he also made several historically important recordings with Charlie Parker for Norman Granz's labels.

After several years as a freelance player, which included engagements with Artie Shaw and Benny Goodman, and recordings with such artists as Lester Young, Milt Jackson, and Cannonball Adderley, in 1959 Jones joined the staff of CBS, where he stayed until the staff was disbanded 17 years later. He worked mostly with big bands such as the Ray Block Orchestra on the "Ed Sullivan Show," but continued touring and recording with leading jazz groups. With his rare combination of talents as a strong soloist, sensitive accompanist, and adept sight-reader, Jones has always been in great demand for recording sessions of all kinds, and may be heard on thousands of albums. By the late 1970s his involvement as pianist and conductor with the Broadway musical *Ain't Misbehavin'* (based on the music of Fats Waller) had informed a wider audience of his unique qualities as a musician.

During the late 1970s and the 1980s Jones continued to record prolifically, as an unaccompanied soloist, in duos with other pianists (including John Lewis and Tommy Flanagan),

(a)

(c)

1. *(a) Hank Jones; (b) the Thad Jones–Mel Lewis Orchestra with Jones (front, conducting) and Lewis (center back, drums) and including (front row) Richard Davis (double bass), Ed Xiques, Jerry Dodgion, and Pepper Adams (saxophones, second and third from left and far right); (middle row) Jimmy Knepper and Eddie Bert (trombones, second from left and far right); (c) Elvin Jones, 1956*

(b)

and with various small ensembles, most notably the Great Jazz Trio. The group took this name in 1976, by which time Jones had already begun working at the Village Vanguard with its original members, Ron Carter and Tony Williams (it was Buster Williams rather than Carter, however, who took part in the trio's first recording session in 1976); by 1980 Jones's sidemen were Eddie Gomez and Al Foster, and in 1982 Jimmy Cobb replaced Foster. The trio has also recorded with other all-star personnel, such as Art Farmer, Benny Golson, and Nancy Wilson. In the early 1980s Jones held a residency as a solo pianist at the Cafe Ziegfeld and made a tour of Japan, where he performed and recorded with George Duvivier and Sonny Stitt.

SELECTED RECORDINGS

As unaccompanied soloist: *Have you Met Hank Jones?* (1956, Savoy 12084); *Tiptoe Tapdance* (1977–8, Gal. 5108); *Satin Doll* (*c*1980, Trio 7131)

Duos: with T. Flanagan: *Our Delights* (1978, Gal. 5113); with J. Lewis: *An Evening with Two Grand Pianos* (1979, Little David 1079)

As leader: *Bop Redux* (1977, Muse 5123); *Just for Fun* (1977, Gal. 5105); of Great Jazz Trio: *The Great Jazz Trio Revisited: at the Village Vanguard* (1980, Ewd 90002, 90005)

As sideman: on B. Carter, J. Hodges, C. Parker, and W. Smith: *Alto Saxes* (1947–54, Norg. 1035), Parker: Star Eyes (1950); on Parker: *The Genius of Charlie Parker*, vii (1949–53, Verve 8009), Blues (1950); S. Stitt and P. Gonsalves: *Salt and Pepper* (1963, Imp. 52); C. Terry and B. Brookmeyer: *Gingerbread Men* (1966, Mstr. 6086); T. Jones and M. Lewis: *Presenting Thad Jones–Mel Lewis and the Jazz Orchestra* (1966, SolS 18003)

BIBLIOGRAPHY

H. P[anassié]: "Hank Jones," *BHcF*, no.75 (1957), 3
"Hank Jones Talking," *CI*, xiii/5 (1974), 16
A. J. Smith: "The Impeccable Hank Jones," *DB*, xliii/11 (1976), 14
"Great Jazz Piano," *SJ*, xxxi/7 (1977), 288 [discography]
C. Battestini and J.-P. Battestini: "Hank Jones," *BHcF*, no.265 (1978), 8 [interview]
L. Feather: "Piano Giants of Jazz: Hank Jones," *CK*, iv/2 (1978), 63
B. Primack and R. Dubin: "Detroit's Triple Gift to the Jazz Piano World," *CK*, v/12 (1979), 12
J. Réda: "Transparence de Hank Jones," *L'improviste: une lecture de jazz* (Paris, 1980), 173
A. Sussman: "Hank Jones: Indefatigable Elegance," *DB*, xlviii/5 (1981), 23
D. Long: "Hank Jones: Interview," *Cadence*, ix/7 (1983), 12

(2) Thad(deus Joseph) Jones (*b* Pontiac, MI, 28 March 1923; *d* Copenhagen, 20 Aug 1986). Cornetist, flugelhorn player, composer, and bandleader. He taught himself trumpet from about the age of 13, and by the time he was 16 was playing professionally with his older brother (1) Hank Jones, and in summer jobs with Sonny Stitt. After performing in army bands (1943–6), with which he toured overseas, he worked in midwestern dance and show bands. From 1950 to 1953 he appeared with his younger brother (3) Elvin Jones in Billy Mitchell's jazz quintet in Detroit. Thereafter he undertook important engagements with Charles Mingus's Jazz Composers' Workshop (1954–5) and Count Basie's orchestra (1954–63).

In December 1965, with Mel Lewis, Jones organized an outstanding 18-piece band (see fig.1*b*) which, beginning in February 1966, played regularly on Monday nights at the Village Vanguard, New York. This arrangement lasted for well over a decade, and gave Jones ample opportunity to display his gifts as a conductor, composer, arranger, and flugelhorn soloist. Later the group performed in nightclubs, appeared at collegiate and festival concerts, and undertook tours of Japan, the USSR, and Europe. At various times its distinguished personnel included Bill Berry, Richard Williams, Snooky Young, Cecil Bridgewater, Jon Faddis, Bob Brookmeyer, Jimmy Knepper, Garnett Brown, Quentin Jackson, Janice Robinson, Jerome Richardson, Jerry Dodgion, Pepper Adams, Eddie Daniels, Joe Farrell, Ed Xiques, Billy Harper, Frank Foster, Roland Hanna, Richard Davis, and George Mraz.

In 1979, after injuring his lip, Jones took up valve trombone. In that same year he ended his partnership with Lewis and settled in Denmark, having already worked there from 1977 to 1978 as the leader of the Radioens Big Band; he formed a new big band, the Thad Jones Eclipse, which recorded in 1979 and 1980. He returned to the USA in 1985 to assume the leadership of the Count Basie Orchestra, a position he retained until February 1986.

Jones played cornet in the bop style with a compact, crisp tone, his improvised melodies often elaborating sequences with striking dissonances. With the Thad Jones–Mel Lewis Orchestra he concentrated on performing sustained, lyrical melodies on flugelhorn. His compositions provided substantial, flexible opportunities for the band's excellent soloists, and have become a staple in the repertory of school stage bands (by 1980 about 40 works by Jones had been published by D'Accord Music, New York). They cover a wide range of styles, exploring waltz rhythms (*The waltz you swang for me*, 1968), boogaloo and ballad combinations (*Central Park North*, 1969), swing with traditional riffs or unpredictable melodies (*The Big Dipper*, 1969; *Tiptoe*, 1970), bossa nova (*It only happens every time*, 1970), bop (*Fingers*, 1970), and jazz-rock (*Greetings and Salutations*, 1975–6). Scores by him are in the George P. Vanier Library of Concordia University, Montreal; *see* LIBRARIES AND ARCHIVES, §2.

SELECTED RECORDINGS

* – composed by Jones

As leader: *The Fabulous Thad Jones* (1954, Debut 12); *The Magnificent Thad Jones* (1956–7, BN 1527, 1546); *Eclipse* (1979, Met. 15652)

As leader with M. Lewis: *Presenting Thad Jones–Mel Lewis and the Jazz Orchestra* (1966, SolS 18003); *Thad Jones–Mel Lewis Live at the Village Vanguard* (1967, SolS 18016), incl. *Little Pixie; *Monday Night* (1968, SolS 18048), incl. *The waltz you swang for me; *Central Park North* (1969, SolS 18058), incl. *The Big Dipper, *Central Park North; *Consummation* (1970, BN 84346), incl. *Consummation, *Dedication, *Fingers, *It only happens every time, *Tiptoe; **Suite for Pops* (1972, 1975, A&M Hor. 701); *New Life* (1975–6, A&M Hor. 707), incl. *Cherry Juice, *Greetings and Salutations; *The Thad Jones–Mel Lewis Quartet* (1977, AH 3)

As sideman: C. Basie: *April in Paris* (1955–6, Verve 8012); T. Monk: *5 by Monk by 5* (1959, Riv. 1150); E. Jones: *Elvin!* (1962, Riv. 9409); D. Gordon: *Ca' purange* (1972, Prst. 10051)

BIBLIOGRAPHY

N. Hentoff: "They're all Talking about the Jones Boy," *DB*, xxii/23 (1955), 9
B. Coss: "Thad Jones: Horn of Plenty," *DB*, xxx/11 (1963), 16
D. Morgenstern: "The Big Bands: in New York . . . Signs of Life," *DB*, xxxiii/8 (1966), 19
I. Gitler: "Thad's Thing," *DB*, xxxv/4 (1968), 18
L. Tomkins: "The Thad Jones Story," *CI*, x (1972), no.10, p.20; no.11, p.14
"Thad Jones Discography," *SJ*, xxviii/2 (1974), 262
A. Smith: "Thad Jones Conducts an Interview," *DB*, xli/20 (1974), 14
C. Sheridan: "Greetings and Salutations," *JJI*, xxxi/6 (1978), 6 [Jones–Lewis discography]
——: "Thad Jones' New Home, New Band, New 'Bone," *DB*, xlvii/1 (1980), 14
W. R. Stokes: "Thad Jones: at the Helm of the Basie Band," *JT* (June 1985), 10
Obituary, J. Simmen, *BHcF*, no.348 (1987), 28

(3) Elvin (Ray) Jones (*b* Pontiac, MI, 9 Sept 1927). Drummer (see fig.1*c*). He began his professional career playing in local groups in Pontiac and Detroit, then, during army service (1946–9), performed in military bands. After returning to Michigan he resumed his professional career working with various bands, including some organized by his brother (2) Thad Jones, and occasionally touring. Of particular importance was his acquaintance with Art Mardigan, whom he eventually replaced as drummer in Billy Mitchell's quintet; this group was the house band at the Bluebird club in Detroit and, as such, accompanied the national jazz artists who were regularly featured there. In 1956 Jones moved to New York, where he began to establish a reputation as a dynamic drummer in the tradition of Art Blakey. Among the most notable groups and individuals with whom he recorded or performed at the time were J. J. Johnson's quintet, Donald Byrd's quintet, Harry Edison, Bud Powell, Sonny Rollins, and Stan Getz.

In 1960 Jones became a member of the John Coltrane Quartet, beginning a five-year association that was to become one of the most significant in jazz history. The innovative performances and recordings of this group, led by Coltrane at the height of his powers, established the standard for excellence in the modal, open-form style of this period. During his years with Coltrane Jones emerged as the premier jazz drummer of the 1960s, and brought his unique style to a state of maturity which irrevocably altered the nature of jazz drumming.

When Coltrane decided in 1966 to add a second drummer (Rashied Ali) to his ensemble, Jones, who found the arrangement incompatible with his musical ideas, left the group and joined Duke Ellington's orchestra briefly for a tour of Europe. He worked in Europe for a short while before returning to the USA, where he formed a series of trios, quartets, and sextets, occasionally in conjunction with Coltrane's former bass player Jimmy Garrison. These groups usually dispensed with a pianist, and characteristically consisted of one and often two saxophonists, a strong bass player, and Jones on drums; among the musicians who were Jones's most frequent sidemen were Joe Farrell, Frank Foster, George Coleman, Garrison, Wilbur Little, and Gene Perla. Jones's ensembles appeared throughout the USA and Europe and conducted major tours of South America and Asia.

In 1970 Jones appeared in the film *Zachariah* and in 1979 he was the subject of a documentary film, *Different Drummer: Elvin Jones*. He has continued to pursue an active performing and recording career into the 1980s.

Jones's style is a logical extension of the bop approach established by Kenny Clarke and Max Roach and modified by Art Blakey. In bop drumming a repeated rhythmic pattern is maintained only on the ride and hi-hat cymbals, the remaining instruments being used to mark the main structural divisions of the performance, to articulate the solo improvisation, and to interject counterrhythmic motifs against the prevailing regular pulse. Blakey, while adhering to this general style, altered it by increasing the level of activity of the accompanying drums and utilizing a greater number of cross-rhythms in his interjected patterns. Jones built on Blakey's techniques and added new ones to the extent that the fundamental role of the drummer changed from that of an accompanist to one of an equal collaborative improviser. Jones played several metrically contrasting rhythms simultaneously, each of which was characterized by irregularly shifting accents that were independent of the basic pulse. Of particular note is Jones's ingenious mixture of playing irregularly accented half-, quarter-, eighth-, and 16th-note triplet subdivisions over an extended period as a means of generating a wide array of polyrhythms. An excellent example of this technique may be heard on *Nuttin' out Jones*, recorded by the Jones–Garrison Sextet in 1963. In addition Jones shaped the background counterrhythmic motifs associated with bop drumming into extended coherent musical statements with a logical internal development of their own (a classic example may be heard in *Part I: Acknowledgement* on Coltrane's *A Love Supreme*).

Jones's techniques resulted in dense percussive textures characterized by greater diversity of timbre, heightened polyrhythmic activity, and increased intensity and volume. Moreover, as the richness of these composite textures made it difficult to discern the basic pulse, they contributed to the development of a new style of "free improvisation" which underplayed or dispensed with regular pulse altogether (as on Coltrane's *Ascension*, 1965). The salient aspects of Jones's style were adopted by many avant-garde drummers of the late 1960s and the 1970s. Ultimately Jones's innovations gave the drummer a broader role in ensemble playing, as a collaborative improviser, and as the principal architect of large-scale, organically evolving percussive textures, while removing the emphasis from his function as a timekeeper.

SELECTED RECORDINGS

As leader: with J. Garrison: *Illumination* (1963, Imp. 49), incl. Nuttin' out Jones; with R. Davis: *Heavy Sounds* (1968, Imp. 9160)

As sideman with J. Coltrane: *Africa/Brass* (1961, Imp. 6); *Live at the Village Vanguard* (1961, Imp. 10); *Impressions* (1961–3, Imp. 42); *Coltrane* (1962, Imp. 21); *Live at Birdland* (1963, Imp. 50); *A Love Supreme* (1964, Imp. 77), incl. Part I: Acknowledgement; *Ascension* (1965, Imp. 95)

As sideman with others: T. Jones and B. Mitchell: *Thad Jones–Billy Mitchell Quintet* (1953, DeeGee 4009) [EP]; S. Rollins: *A Night at the Village Vanguard* (1957, BN 1581)

BIBLIOGRAPHY

B. Jasper: "Elvin Jones and Philly Joe Jones," *JR*, ii/2 (1959), 6
J. Brow: "Elvin Jones," *JM*, viii/3 (1962), 16
R. Kettle: "Re: Elvin Jones: a Technical Analysis of the Poll-winning Drummer's Recorded Solos," *DB*, xxxiii/16 (1966), 17
M. Hennessey: "The Emancipation of Elvin Jones," *DB*, xxxiii/6 (1966), 23
I. Gitler: "Playing the Truth: Elvin Jones," *DB*, xxxvi/20 (1969), 12
L. Tomkins: "Coltrane and I Played without Preparation," *CI*, ix/3 (1970), 10 [interview]
W. Balliett: "A Walk to the Park," *Ecstasy at the Onion* (New York and Indianapolis, 1971) [colln of previously pubd articles and reviews], 146
H. Nolan: "I Play Drums, that's Just What I Do," *DB*, xl/18 (1973), 18 [interview]
B. Cole: *John Coltrane* (New York and London, 1976)
"Elvin Jones," *SJ*, xxx/1 (1976), 280; xxxii/4 (1978), 290 [discography]
F. Kofsky: "Elvin Jones: Rhythmic Displacement in the Art of Elvin Jones," *JJS*, iv (1977), 11
H. Nolan: "Elvin Jones," *DB*, xliv/21 (1977), 13
A. Taylor: "Learn how to Make the Perfect Roll," *Notes and Tones: Musician-to-Musician Interviews* (Liège, Belgium, 1977/R1982), 219
H. Howland: "Elvin Jones," *MD*, iii/4 (1979), 14
G. Endress: *Jazz Podium: Musiker über sich selbst* (Stuttgart, Germany, 1980), 96
K. Rusch: "Elvin Jones: Interview," *Cadence*, vii/2 (1981), 9
R. Mattingly: "Elvin," *MD*, vi/9 (1982), 8

BILL DOBBINS (1), BARRY KERNFELD (2), OLLY WILSON (3)

Jones, Al(bert Francis) (*b* Philadelphia, PA, 18 Dec 1930; *d* *c*1976). Drummer. He played with Lionel Hampton (1949) and Dizzy Gillespie (1951–3), with whom he toured Europe in 1953; he is well represented by *The Champ/Intermission* (1953, Vogue M33310), recorded with Gillespie at a concert in Paris. During this period he also recorded with Milt Jackson, Joe "Bebop" Carroll, Wade Legge, and Miles Davis. He then played with Arnett Cobb (recording in 1956), Billie Holiday, Dinah Washington, and Sarah Vaughan. In 1962 he traveled to Europe with the Living Theater of New York, and decided to settle in Belgium. With the pianist Jean Fanis and the double bass player Roger Van Haverbeke he formed a group to accompany visiting musicians; they played with Dexter Gordon, Clark Terry, and Jackson, among others. He also performed and recorded with Fats Sadi (1965). (*ReclamsJ*)

Jones, Bobby (*b* Louisville, KY, 30 Oct 1928; *d* Munich, 6 March 1980). Tenor saxophonist and clarinetist. He gained experience in big bands before his army service in the early 1950s; thereafter he played in rockabilly groups. In 1959 he joined the Glenn Miller Orchestra under Ray McKinley, playing tenor saxophone. Later he spent several months with Woody Herman (1963) and played clarinet with Jack Teagarden. After teaching in Louisville he worked in 1970–72 with Charles Mingus, undertaking a tour of Japan and making two visits to Europe, where he remained. He eventually settled in Munich, but the climate aggravated his emphysema and he abandoned playing in favor of arranging. Jones's work with Mingus is reasonably well represented on recordings and typically combines a bluesy lyricism with a bop-oriented mobility. These qualities are further displayed on the two albums he made as a leader in the 1970s; one of these, *Hill Country Suite*, also features his affectingly simple clarinet playing, which recalls Jimmy Giuffre's style of the 1950s.

SELECTED RECORDINGS

As leader: *The Arrival of Bobby Jones* (1972, Cob. 9022); *Hill Country Suite* (1974, Enja 2046)

As sideman with C. Mingus: *Pithycanthropus [sic] erectus* (1970, Amer. 6109); *Let my Children Hear Music* (1971, Col. KC31039)

BIBLIOGRAPHY

V. Wilmer: "Bobby Jones: Forced into Jazz," *MM*, xlv (5 Dec 1970), 30
D. Morgenstern: "Inside Mingus with Bobby Jones," *DB*, xxxix/9 (1972), 18
——: "The Arrival of Bobby Jones," *DB*, xxxix/6 (1972), 18
B. Priestley: *Mingus: a Critical Biography* (London, 1982), 182

BRIAN PRIESTLEY

Jones, Buddy [Burgher William] (*b* Hope, AR, 17 Feb 1924). Double bass player. He learned piano as a child and took up the double bass during his time in the navy. After the war he played with Charlie Ventura (1947) and Joe Venuti (1949), and in 1950 moved to New York, where he recorded with Buddy DeFranco (1951) and performed with Lennie Tristano and Stan Getz. He played on Jack Sterling's CBS radio program (1952–64), at first as a member of Elliot Lawrence's quartet. During this period he recorded with Lawrence's big band (1952–7), Al Cohn (1954–5), Sam Most and Gene Quill (both 1955), and Joe Newman, Manny Albam, Andy Kirk, Phil Woods, and Bob Brookmeyer (all 1956); his playing may be heard on Newman's *Salute to Satch* (1956, RCA LPM1324). After playing on television in Hollywood for some time, he returned to New York, where he worked with Bobby Hackett, Al Cohn, and Bill Watrous; he recorded with Cohn in 1965 and Hackett in 1967.

BIBLIOGRAPHY

FeatherE; *Feather '60s*
R. G. Reisner: *Bird: the Legend of Charlie Parker* (New York, 1962/R1975), 123

Jones, (William) Carmell (*b* Kansas City, KS, 19 July 1936). Trumpeter. He took up the trumpet at the age of 11, and after military service spent two years at the University of Kansas; in 1959 he took part in the annual collegiate jazz festival at Notre Dame, Indiana. He led a group in Kansas City, but after being well reviewed by the German jazz critic Joachim-Ernst Berendt he moved in 1960 to California, where he was active until 1964; he recorded as a leader, and with Bud Shank (1961), Gerald Wilson (1961–3), Harold Land, and Curtis Amy. After a year touring with Horace Silver, in August 1965 Jones moved to Europe and joined the SFB Orchestra in Berlin. He made recordings in Europe, but he had faded from prominence when he returned to Kansas City in 1980. Nevertheless, an album that he recorded in 1982 demonstrates that he had lost none of his ability. Jones is a skilled craftsman whose warm tone and melodic ideas are inspired by those of Clifford Brown.

SELECTED RECORDINGS

As leader: *Jay Hawk Talk* (1965, Prst. 7401); *Carmell Jones Returns* (1982, Rev. 44)

As sideman: C. Amy: *Groovin' Blue* (1961, PJ 19); H. Land: *Jazz Impressions of Folk Music* (1963, Imperial 12247); B. Ervin: *The Blues Book* (1964, Prst. 7340); H. Silver: *Song for my Father* (1964, BN 84185)

BIBLIOGRAPHY

J. W. Hardy: Liner notes, *The Remarkable Carmell Jones* (PJ 29, 1961)
J. Tynan: "Trumpet in a Hurry: Carmell Jones," *DB*, xxix/24 (1962), 16
P. Lattes: "Carmell à Juan," *Jh*, no.201 (1964), 6
A. Stevens: "The Scintillating Carmell Jones," *CI*, vi/1 (1967), 18
J. W. Hardy: "Carmell Jones: Interview," *Cadence*, x/2 (1984), 13

MARK GARDNER

Jones, Claude (B.) (*b* Boley, OK, 11 Feb 1901; *d* at sea, 17 Jan 1962). Trombonist. In 1922 he joined the Synco Jazz Band (which later became known as McKinney's Cotton Pickers). He left to work with Fletcher Henderson (1929–31), while also appearing intermittently with Chick Webb. He played with Don Redman (late 1931–September 1933), Henderson (September 1933–*c*September 1934), Alex Hill, and Webb, then from late 1934 to January 1940 worked with Cab Calloway. He played briefly with Coleman Hawkins (twice), Zutty Singleton, and Joe Sullivan (all 1940) and Henderson again (1941–2), but left full-time music in order to manage his own sausage manufacturing firm during which time he performed with Benny Carter (1942) and Redman (1943). In 1943 he returned to Calloway and from 1944 to 1949 was a member of Duke Ellington's orchestra, in which he played valve trombone. He spent further short periods with Henderson (1950) and Ellington (1951), and then became a mess steward aboard the liner *United States*.

Jones's early work was heavily influenced by Miff Mole, as may be heard in the melodic flexibility of his solos with McKinney's Cotton Pickers. Before leaving the band, however, he was beginning to develop a voice of his own, and by the time he was with Henderson he had a big, velvety tone and a refined sense of melody; his solos were propulsive and inventive, and, unlike most of his contemporaries, he frequently employed the upper register of the instrument. He could handle changes of pace in a deft manner (as on *Sugar Foot Stomp*) and his use of upward rips became something of a trademark. *Down in Honky Tonk Town* (1940), which he recorded with Louis Armstrong, reveals traces of the style of J. C. Higginbotham. By the mid-1930s Jones played solos only infrequently and his style was economical and less distinctive, but he was still an original melodist.

For illustration *see* MCKINNEY'S COTTON PICKERS.

SELECTED RECORDINGS

As sideman: McKinney's Cotton Pickers: Put it there (1928, Vic. 38025); Plain Dirt (1929, Vic. 38097); The way I feel today (1929, Vic. 38102); F. Henderson: Chinatown, my Chinatown (1930, Col. 2329D); Just Blues (1931, Mlt. M12239); Sugarfoot Stomp (1931, Vic. 22721); *Connie's Inn Orchestra* (1931, RCA X3013), incl. Sugar Foot Stomp; H. Henderson: Rhythm Crazy (1933, Parl. R1743); J. R. Morton: I thought I heard Buddy Bolden say (1939, Bb 10434); L. Armstrong: Down in Honky Tonk Town (1940, Decca 18091)

BIBLIOGRAPHY

ChiltonW
J. E. Mann: "Claude Jones: Fragment of an Autobiography," *JM*, viii/1 (1962), 3
W. C. Allen: *Hendersonia: the Music of Fletcher Henderson and his Musicians: a Bio-discography* (Highland Park, NJ, 1973)
J. Chilton: *McKinney's Music: a Bio-discography of McKinney's Cotton Pickers* (London, 1978)

BOB ZIEFF

Jones, David [Dave(y)] (*b* Lutcher, LA, *c*1888; *d* Los Angeles, after 1956). Tenor saxophonist. After playing with the Holmes Brass Band in Lutcher (1910), he worked in the Storyville district of New Orleans, on the SS *Capitol* with Fate Marable (1918–21; for illustration *see* NIGHTCLUBS AND OTHER VENUES, fig.3), in California with King Oliver (mid-1921), and in St. Louis with the Record Breakers led by R. Q. Dickerson (1922). He toured with Dickerson in Wilson Robinson's Bostonians and continued to work with the group when it was taken over by the bandleader Andy Preer for an engagement at the New York Cotton Club (1924); it recorded under its new name, the Cotton Club Orchestra, in 1925. He led a band at the Pelican dance hall in New Orleans, then, after a short period with Baba Ridgley's Tuxedo Orchestra, led the JONES AND COLLINS ASTORIA HOT EIGHT with Lee Collins (1928–9). He later moved to the West Coast. Besides his principal instrument Jones also played alto and C-melody saxophones and wrote arrangements. His smooth style is heard to advantage on the Astoria Hot Eight's recording *Damp Weather/Tip Easy Blues* (1929, Bb 10952).

BIBLIOGRAPHY

ChartersJ
A. Rose and E. Souchon: *New Orleans Jazz: a Family Album* (Baton Rouge, LA, 1967, rev. 2/1978, rev. and enlarged 3/1984), 64
C. Hillman: Liner notes, *Harry Cooper, R. Q. Dickerson & the Cotton Club Orchestra* (Collectors Items 006, 1979)

Jones, Dill(wyn Owen) (*b* Newcastle Emlyn, Wales, 19 Aug 1923; *d* New York, 22 June 1984). Welsh pianist. He studied piano and organ at Trinity College of Music, London (1946–8), and began his career as a jazz pianist with Carlo Krahmer and Humphrey Lyttelton (1947–8), performing at the first Nice Jazz Festival (1948). In 1949 he recorded with the BBC Jazz Club band, and during the 1950s introduced the program on both radio and television. After working aboard the liner *Queen Mary* (1950), which allowed him to make regular contact with jazz musicians in New York, he led his own trio in London. In 1961 he settled in New York, where he became associated with many traditional and mainstream players (including Jimmy McPartland and Max Kaminsky) and worked frequently at Condon's, Ryan's and the Metropole. With Budd Johnson, Oliver Jackson, and Bill Pemberton, he formed the JPJ Quartet in 1969, which made several recordings, notably *Montreux '71* (1971, MJR 8111). Jones left the group in 1973 and continued to work as a soloist throughout the 1970s and early 1980s; he occasionally appeared with the Countsmen and the Harlem Blues and Jazz Band. His stride style of playing reflected the influence of James P. Johnson and Luckey Roberts (with whom he studied in 1965), and is best exemplified in his solo recordings, such as *The Music of Bix Beiderbecke* (1972, Chi. 112).

Oral history material in *NjR*.

BIBLIOGRAPHY

Feather–Gitler '70s
H. Lyttelton: *I Play as I Please: the Memoirs of an Old Etonian Trumpeter* (London, 1954)
J. H. Klee: "Dill Jones' Gutter Music," *MR*, vi/4 (1979), 7
S.-A. Worsfold: "'That Hwyl Feeling': Dill Jones," *JJI*, xxxvi/3 (1983), 8

ALYN SHIPTON

Jones, Eddie [Edward; Jonesy] (*b* New York, 1 March 1929). Double bass player. He grew up in Red Bank, New Jersey, close to Count Basie's family home, and studied music education at Howard University, where he played in a student band with Benny Golson, Bill Hughes, and Frank Wess. After touring with Sarah Vaughan (1950) and Lester Young and working for a period as a teacher, he joined Basie's band in mid-1953 and took part in the important "dance session" series of recordings. He had a percussive style influenced by Ray Brown and Milt Hinton, but was sufficiently versatile to be able to scale down his attack and tone to play with smaller groups; his great sensitivity may be heard on recordings made with Joe Newman (1954–60), Milt Jackson (1955, 1958), Ernie Wilkins (1955, 1959), Frank Foster (1956–7), Frank Wess (1956–60), Thad Jones (1957–8), and Putte Wickman (Stockholm, 1958). Jones left Basie in 1962, attracted by the financial security offered by a job with the IBM company. In the late 1980s, while vice-president of an insurance company, he devoted two months of each year to music, playing in a duo with George Wein and with Basie reunion bands.

SELECTED RECORDINGS

As sideman with C. Basie: *Dance Session* (1952–4, Clef 626, 647); *Basie* (1954, Clef 666), incl. Nails; *Chairman of the Board* (1958, Roul. 52032), incl. Speaking of Sounds; *One More Time* (1958–9, Roul. 52024), incl. The Big Walk, Jessica's Day, Meet B. B.; *Kansas City Suite* (1960, Roul. 52056), incl. Katy-Do, Paseo Promenade; *The Kansas City Seven* (1962, Imp. 15)

As sideman with others: E. Wilkins: *Flutes & Reeds* (1955, Savoy 12022); M. Jackson: *Opus de Jazz* (1955, Savoy 12036); C. Hawkins: *Coleman Hawkins Meets the Sax Section* (1958, Savoy 20001); [no leader]: *Basie Reunion* (1958, Prst. 7147); J. Newman: *Jive at Five* (1960, Swingville 2011); *Good 'n' Groovy* (1961, Swingville 2019)

BIBLIOGRAPHY

FeatherE

CHRIS SHERIDAN

Jones, Elvin. *See* JONES family, (3) Elvin.

Jones, Etta (*b* Aiken, SC, 25 Nov 1928). Singer. She was brought up in New York and began her career at the age of 16 on a tour with the rhythm-and-blues group led by the pianist Buddy Johnson. Leonard Feather helped to arrange her first recording, for which he played piano with Barney Bigard's orchestra (1944). Jones recorded with Pete Johnson (1946) and joined J. C. Heard's band in 1948; from 1949 to 1952 she worked and recorded with Earl Hines. Her recording *Don't go with strangers* (1960, Prst. 45-180) won a gold record and led to her making several albums for the Prestige label as a leader (1960–65) and with Gene Ammons (1962). She later toured Japan with Art Blakey (1970) and played at Town Hall, New York, with Billy Taylor (ii). From 1976 into the 1980s she performed with Houston Person, and she recorded for Muse as a sideman with Person and as a leader.

BIBLIOGRAPHY

Feather '60s; *Feather–Gitler '70s*
L. Gourse: *Louis' Children: American Jazz Singers* (New York, 1984), 123

Jones, Fritz. *See* JAMAL, AHMAD.

Jones, Hank. *See* JONES family, (1) Hank.

Jones, Harold (J.) (*b* Richmond, IN, 27 Feb 1940). Drummer. He studied music from the age of 14 and from 1956 worked with such musicians as Wes Montgomery and Freddie Hubbard. While attending the American Conservatory in Chicago (from 1958) he played with the Honeydrippers, led by the blues singer and pianist Roosevelt Sykes, worked with Eddie Harris (recording on his commercially successful track *Exodus*, 1961), and with Paul Winter toured Latin America and performed at the White House (1961–2). He played with Sonny Stitt, Frank Strozier, and Ira Sullivan while working as a freelance in Chicago, and at the end of 1967 joined Count Basie's orchestra, with which he remained for five years. After settling in Los Angeles he worked again as a freelance; he performed and recorded with Marlena Shaw at the Montreux International Jazz Festival (1973), appeared briefly with Basie in the film *Blazing Saddles* (1974), and performed and recorded with Benny Carter in Tokyo (1977, 1979). From 1980 Jones has been a member of Sarah Vaughan's accompanying trio, and in 1981 he played in Carter's quartet in Los Angeles.

SELECTED RECORDINGS

As sideman: E. Harris: *Exodus to Jazz* (1961, VJ 3036), incl. Exodus; P. Winter: *Jazz Premiere: Washington* (1961–2, Col. CS8797); Bunky Green: *Playin' for Keeps* (1965, Cadet 766); C. Basie: *Basie: Straight Ahead* (1968, Dot 25902), incl. The Magic Flea, The Queen Bee; *Afrique* (1970, FD 10138); B. Carter: *Live and Well in Japan!* (1977, PL 2308216)

BIBLIOGRAPHY

Feather–Gitler '70s

CHRIS SHERIDAN

Jones, Isham (*b* Coalton, OH, 31 Jan 1894; *d* Hollywood, FL, 19 Oct 1956). Bandleader, composer, and pianist. He studied piano and saxophone in Chicago, then led and played with various bands in Chicago and Michigan. By the mid-1920s his band had achieved considerable success; it soon traveled to New York, played in London, and toured the USA (1924–5). From 1926 to 1936 it toured extensively and recorded prolifically, becoming famous for its well-disciplined ensemble and large sound, and enjoying a popularity rivaled only by that of Paul Whiteman's band and the Casa Loma Orchestra. Although it was not strictly a jazz band, the group fostered several jazz musicians, among them Jack Jenney, Sonny Lee, Pee Wee Erwin, Howard Smith, and Woody Herman – the last played and sang for a hot sextet called Isham Jones's Juniors, which eventually became the core of Herman's first Herd.

Jones was especially important as a songwriter: among his successes were *On the Alamo* (1922), *Indiana Moon* and *Swingin' down the lane* (both 1923), *I'll see you in my dreams, The One I Love,* and *Spain* (all 1924), *It had to be you* (1925), *I'll never have to dream again* (1932), *Why can't this night go on forever* (1933), and *There is no greater love* (1936).

See also ARRANGEMENT, §2.

BIBLIOGRAPHY

S. Brown: "Down 2: Shies on Jam (anag.)," *Sv*, no.6 (1966), 13
G. T. Simon: *The Big Bands* (New York, 1967, rev. and enlarged 2/1971, rev. 3/1974, 4/1981), 277
A. Wilder: *American Popular Song: the Great Innovators, 1900–1950* (London and New York, 1972)
W. J. Schafer: "'Rhythm King': California Ramblers, Coon–Sanders, Isham Jones," *MR*, v/9 (1978), 7

WAYNE SCHNEIDER

Jones, Jimmy [James Henry] (*b* Memphis, 30 Dec 1918; *d* Burbank, CA, 29 April 1982). Pianist, arranger, and composer. He grew up in Chicago, where he began learning guitar, but he changed to piano as a teenager; he later studied music at Kentucky State College. He first came to prominence in 1943, when he performed in Chicago with Stuff Smith, with whom he traveled to New York (1944) and made several recordings (1944–5). He played with J. C. Heard (1946–7) and accompanied Sarah Vaughan (1947–52, 1954–8). In the 1960s and 1970s he devoted much time to writing and conducting. He conducted Duke Ellington's show *My People* (1963), wrote arrangements for Ellington (until the mid-1970s), and toured Europe as Ella Fitzgerald's music director (1966). He recorded prolifically, with such leaders as Don Byas (1945) and Coleman Hawkins (1946) and with many of Ellington's sidemen, among them Harry Carney (1946), Ben Webster (1947, 1958–9), Rex Stewart (1947), Johnny Hodges (1947, 1960s), Clark Terry (1959), and Paul Gonsalves (1960).

Oral history material in *NjR* (JOHP).

SELECTED RECORDINGS

As leader: Five o'Clock Drag/New World a-Coming (1947, Wax 103); *Jimmy Jones Trio* (1954, Swing 33336), incl. Lush Life
As sideman: S. Smith: Midway/Look at me (1944, Asch 353-1); C. Hawkins: Say it isn't so/Spotlite (1946, Vic. 40-0131)

BIBLIOGRAPHY

FeatherE; Feather '60s; Feather–Gitler '70s
B. Ulanov: "File for the Future," *Metronome*, xi/11 (1945), 22
S. A. Pease: "Bop Harmony: a Contribution of Jimmy Jones," *DB*, xvi/6 (1949), 12
S. Dance: "Portrait of a Professional," *DB*, xxxi/6 (1964), 18
——: *The World of Duke Ellington* (London and New York, 1970/*R*1981) [colln of previously pubd articles and interviews], 212

JAMES M. DORAN

Jones, Jo(nathan) (*b* Chicago, 7 Oct 1911; *d* New York, 3 Sept 1985). Drummer. He grew up in Alabama, and toured as an instrumentalist and tap-dancer with various carnival shows before joining Walter Page's Blue Devils in Oklahoma City in the late 1920s. After playing with the trumpeter Lloyd Hunter in Nebraska he moved in 1933 to Kansas City where, in 1934, he began his long association with Count Basie. Jones left Basie briefly in 1936 to rejoin Page in the Jeter–Pillars Orchestra in St. Louis, but by the end of the year both musicians had returned to Basie's group. When Freddie Green replaced Claude Williams in 1937, Basie's celebrated four-member rhythm section was complete (see illustration, p.632), and soon became the most outstanding and influential of its time (*see* BASIE, COUNT, §2). Jones appeared in the film *Jammin' the Blues* in 1944. Apart from a period in the US Army (1944–6) he remained with Basie until 1948, when he began a varied and active freelance career with many mainstream jazz musicians, revealing an uncommon mastery of swing and modern drumming styles. In 1947 he made the first of several tours with Jazz at the Philharmonic; the organization took him to Europe a number of times and led to his recording with such musicians as Billie Holiday, Teddy Wilson, Duke Ellington, Johnny Hodges, Lester Young, Art Tatum, and Benny Goodman. Later he performed and recorded on many occasions in groups modeled on Basie's "Kansas City" ensembles.

Jones is generally credited with transferring the basic pulse in jazz from the bass drum to the hi-hat, which he left slightly open to produce a light, continuous sound unlike the staccato ideal of earlier jazz drumming. This novel technique, which was fully developed by the time he made his first recordings with Basie in 1936, completely revolutionized the timbre of the jazz rhythm section, making it more subtle and responsive to solo improvisation than had earlier been the case. These recordings also show that he had conceived of the jazz pulse as four evenly stressed beats in a bar, thus helping to establish the four-beat jazz that characterized the later swing period. By concentrating the pulse in the hi-hat, Jones freed his other instruments for irregular accents such as the rim-shots and bass drum bombs for which he became famous (ex.1). Jones

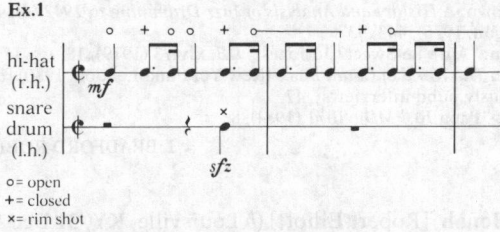

Ex.1

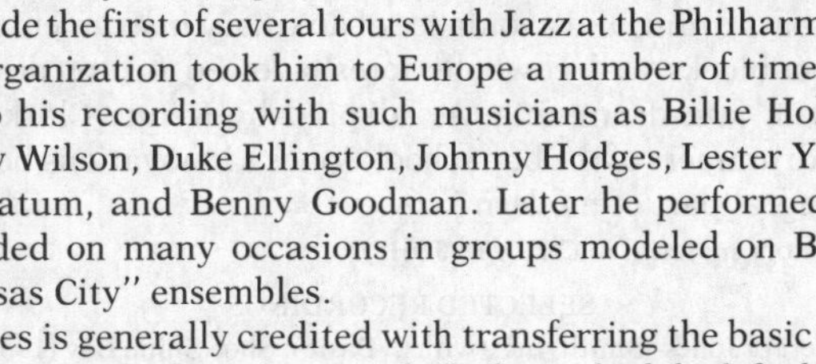

was also among the first jazz drummers to realize the full potential of the brushes, which he used with remarkable facility. Though not given to long solos in the manner of his contemporaries Chick Webb, Gene Krupa, and Cozy Cole, Jones was an expert soloist; his varied phrase lengths, free handling

Count Basie's rhythm section at Decca's recording studios in New York, 1938: (left to right) Freddie Green (guitar), Jo Jones (drums), Walter Page (double bass), and Basie (piano)

of the bass drum, and avoidance of auxiliary instruments such as woodblocks and cowbells foreshadowed future developments in jazz drumming. As adapted by Kenny Clarke and other drummers of the bop school, Jones's innovations became an integral part of modern jazz.

Oral history material in *CtY*, *NjR* (JOHP).

SELECTED RECORDINGS

As leader: of Jones–Smith, Inc. (with C. Basie): Shoe Shine Boy (1936, Voc. 3441); *The Drums* (1973, Jazz Odyssey 008); *The Main Man* (1976, Pablo 2310799)

As sideman: Kansas City Five: I know that you know (1938, Com. 510); C. Basie: Swinging the Blues (1938, Decca 1880); The world is mad (1940, OK 5816); B. Goodman: I found a new baby (1941, Col. 36039)

BIBLIOGRAPHY

"Propos de Jo Jones," *BHcF*, no.40 (1954), 3

W. Balliett: "Jo Jones, Dms.," *Dinosaurs in the Morning* (Philadelphia, 1962/*R*1978) [colln of previously pubd articles and reviews], 61

D. Morgenstern: "Jo Jones: Taking Care of Business," *DB*, xxxii/7 (1965), 15

V. Auvert: "Merveilleux Jo Jones," *BHcF*, no.190 (1969), 6

M. Jones: "Keep Fit Drum Giant," *MM* (7 June 1969), 12

L. K. McMillan, Jr.: "Jo Jones: Percussion Patriarch," *DB*, xxxviii/6 (1971), 16

B. Allibone and M. Gautier: "Jo Jones," *BHcF*, no.218 (1972), 3 [interview]

G. Colombé: "Jo Jones Speaks Out," *JJ*, xxv/12 (1972), 6

——: "The James Joyce of Jazz," *Into Jazz*, i/2 (1974), 14

T. D. Brown: *A History and Analysis of Jazz Drumming to 1942* (diss., U. of Michigan, 1976), 443, 537

R. Brown: "Ain't he Sweet? Jo Jones," *DB*, xlvi/3 (1979), 18

S. Dance: *The World of Count Basie* (New York and London, 1980) [colln of previously pubd interviews], 47

C. Stern: "Papa Jo," *MD*, viii/1 (1984), 8

J. BRADFORD ROBINSON

Jones, Jonah [Robert Elliott] (*b* Louisville, KY, 31 Dec 1909). Trumpeter. He played alto horn in a local band before changing to trumpet. His first professional job was on a Mississippi riverboat, then in 1928 he joined Horace Henderson. After performing in the Midwest with many groups, including that of Jimmie Lunceford (1931), he played with Stuff Smith (1932–4). He worked briefly with Lil Armstrong's big band and McKinney's Cotton Pickers, then rejoined Smith in 1936 for a four-year residency at the Onyx club, for which the group gained much renown. After short periods with Benny Carter (1940) and Fletcher Henderson (1941) Jones became a long-standing member of Cab Calloway's orchestra and Cab Jivers (1941–52; for illustration *see* CALLOWAY, CAB), remaining with Calloway after the band was reduced to a small group. He worked with Earl Hines (1952–3) and toured Europe as a soloist (1954), then formed a quartet that played at the Embers in New York (1955). This group performed tunes from shows, traditional jazz, and standards (which Jones played muted but in a swinging style), and became extremely successful, making several hit recordings. It maintained its popularity throughout the 1960s, and toured Europe, the Far East, and Australia; from 1969 to 1977 the quartet's drummer was Cozy Cole. Jones performed at jazz festivals in Europe in 1978, and continued to work into the 1980s.

Jones was one of the great swing trumpeters. He was able to build a solo gradually until it reached a peak of excitement, often by cleverly distorting his bright, shouting tone with growls or mutes.

Oral history material in *NjR* (JOHP).

SELECTED RECORDINGS

As leader: Hubba hubba hub (1945, Com. 1520); Stompin' at the Savoy (1945, Com. 602); I can't give you anything but love (1946, Swing 228); Jonah's Wail (1946, Swing 243); *Jonah Jones at the Embers* (1956, Groove 1001); *Muted Jazz* (1957, Cap. T839)

As sideman: S. Smith: After You're Gone (1936, Voc. 3201); Here comes the man with the jive (1936, Voc. 3316); Sam the Vegetable Man (1939, Vars. 8063); C. Calloway: Jonah Joins the Cab (1941, OK 6109)

BIBLIOGRAPHY

ChiltonW

J. Jones and H. Panassié: "Jonah Jones par lui-même," *BHcF*, no.32 (1953), 3

D. Gold: "Jonah and the Wail," *DB*, xxv/7 (1958), 17

S. Dance: "Swinging: an Informal Symposium," *JJ*, xxiv (1971), no.1, p.2; no.3, p.2

M. Jones: "Jonah Jones: a Real Good Time Guy," *MM* (26 June 1971), 14

S. Dance: *The World of Swing* (New York, 1974) [colln of previously pubd interviews], 161

E. Townley: "Muted Jazz," *Sv*, no.85 (1979), 5
D. Morgenstern: Liner notes, *Paris* (Swing 8408, 1985)
M. L. Hester: "Jonah Jones: Trumpeter Supreme," *MR*, xiv/11 (1987), 7

SCOTT YANOW

Jones, (Everett) LeRoi. *See* BARAKA, AMIRI.

Jones, (Ronald) Max(well) (*b* London, 28 Feb 1917). English writer. He taught himself to play saxophone and clarinet and worked in dance bands from 1930. After abandoning his career as a performer in 1935 he formed the High Wycombe Rhythm Club and the Challenge Jazz Club in the late 1930s, was the jazz editor of *Challenge* in 1941–2, and worked as a commentator on the BBC's program "Radio Rhythm Club" from 1942 to 1943; he continued to work occasionally in radio during the following decades. He was a founder with Albert McCarthy in 1942 of the journal *Jazz Music* (which he edited in 1944 and again from 1946 to the early 1950s) and the editor in 1944–6 of a series of pamphlets entitled *Jazz Music Books*. Jones had a long association with *Melody Maker*, first as an editor with Rex Harris of "Collector's Corner" (from 1944), then as a critic and feature writer (from early 1945) and author of a weekly column (until his retirement in 1982). At the same time he has contributed articles and reviews to such periodicals as *Jazz Journal* (later *Jazz Journal International*), *Jazz Monthly*, *Jazz Express*, and the *Sunday Times*, and collaborated with John Chilton on a biography of Louis Armstrong based in part on a series of interviews. Jones is a particularly gifted interviewer who has compiled a remarkable collection of oral history material; his close friendships with musicians such as Armstrong have allowed him an insider's view of the art.

WRITINGS

(selective list)

ed. with A. McCarthy: *Piano Jazz* (London, 1945)
with A. McCarthy: *A Tribute to Huddie Ledbetter* (London, 1946)
Jazz Photo Album: a History of Jazz in Pictures (London, 1947)
with J. Chilton and L. Feather: *Salute to Satchmo* (London, 1970)
with J. Chilton: *Louis: the Louis Armstrong Story, 1900–1971* (London, 1971)
Talking Jazz (London, 1987) [colln of previously pubd interviews]

Jones, Oliver (*b* Montreal, 11 Sept 1934). Canadian pianist. He played novelty piano as a youth at clubs in Montreal and studied with Daisy Sweeney, a sister of Oscar Peterson. From 1963 to 1980 he made world tours with the pop singer Ken Hamilton; later he settled in Montreal and resumed his career in jazz. He began touring internationally in the mid-1980s. Jones's recording *The Lights of Burgundy* (1985, Justin Time 6) well illustrates his style, which is swinging and technically involved in the manner of Peterson, Art Tatum, and Erroll Garner.

Oral history material in *CaQMG*.

BIBLIOGRAPHY

M. Miller: "A Legend Comes Home," *Globe and Mail* (Toronto, 28 Jan 1982), §E, p.5
J. Chilton: "The Mature Flair of Oliver Jones," *JJI*, xl/4 (1987), 15
M. Miller: "Oliver Jones," *Boogie, Pete & the Senator: Canadian Musicians in Jazz: the Eighties* (Toronto, 1987), 152

MARK MILLER

Jones, Philly Joe [Joseph Rudolph] (*b* Philadelphia, 15 July 1923; *d* Philadelphia, 30 Aug 1985). Drummer. He played drums from the age of four, studied for three years with Cozy Cole, and was influenced early in his career by Max Roach and Sid Catlett. After serving in the army (from 1941) he moved in 1947 to New York, where as the house drummer at Café Society and other clubs he accompanied such musicians as Fats Navarro, Dexter Gordon, Dizzy Gillespie, and Charlie Parker, and in 1949 moved to Washington, where he worked with Ben Webster; he also played in the late 1940s in a group led by Johnny Griffin and the trumpeter Joe Morris, and with Tiny Grimes and Lionel Hampton. In 1951 he made the acquaintance of Tadd Dameron, who played an important role in advancing his career. He returned in 1952 to New York, worked at the Downbeat club with Miles Davis, Lee Konitz, and Zoot Sims, and in 1953 joined a group led by Dameron, with which he recorded later that year.

From 1955 to 1958 Jones belonged with Paul Chambers and Red Garland to Davis's quintet, and it was for this association that he became best-known; he also worked in the 1950s at Birdland with Duke Ellington, John Coltrane, Jimmy Oliver, and Billie Holiday, and from 1958 performed and recorded as a leader. He lived and taught in London from 1967 to 1969, and in Paris from 1969 until 1972, when he returned to Philadelphia and formed a jazz-rock group, Le Grand Prix. In the late 1970s he worked for a year with Bill Evans (ii) (recording in 1976) and toured with Garland. He became the leader in 1981 of Dameronia, a group dedicated to the performance of music by Dameron; in addition to Jones its members were the saxophonists Frank Wess, Charles Davis, Cecil Payne, and Walter Davis, Jr., the trumpeters Don Sickler and Johnny Coles, the trombonist Britt Woodman, and the double bass player Larry Ridley. In 1984 he took part in a program of jazz and poetry with Archie Shepp and Amiri Baraka.

The volume, aggressiveness, and explosiveness of Jones's playing and the subtlety of his cross-rhythms helped to expand the role of the drums in jazz. A superb timekeeper, he was known especially for his technique with brushes, as well as his cymbal playing and his carefully structured solos.

SELECTED RECORDINGS

As leader: *Blues for Dracula* (1958, Riv. 282); *Philly Mignon* (1977, Gal. 5153); of Dameronia: *To Tadd with Love* (1982, Upt. 2711)
As sideman with M. Davis: *'Round About Midnight* (1955–6, Col. CL949); *Workin'* (1956, Prst. 7150); *Steamin'* (1956, Prst. 7200); *Cookin'* (1956, Prst. 7094); *Milestones* (1958, Col. CL1193)
As sideman with others: T. Dameron: *A Study in Dameronia* (1953, Prst. 159), incl. Philly Joe Jones; J. Coltrane: *Blue Train* (1957, BN 1577); D. Gordon: *Dexter Calling* (1961, BN 84083); A. Shepp: *Archie Shepp and his Band* (1969, Amer. 6102)

BIBLIOGRAPHY

"The Return of Dracula," *DB*, xxvi/5 (1959), 22
R. J. Gleason: "The Forming of Philly Joe," *DB*, xxvii/5 (1960), 28
A. Gerber: "Etude: Philly Joe toujours en tête," *Jm*, no.130 (1966), 42
V. Wilmer: "Ode to Philly Joe," *MM* (13 Jan 1968), 6
A. Romano: "Le Jones de Philadelphia," *Jm*, no.163 (1969), 22
S. Davis: "Philly Joe Jones: Straight Ahead and Rarin' to Go," *DB*, xliii/15 (1976), 18
A. Taylor: "Philly Joe Jones," *Notes and Tones: Musician-to-Musician Interviews* (Liège, Belgium, 1979/*R*1982), 42
R. Mattingly: "Philly Joe Jones," *MD*, vi/1 (1982), 10

MICHAEL ULLMAN

Jones, Preacher. *See* JONES, WARDELL.

Jones, Quincy (Delight, Jr.) [Q] (*b* Chicago, 14 March 1933). Arranger, composer, bandleader, trumpeter, and pianist. He grew up in Seattle, where he started to learn trumpet in 1947. He took some lessons from Clark Terry in 1950, then from 1951 to 1953 was a member of Lionel Hampton's band, with which he traveled to Europe and recorded frequently in Paris. While with Hampton he began to work as a freelance arranger; among those for whom he provided successful arrangements were Oscar Pettiford (1952), Art Farmer, Clifford Brown, and Gigi Gryce (all 1953), Ray Anthony, Tommy Dorsey, James Moody, and Count Basie (all 1953–4), George Wallington (1954), Terry,

Cannonball Adderley, and Jimmy Cleveland (all 1955), Dinah Washington (1955–6, 1961), Paul Quinichette, and Gene Krupa (1956). Jones served as pianist for a recording session with Annie Ross in Stockholm in 1953 and played trumpet in and was music director for Dizzy Gillespie's band for a tour of the Middle East and South America in 1956. The following year he signed a contract with Mercury Records and traveled to Paris, where he spent a year and a half working for Barclay Records as a producer, arranger, and conductor. He returned to New York in 1959, then toured in Europe as music director for Harold Arlen's blues opera *Free and Easy*; after the show finished in Paris in February 1960 he toured Europe and the USA with its band, which included such musicians as Benny Bailey, Terry, Melba Liston, Cleveland, Phil Woods, Sahib Shihab, Jerome Richardson, and Budd Johnson. Later that year he arranged the music for an album by Ray Charles. In 1961 Jones settled in New York as head of the artists and repertory department for Mercury, and in 1964 he became vice-president of the organization, the first Black to hold such a position in a major record company run by Whites. Thereafter he began a successful career writing for films and television (*see* FILMS, §III, 2). From 1969 to 1981 he worked for A&M Records, and in 1980 he founded his own label, Qwest Records.

Jones's compositions and arrangements have been highly influential. His work of the late 1950s was characterized by

Quincy Jones, 1959

use of small-group jazz concepts within a big-band context and was notable for its technical accomplishment. From the 1970s he has made significant contributions to the recordings of several popular singers, notably Aretha Franklin and Michael Jackson. Manuscript scores of his works are in the holdings of the BMI Archives in New York.

SELECTED RECORDINGS

* – composed by Jones

As leader: *The Birth of a Band* (1959, Mer. 20444)

As sideman: L. Hampton: *Kingfish (1951, MGM 11227); D. Gillespie: *Afro* (1954, Norg. 1003)

SELECTED ARRANGEMENTS

* – composed by Jones

As leader: *This is How I Feel about Jazz* (1956, ABC-Para. 149), incl. *Boo's Bloos, *Evening in Paris, *Stockholm Sweetnin'; *Quintessence* (1961, Imp. 11), incl. *For Lena and Lennie, *Hard Sock Dance, *The Quintessence; *Walking in Space* (1969, A&M 3023), incl. *Walking in Space

Recorded by others: A. Farmer: *Work of Art* (1953, Prst. 162); The Champ, I can't get started, *Jessica's Day, on D. Gillespie: *World Statesman* (1956, Norg. 1084); D. Washington: *The Swingin's Miss "D"* (1956, EmA 36104); C. Basie: *Basie One More Time* (1958–9, Roul. 52024), incl. *The Big Walk, *For Lena and Lennie, *I need to be bee'd with, *Jessica's Day, *Meet B. B., *The midnight sun never sets, *Muttnik, *Quince, *Rat Race, *A Square at the Round Table

BIBLIOGRAPHY

J.-E. Berendt: *Das Jazzbuch: Entwicklung und Bedeutung der Jazzmusik* (Frankfurt am Main, Germany, 1953, rev. 2/1959 as *Das neue Jazzbuch*, Eng. trans., New York, 1962; rev. and enlarged 5/1981 as *Das grosse Jazzbuch: von New Orleans bis Jazz Rock*, Eng. trans. as *The Jazz Book: from New Orleans to Fusion and Beyond*, Westport, CT, 1982)

N. Hentoff: "Counterpoint," *DB*, xxi (1954), no.8, p.36; no.9, p.12

R. Horricks: "Portrait of Quincy Jones," *JM*, i/6 (1955), 10

D. Heckman: "Quincy Jones," *JR*, iii/4 (1960), 2

G. Lees: "The Great Wide World of Quincy Jones," *DB*, xxvii/3 (1960), 16

L. Feather: "How to Lose a Big Band without Really Trying," *DB*, xxix/9 (1962), 22

L. Tomkins: "Personally Speaking . . . Featuring Quincy Jones," *Crescendo*, ii/5 (1963), 7; ii/6 (1964), 16

H. Siders: "Keeping up with Quincy Jones," *DB*, xxxvi/24 (1969), 13

——: "Quincy's Got a Brand New (Old) Bag," *DB*, xxxvii/23 (1970), 13

L. Underwood: "Q Lives," *DB*, xlii/17 (1975), 13 [incl. discography]

"Quincy Jones," *SJ*, xxxvi/1 (1982), 252 [discography]

Z. Stewart: "The Quincy Jones Interview," *DB*, lii/4 (1985), 16 [incl. discography]

LEROY OSTRANSKY

Jones, Reunald(, Sr.) (*b* Indianapolis, 22 Dec 1910). Trumpeter. He first performed professionally with local groups in the Midwest, then during the 1930s and 1940s played in several bands, including those of Speed Webb (1930), Fess Williams, Chick Webb (1933–4), Willie Bryant, Teddy Hill, Don Redman (1936–8), Erskine Hawkins, Jimmie Lunceford, and Duke Ellington (1946). After working as the lead trumpeter with Count Basie (1952–7) he toured England with Woody Herman (1959), played in George Shearing's big band, spent four years with Nat "King" Cole's orchestra (1961–5), and worked extensively as a studio musician. He recorded with Sonny Stitt in 1962, but virtually ceased playing jazz from the mid-1960s.

Jones took part in many recording sessions, but after the 1930s rarely played solos, restricting himself mostly to lead parts. His best solos were recorded with Chick Webb (for example, *Let's get together*); his playing on Lil Armstrong's *Harlem on Saturday Night* resembles that of his cousin Roy Eldridge. Jones's wide range and appealing tone made him popular both as a section player and a lead trumpeter.

SELECTED RECORDINGS

As sideman: C. Webb: Let's get together (1934, Col. 741); L. Armstrong: Harlem on Saturday Night (1938, Decca 2234); S. Stitt: *Sonny Stitt and the Top Brass* (1962, Atl. 1395)

BIBLIOGRAPHY

ChiltonW; FeatherE

R. Horricks: *Count Basie and his Orchestra: its Music and its Musicians* (London and New York, 1957), 187

V. Wilmer: "Reunald Jones," *Crescendo*, ii/2 (1963), 12

SCOTT YANOW

Jones, Richard M(ariney) [Richard Myknee] (*b* Barton, nr Donaldsonville, LA, 13 June 1892; *d* Chicago, 8 Dec 1945). Pianist, composer, and arranger. After studying piano (with Richard "Fishin' Bread" Barret), alto horn, and organ he played alto horn and cornet as a member of the Eureka Brass Band (1902) and piano in New Orleans (1908–17). His first composition, *Lonesome Nobody Cares* (1915), was performed by the popular singer Sophie Tucker. In 1918 he played with Papa Celestin and in the following year he moved to Chicago, where he worked for Clarence Williams's music publishing concern and as a promoter of race records. He recorded as an unaccompanied soloist (1921–3), organized sessions for Okeh Records in which he also took part as a performer (1925–8), and worked with Louis Armstrong in groups that accompanied Blanche Calloway (1925) and Chippie Hill (1925–6); he also led the group Jazz Wizards and worked as a sideman with Willie Hightower (recording in 1927) and the cornetist Bernie Young. Later he formed a group for Session Records (1944) and led a jam session of New Orleans jazz at the Zanzibar Cafe in Chicago (March 1945).

SELECTED RECORDINGS

As unaccompanied soloist: Jazzin' Babies Blues/Twelfth Street Rag (1923, Gen. 5174)

As leader: Kin to Kant Blues/Mushmouth Blues (1926, OK 8349); 29th and Dearborn (1944, Session 12006)

As sideman with J. Noone: New Orleans Hop Scop Blues/Keystone Blues (1940, Decca 18095)

BIBLIOGRAPHY

ChiltonW; FeatherE

H. M. Harris and R. Davies: "A Discography of Richard M. Jones," *MM*, xxii (30 March 1946), 4; xxii (6 April 1946), 4

Obituary, G. Hoefer, DB, xiii/2 (1946), 18

JAMES M. DORAN

Jones, Rodney (Bruce) (*b* New Haven, CT, 30 Aug 1956). Guitarist. He took guitar lessons with several teachers and studied improvisation with John Lewis at City College, CUNY. He worked with Jaki Byard (1974) and recorded with Chico Hamilton and as a member of Dizzy Gillespie's quartet (both 1976). He remained with Gillespie until 1979, at the same time playing with his own quartet, with which he recorded (1978, 1980) and toured Europe (1979); he is heard to advantage on *Articulation* (1978, Tim. 125). He also recorded in a quartet with Tommy Flanagan (1981) and in a quartet led by Hank Jones accompanying the vibraphonist Darji (1982). Jones's own group continued to be active, mainly in New York, into the 1980s, but in 1983 he joined the popular singer Lena Horne as her guitarist and arranger, at which point he became less active as a jazz musician. (I. Carr: "Jones, Rodney Bruce," in I. Carr, D. Fairweather, and B. Priestley: *Jazz: the Essential Companion*, London, 1987)

Jones, Rufus [Speedy] (*b* Charleston, SC, 27 May 1936). Drummer. He studied trumpet before taking up drumming at the age of 13. In 1954 he recorded with Lionel Hampton at the Apollo Hall in Amsterdam and in the late 1950s played with Henry "Red" Allen at the Metropole in New York. For four years he belonged to Maynard Ferguson's big band, which he left in 1963 to lead a quartet; this proved unsuccessful commercially, and the following year he joined Count Basie's orchestra. In 1966 he left Basie's band to join that of Duke Ellington, making several important recordings during the next six years.

SELECTED RECORDINGS

As leader: *Five on Eight* (1963, Cameo 1076)

As sideman: L. Hampton: *Apollo Hall Concert, 1954* (1954, Phi. 10157); D. Ellington: *Far East Suite* (1966, RCA LSP3782); *The Intimacy of the Blues* (1967–70, Fan. 9640); *Latin American Suite* (1968, Fan. 8419); *New Orleans Suite* (1970, Atl. 1580)

BIBLIOGRAPHY

R. Barnelle: "Driver's Seat: Rufus "Speedy" Jones," *MD*, vii/11 (1983), 76

CHRIS SHERIDAN

Jones, Rusty [Isham Russell, II] (*b* Cedar Rapids, IA, 13 April 1932). Drummer. Both his parents were professional musicians and he was the great-nephew and godson of Isham Jones. He played with J. R. Monterose then performed and recorded with the pianist Judy Roberts in Chicago (1968–72). He was associated with George Shearing from 1972 to 1978 and made several recordings with him, including *The Reunion* (1976, MPS 68162), recorded in Germany with Stephane Grappelli. He also worked with Lee Konitz, Mose Allison, and Monty Alexander, and recorded with Danny Long and Shearing's sideman Warren Chiasson (1973). In the 1980s he taught workshops and performed at the Fayetteville (Arkansas) Festival. (*Feather–Gitler '70s*)

Jones, Sam(uel) (*b* Jacksonville, FL, 12 Nov 1924; *d* New York, 15 Dec 1981). Double bass player, cellist, and composer. He studied drums and guitar during his school years. He played and recorded on double bass in Cincinnati with Tiny Bradshaw (1953–5), then moved to New York, where he soon became sought after by the leaders of several bop groups, including Kenny Dorham (1956), Cannonball Adderley (1957), Dizzy Gillespie (1958–9), and Thelonious Monk (1959). By 1960 his reputation had grown considerably, and he began recording under his own name on both double bass and cello. He was a member of Adderley's group from 1959 to 1965, and contributed many original compositions, including *Del Sasser* and *Unit 7*, to its repertory. When Ray Brown left Oscar Peterson in 1966 Jones joined the pianist's trio, remaining until 1970. Thereafter he worked with Bobby Timmons, Wynton Kelly, Cedar Walton, Clifford Jordan, Duke Jordan, Lucky Thompson, and Jimmy Heath; a few years before his death he also led a big band with Tom Harrell.

As a jazz cellist Jones must be ranked with Oscar Pettiford and Ray Brown, though his approach to improvisation is more blues-oriented. His soulful perambulations on double bass, even when restricted to basic chord changes, were intrinsically musical, and he sometimes constructed an entire solo from walking-bass patterns.

Oral history material in *NjR* (JOHP).

SELECTED RECORDINGS

As leader: *The Soul Society* (1960, Riv. 324), incl. Deep Blue Cello, Just Friends, Some kind of man, There is no greater love; *The Chant* (1961, Riv. 9358); *Down Home* (1962, Riv. 9432); *Something New* (*c*1980, Sea Breeze 2004)

As sideman: T. Bradshaw: Powder Puff/Ping Pong (1953, King 4687); C. Adderley: *Sophisticated Swing* (1957, EmA 36110), incl. Eddie McLin, Jeanie, Miss Jackie's Delight, Spectacular, Tribute to Brownie; *Them Dirty Blues* (1960, Riv. 322), incl. Del Sasser; *Cannonball Adderley Quintet at the Lighthouse* (1960, Riv. 9344), incl. Sack o'Woe; M. Jackson and W. Montgomery: *Bags Meets Wes* (1961, Riv. 9407), incl. Sam Sack; N. Wilson and C. Adderley: *Nancy Wilson/Cannonball Adderley* (1962, Cap. ST1657), incl. Unit 7; G. Ammons: *Goodbye* (1974, Prst. 10093)

BIBLIOGRAPHY

FeatherE; *Feather '60s*; *Feather–Gitler '70s*
K. Baldock: "Sam Jones," *Crescendo*, iv/12 (1966), 14
B. Gardner: "Along Came Jones," *DB*, xxxiii/5 (1966), 14

LAWRENCE KOCH

Jones, Slick [Wilmore] (*b* Roanoke, VA, 13 April 1907; *d* New York, 2 Nov 1969). Drummer. He played with Fletcher Henderson (1934–6), then joined Fats Waller's band, with which he played and recorded at intervals until 1941; his playing is well represented by an album consisting of material broadcast by Waller's band in 1938 (*Fats Waller Live at the Yacht Club*, Giants of Jazz 1029, 1983 [incl. liner notes by D. Morgenstern]). He also recorded with Emmett Matthews and Putney Dandridge (both 1936), Gene Sedric (1938), Don Redman and Lionel Hampton (both 1939), and Una Mae Carlisle (1940). In the early 1940s he worked with Stuff Smith (1942), Carlisle and Eddie South (both 1943), Redman, and others, and recorded with Don Byas (1945). He was a member of Sedric's band from 1946 to 1954 and also recorded with Sidney Bechet (1949–50); he then played with Wilbur De Paris (1954–5) and Doc Cheatham (in Boston in 1955). In the 1960s he settled in New York, where he worked with Toby Browne and Eddie Durham and recorded with Eddie Barefield (1964). (*ChiltonW*; *FeatherE*; *Feather–Gitler '70s*)

Jones, Snags [Clifford] (*b* New Orleans, 1900; *d* Chicago, 31 Jan 1947). Drummer. He acquired his nickname on account of the gaps between his teeth. He played in New Orleans with Buddy Petit, the trombonist Jack Carey, Papa Celestin, and A. J. Piron, then toured and worked in Chicago with King Oliver (1924). He also recorded with Richard M. Jones, accompanying Chippie Hill and Sara Martin (1926), and with the State Street Ramblers, Junie Cobb, and Jimmy Wade (all 1928). After a period in Milwaukee he returned to Chicago and worked for many years as a freelance, though he also led his own band in 1934. Later he recorded with Punch Miller (1941, 1944) and played with Bunk Johnson and Darnell Howard (both 1946).

BIBLIOGRAPHY

G. Hoefer: "The Hot Box," *DB*, xiv/5 (1947), 12
J. T. Schenck: "Lament for Snags," *Jazz Record*, no.55 (1947), 18

MICHAEL TOVEY

Jones, Speedy. *See* JONES, RUFUS.

Jones, Thad. *See* JONES family, (2) Thad.

Jones, Wallace (Leon) (*b* Baltimore, 16 Nov 1906; *d* New York, 23 March 1983). Trumpeter. He moved to New York in the mid-1930s and played briefly with his cousin Chick Webb and then with Willie Bryant (1936–7). He recorded with Putney Dandridge (1936) and Duke Ellington (1936–43, 1947) and belonged to Ellington's orchestra from 1938 to 1944 (for illustration *see* BANDS, fig.3). He played and recorded with Benny Carter in New York (1945) and played with Snub Mosley (1946) and John Kirby (1947) before abandoning his career in music. The solos Jones recorded with Ellington are mostly brief, beautifully executed muted passages in slow pieces; he is heard to greater advantage, as both a soloist and an accompanist, on Dandridge's *These foolish things* (1936, Voc. 3287).

based on *ChiltonW*

Jones, Wardell [Preacher] (*b c*1905). Trumpeter. He played in 1929 with the trombonist Bill Brown and Benny Carter in ballrooms in New York, and then joined Bingie Madison's band. He was a member of the Mills Blue Rhythm Band (1930–36; for illustration *see* MILLS BLUE RHYTHM BAND), with which he made several recordings (including *Keep that rhythm going*, 1934, Col. 2994D), and briefly of the big bands of Fats Waller and (in 1938) Hot Lips Page. His musical activities ceased after 1940.

based on *ChiltonW*

Jones, Willie [William] (*b* New York, 20 Oct 1929). Drummer. He was largely self-taught. His first important association was with Thelonious Monk, with whom he performed and recorded in 1953. In the mid-1950s he played with Cecil Payne, Charlie Parker, Kenny Dorham, J. J. Johnson, and Lester Young, and recorded with Elmo Hope (1955) and Randy Weston (1956). He was a member of Charles Mingus's first Jazz Workshop (1955–6), with which he recorded three albums, including *Pithecanthropus erectus* (1956, Atl. 1237). (*FeatherE*)

Jones and Collins Astoria Hot Eight. Recording group. Its members were the cornetist Lee Collins, the tenor saxophonist David Jones, the clarinetist Sidney Arodin, the alto saxophonist Theodore Purnell, the pianist Joseph Robichaux, the banjoist Emanuel Sayles, the double bass player Al Morgan, and the drummer Joe Strode. The octet took part in only one recording session, at the Italian Hall in New Orleans on 15 November 1929, during which it recorded the tracks *Astoria Strut/Duet Stomp* (Vic. 38576) and *Damp Weather/Tip Easy Blues* (Bb 10952).

MIKE HAZELDINE

Jones–Smith, Inc. Recording quintet led by Count Basie. Its members were Basie (piano), Carl Smith (trumpet), Lester Young (tenor saxophone), Walter Page (double bass), and Jo Jones (drums). It was named to avoid legal difficulties when it recorded for Vocalion in 1936 after Basie had signed a contract with Decca. The session was supervised by John Hammond, and resulted in *Shoe Shine Boy/Evenin'* (Voc. 3441) and *Boogie Woogie/Lady be Good* (Voc. 3459). The second and third of these tracks include performances by the singer Jimmy Rushing.

FRANK DRIGGS

Jordan, Clifford (Laconia, Jr.) (*b* Chicago, 2 Sept 1931). Tenor saxophonist. He studied piano as a child, but changed to tenor saxophone at the age of 14. His classmates at DuSable High School included Johnny Griffin, John Gilmore, and Richard Davis. After working in and around Chicago with Max Roach, Sonny Stitt, and various rhythm-and-blues groups, he moved in 1957 to New York, where he played first with Roach and then with Horace Silver (with whom he remained until 1958). He spent a year on the West Coast, then returned to New York to work with J. J. Johnson; he also led a quintet with Kenny Dorham (1961–2). During the 1960s Jordan performed with Charles Mingus and again with Roach, and toured Europe, Africa, and the Middle East. He led a group, the Magic Triangle, in the 1970s, and thereafter worked as a freelance, making frequent trips to Europe. In 1972 he played the part of Lester Young in *Lady Day: a Musical Tragedy* at the Brooklyn Academy of Music. He is also a respected teacher.

The most profound influences upon Jordan's style have been the playing of Lester Young and Sonny Rollins, though his album *Glass Bead Games* includes performances in the styles of John Coltrane and Eddie Harris. Nevertheless his playing is highly individual; he combines great control with warmth and passion, and has a distinctive, round tone.

SELECTED RECORDINGS

As leader: *Cliff Craft* (1957, BN 1582); with J. Gilmore: *Blowing in from Chicago* (1957, BN 1549); *Spellbound* (1960, Riv. 9340); *Starting Time* (1961, Jlnd 952); *Glass Bead Games* (1973, SE 19737-8); *Clifford Jordan & the Magic Triangle on Stage* (1975, Ste. 1104); *Repetition* (1984, SN 1084); *Two Tenor Winner!* (1984, Criss Cross 1011)

As sideman: H. Silver: *Further Explorations* (1958, BN 1589); J. J. Johnson: *J. J. Inc.* (1960, Col. CS8406); C. Walton: *Spectrum* (1968, Prst. 7591); *A Night at Boomers* (1973, Muse 5010, 5022)

BIBLIOGRAPHY

FeatherE; *Feather '60s*; *Feather–Gitler '70s*
R. Levin: Liner notes, *Cliff Craft* (BN 1582, 1958)
O. Keepnews: Liner notes, *Spellbound* (Riv. 9340, 1960)
I. Gitler: Liner notes, *Starting Time* (Jlnd 52, 1961)

MARK GARDNER

Jordan, Duke [Irving Sidney] (*b* New York, 1 April 1922). Pianist and composer. He studied classical music privately at an early age and performed with the trombonist Steve Pulliam (at the New York World's Fair, 1939), Al Cooper's Savoy Sultans, and Roy Eldridge's big band (1946). While performing at the Three Deuces in New York in 1946 he was heard by Charlie Parker, who invited him to join a newly formed group with Miles Davis, Max Roach, and Tommy Potter. He played with Parker regularly until autumn 1948 and occasionally thereafter; he also played with Sonny Stitt and Gene Ammons (1950–51). Engagements with Stan Getz (1949, 1952–3) proved unsatisfying because he was given few opportunities to play solos. From 1955 to 1962 he often played in bop groups with Cecil Payne, both as a leader and as a sideman: they performed and recorded with Rolf Ericson in Sweden (1956) and were engaged to play in the theater production *The Connection*, which toured Europe. In the late 1960s Jordan interrupted his musical career; he resumed it, after five years, with a performance in New York (1972). Later he toured Scandinavia (1973–4, 1977–8) and Japan (1976, 1982), and he has lived in Denmark from 1978. Jordan is best known for his introductions to the ballads he recorded with Parker; he developed a lyrical style that owed something to the work of Teddy Wilson and Art Tatum. His compositions include the well-known bop theme *Jordu* and parts of the score to Roger Vadim's film *Les liaisons dangereuses 1960* (1959).

SELECTED RECORDINGS

As unaccompanied soloist: *Midnight Moonlight* (1979, Ste. 1143)

As leader: *Duke Jordan* (1955, Signal 1202), incl. Jordu; *Flight to Jordan* (1960, BN 4046); with S. Hakim: *East and West of Jazz* (1962, CP 805); *The Murray Hill Caper* (1973, Spot. 5); *Two Loves* (1973, Ste. 1024); *Duke's Artistry* (1978, Ste. 1103); *Lover Man* (1979, Ste. 1127); *Change a Pace* (1979, Ste. 1135)

As sideman: C. Parker: Bongo Bop/Embraceable you (1947, Dial 1024); S. Stitt: Nice work if you can get it (1950, Prst. 718); C. Payne: *The Connection* (1962, CP 806)

BIBLIOGRAPHY

M. Gardner: "Duke Jordan: Forgotten Pianist," *JJ*, xvi/11 (1963), 15
R. Baggenaes: "Duke Jordan," *Coda*, xi/3 (1973), 2
S. Peterson: "Flight to Jordan," *Jh*, no.305 (1974), 26
C. Tinder: "Duke Jordan," *DB*, xlviii/2 (1981), 38
T. Sjøgren: *The Duke Jordan Discography* (Copenhagen, 1982, rev. and enlarged 2/1984)

PAUL RINZLER

Jordan, Louis (*b* Brinkley, AR, 8 July 1908; *d* Los Angeles, 4 Feb 1975). Saxophonist, singer, and bandleader. He was taught clarinet and saxophone by his father, who led the band for the Rabbit Foots Minstrels (Jordan toured with them while still in high school). He made his professional début with Jimmy Pryor (1929), then worked with Ruby Williams and other bandleaders in Arkansas until moving to Philadelphia to join the tuba player Jim Winters (1932). He performed with Charlie Gaines (1933–5), the violinist Leroy Smith (1935–6), and Chick Webb (1936–8), and played briefly with Fats Waller and Kaiser Marshall before forming his own ensemble to work in New York. This group, which became known as the Tympany Five, was tremendously popular both in Harlem and throughout the rest of the country until the late 1950s. Jordan also appeared in films with the Tympany Five, including *Follow the Boys* (1944), *Meet Miss Bobby Sox* (1944), *Beware* (1946), *Swing Parade of 1946* (1946), *Reet, Petite and Gone* (1947), and *Look out Sister* (1948). He led a big band briefly (1951–2), made a solo tour of England (1962), and toured Asia (1967–8), and continued to work into the 1970s.

Jordan combined showmanship and musicianship in equal parts and became a widely influential force in music, particularly, in the late 1940s and the 1950s, in the rhythm-and-blues field. As an improviser he is best remembered for his work on alto saxophone, but he also played the soprano, tenor, and baritone instruments. He wrote a number of songs, including *Five Guys Named Moe, Is you is, or is you ain't (ma' baby?), Choo Choo Ch'boogie*, and *Saturday Night Fish Fry*.

See also BLUES, §10, and JUMP.

SELECTED RECORDINGS

Five Guys Named Moe (1943, Decca 8653); Is you is, or is you ain't (ma' baby?) (1943, V-disc 158); Buzz me (1945, Decca 18734); Caldonia (1945, Decca 8670); *Louis Jordan and his Tympany Five* (1945, Cir. [USA] CLP 53), incl. Paper Boy; Beware (1946, Decca 18818); Choo Choo Ch'boogie (1946, Decca 23610); Ain't that just like a woman (1946, Decca 23669); Let the good times roll (1946, Decca 23741); Saturday Night Fish Fry (1949, Decca 24725)

BIBLIOGRAPHY

D. Boyce: "Here Comes Mr. Jordan," *New Beat* (Jan 1950), 12
L. Feather: "Let the Good Times Roll," *DB*, xxxvi/11 (1969), 16
J. Otis: "The Otis Tapes, 1: Louis Jordan," *Blues Unlimited*, no.106 (1974), 12
A. Shaw: *Honkers and Shouters: the Golden Years of Rhythm and Blues* (New York, 1978), 65
S. Harris: *Blues Who's Who: a Biographical Dictionary of Blues Singers* (New Rochelle, NY, 1979)
D. Colebeck: "Louis Jordan Discography," *Blues Unlimited*, no.140 (1982), 14
J. Lubin and D. Garçon: *Louis Jordan Discography, 1929–1974* (Levallois-Perret, France, 1987)

FRANK DRIGGS

Jordan [née Dawson], **Sheila (Jeanette)** (*b* Detroit, 18 Nov 1928). Singer and songwriter. She became interested in jazz as a teenager in Detroit; the work of Charlie Parker influenced her profoundly, and during the 1940s she was a member of a vocal group that sang vocalese to Parker's melodies and improvisations. In 1951 she moved to New York, where she gained more experience of the bop style. From 1952 to 1962 she was married to Duke Jordan, with whom she performed occasionally. She studied jazz theory with Lennie Tristano in the mid-1950s, and in the early 1960s she sang regularly at Page Three, a club in Greenwich Village. In 1962 she was heard by George Russell, who recommended her to Blue Note; he also wrote for her an arrangement of *You are my sunshine*, which she sang on his album *The Outer View*. During the 1960s and 1970s Jordan performed frequently in the USA and Europe. In 1979 she began leading a band with Steve Kuhn and recorded with Steve Swallow, and during the 1980s she has worked in a duo with Harvie Swartz. This setting highlights the diversity and energy of her work. Jordan constantly inflects and interprets texts by varying the timbre, dynamics, and timing of a melodic line. Her varied repertory includes free jazz, settings of contemporary American poetry, scat choruses (such as *Little Willie Leaps* and *Suite for Lady and Prez*), and jazz standards.

SELECTED RECORDINGS

Duos with Arild Andersen: *Sheila* (1977, Ste. 1081)

As leader: *Portrait of Sheila* (1962, BN 9002); *Confirmation* (1975, EW 8024); *The Crossing* (1984, Black Hawk 50501), incl. Little Willie Leaps, Suite for Lady and Prez

As sideman: on G. Russell: *The Outer View* (1962, Riv. 9440), You are my sunshine; R. Rudd: *Numatik Swing Band* (1973, JCOA 1007); *Flexible Flyer* (1974, Ari. 1006); S. Kuhn: *Playground* (1979, ECM 1159)

BIBLIOGRAPHY

R. R. Bennett: "Technique of the Jazz Singer," *Music and Musicians*, xx/6 (1972), 30

S. Harris: "Sheila Jordan," *JJ*, xxvi/6 (1973), 4 [interview]

P. Brodowski: "Music is my Religion: the Sheila Jordan Story," *JF* [intl edn], no.60 (1979), 30 [incl. discography]

L. Jeske: "Sheila Jordan: Working Woman's Blues," *DB*, xlvii/11 (1980), 20 [incl. discography]

L. Tomkins: "Lady of Bracknell: Sheila Jordan," *CI*, xix/1 (1980), 16

R. Riggins: "Sheila Jordan," *Coda*, no.177 (1981), 8 [interview]

S. Placksin: *American Women in Jazz, 1900 to the Present: their Words, Lives, and Music* (New York, 1982), 213

C. Cioe: "The Sheer Need to Sing," *HiFi/MusAm*, xxxiv/5 (1984), 74 [incl. discography]

H. Cutler: "Sheila Jordan," *Cadence*, xiii/11 (1987), 5

MARTY HATCH

Jordan, Stanley (*b* Chicago, 31 July 1959). Electric guitarist. He studied piano from the age of six, changed to guitar when he was 11, and soon after began playing in rock and soul groups; in 1976 he won an award at the Reno (Nevada) Jazz Festival. While studying electronic music, theory, and composition at Princeton University (graduating in 1981) he played with Dizzy Gillespie and Benny Carter. His first album, *Touch Sensitive* (1982), which he recorded as an unaccompanied soloist and produced himself, was an effective display of his virtuosity but in commercial terms was largely a failure. In the following years he gained greater recognition: he performed at the Kool Jazz Festival (1984), the Concord (California) Jazz Festival (1985), and the Montreux International Jazz Festival (1985), and his second album, *Magic Touch* (1985), a recording produced by Al Di Meola on which Jordan plays both without accompaniment and with Onaje Allen Gumbs, the double bass player Charnett Moffett, and the drummer Omar Hakim as sidemen, was a huge commercial success. He also played in the 1980s with Quincy Jones, Michal Urbaniak, and Richie Cole. Jordan's approach to the electric guitar is unprecedented in jazz: although adept at conventional technique he prefers to tap the strings of the instrument with both hands (for illustration *see* GUITAR, fig.3), which allows him to play two independent lines and to comp against his own solos. He has also abandoned the standard guitar tuning in favor of one based entirely on 4ths.

SELECTED RECORDINGS

As unaccompanied soloist: *Touch Sensitive* (1982, Tangent 1001); *Standards*, i (*c*1986, BN 85130)

As leader: *Magic Touch* (1985, BN 85101)

BIBLIOGRAPHY

W. Craig: "Stanley Jordan: Two-handed Jazz Technique," *GP*, xvii/9 (1983), 60

B. Case: "Hammering Out a Magic Touch," *The Wire*, no.18 (1985), 24

J. Ferguson: "Stanley Jordan: Revolutionizing Guitar with the Touch System," *GP*, xix/10 (1985), 82 [incl. transcr.]

B. Milkowski: "Stanley Jordan," *DB*, lii/4 (1985), 29

G. Santoro: "Stanley Jordan: the Man with the Magic Touch," *DB*, liii/5 (1986), 16 [incl. discography]

JIM FERGUSON

Jordan, Steve [Stephen Philip] (*b* New York, 15 Jan 1919). Acoustic guitarist. He studied with Allan Reuss, then played with Will Bradley (1939–42) and Artie Shaw (?1941–2) before joining the navy. In the mid-1940s he recorded with Johnny Bothwell (1945) and Boyd Raeburn (1944–5, 1947), and played and recorded with the Casa Loma Orchestra (*c*1945), Stan Kenton (1947), and Jimmy Dorsey (1947). After a period spent at NBC as a member of the production staff (1950–52) he recorded with Gene Krupa (1953), Mel Powell and Vic Dickenson (1953–4), and Sir Charles Thompson (1954), and worked with Benny Goodman (1954–7); he also recorded with Buck Clayton (1954, 1956) and performed and recorded with Ruby Braff (1956-8). He worked as a tailor for a time, then from 1965 played in Tommy Gwaltney's band at Blues Alley in Washington; he appeared regularly at the Manassas Jazz Festival (1966–*c*1973). His playing may be heard to advantage on an album of duos, *Here Comes Mr. Jordan* (Fat Cat's Jazz 119), which he recorded with the double bass player Billy Goodall in 1971–2.

BIBLIOGRAPHY

ChiltonW

G. W. Kay: "Steve Jordan: Rhythm Man," *JJ*, xix/2 (1966), 16

Jordan, (James) Taft (*b* Florence, SC, 15 Feb 1915; *d* New York, 1 Dec 1981). Trumpeter and singer. He studied baritone horn in Norfolk, Virginia, took up the trumpet, and first worked professionally in Philadelphia (1929). After recording with the Washboard Rhythm Kings and the Washboard Rhythm Band (1932) he joined the orchestra of Chick Webb in 1933 (for illustration *see* WEBB, CHICK), and after Webb's death in 1939 he remained with the orchestra, now led by Ella Fitzgerald, until 1942. He worked as a leader in Harlem and for four years (from 1943) played with Duke Ellington; during the following years he worked in Lucille Dixon's orchestra at the Savannah Club in New York (1949–53), recorded popular music with the singing group the Modernaires and the singer Steve Lawrence (1954), and played briefly with Benny Goodman (1958), with whom he toured Europe. In the 1960s he worked in New York as a freelance and occasionally as the leader of a quintet; he also performed with the Duke Ellington Jazz Society at Town Hall (1963) and from 1964 belonged to the pit orchestra of the musical *Hello, Dolly!*. He continued to work as a freelance in the 1970s, in particular with Earle Warren at the West End. In his early work Jordan was influenced both as a trumpeter and as a singer by Louis Armstrong, whom he often mimicked in his performances. Later he incorporated into his playing growls in the manner of Roy Eldridge, and glissandos and half-valve effects like those of Rex Stewart. His recordings with Ellington are acknowledged to be his best; among the most representative of his style is *Jam-a-ditty* (1946), on which he plays an explosive solo break followed by an improvised chorus.

SELECTED RECORDINGS

As sideman: Washboard Rhythm Kings: Hummin' to myself/Holding my Honey's Hand (1932, Vic. 24065); C. Webb: The Dipsy Doodle/Midnite in a Madhouse (1937, Decca 1587); D. Ellington: It don't mean a thing (1945, Vic. 270054); Suddenly it Jumped (1946, Vic. 203135); Trumpet No End (Blue Skies) (1946, Musi. 484); Jam-a-ditty (1946, Musi. 466)

BIBLIOGRAPHY

ChiltonW; *FeatherE*; *Feather '60s*; *Feather–Gitler '70s*

B. Ulanov: *Duke Ellington* (New York, 1946/*R*1975), 267

S. Dance: *The World of Swing* (New York, 1974) [colln of previously pubd interviews], 77

KEN RATTENBURY

Joyner, George (Leon). *See* NASSER, JAMIL.

JPJ Quartet. Quartet formed by Oliver Jackson, Budd Johnson, DILL JONES, and BILL PEMBERTON in 1969.

Judge, the. Nickname of MILT HINTON.

Judson. Record label. It was founded in the late 1950s as a division of RIVERSIDE, and was used mainly to issue albums of music other than jazz, but the catalogue contained excellent LPs of duos by Kenny Drew and Wilbur Ware, and an item by Herb Strauss that included important work by Mundell Lowe.

MARK GARDNER

Jug. Nickname of GENE AMMONS.

Jug band. An instrumental ensemble developed among black Americans in the early 20th century as a popular novelty entertainment for medicine shows and rural picnics. It takes its name from the use of a jug as a bass instrument, the player making buzzing sounds with the lips and the jug acting as a resonator. Bands with as many as three jugs were noted in Florida in 1904, but generally only one jug is used in each group, which otherwise comprises strings and a melody instrument such as harmonica or kazoo. One of the earliest such bands to record, the Dixieland Jug Blowers from Louisville, occasionally employed two jugs, as on *Skip skat doodle do* (1926, Vic. 20649), and as many as three wind instruments, as on *Southern Shout* (1927, Vic. 20954). Johnny Dodds performed with the Dixieland Jug Blowers on some of their recordings, such as *Memphis Shake* (1926, Vic. 20415), and Clarence Williams also favored the jug, playing it himself on *Chizzlin' Sam* (1933, Col. 2829) and other titles; but despite these jazz connections the jug is mainly associated with folk-blues groups. Will Shade's Memphis Jug Band and Gus Cannon's Jug Stompers, both based in Memphis, were pre-eminent among early jug bands, their recordings featuring an interplay of harmonica or kazoo against strings and jug. The style of Jack Kelly's South Memphis Jug Band was more primitive; members of this loosely formed group were still performing in the 1960s. Similar jug bands existed in other states, including the Birmingham Jug Band from Alabama and the Cincinnati Jug Band. In rural districts the jug continues to be used as a folk instrument, though it lost its popularity on recordings late in the 1930s. During the folk revival of the 1960s jug bands were briefly reintroduced by white performers in the blues idiom.

BIBLIOGRAPHY

S. B. Charters: *The Country Blues* (New York and Toronto, 1959), chap.8
P. Oliver: Liner notes, *Tub Jug Washboard Bands 1924–1932* (Riv. 8802, 1962)
B. Olsson: *Memphis Blues and Jug Bands* (London, 1970)
——: Liner notes, *Cannon's Jug Stompers* (Herwin 208, 1973)
F. E. Cox, J. Randolph, and J. Harris: "Jug Band Ramblings: 1962, Excerpts from the Forthcoming Book 'Jug Bands of Louisville'," *Sv*, no.66 (1976), 204
B. Olsson: Liner notes, *South Memphis Jug Band* (Flyright 113, 1976)
F. E. Cox: "Carl Reid: Jug-blower Non Pareil," *Sv*, no.104 (1982–3), 51
B. Bastin: *Red River Blues: the Blues Tradition in the Southeast* (London, 1986), chap.3

PAUL OLIVER

Jullien, Ivan (*b* France, 27 Oct 1934). French trumpeter and arranger. As a member of groups led by Claude Bolling (1961) and the pianist Jacques Denjean (1961–2) he gained recognition for his trumpet playing, chiefly through recordings; from 1966 to 1967 he led the Paris Jazz All Stars. Later he worked as a leader, performed with Maynard Ferguson (1968) and Ben Webster (1972), and played on a film soundtrack composed and recorded by Lester Bowie (1970). His album *Secret Service* (1971, Riviera 521173) offers a good example of his trumpet playing; of greater importance are his arrangements, which rely heavily on brass instruments and are marked by a strong sense of swing. (J.-L. Ginibre: "Ivan le terrible," *Jm*, no.129 (1966), 33)

MICHEL LAPLACE

Jumbo Jack. Nickname of JACK GARDNER.

Jump. A style of jazz related to swing (*see* SWING (i), (2)). It developed around 1937 and flourished during the 1940s, becoming a precursor of rhythm-and-blues. In a general sense the word "jump" described the compelling energy of the dance music played by the big bands, reflected in such titles as Count Basie's *One o'Clock Jump* (1937, Decca 1363), *Jumpin' at the Woodside* (1938, Decca 2212), and *Do you wanna jump, children?* (1938, Decca 2224), and Earl Hines's *Second Balcony Jump* (1942, Bb 11567). More specifically the term is applied to the small-group style typified by the work of LOUIS JORDAN, the instrumentation of whose group, the Tympany Five, served as the model for all subsequent jump bands (usually trumpet, alto saxophone, and tenor saxophone – with one of the saxophones serving as principal solo instrument – and a rhythm section of piano, double bass, and drums). Jordan's music was characterized by saxophone solos in a relaxed, tuneful swing style; simple swing riffs (played by individual melody instruments); blues and newly composed popular-song structures; and clever lyrics about black-American life. Another important jazz instrumentalist in the style was Pete Brown. Later the emphasis became placed increasingly on lyrics and jump became identified with black-American popular music. Bruce Turner, who led his Jump Band from 1957 to 1965, was a late exponent of the jazz style. (*See also* SAVOY SULTANS (i).)

BIBLIOGRAPHY

N. Haslewood: "The Jump Bands (an Introduction)," *Sv*, no.131 (1987), 164

BARRY KERNFELD

Jungle Kings. Name used in 1928 by an octet that also recorded as the CHICAGO RHYTHM KINGS.

Jungle music. A term used to describe a type of jazz in the 1920s and 1930s that incorporated pseudo-African musical effects – especially pounding tom-toms, unusual harmonies, "primitive" scales (usually pentatonic and whole-tone), and muted, growling brass lines. Although elements of the "jungle style" may be discerned in *March of the Caboceers*, from *In Dahomey* (1902) by Will Marion Cook, and in the Original Memphis Five's recording *Africa* (1924, Pathé 036117), the genre's expressive potential was most fully realized by Duke Ellington. During its residency at the Cotton Club (1927–31) Ellington's orchestra recorded for Brunswick and Melotone as the Jungle Band; for many years it used as its theme *East St. Louis Toodle-o* (1926, Voc. 1064), in which the keening trumpet playing of Bubber Miley is set against a background of dark, sinister reeds. Other compositions by Ellington exploiting the "jungle style" are *The Mooche* (1928, OK 8623), *Jungle Nights in Harlem* (1930, Vic. 23022), *Echoes of the Jungle* (1931, Vic. 22743), and *Ko-Ko* (1940, Vic. 26577).

BIBLIOGRAPHY

G. Schuller: "The Ellington Style: its Origins and Early Development," *Early Jazz: its Roots and Musical Development* (New York, 1968), 318–57
D. Ellington: *Music is my Mistress* (Garden City, NY, 1973)

MARK TUCKER

Juris, Vic (*b* Parsippany, NJ, 1953). Guitarist. He played electric guitar with Lyn Christie (early 1970s). His first recording, made with Eric Kloss in 1975, led to a long association with Barry Miles's jazz-rock group, with which he has toured and recorded. He recorded several hard-bop albums with Richie Cole (1976–8), including *Keeper of the Flame* (1978, Muse 5192); Cole helped him to establish agreements with Muse that resulted in his recording three albums as a leader (1977, *c*1979, 1981). Juris also played with the soul-jazz organists Don Patterson (with whom he recorded in 1977), Wild Bill Davis, and Jimmy Smith, and recorded with Mel Tormé (1977) and Bireli Lagrene (1985). In 1981 he formed a quartet to perform his own compositions; he played acoustic guitar and Mike Nock was among the other members.

BIBLIOGRAPHY

R. Lombreglia: "Jazz Guitarist Vic Juris: Stepping out of the Mainstream," *GP*, xv/2 (1981), 58 [incl. discography]

JVC Grande Parade du Jazz Nice. Festival held annually in Nice, France. Founded in 1974 by George Wein and Simon Ginibre, it was inspired by the Nice Jazz Festival of 1948 and known as the Grande Parade du Jazz until 1984, when the Japanese Victor Corporation became its principal sponsor. The festival is produced by George Wein's Festival Productions, Inc. It takes place over 11 or 12 days in July at several venues in the Jardin des Arènes de Cimiez and has consisted both of informally organized jam sessions, in which many musicians have taken part, and of performances by such established groups as Art Blakey's Jazz Messengers, the Preservation Hall Jazz Band, the Dutch Swing College Band, Soprano Summit, Spyro Gyra, and the orchestras of Count Basie, Thad Jones and Mel Lewis, and Buddy Rich. In 1984 240 musicians performed 180 one-hour sets and 29 two-hour sets before a combined audience of more than 100,000. The festival is widely recognized as one of the most important in the world and receives the most extensive press coverage of any European jazz festival.

PAUL R. LAIRD

JVC Jazz Festival New York. Name by which the NEWPORT JAZZ FESTIVAL became known in 1986.

JWS. *See* JAZZ WORLD SOCIETY.

K

Kahn, Steve. Name by which STEVE KHAN has sometimes (and incorrectly) been identified.

Kahn, Tiny [Norman] (*b* New York, 1923 or 1924; *d* New York, 19 Aug 1953). Drummer and arranger. He began playing harmonica at the age of six; he took up drums when he was 15, and played timpani in his high-school orchestra. He worked with Boyd Raeburn (1948), Georgie Auld, Chubby Jackson, and Charlie Barnet (all 1949), Stan Getz (1951), and Elliot Lawrence (1952–3), and also recorded with Red Rodney and Serge Chaloff (both 1947), Lester Young (1948), and Al Cohn (1950). Some of his finest work was with Jackson, for whom he composed and arranged *Tiny's Blues* and *Father Knickerbopper* and arranged *Godchild*. Barnet, Lawrence, Woody Herman, and others also used his arrangements. Kahn was an excellent timekeeper, and had a light touch and resourceful imagination, but he died just before the LP era and never received the recognition he deserved.

SELECTED RECORDINGS

As sideman: C. Jackson: Tiny's Blues/All Wrong (1949, Col. 38623); Father Knickerbopper/Godchild (1949, Col. 38451); S. Getz: *Jazz at Storyville* (1951, Roost 407, 411, 420)

BIBLIOGRAPHY

FeatherE
I. Gitler: *Swing to Bop: an Oral History of the Transition in Jazz in the 1940s* (New York, and Oxford, England, 1985)

MARK GARDNER

Kalaparush(a). *See* MCINTYRE, KALAPARUSHA MAURICE.

Kalimba. A type of LAMELLAPHONE.

Kaminsky, Max (*b* Brockton, MA, 7 Sept 1908). Trumpeter. He worked in Boston, in Chicago from 1928 with George Wettling and Frank Teschemaker at the Cinderella Ballroom, and in New York for a brief period in 1929 with Red Nichols. For the next five years he worked in commercially oriented dance bands, at the same time recording with Eddie Condon and Benny Carter's Chocolate Dandies (1933) and Mezz Mezzrow (1933–4). He played with Tommy Dorsey (1936, 1938) and Artie Shaw (briefly in 1938), performed and recorded with Bud Freeman (1939–40), and worked again with Shaw (1941–3), who led a navy band with which Kaminsky toured the South Pacific. From 1942 he took part in important concerts in New York that were organized by Condon at Carnegie Hall and Town Hall, and from the following year he played dixieland with various groups; he also worked in the 1940s with Sidney Bechet, Georg Brunis, Art Hodes, Joe Marsala, Willie "the Lion" Smith, and Jack Teagarden. Later he worked in television, toured Europe with Teagarden's and Earl Hines's All Stars (1957), and performed at Ryan's in New York (at intervals from the late 1960s to 1983), the Newport Jazz Festival, and the New York World's Fair (1964–5). In 1975–6 he made recordings as a leader that well illustrate his style, which is full-toned, economical, and swinging in the manner of King Oliver, Freddy Keppard, and Louis Armstrong.

Oral history material in *NjR*.

SELECTED RECORDINGS

As leader: Love Nest/Everybody Loves my baby (1944, Com. 595); *Tea for Two* (1975–6, Fat Cat's Jazz 206), incl. Do you Know what it Means to Miss New Orleans?, I Wish I could Shimmy Like my Sister Kate, You Turned the Tables on me

As sideman: E. Condon: Tennessee Twilight/Madame Dynamite (1933, Bruns. 01690); M. Mezzrow: Old Fashioned Love/35th & Calumet (1934, Vic. 25202); B. Freeman: I've Found a New Baby/Easy to Get (1939, Bb 10370)

BIBLIOGRAPHY

ChiltonW; *FeatherE*; *Feather '60s*; *Feather–Gitler '70s*
W. Miller: *Three Brass: Floyd O'Brien, Maxie Kaminsky, Shorty Sherock* (Melbourne, Australia, 1945)
M. Kaminsky and V. E. Hughes: *My Life in Jazz* (New York, 1963)
J. S. Wilson: "Max Kaminsky," *IM*, lxviii/8 (1970), 10

KEN RATTENBURY

Kamuca, Richie [Richard] (*b* Philadelphia, 23 July 1930; *d* Los Angeles, 22 July 1977). Tenor saxophonist. While in his teens he worked around Philadelphia and made the acquaintance of Roy Eldridge. From 1952 to July 1953 he performed and recorded with Stan Kenton, and took solos on such tracks as *Fascinatin' Rhythm* (1953); he was a principal soloist with Woody Herman from 1954 to 1956. On the West Coast he performed and recorded with Cy Touff (1955), Chet Baker (1956), Art Pepper (1956, 1959), and Shelly Manne (1959–61) and after moving to New York worked with Eldridge (recording in 1965) and belonged to the orchestra of Merv Griffin's television series, with which he moved in 1972 to Los Angeles; he recorded in 1974 and 1976 with Bill Berry's L.A. Big Band. Kamuca's early style was indebted to that of Lester Young; his best recordings, which he made in the 1970s for Concord, display greater individuality and a growing affinity with ballads.

SELECTED RECORDINGS

As leader: *Jazz Erotica* (1958, Hi Fi 604); *Drop me Off in Harlem* (1977, Conc. 39); *Richie* (c1977, Conc. 41); *Charlie* (c1977, Conc. 96)

As sideman: S. Kenton: *Sketches on Standards* (1953, Cap. H426), incl. Fascinatin' Rhythm; W. Herman: *Road Band* (1955, Cap. T658), incl. Captain Ahab, Opus de Funk; C. Touff: *Cy Touff's Octet and Quintet* (1955, PJ 1211); S. Manne: *Shelly Manne and his Men at the Black Hawk* (1959, Cont. 7577–80)

BIBLIOGRAPHY

"Double Exposure," *Record Research*, ii/2 (1956), 24
J. Tynan: "Two Tenor Conversation," *DB*, xxv/10 (1958), 14
A. Morgan: "Woody's Tenors," *JM*, vi (1960–61), no.7, p.4; no.8, p.13; no.12, p.9
D. DeMicheal: "Caught in the Act," *DB*, xxxv/26 (1968), 38
Obituary, *MM*, lii (6 Aug 1977), 6

MICHAEL ULLMAN

Kansas City Five (i). Name used in the mid-1920s for various recording groups led by Elmer Snowden.

Kansas City Five (ii). Quintet led by Eddie Durham and Buck Clayton which recorded in 1938; later that year, augmented by Lester Young, the ensemble recorded as a sextet, the KANSAS CITY SIX.

Kansas City Frank. Pseudonym of FRANK MELROSE.

Kansas City jazz [Southwest jazz]. A style of orchestral jazz developed in the 1920s and 1930s by the territory bands of the American Southwest and bands in Kansas City and St. Louis (*see* TERRITORY BAND). Because this area has strong traditions of orchestral ragtime (which flourished particularly in Missouri) and rural blues, Kansas City jazz evolved along different lines from the urban jazz of New Orleans, Chicago, and New York. Early commentators mention the flexibility of the repertory, the prevalence of eight- and 12-bar blues forms, and an emphasis on the use of saxophones; all these characteristics are evident on the few recordings of groups from the Southwest, which began to appear from the mid-1920s. The bands generally avoided complicated arrangements, preferring simple head arrangements worked out in rehearsal and committed to memory; these gave more freedom to the soloists, and allowed the musicians to concentrate on the rhythmic drive for which the style is noted. Many arrangements were based on the RIFF, which became virtually a trademark of Kansas City jazz. Southwest musicians also played an important part in developing the characteristic rhythmic swing of 1930s jazz through their cultivation of the walking bass technique (exemplified by the playing of Walter Page) and use of the hi-hat (Jo Jones). Although many of the bands also played popular songs in written arrangements, the strength of the tradition lay in its close contact with the vocal blues of the South and Southwest, as may be heard in recordings by the blues shouters Joe Turner (ii), Jimmy Rushing, and Walter Brown.

Undoubtedly the most important early Kansas City group was that of Bennie Moten, which continually attracted the area's most talented musicians and later served as the basis of the Count Basie Orchestra. Other significant early bands were led by Troy Floyd (San Antonio), Page (Oklahoma City), and Alphonso Trent (Dallas). Important later bands included, besides Basie's, those of Andy Kirk, Harlan Leonard, and Jay McShann, and the Jeter–Pillars Orchestra. From the mid-1930s the Kansas City style was incorporated into the swing band movement and entered the mainstream of jazz.

BIBLIOGRAPHY

F. S. Driggs: "Kansas City and the Southwest," *Jazz: New Perspectives on the History of Jazz by Twelve of the World's Foremost Jazz Critics and Scholars* (New York and Toronto, 1959/*R*1974), 189
G. Schuller: *Early Jazz: its Roots and Musical Development* (New York, 1968), 279–319
R. Russell: *Jazz Style in Kansas City and the Southwest* (Berkeley, CA, Los Angeles, and London, 1971/*R*1983, rev. 2/1973)
"Kansas City Revives Jazz Landmark," *New York Times* (2 May 1985)
M. Williams: "Jazz: What Happened in Kansas City," *American Music*, iii (1985), 171
N. W. Pearson, Jr.: *Goin' to Kansas City* (Urbana, IL, and London, 1988)

J. BRADFORD ROBINSON

Kansas City Rockets [Kansas City Sky Rockets]. Big band. It was formed in 1931 by the trombonist Thamon Hayes; several of its members had formerly played with Bennie Moten and George E. Lee. Directed by Jesse Stone, and using his arrangements, it immediately became successful, and was engaged to play for the summer season at Fairyland Park, Kansas City, in 1932. As a result of its frequent tours the band was invited to perform at nightclubs in Chicago, but union regulations prevented it from doing so. In 1934 Hayes resigned, ceding leadership to Harlan Leonard, who directed the ensemble until it disbanded in 1937. Leonard then formed a new band, known simply as the Rockets. (F. Driggs: "Kansas City and the Southwest," *Jazz: New Perspectives on the History of Jazz by Twelve of the World's Foremost Jazz Critics and Scholars*, ed. N. Hentoff and A. J. McCarthy (New York and Toronto, 1959/*R*1974), 210)

FRANK DRIGGS

Kansas City Seven. Septet led by Count Basie that recorded in 1944; some of its members also made recordings around this time that were issued under the name KANSAS CITY SIX.

Kansas City Six. Recording group. Made up of members of Count Basie's band, it grew out of a quintet, the Kansas City Five, which consisted of Eddie Durham, Buck Clayton, and Basie's rhythm section (minus Basie himself). Its earliest recordings (including *Good Morning Blues*, Com. 511), made in March 1938, were among the first to include the electric guitar. Later that year the group recorded again, augmented for several sessions by the addition of Lester Young. As the Kansas City Six this ensemble produced some classic swing recordings (among them *Way down yonder in New Orleans*, Com. 512) which offer some rare examples of Young's clarinet playing. The name was used again in 1944 by a recording sextet that included Bill Coleman, Dicky Wells, Young, and Jo Jones; around the same time Basie himself, Clayton, Wells, Young and Freddie Green made some recordings that were issued under the name Kansas City Seven. Later in his career Basie revived these group titles, recording as the leader of a Kansas City Seven (1962), performing at the Newport Jazz Festival with a Kansas City Six (1967), and touring and recording with all-star swing musicians in a Kansas City Seven (1972), a Kansas City Five (1977), and a Kansas City Six (1981). The name Kansas City Five was also used in the mid-1920s by recording groups led by Elmer Snowden that included Bubber Miley (1924) and Louis Metcalf (1925). (L. Feather and M. Gabler: Liner notes, L. Young: *Kansas City Six and Five*, Com. 14937, 1979)

FRANK DRIGGS

Kansas City Sky Rockets. *See* KANSAS CITY ROCKETS.

Kapstad, Egil (*b* Oslo, 6 Aug 1940). Norwegian pianist, arranger, and composer. He worked professionally from 1960, played with Karin Krog (1962–4), and led groups of which the saxophonists Bjørn Johansen and Bjarne Nerem were often members; he also worked with the double bass players Per Løberg, Sture Janson, and Arild Andersen and the drummers Svein Christiansen and Jon Christensen. As a composer and arranger Kapstad has written music for the stage and orchestral works in addition to jazz; his best-known jazz compositions include *Syner* (Vision), *Children's Waltz*, and *Song of the Bird* (all recorded on the album *Syner*, 1967, Norsk Jazzforum LP1). He received the Buddy Award from the Norwegian Jazz Federation in 1977.

BIBLIOGRAPHY

O. Angell, J. E. Vold, and E. Økland: *Jazz i Norge* (Oslo, 1975)
K. Michelsen, ed.: *Cappelens musikkleksikon* (Oslo, 1978)

VIDAR VANBERG

Karashima, Fumio (*b* Oita, Japan, 9 March 1948). Japanese pianist. He studied piano from the age of three and attended Kyushu University, where his father taught music. After moving to New York in 1973 he returned to Japan the following year, where he joined a group led by the drummer George Otsuka in 1975. From 1980 he belonged to Elvin Jones's Jazz Machine, with which he toured Europe and the USA, performed frequently in New York, and recorded several albums.

SELECTED RECORDINGS

Pirania (1975, Whynot PA7150); *Gathering* (1977, TBM 3004); *Moonflower: Karashima Fumio with Elvin Jones* (1978, Trio PAP9114); *Fusetsu* (1981, Trio–Full House PAP25006); *Round Midnight: Karashimo Trio with Larry Coryell* (1983, Trio–Full House PAP25045); *Autumn in New York* (1985, Pol. H33P20046); *Transparent* (1987, Pol. H33P20149)

YOZO IWANAMI

Kärki, Toivo (*b* Pirkkala, Finland, 3 Dec 1915). Finnish pianist, accordionist, arranger, and composer. From 1933 he played in dance bands, including Klaus Salmi's Ramblers (1935–8), on whose recording of *You can't stop me from dreaming* (1938) he played accordion. His composition *Things happen that way* won a competition sponsored by *Melody Maker* in 1939, and he arranged a series of jazz standards that were recorded by Erkki Aho's swing band in 1944. After World War II he formed his own group, which recorded his compositions *Why nameless* (1945, Rytmi 2114) and *My serenade* (1946, Rytmi 2166); these were the first Finnish jazz works to be issued on record. With K. Kaisla he compiled an encyclopedia of jazz and modern dance music, *Rytmimusiikki* (Turku, Finland, 1946). In the late 1940s Kärki ended his jazz career and became a successful composer of popular songs and film music. (M. Niiniluoto: *Toivo Kärki: siks oon mä suruinen* [Toivo Kärki: The reason why I am sad], Helsinki, 1982)

PEKKA GRONOW

Karolak, Wojciech (*b* Warsaw, 28 May 1939). Polish pianist and organist. He received his first piano lessons as a child, took up alto and tenor saxophone while at the Fryderyck Chopin school of music, then studied composition and music theory at the High School of Music in Kraków. He recorded with Jan Wróblewski's Jazz Believers (1958), Andrzej Trzaskowski (1960), and Andrzej Kurylewicz (1961–3), and from 1962 led his own trio, which accompanied visiting musicians and recorded with Don Ellis (1962) and Annie Ross (1965). In the mid-1960s he worked as a composer and arranger for the orchestra of the Polish Radio Jazz Studio. He took up the Hammond organ in 1965 and in 1970, after hearing Chick Corea, began to play a Fender Rhodes electric piano. In the late 1960s and 1970s he was a member of various jazz-rock groups led by Michal Urbaniak, with whom he toured Europe. In 1973 he returned to playing acoustic jazz and formed the group Mainstream with Wróblewski. Karolak is interested only in what he regards as "pure" jazz, rejecting the experiments made by many Polish players in which jazz is fused with elements of folk and classical music.

SELECTED RECORDINGS

As leader: *The Karolak Trio* (1962, Muza 0200); with J. Wróblewski: *Mainstream* (1973, Muza 1139); *Easy* (1974, Muza 1069)
As sideman: Z. Namysłowski: *Kujawiak Goes Funky* (1975, Muza 1230)

BIBLIOGRAPHY

J. Byrczek: "Eurojazz Personalities: Poland," *JF* [intl edn] no.17 (1972), 85
J. P. Wróblewski: "Wojciech Karolak," *JF* [intl edn], no.27 (1974), 50
W. Karolak: "Jazz and me," *JF* [intl edn], no.50 (1977), 31

WOLFRAM KNAUER

Katz, Dick [Richard Aaron] (*b* Baltimore, 13 March 1924). Pianist and arranger. He studied theory and composition at the Manhattan School of Music and took private piano lessons with Teddy Wilson, then, during the 1950s, worked with Ben Webster, Kenny Dorham, Oscar Pettiford, and Tony Scott (1952–4), and in the quintet led by J. J. Johnson and Kai Winding (1954–5). After periods with Philly Joe Jones and Helen Merrill (for whom he also wrote several arrangements in the West Coast style) he began in 1966 a long association with Roy Eldridge. The same year he was the founder, with Orrin Keepnews, of Milestone Records, for which he produced recordings by Merrill and Lee Konitz. He continued to work as a freelance pianist and returned to full-time playing in 1971, working principally with Konitz and Eldridge. He has an eclectic style that reflects to some degree the classic influence of Wilson but also draws on the inspiration of such modernists as Thelonious Monk and Bill Evans (ii).

SELECTED RECORDINGS

As leader: *Piano and Pen* (1958–9, Atl. 1314); with H. Merrill: *A Shade of Difference* (1965, Mlst. 9019); *In High Profile* (1984, BH 7016)
As sideman: Jay and Kai: *East Coast Jazz*, vii (1955, Beth. 13); B. Carter: *Further Definitions* (1961, Imp. 12); L. Konitz: *Oleo* (1975, Sonet 690)

BIBLIOGRAPHY

FeatherE; *Feather '60s*; *Feather–Gitler '70s*

ANDREW JAFFE

Katz, Fred(erick) (*b* New York, 25 Feb 1919). Cellist. He studied with Pablo Casals and became a professional musician and composer; he was music director for the 7th Army in Europe after World War II and in the early 1950s worked as a piano accompanist to the popular singers Lena Horne and Tony Bennett, among others. He was active in jazz chiefly in the later 1950s. He was a member of Chico Hamilton's quintet from 1955 (for illustration *see* DOLPHY, ERIC) and made recordings with the group until 1959 (including *The Chico Hamilton Quintet with Buddy Collette*, 1955, PJ 1209). He also recorded as an unaccompanied soloist (1956), leader (1956–8), and sideman (with Paul Horn, 1957–8, and Carmen McRae, 1958), and with Ken Nordine created two pioneering albums that combined poetry and jazz (1957). Katz wrote arrangements for a number of jazz musicians, including Horn, Milt Bernhart, and Eric Dolphy.

BIBLIOGRAPHY

FeatherE; *Feather '60s*
M. Weber: "Fred Katz," *Coda*, no.176 (1980), 14 [interview]
R. Gordon: *Jazz West Coast: the Los Angeles Jazz Scene of the 1950s* (London and New York, 1986)

Katzman, Lee (*b* Chicago, 17 May 1928). Trumpeter. He began playing at the age of 13, and later worked with various big bands, including those of Sam Donahue (1947), Buddy Rich (1948), and Claude Thornhill and Jimmy Dorsey (both 1949). After recording in New York with Herbie Fields he moved to California, where in 1956 he joined Stan Kenton; while with the group he toured Europe and the USA and made several recordings. Katzman remained in California and worked with Les Brown (1958) and Terry Gibbs (1959); he also recorded with Med Flory and Pepper Adams (both 1957), a quintet led by Bill Holman and Mel Lewis, Anita O'Day, and Jimmie Rowles (all 1958), Sonny Stitt (1959), Holman (1960), June Christy (1962), Shelly Manne (1965), and Les McCann (1966). He cites his solo on *Between the Devil and the Deep Blue Sea*, from Flory's album *Jazz Wave* (1957, Jub. 1066), as a fine example of his work.

BIBLIOGRAPHY

FeatherE

R. Gordon: *Jazz West Coast: the Los Angeles Jazz Scene of the 1950s* (London and New York, 1986)

Kavka, Arnošt (*b* Prague, 1917). Czechoslovak singer and bandleader. He was a member of the Gramoclub Orchestra under Jan Šima in the 1930s and sang with Karel Vlach's orchestra in 1937. He formed a septet in 1946 that performed on Radio Praha and made recordings; he also led a trio (1956) and sang with Karel Krautgartner's big band (1957). Later he worked as a music-hall entertainer. Kavka's style is well represented by his recording of George Gershwin's *The Man I Love* (1946, first issued on *Česky Jazz, 1920–1960, c*1913–1959, Sup. DV101778H). (S. Titzl: "Pět tváři Arnošta Kavky" [The five faces of Arnošt Kavka], *Hudba pro radost* [Music for joy] (Nov–Dec 1964), 9)

GERHARD CONRAD

Kawaguchi, George (*b* Fukakusa, Kyoto, Japan, 15 June 1927). Japanese drummer and leader. He was brought up in Dairen, Manchuria (now Lü-ten, China), returned to Japan after World War II, and played professionally from 1947. He worked with the Azumanians, a septet, and from 1953 into the 1980s led the group Big Four. In 1981 he recorded as a leader with Art Blakey and won the Nanri Humio prize and the prize of the Geijutsu festival; he gave concerts in Tokyo and Osaka in 1985. Kawaguchi uses two bass drums and is known for his extended solos; he projects strength and vitality as a drummer but is also capable of great delicacy.

SELECTED RECORDINGS

As leader: *Jazz at the Toris* (1957, King K20P6102); *Yesterdays 1: the Original Big Four* (1959, King SKA3003); with M. Hino: *The Drum Battle: George Kawaguchi vs Motohiko Hino* (1975, Tei. GM5005); *Original the Big Four Live* (1977, Phi. FIS7021); *Super Drums* (1979, PW GP3201); *African Hot Dance* (1980, EB K28P6030); with A. Blakey: *Killer Joe* (1981, Union 5001); *Big 2 with Lionel Hampton* (1982, PW K28P61DO)

BIBLIOGRAPHY

FeatherE

YOZO IWANAMI

Kawasaki, Ryo (*b* Tokyo, 25 Feb 1947). Japanese guitarist. He studied physics at Nippon University in Tokyo and first played professionally with the tenor saxophonist Seiichi Nakamura in the 1960s; he also worked with the tenor saxophonist Giro Inagaki and the drummer Takeshi Inomata. He formed a group with Shigeharu Mukai and the alto saxophonist Hedefumi Toki, then moved to New York in 1973, where he played with Gil Evans (1973–5), Joe Lee Wilson (1975), Elvin Jones (1976–7), and JoAnne Brackeen (1977–8) and worked as a leader.

SELECTED RECORDINGS

Prism (1975, EW 8027); *Juice* (1976, RCA AFL1-1855); *Nature's Revenge* (1978, MPS 68191); *Little Touree* (1980, CBS–Sony 25AP1897); *Ryo* (1981, Phi. 30PJ5); *Lucky Lady* (1982, Tei.–Contl C1-5003); *Images/Ryo* (1987, Meldac MED22)

BIBLIOGRAPHY

Feather–Gitler '70s

D. Kastin: "Ryo Kawasaki," *DB*, xliv/15 (1977), 23

A. Berle: "Ryo Kawasaki: Leading Japanese Jazz-rock Soloist," *GP*, xiii/11 (1979), 64 [incl. discography]

YOZO IWANAMI

Kay, Connie [Kirnon, Conrad Henry] (*b* Tuckahoe, NY, 27 April 1927). Drummer. He studied piano with his mother from the age of six and taught himself to play drums. His first professional engagements were with Sir Charles Thompson and Miles Davis (at Minton's Playhouse, 1944–5) and Cat Anderson (1945), with whom he recorded in 1949. After touring the southern USA in a rhythm-and-blues show he joined Lester Young's group in 1949, with which he performed at intervals until 1955; at the same time he played in small groups led by Beryl Booker, Stan Getz, Coleman Hawkins, and Charlie Parker, and recorded with Getz and Hawkins in 1952. In February 1955 he joined the MODERN JAZZ QUARTET as Kenny Clarke's replacement; he belonged to the quartet until it disbanded in 1974. At the same time he recorded with Chet Baker (1959), Cannonball Adderley (1961), Jimmy Heath (1963), and Paul Desmond (1963–74). Later he performed and recorded with Tommy Flanagan, John Lewis, Soprano Summit, and Benny Goodman, from 1975 worked as the house drummer at Eddie Condon's club, and from 1981 belonged again to the Modern Jazz Quartet, which had been re-formed. It is the relaxed, tightly organized music of the quartet to which Kay is best suited; he is reluctant to take solos and in the quartet has only done so regularly in three compositions by Lewis (*La ronde, Fontessa,* and *Sacha's March*). He was one of the first drummers since Sonny Greer to play such percussion instruments as the triangle, chimes, timpani, and finger cymbals in addition to the standard drum set; his mastery of these instruments was exploited by Lewis in his compositions for the Modern Jazz Quartet and inspired other drummers in the 1950s to enlarge their kits.

For illustration *see* MODERN JAZZ QUARTET.

SELECTED RECORDINGS

(recorded for Atlantic unless otherwise indicated)

As sideman with Modern Jazz Quartet: *Fontessa* (1956, 1231), incl. Fontessa; *One Never Knows* (1957, 1284); *The Modern Jazz Quartet* (1957, 1265), incl. La ronde; *Blues at Carnegie Hall* (1966, 1468), incl. Ralph's New Blues; *Echoes* (1984, Pablo 2312142), incl. Sacha's March

As sideman with others: Hollywood Jazz Concert: Bopera (1947, Bop 107-10); L. Young: *Lester's Here* (1953, Norg. 1071); C. Baker: *Chet* (1959, Riv. 1135); J. Lewis: *Improvised Meditations & Excursions* (1959, 1313); C. Adderley: *Know what I Mean?* (1961, Riv. 9433); P. Desmond: *Easy Living* (1963–4, RCA LSP3480); J. McShann: *The Big Apple Bash* (1978, 8804)

BIBLIOGRAPHY

J. S. Wilson: "Connie Kay: One Drummer who doesn't Care to Solo," *DB*, xxvi/5 (1959), 20

W. Balliett: "Like a Marriage," *Ecstasy at the Onion* (New York and Indianapolis, 1971) [colln of previously pubd articles and reviews], 161

C. Brauer: "Connie Kay: Interview," *Cadence*, v/2 (1979), 8

S. Woolley: "Connie Kay," *JJI*, xxxvi/7 (1983), 11

J. Potter: "Connie Kay: Sophisticated Swing," *MD*, xi/2 (1987), 22

WOLFRAM KNAUER

Kaye, Cab [Quaye, Augustus Kwamlake] (*b* Gold Coast, British West Africa [now in Ghana], 1922). Gold Coast singer and pianist. He was educated in England and after working for a time in the diplomatic service in London he became a full-time musician and took the name Cab Kaye. He sang bop with Ted

Heath, Don Byas, Vic Lewis, and James Moody, and recorded with the ensemble Jazz at the Town Hall (1948), the clarinetist Keith Bird (1949), and Ken Moule (1954). In the early 1950s he led his own group, which included such sidemen as Dave Wilkins and the tenor saxophonist Sam Walker; among its many recordings is *School Bop* (1951, Astra Schall AW4005). Kaye also recorded as a leader, accompanied by Gerry Moore's trio and the drummer Norman Burns's quintet (both 1952), and as a sideman with Humphrey Lyttelton (1960). Later he settled in Amsterdam, where he opened Cab's Jazz Piano Bar; a concert he gave there in 1984 was recorded (*Solo Piano*, Kt. 747).

RAINER E. LOTZ

Kazebier, Nate [Nathan Forrest] (*b* Lawrence, KS, 13 Aug 1912; *d* Reno, NV, 22 Oct 1969). Trumpeter. He took up trumpet at the age of nine. He played in dance bands and in Benny Goodman's orchestra (1935–6); while working with Goodman he made some recordings with Gene Krupa in Chicago (1935, including *Blues of Israel*, Parl. R2224). He then went to California and performed with Ray Noble and Spud Murphy among others, played and recorded again with Krupa (1939–40), and worked with Jimmy Dorsey (1940–43; for illustration *see* JAZZ (i), fig.3). After military service he returned to California, where he worked again with Goodman (1946–7) and as a studio musician. He recorded with Ray Bauduc and played with Jess Stacy in the late 1940s and continued to be active into the 1960s. (*ChiltonW*)

Kazoo [bazooka, blue-blower]. An instrument that amplifies the human voice while also imparting a buzzing, rasping quality to it. It consists of a tube of plated metal or plastic, usually about 12 cm long; over a large hole in the upper surface (which is usually flat) a membrane is held in place by a screw-on metal ring or cup. As the player sings or hums into the kazoo, the membrane vibrates; many kinds of sounds, including loud, quacking effects, can be produced. During the 1920s Dick Slevin used the instrument to great effect in recordings with the Mound City Blue Blowers. There are also photographs of Tony Spargo, the drummer of the Original Dixieland Jazz Band, with a large kazoo, though it is not known whether it was regularly used in performance. With a few exceptions, the kazoo and similar membranophones have not otherwise been used in jazz, being more frequently found in blues and skiffle ensembles. (*GroveI*)

Keane, Shake [Ellsworth McGranahan] (*b* St. Vincent, British West Indies, 30 May 1927). West Indian trumpeter and flugelhorn player. After working as a schoolteacher in St. Vincent he moved to London, where he studied English literature at London University (from 1952); his interest in literature and work as a poet earned him the sobriquet "Shake," from Shakespeare. In the mid-1950s he joined the Harlem Allstars, a group led by the pianist Mike McKenzie in which Joe Harriott played as a sideman. From 1954 to 1968 he recorded at intervals as the leader of his own groups (these often included McKenzie and Harriott, as well as sidemen from their bands); he also recorded as a sideman with Harriott (1960–66) and Michael Garrick (1963–5). Keane's playing always retained a singing, shapely sense of melody and he soon became recognized as the most accomplished jazz trumpeter of his generation in England. Later he was associated with several German groups and made recordings with Kurt Edelhagen (1965, 1972), as a member of the Clarke–Boland Big Band (1967–8), and with Peter Trunk (1973).

SELECTED RECORDINGS

As leader: *In My Condition* (1961, Col. SEG8140) [EP]

As sideman: J. Harriott: *Free Form* (1960, Jlnd 949); *Abstract* (1961–2, Col. 33SX1477); *High Spirits* (1964, Col. 33SX1692); on P. Smythe: *Jazz Tete-a-Tete* (1962, Col. 33SX1452), Nardis, Old Devil Moon, Mendacity

BIBLIOGRAPHY

Feather '60s

CHRIS SHERIDAN

Keenan, Norman (Dewey) (*b* Union, SC, 23 Nov 1916; *d* New York, 12 Feb 1980). Double bass player. He first played piano, then, after moving to New York, took up double bass at the age of 15, and studied music while performing in a neighborhood band. He worked with Tiny Bradshaw (*c*1934), Lucky Millinder (1939–40), the trombonist Henry Wells (1940), Earl Bostic, and Cootie Williams; during this period he took part in jam sessions at Minton's Playhouse. After World War II he returned to Williams, then worked with Eddie "Cleanhead" Vinson (1947–9) before joining the house trio at the Village Vanguard, New York, where he stayed until 1957, mainly backing rhythm-and-blues bands. He played in the group accompanying the popular singer Harry Belafonte (1957–62) and worked for three years on the television show "Hootenanny." He returned to jazz in the mid-1960s, playing with Count Basie (1965–74) and recording with Roy Eldridge (1966). Keenan played in an uncomplicated, springy style, somewhat reminiscent of Walter Page's.

SELECTED RECORDINGS

As sideman: C. Williams: You Talk a Little Trash/Floogie Boo (1944, Hit 8089); C. Basie: *Basie . . . Straight Ahead* (1968, Dot 25902); *Have a Nice Day* (1971, Daybreak 2005)

BIBLIOGRAPHY

P. Vacher: "Norman Keenan," *J&B*, i/1 (1971), 12 [interview]

CHRIS SHERIDAN

Keepnews, Orrin (*b* New York, 2 March 1923). Record producer. After graduating from Columbia University (1943) he worked for a publishing company and from 1948 wrote for the *Record Changer*, published by his former classmate Bill Grauer. In 1952 he and Grauer initiated for RCA–Victor's X label a series of 10-inch albums of reissues of important recordings by such artists as Johnny Dodds, Jelly Roll Morton, Bennie Moten, and King Oliver. In the following year they founded the record company and label RIVERSIDE, which at first offered a similar series of reissues, but soon made many important new recordings in bop and related styles, including seminal albums by Thelonious Monk and Bill Evans (ii); Keepnews acted as producer for most of these sessions himself. After a period doing freelance work he ran the company and record label MILESTONE (1966–72) before moving to San Francisco to direct jazz productions for FANTASY; Fantasy acquired the catalogues of Prestige (in 1971), Riverside (in 1972), and Milestone (in 1973), and Keepnews reissued items from these three catalogues on an acclaimed series of double and triple albums. He resigned as a vice-president of Fantasy in 1980 to devote more time to producing albums for that company and others, then in 1985 established a new company and label, LANDMARK. Throughout his career he has also been a prolific writer.

WRITINGS

(selective list)

with B. Grauer, Jr.: *A Pictorial History of Jazz: People and Places from New Orleans to Modern Jazz* (New York, 1956, rev. 2/1966/R1981)

The View from Within: Jazz Writings, 1948–1987 (in preparation)

BIBLIOGRAPHY

Feather–Gitler '70s

J. McDonough: "Orrin Keepnews: 30 Years in Jazz," *BAM Magazine* (1 July 1979), 22

R. Palmer: "Orrin Keepnews' Milestones," *RS* (12 July 1979), 6

Kellaway, Roger (*b* Newton, MA, 1 Nov 1939). Pianist, arranger, and composer. He studied piano as a child, became interested in jazz through the recordings of George Shearing, and taught himself to play double bass. He studied piano, double bass, and composition at the New England Conservatory (1957–9), which he left to play double bass with Jimmy McPartland and the trumpeter Ralph Marterie. In New York he worked for a brief period as the pianist in Kai Winding's group and belonged to quintets led by Al Cohn and Zoot Sims (*c*1963) and Clark Terry and Bob Brookmeyer (1963–5). He made recordings with Ben Webster (1964), Maynard Ferguson (1964), Wes Montgomery (1965), and Sonny Rollins (1966), and in 1966 moved to Los Angeles to play in Don Ellis's big band. There he worked as a music director for the popular singer Bobby Darin (1967–9) and as a performer, arranger, composer, and producer in film, television, and recording studios; at the same time he performed and recorded with Tom Scott (at intervals, 1967–74), toured with the popular singer Joni Mitchell (1974), and recorded with Mundell Lowe (1974), Carmen McRae (1975), for whom he also wrote arrangements and led a backup group, Jimmy Knepper (1977), and a quintet led by Sims and Harry Edison (1978). After returning to New York in 1984 he often performed in a duo with Dick Hyman at Michael's Pub.

Kellaway's compositions and performances make use of several techniques most often associated with contemporary art music, including bitonality, *musique concrète*, and electronic sounds, but his music remains nonetheless firmly rooted in jazz. His works include film scores (*The Paper Lion*, 1968; *A Star is Born*, 1976; *Breathless*, 1983), *PAMTGG* (1971, a ballet commissioned by George Balanchine), *Portraits of Time* (1983, an orchestral work commissioned by the Los Angeles PO), and pieces for the Cello Quartet, a group consisting of cello, piano, double bass, and percussion, of which Kellaway is the leader.

SELECTED RECORDINGS

As unaccompanied soloist: *Say That Again* (1978, Dobre 1045)

As leader: *The Roger Kellaway Trio* (1965, Prst. 7399); *Spirit Feel* (1967, PJ 20122); *Cello Quartet* (1971, A&M 3034); *Come to the Meadow* (1974, A&M 3618); *Nostalgia Suite* (1978, Discwasher 003)

As sideman: C. Terry: *The Happy Horns of Clark Terry* (1964, Imp. 64); S. Rollins: *Alfie* (1966, Imp. 9111); C. McRae: *I am Music* (1975, BN LA462G); Clayton Brothers: *It's All in the Family* (1980, Conc. 138); Richie Cole: *Return to Alto Acres* (1982, PAlt 8023)

BIBLIOGRAPHY

Feather '60s; *Feather–Gitler '70s*

J. S. Wilson: "The Kaleidoscopic Talents of Roger Kellaway," *DB*, xxxii/23 (1965), 15

B. Korall: "Who is Roger Kellaway?," *Saturday Review*, 1 (28 Oct 1967), 66

G. Lees: "Roger Kellaway: a Disciplined Eccentric," *High Fidelity/Musical America*, xxvi/12 (1976), 28

L. Lyons: "The Multifaceted Careers of Two Top LA Jazz Pianists: Roger Kellaway, Clare Fischer," *CK*, iv/4 (1978), 16

L. Feather: "Piano Giants of Jazz: Roger Kellaway," *CK*, v/6 (1979), 68 [incl. transcr.]

GREGORY E. SMITH

Kellens, Christian (*b* Andenne, Belgium, 18 Jan 1925). Belgian trombonist. He first played harmonica, then taught himself trombone and other brass instruments. He played and recorded with the Belgian tenor saxophonist Jack Sels (1951–3), Bobby Jaspar, Martial Solal and Lalo Schifrin (all 1954), Henri Renaud (*Henri Renaud Sextet*, 1955, Vogue 7177 [EP]), Aimé Barelli (1956), and several others. From 1957 to 1958 he performed with Kurt Edelhagen, and in 1958 he appeared at the Newport Jazz Festival as a member of the International Youth Band. He then worked with Fats Sadi and Sels (1959) and performed and recorded with Kenny Clarke and Francy Boland (1960–61). In 1962 Kellens moved to Argentina, where he formed his own quartet, and recorded with the double bass player Jorge Lopez Ruiz (*c*1967), the saxophonist Jorge Anders (1971), and the pianist Bubby Lavecchia (1977). (*FeatherE*)

Kelley, Peck [John Dickson] (*b* Houston, 1898; *d* Houston, 26 Dec 1980). Pianist and bandleader. By the early 1920s he had established himself as a bandleader in the Houston area. He employed a number of significant musicians in his group the Bad Boys, notably Jack Teagarden (1921–3, 1924), Pee Wee Russell (1924), Leon Roppolo (1924), Johnny Wiggs (1927), and the guitarist Snoozer Quinn (1927). Kelley performed in or near Houston throughout his career, although he made short tours to St. Louis (1925), Shreveport (1927), and New Orleans (1934). From 1948 he concentrated on work as a solo pianist. Kelley's style is reputed to have been technically advanced and harmonically adventurous as early as the 1920s. He did not record until 1957, shortly after his retirement from full-time music, but even at this date he displayed a formidable command of the keyboard, with an aptitude for executing long runs in the style of Art Tatum and playing complex figures independently with each hand. The recordings were first issued in 1983 as *Peck Kelley Jam* (Com. 625527-8).

BIBLIOGRAPHY

ChiltonW

K. Kathan: "At Last, the Real Truth! Peck Kelley Tells why he Snubs Name Bands' Offers," *DB*, vii/6 (1940), 3

H. J. Waters, Jr.: *Jack Teagarden's Music: his Career and Recordings* (Stanhope, NJ, 1960), 2

R. Hadlock: *Jazz Masters of the Twenties* (New York, 1965/*R*1985), 174

G. W. Kay: "The Johnny Wiggs Story," *JJ*, xxiii/6 (1970), 12

D. Shannon: "My Friend, Peck Kelley," *MR*, x/5 (1983), 3

ALYN SHIPTON

Kelly, Chris (*b* Deer Range Plantation, Plaquemines Parish, LA, 18 Oct 1885 or 1890; *d* New Orleans, 19 Aug 1929). Cornetist. A pupil of Professor Jim Humphrey, he moved with his family to New Orleans in 1915. He began his career as a full-time musician in the band of the clarinetist Johnny Brown (after 1919), and later took over its leadership; among his regular sidemen were Ikey Robinson and Emile Barnes. A flamboyant and eccentric figure, Kelly became extremely popular and the band was engaged to perform at many dances and social functions; it also often took part in cutting contests. In the late 1920s his behavior grew increasingly erratic as a result of his addiction to alcohol and he frequently failed to fulfill his commitments. His continuing popularity was, however, demonstrated by the enormous crowds that attended his funeral. One of the cornet "kings" of New Orleans and an outstanding blues player, Kelly was best known for his performances of *Careless Love Blues*. His melodies were usually low and limited in range and he often used a plunger mute (he is credited by some with having been the first jazz musician to use a mute); his playing is said to have influenced Louis Armstrong. He never recorded, but an impression of his style may be gained from the playing of his protégé Kid Howard.

BIBLIOGRAPHY

ChartersJ

K. Koenig: "Chris Kelly: Blues King of New Orleans Jazz," *SL*, xxxv (spr. 1983), 4

KARL KOENIG

Kelly, George (*b* Miami, 31 July 1915; *d* Chester, PA, 15 July 1985). Tenor saxophonist. He first played piano, but changed to alto and then tenor saxophone. He led his own group, which included Panama Francis, and worked with other leaders, among them Zack Whyte (*c*1938). In 1941 he moved to New York, where he played with Al Cooper's Savoy Sultans (1941–4), Rex Stewart (1946), the double bass player Lucille Dixon (1948–50), Babs Gonzales, and Tiny Grimes; he also worked as a leader and freelance. In the 1960s he played with Cozy Cole, and in 1970 he toured and recorded in Europe with Jay McShann and Tiny Grimes. From 1970 to 1976 Kelly accompanied the Ink Spots, a popular vocal group. He visited Europe with Ram Ramirez (1976) and worked with Panama Francis's Savoy Sultans (from 1979) and the Harlem Jazz and Blues Band (*c*1980); thereafter he continued to pursue a creative performing and recording career. Kelly's vigorous, swinging style and his abilities as an arranger and leader made him extremely popular in Europe.

SELECTED RECORDINGS

As leader: *George Kelly in Cimiez* (1979, BB 33161); *Fine and Dandy* (1982, Barron 405); *Cotton Club* (1983, Sto. 429); *George Kelly Plays Don Redman* (1984, Stash 240)

As sideman with R. Stewart: on *Rendez-vous with Rex* (1958, Fel. 7001), Pretty Ditty, Tell me more, Tillie's Twist

BIBLIOGRAPHY

D. Brigaud and L. Verdeaux:- "Propos de George Kelly," *BHcF*, no.204 (1971), 12 [interview]

S. Traill: "George Kelly," *JJI*, xxxiii/12 (1980), 6

E. Townley: "Savoy Sultan: George Kelly," *Sv*, no.94 (1981), 124 [interview]

JOHNNY SIMMEN

Kelly, (Edgar) Guy (*b* Scotlandville, LA, 22 Nov 1906; *d* Chicago, 24 Feb 1940). Trumpeter and singer. He played in Toots Johnson's band in Baton Rouge, Louisiana, and with Papa Celestin in New Orleans (1927–8) and toured with the bands of Kid Howard (1929) and Boyd Atkins (1930). In the 1930s, having moved to Chicago, he played with Cassino Simpson (1931), the banjoist Ed Carry (1932), Erskine Tate (early 1930s, 1938), Dave Peyton, Tiny Parham, Carroll Dickerson (1934, 1937–8), Jimmie Noone, and Albert Ammons (1935–6, from 1939). His few recordings (made with Celestin, Frankie "Half Pint" Jaxon, Noone, and Ammons) include Noone's *Blues Jumped a Rabbit* (1936, Parl. 2303). (P. Van Vorst: "Has Anybody Here Seen Kelly?," *MR*, iii/5 (1976), 8)

based on *ChiltonW*

Kelly, Red [Thomas Raymond] (*b* Shelby, MT, 29 Aug 1927). Double bass player. He took up the double bass during World War II and in 1949 he joined Chubby Jackson's big band (Jackson was leading the band at this time, not playing bass). After touring with Charlie Barnet (1950), and Herbie Fields, Red Norvo, and Claude Thornhill (all 1951), he worked with Woody Herman (1953–4). He recorded with Nat Pierce and Dick Collins (both 1954) and Lennie Niehaus (1957), worked with Maynard Ferguson, and performed and recorded with Med Flory (1956–7, 1959) and Stan Kenton (1957–9). In 1960 he recorded the album *Good Friday Blues* (PJ 10) as a member of the Modest Trio with Red Mitchell (piano) and Jim Hall (guitar). From 1961 to 1967 he toured and recorded with Harry James. He later worked in the Pacific Northwest. (*FeatherE*; *Feather '60s*)

Kelly, Wynton (*b* Jamaica, 2 Dec 1931; *d* Toronto, 12 April 1971). Pianist. His family moved to the USA when he was four years old, settling in Brooklyn, New York. As a youth he played professionally in rhythm-and-blues bands. By fusing earthy blues elements with those of the bop style as exemplified by Bud Powell, he developed a highly accessible and personal approach to jazz piano playing which influenced many subsequent performers. After working with Eddie "Lockjaw" Davis and Dinah Washington, Kelly first gained attention as a soloist while performing with Lester Young and Dizzy Gillespie. He was most widely known as a member of Miles Davis's quintet (1959–63), although he frequently led his own trio from the late 1950s until his death. He worked with Paul Chambers and Jimmy Cobb, both former members of Davis's group; the trio performed and recorded with Wes Montgomery. A consistent and sometimes brilliant improviser, Kelly had exceptional skill as an accompanist, though this often overshadowed his rhythmically infectious solo style. His influence is clearly evident in the early work of Victor Feldman, Herbie Hancock, McCoy Tyner, and other young pianists of the 1960s.

See also PIANO, §5.

SELECTED RECORDINGS

As leader: *Kelly Blue* (1959, Riv. 1142); with W. Montgomery: *Smokin' at the Half Note* (1965, Verve 8633); *Full View* (1967, Mlst. 9004)

As sideman with M. Davis: *Someday my Prince will Come* (1961, Col. CS8456); *In Person: Friday and Saturday Nights at the Blackhawk* (1961, Col. C2S820); *Miles Davis at Carnegie Hall* (1961, Col. CS8612)

BIBLIOGRAPHY

G. Lees: "Focus on Wynton Kelly: a Sideman First," *DB*, xxx/l (1963), 16

V. Wilmer: *Jazz People* (New York, 1970/*R*1985)

L. Feather and J. Levin: "Wynton Kelly," *JM*, no.189 (1971), 30

P. Moon: "Wynton Kelly Discography," *DF*, no.32 (1973), 9; no.33 (n.d.), 7; no.34 (n.d.), 11; no.35 (n.d.), 15; no.36 (1976), 7; no.37 (1976), 7; no.38 (1977), 11; no.39 (1977), 13; no.40 (1978), 13; no.41 (1978), 15

R. Horricks: "Wynton Kelly: the Groove Master," *CI*, xxi (1983), no.11, p.24; no.12, p.24

R. Palmer: "Wynton Kelly," *JJI*, xxxix/4 (1986), 15 [incl. discography]

BILL DOBBINS

Kelly's Stable. Nightclub in New York; *see* NIGHTCLUBS AND OTHER VENUES.

Kemp, Hal [James Harold] (*b* Marion, AL, 27 March 1905; *d* California, 21 Dec 1940). Clarinetist, alto saxophonist, and bandleader. He played piano as a child, and later took up clarinet and alto saxophone. While studying at the University of North Carolina he joined, and then led, the Carolina Club Orchestra, a student band, which he took to London in 1924. After returning to the USA and graduating in 1926 he led his own band, which played in New York in 1927, then toured several states and held a residency in Miami; from May to August 1930 it toured Europe. Thoughout the 1930s Kemp continued to lead a highly successful big band: Bunny Berigan was a member for a brief period. Although it was best known for its sweet, smooth playing, the band also played hot jazz on such recordings as *Fraternity Blues* (1930, Bruns. 4988). A collection of his scores and other materials is held in the American Heritage Center of the University of Wyoming in Laramie; *see* LIBRARIES AND ARCHIVES, §2. (G. T. Simon: *The Big Bands* (New York, 1967, rev. and enlarged 2/1971, rev. 3/1974, 4/1981), 287)

based on *ChiltonW*

Kennedy, Charlie [Charles Summer] (*b* New York, 2 July 1927). Alto saxophonist. He joined Louis Prima's band in 1943, and as a tenor saxophonist led his own swing quintet on a recording for Savoy in 1945. From 1945 to 1948 he was with Gene Krupa's band; he may be heard playing an extensive solo on *I should have kept on dreaming* (1947, first issued on *Drummin' Man*, 1938–49, Col. C2L29). He also recorded with Charlie Ventura

(1946), Chubby Jackson (1950), Chico O'Farrill (1951–2), and Flip Phillips and Herbie Fields (both 1952). After moving to the West Coast he recorded with Bill Holman (1957–60) and Art Pepper (1959); he also performed with Med Flory at the Monterey Jazz Festival (1958). From 1959 to 1962 he was a member of Terry Gibbs's orchestra; he also recorded with Jimmy Witherspoon (1961), June Christy and Dizzy Gillespie (both 1962), and Shelly Manne (1964).

BIBLIOGRAPHY

FeatherE

A. J. McCarthy: *Big Band Jazz* (New York and London, 1974), 248

R. Gordon: *Jazz West Coast: the Los Angeles Jazz Scene of the 1950s* (London and New York, 1986), 178

Kenney, Dick [Richard Mathewson] (*b* Albany, NY, 6 July 1920). Trombonist. He learned cello as a youth, then played trombone in an army band with Toots Mondello. Later he performed and recorded with Johnny Bothwell (1946–7), Charlie Barnet (1948–53), and Stan Kenton (1951–2), and recorded with Dizzy Gillespie (1950), Woody Herman (1951), and Maynard Ferguson (1952); his solo playing may be heard on *Charley's Other Aunt*, recorded with Barnet in 1949 (first issued on *Classics in Jazz, 1949–50*, Cap. T624). After touring and recording with Herman (1953–5) Kenney worked in New England as a freelance musician. From 1957 to 1960 he toured and recorded with Les Brown. (*FeatherE*)

Kenton, Stan(ley Newcomb) (*b* Wichita, KS, 15 Dec 1911; *d* Los Angeles, 25 Aug 1979). Bandleader, pianist, and arranger. After playing piano and writing arrangements for various theater and dance bands in the 1930s he formed his own 14-piece big band, the Artistry in Rhythm Orchestra, in 1941. The group immediately drew public attention with its large sound and precise execution, and from 1945, when Pete Rugolo became its staff arranger, it began to dominate jazz popularity polls. In 1949 Kenton appeared in Carnegie Hall with a new 20-piece orchestra, Progressive Jazz, which gave its name to the jazz movement it represented (*see* PROGRESSIVE JAZZ). After retiring briefly in 1949 for reasons of health, Kenton assembled his most ambitious band, the 43-piece Innovations in Modern Music Orchestra, with strings and an expanded wind section. This group conducted two nationwide tours (1950–51), performing monumental "arranger's originals" such as Bob Graettinger's *City of Glass*, but in the end proved too costly to maintain. Thereafter Kenton led a succession of more conventional big bands, with which he frequently recorded and undertook foreign tours.

Kenton established the first of his university "jazz clinics" in 1959, at Indiana and Michigan State universities. Although he continued to produce outstanding big-band recordings (his albums *West Side Story* and *Adventures in Jazz* received Grammy awards), his later career centered on university campuses, where he proved to be an outstanding band trainer and talent scout. In January 1965 he launched his Los Angeles Neophonic Orchestra, a 23-piece concert jazz band with symphonic pretensions (its first concert, at which Friedrich Gulda performed his jazz piano concerto, included transcriptions of works by Wagner), but after two seasons this ensemble also failed. In 1970 Kenton formed his own recording and publishing companies, Creative World Records and Creative World Music, to disseminate the past and current work of his bands. In addition to numerous jazz awards (he was elected to the *Down Beat* Hall of Fame as early as 1954) he received honorary doctorates from Villanova University, Drury College, and the University of Redlands.

Kenton occupies an ambiguous position in jazz history: his own considerable talents as an arranger and pianist were soon overshadowed by those of his superior sidemen and staff arrangers, and his obvious success with the public at large was offset by almost universal condemnation from the jazz critical establishment. At its worst (in his Innovations orchestra) the progressive-jazz movement he initiated was vacuous and pretentious; at its best it served as a vehicle for some of the most sensitive and inventive big-band scores of the post-swing era (by Rugolo, Shorty Rogers, Gerry Mulligan, Neal Hefti, Bill Russo, Johnny Richards, and others). An extraordinarily large number of excellent jazz soloists began their careers in Kenton's groups, among the best being Anita O'Day, June Christy, Lee Konitz, Art Pepper, Stan Getz, Zoot Sims, Pepper Adams, Maynard Ferguson, Kai Winding, Laurindo Almeida, and Shelly Manne. Scores from his library continue to circulate widely among American stage bands; 12 of them were choreographed for a ballet evening at Sadler's Wells, London, in 1954. Kenton's greatest contribution was probably as an educator and trainer of young talent, in which area his influence is still evident in American universities. Arrangements used by his school bands are now held in the library of North Texas State University in Denton; *see* LIBRARIES AND ARCHIVES, §2.

See also PIANO, §4.

SELECTED RECORDINGS

As unaccompanied soloist: *Solo: Stan Kenton without his Orchestra* (1973, CW 1071)

As leader: The Nango (1941, Decca 4037); Reed Rapture (1942, Decca 4319); Eager Beaver/Artistry in Rhythm (1943, Cap. 159); And her tears flowed like wine (1944, Cap. 166); Tampico (1945, Cap. 202); Concerto to End all Concertos (1946, Cap. 382); Jolly Rogers (1950, Cap. 1043); Round Robin (1950, Cap. F15848); City of Glass (1951, Cap. 28062-3); Prologue (1952, Cap. 15966–7); *Stan Kenton in Hi-Fi* (1956, Cap. W724); *Cuban Fire* (1956, Cap. T731); *West Side Story* (1961, Cap. T1609); *Adventures in Jazz* (1961, Cap. T1796); *Live at Redlands University* (1970, CW 1015); *Fire, Fury and Fun* (1974, CW 1073); *Journey to Capricorn* (1976, CW 1077)

BIBLIOGRAPHY

H. J. Dietzel and H. H. Lange: *Stan Kenton* (Berlin, 1959) [H. J. Dietzel: *Stan Kenton Biography* and H. H. Lange: *Stan Kenton Discography* bound together]

D. Schulz-Köhn: *Stan Kenton: ein Porträt* (Wetzlar, Germany, 1961)

J. McKinney: "The Kenton Story: the Rise and Achievements of the Most Controversial Figure in the History of Jazz," *Crescendo*, iv (1965–6), no.3, p.20; no.4, p.17; no.5, p.32; no.6, p.24; no.7, p.12

P. Venudor and M. Sparke: *The Standard Stan Kenton Directory*, i: *1937–1949* (Amsterdam, 1968)

J. Burns: "Stan the Man," *JM*, no.186 (1969), 22

C. A. Pirie: *Artistry in Kenton: the Bio-discography of Stan Kenton and his Music* (Vienna, 1969, enlarged 3/n.d. [?1972])

H. Witt: "Kenton," *JJ*, xxvi/3 (1973), 22

L. Feather: "Stan Kenton, 1912–1979," *CK*, v/11 (1979), 42 [incl. transcr.]

W. F. Lee: *Stan Kenton: Artistry in Rhythm* (Los Angeles, 1980) [incl. discography]

C. Garrod: *Stan Kenton and his Orchestra*, i: *1940–1951*; ii: *1952–1959* (Zephyrhills, FL, 1984)

A. J. Agostinelli: *Stan Kenton: the Many Musical Moods of his Orchestras* (Providence, RI, 1986) [bio-discography]

J. BRADFORD ROBINSON

Kentucky Club. The name of several nightclubs, notably one in New York; *see* NIGHTCLUBS AND OTHER VENUES.

Kenyatta, Robin [Haynes, Prince Roland] (*b* Monck's Corner, nr Charleston, SC, 6 March 1942). Alto saxophonist and bandleader. He grew up in New York, and took the name Kenyatta as a youth. In 1964 he played with Bill Dixon's free-jazz group at the October Revolution in Jazz in New York; he later recorded with the Jazz Composer's Orchestra (1965), Roswell Rudd, Sonny

Members of Stan Kenton's band at Club Harlem, Philadelphia, 1952: (back row, left to right) Conte Candoli, Don Dennis, Buddy Childers, and unidentified player (trumpets); (middle row, far right) Keith Moon (trombone); (front row) Kenton, Ralph Blaze (guitar), Bill Holman, Boots Mussulli, Dick Meldonian, Lee Elliott, and Bob Gioga (saxophones)

Stitt, and Dixon (all 1966), and Barry Miles (*c*1967). He then led his own groups, which combined free-jazz and hard-bop styles, as may be heard on the album *Until* (1967, Vortex 2005); among his sidemen were Walter Booker (1967, 1969), and Wolfgang Dauner and Arild Andersen (Germany, 1970). Kenyatta also recorded with Archie Shepp (1968), Alan Silva (Paris, 1970), and Andrew Hill (1975). (D. Heckman: Liner notes, *Until*, Vortex 2005, 1968)

Keppard, Freddie (*b* New Orleans, 27 Feb 1890; *d* Chicago, 15 July 1933). Cornetist, brother of Louis Keppard. He studied mandolin, violin, and accordion, and was active professionally as a cornetist from about 1906 with his own group (the OLYMPIA ORCHESTRA) and other New Orleans ensembles. In 1914 he moved to Los Angeles to join the Original Creole Band. After touring in vaudeville and performing in Chicago and New York with this group he settled in Chicago; he was prominent there throughout the 1920s with his own groups, including the JAZZ CARDINALS (1926), and those of Doc Cook, Erskine Tate, Ollie Powers, and Charlie Elgar.

Among the leading New Orleans trumpeters who left recordings of their work Keppard is notable for a brusque and staccato style that comes closest to ragtime. Few of the recordings definitely identified as his substantiate either the esteem accorded him by other jazz musicians or his considerable popularity; but he seldom recorded before 1926, by which time his health was failing. Although his stature can never be fully assessed, he was one of the first musicians to lead a New Orleans jazz ensemble in the northern and western USA.

See also TRUMPET, §3; for illustration *see* NELSON, BIG EYE LOUIS.

SELECTED RECORDINGS

As leader: Stock Yards Strut/Salty Dog (1926, Para. 12399)

As sideman: E. Tate: Chinaman Blues (1923, OK 4907); D. Cook: Messin' Around (1926, OK 8390), High Fever/Here Comes the Hot Tamale Man (1926, OK 8369); J. Taylor: Stomp Time Blues/It Must be the Blues (1927, Para. 12409)

BIBLIOGRAPHY

ChartersJ; ChiltonW

O. Spencer: "Trumpeter Freddie Keppard Walked out on Al Capone!," *Music and Rhythm*, ii/6 (1941), 13

W. C. Allen: "Trumpet Giants, 3: Freddie Keppard," *Hot Notes*, ii/3 (1947), 2 [incl. discography]

N. Shapiro and N. Hentoff, eds.: *Hear me Talkin' to ya: the Story of Jazz by the Men who Made it* (New York and London, 1955/*R*1966), 87

S. B. Charters and L. Kunstadt: *Jazz: a History of the New York Scene* (Garden City, NY, 1962/*R*1981)

M. Williams: *Jazz Masters of New Orleans* (New York and London, 1967/*R*1978), 19

D. M. Bakker: "Freddie Keppard," *Micrography*, no.3 (1969), 4; no.5 (1969), 12; no.15 (1971), 3 [discography]

W. J. Schafer: "New Orleans to the World: Freddie Keppard (1889 [*sic*] – 1933)," *MR*, iv/1 (1976), 8

A. Ridley: "The Keppard Brothers," *Fn*, xix/3 (1988), 4

J. R. TAYLOR/R

Keppard, Louis (*b* New Orleans, 2 Feb 1888; *d* New Orleans, 18 Feb 1986). Guitarist and tuba player, brother of Freddie Keppard. As a youth he played guitar with the Cherry Blossom Band and led his own Magnolia Band (with King Oliver and Honore Dutrey among the members). After working with Papa Celestin, Manuel Perez, and in the Olympia Orchestra, led by his brother Freddie, he moved to Chicago in 1917. In the 1920s he played alto horn in New Orleans brass bands; he later performed on guitar as a soloist and in various New Orleans bands (1940s, 1950s) and on tuba in the Gibson Brass Band (from 1953). Keppard was an accomplished chordal guitarist and often used shuffle rhythms in his ensemble work in a manner that recalls Danny Barker's dixieland style; his singing and guitar playing may be heard on Wooden Joe Nicholas's *You made me what I am today* on the album *Wooden Joe's Band* (1949, AM 646). He ceased to play in his last years.

Oral history material in *LNT*.

BIBLIOGRAPHY

ChartersJ
A. Ridley: "Louis Keppard: Reminiscences of a New Orleans Musician," *Sv*, no.40 (1972), 133
Obituary, A. Ridley, *Fn*, xvii/4 (1986), 22
A. Ridley: "The Keppard Brothers," *Fn*, xix/3 (1988), 4

ALYN SHIPTON

Kerr, (Chester) Brooks(, Jr.) (*b* New Haven, CT, 26 Dec 1951). Pianist. At the age of nine he made his début at the Playback Club in New Haven; he was accompanied by Charlie Smith. After moving in 1963 to New York he studied with Sanford Gold and from 1969 to 1973 attached himself to Willie "the Lion" Smith; at the same time he studied theory at the Manhattan School of Music and the Juilliard School (1970–72). He became well-known as a student and interpreter of the work of Duke Ellington, and from 1973 into the 1980s he played with many of Ellington's former sidemen, including Ray Nance, Paul Gonsalves, Russell Procope, and Sonny Greer. He also worked in the 1980s with the double bass players Eric Lemon (at Gregory's in New York) and Al Hall (at the Village Gate, from early in 1987). Kerr has been influenced not only by the music of Ellington but also by that of Fats Waller and Roy Eldridge. His recordings include an album of duos with Greer (*Soda Fountain Rag*, 1975, Chi. 2001) and tributes to Ellington, Waller, and Irving Berlin for the Bluewail label.

Oral history material in *CtY*.

JAMES M. DORAN

Kersey, Kenny [Kenneth Lyons] (*b* Harrow, Ontario, Canada, 3 April 1916; *d* New York, 1 April 1983). Pianist. He received his early musical instruction from his mother, a pianist, and his father, who played cello, then studied piano and trumpet at the Detroit Institute of Musical Arts. After moving to New York in 1936 he worked with Lucky Millinder, Frankie Newton, Roy Eldridge (1939–40), Henry "Red" Allen (1941), and Cootie Williams and Andy Kirk (both 1942). He played trumpet in army bands, then from 1946 to 1949 was a member of the Jazz at the Philharmonic ensemble. He rejoined Eldridge briefly in 1948, worked as a soloist and with Buck Clayton, and performed and recorded with Edmond Hall (1949–50), Allen (1951–2), Sol Yaged (1952–4, 1956–7), and Charlie Shavers (1955), before he was forced by a bone condition to retire in the late 1950s. Kersey also wrote a number of compositions, of which the best known is *Boogie Woogie Cocktail*.

See also Piano, §4.

SELECTED RECORDINGS

As sideman: B. Holiday: Why did I always depend on you? (1939, Voc./OK 4834); Long Gone Blues (1939, Col. 37586); B. Goodman: I can't give you anything but love, baby (1940, Col. 36755); H. Allen: K. K. Boogie (1941, OK 6281); first issued on *The Harlem Jazz Scene* (1941, Eso. 4), D. Gillespie: Stardust; A. Kirk: Boogie Woogie Cocktail (1942, Decca 4381)

BIBLIOGRAPHY

ChiltonW; *FeatherE*

ANDREW JAFFE

Kessel, Barney (*b* Muskogee, OK, 17 Oct 1923). Guitarist. He played with Chico Marx (1943) and performed in the short film *Jammin' the Blues* (1944) before attracting attention as a member of a number of big bands, including that of Artie Shaw (1945). Later he became a freelance studio guitarist in Los Angeles, although he interrupted this work for a lengthy tour with Oscar Peterson's trio (1952–3); he also made several recordings for the Verve and Contemporary labels and in the early 1960s undertook club engagements with his own groups. After a successful tour of Europe with George Wein's Newport All Stars (1968) Kessel moved away from the commercial field. He lived in London from 1969 to 1970, and toured and recorded in Europe before returning to the USA. In 1973, with Charlie Byrd and Herb Ellis, he made a tour of Australia and New Zealand and formed the group Great Guitars, a quintet (with double bass and drums) that has performed and recorded into the 1980s. Kessel has also worked as a leader of other groups and as an unaccompanied soloist, playing in clubs and at concerts, recording widely, leading workshops, and teaching privately. He has published instruction manuals, including *The Guitar: a Tutor* (Hollywood, CA, 1967). Although Kessel has the smooth tone and immaculate technique required of a studio musician, he can also improvise swinging jazz melodies.

Oral history material in *NjR*.

For illustration *see* Shaw, Artie.

SELECTED RECORDINGS

As leader: *To Swing or Not to Swing* (1955, Cont. 3513); *Let's Cook* (1957, Cont. 3603); *Workin' Out* (1961, Cont. 3585); *On Fire* (1965, Emerald 2401); *Feeling Free* (1968, Cont. 7618); with S. Grappelli: *Limehouse Blues* (1969, BL 173); of Great Guitars (with C. Byrd and H. Ellis): *Great Guitars at the Winery* (1980, Conc. 131)

As sideman: C. Parker: Relaxin' at Camarillo (1947, Dial 1012); Norman Granz Jam Session: Jam Blues/Ballad Medley (1952, Clef 4001); H. Edison: *Sweets* (1956, Verve 8097); B. Holiday: *Body and Soul* (1957, Verve 8197)

BIBLIOGRAPHY

N. Hentoff: "Christian my Sole Influence: Kessel," *DB*, xx/12 (1953), 21
G. Lees: "Barney Kessel: Why he Went Back on the Road," *DB*, xxviii/1 (1961), 21
H. Siders: "Kessel '66," *DB*, xxxiii/14 (1966), 28
A. Morgan: "Musicians Talking: Barney Kessel," *JM*, no.171 (1969), 4 [interview]
R. Yelin: "Unbeatable Jazz Trio: Byrd, Kessel and Ellis," *GP*, viii/10 (1974), 20
M. Joyce and J. DeMuth: "Barney Kessel: Interview," *Cadence*, iii/11–12 (1978), 10
"Barney Kessel," *SJ*, xxxvi/7 (1982), 240 [discography]
A. Berle: "Barney Kessel Speaks Out," *GP*, xvi/5 (1982), 70
L. Hollis and E. Ferguson: "Barney Kessel," *Cadence*, xiii/8 (1987), 5

BARRY KERNFELD

Kesterton, Bob [Robert; Dingbod] (*b c*1920). Double bass player. From 1943 to 1945 he played with Harlan Leonard's band in Los Angeles; during this period he also toured and recorded with Stan Kenton (1944–5). He made recordings (including *Cock-a-doodle-doo/Yonder goes my baby*, 1945, Philo 104) with the rhythm-and-blues singer Wynonie Harris, and worked in a band led by Howard McGhee which included Charlie Parker, Teddy Edwards, and Sonny Criss; unfortunately this group did not record, but Kesterton did make recordings with both McGhee (1945–6) and Parker (1946), including two that were issued on one disc – Parker's *Loverman* and McGhee's *Bebop* (1946, Dial 1007). Kesterton later recorded with Preston Love (1953).

BIBLIOGRAPHY

A. McCarthy: *Big Band Jazz* (New York and London, 1974), 149
W. F. Lee: *Stan Kenton: Artistry in Rhythm* (Los Angeles, 1980) [incl. discography]
I. Gitler: *Swing to Bop: an Oral History of the Transition in Jazz in the 1940s* (New York, and Oxford, England, 1985)

Kettledrum. A drum with a hemispherical body that acts as a resonator. The tunable orchestral kettledrums, or timpani, have occasionally been used in the drum set (*see* DRUM SET, §I, 9).

Keyboards, electronic. *See* ELECTRONIC KEYBOARDS.

Keynote. Record company and label. The company was established by Eric Bernay in New York in 1940. It recorded a variety of material – folk and classical music, political songs, and musical theater – but it is best known for its swing and bop recordings produced by Harry Lim between 1943 and 1946. These were made mainly in New York, but also in Chicago, New Orleans, and Los Angeles. After supervising important sessions by Lester Young, Coleman Hawkins, Red Norvo, and a group led by Charlie Shavers that included Earl Hines, Lim established a reputation for his work with excellent musicians who were then less well known. His projects included an album made by sidemen from Woody Herman's First Herd under Chubby Jackson's leadership; Milt Hinton's earliest recordings as a leader; Lennie Tristano's first commercial session; some of the first bop scat singing to be issued on record (by Dave Lambert and Buddy Stewart); and material by Willie Smith, George Barnes, Juan Tizol, and Joe Thomas (iv).

Keynote was also notable for the quality of its discs; when in 1946 it lost the use of a fine pressing plant in Scranton, Pennsylvania, it invested around $250,000 in a plant in California. This, however, proved a failure. John Hammond replaced Lim in 1947, but, other than supervising a second session by Tristano, he shifted the emphasis of the company's policies to classical music. When bankruptcy threatened in 1948 the management sold the company to Mercury. Lim revived the label in 1955 to issue recordings by Nat Pierce. (B. Porter: "Keynote: the Label and the Producer," The Complete Keynote Collection (Key. 830-121-1, 1986) [liner notes])

Keystone Korner. Nightclub in San Francisco; *see* NIGHTCLUBS AND OTHER VENUES.

Khan, Steve (*b* Los Angeles, 28 April 1947). Electric guitarist. After playing piano and drums as a youth he took up guitar at the age of 20. He graduated from UCLA in 1969 with a degree in music, and moved the following year to New York, where he worked as a session musician. He played with George Benson, Hubert Laws, Maynard Ferguson, and Buddy Rich, as well as with the rock group Steely Dan and the singer Billy Joel. In 1975 he began touring and recording with Larry Coryell; he was also the lead guitarist with the Brecker Brothers. These associations ceased in 1977, and Khan then toured Japan with the CBS Jazz All Stars. A book of his transcriptions of solos by Wes Montgomery was published in 1978. In 1981 he formed the group Eyewitness with sidemen Manolo Badrena, the electric bass guitarist Anthony Jackson, and the drummer Steve Jordan. He is the son of the lyricist Sammy Cahn; his name is occasionally misspelled Kahn.

SELECTED RECORDINGS

As unaccompanied soloist: *Evidence* (1980, AN 3023)
Duos with L. Coryell: *Two for the Road* (1977, Ari. 4156)
As leader: *Tightrope* (1977, Col.–Tappan Zee JC34857); of Eyewitness: *Eyewitness* (1981, Ant. 1018), *Casa Loco* (1983, Ant. 1020)

BIBLIOGRAPHY

A. J. Smith: "Steve Khan: Adaptable Tightrope Walker," *DB*, xlv/4 (1978), 18
M. Rozek: "Steve Khan: New York Session Guitarist," *GP*, xiii/3 (1979), 45 [incl. discography]
B. Milkowski: "Steve Khan: Post-fusion Guitarist," *DB*, 1/12 (1983), 27 [incl. discography]
J. Ferguson: "The Double Life of Steve Khan: Session Ace–Fusion Artist," *GP*, xix/11 (1985), 14 [incl. discography]

DIANNA RHYAN

Kick. A word used variously in jazz, mostly in the context of beat. In a fast, lively piece with a heavy beat, to "kick" or "kick out" is to bring out the rhythm very forcefully; a player who drives the music on by his emphatically rhythmic playing is said to "kick along" his fellow musicians (*see also* BEAT, §2, and BOOT). A bandleader "kicks (or stomps) off" by striking the beat of a piece with his heel on the floor; this marks the tempo and gives a signal to the musicians so that they begin playing in time and together. The word is used in a different sense in the expression "to kick around," which in jazz means to improvise in a relaxed, even lazy, fashion, to explore the possibilities of a theme or an idea at length and perhaps unsystematically.

Kid Punch. Nickname of PUNCH MILLER.

Kiffe, Karl (Herman) (*b* Los Angeles, 6 July 1927). Drummer. He played drums from an early age and while at high school led a group which appeared in the film *Junior Jazz Bombers* (1944). He toured and recorded with Jimmy Dorsey (1945–7), then worked with Georgie Auld (1948–50), and Howard Rumsey (*c*1949). After playing with Dorsey again (1950–52) he worked in New York as a freelance musician with Charlie Barnet, Tex Beneke, and Sol Yaged, Jimmy McPartland and Charlie Shavers (1955–56), Stan Getz and Zoot Sims (1956), and Woody Herman (1957). In Los Angeles he performed and made recordings with Red Norvo (including *Helen Humes with Red Norvo and his Orchestra*, 1958, RCA LPM1711), and played with Lionel Hampton and Harry James. After recording with Pee Wee Russell (1958) and Benny Goodman (1960), and performing with June Christy (1959), he moved to Las Vegas where he played again with Barnet (1965). He also toured and performed with Ella Fitzgerald (1964) and Nancy Wilson (1972). (*FeatherE*)

Kikuchi, Masabumi (*b* Tokyo, 23 March 1940). Japanese pianist and composer. He attended the Tokyo National University of Fine Arts and Music, and played jazz from 1958, working with Oya Takatoshi and the Highway Sons, and with a quartet led by the guitarist Shungo Sawada; his early style as a pianist and composer was influenced by Thelonious Monk. He worked as a leader from 1965, and in 1967 formed a quintet with Terumasa Hino of which the two became the leaders; the following year he recorded with Charlie Mariano in Tokyo, toured Japan with Sonny Rollins, and studied at the Berklee College of Music. After returning to Japan in 1969 he led groups of which Gary Peacock was a member and in 1972 moved to New York; with Elvin Jones he toured South America and worked until 1974 and with Gil Evans he played at intervals until 1980. Kikuchi's compositions can be heard on his albums *Dancing Mist* (1970) and *Susuto* (1980), and have also been played by Evans.

SELECTED RECORDINGS

As leader: *Reconfirmation* (1970, Phi. FIX8501); *Doo-sun* (1970, Phi. FIX8506); *Dancing Mist* (1970, Phi. FS6506); *East Wind* (1974, EW 8001); *But not for me* (1978, FDisk VIJ6061); *Susoto* (1980, CBS 25AH1199); *One Way Traveller* (1980, CBS 25AH1402)
As leader with T. Hino: *Hino–Kikuchi Quintet* (1968, Col.–Tact 32C387873)
As sideman with G. Evans: *Live at the Public Theatre* (1980, Trio PAP9233, PAP25016)

BIBLIOGRAPHY

Feather–Gitler '70s

YOZO IWANAMI

Killian, Al(bert) (*b* Birmingham, AL, 15 Oct 1916; *d* Los Angeles, 5 Sept 1950). Trumpeter. At the age of 18 he played in New York as a member of Charlie Turner's Arcadians; he was replaced by Herman Autrey when leadership of the band devolved to Fats Waller. In the following years he worked with Baron Lee (1937), Teddy Hill, and Don Redman, and from 1940 played with Count Basie. Between 1943 and 1947 he worked with Charlie Barnet (on three occasions; for illustration *see* BARNET, CHARLIE), again with Basie, and with Lionel Hampton, Billy Eckstine, the trombonist Earle Spencer, and Boyd Raeburn; he also took part in the series Jazz at the Philharmonic in 1946. Around this time he became interested in bop, which was then emerging as a discernible style, and in 1947 he led a bop group on the West Coast as part of the concert series Just Jazz; but he apparently lacked the technique to play this music convincingly, and the group was short-lived. Late in 1947 he joined the orchestra of Duke Ellington, with which he traveled to Europe; he left the orchestra soon after its return to the USA in 1950.

SELECTED RECORDINGS

As leader: first issued on *Jazz Concert West Coast* (1947, Reg. 6049), Blow, Blow, Blow; first issued on D. Ellington: *Duke Ellington Carnegie Hall Concert, December 1947* (1947, Prst. 24075), Trumpets No End

As sideman: first issued on L. Young and C. Christian: *Lester Young and Charlie Christian, 1939–1940* (1939–40, Jazz Archives 42), C. Basie: Green Bay (1940)

BIBLIOGRAPHY

ChiltonW; *FeatherE*

CHRIS SHERIDAN

Kincaide, (Robert) Deane (*b* Houston, 18 March 1911). Arranger, saxophonist, and clarinetist. He grew up in Decatur, Illinois. After playing with Wingy Manone in Shreveport, Louisiana (1932), he worked with Ben Pollack's band in Chicago (1933–5), during which time he provided some arrangements for Benny Goodman. He was a founding member of Bob Crosby's band (formed in 1935 by disaffected members of Pollack's orchestra) and helped forge its distinctive style with his big-band arrangements of dixieland pieces. He worked with Woody Herman (1937), then again with Crosby (1937–8) and Manone (1938), before being engaged as sideman and arranger by Tommy Dorsey. After leaving Dorsey in 1940 he played with Joe Marsala, Ray Noble, and Muggsy Spanier and wrote some arrangements for Glenn Miller. From 1946 to 1950 he was a member of Ray McKinley's orchestra; he also wrote arrangements for the Glenn Miller Orchestra led by McKinley. Thereafter, until his retirement in 1981, Kincaide arranged music for television shows and continued to play as a freelance. He also made recordings with his own groups, including *The Solid South* (1959, Ev. 5064).

SELECTED ARRANGEMENTS

* – with Kincaide as sideman

B. Goodman: Love me or leave me/Why couldn't it be poor little me (1933, Col. 2871D); B. Crosby: *The Dixieland Band (1935, Decca 479); T. Dorsey: Beale Street Blues (1937, Vic. 36207); *Milenberg Joys (1939, Vic. 26437); M. Spanier: *Columbia: Gem of the Ocean* (1962, Ava 12)

BIBLIOGRAPHY

ChiltonW
H. Johnson: *Tommy and Jimmy: the Dorsey Years* (New Rochelle, NY, 1972)
J. Chilton: *Stomp Off, Let's Go! The Story of Bob Crosby's Bob Cats & Big Band* (London, 1983)

DAVID FLANAGAN

King. Record company and label. The company was formally established in Cincinnati by Syd Nathan in August 1944, though issue began in November the previous year; at first the catalogue consisted solely of country music. A race label, Queen, was established in 1945. Henry Glover, a trumpeter with Lucky Millinder, became director of artists and repertory, and items by several small groups from Millinder's band were among the company's first releases. Recordings were also acquired from 20th Century, and from J. Mayo Williams's labels Southern and Harlem.

In July 1947 the company began issuing recordings by Earl Bostic (derived from the catalogue of Gotham) on Queen, but discontinued the label the following month. Thereafter King itself became the race label, though Queen's numerical series was continued. In September 1948 King acquired DE LUXE, which it operated until 1949 as a separate subsidiary. In 1950, the company established another label, Federal, which was used to release items recorded on the West Coast and reissues of items first put out on Miracle; this continued until the mid-1960s. During the 1950s the most important musicians to record for King were Bostic (who had an exclusive contract with the company from 1949 to 1963), Millinder (1950–55), and Bill Doggett (1952–60).

In 1961 King acquired BETHLEHEM, thus becoming the owner of a well-known catalogue that included highly regarded material recorded in 1956 by Duke Ellington, and much important swing, hard-bop, and West Coast jazz. Later in the decade, however, King was purchased by Starday, which remained the owner until 1973, and instigated a program of reissues; Glover became the vice-president of Starday-King, and continued to direct artists and repertory. The reissue scheme was continued in the later 1970s by the company Gusto, which used both the labels King and Gusto.

BIBLIOGRAPHY

S. Tracy: "King of the Blues: the Story of a Record Label," *Blues Unlimited*, no.87 (1971), 4; no.88 (1972), 7
M. Leadbitter: "De Luxe," *Blues Unlimited*, no.104 (1973), 24
A. Shaw: *Honkers and Shouters: the Golden Years of Rhythm and Blues* (New York, 1978), 275
B. Daniels: "Queen Records," *Whisky, Women, and . . .*, no.11 (1983), 12
M. Ruppli and B. Daniels: *The King Labels: a Discography* (Westport, CT, and London, 1985)

King, Bertie [Albert] (*b* Colón, Panama, 19 June 1912; *d* ? New York, 1980s). Jamaican alto and tenor saxophonist, clarinetist, and flutist. After moving to England in 1935 he played with Leslie Thompson and Ken "Snake Hips" Johnson in the Emperors of Jazz (1936–7), performed and recorded with Benny Carter in The Hague and Paris (1937–8), and made recordings in London with Una Mae Carlisle (1938) and Johnson (1938, 1940). He led his own band in London in 1943 and again in the late 1940s after a spell with Jiver Hutchinson (1944–5). From 1951 to 1956 he recorded as a leader and with Kenny Baker, George Chisholm, and Chris Barber among others, and made recordings of West Indian music (often under the leadership of the clarinetist Freddy Grant); he also took part in Humphrey Lyttelton's experiments with a fusion of Caribbean music and jazz. King's highly idiosyncratic alto saxophone playing may be heard on Barber's *Jazz at the Royal Festival Hall* (1954, Decca DFE6238 [EP]).

JOHN COWLEY, HOWARD RYE

King [Messina], **Morgana** (*b* Pleasantville, NY, 4 June 1930). Singer. She studied at the Metropolitan School of Music in New York, and in 1956 began to sing at clubs in the city and to record swing standards. During the 1960s she developed a distinctive performing and singing style, which gained for her considerable commercial success in the popular-music area.

She realized her ambition to become an actress by appearing in *The Godfather* (1972, 1974). The 1970s also saw her resume a jazz style of singing and return to performing in nightclubs, which she continued to do into the 1980s. After almost a decade when she made no recordings she released the album *Stretchin' Out* (1977, Muse 5166); several more followed up to 1983. She performed in San Francisco in 1986. (*FeatherE*; *Feather '60s*; *Feather–Gitler '70s*)

King, Peter (John) (*b* Kingston upon Thames, England, 11 Aug 1940). English alto saxophonist. At the age of 15 he took up clarinet, but after hearing Charlie Parker he changed to alto saxophone. He led his own quartet, which worked as the house band at Ronnie Scott's, London (1959–60); thereafter he spent a year with John Dankworth's orchestra (1960–61), performed and recorded with Tony Kinsey (1961–3), and led his own group at Annie's Room, London (1962–4). In the early 1960s he played mostly tenor saxophone. He recorded with Tubby Hayes (1964), Philly Joe Jones (1968), and Stan Tracey (1969), and was a founding member of the Bebop Preservation Society, with which he recorded several times during the early 1970s, once accompanying Red Rodney (1975). King has worked successfully with several other American musicians, including Jimmy Witherspoon (with whom he recorded in 1981) and Al Haig (with whom he recorded in 1982). In the early and mid-1980s he led his own group, variously a quartet and a quintet, which recorded three LPs, including *New Beginning* (1982, Spot. 520), and *90% of One Percent* (1985, Spot. 529).

Oral history material in *GBLnsa*.

BIBLIOGRAPHY

Feather '60s
L. Tomkins: "Finding an Identity: Peter King," *CI*, xvii/3 (1978), 12
G. Murphy: "Peter King," *JJI*, xxxvii/7 (1984), 8
S. Britt: "King Alto," *The Wire*, no.16 (1985), 42 [incl. discography]

STAN BRITT

King, Roy. Pseudonym under which ROY CRIMMINS recorded in Germany and Switzerland during the mid-1970s.

King, Stan (*b* Hartford, CT, 1900; *d* New York, 19 Nov 1949). Drummer and percussionist. He went to New York around 1920 with a band led by the drummer Barney Rapp and, after playing regularly with the California Ramblers (1922–6), worked under the bandleaders Roger Wolfe Kahn, Jean Goldkette, Paul Whiteman, Jack Albin (1928), Bert Lown (1929–31), and the Dorsey brothers (in the musical *Everybody's Welcome*). From the early 1930s he was chiefly active in radio and as a studio musician, but he also played with Benny Goodman (1934), Joe Haymes (1935), Frankie Trumbauer and Jack and Charlie Teagarden in the Three Ts (1936), and the bands of Chauncey Morehouse (1938), Bob Zurke (on a tour, 1939–40), and Chauncey Grey (in New York in the 1940s). King made hundreds of recordings between 1923 and 1939; a typical example of his somewhat foursquare playing may be heard on Louis Armstrong's *I'm putting all my eggs in one basket* (1936, Decca 698).

based on *ChiltonW*

King Curtis. *See* CURTIS, KING.

King Jazz. Record company and label. The company was established in New York early in 1945 by John van Beuren, Harry Houck, and Mezz Mezzrow. The first recording, by Sammy Price (both as an unaccompanied soloist and accompanying the blues singer Pleasant Joe), was made on 27 March; on 30 July King Jazz recorded a session by Sidney Bechet and Mezzrow. This proved to be the first of several such sessions, which continued until December 1947 (though the company remained in existence until 1948) and produced the bulk of King Jazz's repertory. Many of the resulting discs are now acknowledged to be classics.

The label name was used in 1951 by Vogue to reissue in the UK some of this material, and also to release items and versions not previously put out by the American company. In the mid-1960s the comprehensive rerelease of the catalogue, and the issue of more of the material not originally released, was undertaken by an Italian company using the label King Jazz, and by the Danish company Storyville. The material has remained available from the latter organization into the late 1980s.

BIBLIOGRAPHY

M. Mezzrow and B. Wolfe: *Really the Blues* (New York, 1946/*R*1972), 331
E. Lambert: "King Jazz," *J&B*, ii (1975), no.5, p.12; no.6, p.20; no.7, p.28; no.8, p.14
J. Chilton: *Sidney Bechet: the Wizard of Jazz* (London and New York, 1987), 174, 187

King Pleasure. *See* PLEASURE, KING.

Kinsey, Tony [Cyril Anthony] (*b* Sutton Coldfield, England, 11 Oct 1927). English drummer. He studied privately with Cozy Cole and took some lessons in composition and orchestration with Bill Russo. He was a founding member of the Johnny Dankworth Seven, with which he performed and recorded from 1950 to 1951. The majority of his playing, however, has been as the leader of his own groups, which have usually included Bill Le Sage; Joe Harriott was a member of the Tony Kinsey Quartet (1954), while Kinsey's quintet has, at various times, numbered Don Rendell, Ronnie Ross, Peter King, and Alan Branscombe among its sidemen. From 1974 Kinsey has played and recorded with his own big band and in 1980 he formed a similar group with Dankworth. He has composed several works for jazz orchestra and has worked as music director for television and films. His playing may be heard to advantage on his recording of his own composition *Starboard Bow* (1955, Decca F10725).

BIBLIOGRAPHY

FeatherE
R. Cotterrell, ed.: *Jazz Now: the Jazz Centre Society Guide* (London, 1976)

NEVIL SKRIMSHIRE

Kirby, John (*b* Baltimore, 31 Dec 1908; *d* Hollywood, CA, 14 June 1952). Double bass player and bandleader. Originally a trombonist, he played tuba and double bass with Fletcher Henderson (1930–33, 1935–6) and Chick Webb (1933–5), attracting attention with his strong pulse and walking bass lines. In 1937 he established his own small group at the Onyx Club, New York, with Frankie Newton and Pete Brown. The following year the band's personnel stabilized into that of a sextet: Charlie Shavers, Russell Procope, Buster Bailey, Billy Kyle, O'Neill Spencer, and Kirby, with the frequent addition of Maxine Sullivan (Kirby's wife). From 1938 to 1942 Kirby's sextet was perhaps the leading small jazz ensemble in the swing style, with a nationwide following from its many recordings and network radio broadcasts. The group concentrated on a "chamber" jazz style, performing intricate arrangements (many supplied by Shavers) at a subdued dynamic level, with a light sense of swing, and achieving an extremely precise ensemble.

John Kirby's sextet in the Pump Room at the Ambassador Hotel, Chicago, 1940: (left to right) O'Neill Spencer (drums), Charlie Shavers (trumpet), Kirby (double bass), Buster Bailey (clarinet), Russell Procope (alto saxophone), Billy Kyle (piano)

In this way it presaged many cool-jazz groups of the late 1940s and early 1950s, particularly those of Lennie Tristano. From 1942 Kirby's group lost its stability as its members were drafted; it disbanded in 1946 and, despite several attempts to reconstitute his sextet, Kirby gradually fell into obscurity.

SELECTED RECORDINGS

Rehearsin' for a Nervous Breakdown (1938, Decca 2367); Undecided (1938, Decca 2216); Blues Petite (1940, OK 5805); Double Talk (1941, Col. 35998); Bugler's Dilemma (1941, Vic. 27568); 9:20 Special (1945, Asch 3571)

BIBLIOGRAPHY

H. Panassié: "Un orchestre méconnu: celui de John Kirby," *BHcF*, no.45 (1955), 5

R. Procope: "Wonderful, Wonderful Jazz," *JJ*, xx/5 (1967), 6

I. Crosbie: "The Biggest Little Band," *JJ*, xxv/3 (1972), 26

R. Stewart: "Flow Gently, Sweet Kirby," *Jazz Masters of the Thirties* (New York and London, n.d. [?1972]), 151

D. Bakker: "John Kirby, 1938–42," *Micrography*, no.29 (1973), 3; no.30 (1974), 1 [discography]

J. BRADFORD ROBINSON

Kirk, Andy [Andrew Dewey] (*b* Newport, KY, 28 May 1898). Saxophonist and bandleader. He spent his childhood in Denver, where he studied piano, singing, alto and tenor saxophone, and music theory with Wilberforce Whiteman (Paul Whiteman's father) and several others. He began playing bass saxophone and tuba in an orchestra led by the violinist George Morrison in 1918 and in 1925 he moved to Dallas, where he joined Terrence Holder's Dark Clouds of Joy. In 1929 he assumed the leadership of the band, which became known as the Clouds of Joy (sometimes the Twelve Clouds of Joy, Original Eleven Clouds of Joy, etc., depending on the number of players taking part in any engagement); he moved with it to Kansas City, where it made its first recordings (1929–30), and became so popular that it rivaled Bennie Moten's band. From 1930 Kirk made several nationwide tours, though the Clouds of Joy continued to be based primarily in Kansas City. The success of *Until the Real Thing Comes Along* (1936) established the band's lasting popularity. Until the group disbanded in 1948 it toured constantly and made many recordings; thereafter Kirk worked occasionally with pickup bands into the 1960s.

Kirk was not a soloist, and rarely played ensemble parts after the early 1930s, but he made an important contribution to jazz through his leadership of the Clouds of Joy. His was the only Kansas City group with a strong reputation both as a jazz orchestra and as a commercial "sweet" band. Its style was largely determined by the compositions and arrangements of Mary Lou Williams, the pianist from 1929 to 1942; though vigorous, her pieces were more subtly orchestrated than those played by most other midwestern bands of the period, and less dependent on riffs. Kirk's outstanding soloists included Williams, Kenny Kersey, Dick Wilson, Don Byas, Shorty Baker, Howard McGhee, and Fats Navarro, and for a brief period Charlie Parker.

Oral history material in *NjR* (JOHP).

See also BLUES, §6; for illustration *see* WILLIAMS, MARY LOU.

SELECTED RECORDINGS

Mess-a-stomp/Blue Clarinet Stomp (1929, Bruns. 4694); Lotta Sax Appeal (1936, Decca 1046); Until the Real Thing Comes Along (1936, Decca 809); Cloudy (1936, Decca 1208); Mary's Idea (1938, Decca 2326); 12th Street Rag (1940, Decca 18123); McGhee Special (1942, Decca 4405)

BIBLIOGRAPHY

F. Driggs: "Kansas City and the Southwest," *Jazz: New Perspectives on the History of Jazz*, ed. N. Hentoff and A. J. McCarthy (New York, 1959/*R*1974), 189

——: "My Story, by Andy Kirk," *JR*, ii/2 (1959), 12

——: "Andy Kirk," *Jazz Panorama*, ed. M. Williams (New York and London, 1962/*R*1979) [colln of previously pubd articles], 119

G. Fernett: "Andy Kirk and his Clouds of Joy," *Swing Out: Great Negro Jazz Bands* (Midland, MI, 1970), 77

A. McCarthy: "Andy Kirk and his Clouds of Joy," *J&B*, i/8 (1971), 18

R. Russell: "Andy Kirk and the Clouds of Joy," *Jazz Style in Kansas City and the Southwest* (Berkeley, CA, Los Angeles, and London, 1971/*R*1983, rev. 2/1973), 163

A. McCarthy: *Big Band Jazz* (New York and London, 1974), 102
L. D. Holmes and J. W. Thomson: *Jazz Greats: Getting Better with Age* (New York, 1986) [colln of interviews]

J. R. TAYLOR/R

Kirk, (Rahsaan) Roland [Ronald T.] (*b* Columbus, OH, 7 Aug 1936; *d* Bloomington, IN, 5 Dec 1977). Tenor saxophonist. He was blind from the age of two. He played bugle and trumpet before taking up clarinet and C-melody saxophone, and by the time he was 15 was working professionally as a tenor saxophonist in rhythm-and-blues bands. While still a teenager he discovered a manzello and a stritch (for illustration *see* SAXOPHONE, fig.4), to which he made ad hoc alterations with tape and rubber bands. By modifying the keys of his tenor saxophone and making use of false fingerings and drones he was able to play all three instruments at once, encompassing most of the tenor's range with his left hand and using his right to finger the manzello or stritch. This technique was fully formed at the time of his first recording, a rhythm-and-blues album made in 1956. By 1960 he was using a siren whistle (a metal hunting horn) to underscore climactic moments in his solos, and in 1963 he adopted the technique of CIRCULAR BREATHING, which allowed him to produce sounds without interruption.

After working in Louisville Kirk moved in 1960 to Chicago, where he recorded his second album, on which Ira Sullivan was a prominent soloist. He toured Germany in April 1961, and later that year spent three months with Charles Mingus. For the next 15 years he led his own groups, drawing on various combinations of lesser-known sidemen; the Vibration Society, as his band was called, toured widely and played in all styles of jazz. In the early 1970s Kirk was the leader of the Jazz and People's Movement, an organization that attempted to open up new avenues for jazz performance; from August 1970, when, with Lee Morgan, he led a group of demonstrators who disrupted the taping of the "Merv Griffin Show," the organization interrupted a number of television and radio shows, protesting the dearth of black music and musicians in the studios.

Roland Kirk playing at the Montreux International Jazz Festival, 1975

Although Kirk was often, and wrongfully, accused of perpetrating nonmusical gimmickry, listeners in the 1960s gradually came to recognize his talents as an improviser, and in the 1970s he even achieved modest commercial success with his speech-song on *Bright Moments*. By that time he had played not only most woodwind and some more unusual instruments, such as nose flute, piccolo, harmonica, and claviette, but also his own homemade creations: the trumpophone (a trumpet with soprano saxophone mouthpiece), slidesophone (a similarly equipped miniature trombone resembling the slide saxophone invented by Snub Mosley), black puzzle flute, and black mystery pipes. Kirk was paralyzed on one side by a stroke in 1975, but, by using his skill in playing more than one instrument with a single hand, he was able to resume performing the following year. Early in 1977 he founded the Vibration School of Music to teach saxophonists in what he called "black classical music," a term he preferred to "jazz."

Oral history material in *NjR*.

SELECTED RECORDINGS

As leader: *Triple Threat* (1956, King 539); *Introducing Roland Kirk* (1960, Argo 669); *Kirk's Work* (1961, Prst. 7210); *We Free Kings* (1961, Mer. 60679); *Reeds and Deeds* (1963, Mer. 60800); *The Roland Kirk Quartet Meets the Benny Golson Orchestra* (1963, Mer. 60844); *Rip, Rig, and Panic* (1965, Lml. 86027); *The Inflated Tear* (1967, Atl. 1502); *Volunteered Slavery* (1968–9, Atl. 1534); *Rahsaan Rahsaan* (1970, Atl. 1575); *Natural Black Inventions: Root Strata* (1971, Atl. 1578); *Bright Moments* (1973, Atl. 2-907); *The Return of the 5000 lb. Man* (1976, WB 2918)

As sideman with C. Mingus: *Oh Yeah!* (1961, Atl. 1377); *Tonight at Noon* (1961, Atl. 1416); *Mingus at Carnegie Hall* (1974, Atl. 1667)

BIBLIOGRAPHY

"The Man who Plays Three Horns," *DB*, xxvii/16 (1960), 13
I. Gitler: "Roland Kirk," *DB*, xxix/13 (1962), 36
D. DeMicheal: "Roland Kirk: the Road to Frustration," *DB*, xxx/12 (1963), 15
L. Feather: "Kirk," *MM*, xxxviii (21 Sept 1963), 7
B. Korall: "I had to Play the Sounds I Heard in my Head," *MM*, xxxviii (9 Feb 1963), 9
A. Morgan: "Roland Kirk," *JM*, ix/9 (1963), 4
B. McLarney: "Telling it Like it is," *DB*, xxxiv/10 (1967), 17 [interview]
M. Cuscuna: "Rahsaan Roland Kirk," *J&P*, x/4 (1971), 32
L. Feather: "TV Soundings," *DB*, xxxviii/7 (1971), 13
T. Barkin: "Rahsaan Speaks his Peace," *DB*, xli/14 (1974), 13
E. Levin: "Rahsaan Roland Kirk Returns," *JM*, i/1 (1976), 26
"Roland Kirk Discography," *SJ*, xxx/12 (1976), 80
C. Welch: "Kirk: Crossing the Barriers," *MM*, lii (17 Dec 1977), 16
Obituary, *JF* [intl edn], no.51 (1978), 12
J. Winter: "Rahsaan Roland Kirk," *Coda*, no.172 (1980), 10 [interview]
P. Cohen: "Vintage Saxophones," *Saxophone Journal*, x/3 (1985), 4

BARRY KERNFELD

Kirkland, Kenny [Kenneth David] (*b* New York, 28 Sept 1955). Keyboard player. He began learning piano at the age of six; his interest in jazz was kindled by taking saxophone lessons in high school. After graduating from the Manhattan School of Music in 1977 he toured with Michal Urbaniak, then in 1979 joined Miroslav Vitous's band; he also played at this time with the percussionist Don Alias. He toured Japan with Terumasa Hino, worked with Elvin Jones, and from 1981 to 1985 played with Wynton Marsalis. He played synthesizers on two highly publicized albums and on tours with the rock singer Sting. Kirkland's training steered him, early in his career, towards sophisticated modernists such as Herbie Hancock; but in the mid-1980s his style began to take on elements of bop (under the influence, notably, of Bud Powell) and rock (in which he gained experience through his work with Sting, the group Crosby, Stills and Nash, and other performers). Kirkland's technical ability, inventiveness, and awareness of tradition mark him as a player of unusual breadth and promise.

SELECTED RECORDINGS

As sideman: M. Urbaniak: *Urbaniak* (1977, IC 1036); M. Vitous: *Miroslav Vitous Group* (1980, ECM 1185); E. Jones: *Earth Jones* (1982, PAlt 8016); W. Marsalis: *Black Codes from the Underground* (1985, Col. FC40009)

BIBLIOGRAPHY

B. Doerschuk: "Kenny Kirkland Straddles the Stylistic Chasm with Wynton Marsalis and Sting," *Keyboard*, xi/12 (1985), 56 [incl. discography]
L. Gourse: "Profile: Kenny Kirkland," *DB*, lii/7 (1985), 50
M. Gilbert: "Kenny Kirkland," *JJI*, xl/6 (1987), 7 [incl. discography]

BOB DOERSCHUK

Kirkpatrick, Don(ald E.) (*b* Charlotte, NC, 17 June 1905; *d* New York, 13 May 1956). Pianist and arranger. In the late 1920s and the 1930s he was associated principally with Chick Webb (intermittently, 1927–37) and Don Redman (1933–7), and while with the latter recorded his arrangement of *No-one loves me like that Dallas man* (1933, Bruns. 6684). During this period he also worked with Harry White (1929–30) and Elmer Snowden (1930), recorded with a group led by Henry "Red" Allen and Coleman Hawkins (1933) and with Benny Morton (1934), and played with Zutty Singleton and Mezz Mezzrow. In the late 1930s and the 1940s Kirkpatrick worked mainly as an arranger, providing scores for Benny Goodman, Alvino Rey, Cootie Williams, Count Basie, and others. Later he performed and recorded with Bunk Johnson (1947) and Wilbur De Paris (1952–5) and worked with Doc Cheatham (1955); he also recorded with Sidney Bechet (1951), and may be heard to advantage on the album *The Fabulous Sidney Bechet and his Hot Six with Sidney De Paris* (BN 7020).

BIBLIOGRAPHY

ChiltonW
A. McCarthy: *Big Band Jazz* (New York and London, 1974)

Kitamura, Eiji (*b* Tokyo, 8 April 1929). Japanese clarinetist. He played in a band at Keio University in Tokyo and worked professionally from the early 1950s. In 1957 he played with Benny Goodman in Tokyo and from 1960 led a quintet. He recorded as a leader with Teddy Wilson (1971, 1973), as a sideman with Woody Herman, John Lewis, Hank Jones, and others, and as a leader of groups of which Wilson was a member (*c*1980, 1981); from 1978 he appeared at festivals in Monterey (California) and elsewhere. Kitamura is chiefly a swing and dixieland player but he has also recorded bop with Harold Land (1980).

SELECTED RECORDINGS

As leader: *Because of you* (1976, Audio Lab J1046); *My Monday Date* (1977, Vic. SPX1037); *Memories of you* (1978, RCA RDC10); *April Date* (1979, CBS–Sony 25AP1035); *3 Degrees North* (1980, CBS–Sony 25AP1861); *Seven Stars* (1981, Toshiba–EMI 1CJ9007)
As leader with others: S. Shoji: *Kitamura Eiji vs Suzuki Shoji* (1976, Tei. GM5001); W. Herman: *We with Woody Herman* (1983, Toshiba–EMI EWJ90026)

BIBLIOGRAPHY

Feather–Gitler '70s

YOZO IWANAMI

Klacto. Record company and label. The company was founded by Mark Gardner in 1968, and was named for Charlie Parker's piece *Klactoveedsedstene* (1947). Three albums of material by Parker were issued in limited editions: these were later licensed to Japan where they were put out by Odeon in a boxed set. Although the reissue of material recorded by Parker in Paris and the release of a new album by Cecil Payne were planned, both were eventually put out on Spotlite.

MARK GARDNER

Klein, Harry [Harold] (*b* London, 25 Dec 1928). English baritone saxophonist. After teaching himself alto saxophone he began playing with dance bands in 1945. He concentrated on baritone saxophone from around 1952 and performed and made several recordings as a leader (1952–5, including *New Sound*, 1955, Nixa 1009 [EP]). He also recorded with Victor Feldman (1952, 1955), Kenny Baker (1952, 1955, 1957), Ronnie Scott and Jack Parnell (both 1952–3), the Melody Maker All Stars (1954–5, 1957), and the Jazz Showcase (1956), among others. In 1956 he toured Europe with Stan Kenton. Klein was voted "top British baritone" by *Melody Maker* in 1957 and was one of the most popular baritone saxophonists in England at that time. From 1960 to 1963 he led a quintet called the Jazz Five with Vic Ash, after which he worked mainly in studios accompanying Ella Fitzgerald, Tony Bennett, Sammy Davis, Jr., and others. From 1980, however, he again worked as a jazz musician in and around London. (*FeatherE*)

DIGBY FAIRWEATHER

Klein, Manny [Emmanuel] (*b* New York, 4 Feb 1908). Trumpeter. One of four brothers who became musicians, he began playing professionally as a teenager; he deputized for Bix Beiderbecke in Paul Whiteman's band, taking a solo on its recording of *Makin' Whoopee*. Klein's many early recordings demonstrate a skillful use of the plunger rare among white musicians of the time and a style similar to that of Bunny Berigan. From 1928 to 1937 he was one of the busiest freelances in New York, playing on hundreds of recordings by Benny Goodman, the Dorsey Brothers, the Boswell Sisters, Red Nichols, and others. He moved in 1937 to California, where he helped to organize and played with a band led by Frankie Trumbauer. Thereafter he established himself as a studio musician; although it is for his work in this capacity that he is best known, Klein was a potent and persuasive stylist in many contexts. He became active in Hollywood, and played both classical music and jazz. He recorded the soundtracks to numerous films, including *From Here to Eternity* (1953) and *The Benny Goodman Story* (1955). He was heard frequently at concerts and festivals during the 1960s, and despite a stroke in 1973 he continued to perform, and made guest appearances at workshops.

SELECTED RECORDINGS

As sideman: P. Whiteman: Makin' Whoopee (1928, Col. 1683D); I. Mills: Barbaric/High and Dry (1929, Bruns. 4920); R. Bloom: The Man from the South/St. James Infirmary (1930, Col. 2103D); Boswell Sisters: It's the Girl/It's You (1931, Bruns. 6151): Dorsey Brothers: Old Man Harlem/By Heck (1933, Bruns. 6624); B. Goodman: Junk Man (1934, Col. 2892D); Adrian Rollini: Davenport Blues/Somebody Loves me (1934, Decca 359); Tutti Camarata: *Tutti's Trumpets* (1957, Dis. 3011)

BIBLIOGRAPHY

ChiltonW

RICHARD SUDHALTER

Klein, Miriam (*b* Basle, Switzerland, 27 March 1937). Swiss singer, wife of Oscar Klein. She was active in jazz from her teenage years, and early in her career performed with Don Byas and the pianist Art Simmons. From 1964 she sang with Klein's dixieland band and also made recordings under her own name. Her imitation of Billie Holiday, recorded with Roy Eldridge, Dexter Gordon, Slide Hampton, and others on the album *Lady Like* (1973, MPS 21218856) had a mixed reception. Klein also recorded with Wild Bill Davison (1975) and made an unaccompanied solo album of swing standards, *By Myself* (*c*1979, L+R 40001). She has appeared at many jazz festivals. (*Feather–Gitler '70s*)

Klein, Oscar (*b* Graz, Austria, 5 Jan 1930). Austrian trumpeter and guitarist. He belonged to Fatty George's band from 1952 until 1957, when he joined the Swiss dixieland group the Tremble Kids; he remained a member of this group for three years. After working with the Dutch Swing College Orchestra (from late 1959 to 1963) he established a guitar school in Innsbruck, Austria, and settled in Basle, Switzerland. He rejoined the Tremble Kids (recording at intervals from 1963 to 1977) and accompanied a number of American musicians, including Albert Nicholas (1969) and Wild Bill Davison (1975). Later he was the host of a Swiss television series, on which he also performed, and made frequent tours with the guitarist Philadelphia Jerry Ricks, with whom he recorded an album of duos (*Low Light Blues*, 1980, L+R 42007). He is married to the singer Miriam Klein.

BIBLIOGRAPHY

Feather–Gitler '70s; ReclamsJ

G. Bielderman and E. Elvers: *Oscar Klein Discography* (Zwolle, Netherlands, 1986)

PETER SCHWALM

Kleindin, Teddy [Franz] (*b* Berlin, 20 July 1914). German clarinetist and alto saxophonist. He studied cello and clarinet at the Hochschule für Musik, Berlin, and in 1934 he began to perform and record on alto saxophone and clarinet with various dance and jazz bands, including those of Teddy Stauffer (1936–7) and Kurt Hohenberger (1938–9). A versatile soloist, whose playing was strongly influenced by Benny Goodman, he was in much demand as a studio musician; he recorded on alto, tenor, and baritone saxophones and clarinet with Kutte Widmann (1939–41), Willy Berking (1940–43), and Freddie Brocksieper (1942, 1947), among others. He also made recordings with his own trio, quartet, and big band (1941–3, including *Klarinettenzauber*, 1941, Tel. 10340, one of his own compositions). He worked as a leader until 1948 and then performed with the dance orchestra of Bayerischer Rundfunk (1948–79).

RAINER E. LOTZ

Kleinschuster, Erich (*b* Graz, Austria, 23 Jan 1930). Austrian trombonist, composer, and bandleader. After studying piano he took up the trombone and began playing professionally in 1953 with Fridl Althaler's Kleines Tanzorchester of Radio Graz. He performed and recorded with the International Youth Band at the Newport Jazz Festival (1958) and with Johannes Fehring's big band (1958–65), and he took part in the Norddeutscher Rundfunk jazz workshops of 1962 and 1965. In 1963 he joined the Clarke–Boland Big Band and in 1965 he worked with Friedrich Gulda's Euro-Jazz Orchestra. He formed his own sextet in Vienna in 1966, which played regularly on Österreichischer Rundfunk with a wide range of soloists; it made a number of recordings, among them *Erich Kleinschuster Sextett Live* (1972, Preiser 9973–4). In 1968 he founded the Jazzinstitut in Vienna. From 1972 Kleinschuster led the big band of Österreichischer Rundfunk, with which he performed on television as well as radio during the 1970s; he also played with Astrud Gilberto, Toots Thielemans, Gerry Mulligan, Stan Getz, Peter Herbolzheimer, and George Gruntz. One of the best bop trombonists in Europe, Kleinschuster has been influenced principally by Bob Brookmeyer and J. J. Johnson. As a composer he has worked in a number of styles, chiefly hard bop; his larger works include *Oberwarter Messe* (1970, EMI 06233026) and *Maurische Anekdoten* (1979, Ego 4017). (*FeatherE*)

KLAUS SCHULZ

Klemmer, John (*b* Chicago, 3 July 1946). Tenor saxophonist. He began to learn guitar at the age of seven, but changed to alto saxophone when he was 11 and to tenor saxophone in his first year at high school; he studied with the saxophonist Joe Daley, led the school stage band, and conducted the concert band. After touring at the age of 16 with a dance band that worked under Ted Weems's name, he played with the dance bands of Les Elgart and Ralph Marterie. He also attended the Interlochen Arts Festival and several of Stan Kenton's summer workshops. He began to record for Cadet in 1967. In the following year he moved west to work with Don Ellis's band; while continuing this association until 1970, he joined a tour of Africa (sponsored by the US State Department) with Oliver Nelson's sextet in 1969 and worked with Alice Coltrane, the Crusaders, and others. After 1970 Klemmer frequently led his own groups, both in performance and in recordings. His own compositions feature in much of his work (he studied orchestration in Los Angeles in 1970–74); recordings such as *Arabesque* achieved commercial success, but his creative potential was more clearly indicated by *Cry* (recorded on solo saxophone with electronic effects) and *Nexus for Duo and Trio*. The recordings he has made in the 1980s include duos with Eddie Harris and a second solo album. Klemmer is most notable for his technical mastery of the saxophone and for his early experimentation with electronics; his recorded output is of uneven quality.

SELECTED RECORDINGS

As unaccompanied soloist: *Cry* (1975, ABC 1106); *Solo Saxophone II: Life* (1985, Elek. Mus. 5E-566)

As leader: *All the Children Cried* (1969, Cadet 326); *Constant Throb* (1971, Imp. 9214); *Arabesque* (1977, ABC 1068); *Nexus for Duo and Trio* (1978, AN 3500)

As sideman: D. Ellis: *Autumn* (1968, Col. CS9721); O. Nelson: *Black, Brown, and Beautiful* (1969, FD 116)

BIBLIOGRAPHY

Feather–Gitler '70s

D. Morgenstern: "John Klemmer: Chicago Find," *DB*, xxxv/7 (1968), 24

L. Tomkins: "Introducing . . . John Klemmer," *CI*, xii/2 (1973), 14

G. Alexander: "Magic in Movement," *DB*, xli/16 (1974), 13

L. Lyons: "John Klemmer: Success and the Echo Complex," *DB*, xlv/19 (1978), 19

L. Underwood: "John Klemmer: Creative Calm," *DB*, xlviii/11 (1981), 24 [incl. discography]

DAVID WILD

Klink, Al(bert) (*b* Danbury, CT, 28 Dec 1915). Tenor and alto saxophonist and clarinetist. From 1939 to 1942 he performed in Glenn Miller's orchestra (during which time he was second tenor saxophonist to Tex Beneke) and he was one of the saxophone duetists on Miller's successful *In the Mood* (1939). He performed and made recordings with Benny Goodman (1942–4) and Tommy Dorsey (1943, 1944–5) and in 1947 he recorded with Billie Holiday as an alto saxophonist in Bob Haggart's orchestra. In the late 1940s and early 1950s he was active as a studio musician. After playing in the Sauter–Finegan Orchestra (1952–3) he became a staff musician at NBC (1954). He joined the World's Greatest Jazz Band in late 1974 and toured

Europe with the group to 1982. From the late 1970s he worked as a freelance and studio musician, recording with George Masso and the trumpeter Glenn Zottola, among others.

For illustrations *see* MILLER, GLENN, and MUTE, fig.3.

SELECTED RECORDINGS

As sideman: G. Miller: In the Mood (1939, Bb 10416); World's Greatest Jazz Band: *The World's Greatest Jazz Band of Yank Lawson and Bob Haggart Plays Rogers and Hart* (1975, World Jazz 7); *The World's Greatest Jazz Band of Yank Lawson and Bob Haggart on Tour* (1975, World Jazz 8, 10)

BIBLIOGRAPHY

ChiltonW; FeatherE

EDDIE COOK

Klook [Klook-mop]. Nickname of KENNY CLARKE.

Kloss, Eric (*b* Greenville, PA, 3 April 1949). Saxophonist and leader. He studied alto saxophone, and later the tenor and soprano instruments, at the Western Pennsylvania School for Blind Children, and began performing professionally in Pittsburgh in the early 1960s. From 1965 he worked with Pat Martino in Philadelphia, and in 1966 he was the subject of a television documentary. He made the first of many recordings as the leader of his own group (variously a quartet and a quintet) at the age of 16. His albums contain an eclectic blend of bop, pop, rock, funk, and free jazz, and in some of his compositions he has experimented with tone rows and classical forms. Kloss's playing is influenced by the work of the musicians with whom he studied, most importantly Lee Konitz, Sonny Stitt, and James Moody. His sidemen have included Jimmy Owens, Booker Ervin, and rhythm sections formed by Cedar Walton, Leroy Vinnegar, and Billy Higgins; Kenny Barron, Bob Cranshaw, and Alan Dawson; and Chick Corea, Martino, Dave Holland, and Jack DeJohnette.

SELECTED RECORDINGS

As leader: *Introducing Eric Kloss* (1965, Prst. 7442); *Life Force* (1967, Prst. 7535); *Sky Shadows* (1968, Prst. 7594); *To Hear is to See* (1969, Prst. 7689); *One, Two, Free* (1972, Muse 5019); *Now* (1978, Muse 5147); with Gil Goldstein: *Sharing* (1981, Omni. 1044)

BIBLIOGRAPHY

M. Cuscuna: "The Exuberance of Eric Kloss," *DB*, xxxvi/19 (1969), 18
Z. Knauss: *Conversations with Jazz Musicians* (Detroit, 1977), 78
C. Berg: "Profile: Eric Kloss," *DB*, xlv/17 (1978), 34
T. Dreibelbis: "Eric Kloss," *IM*, lxxvi (1978), March, 9

BRENDA PENNELL

Kluger, Irv(ing) (*b* New York, 9 July 1921). Drummer and vibraphonist. He played violin as a child, then changed to drums, and later studied music at New York University and elsewhere. At the age of 15 he began playing at local clubs. He worked with Georgie Auld in 1942–3, and recorded with him in 1945. Around this time he also played with Bob Chester, Freddie Slack (1943–4), Boyd Raeburn (1945–7; for illustration *see* RAEBURN, BOYD), Bobby Byrne, and Herbie Fields (1947). After deputizing for Shelly Manne in Stan Kenton's orchestra (1947–8) he worked with Artie Shaw's Gramercy Five (1949–50) and Tex Beneke (?1949). Although it is commonly thought that Manne played in Dizzy Gillespie's early bop sessions of 1945, it has been suggested that the drummer was in fact Kluger. From 1950 to 1953 he played for shows on Broadway. Later he was a member of the house band at the Moulin Rouge, Hollywood, after which he became active as a freelance in California. He also worked briefly with Woody Herman and Benny Goodman.

SELECTED RECORDINGS

As sideman: B. Raeburn: How high the moon (1947, Atl. 860); first issued on S. Kenton: *The Kenton Era* (1940–55, Cap. WDX569), Elegy for Alto (1948); on M. Bernhardt: *Modern Brass* (1955, RCA LPM1123), Tangerine; D. Pell: *Jazz Goes Dancing* (1956, RCA LPM1320)

BIBLIOGRAPHY

FeatherE

JEFF POTTER

Kluger, Jack [Jacob] (*b* Antwerp, Belgium, 23 Jan 1912; *d* Brussels, 26 May 1963). Belgian bandleader. He was brought up in a musical family, and first worked as joint leader of the Collegians, a successful amateur group which recorded as a 12-piece orchestra in 1936; he then joined the saxophonist Maurice Pinto as co-leader of the Pintonians. Kluger subsequently formed his own band with sidemen from both groups; it toured in Europe and made several recordings (1939–41), considered some of the finest to have been made by Belgian jazz musicians, before its activities were interrupted by World War II. Kluger later recorded again as a bandleader (1946, 1951), but thereafter worked principally as a partner of Félix R. Faecq at the International Music Company, where he organized studio bands and became an influential concert promoter, record producer, and publisher.

ROBERT PERNET

Klugh, Earl (*b* Detroit, 16 Sept 1954). Acoustic guitarist. He studied piano for seven years and guitar from the age of ten. In 1970 he played on Yusef Lateef's album *Suite 16*; he then toured with George Benson, played on Benson's recording *White Rabbit* (1971), and in 1973 joined his group. After playing electric guitar with Return to Forever on a tour of the USA in 1974 he ceased touring for a period and from 1976 made recordings as a leader, while continuing to work occasionally as a sideman and as a guest soloist. *One on One* (1979), an album recorded in collaboration with Bob James, received a Grammy Award. Klugh's early style was strongly influenced by the country-music guitarist Chet Atkins and George Van Eps; later he forged a lucid, melodic style that combined elements of mainstream jazz and rhythm-and-blues.

SELECTED RECORDINGS

As leader: *Earl Klugh* (1976, BN LA596G); *Living inside your Love* (1977, BN LA667G); *Finger Painting* (1977, BN LA737H); with B. James: *One on One* (1979, Col.–Tappan Zee FC36251); *Heart String* (1979, UA LA942H); *Dream Come True* (*c*1979, UA LT1026); *Nightsongs* (*c*1983, Cap. ST12372); *Soda Fountain Shuffle* (*c*1985, WB 25262)

As sideman: Y. Lateef: *Suite 16* (1970, Atl. 1563), incl. Michelle; G. Benson: *White Rabbit* (1971, CTI 6015)

BIBLIOGRAPHY

H. Nolan: "Earl Klugh: Man of the Moment," *DB*, xliv/4 (1977), 19
S. Bloom: "Earl Klugh: Lucking out in the Material World," *DB*, xlvii/3 (1980), 20 [incl. discography]
B. Milkowski: "Earl Klugh: Melody Maker," *DB*, l/10 (1983), 14 [incl. discography]
J. Ferguson: "Earl Klugh: Nylon String Pop with Taste and Elegance," *GP*, xix/8 (1985), 54 [incl. discography, transcrs.]

PATRICK T. WILL

Knepper, Jimmy [James M.] (*b* Los Angeles, 22 Nov 1927). Trombonist. He first played alto horn, and at the age of nine began learning trombone; he continued his studies at colleges in Los Angeles. He took his first professional job at the age of 15, and then worked with many big bands, including those of Charlie Spivak (1950–51), Charlie Barnet (1951), Woody Herman, Claude Thornhill (1956), and Stan Kenton (1959). His association with Charles Mingus's group (1957–61) brought him to the attention of the public; he then worked with Gil

Evans (intermittently, 1960–77) and the Thad Jones–Mel Lewis Orchestra (1968–74; for illustration *see* JONES, fig.1*b*). He also toured the USSR with Benny Goodman in 1962. From 1975 to 1981 Knepper played with and wrote arrangements for Lee Konitz's nonet, and from 1979 he toured and recorded with Mingus Dynasty.

Unlike many of his contemporaries Knepper has managed to avoid imitating the playing of J. J. Johnson. His gruff sound and highly distinctive manner of phrasing show him to be a single-minded individualist. He has an excellent technique, but he never allows his playing to be ruled by virtuoso display; the structure and development of his solos have won him many admirers.

SELECTED RECORDINGS

As leader: *A Swinging Introduction to Jimmy Knepper* (1957, Beth. 77); with P. Adams: *Pepper and Knepper* (1958, Metro. 1004); *Cunningbird* (1976, Ste. 1061); *Primrose Path* (1980, Hep 2012)

As sideman with C. Mingus: *Tijuana Moods* (1957, RCA LSP2533); *East Coasting* (1957, Beth. 6019); *Blues and Roots* (1959, Atl. 1305); *Mingus Dynasty* (1959, Col. CS8236)

BIBLIOGRAPHY

C. Albertson: Liner notes, *Idol of the Flies* (Beth. 6031, 1977)
G. Sloan: "Jimmy Knepper: Cunningbird of the Trombone," *JJI*, xxxiii/11 (1980), 6 [incl. discography]
L. Jeske: "Jimmy Knepper," *DB*, xlviii/8 (1981), 14 [incl. discography]
A. Morgan: Liner notes, *Primrose Path* (Hep 2012, 1982)
P. Klasse, M. Gardner, and J. Bernlef: *Jamsession: Portraits of Jazz and Blues Musicians Drawn on the Scene* (Weesp, Netherlands, 1984; Ger. trans., with discography by U. Goeman, Königstein, Germany, 1984)

MARK GARDNER

Koenig, Lester (1918–77). Record producer who in 1951 established the record company and label CONTEMPORARY.

Koffman, Moe [Morris] (*b* Toronto, 28 Dec 1928). Canadian flutist and alto and soprano saxophonist. He played in dance bands in Toronto while in his teens and worked with Sonny Dunham and Jimmy Dorsey in New York (1950–55). In 1957 he played flute on a recording of his composition *Swinging Shepherd Blues* (Jub. 5311), which became a hit single; later he recorded albums not only of jazz but also of pop, funk, and popular arrangements of classical works. He also played regularly at George's Spaghetti House in Toronto for more than 30 years and from 1972 was a principal soloist with Rob McConnell's Boss Brass; in the mid-1980s he toured occasionally with Dizzy Gillespie. (M. Miller: "Koffman, Moe," *Encyclopedia of Music in Canada*, ed. H. Kallmann, G. Potvin, and K. Winters (Toronto, Buffalo, and London, 1981) [incl. discography])

MARK MILLER

Kohlman, Freddie (*b* New Orleans, 25 Aug 1918). Drummer, singer, and bandleader. He received his musical training from Louis Cottrell, Sr., and Manuel Manetta, and began his career playing with the bands of A. J. Piron, Joseph Robichaux, Papa Celestin, and Sam Morgan. In the mid-1930s he moved to Chicago, where he joined a quartet at the Michigan Hotel that included Albert Ammons and Stuff Smith; he also worked with Lee Collins and Earl Hines. He spent a period in Detroit before returning to New Orleans in 1941. From 1944 he led his own band, although in the mid-1950s he spent six months with Louis Armstrong's All Stars. Thereafter he held a long residency at Jazz Limited in Chicago. In the 1960s he moved back to New Orleans and played with Louis Cottrell, Jr., the Dukes of Dixieland, and the Onward Brass Band (ii). He began performing extensively as a soloist in the 1970s and made frequent visits to Europe. His album *Jazz Solos in New Orleans* (1953, MGM 297), recorded with his Mardi Gras Loungers, provides examples of the early fusion of New Orleans jazz and bop, whilst his singing and parade work may be heard on *Take me Back to New Orleans* (1980, BL 157007), recorded by Chris Barber and the singer and pianist Dr. John. In the 1980s he has regularly toured Italy and Switzerland with the Jambalaya Four from Milan.

BIBLIOGRAPHY

T. Fullick: Liner notes, *All of Me* (Camelia TF1, 1977)
T. Stagg: "Freddie Kohlman: a Name Discography," *Fn*, viii/4 (1977), 10
V. Wilmer: "Double Clutching Kohlman," *Time Out*, no.451 (8 Dec 1978), 23
E. Fullick: "Freddie Kohlman," *Fn*, x/6 (1979), 21

ALYN SHIPTON

Koivistoinen, Eero (*b* Helsinki, 13 Jan 1941). Finnish tenor and soprano saxophonist, and composer. He studied at the Sibelius Academy in Helsinki and at the Berklee College of Music with Herb Pomeroy (1971–3). He led his own jazz groups from 1964 and was one of the first to play free jazz in Finland; he also performed and recorded with the rock group Blues Section (1966–7). In the 1970s he played all over Scandinavia, in Poland, and in England, and appeared at the Montreux and Newport jazz festivals; in 1979 he taught jazz in the Faeroes. His playing may be heard to advantage on the album *Valtakunta* (1962, Otava 66). Koivistoinen is a versatile composer; in addition to jazz works he has written children's songs, film scores, and ballet music. (A. Granholm: *Finnish Jazz* (Helsinki, 1974, rev. and enlarged by M. Konttinen 2/1982, rev. and enlarged by J.-P. Vuorela 3/1986), 16)

PEKKA GRONOW

Kok, (Arthur) James (*b* Cernauti, Romania [now Chernovtsy, Ukrainian SSR], 24 Jan 1902; *d* Berlin, 18 Oct 1976). Romanian bandleader. He was taught violin by his father. Although he claimed to have been brought up in the USA, he studied music at the Prague Conservatory. In Berlin in 1923 he organized his own group, which toured Germany and Switzerland and recorded from 1933. Forced to leave Germany in 1935, he returned to Romania and formed a new band, which toured Switzerland (1938) and the Netherlands (1939). He emigrated to Switzerland in 1939 and remained there for two decades; after spending some time in the USA he returned to Berlin (1969). Besides violin, Kok played saxophone, clarinet, and piano; trained in classical music, he was not an outstanding jazz soloist, but his bands (for which Kok made arrangements) played in the style of the Jimmie Lunceford and Casa Loma orchestras.

BIBLIOGRAPHY

A. McCarthy: *Big Band Jazz* (New York and London, 1974), 326
H. H. Lange: *Die grossen Tanz-Orchester, 1930–1950: James Kok* (Pol. 2664260, *c*1978) [liner notes]

RAINER E. LOTZ

Koller, Hans (*b* Vienna, 12 Feb 1921). Austrian tenor saxophonist, composer, and bandleader. He studied at the Academy of Music in Vienna (1936–9) and, after serving in the army (1940–46), joined the group Hot Club Vienna (1947), of which he later became the leader. In 1950 he moved to Germany, where he played for a short time with Freddie Brocksieper and then formed a quartet, which made several successful recordings for Discovery in 1952; he also led the New Jazz Stars, which included Albert Mangelsdorff and Jutta Hipp. He worked with Dizzy Gillespie (1953), Bill Russo (1955), Lee Konitz and

Stan Kenton (both 1956), Eddie Sauter (1957–8), and Benny Goodman (1958). He led a quartet (with Attila Zoller, Oscar Pettiford, and Kenny Clarke or Jimmy Pratt) during the late 1950s, at the same time working in Hamburg as the music director of the Norddeutscher Rundfunk jazz workshops (1958–65) and at the Deutsches Schauspielhaus (1968). In 1970 he returned to Vienna, where he formed Free Sound, the members of which included Wolfgang Dauner, Adelhard Roidinger, and Zbigniew Seifert; from 1975 to 1980 he occasionally led the International Brass Company, which included Kenny Wheeler, Mangelsdorff, and Dauner. He then worked in a duo with Fritz Pauer and performed with Warne Marsh. Koller played all types of saxophone and also clarinet; he was the leading European tenor saxophonist during the cool-jazz era. He performed at many important jazz festivals and was heard on radio and television throughout Europe. He composed several extended pieces, including the ballet *New York City* (1968), which are influenced by contemporary art music.

SELECTED RECORDINGS

As leader: *Hans is Hip* (1952, Dis. 2005); *Hans Koller – exklusiv* (1963, Saba 15024); with A. Zoller and M. Solal: *Zoller–Koller–Solal* (1965, Saba 15061); *Relax with my Horns* (1966, Saba 15088); *New York City* (1968, MPS 68235); *Phoenix* (1972, MPS 2121293-9); *Kunstkopfindianer* (1974, MPS 2122019-2); with W. Dauner: *Hans Koller–Wolfgang Dauner Free Sound and Super Brass* (1975, MPS 68109); *For Marcel Duchamp* (1976, MPS 68171); of Trinity: *Trinity* (1979, L+R 40002); with A. Zoller and G. Mraz: *The K & K 3 in New York* (1979, L+R 40009)

As sideman: O. Pettiford: *In Memoriam Oscar Pettiford* (1959, Phi. B08657L); European All Stars: *The European All Stars 1961* (1961, Tel. 14206)

BIBLIOGRAPHY

FeatherE; *Feather–Gitler '70s*
D. H. Kraner: *Die Hans Koller Discographie, 1947–1966* (Graz, Austria, c1967)
"Free Sound from Vienna," *JP*, xxi/5 (1972), 156
"Hans Koller Free Super," *JF* [intl edn], no.40 (1976), 10
K. Schulz: "The Hans Koller Story," *JF* [intl edn], no.70 (1981), 47

KLAUS SCHULZ

Komeda [Trzciński], **Krzysztof** (*b* Poznań, Poland, 27 April 1931; *d* Warsaw, 23 April 1969). Polish composer and pianist. A doctor by profession, he adopted the pseudonym Komeda to conceal his involvement in jazz, which during his early career was discouraged by the Polish government. His success at the first Sopot Jazz Festival (1956) made him the country's most popular musician; in the 1950s and 1960s he led a free-jazz quintet, for which he also wrote compositions that drew freely on traditional and avant-garde Polish music. His most important work was as a composer of scores for about 40 films, including several directed by Roman Polanski (*Knife in the Water*, 1962; *Cul-de-sac*, 1966; *Rosemary's Baby*, 1968), with whom he was closely associated; from 1967 to 1969 he worked in Hollywood at Polanski's invitation. Komeda's views on jazz as film music, which had a wide influence on the Polish cinema, are expressed in an untitled article that he contributed to *Kwartalnik filmowy* ([Film quarterly], xi/2 (1961), 35; repr. in *JF*, no.2 (1969)).

SELECTED RECORDINGS
(all recorded for Muza)

on *Jazz Festival Sopot* (1956, 0084), Blues in the Corner, Memory of Bach; *Jazz Jamboree 1961* (1961, 0127); *Etiude baletowe* [Ballet études] (1962, 1965, 0558); on *Jazz Jamboree 64* (1964, 0240), Sophia's Tune; *Astigmatic* (1965, 0298)

BIBLIOGRAPHY

Feather–Gitler '70s
J. Radliński: "Komeda," *JF*, no.2 (1969), 55
J. E. Berendt: "We'll Remember Komeda," *Ein Fenster aus Jazz: Essays, Portraits, Reflexionen* (Frankfurt am Main, Germany, 1977), 117

J. BRADFORD ROBINSON

Konitz, Lee (*b* Chicago, 13 Oct 1927). Alto saxophonist. In his youth he studied clarinet with a member of the Chicago SO, which probably helped to form his later "cool" tone on saxophone. After taking up alto saxophone he played briefly with the clarinetist Jerry Wald and, in 1947, with Claude Thornhill's band, at that time the source of much of the talent that shaped cool jazz in New York. This established his contact with Miles Davis, and he took a leading part in the latter's famous nonet performances and recordings of 1948–50. By this time Konitz had already begun his association with Lennie Tristano, under whose influence and tutelage his mature style emerged. After breaking with Tristano he toured Scandinavia (1951) and worked in Stan Kenton's big band (1952–3). Thereafter he mainly led his own small groups, occasionally touring abroad but generally shunning publicity and exposure. In 1954–5 he recorded again with Tristano. He withdrew from music in the early 1960s but re-emerged in the middle of the decade to establish links with the experimental jazz of Paul and Carla Bley. Rejecting the premises of avant-garde jazz, Konitz then returned to improvising over chord sequences, probing and deepening his basic style of the 1950s. He was also active as a private teacher, conducting lessons by tape with students throughout the world and issuing a useful duet series for Music Minus One. In 1975 he joined Warne Marsh, his fellow sideman in earlier sessions with Tristano, to record an important series of albums, and the following year he founded his own nonet modeled on that of Davis. He continued to perform regularly in clubs and at festivals in the 1980s, and made some notable duet recordings with the pianists Hal Galper, Martial Solal, and Harold Danko.

Konitz is the foremost saxophonist in the cool style of jazz, and one of the few alto saxophonists of his generation to create a viable jazz style outside the dominating influence of Charlie Parker. Unlike Parker, he cultivated a smooth sound with few overtones and no vibrato, much like the French classical approach to the instrument. He also rejected Parker's characteristic rhythmic procedures, preferring to play evenly and smoothly over the full range of the instrument without the sudden cross-accents, counterrhythms, and formulae of bop. This enabled him to create long serpentine lines, rich in harmonic implications, with an almost metronomical precision but with varied subdivisions of the beat and a discreet, urgent sense of swing (ex.1). Konitz's concept ideally coincided with

Ex.1 Solo from G. Mulligan: *Lover Man* (1953, PJ 609); transcr. J. Mehegan

Tristano's contrapuntal approach to group improvisation, and it is in performances with adherents of the Tristano school, such as Billy Bauer and Sal Mosca, that Konitz is heard to best advantage, particularly in duet with other like-minded improvisers. Later he broadened his style to include blues inflections and elements of bop. His influence is immediately apparent in the work of the West Coast alto saxophonists Art Pepper, Bud Shank, and Paul Desmond, and also played a decisive role in the emergence of European jazz in the 1950s.

Oral history material in *NjR*.

For illustrations *see* JAZZ (i), fig.6, and TRISTANO, LENNIE.

SELECTED RECORDINGS

Duos: *The Lee Konitz Duets* (1967, Mlst. 9013); with H. Galper: *Windows* (1976, Ste. 1057); with M. Solal: *Live at the Berlin Jazz Days* (1980, MPS 68289); with H. Danko: *Wild as Springtime* (1984, GFM 8002)

As leader: Tautology/Sound-Lee (1949, NewJ 813); Ezz-thetic/Hi-Beck (1951, Prst. 743); Yesterdays/Duet (1951, Prst. 755); with G. Mulligan: Lady be good/Lover Man (1953, PJ 609); *Inside Hi-fi* (1956, Atl. 1258); *The Real Lee Konitz* (1957, Atl. 1273); *Motion* (1961, Verve 8399); *Spirits* (1971, Mlst. 9038); *Lone-Lee* (1974, Ste. 1035); with W. Marsh: *Jazz Exchange* (1975, Sto. 1017, 1020); *Yes Yes Nonet* (1979, Ste. 1119); *Seasons Change* (1979, Cir. [G] 19)

As sideman: C. Thornhill: Anthropology (1947, Col. 38224); Yardbird Suite (1947, Col. 39133); L. Tristano: Subconscious-Lee (1949, NewJ 80001); M. Davis: Move/Budo (1949, Cap. 15404); L. Tristano: Crosscurrent (1949, Cap. 60003); Intuition (1949, Cap. 1224)

BIBLIOGRAPHY

A. Morgan: "Lee Konitz," *JM*, v/4 (1959), 4
M. Harrison and M. James: "Lee Konitz: a Dialogue," *JR*, iii/6 (1960), 10
D. Heckman: "Lee Konitz," *JR*, iii/1 (1960), 28
M. James: *Ten Modern Jazzmen: an Appraisal of the Recorded Work of Ten Modern Jazzmen* (London, 1960), 49
I. Gitler: *Jazz Masters of the Forties* (New York, 1966/*R*1983 with discography), 226–61
L. Goddet: "Lee Konitz," *Jh*, no.288 (1972), 28; no.307 (1974), 7
J. Delmas: "Tristano et ses fils," *Jh*, no.325 (1976), 6; no.326 (1976), 6
P. Manelli: "All the Things you Are," *Musica jazz*, xxxv/11 (1979), 46 [incl. transcr.]
N. Tesser: "Lee Konitz: Searches for the Perfect Solo," *DB*, xlvii/1 (1980), 16
W. Balliett: "Ten Levels," *Jelly Roll, Jabbo and Fats* (New York and Oxford, England, 1983) [colln of previously pubd articles], 177
M. Frohne: *Subconscious-Lee: 35 Years of Records and Tapes: the Lee Konitz Discography, 1947–1982* (Freiburg, Germany, 1983)
H. Hellhund: *Cool Jazz: Grundzüge seiner Entstehung und Entwicklung* (Mainz, Germany, 1985)
G. Schuller: "Lee Konitz," *Musings: the Musical Worlds of Gunther Schuller* (New York, and Oxford, England, 1986) [incl. previously pubd articles], 98

J. BRADFORD ROBINSON

Konopasek, Jan (*b* Prague, 29 Dec 1931). Czechoslovak baritone saxophonist and flutist. He studied piano privately as a youth, then played and recorded in Czechoslovakia with Karel Krautgartner (1957–61), the group Studio 5 (1958–61), and Karel Velebný's group SHQ (1962–5). While playing as a member of the studio orchestra of the radio and television station Sender Freies Berlin, he recorded with Hans Koller (*New York City*, 1968, MPS 68235), Klaus Doldinger (1969), and Oliver Nelson (*Impressions of Berlin*, on the album *Berlin Dialogue for Orchestra*, 1970, FD 10134); he also played with Stan Kenton (1969). He received a scholarship to the Berklee College of Music, where he studied from 1971 to 1973; he then toured and recorded with Woody Herman (1973–4), and performed with him at the Montreux Jazz Festival in 1974. He moved to New York in 1975. (M. Juranek: "Two Interviews from Czechoslovakia: Jan Konopasek and Gustav Brom," *JM*, xi/9 (1965), 17)

Kool Jazz Festival. Name by which the NEWPORT JAZZ FESTIVAL was known from 1981 to 1985. In 1980 it was called the Kool Newport Jazz Festival.

Korner, Alexis (*b* Paris, 19 April 1928; *d* London, 1 Jan 1984). English electric guitarist, pianist, singer, and bandleader. He studied piano from the age of five. Between 1948 and 1950 he led his own band, and in 1949 his blues quartet played for Chris Barber during intermissions. He was a member of Barber's Skiffle Group (1952–4) and also recorded with Ken Colyer (1954–5). While working as a journalist and radio announcer, Korner began an association with the harmonica player Cyril Davies, with whom he led the band Blues Incorporated (1962–8). After working as a soloist (1968) he led the groups New Church (1969–70) and CCS (1970–73) with the singer Peter Thorup, then worked regularly with the bass player Colin Hodgkinson (1973–80). Korner's bands helped to launch the careers of many significant jazz musicians in Britain, including Dick Heckstall-Smith and Art Themen. The strong influence of jazz on his work is evident on his recording *Red Hot from Alex* (1964, Transatlantic 117). His popularity as a broadcaster led to his adoption of the title "Grandfather of British Rhythm and Blues." (S. Loupien: "Alexis Korner: bluesman par adoption," *Jm*, no.284 (1980), 40)

DIGBY FAIRWEATHER

Kőrössy, János [Ianci, Janci, Jancsy, Yanci] (*b* Cluj [now Cluj-Napoca], Romania, 20 March 1926). Romanian pianist. He worked in various Romanian bands, including the studio orchestra of Electrecord. He performed at jazz festivals in Prague (?1960), Warsaw (1961), and Budapest (1962), and made several recordings as a leader with musicians from Czechoslovakia (1961–2, 1965), Sweden and Poland (1961), Hungary (1964), and Romania (1965–6). He also recorded in Warsaw with Bernt Rosengren (1961) and in Germany with J. A. Rettenbacher and Charly Antolini (1969). Kőrössy's style was influenced by Erroll Garner, Oscar Peterson, and Dave Brubeck. His playing may be heard on the solo *Ain't Misbehavin'* from the album *Kőrössy Jànos ès együttes* (1964, Qual. LPX7301).

GÉZA GÁBOR SIMON, RAINER E. LOTZ

Kotick, Teddy [Theodore John] (*b* Haverhill, MA, 4 June 1928; *d* Boston, 17 April 1986). Double bass player. He studied guitar from the age of six, but took up double bass in high school. After working in New England he moved in 1948 to New York, where he played with Johnny Bothwell, Buddy Rich, Tony Pastor, Buddy DeFranco (1949, 1952), Artie Shaw (1950), Stan Getz (1951–3), and Charlie Parker (1951–4). He later played with Bill Evans (ii) (1956), George Wallington (1956–7), and Horace Silver (1957–8), and recorded with René Thomas (1960), Martial Solal (1963), and Teddy Charles (1963). Thereafter Kotick was inactive for many years, but he resumed performing and recording in the late 1970s with J. R. Monterose. Named by Parker as one of his favorite double bass players, Kotick was highly valued by his contemporaries for his impeccable sense of timing, secure choice of notes, and vibrant tone; his supportive bass lines enhanced many bop albums of the 1950s. Although for much of his career he was reluctant to take solos, Wallington, Evans, and Silver prevailed upon him to do so.

SELECTED RECORDINGS

As sideman: S. Getz: *Jazz at Storyville* (1951, Roost 407, 411); C. Parker: *Charlie Parker Plays Cole Porter* (1954, Verve 8007); P. Woods: *Early Quintets* (1954, 1959, Prst. 7673); G. Wallington: *Knight Music* (1956, Atl. 1275); B. Evans: *New Jazz Conceptions* (1956, Riv. 223); G. Wallington: *The New York Scene* (1957, Prst. 16-5); H. Silver: *Further Explorations* (1958, BN 1589); J. R. Monterose: *Live in Albany* (1979, Upt. 2702)

BIBLIOGRAPHY

FeatherE

MARK GARDNER

Kovács, Andor (*b* Budapest, 4 June 1929). Hungarian guitarist. He learned guitar at the age of 15 and at 16 was working in various jazz and dance orchestras, among them those led by Filu, the trumpeter György Kelényi, and the alto saxophonist György Víg. He was a member of Lajos Martiny's quintet (1950–62), which performed at concerts and jazz festivals in the USSR (1956) and Germany (1960–61). He made recordings as a leader (1966–9) and performed with his own quartet in Poland (1966).

In 1983 he became the leader, with the violinist Csaba Deseő, of the group Hot Club Budapest, with which he has performed in Hungary and elsewhere in Europe. He may be heard as a soloist on Deseő's *Blue String* (1983, Krém SLPX17823). Kovács is well known as a teacher; his students have included Gábor Szabó.

GÉZA GÁBOR SIMON, RAINER E. LOTZ

Kovács, Gyula (*b* Budapest, 27 Dec 1929). Hungarian drummer. He studied at the National Conservatory in Budapest. After performing with Filu (1949–50), he was a member of Lajos Martiny's quintet from 1950 to 1962, then played for a year (1962–3) with Mihály Tabányi. He recorded in a duo with Andor Kovács in 1958 (*Gitár–dob párbaj* (Guitar–drum duel), Qual. T7364), as a soloist in 1959 (*Dobfantázia* (Drum fantasy), Qual. T7405), and with Martiny in 1960. He also made recordings with Aladár Pege (*c*1964, 1967–8), in a trio (1964), with the violinist Csaba Deseő (1967–8), and in a quintet led by the pianist János Gonda and the vibraphonist Richard Kruza (1969, 1976). He began teaching jazz at the Béla Bartók Musical Training College (formerly the National Conservatory) in 1965.

GÉZA GÁBOR SIMON, RAINER E. LOTZ

Kowald, Peter (*b* Masserberg, nr Meiningen, Germany, 21 April 1944). German double bass player. He became interested in jazz at the age of 12 after hearing Louis Armstrong; later he studied the music of Ornette Coleman and from 1960 played in local bands. He belonged to Peter Brötzmann's trio (1965–9), toured with Carla Bley's and Mike Mantler's quintet (1966), and was a member of the Globe Unity Orchestra (1966–78), for which he also wrote compositions. From 1968 to 1969 he played in Pierre Favre's trio and quartet in Switzerland; he also performed and recorded with Manfred Schoof (1969) and Robin Kenyatta (1969). On his return to Germany he led groups from 1970 to 1974 of which Günter Christmann, Evan Parker, and Paul Lovens were members, performed and recorded with Karl Berger (1971), and worked with Alex Schlippenbach's quartet (1973–8). At the same time he helped to form several organizations: FMP (1969), which sponsors performances and issues recordings of free jazz, the Wuppertal Free Jazz Workshop, and 360° Spielraum für Ideen, an art gallery and performance space in Wuppertal. He performed and recorded with Michel Pilz (1975) and Derek Bailey (1976), worked as an unaccompanied soloist from the late 1970s, and from 1979 led a trio with Leo Smith and Günter Sommer. With the double bass player William Parker and others he formed Sound Unity, a musicians' cooperative that sponsored a festival in New York. Later he belonged to a quartet led by the pianist Marilyn Crispell (1982–4), made the longest of several tours of the USA in 1984, and played in a trio with Brötzmann and Andrew Cyrille (1984–5).

SELECTED RECORDINGS

(all recorded for FMP)

Duos with B. Phillips: *Die Jungen: Random Generators* (1979, 0680)
As leader: *Peter Kowald Quintet* (1972, 0070)
As sideman: P. Brötzmann: *For Adolph Sax* (1967, 0080); Globe Unity Orchestra: *Globe Unity 73 Live in Wuppertal* (1973, FMP 0160); M. Pilz: *Carpathes* (1975, 0250); L. Smith: *Touch the Earth* (1979, 0730)

BIBLIOGRAPHY

A. Dutilh: "Hans Reichel, Peter Kowald: pas de conversation," *Jh*, no.368 (1979–80), 51
B. Noglik: "Peter Kowald," *Jazzwerkstatt international* (Berlin, 1981), 427 [incl. interview, discography]
M. Chenard: "Peter Kowald: a Global Musician," *Coda*, no.206 (1986), 22

ROBERT J. IANNAPOLLO

Kozlov, Aleksey (Semyonovich) (*b* Moscow, 13 Oct 1935). Russian alto and soprano saxophonist and composer. He is largely self-taught as a musician. From 1959 to 1960 he led a hard-bop quintet and from 1960 to 1966 played baritone saxophone in a group led by the pianist Vadim Sakun, with which he performed at the International Jazz Jamboree Festival in Warsaw (1962). He led groups in Moscow (1961–5, 1969–70) and was a soloist with VIO-66 (the Vocal-instrumental Orchestra, directed by the bandleader Yuri Saulsky), for which he also wrote arrangements. In 1973 he formed the jazz-rock group Arsenal, which toured the USSR, recorded several albums consisting principally of compositions by Kozlov, performed at festivals in Warsaw, Nagykanizsa (Hungary), Bratislava (Czechoslovakia), and Berlin, and in 1984 took part in a television broadcast originating simultaneously in Moscow and California. He also taught at the Moskovskaya exsperimental'naya studiya dzhazovoy muzïki (Moscow experimental jazz studio; 1971–6) and studied music in Moscow (to 1980). Kozlov's playing is exemplified by his recording *Vtoroye dïkhaniye* (Second wind; 1985, Mel. C6023369002). (S. F. Starr: *Red and Hot: the Fate of Jazz in the Soviet Union, 1917–1980* (New York, and Oxford, England, 1983), 313)

WALTER OJAKÄÄR

Krahmer, Carlo (*b* London, 11 March 1914; *d* London, 20 April 1976). English drummer. Born blind, he was self-taught and began playing while he was a teenager; he became professional when in 1937 he joined Claude Bampton's band of all-blind musicians as the percussionist for a variety tour. In 1939 he recorded in a duo and in a trio with George Shearing, and the following year he played for several short engagements at London nightclubs. He then became a member of the Claepigeons, led by trumpeter Johnny Claes, with which he recorded for Columbia (1941–2). Between 1943 and 1945 Krahmer led various ensembles at nightclubs, using such sidemen as Bertie King and Gerry Moore; he also recorded with his Nuthouse Club Band for Parlophone (1945). After a year in which he concentrated on teaching he formed Esquire Records (1947); the first issues on this label were recordings of concerts at Birmingham Town Hall featuring Krahmer and Humphrey Lyttelton. Krahmer's playing may be heard to advantage on *At Sundown* (1947, Esquire 12001), recorded with his band the Chicagoans. (For bibliography *see* ESQUIRE.)

NEVIL SKRIMSHIRE

Kral, Irene (*b* Chicago, 18 Jan 1932; *d* Encino, CA, 15 Aug 1978). Singer, sister of Roy Kral. She sang professionally from the age of 16 and, after short spells with the bands of Woody Herman and Chubby Jackson, joined a vocal group, the Tattle Tales. She then performed as a soloist with Maynard Ferguson (1957–8), recording in 1957. In the early 1960s she worked with Stan Kenton, Herb Pomeroy, and Shelly Manne, then moved to Los Angeles, where she appeared as a freelance into the 1970s. A superior ballad singer of impeccable taste, Kral was influenced by Carmen McRae; Dahl (1984) compared her slightly nasal tone with that of McRae, and wrote that she had "a lovely, resonant voice with a discreet vibrato, flawless diction and intonation . . . . She was a master of quiet understatement."

SELECTED RECORDINGS

As leader: *Steveireneo* (1959, UA 6052); *Better than Anything* (1963, DRG 505); *Wonderful Life* (1965, Mstr. 6058)
As sideman: on M. Ferguson: *Boy with Lots of Brass* (1957, EmA 36114), My Funny Valentine, The Song is You; H. Pomeroy: *Detour Ahead* (1958, UA 4016); L. Almeida: *Guitar from Ipanema* (1964, Cap. T2197)

BIBLIOGRAPHY

FeatherE

L. Dahl: *Stormy Weather: the Music and Lives of a Century of Jazzwomen* (London, Melbourne, Australia, and New York, 1984), 151

REG COOPER

Kral, Roy (Joseph) (*b* Chicago, 10 Oct 1921). Singer, pianist, and arranger, brother of Irene Kral. While working with a quartet in Chicago he met the singer Jackie (Jacqueline Ruth) Cain (*b* Milwaukee, 22 May 1928), with whom he formed a duo, Jackie and Roy. They joined Charlie Ventura in 1948; Kral, who was also Ventura's pianist, contributed many excellent arrangements to the band, including *Flamingo* and *Pennies from Heaven*. After leaving Ventura they married in June 1949, formed a bop sextet, then in 1950 moved to Chicago, where they appeared in their own television show. They returned to Ventura for eight months in 1953 but then worked as a duo in New York, Las Vegas (1957–60), and Los Angeles, and settled in New York in 1963. Kral wrote many television commercials in which they appeared during the 1960s. The duo has continued to perform internationally and to record into the 1980s.

Jackie and Roy were well known in the 1940s and 1950s for their unusual duets and noted particularly for their witty lyrics and skilled vocalese; their style and presentation made their performances acceptable to a wide audience. Jackie was also a strong ballad singer.

SELECTED RECORDINGS

As leader with J. Cain: *Jackie Cain and Roy Kral* (1954, Bruns. 54026); *Jackie and Roy* (1955, Sto. 322); *Sing Baby, Sing* (1955, Sto. 915); *Free and Easy* (1957, ABC-Para. 207); *Jackie & Roy in the Spotlight* (1958, ABC-Para. 267); *Double Take* (1961, Col. CS8501); *Like Sing* (1962, Col. CS8734); *Changes* (1966, Verve 68668); *Lovesick* (1966, Verve 68688); *The Electric Grass* (1968, Cap. ST2936); *Time and Love* (1972, CTI 6019); *A Wilder Alias* (1973, CTI 6040); *East of Suez* (1980, Conc. 149); *High Standards* (1982, Conc. 186)

As sideman with C. Ventura: Deed I Do (1948, National 9077); Pennies from Heaven (1949, Decca 11070); Fine and Dandy (1949, Decca 11073); *Charlie Ventura & his Band in Concert* (1949, Gene Norman 1), incl. Flamingo

BIBLIOGRAPHY

FeatherE; *Feather '60s*; *Feather–Gitler '70s*

H. Frost: "Duo," *DB*, xxx/31 (1963), 22

W. H. Brown: "A Discography of Jacqueline Ruth Cain and Roy Joseph Kral, 1948–73," *JJ* xxix/6 (1976), 20

J. DeMuth: "The Fine Art of Jazz Accompaniment: Insights and Perspectives from Roy Kral of Jackie & Roy," *Keyboard*, xi/11 (1985), 38 [incl. discography]

REG COOPER

Kramer, Gorni. Name that has often been given, incorrectly, as that of KRAMER GORNI.

Krautgartner, Karel (*b* Mikulov, Jihomoravský, Czechoslovakia, 20 July 1922; *d* Cologne, Germany, 20 Sept 1982). Czechoslovak clarinetist, alto saxophonist, arranger, bandleader, and composer. He belonged to the Slavia band in Brno and to Gustav Brom's orchestra (1942–3), led a dixieland band, and performed and recorded on clarinet and alto saxophone with Karel Vlach's orchestra (1944–55), for which he also wrote arrangements. He formed a group in 1956 that took part in festivals in Vienna and Belgrade. For several years he worked in radio: with the group Studio 5 in Prague and from 1960 as the leader of a radio big band that played in Bled, Yugoslavia (1962), Munich (1964), and Cologne (with Kurt Edelhagen's orchestra, 1968). As a result of the political unrest that beset Czechoslovakia in 1968 he left the country; he then led the big band of the Österreichischer Rundfunk in Vienna, and worked as a freelance in Cologne. Krautgartner played an important role in effecting a transition from swing to modern jazz in Czechoslovakia. His playing is well represented by his album *Jazz kolem Karla Krautgartner* (1965, Sup. 9012); among his best-known compositions are *The Lucky Thirteen* and *Eukalyptus*. (*ReclamsJ*)

GERHARD CONRAD

Krazy Kat. Record label. It is owned by Interstate Music; although devoted mainly to blues and rhythm-and-blues, it has also been used to issue important jazz records, among them items from the labels Joe Davis and Gotham.

Kress, Carl (*b* Newark, NJ, 20 Oct 1907; *d* Reno, NV, 10 June 1965). Acoustic guitarist. He first played banjo, then changed to guitar and worked initially with various groups in New York. He played with Paul Whiteman in 1926, then from the late 1920s became much sought after as a session musician, recording with Red Nichols (1927–31), Miff Mole (1928, 1930), and the Dorsey brothers (1928, 1930). In the early 1930s he recorded duets with Eddie Lang and with Dick McDonough. He was one of the owners of the Onyx Club on 52nd Street. During the 1940s and 1950s he continued to work as a session musician, and in the early 1960s he formed a duo with George Barnes. A pioneer rhythm guitarist in the 1920s, Kress matured into an important exponent of swing, using a specially lowered tuning (*B♭'–F–c–g–a–d'*) adapted to his unique chordal style. Numerous soloists were inspired by the rich harmonic support and joyous, buoyant drive that were characteristic of his playing.

SELECTED RECORDINGS

Duos: with E. Lang: Pickin' my Way/Feelin' my Way (1932, Bruns. 6254); with D. McDonough: Danzon/Stage Fright (1934, Bruns. 6917); with G. Barnes: *Town Hall Concert* (1963, UA 6335)

As sideman: R. Nichols: Nobody's Sweetheart/Avalon (1928, Bruns. 3854); Edmond Hall: Blue Interval/Seein' Red (1944, BN 31)

BIBLIOGRAPHY

FeatherE; *Feather '60s*

NORMAN MONGAN

Kriegel, Volker (*b* Darmstadt, Germany, 24 Dec 1943). German electric guitarist. He played from 1962 with Emil Mangelsdorff, Ted Curson, Freddie Hubbard, and Tony Scott and was an original member of the Dave Pike Set (1968–73), a quartet with which he toured internationally. After recording the album *Spectrum* (1971) he formed a group of the same name with Eberhard Weber in 1973, which the following year recorded the album *Mild Maniac* before disbanding; from 1976 he led a jazz-rock group, the Mild Maniac Orchestra. Kriegel is a member of the United Jazz and Rock Ensemble; in addition to his work in jazz he has written music for radio, television, and films.

SELECTED RECORDINGS

As leader: *Inside: Missing Link* (1972, MPS 3321431); *Houseboat* (1978, MPS 15535); of Mild Maniac Orchestra: *Live in Bayern* (1980, MPS 15569); *Schöne Aussichten* (1983, Mood 28636)

As sideman: D. Pike: *Noisy Silence, Gentle Noise* (1969, MPS 15215); United Jazz and Rock Ensemble: *Live im Schützenhaus* (1977, Mood 22666)

BIBLIOGRAPHY

A. J. Smith: "Profile: Volker Kriegel," *DB*, xliv/3 (1977), 32

"Volker Kriegel: the Mild Maniac," *JJI*, xxxi/5 (1978), MPS, p.xiv

L. Jaenichen: "Volker Kriegels Mild Maniac Orchestra," *JP*, xxxiv/1 (1985), 23

I. Carr: "Kriegel, Volker," in I. Carr, D. Fairweather, and B. Priestley: *Jazz: the Essential Companion* (London, 1987)

HEIDI BOULTON

Krog, Karin (*b* Oslo, 15 May 1937). Norwegian singer. She studied singing with Anne Brown (1962–9) and Ivo Knecevic (1969–72) and first came to prominence at the Antibes–Juan-les-Pins Festival in 1964; the same year she made her first recording. She appeared at festivals in Scandinavia, Britain, Eastern Europe, the Netherlands, Switzerland, Germany, and France and in 1967 visited the USA, where she performed and recorded in Los Angeles with Don Ellis's big band and Clare Fischer's trio. In 1969 she recorded in Berlin with the European All Stars (the other members of which were Albert Mangelsdorff, John Surman, Francy Boland, Niels-Henning Ørsted Pedersen, and Daniel Humair) and the same year won *Down Beat*'s poll in the "new star" category; the following year she returned to the USA on a study tour, giving concerts in Massachusetts and New York, and performed with the European All Stars at the world's fair in Osaka, Japan, and around Tokyo. She also played in Hamburg (1970, 1972) and London (1971), taught and performed at the Illini Jazz Festival (1972), and performed again in Japan (1975); later she appeared at the Jazzyatra Festival in Bombay (1978) and toured Australia (1985) and Japan (1988). In addition to her work in jazz Krog has taken part in several programs of classical and avant-garde music, some in collaboration with the composer and pianist Richard Rodney Bennett. She received the Buddy Award from the Norwegian Jazz Federation in 1965.

Oral history material in *SSsv*.

SELECTED RECORDINGS

Duos with B. Hallberg: *A Song for you* (1977, Phon. 7512)

As leader: *By Myself* (1964, Phi. 631062); *Jazz Moments* (1966, Sonet 1404); *Joy* (1968, Sonet 1405); *Some Other Spring* (1970, Sonet 1407); *Different Days, Different Ways* (1970–74, Phi. FDX202); *You must Believe in Spring* (1974, Pol. 2382044); with A. Shepp: *Hi-Fly* (1976, Compendium 2); *Cloud Line Blue* (*c*1978, Pol. 2382093); *With Malice toward None* (1980, Bluebell 115); *I Remember you* (1981, Spot. 22)

BIBLIOGRAPHY

Feather '60s; *Feather–Gitler '70s*

R. Hultin: "Karin Krog," *JF* [intl edn], no.11 (1971), 50

J. Berg and M. Gardner: Discography, *J&B*, ii/8 (1972), 22

M. Gardner: "Karin Krog: Ballads to the Avant-garde," *J&B*, ii (1972), no.8, p.18; no.9, p.20

"Karen [*sic*] Krog," *JF* [intl edn], no.25 (1973), 69

RANDI HULTIN

Kronberg, Günter (*b* Gelsenkirchen, Germany, 26 Sept 1926; *d c*1977). German alto and baritone saxophonist. He first studied piano and clarinet, and played in a local orchestra. He joined a small European jazz group which played in North Africa, and led a hard-bop ensemble at the Frankfurt Jazz Festival (1960). Throughout the 1960s Kronberg performed and recorded with Albert Mangelsdorff, touring Asia, Africa, and the USA; he also recorded with Klaus Weiss (1971) and Joki Freund and the Frankfurt Jazz Ensemble on the album *Frankfurt All Stars* (1975, Tel. 628341). (*ReclamsJ*)

Kroner, Erling (*b* Copenhagen, 16 April 1943). Danish trombonist, bandleader, and composer. He played in dixieland, rock, and free-jazz groups in the early 1960s and attended the Berklee College of Music (1970). From 1967 he worked principally as the leader of a quintet and of a ten-piece group, and led these ensembles on recordings of his own compositions, including *The Forgotten Art* (1977, Sto. 1021), on which both groups perform pieces inspired by Charles Mingus, and *Entre dos cielos* (1982, Music Mecca 109), on which the larger group alone plays in a style influenced by the work of Mingus and by Argentinian tangos. He also belonged to the Radioens Big Band from the late 1970s to the mid-1980s and to Ernie Wilkins's Almost Big Band from 1980.

ERIK WIEDEMANN

Krueger, Benny [Benjamin] (*b* Newark, NJ, 17 July 1899; *d* Orange, NJ, 29 July 1967). Alto and tenor saxophonist, and clarinetist. He is best remembered for his recordings with the Original Dixieland Jazz Band (1920–21); his alto saxophone solo on *Crazy Blues* (1921, Vic. 18729) is a good example of his playing. From the mid-1920s he worked for radio stations as a bandleader and engaged musicians for broadcasts; during the 1930s he was the music director for the singer Rudy Vallee. He recorded with Bing Crosby in 1931 and 1932.

based on *ChiltonW*

Krupa, Gene (*b* Chicago, 15 Jan 1909; *d* Yonkers, NY, 16 Oct 1973). Drummer and bandleader. He first attracted attention on recordings made by McKenzie and Condon's Chicagoans (1927). After playing in numerous commercial orchestras and studio and pit bands in New York he joined Benny Goodman in late 1934, but left in 1938 to form his own big band. Among his sidemen were Sam Donahue, Vido Musso, Corky Cornelius, Shorty Sherock, Roy Eldridge, Leo Watson, and Anita O'Day (for illustration *see* O'DAY, ANITA); with a repertory that included arrangements by Jimmy Mundy and Fred Norman, the band enjoyed great popularity and critical success during the early 1940s. Krupa was forced out of the music business in 1943 when he was accused of contributing to the deliquency of a minor, though he won his case when it came to appeal. He rejoined Goodman briefly later that year, then toured with Tommy Dorsey. In late 1944 he organized another orchestra, this time with Charlie Ventura, Red Rodney, and Don Fagerquist; by the late 1940s the group had developed a superb ensemble sound and had become established as one of the finest big bands. Krupa disbanded his orchestra in 1951 and began touring regularly with Jazz at the Philharmonic, and in 1954, with Cozy Cole, he founded a school of percussion in New York. He spent the last 20 years of his life teaching, studying timpani, classical techniques, and various ethnic drumming concepts, and occasionally leading his own small groups.

Building on the formative influences of Baby Dodds, Zutty Singleton, and, later, the virtuoso drumming of Chick Webb, Krupa soon became the first major jazz soloist on his instrument; thanks to an extraordinary aptitude for showmanship, he was also celebrated as a national idol of the swing era. Although he developed into a superb craftsman, his playing was often marred by a lack of swing, a heavy-handed approach (especially during his years with Goodman), and a tendency towards exhibitionism and vulgar technical display. Nonetheless, paradoxically, his commitment to jazz was genuine and unswerving, as was reflected brilliantly in his own bands. It is ironic that he is remembered more for his bombastic solo on Goodman's *Sing, sing, sing* than for the many tasteful recordings he made with his own groups in later years. Krupa was not only the first major popular drum soloist, but also the ultimate enthusiast; his contribution to jazz drumming remains unique.

SELECTED RECORDINGS

As leader: Blues of Israel (1935, Parl. 2224); Apurksody (1938, Bruns. 8296); Don't be surprised (1939, Bruns. 8412); Drummin' Man (1939, Col. 35324); Blue Rhythm Fantasy (1939, OK 5627); Manhattan Transfer (1940, Col. 35444); Drum Boogie (1941, OK 6046); Let me off uptown (1941, OK 6210); The walls keep talking (1941, OK 6438); Leave us leap (1945, Col. 36802); Tea for Two (1945, Col. 38345); Disc Jockey Jump/Gene's Boogie (1947, Col. 37589); Up an' Atom (1947, Col. 38382); Lemon Drop (1949, Col. 38415); Bop Boogie (1949, Col. B1999); Drum Boogie (1952, Clef 8984); *Gene Krupa Plays Gerry Mulligan Arrangements* (1958, Verve 8292), incl. Mulligan Stew

As sideman: R. Nichols: Indiana (1929, Bruns. 4373); Mound City Blue Blowers: Hello, Lola/One Hour (1929, Vic. 38100); Charleston Chasers: Basin

Street Blues/Beale Street Blues (1931, Col. 2415D); B. Goodman: King Porter (1935, Vic. 25090); After you've gone (1935, Vic. 25115); Who? (1935, Vic. 25181); Swingtime in the Rockies (1936, Vic. 25355); Smoke Dreams (1936, Vic. 25486); Sing, sing, sing (1937, Vic. 36205)

BIBLIOGRAPHY

"Band Business is on Way up Again, Says Krupa," *DB*, xvii/17 (1950), 3
W. Balliett: *Such Sweet Thunder* (Indianapolis, 1966) [colln of previously pubd articles and reviews]
J. Burns: "Lesser Known Bands of the Forties: Gene Krupa & Georgie Auld," *JM*, no.160 (1968), 8
R. Blesh: "Drummin' Man," *Combo, USA: Eight Lives in Jazz* (Philadelphia and London, 1971), 134
G. Hall and S. Kramer: *Gene Krupa and his Orchestra* (Laurel, MD, 1975) [discography]
T. D. Brown: *A History and Analysis of Jazz Drumming to 1942* (diss., U. of Michigan, 1976), 208–99
K. Larcombe: "Gene Krupa: 1909–1973," *MD*, iii/5 (1979), 12 [incl. discography]
K. Stratemann: *Buddy Rich and Gene Krupa: a Filmo-discography* (Lübbecke, Germany, 1980)
C. Garrod and B. Korst: *Gene Krupa and his Orchestra*, i: *1935–1946*, ii: *1947–1973* (Zephyrhills, FL, 1984) [discography]
E. Ronowski: *Gene Krupa: seine Musik auf Schallplatten, 1927–1973: Biographie und Diskographie* (Dassel, Germany, 1985)
S. Woolley: "That Drummin' Man," *JJI*, xxxviii/8 (1985), 12
M. L. Hester: "The Exciting Gene Krupa," *MR*, xiii/10 (1986), 1
B. Crowther: *Gene Krupa* (Tunbridge Wells, England, and New York, 1987) [incl. discography]

GUNTHER SCHULLER

Kühn, Joachim (Kurt) (*b* Leipzig, Germany, 15 March 1944). German pianist and composer, brother of Rolf Kühn. He studied piano and composition with Arthur Schmidt Elsey (1949–61) and performed as a classical pianist (until 1961). He then became the pianist of the S & H Quintet in Prague; he also led a trio (1962–6) and in 1964 began to perform with his brother, an association that continued into the 1980s. He played with his own group around Paris (1969–71), and with Eje Thelin (1970–71), Jean-Luc Ponty (1971–2), and the Dutch group Association PC. In the 1970s he appeared at the Newport Jazz Festival and worked in New York, often in more commercially oriented forms of jazz. Kühn is an intense, virtuoso performer, particularly skilled at exploiting the powerful sonorities to be obtained from playing the interior of the piano. In the early 1960s he was among the most adventurous of the jazz musicians who sought to apply the harmonic devices and structural principles of composed music to improvisation; for example, his use of abruptly changing pulse rates that are mathematically related to one another recalls the metric modulation of the composer Elliott Carter. His approach to such techniques resembles that of Don Ellis. Kühn is also a proficient alto saxophonist.

SELECTED RECORDINGS

As unaccompanied soloist: *Piano* (1971, MPS 2121330-7); *Solos* (1971, Futura 18)
As leader: *Joachim Kühn Trio* (1965, Muza 0285); *Sound of Feelings* (1969, BYG 529317); *Paris is Wonderful* (1969–70, BYG 529346); *Sunshower* (1978, Atl. 19193)
As sideman: R. Kühn: *Transfiguration* (1967, Saba 15118); *The Mad Rockers* (1968, Goody 3005); D. Cherry: *Eternal Rhythm* (1968, MPS 15204); J.-L. Ponty: *Open Strings* (1971, MPS 2121288-2)

BIBLIOGRAPHY

A. Tercinet: "Joachim Kühn," *Jh*, no.273 (1971), 3 [incl. discography]
A. Dutilh and A. Tercinet: "Joachim Kühn Interview," *Jh*, no.306 (1974), 20
L. Lyons: "Joachim Kühn: German Jazz Pianist Explores Rock in America," *Contemporary Keyboard*, iv/7 (1978), 20
K. Kevorkian: "Joachim Kühn: Piano Power Pummels Paris," *Keyboard*, xiii/3 (1987), 34

ROGER T. DEAN

Kühn, Rolf (*b* Cologne, Germany, 29 Sept 1929). German clarinetist and bandleader, brother of Joachim Kühn. He studied piano in Leipzig from 1938, took up the clarinet in 1941, and performed and recorded as a member of several German dance orchestras, including that of Kurt Henkels (1948) and the RIAS-Tanzorchester under Werner Müller (1950). After 1952 he joined a radio big band and worked as a leader; he became well-known in Europe through his radio broadcasts. In 1956 he moved to the USA, where with the encouragement of John Hammond, the booking agent Willard Alexander, and Friedrich Gulda he formed his own group. From 1957 to 1958 he took the place of Benny Goodman, who was unable to play owing to illness, in Goodman's band; he also played in Tommy Dorsey's band under the leadership of Warren Covington (1958) and performed and recorded in a big band led by Urbie Green (1958–60). At the same time he worked in small groups: in 1957 he performed and recorded with Dick Johnson at the Newport Jazz Festival and recorded with Winners Circle (a bop all-star group assembled by Bethlehem Records that included Art Farmer and Oscar Pettiford), and the following year he recorded with Toshiko Akiyoshi. After returning in 1962 to Germany he led the dance and jazz orchestra of the Norddeutscher Rundfunk, Hamburg, recorded with Gulda's Eurojazz Orchestra (1965), and from the 1960s into the 1980s toured and recorded as a member of small groups that at times included his brother Joachim. Kühn's playing has gone through several phases: he worked first in a style influenced by Goodman and Buddy DeFranco, then played successively bop and cool jazz, free jazz (he was perhaps the first clarinetist to explore this style), and jazz-rock. In addition to his work in jazz he has written popular music.

SELECTED RECORDINGS

As leader: *Streamline* (1956, Van. 8510); with J. Kühn: *Impressions of New York* (1967, Imp. A9158); *The Day After* (1972, MPS 21604); with J. Kühn: *Cinemascope* (1974, MPS 2122270-5); *Total Space* (1975, MPS 68065); *Symphonic Swampfire* (1978, MPS 68216); *Don't Split* (1982, L+R 40016)

BIBLIOGRAPHY

FeatherE; *Feather '60s*
H. H. Lange: "Rolf Kuehn: an Introduction and Discography," *JM*, iv/4 (1958), 24
E. T. Vogel: "'Mein Stil ist modern,' sagt Rolf Kühn," *JP*, vii (1958), 261
D. Zimmerle: "Nicht Probleme, Leistungen!," *JP*, xviii (1969), 294 [interview]
"Rolf & Joachim Kühn," *JP*, xvi (1967), 9 [interview]

JOACHIM E. BERENDT/WOLFRAM KNAUER

Kuhn, Steve [Stephen Lewis] (*b* New York, 24 March 1938). Pianist and composer. He played piano from the age of five, studied with Margaret Chaloff (the mother of Serge Chaloff) from 1950, and first played professionally when he was 13. After graduating from Harvard University (1959) he played and recorded with Kenny Dorham (1959–60). He played for two months in John Coltrane's first quartet, but his brief association with Scott La Faro in Stan Getz's quartet in 1961 exerted the greater influence on his playing. After La Faro's death Kuhn remained with the quartet until 1963; while he was a member Getz fashioned a fusion of jazz and bossa nova that achieved great popularity. He performed and recorded with Art Farmer (1964–6), moved to Stockholm, and played and recorded throughout Europe. After returning to the USA in 1971 he performed on the East and West coasts and recorded for ECM as a soloist, as a leader of small groups, and as a leader with Sheila Jordan. In the late 1970s he led a quartet with Jordan, Bob Moses and Harvie Swartz, then became involved with commercial music. In 1986 he returned to playing jazz as the leader of a trio with Swartz (occasionally replaced by Ron Carter) and Al Foster; he recorded with the trio in 1986 and later with Swartz in an album of solos and duos. Kuhn's style ranges from bop to modal jazz and encompasses impressionistic playing and dissonant harmony; he takes a quasi-orchestral approach to the keyboard. His compositions often have fractional time signatures (or no time signature at all) and phrases of unusual length; a good example of his work is *Memory*, which he recorded with his trio on the album *Three Waves* (1966).

SELECTED RECORDINGS

As unaccompanied soloist: *Ecstasy* (1974, ECM 1058)
Duos with H. Swartz: *Mostly Ballads* (*c*1987, New World 351)
As leader: *Three Waves* (1966, Contact 5); *Three Compositions of Gary McFarland* (1966, Imp. 9136); *Watch what Happens* (1968, MPS 15193); *Raindrops: Live in New York* (1972, Muse 5106); *Trance* (1974, ECM 1052); *Motility* (1977, ECM 1094); *Non-fiction* (1978, ECM 1124); *Last Year's Waltz* (1981, ECM 1213); *Life's Magic* (1986, Black-Hawk 522)
As sideman: K. Dorham: *Jazz Contemporary* (1960, Time 52004); S. Getz: *Stan Getz and Bob Brookmeyer* (1961, Verve 68418); P. La Roca: *Pete La Roca* (1965, BN 84205)

BIBLIOGRAPHY

Feather '60s; *Feather–Gitler '70s*
D. Riker: "Steve Kuhn: Now in Season," *Jazz*, iv/11 (New York, 1965), 8
M. Jones: "Kuhn: Let the Listener Make up his Own Mind," *MM* (11 March 1967), 13
L. Lyons: "Steve Kuhn: From Harvard to Coltrane to Sweden and Back," *CK*, v/3 (1979), 14
M. Zipkin: Review of *Non-fiction* (1978), *DB*, xlvi/3 (1979), 25
O. Cordle: Review of *Last Year's Waltz* (1981), *Jazz Times* (July 1982), 13
L. Lyons: "Steve Kuhn," *The Great Jazz Pianists: Speaking of their Lives and Music* (New York, 1983), 229 [incl. interview, discography]
L. Hildebrand: "Jazz Leader: Steve Kuhn Makes Three-way Conversation," *San Francisco Chronicle Datebook* (9 Aug 1987), 22

PAUL RINZLER

Kukko, Sakari (*b* Kajaani, Finland, 8 July 1953). Finnish tenor and soprano saxophonist, flutist, and leader. He played with Jukka Tolonen, the Tapiola Big Band, and other groups in the 1970s. From 1974 he led the small ensemble Piirpauke, which forged a style of ethnic jazz incorporating elements of Finnish and other folk music; it made its first recording, *Piirpauke* (Love 148), in 1975. Kukko performed with the group and as a soloist in the Far East, Africa, and South America, and in the early 1980s in Germany and Spain. (A. Granholm: *Finnish Jazz* (Helsinki, 1974, rev. and enlarged by M. Konttinen 2/1982, rev. and enlarged by J.-P. Vuorela 3/1986), 18)

PEKKA GRONOW

Kulpowicz, Slawomir (*b* Warsaw, 1952). Polish pianist and composer. He was brought up in a musical family and studied in the popular music department of the High School of Music in Katowice. He first played jazz with the big band of the Stodola student club in Warsaw. He won a composition prize given by the Polish magazine *Jazz* (1969) and another for his composition *Utoplashka* at the Jazz on the Odra festival (1973); in 1974 at the same festival he established his reputation as a solo performer by gaining a further award. While studying in Kraków he played works for chamber ensemble by such composers as Stockhausen and Ives. From 1976 he played with Zbigniew Namysłowski, touring Europe and recording five albums. He was a member, with Tomasz Szukalski, Pawel Jarzebski, and Janusz Stefanski, of the cooperative group The Quartet (1978–80) and composed most of its repertory; he is heard to advantage on the group's recording *Loaded* (1979, Leo 010). From 1981 he has led his own group, In/formation, either as a trio, or, with the addition of Tomasz Stańko, as a quartet. His work as a pianist has been influenced by the modal improvisation style of McCoy Tyner; as a composer he acknowledges the influence of John Coltrane and the traditions of classical and contemporary European music.

BIBLIOGRAPHY

K. Czyz: "Slawomir Kulpowicz," *JF* [intl edn], no.58 (1979), 22
K. Brodacki: "Slawomir Kulpowicz: 'The Apprenticeship Has Ended'," *JF* [intl edn], no.73 (1981), 41

WOLFRAM KNAUER

Kurylewicz, Andrzej (*b* Lwów, Poland [now L'vov, Ukrainian SSR], 24 Feb 1932). Polish pianist. He had piano lessons from the age of seven and from 1951 studied piano, music theory, and composition at the High School of Music in Kraków. During this time he played in several dance orchestras and became an important figure in the development of jazz in Poland. In 1955 he formed his own group, the Organ Sextet, which played and recorded both traditional and modern jazz. He performed and recorded with Albert Nicholas (1957), played mellophone in the Jazz Believers (1957–8), and led his own trio (from 1957), with which he toured Europe; he also recorded with his wife, the singer Wanda Warska (1958), played with the Polish All Stars (1958), and accompanied visiting musicians. From 1963 he led the Polish Radio Jazz Big Band, which recorded in 1964. He was one of the founders, in the late 1960s, of the Contemporary Music Foundation, which played aleatory music based on jazz; he led the group from that time into the 1970s. Kurylewicz is an accomplished composer and has written film and theater music and successful pop songs. His talent as a jazz musician is well represented by the album *10 + 8* (1967, Muza 0439), recorded with his own quintet. (J. Byrczek: "Eurojazz Personalities: Poland," *JF* [intl edn] no.17 (1972), 85)

WOLFRAM KNAUER

Kuryokhin, Sergey (Anatol'yevich) (*b* Murmansk, Russian SFSR, 16 June 1954). Russian pianist and composer. He studied choral conducting at a music school affiliated with the Leningrad N. A. Rimsky-Korsakov State Conservatory and piano at the Krupskaya State Institute of Culture in Leningrad but is largely self-taught as a musician. In 1977 he played with various groups led by Anatoly Vapirov; later he played free jazz with Vladimir Chekasin and others, performed as an unaccompanied soloist, and led groups ranging in size from a trio to a septet. He has written music for a 40-piece orchestra (comprising 12 jazz soloists, four rock groups, a folk group, and a string section) and a chorus, and worked with several experimental rock groups, including Kino, Alisa, Strannïye Igrï, Popmekhanika (which he led), and Akvarium (in which he played keyboards). His work can be heard to advantage on his album *The Ways of Freedom* (1981, Leo 107). Kuryokhin is the music director of the Goroshevsky Theatre, which is associated with the Leningrad branch of the Soyuz Pisateley SSSR (Writers' union of the USSR). (A. Khan: "Sergey Kuryokhin Interview," *Cadence*, ix/2 (1983), 10)

WALTER OJAKÄÄR

Kustbandet. Swedish big band. Formed in 1962 by amateur musicians as a New Orleans sextet, it became a 12-piece group in the mid-1960s. In the following decades it made several recordings inspired by the work of Fletcher Henderson, Duke Ellington, and Luis Russell and performed in Sweden, at European festivals, and at the New Orleans Jazz & Heritage Festival (1973). Kustbandet was led until 1977 by the saxophonist Kenneth Arnström.

SELECTED RECORDINGS

(all recorded for Kenneth)

Kustbandet (1972, 2037); *Stardust, Featuring the Great Charlie Holmes* (1974–5, 2039); *Cotton Club Stomp* (1986, 2060)

BIBLIOGRAPHY

B. Scherman: "Kustbandet har hållit stilen i 20 år" [Kustbandet has kept the style for 20 years], *Orkester journalen*, lii/3 (1984), 6

ERIK KJELLBERG

Kuumba. Name used by Albert "Tootie" Heath; *see* Heath family, (3) Albert "Tootie."

Kuznetsov, Aleksey (Alekseyevich) (*b* Chelyabinsk, Russian SFSR, 6 Sept 1941). Russian guitarist. He learned to play guitar from his father, a member of a popular light-music quartet. He studied *dömbra* (a lute) at the Moscow Musical and Pedagogical School (graduated 1962) and belonged to the Estradno-simfonichesky orkestr Vsesoyuznovo radio i tsentral'novo TV (Symphonic variety orchestra of the all-union radio and central TV) from 1962 to 1974. After making his début as a jazz musician at the Moscow Jazz Days (1965) he performed regularly as a leader and soloist at concerts and festivals in the USSR, Warsaw, Bombay, Prague, and Debrecen, Hungary; from 1975 he played in the symphony orchestra of the ministry of cinematography. Kuznetsov has made recordings as a leader (including *Goluboy korall* (The blue coral), 1981, Mel. C60155278) and in a guitar duo with Nikolay Gromin, and has composed music for his own performances.

WALTER OJAKÄÄR

Kyle, Billy [William Osborne] (*b* Philadelphia, 14 July 1914; *d* Youngstown, OH, 23 Feb 1966). Pianist. After playing with local bands he performed with Tiny Bradshaw and the Mills Blue Rhythm Band. From 1938 to 1942 he worked as a pianist and arranger with John Kirby's sextet (for illustration *see* Kirby, John); during this time the group recorded with such musicians as Red Norvo and Midge Williams (1938), Buster Bailey (1938, 1940), and Mildred Bailey (1938–42). After military service (1942–5) Kyle worked intermittently with Sy Oliver (1946–52), whose orchestra often accompanied Louis Armstrong. In 1953 he joined Armstrong's band, with which he remained until his death. Kyle also recorded with many other musicians, among them Lionel Hampton and O'Neill Spencer (1938), Rex Stewart (1940, 1946), Billie Holiday (1946, 1949), Al Hibbler (1950), and Buck Clayton (1954). He credited a saxophone player with whom he had worked in 1934 with the foundation, formation, and development of his right-hand single-note style; he was also strongly influenced by Earl Hines.

SELECTED RECORDINGS

As leader: Sundays are reserved/Havin' a Ball (1937, Var. 574); Finishing up a Date/Between Sets (1939, Decca 2740)

As sideman: O. Spencer: Lorna Doone Shortbread/Baby, won't you please come home? (1938, Decca 1941)

SELECTED ARRANGEMENTS

* – with Kyle as sideman

As leader: Big Boy Blue (1937, Var. 531)

Recorded by others: Mills Blue Rhythm Band: *Callin' your Bluff (1936, Col. 3162); J. Kirby: *From A Flat to C (1938, Decca 2216)

BIBLIOGRAPHY

ChiltonW; *FeatherE*; *Feather '60s*

B. Kyle: "Piano Style: Ace American Swing Pianist Tells you about Himself and his Playing," *Rhythm*, no.142 (1939), 114

A. Guiu: "Billy Kyle," *BHcF*, no.157 (1966), 9

O. J. Astrup: "The Forgotten Ones: Billy Kyle," *JJI*, xxxvii/8 (1984), 10

JOHNNY SIMMEN

Kyner, Sylvester. *See* Red, Sonny.

L

Laakko, Bruno (*b* USA, 19 June 1907). Alto saxophonist and clarinetist of Finnish descent. He played in dance bands in the USA, then in 1938 moved to Finland, where he was engaged by the popular Dallapé dance orchestra; he soon gained a reputation as a fine jazz soloist. He formed his own band in Helsinki in 1939, but returned to the USA the following year. *Jeepers Creepers* and *Alexander's Ragtime Band* (both Col. DY278), recorded by Laakko's band in 1939, are among the best jazz recordings made in Finland in the 1930s. (O. Häme: *Rytmin voittokulku* [The triumph of rhythm] (Helsinki, 1949), 146)

PEKKA GRONOW

LaBarbera. Family of musicians.

(1) Pat [Pascel] **LaBarbera** (*b* Warsaw, NY, 7 April 1944). Tenor saxophonist. He was first taught by his father, Joseph LaBarbera, then attended Potsdam (New York) State Teachers College and the Berklee College of Music (1964–7). While playing with Buddy Rich's band (1967–74) he gained a reputation as a fine soloist; his style is derived principally from that of John Coltrane (as exemplified by the latter's recording of *Giant Steps*), to which he adds his own rhythmic looseness and lyricism. In 1974 LaBarbera settled in Toronto, where he undertook various engagements and worked for television; the following year he joined Elvin Jones, with whom (until 1978, and intermittently thereafter) he performed and recorded extensively. LaBarbera has also made some recordings with his own small groups, notably the album *Pass it on*, for which he composed all the music and on which he demonstrates the range of his abilities, playing flute as well as tenor and soprano saxophones.

SELECTED RECORDINGS

As leader: *Pass it on* (1976, PM 009)
As sideman: B. Rich: *Buddy and Soul* (1969, PJ 20158); *Keep the Customer Satisfied* (1970, Lib. 11006); E. Jones: *The Main Force* (1976, Van. 79372); *Remembrance* (1978, Pausa 7052)

BIBLIOGRAPHY

"Profile: Pat LaBarbera," *DB*, xl/17 (1973), 28
B. Kirchner: "The Odyssey of Pat LaBarbera," *Radio Free Jazz*, xviii (1977), July, 11
G. Quill: "Pat LaBarbera," *Canadian Musician*, iv/2 (1982), 36
K. Alleyne: "A Different View: Pat LaBarbera," *MD*, xi/6 (1987), 68

(2) John LaBarbera (*b* Mount Morris, NY, 10 Nov 1945). Arranger and trumpeter. After studying with his father and at Potsdam (New York) State Teachers College (1962–3) and the Berklee College of Music (1964–5) he played with the Show Las Vegas Revue traveling band. On the recommendation of his brother (1) Pat LaBarbera he joined Buddy Rich in 1968. He began to write arrangements while playing as fourth trumpet and jazz soloist with Buddy DeFranco's Glenn Miller Band (1968–71), then rejoined Rich as an arranger (1971). Among the other bands for which he has provided arrangements are those of Woody Herman, Doc Severinsen, Count Basie, and Bill Watrous. LaBarbera takes an active part in music education as an adjudicator, and also runs workshops.

SELECTED ARRANGEMENTS

Recorded by B. Rich: *Rich in London* (1971, RCA DPS2031); *Stickit!* (1972, RCA LSP4802)
Recorded by B. Watrous: *The Tiger of San Pedro* (1975, Col. PC33701)

BIBLIOGRAPHY

L. Tomkins: "Inside the Miller Band," *CI*, ix/10 (1971), 20
D. Matthews: "I Get Ideas at the Back of the Bus," *CI*, x/6 (1972), 8 [interview]

(3) Joe [Joseph James] **LaBarbera** (*b* Mount Morris, NY, 22 Feb 1948). Drummer. He was taught to play drums by his father and then studied with Alan Dawson at the Berklee College of Music (1966–8). He traveled for a year with the singer Frankie Randall and spent two years in the army, during which time he played occasionally in Buddy Rich's band in New York. He worked with Gap Mangione in Rochester, then joined Woody Herman (1972), but made his name through his recordings and performances with Chuck Mangione (1973–7). He also recorded with his brother (1) Pat LaBarbera. Later LaBarbera worked as a freelance in New York with Jim Hall, Phil Woods, and others, and in 1978 met Bill Evans (ii), with whom he worked until the pianist's death. From 1980 he has toured with Tony Bennett. He is a versatile and lyrical drummer, whose influences include Shelly Manne, Philly Joe Jones, Max Roach, and Elvin Jones.

SELECTED RECORDINGS

As sideman: C. Mangione: *Land of Make Believe* (1973, Mer. 1-684); P. LaBarbera: *Pass it on* (1976, PM 009); B. Evans: *The Paris Concert: Edition One* (1979, Elek. 60164)

BIBLIOGRAPHY

J. LaBarbera: "Big Bands and Small Groups are Closely Related," *CI*, xii/6 (1974), 22
J. Schaffer: "Profile: Joe LaBarbera, Drummer with Chuck Mangione," *DB*, xli/9 (1974), 28
K. Alleyne and J. S. McIntosh: "Joe LaBarbera: Goal Achiever," *MD*, vii/11 (1983), 24

STEVEN STRUNK

Label. *See* RECORD LABEL.

Laboriel, Abe [Abraham] (*b* Mexico City, 17 July 1947). Bass player. He studied composition at the Berklee College of Music in Boston, where he then joined Gary Burton, with whom he recorded in 1973. In the 1970s he played with popular artists and briefly with the Count Basie Orchestra. In 1977 he moved to Los Angeles, where he worked in studios. Laboriel plays double bass and electric bass guitar and has recorded with Al Jarreau (in Europe in 1977), John Klemmer (1977–9), Ella Fitzgerald (1980), Milt Jackson (1980–81), Freddie Hubbard (1981), Tania Maria (1983), Joe Pass (1985), and Lee Ritenour, with whom he recorded eight albums between 1977 and 1985 (including *Sugarloaf Express*, 1977, JVC 2).

BIBLIOGRAPHY

L. Underwood: "Profile: Abraham Laboriel," *DB*, xlvi/9 (1979), 34

R. Carr: "Abraham Laboriel: Session Bassist with Ritenour, Carlton, Benson, Mancini . . .," *GP*, xv/8 (1981), 72 [incl. discography]

Lacy, Steve [Lackritz, Steven Norman] (*b* New York, 23 July 1934). Soprano saxophonist and composer. He was inspired by Sidney Bechet to take up soprano saxophone and to play dixieland jazz with older musicians, including Cecil Scott and Rex Stewart, who in 1952 renamed him "Lacy." Then, in a stylistic leap, from 1955 to 1957 he performed in a quartet led by Cecil Taylor, who was beginning to embrace free jazz. He first performed and recorded with Gil Evans in 1957, and continued to be associated with him into the 1980s. After working with Thelonious Monk (1960, 1963) Lacy was the leader, with Roswell Rudd, of a quartet dedicated to the performance of Monk's music (1961–4). He then played free jazz with Don Cherry, Carla Bley, and others, and toured South America with Enrico Rava, Johnny Dyani, and Louis Moholo. In 1967 he moved to Rome, where he played a hybrid of free jazz, contemporary art music, and electronic music with the group Musica Elettronica Viva and performed with various Italian avant-garde jazz and rock musicians. In 1970 he settled in Paris. During the ensuing years he gradually established a quintet with his wife Irene Aebi (cello), Steven Potts (saxophones), Kent Carter (double bass), and Oliver Johnson (drums) to perform his own avant-garde pieces, which combine elements of formal composition with jazz improvisation, poetry, and dance; Aebi's singing style in particular has been a strong influence on Lacy's writing. Around 1981 the group expanded with the addition of the pianist Bobby Few to become a sextet, and at the same time the double bass player Jean-Jacques Avenel replaced Carter. From 1972 Lacy has also given many solo performances on soprano saxophone, always including some interpretations of Monk's compositions in his repertory. In the 1980s he has worked with Japanese kabuki dancers and Indian musicians and led groups with Misha Mengelberg.

For further illustration *see* JAZZ (i), fig.9.

SELECTED RECORDINGS

As unaccompanied soloist: *Solo* (1972, Emanem 301); *The Kiss* (1986, Lunatic 002)

Duos with M. Waldron: *Snake-out* (1981, HA 2038)

As leader: *Soprano Sax* (1957, Prst. 7125); *The Straight Horn of Steve Lacy* (1960, Can. 8007); *Disposability* (1965, RCA KLVP200); *The Way* (1979, HH 3); *Prospectus* (1983, HA 2001); *Futurities* (1984–5, HA 2022)

As sideman: C. Taylor: *Jazz Advance* (1956, Tran. 19); G. Evans: *Gil Evans & Ten* (1957, Prst. 7120), incl. Just one of those things; T. Monk: *Big Band and Quartet in Concert* (1963, Col. CS8964); C. Bley: *Jazz Realities* (1966, Fon. 881010); Musica Elettronica Viva: *United Patchwork* (1977, Horo 15–16)

RECORDED COMPOSITIONS

(selective list; all recorded as leader)

on *Lapis* (1971, Saravah 10031), The Precipitation Suite; on *Raps* (1977, Adelphi 5004), Stamps; on *Stamps* (1977–8, HH K-L), Wickets; on *The Way* (1979, HH 3), The Tao Suite; on *Troubles* (1979, BS 0035), The Whammies!; on *Capers* (1979, HH 14), Bud's Brother; on *Futurities* (1984–5, HA 2022), Futurities

BIBLIOGRAPHY

I. Gitler: "Steve Lacy," *DB*, xxviii/5 (1961), 15

M. Harrison: "Steve Lacy," *JM*, xii/1 (1966), 7 [incl. discography]

M. Davidson: "The Great Big Beautiful Sounds of Steve Lacy," *Into Jazz*, i/4 (1974), 8

C. France: "Steve Lacy: Interview," *Cadence*, iv/12 (1978), 3

L. Jeske: "Prolific Steve Lacy and his Poly-free Bag," *DB*, xlvii/5 (1980), 20

B. McRae: "Avant Courier," *JJI*, xxxiv/4 (1981), 24

B. Case: "Steve Lacy," *The Wire*, no.1 (1982), 6

T. Johnson: "An American in Paris," *VV*, xxvii (9 March 1982), 74

H. L. Lindenmaier: *25 Years of Fish Horn Recording: the Steve Lacy Discography, 1954–1979* (Freiburg, Germany, 1982) [incl. list of compositions]

C. Preiss: *The Steve Lacy Festival Handbook* (New York, 1982) [incl. discography and interview]

R. Cook: "A Duck is Calling your Name: Some Thoughts on Steve Lacy and the Art of Going Solo on Soprano," *The Wire*, no.19 (1985), 23

K. Whitehead: "Steve Lacy: the Interview," *DB*, liv/12 (1987), 24 [incl. discography]

BARRY KERNFELD, H. L. LINDENMAIER

Ladnier, Tommy [Thomas J.] (*b* Florenceville, LA, 28 May 1900; *d* New York, 4 June 1939). Trumpeter. After moving to Chicago (1917) he worked with various groups and bandleaders in the area, including Ollie Powers (1923), Fate Marable (1924), and King Oliver (1924–5), and made recordings with a number of blues singers. He played in Europe with Sam Wooding (1925) and in the USA with the saxophonist Billy Fowler (1926), then served as principal trumpet soloist in Fletcher Henderson's band (from around October 1926 to the end of 1927). From 1928 to 1929 he was again in Europe with Wooding, and remained there for a while, working with Benny Peyton (1929) and others as well as his own group; he was a member of Noble Sissle's band (1930–31), with which he played in Europe and the USA. After several temporary engagements, he became the leader with Sidney Bechet of the NEW ORLEANS FEETWARMERS, who were active in New Jersey and New York (1932–spring 1933). After the two men briefly ran a tailor shop in New York (1933–4) Ladnier led his own quintet in New Jersey, played and taught in Connecticut, and performed around New York State. In 1938 he recorded with Bechet and Mezz Mezzrow (for illustration *see* MEZZROW, MEZZ).

Ladnier's style of the early 1920s chiefly resembled that of Johnny Dunn, notably in the use of triplets and double-time (he sometimes adapted the latter two elements precisely in the manner identified with Cow Cow Davenport and other midwestern blues pianists); it was also characterized by the cackling muted timbre produced by many trumpeters of the time, and by phrasing reminiscent of King Oliver's. Much of his work is symmetrical and songlike, and lacks melodic adventurousness. He had a fine sense of swing, suggestive of Armstrong's early style, and sometimes played boldly; he was adept at contrapuntal interplay, and in his later work, eschewing the upper register of the instrument, could create an effect at once spirited and relaxed, as the recording of the concert "From Spirituals to Swing" demonstrates.

SELECTED RECORDINGS

As leader: Really the Blues (1938, Bb 10089)

As sideman: O. Powers: Play that Thing (1923, Para. 20263); I. Cox: Ida Cox's Lawdy Lawdy Blues (1923, Para. 12064); M. Rainey: Lucky Rock Blues (1924, Para. 12215); Ma Rainey's Mystery Record (1924, Para. 12200); I. Cox: Kentucky Man Blues (1924, Para. 12220); F. Henderson: The Chant (1926, Col. 817D); Goose Pimples (1927, Har. 545H); S. Bechet: Sweetie

Steve Lacy (soprano saxophone) with Leo Smith (flugelhorn) and Maarten Altena (double bass), London, 1979

Dear (1932, Vic. 23360); M. Mezzrow: Comin' on with the come on (1938, Bb 10085); first issued on *Spirituals to Swing Concert*, i (1938, Van. 8523), New Orleans Feetwarmers: I wish I could shimmy like my sister Kate, Weary Blues

BIBLIOGRAPHY

E. Keartland: "Discography of Tommy Ladnier," *Jazz Forum: Quarterly Review of Jazz and Literature*, no.3 (1947), 17; no.4 (1947), 24
J. L. Anderson: "Evolution of Jazz," *DB*, xix (1952), no.1, p.16; no.2, p.11
A. J. McCarthy: "Tommy Ladnier: a Biography and Assessment," *JM*, ii/7 (1956), 2
H. Panassié: "Tommy Ladnier par le disque," *BHcF* (1964), no.139, p.3; no.140, p.7
J. C. Hillman: "Tommy Ladnier," *JJ*, xviii/8 (1965), 6
——: "Tommy Ladnier: the Sensational Cornetist," *Fn*, xiii/1 (1981), 4; xiii/2 (1981–2), 4
K. G. zur Heide: "Tommy Ladnier: Some Mid-Western Jobs," *Fn*, xiii/6 (1982), 16

BOB ZIEFF

Lady Day. Nickname of BILLIE HOLIDAY.

LaFaro, Scott (*b* Newark, NJ, 3 April 1936; *d* Geneva, NY, 6 July 1961). Double bass player. His family moved to Geneva, New York, when he was five years old. He started playing clarinet at the age of 14; later, in high school, he took up tenor saxophone, and finally studied double bass at Ithaca Conservatory and in Syracuse. In 1955–6 he traveled with Buddy Morrow's band to Los Angeles, where he began his career as a jazz musician as a member of Chet Baker's group (1956–7). After playing briefly in Chicago with Ira Sullivan he accompanied Sonny Rollins and Harold Land in San Francisco (1958) and worked with Barney Kessel and played in a group at the Lighthouse Cafe in Hermosa Beach, California. In 1959 he moved to New York and toured briefly with Benny Goodman, then joined a trio led by Bill Evans (ii) (with Paul Motian). He remained with Evans until his early death in an automobile accident, though he also led his own trio and worked with Stan Getz. His recordings with Evans and Ornette Coleman (1960–61) set the standard for a new generation of jazz bass players who varied their accompaniments by mixing traditional timekeeping bass lines with far-ranging countermelodies in free rhythm.

SELECTED RECORDINGS

As sideman: B. Evans: *Portrait in Jazz* (1959, Riv. 315); G. Schuller: *Jazz Abstractions* (1960, Atl. 1365); O. Coleman: *Free Jazz* (1960, Atl. 1364); *Ornette* (1961, Atl. 1378); B. Evans: *Explorations* (1961, Riv. 9351); *Sunday at the Village Vanguard* (1961, Riv. 9376); *Waltz for Debby* (1961, Riv. 9399)

BIBLIOGRAPHY

FeatherE; *Feather '60s*
M. Williams: "Introducing Scott LaFaro," *JR*, iii/7 (1960), 16
Obituary, *DB*, xxviii/17 (1961), 13

BARRY KERNFELD

Lafayette Theatre. Theater in New York; *see* NIGHTCLUBS AND OTHER VENUES.

Lafertin, Fapy [Jean] (*b* Belgium, *c*1950). Belgian guitarist. After starting his career as a member of the gypsy group WASO, he toured Europe as a soloist in the 1980s, performing at festivals in Mâcon (France), Ghent (Belgium), Edinburgh, and Llangollen (Wales), as well as appearing as one of the main attractions at the Soho Jazz Festival, London, in 1987. He has also recorded widely, and the variety he brings to his solo playing may be heard on the album *Gypsy Swing* (Munich 150246), recorded with Waso in 1979. The principal European guitarist to continue the tradition of Django Reinhardt, Lafertin combines Reinhardt's attack with an exceptionally sweet tone; in addition to using a fluid style of chordal improvisation, he has introduced a delicate and ornamental idiom to his execution of single-string solos. (I. Cruickshank: *The Guitar Style of Django Reinhardt and the Gypsies*, Woodcote, nr Reading, England, 1982, rev. and enlarged 2/1985)

ALYN SHIPTON

Lafitte, Guy (*b* St.-Gaudens, France, 12 Jan 1927). French tenor saxophonist. He played clarinet with gypsy groups in southwestern France before taking up the tenor saxophone in 1947. He moved to Paris, then worked with the blues singer Big Bill Broonzy (1950), toured and recorded with Mezz Mezzrow (1951) and Bill Coleman (1952), and played with Buck Clayton. From 1954 to 1958 he led a small group that performed in Paris at Les Trois Mailletz; later he worked as a freelance, and toured and recorded with Lionel Hampton (1956), Milt Buckner (1977), Wallace Davenport (1978), Bobby Durham, Arnett Cobb (1980), Oliver Jackson, and Jimmy Woode (1981). He was awarded the first Prix Django Reinhardt by the Académie du jazz in 1954 and in 1961 performed with Duke Ellington in Martin Ritt's film *Paris Blues*. Lafitte, who has been strongly influenced by Coleman Hawkins, plays with a lush, full sound that is particularly well suited to ballads.

SELECTED RECORDINGS

As leader: *Blue and Sentimental* (1954, Club français du disque 21); with A. Persiany: *Les classiques du jazz* (1955, 1957, Col. FP1074, FPX145); *Jambo* (1968, RCA LSP10202); *Blues in Summertime* (1970, RCA 730106); with B. Coleman: *Mainstream at Montreux* (1973, Black Lion 212); *Corps et âme* (1978, BB 33128); with W. B. Davis: *Three Men on a Beat* (1983, BB 33181); *Guy Lafitte joue Charles Trenet* (1984, BB 33190)

As sideman: E. Berry: *Swingin' the Berrys* (1956, Col. FP1076); B. Coleman: *Really I Do* (1980, BB 33162)

BIBLIOGRAPHY

L. Malson: "Le jazz en France: Guy Lafitte: un accent bien de chez nous," *Jm*, no.56 (1960), 30

P. Lafargue: "A Guy Lafitte Discography," *JM*, ix (1963), no.7, p.10; no.8, p.24; no.9, p.27

J.-L. Ginibre: "Test: huit pièges pour Guy," *Jm*, no.104 (1964), 33

M. Laverdure: "Lafitte face au free," *Jm*, no.192 (1971), 38

C. Battestini and J.-P. Battestini: "Guy Lafitte," *BHcF*, no.289 (1981), 4

ANDRÉ CLERGEAT

L.A. Four. Quartet formed in 1974 in Los Angeles by the alto saxophonist and flutist Bud Shank, the guitarist Laurindo Almeida, the double bass player Ray Brown, and the drummer Chuck Flores (soon replaced by Shelly Manne, who was in turn replaced in 1978 by Jeff Hamilton). Almeida and Shank had apparently been inspired 20 years earlier to form the group when they recorded in a quartet with the same instrumentation. The group had a varied repertory that included classically oriented pieces for solo guitar and duos, trios, and quartets written by the group's members. Its instrumentation and soft dynamics were particularly well suited to sambas and bossa novas, which became specialties of Almeida and Shank as early as the 1950s. It disbanded around 1985.

SELECTED RECORDINGS

(all recorded for Concord)

The L.A. Four Scores! (1975, 8); *The L.A. 4* (1975, 18); *Live at Montreux* (1979, 100); *Montage* (1981, 156); *Executive Suite* (1982, 215)

BIBLIOGRAPHY

C. Albertson: "The L.A. Four: an Oasis in the Endless Desert of Electronic Aridity," *Stereo Review*, xxxvii/9 (1976), 88

L. Lyons: "The L.A. Four: Journeymen United," *DB*, xliv/15 (1977), 18

F. Nemko-Graham: "The L.A. Four as One," *JT* (1981), Dec, 10

B. Weir: *The L.A. Four Discography* (Cardiff, 1985, rev. 2/1986)

THOMAS OWENS

Lagrene, Bireli (*b* Saverne, France, 4 Sept 1966). French guitarist of gypsy origin. His father and a grandfather were guitarists, and he took up guitar as a young child; by the time he was seven years old he was improvising in a swing style influenced by the work of Django Reinhardt. His first album, *Routes to Django* (1980), evinced a strong technique and a keen musical awareness, and soon brought him recognition. In the following years he appeared at festivals in New York (Kool Jazz Festival) and Europe, performed with Benny Carter, Benny Goodman, and Stephane Grappelli, and in 1984 took part with Larry Coryell and Vic Juris in a tribute to Reinhardt in New York. He played jazz-rock with Jaco Pastorius on a tour of Europe in 1986.

SELECTED RECORDINGS

Routes to Django (1980, Ant. 1002); *15* (1982, Ant. 1009); *Bireli Lagrene Ensemble Live Featuring Vic Juris* (1985, Jazzpoint 1015)

BIBLIOGRAPHY

I. Cruickshank: *The Guitar Style of Django Reinhardt and the Gypsies* (Woodcote, nr Reading, England, 1982, rev. and enlarged 2/1985)

H. Kumpf: "Bireli Lagrene: the Boy Wonder Grows Up," *JF* [intl edn], no.87 (1984), 39

M. Bourne: "Bireli Lagrene," *DB*, lii/4 (1985), 27

G. Giddins: "Gypsy Soul," *Rhythm-a-ning: Jazz Tradition and Innovation in the '80s* (New York, and Oxford, England, 1985) [colln of previously pubd articles], 139

J. Ferguson: "Bireli Lagrene: Stepping Out of Django's Shadow," *GP*, xx/3 (1986), 24 [incl. transcr.]

JIM FERGUSON

Laine, Alfred "Baby" [Pantsy] (*b* New Orleans, 12 July 1895; *d* New Orleans, 1 March 1957). Cornetist and drummer, son of Papa Jack Laine. He played with his father's Reliance Brass Band and also led his own group, the Wampus Cats, which included Raymond Burke.

MARCEL JOLY

Laine, Bob [Lars Robert] (*b* Stockholm, 2 Jan 1910). Pianist. He played with Jay Elfwing in Stockholm before emigrating to the USA in 1928. There he worked as a leader, played with Joe Venuti and Louis Prima, recorded with Wingy Manone (1935), and after moving to California performed and recorded with Ben Pollack (1937–8). In Sweden he performed on radio and recorded with Gösta Törner and Stan Hasselgård (1947) and recorded with Lars Gullin and Ove Lind (1953). Later he recorded with the singer Gene Austin in the USA (1961) and operated an art gallery in California. His recording *Blues Cupol* (1947, Cupol 4011), recorded as a leader with Törner, is a good example of his work.

BIBLIOGRAPHY

FeatherE

H. Nicolausson: "Bob Laine: Stockholmsgrabben som blev amerikansk jazzstjärna" [Stockholm guy who became American jazz star], *Orkester journalen*, xv (1947), April

T. Magnusson: "Bob Laines skivor med Wingy Manone" [Bob Laine's recordings with Wingy Manone], *Orkester journalen*, liii (1985), Jan, 35 [incl. bibliography]

ERIK KJELLBERG

Laine, Cleo [Campbell, Clementina Dinah] (*b* London, 28 Oct 1927). English singer. Born of West Indian and English parents, she began singing at the age of three. In 1952 she joined the John Dankworth Seven; shortly after marrying Dankworth (1958) she left his group and began a very successful stage career, though she remained active as a singer. In 1969 she and Dankworth founded the Wavendon Allmusic Plan, an educational institution devoted to all styles of music. They performed together again in 1971, and in 1972 toured Australia as well as undertaking the first of a series of tours of the USA. Dankworth also worked as her arranger, composer, and music director.

Laine has recorded and performed opera, lieder, and pop music as well as jazz, and in the 1980s was the only singer to have been nominated for Grammy awards in the female popular, classical, and jazz categories. As a jazz singer she is both an interpreter and an improviser, and her scat singing, accompanied by Dankworth on alto saxophone or clarinet, is particularly noteworthy. Her contralto voice is capable of great variety of color, and has an extraordinary upward extension in falsetto to *c''''*, giving her a compass of four octaves.

For further information and illustration *see* DANKWORTH, JOHN.

SELECTED RECORDINGS

As leader: *A Lover and his Lass* (1955, Esquire 15–007); *She's the Tops* (1957, MGM C765); *Cleo's Choice* (1957, Nixa 19024); *Shakespeare and All that Jazz* (1964, Fon. 5209); *If we Lived on Top of a Mountain* (1968, Fon. 5464); *Cleo at Carnegie: the 10th Anniversary Concert* (1983, DRG 2101)

BIBLIOGRAPHY

Feather '60s; Feather–Gitler '70s
C. Mitchell: "Profile: John Dankworth, Cleo Laine," *DB*, xli/13 (1974), 36
G. Collier: *Cleo and John* (London, 1976)
J. Joseph: "Music Education at Wavendon," *Music Teacher*, lxi/2 (1982), 14

PAUL RINZLER (with HENRY PLEASANTS)

Laine, Papa Jack [George Vital] (*b* New Orleans, 21 Sept 1873; *d* New Orleans, 1 June 1966). Drummer, alto horn player, and bandleader. He formed his Reliance Brass Band in New Orleans during the 1890s, and continued to lead it for more than 40 years. It was principally a marching band, and through its ranks passed many young white musicians who subsequently achieved fame, including the Brunies brothers, Tom Brown, Sharkey Bonano, and various members of the Original Dixieland Jazz Band. The success of his first band led Laine to form other similar groups, and at one time he was the music director of five Reliance bands. He also led smaller dance bands, but none of his groups made recordings.

The repertory of Laine's band often included numbers that had jazz associations, but the groups themselves did not specialize in improvisation. Thus the title given to Laine, "the father of white jazz," is misleading; it was bestowed more for Laine's role as an employer and benefactor of jazz musicians than for his musical contributions.

Oral history material in *LNT*.

BIBLIOGRAPHY

C. E. Smith: "White New Orleans," *Jazzmen*, ed. F. Ramsey, Jr., and C. E. Smith (New York, 1939/R1977), 39
G. Hoefer: "Jack Laine Honored by New Orleans Jazz Club," *DB*, xviii/5 (1951), 11
E. Souchon: "The End of an Era," *SL*, xvii (1966), 79
K. Koenig: "Papa Laine, 1873–1966," *MR*, xi/5 (1984), 1

JOHN CHILTON

Laird, Rick [Richard Quentin] (*b* Dublin, 5 Feb 1941). Bass player. He played guitar, then double bass by the age of 18. Having lived in New Zealand and Australia, he moved in 1962 to England, where he worked with Lambert, Hendricks, and Ross, and, as the regular double bass player at Ronnie Scott's jazz club in London (1964–6), with Ben Webster, Art Farmer, Sonny Rollins, Freddie Hubbard, Sonny Stitt, Roland Kirk, and Wes Montgomery; he played with Rollins on the soundtrack to the film *Alfie* (1965). He attended the Berklee College of Music for six semesters from 1966. He began playing electric bass guitar in 1968, and toured with Buddy Rich's band (1969–71), played with the MAHAVISHNU ORCHESTRA (1971–3), then worked in New York as a freelance. In 1978 he played with Chick Corea (for illustration *see* JAZZ (i), fig.8), Stan Getz, and Joe Henderson, and from 1979 he taught and worked again as a freelance in New York. Although Laird has played with bop musicians for most of his career, he is best known for having provided a loud, steady, driving, and rhythmically complex foundation to the jazz-rock of the Mahavishnu Orchestra. He is the author of the methods *Improvising Jazz Bass* (New York, 1978) and *Jazz Riffs for Bass* (New York, 1978).

SELECTED RECORDINGS

As leader: *Soft Focus* (1976, Tim. 104)

As sideman: B. Rich: *Keep the Customer Satisfied* (1970, Lib. 11006); Mahavishnu Orchestra: *The Inner Mounting Flame* (1971, Col. KC31067); *Birds of Fire* (1972, Col. KC31996); *Between Nothingness and Eternity* (1973, Col. KC32766); E. Jefferson: *Still on the Planet* (1976, Muse, 5063)

BIBLIOGRAPHY

J. P. Schaffer: "An Innermost Vision," *DB*, xl/8 (1973), 11
A. Berle: "Rick Laird," *GP*, xiv/7 (1980), 61

JOHN VOIGT

Lake, Oliver (Eugene) (*b* Marianna, AR, 14 Sept 1942). Alto saxophonist. He grew up in St. Louis and began playing drums as a boy, but took up alto saxophone at the age of 18 and later also learned flute. After studies at Lincoln University (BA 1968) he taught in public schools, played in rhythm-and-blues bands, and led the Black Artists Group (BAG). He worked in Paris from 1972 to 1974 with a quintet made up of BAG members, then moved to New York, where he has performed free jazz and classical music with small groups and as a soloist. Lake was a founding member of the WORLD SAXOPHONE QUARTET in 1976 and led a trio with Michael Gregory Jackson and Pheeroan Ak Laff. In 1977 he staged *The Life Dance of Is*, a theatrical piece for which he wrote both music and poetry, and in 1979 he presented a program of compositions for string quartet at Carnegie Hall. As the leader of the commercially successful quintet Jump Up (1981–4), he added a new and startling dimension to his music: the group provided a reggae foundation as a support to his characteristically screaming, chromatic, blues-drenched melodies. Lake played alto, tenor, and soprano saxophones with the quintet, and also sang. In 1984–5 he recorded in Italy and performed in New York with a new free-jazz quintet that included Kevin Eubanks and Ak Laff.

SELECTED RECORDINGS

Duos: with L. Bowie: *In Concert* (1976, Sack. 2010); with J. Hemphill: *Buster Bee* (1978, Sack. 3018)

As leader: *Holding Together* (1976, BS 0009); *Life Dance of Is* (1978, AN 3003); of World Saxophone Quartet (with J. Hemphill, D. Murray, and H. Bluiett): *Steppin' with the World Saxophone Quartet* (1978, BS 0027); *Prophet* (1980, BS 0044); *Clevont Fitzhubert* (1981, BS 0054); *Jump Up* (1982, Gram. 8106); *Plug It* (1982, Gram. 1206); *Expendable Language* (1984, BS 0074); *Gallery* (1986, Gram. 8609)

BIBLIOGRAPHY

D. Jackson: "Profile: Julius Hemphill, Oliver Lake," *DB*, xlii/12 (1975), 32
B. Smith: "The Oliver Lake Interview," *Coda*, no.147 (1976), 2
C. J. Safane: "The World Saxophone Quartet," *DB*, xlvi/16 (1979), 26
B. McRae: "Oliver Lake and Joe McPhee," *JJI*, xxxiii/2 (1980), 25
E. Jost: *Jazzmusiker: Materialen zur Soziologie der afro-amerikanischen Musik* (Frankfurt am Main, Germany, Berlin, and Vienna, 1981), 129
B. Milkowski: "Oliver Lake: Sax in the Hip Pocket," *DB*, l/5 (1983), 22

BARRY KERNFELD

Lallemand, Sadi "Fats." *See* SADI, FATS.

Lamare, Nappy [Hilton Napoleon] (*b* New Orleans, 14 June 1907; *d* Newhall, CA, 8 May 1988). Guitarist, banjoist, composer, and singer. He began playing banjo in New Orleans with such musicians as Monk Hazel, Sharkey Bonano, and the bandleaders Johnny Bayersdorffer and Tony Fougerat, and made his recording début in 1927 playing guitar with John Hyman's Bayou Stompers. In 1930 he joined Ben Pollack, for whom he sometimes sang novelty songs. He was a founding member of

Bob Crosby's orchestra, formed in 1935 from dissatisfied members of Pollack's band, and remained until 1942; he contributed a number of tunes to the band's repertory, including *March of the Bob Cats* (1938). In early 1943 he joined Eddie Miller's band in Los Angeles, and assumed leadership of the group when Miller was drafted in 1944. After World War II Lamare worked as a freelance musician; he appeared in a number of films and played in small groups, often with former sidemen of Crosby's. He was a leader, with Ray Bauduc, of a dixieland band from 1955 until the late 1960s, performed regularly with Joe Darensbourg in 1969 and 1983, and continued to work as a freelance into the 1980s. He also played in the Crosby band for its occasional reunions. Lamare recorded no solos, but was a highly competent, if undistinguished, rhythm guitarist.

Oral history material in *LNT*.

For illustration *see* CROSBY, BOB.

SELECTED RECORDINGS

As leader: South Rampart Street Parade/Mama Inez (1947, Cap. 15050); with R. Bauduc: *Two-beat Generation* (1958, Cap. T1198)

As sideman: J. Hyman: Ain't Love Grand?/Alligator Blues (1927, Vic. 20593); J. Teagarden: Rockin' Chair (1931, Crown 3051); B. Pollack: Got the Jitters (1933, Col. 2870D); W. Manone: No Calling Card/Strange Blues (1934, Bruns. 6911); B. Crosby: March of the Bob Cats (1938, Decca 1865); Don't call me boy/You're bound to look like a monkey (1940, Decca 3431); Way down yonder in New Orleans (1942, Decca 4403)

BIBLIOGRAPHY

ChiltonW

P. Vacher: "Nappy Lamare," *Fn*, vii/3 (1976), 21

E. Townley: "Bob Cat: an Interview with Hilton 'Nappy' Lamare," *Sv*, no.101 (1982), 164

J. Chilton: *Stomp Off, Let's Go! The Story of Bob Crosby's Bob Cats & Big Band* (London, 1983), esp. chap. 18

L. Holmes: "The Jazz Clock: a Look at Aging and Creativity in Jazz," *JT* (1983), April, 12

L. D. Holmes and J. W. Thomson: "Getting Better with Age," *MR*, xv/1 (1987), 8

DAVID FLANAGAN

Lamb, John (*b* Vero Beach, FL, 4 Dec 1933). Double bass player. After playing with Red Garland (1954–5) he led his own sextet in Philadelphia (1957–9), and then worked with the pianists Paul Curry (1960–62) and Johnny Walker (1962–4). In August 1964 he joined Duke Ellington's orchestra, and during his three-year stay with the band made a number of recordings, including *Step in Time* (on the album *Duke Ellington Plays Mary Poppins*, 1964, Rep. 6141) and *La plus belle Africaine* (on the album *Soul Call*, 1966, Verve 68701). Lamb continued to play with Ellington occasionally during the late 1960s.

EDDIE LAMBERT

Lamb, the. Nickname of EDGAR SAMPSON.

Lambert, Dave [Dave Alden] (*b* Boston, 19 June 1917; *d* Westport, CT, 3 Oct 1966). Singer and arranger. As a member of Gene Krupa's band (1944–5) he sang with Buddy Stewart on *What's this?*, which included the first recorded example of a bop vocal line. Leading a small singing group, Lambert made broadcasts with Charlie Parker (1949), and later recorded with him (1953). He worked as a studio contractor and arranger in the 1950s, and collaborated with Jon Hendricks to record *Four Brothers* in 1955. In 1957, with Annie Ross, the two men formed the trio LAMBERT, HENDRICKS, AND ROSS, which quickly became popular for its improvisations and vocalese. The group disbanded in 1964, shortly after Lambert returned to studio work in New York; he also appeared in a film, *Lambert & Co* (1964).

SELECTED RECORDINGS

As leader: A Cent and a Half/Charge Account (1946, Key. 668)

As sideman: G. Krupa: What's this? (1945, Col. 36819); C. Parker: Old Folks (1953, Clef 11100); J. Hendricks: Four Brothers (1955, Decca 29572)

BIBLIOGRAPHY

L. Keating: "The Dave Lambert Singers," *JJ*, xv/4 (1962), 2

Obituary, *DB*, xxxiii/23 (1966), 13

For further recordings and bibliography *see* LAMBERT, HENDRICKS, AND ROSS.

PHILIP GREENE

Lambert, Hendricks, and Ross. Vocal trio. It was formed by Dave Lambert, Jon Hendricks, and Annie Ross, who first sang together in 1957 with ten other singers, recording arrangements of compositions by Count Basie. The sessions proved unsuccessful, however, so Lambert, Hendricks, and Ross recorded all the parts themselves, using overdubbing. The resulting album, *Sing a Song of Basie*, quickly brought them popularity, and the trio became known for its improvisations and settings of lyrics and scat lines to transcriptions of jazz tunes. From 1959 to 1962 it was accompanied by a group that included Gildo Mahones, Ike Isaacs (i), and the drummer Kahil Madi (later Jimmy Wormworth). Ross left the ensemble because of illness in 1962 and after she was replaced by Yolande Bavan the trio became known as Lambert, Hendricks, and Bavan; Mahones was joined by George Tucker and Jimmie Smith. Lambert also left the group, in 1964, and was replaced briefly by Don Chastain, but it soon disbanded. At its best the group offered witty, effective arrangements which were performed with great exuberance and swing; this helped to compensate for the occasionally inaccurate intonation of the singers.

For illustration *see* SINGING, fig.2.

SELECTED RECORDINGS

Lambert, Hendricks, and Ross: *Sing a Song of Basie* (1957, ABC-Para. 223); *The Swingers* (1959, WP 1264); *The Hottest New Group in Jazz* (1959, Col. CL1403); *Lambert, Hendricks, and Ross Sing Ellington* (1960, Col. CS8310); *High Flying* (1961, Col. CS8475)

Lambert, Hendricks, and Bavan: *Lambert, Hendricks, and Bavan at Basin Street East* (1962, RCA LSP2635); *At Newport '63* (1963, RCA LSP2747); *At the Village Gate* (1963, RCA LSP2861)

BIBLIOGRAPHY

G. Lees and J. Hendricks: "Lambert, Hendricks, and Ross and How they Grew," *DB*, xxvi/19 (1959), 16

D. Bittan: "Lambert Exits L-H-B: Replacement Set," *DB*, xxxi/9 (1964), 13

J. Hendricks: "Listening to L-H-R," *The Best of Lambert, Hendricks, and Ross* (Col. KC32911, 1974) [liner notes]

L. Gourse: *Louis' Children: American Jazz Singers* (New York, 1984)

PHILIP GREENE

Lamellaphone. An instrument with a set of tuned lamellae, or tongues, fitted to a resonating box or board. The instrument is usually held in the player's hands while the lamellae are plucked by his thumbs. Many different types exist, particularly in Africa, and it is sometimes referred to as the thumb piano or African thumb piano. In jazz, lamellaphones such as the *mbira*, *kalimba*, and *likembe* have been used to impart an African flavor; a good example of this is the *mbira* solo played by Stanley Cowell on *Smilin' Billy Suite* no.2 from the Heath Brothers' album *Marchin' On* (1975, SE 19766). (*GroveI*)

Lammi, Dick (*b* Red Lodge, MT, 15 Jan 1909; *d* ?1970s). Double bass and tuba player and banjoist. He played banjo in Astoria (Oregon) and Aberdeen (Washington) in the mid-1920s. He was active as a double bass player for five years in Portland (Oregon) before moving in 1936 to San Francisco, where he learned to play tuba. From 1941 to 1950 he performed and recorded on tuba and double bass with Lu Watters's Yerba Buena Jazz

Band (for illustration *see* WATTERS, LU); his playing may be heard on the band's recording *At a Georgia Camp Meeting* (1941, Jazz Man 4). Lammi also recorded with New Orleans revival bands led by Wally Rose (1946), Clancy Hayes (1950), Bob Scobey (1951–5), and Turk Murphy (1949–58). (*FeatherE*)

Lamond, Don(ald Douglas) (*b* Oklahoma City, OK, 18 Aug 1920). Drummer. He grew up in Washington and studied at the Peabody Conservatory in Baltimore. After working with Sonny Dunham (1943) and with Boyd Raeburn's orchestra (1944), he joined Woody Herman in 1945 as Dave Tough's replacement; Herman's Herd broke up in December 1946 but Lamond returned to Herman the following year as a member of the Second Herd. He played on the first recordings that Serge Chaloff made as a leader (1946) and recorded with Charlie Parker (1947). The Second Herd disbanded in 1949 and from the 1950 until the mid-1960s Lamond worked frequently in recording studios. An adaptable player, he recorded traditional jazz with Ruby Braff (1958, 1959) and Bob Crosby (1966), swing with Benny Goodman (1947, 1952, 1955) and Quincy Jones (1959), and bop with such musicians as Stan Getz and Zoot Sims (both 1950), Marian McPartland (1951), Johnny Smith (1952–3, 1967), and Sonny Stitt (1953), and with other musicians and groups as diverse as the Sauter–Finegan Orchestra (1952–3, 1956–8), Dick Hyman (1956), Johnny Guarnieri (1956–7), Jack Teagarden and Willie "the Lion" Smith (both 1958), and George Russell (1960). He was a member of George Wein's Newport Festival All-Stars in the late 1960s; while in Paris with Wein in 1969 he also recorded with Braff, Stephane Grappelli and Joe Venuti, and Red Norvo. He later made recordings with Maxine Sullivan (1971), Bucky Pizzarelli (1972), and his own Big Swing Band, an orchestra of young players from Florida (1977, 1982). He remains best known, however, for his early work with Herman.

SELECTED RECORDINGS

As leader: *Extraordinary* (1977, 1982, Prog. 7067)

As sideman with W. Herman: *One Night Stand with Woody Herman* (1945–6, Joyce 1021); I've got news for you (1947, Col. 38213); The Goof and I (1947, Col. 38369); Four Brothers (1947, Col. 38304); *Road Band, 1948* (1948, Hep 18)

As sideman with others: S. Dunham: *Half Past Jumping Time* (1945, Golden Era 15008); C. Parker: Relaxin' at Camarillo (1947, Dial 1012); W. Bradley, B. Byrne, and B. Freeman: *Dixieland Style, Chicago Style* (c1954, Grand Award 33-313); U. Green: *His Trombone and Rhythm* (1959, RCA LPM1969); Q. Jones: *Birth of a Band!* (1959, Mer. 60129); G. Russell: *Jazz in the Space Age* (1960, Decca 79219), incl. Chromatic Universe, The Lydiot; B. Crosby: *Live at the Rainbow Grill* (1966, Ember 827); G. Wein: *Newport All-Stars* (1967, BL 138)

BIBLIOGRAPHY

FeatherE

J. A. Treichel: *Keeper of the Flame: Woody Herman and the Second Herd, 1947–1949* (n.p. [Zephyrhills, FL], 1978) [bio-discography], 11

G. Villani: "Reflections: Don Lamond," *MD*, iii/4 (1979), 22

SCOTT YANOW

Lancaster, (William) Byard [Thunderbird] (*b* Philadelphia, 6 Aug 1942). Alto saxophonist and flutist. He studied piano and saxophone as a child and, while still in high school, performed with the percussionist and pianist J. R. Mitchell. He studied music at Troy University, the Boston Conservatory, and the Berklee College of Music, and later at Howard University. He performed and recorded with Sunny Murray in New York and Europe (at intervals from 1965 into the 1980s), and performed with Bill Dixon (1966–7), Sun Ra (1968, 1971), and McCoy Tyner (1971–7). From 1977 he performed in diverse styles, including punk rock, blues (with Memphis Slim in Paris), and free jazz. Lancaster acknowledges the influence of Jackie McLean and Ornette Coleman on his saxophone playing, as well as that of the soul singer James Brown. Besides his principal instruments he plays bass clarinet and percussion. Representative examples of his playing may be heard on *Sunny Murray Quintet* (1966, ESP 1032) and an album he made as a leader, *Documentation: the End of a Decade* (1981, Bellows 801).

BIBLIOGRAPHY

V. Wilmer: *As Serious as your Life: the Story of the New Jazz* (London, 1977, rev. 1980)

B. Rusch: "Byard Lancaster: Interview," *Cadence*, vi/3 (1980), 5

L. Jeske: "Profile: Byard Lancaster," *DB*, xlviii/1 (1981), 50

M. Hames: *Albert Ayler, Sunny Murray, Cecil Taylor, Byard Lancaster, and Kenneth Terroade on Disc and Tape* (Ferndown, England, 1983)

DAVID G. SUCH

Land, Harold (de Vance) (*b* Houston, 18 Dec 1928). Tenor saxophonist. He grew up in San Diego, and became interested in music while in high school; he began playing saxophone when he was about 16 years old. After gaining experience with local bands in San Diego he moved to Los Angeles, where he joined the quintet led by Clifford Brown and Max Roach as a replacement for Teddy Edwards. He was with this band for 18 months, but left to play with Curtis Counce (1956–8). Land then led his own groups, or shared leadership with Red Mitchell (1961–2) and Bobby Hutcherson (1967–71); in the 1950s and 1960s he also worked with Gerald Wilson. From 1975 to 1978 he led a quintet with Blue Mitchell, and thereafter has worked as a freelance, mainly in California but also touring overseas.

Land is a fluent modern stylist whose dry tone and individual manner of improvising at first owed little to the work of other musicians. In the late 1960s, however, his playing changed dramatically when he came under the influence of John Coltrane. His tone hardened and his phrasing became more brusque and jagged. His ability and daring are best displayed on his recordings as the leader of small groups including Carl Perkins (1958) and Elmo Hope (1959), and as a sideman with Thelonious Monk.

Land's son Harold C. Land, Jr. (*b* San Diego, 25 April 1950), is a pianist and composer who has worked with Wayne Henderson's Freedom Sounds, Gerald Wilson, Kenny Burrell, Pharoah Sanders, and his father.

SELECTED RECORDINGS

As leader: *Harold in the Land of Jazz* (1958, Cont. 3550); *The Fox* (1959, Hi-Fi 612); *West Coast Blues!* (1960, Jlnd 20); with R. Mitchell: *Hear Ye!* (1961, Atl. 1376); *The Peace-maker* (1967–8, Cadet 813); with B. Mitchell: *Mapenzi* (1977, Conc. 44)

As sideman: C. Brown and M. Roach: *Brown and Roach Incorporated* (1954, EmA 36008); *Clifford Brown and Max Roach* (1954–5, EmA 36036); C. Counce: *Carl's Blues* (1957–8, Cont. 3574); *Exploring the Future* (1958, Dooto 247); T. Monk: *At the Blackhawk* (1960, Riv. 323)

BIBLIOGRAPHY

N. Hentoff: Liner notes, *Harold in the Land of Jazz* (Cont. 3550, 1958)

A. McCarthy and others: *Jazz on Record: a Critical Guide to the First 50 Years: 1917–1967* (London, 1968)

L. Feather: Liner notes, *The Fox* (Cont. 7619, 1969)

M. Harrison and others: *Modern Jazz: the Essential Records: a Critical Selection* (London, 1975), 91

B. Case: "Most Unfortunate, Like a Fox," *The Wire*, no.1 (1982), 8

MARK GARDNER

Lande, Art (*b* New York, 1947). Pianist and leader. Trained in classical piano from the age of four, he studied at Williams College before moving to San Francisco in 1969. During the early 1970s he played electric piano in a jazz quintet with Steve Swallow, and in 1973 recorded in a duo with Jan Garbarek and in Ted Curson's septet. Having already taught privately, he founded a jazz school in about 1975. The following year he formed Rubisa Patrol, a stylistically wide-ranging quartet, which regularly visited Europe and recorded two albums there (including *Rubisa Patrol*, 1976, ECM 1081). He left the group in 1983, then taught for three years at a jazz school in St. Gallen, Switzerland. In 1987 he moved to Boulder, Colorado, to teach at the Naropa Institute. He has made a solo album of swing standards (1977), and has performed and recorded as an unaccompanied soloist in San Francisco; he has also recorded with Gary Peacock (1980) and with his own small groups (1978, 1981).

BIBLIOGRAPHY

B. Ness: "Profile: Art Lande," *DB*, xliv/10 (1977), 38

T. Schnabel: "Art Lande: Interview," *Cadence*, iii/10 (1978), 24

B. Doerschuk: "Art Lande: the Gentle Revolutionary of Jazz Piano," *Keyboard*, x/9 (1984), 32 [incl. discography]

C. Ahlgren: "Art Lande: Solo Pianist Scores Big Home Run," *San Francisco Chronicle Datebook* (18 Oct 1987)

Landers, Wes(ley) (*b* Bermuda, 1925). Drummer. After moving to Chicago in his childhood he began to study violin and later played drums in a number of swing and dixieland bands. He worked with Andy Kirk and, around the end of World War II, played for Earl Hines and Count Basie. In 1948 he began an association with Gene Ammons, recording with him frequently during the next two years. Thereafter Landers made recordings with Sonny Stitt (1950), Buddy DeFranco (1953), and Sonny Clark (1957–8). In New York, and later in New Orleans, he performed in various clubs; he played a mixture of traditional jazz and rhythm-and-blues, most notably with Paul Gayten's orchestra. By 1985 Landers was a member of the New Orleans Blues Serenaders, a traditional jazz band originally formed for the musical play *One Mo' Time*, with which he has toured Europe and the USA. (H. Anrig: "New Orleans Blues Serenaders," *12th Festa New Orleans Music* (Ascona, Switzerland, 1986) [program])

ALYN SHIPTON

Landl, Ernst [Nesty] (*b* Vienna, 12 Feb 1914; *d* Stockholm, 4 Dec 1983). Austrian pianist, leader, and composer. He began playing in the early 1930s with Bobby Sax's orchestra. He accompanied Adelaide Hall in 1935 in Vienna and worked occasionally with Eddie Brunner and Stephane Grappelli in Monte Carlo. During the German occupation of Austria he gave clandestine concerts and led a recording session (1943) with his own quintet. After the war he worked as a pianist and arranger with Horst Winter (1946–7) and made many recordings with his own group, the Hot Club Vienna, including *Nesty Boogie* (one of his own compositions) and *Rug Cutters Swing* (both 1947, ES 8120). He stopped playing jazz in the mid-1950s and moved to Sweden. Landl was an excellent swing pianist in the tradition of Teddy Wilson and Art Tatum.

KLAUS SCHULZ

Landmark. Record company and label. The company was founded by Orrin Keepnews in 1985. Its small catalogue includes recordings by Bobby Hutcherson (1984–5), Jack DeJohnette and Jimmy Heath (both 1985), and Mulgrew Miller (1985–6). (R. Palmer: "The Pop Life: a New Label, Landmark, Records Jazz," *New York Times* (20 Feb 1985), §C, p.17)

Landrum, Richard [Richie, Pablo] (*b* New York, 18 July 1939). Percussionist. He studied at the Juilliard School, and also trained with several Afro-Caribbean and jazz percussionists, including Carlos "Potato" Valdez, Babatunde Olatunji, and Max Roach. As an accompanist for dance classes and companies he has worked with several well-known dancers; he has also been involved with black theater groups. He was much in demand during the late 1960s and early 1970s when many jazz musicians experimented with Afro-Cuban percussion; a good example of his style may be heard on Count Basie's *Afrique* (1970), and his hypnotic bongo playing underpins Leone Thomas's *The Creator has a Master Plan* (1969). After working with the group Pucho and the Latin Soul Brothers (1966–9) Landrum performed in the early 1970s with Randy Weston at the Tangier (Morocco), Monterey, and Newport jazz festivals. He recorded with Groove Holmes (1966), Gato Barbieri (1969), Grant Green and Freddie Hubbard (both 1970), Roland Kirk (1971), and Elvin Jones (1973).

SELECTED RECORDINGS

As sideman: L. Thomas: *Spirits Known and Unknown* (1969, FD 10115), incl. The Creator has a Master Plan; S. Turrentine: *Sugar* (1970, CTI 6005); C. Basie: *Afrique* (1970, FD 10138); E. Jones: *The Prime Element* (1973, BN LA506H2); S. Fortune: *Long Before our Mothers Cried* (1974, SE 7423)

BIBLIOGRAPHY

Feather–Gitler '70s

JEFF POTTER

Lang, Eddie [Dunn, Blind Willie; Massaro, Salvatore] (*b* Philadelphia, 25 Oct 1902; *d* New York, 26 March 1933). Guitarist. He studied violin formally for 11 years and learned guitar from his father, a guitarist and instrument maker. He formed a successful and long-lived partnership with Joe Venuti, his former schoolmate in Philadelphia, and performed with him in the early 1920s in Atlantic City, New Jersey. By 1924, when he recorded with the Mound City Blue Blowers (see illustration), he had moved to New York. There he performed and recorded frequently with, among others, Red Nichols, Jean Goldkette, Frankie Trumbauer, the Dorsey brothers, Paul Whiteman, and above all Venuti, with whom he made a series of duet recordings (1926–8), including the noteworthy *Stringing the Blues*, their recomposition of *Tiger Rag*. He also recorded some duos with Lonnie Johnson (1928–9) and, under the pseudonym Blind Willie Dunn, two titles (1929) with a group called the Gin Bottle Four (which included Johnson and King Oliver). After playing with Whiteman (1929–30) Lang became Bing Crosby's accompanist.

Lang was the first well-known solo jazz guitarist and, from the mid-1920s, was widely influential. His career coincided with the development of recording techniques suited to the acoustic guitar, which partly through his influence supplanted the banjo as a jazz instrument. He was highly regarded for his single-string solos and his accompaniments, which usually interspersed chords and single-string lines in the middle register. Although some contemporary black guitarists were better soloists, Lang's accompaniments resulted in interesting textures (but with rather undirected lines at times); he was a good rhythm guitarist with a fine technique and attained a consistently high level of performance.

See also BLUES, §4; GUITAR, §3; and STRING BAND; for further illustrations *see* FILMS, fig.2, and VENUTI, JOE.

SELECTED RECORDINGS

Duos with J. Venuti: Stringing the Blues (1926, Col. 914D); Doin' Things/ Goin' Places (1927, OK 40825)

Duos with L. Johnson: Guitar Blues/Blue Guitars (1929, OK 8711); A Handful of Riffs (1929, OK 8695)

As leader: Eddie's Twister (1927, OK 40807); Jet Black Blues/Blue Blood Blues (1929, OK 8689)

As sideman with L. Armstrong: Knockin' a Jug (1929, OK 8703)

BIBLIOGRAPHY

F. Trumbauer: "Eddie Didn't Use Music: he Had it in his Pocket," *DB*, vi/ 5 (1939), 17

N. Shapiro and N. Hentoff, eds.: *Hear me Talkin' to ya: the Story of Jazz by the Men who Made it* (New York and London, 1955/*R*1966), 246

R. Hadlock: *Jazz Masters of the Twenties* (New York, 1965/R1985)
A. McCarthy and others: *Jazz on Record: a Critical Guide to the First 50 Years: 1917–1967* (London, 1968), 174
B. McRae: "A B Basics, no.49: Eddie Lang," *JJ*, xxiv/11 (1971), 15
A. McCarthy: *Big Band Jazz* (New York and London, 1974), 172
J. Ferguson: "Eddie Lang: Father of Jazz Guitar," *GP*, xvii/8 (1983), 78 [incl. discography]

JAMES DAPOGNY/R

Lang, Mike [Michael Anthony] (*b* Los Angeles, 10 Dec 1941). Pianist and electronic keyboard player. He began playing piano at the age of five and took up composition when he was 12; later he studied music at the University of Michigan (BM 1963), where he also gained recognition as a jazz musician. He first worked with Paul Horn (1964–5), with whom he recorded his composition *Karen's World* (1966). Thereafter he performed briefly with Stan Kenton's Neophonic Orchestra (1966), Don Ellis (1967), and Tom Scott (1968), and from 1967 led his own trio. From the late 1960s he has been active as a studio musician and has written music for films and television; his writing and playing reflect his studio associations as well as the influence of rock. He has also recorded with such musicians as John Klemmer (1971) and Milt Jackson (1980–81).

SELECTED RECORDINGS

As sideman: P. Horn: *Monday, Monday* (1966, RCA LSP3613), incl. Karen's World; D. Ellis: *Shock Treatment* (1968, Col. CS9668); J. Klemmer: *Constant Throb* (1971, Imp. 9214)

BIBLIOGRAPHY

Feather '60s; *Feather–Gitler '70s*

ANDREW JAFFE

Lang, Ronnie [Langinger, Ronald] (*b* Chicago, 24 July 1927). Alto saxophonist. He first played in Hoagy Carmichael's band, then worked with Ike Carpenter (1947). He played and recorded with Les Brown (1949–50, 1953–6) and led his own West Coast jazz groups for recordings in 1955 and 1956, including *Modern Jazz* (1956, Tops 1521). From 1958 to 1960 he worked in television and film studios on the West Coast. His numerous recordings as a session musician, on some of which he played flute and other reeds besides alto saxophone, include those he made with Dave Pell (1953, 1957), Stan Kenton (1954), John Graas, Pete Rugolo, and Louis Armstrong (all 1956), Don Fagerquist (1957), Manny Klein (1958), Frank Sinatra and Henry Mancini (both 1960), Ella Fitzgerald (1962), Earl Hines (1963), and the producer Bob Thiele (1975). By the 1970s he had begun to perform on recordings for television, films, and advertising jingles, and ceased taking part in jazz or dance band sessions.

BIBLIOGRAPHY

FeatherE
D. Matthews: "First Call Man: ex-Les Brown, Henry Mancini altoist Ronnie Lang tells his story," *CI*, ix/8 (1971), 33; contd as "Studio Woodwind Players Must Cope with Anything, Says Ronnie Lang," ix/9 (1971), 14

Lang–Worth. Record company and label. The company was founded by Cy Langlois, and from the late 1930s into the 1940s it recorded a variety of jazz and popular music, which it issued on large discs that were sold to radio stations. The catalogue included important items by Fats Waller, Count Basie, Jimmie Lunceford, and John Kirby. It was sold to Fred Norman in the mid-1970s, and in August 1981 was purchased by George H. Buck's company Jazzology, which began the first systematic reissue program of Lang–Worth's material. ("Jazzology Acquires Lang–Worth and Riff," *CRC Newsletter*, vii/3 (1981), 2)

Lanigan, Jim [James Wood] (*b* Chicago, 30 Jan 1902; *d* Elburn, IL, 9 April 1983). Double bass and tuba player. His name is spelled Lannigan in some sources. His parents were both musicians and he studied violin and piano from an early age. He played piano and occasionally drums with the Austin High

The Mound City Blue Blowers, New York, 1924: (left to right) Dick Slevin, Jack Bland, Eddie Lang, and Red McKenzie

School Blue Friars before starting to play double bass and tuba. He worked with the bandleaders Husk O' Hare and Bill Paley (1926), with Red McKenzie's Mound City Blue Blowers, and for two years with the clarinetist Art Kassel. He recorded with the McKenzie–Condon Chicagoans (*Nobody's Sweetheart/Liza* (1927, OK 40971), on the two sides of which he plays respectively double bass and tuba), and with the Chicago Rhythm Kings and the Jungle Kings (both 1928). In the 1930s he played as a freelance musician with various groups, and for almost four years worked with the bandleader Ted Fio Rito. He was a staff musician at the NBC studios in Chicago (from 1937) and at the radio station WGN (1948–52); during this period he also recorded with Jimmy McPartland (1939), another group called the Jungle Kings, led by Bud Jacobson (1945), Bud Freeman (1946), and Danny Alvin (1950). From around 1953 to 1968 he played with the Chicago SO, but he continued to play jazz intermittently.

BIBLIOGRAPHY

FeatherE
F. Littler: "Home Cooking," *JM*, xi/6 (1965), 12 [interview]

based on *ChiltonW*

Lanigiros [Lanigiro Syncopating Melody Kings, Lanigiro Hot Players]. Swiss dance and show band. It was formed in Basle in 1924 by the tuba player Hans Philippi as a high school band called the Lanigiro Syncopating Melody Kings, which was also known as the Lanigiros (the name derives from the word "original" spelled backwards). It performed at dances and in theaters, broadcast on radio (from 1926), and was the first band entirely made up of Swiss musicians to record jazz (1929). It became professional in 1932 under the leadership of the alto saxophonist René Schmassmann and was renamed the Lanigiro Hot Players, though it was still referred to as the Lanigiros. During the 1930s it toured Germany, Belgium, and Switzerland, and recorded dance music for Odeon in Berlin (1937). Former sideman Bruno Bandini (tenor saxophone) became leader in 1939 and from 1941 to 1943 the band made several recordings in Zurich (including a version for quartet of *St. Louis Blues*, 1943, Col. ZZ1132). The number of players ranged from four to 15, and the personnel changed frequently: of the original members only the trumpeter and saxophonist Eric Landsrath remained by 1945. Among the principal soloists from 1941 were Rio de Gregori, the clarinetist and tenor saxophonist Fernand Clare, and the double bass player René Bertschi. The group disbanded in 1961. (R. Masopust: "Rheinster Jazz, Swiss Made: die Geschichte der Lanigiros," *Fox auf 78*, no.1 (Munich, 1986), 4; no.3 (1987), 22; no.4 (1987))

RAINER E. LOTZ

Lanoue, Conrad (T.) (*b* Cohoes, NY, 18 Oct 1908; *d* Albany, NY, 15 Oct 1972). Pianist and arranger. He studied at the Troy (New York) Conservatory and played his first engagements at a hotel in Cohoes, before working with Carmen Mastren and his brothers in and around Albany, New York. He recorded with Red McKenzie (1935), performed and recorded with the band of Eddie Farley and Mike Riley (1935–6), and played with Louis Prima; while he was a member of Wingy Manone's orchestra (1936–40) he also played and recorded with Joe Haymes (1937–8) and made arrangements for several big bands. From 1940 until the late 1960s he worked for long periods in the bands of Hal Landsberry, Charles Peterson, and Lester Lanin. His playing is well represented on Manone's *Boogie Woogie* (1939, Bb 10296).

based on *ChiltonW*

Lanphere, Don(ald Gale) (*b* Wenatchee, WA, 26 June 1928). Tenor, alto, and soprano saxophonist. He first achieved recognition in 1949 as the leader of a bop recording group, the other members of which were Fats Navarro, Al Haig, Tommy Potter, and Max Roach. He joined Woody Herman's band in 1949 as a replacement for Jimmy Giuffre, then recorded with Artie Shaw's big band and Gramercy Five (1950). After a period of retirement (1951–7) he worked in Boston with Herb Pomeroy and the trumpeter Joe Gordon, and in 1958–9 toured briefly with Charlie Barnet, Claude Thornhill, Billy May, and Urbie Green. He then re-joined Herman as his tenor saxophone soloist. He ceased playing again in 1961, but resumed in 1982, touring the USA and Europe, and recording several times as the leader of a quintet. Lanphere's playing has always been marked by fluency and control, particularly on faster tunes, such as *Go* (1949); but he also commands a superb lyricism, as in his own composition, *Infatuation*, recorded at the same session. His recordings from 1982 show that he has retained these qualities and acquired a broader, more expressive tone.

SELECTED RECORDINGS

As leader: Wailing Wall/Infatuation (1949, NewJ 819); Go/Stop (1949, NewJ 812); *Out of Nowhere* (1982, Hep 2019); *Into Somewhere* (1983, Hep 2022); *Don Loves Midge* (1985, Hep 2027)
As sideman: A. Shaw: Crumbum/The Shekomeko Shuffle (1950, Decca 27196); W. Herman: *The New Swingin' Herman Herd* (1960, Crown 5180), incl. Darn that Dream

BIBLIOGRAPHY

V. Simosko: "Artie Shaw and his Gramercy Fives," *JJS*, i/1 (1973), 34
A. Morgan: "Woody's Tenors," *JM*, vi (1960), no.7, p.4; no.8, p.13; (1961), no.12, p.9
M. Isherwood: "Out of Nowhere," *JJI*, xl/2 (1987), 6 [incl. discography]
L. Tomkins: "Don Lanphere: an Addiction to Music," *CI*, xxiv/1 (1987), 12
——: "Some Dates to Remember: Don Lanphere," *CI*, xxiv/11 (1988), 8

DAVE GELLY

LaPorta, John (D.) (*b* Philadelphia, 1 April 1920). Saxophonist, clarinetist, and teacher. He was a sideman in the big bands of Bob Chester (1942–4) and Woody Herman (1944–6; for illustration *see* HERMAN, WOODY, fig.1*a*), and studied with Lennie Tristano and other teachers; he also recorded with Tristano in 1947. With Teo Macero, Charles Mingus, and others, he was a founding member in 1953 of the Jazz Composers' Workshop; this established an experimental movement in New York which rivaled that in Los Angeles. LaPorta then began teaching at the Manhattan School of Music, and from 1959 into the 1980s he has served on the faculty at the Berklee College of Music, where he has also been active organizing summer schools.

LaPorta's early work as a clarinetist with Tristano shows not only an impressive instrumental technique but also an ability to realize faithfully the leader's ideas; the same facility is evident (in a different context) on two of Mingus's albums of 1954. LaPorta's own compositions, however, are not compelling, and his high-level involvement with jazz education betokens considerable responsibility for its lop-sided achievements so far.

SELECTED RECORDINGS

As leader: *Conceptions* (1956, Fan. 3228); *The Clarinet Artistry of John LaPorta* (1957, Fan. 3248); *Most Minor* (1958, Ev. 5037)
As sideman with C. Mingus: *The Moods of Mingus* (1954, Savoy 15050); *Jazzical Moods* (1954, Period 1107, 1111)

BIBLIOGRAPHY

FeatherE; *Feather–Gitler '70s*
B. Coss: "John LaPorta: a Clear Voice," *Metronome*, lxxi/2 (1955), 20
"The Two Sides of John LaPorta," *DB*, xxv/21 (1958), 18
J. Burns: "The Forgotten Boppers," *J&B*, ii/3 (1972), 4
B. Priestley: *Mingus: a Critical Biography* (London, Melbourne, Australia, and New York, 1982), 55

BRIAN PRIESTLEY

Larkin, Milt(on) [Tippy] (*b* Houston, 10 Oct 1910). Bandleader, trumpeter, and singer. His name is often misspelled Larkins. After building up a local reputation as a dynamic trumpeter and singer he formed his own big band in Houston in 1936. This toured extensively throughout the Southwest, and secured successful engagements in Kansas City, Chicago (1941–2), and New York (at the Apollo Theater). The group became one of the finest of the territory bands, and included such sidemen as Eddie "Cleanhead" Vinson, Illinois Jacquet, and Arnett Cobb. Larkin served in an army band from 1943 to 1946, then re-formed his big band, but failed to achieve his former success. He made his first recording, *Chicken Blues*, in 1946 (Stinson 455). Thereafter he led small touring groups, and in 1956 settled in New York and played a long residency with his swing septet at the Celebrity Club. In the mid-1970s he retired to Houston.

BIBLIOGRAPHY

F. Driggs: "The Story of Milton Larkin," *JM*, iv/10 (1958), 2
A. McCarthy: *Big Band Jazz* (New York and London, 1974), 109
T. Burke and D. Penny: "Comin' on with the Blues: Arnett Cobb, Milt Larkin, Floyd Ray," *Blues & Rhythm: the Gospel Truth*, no.5 (1984), 20
"Milt Larkin and Arnett Cobb Revisited," *Blues & Rhythm: the Gospel Truth*, no.10 (1985), 21

BOB WEIR

Larkins, Ellis (Lane) (*b* Baltimore, 15 May 1923). Pianist. He studied at the Peabody Conservatory and in 1940 at the Juilliard School; in 1942 he made his début as a jazz musician in a trio led by the guitarist Billy Moore at Café Society in New York, where he later led his own trio. From 1943 to 1952 he worked sporadically in New York at the Blue Angel and in 1945–6 played at Café Society in Edmond Hall's sextet. After working for many years as a vocal coach and as an accompanist for Ella Fitzgerald, Helen Humes, and Joe Williams (on the West Coast from 1968), he performed at Town Hall in New York (1973) and toured South America with Marian McPartland, Teddy Wilson, and Earl Hines (1974). From around 1978 to around 1981 he worked in New York at such clubs as Gregory's, Michael's Pub, the Cookery, and Carnegie Tavern. In his early work (such as his first take of *Caravan*, 1944) Larkins adhered to the conventions of swing. Like Wilson he played long melodies with the right hand that outlined chords and consistently used dotted rhythms. His mature style is subtle and understated, and well suited to accompanying singers. It is characterized by a delicate, even touch, widely spaced chords, dynamics that seldom exceed *mezzo-forte*, and slow to moderate tempos; melodic lines and gestures tend to be brief but intricate and embellished. He often juxtaposes duple meter against triple meter, and simple chord progressions in the left hand (such as I–vi–ii–V) against unexpected nonharmonic tones in the right; this may be heard on his recording *Perfidia* (1974). His tendency to play slightly ahead of the beat when accompanying singers is well illustrated by his recording with Ella Fitzgerald of *Looking for a Boy* (1950).

SELECTED RECORDINGS

As unaccompanied soloist: on M. McPartland, T. Wilson, E. Larkins, and E. Hines: *Concert in Argentina* (1974, Hal. 113), Blues in the Night, Perfidia
Duos: with E. Fitzgerald: on *Ella Sings Gershwin* (1950, Decca 74451), Looking for a Boy, Maybe; on *Ella* (1954, Decca 8068), Nice Work if you can Get it; with R. Braff: *The Grand Reunion* (1972, Chi. 117)
As leader: *A Smooth One* (1977, BB 33123); *Swingin' for Hamp* (1979, Conc. 134)
As sideman: E. Hall: first issued on *Rompin' in '44* (1944, Cir. [US] 52), Caravan [1st take], The Man I Love [3rd take]; R. Braff: *Holiday in Braff* (1955, Beth. 1032)

BIBLIOGRAPHY

J. S. Wilson: "Larkins Weaves Keyboard Moods," *New York Times* (24 June 1972), 19
M. Gardner: "Ellis Larkins: the Melody Comes First," *JJ*, xxix/7 (1976), 8
N. Hentoff: Liner notes, *A Smooth One* (BB 33123, 1977)
J. S. Wilson: "Ellis Larkins Plays Jazz on August Forster Piano," *New York Times* (15 April 1978), 15
W. Balliett: "Einfühlung," *New Yorker*, liv (18 Dec 1978), 41; repr. in *Jelly Roll, Jabbo and Fats* (New York, and Oxford, England, 1983), 129

PAUL S. MACHLIN

La Roca, Pete [Sims, Peter] (*b* New York, 7 April 1938). Drummer. He studied classical percussion at the High School of Music and Art and the Manhattan School of Music. He adopted the name Pete La Roca when he played timbales in Latin bands but prefers the name Peter Sims. He was a member of Sonny Rollins's band from October 1957 to February 1959, then played with a number of leaders, including Jackie McLean, Slide Hampton, Tony Scott, John Coltrane (1960), and Marian McPartland (1962), and, in the later 1960s, Art Farmer, Charles Lloyd, Paul Bley, and Steve Kuhn; he also led his own group (1961–2) and was house drummer at the Jazz Workshop in Boston (1963–4). In 1968, discouraged by the dominance of rock and jazz-rock, he abandoned his musical career and became a lawyer; he resumed playing occasionally in 1979. La Roca's style was somewhat advanced; he used various components of the drum set to keep time, and improvised solos that had changing or imperceptible meters.

Oral history material in *NjR*.

SELECTED RECORDINGS

As leader: *Basra* (1965, BN 84205); *Turkish Women at the Baths* (1967, Douglas 782)
As sideman: S. Rollins: on *A Night at the Village Vanguard* (1958, BN 1581), A Night in Tunisia; J. McLean: *New Soil* (1959, BN 4013), incl. Minor Apprehension; S. Hampton: *Somethin' Sanctified* (1960, Atl. 1362); P. Bley: *Footloose* (1962–3, Savoy 12182); A. Farmer: *Sing me Softly of the Blues* (1965, Atl. 1442); S. Kuhn: *Three Waves* (1966, Contact 5)

BIBLIOGRAPHY

I. Gitler: "Pete La Roca," *DB*, xxxi/8 (1964), 20
D. C. Hunt: "Pete La Roca: is Individuality Futile?" *J&P*, viii/7 (1969), 44
J. Pareles: "Lawyer-Drummer Makes a Case for his Day Gig," *New York Times* (15 Oct 1982), §C, p.6

J. KENT WILLIAMS

LaRocca, Nick [Dominic James] (*b* New Orleans, 11 April 1889; *d* New Orleans, 22 Feb 1961). Cornetist. He was self-taught, and became associated at an early age with other young white musicians in New Orleans, including the Brunies brothers and Eddie Edwards, with whom he was a member of Johnny Stein's Dixie Jass Band. After leaving Stein, Edwards and LaRocca formed with others the group that later became known as the ORIGINAL DIXIELAND JAZZ BAND, which played in Chicago in 1916 and achieved outstanding popularity in New York the following year. LaRocca remained with the group until it disbanded in 1925. Thereafter most of his musical activities revolved around re-creations and revivals of the Original Dixieland Jazz Band, though he also led a 14-piece swing band. After the Original Dixieland Jazz Band disbanded permanently in 1938, LaRocca returned to New Orleans, where he ran his own business; he did not perform again regularly.

There is no doubt about LaRocca's importance as the driving organizational force behind the Original Dixieland Jazz Band. He also instigated a style of cornet playing that was later adopted by Bix Beiderbecke, who was one of the band's admirers; the steady drive and rhythmic freedom of LaRocca's playing on the band's recordings of 1936 are particularly enlightening evidence of this connection. LaRocca also wrote such standards as *At the Jazz Band Ball* and *Clarinet Marmalade* (which was sometimes known as *Clarinet Marmalade Blues*). His collection of scores played by the Original Dixieland Jazz Band, together with other materials, is in the William Ransom Hogan Jazz Archive at Tulane University in New Orleans; *see* LIBRARIES AND ARCHIVES, §2.

SELECTED RECORDINGS

(all recorded for Victor as sideman with the Original Dixieland Jazz Band)

Livery Stable Blues/Dixie Jass Band One-step (1917, 18255); At the Jazz Band Ball (1918, 18457); Skeleton Jangle/Tiger Rag (1918, 18472); Clarinet Marmalade Blues/Mournin' Blues (1918, 18513); Tiger Rag/Skeleton Jangle (1936, 25524); Clarinet Marmalade/Bluin' the Blues (1936, 25525); Barnyard Blues/Original Dixieland One-step (1936, 25502)

BIBLIOGRAPHY

ChiltonW; *FeatherE*

Obituary, *DB*, xxviii/8 (1961), 13

F. Gillis: "Biography of a Jazz Tune: Livery Stable Blues?? Barnyard Blues," *JJ*, xvi/6 (1963), 25

For further bibliography *see* ORIGINAL DIXIELAND JAZZ BAND.

RICHARD SUDHALTER

Larsson, Rolf (*b* Linköping, Sweden, 28 Jan 1918). Swedish pianist. He played in orchestras led by Sune Lundvall, Håkan von Eichwald, Lulle Ellboj (1943–7), and Seymour Österwall and in the late 1950s and early 1960s belonged to Harry Arnold's Swedish Radio Big Band; he recorded as a sideman with Ellboj (1945), Anders Burman (1951, 1954), James Moody (1951), and Gösta Törner (1964) and as a leader from 1954. In the 1960s he performed and made many recordings with Ove Lind and other Swedish swing musicians; he also recorded with Bjarne Nerem (1971). Larsson's piano playing, which recalls the work of Teddy Wilson, may be heard to advantage on his album *Swing and Dance* (1972, Polar 248).

BIBLIOGRAPHY

"Svenskt stjärnalbum" [Swedish star-album], *Orkester journalen*, xii (1944), Dec, 5

A. von Konow: "Rolf Larsson, aktuell pianistveteran," *Orkester journalen*, xxxix (1971), Feb, 10

ERIK KJELLBERG

Lasha [Lawsha], **Prince** [William B.] (*b* Fort Worth, 10 Sept 1929). Alto saxophonist and flutist. He played in a local jazz group with Ornette Coleman. After touring the South with territory bands, he moved to California (1954), where he performed and later recorded two free-jazz albums with Sonny Simmons (including *The Cry*, 1962, Cont. 7610). In New York he led a group at Birdland and played with Eric Dolphy; he recorded with Dolphy and the sextet led by Elvin Jones and Jimmy Garrison (both 1963). In 1965 Lasha recorded as a leader and moved to Europe, where he recorded again the following year. After returning to California, he performed with Harold Land, Bobby Hutcherson, and Charles Moffett, and made recordings with his own band (1967, 1976, *c*1983); he also recorded with Michael White (i) in 1973.

BIBLIOGRAPHY

Feather '60s

E. Romero: "Prince Lawsha: a Short Talk," *Cadence*, vii/6 (1981), 10

Lateef, Yusef [Evans, Bill [William]] (*b* Chattanooga, TN, 9 Oct 1920). Tenor saxophonist and composer. He moved with his family to Detroit at the age of five and in 1938 took up the tenor saxophone, which he studied with Teddy Buckner. He worked with Lucky Millinder (1946), Hot Lips Page, Roy Eldridge, and Herbie Fields (1946–8) and, after moving to Chicago in 1948, with Dizzy Gillespie (for ten months, 1949–50). He returned to Detroit, where he studied flute and composition at Wayne State University. He took the Muslim name Yusef Lateef in the mid-1950s. He led quintets from 1955 to 1959 with Curtis Fuller and Wilbur Harden, and during that period worked with Kenny Burrell (1958), at whose suggestion he began to perform as a flutist. After moving to New York in 1959 he played with Charles Mingus (with whom he recorded in 1960), Donald Byrd, Cannonball Adderley (1962–4), and Grant Green. He continued to perform and record as a leader and sideman during the following decades and in the 1980s taught in Nigeria. Lateef gained recognition early in his career for the use in his groups of Asian and Middle Eastern rhythms and instruments; among the latter were *arghūl* (a double clarinet that sounds similar to a bassoon), *śahnāī* (a North Indian oboe), *algaita* (a West African oboe), and various flutes (including a bamboo flute and a "pneumatic" bamboo flute, both homemade instruments).

Yusef Lateef

In his pursuit of varied tone-colors he also played oboe and bassoon (see illustration), but he was noted above all for his full, sturdy sound on tenor saxophone and tasteful solos on flute. His later performances were characterized by a populist mysticism, as are his later recordings. In addition to his work in jazz Lateef has been active as a painter and writer, and has composed works for flute and piano and for chamber ensemble.

SELECTED RECORDINGS

The Dreamer (1959, Savoy 12139); *Eastern Sounds* (1961, Mdsv. 22); *Club Date* (1964, Imp. 9310); *Psychicemotus* (1965, Imp. 92); *The Golden Flute* (1966, Imp. 9125); *Yusef Lateef* (*c*1968, Cadet 816); *In a Temple Garden* (1979, CTI 7088)

BIBLIOGRAPHY

Feather '60s; *Feather–Gitler '70s*

D. Gold: "Yusef Lateef," *DB*, xxv/9 (1958), 18

J. Cooke: "Yusef Lateef," *JM*, ix/5 (1963), 12 [incl. discography by A. Cooke]

P. Welding: "Music as Color: Yusef Lateef," *DB*, xxxii/11 (1965), 20

L. Feather: *The Pleasures of Jazz: Leading Performers on their Lives, their Music, their Contemporaries* (New York, 1976)

L. Lyons: "Life Begins at 60," *DB*, xlv/6 (1978), 17
A. Groves: "Consistent Craftsman," *JJI*, xxxiii/9 (1980), 14
J. M. Whalen: "Yusef Lateef: Interview," *Cadence*, viii/10 (1982), 9

LEE JESKE/R

Lateral cut recording. A term applied to a sound-recording technique in which, in both recording and playback, the stylus moves from side to side in the spiral groove on a disc; *see* Recording, esp. §I, 1(i).

Latin jazz. A term applied to jazz in which elements of Latin American music, chiefly its dance rhythms, are particularly prominent. In striking contrast to most genres of jazz, in which triple subdivisions of the beat are prevalent, Latin jazz utilizes duple subdivisions. But unlike the rhythms of ragtime and jazz-rock, where the beat also undergoes duple subdivision, Latin-jazz rhythms are constructed from multiples of a basic durational unit, grouped unequally so that the accents fall irregularly in a one- or two-bar pattern. The habanera (or danza) rhythm (ex.1) is the simplest and most common of these

Ex.1 Habanera rhythm

groupings. The rhythmic ostinato may be played by members of a conventional rhythm section (piano, guitar, double bass, and drums) or by Latin American instruments, particularly Afro-Cuban or Brazilian percussion such as the conga drum, bongos, cowbells, and cuíca; the bass line often oscillates between the roots and fifths of chords.

Latin American elements are found in early jazz and related musics. Isolated instances of habanera rhythm, which also formed the basis of the tango, occur in left-hand figurations of some published piano rags (Neil Moret's *Cubanola (Cuban Danza)*, 1902; Scott Joplin and Louis Chauvin's *Heliotrope Bouquet*, 1907; Joe Jordan's *Tango: Two Step*, 1913; and Artie Matthews's *Pastime Rag no.5*, 1918), as well as in the second section of W. C. Handy's famous *St. Louis Blues* (1914). These rhythmic patterns were probably carried over into the earliest jazz, though the lack of recordings from this era makes it difficult to establish the sequence of development. By 1923, at all events, Latin ostinatos were part of Jelly Roll Morton's style: in his recordings of *New Orleans Joys* (also known as *New Orleans Blues*; 1923, Gen. 5486) and portions of *Mamamita* (1924, Gen. 5632) he maintains a habanera rhythm in his left hand. Morton referred to this rhythmic element as the "Spanish tinge," and claimed that it was essential to jazz.

During the 1930s new Latin dances entered the mainstream of American popular music through bandleaders such as Don Azpiazú (who popularized the rumba) and Xavier Cugat. They occasionally found their way into jazz, as in Duke Ellington's recordings of two compositions by his Puerto Rican trombonist Juan Tizol: *Caravan* (1937) and *Conga Brava* (1940). In the 1940s Cuban instruments and instrumentalists became firmly linked to jazz through a reciprocal process. In New York in the early part of the decade Machito formed the Afro-Cubans, in which big-band instrumentation and arranging techniques were combined with Cuban percussion and musical structures; from 1948 to the 1960s he engaged famous jazzmen, including Brew Moore, Charlie Parker, Flip Phillips, Howard McGhee, Cannonball Adderley, Cecil Payne, and Johnny Griffin, as soloists. In 1947 Dizzy Gillespie established his Afro-Cuban jazz orchestra, which included the conga drummer Chano Pozo, and in the same year Stan Kenton introduced the Brazilian guitarist Laurindo Almeida and the bongo drummer Jack Costanzo into his jazz orchestra.

During the 1950s another generation of Latin dances became popular in the USA: the mambo, the merengue, and the cha cha cha were quickly incorporated into the repertories of big bands that played jazz for dancing. In small bop groups Latin tunes regularly supplemented the normal fare of swing standards, ballads, and blues; examples include Parker's *My Little Suede Shoes* (1951, Mer./Clef 11093) and Bud Powell's *Un poco loco* (1951, BN 1577). Latin elements became so integral to the bop style that by the late 1950s their presence was no longer remarkable; but some bop musicians laid particular emphasis on Latin sounds, among them George Shearing, Cal Tjader, Sonny Rollins (a composer of and improviser on calypso tunes), Horace Silver, and Herbie Mann.

The 1960s witnessed the emergence of strong Brazilian influences on jazz. The energetic Samba and the quiet Bossa nova reached a wide audience through the recordings of Stan Getz, Charlie Byrd, Astrud Gilberto, and Antonio Carlos Jobim. Cuban elements continued to be prevalent, both through bop and in the music of Mongo Santamaria and Willie Bobo, whose bands combined popular songs, Cuban vamps, and impassioned hard-bop improvisations. In the late 1960s Airto Moreira initiated a second period of Brazilian influence by introducing Brazilian rhythms and dozens of native instruments into jazz-rock groups in the USA. He recorded with Miles Davis (whose many improvisations on Spanish flamenco music are perhaps related to Latin jazz); during the early 1970s he was the first of a series of Brazilian percussionists in the group Weather Report, and he was a member of the earliest of Chick Corea's groups called Return to Forever, as was his wife, Flora Purim.

Other facets of Latin jazz developed within free jazz, a music that encourages experimentation in various ethnic styles. During the 1970s Gato Barbieri made many recordings in which his wildly energetic tenor saxophone playing is combined with Argentinian rhythmic vamps. In 1978 the Art Ensemble of Chicago recorded a playful distortion of reggae music, *Ja* (on the album *Nice Guys*, ECM 1126), and in 1981 Oliver Lake founded Jump Up, a commercial reggae group. Two musicians embody the continued influence of Latin music on jazz in the 1980s: Naną Vasconcelos has been a member of Pat Metheny's jazz-rock groups and of the free-jazz trio Codona, while Paquito D'Rivera leads small bop groups in performances of Afro-Cuban jazz.

See also Afro-cuban jazz.

BIBLIOGRAPHY

J.-E. Berendt: *Das Jazzbuch: Entwicklung und Bedeutung der Jazzmusik* (Frankfurt am Main, Germany, 1953, rev. 2/1959 as *Das neue Jazzbuch*, Eng. trans., New York, 1962; rev. and enlarged 5/1981 as *Das grosse Jazzbuch: von New Orleans bis Jazz Rock*, Eng. trans. as *The Jazz Book: from New Orleans to Fusion and Beyond*, Westport, CT, 1982)
M. Williams: "Jelly Roll Morton," *Jazz: New Perspectives on the History of Jazz*, ed. N. Hentoff and A. J. McCarthy (New York, 1959/*R*1974)
G. Lees: "Jazz in Latin America," *DB*, xxix/28 (1962), 16
J. S. Roberts: "Latin Persuasions: a Brief Overview of a Vital Musical Genre," *DB*, xliv/8 (1977), 13
——: *The Latin Tinge: the Impact of Latin American Music on the United States* (New York, and Oxford, England, 1979)
E. A. Berlin: *Ragtime: a Musical and Cultural History* (Berkeley, CA, Los Angeles, and London, 1980/*R*1984 with addns), 115

BARRY KERNFELD

Lattimore, Harlan (*b* Cincinnati, 1908). Singer. The son of an opera singer, he began his career performing regularly on radio station WLW in Cincinnati. In 1932 he joined Don Redman, with whom he worked throughout the 1930s, though he also recorded with the bands of Fletcher Henderson (1932) and Victor Young (1934). After World War II he ceased to be active as a professional musician. Lattimore is heard to advantage on Redman's *Who wants to sing my love song?* (1936, Voc. 3354).

based on *ChiltonW*

Laurence, Baby [Jackson, Laurence] (*b* Baltimore, 1921). Singer and tap-dancer. He first sang professionally at the age of 11, touring with Don Redman. During a period at Dickie Wells's club in New York he learned to tap-dance, and from the mid-1930s he performed with several dance groups. He worked steadily during the 1940s, appearing with the bands of Count Basie, Woody Herman, Duke Ellington, Art Tatum, and others. Laurence emphasized footwork, performing tap-dances almost as if they were drum solos; he was one of the few jazz dancers who felt comfortable with the rhythms of bop. Illness prevented him from working for many years, but he later recorded as a leader the album *Dancemaster* (*c*1958–60, CJ 30), accompanied by such all-star musicians as Paul Quinichette, Bobby Jaspar, and Roland Hanna. In 1960 he worked regularly as a tap-dancer with Charles Mingus's quintet at the Showplace in New York. In 1961 he appeared with Count Basie's band at the Apollo Theatre, and the following year he performed at the Newport Jazz Festival. After returning to Baltimore in 1965 he went into semiretirement. (M. Stearns and J. Stearns: "Baby Laurence and the Hoofers Club," *Jazz Dance: the Story of American Vernacular Dance* (New York and London, 1968), 337)

RAINER E. LOTZ

Laurence, Chris(topher Anthony) (*b* London, 6 Jan 1949). English double bass player. He performed with the London Youth Jazz Orchestra (1964–6), studied at the Guildhall School of Music (1966–9), and in the late 1960s played and recorded with Vic Ash and Frank Ricotti. During the 1970s he worked in various groups led by Alan Skidmore (1970–77) and performed and recorded with such musicians as Harry Beckett (1970–72), John Surman and John Taylor (both 1973), Elton Dean (1976–7), and Keith Tippett (1977); he also maintained a long association with Mike Westbrook, with whom he recorded intermittently between 1969 and 1980. Thereafter Laurence has played for Kenny Wheeler (from 1981), in a trio with Tony Coe and Tony Oxley (1983), in a group with Ricotti, Taylor, the keyboard player Tony Hymas, and the saxophonist Stan Sulzmann (1985), and with Coe and Hymas in the trio Three (from 1987). He can be heard as a member of the group Paragonne on the album *Aspects of Paragonne* (1985, MMC 010). Laurence has pursued a parallel career as a classical double bass player.

BIBLIOGRAPHY

R. Cotterell, ed.: *Jazz Now: the Jazz Centre Society Guide* (London, 1976), 142

I. Carr: "Laurence, Chris (Christopher Anthony)," in I. Carr, D. Fairweather, and B. Priestley: *Jazz: the Essential Companion* (London, 1987), 293

SIMON ADAMS

Laurence, Claude. Pseudonym of ANDRÉ HODEIR.

Laurie, Cy(ril) (*b* London, 20 April 1926). English clarinetist. He was self-taught. In 1947 he formed his own band, with which George Melly made his first appearance the following year. After playing with the trumpeter Mike Daniels (1949–50), he began leading the Cy Laurie Four (1950), which included Fred Hunt and the trumpeter and cornetist Les Jowett. From 1951 he ran a club in London, where he performed with his own seven-piece band; among his sidemen were Chris Barber and the trumpeters Alan Elsdon, Al Fairweather, and Colin Smith. He ceased to play between 1960 and the early 1970s, then re-emerged to work with a band of his own. In the late 1970s Laurie resumed an active career as a musician; he toured widely as a guest soloist and occasionally with his own groups, and played with a quintet, which he led with the saxophonist Eggy Ley. He performed in Max Collie's show *New Orleans Mardi Gras*. His recordings as a leader include *Shades of Cy* (1984, Sunstreamer 12LA1).

BIBLIOGRAPHY

R. Harris: *Jazz* (London, 1952, 5/1957), 239

C. Bielderman: *Cy Laurie, Eggy Ley: Discography* (Zwolle, Netherlands, 1986)

D. Fairweather: "Laurie, Cy," in I. Carr, D. Fairweather, and B. Priestley: *Jazz: the Essential Companion* (London, 1987)

NEVIL SKRIMSHIRE

LaVere, Charlie [Johnson, Charles LaVere] (*b* Salina, KS, 18 July 1910; *d* Ramona, CA, 28 April 1983). Pianist, bandleader, and singer. He played alto saxophone, trombone, and trumpet, and sang, but was principally a pianist. In 1933 he played with Wingy Manone, and recorded with Jack Teagarden in Chicago. A recording he made in 1935 with his own all-star group (which included Jabbo Smith and Zutty Singleton) was first issued on an unnumbered disc on the Black Diamond label and later released on *Chicago in the 30s* (Tax M8007); *Boogaboo Blues* from this session well represents his style as a pianist. He played with Paul Whiteman (1937) and Frankie Trumbauer, and recorded with Ben Pollack, Connee Boswell, and Hoagy Carmichael (all 1938), and the Casa Loma Orchestra (1941). From 1939 to 1947 he accompanied Bing Crosby and in the latter year made a hit recording as a popular singer. He also composed several pieces, including *Cuban Boogie Woogie*, which was recorded by Charlie Barnet (1939) and Andy Kirk (1941). He led his own groups from the mid-1940s to the mid-1950s; among his sidemen were Joe Venuti, Matty Matlock, George Van Eps, and Nick Fatool. During this period he also recorded with Billie Holiday (1950) and Louis Armstrong (1951). He played at Disneyland, California (1955–9), then led his own sextet in New York (1960) and worked with Bob Crosby and Wingy Manone (1961–3). (*ChiltonW*)

LaVerne, Andy (*b* New York, ?1948). Pianist and keyboard player. He attended Ithaca College and studied briefly at the Berklee College of Music in Boston. After performing popular music in Boston during the early 1970s, he returned to New York. He toured in Europe and the Americas with Woody Herman from 1973 to 1975 and also recorded with the band. He then played a blend of jazz-rock and free jazz with John Abercrombie and Miroslav Vitous, and recorded bop with Lee Konitz (1976) and Eddie Daniels (1977). From 1977 to 1980 he toured and recorded with Stan Getz; he wrote a symphony for Getz and the Buffalo PO. He has recorded albums with his own groups (including *Another World*, 1977, Ste. 1086) and in 1977 formed a duo with Mike Richmond. In the 1980s he performed and recorded with the Brubeck–LaVerne Trio, the other members of which were the electric bass guitarist Chris Brubeck and the drummer Dan Brubeck. (L. Jeske: "Andy Laverne," *DB*, xlvii/8 (1980), 52)

Lawrence, Arnie [Finkelstein, Arnold Lawrence] (*b* New York, 10 July 1938). Alto saxophonist. He first played the clarinet (from 1951), but while at high school changed to tenor saxophone and then to alto saxophone. After working for two years in Chicago he moved to Los Angeles, where he played with Les McCann and Bob Whitlock. He then returned to the East Coast; he played regularly in a band in the Catskill Mountains, and in 1965 began to work with Clark Terry, Urbie Green, Doc Severinsen, Rusty Dedrick, and Budd Johnson, among others. From 1967 to 1972 he played in Severinsen's orchestra on the television program the "Tonight Show"; around the same time he also performed with Frank Foster (1966), Johnny Richards (1966, 1968), Duke Pearson (1967–8), and Chico Hamilton (from 1967). While continuing to work intermittently with Hamilton until the mid-1970s, he played with Terry's big band (from 1973), Blood, Sweat and Tears (1974), and Chuck Israels's National Jazz Ensemble. At various times Lawrence also led groups under such names as Children of All Ages and Treasure Island. He recorded with Louie Bellson's big band in 1980, and in 1980–81 worked (with support from the National Endowment for the Arts) as jazz artist-in-residence at Shelbyville, Kentucky.

SELECTED RECORDINGS

As leader: *Look Toward a Dream* (1968, Project 3 5028); Renewal (1981, PAlt 8033)

As sideman: C. Hamilton: *The Dealer* (1966, Imp. 9130); J. Richards: *Aqui se habla Español* (1966, Roul. 25351); C. Hamilton: *Peregrinations* (1975, BN LA520G); C. Israels: *National Jazz Ensemble*, i (1976, Chi. 151)

BIBLIOGRAPHY

Feather–Gitler '70s
J. C. Thomas: "Tonight: Arnie Lawrence," *DB*, xxxv/10 (1968), 18
M. Bourne: "Profile: Arnie Lawrence," *DB*, xli/18 (1974), 36

DAVID WILD

Lawrence, Azar (*b* Los Angeles, 3 Nov 1953). Saxophonist. He studied piano and violin from the age of five, abandoned these for alto saxophone around 1965, and took up tenor saxophone in 1970 and soprano saxophone in 1972. He played with Horace Tapscott in Los Angeles and studied informally with Arthur Blythe; later he toured Europe with Clark Terry (1970) and played with Ike and Tina Turner and with the Watts 103rd Street Rhythm Band. In February 1973 he joined Elvin Jones's group, which he left in May to join McCoy Tyner's quartet. During nearly four years with the quartet he also recorded two albums as a leader and performed with Miles Davis. After leaving Tyner in 1976 he recorded a more commercially oriented album, *People Moving*. He has remained active as a leader and a sideman. Like several saxophonists who played with Jones and Tyner, Lawrence has assimilated and simplified somewhat the style of John Coltrane.

SELECTED RECORDINGS

As leader: *Bridge into the New Age* (1974, Prst. 10086); *Summer Solstice* (1975, Prst. 10097); *People Moving* (1976, Prst. 10099)

As sideman: M. Tyner: *Enlightenment* (1973, Mlst. 55001); *Sama Layuca* (1974, Mlst. 9056); E. Jones: *New Agenda* (1975, Van. 79362)

BIBLIOGRAPHY

G. Perla: "Steve Grossman–Azar Lawrence: a Session with Gene Perla," *DB*, xl/15 (1973), 18
L. Lyons: "Moving into Tomorrow: Azar Lawrence," *DB*, xliii/16 (1976), 16 [incl. discography]

DAVID WILD

Lawrence, Elliot(t) [Broza, Elliott Lawrence] (*b* Philadelphia, 14 Feb 1925). Bandleader, arranger, composer, and pianist. After studying music at the University of Pennsylvania, he led a series of dance bands, which gave radio performances (1945–6) and made several recordings (to 1960, including *Elevation*, 1949, Col. 38497); they played arrangements by Lawrence himself and by Gerry Mulligan and Al Cohn. He played piano on cool-jazz recordings by the Four Brothers and Manny Albam (both 1957) and on Woody Herman's recording of Stravinsky's *Ebony Concerto* (1958). During the 1950s he led a small group on Jack Sterling's radio show and in 1959 he visited Moscow and Leningrad on a tour sponsored by the State Department. While continuing to lead his bands, he began in the 1960s to compose, write arrangements, and conduct for television, films, and the Broadway theater.

BIBLIOGRAPHY

FeatherE
G. T. Simon: *The Big Bands* (New York, 1967, rev. and enlarged 2/1971, rev. 4/1981)
C. Garrod: *Elliot Lawrence and his Orchestra* (Spotswood, NJ, and Zephyrhills, FL, 1974) [discography]

Laws, Hubert (*b* Houston, 10 Nov 1939). Flutist, brother of Ronnie Laws. He began his career in Texas with the Crusaders and at the same time studied and performed classical music in Houston. In the 1960s and 1970s he made many recordings for Atlantic and CTI and played for several years in the New York Jazz Sextet (formed *c*1967); his work helped to make the flute popular as a jazz instrument. During this period he was also a member of the Metropolitan Opera Orchestra in New York and played with the New York PO. In the 1980s he took part in several concerts with the classical flutist Jean-Pierre Rampal and continued to record jazz in a largely commercial vein. Laws's clear, full sound and accurate intonation have made him widely popular both in jazz and classical music; in jazz, which is the genre he has emphasized in his work as a soloist, he is one of few musicians to play the flute exclusively (*see* FLUTE, §2 and fig.2).

SELECTED RECORDINGS

The Laws of Jazz (1964, Atl. 1432); *Crying Song* (1970, CTI 1002); *Afro Classic* (1971, CTI 6006); *Morning Star* (1972, CTI 6022); *At Carnegie Hall* (1973, CTI 6025); *How to Beat the High Cost of Living* (1980, Col. JS36741)

BIBLIOGRAPHY

Feather '60s; *Feather–Gitler '70s*
J. Schaffer: "In Review," *DB*, xl/16 (1973), 13
C. Berg: "Pied Piper of Houston," *DB*, xliv/10 (1977), 15

LEE JESKE/R

Laws, Ronnie [Ronald] (*b* Houston, 3 Oct 1950). Tenor saxophonist and leader, brother of Hubert Laws. He played saxophone from the age of 12, studied flute at Stephen F. Austin State University, and attended Texas Southern University. After moving to Los Angeles (1971) he performed with Quincy Jones, Hugh Masekela, and Kenny Burrell, and played and recorded bop with Walter Bishop, Jr. (1973). He then began to play with jazz musicians whose style was influenced by popular music, and recorded with his brother Hubert (1974) and Ramsey Lewis (1977); he also performed with the soul group Earth, Wind and Fire for 18 months. The soulful *Pressure Sensitive* (1975, BN LA452G), his finest album, was the first of his recordings as a leader (1975–8, 1984), though his playing may be heard to advantage during his solos on *Moments Notice* and *Mean Lane* on his brother's album *In the Beginning* (1974, CTI 6065). (J. Coryell and L. Friedman: *Jazz-rock Fusion* (New York and London, 1978), 244)

Lawsha, Prince. *See* LASHA, PRINCE.

Lawson, Harry [Big Jim] (*b* Round Rock, TX, 25 Dec 1904). Trumpeter. He played trombone as well as trumpet for several years, working in circus and carnival bands, before joining Terrence Holder. His principal association was with Andy Kirk, with whom he played regularly until the 1940s and then (after abandoning a full-time career in music) intermittently until 1956.

based on *ChiltonW*

Lawson, (Richard) Hugh (Jerome) (*b* Detroit, 12 March 1935). Pianist, composer, and arranger. From 1956 he performed and recorded as a member of quartets and quintets led by Yusef Lateef, first in Detroit, and from the late 1950s to 1960 in New York, where he later recorded as a sideman with Harry Edison (1962) and Roy Brooks (1963, 1970), again with Lateef (1966, 1968), and with Kenny Burrell (1971). He was a founding member in 1972 of the Piano Choir, a group of seven pianists for which he wrote compositions (including *Ballad for the Beast from Bali Bali*, recorded on the album *Handscapes*, ii, 1974) and arrangements. He toured Europe with Charles Mingus in the autumn of 1975, and, under the sponsorship of the US State Department, Eastern Europe with Mingus in 1977 and the Middle East in 1981–2; he also recorded with Charlie Rouse (1977), his own trio (1977, 1983), and two of Mingus's former sidemen, George Adams and Dannie Richmond, in Milan (1980, 1983). Lawson has taught composition and jazz improvisation at the Henry Street Settlement in New York. He has a formidable technique and a style reminiscent of that of Bud Powell.

SELECTED RECORDINGS

As leader: *Prime Time* (1977, Sto. 4708); *Colour* (1983, SN 1052)
As sideman: Y. Lateef: *The Sounds of Yusef* (1957, Prst. 7122); *Cry! Tender* (1959, NewJ 8234); *The Golden Flute* (1966, Imp. 9125); Piano Choir: *Handscapes*, i (1972, SE 19730); *Handscapes*, ii (1974, SE 19750), incl. Ballad for the Beast from Bali Bali; G. Adams and D. Richmond: *Hand to Hand* (1980, SN 1007)

BIBLIOGRAPHY

Feather E; *Feather–Gitler '70s*
R. Spencer: "Hugh Lawson: *Prime Time*," *JJI*, xxxvi/6 (1983), 30 [review]
W. F. Lee: "Richard Hugh Jerome Lawson," *People in Jazz: Jazz Keyboard Improvisors of the 19th and 20th Centuries* (Hialeah, FL, 1984)

GREGORY E. SMITH

Lawson, Janet (*b* Baltimore, 13 Nov 1940). Singer. Her mother was a singer and her father a drummer. She began performing on radio as a small child, and later appeared on regional television. During her teens she sang in musicals in Baltimore. After performing with local jazz bands she moved in 1960 to New York, where she worked at the Village Vanguard with Art Farmer, and at other clubs with Ron Carter, Duke Pearson, Chick Corea, Eddie Gomez, and others. Thereafter she toured extensively, singing in a jazz-oriented style at nightclubs, visiting the Caribbean, South America, and the Far East. She appeared regularly on Steve Allen's television show (1968–9), then retired temporarily from music and worked in theater, but a performance with Duke Ellington (1971) marked the start of a gradual return to jazz. In the early 1970s she toured with a trio; in 1976 she formed a quintet with which she later recorded two superb albums. She has worked frequently in the 1980s with the singer Judy Niemack, and has also been active as a teacher, serving as head of the vocal jazz program at William Paterson College, New Jersey. Lawson is an expert scat singer and improviser with a four octave range. She augments her technique with such sounds as bird-calls, moans, and tongue-clicks.

SELECTED RECORDINGS

As leader: *The Janet Lawson Quintet* (1980, IC 1116); *Dreams can be* (1983, Omni. 1052)
As sideman: on E. Jefferson: *The Main Man* (1977, IC 1033), Moody's Mood for Love; on David Lahm: *Real Jazz for the Folks who Feel Jazz* (1982, PAlt 8027), Harold's House of Jazz, Shazam

BIBLIOGRAPHY

I. Gitler: Liner notes, *The Janet Lawson Quintet* (IC 1116, ?1982)
L. Gourse: *Louis' Children: American Jazz Singers* (New York, 1984), 341

SCOTT YANOW

Lawson, Yank [John Rhea] (*b* Trenton, MO, 3 May 1911). Trumpeter. After early musical training on piano and saxophone he began playing trumpet in his teens. He later studied at the University of Missouri and in the 1930s worked with Wingy Manone. In 1933 he joined Ben Pollack's band, remaining with it until it broke up late the following year, and in 1935 (along with several other former sidemen of Pollack's) became a founding member of Bob Crosby's band. His distinctive playing on such popular recordings as *Dogtown Blues* and his own composition *Five Point Blues* quickly brought him recognition. In 1938–9 he worked with Tommy Dorsey, his powerful style adding impetus to many recordings, including *Milenberg Joys* and *Hawaiian War Chant*. After a further period with Crosby (1941–2) Lawson played with Benny Goodman (1942), then concentrated on freelance work in television, radio, and recording studios. In 1944 he recorded a superb version of *Stormy Weather* with Frank Sinatra, and from 1951 to 1960 he led a recording band with Bob Haggart. Louis Armstrong selected him in 1957 to play the role of King Oliver on the album *Satchmo: a Musical Autobiography*; Lawson also performed with Armstrong in 1962 at the Newport Jazz Festival. From 1964 to 1966 he played at Eddie Condon's in New York. Reunions of Crosby's band and performances with the Greats of Jazz (1965–9) led Lawson and Haggart to form the WORLD'S GREATEST JAZZ BAND (1968); after this disbanded ten years later its leaders continued to perform together. Lawson has also led his own groups and continued to play at reunions of Crosby's band into the mid-1980s.

Oral history material in *GBLnsa*.

For illustration *see* CROSBY, BOB.

SELECTED RECORDINGS

As leader: *Yank Lawson's Dixieland Jazz* (1943–4, Riv. 2509); with B. Haggart: *South of the Mason-Dixon Line* (1953, Decca 5529); *The Best of Broadway* (1959, Sig. 1014); *Ole Dixie* (1966, ABC-Para. 567); with B. Haggart: *World's Greatest Jazz Band* (1968, Project 5033), *Century Plaza* (1972, World Jazz 1)
As sideman: B. Crosby: Dogtown Blues (1937, Decca 15038); Five Point Blues (1938, Decca 2108); T. Dorsey: Hawaiian War Chant (1938, Vic. 26126); Milenberg Joys (1939, Vic. 26437); F. Sinatra: Stormy Weather (1944, Col. 55037); on L. Armstrong: *Satchmo: a Musical Autobiography* (1956–7, Decca 155), Canal Street Blues, Dippermouth Blues, Snag it (1957); B. Crosby: *Porgy and Bess* (1958, Dot 25193)

BIBLIOGRAPHY

G. T. Simon: "Hall of Fame: John (Yank) Lausen [sic]," *Metronome*, liii/7 (1937), 21
——: "Simon says: Yank is Underrated," *Metronome*, lxxii/9 (1955), 7
H. Sanford: *Tommy and Jimmy: the Dorsey Years* (New Rochelle, NY, 1972)
B. Korall: *The World's Greatest Jazz Band of Yank Lawson and Bob Haggart* (n.p. [Phoenix, AZ], 1973)
D. Morgenstern: Liner notes, *That's A-plenty* (Bob Thiele Music 0941, 1975)
J. Chilton: "Yank Lawson," *Stomp Off, Let's Go! The Story of Bob Crosby's Bob Cats & Big Band* (London, 1983), 245

BRIAN PEERLESS

Lay back. Intentionally to place notes slightly after the beat in a relaxed or hesitating manner; *see* BEAT, §2.

Lay out [stroll]. To cease to play, whether for a few bars, a longer section of a piece, an entire piece, or even a set. The term is used especially of the interruption of conventional roles: for example, a pianist who elects or is instructed to refrain from supplying the normal chordal accompaniment during another player's improvisation is said to "lay out" or "stroll";

the period during which he remains silent may be referred to as a "lay-out."

Lazaroff, Bernard. *See* LEIGHTON, BERNIE.

Lazy Ade. Nickname of ADE MONSBOURGH.

Lead. The principal line (or player) in a band or section of a band. The term is normally used of that line in each of the three wind sections (trumpets, reeds, and trombones) of a big band, jazz orchestra, or stage band; "to take the lead" or "to play lead" or simply "to lead" means to play the melody or lead line. In addition to playing the high part, the lead player decides matters of phrasing and articulation for the section as a whole. Lead playing is a specialty requiring particular skills, and lead players are frequently not as adept at improvisation as others in their sections. In jazz ensembles lacking wind sections, or even a single wind player, other instrumentalists function as "lead" players.

ROBERT WITMER

Leader. The musician who leads, "fronts," or organizes a band. A leader may also be a singer, instrumentalist, or conductor; *see* BANDS, §3(a).

Leaders. Sextet. Formed in 1984, it originally comprised the saxophonists Arthur Blythe and Chico Freeman, the trumpeter Don Cherry, the pianist Kirk Lightsey, the double bass player Cecil McBee, and the drummer Don Moye. The group performed at jazz festivals in Europe, then, with Lester Bowie having replaced Cherry in 1986, toured the USA and recorded the LP *Mudfoot* (1986, Black Hawk 52001). Although oriented towards free jazz, it presents a wide-ranging repertory.

Lead sheet [leadsheet]. A score, in manuscript or printed form, that shows only the melody, the basic harmonic structure, and the lyrics (if any) of a composition (*see* NOTATION, §2). Many performances of jazz are realized from lead sheets, which may be collected and bound together to form a FAKE BOOK. (*GoldJL*)

ROBERT WITMER

Léardée, Ernest (*b* Martinique, 1895). Martinique clarinetist, violinist, and bandleader. In May 1929 he traveled to Paris as a member of Alexandre Stellio's orchestra, with which he recorded later that year. He left Stellio in early 1930 to form his own band with some of Stellio's sidemen (including the pianist Victor Colas and the drummer Orphélien), and was resident for many years at the Bal Colonial (also known as the Bal Nègre). He made numerous recordings with his band (including *La belle Amélie*, 1930, Salabert 2083) and also as a sideman with the tenor saxophonist Félix Valvert, among others. Léardée performed French Creole hot dance music and introduced such jazz instruments as banjo and traps into the traditional beguine orchestra. (A. Boulanger: Liner notes, *Jazz and Hot Dance in Martinique*, Harl. 2018, 1985)

RAINER E. LOTZ

Leary, Ford (*b* Lockport, NY, 5 Sept 1908; *d* New York, 4 June 1949). Trombonist and singer. He worked as a freelance in New York before playing regularly with Bunny Berigan (1936–7), Larry Clinton (1938–40), Charlie Barnet (1940–41), and the trombonist and singer Mike Riley, and briefly with Muggsy Spanier (from spring 1942). He later became a professional actor. Leary's playing and singing are well represented on the recordings made for Variety in 1937 by Phil Napoleon and his orchestra; they include *Blue Bayou* (656, with Leary as singer) and *Swing Patrol* (669, on which he is probably the trombonist).

based on *ChiltonW*

Lee, Alan (Whiteley) (*b* Melbourne, Australia, 29 July 1936). Australian vibraphonist and leader. In 1958 he formed his first group, a quartet consisting of vibraphone, piano, double bass, and drums, which played jazz standards. From that time he led small groups in Melbourne and Sydney, among the members of which have been Brian Brown, Bob Sedergreen, Tony Gould, the trumpeter Keith Hounslow, the double bass players Ray Martin and Derek Capewell, and the drummer Ted Vining; besides vibraphone, Lee has also played guitar and percussion in these ensembles. He made recordings as a guitarist with Bob Barnard (1959), and on vibraphone as a leader (from 1961) and with John Sangster (*Double Vibes*, 1977, Swaggie S1376). He has continued to play both bop and mainstream jazz into the mid-1980s; his style is forceful and highly rhythmic. Lee was one of the first Australian jazz musicians to integrate elements of classical music with jazz and to introduce Latin American rhythms into his work (as on the album *Gallery Concerts*, 1973, Cumquat 12-03).

BIBLIOGRAPHY

A. Bisset: *Black Roots, White Flowers: a History of Jazz in Australia* (Sydney, 1979)
M. Williams: *The Australian Jazz Explosion* (London and elsewhere, 1981), 91
B. Johnson: "Lee, Alan Whiteley," *The Oxford Companion to Australian Jazz* (Melbourne, Australia, 1987)

TONY GOULD

Lee, Baron [Ferguson, Jimmy]. Leader from 1932 to 1933 of the MILLS BLUE RHYTHM BAND.

Lee, Bessie. Pseudonym of TRIXIE SMITH.

Lee, Bill [William James Edwards] (*b* Snow Hill, AL, 23 July 1928). Double bass player. He attended Morehouse College in 1947 and started playing double bass in 1950. After moving to Chicago (1952), he performed with several hard-bop saxophonists, including Clifford Jordan and Frank Strozier. In New York he recorded with Strozier (1960–62), Ray Bryant (1960–61), John Handy (1961), and Harold Mabern (1968); he also made folk-music and blues recordings. In 1968 he formed the Bass Violin Choir (consisting of seven double bass players, a singer, and a rhythm section), which performed several of his works, including the folk opera *The Depot*; from 1972, with Billy Higgins and Bill Hardman, he led the Brass Company, with which he recorded. During the 1970s he made recordings with Jordan (including *Glass Bead Games*, 1973, SE 19737-8), Stanley Cowell (1975), and the Descendants of Mike and Phoebe, a group made up of Lee, his brother the flugelhorn player Cliff Lee, and his sisters the pianist Consuela Lee Moorehead and the singer A. Grace Lee Mims. He assembled a group of well-known bop musicians in 1986 to make the soundtrack for the film *She's gotta have it*, directed by his son Spike Lee. (*Feather–Gitler '70s*)

Lee, David(, Jr.) (*b* New Orleans, 4 Jan 1941). Drummer. He first played professionally in 1954, belonged to army bands, then worked in New Orleans, where he was a founder of the New Orleans Jazz Workshop in 1969. He performed and recorded with Dizzy Gillespie (1969) and Roy Ayers (1971), and played with Sonny Rollins from 1972 until 1975, when he formed a quartet; he continued to work as a sideman, and recorded with the guitarist Yoshioki Masao and Richard Wyands. Lee's straightforward, insistent style can be heard to advantage on Rollins's album *Cutting Edge* (1974).

SELECTED RECORDINGS

As sideman with S. Rollins (all recorded for Milestone): *Next Album* (1972, 9042); *Horn Culture* (1973, 9051); *Cutting Edge* (1974, 9059)

As sideman with others: C. Rouse: *Two is One* (1974, SE 19746); Y. Masao: *111 Sullivan St.* (1975, EW 8020); R. Wyands: *Then, Here, and Now* (1978, Jazzcraft 6)

BIBLIOGRAPHY

Feather–Gitler '70s

PATRICK T. WILL

Lee, Gaby. *See* LINCOLN, ABBEY.

Lee, George E(wing) (*b* Booneville, MO, 28 April 1896; *d* San Diego, *c*Oct 1958). Singer, baritone saxophonist, and bandleader, brother of Julia Lee. He played with an army band (1917) and sang with a vocal quartet, then in 1920 formed his first group, which included his sister, and worked mainly at Lyric Hall in Kansas City. In 1927 he organized a larger band, and two years later engaged Jesse Stone to modernize it so that he could compete on equal musical terms with Bennie Moten; Stone provided new arrangements and recruited musicians who played in a less archaic style, such as Eddie Thompkins, Budd Johnson, Keg Johnson, Tommy Douglas, the saxophonist Herman Walder, and the drummer Baby Lovett. Lee merged his group briefly with that of Moten in 1933–4 and continued touring with a big band into 1935, when he again led a smaller ensemble. He moved to Jackson, Michigan, in 1940, and to Detroit to manage a nightclub in 1942. After World War II he settled in San Diego. Lee's popularity was based primarily on his showmanship and his booming tenor voice. His best bands were recognized as well-drilled units.

SELECTED RECORDINGS

If I could be with you one hour tonight/Paseo Street (1929, Bruns. 7132); Ruff Scufflin' (1929, Bruns. 4684)

BIBLIOGRAPHY

D. Dexter, Jr.: "Moten and Lee are Patron Saints of Kansas City Jazz," *DB*, viii (1941), no.1, p.8; no.2, p.8

F. Driggs: "Kansas City and the Southwest," *Jazz: New Perspectives on the History of Jazz*, ed. N. Hentoff and A. J. McCarthy (New York, 1959/*R*1974), 189–230

R. Russell: *Jazz Style in Kansas City and the Southwest* (Berkeley, CA, Los Angeles, and London, 1971/*R*1983, rev. 2/1973)

F. Driggs and H. Lewine: *Black Beauty, White Heat: a Pictorial History of Classic Jazz, 1920–1950* (New York, 1982), 152

B. Clayton and N. M. Elliott: *Buck Clayton's Jazz World* (London, 1986)

FRANK DRIGGS

Lee, Jeanne (*b* New York, 29 Jan 1939). Singer. She studied modern dance at Bard College (1956–60), where she met Ran Blake, with whom she formed a duo; her concerts and recordings with him were hailed by some critics as showing the first fresh approach to jazz singing since Sarah Vaughan's. She toured Europe with Blake in 1963. In 1964 she moved to California, where she performed with the reed player Ian Underwood and the sound poet David Hazelton (whom she married). While in Europe in 1967 she established a close musical association with Gunter Hampel. She recorded with both Archie Shepp and Sunny Murray in 1969, and later with free-jazz artists such as Marion Brown (1970), Anthony Braxton (1972), Enrico Rava (1973), and Andrew Cyrille (1979); she also worked with Cecil Taylor. In the 1980s she has concentrated on performing her own compositions, which unite her interests in song, dance, and poetry; notable among them is a five-part suite, *Emergence*, and an oratorio in ten acts, *A Prayer for our Time*. The most innovative singer to have emerged from the new music of the 1960s, she improvises dense, complex lines with a precision and flexibility comparable with those of the great instrumentalists, yet she is equally at home in the simple idiom of a spiritual.

SELECTED RECORDINGS

As leader: *Conspiracy* (1974, Earthforms 1)

Duos with R. Blake: *The Newest Sound Around* (1961, RCA LSP2500)

As sideman with G. Hampel: *The 8th of July 1969* (1969, Birth 001); *Spirits* (1971, Birth 007); *Journey to the Song Within* (1974, Birth 017); *Fresh Heat: Live at Sweet Basil* (1985, Birth 0039)

As sideman with others: A. Shepp: *Blasé* (1969, BYG 529318); M. Brown: *Afternoon of a Georgia Faun* (1970, ECM 1004); on A. Braxton: *Town Hall 1972* (1972, Trio 3008–9), W12 B-46 C28-12 4; A. Cyrille: *Nuba* (1979, BS 0030)

BIBLIOGRAPHY

M. Williams: "With Blake and Lee in Europe," *DB*, xxxi/11 (1964), 14

R. Riggins: "Jeanne Lee," *Coda*, nos.164–5 (1979), 4 [incl. discography]

R. Terlizzi, F. Martinelli, and S. Archangeli: "Jeanne Lee and Gunter Hampel," *Coda*, nos.164–5 (1979), 6

RICHARD SCHEININ

Lee, John (Gregory) (*b* Boston, 28 June 1952). Bass player. He began playing professionally while still at high school in Philadelphia, during which time he also began an association with Gerry Brown; in 1970–72 he attended the Philadelphia Musical Academy. Lee and Brown moved in 1972 to the Netherlands to join Chris Hinze's group, with which they toured Europe for two years. Lee then returned to the USA and played in Larry Coryell's band Eleventh House (1974–7). Lee and Brown formed their own jazz-rock group, which toured between 1977 and 1980; it included the guitarists Rodney Jones, Eef Albers, and Darryl Thompson, the keyboard player Rodney Franklin, and the tenor saxophonist Bob Malach. They also toured Europe between 1978 and 1981 with Coryell and Philip Catherine. Lee later performed with McCoy Tyner (1982–4) and joined Dizzy Gillespie's band (1984). His compositions include the title tracks of the LPs *Chaser* and *Mango Sunrise* and the track *That's the Joint* from Eleventh House's album *Level One*.

SELECTED RECORDINGS

As leader with G. Brown: *Mango Sunrise* (1975, BN LA541G); *Still Can't Say Enough* (1976, BN LA701G); *Chaser* (1979, Col. JC36212)

As sideman with Eleventh House: *Level One* (1976, Ari. 4052); *Aspects* (1976, Ari. 4077)

BIBLIOGRAPHY

J. Coryell and L. Friedman: "John Lee," *Jazz-rock Fusion* (New York and London, 1978), 15

J.-E. Berendt: *Das Jazzbuch: Entwicklung und Bedeutung der Jazzmusik* (Frankfurt am Main, Germany, 1953, rev. 2/1959 as *Das neue Jazzbuch*, Eng. trans., New York, 1962; rev. and enlarged 5/1981 as *Das grosse Jazzbuch: von New Orleans bis Jazz Rock*, Eng. trans. as *The Jazz Book: from New Orleans to Fusion and Beyond*, Westport, CT, 1982)

WILLIAM S. BROCKMAN

Lee, Julia (*b* Booneville, MO, 31 Oct 1902; *d* Kansas City, MO, 8 Dec 1958). Pianist and singer, sister of GEORGE E. LEE. She worked predominantly with her brother from 1920 to 1934, then became active as a solo entertainer, playing mainly in Kansas City at Milton's Tap Room and other venues. In the late 1940s she made a tour of the USA and appeared at the White House. She was noted principally for the easy, almost careless, but heartfelt way in which she performed pop standards and, after World War II, songs involving double-entendre. Her piano playing was straightforward, direct, and unadorned except for a few appropriate barrelhouse flourishes.

SELECTED RECORDINGS

Won't you come over to my house? (1929, Bruns. 4761); Julia's Blues (1946, Cap. 320); King Size Papa (1947, Cap. 40087); Draggin' my heart around (1949, Cap. 70051)

BIBLIOGRAPHY

ChiltonW
C. J. Tate: "Julia Lee," *SL*, xi/1–2 (1960), 9
R. Russell: *Jazz Style in Kansas City and the Southwest* (Berkeley, CA, Los Angeles, and London, 1971/*R*1983, rev. 2/1973)
S.-A. Worsfold: "Julia's Blues," *JJ*, xxv/3 (1972), 22
F. Driggs and H. Lewine: *Black Beauty, White Heat: a Pictorial History of Classic Jazz, 1920–1950* (New York, 1982), 152
B. Millar: Liner notes, *Ugly Papa* (Jukebox Lil 603, 1983)

FRANK DRIGGS

Lee, Sonny [Thomas Ball] (*b* Huntsville, TX, 26 Aug 1904). Trombonist. He studied at Texas State Teachers' College, working at the same time with Peck Kelley, then in St. Louis, where he spent much of his career. He played with the Scranton Sirens, with Frankie Trumbauer (1925), occasionally with Charlie Creath (with whom he recorded in 1925), and with the orchestras of the pianists Gene Rodemich and Vincent Lopez and the violinist Paul Specht. He formed a longer association with Isham Jones, with whom he performed and recorded from 1932 to 1936; in that year, having left Jones, he played with Artie Shaw's group and recorded with Charlie Barnet. He then worked in a theater orchestra, with Bunny Berigan (1937–8), and with Jimmy Dorsey's band (1938–46; for illustration *see* JAZZ (i), fig.3). His gruff, rhythmic playing may be heard on a recording made by the singer Teddy Grace in 1939 (*Mama Doo-shee*, Decca 2603).

based on *ChiltonW*

Lee, Tony [Leedham, Anthony] (*b* London, 23 July 1934). English pianist. He taught himself piano at the age of 12 and from 1957 he worked semiprofessionally and then as a full-time musician in various clubs in London. From the early 1960s his trio, which includes Tony Archer, has been resident at the Bull's Head, Barnes, where it has performed with many visiting European and American musicians. In 1968 the group made recordings as London's Gentlemen of Jazz and under Phil Seamen's leadership, and in the mid-1970s played in the *Best of British Jazz* theater show with Kenny Baker, Betty Smith, and the trombonist Don Lusher. Lee has made several recordings as a leader from 1975 (including *Street of Dreams*, 1979, Lee Lambert 102) and has performed at Ronnie Scott's, London, with such musicians as Carmen McRae and Joe Pass. In 1984 he enjoyed a successful engagement at Bradley's restaurant, New York, and played at festivals in Antwerp and Nice.

DIGBY FAIRWEATHER

Lee, Will(iam) (*b* San Antonio, 1952). Bass player. He studied jazz at the University of Miami before moving to New York, where he played with the Brecker brothers in Billy Cobham's group Dreams (1971). From 1973 he worked mainly as a studio musician on electric bass guitar, recording bop, commercial jazz or jazz-rock with Sonny Stitt (1974), the Brecker Brothers (*The Brecker Brothers*, 1975, Ari. 4037), Larry Coryell, Dave Sanborn, and Herbie Mann (all 1975), George Benson (1975, 1976, 1978), Bob James (1976), Earl Klugh (*c*1977), Art Farmer (1977), and Maynard Ferguson (1978). He also made recordings with a number of popular singers.

BIBLIOGRAPHY

M. Rozek: "Will Lee," *DB*, xliv/8 (1977), 42
D. Forte: "Late Night with Sid McGinnis and Will Lee," *GP*, xx/3 (1986), 36 [incl. discography]

Leeman, Cliff(ord) [Mr. Time; the Sheriff] (*b* Portland, ME, 10 Sept 1913; *d* New York, 26 April 1986). Drummer. He first worked in big bands, playing with Artie Shaw (1936–9), Tommy Dorsey (1939), Charlie Barnet (1940–42), and Woody Herman (1942–4), then led his own small band (1944). Later in the 1940s he performed with Don Byas (1944), John Kirby (1944, 1945), Ben Webster, and many others at clubs in New York, and also in the big bands of Barnet (1949) and Bob Chester (1949–50). Besides working regularly on Raymond Scott's radio show "Hit Parade" (broadcast on CBS) throughout the 1950s, he appeared frequently at clubs such as Eddie Condon's and recorded as a member of groups led by Yank Lawson and Bob Haggart (1951–60) and with Ralph Sutton (1953, 1954). Leeman played with Bob Crosby in Las Vegas in 1960, and in 1962 performed and recorded with Wild Bill Davison and toured with Lawson. On later tours he performed in Japan, Australia, and New Zealand with Eddie Condon (1964) and in Europe with the Kings of Jazz (1974) and Davison (1976). In 1974 Leeman recorded with Bud Freeman and a group led by Joe Venuti and Zoot Sims, and in 1976–7 he worked again with Lawson and Haggart as a member of the World's Greatest Jazz Band. He continued to perform at clubs and festivals until his last years. A versatile and highly accomplished drummer, he was equally well equipped to play in big and small bands.

Oral history material in *NjR* (JOHP).

SELECTED RECORDINGS

Duos with R. Sutton: *I Got Rhythm* (1953, Decca DL5498)
As sideman: E. Condon: *Eddie Condon in Japan* (1964, Chi. 154); D. Ewell: *Don Ewell* (1974, Chi. 130)

BIBLIOGRAPHY

ChiltonW; *FeatherE*; *Feather '60s*; *Feather–Gitler '70s*
S. Woolley: "Cliff Leeman: Interview," *Cadence*, iii/3 (1977), 11
H. Kenney: "Sheriff of the Drums," *MR*, viii/2 (1980), 1
W. Vaché, Sr.: "Portraits: Cliff Leeman," *MD*, x/4 (1986), 45
Obituary, J. Simmen, *BHcF*, no.344 (1987), 29

JOHNNY SIMMEN

Lees, Gene [Frederick Eugene John] (*b* Hamilton, Ontario, Canada, 8 Feb 1928). Canadian writer, editor, and lyricist. He received an extensive musical education which included conservatory study at Hamilton (1949) and later at the Berklee College of Music (1961–2) as well as private lessons in theory, composition, singing, piano, and guitar. He began his career as a reporter and critic with the *Hamilton Spectator*, *Toronto Telegram*, and *Montreal Star* (1948–55), after which he became an editor and critic in music and drama for the *Louisville Times* (1955–8). From 1959 to 1961 he held his most important position in jazz, as editor of *Down Beat*. Lees has also been a contributing editor and columnist for *Stereo Review* (1962–5), *High Fidelity* (1966–79), and *American Film* (1977–80). In 1981, in Ojai, California, he founded the *Gene Lees Jazzletter*, a private monthly publication which presents essays on jazz and related topics. Lees has worked extensively as a lyricist; in particular, his translations from Portuguese to English of songs by Antonio Carlos Jobim were important in the popularization of bossa nova during the mid-1960s. He has also served as a music commentator for the Canadian Broadcasting Company and Sveriges Radio Television. (H. Kallmann, G. Potvin, and K. Winters, eds.: *Encyclopedia of Music in Canada*, Toronto, Buffalo, and London, 1981)

Legend. Record label established by Al Aarons.

Legends of Jazz. Traditional-jazz group. Formed in 1973 by the drummer Barry Martyn, its other members were the trumpeter Andy Blakeney (replaced in 1982 by Herbert Permillion), the clarinetist Joe Darensbourg (replaced successively by Joe Thomas (i), 1975–8, Sam Lee, 1978–81, and Floyd Turnham, from 1981), the trombonist Louis Nelson (replaced by Clyde Bernhardt, 1979–86, and Freddy Lonzo, from 1986), the pianist Alton Purnell (replaced in 1984 by Walter Lewis), and the double bass player Ed Garland (replaced by Adolphus Morris, 1977–83, and Chester Zardis, from 1983); the singer Deborah Woodson joined the group in 1984. The group has made annual tours of the USA and Europe, often in conjunction with the stage shows *A Night in New Orleans* (1976–8) and *1000 Years of Jazz* (from 1978). It was the first traditional-jazz group to tour South America and in 1987 toured Australia. Good examples of the group's playing may be heard on two albums entitled *The Legends of Jazz* recorded in 1974 (Crescent 1) and 1980 (Blue Boy 1001). (F. Levin: "Legends of Jazz," *MR*, i/2 (1973), 6)

MIKE HAZELDINE

Legge, Wade (*b* Huntington, WV, 4 Feb 1934; *d* Buffalo, 15 Aug 1963). Pianist. He was born into a musical family and brought up in Buffalo. On Milt Jackson's recommendation he was engaged by Dizzy Gillespie as a double bass player in 1952, then changed to piano two weeks later. He left Gillespie after two years, played with an orchestra led by Johnny Richards, and worked as a freelance in New York; in 1957 he played briefly in Charles Mingus's Jazz Workshop. Later he worked as a freelance in Buffalo.

SELECTED RECORDINGS

As sideman: D. Gillespie: *Dizzy Gillespie Quintet* (1953, Vogue 33310); S. Rollins: *Sonny Rollins Plays for Bird* (1956, Prst. 7095); G. Gryce: *Gigi Gryce and the Jazz Lab Quintet* (1957, Riv. 229); C. Mingus: *The Clown* (1957, Atl. 1260)

BIBLIOGRAPHY

FeatherE; *Feather '60s*

PAUL RINZLER

Leggio, Carmen [Carmelo John] (*b* Tarrytown, NY, 30 Sept 1927). Tenor and alto saxophonist. He studied clarinet from the age of 11 and took up saxophone at 14. In his teens he played with local dance bands. During 1950 and 1951 he performed at Birdland, New York, in jam sessions and with Terry Gibbs. After session work during the mid-1950s, he played with Sol Yaged (1956), Benny Goodman (1957), and Maynard Ferguson, with whom he recorded three albums (1958–9, notably *A Message from Newport*, 1958, Roul. 52012). He later made recordings with Woody Herman (1963) and Jake Hanna (1976), and four albums with his own groups, which included the swing and bop musicians Milt Hinton, George Duvivier, and Mel Lewis (1961–78). In about 1977 he joined the Thad Jones–Mel Lewis Orchestra. (*FeatherE*)

Legrand, Christiane (*b* Aix-les-Bains, France, 21 Aug 1930). French singer, sister of Michel Legrand. Her father, Raymond Legrand, was a noted bandleader. She studied piano from the age of five, and first worked professionally with her brother (1954–8); she also sang with the Blue Stars (1958). In the 1960s she was a member of the Double Six (1960–63) and the Swingle Singers, and made recordings (including *Jazz Cantata*, from the album *Jazz et jazz*, 1963, Fon. 680208) with André Hodeir. She was also active as a studio musician; in the 1980s she taught jazz singing. (*Feather '60s*)

MICHEL LAPLACE

Legrand, Michel (*b* Paris, 24 Feb 1932). French arranger and songwriter, son of the bandleader Raymond Legrand and brother of Christiane Legrand. He studied at the Paris Conservatoire with Nadia Boulanger and from 1951 wrote arrangements for his father, for a number of French singers, and for his own band. In New York he wrote arrangements that were performed by Miles Davis, Ben Webster, John Coltrane, and Bill Evans (ii) on the album *Legrand Jazz* (1958); later he conducted ensembles and wrote material for recordings by Stan Getz (1969), Sarah Vaughan (1972), and Phil Woods (1973, 1975), and performed with Woods in New York, Concord (California), and London. Legrand has also worked as a singer and pianist and achieved recognition as a composer of film scores.

SELECTED RECORDINGS

As leader: *At Shelly's Manne Hole* (1968, Verve 68760); *After the Rain* (1982, Pablo 2312139)

SELECTED ARRANGEMENTS

Recorded by Legrand: *Legrand Jazz* (1958, Col. CL1250); *Michel Legrand Recorded Live at Jimmy's* (1973, RCA BGL1-0850)

Recorded by others: Blue Stars: La légende du pays aux oiseaux [Lullaby of Birdland] (1954, Barclay 70004) [EP]; S. Getz: *Communication '72* (1971, Verve 68807); S. Vaughan: *The Summer Knows* (1972, Mstr. 361)

BIBLIOGRAPHY

FeatherE; *Feather–Gitler '70s*; *Grove6*
L. Tomkins: "Michel Legrand," *CI*, xiii (1975), no.7, p.6; no.8, p.20
L. Lyons: "Profile: Michel Legrand," *DB*, xliii/3 (1976), 34

ANDRÉ CLERGEAT

Lehn, Erwin (*b* Grünstadt, Germany, 8 June 1919). German bandleader, arranger, and vibraphonist. After studying music in Peine, where he learned several instruments, he played piano and wrote arrangements for German radio bands from 1945. With Horst Kudritzki he led the Rundfunk Berlin Tanzorchester, recording in 1948. In the 1950s he began to play vibraphone, and from 1951 into the 1980s led the big band of Süddeutscher Rundfunk, Stuttgart; he produced the jazz program "Treffpunkt Jazz" for the same station in 1955. Lehn has also composed and arranged music for films and performed and made recordings as the leader of a quartet, quintet, and big band (1947–83), including *German Jazz Hurricane* (1956, Col. 33WS1509). In the mid-1980s he served as the director of the big band at the Staatliche Hochschule für Musik, Stuttgart.

BIBLIOGRAPHY

FeatherE; *ReclamsJ*
Liner notes, *German Jazz Hurricane* (Col. 33WS1509, 1956)
H. H. Lange: Liner notes, *Die grossen Tanzorchester, 1930–1950: Erwin Lehn* (Pol. 2437775, 2664252, 1978)

Leibrook, Min [Wilford F.] (*b* Hamilton, OH, 1903; *d* Los Angeles, 8 June 1943). Bass saxophonist and tuba and double bass player. After learning cornet he played bass saxophone and tuba with the Ten Foot Band in Chicago. Later he was a member of the Wolverines (for illustrations *see* RECORDING, fig.3, and WOLVERINES) before moving to New York. From 1927 he performed and made recordings with Paul Whiteman, including *San* (1928, Vic. 24078), on which he plays a bass saxophone solo. Apart from a brief period in 1930 during which his freelance activities included sessions with Bix Beiderbecke, Leibrook remained with Whiteman until 1931. Thereafter he played saxophone and double bass with Lennie Hayton (mid-1930s) and worked with the Three T's, led by Jack and Charlie Teagarden and Frankie Trumbauer (1936). After moving to the West Coast he played double bass in studios and theaters until shortly before his death.

based on *ChiltonW*

Leighton, Bernie [Lazaroff, Bernard] (*b* West Haven, CT, 30 Jan 1921). Pianist. He played with Bud Freeman in the late 1930s and performed and recorded with Raymond Scott (1940) and Benny Goodman (1940–41). After serving in the army he studied at Yale (BMus 1949) and recorded with his own small groups (1946), Dave Tough (1946), and Billie Holiday (1949). He worked as a studio musician, recording swing with his own bands (1950–74, including *The World is Waiting for the Sunrise*, 1951, Mello-Roll 5005), Neal Hefti (1951), Benny Goodman (1953, 1967), Artie Shaw (1953, 1968), and the percussionist Tito Rodriguez (1963), bop with James Moody (1963), and dixieland with the clarinetist and saxophonist Bob Wilber (1969). He toured the USA with Tony Bennett in 1972–3.

BIBLIOGRAPHY

FeatherE
L. Tomkins: "Tony Bennett's new MD: Bernie Leighton," *CI*, xi/6 (1973), 20

Le Lann [Lelann], **Eric** (*b* St. Brieuc, France, 4 Nov 1957). French flugelhorn player. He studied music with his father and played first with dixieland groups, then with René Urtreger, Roger Guérin, the percussionist Bernard Lubat (1980), the Caratini–Fosset Onztet (1980–81), Martial Solal (from 1980), Pepper Adams (1980, 1982), and Glenn Ferris (1981); he has also worked as a leader and in 1983 recorded the album *Night Bird* (JMS 028). In 1986 he appeared with other jazz musicians in Bertrand Tavernier's film *Round Midnight*.

BIBLIOGRAPHY

J. Chesnel: "Eric Lelann: un breton des pistons," *Jh*, no.395 (1982), 28
Y. Thébault: "Lelann sans piston," *Jm*, no.339 (1985), 26 [incl. discography]

MICHEL LAPLACE

Lemer, Pete(r Naphtali) (*b* London, 14 June 1942). English keyboard player. He took some lessons with Paul Bley and Jaki Byard before studying classical piano at the Royal Academy of Music in London (1969–71). His first professional jazz engagement was with Tony Crombie and Jeff Clyne (1963) and his subsequent musical career has been highly varied. He has played and recorded with such diverse groups and musicians as Amalgam, the Spontaneous Music Ensemble (1969), the Don Rendell Five (1974), Harry Beckett (1977), and Barbara Thompson's Jubiaba (1978); in the 1980s he has performed with Macondo, the rock musician Mike Oldfield, Mike Westbrook, In Cahoots, and Thompson's Paraphernalia. Lemer has also worked as a leader from 1963, and his various groups have included Jack Bruce, Jeff Clyne, Johnny Dyani, Barry Guy, Jon Hiseman, John Stevens, Allan Holdsworth, and John Surman. His playing can be heard to advantage on the album *Local Colour* (1966, ESP 1057).

BIBLIOGRAPHY

R. Cotterell, ed.: *Jazz Now: the Jazz Centre Society Guide* (London, 1976), 142
I. Carr: "Lemer, Pete," in I. Carr. D. Fairweather, and B. Priestley: *Jazz: the Essential Companion* (London, 1987), 295

SIMON ADAMS

Lemon, Brian (*b* Nottingham, England, 11 Feb 1937). English pianist. After working with Freddy Randall (1956) and Betty Smith's quintet (1957) he played with a variety of groups, including the Fairweather–Brown All Stars led by Sandy Brown and Al Fairweather, the clarinetist Dave Shepherd's quintet, and Danny Moss's quartet (from 1962). Thereafter he combined playing and recording as a freelance (often in backup groups for visiting American musicians, among them Milt Jackson and Benny Goodman, and such British jazzmen as George Chisholm) with working in bands; he performed with the Randall–Shepherd All Stars (1972–3), Alex Welsh (1977–8), and the Pizza Express All Stars (from 1980). In the 1980s Lemon has led his own trio and small groups, worked as a soloist, and performed his own arrangements with large string ensembles for the BBC. His playing may be heard on *Our Kind of Music* (77 LEU38), a recording he made as a leader in 1970.

BIBLIOGRAPHY

R. Cotterell, ed.: *Jazz Now: the Jazz Centre Society Guide* (London, 1976)
L. Tomkins: "Brian Lemon," *CI*, xxii/3 (1984), 18

DIGBY FAIRWEATHER

Lenz, Günter (*b* Frankfurt am Main, Germany, 25 July 1938). German bass player, leader, and composer. He taught himself guitar in 1952 and played in American clubs from 1954; he later studied harmony and rhythm with Carlo Bohländer (1958). Having taken up double bass in 1959, he played and composed for a military band during his national service in Mittenwald (1959–61). He is well known for his work with the jazz ensemble of Hessischer Rundfunk in Frankfurt am Main (from 1961) and for his playing with the Albert Mangelsdorff Quintet (1961–72). He visited Asia with Mangelsdorff in 1964 on a tour sponsored by the Goethe Institute, and toured in South America with the German All Stars in 1968. After performing with Kurt Edelhagen (1972), he worked as a studio musician in Munich (1973–6). His own band Springtime, formed in 1975, received critical acclaim; he played little in the early 1980s but re-formed the group in early 1986. One of Germany's leading double bass players, Lenz plays with a driving pulse and authoritative swing; his compositions are skillful and refined.

SELECTED RECORDINGS

As leader: with H.-P. Giger and E. Maron: *Beyond* (1976, Nagara 1011); *Roaring Plenties* (1979, L+R 40005)
As sideman: A Mangelsdorff: *New Jazz Ramwong* (1964, CBS 62398); W. Dauner: *Et Cetera* (1972, MPS 2121333); L. Zadlo: *Sting* (1980, Fusion 8001)

GÜNTHER HUESMANN

Leo (i). Record label. It was established in Helsinki by Edward Vesala; issue began in 1978 of recordings made that year. The label has also been used to issue posthumously material recorded by Pekka Pöyry between 1968 and 1980. The catalogue is oriented towards, but by no means restricted to, Finnish free jazz. It also includes albums by American and central European musicians, including Frank Foster, Charlie Mariano, Tomasz Stańko, and a Polish group, the Quartet.

Leo (ii). Record company and label. The company was established in London in 1980 by Leo Feigin, who emigrated to England from the USSR in 1973. The catalogue includes American and English free jazz, but the label is most notable for the issue of around 20 albums by Russian free-jazz musicians, particularly Vyacheslav Ganelin's trio. (A. Turner: "Leo Records," *The Wire*, no.1 (1982), 26)

Leonard, Harlan (Quentin) [Mike] (*b* Kansas City, MO, 2 July 1905; *d* Los Angeles, 1983). Saxophonist and bandleader. He studied music at high school and made his professional début with George E. Lee's band in 1923. Later that year he joined Bennie Moten, with whom he remained as lead saxophonist until late 1931 (for illustration *see* MOTEN, BENNIE). He then joined the Kansas City Sky Rockets (*see* KANSAS CITY ROCKETS), led by the trombonist Thamon Hayes, who had taken over some former members of Moten's band. Leonard became leader of the group on Hayes's resignation in 1934, and when it disbanded in 1937 formed a new ensemble. Harlan Leonard's Rockets became the leading band in Kansas City; it played at the Golden Gate Ballroom in New York in 1940, then worked exclusively in the Midwest until mid-1943, when it moved to Los Angeles. After the band broke up in 1945 Leonard took a job with the Internal Revenue Service.

Leonard's band was noted for its drive and such outstanding sidemen as Fred Beckett, Henry Bridges, Jesse Price, and the trumpeters James Ross and William Smith. Tadd Dameron wrote many of its better arrangements, including *Rock and Ride* and *A la Bridges*.

SELECTED RECORDINGS

Rock and Ride (1940, Bb 10883); A la Bridges (1940, Bb 10899); Mistreated/ Too Much (1940, Bb 11544)

BIBLIOGRAPHY

ChiltonW
F. Driggs: "Kansas City and the Southwest," *Jazz: New Perspectives on the History of Jazz*, ed. N. Hentoff and A. J. McCarthy (New York, 1959/R1974)
J. Simmen: "Harlan Leonard and his Rockets," *JJ*, xvi/8 (1963), 4
L. Feather: Liner notes, *Harlan Leonard and his Rockets* (RCA LPV531, 1966)
R. Russell: *Jazz Style in Kansas City and the Southwest* (Berkeley, CA, Los Angeles, and London, 1971/R1983, rev. 2/1973
D. Penny and T. Burke: "Rockin' with the Rockets: Harlan Leonard and his Kansas City Rockets," *Blues & Rhythm: the Gospel Truth*, no.22 (1986), 10
L. Mallaus: "The Forgotten Ones: Harlan Leonard," *JJI*, xl/7 (1987), 19

FRANK DRIGGS

Leonhart, Jay [James Chancellor] (*b* Baltimore, 6 Dec 1940). Bass player. He attended Peabody Conservatory from 1946 to 1950 and played banjo and double bass in local groups before taking up electric bass guitar. He continued to play jazz while studying at the Berklee College of Music (1959–61) and Oscar Peterson's Advanced School of Contemporary Music (1961–2), performing with Buddy Morrow (1961) and Mike Longo (1962–3). He then worked as a freelance musician and after moving to New York played in a range of styles with, among others, Jim Hall (1973–4) and Urbie Green (1970–75), and accompanied popular singers. He made bop and swing recordings with Marian McPartland (including *A Delicate Balance*, *c*1971, Hal. 105) and Chuck Wayne (1976) and recorded soul jazz with Harold Ousley (1972). In the late 1970s and 1980s he played with Phil Woods, Gerry Mulligan, Lee Konitz, Don Sebesky, Louie Bellson, and others. He formed a duo (1980) and a trio (1985) with the pianist Mike Renzi, with whom he made several albums of his own songs on which he sang and played double bass. (*Feather–Gitler '70s*)

Le Sage, Bill [William A.] (*b* London, 20 Jan 1927). English pianist and vibraphonist. A self-taught pianist, he formed a sextet in 1945 and played with John Dankworth in the same year. After a period in army bands (1945–8), he was a member of the Johnny Dankworth Seven (1950–53) and then of Dankworth's big band (1953–4); he took piano lessons with Lennie Tristano in New York in 1950, and began studying vibraphone in 1953. From 1954 to 1961 he played in Tony Kinsey's trio. He was joint leader of a quartet with Ronnie Ross from 1961 to 1965, and from 1964 also led the ten-piece group Directions in Jazz, which included four cellos; among its recordings is *Directions in Jazz* (1964, Phi. SBL7625). Thereafter Le Sage continued to lead his own ensembles, notably the Bebop Preservation Society (1970–86); he has also performed with Barbara Thompson (1971–8), Dankworth (1979–83), and Charlie Watts (from 1985). His playing is well represented on Martin Drew's LP *Martin Drew and his Band* (1977, Lee Lambert 003). Le Sage is also a composer and arranger who has written scores for several television series.

BIBLIOGRAPHY

FeatherE; *Feather '60s*
R. Cotterell, ed.: *Jazz Now: the Jazz Centre Society Guide* (London, 1976)

SIMON ADAMS

Lesberg, Jack (*b* Boston, 14 Feb 1920). Double bass player. He played violin in Boston clubs in the 1930s, worked with Muggsy Spanier (1940), and then moved to New York (*c*1944), where he played in the New York City SO (1945–8). During a long career he has recorded, and in many instances also performed, with numerous leaders, notably Eddie Condon (1944–50), Sarah Vaughan (1944, 1949), Wild Bill Davison (1945, 1946, 1949), Benny Goodman (1946, 1967), Louis Armstrong (1947, 1949), Jack Teagarden and Coleman Hawkins (both 1947), Peanuts Hucko (1947, 1950, 1953), Sidney Bechet (1949), Tommy Dorsey (1950), Kai Winding (1951), Jimmy McPartland (1952, 1953), Max Kaminsky (1954, 1963), Billy Butterfield (1954, 1956–8), Urbie Green (1956), Bobby Hackett (1963, 1969–70), Ruby Braff (1967), and Joe Venuti (*c*1969). He toured Australia, England, and Africa with Armstrong in 1956 and made two European tours with Teagarden and Earl Hines (1957), and Georgie Auld and Doc Severinsen (1962); after visiting the Pacific with Condon (1964), he returned to Europe in 1965 to play in Iceland with Armstrong. After a period working in classical and jazz ensembles in Australia (1971–4) he returned to the USA and recorded as a leader (1977). In the 1980s he again toured Europe several times, with the group called Tribute to Louis Armstrong, with Braff, and with Yank Lawson. He has been music director at jazz parties in Odessa, Texas (from 1967), Midland, Texas (from 1977), and Minneapolis (from 1985).

SELECTED RECORDINGS

As leader: *Hollywood Swing* (1977, FaD 120)
As sideman: C. Hawkins: Half Step Down Please/Jumpin' Jane (1947, Vic. 20-3143); E. Condon: *Eddie Condon in Japan* (1964, Chi. 154); G. Wein: *The Newport All Stars* (1967, BL 138) B. Hackett: *Live at the Roosevelt Grill* (1970, Chi. 161)

BIBLIOGRAPHY

FeatherE; *Feather '60s*
S. Traill: "Jack Lesberg," *JJ*, xxiii/7 (1970), 24 [interview]
B. Rusch: "Jack Lesberg," *Cadence*, xiii/6 (1987), 11

Leslie. A tremulant loudspeaker system for use with electronic organs, designed by Donald J. Leslie around 1940 and made from the early 1940s by the Electro-Music Co. in Pasadena, California. The tremulant effect is produced by a two-speed rotating curved reflector placed below a downward-facing loudspeaker, and by a rotating treble horn. *See* ORGAN, §2.

Leslie, Sharon. *See* CHRISTY, JUNE.

Le Sony'r Ra. *See* SUN RA.

Lessey, Bob [Robert] (*b* British West Indies, 16 March 1910). Guitarist. His first professional engagement was with the orchestra of the trumpeter Tommy Jones in New York (1931–3). He played under the bandleaders Bill Brown, Sam Wooding (occasionally), Tiny Bradshaw (1934), Fletcher Henderson (1935–6), Don Redman (1937–40), and Lucky Millinder (1941). He then ceased to be active as a full-time musician, though he continued to play for many years. A rhythm guitarist of the first rank, Lessey may be heard playing a fine solo and a fiercely swinging introduction on Tiny Bradshaw's *Shout, sister, shout* (1934, Decca 456).

based on *ChiltonW*

Letman, Johnny [John Bernard] (*b* McCormick, SC, 6 Sept 1917). Trumpeter and bandleader. He worked in Chicago with Nat "King" Cole (1933–4), Horace Henderson (1941–2), and Red Saunders (1942). In 1944 he moved to New York, where he played or recorded with John Kirby, Phil Moore (1944–5), Cab Calloway (1947–9, 1950, 1958), and Milt Buckner (1949). After working briefly with Count Basie in 1951, he played on television and for Broadway shows, and led swing groups in and around New York. He made recordings with Joe Thomas (iv) (including the album *Mainstream*, 1958, Atl. 1303), Stuff Smith (1959), Chubby Jackson (*c*1959), and Panama Francis (1960), and as a leader (including *The Many Angles of John Letman*, 1960, Beth. 6053). During a visit to Paris in 1968 he performed with Buckner and Wallace Bishop, and recorded with his own band and with Tiny Grimes. His work in the 1970s included recordings with Lionel Hampton, Cozy Cole, and Earl Hines (all 1977). In 1985–6 Letman toured Europe and the USA with the New Orleans Blues Serenaders (the band and singers from the stage musical *One Mo' Time*), and appeared at numerous festivals, including the New Orleans Jazz and Heritage Festival; the Oude Stijl Jazz Festival, Breda, the Netherlands; and the Festa New Orleans Music, Ascona, Switzerland.

BIBLIOGRAPHY

ChiltonW
A. J. McCarthy: "Johnny Letman," *JM*, vi/1 (1960), 8
H. Panassié: "Un grand trompette: Johnny Letman," *BHcF*, no.102 (1960), 3

Levallet, Didier (*b* Arcy-sur-Cure, France, 19 July 1944). French double bass player. He studied double bass briefly and from 1969 worked in clubs in Paris with Georges Arvanitas, Ted Curson, Hank Mobley, Mal Waldron, and Chris Woods, among others. He toured with Kenny Clarke, Johnny Griffin, and Slide Hampton, and played with Marc Charig, Tony Coe, Steve Lacy, Byard Lancaster, and Didier Lockwood. He performed with the free-jazz quartet Perception (1970–7, recording in 1972, 1973, and 1976), and was founder (1976) and leader of ADMI, the Association pour le Développement de la Musique Improvisée. He also recorded with Freddie Redd (1971), as the leader of his own group (1975), with Confluence (1975–7), and with Frank Lowe (1976). In the 1980s he played with Chris McGregor's Brotherhood of Breath, Archie Shepp, Tony Oxley (1984–6), and Mike Westbrook (1985–6), performed as the leader of his own trio (1987), and recorded as a leader (*Scoop*, 1983, In and Out 1006). He is also active as a composer and teacher.

BIBLIOGRAPHY

D. Levallet: "En mage (suite): Didier Levallet: raisons et leçons d'un échec," *Jm*, no.235 (1975), 22
D. Soutif: "Ce que dit Levallet," *Jm*, no.286 (1980), 14
I. Carr: "Levallet, Didier," in I. Carr, D. Fairweather, and B. Priestley: *Jazz: the Essential Companion* (London, 1987)

Levey, Stan (*b* Philadelphia, 5 April 1925). Drummer. At the age of 17 he played with Dizzy Gillespie in Philadelphia and then moved to New York, where in the early 1940s he worked at the Onyx Club with Oscar Pettiford. In 1944 he joined Charlie Parker's band at the Spotlite and served as the first drummer in a group led by Coleman Hawkins, which also included Thelonious Monk and Little Benny Harris. Levey's crisp, neat style made him much in demand, and he played with such musicians as Gillespie, Barney Bigard, George Shearing, and Allen Eager. In 1945 he toured with a group consisting of Gillespie, Parker, Milt Jackson, Lucky Thompson, Al Haig, and Ray Brown; he then returned to work at the Spotlite with Gillespie and Leo Parker. The experience he gained in big bands with Charlie Ventura, Georgie Auld, Freddie Slack, and Woody Herman eventually led to a place in Stan Kenton's band (1952–4). Thereafter Levey settled in California, where he was a member of Howard Rumsey's Lighthouse All Stars (1954–8) and played on film and television soundtracks. In the early 1960s he continued to work as a studio musician, and performed with many singers, including Peggy Lee and Ella Fitzgerald, before ceasing to be a professional musician. Levey's playing was clean and accurate; he was at his best when playing fast bop numbers.

SELECTED RECORDINGS

As leader: *Stan Levey Plays Bob Cooper, Bill Holman, Jimmy Giuffre* (1954, Beth. 1017); *This Time the Drum's on me* (1955, Beth. 37); *Grand Stan* (1956, Beth. 71); with M. Roach: *Drummin' the Blues* (1957, Lib. 3064); *Stan Levey Quartet* (1957, Mode 101)

As sideman: first issued on C. Parker: *Yardbird in Lotus Land* (1945–6, Spot. 123), D. Gillespie: Salt Peanuts (1946); Gillespie: Diggin' Diz (1946, Dial 1004); C. Williamson: *Stan Kenton Presents Claude Williamson* (1954, Cap. H6502); F. Rosolino: *Frankly Speaking* (1955, Cap. T6509); L. Levy: *Jazz in Four Colors* (1956, RCA LPM1319); S. Rogers: *Shorty Rogers Plays Richard Rodgers* (1957, RCA LPM1428); Bill Harris (i): *Bill Harris and Friends* (1957, Fan. 3263); P. Lee: *Basin Street East* (1960, Cap. T1520); *I'm a Woman* (1963, Cap. ST1857)

BIBLIOGRAPHY

J. Tynan: "Stan the Man," *DB*, xxv/6 (1958), 23
"Stan Levey," *DB*, xxvi/3 (1959), 13
M. Gibson: "Stan Levey," *JJ*, xiv/10 (1961), 7
A. Morgan: "Stan Levey," *JM*, vii/7 (1961), 18
I. Gitler: *Jazz Masters of the Forties* (New York, 1966/*R*1983 with discography), 188
B. Korall: "Stan Levey, Bop Pioneer," *MD*, xi/4 (1987), 24 [incl. discography]

JEFF POTTER

Leviev, Milcho (*b* Plovdiv, Bulgaria, 19 Dec 1937). Keyboard player. After graduating from the Bulgarian State Music Academy in Sofia (1960) he rose quickly to prominence. He directed the Bulgarian radio and television big band (1962–6), for which he also composed and wrote arrangements, conducted the Sofia PO (1963–8), and led a quartet, Jazz Focus. Among his compositions at this time was *Music for Big Band and Symphony Orchestra* (1966). He worked in Germany with Albert Mangelsdorff in 1970, then moved to the USA. His virtuosity and ability to play effortlessly in complex rhythms (a skill that arose from his familiarity with Bulgarian folk music) were great assets during his association with Don Ellis (1971–7), for whom he also composed and wrote arrangements. During the 1970s Leviev worked with Willie Bobo (1973–4) and John Klemmer (1975–9), recorded with Billy Cobham (three albums, 1974–5) and L. Subramaniam (1979), and led a trio (from 1978). In 1980 he recorded in London as the leader of a bop quartet that included Art Pepper; the following year he wrote arrangements for and recorded with Al Jarreau. From 1980 to 1983 he was a leader of the quartet Free Flight, which played a fusion of jazz-rock and classical music, recording in 1982; during this period he also performed and recorded as a member of Gerald Wilson's big band. Leviev has worked frequently with many important musicians in Los Angeles and elsewhere, playing in duos with Charlie Haden (with whom he recorded around 1986), Dave Holland, Ray Pizzi, and Buddy Collette, and in an all-star septet with Oscar Brashear, Pizzi, Mundell Lowe, and others (from 1986). He wrote two of the chapters in Ellis's *The New Rhythm Book*.

SELECTED RECORDINGS

As leader: *Jazz Focus* (1968, Saba 15219); *Music for Big Band and Symphony Orchestra* (1977–81, Trend 530); *Blues for the Fisherman* (1980, Mole 1)

As sideman: D. Ellis: *Tears of Joy* (1971, Col. CG30927), incl. Bulgarian Bulge; *Connection* (1972, Col. KC31766); *Soaring* (1974, MPS 2125123); B. Cobham: *Total Eclipse* (1974, Atl. 18121); J. Klemmer: *Lifestyle* (1977, ABC

1007); A. Jarreau: *Breakin' Away* (1981, WB BSK3576); Free Flight: *The Jazz/Classic Union* (1982, PAlt 8024); G. Wilson: *Orchestra of the '80s* (1982–?1983, Trend 531, 537)

BIBLIOGRAPHY

Feather–Gitler '70s
F. Nemko: "Milcho Leviev: Playing Unusual Meters," *CK*, ii/3 (1976), 18 [biography, interview]

SCOTT YANOW

Levin, Marc (Leonard) (*b* Bayonne, NJ, 6 Aug 1942). Cornetist and flutist. He studied at Rutgers and the New School for Social Research in New York. From 1964 he was active in New York's free-jazz community, studying with Bill Dixon (1965–6) and playing with Alan Silva (1965), Dixon (1966–7, with whom he also recorded), Perry Robinson (1966), and Burton Greene (1966). In 1973 he moved to Europe where he played with Annette Peacock (1974) and Mal Waldron (1975), and recorded with Joe McPhee (1976). He formed his own band in 1974 with which he recorded three albums during the 1970s; he also played in a trio. Levin plays many instruments besides cornet and flute, and also sings: *Social Sketches* (1975, Enja 2058), for example, displays his abilities on several instruments, including flugelhorn, mellophone, and percussion.

BIBLIOGRAPHY

Feather–Gitler '70s
R. Baggenaes: "Marc Levin: Interview," *Coda*, no.145 (1976), 2
B. Rusch: "Marc Levin: Interview," *Cadence*, iv/11 (1978), 8

Levine, Mark (Jay) (*b* Concord, NH, 4 Oct 1938). Pianist and trombonist. He studied music at Boston University (BA 1960) and privately with Jaki Byard, Hall Overton, and Herb Pomeroy. After playing piano in a big band in Boston (*c*1960) he moved to New York. He performed and recorded (variously on piano and trombone) with Houston Person (1966), Joe Henderson (1973), Gábor Szabó, and Ray Pizzi (1976), and in the Latin bands of Mongo Santamaria (1969–70) and Willie Bobo (1971–4). After moving to San Francisco in the mid-1970s he played in Woody Shaw's band (1975–6), led his own nonet (1975–6, making his first recording as a leader, *Up 'til Now* (Cat. 7614), in 1976), and appeared frequently with Blue Mitchell and Harold Land (1975–9); from 1975 he also worked intermittently with Henderson, Stan Getz, and Bobby Hutcherson, and performed and recorded with Moacir Santos, Luis Gasca, and Cal Tjader (1979–83). In 1977 he received an NEA grant to enable him to compose and write arrangements. He led his own quintet (1981–5) and trio (from 1986) and continued to make recordings, among them *Concepts* (1983, Conc. 234), which includes his own composition *Flame*. Between 1980 and 1983 Levine's principal instrument was trombone, but he then abandoned it in favor of piano. (B. Ness: "Mark Levine," *DB*, xliv/16 (1977), 40)

Levinovsky, Nikolay (Yakovlevich) (*b* Saratov, Russian SFSR, 14 Dec 1944). Russian pianist and composer. He played in jazz and pop groups from 1960, led a sextet (1964–7) and a quartet (1968–9, 1972–5), and belonged to big bands led by Ady Rosner (1970) and the pianist Anatoly Kroll (1971–2). After studying musicology at the Saratov L. B. Sobinov State Conservatory (graduated 1974) he led the Azerbaijan Variety Orchestra from 1975 until 1978, when he formed the octet Allegro, which made several recordings and toured Europe, India, and Sri Lanka. In the 1980s Levinovsky composed several works for his own ensemble, including *Kontrastï* (a concertino in three movements), *V etom mire* (In this world), Fantasy in G major, a concert suite in three movements, Jazz Sinfonietta, and *Triptych*. A good example of his playing is the recording *Sfinks* (Sphinx; 1986, Mel. C6024695003).

WALTER OJAKÄÄR

Levitt, Alan (*b* New York, 11 Nov 1932). Drummer. He first played professionally with Chuck Wayne (*c*1952) and, briefly, with Charlie Parker. After recording with Charles Mingus (1952) and Stan Getz (1953) he performed with Lennie Tristano, Teddy Charles (1953), and Paul Bley (1955). He met Lee Konitz when they were both working with Mingus, and recorded under him in 1954 and 1960. In 1957–8 he lived in Paris, where he recorded with Sidney Bechet and Martial Solal, Stephane Grappelli, and René Urtreger (all in 1957). After touring with Lionel Hampton (1966) Levitt settled in Europe in the early 1970s and resumed his association with Konitz, touring and recording with the quartet led by Konitz and Warne Marsh (1975–6); he also played on Konitz's album *Jazz Confronto* (1976, Horo 101-32) and performed with him in Paris in 1978 and 1982.

BIBLIOGRAPHY

FeatherE; *Feather–Gitler '70s*
A. Levitt: "Chasing the Bird," *JJI*, xxxiii/8 (1980), 6

Levitt, Rod(ney Charles) (*b* Portland, OR, 16 Sept 1929). Trombonist. He toured and recorded with Dizzy Gillespie (1956–7), then recorded with Ernie Wilkins (1957), Kai Winding (1958), and Sy Oliver (1959–60). In 1959 he joined Gil Evans at Birdland, New York, and recorded with Evans's orchestra accompanying Miles Davis. During the same period he performed with the orchestra at Radio City Music Hall in New York (1957–63). Around 1960 he formed an octet which made five albums, including *Insight* (1964, RCA LPM3448); he also recorded with Mundell Lowe (1960), Quincy Jones (1961), and Oliver Nelson (1962). During the 1970s he performed with his octet and with Chuck Israels's National Jazz Ensemble. Besides his activities as a player, Levitt has conducted and written arrangements for Cedar Walton and Blue Mitchell.

BIBLIOGRAPHY

Feather '60s
F. Bouchard: "Caught: Rod Levitt Octet," *DB*, xliv/11 (1977), 37

Levy, Hank [Henry J.] (*b* Baltimore, 27 Sept 1927). Composer, arranger, and baritone saxophonist. He studied at the US Navy School of Music, the College of William & Mary, Peabody Conservatory, the Catholic University of America, and Towson State University. In 1953 he joined Stan Kenton's orchestra, for which he also wrote arrangements; he composed for Sal Salvador (1960–62), Don Ellis (from 1966), and Kenton (from 1969), and his *Opus for Overextended Jazz Ensemble* was given its première by the Baltimore SO in 1971; his compositions are often characterized by unusual meters. Levy joined the faculty of Towson State in 1968 and was one of the original members of Kenton's jazz workshops. Under his leadership the Towson State jazz band won competitions and, from 1976, recorded an album every year.

RECORDED COMPOSITIONS
(selective list)

on D. Ellis: *Live at Monterey* (1966, PJ 20112), Passacaglia and Fugue; on D. Ellis: *Connection* (1972, Col. KC31766), Chain Reaction; on S. Kenton: *Birthday in Britain* (1973, CW 1065), Ambivalence; on S. Kenton: *Kenton '76* (1975, CW 1076), Time for a Change; on S. Kenton: *Journey to Capricorn* (1976, CW 1077), Pegasus

BIBLIOGRAPHY

Feather–Gitler '70s

C. Easton: *Straight Ahead: the Story of Stan Kenton* (New York, 1973)

W. F. Lee: *Stan Kenton: Artistry in Rhythm* (Los Angeles, 1980) [incl. discography]

WILLIAM F. LEE III

Levy, John (O.) (*b* New Orleans, 11 April 1912). Double bass player. In 1944 he recorded in Chicago with Pete Brown, then with Stuff Smith, with whom he moved to New York and made one of his finest recordings (*Look at me*, 1944, Asch 353-1). He performed in New York with Ben Webster, Erroll Garner, and Don Byas, and recorded with Garner, Byas, and Charlie Ventura in 1945. He continued to record with several leaders, including Rex Stewart, Billy Taylor (ii), and Lennie Tristano (all 1947), and Billie Holiday (1948). He joined George Shearing's band in 1948 and began recording with him the following year; he may be heard to advantage on *Strollin'* (1950, MGM 30248), which he also composed. In 1951 he gave up playing to work as a manager for musicians who included Shearing and Sarah Vaughan; he continued to be active in this field into the 1980s. (*FeatherE*)

For illustration *see* SHEARING, GEORGE.

Levy, Lou(is A.) (*b* Chicago, 5 March 1928). Pianist. He studied piano from the age of 12, and listened to the recordings of Charlie Parker and Lester Young. He played with a big band led by Jimmy Dale (1945), worked with Georgie Auld (1947), and accompanied Sarah Vaughan (1947). He played with Chubby Jackson (1947–8), Woody Herman's Second Herd (1948–9), and Tommy Dorsey (1950), and again with Auld, before retiring from music for three years. He resumed his career when he performed at the Blue Note in Chicago as a soloist (1954). In the 1950s he recorded with Conte Candoli, Shorty Rogers, and Stan Getz, and was, at intervals, accompanist for Peggy Lee (for 18 years beginning in 1955) and Ella Fitzgerald (1957–62). He later played and recorded with other singers (June Christy, Anita O'Day, Nancy Wilson) and also played with Getz, Terry Gibbs, and Benny Goodman, and (from 1973) with Supersax. Levy is a fleet-fingered bop pianist known principally as an accompanist. His playing has been influenced by Bud Powell and by the harmonic innovations of Art Tatum.

SELECTED RECORDINGS

As leader: with C. Candoli: *West Coast Wailers* (1955, Atl. 1268); *Tempus Fugue-it* (1977, Inter. 7711)

As sideman: C. Jackson: Crown Pilots/Begin the Beguine (1947, Cupol 4047); S. Rogers: *Martians, Come Back!* (1955, Atl. 1232); S. Getz: *Award Winner Stan Getz* (1957, Verve 8296); E. Fitzgerald: Travelin' Light (1958, Verve 10143); You'll have to Swing it (1961, Verve 10237); Cry me a River (1962, Verve 10241); J. Christy: *Impromptu* (1977, Inter. 7710); Supersax: *Chasin' the Bird* (1977, MPS 68160); A. O'Day: *Mello'Day* (1979, GNP 2126)

BIBLIOGRAPHY

FeatherE; *Feather '60s*; *Feather–Gitler '70s*

S. A. Pease: "Lou Levy: One of Top Pianists in Bop," *DB*, xvi/16 (1949), 12

"Lou Levy," *DB*, xxv/4 (1958), 17

L. Tomkins: "The Most Musical Mr. Levy," *Crescendo*, i/4 (1962), 16

S. Voce: "Lou Levy Talks to Steve Voce," *JJI*, xxxv (1982), no.4, p.16; no.5, p.18

R. Palmer: "Pianos in the Background," *JJI*, xxxviii/8 (1985), 16 [incl. discography]

ANDRÉ BARBERA

Lewis, (Big) Ed [Edward] (*b* Eagle City, OK, 22 Jan 1909; *d* Blooming Grove, NY, 18 Sept 1985). Trumpeter. He began on baritone horn and played with the pianist Jerry Westbrooks in Kansas City in 1924. The following year he changed to trumpet and worked with the pianist Paul Banks, and in 1926 joined the pianist and singer Laura Rucker. From 1926 to 1931 he was a member of Bennie Moten's orchestra (for illustration *see* MOTEN BENNIE), then worked with Thamon Hayes (1932–4), Harlan Leonard (1934–7), and Jay McShann (1937), before joining Count Basie (1937). He remained in Basie's band until 1948 (for illustration *see* FILMS, fig.3), when he left music and became a cab driver. In the mid-1950s, however, he resumed playing, and worked with his own band in the New York area. He toured Europe with the Countsmen in 1984. Lewis was initially influenced by Joe Smith, Red Nichols, and Bix Beiderbecke. He was a featured soloist with Moten's band, but after 1930 he became adept at playing lead, and thereafter was rarely heard in a solo capacity. His compositions include *Justrite* and *It's sand, man!*.

Oral history material in *NjR*.

SELECTED RECORDINGS

As sideman: B. Moten: Moten Stomp (1927, Vic. 20955); Justrite (1928, Vic. 21739); The Jones Law Blues (1929, Vic. 23357); C. Basie: Blue and Sentimental (1938, Decca 1965); Evil Blues (1939, Decca 2922); It's sand, man! (1942, Col. 36647)

BIBLIOGRAPHY

ChiltonW

F. Driggs: "Kansas City Brass: Ed Lewis' Story," *JR*, ii (1959), no.4, p.16; no.9, p.23

FRANK DRIGGS

Lewis, George [Zeno(n), George Joseph François Louis] **(i)** (*b* New Orleans, 13 July 1900; *d* New Orleans, 31 Dec 1968). Clarinetist. He began learning music on fife, then at about the age of 18 taught himself clarinet. He first played with the Black Eagle Band in Mandeville, Louisiana, where he encountered Isidore Fritz, a player he later acknowledged as having had a major influence on his style. During the early 1920s Lewis worked in New Orleans with Buddy Petit and occasionally with Joe Rena, then formed his own band, the New Orleans Stompers, which included Henry "Red" Allen. Later he performed with the Eureka Brass Band, Chris Kelly, Kid Rena (*c*1927), and the Olympia Orchestra (1929). Lewis first played with Bunk Johnson in 1931, in a band led by the trumpeter Evan Thomas; during the 1930s he sometimes appeared with De De and Billie Pierce, though he worked irregularly. From 1942 to 1945 he recorded extensively, usually with Johnson, but also with the trumpeter Kid Shots Madison and as the leader of his own small groups; during this period his playing exhibited a soaring intensity of tone combined with graceful lyric invention. His composition *Burgundy Street Blues* (first recorded in 1944) remains unique in the New Orleans genre, being a solo accompanied by rhythm section only. Despite problems with his embouchure owing to major dental surgery in 1945, Lewis achieved national recognition when he played in New York with Johnson and Baby Dodds in 1945–6 (for illustration *see* JOHNSON, BUNK). After returning to New Orleans he formed the George Lewis Ragtime Band from the nucleus of Johnson's group (Jim Robinson, Lawrence Marrero, and Alcide "Slow Drag" Pavageau), adding the trumpeter Elmer Talbert and Joe Watkins. By 1950 Lewis had become established as the seminal figure of the emerging New Orleans revival. His playing during the following decade almost regained its former timbral purity; a very rapid filigree and seamless registral crossing became hallmarks of his technically fluent and highly individual style. From 1952 to 1954 he toured in Ohio, Illinois, and California, usually in the company of Kid Howard. Later he appeared at the Newport Jazz Festival (1957), made highly successful trips to England, Denmark, and Sweden (1957, 1959), and toured Japan three times (early 1960s). From 1961 until a few weeks before his death he performed regularly at Preservation Hall in New Orleans, leading the PRESERVATION HALL JAZZ BAND; an album recorded in 1964 demonstrates that his playing was still of a very high standard.

Oral history material in *LNT*.

SELECTED RECORDINGS

As leader: Climax Rag/Deep Bayou Blues (1943, Climax 101); *American Music by George Lewis* (1944–5, AM 639), incl. Burgundy Street Blues; Bucket got a hole in it/The girls all like the way I drive (1946, Cir. [USA] 1012); *George Lewis at Herbert Otto's Party* (1949, Jlgy JCE24), incl. Burgundy Street Blues; *George Lewis Jam Session* (1950, Paradox/Pax 6001); *Jazz at vespers* (1954, Riv. 230); *George Lewis at the San Jacinto Hall* (1964, San Jacinto 2)

As sideman with B. Johnson: Tiger Rag/See See Rider (1944, AM 251); Darktown Strutters Ball/Streets of the City (1944, AM 256); Tishomingo Blues/You always hurt the one you love (1945, Decca 25131)

As sideman with others: K. S. Madison: *American Music by George Lewis with Kid Shots* (1944, AM 645), incl. Dumaine Street Drag; G. Guesnon: *Endless the Trek, Endless the Search: George Lewis with George Guesnon's New Orleans Band* (1962, Icon 9)

BIBLIOGRAPHY

C. P. Rogers: "George Lewis and his New Orleans Stompers," *Jazz*, i/2 (1945), 7
G. Lewis: "Play Number Nine," *Jazz Record*, no.40 (1946), 7; repr. in *Selections from the Gutter: Jazz Portraits from "The Jazz Record"*, ed. A. Hodes and C. Hansen (Berkeley, CA, Los Angeles, and London, 1977)
J. Roddy: "Dixieland Jazz is 'Hot' Again," *Look* (6 June 1950)
W. Russell: "The Music of George Lewis and his New Orleans Stompers," *Eureka*, i/1 (1960), 5
J. A. Stuart [pseud. of D. Tait]: *Call him George* (London, 1961)
M. Jones: "Lewis: a Horn with a History," *MM* (17 Sept 1966), 10
M. Harrison: "Backlog 21: George Lewis," *JM*, no.154 (1967), 17
M. Jones: "The Spirit of New Orleans," *MM* (11 Jan 1969), 16
T. Bethell: *George Lewis: a Jazzman from New Orleans* (Berkeley, CA, and London, 1977) [incl. discography]
M. Boyd: "Walking with the King: George Lewis," *Fn*, viii/6 (1977), 4
E. Kraut: *George Lewis: Streifzug durch ein Musiker-Leben* (Menden, Germany, 1980) [incl. discography]
H. Giltrap: "Remembering George Lewis," *Fn*, xvi/1 (1984), 23
L. Fält and H. B. Håkånsson: *Hymn to George: George Lewis on Record and Tape* (n.p. [?Malmö and Stockholm], 1985)
D. Hill: "George Lewis: New Orleans Jazzman," *Cadence*, xiii/1 (1987), 17

ALDEN ASHFORTH

Lewis, George (ii) (*b* Chicago, 14 July 1952). Trombonist and composer. He began studying trombone in 1961; by the age of 12 he was transcribing solos by Lester Young for trombone. He studied theory with Muhal Richard Abrams under the auspices of the Association for the Advancement of Creative Musicians, with which he first became connected in 1971, and played with Douglas Ewart's group Elements. He also studied at Yale University (BA in philosophy 1974) and with Anthony Davis and Fred Anderson. He toured with Count Basie for two months in 1976; a more important association began in May of that year, when he joined Anthony Braxton's group. He belonged to a brass quartet, Quadrisect, with Ewart (1976–7), and from 1980 to 1982 was director of the Kitchen, an avant-garde cultural center in New York. A growing interest in electronic music led to Lewis's working with Richard Teitelbaum, notably on the album *Homage to Charles Parker*, on which Ewart and Davis also played. Lewis has performed with, among others, Roscoe Mitchell, Lester Bowie, Carla Bley, and Derek Bailey; his virtuoso technique and his interest in instrumental and electronic sounds make him a valuable collaborator in a wide range of performing situations. He does not, however, regard himself as a jazz musician. He has written works that combine elements of art music and jazz; some of these, including the *Shadowgraph* series nos.1–3 (1975–8), are scored for standard jazz ensemble; others use electronic sounds, tapes, and (in *Audio Tick*, 1983, for example) computers linked to digital synthesizers and programmed to respond to sounds produced by instrumentalists.

SELECTED RECORDINGS

As unaccompanied soloist: *The George Lewis Solo Trombone Album* (1976, Sack. 3012)

Duos with D. Ewart: *George Lewis/Douglas Ewart* (1978, BS 0026)

As leader: *Homage to Charles Parker* (1979, BS 0029)

As sideman: A. Braxton: *The Montreux–Berlin Concerts* (1975–6, Ari. 5002); B. Altschul: *You Can't Name your own Tune* (1977, Muse 5176); R. Mitchell: *Sketches from Bamboo* (1979, Moers 02024); Evan Parker: *Hook, Drift and Shuffle* (1983, Incus 45)

BIBLIOGRAPHY

J. De Muth: "Anthony Braxton–George Lewis," *Cadence*, ii/2 (1976), 3
J. B. Litweiler: "Profile: George Lewis," *DB*, xliv/14 (1977), 36
C. Flicker: "George Lewis: pas une révolution mais une mutation," *Jm*, nos.266–7 (1978), 38
J. Rockwell: "A New Music Director Comes to the Avant-garde Kitchen," *New York Times* (14 Sept 1980)

CHARLES PASSY/DAVID WILD

Lewis, Herbie (*b* Pasadena, 1941). Double bass player. He recorded with Lennie McBrowne (1959), Harold Land (1959), and Les McCann (1960–61) in California. By 1961 he had moved to New York where he performed and recorded with McCann and played on albums with Dave Pike (1961), Stanley Turrentine (1962), and Jackie McLean (1962). He then returned to California, where he recorded with McCann under the leadership of the tenor saxophonist Clifford Scott (1963), and with Gerald Wilson (1965). In the late 1960s he recorded with many important musicians in and around New York, including Sam Rivers (1966), Bobby Hutcherson (1966, 1969), and Freddie Hubbard (1967). He was a member of the Cannonball Adderley Quintet in 1966, and from 1967 to 1970 he performed with McCoy Tyner; his recordings with Tyner include *Expansions* (1968, BN 84338).

Lewis, Jimmy (*b* Nashville, 11 April 1918). Bass player. He made his first recordings with the rhythm-and-blues singer Ivory Joe Hunter in 1947; he continued to play rhythm-and-blues, recording on electric bass guitar and double bass in the mid-1950s, playing with King Curtis (1956–64), and working with several groups in the 1960s. His career in jazz began with a session with Billie Holiday (1950) and a period in Count Basie's sextet, septet, octet, and orchestra (1950–52). He made a number of recordings with Basie, including four titles with an octet (1950); his playing may be heard to good effect on *Bluebeard Blues* (Col. 38888). From the mid-1960s Lewis worked as a studio musician, recording with the Modern Jazz Quartet in 1965. He also recorded soul jazz with the organists Johnny "Hammond" Smith (1967, 1969, 1971) and Charles Kynard (1969, 1970), Willis "Gator" Jackson (1968, 1976), Horace Silver and Houston Person (both 1970), and Tiny Grimes (1973). Lewis should not be confused with the guitarist Jimmy Lewis, who played with Russ Morgan and Chick Bullock in the 1930s. (K. Mohr: "Jimmy Lewis," *Jazz Statistics*, no.10 (1959), 2)

Lewis, John (Aaron) (*b* LaGrange, IL, 3 May 1920). Pianist and composer. He grew up in Albuquerque, New Mexico, where he began studying piano at the age of seven. His musical studies continued at the University of New Mexico. While in the US Army during World War II he met Kenny Clarke, an early developer of the bop style. After the war Clarke introduced Lewis to Dizzy Gillespie, another bop pioneer, and in 1946 they both joined Gillespie's bop-style big band in New York. There Lewis developed his skills as a composer and arranger, both by writing for Gillespie's band and by studying at the Manhattan School of Music. These studies, which led to a master's degree in 1953, were interrupted in 1948 when the band made a concert tour of Europe. After returning to the USA Lewis worked for Lester Young, Charlie Parker, Miles Davis, Gillespie, Illinois Jacquet, and Ella Fitzgerald. In 1951–2 he served as pianist with the Milt Jackson Quartet, recording on four separate occasions. By the end of 1952 this group was renamed the MODERN JAZZ QUARTET, with Lewis as its music director. For the next two decades Lewis's musical activity centered on the MJQ, for which he wrote many pieces. Lewis also served from 1958 to 1982 as music director of the annual Monterey Jazz Festival, was head of faculty for the summer clinics at the Lenox (Massachusetts) School of Jazz during the late 1950s, and formed the cooperative big band ORCHESTRA U.S.A., which performed and recorded third-stream compositions (1962–5). After the MJQ disbanded temporarily in 1974 he held teaching positions at the City College of New York and at Harvard University. By the early 1980s he was performing with the reunited MJQ and with a sextet, the John Lewis Group, and in 1985, with Gary Giddins and Roberta Swann, he founded the American Jazz Orchestra.

John Lewis, March 1961

Lewis is among the most conservative of bop pianists. His improvised melodies, played with a delicate touch, are usually simple and quiet; the accompaniments are correspondingly light, with Lewis's left hand often just grazing the keys to produce a barely audible sound. His method of accompanying soloists is similarly understated: rather than comping – punctuating the melody with irregularly placed chords – he often plays simple counter-melodies in octaves which combine with the solo and bass parts to form a polyphonic texture. Occasionally Lewis plays in a manner resembling the stride styles of James P. Johnson and Fats Waller, all the while retaining his light touch.

Many of Lewis's solos have a degree of motivic unity which is rare in jazz. For example, in *Bluesology* (1956) each chorus of his solo builds on the previous one by establishing a link from the end of one chorus to the beginning of the next. His 64-bar solo in *Between the Devil and the Deep Blue Sea* (1957) derives almost entirely from its first two bars, which in turn derive from the first four notes of the theme (ex.1). As the solo progresses Lewis subjects its opening motif to inversion (bar 9), chromatic alteration (bars 47 and 57), and a variety of other alterations in pitch and shape (bars 25–6, 41), which nevertheless retain their links with the basic figure.

Ex.1 From *Between the Devil and the Deep Blue Sea*, on *The Modern Jazz Quartet* (1957, Atl. 1265); transcr. T. Owens

Lewis is similarly conservative as a composer, for his music draws heavily on harmonic and melodic practices found in 18th-century European compositions. From the 1950s he has written a number of third-stream works combining European compositional techniques and jazz improvisation. Most of these were written for the MJQ, or for the quartet with instrumental ensembles of various sizes, and are published by MJQ Music. Among his best pieces for the MJQ are *Django* (1960), the ballet suite *The Comedy* (1962), and especially the four pieces *Versailles* (1956), *Three Windows* (1957), *Vendome* (1960), and *Concorde* (1963), all of which combine fugal imitation and nonimitative polyphonic jazz in highly effective ways.

See also PIANO, §5.

SELECTED RECORDINGS

As leader: *Improvised Meditations and Excursions* (1959, Atl. 1313); *Odds Against Tomorrow* (1959, UA 5061); *The Golden Striker* (1960, Atl. 1334); *Preludes and Fugues from the Well-tempered Clavier, Book 1* (1984, Phi. 824381-1); *The Bridge Game* (1984, Phi. 826698-1)

As sideman with C. Parker: on *The Genius of Charlie Parker* (1945–8, Savoy 12009), Parker's Mood (1948); on Charlie Parker (1951–3, Clef 287) [EP], Blues for Alice (1951)

RECORDED COMPOSITIONS

(selective list)

As leader: of Orchestra U.S.A. (with G. Schuller and H. Farberman): *Orchestra U.S.A.* (1963, Colpix 448), incl. Three Little Feelings; *P.O.V.* (1975, Col. PC33534), incl. Mirjana of my Heart and Soul

Recorded by Modern Jazz Quartet with Lewis as sideman: *Modern Jazz Quartet* (1954–5, Prst. 170), incl. Django; *Fontessa* (1956, Atl. 1231), incl. Versailles; *One Never Knows* (1957, Atl. 1284), incl. Three Windows; *Third Stream Music* (1957, 1959–60, Atl. 1345), incl. Sketch for Double String Quartet (1959), Exposure (1960); *European Concert* (1960, Atl. 1385–6), incl. Vendome; *The Modern Jazz Quartet and Orchestra* (1960, Atl. 1359), incl. England's Carol; *Original Sin* (1961, Atl. 1370); *The Comedy* (1962, Atl. 1390); *A Quartet is a Quartet is a Quartet* (1963, Atl. 1420), incl. Concorde; *In Memoriam* (1973, Little David 3001)

BIBLIOGRAPHY

J. E. Berendt: "John Lewis: König des Cool Jazz," *Melos*, xxii/12 (1955), 348
S. Pease: "John Lewis Piano Style," *DB*, xxiii/3 (1956), 46

N. Hentoff: "John Lewis," *DB*, xxiv/4 (1957), 15
J. Lewis: "The Golden Age: Time Future," *Esquire*, li/1 (1959), 112
N. Hentoff: *John Lewis* (New York, 1960)
"John Lewis: Music Master," *Ebony*, xv/5 (1960), 110
G. Schuller: "John Lewis on the Modern Jazz Beachhead," *High Fidelity*, x/10 (1960), 54
F. Thorne: "An Afternoon with John Lewis," *JR*, iii/3 (1960), 6
N. Hentoff: "John Lewis: Success with Integrity," *IM*, lix/6 (1961), 16
M. Williams: "John Lewis and the Modern Jazz Quartet," *Evergreen Review*, vi/23 (1962), 112; repr. in *The Jazz Tradition*, ed. M. Williams (New York, 1970, rev. 2/1983)
T. Owens: *Improvisation Techniques of the Modern Jazz Quartet* (thesis, UCLA, 1965)
M. Williams: "John Lewis," *IM*, lxx/1 (1972), 9
N. Koyama and others: "John Lewis and MJQ Discography," *SJ*, xxviii/3 (1974), 266
R. J. Gleason: *Celebrating the Duke, and Louis, Bessie, Billie, Bird, Carmen, Miles, Dizzy, and other Heroes* (Boston and Toronto, 1975), 109
L. Feather: "John Lewis," *The Pleasures of Jazz: Leading Performers on their Lives, their Music, their Contemporaries* (New York, 1976), 142
T. Owens: "The Fugal Pieces of the Modern Jazz Quartet," *JJS*, iv (1976), 25
L. Feather: "Piano Giants of Jazz: John Lewis," *CK*, iii/7 (1977), 55
B. Korall: "John Lewis: Pianist-Composer-Leader-Teacher," *IM*, lxxv/7 (1977), 8
C. J. Stuessy: *The Confluence of Jazz and Classical Music from 1950 to 1970* (diss., Eastman School, 1978), 348, 402
L. Feather: "MJQ: the Quartet that Wouldn't Die," *Los Angeles Times Calendar* (27 March 1983), 68
I. Gitler: "The Return of the Modern Jazz Quartet," *JT* (1983), March, 10
L. Lyons: *The Great Jazz Pianists, Speaking of their Lives and Music* (New York, 1983), 75
F. Davis: "Back in Time (John Lewis)," *In the Moment: Jazz in the 1980s* (New York, and Oxford, England, 1986) [colln of previously pubd articles], 227
B. Korall: "The American Jazz Orchestra," *IM*, lxxxv/1 (1987), 7

THOMAS OWENS

Lewis, Meade (Anderson) "Lux" (*b* Chicago, 4 Sept 1905; *d* Minneapolis, 7 June 1964). Pianist. Influenced by Fats Waller and Jimmy Yancey, he played at bars and clubs in Chicago before recording his celebrated masterpiece *Honky Tonk Train Blues* (1927), which was not issued until 18 months later. He was rediscovered by John Hammond late in 1935, and recorded this work again. Over the next few years he issued a number of other pieces in the boogie-woogie style, most notably the influential *Yancey Special*, *Bear Cat Crawl*, *Tell your Story*, and *Bass on Top*. His technical ability, energetic cross-rhythms, and remarkable invention made him one of the most important figures of the boogie-woogie craze of the late 1930s. In 1938 he formed a trio with two other important pianists of this school, Albert Ammons and Pete Johnson, but this proved short-lived, and he soon returned to working alone at nightclubs in New York and California. He also performed with such musicians as Sidney Bechet, and was occasionally recorded playing the celesta and harpsichord. He grew increasingly dissatisfied with being identified exclusively as a blues and boogie-woogie player, and his later playing was often rushed and perfunctory.

See also PIANO, §3; for illustration *see* BLUES, fig.2.

SELECTED RECORDINGS

As unaccompanied soloist: Honky Tonk Train Blues (1927, Para. 12896); Honky Tonk Train Blues (1935, Para. R2187); Yancey Special (1936, Decca 819); The Blues (1939, BN 8-9); Bass on Top (1940, BN 16); Tell your Story (1940, BN 15); Self-portrait (1941, BN 19) [hpd]

As leader with A. Ammons and P. Johnson: Boogie Woogie Prayer (1938, Voc. 4606); Bear Cat Crawl (1938, Voc. 4608)

BIBLIOGRAPHY

W. Russell: "Boogie Woogie," *Jazzmen*, ed. F. Ramsey, Jr., and C. E. Smith (New York, 1939/*R*1977), 183
M. Harrison: "Boogie Woogie," *Jazz: New Perspectives on the History of Jazz*, ed. N. Hentoff and A. J. McCarthy (New York, 1959/*R*1974), 105–37
"Meade Lux Lewis: a Blues Man's Story," *DB*, xxvi/4 (1959), 16 [interview]
W. Russell: "Three Boogie Woogie Pianists," *The Art of Jazz: Essays on the Nature and Development of Jazz*, ed. M. Williams (New York, 1959/*R*1979), 104
L. Feather: "Piano Giants of Jazz: Meade Lux Lewis," *CK*, vi/4 (1980), 74 [incl. transcr.]
M. Williams: "Cutting the Boogie," *Jazz Heritage* (New York and Oxford, England, 1985) [colln of previously pubd interviews], 160
D. Hill: "Meade Lux Lewis," *Cadence*, xiii/10 (1987), 16 [interview]

MARTIN WILLIAMS/R

Lewis, Mel [Sokoloff, Melvin] (*b* Buffalo, 10 May 1929). Drummer. His father was a drummer in the Buffalo area. He belonged to the dance bands of Boyd Raeburn (1948), Alvino Rey (1948–9), Ray Anthony (1949–50, 1953–4), and Tex Beneke (1950–53). In 1954 he entered into an association with Stan Kenton, which, apart from brief periods during which he worked with Frank Rosolino's quintet and Hampton Hawes's trio, lasted until he settled in 1957 in Los Angeles. There he led a quintet with Bill Holman (1958), worked frequently in studios, and played in big bands led by Terry Gibbs (with which he recorded in 1959–62) and Gerald Wilson. From 1960 he traveled to New York for engagements with the Gerry Mulligan Concert Jazz Band; at the same time he toured Europe with Dizzy Gillespie (1961) and the USSR with Benny Goodman (1962). After settling in New York he formed the Thad Jones–Mel Lewis Orchestra with Jones in 1965 (for illustration *see* JONES, fig.1*b*); this group performed widely, made many recordings, and achieved great critical success. On Jones's departure from the orchestra in 1979 Lewis became its sole leader; later Bob Brookmeyer assumed the roles of composer, arranger, and music director that Jones previously had filled. Because of his faultless timekeeping, sense of ensemble, and skillful accompaniment of soloists Lewis is widely regarded as one of the greatest drummers in jazz. While known principally for his work with big bands he also plays adeptly in small groups.

SELECTED RECORDINGS

As leader: *Mel Lewis and Friends* (1976, A&M Hor. 716)

As leader with T. Jones: *Live at the Village Vanguard* (1967, SolS 18016); *Central Park North* (1969, SolS 18058); *Consummation* (1970, BN 84346); *Suite for Pops* (1972, 1975, A&M Hor. 701); *The Thad Jones/Mel Lewis Quartet* (1977, AH 3)

As sideman: S. Kenton: *Contemporary Concepts* (1955, Cap. T666); *Cuban Fire!* (1956, Cap. T731); B. Holman: *The Fabulous Bill Holman* (1957, Coral 57188); W. Herman: *Woody Herman's New Big Band at the Monterey Jazz Festival* (1959, Atl. 1328); G. Mulligan: *A Concert in Jazz* (1961, Verve 68415); D. Gillespie: *New Continent* (1962, Lml. 86022)

BIBLIOGRAPHY

J. Tynan: "Time is the Quality Mel Lewis Has," *DB*, xxiv/25 (1957), 22
——: "The Peripatetic Mel Lewis," *DB*, xxix/10 (1962), 24
D. Morgenstern: "Mel Lewis: the Big Band Man," *DB*, xxxiv/6 (1967), 20
A. J. Smith: "Mel Lewis: Staunch but Swinging," *DB*, xlv/11 (1978), 16
I. Gitler: "Mel Lewis and (Just) his Jazz Orchestra," *Radio Free Jazz*, xx/5 (1979), 11
G. Endress: *Jazz Podium: Musiker über sich selbst* (Stuttgart, Germany, 1980), 168
W. F. Lee: *Stan Kenton: Artistry in Rhythm* (Los Angeles, 1980), 196 [interview]
R. Mattingly: "Mel Lewis," *MD*, ix/2 (1985), 8
S. Crouch: "1000 Nights at the Village Vanguard," *VV*, xxxi (4 March 1986), 77

J. KENT WILLIAMS

Lewis, Ramsey (Emmanuel, Jr.) (*b* Chicago, 27 May 1935). Pianist. He studied music at Chicago Musical College and De Paul University. In 1956 he formed a trio with Eldee Young (double bass) and Redd Holt (drums), which became very successful; its album *The In Crowd* sold a million copies and received a Grammy award as the best jazz recording by a small group (1965). In 1958 Lewis also recorded with Max Roach and the vibraphonist Lem Winchester. He has worked with the double bass player Cleveland Eaton (from 1966) and the drummers Maurice White (1966–9) and Morris Jennings (from 1970). In the 1970s he began to play electronic keyboards with larger ensembles and turned towards soul music and funk, though he performed again on piano after 1978. His technically competent but repetitive playing has been criticized as being commercially oriented.

SELECTED RECORDINGS

As leader: *Ramsey Lewis at the Bohemian Caverns* (1964, Argo 741); *The In Crowd* (1965, Argo 757); *Blues for the Night Owl* (n.d., Odyssey PC37019); *Chance Encounter* (1982, Col. FC38294)

As sideman: L. Winchester: *Tribute to Clifford Brown* (1958, Argo 642)

BIBLIOGRAPHY

FeatherE; *Feather '60s*

L. Feather: "'In Crowd': Nothing Succeeds like Success," *DB*, xxxii/25 (1965), 11

B. Gardner: "Ramsey Lewis: Soul Survivor," *DB*, xxxii/10 (1965), 23

M. Bourne: "Ramsey Lewis: . . . those 88 Monsters that I Love . . .'," *DB*, xl/17 (1973), 14

L. Lyons: *The Great Jazz Pianists, Speaking of their Lives and Music* (New York, 1983), 204

STEVE LARSON

Lewis, Sabby [William Sebastian] (*b* Middleburg, NC, 1 Nov 1914). Pianist, bandleader, and arranger. Brought up in Philadelphia, he first played jazz after moving to Boston in 1932. He worked with Tasker Crosson's Ten Statesmen (1934) then formed his own seven-piece band in 1936. From that time until the late 1970s he led big bands and smaller groups, mainly in and around Boston but also in New York; among the prominent musicians who played with him as sidemen were Paul Gonsalves, Sonny Stitt, Cat Anderson, Alan Dawson, Roy Haynes, Al Morgan, Irving "Mouse" Randolph, Idrees Sulieman, and Freddie Webster. A good example of the work of one of his smaller groups is *Edna*, recorded with a nine-piece band (including Lewis as the pianist) in 1946 (Contl 6035).

BIBLIOGRAPHY

B. Porter: "The Sabby Lewis Band," *JJ*, xx/2 (1967), 8

A. McCarthy: *Big Band Jazz* (New York and London, 1974)

"Sabby Lewis: the Boston Legend," *Whiskey, Women, and . . .*, no.15 (1985), 28

based on *ChiltonW*

Lewis, Sylvester (*b* Kansas City, MO, 19 Oct 1908; *d* New York, 1974). Trumpeter. After beginning his jazz career in Kansas City, he played with Kat (Herbert) Cowens's band on tour and in New York (1928), where he also recorded with Jelly Roll Morton in a group led by Wilton Crawley. He played with Aubrey Neal's Ramblers (1929–30) and Claude Hopkins (1930–36), with whom he made recordings (1932–5), among them *Farewell Blues* (1935, issued on *The Golden Swing Years*, Pol. 423269); he then worked in the theater – with Billy Butler's orchestra in *Rhapsody in Black* and with Eubie Blake and Noble Sissle in *Shuffle Along* (from 1941). During his time in the army he led his own band for a tour of the Pacific. He recorded with Roy Eldridge in 1946. Lewis ceased to work as a full-time musician in 1949.

based on *ChiltonW*

Lewis, Ted [Friedman, Theodore Leopold] (*b* Circleville, OH, 6 June 1892; *d* New York, 25 Aug 1971). Bandleader and clarinetist. After working in tent shows and on the vaudeville circuit he settled in New York, where he played in a band led by the pianist Earl Fuller; in 1918 he formed his own group, and in the following year made his first recordings as a leader. In the 1920s his recorded work consisted largely of novelty songs and show tunes; his sidemen included important jazz musicians, however, such as Georg Brunis, Muggsy Spanier, and Jimmy Dorsey, and, between 1929 and 1932, Frank Teschemacher, Benny Goodman, Jack Teagarden, and Fats Waller (who plays piano and sings on *I'm Crazy 'bout my Baby*, 1931). Lewis's style changed little over the years; until the late 1960s he continued to lead groups of various sizes, usually at hotels, resorts, and nightclubs. At the end of his career he still made appearances with a battered top hat and cane performing old vaudeville routines and delivering songs he had popularized many years earlier (including *When my Baby Smiles at me* and *Me and my Shadow*) in his characteristic patter style (more spoken than sung), playing his old Albert system clarinet and asking the audience his favorite, timeworn question, "Is everybody happy?". His private archive is now in the music library of Yale University; *see* LIBRARIES AND ARCHIVES, §2.

Oral history material in *LNT*.

SELECTED RECORDINGS

(all recorded for Columbia)

Maybe – Who Knows? (1929, 1854D); Lewisada Blues (1929, 1916D); Farewell Blues (1929, 2029D); Egyptian-Ella/I'm Crazy 'bout my Baby (1931, 2428D)

BIBLIOGRAPHY

L. Walker: *The Wonderful Era of the Great Dance Bands* (Berkeley, CA, 1964)

B. Rust: *The American Dance Band Discography, 1917–1942* (New Rochelle, NY, 1975)

M. Berresford: "Ted Lewis: a Discography," *Sv*, no.95 (1981), 184; no.96 (1981), 207; no.97 (1981), 5; no.98 (1981–2), 47; no.99 (1982), 93; no.100 (1982), 132

MARK TUCKER/R

Lewis, Vic (*b* London, 29 July 1919). English bandleader, guitarist, singer, and cornetist. He played in a band with George Shearing and Carlo Krahmer in the mid-1930s, and in 1938 visited New York, where he performed with Bobby Hackett. In the same year he led a recording session that included Hackett, Eddie Condon, Zutty Singleton, and other American musicians. While serving in the RAF (1941–4) he performed and recorded as a guitarist with Buddy Featherstonhaugh; his playing may be heard on *Vic Lewis Jam Sessions, 1944–1945: the War Years* (1944–5, Harl. 3008). He then worked with Stephane Grappelli (1944–5) and led a dixieland band with Jack Parnell (1944–6). In 1946 he formed the first of several big bands that toured and recorded frequently; by 1948 their format was based on that of the Stan Kenton Orchestra. Lewis continued to play and record with his own bands during the 1960s, though after 1959 he also worked as a booking agent.

Oral history material in *GBLnsa*.

BIBLIOGRAPHY

FeatherE

"The Vic Lewis Music," *New Beat* (1949), Sept, p.8

S. Voce: "Old Vic," *JJ*, xxix/2 (1976), 22

J. Godbolt: *A History of Jazz in Britain, 1919–50* (London, Melbourne, Australia, and New York, 1984)

T. Middleton: *Vic Lewis: a Discography* (Amsterdam, 1985)

V. Lewis and T. Barrow: *Music and Maiden Overs: My Showbusiness Life* (London, 1987) [autobiography]

Lewis, Willie [William T.] (*b* Cleburne, TX, 10 June 1905; *d* New York, 13 Jan 1971). Alto and baritone saxophonist, clarinetist, singer, and bandleader. He was brought up in Dallas and began his professional career playing in a variety theater. He studied at the New England Conservatory and toured briefly with Will Marion Cook's orchestra before joining Sam Wooding at the Nest Club in New York. From 1925 he toured Europe, South America, and North Africa with Wooding's Symphonic Syncopators, and when the group broke up in 1931 Lewis formed his own band from among its members. During the 1930s he became the most prominent black-American bandleader in Europe, and by 1935 his sidemen included such players as

Herman "Ivory" Chittison, Frank "Big Boy" Goudie, and Benny Carter; later George Johnson and Bill Coleman also joined the group. Lewis disbanded his orchestra in 1941 and returned to New York, where in the 1940s and 1950s he dabbled in acting, though he worked chiefly as a cook and waiter in Harlem.

Lewis was an able showman, singer, and instrumentalist, who engaged the best players he could afford and presented musicianly ensembles. His bands played mostly for royalty and the well-to-do patrons of Europe's best hotels, nightclubs, and ballrooms.

SELECTED RECORDINGS

Christopher Columbus (1936, PAct 898); Swinging for a Swiss Miss (1937, PAct 1296); Happy Feet (1941, ES 4067)

BIBLIOGRAPHY

ChiltonW
J. P. Holloway: "Cross-channel Coloured Rhythm," *MM*, xii (17 Oct 1936), 2
——: "Harlem's Swing Ambassador," *Rhythm*, no.127 (1938), 56
J. Simmen: "Louis Bacon, Henry Mason: Two Trumpet Players," *JJ*, xxi/2 (1968), 12
A. McCarthy: *Big Band Jazz* (London and New York, 1974), 313
H. Langeweg: "Willy [*sic*] Lewis," *Doctor Jazz*, no.91 (1980), 35
F. Driggs and H. Lewine: *Black Beauty, White Heat: a Pictorial History of Classic Jazz, 1920–1950* (New York, 1982), 152
J. Simmen: "Willie Lewis and his Entertainers, 1935–1937," *Sv*, no.115 (1984), 4

FRANK DRIGGS

Liberty Music Shop. Record label. It was established in New York in 1933 by the management of the group of music stores of the same name. The discs were mostly manufactured using the American Record Company's custom recording and pressing facilities. Although the label's catalogue consisted mainly of light music, it also included important recordings by Ethel Waters and Lee Wiley. Issue continued into the 1940s; thereafter the label was used for the release of a series of LPs that included rereleases of the items by Wiley.

BIBLIOGRAPHY

B. Rust: *The American Record Label Book* (New Rochelle, NY, 1978), 177
L. Kunstadt: "Exploratory Discographical Research of the Liberty Music Shop Record," *Record Research*, nos.181–2 (1981), 9; nos.185–6 (1981), 9; nos.187–8 (1981), 9; nos.189–90 (1982), 10; nos.191–2 (1982), 10; nos.195–6 (1983), 12; nos.197–8 (1983), 8; nos.201–2 (1983), 11; nos.203–4 (1983), 9; nos.205–6 (1984), 12; nos.207–8 (1984), 11; nos.209–10 (1984), 12 [addns and corrections in nos.215–16 (1985), 11; nos.217–18 (1985), 2; nos.219–20 (1986), 5; nos.220–21 (1986), 4; nos.227–8 (1987), 10; nos.231–2 (1987), 12]
J. Raymond: "A Numerical Listing of Liberty Music Shop Records," *Record Research*, nos.181–2 (1981), 8

Libraries and archives. This article surveys collections of materials relating to jazz in public and private libraries worldwide. The repositories covered include archives devoted solely to jazz, public and institutional libraries with important jazz holdings, collections of sound recordings, and private collections.

1. History. 2. List.

1. History. Jazz is a relatively young art form and its acceptance as a legitimate subject of systematic study came late in its short history. The assembling of libraries and archives of materials relating to jazz is therefore a recent phenomenon. In the public domain most such materials were at first accumulated as part of the activities of general music libraries rather than through acquisition policies devoted specifically to jazz. Early in its history therefore the most important and comprehensive jazz collections were in private hands, and enthusiasts often owned very significant libraries, particularly of recordings.

By the 1950s the situation had begun to change. As jazz scholarship gained acceptance as a discipline and jazz studies programs were established in educational institutions, academic libraries began actively to acquire relevant materials. At the same time jazz enthusiasts started to give their substantial and sometimes specialized collections to academic and public libraries for general use. The 1950s also saw the first donations and bequests by jazz musicians themselves of primary materials such as manuscripts, correspondence, and memorabilia to libraries and archives.

The first public collections devoted solely to jazz materials were set up in the late 1950s and 1960s: the Archives of New Orleans Jazz, later renamed the William Ransom Hogan Jazz Archive, at Tulane University in New Orleans; the Institute of Jazz Studies at Rutgers in Newark, New Jersey; and the Institut für Jazzforschung in Graz, Austria. The growth of jazz collections has, however, been slow; as in other areas of library development, acquisitions have been affected by changing policies on public funding and tax exemption (the latter pertinent to donations by individuals), and where competition for financial support is strong, jazz (still a subject of comparatively small interest and needing to prove its academic status) has sometimes suffered. For such reasons collections that would be regarded as inadequate in another discipline are, at this stage in its history, important to jazz; this is reflected in the list below, which includes many small collections and private libraries in addition to large, established repositories. By far the majority of important libraries are in the USA, where jazz education and research on jazz are, by and large, better established than elsewhere.

The origins and evolution of jazz are entangled inextricably with the social and cultural history first and foremost of the USA but also of all the places where the music has flourished. Accordingly many areas of the historical and sociological disciplines may be seen as having an important part to play in the study of jazz, and the materials collected by libraries to support those disciplines are thus relevant. Collections covering black social and cultural history, the commercial and cultural history of individual cities, the history and development of sound recording and broadcasting, and union history (particularly in the USA, where the AFM maintained separate local branches for black musicians) contain resources of great significance to jazz. (In general such collections are not listed here.)

Besides the types of holding directly connected with jazz – recordings, books, periodicals, and manuscript and printed music – the materials acquired by libraries and archives include oral history tapes and transcripts, pictures, correspondence and personal papers, and printed ephemera (press clippings, handbills, concert programs, etc., which are usually maintained in loose-leaf files). Items that may not immediately recommend themselves as relevant to the jazz scholar often prove useful in research on specific aspects of the music: for example, city directories give invaluable data on the establishments where jazz was performed, and newspapers dealing with alternative culture and those aimed at specific social groups (notably those produced in the USA for black readers) provide important background and musical information.

2. List. The following list is arranged alphabetically by country, and within each country by city. The full postal address of each library is given where possible. The sigla included here

are those used elsewhere in the dictionary; for most American libraries they are those assigned by the Library of Congress in its publication *Symbols of American Libraries* (Washington, rev. 12/1980). Bibliographies to individual entries list catalogues and published descriptions of the holdings of the libraries concerned; a general bibliography follows the list.

AUSTRIA

GRAZ. Institut für Jazzforschung, Hochschule für Musik und Darstellende Kunst, Leonhardstrasse 15, Palais Meran, A-8010 Graz. The library was formed in 1965 to serve the Institut für Jazz of the Akademie in Graz; the INSTITUT FÜR JAZZFORSCHUNG, to which the library is now attached, was formed after a reorganization in 1969. Its holdings consist of 4650 LP records, 400 items of sheet music, 300 arrangements for small groups and big band, 2400 books, 130 periodicals, and more than 50 videotapes.

BIBLIOGRAPHY
F. Korner: "The History of the Jazz Institute in Graz," *JF* [intl edn], no.19 (1972), 43

CANADA

ISLINGTON. Eugene Miller Collection, 90 Prince George Drive, Islington, Ontario M9B 2X8. This private collection comprises 20,000 recordings (including 500 cylinders and several records issued in Canada by the Berliner label) and 1500 items of sheet music and sheet-music covers (jazz, ragtime, and popular music).

MONTREAL. Concordia University, Montreal, Quebec. In the mid-1980s the Concordia University Archives (1455 De Maisonneuve Boulevard West, Montreal, Quebec H3G 1M8 (*CaQMG*)) acquired several private collections relating to jazz in Montreal. The collection of John Gilmore (three linear meters), accumulated in the course of research into the history of jazz in the city, includes 178 tapes (not indexed or transcribed) of interviews with 86 subjects covering the period up to the 1970s, 100 photographs and 120 negatives from the same period, recordings and posters, and manuscript notes. The collection of the bandleader Johnny Holmes (four linear meters) includes three meters of big-band arrangements (mostly by Holmes), 50 photographs from the 1940s and 1950s (some depicting Oscar Peterson), and 200 tapes of radio broadcasts (each lasting half an hour) made for the CBC by Holmes's big band between 1959 and 1980. The collection of the discographer Alex Robertson (eight linear meters) contains 1300 78 r.p.m. records (on Compo, Berliner, and other labels), 2500 items of sheet music, books and periodicals (some relating to discography), catalogues of record companies, and manuscript notes. The archives also hold 76 photographs from the 1930s in the collection of Myron P. (Mynie) Sutton and 25 from the same period in that of Clyde Duncan, as well as other photographs, scrapbooks, and privately made (unissued) recordings in the collections of Walter Boudreau, Jean Préfontaine, and others.

The university's Georges P. Vanier Library (7141 Sherbrooke Street West, Montreal, Quebec H4B 1R6) holds 900 LP records, 225 scores by Thad Jones, Toshiko Akiyoshi, Bob Brookmeyer, Duke Ellington, and others, 600 books on jazz in the general collection and 50 in the reference collection, 20 catalogues of record companies, 50 videotape recordings, and a small number of instructional materials.

YORK. York University, 4700 Keele Street, North York, Ontario M3J 1P3. The Listening Room (Room 409) of the Scott Library houses the Anne and Robert Levine Recordings Archive of Jazz and Blues, which was acquired in 1985 from the estate of Robert Levine of Cleveland; the archive contains some 6000 LP and 300 EP recordings (mostly of North American jazz). The Scott Library also holds books and more than 80 periodicals relevant to the study of jazz. Two departmental libraries on the campus of York University contain further jazz materials: the Jazz Studies Library holds transcriptions, fake books, and instructional materials, and a graduate students' reading room holds 20 dissertations and theses (on microfilm), newspaper clippings, sheet music, and method books.

FRANCE

VILLEFRANCHE-DE-ROUERGUE. Discothèque Municipale, rue du Sénéchal, 12200 Villefranche-de-Rouergue. The library acquired from his family the collection of Hugues Panassié in November 1979 and made additions to it in the following years. The Panassié collection consists principally of sound recordings: 6000 78 r.p.m. records (dating from 1917 to the 1950s) and 9000 LPs. There are also videotapes, French, British, and American periodicals, discographies, and copies of Panassié's writings. These materials form the substantial proportion of resources that cover all areas of popular music.

GERMANY

BERLIN. Deutsche Bibliothek, Abteilung Deutsches Musikarchiv, Gärtnerstrasse 25–32, D-1000 Berlin 45. The library houses the national sound archive, and new acquisitions to the collection result from a system of compulsory deposit. In 1987 its holdings in jazz consisted of 8000 LP records (all German issues) and 1200 78 r.p.m. records (including 100 V-discs); printed materials include 200 items of jazz and ragtime sheet music from German-speaking countries (notably about 50 works by Scott Joplin and the complete printed works of Claus Ogerman), and 200 discographies, periodicals, and other works of reference.

——. Staatliches Institut für Musikforschung Preussischer Kulturbesitz, Tiergartenstrasse 1, D-1000 Berlin 30. In the area of jazz the library of the institute holds 200 LP records (chiefly from the USA), 120 books, and a small number of periodicals.

BREMEN. Archiv für Populäre Musik, Ostertorsteinweg 3, D-2800 Bremen 1. The archive holds 40,000 recordings of jazz, blues, and popular music (mostly LPs), 4000 books, periodicals, and catalogues of record companies, and newspaper clippings. The archive publishes the quarterly journal *Anschlaege: Zeitschrift des Archivs für Populäre Musik*.

DARMSTADT. Internationales Jazz Zentrum, Internationales Musikinstitut Darmstadt, Nieder-Ramstädter-Strasse 190, D-6100 Darmstadt. This library was formed in 1983 and consists entirely of private collections that were acquired through purchase. It contains 20,000 jazz records, 1800 books, 10,000 numbers of periodicals, films, videotapes, scrapbooks, and files of printed ephemera. The library of the writer and record producer Joachim-Ernst Berendt is being transferred to the institute; in the late 1980s the J.-E. Berendt Archiv contained parts of Berendt's collection of recordings, books, and journals, and photographs of jazz subjects by leading photographers in the field such as Duncan P. Schiedt, Charles H. Stewart, and Yukio Tchikawa.

MUNICH. Amerika-Institut der Universität München, Schellingstrasse 3, D-8000 Munich 40. The institute's collection of jazz materials consists of about 100 records, 50 books, and a small number of periodicals.

GREAT BRITAIN

CROWTHORNE, nr Reading. British Institute of Jazz Studies, 17 The Chase, Edgcumbe Park, Crowthorne, Berkshire RG11 6HT. The institute's library contains around 1400 books, 10,000 numbers of periodicals, 300 concert programs, and several thousand items of printed ephemera.

LONDON. National Sound Archive of the British Library, 29 Exhibition Road, London SW7 2AS (*GBLnsa*). The archive was known as the British Institute of Recorded Sound until April 1984, when it became part of the British Library; it collects recorded sound of all kinds, and jazz is only one of several special areas. Its jazz holdings consist of 25,000 LP records (including the complete issues of many contemporary labels, such as Black Saint, Concord, ECM, Enja, and Incus), 3000–4000 78 r.p.m. records (mostly British issues), recordings of BBC broadcasts, and recordings of concert performances, made specially for the archive; British and European jazz are emphasized, though there is representative coverage of American jazz. A continuing oral history project had by 1987 resulted in taped interviews with about 15 British jazz musicians; a number of recordings of interviews with visiting Americans, conducted in the 1970s by Stan Britt, are also in the collection. Some 50 videotapes include recordings of documentaries and BBC television broadcasts. The archive's printed materials comprise comprehensive holdings of discographies, periodicals, reference books, and record company catalogues, and a collection of newspaper clippings and festival programs. It published the half-yearly journal *Recorded Sound* from May 1961 until 1984.

NETHERLANDS

AMSTERDAM. Nationaal Jazz Archief, Oude Schans 73–77, 1011 KW Amsterdam. The archive was established in April 1980 by Wim van Eyle with the assistance of the Prince Bernhard Fund and the Dutch government and is run by the Stichting Nationaal Jazz Archief; although this organization receives a small subsidy from the government it relies to a great extent on the work of volunteers. The archive's holdings are devoted largely to jazz in the Netherlands and the work of Dutch jazz musicians abroad. They include 400 LP and 200 78 r.p.m. records, 200 hours of oral history interviews, and many recordings of Dutch radio broadcasts; the collection of printed materials consists of 1000 items of sheet music, 700 books, 50 catalogues of record companies, many periodicals, and several hundred items of printed ephemera. The archive also contains several thousand photographs, six hours of film, and 500 hours of videotape recordings. Besides running the archive, the Stichting Nationaal Jazz Archief also assists others in the production of books and recordings.

——. Openbare Muziekbibliotheek, Prinsengracht 587, 1016 HT Amsterdam. The music department of the public library in Amsterdam started a collection of jazz materials in 1972. Its holdings consist of 12,000 LP records, about 300 hours of tape recordings, 1000 items of sheet music, 400 books, and 150 videotapes. A printed catalogue of the collection, *Jazz is Where you Find it*, was published in 1979 (suppls. 1983, 1987).

NORWAY

OSLO. Norsk Jazzarkiv, Toftesgate 69, N-0552 Oslo 5 (*NOnj*). Formed in 1981, the archive holds 300 LP recordings of music by Norwegian jazz musicians, 350 recordings on reel-to-reel and cassette tape, 20 oral history interviews, 70 items of sheet music, 80 books, several Norwegian jazz periodicals, and 40 videotapes. Other materials include photographs, scrapbooks, newspaper clippings, posters, and concert programs. The archive has also published a history of jazz in Norway to 1940 (B. Stendahl: *Jazz hot & swing: jazz i Norge, 1920–1940* (Oslo, 1987) [incl. discography by J. Bergh]).

POLAND

SOPOT. Archiwum Standardów Jazzowych [Archives of Jazz Standards], Ceynowy 5, 81-718 Sopot. Formed in August 1982, the archive is run by the POLSKIE STOWARZYSZENIE JAZZOWE (Polish Jazz Society) and is the only jazz library in Poland with official standing. It holds 2700 items of sheet music and 300 books.

SWEDEN

STOCKHOLM. Svenskt Visarkiv, Centralinstitution för Vis- och Folkmusikforskning, Hagagatan 23A, S-113 47 Stockholm (*SSsv*). The jazz section of the archive was formed in July 1981 and consists principally of material relating to Swedish music and musicians. It holds 1600 LP, 150 EP, and 1300 78 r.p.m. records, as well as some privately made (unissued) wax recordings, 250 hours of reel-to-reel and cassette tapes of music, 600 hours of oral history tapes (some interviews conducted by members of the jazz section and others broadcast on Swedish radio), and 50 videotape recordings of Swedish television broadcasts. Its music and printed materials include 1000 items of sheet music (mostly dance music from 1925 to 1950), printed and manuscript arrangements used by Swedish small groups and bands, among them those of Arne Hülphers, Charles Redland, and Gösta Törner, 800 books, several periodicals (including a complete run of *Orkester journalen*), scrapbooks, newspaper clippings, posters, and concert programs. The archive also owns a large collection of photographs and a film of Thore Ehrling and his orchestra (also on videotape). Among the library's special collections is a large amount of material relating to the career of Alice Babs (donated in 1981), which includes tapes, sheet music, scripts from radio broadcasts, and newspaper clippings; tapes of radio broadcasts made from New York by Claes Dahlgren between 1950 and 1964 (acquired in 1981); and a complete set of recordings (on tape) issued by Metronome between 1949 and 1961 (donated in 1984).

——. Sveriges Radio, Oxenstiernsgatan 20, S-105 10 Stockholm. Founded in 1925, the broadcasting library holds a large collection of Swedish jazz recordings that is comprehensive from around 1930; it includes 23,000 LP and 15,000 78 r.p.m. records (the earliest dating from around 1918). Also held in the library are discographies and a large number of catalogues of European record companies.

SWITZERLAND

WÄDENSWIL. Music of Man Archive, Holzmoosrütistrasse 11, CH-8820 Wädenswil. The archive holds materials on all styles of Afro-American music, including jazz, blues, spirituals, gospel songs, and soul music. Some 1150 LP recordings of music, 30 LP recordings of spoken material (lectures, interviews, etc.), and 200 books are relevant to the study of jazz and blues.

UNION OF SOVIET SOCIALIST REPUBLICS

Several music libraries in the USSR contain jazz materials. Among the important collections are those of the State V. I. Lenin Library of the USSR (Prospekt Kalinina 3, 101000 Moscow), the All-Union State Library of Foreign Literature (Ulanovskaya 1, 109240 Moscow), and the Composers' Union of the USSR (Ogaryovskaya 13, 103009 Moscow).

UNITED STATES OF AMERICA

AMHERST. Music Library, State University of New York at Buffalo, Baird Hall, Amherst, NY 14260. The library of SUNY, Buffalo (now in the nearby town of Amherst), supports a large program of jazz studies. It contains 5000 LP records, more than 100 fake books (indexed by individual work title), more than 100 instrumental methods, and periodicals, bibliographies, discographies, and other works of reference, as well as a sizable collection of biographies of individual musicians. Graphic materials relating to jazz include posters used to promote concerts and festivals and an extensive picture file.

ANN ARBOR. WUOM, 5500 LS&A Building, University of Michigan, Ann Arbor, MI 48109. This radio station holds a large number of jazz recordings made before 1950, including 27,000 78 r.p.m., 6000 LP, and 200 45 r.p.m. records, as well as 100 discographies and other works of reference. The collection is used mainly as a source for the nationally syndicated radio program "Jazz Revisited" and for broadcasts on the university's radio stations, but it is also available for research.

ATHENS. University of Georgia, Athens, GA 30602. The university's Music Recordings Archives hold 78 r.p.m. recordings of jazz and dance music (eight linear meters), which were once owned by a radio station; a manuscript catalogue of the collection is available. Also of some relevance to the study of jazz is the collection of 10,000 items of sheet music held in the Rare Books and Manuscripts Department of the university library.

AUSTIN. University of Texas, Austin, TX 78712 (*TxU*). In January 1981 the university purchased the collection of Ross Russell, the writer on jazz and founder of Dial Records. The university's Fine Arts Library holds the collection's sound materials; these include 3500 LP and 78 r.p.m. records (among which is the world's largest collection of recordings by Charlie Parker, and test pressings made for Dial by Kenny Dorham, Dexter Gordon, and Red Rodney) and reel-to-reel and cassette tape recordings of interviews with Parker, Jesse Price, Jay McShann, and Fats Navarro. Printed materials, which are held in the Humanities Research Center, comprise 265 books on jazz, 400 periodicals (including complete or nearly complete runs of *Down Beat*, *Jazz Review*, *Clef*, *Record Changer*, and *Jazz Record*), and around 200 pamphlets, record catalogues, and concert programs. There are also 15 boxes of correspondence, miscellaneous manuscripts, photographs, unpublished writings, and personal papers.

BIBLIOGRAPHY

R. Lawn: "From Bird to Schoenberg: the Ross Russell Collection," *Library Chronicle* [U. of Texas], new ser., nos.25–6 (1984), 137

BALTIMORE. Milton S. Eisenhower Library, Johns Hopkins University, Charles Street and 34th Street, Baltimore, MD 21218. The Andrew E. Salmieri Jazz Collection, donated by the collector's family, contains 1100 LP, 1200 45 r.p.m., and 750 78 r.p.m. records; the last group dates mostly from the 1940s and 1950s and is indexed by performer.

BERKELEY. Music Library, 240 Morrison Hall, University of California, Berkeley, CA 94720. The library's jazz holdings include 1500 LP records (formerly in private collections) and compact discs, 600 books and periodicals, transcriptions of solos by John Coltrane, and fake books.

BLOOMINGTON. Indiana University Archives of Traditional Music, Morrison Hall, Bloomington, IN 47405 (*InU-Atm*). The holdings of the archives, which were founded at Columbia University by George Herzog in 1936 and transferred to Bloomington in 1948, are strong in jazz: there are 10,000 78 r.p.m. recordings of early jazz, 1500 LPs, 25 recordings of oral history material relating to Hoagy Carmichael and to jazz in Bloomington, and 40 reference books. The Hoagy Carmichael Collection also includes 60 tapes of 78 r.p.m. records from Carmichael's collection (of music by Louis Armstrong, Bob Crosby, Duke Ellington, and others), two letters by Carmichael, and 200 scores.

BIBLIOGRAPHY

P. M. Peek: *Catalog of Afroamerican Music and Oral Data Holdings* (Bloomington, 1970)

A Catalog of Phonorecordings of Music and Oral Data Held by the Archives of Traditional Music (Boston, 1975)

D. S. Lee: *Native North American Music and Oral Data: a Catalogue of Sound Recordings, 1893–1976* (Bloomington, 1979)

M. B. Graf: *A Catalog of Indiana Music and Folklore Held by the Archives of Traditional Music, Indiana University* (Bloomington, 1981)

BOSTON. Berklee College of Music, 150 Massachusetts Avenue, Boston, MA 02125. The library holds core collections in general fields of the humanities and in classical music, but is principally devoted to jazz, rock, and pop, as well as to modern music technology (i.e., electronic instruments and studio recording). Materials on jazz include 11,000 albums, 500 books (a substantial number of them discographies), 25 periodicals, and 60 videos. Of special interest is the extensive collection of notated jazz – 150 books of transcriptions of solos, 300 scores of arrangements and compositions for ensembles ranging in size from small groups to big bands, and, most notably, 5500 lead sheets.

——. Mugar Memorial Library, Boston University, 771 Commonwealth Avenue, Boston, MA 02215. Most of the library's jazz materials are housed in its Department of Special Collections. The Cab Calloway Collection (deposited by Calloway in 1976) consists of six linear meters of material. It contains the typescript with holograph corrections of Calloway's autobiography (*Minnie the Moocher and me* (New York, 1976), written with Bryant Rollins), together with galleys, holograph notes, and tape recorded interviews (with transcripts) used in its preparation. Items of music include manuscript and printed scores of Calloway's own songs and songs played by his band. There are also photographs, scrapbooks, and printed ephemera relating to Calloway, his band and radio program, and the Cotton Club, and correspondence dating from 1929 to 1976.

The Ella Fitzgerald Collection (donated by Fitzgerald between 1965 and 1968) is largely made up of scores written or arranged for Fitzgerald; there are 119 pieces in all (70 arrangements by Buddy Bregman, 25 arrangements by Nelson Riddle, and 24 arrangements by Billy May of songs by Harold Arlen). The collection also includes 15 photographs of Fitzgerald. The materials date from the 1960s.

The Artie Shaw Collection (donated by Shaw in 1980) consists of 15 linear meters of material. It contains printed sheet music (one linear meter), holograph scores and parts of compositions played by Shaw's band (among which are some original compositions and arrangements by Shaw), six holograph notebooks, photographs of Shaw and his family (dating from 1900 to the 1950s), and letters and memorabilia (dating from 1936 to 1955).

The library also holds a small amount of material relating to jazz in the collections of two music critics, Charles Reid (six files of articles and notes based on interviews with Pearl Bailey,

Tony Bennett, Cab Calloway, Lena Horne, George Gershwin, and the wife of George Shearing) and Henry Pleasants (copies of his reviews and of reviews of his books, and letters from Bailey and Marian McPartland).

——. New England Conservatory Libraries, 290 Huntington Avenue, Boston, MA 02115. The Isabelle Firestone Audio Library contains early jazz recordings of note, and the Nellie Chandler Collection includes 100 charts of big-band jazz from the 1920s. The libraries also hold tapes of performances given by the conservatory's jazz ensembles from 1969.

——. Northeastern University, Special Collections, Robert Gray Dodge Library, 360 Huntington Avenue, Boston, MA 02115. Around 1978 Douglass C. Gray donated to the university the Glen Gray and the Casa Loma Orchestra Collection. This comprises nearly 17 linear meters of material, including recordings, correspondence, documents from performances, financial records, photographs, newspaper clippings, and scores. Among the scores are arrangements by Gene Gifford.

Bowling Green. Popular Culture Library and Audio Center, Bowling Green State University, Bowling Green, OH 43402. The center was founded in 1967 in a new library building and has become an important resource for the study of popular culture in the USA. It contains several thousand recordings of rhythm-and-blues and early jazz, donated by William Randle, a disc jockey from Cleveland, and a collection of rare 78 r.p.m. jazz recordings dating from 1925 to 1945, donated by Alfred K. Pearson of Gardner, Massachusetts. The total number of records held by the center (covering all styles of popular music) is about 290,000 (100,000 LPs, 145,000 45 r.p.m. discs, and 45,000 78 r.p.m. discs); there are also 800 cylinders, 14,000 items of sheet music, 500 song folios, and 1250 works of reference (chiefly discographies), as well as journals, dealers' catalogues, auction lists, pictorial materials, and various printed ephemera. The center publishes the journal *Popular Music and Society* (1971/2–).

BIBLIOGRAPHY

W. R. Schurk: "A Description of the Sound Recordings at Bowling Green State University," *ARSCJ*, xiv/3 (1982), 5

B. L. Cooper and W. R. Schurk: "Huntin' for Discs with Wild Bill: William R. Schurk, Sound Archivist," *ARSCJ*, xiv/3 (1982), 9 [interview]

Buffalo. See Amherst.

Chicago. Chicago Public Library. The Music Information Center (78 East Washington Street, Chicago, IL 60602) holds two important jazz collections: the Recorded Sound Collection of Popular Music and Culture, begun in 1987, includes 10,000 78 r.p.m. and 3500 LP records of jazz; the Balaban & Katz Theatre Orchestra Collection (part of the Plitt Theatre Collection, acquired 1975) contains 7500 arrangements for dance band from 1920 to 1955. The center's materials also include 5000 items of sheet music (jazz, ragtime, and blues), and 3000 books and discographies and 50 periodicals having to do with jazz.

The Vivian G. Harsh Research Collection of Afro-American History and Literature in the Woodson Regional Library (9525 South Halsted Street, Chicago, IL 60628) contains about 500 LP jazz records, mostly from the late 1960s and the 1970s (including a large number of issues on Impulse and Blue Note), a picture file, 300 books on jazz, and complete or partial runs of more than 100 black newspapers and periodicals. Of particular interest is the typescript report "The Negro in Illinois: Music and Musicians in Illinois to 1939," prepared by the Writers Project of the WPA, which covers jazz and gospel music in Chicago; associated with it is a complete sequence of the periodical *Negro Music Journal* (1902–3). The collection occasionally prepares bibliographies of its holdings.

——. Columbia College Library, 600 South Michigan Avenue, Chicago, IL 60605. The library's Black Music Research Collection covers all areas of black-American music. Its holdings in recorded sound include 1000 commercially issued jazz recordings, as well as more modest numbers of blues, ragtime, and popular records. Printed materials of jazz interest comprise 120 items of sheet music and the contents of an extensive vertical-file system covering individual musicians. The library also contains more than 700 books and periodicals, 75 dissertations, 30 videotapes, and 100 photographs.

——. Delmark Records, 4243 North Lincoln Avenue, Chicago, IL 60618. The company maintains a collection of materials related to jazz, blues, and folk music, which may be consulted by the public. This consists principally of periodicals (many concerning record collecting and discography), which date from the late 1930s into the 1980s. It also includes recording ledgers of Delmark and of other labels to which Delmark has acquired rights, as well as master recordings (not generally available for public audition) of Delmark and Pearl issues, also of issues on Transition, Apollo, Regal, Lloyd's, Timely, and other labels, a collection of photographs, around 40 hours of film, taped interviews with jazz and blues musicians (not available for public audition), posters, and copies of reviews of recordings issued by Delmark.

——. Joseph Regenstein Library, University of Chicago, 1100 East 57th Street, Chicago, IL 60637 (*ICU*). The library has an extensive collection of discographies, monographs, and other materials on jazz, including a number of record company catalogues. The main holdings in jazz materials are in individual collections established or acquired by the library from the mid-1970s.

The Chicago Jazz Archive, formed in 1976, has a considerable collection of recordings, including more than 4500 78 r.p.m. discs, nearly 3500 LPs, 300 45 r.p.m. discs, more than 400 audio tapes of different kinds, and a small number of videotapes, among them 16 from the Chicago television station WTTW. A continuing oral history project, which aims to chart the history of jazz in Chicago from the earliest days to the present, has resulted in a group of taped interviews. The archive also contains sheet music (mostly ragtime pieces and popular songs), stock arrangements (some modified by the bands that used them), a small number of sets of parts for dance music of the 1920s and 1930s, and around 150 photographs and slides.

In 1982 the most valuable parts of the Don DeMicheal Archives of the Jazz institute of chicago (*ICJic*) were lodged in the Regenstein library. They include extensive oral history material, recordings, photographs, scores, and videotapes, chiefly concerning jazz in Chicago; a catalogue is in preparation.

Other collections held by the library that contain materials pertinent to jazz are those of Bruce Davis, Gordon L. Goodman, Richard W. Manning, Robert G. Peck, Jr., Paul Romaine, Francis Stanton, John F. Steiner, and Henry Temple, and the Milne–Pastore Collection.

Coral Gables. Music Library, University of Miami, PO Box 248165, Coral Gables, FL 33124. The library has a small jazz collection which is intended principally to support research connected with the university's curriculum. It contains 1500 LP and 1000 78 r.p.m. records, as well as discographies, bibliographies, and other works of reference.

DALLAS. Southern Methodist University, Dallas, TX 75275. The Music Library (in the Owen Fine Arts Center) holds 4000 78 r.p.m. jazz recordings (many by big bands), which were donated by Milton J. Kuser; there is also a collection of sheet music, some of which is relevant to jazz.

DEKALB. Northern Illinois University Music Library, Music Building MB175, DeKalb, IL 60115. The library's Kaltenbach–Sorensen Collection (purchased in 1971–2 from the estate of Irwin Kaltenbach of Cherry Valley, Illinois, and from Mervyn Sorensen of Beloit, Wisconsin) consists of 1700 recordings of jazz and dance-band music.

DENTON. North Texas State University, PO Box 5188, Denton, TX 76203. The university's music library holds a large number of 78 r.p.m. jazz records. There are also special collections relating to the careers of Stan Kenton (more than 1600 scores) and Duke Ellington (1000 items dating from the 1920s to the 1960s, including tape and disc recordings, discographies, and biographical material), and the Leon Breeden Jazz Archives (consisting of 780 photographs, 26 large loose-leaf notebooks with four indexes, and a small amount of oral history material). Thousands of sheet-music items and orchestral arrangements from radio stations WFAA in Dallas and WBAP in Fort Worth include material of some relevance to jazz.

EAST BRUNSWICK. Paul Kierney Collection, 271 Old Bridge Turnpike, East Brunswick, NJ 08816. This private collection contains 3000 78 r.p.m. records and 50 cylinder recordings of jazz and other genres of popular music.

EDWARDSVILLE. Lovejoy Library, Southern Illinois University, Edwardsville, IL 62025. The library's main holdings of relevance to jazz are 8000 78 r.p.m. records, dating mostly from before 1945, and about 250 piano rolls. Its other resources, less central but of some interest, are the extremely large collection of sheet music (strong in ragtime and in items published in St. Louis) and band orchestrations (15,000 original and stock arrangements of the period 1910–1960 from radio station KMOX in St. Louis, and a further 15,000 band charts from 1920–1960 used by the dance and theater orchestras of Ben Rader and Russ David in St. Louis).

BIBLIOGRAPHY

L. McKee: *Guide to Research Collections: Lovejoy Library, Southern Illinois University at Edwardsville* (Edwardsville, 1971)

EUGENE. University of Oregon, Eugene, OR 97403. The Department of Special Collections at the university holds the personal papers of Red Nichols; these consist of 3000 items (dating from as early as 1935), including performance materials for his band. There are also some 1500 compositions and arrangements by the trumpeter Axel Stordahl (at one time a member of Tommy Dorsey's orchestra) and more than 1000 stock arrangements from the collection of the dance-band musician Henry J. Beau.

GLEN COVE. Bernard Klatzko Collection, PO Box 306, Glen Cove, NY 11542. This private sound archive contains 2000 recordings (LPs and tape copies of 78 r.p.m. records), a large number of which are of New Orleans jazz (1940–70), blues, ragtime, and barrelhouse piano.

GRAND RAPIDS. Arnold's Archives, c/o Arnold Jacobsen, 1106 Eastwood Avenue Southeast, Grand Rapids, MI 49506. Arnold Jacobsen's private collection contains 200,000 recordings on disc and tape of popular songs; they are classified by subject, and catalogues of different groups of recordings (jazz, blues, dance-band music, etc.) are available.

HAMMOND. Southeastern Louisiana University, Hammond, LA 70401. The library of the music department holds a collection devoted to the work of the pianist Bill Evans (ii), known as the Bill Evans Archives. Begun in the 1980s by Ron Nethercutt, director of the jazz studies program at the university, it was originally based on recordings of Evans's playing, but soon expanded to include other materials relating to him.

ITHACA. Music Library, Lincoln Hall, Cornell University, Ithaca, NY 14853. Cornell's strong collection of jazz materials is the result of a longstanding interest in jazz on the part of the university's librarians and faculty members (who have included Marshall Stearns, the founder of the Institute of Jazz Studies, from 1946 to 1949, and James Patrick in the mid-1970s). The library holds a large number of books and periodicals, 4000 LP records, discographies and record catalogues, American and European dissertations, transcriptions (including those of John Coltrane's solos by Andrew White), and fake books.

KANSAS CITY. Kansas City Museum of History, 3218 Gladstone Boulevard, Kansas City, MO 64123 (*MoKmh*). The archives of the museum hold a small number of transcripts of oral history interviews conducted by Nathan Pearson and Howard Litwak in 1977 with musicians who were active in Kansas City in the 1920s and 1930s; there are also 1300 photographic negatives and items of printed ephemera relating to jazz.

LARAMIE. University of Wyoming, Laramie, WY 82071. The Twentieth Century Music Collections in the American Heritage Center and the Archive Collections of Film Music (established in 1968) contain material associated with a number of jazz musicians. Among these are Rube Bloom (contracts, correspondence, and song lyrics), Les Brown (jazz-band recordings and other materials), Larry Clinton (scores, arrangements, and miscellaneous materials), Bob Crosby (materials dating from 1932 to 1973, including scores, arrangements, sheet music, photographs, printed ephemera, and recordings), Harry James (music manuscripts), Jerry Jerome (music manuscripts, sheet music, and printed ephemera), Hal Kemp (materials dating from 1929 to 1939, including scores and arrangements for dance band, concert programs, and rehearsal records), and Raymond Scott (scores and arrangements). Other items of relevance to jazz are among the large number of works for radio, television, and films.

BIBLIOGRAPHY

E. J. Lewis: *The Archive Collections of Film Music at the University of Wyoming: a Descriptive Guide for Scholars* (MS, 1976)

LAWRENCE. Archives of Recorded Sound, Gorton Music Library, University of Kansas, Lawrence, KS 66045. The archives were formed in August 1982 and specialize in two areas, opera and jazz. The jazz collection, one of the largest in the Midwest, is founded on three private libraries: that of Professor Richard Wright, a member of faculty at the university and a noted authority on jazz (donated 1982), that of Red Nichols (acquired 1984), and that of Howard D. Rittmaster, a local collector (acquired 1986). The archives hold more than 20,000 LP and 5000 78 r.p.m. records of jazz (2500 of the latter are of music by Nichols and others associated with him), and 350 16-inch aluminum discs recorded during the AFM strike in the early 1940s; there are also a number of V-discs and 600 reel-to-reel tapes. This extensive collection includes nearly complete issues by such major record labels as Argo, Atlantic, Blue Note, Columbia, Contemporary, Fantasy, Impulse, Pacific Jazz and World Jazz, RCA Victor, Riverside and Jazzland, and Roulette. Among the musicians who are particularly well represented are (besides Nichols) Charlie Parker, Mary Lou Williams, and Coleman Hawkins. The recorded materials are supplemented by about 2000 books and periodicals, a large collection of discographies, and files of clippings and other ephemera (about one linear meter).

Lawrenceville. John Dixon Library, PO Box 6128, Lawrenceville, NJ 08648. Around 1972 the record producer and entrepreneur Bob Thiele donated to the library his collection of recordings of jazz, blues, and gospel music, which form the holdings of the Robert W. Thiele Center for American Popular Music. The jazz section of the collection consists of 4161 tracks on 78 r.p.m. records, dating from 1918 to 1956 (chiefly the 1930s and 1940s) and representing the work of some 400 leaders, among them Benny Goodman (251 tracks), Duke Ellington (243 tracks), and Louis Armstrong (153 tracks), and 420 LP records, mainly of jazz from the 1950s and 1960s. The contents of the 78 r.p.m. records are also preserved on cassette tapes.

Lincoln. University of Nebraska, Lincoln, NE 68588. The university's music library (30 Westbrook Music Building) holds three collections containing jazz material. The Ruth Etting Collection was acquired in November 1982. Etting was a popular singer whose backup groups included such prominent jazz musicians as Tommy Dorsey and Joe Venuti, and her collection comprises material related to her career: it contains 15 LP, three 45 r.p.m., and 35 78 r.p.m. records by Etting, 29 cassette and 19 reel-to-reel tapes of interviews, radio broadcasts, and performances, 150 sheet-music covers, 300 photographs, two films and four videotapes, and a discography and bibliography compiled by John Moran, as well as scrapbooks, miscellaneous papers, and memorabilia. The Labaree Jazz Collection, acquired in July 1977 from Joseph Labaree, includes 380 45 r.p.m. records of jazz and popular music from the 1950s. The Dick White Louis Armstrong Record Collection (donated by the collector's family in September 1986) includes 47 LP records by Armstrong.

Other material related to jazz is held in the Don L. Love Memorial Library: a collection of popular music from the 1930s and 1940s (received from Mrs. Willard M. Folsom in 1976) contains 80 records by various big bands and singers, and the Benjamin A. Botkin American Folklore Collection (donated by the collector's family in December 1977) contains about 125 records of jazz, blues, and popular music, of which 50 are LPs.

Little Rock. Elizabeth Prewitt Taylor Memorial Library, Arkansas Arts Center, MacArthur Park, PO Box 2137, Little Rock, AR 72203. The library's John D. Reid Collection of Early American Jazz, acquired in 1963, contains about 4000 records (mostly 78 r.p.m.), most of which are of blues and New Orleans jazz, various books, periodicals, and record company catalogues, a small number of photographs, and miscellaneous clippings and memorabilia. Much of the material relates to the career of Sidney Bechet.

BIBLIOGRAPHY

M. McCoy and B. Parker: *Catalog of the John D. Reid Collection of Early American Jazz* (Little Rock, 1975)

Mansfield. Mansfield State College, Mansfield, PA 16933. The college's music library holds 700 78 r.p.m. records, most of which are of jazz. There is also a small collection of sheet music and popular songbooks.

Memphis. Harry Godwin Collection, 796 Reddoch Street, Memphis, TN 38117. This private collection includes 200 78 r.p.m. records (1920–25) and 1200 other records of jazz and blues, unissued master recordings by Johnny Wiggs, Muggsy Spanier, Bing Crosby, and Turk Murphy, and 50 tape recordings (consisting of interviews and privately recorded performances) by such musicians as Frank Assunto, Billie and De De Pierce, Edmond Souchon, Johnny St. Cyr, Phil Napoleon, and W. C. Handy. Iconographic materials include photographs from the early 20th century of Louis Armstrong and other New Orleans jazz musicians and paintings, collages, and manuscript illustrations of jazz musicians by Stephen Longstreet. Among other materials are several hundred items of printed sheet music dating from around 1910 to around 1925 (including 20 by Jelly Roll Morton, 20 by Handy, and some by Clarence Williams) and correspondence, scrapbooks, and memorabilia pertaining to Armstrong, Handy, and other jazz and blues musicians.

Minot. Fred Wolhowe Collection, Highway 52 East, Minot, ND 58701. This private collection contains 25,000 78 r.p.m. recordings of New Orleans jazz, ragtime, and blues, as well as music of other genres. A large number of musical items include some sheet music and dance-band arrangements of some interest to scholars of jazz. There are also about 20 catalogues of record companies from around 1915 to 1940. The collection is eventually to be donated to Luther College in Decorah, Iowa.

Muncie. Department of Library Science, Ball State University, Muncie, IN 47306. The department holds a collection pertaining to the career of John Graas, consisting mostly of instrumental parts to compositions for big band and studio orchestra; these include 16 arrangements for jazz band, 50 jazz compositions by Graas, a jazz symphony, and miscellaneous sketches.

Naperville. Oesterle Library, North Central College, 320 East School Avenue, Naperville, IL 60540. The library's Philip D. Sang Jazz Collection includes 140 books on jazz, 16 record company catalogues, 70 issues of periodicals (1940–44), and a small number of discographies and concert programs. In the late 1980s no additions to the library's jazz holdings were being made and none were planned.

Nashville. Fisk University Library, 17th Avenue and Jackson Street, Nashville, TN 37203 (*TNF*). The Special Collections department of the library contains the following collections: the George Gershwin Memorial Collection of Music and Musical Literature, donated by Carl Van Vechten in 1947; the Scott Joplin Collection, donated by Samuel Brunson Campbell in 1948; the Langston Hughes Jazz and Blues Collection, bequeathed by Hughes and acquired in 1967; the Howard Angel Record Collection, donated by Angel and acquired in 1975; the W. C. Handy Collection, donated by Charles E. Handy in 1979; and the J. C. Johnson Collection, donated by Julie Johnson Ross in 1981. The jazz-related holdings in these collections include more than 400 recordings, 2800 items of sheet music (jazz, blues, and ragtime), more than 50 photographs, miscellaneous correspondence, scrapbooks, newspaper clippings, posters, publishers' contracts, awards, concert programs, and memorabilia. The Black Oral History Collection contains ten interviews with composers and musicians, and the Special Negro Collection of the library contains printed materials concerning black musicians. The main collection holds general reference books of relevance to jazz.

Newark. Institute of Jazz Studies, Rutgers, the State University of New Jersey, Bradley Hall, Newark, NJ 07102 (*NjR*). The Institute of jazz studies was formed as a research center by Marshall W. Stearns at Hunter College, New York, in 1952; it was affiliated with Rutgers in 1966 and moved to the Newark campus the following year. The institute's resources, based on Stearns's library, constitute the most valuable collection of jazz-related materials in the world. Its 75,000 music recordings (many in the John Dale Owen collection) include LPs, 78 r.p.m. and 45 r.p.m. discs, V-discs, transcription discs made from radio broadcasts, audio tapes, cylinders, and piano rolls; there are 120 oral history tapes (including interviews with Fletcher Henderson and Duke Ellington), many of which resulted from the Jazz Oral History Project (JOHP) funded by the NEA. Holdings in the printed word include 4000 books, discographies, and catalogues of record companies (as well as original ledgers from some record companies), a large collection of periodicals from the USA, Canada, Europe, Japan, and Australia (some on microfilm), and several thousand files of newspaper clippings, concert programs, promotional materials, and questionnaires (the last accumulated by Leonard Feather in the course of preparing the second edition (1960) of his *Encyclopedia of Jazz*). Musical materials consist of sheet music, transcriptions of recorded performances, printed and manuscript arrangements, and a number of instrumental methods. The collection also contains photographs, films, videotapes, various musical instruments (including African percussion instruments, and instruments used by Roy Eldridge and Roland Kirk), early phonographs, and memorabilia (paintings, posters, etc.).

BIBLIOGRAPHY

IJS Jazz Register (Newark, 1979–) [microfiche register and indexes]

M. P. Griffin: "The Institute of Jazz Studies: a Unique Resource," *ARJS*, i (1982), 110

NEW HAVEN. School of Music, Yale University, 98 Wall Street, New Haven, CT 06520 (*CtY*). The library of the School of Music acquired the Benny Goodman Archives by Goodman's bequest in 1986; this collection includes the master tapes of all his recordings (400–500 items), 1600 arrangements used by his band, several hundred photographs, a complete set of his films, and printed ephemera. In addition the library holds photographs and printed ephemera in the archives of the pianist and entertainer Alec Templeton (acquired 1983) and in those of Ted Lewis (acquired 1986), which also contain disc recordings of Lewis's radio programs and several arrangements. As part of its wide-ranging project "Oral History, American Music," set up in 1971, the library began the Ellington Project in 1977. This has resulted in the accumulation of more than 80 recorded interviews relating to Duke Ellington's career and in subsidiary research on Ellington's important arranger Billy Strayhorn.

NEW ORLEANS. Al Rose Collection, 3135 Bell Street, New Orleans, LA 70119. This private collection contains a large number of materials relating to ragtime and early jazz; others have been donated by Rose to the Howard–Tilton Memorial Library at Tulane University (see below). The items remaining in Rose's hands include 2500 items of sheet music, 2000 photographs, documents pertaining to a jazz concert given at Mercantile Hall in Philadelphia in 1936, and letters dating from the 1930s written to and by such musicians as Eubie Blake, Perry Bradford, and W. C. Handy.

BIBLIOGRAPHY

A. Rose and E. Souchon: *New Orleans Jazz: a Family Album* (Baton Rouge, LA, 1967, rev. 2/1978, rev. and enlarged 3/1984)

——. Louisiana State Museum, 751 Chartres Street, New Orleans, LA 70116). In 1979 the museum acquired the New Orleans Jazz Club Collection, which constitutes its main holdings in jazz. The collection's recorded items consist of 10,000 records (LP, 45 r.p.m., and 78 r.p.m.), 7000 reel-to-reel tape recordings, and a small number of cylinders and piano rolls. Printed materials include 500 books, 100 periodicals, 2500 items of sheet music, and printed ephemera concerning more than 1000 musicians. The rich holdings in jazz iconography consist of 12,000 photographs, 1000 posters, and 300 films (further items in this category are in the museum's Painting and Graphic Arts Collection, which holds more than 60,000 photographs). There are special collections pertaining to Louis Armstrong and other performers and to individual districts in New Orleans.

——. Periodicals, Arts and Recreation Division, New Orleans Public Library, 219 Loyola Avenue, New Orleans, LA 70140. The division holds 2000 LP records and a number of books, periodicals, and catalogues of record companies; a collection of photographs includes pictures of jazz musicians and events and of the New Orleans Mardi Gras carnival. The Souchon Jazz and Folk Music Collection, donated to the library by Dr. Edmond Souchon in the early 1950s and opened for reference use in 1952, was later transferred to the William Ransom Hogan Jazz Archive at Tulane University (see below). All parts of the public library's collections include material on black history of relevance to the study of jazz.

——. Raymond Barrois Collection, 2711 Ursulines Avenue, New Orleans, LA 70119. The private collection of Ray Burke (Raymond Barrois) contains jazz recordings dating from the 1920s to the 1940s.

——. Tulane University, New Orleans, LA 70118 (*LNT*). The Howard–Tilton Memorial Library (7001 Freret Street, New Orleans) is the repository of most of the university's rich holdings in jazz-related materials. The Amistad Research Center (Tilton Hall, 6823 St. Charles Avenue, New Orleans) also contains materials of jazz interest.

The principal jazz collection in the Howard–Tilton Memorial Library is the William Ransom Hogan Jazz Archive, begun in 1957 by the historian Dr. William Ransom Hogan with the help of a grant from the Ford Foundation; originally named the Archives of New Orleans Jazz and based on a project in oral history, it was established by Hogan with the help of William Russell and Richard B. Allen as a research collection within Tulane University's department of history. In 1965 it became part of the university's library system and it was named after Hogan following his death in 1974. Other collections now part of the archive are those of Nick LaRocca of the Original Dixieland Jazz Band (2800 items of sheet music, scrapbooks, newspaper clippings, correspondence, and advertisements), Al Rose (15,000 items, including sheet music, 2000 records, and 500 photographs), William Russell (published and unpublished writings, films, oral history material, records, and sheet music), Roger C. Guilbrandsen (4500 records), John Robichaux (printed and manuscript scores), Ralston Crawford (600 photographs), and Robert Greenwood (photographs). The Souchon Collection consists of the library of Dr. Edmond Souchon (2000 items, mostly recordings, relating to the early history of New Orleans jazz), formerly held by the New Orleans Public Library but now deposited here, and that of Harry V. Souchon, Sr. (1400 records, including V-discs, as well as 550 tapes, books, periodicals, and photographs), which was acquired in the 1980s. The archive is also the official repository of the records of locals 174 and 496 of the AFM.

The archive's recordings comprise in all 25,000–30,000 discs, 1000 music tapes, a modest collection of cylinders (*c*25) and piano rolls (*c*60), and 1500 tapes of oral history interviews.

Printed and manuscript materials consist of 30,000 scores (including a large amount of sheet music dating from 1830 to 1940, dance-band orchestrations, and big-band arrangements), 1300 books, more than 10,000 numbers of periodicals, and nearly 300 catalogues of record companies. An extensive set of clipping files on individual musicians contain documents, manuscript items, assorted ephemera and memorabilia, and transcripts of oral history interviews. The graphic source materials include more than 8000 photographs, 250 art and advertising posters, and a small but important group of films and videotapes showing jazz performances in New Orleans and related social and cultural events.

The focus of the archive's collection is the tradition of jazz in New Orleans, and related genres such as Creole and Cajun music, rhythm-and-blues, and gospel music. Its holdings are particularly valuable for the study of the early development of New Orleans jazz, but much material covers the spread of the music and its later history. The social and cultural milieu is extensively and fully represented. The archive publishes the half-yearly *Newsletter of the William Ransom Hogan Jazz Archive* (1986–).

Other collections in the Howard–Tilton Memorial Library containing items of relevance to jazz are the Latin American Library, the Louisiana Collection, and the Maxwell Music Library.

The holdings of the Amistad Research Center, formerly at Fisk and Dillard universities, document black American history and culture. Resources related to jazz and popular music include recordings, scores, and miscellaneous materials; the personal papers of Fletcher Henderson are in the collection.

BIBLIOGRAPHY

R. B. Allen: "New Orleans Jazz Archive at Tulane," *Wilson Library Bulletin*, xl (1966), 619

R. Crawford: *Music in the Street* (New Orleans, 1983) [exhibition catalogue]

Catalog of the William Ransom Hogan Jazz Archive (Boston, 1984)

NEW YORK. BMI Archives, 320 West 57th Street, New York, NY 10019. In the area of jazz the archives are principally of interest for their collection of manuscript scores of works by Sy Oliver (for Jimmie Lunceford), Quincy Jones (for Lionel Hampton), Billy May, Benny Golson, Joe Zawinul, Manny Albam, and others. They also contain books, photographs of jazz composers affiliated with BMI, some printed ephemera, a set of the periodical *BMI: the Many Worlds of Music* (formerly *News about BMI Music & Writers*), in which articles about BMI composers have appeared, and an autographed cup mute used by Jonah Jones.

——. Columbia University, New York, NY 10027 (*NNC*). The Oral History Research Office (Room 801, Butler Library) holds a small number of taped interviews with jazz musicians who were active on the South Side of Chicago in the 1920s and 1930s (contributed in 1971 by John Lax).

BIBLIOGRAPHY

E. B. Mason and L. M. Starr: *The Oral History Collection of Columbia University* (New York, 1979)

——. David A. Jasen Collection, 40-21 155th Street, Flushing, NY 13354. Jasen's collection, which is devoted to early jazz and ragtime, has been an important source of material for his discography *Recorded Ragtime, 1897–1958* (Hamden, CT, 1973) and for the book *Rags and Ragtime: a Musical History* (New York, 1978), which he wrote with Trebor J. Tichenor. The collection contains 10,000 items of sheet music, 1500 piano rolls, recordings of early jazz and ragtime, and record catalogues, as well as books, periodicals, photographs, interviews, and printed ephemera.

——. Louis Armstrong Archive, Aaron Copland School of Music, Queens College, Flushing, NY 11367. On the death of Lucille Armstrong in 1983 the Armstrongs' home in Corona, Queens, passed to the City of New York and the trumpeter's personal archive to the Louis Armstrong Educational Foundation; in 1987 both were acquired by Queens College, which administers them in association with the foundation and the New York City Department of Cultural Affairs. Armstrong's collection consists of 500 reel-to-reel and cassette tape recordings, 650 78 r.p.m. records (from 1955 and earlier), 700 LP and 45 r.p.m. records (from 1950 and later), and 240 acetate records (unissued) of radio and television broadcasts, rehearsals, and jam sessions. There are about 100 books relating to music, 80 portraits, framed pictures, plaques, and posters, and 60 scrapbooks and photograph albums (dating from as early as 1926 and especially numerous for the period after 1943), as well as printed sheet music, manuscript scores and parts, and songbooks (three linear meters), and correspondence, newspapers, and miscellaneous photographs and printed ephemera (ten linear meters). The archive also contains an original, unedited manuscript of Armstrong's autobiography (*Satchmo: my Life in New Orleans*, New York, 1954).

——. New York Public Library. The Music Division of the Library and Museum of the Performing Arts at Lincoln Center (111 Amsterdam Avenue, New York, NY 10023) has in its general collection a large number of books, periodicals, and musical items relating to jazz. The Rodgers and Hammerstein Archives of Recorded Sound, the nucleus of which is a considerable body of material donated in 1935 by Columbia Records, contain many jazz recordings; 20,000 of the archive's items (78 r.p.m. and 45 r.p.m. recordings of jazz and popular music dating from before 1967) were given to the library by radio station WNEW. The collection of recordings is supported by discographies and other printed materials documenting the history of sound recording in the USA and Europe. The library publishes a quarterly *Bulletin* (1897–).

Of particular interest is the Schomburg Center for Research in Black Culture (515 Lenox Avenue, New York, NY 10030; *NN-Sc*), which holds resources relating to jazz and black-American music, including books, periodicals, sheet music, photographs, concert programs, posters, and printed ephemera, as well as an index to articles in black periodicals. A special collection is devoted to the career of W. C. Handy. The writer and critic Bob Rusch donated a substantial collection of books (1000) and periodicals (10,000 numbers, 1924–72) to the center, together with an index of articles on composers and performers. The center publishes a *Journal* (1978–).

BIBLIOGRAPHY

Dictionary Catalog of the Schomburg Collection of Negro Literature & History (Boston, 1962; suppls. 1967, 1972)

Dictionary Catalog of the Music Collection, ed. New York Public Library (Boston, 1964; cumulative suppl. 1973; suppl. 1976; annual suppls. as *Bibliographic Guide to Music*, 1976–)

S. P. Williams: *Guide to the Research Collections of the New York Public Library* (Chicago, 1975)

"Listening to the Black Experience: Music at the Schomburg Center," *Schomburg Center for Research in Black Culture: Journal*, i/4 (1978), 12

"Sheet Music at Schomburg," *Schomburg Center for Research in Black Culture: Journal*, i/4 (1978), 8

Dictionary Catalog of the Rodgers and Hammerstein Archives of Recorded Sound (Boston, 1981)

NORFOLK. Old Dominion University, Norfolk, VA 23508. The library of the university holds 2000 78 r.p.m. records of jazz dating from the 1920s, formerly in the collection of Clarence Walton.

PHILADELPHIA. Free Library of Philadelphia, Logan Square, Philadelphia, PA 19103. The library's music department holds the Harvey Husten Jazz Library of 10-inch discs and a collection of 78 r.p.m. records donated by the RCA Victor Company. Large holdings of sheet music contain some items of jazz interest.

PROVIDENCE. Rhode Island Black Heritage Society, 45 Hamilton Street, Providence, RI 02907. The society holds 700 78 r.p.m. records of jazz and blues from the 1920s.

ST. LOUIS. Western Historical Collection and State Historical Society Manuscripts, University of Missouri, Jefferson Library, 8001 Natural Bridge Road, St. Louis, MO 63121 (*MoU-St*). The collection is part of the university's Joint Collection, held at its four campuses in Columbia, Rolla, Kansas City, and St. Louis. Of interest to scholars of jazz are the oral history materials and musical recordings (mostly on reel-to-reel tape) accumulated in the course of the Jazzmen Project, which was devised and largely conducted by the director of the Joint Collection, Irene Cortinovis, during the 1970s. The oral history part of the project is devoted to the reminiscences of jazz and blues musicians connected with St. Louis and transcripts of the interviews have been made. The collection also includes two scrapbooks donated in 1971 – that of the drummer, minstrel-show performer, and union leader Elijah H. Shaw (covering the years 1914–71), and that of the pianist and bandleader Eddie Johnson (covering 1925–55).

SAN FRANCISCO. San Francisco Public Library. The Music Section of the Art and Music Department (Civic Center, San Francisco, CA 94102) holds extensive documentation of musical life in the city (in the form of scrapbooks, and files on topics, organizations, individuals, and groups). The collection of the library's Archives of the Performing Arts (3150 Sacramento Street, San Francisco, CA 94115) is an important resource for the study of theater and other genres; its 2500 78 r.p.m. records include black-American music and jazz and there are also taped oral history interviews. Both departments of the library contain sheet music, books, and periodicals, some of which are relevant to jazz.

SANTA CRUZ. Santa Cruz Public Library, 224 Church Street, Santa Cruz, CA 95060. The Podesta Jazz Collection, held in the music department, was bequeathed to the library by Edward Podesta and began to be acquired in 1977; in the late 1980s the library held about 250 LP records, mostly of jazz performances (but including some blues, brass-band music, work songs, film music, and other related genres), and about 200 books and periodicals from Podesta's collection, the balance of which consists mainly of further recordings. The general music collection has considerable holdings in sheet music (ragtime, boogie-woogie, etc.) from the 1890s to the 1950s.

SIOUX FALLS. George B. German Music Archives, Siouxland Heritage Museum, 200 West 6th Street, Sioux Falls, SD 57105. The Virgil Smith Collection at the archives contains materials pertaining to jazz from as early as 1923; these include 500 78 r.p.m. records and 2000 items of sheet music.

SOUTHFIELD. Michael Montgomery Collection, 17601 Cornell Road, Southfield, MI 48075. This private archive consists largely of piano rolls and related material. It comprises 7000 piano rolls of jazz, blues, ragtime, and popular music by such musicians as Jelly Roll Morton, James P. Johnson, Fats Waller, Jimmy Blythe, Luckey Roberts, Eubie Blake, and J. Russel Robinson, catalogues and promotional material issued by piano roll companies, several photographs of pianists and composers, and a collection of sheet music (photocopies of originals now held at the music library of the University of Michigan).

STANFORD. Stanford Archive of Recorded Sound, Braun Music Center, Stanford University, Stanford, CA 94305. The archive's holdings in jazz consist of some 8000 78 r.p.m. and 2000 LP records (some acquired from Arthur Schalow), and the tape archive of the Monterey Jazz Festival (donated by the festival's board of directors in 1986). To support the recorded materials, there is an extensive collection of discographies, reference works, and early catalogues of record companies.

TALLADEGA. Historical Collections, Talladega College, Talladega, AL 35160 (*ATaT*). The collections contain nine hours of oral history tape recordings with Frank Harrison, a former member of the college's faculty (concerning the evolution of jazz and the "Harlem Renaissance"), and Teddy Wilson.

TALLAHASSEE. Black Archives Research Center and Museum, PO Box 809, Florida A&M University, Tallahassee, FL 32307. A general and wide-ranging collection, the archives contain material relating to all aspects of black-American history from the earliest times. Of interest to scholars of jazz are the Johnnie V. Lee Collection of rare and old recordings of black musicians, and the Cannonball Adderley Collection of selected materials relating to the alto saxophonist's life and career.

TUCSON. University of Arizona, Tucson, AZ 85721. The Music Collection of the University Library includes 13,000 78 r.p.m. records of early jazz from the collection of Louis Belden. The library also has rich holdings of sheet music, including the Historical American Collection of 9000 items (mostly from the 1920s and 1930s).

URBANA. University of Illinois at Urbana-Champaign, 1114 West Nevada Street, Urbana, IL 61801. The university's Music Library is a large general research collection containing more than one million items. It holds 10,000 jazz records (of which 7000 are LPs and 3000 are 78 r.p.m. discs), including important recordings of early jazz from the collection of John Kirker Quinn; the recordings are indexed by performing group, title, and record label. There are also jazz materials in the library's collection of books, periodicals, and sheet music (870,000 items), notably 1400 dance-band and stock arrangements, mostly from the period 1935–46.

BIBLIOGRAPHY

J. A. Major: *Collections Acquired by the University of Illinois Library at Urbana-Champaign, 1897–1974: a Catalog* (Champaign, 1974)

WASHINGTON. Library of Congress, Washington, DC 20540 (*DLC*). The Library of Congress is the copyright deposit library for the USA and therefore contains vast quantities of material relevant to the study of jazz. These resources differ, however, from those of other libraries in two ways: because they have been acquired largely through deposit (and not by selective purchase) the holdings do not form a coherent collection; nor are they classified or stored separately from other areas of music.

The general collection of the Music Division contains most published and copyrighted books and periodicals on jazz. The division's holdings of published scores and sheet music include most works of jazz that appeared in print from the first years of copyright up to 1977; they are strong in ragtime, stock arrangements, published piano solos, etc., in English works from the 1920s, and in European and Latin American works from 1950. The representation is significantly less comprehensive from 1978, when it became possible to establish copyright in music by depositing sound recordings. From 1929, when the deposit of manuscripts became an acceptable method of copyrighting music, large amounts of popular music were lodged with the Copyright Office; these materials include scores and parts for many works and arrangements by Ferde Grofé. The library also possesses a small number of parts formerly used by the Glenn Miller Orchestra, and a few arrangements of classic jazz numbers written for the film-music conductor Hugo Riesenfeld. At different times the Music Division has mounted projects to create, on microfilm, discrete "collections" of its materials on Jelly Roll Morton and Duke Ellington; the Morton project was completed, the Ellington one was not. The division's pictorial materials include a group of original watercolors depicting jazz subjects by Stephen Longstreet.

The collections of the Motion Picture, Broadcasting and Recorded Sound Division (for use by any researcher preparing a work that will be publicly available) include approximately 1,600,000 sound recordings, about 200,000 of which are commercially issued 78 r.p.m. records and 500,000 commercially issued LPs; a substantial number of the recordings are of jazz. The most important holdings are those of unissued recordings: of particular interest are the AFR&TS Collection (more than 150,000 discs), the collection of the entrepreneur Wally Heider, dating mainly from the 1950s and 1960s (1900 discs and 1350 tapes of jazz and dance-band music, including material by Tommy Dorsey and Woody Herman; acquired in 1973), the collection of the radio network Voice of America, which contains among other things recordings of jazz performances at Carnegie Hall and the Newport Jazz Festival, and recordings of broadcasts made on NBC Radio (1933–70) and National Public Radio. The library's recordings of oral history material include the pioneering interviews conducted with Jelly Roll Morton by Alan Lomax in 1938 (and issued commercially in 1948). These rich resources are supported by a substantial collection of record company catalogues, discographies, other books, and periodicals. In the area of film, the division holds about 100,000 motion pictures and recordings of television programs; the collection is particularly strong in Hollywood feature films and television news broadcasts.

Of relevance to some areas of jazz research are the holdings of the Archive of Folk Culture (formerly the Archive of Folk Song), the recorded materials of which are housed in the Motion Picture, Broadcasting and Recorded Sound Division. The general collections of photographs in the Prints and Photographs Division include a significant number of pictures of jazz musicians, many taken during World War II.

BIBLIOGRAPHY
(only those catalogues specific to relevant collections)

The National Union Catalog: Music and Phonorecords, 1953–72 (Washington, 1953–72)

Catalog of Copyright Entries, ser.3, pt xiv: *Sound Recordings*, ed. US Copyright Office (Washington, 1972–7; as ser.4, pt vii, 1980–)

D. L. Leavitt: "Recorded Sound in the Library of Congress," *Library Trends*, xxi/1 (1972), 53

National Union Catalog: Music, Books on Music, and Sound Recordings (Washington, 1973–)

J. C. Hickerson and J. R. Smart: "All that is Audible: Recent Recorded Sound Acquisitions in the Music Division," *Quarterly Journal of the Library of Congress*, xxxii (1975), 51

R. E. Lotz: *The AFR&TS (Gold Label) Transcription Library: a Label Listing* (Menden, Germany, 1978)

Shelflist of the Library of Congress (Ann Arbor, MI, 1979) [in microform; microfiche nos.1511–729 cover the catalogued collections of the Music Division]

A. Melville: *Special Collections in the Library of Congress: a Selective Guide* (Washington, 1980)

J. R. Smart: *Radio Broadcasts in the Library of Congress, 1924–1941: a Catalog of Recordings* (Washington, 1982)

The Rigler and Deutsch Record Index: a National Union Catalog of Sound Recordings (Syracuse, NY, 1985) [pt i: 78 r.p.m. recordings in the holdings of members of the ARSC; in microform]

——. Moorland–Spingarn Research Center, Howard University, Washington, DC 20059. The center takes its name from the Jesse E. Moorland Collection of Negro Life and History, and the Arthur B. Spingarn Collection of Negro Authors. Among the jazz musicians who are represented in the center's holdings are, in the Moorland collection, Eubie Blake, Duke Ellington, and W. C. Handy, and, in the Spingarn collection, Ellington, Handy, Noble Sissle, and Fats Waller.

BIBLIOGRAPHY

D. B. Porter: *A Catalogue of the African Collection in the Moorland Foundation, Howard University Library* (Washington, 1958)

Dictionary Catalog of the Jesse E. Moorland Collection of Negro Life and History (Boston, 1970; suppl. 1976)

WILLIAMSTOWN. Whiteman Collection, Stetson Hall, Williams College, Williamstown, MA 01267. The collection is based on Paul Whiteman's musical memorabilia, donated by Whiteman to the college and acquired between 1935 and 1950. The receipt of items from other sources makes the collection one of popular music in the USA from 1890 to 1950. The holdings include 1500 LP and 2000 78 r.p.m. records of early jazz, tape recordings of radio broadcasts made by Whiteman and his band in the 1930s and 1940s (400 hours), and several taped interviews with Whiteman and members of his orchestra. Printed materials comprise 3000 items of sheet music, 500 books on jazz and popular music, and ephemera concerning Whiteman and other musicians (including George Gershwin, Scott Joplin, Duke Ellington, Louis Armstrong, Benny Goodman, Count Basie, and James Reese Europe). There is a large body of manuscript music consisting of arrangements of 3500 dance tunes and 150 extended works performed by Whiteman's orchestra. The collection also contains several hundred photographs, prints of Whiteman's two principal films (*King of Jazz*, 1930, and *Rhapsody in Blue*, 1945), and 30 videotapes of performances by Whiteman's orchestra from the early 1930s.

BIBLIOGRAPHY

I. Shainman: "The Whiteman Collection at Williams College," *Notes*, 2nd ser., xiv (1956–7), 189

C. Johnson: *Paul Whiteman: a Chronology* (Williamstown, 1977)

GENERAL BIBLIOGRAPHY

Code for Cataloging Music, ed. Music Library Association (n.p., 1941–2, rev. as *Code for Cataloging Music and Phonorecords*, Chicago, 2/1958)

"Notes for Notes," *Notes*, 2nd ser. (1943/4–) [reports new acquisitions and locations]

I. Cazeaux: "Cataloging and Classification," *Manual of Music Librarianship*, ed. C. J. Bradley (Ann Arbor, MI, 1966), 30

R. Benton, ed.: *Directory of Music Research Libraries* (Iowa City, IA, 1967, rev. 2/1983)

C. S. Spalding, ed.: *Anglo-American Cataloging Rules* (Chicago, 1967, rev. P. W. Winkler and M. Gorman 2/1978)

Music Cataloging Bulletin [Music Library Association] (1970–) [reports changes in classification, cataloguing rules, and subject headings]

D. Seaton: "Important Library Holdings at Forty-one North American Universities," *Current Musicology*, no.17 (1974), 7–68

Symbols of American Libraries, ed. Catalog Publication Division, Library of Congress (Washington, rev. 12/1980)

D. W. Krummel and others: *Resources of American Music History: a Directory of Source Materials from Colonial Times to World War II* (Urbana, IL, Chicago, and London, 1981)

D. Richardson: "Black Music Collections in New Orleans," *Black Music Research Newsletter*, ix/1 (1987), 1

Lick. In jazz argot a short motif or formula inserted into an improvisation when the context permits or when invention lapses. Many jazz musicians have at their disposal a repertory of licks, some of their own invention, some borrowed from other players, and an improvisation may be little more than the stringing together of a number of such fragments. In some styles (e.g., slow blues) and for some ubiquitous chord progressions (e.g., I–II–V–I in major or minor keys) a common stock of licks is in circulation. *See also* IMPROVISATION, §4 (iii).

ROBERT WITMER

Lidström, Jack (*b* Södertälje, Sweden, 1 May 1931). Swedish trumpeter. In 1946 he formed the Hep Cats, who became the leading exponents of the New Orleans revival in Sweden, and with whom he performed and recorded in Germany (1959–60). He also played a prominent role as a trumpet soloist, having been inspired by the example of Louis Armstrong, who visited Sweden in 1949. After some years of inactivity in jazz he re-formed the Hep Cats in 1975 with, among others, the trombonist Folke Rabe and recorded the album *Jackpot* (1980, Karusell 1013).

BIBLIOGRAPHY

A. von Konow: "Jack Lidström," *Orkester journalen*, xliv/3 (1976), 12

ERIK KJELLBERG

Liebman, Dave [David] (*b* New York, 4 Sept 1946). Flutist and saxophonist. In the mid-1960s he studied theory and composition with Lennie Tristano, and saxophone and flute with Charles Lloyd. After playing with the rock group Ten Wheel Drive (1970) he worked with Elvin Jones (1971–3) and Miles Davis (1973–4). During his association with Davis he formed his own group, Lookout Farm (1973), with the double bass player Frank Tusa, the pianist Richard Beirach, the tablā player Badal Roy, and the drummer Jeff Williams. With this ensemble Liebman attempted to blend a bop style inspired by the work of John Coltrane with elements of traditional Indian music. He played a fusion of jazz and the popular genre funk in the late 1970s, and in 1978 he toured with Chick Corea, visiting Australia, where he later taught. In the 1980s he has returned to the bop style with the group Quest, which he leads with Beirach, and in collaborations with Jones.

SELECTED RECORDINGS

As unaccompanied soloist: *The Loneliness of a Long Distance Runner* (1985, CMP 24)

As leader: *Open Sky* (1972, PM 001); *Drum Ode* (1974, ECM 1046); *Sweet Hands* (1975, A&M Hor. 702); with R. Beirach: *Quest* (1981, PAlt 8061); *"Lieb": Close-up* (1983, Contempo Vibrato 002); *Sweet Fury* (?1985, From Bebop to Now 1002); *Homage to John Coltrane* (1987, OWL 046)

BIBLIOGRAPHY

Feather–Gitler '70s

C. Berg: "Dave Liebman: the Harmonic Harvest of Lookout Farm," *DB*, xliii/7 (1976), 14

D. Liebman and others: *Lookout Farm: a Case Study of Improvisation for Small Jazz Group* (n.p., 1978)

L. Gicking: "David Liebman's Discography," *Pendulum* (AH 8, ?1980) [liner notes]

M. Williams: *The Australian Jazz Explosion* (London and elsewhere, 1981), 160

L. Gourse: "Richie Beirach and Dave Liebman's 'Quest': What's in a Name?," *JT* (Feb 1985), 5

BILL MILKOWSKI

Lift. (1) A GLISS rising from the end of a note.

(2) To transcribe a part or parts from a recording (*see* TRANSCRIPTION (i)).

Lightfoot, Terry [Terence] (*b* Potters Bar, England, 21 May 1935). English clarinetist and alto saxophonist. He played clarinet in his teens and after working in military bands he began leading the Wood Green Stompers (1952). He became a professional musician in 1956 and in 1959 his band toured the UK as Kid Ory's support group. He has continued to work as a leader, except during the year he spent with Kenny Ball (1967); his sidemen have included Ball, Roy Williams, the trumpeters Colin Smith, Alan Elsdon, Ken Sims, and Dickie Hawdon, the pianist Colin Bates, the drummers Ginger Baker and Johnny Richardson, and his brother the banjoist Paddy Lightfoot. In the late 1970s he was active as a musician only part-time. Lightfoot made several recordings with his own groups (from 1956), among them *Alley Cat* (1964, Col. 33SX1721). He also appeared in the films *It's Trad, Dad!* (1962) and *Plenty* (1985).

BIBLIOGRAPHY

"Looking at Lightfoot," *Jazz News*, iv/37 (1960), 6

I. Berg, I. Yeomans, and N. Brittan: *Trad: an A to Z Who's Who of the British Traditional Jazz Scene* (London and elsewhere, 1962)

B. Matthew: *Trad Mad* (London, 1962), 70

D. Fairweather: "Lightfoot, Terry," in I. Carr, D. Fairweather, and B. Priestley: *Jazz: the Essential Companion* (London, 1987)

DEREK COLLER

Lighthouse Cafe. Nightclub in Hermosa Beach, California; *see* NIGHTCLUBS AND OTHER VENUES. Its best-known resident band, the Lighthouse All Stars, was led by HOWARD RUMSEY.

Lightsey, Kirk (*b* Detroit, 15 Feb 1937). Pianist. He learned piano from the age of five and later played clarinet in high school and an army band. By the mid-1950s he was a committed jazz musician, and during the early 1960s he played briefly in New York with Melba Liston and Ernestine Anderson. He then spent several years in Detroit and California accompanying singers, including Damita Jo, O. C. Smith, and Lovelace Watkins, but in 1965 recorded with Sonny Stitt and made five albums with Chet Baker; his playing may be heard to advantage on *Groovin' with the Chet Baker Quintet*. Lightsey first came to prominence as a sideman in a band led by Dexter Gordon (1979–83), and thereafter he recorded with Jimmy Raney (1983) and Clifford Jordan (1984). In 1986 he appeared at the Jazzfest Berlin with Jabbo Smith and Don Cherry. His style, firmly based in bop, is both diverse and highly individual; his lyrical recordings for Sunnyside contrast strongly with those made as a member of the cooperative group the Leaders during the late 1980s.

SELECTED RECORDINGS

As unaccompanied soloist: *Lightsey* (1982, Sunnyside 1002, 1005)

Duos with Harold Danko: *Shorter by Two* (1982, Sunnyside 1004)

As leader: *Everything Happens to Me* (1983, Tim. 176); *Everything is Changed* (1986, Sunnyside 1020)

As sideman: C. Baker: *Groovin' with the Chet Baker Quintet* (1965, Prst. 7460); H. Land and B. Mitchell: *Mapenzi* (1977, Conc. 44); R. Reid: *Perpetual Stroll* (1980, The. 111); D. Gordon: *American Classic* (1982, Elek. Mus. 60126); Leaders: *Mudfoot* (1986, Blackhawk 52001)

BIBLIOGRAPHY

L. Gourse: "Profile: Kirk Lightsey," *DB*, li/12 (1984), 52

B. McLarney: "Kirk Lightsey," *Coda*, no.200 (1985), 6

SCOTT YANOW

Likembe. A type of LAMELLAPHONE.

Lim, Harry (*b* Batavia, Dutch East Indies [now Jakarta], 23 Feb 1919). Record producer of Javanese birth and Dutch parentage. He was educated in the Netherlands, where he first became acquainted with jazz; he pursued this interest on returning to Batavia and after he moved to the USA in 1939. He worked as a record producer in New York and Chicago, then produced jazz recordings for the KEYNOTE company (1943–

6). In 1949 he recorded Al Haig for his own label, HL. After producing a few sessions for the label Seeco, including one by Wardell Gray, he briefly revived Keynote (1955), and thereafter worked as the principal expert on jazz at Sam Goody's record store in New York (1956–73). In 1972 he founded a new company and label, Famous Door (*see* FAMOUS DOOR (ii)). (B. Porter: "Keynote: the Label and its Producer," *The Complete Keynote Collection* (Key. 830-121-1, 1986) [Liner notes])

Limelight. Record label. It was established in 1962 as a subsidiary of Mercury. Its activities were directed by the producer Jack Tracy; the catalogue included recordings made between 1962 and 1966 by Dizzy Gillespie, Art Blakey, Earl Hines, Milt Jackson, Roland Kirk, Gerry Mulligan, and Oscar Peterson. The albums were packaged in eccentric liners, with intricate folds and cuts; because these were expensive to produce, new recordings ceased to be issued in 1966, although albums on Limelight continued to be available until 1970. Parts of the catalogue were later put out, with conventional liners, by Polydor and by Trip (1974–9), and a Japanese series of reissues began, using the name Limelight, in 1982.

Lincoln. Record label. It was established in 1924. A subsidiary of Cameo, it issued under pseudonyms much material from the parent company's catalogue. Items by the blues singer Viola McCoy were put out under the name Susan Williams. The label was discontinued in 1930 after the formation of the American Record Company. (B. Rust: *The American Record Label Book* (New Rochelle, NY, 1978), 179)

Lincoln, Abbey [Wooldridge, Gaby [Anna Marie]; Anna Marie; Lee, Gaby; Aminata Moseka] (*b* Chicago, 6 Aug 1930). Singer and songwriter. She began performing professionally in the early 1950s, using the names Anna Marie, Gaby Lee, and Gaby Wooldridge. In 1956, after taking the name Abbey Lincoln, she made her first recording, with Benny Carter's orchestra. Shortly afterwards she recorded as the leader of a group that included Sonny Rollins and Max Roach. In the late 1950s she began writing songs, and also started working as an actress. From 1962 to 1970 she was married to Roach, through whom she met many leading musicians, including Thelonious Monk and Charles Mingus. At this time she was influenced by them to explore a wider range of vocal techniques, and began to use a richer poetic style and greater cultural and political content in her songs. She became a strong public advocate for racial equality, and this issue was reflected in her lyrics, and in the energy, boldness, and, at times, violence of her vocal style. In the late 1960s her career as an actress took on new impetus, and she appeared in several films. In 1975 she visited Africa, where the names Aminata and Moseka were conferred on her by politicians in Guinea and Zaire respectively. She continues to perform and tour in the mid-1980s, and has returned to the warm, gentle style that characterized her early work.

SELECTED RECORDINGS

As leader: *That's Him!* (1957, Riv. 251); *Abby is Blue* (1959, Riv. 1153), incl. Let up; *Straight Ahead* (1961, Can. 9015), incl. When Malindy Sings; *People in Me* (1973, IC 6040); *Talking to the Sun* (1983, Enja 4060)
As sideman with M. Roach: *We Insist! Freedom Now Suite* (1960, Can. 9002); *It's Time* (1962, Imp. 16), incl. Lonesome Lover

BIBLIOGRAPHY

Feather '60s; *Feather–Gitler '70s*
B. Gardner: "Metamorphosis: Abbey Lincoln," *DB*, xxviii/19 (1961), 18
A. Lincoln and others: "Racial Prejudice in Jazz," *DB*, xxix (1962), no.6, p.20; no.7, p.22
B. Smith: "Abbey Lincoln," *Coda*, no.170 (1979), 12 [interview]
G. G. Vercelli: "Profile: Aminata Moseka/Abbey Lincoln," *DB*, xlvi/15 (1979), 42
G. Endress: "Soziales Anliegen in der Musik: Abbey Lincoln," *JP*, xxxi/12 (1982), 4
F. Davis: *In the Moment: Jazz in the 1980s* (New York, and Oxford, England, 1986) [colln of previously pubd articles], 197

MARTY HATCH

Lincoln, Abe [Abraham] (*b* Lancaster, PA, 29 March 1907). Trombonist. He played and recorded in New York with Adrian Rollini in several groups, including the California Ramblers, which he joined in 1926. After periods with the bands of Roger Wolfe Kahn, Paul Whiteman, and Ozzie Nelson during the 1930s, he became a studio musician in Los Angeles, recording with Bing Crosby (1937, 1941), Hoagy Carmichael (1938), and Judy Garland (1939). He returned to jazz during the dixieland revival of the 1940s, and recorded with Wingy Manone in 1944. He took part in recordings of traditional jazz more frequently during the 1950s, working with the Rampart Street Paraders (1953), Pete Fountain, Red Nichols, and Bob Scobey (all 1956), and Matty Matlock (1957–8). He performed with Wild Bill Davison in 1967 and appeared at a dixieland festival in Sacramento, California, in 1976. His style is well represented by the tracks he recorded with the Rampart Street Paraders on the album *Jam Session Coast to Coast* (1953, Col. CL547). (*ChiltonW*)

Lincoln Gardens. Ballroom in Chicago; *see* NIGHTCLUBS AND OTHER VENUES.

Lind, Nisse "Bagarn" [Nils] (*b* Stockholm, 27 Oct 1904; *d* Stockholm, 25 Oct 1941). Swedish accordionist and pianist. He played piano as a member of Paramountorkestern (1926–30) and worked with the singer Gösta Jonsson (1933–6) and the tenor saxophonist Frank Vernon (1936–7). In 1934 he made his first recording, *Tiger Rag* (Decca ST44059), on which he played accordion, and two years later he formed a trio with the double bass player Henry Lundin and the guitarist Birger Larsson; this group made a dozen recordings between 1934 and 1939 and toured widely in Sweden. Lind joined the dance orchestra of Swedish Radio in 1938 and in the following years worked frequently in studios and played on many film soundtracks.

BIBLIOGRAPHY

"Svenskt stjärnalbum" [Swedish star-album], *Orkester journalen*, v/11 (1937), 3
B. Englund: "Lind, Nils," *Svenskt biografiskt lexikon* (Stockholm, 1918–).

ERIK KJELLBERG

Lind, Ove (*b* Stockholm, 29 June 1926). Swedish clarinetist. After making his début with Simon Brehm's band in 1949, he joined Thore Swanerud's sextet, with which he recorded in 1949–50. He then played in the Swinging Swedes (1952–4), a cooperative sextet that made recordings (such as *Henderson Stomp*, 1953, Musica 9223) in a modernized swing idiom. In 1954 Lind and the double bass player Gunnar Almstedt formed a quartet (with Bengt Hallberg); this was augmented to a sextet by 1956, but disbanded in 1962. After working in popular music for several years Lind became a leading figure in the Swedish swing revival of the late 1960s and the 1970s, and one of the outstanding exponents of the Benny Goodman school. From this period onwards he made many recordings for Phontastic, notably *Who's Harry Warren? Evergreen!* (1975, Phon. 7412–3) and *Swinging Down the Lane* (with Hallberg; 1977, Phon. 7543). He also recorded with Teddy Wilson (1970).

BIBLIOGRAPHY
"På omslaget" [On the cover], *Orkester journalen*, xxiii/6 (1955), 4
J. Olsson: "Blir nervös av modern jazz" [Get nervous about modern jazz], *Orkester journalen*, xliii/10 (1975), 6

ERIK KJELLBERG

Lindberg, John (Arthur, III) (*b* Detroit, 16 March 1959). Double bass player. After musical studies in Ann Arbor, Michigan, he moved in 1977 to New York, where he played and recorded with Joseph Bowie and Charles "Bobo" Shaw in the Human Arts Ensemble (1978). From 1979 he has worked with Anthony Braxton, performing in Europe and the USA and recording several albums (1978–85). Lindberg is best known for his work with BILLY BANG in the String Trio of New York. He has made recordings with the trio (1979–83, including *First String*, 1979, BS 0031), as well as in a trio led by Jimmy Lyons and Sunny Murray (1980). From 1980 to 1983 Lindberg lived in Paris, where he recorded as a soloist (*Comin' & Goin'*, 1980, Leo 104) and with his own bands. He then moved to Newburgh, New York, where he worked as a leader of small groups, as an unaccompanied soloist, and as a member of an ensemble led by Murray, which also included John Tchicai. (K. Whitehead: "String Trio of New York: a Decade of Perseverance," *DB*, liv/11 (1987), 26 [incl. discography])

Lindberg, Nils (*b* Uppsala, Sweden, 11 June 1933). Swedish composer and pianist. He studied music at Uppsala University (1952–6) and the Royal Swedish Academy of Music, Stockholm (1956–60). While still a student he began playing professionally with Benny Bailey (1957–8) and the Swedes Anders Burman (1958), Ove Lind (1959), and Putte Wickman. In the 1960s he earned a reputation as a composer and arranger with albums such as *Sax Appeald* (1960, Barben 1004) and pieces for jazz orchestra such as *Trisection* (1962). Some of his works, including *7 Dalmålningar* [7 Dalecarlian Paintings] (1972, Swedish Society Discofil 33217), are based on Swedish folk tunes. Lindberg won the Grammis award in 1970 for an album recorded with Jan Allan, and in 1973 he played with Duke Ellington's orchestra in Malmö and Copenhagen. Later he wrote arrangements for and performed with Alice Babs and recorded with Karin Krog (1976) and as a leader (1981). (*FeatherE*; *Feather–Gitler '70s*)

Lindsay [Lindsey], **John(ny)** (*b* New Orleans, 23 Aug 1894; *d* Chicago, 3 July 1950). Double bass player and trombonist. Although he played double bass from his teens, his first professional engagements after army service were as a trombonist: he worked in New Orleans with John Robichaux in the early 1920s, then joined A. J. Piron, with whom he recorded in New York (1923). He then played with Dewey Jackson's band on the riverboat *Capitol*, and in 1925 moved to Chicago; while continuing to play and record on trombone (notably with Willie Hightower), he concentrated increasingly on double bass. For the rest of his career Lindsay remained in Chicago, save for national tours with Louis Armstrong's big band in 1931–2; he also appeared with Armstrong in the short film *Rhapsody in Black and Blue* (1932). Later he recorded frequently with Richard M. Jones, accompanying Jimmie Noone (1940) and Punch Miller (1944); he also made notable recordings with the Harlem Hamfats (1936–7) and Johnny Dodds (1940).

Lindsay may have been influenced by Bob Ysaguirre, who played in Piron's orchestra, though it is likely that he was also inspired by Pops Foster and Henry Kimball (1878–1931); Gunther Schuller also suggests Bill Johnson (i) as a major influence. Lindsay's mature style is well illustrated on the recordings he made with Jelly Roll Morton's Red Hot Peppers (1926), where he makes use of both conventional pizzicato and slapping and displays a varied and flexible approach to the beat.

For illustrations *see* BANDS, fig.1, and DOUBLE BASS, fig.1.

SELECTED RECORDINGS

As sideman on trombone: A. J. Piron: West Indies Blues (1923, Col. 14007D); W. Hightower: Boar Hog Blues (1927, Black Patti 8045)
As sideman on double bass: J. R. Morton: Black Bottom Stomp (1926, Vic. 20221); Grandpa's Spells (1926, Vic. 20431); L. Armstrong: When it's sleepy time down south (1931, OK 41504); The Lonesome Road (1931, OK 41538); Harlem Hamfats: Hamfat Swing (1936, Decca 7262)

BIBLIOGRAPHY
ChiltonW
R. Blesh: *Shining Trumpets: a History of Jazz* (New York, 1946, rev. and enlarged 2/1958/*R*1975)
G. Schuller: *Early Jazz: its Roots and Musical Development* (New York, 1968), 159
A. McCarthy: *Big Band Jazz* (New York and London, 1974)
H. Lyttelton: *The Best of Jazz*, i: *Basin Street to Harlem: Jazz Masters and Masterpieces, 1917–1930* (London, 1978)

ALYN SHIPTON

Lindström. Record company. It was founded in Germany by Carl Lindström early in the history of sound recording: its most important labels in Europe were ODEON and PARLOPHONE. In 1916 Lindström's American interests were transferred to the Otto Heinemann Phonograph Co. (*see* OKEH), though Lindström renewed close relations with the American company after World War I. From 1923 material from Okeh, including much excellent jazz, was issued in Germany on discs bearing the label Lindström American Record. In 1927 these were superseded by Parlophon's A4000 series. Lindström's company was acquired by COLUMBIA in 1925. (H. H. Lange: *Die deutsche Jazz-Discographie: eine Geschichte des Jazz auf Schallplatten von 1902 bis 1955* (Berlin, 1955), 22)

Lindström, Erik (*b* Helsinki, 29 May 1922). Finnish double bass player, vibraphonist, pianist, and composer. He played in amateur swing bands during World War II, and with Ossi Aalto (1945–8), Onni Gideon (1948–52), and his own groups (from 1952). He frequently accompanied visiting musicians and recorded with Peanuts Holland (1950, 1959) and Benny Bailey (1959). His *Main Road 7* was among the first Finnish jazz compositions to be recorded (by Manu Teittinen, 1954). From 1965 Lindström worked principally as a record producer; he recorded an LP of his jazz compositions, *No Money, No Music* (Love 127), in 1974.

PEKKA GRONOW

Lington, Otto [Nitzermaeder, Otto C. J.] (*b* Copenhagen, 5 Aug 1903). Danish violinist and bandleader. He began his career in dance bands and in 1924 formed one of the first Danish jazz groups, Høeg & Lingtons Dixie Boys. He played with Kai Ewans (1927) and in the group We Three with Leo Mathisen and Anker Skjoldborg (1927–8), and made recordings in a duo with Mathisen (including *Wild Cow*, 1929, Col. J26) and as a leader (1929–35) that were inspired by the work of Joe Venuti. He organized the first concert of Danish jazz (1929), at which he conducted symphonic jazz, a genre of which he was a champion; he also made recordings with leading soloists of more conventional jazz, including *Rytme* (1932, Edison Bell DN3193). Lington's published writings include *Jazz skal der til* (Jazz is what we need; Copenhagen, 1941), which is both a memoir and a history of early jazz.

ERIK WIEDEMANN

Linn, Ray(mond Sayre) (*b* Chicago, 20 Oct 1920). Trumpeter. He played with Tommy Dorsey in 1938 and later performed and recorded with him (1940–41). In 1941–2 he toured and recorded with Woody Herman, with whom he later played again on sessions (1945, 1947, 1955–9). From 1942 he was a studio musician (he moved to Los Angeles in 1945), in which capacity he played on numerous recordings, with, among others, Jimmy Dorsey (1942–5), Benny Goodman (1943, 1947), Artie Shaw (1944–6), Boyd Raeburn (1946), Dave Barbour (1946, 1949), Bob Crosby (1950–51), Shorty Rogers (1953), Maynard Ferguson (1955), Buddy DeFranco (1957), and Les Brown (1959). He may be heard to particular advantage on Barbour's *Little boy bop go blow your top/Ensenada* (1949, Cap. 60002) (the latter on muted trumpet). He also made recordings (including *Eastside Jump/Where's Pres?*, Atomic 220) with his own group in 1946. After 1960 he rarely played sessions and worked mainly in television. A versatile musician, Linn worked chiefly with big-band leaders and in the mid-1940s was one of the first trumpeters on the West Coast to develop a bop style; in 1973 he formed a dixieland band and recorded with it twice, in 1978 and 1980. (*FeatherE*)

For illustration *see* DORSEY, TOMMY.

Lion, Alfred (*b* Berlin, 21 April 1908; *d* nr San Diego, 2 Feb 1987). Record producer. He first became interested in jazz at the age of 16 after hearing Sam Wooding's band in Berlin. In 1938 he emigrated to the USA where, inspired by John Hammond's "Spirituals to Swing" concert in New York on 23 December, he founded the Blue Note record company and label on 6 January 1939 (*see* BLUE NOTE (ii)). Lion operated the company (jointly from October 1939 with Francis Wolff) until it was sold to Liberty in 1966; he then continued to work for the label for a further year before retiring owing to ill-health. He was guest of honor at EMI's relaunch of the Blue Note label at Town Hall in New York in February 1985, and visited Japan for a Blue Note festival in August 1986.

BIBLIOGRAPHY

M. Hennessey: "Blue Note," *JJI*, xxxviii/6 (1985), 10
L. Feather: "The Song has Ended: Alfred Lion," *Jazz Express*, no.81 (1987), 9
Obituary, M. Gardner, *JJI*, xl/4 (1987), 19

Lip. (1) The embouchure of a wind player.

(2) To alter the pitch of a note on a wind instrument by means of embouchure and air flow (that is, not by fingering); it is an essential part of the technique of playing most wind instruments and enables the player to tune individual notes perfectly. To lower a note the player slackens the embouchure or decreases the air pressure or both; to raise a note he tightens the embouchure or increases the air pressure or both. Similar techniques are used on brass instruments to execute the lip trill.

(3) A GLISS rising to the beginning or falling from the end of a note, produced by means of an exaggerated form of lipping.

ROBERT WITMER

Liston, Melba (Doretta) (*b* Kansas City, MO, 13 Jan 1926). Trombonist and arranger. At the age of 11 she moved with her family to Los Angeles, where she played with youth bands before starting her career in a pit orchestra (1942). She joined Gerald Wilson's band in 1943 and began to write arrangements; during her time with Wilson she recorded with Dexter Gordon (1947), then when Wilson's orchestra disbanded on the East Coast (1948) she accepted a job with Dizzy Gillespie. She toured with Billie Holiday (1949) but was so profoundly affected by the indifference of the audiences and the rigors of the road that she gave up playing and took a clerical job. In the mid-1950s she enjoyed a brief career as a film extra, appearing in *The Prodigal* and *The Ten Commandments*. She re-joined Gillespie for tours sponsored by the US State Department in 1956 and 1957, and visited Europe (1959) with the show *Free and Easy*, for which Quincy Jones was music director. In the 1960s she worked for a variety of leaders including Randy Weston, then taught at the Jamaica School of Music for six years (1973–9), before returning to the USA to lead her own bands. She is a talented and sensitive arranger, and one of the most accomplished trombonists of her generation.

SELECTED RECORDINGS

As sideman: D. Gordon: Mischievous Lady (1947, Dial 1018); Lullaby in Rhythm (1947, Dial 1038); D. Gillespie: *Dizzy Gillespie at Newport* (1957, Verve 8242)

SELECTED ARRANGEMENTS
(all recorded by D. Gillespie)

Stella by Starlight, on *World Statesman* (1956, Norg. 1084); My Reverie, Annie's Dance (both 1956), on *Dizzy in Greece* (1956–7, Verve 8017)

BIBLIOGRAPHY

J. Burns: "Bopping Bones," *J&B*, ii/7 (1972), 16
S. Placksin: *American Women in Jazz, 1900 to the Present: their Words, Lives, and Music* (New York, 1982), 179
D. Pagani: "Melba Liston: Interview," *Cadence*, xi/9 (1985), 5
S. Woolley: "Melba Liston," *JJI*, xl/2 (1987), 20

STAN WOOLLEY

Little, Booker(, Jr.) (*b* Memphis, 2 April 1938; *d* New York, 5 Oct 1961). Trumpeter. He was born into a musical family and played clarinet for a few months before taking up the trumpet at the age of 12; he took part in jam sessions with Phineas Newborn while still in his teens. While attending the Chicago Conservatory (BM 1958) he played with Johnny Griffin and Walter Perkins's group MJT + 3; he then played with Max Roach (June 1958 to February 1959), worked as a freelance in New York with, among others, Mal Waldron, and from February 1960 worked again with Roach. With Eric Dolphy he took part in the recording of John Coltrane's album *Africa/Brass* (1961) and led a quintet at the Five Spot in New York in July 1961. Little's playing was characterized by an open, gentle tone, a breathy attack on individual notes, and a subtle vibrato. His solos had the brisk tempos, wide range, and clean lines of hard bop, but he also enlarged his musical vocabulary by making sophisticated use of dissonance, which, especially in his collaborations with Dolphy, brought his playing close to free jazz.

SELECTED RECORDINGS

As leader: *Booker Little* (1960, Time 2011); *Out Front* (1961, Can. 9027); *Victory and Sorrow* (1961, Beth. 6061)

As sideman: M. Roach: *Deeds, not Words* (1958, Riv. 280); E. Dolphy: *Far Cry!* (1960, NewJ 8270); first issued on *The Mastery of John Coltrane*, iv: *Trane's Modes* (1961, Imp. 9361–2), Africa [1st version], The Damned don't Cry; M. Roach: *Percussion Bitter Sweet* (1961, Imp. 8)

BIBLIOGRAPHY

FeatherE; *Feather '60s*
Obituary, *DB*, xxviii/29 [*recte* 23] (1961), 11
N. Hentoff: Liner notes, *Booker Little* (Time 2011, 1960)
V. Simosko and B. Tepperman: *Eric Dolphy: a Musical Biography and Discography* (Washington, 1974)
M. Walker: "Booker Little," *JM*, xii (1966), no.5, p.13; no.8, p.26; xiii/2 (1967), 27 [discography]
P.-A. Monti: *Booker Little Discography* (Sierre, Switzerland, 1983)

DAVID WILD

Little, (Weston) Wilbur (*b* Parmele, NC, 5 March 1928; *d* Amsterdam, 4 May 1987). Double bass player. He started playing piano during his military service (1946) but later changed to double bass. He moved in 1949 to Washington, where he worked in the small groups of Sir Charles Thompson and Leo Parker. Thereafter he played rhythm-and-blues, touring with the Griffin Brothers and the singer Margie Day (both 1949–51), and the saxophonist Paul Williams (1951–3). In Washington his bop trio supported guest stars such as Miles Davis, Kenny Dorham, and John Coltrane (1953–5). After studying with Joe Williams of the National SO he became a member of J. J. Johnson's small group (1955–8), with which he made his first tour of Europe in 1957. He worked with Tommy Flanagan (1957, early 1970s), Sonny Stitt, Roland Kirk, Elvin Jones (1969–70, 1973, *c*1977), Kenny Burrell, Al Haig and Jimmy Raney, Clark Terry (1974), and Ellis Larkins (1975), and toured and recorded in Japan with Duke Jordan's trio (1976). He lived in New York from 1967, then in 1977 moved to Amsterdam, from where he toured Europe with Charles Tolliver (1977) and Archie Shepp (1978). In the 1980s he was frequently heard in a quartet including Clifford Jordan and Barry Harris. Inspired by Ray Brown, Little was a strong section player with a steady and reliable sense of rhythm and a large tone; his solos were invariably agile and well shaped. Some of his best work may be heard on *The Tommy Flanagan Trio Overseas*, recorded in Stockholm in 1957.

SELECTED RECORDINGS

As sideman: B. Jaspar: *Bobby Jaspar* (1957, Riv. 240); T. Flanagan: *The Tommy Flanagan Trio Overseas* (1957, Met. 311–13) [EP]; J. J. Johnson: *J. J. In Person!* (1958, Col. CL1161); R. Weston: *Randy Weston Live at the Five Spot* (1959, UA 5066); C. Terry: *Clark Terry's Big B-a-d Band Live* (1974, Van. 79355); A. Haig and J. Raney: *Special Brew* (1974, Spot. 8); A. Shepp: *Little Red Moon* (1985, SN 1112)

BIBLIOGRAPHY

Feather–Gitler '70s
J. De Muth: "Profile: Wilbur Little," *DB*, xlvii/1 (1980), 54

MARK GARDNER

Little Chicks. Instrumental group. It was formed in 1937 by members of Chick Webb's big band, and consisted of Wayman Carver (flute), Chauncey Haughton (clarinet), and a rhythm section. Later that year it recorded four tracks, including *Sweet Sue, just you* (Decca 1759). A later version of the Little Chicks comprised Louis Jordan (alto saxophone), Pete Clarke (clarinet), Teddy McRae (tenor saxophone), and a rhythm section, but it made no recordings and disbanded shortly before Webb's death in 1939.

FRANK DRIGGS

Little Fritz. Nickname of FRITZ TRIPPEL.

Little G. Nickname of HAROLD MCNAIR.

Little Giant. Nickname of JOHNNY GRIFFIN.

Little Jazz. Nickname of ROY ELDRIDGE.

Little T. Nickname of Charlie Teagarden; *see* TEAGARDEN family, (4) Charlie.

Little Turk. Nickname of KID RENA.

Livingston, Fud [Joseph Anthony] (*b* Charleston, SC, 10 April 1906; *d* New York, 25 March 1957). Tenor saxophonist, clarinetist, arranger, and composer. He began working as a performer and arranger with influential jazz groups such as Ben Pollack's band and the California Ramblers. His many recordings of the late 1920s show him to have been a leader of the white jazz avant garde, an influential arranger, and an instrumentalist in the style of his contemporary PeeWee Russell. The recordings of his compositions *Humpty Dumpty* and *Feelin' no Pain* (1927) show, respectively, an advanced harmonic style for that time and an incisive concept of "hot" small-band jazz. Livingston arranged scores for Paul Whiteman (1930–33), Benny Goodman (1934), and Jimmy Dorsey (1935–7); he then turned primarily to commercial music and music publishing.

SELECTED RECORDINGS

As sideman: B. Pollack: 'Deed I do (1926, Vic. 20408); R. Nichols: Riverboat Shuffle/Eccentric (1927, Bruns. 3627); M. Mole: Imagination/Feelin' no Pain (1927, OK 40890); F. Trumbauer: Humpty Dumpty (1927, OK 40926); B. Goodman: Room 1411 (1928, Bruns. 4013); M. Mole: Crazy Rhythm (1928, OK 41098)

JAMES DAPOGNY/R

Livingston, Ulysses (*b* Bristol, TN, 29 Jan 1912). Guitarist. He worked in Buffalo with Lil Armstrong (1936) and in New York with Stuff Smith, Frankie Newton, and Sammy Price before joining Benny Carter (1939). He also recorded with Newton, Blue Lu Barker and Armstrong, and Pete Johnson (all 1939) and Billie Holiday (1940). From 1940 to 1942 he worked regularly with Ella Fitzgerald. After army service he moved to Los Angeles, where he performed and made recordings with Jazz at the Philharmonic (1944), the Spirits of Rhythm, Rex Stewart, Joe Sullivan, and Illinois Jacquet (all 1945), and the pianist and singer Wilbert Baranco (1947, including *Rosetta*, Black & White 857). He also led his own band. Thereafter he worked principally as an electronic engineer, but continued to make recordings as a freelance, notably with Jack McVea (*Nothin' but Jazz* (1962, 77 LA22), including *Soft Winds*). (*ChiltonW*; *FeatherE*)

LJCO. *See* LONDON JAZZ COMPOSERS ORCHESTRA.

Lloyd, Charles (*b* Memphis, 15 March 1938). Tenor saxophonist. He studied informally with Phineas Newborn and was a colleague of Booker Little, George Coleman, Frank Strozier, and Hank Crawford. In the mid-1950s he moved to Los Angeles to attend the University of Southern California, where his major subject was composition; he spent six years at the university, during which he met Harold Land, Eric Dolphy, Buddy Collette, and Ornette Coleman and played alto saxophone and flute with small groups and in Gerald Wilson's big band. In 1961 he joined Chico Hamilton's group, of which he eventually became the manager and principal arranger; the group's repertory included Lloyd's composition *Forest Flower*. After taking up the tenor saxophone in 1962 he joined Cannonball Adderley's sextet (1964), recorded two albums as a leader, and in August 1965 formed a group that included Gábor Szabó, Herbie Hancock, and Don Friedman as sidemen; after he re-formed the group early in 1966 his sidemen were Keith Jarrett, Cecil McBee (later replaced by Ron McClure), and Jack DeJohnette. This group remained in existence for three years, during which it achieved great success not only with jazz audiences at the Monterey Jazz Festival of 1966 (at which the album *Forest Flower* was recorded), in Europe, and in the USSR (1967), but also with rock audiences at such venues as the Fillmore Auditorium in San Francisco, where it performed to the accompaniment of a light-show. By 1969 Jarrett and DeJohnette had left the group, and Lloyd had become less active and his music less inspired; he had few engagements in the 1970s. Later he performed more frequently: he played with Michel Petrucciani in California and toured Europe with Petrucciani, Palle Danielsson, and the drummer Woody Theus. Lloyd's playing in the

1960s and 1970s evoked strong reactions from his listeners: he was acclaimed as a pioneer by some and denounced as a charlatan by others. In fact he was neither; in his best work he was, rather, a powerful improviser, but one whose style was derived largely from that of John Coltrane. His importance lies in his having brought the innovations of free jazz to a wide audience.

SELECTED RECORDINGS

As leader: *Of Course, of Course* (1964–5, Col. CS9212); *Forest Flower* (1966, Atl. 1473); *Charles Lloyd in the Soviet Union* (1967, Atl. 1571); *Charles Lloyd Quartet Montreux 1982* (1982, Elek. Mus. 60220)

As sideman: C. Hamilton: *Man from Two Worlds* (1963, Imp. 59); C. Adderley: *Fiddler on the Roof* (1964, Cap. ST2216)

BIBLIOGRAPHY

B. Korall: "The Charles Lloyd Quartet: Roots and Branches," *DB*, xxxiii/12 (1966), 20
R. J. Wilbraham: "Charles Lloyd," *JM*, xii/10 (1966), 24; no.153 (1967), 28 [discography]
"Dolphins on a Wave: C. Lloyd, Prophet of New Wave Jazz," *Time*, lxxxix (3 Feb 1967), 32
B. McRae: "Charles Lloyd," *JJ*, xx/8 (1967), 4
R. Crocker: "Charles Lloyd: New Journey," *DB*, l/1 (1973), 13
——: "Das Bekenntnis des Charles Lloyd," *JP*, xxxi/11 (1982), 4

DAVID WILD

Lloyd, Jerry [Hurwitz, Jerome] (*b* New York, 17 July 1920). Trumpeter. An early admirer of Charlie Parker and Dizzy Gillespie, he played with Georgie Auld, Buddy Rich, and George Wallington during the 1940s. In 1949 he made recordings with Wallington, Kai Winding, and Brew Moore. After a short absence from music he recorded with Gerry Mulligan (1951), the pianist Harvey Leonard (1955), and Jutta Hipp (1956). In 1956 he was a member of Zoot Sims's group, and the following year he recorded with Wallington again (*The Prestidigitator*, East-West 4004). (R. G. Reisner: *Bird: the Legend of Charlie Parker* (New York, 1962/*R*1982), 136)

Locke, Eddie [Edward] (*b* Detroit, 8 Feb 1930). Drummer. He performed in a duo with Oliver Jackson in Detroit (*c*1948–1953) and then in New York (1954), where he also played with Dick Wellstood and Tony Parenti. In 1958 he began a lasting association with Roy Eldridge, and in 1959 he first played with Coleman Hawkins, with whom he made several recordings between 1962 and 1966 (including *Today and Now*, 1962, Imp. 34). After Hawkins's death in 1969 he played with Eldridge at Ryan's, New York, for nearly 15 years. He also performed with Teddy Wilson, Willie "the Lion" Smith, and Henry "Red" Allen, and led several groups of his own from time to time, including a trio with Roland Hanna and a quintet (1985). He continued to record, with, among others, Ray Bryant (1960), Duke Ellington and Kenny Burrell (both 1962), Earl Hines (1965), Earle Warren (1974), and Lee Konitz and Tiny Grimes (both 1975).

BIBLIOGRAPHY

O. Keller: "Oliver Jackson et Eddie Locke," *BHcF*, no.99 (1960), 3
S. Dance: *The World of Swing* (New York, 1974) [colln of previously pubd interviews], 155

Locked hands. A type of chord voicing for piano in which block chords in close position are played in the right hand and the left doubles the melody at the lower octave. *See* HARMONY (i), §1(iv); PIANO, §§4 and 5, and ex.7; and SHEARING, GEORGE, ex.1.

Lockwood, Didier (*b* Calais, France, 11 Feb 1956). French violinist. He was encouraged to study violin by his father, a teacher at the Conservatoire in Calais, and he undertook formal study in Paris. In 1973 he formed a jazz-rock group with his brother Francis, a keyboard player, and for three years he belonged to another jazz-rock group, Magma. He performed with Stephane Grappelli, Gordon Beck, Tony Williams, and Daniel Humair and from 1975 appeared with them at various festivals. He continued to play in many diverse contexts throughout the 1970s. In the 1980s he led a small group, toured Europe, and performed frequently in the USA. Lockwood's assertive, virtuoso playing is in the tradition of Grappelli and Michel Warlop.

SELECTED RECORDINGS

(recorded for JMS unless otherwise indicated)

As leader: *New World* (1979, MPS 68237); *Didier Lockwood Live in Montreux* (1980, 011); *Fasten Seat Belts* (1981, 016); *The Kid* (1982, 024); *Out of the Blue* (1985, 037); *Live at the Olympia Hall* (1986, 040); with John Blake and M. Urbaniak: *Rhythm and BLU* (1986, Cream 170)

As sideman with H. Texier: *A cordes et à cris* (1979, 06)

BIBLIOGRAPHY

J.-E. Berendt: "Didier Lockwood," *JJI*, xxxii/12 (1979), 15
S. Loupien: "Voix nouvelles: Didier Lockwood," *Jm*, no.281 (1979), 40
L. Jeske: "Profile: Didier Lockwood," *DB*, xlvii/7 (1980), 52
"Entretien avec Didier Lockwood," *Jh*, no.383 (April 1981), 10
P. Brodowski: "The New World of Didier Lockwood," *JF* [intl edn], no.74 (1982), 33
R. Baud: "Didier Lockwood: Le violon sûr de soi," *Jh*, no.409 (April 1984), 16

ANDRÉ CLERGEAT

Loevendie, Theo (*b* Amsterdam, 17 Sept 1930). Dutch saxophonist and composer. He studied at the Sweelinck Conservatory in Amsterdam (1955–60) and in 1961 joined Boy Edgar's big band, of which he became the leader in 1966. He appeared at many festivals in Europe as the leader of a quartet and of the Theo Loevendie Consort (formed 1968). From the early 1970s he wrote several compositions in a style that combined elements of folk music (especially that of Turkey) and free jazz, including *Esperanza* (1971), *Incantations* (1975), and an opera, *Naima* (1985). Loevendie gives lectures on modern music and leads workshops in composition in a number of European countries; he received an Edison Award from the Dutch Gramophone Industries in 1969 and the Dutch National Jazz Prize in 1979. His work as a saxophonist can be heard to advantage on his albums *Orlando* (1977, Waterland 003) and *Quintet* (1986, Varajazz 6218).

WIM VAN EYLE

Loft jazz. A term sometimes applied to the styles of FREE JAZZ which were performed in lofts in New York in the mid-1970s.

Lofton, Tricky [Lawrence Ellis] (*b* Houston, 28 May 1930). Trombonist. He gained his first experience in church and high-school bands and, after moving to Los Angeles in 1946, in small local groups. After serving in the army (1948–53) he toured with blues and rhythm-and-blues musicians, and he continued to work often in these styles. He made his first recording in Cincinnati in 1958 with Bill Doggett. Having returned to Los Angeles he recorded bop and soul jazz with Groove Holmes, Ron Jefferson, and Les McCann (all 1961), and Carmell Jones (1962); he also recorded the album *Tricky Lofton Brass Bag* (1962, PJ 49) with his own group. In 1972 he joined Bill Berry's big band, with which he recorded two albums in 1976; he also played and recorded with Jon Hendricks (1975) and Ray Charles (1978). In the 1980s he led his own quintet in and around San Francisco. (*Feather–Gitler '70s*)

Logan, Giuseppi (*b* Philadelphia, 22 May 1935). Alto saxophonist, bass clarinetist, and flutist. He studied at the New England Conservatory and played in Boston with Earl Bostic.

By 1964 he had moved to New York, where he played free jazz with Bill Dixon, Archie Shepp, and Pharoah Sanders. He performed and recorded with Roswell Rudd in 1966. He also led a quartet with Don Pullen, Eddie Gomez, and Milford Graves which appeared at the October Revolution in Jazz concert series in 1964 and recorded in that year (*Giuseppi Logan Quartet*, ESP 1007) and in 1965.

BIBLIOGRAPHY

Feather '60s
V. Wilmer: *As Serious as Your Life: the Story of the New Jazz* (London, 1977, rev. 1980)

Lombardi, Clyde [Claudio] (*b* New York, 18 Feb 1922; *d* New York, after 1975). Double bass player. He was classically trained, and performed and recorded with Red Norvo (1942–5) and Joe Marsala and Boyd Raeburn (both 1945). He toured and recorded in big bands and small groups led by Benny Goodman in 1945–6, and again in 1948–9 after a period with Charlie Ventura (1946). An accomplished swing player, he also recorded with the bop ensembles of Lennie Tristano (1946), Wardell Gray and Stan Getz (both 1948), and Al Haig (1949). After leaving Goodman he recorded with Zoot Sims (1951), Eddie Bert (1952–3, 1955), Tal Farlow (1953), and George Wallington (1954). On *Home Cookin'*, recorded with Bert in 1955, his swing style may be heard in a bop context. From 1959 Lombardi worked for CBS as a studio musician. He remained active into the mid-1970s, recording with the folk singer Anita Carter (1963), a folk group, the Chad Mitchell Trio (1965), and the tenor saxophonist Tony Graye (in New York, 1975).

SELECTED RECORDINGS

As sideman: on B. Goodman: *Arrangements by Eddie Sauter* (1940–45, Col. GL523), Love Walked in; Goodman: Clarinade (1945, Col. 36823); L. Tristano: I can't get started (1946, Key. 647); S. Getz: Pardon my Bop/As I Live and Bop (1948, SiW 506); B. Goodman: There's a small hotel/Blue Lou (1949, Cap. 60009); E. Bert: *Let's Dig Bert* (1955, Trans World 208), incl. Home Cookin'; T. Graye: *Oh, gee!* (1975, Zim 2001)

BIBLIOGRAPHY

FeatherE

JOHN CURRY

London. Record label. It was established by British Decca (*see* DECCA) in 1947 to issue in the USA items recorded in Britain (and possibly some made elsewhere in Europe); the distribution territory was later expanded to include Canada. London's catalogue was one of the first to include LPs, which were pressed in Britain by Decca and released in the USA from August 1949. In the same year issue began in the UK of the results of recording sessions organized by the label's American management; from 1951 the label was also used as an outlet for material made by small American companies to which British Decca had acquired the British rights. This included a substantial amount of jazz from such labels as Bethlehem, Savoy, Atlantic, Blue Note, and Riverside. In addition the catalogue included a series of ten-inch LPs, Origins of Jazz, which contained reissues of early items from Gennett, QRS, Edison, and other small labels of the 1920s, 1930s, and 1940s. By the time the series ended in 1959 it ran to 65 discs, making it by far the largest reissue project to that date; many issues also appeared on the London label in France and Germany, and on Riverside in the USA. Thereafter the label remained operational, but jazz became less prominent in its catalogue as small American companies found other outlets for their material. In the 1970s the London label was used (to reissue items originally put out on Commodore) by Telefunken in Germany, King in Japan, and British Decca in the UK; after the last-named was purchased by Polygram (1980) it began trading widely under the name London (from 1983).

BIBLIOGRAPHY

H. H. Lange: *Die deutsche Jazz-Discographie: eine Geschichte des Jazz auf Schallplatten von 1902 bis 1955* (Berlin, 1955), 619
C. Fox, P. Gammond, and A. Morgan: *Jazz on Record: a Critical Guide* (London, 1960), 339
B. Lazell: *London Label HL Series Singles Listing*, SMG Special ser., iii (Benfleet, England, 1971)
[P. Pelletier]: *British London Label Complete Listing* (London, 1974–6; Chessington, England, 1982); contd in *Record Information*, nos.1–6 (1983–6)

London Jazz Composers Orchestra [LJCO]. English free-jazz orchestra. It was founded in 1970 by a group of musicians led by BARRY GUY, who later became its director. Its personnel has changed frequently, but the group has included at various times the trumpeters Marc Charig, Dave Spence, and Kenny Wheeler; the trombonists Paul Nieman, Paul Rutherford, and Alan Tomlinson; the reed players Peter Brötzmann, Tony Coe, Karl Jenkins, Evan Parker, Larry Stabbins, and Trevor Watts; the tuba player Melvin Poore; the double bass player Peter Kowald; the pianist Howard Riley; the guitarist Derek Bailey; and the drummers Paul Lytton, Tony Oxley, and John Stevens. As well as jazz musicians, the ensemble has also included instrumentalists with backgrounds in classical music. It has continued to perform at intervals into the late 1980s; its recordings include *Stringer* (1980, FMP SAJ41).

The LJCO aims to resolve the paradox of organizing free music within a large ensemble. Guy first encountered this problem in his composition *Ode* (1970–72), which the ensemble recorded in 1972 (Incus 6–7); he explored solutions to it in this and later works for the LJCO by writing scores in which the playing of particular soloists is given prominence in turn. Several members of the orchestra, including Riley, Rutherford, and Oxley, have written pieces for it, which reflect their different methods and intentions and their varied approaches to group improvisation. The LJCO has performed more than 20 such works. (K. Ansell: "Barry Guy: a Most Ingenious Paradox," *The Wire*, no.8 (1984), 2)

SIMON ADAMS

Long, Slats [Don] (*b* Wichita, KS, 6 Dec 1906; *d* Wichita, 13 March 1964). Clarinetist. He worked with the violinist and bandleader Cass Hagan in 1928 and in the 1930s with the bands led by Eddie Farley and Mike Riley (1935), Red Norvo (1936), the pianist Vincent Lopez (1937), Chauncey Morehouse (1938), and Bud Freeman (at Kelly's Stable, New York, 1939). He made recordings with several of these leaders and many others, including Red McKenzie (1935, 1937), Bunny Berigan (1936–7), and Tommy Dorsey (1937); his playing is well represented on Frank Froeba's *The music goes 'round and 'round/There'll be a great day in the morning* (1935, Col. 3110D). He later played with Bobby Hackett (late 1940), Ted Lewis, and Raymond Scott. He ceased to be active as a musician in 1943.

based on *ChiltonW*

Long Boy. Nickname of CHARLIE GREEN.

Longo, Mike [Michael Joseph] (*b* Cincinnati, 19 March 1939). Pianist and composer. He grew up in a musical family, started piano lessons at the age of three, and gave his first professional performance when he was 15; while in high school in Fort Lauderdale, Florida, he played with Cannonball Adderley. In 1959 he graduated from Western Kentucky University with a BM in music and was awarded a "Hall of Fame" scholarship by *Down Beat*, and the following year he played at the Metropole in New York with Henry "Red" Allen, Coleman Hawkins, and George Wettling. Longo moved in 1961 to Toronto, where he studied with Oscar Peterson and led his own trio. After returning to New York (1962) he worked as an accompanist for various singers, then served as music director, arranger, and pianist for Dizzy Gillespie (1966–73). He continued his studies in 1971, taking lessons in counterpoint from Hall Overton. *Frisco*, recorded by Gillespie, and the title track of the album *Matrix* are good examples of his compositional style. As a pianist, Longo's style is based on those of Peterson and Bud Powell, to which he has added a highly personal, contemplative approach.

SELECTED RECORDINGS

As unaccompanied soloist: *Solo Recital* (*c*1981, Consolidated Artists 100)
As leader: *Matrix* (*c*1971, Mstr. 334), incl. Matrix; *The Awakening* (*c*1972, Mstr. 357); *Talk with the Spirits* (1976, Pablo 2310769)
As sideman with D. Gillespie: *Swing Low, Sweet Cadillac* (1967, Imp. 9149); *The Dizzy Gillespie Reunion Band* (1968, MPS 15207), incl. Frisco

BIBLIOGRAPHY

Feather–Gitler '70s
M. Bourne: "The Musical Maturity of Mike Longo," *DB*, xl/8 (1973), 16

PAUL RINZLER

Long-playing [long-play] **disc** [long player, LP]. A 7-inch, 10-inch, or (most often) 12-inch disc, normally recorded and played back at $33\frac{1}{3}$ (very rarely at $16\frac{2}{3}$) r.p.m. *See* RECORDING, §§I, 3, and II, 3; *see also* ALBUM.

Loose Tubes. English big band. It was established as a 21-piece cooperative ensemble in London in 1984 by several musicians who had formerly been members of a workshop led by Graham Collier. It includes many young English soloists, who draw on a wide range of musical influences – rock, varied ethnic sources, and all styles of jazz – and have an informal and often amusing attitude to stage presentation. The band's repertory is composed by its members; frequent contributors are the keyboard player Django Bates, the bass player Steve Berry, the trumpeters Chris Batchelor and Dave de Fries, and the flutist Eddie Parker. Loose Tubes has achieved immense popularity in Britain as a result of national tours and concert performances in London; it has gained widespread television coverage, including two full-length features for "Jazz Week" (1986), has recorded and broadcast a concert for BBC radio (May 1987), and played in the first jazz Promenade Concert (autumn 1987). The band has also produced albums on its own record label, including *Loose Tubes* (1985, Loose Tubes 001) and *Delightful Precipice* (1986, Loose Tubes 003).

BIBLIOGRAPHY

S. Nicholson: "22 Went to Swing," *The Wire*, no.23 (1986), 21
"Restoring Loose Tubes," *CI*, xxiv/3 (1987), 2
L. Tomkins: "Inside Loose Tubes: a Conversational Cross-section of the Cheer-bringing Conglomerate," *CI*, xxiv/3 (1987), 20

DIGBY FAIRWEATHER

López Fürst, Rubén [Baby] (*b* Buenos Aires, 26 July 1937). Argentine pianist and guitarist. In 1951 he formed a swing group, in which he played guitar, that was modeled after the Quintette du Hot Club de France, and in 1961 he formed a trio in which he played piano. He performed with Roy Eldridge, Louis Armstrong, Jim Hall, and Hermeto Pascoal in Buenos Aires, and recorded with Edmond Hall (1957), Gato Barbieri, and Jim Hall; in 1966 he recorded the albums *Jazz en la universidad* (EDUL 006) and *Jazz argentino* (CBS 8695) as a leader. In 1972 he played guitar in a quartet, with which he recorded, and formed a second trio in which he played piano. He also worked in piano duos with Jorge Navarro and Carlos Franzetti and in the 1980s led a quartet with Andrés Boiarsky.

LAUREANO FERNÁNDEZ, OMAR GARCÍA BRUNELLI

López Ruiz, Jorge (*b* Buenos Aires, 1 April 1935). Argentine double bass player and composer. He belonged to Lalo Schifrin's orchestra (1956) and recorded with Edmond Hall (1957), the Argentina All Stars (1960), and Sergio Mihanovich (1960). Between 1961 and 1980 he recorded nine albums as a leader, on one of which his sidemen included Lew Soloff, Eddie Gomez, and Jorge Dalto, and on others of which he experimented with a fusion of jazz and Argentine popular music. He also recorded with the drummer Pichi Mazzei (1963–4) and Enrique Villegas (1965–8) and performed with Tony Bennett, Ella Fitzgerald, Lionel Hampton, Buddy DeFranco, Larry Coryell, and João Gilberto. While living in the USA (1980–86) he studied composition on the West Coast in 1985; he has written several film scores. López Ruiz may be heard to particular advantage on the albums *El grito* (1968, CBS 9769), and *Viejas raíces* (1975, Odeon EMI8123), both of which he recorded as a leader.

LAUREANO FERNÁNDEZ, OMAR GARCÍA BRUNELLI

Lorber, Jeff (*b* Philadelphia, 4 Nov 1952). Keyboard player, composer, and leader. He played piano from the age of four, and was a member of various soul, rhythm-and-blues, and rock bands while he was in high school. In 1970–71 he studied at the Berklee College of Music, and around this time first heard the work of Herbie Hancock; this inspired him to transcribe and analyze the work of such pianists as Hancock, McCoy Tyner, Chick Corea, Wynton Kelly, Bill Evans (ii), and Horace Silver. He left Berklee to study with Ran Blake and others, and in 1973 he moved to Portland, Oregon, where he played in small clubs and taught jazz improvisation at Lewis and Clark College. In 1977 he recorded his first album, *The Jeff Lorber Fusion*, and from 1979 he led a quartet of the same name; its sidemen included the drummer Dennis Bradford, son of Bobby Bradford. The group made several successful albums, recording mainly Lorber's compositions; Corea, Joe Farrell, and Freddie Hubbard have played as guest soloists with the quartet.

Lorber's style of the late 1970s is well represented by *City*, from the album *Wizard Island*. Here two contrasting sections are juxtaposed, one based on a syncopated, chromatic melody, the other on a sequence of modal chords. The melody is jagged and precise, and the keyboard and saxophone solos combine bop phrases with lines reminiscent of the popular style of funk. In the early 1980s Lorber began singing and playing the guitar, and introduced elements of soul and pop music into his work to attract a wider audience.

SELECTED RECORDINGS

The Jeff Lorber Fusion (1977, IC 1026); *Soft Space* (1978, IC 1056); *Water Sign* (*c*1978, Ari. 4234); *Wizard Island* (*c*1979, Ari. 9516), incl. City; *Galaxian* (*c*1980, Ari. 9545); *It's a Fact* (*c*1981, Ari. 9583); *In the Heat of the Night* (*c*1983, Ari. 8025); *Step by Step* (1984, Ari. 8269)

BIBLIOGRAPHY

C. Stern: "The Jeff Lorber Fusion," *DB*, xlvi/3 (1979), 24 [review of *Soft Space*]
J. Aikin: "The Jeff Lorber Fusion Story: from a $1000 Demo to a Top 10 Jazz LP," *CK*, vi/4 (1980), 18
B. Henschen: "Jeff Lorber: Forging Fusion's Future," *DB*, xlvii/1 (1980), 28
B. Doerschuk: "Jeff Lorber: Keyboard Jazz + Drum Machines = Fusion for the 80s," *Keyboard*, x/8 (1984), 16 [incl. discography]
S. Sutherland: "Lorber Makes 'Heated' Bid for Crossover Success," *Billboard*, xcvi (28 April 1984), 36

B. Doerschuk: "Lorber: Gorgeous Sunsets over the Pacific, Fresh Breezes, a Beautiful Young Wife, Two Precocious Daughters . . . How can Anyone Live so Mellow and Play so Hot," *Keyboard*, xiii/8 (1987), 70 [incl. discography]

DIANNA RHYAN

Louisiana Five. Quintet. Formed in 1918 by the drummer Anton Lada, its other members were the clarinetist Alcide "Yellow" Nuñez, who had belonged to the Original Dixieland Jass Band, the trombonist Charles Panelli, the pianist Joseph Cawley, and the banjoist Karl Berger. The group took part in 18 recording sessions (mostly for Emerson), during which it recorded more than 50 tracks, including *Church Street Sobbin' Blues* (1919, Emerson 9179), and *Slow and Easy* (1919, Col. 2949), on which Doc Behrendson played cornet. The Louisiana Five achieved little influence before disbanding in 1920. (H. H. Lange: *The Fabulous Fives*, Lübbecke, Germany, 1959, rev.2/1978 by R. Jewson, D. Hamilton-Smith, and R. Webb [discography])

MIKE HAZELDINE

Louisiana Rhythm Kings. Recording group led in the late 1920s by RED NICHOLS.

Louiss, Eddy [Louise, Edouard] (*b* Paris, 2 May 1941). French pianist, organist, and leader. As a child he studied piano, vibraphone, and trumpet and by 1954 played occasionally in the band of his father, the Martinique trumpeter Pierre Louise. In Paris he attended the Conservatoire and performed in clubs, and from 1961 to 1963 he sang as a member of the Double Six, with which he toured Canada and the USA. He played piano with Johnny Griffin and the Hammond organ with Art Taylor (1966), Stan Getz (recording in 1971), and Jean-Luc Ponty; he also belonged to a trio with Kenny Clarke and René Thomas (from 1968). In the 1980s he led a big band, Multicolor Feeling. Louiss was awarded the Prix Django Reinhardt by the Académie du jazz in 1964.

SELECTED RECORDINGS

As leader: *Our Kind of Sabi* (1958, Verve 2304041); with J.-L. Ponty and D. Humair: *Trio HLP* (1968, CBS BPG63140); *Eddy Louiss orgue* (1972, Amer. 6127, 6132)

As sideman: Double Six: *Les Double-six* (1961–2, Col. FPX 202); D. Gillespie: *Dizzy Gillespie et les Double Six* (1963, Phi. 652038); J.-L. Ponty: *Jazz Long Playing* (1964, Phi. 77810); B. Kessel: *Barney Kessel* (1969, Mer. 135720); S. Grappelli: *Satin Doll* (1972, Festival 596)

BIBLIOGRAPHY

J.-L. Ginibre: "Les regrets et les espoirs d'Eddy," *Jm*, no.141 (1967), 24
K. Zagrodski: "Eddy Louiss: the Great Unknown," *JF* [intl edn], no.41 (1976), 45
C. Gauffre: "Eddy Louiss: mon big band," *Jm*, no.315 (1983), 36

ANDRÉ CLERGEAT

Loussier, Jacques (*b* Angers, France, 26 Oct 1934). French pianist. He studied classical piano at the Paris Conservatoire with Yves Nat and accompanied such popular singers as Charles Aznavour. With Pierre Michelot and Christian Garros he formed the trio Play Bach in 1959, which played jazz versions of compositions by J. S. Bach. The group recorded four albums of this material between 1960 and 1963 (all issued under the name *Play Bach*, Decca 153905, 153918, 154003; Lon. 3365), on the last of which Loussier played both piano and organ (*see* ORGAN, §2). The trio toured internationally for nearly 15 years, but despite its considerable commercial success it met with little favor from the critics. (L. Tomkins: "Why I Play Bach Jazz: Jacques Loussier," *CI*, x/5 (1971), 14)

ANDRÉ CLERGEAT

Love, Preston (*b* Omaha, NE, *c*1921). Alto saxophonist and bandleader. He played with bands in Omaha led by the trumpeter Lloyd Hunter and by Nat Towles (1941–3), and joined Count Basie in September 1943, replacing Earle Warren for six weeks. He re-joined Hunter, then worked with Lucky Millinder (intermittently, 1944–5) and Harlan Leonard. Basie employed him again from 1945 to 1947; after this engagement Love formed his own rhythm-and-blues group and from 1951 made several recordings as a leader, including *September Song* (1952, Federal 12069). In the early 1960s he formed a recording company with the rhythm-and-blues drummer Johnny Otis, who also played on some of Love's recordings; the two musicians performed together at the Monterey Pop Festival in 1970. Love later returned to Omaha, where he was active as a journalist, teacher, and broadcaster.

BIBLIOGRAPHY

M. Leadbitter and N. Hess: "Preston Love Discography," *Shout*, no.112 (1977), 8.
B. Becker: "Preston Love: on the Omaha and Territory Scene," *Cadence*, v/3 (1979), 10
S. Dance: *The World of Count Basie* (New York and London, 1980) [colln of previously pubd interviews], 151
B. Scherman: Liner notes, *Johnny Otis Presents Preston Love & his Orchestra* (Saxophonograph 501, 1982)

Lovelle, Herbie [Herbert E.] (*b* New York, 1 June 1924). Drummer. He played with Joe Gordon's band at the New York World's Fair (1939), toured the eastern USA with Hot Lips Page (1949), and worked briefly with Buddy Tate. While playing at the Savoy Ballroom in New York (1951–3) he recorded with Eddie Jefferson (1953), then toured with Arnett Cobb and Teddy Wilson (both 1954), Earl Hines (1955), rhythm-and-blues bands, and Buck Clayton (1959), and played with Sam "the Man" Taylor (1958–60). His fluency in styles ranging from dixieland to hard bop led to his recording with artists as diverse as Art Farmer (1954, 1956), Clayton (1958–9), Dicky Wells (1959), Sidney De Paris (1962), Sonny Stitt (1963), Illinois Jacquet (1965), Nat Adderley (1966), Groove Holmes (1968), Snooky Young (1971), Leone Thomas (1973), and Thad Jones (1975–6), as well as with pop, soul, and blues musicians. The most important session in which Lovelle played was probably that with Wells (*Trombone Four-in-hand* (1959, Fel. 7009), including *Heavy Duty*), though *Hard Boiled Rock* on *The Boys from Dayton* (1971, MJR 8130), made with Young, is perhaps more representative of his work.

BIBLIOGRAPHY

FeatherE
V. Wilmer: "Herbie Lovelle," *JJ*, xiii/1 (1960), 4
C. Iero: "Herb Lovelle," *MD*, iii/3 (1979), 13

Lovens, Paul (*b* Aachen, Germany, 6 June 1949). German drummer and percussionist. A self-taught musician, he performed in jazz groups from the age of 14. He worked in a duo, in trios, and in quartets with Alex Schlippenbach from 1969 into the 1980s and also played with the Globe Unity Orchestra (from 1972), Peter Kowald (1972–4), and Michel Pilz (1975). In 1976 he formed Po Torch Records with the percussionist Paul Lytton, played with the pianist Urs Voerkel, and began working as an unaccompanied soloist and with Paul Rutherford; the following year he began to play with Lytton. In 1979 he joined Günter Christmann's group Vario and the Phon trio with Christmann and Maarten Altena; later he worked with the trumpeter Toshinori Kondo (1980) and the pianist Martin Theurer (1981) and collaborated on projects with dancers and actors. Lovens plays a drum set of his own construction.

SELECTED RECORDINGS

Duos: with P. Lytton: *The Fetch* (1980–81, Po Torch 8); with A. Schlippenbach: *Stranger than Love* (1984, Po Torch 12)

As sideman: A. Schlippenbach: *Pakistani Pomade* (1972, FMP 0110); Globe Unity Orchestra: *Evidence*, i (1975, FMP 0220); M. Pilz: *Carpathes* (1975, FMP 0250); G. Christmann: *Vario II* (1980, Moers 01084)

BIBLIOGRAPHY

M. Thiem: "Paul Lovens: so offen wie möglich improvisieren," *JP*, xxvi/3 (1977), 12

G. Rouy: "Paul Lovens, le tambour du Globe Unity," *Jm*, no.272 (1979), 49

ROBERT J. IANNAPOLLO

Lovett, Leroy (*b* Philadelphia, 17 March 1919). Pianist and arranger. He wrote arrangements for Tiny Bradshaw and Luis Russell during the mid-1940s and also led a band in New York. He toured with Noble Sissle and Lucky Millinder, recording with Millinder in 1949. After playing in a rhythm-and-blues band he joined Johnny Hodges. Lovett recorded as a swing pianist with Hodges (1951–2), Harry Carney (1954), Lawrence Brown (1956), Cootie Williams (1957), and Cat Anderson (1959). From 1956 to 1957 he was a record producer for Norman Granz. He then returned to Philadelphia and organized a 13-piece dance band, with which he recorded two albums, including *Jazz Dance Party* (1959, Wynne 108). (*FeatherE*)

Lowe, Curtis (Sylvester, Sr.) (*b* Chicago, 15 Nov 1919). Baritone and tenor saxophonist. He served in the navy (1942–5), playing in a band that included Vernon Alley, Wilbert Baranco, Buddy Collette, Jerome Richardson, and Ernie and Marshall Royal. He toured and recorded with Lionel Hampton (1949–52), played with Dave Brubeck's octet (1952), led his own quintet (1952–3), and played in Gerald Wilson's orchestra (1953–4). He worked again with Hampton (1955–7), then with Earl Hines (1958–68); his playing may be heard to advantage on Hines's tracks from the album *Earl's Backroom and Cozy's Caravan* (1958, Fel. 7002). In the 1980s he continued to play as a freelance musician with groups in the San Francisco area. (*FeatherE*)

Lowe, Frank (*b* Memphis, 24 June 1943). Tenor saxophonist. He studied tenor saxophone from the age of 12 and was influenced first by rhythm-and-blues and the playing of Gene Ammons and King Curtis, then by Ornette Coleman, Eric Dolphy, John Coltrane, and Cecil Taylor. He studied briefly at the University of Kansas, and in San Francisco with Don Garrett. He performed in New York with Sun Ra (1966–8), studied classical music at the San Francisco Conservatory, then returned to New York in 1971 to perform with Alice Coltrane, Rashied Ali, Archie Shepp, Milford Graves, and Don Cherry. From 1973 he led his own groups with such musicians as Charles "Bobo" Shaw, Lester Bowie, and Joseph Bowie, and toured Europe.

SELECTED RECORDINGS

Duos with R. Ali: *Duo Exchange* (1973, Survival 101)

As leader: *Black Beings* (1973, ESP 3013); *Love and Behold* (1977, Musicworks 3002); *Exotic Heartbreak* (1981, SN1032)

As sideman: D. Cherry: *Relativity Suite* (1973, JCOA 1006)

BIBLIOGRAPHY

V. Wilmer: "Lowe: A Breath of Rhythm," *MM*, xlvii (23 Dec 1972), 41

B. Palmer: "Frank Lowe: Chasin' the Trane out of Memphis," *DB*, xli/16 (1974), 18

B. Rusch: "Frank Lowe: Interview," *Cadence*, viii/1 (1982), 5

DAVID G. SUCH

Lowe, (James) Mundell (*b* Laurel, MS, 21 April 1922). Electric guitarist and composer. From 1936 to 1940 he played traditional jazz around New Orleans and country music in Nashville. He then worked in the swing bands of Jan Savitt (1942) and Ray McKinley (1945–7) and in small groups led by Mary Lou Williams (1947–9), Red Norvo, and Ellis Larkins (1949–50). He studied composition with Hall Overton (1948–52) and later with several other eminent teachers. He became a staff musician at NBC in 1950 (he also did some acting), and composed scores for several television programs. He was a member of the Sauter–Finegan Orchestra (1952–3) and in 1952 first played with Benny Goodman, with whom he continued to be associated intermittently until 1984. During the 1950s he formed a quartet, which, with changing personnel, performed and recorded into the 1980s. Lowe moved to California in 1965 and worked mostly as a composer, writing for films and television. He also played in and around Los Angeles with Richie Kamuca, and toured Europe with Betty Bennett (1974–5) and Japan with Benny Carter (1977–8, 1983). From 1970 he was the backing guitarist at the Monterey Jazz Festival and in 1983 he became the festival's music director. He also taught film composition at the Dick Grove School of Music in Los Angeles (1979–85). Lowe was influenced at first by Charlie Christian, then by Jimmy Raney, and like many cool-jazz guitarists he tried to imitate the sound of the tenor saxophone; his polished, understated style, marked by a swinging momentum, is most characteristically exploited in chordal settings of ballads. He is married to the singer Betty Bennett.

SELECTED RECORDINGS

As leader: *A Grand Night for Swinging* (1957, Riv. 238); *California Guitar* (1974, FaD 102)

As sideman with R. Kamuca: *Richie* (*c*1977, Conc. 41)

BIBLIOGRAPHY

FeatherE; *Feather '60s*; *Feather–Gitler '70s*

J. Crockett: "Mundell Lowe," *GP*, vi/4 (1972), 14

"It's Good to Play Again, Says Guitarist/Composer Mundell Lowe," *CI*, xiii/2 (1974), 14

B. Crowther: "Mundell Lowe," *JJI*, xxxvii/8 (1984), 6

P. Elwood: "A Jazzy Convention in Monterey," *San Francisco Examiner* (19 Sept 1986), §D, p.1

NORMAN MONGAN

Lowe, Sammy [Samuel Milton] (*b* Birmingham, AL, 14 May 1918). Arranger and trumpeter. He played trumpet from an early age; while still in high school he began arranging and played with Paul Bascomb and the singer and bandleader Jean Calloway. He led the Tennessee State Collegians, then moved to New York (1936) to join the 'Bama State Collegians, under Erskine Hawkins, with whom he played until 1955; he made numerous arrangements for Hawkins, including one of his own piece *Junction Blues*, which the band recorded in 1940 (Bb 10790). He also worked with Eddie Heywood, Cab Calloway, Earle Warren, Don Redman, Illinois Jacquet, and others. From the 1960s he largely ceased to play, devoting his time instead to writing arrangements and conducting sessions for rhythm-and-blues, soul, and popular musicians; he occasionally recorded as the leader of studio bands.

BIBLIOGRAPHY

S. Lowe: "Samuel Milton Lowe," *BHcF*, no.94 (1960), 6

S. Dance: *The World of Swing* (New York, 1974) [colln of previously pubd interviews], 212 [incl. list of arrangements for Hawkins]

based on *ChiltonW*

Lowther, (Thomas) Henry (*b* Leicester, England, 11 July 1941). English trumpeter. He first played cornet in a Salvation Army band. In 1959 he studied violin at the Royal Academy of Music in London, but resumed playing trumpet the following year. He worked intermittently with Mike Westbrook (1963–1980s), and performed with John Dankworth (1967–77) and John Warren (from 1968). During the 1970s he played with Mike Gibbs (1970–76), Kenny Wheeler (from 1972), Kurt Edelhagen (1974), his own group Quaternity, John Taylor (from 1974), Stan Tracey (from 1976), and Gordon Beck (1978); he also recorded with Gibbs (1972) and Graham Collier (1976, 1978), with whom he made a tour of India (1980). Lowther has worked with blues and rock musicians and in classical ensembles. From 1983 he has been a member of Peter King's quartet (his playing with this group may be heard to advantage on the album *90% of One Percent*, 1985, Spot. 529), and in 1984 he worked with Gil Evans, playing in his English orchestra and film ensembles. He was involved in the reconstruction of John Robichaux' orchestra for a television documentary on Buddy Bolden, organized by Humphrey Lyttelton (1986). Lowther played in the big band led by Charlie Watts in 1986–7 and in 1987 organized his own group Still Waters. (R. Cotterrell, ed.: *Jazz Now: the Jazz Centre Society Guide*, London, 1976)

DIGBY FAIRWEATHER

LP. In popular-music usage the standard abbreviation for "long-playing disc" or "long player." *See* Recording, §§I, 3, and II, 3; *see also* Album.

Lubinsky, Herman (*b* 30 Aug 1896; *d* Newark, NJ, 16 March 1974). Record producer. In 1920 he established the United Radio Company in Newark, New Jersey, first selling electronic parts, then, from the late 1920s, records, and in 1924 he set up New Jersey's first radio station, WNJ. He founded the record company and label Savoy (*see* Savoy (ii)) in late 1942 and remained its sole owner until his death, although production was in the main left to his artists and repertory department.

BIBLIOGRAPHY

A. Shaw: "Savoy Records of Newark, New Jersey," *Honkers and Shouters: the Golden Years of Rhythm-and-Blues* (New York, 1978), 343
M. Ruppli: *The Savoy Label: a Discography* (Westport, CT, and London, 1980)

Lucas, Al(bert B.) (*b* Windsor, Ontario, Canada, 16 Nov 1916; *d* New York, 19 June 1983). Double bass player. After moving to New York he worked with Kaiser Marshall in 1933, then (1933–42) with the Royal Sunset Orchestra, which recorded under the leadership of the pianist Ace Harris (1937) and the trombonist Doc Wheeler (1941–2). He played with many of the leading musicians of the 1940s, including Coleman Hawkins (1942–3), Hot Lips Page (1943), Eddie Heywood (1944–5), Duke Ellington (1945), and Mary Lou Williams (1946). During the early and mid-1940s he recorded with Hawkins, James P. Johnson, and Heywood (all 1944), Williams (1944–5), and Ben Webster (1945); Williams's *Zodiac Suite* (1945) exemplifies his supportive accompaniment, broad sound, and proficient technique. He then worked with Illinois Jacquet (1947–53), again with Heywood (1954–6), and with Teddy Wilson (recording in 1957 and 1959). In the 1960s and 1970s he was active mainly as a studio musician, but he performed (1968) and recorded (1969) with Jacquet and made a tour of Japan with Sam "the Man" Taylor (1970–71). Lucas was best known for a rhythmic and harmonic style that was rooted in swing, and his solos, such as that on Ruby Braff's *Lover come back to me* (1956), show the influence of Jimmy Blanton in their melody and phrase structure.

SELECTED RECORDINGS

As sideman: M. L. Williams: *Zodiac Suite* (1945, Asch 620–21); J. J. Johnson: Boneology/Down Vernon's Alley (1947, Savoy 942); R. Braff: *Ruby Braff, Featuring Dave McKenna* (1956, ABC-Para. 141), incl. Lover come back to me; C. Byrd: *Jazz Recital* (1957, Savoy 12099); I. Jacquet: *Illinois Jacquet Flies Again* (1959, Roul. 52035); *The King!* (1969, Prst. 7597)

BIBLIOGRAPHY

ChiltonW
D. Morgenstern: Liner notes, *Zodiac Suite* (FW 32844, *c*1975)

JOHN CURRY

Lucie, Lawrence [Larry] (*b* Emporia, VA, 18 Dec 1907). Guitarist. He learned banjo, mandolin, and violin in his youth, and played for square dances with a family band. After moving to New York he studied banjo at the Brooklyn Conservatory, but from his first professional job (with June Clark, 1931) he played mainly guitar. He performed briefly with Duke Ellington, worked in Benny Carter's band (1932–4), then played alternately with the Mills Blue Rhythm Band (1934–6; for illustration *see* Mills blue rhythm band) and Fletcher Henderson (1934, 1936–9). In January 1940 he joined Coleman Hawkins, but when Hawkins disbanded a few months later began a four-year tenure with Louis Armstrong. After World War II he led a quartet with his wife, the guitarist and singer Nora Lee (Susan) King, then in the 1950s played with Luis Russell and Cozy Cole. During the 1960s he worked as a freelance and studio musician, taught in New York, and occasionally led small groups. He was a member of the New York Jazz Repertory Company in the 1970s.

Lucie early acquired a thorough knowledge of harmony and an unfailing sense of rhythm. Although he occasionally played a chordal solo (as on Morton's *Climax Rag*), he was primarily a competent and versatile rhythm guitarist, equally at home with the sophisticated swing of Carter's big band and the traditional New Orleans style of Morton.

SELECTED RECORDINGS

As leader: Larry and Leonore: *Traveling Guitars* (1958, Request 10037)
As sideman: B. Carter: Devil's Holiday/Symphony in Riffs (1933, Col. 2898D); F. Henderson: Limehouse Blues/Wrappin' it up (1934, Decca 157); T. Wilson: What a little moonlight can do/A Sunbonnet Blue (1935, Bruns. 7498); Mills Blue Rhythm Band: Merry-go-round/Until the real thing comes along (1936, Col. 3147D); F. Henderson: Moten Stomp (1938, Voc. 4180); J. R. Morton: Climax Rag/West End Blues (1939, Bb 10442); C. Hawkins: Sheik of Araby/My Blue Heaven (1940, Bb10770); L. Armstrong: I cover the waterfront/Long, long ago (1941, Decca 3700)

BIBLIOGRAPHY

ChiltonW
B. McRae: "Lawrence Lucie," *JJ*, xv/2 (1962), 3
W. C. Allen: *Hendersonia: the Music of Fletcher Henderson and his Musicians: a Bio-discography* (Highland Park, NJ, 1973)
S. Dance: "Lawrence Lucie," *The World of Swing* (New York, 1974) [colln of previously pubd interviews], 345
A. Berle: "Lawrence Lucie: Author, Teacher, Big Band Guitarist for over 45 years," *GP*, xiii/2 (1979), 38 [incl. discography]
L. Wright: "Rhythm is my Business: an Interview with Lawrence "Larry" Lucie," *Sv*, no.96 (1981), 218

DAVID FLANAGAN

Ludvik, Emil (*b* Prague, 16 Aug 1917). Bohemian pianist, arranger, composer, and bandleader. He studied music at the Charles University in Prague. Between 1939 and 1944 he led a dance orchestra, and a quintet that played hot jazz and swing; he also made several recordings, including *Sjezd swingaru* (Swing congress) with the orchestra and *Inspiration* with the quintet (both 1940, first issued on *Česky Jazz 1920–1960*, *c*1913–1959, Sup. DV101778H), and composed many dance tunes. (I. Polednák: "Druhý bod krystalizace" [The second crystallization-point], *Tanecní hudba a jazz, 1964–1965* [Dance music and jazz, 1964–1965], ed. L. Dorůžka, J. Hořec, and J. Kotek (Prague, 1965), 2)

GERHARD CONRAD

Luk'yanov, German (Konstantinovich) (*b* Leningrad, 23 Aug 1936). Russian trumpeter and composer. He studied piano from the age of six, trumpet at a music school in Leningrad (graduated 1953), and composition with the composer Aram Khachaturian at the Moscow P. I. Tchaikovsky State Conservatory. He led a trio from 1962 to 1969 and founded a jazz club and studio at the Moscow N. E. Bauman Technical Institute (1967); he then formed a quintet and worked as a soloist with the Kontsertny estradny orkestr Tsentral'novo TV i Vsesoyuznovo Radio (Concert variety orchestra of the central TV and all-union radio) (1970–74) and with the Azerbaijan Variety Orchestra (to 1977), of which he was also the conductor. In 1978 he formed the group Kadans, which made several recordings and appeared at festivals in Warsaw (1980), Székesfehérvár, Hungary (1981), and The Hague (1984). Luk'yanov's playing can be heard to advantage on his album *Kakaya cnezhnaya vesna* (What a snowy spring; 1986, Mel. C60239010). As a composer he displays considerable harmonic invention and skill at writing expressive melodies, and occasionally draws on Russian folk materials; his compositions include *Krest' yanskaya svad'ba* (Peasant wedding), *Ivanushka-durachok* (Ivanushka the fool), and music for films and television. (S. F. Starr: *Red and Hot: the Fate of Jazz in the Soviet Union, 1917–1980* (New York, and Oxford, England, 1983), 253)

WALTER OJAKÄÄR

Lunceford, Jimmie [Jimmy; James Melvin] (*b* Fulton, MO, 6 June 1902; *d* Seaside, OR, 12 July 1947). Bandleader. He learned several instruments as a child in Denver, where he played alto saxophone in the band led by the violinist George Morrison. After studying music at Fisk University (BMus 1926), and at the City College of New York, he taught music at Manassa High School, Memphis. Here, in 1927, he organized a student jazz band, the Chickasaw Syncopators. The group began a professional career in 1929 and issued its first recordings in 1930. After playing for several years in Cleveland and Buffalo, the band began an important engagement at the Cotton Club, Harlem, in 1934. Two "hot" recordings made that year, *Jazznocracy* and *White Heat*, with arrangements by Will Hudson, immediately attracted attention, and by 1935 the group, then called Jimmie Lunceford's Orchestra, had achieved a national reputation as an outstanding black swing band.

Unlike many big bands of the 1930s, Lunceford's group was noted less for its soloists than for its ensemble work, particularly its distinctive two-beat swing at medium tempo. This and its practiced showmanship were widely imitated by other groups, but they seldom achieved the polish and good humor that marked so many of Lunceford's performances. The band drew its early style partly from Alphonso Trent and from the Casa Loma Orchestra, as is most apparent in the crude, insistent riff patterns in the "hot" recordings of 1934. A certain experimental vein is also unmistakable in these years, for instance in Willie Smith's curious recasting of Ellington's *Mood Indigo* (1934). Soon after, however, there emerged a distinctive "Lunceford style," largely the result of the highly imaginative arrangements of the group's trumpeter, Sy Oliver (*see*

Jimmie Lunceford's orchestra at the Fiesta Danseteria, New York, June 1940: (back row, left to right) Russell Bowles, Trummy Young, and Elmer Crumbley (trombones), Jimmy Crawford (drums), Al Norris (guitar), Moses Allen (double bass); (front row) Paul Webster, Snooky Young, and Gerald Wilson (trumpets), Dan Grissom, Willie Smith, Ted Buckner, Joe Thomas (iii), and Jock Carruthers (saxophones); (foreground) Lunceford

ARRANGEMENT, §3, Table 4, and ex.1). The varied interplay of soloists and brass and reed sections in Oliver's best work, such as *For Dancers Only* (1937) and *Margie* (1938), set high standards for dance-band arrangers of the time and proved extremely fruitful for postwar big-band styles. Perhaps even more remarkable was his fusion of novelty effects and bizarre contrasts into coherent musical argument, as in his famous *Organ Grinder's Swing* (1936), which uses woodblocks, celesta, and slap-tongued saxophones. These arrangements, however complex, left ample scope for the group's soloists, the most important of whom were Joe Thomas (iii), Trummy Young, Eddie Durham, and Willie Smith, who also trained and led Lunceford's outstanding reed section from the group's inception in 1929.

After Oliver's departure in 1939 and Smith's in 1942, the group's style became somewhat unfocused, despite some excellent arrangements by Tadd Dameron (1941–2) and George Duvivier (1945–7). The band continued for a year after Lunceford's death under the joint direction of Eddie Wilcox and Joe Thomas, and for several years after that under Wilcox alone. Later attempts to revive the band's sound and Oliver's arrangements with other musicians have been unsuccessful.

See also BLUES, §6.

SELECTED RECORDINGS

White Heat (1934, Vic. 24586); Jazznocracy (1934, Vic. 24522); Mood Indigo (1934, Decca 131); Rhythm is our Business (1934, Decca 369); Organ Grinder's Swing (1936, Decca 908); For Dancers Only (1937, Decca 1340); Margie (1938, Decca 1617); Lunceford Special (1939, Voc./OK 5326); What's your story, mornin' glory? (1940, Col. 33510); Yard Dog Mazurka (1941, Decca 4032)

BIBLIOGRAPHY

H. Panassié: "Jimmy Lunceford and his Orchestra," *Jazz-hot*, 1st ser., no.21 (1937), 3
W. Russo: "Jimmy Lunceford," *Jazz Panorama*, ed. M. Williams (New York and London, 1962/R1979) [colln of previously pubd articles], 132
G. Hoefer: "Hot Box: Jimmie Lunceford," *DB*, xxxi/26 (1964), 35
F. Driggs: "Sy Oliver," *Sounds and Fury*, i (1965), 49
E. Edwards, Jr., G. Hall, and B. Korst: *Jimmie Lunceford* (Whittier, CA, 1965) [discography]
F. Dutton: "Jimmie Lunceford: the Broadcasts and Transcriptions," *Matrix*, no.86 (1969), 3
[G. Hulme]: "In the Wax: Lunceford Broadcasts," *Matrix*, no.93 (1971), 13; no.95 (1971), 14
I. Crosbie: "Lunceford: Message from Memphis," *JJ*, xxv (1972), no.1, p.2; no.2, p.26
S. Dance, ed.: "Willie Smith," *The World of Swing* (New York, 1974) [colln of previously pubd interviews]
A. McCarthy: *Big Band Jazz* (New York and London, 1974), 47
B. Hall and others: "Jimmie Lunceford Broadcasts: Transcriptions and Filmtracks," *Micrography*, no.42 (1976), 15
M. Harrison: *A Jazz Retrospect* (Newton Abbot, England, 1976, rev.2/1977)
S. Dance: "Lunceford Days," *JJI*, xxx/7 (1977), 6

J. BRADFORD ROBINSON

Lundgaard, Jesper (*b* Hillerød, Denmark, 12 June 1954). Danish double bass player. After playing guitar as a child he took up double bass in 1970. He studied at the university in Århus, Denmark, and worked with local groups from 1976. He also accompanied such visiting musicians as Dexter Gordon, Johnny Griffin, and Pepper Adams. In 1978 he toured Europe with the Thad Jones–Mel Lewis Orchestra. The following year he settled in Copenhagen, where he has performed and recorded with many swing and bop ensembles and musicians, including Thad Jones's Eclipse and Benny Carter (both 1980), Doug Raney (1980, 1982, 1984), Eddie "Lockjaw" Davis and Warne Marsh (both 1983), Horace Parlan (1983–4), and Paul Bley (1985). His playing may be heard to advantage on Bley's *My Standard* (Ste. 1214). (J. Arntzen: "Jesper Lundgaard: Mads Vinding," *MM: tidsskrift for rytmisk music m.m.*, xiv/4 (1982), 8)

ROLAND BAGGENAES

Lundstrem, Oleg (Leonidovich) (*b* Chita, Russia, 2 April 1916). Russian composer and bandleader. He lived from 1921 in Harbin, China, where he formed a band in 1934 that played jazz and dance music at dance halls in Shanghai and on the islands of Hangchow Bay; he also studied violin at a local music school, from which he graduated in 1935. In 1947 he moved with his band to Kazan, Russian SFSR, where it played at a workers' club; he also studied composition at the Kazan State Conservatory (graduated 1953). The group became a professional collective in 1956 and played jazz exclusively from 1981; it performed at festivals in Warsaw (1972), Prague (1978, 1986), and Sofia (1986) and made several recordings, including *V stile sving* (In swing time; 1986, Mel. C6023709006). Lundstrem's early compositions include a symphony, a cello sonata, and a suite on Tatar themes; later he turned his attention to big-band jazz, often striving for a distinctly national character in such works as *Mirazh*, *Bukharsky ornament* (Ornament of Bukhara), and *V gorakh Gruzii* (In the Georgian mountains). He was named a Merited Artist (1973) and a People's Artist (1986) of the Russian SFSR. (S. F. Starr: *Red and Hot: the Fate of Jazz in the Soviet Union, 1917–1980*, New York, and Oxford, England, 1983)

WALTER OJAKÄÄR

Luter, Claude (*b* Paris, 23 July 1923). French clarinetist and bandleader. He recorded in Paris with the clarinetist Claude Abadie and the trumpeter Boris Vian (both 1944). From 1946 he led a popular New Orleans revival band which made several recordings with Sidney Bechet (1949–55, including *Riz à la créole*, 1949, Selmer 2971). During the 1950s he recorded in Paris with Mezz Mezzrow (1951), Albert Nicholas (1953), and Barney Bigard (1960), and won wide acclaim there for his interpretations of early jazz; he also performed in the film *Satchmo the Great* with Louis Armstrong (1956). Luter continued to lead revivalist bands in the 1960s and 1970s.

BIBLIOGRAPHY

FeatherE
L. Malson: "Claude Luter ou le salaire de la foi," *Jm*, no.61 (1960), 20
J. P. Binchet and P. Carles: "Entretien avec Claude Luter," *Jm*, no.146 (1967), 35

Lyall, Graeme (William) (*b* Melbourne, Australia, 25 Jan 1942). Australian reed player. He first played at clubs in Melbourne, then worked at El Rocco in Sydney (1961–3). He was a founding member of the Daly–Wilson Big Band in 1969, and toured Japan with Don Burrows's septet in 1970. After working with the ABC Showband in Melbourne from 1974 to 1977 he was a music director for various television programs and tours; in this capacity he accompanied such musicians as Billy Eckstine and Tony Bennett. In 1974 he recorded the album *Lord of the Rings* (EMI EMC2525-6) as a sideman with John Sangster; he may be heard to particular advantage on the track *Grey Haven*. His jazz performances in the late 1970s and 1980s, though less frequent, have retained a clear-cut fluency and lyricism.

BIBLIOGRAPHY

A. Bissett: *Black Roots, White Flowers: a History of Jazz in Australia* (Sydney, 1979)
B. Johnson: "Lyall, Graeme William," *The Oxford Companion to Australian Jazz* (Melbourne, Australia, 1987)

JEFF PRESSING (with JOHN WHITEOAK)

Lyons, Jimmy [James Leroy] (*b* Jersey City, NJ, 1 Dec 1933; *d* New York, 19 May 1986). Alto saxophonist. In his teens he was given an alto saxophone by Buster Bailey and was befriended by Elmo Hope, Bud Powell, and Thelonious Monk; he studied with Rudy Rutherford. He began a long association with Cecil

Taylor in 1960 and over the following decade also worked at nonmusical jobs. He taught music for Narcotic Addiction Control, a drug treatment center in New York (1970–71), was an artist-in-residence with Taylor and Andrew Cyrille at Antioch College (1971–3), and directed the Black Music Ensemble at Bennington College (1975). From 1978 he often performed and recorded as a leader, usually with groups that included the bassoonist Karen Borca and the drummer Paul Murphy. Lyons was influenced by Charlie Parker and by Taylor; he had an energetic, yet lyrical, style and a full, hard-edged tone.

SELECTED RECORDINGS

As leader: *Other Afternoons* (1969, BYG 529309); *Push Pull* (1978, HH YZZ); *Jump up/What to Do about* (1980, HH 21); *Wee Sneezawee* (1983, BS 0067); *Give It Up* (1985, BS 0087)

As sideman with C. Taylor: *Cecil Taylor Live at the Cafe Montmartre* (1962, Debut 138); *Conquistador!* (1966, BN 84260); *One too Many, Salty Swift, and Not Goodbye* (1978, HH 2)

BIBLIOGRAPHY

J. B. Litweiler: "Jimmy Lyons," *DB*, xlii/1 (1975), 34
B. Rusch: "Jimmy Lyons: Interview," *Cadence*, iv/10 (1978), 23

ED HAZELL

Lyons, Len [Leonard S.] (*b* Albany, NY, 24 July 1942). Writer. He studied philosophy at the University of Rochester (BA 1964) and Brown University (MA 1966, PhD 1969) and from 1969 taught philosophy at the University of Santa Clara; he also studied piano with Lennie Tristano. His published writings include *The Great Jazz Pianists, Speaking of their Lives and Music* (New York, 1983), a collection of interviews with 27 jazz pianists that includes biographical material and discographies, and articles for *Down Beat*, *Keyboard*, and *Guitar Player*. He received the first Ralph J. Gleason Memorial Fund Award for Jazz Criticism at the Monterey Jazz Festival in 1976. In the early 1980s he moved from Berkeley, California, to Lexington, Massachusetts.

WRITINGS
(selective list)

The 101 Best Jazz Albums: a History of Jazz on Records (New York, 1980) [listeners' guide]
The Great Jazz Pianists, Speaking of their Lives and Music (New York, 1983)
with D. Perlo: *A Guide to the Jazz Masters* (in preparation)

DANIEL ZAGER

Lyricon. A synthesizer controller in the form of a wind instrument, manufactured from 1975; *see* SYNTHESIZER, §2(iii).

Lystedt, Lars (*b* Umeå, Sweden, 12 Dec 1925). Swedish trombonist, bandleader, and writer on jazz. He played trumpet from 1942 to 1952 then, after taking up valve trombone, led his own quintet (1958–72), which won acclaim at the Zurich Jazz Festival in 1968. In the same year he formed the Umeå Big Band and launched the Umeå Jazz Festival, which became Sweden's largest jazz event. He has recorded with the quintet (1962–4, including *Fanfar!*, 1962, Jazz Records 1401) and the big band (1970–74, including *Swingtime Festival*, 1974, Hitachi 10002). Lystedt became a critic for *Orkester journalen* in 1950 and the Swedish correspondent for *Down Beat* in 1969. (*Feather–Gitler '70s*)

Lytell, Jimmy [Sarrapede, James] (*b* New York, 1 Dec 1904; *d* Kings Point, NY, 28 Nov 1972). Clarinetist. By the age of 14 he was playing professionally in a roadhouse owned by his uncle. From 1922 to 1925 he was a member of the ORIGINAL MEMPHIS FIVE; during this period (until 1924) he also played with the Original Dixieland Jazz Band, as a replacement for Larry Shields. Throughout the 1930s and 1940s Lytell conducted and played on several radio programs. He was a music director for NBC in the mid-1940s and presented his own dixieland show, "The Chamber Music Society of Lower Basin Street" (1940, 1941, 1944). He played with the re-formed Original Memphis Five in 1949 and again in the mid-1950s, and continued to perform and record both as a leader and a freelance until shortly before his death. Lytell's playing was influenced by the work of Benny Goodman and Peanuts Hucko. As a member of the Original Memphis Five he helped to introduce a freer style of improvisation in the dixieland idiom.

SELECTED RECORDINGS

As leader: Basin Street Blues/High Society (1950, Lon. 680); Sugar Foot Stomp/Farewell Blues (1950, Lon. 699)

As sideman with Original Memphis Five: Struttin' at the Strutters' Ball/I wish I could shimmy like my sister Kate (1922, Para. 20161); Jacksonville Gal/'Tain't Cold (1925, Col. 502D)

BIBLIOGRAPHY

ChiltonW
L. Feather: *The Book of Jazz: a Guide to the Entire Field* (New York, 1957, rev. 2/1965)

RAYMOND J. GARIGLIO

Lytle, Johnny [John Dillard] (*b* Springfield, OH, 13 Oct 1932). Vibraphone player. He began his career as a drummer with Ray Charles (1950) and Gene Ammons (1953) before changing to vibraphone and playing with Boots Johnson (1955–7). Thereafter he led his own groups, which often included an organ in their instrumentation, and which played in the propulsive rhythm-and-blues style characteristic of many midwestern organ trios. His ensembles have featured Johnny Griffin, Frank Wess, Joe Farrell, and Ron Carter as sidemen. Lytle has toured widely and received a number of awards for his work as director of the Davey Moore Arts Cultural Center and Davey Moore Foundation in Springfield, Ohio. He is perhaps best known for his composition *The Village Caller*.

SELECTED RECORDINGS

Blue Vibes (1960, Jlnd 22); *Nice and Easy* (1961, Jlnd 67); *The Village Caller* (1964–5, Riv. 9480); *The Soulful Rebel* (1971, Mlst. 9036); *Everything Must Change* (1977, Muse 5158)

BIBLIOGRAPHY

Feather '60s; *Feather–Gitler '70s*

ANDREW JAFFE

Lyttelton, Humphrey (R. A.) (*b* Eton, England, 23 May 1921). English trumpeter, clarinetist, and bandleader. He first played jazz while a schoolboy at Eton and continued to perform during his wartime service with the Grenadier Guards. He began playing professionally when he joined George Webb's Dixielanders in 1947, and the following year he formed his own band. Lyttelton's early outlook, as trumpeter and bandleader, was based on the example of Louis Armstrong, and his group initially adhered to revivalist principles; later, just as his playing reflected the influences of such musicians as Roy Eldridge and Buck Clayton, so his bands moved from the traditional New Orleans style to that used by groups during the swing era. During the mid-1950s Lyttelton introduced saxophonists into his line-up, the first of whom was Bruce Turner, and by 1958 his saxophone section consisted of Tony Coe, Jimmy Skidmore, and Joe Temperley. Thereafter he regularly incorporated in the band such young progressive players as Tony Mann, Dave Green, Mick Pyne, and John Surman. From 1949, when he recorded with Sidney Bechet, Lyttelton collaborated with visiting Americans, and in 1963–6 he toured Europe and recorded with Clayton. He has also played clarinet, and frequently performs duets with his band's regular clarinetists. His band made several international tours for the British Council during the 1970s and also traveled widely in Britain. In 1983 Lyttelton founded his own record label, Calligraph.

Lyttelton is also a talented writer and broadcaster: he has published an autobiography, three semi-autobiographical books, and two volumes of record criticism. For nearly two decades he has broadcast the program "The Best of Jazz" for BBC radio. Throughout his career he has proved a humorous and perceptive figurehead for British jazz.

SELECTED RECORDINGS

As leader: Irish Black Bottom (1949, Parl. R3267); Careless Love Blues (1950, Parl. R3274); I like to go back in the evening (1950, Parl. R3317); Trog's Blues (1951, Parl. R3379); Blue for Waterloo (1953, Parl. R3700); *Humph at the Conway* (1954, Parl. PMC1012); Bad Penny Blues (1956, Parl. R4184); *I Play as I Please* (1957, Decca LK4276), incl. Manhattan; *Triple Exposure* (1959, Parl. PMC1110); *21 Years On* (1969, Pol. 583069–70), incl. Cakewalkin' Babies; *South Bank Swing Session* (1973, BL 2460233); *Spreadin' Joy* (1978, BL 12173); *It Seems Like Yesterday* (1983, Calligraph 01); *Gonna Call my Children Home: the World of Buddy Bolden* (1986, Calligraph 013)

As sideman with S. Bechet: I told you once, I told you twice/Georgia on my Mind (1949, Melo 1105)

WRITINGS

I Play as I Please: the Memoirs of an Old Etonian Trumpeter (London, 1954)
Second Chorus (London, 1958)
Take it from the Top: an Autobiographical Scrapbook (London, 1975)
The Best of Jazz, i: *Basin Street to Harlem: Jazz Masters and Masterpieces, 1917–1930* (London, 1978), ii: *Enter the Giants, 1931–1944* (London, 1981)
Why no Beethoven? (London, 1984)

BIBLIOGRAPHY

FeatherE; *Feather '60s*; *Feather–Gitler '70s*
D. Boulton: *Jazz in Britain* (London, 1958)
S. Traill: "Metamorphosis: Humphrey Lyttelton," *JJ*, xii/4 (1959), 1
I. Berg, I. Yeomans, and N. Brittan: *Trad: A to Z Who's Who of the British Traditional Jazz Scene* (London and elsewhere, 1962)
"Progress of an Individualist," *Crescendo*, i/4 (1962), 13
J. Godbolt: *A History of Jazz in Britain, 1919–50* (London, Melbourne, Australia, and New York, 1984)
J. Purser, J. Wilyman, and P. Schwalm: *Humph: a Discography of Humphrey Lyttelton, 1945–1983* (Walton on Thames, England, 1985)
B. Clayton and N. M. Elliott: *Buck Clayton's Jazz World* (London, 1986)
D. Fairweather: "Lyttelton, Humphrey," in I. Carr, D. Fairweather, and B. Priestley: *Jazz: the Essential Companion* (London, 1987)

CHARLES FOX/DIGBY FAIRWEATHER

M

Mabern, Harold(, Jr.) (*b* Memphis, 20 March 1936). Pianist and composer. He taught himself to play piano as a teenager and after moving to Chicago in 1954 studied harmony with Ahmad Jamal. He joined Walter Perkins's group MJT + 3, then moved to New York in 1959, where he played with Lionel Hampton (*c*1960), Art Farmer's and Benny Golson's Jazztet (1961–2), Donald Byrd, Miles Davis, and J. J. Johnson (1963–5). He was an accompanist for Joe Williams (1966–7), Sarah Vaughan, and Arthur Prysock; he also worked with Sonny Rollins, Freddie Hubbard (1965), and Wes Montgomery (1965). He belonged to the Piano Choir with Stanley Cowell and others and to Walter Bolden's trio (1973–4). He also recorded with Billy Harper in Japan (1977) and performed in England (1978). Mabern has been influenced chiefly by Phineas Newborn and to a lesser degree by George Coleman and John Coltrane. As a composer Mabern is noted for his melodic gifts; he has recorded many of his own compositions, including *Blues for Phineas* and *Rakin' and Scrapin'*.

SELECTED RECORDINGS

As leader: *A Few Miles from Memphis* (1968, Prst. 7568); *Rakin' and Scrapin'* (1968, Prst. 7624); *Workin' and Wailin'* (1969, Prst. 7687)

As sideman: MJT + 3: *Walter Perkins' MJT Plus III* (1959, VJ 1013): A. Farmer and B. Golson: *Here and Now* (1962, Mer. 60698); J. J. Johnson: *Proof Positive* (1964, Imp. 68); Piano Choir: *Handscapes* (1972, SE 19730); B. Harper: *Soran-Bushi – B. H.* (1977, Denon 7522)

BIBLIOGRAPHY

Feather '60s; *Feather–Gitler '70s*

B. Case: "Mabern: Ringing the Changes," *MM*, liv (6 Jan 1979), 12

PAUL RINZLER

Mac, Tommy. *See* MCQUATER, TOMMY.

McBee, Cecil (*b* Tulsa, OK, 19 May 1935). Double bass player. He played clarinet, then double bass from the age of 17. He attended Central State University, Wilberforce, Ohio (at intervals, 1953–62), and early in 1959 worked with Dinah Washington. While serving in the US Army in Fort Knox, Kentucky (1959–61), he led a military band (in which he also played clarinet), studied double bass, and belonged to a trio with the pianist Kirk Lightsey and the drummer Rudy Johnson. After moving in 1962 to Detroit he played with Paul Winter (1963–4), then lived in New York from 1964. During the following years he worked with Grachan Moncur III (1964–5), Jackie McLean (1964–5), Wayne Shorter (1965–6), Charles Tolliver (1965–70), Charles Lloyd (1966), Yusef Lateef (1967–9), Sam Rivers (1967–73), Pharoah Sanders (1969–72), Alice Coltrane (1969–72), Abdullah Ibrahim (from 1973 into the 1980s), Sonny Rollins (1973), and Chico Freeman (from 1976 into the 1980s). From 1976 he also made recordings as a leader, often with Freeman as a sideman; later he played with Art Pepper (1978), McCoy Tyner (1980), Mal Waldron (1981), James Newton (1982–3), and JoAnne Brackeen (1985), and in 1984 joined the LEADERS. McBee is a versatile musician who is equally adept at playing bop, modal jazz, and free jazz; he has a powerful technique, which he uses judiciously, and a rich, full tone.

For illustration *see* JARRETT, KEITH.

SELECTED RECORDINGS

As leader: *Mutima* (1974, SE 7417); *Music from the Source* (1977, Enja 3019); *Flying Out* (*c*1982, IndN 1053)

As sideman: G. Bohanon: *George Bohanon* (1962, Jazz Workshop 207); G. Moncur III: *Some Other Stuff* (1964, BN 84177); J. McLean: *It's Time* (1964, BN 84179); C. Lloyd: *Forest Flower* (1966, Atl. 1473); P. Sanders: *Thembi* (1970, Imp. 9206); S. Rivers: *Streams* (1973, Imp. 9251); C. Freeman: *Chico* (*c*1977, IndN 1031); *Tradition in Transition* (1982, Elek. Mus. 52412); A. Ibrahim: *Ekaya* (1983, Ekapa 005)

BIBLIOGRAPHY

H. West: "Cecil McBee: Reflections," *JT* (1982), March, 10

C. Kuhn: "Cecil McBee, Chico Freeman: Interview," *Cadence*, ix/6 (1983), 5

ED HAZELL

McBrowne, Lennie [Leonard Louis] (*b* New York, 24 Jan 1933). Drummer. He played with local bands in 1945–7 and studied double bass at the New York School of Music (1948) and percussion with Max Roach, Morris Goldenberg, and Sticks Evans. He worked with Pete Brown, Randy Weston, Cecil Payne, and Ernie Henry, performed and recorded with Tony Scott (1956), then moved to Los Angeles to perform with Paul Bley (1957–8); there he later worked with Richie Kamuca, Harold Land, Sonny Rollins, Sonny Stitt, Teddy Edwards, and Benny Golson's and Curtis Fuller's quintet. From 1959 to 1961 he led the Four Souls; after returning to New York he played with Sarah Vaughan, the group Lambert, Hendricks, and Bavan, Carmen McRae, Randy Weston, Ray Bryant, Walter Bishop, Jr., Teddy Wilson, and Toshiko Akiyoshi (all 1964–6), Booker Ervin (1966–9), and Blue Mitchell. He worked with Kenny Burrell in 1971–4 and moved to San Francisco in 1972. The elements of McBrowne's style, including his tendency to play slightly ahead of the beat with the ride cymbal, are strongly characteristic of hard bop.

SELECTED RECORDINGS

As leader: *Lennie McBrowne and the Four Souls* (1959, PJ 1)
As sideman: P. Bley: *Solemn Meditation* (1958, Gene Norman Presents 31); R. Weston: *Alone . . . and Together* (1965, Ari. 1026); B. Ervin: *The In Between* (1968, BN 84283); S. Noto: *Entrance!* (1975, Xan. 103)

BIBLIOGRAPHY

FeatherE; *Feather '60s*; *Feather–Gitler '70s*

J. KENT WILLIAMS

McCall, Mary Ann (*b* Philadelphia, 4 May 1919). Singer. She began her career as a singer and dancer with Buddy Morrow's band in Philadelphia; she joined Tommy Dorsey briefly in 1938, then sang with Woody Herman (1939) and Charlie Barnet (1939–40). After a period of comparative inactivity she rejoined Herman in 1946 and remained with him until 1950 (for illustration *see* HERMAN, WOODY, fig.1*b*); during this time she married Al Cohn. She worked as a solo artist before a short spell with Charlie Ventura (1954–5). Her second marriage, in 1958, took her to Detroit, where she sang in local clubs. Two years later she moved to California and worked occasionally with Nat Pierce, also performing at Chubby Jackson's Estate Club in Hollywood. Although McCall was initially a singer of popular material, by the 1940s she had developed a jazz style and sang with an inflection that owed much to Billie Holiday; discerning critics considered her to be one of the finest jazz singers.

SELECTED RECORDINGS

As leader: *Easy Living* (1956, Reg. 6040); *Detour to the Moon* (1958, Jub. 1078)
As sideman: C. Barnet: You've got me out on a limb/Castle of Dreams (1940, Bb 10644); C. Ventura: *An Evening with Charlie Ventura with Mary Ann McCall* (1954, Norg. 20); J. Hanna: *Jake Hanna's Kansas City Express* (1976, Conc. 22); N. Pierce: *5400 North* (1978, Hep 2004)

BIBLIOGRAPHY

FeatherE
G. T. Simon: *The Big Bands* (New York, 1967, rev. 3/1974, 4/1981)

REG COOPER

McCall, Steve (*b* Chicago, 30 Sept 1933). Drummer and percussionist. He studied music at conservatory and university, and first played professionally with the blues singer Lucky Carmichael. Although he was influenced by Eddie Harris, Ramsey Lewis (with whom he recorded in 1964), and the drummer Wilbur Campbell, his most important early association was with Muhal Richard Abrams, whom he met in 1961; both men became founding members of the Association for the Advancement of Creative Musicians in 1965. McCall played in Chicago with bop bands and also with such free-jazz musicians as Fred Anderson, Anthony Braxton, Leroy Jenkins, Joseph Jarman, Roscoe Mitchell, and Leo Smith. From 1967 to 1970 he lived in Paris, where he performed and recorded with Marion Brown (1968–9) and Braxton (1969–70). After returning to Chicago McCall recorded with Dexter Gordon and Gene Ammons (1970) and formed a trio, Reflection, with Henry Threadgill and Fred Hopkins (1971). He spent a further 13 months in Europe, then went in 1975 to New York, where the trio was re-formed as AIR; he toured extensively with the group, though he later returned to Chicago. He also recorded with Chico Freeman (1976–7), Arthur Blythe (1979), and David Murray (1979–82), and later joined Cecil Taylor's Unit (1985). In the 1980s he has given solo concerts and occasionally led a sextet. His drumming is melodic and coloristic, assertive but flexible, expansive, and dynamically sensitive.

SELECTED RECORDINGS

As sideman: J. Jarman: *Song for* (1966, Del. 410); Creative Construction Company: *Creative Construction Company* (1970, Muse 5071, 5097); G. Ammons and D. Gordon: *The Chase* (1970, Prst. 10010); A. Blythe: *In the Tradition* (1979, Col. JC36300); D. Murray: *Ming* (1980, BS 0045)

BIBLIOGRAPHY

R. Terlizzi: "Steve McCall," *Coda*, xii/2 (1974), 6
J. B. Litweiler: "Air: Impossible to Pigeonhole," *DB*, xliii/21 (1976), 22 [incl. interview]
E. Jost: *Jazzmusiker: Materialen zur Soziologie der afro-amerikanischen Musik* (Frankfurt am Main, Germany, Berlin, and Vienna, 1981), 114
K. Whitehead: "Steve McCall: Interview," *Cadence*, viii/7 (1982), 11
E. Ahonen: "Pheeroan ak Laff ja Steve McCall," *Rytmi*, nos.9–10 (1987), 8

HOWARD MANDEL

McCandless, Paul (*b* Indiana, PA, 24 March 1947). Oboist, english horn player, bass clarinetist, and soprano saxophonist. He played clarinet from the age of nine and in 1967 moved to New York, where he studied oboe with Robert Bloom at the Manhattan School of Music. From 1968 to 1973 he belonged to Paul Winter's group the Winter Consort, and with three of its other members, Ralph Towner, Glen Moore, and Collin Walcott, he formed the group OREGON in 1970. He recorded as the leader of a wind octet (1979), played in the cooperative group Gallery (from 1980), and in 1986 moved to California. McCandless's mastery of the oboe and other wind instruments (including wooden flutes) has contributed much to the distinctive sound and varied timbres of Oregon's music.

SELECTED RECORDINGS

As leader: *All the Mornings Bring* (1979, Elek. 6E196)
As sideman (all recorded for ECM): on R. Towner: *Trios/Solos* (1972, 1025), A Belt of Asteroids, Noctuary, Raven's Wood; A. Lande: *Skylight* (1981, 1208); E. Weber: *Later that Evening* (1982, 1231)

BIBLIOGRAPHY

Feather–Gitler '70s
M. Zipkin: "Oregon: out of the Woods, into the World," *DB*, xlvi/5 (1979), 13 [incl. interview]
L. Lyons: "Goodbye, Oregon," *Musician, Player, and Listener*, no.29 (1981), 56

PAUL RINZLER

McCann, Les(lie Coleman) [Maxie] (*b* Lexington, KY, 23 Sept 1935). Pianist and singer. He grew up in a musical family, and learned tuba and drums as a youth, but was largely self-taught on piano. While at school and in the navy he sang with various groups and developed his skills as a pianist. After winning a navy talent contest as a singer (1956) he appeared on Ed Sullivan's television show. McCann settled in California after being discharged and from 1958 began gaining recognition leading his own trio in nightclubs. He declined an invitation to join Cannonball Adderley's quintet, preferring instead to work on his own music, and signed a contract with the Pacific Jazz label. His two albums of 1960, *Les McCann Plays the Truth* and *The Shout*, displayed the influence of gospel music and brought him considerable fame. He recorded frequently throughout the 1960s, and his soulful funk style influenced many younger players. In 1969 he gave a performance with Eddie Harris at the Montreux International Jazz Festival; this was captured on the album *Swiss Movement*, which yielded a hit song, *Compared to What*. The success of this prompted McCann to emphasize his abilities as a singer. By the early 1970s he was experimenting extensively with electronic keyboards; the album *Live at Montreux* (1972) offers good examples of his work at this time. Later in the decade he gradually ceased playing jazz and concentrated on rhythm-and-blues and soul music. He has made few recordings in the 1980s.

SELECTED RECORDINGS

As leader: *Les McCann Plays the Truth* (1960, PJ 2); *The Shout* (1960, PJ 7); *Les McCann Sings* (1961, PJ 31); *Les McCann in New York* (1961, PJ 45); *The Gospel Truth* (1963, PJ 69); *Live at Shelly's Manne Hole* (1965, Lml. 86036); with E. Harris: *Swiss Movement* (1969, Atl. 1537), incl. Compared to What; *Second Movement* (1971, Atl. 1583); *Invitation to Openness* (1971,

Atl. 1603); *Live at Montreux* (1972, Atl. 2-312); *Layers* (1972, Atl. 1646); *Music Box* (1984, Jam 019)

As sideman: T. Edwards: *It's about Time* (1959, PJ 6); S. Turrentine: *That's where it's at* (1962, BN 84096)

BIBLIOGRAPHY

Feather '60s; *Feather–Gitler '70s*

J. Tynan: "Les McCann & 'the Truth'," *DB*, xxvii/19 (1960), 20

R. Carr: "I Used to Sleep near the Piano!: the Essential Les McCann," *Crescendo*, iii/2 (1964), 16

B. Doerschuk: "Les McCann," *CK*, iv/9 (1978), 26

SCOTT YANOW

McCarthy, Albert (John) (*b* Camborne, England, 1920; *d* London, Nov 1987). English writer. He became interested in jazz in the mid-1930s and established contact with record collectors such as Max Jones, Charles Fox, and Leonard Hibbs. In 1942 McCarthy and Jones founded the Jazz Sociological Society and became the editors of its journal *Jazz Music*; from 1944 to 1946, to circumvent wartime rationing of paper, the journal was temporarily discontinued and instead a series of separate booklets entitled Jazz Music Books was issued. McCarthy then edited the short-lived *Jazz Forum: Quarterly Review of Jazz and Literature* (1946–7), and, with Dave Carey, compiled six volumes of a discography of jazz. From 1955 to 1972 he was editor of the influential periodical *Jazz Monthly*, which, in addition to its catholic coverage of jazz and blues, also included items on related topics such as the record industry; in March 1971 it was expanded and renamed *Jazz and Blues*, of which McCarthy remained editor until December 1972. In 1974 he started another magazine, *Mainstream*, but only one issue was published. He coordinated and contributed to the critical guide *Jazz on Record* (1968) and occasionally worked as a record producer for Atlantic, British RCA, and Black Lion. His *Big Band Jazz* is the definitive survey of black big bands in the era of 78 r.p.m. recordings.

WRITINGS

(selective list)

The Trumpet in Jazz (London, 1945)

ed. with M. Jones: *Piano Jazz* (London, 1945)

ed.: *The PL Jazzbook* (London, 1946)

ed.: *The PL Yearbook of Jazz, 1946* (London, 1946)

with M. Jones: *A Tribute to Huddie Ledbetter* (London, 1946)

ed.: *Jazzbook, 1947* (London, 1947)

with D. Carey: *The Directory of Recorded Jazz and Swing Music* [cover title *Jazz Directory*], i–iv (Fordingbridge, England, 1949–51, ii–iv rev. 2/1955–7); v, vi (London, 1954–7) [discography; A–Longshaw only, later vols. not pubd]

ed.: *Jazzbook, 1955* (London, 1955)

ed. with N. Hentoff: *Jazz: New Perspectives on the History of Jazz by Twelve of the World's Foremost Jazz Critics and Scholars* (New York and Toronto, 1959/*R*1974)

Jazz Discography, i: *an International Discography of Recorded Jazz, Including Blues, Gospel and Rhythm-and-blues for the Year January–December 1958* (London, 1960)

Louis Armstrong (London, 1960)

Coleman Hawkins (London, 1963); repr. in *Kings of Jazz*, ed. S. Green (South Brunswick, NJ, and New York, 1978)

with others: *Jazz on Record: a Critical Guide to the First 50 Years: 1917–1967* (London, 1968) [listeners' guide]

The Dance Band Era: the Dancing Decades from Ragtime to Swing, 1910–1950 (London, 1971/*R*1982)

Big Band Jazz (New York and London, 1974)

BRIAN PRIESTLEY

McClure, Ron(ald Dix) (*b* New Haven, CT, 22 Nov 1941). Bass player and composer. He played piano from the age of five, took up accordion and bass drum, and studied double bass with Joseph Iadone; he attended the Hartt School of Music (BM 1963) and later studied composition with Hall Overton and Don Sebesky. He played with Buddy Rich (1963–4) and performed and recorded with Maynard Ferguson, Herbie Mann, and Marian McPartland (all 1964–5). In 1966 he replaced Paul Chambers in Wynton Kelly's group and the following year joined a group led by Charles Lloyd, which became the first American ensemble to play at a jazz festival in the USSR. In San Francisco he was a founder member of the Fourth Way with Michael White, Mike Nock, and Eddie Marshall in 1968; it played at the Montreux and Newport festivals in 1970 and continued until 1971. Among the leaders with whom McClure played in the 1970s were Joe Henderson (1970–71), Gary Burton and Mose Allison (both 1971), Jack DeJohnette (1976–7), Dave Liebman (from 1978), Thelonious Monk, Tony Bennett, and Keith Jarrett; he recorded with Jerry Hahn, Julian Priester, Cal Tjader, and the Pointer Sisters. From 1973 to 1976 he was a member of Blood, Sweat and Tears. He later performed and recorded with George Russell (1982) and Michel Petrucciani (1985–6).

McClure has a powerful technique on both double bass and electric bass guitar, particularly strong in the upper range; he has an insistent sense of rhythm and often plays rhythmic fills with the left hand alone by striking the strings against the fingerboard. In addition to his work as a performer he has taught at the Berklee College of Music (1971–2) and Long Island University (1983–5) and has led jazz workshops in the USA, Europe, and Australia. His compositions include *No Show* (1975), *Belle* (1978), and *Cold Blues* (1985).

SELECTED RECORDINGS

As leader: *Home Base* (1979, Ode 160)

As sideman: W. Kelly: *Full View* (1967, Mlst. MSP 9004); C. Lloyd: *Love in* (1967, Atl. 1481); *Journey Within* (1967, Atl. 1493); Fourth Way: *The Fourth Way* (1969, Cap. ST317); *Werwolf* (1970, Harvest 666); on J. Henderson: *In Pursuit of Blackness* (1970–71, Mlst. 9034), Invitation; D. Liebman: *If they only Knew* (1980, Tim. 151); A. Farmer: *Art Farmer in Concert* (1984, Enja 4088)

BIBLIOGRAPHY

Feather '60s; *Feather–Gitler '70s*

M. McPartland: "Looking to the Future: Ron McClure, Eddie Gomez: an Appreciation of Two Promising Young Bassists," *DB*, xxxiii/11 (1966), 20; repr. in *All in Good Time* (New York, and Oxford, England, 1987) [colln of previously pubd articles], 113

M. Hennessey: "Bassist Ron McClure: Setting the Scene Alight," *MM*, xlii (9 Sept 1967), 17

"The Blood, Sweat and Tears File," *MM*, xlix (20 July 1974), 31

JOHN VOIGT

McConnell, Rob(ert Murray Gordon) (*b* London, Canada, 14 Feb 1935). Canadian trombonist, bandleader, arranger, and composer. In Toronto he played valve trombone in dance bands and studied with Gordon Delamont (1958–62); he also belonged to Delamont's rehearsal band. He performed and recorded with Maynard Ferguson in New York (1964), then returned to Toronto, where he belonged to Nimmons 'n' Nine Plus Six (1965–9), led by Phil Nimmons, and worked as a studio musician and arranger. In 1968 he formed the group Boss Brass, which at first included no reed instruments and played popular material. A saxophone section was added in 1971, and after Sam Noto joined the group in 1976 it had 22 members. By the late 1970s it was presenting a repertory consisting of jazz standards and compositions by McConnell. It gave occasional performances in the USA and acquired an international reputation in the 1980s, owing in part to McConnell's skillful arrangements; its recording *All in Good Time* (1983) won a Grammy Award in 1984.

SELECTED RECORDINGS

Big band: *Big Band Jazz* (1978, Umbrella 4); *Present Perfect* (1979, MPS 68249); *All in Good Time* (1983, Innovation 00060); *Boss Brass & Woods* (1985, Innovation 0011)

Sextet: *Old Friends, New Music* (1984, Unisson 1001)

BIBLIOGRAPHY

H. McNamara and M. Miller: "McConnell, Rob," *Encyclopedia of Music in Canada*, ed. H. Kallmann, G. Potvin, and K. Winters (Toronto, Buffalo, and London, 1981)
M. Miller: "Rob McConnell: Boss of the Brass," *DB*, 1/6 (1983), 21 [incl. discography]
P. Clatworthy: "Brass Boss," *JJI*, xxxviii/1 (1985), 8 [incl. discography]
M. Miller: "Rob McConnell," *Boogie, Pete & the Senator: Canadian Musicians in Jazz: the Eighties* (Toronto, 1987), 165

MARK MILLER

McCord, Castor (*b* Birmingham, AL, 17 May 1907; *d* New York, 14 Feb 1963). Tenor saxophonist and clarinetist, twin brother of Ted McCord. The brothers played in Edgar Hayes's Blue Grass Buddies in 1924, and Castor then became a member of Horace Henderson's band. At intervals between 1929 and 1934 he played and made recordings with the Mills Blue Rhythm Band (including *Red Devil*, 1931, Banner 32733); during this period he also performed with Eubie Blake and the pianist and bandleader Charles Matson. He went to Europe in 1934 and settled in Paris, where he played in a band that accompanied Louis Armstrong and Coleman Hawkins; between then and 1938, when he returned to the USA, he worked with Leon Abbey for 18 months, twice visiting India (1936), Fletcher Allen (in Paris, 1937), and Walter Rains (in Rotterdam, 1938), and led his own trio (in Amsterdam, 1937). In New York he re-joined Abbey, recorded with Ethel Waters (1938–9), and played and recorded with Benny Carter (1939–40); he then played with the trumpeter and saxophonist Eddie Mallory (from 1940) and Claude Hopkins (1941–2). He ceased to be active as a musician in the 1940s.

based on *ChiltonW*

McCord, Ted [Theodore Jobetus] (*b* Birmingham, AL, 17 May 1907). Clarinetist and saxophonist, twin brother of Castor McCord. With his brother, he played with Edgar Hayes's Blue Grass Buddies (1924), and later recorded with Louis Armstrong (1930), the Mills Blue Rhythm Band (1931), and the bandleader King Carter (1931). He also recorded with McKinney's Cotton Pickers (1929) and with the singer Ollie Shepard (1939).

MARCEL JOLY

McCracken, Bob [Robert Edward] (*b* Dallas, 23 Nov 1904; *d* Los Angeles, 4 July 1972). Clarinetist and saxophonist. He first toured with lesser-known groups; Jack Teagarden was one of his colleagues. He performed and recorded in Chicago and New York from at least 1926 (perhaps as early as 1924) until 1928 with a band led by the composer Willard Robison. He then returned to Texas and worked there until 1935. After periods with Joe Venuti and Frankie Trumbauer he moved to Chicago in 1939. The following year he played with Jimmy McPartland and Wingy Manone, and in 1941 he spent a brief period with Benny Goodman. He then played in dance bands for several years, and he continued to work in Chicago until he toured Europe with Louis Armstrong (1952–3). After settling on the West Coast, McCracken worked with Kid Ory, Ben Pollack, the cornetist Pete Daily, and Jack Teagarden (1954, 1956). He toured Europe with Ory (1959), and later played with Teagarden (1962) and Wild Bill Davison (1967).

SELECTED RECORDINGS

As sideman: W. Robinson: My Melancholy Baby/Lovely Little Silhouette (*c*1927, Per. 14926); K. Ory: Milenberg Joys, Creole Love Call/Bucket's Got a Hole in it, Aunt Hagar's Blues (1953, GTJ EP1041) [EP]; *Storyville Nights* (1961, Verve 68456), incl. Doctor Jazz, Storyville Blues

BIBLIOGRAPHY

ChiltonW
G. Hoefer, Jr.: "The Hot Box," *DB*, xiii/9 (1946), 11

RAYMOND J. GARIGLIO

McCurdy, Roy (Walter, Jr.) (*b* Rochester, NY, 28 Nov 1936). Drummer. After playing and recording with the Jazz Brothers (1960–61), led by Chuck and Gap Mangione, he worked in Art Farmer's and Benny Golson's Jazztet (1961–2), in a trio with Dwike Mitchell and Willie Ruff (which toured Europe, 1962), and with Bobby Timmons (1962), Betty Carter (1962–3), and Sonny Rollins (1963–4), with whom he toured Japan. He is best known for his work in the rhythm section of Cannonball Adderley's group (1965–75), with which he toured widely and made many recordings. Later he played with the guitarist and singer Kenny Rankin (touring in 1975, recording in 1975–7), worked in television and recording studios in California, and performed occasionally with Benny Golson, Jerome Richardson, and Nancy Wilson (from 1982).

SELECTED RECORDINGS

As sideman: S. Rollins: *The Alternative Rollins* (1964, RCA PL43268), incl. Now's the Time; C. Adderley: *Inside Straight* (1973, Fan. 9435); K. Rankin: *The Kenny Rankin Album* (1977, Little David 1013); K. Burrell: *Moon and Sand* (1979, Conc. 121); B. Golson: *One More Mem'ry* (1981, Tim. 180); on [no leader]: *In Performance at the Playboy Jazz Festival* (1982, Elek. Mus. 960298), A. Farmer and B. Golson: I Remember Clifford

BIBLIOGRAPHY

Feather '60s; *Feather–Gitler '70s*
L. Feather: "Blindfold Test: Roy McCurdy," *DB*, xxxvii/21 (1970), 27

JEFF POTTER

McDaniel, Rudy. *See* TACUMA, JAMAALADEEN.

MacDonald, Ralph (*b* ?New York, 1944). Conga player. He learned mainly from listening to his father's calypso band in and around Harlem; he began playing with the popular singer Harry Belafonte in 1961, and remained with him for 10 years before working with Roberta Flack and other pop musicians. The albums he recorded as a leader between 1976 and 1984 demonstrate his interest in the African and West Indian styles that lie at the roots of jazz drumming, as well as in disco. As a session musician he recorded with Roland Kirk (1972, 1975), Grover Washington, Jr. (from 1972), Ron Carter (1973–5, 1978–81), Paul Desmond (1973), Idris Muhammad (1974), the Brecker Brothers (1975), David Sanborn (from 1975), and Steve Khan (1977); much of this work fuses jazz and soul, or jazz and funk, as on the album *The Brecker Brothers* (1975, Ari. 4037).

BIBLIOGRAPHY

M. Ribowski: "Ralph MacDonald," *Sepia*, no.26 (1977), 62
C. Iero: "The New York Scene: Ralph MacDonald," *MD*, iii/3 (1979), 15
R. Santelli: "Ralph MacDonald," *Modern Percussionist*, i/4 (1985), 8

CATHERINE COLLINS

McDonough, Dick [Richard] (*b* 1904; *d* New York, 25 May 1938). Acoustic guitarist and banjoist. During the 1920s and 1930s he was one of the busiest session players in New York; he took part in hundreds of recordings with various leaders, including Miff Mole (1927, 1929, 1931), Red Nichols (1927, 1932), and the Dorsey Brothers (1932–4). In the 1930s he formed an acclaimed partnership with Carl Kress, and also led his own radio and recording band. His playing may be heard to advantage on *Chasing a Buck* (1934), first issued on *Pioneers of the Jazz Guitar* (Yazoo 1057).

based on *ChiltonW*

McDuff, Brother Jack [McDuffy, Eugene] (*b* Champaign, IL, 17 Sept 1926). Organist. A self-taught musician, he began as a double bass player with Denny Zeitlin and Joe Farrell, and studied briefly in Cincinnati before gaining recognition for his work in Chicago with Johnny Griffin. In the 1950s he changed to piano and in 1959, as an organist, he formed his own group. McDuff has made tours of the USA, appeared at major European jazz festivals, and recorded prolifically as a leader with such sidemen as Joe Henderson, George Benson, and Pat Martino. He has also recorded with Jimmy Witherspoon, David "Fathead" Newman, Roland Kirk, Sonny Stitt, and Gene Ammons. His earlier experience of playing other instruments has made a subtle and individual impression on McDuff's style. Although overall his playing (like that of most jazz organists since Jimmy Smith) reflects the influence of the blues, his bop melodies are often pianistic in nature; his remarkably solid bass lines are equaled among organists only by those of Smith.

SELECTED RECORDINGS

Prelude (1963, Prst. 7333); *Dynamic!* (1964, Prst. 7323); *The Concert McDuff* (1964, Prst. 7362); *Double Barrelled Soul* (1967, Atl. 1498); *To Seek a New Home* (1970, BN 84348)

BIBLIOGRAPHY

Feather '60s
D. Morgenstern: "Mellow McDuff," *DB*, xxxvi/9 (1969), 19
G. N. Bourland: "Jack McDuff: Blues – Roots Jazz Organ," *CK*, ii/5 (1976), 8

ANDREW JAFFE

McEachern, Murray (*b* Toronto, 16 Aug 1915; *d* Los Angeles, 28 April 1982). Trombonist and alto saxophonist. He performed on violin at the age of 12 and learned several woodwind and brass instruments at high school. He first played in various local dance bands, then in 1936 he traveled to Chicago, where he worked in a novelty act. He performed as a trombone soloist with Benny Goodman (1936–7) and on both trombone and alto saxophone as a member of the Casa Loma Orchestra (1937–41). After working as assistant conductor of Paul Whiteman's orchestra (1941) McEachern moved to the West Coast, where he began to work in studios; his solo trombone playing may be heard on the soundtracks of a number of films, including *The Glenn Miller Story* (1953) and *The Benny Goodman Story* (1955). He also performed briefly with Harry James (1943), led his own band, and played with Bob Crosby's orchestra. In 1959 he performed on television in the series "Pete Kelly's Blues," and in the 1960s and 1970s he was much in demand as a studio musician. He played with Duke Ellington in 1973 and led Tommy Dorsey's ghost band from 1974 to around 1976. McEachern was an impeccable musician whose style was strongly based on swing throughout his career. His alto saxophone playing is noted for his highly individual use of staccato.

SELECTED RECORDINGS

As leader: Someone (1944), first issued on *Sax Stylists* (Cap. CFF328); *Caress* (*c*1957, Cap. T899)

As sideman: B. Goodman: These foolish things remind me of you/In a Sentimental Mood (1936, Vic. 25351); Bugle Call Rag (1936, Vic. 25467); Casa Loma Orchestra: No Name Jive (1940, Decca 3089); Soft Winds (1940, Decca 3122); Willie Smith: September in the Rain/Willie weep for me (1945, Key. 620)

BIBLIOGRAPHY

FeatherE
J. Tynan: "'Where's the Melody?' asks Mr. McEachern," *DB*, xxv/4 (1958), 19
L. Feather: "Murray's Magnum Opus," *MM*, li (21 Feb 1976), 25
H. Kallmann, G. Potvin, and K. Winters, eds.: *Encyclopedia of Music in Canada* (Toronto, Buffalo, and London, 1981)

LAWRENCE KOCH

Macero, Teo [Attilio Joseph] (*b* Glens Falls, NY, 30 Oct 1925). Tenor saxophonist, composer, and record producer. After leaving the navy he moved in 1948 to New York, where he entered the Juilliard School. In 1953 he graduated (BS and MS) and became a founding member of Charles Mingus's Jazz Composers' Workshop. Playing tenor and baritone saxophones he recorded with Mingus (1953–5) and performed with him at the Newport Jazz Festival (1956). Around this time he also recorded three albums as a leader (1953, 1955, 1957) and worked with the Teddy Charles Tentette (1956). With Mingus, Charles, and Gunther Schuller, he became interested in fusing elements of classical music and jazz; the resulting compositional style came to be known as third stream. In the late 1950s Macero wrote several atonal classical works that showed the influence of jazz. He joined Columbia in 1957 as a music editor, and was soon the company's leading producer of jazz recordings. After producing Miles Davis's album *Kind of Blue* in 1959, he went on to work in this capacity on many outstanding sessions of the 1960s and 1970s. He was responsible for signing Mingus to Columbia, and also supervised recordings by Thelonious Monk, Dave Brubeck, and others. He left Columbia in 1975 and became president of his own company, Teo Productions, but continued to serve as Davis's producer until 1983. In the late 1960s Davis began to rely heavily on tape editing in the studio as part of the production process; Macero's contribution thus became as important as that of a sideman. Macero is the composer of more than a thousand pieces, many of which are oriented towards jazz; among them are film and ballet scores and music for television. He has also written several arrangements of jazz standards, notably *Blues for Amy* and *St. Louis Blues* (both on the album *Something New, Something Blue*, 1959, Col. CS8183). In the 1980s he resumed playing saxophone; his style on this instrument is reminiscent of Lester Young's. In 1983 he directed and produced an album of his own compositions for big band, *Impressions of Charles Mingus*.

Oral history material in *NjR*.

SELECTED RECORDINGS

As leader: *Explorations* (1953, Debut 6); *What's New* (1955, Col. CL842); *Teo Macero with the Prestige Jazz Quartet* (1957, Prst. 7104); *Impressions of Charles Mingus* (1983, PAlt 8046)

As sideman: C. Mingus: Charles Mingus Octet (1953, Debut 450) [EP]; *The Moods of Mingus* (1954, Savoy 15050); *The Jazz Experiments of Charles Mingus* (1954, Period 1107); W. Cirillo: *Wally Cirillo Quartet* (1955, Savoy 15055); M. Legrand: *Legrand Jazz* (1958, Col. CL1250)

BIBLIOGRAPHY

I. Gitler and T. Charles: "Dialogue on Modern Jazz," *Just Jazz*, ed. S. Traill and G. Lascelles (London, 1957), 148
"Meet the A and R Man," *DB*, xxvii/25 (1960), 26
B. Houston: "The Record of the Year almost wasn't!," *MM*, xxxviii (8 June 1963), 7
H. Pekar: "Teo Macero: Tenor Player," *JJ*, xxv/8 (1972), 22
A. Roszczuk: "Teo Macero: 'A Producer Must Encourage the Artist to do New Things'," *JF* [intl edn], no.50 (1977), 38
I. Carr: *Miles Davis: a Critical Biography* (London and New York, 1982), 112
M. Jones: "Thoughts of Chairman Teo," *The Wire*, no.9 (1984), 38

MARK GARDNER

McFadden, Eddie (*b* Baltimore, 6 Aug 1928). Electric guitarist. While studying in Philadelphia he played in rhythm-and-blues bands, and in 1956 he recorded with the rhythm-and-blues tenor saxophonist Al King. He then performed and recorded with the soul-jazz organists Jimmy Smith (1957–8) and Johnny Hammond (1960, 1963, 1966); his solo playing may be heard on *How High the Moon* from the album *A Date with Smith* (1957, BN 1547-8). Later he recorded with Sonny Phillips (1977) and Don Patterson (1978). (*FeatherE*)

McFall, Reuben (*b* Los Angeles, 1 Feb 1931). Trumpeter. He attended the Westlake (California) College of Music, then played with Freddie Slack and Vido Musso and recorded with Roy Porter (1949). After touring and recording with Stan Kenton (1952–3) he worked with Woody Herman (1953–5), for whom he composed and arranged *Mambo the Most* (1954, Mars 1006). (*FeatherE*)

McFarland, Gary (*b* Los Angeles, 23 Oct 1933; *d* New York, 3 Nov 1971). Composer, arranger, and vibraphonist. His family moved to Grants Pass, Oregon, in 1948, and McFarland's interest in jazz developed while he was attending Oregon State University. During his army service he learned vibraphone and around 1954 he began to pursue his jazz studies seriously, showing an aptitude for composition. In 1957 he entered San Jose City College, and in the summers of 1959 and 1960 he attended the jazz workshops in Lenox, Massachusetts, where he was greatly encouraged by John Lewis. He was awarded a scholarship to study at the Berklee College of Music, which he attended in 1959–60; he then moved to New York to work as a composer (September 1960). In 1961 two of his compositions were recorded by Gerry Mulligan, he wrote arrangements and conducted an album for Anita O'Day, and he recorded as a leader. His main activities thereafter were as a composer and arranger for many musicians, among them Stan Getz and Lewis, but he also toured with his own quintet (1965) and founded the short-lived label Skye Records.

SELECTED RECORDINGS

As leader: *The Jazz Version of "How to Succeed in Business Without Really Trying"* (1961, Verve 68443); *Point of Departure* (1963, Imp. 46)

RECORDED COMPOSITIONS

(selective list)

* – with McFarland as conductor

Recorded by others: on G. Mulligan: *A Concert in Jazz* (1961, Verve 68415), Chuggin', Weep; on Modern Jazz Quartet: *Lonely Woman* (1962, Atl. 1381), Why are you blue?; J. Lewis: **Essence* (1962, Atl. 1425); on S. Getz: **Big Band Bossa Nova* (1962, Verve 68494), Night Sadness

SELECTED ARRANGEMENTS

(all with McFarland as conductor)

Recorded by A. O'Day: *All the Sad Young Men* (1961, Verve, 68442)
Recorded by S. Getz: on *Big Band Bossa Nova* (1962, Verve 68494), One Note Samba

BIBLIOGRAPHY

Feather '60s; *Feather–Gitler '70s*
D. Cerulli: Liner notes, *Big Band Bossa Nova* (Verve 68494, 1962)
M. Williams: "New Writer in Town," *DB*, xxix/5 (1962), 24
R. F. Thompson: "The Young Art of Gary McFarland," *Saturday Review*, xlviii/7 (1965), 58

LAWRENCE KOCH

McFarlane, Howard (Osmond) (*b* London, 13 Nov 1894; *d* London ?6 March 1983). English trumpeter. He worked in film theaters in London from 1919 and joined Alex Hyde's band, with which he toured and made recordings in Germany in 1924 (including *Mama Loves Papa, Papa Loves Mama*, Vox 01622). When the group disbanded he remained in Germany, where he played and recorded with the dance orchestras of Bernard Etté (1924–6) and the violinist Dajos Béla (1925–32), among others. He also made recordings of hot jazz with his own small groups (1926–7). He returned to England and worked with the trumpeter Jack Jackson (1933–4); then, after playing with Béla in Argentina (1935–7), he toured Europe (1937–40). From 1940 until his retirement in 1957 he was a member of the dance orchestra of the BBC. McFarlane played with a light, cantabile tone and may be heard to best advantage on his recordings as a leader, for example *Ace in the Hole* (1927, Odeon O2078).

BIBLIOGRAPHY

R. E. Lotz: "Howard Osmond McFarlane: Trumpet," *Sv*, no.81 (1979), 89 [incl. discography]
——: Liner notes, *Hot Dance and Doo-wacka-doo from Germany, 1924: Alex Hyde*, i (Harl. 2033, 1985)

RAINER E. LOTZ

McFerrin, Bobby (*b* New York, 11 March 1950). Singer. The son of the opera singers Robert and Sara McFerrin, he first trained as a pianist, studying at the preparatory division of the Juilliard School and later at Sacramento State College. By the mid-1970s he was working as an accompanist and as a pianist and singer in popular groups. Singing, especially improvised singing, became his principal interest in 1977, and from 1983 he worked mainly as a soloist. In the mid- to late 1980s he began to mix his solo work in concerts with improvised and composed dialogues with musicians from various styles (including Wynton Marsalis, Wayne Shorter, Robin Williams, and the Manhattan Transfer). McFerrin was the winner in 1984 and 1985 of the *Down Beat* poll for "best male vocalist" and in 1985 and 1986 of the Grammy Award for "best male jazz vocalist."

In early performances and in his first recording he usually sang with accompaniment, and his style at this period drew heavily on Lambert, Hendricks and Ross. But after 1983 he took a new direction, singing mostly improvised lines that explore timbre, attack, and resonance within a framework of established harmonies, meters, and repetitive rhythmic patterns; he uses elements of a wide variety of vocal styles, sometimes encompassing several within a single song. In unaccompanied songs he performs, consecutively, several parts of a multipartite texture (percussion, bass, solo voice, and sometimes inner voices), exploiting all kinds of vocal sound from popping noises and grunts to swooping falsetto. He has an astonishing range (usually from *D* to *f″*, but occasionally up to *f‴*) and accuracy of pitch, and a solid but fluid, agile control in all registers. His deep conviction that everyone has the potential to make music leads him to involve audiences in his performances, asking them to maintain ostinato choral parts against which he sings a lively counterpoint. The same theme is present in the lyrics of the song, which he composed himself, *I'm my own Walkman*.

SELECTED RECORDINGS

As unaccompanied soloist: *The Voice* (1984, Elek. Mus. 60366), incl. I'm my own Walkman
As leader: *Bobby McFerrin* (1982, Elek. Mus. 60023); *Spontaneous Inventions* (1985, BN BT85110), incl. Walkin'
As sideman: B. Dorough: *That's the Way I Feel Now* (*c*1984, A&M 6600), incl. Friday the Thirteenth

BIBLIOGRAPHY

L. Gourse: *Louis' Children: American Jazz Singers* (New York, 1984), 52
G. Lock: "The Voice Inside," *The Wire*, no.18 (1984), 7
M. Bourne: "Bobby McFerrin: the Voice," *DB*, lii/5 (1985), 20 [incl. discography]
J. Potter: "Bobby McFerrin: the Unpredictable Voice," *JT* (Dec 1985), 11
F. Davis: "Heeding Inner Voices," *In the Moment: Jazz in the 1980s* (New York, and Oxford, England, 1986) [colln of previously pubd articles], 51
L. Van Tuyl: "A One-man Pop/Jazz/Blues Band – a cappella and ad lib," *Christian Science Monitor* (17 April 1987), 1

MARTY HATCH

McGarity, (Robert) Lou(is) (*b* Athens, GA, 22 July 1917; *d* Alexandria, VA, 28 Aug 1971). Trombonist. He played violin from the age of seven, and took up trombone some ten years later. After working with lesser-known bands he played with Benny Goodman (1940–42) and Raymond Scott (1942–4). He rejoined Goodman in 1946 after military service, but left the band in

Los Angeles and became a studio musician. In 1947 he returned to New York, where his spirited playing, with its secure upper register, was much in demand for radio, television, and performances in clubs. A heart disorder restricted his activities from 1957, but in the 1960s he resumed full-time work, playing with Bob Crosby (1964, 1966) and others. He was a founding member of the World's Greatest Jazz Band, with which he performed from 1968 to 1970; thereafter illness meant that he worked only occasionally.

SELECTED RECORDINGS

As leader: *Blue Lou* (1959, Argo 654)

As sideman: Cootie Williams: West End Blues (1941, OK 6370); B. Goodman: Limehouse Blues (1941, OK 6486); V-disc All Stars: Jack Armstrong Blues (1944, V-disc 834); B. Goodman: Oh Baby (1946, Col. 55039); Y. Lawson and B. Haggart: *Jelly Roll's Jazz* (1951, Decca 5368); E. Condon: *Jammin' at Condon's* (1954, Col. CL616), incl. Tin Roof Blues; All Stars: *Session at Riverside* (1956, Cap. T761); Ten Greats of Jazz: *Jazz in the Troc* (1969, WCS 3330)

BIBLIOGRAPHY

G. Hoefer: Liner notes, *Blue Lou* (Argo 654, ?1959)
T. O. Gwaltney: Liner notes, *Jazz Master* (Fat Cat's Jazz 124, ?1970)
D. Coller: "Who is Lou McGarity?," *Pieces of Jazz* (Canterbury, England, 1971), 13 [incl. discography]
J. L. Fell: Liner notes, *In Celebration* (IAJRC 36, 1981) [incl. discography]

For further recordings and bibliography *see* WORLD'S GREATEST JAZZ BAND.

BRIAN PEERLESS

McGhee, Andy [Andrew] (*b* Wilmington, NC, 3 Nov 1927). Tenor saxophonist. He graduated from the New England Conservatory in 1949, worked briefly with Roy Eldridge (1949), and then played with bands in Boston. From 1957 to 1963 he played for Lionel Hampton, with whom he toured the USA, Europe, and the Far East; among the recordings he made with Hampton is *The Many Sides of Lionel Hampton* (*c*1960, Glad Hamp 1001), which includes his own composition *McGhee*. He worked with Woody Herman in 1963–6, making recordings in 1964–5. In 1966 he was appointed to the faculty of the Berklee College of Music and thereafter devoted much of his time to teaching; he continued to play in and around Boston, however, with Phil Wilson (with whom he recorded in 1977), Sammy Price, and Alan Dawson. (*Feather '60s*)

McGhee, Howard (B.) [Maggie] (*b* Tulsa, OK, 6 March 1918; *d* New York, 17 July 1987). Trumpeter and composer. He played clarinet and tenor saxophone before taking up trumpet in 1935. After working with territory bands in the Mid- and Northwest in the late 1930s, he joined Lionel Hampton (1941), then played as a principal soloist with Andy Kirk (1941–2), for whom he also provided compositions and arrangements. In 1942 he participated in jam sessions at Minton's Playhouse and Monroe's Uptown House which contributed to the emergence of the bop style. After playing with Charlie Barnet (1942–3), Kirk (1943–4), Georgie Auld (1944), and briefly with Count Basie he went with Coleman Hawkins to Los Angeles (1945). McGhee remained in California for two years, recording *How High the Moon* with Jazz at the Philharmonic (JATP) and taking part in Charlie Parker's sessions for *Lover Man* (which was originally issued under McGhee's name) and *Relaxin' at Camarillo*. In 1947 he joined the JATP touring group, and thereafter toured frequently and recorded prolifically as the leader of his own groups. By the end of the decade he was one of the most highly regarded musicians in the bop movement; he was named "best trumpeter" by *Down Beat* in 1949. During most of the 1950s he was relatively inactive, but after 1960 he performed frequently; he formed a big band in the mid-1960s, and participated in jazz services at St. Peter's Lutheran church in New York. McGhee had a thin tone and an agile style, which he traced to his early familiarity with the clarinet. He also wrote several pieces for his own groups, among them *Dorothy* and *Night Mist*.

Oral history material in *GBLnsa*, *NjR* (JOHP).

For illustrations *see* NIGHTCLUBS AND OTHER VENUES, fig.6, and PETTIFORD, OSCAR.

SELECTED RECORDINGS

As leader: Bebop (1946, Dial 1007); Dialated Pupils/Midnight at Minton's (1946, Dial 1011); Dorothy/Night Mist (1947, Dial 1027); Double Talk (1948, BN 557); *The Howard McGhee Sextet with Milt Jackson* (1948, Savoy 12026), incl. Down Home; with T. Edwards: *Together Again!* (1961, Cont. 7588); *Cookin' Time* (1966, Zim 2004)

As sideman: A. Kirk: McGhee Special (1942, Decca 4405); C. Hawkins: Sportsman's Hop/Ready for Love (1945, Asch 3533); Too Much of a Good Thing/Bean Soup (1945, Cap. 15855); Jazz at the Philharmonic: How High the Moon (1945, Asch 4531–2); L. Young: Jammin' with Lester (1946, Ala. 128); C. Parker: Lover Man (1946, Dial 1007); Relaxin' at Camarillo (1947, Dial 1012)

BIBLIOGRAPHY

J. Sippel: "Faster Trumpet Work Tabs 'McGhee' Special," *DB*, xi/18 (1944), 4
R. Boenzli: *Discography of Howard McGhee* (Basle, Switzerland, 1961)
B. Coss: "Back to Stay: Howard McGhee," *DB*, xxix/2 (1962), 20
G. Hoefer: "The Early Career of Howard McGhee," *DB*, xxx/23 (1963), 33
V. Wilmer: "Maggie's Back in Town," *Jazz People* (London, Indianapolis, and New York, 1970/R1985), 131
S. DeVeaux: *Jazz in Transition: Coleman Hawkins and Howard McGhee, 1935–1945* (diss, U. of California, Berkeley, 1985)
Obituary, M. Gardner, *The Independent* (23 July 1987)

SCOTT DEVEAUX

McGrath, (David) Fulton [Fidgey] (*b* Superior, WI, 6 Dec 1907; *d* Los Angeles, 1 Jan 1958). Pianist. He played and recorded with Red Nichols in New York (1931–2) and was a studio musician in the bands of the American Radio Corporation. He performed regularly with the Dorsey Brothers Orchestra, with which he recorded from 1932 to 1934. During the 1930s he also made recordings with Mildred Bailey and Red Norvo (both 1933), Chick Bullock (1933, 1936), Adrian Rollini (1933–4, 1937), and Joe Venuti (1934, 1935, including *Mystery/Tap Room Blues*, 1935, Decca 625). He was a member of Lennie Hayton's studio orchestra (1935–7) and after playing briefly with Bunny Berigan at the beginning of 1938, he joined Chauncey Morehouse (with whom he recorded, 1938). He worked as a session musician for NBC from 1939 until 1943, when he moved to Hollywood to work in film studios.

based on *ChiltonW*

McGregor, Chris (*b* Umtata, South Africa, 24 Dec 1936). South African pianist and bandleader. He studied piano at the South African College of Music, Cape Town, and in 1960–62 led two big bands that played a type of jazz influenced both by urban popular music and classical music. With Johnny Dyani, Dudu Pukwana, the alto saxophonist Nick Moyake, the tenor saxophonist Ronnie Beer, Louis Moholo, and Mongezi Feza he formed the Blue Notes in 1963; the group left South Africa in 1964, traveling first to France to play at the Antibes–Juan-les-Pins Jazz Festival and then settling in London. The same players, without Moyake, recorded an album (*Very Urgent*) in 1967 and formed the nucleus of the big band Brotherhood of Breath, formed by McGregor in 1970, which also included many of the leading free-jazz musicians in London; it made four albums over the next ten years. McGregor moved to France in 1974 and in the late 1970s recorded three albums as a soloist. In 1975 he re-formed the Blue Notes and with them recorded a spontaneous tribute to Mongezi Feza, who had died that year.

In the 1980s he led small groups, in which his playing was more prominent than in the big-band setting. He also performed with the Brotherhood of Breath in Mozambique and Europe in 1984 and in 1985 performed frequently with the Ghanaian alto saxophonist George Lee.

SELECTED RECORDINGS

Very Urgent (1967, Pol. 184137); *Live at Willisau* (1974, Ogun 100); *Blue Notes for Mongezi* (1975, Ogun 001–2); *In his Good Time* (1977, Ogun 521); *Procession* (1977, Ogun 524); *Blue Notes in Concert* (1978, Ogun 800)

BIBLIOGRAPHY

V. Wilmer: "McGregor's Mission," *JB*, ii/10 (1965), 20
R. Cotterell, ed.: *Jazz Now: the Jazz Centre Society Guide* (London, 1976)
R. Cotterell: "Chris McGregor: African Roots," *JF* [intl edn], no.46 (1977), 41
G. Rouy: "Chris McGregor: le second souffle," *Jm*, no.297 (1981), 22
C. de Ledesma: "Afro Jazz: Evolution and Revolution," *The Wire*, no.12 (1985), 26, esp. 37f, 40ff

CHARLES DE LEDESMA

McGriff, Jimmy [James Harrell, Jr.] (*b* Philadelphia, 3 April 1936). Organist and bandleader. He studied double bass, drums, saxophone, and vibraphone in his teens, attended Combe College of Music in Philadelphia and the Juilliard School, and studied electric organ with Jimmy Smith, Milt Buckner, and Groove Holmes. In the early 1960s he formed a soul-jazz trio which performed in the USA and Europe, then led blues bands as well as big bands and other groups. From 1963 to 1973 he made at least one recording as a leader each year (including *Blues for Mr. Jimmy*, 1965, Sue 1039), and led sessions again in 1976 and 1981. He also recorded with the blues singer Little Junior Parker (*c*1968 and 1971), Groove Holmes (1973), and Buddy Rich (1974).

BIBLIOGRAPHY

Feather '60s
B. Doerschuk: "Jimmy McGriff: 'Jazz Organ is Alive and Growing'," *Keyboard*, x/1 (1984), 28

Machito [Grillo, Frank Raul] (*b* Havana, 16 Feb 1912; *d* London, 15 April 1984). Cuban bandleader, singer, and maraca player. Although he was already a professional musician when he arrived in the USA in 1937, his musical maturity and influence date from 1940. In that year, after working in and around New York and recording with several local dance bands, Machito formed the first of his groups known as the Afro-Cubans. The following year he was joined by his brother-in-law Mario Bauzá, who engaged black arrangers to give jazz voicings to the Cuban melodies of Machito's band. As a result the Afro-Cubans became one of the most influential forces in the music later to be called salsa. By the mid-1940s the Afro-Cubans had performed at concerts with Stan Kenton's big band, and had recorded or played with most of the leading bop musicians, giving rise to a fusion style known as AFRO-CUBAN JAZZ or "cubop." Soloists on recordings by the band included Charlie Parker, Dizzy Gillespie, Flip Phillips (1948–9), Howard McGhee, Brew Moore, and Armando Peraza (1949), Cannonball Adderley (1957), Curtis Fuller, Herbie Mann, and Johnny Griffin (1958), and Aaron Sachs (*c*1960). Machito's preeminence continued during the mambo era of the 1950s and 1960s, when his was one of three big bands playing regularly at the Palladium in New York. He continued to work frequently into the 1980s, mainly in New York, performing in both salsa and jazz-oriented clubs and concerts. Carlo Ortiz's film documentary *Machito: a Latin Jazz Legacy* (1987) includes photographs and newsreel material of Machito's work in New York in the 1930s and 1940s, and interviews and performances filmed in the last years of his life.
Oral history material in *NjR* (JOHP).

SELECTED RECORDINGS

As leader: No Noise (1948, Mer./Clef 11012); *Afro-Cubop* (1949, Spot. 138); Cubop City (1949, Roost 502); *Kenya* (1957, Roul. 52006); *With Flute to Boot* (1958, Roul. 52026); *Machito at the Crescendo* (*c*1960, GNP 58); with D. Gillespie: *Afro-Cuban Jazz Moods* (1975, Pablo 2310771); *Live at North Sea '82* (1982, Tim. 168)

As sideman: S. Kenton: Cuban Carnival (1947, Cap. F661); The Peanut Vendor (1947, Cap. 904); C. Parker: Mango mangue/Okiedoke (1948–9, Mer./Clef 11017)

BIBLIOGRAPHY

D. Cerulli: "Machito Maps an Attack on Juvenile Delinquency," *DB*, xxiii/2 (1956), 11
J. Burns: "Lesser Known Bands of the Forties: Illinois Jacquet, Roy Porter, Machito," *JM*, no.164 (1968), 7
A. J. Smith: "Sounds from the Salsa Source: Tito and Machito," *DB*, xliii/8 (1976), 16
S. Woolley: "Machito: Making Musical Earthquakes," *JJI*, xxx/11 (1977), 36
J. S. Roberts: *The Latin Tinge: the Impact of Latin American Music on the United States* (New York, and Oxford, England, 1979)
L. Birnbaum: "Machito: Original Macho Man," *DB*, xlvii/12 (1980), 25
"Machito," *CBY 1983*
Obituary, J. Pareles, *New York Times* (17 April 1984)
S. Woolley: "The Spanish Tinge," *JJI*, xxxviii/7 (1985), 9
J. Hamlin: "Film: Life and Times of a Latin Musical Giant," *San Francisco Chronicle Datebook* (16 Aug 1987), 39

JOHN STORM ROBERTS/R

McIntosh, Tom [Thomas S.] (*b* Baltimore, 6 Feb 1927). Composer and trombonist. He studied singing at the Peabody Conservatory, played trombone in an army band, and graduated from the Juilliard School in 1958. The following year he played trombone in James Moody's bop group, for which he wrote his first original jazz composition, *With Malice Toward None*; this work reflects his interest in jazz and gospel music as well as his classical training. He then worked with the Art Farmer–Benny Golson Jazztet (1960–61) and again with Moody (1962–3). From 1964 to 1969 McIntosh was a member of the New York Jazz Sextet, which performed his extended suite *Whose Child are You? (A Riddle for Everybody's Children)*. He also performed and recorded with the Thad Jones–Mel Lewis Orchestra (1966–9) and took part in recording sessions with Jimmy Heath (1960), Milt Jackson (1960, 1962–3), Hubert Laws (1965), Dizzy Gillespie (1968), and Lionel Hampton (1980–81). McIntosh arranged many of his own compositions for these bands. In 1969 he moved to the West Coast, where he has concentrated on scoring for films.
See also SCEPTER.

RECORDED COMPOSITIONS
(selective list; all with McIntosh as sideman)

Recorded by others: J. Moody: on *James Moody* (1959, Argo 648), With Malice Toward None; A. Farmer and B. Golson: *Big City Sounds* (1960, Argo 672); D. Gillespie: on *Something Old, Something New* (1963, Phi. 600091), The Cup Bearers; J. Moody: on *Great Day* (1963, Argo 725), Great Day; New York Jazz Sextet: *New York Jazz Sextet* (1965–6, Scepter 526); T. Jones and M. Lewis: on *Presenting Thad Jones–Mel Lewis and the Jazz Orchestra* (1966, SolS 18003), Balanced Scales = Justice

BIBLIOGRAPHY

Feather '60s; Feather–Gitler '70s
V. Wilmer: "The Youngest Forty-year-old in Jazz," *DB*, xxxiv/4 (1967), 20
L. Feather: "From Screen to Pen: Tom McIntosh," *IM*, lxxii (1973), Oct, 9

DAVID FLANAGAN

McIntyre, Hal [Harold W.] (*b* Cromwell, CT, 29 Nov 1914; *d* Los Angeles, 5 May 1959). Bandleader, alto saxophonist, and clarinetist. He led a swing band from 1935 to 1936, then joined Glenn Miller as saxophonist and clarinetist in 1937. He remained with Miller until 1941 (for illustration *see* MUTE, fig.3), when he formed a dance band. This recorded frequently and enjoyed popular success throughout the 1940s; its best-known members were Eddie Safranski (1941–5), Helen Ward, and Allen Eager (both 1943). McIntyre continued to lead bands into the 1950s.

BIBLIOGRAPHY

FeatherE

G. T. Simon: *The Big Bands* (New York, 1967, rev. and enlarged 2/1971, rev. 3/1974, 4/1981)

C. Garrod: *Hal McIntyre and his Orchestra* (Spotswood, NJ, and Zephyrhills, FL, 1974) [discography]

McIntyre, Kalaparusha Maurice [Difda, Kalaparusha Ahrah; Kalaparush(a); McIntyre, Maurice (Benford)] (*b* Clarksville, AR, 24 March 1936). Tenor saxophonist. He grew up in Chicago and played drums from the age of seven; he changed to clarinet and saxophone when he was nine and took lessons from the reed player Warren Smith, Sr. As Maurice McIntyre he was a founding member of the Association for the Advancement of Creative Musicians (AACM) in 1965 and made his first recording, as a sideman on Roscoe Mitchell's album *Sound*, the following year; he also performed and recorded with many other members of the AACM, including Muhal Richard Abrams, and worked with Jerome Cooper in 1968. In 1969 he took his Muslim name and moved to New York, where he played with Warren Smith (ii); he returned to Chicago in 1970 and in 1974 moved again to New York and resumed his association with Cooper, with whom he performed and recorded into the 1980s. He also worked in a quartet with Warren Smith (ii), the pianist Sonelius Smith, and the double bass player Wilber Morris and led other groups. McIntyre's tone is hard and dry; he uses many of the free-jazz techniques devised by John Coltrane, Albert Ayler, and members of the AACM.

SELECTED RECORDINGS

As leader: *Humility in the Light of the Creator* (1969, Del. 419); *Kalaparusha* (1975, Trio 7167); *Peace and Blessing* (1979, BS 0037); *Ram's Run* (1981, Cadence 1009)

As sideman: R. Mitchell: *Sound* (1966, Del. 408); M. R. Abrams: *Levels and Degrees of Light* (1967, Del. 413); J. Cooper: *Positions 369* (1977, Karma 3–4)

BIBLIOGRAPHY

V. Wilmer: *As Serious as your Life: the Story of the New Jazz* (London, 1977, rev. 1980)

B. Rusch: "Kalaparusha: Interview," *Cadence*, viii/10 (1982), 5

ED HAZELL

McIntyre, Ken(neth Arthur) (*b* Boston, 7 Sept 1931). Alto saxophonist, reed player, and teacher. He studied piano, then alto saxophone; the music of Charlie Parker, which he first heard in 1946, influenced him strongly. After serving in the army, during which time he played piano in jazz groups, he studied at the Boston Conservatory (BA 1958, MA 1959). In the early 1960s he became an important figure in free jazz and began performing and recording as a leader; Eric Dolphy played on his first album, *Looking Ahead* (1960). He was unable to earn a living in jazz, however, and began teaching in public schools in 1961; he received the doctorate in education from the University of Massachusetts in 1971, and then became a professor at SUNY, Old Westbury. At the same time he continued to play jazz occasionally: on a highly acclaimed recording with Cecil Taylor (1966), in loft sessions in New York and on albums for Steeplechase as a leader (mid-1970s), on tour with the 360 Degree Music Experience (1979), and on a recording with Craig Harris (1983).

SELECTED RECORDINGS

As leader: *Looking Ahead* (1960, NewJ 8247); *Introducing the Vibrations* (1976, Ste. 1065)

As sideman: C. Taylor: *Unit Structures* (1966, BN 84237)

BIBLIOGRAPHY

Feather '60s

B. Case: "Days with Dolphy," *MM*, liv (23 June 1979), 57

M. Ullman: *Jazz Lives: Portraits in Words and Pictures* (Washington, 1980), 153

DAVID G. SUCH

McKay, Cliff(ord John) (*b* Seaforth, nr Stratford, Ontario, Canada, 1909; *d* Nikšić, Yugoslavia, 26 March 1987). Canadian clarinetist, saxophonist, and bandleader. He gained his first experience in the orchestras of Harry Rich in Toronto (*c*1926) and Joe DeCourcy in Ottawa. He led his own dance band for a time, worked in radio and the theater, and played in hotels with the orchestras of Percy Faith and the pianists Horace Lapp and Rex Battle. He was a member of the group that performed popular music on the daily variety show "The Happy Gang" on CBC radio (1941–52); the group made a few recordings which included jazz. He continued to play on radio and television until 1958 and presented his own program for CBC TV (1952–8). He then led small groups in Toronto nightclubs and played with Trump Davidson (1969–71). His recordings (1945–71) include several made as the leader of a swing quartet and quintet playing swing and dixieland repertory (1949, 1958).

BIBLIOGRAPHY

M. Miller and H. McNamara: "McKay, Cliff," *Encyclopedia of Music in Canada*, ed. H. Kallmann, G. Potvin, and K. Winters (Toronto, Buffalo, and London, 1981)

JACK LITCHFIELD

Mackay, Dave [David Owen] (*b* Syracuse, NY, 24 March 1932). Pianist. He attended Trinity College, Hartford, Connecticut (1950–54), and Boston University (1956–8), and was helped to come to terms with his blindness by meeting George Shearing and studying with Lennie Tristano. He played in Boston with Bobby Hackett, Sonny Stitt, Charlie Mariano, Bob Wilber, and Serge Chaloff, and in New York with Jim Hall and his own group. After leading a group in Chicago he settled on the West Coast and joined Don Ellis, with whom in 1966 he made two albums, one of which was a recording of a performance (with Mackay playing piano and organ) at the Monterey Jazz Festival (*Live at Monterey*, PJ 20112). He performed and recorded with Emil Richards in 1968, and recorded with his own group (which included his wife, the singer Vicky Hamilton) the following year. Mackay also played with Shelly Manne, Paul Horn, Chet Baker, and Joe Pass, and later recorded on piano and electric piano with Bill Henderson (1975, 1979, and 1981). He led a trio (1976–83) and played in a duo with the flutist Lori Bell (from 1982). He has also been active as a composer and teacher. (*Feather–Gitler '70s*)

Mackel, Billy [John William] (*b* Baltimore, 28 Dec 1912). Electric guitarist. He was at first a professional banjoist, playing in and around Baltimore in the early 1930s, but later changed to guitar. He led his own group from 1940, then in 1944 joined that of Lionel Hampton, with which he toured and recorded steadily from that time with only brief interruptions until at least the late 1970s. In the mid-1940s he recorded with Milt Buckner, Arnett Cobb, Herbie Fields, and other musicians associated with Hampton, and in the 1960s divided his time between working with Hampton and accompanying a vocal quartet led by Billy Williams. His playing is well represented on a recording made in 1953 with Hampton's group under the name Lionel Hampton and his Paris All Stars (issued on three 10-inch LPs, Vogue LD166-8).

BIBLIOGRAPHY

ChiltonW; *FeatherE*
S. Dance: *The World of Swing* (New York, 1974) [colln of previously pubd interviews], 279
B. Mackel: "Hamp's Playing Inspires me," *CI*, xii/2 (1974), 22

McKenna, Dave [David J.] (*b* Woonsocket, RI, 30 May 1930). Pianist. He took piano lessons as a child, but learned to play jazz chiefly from listening to the radio and recordings. At the age of 12 he began to play with pickup groups at weddings and other occasions, and when he was 15 joined the musicians' union. By 1947 he was performing in and around Boston with a group led by Boots Mussulli. In 1949 he joined Charlie Ventura's band, then played with Woody Herman (1950–51) before serving for two years in the US Army. He rejoined Ventura's band in 1953 for 18 months, but thereafter worked mostly with smaller groups, playing with Gene Krupa, Stan Getz, Zoot Sims, Al Cohn, Bobby Hackett, and others. In 1967 he moved from New York to South Yarmouth on Cape Cod, Massachusetts, and from 1970 has worked regularly as a solo player in piano bars, chiefly in Boston and on the Cape. In 1978 he renewed an earlier association with Bob Wilber, playing in the Boston area, touring in England and Sweden, and recording two albums. McKenna has also made a number of albums for the Concord label, recording as an unaccompanied soloist, in a duo with Dick Johnson, as the leader of a trio including Jake Hanna, as a member of several Concord all-star groups, and as a sideman with such swing musicians as Johnson and Scott Hamilton (both 1979) and the tenor saxophonist Fraser McPherson (1984).

McKenna's style combines enormous rhythmic drive with melodic inventiveness and a profound strain of lyricism; while playing a wide range of tunes, he especially favors Tin Pan Alley standards. He treats ballads lovingly, drawing on his command of the rich harmonic idiom of the progressive jazz of the 1940s and 1950s, and paying close attention to details of sound. At faster tempos he seems to ride along on the energy of his powerful left hand, which may play single-note lines, strummed chords or, more rarely, stride figures. At its best, his music maintains the coherence and conviction that mastery of a classic style can confer, but without sacrificing vitality and excitement.

SELECTED RECORDINGS

As unaccompanied soloist: *Solo Piano* (1955, ABC-Para. 104); *Solo Piano* (1973, Chi. 119); *Giant Strides* (1979, Conc. 99); *Left Handed Complement* (1979, Conc. 123); *A Celebration of Hoagy Carmichael* (1983, Conc. 227)
Duos: with J. Venuti: *Alone at the Palace* (1977, Chi. 160); with D. Johnson: *Spider's Blues* (1980, Conc. 135)
As leader: *Piano Scene* (1958, Epic 3558); *No Bass Hit* (1979, Conc. 97); *The Dave McKenna Trio Plays the Music of Harry Warren* (1981, Conc. 174)
As sideman: Z. Sims: *Down Home* (1960, Beth. 6051); B. Wilber: *New Clarinet in Town* (1960, CJ 8); S. Hamilton: *Tenorshoes* (1979, Conc. 127)

BIBLIOGRAPHY

M. Jones: "Quiet Man of the Keyboard," *MM*, liii (20 May 1978), 47
B. Doerschuk: "Dave McKenna Carrying on the Jazz Piano Tradition," *CK*, vi/10 (1980), 20
L. Tomkins: "Dave McKenna: Home-grown Swing Man of the Piano," *CI*, xix/6 (1981), 6 [interview]
W. Balliett: *Jelly Roll, Jabbo and Fats* (New York, and Oxford, England, 1983) [colln of previously pubd articles], 153
B. Wilber and D. Webster: *Music was not Enough* (London and New York, 1987)

RICHARD CRAWFORD

McKenzie, Red [William] (*b* St. Louis, 14 Oct 1899; *d* New York, 7 Feb 1948). Singer, entertainer, and promoter. Although McKenzie played no instrument and was only a mediocre singer, he became an important figure in the Chicago jazz movement of the 1920s. His activities as a talent scout resulted in recording contracts for Bix Beiderbecke, the Chicago Rhythm Kings, the New Orleans Rhythm Kings, the Spirits of Rhythm, and others. In 1924 he formed the MOUND CITY BLUE BLOWERS (for illustration *see* LANG, EDDIE) with the banjoist and guitarist Jack Bland and the kazoo player Dick Slevin; McKenzie himself played comb-and-paper. Among his better tracks as the leader of the Mound City Blue Blowers are his own composition *Hello Lola* (1929, Vic. 38100) and *The Darktown Strutter's Ball* (1931, OK 41526). McKenzie also made recordings with Red Nichols (1929–31), Adrian Rollini (1933), and a new version of the Mound City Blue Blowers (1935–6), and sang with Paul Whiteman (1932–3) and other leaders. Later he led a band with the trombonist Mike Riley and the trumpeter Eddie Farley, and ran a club on 52nd Street in New York. He retired from music from 1939 to 1944, then returned to New York and sang with Eddie Condon at Town Hall. He also recorded again as a leader: *It's the Talk of the Town* (1944, Com. 562) offers a good example of his style at this time.

BIBLIOGRAPHY

ChiltonW
"Immortals of Jazz: Red McKenzie," *DB*, vi/11 (1939), 22
M. Mezzrow and B. Wolfe: *Really the Blues* (New York, 1946/*R*1972)
R. Hadlock: *Jazz Masters of the Twenties* (New York, 1965/*R*1985), 120

RAINER E. LOTZ

McKibbon, Al(fred Benjamin) (*b* Chicago, 1 Jan 1919). Double bass player. He began his career working with local bands in Detroit in the late 1930s (his brother Alphonso played guitar with McKinney's Cotton Pickers briefly in 1935). During the mid-1940s he established himself in New York as a musician with a full tone and metronomic beat, and recorded with Lucky Millinder (1944), Tab Smith (1944–5), and J. C. Heard and Coleman Hawkins (both 1946). His reputation was further enhanced when he replaced Ray Brown in Dizzy Gillespie's orchestra in 1947; he played with Gillespie intermittently until 1950 and during that time also performed and recorded with Miles Davis, taking part in the important "Birth of the Cool" recording sessions. In the 1950s McKibbon performed with Thelonious Monk at Minton's Playhouse, recorded with Earl Hines and Count Basie (both 1950) and Johnny Hodges and Monk (both 1951), and readily adapted to the Latin style as a member of George Shearing's quintet (1951–8) and for two years with Cal Tjader's group; he also recorded with Herbie Nichols (1955) and at the Newport Jazz Festival with Coleman Hawkins (1957). After working as a freelance musician on the West Coast in the 1960s, he played on Monk's last album (1971) and toured and recorded with the Giants of Jazz (1971–2). He recorded with Benny Carter in 1976, and in the 1980s continued to perform in Los Angeles.

SELECTED RECORDINGS

As sideman: D. Gillespie: Two Bass Hit/Stay on it (1947, Vic. 202603); *Salle Pleyel Concert* (1948, Swing 33301); on M. Davis: *Classics in Jazz* (1949–50, Cap. H459), Deception, Moondreams, Rocker; G. Shearing: Don't Blame Me (1951, MGM 11046); I Hear Music (1953, MGM 30624); I've Never Been in Love Before (1954, MGM 11754); C. Tjader: *In a Latin Bag* (1961, Verve 68419); Giants of Jazz: *Giants of Jazz* (1971, Atl. 2-905); B. Carter: *Carter, Gillespie, Inc.* (1976, Pablo 2310781)

BIBLIOGRAPHY

ChiltonW; *FeatherE*; *Feather '60s*; *Feather–Gitler '70s*
B. Rusch: "Al McKibbon," *Cadence*, xiii/3 (1987), 13

STAN WOOLLEY

McKinley, Ray(mond Frederick) (*b* Fort Worth, 18 June 1910). Drummer and singer. His first significant engagement was with Smith Ballew (1932), after which he joined the Dorsey Brothers

Orchestra (1934). When the brothers split up the following year, he remained with the group led by Jimmy Dorsey, but left in mid-1939 to form a band with Will Bradley. This band, under Bradley's name, achieved considerable commercial success with a series of recordings in a boogie-woogie style, which owed much to McKinley's rhythmic and relaxed singing. In 1942 he led his own big band, then, during wartime service, toured Europe as a member of Glenn Miller's orchestra. At this time he also led a small group from Miller's band, Swing Shift, which included Mel Powell, Peanuts Hucko, and Trigger Alpert, and attained great popularity through its daily broadcasts to the forces. After Miller's death in 1944 McKinley shared the leadership of the main dance band with Jerry Gray. Later he led his own band (1946–50) and worked as a freelance singer before organizing a new Glenn Miller Orchestra, which performed much of the original repertory and toured throughout the world (1956–66). Thereafter he led his own big bands (1966–8) and a small group which performed in New York (1968–70). In 1973 he took over from Tex Beneke as the leader of another big band devoted to Miller's music, remaining until 1978. McKinley's swinging, tasteful drumming was the driving force behind many important groups and his bubbly, buoyant character and infectious good humor, evident in both drumming and singing, were qualities which proved considerable assets both musically and commercially.

SELECTED RECORDINGS

As leader: Love in the First Degree/New Orleans Parade (1936, Decca 1019); Sugar/After You've Gone (1945, Jazz Club of France 130); Down the Road Apiece (1946, Majestic 7189); with P. Hucko: *The Swingin' 30s* (1955, Grand Award 33-333), incl. Scrub me mama with a boogie beat, Hard Hearted Hannah

As sideman: Dorsey Brothers: Anything Goes/All Through the Night (1934, Decca 318); Footloose and Fancy Free/You're All I Need (1935, Decca 482); No Strings/Top Hat, White Tie, and Tails (1935, Decca 516); W. Bradley: Beat me daddy, eight to the bar (1940, Col. 35530); Scrub me mama, with a boogie beat (1940, Col. 35743); G. Miller: *Glenn Miller and his Army Airforce Orchestra ('I Sustain the Wings' Shows)* (1944, Soundcraft 1004), incl. Flying Home

BIBLIOGRAPHY

ChiltonW

R. Harris and B. Rust: *Recorded Jazz: a Critical Guide* (Harmondsworth, England, 1958), 122

C. Popa: *Ray McKinley and his Orchestra* (Zephyrhills, FL, 1979) [discography]

B. Korall: "Ray McKinley: Swing Pioneer," *MD*, x/4 (1986), 30

KEN RATTENBURY

McKinney, Bernard (Atwell) *See* ZAWADI, KIANE.

McKinney, William [Bill] (*b* Cynthiana, KY, 17 Sept 1895; *d* Cynthiana, 14 Oct 1969). Bandleader and drummer. He performed as a circus drummer after World War I and then settled

McKinney's Cotton Pickers at the Graystone Ballroom in Detroit, 1929: (back row, left to right) Todd Rhodes (piano), Cuba Austin (drums), Prince Robinson (clarinet, tenor saxophone), Ralph Escudero (tuba), Claude Jones (trombone), Fathead Thomas (alto saxophone, voice), and John Nesbitt (trumpet); (front row) Joe Moxley (alto saxophone), Langston Curl (trumpet), Dave Wilborn (banjo), and (standing) Don Redman (alto saxophone)

in Springfield, Ohio, where he assumed leadership of the Synco Septet, a group which later became known as the Synco Jazz Band. In 1923 he ceased playing drums to become the band's conductor and manager. As McKinney's Cotton Pickers it held several long-term engagements, the most successful being its residency at the Graystone Ballroom, Detroit (1927–30), and toured throughout the USA. McKinney's recordings with the band include *The way I feel today* (1929, Vic. 38102). The group disbanded in 1934, but McKinney re-formed it the following year and continued working as a leader and manager until the early 1940s, when he ceased to be active in the music business. (J. Chilton: *McKinney's Music: a Bio-discography of McKinney's Cotton Pickers*, London, 1978)

based on *ChiltonW*

McKinney's Cotton Pickers. Big band. It was formed in Springfield, Ohio, from the Synco Jazz Band, a group organized by William McKinney shortly after World War I. In 1923 McKinney decided to conduct the band himself, and consequently engaged Cuba Austin as the band's percussionist. At the behest of its agent, in 1926 the band became known as McKinney's Cotton Pickers. With their musical versatility and inspired showmanship the musicians blended comedy routines and light music with jazz numbers arranged by their trumpeter, John Nesbitt. From 1927, when DON REDMAN became music director and principal arranger, the band developed its own distinctive style, which highlighted the precision of the saxophones and brass and emphasized the buoyancy of the rhythm section.

The band's first recordings, in July 1928, helped establish the group nationally, and brought widespread praise for the brilliance of Redman's arrangements and the solo improvisations of Prince Robinson. The Cotton Pickers' golden era took place during the group's long residency at the Graystone Ballroom in Detroit (beginning in 1927; see illustration, p.67), where it gained a reputation equal to that of the two other leading black bands of that era, those of Duke Ellington and Fletcher Henderson. Claude Jones, who at various times played in all three groups, later claimed that McKinney's Cotton Pickers was the best of the three. Bright-sounding ensembles, good intonation, and effective soloists were the band's principal strengths; these assets, combined with the appealing singing of Fathead Thomas, Dave Wilborn, and Redman, made the Cotton Pickers popular with dancers, listeners, and other musicians.

In 1931 the band suffered a serious setback when Redman left to form his own big band, taking some key sidemen with him. The Cotton Pickers re-formed, and even found superior replacements in the new members Joe Smith, Benny Carter, and Rex Stewart; but the group never regained its former popularity. Internal dissension caused many personnel changes during the mid-1930s, and by 1936 almost all the original members had left. McKinney continued to lead the band until the early 1940s, engaging various musicians to direct while he concentrated on administration. Unfortunately the group made no recordings after September 1931.

SELECTED RECORDINGS

Crying and Sighing (1928, Vic. 38000); Peggy (1929, Vic. 38133); I'll make fun for you (1930, Vic. 38142); If I could be with you one hour tonight (1930, Vic. 38118); Do you believe in love at sight? (1931, Vic. 22811)

BIBLIOGRAPHY

B. Howard: "Old Cotton Pickers Could Outrock Modern Jazz Orchestras," *DB*, ix/11 (1942), 8
T. Grove and M. Grove: "McKinney's Cotton Pickers," *Record Changer* (1951), Nov, 3
H. P[anassié]: "Notes discographiques sur les McKinney's Cotton Pickers," *BHcF*, no.88 (1959), 40
G. Blonston: "Stompin' at the Pontch," *Detroit Free Press* (11 Feb 1973)
J. Chilton: *McKinney's Music: a Bio-discography of McKinney's Cotton Pickers* (London, 1978)
N. Gentieu: "Don Redman's Masterpiece," *IAJRCJ*, xiv/1 (1981), 8

JOHN CHILTON

McKusick, Hal [Harold Wilfred] (*b* Medford, MA, 1 June 1924). Alto saxophonist. He first worked as a sideman and a principal soloist with a number of big bands, including those of Les Brown, Woody Herman (both 1943), Boyd Raeburn (1944–5), the guitarist Alvino Rey (1946), Al Donahue, Buddy Rich, and Claude Thornhill (1948–9). During the 1950s he played with Terry Gibbs (1950–51, 1955–6), Bill Harris (i) (1952), and Elliot Lawrence (1952–7), and also worked as a studio musician and led his own groups. In 1958 he joined the staff of CBS in New York, but continued to perform and record as a freelance. McKusick is noted for his experiments in the 1950s with novel time signatures, modes, and counterpoint; the influence of Lester Young may be discerned in his delicate tone and phrasing, both well suited to the cool-jazz style.

SELECTED RECORDINGS

As leader: *The Hal McKusick Quartet* (1955, Beth. 16); *Jazz Workshop* (1956, RCA LPM1366); *Hal McKusick Quintet* (1957, Coral 57131); *Triple Exposure* (1957, Prst. 7135); *Cross Section: Saxes* (1958, Decca 9209)
As sideman: B. Raeburn: Yerxa (1945, Jwl 10001); E. Lawrence: *Elliot Lawrence Plays Gerry Mulligan Arrangements* (1955, Fan. 3206)

BIBLIOGRAPHY

FeatherE; *Feather '60s*
M. Harrison: "Backlog 16: Hal McKusick," *JM*, xi/1 (1965), 24
J. Postgate: "Hal McKusick," *JJI*, xxxv/11 (1982), 33

DIANNA RHYAN

McLaughlin, John (*b* Yorkshire, England, 4 Jan 1942). Guitarist and bandleader. He is essentially self-taught on his instrument, and was early influenced by the recordings of Django Reinhardt. In the 1960s he was active in London, where he played with such rock musicians as Jack Bruce, Mick Jagger, and Eric Clapton. He emigrated to the USA in 1969 and joined Tony Williams's group Lifetime; in the same year he began an association with Miles Davis, and took part in the recording sessions for the albums *In a Silent Way* and *Bitches Brew*. McLaughlin became a disciple of the guru Sri Chinmoy in 1970, and the following year he formed the MAHAVISHNU ORCHESTRA, adopting the name suggested by his spiritual mentor; the ensemble was influential in blending jazz with rock and Indian music. After a second version of the orchestra disbanded in 1975, McLaughlin concentrated on working with the group SHAKTI, in which he played acoustic guitar. He settled in Paris in the late 1970s and resumed playing electric guitar briefly, then again took up the acoustic instrument. During the early 1980s he performed in guitar duos and trios, most frequently with the Spanish flamenco player Paco de Lucia and Al Di Meola, but also with Larry Coryell and Christian Escoudé. In 1984 McLaughlin toured and recorded with a new Mahavishnu Orchestra. He has written a guitar concerto, which received its première (with the Los Angeles PO) in 1985.

McLaughlin is noted for his considerable technical proficiency, and is probably the most influential jazz guitarist since Wes Montgomery. His improvised solos usually involve far less of the pronounced syncopation and relaxed swing common to jazz. Indeed, his work is different in concept from that of Charlie Christian and Kenny Burrell, whose improvisations were of a bouncy, twisting, and turning character, but it is also devoid of the gentle lyricism of Jim Hall. McLaughlin prefers the hard, metallic, and cutting tone obtained by rock guitarists, and he frequently alters the sound he produces by means of a wa-wa pedal or phase shifter. Some of his solos are built of long passages of 16th-notes with interludes of held notes that are distorted in waveform and expressively bent in pitch. His choice of notes is reminiscent of the modal approach of John Coltrane (both musicians studied Indian music).

John McLaughlin playing a solid-bodied double-necked electric guitar (with 12 strings on the upper neck and six strings on the lower), July 1972

In the early 1970s McLaughlin played a specially built electric guitar with two necks, one having six and the other 12 strings (see illustration). Later, for the group Shakti, he designed a guitar based on the Indian *vīṇā*, which had a second set of strings running diagonally across the soundhole and attached at either end to plates on the instrument's table. In the 1980s he has employed the Synclavier guitar synthesizer.

SELECTED RECORDINGS

As unaccompanied soloist: *My Goal's Beyond* (1970, Douglas 9)

As leader: *The Inner Mounting Flame* (1971, Col. KC31067); *Birds of Fire* (1972, Col. KC31996); *Apocalypse* (1974, Col. KC32957); *Shakti* (1975, Col. PC34162); *Johnny McLaughlin, Electric Guitarist* (*c*1979, CBS 82702); *Belo Horizonte* (1981, WB DSK3619); *Mahavishnu* (1984, WB 25190)

As sideman: M. Davis: *In a Silent Way* (1969, Col. CS9875); *Bitches Brew* (1969, Col. GP26); T. Williams: *Emergency* (1969, Pol. 253001); M. Davis: *A Tribute to Jack Johnson* (1970, Col. KC30455); T. Williams: *Turn it Over* (1970, Pol. 244021); L. Coryell: *Spaces* (1970, Van. 6558); on M. Davis: *You're Under Arrest* (*c*1984, Col. FC40023), Katia

BIBLIOGRAPHY

M. Delorme and A. Tercinet: "Discographie de John McLaughlin," *Jh*, no.269 (1971), 14

B. Korall: "Extending Beyond Mahavishnu," *DB*, xl/11 (1973), 18

J. E. Berendt: "Mahavishnu John McLaughlin," *JF* [intl edn], no.27 (1974), 43

J. Schaffer: "Mahavishnu's Apocalypse," *DB*, xli/11 (1974), 4

C. Berg: "John McLaughlin: Evolution of a Master," *DB*, xlv/12 (1978), 14

D. Menn and C. Stern: "John McLaughlin: After Mahavishnu and Shakti, a Return to Electric Guitar," *GP*, xii/8 (1978), 40

S. Rosen: "John McLaughlin," *The Guitar Player Book* (Saratoga, CA, and New York, 1978, 2/1979) [colln of previously pubd articles]

L. Jeske: "Johnny McLaughlin: Acoustic Guitarist," *DB*, xlix/4 (1982), 15

J. Ferguson: "John McLaughlin: from the Symphonic Stage to the Frontiers of Technology," *GP*, xix/9 (1985), 82 [incl. discography]

H. Mandel: "John McLaughlin: Spirit of the Sine Wave," *DB*, lii/3 (1985), 17

J. Ferguson: "John McLaughlin, Al Di Meola, Frank Zappa: Synclavier," *GP*, xx/6 (1986), 122

I. Carr: "McLaughlin, John," in I. Carr, D. Fairweather, and B. Priestley: *Jazz: the Essential Companion* (London, 1987)

MARK C. GRIDLEY/R

McLean, Jackie [John Lenwood, Jr.; Abdul Kareem, Omar Ahmed] (*b* New York, 17 May 1932). Alto saxophonist, father of Rene McLean. His father, John McLean, was a guitarist in Tiny Bradshaw's orchestra. He played alto saxophone from the age of 15, studying briefly with Foots Thomas and Cecil Scott, then worked with Sonny Rollins (1948–9), Miles Davis (at intervals, 1951–2), with whom he made his first recordings, Paul Bley and George Wallington (1955), and Charles Mingus (1956, 1958–9); he also belonged to Art Blakey's Jazz Messengers (1956–8; for illustration *see* BANDS, fig.5) and worked occasionally as a leader. From 1958 he led a quintet, with which he made several recordings and toured Japan in 1965. In 1968 he joined the faculty of the Hartt School of Music, and in the following summers he made tours (sometimes with his son Rene) and taught in Europe. In the early 1980s he appeared in Ken Levis's documentary film *Jackie McLean on Mars*, in which he is seen teaching, playing, and discoursing on life and music. McLean has a raw, urgent style that is grounded in bop but also greatly affected by free jazz.

SELECTED RECORDINGS

As leader: with J. Jenkins: *Alto Madness* (1957, Prst. 7114); *New Soil* (1959, BN 4013); *Capuchin Swing* (1960, BN 4038); *Bluesnik* (1961, BN 84067); *Destination Out* (1963, BN 84165); *'Bout Soul* (1967, BN 84284); with D. Gordon: *The Meeting* (1973, Ste. 1006); on [no leader]: *One Night with Blue Note*, ii (1985, BN 85114), with M. Tyner: Blues on the Corner, Sweet and Lovely

BIBLIOGRAPHY

M. James: "Jackie McLean: an Introduction," *JM*, v/10 (1959), 4

R. Atkins and M. James: "Jackie McLean Discography," *JM*, v/11 (1960), 24

M. James: "A Progress Report on Jackie McLean," *JM*, viii/3 (1962), 5

I. Gitler: "Jackie McLean," *DB*, xxx/25 (1963), 22

A. B. Spellman: *Four Lives in the Bebop Business* (New York, 1966/*R*1970 as *Black Music: Four Lives*)

R. Wilbraham: *Jackie McLean: a Discography with Biography* (London, 1968)

V. Wilmer: *Jazz People* (London, Indianapolis, and New York, 1970/*R*1985)

H. Nolan: "The Connection between Today and Yesterday," *DB*, xlii/7 (1975), 11

R. Brown: "Ah! Unh! Mr. Funk," *DB*, xlvi/16 (1979), 22

B. Case: "Doctor Jackie & Mister Bop," *MM*, liv (10 Nov 1979), 47

L. Jeske: "Jackie and Rene McLean," *DB* l/9 (1983), 53

LEE JESKE/R

McLean, Rene (*b* ?New York, *c*1947). Saxophonist and flutist, son of Jackie McLean. He studied privately with Sonny Rollins and his father, and played baritone, then alto, saxophone with Tito Puente for three years in the early 1970s. He then worked with Sam Rivers, Lionel Hampton, and the keyboard player Doug Carn, with whom he recorded in 1973. From 1970, with his father, he led the Cosmic Brotherhood, recording with the group once in 1974. He also recorded with the tenor saxophonist Tyrone Washington (*c*1974), and as a leader (1975). He was a member of the quintet led by Woody Shaw and Louis Hayes, and played on recordings credited to each leader individually (including Hayes's album *The Real Thing*, 1977, Muse 5125). In the early 1980s he led his own quintet and a bop sextet with his father.

BIBLIOGRAPHY

J.-R. Masson and G. Rouy: "Rene McLean," *Jm*, no.216 (1973), 26

B. Primack: "Rene McLean," *DB*, xlv/5 (1978), 35

C. J. Jennings: "Focus on Rene McLean: the Dynamics of Leadership and Followership," *JSN*, i/5 (1980), 3

McLeod, Alice. *See* COLTRANE, ALICE.

McLin, Jimmy [James A.] (*b* Brookesville, FL, 27 June 1908; *d* St. Petersburg, FL, 15 Dec 1983). Guitarist. He played banjo and guitar until the early 1930s, after which he concentrated on guitar. After beginning his career in Jacksonville, Florida (*c*1926), he moved in 1928 to New York, where he worked with James P. Johnson (1931–4) and briefly with Ward Pinkett, Roy Eldridge, and others. McLin's subtle and varied accompaniments are well represented by *The swampland is calling me* (Decca 1291), recorded with Willie "the Lion" Smith in 1937; he also recorded with Buster Bailey (1937–8) and Billie Holiday (1939), and played with Sidney Bechet (1940), Dave Nelson (1941), and Claude Hopkins (1941–2). While serving in the navy he continued to perform regularly, playing mainly trombone and mellophone. He re-joined Hopkins (as a guitarist) in 1945 and again in 1950, after studying music for three years; he recorded with Hopkins in 1950. He then returned to freelance work before becoming an accompanist to the Ink Spots, a popular vocal group.

based on *ChiltonW*

McNair, Harold [Little G] (*b* Kingston, Jamaica, 5 Nov 1931; *d* London, 7 March 1971). Jamaican tenor and alto saxophonist, and flutist. He traveled to Europe in 1959, and worked with Kenny Clarke in France. In 1960–61 he performed and recorded as the leader of his own group. Thereafter he returned to France, where he worked with Quincy Jones. During the mid-1960s he worked in England, the Bahamas, and New York before settling in London. He performed and made recordings (including the album *Affectionate Fink*, 1965, Isl. 926) leading his own ensembles, some of which included Ian Carr. He was also active as a studio musician and participated in sessions by Zoot Sims (1967), Philly Joe Jones (1968), and Blossom Dearie, Alexis Korner, and Jon Hendricks (all 1970). (*Feather '60s*; *Feather–Gitler '70s*)

SALLY-ANN WORSFOLD

McNeely, Jim [James Harry] (*b* Chicago, 18 May 1949). Pianist. After studying at the University of Illinois (BMus 1975) he performed and recorded with Ted Curson (1976–8). From 1978 to 1984 he was associated with Mel Lewis (initially in the Thad Jones–Mel Lewis Orchestra). During the same period he worked with Stan Getz (1981–5) and led a trio with Adam Nussbaum and the double bass player Marc Johnson (from 1983); he also recorded with Art Farmer and Bobby Watson (both 1984). From 1985 he has worked with Joe Henderson. McNeely has made several albums as a leader (from 1976); *The Plot Thickens* (1979, Gatemouth 1007) includes some of his own compositions. He has taught at New York University, William Paterson College of New Jersey, and the New England Conservatory.

BIBLIOGRAPHY

J. Olsson: "Intressant nykomling" [Interesting newcomer], *Orkester journalen*, xlvi/11 (1978), 8

[J.] Balleras: Review of *The Plot Thickens* (1979), *DB*, xlvii/10 (1980), 35

McPartland, Dick [Richard George] (*b* Chicago, 18 May 1905; *d* Elmhurst, IL, 30 Nov 1957). Acoustic guitarist and banjoist, brother of Jimmy McPartland. He was a member of the circle of young white musicians in Chicago known as the Austin High School Gang (for illustration *see* TESCHEMACHER, FRANK). In the 1920s he toured with Red McKenzie as a replacement for Eddie Lang. Thereafter he remained in Chicago playing with local bands until illness forced him to cease working as a full-time musician. He recorded only occasionally; his sessions with Irving Mills (1928) and Jack Teagarden (1928) gave him little prominence. He may be heard to advantage, however, on the recordings he made with his brother in 1939. The two tracks issued on Decca 18403 are particularly representative; his rhythm work on *The world is waiting for the sunrise* shows him to be an efficient timekeeper, and his introduction to *Sugar* is simple and pleasing. (*FeatherE*)

RICHARD SUDHALTER

McPartland, Jimmy [James Dougald] (*b* Chicago, 15 March 1907). Cornetist, brother of Dick McPartland. He was a member of the circle of young white musicians known as the Austin High School Gang (for illustration *see* TESCHEMACHER, FRANK). At the age of 17 McPartland was invited to replace Bix Beiderbecke in the Wolverines. He remained with this group for just over a year, then worked with the bandleader Art Kassel and others before joining Ben Pollack in 1927. Later that year, with members of the Austin High School Gang (using the name McKenzie and Condon's Chicagoans), he made recordings for Okeh that introduced and defined the exciting, nervously energetic style that was later termed Chicago jazz. With Pollack he achieved considerable fame; his colleagues included Benny Goodman and Jack Teagarden. After leaving Pollack in 1929 he worked as a freelance in and around New York. From the mid-1930s McPartland performed in Chicago, mostly leading small groups, sometimes with his brother. During military service (1942–4) he played in Europe, where he met and married the English pianist Marian Turner. After returning to the USA he led a quartet in Chicago and elsewhere. From 1953 he began playing regularly in New York, performing frequently at Nick's. He has remained active into the 1980s, playing with his own ensembles and with others (including Tony Parenti, 1969). Although he and his wife were later divorced, they have continued to work together occasionally, and performed together at the Newport Jazz Festival in 1978.

McPartland's playing was much admired by Beiderbecke, and, particularly in his early years, his work owed something to the latter's ringing lyricism and balanced phrasing. However it later developed a rather more astringent quality which was wholly individual.

Oral history material in *CtY*, *GBLnsa*, *NjR* (JOHP), and *NjR*.

SELECTED RECORDINGS

As leader: Eccentric/Original Dixieland One-step (1936, HRS 1004); I'm all bound round with the Mason–Dixon Line/Panama (1936, HRS 1003); Jazz me Blues/China Boy (1939, Decca 18042); The world is waiting for the sunrise (1939, Decca 18043); *Shades of Bix* (1953, Bruns. 58049); *Jimmy McPartland's Dixieland* (1957, Epic 3371); with M. McPartland: *The McPartlands Live at the Monticello* (1972, Hal. 107)

As sideman: Wolverines: When my sugar walks down the street/Prince of Wails (1925, Gen. 5620); McKenzie and Condon's Chicagoans: Sugar/China Boy (1927, OK 41011); Nobody's Sweetheart/Liza (1927, OK 40971); I. Mills: Since you went away (1928, Bruns. 4122); B. Pollack: Buy, buy for baby/She's one sweet show girl (1928, Vic. 21743); Louise (1929, Vic. 21941)

BIBLIOGRAPHY

ChiltonW; *FeatherE*; *Feather '60s*; *Feather–Gitler '70s*

J. McPartland: "My Thirty Years in Jazz," *MM*, xxx (11 Sept 1954), 3; (18 Sept 1954), 5; (25 Sept 1954), 4; (2 Oct 1954), 6; (9 Oct 1954), 4; (16 Oct 1954), 7; (30 Oct 1954), 7; (13 Nov 1954), 5; (27 Nov 1954), 13; repr. in M. Jones: *Talking Jazz* (London, 1987)

S. Traill: "Jimmy McPartland: Just a Jazzman," *JJ*, vii/9 (1954), 1

G. Hoefer: "With Jimmy McPartland: Swing's the Thing," *DB*, xxvi/7 (1959), 16

Z. Knauss: *Conversations with Jazz Musicians* (Detroit, 1977), 98

B. Rusch: "The McPartlands: Interview," *Cadence*, vi/3 (1980), 11

C. Deffaa: "Jimmy McPartland's Story," *MR*, xiv (1987), no.9, p.1; no.10, p.13

RICHARD SUDHALTER

McPartland [née Turner], **Marian (Margaret)** (*b* Windsor, England, 20 March 1920). Pianist. She left the Guildhall School of Music, London, to join a four-piano vaudeville act, and later performed for British and American troops during World War II. In Belgium in 1944 she met Jimmy McPartland, whom she married; the couple moved to the USA in 1946. Gradually overcoming the resistance of American jazz musicians to her nationality and sex, she established her own trio, which first played in New York at the Embers Club (1950) and later at the Hickory House (1952–60). Known for her elegant modern style and remarkable technique, she has performed at many important jazz venues, acted as host and producer of a nationally syndicated radio series, "Jazz Piano," and established her own record company, Halcyon. From 1955 she has spent much time introducing jazz to schoolchildren. Although she and Jimmy McPartland were later divorced they have continued to work together occasionally; in 1978 they performed at the Newport Jazz Festival. In the early 1980s she returned to classical music, performing Grieg's Piano Concerto throughout the USA, but she has remained active performing and recording jazz. Among her best-known compositions are *In the Days of our Love, Twilight World, So Many Things, With You in my Mind,* and *Ambiance*. A collection of her writings, *All in Good Time* (New York, and Oxford, England), was published in 1987.

SELECTED RECORDINGS

Duos with G. Shearing: *Alone Together* (1981, Conc. 171)
As leader: *Jazz at the Hickory House* (1952–3, Savoy 8032); *With You in Mind* (1957, Cap. T895), incl. With You in my Mind; *At the London House* (1958, Argo 640), incl. So Many Things; *Ambiance* (1970, Hal. 703); *Marian McPartland Plays the Music of Alec Wilder* (1973, Hal. 109); *From this Moment on* (1978, Conc. 86), incl. Ambiance; *At the Festival* (1979, Conc. 118), incl. In the Days of our Love

BIBLIOGRAPHY

D. Cerulli: "Marian McP.: What's it Like to be a Woman in a Man's Jazz World? It has Problems," *DB*, xxiv/19 (1957), 17
——: "Meet Maid Marian," *DB*, xxiv/18 (1957), 32
M. Gardner: "Marian McPartland," *JJ*, xxvi/4 (1973), 4
W. Balliett: "The Key of D is Daffodil Yellow," *Alec Wilder and his Friends* (Boston, 1974) [colln of previously pubd articles], 1
"McPartland, Marian," *CBY 1976*
L. Feather: "Marian McPartland," *CK*, iii/12 (1977), 63
J. Waz: "Marian McPartland: a Fine Romance," *JF* [intl edn], no.52 (1978), 34
B. Rusch: "The McPartlands: Interview," *Cadence*, vi/3 (1980), 11
M. Ullman: *Jazz Lives: Portraits in Words and Pictures* (Washington, 1980)
L. Lyons: *The Great Jazz Pianists: Speaking of their Lives and Music* (New York, 1983), 167 [incl. interview, discography]
S. Voce: "Marian McPartland," *JJI*, xl/3 (1987), 6

KAREN MONSON

McPhee, Joe (*b* Miami, 3 Nov 1939). Saxophonist and leader. He made his first recording on trumpet with Clifford Thornton in 1967; the following year he taught himself to play saxophone and in 1969 he recorded the first of the many free-jazz albums he made as a leader of small groups and as an unaccompanied soloist, on some of which he played exotic percussion and wind instruments as well as saxophones. He lectured on jazz at Vassar College (1969–71) and played in New York with Don Cherry (*c*1972). From 1975 to 1977 he lived in Europe. His playing is well represented on his solo album *Graphics* (1977, HH I/J) and also on the album *Topology* (1981, HA 1987/88), which includes his own arrangements.

BIBLIOGRAPHY

B. Rusch: "Rapping with Joe McPhee," *Cadence*, ii/3–4 (1977), 3
B. McRae: "Oliver Lake and Joe McPhee," *JJI*, xxxiii/2 (1980), 25
P. Davison: "Joe McPhee," *DB*, xlviii/10 (1981), 58
G. Cerutti: *Joe McPhee Discography* (Sierre, Switzerland, 1983)

McPherson, Charles (*b* Joplin, MO, 24 July 1939). Alto and tenor saxophonist. By the time he was 17 years old he was playing professionally in Detroit with Barry Harris and Lonnie Hillyer. He moved to New York in 1959, and the following year he joined Charles Mingus's Jazz Workshop; he performed intermittently with Mingus until 1974. In 1966 he and Hillyer, who had also worked with Mingus, led a quintet, which replaced Mingus's group at the Five Spot, New York, and in 1968 he performed in the documentary film *Mingus*. During the 1970s and 1980s he worked as a freelance (he settled in San Diego in 1978), mainly with his own groups and in association with Harris and Billy Higgins; he also performed at various jazz festivals and toured internationally. In 1988 he worked with the bop quintet Uptown Express, which included his son, the drummer Chuck McPherson, and Tom Harrell.

McPherson's early awareness of the playing of Johnny Hodges was supplemented by the strong influence of Charlie Parker. Paradoxically his thorough absorption of Parker's rhythmic and harmonic ideas enabled him to develop an individual style. His interpretations of such standard pieces as *They say it's wonderful* (1975) are imbued with a characteristic dulcet warmth, and a similarly emotional vein runs through idiomatic workings of Parker's themes *Si si* (1964) and *An Oscar for Treadwell* (1983). In the 1980s he became known for his planned approach to collective improvisation, the results of which are exemplified by the album *The Prophet* (1983).

SELECTED RECORDINGS

As leader: *Bebop Revisited!* (1964, Prst. 7359), incl. Si si; *Siku ya bibi (Day of the Lady)* (1973, Mstr. 365); *Today's Man* (1973, Mstr. 395); *Beautiful!* (1975, Xan. 115), incl. They say it's wonderful; *New Horizons* (1977, Xan. 149); *The Prophet* (1983, Dis. 882), incl. An Oscar for Treadwell
As sideman: C. Mingus: *My Favorite Quintet* (1965, Charles Mingus 009); *Charles Mingus* (1965, Charles Mingus 0013–14); B. Harris: *Bull's Eye* (1968, Prst. 7600)

BIBLIOGRAPHY

Feather '60s; *Feather–Gitler '70s*
C. Albertson: "Charles McPherson: Ornithologist," *DB*, xxxv/10 (1968), 19
M. Gardner: "Charles McPherson Discography," *JM*, no.183 (1970), 25; no.185 (1970), 26 [addns and corrections]
L. Tomkins: "Charles McPherson," *CI*, xvii/4 (1978), 6
R. Lesnik: "Charles McPherson: Interview," *Cadence*, vii/2 (1981), 5
M. Wisckol: "Profile: Charles McPherson," *DB*, xlviii/6 (1981), 52
B. Priestley: *Mingus: a Critical Biography* (London, Melbourne, Australia, and New York, 1982)

MICHAEL JAMES

MacPherson, (John) Fraser (*b* Winnipeg, Canada, 10 April 1928). Canadian saxophonist. He began his career in 1951 in Vancouver, Canada, where for more than 25 years he played in dance bands and studios; at the same time he played jazz alto saxophone and clarinet on broadcasts of the CBC with Ray Norris, the pianist Chris Gage, the trombonist Dave Robbins, and his own nonet. He acquired an international reputation in the late 1970s and toured the USSR in 1978, 1981, 1984, and 1986. MacPherson is a versatile musician who plays several instruments in styles ranging from traditional jazz to bop; he is best known for his work as a tenor saxophonist in a style derived from that of Lester Young. His recordings include *Indian Summer* (1983, Conc. 224).

BIBLIOGRAPHY

M. Miller: "Fraser MacPherson," *DB*, xlvii/5 (1980), 56
——: "MacPherson, Fraser," *Encyclopedia of Music in Canada*, ed. H. Kallmann, G. Potvin, and K. Winters (Toronto, Buffalo, and London, 1981)
——: "Fraser MacPherson," *Boogie, Pete & the Senator: Canadian Musicians in Jazz: the Eighties* (Toronto, 1987), 158

MARK MILLER

McQuater, Tommy [Thomas Mossie, Sr.; Mac, Tommy] (*b* Maybole, Scotland, 4 Sept 1914). Scottish trumpeter. Although he received tuition in a brass band, he was largely self-taught. He began playing professionally with Louis Freeman, whose band performed on transatlantic liners, then worked with the bandleaders Jack Payne (1934) and Lew Stone (1934–5). He spent two years with Bert Ambrose (1936–8) before playing briefly with the Heralds of Swing (1939); he returned for a short time to Ambrose, then during and after the war played with the Squadronaires, making several recordings. After performing with a pit band called the Skyrockets (1952–3), he played mainly in radio and television, at first as a member of Cyril Stapleton's BBC Showband, then as a staff musician in television under Jack Parnell. He continued to work as a freelance player into the 1980s. Among the many leaders with whom McQuater recorded were Benny Carter (1936–7), Danny Polo (1937), George Chisholm (1938, 1944–5, 1961), John Dankworth (1955, 1961), and Benny Goodman (1969); his playing is well represented on Chisholm's *Rosetta* (1938, Decca F7015).

BIBLIOGRAPHY

D. Boulton: *Jazz in Britain* (London, 1958)
J. Godbolt: *A History of Jazz in Britain, 1919–50* (London, Melbourne, Australia, and New York, 1984)

NEVIL SKRIMSHIRE

McRae, Barry [Barrington Donald] (*b* London, 25 Feb 1935). English writer. From 1960 he wrote regularly for *Jazz Journal* (from May 1977 known as *Jazz Journal International*), to which he later contributed a feature on free jazz called "Avant Courier" that ran for many years; he also worked as a freelance for *Music Maker*, *Jazz Down Under*, *Jazz Forum*, and *The Wire*. His book *The Jazz Cataclysm* (1967) traces the history of jazz to the late 1950s and examines the ways in which Sonny Rollins, John Coltrane, Charles Mingus, and Ornette Coleman effected a transition from bop to free jazz. McRae is an insightful writer with a clear, concise style; his work displays a sympathy towards musicians for whom self-expression is more important than commercial success.

WRITINGS
(selective list)

The Jazz Cataclysm (London, South Brunswick, NJ, and New York, 1967/*R*1985)
The Jazz Handbook (Harlow, England, 1987)
Miles Davis (London, 1988) [incl. discography]
Dizzy Gillespie (Tunbridge Wells, England, in preparation) [incl. discography]
Ornette Coleman (London, in preparation)

ROBERT GANNON

McRae, Carmen (*b* New York, 8 April 1922). Singer. She studied piano privately in her early years and began her career as a singer with Benny Carter's orchestra (1944). Her early and enduring influence was Billie Holiday. After performing with the bands led by Count Basie and Mercer Ellington (1946–7) she worked as an intermission singer and pianist at Minton's Playhouse and other clubs in New York, where she listened to and absorbed the sounds of bop, and came under the influence of Sarah Vaughan. In 1954 she made her first recordings as a leader and was named "best new female singer" by *Down Beat*; the following year she signed a recording contract with Decca, which issued her superb renditions of *Suppertime*, *Yardbird Suite*, and *You took advantage of me*. From that time she has pursued an active career as a solo singer, performing in clubs, at concerts, and at festivals; she made several tours of Europe and Japan from the 1960s into the 1980s. In 1967 she settled in Los Angeles. She was married to Kenny Clarke and to Ike Isaacs (ii). In 1988 she recorded an album of vocalese versions of compositions by Thelonious Monk at the Great American Music Hall in San Francisco.

McRae is an important figure among the group of singers that was directly influenced by the emergence of bop. Her voice has an immediately recognizable "smoky" timbre, and she performs popular ballads and jazz numbers with bop phrasing and inflections. She is especially inventive as a scat singer and has an instinctive feeling for rhythm. She is also a thoroughly competent pianist.

SELECTED RECORDINGS

By Special Request (1955, Decca 8173), incl. Suppertime, Yardbird Suite; You took advantage of me (1955, Decca ED2281); *After Glow* (1957, Decca 8583), incl. Exactly Like You, Little things mean a lot; *Something to Swing About* (1959, Kapp, 1169), incl. Falling in love with you, Love is a simple thing; *The Great American Songbook* (1971, Atl. 2-904); *As Time Goes By* (1973, Cat. 7904); *You're Lookin' at Me* (1983, Conc. 235)

BIBLIOGRAPHY

"Carmen McRae Looks Back on her First Big Year," *DB*, xxii/1 (1955), 17
B. Gardner: "On the Threshold: Singer's Singer Carmen McRae," *DB*, xxix/24 (1962), 19
R. J. Gleason: *Celebrating the Duke, and Louis, Bessie, Billie, Bird, Carmen, Miles, Dizzy, and other Heroes* (Boston and Toronto, 1975), 118
A. Taylor: *Notes and Tones: Musician-to-Musician Interviews* (Liège, Belgium, 1977/*R*1982)
G. Endress: *Jazz Podium: Musiker über sich selbst* (Stuttgart, Germany, 1980), 74
L. Lyons: *The 101 Best Jazz Albums: a History of Jazz on Records* (New York, 1980) [listeners' guide]
"Carmen McRae," *SJ*, xxxv/2 (1981), 192 [discography]
L. Gourse: *Louis' Children: American Jazz Singers* (New York, 1984), 262, 278
L. Tomkins: "Carmen McRae: Good New Songs are Hard to Come by," *CI*, xxii/3 (1984), 6 [interview]
G. Giddins: *Rhythm-a-ning: Jazz Tradition and Innovation in the '80s* (New York, and Oxford, England, 1985) [colln of previously pubd articles], 211

ED BEMIS

McRae, Teddy [Theodore; Mr. Bear] (*b* Philadelphia, 22 Jan 1908). Tenor saxophonist, arranger, and composer. He performed locally with his brothers in the mid-1920s and briefly studied medicine. From 1926 he played intermittently with June Clark and in 1927 he led his own group in New York. He worked with various leaders in the early 1930s, among them Chick Webb, Charlie Johnson, Elmer Snowden (1932), Stuff Smith (1934), and Lil Armstrong (1935); he first recorded in 1934 with Benny Morton. He then spent three years with Webb (1936–9; for illustration *see* WEBB, CHICK), during which time he also made recordings with Teddy Wilson and Henry "Red" Allen (both 1936). When Webb died (1939) McRae remained with the band under Ella Fitzgerald's leadership (until 1941), acting as its music director for a short time. Thereafter he performed with Cab Calloway (1941–2), Jimmie Lunceford (1942), and Lionel Hampton (1943), and worked as staff arranger for Artie Shaw (1943) and music director of Louis Armstrong's big band (1944–5). After touring with his own band (1945) McRae played with small groups and concentrated on writing arrangements; he also formed Raecox, a record company, with Eddie Wilcox. His compositions include *Back Bay Shuffle*, recorded by Shaw in 1938 (Bb 7759).

Oral history material in *NjR* (JOHP).

SELECTED RECORDINGS

As leader: Pluggin' Jone/To satisfy you (1946, Chicago 106); [Mr. Bear:] Peek-a-bop/The Bear Hug (1955, Groove 0138)
As sideman: B. Morton: Tailor Made (1934, Col. 2924D); T. Wilson: Rhythm in my Nursery Rhymes (1936, Bruns. 7612); C. Columbus (1936, Bruns. 7640)

BIBLIOGRAPHY

ChiltonW; *FeatherE*

LAWRENCE KOCH

McShann, Jay [James Columbus; Hootie] (*b* Muskogee, OK, 12 Jan 1916). Pianist. He is largely self-taught as a pianist. He worked with Don Byas in 1931, attended the Tuskegee Institute, and played in Tulsa, Oklahoma (1934), and in Arkansas; from December 1936 he belonged to a trio in Kansas City with Oliver Todd and the drummer Elmer Hopkins. After working in a group with Buster Smith and the trumpeter Dee Stewart he formed his own sextet in 1937, which became popular in the Country Club district. In late 1939 he formed a big band, which in the following year performed at the Century Room and Fairyland Park, and from 1941 he made recordings for Decca that featured the blues singing of Walter Brown. His band, which now included Charlie Parker, Gene Ramey, Gus Johnson, and the trumpeters Buddy Anderson and Orville Minor, made its first appearance in New York at the Savoy Ballroom in February 1942; in 1942–3 Jimmy Forrest and Paul Quinichette were members. After serving in the army (1943–4) he re-formed his big band, which he led at the Savoy, at other clubs on 52nd Street in New York, and in California, where in the late 1940s he led a small group that included Jimmy Witherspoon. Later he moved again to Kansas City (after 1950), performed in the Midwest, and from 1969 into the 1980s appeared at festivals in the USA and abroad; he often toured as the leader of a trio, which included as his sidemen Claude Williams and the drummer Paul Gunther. McShann is noted for his percussive piano playing, which draws on elements of the blues and boogie-woogie; he also sings the blues in a nasal style reminiscent of that of Brown. He is the subject of Bart Becker's and Michael Farrell's film *Hooties Blues* (1978), and his performances figure prominently in the film *The Last of the Blue Devils* (1979).

Oral history material in *GBLnsa*, *NjR* (JOHP), and *TxU*.

SELECTED RECORDINGS

Swingmatism/Vine Street Boogie (1941, Decca 8570); Hootie Blues/Confessin' the Blues (1941, Decca 8559); Dexter Blues (1941, Decca 8583); The Jumpin' Blues (1942, Decca 4418); Sepian Bounce (1942, Decca 4387); *McShann's Piano* (1966, Cap. ST2645); *Confessin' the Blues* (1969, BB 33022); *The Man from Muskogee* (1972, Sack. 3005); *The Last of the Blue Devils* (1977, Atl. 8800)

BIBLIOGRAPHY

F. Driggs: "Jay McShann Relates his Musical Career," *JM*, iv/1 (1958), 5
R. G. Reisner: *Bird: the Legend of Charlie Parker* (New York, 1962/R1975), 146
B. Niquet: "Jay McShann ou la légende de K.C.," *Jh*, no.235 (1967), 23 [incl. discography]
R. Russell: "Jay McShann, New York: 1208 Miles," *J&P*, vii/9 (1968), 18
R. Morris: "Jay McShann: Then and Now," *MR*, i/8 (1974), 12
——: "The Great Band," *MR*, iii/1 (1975), 7
B. Becker: "Jay McShann: Interview," *Cadence*, v (1979), no.9, p.12; no.10, p.8
S. Dance: *The World of Count Basie* (New York and London, 1980) [colln of previously pubd interviews], 247
M. Jones: "Oiling the Blues," *MM*, lv (16 Feb 1980), 36
L. Gourse: "Jay McShann," *CK*, vii/6 (1981), 24
T. Burke and D. Penny: "Jay McShann 'Hold 'em Hootie,' 1940–1959," *Blues & Rhythm: the Gospel Truth*, no.6 (1985), 14 [incl. discography]
J.-P. Battestini: "Jay McShann: pianiste, chanteur et chef d'orchestre," *BHcF*, no.340 (1986), 3
E. Townley: "Jay McShann," *JJI*, xxxix/10 (1986), 6 [incl. discography]
D. Koechlin: *Liste des enregistrements réalisés avec Jay McShann* (n.p., n.d.)

FRANK DRIGGS

McVea, Jack (*b* Los Angeles, 5 Nov 1914). Tenor saxophonist and bandleader. He first played banjo (1925–7), then took up the alto saxophone. He performed with his father, the banjoist Satchel (Isaac) McVea (to 1932), the trumpeters Dootsie (Walter) Williams (1932), and Charlie Echols (1934, 1935), and Eddie Barefield (1936). He joined Lionel Hampton's band in 1940 as a baritone saxophonist, but left in 1943 to play with Snub Mosley. He played in the first Jazz at the Philharmonic concerts (1944) and recorded with Dizzy Gillespie and Charlie Parker in a band led by Slim Gaillard (1945). From 1944 he led his own group, which sometimes included Buster Bailey and Teddy Buckner; he enjoyed a period of great popularity from 1946 to 1948 following the worldwide success of *Open the Door, Richard* (1946, Black and White 792). Thereafter he worked steadily, mostly as a leader of small groups but also briefly with Benny Carter (*c*1956) and the organist Perry Lee Blackwell (1959). Although he recorded with many established jazz musicians, his own band played in a style that was closer to rhythm-and-blues. From 1966 until the 1980s he led a trio at Disneyland in Anaheim, California, playing clarinet rather than his principal instrument.

For illustration *see* TURNER, JOE (ii).

BIBLIOGRAPHY

ChiltonW; *FeatherE*
D. Hague: Interview, *JJ*, xvii/2 (1964), 7
T. Burke and D. Penny: "Opening the Door on Richard," *Blues & Rhythm: the Gospel Truth*, no.17 (1986), 28
B. Rusch: "Jack McVea: Interview," *Cadence*, xii/4 (1986), 11

ERIC THACKER

McWashington, Willie. *See* WASHINGTON, MACK.

Madison, Bingie (S.) (*b* Des Moines, IA, 1902; *d* New York, 1978). Tenor saxophonist and clarinetist. He worked as a pianist in clubs in Des Moines (from 1919) and in California and Canada (during 1921), and played with the alto saxophonist Bobby Brown (1922–5) and Bernie Davis (on piano and tenor saxophone). He formed his own band in 1926 and after a brief spell with Cliff Jackson he became a member of a band led by the trombonist Lew Henry, of which he later became leader. When the group disbanded in about 1930 Madison played with Elmer Snowden and then formed another big band (*c*1931). In the early 1930s he joined Luis Russell, whose group began accompanying Louis Armstrong and recording under the latter's name in 1935. Madison remained until 1940, after which he played with such leaders as Edgar Hayes, Ovie Alston, and Alberto Socarras (1943–7), recorded in Hank Duncan's trio (1944), and led his own small band. His clarinet and tenor saxophone playing may be heard on Russell's *At the Darktown Strutters' Ball* (1934, Ban. 33179). (M. B. Demeusy: "Bingie Madison: Biography of a Career," *JM*, x/7 (1964), 7)

based on *ChiltonW*

Maeda, Norio (*b* Osaka, Japan, 6 Dec 1934). Japanese composer, arranger, and pianist. He worked in the Osaka area before moving to Tokyo in 1955, then played with the Double Beats Five, led by the guitarist Shungo Sawada, and worked as a pianist and arranger for the West Liners (from 1959), led by the tenor saxophonist Konasuke Saijo, and his own group, the Wind Breakers. He has written compositions for many bands, including the Blue Coats (*With Happy Feeling*), Tatsuya Takahashi's Tokyo Union (*Confusion*), Nobuo Hara's Sharps and Flats, and Toshiyuki Miyama's New Herd, and arrangements for about 150 albums, among them Miki Sato's *I'm a Woman* (1981, Phi. 28PJ1002) and Fumio Miyamoto's *Jazzy Wind* (1983, CBS–Sony 36CD182).

SELECTED RECORDINGS

Alfa Ray (1975, Col.–Tact YS7513); *Happy Mama on Green Dolphin Street* (1976, Offbeat 1011); *Norio Maeda and West Liners* (1977, King SKA3007); *Rhapsody in Blue* (1978, Toshiba–EMI–Express ETJ85004); *I Remember April* (1981, Discomate DSP8106)

YOZO IWANAMI

Maggie. Nickname of HOWARD MCGHEE.

Magnetic tape recording. A term applied to a sound-recording technique in which signals are converted into variations of magnetic flux along a length of magnetic tape; *see* RECORDING, §§I, 3, and II, 7.

Magnusson, Bob [Robert William] (*b* New York, 24 Feb 1947). Double bass player. He grew up in a musical family (his father was principal clarinetist in the San Diego SO), studied french horn for 12 years, and in 1967 took up double bass. The following year he toured Europe with Buddy Rich's big band, then played with the San Diego SO (1968, 1972–3) and in a backup trio for Sarah Vaughan (1971–2, 1975–6). He performed and recorded with Art Pepper (intermittently 1977–80), Benny Golson (intermittently, 1977–82), John Klemmer (1978), Joe Farrell (1978–80), and in Nelson Riddle's orchestra accompanying the pop singer Linda Ronstadt (1983–5). As a studio musician he recorded for the Concord label with such leaders as Bud Shank (1977), Laurindo Almeida (1978–83), and Shank and Shorty Rogers (1983). From 1979 to 1982 Magnusson played in the cooperative group Road Work Ahead with the drummer Jim Plank, the pianist Bill Mays, and the guitarist Peter Sprague; albums were issued under Magnusson's name.

SELECTED RECORDINGS

As leader: *Revelation* (1979, Dis. 804); *Road Work Ahead* (1980, Dis. 824); *Song for Janet Lee* (1984, Dis. 912)

As sideman: B. Rich: *Buddy and Soul* (1969, PJ 20158); S. Vaughan: *A Time in my Life* (1971, Mstr. 340); J. Klemmer: *Nexus* (1978, AN 3500)

BIBLIOGRAPHY

L. Underwood: "Profile: Bob Magnusson," *DB*, xlvii/5 (1980), 57

WILLIAM S. BROCKMAN

Magpie. Record label. It is owned by Interstate Music; although not devoted to jazz, some items in its wide-ranging series Piano Blues are of considerable jazz interest.

Mahavishnu Orchestra. Fusion group. It was formed in summer 1971 by JOHN MCLAUGHLIN; Mahavishnu was the spiritual name bestowed on McLaughlin by his guru. The group made its début in New York as a quintet with the sidemen Jerry Goodman (violin), Jan Hammer (keyboards), Rick Laird (electric bass guitar), and Billy Cobham (drums). Its music incorporated various elements: the biting electronic sound, sustained high volume, and dance rhythms of hard rock; the virtuoso improvisation and complex meters of jazz; and spiritual, mantra-like ostinatos borrowed from Indian religious traditions. A second, 11-piece, group was formed in May 1974 – brass, reeds, and strings being added to a central core whose members were, with the exception of the violinist Jean-Luc Ponty, weaker than before. Ponty left over a dispute about royalties in spring 1975, McLaughlin dismissed the additional players the following July, and the group completed its concert and recording commitments as a quartet. McLaughlin formed a new Mahavishnu Orchestra that included Cobham, Bill Evans (iii), and Danny Gottlieb in 1984.

SELECTED RECORDINGS

The Inner Mounting Flame (1971, Col. KC31067); *Birds of Fire* (1972, Col. KC31996); *Apocalypse* (1974, Col. KC32957); *Mahavishnu* (1984, WB 25190)

BIBLIOGRAPHY

B. Korall: "My Goal's Beyond," *MM*, xlviii (17 Feb 1973), 13
J. P. Schaffer: "An Innermost Vision," *DB*, xl/8 (1973), 11
C. Welch: "Music of the Gods," *MM*, xlviii (23 June 1973), 13
L. Cauffiel: "Mahavishnu Demystifies: McLaughlin Fires Orchestra," *RS*, no.204 (15 Jan 1976), 14

BARRY KERNFELD

Mahones, Gildo (*b* New York, 2 June 1929). Pianist. One of his first professional engagements was with the trumpeter Joe Morris (1948). He performed at Minton's Playhouse with Milt Jackson, and after serving in the army played with Lester Young (1953–6). He worked in and around New York with the Jazz Modes and Sonny Stitt and then joined a trio led by Ike Isaacs (i) which accompanied Lambert, Hendricks, and Ross from 1959 to 1962. The Gildo Mahones Trio, with George Tucker and Jimmie Smith, was formed in 1962 and accompanied the singers (Yolande Bavan working as Ross's replacement) until 1964. After the group disbanded Mahones moved to Los Angeles, where he worked with the soul singers O. C. Smith and Lou Rawls. He continued to play jazz, leading his own trio and working as a sideman for several musicians, including Stitt, James Moody, Abbey Lincoln, Leone Thomas, Jim Hall, Joe Turner (ii), and others. In 1973 he played with Benny Carter at the Yamaha Jazz Festival in Japan. He toured the Middle East in the mid-1970s, performed occasionally with Carter in the early 1980s, and played in an all-star bop concert in Oakland, California in 1987.

SELECTED RECORDINGS

As leader: *Shooting High* (1963, Prst. 16004); *The Soulful Piano of Gildo Mahones* (1963–4, Prst. 7339)

As sideman: J. Hendricks: *A Good Git-together* (1959, WP 1283); B. Ervin: *The Blues Book* (1964, Prst. 7340)

BIBLIOGRAPHY

FeatherE; *Feather–Gitler '70s*

For further recordings and bibliography *see* LAMBERT, HENDRICKS, AND ROSS.

PHILIP GREENE

Maiden, Willie [William Ralph] (*b* Detroit, 12 March 1928; *d* Los Angeles, 29 May 1976). Composer, arranger, and tenor and baritone saxophonist. He studied piano from the age of five and saxophone from the age of 11. He began writing arrangements for Maynard Ferguson in 1952; later he became Ferguson's principal soloist on tenor saxophone and in 1966 played briefly with Charlie Barnet. He composed, wrote arrangements, and played baritone saxophone for Stan Kenton from 1969 to 1973, when he began teaching at the University of Maine, Augusta. Maiden's saxophone playing can be heard to advantage on Ferguson's album *A Message from Newport* (1958), in particular on the track *Humbug*.

RECORDED COMPOSITIONS

(selective list; all with Maiden as sideman)

Recorded by M. Ferguson: on *A Message from Newport* (1958, Roul. 52012), Tag Team

Recorded by S. Kenton: on *Stan Kenton Live at Redlands University* (1970, CW 1015), A Little Minor Booze; on *Stan Kenton Live at Brigham Young University* (1971, CW 1039), April Fool, Kaleidoscope; on *Stan Kenton Live at Butler University* (1972, CW 1058), Boilermaker, Height of Ecstasy; on *Birthday in Britain* (1973, CW 1065), No Harmful Slide Effects

BIBLIOGRAPHY

FeatherE; *Feather–Gitler '70s*
L. Tomkins: "Kenton '72 in Depth," *CI*, x/8 (1972), 22
C. Easton: *Straight Ahead: the Story of Stan Kenton* (New York, 1973)
W. F. Lee: *Stan Kenton: Artistry in Rhythm* (Los Angeles, 1980) [incl. discography]

WILLIAM F. LEE III

Maini, Joe [Joseph, Jr.] (*b* Providence, RI, 8 Feb 1930; *d* Los Angeles, 8 May 1964). Alto saxophonist. He grew up in a musical family. After touring with bands led by Alvino Rey and Johnny Bothwell (1948) he spent a few weeks with Claude Thornhill (1951). He then moved to Hollywood, where he appeared in the short film *Birth of a Band* (1955), played on the soundtrack of *I Want to Live* (1958), and performed in bands at clubs in which his close friend the comedian Lenny Bruce was the compère. In the 1960s Maini worked as a sideman with many orchestras, including those led by Gerald Wilson, Bill Holman, Terry Gibbs, Shelly Manne, and Louie Bellson. He was a fine player, influenced by Charlie Parker, but he never quite fulfilled his potential; he may be heard at his best on two albums recorded during a jam session with Clifford Brown and Max Roach (1954). He died after losing a game of Russian roulette.

SELECTED RECORDINGS

As sideman: C. Brown: *Best Coast Jazz* (1954, EmA 36039); *Clifford Brown All-Stars* (1954, EmA 36102); on [no leader]: *Jazz West Coast* (c1955, PJ 501), J. Sheldon: Contour (1955); Red Mitchell: *Jam for your Bread* (1955, Beth. 38); K. Drew: *Talkin' and Walkin'* (1955, Jazz West 4); J. Knepper: *Jimmy Knepper Quintet* (1957, Debut 129)

BIBLIOGRAPHY

FeatherE; *Feather '60s*
A. Levitt: "Joe Maini," *Jm*, no.280 (1979), 32
R. Gordon: *Jazz West Coast: the Los Angeles Jazz Scene of the 1950s* (London and New York, 1986)

SCOTT YANOW

Mainieri, Mike [Michael, Jr.] (*b* New York, 24 July 1938). Vibraphonist, keyboard player, arranger, and composer. He first played professionally at the age of 14, touring with Paul Whiteman, and from 1956 to 1962 he was the vibraphonist in Buddy Rich's band. Later he worked as a session musician with Billie Holiday, Benny Goodman, Coleman Hawkins and Wes Montgomery, recording with the last in 1967–8. In the late 1960s and early 1970s Mainieri led two groups: White Elephant (a rehearsal band for studio musicians that included Mike and Randy Brecker, Jon Faddis, and Steve Gadd) and L'image. In 1979 he founded the group Steps (later known as STEPS AHEAD), which received considerable critical acclaim for its sophisticated jazz-rock. Mainieri writes much of the group's music; he has also composed music for commercials and films and worked as a record producer. He was one of the inventors of the Synthivibe, which consists of a series of copper percussion bars powered by static electricity.

SELECTED RECORDINGS

Duos with W. Bernhardt: *Free Smiles* (1978, AN 3009)
As leader: *Wanderlust* (1981, WB 3586)
As sideman: B. Rich: *Blues Caravan* (1961, Verve 68425)

BIBLIOGRAPHY

B. Primack: "Mike Mainieri: Good Vibes Unlimited," *DB*, xlv/8 (1978), 17
H. Mandel: "Steps Ahead," *DB*, l/8 (1983), 18 [incl. interview]
J. Sabins: "Mike Mainieri," *Modern Percussionist*, ii/3 (1983), 8
M. Gilbert: "Mike Mainieri," *JJI*, xxxvii/12 (1984), 10 [interview]

PAUL RINZLER

Mainstream jazz. A term coined in the 1950s by Stanley Dance to describe the work of contemporary musicians working in the swing idiom of the 1930s and 1940s. However, it is now more widely used of any jazz improvised on chord sequences in the essentially solo style developed by Louis Armstrong and others in the late 1920s. As time goes on and new styles of jazz lend elements to the mainstream, the term has come to be used more broadly, though most writers would still exclude the free or aleatory jazz of the avant garde, fusion styles (notably jazz-rock), and dixieland and other traditional forms from any definition of mainstream jazz. *See also* JAZZ (i), §V, 9.

JAMES LINCOLN COLLIER

Maize, Bob [Robert] (*b* San Diego, 15 Jan 1945). Double bass player. He studied piano from the age of seven, then took up the double bass; he first played professionally at the age of 13 in a band led by his father. In 1963 he moved to San Francisco, where he worked in house bands at the Soulville and Bop City clubs and with Sonny Stitt at the Jazz Workshop (c1964). He toured the West Coast with Philly Joe Jones (1965) and the USA and Canada with Jon Hendricks (1966). After playing electric bass guitar in a progressive rock band for several years he remained in the San Francisco area and worked as a freelance musician, playing double bass with Mose Allison, Herb Ellis, and Jerome Richardson (all c1972–5); in the mid-1970s he toured with Monty Alexander (1975) and Anita O'Day (Japan, 1976). He recorded for the Concord label with a number of leaders, including Cal Collins (1979), Dave McKenna (1980), and Scott Hamilton (1981), and with the Concord Jazz All-Stars (1981). He performed on public television with Buddy DeFranco, Terry Gibbs, and Ernestine Anderson (1982), played and recorded with Horace Silver (1983–4), and toured Japan with Sarah Vaughan (1985). In the late 1980s he was active in Los Angeles, playing with artists such as Billy Eckstine (1986) and Ross Tompkins (1987); in 1987 he toured with Mel Tormé.

Maize's legato walking bass lines and relaxed swing contribute to a contemporary form of the West Coast style. His outstanding work as a soloist, heard to advantage on *I Can't Get Started*, recorded with Tal Farlow (1984), demonstrates technical facility and a lyrical conception influenced by Red Mitchell and Oscar Pettiford.

SELECTED RECORDINGS

(recorded for Concord unless otherwise indicated)

As sideman: C. Collins: *Blues on my Mind* (1979, 95); D. McKenna: *Piano Mover* (1980, 146); on S. Hamilton: *Apples and Oranges* (1981, 165), Ham Fat, Royal Orchid Blues, Silk Stockings; Concord Jazz All-Stars: *At the North Sea Jazz Festival* (1981, 182); H. Silver: *There's No Need to Struggle* (1983, Silveto 103); T. Farlow: *The Legendary Tal Farlow* (1984, 266), incl. I Can't Get Started

BIBLIOGRAPHY

J. L. Ginibre and P. Carles: "Dictionnaire de la Contrebasse," *Jm*, no.166 (1969), 27

JOHN CURRY

Majewski, Henryk (*b* Poland, 13 April 1936) Polish trumpeter. A self-taught musician, he began his jazz career in amateur dixieland bands. In the late 1950s he played with the New Orleans Stompers, later known as the Warsaw Stompers, and recorded with them between 1959 and 1964. From 1965 he led his own group, the Old Timers, with which he played regularly at the Stodola student club in Warsaw, in festival concerts, and on tours. The group accompanied several visiting musicians to Poland, including Beryl Bryden and Sandy Brown (both 1968), Albert Nicholas, and Wild Bill Davison (it recorded under Davison's name in 1976). Majewski's *Hello! Hold the Line* (1972, Muza 0842) was one of the most successful jazz recordings issued in Poland.

BIBLIOGRAPHY

J. Byrczek: "Eurojazz Personalities: Poland," *JF* [intl edn], no.17 (1972), 85
K. Brodacki: "Old Timers," *JF* [intl edn], no.46 (1977), 49

WOLFRAM KNAUER

Makowicz [Matyszkowicz], **Adam** (*b* Hnojnik, nr Český Těšín, Czechoslovakia, 18 Aug 1940). Pianist. He studied classical music at the Fryderyck Chopin school of music in Kraków, Poland, but left after coming into contact with jazz. During the early 1960s he played with Andrzej Kurylewicz and Jan Wróblewski, then, with Tomasz Stańko, formed Jazz Darings, one of the first free-jazz groups in Europe. In 1965 he moved to Warsaw, where he led his own trio and played in groups led by Michal Urbaniak and Zbigniew Namysłowski. With the Novi Singers he recorded (1965–8) and toured New Zealand, Australia, and

India (1969). At about this time he began to use the name Makowicz. In 1970, having also taken up electric keyboard instruments, he became a member of Urbaniak's new group, and from 1972 concentrated more on composition. He worked closely with Urszula Dudziak (to 1973), and with Stańko as joint leader of the group Unit (to 1976). He played piano with Duke Ellington's orchestra in a concert in Warsaw (1976) and the following year made his début in the USA as an unaccompanied soloist at the Cookery, New York. In 1978 he moved to New York and in 1986 he became an American citizen.

Makowicz is best known for his work in the late 1970s as a solo pianist; he acknowledges Art Tatum, Keith Jarrett, and composers of the European Romantic tradition, such as Chopin, as the major influences on his playing. He has an outstanding technique that incorporates both stride and free-jazz styles; his swinging improvisations and talent for Romantic composition put him on a level with the very best jazz pianists.

SELECTED RECORDINGS

As unaccompanied soloist: *Live Embers* (1975, Muza 1218); *Adam* (1977, Col. JC35320); *Winter Flowers* (1978, Sup. 1151987); *From My Window* (1980, Choice 1028)

Duos with U. Dudziak: *Newborn Light* (1972, Cameo 101)

As leader: with T. Stańko: *Stańko-Makowicz Unit* (1975, Pronit 06060); *Naughty Baby* (1987, RCA/Novus 3022-1-N)

BIBLIOGRAPHY

Feather–Gitler '70s

J. Byrczek: "Eurojazz Personalities: Poland," *JF* [intl edn], no.17 (1972), 85

K. Czyz: "Adam Makowicz: Conviction to Create," *JF* [intl edn], no.32 (1974), 38 [incl. discography]

B. Primack: "Adam Makowicz: the Polish Prince of Jazz," *CK*, v/10 (1977), 12

A. J. Smith: "Spotlight Gazette: Adam Makowicz," *DB*, xliv/15 (1977), 23

J. Szprot: "Adam Makowicz," *JF* [intl edn], no.45 (1977), 42 [incl. discography]

B. Doerschuk: "Getting the Jazz Feel: an Informal Lesson with Adam Makowicz," *Keyboard*, xiii/9 (1987), 78

M. Bourne: "Adam Makowicz," *DB*, lv/2 (1988), 14

WOLFRAM KNAUER

Malachi, John (*b* Red Springs, NC, 6 Sept 1919; *d* Washington, 11 Feb 1987). Pianist. He taught himself music. His first engagement was with Trummy Young in 1943. After recording with Young (1944) he played in Billy Eckstine's big band (1944–5), for which he wrote arrangements, and worked as Eckstine's accompanist (1947). He played with Illinois Jacquet (1948) and then accompanied singers who included Pearl Bailey (1950), Dinah Washington (1951), Louis Jordan (1951), Sarah Vaughan (1952–4), Al Hibbler (1955–8), and Joe Williams. Later he worked as a freelance in Washington. In the mid-1970s he made a recording for the Smithsonian Institution, *Classic Rags and Ragtime Songs*, under the conductor T. J. Anderson (Smithsonian 001).

Oral history material in *NjR* (JOHP).

SELECTED RECORDINGS

As sideman: B. Eckstine: Opus X (1944, De Luxe 2002); The Real Thing Happened to me (1944, De Luxe 2003); *Together!* (1945, Spot. 100), incl. Blue 'n Boogie; S. Vaughan: *Swingin' Easy* (1954, EmA 36109), incl. Lover Man

BIBLIOGRAPHY

Feather–Gitler '70s

B. S. Page: "John Malachi," *DB*, xxxiv/21 (1967), 26

G. V. Johnson: "John Malachi," *JSN*, ii/4 (1982), 120 [interview]

PAUL RINZLER

Malik, Ahmed Abdul. *See* ABDUL-MALIK, AHMED.

Mallet. A beater consisting of a wooden, plastic, or rattan handle and a head made of hard felt, wood, soft cotton, or plastic. Mallets are employed as an alternative to sticks for special drum effects (*see* DRUM SET, §I, 8); they are also used for playing the xylophone and VIBRAPHONE.

Malmstén, Eugen (*b* Helsinki, 16 Feb 1907). Finnish trumpeter, singer, and bandleader. He started his career in a navy band, then played with the Flappers Dance Band, the Hot Five, and other dance bands (1926–34). In 1935–9 he led his own band, Rytmi-pojat (Rhythm boys), which recorded a large number of popular songs (including *My Baby*, 1935, first issued on *Jazz and Hot Dance in Finland*, 1985, Harl. 2017). In its performances it displayed a swinging style similar to that of contemporary British big bands. Malmstén, an admirer of Louis Armstrong, was one of the first trumpeters in Finland to play hot jazz, and his article "Hiukan hot-äänistä" (About hot notes, published in *Rytmi*, i/7–8 (1934), 98) was among the earliest treatments of jazz improvisation published in Finland. (O. Häme: *Rytmin voittokulku* [The triumph of rhythm] (Helsinki, 1949), 152)

PEKKA GRONOW

Malneck, Matty [Matt] (*b* Newark, NJ, 9 Dec 1903; *d* Hollywood, CA, 25 Feb 1981). Violinist and songwriter. He played in dance bands in the early 1920s, then performed and recorded with Paul Whiteman (1926–37; his playing is well represented by *San*, 1928, Vic. 24078); he also wrote arrangements for the orchestra. During the same period he recorded with Frank Signorelli (1927), Frankie Trumbauer (1928–31), Mildred Bailey (1931–2), and Chick Bullock (1932). In the mid-1930s he earned a reputation as a composer of such songs as *Goody-goody* (recorded by Benny Goodman in 1936) and *Eeny meeny miney mo* (recorded by Goodman, Billie Holiday, Joe Venuti, Bob Crosby, and others). After leaving Whiteman, Malneck led a big band that recorded twice (1938–9). He appeared in the documentary film on Bix Beiderbecke *Bix: "ain't none of them play like him yet"* (1981).

BIBLIOGRAPHY

FeatherE

R. M. Sudhalter, P. R. Evans, and W. Dean-Myatt: *Bix: Man & Legend* (New Rochelle, NY, and London, 1974)

Malone, Tom [Thomas Hugh] (*b* Honolulu, 16 June 1947). Trombonist and arranger. He was brought up in Mississippi and attended the University of Southern Mississippi (1965–7) and North Texas State University (BS 1969), where he played and recorded with the NTSU Lab Band. He then joined Woody Herman (1969), Duke Pearson (1970), Louie Bellson (1972), Doc Severinsen, and Blood, Sweat and Tears (1973). From 1973 to 1976, and again in 1978 and 1982, he performed and recorded with Gil Evans. He has recorded in studio brass sections with David Sanborn and Phil Woods (both 1975), Buddy Rich and Stanley Turrentine (both 1976), and Ron Carter (1979). He wrote arrangements for Evans (including *Angel*, recorded on *The Gil Evans Orchestra Plays the Music of Jimi Hendrix*, 1974, RCA CPL1-0677), the Blues Brothers, and his own group, and was the arranger for the television program "Saturday Night Live" from 1975 to 1985. In 1974 he published *Alternate Position System for Trombone*. (*Feather–Gitler '70s*)

Maly. Nickname of CZESŁAW BARTKOWSKI.

Mance, Junior [Julian Clifford, Jr.] (*b* Chicago, 10 Oct 1928). Pianist. As a child he learned piano from his father, who was a stride and boogie-woogie pianist; later more formal studies (which included two years at Roosevelt College, Chicago) developed his awareness of contemporary styles. He played professionally from the age of 10; his first important association was with Gene Ammons (1947–9). After working with Lester Young for a year he re-joined Ammons, then played in an army band at Fort Knox, Kentucky (1951); among his fellow musicians there were Cannonball and Nat Adderley and Curtis Fuller. As the house pianist at the Bee Hive in Chicago (1953–4) he performed with many important jazz musicians; he then spent 18 months as Dinah Washington's accompanist. In 1956–7 he worked with the first band led by the Adderley brothers, and from March 1958 to July 1960 he was a member of Dizzy Gillespie's quintet; he then played with a group led by Eddie "Lockjaw" Davis and Johnny Griffin. In February 1961 he appeared as the leader of a trio at the Village Vanguard, New York. From that date he performed almost exclusively with his own groups (his sidemen have included Billy Cobham, Shelly Manne, and Pete Candoli); in the 1970s and 1980s he appeared regularly in such clubs as Boomer's, the Knickerbocker Saloon, the Angry Squire, Griff's Plaza Café, and Zinno's. Mance's highly rhythmic style is a technically polished blend of the blues and styles that developed from bop.

SELECTED RECORDINGS

As leader: *The Soulful Piano of Junior Mance* (1960, Jlnd 930); *Junior Mance Trio at the Village Vanguard* (1961, Jlnd 941); *Holy Mama* (1976, IC 6018); *For Dancers Only* (1983, Sack. 3031)

As sideman: E. Davis and J. Griffin: *Tough Tenors* (1960, Jlnd 931)

BIBLIOGRAPHY

B. Dawbarn: "It's Always been the Blues, says Julian Mance," *MM*, xxxiv (10 Oct 1959), 14 [interview]
F. Manskleid: "Junior Mance," *JM*, ix/10 (1963), 13 [interview]
C. H. Greene: "Life Begins at Forty: Junior Mance," *DB*, xxxvi/21 (1969), 16
M. Jones: "Junior Mance: Man of Montreux," *MM* (11 July 1970), 14
C. Renninger: "Junior Mance," *Radio Free Jazz*, xv/6 (1975), 8 [interview]
J. Norris: Liner notes, *For Dancers Only* (Sack. 3031, 1983)
R. Palmer: "Pianos in the Background," *JJI*, xxxviii/8 (1985), 16 [incl. discography]

BOB DOERSCHUK

Mandel, Johnny [John Alfred] (*b* New York, 23 Nov 1925). Composer, arranger, and trombonist. A child prodigy who learned many instruments, he began writing arrangements at the age of 13. From 1943 to 1953 he played trumpet (later trombone and bass trumpet) with a series of bands, including those of Joe Venuti (1943), Boyd Raeburn and Jimmy Dorsey (both 1945), Buddy Rich, Georgie Auld, and Alvino Rey (all 1946), Chubby Jackson (1949), Elliot Lawrence (1951–3), and Count Basie (1953). He first came to prominence as an arranger for Woody Herman (1948), but he also wrote for Artie Shaw (1949) and Basie (1952–6); the last named recorded his well-known composition *Straight Life* in 1953. That same year Mandel settled in Los Angeles to pursue a full-time career writing music; he provided arrangements for numerous jazz musicians and singers in the 1950s and wrote the successful jazz score for the film *I Want to Live* (1958; *see* FILMS, §III, 2). His most successful film composition was the song *The Shadow of your Smile* (in *The Sandpiper*, 1965). Despite gradually moving away from jazz and taking on a broader range of work in films and television, Mandel has maintained his reputation as a superior craftsman.

SELECTED ARRANGEMENTS

As leader: *I Want to Live* (1958, UA 4005)

Recorded by others: W. Herman: Not really the Blues (1949, Cap. 837); on C. Basie: *Dance Session* (1953, Clef 626), Straight Life; M. Tormé: *I Dig the Duke, I Dig the Count* (1960–61, Verve 68491)

BIBLIOGRAPHY

J. Tynan: "Mandel," *DB*, xxiii/17 (1956), 15

STEVEN STRUNK

Mandolin. A plucked string instrument with a fingerboard and a rounded body. The instrument used in jazz usually has four or six courses of double strings; the tuning of the instrument with four courses, which is more common, follows that of the violin. The instrument is usually played with a plectrum and has an incisive tone; some mandolinists produce tremolos by rapidly strumming a single note or chord. The mandolin was used in early string bands to carry a solo line against a chordal accompaniment played by other instruments (*see* STRING BAND); the use of the mandolin in this fashion is well illustrated by the recordings of the Six and Seven Eighths Band, formed by Edmond Souchon to re-create the style of the early string bands. In Britain the instrument found favor during the skiffle movement and was played with some success by Sammy Rimington in Ken Colyer's Skiffle Group (on, for example, the recording *Wandering*, 1965, KCS 1001); in the USA, where the mandolin has long been a bluegrass instrument, it came to be used in fusions of bluegrass and jazz, particularly in the work of Dave (David) Grisman (*b* Hackensack, NJ, 23 March 1945), who in the late 1970s undertook a collaboration with Stephane Grappelli that resulted in the recording *Live* (1979, WB 3550). Perhaps the only free-jazz musician to have turned his attention to the instrument is Ornette Coleman, who in 1986 wrote a composition for unaccompanied mandolin entitled *Notes Talking*. (L. Tomkins: "Making the Mandolin Swing: David Grisman," *CI*, xix/12 (1981), 20; xx/1 (1982), 6)

BARRY KERNFELD, ALYN SHIPTON

Manetta, Manuel [Fess] (*b* New Orleans, 3 Oct 1889; *d* New Orleans, 10 Oct 1969). Pianist, cornetist, and saxophonist. He started as a violinist, working with Tom Albert and Buddy Bolden (1906). From 1908 he performed as a solo pianist and became a popular entertainer in the brothel district of New Orleans. He played various instruments with the Tuxedo Orchestra, with King Oliver and Kid Ory (1916), and in Ory's band in Los Angeles (1919), and piano and calliope on the SS *Capitol* (1922). He first recorded on piano in 1925 when working with Papa Celestin, and plays a notable break on *Original Tuxedo Rag* (OK 8215). He also recorded as a soloist (1957, first issued on *Whorehouse Piano*, Jlgy JCE6). Manetta spent the last 40 years of his life teaching; among his pupils were Henry "Red" Allen and Buddy Petit.

Oral history material in *LNT*.

BIBLIOGRAPHY

ChartersJ
B. Thompson and C. De Vore: "Recollections of a New Orleans Professor," *MR*, i/6 (1974), 1
W. Russell: "'Fess' Manuel Manetta (1889–1969)," *Whorehouse Piano* (Jlgy JCE6, 1985) [liner notes]
T. Dash: "Charlie De Vore," *Fn*, xvii/2 (1986), 4

BILL RUSSELL

Mangelsdorff, Albert (*b* Frankfurt am Main, Germany, 5 Sept 1928). German trombonist and leader, brother of Emil Mangelsdorff. After studying violin and working as a jazz guitarist (1947) he took up the trombone in 1948. He played with the pianist Joe Klimm (1950), Hans Koller's New Jazz Stars (1953–4), the Frankfurt All Stars (1955–6), and hard-bop quintets of which Joki Freund was a leader and a sideman (*c*1955–*c*1958). In the 1950s he was a regular member of the orchestra of the Hessischer Rundfunk, Frankfurt am Main; in 1958 he played in Marshall Brown's International Youth Band at the Newport Jazz Festival, and from the same year he performed throughout Europe as the leader of quartets and quintets, in concerts and on radio and television, into the 1980s. He recorded the album

Animal Dance (1962) with John Lewis in Germany, as a result of which his international reputation grew considerably. After touring Asia on behalf of the Goethe Institute in 1964 he recorded the album *New Jazz Ramwong* later that year with the sitarist Ravi Shankar and incorporated elements of Eastern music into his playing; he also toured the USA and South America. Later he performed as an unaccompanied soloist (from 1972), performed and recorded with a trio consisting of Barre Phillips, John Surman, and the drummer Stu Martin (1977), and worked with such large groups as the Globe Unity Orchestra (from 1967 into the 1980s), Free Sound & Super Brass (1975–6), led by Hans Koller and Wolfgang Dauner, and the United Jazz & Rock Ensemble (from 1975 into the late 1980s). In the 1980s he was a leading figure in the Union Deutscher Jazzmusiker,

Albert Mangelsdorff (trombone) and Larry Ridley (double bass) at the Newport Jazz Festival, late 1960s

and, with Jean-François Jenny-Clark, led the German–French Jazz Ensemble, sponsored by that organization. Mangelsdorff is one of the most important trombonists in jazz. Like most German jazz musicians in the 1950s he was at first influenced by the cool jazz of Lee Konitz and Lennie Tristano; later he developed a highly individual style of free jazz characterized by wide-ranging melodic lines. He has an imposing technique and is, among trombonists, the most innovative player of multiphonics (on, for example, the album *Trombirds*, 1972). He is the author of *Anleitung zur Improvisation für Posaune* (Mainz, Germany, 1965).

SELECTED RECORDINGS

As unaccompanied soloist: *Trombirds* (1972, MPS 2121654-3); *Solo* (1982, MPS 68287)

Duos with D. Cherry, L. Konitz, Elvin Jones, K. Berger, and W. Dauner: *Albert Mangelsdorff and his Friends* (1967–9, MPS 15210)

As leader: with J. Lewis: *Animal Dance* (1962, Atl. 1402); *Tension* (1963, CBS 62336); *Live in Tokyo* (1971, Enja 2006); *The Wide Point* (1975, MPS 2022569-0); *A Jazz Tune I Hope* (1978, MPS 68212); with P. Brötzmann and G. Sommer: *Pica* (1982, FMP 1050)

As sideman with United Jazz & Rock Ensemble: *Live in Berlin* (1981, Mood 28628); *United Live Opus Sechs* (1984, Mood 28642)

BIBLIOGRAPHY

FeatherE; *Feather '60s*; *Feather–Gitler '70s*; *ReclamsJ*

J. E. Berendt: "Jazz für den Fernen Osten: Joachim Ernst Berendt berichtet über die Asien Tournee des Albert Mangelsdorff-Quintetts," *JP*, xiii (1964), 138; Eng. trans. as "Teutonic Tour: through Asia with the Albert Mangelsdorff Quintet," *DB*, xxxi/25 (1964), 13

D. Glawischnigg: "Motivische Arbeit im Jazz," *Jazzforschung*, i (1969), 133 [incl. transcrs.]

W. Sandner: "Anmerkungen zur Improvisationstechnik von Albert Mangelsdorff," *Jazzforschung*, iii–iv (1971–2), 166 [incl. transcrs.]

G. Rouy: "Albert Mangelsdorff," *Jm*, no.234 (1975), 14

J. E. Berendt: "Albert Mangelsdorff: Big Noise from Frankfurt," *DB*, xliv/3 (1977), 16

——: "Wiederentdecken, was Jazz in Wirklichkeit ist," *Ein Fenster aus Jazz* (Frankfurt am Main, Germany, 1977), 61 [interview]

D. J. Noll: *Zur Improvisation im deutschen Free Jazz* (Hamburg, Germany, 1977)

B. Rusch: "Albert Mangelsdorff: Interview," *Cadence*, iii/4–5 (1977), 10

L. Tomkins: "John Surman and Albert Mangelsdorff," *CI*, xvi (1978), no.6, p.23; no.7, p.14

B. Smith: "Albert Mangelsdorff," *Coda*, no.168 (1979), 4

L. Jeske: "Free Jazz Players from Many Lands Form Globe Unity Orchestra," *DB*, xlvii/9 (1980), 25

B. Noglik: "Albert Mangelsdorff," *Jazzwerkstatt international* (Berlin, 1981), 65 [incl. interview, discography]

A. Bausch: *Jazz in Europa* (Echternach, Luxembourg, 1985) [colln of interviews]

JOACHIM E. BERENDT/WOLFRAM KNAUER

Mangelsdorff, Emil (*b* Frankfurt am Main, Germany, 11 April 1925). German alto saxophonist, brother of Albert Mangelsdorff. He was a founder of the Hot Club of Frankfurt and played accordion as a member of the Hot Club Combo. He worked with his brother, with Jutta Hipp, and with Joki Freund (1954–5), and led two quintets, of one of which Freund was also a leader; he also played clarinet in a traditional-jazz group, Werner Rehm's Two-beat Stompers. Later he was the music director for the show "History of Jazz" and belonged to the jazz orchestra of the Hessischer Rundfunk; from 1960 to 1966 he taught jazz in Frankfurt am Main. With the German All Stars he toured South America (1968) and Asia (1971), and he worked as a sideman with Stan Getz, Sonny Rollins, Slide Hampton, Tony Scott, Sahib Shihab, and Joe Henderson; from 1974 he led a quartet. Mangelsdorff is the author of *Anleitung zur Improvisation für Saxophon* (Mainz, Germany, 1965).

SELECTED RECORDINGS

As leader: *Like a Drop of Oil* (1966, CBS S63058); *Old Fashion, New Sound* (1969, Europa 386); *Interaction Jazz* (1977, Tel. 623282); *10 Jahre Interaction Jazz* (1984, L+R 40021)

As sideman: J. Freund: *Yogi Jazz* (1963, CBS BPG62273); German All Stars: *Live at the Domicile, Munich* (1971, CBS S66217)

BIBLIOGRAPHY

ReclamsJ

E. Walter: "Emil Mangelsdorff, Martin Mosebach," *JP*, xxxii/12 (1983), 19

——: "Gespraechskonzert mit dem Emil Mangelsdorff Quartett," *JP*, xxxiv/6 (1985), 31

HEIDI BOULTON

Mangione, Chuck [Charles Frank] (*b* Rochester, NY, 29 Nov 1940). Trumpeter, flugelhorn player, composer, and bandleader, brother of Gap Mangione. As a teenager he played informally in Rochester with such musicians as Dizzy Gillespie, Kai Winding, Jimmy Cobb, Ron Carter, and Sam Jones. He studied music at the Eastman School (BA 1963) and between 1960 and 1965, when he moved to New York, he led a hard-bop group, the Jazz Brothers, with his brother. He first gained notice as a trumpeter in the bands of Woody Herman (1965), Maynard Ferguson (1965), and Art Blakey (1965–7), playing in the style of Miles Davis and Clifford Brown. Mangione formed a quartet, which included Gerry Niewood, in 1968, and in the 1970s attracted a large following with performances of catchy original melodies – particularly *Feels So Good* and *Land of Make Believe* – that involved little improvisation and made use of only elementary accompaniments; his album *Feels So Good* sold more than two million copies, making Mangione's name a byword for jazz in the popular imagination. Equally successful was his score for the film *Children of Sanchez* (1978; the album sold about 673,000 copies), in which soft tone-colors, uncomplicated melodies, and Latin American rhythms were combined with a jazz flavor. Mangione began to tour widely with his group in 1972, and appeared at numerous festivals in the USA and Europe.

Mangione's greatest contributions have been to make jazz palatable to a large nonspecialist audience and to extend the popularity of the flugelhorn as a jazz instrument (he gave up the trumpet to play flugelhorn alone). He has been active as a teacher, and from 1968 to 1972 served on the faculty of the Eastman School; he also organized a jazz program at the Hochstein School of Music in Rochester.

SELECTED RECORDINGS

As leader: with G. Mangione: *The Jazz Brothers* (1960, Riv. 335); *The Chuck Mangione Quartet* (1972, Mer. SRM1631), incl. Land of Make Believe; *Bellavia* (1975, A&M 4557); *Feels So Good* (1977, A&M 4658); *Children of Sanchez* (1978, A&M 6700); *Love Notes* (1982, Col. FC38101); *Disguise* (1984, Col. FC39479)

As sideman with A. Blakey: *Buttercorn Lady* (1966, Lml. 86034)

BIBLIOGRAPHY

J. Szantor: "Chuck Mangione: in Love with Music," *DB*, xxxviii/20 (1971), 12

L. Tomkins: "The Way Chuck Mangione Sees it," *CI*, xi/1 (1972), 20

J. Schaffer: "Chuck Mangione: 'the Whole Feeling!'," *DB*, xl/10 (1973), 18

L. Underwood: "Chuck Mangione: an Open Feeling, a Sound of Love," *DB*, xlii/9 (1975), 11

B. Rusch: "Chuck Mangione: Interview," *Cadence*, iii/6 (1977), 7

G. Brown: "Thou Shalt Always Have a Good Time and Groove with the Music: the Chuck Mangione Story," *Black Music and Jazz Review*, i/12 (1978), 12

H. Nolan: "Chuck Mangione: Mr. Good Feel," *DB*, xlv/6 (1978), 13

L. Tomkins: "The Gratifying Rise of Chuck Mangione," *CI*, xvii (1979), no.8, p.20; no.9, p.16 [interview]

MARK C. GRIDLEY/R

Mangione, Gap [Gaspare Charles] (*b* Rochester, NY, 31 July 1938). Pianist and bandleader, brother of Chuck Mangione. At first mainly self-taught, in his 20s he studied music at Syracuse University (BA 1965). With his brother he led a hard-bop group, the Jazz Brothers, which at various times included Ron Carter, Steve Davis, Roy McCurdy, and Sal Nistico (ii); its recording *Hey Baby!* (1961, Riv. 9371) well represents Mangione's playing. The brothers re-formed the group in 1963 but Chuck left for New York in 1965 and Gap then led his own trio; he recorded with Chuck (1970) and as a leader (1971, 1972), and in the mid-1970s he played in Chuck's band at several concerts. He also taught piano in Rochester. In 1986, to celebrate the 25th anniversary of the group's first recording, the Mangiones re-formed the Jazz Brothers and toured the USA.

BIBLIOGRAPHY

Feather '60s; *Feather–Gitler '70s*

A. Duncan: "Mangiones on Tour Marking 25th Year," *Christian Science Monitor* (26 Aug 1986)

Manhattan Transfer. Vocal group. It was formed in New York in 1972 by four singers: Tim Hauser (*b* Troy, NY, *c*1943), Janis Siegel (*b* Buffalo, *c*1954), Alan Paul (*b* Newark, NJ, *c*1950), and Laurel Massé (*b c*1954); Cheryl Bentyne (*b* Seattle, *c*1956) replaced Massé in 1979. The group achieved critical and public acclaim for its recordings and performances of vocalese, accompanied by ensembles that ranged in size from small groups to large studio orchestras. In 1976 it was given its own television program on CBS. The album *Extensions* (*c*1979), which included versions of *Body and Soul* and *Birdland*, established Manhattan Transfer as one of the foremost jazz vocal groups. *Birdland*, which was arranged by Siegel and included lyrics by Jon Hendricks, won two Grammy awards in 1981, and the album *Vocalese* won a further three in 1986. The group works in a variety of styles, including pop, swing, bop, and jazz-rock.

SELECTED RECORDINGS

(all recorded for Atlantic)

The Manhattan Transfer (1974–5, 18133); *Pastiche* (1976–7, 19163); *Extensions* (*c*1979, 19258), incl. Birdland, Body and Soul; *Mecca for Moderns* (*c*1981, 16036); *Bodies and Souls* (*c*1982, 80104); *Bop doo-wopp* (1983, 81233); *Vocalese* (1985, 81266)

BIBLIOGRAPHY

L. Feather: "Manhattan Transfer: Sings the Songs of Birdland," *DB*, xlvii/3 (1980), 16 [incl. discography]

R. B. Dold: Review of *Mecca for Moderns* (*c*1981), *DB*, xlviii/12 (1981), 34

M. Bourne: "Manhattan Transfer: from Doo-wop to Bebop," *DB*, lii/11 (1985), 22 [incl. discography]

PAUL RINZLER

Mann, Herbie [Solomon, Herbert Jay] (*b* New York, 16 April 1930). Flutist. He studied clarinet from the age of nine and later took up the flute and saxophone. He gained experience of playing during his three years' army service in Trieste, Italy, and after returning to the USA played and recorded with Mat Mathews (1953–4) and Pete Rugolo (1954). He toured France and Scandinavia in 1956, and in 1960 led a group which, under the sponsorship of the US State Department, visited 15 African countries; he became familiar with the bossa nova style on two tours of Brazil (1961–3) and in 1964 toured Japan. He then established a big band in which he played tenor saxophone and which was enthusiastically received when it appeared at the Newport Jazz Festival in 1965. Over the next few years he used elements of ethnic music and blues in his compositions.

In 1969 Mann became a record producer for Embryo, a subsidiary of Atlantic Records. An astute sense of musical trends led him to begin playing rock music in 1971 and by 1973 he had formed his own group, Family of Mann, which incorporated sounds from many kinds of music, including Japanese court music, into its performances. In England in 1974 he experimented with rock once more and also played reggae; his disco recording *Hi-jack* was a hit in the USA in 1975, but after this success he immediately reverted to the style in which he had played in the early 1960s. Atlantic terminated his contract in 1979 and Mann started his own recording company, Herbie Mann Music, in 1981.

Mann is a prodigiously versatile instrumentalist and one of the most talented of jazz flutists, playing Latin jazz, bop, cool jazz, and jazz-rock with equal brilliance. He has restlessly explored many other popular and ethnic styles, mixing them and changing from one to another as musical fashion and his own developing interests dictate.

SELECTED RECORDINGS

(recorded for Atlantic unless otherwise indicated)

As leader: *Yardbird Suite* (1957, Savoy 12108); *Herbie Mann at the Village Gate* (1961, 1380); *Memphis Underground* (1968, 1522); *Stone Flute* (1970, Embryo 520); *London Underground* (1973, 1648); *Reggae* (1973, 1655); *Gagaku and Beyond* (1974, Finnadar 9014); *Discotheque* (1974–5, 1670), incl. Hi-jack; *Astral Island* (1983, 80077)

As sideman: C. McRae: *Easy to Love* (1954, Beth. 1023); Bill Evans (ii): *Nirvana* (1961–2, 1426)

BIBLIOGRAPHY

I. Gitler: "The Family of Mann," *DB*, xxxv/24 (1968), 15

D. Morgenstern: "Herbie's Mann-made World," *DB*, xxxvii/25 (1970), 14

P. Willard: "The Essence of Mann," *DB*, xli/16 (1974), 17

L. Feather and H. Mandel: "Herbie Mann's Independent Flute and the Blues," *DB*, xlvii/12 (1980), 20
K. Dallas: "Jazz: Behind the Real Mann," *MM*, lvii (6 Feb 1982), 23

LEROY OSTRANSKY

Mann, Tony [Anthony] (*b* Frome, England, 31 Jan 1942). English drummer. He began playing as a child and took lessons for a year when he was 14. In 1960 he became a professional musician, joining first a quintet led by Peter King and Gus Galbraith, then a quartet led by Tubby Hayes. After performing on the Cunard liner *Mauretania* (1961) he worked with Tony Lee at the Bull's Head in Barnes, London (1962–70), Humphrey Lyttelton (1970–78), and Kathy Stobart (1979). He recorded with Lyttelton (1972–6), Stobart (1976, 1978), Al Haig (1978), and Chet Baker (1979); his playing may be heard on *All Blues* (1979, Bingow 03), which he recorded with Baker's group and the singer Rachel Gould. In 1980 Mann joined the radio orchestra of Westdeutscher Rundfunk in Cologne, Germany. After returning to England he ceased full-time performing (1983), but worked as a freelance with his own group and accompanied visiting musicians.

NEVIL SKRIMSHIRE

Manne, Shelly [Sheldon] (*b* New York, 11 June 1920; *d* Los Angeles, 26 Sept 1984). Drummer. He first played saxophone, and changed to drums at the age of 18. Having deputized for Dave Tough in Benny Goodman's orchestra he replaced Tough in Joe Marsala's group, with which he recorded in 1941. The following year he played in the big bands led by Will Bradley, Raymond Scott, and Les Brown, and later he took part in Coleman Hawkins's famous recording of *The Man I Love* (1943). It is commonly held that he participated in Dizzy Gillespie's first bop sessions (1945); some historians, however, assert that the drummer was Irv Kluger. From 1946 to 1952 Manne enjoyed a productive association with Stan Kenton, though during the same period he also worked with Johnny Bothwell (1946), George Shearing, Charlie Ventura (1947), Bill Harris (i) (1948–9), and Woody Herman (1949), as well as touring with Jazz at the Philharmonic (1948–9). After moving to Los Angeles he became a central figure in the carefully arranged, cool derivative of bop known as WEST COAST JAZZ, and from 1955 was the leader of a remarkably stable series of small groups. In 1956 his quintet, with Stu Williamson, Russ Freeman, Leroy Vinnegar, and Charlie Mariano as a replacement for Bill Holman, worked in Boston; by the end of the decade the group's members were Joe Gordon, Richie Kamuca, Freeman, and Monty Budwig, and in 1961 Gordon was replaced by Conte Candoli. From the late 1960s, however, Manne was employing lesser-known sidemen such as Gary Barone. He was also the leader, with Barney Kessel and Ray Brown, of the trio the Poll-Winners (1957–60, 1975), and a member of André Previn's trio; with Previn he recorded instrumental versions of songs from *My Fair Lady* (1956), the first of a series of jazz interpretations of material from Broadway musicals. From 1960 to 1974 he ran a jazz club, Shelly's Manne-Hole, and from 1974 to 1977 was a member of the L. A. FOUR. He led a quartet that included Lew Tabackin in 1977, and in 1980 made a tour of Japan with the Gentlemen of Swing (Benny Carter, Harry Edison, Teddy Wilson, and Milt Hinton). Manne was a traditional drummer who possessed a strong sense of swing. He was opposed to ostentatious displays of technical skill, and his sensitivity to percussive pitches allowed him to develop a restrained, "melodic" approach to his instruments.

Oral history material in *GBLnsa, NjR*.

SELECTED RECORDINGS

As leader: *The Three* (1954, Cont. 2516); *My Fair Lady* (1956, Cont. 3527); with B. Kessel and R. Brown: *The Poll-Winners* (1957, Cont. 3535); *At the Black Hawk* (1959, Cont. 3577–80); *2-3-4* (1962, Imp. 20); *Outside* (1969, Cont. 7624); of L. A. Four (with B. Shank, L. Almeida, and R. Brown): *The L. A. Four Scores!* (1975, Conc. 8); *French Concert* (1977, Gal. 5124)

As sideman: C. Hawkins: The Man I Love (1943, Sig. 9001); S. Kenton: Artistry in Percussion (1946, Cap. 289); Shelly Manne (1950, Cap. 28008); A. Previn: *Pal Joey* (1957, Cont. 3543); D. Menza: *Hip Pocket* (1981, PAlt 8010)

BIBLIOGRAPHY

FeatherE; *Feather '60s*; *Feather–Gitler '70s*
"Shelly Manne," *DB*, xxi/13 (1954), 113
J. Tynan: "Portrait of a Jazz Success: Shelly Manne," *DB*, xxix/14 (1962), 20
L. Feather: "Shelly: the Whole Manne," *DB*, xxxvii/25 (1970), 16
L. Tomkins: "In Depth: the Shelly Manne Sextet," *CI*, ix/2 (1970), 8
——: "The Shelly Manne Story," *CI*, ix/7 (1971), 20
S. Traill: "The Shelly Manne Story," *JJI*, xxxii/8 (1979), 21
D. Levine: "Shelly Manne," *MD*, v/7 (1981), 10
C. Bernstein: "Shelly Manne: the Last Interview," *MD*, ix/1 (1985), 14 [incl. discography by D. Levine]

BARRY KERNFELD

Manone, Wingy [Joseph Matthews] (*b* New Orleans, 13 Feb 1900; *d* Las Vegas, NV, 9 July 1982). Trumpeter, singer, and bandleader. As a child he lost his right arm in an accident. He began playing trumpet on riverboats at the age of 17, then worked briefly in Chicago and New York before joining the Crescent City Jazzers in Mobile, Alabama. After traveling with this ensemble to St. Louis (where it took the name the Arcadian Serenaders) he played with various bands in Texas, and also made his first recordings in Chicago, although these were never released. He then played with Jack Teagarden in a band led by the drummer Doc Ross which toured Texas, New Mexico, and California. Thereafter Manone led a band in Biloxi, Mississippi (1926), recorded in New Orleans and New York (both 1927), and worked in Chicago. He recorded with Benny Goodman in 1929 in New York before touring extensively with theater companies. From late 1934 he led a band in New York. His recording of *The Isle of Capri* (1935) rapidly became a hit, and its reputation brought him regular work, both performing and recording, into the 1940s. He moved in 1940 to Hollywood, where he appeared in the film *Rhythm on the River*. Later he played regularly on radio broadcasts with Bing Crosby. In 1954 he settled in Las Vegas, and continued to work there into the 1970s.

Comedy was always an element of Manone's work, from the early parody of the words to *The Isle of Capri* and the painfully accurate imitation of *The Broken Record* to his work with Crosby. This has tended to obscure his importance as a musician. Although he was not noted for his technical prowess he was a fine lead trumpeter, and his ringing tone was unrivaled among his generation of white trumpeters who played in the New Orleans style. His surname has occasionally been misspelled Mannone.

SELECTED RECORDINGS

As leader: Up the Country Blues/Ringside Stomp (1927, Col. 1044D); Tar Paper Stomp/Tin Roof Blues (1930, Champion 16153); The Isle of Capri (1935, Voc. 2913); The Broken Record (1936, Voc. 3158); Memphis Blues (1944, Bruns. 80106); with S. Bechet: At the Jazz Band Ball, St. Louis Blues, first issued on *Wingy Manone/Sidney Bechet – Together at Town Hall, 1947* (1947, Jazz Archives 29); with Papa Bue: *A Tribute to Wingy Manone* (1967, Sto. 210)

BIBLIOGRAPHY

W. Manone and P. Vandervoort: *Trumpet on the Wing* (Garden City, NY, 1948) [autobiography]
B. Whyatt: "Discography of Joseph 'Wingy' Manone," *JJ*, iii (1950), no.9, p.18; no.10, p.15; iv/5 (1951), 17 [addns and corrections]
"Stay Solid, Hip as can be: an Appreciation of Joseph 'Wingy' Manone," *Sv*, no.7 (1966), 4

L. Wright and J. Harvey: "Wingy Manone," *Sv*, no.10 (1967), 33 [interview]
A. Hodes: "Playing for Kicks," "Wingy, Louis, and me," *Selections from the Gutter: Jazz Portraits from "The Jazz Record"* (Berkeley, CA, and London, 1977)
L. Page: "The Strange Case of Wingy, Bunk, Wooden Joe & the Kid," *Fn*, xvi/2 (1984–5), 4
——: "Doing a Bunk," *Fn*, xvii/2 (1985–6), 15

MICHAEL TOVEY

Manor. Record label. It was established in 1944 or 1945 by the Clark Record Co. of Newark, New Jersey, and was managed by Irving Berman. It maintained the artists and repertory, and the matrix series, of his earlier label Regis; the race catalogue included the work of such musicians as Tiny Bradshaw, Paul Bascomb, Jimmie Lunceford, and the International Sweethearts of Rhythm, as well as material by Coleman Hawkins and Dizzy Gillespie. The general series included two discs by Sid Catlett. Manor had been phased out by early 1950, when Berman started the label Arco. ("Regis–Manor–Arco," *Blues Research*, no.15 (n.d. [?1966]), 2)

Mantilla, Ray(mond) (*b* New York, 22 June 1934). Percussionist. He accompanied the popular singer Eartha Kitt in 1955, then played in numerous Latin bands. He toured and recorded with Herbie Mann and also recorded with Max Roach (1960) and Al Cohn (1961). From 1963 to 1969 he lived in Puerto Rico, where he led a Latin band. In 1970 he was a founding member of Roach's M'BOOM RE: PERCUSSION. After two years with Art Blakey (during which he toured Europe and Japan) he played on sessions with Gato Barbieri and Joe Farrell (both 1974), Richie Cole and Don Pullen (both 1976–7), Blakey (1977–8, including *In my Prime*, 1978, Tim. 114, 118), Charles Mingus (1977–8), Walter Bishop (1978), M'Boom Re: Percussion (1979), and Morgana King (1979). He also recorded as a leader (*Mantilla*, 1978, IC 1052). In 1979 he formed the group Space Station, with which in the 1980s he made several European tours; he also played with Muhal Richard Abrams and continued to work with Roach.

BIBLIOGRAPHY

A. J. Smith: "Ray Mantilla," *DB*, xliv/21 (1977), 44
M. Ullman: *Jazz Lives: Portraits in Words and Pictures* (Washington, 1980), 189

Mantler, Mike [Michael] (*b* Vienna, 10 Aug 1943). Composer, trumpeter, and bandleader. He took up the trumpet at the age of 12, attended the Akademie in Vienna, and in the autumn of 1962 moved to the USA and settled in the Boston area. Two years later he went with the pianist Lowell Davidson to New York, where the two performed at such venues as the Cellar Café, Judson Hall, and Town Hall. He became well known chiefly through his collaborations with Carla Bley, whom he married; they belonged to the Jazz Composers Guild and together led the Jazz Composers Guild Orchestra (1964) and the Jazz Composer's Orchestra (July 1965), and formed the JAZZ COMPOSER'S ORCHESTRA ASSOCIATION (1966). They traveled to Europe, where with Steve Lacy they formed the quintet Jazz Realities in the autumn of 1965, which toured Germany and Austria. After their return in February 1966 to the USA Mantler composed and recorded several unusual orchestral works notable for their slow tempos and their bleak, eerie quality. He also belonged to Charlie Haden's Liberation Music Orchestra from its formation in 1969 and again from its re-formation (for a recording) in 1982, and he toured with the orchestra from 1983. With Bley he formed the record companies JCOA Records and Watt Works, which issue his compositions, and made tours and recordings into the late 1980s.

SELECTED RECORDINGS

(recorded for Watt unless otherwise indicated)

Duos with D. Preston: *Alien* (1985, 15)
As sideman: G. Burton: *A Genuine Tong Funeral* (1967, RCA LSP3988); C. Haden: *Liberation Music Orchestra* (1969, Imp. 9183); C. Bley: *European Tour 1977* (1977, 8); *Social Studies* (1980, 11)

RECORDED COMPOSITIONS

(selective list; recorded for Watt unless otherwise indicated)

As leader: of Jazz Composer's Orchestra (with C. Bley): *The Jazz Composer's Orchestra* (1968, JCOA 1001–2), incl. Communications nos.8–11, Preview; *No Answer* (1973, 2), incl. Number Six, Number Twelve; *The Hapless Child* (1975–6, 4); *Silence* (1976, 5); *Movies* (1977, 7); *Something There* (1982, 13)
As leader with C. Bley: on *13–3/4* (1975, 3), 13 for Piano and Two Orchestras

BIBLIOGRAPHY

Feather–Gitler '70s
B. Smith: "An Interview with Carla Bley & Mike Mantler," *Coda*, x/9 (1972), 11
A. Trzaskowski: "Carla Bley, Mike Mantler," *JF* [intl edn], no.55 (1978), 37
J. Carey: "The High-watt Energy of Mike Mantler," *DB*, l/11 (1983), 17 [incl. discography]
I. Carr: "Mantler, Michael," in I. Carr, D. Fairweather, and B. Priestley: *Jazz: the Essential Companion* (London, 1987)

GARY THEROUX

Manzello. A modified version of the saxello, used and named by Roland Kirk; *see* SAXOPHONE, §6(vi).

Marable, Fate (*b* Paducah, KY, 2 Dec 1890; *d* St. Louis, 16 Jan 1947). Pianist and bandleader. Beginning in 1907 he played piano and calliope aboard the Mississippi steamer *J. S.* A decade later he formed his own riverboat band, the Kentucky Jazz Band (for illustration *see* NIGHTCLUBS AND OTHER VENUES, fig.3); although this was based in St. Louis, Marable made a point of recruiting his key musicians in New Orleans. So many of his sidemen later achieved fame that his group became known as "the floating conservatoire"; Louis Armstrong, Henry "Red" Allen, Baby Dodds, and Jimmy Blanton were all former members of Marable's band. He continued to direct bands (sharing leadership duties in the 1930s with Charlie Creath) until the early 1940s, when illness restricted his activities. Despite Marable's reputation among fellow musicians, his band recorded only two titles: *Frankie and Johnny* and *Pianoflage* (1924, OK 40113); neither of these recordings captures exceptional performances.

BIBLIOGRAPHY

G. Fernett: *Swing Out: Great Negro Jazz Bands* (Midland, MI, 1970), 17
P. Vandervoort, II: "The King of Riverboat Jazz," *JJ*, xxiii/8 (1970), 12
W. Dobie: "Remembering Fate Marable," *Sv*, no.38 (1971–2), 44
A. McCarthy: *Big Band Jazz* (New York and London, 1974), 113

JOHN CHILTON

Marable, Larry [Lawrence; Larance Norman] (*b* Los Angeles, 21 May 1929). Drummer. He came from a musical family and was largely self-taught. He lived in Los Angeles and in the 1950s played bop with Stan Getz, Hampton Hawes, Zoot Sims, Charlie Parker, and many others. Musicians he recorded with included Hawes (1952), Wardell Gray (1952–3), Dexter Gordon (1955, 1960), Chet Baker (1956), Sonny Stitt (1959), George Shearing (1959), Wes Montgomery (1960), and Vic Feldman (1962); he also recorded as a leader with the tenor saxophonist James Clay (*Lawrence Marable: Tenorman*, 1956, Jazz West 8). After an interval during which he played little he toured with Supersax (1976) and Bobby Hutcherson (1979–80) and played and recorded (1980) with Milt Jackson. In 1986 he toured again with Supersax and played on the West Coast with Johnny Griffin.

BIBLIOGRAPHY

FeatherE

R. Gordon: *Jazz West Coast: the Los Angeles Jazz Scene of the 1950s* (London and New York, 1986)

Marathon. Record label. On it were issued seven-inch records with close grooving; these were pressed by the Nutmeg Record Corp. for a short period from November 1928, and offered the same playing time as ordinary ten-inch discs. The recordings were made by Emerson; Marathon's catalogue included items by Rosa Henderson and one fine recording by a black band, Jackson and his Southern Stompers. The members of this ensemble have not been conclusively identified.

BIBLIOGRAPHY

B. Rust: *The American Record Label Book* (New Rochelle, NY, 1978) , 186

C. Kendziora: "Behind the Cobwebs: the Nutmegs," *Record Research*, nos.195–6 (1983), 12

Marcus, Steve [Stephen] (*b* New York, 18 Sept 1939). Tenor and soprano saxophonist. He attended the Berklee College of Music (1959–61) and then joined Stan Kenton as a tenor saxophonist (1963). From 1967 to 1970 he played with Herbie Mann, while also working occasionally with Woody Herman. He recorded with Gary Burton (1966), the Jazz Composer's Orchestra (1968), and his own groups in the USA (1967–70) and Japan (1971). He played and recorded jazz-rock with Larry Coryell (1971–3), then formed another group of his own, the Count's Rock Band. From 1975 he toured as a soloist with Buddy Rich, making recordings from 1976 (including *'Round Midnight*, on *Buddy Rich Plays and Plays and Plays*, 1977, RCA CPL1-2273).

BIBLIOGRAPHY

Feather–Gitler '70s

B. Rusch: "A Conversation with Steve Marcus," *Cadence*, ii/12 (1977), 8

L. Tomkins: "Rich Reeds," *CI*, xviii/10 (1980), 14

Mardigan, Art(hur) (*b* Detroit, 12 Feb 1923; *d* Detroit, ?Aug 1977). Drummer. In 1945–6 he performed and recorded with Georgie Auld in New York, where he settled, sharing an apartment with Stan Levey and Max Roach. He played with Charlie Parker, Allan Eager, Elliot Lawrence, and Kai Winding, and made recordings with Fats Navarro in Dexter Gordon's bop quintet, including *Dextrose* (1947, Savoy 955); he also recorded with Wardell Gray (1950) and Nat Pierce (1952). After touring and recording with Woody Herman (1952–3) he played with Pete Rugolo, and in 1954 recorded with Med Flory, Bill De Arango, Nick Travis, Jimmy Raney, George Handy, Chris Connor, Jimmie Rowles, Stan Getz, and his own sextet (including Al Cohn and Teddy Kotick). The following year he recorded with Bob Hardaway, Pete Jolly, and Marty Paich on the West Coast, then returned to Detroit. In 1963 he recorded with Jack Brokensha; shortly before his death he played again with Getz and with Brokensha.

BIBLIOGRAPHY

FeatherE

I. Gitler: *Jazz Masters of the Forties* (New York, 1966/*R*1983 with discography), 188

Obituary, A. Morgan, *JJI*, xxx/12 (1977), 30

Mares, Joe [Joseph P.] (*b* New Orleans, 20 Aug 1908). Clarinetist, brother of Paul Mares. In his youth he played informally with the New Orleans Rhythm Kings. Later he formed his own record company, Southland, and during the 1950s recorded many New Orleans musicians. (G. Kay: "Joe Mares's Southland," *MR*, xi/9 (1984), 1)

Oral history material in *LNT*.

MARCEL JOLY

Mares, Paul (Joseph) (*b* New Orleans, 15 June 1900; *d* Chicago, 18 Aug 1949). Trumpeter, brother of Joe Mares. He was self-taught and during his teens played with Tom Brown's band on the riverboat *Capitol*. After moving to Chicago in late 1919 he worked at Camel Gardens with the drummer Ragbaby Stevens and at the Blatz Beer Garden with Georg Brunis, Jack Pettis, the drummer Frank Snyder, Elmer Schoebel, and Lou Black. In 1921, with the latter group of musicians, Mares organized the Friars Society Orchestra, adding Leon Roppolo and, on double bass, Arnold Loyocano. This ensemble first recorded in 1922 and the following year was renamed the NEW ORLEANS RHYTHM KINGS, but in 1924 it disbanded and Mares and Roppolo went to work in New York. The two men returned to New Orleans in 1925 and, having recruited new personnel, recorded under the name New Orleans Rhythm Kings; Mares used the same name, and the name Friars Society Orchestra, for further recordings made in 1925 and 1935 respectively, but, except for himself, no member of the original group played on either. He ceased to be a full-time musician after 1925, but he played occasionally in Chicago between 1945 and 1948. Although his career was short-lived Mares exerted a certain influence on other trumpeters.

SELECTED RECORDINGS

As leader: of Friars Society Orchestra: Farewell Blues/Oriental (1922, Gen. 4966); of New Orleans Rhythm Kings: Shimmeshawabble (1923, Gen. 5106); Wolverine Blues (1923, Gen. 5102); Milenberg Joys (1923, Gen. 5217); I never knew what a gal could do (1925, OK 40422); She's Crying for me Blues (1925, OK 40327); Reincarnation/The Land of Dreams (1935, OK 41575)

BIBLIOGRAPHY

ChiltonW

D. Gayer: "There is a Chicago Style! – Mares," *DB*, x/4 (1943), 4

G. Avakian: "Paul Mares, New Orleans Rhythm King," *Record Changer*, viii/11 (1949), 17

M. Williams: "N. O. R. K.," *Jazz Masters of New Orleans* (New York and London, 1967/*R*1978), 122

LAWRENCE KOCH

Margolis, Sam(uel D.) (*b* Boston, 1 Nov 1923). Tenor saxophonist and clarinetist. He was largely self-taught. He played in and around Boston with Vic Dickenson, Shad Collins, Bobby Hackett, Rex Stewart, and Nat Pierce. He became the friend of Ruby Braff and first recorded with him in Boston in 1954; the two then worked together in New York and at the Newport Jazz Festival (1957). Margolis returned to Boston in 1958. Among the albums Margolis recorded between 1954 and 1957 several were made as Braff's sideman (including *Ruby Braff Special* (1955, Van. 8504), on which Margolis played both clarinet and saxophone) and on the rest the two were sidemen under other leaders. He recorded again in 1973 with Braff's International Jazz Quartet Plus Three and continued to play with Braff and others into the 1980s. (*FeatherE*)

Margulis, Charlie [Charles A.] (*b* Minneapolis, 24 June 1903; *d* Little Falls, MN, 24 April 1967). Trumpeter. He joined Jean Goldkette's Book–Cadillac Hotel Orchestra in Detroit in 1924 (at which time the orchestra was directed by Joe Venuti), then played with Russ Morgan briefly before joining Paul Whiteman's band in 1927. During the 1930s he was active as a studio musician in New York and played in many sessions with the Dorsey brothers. He formed his own band in 1937 and the following year joined Glenn Miller's orchestra. In 1940 he temporarily adopted the name Charlie Marlowe and formed a new group, with which he played several residencies in California during 1941; he returned to New York in 1942, resumed his studio work, and continued to play as a freelance for many years. He also recorded with Artie Shaw (1940, 1950) and as a leader (1958).

based on *ChiltonW*

Maria, Tania [Correa Reis [Reis Leite], Tania Maria] (*b* São Luís, Brazil, 9 May 1948). Brazilian pianist and singer. She studied classical piano from the age of seven. After recording five albums while still in her teens she moved in 1974 to Paris, where she played for seven years in clubs and made recordings for French and Dutch labels. She performed in 1975 at the Newport Jazz Festival, moved in 1981 to the USA, and settled in 1983 in New York. Her recording *Come with me* (1982) was the most commercially successful album issued by Concord. Maria's style combines jazz, energetic Latin rhythms, and other characteristics of Brazilian music; she often scat-sings in unison with a piano line. In her early work she was influenced by Oscar Peterson and Nat "King" Cole; after she began an association with the record label Manhattan her music took on a more commercial orientation and came to include elements of pop, funk, and rock.

SELECTED RECORDINGS

(recorded for Concord unless otherwise indicated)

Piquant (1980, 151); *Taurus* (1981, 175); *Come with me* (1982, 200); *Love Explosion* (1983, 230); *The Real Tania Maria: Wild!* (1984, 264); *Made in New York* (1985, Manhattan 53000)

BIBLIOGRAPHY

F. Bouchard: "Profile: Tania Maria," *DB*, l/2 (1983), 49
S. Holden: "Brazilian Pianist on Expatriate Road to Stardom," *New York Times* (19 Aug 1983), §C, p.4
L. Gourse: *Louis' Children: American Jazz Singers* (New York, 1984), 348
——: "Tania Maria's Perpetual Motion," *JT* (1984), Feb, 4 [incl. discography]

PAUL RINZLER

Mariano, Charlie [Charles Hugo] (*b* Boston, 12 Nov 1923). Alto saxophonist. After studying music for three years in Boston he played with Shorty Sherock (1948), Larry Clinton, and Nat Pierce (1949–50), and led a quintet (1950–51). Later he worked with the group led by Chubby Jackson and Bill Harris (i) (1953), then spent two years with Stan Kenton. In 1956 he moved to Los Angeles, where he worked with Shelly Manne's group. Thereafter he returned to Boston (1958) and played with Herb Pomeroy and taught at the Berklee College of Music. In 1959 he worked again with Kenton, and married Toshiko Akiyoshi, with whom in 1960 he formed a cooperative group which existed for around seven years; during much of this time they lived in Japan. In 1962–3 Mariano worked with a ten-piece band led by Charles Mingus. Later he taught again at Berklee (1965–6, 1967–8, 1975) and formed a jazz-rock group, Osmosis (1967). He also traveled in India and the Far East in order to study ethnic music. In the early 1970s he settled in Europe, where he led the group Pork Pie with Philip Catherine and Jasper van 't Hof (1973–5) and worked with fusion bands. During this period he often played Indian instruments, and attempted to combine the principles of non-Western music with bop. In 1975 he was a founding member of the United Jazz and Rock Ensemble, with which he has performed and recorded into the mid-1980s; he has also recorded with Eberhard Weber (1975–80) and many jazz-rock musicians. In 1987, however, in a performance in England with former members of Kenton's band, his biting tone and flowing, inventive solos demonstrated his continuing ability in the style that earned him popularity with jazz audiences.

SELECTED RECORDINGS

As leader: *Charlie Mariano with his Jazz Group* (1950–51, Imperial 3006); *The Modern Saxophone Stylings of Charlie Mariano* (1950–51, Imperial 3007); *Johnny One-note* (1954, Beth. 25); with T. Akiyoshi: *Toshiko–Mariano Quartet* (1960, Can. 9012), *Toshiko–Mariano Quartet* (1963, Takt Jazz 12); *A Jazz Portrait of Charlie Mariano* (1963, Regina 286); *Tea for Four* (1980, Leo 012)

As sideman: S. Kenton: *Contemporary Concepts* (1955, Cap. T666); S. Manne: *The Gambit* (1957–8, Cont. 3557); C. Mingus: *The Black Saint and the Sinner Lady* (1963, Imp. 35); M. Tyner: *McCoy Tyner Live at Newport* (1963, Imp. 48); C. Mingus: *Mingus, Mingus, Mingus, Mingus, Mingus* (1963, Imp. 54); E. Jones: *Dear John C.* (1965, Imp. 88)

BIBLIOGRAPHY

Feather E; *Feather '60s*; *Feather–Gitler '70s*
N. Hentoff: Liner notes, *Toshiko–Mariano Quartet* (Can. 9012, 1961)
M. McPartland: "Focus on Toshiko and Charlie Mariano," *DB*, xxviii/22 (1961), 18
M. Fega: Liner notes, *A Jazz Portrait of Charlie Mariano* (Regina 286, 1963)
D. Heckman: Liner notes, E. Jones: *Dear John C.* (Imp. 88, 1966)
M. Jones: "Mariano: Who Wants Pleasant Music Today?," *MM* (3 Sept 1966), 6
C. Mariano: "My Japanese Influence," *Crescendo*, v/3 (1966), 8
J.-E. Berendt: "Charlie Mariano: Stationen eines Leben," *JP*, xxix/10 (1980), 9

MARK GARDNER

Marimba. A tuned percussion instrument, probably of African origin. The modern orchestral instrument consists of a set of wooden bars arranged in two ranks similar to a keyboard configuration, each bar suspended over a tube resonator. The marimba has a compass of three or more octaves ascending from *c*; the bass marimba has a similar range ascending from *C*. It is usually played with soft-headed mallets, producing a more mellow and resonant sound than the xylophone, to which it is closely related. Red Norvo recorded solos on the marimba in 1933 (*In a Mist/Dance of the Octopus*, Bruns. 6096). Later several other vibraphonists played marimba as a second instrument, including Bobby Hutcherson (from the 1960s), Gary Burton (on *Hotel Hello*, 1974, ECM 1055, an album of duos with Steve Swallow), Dave Samuels (on the title track of Spyro Gyra's album *Morning Dance*, 1979, Infinity 9004, and with David Friedman in the quartet Double Image, 1977–80), and Mike Mainieri (both as a leader and as a member of Steps Ahead). A solo on unaccompanied bass marimba is played by Sun Ra at the beginning of *Of Heavenly Things* from his album *The Heliocentric Worlds of Sun Ra* (1965, ESP 1014). The marimba has also been used occasionally by free-jazz ensembles to add an African quality to their work; it was, for example, one of the many instruments played by Joseph Jarman as a member of the Art Ensemble of Chicago between 1969 and 1972.

BIBLIOGRAPHY

L. Feather: *The Book of Jazz: a Guide to the Entire Field* (New York, 1957, 2/1965 as *The Book of Jazz from Then till Now: a Guide to the Entire Field*)
J. Blades: *Percussion Instruments and their History* (London, 1970, rev. [3]/1984)

CLIFFORD BEVAN

Markham, John (Gordon) (*b* Oakland, CA, 1 Nov 1926). Drummer. He performed and recorded with Charlie Barnet (1950–52) and then worked with Billy May (1952–3). From 1955 to 1959 he was a member of the staff orchestra of KGO television in San Francisco, while also recording with Brew Moore and Eddie Duran (both 1957) and others. In 1959 he toured Australia with Red Norvo and Europe with Benny Goodman. He also made recordings with Goodman (1959–60, including *The Sound of Music*, 1959, MGM 3810). During the 1960s he worked in television studios and with various bandleaders, including Ralph Sharon, and recorded with Jack Sheldon (1961). He recorded again with Goodman (1980) and remained active into the late 1980s, playing mostly in big bands accompanying singers. (*FeatherE*)

Markowitz, Marky [Markie; Markowitz, Irv(ing)] (*b* Washington, 11 Dec 1923; *d* New York, 11 Nov 1986). Trumpeter. He played first with Charlie Spivak (*c*1941–2), then Jimmy Dorsey (1943–4), Boyd Raeburn (1944), Woody Herman's First Herd (1946), Buddy Rich (1946–7), and Herman's Second Herd (1947–8; for illustration *see* HERMAN, WOODY, fig.1*b*). During the 1950s he performed mainly in New York and Washington, where he recorded with Dizzy Gillespie (1955). In New York he worked as a studio musician, recording with Gene Krupa (1958), Herman, Lee Konitz, and Art Farmer (all 1959), George Russell (1960), Al Cohn (1962), Herbie Mann (1966), Paul Desmond (1969), Eumir Deodato (1972), and Bill Evans (ii) (1974); a good example of his playing may be heard on *Day in, day out* on Ralph Burns's album *Where There's Burns There's Fire* (1960, Warwick 5001). On the West Coast Markowitz recorded with Gato Barbieri (1976) and Maynard Ferguson (1978). (*FeatherE*)

Marmarosa, Dodo [Michael] (*b* Pittsburgh, 12 Dec 1925). Pianist. He studied classical piano, but was mainly inspired by the styles of Art Tatum and Teddy Wilson. After playing in and around Pittsburgh he was a member of Gene Krupa's band in 1942–3; he then worked with Tommy Dorsey (1944) and Artie Shaw (1944–5), with whose big band and quintet he made several important recordings. The influence of bop began to show in Marmarosa's work during the mid-1940s. In 1946 he moved to Los Angeles, where he became the house pianist for the recording company Atomic; he also recorded with Boyd Raeburn's orchestra and played on sessions with Charlie Parker. He won wider acclaim among jazz audiences in 1947, but illness forced him to return to Pittsburgh the following year; apart from brief tours with the singer Johnny "Scat" Davis and Shaw, he was inactive as a player for more than a decade. In 1961 he recorded the album *Dodo's Back!*, and in 1962 gave a concert at the University of Chicago; his return was short-lived, however, and he retired to Pittsburgh.

Although Marmarosa generally followed the normal practice of bop pianists in playing single-line solos and sparse left-hand accompaniments, he infused his work with a rhythmic approach rooted in swing and a remarkable melodic inventiveness, which established him as one of the most imaginative ensemble pianists of his day. He was one of the first white musicians to be recognized as a bop innovator.

For illustration *see* SHAW, ARTIE.

SELECTED RECORDINGS

As leader: *Dodo's Back!* (1961, Argo 4012); with G. Ammons: *Jug & Dodo* (1962, Prst. 24021)

As sideman: A. Shaw: Mysterioso/Hop, Skip and Jump (1945, Vic. 201800); L. Young: D. B. Blues/Lester Blows Again (1945, Ala. 123); C. Parker: Moose the Mooche/Yardbird Suite (1946, Dial 1003)

BIBLIOGRAPHY

R. A. Horricks: "Dodo Marmarosa," *JJ*, iv/10 (1951), 7

M. Harrison: "A Note on Dodo Marmarosa," *JM*, viii/7 (1962), 16

F. Gibson: "Dodo Marmarosa Discography," *JJ*, xviii (1965), no.5, p.37; no.6, p.25; no.12, p.43; xix/6 (1966), 25

G. Hoefer: "The Recorded Flights of Dodo," *DB*, xxxiii/26 (1966), 25

O. Peterson: "The Consummate Artistry of Dodo Marmarosa," *J&B*, ii (1972), no.1, p.4; no.2, p.7

BOB DOERSCHUK

Marrero, Lawrence (Henry) (*b* New Orleans, 24 Oct 1900; *d* New Orleans, 6 June 1959). Banjoist. He was taught by his father, Billy Marrero (*b* New Orleans, *c*1874), a double bass player who led the Superior Orchestra (1910–13) and played in Manuel Perez's Imperial Orchestra (1905–08), the Olympia Orchestra (1913), and the Camelia Dance Orchestra (1918). Lawrence began to work as a professional musician around 1918, playing with his father in the Camelia Dance Orchestra and then with Chris Kelly and Kid Rena. In 1920 he led the Young Tuxedo Orchestra, in which his brother Eddie (*b* New Orleans, 4 Aug 1902) played double bass (for illustration *see* BANJO). He worked in John Robichaux' orchestra (1926) and in the late 1930s began to perform regularly with George Lewis (i), sometimes playing bass drum in marching bands, and also occasionally playing electric guitar. He became well known as the mainstay of Lewis's rhythm section and concentrated on being a dependable accompanist; Lewis said of him, "The banjo is supposed to be steady, and that's what Lawrence was . . . he could make the banjo ring and get that tone." Both men took part in Bunk Johnson's first recording session in 1942, and Marrero also played with Johnson in New York (1945–6). Although sources consistently give Marrero's forename as Lawrence, he himself used the spelling Laurence.

Marrero's two elder brothers were also musicians. John Marrero (*b* New Orleans, *c*1895) was a banjoist who played with Rena (1919), A. J. Piron (1920), and William "Baba" Ridgley and Papa Celestin's Original Tuxedo Orchestra, with which he recorded from 1925 to 1927 (*see* BANJO). Simon Marrero (*b* New Orleans, *c*1897), a tuba and double bass player, worked with Rena and Celestin during the 1920s (recording with the latter in 1927–8), and briefly with King Oliver (1931); he later moved to New York.

Oral history material in *LNT*.

SELECTED RECORDINGS

As sideman: G. Lewis: Burgundy Street Blues/A Closer Walk with Thee (1944, AM 531); B. Johnson: Tiger Rag/Weary Blues (1945, Met. B530); G. Lewis: *Ragtime Band* (1953, Del. 105–6), incl. Mama don't allow; *Concert!* (1954, BN 1208); *Live Concert* (1954, Sto. 106), incl. The world is waiting for the sunrise

BIBLIOGRAPHY

T. Bethell: *George Lewis: a Jazzman from New Orleans* (Berkeley, CA, 1977), 109

J. Vincent: "The Banjo in Jazz," *JJ*, xxx/3 (1977), 20

L. Page: "A Tribute to Little Laurence Marrero," *Fn*, xv/4 (1984), 16

DAVID FLANAGAN

Marsala, Joe [Joseph Francis] (*b* Chicago, 4 Jan 1907; *d* Santa Barbara, CA, 3 March 1978). Clarinetist and bandleader, brother of Marty Marsala. He started to play clarinet in 1925 and began performing in and around Chicago. He moved to Akron, Ohio, in 1929 to join Wingy Manone, with whom he worked only briefly; he played with a band in Cleveland before returning to Chicago, where he worked as a freelance, occasionally with Ben Pollack. He toured with a circus band in 1931 and again played with Manone in 1933. After working in Florida (1934) he re-joined Manone, with whom he recorded on clarinet and alto and tenor saxophone; the group was resident at Adrian's Tap Room, New York, and then at the Hickory House. When Manone left in 1936 Marsala became the leader of a small group, which included Henry "Red" Allen, Joe Bushkin, and Eddie Condon. In 1937 he married the harpist Adele Gerard, who thereafter performed and recorded in his groups. He returned to the Hickory House as a leader in 1937 and worked there regularly until 1948, when he ceased full-time performing. He occasionally led big bands, but preferred to work with small groups; among his sidemen were Buddy Rich, Dave Tough, and Shelly Manne. On clarinet Marsala developed a dark and smoky timbre and his playing was particularly strong in the lower register.

SELECTED RECORDINGS

As leader: Wolverine Blues/Jazz me Blues (1937, Var. 565); Mighty like the Blues/Hot String Beans (1938, Voc. 4168); Three o'Clock Jump/Reunion in Harlem (1940, General 3001); Lower Register/I know that you know (1941, Decca 3764); Chimes Blues/Sweet Mama (1942, Decca 27074); Walkin' the Dog/Lazy Daddy (1942, Decca 27075)

As sideman: A. Rollini: Nagasaki/Jazz o' Jazz (1935, Vic. 25085); W. Manone: Every Now and Then/I've Got a Note (1935, Voc. 3071); Shoe Shine Boy/West Wind (1936, Voc. 3192); Dallas Blues/Swingin' at the Hickory House (1936, Bb 6375); Formal Night in Harlem/Sweet Lorraine (1937, Bb 6816); Down Stream/Where's the Waiter? (1938, Bb 7391)

BIBLIOGRAPHY

ChiltonW; *FeatherE*

P. Tanner: "New Wine from an Old Bottle: Joe Marsala Flows Again," *JJ*, xxiii/10 (1970), 22 [incl. discography]

Arnold Shaw: *The Street that Never Slept: New York's Fabled 52nd Street* (New York, 1971/*R*1977 as *52nd Street: the Street of Jazz*)

WARREN VACHÉ, SR.

Marsala, Marty [Mario Salvatore] (*b* Chicago, 2 April 1909; *d* Chicago, 27 April 1975). Trumpeter, brother of Joe Marsala. He began working in Chicago as a drummer, but changed to trumpet in the late 1920s. He moved to New York in 1936 to join his brother's band, with which he recorded; he also made a series of recordings with the violinist Tempo King (1936–7). Marsala worked briefly with Will Hudson in 1937 and played again with his brother until 1941, when he led his own group at Nick's. He performed in the comedian Chico Marx's band (1942–3) and led his own quintet in Chicago (1943). After serving in the army (1944–5), he played with his brother (1945) and Miff Mole and Tony Parenti (both 1946). From the mid-1940s and through the 1950s he led his own groups; after moving to San Francisco in 1955 he also played with Earl Hines and recorded with Kid Ory, but owing to ill health he performed only intermittently from the late 1950s. Marsala, whose abilities have been underrated, played trumpet in a hot Chicago style.

SELECTED RECORDINGS

As sideman: T. King: Swing High, Swing Low/Floating on a Bubble (1937, Bb 6880); B. Howard: Spring Cleaning/You're just a little different (1937, Decca 1195); J. Marsala: Wolverine Blues/Jazz me Blues (1937, Var. 565); E. Condon: Georgia Grind/Dancing Fool (1940, Com. 536); E. Hines: *Live at Club Hangover*, v (1955, Sto. 263)

BIBLIOGRAPHY

ChiltonW; *FeatherE*; *Feather '60s*; *Feather–Gitler '70s*

WARREN VACHÉ, SR.

Marsalis, Branford (*b* Breaux Bridge, LA, 1960). Tenor and soprano saxophonist, brother of Wynton Marsalis. His father, Ellis Marsalis, was a pianist in the New Orleans modern bop movement, and his younger brother Delfeayo is a trombonist. While attending Southern University, Louisiana, for a year, he took lessons from Alvin Batiste. He then studied for several years at the Berklee College of Music. After his graduation he worked for five months with his brother Wynton in Art Blakey's Jazz Messengers and toured with Clark Terry's orchestra. He spent three years as a member of Wynton's quintet, during which time he also recorded with such musicians as Dizzy Gillespie and Miles Davis (he was a member of Davis's group in 1984–5), and in 1983 he toured with the quintet V.S.O.P. II. In 1985 he was a founding member of a band led by the English rock singer and electric guitarist Sting, which played a combination of bop, rock, and soul; the other members were Kenny Kirkland, the electric bass guitarist Daryl Jones, and Omar Hakim. Marsalis then worked with his own quartet, achieving popular acclaim in 1987 with a video of his bop version of *Royal Garden Blues*, in which he played soprano saxophone. Later he renewed his association with Sting for further recordings (1987) and an international tour (1988). Marsalis is a versatile and skillful performer (he has also given classical performances with the English Chamber Orchestra); although initially overshadowed by his brother, he has become a major figure in his own right.

SELECTED RECORDINGS

As leader: *Scenes in the City* (1983, Col. FC38951); *Royal Garden Blues* (1986, Col. FC40363)

As sideman: W. Marsalis: *Wynton Marsalis* (1981, Col. FC37574); M. Davis: *Decoy* (1983–4, Col. FC38991); D. Gillespie: *New Faces* (1984, GRP 91012); W. Marsalis: *Black Codes (from the Underground)* (1985, Col. FC40009); Sting: *Bring on the Night* (*c*1986, A&M Bring 1)

BIBLIOGRAPHY

A. J. Liska: "Wynton and Branford Marsalis: a Common Understanding," *DB*, xlix/12 (1982), 14 [interview; incl. discography]

A. Lange: "Sting & Band: Blue Turtles and Blue Notes," *DB*, lii/12 (1985), 16 [incl. interview]

F. Davis: *In the Moment: Jazz in the 1980s* (New York, and Oxford, England, 1986) [colln of previously pubd articles], 29

M. Gilbert: "Branford Marsalis," *JJI*, xxxix/6 (1986), 18

K. Whitehead: "The Many Sides of Branford Marsalis," *DB*, liv/3 (1987), 16 [incl. discography]

DAVID WILD

Marsalis, Wynton (*b* New Orleans, 18 Oct 1961). Trumpeter, brother of Branford Marsalis. From an early age he studied both jazz and classical music: at about the age of eight he belonged to a children's marching band led by Danny Barker that performed at the New Orleans Jazz and Heritage Festival, and when he was 14 he performed Haydn's Trumpet Concerto with the New Orleans PO. He attended the Berkshire Music Center at Tanglewood (near Lenox, Massachusetts) and while

Wynton Marsalis, 1987

a student at the Juilliard School he joined Art Blakey's Jazz Messengers (1980). He toured in a quartet with Herbie Hancock, Ron Carter, and Tony Williams and recorded his first album as a leader (1981), then in early 1982 left the Jazz Messengers to form a quintet with his brother Branford, Kenny Kirkland, the double bass player Charles Fambrough, and the drummer Jeff Watts; he also toured with Hancock in 1983 as a member of the quintet V.S.O.P.II (for illustration see HANCOCK, HERBIE). In 1984 he became the first musician to win Grammy awards for both a jazz recording and a classical recording (for his album *Think of One* (1982) and his recording of trumpet concertos by Haydn, Johann Nepomuk Hummel, and Leopold Mozart). Marsalis won great critical acclaim in the early 1980s for his dazzling technique, emotional intensity, and gift for improvisation; his playing is firmly rooted in bop and hard bop and makes no use of free-jazz elements.

SELECTED RECORDINGS

As leader: *Wynton Marsalis* (1981, Col. FC37574); *Think of One* (1982, Col. FC38641); *Black Codes (from the Underground)* (1985, Col. FC40009)

As sideman with A. Blakey: *Recorded Live at Bubba's* (1980, Who's Who in Jazz 21019); *Straight Ahead* (1981, Conc. 168); *Keystone 3* (1982, Conc. 196)

BIBLIOGRAPHY

B. Rusch: "Wynton Marsalis: Interview," *Cadence*, vii/7 (1981), 5

A. J. Liska: "Wynton and Branford Marsalis: a Common Understanding," *DB*, xlix/12 (1982), 14 [interview; incl. discography]

C. Murray: "Wynton Marsalis," *The Wire*, no.1 (1982), 28

M. Seidel: "Profile: Wynton Marsalis," *DB*, xlix/1 (1982), 52

L. Jeske: "Who is Wynton Marsalis?," *Jazz*, no.3 (Basle, Switzerland, 1983), 4

H. I. West: "Wynton Marsalis: Blowing his Own Horn, Speaking his Own Mind," *JT*, vi (1983), July, 10

H. Mandel: "The Wynton Marsalis Interview," *DB*, li/7 (1984), 16

"Marsalis, Wynton," *CBY 1984*

J. Pareles: "Jazz Swings Back to Tradition," *New York Times Magazine* (17 June 1984), 22

G. Giddins: "Wynton Marsalis and Other Neoclassical Lions," *Rhythm-a-ning: Jazz Tradition and Improvisation in the '80s* (New York, and Oxford, England, 1985) [colln of previously pubd articles], 156, esp. 158ff

S. Crouch: "Wynton Marsalis: 1987," *DB*, liv/11 (1987), 17 [incl. discography]

LEE JESKE/R

Marsh, Arno (Leroy) (*b* Grand Rapids, MI, 28 May 1928). Tenor saxophonist. He played in dance bands from the age of 18, then in 1951 joined Woody Herman; while with Herman's group he contributed notable solos to several recordings on the Mars label, including *Perdido* (1952, 400), *Moten Stomp* (1952, 900), *Mother Goose Jumps* (1952, 500), and *Blue Lou* (1953, 700). After leaving Herman in 1953 Marsh led the resident big band at the Rose Hotel, Grand Rapids, and later played with hotel orchestras in Las Vegas. He recorded in Los Angeles with Med Flory (1956), and again with Herman (1956, 1958), then performed and recorded in New York with Harry James (1966), and in Las Vegas with Nancy Wilson (1968).

BIBLIOGRAPHY

FeatherE

A. Morgan: "Woody's Tenors," *JM*, vi (1960–61), no.7, p.4; no.8, p.13; no.12, p.9

DAVE GELLY

Marsh, George (W.) (*b c*1900; *d* Los Angeles, April 1962). Drummer. In 1924 he joined Paul Whiteman's band, in which he worked, with occasional interruptions, until the late 1920s. He made recordings with Frankie Trumbauer, Eddie Lang (including *What kind o' man is you*, 1929, Parl. R840), and others, and after playing in the orchestra led by Ferde Grofé (*c*1932–1934) moved to California, where he worked in film studios.

based on *ChiltonW*

Marsh, Warne (Marion) (*b* Los Angeles, 26 Oct 1927; *d* North Hollywood, CA, 18 Dec 1987). Tenor saxophonist. He began playing professionally in 1944 and the following year he worked with Hoagy Carmichael's Teenagers. Towards the end of his military service (1946–7) he was stationed near New York, where he was first exposed to the teachings of Lennie Tristano. After working as a freelance in Los Angeles and touring with Buddy Rich he moved to New York (1948) and established himself as one of Tristano's students and sidemen (for illustration *see* TRISTANO, LENNIE). He played briefly with Lee Konitz (1955) and in 1956–7 he performed intermittently as a leader in California. He returned to New York shortly afterwards, but in 1966 he moved back to the West Coast and began to work mainly as a teacher. He was a member of Supersax from 1972 to around 1977, during which time he also toured Europe and recorded with Konitz (1975–6). He then settled in New York, where he continued to teach.

Marsh's ideal was to create linear improvisations that achieved clarity and continuity without sacrificing spontaneity; his melodic lines are underpinned by metrical and harmonic complexities, but the basic ground beat, though supple, is regular and undecorated. *Crazy she calls me* (1956), *It's all right with me* (1957), and *Tracery* (1960) represent the realization of his intentions at various tempos, and also suggest that his individual tone and characteristic inflections resulted from the pursuit of his higher goals and were not developed for their own sake as hallmarks of his style. From the mid-1960s his solo conception was combined with rhythmic support of greater complexity, as may be heard on *Ne plus ultra* (1969) and *All Music* (1976).

SELECTED RECORDINGS

As leader: with L. Konitz: *Lee Konitz with Warne Marsh* (1955, Atl. 1217); *Warne Marsh* (1957–8, Atl. 1291), incl. It's all right with me; *The Art of Improvising* (1959, Rev. 22, 27); *Jazz from the East Village* (1960, Wave 10), incl. Tracery; *Ne plus ultra* (1969, Rev. 12); *All Music* (1976, Nessa 7); *Warne Out* (1977, Inter. 7709); *Star Highs* (1982, Criss Cross 1002)

As sideman: Ted Brown: *Free Wheeling* (1956, Van. 8515), incl. Crazy she calls me; A. Pepper: *The Way it Was!* (1956–7, 1960, Cont. 7630); J. Albany: *The Right Combination* (1957, Riv. 270); Bill Evans (ii): *Crosscurrents* (1977, Fan. 9568)

BIBLIOGRAPHY

A. Morgan: "Warne Marsh," *JM*, vii/4 (1961), 7 [incl. discography]

J. Delmas: "Warne Marsh," *Jh*, no.326 (1976), 14 [discography]

L. Goddet: "Interview: Warne Marsh," *Jh*, no.325 (1976), 18

L. Tomkins: "The Warne Marsh Story," *CI*, xiv/10 (1976), 20; contd as "Supersax, the Sound of Success, by Warne Marsh," xiv/11 (1976), 16

W. van Eyle: "Warne Marsh discografie," *Journal of Jazz Discography*, no.1 (1976), 5; no.2 (1977), 2 [addns and corrections]

F. Davis: "Warne Marsh's Inner Melody," *DB*, l/1 (1983), 27 [incl. discography]; repr. in F. Davis: *In the Moment: Jazz in the 1980s* (New York, and Oxford, England, 1986), 157

W. Balliett: "Jazz: a True Improvisor," *New Yorker*, lxi (14 Oct 1985), 109

MICHAEL JAMES

Marshall, Eddie (*b* Springfield, MA, 13 April 1938). Drummer. By 1960 he had moved to New York, where he performed with Sam Rivers and Stan Getz; he also played and recorded with Charlie Mariano (1960) and Toshiko Akiyoshi (1961). He joined several groups led by Mike Nock, including Almanac (1967) and the Fourth Way (1968–71). He then worked as house drummer at the Keystone Korner in San Francisco (1971 to the early 1980s), accompanying Dexter Gordon, George Benson, and others. He has recorded with John Klemmer (1972), Bobby Hutcherson (1974–8), Kenny Burrell and Jon Hendricks (both 1975), the pianist Larry Vukovich (1981), and the sextet Bebop and Beyond and Bruce Forman (both 1984), and also as a leader (*Dance of the Sun*, 1977, Tim. 109).

BIBLIOGRAPHY

R. Tolleson: "Eddie Marshall," *DB*, xlviii/5 (1981), 48

F. Kofsky: "Eddie Marshall: Covering the Jazz Spectrum," *MD*, v/5 (1982), 22

Marshall, John (Stanley) (*b* Isleworth, England, 28 Aug 1941). English drummer. After playing drums at school and university, he joined Alexis Korner's Blues Incorporated in 1964, and later worked with Graham Collier (1965–70) and other prominent musicians. He was a founding member of Ian Carr's Nucleus, with which he played in 1969–71, and also worked with Mike Gibbs (1969–72), Jack Bruce (1971–2), and SOFT MACHINE (1972–81), of which he was joint leader with Karl

Jenkins from 1977. At the Free Jazz Meeting at Baden-Baden, Germany, in 1973, he played for the first time with Charlie Mariano and Jasper van 't Hof; he later performed with them in the group Pork Pie (1975). He played with Eberhard Weber's Colours in 1977–81. Notable among the other musicians with whom he has worked in the 1970s and 1980s are Anthony Braxton, Gil Evans, John Surman, Sarah Vaughan, and Ben Webster. A versatile drummer, Marshall has been a mainstay of British and European jazz for more than 20 years, showing himself equally skilled in bop, modal jazz, jazz-rock, free jazz, and concert music. Although informed by American music, his work owes much to European influences; he himself stresses that intensity is more important than style or genre in his performances.

SELECTED RECORDINGS

As sideman: J. Bruce: *Harmony Row* (1971, Pol. 2310107); Pork Pie: *The Door is Open* (1975, MPS 228754); Soft Machine: *Bundles* (1975, Harvest 4044); *Softs* (1976, Harvest 4056); E. Weber: *Silent Feet* (1977, ECM 1107)

BIBLIOGRAPHY

R. Cotterrell, ed.: *Jazz Now: the Jazz Centre Society Guide* (London, 1976)
H. Logan: "John Marshall: Astute Musicianship," *MD*, vii/3 (1983), 14
I. Carr: "Marshall, John Stanley," in I. Carr, D. Fairweather, and B. Priestley: *Jazz: the Essential Companion* (London, 1987)

For further recordings and bibliography *see* SOFT MACHINE.

SIMON ADAMS

Marshall, Kaiser [Joseph] (*b* Savannah, GA, 11 June 1899; *d* New York, 3 Jan 1948). Drummer. He was brought up in Boston, where he studied with George L. Stone, one of the most important drum teachers, and played with Charlie Dixon before they both moved to New York in the early 1920s. After playing briefly with the violinist Ralph "Shrimp" Jones in 1923, he joined Fletcher Henderson and other former members of Jones's group in the Club Alabam house band (1924). Marshall remained with Henderson's band during its formative period, playing for many years at the Roseland Ballroom (for illustration *see* JAZZ (i), fig.2), but left in 1930. Over the next 20 years he played and recorded with, among others, Duke Ellington, Cab Calloway, Bill McKinney, Bobby Martin (1937), Edgar Hayes (1939), Wild Bill Davison (1943), Art Hodes (1943, 1944, 1946, 1947), Garvin Bushell (1944), Sidney Bechet (1945), Bunk Johnson (1946), Mezz Mezzrow, and Lionel Hampton. He led several groups in the early 1930s, but made no recordings with them. Except for his early sessions with Henderson, Marshall's recordings of the 1920s generally show little of the free, improvisatory drumming style that is so evident on his recording of *Knockin' a Jug* with Armstrong (1929). This is probably because Henderson's evolving big-band style left little room for extemporary embellishments.

SELECTED RECORDINGS

As sideman: F. Henderson: Shanghai Shuffle (1924, PAct 036157); Rocky Mountain Blues (1927, Col. 970D); Whiteman Stomp (1927, Col. 1059D); Easy Money (1928, Col. 14392D); L. Armstrong: Knockin' a Jug (1929, OK 8703)

BIBLIOGRAPHY

ChiltonW
M. Jones: "The Man who Knocked that Jug Around is Dead," *MM*, xxiv (14 Feb 1948), 2
J. Simmen: "Carnet de notes, xvii: Mrs. Emily Kraft-Banga and Mr. Kaiser Marshall," *BHcF*, no.208 (1971), 4; no.209 (1971), 7; rev. version in *Sv*, no.41 (1972), 176
W. C. Allen: *Hendersonia: the Music of Fletcher Henderson and his Musicians: a Bio-discography* (Highland Park, NJ, 1973)
K. Marshall: "When Armstrong Came to New York," *Selections from the Gutter: Jazz Portraits from "The Jazz Record"*, ed. A. Hodes and C. Hansen (Berkeley, CA, Los Angeles, and London, 1977), 83

T. DENNIS BROWN

Marshall, Wendell (*b* St. Louis, 24 Oct 1920). Double bass player. He was inspired to play double bass by his cousin Jimmy Blanton, from whom he received his first lessons; he also inherited Blanton's instrument. After attending Lincoln University, Jefferson City, Missouri, and serving in the army (1943–6) he played briefly in the area around St. Louis. In 1948 he moved to New York and joined Mercer Ellington, and later the same year transferred to Duke Ellington's band, with which he remained for seven years. From 1955 Marshall worked as a freelance. In that year he recorded with Mary Lou Williams, Carmen McRae, Hank Jones, and Louie Bellson, and made an album with Billy Byers on which he was featured as a soloist. Later he recorded with Art Blakey (1957–8) and Mercer Ellington (1958–9) and played in pit bands for Broadway shows, his principal source of work before his early retirement in 1968.

Marshall's strong technique and opulent tone place him among the finest double bass players of the 1950s. Some of his best solo work, notable for the consistency of his rhythmic ideas and the ingenious use he made of rising and falling lines, may be heard on the album *A Keyboard History*, recorded with Williams in 1955.

SELECTED RECORDINGS

As leader: *Wendell Marshall with the Billy Byers Orchestra* (1955, RCA LPM1107), incl. Careless, The Continental, How blue was my bass, Tenderly
As sideman with D. Ellington: *Duke Ellington* (1949–51, FDC 1022), incl. Duet; *Seattle Concert* (1952, RCA LJM1002); *Duke Ellington Plays Ellington* (1953, Cap. H477)
As sideman with others: L. Bellson: *Just Jazz All Stars* (1952, Cap. H348); M. L. Williams: *A Keyboard History* (1955, Jzt. 1206), incl. Amy, I love you, Lullaby of the Leaves; C. McRae: *By Special Request* (1955, Decca 8173), incl. Sometimes I'm happy

BIBLIOGRAPHY

FeatherE
B. Ulanov: *A Handbook of Jazz* (New York, n.d. [?1957]/*R*1975)
C. Carrère: "Pitter Panther Patter: les bassistes de Duke Ellington," *Jh*, no.316 (1975), 10

LAWRENCE KOCH

Marsh Laboratories. Record company. It was established before 1922 in Chicago by O. B. Marsh. Recordings made by the company were issued on many small contemporary labels, including Rainbow, Rialto, Paramount, and Gennett, as well as on its own label, AUTOGRAPH. From autumn 1924 the company used a primitive form of electric recording. It remained active into the late 1920s.

BIBLIOGRAPHY

B. Rust: "A Glimpse into the Past: Autograph," *Sv*, no.40 (1972), 124
B. Englund: "Wallin's Svenska Record," *Sv*, no.46 (1973), 134

Martin, Bobby [Robert] (*b* Long Branch, NJ, 15 May 1903). Trumpeter. He played with Sam Wooding at the Club Alabam, New York, in 1925, and remained with him, working in Europe and the USA, until 1931. From 1932 to 1936 he was a member of Willie Lewis's orchestra, which was based in Europe; his solo playing may be heard to advantage on Lewis's *Nagasaki* (1935, PAct 591). Martin returned to New York in 1936 and formed his own band, among the members of which were Ram Ramirez and Kaiser Marshall; while touring Europe in 1937–9 it made a recording in the Netherlands (1938). From 1939 Martin led his own groups in New York and New Jersey; he ceased full-time playing after 1944. (A. McCarthy: *Big Band Jazz*, New York and London, 1974)

based on *ChiltonW*

Martin, Chink [Abraham, Martin, Sr.] (*b* New Orleans, 10 June 1886; *d* New Orleans, 7 Jan 1981). Tuba and double bass player. He first played guitar, then changed to tuba, and also played sousaphone. He worked with Papa Jack Laine's Reliance Brass Band from around 1910, and from 1923 to 1925 he performed and recorded with the New Orleans Rhythm Kings in Chicago and New Orleans; he also made recordings with Abbie Brunies's Halfway House Orchestra. One of these, *When I'm Blue* (1927, Col. 1263D), is a fine example of his intricate and agile sousaphone playing. After working during the 1930s as a staff musician at radio station WSMB, New Orleans, he performed and recorded as a freelance in the 1940s and 1950s with such musicians as Sharkey Bonano and Santo Pecora; he played frequently with the Crawford–Ferguson Night Owls in the 1960s. Throughout the following decade he worked at Preservation Hall, New Orleans, playing mainly double bass. On the latter instrument he displayed a strong slapping style, comparable with that of Chester Zardis. His son, Martin "Little Chink" Abraham, Jr., is a double bass player.

Oral history material in *LNT*.

BIBLIOGRAPHY

G. W. Kay: "Happy Birthday Chink," *SL*, xxiv (sum. 1972), 19
——: "Chink Martin," *JJ*, xxv/4 (1972), 18 [interview]

based on *ChiltonW*

Martin [Dunn], **Sara** (*b* Louisville, KY, 18 June 1884; *d* Louisville, 24 May 1955). She sang on a vaudeville circuit based in the Chicago area (around 1915), then performed in New York (1922). There her robust, extrovert style of singing the blues was noticed by Clarence Williams, who booked accompanists for her and arranged recordings; she was one of the first female blues singers to be recorded. During this time she also toured with Fats Waller (1922–3) and W. C. Handy (1923) and in several revues, and traveled widely as a soloist. She later worked in Chicago with the gospel musician Thomas Dorsey. Her vocal tone was hard and often abrasive and she lacked the warmth and worldly-wise ambience transmitted by such singers as Bessie Smith and Ma Rainey. According to Williams, however, she possessed a fine sense of drama, and, in addition to her customary blues repertory, excelled in the performance of vaudevillian ditties, with or without risqué elements.

SELECTED RECORDINGS

Sugar Blues/Achin' Hearted Blues (1922, OK 8041); Graveyard Dream Blues (1923, OK 8099); Yes, sir, that's my baby (1925, OK 8262); Death Sting me Blues/Mistreatin' Man Blues (1928, QRS 7042); Mean Tight Mama (1928, QRS 7043)

BIBLIOGRAPHY

S. Harris: *Blues Who's Who: a Biographical Dictionary of Blues Singers* (New Rochelle, NY, 1979)
"Sara Martin," *Living Blues*, no.52 (1982), 23

KEN RATTENBURY

Martin, Skip(py) [Lloyd] (*b* Robinson, IL, 14 May 1916). Saxophonist and arranger. He played and recorded with or worked as an arranger for several big bands, including those of Count Basie (1937, 1941), Charlie Barnet (in which he played both clarinet and saxophone, 1939–40), Benny Goodman (1940–41), Glenn Miller (1941–2; for illustration *see* MILLER, GLENN), and Les Brown (*c*1945, 1949). Basie recorded his arrangement of *Our love was meant to be* in 1937 (Decca 1446). Martin also made recordings with Cootie Williams's septet: a baritone saxophone solo on *G-men* (1941, OK 6370) is a good example of his playing. In the 1950s he moved to Los Angeles, where he worked as a conductor, wrote arrangements of popular music, and recorded three commercially oriented jazz albums as a leader. (*FeatherE*)

Martinez, Sabu [Luis] (*b* New York, 14 July 1930; *d* Sweden, 13 Jan 1979). Percussionist. He performed and recorded with Dizzy Gillespie (1948) and Benny Goodman (1949), and played with Charlie Parker and others in the mid- and late 1940s. From 1949 to 1961 he was associated intermittently with Art Blakey, recording with him in 1953, 1957, and 1958, and during the 1950s and 1960s he worked with the popular musicians Tony Bennett, Xavier Cugat, and Sammy Davis, Jr. He moved to Sweden in 1967, and soon became an important, and sometimes controversial, member of the jazz community there. He led his own groups, including one called New Burnt Sugar, and also played with several Swedish bands. In 1972 Martinez worked with Peter Herbolzheimer's big band Rhythm Combination & Brass, and the following year he published a book of exercises for conga players.

SELECTED RECORDINGS

As leader: *Palo Congo* (1957, BN 1561); *Afro Temple* (1973, Grammofonverket 7361)

As sideman: A. Blakey: *Orgy in Rhythm* (1957, BN 1554–5); G. Russell: *Vertical Form VI* (1977, SN 1019)

BIBLIOGRAPHY

Feather–Gitler '70s
L. Mattsson: "Sabu Martinez: Levnadsglad slagverkare" [Percussionist who is happy to be alive], *Orkester journalen*, xxxvi (1968), April, 8
Obituary, H. Nicolausson, *Orkester journalen*, xlvii (1979), Feb, 5

ROLAND BAGGENAES

Martino [Azzara], **Pat** (*b* Philadelphia, 25 Aug 1944). Electric guitarist. He played professionally from the age of 15 with the saxophonists Willis "Gator" Jackson and Red Holloway, and later performed in several ensembles led by the organists Don Patterson, Jimmy Smith, Jack McDuff, Richard "Groove" Holmes, and Jimmy McGriff. In 1966 he attracted critical attention as a member of John Handy's group, and from the late 1960s has led his own bands with such sidemen as Cedar Walton, Richard Davis, and Billy Higgins. He has also taught privately; with T. Baruso, he wrote a guitar method, *Linear Expressions* (1983). In the 1970s Martino showed an interest in the music of the classical composers Karlheinz Stockhausen and Elliott Carter. He suffered a seizure in 1980 and an aneurysm was discovered; an operation to correct his condition caused a temporary loss of memory, and he did not resume playing until 1984. Although he has not been particularly influential, Martino has a high reputation as a strong and consistently tasteful improviser with excellent technique. He has cited Johnny Smith and Wes Montgomery as his principal influences. With Montgomery, Barney Kessel, and George Benson, he is one of the better-known guitarists often to improvise lines in octaves. With the jazz-rock guitarists John McLaughlin and Pat Metheny, Martino is also one of the contemporary figures to employ the electric 12-string guitar.

SELECTED RECORDINGS

El Hombre (1967, Prst. 7513); *East* (1968, Prst. 7562); *Footprints* (1972, Cob. 9015); *Consciousness* (1974, Muse 5039)

BIBLIOGRAPHY

K. Hazen: "Lightning Bug in Eclectic Jar," *DB*, xlii/16 (1975), 16
V. Trigger: "Pat Martino," *The Guitar Player Book* (Saratoga, CA, and New York, 1978, 2/1979) [colln of previously pubd articles]
F. Davis: "Playing without Memory," *JT* (1985), March, 9

MARK C. GRIDLEY/R

Martiny, Lajos (*b* Budapest, 11 June 1912; *d* Budapest, 14 Sept 1985). Hungarian pianist and bandleader. He learned violin and piano as a child and performed in local cafés when he was studying music in Budapest (from 1928). After playing in Hungary, Denmark, and Germany with the Blue Boys (1932–6), he led his own group in Switzerland (1936–9) and Hungary (1940–44). From 1946 he performed as a bandleader in Budapest, where in 1948–9 he led the big band of Magyar Rádió. He worked with his own quartet (1950–62), which toured Poland, East Germany, and the USSR (1956), and West Germany (1958), and later led a quartet with Jenő Beamter (1981–4). Martiny made many recordings as a leader from 1940 into the 1960s, among them *Perzsa vásár* (In a Persian market, 1960, Qualiton LPT7097). His works as an arranger include the soundtrack to the film *Karussell* (1941).

BIBLIOGRAPHY

G. G. Simon: "Egy magyar jazzpionír: Martiny Lajos," *Jazz*, no.1 (Budapest, 1986), 16
——: "A Hungarian Jazz-pioneer: Lajos Martiny," *It's a Hap-hap-happy Day: Recordings from the 40's* (Black Jack 3017, 1987) [liner notes]
——: *Lajos Martiny: a Discography* (in preparation)

GÉZA GÁBOR SIMON, RAINER E. LOTZ

Martyn, Barry [Kid; Godfrey, Barry Martin] (*b* London, 23 Feb 1941). Drummer. He began playing in 1955 and the following year formed his own band; he made his first recordings in 1959. In 1961 he visited New Orleans, where he studied with Cié Frazier and made the first of a series of documentary recordings for his label Mono. He subsequently recorded in New Orleans with such players as Kid Sheik Colar (1963) and Capt. John Handy and Percy Humphrey (both 1966), and accompanied American musicians who toured in Europe, notably George Lewis (i) (1965) and Colar, Handy, Albert Nicholas, and Louis Nelson (all 1966). Martyn settled in Los Angeles in 1972. The following year he founded the LEGENDS OF JAZZ, a band of elderly traditional jazz musicians, with which he toured extensively. He moved in 1984 to New Orleans, where he has continued to play and record; he has also conducted oral history interviews with more than 40 musicians for the archives at Tulane and Rutgers universities and has written extensively on early jazz. Martyn's small-group drumming is best heard in his trio with Barney Bigard and Duke Burrell on *Barney Bigard & the Pelican Trio* (1976, Crescent 5) and his work with brass bands on *Last of the Line* (1983, GHB 170), recorded by the Eagle Brass Band.

BIBLIOGRAPHY

Feather–Gitler '70s
D. Pawson: "Barry Martyn's Mono Label," *Fn*, xiv/2 (1982–3), 13
A. Ashforth: "The Eagle Brass Band in Los Angeles," *Fn*, xv/2 (1983–4), 4

ALYN SHIPTON

Masekela, Hugh (Ramopolo) (*b* Witbank, South Africa, 4 April 1939). South African trumpeter, flugelhorn player, and singer. At the age of 19 he joined Alfred Herbert's African Jazz Revue, which played an amalgam of jazz and *mbaqanga*, a type of popular music from the South African townships. With Dollar Brand, the drummer Makaya Ntshoko, the trombonist Jonas Gwanga, and the alto saxophonist Kippie Moeketsi, he formed the Jazz Epistles (1959) to play "township bop." In 1961 he left South Africa with his wife, the folksinger Miriam Makeba, and moved to the USA; he studied at the Manhattan School of Music, then moved to California, where over the next ten years he recorded eight albums on his own label, Chisa, in a style that may be described as African cool jazz. He recorded the impressive album *Home is where the Music is* with Ntshoko and Dudu Pukwana in 1972, then toured Guinea with the Ghanaian band Hedzollah Zoundz and took it to California to make a series of recordings; the best of these, *I am Not Afraid* (1974), includes the song *Stimela* (Coal train), which is notable for Masekela's plaintive, passionate flugelhorn playing. He left the USA in 1982 for Botswana, joined the Kalahari Band, a group based in South Africa, and recorded two jazz-funk albums. In the mid-1980s he was associated with the popular singer Paul Simon, recorded several albums as a leader, and produced recordings by Makeba.

SELECTED RECORDINGS

As leader: *Home is where the Music is* (1972, Chisa 6003); *I am Not Afraid* (1974, Chisa 6015); with Herb Alpert: *Main Event* (1978, A&M Hor. 4727); *Technobush* (1984, Jive 64); *Waiting for the Rain* (1985, Jive 25)

BIBLIOGRAPHY

H. Mandel: "Hugh Masekela: the Colonialization of the Ooga-booga Man," *DB*, xliii/9 (1976), 18 [incl. discography]
C. de Ledesma: "Hugh Masekela," *The Wire*, no.10 (1984), 40 [incl. discography]

CHARLES DE LEDESMA

Masetti, Glauco (*b* Milan, 19 April 1922). Italian alto saxophonist and clarinetist. He studied violin at the conservatories of Milan and Turin (to 1940) and taught himself to play clarinet and alto saxophone. He recorded with Gil Cuppini's sextet in 1947 and 1949, and as a studio musician worked with many groups from 1950 to 1955, effecting a smooth transition from dixieland to bop. He performed with Cuppini, Gianni Basso, and Oscar Valdambrini, then formed a swing sextet in 1955 (with which he made some recordings), and played in the Sestetto jazz moderno with Cuppini and Eraldo Volonté (1956–8); he also worked as a leader (1956–61) and recorded with Chet Baker (1959). From 1962 to 1969 he worked principally with Cuppini and Giorgio Gaslini; later he played alto saxophone for RAI in Milan, worked in big bands, and again formed a swing sextet that recorded in 1974. Masetti can be heard playing alto saxophone on the track *Laura* from Cuppini's album *A New Day* (1980, RR 154).

ADRIANO MAZZOLETTI

Masman, Theo Uden (*b* Tjirebon, Dutch East Indies [now Cirebon, Indonesia], 15 March 1901; *d* The Hague, 27 Jan 1965). Dutch bandleader and pianist. He studied piano at the Rotterdam Conservatory in the Netherlands, wrote compositions from the early 1920s, and played piano in the Queen's Melodists; he first worked professionally as a member of the Resonance Seven (1926). Masman is best known for his association with the RAMBLERS, which he formed in September 1926 and led until 1964. His work as a pianist is well represented by the recording *Ramblers Alabama Swing* (1933–5, Panachord 2004).

WIM VAN EYLE

Mason, Harvey (, Sr.) (*b* Atlantic City, NJ, 22 Feb 1947). Drummer. He attended the Berklee College of Music for a year and a half and received a degree in music education from the New England Conservatory. He toured for four months with Erroll Garner (1970) and worked for 13 months with George Shearing (1970–71), with whom he recorded. After moving to Los Angeles he worked in television and films and recorded with Quincy Jones and Herbie Hancock (both 1973), Donald Byrd, Gerry Mulligan (at Carnegie Hall), Freddie Hubbard, and Grover Washington, Jr. (all 1974), Lee Ritenour (1977), and Victor Feldman (*c*1983); he also played as a sideman with Duke Ellington, Bob James, and George Benson. One of the most sought-after studio musicians in Los Angeles, Mason has worked in a range of popular music styles; his clear, rhythmic playing is well suited to jazz-funk, and was an important element in the success of such innovative hit recordings as Hancock's *Chameleon* (1973), Washington's *Mister Magic* (1974), and Benson's *Breezin'* (1976).

SELECTED RECORDINGS

As leader: *Marching in the Streets* (1975, Ari. 4054); *World Class* (1981, Ari. 4283)

As sideman: H. Hancock: *Headhunters* (1973, Col. KC32731), incl. Chameleon; G. Washington, Jr.: *Mister Magic* (1974, Kudu 20); G. Benson: *Breezin'* (1976, WB 3111)

BIBLIOGRAPHY

Feather–Gitler '70s
L. Underwood: "Profile: Harvey Mason," *DB*, xlii/14 (1975), 32
L. Feather: "Blindfold Test: Harvey Mason," *DB*, xliii/3 (1976), 33
R. Flans: "Harvey Mason," *MD*, v/5 (1981), 10

JEFF POTTER

Mason, Rod (*b* Plymouth, England, 28 Sept 1940). English trumpeter and bandleader. He made his professional début playing with Cy Laurie (1959) and later worked with Monty Sunshine (1962–6) and Acker Bilk (1970–71). Mason took part in sessions with such musicians as the reed player Ian Wheeler and the pianist Ray Foxley (both 1974), and has recorded ten albums as a leader (1974–85); his playing may be heard to advantage on the album *Rod Mason–Ian Wheeler Band* (1974, WAM LP5008) and, with Foxley, on *Six for Two* (1979, Jeton 1003309). During the 1980s he performed as a member of the Dutch Swing College Band, but left the group in 1985 to work throughout Europe as a freelance bandleader. Mason has a wide range and great stamina; his playing, particularly during the time he spent with Bilk, is reminiscent of Louis Armstrong. (D. Fairweather: "Mason, Rod," in I. Carr, D. Fairweather, and B. Priestley: *Jazz: the Essential Companion*, London, 1987)

Massey, Cal (*b* Philadelphia, 11 Jan 1927 or 1928; *d* New York, 25 Oct 1972). Composer. He studied trumpet with Freddie Webster and played in the big bands of Jay McShann, Jimmy Heath, and Billie Holiday. From the mid-1950s, however, he concentrated on composition, and between 1956 and 1958 led an ensemble in Philadelphia that performed his own music; its sidemen included Jimmy Garrison, McCoy Tyner, and Al "Tootie" Heath, and it featured such guest artists as John Coltrane and Donald Byrd. Among other musicians who recorded Massey's compositions are Jackie McLean, Philly Joe Jones, Lee Morgan, Freddie Hubbard, Coltrane, and Archie Shepp. Massey worked and toured extensively with Shepp from 1969 to 1972, and in 1970, with the keyboard player Romulus Franceschini, founded the Romas Orchestra, which also performed his own compositions. His last work was for a musical play about Billie Holiday, *Lady Day: a Musical Tragedy* (1972).

RECORDED COMPOSITIONS
(selective list)

J. Coltrane: on *Coltrane* (1957, Prst. 7105), Bakai; P. J. Jones: on *Blues for Dracula* (1958, Riv. 282), Fiesta; F. Hubbard: on *Here to Stay* (1962, BN 84135), Assunta, Father and Son; J. McLean: on *Demon's Dance* (1967, BN 84345), Message from Trane, Toyland

BIBLIOGRAPHY

Feather–Gitler '70s
J. Welch: "Cal Massey's Odyssey," *DB*, xxxix/2 (1972), 20

ANDREW JAFFE

Masso, George (*b* Cranston, RI, 17 Nov 1926). Trombonist. He worked with Jimmy Dorsey in 1948, then from the mid-1950s until 1973 taught music, first in public schools and later at the University of Connecticut. Thereafter he resumed playing professionally, touring Europe with Benny Goodman's sextet (1973) and touring and recording with the World's Greatest Jazz Band (1975–6). He also recorded with Buck Clayton (*Buck Clayton Jam Session*, 1975, Chi. 143), Goodman (1978), Scott Hamilton and Warren Vaché (1979), and Woody Herman (1983), and as a leader (1978–83). He continued to play with the World's Greatest Jazz Band on occasion into the mid-1980s.

BIBLIOGRAPHY

Feather–Gitler '70s
E. Cook: "George Masso," *JJI*, xxxviii/3 (1985), 13
D. Herdegen: "George Masso," *Cadence*, xiii/9 (1987), 5
W. V. Vaché, Sr.: "Transcendent Trombone," *MR*, xiv/8 (1987), 1

Master (i). The original circular block, magnetic tape, or digital disc on which a sound recording is made; the word is also applied, adjectivally (and more broadly), to any image of the recording in the early stages of the pressing process from which further copies are made, and in this sense it may be synonymous with the terms "matrix" and "mother" (*see* Recording, §I, 1(i)). Consequently, throughout the pre-tape era, the term "master number" is synonymous with Matrix number. With the advent of mastering on magnetic tape, the notion of a matrix number lost its meaning, but the term "master number" continued to be used sometimes, identifying not an independent object (the disc), but instead a section of a reel of tape on which a performance of a particular title is preserved. An example of this usage may be found in the numbering system of Atlantic Records, which continued to assign master numbers to individual titles (and sometimes, new master numbers to edited versions of those titles) throughout the microgroove era. A "master pressing" is one made from a master cut directly from a microphone or recording horn, as opposed to a "dub pressing," which is one made from a master cut from a pre-existing pressing.

Master (ii). Record label. It was founded in February 1937 by Irving Mills to issue recordings by musicians under his management, including Duke Ellington. The material was recorded and pressed by Brunswick, and the catalogue consisted of 40 items that were put out between 1 April and 16 July 1937. Reissues began shortly thereafter on Brunswick, to which artists and repertory had been transferred by the end of the year. Mills also established a low-price label, Variety (*see* Variety (ii)).

BIBLIOGRAPHY

B. Whyatt: "Discography: Master and Variety," *Vintage Jazz Mart* (April 1970), 2
B. Rust: *The American Record Label Book* (New Rochelle, NY, 1978), 187

Master Jazz Recordings. Record company and label. The company was established in 1967 by Bill Weilbacher and Don Kanter, and was devoted to recording mainstream jazz. The catalogue included several important albums by artists such as Earl Hines, Jimmy Rushing, and Buddy Tate, and several anthologies of piano music under the series title Master Jazz Piano. The label was also used to re-release the recordings made by Stanley Dance for Felsted in 1958–9. Operations ceased in the mid-1970s, but much of the catalogue has remained available on the labels Swaggie (in Australia) and Bittersweet. (S. Dance: "Lightly and Politely, 1112: MJR," *JJ*, xx/12 (1967), 14)

Master rhythm part. A score usually notated on two staves and showing the melody, bass line, chord symbols, lyrics (if any), and essential elements of the inner lines; *see* Notation, §2.

Mastersounds. Quartet. It was formed in California in 1957 by two of the Montgomery brothers, Buddy and Monk, with the pianist Richie (Richard Arthur) Crabtree (*b* Sidney, MT, 23 Feb 1934) and the drummer Benny (Ben Caldwell) Barth (*b* Indianapolis, 16 Feb 1929). Its instrumentation was modeled on that of the Modern Jazz Quartet (with electric bass guitar rather than double bass), and it specialized in the performance of mild bop versions of songs from the musical theater – a fashion initiated by André Previn and Shelly Manne. Wes Montgomery also played on the album *Kismet* (1958). After disbanding as a working group in 1960 the quartet continued to record (1960–61); it re-formed briefly in 1965. (*See also* MONTGOMERY.)

BARRY KERNFELD

Mastren, Carmen (Nicholas) [Mastandrea, Carmine Niccolo] (*b* Cohoes, NY, 6 Oct 1913; *d* Valley Stream, NY, 31 March 1981). Acoustic guitarist and arranger. In his youth he learned banjo and violin, and played in a family band with his brothers John, Frank, Eddie, and Al. By 1931 he was working as a professional musician, and in 1935 he moved to New York, where he soon joined Wingy Manone. From 1936 to 1940 he played with Tommy Dorsey, during which time he was named "best guitarist" by *Down Beat* (1937) and *Metronome* (1939, 1940). He also wrote arrangements for Dorsey's orchestra, and his version of Anton Rubinstein's *Melody in F* reveals a competent, if conventional, hand. After working with Joe Marsala (1940–41) he became a staff musician for NBC. His army service (1943–5) included a tour of Europe with Glenn Miller's band, after which he did freelance studio work as a guitarist, conductor, and arranger. He rejoined NBC (1953–70), then during the 1970s worked with the New York Jazz Repertory Company. Mastren's solos on *Squeeze me* (recorded with the Bechet–Spanier Big Four, 1940) and *There's frost on the moon* (with Dorsey, 1936) are fine examples of the chordal solo style that was eclipsed by the single-string solo style of Charlie Christian.

Mastren's younger brother Al Mastren was a trombonist who recorded with the big bands of Red Norvo (1936–8), Miller (1939), Bob Chester (1940–43), Woody Herman (1943–4), Benny Goodman (intermittently, 1943–5), and Dorsey (1946–7).

SELECTED RECORDINGS

As sideman with T. Dorsey: There's frost on the moon (1936, Vic. 25482); Melody in F (1937, Vic. 25519); After I say I'm sorry (1940, Vic. 26518)
As sideman with others: Delta Four: Swingin' on that Famous Door (1935, Decca 737); Bechet–Spanier Big Four: Squeeze me (1940, HRS 2003)

BIBLIOGRAPHY

ChiltonW; *FeatherE*; *Feather–Gitler '70s*
A. Berle: "Carmen Mastren: from Big Bands to the Today and Tonight Shows," *GP*, xii/7 (1978), 32
M. Grosz and L. Cohn: Liner notes, *The Guitarists* (TL 12, 1980)

DAVID FLANAGAN

Masuda, Ichiro (*b* Tokyo, 23 May 1933). Japanese vibraphonist. He studied at Maiji University in Tokyo and played guitar before taking up vibraphone. He played with the double bass player Mitsuru Ono and his six brothers and with a quintet led by Eiji Kitamura (from 1956), and formed a quartet in 1976. His playing has been influenced most strongly by Milt Jackson, but in his performances with such swing groups as Kitamura's quintet it has also recalled the work of Lionel Hampton. In addition to his career as a performer he has worked occasionally as a sound engineer.

SELECTED RECORDINGS

As leader: *So Sorry Please* (1976, Toho–Maslafon YX6102); *Song is Ended* (1976, Vic. SPX1036) [with Hank Jones as sideman]; with R. Brown: *The Most Special Joint* (1977, Vic. SGS6); with H. Matsumoto: *The Blues* (1980, Nippon Phonogram–Next Wave 25PJ1009); *The Swing Session* (1982, Tei. 5002); *Duology* (1983, Lobster LFIA1042)

YOZO IWANAMI

Masuda, Mikio (*b* Osaka, Japan, 14 Aug 1949). Japanese pianist and leader. He is self-taught, and played in Osaka before moving to Tokyo in 1969. He worked at clubs with Isao Suzuki and the trombonist Hiroshi Suzuki, and performed at jazz festivals in Japan, Europe, and the USA. In 1973 he performed, toured Europe, and recorded with Terumasa Hino's hard-bop group. After moving to New York he played with Art Blakey and recorded the album *Trace* (EW 7004) as a leader (both 1974). Thereafter he recorded with Hino (on piano and electric piano, 1975), with the tenor saxophonist Kohsuke Mine (1975, 1976), and again as a leader (1976). (*Feather–Gitler '70s*)

Masuo, Yoshiaki (*b* Tokyo, 12 Oct 1946). Japanese guitarist. His father was a pianist with the group Old Boys. He took up guitar while in his teens and was strongly influenced by Grant Green. He attended Waseda University, Tokyo, which he left after joining Sadao Watanabe's quintet in 1968; he then settled in New York (1971), where he played with Lee Konitz (1972–3) and Mike Brecker and belonged to Sonny Rollins's group (1973–5).

SELECTED RECORDINGS

Wind of Barcelona (1969, CBS–Sony 23AP1076); *111 Sullivan St.* (1975, EW 8020); *Sailing Wonder* (1977, King–EB SKS8001); *Sunshine Avenue* (1979, King–EB 8005); *Good Morning* (1979, King–EB SKS8013); *Mellow Focus* (1982, Casablanca 28P29)

BIBLIOGRAPHY

Feather–Gitler '70s

YOZO IWANAMI

Mathews, Emmett (*b* St. Louis, *c*1902). Saxophonist and singer. After working in St. Louis in the early 1920s he moved to New York, where he played with Edgar Hayes (1928) and Bill Benford (1930); he led his own bands there (1930) and in Chicago (1931). He then returned to New York and joined the band of the double bass player Charlie Turner, which later accompanied Fats Waller; Mathews may be heard playing soprano saxophone on Waller's *Fat and Greasy* (1935, first issued on an untitled album on the Rarest Fats Waller label, RFW1, *c*1966). In 1936 he recorded with a group of Waller's sidemen; Mathews led the sessions and played alto saxophone and sang. He remained with Waller until 1937, when he re-formed his own band, which played in theaters in New York. During the 1940s and 1950s he worked with a vocal group led by Steve Gibson. His name is sometimes spelled Matthews.

based on *ChiltonW*

Mathews, Mat [Schwartz, Matthieu] (*b* The Hague, 18 June 1924). Dutch accordionist. After playing in a Dutch group, the Millers (1947–50), and performing on BBC radio he moved to New York in 1952 and formed a quartet. From 1953 to 1961 he recorded several albums (including *Mat Mathews Quintet*, 1953–4, Bruns. 54013) in a bop style with such sidemen as Kenny Clarke, Art Farmer, Percy Heath, Herbie Mann, and Oscar Pettiford. He also recorded with Carmen McRae (1954–5) and Joe Puma and Rita Reys (both 1957), and worked frequently in studios in New York. In 1964 he returned to the Netherlands, where he arranged and produced music for television, radio, and films. He worked with the Millers again from 1968 to 1984. (*FeatherE*)

Mathews, Ronnie [Ronald Albert] (*b* New York, 2 Dec 1935). Pianist. He studied piano, theory, and composition at Brooklyn College and the Manhattan School of Music (BM 1959). After brief periods with Kenny Dorham and Roy Haynes he worked with Max Roach (1963–8), Freddie Hubbard (1964–*c*1966), and Art Blakey (1968–9, 1975), making tours of Europe and Japan with both Roach and Blakey. He played with Louis Hayes (from 1972) and Clark Terry, then joined Hayes and Woody Shaw to accompany Dexter Gordon when the saxophonist returned to the USA from Europe in 1976. (Shaw recorded Mathews's composition *Jean-Marie* in the same year.) Thereafter Mathews toured and recorded (1978) with Johnny Griffin and made a number of recordings under his own name. His playing style reflects the influence of the major pianists of the modal-jazz period, notably McCoy Tyner and Herbie Hancock.

SELECTED RECORDINGS

As leader: *Legacy* (1958, 1979, BH 7011); *Roots, Branches, and Dances* (1978, BH 7008); *So Sorry Please . . .* (1985, Nilva 3414)

As sideman: W. Shaw: *Little Red's Fantasy* (1976, Muse 5103), incl. Jean-Marie; J. Griffin: *Return of the Griffin* (1978, Gal. 5117)

BIBLIOGRAPHY

Feather–Gitler '70s

H. Saunders: "Ronnie Mathews: Quiet Determination," *JSN*, i/5 (1980), 35

ANDREW JAFFE

Mathewson, Ron [Rognvald Andrew] (*b* Lerwick, Scotland, 19 Feb 1944). Scottish bass player. Born into a musical family, he played piano from the age of eight and took up double bass when he was 15. His first professional engagement was in Germany in 1962 with a dixieland band, the Clyde Valley Stompers; he later played in London with Alex Welsh's band and various other rhythm-and-blues and traditional bands, and recorded with Wild Bill Davison (1965) and with Earl Hines, Rex Stewart, and Bud Freeman (all 1966). From 1966 to 1973 he worked with Tubby Hayes, recording with him in 1966–7 and 1969. Thereafter he was associated with Philly Joe Jones (recording in 1968), Ronnie Scott (from 1968), the Clarke–Boland Big Band (recording in 1969), Ray Nance (recording in 1971), Charles Tolliver (recording in 1972), Francy Boland's orchestra, Stan Getz, the Brecker Brothers, Roy Eldridge, Bill Evans (ii), Joe Henderson, Oscar Peterson, and Ben Webster; he toured with Stan Getz in Scandinavia (1970) and with Phil Woods in the USA (1971), and recorded with Woods at the Montreux International Jazz Festival (1972). Mathewson has played with British groups led by Gordon Beck, the saxophonist Stan Sulzmann (recording in 1977), the rock drummer Charlie Watts, John Taylor, and Kenny Wheeler, and has been a member of Paz. He has occasionally led his own ensembles, notably the Ron Mathewson Six Piece (which recorded with Shorty Rogers in 1984). A versatile and thoughtful musician, he is at home in many different styles and has an accomplished and highly accurate technique.

For illustration *see* Nightclubs and other venues, fig.2.

SELECTED RECORDINGS

As sideman: T. Hayes: *Mexican Green* (1967, Fon. 911); F. Boland: *Blue Flame* (1976, MPS 229106); [no leader]: *Seven Steps to Evans* (1979, MPS 68248)

BIBLIOGRAPHY

R. Cotterrell, ed.: *Jazz Now: the Jazz Centre Society Guide* (London, 1976)

I. Carr: "Mathewson, Ron," in I. Carr, D. Fairweather, and B. Priestley: *Jazz: the Essential Companion* (London, 1987)

SIMON ADAMS

Mathisen, (Hans) Leo (*b* Copenhagen, 10 Oct 1906; *d* Copenhagen, 16 Dec 1969). Danish pianist, singer, bandleader, composer, and arranger. He played in the group We Three with Otto Lington and Anker Skjoldborg (1927–8), toured Germany and Sweden (1928–31), and worked with Kai Julian (1932) and Erik Tuxen (1932–6). From 1936 to 1951 he worked as a leader (his bands were especially prominent during World War II), and recorded prolifically as a soloist (*A Wee Bit of Swing*, 1941, Odeon D515), as a singer and leader of a small group modeled after the groups of Fats Waller (*Take it Easy*, 1941, Odeon D504), and with big bands (*Jungle Party*, 1942, Odeon D792); many of his recordings were of his own compositions. He worked as a lounge pianist in 1951–3, then became inactive owing to failing health. (B. Jørgensen: *Leo Mathisen*, Copenhagen, 1962)

ERIK WIEDEMANN

Matlock, Matty [Julian Clifton] (*b* Paducah, KY, 27 April 1907; *d* Los Angeles, 14 June 1978). Clarinetist and arranger. He learned to play clarinet at the age of 12 and gained early experience in the orchestras led by the pianist Beasley Smith, Jimmy Joy, and the tuba player Frank Tracy and the violinist and saxophonist Nelson Brown. In 1929 he joined Ben Pollack's group in New York and he stayed on when Pollack left in 1934 and Bob Crosby became the leader in 1935; from 1938 Matlock played and toured with the band only intermittently, concentrating instead on writing arrangements for it. When it broke up in 1942 he moved to the West Coast, where he became active as a studio musician. He led his own groups, wrote arrangements for a number of bands, and played with several leaders, including Red Nichols, Pollack, and Rex Stewart; he also led a small group on radio and television programs about the fictional character Pete Kelly and in the film *Pete Kelly's Blues* (1955). He made many recordings as a member of Crosby's reformed bands (1950–52, 1956–7, 1960, 1966) and of the Rampart Street Paraders (1953–4, 1957); he continued to perform until 1975. Matlock was a fine clarinetist and an expert arranger in the dixieland and Chicago styles.

SELECTED RECORDINGS

* – arranged by Matlock

As leader: *Pete Kelly's Blues* (1955, Col. CL690); *Dixieland* (*c*1957, Tops 1569); *The Dixieland Story* (1958, WB 1202); *And they Called it Dixieland* (1958, WB 1262); *Four-Button Dixie* (1958, WB 1280); *Gold Diggers in Dixieland* (1960, WB 1374)

As sideman: B. Pollack: Got the Jitters/I'm full of the Devil (1933, Col. 2870D); Deep Jungle/Swing Out (1933, Col. 2879D); B. Crosby: *Panama (1937, Decca 1615); *Wolverine Blues (1938, Decca 2032); *Honky Tonk Train Blues (1938, Decca 2208); *Mama's Gone, Goodbye/*A vous tout de vey, à vous? (1940, Decca 3056); B. Hackett: *Coast Concert* (1955, Cap. T692); Pete Kelly's Big Seven: *Pete Kelly at Home* (1957, RCA LPM1413)

BIBLIOGRAPHY

FeatherE; *Feather '60s*; *Feather–Gitler '70s*

J. Chilton: *Stomp Off, Let's Go! The Story of Bob Crosby's Bob Cats & Big Band* (London, 1983), 219

WARREN VACHÉ, SR.

Matrix number. A number, or a combination of numbers and letters, assigned by a record company to a master at one of the early stages of the recording process; the term may be used, strictly, only of recordings made before the introduction of magnetic tape. It was derived in the following way: a single number was allocated to a unified body of recorded performances on a single title by a single individual or group. Each separate Take was assigned its own distinct letter or number – called in either case the "take number" – which is considered to be a part of the matrix number. (Some companies assigned an entirely new matrix number to each take.) Thus, for example, on 26 November 1945 Charlie Parker's quintet attempted five takes of *Billie's Bounce*: Savoy Records assigned the letter and numbers S5850 to this title, and the numbers one through five to each take; the full matrix numbers identifying each of the takes thus are S5850-1, S5850-2, S5850-3, S5850-4, S5850-5.

The matrix number might be assigned to the original, fragile master, or to the sturdy disc known as the "matrix" (also called the "mother"; *see* RECORDING, §I, 1(i)). The matrix number was usually etched, embossed, or stamped near the center of the disc and in the final marketed product it usually remained visible in the smooth portion of the disc between the end of the spiral groove and the label, though it was sometimes covered by the label; some record companies printed it on the label itself (*see* RECORDING, fig.4). During the pre-tape era the terms "matrix number" and "master number" are used synonymously (*see also* MASTER (i)). In the 1930s the discographer Charles Delaunay was the first to recognize the significance of this number, which uniquely identifies a take (it thus provides a more accurate means of identifying the recording than the ISSUE NUMBER, which was sometimes the same for different takes).

Although record companies ceased to use matrices with the advent of mastering on magnetic tape, they have continued to assign numbers to masters of distinct sessions, distinct performances of titles, and, sometimes, distinct takes, and they have continued to etch, emboss, or stamp numbers onto discs at various stages in the recording process. These various types of number may appear to be matrix numbers, and have been so called, but such usage is incorrect. A number identifying a master tape may more properly be referred to as a "session number" (if individual titles are not differentiated) or a "master number" (if each title has its own number). A number identifying various stages in the pressing process might be referred to as a "pressing number," "stamper number," or "transfer number." (D. C. Black: *Matrix Numbers, their Meaning and History*, Melbourne, Australia, n.d. [1940s])

Matsumoto, Sleepy [Hidehiko] (*b* Okayama, Tamashimacho, Japan, 12 Oct 1926). Japanese tenor saxophonist. He joined the CB Nine, the first Japanese bop group, in 1949, played with the Six Joes, then formed the Big Four with George Kawaguchi, the pianist Hachidai Nakamura, and the double bass player Mitsuru Ono; in 1959 he joined a quintet led by the drummer Hideo Shiraki. He recorded as a guest soloist with Gerald Wilson's big band at the Monterey (California) Jazz Festival in 1963 and worked as a leader from the following year.

SELECTED RECORDINGS

As leader: *Sleepy* (1976, TBM 74); of Swing Beavers (with M. Ono): *When you are Smiling* (1978, Vic. SJV940); *Great Tenor Sax* (1979, CBS–Sony 28AG413); with I. Masuda: *The Blues* (1980, Nippon Phonogram–Next Wave 25PJ1009); *Rio-Manhattan* (1981, Seven Seas K28P6120); *Hot Jazz* (1983, Union 7005); *Bolero* (1983, RVC–Carnival RJL8078); *40 Years Anniversary* (1987, BGM Vic. R32H-1059)

BIBLIOGRAPHY

FeatherE; *Feather '60s*

YOZO IWANAMI

Matthews, Dave [David] (*b* Chagrin Falls, OH, 6 June 1911). Tenor and alto saxophonist and arranger. He grew up in McAlester, Oklahoma, and studied at Oklahoma University and at Chicago Musical College (to 1930). He played alto saxophone as a sideman with Ben Pollack (1935–6), Jimmy Dorsey (1936–8), and Benny Goodman (1938–9). After leaving Goodman he joined Harry James's first band, and remained until 1940; among his arrangements for this ensemble was *Two o'Clock Jump* (1939). By the time he returned to James in 1941 he had changed permanently to tenor saxophone. As a section player with Hal McIntyre (1941–2), Woody Herman (1942–3), Stan Kenton (1944), and Charlie Barnet (periodically, 1944–9), Matthews took solos only occasionally; he wrote arrangements for all these leaders, notably *Portrait of Edward Kennedy Ellington* for Barnet. He led his own band on the West Coast during the latter half of the 1940s, then worked mostly as an arranger during the next two decades. In the early 1970s he led a band at Lake Tahoe, Nevada. Matthews had an impressive technique, and his alto saxophone playing was inspired by the work of Johnny Hodges; his robust playing on the tenor instrument recalled Coleman Hawkins's style of the mid-1930s. He should not be confused with the pianist and arranger David Matthews (*b* Sonora, KY, 3 April 1942), who led a big band in New York in 1974–5.

SELECTED RECORDINGS

As sideman: B. Goodman: Wrappin' it up (1938, Vic. 25880); B. Freeman: Tappin' the Commodore Till/Memories of you (1938, Com. 508); Life Spears a Jitterbug/What's the Use? (1938, Com. 507); H. James: Two o'Clock Jump (1939, Bruns. 8337); Capitol Jazzmen: Clambake in B Flat (1943, Cap. 10009); In my Solitude (1943, Cap. 10010); on H. L. Page: *Tooting Through the Roof* (1945–6, Onyx 209), Bloodhound [2 versions], You come in here, woman (all 1945); C. Barnet: Portrait of Edward Kennedy Ellington (1949, Cap. 60010)

BIBLIOGRAPHY

ChiltonW; *FeatherE*

SCOTT YANOW

Matthews, Emmett. Form of name by which EMMETT MATHEWS is referred to in some sources.

Matthews, George (*b* Dominica, British West Indies, 23 Sept 1912; *d* New York, 28 June 1982). Trombonist. His family settled in New York during his childhood; after studying at the Martin Smith School of Music there (1927–31) he began to play professionally. In 1934 he joined Tiny Bradshaw, with whom he made his first recording. He went on to perform and record with Willie Bryant (1935–7), Louis Armstrong (1937), Chick Webb and Ella Fitzgerald (1938–41; for illustration *see* WEBB, CHICK), and Lucky Millinder (1945). He spent the next four years with the Count Basie Orchestra, during which time he made many recordings; when Basie disbanded the orchestra in 1950, Matthews joined Erskine Hawkins. From the mid-1950s he worked as a freelance musician, playing with Ray Charles, Clark Terry, and others. Although principally a big-band section player, Matthews made a few recordings with small groups, including Chu Berry's octet (1937) and a nonet drawn from the Count Basie Orchestra (1947). He may be heard as a soloist on *Katy*, recorded with Basie in 1949.

SELECTED RECORDINGS

As sideman: T. Bradshaw: The Darktown Strutters' Ball/The Sheik of Araby (1934, Decca 194); C. Berry: Indiana/Limehouse Blues (1937, Var. 587); C. Basie: Backstage at Stuff's/My Buddy (1947, Vic. 202693); on Basie: *Count Basie and his Orchestra* (1947–50, RCA LPM1112), Katy (1949); E. Hawkins: After Hours/Tuxedo Junction (1950, Coral 60361)

BIBLIOGRAPHY

ChiltonW
P. Carr: "George Matthews," *Mainstream*, no.1 (1974), 21

LAWRENCE KOCH

Matuszkiewicz, Jerzy [Duduś] (*b* Jasło, Poland, 10 April 1928). Polish saxophonist, clarinetist, composer, and leader. An influential figure in the Polish postwar jazz movement, he was the leader of Melomani (formed 1951), a famous group active during the so-called catacomb era of the Stalinist years (1949–55), when jazz was officially banned as a decadent, bourgeois American style and was played only in secret. The group's other members were Andrzej Wojciechowski (trumpet), Witold

Sobocinski (trombone, drums), Andrzej Trzaskowski (piano), and Witold Kujawski (double bass); its repertory ranged from traditional jazz to modern standards. The gradual liberalization in Poland (from 1955) led to a surge of jazz activity, and Melomani began performing at concerts throughout the country and enjoying a massive popular following. Along with Krzysztof Komeda, the group was the main feature at the first Sopot Jazz Festival (1956). It worked as the Hot Club Melomani before disbanding in 1958. Matuszkiewicz later led the Polish All Stars, the Traditional Jazz Makers, the Swingtet, and Big Band Hybrydy; he retired from jazz performance in 1966 to pursue a successful career as a composer of film music.

PAWEL BRODOWSKI

Matyszkowicz, Adam. *See* MAKOWICZ, ADAM.

Maupin, Bennie (*b* Detroit, 29 Aug 1940). Saxophonist and bass clarinetist. He took up saxophone in high school and later attended the Detroit Institute for Musical Arts, though he considers he gained his most significant education through his contact with such musicians as Yusef Lateef, Alice McLeod (later Coltrane), Hugh Lawson, and Barry Harris. In 1963 he moved to New York, where he combined work in soul-jazz organ trios, rock groups, soul groups, and calypso bands with rehearsals and occasional performances with Marion Brown (with whom he later recorded) and Pharoah Sanders. He next played with Roy Haynes (1966–8) and Horace Silver (1968–9). Through contact with Jack DeJohnette he joined the studio group for Miles Davis's album *Bitches Brew* (1969); he also worked with groups led by McCoy Tyner (recording in 1968) and Lee Morgan (recording in 1970). In 1970 he replaced Joe Henderson in Herbie Hancock's sextet; he stayed in the group for most of the decade, though he also recorded with Woody Shaw (1970, 1972) and worked with Hancock's sidemen in the Headhunters, a group that played a fusion of jazz and the popular genre funk. After settling in Los Angeles in 1972 Maupin has both performed and recorded as a leader. A strong soloist, he is best known for his work on saxello and bass clarinet.

SELECTED RECORDINGS

As leader: *The Jewel in the Lotus* (1974, ECM 1043); *Slow Traffic to the Right* (*c*1976–7, Mer. SRM-1-1148)

As sideman: M. Tyner: *Tender Moments* (1967, BN 84275); on H. Silver: *Serenade to a Soul Sister* (1968, BN 84277), Jungle Juice, Kindred Spirits; M. Davis: *Bitches Brew* (1969, Col. GP26); C. Corea: *Sundance* (1969, GM 2202); A. Hill: *One for One* (1969–70, BN LA459H2); J. DeJohnette: *Have You Heard?* (1970, Mlst. 9029); M. Brown: *Afternoon of a Georgia Faun* (1970, ECM 1004); H. Hancock: *Mwandishi* (1971, WB 1898); *Headhunters* (1973, Col. KC32731)

BIBLIOGRAPHY

Feather–Gitler '70s

P. Carles: "Béni soit Maupin," *Jm*, no.162 (1969), 12

E. Meadow: "Meet Benny Maupin," *DB*, xl/1 (1973), 16

R. Townley: "Bennie Maupin: not to be Confused with Bernie Taupin," *DB*, xlii/10 (1975), 17 [incl. discography]

DAVID WILD

Mavounzy, Robert (*b* Panamá, 1917; *d* Paris, March 1974). Guadeloupe clarinetist and alto saxophonist. He was brought up in Guadeloupe from 1928. In 1930 he settled in France and began working in Paris as a drummer in Alexandre Stellio's orchestra. After 1938 he performed with such visiting American musicians as Bill Coleman and led his own band at La Cigale for some time. He made recordings as a clarinetist and alto saxophonist with the Ensemble Swing du Hot Club Colonial (*c*1943), Django Reinhardt (1943), and Harry Cooper (1943, 1946, including *China Boy*, 1946, Swing 236, in the group Jam Session no.6), among others. He also recorded on alto saxophone with his own orchestra (1947, 1954), which included André Persiany. One of the outstanding performers of antillean jazz, Mavounzy was, however, influenced by Benny Carter (1930s) and Charlie Parker (1940s). (A. Boulanger: Liner notes, *Jazz and Hot Dance in Martinique*, Harl. 2018, 1985)

RAINER E. LOTZ

Maxey, Leroy (*b* Kansas City, MO, 6 June 1904). Drummer. In the early 1920s he played with Bennie Moten and Dave Lewis's Jazz Boys. He moved to St. Louis in 1923 to join the Syncopators, a band led by the violinist Wilson Robinson. After touring widely, the band was resident at the Cotton Club, New York; it changed its name to the Missourians before becoming Cab Calloway's orchestra (1930). Maxey made several recordings under Calloway (including *Queen Isabella/Savage Rhythm*, 1937, Var. 662), and remained with the band until 1938, when he became seriously ill and had to cease full-time playing.

based on *ChiltonW*

Maxie. Nickname of LES MCCANN.

Maxted, Billy [William George] (*b* Racine, WI, 21 Jan 1917). Pianist and arranger. From 1937 to 1940 he played with and wrote arrangements for Red Nichols (the band recorded his version of *A pretty girl is like a melody* (Bb 10522) in 1939), and also studied at the Institute of Musical Art. He then worked as a pianist and arranger for Will Bradley (1941–2). After serving in the navy he returned to New York, recorded with Bradley (1946), wrote arrangements for Benny Goodman and Claude Thornhill, and led his own groups, including a band with Ray Eberle (1947–8). From 1949 to 1960 Maxted worked mostly as the resident pianist at Nick's, where he played traditional jazz and specialized in boogie-woogie. He also made recordings with Pee Wee Erwin (1950, 1955), Bob Crosby (*Crosby's Great Hits*, 1960, Dot 25278), and Nichols (1960), and as a leader (1950–66). (*FeatherE*)

Maxwell, Jimmy [James Kendrick] (*b* Stockton, CA, 9 Jan 1917). Trumpeter. He came from a musical family and studied cornet as a child, then trumpet; from the age of 15 he worked professionally and soon after he played with Gil Evans. During the following years he worked with Jimmy Dorsey (1936), Maxine Sullivan (1937), the drummer Skinnay Ennis (1938), and Benny Goodman (1939–43). In 1943 he joined the staff orchestra of CBS and for the next 30 years worked in radio and television; at the same time he belonged to the NBC SO and played occasionally in the bands of Woody Herman (recording in 1958), Count Basie, and Duke Ellington, and later worked with Quincy Jones (recording in 1961 at the Newport Jazz Festival), Oliver Nelson, and Gerry Mulligan; in 1962 he toured the USSR with Goodman. He performed in the 1970s with the New York Jazz Repertory Company and the National Jazz Ensemble and appeared at many festivals into the 1980s. Maxwell's work as the leader of a section is highly regarded; his style as a soloist is reminiscent of that of Cootie Williams.

Oral history material in *NjR* (JOHP).

SELECTED RECORDINGS

As sideman: B. Goodman: The Man I Love (1940, Col. 55001); After you've Gone (1942, Col. 36699); first issued on *Benny and Sid "Roll 'em"* (1942, Honeysuckle Rose 5004-5), Roll 'em; C. Israels: *National Jazz Ensemble*, ii (1976, Chi. 151)

BIBLIOGRAPHY

ChiltonW; *Feather–Gitler '70s*

S. Levy: "Jimmy Maxwell: How my Ducal Dream Came True," *JJI*, xxx/10 (1977), 35

The Battestinis: "Jimmy Maxwell," *BHcF* (1980), no.280, p.16; no.284, p.26 [interview]
E. Townley: "Big Jim," *Sv*, no.98 (1981–2), 60 [interview]

EDDIE LAMBERT

May, Billy [William E.] (*b* Pittsburgh, 10 Nov 1916). Arranger, composer, and trumpeter. He played with and wrote arrangements for Charlie Barnet (1938–40), Glenn Miller (1940–42; for illustration *see* MUTE, fig.3), and Les Brown (1942). In the early 1940s he also worked in studios and as an arranger for NBC; later in the decade he settled in Hollywood, where he provided arrangements for bands led by Phil Harris, Ozzie Nelson, and others, and for Capitol studio orchestras. From 1951 to 1954 he made recordings with his own studio band. He has also written music for television (notably the series *Naked City*), advertisements, films (such as *Nightmare*, 1956, in which he also acted), and recordings (including several albums for Frank Sinatra). Manuscript scores of his works are in the holdings of the BMI Archives in New York.

May is probably best known for his arrangements for Charlie Barnet, which were characterized by wailing, "scooping" saxophones voiced in thirds. His version of Ray Noble's *Cherokee* became a standard of the swing era and also Barnet's signature tune. While with Miller, however, he was more prominent as a trumpeter; good examples of his playing may be heard on *I dreamt I dwelt in Harlem* (1941, Bb 11063) and *American Patrol* (1942, Vic. 27873).

SELECTED ARRANGEMENTS

As leader: *Sorta Dixie* (1955, Cap. T677); *The Great Jimmie Lunceford* (1957, Cap. T924)
Recorded by C. Barnet: In a Mizz (1939, Bb 10191); Cherokee (1939, Bb 10373); D. Ellington and F. Sinatra: *Francis A. and Edward K.* (1964, Rep. 1024)

BIBLIOGRAPHY

A. McCarthy: *Big Band Jazz* (New York and London, 1974)
G. T. Simon: *Glenn Miller and his Orchestra* (New York, 1974)
S. Dance: "Big Band Memories," *JJI*, xxxv/5 (1982), 6
L. Tomkins: "Billy May," *CI*, xx (1985), no.11, p.20; no.12, p.6; xxi/1 (1985), 23

WAYNE SCHNEIDER

May, Earl (Charles Barrington) (*b* New York, 17 Sept 1927). Double bass player. He worked in New York with Gene Ammons, Miles Davis, Sonny Stitt, and Mercer Ellington (all 1951), then played with the trio led by Billy Taylor (ii) (1951–9). Thereafter he played, wrote arrangements, and acted as music director for the singer Gloria Lynne (1959–63). He also recorded with John Coltrane (1957), Chet Baker (1959), Dave McKenna (1960), and Herman Foster (1960–61). After recording with Herbie Mann (1965–7) he toured with Dizzy Gillespie (1971–4), performing in his *Sacred Concert for Jazz Quartet and Chorus* (1974). Around this time he began playing electric bass guitar, working with Joe Newman (1972–3) and Johnny Hartman (1973). Later he performed with Frank Foster in New York, Japan (1977), and Europe (1978–9), and recorded with Archie Shepp (1977) and George Benson. Also involved in musical theater, he played for the shows *Sophisticated Ladies* (on Broadway and national tours, 1981–5) and *Big Deal* (1986). A skilled technician, May is a supportive accompanist with a good sense of swing. His style most closely resembles the work of his contemporaries of the 1950s, notably Oscar Pettiford, Paul Chambers, and Percy Heath.

SELECTED RECORDINGS

(all recorded for Prestige unless otherwise indicated)

As sideman: S. Stitt: For the Fat Man (1951, 831); B. Taylor: Lover (1952, 849); *A Touch of Taylor* (1954, 7001); on J. Coltrane: *Lush Life* (1957–8, 7188), I Love You, Like Someone in Love, Trane's Slow Blues (all 1957); J. Hartman: *Today* (1973, Perceptions 30); G. Benson: *20/20* (?1984, WB 125178)

BIBLIOGRAPHY

Feather '60s
C. Albertson: Liner notes, *A Touch of Taylor* (Prst. 7001, 1955)

JOHN CURRY

Maycock, George (*b* Panama, 9 Sept 1917; *d* New York, 20 Aug 1979). Panamanian pianist. He emigrated to Germany and in 1948 organized the Chic Combo, a bop quintet composed of black musicians from the Caribbean. It recorded five titles (1956, 1959), including *Maycock's Bop* (1956, Phi. 47001), and also the soundtrack for the film *Jazz: Rhythmus der Zeit* (1956). When the group disbanded in the 1960s Maycock continued as a solo entertainer, then, during the 1970s, led and recorded with the Downtown Trio and Quartet. Maycock was influenced by Bud Powell; his groups were modeled after the quintets led by Miles Davis and by Max Roach and Clifford Brown, though they played with strong overtones of the blues. (R. Böttger: Obituary, *JP*, xxviii/10 (1979), 13)

RAINER E. LOTZ

Mayers, Lloyd (G.) (*b* New York, 11 Nov 1929). Pianist. He worked with Eddie "Cleanhead" Vinson (1949), attended the Manhattan School of Music, and played with Dinah Washington (1954–5). In 1956 he recorded with Arnett Cobb and Bennie Green, and during the following years he worked with the singer Josephine Baker (1959–60), Joe Newman (1961, 1965–6), Johnny Griffin (1961), Eddie "Lockjaw" Davis (recording in 1961), Etta Jones and Sam Taylor (recording with both in 1962), and Nancy Wilson (1962–3). After working from 1967 to 1972 as a pianist and arranger for the popular singer Sammy Davis, Jr., he performed and recorded as a member of Mercer Ellington's orchestra from 1974; he also worked as a performer, arranger, and conductor for several Broadway shows from the mid-1970s, including *Bubbling Brown Sugar* (1976), *Comin' Uptown* (1979), and *Sophisticated Ladies* (1981). He performed and recorded with the singer Anita Moore in 1983–4 and worked in Claudio Segovia's and Hector Orezzoli's revue *Black and Blue* in Paris in 1985–6.

SELECTED RECORDINGS

As leader: *A Taste of Honey* (1962, UA 15018)
As sideman: B. Green: *Walking Down* (1956, Prst. 7049); J. Newman: *Live at Count Basie's* (1961, Mer. 60696); M. Ellington: *Continuum* (1974–5, Fan. 9481); A. Moore: *The Lady* (1983, Zeus 1000); T. Brewer and M. Ellington: *Cotton Connection* (1985, Doctor Jazz 40031)

BIBLIOGRAPHY

Feather–Gitler '70s
W. F. Lee: "Lloyd G. Mayers," *People in Jazz: Jazz Keyboard Improvisors of the 19th and 20th Centuries* (Hialeah, FL, 1984)

GREGORY E. SMITH

Mayl, Gene (*b* Dayton, OH, 30 Dec 1928). Double bass and tuba player, and singer. He played with Claude Luter, Claude Bolling, and Don Byas in France (1948–9). In 1948 he founded the Dixieland Rhythm Kings, a traditional jazz band that performed frequently in the USA and Canada into the 1970s and recorded several albums, including *Gene Mayl Dixieland Rhythm Kings* (1953, Riv. 210). Mayl has also performed with Bob Scobey, Muggsy Spanier, Billy Maxted, Wild Bill Davison, and Georg Brunis: he recorded three albums with Brunis (1964, 1965, and 1973). Later he was active in dixieland bands in the Midwest. (*Feather–Gitler '70s*)

Mays, Bill [William Allen] (*b* Sacramento, CA, 5 Feb 1944). Pianist. After studying music at San Diego State College (1965) and elsewhere he worked in Los Angeles as an accompanist to Sarah Vaughan (1972–3) and Al Jarreau (1975). Later he worked with Bobby Shew (1975–83), led his own quartet (1976–7), and performed and recorded with Bud Shank (1976–83), Howard Roberts (1977–80), Shelly Manne (1980, 1982–3), and Benny Golson (1980–83). He also played and recorded with Bob Magnusson and others in the group Road Work Ahead (1979–82). In 1982 he formed a trio, began working as an accompanist to Mark Murphy, and recorded in a duo with Red Mitchell in New York. The following year he made the album *Tha's Delights* (Trend 532) in Los Angeles as the leader of a quintet that included Tom Harrell and Manne, then settled in New York. As well as continuing to lead a quintet, work with Murphy, and play in duos with several distinguished double bass players, Mays has also worked as a sideman with Gerry Mulligan and others. From the early 1980s he has also been active as a composer and arranger.

Mays, Lyle (David) (*b* Wisconsin, 1953). Keyboard player and composer. He studied piano, played with various stage bands in the Midwest, and attended North Texas State University. He toured the USA and Europe with Woody Herman's big band from 1975 until 1976, when he joined Pat Metheny's quartet. During the following decade he worked as a sideman with Metheny, Eberhard Weber, and the singer Joni Mitchell; in 1986 he recorded his first album as a leader. Mays was among the first keyboard players to employ polyphonic synthesizers in concert, which enabled him to provide a rich, complex backing to Metheny's playing; as a soloist he prefers to play acoustic piano. His compositional style is well illustrated by the album *As Falls Wichita, so Falls Wichita Falls* (1980), a collaboration with Metheny that was a critical success.

SELECTED RECORDINGS
(recorded for ECM unless otherwise indicated)

As leader: with P. Metheny: *As Falls Wichita, so Falls Wichita Falls* (1980, 1190); *Lyle Mays* (1986, Geffen 24097)
As sideman with P. Metheny: *Watercolors* (1977, 1097); *The Pat Metheny Group* (1978, 1114); *American Garage* (1979, 1155); *Offramp* (1981, 1216); *Travels* (1982, 1252–3)
As sideman with E. Weber: *Later that Same Evening* (1982, 1231)

BIBLIOGRAPHY

C. Welch: "Lyle: the Young Lion of the Herd," *MM*, li (28 Feb 1976), 41
M. Davis: "Lyle Mays," *CK*, vi/10 (1980), 12
J. Diliberto and K. Haas: "Lyle Mays: Straight Talk on Synths," *DB*, l/7 (1983), 25 [incl. discography]
T. Greenwald: "Lyle Mays: at the Horizons of Jazz with and without Pat Metheny," *Keyboard*, xii/7 (1986), 76 [incl. discography]
G. Santoro: "Lyle Mays: Catching a (Sound) Wave," *DB*, liv/7 (1987), 16 [incl. discography]

PATRICK T. WILL

Mayuto. *See* CORREA, MAYUTO.

Mazur, Marilyn (*b* New York, 8 Jan 1955). Danish drummer, percussionist, bandleader, and composer. She moved to Denmark with her family when she was six. By 1970 she was writing her own compositions, and she took up drums and percussion while working with the group Zirenes (1973–8). From the early 1980s she belonged to the Six Winds, to Finn Savery's trio, and to the New Jungle Orchestra under Pierre Dørge; at the same time she made recordings as the leader of a quartet with the saxophonist Uffe Markussen (*MM4*, 1984, Rosen 28, which includes her composition *Våd vinkel* (Wet corner)) and of the Primi Band, a group comprising ten women (*Primi*, 1984, Rosen 29, which includes her *Ocean Suite*). She later played percussion with Miles Davis (1985–6) and Wayne Shorter (1987).

ERIK WIEDEMANN

Mbira. A type of LAMELLAPHONE.

M' Boom Re: Percussion. Percussion ensemble formed by Max Roach in 1970. It was originally a septet, the members of which were, besides Roach, Roy Brooks, Joe Chambers, Omar Clay, Fred King, Ray Mantilla, and Warren Smith (ii); later it became a group of around ten pieces, including Freddie Waits from 1971. Between them the group's members play more than a hundred percussion instruments, drawn principally from the instrumentaria of Western orchestral, African, and Latin music. By the late 1980s the ensemble had recorded three albums, the first a performance in the Netherlands at the Laren Internationaal Jazz Festival in 1973. For the most part it presents complex improvisations on newly composed themes, but the album *M' Boom Re: Percussion* (1979, Col. IC36247) includes a version of Thelonious Monk and Kenny Clarke's composition *Epistrophy*.

BIBLIOGRAPHY

R. Mattingly and S. Fish: "M' Boom," *MD*, vii/9 (1983), 8 [incl. interviews with Brooks, Chambers, Mantilla, Roach, Smith, and Waits]
C. Fox: "Sit Down and Listen: the Story of Max Roach," *Repercussions: a Celebration of African-American Music*, ed. G. Haydon and D. Marks (London, 1985), 80

Meadowbrook Inn. Ballroom in Cedar Grove, New Jersey; *see* NIGHTCLUBS AND OTHER VENUES.

Medallion. Record label. It was established in 1919 by the Baldwin Piano Co., Cincinnati. Its catalogue was derived entirely from that of the Emerson label, and included early jazz recordings by the Louisiana Five and Eubie Blake.

BIBLIOGRAPHY

C. Kendziora: "Behind the Cobwebs: Medallion," *Record Research*, no.85 (1967), 6
B. Rust: *The American Record Label Book* (New Rochelle, NY, 1978), 189

Mega mute. A type of double mute; *see* MUTE, §2(b).

Meldonian, Dick [Richard Anthony] (*b* Providence, RI, 27 Jan 1930). Alto and tenor saxophonist. He played and recorded in California and on the East Coast with Charlie Barnet (1950–51), then toured and recorded with Stan Kenton (1952; for illustration *see* KENTON, STAN). In 1953 he began to work as a session musician in and around New York, and played in studio bands with Erroll Garner (1957), Gene Roland (1959), and Gerry Mulligan and Bill Russo (both 1960), among others. He led his own small groups in the 1960s and 1970s, and appeared with a quartet at the Newport Jazz Festival in 1964. Besides saxophones, he played clarinet, flute, and oboe; he recorded on tenor saxophone as the leader of a quartet, the Jersey Swingers, in 1978 (*Some of these Days*, Prog. 7033). In the early 1980s he formed a big band with Sonny Igoe, which made recordings in 1982 and 1983, and continued to lead small groups, including a duo and trio with Marty Grosz. (*FeatherE*; *Feather '60s*)

Melillo, Mike [Michael Cosimo] (*b* Newark, NJ, 9 June 1939). Pianist and composer. He studied at Rutgers for four years, then from 1962 to 1964 led the house trio at the Tap Room in Clifton, New Jersey, backing visiting artists such as Sonny Rollins, Phil Woods, Freddie Hubbard, and Grachan Moncur III. He then played with Rollins (1965–7), a musician whom he admires greatly and considers an important influence. He formed his own group with the guitarist Harry Leahey in 1967, but moved initially to a farm in western New Jersey, then in 1973 deep into the Poconos in Pennsylvania to concentrate on composition and the study of music theory. Woods, Steve Gilmore, and Bill Goodwin were all close neighbors, and, with Melillo, formed the Phil Woods Quartet, a successful group that recorded and played together until 1979, when Melillo left to go to Italy. Thereafter he has performed and recorded mostly as a solo pianist, developing a style influenced as much by contemporary classical music as by bop. Among his compositions are *Gee*, *A Little Peace*, and *Sepia (for Charles Ives)*.

SELECTED RECORDINGS

As unaccompanied soloist: *Sepia* (1984, RR 170)
As sideman with P. Woods: *"Live" from the Showboat* (1976, RCA BGL2-2202); *The New Phil Woods Album* (1976, Gryphon BGL1-1391); *Songs for Sisyphus* (1977, Gryphon 782)

BIBLIOGRAPHY

Liner notes, *"Live" from the Showboat* (RCA BGL2-2202, 1976)
J. De Muth: "Phil Woods Quartet: Mike Melillo, Steve Gilmore, Bill Goodwin," *DB*, xlvi/1 (1979), 35

STEVEN STRUNK

Mellophone [tenor cor]. A valved brass instrument, similar in appearance to the orchestral horn, which combines elements of the horn (*see* HORN (2)) and the E♭ alto or tenor horn (*see* SAXHORN). It is built in E♭ or F, an octave higher than the horn; its three valves are operated by the player's right hand, while the left rests in the bell. The mellophone is less technically demanding than the horn and has been used as a substitute for it in jazz: the lip technique is easier to master, the instrument "speaks" more readily, and with skillful manipulation of the left hand it can produce a horn-like sound.

The mellophone was used in marching bands in place of the horn and was taken over, like other brass instruments, into early jazz bands. It formed part of the instrumentation in Fate Marable's riverboat band of 1918 (played by Dave Jones; for illustration *see* MARABLE, FATE), the Friars Society Orchestra (later renamed the New Orleans Rhythm Kings) of 1922 (played by Paul Mares), Doc Cook's orchestra of the 1920s (played by Freddie Keppard and Jerome Don Pasquall), Hot Lips Page's small group of 1938, and Don Elliott's band of the 1960s. In the 1950s C. G. Conn of Elkhart, Indiana, introduced the mellophonium, a variant of the mellophone with the bell facing forwards (instead of upwards), and in 1962–3 Stan Kenton included a section of four of these instruments in his band. The mellophone has always been regarded in jazz as a second instrument for trumpeters, who have used it to provide a contrasting mellow brass sound; but from the 1960s this function seems to have been taken over by the flugelhorn, which trumpeters find more compatible technically with their main instrument.

For bibliography *see* HORN.

CLIFFORD BEVAN

Melly, (Alan) George (Heywood) (*b* Liverpool, England, 17 Aug 1926). English singer. He took up blues singing in the late 1940s and joined Mick Mulligan's Magnolia Jazz Band, with which he performed and recorded until the early 1960s. During this period his repertory was built around the classic blues and vaudeville songs of Bessie Smith. *Gulf Coast Blues* (1957, Decca LK4226) is a fine example of his work at this time. Thereafter he concentrated on journalism and criticism, contributing articles on art and music to many English newspapers and periodicals. He also appeared on a series of television programmes about art. In 1971 he began singing again, and the following year formed a highly successful association with John Chilton's Feetwarmers which has continued into the mid-1980s. He has toured widely in Europe and performed in New York, Australia, and China. The passionate blues style of his early work has been replaced by an ostentatious but highly effective showmanship, which may be heard to advantage on the album *Nuts* (1972, WB K46188). Melly has written three volumes of autobiography, of which *Owning Up* (London, 1965) is an account of his early career as a jazz singer.

BIBLIOGRAPHY

P. Devlin: "Mellymania," *Vogue*, cxxx/5 (1973), 118
A. Shipton: "George Melly," *Isis* (4 May 1973), 18
R. Cotterell, ed.: *Jazz Now: the Jazz Centre Society Guide* (London, 1976), 149
D. Fairweather: "Melly, George," in I. Carr, D. Fairweather, and B. Priestley: *Jazz: the Essential Companion* (London, 1987)

CLARRIE HENLEY

Melotone. Record label. It was established by Warner Bros. in November 1930 as a subsidiary of Brunswick, and was continued by Consolidated Film Industries after it acquired Brunswick in December 1931. Its catalogue included much popular music; most of the jazz items were commercially oriented, and included a series of dance records made under Benny Goodman's leadership. From November 1932 Melotone was operated by the AMERICAN RECORD COMPANY as one of five "dime-store" labels, being used to issue cheap records. As well as jazz records in a popular series, the repertory also included a substantial race catalogue. CBS purchased ARC–BRC in February 1938 and discontinued Melotone shortly thereafter.

BIBLIOGRAPHY

J. Godrich and R. M. W. Dixon: *Blues & Gospel Records, 1902–1942* (Hatch End, nr London, 1964, rev. 2/1969, rev. and enlarged 3/1982 as R. M. W. Dixon and J. Godrich: *Blues & Gospel Records, 1902–1943*), 20
R. M. W. Dixon and J. Godrich: *Recording the Blues* (London, 1970)
R. D. Kinkle: "Melotone Numerical List," *The Complete Encyclopedia of Popular Music and Jazz, 1900–1950*, iv (New Rochelle, NY, and Westport, CT, 1974), 2222
B. Rust: *The American Record Label Book* (New Rochelle, NY, 1978), 192

Melrose, Frank(lyn Taft) (*b* Sumner, IL, 26 Nov 1907; *d* nr Hammond, IN, 1 Sept 1941). Pianist and bandleader. He was active mainly in and around Chicago; he first recorded with Junie and Jimmy Cobb (1928) and as a leader (1929–30), sometimes using the pseudonyms Kansas City Frank and Broadway Rastus, and also recorded with Johnny and Baby Dodds in the Beale Street Washboard Band, and with the Cobbs in the Windy Rhythm Kings and Kansas City Tin Roof Stompers (all 1929). He also worked in Kansas City, New York, Detroit, and St. Louis, occasionally on violin, but more often playing piano in a vigorous barrelhouse style; *Jelly Roll Stomp* (1929, Bruns. 7062) is a good example of his work in this vein. After recording in 1930 with the Cellar Boys (a group that included Wingy Manone, Frank Teschemacher, and Bud Freeman) he played with the clarinetist Bud Jacobson in 1933 at the World's Fair in Chicago, where he then remained, working in various clubs.

BIBLIOGRAPHY

ChiltonW; *FeatherE*
J. Steiner: "Kansas City Frank," *Jazz*, i/8 (1943), 5
P. Daily: "Barrelhouse Frank Melrose," *Piano Jazz*, i (London, 1945); repr. in *Selections from the Gutter: Jazz Portraits from "The Jazz Record"*, ed. A. Hodes and C. Hansen (Berkeley, CA, Los Angeles, and London, 1977)
E. H. Newberger: "The Development of New Orleans and Stride Piano Styles," *JJS*, iv/2 (1977), 43 [incl. transcr. of part of *Jelly Roll Stomp*]

Melvoin, Mike [Michael] (*b* Oshkosh, WI, 10 May 1937). Pianist and organist. He began playing piano at the age of three. He studied English at Dartmouth College (BA 1959), and first played professionally in New York in 1959. After moving to the West Coast in 1961 he worked with Frank Rosolino, Leroy Vinnegar, Gerald Wilson, Paul Horn, and Terry Gibbs; he recorded with Vinnegar in 1963–4 and Gibbs in 1966. In 1964 Melvoin toured New Zealand as an accompanist to the singer Gene McDaniels; he also worked with Joe Williams and Peggy Lee. Later he recorded with a sextet led by Herb Ellis and Ray Brown, and with Plas Johnson (1975–6). Although Melvoin's performances are in the mainstream style, his influences include hard bop, the West Coast school, and the playing of Bill Evans (ii).

SELECTED RECORDINGS

As sideman: L. Vinnegar: *Walker* (1964, VJ 2502); Milt Jackson: *Memphis Jackson* (1969, Imp. 9193); H. Ellis and R. Brown: *Hot Tracks* (1975, Conc. 12)

BIBLIOGRAPHY

Feather '60s

PAUL RINZLER

Mengelberg, Misha [Misja] (*b* Kiev, Ukrainian SSR, 5 June 1935). Dutch pianist and composer of Ukrainian birth. His father, Karel Mengelberg, and great-uncle, Willem Mengelberg, were conductors. He studied at the Royal Conservatory in The Hague (1958–64) and won a first prize at the jazz festival in Loosdrecht, near Hilversum (1959). He played on Eric Dolphy's last album (1964) and with Piet Noordijk led a quartet that appeared at the Newport Jazz Festival in 1966; the same year he was awarded the Dutch National Jazz Prize. In 1967 he was a founder of the Instant Composers Pool, a nonprofit organization that sponsors performances and recordings by members of the Dutch avant garde, and the following year he formed a duo with Han Bennink, which made several recordings and gave frequent performances (often of a theatrical nature) into the 1980s. Among Mengelberg's compositions are *Muziek voor 17 instrumenten* (1961), *Vietcong* (1966), and *Een behoorlijk kabaal* (A proper noise; 1975); his representative recordings include *Driekusman, Total Loss* (1964, 1966, Varajazz 210) and *Pech onderweg* (Bad luck on the way; 1978, BVHaast 016). (G. Rouy: "Misha Mengelberg: '. . . comme des chiens de garde'," *Jm*, no.295 (1981), 30)

WIM VAN EYLE

Menza, Don (*b* Buffalo, 22 April 1936). Tenor saxophonist and composer. He began playing tenor saxophone at the age of 15 and taught himself composition and arranging while serving in army bands. He toured with Maynard Ferguson's big band (1960–62), then after a short period with Stan Kenton returned to Buffalo and played in a bop quintet (1962–3). From 1964 to 1968 he lived in Munich, where he worked in jazz clubs and played as a studio musician under Max Greger; during this period he also took up other saxophones and flute. After returning to the USA Menza joined Buddy Rich's big band. He received critical acclaim for his solo playing on Rich's recording of *Channel One Suite* (1968), on which his urgent, full tone may be heard to good effect; his rapid and precise style of improvisation was patterned after the manner, during the late 1950s, of John Coltrane. Menza then settled in California and played briefly with Elvin Jones (1969) before working for Louie Bellson as both performer and composer (1969–79). In the 1980s he toured Scandinavia (*c*1984) and England (1986, 1987), performing with local rhythm sections. During this period, however, he worked mostly outside jazz, playing the flute in Los Angeles for the musical *Cats*. In his compositions, especially *Groovin' Hard* and *Time Check*, Menza succeeds in transferring to the big-band idiom the spirit of small-group jazz, notably through his use of exciting choruses written for the saxophone section.

SELECTED RECORDINGS

As leader: *Burnin'* (1980, RT 301)
As sideman: S. Kenton: *Adventures in Time* (1962, Cap. ST1844); B. Rich: *Mercy, Mercy* (1968, PJ 20133), incl. Channel One Suite

RECORDED COMPOSITIONS

(selective list)

* – with Menza as sideman

Recorded by B. Rich: on *Keep the Customer Satisfied* (1970, Lib. 11006), Groovin' Hard; on *The Roar of '74* (1973, GM 528), Time Check
Recorded by L. Bellson: on **The Louis Bellson Explosion* (1975, Pablo 2310755), Groove Blues

BIBLIOGRAPHY

"Don Menza Talking," *CI*, vi/11 (1968), 12
L. Feather: "Blindfold Test: Don Menza," *DB*, xxxviii/21 (1971), 26
L. Tomkins: "The Importance of Jazz Work: Don Menza," *CI*, xviii/6 (1980), 18
——: "Making the Most of the Single Life," *CI*, xxiv/5 (1987), 8

BARRY KERNFELD

Mercer, Johnny [John Herndon] (*b* Savannah, GA, 18 Nov 1909; *d* Los Angeles, 25 June 1976). Lyricist and singer. He went to New York in 1927 as a member of an acting troupe from Savannah, and also began writing lyrics. Later he became one of the most prolific songwriters of all time: he contributed the lyrics (and in some cases the music) to hundreds of popular, film, and theater songs, many of which became standards. Among the finest are *Lazybones* (1933), *Jeepers Creepers* (1938), *Fools Rush in* (1940), *Blues in the Night* (1941), *Skylark* (1942), *That Old Black Magic* (1942), *Moon River* (1961), and *The Days of Wine and Roses* (1962). He also worked in radio and later in television, and in 1942, with Glen Wallichs and Buddy DeSylva, he established the record company CAPITOL.

Mercer was a successful jazz singer with a distinctive, engaging style; he cultivated a relaxed manner of delivery, which emphasized his southern roots. He was well known for his work with Paul Whiteman (from 1932), and also sang with Frankie Trumbauer (recording in 1932), Jack Teagarden, Wingy Manone (recording in 1935, 1944, and 1947), and Benny Goodman; his recording with Goodman's orchestra of *Sent for you yesterday and here you come today* (1939) was modeled on the famous version recorded in 1938 by Jimmy Rushing and Count Basie's orchestra. He continued to make recordings into the 1970s.

SELECTED RECORDINGS

As sideman: Dorsey Brothers: Dr. Heckle and Mr. Jibe (1933, Bruns. 01834); P. Whiteman: Fare-thee-well to Harlem (1934, Vic. 24571); Pardon my southern accent (1934, Vic. 24704); B. Crosby: Small Fry/Mr. Crosby and Mr. Mercer (1938, Decca 1960); B. Goodman: Sent for you yesterday and here you come today (1939, Vic. 26170)

BIBLIOGRAPHY

FeatherE
R. Bach and G. Mercer: *Our Huckleberry Friend: the Life, Times and Lyrics of Johnny Mercer* (Secaucus, NJ, 1982)
D. Fairweather: "Mercer, Johnny," in I. Carr, D. Fairweather, and B. Priestley: *Jazz: the Essential Companion* (London, 1987)

SAMUEL S. BRYLAWSKI/WARREN VACHÉ, SR.

Mercury. Record company and label. The company was established around 1945 in New York, and was involved in recording both jazz and popular music. Among the first jazz musicians to record for the label were Erroll Garner (1945–6, 1949), Albert Ammons and Gene Ammons (both late 1940s), and, most importantly, Dinah Washington (1949–61), but in its early years the organization was better known as the distributor of recordings made by Norman Granz's company Clef (1946–53). Mercury also acquired the catalogue of the label Keynote in 1948. After Granz terminated his association with the company its president, Irv Green, engaged the producer Bob Shad to establish a new subsidiary label, EmArcy (an acronym for Mercury Record Corp.), which was devoted exclusively to jazz; issue began in 1954. The catalogue was mainly oriented towards bop styles, and included the results of new sessions by the Clifford Brown–Max Roach Quintet, Cannonball Adderley, Jimmy Cleveland, Maynard Ferguson, Garner, Herb Geller, Sarah Vaughan, and Washington. Other recordings by some of these musicians were released on the Mercury label itself, and in general there was no firm stylistic distinction between the two catalogues. Vaughan's contract, however, required her to record jazz for the subsidiary, pop for the parent.

In 1955 Quincy Jones began arranging material for Washington's sessions for the company; he joined the staff the following year, and worked variously as an arranger, bandleader, composer, and producer until 1966, becoming director of artists and repertory in 1961. After Shad turned his attentions to popular music his place at EmArcy was taken in 1958 by Jack Tracy, but the label's activities slowly declined. During this period, however, the company issued a considerable amount of jazz on the Mercury label itself, including material by Ernestine Anderson, Adderley, Al Cohn, and Buddy Rich. After EmArcy ceased to operate altogether Tracy founded another subsidiary, Limelight, in 1962, but this was only short-lived. By the 1970s Mercury had been acquired by Polydor, and much of its catalogue was reissued on Trip; ownership of the repertory was later transferred to Polygram. Facsimile reissues of EmArcy albums, manufactured in the Netherlands and Japan, appeared in the mid-1980s. (L. Feather: Liner notes, *Mercury 40th Anniversary V.S.O.P. Album*, Mer. 824116, 1985)

Meritt (i). Record company and label. It was established by the owner of a music store, Winston M. W. Holmes, in Kansas City in 1925. It concentrated on race records, and only issued five or six titles; these were pressed in very limited quantities and sold only in the store. Holmes's studio was also used by other companies based elsewhere in the USA when they were recording in Kansas City. The company ceased to operate in 1929.

BIBLIOGRAPHY

J. Randolph: "A Pioneer Race Recorder," *JJ*, x/2 (1957), 11
D. Jydstrup: "Winston Holmes: Kansas City Promoter," *78 Quarterly*, i/2 (1968)

Meritt (ii). Record label. It was established in 1979 by Jerry Valburn. Its catalogue contains previously unissued recordings of early jazz; these are presented on albums that are pressed in limited quantities and made available only by mail order to members of the Meritt Record Society. Valburn has also launched three similar labels, Blu-disc, Up-to-date, and Everybody's, which are all devoted to reissuing recordings of early jazz; like Meritt, these are all named after small labels of the 1920s. The society also produces the Duke Ellington Treasury Series, which consists of reissues of broadcasts made in 1945–6 by Ellington's orchestra for the US Treasury Department. The *Meritt Rag*, a magazine edited by Valburn which contains discographical and historical information about the label's issues, is published regularly for members of the society.

Merrill [Milcetic], **Helen** (*b* New York, 21 July 1929 or 1930). Singer. In the late 1940s she sang with Charlie Parker, Miles Davis, Bud Powell, and J. J. Johnson. During her marriage to Aaron Sachs (early to mid-1950s) she worked only occasionally, singing with Earl Hines briefly in 1952 and recording her first album, which was arranged by Quincy Jones and featured Clifford Brown as a soloist, in 1954. She toured Brazil early in 1957 (shortly after her divorce) and in 1959 moved to Europe and settled in Italy. She toured widely, performing in Scandinavia with Stan Getz, in Lebanon with Jamil Nasser, in Japan, and at major European festivals. Her return to the USA in 1963 brought her little work, but in 1965 she led sessions in New York, accompanied by Thad and Elvin Jones, Jim Hall, and Ron Carter, among others. She lived in Japan for a period (1967–73), during which she performed with Gary Peacock and Teddy Wilson. Once more in the USA she again worked infrequently, and it was not until around 1977 that she resumed recording.

Although she is much admired by leading American jazzmen, Merrill has been less successful in the USA than in Japan and Europe. She is noted for her soft, smoky timbre, precise intonation, and sophisticated sense of harmony. She has worked most often with bop musicians but does not employ the scat technique, preferring a careful interpretation of the lyrics of popular songs; her approach is well represented by *Chasin' the Bird* (1979), an album of songs by George Gershwin on which Pepper Adams contributes a counterpoint to the vocal line consisting of carefully selected bop melodies by Charlie Parker.

SELECTED RECORDINGS

As leader: *Don't Explain* (1954, EmA 36006); *The Feeling is Mutual* (1965, Mlst. 9003); with D. Katz: *A Shade of Difference* (1965, Mlst. 9019); with G. Peacock: *Sposin'* (1971, RCA SMJX10132); with T. Wilson: *Helen Sings, Teddy Swings* (?early 1970s, Cat. 7903); with John Lewis: *Helen Merrill/ John Lewis* (1977, Mer. 1150); *Chasin' the Bird* (1979, IC 1080)
As sideman with E. Hines: A Cigarette for Company (1952, D'Oro 102)

BIBLIOGRAPHY

D. Gold: "Meet Miss Merrill," *DB*, xxv/3 (1958), 17
J. Tynan: "On the Road with Helen Merrill," *DB*, xxx/27 (1963), 18
M. McPartland: "The Essential Helen Merrill," *Crescendo*, iii/12 (1965), 10
H. Nolan: "Profile: Helen Merrill," *DB*, xliii/9 (1976), 36
L. Gourse: *Louis' Children: American Jazz Singers* (New York, 1984), 127

BARRY KERNFELD

Merritt, Jymie [James] (*b* Philadelphia, 3 May 1926). Double bass player. He was classically trained, and first worked with John Coltrane, Benny Golson, and Philly Joe Jones in Philadelphia (all 1949). After playing electric bass guitar on tours with the rhythm-and-blues musicians Bull Moose Jackson (1951–3) and B. B. King (1955–7), Merritt returned to jazz and the acoustic instrument when he joined Art Blakey's Jazz Messengers (1958). This association lasted until 1962 and consolidated his reputation as one of the foremost double bass players of the hard-bop movement. Thereafter he recorded with Chet Baker (1964) and played electric bass guitar with Max Roach (1965–8), Dizzy Gillespie (1969), and Lee Morgan (1970–72). Merritt and others formed the Forerunners, a loosely knit group of musicians and practitioners in other disciplines, in 1962; this later became Forerunner, a constantly evolving cooperative organization that has performed intermittently in and around Philadelphia, and has remained active, under Merritt's artistic directorship, into the late 1980s. Its repertory includes his extended composition *The Spiritual Impulse*. Among his other works is *Nommo*, which he recorded with Roach in 1966. Merritt's propulsive rhythmic style, which he achieves by placing notes ahead of the beat, and by frequent use of triplet figures and grace notes, was particularly appropriate to Blakey's drumming.

SELECTED RECORDINGS

As sideman: A. Blakey: *Moanin'* (1958, BN 4003); *A Night in Tunisia* (1960, BN 84049); C. Baker: *The Most Important Jazz Album of 1964–65* (1964, Colpix 476); M. Roach: *Drums Unlimited* (1966, Atl. 1467), incl. Nommo; L. Morgan: *Live at the Lighthouse* (1970, BN 89906)

BIBLIOGRAPHY

FeatherE; *Feather '60s*
M. Hennessey: "The Enduring Jazz Message of Abdullah ibn Buhaina," *JJI*, xxx/9 (1977), 6

JOHN CURRY

Mertz, Paul (Madeira) (*b* Reading, PA, 1 Sept 1904). Pianist and arranger. He first played in local groups, then, after touring with the Dorsey Brothers' Wild Canaries (1922), performed and recorded with various bands led by Jean Goldkette (1923–7). He also wrote arrangements for Goldkette and Red Nichols. He recorded with Goldkette's sidemen Bix Beiderbecke (*Toddlin' Blues/Davenport Blues*, 1925, Gen. 5654) and Frankie Trumbauer (1927), and played with Fred Waring's Pennsylvanians before rejoining Goldkette for several months (1929). He then moved to Hollywood, where he worked as an arranger in the Paramount studios. In the early 1930s he performed in New York with various groups, including Nichols's orchestra, but he returned to Hollywood in 1933 and concentrated on composing and arranging film music, working for Paramount, Columbia, and MGM. He wrote the song *I'm Glad there is You* (1941, Decca 4197), which was a hit in 1942.

based on *ChiltonW*

Metcalf, Louis (, Jr.) (*b* Webster Groves, MO, 28 Feb 1905; *d* New York, 27 Oct 1981). Trumpeter. He played for Charlie Creath in St. Louis (*c*1918–1923) before touring with Jimmie Cooper's Black and White Revue (1923–4). He then settled in New York, where he made his first recordings, accompanying classic blues singers (from 1924). He performed with Willie "the Lion" Smith and Sidney Bechet (1924), Elmer Snowden (1925), Charlie Johnson (1926), and Sam Wooding (1927); he also played for the show *4-11-44* and recorded with Duke Ellington (1926). From 1927 to 1928 he was a member of Ellington's Cotton Club Orchestra, where he made fluent use of muted and bluesy effects and, through his high range, bright timbre, and precise articulation, supplied a contrast to Bubber Miley's growling trumpet playing. He performed with Jelly Roll Morton (1928) and the Luis Russell Orchestra, with which he recorded under the leadership of both Russell and King Oliver (1929). In the early 1930s Metcalf formed a band in Montreal, then traveled around the Midwest, leading bands and working briefly with Fletcher Henderson. In 1936 he returned to New York, where he formed a band which included Lester Young, Billie Holiday, and Hot Lips Page. During World War II he ran a social club and supported the *Music Dial*, a magazine dedicated to civil rights. He resumed playing as leader of the International Band in Montreal (1946–*c*1952), and spent the remainder of his career performing in clubs in New York.

Oral history material in *CtY*.

SELECTED RECORDINGS

As leader: *Louis Metcalf at the Alibaba* (1966, Spivey 1007)
As sideman: Rosa Henderson: Twelfth Street Blues (1924, Ajax 17081); Cotton Club Orchestra: Down and Out Blues/Snag 'em Blues (1925, Col. 287D); Harry's Happy Four [H. Cooper]: Western Melody/Blue, that's all (1925, OK 8266); D. Ellington: Jubilee Stomp (1928, Bruns. 4044); Yellow Dog Blues/Tishomingo Blues (1928, Bruns. 3987); K. Oliver: West End Blues (1929, Vic. 38034); Call of the Freaks (1929, Vic. 38039); Bessie Smith: In the House Blues/Blue Blue (1931, Col. 14611D)

BIBLIOGRAPHY

L. Kunstadt: "The Story of Louie Metcalf," *Record Research*, no.46 (1962), 3
D. Stewart-Baxter: "Louis Metcalf," *JJ*, xix (1966), no.11, p.15; no.12, p.20; xx/1 (1967), 19
L. Kunstadt: "Louis Metcalf," *Record Research*, no.86 (1967), 3
A. Vollmer: "Some Notes on Clarence M. Jones . . . and Others," *Sv*, no.51 (1974), 84

BARRY KERNFELD

Meter. In measured music the grouping of beats (in jazz most often four, three, or two) into a recurring pattern (the bar) defined by accentuation. An entire piece or section of a piece is constructed of a succession of bars, and the recurring accentual pattern, whether explicitly stated or present only by implication, is the framework within which rhythm is established and perceived. For a discussion of meter in jazz *see* BEAT, esp. §1.

Metheny, Pat(rick Bruce) (*b* Lee's Summit, MO, 12 Aug 1954). Electric guitarist and composer. While a teenager he played informally with Gary Burton, who engaged him in 1974 for his quartet. He also taught at the University of Miami and the Berklee College of Music in the early 1970s, and from the mid-1970s he has played and toured widely with his own groups. The excellent sales of his album *The Pat Metheny Group* (1978) gained him, during the late 1970s and early 1980s, a larger and wider audience than that attained by all but the most successful jazz musicians. Among his sidemen have been such notable players as Jaco Pastorius, Dewey Redman, Jack DeJohnette, and Nana Vasconcelos. In 1983 he organized a trio with Charlie Haden and Billy Higgins (both former members of Ornette Coleman's group), and from 1984 he has led a quintet. He has written music for a number of films, including *Twice in a Lifetime* and *The Falcon and the Snowman* (both 1985).

Metheny is a highly proficient player of both standard and 12-string electric guitar, on which he performs quick passages with ease. He makes tasteful use of electronic sound-delay devices for "slap-back echo," and from the 1980s has frequently employed the Synclavier guitar synthesizer. His approach is more lyrical than that of his contemporaries John McLaughlin and Larry Coryell, and, unlike many guitarists with similar dexterity, he seems to strive for simplicity in his improvisations. In the early 1980s he incorporated the tunes and improvisational attack of Coleman into his performances, which clearly distinguishes his style from that of guitarists whose work has come under the sway of McLaughlin. Metheny cites Jim Hall and Wes Montgomery as having influenced his playing.

SELECTED RECORDINGS

(all recorded for ECM unless otherwise indicated)

As leader: *Bright Size Life* (1975, 1073), incl. Midwestern Night's Dream, Missouri Uncompromised, Unity Valley; *Watercolors* (1977, 1097), incl. River Quay; *The Pat Metheny Group* (1978, 1114), incl. April Joy; *80/81* (1980, 1180–81); *Offramp* (1981, 1216); *Rejoicing* (1983, 1271); *The Falcon and the Snowman* (1984–5, EMI 240305-1)
As sideman with G. Burton: *Ring* (1974, 1051); *Passengers* (1976, 1092)

BIBLIOGRAPHY

N. Tesser: "Profile: Pat Metheny," *DB*, xlii/15 (1975), 36
J. A. Simon: "Pat Metheny: Ready to Tackle Tomorrow," *DB*, xlv/13 (1978), 23
L. Tomkins: "Today's Jazz Guitarist: Pat Metheny," *CI*, xvi (1978), no.10, p.14; no.12, p.6 [interview]
F. Bourque and N. Tesser: "Pat Metheny: Musings on Neo-fusion," *DB*, xlvi/6 (1979), 12

L. Feather: *The Passion for Jazz* (New York, 1980), 105
D. Forte: "Pat Metheny," *GP*, xv/12 (1981), 90
T. Schneckloth: "Pat Metheny: a Step Beyond Tradition," *DB*, xlix/11 (1982), 14
J. Fordham: "Pat Metheny," *The Wire*, no.15 (1985), 28
G. Giddins: *Rhythm-a-ning: Jazz Tradition and Innovation in the '80s* (New York, and Oxford, England, 1985) [colln of previously pubd articles], 56
B. Milkowski: "Pat Metheny's Digital Manifesto," *DB*, lii/1 (1985), 16

Metrojazz. Record label. Established as a subsidiary of MGM in 1958, it was used to issue a series of excellent material produced by Leonard Feather; this included albums led by Randy Weston and the vibraphonist Lem Winchester, Sonny Rollins, Pepper Adams and Jimmy Knepper, Sonny Rollins and Teddy Edwards, Thad Jones, Gigi Gryce, Red Callender, and Toshiko Akiyoshi. Some of these were rereleased in the 1960s on Verve (which was then owned by MGM); the label was revived in the 1970s for cheap reissues. Many of the early albums in the Metrojazz catalogue were put out in Japan in the early 1980s in replicas of the original liners.

MARK GARDNER

Metronome. Record company and label. The company was established in Sweden in 1949 by Lars Burman, Börje Ekberg, and the drummer Anders Burman. It quickly became the most important source of modern jazz in the country, issuing both 78 r.p.m. discs and EPs. Some of the material in the catalogue was drawn from such American companies as Prestige and Atlantic. Around 1950 Metronome began recording both popular and classical music, and, after the advent of LPs in Sweden in the mid-1950s, the recording policy became more commercially oriented. Nevertheless the catalogue included notable material by such leaders as Arne Domnérus (1949–50, 1959–60), Zoot Sims (1950), Toots Thielemans (1950–51, 1959, 1961), Bengt Hallberg (1950–53, 1962), Lars Gullin (1951–6), Alice Babs (1951, 1954, 1957), Rolf Ericson and Jan Johansson (both 1956), Eje Thelin (1964), and Svend Asmussen and Stephane Grappelli (1965). A complete set of recordings (on tape) issued by the company between 1949 and 1961 is in the Svenskt Visarkiv, Stockholm (*see* LIBRARIES AND ARCHIVES, §2).

ERIK KJELLBERG

Metronome All Stars. Name of several recording groups. The American magazine *Metronome* organized an annual poll of its readers' favorite instrumentalists and bands from 1939 until it ceased publication in 1961; in most years from 1939 to 1956 the individual winners (or substitutes in cases of contractual or logistical unavailability) were assembled for recording sessions. Although overall the results are uneven, the sessions provide a useful survey of the prevailing styles and tastes in jazz during a period of rapid change. Among notable recordings are *Bugle Call Rag* (1941, Vic. 27314), featuring Cootie Williams, Benny Carter, and Coleman Hawkins, and *Double Date* (1950, Col. 38734), on which Dizzy Gillespie and Serge Chaloff take fine solos. (J. Burns: "Metronome Riff," *JJ*, xxix/9 (1976), 4)

BOB WEIR

Metropole. Bar in New York; *see* NIGHTCLUBS AND OTHER VENUES.

Mettome, Doug(las Voll) (*b* Salt Lake City, 19 March 1925; *d* Salt Lake City, 17 Feb 1964). Trumpeter. He studied piano as a child, then took up trumpet, and led his own 12-piece band in Salt Lake City. After military service he worked with big bands, including those of Billy Eckstine (1946–7), Benny Goodman (1948–9), Woody Herman (1950–52), and Tommy Dorsey (1953). He recorded with, among others, Eckstine, Goodman, Herman, Urbie Green (1953, 1955), Johnny Richards (1957), and Sam Most.

Mettome was initially inspired by Roy Eldridge and later influenced by Dizzy Gillespie and Fats Navarro. He was greatly admired by Goodman, who employed him as a soloist on such recordings as *Undercurrent Blues* and *The Huckle-buck*, made with his big band, and *Bedlam* and *Blue Lou*, with his septet. He was an inspired soloist, but unfortunately spent most of his career as a section player in large ensembles. He did not record as a leader, and the recordings he made in small groups with Goodman and Most are therefore especially valuable.

SELECTED RECORDINGS

As sideman: B. Goodman: Undercurrent Blues (1949, Cap. 15409); The Huckle-buck (1949, Cap. 576); Bedlam (1949, Cap. 621); Blue Lou (1949, Cap. 60009); S. Most: *Introducing a New Star* (1953, Prst. 1322); *Sam Most Plays Bird, Bud, Monk and Miles* (1957, Beth. 75)

BIBLIOGRAPHY

I. Gitler: *Jazz Masters of the Forties* (New York, 1966/*R*1983 with discography), 92
J. Burns: "Doug Mettome," *JJ*, xxviii/6 (1975), 21 [incl. discography]

MARK GARDNER

Meyer, Johnny (*b* Amsterdam, 1 Oct 1912). Dutch accordionist. After studying accordion (1919–25) and piano (1924–6) he played swing on radio broadcasts and recordings with the popular singers Maurice Chevalier, Hans Moser, and Josephine Baker. He toured Denmark, England, and Switzerland (1952–3), made recordings as a leader (*c*1947–1957), and played in Paris; later he recorded again as a leader (*The Swinging Accordeon of Johnny Meyer*, 1972, Park 3031), played with Joe Venuti (1973), and recorded dixieland with the Dutch Swing College Orchestra (1974).

WIM VAN EYLE

Mezzrow, Mezz [Mesirow, Milton] (*b* Chicago, 9 Nov 1899; *d* Paris, 5 Aug 1972). Clarinetist. In the early 1920s he played occasionally with the Austin High School Gang in Chicago. Later he worked as a freelance musician in New York, where in the 1930s and 1940s he organized many recording sessions; he also founded one of the earliest interracial jazz bands (1937). During the early 1950s he moved to France and worked as an entrepreneur, organizing all-star touring bands. He continued to make guest appearances in Europe throughout the 1960s.

The success that Mezzrow achieved with *Really the Blues*, the lurid story of his life, has placed undue importance on his clarinet playing, which was marred by a shrill tone, trivial ideas, and a limited sense of rhythm and harmony. Because he frequently recorded in superior company, the results generally show up his technical deficiencies; on the album *Mezz Mezzrow à la Schola Cantorum* (1955, Ducretet-Thomson 300V010), however, his playing may be heard to good effect. His greatest contribution to jazz was doubtless the many worthwhile recording sessions he organized, particularly those with Sidney Bechet and the previously neglected trumpeter Tommy Ladnier (see illustration, p.102). Mezzrow rarely played clarinet in public during the last years of his life, but often promulgated his candid evaluations of jazz performances; he

Mezz Mezzrow (clarinet) with James P. Johnson (piano), Hugues Panassié, and Tommy Ladnier (trumpet) during a recording session for Bluebird at the Victor studios in New York, 21 November 1938

remained a staunch devotee of black music in general and of Louis Armstrong's work in particular.

BIBLIOGRAPHY

M. Mezzrow and B. Wolfe: *Really the Blues* (New York, 1946/R1972)
L. Armstrong: "Vive Mezzrow et Joe Oliver," *BHcF*, no.23 (1952), 1
H. Panassié: *Quand Mezzrow enregistre* (Paris, 1952)
——: "La tournée de Mezz," *BHcF*, no.42 (1954), 3
E. P. Townley: "Blue Clarinet: a Study and Discography of Mezz Mezzrow," *JM*, ii (1956), no.6, p.26; no.7, p.26
G. E. Lambert: "Mezz Mezzrow: an Assessment," *JM*, vi/10 (1960), 10
K. Palmer: "Mezz Mezzrow at Sixty-five," *JM*, x/9 (1964), 2
M. Hennessey: "Mezz Mezzrow: Alive and Well in Paris," *DB*, xxxv/11 (1968), 24
H. Panassié: "Mezz," *BHcF*, no.192 (1969), 3
R. Peronnet: "Swinging with Mezz," *BHcF*, no.196 (1970), 29
Obituary, M. Gautier, *BHcF*, no.220 (1972), 3
P. Andreota: "Il y a un an: Mezz, un homme libre," *BHcF*, no.229 (1973), 3
J. Poinsot: "Une interview de Mezz," *BHcF*, no.229 (1973), 5
——: "Swinging with Mezz," *BHcF*, no.264 (1978), 5

JOHN CHILTON

Mica mute. *See* MUTE, §2(d).

Michelot, Pierre (*b* St.-Denis, Seine–St.-Denis, France, 3 March 1928). French double bass player. He studied piano from his early childhood and classical double bass from the age of 16. Having taken an interest in jazz through the work of Jimmy Blanton and Oscar Pettiford he played with Rex Stewart (1948) and toured France and Germany with Kenny Clarke (1949–50); he also recorded with Coleman Hawkins (1949). During the following years he played frequently in Paris: at the Club Saint-Germain with Django Reinhardt (1950) and Stephane Grappelli (1955), at Ringside in the early 1950s with Don Byas, John Lewis, and Thelonious Monk, and at the Blue Note in 1956–60 with Lester Young, Dexter Gordon, Stan Getz, and Bud Powell. At the same time he made recordings with James Moody (1950–51), Zoot Sims (1950), Kenny Clarke (1950–59), Lewis (1950, 1956), Reinhardt (1951, 1953), Gillespie (1952, 1963), Martial Solal (1953–68), Young (1956), Miles Davis (1957), and Powell (1960–61), and wrote arrangements for Chet Baker (1956), Clarke, and his own big band. For nearly 15 years beginning in 1959 he belonged to Jacques Loussier's trio Play Bach, with which he toured internationally. Michelot received the Prix Django Reinhardt from the Académie du jazz in 1963 and in 1986 performed in Bertrand Tavernier's film *Round Midnight*.

SELECTED RECORDINGS

As leader: with R. Urtreger and D. Humair: *HUM* (1960, Vega 837); *Round about a Bass* (1963, Mer. 125500)

As sideman: Z. Sims: *Zoot Goes to Town* (1950, Vogue 185); D. Reinhardt: Blues for Ike (1953, BStar 12008) [EP]; K. Clarke: *When Lights are Low* (1956, Phi. 77312); B. Powell: Memorial Oscar Pettiford (1960, Vogue 7942) [EP], incl. Buttercup; D. Gordon: *Our Man in Paris* (1963, BN 84146); D. Gillespie: *Dizzy Gillespie et les Double-six* (1963, Phi. 200106)

BIBLIOGRAPHY

H. Olier: "Le jazz en France: Pierre Michelot," *Jh*, no.95 (1955), 42
L. Malson: "Pierre Michelot ou notre sommet de la basse," *Jm*, no.60 (1960), 28
M. Howlett and D. Roustain: "Michelot: le bassiste du Blue Note," *Jm*, no.344 (1985), 31

ANDRÉ CLERGEAT

Microgroove recording. A sound-recording standard that utilizes a groove spacing of about 100 grooves to the centimeter; *see* RECORDING, §I, 3(ii).

Middlebrooks, Wilfred (Roland) (*b* Chattanooga, TN, 17 July 1933). Double bass player. He was brought up in a musical family, and from the age of 15 toured with a vaudeville show. He then played in a rhythm-and-blues group led by Tab Smith (1950–53), and after a period of military service briefly rejoined Smith for a tour of California (1955) before settling in Los Angeles. He played in Buddy Collette's quintet for two years, recorded with Frank Rosolino (1956, 1957) and a group led by Mel Lewis and Bill Holman (1958), and worked with Eric Dolphy and Art Pepper. From 1958 he toured internationally in Ella Fitzgerald's backup group, then in the mid-

1960s resumed freelance work in California. Inspired by Ray Brown, Middlebrooks plays in a sturdy, swinging style, and, although he ceased to work as a full-time musician, in the 1980s continued to play with the alto saxophonist Curtis Peagler, among others.

SELECTED RECORDINGS

As sideman: T. Smith: Because of You/Dee Jay Special (1951, United 104); F. Rosolino: *I Play Trombone* (1956, Beth. 26); B. Collette: *Buddy's Best* (1957, Dootone 245); J. Hodges: *Masters of Jazz*, ix: *Johnny Hodges* (1960–61, Sto. 4109); E. Fitzgerald: *Ella in Berlin: Mack the Knife* (1960, Verve 4041); *Ella in Hollywood* (1961, Verve 4052)

BIBLIOGRAPHY

FeatherE; *Feather '60s*
P. Vacher: "Ella's Bassist," *JM*, viii/12 (1963), 11

PETER VACHER

Middle eight. The penultimate section in the refrain of a popular song, leading to the final repeat of the opening section (section *b* in the form *aaba*); it is so called because the phrases of such a song are commonly eight bars long. It provides a contrast, often tonal as well as harmonic and melodic, with the opening section. *See* FORMS, esp. §1(i)(a).

Middleton, Velma (*b* St. Louis, 1 Sept 1917; *d* Freetown, Sierra Leone, 10 Feb 1961). Singer. She gained experience performing in clubs in the 1930s then from 1942 sang with Louis Armstrong, at first in his big band and later with the All Stars. Her comic romantic duets with Armstrong, such as *That's my desire* (1947, Decca 28372), became famous, though some listeners found them distasteful. She made many recordings with Armstrong and is heard to advantage on *Baby, it's cold outside* (1951, Decca 928172); she also recorded two albums as a leader (1948, 1951), on the first of which she was joined by Earl Hines and Cozy Cole. She died while touring Africa with Armstrong.

BIBLIOGRAPHY

ChiltonW; *FeatherE*; *Feather '60s*
Obituary, *SL*, xi/3–4 (1961), 27
H. Panassié and M. Gautier: "Il y a cinq ans mourait Velma Middleton," *BHcF*, no.155 (1966), 3
L. Gourse: *Louis' Children: American Jazz Singers* (New York, 1984), 29
B. Bigard: *With Louis and the Duke*, ed. B. Martyn (London, 1985)

Midnite Follies Orchestra. Orchestra directed from 1978 by KEITH NICHOLS and Alan Cohen.

Migliori, Jay [James] (*b c*1930). Tenor saxophonist. He recorded with his own quintet in Boston in 1955, and in March 1957 he joined Woody Herman's band. His 18-month association with Herman included a tour of South America (1958); his playing is well represented by his solos on *The Preacher* and *Bar Fly Blues* on *Woody Herman '58, Featuring the Preacher* (1957, Verve 8255). He later settled on the West Coast, where he worked as a freelance in the 1960s. He made recordings with Si Zentner (1960), Gene Ammons (1973–4), and the group Supersax (1972–84), and as the leader of his own small group (1975, 1980–81, including the acclaimed album *Count the Nights and Times* (1975, PBR 5), recorded with a quartet). (A. Morgan: "Woody's Tenors," *JM*, vi (1960–61), no.7, p.4, esp. p.7; no.12, p.9, esp. p.10)

Mikkelborg, Palle (*b* Copenhagen, 6 March 1941). Danish trumpeter, flugelhorn player, leader, and composer. He taught himself to play trumpet from 1956 and first worked professionally in 1960. In 1963 he joined the Danish Radiojazzgruppen, which he led from 1967 to 1972 (during which time it was known by the name Opportunity; *see* RADIOJAZZGRUPPEN (i)), and from 1964 to 1971 he belonged to the Radioens Big Band, which he later led on several occasions. With Alex Riel he led a quintet that performed at the Montreux and Newport jazz festivals (1968) and the octet V8 (1970–75); he also led the group Entrance (1975–85) and a trio with a rhythm section consisting of Thomas Clausen and Niels-Henning Ørsted Pedersen (1983–5). He toured and recorded with big bands led by Peter Herbolzheimer and George Gruntz and with Terje Rypdal, and in the mid-1980s he performed in a trio with Ørsted Pedersen and the keyboard player Kenneth Knudsen. Mikkelborg has also played at various times with many other musicians, including Abdullah Ibrahim, Jan Garbarek, Gil Evans, Eje Thelin, and Karin Krog. As a composer and arranger he worked from the late 1960s with Bill Evans (ii) and Dexter Gordon, and in films, television, and radio; in 1969 he recorded his composition *Tempus incertum remanet* as a member of the Radioens Big Band and in 1985 recorded his suite *Aura* with Miles Davis. Mikkelborg's instrumental style and use of electronic effects bear the influence of Davis; his orchestral compositions, which have been influenced by Gil Evans and the composers Olivier Messiaen and Charles Ives, are often cast in the form of suites and reflect Mikkelborg's interest in Eastern philosophy.

SELECTED RECORDINGS

As leader: of Radiojazzgruppen: *The Mysterious Corona* (1967, Debut 150); *Ashoka Suite/Guadiana* (1970, Met. 15374); of Entrance: *Entrance* (1977, Met. 15612), *Live as Well* (1978, Met. 15631), *Journey to* (1984, Met. 15826)
As sideman: Radioens Big Band: *Brownsville Trolley Line* (1969, Sonet 1520), incl. Tempus incertum remanet; T. Rypdal: *Waves* (1977, ECM 1110); *Descendre* (1979, ECM 1144); Lakshinarayana Shankar: *Vision* (1983, ECM 1261); D. Saluzzi: *Once upon a Time* (1985, ECM 1309)

BIBLIOGRAPHY

Feather–Gitler '70s

ERIK WIEDEMANN

Miles, Barry (*b* Newark, NJ, 28 March 1947). Keyboard player. He began learning drums at the age of seven, and three years later he played informally with Woody Herman's band. He also studied classical piano, and (with John Mehegan) jazz piano and theory. Radio broadcasts, a tour of Europe sponsored by the US State Department, and his first album, *Miles of Genius* (1961), earned him considerable public attention before he had reached the age of 14. He formed his first group in 1964, and during his first year at Princeton University he changed from drums to piano. In 1966 he began integrating rock elements into his playing (which has always owed most to bop); he first recorded on electric piano in 1969, and shortly afterwards he began playing synthesizer. After leading his own group, Silverlight, for several years (with such sideman as John Abercrombie, Al Di Meola, Jimmy Owens, and Woody Shaw), in 1981 he became the music director for the popular singer Roberta Flack and began working as a session musician in New York. Although he is often thought of as a jazz-rock player, Miles has retained his love of complex chord changes and remains essentially a bop musician.

SELECTED RECORDINGS

As leader: *Miles of Genius* (1961, CP 804); *Barry Miles* (1969, Poppy 40009); *White Heat* (1971, Mstr. 353); *Barry Miles and Silverlight* (1974, Lon. 651); *Fusion is* (1977, Cen. 1070).
As sideman: M. Santamaria: *Red Hot* (1979, Col.–Tappan Zee JC35696)

BIBLIOGRAPHY

B. Coss: "Young Veteran," *DB*, xxx/8 (1963), 24
G. Perla: "Profile: the Miles Brothers," *DB*, xli/7 (1974), 30
Z. Knauss: *Conversations with Jazz Musicians* (Detroit, 1977), 118–49

BOB DOERSCHUK

Miles, Butch [Thornton, Charles J., Jr.] (*b* Ironton, OH, 4 July 1944). Drummer. He studied music at West Virginia State College (1962–6) and after working with small groups in West Virginia he toured with Iris Bell's trio (late 1960s) and performed with Mel Tormé (1972–4). As a member of Count Basie's orchestra (1975–9) he made several recordings and appeared in the film *The Last of the Blue Devils* (1979). In 1979 he performed for several months with Dave Brubeck and he then spent almost a year with Tony Bennett (1980). He worked as a freelance with many musicians, among them Gerry Mulligan, Harry Edison, Al Cohn, Zoot Sims, Sal Nistico (ii), Woody Herman, Peanuts Hucko, Wild Bill Davison, Clark Terry, Al Grey, Buddy Tate, Arnett Cobb, Eddie "Lockjaw" Davis, Scott Hamilton, Warren Vaché, Joe Bushkin, the popular singer Lena Horne, and Bob Wilber's Bechet Legacy. Miles began to record as a drummer and singer with his own groups in the late 1970s. He has played at festivals and taken part in numerous concerts and workshops for the Ludwig Drum Co. His big-band style is strongly influenced by Buddy Rich; he also plays dixieland jazz.

SELECTED RECORDINGS

As leader: *Butch Miles Salutes Chick Webb* (1979, FaD 132); *Hail to the Chief! Butch Miles Salutes Basie* (1982, FaD 145)

As sideman: M. Tormé: *Live at the Maisonette* (1974, Atl. 18129); C. Basie: *Montreux '77* (1977, PL 2308207); D. Brubeck: *Back Home* (1979, Conc. 103)

BIBLIOGRAPHY

Feather–Gitler '70s
L. Tomkins: "Butch Miles Talks on Drums," *CI*, xiv/6 (1976), 20
G. Villani: "Butch Miles: Drivin' the Basie Rhythm Machine," *MD*, i/3 (1977), 12
E. Cook: "Butch Miles," *JJI*, xxxvii/1 (1984), 6

RICK MATTINGLY

Miles, Lizzie [Pajaud [née Landreaux], Elizabeth Mary] (*b* New Orleans, 31 March 1895; *d* New Orleans, 17 March 1963). Singer. From 1909 to 1911 she sang with King Oliver, Kid Ory, Bunk Johnson, and A. J. Piron, then toured the South in theaters, circuses, and with minstrel shows. She sang with Manuel Manetta (*c*1918), and later with Oliver, Freddie Keppard, and Charlie Elgar in Chicago before moving to New York (all 1921). The following year she made her first recordings, which were in a blues style. She sang with Piron (1923) and Sam Wooding (1924), and toured Europe (1924–5), then worked at clubs in New York (1926–31). During this period she recorded as the leader of a trio with Oliver and in a duo with Jelly Roll Morton. From 1931 she was largely inactive because of illness, but she appeared in two films in the early 1930s. In 1935 she resumed regular work, performing with Paul Barbarin at the Strollers Club, New York. After singing with Fats Waller in 1938 she worked mainly in Chicago until 1942, when she left music for some years. In 1950 she began singing again and worked in New Orleans, Chicago, Las Vegas, and California. She participated in several recording sessions and broadcasts before retiring to New Orleans in 1959.

Oral history material in *LNT*.

SELECTED RECORDINGS

Duos: with J. R. Morton: I hate a man like you/Don't tell me nothin' 'bout my man (1929, Vic. 38571); with Red Camp: *Torchy Lullabies my Mother Sang me* (*c*1955, Cook 1184)

As leader: Muscle Shoals Blues/She walked right up and took my man away (1922, OK 8031); That's all right, daddy (1939, Voc. 06165); Stranger Blues/Twenty Grand Blues (1939, Voc. 05392); on G. Lewis (i): *George Lewis Live at the Hangover Club* (1953–4, Dawn Club 12008), Careless Love, You made me love you; *Moans and Blues* (*c*1954, Cook 1182)

As sideman: on G. Lewis (i): *George Lewis Live at the Hangover Club* (1953–4, Dawn Club 12008), Darktown Strutters' Ball (1954)

BIBLIOGRAPHY

B. Wood: "Lizzie Miles from New Orleans," *JJ*, x/6 (1957), 1
L. Goreau: "An Evening with Lizzie Miles," *JJ*, xvii/1 (1964), 8
S. Harris: *Blues Who's Who: a Biographical Dictionary of Blues Singers* (New Rochelle, NY, 1979)

MICHAEL TOVEY

Milestone. Record company and label. The company was established by Orrin Keepnews and Dick Katz in New York in 1966. Among the musicians who have recorded regularly for the label are Lee Konitz (1967–74), Joe Henderson (1967–75), McCoy Tyner (1972–80), Sonny Rollins (from 1972) and Ron Carter (from 1976). By 1972 the label had been acquired by Audio Fidelity, and the following year it was sold to FANTASY. Milestone remained an important subsidiary into the late 1980s, but by that time was far better known for its reissues of material from Keepnews's earlier label Riverside than for any new recordings.

In 1978 the company sponsored the Milestone Jazzstars, a quartet comprising Rollins, Tyner, Carter, and Al Foster, which toured the USA and recorded.

Miley, Bubber [James Wesley] (*b* Aiken, SC, 3 April 1903; *d* New York, 20 May 1932). Trumpeter. He moved to New York at the age of six, and studied trombone before learning cornet. He was active professionally from 1920 with the pianist Willie Gant, Mamie Smith, and others, and in 1923 joined Elmer Snowden's Washingtonians, which shortly afterwards came under the leadership of Duke Ellington (for illustration *see* WASHINGTONIANS). Miley remained with Ellington until early 1929, and then worked with Noble Sissle, with whom he traveled to Paris in 1929, Zutty Singleton, and others. In the last months of his life he led his own orchestra.

Miley's melodic and rhythmic styles were influenced by King Oliver and Johnny Dunn; he is noted for having begun the practice of using a plunger mute in conjunction with a straight mute, thus combining two techniques employed separately by Oliver to achieve a wa-wa effect. His growl effect was adopted by Sidney De Paris, Cootie Williams, Ray Nance, and many other jazz trumpeters, and formed an important element of Ellington's style. He was the most impressive of the early Ellington soloists, and collaborated on or strongly influenced many of Ellington's early compositions; the better sections of *Black and Tan Fantasy*, *East St. Louis Toodle-oo*, and *Doin' the Voom-voom* are thought to be Miley's work.

See also BLUES, §5, and TRUMPET, §3.

SELECTED RECORDINGS

(all as sideman with Duke Ellington)

Choo-choo (1924, Blu-Disc T1002); Animal Crackers (1926, Gen. 3342); East St. Louis Toodle-oo (1926, Voc. 1064); Immigration Blues (1926, Voc. 1077); Black and Tan Fantasy (1927, Bruns. 3526); Creole Love Call (1927, Vic. 21137); Jubilee Stomp (1928, Vic. 21580); The Mooche (1928, Bruns. 4122); Doin' the Voom-voom (1929, Vic. 38035)

BIBLIOGRAPHY

ChiltonW
R. Dodge: "Harpsichords and Jazz Trumpets," *Frontiers of Jazz*, ed. R. de Toledano (New York, 1947, rev. 2/1962), 13
——: "Bubber Miley," *JM*, iv/3 (1958), 2
G. Schuller: *Early Jazz: its Roots and Musical Development* (New York, 1968), 320
B. McRae: "A B Basics: Bubber Miley," *JJ*, xxiii/2 (1970), 39
D. Ellington: *Music is my Mistress* (Garden City, NY, 1973), 106

J. R. TAYLOR

Miller, Eddie [Müller, Edward Raymond] (*b* New Orleans, 23 June 1911). Saxophonist, clarinetist, and singer. As a youth he sold newspapers in order to be eligible to play in a newsboys' band. By the age of 16 he was working professionally, and he made his first recording in New York with the bandleader Julie Wintz (1930). Thereafter he was a principal soloist with Ben Pollack (1930–34) before becoming a founding member of Bob Crosby's band (1935). His eloquent clarinet playing may be heard on such recordings as *South Rampart Street Parade* and *Dogtown Blues*, and his emotionally charged work on tenor saxophone is particularly effective on recordings by the Bob Cats, among them *I hear you talking* and *Call me a taxi*. He also played a masterful solo on the ballad *Slow Mood*, his own composition.

Before being drafted Miller led a band on the West Coast (1943–4); he revived this ensemble in 1945 after leaving the army because of illness. From 1945 to 1954 he worked as a studio musician for 20th Century-Fox. He played on many soundtracks and also took part in the film *Pete Kelly's Blues* (1955) and the subsequent television series of the same name. Thereafter he participated in many reunions of Crosby's band, with which he traveled to Japan and Australia in 1964. He toured the UK as a soloist (1967), then returned to New Orleans and worked with Pete Fountain (1967–76). He has continued to work as a freelance into the mid-1980s, touring Europe with Yank Lawson and Bob Haggart (1978, 1984).

Oral history material in *LNT*.

For illustration *see* CROSBY, BOB.

SELECTED RECORDINGS

As leader: Yesterdays (1944, Cap. 170); Cajun Love Song (1945, Cap. 10023); on Tenor of Jazz: *Tenor of Jazz* (1967, Fon. 5453), Bud meets Eddie, Little Girl Blue; *A Portrait of Eddie* (?1970, Blue Angel 509); *It's Miller Time* (1981, FaD 131)

As sideman: B. Pollack: Two Tickets to Georgia (1933, Vic. 24284); B. Berigan: You took advantage of me/Chicken and Waffles (1935, Decca 18117); I'm Coming Virginia/Blues (1935, Decca 18116); W. Manone: Dallas Blues/Swingin' at the Hickory House (1936, Bb 6375); B. Crosby: South Rampart Street Parade/Dogtown Blues (1937, Decca 15038); Wolverine Blues (1938, Decca 2032); Slow Mood (1938, Decca 2011); I hear you talking/Call me a taxi (1938, Decca 2207);

BIBLIOGRAPHY

"Hall of Fame: Eddie Miller," *Metronome*, lii/7 (1936)
B. Esposito: "Eddie Miller," *JJ*, xxvi/4 (1973), 13
J. Gordon: "Some Notes on Some Crosby Ex-Bobcats," *Sv*, no.75 (1978), 85
E. Cook: "Eddie Miller," *JJI*, xxxiv/12 (1981), 6; xxxv/1 (1982), 11
J. Chilton: "Eddie Miller," *Stomp Off, Let's Go! The Story of Bob Crosby's Bob Cats & Big Band* (London, 1983), 161
M. L. Hester: "Master of the Sax," *MR*, xi/8 (1984), 1
W. Warner: Liner notes, B. Crosby: *Bob Crosby's Camel Caravan* (Giants of Jazz 1037, 1984)
L. D. Holmes and J. W. Thomson: *Jazz Greats: Getting Better with Age* (New York, 1986)

BRIAN PEERLESS

Miller, (Alton) Glenn (*b* Clarinda, IA, 1 March 1904; *d* between London and Paris, ?15 Dec 1944). Bandleader and trombonist. He grew up in Fort Morgan, Colorado, where he studied music. He played with the locally popular Boyd Senter Orchestra in

Members of Glenn Miller's band at the Great Lakes Naval Training Station, Great Lakes, Illinois, 2 June 1942: (front, left to right) Paul Tanner and Miller (trombones), Wilbur Schwartz (alto saxophone), Al Klink (tenor saxophone), and Skip Martin (alto saxophone); (back) R. D. McMickle (trumpet), Moe Purtill (drums), Ed "Doc" Goldberg (double bass), and Bobby Hackett (cornet)

1921, attended the University of Colorado briefly, and in 1924 joined Ben Pollack's band on the West Coast. After moving to New York with Pollack in 1928 he performed as a freelance for several years, working at times with Red Nichols, Smith Ballew, and the Dorsey brothers, as both arranger and trombonist.

In 1934 Miller helped organize an orchestra for Ray Noble which later became popular through its radio broadcasts. By the mid-1930s he was well known in dance-band circles, and in 1937 organized an orchestra of his own. Although it made a few recordings for Decca, it failed to interest the public, and Miller disbanded it. In 1938 he organized a second group; again public interest was slow to develop, and the band's records did not sell well. Eventually, in March 1939, the group was chosen to play the summer season at the prestigious Glen Island Casino in a suburb of New York, which led to another important engagement, at Meadowbrook, in New Jersey, in spring of the same year. Both places offered frequent radio broadcasts, and by midsummer the Miller orchestra had developed a nationwide following. In autumn 1939 it began a series of radio broadcasts for Chesterfield cigarettes, which increased its already great popularity. Thereafter the band was in constant demand for recording sessions, and appeared in two films, *Sun Valley Serenade* (1941) and *Orchestra Wives* (1942; *see* FILMS, §I, 2).

In October 1942, as a patriotic gesture, Miller disbanded his group and joined the US Army Air Force with the rank of captain. He assembled a high-quality dance band to play for the troops, which in 1944 moved its base to England. On 15 December Miller set off by airplane in bad weather for Paris to arrange for his band's appearance there, but the airplane never arrived, and no trace of it was found. Miller was mourned internationally and attained the status of a war hero. His recordings remain popular in the USA and also in Britain, and at times various Glenn Miller orchestras, under several leaders, have been formed to play his music.

Miller led one of the most popular and best-remembered dance bands of the swing era. In his lifetime he was seen as an intense, ambitious perfectionist, and his success was built on the precise playing of carefully crafted arrangements, rather than propulsive swing or fine jazz solo improvisation (his only important jazz soloist was Bobby Hackett). He was particularly noted for the device of doubling a melody on saxophone with a clarinet an octave higher. His arrangements were seamless and rich. Paradoxically, however, although he had many hits with sentimental ballads performed by such singers as Ray Eberle and Marion Hutton, it was his swinging riff tunes, for example *In the Mood* and *Tuxedo Junction*, which became most famous. In 1943 he published *Glenn Miller's Method for Orchestral Arranging*.

For further illustration *see* MUTE, fig.3.

SELECTED RECORDINGS

(all recorded for Bluebird unless otherwise indicated)

Moonlight Serenade (1939, 10214B); Little Brown Jug (1939, 10286A); In the Mood (1939, 10416A); My Prayer (1939, 10404B); Tuxedo Junction (1940, 10612A); Pennsylvania 6-5000 (1940, 10754A); Chattanooga Choo Choo (1941, 11230B); A String of Pearls (1941, 11382B); Kalamazoo (1942, Vic. 27934A)

BIBLIOGRAPHY

S. F. Bedwell: *A Glenn Miller Discography and Biography* (London, 1955)
J. Burns: "Briefly Glenn Miller," *JM*, no.192 (1971), 6
J. Flower: *Moonlight Serenade: a Bio-discography of the Glenn Miller Civilian Band* (New Rochelle, NY, 1972)
G. T. Simon: *Glenn Miller and his Orchestra* (New York, 1974)
J. Green: *Glenn Miller and the Age of Swing* (London, 1976)
G. Butcher: *Next to a Letter from Home: Major Glenn Miller's Wartime Band* (Edinburgh, 1986) [incl. discography]

JAMES LINCOLN COLLIER

Miller, Harry [Harold Simon] (*b* Cape Town, 25 April 1941; *d* Netherlands, 16 Dec 1983). South African double bass player. He moved to London in 1961 and joined the group Sounds Five, which was led by the West Indian drummer Don Brown. In 1967–70 he was the pre-eminent double bass player of the developing free-jazz movement in London; he played with John Surman, Alan Skidmore, Mike Westbrook, the Brotherhood of Breath, and, most notably, as a member of Mike Osborne's trio with Louis Moholo. In 1973, with others, he formed the record company OGUN; during the mid-1970s he led his own band, Isipingo, which at times included Moholo and Keith Tippett. He played with Peter Brötzmann in Berlin early in 1977, and later that year moved to the Netherlands, where he formed a quintet. Miller's versatility and range of expression as a player were remarkable: his solo album *Children at Play* is characterized by a gentle beauty, while with Irène Schweizer he played a racy style of free jazz and with Dudu Pukwana's group Spear a rhythmic form of *kwela* (urban popular music from South Africa) influenced by funk.

SELECTED RECORDINGS

As unaccompanied soloist: *Children at Play* (1973, Ogun 200)
As leader: of Isipingo: *Family Affair* (1977, Ogun 310); *Down South* (1983, Vara 4213)
As sideman: M. Osborne: *Border Crossing* (1974, Ogun 300); *All Night Long* (1975, Ogun 700)

BIBLIOGRAPHY

D. Constant: "Harry Miller: le tropique d'Ogun," *Jm*, no.239 (1975), 19
R. Cotterrell, ed.: *Jazz Now: the Jazz Centre Society Guide* (London, 1976)
C. de Ledesma: "Afro Jazz: Evolution and Revolution," *The Wire*, no.12 (1985), 26, esp. 28

CHARLES DE LEDESMA

Miller, Marcus (*b* New York, 14 June 1959). Electric bass guitarist and record producer. He took up electric bass guitar as a teenager, and first played professionally at the age of 15 with the soul group Harlem River Drive. Later he played with the flutist Bobbi Humphrey (1977) before touring with Lenny White. Thereafter he became active as a studio musician in New York, working with Bob James, Grover Washington, Jr., and the soul singers Roberta Flack and Aretha Franklin, among others. He joined Miles Davis's new band in 1980 and remained with it until 1982. During this period he also began collaborating with David Sanborn, contributing to his album *Voyeur* as both a player and a composer. At this time he recorded the first of his albums as a leader, which was highly influenced by pop and soul music. Later he produced, with others, Sanborn's album *Backstreet*, on which he also played electric bass guitar, keyboards, and percussion, sang, and for which he wrote arrangements. In 1986 he played many of the instruments on and composed, produced, and arranged much of the music for Davis's album *Tutu*. Miller leads a band, the Jamaica Boys, with White, and has remained active into the mid-1980s as a studio musician, working with Kazumi Watanabe (1983–4), a quintet led by McCoy Tyner and Jackie McLean (1985), Kevin Eubanks (1986), and numerous pop and soul musicians, including Luther Vandross.

SELECTED RECORDINGS

As sideman with M. Davis: *The Man with the Horn* (1980–81, Col. FC36790); *We want Miles!* (1981, Col. C2-38005); *Tutu* (1986, WB 254904)
As sideman with others: D. Sanborn: *Voyeur* (*c*1980, WB 3546); *Backstreet* (*c*1982, WB 23906); K. Watanabe: *Mobo I* (1983–4, Gram. 8404); M. Tyner and J. McLean: *It's about Time* (1985, BN 85102)

BIBLIOGRAPHY

S. Freedman: "Marcus Miller: the Thumbslinger Bassist for Hire," *DB*, 1/4 (1983), 17 [incl. discography]

T. Mulhern: "Marcus Miller: Solo Bassist, Stellar Sideman," *GP*, xvii/11 (1983) [incl. discography]
B. Milkowski: "Marcus Miller: Miles' Man in the Studio," *DB*, liv/4 (1987), 20 [incl. discography]

BILL MILKOWSKI

Miller, Mulgrew [Mug] (*b* Greenwood, MS, 13 Aug 1955). Pianist. He studied music at university and first played in gospel and rhythm-and-blues groups. In the late 1970s he was a member of Mercer Ellington's band, touring Europe in 1977, then worked with Betty Carter (1980), Woody Shaw's quintet (1981–3), and Art Blakey's Jazz Messengers (1983–6). These associations established him as mainly a hard-bop player. In his active career as a session musician he has recorded with numerous leaders, including Johnny Griffin and Branford Marsalis (both 1983), Terence Blanchard and Donald Harrison (1983, 1984), John Stubblefield (1984), and Tony Williams and Bobby Hutcherson (both 1985); he has also recorded as the leader of a trio.

SELECTED RECORDINGS

As leader: *Keys to the City* (1985, Landmark 1507); *Work!* (1986, Landmark 1511)
As sideman: W. Shaw: *Master of the Art* (1982, Elek. Mus. 60131); A. Blakey: *Blue Night* (1985, Tim. 217); F. Hubbard and W. Shaw: *Double Take* (1985, BN 85121)

BIBLIOGRAPHY

I. Gitler: Liner notes, A. Blakey: *Art Blakey Live at Sweet Basil* (1985, PW 6357)
B. Doerschuk: "Mulgrew Miller: Riding the Crest of the New Jazz Piano Wave," *Keyboard*, xii/11 (1987), 64 [incl. discography]
B. Priestley: "Miller, Mulgrew," in I. Carr, D. Fairweather, and B. Priestley: *Jazz: the Essential Companion* (London, 1987)
G. Kalbacher: "Profile: Mulgrew Miller," *DB*, lv/3 (1988), 45

Miller, Punch [Ernest; Burden, Ernest; Kid Punch] (*b* Raceland, LA, 10 June 1894; *d* New Orleans, 2 Dec 1971). Trumpeter and singer. Deserted by his father as a baby, he adopted his mother's maiden name. As a teenager he specialized on cornet and worked with local groups. During military service he played in army bands, and after being discharged (1919) he traveled to New Orleans, where he worked with the trombonist Jack Carey. He then spent a long period touring with a vaudeville revue before moving to Chicago in 1926. He played with Al Wynn, Tiny Parham, and Freddie Keppard, and toured with Jelly Roll Morton. Thereafter he worked regularly with the drummer Frankie Franko (François Moseley) and others (1929–35), then led groups and performed in and around Chicago until the mid-1940s. On tour with a carnival show he arrived in New York in 1947 and played on the radio program "This is Jazz." In 1956 he returned to New Orleans, and after a serious illness in 1959 he resumed playing in 1960. He toured Japan with George Lewis (i) in 1963, and was the subject of a film, *New Orleans: 'Til the Butcher Cuts him Down*, in 1971. Miller is best remembered for his fast fingering and his exceptional work in the blues style.
Oral history material in *LNT*.

SELECTED RECORDINGS

As leader: *The Wild Horns* (1941, Para. 102); West End Blues (1944, Session 12014); Weary Blues (1947, Cen. 4019); *Preservation Hall* (1962, Atl. 1410); *The River's in Mourning* (1962, Icon 7)
As sideman: A. Wynn: Down by the Levee/Parkway Stomp (1928, Voc. 1220); F. Franko: Somebody stole my gal (1930, Mlt. 12009); G. Lewis: *George Lewis and his New Orleans All Stars in Tokyo* (1963, King 3009)

BIBLIOGRAPHY

W. C. Allen: "Trumpet Giants, 4: 'Punch' Miller," *Hot Notes*, ii/4 (1947), 2 [incl. discography]
B. Grauer: "Kid Punch," *Record Changer*, vii/6 (1948), 10
P. Spalding: "Just Call me Punch Miller," *MM* (18 Dec 1971), 54
P. Haby: "Punch Miller, 1894–1971," *Fn*, xiv/1 (1982), 4 [incl. discography]
C. Hillman: "Punch Miller: the Chicago Recordings," *Fn*, xiv/5 (1983), 4
M. Tovey: "Punch Miller: a Checklist of Recordings, 1925–1947," *Fn*, xix/3 (1988), 21

BRIAN PEERLESS

Miller, Sing [James Edward] (*b* New Orleans, 17 June 1914). Pianist. As a youth he sang with the Harmonizing Browns Quartet. He first played ukulele and banjo, but by the late 1920s was concentrating on piano. In the mid-1930s he worked with several bands, principally that of Percy Humphrey, while also performing as a soloist. After army service (1942–5) he was a member for 16 years of the band led by the drummer Earl Foster. From 1961 Miller has toured and recorded with various bands emanating from Preservation Hall, including those of Kid Sheik Colar (1961–3, 1967), Kid Thomas (1963–4), and Humphrey (from 1968). He has also made recordings with Jim Robinson and Polo Barnes (both 1973) and as a leader (including *Old Times with Sing Miller*, 1975, Smoky Mary 1975S). He toured Europe as a soloist in 1979 and 1981.
Oral history material in *LNT*.

BIBLIOGRAPHY

F. Demond: Liner notes, *Old Times with Sing Miller* (Smoky Mary 1975S, 1975)
J. DeDonder: "Music is a Medicine: James Edward 'Sing' Miller," *Fn*, xi/3 (1980), 4
C. Strickland: "Recording in New Orleans, 1981," *Fn*, xii/4 (1981), 4

ALYN SHIPTON

Millinder, Lucky [Lucius Venable] (*b* Anniston, AL, 8 Aug 1900; *d* New York, 28 Sept 1966). Bandleader. He grew up in Chicago, and worked at cabarets on the South Side for several seasons as a dancer and compère before becoming a bandleader in 1931; during this period he used the name Lucius Venable. The following year he moved to New York, and in 1933 led his band on the south coast of France. He returned to New York later that year and in 1934 he began leading the Mills Blue Rhythm Band, with which he remained until 1938 (for illustration *see* MILLS BLUE RHYTHM BAND). Thereafter his career faltered until 1940, when he formed a new band which worked regularly at the Savoy Ballroom and included such musicians as Eddie "Lockjaw" Davis, Dizzy Gillespie, Freddie Webster, and Sister Rosetta Tharpe. In the mid-1940s this ensemble was partly responsible for the popularization of rhythm-and-blues. It appeared in a number of films, including *Paradise in Harlem* (1939) and *Boarding House Blues* (1948), and remained active into the 1950s. Millinder composed many of his bands' hits, including *Ride, Red, Ride*, which he wrote in collaboration with Irving Mills. He later pursued a variety of occupations, working for a while as a disc jockey. He was noted for his ebullient personality and acrobatic showmanship. Although unable to read music, he was an exceptional conductor.

SELECTED RECORDINGS

Spitfire (1935, Col. 3020D); Ride, Red, Ride (1935, Col. 3087D); Algiers Stomp (1936, Col. 3158D); Jammin' for the Jackpot (1937, Var. 634); Trouble in Mind/Big Fat Mama (1941, Decca 4041); Shout, Sister, Shout/I want a tall, skinny papa (1941–2, Decca 18386); Savoy (1942, Decca 18353); Mason Flyer/Little John Special (1942, Bruns. 03406); Shipyard Social Function (1943, Decca 18674); Let it Roll (1947, Decca 24182)

BIBLIOGRAPHY

Discography of Lucky Millinder (Basel, Switzerland, 1962)
A. McCarthy: *Big Band Jazz* (New York and London, 1974), 289
A. Gerber: Liner notes, *Lucky Millinder's Orchestra with Sister Rosetta Tharpe: Lucky Days 1941–1945* (MCA 1319, 1980)
T. Burke and D. Penny: "Big Band Blues: Lucky Millinder's Orchestra: 'Let me off Uptown'," *Blues & Rhythm: the Gospel Truth*, no.2 (1984), 9 [incl. discography]; no.6 (1985), 40 [addns and corrections]
D. Barker: *A Life in Jazz*, ed. A. Shipton (London and New York, 1986)

FRANK DRIGGS

Mills, Irving (*b* New York, 16 Jan 1884; *d* Palm Springs, CA, 21 April 1985). Impresario, music publisher, composer, lyricist, and singer. He worked as a song demonstrator and dance-band singer while in his teens. In 1919, with his brother Jack, he established Jack Mills, Inc., a music-publishing business that specialized in the work of black artists. The firm was renamed Mills Music, Inc., in the mid-1920s and flourished under Irving Mills's direction. Mills also worked as a talent scout, record producer, and band manager, and in 1926 became manager for the Duke Ellington Orchestra. Among the other bandleaders whose careers he promoted were Cab Calloway, Benny Carter, Fletcher Henderson, Jimmie Lunceford, and Don Redman. He also organized pick-up bands for recording sessions – such as Irving Mills and his Hotsy Totsy Gang (1928–30) and the Whoopee Makers (1929) – and usually engaged the best white musicians, including Jack Teagarden and Benny Goodman. Mills participated as singer in many of these sessions, as well as some of Ellington's; he also composed a number of pieces in collaboration with the artists whom he promoted, and provided the lyrics for such standards as *Sophisticated Lady, Mood Indigo*, and *It don't mean a thing if it ain't got that swing.* In 1931 he took over the Cocoanut Grove Orchestra, initially to act as a relief band at the Cotton Club while Ellington and Calloway were on tour; this group soon became known as the MILLS BLUE RHYTHM BAND. In 1936 Mills founded the Master and Variety record labels, and in 1943 he assembled the all-star cast for the film *Stormy Weather*, for which he also composed some music. He continued to be active in management and music publishing into the 1960s.

Oral history material in *CtY, NjR*.

SELECTED RECORDINGS

As sideman with Duke Ellington: Doin' the New Lowdown (1928, OK 8602); Diga diga do (1928, Vic. 38008); A Nite at the Cotton Club (1929, Pirate MPC524) [EP]

SELECTED ARRANGEMENTS

As leader: Futuristic Rhythm/Out where the blues begin (1929, Bruns. 4200)

BIBLIOGRAPHY

I. Mills and C. Emge: "I Split with Duke when the Music Began Sidetracking," *DB*, xix/22 (1952), 6

L. Feather: *The Passion for Jazz* (New York, 1980), 161

D. Carey: "Irving Mills: Musical Dynamo," *Irving Mills and his Hotsy Totsy Gang, 1928–29* (Retrieval FJ122, 1984) [liner notes]

EDDIE LAMBERT

Mills, Jackie (*b* New York, 11 March 1922). Drummer. He grew up in a musical family and changed from guitar to drums at the age of ten. His first professional engagements were with the big bands of Charlie Barnet, Benny Goodman, and Boyd Raeburn in the 1940s. During this period he became attracted to the bop style and developed a drumming technique based on that of Max Roach. In 1949 he began an association with Harry James which was to occupy him for most of the 1950s. He also recorded as a studio musician at this time. In the 1960s he began working as a record company executive, and from that time he has performed and recorded only rarely.

SELECTED RECORDINGS

As sideman: C. Barnet: Ya-lu-blu/Night of nights (1942, Bb 11446); D. Marmarosa: Mellow mood/How high the moon (1946, Atomic 225); R. Norvo: I'll follow you/Bop (1947, Cap. 15233); G. Wiggins: *Relax and Enjoy it* (1956, Cont. 7595)

BIBLIOGRAPHY

FeatherE

D. Gillespie and A. Frazer: *To be, or not . . . to Bop: Memoirs* (Garden City, NY, 1979; Ger. trans., Vienna, 1984), 243

SCOTT DeVEAUX

Mills Blue Rhythm Band [Blue Rhythm Band]. Big band. It was formed in 1930 in New York as the Blue Rhythm Band by the drummer Willie Lynch. During the same year it was known for a time as the Cocoanut Grove Orchestra and it accompanied Louis Armstrong on several recordings. When Irving Mills joined as manager in 1931 it became the Mills Blue Rhythm Band, although on early recordings it appears under a variety of titles, including Mills Music Masters and Blue Rhythm Boys. When Lynch left the band (1931) Baron Lee was chosen to act as leader (1932), and he was followed for a brief period by the trumpeter Eddie Mallory; Lucky Millinder assumed leadership in 1934, and remained with the group until it disbanded in 1938 (see illustration). Among the band's principal members were Wardell Jones, Shelton Hemphill, and Ed Anderson (trumpet), Harry White (trombone), Crawford Wethington (clarinet and alto and baritone saxophone), Ted and Caster McCord (clarinet and tenor saxophone), Edgar Hayes (piano), and Hayes Alvis (double bass). J. C. Higginbotham and Henry "Red" Allen joined in 1934, and the group later included Charlie Shavers, Harry Edison, Wilbur De Paris, and Danny Barker. It was most creative and successful in 1931–2, when its arrangements were written by Harry White, Edgar Hayes, and Nat Leslie, and again in 1935–6, when the arrangers included Billy Kyle, Hayes, Alex Hill, and Tab Smith. Although Mills originally used the group to substitute for Cab Calloway's and Duke Ellington's orchestras (which he also managed), it developed into an important band, and its best performances showed much originality and sound musicianship.

SELECTED RECORDINGS

Moanin' (1931, Bruns. 6156); Blue Rhythm/Blue Flame (1931, Bruns. 6143); Futuristic Jungleism (1931, Ban. 32240); Rhythm Spasm (1932, Mlt. 12418); White Lightning (1932, Mlt. 12414); Wild Waves (1932, Ban. 32493); Back Beats/Spitfire (1935, Col. 3020D); Balloonacy/Barrel House (1936, Col. 3156D); Big John Special/Callin' your Bluff (1936, Col. 3162D)

For further recordings *see* MILLINDER, LUCKY.

BIBLIOGRAPHY

F. Littler: "The Blue Rhythm Band," *JM*, iii/7 (1957), 7

"Lucky Millinder and the Mills Blues [sic] Rhythm Band: Personnel???," *Record Research*, no.88 (1968), 9

A. McCarthy: *Big Band Jazz* (New York and London, 1974), 255

F. Dutton and others: "Mills Blue Rhythm Band: a Discography and Solography," *Sv*, no.108 (1983), 204; no.109 (1983), 6; no.117 (1985), 109 [addns and corrections]

JOHNNY SIMMEN

Mills Brothers. Vocal quartet. Its principal members were the three brothers Herbert Mills (*b* Piqua, OH, April 1912), Harry Mills (*b* Piqua, 19 Aug 1913; *d* Los Angeles, 28 June 1982), and Donald Mills (*b* Piqua, 29 April 1915). A fourth brother, John Mills, Jr. (*d* Bellefontaine, OH, 1935), played guitar and sang bass in the group until his death, after which his place was taken by his father John Mills, Sr. (*b* Bellefonte, PA, 11 Feb 1882; *d* Bellefontaine, 9 Dec 1967). The group began singing in small-town vaudeville and tent shows, then in the late 1920s was featured for ten months on radio station WLW in Cincinnati. By 1930 the brothers were in New York performing in theaters, in clubs, and on radio, and soon began recording for Brunswick and appearing in films. During the 1930s and 1940s they had many hit songs; *Paper Doll* (1943) was their biggest success, selling some six million copies. John Mills, Sr., retired in 1957, but Herbert, Harry, and Donald continued to perform together throughout the 1970s.

The quartet was one of the first vocal groups to achieve great commercial success, and among the earliest black ensembles to attract a nationwide following. Early in their career the brothers sang accompanied only by guitar. Later they were

The Mills Blue Rhythm Band, New York, 1936: (back row, left to right) Lawrence Lucie (guitar), J. C. Higginbotham and George Washington (trombones), O'Neill Spencer (drums), and Elmer James (double bass); (middle row) Shelton Hemphill, Wardell Jones, and Henry "Red" Allen (trumpets); (front row) Lucky Millinder (leader), Crawford Wethington and Gene Mikell (alto saxophones), Buster Bailey (clarinet), Joe Garland (tenor saxophone), and Edgar Hayes (piano)

backed by orchestras and big bands, but their trademark remained a smooth and mellow three- or four-part harmony, closer to white popular music traditions than to Afro-American singing styles. The Mills Brothers recorded with the orchestras of Don Redman, Duke Ellington (1932), and Benny Carter (1940); their importance to jazz, however, is demonstrated more by their spectacular forays into scat singing, as on their quartet recording of *Tiger Rag/Nobody's Sweetheart* (1931, Bruns. 6197).

BIBLIOGRAPHY

FeatherE
J. R. T. Davies: "The Mills Brothers 1931–1934," *Sv*, i/6 (1966), 14
D. Ewen: *All the Years of American Popular Music* (Englewood Cliffs, NJ, 1977)

MARK TUCKER/R

Mince, Johnny [Mussenger [Muenzenberger], John Henry] (*b* Chicago Heights, IL, 8 July 1912). Clarinetist and saxophonist. His first important job was with Joe Haymes (?1929–1934). Shortly thereafter he became a member of Ray Noble's first American band (1935–7, interrupted by a brief period with Bob Crosby in 1936). In Glenn Miller's arrangements for Noble's band Mince played (on clarinet) the high trumpet parts originally written for Pee Wee Erwin and helped to establish the distinctive reed sound associated with Miller, in which a melody played on tenor saxophone was doubled by a clarinet an octave higher. He rose to fame as a clarinet soloist with Tommy Dorsey's orchestra (for illustration *see* DORSEY, TOMMY) and Clambake Seven (1937–41). After playing in an army band (1941–5) he commenced studio work. From 1966 he lectured and taught woodwinds privately and led his own small groups in and around New York. He appeared with Warren Covington's Tommy Dorsey Orchestra (1974), the Kings of Jazz (1974, in the UK), and the New Paul Whiteman Orchestra (1976); toured with Yank Lawson and Bob Haggart (1982); and performed at Dick Gibson's Colorado Jazz Party and many festivals, including the Festival of Traditional Jazz (Chicago, 1980) and the Grande Parade du Jazz Nice (1984).

Mince's superlative technique, fondness for flurries of notes, and bright, clean, even sound on the clarinet provided a foretaste of the style of Buddy DeFranco. Within one chorus his solos were often limited to a narrow range and his improvisation sometimes seemed busy, but he could project above a band through sheer power and rhythmic energy. His best solos are stellar examples of clarinet playing in the swing era.

SELECTED RECORDINGS

As leader: *Summer of '79* (1979, MonE 7090); *The Master Comes Home* (1983, Jlgy J126)

As sideman: R. Norvo: Honeysuckle Rose (1935, Col. 3059D); G. Miller: Solo Hop (1935, Col. 3058D); R. Noble: Chinatown, my Chinatown (1935, Vic. 25070); T. Dorsey: Blue Danube (1937, Vic. 25556); Panama (1938, Vic. 26185); Old Black Joe (1938, Vic. 26145); Milenberg Joys (1939, Vic. 26437); *The Sentimental Gentleman* (1940–42, RCA LPM6003), incl. Hallelujah (1940)

BIBLIOGRAPHY

ChiltonW; *FeatherE*; *Feather–Gitler '70s*
J. Dawson: "Clubbing Around," *MM*, xlix (13 April 1974), 20
G. T. Simon: *Glenn Miller and his Orchestra* (New York, 1974)
S. Traill: "Mince's Words," *JJI*, xxxiii/11 (1980), 18

JEFFREY COOPER

Minerve, Geezil [Harold "Geezil"] (*b* Havana, 3 Jan 1922). Alto saxophonist and clarinetist. He grew up in Florida and studied music from the age of 12. After working with the drummer Jeff Gibson and Ida Cox he belonged to a band in New Orleans. In the early 1940s he played under the bandleader Clarence Love and with Ernie Fields; after serving in the US Army (1943–6) he again worked with Fields, recording around 1949. He performed and recorded with Buddy Johnson (1949–57), worked as a freelance in New York, then played with Mercer Ellington (1960) and Ray Charles (1962–4); he also worked as a music director for the singer Arthur Prysock. Minerve also played flute and piccolo. From 1971 he belonged to Duke Ellington's orchestra; after Ellington's death in 1974 he played again with Mercer Ellington and worked as a freelance in and around New York.

SELECTED RECORDINGS

As sideman: B. Johnson: Root Man Blues (1951, Decca 27998); D. Ellington: *Toga brava Suite* (1971, UA 92), incl. Addie; on *Up in Duke's Workshop* (1969–72, Pablo 2310815), Blem (1972); *Eastbourne Performance* (1973, RCA APL1-1023), incl. Don't you know I care?

BIBLIOGRAPHY

Feather–Gitler '70s
S. Dance: "Harold 'Geezil' Minerve," *JJ*, xxvi/10 (1973), 8

EDDIE LAMBERT

Mingus, Charles(, Jr.) (*b* Nogales, AZ, 22 April 1922; *d* Cuernavaca, Mexico, 5 Jan 1979). Double bass player, pianist, composer, and bandleader.

1. Life. Mingus grew up in the Watts area of Los Angeles. He first attempted to learn trombone and cello, but after being frustrated by poor teachers he took up double bass in high school, studying with Red Callender and a former bass player with the New York PO, Herman Rheinschagen. He also studied composition with Lloyd Reese, writing *What Love* in 1939 and *Half-mast Inhibitions* in 1940–41 (both were recorded in the 1960s). He played with Kid Ory in Barney Bigard's ensemble (1942), and toured as bass player in the big bands of Louis Armstrong (*c*1943) and Lionel Hampton (1947–8). In his first recordings he accompanied jazz musicians and rhythm-and-blues singers, and as "Baron Mingus" led diverse ensembles. He gained national attention as a member of Red Norvo's trio (with Tal Farlow) in 1950–51 (see illustration). Thereafter he settled in New York, where in the early 1950s he worked with Billy Taylor (ii), Duke Ellington, Stan Getz, Art Tatum, and Bud Powell. Some of his performances during this period, including the famous concert at Massey Hall in Toronto with Charlie Parker and Dizzy Gillespie, and several of his early Jazz Workshop sessions, are preserved on recordings issued by Mingus's own company, Debut Records (1952–5).

In the mid-1950s Mingus's activities as a composer became increasingly important. Along with Teo Macero, Teddy Charles, and other experimenters, he contributed written works to a Jazz Composers' Workshop from 1953 to 1955. Realizing that musical notation was inadequate for his approach to composition, he founded a new workshop in 1955 in which he transmitted the details of his works by dictating lines to each player. Over the years this four- to 11-piece group included such musicians as Jimmy Knepper, Booker Ervin, John Handy, Eric Dolphy, Roland Kirk, Jaki Byard, and Mingus's lasting associate, the drummer Dannie Richmond.

The early 1960s saw the birth of Mingus's most complex musical creations – his compositions *The Black Saint and the Sinner Lady* and *Meditations on Integration*, and his many performances with Dolphy. In the same years he endeavored, unsuccessfully, to free himself from economic dependence on the white commercial jazz scene. In 1960 he arranged some concerts in competition with the Newport Jazz Festival; from these came the Jazz Artists Guild, a short-lived organization intended to provide jazzmen with means for promoting their own businesses. He presented a disastrous rehearsal-concert at Town Hall, New York, in 1962, and was unable to find a publisher for his remarkable autobiography, *Beneath the Underdog*; his second recording company, the Charles Mingus label, issued only a few titles in 1964–5 before collapsing. By then Mingus was in dire financial straits and suffering from deep-seated psychological problems. Rarely performing, he essentially withdrew from public life from 1966 to 1969; Thomas Reichman's film *Mingus* (1968) documented his sad eviction from a New York apartment.

Financial pressures forced Mingus to resume his career in June 1969; his enthusiasm was rekindled in 1971 by the granting of a Guggenheim fellowship in composition and the publication of his autobiography. During his remaining years he wrote big-band music and two suites for films and collaborated on an LP with the pop singer Joni Mitchell. He traveled extensively with his workshop until 1977, when he fell seriously ill; he supervised his last recording session (January 1978) from a wheelchair.

2. Music. Mingus's accomplishments surpass in historic and stylistic breadth those of any other major figure in jazz. As a double bass player he commanded an awesome technique and was thoroughly conversant with all styles of jazz extant during his lifetime. He developed a new "conversational" approach to his instrument in his dialogues with Dolphy (*What Love*, 1960; *Epitaph*, 1962), and also a "pianistic" approach that simultaneously combined the bass line, inner harmonies, and improvised countermelodies (*Stormy Weather*, 1960). Other fine examples of his double bass solos may be heard on *Cryin' Blues*, *Tensions* (both 1959), *Mood Indigo* (1963), *Orange was the color of her dress*, *Sophisticated Lady*, *I got it bad*, *Meditations on Integration*, and *New Fables* (all 1964).

Mingus's bop works are a coherent blend of New Orleans jazz, blues, and black gospel music; he also made use of material from pieces by Duke Ellington. In almost every composition he modified conventional blues and popular-song forms by adding rhythmic contrasts: double-, half-, or stop-time passages, shifting tempos or meters, and walking, shuffle, two-beat, or Latin patterns. (*Fables of Faubus*, 1959, and *The Black Saint and the Sinner Lady*, 1963, summarize these procedures; for a further discussion of *Fables of Faubus*, *see* Forms, §5.) He frequently changed textures, and had a particular preference for dense sonorities generated by low-pitched instruments (double bass, trombone, baritone saxophone, tuba), striking dissonances (most obvious in his reharmonization of the melody of *Ladybird*, 1955), collective improvisation (*Wednesday Night Prayer Meeting*), and overlapping riffs. These traits are all present in the 12-bar blues *Hora decubitus*, the first four bars of which are given in ex.1. The numbers to the left of the example refer to the entries of instruments in successive choruses (2–7), reading from bottom to top; the walking patterns on the double bass are varied, but the other parts remain constant. Mingus's rhythmic and textural devices often prefigured features associated with free jazz, just as his use of pedal points and oscillating chords (*Love Chant*, 1955; *Ysabel's Table Dance*, 1957) prefigured Miles Davis's influential compositions of the late 1950s. The theatrical side of his art emerged in humorous or biting vocal pieces such as *Eat that chicken* (1961) and *Freedom* (1962).

In the Jazz Workshop Mingus was not especially concerned with creating perfect, polished performances. Instead he experimented, continually revising a central core of compositions. The results were chains of related pieces. Some were obviously linked by title and substance: *My Jelly Roll Soul* (1959), *Jelly Roll* (1959); *Fables of Faubus* (1959), *Original Faubus Fables* (1960), *Fables of Faubus* (1964), *New Fables* (1964); *Song with Orange* (1959), *Orange was the color of her dress* (1963, 1964). Retitling disguised others: *Haitian Fight Song* (1955), *II B. S.* (1963); *E's flat, Ah's flat too* (1959), *Hora decubitus* (1963); *Goodbye pork pie hat* (1959), *Theme for Lester Young* (1963); and the *Meditation* pieces (1964, 1965), initially entitled *Praying with Eric* because of Dolphy's death (1964). Others shared themes but included substantial sections of new material: *Pithecanthropus erectus* (1956), *Epitaph* (1962), *Opus 3* (1973); *Nourogg* (1957), *Open Letter to Duke* (1959), *Don't come back* (1962), *I X Love* (1963); *Wednesday Night Prayer Meeting* (1959), *Better git it in your soul* (1959), *Slop* (1959). Among these evolving works the two series *Fables* and *Meditations* demonstrate Mingus's

Ex.1 Bars 1–4 of *Hora decubitus*, on *Mingus, Mingus, Mingus, Mingus, Mingus* (1963, Imp. 54); transcr. B. Kernfeld

greatest achievement; he obliterated the standard distinctions between improvisation and composition and brought the spontaneity of improvised jazz to complex structures.

Although Mingus continued to notate big-band music and compositions containing sections of art music, his finest works were dictated. He used the piano in rehearsals to outline structures, assign individual lines, and set limitations on improvised sections. In nightclubs he directed from the bass, playing

Red Norvo's trio at Fazio's Towne Room, Milwaukee, 1951: Tal Farlow (guitar), Charles Mingus (double bass), and Norvo (vibraphone)

while shouting instructions. In 1961–2 he engaged other double bass players and performed as the workshop's pianist. He frequently stopped in mid-tune to correct mistakes and to upbraid inattentive audiences; his several explosive confrontations with the public brought him considerable notoriety. Nevertheless in his performances he generally managed to convey his lofty musical standards and a sense of jazz history.

Oral history material in *NjR* (JOHP).

See also BLUES, §12.

SELECTED RECORDINGS

* – composed by Mingus

AS LEADER

Charles Mingus Quintet (1955, Debut 139), incl. *Haitian Fight Song, Ladybird, *Love Chant; *Pithecanthropus erectus* (1956, Atl. 1237), incl. *Pithecanthropus erectus; *The Clown* (1957, Atl. 1260), incl. *Reincarnation of a Lovebird; *Tijuana Moods* (1957, RCA LSP2533), incl. *Ysabel's Table Dance; *A Modern Jazz Symposium of Music and Poetry* (1957, Beth. 6026), incl. *Nourogg; *Blues and Roots* (1959, Atl. 1305), incl. *Cryin' Blues, *E's flat, Ah's flat too, *My Jelly Roll Soul, *Tensions, *Wednesday Night Prayer Meeting; *Mingus Ah Um* (1959, Col. CL1370), incl. *Better git it in your soul, *Fables of Faubus, *Goodbye pork pie hat, *Jelly Roll, *Open Letter to Duke; *Mingus Dynasty* (1959, Col. CS8236), incl. *Slop, *Song with Orange

Pre-Bird (1960, Mer. 20627), incl. *Half-mast Inhibitions; *Charles Mingus Presents Charles Mingus* (1960, Can. 9005), incl. *Original Faubus Fables, *What Love; *Mingus!* (1960, Can. 9021), incl. Stormy Weather; *Oh Yeah* (1961, Atl. 1377), incl. *Eat that chicken, *Ecclusiastics, *Oh Lord, don't let them drop that atomic bomb on me; *Tonight at Noon* (1961, Atl. 1416), incl. *Peggy's Blue Skylight; *Town Hall Concert* (1962, UA 15024), incl. *Epitaph, *Freedom; **The Black Saint and the Sinner Lady* (1963, Imp. 35); *Mingus Plays Piano* (1963, Imp. 60), incl. *Orange was the color of her dress; *Mingus, Mingus, Mingus, Mingus, Mingus* (1963, Imp. 54), incl. *Hora decubitus, *I X Love, Mood Indigo, *Theme for Lester Young, *II B. S.

Town Hall Concert (1964, Charles Mingus 005), incl. *Praying with Eric; *The Great Concert of Charles Mingus* (1964, Amer. 003–5), incl. *Fables of Faubus, *Orange was the color of her dress, Sophisticated Lady; *Right Now* (1964, Fan. 86017), incl. *Meditation for a Pair of Wire Cutters, *New Fables; *Mingus at Monterey* (1964, Charles Mingus 001–2), incl. I got it bad, *Meditations on Integration, *Orange was the color of her dress; *Charles Mingus* (1965, Charles Mingus 0013–14), incl. *Meditation on Inner Space; *Mingus Moves* (1973, Atl. 1653), incl. *Opus 3; *Cumbia and Jazz Fusion* (1976–7, Atl. 8801), incl. *Cumbia and Jazz Fusion; *Three or Four Shades of Blues* (1977, Atl. 1700), incl. *Three or Four Shades of Blues

AS SIDEMAN

L. Hampton: *Mingus Fingers (1947, Decca 24428); R. Norvo: Godchild (1951, Dis. 167); Jazz at Massey Hall: *Quintet of the Year* (1953, Debut 2, 4), incl. Hot House

BIBLIOGRAPHY

N. Hentoff: "Charlie Mingus: Cafe Bohemia, New York," *DB*, xxiii/1 (1956), 8

I. Gitler: "Mingus Speaks, and Bluntly," *DB*, xxvii/15 (1960), 29

G. Lees: "Newport: the Trouble," *DB*, xxvii/17 (1960), 20

N. Hentoff: *The Jazz Life* (New York and London, 1961/*R*1975) [incl. previously pubd articles], 157

T. White: "Mingus at Town Hall," *Jazz*, i/3 (1963), 13

J. Berendt: "Mingus and the Shadow of Duke Ellington," *Jazz*, iv/4 (1965), 17; repr. in *Ein Fenster aus Jazz: Essays, Portraits, Reflexionen* (Frankfurt am Main, Germany, 1977), 148

I. Goldberg: *Jazz Masters of the Fifties* (New York and London, 1965/*R*1980)

D. Locke: "Jazz Paradox," *JM*, xi/9 (1965), 23

R. J. Wilbraham: *Charles Mingus: a Biography and Discography* (London, 1967) [incl. list of compositions]

W. Balliett: *Ecstasy at the Onion* (New York and Indianapolis, 1971) [colln of previously pubd articles and reviews], 263

C. Mingus: *Beneath the Underdog*, ed. N. King (New York and London, 1971; Ger. trans. as *Autobiographie*, Hamburg, Germany, 1980, 2/1986)

E. Jost: *Free Jazz* (Graz, Austria, 1974)

J. Litweiler: "There's a Mingus among us," *DB*, xlii/4 (1975), 12

G. Giddins: "Three or Four Shades of Mingus," *VV*, xxiii (3 July 1978), 53

B. Primack: "The Gospel According to Mingus: Disciplines Carry the Tune," *DB*, xlv/20 (1978), 12

B. Sidran: "Charles Mingus Finds a New Voice," *RS*, no.282 (28 Dec 1978–11 Jan 1979), 33

L. Feather: "Joni Mitchell Makes Mingus Sing," *DB*, xlvi/15 (1979), 16

D. Morgenstern: "Charles Mingus, 1922–1979," *Radio Free Jazz* (1979), Feb, 14

B. Priestley: *Mingus: a Critical Biography* (London, Melbourne, Australia, and New York, 1982)

M. Ruppli: *Charles Mingus Discography* (Frankfurt am Main, Germany, 1982)

H. L. Lindenmaier and H. J. Salewski: *The Man who Never Sleeps: the Charles Mingus Discography 1945–1978* (Freiburg, Germany, 1983)

H. Weber and G. Filtgen: *Charles Mingus: sein Leben, seine Musik, seine Schallplatten* (Gauting, Germany, 1984)

BARRY KERNFELD

Mingus Dynasty. Group formed by Susan Graham Ungaro Mingus shortly after Charles Mingus's death in 1979, for the purpose of giving performances of Mingus's compositions. The group has usually had six or seven members, many of whom have been musicians who worked as Mingus's sidemen; it has recorded three albums, including *Chair in the Sky* (1979, Elek. 248) and *Reincarnation* (1982, SN 1042), which represent an interesting selection of material. Both Dannie Richmond and Jimmy Knepper have worked as Mingus Dynasty's music director.

BRIAN PRIESTLEY

Minor, Dan [Slamfoot] (*b* Dallas, 10 Aug 1909; *d* New York, 11 April 1982). Trombonist. He played in a church orchestra in 1926 and soon after joined the Blue Moon Chasers, a local group that included the brothers Keg and Budd Johnson. He performed with many of the prominent bands in the Southwest, including those led by Walter Page (1927–9), Ben Smith (1929–30), Earl Dykes (1930), Gene Coy, Lloyd Hunter, and Alphonso Trent (all 1931), and Bennie Moten (1931–4). In 1934 Minor was a member of Count Basie's first group, which was formed as a subsidiary of Moten's band; he re-joined Basie in Kansas City in 1936 and remained with him until 1941. Although Minor was a strong player he was overshadowed in Basie's orchestra by Dicky Wells, Benny Morton, and Vic Dickenson, and had little opportunity to play solos. In the 1940s Minor performed and recorded with Buddy Johnson (1941–4), Mercer Ellington and Lucky Millinder (both 1945), and Willie Bryant (1946). After working as a freelance player he left the profession, though he continued to play part-time.

SELECTED RECORDINGS

As sideman: W. Page: Blue Devil Blues/Squabblin' (1929, Voc. 1463); B. Moten: Toby/Moten Swing (1932, Vic. 23384); The Blue Room/Milenberg Joys (1932, Vic. 24381); New Orleans Feetwarmers: Weary Blues/I wish I could shimmy like my sister Kate (1938, Top Rank 35064); C. Basie: Gone with what Wind? (1940, OK 5629); You Can't Run Around (1940, OK 5673); B. Johnson: I'm Steppin' Out/Toodle-oodle-oo (1941, Decca 8599)

BIBLIOGRAPHY

ChiltonW

R. Horricks: *Count Basie and his Orchestra: its Music and its Musicians* (London and New York, 1957), 169

LAWRENCE KOCH

Minton's Playhouse. Nightclub in New York; *see* NIGHTCLUBS AND OTHER VENUES.

Missourians. Big band. It grew out of an ensemble founded as the violinist Wilson Robinson's Syncopators in the early 1920s. This later worked as the violinist Andrew Preer's Cotton Club Orchestra (1925–7) at the Cotton Club, New York. While touring with Ethel Waters in 1927 it took the name the Missourians to avoid confusion with Duke Ellington's Cotton Club Orchestra. Later it became the house orchestra at the Savoy Ballroom in Harlem (1928–9) under the leadership of the alto saxophonist and clarinetist George Scott. It made recordings in 1929–30, including *Ozark Mountain Blues* (1929, Vic. 38071) and *Two Hundred Squabble* (1930, Vic. 38145), which are notable for their driving ensemble passages and exciting solos. In 1930 CAB CALLOWAY, who had directed the band at intervals in

1929, became its leader, and thereafter it achieved great success performing and recording under his name. (E. P. Townley: "The Missourians," *JM*, iv/5 (1958), 6)

FRANK DRIGGS

Mr. B. Nickname of BILLY ECKSTINE.

Mr. Bear. Name under which TEDDY MCRAE occasionally recorded.

Mr. Eli. Nickname of ELI ROBINSON.

Mr. Five by Five. Nickname of JIMMY RUSHING.

Mr. Tailgate. Nickname of SANTO PECORA.

Mr. Time. Nickname of CLIFF LEEMAN.

Mitchell, Billy (*b* Kansas City, MO, 11 March 1926). Tenor saxophonist. He first worked in Detroit with Nat Towles, and in the late 1940s went to New York with Lucky Millinder's orchestra. In 1949 he recorded solos under Milt Jackson's leadership, worked with the big bands of Milt Buckner and Gil Fuller, and spent two months in Woody Herman's Second Herd. He then returned to Detroit, where from 1950 to 1953 he led a bop quintet which included Thad and Elvin Jones; the group recorded an album during this period, but the date of the session is erroneously given in standard discographies as 1948. After touring with Dizzy Gillespie (1956–7) Mitchell became a member of Count Basie's orchestra; he made several recordings with the band, though few of these feature him as a soloist. He left Basie in 1961 and, with Al Grey, formed a sextet; this ensemble, in its use of swinging riffs and bop improvisation, captured in a small-group context the essence of Basie's orchestral approach. Mitchell recorded in Germany with the Clarke–Boland Big Band (1963), and later played with the group briefly (1970). He also worked with Basie again (mid-1966 to mid-1967). During the 1970s he performed and taught in the New York area, recording with the Xanadu All Stars (1978) and as a leader (1980).

Oral history material in *NjR*.

SELECTED RECORDINGS

As leader: with T. Jones: Thad Jones–Billy Mitchell Quintet (1953, Dee Gee 4009) [EP]; with A. Grey: *Al Grey with Billy Mitchell* (1961, Argo 689); *A Little Juicy* (1963, Smash 67042); *De Lawd's Blues* (1980, Xan. 182)

As sideman: M. Jackson: Junior/Bubu (1949, Savoy 946); T. Jones: *Detroit–New York Junction* (1956, BN 1513); R. Charles: *Soul Brothers* (1957, Atl. 1279); C. Basie: *Basie One More Time* (1958–9, Roul. 52024), incl. Rat Race; K. Clarke and F. Boland: *Clarke–Boland Big Band* (1963, Atl. 1404); Xanadu All Stars: *Xanadu at Montreux* (1978, Xan. 163–5)

BIBLIOGRAPHY

P. Welding: "Difficulties Facing a New Group: the Al Grey–Billy Mitchell Sextet," *DB*, xxix/13 (1962), 16

V. Wilmer: "Prickly Billy's among his Peers," *MM*, xlv (31 Oct 1970), 28

BARRY KERNFELD

Mitchell, Blue [Richard Allen] (*b* Miami, 13 March 1930; *d* Los Angeles, 21 May 1979). Trumpeter. He took up trumpet in high school, where he acquired his nickname. He toured with rhythm-and-blues bands led by Paul Williams (1951–2), Earl Bostic (1952–5), and Chuck Willis. After returning to Miami he was heard by Cannonball Adderley, who took him to New York to record for Riverside (1958). He made his name as a member of Horace Silver's quintet (1958–63), where his lyrical playing and beautiful timbre perfectly complemented Silver's simplified, soulful brand of bop. When Silver disbanded his group the members – Junior Cook, Gene Taylor, and Roy Brooks – stayed together under Mitchell's leadership; Silver and Brooks were replaced by Chick Corea and Al Foster, whose places were later taken by Harold Mabern and Billy Higgins. Mitchell then returned to popular music, recording soul-jazz albums (1967–9) and touring with Ray Charles (1969–71) and the blues-rock bandleader John Mayall (1971–3). From 1974 he worked as a freelance in Los Angeles, and played as a principal soloist with Tony Bennett and Lena Horne. He also performed in the big bands of Louie Bellson, Bill Holman, and Bill Berry, and in bop groups, including a quintet with Richie Kamuca. During his final years he recorded a number of disco-jazz albums (1975–7) and played in a bop quintet with Harold Land (1975–8).

SELECTED RECORDINGS

As leader: *Big Six* (1958, Riv. 273); *Blue Soul* (1959, Riv. 309); *The Thing to Do* (1964, BN 84178); *Blue Mitchell* (1970, Mstr. 315); *True Blue* (1976, Xan. 136); with H. Land: *Mapanzi* (1977, Conc. 44)

As sideman: H. Silver: *Finger Poppin'* (1959, BN 4008); *Horace-scope* (1960, BN 4042); J. McLean: *Jackie's Bag* (1960, BN 4051); H. Silver: *Doin' the Thing* (1961, BN 84076); D. Patterson: *Opus de Don* (1968, Prst. 7577); J. Mayall: *Jazz Blues Fusion* (*c*1971, Pol. 5027)

BIBLIOGRAPHY

K. Mohr: "Richard 'Blue' Mitchell," *Jazz Statistics*, no.10 (1959), 4

M. Gardner: "Blue Mitchell on Blue Note," *JJ*, xxiii/2 (1970), 2

H. Nolan: "Blue Mitchell: Able to Leap all Genres with a Single Blast," *DB*, xliii/10 (1976), 19

H. Siders: "Gilt by Association: Blue Mitchell," *Radio Free Jazz*, xix (1978), Dec, 7

BARRY KERNFELD

Mitchell, Bob(by) [Robert Andrew] **(i)** (*b* Houston, 3 April 1920). Trumpeter. He attended college in Alabama and worked with Jimmie Lunceford (1941–7), Louis Jordan (1949–56), and Count Basie (early 1950s). He also led a sextet in New York that included Billy Taylor (ii) as a sideman, and worked in the backup groups of many popular and rhythm-and-blues singers. In the 1980s he led a nine-piece band.

Mitchell, Bob(by) [Robert E., Jr.] **(ii)** (*b* Birmingham, AL, 23 May 1935). Trumpeter. He attended the Juilliard School (1964–7) and later played with Earl Hines (1972–4) and worked as a freelance in Los Angeles. In 1974 he joined Count Basie's band, with which he toured and recorded and performed at the Montreux Jazz Festival in 1977. He may be heard playing a solo on *Freckle Face* on the album *Basie Big Band* (1975, Pablo 2310756). He should not be confused with the trumpeter of the same name (*see* MITCHELL, BOB (i)) nor with the clarinetist Bob Mitchell (*c*1931–1982), who played with Eddie Condon and others. (*Feather–Gitler '70s*)

Mitchell, Dwike [Ivory, Jr.] (*b* Dunedin, FL, 14 Feb 1930). Pianist. From the age of five he took piano lessons and played for church services. He served in the army (1946–9), and performed in bands at the Lockbourne (Ohio) Air Force Base. Mitchell studied at the Philadelphia Musical Academy, then in 1954 joined Lionel Hampton's band. The following year he formed the Mitchell–Ruff Duo with WILLIE RUFF, whom he had first met at Lockbourne, and who also played for Hampton. They have performed and lectured throughout the USA, and in the USSR, Mexico, and China. Mitchell's playing is elegant and stylish, and he possesses a prodigious technique.

For recording-list and bibliography *see* RUFF, WILLIE.

PHILIP GREENE

Mitchell, George [Little Mitch] (*b* Louisville, KY, 8 March 1899; *d* Chicago, 27 May 1972). Cornetist. He worked in dance, theater, and brass bands in Louisville, then toured in the South with a minstrel show and played in Chicago with Tony Jackson (1920). After a tour of Canada (1921–2) and a period in Milwaukee he returned to Chicago, where he worked with Carroll Dickerson (1923–4), Doc Cook and Jimmie Noone (both 1924–5), Lil Armstrong (1925–6), Cook again (1927–9), and Earl Hines (1929–31). Thereafter he played only occasionally. Mitchell was perhaps the most significant classic-jazz cornetist, apart from Louis Armstrong and King Oliver, to have recorded; his fame rests on the excellent recordings he made as a member of the New Orleans Wanderers and the New Orleans Bootblacks (both 1926), under his own name (1927), and, especially, those with Jelly Roll Morton's Red Hot Peppers (1926–7; for illustration *see* MORTON, JELLY ROLL). Morton's *Black Bottom Stomp* demonstrates Mitchell's finest qualities: as lead cornetist, he carefully articulates the ragtime melodies; as soloist against a stop-time accompaniment, he maintains a propulsive, swinging line. Mitchell displayed great tonal variety and used mutes to good effect. The two-cornet team he established with Natty Dominique (in the sessions with Dodds) drew on both the brass-band tradition and the model of Oliver's Creole Jazz Band; the two men's ensemble work and finely executed breaks are well illustrated on *Joe Turner Blues*.

Oral history material in *LNT*.

SELECTED RECORDINGS

As sideman: New Orleans Wanderers: Perdido Street Blues/Gatemouth (1926, Col. 698D); J. R. Morton: Black Bottom Stomp/The Chant (1926, Vic. 20221); Dead Man Blues (1926, Vic. 20252); Grandpa's Spells (1926, Vic. 20431); Beale Street Blues/The Pearls (1927, Vic. 20948); J. Dodds: Come on and stomp, stomp, stomp (1927, Bruns. 3568); Joe Turner Blues (1927, Bruns. 3696)

BIBLIOGRAPHY

W. C. Allen: "Trumpet Giants, 1: George Mitchell," *Hot Notes*, ii/1 (1947), 2

"George Mitchell Discography," *Hot Notes*, ii/1 (1947), 3

G. M. Erskine: "Little Mitch," *DB*, xxx/29 (1963), 22

G. Schuller: *Early Jazz: its Roots and Musical Development* (New York, 1968), 155

P. Bright: "Little Mitch: an Appreciation of George Mitchell," *JJ*, xx/3 (1969), 12

R. von Arx: "George Mitchell Revisited," *Sv*, no.52 (1974), 136

BARRY KERNFELD, ALYN SHIPTON

Mitchell, Grover (*b* Whatley, AL, 17 March 1930). Trombonist and bandleader. He grew up in Pittsburgh from the age of eight and was influenced first by the blues recordings of Blind Lemon Jefferson and Peatie Wheatstraw, then by the work of such jazz musicians as Tommy Dorsey, Lawrence Brown, Jack Teagarden, J. J. Johnson, and especially Bennie Green. After working in the territory band of the trumpeter King Kolax (from 1946) he moved in the 1950s to the West Coast, where he led bands in the San Francisco Bay area with Cedric Haywood. He joined Duke Ellington's group in 1961, in the following year worked briefly with Lionel Hampton, then joined the orchestra of Count Basie, with which he remained for eight years. From 1970 he worked in television (for NBC), films (including *Lady Sings the Blues*, 1972), and studios. Later he led his own band (from 1978), and worked again with Basie (1980–84) and as a leader (from 1984).

SELECTED RECORDINGS

As leader: *Meet Grover Mitchell* (1979, Jazz Chronicles 104); *The Devil's Waltz* (1980, Jazz Chronicles 1)

As sideman: C. Basie: *Lil' Ol' Groovemaker* (1962, Verve 68549); R. Eldridge: *The Nifty Cat Strikes West* (1966, MJR 8121); C. Basie: *Basie: Straight Ahead* (1968, Dot 25902); B. Collette: *Now and Then* (1973, Legend 1004)

BIBLIOGRAPHY

Feather '60s; *Feather–Gitler '70s*

P. Vacher: "The Grover Mitchell Story," *JM*, no.183 (1970), 13

B. Rusch: "Grover Mitchell: Interview," *Cadence*, x (1984), no.10, p.5; no.12, p.10

CHRIS SHERIDAN

Mitchell, John (*b* Baltimore, 1902). Guitarist and banjoist. He moved to New York in 1921 and made several recordings on banjo with Johnny Dunn's band (including *Ham and Eggs*, 1928, Col. 14358D). He also recorded with W. C. Handy and Ethel Waters (both 1923). He joined Sam Wooding's orchestra and traveled with it to Europe in 1925 and again in 1931; when it disbanded (late 1931), he remained in Europe and worked as a guitarist with Willie Lewis (1931–41), making a number of recordings. After returning to the USA (1944), he performed and recorded with Jimmie Lunceford's orchestra until 1946, when he abandoned his musical career. The assertive rhythm playing characteristic of Mitchell's mature style may be heard on Bill Coleman's *Way Down Yonder in New Orleans* (1938, Swing 214).

based on *ChiltonW*

Mitchell, Louis (A.) (*b* New York, 17 Dec 1885; *d* Washington, 12 Sept 1957). Drummer and bandleader. He first worked in vaudeville and in 1912 moved to New York, where he led the Southern Symphony Quintet. His band was resident in London in 1914, after which he toured the USA with the Clef Club Orchestra led by the cellist Walter Kildaire. The following year Mitchell returned to London with the band led by Kildaire's brother Dan, a pianist; he also performed in a variety act with the pianist Joe Jordan and as a solo drummer. Mitchell then formed the Syncopating Sextette, which played in Glasgow in February 1917, and later that year he led the Seven Spades in London and on tour. In 1918 he organized in the USA a new band called Mitchell's Jazz Kings, which he took to Europe; his sidemen included Crickett Smith. In the 1920s the band held a long-term engagement in Paris and made many recordings (including *Now and Then*, 1922, Pathé 6550). Mitchell ceased full-time performing in the 1930s.

BIBLIOGRAPHY

ChiltonW

R. Goffin: *Jazz: from the Congo to the Metropolitan* (Garden City, NY, 1944/*R*1975, rev. [2]/1946 as *Jazz: from Congo to Swing* [in Eng. trans.]; Fr. orig. pubd as *Histoire du jazz*, Montreal, 1945, rev. [2]/1948 as *Nouvelle histoire du jazz: du Congo au bebop*)

L. Gutteridge: "The First Man to Bring Jazz to Britain," *MM*, xxxi (14 July 1956), 6

Obituary, *Amsterdam News* (21 Sept 1957), 13

A. V. Gillet: *The European Recordings by Louis A. Mitchell* (Brussels, 1957, rev. 2/1957)

——: *Louis A. Mitchell: bio-disco-bibliographie* (Brussels, 1966)

——: *The Mitchell's Jazz Kings (discographie critique)* (Brussel, 1966)

HOWARD RYE

Mitchell, Red [Keith (Moore)] (*b* New York, 20 Sept 1927). Double bass player, brother of Whitey Mitchell. He studied piano for nine years before changing to double bass while a member of an army band in Germany. After working with Jackie Paris (1947–8) and Mundell Lowe (1949) he played both piano and double bass with Chubby Jackson's big band, then bass with Charlie Ventura (both 1949), and toured and recorded with Woody Herman (1949–51) and Red Norvo's trio (1952–4). While in Europe with Norvo he recorded with Billie Holiday and Jimmy Raney, then joined Gerry Mulligan's quartet (all 1954). During a period in Los Angeles (1954–68) Mitchell performed and recorded with Hampton Hawes (1955–7, 1966),

Holiday (1956–7), and Ornette Coleman (1959), and recorded film and television soundtracks as the principal double bass player in the studio orchestra at MGM (1959–68). He also led his own quartet (1957) and a quintet with Harold Land (1961–2), both of which made prominent use of the double bass as a principal melody instrument on such pieces as *Rainy Night* and *Triplin' Awhile*.

Seeking a political and social outlook closer to his own, Mitchell moved in 1968 to Stockholm. He performed exclusively in Europe for ten years, working with such musicians as Dizzy Gillespie (on tour, 1968–9), Phil Woods (1969), the Swedish Radiojazzgruppen (1973), and the pianist Guido Manusardi (1974). Around 1976 he formed a group, Communication, that has included such musicians as Nisse Sandström, the drummer Rune Carlsson, and Horace Parlan; Mitchell has continued to work with this ensemble into the mid-1980s. He has returned occasionally to the USA, where he recorded with Jim Hall (1978) and toured with Communication (1979). He has also recorded with Tommy Flanagan (1980) and Jimmie Rowles (1985). In 1966 he began tuning his instrument in fifths – *C'–G'–D–A* – and his open sound, expanded range, and almost pianistic use of double-stopping are attributable in part to this practice. His phrasing and articulation, often reminiscent of vocal inflections, are evident on *Osaka Express*, and convey a musicality and virtuosity of the highest rank.

SELECTED RECORDINGS

As unaccompanied soloist: *Home Suite* (1985, Caprice 1313)

Duos: with L. Konitz: *I Concentrate on You* (1974, Ste. 1018); with J. Hall: *Jim Hall/Red Mitchell* (1978, AH 5), incl. Osaka Express; with T. Flanagan: *You're me* (1980, Phon. 7528)

As leader: *Presenting Red Mitchell* (1957, Cont. 3538), incl. Rainy Night; with H. Land: *Hear Ye!* (1961, Atl. 1376), incl. Triplin' Awhile; of Communication: *Blues for a Crushed Soul* (1976, Sonet 762), *Home Cookin'* (1980, Phon. 7530); *The Jimmy Rowles/Red Mitchell Trio* (1985, Cont. 14016)

As sideman: R. Norvo: *The Red Norvo Trio* (1952, Fan. 312); H. Hawes: *This is Hampton Hawes* (1955–6, Cont. 3515); B. Holiday: *Body and Soul* (1957, Verve 8197); A. Pepper: *Straight Life* (1979, Gal. 5127)

BIBLIOGRAPHY

P. Harris: "Red Mitchell, an Amazing Bassist," *DB*, xvii/8 (1950), 2
L. Feather: "Who's Who with Mulligan," *MM*, xxx (29 May 1954), 2
J. Tynan: "The Red and Whitey Blues," *DB*, xxv/11 (1958), 19
J. P. Binchet: "Jazz dans le monde: Portrait: L'homme aux bras d'or," *Jm*, no.94 (1963), 32
B. Primack: "News: Bassist Red Mitchell Tours US: an Exile after Communication," *DB*, xlvi/11 (1979), 9
Liner notes, J. Hall and R. Mitchell: *Jim Hall/Red Mitchell* (AH 5, 1979) [incl. transcrs. and discography]
C. E. Lindgren: "Red Mitchell," *Orkester journalen*, lii/1 (1984), 10

JOHN CURRY

Mitchell, Roscoe (Edward, Jr.) (*b* Chicago, 3 Aug 1940). Reed player, composer, and leader. He played clarinet, baritone saxophone, and alto saxophone in high-school and army bands. In Chicago from 1961 he led a hard-bop sextet, which included Joseph Jarman and Henry Threadgill, and played in a free-jazz quartet with Jack DeJohnette and in Muhal Richard Abrams's Experimental Band. A founding member of the Association for the Advancement of Creative Musicians (AACM; 1965), he led a sextet and then a series of quartets and trios made up of members of the association, notably Malachi Favors, Lester Bowie, and Phillip Wilson; these three performed and recorded with Mitchell in 1967 as the Roscoe Mitchell Art Ensemble. Jarman (who played reed instruments and percussion) replaced Wilson when the group moved to Paris and was renamed the ART ENSEMBLE OF CHICAGO (AEC; 1969). Mitchell is best known for his work with the AEC but he has also pursued independent activities. From 1967 he performed and recorded as a solo saxophonist. After returning to the USA in 1971 he played briefly in St. Louis and then settled again in Chicago. Around 1974 he established the Creative Arts Collective, modeled on the AACM, in East Lansing, Michigan; several of its members later joined the Roscoe Mitchell Sound Ensemble, which recorded in Chicago in 1980 and Milan in 1981.

Besides saxophones, Mitchell plays flutes, homemade wind instruments, and many percussion instruments, and employs a variety of vocal sounds and effects. His improvisations and compositions are centered on the idioms of free jazz and show the influence of Eric Dolphy; these elements are, however, combined with an eclectic and wide-ranging approach, and Mitchell's music consequently defies conventional stylistic categorization.

SELECTED RECORDINGS

As unaccompanied soloist: *Solo Saxophone Concerts* (1973–4, Sack. 2006), incl. Nonaah

Duos with A. Braxton: *Duets with Anthony Braxton* (1977, Sack. 3016)

As leader: *Sound* (1966, Del. 408); *Old/Quartet* (1967, Nessa 5), incl. Solo; *Snurdy McGurdy and her Dancin' Shoes* (1980, Nessa 20); *3 × 4 Eye* (1981, BS 0050); *Roscoe Mitchell* (1983, BS 0070)

As sideman: L. Bowie: *Numbers 1 and 2* (1967, Nessa 1); George Lewis (ii): *Shadowgraph* (1977, BS 0016)

RECORDED COMPOSITIONS

(selective list; all recorded by Mitchell as leader)

Congliptious (1968, Nessa 2); *Nonaah* (1976–7, Nessa 9–10); *L-R-G*, *The Maze*, *S II Examples* (1978, Nessa 14–15)

For further recordings *see* ART ENSEMBLE OF CHICAGO.

BIBLIOGRAPHY

T. Martin: "Blowing Out in Chicago: Roscoe Mitchell," *DB*, xxxiv/7 (1967), 20
T. Mitchell: "Roscoe Mitchell Art Ensemble," *DB*, xxxiv/18 (1967), 28
J. Litweiler: "Roscoe Mitchell," *DB*, xxxv/15 (1968), 29
B. Smith: "Roscoe Mitchell," *Coda*, no.141 (1975), 2 [interview; incl. discography]
J. Litweiler: "The Art Ensemble of Chicago: Adventures in the Urban Bush," *DB*, xlix/6 (1982), 19 [incl. discography]
E. Janssens and H. de Craen: *Art Ensemble of Chicago Discography: Unit and Members* (Brussels, 1983) [incl. list of compositions]
F. Davis: "Maintaining the Structure (Roscoe Mitchell)," *In the Moment: Jazz in the 1980s* (New York, and Oxford, England, 1986) [colln of previously pubd articles], 177

BARRY KERNFELD

Mitchell, Whitey [Gordon B.] (*b* Hackensack, NJ, 22 Feb 1932). Double bass player, brother of Red Mitchell. From 1954 to 1965 he performed frequently at clubs in New York. In 1955 he recorded with Gene Krupa at a concert in Chicago sponsored by Jazz at the Philharmonic. Thereafter he made recordings with Herbie Mann and Betty Roche (both 1956), Joe Puma and Oscar Pettiford's big band (both 1956–7), and Gene Quill (1958). He also led a sextet for recording sessions that included Steve Lacy (1956), and a trio with Red Mitchell and Blue Mitchell, the Mitchells, which recorded the album *Get those Elephants outa Here!* (1958, Metro. 1012). With Mann, Puma, and Mat Mathews he performed and recorded as a member of a quartet. In 1961 he wrote a satirical essay that was published in *Down Beat* magazine ("My First 50 Years with Society Bands," *DB*, xxviii/3 (1961), 20). After touring with Benny Goodman (1963–4) and playing in André Previn's trio (1964–5) Mitchell settled in Los Angeles, where he began working as a writer and producer for television programs.

BIBLIOGRAPHY

FeatherE; *Feather '60s*
D. Cerulli: "The Red and Whitey Blues," *DB*, xxv/11 (1958), 18

JOHN CURRY

Mixon, Danny [Daniel Asbury] (*b* New York, 19 Aug 1949). Pianist. He played at clubs in Atlantic City, New Jersey (1966), and then accompanied Joe Lee Wilson (1967–70). From 1971 to 1974 he toured and made recordings (including *Betty Carter Album*, *c*1972, Bet-Car 1002) with Betty Carter, who was his wife at the time. He led a trio from 1972, and recorded with the Piano Choir (*c*1973). Mixon also accompanied the singers Joe Williams, Eddie Jefferson, Big Maybelle, and Dee Dee Bridgewater, and played with Kenny Dorham (1970), Art Blakey, Frank Foster, Grant Green, and Pharoah Sanders (1975). He toured with Charles Mingus in 1976, and recorded with Dannie Richmond, who had been the drummer in Mingus's band, in 1979.

BIBLIOGRAPHY

Feather–Gitler '70s
B. Priestley: *Mingus: a Critical Biography* (London, Melbourne, Australia, and New York, 1982)

Miyama, Toshiyuki (*b* Chiba, Japan, 31 Oct 1921). Japanese clarinetist and bandleader. He belonged to a navy band from 1939 and after World War II played with the Lucky Puppy Orchestra. In 1950 he formed a band, Jive ACE, that in 1958 became a 16-piece group known as New Herd, the principal arranger of which was the guitarist Kozaburo Yamaki. With the group Miyama recorded with Charles Mingus (1971) and other American musicians, and from 1974 appeared at festivals in Newport (Rhode Island), Monterey (California), and The Hague. As a leader Miyama favors a driving, swinging style that recalls the work of Dizzy Gillespie's big bands; his repertory includes such jazz standards as *Donna Lee*, *Fiesta*, and *Naima*.

SELECTED RECORDINGS

At Monterey (1974, Nadja PA3038–9); *Live at Newport '75* (1975, RVC–RCA 6332); *Orchestrane* (1977, Denon YX7566); *So Long Charlie* (1979, Denon YX7594); *Misty* (1982, SMS SE25–5003)

BIBLIOGRAPHY

Feather–Gitler '70s

YOZO IWANAMI

Miyazawa, Akira (*b* Matsumoto, Japan, 6 Dec 1927). Japanese tenor saxophonist. He joined an army brass band in 1944 and began playing professionally after World War II. He performed with, among others, the pianist Shotaro Moriyasu, Toshiko Akiyoshi, and Sadao Watanabe and recorded with Akiyoshi (1954–64), Hampton Hawes (1968), Helen Merrill (1969), and Mal Waldron (1982). Miyazawa is among the most creative tenor saxophonists in Japan; he also plays flute on occasion.

SELECTED RECORDINGS

Yamame (1962, King K20P6110); *Iwana* (1969, Vic. SJX20181); *My Piccolo* (1981, Nippon Phonogram–Next Wave 28PJ1003); *Green Dolphin* (1982, Tei.–Union 7002); *Round Midnight* (1985, PW K326025)

YOZO IWANAMI

MJQ. *See* MODERN JAZZ QUARTET.

MJT + 3. Hard-bop group led by WALTER PERKINS from the mid-1950s until 1962.

Mobiglia, Tullio (*b* Carezzano, Alessándria, Italy, 12 April 1911). Italian alto and tenor saxophonist and bandleader. He studied violin and from the late 1920s performed with Romero Alvaro, the tenor saxophonist Bruno Martelli, and others. He played on the SS *Il Conte di Savoja* and led his own groups from the 1930s, including a septet that performed and recorded in Berlin during World War II. From the late 1940s he led a big band in Milan, performed at "hot clubs" in northern Italy, and recorded frequently. Later he settled in Helsinki, where he taught violin into the 1980s. Mobiglia's playing is well represented by his recording *Tullio's Rhythmen* (1941, Bruns. 82237).

ADRIANO MAZZOLETTI

Mobley, Hank [Henry] (*b* Eastman, GA, 7 July 1930; *d* Philadelphia, 30 May 1986). Tenor saxophonist. After playing with Paul Gayten's rhythm-and-blues band (1950) he performed intermittently with Max Roach (1951–3) and with Dizzy Gillespie (1954). He was one of the founding members of the Jazz Messengers with Horace Silver and Art Blakey (1954) and remained with the group until 1956. He worked with Silver's own quintet (1956–7), again with Blakey (1959), and with Dizzy Reece (1960) and Miles Davis (1961–2). He continued to record throughout the 1960s and worked as a freelance, mainly with his own groups; among his distinguished sidemen were Wynton Kelly, Philly Joe Jones, Lee Morgan, and Billy Higgins. He toured Europe from 1968 to 1970, but from the early 1970s his activities were restricted by ill health.

The hallmark of Mobley's playing is his precise and idiosyncratic use of rhythm. Initially this led him to produce very intricate improvised melodies whose impact was sometimes jeopardized by the extreme strain they imposed on his technique and timing. But he soon evolved a style in which his harmonic and rhythmic inventiveness was matched by an immaculate adherence to the beat, a subtly expressive use of tone, and beautifully relaxed delivery. His playing in the period 1960–61, exemplified by *This I dig of you* (1960), shows how his keen understanding of rhythmic structure enabled him to interact effectively with the finest drummers of his day; though his work of the early 1960s arguably represents the peak of his achievement, his later exploration of rhythmic complexities in a group context, which resulted in such densely multilayered works as *Dippin'* (1965), also merits close study.

For illustration *see* BYRD, DONALD.

SELECTED RECORDINGS

(recorded by Blue Note unless otherwise indicated)

As leader: *Mobley's Message* (1956, Prst. 7061); *Hank Mobley Sextet* (1957, 1568); *Soul Station* (1960, 4031), incl. This I dig of you; *Roll Call* (1960, 84058); *Workout* (1961, 84080); *Another Workout* (1961, 84431); *No Room for Squares* (1963, 84149); *Dippin'* (1965, 84209); *A Slice of the Top* (1966, LT995); *Thinking of Home* (1970, 84367)

As sideman with A. Blakey: *The Jazz Messengers at the Café Bohemia* (1955, 1507–8)

BIBLIOGRAPHY

FeatherE; *Feather–Gitler '70s*
M. James: "Hank Mobley," *JM*, vii/8 (1961), 6
——: "Out of the Bag, 4: Hank Mobley," *JM*, viii/10 (1962), 14
J. Litweiler: "Hank Mobley: the Integrity of the Artist," *DB*, xl/6 (1973), 14
C. Lauder: "Hank Mobley: Yesterday and Forever," *JSN*, ii/1 (1980), 2
C. Schlouch: *Come Back! Hank Mobley: a Discography* (n.p. [?Marseille, France], 1983)

MICHAEL JAMES

Mobo Band. Group formed in 1983 by KAZUMI WATANABE.

Modal jazz. A style of jazz, developed in the late 1950s, in which modal scales (or their general characteristics) dictate the melodic and harmonic content. Modal jazz rarely adheres strictly to the classical modes (dorian, phrygian, etc.), but it creates their flavor, or in some cases that of other nondiatonic scales, such as those of Spanish or Indian music. The term "modal jazz" has also been applied, somewhat misleadingly, to performances based on the major or minor modes. The style has attracted musicians partly because it is relatively undemanding by comparison with those based on chord progressions. Because it is free of frequent harmonic interruption it can more easily create an unhurried and meditative feeling.

Many performances are based on a two-chord sequence or a drone. The absence of frequent chord changes alone is sometimes regarded as defining modal jazz.

The first widely known jazz piece based on modes was Miles Davis's *Milestones*, on the album of the same name (1958, Col. CL1193); it has the form *aabba*, in which the *a* section uses the dorian mode in G (with a prominent C reiterated by the piano in the bass register) and the *b* section the aeolian mode on A (ex.1). The themes of the two sections are chordal successions

Ex.1 Modal bases of *Milestones*, on M. Davis: *Milestones* (1958, Col. CL1193)

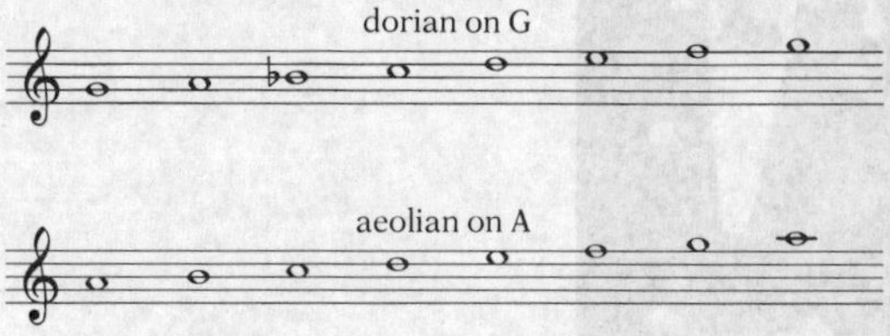

based strictly on their respective modes, and the pianist Red Garland plays literal repeats of these patterns throughout the piece. Among the soloists, although Davis adheres closely to the notes of the mode in his improvisation, the saxophonists (Cannonball Adderley and John Coltrane) explore more freely. *Milestones* was followed in 1959 by Davis's collaboration with Bill Evans (ii) on the album *Kind of Blue* (1959, Col. CL1355). *Flamenco Sketches* (often mistakenly identified as *All Blues*) on *Kind of Blue* developed an idea that had appeared in Evans's *Peace Piece* (on the album *Everybody Digs Bill Evans*, 1958, Riv. 291); it is not based on an existing theme, but consists solely of improvisations on a succession of five scales, three of which are outside the major-minor tonal system (*see* DAVIS, MILES, §2). Another piece on the album, *So What*, the melody of which is stated by pizzicato bass, has a 32-bar *aaa'a* structure; the solo improvisations in the *a* section are in D dorian, while in the *a'* section the mode is simply shifted up a half-step (ex.2). The form and modal bases of *So What* were followed by John Coltrane in his piece *Impressions* (on the album of the same name, 1961–3, Imp. 42).

Ex.2 Modal bases of *So What*, on M. Davis: *Kind of Blue* (1959, Col. CL1355)

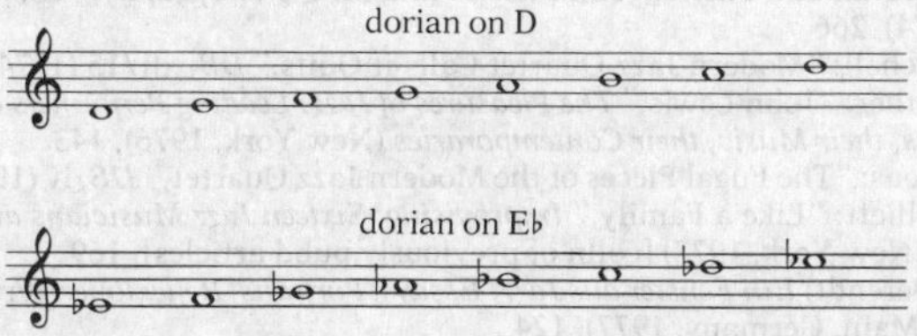

Another pioneering modal performance is Davis's trumpet solo in *Solea* on *Sketches of Spain* (1959–60, Col. CS8271), which rests on an ostinato bass figure and a drum pattern. Popularization of modal techniques in jazz was substantially aided by the enthusiastic reception that greeted Coltrane's version (1960) of *My Favorite Things* (on the album of the same name, Atl. 1361) by Rodgers and Hammerstein, in which his improvisations did not follow the tune's chord progressions; the pianist McCoy Tyner accompanied Coltrane with a two-bar, two-chord pattern, which he repeated at length in E dorian and then in E major. This became a much imitated technique (as did the accompaniment voicings used by Evans and Tyner on various recordings). During the 1960s Davis concentrated more on chord progressions, but he eventually adopted improvisational techniques based almost exclusively on modes when he began to combine jazz and funk, beginning with his influential albums *In a Silent Way* and *Bitches Brew* (both recorded for Columbia in 1969; CS9875; GP26). The group's harmonies are usually founded on a repeating bass figure, but the improvisations often imply more changes of harmony that are played because the soloists (using an approach pioneered by Coltrane) conceptually juxtapose distantly related chords. Davis and many other bandleaders continued to use these techniques into the 1980s. Besides those already mentioned, an influential figure in modal jazz is Pharoah Sanders.

Modal jazz and free jazz are in some cases difficult to distinguish largely because the lack of a predetermined harmonic structure in modal jazz may be easily confused with the avoidance of a tonal center in free jazz; moreover, free jazz sometimes acquires a modal orientation in the course of improvisation. Coltrane's *Ascension* (1965, Imp. 95), for example, is a sterling example of free jazz, but it is loosely based on four modes.

See also IMPROVISATION, §4(vi), and JAZZ (i), §VI, 2.

BIBLIOGRAPHY

E. Jost: *Free Jazz* (Graz, Austria, 1974), chap.1
J. Pressing: "Towards an Understanding of Scales in Jazz," *Jf*, ix (1977), 25
B. Kernfeld: *Adderley, Coltrane, and Davis at the Twilight of Bebop: the Search for Melodic Coherence (1958–59)* (diss., Cornell U., 1981)

Modern. Record company and label. The company was established in Los Angeles early in 1945 by the brothers Jules, Joe, Lester, and Saul Bihari. At first it was called Modern Music; after a short time, however, the second word of the title was dropped. The catalogue included all kinds of Afro-American music, but its importance to jazz derives chiefly from its recordings made at concerts on the West Coast and credited to Gene Norman's Just Jazz; it is also notable for many discs by Jimmy Witherspoon. A separate dixieland series was issued briefly in 1950.

The company was one of the first to issue cheap LPs; the subsidiary Crown was established for this purpose in 1949. As well as releasing material first put out on Modern, Crown was used in 1959–60 for a series of big-band LPs directed by Maxwell Davis; the company later set up the label United for further reissues. In 1950 Modern also founded a blues label, RPM.

BIBLIOGRAPHY

A. Rotante and P. B. Sheatsley, eds.: "Modern Records, Hollywood," *Blues Research*, no.7 (1962) [complete issue]
A. Shaw: *Honkers and Shouters: the Golden Years of Rhythm and Blues* (New York, 1970), 194
E. M. Bakker and C. Hoffman: "Crown Research," *Names & Numbers*, no.1 (1985), 25
"Jules Bihari," *Blues & Rhythm: the Gospel Truth*, no.6 (1985), 25 [obituary]

Modern jazz. A term used collectively of the jazz styles developed between the early 1940s and the 1960s; it covers mainly bop and its offshoots. (It is not applied to free jazz, despite the fact the the latter developed during this period.) *See* JAZZ (i), §V.

Modern Jazz Quartet [MJQ]. Jazz ensemble. Its original members – MILT JACKSON (vibraphone), JOHN LEWIS (piano and director), Ray Brown (double bass), and Kenny Clarke (drums) – first performed together in 1946 in Dizzy Gillespie's big band. In 1951–2 these four players made recordings under the name of the Milt Jackson Quartet. By 1952, when the first recordings under the name Modern Jazz Quartet were issued, Percy Heath had replaced Brown as bass player. The group began performing regularly in concert halls and nightclubs from 1954. In the following year Clarke was replaced by Connie Kay, thus estab-

The Modern Jazz Quartet, c1955: (left to right) Percy Heath (double bass), Connie Kay (drums), John Lewis (piano), and Milt Jackson (vibraphone)

lishing the group's present membership (see illustration). By virtue of its recordings and international concert tours the MJQ soon acquired a reputation as a superior jazz ensemble. Beginning in the early 1960s the group disbanded during the summer months, enabling Lewis to pursue his activities as a composer and teacher, and the other members to perform in different jazz contexts. In 1974, primarily because of Jackson's desire to perform full-time as a leader, the MJQ broke up. For several years its members pursued separate careers, reuniting occasionally for short concert tours, but in the early 1980s they resumed playing together for several months each year.

The MJQ plays in a restrained, conservative bop style that is sometimes referred to as cool jazz. In its best moments it has a finely honed ensemble sound, owing in part to the long-standing association of the four excellent players and in part to Lewis's compositions, which include some of the most carefully organized works in jazz history. The main soloist is Jackson, whose exuberant and rhythmically complex solos contrast effectively with Lewis's restrained and deceptively simple manner of playing. By frequently accompanying Jackson with subsidiary countermelodies rather than the usual chordal punctuations of bop, Lewis creates a distinctive contrapuntal texture seldom heard in other bop performances.

Throughout its long career the MJQ has also performed and recorded much third-stream music, combining techniques of European art music and jazz improvisation. These works, written by Lewis, Gunther Schuller, André Hodeir, and others, are uneven in quality, some suffering from disparities between the composed and improvised sections, others from pretentiousness. Among the best are Lewis's *England's Carol* and his fugal pieces *Versailles*, *Concorde*, *Vendome*, and *Three Windows*.

SELECTED RECORDINGS

As the Milt Jackson Quartet: Softly as in a Morning Sunrise/True Blues (1952, Hi-Lo 1412)

As the Modern Jazz Quartet: *Fontessa* (1956, Atl. 1231), incl. Versailles; *The Modern Jazz Quartet* (1957, Atl. 1265); *One Never Knows* (1957, Atl. 1284), incl. Three Windows; *Third Stream Music* (1957, 1959–60, Atl. 1345); *The Modern Jazz Quartet and Orchestra* (1960, Atl. 1359), incl. England's Carol; *European Concert* (1960, Atl. 1385–6), incl. Vendome; *The Comedy* (1962, Atl. 1390); *A Quartet is a Quartet is a Quartet* (1963, Atl. 1420), incl. Concorde; *Blues at Carnegie Hall* (1966, Atl. 1468); *In Memoriam* (1973, Little David 3001); *The Last Concert* (1974, Atl. 2-909); *Together Again* (1982, PL 2308244)

BIBLIOGRAPHY

N. Hentoff: "Jazz Reviews: Modern Jazz Quartet," *DB*, xx/22 (1953), 16

——: "The Modern Jazz Quartet," *High Fidelity*, v/3 (1955), 36

M. Harrison: "Looking Back at the Modern Jazz Quartet," *JM*, v/4 (1958); repr. in *The Art of Jazz: Essays on the Nature and Development of Jazz*, ed. M. Williams (New York, 1959/*R*1979), 219

M. Williams: "Closing Chorus for the MJQ," *Saturday Review*, xlv (14 July 1962), 34

G. Marne: "The Modern Jazz Quartet," *IM*, lxii/1 (1964), 8

M. Williams: "Early MJQ: an Appreciation," *Kulchur*, iv (spr. 1964), 94

J. Goldberg: *Jazz Masters of the Fifties* (New York and London, 1965/*R*1980), 113

T. Owens: *Improvisation Techniques of the Modern Jazz Quartet* (thesis, UCLA, 1965)

M. Williams: *The Jazz Tradition* (New York, 1970, rev. 2/1983)

N. Koyama and others: "John Lewis and MJQ Discography," *SJ*, xxviii/3 (1974), 266

C. Mitchell: "Modern Jazz Quartet Calls it Quits," *DB*, xli/15 (1974), 9

L. Feather: "John Lewis," *The Pleasures of Jazz: Leading Performers on their Lives, their Music, their Contemporaries* (New York, 1976), 143

T. Owens: "The Fugal Pieces of the Modern Jazz Quartet," *JJS*, iv (1976), 25

W. Balliett: "Like a Family," *Improvising: Sixteen Jazz Musicians and their Art* (New York, 1977) [colln of previously pubd articles], 169

J. E. Berendt: *Ein Fenster aus Jazz: Essays, Portraits, Reflexionen* (Frankfurt am Main, Germany, 1977), 124

L. Feather: "MJQ: the Quartet that Wouldn't Die," *Los Angeles Times Calendar* (27 March 1983), 68

I. Gitler: "The Return of the Modern Jazz Quartet," *JT* (1983), March, 10

THOMAS OWENS

Modern Jazz Sextet (i). Name used by the CRUSADERS in the mid-1950s.

Modern Jazz Sextet (ii). Group that recorded for Norgran in 1956. Its members were Dizzy Gillespie, Sonny Stitt, Charli Persip, Skeeter Best, Charlie Heath, and John Lewis.

Modes. Name under which the bop quintet Jazz Modes was formed by Charlie Rouse and JULIUS WATKINS in 1956.

Moeckel, Thomas (*b* Basle, Switzerland, 22 Feb 1950). Swiss trumpeter, flugelhorn player, and guitarist. He came from a musical family (his father was for many years the leader of the Swiss Radio Big Band) and won awards at jazz festivals in Zurich in 1969, 1970, and 1971; his first professional engagements, which he fulfilled as a freelance, were in 1970. He worked as a leader and sideman with such groups as Caleidoscope (recording in 1971), Jazz-rock Experience, and Fasten Belts; he also led the group Centrifuge, which recorded an album of the same name around 1975 (Meteor 32014). Moeckel has worked as a soloist, composer, and arranger for the Swiss Radio Big Band, the trombonist Jiggs Whigham, Charles Tolliver, Franco Ambrosetti, and Toots Thielemans.

PETER SCHWALM

Moer(schbacher), Paul (E.) (*b* Meadville, PA, 22 July 1916). Pianist. He studied music at the University of Miami (BA 1951) and composition at the University of Southern California (to 1953). He settled in Los Angeles, where he played with Benny Carter and Vido Musso (both 1953), Zoot Sims and Stan Getz (both 1954), Jerry Gray and Bill Holman (both 1955), and Shorty Rogers, Ben Webster, Maynard Ferguson, Buddy DeFranco, and Jack Sheldon. He made recordings with Bob Gordon (1954), Jack Montrose (*Jack Montrose with Bob Gordon*, 1955, Atl. 1223), Dave Pell (1957), and John Graas (1957–8), and, jointly with Montrose, Paul Chambers, and Bill Perkins, led a session in 1957. In 1960 he toured Australia with Benny Carter and first played with Paul Horn's quintet, with which he remained until 1968 and for which he wrote a number of pieces. He performed with Les Brown for ten years from 1965 and appeared on television with him. He also wrote arrangements for Sheldon and Rosemary Clooney, among others, and was Clooney's conductor on several tours (1965–80).

BIBLIOGRAPHY

FeatherE; *Feather '60s*
R. Gordon: *Jazz West Coast: the Los Angeles Jazz Scene of the 1950s* (London and New York, 1986)

Moers Music. Record label. It was established in Moers, Germany, in 1974, by Moers Music Verlag. At first it was called Ring, but there were objections from a Canadian label of the same name, and around 1977, after issue number 01032, the label title was changed. The company specializes in free jazz, and the catalogue includes studio recordings by the World Saxophone Quartet, James Newton and Anthony Davis, John Carter, Leo Smith, Barry Altschul, Anthony Braxton, Roscoe Mitchell, the Vienna Art Choir, and the Vienna Art Orchestra. In addition, a number of recordings, especially those originally put out on Ring, were made at concerts given as part of the INTERNATIONAL NEW JAZZ FESTIVAL MOERS (which is organized by the parent company) by such musicians as Braxton, John Surman and Tony Levin, Günter Christmann and the drummer Detlef Schönenberg, the European Jazz Quintet, Sunny Murray, and Phillip Wilson.

Moffett, Charles (Mack, Sr.) (*b* Fort Worth, 11 Sept 1929). Drummer. He played trumpet in Jimmy Witherspoon's group and other rhythm-and-blues ensembles as a teenager, and started to play drums while at college. After navy service he attended university in 1950–53, gaining a BA in music education. While working as a high school teacher in Texas (1953–61) he played with jazz bands and with the rhythm-and-blues singer Little Richard (1953). In 1961 he joined Ornette Coleman in New York; during Coleman's retirement from public performance (1962–5) he worked in his rehearsals, and in 1965–7 he toured and recorded with him and David Izenzon. Moffett also played with Sonny Rollins (1963) and led his own group, which included Pharoah Sanders, the trumpeter Alan Shorter, and Carla Bley (1964). In 1970 he moved to Oakland, California, where he directed a music school and led two bands, one of them featuring his children and the other, the Moffettes, made up of students; he also performed with Steve Turre, the saxophonist Keshavan Maslak, and Prince Lasha. Later he returned to New York, where he has continued to perform (with Frank Lowe, Maslak, and others) and to teach. His playing has an individual, swinging style that reflects Coleman's free-jazz ideas.

Moffet's son Charnett Moffett is a double bass player who has recorded as a sideman with Branford Marsalis (1983) and Stanley Jordan (1984) and also as a leader.

SELECTED RECORDINGS

As leader: *The Gift* (1969, Savoy 12194); *The Charles Moffett Family* (*c*1974, LRS 6142)

As sideman: O. Coleman: *Town Hall, 1962* (1962, ESP 1006); A. Shepp: *Four for Trane* (1964, Imp. 71); O. Coleman: *Ornette Coleman at the Golden Circle* (1965, BN 84224–5); K. Maslak: *Blaster Master* (1981, BS 0079)

BIBLIOGRAPHY

V. Wilmer: "Charles Moffett: Gettin' out There," *DB*, xxxiv/9 (1967), 18
G. Giddins: "The Moffett Family: Prodigal Kids," *VV* (23 July 1979), 51
"Talent's All in the Family Moffett," *DB*, xlvi/5 (1979), 12
G. Coppens: "Charles Moffett: Interview," *Coda*, no.191 (1983), 12

ED HAZELL

Moholo, Louis (T.) (*b* Cape Town, 10 March 1940). South African drummer. In 1963 he joined the Swinging City Six, led by the tenor saxophonist Ronnie Beer in Cape Town, and in 1964 became a member of Chris McGregor's Blue Notes and moved with the group to London, where he also recorded many albums with the Brotherhood of Breath. He played with Steve Lacy and John Tchicai and recorded in a trio led by Irene Schweizer (1975, 1977), as the leader of an octet (1978, *Spirits Rejoice*, Ogun 520) and of a trio (1982), with Interjazz (1979), in a trio with Peter Brötzmann and Harry Miller (1979, 1980), in a quintet led by Elton Dean (1980), and in a duo with Keith Tippett (1980); later he played with Brötzmann in Germany and Tippett in England. Moholo's style is reminiscent of that of Elvin Jones, but is imbued with rhythms that are distinctively South African.

BIBLIOGRAPHY

R. Cotterrell, ed.: *Jazz Now: the Jazz Centre Society Guide* (London, 1976)
G. Rouy: "Louis Moholo, le rythme de souffle," *Jm*, no.239 (1975), 20
C. de Ledesma: "Afro Jazz: Evolution and Revolution," *The Wire*, no.12 (1985), 26, esp. 34

CHARLES DE LEDESMA

Mojoli, Franco (*b* Milan, 1914; *d* *c*1970). Italian alto saxophonist, clarinetist, organist, accordionist, pianist, arranger, and bandleader. He studied piano and composition, then saxophone, and recorded as a pianist, accordionist, and saxophonist in the Orchestra nuovo ritmo, led by the double bass player Michele d'Elia; he also recorded in a trio with d'Elia and the guitarist Cosimo Di Ceglie (1937) and played in an orchestra led by the clarinetist Piero Rizza. He wrote arrangements for the Odeon record label (from 1938) and for the group I Maestri del ritmo (1942–3), which recorded several of them. From 1940 to 1945 he led the Quintetto del delirio (also known as the Complesso del delirio), with which he also recorded as a soloist; with the drummer Claudio Gambarelli and the pianist Giampiero Boneschi he formed a trio that in 1945 made outstanding recordings. In the 1950s he recorded as a pianist and wrote arrangements that were recorded by others. A good example of Mojoli's work is his recording *I Saw Stars* (1937, HMV GW1415).

ADRIANO MAZZOLETTI

Molde International Jazz Festival. Festival held annually from 1961 in Molde, Norway. It was first organized by the Storyville Jazz Club in Molde, which continued as a sponsor into the late 1980s; from 1970 it also received funds from the Norwegian government. The festival takes place over six days in July or August and consists of about 50 performances at various clubs and concert halls, as well as exhibits and showings of jazz films. The combined attendance at the events of a single festival has reached 15,000 persons. The styles of music range from traditional jazz to the avant garde; among those who have performed at the festival are Gary Burton, Ornette Coleman, Miles Davis, Panama Francis and the Savoy Sultans, Herbie Hancock, the Modern Jazz Quartet, and Oscar Peterson. (T. Mosnes: *Jazz i Molde*, Ålesund, Norway, 1980)

PAUL R. LAIRD

Mole. Record company and label. The company was established in London in 1980, and called after the record store of the same name. The owners of both enterprises, Ed Dipple, Graham Griffiths, and Peter Bould, have pursued a policy of recording only the work of musicians whom they admire; the catalogue includes material by Art Pepper, Gil Evans, Stan Tracey, Bill Watrous, and Bud Shank. Mole has also reissued classic albums by Tubby Hayes, and made available previously unreleased material by Bobby Jaspar. In 1986 a subsidiary label, Hot House, was established, and used to issue new albums recorded in London by Nathan Davis and Dusko Goykovich, with a rhythm section of Kenny Drew, Alan Levitt, and Jimmy Woode. Mole also has excellent distribution arrangements throughout Europe, but rarely makes leasing arrangements other than with Japanese companies. The company released its first compact discs, by Pepper and Evans, in 1986.

MARK GARDNER

Mole, Miff [Irving Milfred] (*b* Roosevelt, NY, 11 March 1898; *d* New York, 29 April 1961). Trombonist. He played violin, alto horn, and piano before learning trombone. Based in New York, he made hundreds of recordings with many groups, the most influential being those with the ORIGINAL MEMPHIS FIVE and with Red Nichols's innovative groups in the 1920s. In these years he fashioned the first distinctive and influential solo jazz trombone style, free from the glissandos and rudimentary bass-line paraphrases of tailgate playing and characterized by precise execution, wide leaps and short rhythmic values. This style was already formed by the time he recorded his own composition *Slippin' Around* with Nichols (1927). In 1929 he joined the NBC radio orchestra, where he remained for most of the 1930s. After playing with Paul Whiteman (1938–40) and Benny Goodman (1943) he returned to small-group jazz, sometimes with Muggsy Spanier. Illness prevented him from playing regularly in the mid-1950s, but he continued to work sporadically until his death.

SELECTED RECORDINGS

As leader: with R. Nichols: Davenport Blues (1927, Vic. 20778), Slippin' Around (1927, Vic. 21397); Shim-me-sha-wabble (1928, OK 41445); Crazy Rhythm (1928, OK 41098); I've got a feeling I'm falling (1929, OK 41232)

As sideman with E. Condon: A good man is hard to find (1940, Com. 1504–5)

BIBLIOGRAPHY

ChiltonW

J. L. Anderson: "Evolution of Jazz," *DB*, xvii/20 (1950), 11

N. Shapiro and N. Hentoff, eds.: *Hear me Talkin' to ya: the Story of Jazz by the Men who Made it* (New York and London, 1955/*R*1966), 244

A. C. Webber: "The Man Behind Miff's Horn," *SL*, xii/7–8 (1961), 3

M. Harrison: "Miff Mole on Okeh," *J&B*, ii/10 (1973), 6

——: *A Jazz Retrospect* (Newton Abbot, England, 1976, rev. 2/1977)

B. Harrington: "Miff Mole," *MR*, v/12 (1978), 6

JAMES DAPOGNY/R

Moncur, Grachan (*b* Miami, 2 Sept 1915). Double bass player, father of Grachan Moncur III and half-brother of Al Cooper. He began playing double bass, tuba, and trombone in his early teens and performed with George Kelly in Miami. He moved with his family to Newark, New Jersey, where John Hammond heard him play double bass on local radio and arranged for him to record with Bud Freeman, Putney Dandridge, Bunny Berigan, and Mildred Bailey (all 1935), and Teddy Wilson (1935–6). Moncur was one of the original members of Cooper's Savoy Sultans (formed 1937) and he remained with the group until 1945. He led a band with the pianist Ace Harris in 1947 and the following year played with Joe Thomas (iii). In the 1950s he moved to Miami, where he continued to perform into the late 1960s. His solo playing and skillful rhythm accompaniments may both be heard on Ike Quebec's *Topsy* (BN 515), recorded in 1945.

based on *ChiltonW*

Moncur, Grachan, III (*b* New York, 3 June 1937). Trombonist, son of Grachan Moncur. After playing piano and cello briefly as a child he took up the trombone at the age of 11. He played in Newark, New Jersey, in an orchestra led by the pianist Nat Phipps, of which Wayne Shorter was also a member, and attended the Manhattan School of Music and the Juilliard School for brief periods. He played with Ray Charles (1959–62), belonged to the Jazztet (1962), then worked for six months as Charles's music director. In 1963 he belonged to a group led by Jackie McLean that played an amalgam of hard bop and free jazz; he then worked as a leader and as a sideman in groups that included Herbie Hancock (recording in 1963), Tony Williams, Bobby Hutcherson, and Wayne Shorter (recording in 1965). In New York and London he appeared as an actor in James Baldwin's play *Blues for Mr. Charlie* (1964–5), for which he also wrote incidental music. He toured with Sonny Rollins (1964), played with Marion Brown (recording in 1966) and in Joe Henderson's sextet (recording in 1967), and in 1968 formed the cooperative group 360 Degree Music Experience, with Beaver Harris and Dave Burrell, of which he was also the music director. In Europe he performed with Archie Shepp at the Actuel and Donaueschingen festivals and recorded as a leader (1969); after returning to the USA he composed and took part in the recording of *Echoes of Prayer* (1974), a work commissioned by the Jazz Composer's Orchestra that incorporated elements of West Indian, Latin and classical music. He collaborated with the choreographer Keith Lee in 1978 and in the following year re-joined the 360 Degree Music Experience. Later he became a composer-in-residence at the Newark Community School of the Arts (from 1983), performed with the group Blue Ark and the poet Amiri Baraka, and toured and recorded with Frank Lowe (1984–5), the singer Cassandra Wilson (1985), and Nathan Davis's Paris Reunion Band (1986). He received a grant from the NEA's jazz program in 1970 and a Mason Gross Award from the New Jersey Council for the Arts in 1978.

SELECTED RECORDINGS

As leader: *Evolution* (1963, BN 84153); *Some Other Stuff* (1964, BN 84177); *New Africa* (1969, BYG 529321); *Echoes of Prayer* (1974, JCOA 1009)

As sideman: Jazztet: *Another Get Together* (1962, Mer. 60737); J. McLean: *Destination Out* (1963, BN 84165); J. Henderson: *The Kicker* (1967, Mlst. 9008); A. Shepp: *Archie Shepp Live at the Donaueschingen Music Festival* (1967, Saba 15148); B. Harris: *Beautiful Africa* (1979, SN 1002); F. Lowe: *Decision in Paradise* (1984, SN 1082)

BIBLIOGRAPHY

Feather '60s; *Feather–Gitler '70s*
A. B. Spellman: Liner notes, G. Moncur III: *Evolution* (BN 84153, 1964)
V. Wilmer: "Grachan Moncur 3rd," *JM*, xi/5 (1965), 21
G. Bright: "Getting into it: Grachan Moncur III," *DB*, xxxii/2 (1965), 14
G. Endress: "Grachan Moncur," *JP*, xvi (1967), 314

ED HAZELL

Mondello, Toots [Nuncio M.] (*b* Boston, 1912). Alto saxophonist. He was lead alto saxophonist with Benny Goodman from 1934 to 1935, and again from 1939 to 1940, and also worked with Joe Haymes (1934–5), Ray Noble (1935), and his own band (1937–9). His prolific studio work included sessions with Chick Bullock (1935, 1937), Bunny Berigan (1936), Miff Mole, Larry Clinton, Claude Thornhill (all 1937), Teddy Wilson (1938), Louis Armstrong (1938–9), and Lionel Hampton (1939–40), with whom he recorded *Gin for Christmas* (1939, Vic. 26423). He then worked with the Metronome All Stars (1940–41), and, after military service, recorded with Pearl Bailey (1946), Billie Holiday (1947), Sarah Vaughan (1949), Toots Thielemans (1954–5), Billy Butterfield (1950, 1956–8), Artie Shaw (1963), and Goodman again (1967). (*ChiltonW*; *FeatherE*)

Mondragon, Joe [Joseph] (*b* Antonito, CO, 2 Feb 1920). Double bass player. A self-taught musician, he first worked with dance bands in and around Los Angeles. He continued to play while in the army, but his first major engagement was with Woody Herman (1946). In the next two decades he was much in demand as a session musician: he recorded with June Christy (intermittently, 1949–62), Shelly Manne (1953–4), Shorty Rogers (1953–62), Harry Edison (1956), Buddy Rich (1956–7), Buddy DeFranco, Paul Smith, and Herman (all 1957), Marty Paich (1959–60), and Claude Williamson (1961). He also played on a number of film soundtracks, including *The Wild One* with Rogers (1953), and *Pete Kelly's Blues* with Ella Fitzgerald (1955). Mondragon's work is characterized by an outstanding technique, a full, resonant sound, and a fine sense of swing.

SELECTED RECORDINGS

As sideman: W. Herman: Woodchopper's Ball (1946, Col. 37238); S. Rogers: *Shorty Rogers and his Giants* (1953, RCA LPM3137); S. Manne: *New Works* (1953–4, Cont. 2511); B. Holiday: *All or Nothing at All* (1956–7, Verve 8329): E. Fitzgerald: *Ella Fitzgerald Sings the Duke Ellington Songbook* (1956–7, Verve 4008–9); M. Paich: *I Get a Boot out of You* (1959, WB 1349)

BIBLIOGRAPHY

FeatherE

BRENDA PENNELL

Monk, Thelonious (Sphere) [Thelious Junior] (*b* Rocky Mount, NC, 10 Oct 1917; *d* Weehawken, NJ, 17 Feb 1982). Pianist and composer. Although he remained long misunderstood and little known, both his playing and his compositions had a formative influence on modern jazz.

1. Life. 2. Compositions. 3. Piano style.

1. Life. When Monk was four his family moved to New York, which was his home until he retired. In the early 1940s he worked as a sideman in jazz groups and became house pianist at Minton's Playhouse in Harlem. Here he encouraged the young jazz pianist Bud Powell (who achieved success far earlier than Monk himself) and was first recorded in 1941 in Minton's house quartet, when Charlie Christian was making a guest appearance. In these and similar performances with visiting musicians, such as Don Byas, Roy Eldridge, and Helen Humes, Monk helped to formulate the emerging bop style.

In 1944 Monk made his first known visit to a recording studio, as a member of the Coleman Hawkins Quartet; in the same year his well-known tune *'Round about Midnight* was recorded by Cootie Williams, who collaborated with him in its composition. By this time Monk was playing at the Spotlite Club on 52nd Street with Dizzy Gillespie's orchestra. Three years later, in 1947, Monk made the first recordings under his own name in a sextet session for Blue Note, which included his compositions *Humph* and *Thelonious*. These and five other recordings issued by Blue Note between 1947 and 1952, including such masterpieces as *Evidence*, *Criss Cross*, and a bizarre arrangement of *Carolina Moon*, are regarded as the first characteristic works of Monk's output, along with the recordings he made as a sideman for Charlie Parker in 1950, which included *Bloomdido* and *My Melancholy Baby*.

In 1952 Monk acquired a contract from Prestige Records, with which he remained associated for three years. Although this was perhaps the leanest period in his career in terms of live performances, he recorded such notable works as the remarkable *Little Rootie Tootie* (dedicated to his son), a daring version of Jerome Kern's *Smoke gets in your eyes*, and perhaps his finest solo performance, *Bags' Groove*, in a memorable session with the Miles Davis All Stars on Christmas Eve 1954. Two months earlier he had recorded an album with Sonny Rollins, and in June 1954 he made his first solo album, in Paris for Swing Records. This album offers great insight into the audacity of Monk's music, his version of *Eronel* in particular being outstanding for its considerable pianistic demands.

In 1955 Prestige, dissatisfied with the low sales of Monk's recordings, sold his contract to Riverside Records. Monk remained with Riverside until 1961. His first two recording sessions were conceived with the intent of introducing his music to a wider audience, and were given a lukewarm reception by the critics. Between these two dates Monk also recorded his highly complex piece *Gallop's Gallop* with Gigi Gryce for Signal Records (1955) and made an album with Art Blakey for Atlantic (1957). This latter recording and three of his next albums for Riverside (*Brilliant Corners*, *Thelonious Himself*, and *Thelonious Monk with John Coltrane*) were masterpieces, and Monk became the most acclaimed and controversial jazz improviser of the late 1950s almost overnight.

Monk's professional career now took a dramatic turn for the better, and in 1957 he began appearing regularly with Coltrane, Wilbur Ware, and Shadow Wilson at the Five Spot in New York. During the next few years his group included such noteworthy musicians as Johnny Griffin, Roy Haynes, and Charlie Rouse, his lifelong associate. He began to tour the USA regularly and also to appear in Europe. Perhaps his most memorable performance of this period was in 1959 at Town Hall, New York, where he appeared with an orchestra playing his compositions in skillful arrangements by Hall Overton. He also continued to issue albums for Riverside.

In 1962 Monk's popularity was such that he was put under contract by Columbia records. He was also made the subject of a cover story by *Time* (1964), an honor bestowed on only three other jazz musicians. He made several overseas tours, including visits to Mexico and Japan. Around 1970 he disbanded his group and in 1971–2 worked in the Giants of Jazz together with Dizzy Gillespie, Kai Winding, Sonny Stitt, Al

Thelonious Monk

McKibbon, and Art Blakey. In November 1971 he made solo and trio recordings for Black Lion Records in London, which some critics felt heralded a new era in his development, but shortly afterwards he suddenly retired from public view. He made three final performances with an orchestra at Carnegie Hall, and appeared with a quartet at the Newport Jazz Festival New York in 1975 and 1976, but otherwise spent his final years in seclusion in Weehawken, New Jersey, at the home of the Baroness Pannonica de Koenigswarter, his lifelong friend and patron.

2. Compositions. Monk's compositions fall into three periods: those recorded for Blue Note in the 1940s, his works in the 1950s for Riverside and Signal, and a few tunes written after 1960 for Columbia. Most critics consider those of his first two periods the most significant. Of the first-period works, *'Round about Midnight* is his most popular, both with the public and with musicians. *Evidence*, *Misterioso*, and particularly *Criss Cross* are considered his masterpieces in purely instrumental terms; quite different from each other, they are united by vigorous, angular melodies of a strongly pianistic character. The first eight bars of *Criss Cross*, for example, consist of two contrasting motifs and demonstrate Monk's highly personal use of rhythmic displacement (ex.1). Each piece of this period reveals

Ex.1 *Criss Cross* (1951, BN 1590)

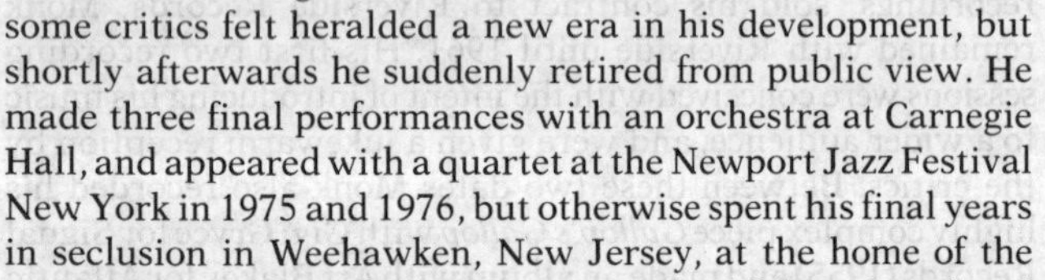

fresh facets of his thinking: *Eronel* demonstrates his affection for bop, and *Hornin' In* his fascination with the whole-tone scale, which allowed him to suspend the work's tonality for

Ex.2 *Hornin' In* (1952, BN 1603)

bars at a time (ex.2). Another aspect of Monk's first-period pieces is his reworking of standard tunes, such as *Smoke gets in your eyes* and *Carolina Moon*, in which he dramatically alters and develops familiar material in an unorthodox and entirely characteristic fashion; his version of the latter (1952) is an early example of the "bop waltz."

In his second period Monk produced many carefree popular pieces such as *Jackie-ing*, but also substantial works, including *Pannonica*, the highly dissonant *Crepuscule with Nellie*, and *Gallop's Gallop*, a tour de force of "wrong" notes which unexpectedly interrupt the conventional harmonies. His most important composition of the 1950s, and perhaps the most unorthodox work of his career, was *Brilliant Corners*, whose melody skirts the whole-tone, chromatic, and Lydian scales and is furthest removed from his Afro-American roots.

3. Piano style. It is as a performer that Monk was most misunderstood. He did not always exhibit the customary right-hand dexterity of most jazz pianists and, more importantly, his fellow jazz musicians quite often disagreed with his choice of notes. But his style, based on the Harlem stride tradition, had many strengths: a highly distinctive timbre, an ability to provide uncanny rhythmic surprises, and a wide variety of articulation. More importantly, Monk invented and developed ideas rather than merely embroidering chord changes. Some of his performances, such as *I Should Care* (1957), show a fresh use of rubato quite different from that of other jazz or lounge pianists. Monk also favored "crushed" notes and clusters which "evaporated" to leave a few key pitches. But his most important contribution as a pianist was his remarkable ability to improvise a coherent musical argument with a logic and structure comparable to the best of his notated compositions. Brilliant examples can be found in his solos and accompaniments on the recordings of *Misterioso* (1948) and especially *Bags' Groove* (1954), both with Milt Jackson. Although several young musicians of the 1970s and 1980s have borrowed and reinterpreted Monk's melodies for their own improvisations, most jazz pianists seem incapable or unwilling to pursue the introverted,

quirky, yet meticulous thought processes that inspired Monk's greatest solos.

See also HARMONY (i), §1(iv), and Table 1 and ex.9; IMPROVISATION, §4(iv) and ex.5; and PIANO, §4; for further illustration *see* NIGHTCLUBS AND OTHER VENUES, fig.6.

SELECTED RECORDINGS

* – composed by Monk

AS UNACCOMPANIED SOLOIST

Thelonious Monk (1954, Swing 33342), incl. *Eronel; *Thelonious Himself* (1957, Riv. 235), incl. I Should Care, *'Round Midnight; *Solo Monk* (1964, Col. CS9149), incl. I Should Care, Ruby, my Dear

AS LEADER

*Humph/*Misterioso (1947–8, BN 560); Evonce (1947, BN 547); Suburban Eyes/*Thelonious (1947, BN 542); Ruby, my Dear/*Evidence (1947–8, BN 549); *'Round about Midnight (1947, BN 543); *Criss Cross/*Eronel (1951, BN 1590); Carolina Moon/*Hornin' In (1952, BN 1603); *Little Rootie Tootie (1954, Prst. 850); *Thelonious Monk Quintet* (1954, Prst. 180), incl. Smoke gets in your eyes; *Brilliant Corners* (1956, Riv. 226), incl. *Brilliant Corners, *Pannonica

Monk's Music (1957, Riv. 242), incl. *Crepuscule with Nellie, Ruby, my Dear; *Thelonious Monk with John Coltrane* (1957, Jlnd 946); *The Thelonious Monk Orchestra at Town Hall* (1959, Riv. 1138), incl. *Crepuscule with Nellie; *5 by Monk by 5* (1959, Riv. 1150), incl. *Jackie-ing; *Straight, No Chaser* (1966–7, Col. CS9451), incl. *Straight, No Chaser; *Something in Blue* (1971, BL 152), incl. Nice work if you can get it, *Something in Blue; *The Man I Love* (1971, BL 197)

AS SIDEMAN

first issued on C. Christian: *Jazz Immortal* (1941, Eso. 1), Swing to Bop; C. Hawkins: Drifting on a Reed/Flyin' Hawk (1944, Joe Davis 8250); C. Parker: Bloomdido/My Melancholy Baby (1950, Mer./Clef 11058); S. Rollins: *Sonny Rollins Quintet* (1954, Prst. 190); M. Davis: *Miles Davis All Stars* (1954, Prst. 196), incl. Bags' Groove; *Miles Davis All Stars* (1954, Prst. 200), incl. *Bemsha Swing/The Man I Love; on G. Gryce: *Gigi Gryce Quartet* (1955, Signal 1201), *Gallop's Gallop; A. Blakey: *Art Blakey's Jazz Messengers and Thelonious Monk* (1957, Atl. 1278); Giants of Jazz: *The Giants of Jazz* (1971, Atl. 2-905)

BIBLIOGRAPHY

O. Keepnews: "Thelonious Monk," *Record Changer*, ii/4 (1948), 5
L. Malson: *Les maîtres du jazz* (Paris, 1952, rev. 6/1972)
G. Schuller: "Thelonious Monk," *JR*, i/1 (1958), 22; iii/6 (1960), 26; repr. in *Jazz Panorama*, ed. M. Williams (New York and London, 1962/*R*1979)
M. Harrison: "Thelonious Monk," *Just Jazz*, iii, ed. S. Traill and G. Lascelles (London, 1959), 14
N. Hentoff: "The Private World of Thelonious Monk," *Esquire*, liii/4 (1960), 133
M. James: "Thelonious Monk," *Ten Modern Jazzmen: an Appraisal of the Recorded Work of Ten Modern Jazzmen* (London, 1960), 81
N. Hentoff: *The Jazz Life* (New York and London, 1961/*R*1975) [incl. previously pubd articles]
A. Hodeir: *Toward Jazz* (New York, 1962/*R*1976)
"Loneliest Monk," *Time*, lxxxiii (28 Feb 1964), 84
J. Goldberg: *Jazz Masters of the Fifties* (New York and London, 1965/*R*1980)
J. G. Jepsen: *A Discography of Thelonious Monk & Bud Powell* (Copenhagen, 1969)
J. Langford: Monk's Horns," *JJ*, xxiii/11 (1970), 2
M. Williams: *The Jazz Tradition* (New York, 1970, rev. 2/1983)
M. Harrison: *A Jazz Retrospect* (Newton Abbot, England, 1976, rev. 2/1977)
M. Ruppli: "Discographie de Thelonious Monk," *Jh*, no.331 (1976), 22
J. Réda: *L'improviste: une lecture de jazz* (Paris, 1980), 128
J. R. Mitchell: "Thelonious Monk: the Man and his Music," *JSN*, ii/3 (1981), 51
L. Bijl and F. Canté: *Monk on Records: a Discography of Thelonious Monk* (Amsterdam, 1982, 2/1985) [incl. list of compositions]
M. F. Hopkins: "Monk the High Preachment," *JSN*, ii/4 (1982), 17
R. Blake: "Thelonious Monk: the Music," *The Wire*, no.10 (1984), 29
T. Fitterling: *Thelonious Monk: sein Leben, seine Musik, seine Schallplatten* (Waakirchen, nr Bad Tölz, Germany, 1987)
L. Tomkins: "The Classic Interview: Thelonious Monk," *CI*, xxiv/6 (1987), 12

RAN BLAKE

Monroe's Uptown House. Nightclub in New York, properly known as Clark Monroe's Uptown House; *see* NIGHTCLUBS AND OTHER VENUES.

Monsbourgh, Ade [Adrian Herbert; Lazy Ade] (*b* Melbourne, Australia, 17 Feb 1917). Australian reed player and bandleader. He studied piano as a child, and later took up saxophones, clarinet, valve trombone, trumpet, and recorder. In 1930 he began a long association with Graeme Bell, with whom he toured Europe (1947–8, 1949), and made many recordings (1944–52, 1958, 1962) in several countries, including Czechoslovakia; the band accompanied Rex Stewart in Australia in 1949. During visits to England, Monsbourgh performed and recorded with Humphrey Lyttelton (1951, 1952). He also played and recorded in Australia with Roger Bell (intermittently 1943–71), Dave Dallwitz (1950, 1972–4), Len Barnard (1952–5, 1967–8), and Frank Traynor (1959–63), and from 1944 to 1971 led his own bands on recordings, including *Recorder in Ragtime* (1956, Swaggie 4503) and *Lazy Ade and his Late Hour Boys* (1956, Swaggie 4501); among his sidemen were Bob Barnard, the reed player Neville Stribling, the tuba player Ron Williamson, and the banjoist Peter Cleaver. Although he retired from full-time playing in the 1970s, Monsbourgh has continued to perform occasionally in Australia, both as a leader and as a sideman.

BIBLIOGRAPHY

A. Bisset: *Black Roots, White Flowers: a History of Jazz in Australia* (Sydney, 1979), 114, 121, 164
B. Johnson: "Monsbourgh, Ade," *The Oxford Companion to Australian Jazz* (Melbourne, Australia, 1987)

TONY GOULD

Monterey Jazz Festival. Festival held annually from 1958 near Monterey, California. It was founded by Ralph J. Gleason and the disc jockey Jimmy Lyons, partly at the suggestion of George Wein and Louis Lorillard (the founders of the Newport Jazz Festival). Gleason was an adviser to the festival's organizers during its early years and Lyons was its general manager into the 1980s; its music directors have been John Lewis (to 1983) and Mundell Lowe. The festival takes place over three days in September (including the third weekend of the month) at three venues on the Monterey County Fairgrounds (seating 7000) and usually offers performances by well-known swing and bop musicians; Louis Armstrong and Thelonious Monk appeared regularly, as have Dizzy Gillespie, Gerry Mulligan, and Dave Brubeck. A blues concert has also been included in most years. Proceeds from the festival have been used for educational purposes, including the awarding of grants and scholarships (from 1961) and the administration of the Annual California High School Jazz Competition (from 1971), the winners of which perform on the last day of the festival with its featured performers. The Monterey Jazz Festival was acclaimed during its early years for its innovative programming; in 1959, for example, it included the premières of works by Jimmy Giuffre, John Lewis, and Gunther Schuller (all performed by an ensemble directed by Schuller) and performances by an all-star band assembled for the occasion by Woody Herman. Later, however, it drew criticism for its indifference towards free jazz and other modern styles. The tape archive of the festival is held by the Stanford Archive of Recorded Sound at Stanford University; *see* LIBRARIES AND ARCHIVES, §2.

BIBLIOGRAPHY

L. Tomkins: "The Man behind Monterey: Jimmy Lyons," *CI*, xi/1 (1972), 6
L. Lyons: "Monterey, 19 Years Healthy," *DB*, xliii/19 (1976), 16
J. Lyons and I. Kamin: *Dizzy, Duke, the Count, and me: the Story of the Monterey Jazz Festival* (San Francisco, 1978)

SARA VELEZ/PAUL R. LAIRD

Monterose, J. R. [Frank Anthony, Jr.] (*b* Detroit, 19 Jan 1927). Tenor saxophonist. He played in territory bands in the late 1940s, then moved to New York, where he worked with Buddy

Rich (1952) and Claude Thornhill (1954). In 1955 he recorded in bop groups led by Teddy Charles, Jon Eardley, Ralph Sharon, and Eddie Bert, and the following year he was a member of Charles Mingus's Jazz Workshop and Kenny Dorham's Jazz Prophets. Beginning in 1956 he made several recordings as a leader, including the album *The Message* (1960, Jaro 5004). Monterose also recorded with Sharon (1956), George Wallington (1957), René Thomas (1960), and Rein De Graaff (1970). He continued to perform in New York state into the 1980s; his later work is well represented by his solo on *Just Friends* from the album *Live in Albany* (1979, Upt. 2702).

BIBLIOGRAPHY

M. Gardner: "J. R. Monterose," *JM*, no.157 (1968), 2 [incl. discography]

J. Jeremy: "J. R. Monterose: Something with Music in it." *Coda*, xii/1 (1974), 2

P. Adamson: "J. R.: Alive and Well!," *JJI*, xxxiv/3 (1981), 22

Montgomery. Family of musicians.

(1) Monk [William Howard] **Montgomery** (*b* Indianapolis, 10 Oct 1921; *d* Las Vegas, NV, 20 May 1982). Bass player. He began to play double bass at the age of 30, but changed to electric bass guitar in order to make an international tour with Lionel Hampton's big band (1951–3), and became the first jazz musician to specialize and record on the instrument (1953). He then played in the Montgomery–Johnson Quintet with his brothers (2) Wes and (3) Buddy Montgomery, the tenor saxophonist Alonzo Johnson, and the drummer Robert Johnson (1955–6). Thereafter he moved to Seattle, where he was soon joined by Buddy. The two musicians then moved to San Francisco, where they continued to play together (occasionally with Wes) in the MASTERSOUNDS (1957–60) and the Montgomery Brothers (1960–61); the latter was a quartet involving a number of different drummers. During the early 1960s he again played double bass, but returned to electric bass while with Cal Tjader (1966). In 1970 he settled in Las Vegas, where he worked with Red Norvo's trio (1970–72), founded the Las Vegas Jazz Society (1975), and promoted jazz as a disc jockey. He visited South Africa in 1974 as the leader of a black-American jazz group.

Oral history material in *NjR* (JOHP).

SELECTED RECORDINGS

As leader of Mastersounds (with B. Montgomery): *Jazz Showcase* (1957, PJ 403); of Montgomery Brothers (with B. Montgomery and W. Montgomery): *Groove Yard* (1961, Riv. 9362); *It's Never too Late* (*c*1969, Chisa 801); *Reality* (1974, Philadelphia International KZ33153)

As sideman: L. Hampton: *He Swings the Most* (1953, Vogue 167–8); W. Montgomery: *Montgomeryland* (1958–9, PJ 5); H. Hawes: *The Green Leaves of Summer* (1964, Cont. 7614)

BIBLIOGRAPHY

F. R. Nemko: "Monk Montgomery: Pioneer's Dues," *DB*, xlii/8 (1975), 16 [incl. discography]

M. Newman: "Monk Montgomery: the First Man to Record on Bass Guitar," *GP*, xi/9 (1977), 26 [incl. discography]

(2) Wes [John Leslie] **Montgomery** (*b* Indianapolis, 6 March 1923; *d* Indianapolis, 15 June 1968). Guitarist, brother of (1) Monk and (3) Buddy Montgomery. He began to teach himself guitar about 1943 and soon played in local bands. He toured and recorded with Lionel Hampton from 1948 until the beginning of 1950, playing brief solos on live broadcasts and also recording with the tenor saxophonist Gene Morris and one of Hampton's vocalists, Sonny Parker. After returning to Indianapolis he worked in obscurity until joining the Montgomery–Johnson Quintet in 1955; he recorded his first extended solos while playing in several groups with his brothers. In 1959 he organized his own trio with organ and drums, and its first recording, *The Wes Montgomery Trio*, initiated a series of albums for Riverside. These represent Montgomery at his peak, accompanied by the finest rhythm sections available, including Tommy Flanagan, Hank Jones, Ron Carter, Albert "Tootie" Heath, and Louis Hayes, and brought him belated recognition; he soon began to dominate the *Down Beat* and *Playboy* jazz polls.

In 1960 Montgomery moved to the San Francisco Bay area, where he continued to perform with his brothers, though he also appeared with John Coltrane (1961–2). He returned to Indianapolis in 1962 and resumed touring in March 1963, now with his trio. The following year he began recording for Verve, using backing arrangements for string orchestras and large jazz bands. Though unrepresentative of his talents, these

Wes Montgomery, Indianapolis

recordings considerably broadened his audience; his rendition of *Goin' out of my Head* (1965) won a Grammy Award, and the album *A Day in the Life*, recorded for the A&M label, was the best-selling jazz LP of 1967. In live performances, however, Montgomery continued to appear in small groups, notably with the Wynton Kelly Trio and in a quintet that included his brothers. He died unexpectedly at the height of his career.

Critics generally consider Montgomery the most important and influential jazz guitarist after Charlie Christian. Like Christian, whose recorded solos he memorized in his youth, Montgomery invented perfectly shaped phrases with tremendous rhythmic drive. But he also took advantage of recent developments in jazz harmony and melody, as well as improvements in the construction of electric guitars, to create a unique style. He used his thumb instead of a plectrum, achieving a soft attack and freeing his fingers for the playing of octaves and chordal passages, and for various kinds of strumming. His mastery of these techniques created a sensation among younger guitarists, and the playing of octaves, in particular, became a trademark of the Montgomery style.

Montgomery tended to build his solos from melodies in single notes to octave passages and finally to chords. He had a highly original melodic imagination and, at his best, constantly produced refreshing ideas that broke off unexpectedly. Even when he paraphrased a melody he managed to invest it with

Ex.1

(a) Opening of T. Dameron: *If you could see me now*

(b) Montgomery's improvisation on the opening of *If you could see me now* from *Smokin' at the Half Note* (1965, Verve 68633); transcr. L. Porter

rhythmic excitement; ex.1 shows a melody of quarter-notes used as the starting point of a long line of triplet eighth-notes spanning more than three octaves, in which interesting ambiguities of phrasing (bracketed) are created. Montgomery's playing abounded in subtle embellishments, deep blues sentiment, and a highly expressive use of portamento, tremolo, and other effects. In his sincere, unsensational way, he expanded the resources of jazz guitar, and his influence has been acknowledged by many later guitarists, including George Benson and Pat Martino.

Two volumes containing transcriptions of Montgomery's solos have been published: *The Wes Montgomery Guitar Method* (including pedagogical text), by L. Garson and J. Stewart (New York, 1968); and *The Wes Montgomery Guitar Folio: Improvisations and Interpretations*, transcribed by Steve Khan (New York, 1978).

Oral history material in *NjR*.

SELECTED RECORDINGS

As leader: of Montgomery Brothers (with B. Montgomery and M. Montgomery): first issued on *Almost Forgotten* (1955–62, Col. FC38509), Love for Sale (1955); *The Montgomery Brothers and Five Others* (1957, WP 1240); Finger Pickin' (1957, PJ 301); *Montgomeryland* (1958–9, PJ 5), incl. Far Wes'; *The Wes Montgomery Trio* (1959, Riv. 310); *The Incredible Jazz Guitar of Wes Montgomery* (1960, Riv. 320); *Movin' Along* (1960, Riv. 9342); *So Much Guitar!* (1961, Riv. 9382); *Full House* (1962, Riv. 9434); with W. Kelly: *Smokin' at the Half Note* (1965, Verve 68633), incl. If you could see me now; *Goin' out of my Head* (1965, Verve 68642); *A Day in the Life* (1967, A&M 3001)

As sideman: L. Hampton: *Hot House* (1948, Alamac 2419), incl. Adam blew his hat, Brant Inn Boogie; Mastersounds: *Kismet* (1958, WP 1243); M. Jackson: *Bags Meets Wes* (1961, Riv. 9407)

BIBLIOGRAPHY

R. J. Gleason: "Wes Montgomery," *DB*, xxviii/15 (1961), 23
I. Gitler: "Wes Montgomery: Organ-ic Problems & Satisfaction," *DB*, xxxi/21 (1964), 19
V. Wilmer: "Wes Montgomery," *JM*, xi/3 (1965), 23
Obituary, H. Panassié, *BHcF*, no.180 (1968), 11
B. Quinn: "The Thumb's up, or What the View is Like from the Top," *DB*, xxxv/13 (1968), 17
L. Tomkins: "Last Words of a Great Jazzman: Wes Montgomery," *CI*, vi/12 (1968), 18
R. J. Gleason: "Wes Montgomery, 1925 [sic] –1968," *GP*, vii/5 (1973), 22; repr. in *Jazz Guitarists: Collected Interviews from Guitar Player Magazine* (Saratoga, CA, 1978), 75
"Wes Montgomery," *SJ*, xxxii/8 (1978), 314 [discography]
D. Wild: "Wes and Trane: an Unrecorded Sextet," *Disc'ribe*, no.1 (1980), 3
A. Ingram: *Wes Montgomery* (Gateshead, England, 1985) [bio-discography]
——: "Wes Montgomery," *JJI*, xxxix/7 (1986), 10 [incl. discography]

(3) Buddy [Charles F.] **Montgomery** (*b* Indianapolis, 30 Jan 1930). Pianist and vibraphonist, brother of (1) Monk and (2) Wes Montgomery. He began playing piano in a group with Slide Hampton in Indianapolis, and during army service performed in a quartet with the double bass player Roy Johnson (1954). In 1955 he joined the Montgomery–Johnson Quintet with his brothers, then from 1957 to 1960 played vibraphone with the Mastersounds. During the 1960s he worked with the Montgomery Brothers (1960–61) and other groups, performing on both his instruments, but after settling in Milwaukee in 1969 he concentrated on piano. As a leading jazz musician in the city he worked regularly as a soloist and as the leader of bop and soul-jazz groups. In the early 1980s he settled in Oakland, California, and continued to perform, working throughout the San Francisco Bay area; he also toured and recorded with the singer Marlena Shaw. Montgomery organized the first Oakland Jazz Festival at the Calvin Simmons Theater of the Kaiser Convention Center on 4 October 1987, bringing in such distinguished soloists as Kenny Burrell, Ron Carter, Junior Cook, Slide Hampton, Marvin "Smitty" Smith, and Mel Lewis.

SELECTED RECORDINGS

As leader: of Montgomery Brothers (with M. Montgomery and W. Montgomery): *The Montgomery Brothers and Five Others* (1957, WP 1240); of Mastersounds (with M. Montgomery): *Swinging with the Mastersounds* (1960, Fan. 3305); *The Two-sided Album* (1968, Mlst. 9015); *Ties* (1976, Bean 102)

As sideman: J. Griffin: *Do Nothin' till you Hear from me* (1963, Riv. 9462)

BIBLIOGRAPHY

FeatherE; *Feather '60s*
J. De Muth: "Buddy Montgomery," *DB*, xlvii/4 (1980), 55
P. Elwood: "Proving there's Jazz in Oakland," *San Francisco Examiner* (2 Oct 1987)
L. Hildebrand: "Buddy Montgomery: the Man's been Flying on Jazz for 40 Years," *San Francisco Examiner* (3 May 1987)

BARRY KERNFELD (1, 3), LEWIS PORTER (2)

Montgomery, Little Brother [Eurreal Wilford] (*b* Kentwood, LA, 18 April 1906; *d* Chicago, 6 Sept 1985). Pianist, singer, and bandleader. He was self-taught, and began playing at the age of five; six years later he left home to work as a blues pianist in Holton, Louisiana. During the early 1920s he traveled extensively in Louisiana and Mississippi, and formed his own band and worked with Buddy Petit (*c*1925). Thereafter he toured logging camps with the blues singer and guitarist Big Joe Williams (*c*1926) and with Danny Barker (*c*1927). After moving to Chicago, where he made his first recordings in 1930, he returned to Jackson. He led a touring band of up to 14 members, the Southland Troubadours, from 1931 to 1939. During this period he recorded in New Orleans (1935–6). He continued to work in Mississippi, and also played in Texas, until he returned to Chicago in 1942. After World War II he made several recordings, toured with Kid Ory, and worked with Franz Jackson from around 1950 into the 1970s. He also performed and recorded frequently as an unaccompanied soloist. He toured England (1960, 1980) and Europe (1966, 1972), and performed at the Berliner Jazztage (1974) and the New Orleans Jazz and Heritage Festival (1976).

Oral history material in *ICU, LNT*.

SELECTED RECORDINGS

As unaccompanied soloist: Vicksburg Blues (1930, Para. 13006); Crescent City Blues/Shreveport Blues (1936, Bb 6733); *Deep South Piano* (1972, Sto. 228); *Tishomingo Blues* (1980, JSP 1015)

Duos: with Irene Scruggs: Must get Mine in Front (1930, Para. 13023); with V. Spivey: *The Queen and her Knights* (1965, Spivey 1006), incl. West Texas Blues

As leader: El ritmo/Long Time ago (1947, Cen. 4009)

BIBLIOGRAPHY

T. Standish: "Billed out and Bound to go: the Story of Little Brother Montgomery," *Eureka*, i/5 (1960), 18

D. Stewart-Baxter: "Blues," *JJ*, xx/4 (1967), 14

K. Gert zur Heide: *Deep South Piano: the Story of Little Brother Montgomery* (London, 1970)

T. Kent: "Down there in Vicksburg," *Sv*, no.55 (1974), 4

P. van Vorst: "Little Brother Montgomery: a Jazzman Sings the Blues," *MR*, i/6 (1974), 10

"Little Brother Tells his Story," *MR*, ii/3 (1975), 1

E. Montgomery: "Little Brother," *Selections from the Gutter: Jazz Portraits from "The Jazz Record"*, ed. A. Hodes and C. Hansen (Berkeley, CA, Los Angeles, and London, 1977), 51

D. von Staden: "Little Brother Montgomery," *Sv*, no.111 (1984), 94; no.112 (1984), 147; no.113 (1984), 169; no.114 (1984), 206 [discography]

Obituary, C. Hillman, *Fn*, xvii/2 (1985–6), 23

D. Barker: *A Life in Jazz*, ed. A. Shipton (London and New York, 1986)

P. Oliver: "Montgomery, Little Brother," *GroveAM*

MICHAEL TOVEY

Montgomery, Marian (Maud Runnels) (*b* Natchez, MS, 17 Nov 1934). Singer. After studying music and drama she worked throughout the USA and by 1965 was performing at such venues as the Sands Hotel, Las Vegas, and Basin Street East, New York. During the same year, following a season working at the Cool Elephant Club in London, she moved to England and married the pianist and director Laurie Holloway. Thereafter Montgomery has maintained a flourishing international career which has included performances at important London concert halls and nightclubs (including Ronnie Scott's) and at festivals. She has appeared frequently on television, notably in a feature program "A Dream of Alice" with Holloway in 1979, staged a one-woman show, and performed in musicals and cabaret. Montgomery has also gained wide press coverage for her collaborations with the composer Richard Rodney Bennett; they have worked together regularly in concerts, on television, and in recordings. Her singing can be heard to advantage on the album *On Stage* (1979, Cube 29). (*Feather '60s*)

DIGBY FAIRWEATHER

Montgomery Ward. Record label. It was established in the 1930s by the mail-order company of the same name. Most items in its catalogue (which included a high proportion of jazz and race records) were pressed by Victor from the latter's own repertory. Later issues (1938–9) were taken from the Varsity label. (B. Rust: *The American Record Label Book* (New Rochelle, NY, 1978), 199)

Montmartre (Jazzhus). Nightclub in Copenhagen; *see* NIGHTCLUBS AND OTHER VENUES.

Montoliu, Tete [Vincente] (*b* Barcelona, 28 March 1933). Spanish pianist. His father was a professional oboist. Born blind, Montoliu learned to read music in Braille when he was seven years old. At the age of 13, while beginning classical studies at the Barcelona Conservatory, he practiced and performed with Don Byas. He recorded with Lionel Hampton in Madrid (1956) and first left Spain to appear at a jazz festival in Cannes, France, with Doug Watkins and Art Taylor (1958). He worked with Archie Shepp in Copenhagen (1963–4) and later recorded two albums of bop standards with Anthony Braxton (1974). Generally, however, he played with more traditional swing and bop musicians, touring with Roland Kirk (1964) and recording with Kirk, Kenny Dorham (1963), Dexter Gordon (1964, 1975), Ben Webster (1968, 1972), and Lucky Thompson (1970). He worked as a soloist in New York at the Top of the Gate (1967). From the mid-1970s Montoliu began to acquire an international reputation through a series of albums recorded as a soloist and as leader of trios with Niels-Henning Ørsted Pedersen and Al "Tootie" Heath, and George Mraz and Al Foster. His repertory consists principally of bop tunes, but he also makes use of Catalan folk music. His improvisation on John Coltrane's rapid, harmonically challenging composition *Giant Steps* (1974), one of the most relaxed and imaginative interpretations recorded, demonstrates his impeccable technique, rhythmic drive, and gift for melody.

SELECTED RECORDINGS

As unaccompanied soloist: *Music for Perla* (1974, Ste. 1021); *Catalonian Folksongs* (1977, Tim. 116); *Lunch in LA* (1980, Cont. 14004)

As leader: *Catalonian Fire* (1974, Ste. 1017); *Tete!* (1974, Ste. 1029), incl. Giant Steps; *Tete à Tete* (1976, Ste. 1054); *I Wanna Talk about You* (1980, Ste. 1137)

As sideman: B. Webster: *Ben Webster Meets Don Byas in the Black Forest* (1968, Saba 15159); G. Coleman: *Meditation* (1977, Tim. 110)

BIBLIOGRAPHY

F. Marmande and G. Rouy: "Tete Montoliu," *Jm*, no.216 (1973), 25

C. J. Safane: "Tete Montoliu: Catalan Jazz Piano Virtuoso," *CK*, vi/9 (1980), 24

A. Papo: "Spanish Blues: Pianist Tete Montoliu," *JJI*, xxxiv/2 (1981), 13

R. Latxague: "Montoliu: bop en Tete," *Jm*, no.321 (1983), 40

BARRY KERNFELD

Montreux International Jazz Festival. Festival held annually from 1967 in Montreux, Switzerland. It was first organized by Claude Nobs, who continued as its director into the late 1980s. The festival takes place over 17 days in July at the Montreux Casino, and offers not only jazz but a large amount of popular music (for some time in the mid-1970s it was known simply as the Montreux International Festival). The concerts feature professional and student groups, many from the USA, in performances of swing, bop, and jazz-rock. The festival has benefited greatly from the sponsorship of record companies (particularly Pablo), for which it has been an important source of jazz recordings. The festival is associated with the Montreux–Detroit Kool Jazz Festival, which includes performances by the winner of the band contest at the Swiss festival and other Swiss artists. *See also* FESTIVALS, §3 (USA, Detroit).

BIBLIOGRAPHY

L. Lyons: "Perspective: Claude Nobs: Chef de Festival," *DB*, xliii/16 (1976), 49

On Stage, Backstage: Montreux Jazz Festival (Lausanne, Switzerland, 1986) [photographs]

PAUL R. LAIRD

Montrose, Jack (*b* Detroit, 30 Dec 1928). Tenor saxophonist. He played clarinet and alto saxophone in a high-school band in Chattanooga, Tennessee. He studied at Los Angeles State College (BA 1953) and played frequently on the West Coast throughout the 1950s as a soloist on tenor saxophone; he worked with Jerry Gray (1953), Art Pepper (1954), Red Norvo, Shorty Rogers, Mel Tormé, and others. The decline in the popularity of West Coast jazz affected his career and by the early 1960s Montrose was playing mainly at strip clubs in Los Angeles and as a studio musician on rock recordings. In 1966 he moved to Nevada, where he played in bands that accompanied performers at casinos in Lake Tahoe, Reno, and Las Vegas. After 1960, apart from a brief period with Frank Butler in the mid-1970s, Montrose played very little jazz until 1986, when he made an album with a group that included Pete Jolly. Montrose combines considerable creative abilities with a strong sound and a smooth, flowing style.

SELECTED RECORDINGS

As leader: *Jack Montrose with Bob Gordon* (1955, Atl. 1223); *Jack Montrose Sextet* (1955, PJ 1208); *Blues and Vanilla* (1956, RCA LPM1451); *Horn's Full* (1956–7, RCA LPM1572); *Better Late than Never* (1986, Slingshot 1001)

As sideman: J. Gray: Oomp chuck (1953, Decca 28986); Coronado Cruise (1953, Decca 29038); B. Gordon: *Meet Mr. Gordon* (1954, PJ 12); A. Pepper: *Art Pepper Quintet* (1954, Dis. 3023)

BIBLIOGRAPHY

FeatherE

R. Gordon: *Jazz West Coast: the Los Angeles Jazz Scene of the 1950s* (London and New York, 1986)

SCOTT YANOW

Moodsville. Record label founded in 1960 as a subsidiary of PRESTIGE.

Moody, James (*b* Savannah, GA, 26 Feb 1925). Alto and tenor saxophonist and flutist. He grew up in Reading, Pennsylvania, and in Newark, New Jersey, where at the age of 16 he took up the alto saxophone before changing to tenor saxophone. While serving in the air force (1943–6) he belonged to a military band and played in Dizzy Gillespie's orchestra during a performance in Greensboro, North Carolina; after his discharge he played tenor saxophone with Gillespie from late 1946 (for illustration *see* GILLESPIE, DIZZY). In late 1948 he traveled to Europe, where he toured France, Scandinavia, and Switzerland, again took up the alto saxophone, and recorded a version of *I'm in the Mood for Love* (1949) that became a hit recording when it was issued in the USA by Prestige. After moving late in the summer of 1951 to New York he formed a septet that played a style of jazz strongly influenced by rhythm-and-blues; he toured and recorded as the leader of this group for five years. He made a series of outstanding recordings for Argo (1956–63), formed a second group, in which he played flute, and worked briefly with Gene Ammons and Sonny Stitt; from 1962 to 1969 he played in a small group with Gillespie. Later he worked as a leader and as a freelance, made frequent visits to Europe, and occasionally rejoined Gillespie, with whom he toured in 1980. Moody is a fluent soloist on all three of his instruments; he has a strong sense of swing and a feeling for the blues, and is an unsentimental interpreter of ballads. On the tenor saxophone his playing is reminiscent of that of Lester Young, but the harder tone that he adopted in the 1960s was doubtless inspired by the work of John Coltrane; as an alto saxophonist his style owes much to that of Charlie Parker. He has made his most effective recordings with small groups.

SELECTED RECORDINGS

As leader: *James Moody and his Modernists* (1948, BN 5006); I'm in the Mood for Love (1949, Met. 8502); *Wail, Moody, Wail* (1955, Prst. 7036); *Flute 'n the Blues* (1956, Argo 603); *Last Train from Overbrook* (1958, Argo 637); *Cookin' the Blues* (1961, Argo 756); *Running the Gamut* (1964, Scepter 525); *Don't Look Away Now!* (1969, Prst. 7625); *Feelin' it Together* (1973, Muse 5020)

As sideman: D. Gillespie: *Dizzy Gillespie at the Downbeat Club, Summer 1947* (1947, Phon. 7629); H. McGhee: *Howard McGhee Sextet* (1947, Dial 209); D. Gillespie: *Something Old, Something New* (1963, Phi. 600091); D. Gordon: on *The Tower of Power!* (1969, Prst. 7623), Montmartre; T. Swanerud: *More than you Know* (1984, Dra. 85)

BIBLIOGRAPHY

I. Gitler: "New Mood for Moody," *DB*, xxvii/22 (1960), 23

A. Gerber: "Pourquoi j'aime Moody," *Jm*, no.180 (1970), 30

C. Suber: "James Moody: Versatile Virtuoso," *DB*, xxxix/10 (1972), 14

L. Jeske: "James Moody's Move," *DB*, xlvii/7 (1980), 19 [incl. discography]

D. Long: James Moody: Interview," *Cadence*, vii/8 (1981), 5

S. Voce: "James Moody," *JJI*, xxxvi/6 (1983), 12

MARK GARDNER

Mooney, Joe (*b* Paterson, NJ, 14 March 1911; *d* Fort Lauderdale, FL, 12 May 1975). Accordionist, organist, and singer. In the 1920s he sang and played piano on radio with his brother Dan; the two recorded as the Sunshine Boys in 1929–31. He played accordion and wrote arrangements for Frank Dailey (1937), Paul Whiteman, Larry Clinton, and other big-band leaders. He played accordion and sang as leader of a swing quartet (1946–7; re-formed as a quintet, 1963–5) which made several recordings (including *Just a Gigolo*, 1946, Decca 23790); he also played accordion on a recording with Buddy Rich and Ella Fitzgerald (1947). Mooney later recorded as a singer with the Sauter–Finegan Orchestra (1952). From the late 1940s he worked principally as an organist; he performed in Florida and recorded as a leader (1951, 1956) and with Johnny Smith (1953).

BIBLIOGRAPHY

FeatherE; *Feather '60s*; *Feather–Gitler '70s*

A. Shaw: *The Street that Never Slept* (New York, 1971/*R*1983 as *52nd Street: the Street of Jazz*), 330

D. Salemann: "Joe Mooney, 1911–1975: a Sunshine Boy?," *Pj*, no.15 (1979), 29 [incl. discography]

Moore, Alton ("Slim") [Slim] (*b* Selma, AL, 7 Oct 1908; *d* New York, 1978). Trombonist. He began playing professionally in 1925 and toured with various shows (1926–9). In 1931 he became the principal trombonist with Blanche Calloway, with whom he made several recordings; on leaving Calloway (1934) he moved to New York, where he joined Jack Butler. He worked with many musicians, including Hot Lips Page, Charlie Johnson, and Tiny Bradshaw (all 1939), Fats Waller (1940), Coleman Hawkins and Horace Henderson (both 1941), Ella Fitzgerald (1941–2), Benny Carter (1942–6), Louis Armstrong (1946–7), and Lucky Millinder and Rex Stewart (mid-1940s). Among the players with whom Moore recorded were Carter, Dizzy Gillespie (1946), Armstrong (1947), and Herbie Fields (1947); his obbligato and ensemble playing may be heard on Fats Waller's *That Ain't Right* (1943, V-disc 165). Although Moore ceased full-time performing in 1952, he later worked in the Fletcher Henderson reunion bands (1957) and with Puddinghead Battle (1960s).

based on *ChiltonW*

Moore, Big Chief [Russell] (*b* nr Sacaton, AZ, 13 Aug 1912; *d* Nyack, NY, 15 Dec 1983). Trombonist. He was an American Indian of the Pima tribe. In 1924 he moved to Chicago where he was taught trombone and piano by his uncle, after which he studied music in California. He played with Lionel Hampton's band (1935) and briefly with Eddie Barefield (1936), then worked in California for three years as a freelance musician and in New Orleans with Papa Celestin (1939). He also played with Kid Rena, A. J. Piron, Joe Robichaux, Paul Barbarin, Ernie Fields, Harlan Leonard, and Noble Sissle. From 1944 to 1947 Moore was a member of Louis Armstrong's orchestra, with which he appeared in the film *New Orleans* (1946). Thereafter he played intermittently with Sidney Bechet at Jimmy Ryan's, New York, worked with Ruby Braff and Pee Wee Russell, and performed with numerous dixieland musicians such as Tony Parenti, Eddie Condon, and Wild Bill Davison. In 1949 he performed at the Festival International de Jazz, Paris, and in 1953 he toured Europe with Mezz Mezzrow, taking part in recording sessions in Paris with Mezzrow, Bechet, and Buck Clayton;

later he toured internationally with Armstrong's All Stars (1964–5). After a period of illness he toured with his own group, establishing an enthusiastic following in Canada. He recorded as a leader in 1973 and with Cozy Cole in 1977, and in 1981 toured England with a band led by Keith Smith and made up of former Armstrong sidemen.

Moore had a good technique and a fine tone with a warm, if somewhat pronounced, vibrato. His phrasing was influenced by that of Armstrong and he was at his most effective when contributing to the improvised counterpoint of a standard New Orleans ensemble of trumpet, clarinet, and trombone.

Oral history material in *NjR* (JOHP).

SELECTED RECORDINGS

As leader: *Russell "Big Chief" Moore* (1953–74, Jazzart 520472) [incl. previously unissued tracks]

As sideman with M. Mezzrow: Swingin' with Mezz/Wabash Blues (1953, Vogue 5161)

BIBLIOGRAPHY

ChiltonW; *FeatherE*; *Feather '60s*

E. Cook: "The Wonderful World of Louis Armstrong," *JJI*, xxxiv/9 (1981), 9

P. Vacher: "Big Chief Russell Moore," *MR*, x/8 (1983), 8

KEN RATTENBURY

Moore, Bill [William Henry] (*b* New York, 1901; *d* New York, 17 June 1964). Trumpeter. He played in the California Ramblers in the 1920s and performed solos on many of their recordings, including *Charleston Cabin* (1924, Col. 171D); as a studio musician he worked in small groups drawn from the California Ramblers (the Five Birmingham Babies and the Goofus Five, both 1924–5, and the Lumberjacks, 1928). He was also a member of the violinist Ben Bernie's orchestra and of bands led by Don Voorhees, Bert Lown, and Lester Lanin, and he recorded with Bernie (1925–7), Jack Pettis (1926–9), Irving Mills (1929–30), Fred Rich (1930), and the Dorsey brothers (1930). He then worked in radio and studio orchestras.

based on *ChiltonW*

Moore, Billy [William, Jr.] (*b* Parkersburg, WV, 7 Dec 1917). Arranger and pianist. In 1939 he replaced Sy Oliver as the arranger in Jimmie Lunceford's band. His work in this capacity may be heard to advantage on *Belgian Stomp* (*Dutch Kitchen Stomp, State and Tioga Stomp*) (1939, Voc./OK 5207). After leaving Lunceford he wrote arrangements for Charlie Barnet and Jan Savitt (both 1940–44) and Tommy Dorsey. During the late 1940s he worked in New York as a music publisher. After moving to Europe in the early 1950s, Moore wrote music for French bands and toured as the music director and pianist with a popular vocal group, the Peters Sisters (1953–60). He then worked as a staff arranger for a radio station in Berlin (1960–63) and toured Europe with the Delta Rhythm Boys, a popular group. Later he settled in Copenhagen and in the 1970s worked as a freelance arranger. (*ChiltonW*; *FeatherE*; *Feather '60s*; *Feather–Gitler '70s*)

Moore, Brew [Milton Aubrey, Jr.] (*b* Indianola, MS, 26 March 1924; *d* Copenhagen, 19 Aug 1973). Tenor saxophonist. From the age of 12 he played clarinet and, briefly, trombone, but while at high school he changed to tenor saxophone. From around 1942 to 1948 he played in New Orleans and Memphis and made several unsuccessful attempts to break into jazz circles in New York; the new bop style was in fashion at the time, but Moore was a driving, lyrical swing soloist. Finally he moved to New York (1948) and found a place in Claude Thornhill's orchestra (1948–9). In 1949 he played as a principal soloist with Machito and performed in Kai Winding's bop group; he also recorded with Stan Getz's Five Brothers, a group of tenor saxophonists devoted to reproducing in their own playing the smooth, airy timbre of Lester Young, of whom Moore, in particular, was a great admirer. In 1954 he moved to San Francisco, where he worked with Cal Tjader and as a leader. Moore traveled to Paris in 1961 to play with Kenny Clarke and then settled in Copenhagen, though he continued to perform intermittently in the USA (1964–5, 1967–70, 1972–3).

SELECTED RECORDINGS

As leader: Lestorian Mode (1949, Savoy 953); *Brew Moore Quintet* (1955–6, Fan. 3222); *Danish Brew* (1959, *c*1961, Jazz Mark 101); *Brew's Stockholm Dew* (1971, Sonet 624)

As sideman: Machito: Cu-bop City (1949, Roost 502); S. Getz: Four and one Moore/Five Brothers (1949, NewJ 802); K. Winding: *Arrangements by Gerry Mulligan* (1951, Roost 408)

BIBLIOGRAPHY

J. S. Wilson: "Brew Brews Bop on Pres Kick," *DB*, xvi/12 (1949), 7

I. Gitler: "Home Brew: Brew Moore Returns," *DB*, xxxvi/15 (1969), 16

J. Burns: "Some New York Jazz: 1949," *JJ*, xxiii/2 (1970), 6

——: "Cool Sounds," *JJ*, xxiii/6 (1970), 2

S. Woolley: "Brew Moore," *Coda*, no.142 (1975), 25

BARRY KERNFELD

Moore, Danny [Daniel William] (*b* Waycross, GA, 6 Jan 1941). Trumpeter. He first heard jazz attending Florida Agricultural & Mechanical University, when Cannonball Adderley performed in Fort Lauderdale, and he immediately began practicing and listening to jazz; he was especially influenced by Clifford Brown, Fats Navarro, and Dizzy Gillespie. In the early 1960s Moore played with the singer Ruth Brown, Quincy Jones, and the house band at the Apollo Theatre, New York. He toured with the saxophonist Paul Williams (1962) and played with Art Blakey (1964) and briefly with Count Basie (1966). From 1968 he worked with the Thad Jones–Mel Lewis Orchestra and on leaving the band in 1972 he joined George Coleman's octet, with which he played flugelhorn; his association with Coleman continued into the 1980s. Moore has played with Johnny Hammond, Wes Montgomery, the soul singer Aretha Franklin (1971), Oliver Nelson (at the Montreux International Jazz Festival, 1973), and Dizzy Gillespie (1975). He worked as a studio musician with Charles Earland (1973) and Al Grey and Frank Strozier (both 1976), and by 1981 he was leading his own quintet.

SELECTED DISCOGRAPHY

As sideman: T. Jones and M. Lewis: *Central Park North* (1969, SolS 18058); C. Earland: *The Dynamite Brothers* (1973, Prst. 10082); A. Grey: *Struttin' and Shoutin'* (1976, Col. FC38505); F. Strozier: *Remember me?* (1976, Ste. 1066); G. Coleman: *Big George* (1977, Affinity 52)

BIBLIOGRAPHY

R. Williams: "Big Band Veteran," *MM* (6 Sept 1969), 8

L. Tomkins: "Sound Matters more than Range: Danny Moore," *CI*, xix/8 (1981), 12

FREDERICK A. BECK

Moore, Don (*b* New York, 1932). Double bass player. He first played piano, then in 1959 changed to double bass. In 1962 he recorded and toured Europe in a quartet led by Archie Shepp and Bill Dixon. The following year, as a member of the New York Contemporary Five, he recorded four albums, two each in New York and Copenhagen (including *The New York Contemporary Five*, Fon. 881013); one of these was released under the names of Shepp and John Tchicai. While in Copenhagen he also recorded with Roland Kirk. He later played hard bop with Sonny Rollins, Jackie McLean, Frank Foster, and Lee Morgan, and recorded with Elvin Jones (1966) and Clifford Thornton (1967), then ceased working as a musician. Moore should not be confused with the trumpeter of the same name who recorded with Red Nichols in 1931. (V. Wilmer: *As Serious as your Life: the Story of the New Jazz* (London, 1977, rev. 1980), 165, 275)

Moore, Dudley (*b* London, 19 April 1935). English pianist. He played jazz in various clubs while at school, and after graduating from Oxford University (BMus 1957) joined Vic Lewis's band. In 1960 he performed and recorded with John Dankworth. He then formed his own trio, which first recorded in 1961; it performed in London and New York in the revue *Beyond the Fringe,* in which Moore also acted. From 1964 he became well known for his work as a television comedian and film actor. He has composed music for films, plays, ballets, and television, and has made several recordings with his trio. His playing may be heard to advantage on the album *Dudley Moore at the Wavendon Festival* (1976, BL 12151).

BIBLIOGRAPHY

Feather–Gitler '70s

L. Tomkins: "Music and Moore," *Crescendo,* iv/12 (1966), 18; v/1 (1966), 18

M. McPartland: "Dudley (Moore): Serious Music from a Colossus of Comedy," *All in Good Time* (New York, and Oxford, England, 1987) [colln of previously pubd articles], 129

Moore, Eddie (*b* San Francisco, 14 Sept 1940). Drummer. After starting his career in a band led by his cousin, the organist Merl Saunders, he worked with the Montgomery brothers in the Mastersounds and with Dewey Redman, with whom he recorded in 1966. In 1968 he toured Vietnam with the singer Barbara Virgil, then traveled to Europe; he became house drummer at the Montmartre Jazzhus, Copenhagen, and played with Dexter Gordon. He moved to New York in 1970 and worked with Stanley Turrentine (1971–4) and Sonny Rollins (1974–7). During the 1970s he made recordings with Turrentine and Rollins, Redman (1973, 1974, 1978), Woody Shaw (1976), and Bennie Wallace (1978). Having returned to San Francisco, he played with Bobby Hutcherson, led his own band, and worked as a freelance musician. He performed with Rollins in India (1978) and toured with Redman (1981); in 1983 he made a recording with the guitarist Peter Sprague. The influence on Moore's playing of Philly Joe Jones, Roy Haynes, and Elvin Jones can be heard in the free style of his performances with such musicians as Redman.

SELECTED RECORDINGS

As sideman: D. Redman: *The Ear of the Behearer* (1973, Imp. 9250); S. Turrentine: *Pieces of Dreams* (1974, Fan. 9465); S. Rollins: *Nucleus* (1975, Mlst. 9064); B. Wallace: *The Fourteen Bar Blues* (1978, Enja 3029); P. Sprague: *Musica del mar* (1983, Conc. 237)

BIBLIOGRAPHY

B. Primack: "Eddie Moore," *DB,* xlvi/4 (1979), 37

RICK MATTINGLY

Moore, Freddie (*b* Washington, NC, 20 Aug 1900). Drummer and singer. He played drums from the age of 12 and first worked in traveling shows. Later he performed with Charlie Creath in St. Louis (*c*1927) and led his own seven-piece band at the Savoy, Detroit. After playing in New York with Wilbur Sweatman (1928–31) he toured with King Oliver (1931–2); his drumming may be heard to advantage on Oliver's *Nelson Stomp* (1930, Vic. 23388). From 1933 to 1937 Moore led his own trio (with Pete Brown and Don Frye), and worked mainly at the Victoria Café in New York. He then played with John Kirby, Lem Johnson, Art Hodes (mid-1940s, 1950), Sidney Bechet (1945, 1947), Wilbur De Paris (*c*1948, 1952–4), Bob Wilber (1948), and the trombonist Conrad Janis (1951). He toured Europe with Mezz Mezzrow (1954–5) and again with Sammy Price (1955). Moore's style in the 1950s is well represented by *Emmett Berry and his Orchestra* (1956, Col. 33FP1076). He continued to work as a freelance into the early 1980s, performing with such musicians as Tony Parenti (1968–70) and Roy Eldridge (1971). Unable, on account of ill-health, to play a full drum set in the mid-1980s, he concentrated on washboard.

Oral history material in *LNT, NjR* (JOHP).

BIBLIOGRAPHY

F. Moore: "King Oliver's Last Tour," *Jazz Record,* no.31 (1945), 10; repr. in *Selections from the Gutter: Jazz Portraits from "The Jazz Record",* ed. A. Hodes and C. Hansen (Berkeley, CA, Los Angeles, and London, 1977), 86

G. Clamer: "Freddy Moore," *Record Changer,* ix (Dec 1950), 9

G. Hoefer: "The Hot Box: ex-King Oliver Drummer at Blue Note with Hodes," *DB,* xvii/5 (1950), 10

H. Panassié: "La tournée de Mezz," *BHcF,* no.42 (1954), 3

C. Hillman: "Facts and Fancies," *Fn,* iv/3 (1973), 17

A. Vollmer: "Some Notes on Clarence M. Jones . . . and Others," *Sv,* no.51 (1974), 84

W. Balliett: *Jelly Roll, Jabbo and Fats* (New York, and Oxford, England, 1983) [colln of previously pubd articles], 42

based on *ChiltonW*

Moore, Gerry [Gerald Asher] (*b* London, 8 Oct 1903). English pianist. From 1919 to 1939 he worked in London as a freelance musician and as a pianist in cinemas and clubs, including Sherry's (1925–6), the Empress Rooms (1927), Chez Rex Evans (1933–4), the Bag O' Nails and the 43 Club (both 1934–5), and Mema's (1934–9). Later he played in Southsea with Buddy Featherstonhaugh (1939) and performed in various clubs, notably the Florida Club (with Adelaide Hall, 1940–42) and the Nut House (1944). In the late 1940s Moore worked with the bandleaders Max Geldray (in Germany, 1947) and Carlo Krahmer (at the Paris Jazz Fair, 1949); during this period he also played at the Palm Beach Hotel in Cannes (1948–*c*1950) as well as regularly in nightclubs. Thereafter he performed with the saxophonists Harry Gold and Laurie Gold (1954–7), and as a solo pianist on the liners *Queen Mary* (1957) and *Caronia* (1959–63). From the 1960s he again worked in clubs, including the Living Room in London (1963–5), and from 1984 he has played at the Royal Lancaster Hotel. Moore is featured in the duo *Mean to Me,* issued on the anthology *Vic Lewis Jam Sessions,* ii: *1945: the War Years* (Harl. 3009).

Oral history material in *GBLnsa.*

DIGBY FAIRWEATHER

Moore, Glen (R.) (*b* Portland, OR, 28 Oct 1941). Double bass player. He first played piano, and learned double bass from the age of 13, undertaking his first professional engagement a year later. After further study in Copenhagen he moved to New York, where he worked with Ted Curson, Jake Hanna, Zoot Sims, and others. He also recorded with Nick Brignola (1967), and played intermittently with the Paul Bley Synthesizer Show (1969–71). Moore's most important association began after he joined the Paul Winter Consort in 1970; later that year, with other members of the group, he formed the ensemble Oregon. Its improvisations drew on classical music, jazz, and ethnic music, and Moore's role was accordingly more interactive than that of a traditional jazz double bass player. He also expanded his instrument's range by altering its tunings. In 1979 he returned to live in Oregon; he recorded his first LP as a leader in the same year. Moore has taught at UCLA, the University of Miami, and the Naropa Institute at Boulder, Colorado.

SELECTED RECORDINGS

As leader: with P. Warren, D. Holland, and J. Faunt: *Bass is* (1970, Enja 2018); *Introducing Glen Moore* (1979, Elek. 6E197)

As sideman: on P. Bley: *The Paul Bley Synthesizer Show* (1970–71, Mlst. 9033), Gary, Mr. Joy (both 1971); R. Towner: *Trios/Solos* (1972, ECM 1025)

For further recordings *see* Oregon.

BIBLIOGRAPHY

Feather–Gitler '70s
Freff: "Book-ends: Oregon's Collin Walcott and Glen Moore," *Musician*, no.70 (1984), 68 [interview]

PAUL RINZLER

Moore, Mel(vin) (*b* Chicago, 15 June 1923). Trumpeter. He played and recorded with Jimmie Lunceford (1942–5), then worked with Lucky Millinder (1947) and briefly with Duke Ellington (1948, 1950). After playing in rhythm-and-blues groups on the West Coast he performed with Charles Mingus and Thelonious Monk at the Monterey Jazz Festival in 1964; a recording was issued as *Mingus at Monterey* (1964, Charles Mingus 001, 002). The following year he played at Monterey with Gil Fuller. Later he recorded with Fuller and Gerald Wilson in Los Angeles (both 1965–6) and played violin on a recording by Bobby Bryant (1969). He continued to perform and record into the 1970s, but remained associated mainly with rhythm-and-blues groups. He should not be confused with the singer Melvin Moore (*b* Oklahoma City, OK, *c*1928), who performed with Don Albert (1936–7), Dizzy Gillespie (1949–50), Fletcher Henderson (*c*1950), and Lucky Millinder (*c*1950–*c*1952), and later sang in Panama Francis's re-creation of Millinder's band (1975). (*Feather '60s*)

Moore, Michael (Watson) [Mike] (*b* Glen Este, nr Cincinnati, 16 May 1945). Double bass player. He took up double bass at the age of 15, played in local clubs with his father, a guitarist, then studied at the Cincinnati College-Conservatory and performed at the Playboy Club in Cincinnati with Cal Collins and the pianist Woody Evans. In 1966 he toured Africa and Eastern Europe with Woody Herman's big band; he recorded as Mike Moore in New York with Herman and in Belgrade with Dusko Goykovich. His work has sometimes been conflated in discographies with that of the electric bass guitarist Mike Moore, who recorded with the soul singer James Brown. From 1968 Moore lived in New York, where he played with Marian McPartland, Freddie Hubbard, Jim Hall, and Benny Goodman (1978), and in the quartets led by Ruby Braff and George Barnes, and Chet Baker and Lee Konitz. In the late 1970s he began a long association with the guitarist Gene Bertoncini, for which he is best known; their performances and recordings together have included a mixture of jazz standards and classical pieces. He has also recorded with Jake Hanna (1976), Warren Vaché and Herb Ellis (both 1979), Zoot Sims (1979–80), Michal Urbaniak (1981), and Kenny Barron (1984). Noted for his melodic sensitivity, in the 1980s Moore has frequently performed to critical acclaim in New York clubs.

SELECTED RECORDINGS

Duos with G. Bertoncini: *Close Ties* (1984, Omni. 3334); *O grande amor: a Bossa Nova Collection* (1986, Stash 258)
As sideman: M. McPartland: *Ambiance* (1970, Hal. 103); R. Braff and G. Barnes: *Live at the New School* (1974, Chi. 126); L. Konitz: *Tenorlee* (1977, Choice 1019)

BIBLIOGRAPHY

B. Kirchner: "Fundamental Advocate: Mike Moore," *DB*, xliv/9 (1977), 18
W. Balliett: "Good, Careful Melody," *New Yorker*, lv (14 Jan 1980), 39; repr. in *American Musicians: Fifty-six Portraits in Jazz* (New York, and Oxford, England, 1986), 387
J. E. Siegel: "Michael Moore," *Radio Free Jazz*, xxi (March 1980), 11

WILLIAM S. BROCKMAN

Moore, Monette (*b* Gainesville, TX, 19 May 1902; *d* Garden Grove, CA, 21 Oct 1962). Singer. She worked in New York in the early 1920s and in 1923 made the first of numerous recordings, many of which were issued under pseudonyms. She sang regularly with Charlie Johnson at Smalls' Paradise, New York; their recordings include *Don't you leave me here* (1927, Vic. 20653). In the 1930s and 1940s Moore worked in theaters and clubs in New York, Chicago, and Hollywood (1942–6); she sang with Sidney Bechet in New York (1946) and recorded there with Sammy Price's trio (1947). After returning to the West Coast she ceased to work as a full-time singer, though she continued to perform locally. Moore appeared in a number of films, including *Yes Sir, Mr. Bones* (1951) and *The Outsider* (1967).

BIBLIOGRAPHY

D. Hague: "The Story of Monette Moore," *JJ*, xvi/4 (1963), 7
S. Harris: *Blues Who's Who: a Biographical Dictionary of Blues Singers* (New Rochelle, NY, 1979)

based on *ChiltonW*

Moore, Oscar (Frederic) (*b* Austin, TX, 25 Dec 1912; *d* Las Vegas, NV, 8 Oct 1981). Guitarist. He performed with the Nat "King" Cole Trio from 1937 to 1947, recording with the group from 1939; during the same period he also recorded with Lionel Hampton (1940), Art Tatum (1941), the Capitol Jazzmen (who included Benny Carter and Coleman Hawkins, 1945), and Lester Young (1946). From 1947 to the mid-1950s Moore lived in Los Angeles, where he played with the Three Blazers, a group led by his brother Johnny Moore, also a guitarist. He recorded three albums as a leader (1953–4), but shortly afterwards left music and found work as a bricklayer. In the 1960s, however, he resumed playing occasionally, and in 1965 recorded an album dedicated to Cole. Moore was one of the first bop guitarists, and his single-note solo lines were strongly influenced by Charlie Christian: he had a bright, but rounded, timbre and blended clean, fleet passages with blues riffs.

SELECTED RECORDINGS

As leader: *The Oscar Moore Quartet* (1954, Tampa 10); *Tribute to Nat King Cole* (1965, Surrey 1013)
As sideman: L. Hampton: Central Avenue Breakdown (1940, Vic. 26652); N. Cole: Sweet Georgia Brown (1945, Cap. 239)

BIBLIOGRAPHY

ChiltonW; *FeatherE*
B. Kessel: "Allen Reuss and Oscar Moore," *GP*, xi/7 (1977), 10
Obituary, J. McAffee, Jr., *JSN*, ii/4 (1982), 21

BARRY KERNFELD

Moore, Pee Wee [Numa "Pee Wee," Numa Smith] (*b* Raleigh, NC, 5 March 1928). Baritone saxophonist. He played and recorded with Lucky Millinder (1950–51) and Louis Jordan (1951), and recorded with Wynonie Harris and other rhythm-and-blues musicians. After a brief association with Illinois Jacquet (1952) he played and recorded bop with James Moody (1954–6). In 1957 he joined Dizzy Gillespie's group and made recordings with Gillespie and Mary Lou Williams; he later recorded with Bill Doggett (1965). (*FeatherE*)

Moore, Slim. Nickname of ALTON MOORE.

Morand, Herb (*b* New Orleans, 1905; *d* New Orleans, 23 Feb 1952). Trumpeter and singer. He first worked professionally in New Orleans and Oklahoma with Nat Towles. Later he moved to New York and accompanied his step-sister Lizzie Miles and performed with Cliff Jackson. After returning to New Orleans he played with Chris Kelly and led his own band, then in the late 1920s moved to Chicago, where he worked with the pianist William Barbee and recorded (*Forty and Tight*/*Piggly Wiggly*, 1929, Voc. 1403) with Baby and Johnny Dodds and Frank Melrose in the Beale Street Washboard Band. From the mid- to late 1930s Morand performed and made recordings (including

Lake Provinces Blues, 1936, Decca 7182) with the Harlem Hamfats and played with Meade "Lux" Lewis. After working with Jimmy Bertrand in 1941 he returned to New Orleans, where he again led his own band; he also played with George Lewis (i), becoming a member of his group in 1948. In 1950, shortly before illness forced him to retire, he recorded as a leader and also with Lewis. (P. Van Vorst: "The Harlem Hamfats," *MR*, iv/4 (1977), 5)

Oral history material in *LNT*.

based on *ChiltonW*

Morehouse, Chauncey (*b* Niagara Falls, NY, 11 March 1902; *d* Philadelphia, 3 Nov 1980). Drummer. In 1906 his family moved to Chambersburg, Pennsylvania, where he played drums in the school orchestra and town band; he later worked with his father, who accompanied silent films at the piano, and while still in high school he formed the Versatile Five. In 1922–4 he performed and recorded with the violinist Paul Specht, visiting London in 1923. As a member of Jean Goldkette's orchestra in 1925–7 he performed widely and made many recordings; he then worked briefly with Adrian Rollini (1927) and the orchestra leader Don Vorhees (1928–9), during which period he also recorded with Bix Beiderbecke (1927), Frankie Trumbauer (1927–8), Red Nichols (1927–9), the Dorsey Brothers (1928–9), and Joe Venuti (1928–9). From 1929 until the late 1960s he was a studio percussionist, active in radio and later in television; although he recorded with a number of jazz musicians, he became best known as a studio player. After his retirement from studio work, however, he continued to play in jazz groups.

Morehouse's early playing, typical of drumming in the 1920s, combines hot rhythms on cymbals and subtle syncopated accompanimental patterns; his later work reflects swing techniques, making much use of the cymbals and of syncopated fills. In two of his recordings, *Ku-li-a* and *Mazi-pani*, he played the "n'goma drums," a set of 14 chromatically tuned snare drums mounted on a circular bar, which he designed around 1932. These, like modern steel drums, allowed the drummer to play melodies, but they proved difficult to tune accurately.

Oral history material in *NjR* (JOHP).

SELECTED RECORDINGS

As leader: Blues in B Flat/On the Alamo (1937, Var. 608); Plastered in Paris/Mazi-pani (1938, Bruns. 8122); Ku-li-a/Oriental Nocturne (1938, Bruns. 8142)

As sideman: J. Goldkette: After I Say I'm Sorry/Dinah (1926, Vic. 19947); B. Beiderbecke: At the Jazz Band Ball/Jazz me Blues (1927, OK 40923); R. Nichols: Harlem Twist/Five Pennies (1928, Vic. 21560)

BIBLIOGRAPHY

ChiltonW; *FeatherE*

J. Kline: "Chauncey Morehouse," *MR*, vi/7 (1980), 1

W. Vaché, Sr.: "The Forgotten Ones: Chauncey Morehouse," *JJI*, xxxv/8 (1982), 19

T. DENNIS BROWN

Moreira, Airto (Guimorva) [Airto] (*b* Itaiópolis, Brazil, 5 Aug 1941). Brazilian percussionist. He played tambourine and sang as a child, and lived from the age of 16 in São Paulo and later in Rio de Janeiro. After leading a quartet in the mid-1960s that included the pianist and flutist Hermeto Pascoal he moved in 1968 to Los Angeles and in 1970 to New York. He made several recordings with Miles Davis (from 1970), played on Weather Report's first album (1971), and was the first percussionist and drummer in RETURN TO FOREVER. In the 1970s he became one of the best-known percussionists in jazz. He skillfully manipulated such small instruments as the tambourine and bongos, and introduced to jazz such exotica as the cuíca and berimbau. From 1973 into the 1980s he performed with his own bands and with his wife, Flora Purim, for whom he has also written arrangements.

See also LATIN JAZZ.

SELECTED RECORDINGS

As leader: *Seeds on the Ground* (1970, Buddah 5085); *Free* (1972, CTI 6020); *Fingers* (1973, CTI 6028); *Identity* (1975, Ari. 4068); *Touching you, Touching me* (1979, WB 3279)

As sideman: M. Davis: *Miles Davis at Fillmore* (1970, Col. KG30038); Weather Report: *Weather Report* (1971, Col. KC30661); Return to Forever: *Return to Forever* (1973, ECM 1022); F. Purim: *Five Hundred Miles High at Montreux* (1974, Mlst. 9070)

BIBLIOGRAPHY

R. Williams: "Percussion by Airto Moreira," *MM* (4 Nov 1972), 53

D. Morgenstern: "Music is a Beautiful Game," *DB*, xl/5 (1973), 18

C. Mitchell: "Bim, bang, boing, slam, pop, z-i-i-ing!: the Anatomical Signatures of Airto," *DB*, xli/18 (1974), 18

L. Underwood: "Airto and his Incredible Gong Show," *DB*, xlv/8 (1978), 15

R. Flans: "Airto," *MD*, vii/8 (1983), 8

R. Palmer: "Another Boost for Pan-American Fusion Music," *New York Times* (30 March 1984), §C, p.20

MICHAEL ULLMAN

Morell, John (E.) (*b* Niagara Falls, NY, 2 June 1946). Guitarist. On the West Coast he played with Les Brown (1967–70) and the Gil Evans–Miles Davis Orchestra (1968). He toured Europe with Shelly Manne in 1970, then played in Los Angeles with Manne (1970–74) and with his own groups (from 1975). He recorded with Manne in 1970 (*Alive in London*, Cont. 7629) and 1972, with Ray Pizzi in 1976, and as a leader in 1983.

BIBLIOGRAPHY

Feather–Gitler '70s

L. Tomkins: "In Depth: the Shelly Manne Sextet," *CI*, ix/2 (1970), 8

Morell, Marty [Martin Matthew] (*b* New York, 15 Feb 1944). Drummer and percussionist. He studied at the Manhattan School of Music (1960), and in 1966 played with the quintet led by Al Cohn and Zoot Sims and recorded with Henry "Red" Allen, Gary McFarland, and Steve Kuhn; in 1967 he recorded with Gábor Szabó. From 1968 to 1975 he toured and recorded regularly with Bill Evans (ii); his playing is well represented on *The Bill Evans Album* (1971, Col. C30855), which received a Grammy Award. Based in Toronto from 1974, he worked as a studio percussionist (recording with, among others, Jeremy Steig (1974)), led his own Latin-jazz bands (in which he played vibraphone), and played percussion in Rob McConnell's band Boss Brass (1978–81). (*Feather–Gitler '70s*)

Morello, Joe [Joseph A.] (*b* Springfield, MA, 17 July 1928). Drummer. He studied violin as a child but changed to drums in high school and played with Phil Woods and Sal Salvador. After moving to New York (1952) he worked with Johnny Smith and briefly with Stan Kenton, then performed and recorded with the saxophonist Gil Melle (1953). From 1953 to 1956 he was a member of Marian McPartland's trio, though he also recorded as a freelance with Tal Farlow, the pianist John Mehegan, Jimmy Raney, and Woods (all 1954), Jackie Cain and Roy Kral (1955), and Salvador (1956). Morello joined the Dave Brubeck Quartet in late 1956, remaining with the group until 1967. Thereafter he worked principally as a drum instructor, making international tours for the Ludwig company, though he continued to play occasionally – notably in reunions with Brubeck (1976) and McPartland (1977). He recorded again with Salvador (1978) and also led his own groups in and around New York. Among his pupils in the 1980s was Danny Gottlieb.

Morello's playing is characterized by delicacy, clarity, and sensitivity. He is widely admired for his work with Brubeck, especially for his skill in imparting a sense of swing to such pieces as *Take Five* (written in 5/4 time), where he consistently wove calm, melodic, supple solos around the tune's rigid ostinato.

SELECTED RECORDINGS

As leader: *It's about Time* (1961, RCA LSP2486)

As sideman with D. Brubeck: *Jazz Impressions of the USA* (1956, Col. CL984), incl. Sounds of the Loop; *Time Out* (1959, Col. CL1397), incl. Take Five; *The Dave Brubeck Quartet at Carnegie Hall* (1963, Col. C2S826), incl. Take Five; *The Dave Brubeck Quartet 25th Anniversary Reunion* (1976, A&M Hor. 714)

As sideman with others: M. McPartland: *Jazz at the Hickory House* (1953, Savoy 15032); T. Farlow: *The Tal Farlow Album* (1954, Norg. 19); J. Raney: *Jimmy Raney Quintet* (1954, NewJ 1103); M. McPartland: *The Marian McPartland Trio* (1956, Cap. T785); S. Salvador: *Juicy Lucy* (1978, BH 7009)

BIBLIOGRAPHY

J. Tracy: "Joe Morello" *DB*, xxii/18 (1955), 13
L. Tomkins: "Joe Morello," *Crescendo*, i/6 (1963), 24
J.-L. Ginibre: "Entretiens avec Joe Morello," *Jm*, no.146 (1967), 32
A. J. Smith: "A Quarter of a Century Young: the Dave Brubeck Quartet," *DB*, xliii/6 (1976), 18 [incl. discography]
S. K. Fish: "Joe Morello," *MD*, iii/2 (1979), 24
R. Mattingly: "Joe Morello," *MD*, x/11 (1986), 16
M. McPartland: "The Fabulous Joe Morello," "Joe Morello: with a Light Touch," *All in Good Time* (New York, and Oxford, England, 1987) [colln of previously pubd articles], 31, 43

BARRY KERNFELD

Morgan. Family of musicians.

(1) Sam Morgan (*b* Bertrandville, LA, 18 Dec 1887; *d* New Orleans, 25 Feb 1936). Trumpeter. His parents sang in a Baptist choir, and he grew up in a musical family. From the 1910s he played in brass bands in Plaquemines Parish, then around 1915 moved to New Orleans, where he led the Magnolia brass and dance bands. He suffered a stroke in 1924, but recovered; the following year he joined the band organized by his brother (2) Isaiah Morgan, and soon afterwards took over leadership of the group. The band played with a swinging beat and provided its audiences with perfect dance tempos, and it became one of the most popular in the city. In 1927 it recorded eight titles (including the first spirituals to be recorded by a jazz band), which, according to Charters, are "the only recordings of a first-rate [early New Orleans] band playing anywhere near its prime." Morgan was a member of the WPA band in 1934 but retired on account of ill-health in 1935.

SELECTED RECORDINGS

(all recorded in 1927 for Columbia)

Everybody's talking about Sammy/Sing on (14213D); Short Dress Gal/Bogalousa Strut (14351D); Down by the Riverside (14539D); Over in the Gloryland (14267D)

BIBLIOGRAPHY

ChartersJ
G. Schuller: *Early Jazz: its Roots and Musical Development* (New York, 1968), 75
R. Allen: "Notes on Sam Morgan for VJM," *Sam Morgan's Jazz Band/The Get-Happy Band/The Blue Ribbon Syncopators* (VJM 32, 1972) [liner notes]
W. J. Schafer: "Hot Dancing in New Orleans: the Black Bands," *MR*, vii/9 (1980), 6
K. Koenig: "Four Country Brass Bands," *SL*, xxxvi (aut. 1984), 13

(2) Isaiah Morgan (*b* Bertrandville, LA, 7 April 1897; *d* New Orleans, 11 May 1966). Trumpeter. He began playing in Plaquemines Parish before 1915, and then moved to New Orleans. In 1922 he organized the Young Morgan Band, which was later led by his brother (1) Sam Morgan. He retired in 1956.

Oral history material in *LNT*.

(3) Andrew Morgan (*b* Pensacola, FL, 13 March 1901; *d* New Orleans, 19 Sept 1972). Clarinetist and saxophonist. After playing clarinet in the Imperial Band, in 1925 he joined the group led by his brother (2) Isaiah Morgan; he was in the band in 1927 when it recorded under the leadership of (1) Sam Morgan. Later he played with Kid Howard, Kid Rena, and Kid Thomas. In 1967 he became the leader of the Young Tuxedo Brass Band, and in 1969 he recorded an album as a leader (*Andrew Morgan/Kid Martyn: Down by the Riverside*, Dixie 2).

Oral history material in *LNT*.

(4) Al(bert) Morgan (*b* New Orleans, 19 Aug 1908; *d* Los Angeles, 14 April 1974). Double bass player. He was a pupil of Simon Marrero, and first played with bands led by his brother (2) Isaiah Morgan. In 1923 he joined Lee Collins on a tour of Florida, then worked in New Orleans with the saxophonist David Jones, occasionally performing on tuba. From 1925 to 1929 he played with Fate Marable on the riverboat *Capitol* (following Pops Foster, whose style he emulated). In 1929 his association with Collins and Jones culminated in the celebrated recording session in New Orleans with the JONES AND COLLINS ASTORIA HOT EIGHT, and he also made his first recordings (in New York) with Fats Waller. Morgan's powerful playing on the titles he recorded with Billy Banks's Rhythmakers in 1932 shows a certain insecurity of intonation and a relentless slapping, in contrast to his lighter work on Jones and Collins's *Duet Stomp*. In June 1932 he joined Cab Calloway's big band, with which he made several recordings; he contributed immense drive to the band's rhythm section, but lacked the flexibility of pitch and tone of Milt Hinton (who succeeded him). While with Calloway, Morgan appeared in films, including *The Big Broadcast* (1932) and *The Singing Kid* (1936). He then worked at the Club Alabam, Los Angeles, with Eddie Barefield (1936–7), and later played with Les Hite (1939–41). For much of the next 15 years he was a member of Sabby Lewis's band in Boston, though he spent a period with Louis Jordan (1944–5) and occasionally worked as a freelance. By the time he settled on the West Coast in 1957 his style was lighter and more suited to the smaller ensembles (including Joe Darensbourg's band and a duo with the pianist Buddy Banks) with which he played.

Oral history material in *LNT*.

SELECTED RECORDINGS

As sideman: D. Jones and L. Collins: Astoria Strut/Duet Stomp (1929, Vic. 38576); B. Banks: Oh Peter (1932, Ban. 32462); C. Calloway: Nagasaki (1935, Bruns. 7504); F. Waller: Every day's a holiday (1937, Vic. 25749); C. Berry: Blowing up a Breeze (1941, Com. 541)

BIBLIOGRAPHY

ChiltonW
H. Panassié: *Le jazz hot* (Paris, 1934; Eng. trans., rev. Panassié, London and New York, 1936/R1970), 129
N. Hentoff: "Morgan: Riverboat Bass," *Jazz Record* (1946), Feb, 11
P. Foster, T. Stoddard, and R. Russell: *Pops Foster: the Autobiography of a New Orleans Jazzman* (Berkeley, CA, Los Angeles, and London, 1971)
A. McCarthy: *Big Band Jazz* (New York and London, 1974)
F. Driggs and H. Lewine: *Black Beauty, White Heat: a Pictorial History of Classic Jazz, 1920–1950* (New York, 1982)

BILL RUSSELL (1–3), ALYN SHIPTON (4)

Morgan, Alun (*b* Pontypridd, Wales, 24 Feb 1928). Welsh writer and broadcaster. He began writing on jazz in about 1950 and contributed articles, discographies, and reviews to *Melody Maker* (from 1951), *Jazz Journal* (1951–5), and *Jazz Monthly* (1955–71). He has also furnished liner notes for about 2000 albums and has written, collaborated on, or contributed to some dozen books; *Modern Jazz* (1956) is looked upon as the first thorough survey of bop published in England. He has provided scripts for radio and television and from 1954 worked regularly for the BBC. He has also lectured on jazz and from 1969 has written a weekly jazz column for the *Kent Evening Post*.

WRITINGS
(selective list)

with R. Horricks: *Modern Jazz: a Survey of Developments since 1939* (London, 1956/R1977)
——: *Gerry Mulligan: a Biography, Appreciation, Record Survey and Discography* (London, 1958)
with C. Fox and P. Gammond: *Jazz on Record: a Critical Guide* (London, 1960) [listeners' guide]
with A. McCarthy and others: *Jazz on Record: a Critical Guide to the First Fifty Years: 1917–1967* (London, 1968) [listeners' guide]
with M. Harrison and others: *Modern Jazz: the Essential Records: a Critical Selection* (London, 1975) [listeners' guide]
Count Basie (Tunbridge Wells, England, 1984)

ROBERT GANNON

Morgan, Frank (*b* Minneapolis, 23 Dec 1933). Alto and soprano saxophonist. The son of a guitarist, he grew up in Milwaukee; he took up the clarinet at the age of seven and the alto saxophone at the age of ten. In 1947 his family moved to Los Angeles, where he won a talent contest and recorded a solo with the bandleader Freddie Martin when he was 15. Having become involved in the underground bop movement in Los Angeles, he recorded with the visiting musicians Teddy Charles (1953) and Kenny Clarke (1954), and in 1955 made his own album. During a jail term (for drug abuse, from 1955) he played with Art Pepper and other fellow prisoners. Although he performed locally in the late 1970s, Morgan did not return to national prominence until 1985. His recordings reveal him as a passionate and sometimes inspired soloist in the tradition of Charlie Parker.

SELECTED RECORDINGS

As leader: *Introducing Frank Morgan* (1955, GNP Crescendo 12); *Easy Living* (1985, Cont. 14013)

BIBLIOGRAPHY

L. Hildebrand: "He Played Some of his Best Notes Behind Bars: Frank Morgan Kicks Heroin, Comes Back with Hot Album," *San Francisco Examiner* (23 March 1986)

BRIAN PRIESTLEY

Morgan, Lanny [Harold Lansford] (*b* Des Moines, IA, 30 March 1934). Alto saxophonist. He studied violin from the age of six, and later took up alto saxophone. In 1944 he moved with his family to Los Angeles. After playing in the stage band at Los Angeles City College he worked in big bands led by Charlie Barnet (1954), Si Zentner, Terry Gibbs, and Bob Florence. In 1960 he traveled to New York, where he played for five years as a principal soloist with Maynard Ferguson, touring Europe in 1962. After leaving Ferguson Morgan worked as a lead alto saxophonist with other distinguished bandleaders and became active as a studio musician. He has continued to perform regularly – often with Bill Berry, Ed Shaughnessy, Florence, and Bill Holman – and for several years has been a member of Supersax. He has also taught and led workshops and given master classes at Stanford University and other institutions. Morgan recorded as the leader of his own small group in 1981 and as a member of Jeff Hamilton's quintet in 1982.

SELECTED RECORDINGS

As leader: *It's About Time* (1981, PAlt 8007)
As sideman: M. Ferguson: *Let's Face the Music & Dance* (1960, Roul. 52055); *Maynard '64* (1964, Roul. 52107); *The Blues Roar* (1964, Mstr. 6045); *Maynard Ferguson Sextet* (1965, Mstr. 6060); B. Berry: *Hello Rev.* (1976, Conc. 27); Supersax: *Dynamite!* (1978, MPS 68210); J. Hamilton: *Indiana* (1982, Conc. 187); Supersax: *Supersax & L. A. Voices* (*c*1984, Col. FC39925)

BIBLIOGRAPHY

Feather '60s
O. Cordle: "Lanny Morgan: it's about Time," *DB*, xlix/9 (1982), 36

STAN BRITT

Morgan, Lee (*b* Philadelphia, 10 July 1938; *d* New York, 19 Feb 1972). Trumpeter. He began playing professionally in Philadelphia at the age of 15 and in 1956 he joined Dizzy Gillespie's orchestra in New York, with which he remained until it disbanded in 1958. He was a member of Art Blakey's Jazz Messengers from 1958 to 1961; after playing mainly in Philadelphia he returned to New York (1963), where he again worked with Blakey (1964–5) and then as a freelance, generally with his own groups. In 1970–71 he was active in the Jazz and People's Movement. He was shot dead by his mistress at Slugs, a nightclub in New York.

As early as his time with Gillespie's band, Morgan began increasingly to place his high-spirited approach at the service of expressive ends, and this adaptation of his style continued in intensified form during his association with Blakey. His playing was at first heavily indebted to Clifford Brown but, as the album *The Freedom Rider* (1961) shows, this influence weakened as Morgan's style became more personal; his work of the early 1960s is marked by highly irregular phrase lengths underpinning exuberant virtuoso display, in which half-valving techniques play a prominent part. The new-found poise and controlled intensity of *Totem Pole* (1963) set the tone for the last stage of his career, during which he made many notable recordings under his own name and with Hank Mobley, whose techniques of improvisation found echoes in Morgan's own style. In this last phase the tense sensitivity of ballads such as *What now my love?* (1966) complements and contrasts with the flashing trumpet lines set against the churning polyrhythms of Mobley's *Dippin'* (1965); both works confirm that Morgan was one of the most individual stylists of his time.

SELECTED RECORDINGS
(recorded for Blue Note unless otherwise indicated)

As leader: with H. Mobley: *Peckin' Time* (1958, 1574); *Leeway* (1960, 4034); *Take Twelve* (1962, Jlnd 980); *The Sidewinder* (1963, 84157), incl. Totem Pole; *Cornbread* (1965, 84222); *The Rajah* (1966, 84426), incl. What now my love?
As sideman: J. Coltrane: *Blue Train* (1957, 1577); A. Blakey: *The Freedom Rider* (1961, 84156); H. Mobley: *Dippin'* (1965, 84209)

BIBLIOGRAPHY

Feather '60s; *Feather–Gitler '70s*
M. James: "Trumpet Trio: Bill Hardman, Freddie Hubbard, Lee Morgan," *JM*, vii/10 (1961), 4
——: "Lee Morgan: in the Ascendant," *JM*, x/10 (1964), 13
M. Bourne: "Lee Morgan: the Last Interview," *DB*, xxxix/8 (1972), 11
Obituary, *DB*, xxxix/6 (1972), 11
R. Wernboe: *Lee Morgan Discography* (Saltsjöbaden, Sweden, 1985)

MICHAEL JAMES

Morgan, Russ (*b* Scranton, PA, 28 April 1904; *d* Las Vegas, NV, 7 Aug 1969). Trombonist and arranger. He sold his first arrangements while still in his teens, and toured and recorded with Paul Specht in the early 1920s. He then became music director for Jean Goldkette's organization, and led the Book-Cadillac Hotel Orchestra and the Capitol Theatre Orchestra. Later he worked as a freelance arranger for various bands, including that of Fletcher Henderson; he also wrote an arrangement of *Body and Soul* (1930, OK 41468) for Louis Armstrong. In the early 1930s Morgan worked as a record company executive, and from 1935 he led his own big band, with which he made several recordings (including *Midnight Oil*, 1935, Col. 3050D). (G. T. Simon: *The Big Bands* (New York, 1967, rev. and enlarged 2/1971, rev. 3/1974, 4/1981), 375)

based on *ChiltonW*

Morgan, Sonny [Howard] (*b* Philadelphia, 17 July 1936). Percussionist. He studied flute, drums, and African percussion and the music, dance, and languages of West Africa and the Caribbean. From 1953 to 1960 he led a band in Philadelphia, with which he played flute and percussion; he also worked with several jazz and Latin musicians, including Willie Bobo, the percussionist Montego Joe, Mongo Santamaria, Max Roach, Milford Graves (with whom he recorded an album of duos in 1964), and Leone Thomas (1970–73). In addition to his work as a performer he has composed and arranged works for dance companies (including that of Geoffrey Holder and the Negro Ensemble Co.) and theatrical productions. He performed on the soundtrack to Herbert J. Biberman's film *Slaves* (1969). Morgan is a versatile player with a keen sense of rhythm and timbre.

SELECTED RECORDINGS

Duos with M. Graves: *Percussion Duo* (1964, ESP 1015)

As sideman: Montego Joe: *Wild and Warm* (1965, Prst. 7413); C. Basie: *Afrique* (1970, FD 10138); L. Thomas: *Gold Sunrise on Magic Mountain* (1971, Mega 51-5003); W. Jackson: *West Africa* (1973, Muse 5036)

BIBLIOGRAPHY

Feather–Gitler '70s

J. KENT WILLIAMS

Morgenstern, Dan (Michael) (*b* Munich, 24 Oct 1929). Writer. After moving to the USA in 1947 he studied history at Brandeis University (1953–6). From 1958 to 1961 he was the New York correspondent for *Jazz Journal*. He then served as editor of *Metronome* (1961), *Jazz* (1962–3), and *Down Beat* (1964–73) magazines, and during the 1960s also produced jazz concerts in New York and for television. In the mid-1970s he held appointments as visiting lecturer in jazz at Brooklyn College and the Peabody Institute, and in 1976 he became director of the Institute of Jazz Studies at Rutgers, in which capacity he has also worked as an editor of the *Journal of Jazz Studies* (from 1982 the *Annual Review of Jazz Studies*). Morgenstern considers his writing of album notes to be an important part of his work, and won Grammy awards for his contributions in 1973, 1974, 1976, and 1981. In addition to the book *Jazz People* (New York, 1976), which received the ASCAP–Deems Taylor Award in 1977, he has published articles in numerous newspapers and periodicals; he also translated and edited Joachim Berendt's *Das neue Jazzbuch* (1962). (B. Rosenberg and E. Goldstein: *The Creators and Disturbers: Reminiscences by Jewish Intellectuals of New York*, New York, 1982)

PAULA MORGAN/R

Morks, Jan (*b* The Hague, 14 Oct 1925; *d* The Hague, 4 Sept 1984). Dutch reed player. He taught himself to play clarinet and tenor and soprano saxophones, then played with the Dixieland Pipers (1945–50, 1952–4), the Dutch Swing College Orchestra (1954–61), John's Jazz Men (1961–3), the drummer Ted Easton (1968–72), the New Orleans Syncopators (1973–6), and again with the Dixieland Pipers (1978–82). He also performed and made recordings as a leader (including *Swing 'n Sweet*, 1976–7, Phi. 6413102, and *Strike up the Band*, 1984, Zero One 822496-1), appeared at many festivals, and toured Europe; he received an Edison Award from the Dutch Gramophone Industries in 1964. (G. Bielderman: *Jan Morks Discography*, Zwolle, Netherlands, 1986)

WIM VAN EYLE

Moro, Joe [Casas, José Moro] (*b* Portugalete, Spain, 1910; *d* Madrid, 19 May 1980). Spanish trumpeter. After studying law he decided to become a musician, and toured many countries with commercial bands before settling in Madrid. He played with big bands and small groups, and was also active as a studio musician. On several occasions he performed on television; he also provided help and encouragement for several young musicians in Madrid. A particularly fine solo by Moro may be heard on *Bad Feeling*, from the album *Bloque 6* (1968, Hispavox-Clave 187012) by the pianist Juan Carlos Calderón. During the last ten years of his life he played traditional jazz with the group Canal Street at the Whisky Jazz Club.

ALFREDO PAPO

Morris, Lawrence "Butch" (*b* Los Angeles, *c*1940). Cornetist. He performed with J. R. Monterose, George Morrow, Frank Lowe, and Don Moye in California, and around 1975 moved briefly to New York, where he played free jazz with Charles Tyler, Hamiet Bluiett, David Murray, Stanley Crouch, and Lowe. From 1976 to 1977 he lived in Paris, recording with Jef Gilson, Steve Lacy, and Lowe, and performing with Alan Silva, Frank Wright, and his own group. From 1977 Morris made recordings (including the album *Ming*, 1981, BS 0045) with Murray, and performed with him in the USA and in Europe. He recorded with Lowe again in 1981, and as co-leader of a trio in 1982. He has also performed experimental music at lofts in Manhattan.

BIBLIOGRAPHY

R. Riggins: "Butch Morris," *Coda*, no.157 (1977), 12

H. Mandel: "Butch Morris: Conducting the New Tradition," *DB*, liii/10 (1986), 26 [incl. discography]

Morris, Marlowe (*b* New York, 16 May 1915; *d* New York, *c*1977). Pianist, organist, and arranger. He learned drums, harmonica, and ukulele before taking up piano. He played with June Clark from 1935 to 1936 and Coleman Hawkins from 1940 to 1941, spending much of the intervening period performing as a solo pianist. After army service (1941) he worked with Toby Browne, Al Sears (1943), Sid Catlett (1944), and Tiny Grimes (1946), and also led his own trio. He then played only part-time and took a job in the post office; from 1949, when he returned to music full-time, he worked mainly as a solo organist. His album *Play the Thing* won the Grand Prix du Disque of the Hot Club de France. Morris is best known for his appearance in the film *Jammin' the Blues* (1944). He was the nephew of Thomas Morris.

SELECTED RECORDINGS

As leader: *Play the Thing* (1961–2, Col. CS8619)

As sideman: S. Catlett: Sleep/Linger awhile (1944, Com. 546); Memories of You/Just a Riff (1944, Com. 1515); B. Clayton: Basic Organ Blue/'S wonderful (1952, Epic 7009) [EP]

BIBLIOGRAPHY

ChiltonW; *Feather '60s*

J. Simmen: "Marlowe Morris," *BHcF*, no.178 (1968), p.4; no.179 (1968), p.6

ANDREW JAFFE

Morris, Thomas [Tom] (*b* New York, *c*1898; *d* after 1940). Cornetist. In the 1920s he worked as a leader in New York and his band, the Hot Babies, recorded with Fats Waller (1927). A fine example of his blues style may be heard on *P. D. Q. Blues* (1926, Vic. 20330). He also made recordings with Clarence Williams (1923, 1926) and (often as a member of Williams's group) with numerous important blues singers, among them Eva Taylor, Sara Martin, and Rosa Henderson. Morris ceased playing in the late 1930s. He was the uncle of Marlowe Morris. (R. Cooke: Liner notes, *Fats Waller with Morris's Hot Babies*, RCA 741062, 1972)

based on *ChiltonW*

Morrison, Peck [John A.] (*b* Lancaster, PA, 11 Sept 1919; *d* New York, 25 Feb 1988). Double bass player. After conservatory training he served in a military band in Italy, then worked in New York with Lucky Thompson (1949–53); he also played with Bill Graham (1953–4), and recorded with Joe "Bebop" Carroll and King Pleasure (both 1952), Zoot Sims and Eddie Jefferson (both 1953), and a quintet led by J. J. Johnson and Kai Winding (1954). In 1955 he performed briefly with Duke Ellington and recorded with Lou Donaldson and Gerry Mulligan. After playing with Johnny Smith (1956) he worked as house bass player at the Five Spot Café (1957–9) and recorded again with Donaldson (1957, 1958) and Jefferson (1959) and with Randy Weston (1957, 1959) and Babs Gonzales (1958–9). Later he appeared with the Newport Rebels at the Cliff Walk Manor Festival (1960) and recorded with Dave Bailey and Charlie Rouse (both 1960), Shirley Scott and Johnny Coles (both 1961), Red Garland (1961, 1971), Weston (1963), Ellington (1964), and Charles McPherson (1968). He also performed and recorded on electric bass guitar with Sy Oliver in Paris in 1973. Morrison continued to work as a freelance in the New York area, appearing frequently with the Harlem Blues and Jazz Band in 1986.

Morrison's accompanimental playing is heard to advantage on *Tain't Nobody's Bizness if I Do* on the Jazz Artists Guild's album *Newport Rebels* (1960, Can. 9022); his clear articulation contrasts sharply with the smoother playing of his fellow double bass player on the recording, Charles Mingus. His bop style is also exemplified on the album *Presenting the Gerry Mulligan Sextet* (1955, EmA 36056), which includes brief walking bass solos on *Mud Bud, Apple Core, Broadway*, and *Bernie's Tune*. (*FeatherE*)

Oral history material in *CtY*.

Morrissey, Dick [Richard Edwin] (*b* Horley, England, 9 May 1940). English tenor saxophonist. After playing clarinet with Gus Galbraith at the age of 17, he changed to tenor saxophone and quickly established a reputation. His first full-time professional engagement was with Harry South in India (1960–61), and in 1961 he recorded his first album as a leader, *It's Morrissey, Man!* (Fon. 5194). During the mid-1960s he recorded several times with his own quartet, and in 1966 he made an album with Jimmy Witherspoon. He was a founding member of the jazz-rock group If, with which he made a number of recordings and toured the USA several times in the early 1970s. After the band broke up in 1974 Morrissey lived for a year in Sweden, then worked with Herbie Mann, and with the soul and funk group the Average White Band. In the mid-1970s, with Jim Mullen, he formed a small jazz-funk group, Morrissey–Mullen, which toured and recorded successfully until 1985. During this period Morrissey also made recordings as the leader of other groups: *After Dark* (1983, Coda 2) proved his status as one of the very finest British tenor saxophonists.

BIBLIOGRAPHY

J. Shirley: "Dick Morrissey," *JJ*, xvii/4 (1964), 7
R. Cotterell, ed.: *Jazz Now: the Jazz Centre Society Guide* (London, 1976)

STAN BRITT

Morrow, Buddy [Zudekoff, Moe [Muni]] (*b* New Haven, CT, 8 Feb 1919). Trombonist and bandleader. He began learning trombone at the age of 12 and by 1933 he was playing with local bands, including the Yale Collegians. The following year he moved to New York and studied at the Institute of Musical Art. He made his first recordings in 1936 with the singer Amanda Randolph and Sharkey Bonano, then performed and recorded with Artie Shaw (1936–7), Bunny Berigan and Frank Froeba (both 1937), the pianist Eddie Duchin and Tommy Dorsey (both 1938), and Paul Whiteman (1939). In the late 1930s he worked both as Moe Zudekoff and under the assumed name Buddy Morrow, but in the early 1940s he abandoned the former name. After performing as a studio musician (1940) he played with Bob Crosby (1941–2) and Jimmy Dorsey (1945) and recorded with Lee Wiley (1943) and Red McKenzie (1944). When his attempt to lead his own band failed (1945), he returned to studio work. In 1950, however, RCA decided to promote Morrow as a bandleader and he achieved a certain amount of success; his ensemble played mainly a rocking style of rhythm-and-blues rather than jazz. In the 1960s Morrow again performed in studios and worked with his own group, and from the late 1970s to the 1980s he has led Tommy Dorsey's ghost band.

SELECTED RECORDINGS

As leader: *Night Train* (? early 1950s, RCA LPM1497)
As sideman: S. Bonano: Mister Brown goes to town/When you're smiling (1936, Voc. 3400); E. Duchin: Between the Devil and the Deep Blue Sea (1938, Bruns. 8155); B. Crosby: Black Zephyr (1942, Decca 4415); I'll keep the lovelight burning (1942, Decca 4290)

BIBLIOGRAPHY

ChiltonW; *FeatherE*
L. Walker: *The Wonderful Era of the Great Dance Bands* (Berkeley, CA, 1964)
G. T. Simon: *The Big Bands* (New York, 1967, rev. and enlarged 2/1971, rev. 3/1974, 4/1981)

LAWRENCE KOCH

Morrow, George (Washington) (*b* Pasadena, CA, 15 August 1925). Double bass player. He learned violin from an early age but changed to cello at the age of 13 and then took up double bass while studying at the Fine Arts Conservatory in Los Angeles. After his military service (1943–6) he returned to Los Angeles, where he worked with Charlie Parker, Hampton Hawes, Sonny Criss, Chuck Thompson, and Teddy Edwards, among others. In 1948 he moved to San Francisco and frequently appeared at Bop City, accompanying Billie Holiday, Wardell Gray, Dexter Gordon, Sonny Clark, and Edwards (1948–53). He joined the quintet led by Clifford Brown and Max Roach in 1954 and stayed with it until it disbanded after the deaths of Brown and Richie Powell (1956); when Roach re-formed the group Morrow became a member, and remained so until 1958. Thereafter he worked intermittently with Anita O'Day (1958–75), touring Europe in 1975 and appearing at the Grande Parade du Jazz, Nice, France. In 1976 he moved to Florida, where he became a member of the house band at Disney World; he also accompanied visiting soloists, including Art Farmer, Barney Kessel, and Charlie Byrd. Morrow was originally inspired by Jimmy Blanton, whom he met in 1942; he was also influenced by Ray Brown and Oscar Pettiford, who helped him technically during the period when they worked together in San Francisco. Morrow is an assured soloist and a fine player of walking bass; his contribution to the music of the much admired Brown and Roach quintet, through his resilient beat and judicious choice of notes, has been underestimated.

SELECTED RECORDINGS

As sideman with C. Brown and M. Roach: *Max Roach and Clifford Brown in Concert* (1954, GNP 6); *Brown and Roach Incorporated* (1954, EmA 36008); *Study in Brown* (1955, EmA 36037); *At Basin Street* (1956, EmA 36070)
As sideman with S. Rollins: *Work Time* (1955, Prst. 7020); *Sonny Rollins Plus Four* (1956, Prst. 7038)
As sideman with M. Roach: *Jazz in 3/4 Time* (1957, EmA 36108); *Max* (1958, Argo 623)

BIBLIOGRAPHY

G. Henderson: "George Morrow: Interview," *Cadence*, vii/1 (1981) 5

MARK GARDNER

Morton, Benny [Henry Sterling] (*b* New York, 31 Jan 1907; *d* New York, 28 Dec 1985). Trombonist. As a member of Fletcher Henderson's orchestra (1926–8, 1931), he first attracted attention when he displayed his precocious talents on a recording of *Jackass Blues* (1926). After distinguished periods performing in big bands led by Chick Webb (1930–31), Don Redman (1931–7), and Count Basie (1937–40; for illustration *see* BASIE, COUNT) Morton concentrated on playing in small groups, where his unfailing reliability and thoughtful musicianship were always apparent. From 1940 to 1943 he worked with Teddy Wilson's sextet (for illustration *see* WILSON, TEDDY), then spent a short time in Edmond Hall's sextet before forming his own group in September 1944. From January 1946 he worked for several years in Broadway theater orchestras; he also played as a freelance with, among others, Henry "Red" Allen (1960), Ted Lewis (1964), the Saints and Sinners (1967, 1970), Wild Bill Davison (1968), and Sy Oliver (1970–71). He toured with the World's Greatest Jazz Band in 1973–4 and, after a period of illness, resumed playing in the late 1970s.

A disciple of Jimmy Harrison, Morton was by nature a sideman rather than a leader; he did, however, organize his own recording bands with considerable success, notably on *The Gold Digger's Song* and *Conversing in Blue*. Although he was not an outstanding innovator, he was always capable of improvising interesting solos, and every performance was graced with feeling and an exquisite tone.

Oral history material in *NjR*.

SELECTED RECORDINGS

As leader: The Gold Digger's Song (1934, Col. 2924D); Conversing in Blue (1945, BN 46)

As sideman: F. Henderson: Jackass Blues (1926, Col. 654D); D. Redman: I got rhythm (1932, Bruns. 6354); E. Hall: Big City Blues (1944, BN 36); on B. Clayton: *Buck Meets Ruby* (1954, Van. 8008), Kandee

BIBLIOGRAPHY

G. Schuller: *Early Jazz: its Roots and Musical Development* (New York, 1968), 263 [incl. transcr.]

R. Bolton: "A Study in Excellence," *JJ*, xxvii/2 (1974), 4

S. Dance: *The World of Swing* (New York, 1974) [colln of previously pubd interviews], 283

L. Tomkins: "The Bennie Morton Story," *CI*, xiii (1975), no.6, p.14; no.10, p.10; no.12, p.10

M. Collier: "Talking Trombone," *JJI*, xxxviii/6 (1985), 18

JOHN CHILTON

Morton, Jelly Roll [Lemott [La Menthe, La Mothe], Ferdinand Joseph] (*b* New Orleans, 20 Oct 1890; *d* Los Angeles, 10 July 1941). Composer and pianist.

1. Life. 2. Achievement.

1. LIFE. He grew up in New Orleans, starting to learn piano at the age of ten. By 1902 he was working in the bordellos of Storyville, playing ragtime, French quadrilles, and other popular dances and songs as well as a few light (mostly operatic) classics. Nothing is known of his formal musical training, but his major youthful influence appears to have been Tony Jackson. Around 1904 Morton became an itinerant pianist, working in many cities in Louisiana, Mississippi, Alabama, and Florida. He was also apparently quite active as a gambler, pool player, and procurer, though music remained his first "line of business." Retaining New Orleans as his base, he later extended his travels to Memphis, St. Louis, and Kansas City, frequently working for prolonged periods in minstrel shows; eventually he traveled as far east as New York (where James P. Johnson heard Morton play his *Jelly Roll Blues* in 1911), and as far west as Los Angeles, where he arrived in 1917. During these dozen years of travel Morton apparently fused a variety of black musical idioms – ragtime, vocal and instrumental blues, items from the minstrel show repertory, field and levee hollers, religious hymns, and spirituals – with Hispanic music from the Caribbean and white popular songs, creating a musical amalgam that bore a very close resemblance to the music then beginning to be called "jazz."

Morton enjoyed such success in Los Angeles that he remained there for five years. In 1922, however, he moved to Chicago, the new center of jazz activity. His first recordings were made there in 1923: two performances with a sextet (*Big Foot Ham* and *Muddy Water Blues*) and a series of solo piano renditions of his own works. The compositional maturity and the advanced conception of the ensemble and solo writing revealed in these recordings suggest that Morton's style must have crystallized many years previously. By 1926–7 Morton was recording with his RED HOT PEPPERS (see illustration, p.138), a seven- or eight-piece band organized for recording purposes and comprising colleagues well-versed in the New Orleans style and familiar with Morton's music. The resultant recordings were a triumphant fusion of composition and improvisation. Pieces like *Grandpa's Spells*, *Black Bottom Stomp*, and *The Pearls* are masterly examples of Morton's creative talents, not only as a composer and arranger (*see* ARRANGEMENT, §2 and Table 1) but also as a pianist. These works were ingeniously conceived so as to yield a maximum variety of texture and timbre without sacrificing clarity of form (see ex.1); furthermore, unlike most jazz performances in those days, they were carefully rehearsed. Particularly noteworthy is the manner in which Morton provides opportunities for all the performers to contribute significant solos (usually climaxing in exultant two-bar breaks) without losing sight of overall structural unity and a balance between solo and ensemble. As a pianist Morton contributed not only some of his most inspired solos, such as those on *Smoke-house Blues* and *Black Bottom Stomp* (see ex.2), but also sensitive countermelodies that were without precedent in 1920s jazz; similar ideas were taken up only by Earl Hines and, some years later, Art Tatum.

In 1928 Morton moved to New York. There he continued to record such pieces (not necessarily his own) as *Kansas City Stomp*, *Tank Town Bump*, *Low Gravy*, and *Blue Blood Blues*. He gradually made use of such "modern" devices as homophonically harmonized ensembles and laid a greater emphasis on solo improvisation. However, he remained at heart true to the New Orleans spirit of collective improvisation and was never able to assimilate the new orchestral styles advanced in the late 1920s by Don Redman, Fletcher Henderson, and John Nesbitt. By 1930 Morton's style, both as arranger and pianist, came to be regarded as antiquated. Ironically, some of his compositions, such as *Wolverine Blues*, *Milenberg Joys*, and especially *King Porter Stomp*, continued to be performed regularly, remaining as influential pieces in the repertory throughout the 1930s. Indeed, it was Benny Goodman's performance of the last-named title, in Fletcher Henderson's updated arrangement (1935), that was largely responsible for ushering in the swing era.

In the early 1930s Morton drifted into obscurity. He settled in Washington, where he managed a jazz club and also played intermittently. In 1938 the folklorist Alan Lomax, later Morton's biographer, recorded him in an extensive series of interviews held at the Library of Congress (issued on disc in 1948 and reissued in 1957). In this invaluable oral history Morton recalled in words and performances his early days in New Orleans, re-creating the styles of many of his turn-of-the-century contemporaries. His accounts, both verbal and pianistic, have the ring of authenticity, and revealed Morton as jazz's earliest musician-historian and a perceptive theorist and analyst of the music. The Library of Congress recordings rekindled public interest in Morton, eventually leading to further recording sessions in 1939–40 and, in tandem with the New Orleans revival, a renewed career; this was cut short in 1940, however, owing to his ill-health.

Ex.1 From *Grandpa's Spells*, recorded by the Red Hot Peppers (1926, Vic. 20431); transcr. G. Schuller

Ex.2 Morton's solo chorus from *Black Bottom Stomp* (1926, Vic. 20221); transcr. G. Schuller

Jelly Roll Morton and his Red Hot Peppers, Chicago, 1926: (left to right) Omer Simeon, Andrew Hilaire, John Lindsay, Morton (seated), Johnny St. Cyr, Kid Ory, and George Mitchell

2. ACHIEVEMENT. Morton was the first important jazz composer. His compositions, many written long before he began recording, represent a rich synthesis of Afro-American musical elements, particularly as embodied in the pure New Orleans collective style which he helped to develop to its finest expression. Paradoxically, his emphasis on composition and well-rehearsed, coordinated performances was unique and antithetical to the primarily extemporized, polyphonic New Orleans style. In his best ensemble work, especially with the Red Hot Peppers, Morton showed that composition and meticulously rehearsed arrangements were not incompatible with the spontaneity of improvised jazz but could in fact retain and enhance it. In this respect Morton's achievement may be ranked with that of Duke Ellington, Thelonious Monk, Charles Mingus, and Gil Evans.

Morton's sophisticated conception of jazz is all the more remarkable since the origins of his style lie primarily in classic midwestern ragtime and simple instrumental blues. His piano pieces (such as *Grandpa's Spells* and *Kansas City Stomp*) strongly resemble ragtime in their form, but by elaborating these works with composed and improvised variation Morton was able to transcend ragtime's formal conventions. Ultimately he freed ragtime from its narrow strictures by developing within it an ensemble style embracing homophony, improvised polyphony, solo improvisations, breaks, and a constant variation of texture and timbre.

Oral history material in *DLC*.

See also BLUES, §5; FORMS, §§2 and 3; and PIANO, §1.

WORKS

(selective list; dates of composition are mostly conjectural)

© – date of copyright

Edition: *The Collected Piano Music of Ferdinand "Jelly Roll" Morton*, ed. J. Dapogny (Washington, 1982)

New Orleans Blues, 1902, © 1925; Jelly Roll Blues, 1905, © 1915; King Porter Stomp, 1906, © 1924; Buffalo Blues, 1907, © 1928; Georgia Swing, 1907, © 1928; Frog-i-more Rag (Sweetheart o' Mine), 1908, © 1918; The Crave, 1910–11, © 1939; Bert Williams, 1911, © 1948; Grandpa's Spells, 1911, © 1923; Wolverine Blues, 1915–16, © 1923; Mamanita, 1917–22, © 1949; Kansas City Stomp, 1919, © 1923; The Pearls, 1919, © 1923; Big Foot Ham, 1923, © 1923; London Blues (Shoe Shiner's Drag), 1923, © 1923; Mr. Jelly Lord, 1923, © 1923

Milenberg Joys, 1923, © 1925; Perfect Rag (Sporting House Rag), 1924, © 1939; Shreveport Stomp, 1924, © 1925; Black Bottom Stomp (Queen of Spades), 1925, © 1925; Dead Man Blues, 1926, © 1926; Fickle Fay Creep, 1926, © 1930; Hyena Stomp, 1927, © 1927; Jungle Blues, 1927, © 1927; Sweet Peter, 1929, © 1933

SELECTED RECORDINGS

As unaccompanied soloist: Smoke-house Blues (Beale Street Blues) (1926, Vic. 20296)

As leader: Muddy Water Blues (1923, Para. 12050); Tank Town Bump (1929, Vic. 38075); Low Gravy (1930, Vic. 23334); Blue Blood Blues (1930, Vic. 22681)

RECORDED COMPOSITIONS

(selective list)

AS UNACCOMPANIED SOLOIST

King Porter Stomp/Wolverine Blues (1923, Gen. 5289); New Orleans Joys (New Orleans Blues) (1923, Gen. 5486); Grandpa's Spells/Kansas City Stomp (1923, Gen. 5218); The Pearls (1923, Gen. 5323); Mamanita (1924, Para. 12216); Shreveport Stomp (1924, Gen. 5590); Jelly Roll Blues/Big Foot Ham (1924, Gen. 5552); Froggie Moore (Frog-i-more Rag) (1924, Para. 14032); Perfect Rag (1924, Gen. 5486); London Blues (Shoe Shiner's Drag) (1924, Rialto [unnumbered])

Mr. Jelly Lord (1924, Vocal Style Song Roll 12973); Dead Man Blues (1926, QRS 3674); Fickle Fay Creep/Jungle Blues (1938, Cir. [USA] 32-46); Sweet Peter (1938, Cir. [USA] 73-69); Hyena Stomp (1938, Cir. [USA] 8-55); Bert Williams (1938, Cir. [USA] 45-71); The Crave (1938, Cir. [USA] 31)

AS LEADER

Big Foot Ham (1923, Para. 12050); London Blues (Shoe Shiner's Drag) (1923, OK 8105); Mr. Jelly Lord (1923, Para. 20332); King Porter Stomp (1924, Aut. 617); Wolverine Blues (1925, Aut. 623); Black Bottom Stomp (1926, Vic. 20221); Dead Man Blues (1926, Vic. 20252); Grandpa's Spells (1926, Vic. 20431); Original Jelly Roll Blues (1926, Vic. 20405); Hyena Stomp (1927, Vic. 20772); Jungle Blues (1927, Vic. 21345); The Pearls (1927, Vic. 20948)

Georgia Swing (1928, Vic. 38024); Kansas City Stomps (1928, Vic. 38010); Shreveport (Stomp) (1928, Vic. 21658); Sweet Peter (1929, Vic. 23402); Fickle Fay Creep (1930, Vic. 23019)

BIBLIOGRAPHY

J. R. Morton: "I Created Jazz in 1902," *DB*, v/8 (1938), 3
K. Hulsizer: "Jelly Roll Morton in Washington," *Jazz Music*, ii/6–7 (1944), 109; repr. in *This is Jazz*, ed. K. Williamson (London, 1960), 202
J. R. Morton: "Fragment of an Autobiography," *Record Changer*, iv (1944), March, 15; April, 27
C. E. Smith: "Oh, Mr. Jelly!," *Jazz Record*, no.17 (1944), 8
O. Simeon: "Mostly about Morton," *Jazz Record*, no.37 (1945), 5
P. E. Miller, ed.: *Esquire's 1946 Jazz Book* (New York, 1946)
R. J. Carew: "New Orleans Recollections," *Record Changer*, vii (1948), Dec, 12
R. Blesh and H. Janis: *They all Played Ragtime* (New York, 1950, rev. 4/1971)
A. Lomax: *Mister Jelly Roll: the Fortunes of Jelly Roll Morton, New Orleans Creole and "Inventor of Jazz"* (New York, 1950, 2/1973)
R. Carew: "1211 U Street, Northwest," *JM*, i/1 (1955), 8
——: "Of This and That and Jelly Roll," *JJ*, x/12 (1957), 10
M. Williams: Liner notes, *Jelly Roll Morton: the Library of Congress Recordings* (Riv. 9001-12, 1957)
R. Hadlock: "Morton's Library of Congress Albums," *Jazz: a Quarterly of American Music*, no.2 (1959), 133
W. Russell: "Morton and *Frog-i-more Rag*," *The Art of Jazz: Essays on the Nature and Development of Jazz*, ed. M. Williams (New York, 1959/*R*1979)
J. Butler and J. Poinsot: "Harlem en 1928," *BHcF*, no.100 (1960), 4
D. Locke: "Jelly Roll Morton: the Library of Congress Recordings," *JJ*, xiii/1 (1960), 15
K. Kramer: "Jelly Roll in Chicago (1927)," *SL*, xi (1961), nos.1–2, p.1; nos.3–4, p.19
G. Waterman: "Jelly Roll Morton," *Jazz Panorama*, ed. M. Williams (New York and London, 1962/*R*1979) [colln of previously pubd articles], 31
M. Williams: *Jelly Roll Morton* (London, 1962); repr. in *Kings of Jazz*, ed. S. Green (South Brunswick, NJ, and New York, 1978)
C. E. Smith: Liner notes, *Stomps and Joys* (RCA LPV508, 1964)
K. Kramer: "Jelly Roll in Chicago: the Missing Chapter," *The Ragtimer*, vi/1 (1967), 15
M. Williams: *Jazz Masters of New Orleans* (New York and London, 1967/*R*1978)
J. R. T. Davies and L. Wright: *Morton's Music* (London, 1968)
J. R. Morton: "Final Years of Frustration (1939–41)," *JJ*, xxi (1968), no.11, p.2; no.12, p.8 [letters to R. Carew]
G. Schuller: *Early Jazz: its Roots and Musical Development* (New York, 1968)
B. Kumm and H. Smith: "The Strange Case of Jelly's Will," *Sv*, no.25 (1969), 8
M. Williams: *The Jazz Tradition* (New York, 1970, rev. 2/1983)
M. A. Hood and H. N. Flint, eds.: *"Jelly Roll" Morton: the Original Mr. Jazz* (New York, 1975)
M. Hill and E. Bryce: *Jelly Roll Morton: a Microgroove Discography and Musical Analysis* (Salisbury East, South Australia, 1977)
L. Wright: *Mr Jelly Lord* (Chigwell, England, 1980)
L. Gushee: "Would you Believe Ferman Mouton?," *Sv*, no.95 (1981), 164; no.98 (1981–2), 56
W. Balliett: "Ferdinand La Menthe," *Jelly Roll, Jabbo and Fats* (New York, and Oxford, England, 1983) [colln of previously pubd articles], 16
J. Dapogny: "Jelly Roll Morton and Ragtime," *Ragtime: its History, Composers, and Music*, ed. J. E. Hasse (New York and London, 1985), 257
L. Gushee: "A Preliminary Chronology of the Early Career of Ferd "Jelly Roll" Morton," *American Music*, iii (1985), 389; repr. in *Sv*, no.127 (1986), 11

GUNTHER SCHULLER

Mosaic (i). Record company and label. The company was established by Graham Collier in London in 1974. By 1987 it had issued 14 albums, the majority of which are of his own music. Others are by such English musicians as Howard Riley (1975–6), Elton Dean, and the reed player Stan Sulzmann.

SIMON ADAMS

Mosaic (ii). Record company and label. The company was formed around 1982 in Santa Monica, California, by Michael Cuscuna. It issues items intended for dedicated listeners and collectors; its recordings are available only by mail order, and only one edition of each is made. The majority of Mosaic's releases consists of carefully prepared and well recorded boxed sets of material drawn mainly from the Blue Note and Pacific Jazz labels. The first issue, for example, presented all of Thelonious Monk's recordings for Blue Note from 1947 to 1952, including 15 new performances discovered by Cuscuna; the albums were accompanied by a booklet providing extensive commentary, as well as a discography of Monk's commercial recordings. Among the subjects of later collections are Gerry Mulligan and Chet Baker, Clifford Brown, Albert Ammons and Meade "Lux" Lewis, and Art Pepper. It announced the issue, in 1988, of the complete recordings of the Commodore label in chronological order.

BIBLIOGRAPHY

B. Davis: "Mosaic Records," *JJI*, xxxvii/5 (1984), 18
B. Priestley: "Records: Mosaic Moves on," *Jazz Express*, no.73 (1986), 16

Mosca, Sal(vatore Joseph) (*b* Mount Vernon, NY, 27 April 1927). Pianist. He studied bop piano with Lennie Tristano (1947–55) and attended New York University and the New York College of Music (1947–50). He worked principally with Lee Konitz (1949–65), making recordings with him at intervals (including *Very Cool*, 1957, Verve 8209); he also recorded as a leader (1955, 1959). In the 1970s he performed in New York with a quintet led by Konitz and Warne Marsh. As a soloist he gave concerts in New York (1977, 1979) and in 1981 toured the Netherlands. He led groups with Marsh and others in the late 1970s and 1980s, and alone for engagements in New York (1980–83). He has also been active as a teacher.

BIBLIOGRAPHY

FeatherE
J. Mulder: "Pianist Sal Mosca: er gebeurt wat als Sal Mosca speelt," *Jazz Freak*, ix/1 (1981), 14 [incl. discography]

Moseholm, Erik (*b* Fredericia, Denmark, 13 May 1930). Danish double bass player. He performed and recorded with the baritone saxophonist Max Brüel and the trumpeter Jørgen Ryg in the early 1950s and belonged to the Radio Jazz Dance Band (1954–5), Ib Glindemann's big band (1957), and Finn Savery's trio (1957–8, 1960). From 1959 he worked in duos and led trios, one of which performed at festivals in Antibes–Juan-les-Pins and Comblain-la-Tour in 1960; he also led the band Radiojazzgruppen from its inception in 1961 until 1966, when he began working in programming for Danmarks radio (*see* RADIOJAZZGRUPPEN, (i)). Moseholm was the leading double bass player in Denmark in the 1950s; his playing may be heard to advantage on the album *Trio Suite* (Artist 505), recorded in 1970 with the drummer Jørn Elniff and the pianist Arne Forchhammer. In addition to his work as a performer he has been active in music organizations. (J. Schoustrup Thomsen: *Erik Moseholm* (Copenhagen, 1962) [incl. discography])

ERIK WIEDEMANN

Moseka, Aminata. *See* LINCOLN, ABBEY.

Moses, Bob [Moses, Rahboat Ntumba; Robert Laurence] (*b* New York, 28 Jan 1948). Drummer, percussionist, and composer. He played vibraphone in Latin bands in New York while still in his teens, and formed the group Free Spirits with Larry Coryell in 1966. The following year he played and recorded with Roland Kirk for six months and joined Gary Burton's quartet, with which he remained until 1968; he then joined Jack DeJohnette's group Compost and worked as a freelance in New York. With Dave Liebman he formed the trio Open Sky in the late 1960s, which recorded two albums (1972, 1974) and performed at intervals until 1984; he also recorded with Burton (1974–5) and in 1975 toured with Burton, recorded with Mike Gibbs, and performed and recorded with Pat Metheny. He rejoined Burton's group and recorded with Hal Galper and the pianist Gil Goldstein (1978), then recorded with Steve Swallow and joined Steve Kuhn's and Sheila Jordan's band (1979), with which he toured and recorded until 1982; he also toured and recorded with George Gruntz's Concert Jazz Band (1983) and Emily Remler (1983–4), and in the early 1980s recorded with the group Mister Spats, led by the keyboard player Steve Evans and the singer June Bisantz. Moses' drumming, based solidly on the jazz tradition, incorporates Latin, funk, and African elements; his work as a composer is well represented by *Bittersweet in the Ozone* (1975), the first album he recorded as a soloist. He is the author of a drumming method, *Drum Wisdom* (Clifton, NJ, 1984).

SELECTED RECORDINGS

As leader: *Bittersweet in the Ozone* (1975, Mozown 001); *Visit with the Great Spirit* (1983, Gram. 8307)

As sideman: G. Burton: *Lofty Fake Anagram* (1967, RCA LSP3901); M. Gibbs: *The Only Chrome Waterfall Orchestra* (1975, Bronze 2012); P. Metheny: *Bright Size Life* (1975, ECM 1073); S. Swallow: *Home* (1979, ECM 1160)

BIBLIOGRAPHY

R. Brown: "Bob Moses," *Into Jazz*, i/5 (1974), 9 [interview]
C. Mitchell: "Bob Moses: Percussion Bittersuite," *DB*, xlii/20 (1975), 18
C. Iero: "Bob Moses: Beneath the Surface," *MD*, iii/6 (1979), 18
H. Mandel: "Bob Moses: Surreal Swing," *DB*, l/5 (1983), 25 [incl. discography]
C. Stern: "Bob Moses, Dreamer," *MD*, viii/8 (1984), 18

RICK MATTINGLY

Moses, J(ohn) C(urtis) (*b* Pittsburgh, 18 Oct 1936; *d* 1977). Drummer. As a freelance in New York he recorded with Clifford Jordan (*c*1962), Kenny Dorham (1962), and Eric Dolphy (1963). He then toured and recorded in Denmark (1963), playing free jazz as a member of the New York Contemporary Five with Archie Shepp, John Tchicai, Don Cherry, and Don Moore; his playing may be heard to advantage on the album *New York Contemporary Five* (1963, Fon. 881013). After returning to New York Moses worked with the New York Art Quartet (1964) and toured with Charles Lloyd (1964) and Roland Kirk (1965–7). He continued his association with Shepp, recording with him in 1965; the following year he recorded as a member of a quartet led by Andrew Hill and Sam Rivers. In 1969 he traveled to Copenhagen, where he worked as a house drummer at the Montmartre Jazzhus, accompanying such swing and bop musicians as Ben Webster, Coleman Hawkins, Dexter Gordon, and Booker Ervin. Illness forced him to curtail his activities in the early 1970s, but he continued to work occasionally in Pittsburgh with Nathan Davis and Eric Kloss. (V. Wilmer: *As Serious as your Life: the Story of the New Jazz,* London, 1977, rev. 1980)

Mosley, Snub [Mosely, Lawrence Leo] (*b* Little Rock, AR, 29 Dec 1905; *d* New York, 21 July 1981). Trombonist, slide saxophonist, singer, leader, and composer. He learned to play trombone in high-school bands. From 1926 to 1933 he was a principal soloist with Alphonso Trent's orchestra, in which he also sang. During this period his preference for playing short, rapid phrases in the trombone's high register led to his developing a slide saxophone (*see* SAXOPHONE, §6 (viii)); this instrument had a saxophone mouthpiece and a small slide for altering pitch, and its sound resembled that of a soprano saxophone. Mosley was a founding member of the Jeter–Pillars Orchestra (1934). After playing with Claude Hopkins (1934–5) and Fats Waller (1935) he worked in the Luis Russell Orchestra, which was accompanying Louis Armstrong (1936–7), and thereafter led his own groups. He made several tours with the USO during World War II and the Korean War, but worked mostly in and around New York. From 1978 he performed annually in England. Mosley usually played trombone with a mute, often employing a combination of a straight mute and a plunger; he tended to reserve the slide saxophone for performing ballads. He composed several songs, including *Pretty Eyed Baby* (with Mary Lou Williams), *Gilded Kisses*, and *Amen*; others, such as *Juice Head Willie*, were vehicles for his blues-oriented singing.

Oral history material in *NjR* (JOHP).

SELECTED RECORDINGS

As leader: The Man with the Funny Little Horn (1940, Decca 7728); Hey man, hey man! (Amen) (1941, Decca 8586); *Snub Mosley Live at Pizza Express* (1978, Pizza 5502), incl. Juice Head Willie

As sideman: A. Trent: Louder and Funnier/Gilded Kisses (1928, Gen. 6664); Clementine/I've found a new baby (1933, Champion 16587)

BIBLIOGRAPHY

F. Manskleid: "Portrait of Two Musicians: 1: Snub Mosley," *JM*, vi/1 (1960), 8
S. Dance: *The World of Count Basie* (New York and London, 1980) [colln of previously pubd interviews], 326
P. Vacher: "Snub Mosley's Music," *MR*, vii/8 (1980), 1
——: "Snub Mosley," *JJI*, xxxiv/10 (1981), 20
L. Wright: "(Very) Young Man with a Horn," *Sv* (1981), no.97, p.26; no.98, p.53 [incl. illustration of slide saxophone]
F. Driggs: "The Man with the Funny Horn: Snub Mosley," *Whiskey, Women, and . . .*, nos.12–13 (1983), [43]

BARRY KERNFELD

Moss, Danny [Dennis] (*b* Redhill, England, 16 Aug 1927). English tenor saxophonist. He began playing professionally at the age of 16 and rapidly established himself as an important musician. From the late 1940s he performed and recorded with many of the leading British big bands, including those led by the violinist Oscar Rabin, Vic Lewis, Ted Heath (1953–5), John Dankworth (1957–61), and Humphrey Lyttelton (1962). Thereafter he formed his own quartet, and also recorded with Buck Clayton (1963) and Adelaide Hall (*c*1969). He toured with a band led by Freddy Randall and the clarinetist Dave Shepherd in 1972–3, then began working as a freelance. As well as recording with Tony Bennett, Bing Crosby, Ella Fitzgerald, Sarah Vaughan, and Rosemary Clooney he has played in symphony orchestras. In 1979 he was a founding member of the educational ensemble Jazz College, and in the 1980s he has played with the Pizza Express All-Stars. Moss is married to the singer Jeannie Lamb, with whom he has twice toured Australia and the USA.

BIBLIOGRAPHY

R. Cotterrell, ed.: *Jazz Now: the Jazz Centre Society Guide* (London, 1976), 151
D. Fairweather: "Strictly Instrumental," *JJI*, xxxiv/5 (1981), 12
——: "Moss, Danny," in I. Carr, D. Fairweather, and B. Priestley: *Jazz: the Essential Companion* (London, 1987)

CLARRIE HENLEY

Mosse, Sandy [Sanford] (*b* Detroit, 29 May 1929; *d* Amsterdam, 1 July 1983). Tenor saxophonist. After early professional experience as a clarinetist and alto saxophonist he took up the tenor instrument in 1950. At the age of 22 he moved to Paris, where he worked with Wallace Bishop (1951), Henri Renaud (including recordings, 1951–2), and Django Reinhardt; he then toured as a soloist with Woody Herman (1953). After returning to Chicago he recorded with Bill Russo (1955), Chubby Jackson (1957), and Cy Touff (1958), and made two albums as a leader, including *The Chicago Scene* (1956, Argo 609). He also played briefly with Maynard Ferguson (1956) and Buddy Rich (1958). Later, in Chicago, he recorded in a big band led by the trombonist Dave Remington (1968).

BIBLIOGRAPHY

FeatherE

D. Gold: "Mosse Grows: a Warm, Fluent Tenor Saxist is Finally being Heard after Long Struggle," *DB*, xxiv/9 (1957), 18

A. Morgan: "Woody's Tenors," *JM*, vi (1960–61), no.7, p.4; no.8, p.13; no.12, p.9

H. Kleinhout and W. van Eyle: *The Wallace Bishop Story* (Alphen aan de Rijn, Netherlands, 1981)

DAVE GELLY

Most, Abe [Abraham] (*b* New York, 27 Feb 1920). Clarinetist, brother of Sam Most. He began playing professionally at the age of 16 and later led his own group at Kelly's Stable, New York. In 1939 he joined Les Brown, with whom he recorded on alto saxophone and as a singer. After military service (1942–5) he played as a leader in Los Angeles and worked briefly with Tommy Dorsey (1946); then he again led his own band at the Hickory House, New York. He re-joined Brown on the West Coast in the late 1940s but left to play in the film studios of 20th Century-Fox. Most continued working as a studio musician in Los Angeles into the 1980s. His playing is well represented on *Mr. Clarinet* (*c*1955, Lib. 6004).

BIBLIOGRAPHY

FeatherE

H. Lucraft: "Abe is the Most," *MM*, xxx (11 Sept 1954), 7

J. Staples: "The Winning Clarinet of Abe Most," *CI*, xx/2 (1981), 16

WARREN VACHÉ, SR.

Most, Sam(uel) (*b* Atlantic City, NJ, 16 Dec 1930). Flutist, clarinetist, and alto saxophonist, brother of Abe Most. He was brought up in a musical family and began his career as a reed player working with Tommy Dorsey (1948), Boyd Raeburn, and Don Redman before changing to flute, finding that it was better suited to the new ideas he wanted to express. In 1953 he made his first recording, *Undercurrent Blues*, and became established as the first bop flutist. Throughout the 1950s he led his own groups and in 1954 won the *Down Beat* critics' "New Star" award. He also worked with players of such diverse styles as Chris Connor, Calvin Jackson, Paul Quinichette, and Teddy Wilson. From 1959 to 1961 he played in Buddy Rich's orchestra, touring India, the Far East, and South America. On his return to the USA he joined his brother Abe in Los Angeles and performed (mostly on alto saxophone) with Louie Bellson. Later he divided his time between working with Red Norvo in Las Vegas and as a freelance musician in California. In the mid-1970s Most returned to prominence following the release of recordings on the Xanadu label.

SELECTED RECORDINGS

As leader: Sam Most Sextet (1953, Prst. 1322) [EP], incl. Undercurrent Blues; *Mostly Flute* (1976, Xan. 133), incl. Rio Romance; *Flute Flight* (1976, Xan. 141); *From the Attic of my Mind* (1978, Xan. 160)

As sideman: B. Rich: *Playtime* (1960, Argo 676); L. Bellson: *Thunderbird* (1965, Imp. 9107)

BIBLIOGRAPHY

FeatherE; *Feather '60s*; *Feather–Gitler '70s*

J. Burns: "The Forgotten Boppers," *J&B*, ii/3 (1972), 4

CHRIS SHERIDAN

Moten, Bennie [Benjamin] (*b* Kansas City, MO, 13 Nov 1894; *d* Kansas City, 2 April 1935). Pianist and bandleader. He studied piano with two of Scott Joplin's pupils and by 1918 was working professionally as the leader of the ragtime trio B. B. & D. By 1922 his group had expanded to six members, and in the next year they issued their first recordings, playing mostly blues with a heavy, stomping beat. Within ten years Moten's ensemble included among its members such outstanding performers as Walter Page, Hot Lips Page, Eddie Durham, Ben Webster, Buster Smith, Count Basie, and Jimmy Rushing, and had largely established the Kansas City or southwest style of orchestral jazz (*see* KANSAS CITY JAZZ). This style was based on a four-beat rhythmic pattern that emphasized horizontal "flow," on a flexible and texturally well-integrated rhythm section, and on frequent use of instrumental riffs and blues chord sequences. The arrangements (by Durham, Eddie Barefield, and Basie) were, except for Ellington's, the most advanced of their time, offering highly virtuoso performances, often at breakneck tempos, which effectively blended solo and ensemble passages into organic compositions. These characteristics

Bennie Moten and his band at the Pearl Theater, Philadelphia, 1931: (back row, left to right) Hot Lips Page, Booker Washington, and Ed Lewis (trumpets), Thamon Hayes and Eddie Durham (trombones), and Vernon Page (sousaphone); (front row) Count Basie (piano), Jimmy Rushing (voice), Mack Washington (drums), Leroy "Buster" Berry (banjo), Harlan Leonard, Jack Washington, and Woodie Walder (saxophones), and Bennie and Buster Moten

are well represented in a series of ten performances from the group's final recording session in 1932. On Moten's death his group was led briefly by Basie and Buster Moten (Ira Alexander Smith, a brother or perhaps a nephew of Moten's). From 1936 its personnel and style went on, through the Count Basie Orchestra, to become an important force in big-band swing, and a formative influence on bop and other styles of modern jazz.

SELECTED RECORDINGS

Elephant's Wobble/Crawdad Blues (1923, OK 8100); The New Tulsa Blues (1927, Vic. 21584); Moten Stomp (1927, Vic. 20955); Kansas City Breakdown (1928, Vic. 21693); When I'm Alone (1930, Vic. 22734); Toby/Moten Swing (1932, Vic. 23384); Lafayette (1932, Vic. 24216); Prince of Wales (1932, Vic. 23393)

BIBLIOGRAPHY

F. Driggs: "Kansas City and the South West," *Jazz: New Perspectives on the History of Jazz*, ed. N. Hentoff and A. J. McCarthy (New York and Toronto, 1959/*R*1974), 189–230
G. Schuller: *Early Jazz: its Roots and Musical Development* (New York, 1968), 283
B. Rust: "The Bennie Moten OKehs," *Sv*, no.22 (1969), 138
R. Russell: *Jazz Style in Kansas City and the Southwest* (Berkeley, CA, Los Angeles, and London, 1971/*R*1983, rev. 2/1973)
D. Bakker: "Bennie Moten, 1923–1932," *Micrography*, no.24 (1973), 2; no.26 (1973), 1 [discography]
A. McCarthy: *Big Band Jazz* (New York and London, 1974), 33

GUNTHER SCHULLER

Moten, Benny [Clarence Lemont] (*b* New York, 30 Nov 1916; *d* New Orleans, 27 March 1977). Double bass player. After beginning his career in 1941 with Hot Lips Page and Jerry Jerome he worked with Henry "Red" Allen (1942–9), Eddie South (1949), Stuff Smith (1950–51), and Arnett Cobb (1953–4). He rejoined Allen's group, with which he recorded in 1955 and occasionally afterwards, and in 1956 played with Ella Fitzgerald and performed and recorded at the Newport Jazz Festival with Buck Clayton. Later he worked with Wilbur De Paris (accompanying Jimmy Witherspoon on recordings, 1956, and touring Africa, 1957), recorded with Buster Bailey (1959) and Roy Eldridge (1959–60), and played with Dakota Staton (1961–3) and again with Allen (1963–5). He worked frequently as a freelance in New York until the end of his life. Moten has sometimes been confused with the well-known pianist and bandleader Bennie Moten.

SELECTED RECORDINGS

As sideman: H. Allen and C. Shavers: *Jazz at the Metropole* (1955, Beth. 21); on B. Clayton: *Duke Ellington and the Buck Clayton All-stars at Newport* (1956, Col. CL933), Newport Jump; W. De Paris and J. Witherspoon: *New Orleans Blues* (1956, Atl. 1266); R. Eldridge: *Swingin' on the Town* (1960, Verve 68389); H. Allen: *Nice!* (1963, Phoenix Jazz 24), incl. Fidgety Feet

BIBLIOGRAPHY

ChiltonW; *FeatherE*; *Feather '60s*

Motian, (Stephen) Paul (*b* Philadelphia, 25 March 1931). Drummer and composer. After moving to New York in 1955 he accompanied a variety of musicians, including Gil Evans, George Russell, Stan Getz, Lennie Tristano, Thelonious Monk, Coleman Hawkins, and Roy Eldridge. He made his first contributions to the evolution of jazz drumming, however, when he was a member of a trio led by Bill Evans (ii) (1959–*c*1964). In this group Motian created a highly interactive style of playing in which his phrasing became less closely related to the meter of the composition than to the phrasing implied by the other group members; he also made effective use of varied textures and tone colors as elements of musical interest in themselves. By the time he was playing with Paul Bley (1963–4) and Keith Jarrett (1966–77), Motian had nearly eliminated the ostinato timekeeping patterns typically played on the ride cymbal and hi-hat and had developed an unusually spontaneous approach in which the use of cliché figures was kept to a minimum.

In the 1970s Motian began composing, first for the film makers Peter Watkins and Stan Vanderbeek, and later for his own groups. His writing, like Jarrett's, is eclectic, but tends to be more abstract, favoring structures that are paradoxically at once open and well organized. Like Motian himself in his drumming style, his groups employ varied textures of sound and an unusual diversity of musical concepts.

SELECTED RECORDINGS

As leader: *Tribute* (1974, ECM 1048); *It Should've Happened a Long Time Ago* (1984, ECM 1283)

As sideman: B. Evans: *New Jazz Conceptions* (1956, Riv. 223); *How my Heart Sings!* (1962, Riv. 9473); P. Bley: *Turns* (1964, Savoy 1192); K. Jarrett: *Life Between the Exit Signs* (1967, Vortex 2006); *Mysteries* (1975, Imp. 9315); C. Haden: *The Ballad of the Fallen* (1982, ECM 1248)

BIBLIOGRAPHY

Feather–Gitler '70s
G. Lees: "Inside the New Bill Evans Trio," *DB*, xxix/29 (1962), 24
M. Henaels: "Paul Motian: I'd Like to Bring Back the Art of Playing the Drum Set," *JF* [intl edn], no.56 (1978), 30
S. K. Fish: "Paul Motian: Drawing from Tradition," *MD*, iv/2 (1980), 16
S. Cotta: "La grande oreille de Paul Motian," *Le monde de la musique*, no.61 (1983), 68
D. Soutif: "Motion + Emotion = Motian," *Jm*, no.323 (1983), 24
S. Lake: "Paul Motian," *The Wire*, no.25 (1986), 7
H. Mandel: "Poetry in Motian," *DB*, liii/5 (1986), 23 [incl. discography]
J. Bloom: "Paul Motian: Conversation with a Drummer," *JT* (Oct 1987), 15

CHUCK BRAMAN

Moule, Ken(neth John) (*b* Barking, England, 26 June 1925; *d* Marbella, Spain, 27 Jan 1986). English composer and arranger. He first played piano, touring and recording with his own septet in 1954–6. Thereafter he worked for three years as an arranger for Ted Heath's orchestra. During this period he also composed and arranged a jazz suite, *Jazz at Toad Hall* (1958, Decca 4261). Based on the children's book by Kenneth Grahame *Wind in the Willows*, it was immediately recognized as a brilliant work that both captured the essence of the story and displayed an original and innovatory approach to jazz arranging. His work for Heath's band was by necessity more conventional, but Moule's craftsmanship was often apparent. He began working as a freelance, in particular arranging and conducting works by the composer Lionel Bart (notably *Fings Ain't Wot they Used t'Be*, 1960–62, and *Twang!!*, 1965–6). In 1970, with the London Jazz Chamber Group, he recorded his *Adam's Rib Suite* (Ember CJS823), which fused elements of classical music and jazz and included performances by Kenny Wheeler. Later he scored several compositions by the songwriter Cole Porter for the show *Cole!* (1974) at the Mermaid Theatre, London, and wrote for John Dankworth's collaborations with the London SO. In the late 1970s he worked frequently in Germany. (*Feather '60s*)

CLARRIE HENLEY

Mound City Blue Blowers. Dixieland group formed as a novelty trio in 1924 by RED MCKENZIE (comb-and-paper, voice), Jack Bland (banjo and guitar), and Dick Slevin (KAZOO and other homemade instruments). The term blue-blowing, derived from the band's name, later came to be used of any dixieland jazz played on homemade or non-standard instruments. The group's first recording, *Arkansaw Blues* (1924, Bruns. 2581), made in Chicago, reputedly sold a million copies. After moving to New York the three made further recordings (July 1924), then, with Eddie Lang (guitar), they played in London (winter 1924–5) and recorded under the group's original name and as McKenzie's Candy Kids (1924–5).

Between 1929 and 1936 McKenzie used the name Mound City Blue Blowers for various groups of up to ten players, including at different times Eddie Condon, Coleman Hawkins, Gene Krupa, Glenn Miller, Pee Wee Russell, Muggsy Spanier, and Jack Teagarden, all of whom recorded with him in 1929–31; Bland continued to play with the groups until around 1931, but Slevin was not apparently connected with McKenzie after 1925. Besides recording, the Mound City Blue Blowers appeared in *The Opry House* (1929), a short film made by Warner Bros. (E. Condon and T. Sugrue: *We Called it Music: a Generation of Jazz*, New York, 1947/*R*1985)

For illustration *see* LANG, EDDIE.

Mousie. Nickname of ART ROLLINI.

Mouth organ. *See* HARMONICA.

Mouzon, Alphonse (*b* Charleston, SC, 21 Nov 1948). Drummer. After moving to New York in 1966 and playing in the musical *Promises, Promises* by Hal David and Burt Bacharach, he worked as a freelance with Roy Ayers, the popular singer Roberta Flack, and the guitarist Gene McDaniels. In 1971 he joined Weather Report, with which he remained for one year, then worked with McCoy Tyner (1972–3) and belonged to Larry Coryell's group Eleventh House (1973–5). Over the next several years he performed and recorded in the USA and Europe with his own group, as a leader with Coryell, and with Al Di Meola and George Benson. From 1979 to 1982 he performed and recorded with Herbie Hancock, while continuing to record as a leader. With Billy Cobham and Lenny White, Mouzon helped fashion a jazz-rock style of drumming by combining the volume, pulse, and energetic style of rock playing with jazz polyrhythms and technique.

SELECTED RECORDINGS

As leader: *Mind Transplant* (1974, BN LA398G); *Back to Jazz* (1986, Pausa 7196)

As sideman: Weather Report: *Weather Report* (1971, Col. KC30661); M. Tyner: *Sahara* (1972, Mlst. 9039); L. Coryell: *Introducing the Eleventh House* (1973, Van. 79342); H. Hancock: *Mr. Hands* (1980, Col. PC36578)

BIBLIOGRAPHY

M. Hohman: "Do the Funky Renaissance with Alphonse Mouzon," *DB*, xlii/20 (1975), 15 [incl. discography]

L. Perry, Jr.: "Alphonse Mouzon: Marked Man," *MD*, iii/2 (1979), 28

RICK MATTINGLY

Mover, Bob [Robert Alan] (*b* Boston, 22 March 1952). Alto and soprano saxophonist. He grew up in a musical family in Miami, where by the age of 16 he was playing with Ira Sullivan. Around 1969 his family moved to New York, where he studied with Richie Kamuca and played informally with Roy Eldridge, Brew Moore, and others. In 1973, after working briefly with Charles Mingus, he began playing with Chet Baker, and remained with him until 1975. Mover has led his own groups from 1976, recording four albums between 1977 and 1982, including *Bob Mover* (1977, Van. 79408). He also recorded with Lee Konitz in 1977, and in 1981 rejoined Baker for a European tour and a recording session.

BIBLIOGRAPHY

Feather–Gitler '70s

E. Hazell: "Bob Mover: Interview," *Cadence*, viii/4 (1982), 9

Moye, Don [Famoudou Don, Dougaufana Famoudou] (*b* Rochester, NY, 23 May 1946). Drummer and percussionist. He studied percussion at Wayne State University and then joined the group Detroit Free Jazz, which toured Europe (1968–9). After performing with Steve Lacy in Rome, he became a member of the ART ENSEMBLE OF CHICAGO (AEC) in Paris (1970), playing "sun percussion," a collection of conventional, ethnic, and homemade instruments. Moye is best known for his varied work with the AEC but he has also pursued other activities. He played and recorded with members of the Black Artists Group in St. Louis before settling in Chicago in 1971. During the 1970s he performed at the Montreux International Jazz Festival with Randy Weston (1974), performed in a duo with Steve McCall, worked as a drummer with the big band of the Association for the Advancement of Creative Musicians, led the percussion ensemble Malinke Rhythm Tribe, and played in clubs with bop, modal-jazz, and free-jazz groups. By 1975 he had added the prefix Famoudou to his name and around 1979 he used the name Dougaufana Famoudou Moye for a time. Besides performing, Moye recorded as a soloist (1975) and with Joseph Jarman (1978–81) and Don Pullen (1978–9) in duos and as the joint leader of two trios and a quartet; he also played on sessions with Cecil McBee (1977, 1979), Hamiet Bluiett and Julius Hemphill (both 1977), Chico Freeman (1979), and Jay Hoggard (1981). In 1984 he became a member of the LEADERS. He composed the music for his solo album as well as some of the material performed by his duos and groups with Jarman and Pullen.

SELECTED RECORDINGS

As unaccompanied soloist: *Sun Percussion* (1975, AECO 001)

Duos with D. Pullen: *Milano Strut* (1978, BS 0028)

As leader with J. Jarman: *Black Paladins* (1979, BS 0042)

As sideman: R. Weston: *Live Montreux 74 "Carnival"* (1974, Fre. 40148); C. McBee: *Music from the Source* (1977, Enja 3019); H. Bluiett: *We have Come to Save you from yourselves* (1977, IndN 1039); C. Freeman: *Spirit Sensitive* (1979, IndN 1045); J. Hoggard: *Mystic Winds, Tropic Breezes* (1981, IndN 1049)

For further recordings *see* ART ENSEMBLE OF CHICAGO.

BIBLIOGRAPHY

Feather–Gitler '70s

B. Rusch: "Don Moye: Interview," *Cadence*, v/10 (1979), 14

R. Mattingly: "Famoudou Don Moye: Drawing on Tradition," *MD*, v/2 (1981), 14

J. Litweiler: "The Art Ensemble of Chicago: Adventures in the Urban Bush," *DB*, xlix/6 (1982), 19 [incl. discography]

E. Janssens and H. De Craen: *Art Ensemble of Chicago Discography: Unit and Members* (Brussels, 1983)

BARRY KERNFELD

MPS [Musik Produktion Schwarzwald]. Record company and label. The company was established in 1968 by Hans Georg Brunner-Schwer, who had previously owned the SABA record label, in Villingen-Schwenningen, Germany. It quickly established one of the largest, most varied catalogues of any European label, and retained its importance throughout the 1970s; by the end of the decade MPS had issued more than 500 albums. Sessions took place not only in Villingen-Schwenningen but also at clubs, festivals, and studios in other parts of Europe and in the USA; the catalogue included material produced by Joachim-Ernst Berendt elsewhere in Germany, and by Don Schlitten in New York. Among the company's principal musicians were Monty Alexander, Albert Mangelsdorff, George Shearing, Oscar Peterson, Volker Kriegel, George Duke, Martial Solal, and the Clarke–Boland Big Band. The preponderance of pianists reflects Brunner-Schwer's interest in the piano; his experience as an amateur player contributed to his particular professional expertise in recording the instrument. MPS greatly reduced its activities in the early 1980s; a duo by Hank Jones and Tommy Flanagan of 1983 appears to have been one of the company's last recordings. ("The MPS Decade 1968–1978," *JJI*, xxxi/5 (1978), suppl.)

Mraz, George [Jiří] (*b* Písek, Czechoslovakia, 9 Sept 1944). Double bass player. He studied violin and alto saxophone as a youth, but concentrated on double bass at the Prague Conservatory (1961–6). He recorded with Karel Velebný (1964–6) and played at a club in Munich for a year. At the time of the Soviet invasion of Czechoslovakia (1968) he emigrated to the USA, and (having changed his forename to George) he became an American citizen in 1973. On his arrival in the USA he entered the Berklee College of Music, where he studied composition and arranging. He toured and recorded with Oscar Peterson (1970–72) before moving to New York and becoming a member of the Thad Jones–Mel Lewis Orchestra, with which he remained until 1976; he interrupted this association to perform and record with Stan Getz in Europe (1974–5) and Walter Norris (1974–5). He has also performed and recorded with Pepper Adams and Roland Hanna (both from 1973), Zoot Sims (1975–83), Tommy Flanagan and the New York Jazz Quartet (both from 1977), and John Abercrombie (from 1978). In 1988 Mraz performed and recorded compositions by Thelonious Monk with Carmen McRae in San Francisco.

During his time with Jones and Lewis, Mraz established himself as one of the finest double bass players in jazz; a sensitive accompanist and improviser, he has otherwise rarely worked in ensembles larger than a quartet. Although he plays ably in free-jazz and jazz-rock styles, notably with Abercrombie, he is principally a bop musician, praised for his penetrating but smooth timbre, precise intonation, and impeccable sense of rhythm.

SELECTED RECORDINGS

Duos: with W. Norris: *Drifting* (1974, Enja 2044); with R. Hanna: *Sir Elf + 1* (1977, Choice 1018); with T. Flanagan: *Ballads and Blues* (1978, Enja 3031)

As sideman: S. Grappelli: *Stephane Grappelli Meets the Rhythm Section* (1973, BL 183); New York Jazz Quartet: *Surge* (1977, Enja 2094); Z. Sims: *Warm Tenor* (1978, Pablo 2310831); T. Montoliu: *I Wanna Talk About you* (1980, Ste. 1137); J. Abercrombie: *M* (1980, ECM 1191); P. Adams: *Urban Dreams* (1981, PAlt 8009)

BIBLIOGRAPHY

Feather–Gitler '70s
J. Solothurnmann: "Into Different Things: an Interview with George Mraz," *JF* [intl edn], no.29 (1974), 46
H. Nolan: "Profile: George Mraz," *DB*, xlii/6 (1975), 26

BARRY KERNFELD

Mucci, Lou(is Raphael) (*b* Syracuse, NY, 13 Dec 1909). Trumpeter. He studied baritone horn, played professionally from the age of ten, and took up trumpet six years later. He played and recorded in Chicago with Red Norvo and Mildred Bailey (1937), then joined Glenn Miller as lead trumpeter (1938–9). He performed and recorded with Bob Chester (1941–2), Claude Thornhill (1942, 1946–*c*1948), and Hal McIntyre (1942–3), and recorded with Benny Goodman (1945). He made recordings as a member of orchestras led by Artie Shaw (1950) and Buddy DeFranco (1951), belonged to the music staff at CBS for four years (from 1951), then recorded with Gunther Schuller (1957), Billy Butterfield (1957–8), and John Lewis (1962), and as a soloist in small groups led by John LaPorta (1954–6, including *Conceptions*, 1956, Fan. 3228). As a member of the Gil Evans Orchestra he recorded with Helen Merrill (1956), Miles Davis (1957–62), and Kenny Burrell (1964). (*FeatherE*)

Muffle Jaws. Nickname of ELMER CHAMBERS.

Mug. Nickname of MULGREW MILLER.

Muhammad, Idris [Morris, Leo] (*b* New Orleans, 13 Nov 1939). Drummer. He began playing drums when he was eight years old, and was performing in jazz bands by the age of 16. From 1962 to 1967 he played soul music, working with the singers Sam Cooke and Jerry Butler (1962–5), and performing with the group the Impressions; he was also a member of Lou Donaldson's groups (1965–7). He played for the musical *Hair* (1969–73) and at the same time was drummer in the house band for the Prestige label (1970–72), playing mainly soul jazz, and recording as both a sideman and a leader. Later he recorded rhythm-and-blues and jazz albums for other companies, accompanied the popular singer Roberta Flack (1973–7), led his own band (1977–8), and worked with Johnny Griffin (1978–9) and Pharoah Sanders (from 1980). Muhammad was one of the most innovative drummers in black popular music of the 1960s; his playing is always rhythmically infectious, whatever the style.

SELECTED RECORDINGS

As leader: *Kabsha* (*c*1980, The. 110)

As sideman: J. Griffin: *NYC Underground* (1979, Gal. 5132); P. Sanders: *Journey to the One* (*c*1980, The. 108–9)

BIBLIOGRAPHY

Feather–Gitler '70s

Muhiddin, Ahmed. *See* RATIP, AHMED.

Mukai, Shigeharu (*b* Nagoya, Japan, 21 Jan 1949). Japanese trombonist. He left Doshisha University, Kyoto, to embark on a career as a musician, working with the alto saxophonist Yoshio Otomo, Ryo Kawasaki, and Hiroshi Fukumura. He then formed his own group and won the prize of the first Shinjuku Jazz Festival. Later he worked with the group Spik and Span, recorded with Terumasa Hino in 1975, and played with Kazumi Watanabe in the 1980s.

SELECTED RECORDINGS

(recorded for Columbia–Better Days unless otherwise indicated)

For my Little Bird (1974, Col. YZ7010); *Mukai Kaze* (1975, Col. YQ7516); *Favorite Time* (1976, Tei. GM5007); *Spacing Out* (1977, UX7582); *Hip Cruiser* (1978, YX7588); *Pleasure* (1980, YX7266); *Orissa* (1982, YF7053); *Japonesia* (1984, YF7087)

YOZO IWANAMI

Muldaur [née D'Amato], **Maria (Grazia Rosa Domenica)** (*b* New York, 12 Sept 1943). Singer. From 1964 to 1969 she toured and recorded with a jug band led by the guitarist and singer Jim Kweskin, singing and playing kazoo and blues fiddle. Although she was known primarily as a pop singer she made several recordings in the 1970s that were influenced by jazz; the sidemen for her album *Waitress in a Donut Shop* (1974, Rep. 2194) included Harry Edison, Dennis Budimir, Red Callender, Roger Kellaway, Snooky Young, Bud Shank, and Ray Brown. In 1974 Muldaur sang in an all-star band led by Benny Carter, and the following year performed with him at the Newport (New York) and Montreux jazz festivals. Her later work as a leader has been only indirectly related to jazz although in 1987 she sang in a jazz festival in San Francisco.

BIBLIOGRAPHY

Feather–Gitler '70s
N. Hentoff: "Her Heart Belongs to Pop – and Jazz, Folk, Rock, Country, Blues . . .," *New York Times* (8 Dec 1974), §2, p.1

Mule (i). Nickname of PERRY BRADFORD.

Mule (ii). Nickname of MAJOR HOLLEY.

Mullen, Jim [James] (*b* Glasgow, 2 Nov 1945). Scottish electric guitarist. He first worked professionally as a double bass player, performing and recording commercially-oriented music. In the mid-1960s he played his first important engagements as a guitarist with his own trios in Glasgow. He traveled in 1969 to London, where he worked chiefly with rhythm-and-blues and pop musicians. Later he toured the USA with a soul and funk group, the Average White Band, worked with Herbie Mann (1975–6), then returned to the UK. With Dick Morrissey, a former colleague from the Average White Band, he formed Morrissey–Mullen in the mid-1970s; this group gained a large following and made several recordings (including *Badness*, 1981, Beggar's Banquet 27) before disbanding in 1985. He also worked with the group PAZ and recorded with Mike Carr (1979) and Hal Singer and Jimmy Witherspoon (both 1981). Mullen plays with his thumb in a manner indebted to Wes Montgomery; his style contains elements of bop and the blues.

BIBLIOGRAPHY

D. Sigerson: "Mullen/Morrissey: Collegiate Theatre, London," *MM*, liii (9 Dec 1978), 49 [review]

C. May: "Chitterlings, Hog Maws . . .," *Black Music & Jazz Review*, ii/5 (1979), 22

S. Britt: "Jim Mullen," *The Wire*, no.15 (1985), 36

STAN BRITT

Mullens, Moon [Ed(ward)] (*b* Mayhew, MS, 11 May 1916; *d* 7 April 1977). Trumpeter. He grew up in Chicago, where he played with many local bands, including one led by Frankie "Half Pint" Jaxon. After moving to New York he worked with Chris Columbus and joined Hot Lips Page's big band, with which he made his first recordings, in 1938. He then played with Earl Bostic, but rejoined Columbus in 1941. A period with Benny Carter was interrupted by military service; after leaving Carter he was a member of Louis Armstrong's big band (1946–7). Thereafter Mullens played with Cab Calloway and Joe Thomas (iii), and from 1949 to 1959 worked intermittently with various groups led by Lionel Hampton. He played on the album *Lionel Hampton Big Band* (1955, Clef 670), and for the same session arranged the piece *G. H. Q.*, later issued on *The Genius of Lionel Hampton* (Verve 8215). His last major association was with Duke Ellington (1959–61), after which he left music to run a photography business. Mullens was a well-respected player, but he never led his own groups, and as a sideman he rarely took solos. (*ChiltonW*; *FeatherE*)

SCOTT YANOW

Müller, Werner (*b* Berlin, 2 Aug 1920). German bandleader, arranger, and trombonist. He studied violin and trombone and after military service he joined Kutte Widmann as trombonist and arranger (1946); *Flamingo* (1947, Odeon 31833) is a notable example of Widmann's recordings of Müller's arrangements. In 1948 he was appointed leader of the RIAS Tanzorchester, with which he made recordings (including *How High the Moon*, 1951, Pol. 48557); among its members were the soloists Rolf Kühn (clarinet), Hans Berry and Macky Kaspar (trumpet), Bon Henders (trombone), and, in the early 1950s, Fritz Schulz-Reichel (piano). Müller toured Japan in 1958 and later became leader of the Cologne WDR Tanzorchester (1967). His best jazz recordings date from the period 1950 to 1957. (Liner notes, *Werner Müller und sein Orchester*, Pol. 2459031, *c*1978)

RAINER E. LOTZ

Mulligan, Gerry [Gerald Joseph; Jeru] (*b* New York, 6 April 1927). Baritone saxophonist and arranger. He grew up in Philadelphia, and first learned piano, which he still plays in public

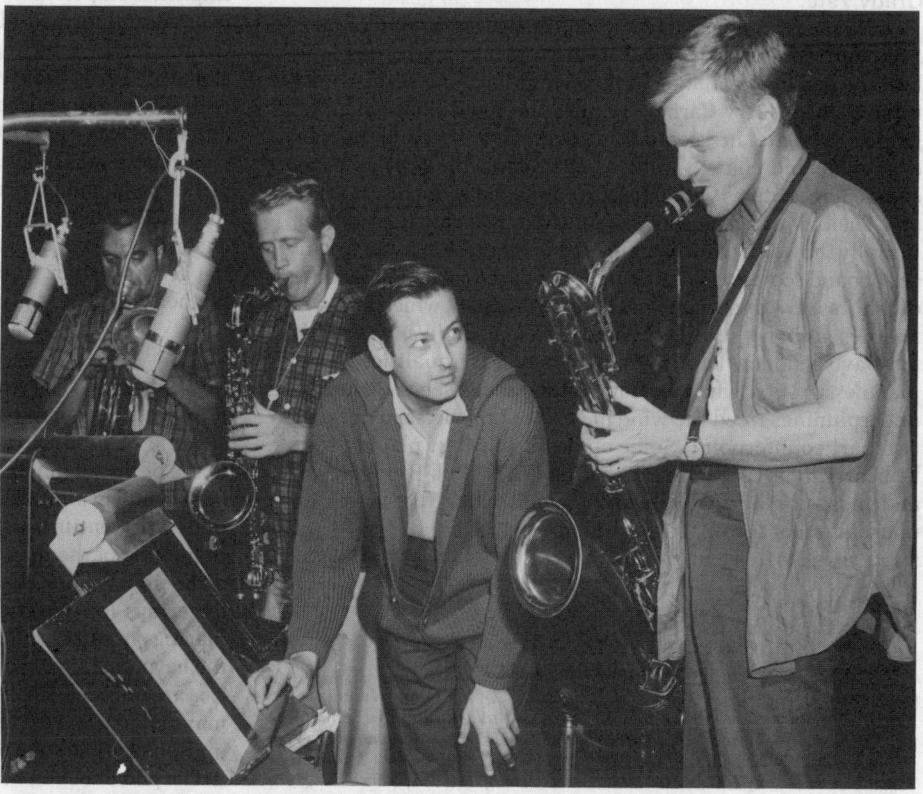

Gerry Mulligan (baritone saxophone) with (left to right) Buddy Childers (valve trombone), Bill Perkins (tenor saxophone), and André Previn at a recording session, 1957

occasionally. While in his teens he wrote arrangements for Johnny Warrington's radio band (1944) and played reed instruments professionally. After moving to New York in 1946 he joined Gene Krupa's big band as staff arranger, attracting attention with his *Disc Jockey Jump* (1947, Col. 37589). He then became involved with the nascent cool-jazz movement in New York, taking part in the performances (1948) and recording sessions (1949–50) of Miles Davis's nonet and contributing scores to the big bands of Elliot Lawrence and Claude Thornhill. By this time he was specializing on baritone saxophone and playing in groups with Kai Winding and others. He also wrote scores for Stan Kenton's band and recorded with his own tentet (1951), which was modeled on Davis's ensemble.

In 1952 Mulligan, then based in Los Angeles, formed his first "pianoless" quartet, with Chet Baker on trumpet. The group was instantaneously successful, and brought Baker and Mulligan international acclaim. Mulligan led a new tentet and various versions of the quartet throughout the mid-1950s; he made a sensational appearance at the Salle Pleyel, Paris, in 1954 and began dominating jazz opinion polls for his instrument. In 1960 he organized his own 13-piece concert jazz band with which he toured Europe in that year and Japan in 1964. After it disbanded he became an active sideman, working often with Dave Brubeck (1968–72) and as a freelance arranger for other jazz groups. He formed a new 14-piece big band, the Age of Steam, in 1972, and was artist-in-residence at Miami University in 1974. From 1974 to 1977 Mulligan led a sextet that included Dave Samuels, and during this period he worked regularly in New York and Italy; around the same time he began playing soprano saxophone. He formed a 14-piece band in 1978, and toured with it into the following year. During the early 1980s he made recordings as a leader in New York that involved experiments with a 20-piece big band (1980) and electronic instruments (1982–3), but in 1986 he returned to a more familiar format as the leader of a quintet with Scott Hamilton and Grady Tate.

Mulligan is among the most versatile figures in modern jazz. Although slow to develop as an instrumentalist, he has long been recognized as the most important baritone saxophonist in jazz since Harry Carney. Besides the cool idiom which he helped to create, he is equally at home in a big-band, bop, or even dixieland context (playing clarinet in the last), and his excellent recordings with musicians as varied as Johnny Hodges and Thelonious Monk show an unusual musical adaptability. Initially, however, Mulligan made his reputation as an arranger of band scores with intricate inner parts, careful balancing of timbres, low dynamics, and light swing, all of which features are present in his settings of *Jeru*, *Godchild*, and *Venus de Milo* for Davis's nonet. Later he abstracted these qualities in his pianoless groups, where the low volume and absence of chordal underpinnings freed the wind players to improvise in delicate two-part counterpoint. Some of Mulligan's best playing may be heard in his recordings with Chet Baker, Bob Brookmeyer, and most notably Paul Desmond, with whom he shares an unusual talent for improvised countermelody.

See also BLUES, §11; for further illustrations *see* JAZZ (i), fig.6, and RECORDING, fig.5.

SELECTED RECORDINGS

* – composed by Mulligan

† – arranged by Mulligan

As leader: *Line for Lyons/Carioca (1952, Fan. 522); My Funny Valentine/*Bark for Barksdale (1952, Fan. 525); *Gerry Mulligan and his Ten-tette* (1953, Cap. H439), incl. *Rocker, *Walkin' Shoes; [*Paris Concert*] (1954, Vogue 7381, 7383), incl. *Five Brothers; *Presenting the Gerry Mulligan Sextet* (1955, EmA 36056); *Desmond Meets Mulligan* (1957, Verve 8246); *Concert Jazz Band* (1960, Verve 68388), incl. *Bweebida, bwobbida, *Django's Castle; *Jeru* (1962, Col. CS8732); *Idle Gossip* (1976, Chi. 155); *Little Big Horn* (c1983, GRP 91003); *Gerry Mulligan Meets Scott Hamilton* (1986, Conc. 300)

As sideman: M. Davis: *Jeru/†Godchild (1949, Cap. 60005); Boplicity/Israel (1949, Cap. 60011); *Venus de Milo/†Darn that Dream (1949–50, Cap. 1221); P. Desmond: *Two of a Mind* (1962, RCA LSP2624)

BIBLIOGRAPHY

A. Morgan and R. Horricks: *Gerry Mulligan: a Biography, Appreciation, Record Survey and Discography* (London, 1958)

M. Harrison: "An Ensemble Style for Jazz," *These Jazzmen of our Times*, ed. R. Horricks and others (London, 1959), 68

L. Feather: "Gerry Mulligan," *DB*, xxvii (1960), no.11, p.22; no.12, p.20

M. Harrison: "Gerry Mulligan," *JR*, iii/7 (1960), 23

M. James: *Ten Modern Jazzmen: an Appraisal of the Recorded Work of Ten Modern Jazzmen* (London, 1960), 93

G. Lees: "Gerry Mulligan: a Writer's Credo," *DB*, xxx/2 (1963), 19

H. Frost: "Big Band, Soft Sell," *DB*, xxxi/10 (1964), 19

W. F. Mellers: *Music in a New Found Land: Themes and Developments in the History of American Music* (London, 1964/R1975), 357

J. Goldberg: *Jazz Masters of the Fifties* (New York and London, 1965/R1980), 9

L. Tomkins: "The Gerry Mulligan Story," *CI*, vii (1969), no.8, p.6; no.9, p.17; no.10, p.13

J. Burns: "Gerry Mulligan: the Formative Years," *J&B*, i/1 (1972), 9

P. Willard: "Mulligan Full Steam Ahead," *DB*, xli/17 (1974), 18

A. Smith: "Jeru's Views," *DB*, xliii/13 (1976), 13

A. Tercinet: "Discographie de Gerry Mulligan," *Jh*, no.335 (1977), 25; no.336 (1977), 21

I. Kendall: "Mulligan's Due," *JJI*, xxxi/1–2 (1978), 30

R. Brown: "Gerry Mulligan: Cool Charts, Bearish Tone," *DB*, xlvi/11 (1979), 12

G. Endress: *Jazz Podium: Musiker über sich selbst* (Stuttgart, Germany, 1980), 144

H. Hellhund: *Cool Jazz: Grundzüge seiner Entstehung und Entwicklung* (Mainz, Germany, 1985), 149–204, 262

R. Horricks: *Gerry Mulligan's Ark* (London, 1986) [incl. discography by T. Middleton]

——: "Gerry Mulligan: Three Frontier Posts," *JJI*, xxxix/7 (1986), 8

L. Tomkins: "The Classic Interview: Gerry Mulligan," *CI*, xxiv/10 (1987), 16

J. BRADFORD ROBINSON

Mulligan, Mick [Michael] (*b* Harrow, England, 24 Jan 1928). English trumpeter and bandleader. He taught himself trumpet in 1948 and formed his Magnolia Jazz Band, which featured George Melly, later that year. After the band became professional in 1950 it toured, broadcast, performed on television, and made many successful recordings (including *Young and Healthy*, 1958, Saga 7020); it also worked with visiting American blues and gospel singers. It was later re-formed as a six-piece group and known as Mick Mulligan's Jazz Band, and by the late 1950s it had become one of the most popular and charismatic jazz bands in Great Britain. Mulligan disbanded the group in 1962 and worked as a part-time musician for a further year. (G. Melly: *Owning Up*, London, 1965)

DIGBY FAIRWEATHER

Multiphonics. The simultaneous sounding of several (usually no more than four) notes on an instrument normally considered capable of producing only one at a time, or with the voice. Some of the techniques needed to produce multiphonics were known and exploited by woodwind and brass players from the mid-19th century. These include exceptional relaxation or tightening of the lips, a change or unconventional positioning of the embouchure, a decrease or increase of air pressure, unusual fingerings (on woodwind instruments, *see* FALSE FINGERING), playing one pitch while humming another, and blowing between the harmonics (on brass instruments). The additional frequencies are not necessarily a fundamental and upper partials: they may or may not be accompanied by the production of summation or difference tones.

The phenomenon has been used in jazz since Illinois Jacquet

pioneered it in the 1940s. The most important exponent is the trombonist Albert Mangelsdorff, a startling example being his playing of the theme of Duke Ellington's *Mood Indigo* in three-part harmony on the album *The Wide Point* (1975, MPS 2022569-0). Among others who have employed multiphonics in their playing are Albert Ayler, Anthony Braxton, Roland Kirk, Yusef Lateef, Pharoah Sanders, and Archie Shepp (reeds) and Roswell Rudd and Paul Rutherford (brass). Bobby McFerrin sings multiphonics, producing, for example, a descending phrase in parallel 6ths.

BIBLIOGRAPHY

B. Bartolozzi: *New Sounds for Woodwind*, ed. R. Smith Brindle (London, New York, and Toronto, 1967, 2/1982)
A. Blatter: *Instrumentation/Orchestration* (New York and London, 1980)

CLIFFORD BEVAN

Multitrack recording. A term applied to sound-recording techniques in which separate tracks are recorded simultaneously or successively and then combined in the studio; *see* RECORDING, §§I, 3, and II, 7.

Mumbles. Nickname of CLARK TERRY.

Mumford, John (T.) (*b* London, 22 Sept 1940). English trombonist. A self-taught musician, he first played in bands led by the clarinetist Teddy Layton and the trumpeter Trevor Williams, and in 1959 joined Bruce Turner's Jump Band, with which he recorded (1959–61) and appeared in the film *Living Jazz* (1961). He then turned to freelance work and played with the drummer John Cox (recording in 1962), Graham Collier, the New Jazz Orchestra, and others. From 1969 he worked with cabaret bands and popular singers, later touring Europe and the USA. He performed and recorded with the trumpeter Bob Wallis in Zurich (1975), where he later made his home (1980–84). In the mid-1980s he has worked in both London and on the Continent. A good example of Mumford's playing may be heard on the album *From the First Time I Met You* (1977, Affinity 5), recorded with the saxophonist Jimmy Jewell and his group Ears.

NEVIL SKRIMSHIRE

Mundy, Jimmy [James] (*b* Cincinnati, 28 June 1907; *d* New York, 24 April 1983). Arranger and tenor saxophonist. He first trained as a classical violinist, and when still in his teens toured with an evangelist's orchestra, playing violin and tenor saxophone. From 1926 he worked in Washington, where he first learned to arrange music for big bands. In 1932, while a member of a band led by the drummer Tommy Myles, he was engaged by Earl Hines, who heard the band perform Mundy's composition *Cavernism* (later credited on recordings to Hines). The solos Mundy recorded on tenor saxophone with Hines exhibit a gruff and impassioned tone resembling that of Coleman Hawkins, and his arrangements offered imaginative, detailed variations on swinging riffs. In 1936 Mundy became staff arranger for Benny Goodman (who had recorded his version of *Madhouse* the previous year) and wrote many fine pieces for the band, such as *Swingtime in the Rockies* (1936) and *Solo Flight* (1941). His arrangements were also recorded by other leaders, including Gene Krupa (1938–9), Count Basie (1940–47), and Dizzy Gillespie (1949). In 1937 Mundy recorded as the leader of a small group (*I surrender, dear/Ain't Misbehavin'*, Var. 598), and in 1939 he briefly led his own band. From the 1950s he was active in jazz only occasionally, but wrote arrangements for and led studio orchestras in undistinguished recordings with famous swing and bop soloists.

SELECTED ARRANGEMENTS

* – with Mundy as sideman

Recorded by E. Hines: *Copenhagen (1934, Decca 337); Cavernism (1934, Decca 183)
Recorded by B. Goodman: Madhouse (1935, Vic. 25268); Swingtime in the Rockies (1936, Vic. 25355); Sing, sing, sing (1937, Vic. 36205); Solo Flight (1941, Col. 36684)
Recorded by C. Basie: Feather Merchant (1941, Col. 36845)

BIBLIOGRAPHY

ChiltonW
Arnold Shaw: *The Street that Never Slept: New York's Fabled 52nd Street* (New York, 1971/R1977 as *52nd Street: the Street of Jazz*), 94
S. Dance: *The World of Earl Hines* (New York, 1977) [interviews], 197
H. Panassié and M. Gautier: *Dictionnaire du jazz* (Paris, rev. and enlarged 3/1980)
D. R. Connor: *The Record of a Legend: Benny Goodman* (n.p. [New York], 1984)

BARRY KERNFELD

Muniak, Janusz (*b* Kraków, Poland, June 1941). Polish tenor and soprano saxophonist and flutist. He played violin at school and took up tenor saxophone in 1959. He made his professional début in Tomasz Stańko's free-jazz group Jazz Darings (1963), then played with Andrzej Trzaskowski, recording with his quintet (1964–5) and sextet (1966). In 1965 he moved to Warsaw, where he became a regular member of the orchestra of the Polish Radio Jazz Studio led by Jan Wróblewski, recording with it in 1969. From 1970 to 1974 he often played and recorded with Stańko. He has made many tours of Europe, and in 1976 accompanied Charlie Ventura on a tour of Poland. From that year he has led his own quintet, with which he recorded *Question Mark* (1978, Muza 1616); in 1982 he recorded as the leader of a quartet. Muniak is at home both in modern mainstream jazz and in free jazz.

BIBLIOGRAPHY

J. Byrczek: "Eurojazz Personalities: Poland," *JF* [intl edn], no.17 (1972), 85
K. Brodacki: "Janusz Muniak Now," *JF* [intl edn], no.49 (1977), 40 [incl. discography]

WOLFRAM KNAUER

Munn, Billy [William] (*b* Glasgow, 12 May 1911). Scottish pianist and arranger. After conservatory training he joined Jack Hylton's big band as a pianist and arranger (1929); he remained with Hylton until 1936, making a number of recordings. He also recorded during the 1930s with Spike Hughes (1932) and Benny Carter (1936). He played with the band of Sydney Lipton (1936–40), toured with Stephane Grappelli, and accompanied Louis Armstrong and Coleman Hawkins in England and Wingy Manone in the USA (1935–9). Munn recorded with such musicians as George Chisholm (1944) and, after the war, led his own group at the Orchid Room, Mayfair (1945–8). He directed Maurice Winnick's orchestra at Ciro's, London (1948–9), and worked again as a leader at the Imperial Hotel, Torquay (1949–79); his recordings are well represented by *St. Louis Blues* (1949, Harmony A1008). From 1979 he played mainly as a soloist. Munn was a joint founder, with Mark White and Harry Parry, of the BBC radio program "Jazz Club," of which he was also, for a short period, music director (1946–9).

Munn should not be confused with the American soul-jazz organist and electric pianist of the same name, who recorded with Johnny Lytle in New York (1969 and 1971).

DIGBY FAIRWEATHER

Munro, Charlie [Charles Robert] (*b* Christchurch, New Zealand, 22 May 1917; *d* Sydney, 9 Dec 1985). Australian reed player. He became a professional musician at the age of 17 and settled in Sydney in 1938. He joined the bands of Myer Norman and Wally Parks, and played on ships, in nightclub and theater groups, and then in army entertainment units. After he was discharged he played with the trumpeter and trombonist Wally Norman at the Roosevelt club in Sydney. In 1950 he left to work with the bandleader Bob Gibson and at this time resumed his study of the cello. He was associated with the dance band of the Australian Broadcasting Company as a performer, composer, and arranger (1954–76). At the same time he participated in important experimental jazz workshops, which combined free and modal jazz with non-Western music in performances and recordings; he is heard to advantage on *Eastern Horizons* (1967, Phi. JS020). At the end of his career he led his own groups and worked with the singer Georgina de Leon. Besides his main instruments, Munro also played flute and cello.

BIBLIOGRAPHY

A. Bisset: *Black Roots, White Flowers: a History of Jazz in Australia* (Sydney, 1976), 145

B. Johnson: "Munro, Charles Robert (Charlie)," *The Oxford Companion to Australian Jazz* (Melbourne, Australia, 1987)

BRUCE JOHNSON

Muranyi, Joe [Joseph Paul] (*b* Martins Ferry, OH, 14 Jan 1928). Clarinetist, soprano saxophonist, and singer. He studied with Lennie Tristano and later played clarinet for three years in an air force band. After his discharge he worked in New York with many prominent dixieland groups, including those of Jimmy McPartland, Yank Lawson, Max Kaminsky, Bobby Hackett, and Eddie Condon. He recorded with the Red Onion Jazz Band (1952–4) and in a quintet with Danny Barker (1958), where his playing may be heard to good effect. In 1963 he formed the Village Stompers, a traditional jazz group that toured the USA and Japan. He also toured extensively with the Louis Armstrong All Stars (1967–71) and was the last clarinetist to perform and record regularly with this group. After leaving Armstrong Muranyi returned to New York to work and record with Roy Eldridge. In 1975 he played and sang with the World's Greatest Jazz Band, and in 1977 he recorded with Cozy Cole and Lionel Hampton. Muranyi has also worked as producer for several major record companies.

SELECTED RECORDINGS

As leader with H. Hall: *Clarinet Wobble* (1970, Fat Cat's Jazz 118)

As sideman: Red Onion Jazz Band: *New Orleans Encore* (1952, Riv. 2503) incl. Creole Belles, Misery Blues; D. Barker: *Fabulous Banjo* (1958, Period 1205); L. Armstrong: *Louis Armstrong and the All Stars* (1968, Bruns. 754169)

BIBLIOGRAPHY

FeatherE; *Feather '60s*; *Feather–Gitler '70s*

C. Deffaa: "Joe's Jazz Journey," *MR*, xii/11 (1985), 1

RAYMOND J. GARIGLIO

Murphy, Mark (Howe) (*b* Syracuse, NY, 14 March 1932). Singer. He grew up in a musical family, and began performing at the age of 16. He toured and recorded in the USA during the late 1950s and early 1960s, and by 1962 had appeared in several television shows, including Steve Allen's "Jazz Scene USA." That same year he recorded the album *That's how I Love the Blues* (Riv. 9441) with Al Cohn as his arranger and director. In 1963 Murphy moved to London, and during the 1960s toured in Europe; he occasionally made radio and television broadcasts and recorded under his own name. After returning to the USA in 1973 he continued to perform, record, and tour internationally into the 1980s. Murphy is also a scat singer; he has composed and recorded vocalese, including *Stolen Moments*, which was issued on the album of the same name (1978, Muse 5102).

BIBLIOGRAPHY

Feather '60s; *Feather–Gitler '70s*

G. Lees: "Mark Murphy: the Slow Way up," *DB*, xxx/29 (1963), 20

T. Schnabel: "Mark Murphy," *DB*, xlvii/2 (1980), 52

Murphy, Spud [Lyle] (*b* Salt Lake City, 19 Aug 1908). Arranger, composer, and alto saxophonist. He played in dance bands from 1927 and recorded as an oboist with Slim Lamar (1928). He was an arranger and saxophonist for Austin Wylie (1930–31), Jan Garber (1931–2), Mal Hallett (1933), and Joe Haymes (1934), and a staff arranger for Benny Goodman (1935–7); he also wrote arrangements for Glen Gray (1935–7). From 1938 he led a conventional swing orchestra that made several recordings in 1938–9, including his version of *Quaker City Jazz* (1938, Decca 2040). Around the early 1940s he led an avant-garde big band that was commercially unsuccessful. He then devoted most of his time to arranging, working for Goodman, among others, but in the 1950s he led a small ensemble that recorded his own third-stream jazz compositions (1955, 1957, with Murphy playing celesta).

BIBLIOGRAPHY

FeatherE; *Feather '60s*

A. McCarthy: *Big Band Jazz* (New York and London, 1974), 292

Murphy, Turk [Melvin Edward Alton] (*b* Palermo, CA, 16 Dec 1915; *d* San Francisco, 30 May 1987). Trombonist and bandleader. A stalwart of traditional jazz in California, he first came to fame in the band led by Lu Watters in the early 1940s (for illustration *see* WATTERS, LU). Murphy formed his own band in 1947 and continued to lead it into the 1980s. The band was based in San Francisco, where it had a permanent booking for many years at a club called Earthquake McGoon's. It also worked occasionally on the East Coast, toured Australia and Europe in 1974, appeared in the Netherlands at the Oude Stijl Jazz Festival, Breda, in 1981, and performed in Carnegie Hall in 1987. Murphy's trombone playing was robust and full of good humor; the repertory of his band blended jazz classics of the 1920s with well-known ballads and original compositions. The consistency of Murphy's style is clearly apparent on the huge number of recordings that his band, with various changes of personnel, made from 1950 to 1980. In 1986 he opened his Traditional Jazz Museum in the Front Page, San Francisco.

SELECTED RECORDINGS

Sidewalk Blues (1953, Col. CL6324); Maryland, my Maryland (1955, Col. 40586); *Music for Losers* (1957, Verve 1013), incl. The Yama Yama Man; *Turk Murphy at the Newport Jazz Festival 1957* (1957, Verve 8232), incl. Weary Blues; *Turk Murphy* (1972, GHB 93), incl. Wild Man Blues

BIBLIOGRAPHY

E. Condon and R. Gehman, eds.: *Eddie Condon's Treasury of Jazz* (New York, 1956/*R*1975), 176

R. J. Gleason, ed.: *Jam Session: an Anthology of Jazz* (New York and London, 1958), 116

R. D. Johnson: "Turk," *MR*, iv/9 (1977), 6

J. Goggin: *Turk Murphy: Just for the Record* (San Leandro, 1982) [incl. discography]

JOHN CHILTON

Murray, David (*b* Berkeley, CA, 19 Feb 1955). Tenor saxophonist and leader. He first took lessons in stride and ragtime piano, then from the age of nine played alto saxophone, accompanying his mother, a renowned gospel pianist, in church. As a teenager he was one of the leaders of a soul group and emulated bop and swing tenor saxophonists. At Pomona College he studied and played with Stanley Crouch, Bobby Bradford, and Arthur Blythe, who introduced him to free jazz (1973–5). After moving to New York (1975) he formed the WORLD SAXO-

PHONE QUARTET in late 1976 with Oliver Lake, Julius Hemphill, and Hamiet Bluiett. Besides his activities with this group he has led a number of others, which have made international tours; among the avant-garde jazz musicians who have worked with him are Olu Dara, Lawrence "Butch" Morris, Art Davis, Ed Blackwell, and members of the group Air. As a sideman he performed and recorded with Sunny Murray (1976) and James "Blood" Ulmer (1978–81), and has formed lasting associations with Jack DeJohnette's group Special Edition (from 1979) and John Carter's quartet Clarinet Summit (from 1981), in which he plays bass clarinet.

Murray was at first compared with Albert Ayler, but whereas Ayler found the synthesis of different styles difficult Murray has succeeded in amalgamating soul jazz and free jazz in his playing without weakening either. Murray is not afraid to employ conventional bop formulas or to repeat and develop a tuneful, bluesy motif, but he effectively combines such elements with noise, wide leaps, harsh dissonances, and other extreme devices to achieve contrasts and climaxes, as for example in his tenor saxophone solo on the title track of the album *Murray's Steps*.

SELECTED RECORDINGS

As unaccompanied soloist: *Solo Live* (1977, Cecma 1001–2); *Sur-real Saxophone* (1978, Horo 09)

Duos with J. Newton: *Solomon's Sons* (1977, Cir. [G] 5)

As leader: *Flowers for Albert* (1976, IndN 1026); *3D Family* (1978, HH U–V); *Sweet Lovely* (1979, BS 0039); *Home* (1981, BS 0055); *Murray's Steps* (1982, BS 0065); *Live at Sweet Basil* (1984, BS 0085)

As sideman: S. Murray: *Live at the Moers Festival* (1979, Moers 1054); J. Carter: *Clarinet Summit* (1981, IndN 1062); J. DeJohnette: *Album Album* (1984, ECM 1280)

BIBLIOGRAPHY

P. Occhiogrosso: "Profile: Stanley Crouch–David Murray," *DB*, xliii/6 (1976), 38

L. Goddet: "David Murray," *Jh*, no.343 (1977), 11

F. Davis: "David Murray: Tenor Energy," *DB*, l/6 (1983), 24 [incl. discography]

G. Giddins: *Rhythm-a-ning: Jazz Tradition and Innovation in the '80s* (New York, and Oxford, England, 1985) [colln of previously pubd articles], 171

F. Davis: "The Tenor of these Times (David Murray)," *In the Moment: Jazz in the 1980s* (New York, and Oxford, England, 1986) [colln of previously pubd articles], 42

For further recordings and bibliography *see* WORLD SAXOPHONE QUARTET.

BARRY KERNFELD

Murray, Don(ald Leroy) (*b* Joliet, IL, 7 June 1904; *d* Los Angeles, 2 June 1929). Clarinetist and saxophonist. He played tenor saxophone with the New Orleans Rhythm Kings (*c*1923), then moved to Detroit, where until 1927 he played for Jean Goldkette (for illustration *see* BEIDERBECKE, BIX). During this period he also made recordings with Bix Beiderbecke (1925, 1927) and Frankie Trumbauer (including *Riverboat Shuffle*, 1927, OK 40822). His later work as a freelance included sessions with Joe Venuti (1927–8). He was a member of Adrian Rollini's short-lived big band (1927) and also played in theater orchestras on Broadway. Murray was performing in Ted Lewis's band for the film *Is Everybody Happy* at the time of his death. (W. K. Plath: "Don Murray: the Early Years (1904–1923)," *Sv*, no.122 (1985), 51)

based on *ChiltonW*

Murray, Sunny [James Marcellus Arthur] (*b* Idabel, OK, 21 Sept 1937). Drummer. He grew up in Philadelphia, played drums from the age of nine, and in 1956 moved to New York, where he worked with Henry "Red" Allen, Willie "the Lion" Smith, Jackie McLean, and Ted Curson. In 1959 he made the acquaintance of Cecil Taylor, under whose influence his playing moved closer to free jazz, but it was only after he heard John Coltrane's quartet and played with it informally in 1963 that he developed his own style. He performed with Albert Ayler (at intervals from around 1965 to around 1967) and made recordings as a leader from 1966. In the late 1970s, most notably on the LP *Apple Cores*, he modified his style somewhat, moving towards bop in an attempt to reach a wider audience. In the 1980s he led a quintet that included Grachan Moncur III, the alto saxophonist Steve Coleman, the pianist Curtis Clark, and the double bass player William Parker, another quintet that included two violins and two tenor saxophones, and various groups known as the Untouchable Factor. He also recorded again with Taylor (1980), and with the cellist David Eyges. Murray's playing, which is aggressive, fluid, and characterized by waves of cymbal sound and heavy punctuation by the bass drum and tom-toms, has exerted a strong influence on younger musicians. More than anyone else Murray was responsible for the development of the coloristic, unmetered style of free-jazz drumming in which the player, rather than marking time, contributes to the collective improvisation by accentuating freely and by exploring the timbres and pitches of the various components of the drum set.

SELECTED RECORDINGS

As leader: *Sunny Murray Quintet* (1966, ESP 1032); *Homage to Africa* (1969, BYG 529303); *Sunshine* (1969, BYG 529348); *Never Give a Sucker an Even Break* (1969, BYG 529332); *Apple Cores* (1978, Philly Jazz 1004)

As sideman: C. Taylor: *Live at the Cafe Montmartre* (1962, Fan. 86014); A. Ayler: *Bells* (1965, ESP 1010); A. Shepp: *Yasmina, a Black Woman* (1969, BYG 529304); D. Eyges: *Crossroads* (1981, Music Unlimited 7432)

BIBLIOGRAPHY

J. Cooke: "New York Nouvelle Vague, 8: Sunny Murray," *JM*, xiii/9 (1967), 13

L. Jones: *Black Music* (New York, 1967/*R*1980)

V. Wilmer: "Controlled Freedom is the Thing this Year," *DB*, xxxiv/6 (1967), 16

R. Levin: "Sunny Murray: the Continuous Crackling of Glass," *Black Giants*, ed. P. Rivelli and R. Levin (New York and Cleveland, 1970/*R*1980 as *Giants of Black Music*), 56

J. Cooke: "Sunny Murray in Paris," *J&B*, ii/10 (1973), 17

V. Wilmer: *As Serious as your Life: the Story of the New Jazz* (London, 1977, rev. 1980)

S. Weston: "Interview with Sunny Murray," *Cadence*, v/6 (1979), 14

M. Hames: *Albert Ayler, Sunny Murray, Cecil Taylor, Byard Lancaster and Kenneth Terroade on Disc and Tape* (Ferndown, England, 1983)

MICHAEL ULLMAN

Muse (i). Record label. It was established by the American Record Manufacturing Co. in Framingham, Massachusetts, in 1922. Its catalogue was derived chiefly from that of Cameo, but also contained material first issued on Banner, Emerson, and Grey Gull. (B. Rust: *The American Record Label Book*, New Rochelle, NY, 1978)

Muse (ii). Record company and label. A subsidiary of Blanchris, Inc., the company was established in New York in 1972 by Joe Fields. Don Schlitten, formerly the executive producer with Fields's earlier label, Cobblestone, joined Muse in the same capacity. The company has continued into the late 1980s to make new recordings of bop and related music; the catalogue includes important material by Mark Murphy and Sonny Stitt (both from 1972), Kenny Barron (1973-80), Willis "Gator" Jackson (from 1973), Woody Shaw (from 1974), Red Rodney (1975–9), Richie Cole and Houston Person (both from 1976), Morgana King (from 1977), Kenny Burrell, and Ricky Ford (from 1978). In 1973 Fields and Schlitten also founded ONYX, and recordings made by that company were issued by Muse until a disagreement between the two men caused the termination of the partnership in 1978. Thereafter Schlitten established Xanadu, and Fields managed Muse alone, engaging on a freelance basis such noted producers as Michael Cuscuna and Bob Porter. Around 1985 Muse acquired from Arista the Savoy catalogue, from which it has maintained an active programme of reissues; the company is also the distributor in the USA for the labels Enja and Sunnyside.

Musette. A small oboe of conical bore, without a reed-cap, pitched a 5th above the conventional oboe. It is 31 to 36 cm long, is made in two joints, and has seven finger-holes, a thumb-hole, and two vents in the bell. The musette employs a double reed that is thinner than that of the oboe and a fingering system similar to that of the saxophone and flute. It has a piercing, nasal sound; tightening or loosening of the embouchure produces wide variations in pitch. The best-known player of the musette in jazz is Dewey Redman; his approach to the instrument, which is characterized by many bent notes and glissandos, and, more generally, a non-Western conception of intonation, is well illustrated by the track *Image in Disguise* from his album *The Ear of the Behearer* (1973, Imp. 9250). An earlier, but undistinguished, example of musette playing may be heard on Albert Ayler's *The Last Album* (1969, Imp. 9208); on the track *Untitled duet* he improvises on the "bagpipe chanter" in a middle-eastern style which contrasts sharply with the rock electric guitar playing of Henry Vestine. The oboe known as the musette is unrelated to a small bagpipe of the same name, which has not been used in jazz.

BARRY KERNFELD

Musica Elettronica Viva. Group formed in Rome in 1966 by RICHARD TEITELBAUM and others for the production and performance of live electronic music.

Music, Inc. A cooperative bop quartet formed in 1969 by CHARLES TOLLIVER.

Musicraft. Record company and label. Founded in New York in 1937, the company recorded only classical music in the first four years of its existence, but during World War II began marketing popular styles. Jazz became an important element of the repertory after Albert Marx (a record producer who had directed Art Tatum's first sessions) joined the company as its artistic director in 1944. Musicraft bought Guild's catalogue in 1945, and reissued most of it the following year, thus making some of the earliest small-group and big-band bop sessions available to a wider audience. Among the many musicians who recorded new material for the company were Teddy Wilson, Artie Shaw, Duke Ellington, Georgie Auld, Dizzy Gillespie, and Slam Stewart. Sarah Vaughan had a contract with Musicraft for three years from 1946. During this period she made several recordings, including a remarkable pairing taken from a session of 1948 which, in order to circumvent the recording ban on instrumentalists then current, had only vocal accompaniment. By 1949 Musicraft had recorded more than a thousand items, most of which were jazz. The catalogue was sold in the early 1950s, and was eventually acquired by Pickwick International; some of the material appeared on cheap reissues in both the USA and the UK, but the selections were often chaotically ordered and contained little liner information. In the 1970s, however, the items by Gillespie were reissued by Phoenix, and later in the decade the label was revived by Marx, by then president of Trend and Discovery in Los Angeles. Many of the early sessions were then put out on LPs; two albums were devoted to valuable material by Auld which had to that date been hard to obtain.

MARK GARDNER

Musik Produktion Schwarzwald. *See* MPS.

Musso, Vido (William) (*b* Carrini, Sicily, 13 Jan 1913; *d* Rancho Mirage, CA, 9 Jan 1982). Tenor saxophonist. In 1920 his family emigrated to the USA and settled in Detroit, where he took up clarinet. He moved to Los Angeles in 1930 and played with Stan Kenton in several local orchestras. The two men founded a big band in 1936, but Musso left later the same year to work first with Benny Goodman (1936–7) and then with Gene Krupa (1938). He made repeated attempts between 1938 and 1947 to establish himself as a bandleader, but also played again with Goodman (1939, 1941–2) and with Harry James (1940–41), Woody Herman (1942–3), and Tommy Dorsey (1945). Most importantly, he spent two further periods with Kenton (1945–6, 1947), where his exuberant and uncomplicated improvisations and gruff, aggressive style made him extremely popular. After leaving Kenton, Musso played in southern California, and from 1957 worked in Las Vegas.

SELECTED RECORDINGS

As leader: Moose on the Loose/Vido in a jam (1946, Savoy 599)

As sideman: B. Goodman: Did you mean it? (1936, Vic. 25469); S. Kenton: Artistry Jumps (1945, Cap. 299); Painted Rhythm (1945, Cap. 250); Willie Smith: Glandular Activity (1945, Monarch 202); S. Kenton: Come back to Sorrento (1946, Cap. 286)

BIBLIOGRAPHY

ChiltonW

J. Burns: "Swing Tenors," *JJ*, xix/12 (1966), 13

W. F. Lee: *Stan Kenton: Artistry in Rhythm* (Los Angeles, 1980) [incl. discography]

BARRY KERNFELD

Mussolini [Full], Romano (*b* Carpena, Forlì, Italy, 26 Sept 1927). Italian pianist. His father was the Italian dictator Benito Mussolini; for this reason he found it expedient during the early part of his career to work under the pseudonym Romano Full. After recording with a group led by Nunzio Rotondo (1954) he gave a successful performance at the first Festival Internazionale del Jazz, San Remo, in a quintet with Rotondo and Gil Cuppini (1955). He led bop groups from 1956 to 1962 and performed and recorded with Carlo Loffredo (1957), Lars Gullin (1959), and others (from 1973). He also played with a number of American musicians and toured the USA. Mussolini is a refined, sensitive pianist who has been influenced chiefly by Oscar Peterson. A good example of his playing is his recording *Topsy* (1957, RCA LPM10010). (*FeatherE*)

ADRIANO MAZZOLETTI

Mussulli, Boots [Henry W.] (*b* Milford, MA, 18 Nov 1917; *d* Norfolk, MA, 23 Sept 1967). Alto and baritone saxophonist. He played with Teddy Powell (1943–4), and from 1944 to 1947 was alto saxophone soloist in the orchestra of Stan Kenton, with whom he toured in 1952 and 1954 (for illustration *see* KENTON, STAN). He performed and recorded with Vido Musso (1946–7) and, after joining Gene Krupa's group (1948), with Charlie Ventura's octet (1949). He also made recordings as the leader of a quintet and two quartets in 1954 (including *Stan Kenton Presents Boots Mussulli*, Cap. H6506), and performed and recorded in Boston with Serge Chaloff (1954), Toshiko Akiyoshi (1955), and Herb Pomeroy (1957). He later taught in Milford and formed the Milford Youth Band, which appeared at the Newport Jazz Festival in 1967. (*FeatherE*)

Mustafa-Zade, Vagif (*b* Baku, Azerbaijan SSR, 16 March 1940; *d* Tashkent, Uzbek SSR, 17 Dec 1979). Azerbaijan pianist and composer. He attended music school in Baku (graduated 1959), formed the trio Kavkaz in Tbilisi, Georgian SSR, and first gained prominence at the jazz festival in Tallinn, Estonian SSR (1967). He led the Azerbaijan Variety Orchestra (1969–70), with which he also performed as a soloist; in Baku he formed and led the groups Leili (1970–71), Sevil (1972–7), and Mugam (1977–9). His piano piece *Expecting Aziza* won the first prize at the competition for jazz compositions in Monaco (1979); he has also written two piano concertos and music for the theater and films. A good example of Mustafa-Zade's work is the album *Dzhazovïye kompozitsii* (Jazz compositions; 1980, Mel. C601227780). He was named a Merited Artist of the Azerbaijan SSR in 1979. (S. F. Starr: *Red and Hot: the Fate of Jazz in the Soviet Union, 1917–1980* (New York, and Oxford, England, 1983), 310)

WALTER OJAKÄÄR

Mute. A device used on a musical instrument to modify its timbre by reducing the intensity of certain partials and amplifying others. Additional effects of muting may include changes in pitch, reduction of volume, and increased directivity.

1. Introduction. 2. Mutes and muting techniques. 3. Use in jazz.

1. Introduction. In jazz the mute is associated principally with brass instruments, in particular the trumpet, cornet, and trombone, and several types of mute and methods of muting have been invented specifically for the playing of jazz. The muting of brass instruments is thus the subject of this article.

In instruments of the violin family, the mute takes the form of a weight (usually a pronged clamp) attached to the bridge, which creates a veiled sound. Muting of woodwind instruments is comparatively rare, though clarinetists, bassoonists, and saxophonists occasionally apply a cloth or other absorbent material to the bell of the instrument to achieve a muffled effect. Drums may be muted by employing an internal damper mechanism or by placing a cloth on the head; the latter method may also be used with the vibraphone, while felt dampers are employed with the celesta and tubular bells. The piano is "muted" by means of dampers or the una corda pedal. It is a common misconception that the purpose of a mute is to effect a reduction in volume; the only kind of mute of which this is strictly true is the "practice" mute, which decreases volume to a fraction of normal and which is not intended for use in performance.

2. Mutes and muting techniques. The brass instruments most commonly muted in jazz are the trumpet, cornet, and trombone; horns, flugelhorns, and tubas are seldom muted, though straight and bucket mutes are available for all three kinds of instrument and cup and harmon mutes for the flugelhorn. Mutes for brass instruments are inserted into or held over the end of the bell and function by obstructing in different ways the oscillations of the air column inside or outside the body of the instrument (or both). They are made from aluminum, brass, copper, wood, papier-mâché, cardboard, fiber, composition, polystyrene, or rubber, and some types are lined with plaster or stone. Methods of muting other than with a purpose-made mute involve the use of the player's hand, a piece of cloth, or some other device (see (k) to (n), also (i) and (j), below). The player positions his collection of mutes around him on the floor or hangs them on a stand in front of him.

Of the mutes described below, (a), (c), and (f) are in standard use, while (b), (d), and (g) to (k) are less common.

(a) Straight mute. The straight mute is conical (or when made of metal often pear-shaped), with the wider end closed; it is often lined with stone. It is inserted into the bell of the instrument, where longitudinal strips of cork hold it in position, allowing some air to pass between the walls of the instrument and those of the mute. The sound is pure, incisive when the player blows hard.

(b) Double mute. The double mute has the appearance of two straight mutes, one projecting from the other. It functions in a similar way to the straight mute, but the second tier, protruding from the instrument, means that the mute interferes

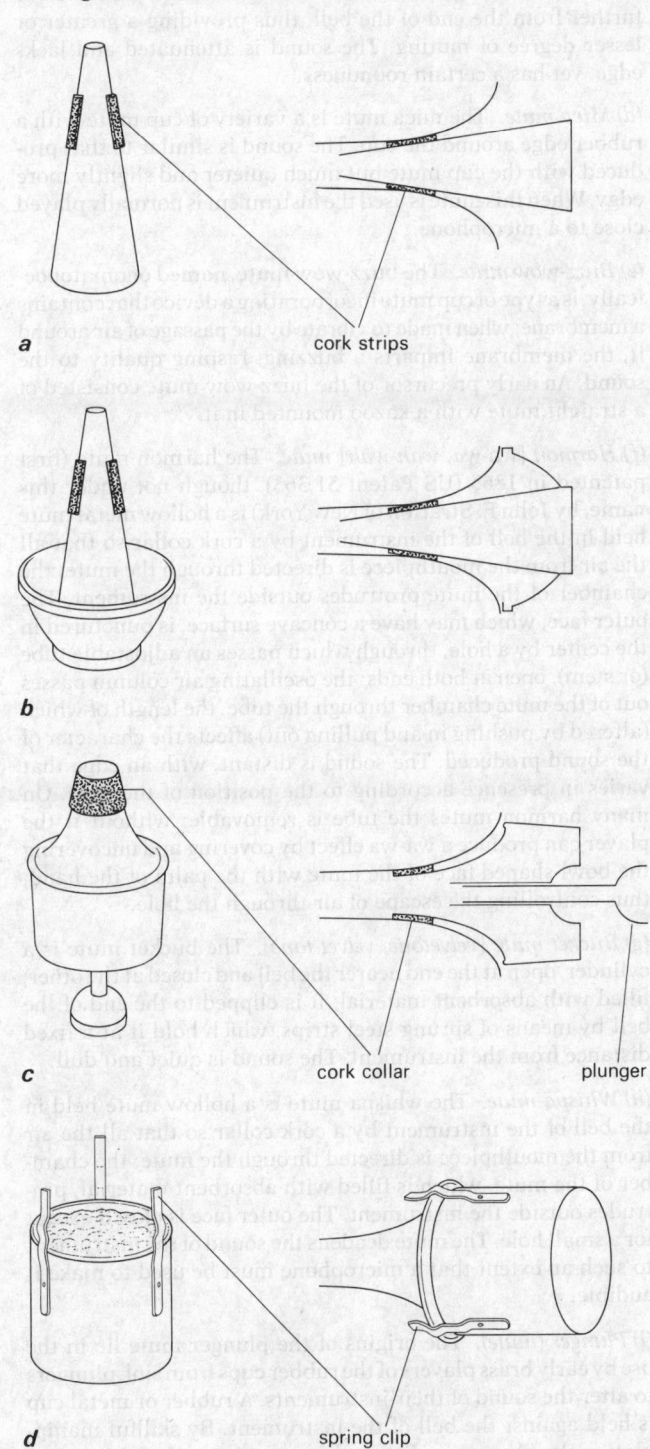

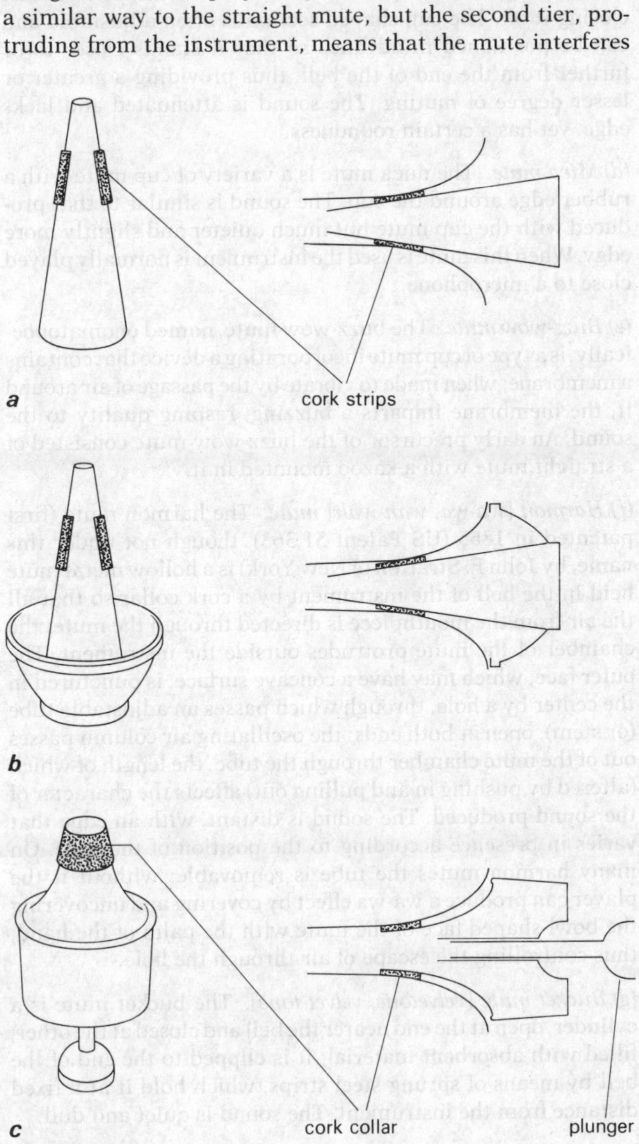

1. Standard mutes for brass instruments: (a) straight mute; (b) cup mute; (c) harmon mute; (d) bucket mute

with the air column outside as well as inside the bell. It produces a nasal yet resonant timbre. Various firms have manufactured double mutes under such names as clear-tone, solo-tone, and mega mute.

(c) Cup mute. The cup mute is essentially a straight mute, to the wide end of which is attached a cup-shaped section (usually lined with felt), which more or less covers the bell, almost closing it off. The cup-shaped section is often adjustable and can be positioned in advance so that it stands closer to or further from the end of the bell, thus providing a greater or lesser degree of muting. The sound is attenuated and lacks edge, yet has a certain roundness.

(d) Mica mute. The mica mute is a variety of cup mute with a rubber edge around the cup. The sound is similar to that produced with the cup mute but much quieter and slightly more edgy. When this mute is used the instrument is normally played close to a microphone.

(e) Buzz-wow mute. The buzz-wow mute, named onomatopoeically, is a type of cup mute incorporating a device that contains a membrane; when made to vibrate by the passage of air around it, the membrane imparts a buzzing, rasping quality to the sound. An early precursor of the buzz-wow mute consisted of a straight mute with a kazoo mounted in it.

(f) Harmon [*wa-wa, wah-wah*] *mute.* The harmon mute (first patented in 1865 (US Patent 51,363), though not under this name, by John F. Stratton of New York) is a hollow metal mute held in the bell of the instrument by a cork collar so that all the air from the mouthpiece is directed through the mute; the chamber of the mute protrudes outside the instrument. The outer face, which may have a concave surface, is punctured in the center by a hole, through which passes an adjustable tube (or stem), open at both ends; the oscillating air column passes out of the mute chamber through the tube, the length of which (altered by pushing in and pulling out) affects the character of the sound produced. The sound is distant, with an edge that varies in presence according to the position of the tube. On many harmon mutes the tube is removable; without it the player can produce a wa-wa effect by covering and uncovering the bowl-shaped face of the mute with the palm of the hand, thus controlling the escape of air through the hole.

(g) Bucket mute [*velvetone, velvet-tone*]. The bucket mute is a cylinder, open at the end nearer the bell and closed at the other, filled with absorbent material; it is clipped to the end of the bell by means of sprung steel strips, which hold it at a fixed distance from the instrument. The sound is quiet and dull.

(h) Whispa mute. The whispa mute is a hollow mute held in the bell of the instrument by a cork collar so that all the air from the mouthpiece is directed through the mute; the chamber of the mute, which is filled with absorbent material, protrudes outside the instrument. The outer face is closed except for a small hole. The mute deadens the sound of the instrument to such an extent that a microphone must be used to make it audible.

(i) Plunger (mute). The origins of the plunger mute lie in the use by early brass players of the rubber cups from sink plungers to alter the sound of their instruments. A rubber or metal cup is held against the bell of the instrument. By skillful manipulation the player can distort the natural sound of the instrument in such a way that it seems almost to speak. The plunger is sometimes used in conjunction with the straight mute.

(j) Derby (mute) [*hat*]. The derby mute originated in the use by brass players of their derby (bowler) hats to alter the sound of their instruments. The metal or fiber mute (usually lined with stone) is shaped like a derby hat and is held by the "brim" over the bell. It has little effect on the tone of the instrument but reduces the volume. In the 1920s and 1930s it was often fitted to the top of the mute stand so that players could easily employ it simply by positioning the bell of the instrument inside it.

(k) Felt mute. Some players, mostly trumpeters, hang a felt beret over the bell of the instrument to produce a remote sound, less intense than the instrument's natural tone. The same effect may be achieved using a handkerchief or other cloth.

(l) Beer glass. The use of a beer glass as a mute is one of the first known types of muting in jazz; its introduction is attributed to King Oliver, and it is usually limited to the trumpet and cornet. By holding the glass in the left hand and varying the angle between the glass and the bell, the player can distort the sound at will, much as with the plunger. Various other types of glass have also been used in this way.

(m) Hand over bell. The effect of placing the hand over the bell of the instrument is slightly to diminish the volume of sound. This method of muting was characteristic of the Glenn Miller Orchestra, whose brass players could produce a subtle "wa" in precise rhythmic synchronization.

(n) Hand in bell. The use of the right hand, placed inside the bell of the instrument, is a standard technique in horn playing, essential to the correct tuning of certain notes. As a method of muting it is employed chiefly on the horn, seldom with the trumpet. The further inside the bell the hand is positioned the more muffled becomes the tone and the lower the pitch of the notes; when the instrument is fully stopped, however, the pitch rises.

3. USE IN JAZZ. Brass instruments have been used in jazz with a variety of mutes since the early years of the century. Oral histories credit the cornetist Chris Kelly with having been the first jazz musician to play with a mute; he used a plunger as an extension of "hand in bell" techniques to produce a wa-wa effect. The first major figure, though, to employ a wide range of mutes was King Oliver. Although Oliver's important recordings with his Creole Jazz Band date from 1923, contemporary accounts suggest he used muted effects well before that. Many of the Creole Jazz Band recordings contain lead and duet passages in which both Oliver and Louis Armstrong employ straight mutes; these are exemplified by *Snake Rag* (1923, Gen. 5184), where the sequence of unison breaks played by the two cornetists is the more effective for the incisive sound produced by their mutes. Oliver's famous solo chorus on *Dipper Mouth Blues* (1923, Gen. 5132) shows his mastery of plunger-mute technique. Oliver also pioneered the early versions of what became known as the harmon mute, and this may be heard on *Stingaree Blues* (1930, Vic. 23009). As a soloist he employed muted effects using all the mutes then available. His playing with a cup mute on *Sugar Blues* (1931, Bruns. 6065) is an early example of the effect known as "talking trumpet," which was popularized by Clyde McCoy. In the big bands he led from late 1924 the brass sections used mutes when accompanying solo players, as in *Someday, Sweetheart* (1926, Voc. 1059).

The variety of mutes used by Oliver covers almost all the types described in 1923 by the novelty cornetist Louis Panico, including a glass cup mute used for "talking trumpet" effects. Panico also shows a precursor of the buzz-wow mute, consist-

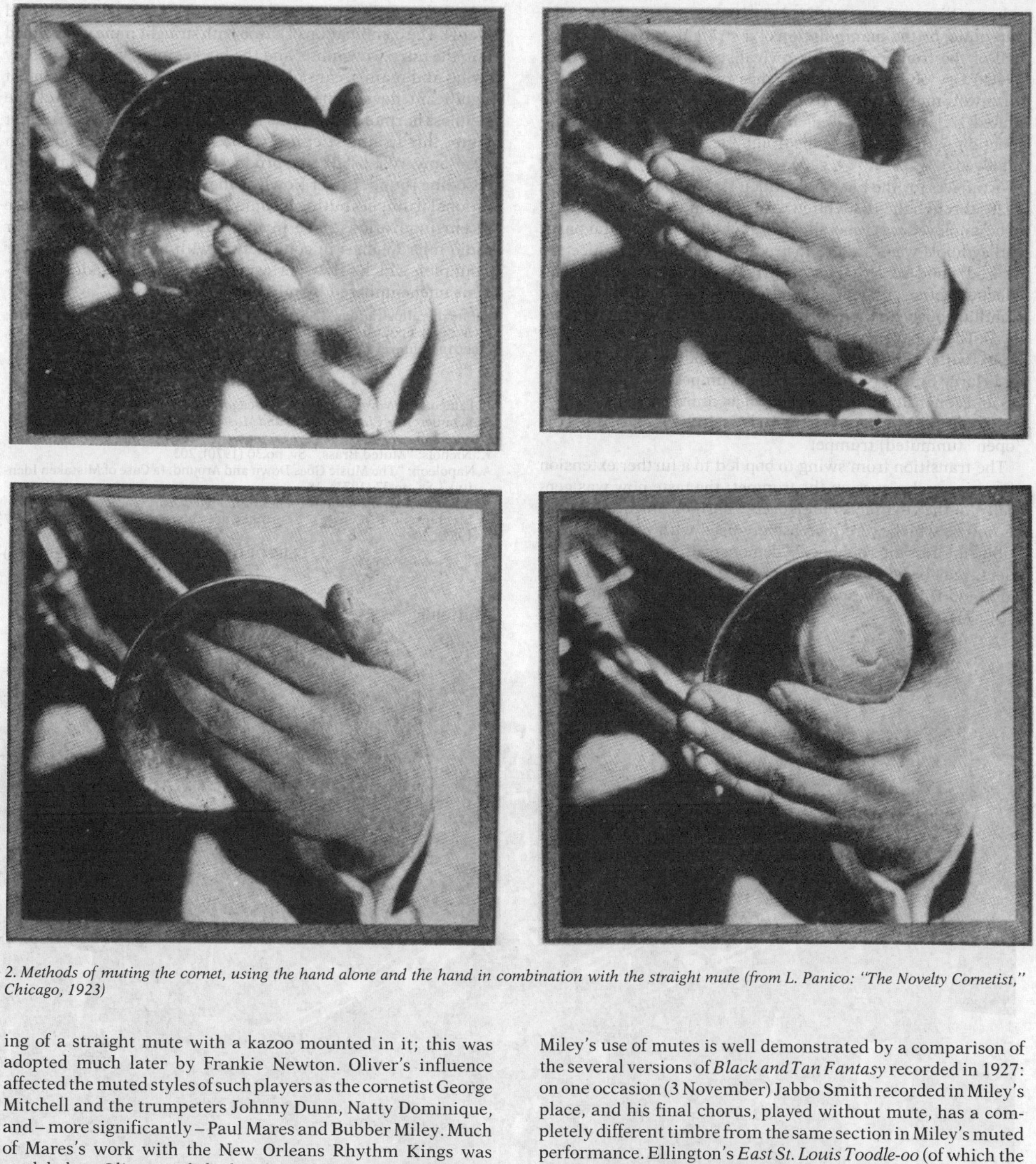

2. Methods of muting the cornet, using the hand alone and the hand in combination with the straight mute (from L. Panico: "The Novelty Cornetist," Chicago, 1923)

ing of a straight mute with a kazoo mounted in it; this was adopted much later by Frankie Newton. Oliver's influence affected the muted styles of such players as the cornetist George Mitchell and the trumpeters Johnny Dunn, Natty Dominique, and – more significantly – Paul Mares and Bubber Miley. Much of Mares's work with the New Orleans Rhythm Kings was modeled on Oliver, and the band regularly employed muted effects: indeed mutes are shown in their Friar's Inn publicity photographs of 1921, where both Mares and Georg Brunis are using straight mutes.

Miley, through his work with Ellington, became the most important figure in the development of muted effects on the trumpet. His "growl and plunger" technique, involving the use of a cornet straight mute (smaller than that for the trumpet) together with a trumpet plunger mute, was regularly adopted as an integral part of Ellington's arrangements. The effect of Miley's use of mutes is well demonstrated by a comparison of the several versions of *Black and Tan Fantasy* recorded in 1927: on one occasion (3 November) Jabbo Smith recorded in Miley's place, and his final chorus, played without mute, has a completely different timbre from the same section in Miley's muted performance. Ellington's *East St. Louis Toodle-oo* (of which the band made several recordings in 1926–7) was a perfect vehicle for Miley and the trombonist Tricky Sam Nanton, who developed the growl and plunger technique for the trombone, using a trumpet straight mute with a trombone plunger. (*See also* Growl.)

Muted trombone effects had been used before, but generally players used only the straight mute (as Honore Dutrey did to balance the muted tone of Armstrong and Oliver). Kid Ory used the straight mute effectively both as an ensemble player (particularly with Jelly Roll Morton) and also as a soloist. His solo on Oliver's *Snag it* (1926, Voc. 1007) suggests the use of a cup mute, or the manipulation of a straight mute within the bell of the trombone. In his revivalist phase (from the mid-1940s) Ory often employed a range of mutes, including the buzz-wow mute. Another trombonist to develop an identifiable muted style was Jack Teagarden, who used a glass in conjunction with the slide of his trombone, the bell having been removed.

Arrangers for the big bands which flourished from the mid-1920s through the 1930s often wrote for muted brass; the mute to be employed was generally named on the instrumental parts, and symbols were used to instruct the player to produce the desired sound (*see* NOTATION). A striking visual (as well as aural) effect was often created when the entire brass section of a band simultaneously applied derby mutes to their instruments (see fig.3). The solo trumpet tradition was continued by Cootie Williams (with Ellington), and, in the late 1930s, by Buck Clayton and Harry Edison (with Basie). The trumpeters Charlie Shavers and Jonah Jones became known as mute specialists in the swing period; Shavers, particularly, seldom recorded on the "open" (unmuted) trumpet.

The transition from swing to bop led to a further extension of muting techniques on the trumpet; the taste now was generally for the "tighter" sounds of cup, harmon, mica, and whispa mutes, which were increasingly used with recording and public-address microphones. A demonstration of many of these effects may be heard in the duet recordings made by Roy Eldridge and Dizzy Gillespie in 1954 (*Roy and Diz*, Clef MGC641, MGC671).

Very few technical changes in muting occurred after World War II. The combination of kazoo with straight mute was refined into the buzz-wow mute, and the bucket mute was adopted by swing and mainstream players such as Ruby Braff. The most significant development has been the establishment of the stemless harmon mute as the most widely used type of trumpet mute; this is almost entirely due to Miles Davis, who, from 1954 onwards, used it to produce his characteristic remote, brooding sound. Lester Bowie is the principal exponent of traditional trumpet-muting techniques in the free-jazz style. More recent innovations have involved the use of transducers or radio microphones in conjunction with mutes (by Davis, for example), which allow performers to use public-address systems unencumbered by microphone placings.

For further illustrations *see* ELDRIDGE, ROY; KIRBY, JOHN; NAPOLEON, fig.1*a*; ORIGINAL DIXIELAND JAZZ BAND; TRUMPET (plunger mutes); and WILLIAMS, COOTIE (plunger mute).

BIBLIOGRAPHY

L. Panico: *The Novelty Cornetist* (Chicago, 1923)
G. Schuller: *Early Jazz: its Roots and Musical Development* (New York, 1968), esp. 328ff
K. Nichols: "Muted Brass," *Sv*, no.30 (1970), 203
A. Napoleon: "The Music Goes Down and Around: (a Case of Mistaken Identity)," *Sv*, no.37 (1971), 18
A. Blatter: *Instrumentation/Orchestration* (New York and London, 1980)
B. Sluchin and R. Caussé: "Sourdines des cuivres," *Brass Bulletin*, no.57 (1987), 20

CLIFFORD BEVAN (1, 2), ALYN SHIPTON (3)

Muttonleg. Nickname of TED DONNELLY.

3. Glenn Miller's band, Hollywood, May 1941, showing the brass section using derby mutes: personnel includes (back row, left to right) Johnny Best and Billy May (trumpets), Moe Purtill (drums), Trigger Alpert (double bass), and Tex Beneke and Al Klink (tenor saxophones); (middle row) Ray Anthony (trumpet, left); (front row) Paul Tanner (trombone, left) and Ernie Caceres, Hal McIntyre and Wilbur Schwartz (alto saxophones); Miller (trombone, center front)

Myers, Amina Claudine (*b* Blackwell, AR, 21 March *c*1943). Pianist, organist, and singer. She studied music formally from the age of seven and directed and performed with gospel groups throughout her school years. She played in jazz and rock groups before moving to Chicago, where she taught in the public schools, performed with Sonny Stitt and Gene Ammons, and joined the Association for the Advancement of Creative Musicians. In 1976 she traveled to New York, but continued to work extensively with various members of the AACM; these collaborations continued after she moved around 1980 to Europe, where she remained for some years before returning to New York. Myers has recorded free jazz with Lester Bowie (1978), Muhal Richard Abrams (1978–9, 1981), and Frank Lowe (1981), and in a gospel group with Martha Bass, Fontella Bass, and David Peason (1980); recordings under her own name often combine these two distinct styles of performance. She has also issued an album of blues dedicated to Bessie Smith. Most of Myers's recordings, including those made in New York, have been issued on European labels.

SELECTED RECORDINGS

As unaccompanied soloist: *Poems for Piano: the Music of Marion Brown* (1979, Sweet Earth 1005)

Duos with P. Ak Laff: *Song for Mother E* (1979, Leo 100)

As leader: *Amina Claudine Myers Salutes Bessie Smith* (1980, Leo 103); *The Circle of Time* (1983, BS 0078); *Country Girl* (1986, Minor Music 1012)

BIBLIOGRAPHY

V. Wilmer: *As Serious as your Life: the Story of the New Jazz* (London, 1977, rev. 1980)

Myers, Bumps [Hubert Maxwell] (*b* Clarksburg, WV, 22 Aug 1912; *d* Los Angeles, 9 April 1968). Tenor saxophonist. He began playing professionally at the age of 17 and in the early 1930s he worked with many bandleaders in Los Angeles. He traveled to Shanghai with Buck Clayton's big band (1934) and after returning to Los Angeles (1936) he performed with Lionel Hampton, Les Hite, Lee and Lester Young (*c*1941, with whom he again worked in New York in 1942), Jimmie Lunceford (1942, 1945), and Benny Carter (1943). He recorded as a leader (1949) and with various musicians, including Carter (1943, 1944–6, 1947–8), Sid Catlett (1945), Benny Goodman (1947), Red Callender (1952–4), Louie Bellson (1953), and the popular singer Harry Belafonte (1958). In 1961–2 he toured with Horace Henderson, but he then ceased working because of ill health. Myers's tenor saxophone style is well represented by his long solo on Catlett's *Love for Sale* (1945, Cap. 10032); he also played alto and baritone saxophones.

BIBLIOGRAPHY

J. Simmen: "Un vrai disciple de Coleman Hawkins: Hubert 'Bumps' Myers," *BHcF*, no.187 (1969), 5

A. McCarthy: *Big Band Jazz* (New York and London, 1974)

B. Clayton and N. M. Elliott: *Buck Clayton's Jazz World* (London, 1986)

based on *ChiltonW*

Myers, Wilson (Ernest) [Serious] (*b* Germantown, PA, 7 Oct 1906). Double bass player, singer, and arranger. He played drums and then (from 1925) guitar and banjo; after changing to double bass he performed with various bands, among them the New Orleans Feetwarmers led by Sidney Bechet and Tommy Ladnier (1932–3) and the Spirits of Rhythm (1933–7). From 1937 he worked in Europe; he recorded in Paris with Bill Coleman (1937, in a quintet that included Django Reinhardt and Stephane Grappelli, and 1938), Willie Lewis, for whom he played and wrote arrangements (1937, 1938), Oscar Alemán (*Russian Lullaby*, 1939, Swing 59), and several others. He led his own band in 1938–9. After returning to the USA (1939) he played with many musicians, including Sidney Bechet (1940), Everett Barksdale (1942), Mezz Mezzrow (1943), and the De Paris brothers (1944), and led his own small groups. He also wrote arrangements for Jimmy Dorsey (1940) and made a number of recordings, with Bechet (1940, 1941), Rex Stewart (1946), and Duke Ellington (1946), among others. From 1946 for many years he led his own small band in Philadelphia. (J. Chilton: *Sidney Bechet: the Wizard of Jazz*, London and New York, 1987)

based on *ChiltonW*

N

Nāgasvaram. Conical, double-reed woodwind instrument of south India, generically a type of OBOE.

NAJE. *See* NATIONAL ASSOCIATION OF JAZZ EDUCATORS.

Nakamura, Teruo (*b* Tokyo, 3 March 1942). Japanese bass player and record producer. He attended Nippon Geijutsu University in Tokyo and in 1964 moved to New York. He studied double bass with Reggie Workman, then formed the Rising Sun Band and performed at many venues in New York, including The Kitchen, the Bottom Line, and the Village Gate; in 1979 he performed and recorded at Carnegie Hall. He worked principally as a record producer in the 1980s.

SELECTED RECORDINGS

Unicorn (1973, TBM 2518); *Rising Sun* (1976, Pol. 6097); *Songs of the Birds* (1977, Kitty MFK1014); *Big Apple* (1979, Agharta C25R002D); *Route 80* (1980, Agharta C28R0064); *At Carnegie Hall* (1979, Agharta C25R0026); *Super Friends* (1985, Ewd 90039)

YOZO IWANAMI

Namaro, Jimmy [James J.] (*b* La Rosita, Mexico, 14 April 1915 or 1919). Canadian vibraphonist, marimba player, and bandleader. In 1921 he moved with his family to Hamilton, Canada, where he learned piano; he became a Canadian citizen around 1945. He made his début playing marimba on radio station CHML in Hamilton and continued to work in radio as a performer and composer. In 1936 he was engaged to play at the Club Esquire in Toronto and he later led groups (usually a trio or a quartet) that played light jazz in Toronto and New York; he made a number of recordings with small groups, sometimes accompanied by a big band (1947–72). He moved to California in the 1970s.

BIBLIOGRAPHY

M. Miller: "Namaro, Jimmy," *Encyclopedia of Music in Canada*, ed. H. Kallmann, G. Potvin, and K. Winters (Toronto, Buffalo, and London, 1981)

JACK LITCHFIELD

Namysłowski, Zbigniew (*b* Warsaw, 9 Sept 1939). Polish alto saxophonist and composer. He played piano from the age of four and cello from the age of 12, then studied music theory in Warsaw. He made his début as a jazz musician playing trombone in a traditional band led by the pianist Witold Krotochwil (1956); his first involvement with contemporary jazz was as a cellist with Krzysztof Sadowski's Modern Combo (1957). Namysłowski toured Denmark with the Polish All Stars (1957) and France with Krotochwil, and established a reputation as Poland's leading trombonist while a member of the dixieland group the New Orleans Stompers. In 1960 he took up alto saxophone and joined Andrzej Trzaskowski's hard-bop group the Jazz Wreckers. In 1963 he formed a quartet, with which he regularly toured Europe. He recorded with the New Orleans Stompers (1961), his own bop group the Jazz Rockers (1961–2), Krzysztof Komeda (1962, 1965, 1967), and the Novi Singers (1965, 1968, 1973), and was active as both instrumentalist and composer with the orchestra of the Polish Radio Jazz Studio. Later he made tours of India, Australia, and New Zealand (1969, leading his own group and playing as a sideman with the Novi singers), the USA (1977, 1979, with Michal Urbaniak), and India (1977, with his own group).

Namysłowski cites John Coltrane, Sonny Rollins, Wayne Shorter, and Joe Henderson as his favorite musicians but also draws inspiration from other sources, including blues, rock, and traditional Polish, Balkan, and Indian music; he plays in a modern idiom, incorporating elements of free jazz. He is one of the best-known musicians in his country and his album *Winobranie* (*Wine feast*), recorded in 1973, became a best-seller.

SELECTED RECORDINGS

As leader: *Lola* (1964, Decca SLK4644); *Winobranie* (*Wine feast*) (1973, Muza 0952); *Kujawiak Goes Funky* (1975, Muza 1230); *Air Condition* (1981, IC 1130)

As sideman: A. Trzaskowski: *The Wreckers* (1960, Muza 0133); M. Urbaniak: *Urbaniak* (1977, IC 1036)

BIBLIOGRAPHY

Feather–Gitler '70s

J. Byrczek: "Eurojazz Personalities: Poland," *JF* [intl edn], no.17 (1972), 85

K. Czyz: "Zbigniew Namyslowski: Diversity of Inspirations," *JF* [intl edn], no.36 (1975), 39 [incl. discography]

L. Tomkins: "From Poland with Jazz: Zbigniew Namyslowsky," *CI*, xvi/1 (1977), 6

K. Czyz: "Zbigniew Namyslowski: Forging a Folk-jazz Fusion," *JF* [intl edn], no.53 (1978), 39

B. Primack: "Zbigniew Namyslowski," *DB*, xlv/18 (1978), 44

WOLFRAM KNAUER

Nance, Ray [Willis] (*b* Chicago, 10 Dec 1913; *d* New York, 28 Jan 1976). Trumpeter, cornetist, violinist, singer, and dancer. He studied piano from the age of six, took lessons on violin, taught himself trumpet, and marched as a drum master in high school. From 1932 to 1937 he led a sextet in Chicago, then worked, principally as a trumpeter, with Earl Hines (1937–8) and Horace Henderson (1939–40). In 1940, after spending eight months performing as a solo act – singing, dancing, and playing both trumpet and violin – he joined Duke Ellington, with whom he remained (apart from a few brief periods) until 1963 (for illustrations *see* BANDS, fig.3, and ELLINGTON, DUKE, fig.2). While with Ellington, Nance continued to make use of all his talents. He often performed as a singer and dancer, and the full and penetrating tone he obtained on violin was the highlight of many of the band's recordings, including *Moon Mist* (1942) and *Come Sunday* (1958). On trumpet he inherited the role, created by Bubber Miley and continued by Cootie Williams (whom he replaced), of playing with a muted, wa-wa tone, and immediately created a notable solo on *Take the "A" Train* (1941) that was widely imitated. In 1961 he changed to cornet. Although he continued to work intermittently for Ellington, he also played with Paul Lavelle's orchestra at the New York World's Fair (1964–5) and with Sol Yaged (1966–9) and Brooks Kerr (1973). He toured England with Chris Barber in 1974 and thereafter worked in clubs in New York.

Oral history material in *NjR*.

SELECTED RECORDINGS

As leader: *Body and Soul* (1969, SolS 18062); with P. Gonsalves: *Just a-Sittin' and a-Rockin'* (1970, BL 191); *Huffin' 'n' Puffin'* (1971, MPS/BASF 5057)

As sideman: E. Hines: Solid Mama (1938, Voc. 4143); Jack climbed the beanstalk (1938, Voc. 4272); H. Henderson: Kitty on Toast (1940, Voc./OK 5433); D. Ellington: Take the "A" Train (1941, Vic. 27380); Perdido (1942, Voc. 27880); Moon Mist/C-Jam Blues (1942, Vic. 27856); Tulip or Turnip (1946, Musi. 483); J. Hodges: *Duke's in Bed* (1956, Verve 8203); D. Ellington: *Duke Ellington Presents* (1956, Beth. 6005), incl. I can't get started; *Black, Brown and Beige* (1958, Col. CL1162), incl. Come Sunday; *Will the Big Bands Ever Come Back?* (c1965, Rep. 6168)

BIBLIOGRAPHY

ChiltonW

M. Jones: "Ray Nance: the Cat on a Hot Fiddle," *MM*, xl (27 Feb 1965), 8

D. Morgenstern: "Jazz Fiddle," *DB*, xxxiv/3 (1967), 16

S. Dance: *The World of Duke Ellington* (London and New York, 1970/*R*1981) [colln of previously pubd articles and interviews], 131

B. Niquet: "Le retour de Ray Nance," *Jh*, no.277 (1971), 18

M. G. P. [M. Gautier Panassié]: "Ray Nance," *BHcF*, no.251 (1976), 5 [obituary]

H. Panassié and M. Gautier: *Dictionnaire du jazz* (Paris, rev. and enlarged 3/1980), 225

BARRY KERNFELD

Nanton, Tricky Sam [Joe; Irish, Joseph N.] (*b* New York, 1 Feb 1904; *d* San Francisco, 20 July 1946). Trombonist. After playing in the early 1920s with Cliff Jackson and Elmer Snowden, in mid-1926 he joined Duke Ellington's orchestra, replacing Charlie Irvis. He soon mastered the novel "growl and plunger" techniques pioneered by Ellington's trumpeter Bubber Miley, thus earning his unusual nickname and becoming a key figure in producing the familiar "jungle" sound of Ellington's early recordings. Nanton remained with Ellington for the whole of his career (for illustrations *see* BANDS, fig.3, and TROMBONE), contributing numerous excellent "talking" solos to Ellington's recorded output. Although limited in dexterity and range (his solos seldom span more than an octave and often merely elaborate two or three pitches), Nanton's performances have an earthy, poignant sincerity, which is heightened by the complexity of their musical surroundings.

SELECTED RECORDINGS

As sideman with D. Ellington: East St. Louis Toodle-oo (1926, Voc. 1064); Black and Tan Fantasy (1927, Bruns. 3526); Yellow Dog Blues (1928, Bruns. 3987); Harlem Flat Blues (1929, Bruns. 4309); Saddest Tale (1934, Bruns. 7310); Ko-Ko (1940, Vic. 26577); Bojangles/A Portrait of Bert Williams (1940, Vic. 26644); Blue Serge (1941, Vic. 27356)

As sideman with others: Cootie Williams: I can't believe that you're in love with me/Diga diga doo (1937, Var. 555); R. Stewart: San Juan Hill (1939, Voc./OK 5510)

BIBLIOGRAPHY

C. Fox: "An Appreciation of Joe 'Tricky Sam' Nanton," *Hot Notes*, ii/5 (1947)

B. McRae: "Joe 'Tricky Sam' Nanton," *JJ*, xiii/6 (1960), 14

R. Stewart: "Tribute to Tricky Sam (Joe Nanton)," *Jazz Masters of the Thirties* (New York and London, n.d. [?1972]), 103

J. BRADFORD ROBINSON

Napoleon. Family of musicians.

(1) Phil Napoleon [Filippo Napoli] (*b* Boston, 2 Sept 1901). Trumpeter and bandleader (see fig.1*a*). He was the leader of the ORIGINAL MEMPHIS FIVE, which was formed in 1917 and enjoyed considerable popularity during the mid-1920s. He also recorded with the Cotton Pickers (1922–3) and the Charleston Chasers (1929–30), and as the leader of his own bands; all these groups drew on a pool of white jazz musicians in New York, which included Jimmy and Tommy Dorsey, Joe Venuti, and Eddie Lang. When, in the early 1930s, public interest in small-group jazz waned, Napoleon concentrated on playing in radio orchestras; later in the decade he briefly led a big band, but it proved unsuccessful and he went into the musical instrument business. In 1949, however, he returned to professional playing; until 1956, when he moved to Florida, he led an excellent dixieland group at Nick's, New York. He played at the Newport Jazz Festival in 1959, and in 1966 opened his own club, Phil Napoleon's Retreat, near Miami, and led the band there. He has remained active into the 1980s.

Napoleon's recordings of the 1920s suggest that he was a solid, workmanlike player, and – by their quantity – they helped to popularize jazz. As a soloist, however, he was not as influential as his contemporaries Louis Armstrong, Bix Beiderbecke, and Red Nichols. He belongs to a large family of musicians whose members include his brothers George, Joe (both professional saxophonists), Ted (a drummer who played on some of the later recordings by the Original Memphis Five), and Matthew (a guitarist, and father of (2) Teddy and (3) Marty Napoleon).

SELECTED RECORDINGS

As leader of the Original Memphis Five: My Honey's Lovin' Arms (1922, Arto 9140); Lonesome Mama Blues (1922, Para. 20131); Farewell Blues (1923, Arto 9210); Static Strut (1926, Vic. 20039); I'm More than Satisfied (1928, Voc. 15712); Jazz me Blues (1931, Col. 2588D)

As leader of other groups: Tiger Rag (1926, Edison 51908); Mean to Me (1929, Vic. 38057); That's a Plenty (1937, Var. 669); Royal Garden Blues (1946, Swan 7506); When the saints go marching in (1950, Decca 27039); *Phil Napoleon and his Memphis Five* (1959, Cap. T1344)

As sideman with M. Mole: After you've Gone (1929, OK 41445)

BIBLIOGRAPHY

ChiltonW

S. B. Charters and L. Kunstadt: *Jazz: a History of the New York Scene* (Garden City, NY, 1962/*R*1981)

G. T. Simon: *Simon Says: the Sights and Sounds of the Swing Era, 1935–1955* (New Rochelle, NY, 1971)

(2) Teddy Napoleon [George Napoli] (*b* New York, 23 Jan 1914; *d* Elmhurst, NY, 5 July 1964). Pianist, nephew of (1) Phil Napoleon (see fig.1*b*). He first played in a band with Lee Castaldo in a Chinese restaurant in 1933, then toured for several years with Tommy Tompkins, and in the late 1930s worked in and around New York. After playing in dance orchestras led by Johnny Messner and Bob Chester in the early 1940s, in 1944 he began an association with Gene Krupa that lasted sporadically for 14 years. He worked with Krupa's big band and trio, and played on many of his best-known recordings, including *Leave us Leap* and *Dark Eyes*; he toured the USA, and went with the trio to Japan and Sweden (1952) and Australia (1954). He also worked with Eddie Shu, Flip Phillips, and Bill Harris (i),

(a)

(b)

(c)

1. Members of the Napoleon family: (a) Phil Napoleon, 1937; (b) Teddy Napoleon, c1943; (c) Marty Napoleon, 1953

and, in 1955, with his brother (3) Marty Napoleon. In 1959 he moved to Florida, where he led a trio. His forceful playing was in the swing style of such pianists as Mel Powell.

SELECTED RECORDINGS

As sideman with G. Krupa: Leave us Leap/Dark Eyes (1945, Col. 36802); Boogie Blues/Lover (1945, Col. 36986); *The Rocking Mr. Krupa* (1953, Clef MGC627), incl. Sing, sing, sing; *Krupa Rocks* (1957, Verve 8276)

BIBLIOGRAPHY

FeatherE

(3) Marty Napoleon [Matthew Napoli] (*b* New York, 2 June 1921). Pianist, nephew of (1) Phil Napoleon (see fig.1*c*). By the age of 12 he had decided to become a trumpeter, but a heart ailment caused him to change to piano. In the 1940s he worked in big bands led by Chico Marx, Joe Venuti, Lee Castle, and Charlie Barnet, and in 1945 he briefly replaced his brother (2) Teddy Napoleon in Gene Krupa's band. His first attempt at playing small-group traditional jazz was in 1950, when he joined his uncle's new Memphis Five, and the following year he was a member of the highly acclaimed Big Four led by Charlie Ventura. After playing with Louis Armstrong's All Stars (1952–3) Napoleon formed a quartet with his brother (1955), then worked with Coleman Hawkins and Charlie Shavers in New York (1958–9). From that time he has mostly led his own trios or performed as a soloist, although from 1966 to 1968, and occasionally thereafter, he worked with Armstrong. In 1983 he recorded with Peanuts Hucko, and in 1986 he played in a memorial concert for Armstrong in New York. Because of his association with his uncle, Napoleon is often thought of as a traditional-jazz musician; his preference, however, is for more modern forms (as may be heard on his recordings with Charlie Ventura), and he gained a reputation for his ability to perform in both genres. He has absorbed elements of the work of Erroll Garner and Oscar Peterson into his playing, but his style is readily identifiable as his own.

SELECTED RECORDINGS

As sideman: A. Killian: You're the One (1945, Manor 1098); G. Krupa: Tea for Two (1945, Col. 38345); C. Ventura: After you've Gone (1951, Clef/Mer. 8957); Big Four Blues (1951, Clef/Mer. 8965); L. Armstrong: Kiss of Fire (1952, Decca 28177); Your Cheating Heart (1953, Decca 28628); R. Braff: *Little Big Horn* (1955, Concert Hall 1210); H. Allen: *Ride, Red, Ride in Hi-fi* (1957, RCA LPM1509), incl. Ride, Red, Ride; L. Armstrong: *Louis* (1966, Mer. 61081), incl. Mame, Tin Roof Blues; *I will Wait for you* (1967–8, Bruns. 754136), incl. Talk to the Animals

BIBLIOGRAPHY

FeatherE; Feather '60s; Feather–Gitler '70s
G. Simon: "Napoleon Flying High," *New York Post* (16 Jan 1981)
J. S. Wilson: "'Hard Times, Good Times' of Marty Napoleon," *New York Times* (23 March 1984), §C, p.16

CHIP DEFFAA

Napper, Kenny [Kenneth] (*b* London, 14 July 1933). English double bass player, arranger, and composer. After conservatory training in the early 1950s he recorded with Mary Lou Williams (1953), then played with Jack Parnell (1953–4). From the late 1950s he worked with many of the most important British bop musicians, including Ronnie Scott (1957, 1961), Stan Tracey (1958, 1959), Tubby Hayes (1959, 1961), and John Dankworth (1961, *c*1964); he may be heard to advantage on Tracey's album *Little Klunk* (1959, Vogue 160155). In the early 1960s he was a member of the house band at Scott's club, where he recorded with Zoot Sims (1961). He also took part in sessions with such visitors as Carmen McRae (1961), Paul Gonsalves (1963, 1969), Barney Kessel (1968), and Stephane Grappelli (1970), and composed and wrote arrangements for the bands of Parnell and Dankworth and for films and television. Later he moved to Germany, where he worked with Kurt Edelhagen (1970–72). Thereafter he began to concentrate on composing and arranging, and in the late 1970s settled in the Netherlands, where he wrote extensively for radio bands.

SALLY-ANN WORSFOLD

Narell, Andy (*b* New York, 18 March 1954). Steel drummer, percussionist, pianist, and composer. He graduated from the University of California, Berkeley, in 1973 and formed a band in California (1978) and a record company, Hip Pocket. He performed with his band in Europe from 1981, appearing at festivals in Berlin, Cologne, Balve, and Neuwied (all in Germany), The Hague, Vienna, and Montreux (Switzerland); in June 1986 the group performed in Japan. Narell has also played on film soundtracks and as a sideman on albums by the Manhattan Transfer, the drummer Narada Michael Walden, the soul singer Aretha Franklin, and the vocal groups LaBelle and the Pointer Sisters. Narell has enabled the steel drum to transcend its traditional role as a Caribbean folk instrument by incorporating influences from jazz, popular, ethnic, and classical music into his playing. As a composer he has written repertory for his own band, television and film scores, and modern dance scores.

SELECTED RECORDINGS

(all recorded for Hip Pocket)

Stickman (1980, 101); *Light in your Eyes* (1983, 103); *Slow Motion* (1985, 105)

BIBLIOGRAPHY

L. Underwood: "Andy Narell," *DB*, xlvii/6 (1980), 56

JEFF POTTER

Naret, Bobby [Robert] (*b* Loncin, Belgium, 14 Aug 1914). Belgian alto saxophonist and clarinetist. He studied clarinet from the age of 11 and took up saxophone after playing informally with a local group. In Brussels he worked with the alto saxophonist Jo Magis and the bandleader Lucien Hirsch. After leaving Hirsch in 1934 he formed an association with Fud Candrix, with whom he worked at a number of clubs in Brussels, in Westende on the Belgian coast, with Coleman Hawkins in The Hague, and in Heliopolis, Egypt. He left Candrix in 1943, having formed his own band, with which he recorded in 1942–4 and 1953; at one time this group included seven saxophonists. Naret also recorded with Hirsch (1931), Candrix (1937–43), the violinist Chas Dolne (1940–42), Hubert Rostaing (1942), Robert De Kers and Aimé Barelli (both 1943), and Gus Clark and Ernst van 't Hoff (both 1944). He continued to play throughout the 1950s and 1960s.

ROBERT PERNET

Nascimento, Milton (*b* Rio de Janeiro, 1942). Brazilian singer, bandleader, and composer. He grew up in Três Pontas, and played guitar with local groups before moving to São Paolo in 1965. Two years later he achieved acclaim as a songwriter at the first International Pop Song Festival in Rio de Janeiro, and recorded with the Tamba Trio. He performed and recorded as a leader frequently in the 1970s and 1980s, working with the music director and keyboard player Wagner Tiso and the drummer Ricardo Silva. His albums include *Minas* (1975, EMI-Odeon 82325), and he may be heard to advantage on Wayne Shorter's *Native Dancer* (1974, Col. PC33418). He has also recorded with Flora Purim (1974), Airto Moreira (1976), and George Duke (1980), performed at Carnegie Hall, New York (1984), written film scores, and worked as an actor.

BIBLIOGRAPHY

C. Cooper: "Milton Nascimento," *DB*, li/9 (1984), 21 [incl. discography]
L. Jeske: "On Jazz: Nascimento," *Cash Box* (15 June 1984)

Nash, Dick [Richard Taylor] (*b* Somerville, MA, 26 Jan 1928). Trombonist, brother of Ted Nash. He played with Sam Donahue (from 1947), Glen Gray, and Tex Beneke, and, during his military service in Japan and Korea, with an army band (1950–52). After working with Billy May (1953) he became a freelance musician on the West Coast. His playing may be heard on *Ken Hanna and his Orchestra* (1954, Trend 1007) and on *The Swing Era: the Music of 1936–1937* (*c*1970, TL 341) for which he re-created solos originally played by Tommy Dorsey (including that on *Marie*). His son the saxophonist Ted Nash (*b* Hollywood, CA, 28 Dec 1959) performed with Louie Bellson and toured and recorded with Don Ellis in 1977.

BIBLIOGRAPHY

FeatherE
L. Tomkins: "Trombone Talk with Dick Nash and Don Lusher," *CI*, xii/10 (1974), 14

WARREN VACHÉ, SR.

Nash, Ted [Theodore Malcolm] (*b* Somerville, MA, 31 Oct 1922). Tenor saxophonist, brother of Dick Nash. He became known for his work with Les Brown (1944–6), with whom he played alto as well as tenor saxophone, and Jerry Gray (1947–52). An excellent soloist and proficient on several reed instruments, he recorded prolifically and played with a large number of bands, including those led by Bob Crosby (1947), Sonny Burke (1948), Dave Barbour and Skippy Martin (both 1949), Pete Rugolo (1950), and Billy May and Ray Anthony (both 1953). He also recorded with his own group in the mid-1940s and 1950s. He worked on the West Coast in radio, television, and film studios, and in the 1960s and 1970s he played regularly on television as a member of Mort Lindsey's big band. Nash published a book on playing high harmonics on the saxophone.

SELECTED RECORDINGS

As leader: *The Music of Frank Comstock* (*c*1954, Starlight 6001); *Star Eyes* (*c*1956, Col. CL989)
As sideman: L. Brown: Lover's Leap/High on a Windy Trumpet (1946, Col. 37061); I've got my love to keep me warm (1946, Col. 38324)

BIBLIOGRAPHY

FeatherE

WARREN VACHÉ, SR.

Nasser, Jamil (Sulieman) [Joyner, George (Leon); Sulieman, Jamil] (*b* Memphis, 21 June 1932). Double bass player. He studied piano with his mother and took up double bass at the age of 16. At Arkansas State University (1949–52) he led the band, and during his army service (1953–5) played tuba and double bass. After his discharge he played electric bass guitar with the blues singer and guitarist B. B. King (1955–6), then, in New York, worked with Phineas Newborn (with whom he recorded in 1956 and 1958), Sonny Rollins, and other bop musicians. He toured Europe and North Africa with Idrees Sulieman (from February 1959) and recorded with Lester Young in Paris (1959). After living in Milan (1961) he returned to the USA, where he led a trio (1962–4). Under the name Jamil Sulieman he played with Ahmad Jamal (1964–72); he then worked with Al Haig (at intervals, 1975–8), as a freelance in New York, and with Clifford Jordan (1983).

SELECTED RECORDINGS

As sideman: A. Jamal: *At the Top: Poinciana Revisited* (1968, Imp. 9176); *The Awakening* (1970, Imp. 9194); *Free Flight*, i (1971, Imp. 9217); A. Haig and J. Raney: *Strings Attached* (1975, Choice 1010); Louis Smith: *Just Friends* (1978, Ste. 1096)

BIBLIOGRAPHY

FeatherE; *Feather '60s*; *Feather–Gitler '70s*

JOHN VOIGT

Nationaal Jazz Archief. Archive founded in Amsterdam in 1980; *see* LIBRARIES AND ARCHIVES, §2.

National (i). Record label. It was used in the 1920s by the National Certificate Co. of New York and drew its repertory from the labels owned by the Bridgeport Die & Machine Co. Because of the latter group's links with the New York Recording Laboratories, National also issued important jazz first put out by Paramount.

BIBLIOGRAPHY

B. Rust: *The American Record Label Book* (New Rochelle, NY, 1978), 203
M. E. Vreede: "Puritan-ism in Discography," *Sv*, no.89 (1980), 178

National (ii). Record label. It was owned in the 1920s by the National Record Exchange Co. of Iowa City, Iowa, and drew its repertory from the labels owned by the New York Recording Laboratories. It was thus used to issue some important jazz first put out by Paramount. Given the close connections between the NYRL and the Bridgeport Die & Machine Co., the catalogue was very similar to that of National (i).

BIBLIOGRAPHY

B. Rust: *The American Record Label Book* (New Rochelle, NY, 1978), 203
M. E. Vreede: "Puritan-ism in Discography," *Sv*, no.89 (1980), 178

National (iii). Record company and label. The company was established in 1944 in New York by A. B. Green. Artists and repertory were supervised by Herb Abramson (later one of the founders of Atlantic), who built a substantial jazz and race catalogue. Among the first issues were discs by Emmett Berry, Pete Johnson and Joe Turner (ii), and Billy Eckstine's orchestra; in the late 1940s the company put out many recordings by Charlie Ventura's group. Abramson was succeeded by Lee Magid, who concentrated on music with a more commercial orientation. Around 1950 Magid joined Savoy, which shortly thereafter acquired National. (A. Shaw: *Honkers and Shouters: the Golden Years of Rhythm and Blues* (New York, 1978), 133, 359)

National Association of Jazz Educators [NAJE]. An associate organization of the Music Educators National Conference (MENC) with the purpose of furthering the teaching of jazz at schools and fostering jazz appreciation. It was founded in 1968 as a result of the MENC's Tanglewood Symposium of 1967, one of its founders being Stan Kenton. Besides holding an annual convention, the NAJE publishes various anthologies and works in book and booklet form as well as a quarterly *Jazz Educators Journal* (formerly *NAJE Educator*) and the *Proceedings of Jazz Research*, an annual periodical derived from papers presented at its research sessions. In August 1987 the International Foundation for Jazz was established to support, develop, and raise funds for the NAJE's educational programs.

BIBLIOGRAPHY

M. L. Mark: *Contemporary Music Education* (New York and London, 1978, rev. 2/1986)
D. A. Herfort: *A History of the National Association of Jazz Educators and a Description of its Role in American Music Education, 1968–1978* (diss., U. of Houston, 1979)

LEE BASH

National Jazz Ensemble. Group formed in 1973 by CHUCK ISRAELS.

National Jazz Service Organization [NJSO]. Organization dedicated to the promotion and advancement of jazz. It was formed in 1984 by 15 leading members of the American jazz community at a meeting in Racine, Wisconsin, and by 1985 a grant from the NEA had allowed it fully to establish its operations. Among its founding members were David Baker (who became president), Donald Byrd (vice-president), James Jordan (secretary), and Dave Bailey (treasurer); the first executive director was Eunice Lockhart-Moss. The NJSO offers various services to its membership, which includes musicians, patrons, and organizations: it encourages and supports the entrepreneurial activities of musicians, aids the creation of new audiences and consumer markets for jazz, and distributes throughout the USA educational material and information concerning the contemporary performance of jazz. The objectives of the organization include the representation of jazz at various events and the establishment of the National Center for Jazz, which will house a library, archives, recording studios, and performance facilities. In 1986 the NJSO held the conference New Perspectives on Jazz at Racine; this was attended by several major American jazz figures, including Gunther Schuller, Stanley Crouch, and Billy Taylor (ii), who assessed the current place of jazz in American music and considered its future. In the same year the organization published *The American Jazz Music Audience*, which contained the results of a survey carried out by the NEA and the US Census Bureau.

National Youth Jazz Orchestra. Group organized in 1965 as the London Schools Jazz Orchestra by BILL ASHTON.

Natoli, Nat (*b* Boston, *c*1902; *d* after 1950). Trumpeter. He traveled to Montreal with the Original Memphis Five (*c*1924) and played with Jean Goldkette in Kansas City (1927–8). From 1930 to 1934 he was a member of Paul Whiteman's band, but left to work in studio orchestras. He continued to play steadily throughout the 1940s, then became more active as a contractor for studio musicians. Although Natoli made several recordings, his contributions were as a section player, not as a soloist.

based on *ChiltonW*

Naude, Jean-Claude (*b* Amiens, France, 7 March 1933). French trumpeter and bandleader. He studied piano and trumpet at the Conservatoire in Amiens and made his début in the orchestra of Georges Arvanitas. He performed and recorded regularly with Maxim Saury (1955–65) and Claude Bolling (1972–5) and is best known as a leader of big bands (1965–8, and at intervals from 1970). Naude is an adept swing player influenced by Louis Armstrong and an effective arranger; a good example of his work is his album *Special Blend* (1971, Blue Swan 51171).

BIBLIOGRAPHY

J.-L. Ginibre: "Au risque de se perdre," *Jm*, no.128 (1966), 30 [interview]
C. Bonnet: "Jean-Claude Naude," *Jh*, no.262 (1970), 24 [interview]

MICHEL LAPLACE

Naughton, Bobby [Robert] (*b* Boston, 25 June 1944). Vibraphonist, pianist, and composer. He is self-taught as a performer and composer. After playing piano in rock-and-roll groups he took up vibraphone in 1966, and in the late 1960s played with Perry Robinson, Sheila Jordan, and others. He continued to work intermittently with Robinson while recording as a leader from 1969 on his own label, Otic; in 1971 he wrote a score for Hans Richter's silent film *Everyday* (1929). He played with the Jazz Composer's Orchestra in 1972 and Leo Smith (from the mid-1970s), and joined the Creative Music Improvisers Forum in New Haven, Connecticut. Naughton's vibraphone playing, like that of Gunter Hampel, emphasizes the instrument's role in group improvisation rather than its possibilities as a solo vehicle. He plays fluently with four sticks, exploits the vibraphone's overtones, and sometimes controls manually the instrument's vanes (which vary its sound intensity). His piano playing (which may be heard on the first of his own albums) has a melodic strength and terseness reminiscent of Paul Bley.

SELECTED RECORDINGS

As leader: *Nature's Consort* (1969, Otic 1001); *Understanding* (1971, Otic 1003); *The Haunt* (1976, Otic 1005)
As sideman with L. Smith: *Divine Love* (1978, ECM 1143)

BIBLIOGRAPHY

R. T. Dean: "Jazz Vibes: Bebop and After," *JJ*, xxx/4 (1977), 4
J. Waz: "Bobby Naughton: the Mission of the Small Label," *JF* [intl edn], no.52 (1978), 37

ROGER T. DEAN

Naura, Michael (*b* Memel, Memel territory [now Klaipėda, Lithuanian SSR], 19 Aug 1934). German pianist of Memel birth. He belonged to a swing band and in 1953 formed a quintet consisting of piano, vibraphone, guitar (from 1956 alto saxophone), double bass, and drums, which performed at festivals and clubs and on radio broadcasts. He interrupted his career in 1963 owing to ill health; after resuming it in 1966 he belonged to trios and quartets and recorded jazz and poetry with Wolfgang Schlüter and the poet Peter Rühmkorf. As the head of the jazz department of the Norddeutscher Rundfunk (from 1971) he started a series of jazz workshops.

SELECTED RECORDINGS

(recorded for ECM unless otherwise indicated)

Duos with W. Schlüter: *Country Children* (1977, 5803)
As leader: *Down to Earth* (1958, Tel. 4880); *Vanessa* (1974, 1053); with P. Rühmkorf: *Kein Apolloprogram für Lyrik* (1976, 5801); *Phönix voran* (1978, 5802)

BIBLIOGRAPHY

FeatherE; *Feather–Gitler '70s*; *ReclamsJ*
H.-W. Schneider: "Das Michael Naura Quartett," *JP*, iv/3 (1955), 14
H. Holzer: "Erlebter Jazz," *JP*, viii/9 (1959), 211
M. Naura: "Zwischen Licht- und Schattenseiten des Jazz," *JP*, x/3 (1961), 70
"Spree City Stompers in England," *JP*, xii/6 (1963), 123
J. Engelhardt: "Jazz und Lyrik mit Naura und Ruehmkorf," *JP*, xxxi/6 (1982), 30
I. Carr: "Naura, Michael," in I. Carr, D. Fairweather, and B. Priestley: *Jazz: the Essential Companion* (London, 1987)

HEIDI BOULTON

Navarro, Fats [Theodore] (*b* Key West, FL, 24 Sept 1923; *d* New York, 7 July 1950). Trumpeter. As a youth he played piano and tenor saxophone, but by the age of 17 he was touring with dance bands as a trumpeter. Three years later, in 1943, he joined Andy Kirk's nationally known jazz band, which then included Howard McGhee. In January 1945 Navarro replaced Dizzy Gillespie in Billy Eckstine's band. As the principal trumpet soloist in this important group he was among the foremost players in the new bop idiom. In autumn 1946, physically unequal to the heavy touring schedule and restricted musically by the big-band format, he left Eckstine. He spent the remainder of his brief career working mostly in small bop groups in New York, where he died of tuberculosis exacerbated by heroin addiction.

Although Navarro recorded a few solos with Eckstine's band, his main legacy is the approximately 150 small-group recordings he made between 1946 and 1950, mostly as a sideman in groups led by Kenny Clarke, Coleman Hawkins, Bud Powell, Charlie Parker, and especially Tadd Dameron. These recordings, of which one third originated as radio broadcasts, reveal Navarro to be the rival of Gillespie as the leading bop trumpeter of the 1940s. Gillespie was clearly one of his models, for Navarro used many of the older player's favorite phrases. Compared with that of Gillespie, however, Navarro's tone was

Fats Navarro (left) with Miles Davis (center) and Kai Winding, January 1949

Ex.1 Navarro's solo on B. Powell, *Wail* [3rd take] (1949, BN 1567); transcr. T. Owens

sweeter; his style was also less dramatic, employing fewer passages of fast notes and fewer notes played in the upper register of the instrument. At times Navarro seemed to be more heavily influenced by the acknowledged leader of the bop school, Charlie Parker. Certain motifs in *Wail* (ex.1, marked *s–z*) were frequently used by Parker as building blocks for solo improvisations; the nearly continuous flow of eighth-notes with an unpredictable sprinkling of accents between the beats was also typical of Parker. The effective recurrence of motif *s*, however, which connects by chromatic descent the 13th and raised 11th of each chord, is a characteristic Navarro touch, as is the scale passage that ends the phrase. Navarro's recordings are of a consistently high quality. *The Street Beat* and *Ornithology*, made with Parker in 1950, are particularly intriguing: if discographers have dated these pieces accurately, Navarro, emaciated and gravely ill, made these fine recordings just one week before he died.

Oral history material in *TxU*.

See also TRUMPET, §5.

SELECTED RECORDINGS

As leader: Nostalgia (1947, Savoy 955); Barry's Bop (1947, Savoy 959); on *Fat Girl* (1947, Savoy 2216), Barry's Bop, Nostalgia [alternative takes]

As sideman: on B. Eckstine: *Together!* (1945, Spot. 100), Air Mail Special; T. Dameron: Our Delight (1947, BN 540); Our Delight [alternative take] (1947), first issued on F. Navarro: *Fabulous Fats Navarro* (1947, 1949, BN 1531); on B. Ulanov: *Anthropology* (1947, Spot. 108), Fats' Flats, Koko; on T. Dameron: *The Tadd Dameron Band 1948* (1948, Jlnd 68), Good Bait; B. Powell: Wail [take 2] (1949), first issued on F. Navarro: *Fabulous Fats Navarro* (1947, 1949, BN 1531); Wail [take 3] (1949, BN 1567); on C. Parker: *Charlie Parker in Historical Recordings*, i (1948, 1950, Le Jazz Cool 101), Ornithology (1950); on *Charlie Parker in Historical Recordings*, ii (1948–50, Le Jazz Cool 102), The Street Beat (1950)

BIBLIOGRAPHY

J. G. Jepsen: *Discography of Fats Navarro, Clifford Brown* (Brande, Denmark, 1960)
I. Gitler: *Jazz Masters of the Forties* (New York, 1966/*R*1983 with discography), 97
G. Hoefer: "The Significance of Fats Navarro," *DB*, xxxiii/2 (1966), 16
J. Burns: "Theodore 'Fats' Navarro," *JJ*, xxi/5 (1968), 12
R. Russell: "Fat Girl: the Legacy of Fats Navarro," *DB*, xxxvii/4 (1970), 14
W. Balliett: "Jazz: Fat Girl," *New Yorker*, liv (12 June 1978), 116
J. L. Collier: *The Making of Jazz: a Comprehensive History* (New York and London, 1978), 398
M. Ruppli: "Fats Navarro Discography," *DF*, no.42 (1979) – no.45 (1982)

THOMAS OWENS

Navarro, Jorge [Pampero] (*b* Buenos Aires, 20 Jan 1940). Argentine pianist. He played with the Swing Timers (1956) and after receiving a favorable notice from the writer Gene Lees in 1960 joined the Agrupacíon nuevo jazz later that year, of which Gato Barbieri was also a member; he recorded with this group in 1961, and as the leader of his own trio in 1964. During the following years he performed at the International Jazz Festival of Santiago (1966), worked with Jim Hall, Ella Fitzgerald, and Roy Eldridge in Buenos Aires, and from 1969 to 1975 lived in the USA. Later he recorded with Jorge Anders's quartet (1976), recorded as a leader the album *Con polenta* (1977, Aleluya 17001), performed and recorded with Buddy DeFranco (1980), and recorded with Andrés Boiarsky (1982). He was a founding member in 1984 of the TRÍO ARGENTINA. In 1987 he recorded the album *El loco son ustedes* (CBS 8695), on which he may be heard to advantage leading his own group.

LAUREANO FERNÁNDEZ, OMAR GARCÍA BRUNELLI

Ndugu [Chancler, Leon; Chancler, Ndugu Leon] (*b* Shreveport, LA, 1 July 1952). Drummer and percussionist. His family moved to Los Angeles in 1960 and he began drumming when he was 12 or 13. He studied music in high school, and at the same time performed with Willie Bobo and Gerald Wilson; he then attended a California State college for two years and played with Hugh Masekela, Herbie Hancock, Eddie Harris, and Thelonious Monk. Thereafter he played briefly in the bands of Freddie Hubbard and Miles Davis before joining George Duke, with whom he played intermittently from 1972 to 1980. He toured with Carlos Santana from 1974 to 1976, and formed his own group, Chocolate Jam Co., in 1978. During the 1980s Ndugu has worked mostly as a record producer for several pop musicians, including Kenny Rogers and Michael Jackson, and as a session musician. Around 1983 he was associated with the Crusaders. Although he has seldom recorded in a jazz context, Ndugu's execution of the rhythms of pop music is unusually loose and imaginative.

SELECTED RECORDINGS

As sideman: E. Harris: *Excursions* (1973, Atl. 2-311); J. Priester: *Love, Love* (1973, ECM 1044); Weather Report: *Tale Spinnin'* (*c*1975, Col. PC33417); G. Duke: *Reach for it* (*c*1977, Epic 34883)

BIBLIOGRAPHY

Feather–Gitler '70s
R. Tolleson: "Ndugu Leon Chancler," *MD*, vii/11 (1983), 14

CHUCK BRAMAN

Neidlinger, Buell (*b* New York, 2 March 1936). Bass player. He studied cello with Luigi Silva and Gregor Piatigorsky, and at the age of 12 won a competition to play with the New York PO. In his mid-teens he began to perform on double bass with such famous dixieland and swing musicians as Joe Sullivan, Vic Dickenson, Ben Webster, and Billie Holiday. Leaping the boundary between genres once again, in 1955 he joined Cecil Taylor's group, with which he remained until the early 1960s, thereby playing a prominent role in the development of free jazz; he also recorded under the leadership of his fellow sideman Steve Lacy. In the mid-1960s he performed in major American symphony orchestras, then in 1969 went to Los Angeles for a jazz-rock recording session with Frank Zappa and Jean-Luc Ponty. After settling in the city Neidlinger taught at the California Institute for the Arts (1970–82) and worked as a studio musician, recording prolifically on both double bass and electric bass guitar. He was also the principal bass player of the Los Angeles Chamber Orchestra from 1972 to 1978. From the late 1970s he has been a leader, with the tenor saxophonist Marty Krystall, of several jazz-rock bands, and has played with his own bluegrass group, Buellgrass.

SELECTED RECORDINGS

As sideman: C. Taylor: *Jazz Advance* (1956, Tran. 19); *The Gigi Gryce–Donald Byrd Jazz Lab & Cecil Taylor at Newport: Jazz Lab* (1957, Verve 8238); S. Lacy: *Soprano Sax* (1957, Prst. 7125); C. Taylor: *Looking Ahead!* (1958, Cont. 3562); S. Lacy: *Reflections* (1958, NewJ 8206); C. Taylor: *The Cecil Taylor All Stars Featuring Buell Neidlinger* (1961, CBS Sony 01107); J.-L. Ponty: *King Kong* (1969, PJ 20172)

BIBLIOGRAPHY

A. B. Spellman: "Cecil Taylor," *Four Lives in the Bebop Business* (New York, 1966/*R*1970 as *Black Music: Four Lives*), 1–76
Z. Stewart: "Buell Neidlinger," *DB*, xlviii/6 (1981), 21
J. Weiss: "Buell Neidlinger," *Coda*, no.188 (1983), 8
B. Rusch: "Buell Neidlinger: Interview," *Cadence*, xii/6 (1986), 5

BARRY KERNFELD

Neloms, Bob [Robert James] (*b* Detroit, 2 March 1942). Pianist. He attended the Berklee College of Music in Boston on a scholarship awarded by *Down Beat* (1959) and, after working in Motown's studios in Detroit (1961–3), he led his own small groups on the West Coast and in Boston; his sidemen included Eddie Henderson, Ricky Ford, and Bob Mover. He again studied at Berklee in 1969–70 and in 1973 he moved to New York, where he appeared with, among others, Roy Haynes and Freddie Waits. From 1977 to 1978 he played and recorded with Charles Mingus. He also made recordings with James Newton, Hamiet Bluiett, and Dannie Richmond (including *Dannie Richmond Quintet*, 1980, Gatemouth 1004), and as a soloist (*Pretty Music*, 1982, IndN 1050). Neloms has been active as a music teacher and therapist and has continued leading small groups; although he is best known as a pianist, he also plays organ and trombone.

Big Eye Louis Nelson (left) and Freddie Keppard, New Orleans, c1911

Nelson, Big Eye Louis [DeLisle, Louis Nelson] (*b* New Orleans, 28 Jan 1880 or 1885; *d* New Orleans, 20 Aug 1949). Clarinetist. He learned to play accordion, guitar, banjo, violin, and double bass. Largely self-taught as a clarinetist, he received some lessons from Luis Tio and Lorenzo Tio, Sr., in 1904. Remaining in New Orleans for most of his life, he performed with many well-known musicians there, including King Oliver, Jelly Roll Morton, and Papa Celestin; he also played with the Imperial Orchestra (*c*1905), the Golden Rule Orchestra (*c*1907), the Imperial Band (*c*1910), and the Superior Orchestra. Marquis attests that Nelson was a member of the last-named group as early as 1907; Chilton, however, gives 1912, and also asserts that he played with Buddy Bolden. In 1916 Nelson went to Chicago to work with Freddie Keppard, but in 1918 he returned to New Orleans and until 1924 played with John Robichaux' orchestra. After working with Sidney Desvigne in the late 1920s he led his own quartet at Luthjen's from 1939 until 1948.

Nelson was one of the foremost exponents of the early New Orleans clarinet style and is remembered for his warm, pure, full tone, imaginative phrasing, and fluid technique. He recorded with Kid Rena in 1940. The other clarinetist on these numbers is Alphonse Picou, and although both musicians were perhaps past their prime they demonstrate the role of the clarinet in early jazz ensembles. In 1949 Nelson took part in two sessions for the American Music label, one with Wooden Joe Nicholas and the other under his own name (as Louis Delisle). These recordings show his clear, liquid tone and considerable facility of technique, notably in the arpeggios he plays on Nicholas's *Holler Blues*; on his own titles he frequently takes over the ensemble lead from the trumpeter Charlie Love. Nelson taught Sidney Bechet, and his style influenced Johnny Dodds and Jimmie Noone.

Oral history material in *LNT*.

For futher illustration *see* BANDS, fig.2.

SELECTED RECORDINGS

As leader: *Louis Delisle's Band* (1949, AM 646), incl. Clarinet Marmalade, Dinah

As sideman: K. Rena: Panama (1940, Delta 800); Milenberg Joys/Clarinet Marmalade (1940, Delta 802/805); W. J. Nicholas: *Wooden Joe's Band* (1949, AM 646), incl. B-flat Blues, Holler Blues

BIBLIOGRAPHY

ChiltonW
R. Goffin: " 'Big Eye' Louis Nelson," *Jazz Record*, no.45 (1946), 7; repr. in *Selections from the Gutter: Jazz Portraits from "The Jazz Record"*, ed. A. Hodes and C. Hansen (Berkeley, CA, Los Angeles, and London, 1977), 126
A. Lomax: *Mister Jelly Roll: the Fortunes of Jelly Roll Morton, New Orleans Creole and "Inventor of Jazz"* (New York, 1950, 2/1973)
M. Williams: *Jazz Masters of New Orleans* (New York and London, 1967/*R*1978)
T. Bethell: *George Lewis: a Jazzman from New Orleans* (Berkeley, CA, and London, 1977)
D. M. Marquis: *In search of Buddy Bolden, First Man of Jazz* (Baton Rouge, LA, and London, 1978)
J. Chilton: Sidney Bechet: the Wizard of Jazz (London and New York, 1987)

RAYMOND J. GARIGLIO

Nelson, Dave [Davidson C.] (*b* Donaldsonville, LA, 1905; *d* New York, 7 April 1946). Trumpeter, pianist, and arranger. He had early formal training on violin and piano before taking up trumpet, and later studied arranging informally with Richard

M. Jones. As a protégé of King Oliver, he went to Chicago with the latter's band, although he did not play in the group; his first professional work was at the Lincoln Gardens with the Marie Lucas Orchestra. Thereafter he played with Ma Rainey (for illustration *see* BLUES, fig.1), Jelly Roll Morton, Edgar Hayes (1927), Jimmie Noone, the violinist Leroy Pickett (1928), and Luis Russell (1929), as well as with his own band. In autumn 1929 he joined Oliver and arranged many of the titles the band recorded for Victor during the following year. In the 1930s and early 1940s Nelson played both trumpet and piano in various groups of his own. His last years were spent as a staff arranger for the Lewis Publishing Co.

Nelson had a big and brassy trumpet tone in the manner of Oliver, and was often mistaken for his mentor on recordings that they made together. He also assimilated Oliver's muting techniques and used them creatively. He was a skilled arranger with a sound knowledge of harmony.

SELECTED RECORDINGS

As leader: I ain't got nobody/When day is done (1931, Vic. 22639)

As sideman: M. Rainey: Broken Hearted Blues/Jealousy Blues (1926, Para. 12364); K. Oliver: Sweet like this/I want you just myself (1929, Vic. 38101); New Orleans Shout/Nelson Stomp (1929–30, Vic. 23388); Willie "the Lion" Smith: More than that/I'm all out of breath (1937, Decca 1308)

BIBLIOGRAPHY

ChiltonW

M. Williams: "Papa Joe," *Jazz Masters of New Orleans* (New York and London, 1967/R1978), 112

C. Hillman: "Some Ambiguous Cornet Players," *Sv*, no.43 (1972), 28

A. McCarthy: *Big Band Jazz* (New York and London, 1974)

D. Nelson: "The King's Nephew," *Selections from the Gutter: Jazz Portraits from "The Jazz Record"*, ed. A. Hodes and C. Hansen (Berkeley, CA, Los Angeles, and London, 1977), 139

F. Driggs: *Black Beauty, White Heat: a Pictorial History of Classic Jazz, 1920–1950* (New York, 1982)

C. Hillman: "A Paramount Cornettist," *Sv*, no.113 (1984), 164

L. Wright and others: *Walter C. Allen & Brian A. L. Rust's "King" Oliver* (Chigwell, England, 1987) [completely rev. version of Allen and Rust: *King Joe Oliver* (Belleville, NJ, 1955)]

LAWRENCE KOCH

Nelson, George (*b* New Orleans, *c*1905; *d* New Orleans, May 1981). Saxophonist, brother of Louis Nelson. He played with Buddy Petit on the SS *Madisonville* in the late 1920s, remaining with the band when, after Petit's death in 1931, it was taken over by the banjoist Reuben McClennon. Nelson ceased playing in 1936.

MARCEL JOLY

Nelson, Louis (*b* New Orleans, 17 Sept 1902). Trombonist, brother of George Nelson. He began playing alto horn but had changed to trombone by the early 1920s. He worked in New Orleans with Kid Rena and Sidney Desvigne (1930s), among others, and from 1944 he played regularly with Kid Thomas, with whom he later made several recordings (including *Kid Thomas at Moulin Rouge*, *c*1955, Center 14). In the 1960s Nelson toured Japan and Europe with George Lewis (i) and performed in Europe as a soloist. He has played frequently at Preservation Hall, New Orleans, with such musicians as Punch Miller and Percy Humphrey and at the New Orleans Jazz and Heritage Festival (from 1969), and in the 1970s and 1980s he performed on tour with Humphrey and the New Orleans Joymakers, with the LEGENDS OF JAZZ, as a soloist, and with Kid Thomas and Sammy Rimington. Nelson has made many recordings as a leader (including *Louis Nelson Big Four*, 1963, GHB 25–6) and with other musicians, among them Miller (1962) and Humphrey (1966). His performances exemplify the New Orleans ensemble trombone style, and his solos are characterized by the use of a number of stock phrases as trademarks.

Oral history material in *LNT*.

BIBLIOGRAPHY

E. Kennedy: "Been Here and Gone: Louis Nelson in Europe," *Fn*, iii/5 (1972), 12

P. Vacher: "Louis Nelson and 'the New Orleans Navy'," *JJI*, xxx/10 (1977), 38

based on *ChiltonW*

Nelson, Oliver (Edward) (*b* St. Louis, 4 June 1932; *d* Los Angeles, 28 Oct 1975). Composer, arranger, and alto and tenor saxophonist. He studied piano, then saxophone, and in the late 1940s was a lead alto saxophonist in the Jeter–Pillars Orchestra and the big band led by George Hudson (both of which he worked with in St. Louis), and an orchestra led by Nat Towles (with which he traveled through Nebraska and Iowa). After working in New York with Louis Jordan's group and completing military service he studied composition and theory at Washington University (BM 1957) and at Lincoln University in Missouri (MM 1958), then returned to New York. He performed and recorded in the orchestras of Louie Bellson (1959), Eddie "Lockjaw" Davis (1960), and Duke Ellington (1961) and recorded frequently as the leader of small groups, for which he also wrote compositions. From the mid-1960s he gave fewer performances and concentrated his efforts on teaching, arranging, leading big bands, writing music for television and films, and, above all, composing works that combine aspects of jazz and Western art music. In 1967 he settled in Los Angeles and in 1969 toured Africa as the leader of a septet.

Nelson aspired towards legitimacy as a composer, but his serious works are saccharine, and his playing of rhythm-and-blues, hard bop, and modal jazz and his compositions in these styles are of far greater importance. His best work as a performer consists of three albums that he recorded in 1960–61 as the leader of a group that included Eric Dolphy. Among his more effective compositions is the suite *Afro/American Sketches*, which he recorded in 1961; this combines blues forms, swing riffs, a simulation of African drumming, a brass chorale, tender, lamenting melodies, and his own raucous, violent alto and tenor saxophone improvisations. The manuscript score of his composition *Stolen Moments* was published in *Down Beat*, xxix/14 (1962), 14. He is the author of *Patterns for Saxophone* (Hollywood, CA, 1966), a compendium of improvisatory formulas that has become widely used.

SELECTED RECORDINGS

Screamin' the Blues (1960, NewJ 8243); *Straight Ahead* (1961, NewJ 8255); *More Blues and the Abstract Truth* (1964, Imp. 75)

RECORDED COMPOSITIONS

(selective list; all recorded by Nelson)

Stolen Moments, on *Blues and the Abstract Truth* (1961, Imp. 5); *Afro/American Sketches* (1961, Prst. 7225); *Black, Brown, and Beautiful* (1969, FD 116); *Berlin Dialogue for Orchestra* (1970, FD 134)

SELECTED ARRANGEMENTS

Recorded by J. Smith: Walk on the Wild Side, on *The Unpredictable Jimmy Smith: Bashin'* (1962, Verve 68474)

Recorded by G. Barbieri: *Last Tango in Paris* (*c*1972, UA LA045F)

BIBLIOGRAPHY

J. Goldberg: "Focus on Oliver Nelson," *DB*, xxix/4 (1962), 17

R. Williams: "Straight Ahead: the Early Work of Oliver Nelson and Eric Dolphy," *JJ*, xx/7 (1967), 4

W. L. Fowler: "New Hope for the Abstract Truth: Oliver Nelson," *DB*, xlii/8 (1975), 10 [incl. discography]

"Oliver Nelson," *SJ*, xxx/2 (1976), 262 [discography]
D. N. Baker, L. M. Belt, and H. C. Hudson, eds.: *The Black Composer Speaks* (Metuchen, NJ, and London, 1978), 203–38 [incl. list of compositions]

BARRY KERNFELD

Nerem, Bjarne (Arnulf) (*b* Oslo, 31 July 1923). Norwegian tenor saxophonist. He studied clarinet with his father and took part in jam sessions during the early 1940s. He started working professionally with the pianist Willy Andersen (1947) and the trumpeter Nisse Skoogh (1948) in Norway, then played on a transatlantic liner (1949). In the 1950s he performed with Ernie Englund (1954), Ove Lind (1958), and the Swedish bandleaders Anders Burman and Åke Persson (both 1959). He played on many bop and swing albums; among those with whom he recorded were Persson and Benny Bailey (1959), Harry Arnold's Radiobandet (1957–8, 1960–61), the American leaders Roy Haynes (1954) and Stan Getz (1958), and Karin Krog (1973–4). He also recorded an album as leader, *How Long has This been Going On?* (1971, Odeon E062-34320). (*FeatherE*)

Nesbitt, John (*b* Norfolk, VA, *c*1900; *d* Boston, 1935). Trumpeter and arranger. He began playing with William McKinney around 1925 and made several recordings with McKinney's Cotton Pickers (1928–31; for illustration *see* MCKINNEY'S COTTON PICKERS), including *Plain Dirt* (1929, Vic. 38097), which was one of many arrangements he wrote for the band; the group also recorded as the Chocolate Dandies (1928) and with Jean Goldkette (1929). Nesbitt then worked as an arranger with Fletcher Henderson (with whom he recorded in 1930) and Luis Russell, among others, and performed with Zack Whyte's Chocolate Beau Brummels, Speed Webb, and Earle Warren (early 1930s). (J. Chilton: *McKinney's Music: a Bio-discography of McKinney's Cotton Pickers*, London, 1978)
See also ARRANGEMENT, §2 and Table 2.

based on *ChiltonW*

Nessa. Record company and label. The company was established in 1967 in Chicago by Chuck (Charles T.) Nessa. It issued important early albums by Lester Bowie and Roscoe Mitchell. After lying dormant until 1975 it was active once more during the late 1970s, and continued to concentrate on the work of free-jazz musicians from Chicago, recording them both there and in New York. Nessa also put out new bop recordings by Warne Marsh and Von Freeman. (J.-L. Bourget: "Nessa," *Jm*, no.264 (1978), 30)

Nestico, Sammy [Sam(uel Louis); Nistico, Sal] (*b* Pittsburgh, 6 Feb 1924). Arranger and composer. He taught himself to play trombone and, at the age of 17, worked in Pittsburgh as a member of the ABC staff orchestra. After military service he studied music at Duquesne University (BS 1950). He was then appointed staff arranger for the US Air Force Band (1951) and moved to Washington, where he attended the Catholic University of America (1951–2); from 1963 he also provided arrangements for the US Marine Band and led the orchestra at the White House. In 1967 he was recommended to Count Basie as an arranger by his cousin Sal Nistico (ii) and Grover Mitchell, both members of Basie's band. The following year he moved to Hollywood to compose and conduct for Basie, and the several recordings he made with the group are probably his best-known work. He also composed music for films and television and recorded an album as the leader of his own studio orchestra (1982). Nestico has been active in jazz education, writing many arrangements for school bands and presenting workshops.

SELECTED ARRANGEMENTS

As leader: *Dark Orchid* (1982, PAlt 8081), incl. Dark Orchid
Recorded by C. Basie: *Basie Big Band* (1975, Pablo 2310756); *Prime Time* (1977, Pablo 2310797); *Warm Breeze* (1981, Pablo 2312131)

BIBLIOGRAPHY

L. Feather: "Sammy Nestico: Basies graa eminens," *Orkester journalen*, xl (1972), Sept, 6
H. Wong: "Professional Spotlight on Sammy Nestico," *NAJE Educator*, x/4 (1978), 12
D. Davis: "Taking a Break with Sammy Nestico," *The Instrumentalist*, xxxiv/1 (1979), 12

STEVEN STRUNK

Neves, Oscar. *See* CASTRO-NEVES, OSCAR.

New Air. Name under which the trio AIR was re-formed in the 1980s.

New Artists Guild. Informal cooperative organization, founded in Berlin in the mid-1960s, which in 1969 developed into the company FMP.

New Black Eagle Jazz Band. Traditional jazz band. It was formed in September 1971 by the cornetist Tony Pringle (*b* Greasty, Cheshire, England, 21 Dec 1936) and has been active principally in New England. With an instrumentation of a conventional dixieland band – its personnel includes the tuba player Eli Newburger (*b* New York, 26 Dec 1940) and the pianist Bob Pilsbury (*b* Boston, 28 Dec 1926) – the group's repertory is drawn from early and classic jazz. It has made many appearances at international festivals, and among its several recordings are *Classic Jazz* (1976, 1978, Phi. 9198784) and *The New Black Eagle Jazz Band at Symphony Hall* (1981, Philo 1086).

BIBLIOGRAPHY

B. Byler: "Flying High," *MR*, iv/4 (1977), 1
F. Hollander: Liner notes, *The New Black Eagle Jazz Band at Symphony Hall* (Philo 1086, 1982) [incl. chronology]

ALYN SHIPTON

Newborn, (Edwin) Calvin (*b* Memphis, 27 April 1933). Guitarist, brother of Phineas Newborn. He made recordings with his brother from 1953 to 1958 (including *Phineas Newborn*, 1956, Atl. 1235) and in 1959 joined Earl Hines's group, with which he recorded the following year (*Earl's Pearls*, MGM SE3832). He also recorded swing and bop with Lionel Hampton (in New York and Paris, 1960–61), Jimmy Forrest (1961), Wild Bill Davis (1962), Al Grey (1963), and Freddie Roach (1964).

BIBLIOGRAPHY

FeatherE
S. Dance: "Earl's Four," *JJ*, xiii/7 (1960), 9

PAUL RINZLER

Newborn, Phineas(, Jr.) (*b* Whiteville, TN, 14 Dec 1931). Pianist, brother of Calvin Newborn. He was born to a musical family and while in high school studied piano, theory, alto saxophone, and several brass instruments. He played in local bands in Memphis (1945–50), with Lionel Hampton (1950, 1952), and in a military band (1953–5), then moved in 1956 to New York, where he drew the favorable attention of critics. He formed a duo with Charles Mingus (1958) and toured Europe (1958, 1959). After moving to Los Angeles in 1960 his appearances became less frequent owing to illness and a hand injury, but later his career again became more active, and in 1975 he performed at a concert sponsored by the World Jazz Association in Los Angeles. Newborn's prodigious technique and extraordinary speed have been likened to those of Art Tatum.

SELECTED RECORDINGS

As unaccompanied soloist: *Solo Piano* (1974, Atl. 1672)
As leader: *Here is Phineas* (1956, Atl. 1235); *Fabulous Phineas* (1958, RCA LPM1873); *Piano Portraits* (1959, Roul. 52031); *A World of Piano* (1961, Cont. 7600); *Please Send me Someone to Love* (1969, Cont. 7622)
As sideman: R. Haynes: *We Three* (1958, NewJ 8210); T. Edwards and H. McGhee: *Together Again* (1961, Cont. 7588)

BIBLIOGRAPHY

D. Hunt: "Phineas Newborn Jr.: Problems of a Virtuoso," *J&P*, ix/6 (1970), 22
H. Siders: "Phineas Newborn, Jr.: *Please Send me Someone to Love*," *DB*, xxxvii/16 (1970), 24 [review]
L. Lyons: "Phineas Newborn: a Jazz Self Portrait," *CK*, ii/3 (1976), 16
L. Feather: "Piano Giants of Jazz: Phineas Newborn Jr.," *CK*, v/8 (1979), 62 [incl. transcr.]
P.-A. Monti: *Discographie de Phineas Newborn* (Sierre, Switzerland, n.d. [?1980])
P. Palmer: "Pianos in the Background," *JJI*, xxxvii/11 (1984), 17
K. Hodges: "The Forgotten Ones: Phineas Newborn," *JJI*, xxxix/9 (1986), 22 [incl. discography]

PAUL RINZLER

New Dalta Ahkri. A two- to five-piece group formed in 1970 by LEO SMITH.

New Herd. Name by which a big band led by TOSHIYUKI MIYAMA was known from 1958.

New Hot Players. Swiss swing orchestra. An amateur group, it was formed in Neuchâtel, Switzerland, and modeled on Bob Crosby's Bob Cats. Although the members of the group played together from 1930 and first appeared in public in 1934, the name New Hot Players was not adopted until 1936. The group was awarded a prize at an amateur jazz festival in Brussels (1938) and it made about 20 recordings for Elite Special in Zurich in 1940 and 1943 (including *Swinging Upstairs*, 1940; all reissued on *New Hot Players*, ES SJ6304). At the first session the musicians were Claude de Coulon (trombone), Henri du Pasquier (tenor saxophone, clarinet), Charles Wilhelm (clarinet), Marco Junod (piano), Paul Girard (double bass), Roger du Pasquier (guitar), and Giovanni Marcozzi (drums); in 1943 the musicians included Charles Matthey (trumpet), Raymond Blum (trombone), and Paul Junod (double bass). The group was occasionally revived by its former members: unissued recordings exist of a concert given in 1948 and a radio broadcast of 1954 called "Jazz partout," both of which took place in La Chaux-de-Fonds, near Neuchâtel.

BIBLIOGRAPHY

R. Quenet: "Die Geschichte der New Hot Players/L'histoire des New Hot Players," *New Hot Players* (ES SJ6034, 1966) [liner notes]
J.-R. Hippenmeyer: *Le jazz en Suisse, 1930–1970* (Yverdon, Switzerland, 1971)

RAINER E. LOTZ

New Jazz. Record label operated by the PRESTIGE company.

New Jazz Orchestra. Ensemble formed in 1963 by Clive Burrows and directed from 1964 to 1968 by NEIL ARDLEY.

Newk. Nickname of SONNY ROLLINS.

Newman, David "Fathead" (*b* Dallas, 24 Feb 1933). Tenor saxophonist. He played professionally in Dallas with Buster Smith while still in his teens, and later played with Ornette Coleman in a band led by the saxophonist Red Connors; he also worked with such rhythm-and-blues musicians as Lowell Fulson, T-Bone Walker, and, from 1952, Ray Charles, who had been Fulson's pianist. From 1954 he played in Charles's band, first as a baritone saxophonist, then as the tenor saxophone soloist, and in 1958 he made his first recording as a leader, with Charles and Hank Crawford among his sidemen. After leaving Charles's band in 1964 he played for two years in Dallas, then moved to New York. He worked again with Charles (for a brief period in 1970–71) and played with Red Garland and Herbie Mann (1972–4). Later he performed and recorded as a leader and recorded with Junior Mance (1983).

SELECTED RECORDINGS

As leader: *Ray Charles Presents "Fathead"* (1958, Atl. 1304); *Lonely Avenue* (1971, Atl. 1600); *Resurgence* (1980, Muse 5234)
As sideman: R. Charles: *Ray Charles at Newport* (1958, Atl. 1289)

BIBLIOGRAPHY

FeatherE; *Feather '60s*; *Feather–Gitler '70s*
F. Postif: "Marjorie Hendricks, David Newman et John Hunt nous aident à mieux connaître les véritables débuts de Ray Charles," *Jh*, no.170 (1961), 15
M. Cuscuna: "Fathead Newman: King of the Texas Panhandle," *DB*, xli/20 (1974), 16

DAVID WILD

Newman, Joe [Joseph Dwight] (*b* New Orleans, 7 Sept 1922). Trumpeter. His father, Dwight Newman (1902–*c*1942), played piano with the Bocage brothers in the Creole Serenaders. After playing with bands at Alabama State Teachers College Joe Newman joined Lionel Hampton in 1941, then played intermittently with Count Basie from 1943 to 1946. He spent brief periods with Illinois Jacquet and J. C. Heard in 1946, and the following year rejoined Jacquet, remaining until 1950. By the time he returned to Basie once more in 1952 he was one of the leading trumpet soloists in the swing style; he assumed the position in the band that had previously been held by Harry Edison, and played very much like his predecessor. He toured Europe with Basie (1954) and took solos in numerous arrangements. After leaving the band (1961) he toured the USSR with Benny Goodman (1962). In the early 1960s he was a founder of Jazz Interactions, Inc., an organization formed in New York to promote the appreciation of jazz, particularly in schools; in 1967 he became its president. From 1974 he worked with the New York Jazz Repertory Company, with which he toured the USSR and Europe in 1975. He has continued to record and perform into the 1980s. Newman is one of the most powerful trumpeters in jazz: his style in the mid-1980s consisted of strong attacks, forceful runs, and slow melodies reminiscent of Basie's. The energy and quiet strength of his playing have been praised by critics and musicians alike.

SELECTED RECORDINGS

As leader: *Joe Newman and his Band* (1954, Van. 8007); *I'm Still Swinging* (1955, RCA LPM1198); *Salute to Satch* (1956, RCA LPM1324); *Happy Cats* (1957, Coral 57121); with J. Wilder: *Hangin' out* (1984, Conc. 262)
As sideman: B. Holiday: My Man/He's Funny that Way (1952, Clef 89089); N. Pierce: *Kansas City Memories* (1956, Coral 57091); C. Basie: *Basie* (1957, Roul. 52003); *Count Basie/Sarah Vaughan* (1960, Roul. 52065); L. Hampton: *Newport Uproar!* (1967, RCA LSP3891)

BIBLIOGRAPHY

FeatherE; *Feather '60s*; *Feather–Gitler '70s*
R. Horricks: "Joe Newman Continues a Tradition," *JM*, ii/3 (1956), 2
——: *Count Basie and his Orchestra: its Music and its Musicians* (London and New York, 1957), 192
L. Tomkins: "The Joe Newman Story," *CI*, xvi (1977), no.3, p.22; no.4, p.14
S. Dance: *The World of Count Basie* (New York and London, 1980) [colln of previously pubd interviews], 142

LEROY OSTRANSKY

New Orleans Bootblacks. Name under which the personnel of the NEW ORLEANS WANDERERS also recorded.

New Orleans Feetwarmers. Sextet. Formed in September 1932, it was led by the soprano saxophonist and clarinetist Sidney Bechet and the trumpeter Tommy Ladnier and included as its other members the trombonist Teddy Nixon, the pianist Hank Duncan, the double bass player Wilson Myers, and the drummer Morris Morland. The group recorded six tracks for Victor on 15 September 1932 (of which *Maple Leaf Rag*, *I've Found a New Baby*, and *Shag* are particularly outstanding), performed at the Savoy Ballroom and the Saratoga Club in New York until early 1933, and took part in the concert "Spirituals to Swing" in 1938. Between February 1940 and October 1941 Bechet recorded 40 tracks during eight sessions with various other groups known as the Feetwarmers; among the best-known of these recordings are *Shake it and Break it* with Sidney De Paris and Sandy Williams, *Save it Pretty Mama* (1940, 27240) with Rex Stewart and Earl Hines, and *Egyptian Fantasy* (1941, 27337) with Henry "Red" Allen.

SELECTED RECORDINGS

(all recorded for Victor)

Sweetie Dear/Maple Leaf Rag (1932, 23360); I've Found a New Baby/Shag (1932, 24150); Shake it and Break it/Wild Man Blues (1940, 26640)

BIBLIOGRAPHY

G. Hoefer: Liner notes, S. Bechet: *Bechet of New Orleans* (RCA LPV510, 1965)
——: Liner notes, S. Bechet: *The Blue Bechet* (RCA LPV535, 1967)

MIKE HAZELDINE

New Orleans jazz. A style of small-ensemble jazz that originated shortly before World War I, became internationally known through recordings in the 1920s, and underwent a revival in the 1940s (*see* TRADITIONAL JAZZ). It now exists as an interrelated group of performance styles with fixed instrumentation and a relatively restricted repertory. Some writers distinguish it from DIXIELAND JAZZ, a label that they reserve for white musicians and orchestras.

The earliest New Orleans "hot" players in the first two decades of the century thought of their music as ragtime, albeit with a local accent. This music was for the most part learned and played by ear by amateurs or semiprofessionals, though some players were musically literate; it usually used a rhythm section of drums (not always present before 1910), guitar, and double bass (often bowed rather than plucked) and an unusually wide variety of timbres, and emphasized a continuous ensemble polyphony, in which the wind players rarely rested. The early repertory consisted of old-fashioned schottische, mazurka, and quadrille dance tunes as well as a number of local specialties, such as *Tiger Rag* and *Don't go way nobody*; other tunes were probably taken from a general southern repertory (*Make me a pallet on the floor*, *Easy Rider*, *Bucket got a hole in it*), while certain pieces that have become "New Orleans standards" (e.g., *High Society*, *Panama*, and *Moose March*) were nationwide hits which simply remained current in New Orleans.

The large dance bands before 1920 comprised violin, cornet, clarinet, trombone, drums, double bass, guitar, and sometimes piano. Many musicians gained their first experience in smaller, so-called string bands: violin, guitar, double bass, and one or two wind instruments. New Orleans bands followed a national fashion in dropping the violin and exchanging guitar and double bass for banjo and tuba; they also adopted the saxophone family, contrary to a longstanding jazz myth. The use of two cornets – which was thought on the evidence of King Oliver's recordings of 1923 to be essential to the authentic New Orleans style – was virtually never a feature of the older orchestras. Furthermore, though often imitated during the 1920s, the instrumentation of the Original Dixieland Jazz Band (cornet, trombone, clarinet, piano, and drums) was not common in New Orleans itself – except possibly for bands that performed for ballyhoos (*see* BATTLE OF BANDS) and at prize fights – and was perhaps fostered by the Chicago cabarets that used jazz bands between 1915 and 1918. Musicians active before World War I sometimes employed a typology that distinguished between orchestras whose players could read music, those in which they both read and played by ear, and those whose members could play only by ear.

In early New Orleans groups, the melody was often shifted from instrument to instrument. By the early 1920s, however, it was generally assigned to the cornetist, who most often functioned as leader – a role previously taken by the violinist. New Orleans cornetists born before about 1895 played the lead with relatively little variation, unlike later jazz trumpeters; they made use of clipped articulation with relatively precise binary subdivisions of the beat, cultivating the middle register to f'' and employing a forceful tone, often with a "whinnying" rapid vibrato. The clarinetist supplied a countermelody in eighth-notes over a wide range, and characteristically used a more limpid timbre than later players, perhaps because of a French bias in the training of early New Orleans clarinetists. (Some timbral differences resulted from an ingrained preference, persisting to the present day, for Albert-system clarinets with wide bores and undercut tone-holes.) While clarinets and their idiom were underemployed in American dance orchestras before 1920, trombones were ubiquitous from 1910 on; hence the so-called TAILGATE style, with its many glissandos and its flexible mixture of tenor countermelody and doubling of the bass line, was perhaps the least local feature of New Orleans jazz. In general, the earliest recordings by King Oliver, Sidney Bechet, and others show New Orleans players as the first to integrate blue notes as well as portamento and strong vibrato into an expressive melodic instrumental style.

New Orleans drummers used very large and resonant bass drums and employed the press roll on the snare drum, probably with comparatively little reliance on other percussion accessories (*see* DRUM SET, §II, 3). The much-discussed question of two-beat versus four-beat rhythm is related to the transition from ragtime to jazz: the first New Orleans jazz drummer to be recorded, Tony Sbarbaro of the Original Dixieland Jazz Band in 1917–18, freely shifted from one to the other. Some early recordings indicate a predilection in New Orleans for somewhat slower tempos and a less assertive and heavily accented manner than elsewhere in the USA. Perhaps the most distinctive rhythmic feature was a pervasive but relaxed playing off the beat, particularly at the slower foxtrot or slow drag tempo.

The repertory and instrumentation of the white dixieland tradition became fixed to a far greater degree than that of the black tradition. Particularly with the onset of the "revival" in the late 1930s, many hymn tunes and various Creole folk or popular songs entered the repertory of black New Orleans jazz, often at the behest of recording directors and jazz historians. The harmony of New Orleans jazz is often simpler than the ragtime progressions that underlie it: chords more complex than the dominant seventh and diminished seventh are seldom used; there is little modulation, except between the strains of march tunes; and keys with more than one sharp or four flats are avoided. Solo playing is generally confined to the recurring two-bar breaks or to brief moments when one player dominates the ensemble, though there are frequent duets for wind instruments. In general there is little improvisation in the sense that term acquired after the early 1920s; routines, once learned, are quite stable.

The classic bands of the early 1920s New Orleans style were King Oliver's Creole Jazz Band and the New Orleans Rhythm Kings, though some critics find them much influenced by midwestern taste; later recordings of bands led by Jelly Roll Morton, Lil and Louis Armstrong, and Johnny Dodds are also prized as early examples of New Orleans jazz. These were all recorded in Chicago for the so-called race record market. Recordings made in the 1920s in New Orleans itself, especially by Sam Morgan's band and the Jones and Collins Astoria Hot Eight, are somewhat different in character from the groups recorded in the North, and no doubt reflect the contemporary local style.

The strong association in the public's mind between New Orleans jazz and the music of the marching-band tradition is somewhat exaggerated: the custom of employing wind bands to play at the funerals of members of fraternal orders (*see also* BRASS BAND) is a picturesque survival of one widespread in the USA during the 19th century. Many musicians and historians also hold that certain features of New Orleans jazz derive from or are common to musics of the West Indies. However, despite New Orleans's long history of close contact with the West Indies, this "Spanish tinge" (the term is Jelly Roll Morton's) has yet to receive thorough study.

See also BANDS, §§4(i) and (ii); FORMS, §2; and JAZZ (i), §§II, 3, 5, 6, III, 2, IV, 7.

BIBLIOGRAPHY

ChartersJ

B. King: "A Reassessment of New Orleans Jazz on American Music Records," *JM*, v (1959), no.1, p.2; no.2, p.6

H. Panassié: "Sur le style Nouvelle-Orléans," *BHcF*, no.120 (1962), 3

L. A. Pyke: *Jazz, 1920 to 1927: an Analytical Study* (diss., U. of Iowa, 1962)

B. King: "New Orleans Jazz: Some Speculations," *JM*, xii/5 (1967), 12

A. Rose and E. Souchon: *New Orleans Jazz: a Family Album* (Baton Rouge, LA, 1967, rev. 2/1978, rev. and enlarged 3/1984)

M. Williams: *Jazz Masters of New Orleans* (New York and London, 1967/*R*1978)

M. Dorigné: *Jazz, i: Les origines du jazz: le style Nouvelle-Orléans et ses prolongements* (Paris, 1968)

G. Schuller: *Early Jazz: its Roots and Musical Development* (New York, 1968)

O. Smith: "The 'New' New Orleans Revival," *JJ*, xxii/7 (1969), 18

[G. M. Foster], T. Stoddard, and R. Russell: *Pops Foster: the Autobiography of a New Orleans Jazzman* (Berkeley, CA, Los Angeles, and London, 1971) [incl. discography by B. Rust]

R. J. Martinez, ed.: *Portraits of New Orleans Jazz: its People and Places* (Jefferson, LA, 1971)

C. G. Herzog zu Mecklenburg: *Stilformen des Jazz*, i: *Vom Ragtime zum Chicago-Stil* (Vienna, 1973) [incl. discography by M. Scheffner]

W. J. Schafer and R. B. Allen: *Brass Bands and New Orleans Jazz* (Baton Rouge, LA, and London, 1977)

F. Turner: *Remembering Song: Encounters with the New Orleans Jazz Tradition* (New York, 1982)

LAWRENCE GUSHEE

New Orleans Jazz & Heritage Festival. Annual festival dedicated to the forms of jazz and popular music cultivated in New Orleans. It began in May 1968 as the New Orleans International Jazz Festival, and formed part of the city's 250th-anniversary celebrations. It was repeated in June 1969 under the sponsorship of Willis Conover, who had served as master of ceremonies the previous year. In 1970 George Wein, Quint Davis, and the New Orleans Jazz & Heritage Foundation took over as sponsors, and from 1972 the festival has taken place during a ten-day period in April and May at the New Orleans Fairgrounds Race Track and other local venues, such as the SS *President*, the Theater for the Performing Arts, and various clubs. It presents local musicians together with artists of international fame (such as Ella Fitzgerald and the soul singer Stevie Wonder); in 1985 there were 3000 participants, who performed on 14 separate stages before an audience estimated to comprise 300,000 people. The festival features a wide range of musical genres, among them traditional jazz, later forms of jazz, blues, soul, and Cajun music.

PAUL R. LAIRD

New Orleans Jazz Club [NOJC]. Organization of jazz musicians and jazz enthusiasts in New Orleans. It was established on Mardi Gras, 1948, by Johnny Wiggs, Gilbert Erskine, George Blanchin, Pete Miller, Don Perry, Al Diket, and Freddie King. The club's early activities, which were designed to preserve and promote New Orleans jazz, included monthly jam sessions, a weekly radio program, and summer concerts. The radio program, "Jazz from Congo Square," was first broadcast on WTPS but transferred to WWL in 1949; the jam sessions reached a height of popularity in the 1950s, when such musicians as Johnny St. Cyr and Pete Fountain took part. In the same decade the NOJC founded the New Orleans Jazz Museum, which by 1973 contained 20,000 photographs and 15,000 recordings as well as books, documents, and memorabilia; in 1979 the collection was transferred to the Louisiana State Museum, with Don Marquis as curator (*see* LIBRARIES AND ARCHIVES, §2).

The NOJC's most prominent activity has been the publication of its journal *Second Line*. Founded in 1950 as a monthly newsletter (its original title was the *Jazz Club Bulletin*), this was issued bimonthly as early as 1952; its first editor, Myra Menville, was succeeded in 1951 by Edmond Souchon, who led it through a period of growth and increasing popularity until his death in 1968. The journal was published quarterly from 1971. The NOJC, which is a member of the American Federation of Jazz Societies, had more than 1000 members in 1973.

BIBLIOGRAPHY

A. Rose and E. Souchon: *New Orleans Jazz: a Family Album* (Baton Rouge, LA, 1967, rev. 2/1978, rev. and enlarged 3/1984)

M. Menville: "The Jazz Club History," *SL*, xxv (spr. 1973), 7

K. Koenig: "A Brief History of the New Orleans Jazz Club, 1948–1985," *Federation Jazz*, i/2 (1985), 4

New Orleans Jazz Club of California [NOJCC, NOJCOC]. Organization of jazz enthusiasts. It was established in 1963 by Bill Bacin (who continued as its president into the late 1980s) to foster the playing and preservation of dixieland jazz; Bacin took as his model the New Orleans Jazz Club. The club's name was at first abbreviated to NOJCOC, but later to NOJCC. The members met regularly until 1968, but meetings were then discontinued and the club pursued its goals by sponsoring performances, gaining publicity for dixieland jazz, and publishing the journals *The Jazzologist* (1963–83) and *Jazz Newsletter* (1984–6). A highlight of the club's activities was the performance by the NOJCC All-Stars (including Ben Pollack, Barney Bigard, Alton Purnell, Dick Cary, and Wingy Manone) at the Monterey Jazz Festival in 1968. The organization's headquarters were originally in Orange, California, but moved in 1972 to Kerrville, Texas. A number of local jazz clubs are affiliated with the NOJCC and in 1987 the total membership was 4300.

New Orleans Rhythm Kings [NORK]. Jazz band. Its three principal members, PAUL MARES, Georg Brunis (*see* BRUNIES family, (4) Georg), and LEON ROPPOLO, were boyhood friends from New Orleans who had played together in various bands during their adolescence. After moving separately to the North, these three musicians reunited in Chicago in the early 1920s to form a band for a 17-month residency at the Friar's Inn

The New Orleans Rhythm Kings, Chicago, 1923: (left to right) Paul Mares (trumpet), Georg Brunis (trombone), Ben Pollack (drums), Steve Brown (double bass), Lou Black (banjo), Mel Stitzel (piano), Leon Roppolo (clarinet), and Volly DeFaut (C-melody saxophone)

nightclub. Originally their colleagues in the band were Jack Pettis, Elmer Schoebel, Arnold Loyocano (double bass), Lou Black, and Frank Snyder (drums). The group's first recordings (for Gennett in August 1922) were issued under the name of the Friar's Society Orchestra, but by 1923 it was known as the New Orleans Rhythm Kings. Loyocano's place on bass was taken by Steve Brown, who was in turn replaced by Chink Martin. Ben Pollack replaced Snyder as drummer, and Schoebel's place at the piano was taken by Mel Stitzel (see illustration).

The instantaneous success of the New Orleans Rhythm Kings' recordings and live performances made it the most important white New Orleans group after the Original Dixieland Jazz Band. Though the players never achieved the same widespread fame, and despite the fact that they partly based their style and repertory on those of the earlier band, on several counts they were superior to it. Their originality lay in blending the influences of the Original Dixieland Jazz Band with inspiration derived from the black New Orleans music of King Oliver's Creole Jazz Band. The New Orleans Rhythm Kings exuded a sense of relaxation that was rare among its contemporaries; the musicians avoided the nearly ubiquitous jerky phrasing, and with no loss of expression concentrated on legato playing. The final choruses of their performances are stirring without seeming frantic.

Mares, the group's leader, was heavily influenced by King Oliver's cornet playing. He usually remained in the middle register and established an emphatic lead part; during his solos he seldom departed from the melody, relying on subtle rhythmic and tonal inflections for variation. The group's foremost improviser was Roppolo, a highly original clarinetist whose solos on *Panama*, *Tiger Rag*, and *She's Crying for me Blues* are superb. His playing on the ingeniously arranged *Wolverine Blues* was much copied. Georg Brunis also played confident, adept solos, but his strength lay in creating clever "tailgate" patterns, many of which were rigorously imitated by other trombonists for decades afterwards. The band's front line inspired a school of young white Chicago jazz musicians, and it is regrettable that so few of its recordings are satisfactorily balanced.

After leaving the Friar's Inn the group enjoyed brief residencies at two Chicago dance halls before disbanding altogether. In 1924 Mares moved back to New Orleans, as did Roppolo and Martin; these three formed the nucleus of a revived New Orleans Rhythm Kings, which included Santo Pecora. The new band made a series of recordings in January 1925 which show that Mares was ever improving and that Roppolo was still a consummate improviser; but there are few signs that the band was attempting to broaden or develop its musical style. The same can be said of the titles recorded two months later when Roppolo's place on clarinet was taken by Charlie Cordilla. The group disbanded permanently soon afterwards, Mares leaving music for a decade and Roppolo beginning the first of several long stays in a Louisiana asylum. Brunis, who remained in the North, later became a key figure in the New Orleans revival movement from the late 1930s, particularly with Muggsy Spanier and Eddie Condon.

SELECTED RECORDINGS

(all recorded for Gennett unless otherwise indicated)

Eccentric (1922, 5009); Bugle Call Blues (1922, 4967); Panama/Tiger Rag (1922, 4968); Weary Blues/Wolverine Blues (1923, 5102); Maple Leaf Rag (1923, 5104); Tin Roof Blues (1923, 5105); She's Crying for me Blues (1925, OK 40327)

BIBLIOGRAPHY

G. Beall: "The New Orleans Rhythm Kings," *Frontiers of Jazz* (New York, 1947, rev. 2/1962), 82

G. Erskine: "Last of the New Orleans Rhythm Kings," *DB*, xxix/10 (1962), 22
M. Williams: "N.O.R.K.," *Jazz Masters of New Orleans* (New York and London, 1967/*R*1978), 121
D. Bakker: "N.O.R.K. 1922–1925," *Micrography*, no.19 (1972), 4
D. Coller: "Frank Snyder," *MR*, x/6 (1983), 7

JOHN CHILTON

New Orleans Wanderers. Recording group. Formed in 1926 by the pianist Lil Hardin (who later used her married name, Lil Armstrong), its other members were the clarinetist Johnny Dodds, the trombonist Kid Ory, the banjoist Johnny St. Cyr, the cornetist George Mitchell, and the alto saxophonist Joe Clark; all except Mitchell and Clark had been members of the Hot Five with Hardin. The group recorded four compositions by Louis Armstrong on 13 July 1926 and, as the New Orleans Bootblacks, four more on the following day; it made no other recordings. Such tracks as *Gate Mouth*, *Papa Dip*, and *Mad Dog* are particularly revealing of Ory's playing; Dodds's work is shown to advantage on *Perdido Street Blues* and *Too Tight*.

RECORDINGS

(all recorded in 1926 for Columbia)

As New Orleans Wanderers: Perdido Street Blues/Gate Mouth (698D); Too Tight/Papa Dip (735D)

As New Orleans Bootblacks: Mixed Salad/I Can't Say (14465D); Flat Foot/Mad Dog (14337D)

BIBLIOGRAPHY

G. E. Lambert: *Johnny Dodds* (London, 1961)
B. Rust: Liner notes, J. Dodds: *The Immortal Johnny Dodds* (VJM 48, 1981)

MIKE HAZELDINE

Newport Jazz Festival. Festival held annually from 1954. It is one of the oldest annual jazz festivals in virtually continuous operation. The festival was first organized in Newport, Rhode Island, by Louis Lorillard and Elaine Lorillard, who administered it through a nonprofit corporation and engaged as its director George Wein, then the owner of the Storyville Club in Boston. It was held in its first year in the grounds of the Newport Casino and in the following years at various locations in Newport; in 1958 it was the subject of the film *Jazz on a Summer's Day* (*see* FILMS, §II, 4). The festival was canceled in 1961 by the Newport City Council owing to unruly crowds in previous years, but it resumed in 1962, by which time Wein was the director and producer of a profit-making venture rather than a nonprofit one. Wein's activities expanded considerably during this period: in 1958 he produced (with the cooperation of the US Department of State) a week-long jazz festival with artists from Newport at the World's Fair in Brussels, and by 1961 he had also organized festivals in Boston, Buffalo, Philadelphia, Toronto, and French Lick (Indiana). In 1962 he produced the Newport Jazz Festival in Europe, a tour of eleven countries. In the 1960s the Newport All-Stars toured widely with Wein as their pianist. At the same time the Newport Jazz Festival grew considerably, in part because popular music came to be included in its programs in addition to jazz (Chuck Berry appeared as early as 1958, Ray Charles made several appearances in the 1960s, and in 1969 the performers included Blood, Sweat and Tears and the rock groups Jethro Tull and Sly and the Family Stone), and in part because of the sponsorship of such corporations as the Jos. Schlitz Brewing Co., which subsidized many festivals in the 1960s and 1970s. The festival was ended prematurely by a riot in 1971 and in the following year was moved to New York, where it became known as the Newport Jazz Festival/New York.

From the 1970s the festival also sponsored events in other cities, including a tribute to Charlie Parker at the Salle Pleyel in Paris (1974) and a concert at the White House celebrating the festival's 25th season (1978). Between 1975 and 1985 musicians who took part in the festival in New York also made a tour of the USA under the festival's name; in 1983 the tour brought performances to 20 American cities between June and October. The festival received the backing in 1980 of the manufacturer of Kool cigarettes (the Brown & Williamson Tobacco Co.), and its name was changed first to the Kool Newport Jazz Festival (1980), then to the Kool Jazz Festival (1981). In 1982 the Newport All-Stars resumed touring, again with Wein as their pianist. The festival's name changed again in 1986 when the Japanese Victor Corporation became its principal sponsor; it was now known as the JVC Jazz Festival/New York. By this time the festival had evolved from a series of concerts held over three to five days at one outdoor location to an urban festival lasting ten days and held at many venues, most of which were indoors. Performances were given in New York at Carnegie Hall, Avery Fisher Hall, Town Hall, Radio City Music Hall, Roseland Ballroom, the City Center, and the Staten Island Ferry, and outside the city in Saratoga Springs (New York, where they were presented under the name JVC Salutes Newport at Saratoga), Purchase (near White Plains, New York), and Waterloo Village (near Stanhope, New Jersey). Most musicians who take part in the festival are established, internationally known figures; in 1987 these included Miles Davis, Dizzy Gillespie, Herbie Hancock, Wynton Marsalis, Oscar Peterson, George Shearing, and Sarah Vaughan.

At the same time Wein and his firm Festival Productions, Inc., have continued to produce festivals under the name Newport Jazz in many other cities, including Philadelphia, Pittsburgh, and Hampton, Virginia (all of which were visited regularly during the tours of 1975–85), as well as Rochester (New York) and Madarao (a mountaintop near Tokyo). With the Japanese Victor Corporation he has also resumed production of a festival in Newport.

BIBLIOGRAPHY

A. J. Agostinelli: *The Newport Jazz Festival, Rhode Island, 1954–1971: a Bibliography, Discography, and Filmography* (Providence, RI, 1977)
B. Goldblatt: *Newport Jazz Festival: the Illustrated History* (New York, 1977)
K. Frankling: "George Wein's Long Run," *JT* (1985), Oct, 12

SARA VELEZ/PAUL R. LAIRD

Newsom, Tommy [Thomas Penn] (*b* Portsmouth, VA, 25 Feb 1929). Alto and tenor saxophonist, and arranger. He studied at the Peabody Conservatory and Columbia University Teachers College. During the 1950s he worked mainly as a studio musician in New York; he also toured Europe and North Africa with a US Air Force dance band. After touring Latin America (1961) and the USSR (1962) with Benny Goodman, he recorded with Goodman's big band (1962, 1964, 1967). He also recorded with a swing sextet led by Ruby Braff and Marshall Brown (*Ruby Braff–Marshall Brown Sextet*, 1961, UA 4093). In 1962 he joined NBC's music staff and from 1963 played in the band on "The Tonight Show," becoming its assistant conductor in 1968. His arrangements have been recorded by Billy Butterfield, Goodman, and Charlie Byrd (*Brazilian Byrd*, 1965, Col. CS9137).

New Thing. Term applied in the 1960s to FREE JAZZ.

Newton, Frankie [William Frank] (*b* Emory, nr Glade Springs, VA, 4 Jan 1906; *d* New York, 11 March 1954). Trumpeter. After touring in the West and playing in New York with the drummer Lloyd Scott (1927–9) he then settled in New York, where he worked with various musicians, including Cecil Scott (1929–

30), Chick Webb, Elmer Snowden (1931), Charlie Johnson (*c*1931, 1933–5), Garland Wilson, and Sam Wooding; he also recorded with Bessie Smith (1933) and Mezz Mezzrow (1936). He was a member of Teddy Hill's band (1936–7) and he performed with John Kirby's small group (1937) and Lucky Millinder (1937–8). In 1939 Newton formed his own group, which played at the Café Society, Kelly's Stable, and other clubs, and in the 1940s he continued to lead both small and large bands. He also worked with other leaders, among them James P. Johnson (1944–5), but in later years he devoted himself to painting and performed only occasionally. Newton, whose career was frequently interrupted by illness, was an inventive improviser. He often used a buzz-wow mute for contrast and to highlight his own ideas, many of which were highly individual and unusual.

SELECTED RECORDINGS

As leader: You showed me the way/Please don't talk about me when I'm gone (1937, Var. 518); I found a new baby/The Brittwood Stomp (1937, Var. 571); Tab's Blues (1939, Voc. 4821)

As sideman: B. Smith: Gimme a pigfoot/Take me for a buggy ride (1933, OK 8949); M. Mezzrow: Mutiny in the Parlor/The panic is on (1936, Bb 6319); J. P. Johnson: Four o'Clock Groove (1944, Asch 551–2)

BIBLIOGRAPHY

ChiltonW

A. McCarthy: "Frank Newton," *JM*, vii/5 (1961), 4

J. Evensmo: *The Trumpets of Bill Coleman, 1929–1945, Frankie Newton* (n.p. [Oslo], n.d. [?1978]) [discography]

G. Murphy: "The Forgotten Ones: Frankie Newton," *JJI*, xxxiii/12 (1980), 17

JOHNNY SIMMEN

Newton, James (*b* Los Angeles, 1 May 1953). Flutist. In high school he played electric bass guitar, alto and tenor saxophone, bass clarinet, and, from the age of 17, flute. He attended a junior college in California, where his major subject was music, and he also studied under Buddy Collette. At the same time he played flute and saxophone in a funk band, and performed in and around Pomona with Arthur Blythe, David Murray, and other young free-jazz musicians in Stanley Crouch's group Black Music Infinity (1972–5). From 1977 he dedicated himself exclusively to the flute. The following year he moved to New York and led a small ensemble with Anthony Davis, marking the beginning of an association that has continued into the 1980s. He has also performed in a trio with a Japanese koto player, a flute quartet with Frank Wess, and a woodwind quintet, and has made recordings regularly as an unaccompanied soloist and as a leader, including an album devoted to the music of Duke Ellington (1985). When improvising, Newton modifies his essentially pure, classical flute timbre with such special effects as multiphonics, flutter tonguing, harmonics, humming, and glissandos. His compositions include *Monk's Notice* and *Forever Charles*; transcriptions of his solos and scores of his compositions have been issued by his own company in Los Angeles, Janew Music Publications.

SELECTED RECORDINGS

As unaccompanied soloist: *Axum* (1981, ECM 1214)

Duos with D. Murray: *Solomon's Sons* (1977, Cir. [G] 5), incl. Monk's Notice

As leader: *Paseo del mar* (1978, IndN 1037), incl. Monk's Notice; with A. Davis: *Hidden Voices* (1979, IndN 1041), incl. Forever Charles; with C. Freeman: *Peaceful Heart, Gentle Spirit* (1980, Cont. 14005); *Portraits* (*c*1982, IndN 1051); *James Newton* (*c*1983, Gram. 8205); *The African Flower* (1985, BN 85109)

BIBLIOGRAPHY

H. L. Lindenmaier: "James Newton: Interview," *Cadence*, vi/2 (1980), 5

C. J. Safane: "Profile: James Newton," *DB*, xlvii/3 (1980), 54

"James Newton: Young Lion," *JT* (1982), Dec, 10

L. Jeske: "James Newton," *DB*, 1/4 (1983), 24 [incl. discography]

R. Hershon: "James Newton: Learning from Other Cultures," *JJI*, xxxix/6 (1986), 14

BARRY KERNFELD

New York Art Quartet. Free-jazz group. It was formed in 1964 by Roswell Rudd (trombone), John Tchicai (saxophone), and Milford Graves (drums); Lewis Worrell was the first and best of the group's many double bass players. The quartet disbanded in 1965. (J. Cooke: "New York Nouvelle Vague, 5: the New York Art Quartet," *JM*, xii/9 (1966), 2)

New York Contemporary Five. Group organized in 1963 by the trumpeter Don Cherry, the alto saxophonist John Tchicai, and the tenor saxophonist Archie Shepp; the other members of the quintet, which recorded five albums in 1963–4, were the double bass player Don Moore and the drummer J. C. Moses.

New Yorkers (i). Dance orchestra. In 1927 the banjoist and guitarist George Carhart organized a group of American musicians to play jazz and dance music in Europe; among the personnel were Jack Purvis (trumpet), Danny Polo (alto saxophone and clarinet), Babe Russin (tenor saxophone), Spencer Clark (bass saxophone), Jack O'Brien (piano), and Dave Tough (drums). The band made recordings in Berlin, including *Sunny Disposish* (1927, Homocord 4-2420) and *Ostrich Walk* (1927, Tri Ergon 5134), and one of the first soundtracks for the Universum Film Aktiengesellschaft studios (1928). Although it was short-lived (it disbanded early in 1929), the group was important for having disseminated, and perhaps even introduced, Chicago jazz in Europe.

BIBLIOGRAPHY

J. Considine: "I'm away ahead of Peck Kelley," *DB*, vii/14 (1940), 9

B. Harrington: "Life was a Cabaret," *MR*, iv/2 (1976), 6

R. E. Lotz: *Tony Morello* (Menden, Germany, 1981) [incl. discography]

HAROLD S. KAYE, RAINER E. LOTZ

New Yorkers (ii). Name used on recordings by an orchestra led by the Dorsey brothers in 1931, by Gene Kardos and his Orchestra in 1932, and by others.

New York Jazz Quartet. Quartet formed by the pianist Roland Hanna around 1971; its other members were the flutist and saxophonist Hubert Laws, the double bass player Ron Carter, and the drummer Billy Cobham, all of whom had played in Hanna's New York Jazz Sextet (formed *c*1967). In 1974 Hanna re-formed the quartet as a cooperative, replacing Laws with Frank Wess and Cobham with Ben Riley; Carter was later replaced by George Mraz. This ensemble proved more successful and has worked intermittently into the 1980s (Richard Pratt and Grady Tate have sometimes substituted for Riley). The quartet's bop repertory, much of which is composed by the members, reflects their musical personalities as well as their technical skill. The ensemble should not be confused with a group of the same name (comprising Herbie Mann, Mat Mathews, Joe Puma, and Whitey Mitchell) that recorded around 1956–7.

SELECTED RECORDINGS

The New York Jazz Quartet in Concert in Japan (1975, Salvation 703); *Surge* (1977, Enja 2094); *Song of the Black Knight* (1977, Sonet 753); *Blues for Sarka* (1978, Enja 3025); *Oasis* (1981, Enja 3083); *The New York Jazz Quartet in Chicago* (1981, BH 7013)

SCOTT YANOW

New York Jazz Repertory Company [NYJRC]. Big band formed in 1974 by George Wein. The NYJRC performed during the 1970s at the Newport Jazz Festival in New York and at concerts. Among those who led the band at various times were

George Russell, in performances of his own compositions; Gil Evans, who performed his own compositions and his arrangements of pieces by the rock singer and guitarist Jimi Hendrix, which he later recorded; Paul Jeffrey, who performed music by Thelonious Monk with Monk as a soloist; Dick Hyman, who led the band in performances of works by Louis Armstrong (recorded on the album *Satchmo Remembered*, 1974, Atl. 1671, and performed in the following year in the USSR), Duke Ellington (including his composition *Black, Brown and Beige*), and Jelly Roll Morton; and Sy Oliver and Budd Johnson, who performed arrangements of swing tunes. The NYJRC received grants from the New York State Council on the Arts and the New York City Department of Cultural Affairs. Its example inspired the formation of other groups such as the National Jazz Ensemble, the Smithsonian Repertory Orchestra, and the American Jazz Orchestra.

BIBLIOGRAPHY

S. Dance: "Lightly and Politely, 1358: NYJRO," *JJ*, xxvii/4 (1974), 14
A. J. Smith: "Russian Tour for NYJRC," *DB*, xlii/14 (1975), 10

BRIAN PRIESTLEY

New York Jazz Sextet. Name used by two ensembles. The first was an all-star group which, at the time of its only recording (1965–6), consisted of Art Farmer, James Moody, Tom McIntosh, Tommy Flanagan, Richard Davis, and Albert "Tootie" Heath. The other was established by Roland Hanna around 1967; some of its members later joined Hanna's NEW YORK JAZZ QUARTET.

New York Recording Laboratories [NYRL]. Record company. The principal recording subsidiary of the Wisconsin Chair Co. of Port Washington, Wisconsin, it operated from 1916 to 1932. NYRL sponsored recordings and manufactured records for issue on its labels PARAMOUNT, FAMOUS, and Puritan, and also some for Broadway. Some masters made by the company were also pressed for issue on Claxtonola and one of the two National labels of the 1920s (*see* NATIONAL (ii)), and by leasing agreements were also put out on several others, most notably those of the Bridgeport Die & Machine Co. In addition the company also supplied material for the label Blue Bird, based in Los Angeles. (B. Rust: *The American Record Label Book* (New Rochelle, NY, 1978), 38)

New York Saxophone Quartet. Ensemble formed in 1980 by RAY BECKENSTEIN, Dennis Anderson, Bill Kerr, and Wally Kane (respectively soprano, alto, tenor, and baritone saxophonists).

Nicholas, Albert [Nick] (*b* New Orleans, 27 May 1900; *d* Basle, Switzerland, 3 Sept 1973). Clarinetist and saxophonist. He studied with Lorenzo Tio, Jr., and played in the bands of Buddy Petit, King Oliver, and Manuel Perez while still in his teens. After spending three years in the Merchant Marine (1916–19) he joined Perez's band (1922) and led his own six-piece group at Tom Anderson's New Cabaret and Restaurant (1923), then spent two years with King Oliver in Chicago (1924–6). He played with various groups in Shanghai, China; Cairo and Alexandria, Egypt; and Paris (August 1926–November 1928), then worked with Luis Russell (1928–33). Nicholas spent the next two decades as a sideman for such renowned leaders as Chick Webb (1934), John Kirby, Louis Armstrong (1937–9), and Rex Stewart (1953), but also led his own group intermittently. From 1953 until his death he lived and toured in Europe, although he occasionally returned to the USA to play and record (1959, 1960).

Nicholas must be considered one of the outstanding clarinetists in the New Orleans tradition, and the recordings from the last two decades of his life show a sensitivity to the changes that had taken place in jazz. His style was influenced by the blues: he frequently made use of the rich, lower register of his instrument and, in the higher register, dirty "whiskey-toned" inflections. Both elements may be heard on *Basin Street Blues* (1953). Nicholas was a nephew of Wooden Joe Nicholas.

Oral history material in *LNT*.

SELECTED RECORDINGS

As leader: Les oignons/Creole Blues (1947, Cir. [USA] 1019); *Albert Nicholas Quartet* (1959, Del. 207)

As sideman: R. M. Jones: New Orleans Shags (1925, OK 8290); K. Oliver: Sugarfoot Stomp/Wa wa wa (1926, Voc. 1033); L. Russell: Louisiana Swing (1930, OK 8811); R. Stewart: Basin Street Blues (1953, Jzt. 704)

BIBLIOGRAPHY

ChiltonW
C. Shain: "Albert Nicholas: New Orleans Clarinetist," *Jazz Session* (1946), July, 4
M. Mezzrow: "Albert Nicholas," *BHcF*, no.35 (1954), 3
M. Jones: "Nicholas of New Orleans," *MM* (7 Jan 1956), 2
——: "Papa Tio Made Cigars and Jazzmen," *MM* (14 Jan 1956), 7
——: "Nick: Concluding the Albert Nicholas Story," *MM* (21 Jan 1956), 5
B. King: "Albert Nicholas: Artist in Exile," *JM*, vii (1961), no.7, p.8; no.8, p.17
M. Casimir: "Albert Nicholas," *Jazz Times*, iv (1967), no.3, p.7; no.4, p.7; no.5, p.9; no.6, p.23; no.7, p.25; no.8, p.10 [interview]
A. Nicholas: "Propos et souvenirs," *BHcF*, no.180 (1968), 3
M. Casimir: "Albert Nicholas Talking," *Fn*, iii (1972), no.5, p.2; no.6, p.9
M. Jones: "Albert Nicholas: Classic Clarinet," *MM* (15 Sept 1973), 48
M. Mezzrow: "Albert Nicholas," *BHcF*, no.231 (1973), 6
R. Richard: "Albert Nicholas," *Sv*, no.57 (1975), 86
B. Bigard: *With Louis and the Duke*, ed. B. Martyn (London, 1985)
D. Barker: *A Life in Jazz*, ed. A. Shipton (London and New York, 1986)

LAWRENCE KOCH

Nicholas, Big Nick [George Walker] (*b* Lansing, MI, 2 Aug 1922). Tenor saxophonist and singer. He studied piano and clarinet as a child and in his teens played saxophone in a band with Hank and Thad Jones. He worked with Earl Hines (1942) and Tiny Bradshaw (1943), then, after army service, with Sabby Lewis, J. C. Heard (1946–7), and Lucky Millinder. In 1947 he began an association with Hot Lips Page that lasted until 1954, and also joined Dizzy Gillespie's big band; his warm, round tone may be heard on Gillespie's recording of *Manteca* (1947). From 1950 to 1951 Nicholas led jam sessions at the Paradise Club in Harlem, where he developed a joyous, booming style of singing. He played with Jonah Jones in a group led by the singer Timmie Rogers (1953) and then with Buck Clayton (1955). During the late 1950s and the 1960s, despite the modest fame he achieved through *Big Nick*, a song composed and recorded in 1962 by John Coltrane, Nicholas found little work. In the 1970s, however, he performed and taught in Virginia. After a successful appearance in New York (1979) he toured Europe with Walter Booker, Jimmy Cobb, and the pianist John Hicks (1980), and later recorded his first albums as a leader.

Oral history material in *NjR* (JOHP).

SELECTED RECORDINGS

As leader: *Big and Warm* (*c*1984, IndN 1061); *Big Nick* (*c*1985, IndN 1066)

As sideman: L. Millinder: The Spider and the Fly (1947, Decca 23949); D. Gillespie: Manteca (1947, Vic. 203023); Ool-ya-koo (1947, Vic. 202878); H. L. Page: Take your shoes off baby (1947, Har. 1069); U. M. Carlisle: Gone (1950, Col. 38881); B. Clayton and Frankie Laine: *Jazz Spectacular* (1955, Col. CL808)

BIBLIOGRAPHY

D. Morgenstern: "Big Nick's Story," *Jazz*, ii/8 (1963), 9
J. Simmen: "George 'Big Nick' Nicholas," *JJ*, xxv/9 (1972), 6
B. Cataliotti: "Big Nick Nicholas," *DB*, xlviii/3 (1981), 50

BARRY KERNFELD

Nicholas, Wooden Joe [Joseph] (*b* New Orleans, 23 Sept 1883; *d* New Orleans, 17 Nov 1957). Cornetist and clarinetist, uncle of Albert Nicholas. He played clarinet as a boy and took up cornet while he was with King Oliver (1915), modeling his style on that of Buddy Bolden and Bunk Johnson. In 1918 he formed the Camelia Band. He earned his nickname from the power and stamina he displayed as a street cornetist. He recorded on trumpet (and occasionally clarinet) as leader (1945, 1949), and under Raymond Burke with Johnny St. Cyr (1949).

Oral history material in *LNT*.

BIBLIOGRAPHY

ChartersJ; *FeatherE*
Obituary, B. Morris, *SL*, viii/11–12 (1957), 7

LAWRENCE KOCH

Nicholas Brothers. Vaudeville duo. Its members were the brothers Fayard (*b* 1918) and Harold (*b* 1924) Nicholas, who grew up in Philadelphia. From 1932 to 1934 they worked at the Cotton Club, New York, where they sang and danced with Cab Calloway, Lucky Millinder, Jimmie Lunceford, and Duke Ellington. While Harold was the better singer, Fayard was more accomplished as a dancer; his style combined acrobatic jazz steps with dramatic gestures of the arms and hands. After traveling to Hollywood to appear in the film *Big Broadcast of 1936* the duo toured England with a revue. In 1938 the brothers returned to the Cotton Club. They continued to work with great success, performing at nightclubs, concerts, and Broadway shows, appearing in films (including *Sun Valley Serenade*, 1941), and touring South America, Africa, and Europe. From 1958 to 1964 they worked apart, Harold in Paris and Fayard in the USA and Mexico. Thereafter they reunited and performed frequently on television. They made a few recordings, including *Keep a Twinkle in your Eye* (1936, HMV BD373), but are best remembered for their work in films.

BIBLIOGRAPHY

M. Stearns and J. Stearns: *Jazz Dance: the Story of American Vernacular Dance* (New York and London, 1968)
D. Bogle: *Toms, Coons, Mulattoes, Mammies, and Bucks: an Interpretive History of Blacks in American Films* (New York, 1973)

RAINER E. LOTZ

Nichols, Bobby [Robert Joseph] (*b* Boston, 15 Sept 1924). Trumpeter. He studied trumpet from 1933 and attended the New England Conservatory. He played with Vaughn Monroe from 1940 to 1943, then served three years in the army, during which he performed and recorded with Glenn Miller's Army Air Force Band (1943–5). Through the late 1940s he worked with Tex Beneke (1946–7), his own group (1947–8), and Ray McKinley (1948). He performed with Tommy Dorsey in 1951 (touring Brazil) and played on many of the Sauter–Finegan Orchestra's recordings between 1952 and 1961; his playing is well represented by his solo on *New York, 4 a.m.* (from *Inside Sauter–Finegan*, 1953, RCA LPM1003). He first performed with the Roxy Theater Orchestra of Hollywood in 1953; having left the orchestra he rejoined it in 1956.

Nichols, Herbie [Herbert Horatio] (*b* New York, 3 Dec 1919; *d* New York, 12 April 1963). Pianist and composer. He studied piano from the age of nine and attended the City College of New York. In 1938, at Monroe's Uptown House, he took part in some of the jam sessions that led to the new bop music. But although Nichols was the musical equal of the other players there, his education made him feel ill at ease in their company. As a result he worked infrequently and generally not in his preferred style; when he did find employment (from the mid-1940s to the mid-1950s) it was not in bop groups but in dixieland and swing bands with such musicians as Danny Barker, Illinois Jacquet, John Kirby, Snub Mosley, Edgar Sampson, Lucky Thompson, Arnett Cobb, and Wilbur De Paris. He composed many tunes, though none were recorded until 1951, when Mary Lou Williams included *Stennell* (retitled *Opus Z*) and *The Bebop Waltz* (retitled *Mary's Waltz*) on her album *Mary Lou Williams Trio* (Atl. 114). Nichols recorded three albums as a leader (1955–7), which received critical acclaim but sold poorly. Like Thelonious Monk, he enhanced his playing of conventional bop by the addition of unusual rhythms and gestures derived from swing.

SELECTED RECORDINGS

Herbie Nichols Trio (1955, BN 5068–9); *Herbie Nichols Trio* (1955–6, BN 1519); *Love, Gloom, Cash, Love* (1957, Beth. 81)

BIBLIOGRAPHY

J. Cooke: "Herbie Nichols," *JM*, vi/9 (1960), 9
A. B. Spellman: "Herbie Nichols," *Four Lives in the Bebop Business* (New York, 1966/*R*1970 as *Black Music: Four Lives*), 151
R. Rudd: Liner notes, *The Third World* (BN LA85H2, 1975)
J. Litweiler: *The Freedom Principle: Jazz after 1958* (New York, 1984), 21
G. Giddins: *Rhythm-a-ning: Jazz Tradition and Innovation in the '80s* (New York, and Oxford, England, 1985) [colln of previously pubd articles], 168

BARRY KERNFELD

Nichols, Keith (*b* London, 13 Feb 1945). English trombonist, pianist, vibraphonist, and arranger. He formed his first band, with which he played trombone, while still at high school. In 1964 he joined a group led by the trumpeter Mike Daniels, with whom he made his first recordings. Thereafter he established his own swing band, with which he played variously piano, trombone, and vibraphone; during this period he also worked as a freelance. Later he performed and recorded as a member of the cornetist Dick Sudhalter's Anglo-American Alliance, and his playing may be heard to advantage on the album *The Anglo-American All Stars* (1967–8, 77 LEU25, LEU28). From 1967 to 1974 he was a member of a vaudeville band, the Levity Lancers. During a visit to the USA (1974) he performed and recorded on trombone with the New Paul Whiteman Orchestra and wrote arrangements for the New York Jazz Repertory Company. From 1978 he has directed the Midnite Follies Orchestra with Alan Cohen, touring, recording, and broadcasting frequently. Nichols has also organized tributes to King Oliver, Louis Armstrong, and Jelly Roll Morton. He continues to work as a freelance, and leads a variety of ensembles of different sizes.

BIBLIOGRAPHY

R. Cotterrell, ed.: *Jazz Now: the Jazz Centre Society Guide* (London, 1976), 152
L. Tomkins: "The Evolution of a Jazz Historian," *CI*, xxii/5 (1984), 10 [interview]

SALLY-ANN WORSFOLD

Nichols, Red [Ernest Loring] (*b* Ogden, UT, 8 May 1905; *d* Las Vegas, NV, 28 June 1965). Cornetist and bandleader. He studied cornet with his father, a college music teacher, and acquired a sure technique. In 1923 he moved to New York, where he soon became a highly regarded sideman and the most prolifically recorded white jazz bandleader of the late 1920s. For the Brunswick label he recorded under the name Red Nichols and his Five Pennies, though for recordings with other companies he used many different names for the group: the Arkansas Travelers, the Red Heads, the Louisiana Rhythm Kings, and the Charleston Chasers. He toured the West Coast in 1928–9, and in the 1930s led a big band as well as working for radio; in the late 1930s he returned to small-group jazz. In 1959 he played for the soundtrack of *The Five Pennies*, a film based loosely on his life, as a result regaining much of his earlier popularity. He toured Europe in 1960 and 1964. His personal papers are in the University of Oregon at Eugene, and his private collection is in the Archives of Recorded Sound at the University of Kansas in Lawrence; *see* LIBRARIES AND ARCHIVES, §2.

Nichols's playing has often been compared with that of Bix Beiderbecke, with whom he shared a strong attack and clear tone, though his style was more rhythmically incisive, angular, and polished, and of a narrower emotional range. His many recordings of 1926–8 are the most progressive white jazz of the period in concept and execution, with wide-ranging harmonies and balanced ensemble; at this time his groups included such important musicians as Joe Venuti, Eddie Lang, Vic Berton, Jimmy Dorsey, Adrian Rollini, Fud Livingston, Pee Wee Russell, and Miff Mole; later bands featured Benny Goodman, Jack Teagarden, Glenn Miller, and Artie Shaw at formative stages of their careers. The innovative style of these groups was almost entirely superseded by the swing style of the 1930s, to which Nichols turned as a bandleader and occasionally as a performer. His later small groups attempted to recapture the sound of his performances from the 1920s.

SELECTED RECORDINGS

As leader: That's no Bargain (1926, Bruns. 3407); with M. Mole: Delirium (1927, Vic. 20778); China Boy (1930, Bruns. 4877); *Syncopated Chamber Music* (1953, Audiophile 7–8)

As sideman with M. Mole: Imagination/Feelin' no Pain (1927, OK 40890)

BIBLIOGRAPHY

ChiltonW

O. Ferguson: "The Five Pennies," *Jazzmen*, ed. F. Ramsey, Jr., and C. E. Smith (New York, 1939/*R*1977), 221

R. Venables and C. White: *A Complete Discography of Red Nichols and his Five Pennies* (Melbourne, Australia, 1946, 2/1947)

N. Shapiro and N. Hentoff, eds.: *Hear me Talkin' to ya: the Story of Jazz by the Men who Made it* (New York and London, 1955/*R*1966), 248

H. H. Lange: *Loring "Red" Nichols: ein Porträt* (Wetzlar, Germany, 1960)

R. Hadlock: *Jazz Masters of the Twenties* (New York, 1965/*R*1985)

A. McCarthy: *Big Band Jazz* (New York and London, 1974), 124

J. R. T. Davies: "Re-minting the Pennies," *Sv*, no.75 (1978), 107; contd as "Re Re-minting the Pennies," *Sv* (1978), no.76, p.128; no.77, p.176; no.78, p.224; no.79, p.16; no.80, p.56; (1979), no.81, p.107; no.82, p.145 [discography]

JAMES DAPOGNY/R

Nick's (Tavern). Nightclub in New York; *see* NIGHTCLUBS AND OTHER VENUES.

Nicolosi, Roberto (*b* Genoa, Italy, 16 Nov 1914). Italian arranger, double bass player, and bandleader. He studied piano and violin as a youth and trumpet from 1936. From 1945 to 1949 he wrote arrangements for and played guitar, double bass, and vibraphone with Aldo Rossi, Kramer Gorni, and others. He performed frequently in the early 1950s and made recordings of his own bop and cool-jazz arrangements in 1951 and 1953 (including *Morbido*, 1953, Col. CJ1005); among his sidemen were Franco Cerri, Gil Cuppini, Oscar Valdambrini, and Glauco Masetti. He wrote reviews of concerts and recordings for the periodicals *Illustrazione italiana* and *Settimo giorno*, composed film scores (from 1954), and took part in many jam sessions (to 1957). In 1978 he played double bass with the Roman New Orleans Jazz Band.

ADRIANO MAZZOLETTI

Nicols, Maggie (*b* Edinburgh, 24 Feb 1948). Scottish singer. She first achieved recognition in the late 1960s, performing in a style that effectively synthesized her experience of cabaret, theater, rock, and jazz. She sang with Denis Rose in 1965–7 and from 1969 worked intermittently with the Spontaneous Music Ensemble. She also performed with Keith Tippett's bands Centipede (1971) and Ark (1978), and with the group Talisker led by the drummer Ken Hyder (1977). In the mid-1970s she became involved with the feminist movement and helped to establish the ensembles Ova (1976), the Feminist Improvising Group (FIG), which included Irène Schweizer (1977), and Contradictions (1980). Nicols has worked increasingly as a soloist in the 1980s, but has also sung with such ensembles as Very Varied and Trevor Watts's Moiré Music, and the pianist Pete Nu, with whom she recorded an album of duets (*Nicols 'n' Nu*, 1985, Leo 127).

BIBLIOGRAPHY

S. Loupien: "La voix quotidienne de Maggie Nicols," *Jm*, no.288 (1980), 46

H. Charlton: "Maggie Nicols: Liberating Women's Music," *JF* [intl edn], no.76 (1982), 40

S. May: "Maggie's Mix," *JJI*, xxxviii/5 (1985), 13

D. Ilic: "Maggie Nicols: Living out your Contradictions," *The Wire*, no.24 (1986), 22 [incl. discography]

MARK GILBERT

Niebergall, Buschi [Johannes] (*b* Marburg, Germany, 18 July 1938). German double bass player. He played trombone in an amateur group with Manfred Schoof in 1955 and studied medicine until 1963. After changing to double bass he worked with Tete Montoliu in Spain (1962) and played free jazz as a member of Gunter Hampel's quartet (from 1964) and Schoof's quintet (1965–7). He also belonged to the Globe Unity Orchestra (1966–81), performed and recorded with Peter Brötzmann (1968–9), and played with Marion Brown (1968), Alex Schlippenbach (1969), Albert Mangelsdorff's quintet (1972–5), and Gerd Dudek (1977). A performance at the International New Jazz Festival Moers (1978) in a trio with Michel Pilz and the drummer Uwe Schmidt was one of the few occasions on which he worked as a leader.

SELECTED RECORDINGS

As sideman: Globe Unity Orchestra: *Globe Unity* (1966, Saba 15109); M. Schoof: *The Early Quintet* (1966, FMP 0540); P. Brötzmann: *Machine Gun* (1968, FMP 0090); *Nipples* (1969, Calig 30604); A. Mangelsdorff: *Birds of Underground* (1972, MPS 2121746); Globe Unity Orchestra: *Compositions* (1979, Japo 60027)

BIBLIOGRAPHY

ReclamsJ

W. Liefland: "Vom Jazz, der Freiheit und der Wurde: Niebergall, Pilz, Schmidt," *JP*, xxviii/6 (1979), 28

ROBERT J. IANNAPOLLO

Niehaus, Lennie [Leonard] (*b* St. Louis, 1 June 1929). Alto saxophonist, composer, and arranger. He studied music at California State University, Los Angeles, then worked with Stan Kenton (1951–2). After service in the US Army (1952–4) he rejoined Kenton in 1954, with whom he performed and recorded to 1960. He also recorded West Coast jazz with Shorty Rogers (1954) and wrote compositions and arrangements for his own albums (1954–7) and for Kenton (to the late 1960s); his playing is well represented on the track *Who's Blues* from his album *The Quintet*, i (1954, Cont. 2513). In the 1960s he performed and recorded with Lalo Schifrin, but from that time worked principally as a commercial arranger and composer; he worked in television in the 1970s and wrote the scores to the films *Tightrope* and *City Heat* (1984), *Pale Rider* (1985), and *Heartbreak*

Ridge (1986). Niehaus has published numerous stage-band compositions and several texts on saxophone pedagogy.

BIBLIOGRAPHY

FeatherE; Feather–Gitler '70s

W. F. Lee: *Stan Kenton: Artistry in Rhythm* (Los Angeles, 1980) [incl. discography]

A. Groves: "The Forgotten Ones: Lennie Niehaus," *JJI*, xxxviii/1 (1985), 15

R. Gordon: *Jazz West Coast: the Los Angeles Jazz Scene of the 1950s* (London and New York, 1986)

Nielsen, Kai (Peter Anthon). *See* EWANS, KAI.

Niewood, Gerry [Nevidosky, Gerard J.] (*b* Rochester, NY, 6 April 1943). Soprano and tenor saxophonist. While at the University of Buffalo he played tenor saxophone and flute and sang in a show band. He then went to New York, where he joined Chuck Mangione's quartet (1968) and also studied at the Eastman School of Music (BM 1970). He was the strongest soloist in Mangione's group, and was particularly adept at inventing clean, rapid, driving soprano saxophone melodies over Latin-jazz ostinatos. After leaving Mangione in 1976 Niewood formed a bop quartet with Dave Samuels, Mike Richmond, and the drummer Ron Davis; its albums (*c*1976–7) were, however, poorly received. In the early 1980s he led the Sunday Morning Jazz Band, and in 1985 he recorded as the leader of a jazz-rock septet which included Joe Beck.

SELECTED RECORDINGS

(all as sideman with C. Mangione)

The Chuck Mangione Quartet (1972, Mer. 1-631); *Together* (1973, Mer. 2-7501); *Bellavia* (1975, A&M 4557)

BIBLIOGRAPHY

Feather–Gitler '70s

"Gerry Niewood," *DB*, xl/19 (1973), 32

R. Ricker: "An Interview with Gerry Niewood," *The Instrumentalist*, xxxi/3 (1976), 68

BARRY KERNFELD

Nightclubs and other venues.

I. Introduction. II. List and Index.

I. Introduction. The history of jazz in terms of the venues that have fostered it is as yet largely unwritten. It is the history of nightlife in different cities, and thus has as much to do with social, general cultural, commercial, and political history as with musical history. The list presented here, organized geographically, is the first published attempt at an international and historical catalogue of significant, enduring settings for the presentation of jazz. These diverse settings include nightclubs (or clubs), cabarets, casinos and gambling clubs, restaurants, bars, cafés and coffee houses, pubs, taverns, saloons, and speakeasies; ballrooms and dance halls; cinemas, music halls, theaters, concert halls, entertainment centers, and lofts; hotels, inns, roadhouses, and brothels; cruise ships and riverboats; and parks, gardens, and lakesides. The list does not include those sites used exclusively for jazz festivals, which are identified in the article FESTIVALS. Nor can it include whole groups of venues and locations used for certain kinds of performance: for example, the apartments in Harlem where rent parties and jam sessions were held, the streets of New Orleans down which brass bands paraded, the outdoor sites where bands touring on wagons stopped to engage each other in battles of skill, and the dance halls in small towns and on college campuses at which countless groups have played one-night stands.

Comprehensive research has been carried out on the popular music life of a small number of cities, chiefly in the USA, and in a few cases on individual venues; but the majority of information in the enormous field of jazz performance venues worldwide must be sifted from general histories of the music, memoirs of players and impresarios, record liner notes, specialist articles, and nonmusical sources of the kinds mentioned above. The following list is based on material of these kinds and in some cases on the specialist knowledge of jazz scholars. The uneven nature of the sources is reflected in the amount of information presented here: the number and length of entries on, for example, New York, Paris, and London is commensurate with the importance of these cities in the history of the music, but the absence of information on many cities and indeed whole countries does not mean that they have no traditions of jazz performance, rather that published material on those traditions is lacking.

II. List and Index. The list is arranged alphabetically by country, by city within country, and by name of venue (the definite article in all languages is ignored for purposes of alphabetical ordering); the only exception to this arrangement is the category of American riverboats, which are entered under the names of the rivers on which they traveled. Addresses are given where possible, and the dates between which a certain address was current are supplied if they are known. Where the nature of a venue is not evident from its title, an effort has been made to supply a definition. Dates of operation are supplied when they are known, but if they are not available some indication is usually given of the period during which the venue is known to have flourished: this should not be taken to mean that it was in existence at no other time, simply that the sources consulted contain information only on the period indicated.

Many venues change performers constantly, and thus any attempt at full listings, even if that were possible, would be of questionable value; this is especially true of large cities, where the number of venues and the community of resident musicians are sufficiently large to allow owners and bandleaders to change programs and players, sometimes even on a daily basis. The list therefore aims primarily to identify extended residencies and isolated performances of particular importance or at least to offer selective lists of musicians who worked at a venue so as to give a sense of its stylistic orientation. Whenever possible, dates of performances are provided, but the appearance of such a date by no means excludes the possibility that the musician concerned performed at the venue on other occasions as well.

Items of bibliography are cited at the ends of individual entries, after a group of entries on venues in a particular city, or after a group of entries for a country, as appropriate; a general bibliography listing sources of relevance to more than one country appears at the end of the list. An alphabetical index of venues by name follows the list.

The scholars and specialists named below have contributed significant material to the sections indicated, but in no case is any of them wholly responsible for the selection of venues covered or for all the information supplied: Bruce Johnson (Australia), Mark Miller (Canada), Wolfram Knauer (Germany), Howard Rye (with Alyn Shipton) (Great Britain, London), Wim van Eyle (with Alyn Shipton) (Netherlands), Bob Blumenthal (USA, Boston and Cambridge), James Patrick (USA, Buffalo), Howard Rye (USA, Chicago), Bill Russell (USA, New Orleans), Barry Kernfeld (USA, Detroit, New York (with Dan Morgenstern), and San Francisco), and Harrison Ridley, Jr. (USA, Philadelphia).

ARGENTINA

BUENOS AIRES. **La Chaumière.** This club presented jazz from at least the mid-1930s. The alto saxophonist and clarinetist Booker Pitman, whose influence on Argentine players was considerable, performed there during the time he led his own big band, the Swing Stars, in Buenos Aires (1939–42).

——. **Novelty Club.** In operation from the early 1930s, it offered performances by a number of visiting American musicians. Herb Flemming and his International Rhythm Aces, which included Crickett Smith and Roy Butler, were resident there in 1933. Flemming himself (in E. Biagioni: *Herb Flemming: a Jazz Pioneer around the World*, Alphen aan de Rijn, Netherlands, n.d. [?1977]) mentioned that his band played in Buenos Aires at the Ta-Ba-Ris Club, where it was "a novelty for the aristocracy"; it appears that this might be the same venue.

——. **La Oreja.** Paraná 330, Buenos Aires 1017. One of several nightclubs run by Jorge Gonzalez (others include La Trastienda, El Fonografo, and Jazz & Pop), it is the principal venue in the city for modern jazz.

——. **Ta-Ba-Ris Club.** See Novelty Club.

AUSTRALIA

ADELAIDE. **Tivoli Theatre.** In the 1950s Bill Holyoak, the owner of the Memphis Record Co., organized a series of jazz concerts at the theater; the music presented was mainly traditional, dixieland, and mainstream jazz. The venue is now known as Her Majesty's Theatre.

MELBOURNE. **Fat Black Pussycat.** 90 Toorak Road, South Yarra. It was founded in 1963 by Ali Sugerman and functioned as a jazz club (under the ownership of Adrian Rawlins from 1965) until 1966, when it became a discothèque. The club opened with a group led by Barry McMinn and Heinz Mendelson and went on to engage other important musicians of the younger generation of modernists, including Brian Brown and Bernie McGann. The Fat Black Pussycat was the most important center in Melbourne for contemporary and experimental jazz after Jazz Centre 44 (see below) began to present mainly traditional jazz.

——. **Fawkner Park Kiosk.** Fawkner Park. Built as the pavilion for the adjacent tennis courts, it became in 1936 the venue for Sunday afternoon jam sessions. It provided a forum for the most important prewar jazz musicians, including Bob and Ern Tough and Benny Featherstone, whose performances inspired younger musicians such as Roger and Graeme Bell. It ceased to be used for jazz performances around 1941.

——. **Jazz Centre 44.** Ackland Street, St. Kilda. It was founded by Horst Liepolt in 1957 and was managed by him until he moved to Sydney in 1960. Particularly during the late 1950s, it was the most important jazz venue in Melbourne and presented performances in a wide range of styles: among the prominent Australian groups and musicians who performed there were the Yarra Yarra Jazz Band (playing traditional jazz) and important modernists such as Brian Brown. Many of the jazz musicians active in Melbourne into the 1980s first became known through their appearances at Jazz Centre 44. After Liepolt left Melbourne the club's repertory increasingly emphasized traditional jazz and it ceased operation around 1966.

BIBLIOGRAPHY

M. Murphy: "Mike Murphy Recalls Jazz Centre 44," *Jazz Down Under* (Nov 1975)
"Australian Jazz Today: Jazz Centre 44," *Jazz Australia*, no.1 (1976)

——. **Royal Terminus Hotel.** Brighton. Frank Johnson's Fabulous Dixielanders were among the musicians to perform there.

——. **Uptown Club.** Queensbury Road, North Melbourne. It was founded in 1946 by Roger and Graeme Bell and continued until 1947. Although relatively short-lived, the Uptown was active at a time when the jazz movement in Melbourne was becoming firmly established, and it rapidly developed into a center for musicians, painters, and writers who valued jazz as a legitimate modern art form.

SYDNEY. **The Basement.** 29 Reiby Place, Circular Quay. It was established in 1973 by a group that included Bruce Viles and Tom Hare. In its early years it provided an important venue for contemporary and experimental jazz and featured several of the main contemporary jazz groups of the 1970s, including the Last Straw and Jazz Co-op; it also ran a public workshop to explore ideas raised by the newly established course in jazz at the New South Wales Conservatorium. The club has given increasing exposure to fusion groups and has become the best-known jazz venue in Australia. From its opening its house band has been Galapagos Duck.

BIBLIOGRAPHY

G. Gilbert: "Jazz on a High Note," *Jazz Australia*, no.1 (1976)
P. Tripp: "Ten Years of The Basement," *Jazz: the Australasian Contemporary Music Magazine* (spring 1983)

——. **El Rocco.** Brougham Street, Kings Cross. The club was opened in 1955 by Arthur James and began to present jazz in October 1957; from then until it closed in 1969 it was the main venue for the various forms of progressive jazz performed in Australia. It saw many early experiments in free jazz and provided a meeting place for the new generation of musicians, who were to carry the music into the 1980s. Many musicians from abroad and from other places in Australia played there, and the club's success inspired the founding of similar establishments elsewhere in the country. The El Rocco was in its time the most important club in Australia.

BIBLIOGRAPHY

D. Fisher: "Modern Jazz or . . . ," *Music Maker* (Sept 1963)
B. Johnson: "The El Rocco: an Era in Sydney Jazz," *Jazz: the Australasian Contemporary Music Magazine* (Jan–Feb, March–April, May–June 1983)

——. **Rock's Push.** It flourished as a center for jazz during the 1980s, when Graeme Bell was among the notable resident musicians.

——. **Soup Plus Restaurant.** 383 George Street. It was founded in 1974 by James Dupree, who introduced jazz in 1975 with a performance by Bill Haesler's Washboard Band. It became one of the best known and most consistent jazz venues in Sydney, with performances on six nights of the week and resident groups that changed monthly: while other clubs concentrated on a narrow range of styles it offered a broad cross-section of all kinds of jazz. Performances at the club have frequently been recorded for later broadcast.

——. **Vanity Fair Hotel.** Goulburn Street and Wentworth Street. Pub. Jim Hourigan first put on jazz performances there in 1970 and later licensees continued his policy. The Vanity Fair was the most stable venue in Sydney for traditional and mainstream jazz and its durability gave it an international reputation. In addition to presenting different resident bands on various nights of the week, the club employed the Eclipse Alley Five for Saturday afternoon performances from 1970 until it closed in 1986 (this constituted the longest band residency in the history of Australian jazz). The pub also served as the unofficial headquarters for the Sydney Jazz Club. (C. Lindley: *Goodbye Vanity Fair*, Sydney, 1986)

BIBLIOGRAPHY

Australia

B. Johnson and others: *The Oxford Companion to Australian Jazz* (Melbourne, Australia, 1987)

AUSTRIA

VIENNA. **Jazzland.** 29 Franz Josefs Kai. This jazz club on the Danube Canal was in operation from at least 1973, when Max Kaminsky worked there with the Austrian traditional group the Barrelhouse Jazzband.

——. **Weinberg Bar.** It presented jazz from at least the 1920s. Among the jazz musicians who performed there were Arthur Briggs with the Savoy Syncops Orchestra (1924–6), which was one of the first jazz ensembles to play arrangements by Spike Hughes.

——. **Wiener Metropol.** Hernalser Hauptstrasse 55, A-1170 Vienna. Theater. It opened as a general arts center early in 1981 under the artistic direction of Alf Krauliz. As part of its highly varied program of events the Wiener Metropol has offered performances of many kinds of music, among them jazz, rock, and pop; its other activities include theater, dance, and cabaret, and the center emphasizes entertainment for children and young people. Many notable American and European jazz musicians have performed there, including Bireli Lagrene, Jan Garbarek, Chet Baker, Art Blakey, Lester Bowie, Aladár Pege, Carla Bley, Charlie Mariano, and Baden Powell. The Wiener Metropol publishes a youth magazine, *Metropol.*

WIESEN. **Jazz-Pub-Wiesen.** Hauptstrasse 140, A-7203 Wiesen. It was founded as a discothèque in the early 1970s by Franz Bogner and took the name Jazz-Pub-Wiesen in 1976 when it staged the first International Jazzfest Wiesen (*see* FESTIVALS). One of the first discothèques to include jazz in its program, the club has favored fusion (particularly jazz-rock and jazz-funk) though all styles of jazz are presented (including, occasionally, avant-garde improvised music). Notable jazz musicians who have appeared there include Barbara Thompson, Jon Hiseman, Jasper van 't Hof, and Larry Coryell.

BELGIUM

ANTWERP. **King-Kong.** Keizerstraat 38, B-2000 Antwerp. This nightclub was active from at least the early 1970s. From 1974 it played host to the festival Free Music Antwerpen, which presents avant-garde improvised and composed music and free jazz (*see* FESTIVALS).

BRUSSELS. **Alhambra.** The club presented revues that featured jazz from at least 1919; bands that appeared there included Louis Mitchell's Jazz Kings (23 January 1920 to April 1921) and a group led by the drummer Hughes Pollard (1922).

——. **Le Boeuf sur le Toit.** Named after the famous nightclub in Paris, this venue was opened by Jean Omer around 1940. It became an important center for jazz performance by Belgian musicians and Omer himself led a band there until the early 1960s.

——. **Gaieté Théâtre.** Rue Fosse-aux-loups. It was used for dancing from the 1920s. Among the bands that played residencies there were one led by a drummer named Wilson, which included the trumpeter Bobby Jones and the trombonist Frank Withers (1921–2), and Johnny Dunn's New Yorkers (1932); Wilson's band apparently also played at a club called Chez Pan in Ostend.

——. **Grand Café Corso.** Boulevard Adolphe Sax. Jazz was performed at the café from at least the early 1940s; a band led by Fud Candrix played there in 1942.

——. **Merry Grill.** Place du Samedi. Restaurant. It offered performances of jazz from at least the early 1930s. Sam Wooding's group played there in 1931, then, when it disbanded (November), Willie Lewis took over as the resident bandleader, forming a group that consisted of several of Wooding's American sidemen and Belgian musicians.

——. **Palais des Beaux-Arts.** Arts complex. It contains facilities for music, theater, cinema, and art exhibitions. One of the earliest rhythm clubs, the Sweet and Hot Club, founded in 1932, met in a lecture room there. It has continued to be used for jazz concerts, as in January 1955, when during an extensive tour Sidney Bechet played there with Claude Luter's band.

——. **Pol's Club.** Founded by and named for the entrepreneur Pol, it flourished during the 1960s and 1970s. Sam Woodyard's band, made up of former sidemen of Duke Ellington, played there in 1977 and Pol frequently engaged major American bands.

——. **Théâtre des Galeries.** It was used for jazz performances from at least the 1940s when, under the auspices of the Belgian Hot Club and its president Willy de Cort, weekly jazz concerts were given there.

DENDERMONDE. **Jazzclub Honky Tonk.** Bastion V, Leopold II laan, B-9330 Dendermonde. It was founded and is managed by Piet Heuvinck. It originally specialized in traditional jazz, but later incorporated various other styles into its repertory; the club has its own swing big band. In 1971 Heuvinck and others founded the Dendermonde jazz festival (*see* FESTIVALS).

GHENT. **Lazy River Jazz Club.** Stadhuissteeg 5, B-9000 Ghent. Established in cellar premises in nearby Gentbrugge in 1966, it at first presented jazz on Friday evenings. It became more active on its moving to the Stadhuissteeg premises. Although it is best known for traditional jazz the club also offers most other styles (except free jazz) and also ragtime, blues, and rhythm-and-blues. From 1969 it mounted an annual jazz festival (*see* FESTIVALS) and it publishes a monthly newsletter, *Lazy River News*.

KNOKKE. **Casino.** The casino at Knokke presented jazz during its summer season from at least the mid-1930s.

KORTRIJK. The town's jazz club has been a center for traditional and mainstream jazz from the early 1970s. It has engaged many of Belgium's leading bands, including the Cotton City Jazz Band (under the leadership of Rudy Balliu and later Jacques Cruyt) and the Jegg Papp Jazz Band; it has also offered performances by other leading European musicians.

OOSTAKKER. **Cotton Fields Jazzclub.** Pegasus-Hoeve, Nieuwstraat 11. It flourished during the mid-1970s, when it was an important venue for visiting American and European artists. Most of the music performed was traditional or mainstream jazz.

RUISELEDE. **Banana Peel Club.** Run by the discographer Erik Karette, this club has presented jazz and rhythm-and-blues during the 1970s and 1980s. As well as visiting American musicians, it presents European players such as Sammy Rimington.

WILLEBROEK. **Jazzclub het Veerhuis.** Hoofd 2, B-2660 Willebroek. It was founded by Camiel van Breedam, Johnny van Breedam, and Marc Vandevelde in 1970 and opened on 1 June. It specializes in New Orleans jazz and has regularly engaged American musicians who developed the style early in the century, including Kid Thomas and Emanuel Sayles. The resident band is the Fondy Riverside Bullet Band. The club has its own record label, Fondy, on which Alvin Alcorn recorded the album *Alvin Alcorn Meets his Friends in Belgium* (Fondy 7771) in 1976.

CANADA

EDMONTON. **Yardbird Suite.** A venue of this name, run by a musicians' cooperative, functioned at several addresses for a decade from around 1957. The name was revived by the Edmonton Jazz Society in 1984 for a nightclub at 1023 86 Street.

MONTREAL. **Alberta Lounge.** It offered jazz performances from at least the 1940s, when Oscar Peterson appeared there.

——. **Café St.-Michel.** The performances given there by American musicians in the 1930s and 1940s, including Louis Metcalf, were important in maintaining jazz activities in Canada at that period.

——. **Rendez-Vous.** Dance hall. In the early 1940s Montreal's leading black jazz band, George Sealey's Orchestra, played for dancing there. (J. Litchfield: Liner notes, *Jazz and Hot Dance in Canada*, Harl. 2023, 1986)

——. **Rising Sun.** One of the principal nightclubs in the city, it pursued a policy of presenting visiting American groups.

——. **Rock Head's** [Rockhead's] **Paradise.** It was in operation by the late 1920s and became Canada's longest-running jazz club, remaining active until the early 1980s. In the early 1930s it was under black ownership and managements, and was a leading venue in the city for black bands. It became known for presenting almost exclusively Canadian musicians.

TORONTO. **Basin Street.** 180 Queen Street West. It occupied premises upstairs in the same building as Bourbon Street (see below) and similarly favored visiting American musicians. In a short period in the spring of 1980, for example, players of the standing of Benny Carter, Stan Getz, and Joe Williams were billed to appear at the club.

——. **Blues Alley.** 110 Lombard Street. It opened in 1973 and in the autumn of that year a trio consisting of Jim Galloway, Dick Wellstood, and the drummer Peter Magadini performed there.

——. **Bourbon Street.** 180 Queen Street West. This nightclub was opened in 1971 by Doug Cole, who had long owned George's Spaghetti House (see below). Under the management of Jim Galloway and later Paul Grosney it gained international renown as a venue for solo and small-group jazz performed by both Canadian and visiting foreign musicians. Many American players, in particular, appeared there, often performing as guest soloists with Canadian rhythm sections; among them were Benny Carter (1973), Junior Cook (1974), Flip Phillips (1975), and Zoot Sims and Herb Ellis (both 1980). Notable recordings were made at the club by Jim Hall (June 1975), Paul Desmond (October–November 1975), Frank Rosolino (April 1976), and Lenny Breau (an album released posthumously). A second nightclub, Basin Street (see above), operated intermittently in the same building. Bourbon Street closed in 1986 and the premises were taken over by a striptease club.

——. **Colonial Tavern.** 201 Yonge Street. It was active from the 1950s until 1984; in the early 1960s its activities were in the hands of Goodie Lichtenstein. An important venue for Canadian musicians, it was also on the touring circuit for visiting jazzmen and thus presented performances by many internationally known soloists and groups. Among those who appeared there in the 1960s were Buck Clayton (1962) and Eddie Condon (1968).

——. **George's Spaghetti House.** 290 Dundas Street East. Restaurant. It was opened in 1956 by Doug Cole and at first offered jazz at weekends only; from 1960 the program was extended to cover six evenings a week. In the mid-1960s American musicians appeared there often, but George's later became known as the principal venue in the city for hearing Canadian jazz. Among the bands that have played there regularly is that of Moe Koffman, who became the manager in 1960; Ed Bickert recorded there in 1975, and broadcasts have frequently been made from the restaurant. In 1984 it moved from a downstairs to an upstairs room in the same building.

——. **Jungle Temple.** Everett Highway. Roadhouse. Under the direction of Fred Owens, it presented jazz from the late 1920s. Joe Darensbourg played there around 1929 with his Jungle Temple Syncopators.

——. **Malloney's Club.** 85 Grenville Street. It has presented performances by Canadian and visiting foreign musicians from at least the 1970s. The Australian pianist Graeme Bell led a band of Canadian musicians there in 1975 under the name Climax Jazz Band; their album *Live at Malloney's* (1975, Tormax 33004) includes the numbers *Malloney's Boogie* and *Grenville Street Blues*.

——. **Massey Hall.** Shuter Street. Concert hall. Opened in 1894 as Massey Music Hall (the name changed in 1933), it was for many years the only purpose-built concert hall in the country. It has been the venue for numerous popular-music performances and recording sessions. The most important jazz event to take place there was the concert given on 15 May 1953, under the auspices of the New Jazz Society, by a quintet consisting of Charlie Parker, Dizzy Gillespie, Bud Powell, Charles Mingus, and Max Roach; a landmark in the history of bop, the performance was preserved on record though the recording quality is poor.

——. **Music Gallery.** It was opened in warehouse premises in 1975 by the Canadian Creative Music Center (CCMC), an improvising ensemble, formed in 1974, some of whose music is close to free jazz. The group played at the Music Gallery twice a week and the venue also mounted avant-garde performances in other areas of music. In 1976 the record company Music Gallery Editions was launched; folk music, avant-garde improvised music, and jazz have been issued on its label. From 1978 the venue produced a quarterly newsletter, *Musicworks*. Around 1984 the Music Gallery moved to a building formerly occupied by the YMCA.

——. **Town Tavern.** Queen Street East. It flourished for 20 years from the mid-1950s, presenting both Canadian and visiting (mostly American) musicians. Oscar Peterson recorded there in 1958.

VANCOUVER. **The Cellar.** Managed by musicians, it was in operation from 1956 until 1964. It regularly engaged visiting American players.

——. **Classical Joint.** Café. It opened around 1970 and quickly became the principal venue for jazz in the city.

BIBLIOGRAPHY

Canada

H. Kallmann, G. Potvin, and K. Winters, eds.: *Encyclopedia of Music in Canada* (Toronto, Buffalo, and London, 1981)

J. Litchfield: *The Canadian Jazz Discography, 1916–1980* (Toronto, Buffalo, and London, 1982)

DENMARK

COPENHAGEN. **La Fontaine.** Kompagnistrade 11. It presents mainly small-group jazz and performances by unaccompanied soloists.

——. **Hollaenderbyen.** Restaurant. From 1935 until 1960 it was managed by Thorkild and Agnete Larsen, and it offered jazz performances from at least the late 1930s, when Richard Stangerup's Jazzband was the resident group. A large venue, with seating for more than 700, it was regularly packed during the residency played there by Leon Abbey's band in October 1938, when among the Danish musicians who heard the visiting band was Svend Asmussen. Abbey and his group made a triumphant return visit the following year for a residency of six weeks, during which they also broadcast on Danish Radio.

——. **Jazzhus Slukefter.** Tivoli Gardens. Principally a summer venue (it is open only occasionally between September and May), it has engaged many visiting American musicians, including Count Basie, Benny Carter, Benny Goodman, Buddy Rich, Teddy Wilson, and Milt Jackson. The house band, led by Papa Bue, plays traditional jazz.

——. **Loppen Christiania.** Baadmandsstraede 43. Nightclub and discothèque. Its repertory covers a broad range of styles, from blues and jazz to rock and funk.

——. **Montmartre (Jazzhus).** Dahlerupsgade; Store Regnegade; Nørregade 41, 1165 Copenhagen K (1976–). It was founded in the late 1950s and operated under Anders Dyrup at premises on Dahlerupsgade and under Herluf Kamp-Larsen and Per Svensson on Store Regnegade, before opening at Nørregade 41 on 15 September 1976. It became the foremost jazz club in Scandinavia, presenting all kinds of jazz from bop and Latin jazz to fusion, and has made a point of fostering experimental styles; it also functions as a discothèque. The Montmartre has engaged many Scandinavian and visiting foreign musicians. Niels-Henning Ørsted Pedersen and other Danish musicians began their careers there, and among those who have played long residencies are the Americans Dexter Gordon, Idrees Sulieman, Horace Parlan, and Thad Jones, all of whom as expatriates settled for some time in or near Copenhagen. Many performers have recorded there, including Jackie McLean and Gordon, Ben Webster, Charles Lloyd, Stan Getz, Cedar Walton, and Tania Maria; Danish Radio has made numerous broadcasts of important performances. The house players have included the drummer Alex Riel and the pianist Kenny Drew. The club publishes a bi-monthly newsletter, *Jazz & Rock*, and in 1986 issued a book to mark the club's ten years in the Nørregade premises, *Montmartre gennem 10 år*, written by the jazz journalist Jens Jørn Gjedsted with the assistance of Montmartre's music directors Niels Christensen and Lars Thorborg.

——. **My Blue Heaven.** It was opened in 1943 by Svend Asmussen.

——. **De Tre Musketerer.** Nikolaj Plads 25. Owned and managed by Bodil and Hans-Henrick Humleback, this club presents dixieland jazz, mostly played by Danish musicians.

ENGLAND. See Great Britain.

FRANCE

BIARRITZ. **Bricktop's.** At the Merry Sol (near the Grand Casino). One of several clubs set up by the singer Bricktop (Ada Smith) in different cities (others were in Paris, Mexico City, and Rome), it operated only for the 1932 season. Among the resident artists were Charlie Lewis and his band, Mabel Mercer, and Bricktop herself. The following year Bricktop took new premises for the season, which were less successful. An attempt to run a similar club during the 1950 season lasted only four nights.

CANNES. **Palm Beach Casino.** It was opened in 1932 and its cabaret mounted performances of jazz from that time; Django Reinhardt appeared in the early 1930s, and in 1953 Big Chief Moore led a band there, which included Geo Daly (vibraphone), Raymond Fol (piano), and the singer Anita Love. Among the club's managers was the impresario Leon Voltera.

JUAN-LES-PINS. **Le Vieux Colombier.** Boulevard de la Pinède (near the casino). It was owned and managed by Annet Badel and modeled on his Parisian club of the same name. Claude Luter's band, featuring Sidney Bechet, was resident there for several seasons in the 1950s.

NICE. **Negresco Hotel.** Among the jazz musicians who played in resident bands there were Dave Tough and the baritone saxophonist Spencer Clark (both in the late 1920s).

——. **Palais de la Méditerranée.** Jazz musicians played there for dancing during the venue's heyday in the 1920s and 1930s. Among them were Benny Peyton and his band, which for its residency in Nice included June Cole and Tommy Ladnier.

PARIS. **Abbaye Thélème.** Place Pigalle, Paris 9. It offered performances by European and American jazz musicians from at least the mid-1920s. Among those who appeared there were Léo Vauchant (1925), the pianist Jack O'Brien with Dave Tough (1929), and in 1929–30 the Plantation Orchestra, led at first by Joe Hayman and Edwin Swayze, later by Herb Flemming.

——. **ABC Music Hall.** Boulevard Poissonnière, Montmartre. One of the leading variety venues in Paris, its presentations included performances by jazz musicians. Django Reinhardt appeared there intermittently from 1938 for a decade, and the recording *ABC*, which he made with his orchestra in 1942 (Swing 180), is named after the theater. It was later converted to a cinema.

——. **Ad Lib.** Rue Fontaine, Paris 9. It flourished as a center for jazz until at least 1930; during the period of its greatest importance it was managed by Joe Zelli, who was manager of several clubs in the city (see Royal Box, Tempo Club, and Zelli's below).

——. **Les Ambassadeurs.** 1 avenue Gabriel, off avenue des Champs-Elysées, Paris 8. This large venue presented variety acts, revues, and the like, as well as performances by jazz and popular musicians in its several rooms. In its heyday in the late 1920s it was one of the most fashionable and exclusive venues in Paris, attracting a clientèle that included foreign royalty and the "international set." Among the jazzmen who appeared there were Leon Abbey (mid-1920s, 1929), Sam Wooding (*c*1925), Paul Whiteman (1928, with the Rhythm Boys, a vocal group led by Bing Crosby), Noble Sissle (1928–31, at first with the pianist Harry Revel, then with his own band, which included Sidney Bechet, Johnny Dunn, and the pianist

Charlie Lewis), and Fred Elizalde (1928); George Gershwin was also to be heard there as a solo pianist and with duo partners, playing his own music. The club continued to offer jazz after the war: in the late 1950s André Ekyan and his orchestra made regular appearances there on Sundays.

——. **Apollo.** Rue de Clichy, Paris 9. An early venue for jazz in Paris, the club presented a brief residency by Louis Mitchell's Jazz Kings (which included Sidney Bechet) in October 1921.

——. **La Bagatelle.** Rue de Clichy (next to the Casino de Paris), Paris 9. It presented jazz from at least the 1930s; Eddie Brunner performed there around 1938.

——. **Barclay's Club.** Near avenue des Champs-Elysées, probably in rue Pierre-Charron, Paris 8 (to 1951); 34 rue du Colisée, Paris 8 (from 1951). The original Barclay's Club was a musicians' rehearsal room owned by the French jazz pianist and entrepreneur Eddie Barclay, who also ran the record companies Blue Star and Barclay, and edited the journals *Jazz News: Blue Star Revue* (1948–50) and *Jazz magazine* (from 1954). It was active in the 1940s and closed shortly after the turn of the decade. In 1951 Barclay reopened in new premises lately vacated by Le Boeuf sur le Toit (see below).

——. **Bar Gaya.** This small nightclub was in operation in the years following World War I, when the pianist Jean Wiener played American music – ragtime and Broadway songs, which were at that time spoken of as jazz – to a bohemian clientèle. Its management took larger premises in 1921 and opened Le Boeuf sur le Toit (see below).

——. **Blue Note.** Off rue de Berri, behind avenue des Champs-Elysées, Paris 8. Active in the 1950s and 1960s, it was managed first by Ben Benjamin, later by George Gainford (the former manager of the boxer Sugar Ray Robinson). Many visiting American musicians played there, including Buck Clayton and Don Byas. Lester Young played his final engagements there in January–March 1959.

——. **Le Boeuf sur le Toit.** 28 rue Boissy-d'Anglas (1921–8); rue de Penthièvre (1928–?); 43bis avenue Pierre-1er-de-Serbie (by July 1937); 34 rue du Colisée (by 1951–?). The club occupied a succession of premises in the seventh and eighth arrondissements. It was opened on 21 December 1921 by Louis Moyses and named after a popular Brazilian song (on which the composer Darius Milhaud later based a work). In its early days the club was the haunt of French writers, artists, and musicians, including Jean Cocteau, Erik Satie, René Clair, and Maurice Ravel, and the influence of jazz on the music of Parisian composers at this time was in some part due to what they heard there. The first resident pianist was Jean Wiener, who performed both as an unaccompanied soloist and with other musicians, including Clément Doucet. Among the many French and visiting musicians who performed there were Léo Vauchant (1924), Leon Abbey (before 1935), Una Mae Carlisle (1937, 1939), Bobby Martin (1937–8), Benny Carter (15 October 1937 to April 1938), and Django Reinhardt (late 1930s, 1944, 1947, 1948). Carter's residency, as the leader of the seven-piece band that played for dancing in a downstairs room, coincided with performances by Reinhardt, who played upstairs in the dining room and often joined Carter for jam sessions between sets. In the 1930s and again in the 1950s Le Boeuf sur le Toit was the Parisian home of Garland Wilson: he led the resident band there from July 1937 to December 1938 and was host in his own room at the club in January–May 1954.

——. **Bricktop's.** Rue Pigalle, Paris 9 (*c*1928–1939); 26 rue Fontaine, Paris 9 (from 1950). The singer Bricktop (Ada Smith) first sang in Paris at Le Grand Duc (see below), owned by George Jamerson and his wife, in 1924; after running that club for about a year, by 1928 she had taken new premises in the rue Pigalle and opened Bricktop's, which became one of the most fashionable clubs in Paris. From November 1931 her partner was Mabel Mercer and the club was at 66 rue Pigalle where it remained until Bricktop fled Paris in 1939. She opened a new club on the rue Fontaine in May 1950. Many important musicians performed for Bricktop and her patrons included the cream of Parisian society. She also opened clubs in Biarritz, Mexico City, and Rome at different times. (Bricktop and J. Haskins: *Bricktop*, New York, 1983).

——. **Calvados.** 40 avenue Pierre-1er-de-Serbie, Paris 8. It was an important venue for solo pianists, notably Joe Turner (i).

——. **Casanova Club.** Rue Fromentin, Paris 9. A fashionable venue for jazz in Paris before the war, it offered performances by the Quintette du Hot Club de France in the 1930s (for illustration *see* JAZZ (i), fig.4).

——. **Casino de Paris.** 16 rue de Clichy, Paris 9. Jazz formed part of the entertainment from late 1918, when Louis Mitchell appeared there (perhaps as a soloist, perhaps with a band); he returned with the septet the Jazz Kings on 4 July 1919, and played a five-year residency in the 1920s. In the spring of 1933 the singer and actress Josephine Baker performed in a revue at the casino. (Le Perroquet (see below) occupied part of the same building.)

——. **Caveau de l'Huchette.** 5 rue de la Huchette, Paris 5. The oldest of the jazz "caves" on the Left Bank, it was in existence by 1951. In the mid-1960s it offered traditional jazz by musicians such as Raymond Fonsèque. It was later owned by the vibraphonist Dany Doriz, who presented a range of styles there; Hal Singer and Benny Waters both appeared often from the late 1970s, and other important performers in that period included Bill Coleman (1979), the trombonist Gene Connors (1981), Wild Bill Davis (1982), and Maxim Saury (1983). The big band of Roger Guérin was resident in the mid-1980s.

——. **Cave du Hot Club de France.** 9 rue Pavée, Paris 4. It is the Paris home of the HOT CLUB DE FRANCE. The premises were acquired in late 1969 and were initially used for concerts. Since the completion of renovations in December 1970 regular jazz performances have been given there; among the French and resident American musicians to appear have been Benny Waters and Joe Turner (i). The club is also used as a rehearsal room and for record recitals.

——. **Le Chat qui Pêche.** Rue du Chat qui Pêche, off rue de la Huchette, Paris 5. This cellar nightclub on the Left Bank flourished from the late 1950s until 1970, when the owner Madame Ricard sold her license.

——. **Chez Boudon.** Rue Fontaine and rue Mansart, Paris 9. Restaurant and bar. Open day and night, it was a favorite haunt of local and visiting musicians, though in all likelihood no jazz was performed there. In 1937 Dicky Wells recorded a number (*Hangin' around Boudon*, Swing 16) named for the bar.

——. **Chez Django Reinhardt.** Rue Pigalle, Paris 9. In the spring of 1944 the nightclub Roulotte was temporarily given this name for a residency by Reinhardt under the management of Lulu de Montmartre. It was frequented, after the curfew, both by members of the Gestapo and by British agents, and Reinhardt's band was often requested (and permitted) to play *God save the King*. The engagement apparently ended before the Liberation, but the name remained over the door for some time afterwards.

——. **Chez Florence.** Rue Pigalle, Paris 9 (? to 1926); rue Blanche, Paris 9 (? from *c*1927). It was founded as Mitchell's by Louis Mitchell in the 1920s, but renamed for the singer and hostess Florence Embry Jones (*d* New York, early January 1932). The original premises were closed in autumn 1926 but the club was in operation again by 1928 when the International Five played there. Among the musicians who played at the club from the 1930s were Willie Lewis (1935–6, with a band that included Benny Carter), Wilson Myers (1937, in a band led by Roger Devereaux), the Quintette du Hot Club de France (1938), and a number of others, including a group led by Bobby Martin (1937); after the war Arthur Briggs led the house band from 1946 to 1951.

——. **Chez Jane Stick.** It is known chiefly for a series of performances given in 1941 by Django Reinhardt with the drummer Pierre Fouard, Hubert Rostaing, and others.

——. **Chez Josephine.** Rue Fontaine, Paris 9. It was opened in December 1926 by the singer and actress Josephine Baker, who continued to run nightclubs in Paris through the 1930s. Her establishments were favored by the haut monde, whose darling Baker became through her own colorful and exotic performances.

——. **Chez Sidney Bechet.** 67 rue Pierre-Charron, Paris 8. Opened on 23 December 1953 by Bechet with the band led by the clarinetist and soprano saxophonist André Réwéliotty, the club was large enough for dancing. For a short time early in 1954 Bechet performed as resident musician both in his own club and at Métro Jazz (see below) but his operation on the rue Pierre-Charron was short-lived and closed after a few months.

——. **La Cigale.** 124 boulevard Rochechouart, near Place Pigalle, Paris 9. Café. It was named after a nearby music hall. In the early 1940s it flourished as a venue for West Indian and Madagascan music – Harry Cooper led a group of French-Antillean musicians there during this period. Then after the war it became a meeting place for jazz musicians (particularly American servicemen), who regularly played jam sessions. Among the musicians to perform at the café in the 1950s and 1960s were Benny Waters and Jacques Butler, who was resident from 1951 until he returned to the USA in 1968. La Cigale ceased to offer music in the 1970s.

BIBLIOGRAPHY

P. Vacher: "Montmartre Mainstream," *JJ*, xvi/2 (1963), 15

——: "La Cigale, 1963," *JM*, ix/11 (1964), 10

——. **Ciro's.** The entrepreneur Ciro founded a number of exclusive restaurant clubs from the 1910s, notably those in Paris, London, Deauville, and Monte Carlo, which were frequented by the cream of society, including the British royal family. His establishments were first and foremost restaurants, but they were important jazz venues and Ciro built up a long-standing association with black-American musicians. The Paris club was in existence before April 1915, when Ciro opened in London; among the musicians who led bands there were Noble Sissle (summer 1930), the British violinist James Boucher (1931), the double bass player Louis Vola (1932), Django Reinhardt (1940), and Nat Gonella.

——. **Club l'Arlequin.** 1 rue du Four, Paris 6. It flourished at the period (from the early 1950s) when the Left Bank enjoyed a renaissance, thanks to the lively artistic and student community centered on the Sorbonne. Native and visiting musicians played there, including Don Byas and his quintet (1951), Claude Bolling (1953), and Jef Gilson.

——. **Club Saint-Germain.** 13 rue Saint-Benoît, Paris 6. This nightclub on the Left Bank opened in 1949 and continued as a center for jazz during the 1950s and 1960s. During its early days it typified the intense, sophisticated atmosphere of the area, where a highly intellectual café society flourished. It was at first the club where the clarinetist and soprano saxophonist André Réwéliotty was based, and in 1951 Django Reinhardt staged a brief comeback there, performing with Hubert Fol; Claude Bolling's band (which included Bill Coleman) played lengthy engagements in 1951 and 1952, and in April 1954 Stephane Grappelli began a residency there, establishing an association with the club that lasted for many years. Other notable musicians to perform in the 1950s were Lester Young (1956), Miles Davis (1957), and Kenny Clarke, who was resident for some time around 1958.

——. **Club des Trois Mailletz** [Maillets]. See Les Trois Mailletz.

——. **Club du Vieux Colombier.** See Le Vieux Colombier.

——. **Le Croix du Sud.** Montparnasse. It presented jazz as early as 1918, when the pianist Alain Romans was the resident musician for a year. The club became a lively bohemian haunt, popular with the more exotic elements of Parisian society. It was also a favorite haunt of visiting musicians – Jimmy Dorsey and Muggsy Spanier were among those who in the early 1930s occasionally jammed there with the resident band. André Ekyan led the house ensemble at that time, with Stephane Grappelli among his sidemen, and it was supposedly there that Grappelli first met Django Reinhardt late in 1931.

——. **Le Doyen** [L'Impératrice]. Champs-Elysées gardens, Paris 8. Restaurant. It offered musical entertainment from at least the early 1940s. In the spring of 1941 Django Reinhardt performed there daily for the afternoon *thé dansant* (before going on to perform in the evenings at Chez Jane Stick).

——. **Ecole Normale de Musique.** 78 rue Cardinet, at boulevard Malesherbes, Paris 17. The hall of the school was used by the Hot Club de France for many of its concerts in the 1930s and 1940s, beginning with the first performance by the Quintette du Hot Club de France (2 December 1934). Among the musicians whom the club presented were Coleman Hawkins (February 1935), Garland Wilson (1935, 1937), Bill Coleman (1935, 1938), Benny Carter (1937), and Eddie South (1937, 1938). In November 1944 Arthur Briggs appeared at a special performance there to celebrate his release from internment.

——. **Embassy Club.** Avenue des Champs-Elysées, Paris 8. It came to prominence as a venue for jazz in the 1920s, when the bands of Sam Wooding and Leon Abbey (both 1929), and Paul Whiteman, among others, played there. The double bass player Louis Vola led a group there in late 1932, standing in for Arthur Briggs, the current resident, while he played a winter season elsewhere.

——. **L'Ermitage Muscovite.** Rue Caumartin, Paris 9. Jazz was performed there from at least the late 1920s; Mezz Mezzrow's quartet appeared in March 1929.

——. **Florida Night Club.** The Florida was an exclusive club, which flourished from the 1920s; Leon Abbey led a resident group in 1929 and the band of Benny Peyton also appeared there.

——. **Gill's Club.** 7 rue Sainte-Croix-Bretonnerie, Paris 4. Active in the 1970s, it presented various French and visiting traditional musicians, such as the trumpeter Irakli de Davrichewy.

——. **Le Grand Duc.** 52 rue Pigalle, at rue Fontaine, Paris 9. A small nightclub, barely bigger than a bar, it was opened in the early 1920s by Mr. and Mrs. George Jamerson; its managers during the 1920s included Gene Bullard, who worked for the Jamersons and then for the singer Bricktop, who, having sung there from 1924, ran the club for about a year from 1926 (see also Bricktop's).

——. **Le Grand Ecart.** Rue Fromentin, Paris 9. Cabaret. It was in operation by 1930 and in 1931 the house band there was led by the double bass player Dan Parrish. The same premises later housed the Nuits Bleues club (see below).

——. **Harlem Club.** Although it was short-lived the Harlem was an important venue while it lasted. It was opened in 1937 by the trumpeter, singer, guitarist, and dancer Freddy Taylor and was run by Taylor (who led the house band) with James Monroe (later the first husband of Billie Holiday). It closed in 1938.

——. **Hôtel Claridge.** Jazz was played there from at least 1923, when the Georgians under the leadership of Frank Guarente were the resident band. Among the groups that played at the hotel were those led by Paul Gason (1928–9) and the double bass player Louis Vola (1934). Vola's orchestra accompanied the daily *thé dansant* between five and seven in the evening; Django Reinhardt and Stephane Grappelli, who were members of Vola's ensemble, spent time between sets jamming backstage, and it was out of this activity that the Quintette du Hot Club de France was born. Grappelli returned to the hotel 20 years later to play a long season in 1956.

——. **Hôtel Hilton.** See Le Toit de Paris.

——. **Hôtel Meridien.** 81 boulevard Gouvion-Saint-Cyr, Paris 17. Jazz has been promoted there by the entrepreneur Moustache Galipedes, who was earlier active as a jazz drummer; it is reputed to be one of the most expensive jazz venues in Europe. Among those who have appeared there are Buddy Tate (1982, 1983), Eddie "Lockjaw" Davis (1983, 1984, 1986), John Collins's trio, Al Grey, Arnett Cobb, and Buck Clayton (all 1983), Panama Francis and his Savoy Sultans (1986, 1987), Joe Newman and Jimmy Witherspoon (both 1986), and Doc Cheatham and Jimmy Smith (both 1987). In the mid-1980s the orchestra of Claude Bolling performed regularly at Sunday brunch.

——. **Hot Feet.** Rue Notre-Dame-de-Lorette, Paris 9. It opened in 1939 with performances by Django Reinhardt, and Duke Ellington played informally with him there in the late summer of that year.

——. **L'Impératrice.** See Le Doyen.

——. **Jimmy's Bar.** Rue Huyghens, Paris 14. The club was opened by an English barman, Jimmy Charles, and offered jazz from at least the late 1930s. A band that included Django Reinhardt, Alix Combelle, the pianist Charlie Lewis, and Philippe Brun played a residency there in the winter of 1939–40. The club later reopened as New-Jimmy's in more prominent premises a short distance away at 124 boulevard du Montparnasse.

——. **Le Lorientais.** Rue des Carmes, Paris 5. It was from this cellar nightclub that Claude Luter et ses Lorientais launched the traditional jazz revival in France late in 1945; the group continued to play there into the late 1940s. Jacques Brecker's film *Rendez-vous de juillet* (1949), made at the club and featuring Rex Stewart, became the seminal document of the youth culture of the Latin Quarter in the 1950s, dubbed "le Désordre."

——. **Métro Jazz.** 56 rue Galande, Paris 5 (to 1953); beneath the Théâtre du Quartier Latin, 9 rue Champollion, Paris 5 (from 1953). The earlier club, though it had presented musicians of the stature of Lil Armstrong and Peanuts Holland, was eclipsed by the new establishment, which opened in autumn 1953 on the rue Champollion in cellar premises dating back to the 12th century. The house ensemble was led by Michel Attenoux and accompanied such important visiting musicians as Sidney Bechet, who played there in 1953–4. The premises on the rue Galande were taken over by Les Trois Mailletz (see below).

——. **Mitchell's.** See Chez Florence.

——. **Musée d'Art Moderne.** 11 avenue du Président-Wilson, Paris 16. Under the auspices of l'ARC (Animation-recherche-confrontation) Daniel Humair organized a series of jazz concerts at the museum on Monday afternoons from 1967 to 1972. All styles of jazz were presented and among the principal performers were Maxim Saury and Sunny Murray; others who appeared included Tony Scott, Gato Barbieri, Jimmy Owens, and Karl Berger. An important retrospective exhibition covering l'ARC's activities was mounted at the museum in 1972.

——. **Music Box.** Rue Pigalle, Paris 9. A short-lived but successful nightclub run by the singer Bricktop with the help of Louis Mitchell, it opened in October 1926 and closed soon afterwards, owing to the refusal by the authorities to grant it a permanent license. A second club of this name, also in Montmartre, operated in the 1930s; among the jazz musicians to perform there were Herb Flemming (autumn 1930), the cabaret singer Zaidee Jackson (1931), and Fats Waller, whose band included Spencer Williams.

——. **New-Jimmy's.** See Jimmy's Bar.

——. **Nuits Bleues.** Rue Fromentin, Paris 9. It was opened in late summer 1935 under the direction of Mme. Moises in the premises formerly occupied by Le Grand Ecart. The resident bands included the Quintette du Hot Club de France, with which Bill Coleman occasionally played informally.

——. **Olympia.** 28 boulevard des Capucines, Paris 9. Music hall, later theater. In 1929 Gregor and his Gregorians appeared there and during the war it offered performances by the Quintette du Hot Club de France (1941, 1944). But it was most important as a venue for jazz from the 1950s, when its director, the musician and impresario Bruno Coquatrix, began to present concerts of jazz, many of them by visiting American musicians. A successful performance by Sidney Bechet with Claude Luter's band in December 1954 was recorded on the Vogue label, and Bechet appeared there again at a concert in March 1955 to celebrate the 20th anniversary of the founding of the journal *Jazz hot*. Among other musicians who performed at the Olympia were Louis Armstrong and his All Stars, Mezz Mezzrow (1955), Lionel Hampton (1955, 1961), Jack Teagarden, Earl Hines, Cozy Cole, and Erroll Garner (all 1957), Count Basie (1957, 1959, 1960), and Johnny Hodges, Ella Fitzgerald, and Ruby Braff (all 1961). Buck Clayton made well-known recordings there in 1959 with Jimmy Rushing and in 1961 with Jimmy Witherspoon. (The Ten Gallons (see below) operates in a cellar beneath the theater.)

——. **Le Perroquet.** 16 rue de Clichy, Paris 9. It occupied premises above the Casino de Paris (see above). Among the bands that played residencies there were Louis Mitchell's Jazz Kings (1922–3), which became the Real Jazz Kings under Crickett Smith when Mitchell left in 1923, André Ekyan's band, and Lud Gluskin's orchestra, which was the house ensemble in the last few years of the decade.

——. **Le Petit Journal.** 71 boulevard Saint-Michel, Paris 6. It is one of the principal venues in the city for traditional jazz in the 1980s, though its repertory ranges somewhat more widely. Claude Bolling has appeared regularly at the club, which has also engaged many prominent Americans, including Bill Coleman and Benny Waters (1981), the pianist Champion Jack Dupree (1982), Kenny Burrell, Joe Turner (i), Carrie Smith, Buddy Tate, and Harry Edison (all 1983), Sam Woodyard (1984), and Benny Bailey (1986).

——. **Ringside.** Rue Thérèse, Paris 1; 23 rue d'Artois, Paris 8 (by 1953). A venue that presented small groups, it was in operation from at least 1951, when Nelson Williams appeared there and Don Byas, accompanied by a rhythm section that included Pierre Michelot and the pianist Art Simmons, gave a series of after-hours performances. Byas returned to the club after it moved to new premises, performing with Buck Clayton backed by a rhythm section.

——. **Roulotte.** See Chez Django Reinhardt.

——. **Royal Box.** 16 rue Fontaine, Paris 9. It flourished as a center for jazz performance during the 1920s and 1930s, when it was directed by Joe Zelli (the manager of several Parisian nightclubs at this period – see Ad Lib, Tempo Club, and Zelli's). The house band was led for many years by the ragtime pianist J. Glover Compton and included the trumpeter Crickett Smith, the tenor saxophonist and clarinetist Frank "Big Boy" Goudie, and the drummer Gene Bullard (see fig.1), who had earlier worked as the manager of Le Grand Duc (see above).

——. **Salle Gaveau.** Concert hall. It was regularly used for jazz concerts. Pierre Nourry organized an appearance by the Quintette du Hot Club de France there on 20 October 1937 and the group performed again in March the following year. It was also the venue for an important concert on 19 December 1940, at which many notable French jazz musicians, including Django Reinhardt and Hubert Rostaing, performed.

——. **Salle Pleyel.** 252 rue du Faubourg-Saint-Honoré, Paris 8. One of several concert halls in the same building (the others are the Salles Chopin, Rameau, and Debussy), it has been the venue for many important jazz performances from before World War II. Among those who played there in the prewar period were Louis Armstrong (two concerts, November 1934), Duke Ellington (two concerts), and the Quintette du Hot Club de France. (Coleman Hawkins appeared at the Salle Rameau in 1935.) During and after the war the hall presented performances by Fud Candrix (1942), André Ekyan, Eddie Barclay, and others (1942), the reunited Quintette du Hot Club de France (1947), Dizzy Gillespie (1948), Mezz Mezzrow (1951, 1952), Bill Coleman (1952), Sidney Bechet (1952), Art Tatum (1955), Sammy Price (1956), Kid Ory (1956, 1959), and Duke Ellington (1958). In 1949, 1952, and 1954 the Festival International de Jazz (popularly known as the Paris Jazz Fair), organized by Charles Delaunay, was held in the hall; Charlie Parker, Miles Davis, and Tadd Dameron, among others, appeared at the festival in 1949 (*see* FESTIVALS). In 1954 Gerry Mulligan gave an electrifying performance there, which was recorded and released as a double album ([*Paris Concert*], Vogue 7381, 7383). A gala evening to celebrate Stephane Grappelli's 75th birthday was held at the Salle Pleyel on 29 March 1983.

——. **Slow Club.** 130 rue de Rivoli, Paris 1. It presented various French jazz musicians from at least the early 1970s, including Claude Luter; in the mid-1980s a sextet led by the vibraphonist Dany Doriz appeared there.

——. **Le Spaghetti Club.** Rue du Colisée, Paris 8. Opened in 1958, this nightclub's programs were devoted to traditional jazz. The trombonist Mowgli Jospin and Raymond Fonsèque were among the leading revivalists who performed there.

——. **Swing Time.** Rue Fromentin, Paris 9. It was the base for André Ekyan and his band in the late 1930s. Many French and

1. The Royal Box, Paris, 1927: (the band, left to right) J. Glover Compton (piano), Ferdie Allen (banjo), Crickett Smith (trumpet), Frank "Big Boy" Goudie (tenor saxophone), unidentified trombonist, and Gene Bullard (drums); the proprietor, Joe Zelli, is seated immediately in front of the piano

American musicians dropped in at the club to play in jam sessions with Ekyan, among them Benny Carter, Coleman Hawkins, Bill Coleman, and Django Reinhardt.

——. **Tempo Club.** Rue Caumartin, Paris 9. It occupied premises above Zelli's (see below) and was probably an after-hours club. It was active in the 1920s and among the groups that appeared there was Louis Mitchell's band the Jazz Kings.

——. **Ten Gallons.** 28 boulevard des Capucines, Paris 9. Cellar bar and nightclub in premises beneath the Olympia theater (see above). The pianist Bob Vatel, active for many years in Parisian clubs and bars, made it his base; his connection with the club is honored in Jaki Byard's *Dedicated to Bob Vatel of the "Ten Gallons"* on his solo album *Parisian Solos* (Futura Swing 05).

——. **Le Toit de Paris.** Hôtel Hilton, 18 avenue de Suffren, Paris 7. The bar and restaurant of the Paris Hilton has presented notable performances of jazz on an occasional basis from the mid-1960s. Stephane Grappelli led a resident quintet there for five years from 1967, recording the album *Sur le Toit de Paris* (RCA 740038) in January 1969.

——. **Les Trois Mailletz** [Maillets]. 56 rue Galande, Paris 5. It opened in 1953 in the premises on the Left Bank that had formerly housed the Métro Jazz club (see above), and was managed by Mme. Calvet. Bill Coleman played a notable residency there from 1955 to 1960 (with occasional absences), and other important musicians to appear included Mezz Mezzrow (with Nelson Williams and André Persiany, 1959), Stephane Grappelli (with a band led by the soprano saxophonist Michel Attenoux, 1960), Peanuts Holland (again with Attenoux, 1961), and Buck Clayton (*c*1967). (C. Roby: "Blue Stomping at the Trois Mailletz," *JB*, ii/11 (1965), 4)

——. **Le Vieux Colombier** [Vieux-Cô]. 21 rue du Vieux-Colombier, Paris 6. In existence by 1951 at the latest, this cellar club, owned and managed by Annet Badel, was an important venue for jazz. Badel operated a second club of this name, modeled on his Paris operation, at Juan-les-Pins near Antibes. At both venues his most important performers were Sidney Bechet with Claude Luter's orchestra. Among the other musicians who appeared in at the Paris club were Mezz Mezzrow, Hot Lips Page, Lionel Hampton, the clarinetist and soprano saxophonist André Réwéliotty, and Big Chief Moore.

——. **Villa d'Este.** 4 rue Arsène-Houssaye, Paris 8. Directed by Sacha de Horn, the club was active as a center for jazz performance from at least the 1930s. Freddy Taylor's Swing Men from Harlem, which included Billy Taylor (i) and Fletcher Allen and featured Bill Coleman, played there in 1935. The resident band in the mid-1940s was the Jazz de Paris led by the drummer Jerry Mengo.

——. **Zelli's.** Rue Caumartin, Paris 9. It was one of several Parisian clubs owned and run by Joe Zelli, and was in operation by around 1920. Among the musicians who played there were Crickett Smith, the pianist and accordionist Tom Waltham, and the black trumpeter Bobby Jones.

BIBLIOGRAPHY

Paris

L. Feather: "Vive le hot! Snapshots of Paris and its Dance Music," *MM*, x (17 Nov 1934)

——: "Tempo di Jazz," *Radio Times* (23 July 1937)

C. Delaunay: *Django Reinhardt: souvenirs* (Paris, 1954; Eng. trans., London, 1961/*R*1981, 1982, rev. 2/1981)

M. Dorigné: "Petite chronique du jazz New Orleans en France," *Jazz*, i: *Les origines du jazz, le style Nouvelle-Orléans et ses prolongements* (Paris, 1968), 140

P. Lafargue: Liner notes, *Le jazz parisien . . . libéré* (Barclay 81004-5, 1976)

K. Henriques: "Jazz sur Seine," *Jazz Express* (Feb 1987), 7

GERMANY

BERLIN. **Barbarina Cabaret.** Its program included jazz from at least 1927, when an all-star group, the New Yorkers (i), led by the guitarist and banjoist George Carhart played at the club; among Carhart's players were Danny Polo and Dave Tough.

——. **Delphi** [Delphi-Palast]. Kantstrasse 12, D-1000 Berlin. It flourished as an important venue for jazz from the 1920s and was particularly noted for its jam sessions during the 1930s and 1940s; it continued to present jazz, under other guises, throughout the period of Nazi rule. By the 1980s the building had become a cinema, occasionally used as a concert hall; jazz performances take place there only during the Jazzfest Berlin (*see* FESTIVALS).

——. **Haus der Jungen Talente.** Klosterstrasse 68-70, DDR-1020 Berlin. Youth club. Its various programs include modern, mainstream, and free jazz and free improvised music; jazz is normally presented on Monday evenings.

——. **Haus Gurmenia.** It offered performances of jazz from at least 1929, when Lud Gluskin's band performed there.

——. **Haus Vaterland.** Entertainment complex. This vast establishment was built on six floors and offered entertainment of many different kinds. At any one time at least six bands were playing in its various restaurants and nightclubs. One of the jazz musicians to perform there (mainly in the Wild West Bar) was Sidney Bechet, who in 1930–31 was engaged as the principal soloist in small bands that played for dancing and cabaret acts. The Haus Vaterland issued its own magazine, *Berolina*.

DRESDEN. **Jazzclub Tonne.** Tzschirnerplatz 3, DDR-8010 Dresden. It opened in 1981 as the premises for the jazz club IG Jazz Dresden, founded in 1977. It presents all styles of jazz, from dixieland to free improvised music.

FRANKFURT AM MAIN. **Der Jazzkeller** [Domicile]. Bockenheimer Landstrasse (1947–52); Kleine Bockenheimer Strasse 18a, D-6000 Frankfurt am Main (1952–). It was founded (as Der Jazzkeller) in cellar premises on Bockenheimer Landstrasse in 1947 by the trumpeter and writer Carlo Bohländer; later known for a time as the Domicile, it eventually reverted to its original name. The club at first specialized in traditional and contemporary styles of jazz, though little live jazz was presented at the earlier of the two locations. After it moved, however, the club became the venue in which the most important Frankfurt musicians, who have been among the foremost German jazzmen, met and played together; under the ownership of Willi Geipel, in the late 1980s Der Jazzkeller was known mostly for modern styles, from mainstream to avant-garde jazz.

——. **Schumann Café.** In spite of the restrictions imposed under Nazi rule, jazz performances continued at the café during World War II, when the trumpeter and writer Carlo Bohländer was among the musicians who played there.

HAMBURG. **Onkel Pö's Carnegie Hall** [Onkel Pö]. Lehmweg 44, D-2000 Hamburg 20 (?1970–1985). It was founded in 1968 by Peter Marxen under the name Onkel Peu à Peu; Marxen managed the club until 1979, when Holger Jass took over. One of the principal jazz clubs in Germany during the 1970s, Onkel

Pö presented mainly modern jazz and popular music; besides German jazz musicians, Al Jarreau, Pat Metheny, and other Americans performed there early in their careers. The repertory became increasingly popular and by the time the club closed in 1985 little jazz was being performed. (K. Berger: "Pö à Pö abwärts," *JP*, xxxv/2 (1986), 18)

MUNICH. **Domicile.** Siegesstrasse 19/1, D-8000 Munich (to late 1970s); Leopoldstrasse 19, D-8000 Munich (late 1970s–). It played an important role in the jazz scene in Munich and was a favorite venue for visiting American musicians; the Thad Jones–Mel Lewis Orchestra played a noted engagement there in the mid-1970s. In the 1980s the club became better known for the performance of rock music.

——. **Jazzclub Unterfahrt.** Kirchenstrasse 96, D-8000 Munich 80. Founded in 1978 by the Förderkreis für Jazz und Malerei, it presents mostly modern styles of jazz (mainstream and free jazz and Latin music) under the direction of the program manager Josef M. Dachsel. Different performers appear every evening, and they regularly include musicians of international standing; an open jam session takes place on Sunday.

NUREMBERG. **Jazz-Studio Nürnberg.** Paniersplatz 27-9, D-8500 Nuremberg 1. It was founded by a group of 13 people as a nonprofit organization on 4 April 1954; it is run by a council elected annually. The studio promotes the performance of all styles of jazz and musicians from all over the world have appeared there; another aspect of its activities is to support local jazz musicians, by providing rehearsal facilities and devoting one night a week to performances by local players. It also sponsors the festival Jazz Ost-West (*see* FESTIVALS) and presents a weekly radio program, "Jazztime Nürnberg," in cooperation with a private station, Radio Franken.

BIBLIOGRAPHY

Germany

H. H. Lange: *Jazz in Deutschland: die deutsche Jazz-Chronik, 1900–1960* (Berlin, 1966)

J. Oehlmann, ed.: *Jazzaz: Texte zur Jazzmusik* (Giessen, Germany, 1982)

GREAT BRITAIN [GB]

BARNEHURST. **Red Barn.** Barnehurst Road, Barnehurst, Kent. It was founded by the Bexleyheath and District Rhythm Club in 1943. The first important postwar British revival jazz club, it flourished until around 1950. The performances given there in the mid-1940s by the resident band, George Webb's Dixielanders, are usually regarded as having sparked off the traditional revival in Britain; a plaque commemorating their association with the Red Barn was unveiled there on 4 July 1985.

BIRMINGHAM. **Palais de Dance.** Monument Road. Dance hall. It opened on 21 December 1920 with a performance by the Frisco Jazz Band. After the summer recess in 1921 Benny Peyton's Jazz Kings, which included Sidney Bechet, played there (1–10 September); the band returned for a residency of a month in February 1922, and during that year the Paramount Six also appeared. Emile Christian was a member of the house band in late 1921 and early 1922. (E. S. Walker: "Saturday Night at the Palais, '21," *Sv*, no.105 (1983), 108)

LONDON. **Bag o' Nails.** Kingly Street, London W1. It flourished as a venue for jazz in the 1930s, when Gerry Moore was among the important musicians who performed there. Towards the end of the decade it was the meeting place of the No. 1 Rhythm Club.

——. **Barbican.** London EC2. Arts complex. It opened in 1982 and has developed a lively program of pop and jazz performance, both in the concert hall and in the foyer and public areas. Among the jazz musicians who have appeared in concert are Keith Jarrett, Buddy Rich, Louie Bellson, John Dankworth, Cleo Laine, Carmen McRae, Billy Eckstine, Sarah Vaughan, Oscar Peterson, Stephane Grappelli, George Shearing, Marian Montgomery, Clark Terry, and the Preservation Hall Jazz Band. Free performances are given in the foyer every Sunday lunchtime.

——. **Bass Clef.** 1 Hoxton Square, London N1. It was founded by Peter Ind around 1984 and rapidly became one of the city's most popular clubs; it presents mostly modern repertory, including free improvised music. In another part of the same building are the studios for Ind's record company, Wave; these are linked to the club, and performances are sometimes recorded.

——. **Bull's Head.** Lonsdale Road, Barnes, London SW13. Pub. The manager, Albert Tolley, began presenting jazz in 1960; performances (mostly of bop and associated styles) have continued every night of the week into the late 1980s, by which time the manager was Dan Fleming and the venue was among the most renowned in Britain. As well as engaging some of the country's most important musicians (Tony Lee's trio has been resident from the early 1960s, and Humphrey Lyttelton's band and Bill Le Sage's trio have appeared regularly), the Bull's Head has also booked important visiting musicians, including Jimmy Witherspoon, Al Casey, Snub Mosley, Don Ewell, Benny Waters, George Coleman, Lanny Morgan, Hal Singer, and Mundell Lowe.

——. **Café de Paris.** 3 Coventry Street, London W1. One of the fashionable establishments for dining and dancing in London, it presented jazz from at least the late 1920s; Ethel Waters was resident there in 1929–30. It became known especially as a center for Afro-Caribbean bands; these included the West Indian Swing Band, led by Ken "Snake Hips" Johnson, which opened in October 1939; Johnson was killed when the premises were destroyed by a bomb on 8 March 1941.

——. **Carlton Dance Hall.** See Rector's.

——. **Casino de Danse.** 160 Finchley Road, London NW3. These premises operated as a dance hall from 1919 and took the name Casino de Danse around 1922. Jazz was played for dancing from at least the mid-1930s, when bands led by Cyril Blake and others played there.

——. **Ciro's.** Orange Street, London WC2. It was opened in April 1915 by the French entrepreneur Ciro, and was modeled on his sophisticated and expensive restaurant club in Paris; he later set up other such clubs in Deauville and Monte Carlo. Although he insisted (perhaps for licensing reasons) that his establishments were restaurants, they offered musical entertainment from the start; the London Ciro's opened with Dan Kildare's Clef Club Orchestra as the resident band. The club was frequented by the haut monde, and its patrons included members of the British royal family. It closed between 1917 and 1919, then reopened, and continued until 1939. Among the musicians to perform there were Noble Sissle, with a band that included Arthur Briggs and Tommy Ladnier (1930), and Art Tatum (March 1938).

——. **Club Eleven.** 41 Great Windmill Street, London W1 (1948–50); 50 Carnaby Street, London W1 (1950). It was established in 1948; its 11 founders were, apart from the business manager Harry Morris, all bop musicians. They included Ronnie Scott and John Dankworth, each of whom led a resident band, with such players as Tony Crombie, Lennie Bush, Hank Shaw, and others. The club became an important center for early experiments with the bop style in London, but closed only months after moving to new premises in 1950. (J. Fordham: *Let's Join Hands and Contact the Living: Ronnie Scott and his Club*, London, 1986)

——. **Cook's Ferry Inn.** Angel Road, Edmonton, London N18. Pub. It was one of the principal venues for traditional jazz in London in the late 1940s and 1950s. Rex Stewart performed there in 1949 and the resident band was led for some time by Freddy Randall. It was the home of the Cleveland Jazz Club.

——. **Cossack.** Restaurant. 40 Jermyn Street, London SW1. In the early 1930s the orchestra African Polyphony led by the conductor and clarinetist Rudolph Dunbar appeared there, also making broadcasts for the BBC; among the jazz musicians who played in Dunbar's orchestra was Cyril Blake.

——. **Embassy Club.** 6–8 Old Bond Street, London W1. It was one of the first nightclubs to be established in London, and from December 1919 to August 1920 Benny Peyton's group the Jazz Kings (made up of former members of Will Marion Cook's Southern Syncopated Orchestra, and at first including Sidney Bechet) was the resident band. Jazz and dance bands continued to play there into the 1950s; Bert Ambrose was music director in 1920–26 and 1933–6, and Reginald Foresythe led the resident band in 1940. The premises later served principally as a discothèque.

——. **Feldman Swing Club.** See 100 Oxford Street.

——. **'51 Club.** See Studio 51.

——. **Flamingo.** Beneath Mapleton Restaurant, Leicester Square, London W1 (1953); Café Anglais, Leicester Square (early 1950s); Wardour Street, London W1 (from mid-1950s). Under the management of Sam Kruger it became one of the better-known venues for bop in London, employing as resident musicians Tony Kinsey, Dizzy Reece, Bill Le Sage, Wilton "Bogey" Gaynair, Tommy Whittle, and Ronnie Ross, among others. In the early 1950s the club operated at both venues in Leicester Square, but its most important activities began with the move to Wardour Street, where it flourished until the mid-1960s.

——. **Florida Club** [Old Florida]. 5 South Bruton Mews, London W1. One of London's most luxurious and exclusive clubs, it opened in the mid-1920s. Ronnie Monroe led the first resident band (with Ben Davis, saxophones, Frank Wilson, trumpet, and Max Bacon, drums), which played hot dance music. The club quickly became important for the presentation of Afro-Caribbean jazz and was the venue at which Ken "Snake Hips" Johnson and his Rhythm Swingers undertook their first London residency in 1936–8. Adelaide Hall sang there for several years accompanied first by Fela Sowardi's band (1938–40), then by Gerry Moore (1940–42).

——. **Hammersmith Palais (de Danse).** Brook Green Road, London W6. Dance hall. It opened in 1919 and from October of that year to June of the next the Original Dixieland Jazz Band played there, giving some of the first jazz performances in London. Other early jazz bands to appear included Benny Peyton's Jazz Kings (their first residency beginning on 3 October 1920). For a time in the 1930s the venue was used as an ice-rink. In 1950 the National Federation of Jazz Organisations hired the hall for a special event, the Jazz Band Ball. After several years as a discothèque and a venue for rock concerts, the Hammersmith Palais began, in addition, to promote jazz again on an occasional basis following a concert given in 1984 by Kid Thomas and the Preservation Hall Jazz Band.

——. **Havana Club.** 6 New Compton Street, London W1 (1938); 4 Denman Street, London W1 (1938–?1940; 1942–3). It was chiefly associated with Afro-Caribbean jazz bands, including that led by the double bass player Jack Davis. The club also engaged Una Mae Carlisle during her visit to Europe in the late 1930s. It closed in 1943.

——. **Hippodrome.** Charing Cross Road at Cranbourn Street, London WC2. Theater and ballroom. It was the site of the first performance by a jazz band in Britain, when the Original Dixieland Jazz Band played in the revue *Joy Bells* on 7 April 1919. It continued to promote jazz throughout the 1920s, engaging Paul Whiteman's orchestra in 1923 and 1926. In the 1930s the Hippodrome functioned as a theater and concerts of jazz were given there on Sundays: Garland Wilson appeared at one of these in 1935 and Benny Carter in 1937. From 1958 until the mid-1980s the premises housed a nightclub, the Talk of the Town, where a number of jazz musicians, including Louie Bellson, performed. Thereafter the entrepreneur Peter Stringfellow opened a discothèque there, using the building's original name.

——. **Humphrey Lyttelton Club.** See 100 Oxford Street.

——. **Jazzshows.** See 100 Oxford Street.

——. **Jig's Club.** 124-6 Wardour Street, London W1. It flourished as a center for jazz from at least the early 1930s, when it was managed by Alec and Rose Ward. Its name derived from an American slang word for Black, and its clientèle was mostly West Indian. In the early 1940s the club band included Cyril Blake; four recordings were made by the band for the Regal–Zonophone label in December 1941.

——. **Ken Colyer's.** Great Newport Street, London WC2. A small cellar nightclub on the fringes of Soho, it was an important venue for traditional jazz in the early 1960s. Colyer's own band, the New Orleans Jazzmen, playing a faithful form of classic jazz, was joined there by a dixieland band, the Original Downtown Syncopators, and the Delta Jazzmen.

——. **Kit Kat.** Haymarket, London SW1. Its name was taken from an 18th-century Whig club founded by Christopher Catt. It presented jazz from the mid-1920s, when Noble Sissle and Eubie Blake appeared there. The club was a favorite haunt of Duke Ellington and his band members during their visit to London in 1933. Cab Calloway performed at the Kit Kat in 1934 and other musicians to play there included Léo Vauchant and Jack Hylton. The club closed about 1935 and the premises later became a cinema. Another club of the same name operated on Regent Street around the turn of the decade; among the musicians it engaged were the reed player and bandleader Teddy Joyce and Al Jennings, whose band included Joe Appleton.

——. **Leicester Square Jazz Club.** Above Café de l'Europe, Leicester Square, London W1. It operated on Monday nights in 1947–8 in premises rented from the National Society for the Prevention of Cruelty to Children. It was the first jazz club in London to offer traditional jazz for dancing. Humphrey Lyttelton's band played regularly and Graeme Bell's Australian Jazz Band was also resident for a time.

——. **London Jazz Club.** Great Windmill Street, London W1 (1948–?1951); 100 Oxford Street, London W1 (?1951–1958). At first the London Jazz Club operated twice weekly in a large rehearsal room beneath a gymnasium in Great Windmill Street. Among the musicians who performed at the club was Humphrey Lyttelton, whose band (including Wally Fawkes) was resident there from around 1949 and played with guest musicians such as Rex Stewart and Jimmy McPartland. In 1950 or 1951 the club moved to 100 Oxford Street (see below), where it coexisted for a time with the Humphrey Lyttelton Club, closing in 1958.

——. **London Palladium** [Palladium Theatre]. 8 Argyll Street, London W1. Variety theater. An important venue for concert performances of popular music, the Palladium first presented jazz in April 1919, when the Original Dixieland Jazz Band played there during its first visit to London. Will Marion Cook's Southern Syncopated Orchestra gave performances in the following year. From the 1930s many eminent musicians and big bands played short residencies at the theater, including Duke Ellington (1933), Cab Calloway (1934), Coleman Hawkins (1934), Garland Wilson (1936), Teddy Hill (1937), and Fats Waller (1938); Louis Armstrong led his group there in 1932 and 1933, and Joe Venuti and the guitarist Frank Victor appeared in August 1934. During the 1940s and 1950s such engagements continued, with many notable performances, such as those of Ellington with Ray Nance and Kay Davis (1948), Benny Goodman (1949), Ellington with his orchestra (1957), Count Basie's orchestra (November 1957), and Bob Crosby (1958); from 1944 Ted Heath gave regular monthly concerts.

——. **Lyons Corner House.** Shaftesbury Avenue at Coventry Street, London W1. Café. Jazz was played there from at least the early 1920s; the Georgians, led by Paul Specht and including Chauncey Morehouse and Arthur Schutt, was the resident band in 1923.

——. **Lyttelton Club.** See 100 Oxford Street.

——. **Mack's.** See 100 Oxford Street.

——. **Marquee Club.** 165 Oxford Street (at Poland Street), London W1 (1958–64); Wardour Street, London W1 (from 1964). It was established by the National Jazz Federation and opened early in 1958 with a performance by Kenny Baker. The club espoused a fairly broad programming policy, offering mainly traditional and mainstream jazz together with blues and rhythm-and-blues; indeed, it made an important contribution to the development of the blues scene in London. Among the bands that performed were those of Chris Barber, Humphrey Lyttelton, John Dankworth, Joe Harriott, and Harold McNair; Alexis Korner's Blues Incorporated was resident there in 1962, often accompanying guest singers. After the club moved in 1964 to premises owned by Harold Pendleton, it concentrated on blues and rock music, and by the late 1960s it was no longer thought of as a jazz venue. ("Mainstream at the Marquee," *Jazz News*, iii (March 1958), 4)

——. **Mayfair Hotel.** Berkeley Street, London W1. Music was played for dancing from at least the 1920s. Bert Ambrose's band was resident there in 1927–33 and from 1928 made fortnightly broadcasts from the hotel's ballroom; Ambrose returned to the Mayfair in 1937–8 and 1939–40.

——. **Moody's Club.** 71 Tottenham Court Road, London W1. It flourished from about 1922 to about 1927; many black groups performed there regularly and of particular importance were the several ensembles that grew out of Will Marion Cook's Southern Syncopated Orchestra.

——. **Nest Club.** Little Pulteney Street (now Brewer Street), London W1; Kingly Street, London W1 (by mid-1930s). The Nest Club at Kingly Street was an important venue before the war for visiting American jazzmen, including Coleman Hawkins, Fats Waller, and Benny Carter. In 1937 Dizzy Gillespie sat in at the club with local musicians; at that time the house band included the trumpeter Duncan Whyte and George Chisholm.

——. **Old Florida.** See Florida Club.

——. **Olympia Ballroom.** Dance hall. It was active from at least the 1920s. Leon Abbey and his band performed there in 1927–8.

——. **100 Club.** See 100 Oxford Street.

——. **100 Oxford Street.** London W1. In the 1930s the premises housed a dance hall. From the early 1940s a succession of clubs operated at this address, making 100 Oxford Street the longest-running venue for traditional and mainstream jazz in London; a number of broadcasts have been made from the club and many musicians have recorded there.

In 1942 Joseph Feldman took over the premises and started a Sunday jazz club to promote the work of his sons Robert (clarinet), Monty (accordion), and Victor (drums). The club presented traditional jazz and swing, and the bands of Vic Lewis and Jack Parnell, Freddy Randall, and others played there, as did several American forces ensembles. The Feldman Swing Club continued until 1954. By 1951 the London Jazz Club (see above) and the Humphrey Lyttelton Club were also offering sessions, on different nights of the week, at 100 Oxford Street. By 1953 Humphrey Lyttelton was appearing twice weekly, and the number of evenings on which jazz was presented gradually increased until 1955 (by which time the venue itself was known as Mack's); Lyttelton's organization issued a regular newsletter called the *Humphrey Lyttelton Club Bulletin*. The London Jazz Club ceased to function in 1958 and from December of that year the premises were called The 100.

In September 1959 Ted Morton opened the Jazzshows Jazz Club at 100 Oxford Street with Don Kingswell as his manager (Morton also presented jazz at other locations under the name Jazzshows). In 1964 the venue became the 100 Club and the following year Roger Horton replaced Don Kingswell. Horton and Morton together continued to run the club into the 1980s; it publishes a bimonthly newsletter *Jazz at the 100 Club*.

——. **Palais de Danse.** East Ham. Dance hall. It was active during the 1920s; Victor Vorzanger's Broadway Band, which included the trombonist Ellis Jackson, was resident there in 1922–3.

——. **Palladium Theatre.** See London Palladium.

——. **Palm Beach.** Frith Street, London W1. A number of visiting American jazz musicians performed at this Soho club, including Fats Waller (1938) and Coleman Hawkins (1939). The banjoist Ike Hatch was the principal resident musician there at that time and the house band was led by the pianist Hettie Booth (1938–40).

——. **Pizza Express.** 10 Dean Street, London W1. Restaurant. In the mid-1970s Peter Boizot began to engage jazz musicians to play in the restaurant, which under his direction (and later that of K. C. Sulkin and Dave Bennett), became an important location for small-group jazz of all traditions and styles. A number of visiting American and European musicians have played there, including Bob Wilber and Bud Freeman. Around 1978 Boizot began to publish the news sheet *Jazz at the Pizza Express*, which developed into a monthly journal (from 1984 *Jazz Express*).

——. **Pizza on the Park.** Knightsbridge, London SW1. Restaurant. It was established in the mid-1970s and is managed by Peter Boizot, who has presented mostly solo and duo performances there. The venue has two pianos and among the resident pianists have been Ralph Sutton and Eddie Thompson.

——. **Purcell Room.** See South Bank.

——. **Queen Elizabeth Hall.** See South Bank.

——. **Rainbow Roof.** See Shim Sham Club.

——. **Rector's.** 31 Tottenham Court Road, London W1. It was one of the London venues at which the Original Dixieland Jazz Band performed during its visit to the city in 1919. In the 1920s it was a fashionable nightspot and was associated with several of the small ensembles to grow out of Will Marion Cook's Southern Syncopated Orchestra. Between 1920 and 1922 resident groups at the club included Benny Peyton's Jazz Kings and the Red Devils; the personnel of both of these bands originated from the SSO and the first included Sidney Bechet. In 1928 the Tottenham Court Road premises became the Carlton Dance Hall. A later club under the name Rector's operated at 207 Regent Street from the late 1930s; Al Jennings led a band there which included Joe Appleton.

——. **Red Barn.** See Great Britain, Barnehurst.

——. **Ronnie Scott's.** 39 Gerrard Street, London W1 (1959–67); 47 Frith Street, London W1 (from 1967; see fig.2). It was founded in 1959 by Ronnie Scott, who continues to manage it with Peter King. It became the most important venue for jazz performance in London, especially after it moved to Frith Street, and has frequently been used for recordings and broadcasts. Numerous eminent performers have appeared there: the club has accommodated big bands such as those of Count Basie, Buddy Rich, and Maynard Ferguson, but it is equally suited to solo performers and small groups. For many years it had a house rhythm section led by Stan Tracey, who worked with visiting soloists such as Sonny Rollins and Ben Webster; other Americans to play there have included Illinois Jacquet and Panama Francis. Its promotion of British jazz has been of supreme significance and many British musicians appear regularly, among them Ronnie Scott's own trio.

BIBLIOGRAPHY

K. Grime: *Jazz at Ronnie Scott's* (London, 1979)

J. Fordham: *Let's Join Hands and Contact the Living: Ronnie Scott and his Club* (London, 1986)

——. **Royal Festival Hall.** See South Bank.

——. **Savoy Hotel.** The Strand, London WC2. To celebrate the armistice that ended World War I the hotel gave a ball in 1919, the Peace Ball, at which the Original Dixieland Jazz Band played. During the first two decades of the century the resident dance bands in the hotel ballroom at times included notable jazz musicians: the Savoy Quartet (1915–20) and the Savoy Orpheans (from mid-1920s) made numerous recordings, some of which contain points of jazz interest; in 1927–9 Fred Elizalde led the Savoy Hotel Band, among the members of which were Adrian Rollini and Fud Livingston.

——. **Shim Sham Club.** 37 Wardour Street, London W1. It opened in March 1935 and by late 1936 Garland Wilson was leader of the resident band. Benny Carter performed there in 1936 and Una Mae Carlisle the following year; such jazz-oriented dance-band players as the trumpeter Duncan Whyte, the guitarists Alan Ferguson and Ivor Mairants, the drummer Maurice Burman, and Edgar Jackson also appeared during the 1930s. In 1937 Joe Appleton became the bandleader and late that year the club's name was changed to the Rainbow Roof; it had reverted to the original name by April 1938. (R. Dunbar: "Harlem in London," *MM*, xii (7 March 1936), 2)

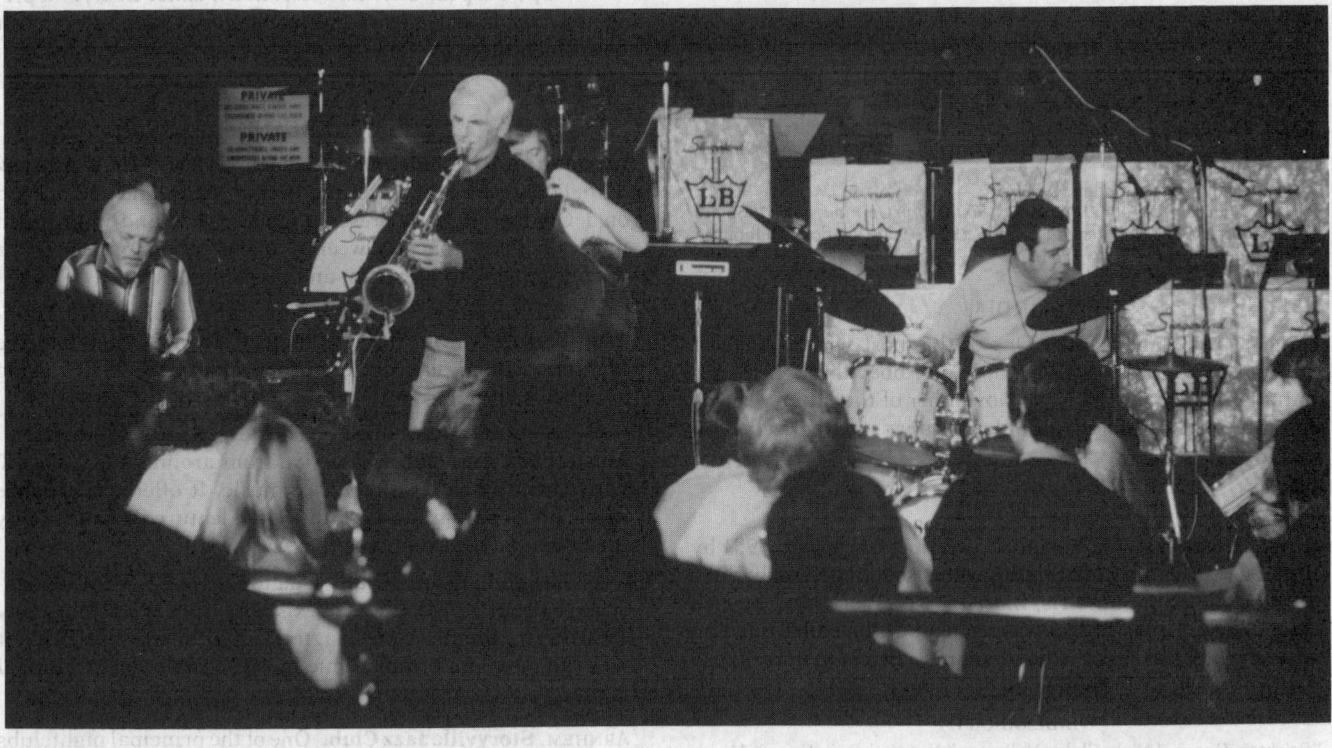

2. Ronnie Scott with his quartet playing at Ronnie Scott's, London, October 1979: (left to right) John Critchenson (keyboards), Scott (tenor saxophone), Ron Mathewson (double bass), and Martin Drew (drums)

——. **Six Bells.** King's Road, Chelsea. Pub. A large upstairs room was used for jazz performances and jam sessions from the 1930s until the early 1960s. Spike Hughes's composition *Six Bells Stampede* (1932, Decca F2844) was dedicated to the venue. In the 1950s and 1960s it was used as a recording studio by Decca, and sessions by such leaders as Ken Colyer and Mick Mulligan took place there. In 1961 Bruce Turner's Jump Band, which included John Chilton and John Mumford, which was then resident there, used the pub as a location in Jack Gold's film *Living Jazz*. Other notable British bands to appear included Wally Fawkes's Troglodytes, who also recorded there for Decca.

——. **South Bank.** SE1. Arts complex. The Royal Festival Hall, the Queen Elizabeth Hall, and the Purcell Room, which form part of the complex, are among the principal concert halls in London. The first major jazz concert at the Royal Festival Hall took place on 14 July 1951 under the auspices of the National Federation of Jazz Organisations. By the 1980s jazz was part of the program in all three halls and free performances were regularly given in the Royal Festival Hall foyer. Particularly important are the series of jazz events held mostly in the summer, notably the JVC–Capital Radio Jazz Parade in June (*see* FESTIVALS).

——. **Studio 51** ['51 Club]. London W1. Founded around 1956 by Ken Colyer it was an important venue for traditional jazz in the 1950s and 1960s. Parts of the film *West 11* (1963) were set in the club and its soundtrack was played by Colyer, Acker Bilk, and Tony Kinsey.

——. **Suzi-Q.** Gerrard Street, London W1. It was run by the banjoist Ike Hatch and was active in the late 1930s.

——. **Talk of the Town.** See Hippodrome.

——. **Wolsey's.** Wells Street, London W1. It opened in June 1987 with a performance by Betty Bennett, accompanied by a trio led by her husband Mundell Lowe. Its size makes it appropriate for solo and small-group performances.

BIBLIOGRAPHY

London

A. Gray: "London's After-dark Swing Spots," *MM*, xiii (17 April – 10 July 1937, 24 July 1937, 17 Sept 1937) [series of 14 articles]

H. Lyttelton: *I Play as I Please: the Memoirs of an Old Etonian Trumpeter* (London, 1954)

——: *Second Chorus* (London, 1958)

P. Green: "Jazz in London, June 1962," *Sixth Form Opinion*, no.5 (1962), 11

J. Godbolt: *A History of Jazz in Britain, 1919–1950* (London, Melbourne, Australia, and New York, 1984)

INDIA

BOMBAY. **Taj Mahal Hotel.** One of the most widely traveled jazz musicians of the swing era, Leon Abbey, brought bands to India in 1935 and 1936; in November of the latter year his ensemble, which included Emile Christian, played at the Taj Mahal.

ITALY

ROME. **Bricktop's.** Via Veneto. It was opened early in 1951 by the singer Bricktop (Ada Smith), who also founded nightclubs of the same name in Paris, Biarritz, New York, and Mexico City. Charlie Lewis's band was resident at the club's opening and Ralph Burns was the house pianist; Bricktop herself also performed often. The club closed in March 1964.

BIBLIOGRAPHY

"Bricktop, Queen of Night Clubs, Abdicates," *New York Daily News* (6 March 1964)

Bricktop and J. Haskins: *Bricktop* (New York, 1983)

——. **Fonclea.** Via Crescenzio 82A, 00193 Rome. It was founded in 1978 and from 1979 it was directed by Claude Mage, Francesco Ghidoli, Massimo Altano, and Marco Caroni. The club has presented not only many styles of jazz (including swing, dixieland, and fusion) but also funk, easy listening, and Latin music. It was used for two years as the venue for a drum school directed by Marvin Boogaloo Smith. Among the musicians who have played at the club are Chet Baker, Tony Esposito, Joe Bonner, and the alto saxophonist Massimo Urbani.

——. **Manuia.** Vicolo del Cinque 54-6, 00153 Rome. Restaurant and bar. It was opened on 1 April 1971 by Sandro and Tony Melaranci, who own and manage the venue. It soon became a favorite meeting place for musicians, specializing in Brazilian music and jazz. Among the jazz musicians who have appeared there are Chet Baker and Pat Metheny; the pianist and singer Jim Porto was engaged as the resident performer in 1979.

——. **Mississippi Jazz Club.** Borgo Angelico 16. It was founded in 1979 by Luigi and Roberto Toth and Rodi Adele and has presented mainly small-group jazz in traditional and modern styles. Prominent visiting musicians to the club have included John Lewis, Chet Baker, Elvin Jones, Max Roach, Archie Shepp, Barney Kessel, Attila Zoller, Abbey Lincoln, Buck Clayton, Wild Bill Davison, and Abdullah Ibrahim. Luigi Toth and his Old Time Jazz Band perform as the house band.

——. **Open Gate.** This exclusive nightspot offered jazz from around 1950, when it was regarded as a fashionable form of entertainment in Rome. In 1950 Svend Asmussen played a residency and he was followed into the club by Django Reinhardt and André Ekyan; Reinhardt's services were secured by Christian Livorness, a jazz enthusiast and founding member of the Open Gate. In 1953 the singer Thelma Carpenter appeared there.

——. **Rupe Tarpea.** Restaurant. It had a dance floor, and presented jazz from at least the late 1940s; Django Reinhardt performed there in 1948.

NETHERLANDS

AMSTERDAM. **BIM-huis.** Oude Schans 73–7, 1011 KW Amsterdam. Founded by the Stichting Jazz in Nederland and opened on 1 October 1973, it presents modern jazz and improvised music in three concerts weekly. It has become a center for visiting American, German, and French musicians.

——. **Carlton Hotel.** Jazz was played there for the entertainment of guests from the late 1920s. Edwin Swayze and the Plantation Band played there in the summer of 1930, during a tour of Europe.

——. **La Gaité.** Tusschinsky Theater, Reguliersbreestraat, Amsterdam. The club was active from around 1923 to 1940 with Max Tak as its director of music. It offered hot dance music and small-group jazz. In 1934 it featured a band led by the Surinamese saxophonist Lex Van Spall.

——. **Joseph Lam Jazz Club.** Laagte Kadijk 35; Van Diemenstraat 8 (from ?1984). It was in existence from at least the early 1980s in its premises on Laagte Kadijk. In the mid-1980s it was the most important venue in Amsterdam for traditional jazz.

ARNHEM. **Storyville Jazz Club.** One of the principal nightclubs in the Netherlands, it engages many American and British musicians.

BREDA. **Roaring Twenties Jazzclub.** It is best known as one of the main venues for traditional jazz in the Netherlands. Several members of its organizing committee are active in the management of the Oude Stijl Jazz Festival Breda (*see* FESTIVALS).

EINDHOVEN. The town's jazz club plays host to a small annual festival of traditional jazz and for its day-to-day performances frequently presents visiting American and British musicians.

HAARLEM. **Zanderzaal.** Groot Heiligland 37, 2001 DG Haarlem. It was founded in 1949 by Han Baas, John Easton, and Cas Jeekel and opened on 24 September. It is run by the Stichting Haarlemse Jazz Club and is one of the oldest jazz clubs in the Netherlands. Its Friday-night concerts offer traditional, mainstream, and avant-garde jazz, and blues. The Haarlemse Jazz Club regards itself as the direct descendant of the Haarlemse Hot Club, established in 1932 by Eddie C. Commelin. In 1934 the club promoted a recording session by Freddy Johnson and the Surinamese saxophonist Lex Van Spall at the Casino Hamdorff in Laren (see below); one of the numbers recorded was *Haarlem Hot Club Stomp*, on which Rosy Poindexter was the singer (Decca F42045).

BIBLIOGRAPHY

J. Trabsky: Liner notes, F. Johnson and L. Van Spall: *Haarlem Hot Club: 20 Years Haarlemse Jazz Club* (Cat 3, 1969) [commemorative EP]

H. Openeer: Liner notes, B. Carter, C. Hawkins, and F. Johnson: *Made in Holland, 1934–'37* (Panachord H2005, 1982)

THE HAGUE. **Tabaris (Dancing).** Dance hall. It was a major venue for American jazz musicians in the 1930s. Among the ensembles that played there were Freddy Johnson's Harlemites (1934), and the bands led by Willie Lewis (1933, 1936) and Leon Abbey (1938). Between visits by foreign bands the club featured European groups playing hot dance music. It closed probably in 1940.

BIBLIOGRAPHY

R. Z.: "How they Swing at The Hague," *MM*, x (12 May 1934), 3

J. P. Holloway: "Cross-Channel Coloured Rhythm," *MM*, xii (17 Oct 1936), 2

LAREN. **Casino Hamdorff.** Associated with the Hotel Hamdorff, the casino flourished from about 1913 until 1950. The repertory it offered was chiefly hot dance music and one of the ensembles that performed there regularly was the Ramblers; the group recorded at the casino with Coleman Hawkins in 1935 and 1937. The Dutch Decca company set up another recording session at the casino in 1934, with a band led by Freddy Johnson and the saxophonist Lex Van Spall. A number of visiting American and European musicians were engaged to play at the Hamdorff including Benny Carter in 1936.

ROTTERDAM. **Harbour Jazz Club.** One of the largest jazz clubs in the Netherlands, it flourished in the 1970s and early 1980s, regularly presenting traditional and mainstream jazz; among the groups that performed there was Chris Barber's band.

——. **Pschorr.** Dance hall. The music played for dancing there from around 1924 until 1940 included hot dance music and small-group jazz. During this period the establishment was directed by Dick Reese and among the notable jazz musicians who performed was Freddy Johnson (1934).

SCHEVENINGEN. **Kurhaus Hotel.** This hotel in a popular seaside resort near The Hague engaged jazz musicians from at least the mid-1930s. Benny Carter played two notable residencies there, in 1936 and 1937; for the latter he was supported by a band of internationally known musicians, including George Chisholm and Bertie King. These performances received extensive coverage in the Netherlands' leading jazz journal of the time, *De jazzwereld*.

NORWAY

MOLDE. **Storyville Jazz Club.** A nonprofit organization, its principal activity is to present the annual Molde International Jazz Festival (*see* FESTIVALS).

OSLO. **Amalienborg Jazzhus.** It was active from at least the mid-1970s, when it offered jazz six nights a week.

——. **Saga-Cinema.** Movie theater. From the 1930s it engaged musicians of international repute to perform before the films during a summer season. Leon Abbey's band played there for that purpose for most of June in 1938, also making a broadcast of dance music over Norwegian Radio.

POLAND

WARSAW. **Akwarium.** Ulica Emilii Plater 49, Warsaw. It was founded in April 1977 and has been supported by sponsorship from the Polskie Stowarzyszenie Jazzowe. Besides presenting performances by Polish players such as Tomasz Stańko, it has engaged visiting foreign musicians, including the L. A. Four, Sheila Jordan, the Thad Jones–Mel Lewis Orchestra, and the Toshiko Akiyoshi–Lew Tabackin Big Band.

——. **Café Bodega.** Between Chmienla and Nowy Świat streets. It flourished as a center for jazz during World War II, when among the musicians who performed there was the big band of George Scott.

——. **Hybrydy.** Ulica Mokotowska 48, Warsaw. It opened as a student club in 1970 with a performance given by Urszula Dudziak and Michal Urbaniak.

——. **Jazz Club Remont.** Warynskiego 12. A student club under the direction of Waldemar Deska, among others, it has offered performances by European and American groups and musicians, including Gunter Hampel, Manhattan Transfer, and Buddy Rich.

——. **Latawiec.** Ulica Stanow Zjednoczonych 26, Warsaw. It is one of several venues in the city to offer principally a traditional jazz repertory.

——. **Rio Rita.** Krakowskie Przedmiescie Street. Café. Among the jazz musicians to be resident performers there were the pianists Marek Cybulski and Stefan Kisielewski, who both played at the café during the period of German occupation.

——. **Stodola.** Ulica Trebacka 7, Warsaw; 10 Batorego, Warsaw. This student club was founded in 1964 and has presented mostly traditional and mainstream jazz. Among the Polish musicians to have appeared with the resident big band (which has made a number of recordings) are Zbigniew Jaremko and Slawomir Kulpowicz; Henryk Majewski's group the Old Timers played there regularly.

——. **V Wandy Warskiej.** Rynek Staromiejski 19, Warsaw. Jazz has been played there from the time of its opening in 1967 by the singer Wanda Warska.

PORTUGAL

LISBON. **Hot Clube de Portugal.** Praça da Alegria 39, 1200 Lisbon. Founded in 1950, it is the most important and longest-lived nightclub in Portugal. It presents jazz nightly during the summer months and on three nights a week in the winter. Besides Portuguese musicians it has engaged numerous visiting jazz performers; Dexter Gordon, Count Basie, Charlie Mariano, Charlie Haden, Enrico Rava, Atilla Zoller, and Tete Montoliu, among others, have appeared there.

SWEDEN

STOCKHOLM. **Bern's Restaurant.** Jazz was played regularly in this restaurant in the 1960s. A performance there by Count Basie in July 1968 was recorded by Swedish Radio and transmitted later in that year under the title "We go to the Jazz Concert."

——. **China Theatre.** It offered jazz from at least the early 1940s. Svend Asmussen's quintet played as the resident band there in 1942.

——. **Fasching.** Kungsgatan 63, Stockholm. Opened in 1975, this club has engaged many internationally known jazz musicians, playing mostly free jazz and jazz-rock. Among those who have performed there are Ornette Coleman, the Art Ensemble of Chicago, Don Pullen and George Adams, Tomasz Stańko, Steve Lacy, James Moody, John Tchicai, Bobo Stenson, Joe Henderson, Carla Bley, Wayne Shorter, and Rena Rama.

——. **Gamlingen.** See Stampen.

——. **Gazell Club.** It took the name of Dag Haeggqvist's record label, Gazell, and similarly promoted traditional jazz, becoming an important center for this style in Stockholm. It closed in 1971.

——. **Gyllene Cirkeln** [Golden Circle]. The best-known nightclub in the city, it presented performances by both Scandinavian and visiting American musicians, among them Coleman Hawkins, Bud Powell, Sonny Rollins, Bill Evans (ii), Albert Ayler, Johnny Griffin, and George Russell. A number of recordings were made there, including *The Ornette Coleman Trio at the Golden Circle* (1965, BN 84224-5). It closed around 1967.

——. **Nalen** [Nationalen]. It was active in the 1950s and early 1960s, until around 1963. Among the Swedish musicians who played there was Hacke Björksten, who played a long residency from 1954 to 1959 with a small group that included Åke Persson.

——. **Nojesfaltet.** Djurgården island. Amusement park. In the late 1930s it was under the direction and ownership of J. E. Lindgren, who engaged the band of Leon Abbey to perform and play for dancing there in the summer of 1938; Emile Christian was among Abbey's sidemen.

——. **Stampen.** Stora Gråmunkegränd 7, Stockholm; Stora Nygatan 5. This nightclub presented jazz from the late 1960s until around 1981. Its premises were then taken over by another club, the Gamlingen.

SWITZERLAND

GENEVA. **Maxim's.** 2 avenue Thalberg and Place des Alpes. Dance hall. The music played for dancing included jazz from at least the early 1940s. The French trumpeter Philippe Brun led his bands there from time to time between 1941 and 1955.

——. **Palladium.** Sidney Bechet played a month's residency there with the band of the Swiss soprano saxophonist Claude Aubert in spring 1954; he returned to the club in December for a performance in which he was reunited with another New Orleans clarinetist, Albert Nicholas.

ZURICH. **Casa Bar.** 30 Münster-Gasse. This nightclub, owned by Maurice Berger, has concentrated chiefly on presenting traditional jazz. Bill Coleman, Albert Nicholas, and Wallace Bishop are among the musicians who performed there; the groups most often engaged to play are the British bands Piccadilly Six and Bob Wallis's Storyville Jazzmen.

——. **Embassy Club.** Active from at least the mid-1950s, it presented performances by Sammy Price with the band of George Johnson in 1957.

——. **Widder-Bar.** 6 Widdergasse. Active at least from the early 1980s, it has presented jazz in various styles; among the American visitors who have appeared there are Wild Bill Davis and Oliver Jackson, who each played a short residency in 1983. (J. Simmen: "Jazz au Widder-Bar," *BHcF*, no.306 (1983), 9)

UNION OF SOVIET SOCIALIST REPUBLICS [USSR]

LENINGRAD. **Café in the Cultural Palace of Seamen.** 2 Vindavskaya Street. Active as a center for jazz from 1986, it presents principally mainstream jazz; the house band is led by David Goloshchokin. Important Western musicians such as Dave Brubeck, who visited the club with his quartet in April 1987, have worked with local musicians there.

——. **Kvadrat** [Chorus]. Leningrad Palace of Culture (1965–86); 47 Professor Popov Street. Founded by the city's Komsomol committee in January 1965, it has operated without interruption into the late 1980s, when the president was N. Leites. It presents mostly dixieland and mainstream jazz and bop, with occasional free-jazz performances. All the leading Soviet jazz musicians have appeared there and it is the major venue for Leningrad players; the Leningrad Dixieland Band was the resident ensemble for the first year of the club's existence. Kvadrat was associated with the first two jazz festivals to take place in the city, in 1965 and 1966 (*see* FESTIVALS), and in 1986 it organized a festival of traditional jazz, Jazz on the Neva. Between 1965 and 1985 about 40 lectures were given there on jazz-related topics and the club also issues its own journal.

——. **Vostok.** 10 Pravda Street. Café. It opened in the Leningrad Palace of Culture in September 1985, under the management of Anatoly Popov and Yakov Zeitlin. The resident band, playing mainstream jazz, is led by the drummer Valery Myssovsky. The venue also runs the only jazz workshop in Leningrad.

MOSCOW. **Dmitrovka Cinema.** One of the earliest performances of jazz in the USSR was given there on 22 February 1926 by a black band organized by the trombonist Frank Withers; among the musicians were Sidney Bechet, Benny Peyton, and Crickett Smith.

——. **Sinyaya Ptitsa** [Bluebird]. 23 Chekhov Street. Café. A club of this name was first active there in the 1960s. In the mid-1980s the Sinyaya Ptitsa operated in the workshop of the sculptor Sergey Gadjukov; the journalist Vartan Tonoyan established the club as a publicly owned operation in its premises on Chekhov Street in 1986 and it was officially opened on 5 April 1987 with Eric Avagimov as its commercial director. It offers a wide range of styles from traditional to avant-garde jazz and jazz-rock, and celebrates the birthdays of prominent musicians with special programs. Among the visiting Americans who have appeared at the club are Grover Washington, Jr., Dave Brubeck, Pat Metheny, and Billy Taylor (ii); the Sinyaya Ptitsa is also a center for Soviet musicians from other cities and runs regular jam sessions.

RIGA, LATVIAN SSR. **Do-re-mi.** 1 Sverdlov Street, Riga. Café. It has operated as a venue for jazz performance from 1984 and specializes in mainstream jazz. The house duo consists of the pianist Ilga Berzinya and the double bass player Boris Bannykh.

TALLINN, ESTONIAN SSR. **Kiko.** 12 Vaike-Karja Street. This café and bar, which is part of the publishing house Valgus, began to present jazz in 1981. Its program takes place on every second and fourth Monday of the month and features mainstream and modern jazz, including jam sessions with visiting musicians.

UNITED KINGDOM. See Great Britain.

UNITED STATES OF AMERICA [USA]

ANAHEIM, CA. See Los Angeles (metropolitan area).

ARKANSAS RIVER. **SS *J. S.*** This steamer, owned by the Streckfus Line, was purpose built for the excursion trade and named after Captain John Streckfus, who had founded the line in 1884; the boat was launched in 1901 and plied out of Little Rock. 175 feet long, it had a ballroom with a dance floor 100 feet by 27 feet and could carry 2000 passengers. It was the first riverboat on which Fate Marable performed – he joined the band of the violinist Emil Flindt (or Flint) around 1907, and by 1910 was leading his own small ragtime band on the boat. The *J.S.* was destroyed by fire in 1910; its namesake, the *J. S. Deluxe* (often, confusingly, referred to simply as the *J. S.*) traveled on the Mississippi River (see below) from 1919.

ASBURY PARK, NJ. **Smile-a-While Café.** One of many resorts near Atlantic City, Asbury Park was sometimes included on the itinerary of touring jazz musicians. Claude Hopkins's band worked at the Smile-a-While Café around 1924.

ASTORIA, NY. **Momart Café.** In 1939 Sidney Bechet played there in a trio with Willie "the Lion" Smith and the drummer Dinah Taylor.

ATLANTIC CITY, NJ. **Paradise Club.** In operation by at least the early 1930s, it engaged important jazz musicians to perform during the summer season. Lucille Hegamin worked there in 1933–4 and Count Basie was resident from June to August 1947.

——. **Silver Slipper.** One of the earlier clubs in Atlantic City, it was open by the early 1920s. Joe Venuti and Eddie Lang regularly led a band there for summer seasons through the decade.

BALTIMORE. **Carlin's Park.** Tommy Ladnier played there in the band of Billy Fowler in 1926, and Cuba Austin's Original Cotton-Pickers, which toured widely in the USA, played one of its last engagements there in 1934.

BATON ROUGE, LA. **Bernard Hall.** Dance hall. It was used as a venue for minstrel shows and was on the TOBA circuit. The hall did not employ a permanent music director but relied on each group that played there to administer the running of the establishment during its residency. Among the musicians who appeared at the hall were Joe Darensbourg and Kid Ory with his band.

BERWYN, IL. **Red Arrow Club.** 6927 Pershing Road, Berwyn. This nightclub in the metropolitan area of Chicago was active from at least the mid-1950s under the ownership of Otto Kubik. Franz Jackson's Original Jass All-Stars, which included Bob Shoffner, Al Wynn, and Lawrence Dixon, played a ten-year residency there from 1957.

BOSTON. **Copley Square Hotel.** See Mahogany Hall and Storyville Club.

——. **Crescent Club.** This nightclub was in existence from at least the early 1930s. During an extended stay in Massachusetts Pee Wee Russell played a residency at the Crescent with Bobby Hackett and Teddy Roy in the winter of 1933–4.

——. **Hi Hat.** Columbus Avenue and Massachusetts Avenue. Nightclub. Situated at the intersection of the two avenues, it was in operation from the late 1940s into the 1950s. It was the first club to offer bop to Boston audiences. In 1953 Charlie Parker made a number of broadcasts from the club, selections from which were later issued as the album *New Bird: Hi Hat Broadcasts, 1953* (Phoenix Jazz 10).

——. **Howard Johnson's Motor Inn.** See Starlight Roof.

——. **Izzy Ort's.** Tremont Street. It was a favorite venue for local musicians, who gathered there to listen to and take part in jam sessions. Quincy Jones was among those who played there around 1950.

——. **Jazz Workshop.** 733 Boylston Street. It was opened in 1964 and managed by Fred Taylor and Tony Mauriello. In an adjacent room in the same basement premises, and also under the direction of Taylor and Mauriello, was a separate club, Paul's Mall. The two venues offered similar repertories, though the Jazz Workshop leaned more towards jazz and Paul's Mall towards jazz-rock and popular music. Among the many prominent musicians to appear at the Workshop were Charles Mingus, Roland Kirk, Elvin Jones, Miles Davis, and Ted Curson; Davis also played at the Mall. The clubs closed in 1978.

——. **Ken Club.** Warrenton Street. It was in operation from at least the early 1940s. Henry "Red" Allen and his band were resident there during 1942, when among the guest musicians who appeared with them was Sidney Bechet.

——. **Lulu White's.** 3 Appleton Street. Although it was in operation for only three years (1977–80), it presented performances by many well-known musicians, including Dizzy Gillespie, Illinois Jacquet, Lionel Hampton, the Art Ensemble of Chicago, Harry Edison, Eddie "Lockjaw" Davis, Clifford Jordan, Zoot Sims and Al Cohn, and Henry Threadgill's group Air.

——. **Mahogany Hall.** Copley Square Hotel. This venue in the basement of the hotel was opened in the early 1950s by George Wein and specialized in the presentation of dixieland jazz. Wein himself recorded there in 1953 with a group known as the Mahogany All Stars, which included Vic Dickenson and Doc Cheatham. The hotel was also the site of the second location of the Storyville Club (see below).

——. **Michael's.** 52 Gainsborough Street. It was active as a jazz venue from the 1970s. Among the players who have performed there are Miroslav Vitous, Ricky Ford, and Jaki Byard.

——. **Paul's Mall.** See Jazz Workshop.

——. **Savoy Café.** 410 Massachusetts Avenue. It was an important venue for jazz by the mid-1940s, when the manager was Steve Connelly. In 1945, through the intervention of the president of the Boston Jazz Society, Dick Schmidt, Connelly engaged Sidney Bechet's New Orleans Rhythm Kings to play there; this group consisted of Bechet, Pops Foster, Ray Parker (piano), George Thompson (drums), and (perhaps the greatest attraction) Bunk Johnson, lately rediscovered in Louisiana and brought to the East Coast by Bechet. In spite of difficult relationships among the players and the ultimate failure of Bechet's intention to re-create authentic New Orleans jazz, the residency (which began on 12 March and continued through the spring) was a success, and the group made a number of broadcasts and recordings. Other jazz musicians who played at the club included Sabby Lewis, and a band led by Bob Wilber and later by Jimmy Archey, which played a long residency starting in December 1948 and continuing into the spring of 1950. George Wein, who was just beginning to be active on the Boston jazz scene at this time, organized some of the performances there in 1950. (M. Hazeldine: "Dear Wynne: a Review of the Events of 1945–6 Concerning Bunk Johnson, Sidney Bechet, Boston, and Beyond," *Fn*, xv/5 (1984), 4)

——. **Southland Casino.** 76 Warrenton Street. It opened in the 1930s and flourished into the next decade. Blanche Calloway's last big band (which included Ray Perry and Frank Wess) played at the casino in early autumn 1940 during a short tour of East Coast cities. Charlie Barnet's recording *Southland Shuffle* (1940, Bb 10602) was named for the venue.

——. **The Stable(s).** Huntington Avenue. Located not far from the Storyville Club, it opened in 1953 and remained active until 1962 as a venue for swing and bop played by local musicians. Herb Pomeroy and the saxophonist Varty Haroutunian led a big band there for a protracted residency from 1956 until 1960; Benny Golson's number *Stablemates* was written for the band. Other performers to appear there were Jaki Byard and Dick Twardzik, who played solo piano during intermissions.

——. **Starlight Roof.** Howard Johnson's Motor Inn, Kenmore Square. During its short period of activity (1984–6) this nightclub within the motel engaged several prominent jazz musicians; among those who appeared there were Art Farmer, Kenny Burrell, Jay McShann, James Moody, Jimmy Smith, Phil Woods, and Sheila Jordan.

——. **Storyville Club.** Kenmore Square; Copley Square Hotel. It was opened by George Wein in 1950 and specialized in the presentation of dixieland jazz and swing. It operated at two locations, the second being the Copley Square Hotel, where it coexisted with Mahogany Hall (see above). During the early 1950s Sidney Bechet established an association with the club, performing there in October and December 1951 and again in October 1953. The first of these engagements was shared with a quartet led by Jo Jones and for the second Bechet was accompanied by a trio led by Wein. Wein made a number of recordings at his club – with Wild Bill Davison (1951), as a replacement for Claude Hopkins in a session with Bechet (25 October 1953), and with Jo Jones (*c*1953) – as did Ruby Braff, Pee Wee Russell, Vic Dickenson, and others; several of the resulting albums were released under the title *Jazz at Storyville*. Among other important musicians to appear at the Storyville were Duke Ellington, Count Basie, Billie Holiday, and Charlie Parker.

——. **Tic-Toc Club.** Jazz was played there from at least the early 1940s. In Boston for his last important show, *Early to Bed*, which opened in May 1943, Fats Waller also played a residency at the Tic-Toc. Among other bandleaders to appear at the club was Lionel Hampton, who led a group there that included Joe Williams.

——. **Wally's Paradise.** Massachusetts Avenue. Known chiefly as a venue for local musicians, its repertory emphasizes soul jazz and it has often presented performances by organ trios.

For other venues in the metropolitan area of Boston see Cambridge, Peabody, and Somerville.

BIBLIOGRAPHY

Boston

M. Hazeldine: "Dear Wynne: a Review of the Events of 1945–6 Concerning Bunk Johnson, Sidney Bechet, Boston and Beyond," *Fn*, xv/5 (1984), 4

BUFFALO. **Anchor Bar.** Main Street. Successive owners of this bar and club have pursued a policy of presenting jazz from the 1930s into the 1980s. From 1942 to 1954 George Clarke's band was resident there. Latterly the club has engaged renowned musicians to play as guest soloists with a house band of local professionals.

——. **Casino.** Main Street. It became an important venue for jazz in the 1950s, when such major bop musicians as Charlie Parker played there.

——. **Colored Musicians' Club.** Broadway Street. The premises housed the black local of the AFM until 1969 (when black and white branches of the union amalgamated), and jazz musicians had played in jam sessions there for decades. When the AFM had no further use for the building a social club opened and more formal jazz performances were given. Among the leading visiting artists to appear there were Sarah Vaughan, Art Tatum, and Zoot Sims; rehearsal bands also play at the club.

——. **Davio's.** Sheridan Drive. It flourished in the late 1970s and early 1980s as a venue for bop. The musicians who have played there include Sonny Stitt, Phil Woods, and Mark Murphy.

——. **Downtown Room.** Statler Hotel. Jazz was performed there from at least the 1970s. The first programs in the "Jazz Alive" series broadcast on National Public Radio were made there.

——. **Eduardo's.** Bailey Avenue. Restaurant. It offered jazz for the entertainment of patrons from the 1970s and sometimes engaged big bands; the bands of Maynard Ferguson and Woody Herman were among those that played there.

——. **Joe Rico's Milestones.** Main Street and Fillmore Street. Around 1986 the disc jockey Joe Rico opened this nightclub in the premises formerly occupied by the Tralfamadore Café (see below).

——. **Little Harlem Club.** It was in operation by around 1930. Stuff Smith was resident in 1931, and Jonah Jones joined Smith's band during this engagement.

——. **Lloyd's Lounge.** Ferry Street. It flourished in the 1950s and 1960s, presenting a repertory that focused on soul jazz.

——. **Memorial Auditorium.** This downtown venue, on the lakeside, was an important location for major bands visiting Buffalo from the 1930s to the 1960s.

——. **Milestones.** See Joe Rico's Milestones.

——. **Moonglow.** Williams Street. It was a prominent venue for jazz in the city during the swing era. From the 1930s to the 1950s most of the leading American black bands appeared there.

——. **Nietzsche's.** Allen Street. It opened around 1985 and offers a repertory of jazz and blues.

——. **Paradise Ballroom.** Jazz big bands and dance bands played there from at least the late 1920s. Bennie Moten's was among the resident ensembles there at that period.

——. **Pine Grill.** Restaurant. Active in the 1970s, it mostly presented performances by soul-jazz players.

——. **Rainbow Ballroom.** Dance hall. Jazz was played for dancing there from at least the 1930s.

——. **Rebelot.** It flourished in the 1970s as a venue for soul jazz.

——. **Renaissance II.** Bailey Avenue. Owned by Sam Noto, it operated for about two years in the early 1980s. Among the musicians who played there were Chet Baker, Scott Hamilton, Sal Nistico (ii), and David Schnitter.

——. **Royal Arms.** Main Street and West Utica Street. It was an important venue for bop in the 1950s and 1960s. Miles Davis and many other prominent musicians appeared there.

——. **Shea's Buffalo Theater.** Main Street. Built in 1926, this opulent theater presented variety performances into the 1940s; leading jazz bands occasionally played for the stage acts that formed part of these programs – Jimmie Lunceford's orchestra appeared there in 1935. The theater continues to be used for jazz concerts and other musical performances.

——. **Silver Grill.** Restaurant. Jazz was played there during the 1930s; among the groups who performed at that period was Stuff Smith's band, which included Jonah Jones.

——. **Statler Hotel.** See Downtown Room.

——. **Tralfamadore Café.** Main Street and Fillmore Street (to 1980); Main Street at Theater Place (from 1983). Opened by Ed Lawson in the 1970s this cellar club became the principal venue for jazz in the city, presenting renowned bop, free-jazz, and jazz-rock musicians. (Its programs also occasionally included poetry and comedy acts.) In 1980 Lawson sold the name to a corporation, which after an interval opened a new Tralfamadore, where the repertory was broadened to include other kinds of music besides jazz.

——. **Vendome Hotel.** Among the musicians who performed at this venue were Stuff Smith's group (early 1930s), a band led by Clarence Olden (1934), and Count Basie's orchestra, which played there around 1936.

CAMBRIDGE, MA. **Charles Hotel.** See Regattabar.

——. **Charlie's Tap.** Green Street. During its short existence (1985–6) it presented a large number of performances by nationally known figures. Among those who appeared there were Dave Holland, Lester Bowie's Brass Fantasy, Henry Threadgill, Oliver Lake, Jaki Byard, Abbey Lincoln, David Murray, Hamiet Bluiett, Stanley Cowell, Ran Blake, Kenny Barron and Bill Barron, Amina Claudine Myers, Ricky Ford, and Frank Lowe.

——. **Nightstage.** Central Square, Main Street. This club, which opened in 1985, presents a varied repertory of black music – blues, reggae, and African music in addition to jazz. Jazz performances have been given there by Dizzy Gillespie, Wynton Marsalis, the World Saxophone Quartet, Steve Lacy's sextet, Lacy and Mal Waldron, Archie Shepp and Horace Parlan, Sun Ra, Abdullah Ibrahim, Tal Farlow, Jan Garbarek, Gato Barbieri, Carla Bley, Gil Evans, Vyacheslav Ganelin's trio, Art Blakey, and Ran Blake.

——. **1369 Club.** 1369 Cambridge Street. Jazz was first performed there in 1980 and it has continued to flourish as a venue for contemporary jazz. Among those to have played at the club are Archie Shepp, New Air, Kenny Burrell, Barry Harris, Mark Helias, Lew Tabackin, Clifford Jordan, George Adams and Don Pullen, Jack Walrath, Mulgrew Miller, Gary Bartz, Steve Lacy, Roscoe Mitchell, Bill Frisell, JoAnne Brackeen, Paul Motian, Dave Liebman, Bobby Watson, Roswell Rudd, and a number of organists including Brother Jack McDuff, Lonnie Smith, Charles Earland, and Don Patterson.

——. **Regattabar.** Charles Hotel, Harvard Square. The nightclub of the hotel opened in 1985 and has engaged many notable jazz musicians, including Stan Getz, J. J. Johnson, Branford Marsalis, Milt Jackson, McCoy Tyner, Ahmad Jamal, Sphere, Phil Woods, Tommy Flanagan, Astrud Gilberto, the Jazztet, the Timeless All-Stars, Bobby Hutcherson, Donald Harrison and Terence Blanchard, Tony Williams, Art Blakey, Gary Burton, James Moody, Richie Cole, Morgana King, and Cedar Walton. Jazz is also played in the hotel's ballroom, where Sonny Rollins and the Modern Jazz Quartet, among others, have appeared.

——. **Ryles.** Inman Square, Hampshire Street. It has been active from the mid-1980s and has engaged such musicians as Pat Metheny, Mal Waldron, Julius Hemphill, Charlie Haden, Paul Motian, and Dewey Redman.

CEDAR GROVE, NJ. **Meadowbrook Inn.** Pompton Turnpike. Ballroom. Owned by Frank Dailey, it was an important venue during the swing era. Numerous bands, both black and white, played there between 1935 and 1945, including Fats Waller's big band (1935) and the orchestras of Charlie Barnet and Count Basie. The ballroom was later converted into a restaurant and theater performance space, and was known variously as the Meadowbrook Lounge and Meadowbrook Theater.

CHICAGO. *Note.* Addresses are given as precisely as possible, though sources do not consistently use the locations "North," "South," "East," and "West." The names of a number of streets in Chicago have been changed during the 20th century. For the purposes of this list the following changes are important: East 55th Street became East Garfield Boulevard; Grand Boulevard became South Parkway Boulevard (1926) and later Dr. Martin Luther King Drive (31 July 1968).

——. **Ace of Clubs.** See Dave's Café.

——. **Alabam.** See Club Alabam.

——. **Al Turner's Café.** See Plantation Café.

——. **Alvadere.** See Club Alvadere.

——. **Ambassador.** See Club Ambassador.

——. **Ambassador Hotel.** See Pump Room.

——. **Andy's.** 11 East Hubbard Street. This restaurant began to present jazz in 1977 when, under Penny Tyler's management, it absorbed the weekly "Jazz at Noon" program of concerts which had begun at Marina Towers. In 1981 it assimilated the similar "Jazz at Five" series, also begun at Marina Towers. Tyler has expanded both, presenting music every weekday as well as on Saturday nights and Sunday afternoons in styles ranging from early jazz and swing (for example, Truck Parham) to bop. The resident band, Ears, includes Cy Touff.

——. **The Annex.** 2840 South State Street; 2300 South State Street (from October 1934). Entertainment center. It flourished in the 1930s. Among the bands that played there were Chippie Hill's, which was resident from 1934 (at both locations) until 1936, Jimmy Cobb's Annex Syncopators, which played a residency in the café from April to October 1936, Jack Ellis's Musical Wildcats (June 1937), and a band led by Zinky Cohn (1937). The venue may have closed in the late 1930s since in 1939 the opening was announced of the New Annex on South Parkway Boulevard (see below).

——. **Apex Café.** See Apex Tavern.

——. **Apex Chateau.** See Robbins, IL.

——. **Apex Club.** East 35th Street between South Prairie Avenue and South Calumet Avenue. The first owner of the Apex Club was Julian Black, who was a close friend of the politician Dan Jackson. The premises, which had earlier operated as the Club Alvadere and the Nest Club (see below), were bought by Black in 1926, renovated, and opened in the autumn as a luxurious supper club. The most important residency was that of Jimmie Noone, who had led a small group at the venue before Black's time; his Apex Club Orchestra, which at different times included Earl Hines, Johnny St. Cyr, Dave Nelson, Joe Poston, and Johnny Wells, was the resident band from 1926 until the club closed in the spring of 1928.

——. **Apex Grill and Road House.** See Robbins, IL.

——. **Apex Tavern.** 354½ East 51st Street. It was in operation at least from 1934, when it was advertised in June as having been lately refurbished; at this time the club was owned by Doc Jennings and managed by Harry Boyd. The resident band was Duke Patterson and his Syncopators, with Art Campbell on piano and the singer Lil Christian. By October of that year the Apex Café, owned by Jennings (presumably the same venue), was under the direction of Charles Christian, with the Apex Continental Syncopators as the house band. The New Apex Café (see below) opened in 1935.

——. **Apollo Theater.** 526 East 47th Street. During the 1920s it presented shows in which the music was sometimes provided by jazz musicians. Frankie "Half Pint" Jaxon, for example, played there in March 1927. By 1930 the theater had become a cinema.

——. **Aragon Ballroom.** 1100 West Lawrence Avenue. Jazz began to be played for dancing there in the mid-1920s; the first jazz-oriented group to appear was one led by Wingy Manone, which included Art Hodes, Bud Freeman, Floyd O'Brien, and Gene Krupa. During the swing era the ballroom regularly engaged big bands, and live broadcasts were frequently made on Chicago radio stations.

——. **Arcadia Ballroom.** This venue, on the West Side, was owned (like the later Dreamland Ballroom, see below) by Paddy Harmon and offered jazz from at least 1917 when Darnell Howard led a band there. During the 1920s the resident bands included one from St. Louis, led by Joe Kayser and including Jess Stacy among the members (1926), the Creole Orchestra led by Charlie Elgar (early 1926; September 1926–February 1927), and Walter Barnes's Royal Creolians (April 1928 into 1929).

——. **Arsonia Café.** Around 1915 it engaged Charlie Elgar's band, which included the trombonist George Filhe and a number of New Orleans players, among them Manuel Perez, Lorenzo Tio, Jr., and Louis Cottrell, Sr. Small groups made up of these and other players continued to be resident at the club under different leadership for several years; for example, Perez led a quintet there around 1917, which included Alphonse Picou.

——. **Ascher's Metropolitan Theater.** See Metropolitan Theater.

——. **Athenia Café.** Around the beginning of 1917 the management hired the Louisiana Five, a New Orleans band led by the drummer Anton Lada, to play a six-month engagement there; this was among the first residencies by a jazz-oriented ensemble in the city.

——. **Avenue Theater.** 3108 South Indiana Avenue, at East 31st Street. Variety theater. It opened in August 1913 and like several theaters in the city maintained separate seating areas for Blacks and Whites. Its revues, vaudeville shows, and other theatrical productions provided work for many musicians. Many of the great singers of the vaudeville tradition played there in touring companies, including Lucille Hegamin and Ethel Waters (both December 1923), Bessie Smith (May 1924 and October 1932), and Sara Martin (February 1925). In the mid-1920s the resident orchestra was directed by Hugh Swift. The venue was still active in the mid-1930s.

——. **Bacon's Casino.** East 49th Street and South Wabash Avenue. It occupied premises on the northeast corner of the intersection which had been built as a garage. In 1927 the Bacon brothers, Robert and Ernest, opened a dance hall in the building, which came in time to be used for functions of many kinds, such as lectures, public meetings, and charity events. The venue flourished until 1945, and a number of jazz musicians performed there; Jimmie Noone's orchestra played for a cabaret party in 1935 and the singer Joe Williams appeared with Floyd Campbell's orchestra (of which Scoops Carry was also a member) during the late 1930s and early 1940s.

——. **Bee Hive Club.** East 55th Street and South Harper Avenue. This nightclub opened in 1948 at a time when the jazz scene in the city was flourishing. It engaged a number of older musicians, including Chippie Hill, Art Hodes, Doc Evans, Baby Dodds, Miff Mole, and Darnell Howard. Lester Young also performed there during the month he spent in Chicago in 1949 (February–March). Norman Simmons was the house pianist from 1953 to 1956, and Charlie Parker played his last engagement in Chicago at this venue. The club closed in 1956. In 1977 the record producer Jim Neumann adopted the club's name for a newly founded record label (*see* BEE HIVE).

——. **Bert Kelly's Stables.** See Kelly's Stables.

——. **Big House.** See New Apex Café.

——. **Blackhawk Restaurant.** 139 North Wabash Avenue, south of East Randolph Street. It presented jazz performances from the 1920s. In 1924 Joe Sanders and Carleton Coon brought their band, the Coon–Sanders Nighthawks, to Chicago and from 1926 it was resident at the restaurant; the band continued to appear regularly through the 1930s and Sanders occasionally returned there in the 1940s. Other important bands to play residencies at the venue were those of Ben Pollack (from May 1927), Red Norvo, Bob Crosby (1938; for illustration *see* CROSBY, BOB), Jack Teagarden (1939), and Raymond Scott (1940).

——. **Blatz Palm Gardens.** Ballroom. Jazz was played there from at least the end of World War I. From 1919 Elmer Schoebel led a resident group that included Paul Mares, Georg Brunis, and Jack Pettis, who later became the nucleus of the New Orleans Rhythm Kings. Schoebel was still at the ballroom in 1921, when Muggsy Spanier joined his band.

——. **Blue Note Club.** 3 North Clark Street, at West Randolph Street. The club flourished in the 1940s and early 1950s under the direction of Frank Holzfeind. Among the notable jazzmen who led resident bands there were Doc Evans (1940s), Muggsy Spanier (1947), Paul Mares (1948), Miff Mole (around the turn of the decade), and Sidney Bechet (during an American tour in 1951); Count Basie regarded the Blue Note as his Chicago headquarters and played there regularly from 1949 to 1958, and Gene Ammons performed his last engagement with Woody Herman's Herd there in 1949. The venue also engaged a number of important singers, including Billie Holiday, who appeared in December 1949, Chippie Hill, who gave her last Chicago performance at the club in 1950, and Mildred Bailey, who performed there with Joe Marsala in 1950.

——. **The Bottom.** See Dusty Bottom.

——. **Brass Rail.** This downtown venue was in existence from at least 1950; Count Basie played short residencies there in February to March of that year and in December to January of the following winter. A nightclub of the same name (apparently a different location) flourished before World War II.

——. **Breakfast Club.** See Liberty Inn.

——. **Café de Paris.** See Lincoln Gardens.

——. **Camel Gardens.** It offered performances of jazz from around 1920. Georg Brunis and Paul Mares played in the resident band, led by the drummer Ragbaby Stevens, in 1920–21, and in 1922 Eddie Condon appeared there as a member of a sextet.

——. **Capitol Lounge.** It flourished from at least 1940 as a venue for small groups and soloists. Roy Eldridge led a combo there in late 1940, and in 1951 Dizzy Gillespie and Count Basie both played residencies with small groups.

——. **Cascade Gardens** [Cascades Ballroom]. North Sheridan Road and West Argyle Street. Owned by Palmer Cody, this dance hall on an upper floor of a building on the north side of the intersection was in operation from the early 1920s. The Wolverines played there early in 1924.

——. **Casino Gardens.** North Clark Street, north of West Kinzie Street. Dance hall. It was part-owned by the promoter Harry James, who also managed the Schiller Café (see below) at the time when Johnny Stein led his band of New Orleans musicians there in 1916. The Original Dixieland Jazz Band, which grew out of Stein's group, opened at the Casino Gardens on 6 July 1916, after a residency at the Del'Abe Café (see below), and continued to play there for the rest of the year.

——. **The Cellar** [My Cellar]. 222 North State Street. During the late 1920s Wingy Manone led a band (which included Joe Marsala) at this nightclub; the musicians associated with the so-called Austin High School Gang, including Frank Teschemacher, Bud Freeman, and Bix Beiderbecke, often dropped into the club to play in jam sessions with Manone's group. The premises were later the site of the Three Deuces (see below).

——. **Cinderella Ballroom.** It offered jazz for dancing from at least the mid-1920s. Among the bands that performed there were those led by Joe Sullivan (1927) and George Wettling (1928).

——. **Circle Inn.** East 63rd Street and South Cottage Grove Avenue. The trumpeter George Dixon led a combo in a long residency there beginning in April 1946; among the notable musicians who played with him was Roy Eldridge.

——. **Civic Opera House.** Opened in 1929, the theater seats 3500. It has sometimes been used for concerts of jazz, including one in October 1946, at which Dizzy Gillespie, Sidney Bechet, Gene Sedric, Jimmy McPartland, and Bud Freeman, among others, appeared.

——. **Claremont.** East 39th Street and South Indiana Avenue. This nightclub occupied premises in a building on the northwest corner of the intersection. It was opened around 1922 by the trumpeter and pianist Jimmy Wade and provided a platform for numerous bands. It closed in 1938 with a performance by Albert Ammons.

——. **Club Alabam.** 747 North Rush Street, at West Chicago Avenue. A small venue downtown, it was in existence from at least the mid-1920s. Eddie South's Alabamians played there in 1927.

——. **Club Alvadere.** East 35th Street between South Prairie Avenue and South Calumet Avenue. This was the first of at least three clubs to operate in premises on an upper floor of the building (which was two doors away from the Plantation Café, see below); it was in existence by the turn of the 1920s, when Junie Cobb led a band there (1920–21). By 1922 the venue was known as the Nest Club (see below) and by autumn 1926 as the Apex Club (see above).

——. **Club Ambassador.** Situated on Chicago's North Side, it was offering jazz by the late 1920s. Musicians who performed there at that period were Darnell Howard (summer 1928), Jimmie Noone (1928–31), Junie Cobb, and Jerome Don Pasquall, who led a quintet at the club (1929–30).

——. **Club Congo.** 35th Street and South State Street. It was active at least around 1930; in 1931 bands led by Dave Peyton (September) and Walter Barnes (December) appeared there.

——. **Club DeLisa.** 5516 South State Street (1933–41); 5521 South State Street (1941–?). This nightclub was opened during the 1933 World's Fair by the brothers Mike De Lisa, Louie De Lisa, and Jim De Lisa. After the original premises were destroyed by fire on 11 February 1941 the club opened again on Sunday 27 April 1941 at a large new location (with seating for more than a 1000) on South State Street under the name the New Club DeLisa; its activities were under the direction of the producer and choreographer Sam Dyer. Many bands played long residencies at the DeLisa, including Junie Cobb's (early 1930s), the Rhythm Kings led by Albert Ammons and later by Red Saunders (1935–6), and ensembles led by Saunders, whose group was resident for 18 years from 1937, Billy Eckstine (1938), Jimmie Noone (1939), and Fletcher Henderson (1946–7). Other musicians who worked there included a number of singers; Chippie Hill was resident for a long period in the early 1940s and it was at the DeLisa that Count Basie first heard Joe Williams sing in the 1950s. (D. J. Travis: "Club DeLisa," *An Autobiography of Black Jazz* (Chicago, 1983), 123)

——. **Club Deluxe.** See Joe's Deluxe Club.

——. **Club Dixie.** Jazz was played there from at least the early 1930s. The club was one of the many venues where Jimmie Noone played during his years in Chicago; he was resident there in 1932.

——. **Club Metropole.** It was active as a venue for jazz from the end of the 1920s; among the musicians who led bands there in the following decade was Junie Cobb.

——. **Club 29.** It flourished in the 1930s, when Albert Ammons and his Rhythm Kings and a small band led by Johnny Dodds appeared there.

——. **Coach Club.** It was in existence by 1940, in the winter of which year Jimmie Noone began a residency there with a band that included Baby Dodds; the engagement ended in spring 1941.

——. **Coliseum.** East 15th Street and South Wabash Avenue. Theater. This large venue was the site of two sensational events in 1926, when, under the auspices of the record company Okeh, numerous prominent jazz musicians were brought together to entertain audiences of several thousands. On 27 February Clarence Williams, Louis Armstrong, Sara Martin, Chippie Hill, Doc Cook, Blanche Calloway, Sippie Wallace, and Bennie Moten, among others, performed at a concert billed as Okeh Race Records Artists Night. On 12 June a great battle of bands was staged between many of the most notable ensembles of the day, including those led by Charlie Elgar, Carroll Dickerson, Dave Peyton, Cook, King Oliver, Armstrong, Al Wynn, and Erskine Tate, all of which were currently based in the city.

The Coliseum Annex (at the same address) engaged Tate's orchestra to appear in October 1923 and Ollie Powers's in December of that year. 1 May 1924 saw a competition between the bands of Cook, Sammy Stewart, Dickerson, and Jimmy Wade, and Honore Dutrey's Creole Jazz Band, which was currently playing at Lincoln Gardens; Fletcher Henderson's orchestra gave an acclaimed performance for a dance there on 17 September 1927.

——. **College Inn.** See Sherman Hotel.

——. **Colosimo Café.** 2126 South Wabash Avenue. It was one of the numerous venues where Billie Holiday appeared as a soloist in the last decade of her career; she was resident there in the early part of 1947.

——. **Congress Hotel.** South Michigan Avenue north of East 22nd Street. The hotel engaged jazz and dance bands from at least the mid-1920s. An orchestra led by Fletcher Henderson played there in the summer of 1927, making nightly broadcasts on radio station KYW. Eddie South led a group there in 1932, playing in the hotel lobby to entertain the members of the Democratic National Convention. Benny Goodman's band was resident from 6 November 1935 to May 1936 and it was followed by Duke Ellington's in May–June 1936; Henderson played at the hotel again in the same year.

——. **Cotton Club.** 1213-19 South Blue Island Avenue, at West Roosevelt Road. It opened in late 1937 or early 1938 under the direction of the Pintozzi brothers; its programs consisted of fully fledged floor shows that included dancers, a chorus line, comedy acts, and music by a large band.

——. **Cotton Club Ballroom.** 35th Street and South State Street. This venue on the top floor of the Arcade Building opened on 9 September 1933 with Walter Barnes's band playing for the dancing. Erskine Tate led a 12-piece group in a long residency there in the 1930s.

——. **Crown Propellor Lounge.** East 63rd Street. It flourished in the 1950s, engaging small groups and also dancers and entertainers. Nancy Wilson sang there in 1956 with a band led by Rusty Bryant, and the following year Johnny Griffin, Gene Ammons, and Lester Young played a residency.

——. **Dave's Café.** East 51st Street and South Michigan Avenue (to 1934); 343 East 55th Street (from June or July 1934). It was one of several nightclubs to occupy premises in the Ritz Building on the northwest corner of the intersection; earlier the Ace of Clubs had operated there. Owned by Dave Heighly, Dave's Café opened in the early 1930s, but it was burned out by gangsters and Heighly moved into a new venue close by in 1934. In 1933 a band led by George McClennon and Ray Nance's sextet were simultaneously in residence; Nance and his Rhythm Barons were still playing for Heighly in April 1934, and in the same year May Alix (ii), Carroll Dickerson, and Fletcher Henderson (with Coleman Hawkins in his band) all appeared. Other bands to perform at the club included François' Louisianians (1935–6). Under new management the club was renamed the Swingland Café in August 1936 (see below).

——. **Del'Abe Café** [De Labbie Café]. Hotel Normandy, North Clark Street and West Randolph Street. In the mid-1910s it was managed by Sam Rothschild, who presented the first performances by the Original Dixieland Jazz Band; the group was resident there from 2 June 1916 until the beginning of July, when it moved on to the Casino Gardens (see above).

——. **De Lisa Club.** See Club DeLisa.

——. **De Luxe Café.** 3503 State Street, south of 35th Street. Under the management of Isidore Schorr, it flourished before the 1920s and was among the first venues in Chicago to offer jazz consistently; the club included a billiard hall, bar, and dance hall. A number of important early jazz musicians played there, including Jelly Roll Morton, King Oliver, Manuel Perez, and Lawrence Duhé, whose band included Wellman Braud, Sidney Bechet, Louis Keppard, Roy Palmer, Minor Hall (who replaced his brother Tubby Hall), and Lil Hardin. At the turn of the decade Freddie Keppard brought a group to the De Luxe, which remained there some time under the leadership successively of Perez, the trombonist George Filhe, Lorenzo Tio, Jr., and Bechet. This venue should not be confused with Joe's Deluxe Club (see below).

——. **Disc Jockey Lounge.** See McKee's Disc Jockey Show Lounge.

——. **Dreamland Ballroom (i).** 3518–20 South State Street, at 35th Street. It was opened in 1912 by Elijah Johnson and for a time in the mid-1910s the managers and dance instructors were Robert and Ernest Bacon, who later opened Bacon's Casino (see above); the manager late in the decade was Bill Bottoms. Among the bands that played there was one led by Lawrence Duhé (which included King Oliver and Sidney Bechet) in 1918. In the 1920s the premises were renovated and reopened as the Dreamland Café (see below).

——. **Dreamland Ballroom (ii)** [Harmon's Dreamland Ballroom]. South Ashland Avenue and West Van Buren Street. This venue on the city's North Side was active by at least 1915 and offered dancing for a white clientèle accompanied by black bands. Under the management of Paddy Harmon a number of prominent early jazz musicians played there, including Charlie Elgar with a 15-piece band (1916–22), and Doc Cook, who led the resident group for about six years from 1922; Cook's sidemen at different times included Freddie Keppard, Jimmie Noone, and Johnny St. Cyr. Jerome Don Pasquall led a band there in 1929.

——. **Dreamland Café** [Dreamland Gardens]. 3518–20 South State Street, at 35th Street (to 1928); 4700 South State Street (1933–46). An opulent nightclub with a mirror-hung dance floor, it opened in the early 1920s and was managed during its heyday by J. H. Carlis (1923–4), Walter J. Burton (1924), Bill Bottoms (1924), and Warren La Rue (by 1928). It was closed in October 1928 for violating the prohibition laws. The club reopened further down South State Street on 25 November 1933 under the proprietorship of Saul Ruben with Raymond "Sheeny" Barnett as its manager; Barnett was succeeded by Billy Page and Fess Wade (both 1934) and Joe Peterson (1935). Among the jazz musicians to appear there were Mae Brady (1921), Ollie Powers and his Harmony Syncopators, which included Louis Armstrong (1924), Honore Dutrey, whose band included Baby and Johnny Dodds (1924), Lil Armstrong (1925–6), Cab Calloway (1927), Freddie Keppard (1928), and Tiny Parham (1928).

——. **Dusty Bottom.** South Wabash Avenue and East 33rd Street. Open-air café. It had a freestanding wooden dance floor, the dust from which gave the venue its name. Among the jazz musicians who played residencies there in the 1930s was Albert Ammons.

——. **Elite Club** [Elite Café]. 3030 South State Street; State Street between 26th Street and 31st Street. An early venue for jazz in Chicago, the club flourished between around 1910 and 1928 at two locations on State Street (usually referred to as Elite #1 and Elite #2), where the managers were (respectively) Dan Gain and Teenon Jones. The pianists J. Glover Compton and Tony Jackson played as a duo there around 1912, and Jelly Roll Morton was the resident pianist when he first arrived in Chicago around 1914.

——. **Entertainers' Café** [Entertainers' Club]. East 35th Street and Michigan Avenue; East 35th Street between South Indiana

Avenue and South Prairie Avenue. This club functioned at two locations close to each other on 35th Street. Before 1920 Freddie Keppard led a band of New Orleans musicians there and Carroll Dickerson performed regularly from 1921 with an ensemble that included Natty Dominique. Earl Hines played in the resident band (led by the violinist Vernie Robinson) in 1924 and later returned to the club with a group of his own.

——. **Fiume Café.** State Street north of 35th Street. It engaged jazz musicians from at least 1919, when a band led by Freddie Keppard and including Buster Bailey played there.

——. **Fountain Inn.** West 63rd Street and South Halsted Street. It was one of many venues in the city to engage New Orleans musicians in the 1910s. Charlie Elgar led a quintet there in 1914 and the trombonist George Filhe a sextet in 1916.

——. **Friar's Inn.** South Wabash Avenue and East Van Buren Street. This nightclub on the North Side is remembered chiefly because of its connection with the white jazz band that became known as the New Orleans Rhythm Kings. The nucleus of this group played at the club for 17 months from autumn 1921 and recorded in 1922 as the Friars Society Orchestra; their performances and recordings provided a model for a generation of white jazz musicians in Chicago. Merritt Brunies followed the New Orleans Rhythm Kings into the club, playing a long residency from 1923 to 1926. Other bands to appear there included Bill Paley's Rhythm Kings (*c*1926), among the members of which were Jimmy McPartland and Jim Lanigan.

——. **Garfield Hotel.** See El Rado Café.

——. **Garrick Stage Bar** [Garrick Lounge]. West Randolph Street and North Clark Street. Situated next door to the Garrick Theater, the bar was owned from the 1940s by Joe Sherman. Long residencies were played by Henry "Red" Allen (1942–6), with whom Ben Webster played as a guest soloist, Lil Armstrong, and Eddie South; Webster also led a small group there in the mid-1940s, as did Stuff Smith and Al Casey (both 1943). Other notable performers who appeared included Alberta Hunter and Ethel Waters.

——. **George's.** 230 West Kenzie Street. Dinner club. Jazz has been played in the club from the early 1980s. Following the policy established at London House (see below) and then at Rick's Café Americain (see below), George's has presented such musicians as the pianists George Shearing and Ahmad Jamal and the singer Joe Williams, and, less often, noted performers on other instruments, notably the saxophonist Eddie Harris.

——. **Goat's Nest.** See Three Deuces.

——. **Golden Lily (Tavern).** 309 East 55th Street. A Chinese restaurant opened on the second floor of the building in September 1926 and jazz was offered there from the start: on the opening night Tiny Parham and Ikey Robinson led a performance by the Victor Recording Orchestra. From 1929 to at least 1935 a band led by the drummer François Moseley (known variously as Frankie Franko and his Louisianians, the Louisiana Stompers, and François' Louisianians), played a long residency there; among the sidemen were Teddy Wilson, Albert Ammons, and Punch Miller. The venue was sold in 1939 and its name was changed to White's Emporium. Coleman Hawkins gave a series of performances there beginning in February 1941.

——. **Golden Pumpkin.** This venue included jazz performance from the late 1920s. The double bass player Thelma Terry and her Playboys, which included Gene Krupa, was resident there in 1929–30.

——. **Grand Terrace** [New Grand Terrace]. 3955 South Parkway Boulevard (28 December 1928 to 24 January 1937); 315–17 East 35th Street, at South Calumet Avenue (from 19 June 1937). Ballroom. It opened on 28 December 1928 in a building that had formerly been the Peerless Theater (from 1917), a movie theater where jazz was played during intermissions (Dave Peyton bought partial control of the Peerless Theater in April 1926 and led an orchestra there, but the venue failed that summer); these premises were reconverted to a theater when the Grand Terrace closed, and were renamed The Park. The ballroom's second location was in premises formerly occupied by the Sunset Cafe (see below). Its change of name clearly did not coincide with the move since it was known as the New Grand Terrace by at least 1932. Activities at the Grand Terrace were directed by Edward Fox and the producer of the musical shows was Ralph Cooper, but the venue is supposed to have been controlled for some time by Joe Fusco, a henchman of the gangster Al Capone. Among the resident performers were Tiny Parham (*c*1931), Earl Hines (1928–38), Carroll Dickerson (1934), Fletcher Henderson (1936–9, 1941–2), Count Basie (from 1936), and Horace Henderson (from January 1939); Billie Holiday appeared in the summer revue there in 1936. The ballroom was the site of Hines's first real success as a bandleader and the long residencies by his band throughout the 1930s, together with his appearances on many of the radio broadcasts made from there, gained him a large following. Other musicians who performed at the Grand Terrace included George Dixon, Walter Fuller, Reginald Foresythe, and Chu Berry.

——. **Grand Theater.** 3110–12 South State Street, at 31st Street. Vaudeville theater. In the heart of the city's vaudeville district, it was opened in the early days of the century. Although it presented mostly variety acts until at least 1914, some early jazz bands played there: Wilbur Sweatman's trio, which included Dave Peyton, was resident between 1908 and 1912, and in the latter year the theater was on the itinerary of a tour by the Original Creole Band. Peyton was directing the pit band by 1915 and he continued to do so for about 12 years; latterly his groups included, at different times, Charlie Allen, George Mitchell, Bob Shoffner, Reuben Reeves, Kid Ory, Bud Scott, Jimmy Bertrand, Zue Robertson, and Baby Dodds. *Plantation Days*, one of the most successful musical shows of the 1920s, played to ecstatic receptions at the Grand in August 1927; among the cast were Blanche and Cab Calloway. In the 1920s the theater was often used for performances by singers; almost all the prominent vocalists who recorded in that decade appeared there, including Clara Smith and Bessie Smith. The theater's fortunes declined with the shifting of the black entertainment center downtown in the late twenties; it seems to have ceased to operate as a venue for jazz in 1930, and the building was eventually demolished to make way for a program of urban renewal.

——. **Green Mill Ballroom.** 4802 North Broadway Street. The Green Mill engaged jazz musicians to play for the dancing from around 1920. Isham Jones (*c*1920) and Charlie Elgar (1922) both led orchestras there. The venue continued to be active into at least the 1940s. It reopened under new ownership in the 1980s, retaining the original decor from the 1920s. Jazz (bop and newer styles) is played there every night of the week.

——. **El Grotto.** 6412 South Cottage Grove Avenue, at East 64th Street. Supper club. It occupied a large room with a dance floor in the basement of the Pershing Hotel (see below). Charlie Cole and Harry Fields took out a lease on the club in autumn 1944, then, after entering into part-ownership, Earl Hines finally bought it in April 1947. Hines played there himself from 1945, and other prominent musicians who appeared included Johnny Griffin, a band led by the electric guitarist T-Bone Walker, and Roy Eldridge and Eddie "Lockjaw" Davis (1947).

——. **Harlem Café.** 346 East 31st Street. It was active as a venue for jazz in the 1930s. Sammy Price was among the musicians who played there.

——. **Harmon's Dreamland Ballroom.** See Dreamland Ballroom (ii).

——. **Hotel Normandy.** See Del'Abe Café.

——. **It Club.** 5450 South Michigan Boulevard. This basement nightclub, which flourished in the 1930s, was in the middle of a lively area of Chicago's nightlife at the intersection of Michigan and Garfield boulevards. A small group led by Albert Ammons played a residency there in the mid-decade and Tommy Powell and his Hi-de-ho Boys appeared from December 1938.

——. **Jazz Ltd.** 11 East Grand Avenue. Founded by Bill Reinhardt and his wife Ruth Reinhardt, this nightclub on the North Side opened in June 1947. It flourished until at least the late 1960s. Reinhardt led the five-piece house band, which at different times included Munn Ware, Danny Alvin, Sidney Bechet, Floyd Bean, Big Chief Moore, Sid Catlett, and Barrett Deems. In order to avoid tax regulations singers were not engaged. Among the guest musicians who played at Jazz Ltd. were Doc Evans, Miff Mole, and Muggsy Spanier with Georg Brunis (all in the late 1940s), Art Hodes (1950s and 1960s), Zinky Cohn (who had a regular engagement on Monday evenings from 1950 to 1952), and Marty Marsala (1962).

——. **Jazz Showcase.** See Joe Segal's Jazz Showcase.

——. **Jeffrey's Tavern.** Nightclub on the South Side. In the mid-1920s a band, fronted by Hugh Swift, was featured in nightly broadcasts from the club on radio station WBJC. The saxophonist Vernon Roulette played a residency there in 1926 with a band that included Zutty Singleton (substituting for Baby Dodds) and George Mitchell.

——. **Joe's Deluxe Club** [Joe's De Luxe Café]. 6323 South Parkway Boulevard, at East 63rd Street. It opened in April 1939 under the direction of its owner Joe Hughes. By December of that year Hughes was advertising a weekly "Swing Session" with a different band every week. The club's principal attraction became its celebrity night on Monday, to which many famous jazz musicians came, among them Duke Ellington, Earl Hines, Cab Calloway, Nat "King" Cole, Sarah Vaughan, and Dizzy Gillespie. Others who appeared at the club included the bandleader Ted Weems, Joe Williams, Johnny Letman, Johnny Griffin, Ray Nance, and the dancer and producer Joe "Ziggy" Johnson. Joe's Deluxe Club should not be confused with the Deluxe Café (see above).

——. **Joe Segal's Jazz Showcase.** North Clark Street; Rust Street; 636 South Michigan Street, in the Blackstone Hotel (from the 1970s). Owned and managed by Joe Segal, it was established in the late 1940s and has been the most important club in Chicago since the demise of the Bee Hive Club in 1956. Many leading bop musicians have played there.

——. **Joe's Paradise.** East 35th Street and South Prairie Avenue. The club was situated on the southeast corner of the intersection, and was active in the 1920s. Among the jazz musicians who led bands there were Jimmie Noone and Jimmy O'Bryant.

——. **Kelly's Stables** [Bert Kelly's Stables]. 431 North Rush Street, at East Kinzie Street. A small, intimate venue, it was opened by Bert Kelly during the first heyday of Chicago jazz in the 1920s. Several musicians had long associations with the club: from 1924 Freddie Keppard, Johnny Dodds, and Baby Dodds worked there together in a group which Johnny Dodds took over and led as the house band for six years; Dodds's sidemen included his brother, Honore Dutrey, and Charlie Alexander, and Keppard returned frequently as a guest soloist. The venue was destroyed by fire in the late 1920s.

——. **Kimball Hall.** Concert hall. Jazz concerts were given in this small hall (capacity 450) from at least the mid-1940s. On 1 December 1946 the author and raconteur Studs Terkel acted as compère at a concert that included performances by Mezz Mezzrow and Sidney Bechet backed by local musicians; Bechet returned on 26 January 1947, when the program also included Bill Harris (i), Fletcher Henderson, and the tenor saxophonist Otis Finch. Bechet made further appearances in May and June 1947, the latter with Max Kaminsky.

——. **Lamb's Café.** North Clark Street and West Randolph Street. It was an early venue for jazz-oriented music in the city and among the groups to play there before 1920 was Tom Brown's Ragtime Band, which was resident from May to September 1915; Brown's was probably the first white jazz band to appear in Chicago. The club came into its own during the first flowering of jazz in Chicago in the 1920s and continued to flourish into the 1930s. In the mid-thirties Jabbo Smith played a brief residency and Johnny Dodds led his small band there.

——. **Liberty Inn.** North Clark Street and West Erie Street. Owned by the Irish-American Johnny McGovern, it was known as the Breakfast Club during the Prohibition era. Boyce Brown formed a connection with the venue, leading his own trio there for a long period from the late 1930s and returning intermittently until the early 1950s. The Liberty Inn was a favorite venue for jam sessions and among the musicians who played in these was Art Hodes.

——. **Lincoln Gardens** [Royal Gardens]. 459 East 31st Street, at South Cottage Grove Avenue. Dance hall. A huge venue, it could accommodate around 1000 dancers and was open from the early years of the century. It was originally known as the Royal Gardens, but the name was changed to Lincoln Gardens between February and July 1921. After a fire late in 1924 the hall was magnificently refurbished for its reopening on 28 October 1925, when the name was changed to the New Charleston Café; it later became known as the Café de Paris. Dave Peyton led a band there from late November 1926, but in June 1927 it was bombed – perhaps in gang warfare – and closed.

The residency at the Royal Gardens in 1918 of the Original Creole Band, led by Bill Johnson (i), established the dance hall's reputation as a venue for jazz, and initiated a series of appearances by New Orleans musicians that were of great significance for the development of the music in Chicago. King Oliver's Creole Jazz Band played a residency from 17 June 1922 until February 1924, when Oliver left and his former sidemen Johnny Dodds, Baby Dodds, and Honore Dutrey formed a new resident group with Bob Shoffner on trumpet; Oliver returned in June, with different personnel and remained until the fire closed the hall at the end of the year.

——. **London House.** 360 North Michigan Avenue. Dinner club. It opened in 1951 and flourished into the 1970s. The owner, George Marianthal, presented for the most part piano trios, sometimes together with a singer. Oscar Peterson and George Shearing performed there regularly, and the house band included such distinguished local musicians as the pianist Norman Simmons.

——. **Lucky Spot.** See Roberts Show Club.

——. **McKee's Disc Jockey Lounge.** East 63rd Street and South Cottage Grove Avenue. It was directed around 1950 by the dance promoter McKee Fitzhugh, who had been associated in the 1940s with several of the major ballrooms in Chicago. He engaged the saxophonist Johnny Board as the house bandleader, and Board formed an organ trio, which accompanied various visiting artists, among them Gene Ammons and Sonny Stitt. The club became well known for the exciting jam sessions that developed when such players were in residence. It remained active at least into the early 1960s, presenting Ammons and Dexter Gordon in 1961 and Ammons and Stitt the following year.

——. **The Macomba.** East 39th Street and South Cottage Grove Avenue. It was owned by the brothers Leonard Chess and Philip Chess of Chess Records and flourished in the 1940s. In addition to various local bands, it engaged guest soloists such as Louis Armstrong, Lionel Hampton, and Ella Fitzgerald.

——. **Mark Twain Lounge.** Active in the 1940s and 1950s it was one of the clubs where Lil Armstrong played long residencies as an unaccompanied soloist.

——. **Merry Gardens.** It was in operation by the mid-1920s. In 1927 Detroit Shannon's band, which included Walter Barnes, was in residence; Barnes took over the band, and under the name the Royal Creolians it returned to the Merry Gardens the following year. Other bands to appear were Joe Kayser's (1928), which included Muggsy Spanier, the Alabamians, with Cab Calloway as master of ceremonies (from April 1929), and Tiny Parham's big band (1931–2).

——. **Metropolitan Theater** [Ascher's Metropolitan Theater]. 4644 South Grand Boulevard. It flourished as a venue for jazz performance from 1917 until around 1930, when it fell victim to the enormous popularity of the Regal Theater and Savoy Ballroom, and the consequent removal downtown of the black entertainment area; the building then became a movie theater and was eventually demolished to make way for a program of urban renewal. The managers of the Metropolitan when its jazz activities were at their height in the late 1920s were Cary Lewis (1927) and Matt Taylor, Jr. (1928). Among the musicians who played there were Sammy Stewart (who appeared regularly in the late 1920s), Fats Waller (1927), Erskine Tate (1928–30), whose orchestra included Bob Shoffner, Omer Simeon, Quinn Wilson, and Wallace Bishop, and Clarence Jones's Syncopators, with which Louis Armstrong played in February 1928.

——. **Michigan Theater.** East 55th Street and South Michigan Avenue. It became known for its presentation of jazz late in the 1920s. Sammy Stewart performed there in November 1929 (when his sidemen included Chu Berry and Sid Catlett) and Boyd Atkins in 1930; Erskine Tate was music director from 1930 to 1932. In the 1930s the venue functioned mainly as a movie theater.

——. **Midnite Club.** 3140 South Indiana Avenue. It was in operation by at least the mid-1930s. Among the musicians who appeared there at that period were Jimmie Noone (1934), Ray Nance and his Rhythm Boys (March 1935), and Frankie "Half Pint" Jaxon (June 1935).

——. **Midway Garden Ballroom** [Midway Gardens]. South Cottage Grove Avenue between East 55th Street and East 63rd Street. Active as a jazz venue from at least the early 1920s, it engaged a number of prominent musicians. Elmer Schoebel's band played there around 1923 and in 1927 the reed player Art Kassel led a resident group that included Benny Goodman, Schoebel, and Frank Teschemacher; others who played there included Boyce Brown and Muggsy Spanier. It became renowned for the staging of battles of bands in which as many as 15 ensembles might take part on a single night.

——. **Monogram Theater.** 3435–40 South State Street, north of 35th Street. Vaudeville theater. One of the foremost variety venues in the city, it was located in the heart of the black nightlife area and flourished from the early years of the century. Besides important vaudeville singers such as Ma Rainey and Ethel Waters, a number of jazz musicians appeared there, including a band from New Orleans (1917), of which Sidney Bechet was a member, and Lovie Austin, who was music director at the theater for 20 years from the mid-1920s.

——. **El Morocco.** 55th Street. This nightclub was active from at least the 1930s. It was among the several venues where Jesse Stone led residencies by his band, the Cyclones, in the mid-decade.

——. **Moulin Rouge Café.** South Wabash Avenue north of East Van Buren Avenue. It offered jazz from at least the early 1920s, when among the resident performers were the pianist Clarence Jones and his Wonder Orchestra (1922), a band led by Jimmy Wade (1923–6) with Eddie South as front man and music director, and Izzy Friedman's group (*c*1923).

——. **My Cellar.** See The Cellar.

——. **Nest Club.** East 35th Street between South Prairie Avenue and South Calumet Avenue. A club functioned on an upper floor of a building at this location from at least 1920 (see Club Alvadere above) and by 1922 had become a luxurious supper club under the name of the Nest Club. Jimmie Noone led a small band there from summer 1926 and continued to be associated with the venue when it became the Apex Club (see above) in autumn of that year.

——. **New Annex.** 6323 South Parkway Boulevard, at East 63rd Street. Its opening, in premises that also housed Joe's Deluxe Club (see above), was announced in April 1939. The club's management may have been connected with that of the Annex (see above).

——. **New Apartment Lounge.** 504 East 75th Street. The venue has flourished in the 1980s presenting soul-jazz groups, including those of Hank Crawford and Jimmy McGriff. Von Freeman has also appeared there.

——. **New Apex Café.** 4311–17 South Indiana Avenue. It occupied premises where a venue called the Big House had operated earlier. Managed by Doc Jennings, it opened in January 1935, by which time his Apex Café (see Apex Tavern above) may have closed. At the time it opened the resident band was Georgia Gorham and her Syncopators, with the singer Dan Grisson and the guitarist John Collins; by the end of January Elbert Topps and his Famous Orchestra had begun a residency there.

——. **New Charleston Café.** See Lincoln Gardens.

——. **New Club DeLisa.** See Club DeLisa.

——. **New Deal Tavern.** West 55th Place at the Loop. Active by at least the mid-1930s, it was owned by Warren La Rue, who was associated with a number of clubs in Chicago. The resident pianist from March 1936 until at least the end of 1939 was Laura Rucker.

——. **New Grand Terrace.** See Grand Terrace.

——. **New Pekin Theater.** See Pekin Theater.

——. **New Plantation Café.** 5060 South Michigan Avenue, at East 51st Street. Nightclub. It flourished in the mid-1930s and may have been connected with the Plantation Café, active earlier on East 35th Street (see below). In 1934 the Rhythm Kings, led by Johnny Dodds and Natty Dominique, played a residency at the New Plantation.

——. **New Regal Theater.** 79th Street and Stony Island Street. The old Avalon Theater was renovated and reopened in 1987 as the New Regal Theater. Performers have included Count Basie's orchestra under the direction of Frank Foster, and Bobby McFerrin.

——. **Nob Hill Club.** It was probably in operation by around 1940. It was one of the venues at which Lil Armstrong appeared as an unaccompanied soloist during the 1940s and early 1950s.

——. **North American Restaurant.** North State Street and West Monroe Street, on the northwest corner of the intersection. The performances given there by the Original Creole Band, led by Bill Johnson (i), around 1914, were among the first by black jazz musicians in the city.

——. **100 Club.** It offered performances of jazz from at least 1930. Danny Alvin led the resident band from around 1930 until 1933.

——. **Orchestra Hall.** 216 South Michigan Avenue. Concert hall. It was used from time to time as a venue for jazz, beginning in the late 1910s with a concert by Charlie Elgar's band. Other musicians who appeared there included Will Marion Cook's New York Syncopated Orchestra (1919), Chippie Hill, and Kid Ory and Joe Darensbourg (late 1940s).

——. **Oriental Café.** 3532 State Street, south of 35th Street. It appears to have occupied premises where the Panama Club (see below) functioned earlier. In the mid-1920s resident musicians included the pianist J. Glover Compton with his band, the Syncopators (1924–5), and Reuben Reeves (1925).

——. **Oriental Theater.** This downtown venue engaged a number of prominent big bands in the 1930s. Duke Ellington's orchestra appeared there in 1930 and 1934, Erskine Hawkins's band in 1938, and Earl Hines's in 1939.

——. **Owl Theater.** 4653 South State Street. It was used as a movie theater and also as a venue for other kinds of performance, including vaudeville acts, from around 1914; jazz formed part of many of the presentations. From about 1919 to 1927 the pianist Clarence Jones directed a small band there, which included Clarence Williams and the drummer Jasper Taylor. Others to appear there later were Williams's protégée Sara Martin and (in 1927) George Mitchell.

——. **Panama Café (Nite Club).** 307 East 58th Street, at South Prairie Avenue. Nightclub. It was opened by Ben Tolliver after Prohibition was repealed in February 1933; he had previously run a gambling house on the premises, which he renovated when he converted them to a nightclub. The club was initially known as the Panama Tavern, but in December 1933 the name was changed to Panama Café Nite Club. The saxophonist Billy Paige, who had earlier worked with King Oliver, ran the Panama's activities. Jabbo Smith and the drummer and singer Floyd Campbell were resident musicians for two years from shortly after the club opened, and Budd Johnson also performed there in 1933. Nat "King" Cole appeared in a band led by his brother Eddie in 1935, then returned for a six-month period the following year.

——. **Panama Club.** 3532 State Street, south of 35th Street. Around 1914 it was owned and directed by Isadore Levine, who engaged a number of prominent singers to perform there, including Bricktop (Ada Smith), Florence Mills, Cora Green, and the young Alberta Hunter. In the 1920s the Oriental Café (see above) seems to have operated in the same premises.

——. **Panther Room.** See Sherman Hotel.

——. **The Park.** See Grand Terrace.

——. **Parkway Ballroom.** 4457 South Parkway Boulevard. It opened on 9 March 1940 under black ownership, with performances by Floyd Campbell's orchestra, which played there regularly. In 1941 Gene Ammons appeared as the star attraction of a band led by the trumpeter King Kolax. During the 1940s the dances there were promoted by McKee Fitzhugh, who was associated with a number of ballrooms in the city.

——. **Paul Mares Barbecue.** 935 North State Street. Restaurant and bar. It was owned and run by Paul Mares, formerly a member of the New Orleans Rhythm Kings, and was in operation from at least the late 1930s. Among its activities were after-hours jam sessions. Mares sold the restaurant when he embarked on war work in the 1940s.

——. **Peerless Theater.** See Grand Terrace.

——. **Pekin Theater.** 2700 South State Street, at 27th Street. Early in the century Robert T. Motts, a black entrepreneur, ran a saloon and gambling house in the building. On 18 June 1905 he opened the Pekin Temple of Music for variety performances in an upstairs room at the north end of the premises, and barely a year later he refurbished the venue and reopened it as the New Pekin Theater. The shows presented consisted essentially of vaudeville and cabaret acts, but a number of early jazz musicians appeared there. Manuel Perez led a quintet there before 1920, and Tony Jackson's band (which included Sidney Bechet) performed regularly until shortly before Jackson's death in 1921. King Oliver was also a resident bandleader around 1920. The venue is variously referred to as the Pekin Theater, the Pekin Café, and the Pekin Cabaret.

——. **Pershing Hotel.** East 64th Street west of South Cottage Grove Avenue. The hotel offered music for the entertainment of its patrons in at least three venues – the Pershing Lounge (the hotel's main bar), the Pershing Ballroom, and the El Grotto supper club (see above). Among the musicians to appear in the lounge were the tenor saxophonist and organist Lonnie Simmons, whose ten-piece band was resident for long periods in the mid-1940s, and the pianist Ahmad Jamal. Around this time the dance promoter McKee Fitzhugh was responsible for the activities of the ballroom, which began to admit black patrons when the lease of the hotel was taken over by black owners in 1944. Private recordings survive of Charlie Parker's group performing in the ballroom in 1949 and ?1950.

——. **Plantation Café.** 338 East 35th Street, at Grand Boulevard. Nightclub. It was opened on 29 October 1924 under the ownership of Edward Fox and Al Turner, in premises formerly occupied by Al Turner's Café; it was controlled, like other clubs in which Fox had an interest, by the Capone syndicate. One of the most popular "black and tan" venues in Chicago in the twenties, it offered all-night dancing and drinking. A dance orchestra led by Dave Peyton opened the club, and King Oliver's Dixie Syncopators played a long residency from February 1925 until spring 1927. It may have ceased operations in the 1930s since a New Plantation Café (see above) had opened by 1934.

——. **Platinum Lounge.** Vincennes Hotel, 601 East 36th Street, at South Vincennes Avenue. A room in the basement of the hotel, it was run by Pops Lewis, a prominent gambling operator on the South Side, who was the husband of the hotel's owner, Elizabeth B. Lewis. The lounge opened on 3 December 1936 and the following year Jimmie Noone brought a band there for a residency; among his sidemen were Franz Jackson and Joe Williams. Broadcasts were frequently made from the club in the late 1930s. The hotel was demolished in the course of a program of urban renewal.

——. **Plugged Nickel.** North Wells Street. Many leading modern-jazz musicians played in the club. Miles Davis's quintet made a series of acclaimed recordings (portions of which were first issued in Japan in 1976) during the beginning of a two-week residency from 21 December 1965 to 2 January 1966, and in 1969 Gene Ammons returned to public performance leading a quintet there. It closed in the 1970s.

——. **Premier Studio.** See Rhumboogie Club.

——. **Pump Room.** Ambassador Hotel. It was active in the 1930s and offered performances mostly by soloists and small groups. Among the musicians to appear there were Maxine Sullivan with John Kirby's sextet (for illustration *see* KIRBY, JOHN), Teddy Wilson, and Caspar Reardon, who played a residency in the mid-1930s.

——. **El Rado Café.** Garfield Hotel, 231 East 55th Street, at South Prairie Avenue. The café was in the basement of the hotel, which was in the area at the hub of Chicago's South Side nightlife in the 1920s. After the closure of the Apex Club in 1928 Jimmie Noone led his Apex Recording Orchestra in a residency at the El Rado (1928–31).

——. **Rainbow Café** [Rainbow Gardens]. It flourished around 1920. Among the jazz musicians who played there were Isham Jones and his orchestra and Art Hodes (1924).

——. **Red Mill Café.** East 39th Street between South Parkway Boulevard and South Cottage Grove Avenue. It was active in the early 1920s as a venue for jazz. The resident bandleaders included Roy Palmer and Tommy Ladnier.

——. **Regal Theater.** 4719 South Parkway Boulevard. Variety theater. Built in a Moorish style and opulently, even garishly, decorated, with chandeliers, rhinestone-studded stage curtains, and silk and velvet drapery, the theater itself could seat 3500 and the spacious foyer could accommodate 1500. With the Savoy Ballroom, it occupied the block on the east side of 47th Street and the boulevard.

The Regal opened on 4 February 1928 and its glitter and glamor soon lured audiences away from the older Chicago theaters. The resident band for more than a year after the opening was conducted by Fess Williams, who also served as master of ceremonies for the show. In the early years the programs consisted of variety acts and musical numbers, and the Regal engaged famous singers and dancers such as Blanche Calloway, Josephine Baker, Buck and Bubbles, and the Mills Brothers; the show producer at that time was Percy Venable, uncle of Lucky Millinder. The numerous famous jazz musicians to appear in the 1930s and 1940s included Louis Armstrong, Duke Ellington, Count Basie, Jimmie Lunceford, Lucky Millinder, Lionel Hampton, Woody Herman, and Jay McShann. Later the theater offered jazz concerts among its other events and in the 1950s and 1960s leading bop and cool-jazz players appeared, including Miles Davis, Dizzy Gillespie, and Sonny Stitt. The manager of the Regal for 20 years (1939–59) was Ken Blewett, whose successful operation did much to maintain live entertainment on Chicago's South Side. The New Regal Theater (see above), which opened in 1987, is not connected with this venue. (D. J. Travis: "The Regal Theater that I Remember," "Ken 'Mr. Regal' Blewett," *An Autobiography of Black Jazz* (Chicago, 1983), 145, 157)

——. **Rendezvous.** 622 West Diversey Avenue, at North Broadway. It was active in the mid-1920s, when bands led by Charlie Straight (with Bix Beiderbecke among the members) and Ben Pollack played there.

——. **Rhumboogie Club.** 343 East Garfield Boulevard. It occupied premises on the first floor of the Ritz Building, where the Swingland Café (see below) had been located in the 1930s; its principal feature was its balcony bar. The venue was owned by Joe Louis and managed by Leonard Reed and Pat Brooks, and the show producer was Joe "Ziggy" Johnson. It was active from the early 1940s until April 1947, when it was closed by the revenue service for nonpayment of taxes.

Among the jazz musicians who appeared at the Rhumboogie were Milt Larkin (as leader of the house band in 1941–2, and resident bandleader in 1946), Fletcher Henderson (1945), the drummer and singer Floyd Campbell (1946–7), Walter Fuller, Horace Henderson, Sarah Vaughan, and George Dixon. A new club, the Premier Studio, opened in the Rhumboogie's place in August 1949; aided financially by a number of jazz musicians (among them Joe Dixon, Chester Lewis, and George Johnson), it functioned for three nights a week for 15 months before it closed.

——. **Rick's Café Americain.** 910 North Lakeshore Drive, at the Holiday Inn. It was modeled after the club of the same name in the film *Casablanca* and opened in 1976 after the demise of London House (see above); it presented pianists who would have worked at the earlier venue and soon became the major competition for Joe Segal's Jazz Showcase. The excellent quality of its piano elicited memorable performances from such players as Oscar Peterson, Teddy Wilson, Hank Jones, and Bill Evans (ii). Benny Carter, Red Norvo, Joe Williams, and Clark Terry were among other musicians who worked there. It closed in the early 1980s.

——. **Riverview Park Ballroom.** Western Avenue and West Madison Street. Dance hall. Active from before 1920, it presented jazz-oriented bands to accompany the dancing. Doc Cook was the music director for three years from 1918 to 1921. The hall is of jazz interest mainly for the staging of battles of bands. A notable event of this kind took place on 11 September 1927, when 12 groups assembled to compete with one another.

——. **Roberts Show Club.** 6222 South Parkway Boulevard. It was owned and managed by Herman Roberts, who began his career as the owner of a fleet of taxi cabs. He first ran a nightclub called the Lucky Spot (renamed the Roberettes) at 605 East 71st Street, which was so successful that it soon outgrew its premises. Roberts decided to relocate his club to the garage from which his cab company functioned on South Parkway Boulevard, and after completely renovating the building he opened a large dance hall there, which shortly afterwards he refurbished as a nightclub, able to seat 1000 people, under the name Roberts Lounge and Liquor. In 1957 Roberts sold his cab franchise to devote himself to his club, which by now was known as Roberts Show Club. Among the many prominent performers he engaged were Dinah Washington, who appeared regularly three times a year, Sarah Vaughan, Count Basie, Sammy Davis, Jr., Billy Eckstine, Ray Charles, and Louis Jordan; Red Saunders directed the house band. (D. J. Travis: "Roberts Show Club," *An Autobiography of Black Jazz* (Chicago, 1983), 191)

——. **Royal Gardens** [Royal Garden Café]. See Lincoln Gardens.

——. **Savoy Ballroom.** South Parkway Boulevard and East 47th Street. The opening of the Savoy on 23 November 1927 and of the Regal Theater (see above) on the same block in 1928 marked the removal downtown of Chicago's center of black entertainment and commerce, and the consequent decline of the area around 35th Street and State Street. The Savoy's fortunes rose and fell several times in its 20-year existence. Until the collapse of the New York stock exchange in 1929 the ballroom flourished, offering music and dancing seven nights a week; thereafter it was found expedient to introduce such activities as boxing and skating. The ballroom was partly refurbished in 1938 and when it reopened its policy was to present dances on four nights; but this lasted no more than a year before the management decided that it could afford only one dance night – Sunday. The ballroom closed in summer 1948 and the building was later demolished.

Despite its checkered commercial history, the Savoy was a major center for jazz in Chicago for two decades. Among the bands that appeared there in its first few sensational years were those led by Carroll Dickerson (which included Louis Armstrong and Zutty Singleton), Charlie Elgar, Fletcher Henderson, and the violinist Clarence Black. From the 1930s virtually all the prominent bandleaders of the day were engaged by the Savoy, notably Henderson (1936–9, 1941, 1943–5), Duke Ellington, Count Basie, Horace Henderson, Andy Kirk, Jimmie Lunceford, Chick Webb, Earl Hines, Erskine Tate, Tiny Parham, Willie Bryant, and many others. After the renovation in 1938 the ballroom reopened on 16 May with a gala performance by 25 swing bands and from that time live broadcasts were regularly made. In its later years the Savoy continued to present the greatest jazz performers: among those who appeared were Basie, Ellington, Stan Kenton, Dizzy Gillespie, Ella Fitzgerald, Gene Krupa, Woody Herman, Louis Jordan, and the International Sweethearts of Rhythm. (D. J. Travis: "Jumping at the Savoy," "The Many Faces of Lady Savoy, 1927 to 1948," *An Autobiography of Black Jazz* (Chicago, 1983), 77, 93)

——. **Schiller Café.** 318 East 31st Street, at South Calumet Avenue. Like the Casino Gardens (see above), this venue was managed by the promoter Harry James and offered some of the earliest performances by New Orleans players in Chicago. In March 1916 a band consisting of Johnny Stein, Alcide "Yellow" Nuñez, Eddie Edwards, Henry Ragas, and Nick LeRocca began a long engagement there (as Stein's Band from Dixie, and later Stein's Dixie Jass Band); Edwards, Ragas, and LaRocca left on 26 May to form the Original Dixieland Jazz Band, and Stein was obliged to form a new group to fulfill his contract at the club.

——. **Sherman Hotel.** West Randolph Street and North Clark Street. Jazz was played for the entertainment of patrons in several rooms in the hotel. Paul Whiteman's band was resident in the College Inn in 1933, and in the late 1930s the Old Town Room engaged a number of important peformers. The Panther Room, lavishly decorated with panther-skin patterning (for illustration *see* SPANIER, MUGGSY), was the hotel's principal venue for the presentation of jazz and a fashionable nightspot. Count Basie's orchestra undertook an engagement in June 1939 and most of the best-known big bands of the 1940s played there, but it also offered performances by small groups led by Bud Freeman, Fats Waller, Hot Lips Page, and Muggsy Spanier. Other prominent jazzmen who played at the Sherman included Jimmy McPartland, Joe Sullivan in a duo with Meade "Lux" Lewis, and Caspar Reardon. Live radio broadcasts were frequently made from its various venues.

——. **Showboat Cabaret.** North Clark Street. A speakeasy on the Chicago Loop, it was owned in the early 1930s by Sam Beers and controlled by the Capone syndicate. Bands led by Jabbo Smith and Cassino Simpson played residencies there, and Louis Armstrong appeared in 1931.

——. **Southmoor Hotel.** See Venetian Room.

——. **Studio Club.** One of several Chicago nightclubs owned and run at different times by Earl Hines, it opened in the spring of 1940; the operation lasted only until October, when Hines reorganized his band for engagements in California.

——. **Sunset Cafe.** 315–17 East 35th Street, at South Calumet Avenue. Nightclub. It was opened on 3 August 1921 by Edward Fox and Sam Dreyfus, though it was under the control of Al Capone's gangster syndicate. Situated in the center of Chicago nightlife in the 1920s, close to the Apex Club and the Plantation Café, it became one of the most popular "black and tan" clubs on the South Side. It came into its own as a jazz venue when Carroll Dickerson became the resident leader in 1922; after a residency by Sammy Stewart's band (1924–6) Dickerson returned for another long period in 1926–7. His band, which latterly included Louis Armstrong and Earl Hines, was a phenomenal success, and drew jazz musicians from all over Chicago to hear it. When Dickerson left the club in February 1927 Armstrong led the Sunset Stompers there, with Hines as music director; it is supposed to have been at the Sunset that he first met Joe Glaser, who later became his manager. The club continued to flourish for the remainder of the decade, engaging bands led by Charlie Elgar (1929–30), Boyd Atkins (1929–30), and Tiny Parham (1930). Dickerson returned in the mid-1930s for a further residency, but the Sunset was by that time in financial difficulty and it closed in 1937. The premises were taken over by the Grand Terrace, which was also owned and run by Fox (see above).

——. **Sutherland Show Lounge.** Sutherland Hotel, South Drexel Boulevard and East 47th Street. The nightclub and bar of the Sutherland Hotel offered jazz performances from at least the late 1950s. It engaged mainly soloists and small groups, and among those who appeared there were Cannonball Adderley, Nancy Wilson, John Coltrane, and Miles Davis.

——. **Swingland Café.** 343 East Garfield Boulevard. In August 1936 Benny Skoller took over these premises in the Ritz Building from Dave Heighly, who had run them as Dave's Café (see above). Among the prominent musicians to perform at the Swingland were Horace Henderson's orchestra (1937–8) with the singer Viola Jefferson. From the 1940s the same building housed the Rhumboogie Club (see above).

——. **Swing Room.** See Three Deuces.

——. **Tejar's Slipper Lounge.** 1321 South Michigan Avenue. It was active in the 1960s under the ownership of Ahmad Jamal. Besides Jamal himself, a number of soloists and small groups played there. It had closed by March 1971, when the blues club Pepper's Lounge opened in its place.

——. **Three Deuces.** 222 North State Street. Nightclub. It occupied premises that formerly housed clubs called the Goat's Nest and The Cellar (see above). It was in operation by the mid-1930s and by 1936 was owned and managed by Sam Beers. Zutty Singleton led a sextet at the club from May 1935 and stayed to play in Roy Eldridge's band, which began a long and highly successful residency in September 1936; among Eldridge's other sidemen were Dave Young, Scoops Carry, and Tiny Parham. During this period the club enjoyed enormous popularity; simultaneously with Eldridge's residency, Art Tatum was the pianist in the Swing Room, a small venue downstairs from the main club. Among other important musicians to play at the Three Deuces in the late 1930s were Art Hodes, Jimmy McPartland (*c*1937), Baby Dodds (who was the house drummer, 1936–9), Johnny Dodds (late 1930s), Lonnie Johnson (*c*1937–1939), Julia Lee (1939), and Anita O'Day (with Max Miller's band, 1939–40). Broadcasts were frequently made from the club during these years.

——. **Trianon Ballroom.** 6201 South Cottage Grove Avenue. Like other ballrooms in the city, it enjoyed its greatest celebrity in the 1930s when major swing bands played for dancing there and broadcasts brought a wide audience for the music it offered. The dance promoter McKee Fitzhugh organized its activities in the mid-1930s. It operated a strict segregationist policy until 1950, admitting Whites only. The ballroom closed in 1954 and the building was demolished in the late 1960s.

——. **Vendome Theater.** 3145 South State Street, at 32nd Street. Built in 1909, it was one of many vaudeville theaters in the area where Chicago's nightlife was busiest early in the century. By the time jazz emerged in the city in the 1910s the Vendome was directed by the Hammond brothers and the theater was offering silent movies with musical accompaniment and an hour-long floor show in the intermissions. The venue is of jazz interest principally for the long connection with it of Erskine Tate, whose Vendome Theater Symphony Orchestra opened there in 1919 and remained the resident band until 1928; Tate returned to the theater in the 1930s. The most important of his sidemen was Louis Armstrong, who was a member of the band in 1926. Among the other jazz musicians to appear there was Fats Waller, who was the house organist in 1927. In the late 1920s, when the success of the Regal Theater was threatening older theaters on the South Side, the pianist Clarence Jones and Armstrong moved from the Metropolitan to the Vendome in an attempt to restore audiences there, but the ploy failed and the decline continued. The theater was eventually demolished in 1949.

——. **Venetian Room.** Southmoor Hotel. Jazz was offered in the hotel's nightclub from at least 1926, when Ben Pollack and his Sunkist Serenaders (later renamed the Californians) began a residency that lasted a year; among Pollack's sidemen was Benny Goodman.

——. **Victory Club.** 644 North Clark Street. It was founded and directed by Werlie Catanese and flourished during the 1940s and 1950s, when it became known as a venue for traditional and mainstream jazz. Among the resident performers employed by the club was Lee Collins, who worked there in 1945 and again from November 1951.

——. **Vincennes Hotel.** See Platinum Lounge.

——. **White City Ballroom.** East 63rd Street and South Parkway Boulevard. It was situated in the White City Amusement Park at 6300 South Parkway Boulevard, and offered jazz for dancing from at least the early 1920s. Among the resident groups during the twenties were Sig Meyers's band in which Muggsy Spanier gained his first professional experience in 1922, the Wolverines (1925), and Doc Cook's band (spring 1927–spring 1930). The ballroom was still in operation in the mid-1930s, when McKee Fitzhugh promoted the dances there.

——. **White's Emporium.** 309 East 55th Street. It opened in 1939 under the ownership of one White in the premises that had formerly been occupied by the Golden Lily. Coleman Hawkins played a residency of several months there from February 1941.

——. **Zeppelin Inn.** South Indiana Avenue and East 31st Street. It was a small venue and flourished only briefly, around 1930, under the management of "Big Boy" Mills. Frankie "Half Pint" Jaxon's quintet was in residence in 1930 and Freddie Keppard's band played there as a guest attraction.

For other venues in the metropolitan area of Chicago see Berwyn, Cicero, and Robbins.

BIBLIOGRAPHY

Chicago

P. E. Miller: "Thirty Years of Chicago Jazz," with G. Hoefer: "Chicago Jazz History," *Esquire's Jazz Book*, ed. P. E. Miller and R. Venables (London, 1947) [abridged edn of three vols., previously pubd (New York, 1944–6)]

C. Sengstock: "Chicago Jazz Landmarks Crumble," *SL*, xi/5–6 (1961), 3

T. J. Hennessey: "The Black Chicago Establishment 1919–1930," *JJS*, ii/1 (1974), 15–45

S. Dance: *The World of Earl Hines* (New York, 1977) [interviews]

D. J. Travis: *An Autobiography of Black Chicago* (Chicago, 1981)

——: *An Autobiography of Black Jazz* (Chicago, 1983) [incl. interviews]

CICERO, IL. **Cotton Club.** One of several establishments named after the famous nightclub in New York, it was owned by Ralph Capone, the brother of Al Capone. Among the jazz musicians to play there were Lucky Millinder (then working as Lucius Venable), who was probably connected with the club around 1928, and Walter Barnes, whose band was resident from late 1929; the Barnes band became a favorite with radio listeners as a result of its broadcasts from the club. The venue closed in July 1930 when the federal authorities prosecuted Ralph Capone.

CINCINNATI. **Doyle's Dance Hall** [Dancing Academy]. Court Avenue and Central Avenue. It occupied premises on the third floor of the building on the north-west corner of the intersection. Jazz was played there for dancing from at least the early 1920s; the Wolverines with Bix Beiderbecke played a three-month residency in 1924, which attracted as many local musicians as it did dancers.

——. **Moonlight Gardens Ballroom.** In 1936 Noble Sissle's band, which included Sidney Bechet, Billy Banks, and Lena Horne, was engaged to perform there; it was the first black band to do so. In the event Sissle was unable to appear, owing to an automobile accident on the journey to Cincinnati, and Horne fronted the band in his place.

COVINGTON, KY. **Look Out House.** This sophisticated nightclub was active from at least the mid-1930s. In the autumn of 1937 Noble Sissle's band, which at that time included Sidney Bechet and Erskine Butterfield, was engaged to appear there for a month.

CULVER CITY, CA. See Los Angeles (metropolitan area).

DALLAS. **Adolphus Hotel.** Jazz was played for the entertainment of patrons from at least the mid-1920s, and bands continued to perform there through the 1930s. Alphonso Trent's orchestra played a long residency of 16 months from 1924, during which time it made highly successful broadcasts from the hotel on radio station WFAA.

——. **Cain's Hitching Post.** It was in existence by around 1950 as a venue for jazz. Sammy Price played a long residency there in the early 1950s.

——. **Tip Top Inn.** It featured jazz from around 1925 when the resident group was Lee Collins's band. New Orleans musicians were in great demand at that time and the Tip Top was regarded as the principal venue for black bands in Dallas.

DENVER. **Navarre.** Built as a school in 1879, the premises were used for various purposes before becoming a restaurant in the 1920s. It flourished as a venue for jazz performance during the 1960s and early 1970s, when among the musicians who played there were the World's Greatest Jazz Band, Peanuts Hucko, and Ralph Sutton. It closed in January 1974.

——. **Tivoli Terrace.** West 32nd Street and Shoshone Street. It featured jazz from at least the mid-1930s, when Hymie Hirschorn was the manager and an engagement at the club was regarded by musicians as the best in the city. The drummer Kenney "Sticks" McVey led the house band from 1934 to 1940; it made regular broadcasts on local radio and gained a high reputation for its supple swing playing.

——. **Trocadero Ballroom.** The venue was managed by Jack Gurtler, who put on jazz performances there from at least the 1960s. In collaboration with the businessman Dick Gibson he engaged a band organized by Gibson, which with varying personnel played at the Trocadero every year between 1965 and 1971. In 1968 it crystallized into the World's Greatest Jazz Band of Yank Lawson and Bob Haggart, and the following year recorded the album *Jazz in the Troc* (WCS 3330) at the ballroom.

DES MOINES, IA. **Riverview Park.** Jazz musicians played summer engagements in the park from at least the mid-1920s. Husk O'Hare's Wolverines, which was led by Jimmy McPartland and included Frank Teschemacher, Bud Freeman, and Dave Tough, played there in 1926.

DETROIT. **Arcadia Ballroom.** Dance hall. Touring jazz groups performed there from at least the mid-1920s. Among the bands that appeared were McKinney's Cotton Pickers in 1926, Paul Whiteman's orchestra in 1928, and Benny Carter's band, which played for a Thanksgiving Day ball on 29 November 1934.

——. **Baker's Keyboard Lounge.** Livernoia Street and Eight Mile Street. It was opened in 1934 by Chris Baker and was managed for 45 years by his son Clarence before coming under new direction late in 1985. Despite its name, it has presented not only pianists and organists but also other leading instrumentalists and singers. Among the diverse performers who have worked there are John Coltrane, Art Pepper, Yusef Lateef, Kenny Burrell, Groove Holmes, Jimmy McGriff, the Modern Jazz Quartet, George Benson, Gene Krupa, Eddie "Lockjaw" Davis and Harry "Sweets" Edison, Bobby Hutcherson, Woody Shaw, and Herb Ellis.

——. **Bluebird Inn.** Frank Rosolino played at jam sessions there in the early 1940s and by the end of the decade it had become the most important venue in Detroit during the heyday of bop, presenting groups every week from Tuesdays to Sundays. From 1949 Billy Mitchell's group, which at times included Tommy Flanagan, Barry Harris, Thad and Elvin Jones, and Pepper Adams, began a long residency, during which it accompanied such guest soloists as Charlie Parker, Wardell Gray, Sonny Stitt, and Miles Davis. This small black-owned venue was noted for its delicious food.

——. **Bowlerdrome.** Barry Harris and Frank Rosolino worked there in the mid-1940s, and later Pepper Adams played at the Bowlerdrome for six nights a week. It is unclear whether this venue is the same as the Drome (see below).

——. **Broadway Capitol Theater.** Around the late 1940s Billy Mitchell led a group that gave concerts on Saturday nights at the theater. Tommy Flanagan was among his sidemen and on one occasion Charlie Parker played as a guest soloist.

——. **Club Juana.** Dizzy Gillespie played a month-long engagement at this venue early in 1951; Kenny Burrell was among his sidemen.

——. **Club Sudan.** It was active in the late 1940s, when jam sessions lasting from midnight to 4 a.m. were held there. Among the participants were Kenny Burrell, Lucky Thompson, and Illinois Jacquet.

——. **Club Zombie.** This was a noted venue in the 1930s.

——. **Drome.** This venue flourished in the 1960s, when Dorothy Ashby and Yusef Lateef held residencies there.

——. **Freddie Guignards'.** After-hours club. It was situated in the basement of Guignards's home, near the Paradise Theater, from which such visiting musicians as Jimmie Lunceford, Earl Hines, Fats Waller, and Art Tatum came to play.

——. **Graystone** [Greystone] **Ballroom.** 4237 Woodward Avenue. Dance hall. It was built by the bandleader and entrepreneur Jean Goldkette in the mid-1920s. Goldkette also managed the ballroom and directed the resident band, the Jean Goldkette Victor Recording Orchestra, making numerous radio broadcasts; among his sidemen were Bix Beiderbecke and Frankie Trumbauer. After a successful residency at the ballroom by the Fletcher Henderson Orchestra, Goldkette wished to engage a black band that would play in a style reminiscent of Henderson's; he chose McKinney's Cotton Pickers, which established a close association with the ballroom from 1926 until it disbanded (for illustration *see* MCKINNEY'S COTTON PICKERS). A number of "battles" between bands were staged at the Graystone, including one between McKinney's Cotton Pickers and Benny Carter's band in 1928 and another between bands led by Count Basie and Stan Kenton in 1955. At one point in the late 1940s, several of the finest young bop musicians in the city had their first opportunity to play with Charlie Parker there.

——. **Klein's Showbar.** 12th Street and Pingree Street. This showbar (in which the stage or bandstand is directly behind the bar) was a rival to the Bluebird Inn (see above); owned by whites, it was comparatively more formal and expensive. Pepper Adams, Kenny Burrell, Tommy Flanagan, Paul Chambers, and Elvin Jones played there, and later Yusef Lateef was resident to 1959.

——. **Mirror Ballroom.** Frank Rosolino was one of the participants in the jam sessions that took place in the ballroom every Sunday afternoon around the early 1940s.

——. **Paradise Club.** It flourished in the 1940s as a dance hall for teenagers; hence no alcohol was served. Pepper Adams, Frank Foster, Barry Harris, Buddy Johnson, and Yusef Lateef played there.

——. **Paradise Theater.** It was an important venue for renowned touring swing musicians in the 1930s.

——. **Parrot Lounge.** In the late 1940s Tommy Flanagan played there with Rudy Rutherford.

——. **Rouge Lounge.** Bar and bowling alley. In the 1950s it was run by Ed Sarkesian, who presented both local and touring musicians. As the house pianist, Barry Harris accompanied Lester Young and Flip Phillips there, and, after leaving his job at the Bluebird Inn (see above) late in 1954, Elvin Jones joined Kenny Burrell as an accompanist to Carmen McRae.

——. **El Sino.** St. Antoine Street. This downtown club was opened in 1947. Paul Bascomb led a group there for seven years from the early 1950s; other notable bands to appear were those led by Andy Kirk, Dizzy Gillespie, Henry "Red" Allen, and Illinois Jacquet.

——. **Three Sixes.** It was a noted venue in the 1930s.

——. **West End Hotel.** It was situated on the far side of the railroad tracks, near the Cadillac Fleetwood plant. After-hours jam sessions (from 2.30 to 7 a.m.) were held there on Saturday and Sunday mornings around the late 1940s and early 1950s. Pepper Adams was among the participants.

——. **World Stage.** Woodward Street near Davidson Street. Theater. In the mid-1950s concerts were presented there on Tuesday nights under the auspices of the New Music Society, for which Kenny Burrell served as both president and concert manager. The society's members, which at times numbered more than 5000, heard performances by many leading young bop musicians, including Pepper Adams, Roy Brooks, Burrell, Donald Byrd, Barry Harris, Lonnie Hillyer, Yusef Lateef, Charles McPherson, Bernard McKinney (Kiane Zawadi), and Lucky Thompson; some of these were recorded for the label Transition.

El Cerrito, CA. **Hambone Kelly's.** 204 San Pablo Avenue. Restaurant and bar. It was in operation by at least the 1940s when Paul Lingle was the house pianist there for a long period. By the late decade it was offering jazz performances on Friday, Saturday, and Sunday evenings; Lu Watters's Yerba Buena Jazz Band, performing traditional jazz, was resident for several years from 1947, and recorded at the club in 1950.

Fonda, NY. **Log Cabin.** Route 5, 6 miles west of Fonda. Roadhouse. The proprietor of this establishment, Allen Armstrong, presented jazz performances from at least the late 1930s. Sidney Bechet performed there from 8 September 1939 to January 1940 with a group that latterly included Sonny White, Kenny Clarke, and Wilson Myers. In spite of difficulties with Armstrong, Bechet returned to the Log Cabin in October 1940 for a further three-month engagement; among his sidemen on this occasion were Wellman Braud and Cliff Jackson.

Fort Worth. **Caravan of Dreams.** Houston Street. Directed by Ed Bass, it has been active from the 1970s as a venue for avant-garde performances of dance, theater, and music, including jazz. Ornette Coleman first recorded for its label, Caravan of Dreams Productions, in 1985.

Hermosa Beach, CA. See Los Angeles (metropolitan area).

Hollywood, CA. See Los Angeles (metropolitan area).

Hudson Lake, IN. **Blue Lantern Inn.** Roadhouse. It was built by Victor Smith on Hudson Lake, between South Bend and Michigan City, and opened in 1922 as the Hudson Lake Casino. After Smith's death in 1926 it was taken over by Jean Goldkette, who renamed it the Blue Lantern Inn (he ran a similar establishment under the same name at Island Lake, near Detroit). Goldkette continued Smith's policy of opening only in spring and summer; in 1926 a unit from his Victor Recording Orchestra, led by Frankie Trumbauer and including Bix Beiderbecke, alternated at the Blue Lantern with Joe Dockstader's Indianans.

Hudson River. From at least the 1930s jazz was played on the steamers that worked the Hudson between New York and Albany during the summer season. Among the famous musicians who played in the bands from time to time was Lorenzo Tio, Jr.

Island Lake, MI. **Blue Lantern Inn.** It offered jazz for dancing from at least 1925, when Jean Goldkette's Breeze Blowers (the nucleus of what became his Victor Recording Orchestra) played the summer season there. Bix Beiderbecke joined the band during that summer. Goldkette later organized further residencies there for his musicians, dividing his band between the Island Lake venue and its namesake in Hudson Lake, Indiana (see above).

Jefferson Parish, LA. **Club Forest.** 407 Jefferson Highway. Supper and gambling club. Situated just outside the boundaries of New Orleans, this club was active by the late 1920s. Among the jazz bands that played there were the orchestra of Louis Prima and Sharkey Bonano (1928) and Abbie Brunies's orchestra.

——. **Suburban Gardens.** Jefferson Highway, near the Huey Long Bridge. Supper and gambling club. It was probably controlled by the mafia. Here in 1931 Louis Armstrong held his only extended engagement in the New Orleans area after leaving the city in 1922 to join King Oliver in Chicago. He performed there through the summer, broadcasting regularly. It became known as the Beverly Gardens perhaps in the 1940s, but neither then nor later was it known for jazz performances.

Kansas City. **Band Box.** See Lucille's Band Box.

——. **Cherry Blossom.** 12th Street and Vine Street. It was opened around 1933 on the site of the old Eblon Theatre and during the next few years presented performances by the most eminent Kansas City bands. The merged bands of George E. Lee and Bennie Moten were resident in 1933, and Count Basie led his Cherry Blossom Orchestra at the club later in the decade. It was also the venue of a spectacular cutting contest between Coleman Hawkins, Ben Webster, Herschel Evans, and Lester Young on 18 December 1933.

——. **College Inn.** It offered jazz probably from the 1930s. Milt Larkin was the resident bandleader there at the turn of the decade and the tenor saxophonist and clarinetist Jimmy Keith led his sextet at the club in 1945.

——. **Cuban Room.** See Milton's Tap Room.

——. **Fairyland Park.** During summer seasons from at least the 1930s jazz was played for dancing in a pavilion in the park. Among the bands that appeared there were Bennie Moten's (resident in 1930–31), the Kansas City Rockets (1932), and Andy Kirk's Twelve Clouds of Joy (1935). From 1940 Jay McShann's big band often performed at Fairyland Park between tours.

——. **Harlem Club.** 15th Street and Paseo Street. Known at first as the El Paseo Ballroom, its name had changed by 1933. Around that time the amalgamated bands of Bennie Moten and George E. Lee moved there after playing at the Cherry Blossom (see above) and were resident until 1934. The orchestras of Count Basie and Duke Ellington engaged in a "battle of bands" at the Harlem Club on 31 October 1936.

——. **Lone Star.** 12th Street. This nightclub was in existence by the mid-1930s, catering for a black clientèle. Its indoor rooms included a bar and pool hall, and dancing and cabaret acts took place in the garden under canvas. Pete Johnson played there in 1937.

——. **Lucille's Band Box.** 18th Street. It was owned by a Miss Lucille, and was in operation by the late 1920s. It offered performances by Kansas City musicians, including Bennie Moten's band, whose *Band Box Shuffle* (1929, Vic. 23007) was named for it.

——. **Lyric Hall.** Jazz was regularly presented there from at least the early 1920s. At the beginning of his career the prominent Kansas City musician George E. Lee led his own trio there for a long residency in the 1920s.

——. **Milton's Tap Room.** It was active from the early 1930s. The singer Julia Lee, sister of George E. Lee, formed a long association with the club, opening there in 1934 and continuing to perform as the resident artist until 1948. She moved from Milton's to the Cuban Room, where she began a residency in late 1950.

——. **El Paseo Ballroom** [Paseo Hall]. See Harlem Club.

——. **Playmates Club.** It was in existence from at least the 1950s. The tenor saxophonist and clarinetist Jimmy Keith was the resident leader there for many years into the 1960s.

——. **Reno Club.** 12th Street, between Cherry Street and Locust Street. It flourished during the 1930s but was closed for tax evasion in 1938. The club's activities, directed by Papa Sol Epstein, were segregated, and separate dance floors, bars, and dining areas were reserved for black and white patrons. Bennie Moten played there in the early 1930s, and in 1935 Count Basie formed a nine-piece group, the Barons of Rhythm, for a residency; it was in this venue that Basie was discovered by John Hammond in 1936. Nightly broadcasts from the club were relayed on radio station W9XBY. In 1938 Jesse Price's big band played there, and the following year George E. Lee, whose career passed through a decline in the mid-1930s, brought his new band (formed the preceding year for a residency at the Brookside Club) to play an engagement at the Reno. The club was as important for after-hours jam sessions by the many jazz musicians playing in the city at that time as it was for the music that was played to entertain the clientèle.

——. **Roscoe Hall.** 18th Street and Prospect Street. Among the jazz musicians who were resident performers at this venue in its heyday in the 1930s was Tommy Douglas.

——. **Subway Club.** 18th Street and Vine Street. In the 1930s it was owned by Felix Payne and managed by Piney Brown. It was noted for its all-star jam sessions, which attracted important musicians who were playing in the bands of leaders such as Fletcher Henderson and Count Basie at other clubs in the city.

——. **Sunset Crystal Palace** [Sunset Club]. 12th Street and Woodlawn Street. Like the Subway Club it was owned by Felix Payne and managed by Piney Brown; it too was a favorite after-hours venue for musicians and it was the site of many cutting contests between such players as Irving "Mouse" Randolph, Ben Webster, Herschel Evans, Dick Wilson, Lester Young, Chu Berry, and Coleman Hawkins. During the mid-1930s Pete Johnson was a resident performer and played here with an octet until 1938. Joe Turner (ii) had one of his first jobs at this club, where he was engaged as a barman and singer.

——. **El Torreon Ballroom.** 31st Street and Gillham Street. Phil Baxter's Texas Tommies opened this venue and became the house band. Among those who led ensembles for dancing there during the 1920s was Bennie Moten.

——. **Yellow Front Cafe.** Jazz was played there from at least 1930. During his stay in Kansas City from 1930 to 1933 Sammy Price played a long residency at the Yellow Front, performing for a brief time with Bunk Johnson.

BIBLIOGRAPHY

Kansas City

R. Russell: *Jazz Style in Kansas City and the Southwest* (Berkeley, CA, Los Angeles, and London, 1971/*R*1983, rev. 2/1973)

N. W. Pearson, Jr.: *Goin' to Kansas City* (Urbana, IL, and London, 1988)

Las Vegas. **Blue Room.** Hotel Tropicana. Like many of the hotels, casinos, and supper clubs in the city it offered popular music and jazz for the entertainment of its patrons. Among the important bands that played there was Count Basie's orchestra, which appeared often in the late 1960s and early 1970s.

——. **Cinderella Club.** It flourished in the 1960s, when Charlie Teagarden, who lived in Las Vegas for the last 25 years of his life, led his band in several long residencies there.

Long Beach, CA. See Los Angeles (metropolitan area).

Los Angeles (metropolitan area). **Ambassador Hotel.** See Cocoanut Grove.

——. **Apex Club.** See Club Alabam.

——. **Aragon Ballroom.** Ocean Park. This venue, close to Santa Monica, was active during the swing era and engaged a number of big bands to play for dancing. Count Basie's orchestra appeared there for a short residency in summer 1943.

——. **Bal Tabarin.** Western Avenue. A large dance hall some way out of the center of the city, it engaged jazz bands from at least the 1940s. Jack Teagarden played there in 1944 and Louis Armstrong at the end of the decade.

——. **Beverly Cavern.** It flourished from the 1940s into the 1970s. At first its repertory emphasized dixieland – the club opened with performances by a dixieland band led by the trombonist Ted Vesely. In the late 1940s it was owned by Sam Rittenberg and Rose Stanman. Among the jazzmen who played there were Jim Robinson, Kid Ory's band (1949), Ward Kimball's Firehouse Five Plus Two, a sextet led by Ben Pollack (*c*1950), and Teddy Buckner, whose band was resident for a long period in the 1970s.

——. **Billy Berg's Swing Club.** Vine Street, Hollywood. This nightclub, one of the most important in the Los Angeles area, was owned by Billy Berg and flourished from the 1940s, when it concentrated on the presentation of swing and bop; Berg had earlier run a club called the Waldorf Cellar (see below). Among the first jazz groups to play at the Vine Street club were one led by Lester and Lee Young (1941) and Benny Carter's orchestra (1943), which was the first big band that Berg engaged. Thereafter, many prominent jazz musicians worked there, including Zutty Singleton (spring 1943), Slim Gaillard (1945–6), Dizzy Gillespie and Charlie Parker (1945–6), and Vic Dickenson (1947–8). On 13 August 1947 Berg presented the official début of Louis Armstrong's All Stars. Other performers who worked for him included Coleman Hawkins, who appeared with Howard McGhee and Boyd Raeburn, Edgar Hayes, Teddy Bunn, the Mills Brothers, Kid Ory, Lucky Thompson, Billie Holiday, and Wingy Manone.

——. **Cadillac Café.** Central Avenue, between 6th and 7th streets. One of the first venues in the city to present hot music, it was the scene of some of Jelly Roll Morton's early activities as an impresario and player during his successful stay in Los Angeles from 1917. He staged shows there, in which both he and the singer Bricktop (Ada Smith) performed.

——. **Calabassas Inn.** A large venue in Hollywood, it was active in the 1960s and 1970s. Joe Darensbourg led his own trio for a residency there in 1970; they were often joined for jam sessions by other musicians, including Barney Bigard, Matty Matlock, and Eddie Miller.

——. **Casablanca.** An after-hours club, it was owned and run by the guitarist Stanley Morgan, father of Frank Morgan; it was in existence at least by the mid-1940s. Its repertory included West Coast jazz and bop; Charlie Parker was a frequent attraction there during his stay in California from 1945.

——. **Century Plaza Hotel.** See Hong Kong Bar.

——. **Ciro's.** Sunset Boulevard. This nightclub staged the first performance by a black group in the locality, when Duke Ellington's orchestra played there for a two-week engagement in 1945.

——. **Civic Auditorium.** Pasadena. The city's principal performance venue was the site of jazz concerts from at least the late 1940s. Gene Norman's "Just Jazz" concerts occasionally used the auditorium, as on 4 August 1947 and 2 February 1952; the musicians who played at these two events included Charlie Shavers, Barney Kessel, Slam Stewart, and Dexter Gordon. The venue also staged a performance in June 1956 by Kid Ory and Louis Armstrong; among the musicians were Trummy Young, Edmond Hall, Barrett Deems, Billy Kyle, and Arvell Shaw.

——. **Club Alabam.** Central Avenue. It was founded (as the Apex Club) by the drummer and bandleader Curtis Mosby in the 1920s. A large, luxurious room, with a spacious dance floor and a bar, it featured dancing and musical entertainment nightly. It became the focal point of the jazz scene in Los Angeles, which in the 1930s and 1940s was centered in this area. Among the musicians that played there when the club's activities were at their height were the Dixie Aces led by the reed player Floyd Turnham and Edythe Turnham (*c*1932), and the bands of Eddie Barefield (1936–7), and Lee Young (during the war years); among the regular members of Young's band were Dexter Gordon and Art Pepper, and Charles Mingus played with it intermittently.

——. **Club Finale.** This was an after-hours "bottle" club (that is, a club to which the patrons brought their own drinks) in the Little Tokyo area of Los Angeles; it was opened by the dancer and vaudevillian Foster Johnson, who ran it as a sideline and sometimes gave impromptu performances to the jazz that the musicians played. Charlie Parker and Miles Davis were resident there in spring 1946, and many of the most prominent West Coast musicians dropped by to hear them and sometimes to play in jam sessions with them; Ross Russell heard Parker play there and contracted him to record for Dial as a result. Johnson closed the club abruptly in the middle of Parker's engagement, but it was reopened shortly afterwards by Howard McGhee and Parker continued to play there into the summer of that year.

——. **Club 47.** Ventura Boulevard, Studio City. This club was opened in the late 1940s by Nappy Lamare and Doc Rondo. It became a popular venue with musicians, who congregated there to hear each other play and to take part in frequent jam sessions; sometimes these were organized but more often they took place informally. The many musicians who played there included Eddie Miller, Matty Matlock, Sharkey Bonano, Zutty Singleton, Joe Darensbourg, and the owners themselves.

——. **Club Plantation.** See Plantation Club.

——. **Cocoanut Grove.** Ambassador Hotel, Wilshire Boulevard. The hotel's ballroom engaged jazz musicians to play for dancing from at least the early 1920s. The drummer Abe Lyman led a fine band there for a long residency from 1924 to 1927. Later the venue took on more the character of a nightclub and among the bands that performed there were those of Benny Goodman (spring 1940) and Billy Kyle (1962).

——. **Concerts by the Sea.** Redondo Beach. This nightclub was opened in 1972 by Howard Rumsey, who had formerly managed the Lighthouse Cafe in Hermosa Beach (see below). Like its predecessor it was an important venue for musicians on the West Coast, though Rumsey presented a somewhat broader spectrum of styles there than at the Lighthouse.

——. **Cotton Club.** Culver City. One of the many clubs in the USA named after the famous establishment in New York, it was active from the 1920s under the direction of Frank Sebastian; it presented not only jazz but fully fledged floor shows. Paul Howard's Quality Serenaders, which included Lionel Hampton, played there for two years in the late 1920s, and when that group disbanded Hampton returned to join the house band, led at first by the trumpeter Vernon Elkins then by Les Hite. Hite continued as the bandleader at the club (except during summers, when he went on tour) until its closure in 1939. Louis Armstrong performed with the band as a guest soloist, first in July 1930 and again for three months in 1932. Among the other jazz musicians who performed there were Ivie Anderson (mid-1920s), McKinney's Cotton Pickers (from May 1931), Fats Waller (June 1935), and Buck Clayton (1936).

The premises later housed clubs called Casa Mañana and the Meadowbrook Club.

——. **Crescendo Club.** It presented jazz from at least the mid-1950s. In June 1958 Count Basie and his orchestra made an important series of recordings there.

——. **Disneyland.** Anaheim. Amusement park. It was opened in 1955 by the film maker Walt Disney. Jazz of various styles is played in numerous locations in the park and big bands regularly perform there. Among the many "environments" is a replica of a Mississippi riverboat, the *Mark Twain*, on which a band of jazz musicians plays New Orleans jazz; the original resident band, called the Young Men from New Orleans, included Joe Darensbourg, Johnny St. Cyr, Mike DeLay, and Harvey Brooks. Among the numerous important musicians who have appeared at Disneyland are Benny Goodman, the singer Monette Moore, Kid Ory, Earl Hines, Streamline Ewing, Nappy Lamare, Jack McVea, and Louie Bellson.

——. **Down Beat Club.** Central Avenue. Two doors away from Club Alabam at the center of the principal area for jazz in the city, the club was in existence from at least the mid-1940s. In spring 1946 Charles Mingus and Buddy Collette led a co-operative septet there known as the Stars of Swing.

——. **Embassy Theater.** Jazz at the Philharmonic used the theater for a single concert on 22 April 1946. The performers who appeared included Slim Gaillard, Meade "Lux" Lewis, and Billie Holiday.

——. **Finale Club.** See Club Finale.

——. **400 Club.** 8th Street. It was in existence by the early 1920s when Larry Shields led a band there. During the 1950s the club featured long residencies by Teddy Buckner's band (1954–7) and an ensemble led by Andy Blakeney. Buckner returned for a further residency in the 1970s.

——. **The Haig.** Wilshire Boulevard. Owned by John Bennett it was a leading venue for West Coast jazz in the 1950s; its publicity officer was Richard Bock, who became the principal figure in the record company Pacific Jazz. The premises were small (they consisted of a converted bungalow) and were suited only to performances by combos; a regular jam session was held there on Monday nights, which attracted many of the most important jazz musicians active in Los Angeles at that time. Among the players who fulfilled engagements at the club were Red Norvo's trio (1950), Gerry Mulligan's quartet (1952–3), a quartet led by Laurindo Almeida and Bud Shank (1953), Shorty Rogers (1954, 1955), Hampton Hawes, Zoot Sims, and Curtis

Counce (1956). Many significant recordings were also made there.

——. **Hangover Club.** Jazz was played there from at least the early 1940s. Bob Zurke led his band for a long residency from 1942 until his death in 1944, and the cornetist Pete Daily was the house bandleader for many years, playing dixieland jazz.

——. **Hollywood Bowl.** Open-air concert arena. It has often been used for jazz performances, and regular jazz concert series have been part of its programs from at least the 1970s; it was the site of the Los Angeles Jazz Festival in 1959–60, and the Playboy Jazz Festival, a mainstream event that attracts very large audiences, takes place there. The jazz musicians and groups that have performed at the Bowl include Teddy Buckner's band, Louis Armstrong's All Stars, Count Basie, and a quintet led by Cannonball Adderley. Art Tatum's last important performance was given there on 15 August 1956 as part of a concert by Jazz at the Philharmonic (under the banner "Jazz at the Hollywood Bowl"); the All Stars also appeared on that occasion.

——. **Hong Kong Bar.** Century Plaza Hotel. Jazz was played for the entertainment of the hotel's patrons from at least 1970. The World's Greatest Jazz Band led by Yank Lawson and Bob Haggart played there in the early 1970s.

——. **Humming Bird Cafe.** 12th Street and Central Avenue. The Humming Bird was one of the principal venues in the city for black performers in the 1930s. Among the jazz bands that performed there was one led by the drummer Curtis Mosby.

——. **Jackson's Cafe.** 1271 East 33rd Street. It was active as a venue for jazz from at least the 1940s. Teddy Bunn and his group, which included Pony Poindexter and Curtis Counce, was in residence there at the time it recorded *Jackson's Nook* (Selective 114) in 1949.

——. **Jade Palace.** Hollywood. A luxurious club with beautiful décor, it was a favorite haunt of jazz musicians, who went there to listen to the playing of the resident bands. Jimmie Noone led a small group there in the early 1940s and Kid Ory's band played a residency in 1945.

——. **Kentucky Club.** Central Avenue. It featured jazz from around the late 1920s. Paul Howard's Quality Serenaders, one of the finest bands working on the West Coast at that time, played a residency there.

——. **Kid Ory's Club.** Vine Street. This club, in a large building on Vine Street, was opened by Kid Ory, with financial help from Billy Berg (see Billy Berg's Swing Club, above), in 1947; the trumpeter Sidney Desvigne, who by then was no longer playing full-time, was in charge of the catering. The venue survived for only a month before the AFM closed it owing to contravention of union rules by Berg at his own club.

——. **Liberty Dance Hall.** East 3rd Street. Taxi-dance hall. Among the groups who played for the dancing there was Mutt Carey's Liberty Syncopators, which was resident in 1927; Carey's sidemen for this engagement included Joe Darensbourg and Minor Hall.

——. **Lighthouse Cafe.** Hermosa Beach. 30 Pier Avenue. It was owned by John Levine, who, on the suggestion of HOWARD RUMSEY, began to present jazz in the spring of 1949; a group led by Rumsey opened there on 29 May, initiating a policy of jazz performances at weekends, which in time was extended; a weekly jam session was held on Sundays. Rumsey continued to be closely connected with the club for the 20 years during which it flourished as a jazz venue, eventually becoming its manager and part owner; in 1951 he formed the Lighthouse All Stars, which performed there regularly and made a number of recordings at the club. The Lighthouse became a leading venue for West Coast jazz; among the important players to appear were Max Roach (1954), Art Pepper (1959), Shorty Rogers, Jimmy Giuffre, and Shelly Manne.

——. **Montmartre Café.** Hollywood Boulevard. Owned by Eddie Brandstatter, this was an exclusive venue for jazz in the late 1920s. Paul Howard's Quality Serenaders played there around the turn of the decade, after they had completed their engagement at the Kentucky Club (see above); by this time the band included Lawrence Brown and Lionel Hampton.

——. **Nap Moore's.** Named for its owner, this café was open 24 hours a day; it became a meeting place for musicians, who jammed informally round the café's piano. Among those who spent their off-hours there in the late 1920s were Lionel Hampton, Alex Hill, and Joe Darensbourg, who were all playing engagements elsewhere in the city.

——. **111 Dance Hall.** 111 West 3rd Street (near Main Street). Jazz was played for dancing there from the 1920s. Ed Garland's band was resident for a long period from around 1927; in 1930 Paul Howard joined the band after the breakup of his Quality Serenaders.

——. **Palomar Ballroom.** Vermont Street, at 2nd Street. It was the scene in 1935 of the sensational success of Benny Goodman's big band, and he returned there in subsequent years; a number of films were made at the ballroom, including Goodman's *The Big Broadcast of 1937*, filmed during his residency in 1936, and *Dancing Coed* (1939), which starred Artie Shaw. Charlie Barnet's band played at the Palomar in 1939, but during their stay there the ballroom was destroyed by fire.

——. **Paradise Club.** Hollywood. It presented jazz from at least the mid-1930s. The big band of Lionel Hampton (later taken over by one of the sidemen, Teddy Buckner) played there in 1936.

——. **Philharmonic Auditorium.** This venue, which seats 2600, was inaugurated in 1906 as The Auditorium and later known as the Clune Auditorium (from 1915) before taking its current name in 1920. Norman Granz launched his concert series Jazz at the Philharmonic there on 2 July 1944 and continued to use the auditorium until early in 1946, when its administration banned the concerts owing to audience disturbances. The performances given under the JATP's banner are preserved on scores of recordings.

——. **Plantation Club.** Hollywood. An important venue for big bands in the 1940s, it engaged Count Basie's orchestra (1944, 1945, 1949) and Horace Henderson's re-formed big band (1945), among others.

——. **Quality Café** [Quality Club]. 12th Street at Central Avenue. Paul Howard formed a quartet to play there in 1924; the group soon became known as the Quality Serenaders and went on to play successful residencies at a number of other clubs in the city. Among the jazz musicians who performed as guests with them at the Quality Café was the singer Jimmy Rushing.

——. **Randini's.** 600 South Western Avenue. During the 1940s it was active as a venue for small groups. Meade "Lux" Lewis performed there as a soloist, and among the combos to appear was Al Casey's trio.

——. **Royal Room.** Hollywood Boulevard. In operation from at least the 1950s, it was owned by Abe Bush. It was known principally for jam sessions, in which as many as 30 musicians might play together; Louis Armstrong took part in one of the Sunday sessions by invitation in 1950. The Royal Room also offered more formal performances – Kid Ory led a band there for a 12-week residency in 1950, and he was followed into the club by the cornetist Pete Daily. Other musicians who appeared there included Zutty Singleton.

——. **Sardi's** [Zardi's] **(Jazzland).** Hollywood Boulevard. It was a popular jazz venue from the late 1940s. Among the musicians who played there were Benny Carter and his orchestra, the singers Monette Moore and Anita O'Day, Red Nichols, Eddie Miller, Pete Fountain, and Joe Darensbourg, who led a band there on Sundays during the time he was playing an engagement at the Beverly Cavern. In the mid-1950s notable appearances were made by Louis Jordan (1956), Dinah Washington (1957), and Lizzie Miles with Bob Scobey's band (1957).

——. **Shelly's Manne-Hole.** Hollywood. It was opened in 1960 by Shelly Manne and became a leading venue for West Coast jazz; Manne's own group appeared there regularly. In 1972 Manne was forced to close the club at its original premises, because the music was disrupting the work of Wally Heider's recording studio in the adjacent building. Manne reopened the Manne-Hole in the Wilshire area of Los Angeles in 1973 but the new operation was short-lived and the club closed for good the following year.

——. **Shrine Auditorium.** Built in 1927, this enormous auditorium seats nearly 7000 people. It has been used for the presentation of jazz from at least the 1940s. Gene Norman mounted one of his "Just Jazz" series of concerts there in December 1947; the musicians who played on that occasion included Barney Kessel, Ernie Royal, and Arnold Ross, and the performance was recorded and issued on the Crown label. A concert by Jazz at the Philharmonic was given in the auditorium on 19 November 1950 and in September 1952 Count Basie's orchestra played there; Stan Getz's performance in 1954 was recorded and released as *Stan Getz at the Shrine Auditorium* (1954, Norg. 2000). The Dixieland Jubilee (*see* FESTIVALS) took place there from 1948 to 1960.

——. **Streets of Paris.** Hollywood. A venue that specialized mainly in solo and small-group jazz, it flourished in the 1940s and 1950s. Jimmie Noone played there in 1943 with a small ensemble, Monette Moore was the resident singer from 1945, and Zutty Singleton led a group at the club after 1945. In the mid-1950s Wingy Manone led the house band for a period.

——. **Strollers.** Long Beach. It was founded, probably in 1955, by Harry Rubin, who had owned several clubs in and around Los Angeles. Shortly after it opened Rubin engaged a quintet led by Chico Hamilton and during its residency at the club Fred Katz played cello between sets; from this conjunction of circumstances Hamilton's innovative "pianoless" quintet resulted.

——. **Suzi-Q.** Hollywood. It was in operation from at least the late 1930s, featuring mostly performances by small groups. Red Callender's trio appeared there around the turn of the decade and Charlie Teagarden led a band for a short residency in December 1946. In the late 1940s when a vogue for blues-oriented styles overtook the jazz scene in Los Angeles Jimmy Witherspoon appeared at the Suzi-Q with a backup group consisting of Benny Bailey, Addison Farmer, and the drummer Pete McShann.

——. **331 Club.** 8th Street. It flourished from around the late 1930s, when Nat "King" Cole performed there. The saxophonist Billy Myles appeared at the club around 1950 and Kid Ory led a band in 1951.

——. **Tiffany Club.** 8th Street. The Tiffany, which was close by the 400 Club, offered jazz from at least the late 1940s. Sharkey Bonano played a residency there before 1950 and in 1956 Shelly Manne brought his newly formed quintet to the club.

——. **Tip Toe Inn.** Whittier Boulevard. In late 1943 Kid Ory led a quartet drawn from his band for a residency there; Bunk Johnson sat in with the group occasionally. The Tip Toe was frequented by the record producer Nesuhi Ertegun and others who were prominent in the Los Angeles jazz industry. Among the celebrity visitors was Orson Welles, on whose radio show Ory's band played in 1944.

——. **Trianon Ballroom.** Firestone Boulevard. Under the direction of Horace Heidt, it engaged jazz musicians to accompany the dancing from at least the 1940s. Joe Sanders led a band there in 1940 and in 1942 Count Basie's orchestra used the ballroom to record its part in the film *Reveille with Beverley* (1943). Basie returned to the Trianon around 1945 and in 1946 Ike Carpenter's band began a long residency there.

——. **Trocadero.** Sunset Boulevard. It presented jazz, in competition with Ciro's (see above), in the 1940s. The blues guitarist T-Bone Walker held a long solo residency there early in the decade; the jazz musicians who appeared included Benny Carter, who brought his orchestra to the club for a week's engagement in 1945, and Eddie South, who led a group there for some time.

——. **Tudor Inn.** Norwalk. It was in operation by the 1960s. Among long-time residents there was the duo of Al Morgan and the pianist Buddy Banks, who played throughout the latter part of the decade.

——. **Waldorf Cellar.** Main Street. Situated in the downtown area of the city, the Waldorf was owned by Billy Berg; its activities had ceased by the time he opened his successful club on Vine Street (see Billy Berg's Swing Club).

——. **Zanzibar Club.** It was in operation by the early 1940s. Fats Waller played his last residency there from early autumn to December 1943.

——. **Zardi's (Jazzland).** See Sardi's.

BIBLIOGRAPHY

Los Angeles

R. Gordon: *Jazz West Coast* (London and New York, 1986)

MILNEBURG, NEW ORLEANS. An incorporated village on Lake Pontchartrain, it was an active resort from the 19th century. It was the site of the Pontchartrain Amusement Park until 1984, and during its heyday (to the mid-1930s) it boasted numerous venues, both public and private, which engaged jazz bands to play residencies or for individual functions. On the pier, for example, were Morgan's Saloon, the Joy Club, Romer's Café, The Inn, Quarelles, Nick's Restaurant, and The Lighthouse, and there were 100 more such venues close by. Its memory is preserved (though its name is misspelled) in the often performed and recorded tune *Milenberg Joys*.

MILWAUKEE. **Crystal Ballroom.** It was one of the many venues in the city where Jabbo Smith played from the mid-1940s, mostly as a part-time musician; he led a sextet there for a residency late in the decade.

——. **Down Under.** This nightclub was in existence from at least the mid-1950s; Jabbo Smith played a residency there in 1958.

——. **Eagle Ballroom.** Jazz was played there for dancing from at least the mid-1920s. Charlie Elgar's band, which included Omer Simeon, was resident in the summer of 1927.

——. **East Town Bar.** It flourished as a venue for jazz in the 1940s. Lil Armstrong played a long residency there as an unaccompanied soloist during the time she was based in Chicago (1940s to early 1950s).

——. **Roof Ballroom.** Wisconsin Theater. The resident bands in the 1920s, which included the Creole Roof Orchestra led first by Arthur Sims and later (as the Wisconsin Roof Orchestra) by Bernie Young, numbered several jazz-oriented musicians among their personnel: such players as Cassino Simpson, Preston Jackson, and Zilner T. Randolph played in the band between 1926 and the early 1930s, and Buster Bailey, Wallace Bishop, and Quinn Wilson all spent short periods as members under Young.

——. **Tina's Lounge.** It offered jazz performances from the 1960s at least. Jabbo Smith played a residency there as a trombonist (playing the valve instrument) and pianist in 1966.

——. **Wisconsin Theater.** See Roof Ballroom.

MINNEAPOLIS. **Cotton Club.** Named after the famous venue in New York, it was open by at least the late 1930s, when Boyd Atkins's band played a long residency there.

——. **Nest Club.** It was in existence by 1930. In 1931–2 Lester Young played there in bands led by Frank Hines, Eddie Barefield, and Leroy White; during this period he also worked with Paul Cephas at the South Side Club.

——. **White House Restaurant.** Jazz was offered for the entertainment of the diners from at least the 1960s. The performances were often given by a solo pianist: Meade "Lux" Lewis was playing a residency at the restaurant at the time of his death.

MISSISSIPPI RIVER. The Streckfus Line of Mississippi steamboats was started in 1884 by Captain John Streckfus and for a time its activities were restricted to the carrying of freight. With the launching of the SS *J.S.* in 1901 (see Arkansas River, above) the line entered the excursion trade for which its name is now remembered. After the death of John Streckfus, Sr. (1925), his sons Joe (*d* 1959), Roy (*d* 1967), John, Jr., and Verne directed the business, which was still active in the 1970s; in 1980 the family dissolved the Streckfus business, selling it to the New Orleans Steamboat Co. and an agency in St. Louis. The Streckfus boats mainly traveled the Mississippi, but their routes also took them onto the Illinois, the Ohio and the Arkansas rivers and some were based in cities not on the Mississippi. Some appear not to have traveled at all but were moored for use as floating clubs or ballrooms. The excursion season lasted from Memorial Day (late in May) until Labor Day (in early September).

Musicians were employed on the pleasure craft from the beginning, though Joe Streckfus apparently promoted this aspect of the entertainment with particular zeal; he engaged the individual players himself, insisting that they be able to read music. Many early jazz musicians gained invaluable experience playing in riverboat bands; the name most strongly associated with the Mississippi vessels is that of Fate Marable, who spent all his professional life in the employ of the Streckfus line and directed bands that at different times included such musicians as Louis Armstrong, Henry "Red" Allen, Jimmy Blanton, Pops Foster, and the Dodds brothers. Other bandleaders to work for Streckfus were A. J. Piron, who played for long periods on the riverboats from 1934 until his death in 1943, Alphonso Trent, Sidney Desvigne, Carlisle Evans, Dewey Jackson, and Charlie Creath.

Streckfus Steamers was not the only concern to be active in the pleasure boat business. Another company that ran a similar service was General Excursion, which was based in St. Louis. It was generally acknowledged by musicians, however, that the Streckfus boats were the more notable for their presentation of jazz.

——. **SS *Admiral*.** Launched around 1940, it was reputed to be the largest inland steamer in the world. It worked out of St. Louis for more than 30 years, and in October 1971 it carried the "Jazz on the River" excursion, at which bands based in St. Louis played to audiences of about 3000. It was later moored at the waterfront in St. Louis, and in 1984 it was converted into a floating mall of shops and restaurants.

——. **SS *Capitol*.** Perhaps the Streckfus boat most celebrated in jazz history, it was launched as a pleasure steamer in 1920 after conversion from the sternwheel packet boat the *Dubuque*. It spent summers in St. Paul, Minnesota, and winters in New Orleans. Among the bandleaders associated with the *Capitol* were Fate Marable (from 1917; see fig.3), Carlisle Evans (*c*1919), Albert "Doc" Wrixon (*c*1921), Tony Catalano (early 1920s), Dewey Jackson (1924–6, 1935), and Fats Pichon (1930s). Bix Beiderbecke played briefly with Wrixon in 1921, and Marable's sidemen included Johnny Dodds, Al Morgan, Amos White, Emanuel Sayles, and Charlie Creath. The steamer was dismantled in 1945.

——. **SS *Island Queen*.** It was owned by General Excursion and traveled between St. Louis and Cincinnati. By way of music on board there was usually a large orchestra that played band arrangements for dancing. Sidney Desvigne led the Southern Syncopators for a long period from the mid-1920s, numbering among his sidemen at different times Al Morgan and the reed player Warner A. Seals.

——. **SS *J. S. Deluxe*.** It was named for Captain John Streckfus in 1919 on its conversion from the sternwheel packet boat the *Quincy*. It worked out of St. Louis throughout the 1920s and was finally taken out of commission and dismantled in 1938. Fate Marable, Dewey Jackson, Charlie Creath, and Harry Dial were among the jazz musicians who entertained on board the boat. It should not be confused with the earlier steamer of the Streckfus line, the SS *J.S.*, which sailed on the Arkansas River.

——. **SS *Majestic*.** It was a large sternwheeler with five decks, capable of accommodating as many as 2500 passengers. Its route took it out of St. Louis and along the upper Mississippi to Winona, Minnesota. Among the jazz musicians who played on board the *Majestic* was Bix Beiderbecke, who served as a temporary member of the resident band in 1921.

——. **SS *President*.** A sidewheeler, it cruised out of New Orleans from at least the 1910s. Beginning around 1918, jazz bands played for its moonlight river excursions; Fate Marable led a group on board the *President*, which at different times included Louis Armstrong, Baby Dodds, Pops Foster, and Johnny St. Cyr. The steamer continued to offer performances of jazz until about 1970, when the repertory changed to rock music. It was still in operation in the late 1980s, when it was docked on the river at Canal Street in New Orleans.

——. **SS *St. Paul*.** Converted from a sidewheel packet boat of the same name, it was put into service as a pleasure steamer in 1917 and was based in St. Louis. In 1939 it went out of commission and was refitted, starting work again in 1940 as

3. Fate Marable's riverboat band aboard the SS Capitol, New Orleans, 1919: (left to right) Henry Kimball (double bass), Boyd Atkins (violin), Marable (piano), Johnny St. Cyr (banjo), David Jones (C-melody saxophone), unidentified saxophonist, Louis Armstrong (cornet), James Brashear (trombone), and Baby Dodds (drums)

the SS *Senator* (see below). Fate Marable played on the boat as a solo pianist in 1918 and the following year led a band that included Louis Armstrong, Joe Howard, David Jones, Johnny St. Cyr, and Baby Dodds. Marable maintained his connection with the *St. Paul*, playing every spring during the 1930s on a cruise up the Ohio to Pittsburgh. Charlie Creath formed his association with the vessel in the 1920s, when his Jazz-o-Maniacs was the resident band; he too returned regularly to the boat in the following decade. Other bandleaders on the *St. Paul* included Dewey Jackson and Sidney Desvigne.

——. **SS *Senator*.** Formerly named the SS *St. Paul*, it was renamed after being rebuilt in 1939–40. In its new guise it had a short career as an excursion craft: in 1942 it was put to use in the coastguard service, and it was scuttled in 1953. Fate Marable was the bandleader on board in 1942, when his sidemen included Dewey Jackson.

——. **SS *Sidney*.** This sidewheeler was in operation from at least 1918, by which time Fate Marable was the bandleader on board; he remained with the vessel until 1921, when it was withdrawn from service, rebuilt, and renamed the SS *George Washington* (see Ohio River). Tony Catalano also played on the *Sidney*, probably in 1919 or 1920. Marable's sidemen included Baby Dodds, and Emmett Hardy worked with Catalano.

BIBLIOGRAPHY
Mississippi River

W. Dobie: "Remembering Fate Marable," *Sv*, no.38 (1971), 44
P. Foster, T. Stoddard, and R. Russell: "On the Boats," *Pops Foster: the Autobiography of a New Orleans Jazzman* (Berkeley, CA, Los Angeles, and London, 1971), 105
D. Coller: "Jazz on the Mississippi River," *Fn*, vi/6 (1975), 4
C. Landrum: "From Quincy's Past: when the Excursion Boat was Queen of the Mississippi," *Quincy Herald-Whig* (14 Oct 1984), 4E
"Operator of Steamship Fleet, Capt. [Verne Walter] Streckfus, Dies at 89," *New Orleans Times-Picayune* (16 Oct 1984)

NATCHEZ, MS. **Rhythm Club.** This dance hall, which occupied premises that had once been a church, was in operation by the early 1920s and was one of the better venues in the South on the regular circuit for touring bands. Walter Barnes's big band was playing an engagement there on 23 April 1940, when fire destroyed the building, killing most of the people inside.

NEWARK, NJ. **Adams Theater.** It was used for concerts of jazz from at least the 1930s and during the swing era, particularly, prominent bands such as those of Duke Ellington, Jimmie Lunceford, Woody Herman, and Stan Kenton appeared.

——. **Alcazar.** This small venue was open from at least the 1930s. In the late thirties the trumpeter and singer Leon Eason led a band there, and Jabbo Smith played a long residency from around 1940, first with his own trio and then (1944) with the band of the saxophonist, trumpeter, and pianist Larry Ringold. In the 1980s the guitarist Bill Johnson owned and managed the New Alcazar, where Ringold also played.

——. **Front Room.** Active in the 1950s, it was an important venue for contemporary jazz. Among the musicians who appeared at this and other similar clubs in the city were Miles Davis, Art Blakey, and John Coltrane. In the 1960s, however, it fell victim to a general decline in interest in jazz and it had closed by the middle of the decade.

——. **Key Club.** It was in operation by the 1950s and continued to be active into the 1970s. It weathered the lean years of the Newark jazz scene in the 1960s and by the middle of the decade was the only important nightclub still open. In the 1970s it became the center for the revival of jazz in the city.

——. **Lynn & Lynn's.** In the early 1960s it mounted regular jam sessions on Tuesday nights; among the musicians to play on these occasions was Johnny Griffin. The club closed around the middle of the decade.

——. **New Alcazar.** See Alcazar.

——. **Paramount Theater.** One of several large halls in the city, built early in the century, it came into its own as a jazz venue in the swing era, when notable big bands performed there.

——. **Pere's East.** It was active as a jazz venue from at least the 1970s, when its weekly jam sessions formed an important element in the jazz revival in Newark.

——. **Pitt's Place.** It was open by the mid-1950s. The trumpeter and singer Leon Eason, whose career was intimately bound up with Newark's nightclubs – in the late 1930s he played at the Park Rest, the Miami Club, and the Alcazar (see above) – led his trio in a long residency there from 1956 to 1967.

——. **Powell's Lounge.** It was one of many flourishing small venues in the 1950s. Some of the most prominent American musicians of the period, including Miles Davis and John Coltrane, appeared there. It was closed some time in the 1960s.

——. **Savoy Ballroom.** Jazz was played there for dancing from at least the 1930s. Besides visiting bands, two local groups, the Savoy Dictators (of which Bobby Plater was a member) and Gil Fuller's Barons of Rhythm, played there regularly.

——. **Sparky J's.** It opened in the 1970s at a time when jazz began to re-establish itself in the city. Along with those of the Key Club and Pere's East (see above), its activities made an important contribution to the revival of the music during that decade.

BIBLIOGRAPHY

Newark

K. D. Wright: "Jazz in Newark, 1930–1970," *JSN*, ii/1 (1980), 14

New Orleans. *Note.* Addresses are given as precisely as possible in the historically correct form. The names of a number of streets have been changed during the 20th century. For the purposes of this list the following changes are important: Basin Street became Saratoga Street for a period, then in 1945 reverted to its original name; Customhouse Street became Iberville Street (*c*1912); Franklin Street became Crozat Street (*c*1912); Howard Street became LaSalle Street; and Liberty Street became Treme Street.

——. **Abadie's.** 1501 Bienville Street, at Marais Street. Cabaret. Owned by Eloise Blankenstein and Louis Abadie, it was active between 1906 and 1917. Richard M. Jones led his Four Hot Hounds in a residency there around 1912, with King Oliver and Wooden Joe Nicholas among his sidemen.

——. **Absinthe House.** See Old Absinthe House.

——. **Amis de l'Espérance Hall.** See Hopes Hall.

——. **Anderson's Annex** [Tom Anderson's Annex]. 201 North Basin Street, at Iberville Street. Saloon. From 1901 to around 1925, it was the headquarters of Tom Anderson, from where he controlled the brothel district of New Orleans. The venue was managed by Billy Struve, who also produced the famous Blue Book (a guidebook to the district), which advertised it somewhat misleadingly as a "café and restaurant." From about 1905 it was sometimes known as the Arlington Annex, after Josie Arlington's whorehouse, one of the three largest and most popular on Basin Street. The saloon offered music on a modest scale, presenting small bands, such as string trios (mandolin or violin, guitar, and double bass); among the musicians who played there were Bill Johnson (i) (before 1908), the black guitarist Tom Brown, and Wellman Braud, playing violin. In published accounts such famous musicians as Louis Armstrong and Albert Nicholas are said to have played at Anderson's Annex, but they actually worked at Tom Anderson's New Cabaret and Restaurant (see below).

——. **Anderson's Café.** 110–12 North Rampart Street. Owned by Tom Anderson, it presented music during the early years of the century until some time after 1912, when the original venue was closed and Tom Anderson's New Cabaret and Restaurant was opened in premises further down the street (see below).

——. **Anderson's Saloon.** See Tom Anderson's New Cabaret and Restaurant.

——. **Antoine's.** Restaurant. Probably the most famous French restaurant in the city, because of the novel *Dinner at Antoine's* by Frances Parkinson Keyes, it has several private dining-rooms, where jazz bands have often performed at functions and parties. John Robichaux' orchestra played there as early as about 1906, and jazz groups have continued to be engaged on such occasions into the 1980s.

——. **Arlington Annex.** See Anderson's Annex.

——. **Artisan Hall.** 1460 North Derbigny Street. It served regularly as a venue for dances and banquets, at which jazz musicians often performed; those who appeared there early in the century included Chris Kelly, Sidney Bechet, Manuel Perez, Big Eye Louis Nelson, and Johnny St. Cyr. On at least two occasions recordings were made at the hall: Wooden Joe Nicholas recorded for the American Music label in 1945, and George Lewis (i) for Decca in 1952.

——. **Astoria.** 235–43 South Rampart Street. Dance hall. It flourished during the 1920s and 1930s and often engaged jazz musicians to accompany the dancing. Among the bands that played there were Kid Rena's and one led by David Jones and Lee Collins, which recorded as the Jones and Collins Astoria Hot Eight in 1929. The venue is variously referred to as the Astoria Dance Hall, the Astoria Ballroom, and the Astoria Gardens.

——. **Autocrat (Social and Pleasure) Club.** 1725 St. Bernard Avenue. Once one of many clubs of its kind, by the 1980s the Autocrat was among the very few remaining active in the city. It was not often used for public dances, but private functions and Mardi Gras balls were held there at which musicians were engaged to play.

——. **Betsy Cole's.** Josephine Street and Willow Street. Betsy Cole for many years in the 1910s and 1920s held lawn parties in the yard behind her house. Jazz bands played there regularly for dancing.

——. **Bienville Roof Gardens.** Bienville Hotel, St. Charles Avenue at Lee Circle. This venue, on the roof of a large hotel, offered jazz for dancing during the 1920s and 1930s. Monk Hazel led the Bienville Roof Orchestra there in the late 1920s and early 1930s; in December 1928 the band, directed by Sharkey Bonano, recorded four sides for Brunswick.

——. **Big 25** [The 25, Johnny Lala's]. Near the intersection of North Franklin Street and Customhouse Street. Gambling house and bar. Established by the beginning of the century, its activities were directed by Johnny (John T.) Lala. It served exclusively a colored clientèle, and became the most popular meeting place for musicians in the red-light district. Big Eye Louis Nelson stated that he played there in Buddy Bolden's band around 1900, and among those who at different times performed or rehearsed in a small room separating the gambling house from the bar were Bunk Johnson and Tony Jackson, and Manuel Manetta and Jelly Roll Morton. By 1940 musicians were no longer hired to perform there and the building was demolished in the mid-1950s.

——. **Blue Angel.** 225 Bourbon Street. Nightclub. It was presenting jazz by at least the early 1970s, since Pud Brown appeared there in 1973. For several years it employed more than one band, offering afternoon and evening performances, but by the mid-1980s the afternoon sessions had been discontinued. It has often employed the city's younger jazz musicians.

——. **Blue Room.** Roosevelt Hotel, later Fairmount Hotel, University Place. The hotel was formerly known as the Grunewald and its nightclub as The Cave (see below). The Blue Room was opened in the 1930s, when the bands that performed included one led by Sharkey Bonano. At some stage in its existence it became known as the New Blue Room and it has continued to present jazz into the 1980s, engaging leading musicians such as Lionel Hampton, who appeared there in December 1987.

——. **Buddy Bartley's Club.** See Toodlum's Bar.

——. **Budweiser Dance Hall.** See Fern Dance Hall.

——. **Bulls Club.** 1913 8th Street, at Danneel Street. One of the more important uptown venues during the early part of the century, it numbered among its members many butchers, and the name of the club probably derives from their practice of leading a bull around in their parades. Music was presented both indoors and in an adjacent vacant lot on the corner of the two streets; the latter served as an outdoor beer garden, at which two bands played, one at each end. The club's programs included jazz from at least 1918, when Chris Kelly and Mutt Carey played there; in the 1920s Kid Rena's band appeared regularly. By around the 1940s the venue had been taken over by the Elks Club, and music was no longer presented.

——. **Cadillac Café** [Cadillac Club]. 342 Rampart Street. It was active from at least the 1910s. Willie Hightower led his band the American Stars there in 1914–15, and in the early 1920s the orchestra of Arnold Du Pas, which included Luis Russell and Albert Nicholas, played a residency.

——. **The Cave.** Hotel Grunewald, University Place. This nightspot within the hotel was suitably dimly lit and decorated with imitation stalagmites and stalactites. It was an important jazz venue from around 1912 until 1926. A band led by the cornetist Johnny De Droit, which included Tony Parenti, played there about 1916. The Fountain Lounge (see below) was also in the Grunewald. The hotel's name was later changed successively to the Roosevelt and the Fairmount, and the nightclub was known as the Blue Room (see above).

——. **Claiborne Theatre.** Claiborne Avenue and St. Louis Street. It was one of several venues owned by Pete Lala that was used for jazz performances. Sidney Bechet and King Oliver played there regularly around 1916, and according to Bechet it was in use as a movie house in 1917. Manuel Manetta stated that at some point Kid Ory had a controlling interest in the theater.

——. **Club Lavida.** See La Vida Dance Hall.

——. **Cooperators Hall.** See Hopes Hall.

——. **Dew Drop Inn.** 2836 La Salle Street. For 30 or 40 years it was the most popular uptown venue for Blacks. Its favored repertory was rhythm-and-blues and many bands and popular entertainers played there.

——. **Dixieland Hall.** 552 Bourbon Street; 616 Bourbon Street. Concert hall. The first of the two venues to use this name opened in 1962. Both presented commercial dixieland jazz, performances of which provided a popular tourist attraction. Kid Howard played regularly at Dixieland Hall in the 1960s.

——. **Eagle Saloon.** 401 South Rampart Street. It was a favorite haunt of the many musicians who played at the Masonic Hall next door on Perdido Street, and gave its name to Frankie Dusen's Eagle Band. It was not itself a venue for jazz performance.

——. **Economy Hall.** 1422 Ursuline Street. Dance hall. It flourished from perhaps as early as 1885 until about 1942; the building was then used as a church, and was finally demolished after being damaged severely by Hurricane Betsy in 1965. Kid Ory played there regularly, and at one time held a lease on the hall so that no other band could perform without his agreement. Among other musicians who played there were King Oliver, who was a member of Ory's band, and Johnny Dodds (both before World War I), and in the 1920s George Lewis (i) and Chris Kelly. The name was revived during the 1970s for a nightclub in the basement of the Royal Sonesta Hotel, at the downtown end of the 300 block on Bourbon Street; it was associated with the New Orleans Jazz Club Museum, which was located in the hotel at that time.

——. **Entertainers Club.** 206 Franklin Street. It occupied premises known variously in the early years of the century as the 101 Ranch (see below), the 102 Ranch, and Phillips Café. The name seems to have been changed to the Entertainers Club by the mid-1920s, by which time the venue was under new management. Around this time Lee Collins's quartet played there and Capt. John Handy led a resident band.

——. **Espérance Hall.** See Hopes Hall.

——. **Fairgrounds.** See New Orleans Fairgrounds Race Track.

——. **Fairmount Hotel.** See Blue Room.

——. **Famous Door.** Bourbon Street and Conti Street. An important venue for dixieland jazz, it was in existence by the 1940s and has continued to be active into the 1980s; among its managers was Hyp Guinle. In the early 1940s Alton Purnell played there, and later in the decade Sharkey Bonano; Pete Fountain worked at the club in 1953 and around 1960 the bandleader for several years was Santo Pecora.

——. **Fern Dance Hall.** 1017 Iberville Street. In the mid-1920s Armand Hug made his professional début there at the age of 15. It was in operation until at least 1940, when Kid Rena led a resident band; by that time the hall was known officially as the Budweiser Dance Hall, a name derived from the beer advertisement outside the door. It was also known as the Fern Café and Dance Hall.

——. **Fewclothes Cabaret.** 135 North Basin Street. Its name was probably a corruption of that of its owner, George Foycault. Opened in about 1902, it flourished as a center for jazz performance until 1917. Many of the leading New Orleans musicians performed there, among them Big Eye Louis Nelson, Freddie Keppard, King Oliver, Baby Dodds, and Sidney Bechet, who appeared in a group led by Richard M. Jones, which also included Keppard and Oliver on occasions, and in the Eagle Band (*c*1917).

——. **Fountain Lounge.** Hotel Grunewald, University Place. It offered jazz performances from at least 1923, when the New Orleans Owls played there. Its activities complemented those of The Cave (see above), another nightclub in the hotel.

——. **Francs Amis Hall.** 1820 North Robertson Street. The hall was owned by an exclusive creole social, aid, and pleasure club; its social activities included dances, organized strictly by invitation only. From about 1940 the building was used as a church.

——. **The Frenchman's.** Villere Street and Bienville Street. In the early years of the century it was a lively venue where the best pianists and entertainers of the brothel district gathered after hours to perform.

——. **Friends of Hope Hall.** See Hopes Hall.

——. **Funky Butt Hall.** 1319 Perdido Street. From 1866 it was owned by the Union Sons Relief Association of Louisiana and was properly known as Union Sons Hall; it was popularly referred to as Funky Butt Hall from the 1890s, when Buddy Bolden played there. It was also known as Kenna's or Kinney's Hall. It played an important part in the development of jazz in the city from the 1890s until about 1910. Besides Bolden, the musicians who played there included the Eagle Band (with Sidney Bechet) and Louis Armstrong. On Sunday mornings the hall was used for Baptist services and in the 1920s it became exclusively a church; it was demolished in the 1950s to make way for new civic buildings.

——. **Globe Hall.** St. Claude Street and St. Peter Street. Dance hall. Situated at the end of the old Basin Canal, near Basin Street, it was active until about 1920. In the period from 1900 to 1906 Buddy Bolden's band frequently played there for dances.

——. **Grunewald Hotel.** See The Cave and Fountain Lounge.

——. **Guidrey and Allen's Upstairs Club.** Perdido Street. It flourished in the 1910s, when among the musicians who played there were Minor Hall and Sidney Bechet.

——. **Gypsy Tea Room.** 1432 St. Ann Street. The premises consisted of a large bar room in the front, and a room behind which was advertised as "the largest nightclub in the South." Jazz was played there from at least 1936 when Kid Rena's band appeared; George Lewis (i) led his band for a residency at the club in 1943.

——. **Halfway House.** City Park Avenue and Pontchartrain Boulevard. It was active as a venue for jazz performance from at least 1914 until 1930. The cornetist Abbie Brunies had a long connection with the club; among the bands he led there was the Halfway House Orchestra, which made a number of recordings from 1925 to 1928.

——. **Hopes Hall** [Friends of Hope Hall, Amis de l'Espérance Hall, Cooperators Hall]. 922 North Liberty Street. It was named after the Society of Friends of Hope, one of many early black social and benevolent clubs in New Orleans. Jazz regularly formed part of the activities there from around the beginning of the century. It should not be confused with Hopes Hall at Burgundy Street and Spain Street.

——. **Hotel Grunewald.** See The Cave and Fountain Lounge.

——. **Italian Hall.** 1020 Esplanade Avenue, near North Rampart Street. A handsome building, it was later converted into an apartment house. The New Orleans Rhythm Kings played for a dance in the early 1920s, and the recording session by the Jones and Collins Astoria Hot Eight for Victor took place there in 1929.

——. **Jackson Hall.** See Longshoremen's Hall.

——. **Johnny Lala's.** See Big 25.

——. **Johnson Park.** Adjacent to Lincoln Park (see below). One of several outdoor sites in New Orleans where jazz was played, it presented performances by Buddy Bolden's band from around 1902.

——. **Kenna's Hall** [Kinney's Hall]. See Funky Butt Hall.

——. **Kolb's Restaurant.** 125 St. Charles Avenue. A well-known German restaurant, it was open from at least the early years of the century. In the 1910s and 1920s the cornetist Johnny De Droit fulfilled a long engagement there; in May 1983 the restaurant's managers mounted a night of music by the group Tulane Hot Jazz Classic to honor De Droit as a special guest.

——. **La Vida Dance Hall.** 1014 Iberville Street; 66 St. Charles Avenue at Canal Street; Burgundy Street. The premises on Iberville Street formerly housed Pup's Café. A number of jazz musicians played for dancing at this establishment, including Lee Collins (mid-1920s), Tony Parenti (1924), and Capt. John Handy, Jim Robinson, and Kid Howard, who all led resident bands for long periods in the 1930s. The venue has sometimes been referred to as the Club Lavida.

——. **Liberty Hall.** Dance hall. The promoter of dances at this establishment was the trombonist Frankie Dusen, whose Eagle Band played here three times a week in the 1910s.

——. **Lincoln Park.** Carrollton Avenue at Oleander Street. A popular colored resort, in the early years of the century it presented performances by the bands of John Robichaux and Buddy Bolden.

——. **Little Club.** Rampart Street near Common Street. Under the direction of Tony Dinapolis, it presented jazz from at least the late 1920s, when the Prima–Sharkey Orchestra, led by Leon Prima and Sharkey Bonano, performed there.

——. **Longshoremen's Hall** [Jackson Hall]. 2059 Jackson Avenue. It was one of the most important halls in the uptown area of the city. Although its function was principally that of headquarters for the musicians' union, many dances were given there from the time of Buddy Bolden, and jazz bands played there regularly. The building was razed in the late 1970s.

——. **Luthjens'.** Marais Street and Almonaster Avenue (to January 1960); 2300 Charters Street (mid-1970s). Owned by Mrs. Luthjens, this small venue flourished from the late 1930s. The clarinetist Big Eye Louis Nelson formed a long and important association with the club, leading a quartet for a residency that lasted from 1939 to 1948. The duo of Billie and De De Pierce performed there from around 1949 into the 1950s and in 1953 recorded for the documentary series on New Orleans clubs made by Center Records (*Billie and De De Pierce at Luthjens'*, 1953, Center 15). The original premises were destroyed by fire in January 1960. The name was revived in the mid-1970s for a bar and bistro. (H. Friedwald: Liner notes, B. Pierce and D. D. Pierce: *Vocal Blues & Cornet in the Classic Tradition*, Riv. 9390, 1961)

——. **Lyric Theater.** 201 Burgundy Street. It was one of the establishments on the TOBA circuit, and presented performances by a number of jazz musicians; Bessie Smith sang there in 1921. A band led by John Robichaux was in residence from 1918 until 1927, when the theater was destroyed by fire.

——. **Mahogany Hall.** 235 Basin Street, at Bienville Street. Brothel. It functioned from at least the beginning of the century until 1917, when legal prostitution was abolished in the Storyville district; the building was demolished in the 1950s. The name was revived in the mid-1980s when it was taken up by the venue formerly known as the Paddock Lounge (see below). The establishment's musical and other activities were directed by Lulu White, known variously as "the Queen of the Demimonde" and "the Queen of Diamonds"; she was the aunt of the composer Spencer Williams. By way of providing background music White employed pianists: Kid Ross appeared regularly, and of the others she engaged the finest were Tony Jackson, Jelly Roll Morton, and Manuel Manetta; Richard M. Jones and Clarence Williams also played there.

——. **Maison Bourbon.** It was in existence by at least the 1960s; Danny Barker began a residency there in autumn 1969.

——. **Mama Lou's.** Off Little Woods Road. It was a wooden building erected on piles and set about 75 feet out from the shore of Lake Pontchartrain. Jazz was played there from at least the 1940s: Herb Morand led his band in a residency that lasted for much of the decade and the trumpeter Louis "Kid Shots" Madison appeared in the mid-1940s. The club remained in operation until at least 1961, but was closed by the time that Hurricane Betsy damaged the area in 1965.

——. **Manny's Tavern.** 3129 St. Roch Avenue. George Lewis (i) played there intermittently between 1946 and 1952.

——. **Maple Leaf Bar.** 8316 Oak Street. It opened around 1970, and became one of the most important venues in the city, presenting music on five or six nights each week. Its programs cover a wide range of styles, including jazz, folk music, and Cajun music.

——. **Mardi Gras Lounge.** 333 Bourbon Street. This nightclub was owned by the clarinetist Sid Davilla. Among the jazz musicians who appeared there were Alphonse Picou and Paul Barbarin; it was probably the only venue in New Orleans at which Lizzie Miles worked in the 1950s, during her last active years.

——. **Masonic Hall** [Odd Fellows Hall]. 1116 Perdido Street. One of several Masonic halls in the city, it was located uptown, in the heart of the colored prostitution district; a number of published photographs mistakenly represent other halls as the Perdido Street venue. It was built in 1850 and consisted of a dance hall, a dining area, and a pool room. Because it was used (and may have been partly owned) by the Odd Fellows Lodge, it was also known as Odd Fellows Hall; it should not be confused with the Odd Fellows Hall on Camp Street, a white venue where the Carnival French Balls, sponsored in part by Tom Anderson, were held. Masonic Hall was a flourishing venue for jazz from the early days of the century, in particular in its function as a dance hall; music for dancing was supplied by Buddy Bolden's band between 1900 and 1906, and later by the Eagle Band, formed by Bolden's sideman Frankie Dusen.

——. **Matranga's.** Franklin Street and Perdido Street. This club, named after its owner, presented jazz from at least 1915; Louis Armstrong, who made his professional début there, was one of its resident performers around that date.

——. **El Morocco.** 200 Bourbon Street. It was active in the 1940s, when it played a part in the revival of New Orleans jazz. Among the musicians who performed there was George Lewis (i), who appeared frequently in the period 1949–51. The club was featured in the 20-minute film documentary *Night Clubs Boom* (1946), in Louis de Rochemont's series *The March of Time* (made by Time and RKO Radio).

——. **Moulin Rouge.** Bourbon Street and Bienville Street. Jazz musicians were engaged to play there from at least 1923, when the resident band was led by the tuba and double bass player Octave Gaspard. Sharkey Bonano performed at the club late in 1939 and from that year until around 1941 Percy Gabriel led small groups there. Around 1954 Kid Thomas recorded at the club for a documentary series on New Orleans venues made by Center Records (*Kid Thomas at Moulin Rouge*, *c*1954, Center 14).

——. **Municipal Auditorium.** Saratoga Street (formerly and later Basin Street). Concert hall. It has been used for jazz performances from at least December 1944, when the National Jazz Foundation arranged a concert by Benny Goodman and various New Orleans musicians. The same local organization, which flourished before the founding of the New Orleans Jazz Club, staged an event there on 17 January 1945, which was broadcast live; the concert presented stars from *Esquire* magazine's 1945 All-American Band, including Louis Armstrong, Paul Barbarin, Sidney Bechet, J. C. Higginbotham, Bunk Johnson, and James P. Johnson. (It was at this time that the name of the street reverted to Basin Street.) From the 1950s to the early 1970s the auditorium was used for jazz festivals sponsored by several local organizations and then for the New Orleans International Jazz Festival (during its early years), which became the New Orleans Jazz and Heritage Festival. It was also used for concerts by Louis Armstrong, the gospel singer Mahalia Jackson, and others.

——. **New Blue Room.** See Blue Room.

——. **New Orleans Fairgrounds Race Track.** Near City Park. In the early years of the century, bands played there for picnics and special events, as well as at the horse races. From 1972 it has been the principal site of the New Orleans Jazz and Heritage Festival.

——. **New Slipper Night Club** [Silver Slipper]. 426 Bourbon Street. Active in the 1930s, it was one of several clubs where Abbie Brunies, one of the city's more successful bandleaders during the lean years of the Depression, played residencies.

——. **Odd Fellows Hall.** The name of two venues in New Orleans: see Masonic Hall.

——. **Old Absinthe House** [Absinthe House]. 238 Bourbon Street, at Bienville Street. This venue (which remains open in the 1980s) presented jazz performances from the 1920s into the 1950s. It specialized in solo and small-group jazz and engaged many outstanding pianists among its resident musicians. Jazz performers who played there included Ray Bauduc (before 1924), the Creole Serenaders (during most of the 1930s), Fats Pichon (regularly in the 1940s and 1950s), and various four- or five-piece bands often numbering Sweet Emma Barrett and the Humphrey brothers among the members (1950s).

——. **101 Ranch.** 206 Franklin Street. Dance hall. Under the ownership of Billy Phillips and Harry Parker, it was one of the largest and most popular dance halls in the red-light district early in the century. In 1909 Phillips bought out his partner and changed the name of the hall to the 102 Ranch (it was also known as Phillips Café and the Entertainers Club (see above)); Parker opened the Tuxedo Dance Hall across the street (see below). Jazz was played for dancing and entertainment at this venue under its different guises from 1902 until the early 1930s; among the musicians who performed there in the early period were Freddie Keppard, Kid Ory, Mutt Carey, and King Oliver.

——. **Paddock Lounge.** Bourbon Street. It flourished from at least the 1940s as a venue for jazz. Papa Celestin led a band in a long residency there from 1949 into the 1950s; the group continued to be connected with the club into the 1960s under the leadership (successively) of the trombonist Bill Matthews and the pianist Octave Crosby. Alphonse Picou, who played with Celestin for a year at the turn of the decade, led his own small group at the Paddock in the 1950s, with Johnny St. Cyr among his sidemen. In the mid-1980s the venue took the name of a former brothel in the Storyville district, Mahogany Hall (see above).

——. **Parisian Room.** 124 Royal Street. Nightclub. Occupying premises above Gluck's Restaurant, it was opened by Tony Almerico in 1948 and remained active as a jazz venue until his death in 1961. Weekly coast-to-coast radio broadcasts were made from the club in the 1950s.

——. **Pelican Roof Ballroom** [Pelican Club Roof Garden]. 407 South Rampart Street. It flourished from the 1920s. Among the jazz groups that played there were one led by Manuel Perez, Sam Morgan's Jazz Band, Sidney Desvigne's Southern Syncopators, and Papa Celestin's band (1939).

The owners of the ballroom ran other venues in New Orleans. References occur in the literature to the Pelican Annex (where Alton Purnell played in the late 1920s), the Pelican Café (where Fats Pichon led a band in 1927), and the Pelican Dance Hall at the intersection of Rampart Street and Gravier Street; it is not clear whether different venues or alternative names for one or more venues are involved.

——. **Perseverance Hall.** 1642 North Villere Street. The hall was the headquarters of the Benevolent Mutual Aid Association (founded 13 November 1853). Much fine jazz was presented there in the early decades of the century. The venue was later used as a church. It should not be confused with the Perseverance Hall (a Masonic hall) at 907 St. Claude Avenue and Dumaine Street (now in Louis Armstrong Park).

——. **Pete Lala's.** 1300 Customhouse Street, at Marais Street. The premises included a bar room in front and a dance hall behind, and operated variously as a nightclub, café, and dance hall. Named after its owner (whose real name was Pete Ciaccio), it flourished from 1906 until 1917, and according to the Blue Book (the guidebook to the black brothel district) operated a nonsegregationist policy. Among the musicians who played there were Freddie Keppard, Kid Ory, King Oliver, Sidney Bechet, Manuel Manetta, Zue Robertson, and Big Eye Louis Nelson.

——. **Phillips Café.** See 101 Ranch.

——. **Poodle Dog.** Liberty Street and Bienville Street. Cabaret. Active in the 1910s, it provided an early engagement for Buddy Petit around 1916; Sidney Bechet played with Petit's band during its residency.

——. **Preservation Hall.** 726 St. Peter Street. It opened in June 1961 in premises adjacent to Larry Borenstein's art gallery (for illustration *see* HUMPHREY), where Borenstein had been mounting informal performances by veteran jazz musicians during the 1950s. Its activities were directed variously by Borenstein and Grayson Mills, and Allan and Sandra Jaffe, and its presentation of New Orleans jazz quickly became internationally renowned. The resident band, known as the PRESERVATION HALL JAZZ BAND, has been led by such musicians as Punch Miller, Kid Thomas, and George Lewis (i).

——. **Providence Hall.** 2241 South Liberty Street. It was probably in existence by the 1890s and offered jazz performances from an early period: it was one of the venues where Buddy Bolden led his band. The building was demolished in 1937 and a church built in its place.

——. **Puppy House.** Jazz was performed there from at least 1939, when Sidney Arodin was resident for a year's engagement.

——. **Pup's Café.** See La Vida Dance Hall.

——. **Red Onion.** 762 South Rampart Street. This low-class nightclub was situated in a dangerous area and was regarded by musicians as an unpleasant venue to work at. Jelly Roll Morton, Louis Armstrong, Johnny Dodds, Sidney Bechet, and Lee Collins were among those who played there. Later, in New York in 1924, Armstrong recorded in several groups called the Red Onion Jazz Babies, the last of which included Bechet.

——. **Rhythm Club.** 3000 Jackson Avenue. A large venue in the uptown area, it offered jazz from at least the late 1930s. Joseph Robichaux' New Orleans Rhythm Boys appeared there in 1938.

——. **Rice's Café.** Marais Street and Customhouse Street. Cabaret. It was situated on the downtown side of the intersection, opposite Pete Lala's; it catered for an exclusively white clientèle. Manuel Perez played there regularly.

——. **Ringside Club** [Ringside Café]. Dauphine Street and Bienville Street. In existence by the early 1920s, it was run by the bantamweight champion prizefighter Pete Herman. The New Orleans Rhythm Kings played there in 1927, and others who appeared during the 1920s included Sidney Arodin and Wingy Manone.

——. **Roosevelt Hotel.** See Blue Room.

——. **St. Katherine's Hall.** South Liberty Street near Tulane Avenue. It was around the corner from St. Katherine's Church (which was at 1509 Tulane Avenue), and was probably connected with the church. It was an important venue for dancing and many jazz groups played there, including those of Kid Ory, Bunk Johnson, King Oliver, and John Robichaux, as well as the Crescent Band, led by Mutt Carey's brother, the trombonist Jack Carey. The entire block was razed in the 1960s to make way for the Tulane University Medical Center.

——. **San Jacinto Hall.** 1422 Dumaine Street. It was one of a score of halls in the city that were hired by social clubs for their dances, and jazz was played there from at least the early 1920s until the 1960s; it was destroyed by fire on 9 January 1967. The hall became noted for the presentation of battles of bands between such groups as Sidney Desvigne's Southern Syncopators (which was resident around 1928) and those led by Papa Celestin and Joseph Robichaux. Other musicians to appear there included Bunk Johnson. It was also used for a number of recordings made by Bill Russell's American Music label; the last of these sessions took place in December 1965.

——. **Silver Slipper.** See New Slipper Night Club.

——. **Snug Harbor.** 626 Frenchmen Street. Nightclub. Opened in the 1980s, it has become one of the city's most important venues for the presentation for jazz in modern styles, both by local and visiting musicians.

——. **Storyville Jazz Hall.** 1104 Decatur Street. Situated near the French Market, this hall opened in the mid-1980s. It presents music on almost every night of the week and offers a wide repertory of jazz and rock styles.

——. **Tin Roof Café** [Tin Roof Dance Hall]. There are conflicting accounts of its name and location. According to Abbie Brunies and other musicians, it was situated at Washington Avenue and Claiborne Avenue in a large old building which by the mid-1950s had become a vinegar factory; Brunies's identification is probably correct, but others give Tchoupitoulas Street and Napoleon Avenue as the location. The Tin Roof was active as a venue for jazz performance until 1910, and later lent its name to the *Tin Roof Blues*, which became a standard after being recorded by the New Orleans Rhythm Kings in 1923 (Gennett 5105).

——. **Tipitina's.** 500 Napoleon Avenue. Nightclub. Active from the 1960s, it has presented both local and visiting musicians playing in a variety of styles, including jazz and rock.

——. **Tokyo Gardens.** Ballroom. It was situated in the resort at Spanish Fort, near where the Bayou St. John runs into Lake Pontchartrain. Among the jazz groups that performed there was a band led by the cornetist Johnny Bayersdorffer, which was resident in the summer of 1924.

——. **Tom Anderson's Annex.** See Anderson's Annex.

——. **Tom Anderson's New Cabaret and Restaurant** [Tom Anderson's Saloon]. 122–6 North Rampart Street. It opened some time after 1912 as a successor to Anderson's Café (see above); owned by Tom Anderson, who controlled the black brothel district of the city, it was run by his son-in-law George Delsa. Among the leading jazz musicians who worked there were Louis Armstrong, who was associated with the club in the early 1920s before he left New Orleans to join King Oliver in Chicago, and Albert Nicholas (1923–4), whose six-piece resident band included Luis Russell, Paul Barbarin, and Barney Bigard.

——. **Toodlum's Bar.** It occupied premises near Perdido Street in the Storyville district, which had formerly housed Buddy Bartley's Club. Its owner, Toodlum, also organized lawn parties and hired jazz musicians for these as well as for work in the bar. Among the performers he engaged in the 1910s were Sidney Bechet and King Oliver.

——. **Tranchina's Restaurant.** It was situated in the resort at Spanish Fort, near where the Bayou St. John runs into Lake Pontchartrain. Jazz was performed there from at least 1918, when A. J. Piron formed an orchestra to begin an engagement at the restaurant, which continued intermittently until 1923 (for illustration *see* BANDS, fig.1).

——. **Tuxedo Dance Hall.** 219 Franklin Street. It was opened in 1909 by Harry Parker, who had been the partner of Billy Phillips at the 101 Ranch (see above). A band led by Papa Celestin, which included Peter Bocage, accompanied the dancing there from 1910 until 1913. On the day after Easter that year Parker and Phillips were murdered in a brawl arising from their business rivalry and the hall was closed by the police. The Villa Café opened shortly afterwards in the same building.

——. **The 25.** See Big 25.

——. **Tyler's.** 5234 Magazine Street. Active from at least the 1980s, it is one of the most thriving venues in the city for the performance of modern styles of jazz.

——. **Villa Café** [Villa Cabaret]. 221 Franklin Street. Situated in the same building as the Tuxedo Dance Hall, it opened some time shortly after the Tuxedo's activities were discontinued in 1913. The jazz musicians who appeared there in its early years included Papa Celestin and Manuel Manetta.

For other venues in the New Orleans area see Jefferson Parish and Milneburg. For riverboats that plied into and out of the city see Mississippi River.

BIBLIOGRAPHY

New Orleans

A. Rose and E. Souchon: *New Orleans Jazz: a Family Album* (Baton Rouge, LA, 1967, rev. 2/1978, rev. and enlarged 3/1984)

R. J. Martinez, ed.: *Portraits of New Orleans Jazz: its People and Places* (Jefferson, LA, 1971)

A. Rose: *Storyville, New Orleans: being an Authentic Illustrated Account of the Notorious Red-light District* (University, AL, 1974)

R. Spedale, Jr.: *A Guide to Jazz in New Orleans* (New Orleans, 1984)

K. Koenig: *Jazz Map of New Orleans* (New Orleans, 1985) [annotated map]

——: *"Just a Closer Walk": the Walker's Guide to Jazz's History in the French Quarter* (New Orleans, 1988)

NEW ROCHELLE, NY. **Glen Island Casino.** Shore Road. Dance hall. It offered jazz for dancing by the late 1920s. The Casa Loma Orchestra was resident there in 1931 and during the 1930s numerous swing bands appeared, including those led by Tommy Dorsey, Jimmy Dorsey, Benny Goodman, Glenn Miller, and Alberto Socarras.

NEW YORK. **Adrian's Tap Room.** President Hotel. It was opened, probably in November 1934, by Adrian Rollini, who also directed its activities; it was situated in a basement room in the hotel and quickly became a fashionable venue, both with New York society and with musicians. Throughout the 1930s Rollini engaged numerous prominent swing performers to play there, including Fats Waller, Willie "the Lion" Smith, John Kirby's quartet, Wingy Manone, Joe Marsala, and Albert Nicholas.

——. **Alhambra Theater.** West 126th Street between 7th Avenue and 8th Avenue. The theater was opened in the 1920s and directed by Milton Gosdorfer, who made it an important circuit venue (originally on the B. F. Keith circuit), rivaling the Lafayette Theater in popularity. He staged variety shows that often included musical acts, and among the jazz musicians who performed for him were Bessie Smith (1927) and Cab Calloway (1931); Edgar Hayes led the resident orchestra there from August 1927 until 1930, when a band led by Emmett Mathews took over. The Alhambra Ballroom referred to in some sources as being at the same location may or may not have been the same venue.

——. **Ali's Alley.** North Greene Street between Spring Street and Broome Street. It was opened by Rashied Ali around 1973 in a village loft under the name Studio 77, which he shortly changed to Ali's Alley. It presented mainly free jazz, and to begin with Ali was the principal performer; once the club became established, however, other major free-jazz musicians led groups there, including Gunter Hampel, Archie Shepp, and Perry Robinson. By 1976 Ali had converted the premises into a bar, restaurant, and club. The venue closed in summer 1979.

——. **Angry Squire.** 216 Seventh Avenue, at West 23rd Street. Bar and restaurant. It opened in 1981 in premises that had formerly been used as a factory. It has presented performances by many prominent contemporary-jazz musicians, including Junior Mance (1981), Hal Galper, Walter Bishop (1983), Barry Harris and Jaki Byard (1984), Scott Hamilton and Harold Ousley (1985), and Dakota Staton (1987).

——. **Apollo Theatre.** 253 West 125th Street. Variety theater. It was opened in 1913 under the direction of Frank Schiffman and Leo Brecher, who had earlier owned the Lafayette Theatre. In the 1920s it staged various shows in which jazz played some part, but it came into its own as a venue for jazz only in the 1930s. The building was bought by Sidney Cohen late in 1933, and structural renovations were set in train. The theater reopened on 26 January 1934 under the management of Morris Sussman and quickly became the center of Harlem entertainment and an internationally known venue.

During the 1930s and 1940s, particularly, the Apollo offered performances by all the leading jazz musicians, and an engagement there was regarded as an important landmark in a musician's career. The great swing bands (among them those of Duke Ellington, Fletcher Henderson, Chick Webb (for illustration *see* WEBB, CHICK), Count Basie, Cab Calloway, and Benny Carter), singers (Bessie Smith, Lena Horne, Ella Fitzgerald, and Sarah Vaughan), pianists (James P. Johnson, Lil Armstrong, and Fats Waller), and jazz dancers and entertainers (Buck and Bubbles and Bill Robinson) all appeared on the Apollo's stage. The theater also played an important role in the discovery of new talent; it mounted competitions and weekly sessions specifically for amateur musicians. Although it continued to be active after the 1940s, its heyday as a jazz venue was over and it later specialized in presenting rhythm-and-blues, gospel, and soul music.

4. 52nd street at night

The Apollo Theatre on 125th Street should not be confused with that on 42nd Street, usually referred to as the old Apollo, which flourished in the 1920s.

BIBLIOGRAPHY

J. Schiffman: *Uptown: the Story of Harlem's Apollo Theatre* (New York, 1971)
T. Fox: *Showtime at the Apollo* (New York, 1983)
J. Schiffman: *Harlem Heyday: a Pictorial History of Modern Black Show Business and the Apollo Theatre* (Buffalo, 1984)

——. **Arcadia Ballroom.** Broadway and West 53rd Street. It was opened in 1924 by the brothers Jay and John Faggin (or Fagin) and flourished until at least the late 1930s. By 1929 the manager was H. M. Corrigan. Among the numerous jazz musicians and groups who worked there were the Mound City Blue Blowers, Frankie Trumbauer and Bix Beiderbecke (1925), Isham Jones, Benny Carter (from 1928), Luis Russell (late 1920s), Sammy Stewart (1930), Sam Wooding (early 1930s), Charlie Turner (1934), and Roy Eldridge (1939). Coleman Hawkins formed a big band for a residency there beginning in November 1939. Jay Faggin also owned the Harlem Uproar House (see below).

——. **Arthur's Tavern.** 57 Grove Street. This club in Greenwich Village presented trios of piano, double bass, and drums in the 1950s, including a lengthy residency by the pianist Loumell Morgan; frequently modern jazz players such as Brew Moore sat in. From the 1960s into the 1980s the repertory centered on traditional jazz. The resident band is the Grove Street Stompers.

——. **Audubon.** A small venue, it offered bop performances in the 1940s. In January 1949 a sextet that included Sonny Rollins, Art Blakey, J. J. Johnson, and Miles Davis played there. The club is celebrated in the title of Rollins's composition *Audubon*, recorded by Johnson in 1949 (Savoy 947).

——. **Bamboo Inn.** Seventh Avenue between West 139th Street and West 140th Street. It was founded in the 1920s by Honey Brown in a building that was under Chinese ownership (hence the name); the Palace Gardens Club (see below) had occupied the premises earlier, but it was closed by the police and the Bamboo Inn opened in its place. Brown played at the club in his own band, which was led by the pianist Willie Wilkins and included the banjoist John Marrero and the trombonist Clyde Bernhardt. Among other jazz musicians who performed there were Jimmy Archey (intermittently, 1926–9), Harry Carney, Ward Pinkett, and Russell Procope in a band led by Henri Saparo (1927), and Elmer Snowden, who worked there before moving to Smalls' Paradise. The Bamboo Inn closed in late 1929 and a new club, the Dunbar Palace, took over the premises.

——. **Bamville Club.** 65 West 129th Street, near Lenox Avenue. It opened in 1942 in premises that had formerly housed the Rendezvous Cabaret (see below). It took its name from the title of the successful show *In Bamville* by Noble Sissle and Eubie Blake.

——. **Band Box.** 161 West 131st Street, between Seventh Avenue and Lenox Avenue. It was active during the late 1920s in premises on the second floor of a building that contained several rehearsal rooms; it was directed by the cornet player Addington Major, who had earlier played with Mamie Smith. The Band Box became a popular after-hours venue with musicians playing engagements elsewhere in the city; among those who played in the impromptu jam sessions there was Jabbo Smith.

——. **Bandbox.** Near Broadway north of 52nd Street. A basement venue close to Birdland, it was opened in summer 1953. During its short existence (it lasted only a matter of months) it engaged a number of prominent jazz musicians to lead bands for short residencies; they included Sidney Bechet (with Herb Flemming, Panama Francis, and Dick Wellstood), Earl Hines, Muggsy Spanier, Count Basie, and Machito. Art Tatum also played there.

——. **Barron's Club** [Barron Wilkins' Club]. 2259 Seventh Avenue, at West 134th Street. It was opened by Barron Wilkins at this location around 1915 and was one of the first large clubs in Harlem. James P. Johnson appeared around 1918 and Mamie Smith sang there before 1920, but it enjoyed its best years in the early to mid-1920s; among the musicians whom Wilkins engaged were Sam Wooding and his Society Syncopators (early 1920s), Duke Ellington (as a solo pianist, 1923), the Washingtonians led by Elmer Snowden (1923), and Joe Turner (i) with Hilton Jefferson. The club's activities seem to have ceased around the time of Wilkins's death in the mid-decade.

——. **Basin Street.** Broadway and West 51st Street. Situated in the Roseland Theater building, it was active in the early 1950s under the direction of Ralph Watkins. Buck Clayton (1953–4) and Erroll Garner (1954–5) were among the musicians who played there. The club had closed by 1959 and the building was eventually demolished to make way for the City Squire Motel.

——. **Basin Street East.** 137 East 48th Street. It was founded as the Casa Cugat in 1959, after the closure of Basin Street, and was managed by Ralph Watkins. It flourished into the 1960s, engaging some of the most important names in jazz of the day, including Lionel Hampton, Dicky Wells, and Rex Stewart (all 1959), Erroll Garner (1960–61), Count Basie (1962, 1964), and Duke Ellington (1965); Louis Armstrong was also frequently heard there.

——. **Bechet's.** 1319 Third Avenue, at East 76th Street. It was active for a short period in the early 1980s as a venue for traditional jazz and swing. Among the musicians who played there were Kenny Davern and Warren Vaché.

——. **Bemelmans Bar.** Hotel Carlyle, Madison Avenue at East 76th Street. One of the several venues within the hotel to offer music for the entertainment of patrons, it was active as a jazz lounge by the early 1970s. It has presented mostly solo performers, notably Marian McPartland (from 1974) and Barbara Carroll (from 1976) – both of whom formed lasting connections with the venue and continued to appear on a regular basis into the late 1980s – and George Shearing (from 1984).

——. **Birdland.** 1678 Broadway, north of 52nd Street. It occupied premises that had earlier housed clubs called the Ebony (in the late 1920s), the Ubangi, and the Clique (1948–9). It took its name from Charlie Parker's nickname "Bird" and opened on 15 December 1949 with Parker playing. Under the direction of Morris Levy it became known as one of the foremost venues for bop, and offered performances by all the leading players in the style; Parker appeared there regularly (for illustration *see* PARKER, CHARLIE, fig.2), and the club also became Count Basie's New York headquarters during the 1950s. From the early days Birdland maintained its own radio wire and booth (nationwide broadcasts were later made from the club in conjunction with NBC); the resident disc jockey was the renowned Symphony Sid (Torin). Many of the broadcasts were also recorded and later issued on record labels owned by Boris Rose. Numerous other recordings were made at the club, including one in 1955 at which Basie recorded George Shearing's composition *Lullaby of Birdland*; performances given in 1963 by John Coltrane's quartet, which was resident at the club for several periods from 1963 to 1965, were recorded and issued as the highly acclaimed album *Live at Birdland* (Imp. 50).

Birdland's fortunes declined in the 1960s and the premises were eventually taken over by the rhythm-and-blues and rock-and-roll singer Lloyd Price, who opened the Turntable there. But the venue's old name continued to be celebrated, largely through the enormous popularity of Joe Zawinul's composition *Birdland*, which was recorded by Weather Report (1976) as an instrumental piece and was later supplied with lyrics by Manhattan Transfer.

——. **Black Cat.** West Broadway. It was active during the 1930s and presented jazz performances by many leading bands and musicians. Kenny Clarke's quintet, one of the members of which was Freddie Green, played there in 1937.

——. **Blue Note.** 131 West 3rd Street, near Sixth Avenue. It opened in 1981 and quickly established itself as an important venue for mainstream jazz and bop, offering major musicians the opportunity to play residencies in a club ambience. Numerous well-known players have appeared there, including Dizzy Gillespie, Tal Farlow, Oscar Peterson, Gerry Mulligan, Johnny Griffin and Eddie "Lockjaw" Davis, Toshiko Akiyoshi, Jaco Pastorius, the Modern Jazz Quartet, Phil Woods, and Illinois Jacquet.

——. **Blue Room.** Lincoln Hotel, Eighth Avenue at West 44th Street. This small venue within the hotel engaged combos, solo performers, and big bands; Count Basie played three extended engagements there between 1943 and 1945.

——. **Boomer's.** 340 Bleecker Street, at Christopher Street. Established in 1971, it specialized in the presentation of bop and soul jazz, offering performances by Barry Harris, Junior Mance, Joe Newman, Junior Cook, Cedar Walton, and Woody Shaw, among others; Walton recorded there in 1973 (*A Night at Boomer's*, Muse 5010, 5022). It closed in 1977.

——. **Bop City.** 1619 Broadway, at West 49th Street. It opened in 1948, but it was soon overshadowed by the nearby Birdland, which was founded the following year, and it survived only into the early 1950s. The club's activities were directed briefly by Ralph Watkins, who promoted programs of bop, swing, traditional jazz, rhythm-and-blues, and pop music there; among the jazz musicians to appear were Fletcher Henderson (1948), Artie Shaw (1949), Mary Lou Williams (early 1950s), and Louis Armstrong's All Stars, who gave a number of successful performances.

——. **Bottom Line.** 15 West 4th Street, at Mercer Street. In spacious premises in Greenwich Village, it was opened in 1974 as a rock and folk club, though jazz was occasionally presented there from the beginning – Grover Washington, Jr., appeared in 1974 and Charles Mingus also worked there in the mid-1970s. In the 1980s jazz has formed a small but constant element of the repertory, and performers have included Sun Ra and Dexter Gordon (both 1980), Andrew Cyrille and Lester Bowie (both

1983), Sonny Rollins (1984), Ralph Towner, John Abercrombie and Makoto Ozone (1985), and John Scofield (1987).

——. **Bradley's.** 70 University Place, at East 11th Street. Piano bar. Named for its owner, it flourished as a venue for mainstream jazz and bop from the 1970s into the late 1980s. It has specialized in the presentation of duos consisting of piano and double bass, piano and guitar, or guitar and double bass. Among those who have appeared there are the pianists Cedar Walton, Duke Jordan, Barry Harris, Jimmie Rowles, Tommy Flanagan, JoAnne Brackeen, Hank Jones, and Kirk Lightsey, and the double bass players Red Mitchell, George Mraz, and Calvin Hill.

——. **Breakfast Club.** See Lenox Club.

——. **Brittwood.** 594 Lenox Avenue, at West 140th Street. Bar and grill. It offered jazz from around 1932 to 1942. Among the musicians who played residencies there were the pianist Willie Gant, Frankie Newton, Pete Brown, and Clyde Hart; the house pianist for a considerable period was Don Frye.

——. **Broadway Joe's.** 315 West 46th Street, near Eighth Avenue. Bar. It offered jazz performances from around 1980; Warren Vaché played a residency there in 1983.

——. **Café Bohemia.** 15 Barrow Street. Located in premises formerly occupied by the Pied Piper (see below), it was owned by Jimmy Giarofolo and opened in the spring of 1955 with Oscar Pettiford as director of music. Pettiford himself led a band there, and it was the site of Cannonball Adderley's New York début in 1955. The name of the club is commemorated in Kenny Clarke's tune *Bohemia after Dark*, recorded on the album of the same name (1955, Savoy 12017) with Adderley among the sidemen.

——. **Café Carlyle.** Hotel Carlyle, Madison Avenue at East 76th Street. Like the rather less well-known Bemelmans Bar in the Hotel Carlyle (see above), the Café Carlyle specializes in presenting solo pianists, duos, and small groups. The performer most closely associated with the club is the pianist Bobby Short, who first appeared there in the 1970s and continued to do so into the late 1980s; others who have played extended residencies are Marian McPartland (1979–82), George Shearing and Brian Torff (1979–81), and Joe Bushkin (1983).

——. **Café Pierre.** Pierre Hotel, Fifth Avenue at East 61st Street. Restaurant. This venue within the hotel offered jazz from at least the late 1970s. Bucky Pizzarelli played there regularly between 1979 and 1983, as did Hank Jones.

——. **Café Society (Downtown).** 2 Sheridan Square. It opened in January 1939 under the direction of Barney Josephson, who presented Billie Holiday (in one of her most important engagements), Frankie Newton's band, and the Boogie-woogie Trio of Albert Ammons, Pete Johnson, and Meade "Lux" Lewis (making their New York nightclub début). Lena Horne followed Holiday into the club, remaining until 1941. Among other jazz musicians who appeared there were James P. Johnson (June 1940), Kenny Kersey (*c*1940), Teddy Wilson (1941), Lee Young's sextet (September 1942), Eddie Heywood's sextet (mid-1940s), J. C. Heard (1946), and Hayes Alvis, Art Tatum, and Sarah Vaughan (all *c*1947). Fletcher Henderson played his last engagement there, leading a sextet in 1950. The club also staged jam sessions in 1941, directed by George Simon and Leonard Feather.

——. **Café Society (Uptown).** 128 East 58th Street. Following the success of his downtown venue, in October 1940 Barney Josephson opened a second club uptown, between Lexington and Third avenues on East 58th Street. A number of musicians played at both Josephson's clubs, among them Edmond Hall, who led a sextet (1944–6), and Mary Lou Williams (1944–8). Those who appear to have played only at the uptown venue include John Kirby, Mildred Bailey, and Count Basie.

——. **Café Zanzibar.** See Zanzibar.

——. **Capitol Palace.** 575 Lenox Avenue, between West 139th Street and West 140th Street. Owned by Johnny Powell, it was opened in 1922 under the managership of Rudolph Brown. Among the musicians who played there were Fats Waller (early 1920s), Willie "the Lion" Smith (1920s), the Broadway Syncopators led by the reed player Billy Paige (1924), Lizzie Miles (1926), Cliff Jackson (late 1920s), and the banjoist Bernie Robinson (1927). The Capitol Palace closed in 1929 and the venue reopened as the Saratoga Club (see below).

——. **Carlos I.** 432 Sixth Avenue, at West 10th Street. Restaurant. It offered jazz performances for the entertainment of diners from the 1980s. The jazz musicians who have appeared there include Chico Freeman, Bobby Watson, Benny Carter, David Murray, and Clark Terry.

——. **Carnegie Hall.** West 57th Street and Seventh Avenue. Concert hall. It opened on 5 May 1891 and has offered performances in all styles of music by musicians from all over the world to audiences that can number nearly 3000. Concerts related to jazz and its origins have been given there from the first years of the 20th century. From around 1912 to 1914 James Reese Europe organized events in aid of the Clef Club, which aimed to promote black performers. A number of commemorative and celebratory concerts have taken place in the hall. In 1928 a tribute to W. C. Handy featured James P. Johnson and Fats Waller. The most notable event of this kind was the first "From Spirituals to Swing" concert (23 December 1938), organized by John Hammond in memory of Bessie Smith. Among the musicians who participated were Sidney Bechet, who played in a sextet with James P. Johnson, Jo Jones, Tommy Ladnier, Walter Page, and Dan Minor; appearances by the boogie-woogie pianists Meade "Lux" Lewis, Albert Ammons, and Pete Johnson inspired a general kindling of interest in the boogie-woogie style. The great impact made by Hammond's first venture led to the staging of a second event in 1939 (24 December), and in 1955 Count Basie adapted Hammond's title for his concert "Spirituals to Jazz Hour" on 6 May; Hammond presented a further "Spirituals to Swing" concert in 1967. The hall was also used regularly between 1949 and 1953 for performances in Norman Granz's Jazz at the Philharmonic series.

Many of the greatest jazz musicians have appeared at Carnegie Hall, which has been at the center of the presentation of jazz as a concert music. Benny Goodman's first performance there (16 January 1938) was highly acclaimed and was brought to a wide audience through the later release of a number of recordings; Goodman returned to the hall on 17 January 1978 to celebrate the 40th anniversary of the original concert, and in 1988 its 50th anniversary was marked by a re-creation of the first program by a big band led by Bob Wilber. Duke Ellington's orchestra played his suite *Black, Brown and Beige* on 23 January 1943, and gave six further concerts between 1943 and 1948. In March 1946 Woody Herman and his Herd gave the first performance of the *Ebony Concerto*, written for Herman by Igor Stravinsky. Charlie Parker established a link with the venue in the late 1940s and his numerous performances between 1949 and 1954 were often broadcast. Important events from the 1960s onwards have included a concert given by Miles Davis on 19 May 1961 in which his quintet was accompanied by Gil Evans's orchestra (recorded and issued as *Miles Davis at Carnegie Hall*, Col. CS8612), a performance by John Coltrane's quartet (1961), and Charles Mingus's concert on 19 January 1974. The presentation of leading figures of the jazz world has continued into the 1980s, when Jean-Luc Ponty was among those who played in the hall. Carnegie Hall also became one of the principal venues for the Newport Jazz Festival after its move to New York in 1972 (*see* FESTIVALS).

——. **Carnegie Tavern.** 165 West 56th Street. Restaurant. It was in existence by the late 1970s. Ellis Larkins performed there regularly from 1979 to 1985, when its name was changed to the Chinese Tea Room.

——. **The Carousel.** See Downbeat.

——. **Casa Cugat.** See Basin Street East.

——. **Central Plaza.** 111 Second Avenue. Dance hall complex. The building, owned by Bernie Birns, contained five separate ballrooms on five floors, the largest of which was used for jam sessions and held an audience of 700. Regular jazz concerts were staged at this establishment every Friday and Saturday night under the direction of Jack Crystal (the manager of Milt Gabler's Commodore Music Shop), and from the late 1940s into the 1960s Central Plaza was an important venue for traditional and mainstream jazz in the city. Numerous prominent jazz musicians appeared there, including Willie "the Lion" Smith, Roy Eldridge, Jo Jones, and Sidney Bechet, who played at a jam session organized by Gabler on 21 January 1949 and from December of that year gave a series of weekly performances. Bechet was also among the many players who made guest appearances in the 1950s and 1960s; others included Wild Bill Davison, J. C. Higginbotham, Dick Wellstood, Zutty Singleton, Panama Francis, Buck Clayton, Eldridge, Charlie Shavers, Hot Lips Page, Coleman Hawkins, James P. Johnson, Henry "Red" Allen, Vic Dickenson, Herb Flemming, Russell Moore, Ralph Sutton, and Sammy Price. Central Plaza was used by the producer Roger Tilton as the location for the film *Jazz Dance* (1954), which includes performances by Willie "the Lion" Smith, Pops Foster, George Wettling, Jimmy McPartland, Pee Wee Russell, and Jimmy Archey.

——. **Childs' Paramount.** Times Square at Broadway and West 48th Street. It occupied premises earlier used as the Cinderella Ballroom (see below) and was active as a venue for jazz in the late 1940s and early 1950s. Wilbur De Paris's band, which included Buster Bailey and Sidney De Paris, was resident there in 1948–9.

——. **Chinese Tea Room.** See Carnegie Tavern.

——. **Cinderella Ballroom.** Times Square at Broadway and West 48th Street. It was established in September 1923 by Robert Blum and the Joseph brothers. Between September and November 1924 the Wolverines (with Bix Beiderbecke) played there, and from early 1925 Tony Sbarbaro led the Original Dixieland Jazz Band in a residency. The premises later housed a club known as Childs' Paramount (see above).

——. **Cinderella Club.** It is unclear whether this nightclub, which flourished in the 1940s and 1950s, occupied the same premises as the Cinderella Ballroom (see above). The jazz musicians who appeared there included Cliff Jackson, who led his own trio in the early 1940s, Shirley Clay (1944), and the trumpeter Harvey Davis, whose band (which included Sonny White and Herb Hall) played a long residency from 1947 to 1954.

——. **Ciro's Club.** Probably named for the prestigious restaurant clubs established in London and Paris in the 1910s, it was in operation from the early 1920s. In the mid-decade it engaged a number of important jazz musicians, including Blanche Calloway and Duke Ellington's Washingtonians.

——. **The Clique.** 1678 Broadway, north of 52nd Street. It was opened in December 1948 by Sammy Kay and Irving Alexander in premises earlier occupied by the Ebony club (see below). During its short existence it engaged some notable performers, including a sextet led by Lennie Tristano. The operation failed in 1949 and Birdland opened in the venue late that year (see above).

——. **Club Alabam.** 216 West 44th Street, between Seventh Avenue and Eighth Avenue. It was situated beneath the Nora Baye Theater in basement premises that had formerly housed the Little Club (from at least 1921 until April 1923) and the Club Balagan, which specialized in the presentation of Russian music. It opened in 1923 or 1924, and in the first few years of its existence offered performances by notable jazz musicians, including Fletcher Henderson, whose ten-piece band accompanied the singer Edith Wilson (1924), Lovie Austin, Sam Wooding and Garvin Bushell (early 1925), and Jimmy Wade (1927).

——. **Club Balagan.** See Club Alabam.

——. **Club Basha.** 2493 Seventh Avenue at West 145th Street. Owned and run by Sidney Bechet and a partner, its name was derived from Bechet's surname (in the corrupt pronunciation used by his New York friends). The club opened in summer 1925 in basement premises that in the preceding year had housed a venue called Hermit's End. Bechet led the house band, which included Johnny Hodges and Tommy Benford, and his enterprise quickly became a success; however, owing to a quarrel with his fellow manager, Bechet withdrew and by September 1925 was on his way to Europe. The club continued to prosper at least into 1926.

——. **Club Condon.** See Eddie Condon's.

——. **Club Deluxe.** See Cotton Club.

——. **Club 18.** 18 West 52nd Street; 20 West 52nd Street. Owned by Jack White, it flourished as a venue for burlesque shows and comedy acts. Jack Purvis led a quartet there in 1935 but the club is principally of jazz interest for the long residency (1935–44) played by Frank Froeba's band.

——. **Club Riviera.** See Riviera Club.

——. **Club Samoa.** 62 West 52nd Street. It was situated in the building where the Onyx club had premises between 1937 and 1939 (see below). Active as a venue for jazz in the early 1940s, it was owned by Leo Bernstein and directed by Henry Fink. Elmer Snowden led a trio there around 1940. From 1943 into the 1950s it operated as a striptease club.

——. **Club Zanzibar.** See Zanzibar.

——. **Cocoanut Grove.** 253 West 125th Street. It operated for a period around 1930 in a room in the basement of the Apollo Theatre; its owner and manager was Joe Ward. Louis Armstrong performed there from February 1930. The venue was later known as the Rathskeller, and eventually it reverted to use as a rehearsal room.

——. **College Arms Cabaret.** See College Inn.

——. **College Inn.** Coney Island. Situated in a popular resort in Brooklyn it was an early venue for jazz in the area. George Baquet worked there between 1916 and 1923. In 1915 Ted Lewis played at the College Arms Cabaret, which may be the same venue.

——. **Condon's.** See Eddie Condon's.

——. **Connie's Inn.** 2221 Seventh Avenue, at West 131st Street (to 1933); 200 West 48th Street (1933–6). The Seventh Avenue venue, which consisted of basement premises next door to the Lafayette Theatre, had earlier functioned as the Shuffle Inn; this opened in November 1921 and was directed by Jack Goldberg. In June 1923 Connie and George Immerman opened Connie's Inn there, with performances by Wilbur Sweatman's band, which included Coleman Hawkins. From September 1923 until February 1926 the house band was led by the violinist Leroy Smith, and thereafter until late 1927 by the clarinetist and saxophonist Allie Ross, with whom Zutty Singleton later played; in 1929 the pianist Leroy Tibbs was in residence there.

Connie's Inn enjoyed its greatest success in the 1920s and early 1930s and established a strong rivalry for audiences and performers with the Cotton Club. The numerous important groups engaged to play at the club included Horace Henderson's Dixie Stompers (late 1920s), and bands led by Luis Russell (late 1920s, 1932), Louis Armstrong (1929–30), Fletcher Henderson (November 1930 into 1931), Fats Waller (1931), and Don Redman (1932–*c*1935); in the early 1930s a number of performances were broadcast from the club on radio station WBC. In 1935–6 the revue *Stars over Broadway*, which featured Fats Waller and Billie Holiday among others, was staged there. In 1933 Connie's Inn moved downtown to 200 West 48th Street, a building formerly occupied by the Palais Royal. It apparently continued in operation until some time in 1936, since the Cotton Club took over the premises in September of that year (see below).

——. **Cookery.** 21 University Place, at East 8th Street. It was owned by Barney Josephson, who had formerly run the celebrated Café Society clubs (see above). Originally opened as a restaurant, it offered music from the early 1970s and quickly became a flourishing venue for jazz performance. It specialized in solo and small-group jazz, and among the important performers to appear there were Mary Lou Williams (1970–71, 1976), Blossom Dearie, Helen Humes, Jimmie Rowles, Sammy Price (1971), Teddy Wilson (1973, 1983), Alberta Hunter (1977), and Carrie Smith (1984).

——. **Cotton Club.** 644 Lenox Avenue, at West 142nd Street (to 16 February 1936); 200 West 48th Street (September 1936 – 10 June 1940). The venue on Lenox Avenue was first opened in 1920 as the Club Deluxe, under the ownership of the former heavyweight boxing champion Jack Johnson. Owney Madden took it over and in 1922 changed its name to the Cotton Club; the club's manager in the early 1920s was Don Healy and the stage manager was Herman Stark. After race riots in Harlem in 1935, the area was considered unsafe for Whites (who formed the Cotton Club's clientèle) and the club was forced to close (16 February 1936). It reopened in September 1936 downtown on West 48th Street, in premises that had formerly housed the Palais Royal and Connie's Inn (1933–6); the Cotton Club continued to operate at this location until June 1940.

The Cotton Club was the most famous of the city's nightclubs in the 1920s and 1930s, attracting an audience that often included the cream of New York society. Its glittering revues provided a medium for performances by the most prominent jazz musicians of the day, and the club's activities were brought to a wide audience by frequent broadcasts. The house band when the venue first opened was Andy Preer's Cotton Club Syncopators; after Preer's death in 1927 Duke Ellington's orchestra was engaged and its residency became the most celebrated in the club's history, lasting until 1931. Cab Calloway and his Missourians, who had first appeared with great success in 1931, then took over, and Calloway's time as the Cotton Club's bandleader (which extended to 1934, when Jimmie Lunceford succeeded him) was to make his reputation. Both Ellington and Calloway returned after the club moved downtown. Most of the principal jazz musicians, singers, and dancers of the period appeared at the Cotton Club at some stage, including Louis Armstrong, Ethel Waters, Ivie Anderson, Bill Robinson, and the Nicholas Brothers. The heyday of the club's existence was re-created in Francis Ford Coppola's film *The Cotton Club* (1984). (J. Haskins: *The Cotton Club*, New York, 1977)

——. **Count Basie's (Club)** [Count Basie's Lounge]. 2245 Seventh Avenue, at West 132nd Street. A small, comfortable venue, it was opened by Count Basie in the mid-1950s. Although it was not his primary purpose to create a club where he could play, he sat in from time to time; in October 1956 he recorded at the club as a member of a mainstream sextet, with Emmett Berry, Vic Dickenson, Aaron Bell, Bobby Donaldson, and Joe Williams. Among the other musicians who played there were Eddie "Lockjaw" Davis and Shirley Scott (1959).

——. **Crawdaddy.** Vanderbilt Avenue at East 45th Street. It was active from around the mid-1970s. Among the musicians who played residencies there were Buddy Tate and Vic Dickenson (both 1978) and Warren Vaché (1979–80).

——. **Delmonico's.** See Harlem Uproar House.

——. **Diamond Horseshoe.** It was owned and managed by Billy Rose, and was opened in the 1930s. Among the musicians who worked there were Billy Banks, who played an unbroken series of more than 7000 performances between December 1938 and June 1948, and Noble Sissle, whose orchestra was resident at the club in 1938–42 and again from 1945 to the mid-1950s.

——. **Dickie Wells's Shim Sham Club.** 169 West 133rd Street. It was opened by Wells (who should not be confused with the famous trombonist of the same name) in 1933 in premises that had previously housed the Nest Club (see below). It operated successfully for several years at least, and the musicians who performed there included Billie Holiday (1936).

——. **Downbeat.** 66 West 52nd Street (1944–8); West 54th Street (from 1952); Lexington Avenue at East 42nd Street (by the late 1960s). At least three different clubs have used this name in New York. The first opened on 52nd Street in premises that had earlier been occupied by the Yacht Club (see below). It was managed to begin with by Morris Levy, and then (when he moved to the Royal Roost) by his brother Irving Levy. It became one of the most flourishing venues in the city, engaging many major musicians. Dizzy Gillespie, who had played at the Yacht Club, appeared regularly at the Downbeat, as did Coleman Hawkins from its early days. Others who worked there were Red Norvo and the Bascomb brothers (both 1944), Art Tatum, Tiny Grimes, and Sid Catlett (all 1944–6), Jay McShann (1945), Billie Holiday (1945, 1947), Sarah Vaughan (*c*1946), and Eddie Heywood, Gillespie, Ella Fitzgerald, and Lester Young (all 1947). In 1948 the 52nd Street venue became a striptease club called the Carousel. In 1952 a new club, called Le Downbeat, opened on West 54th Street, and it remained active until at least 1954; Mary Lou Williams, Billy Taylor (ii), and Terry Gibbs were among those who played there. The third Downbeat was opened in the late 1960s on Lexington Avenue at 42nd Street. The musicians it engaged included Maxine Sullivan with the World's Greatest Jazz Band, Roy Eldridge (1969), and Anita O'Day (1970). The venue became a rock club in 1970.

——. **Dunbar Palace.** See Bamboo Inn.

——. **East.** 10 Claver Place, Brooklyn. It was active from at least the 1970s as a venue for free jazz.

——. **Ebony.** 1678 Broadway, north of 52nd Street. Owned by Dickie Wells (who should not be confused with the trombonist of the same name), it was opened around 1944 and was run by Wells with the help of John Levy and Al Martin. In December 1948 the Clique opened in the same premises, and a year later Birdland took its place (see above).

——. **Eddie Condon's.** 47 West 3rd Street (from 20 December 1945 to 1957); 330 East 56th Street (1958–mid-1967); 144 West 54th Street (March 1975 to 31 July 1985). It was opened by Eddie Condon in December 1945 and managed by him in association with Pete Pesci. It remained on West 3rd Street until 1957, then the following year Condon took new premises uptown on East 56th Street. This second venue closed in mid-1967. In 1975, after Condon's death, a new club on West 54th Street, next to Jimmy Ryan's, was opened by Red Balaban, who led its house band, Balaban and Cats, from that time; their playing was recorded and issued on the LP *A Night at the New Eddie Condon's* (1975, CJ 17). It closed on 31 July 1985. The original Eddie Condon's was one of the clubs featured in the 20-minute film documentary *Night Clubs Boom* (1946), in Louis de Rochemont's series *The March of Time* (made by Time and RKO Radio).

Condon's specialized in the presentation of Chicago jazz, and all the principal players in the style appeared there. The club's resident band (see fig.5) always bore Condon's name during his lifetime, even during those periods when he seldom played with it. Among his regular sidemen were Sammy Price (1940s), George Wettling (1940s–1950s), Walter Page (early 1950s), Pee Wee Russell (1955–6), Herb Hall (for several years in the mid-1950s), Tony Parenti (1962–3), and Yank Lawson; Wild Bill Davison was resident at the West 3rd Street location for much of its existence and played again at the club in its uptown venue in 1983. James P. Johnson worked there as an intermission pianist (1946), as did Ralph Sutton and Dick Wellstood.

BIBLIOGRAPHY

E. Condon and T. Sugrue: *We Called it Music: a Generation of Jazz* (New York, 1947/*R*1975)

E. Condon and H. O'Neal: *The Eddie Condon Scrapbook of Jazz* (New York, 1973)

——. **Edwardian Room.** Plaza Hotel, Fifth Avenue at 59th Street. Jazz was played in this venue within the hotel from at least the 1980s. Bucky Pizzarelli played regularly there in 1984–5.

——. **The Embers.** East 54th Street. It flourished as a venue for soloists and small groups from the late 1940s into the 1960s. Its activities were directed briefly by Ralph Watkins, who worked there between his appointments at Bop City and Basin Street. Among the musicians who played at the club were Roy Eldridge, Louis Metcalf, Charlie Shavers, Mary Lou Williams, Buck Clayton, Joe Bushkin (who was the house pianist in the early 1950s), Art Tatum, Stuff Smith, and Tyree Glenn. Earl Hines and Eddie Heywood were resident in 1959–60, and they were succeeded by a quartet led by Jonah Jones (from 3 January 1960); Jones's group formed a lasting association with the Embers, playing there again in 1961, opposite a quartet led by Erskine Hawkins, and in 1963.

——. **Empire Ballroom.** West 48th Street and Broadway. Jazz bands were engaged to accompany the dancing from at least the 1930s. Among the prominent orchestras that appeared there were those of Fletcher Henderson (1933), Benny Carter (1933), and Rex Stewart (1933–4). A number of performances by the Henderson band were broadcast on radio stations WINS and WMCA.

——. **Empire Room.** See Waldorf Astoria.

5. Eddie Condon's, New York, June 1954: (on stage, left to right) Condon (guitar), Urbie Green (trombone), Dick Cary (trumpet), Bobby Donaldson (drums), Ernie Caceres (clarinet), Al Hall (double bass), and Gene Schroeder (piano)

——. **Enduro Restaurant.** Brooklyn. It presented jazz for the entertainment of the diners from at least 1940, when Sidney Bechet and Sidney De Paris both played there every Monday night throughout the summer. Bechet returned between August and November of the same year as the leader of a quintet.

——. **Essex House Hotel.** Central Park South. It was in operation from at least the early 1930s. The Casa Loma Orchestra played a residency of almost two years in the hotel in 1933–4 (for illustration *see* CASA LOMA ORCHESTRA), and during that time made pioneering broadcasts on radio.

——. **Famous Door.** 35 West 52nd Street (1 March 1935 – 10 May 1936); 66 West 52nd Street (December 1937 – November 1943); 201 West 52nd Street at Seventh Avenue (November 1943 – early 1944); 56 West 52nd Street (1947–50); West 52nd Street, between Sixth Avenue and Seventh Avenue (1960s). The club was opened at the first of its many locations on 1 March 1935 as a cooperative venture financed by, among others, Lennie Hayton and his manager Jack Colt, Glenn Miller, and Jimmy Dorsey. Its name derived from an autographed door, which was set on a dais next to the bar; it bore the signatures of the original investors and in time those of many celebrities who visited or played at the club. Founded principally as a venue where musicians employed by other New York clubs could meet to eat, drink, and play together, it rapidly gained popularity with theater and film actors as well. On its opening night Louis Prima and his New Orleans Gang (which included Pee Wee Russell) played at the Famous Door; following Prima, Georg Brunis, Max Kaminsky, Bobby Hackett, Billie Holiday, Red Norvo, and Wingy Manone (all 1935) and Bunny Berigan (1935–6) were among the various musicians who etablished its reputation as a venue for dixieland jazz and swing. It was the venue chosen by Bessie Smith in February 1936 for her only performance on 52nd Street. The original purpose of the Famous Door was not neglected, however, and regular jam sessions were held in an upstairs room. Despite its successful beginning the club ran into financial difficulties and was forced to close on 10 May 1936.

The second club of the name was opened in December 1937 at 66 West 52nd Street (premises that were later used by the Downbeat (see above)); it was directed initially by Al Felshin and Jerry Brooks, and later by various other managers, including Arthur Jarwood (1940–43). Prima was again engaged as the first resident bandleader, and Art Tatum played solo piano between sets. Although its bandstand was small, the club presented some of the leading bands of the period, including those of Count Basie (1938, 1939; for illustration *see* BASIE, COUNT), Red Norvo (regularly from 1938 into the 1940s), Mildred Bailey (1938), John Kirby, Charlie Barnet, Red Nichols, and Ella Fitzgerald (all 1939), Teddy Powell (1939–40), Woody Herman (1939, *c*1941), Benny Carter (1940–42), Andy Kirk (1941), and Hot Lips Page (1943); CBS made regular broadcasts from the venue during the late 1930s. The club was closed temporarily from June 1940 because of failure to pay the musicians' wages, but it reopened on 25 September.

In November 1943 the Famous Door moved to another location on 52nd Street, where it operated for little more than a month. During this time John Kirby and Lionel Hampton were among the musicians who played there. A fresh start was made in 1947, when a new venue was opened at 56 West 52nd Street; the Famous Door at this location was active until 1950. It featured a repertory of swing and bop, as before staging performances by the most prominent musicians of the day, including Henry "Red" Allen, Ella Fitzgerald, Lester Young, Sid Catlett, Art Tatum, Roy Eldridge, Dizzy Gillespie, Ben Webster, and Jack Teagarden. After the closure of the club in 1950 this venue became a striptease club. The last of the venues to take the illustrious name of the Famous Door was active on 52nd Street in the 1960s; clubs in other American cities have also used the name, including one in New Orleans. (A. Shaw: "Swingin' at the Famous Door," "The Big Bands and the Famous Door," "Cracks in the Door," *The Street that Never Slept: New York's Fabled 52nd Street* (New York, 1971/*R*1983 as *52nd Street: the Street that Never Slept*), 105, 125, 312)

——. **Fat Tuesday.** 190 Third Avenue, at East 17th Street. It was founded in 1979 and flourished as a venue for bop, blues, and mainstream jazz during the 1980s. Among the many important musicians who have played there are Gerry Mulligan, Jack DeJohnette, Eddie Gomez, and Hilton Ruiz (all 1980), Helen Merrill and Sheila Jordan (both 1983), McCoy Tyner and Joe Henderson (1987), and Jay McShann, Zoot Sims, Joe Turner (ii), Stan Getz, Dexter Gordon, Buddy DeFranco, Ahmad Jamal, Freddie Hubbard, and the Jazztet. From the mid-1980s the guitarist Les Paul played a regular engagement on Monday nights.

——. **Fiesta Danceteria.** West 42nd Street and Broadway. Restaurant. This venue, which opened in November 1939, was situated on the second floor of the Rialto Theater and consisted of a self-service restaurant, glass-covered roof garden, and dance floor. Joe Marsala led a big band there late in 1939 and Jimmie Lunceford's orchestra was resident in 1940 (for illustration *see* LUNCEFORD, JIMMIE).

——. **Five Spot (Café).** 5 Cooper Square (to 1962); Third Avenue and East 7th Street (1962–72); 2 St. Marks Place, east of Seventh Avenue (from 1972). It was owned by Joe and Iggy Termini and opened at its first location on the edge of the Bowery by the mid-1950s. From the start it was noted for the uncompromising presentation of the latest styles of music. In 1956 an all-star sextet, including Phil Woods, Duke Jordan, Art Taylor, and Cecil Payne, recorded a tribute to Charlie Parker at the club (released on the Signal label). Landmarks in the Five Spot's history were the long residencies played from 1956 by Cecil Taylor and in 1957–9 by Thelonious Monk as the leader of a quartet of changing personnel, including, most notably, John Coltrane (1957). Ornette Coleman made his controversial New York début there and played a series of residencies at the club between 1959 and 1961. In the latter year Eric Dolphy gave important performances there; these were recorded and issued as *Live! at the Five Spot* (NewJ 8260; Prst. 7294). Monk returned to the club in 1963 after it had moved to its new location on the West side. Another influential connection was that with Charles Mingus, who first appeared at the Five Spot in its early days and played for an extended period in 1964–5.

In 1972 the club's management took a new direction, opening premises on St. Marks Place under the name the Two Saints and presenting a repertory that emphasized jazz-rock. The original name was resumed, however, in 1975 and the Five Spot reopened with Art Blakey's Jazz Messengers. Among others who performed there were Coleman again (1975) and Jackie McLean. The club was forced to close after losing its cabaret license. The Termini brothers also ran the Jazz Gallery in Greenwich Village (see below).

——. **Flamingo Club** [Club Flamingo]. 38 West 52nd Street. It was active in the 1940s, when among the resident leaders was the cornetist Johnny Bayersdorffer. The venue became a striptease club in the 1950s.

——. **Garden of Joy.** Seventh Avenue and West 140th Street. This open-air cabaret occupied an entire block on Seventh Avenue; the site had a dance floor, illuminated at night by Japanese lanterns. It was in operation from at least 1920, when Willie "the Lion" Smith played the first of a series of long residencies there. During the early 1920s Sidney Bechet, James P. Johnson, Bubber Miley, and Coleman Hawkins played there as sidemen with Mamie Smith, and in the mid-decade Hawkins was a member of a band led by the pianist Ginger Jones. Other jazzmen to appear there included Charlie Gaines, who played with several different leaders.

——. **Gaslight (Club).** It flourished in the 1950s and 1960s. Clarence Hutchenrider's successful trio played a long residency (from 1958), and one of his sidemen, George Wettling, subsequently led a trio of his own there in the mid-1960s. Sol Yaged's quintet, which included Ray Nance, also appeared at the Gaslight in the mid-1960s.

——. **Ginger Man.** 51 West 64th Street. Restaurant. For a short time in the early 1980s (*c*1981–2) it presented performances by the Harlem Blues and Jazz Band.

——. **Golden Gate Ballroom** [Golden Gate Club]. 46–8 West 135th Street. It was founded by Earl Dancer, probably in the 1930s, when its activities were directed by Moe Galewski. Among the big bands that worked there were those led by Coleman Hawkins (late 1930s), Hot Lips Page (1939), and Count Basie, Teddy Wilson, Harlan Leonard, and Les Hite (all 1940). Sammy Stewart played organ at the ballroom in the early 1940s.

——. **Golden Triangle.** See Village Vanguard.

——. **Greene Street.** 101 Greene Street, near Prince Street. Bar and restaurant. Occupying premises that had been converted from a warehouse, it opened in 1980 and was still flourishing late in the decade. It has become known particularly for the presentation of ensembles that do not use a drummer. The musicians who have played there include Lee Konitz, John Hicks, Mal Waldron, Hilton Ruiz, Art Davis, John Abercrombie, Andy Laverne, Rufus Reid, and Amina Claudine Myers.

——. **Gregory's.** 1149 First Avenue, at East 63rd Street. It was established in 1972 and continued to be active into the late 1980s. Ellis Larkins, Brooks Kerr, Lee Konitz, Jimmy Raney, Don Friedman, Chuck Wayne, Mike Longo, and Bob Dorough, among others, have performed there.

——. **Griff's (Plaza Café).** Third Avenue and East 37th Street. Restaurant. Jazz was performed to entertain the diners from at least the early 1980s. John Bunch, Major Holley, and Junior Mance appeared there around 1981–2.

——. **Half Note.** 289 Hudson Street, near Spring Street (1957–72); 149 West 54th Street (October 1972–1974). The venue in Greenwich Village, operated by the Canterino family, was active from 1957 to 1972 and quickly established a name as a center for contemporary styles of jazz. Many of the most prominent musicians of the 1950s and 1960s performed there, notably Charles Mingus (1957–8), Lennie Tristano (1958–9), John Coltrane with his quartet (1960–65), and the Modern Jazz Quartet (1966); Al Cohn and Zoot Sims appeared there together throughout the 1960s and then, during the 1970s, each returned with his own group. Others who played at the Half Note were Ben Webster (1962), Jimmy Rushing (1965–6, 1971), and Anita O'Day (1969).

In October 1972 the Half Note opened in larger premises at 149 West 54th Street, across the street from Jimmy Ryan's. Among those who played there were Woody Herman, Dizzy Gillespie, Bill Evans (ii), and Zoot Sims. It closed in late 1974.

——. **Hanratty's.** 1754 Second Avenue, at East 91st Street. Bar. Opened in 1979, it remained active until 1986. Dick Wellstood played there regularly in 1979–80 and 1983–4, and was responsible for booking other pianists, including John Coates (1980), Don Ewell (1981), Ralph Sutton (1982), Roland Hanna (1985), Dick Hyman (1986), Dave McKenna, Tommy Flanagan, and Judy Carmichael.

——. **Harlem Club.** West 116th Street between Lenox Avenue and Seventh Avenue. This nightclub flourished during the 1930s. It was a favorite haunt of Dizzy Gillespie, who sat in with various bands there early in his career.

——. **Harlem Opera House.** 211 West 125th Street, west of Seventh Avenue. It was opened in 1889 as an opera house, but by the early years of the 20th century it was used for variety performances. Its most active period as a jazz venue occurred in the mid-1930s but it was short-lived: on 9 June 1934 Frank Schiffman and Leo Brecher, the owners of the rival Apollo Theatre, took over the opera house and in the late spring of 1935 discontinued its stage policy, converting it to a movie theater. After the cessation of jazz performances at the Harlem Opera House the Apollo was the only theater in Harlem presenting variety acts.

Among the jazz musicians who appeared at the Harlem Opera House during its brief golden era were Tiny Bradshaw, Don Redman, Teddy Hill, Chick Webb, Benny Carter, Fletcher Henderson, and Charlie Turner's Arcadians. Ella Fitzgerald won an amateur contest there early in 1935, before her success at a similar competition staged at the Apollo Theatre, which launched her career.

——. **Harlem Uproar House.** 52nd Street. It was at least the third club to occupy the premises, which had earlier housed Delmonico's and then the Uptown Lowdown Club. The dates at which the name of the venue changed are not clear but it was known as the Harlem Uproar House by 1937. At that time the club was owned by Jay Faggin (or Fagin), who also owned the Arcadia Ballroom (see above), and it offered an elaborate floor show every night. Among the bands that appeared there were those led by Lucky Millinder (1932), Kaiser Marshall (1935), Coleman Hawkins (1937), Alberto Socarras (1937), and Mezz Mezzrow (1937); Mezzrow's 14-piece ensemble included Zutty Singleton, Dicky Wells, Frankie Newton, and Sidney De Paris. During the same period Hazel Scott played piano during intermissions and the club also presented a trio led by the violinist Emilio Caceres (brother of Ernie Caceres).

——. **Heat Wave.** West 145th Street. The club was active in the 1930s and 1940s under the direction of Louis Metcalf, who also played there until 1946.

——. **Hermit's End.** 2493 Seventh Avenue. It was in operation by the early 1920s. Cecil Scott and Lloyd Scott led the resident band there in 1924. The premises were taken over in 1925 by the Club Basha (see above).

——. **Hickory House.** 144 West 52nd Street. Restaurant and club. One of the longest-lived jazz venues on 52nd Street, it was opened in 1933 and under the direction of John Popkin soon became known for the presentation of dixieland jazz and swing; later it was also a major venue for bop. Wingy Manone was the resident leader from late 1934 and when he left the club in 1936 one of his sidemen, Joe Marsala, took his place, establishing a connection with the Hickory House that lasted on and off to the mid-1940s. Other notable residencies were played by Art Hodes (1938, 1944), John Kirby's sextet (late 1930s), Hot Lips Page (1940), Eddie South (1942), Red Norvo (intermittently until 1944), Billy Taylor (ii), Marian McPartland (1952–60), and Mary Lou Williams. The club also mounted regular jam sessions on Sunday afternoons; Sidney Bechet played as a guest soloist at a number of these in the late 1930s. The club's activities featured in a number of broadcasts. The Hickory House closed in 1968.

BIBLIOGRAPHY

A. Shaw: "Hickory-broiled Steaks and Jazz," *The Street that Never Slept: New York's Fabled 52nd Street* (New York, 1971/*R*1983 as *52nd Street: the Street that Never Slept*), 141

M. McPartland: "Halcyon Days: Remembering the Hickory House," *All in Good Time* (New York, and Oxford, England, 1987) [colln of previously pubd articles], 19

——. **Hickory Log.** It was in operation by the late 1940s. Ernie Caceres led his own quartet there in 1949 and John Kirby worked at the club with Henry "Red" Allen in the 1950s.

——. **Hollywood Club.** 203 West 49th Street. It was opened in 1923 by Leonard Bernstein (not the composer, conductor, and pianist of that name), but was active under this name only until the following year, when the premises were renamed the Kentucky Club (see below). The Washingtonians, first led by Elmer Snowden, then by Duke Ellington, were the resident band from 1923, and in spring 1924 James P. Johnson led a band at the Hollywood with Benny Carter and Sidney Bechet among his sidemen.

——. **Hoofers Club.** See Rhythm Club.

——. **Hotel Carlyle.** See Bemelmans Bar and Café Carlyle.

——. **Hot Feet Club.** West Houston Street. The principal bandleaders at this downtown venue, which flourished in the late 1920s and 1930s, were Otto Hardwick and Elmer Snowden; among the musicians who played with them there were Al Morgan and Fats Waller.

——. **Hurricane Club.** Broadway and West 51st Street. It was in operation by the early 1940s. In 1943 Duke Ellington's orchestra played there from April to September and in the spring of that year Sidney Bechet led a small group at the club on the orchestra's nights off.

——. **International.** Broadway. It was active from at least 1960, when Doc Cheatham began the first of a series of residencies there. He continued to be connected with the club until 1965.

——. **Jasmine.** 168 West 96th Street. A short-lived nightclub on the upper West side, it functioned in the mid-1980s. Among the musicians engaged to play there in 1984 were John Hicks and Steve Grossman.

——. **Jazz Gallery.** 80 St. Marks Place, at First Avenue. It was founded around December 1959 by Joe and Iggy Termini (who also owned the Five Spot, see above); the groups that played there in its early days included the Jazztet (1959–60) and John Coltrane's first quartet (May–June 1960). In 1961 the club featured an orchestra led by Gil Evans, among the sidemen in which were Budd Johnson, Keg Johnson, and Ray Crawford. During the same year the singer Joe Williams appeared, accompanied by Harry Edison, and in 1962 Charles Mingus performed there.

——. **Jazzmania Society.** 14 East 23rd Street; 40 West 27th Street. It was opened in 1978 as Jazzmania, but by late the following year, when it was owned by the saxophonist Mike Morgenstern, it was known as Jazzmania Society. It originally occupied a room on the fourth floor of the 23rd Street building, but later moved to a more spacious loft on West 27th Street. Lee Konitz played regularly at the club in 1980 and 1982 and Sun Ra also appeared there in the latter year.

——. **Jimmy Ryan's (Club).** 53 West 52nd Street (1940–62); 154 West 54th Street (from 1962). Named for its owner, it was opened in 1940 and became one of the most celebrated of all New York clubs. Ryan managed the venue in collaboration with Matty Walsh, and Milt Gabler was responsible for organizing its jam sessions, which formed an important part of its activities. After Ryan's death in 1963 the club continued to be active until December 1983.

Jimmy Ryan's has been perhaps the most successful location in the city for the performance of dixieland jazz and swing. All the most famous musicians in these styles have played there at one time or another; resident musicians from the 1940s included Mezz Mezzrow (*c*1943), James P. Johnson (1943), Art Hodes (1945–9), J. C. Higginbotham (1946), Henry "Red" Allen (1946), Sidney De Paris (1947–57), Sidney Bechet (1948), Max Kaminsky (1948–9), Wilbur De Paris (1951–62), Zutty Singleton (1963–70), and Roy Eldridge (1970–80). Among the prominent participants in the jam sessions were Bechet, Pops Foster, Hot Lips Page, Pee Wee Russell, Eddie Condon, Mezzrow, Kaiser Marshall, Hank Duncan, Sandy Williams, Brad Gowans, Ben Webster, Chu Berry, and Coleman Hawkins.

——. **Joanna.** See Whippoorwill.

——. **Jock's Place.** See Yeah Man.

——. **J's.** 2581 Broadway, at West 97th Street. Bar and restaurant. It occupies premises on the second floor of the building and has been active from the mid-1980s, favoring a repertory of mainstream jazz. Those who played there in 1987 included John Pizzarelli, Dick Hyman, and a duo consisting of Jay Leonhart and Joe Beck.

——. **Kelly's Stable.** 141 West 51st Street (to 1940); 137 West 52nd Street (1940–47). Named for Bert Kelly's club in Chicago (see Chicago, Kelly's Stables), it was opened during the 1930s by Ralph Watkins, who directed its activities himself; Watkins's interest in the venue waned in the mid-1940s when he opened the Royal Roost (see below) with Morris Levy, and he sold Kelly's Stable in 1947.

At its first location the club presented such musicians as Hot Lips Page, Bud Freeman, Coleman Hawkins, Stuff Smith, the Spirits of Rhythm, and Baby Laurence; it was at Kelly's that Hawkins worked up his famous rendering of *Body and Soul* (1939). After the removal to new premises in 1940, Watkins engaged a stream of notable players, including Roy Eldridge and Slam Stewart (both 1940), Benny Carter, Lester Young, and Benny Waters (all 1941), Kenny Clarke (1942, with Thelonious Monk in his band), Mezz Mezzrow (1943), Henry "Red" Allen, Nat "King" Cole, Art Tatum, J. C. Higginbotham, Billie Holiday, Una Mae Carlisle, Dizzy Gillespie, and Dinah Washington. A particular feature of the club's programs were the all-star jam sessions staged there, in which such musicians as Young, Chu Berry, and Hawkins took part. (A. Shaw: "Cats in a Stable," *The Street that Never Slept: New York's Fabled 52nd Street* (New York, 1971/*R*1983 as *52nd Street: the Street that Never Slept*), 200)

——. **Kentucky Club.** 203 West 49th Street. This venue, formerly known as the Hollywood Club (see above), had taken the name Kentucky Club by the summer of 1924. The new venue continued to present Duke Ellington and his Washingtonians, who had been in residence at the Hollywood, until 1927. Other bandleaders to work at the Kentucky were Red Nichols (1929), Jimmy Reynolds, who remained for many years in the 1930s and 1940s, and Lester Boone, who led a quartet there in 1940.

——. **King Cole Room.** See St. Regis Hotel.

——. **Knickerbocker Saloon.** 33 University Place, at East 9th Street. Restaurant and bar. It was opened in 1978 and continued to be active through the 1980s. It presented piano duos and trios, engaging the following musicians, among others: Billy Taylor (ii) (1978–9), Junior Mance (regularly), Tommy Flanagan (1981), and Jay Leonhart, Bill Mays, and a duo consisting of Steve Kuhn and Ron Carter (all 1987).

——. **Lafayette Theatre.** 2227 Seventh Avenue, at West 131st Street. Variety theater. It opened around 1915 under the ownership of the Coleman brothers and became one of the principal venues of its kind in Harlem. In the 1920s it was taken over by Frank Schiffman and Leo Brecher, who by the mid-1930s also owned the Apollo Theatre and the Harlem Opera House; like the opera house, the Lafayette's activities as a variety theater were discontinued by its owners in 1935 and it became a movie theater. As a venue for jazz performance the Lafayette flourished in the 1920s and 1930s; many of the most important musicians of the day played in the bands that accompanied its shows. Wilbur Sweatman topped the bill there in 1923, with Duke Ellington, Otto Hardwick, and Sonny Greer in his band; Ellington later returned with the Washingtonians (*c*1927). Other prominent bandleaders who appeared included Fletcher Henderson (intermittently 1928–34), Zutty Singleton (1929), Louis Armstrong fronting Carroll Dickerson's band (June 1930), Blanche Calloway and Noble Sissle (both 1931), Bennie Moten (1931–4), and Chick Webb (1933). Fats Waller worked there as an organist with James P. Johnson in the show *Fireworks of 1930*.

——. **Lenox Club.** 652 Lenox Avenue. Owned by Caspar Holstein, it was opened in the 1920s; its location was close to that of the Cotton Club's Harlem venue (see above). The main feature of the Lenox's programs were its Sunday morning breakfast dances, beginning at 7 a.m. and continuing until 11; the popularity of these events led to the venue's informal adoption of the name Breakfast Club. Among the jazz musicians who played there during the early 1930s were Cliff Jackson and Johnny Russell.

——. **Leroy's.** 135th Street and Fifth Avenue. This basement club was founded around 1910 by Leroy Wilkins, the elder brother of Barron Wilkins (see Barron's Club, above), and was one of the earliest jazz venues in the city. It frequently presented pianists, among them James P. Johnson (*c*1918), Willie "the Lion" Smith (from 1920), and Fats Waller (early 1920s). Other jazz musicians who appeared included Mamie Smith (before 1920) and Cyrus St. Clair (*c*1925).

——. **Lido Ballroom.** 160 West 146th Street. Active from at least the early 1930s, it offered music for both dancing and concerts. Jelly Roll Morton led a band there in October 1932 and on 19 August 1944 Mamie Smith (singing one of her last engagements), Billie Holiday, and others gave a benefit concert in the ballroom.

——. **Lincoln Hotel.** See Blue Room.

——. **Lincoln Theater.** 58 West 135th Street. Variety theater. A small theater was opened at this address by Marie Downs in 1909; it was later demolished and the Lincoln was built in its place in 1915. The theater was run for a short time by Frank Schiffman and Leo Brecher (see also Apollo Theatre, Harlem Opera House, and Lafayette Theatre, above). The Lincoln Theater belonged to the TOBA circuit and presented many jazz performances as part of its variety programs. Fats Waller was the house organist there in the mid-1920s, doubling at the same time at the Lafayette. In 1927 Victoria Spivey sang a highly successful residency there.

——. **Little Club.** A number of venues in New York, apparently unconnected, have gone by this name. Between 1921 and 1923 the premises later occupied by the Club Alabam (see above) were known as the Little Club. The venue at which Ben Pollack played in 1928 was probably the speakeasy on West 44th Street, between Broadway and Seventh Avenue, run by John Popkin, who later directed activities at the Hickory House (see above). During the 1950s a Little Club was in operation at 70 East 55th Street; although this was not essentially a jazz venue, Bud Freeman played there on 31 December 1959.

——. **Log Cabin.** See Pods' and Jerry's.

——. **Luckey's Rendezvous** [Rendezvous Inn, Rendezvous Club]. 773 St. Nicholas Avenue. It was opened by Luckey Roberts in 1940 and was active as a venue for many styles of music, from opera (sung by the waiters) to jazz, until around 1954, when Roberts gave up its ownership. The highpoint of each evening's entertainment was Roberts's own solo piano spot.

——. **Lush Life.** 184 Thompson Street, at Bleecker Street. It was opened in 1982 by Horst Liepolt and Mel Litoff, the managers of Sweet Basil (see below), and was active until 1984. During its brief existence it presented performances by Bob Moses and Don Cherry (both 1982), Red Garland, Charlie Rouse, and Paquito D'Rivera (all 1983), and the Toshiko Akiyoshi–Lew Tabackin Big Band (1984).

——. **Mark Twain Riverboat.** Empire State Building, Fifth Avenue at 34th Street. Situated in the basement of the building this nightclub was open by the early 1960s. It was a venue for big bands, including those of Woody Herman and Harry James. Count Basie played a number of short residencies there between 1964 and 1968, and returned to the club in 1978.

——. **Martin's Tavern.** See Saratoga Club.

——. **Marty's.** 1265 Third Avenue at East 73rd Street. It flourished from the late 1970s into the early 1980s and presented performances principally by jazz and popular singers. The jazz-oriented performers who appeared there included Joe Williams (1980) and Mel Tormé (1982).

——. **Metropole.** Seventh Avenue and West 48th Street. Although it was active as a cabaret, the Metropole did not offer jazz until the early 1950s, when it began to put on afternoon sessions at which Tony Scott, Max Kaminsky, and Sol Yaged, among others, appeared. Henry "Red" Allen introduced evening performances and was resident there himself from 1954 until shortly before his death in 1967 (for illustration *see* ALLEN, HENRY "RED"). In its heyday from the late 1950s until the mid-1960s the club featured trios in the afternoon (Zutty Singleton and Tony Parenti each led groups for long periods) and two bands, alternating, in the evening (Allen's was one, the other was often led by Roy Eldridge or Coleman Hawkins). Resident players included Cozy Cole, Claude Hopkins, Buster Bailey, J. C. Higginbotham, and Charlie Shavers. Occasionally the Metropole presented single performances by such musicians as Louis Armstrong and Gene Krupa, and it also engaged big bands from time to time, including those of Lionel Hampton and Woody Herman. While the club's repertory was essentially mainstream jazz, it also offered modern jazz in an upstairs room for a short period during the 1960s; among the musicians to play in this venue was Sonny Rollins.

——. **Michael's Pub.** 211 East 55th Street. Restaurant and club. This venue was established in 1972 and flourished during the 1970s and 1980s. It presented swing and traditional jazz from

9 p.m. to 1 a.m., specializing in small groups. Among the many well-known musicians to have played residencies there are Benny Carter, Ray Bryant, George Melly, Dave McKenna, Ruby Braff, Teddy Wilson, Terry Gibbs, George Shearing, Dick Hyman, Pee Wee Erwin, Bobby Rosengarden, Milt Hinton, and Dick Wellstood. By the late 1980s the venue was better known for the presentation of Broadway show music than jazz.

——. **Mikell's.** 760 Columbus Avenue, at West 97th Street. It was active in the 1970s and 1980s, and engaged such musicians as McCoy Tyner (1985); both Art Blakey and Randy Weston played there regularly.

——. **Mimo Club.** 132nd Street. It was partly owned by the dancer Bill Robinson and was in operation from the late 1930s. Sidney Bechet led a quartet there in 1939 and later returned with a nine-piece band. In the early 1940s Hot Lips Page was the resident bandleader, and Earl Bostic, who first played at the Mimo Club with Page, also led a group there.

——. **Minton's Playhouse.** 210 West 118th Street. It was opened in 1938 by the tenor saxophonist Henry Minton. In 1940 the club's management was taken over by the former bandleader Teddy Hill (see fig.6), who concentrated much of his energy on the regular Monday-night jam sessions, in which visiting musicians took part; among the guest performers who played there often were Dizzy Gillespie, Hot Lips Page, Roy Eldridge, Charlie Christian, and Don Byas. The resident musicians included Thelonious Monk (from 1939), Kenny Clarke, Joe Guy (who led the house band), and Rudy Williams (1945). The weekly jam session and after-hours playing at Minton's provided an opportunity for musicians such as Gillespie and Monk to explore new ideas together, and their experiments played an important part in the development of bop. In the 1950s Tony Scott and Jerome Richardson held long engagements there.

——. **Monette's Supper Club.** 133rd Street. This short-lived nightclub was named after Monette Moore, who sang there. It was here that John Hammond first heard Billie Holiday in 1933.

——. **Monroe's Uptown House.** 198 West 134th Street; 52nd Street (from 1943). It was opened by Clark Monroe in the 1930s in premises formerly occupied by the Theatrical Grill. It became known for the presentation of swing (Billie Holiday sang there for three months early in 1937) and (from the mid-1940s) bop, and staged jam sessions that rivaled those at Minton's Playhouse (see above); Charlie Parker was the featured soloist in 1943. In December 1944 Monroe opened a second club on 52nd Street, the Spotlite (see below). (*See also* TINNEY, AL.)

——. **Music Hall.** Broadway. This club was owned by Billy Rose and presented jazz from at least 1934, when Benny Goodman's big band played its first engagement there.

——. **Nest Club.** 169 West 133rd Street. It was opened in the early 1920s by John Carey and Mel Frazier, and managed by Johnnie Cobb (1923) and Jeff Blood (1927). Among the jazz musicians who led bands there were Sam Wooding (*c*1923), Elmer Snowden (mid-1920s to early 1930s), George Howe (1927–8), Luis Russell (1928), and Lorenzo Tio, Jr. (1933). In 1932 the Rhythm Club (see below), which had functioned at 168 West 132nd Street, closed at that venue and began to operate in a room behind the Nest Club. The Nest Club itself closed in 1933, and Dickie Wells's Shim Sham Club (see above) took over the venue.

——. **New Garden Ballroom** [New Gardens]. Jazz was played there from at least the 1940s. The venue is chiefly of interest for the long residency of a band led by the pianist Benton Heath

6. Thelonious Monk, Howard McGhee, Roy Eldridge, and Teddy Hill outside Minton's Playhouse, New York

(from the early 1940s to the mid-1960s). Heath's sidemen at different times included Abe Bolar, Ed Allen, Floyd Casey, and Rudy Powell.

——. **Nick's (Tavern).** 140 Seventh Avenue South (?1936–1937); West 10th Street and Seventh Avenue (from 1937). Steak restaurant. It was opened by Nick Rongetti, probably in 1936, and quickly became known for the presentation of dixieland jazz. By late 1938 the term "Nixieland" (or "Nicksieland") was used to refer to music heard at the club, which was one of the main haunts of major jazz musicians during the 1930s. In the early years of the club's existence the resident band was led by Bobby Hackett and featured Eddie Condon, Pee Wee Russell, and Zutty Singleton; Russell and Singleton continued to play there with their own groups – Singleton leading a trio in 1939 and Russell several ensembles throughout the 1940s. Sidney Bechet, who first appeared as a guest musician with the venue's intermission group, the Spirits of Rhythm, remained at the club as the leader of a quartet until 1940. The numerous important resident performers there also included Georg Brunis (1936–8, 1941–2), Meade "Lux" Lewis (as intermission pianist *c*1936), Muggsy Spanier (1939, mid-1940s to 1948), Wild Bill Davison (1941), Brad Gowans and Bob Casey (both 1942–3), Miff Mole (1943–7), Billy Butterfield (from late 1947), Hank Duncan (1947–63), Phil Napoleon (1949–55, alternating with Pee Wee Erwin during the early 1950s), and Kenny Davern (1961). Others who played less regularly at Nick's were Cliff Jackson and Buster Harding (both as intermission pianists) and Sidney De Paris. The club closed in 1963.

BIBLIOGRAPHY

J. Harris: "Bobby Hackett at Nick's," *Jazz Session*, no.9 (1945), 11
M. Peart: "Home of Dixieland Jazz," *Jazz Session*, no.9 (1945), 3

——. **One Fifth Avenue.** Fifth Avenue and 8th Street. Lounge. In the late 1970s and early 1980s it offered jazz performances by such musicians as Al Haig and Freddie Moore.

——. **Onyx.** 35 West 52nd Street (1927–34); 72 West 52nd Street (4 February 1934 – spring 1937); 62 West 52nd Street (April 1937 – December 1939); 57 West 52nd Street (1942–*c*1949). The first club of this name was a speakeasy which opened in 1927 and was managed by Joe Helbock; among those who performed there were Joe Sullivan, as an unaccompanied soloist (1933), and the Spirits of Rhythm. After the repeal of Prohibition in 1933, a new Onyx opened on 4 February 1934 as a legitimate nightclub at 72 West 52nd Street, still under Helbock's direction. Art Tatum was employed there as the club's intermission pianist and the Spirits of Rhythm returned; other jazz musicians to appear were Stuff Smith and Billie Holiday (both 1936) and the participants in the Onyx's organized jam sessions, who included Jack Teagarden, the Dorsey brothers, and Bud Freeman. A fire on 28 February 1935 closed the premises until 23 July, but the club resumed its activities at the same address and remained there until 1937. In that year the Onyx moved along West 52nd Street to no.62, where it was managed by Helbock in association with Carl Kress. The most notable performances at this location were those of John Kirby's sextet with Maxine Sullivan. This venue closed in its turn in the final week of 1939 but, in 1942, Irving Alexander opened another Onyx club, the last to bear the name, at 57 West 52nd Street, which was active under various managers until around 1949, when it became a striptease club.

At its last address, the Onyx became well known for the presentation of swing, bop, and dixieland jazz, offering performances by many illustrious musicians and groups. Among them were a trio led by Al Casey (1943), Dizzy Gillespie's small group, which included Lester Young, Oscar Pettiford, and Budd Johnson (winter 1943–4), Billie Holiday (1943–4), Cozy Cole (to 1944), Barney Bigard (1944), Hot Lips Page (1944–5), Roy Eldridge, Ben Webster, Sarah Vaughan (1946), and Gillespie and Charlie Parker (both 1948). (A. Shaw: "Tape 4: the Onyx Club Review," "Onyx III," *The Street that Never Slept: New York's Fabled 52nd Street* (New York, 1971/*R*1983 as *52nd Street: the Street that Never Slept*), 75, 296)

——. **Open Door.** West 3rd Street and Washington Square South. Saloon. In spring 1953 Robert Reisner, assisted by Dave Lambert, began to present bop sessions on Sunday nights in the spacious room behind the bar; among the illustrious players they engaged were Charlie Parker, Bud Powell, Charles Mingus, Max Roach, Sonny Rollins, Milt Jackson, and Brew Moore. Reisner introduced a more extensive program of jazz, running from Sunday to Thursday, in October 1953, but this proved short-lived even though he presented fine groups led by Jackson, Roach, and others. After Reisner left the Open Door it became a venue for jam sessions: Moore, the trumpeter Tony Fruscella, the guitarist Ronnie Singer, and the drummer Freddie Gruber formed the resident band and such players as Cecil Taylor sat in on the sessions. Fruscella and Moore recorded the album *Fru 'n Brew* at the club in 1953 (Spot. 151). By early 1954 jazz was no longer offered there.

——. **Palace Gardens Club.** Seventh Avenue between West 139th Street and West 140th Street. At its grand opening on 14 March 1925 Fletcher Henderson's band and June Clark's Creole Orchestra played there. The club appears to have been short-lived, for by the following year at the latest the Bamboo Inn had taken over the premises (see above).

——. **Palais Royal.** 200 West 48th Street, at Broadway. It was in operation from at least 1920: Paul Whiteman led a nine-piece orchestra there from 1 October of that year. The venue was later used first by Connie's Inn and then by the Cotton Club (see above). There was apparently another Palais Royal in operation about a decade later, since the Dorsey Brothers Orchestra played at a club of that name in 1934.

——. **Palsson's.** 158 West 72nd Street. Bar. The venue consisted of a bar room and a separate room for jazz performances. It was active in 1981, when Anthony Davis and Chico Freeman appeared there.

——. **Paramount Hotel Grill.** This restaurant within the hotel offered jazz performances from at least the early 1930s. Charlie Barnet led a band there in 1933 and 1939.

——. **Paramount Theater.** Situated on Broadway downtown, by the time it became known in the 1930s as the mecca of swing bands in New York, it had a dual function as a theater for movies and stage shows. All the best-known big-band leaders appeared there, including Artie Shaw and Glen Gray (both December 1936), Ray Noble (January 1937), Benny Goodman (March 1937), and Cab Calloway.

——. **Park Central Hotel.** Seventh Avenue and West 55th Street. Jazz was offered for the diversion of the hotel's clients from at least the late 1920s. Ben Pollack appeared there in 1928, and in 1931 Noble Sissle and Red Nichols were both resident bandleaders (Artie Shaw was one of the latter's sidemen); Nichols continued to be associated with the hotel during the early years of the decade.

——. **Park Lane Hotel.** Regular jam sessions, organized by Paul Smith, Ernie Anderson, and Eddie Condon, took place in a venue in the hotel in the late 1930s. Among the musicians who took part in them was Sidney Bechet (early 1939).

——. **Patagonia.** See Pods' and Jerry's.

——. **Peacock Alley.** See Waldorf Astoria.

——. **Pied Piper.** 15 Barrow Street. This venue in Greenwich Village was active during the war years. James P. Johnson played an extended residency there in 1944–5, engaging Pee Wee Russell and Frankie Newton, among others, as members of his band. Ensembles led by Max Kaminsky and Willie "the Lion" Smith also performed at the club. On 26 December 1944 Wilbur De Paris presented a public jam session there, in which, besides De Paris himself, Sidney Bechet, Hank Duncan, Eddie Dougherty, Bob Wilber, Mary Lou Williams, Al Hall, and Bill Coleman took part; it was billed as a "Swing Soiree". The premises were later taken by the Café Bohemia (see above).

——. **The Plantation.** 50th Street and Broadway. The name Plantation was used at various times for venues in different parts of New York. It is not always possible to distinguish from references in the literature which of them is meant. The Plantation at which Duke Ellington's orchestra played between April and June 1926 seems likely to be the Plantation Theater Restaurant (see below).

——. **Plantation Café.** Winter Garden Theater. The restaurant above the theater offered jazz performances from at least 1927, when Duke Ellington's orchestra appeared there in the revue *Messin' Around*. It may or may not be the same venue as those referred to in different sources as the Plantation (see above) and the Plantation Theater Restaurant (see below).

——. **Plantation Club.** At least three venues in the city were known by this name. The principal Plantation Club opened at 644 Lenox Avenue (at West 142nd Street), in the premises occupied until February 1936 by the Cotton Club; it flourished until the early 1940s. Among the bands that appeared there were those led by Willie Bryant (1937), Ovie Alston (1937), and Hot

Lips Page (1938). Una Mae Carlisle performed at the club in the early 1940s, after her return from Europe.

Around 1930 Connie and George Immerman (who also owned and ran Connie's Inn, see above) took over a venue on Lenox Avenue and West 126th Street, intending to extend the rivalry that Connie's Inn already posed to the Cotton Club; Cab Calloway was to have been the resident bandleader. But their Plantation Club was destroyed, probably on its opening night, by gangsters hired by the Cotton Club's proprietor Owney Madden.

A third club of this name existed at 72 West 52nd Street (in premises lately vacated by the Onyx club) between about 1940 and 1943; the location was then taken over by the Three Deuces (see below). The Plantation Club on this site was owned by Arthur Jarwood.

——. **Plantation Theater Restaurant** [Plantation Room]. Broadway. This venue was opened in 1922 by Sam Salvin for the express purpose of staging a revue starring the singer Florence Mills; when the show subsequently went on tour it was named *The Plantation Revue.* Salvin's first venture was so successful that the theater restaurant continued to flourish for several years (to at least 1926).

——. **Pods' and Jerry's.** 168 West 132nd Street. It was formally named the Patagonia but was known by the nicknames of its owners, Pods (Charles) Hollingsworth and Jerry (Jeremiah) Preston; after the repeal of Prohibition in 1933 it was renamed the Log Cabin. Occupying premises earlier used by the Rhythm Club (see below) and for a short time in 1932 by the Hoofers Club, it flourished as a venue for small groups from 1932. It featured such musicians as Willie "the Lion" Smith, Jelly Roll Morton, Fats Waller, Sidney Bechet, and Billie Holiday.

——. **Prelude.** 3219 Broadway, at West 129th Street. It was active from at least the 1950s. Mary Lou Williams played there in December 1959.

——. **President Hotel.** See Adrian's Tap Room.

——. **Primrose Dancehall.** 125th Street. This Harlem venue engaged jazz bands to play for dancing during the 1930s. Cozy Cole and his Hot Cinders were among the groups that worked there.

——. **Rainbow Room.** RCA Building, 30 Rockefeller Plaza, Sixth Avenue. At the top of the RCA Building, the club consists of a bar, restaurant, and dance floor. It offered jazz performances from at least the late 1930s and continued to flourish through the 1980s. Landmarks in its history as a jazz venue included residencies by the Casa Loma Orchestra (1937), Sy Oliver's band (1970s and 1980s), and Panama Francis and his Savoy Sultans (1980–85). Other musicians who have played there are Jonah Jones (1950s), Bob Wilber, Woody Herman, Bob Haggart (1984), and Bobby Rosengarden (1985).

——. **Rathskeller.** See Cocoanut Grove.

——. **Reisenweber's Restaurant.** West 58th Street and Eighth Avenue, south of Columbus Circle. It was open by the mid-1910s, when its activities were directed by Max Hart. It is of jazz interest chiefly because it was the scene of the first sensational success of the Original Dixieland Jazz Band in January 1917. It continued to engage jazz musicians now and again into the 1920s; Bubber Miley played for cabaret acts there around 1923.

——. **Renaissance Ballroom and Casino.** 150 West 138th Street. It was active from the early 1920s into the early 1950s in large premises in a two-storey building at an intersection; the entertainment it offered, besides gambling and dancing, included cabaret acts, and there was always a call for jazz musicians. Vernon Andrade was resident for a period of 15 years from around 1923; among his sidemen at different times were Happy Caldwell, George Washington, and Zutty Singleton. Fletcher Henderson led his band there regularly in the late 1920s, Chick Webb's orchestra played in 1928–9, and Edgar Hayes's in 1937–8. In the early 1940s Al Sears led a big band at the Renaissance, of which Lester Young was a member early in 1943.

——. **Rendezvous Cabaret.** 65 West 129th Street, near Lenox Avenue. It opened on 11 September 1923 under the direction of Broadway Jones. Horace Henderson's Collegians played there in 1924. After a temporary closure, the club was reopened in November 1926 by the orchestras of Fletcher Henderson, Jimmy Wade, and Fess Williams; Elmer Snowden led successful residencies there in the late 1920s and early 1930s. In 1942 the Bamville Club opened at the same location (see above).

——. **Rendezvous Inn** [Rendezvous Club]. See Luckey's Rendezvous.

——. **Reno Sweeney.** See Zinno's.

——. **Rhythm Club.** 168 West 132nd Street, at Seventh Avenue (to 1932); 169 West 133rd Street (from 1932). It was opened in the early 1920s and managed by Bert Hall, a trombonist from Chicago. An informal venue in a basement room, it became a favorite haunt of musicians, who often jammed with the house band there. Sidney Bechet, Buddy Christian, Tommy Benford, and Louis Metcalf worked together at the club in 1924 and Bechet returned as resident bandleader the following year. The Rhythm Club was apparently still active in the early 1930s, for in 1932 it moved to a room at the back of the Nest Club on 133rd Street and the old venue was renamed the Hoofers Club. Pods' and Jerry's (see above) operated at the 132nd Street venue in the 1930s. For a time the Rhythm Club published its own newsletter, the *Rhythm Club News.*

——. **Riviera Club** [Club Riviera]. There appear to have been at least two venues of this name in the New York area at different times. The first, which may have been some way out of the city, was managed by Ben Marden and presented jazz from at least the mid-1930s. The short-lived Dorsey Brothers Orchestra appeared there in 1934. The following year the violinist Eddie South led a big band there opposite Paul Whiteman's orchestra; among South's sidemen were Don Pasquall, Everett Barksdale, Milt Hinton, and Tommy Benford.

Somewhat later a Riviera Club was active in Greenwich Village on Seventh Avenue South. Pee Wee Russell, Art Hodes, and Willie "the Lion" Smith appeared there in 1949, and between that time and 1951 other performers included Hot Lips Page, Vic Dickenson, Jonah Jones, Gene Roland, and Frank Orchard. The club later engaged a resident trio of lesser-known players led by the clarinetist Ben Parrish and became a venue for informal jam sessions.

——. **Rockland Palace.** Dance hall. This Harlem venue engaged jazz bands from at least 1928, when the Royal Garden Orchestra, led by the drummer Herbert Cowens, played there. In late 1930 Noble Sissle's band, with Sidney Bechet, undertook its first New York engagement at the Rockland. Other groups to perform at the dance hall during its long existence were Horace Henderson's Dixie Stompers (1931), Fletcher Henderson's Orchestra (1932), and a band led by Happy Caldwell (1957).

——. **Rose Danceland.** A small venue, established in a former dancing school, it was in operation from at least 1927. In that year Tony Sbarbaro and Chick Webb played there, and Jelly Roll Morton began a residency that lasted into 1928, with a group that included at various times Lee Blair, Russell Procope, Omer Simeon, and Ed Anderson. In the early 1930s Bingie Madison (1931) and the pianist Earle Howard (1932) were both resident at the club.

——. **Roseland Ballroom.** Two venues in the New York area used this name. After the success of his Roseland Ballroom in Philadelphia (see below), Louis J. Brecker opened the New York Roseland Ballroom at 1658 Broadway (at West 51st Street) on New Year's Day 1919. One of the largest ballrooms in New York, it was sumptuously decorated and beautifully maintained (it was thoroughly refurbished in 1930), and became the center for hot music and jazz dancing in the downtown area.

Early in its existence it began to engage black bands (the clientèle was exclusively white): A. J. Piron's orchestra appeared there in 1924 and in that year Fletcher Henderson started his long and influential association with the ballroom, which was to last intermittently until 1942. Jean Goldkette's band (with Bix Beiderbecke) also played at the Roseland (1926–31), and in 1926 engaged in a battle of bands with the Henderson ensemble (the two groups also played in alternation at the Graystone Ballroom in Detroit, see above).

From the late 1920s all the major swing bands took their turn at the Roseland, including McKinney's Cotton Pickers (1928), the Casa Loma Orchestra (1929), Marion Hardy's Alabamians (1931), and ensembles led by Claude Hopkins (late 1920s, 1931–4), Andy Kirk (1930), Chick Webb (intermittently 1930–31), Cab Calloway (1932), Luis Russell (1933), Count Basie (1936–9), Benny Carter (1939), and Ovie Alston (1942–7). Live broadcasts were made regularly from the venue by landline and transmitted throughout the USA. The ballroom closed on 27 December 1956 and the magnificent venue was demolished shortly afterwards. A new and even larger ballroom, Roseland Dance City, opened in the same year at 239 West 52nd Street. Among the bands that worked there was Count Basie's, which appeared several times in the 1970s (1972, 1973, 1979).

The success of the main Roseland Ballroom in Manhattan led to the opening in Brooklyn of another venue of the same name around 1930. Woody Herman's band made its official début there in 1936.

——. **Roseland Dance City.** See Roseland Ballroom.

——. **Ross Tavern.** West 51st Street and Sixth Avenue. After-hours club. This basement venue, active in the 1930s, was a favorite meeting place for jazz musicians. Among those who played there was Art Hodes (1939).

——. **Roundtable.** 151 East 50th Street. It was in operation by at least the late 1950s. Muggsy Spanier appeared there in 1959, as did Jimmy Rushing and Cootie Williams, and in December of the same year Jack Teagarden played with the trumpeter Don Goldie; a quintet led by Cootie Williams was resident in 1960–61 and Tyree Glenn led a group at the club in 1969.

——. **Royal Roost.** 1674 Broadway at West 47th Street. It was owned by Ralph Watkins (who had earlier run Kelly's Stable, see above) and Morris Levy (later the proprietor of Birdland (see above) and director of the record company Roulette), and was managed by Monte Kay; it probably opened in 1945. The venue originated as a chicken restaurant, but by 1946 was known principally as a venue for jazz. After an initial residency by Jimmie Lunceford's orchestra, the club's repertory turned increasingly to bop and cool jazz. This tradition was well established by the late 1940s, when among the musicians featured at the Royal Roost were Miles Davis, Lester Young, Charlie Parker, and Lennie Tristano. Watkins left the club in 1948 to open a new club called Bop City (see above), but the Royal Roost continued to be active into the 1950s; Buck Clayton was among the resident players around 1953.

——. **Ryan's.** See Jimmy Ryan's.

——. **St. James Infirmary.** 22 Seventh Avenue South, at Leroy Street. Active from at least the mid-1970s, the club has presented such musicians as Roswell Rudd (1974–5), Beaver Harris, and the pianist Hod O'Brien.

——. **St. Regis Hotel.** Fifth Avenue and 55th Street. Its name was later changed to the St. Regis–Sheraton Hotel. Jazz has been performed in various parts of the hotel from at least the late 1930s. In 1938 a jam session involving Sidney Bechet, Max Kaminsky, Yank Lawson, Hot Lips Page, Bobby Hackett, Mezz Mezzrow, Pee Wee Russell, Tommy Dorsey, Bud Freeman, Eddie Condon, Zutty Singleton, Dave Tough, and others was organized in the Viennese Roof Room by Joe Marsala; it was broadcast in both the USA and England. This venue was still in operation in 1973, when Count Basie appeared there. In the 1980s jazz was occasionally presented in the King Cole Room: Doc Cheatham (1984), Woody Herman (1985), and Joe Bushkin (1986) were among those who played there.

——. **Saratoga Club.** 575 Lenox Avenue, between West 139th Street and West 140th Street. Opened in 1929 in premises formerly occupied by the Capitol Palace (see above), it was directed by Johnny Carey and Sandy Thompson. It was one of the earliest cabarets in Harlem to adopt a jazz policy; Sidney Bechet's New Orleans Feetwarmers and a band led by Luis Russell both appeared there before the turn of the decade. In the 1930s resident musicians included Charlie Green and the pianist Earle Howard (both 1930) and Reggie Johnson, whose band included Cedric Wallace (1932). The venue was renamed Martin's Tavern in 1933.

——. **Savoy Ballroom.** 596 Lenox Avenue, between West 140th Street and West 141st Street. It was opened on 12 March 1926 by Moe Gale (Moses Galewski), Charles Galewski, and a Harlem real-estate businessman called Charles Buchanan, who functioned as the ballroom's manager. The Savoy was billed as the world's most beautiful ballroom; it occupied the second floor of a building that extended along the whole block between 140th and 141st streets, and featured a large dance floor (200 feet by 50 feet), two bandstands, and a retractable stage. It swiftly became the most popular dance venue in Harlem and many of the jazz dance crazes of the 1920s and 1930s originated there; it enjoyed a long and glittering career that lasted well into the 1950s, before a decline in its fortunes set in.

On its opening night the Savoy featured Fess Williams and his Royal Flush Orchestra, the Charleston Bearcats, fronted by Leon Abbey, and, as a guest band, Fletcher Henderson's Roseland Orchestra; the Charleston Bearcats formed a lasting connection with the venue and later changed its name to the Savoy Bearcats. Except on special occasions, the ballroom engaged two bands, which played alternate sets, and this policy led to its becoming a famous venue for battles of bands. Elaborate events of this kind were also organized by the management: on 15 May 1927 the Savoy presented a "Battle of Jazz," which featured King Oliver's Dixie Syncopators, a band led by Williams, Chick Webb's Harlem Stompers, and Henderson's Roseland Orchestra; other battles were fought between bands led by Lloyd Scott, Webb, Alex Johnson, Charlie Johnson, Williams, and Henderson (6 May 1928) and between Cab Calloway's Missourians and groups led by Duke Ellington, Henderson, Cecil Scott, Lockwood Lewis, and Webb (14 May 1930).

From the 1930s a number of bandleaders formed long and influential associations with the ballroom. By the mid-1930s Chick Webb's name was inextricably linked with the Savoy's and he continued to lead his band there through the decade; his singer from 1934 was Ella Fitzgerald, who took over leadership of the ensemble after Webb's untimely death in 1939. Al Cooper's Savoy Sultans first appeared at the ballroom in 1937 and remained for many years. The Erskine Hawkins Orchestra enjoyed a similar connection with the venue, playing extended residencies from the 1940s through the 1950s. Besides those who played there regularly, most of the important bands and musicians of the swing era appeared at the Savoy at some time: Andy Kirk, the Mills Brothers, Sidney Bechet, Count Basie, Coleman Hawkins, Roy Eldridge, and many others played single engagements or short residencies there. Benny Carter's big band made its début in the ballroom in March 1939 and Carter continued to work there intermittently until January 1941. As was the case with several of the city's most famous nightspots, the Savoy was connected by landline with a New York radio station, which allowed its music to be broadcast throughout the nation.

——. **Seventh Avenue South.** 21 Seventh Avenue South, at Leroy Street. This small venue was opened in 1978 and remained active until 1985. It was owned by Mike and Randy Brecker, whose band, the Brecker Brothers, often played there. Until the early 1980s it offered a repertory that emphasized jazz-rock, but the range of styles gradually broadened; in 1984, for example, Lew Soloff and Gil Evans's big band appeared there.

——. **Sherwood Inn.** It was active from at least the late 1950s, when Billy Bauer first played there; his connections with the club continued into the next decade. Other musicians who performed at the Sherwood included Miff Mole and Pee Wee Russell in 1960.

——. **Showplace.** 146 West 4th Street. Its importance to jazz rests largely on the performances given there between December 1959 and October 1960 by Charles Mingus. After Mingus left the club, his former sidemen Lonnie Hillyer and Charles McPherson led a band there.

——. **Shuffle Inn.** See Connie's Inn.

——. **Slugs.** 242 East 3rd Street. It was opened early in 1966 and specialized in (but was not restricted to) the presentation of hard bop. During its first year of operation the performers who appeared there included Jackie McLean, Joe Henderson, Philly Joe Jones, Yusef Lateef, Stanley Turrentine, Charles Lloyd, and Ornette Coleman (who led a trio in September 1966). The club later engaged other such prominent players as Freddie Hubbard (1967), Sun Ra (1967–8), Art Blakey (1969), McCoy Tyner (1969), Elvin Jones (1970–71), Lee Morgan (1971–2), and Gato Barbieri (1972). Performances given by Charles Tolliver at Slugs in 1970 were recorded and issued on the LP *Live at Slugs* (SE 1972). The club closed shortly after Lee Morgan was murdered there in 1972.

——. **Smalls' Cafeteria.** Fifth Avenue and 135th Street. The history of the jazz venues run by Ed Smalls is not altogether clear. A club or clubs known variously as Smalls' Cafeteria, Smalls' Cabaret Club, and Smalls' Paradise Lounge apparently predated the famous Smalls' Paradise (see below), as did the Sugar Cane Club (see below). Willie "the Lion" Smith was first engaged by Ed Smalls in 1920 and Rex Stewart in 1923; in 1924 Chas and Perry Smith led Smiths Creole Five, with June Clark among the members, at Smalls' Cafeteria.

——. **Smalls' Paradise.** 2294½ Seventh Avenue, at West 135th Street. It was opened on 22 October 1925 by Ed Smalls in basement premises, where he offered music and dancing. It became one of the most successful clubs in Harlem, surviving the Depression and then the difficult postwar years, when most venues in the area felt the pinch and many closed. It continued to be active into the 1980s and ceased operations only in 1986.

Smalls' enjoyed its heyday in the 1920s and early 1930s, when many of the most important groups and musicians of the period occupied its bandstand. Willie "the Lion" Smith, Jimmy Archey, Fletcher Henderson, and Charlie Johnson all first played there in the late 1920s, and Smith and Johnson both returned to the club for long residencies; Elmer Snowden led the Smalls' Paradise Orchestra there during the early 1930s and the group made the film *Smash Your Baggage* in 1932. During the Depression Smalls cut back his operation, and in 1934–5 James P. Johnson led a band of reduced size; after 1935, however, the club's resources were restored and by 1937 Hot Lips Page was leading a big band there. In the 1940s and 1950s resident bandleaders included Gene Sedric (late 1940s), Harry Dial (1947–55), Happy Caldwell (1950–53), and Gus Aitken (1950).

——. **Spotlite (Club).** 56 West 52nd Street. It was opened in December 1944 by Clark Monroe (also the proprietor of Monroe's Uptown House, see above) and operated for about two years as a venue for swing and bop. Among the leading musicians he engaged were Coleman Hawkins, Hot Lips Page, Billie Holiday, Ben Webster, Charlie Parker, Dizzy Gillespie, and Oscar Pettiford.

——. **Star and Garter.** 105 West 13th Street, near Sixth Avenue. Bar and restaurant. Active around 1980, it presented jazz at weekends and specialized in piano and double bass duos. The musicians who appeared there included Tommy Flanagan and Cedar Walton.

——. **Storytowne.** See Storyville.

——. **Storyville.** 41 East 58th Street. Named, like the club he founded earlier in Boston (see above), for the red-light district of New Orleans, it was opened by George Wein in 1976. By 1979 it had been renamed Storytowne. The musicians who played there included the quintet led by Harry Edison and Eddie "Lockjaw" Davis, Joe Newman, and Gerry Mulligan.

——. **Stryker's.** 103 West 86th Street, at Columbus Avenue. Bar. It was established in 1972 and offered performances by some notable musicians, among them Jimmy Garrison, Warren Chiasson, Chet Baker, Lee Konitz, and the duo of Chuck Wayne and Joe Puma. It had closed by 1982.

——. **Studio Rivbea.** Situated in the SoHo district, it was opened in 1970 by Sam and Bea Rivers and specialized in free jazz. It remained active throughout the decade.

——. **Studio 77.** See Ali's Alley.

——. **Stuyvesant Casino.** 140 Second Avenue, near East 9th Street. Ballroom. This large venue flourished during the 1940s and 1950s, offering dancing, jazz performances, and jam sessions. Bunk Johnson's New Orleans band (for illustrations *see* JOHNSON, BUNK) made its New York début there on 28 September 1945, a performance that precipitated an upsurge of interest in New Orleans jazz. Later the promoter Bob Maltz rented the venue on Friday and Saturday nights to present traditional and mainstream jazz; he engaged, among others, Sidney Bechet, Art Hodes (1945–9), Henry "Red" Allen (1950), Zutty Singleton, and Buck Clayton.

——. **Sugar Cane Club.** Fifth Avenue. It was opened by Ed Smalls in the early 1920s, before the founding of Smalls' Paradise. It continued to be active until at least the late decade, since Pete Brown appeared there in 1927–8. (But see Smalls' Cafeteria, above, for a discussion of the difficulty of identifying the various venues run by Smalls.)

——. **Sweet Basil.** 88 Seventh Avenue, at Bleecker Street. It was opened in January 1975 by Horst Liepolt and Mel Litoff, and it continued to flourish throughout the 1980s, offering a wide-ranging repertory. Musicians who have appeared there include Gil Evans, Bucky Pizzarelli, John Abercrombie, Ron Carter, Junior Mance, Lester Bowie, Pharoah Sanders, David Murray, Doc Cheatham, Jim Hall and Red Mitchell (as a duo), Abdullah Ibrahim, George Russell, and the Leaders. For several years into the mid-1980s Doc Cheatham's band played there regularly on Sunday afternoons. Until shortly before his death Evans led a band at the club on Mondays; performances by this ensemble were recorded in 1984 and issued on the Japanese label Electric Bird as *The Monday Night Orchestra Live at Sweet Basil*. From 1983 Liepolt's Music is . . . an Open Sky festival took place at the club (*see* FESTIVALS).

——. **Syncopation.** 15 Waverly Place, at Mercer Street. Loft. It was active as a venue for bop from at least 1980, when John Lewis appeared there.

——. **Tango Gardens.** Ballroom. It was active from the late 1920s, when a band led by June Clark, with Jimmy Harrison and Charlie Green among the members at different times, played there. From 1947 to 1953 Bingie Madison led a small group at the Tango Palace, which may or may not be the same venue as the Tango Gardens.

——. **Tap Room.** See Adrian's Tap Room.

——. **Three Deuces.** 72 West 52nd Street. It opened in premises vacated in 1937 by the Onyx club (see above) and was active as a jazz venue until around 1950. Among the managers were Sammy Kay and Irving Alexander. The club presented a range of styles and in the 1940s particularly engaged many notable musicians, including Art Tatum, the Spirits of Rhythm, John Kirby, Maxine Sullivan, Slim Gaillard, Ben Webster, Eddie Heywood, Johnny Guarnieri, Billy Taylor (ii), Georgie Auld, Slam Stewart, Sid Catlett, Lennie Tristano, Erroll Garner, Don Byas, Shelly Manne, Charlie Parker, Dizzy Gillespie, Ella Fitzgerald, George Shearing, and Kai Winding. In 1950 the venue became a striptease club, and it closed around 1954. (A Shaw: "The Three Deuces," *The Street that Never Slept: New York's Fabled 52nd Street* (New York, 1971/*R*1983 as *52nd Street: the Street that Never Slept*), 284)

——. **Tin Palace.** 325 Bowery, at 2nd Street. This jazz room was opened in 1979; Art Davis, Hilton Ruiz, and Gary Bartz played there in that year.

——. **Top of the Gate.** See Village Gate.

——. **Town Hall.** 123 West 43rd Street. It opened in 1921 as a public meeting house, seating nearly 1500 people (for illustration *see* JAZZ (i), fig.5). The hall was acquired by New York University in 1958 and closed temporarily between 1978 and 1980. Concerts of jazz were held there from the 1940s and Eddie Condon regularly organized jam sessions early in the decade. Among the important events held at Town Hall were several concerts given by Sidney Bechet (the first of which took place on 21 February 1941), a gala performance staged by the Blue Note record label (15 December 1945), a series of midnight concerts of blues (1947), an appearance by Louis Armstrong (17 May 1947), and an all-star concert in which Bunk Johnson, Muggsy Spanier, Albert Nicholas, James P. Johnson, and other New Orleans jazz musicians took part (4 October 1947). Among the promoters who used the venue at this time was "Symphony Sid" Torin.

A number of important recordings were made at Town Hall. Condon's concerts were transcribed for radio broadcasts, and many subsequently were issued on commercial discs. A performance given on 9 June 1945 by Don Byas with Slam Stewart, Teddy Wilson, Red Norvo, and Stuff Smith was recorded in its entirety. Concerts given by Charlie Ventura in 1945, and by an all-star group that included Sidney Bechet, James P. Johnson, and Baby Dodds in 1946, were also recorded, as were two given later by Charles Mingus (12 October 1962 and 4 February 1972).

——. **Two Saints.** See Five Spot.

——. **Ubangi Club.** 2221 Seventh Avenue, at West 131st Street (1936 or later to early 1940s); 1678 Broadway, north of 52nd Street (early 1940s to *c*1948). It opened some time after 1936 in the premises formerly occupied by Connie's Inn (see above) in Harlem, and was the only other club to succeed at that venue. Some time in the early 1940s it moved downtown to a building on Broadway that later housed the Clique and Birdland (see above). Before the move bands led by Teddy Hill, Kaiser Marshall (1935) and Ovie Alston played at the club. In the 1940s resident bandleaders included Leon Abbey, Cecil Scott (1942–3), and Erskine Hawkins. The successful floor shows at the downtown venue were written by Chappie Willett.

——. **Uptown Lowdown Club.** See Harlem Uproar House.

——. **Victoria Café.** West 141st Street and Seventh Avenue. It presented jazz from at least the 1930s, when among the groups to perform there was a trio led by Freddie Moore (1933–6).

——. **Viennese Roof Room.** See St. Regis Hotel.

——. **Village Fair.** See Village Vanguard.

——. **Village Gate.** 160 Bleecker Street, at Thompson Street. It opened in 1958 and continued to be active through the late 1980s. The club contains separate venues: in the basement is the main club, on the ground floor the Terrace Bar, and upstairs a room known as the Top of the Gate. During the 1960s and 1970s the Village Gate presented mostly bop and hard-bop performers, though other styles were also represented; among the numerous internationally known musicians who performed there were Miles Davis, Erroll Garner, Cecil Taylor, Horace Silver, Gerry Mulligan, Earl Hines, Jaki Byard, Bill Evans (ii), Lee Konitz, Ahmad Jamal, Roland Kirk, McCoy Tyner, and Art Blakey. During the 1980s the stylistic emphasis at this establishment changed from bop to jazz-rock and salsa. Among performers in the Terrace Bar in the late 1980s were Patti Bown, and duos of Bill Mays and Michael Formanek and Allan Botschinsky and Niels-Henning Ørsted Pedersen.

——. **Village Vanguard.** Charles Street and Greenwich Avenue (26 February 1934 – 1935); 178 Seventh Avenue (from 1935). In 1932 Max Gordon opened a club, the Village Fair, on Sullivan Street in Greenwich Village, which provided a forum for poets to meet and read their work. The first Village Vanguard, opened in a basement on Charles Street at Greenwich Avenue, also functioned as a meeting place for local poets; when he wanted to introduce music at the club, Gordon was refused a cabaret license because of the shortcomings of the premises and was therefore obliged to move again. He opened a third club early in 1935 in another basement on Seventh Avenue, where a speakeasy called the Golden Triangle had operated earlier. The new venue offered poetry and jazz, but it was not until the mid-1950s that it became known mainly as a jazz venue.

During its long and distinguished career the Village Vanguard has offered jazz in many styles, popular music, folk music, dancing, cabaret acts, and performances by comedians. In the 1930s and 1940s, though not yet fully established as a jazz venue, it engaged performers of the standing of Sidney Bechet, Una Mae Carlisle, Art Hodes, and Mary Lou Williams; during the 1940s Eddie Heywood, Zutty Singleton, and Jimmy Hamilton were the resident trio, playing for dancing and accompanying visiting musicians. After it made its name as one of New York's main jazz venues, such musicians as Dizzy Gillespie, Art Blakey, Miles Davis, Sonny Rollins, Coleman Hawkins, Charles Mingus, Gerry Mulligan, the Modern Jazz Quartet, Thelonious Monk, Keith Jarrett, Chick Corea, J. J. Johnson, Frank Morgan, and Sphere played at the Village Vanguard. The most significant of the venue's events were perhaps the many performances given by John Coltrane's groups, which resulted in some of his finest recordings, among them *Live at the Village Vanguard* (1961, Imp. 10) and *Live at the Village Vanguard Again* (1966, Imp. 9124). The Thad Jones–Mel Lewis Orchestra (from 1979 the Mel Lewis Orchestra) played there every Monday night from February 1966 into the 1980s. The club marked its 50th anniversary in 1985 with a year of celebratory performances by musicians who included Gillespie, Wynton Marsalis, and Annie Ross. (M. Gordon: *Live at the Village Vanguard*, New York, 1980)

——. **Village West.** 577 Hudson Street, near Bank Street. Bar. It was active for a short time around 1982–4. Among the soloists and small groups who performed there were Jaki Byard, Barney Kessel, and JoAnne Brackeen, and the duo of Ron Carter and Jim Hall, which appeared regularly in 1984.

——. **Waldorf Astoria.** Park Avenue at East 49th Street and East 50th Street. The hotel opened on this site, occupying the entire block between Park Avenue and Lexington Avenue, in November 1931, and jazz was performed in its various venues from the mid-1930s. The violinist Leo Reisman led a popular orchestra in the hotel for long periods in the 1930s and 1940s, during which time residencies were also played by major big bands, including Benny Goodman's, which fulfilled an engagement in the Empire Room from October 1939 until New Year's Day 1940 (for illustration *see* BANDS, fig.4). On 23 February 1949 Rudi Blesh organized a battle of bands there, and Charlie Parker and Sidney Bechet played for a youth conference; a performance by Parker on 5 March of the same year was broadcast. Among the other musicians who performed at the Waldorf was Count Basie, who worked there in June 1957, June 1959, and June 1960. During the 1970s jazz pianists played regularly at Peacock Alley, a lounge in the hotel.

——. **West Boondock.** 114 Tenth Avenue, at West 17th Street. Restaurant. It was in existence from around the late 1970s until the mid-1980s and regularly engaged solo pianists. Among those who appeared there was Sadik Hakim (1981, 1983).

——. **West End.** 2911 Broadway, at West 113th Street. Restaurant. Situated near Columbia University, it opened in 1973 and continued to be active through the late 1980s. Until the early 1980s its activities were directed by Phil Schaap, who engaged numerous veteran swing musicians. Among those who appeared there were the Countsmen, Jo Jones, Sonny Greer, Russell Procope, Eddie Durham, Sammy Price, Harold Ashby, Franc Williams, and George Kelly. During the mid-1970s, in a departure from its usual activities, the club presented performances by the bop alto saxophonist Lee Konitz. In the 1980s among the musicians to appear at the West End were Dizzy Gillespie, Benny Carter, and David "Fathead" Newman.

——. **Whippoorwill.** 18 East 18th Street. This venue consisted of the main nightclub on the ground floor and an upstairs restaurant named Joanna. Donald Byrd and Jimmy Owens were among the musicians who appeared there during 1986, its only year of operation.

——. **Yacht Club.** 38 West 52nd Street (1934–8); 150 West 52nd Street (1938–44); 66 West 52nd Street (1944). The first club of this name was a speakeasy, which operated in the 1920s at an unknown address. After the repeal of Prohibition a supper club of this name opened in 1934 at 38 West 52nd Street; it moved to no.150 in 1938. Early in 1944 it took over premises (at no.66) vacated in November 1943 by the Famous Door (see above); however, it lasted only a few months at this location, closing in May 1944, and the venue was taken over by the Downbeat club (see above). The Yacht Club was noted for the presentation of popular music, swing, and bop. During its ten years' existence it featured such musicians as Red McKenzie (1936), Fats Waller (1938), Trummy Young, Billy Eckstine (1944), and Coleman Hawkins; Dizzy Gillespie's and Oscar Pettiford's quintet was resident in 1944, and when the group disbanded Gillespie remained at the club, and continued to play there when it opened as the Downbeat.

——. **Yeah Man.** Seventh Avenue and West 137th Street (1925–33); ?1350 Seventh Avenue (from 1933). It began as a speakeasy, then after the repeal of Prohibition opened as a legitimate club in new premises further down Seventh Avenue. The house pianist at the second location was Don Lambert, and from the late 1930s the club featured a number of small groups. Yeah Man was taken over in the mid-1940s by John Velasco and it was later renamed Jock's Place.

——. **Ye Old Nest.** This club in Harlem was active in the 1930s, when it was a noted venue for jam sessions.

——. **Zanzibar** [Club Zanzibar, Café Zanzibar]. West 49th Street and Broadway. It was opened in July 1943 and became an important venue during and after World War II for black shows and performances by big bands. Many of the most important ensembles of the period played there, including those led by Don Redman (1943), Sabby Lewis (1944), Claude Hopkins (1944–6), Duke Ellington (1945), and Sy Oliver (1946).

——. **Zinno's.** 126 West 13th Street. Bar and restaurant. It was opened in 1982 in premises that housed a speakeasy in the 1920s and a club called Reno Sweeney in the 1970s; it continued to be active throughout the decade. Performers who have appeared there include George Mraz, Michael Moore, Hilton Ruiz, and Major Holley (all 1982), Ray Bryant, Jimmy Rowser, and Milt Hinton (all 1986), and Ruby Braff (1987). The club specializes in the presentation of piano and double bass duos: Junior Mance and Marty Rivera, Ruiz and Rowser, and Moore and Gene Bertoncini played as duos at Zinno's.

——. **Zombie.** Flushing Meadows. Bar and restaurant. It was one of the stands at the World's Fair in 1940. Among the jazz ensembles that played there was John Kirby's sextet.

See also Hudson River.

BIBLIOGRAPHY

New York

S. B. Charters and L. Kunstadt: *Jazz: a History of the New York Scene* (Garden City, NY, 1962/R1981)
J. H. Clarke, ed.: *Harlem, U.S.A.* (Berlin, 1964)
A. Shaw: *The Street that Never Slept: New York's Fabled 52nd Street* (New York, 1971/R1983 as *52nd Street: the Street that Never Slept*)
W. C. Allen: *Hendersonia: the Music of Fletcher Henderson and his Musicians: a Bio-discography* (Highland Park, NJ, 1973)
T. Fox: *Showtime at the Apollo* (New York, 1983)
J. Schiffman: *Harlem Heyday: a Pictorial History of Modern Black Show Business and the Apollo Theatre* (Buffalo, 1984)

NORWALK, CA. See Los Angeles (metropolitan area).

OAKLAND, CA. **Big Bear Tavern.** Redwood Canyon, near Oakland. Roadhouse. Jazz was presented there from at least the late 1930s and the management developed a policy of mounting all-night jam sessions. The musicians who regularly took part included Lu Watters and some of the sidemen from his big band, with whom in 1940 he formed his Yerba Buena Jazz Band.

——. **Koncepts Cultural Gallery.** Jenny Lind Hall, 2267 Telegraph Avenue (1984–7); 480 Third Street (at Washington Street) (1987–). It was opened in June 1984 by Edsel Matthews and Kimathe Asante for the performance of rhythm-and-blues, jazz (styles from bop to free jazz), and blues. Art Sato directed its "Masters of Jazz" series, which included concerts by such musicians as Sun Ra, Teddy Edwards, Joe Henderson, and Randy Weston. The club moved to new premises, formerly the Western Pacific railway station in Jack London Square, in 1987, opening on 5 November with a performance by James Newton and his group, with Bobby Hutcherson as a guest soloist. (D. Richardson: "The Grass Roots of Jazz," *San Francisco Bay Guardian* (11 Nov 1987), 21)

——. **Yoshi's (Night Spot).** 6030 Claremont Avenue. Jazz has been played at this Japanese restaurant from the mid-1980s, under the music director Charles Lapaglia. The favored repertory is bop and the restaurant has become the principal venue in the San Francisco Bay area following the demise of Keystone Korner in San Francisco. It has engaged numerous important players in different styles, including Jimmy Smith, Joe Henderson, Steve Lacy, Phil Woods, Ray Brown and Milt Jackson, Horace Silver, Randy Weston, Stan Getz, McCoy Tyner, Toots Thielemans, Chico and Von Freeman, Art Blakey, and Tommy Flanagan.

OCEAN PARK, CA. See Los Angeles (metropolitan area).

OHIO RIVER. **SS *George Washington.*** This pleasure steamer, formerly named the SS *Sidney* (see Mississippi River, above), belonged to the Streckfus line and became the *George Washington* in 1921 after major refitting. It plied the Ohio River throughout the 1920s and for much of the 1930s until it was removed from service and dismantled in 1938. In 1922 Clarence W. Elder joined the boat's band to play calliope and banjo, and he later became the *Washington*'s bandleader and ultimately its captain; Claude Thornhill played with him in 1925.

PASADENA, CA. See Los Angeles (metropolitan area).

PEABODY, MA. **Lenny's on the Turnpike.** It was active from 1963 to 1971, during which time it presented performances by some of the most important American jazz musicians of the period. Among those who appeared there were Miles Davis, Charles Mingus, Thelonious Monk, Buddy Rich, Weather Report, Cannonball Adderley, Stan Getz, Zoot Sims and Al Cohn, and Henry "Red" Allen.

PHILADELPHIA. **Aqua Lounge.** 52nd Street and Chancellor Street, West Philadelphia. It was active as a venue for jazz for about eight years in the 1960s.

——. **Benny the Bum.** 53rd Street and Market Street. It was in operation from the mid-1970s until the early 1980s and mounted performances by both local groups and nationally known musicians.

——. **Blue Note.** 15th Street and Ridge Avenue; Washington Lane and Limekiln Pike. At least two venues in Philadelphia have been known as the Blue Note. The first was the city's principal nightclub in the 1950s and offered performances of bop and related styles. The resident pianist for a period from 1953 was Ray Bryant, and Jimmy Bond was the resident double bass player around that time; the other musicians who appeared there included Charlie Parker, Miles Davis, Lester Young, Clifford Brown, Dizzy Gillespie, Sonny Rollins, Kenny Dorham, Eddie Jefferson, and James Moody. The club was destroyed by fire. The new Blue Note has engaged such performers as Donald Byrd and Oscar Brown, Jr., and features open jam sessions on Monday evenings.

——. **Borgia Café.** 406 South 2nd Street. Principally a venue for local musicians, this nightclub has presented a wide range of jazz styles from the early 1980s.

——. **Broad Street Tavern.** 4638 North Broad Street. Active in the 1980s, the tavern features bop, played mostly by local performers.

——. **Carl Drew's Lounge.** 52nd Street and Media Street. Among the players who have appeared there are many local bands and such nationally known musicians as Cat Anderson.

——. **Chestnut Cabaret.** 38th Street and Chestnut Street. It offered jazz, blues, and folk music from the mid-1970s. Jon Faddis, Jimmy Heath, Slide Hampton, Eddie "Lockjaw" Davis, and Clark Terry have performed there. In the late 1980s the house big band was led by the baritone saxophonist Joe Sudler.

——. **Down Beat Club.** It was in existence by at least the early 1940s. Dizzy Gillespie led his own small group there in 1942.

——. **Dunbar Theatre.** South Street near 15th Street. Its programs included jazz from at least the early 1920s. In 1923 the show *How Come,* which starred Sidney Bechet and also included Bessie Smith in the cast, was staged there. Eubie Blake performed frequently in the theater during the 1920s. In the early 1930s the Dunbar was converted to a movie house.

——. **George Wilson's Café.** See Wilson's Café.

——. **Gino's Empty Foxhole.** 40th Street and Locust Walk. This nightclub was in existence for about ten years from the early 1970s. It presented leading bop and free-jazz musicians such as Sunny Murray, Cecil Taylor, Sun Ra, and Byard Lancaster.

——. **Gleason's Musical Bar.** A small venue, it was active by the mid-1940s. Herman Autrey led a combo there for a residency of several years from 1945.

——. **Hotel Senator.** See Swing Rendezvous.

——. **International House.** 36th Street and Chestnut Street. Established in the 1960s, it presented a broadly based repertory, including blues, folk music, and jazz. Among the jazz musicians who appeared there is Jimmy Heath.

——. **Jewel's.** 679 North Broad Street. It was opened around 1980 and has offered performances by Clark Terry, Frank Wess, Joe Newman, Dakota Staton, and Etta Jones, among others.

——. **Just Jazz.** 2121 Arch Street. It operated under this name for a short time from the late 1960s into the early 1970s. Its repertory was mainly hard bop, and among the musicians who performed there were Elvin Jones, Milt Jackson, and Art Blakey. A new club, named the Memphis, later opened in the same premises.

——. **Lincoln Theater.** South Broad Street and Lombard Street. One of many theaters in the city to present jazz performances as part of its variety programs, it flourished in the 1930s. Fletcher Henderson (1934–6) and Noble Sissle were regularly engaged there, and Duke Ellington, Don Redman, and Jimmie Lunceford also appeared.

——. **Memphis.** See Just Jazz.

——. **Natalie's Lounge.** 4003 Market Street. This nightclub was opened in the late 1960s and included jazz in its repertory from the early 1980s. Philly Joe Jones and Johnny Coles are among the musicians to have played there. Open jam sessions are held on Saturday afternoons.

——. **Night Owl.** Temple University. A nightspot on the university campus, it offers all styles of jazz as well as Latin music. Performances are often broadcast on radio station WRTI.

——. **Painted Bride.** 4th Street and Arch Street. It was opened in the late 1970s and flourished into the 1980s. Among the musicians to have appeared there are Mal Waldron, Odeon Pope, and Sun Ra.

——. **P & T Club.** Broad Street and Arch Street. Active from the early 1980s, the club has featured Donald Byrd and Philly Joe Jones, among others.

——. **Pearl Theater.** Ridge Avenue near 23rd Street. Jazz was performed there from at least the late 1920s and appears to have formed part of the entertainment until well into the 1940s. Wilbur De Paris was manager of the resident orchestra in 1927–8. In 1930 Noble Sissle's band appeared, and the following year Andy Kirk's Clouds of Joy played a residency there under the leadership of Blanche Calloway. Other important bands to visit the Pearl were those of Bennie Moten (for illustration *see* MOTEN, BENNIE) and Count Basie.

——. **Pep's Musical Bar.** Broad Street and South Street. The bar was in existence from the 1940s until the mid-1960s and offered performances by many of the principal musicians of the period. Herman Autrey led his own group for a long residency there from 1945; among the other jazz players who performed there were John Coltrane, Dizzy Gillespie (as the leader of a small group), Sonny Rollins, Max Roach, Clifford Brown, Dinah Washington, and Benny Golson. A performance by Yusef Lateef was recorded at the club in 1964 (*Live at Pep's*, Imp. 69).

——. **Prince Total Experience Lounge.** 1410 Hunting Park Avenue. This nightclub was opened in the mid-1980s, offering jazz on Sunday and Monday nights. Among the performers who have appeared there are McCoy Tyner and Ray Bryant.

——. **Roseland Ballroom.** 12th Street and Chestnut Street. It was opened in 1918 by Louis J. Brecker. Its successful operation led to his opening a second ballroom of that name in New York the following year.

——. **Showboat.** Broad Street and Lombard Street. The many famous jazz musicians to play at this venue have included John Coltrane, Thelonious Monk, Ahmad Jamal, Horace Silver, Miles Davis, J. J. Johnson, Stan Getz, and Sonny Rollins.

——. **Spider Kelly's.** It was active from at least the 1950s as a venue for solo and small-group jazz. Among the musicians who worked there was Ray Bryant, who appeared at the club in 1958.

——. **Sterling's Place at Dino's.** 135 South 46th Street. This nightclub has presented a repertory that emphasizes bop and related styles. Milt Jackson, Art Blakey, Dakota Staton, and Junior Cook, among others, have performed there.

——. **Strand Ballroom.** From 1928 to 1930 Fletcher Henderson's orchestra played there several times for dances, sharing the bandstand with the Ten Arcadians (1928–9) and Wilbur De Paris's orchestra (1928). The venue was active at least to the end of 1938, when Henderson returned.

——. **Swing Rendezvous.** This nightspot within the Hotel Senator was in existence by the 1950s, employing solo performers and small groups. Sidney Bechet led a group there regularly around 1950 and Dick Wellstood was the resident pianist for a time.

——. **Watusi Club.** 46th Street and Walnut Street. Although it opened in the 1950s it first offered performances of jazz in the mid-1980s.

——. **Wilson's Café.** Named for its owner, George Wilson, it was a venue for jazz performances from at least the 1920s. George Baquet led a band there for more than 14 years in the 1920s and 1930s.

PHOENIX, AZ. **Bud Brown's Barn.** Situated on the outskirts of Phoenix, this venue, owned by Bud Brown, specialized in country music and was used for barn dances and barbecues. Its musical programs often included dixieland jazz and Kid Ory's band performed there regularly.

POTOMAC RIVER. Jazz formed part of the entertainment offered on the pleasure craft that worked the river during the summer season. Around 1920 Rex Stewart gained his first professional experience playing in one of the riverboat bands.

REDONDO BEACH, CA. See Los Angeles (metropolitan area).

ROBBINS, IL. **Apex Chateau.** West 136th Street and South Kedzie Avenue (1936–*c*1940); 13614 Clair Boulevard (from *c*1940). On the extreme south side of Chicago, the location of this venue testifies to the steady drift of the black population from the center of the city to the suburbs, starting in the 1930s. It was in operation by June 1936 and by 1940 had moved its premises and changed its name to the Apex Grill and Road House. In May 1940 the pianist Sonny Thompson and his Swingsters were the resident band and the following summer Rosetta Howard appeared there. The proprietors at that time were Jesse "Fats" Robinson and Walter Flowers and the venue continued to be active into at least the mid-1940s. In 1959 the comedian Dick Gregory opened a club on the site formerly occupied by the Apex.

ST. LOUIS. **Arcadia Ballroom.** 3515–23 Olive Street. It was built before World War I as the Dreamland Ballroom and took its new name shortly after the war, when Joe Ternes became the owner. A six-piece New Orleans group played there in the mid-1920s; originally using the name Crescent City Jazzers, it soon became the Arcadian Serenaders and recorded under that name in St. Louis, with Wingy Manone as the trumpeter in 1924 and Sterling Bose in 1925. In the ballroom the Arcadian Serenaders played alongside a group led by Frankie Trumbauer (resident 8 September 1925 to 3 May 1926), which included Bix Beiderbecke and Pee Wee Russell. The Arcadia continued to be active in the 1930s: Charlie Creath led a band there in 1933. The venue was later known as the Tune Town Ballroom; it was demolished in 1966.

——. **Chauffeur's Club.** 3133 Pine Boulevard. It offered performances of jazz from at least 1918, when De Priest Wheeler played in the resident band. In the 1920s Charlie Creath, Ed Allen (1923–4), and Dewey Jackson (*c*1927) all led bands there.

——. **Club Plantation.** See Plantation Club.

——. **Club Riviera.** Billy Eckstine's orchestra, including Dizzy Gillespie and Charlie Parker, performed there in 1944.

——. **Dreamland Ballroom.** See Arcadia Ballroom.

——. **Elk's Club.** It was used during the 1930s and 1940s for after-hours jam sessions. Although he had met Miles Davis earlier, it was there that Clark Terry first appreciated the latter's talent as an improviser.

——. **Jazzland.** 22nd Street and Market Street. It may have been owned by Charlie Creath, who from the mid-1920s played a long residency there, which lasted into the 1930s. In the summer of 1925 he led a pickup band at the club in a recording session for Okeh.

——. **Plantation Club.** Active from at least the early 1930s, it appears to have opened only during the winter. In 1932–3 the house band was led by the trumpeter Walter Stanley; his ensemble was followed into the club by the Jeter–Pillars Orchestra, which played an extended residency from 1934 until the mid-1940s.

——. **Red Inn.** Jimmy Blanton played there in the late 1930s.

——. **Rhumboogie Club.** It flourished at least during the early 1940s, when Tiny Bradshaw's orchestra, including Sonny Stitt, performed there.

——. **Tune Town Ballroom.** See Arcadia Ballroom.

See also Mississippi River.

San Diego, CA. **Club Royal.** It was in existence from at least the mid-1940s. The trumpeter and singer Walter Fuller led his own band there for a 12-year residency from 1946.

——. **Honeybucket Club.** It was active from the 1950s. Late in the decade and into the 1960s Johnny Best played there five nights a week.

San Francisco. **Basin Street West.** Broadway Street and Montgomery Street. Named after the club Basin Street East in New York, it flourished in the 1960s. Its policy was to engage major musicians for short residencies: Duke Ellington, Count Basie, Woody Herman, Oscar Peterson, and Erroll Garner played there when the club's activities were at their height in the mid- to late decade.

——. **Blackhawk.** It was, with the Jazz Workshop, the principal jazz club in the city in the 1950s and early 1960s. The repertory it offered was mainly bop. Art Tatum played one of his last residencies there in 1955, and Miles Davis recorded an album with his quintet in 1961 (*In Person: Friday and Saturday Nights at the Blackhawk*, Col. C2S820).

——. **Bop City.** See Jimbo's Bop City.

——. **Both/And.** Divisidero Street. It was active in the 1950s and 1960s as a venue chiefly for bop and (later) free jazz. Dexter Gordon, John Handy, and Ornette Coleman were among the prominent musicians who performed there.

——. **The Cellar.** See Jazz Cellar.

——. **Club Hangover.** 729 Bush Street. It was in operation from at least the 1940s, when it was owned by Doc Dougherty. Ted Buckner's band made weekly broadcasts from the club on Saturday evenings and Kid Ory also led a band there (until 1949). In the early 1950s notable residencies included those of George Lewis (i) with Lizzie Miles (1952), Don Ewell, and Earl Hines (1952), the last of whom returned for a long period beginning in September 1955. Among other musicians who performed at the Hangover were Joe Sullivan (who played solo piano between band sets, from 1955), Jimmy Rushing, Joe Darensbourg, who led an all-star sextet there in 1960, Marty Marsala (1962), and Muggsy Spanier (early 1960s). The club closed in the 1960s and the premises were taken over by a Japanese restaurant called Ginza West.

——. **Coffee Gallery.** Grant Street at Green Street. Coffee house. It opened in 1950 and was directed by Leo Riegler. At first its activities centered on poetry, but its programs soon included, and later concentrated exclusively on, jazz. Pony Poindexter led the house band there after leaving the Jazz Cellar. It survived for a time the decline of the jazz scene in San Francisco in the late 1960s but closed in 1971.

——. **Dawn Club.** 20 Annie Street. It was active in the 1940s in the basement of the Monadnock Building. Lu Watters's Yerba Buena Jazz Band played a long residency there from 1940 to 1947 (for illustration *see* Watters, Lu), and around the latter date Kid Ory's band appeared. The Front Page club (see below) later opened in the same premises.

——. **Down Beat Club.** 90 Market Street. Open from at least 1950 it became an important venue for modern jazz. Among the musicians who appeared there were Buddy DeFranco (around 1951) and, later, Miles Davis.

——. **Earthquake McGoon's.** It was managed by Turk Murphy, who led the resident band there from September 1960 to February 1978. The club had reopened at a new address by the 1980s.

——. **Fairmont Hotel.** It offered jazz for the entertainment of patrons from at least the 1950s. Notable jazz musicians who have appeared there include Louis Armstrong, who brought a band to the hotel for a residency (early 1962), and Ella Fitzgerald.

——. **Front Page.** 20 Annie Street. It opened in the 1980s in the premises that formerly housed the Dawn Club (see above). In 1986 Turk Murphy opened his Traditional Jazz Museum there.

——. **Great American Music Hall.** 859 O'Farrill Street. It flourished in the 1970s and 1980s, and in 1987 founded its own record label, on which recordings of performances given at the club have been issued. It has offered a great variety of performances in jazz and popular styles; among the numerous jazz musicians who have appeared there are Lee Konitz, Bobby McFerrin, the Preservation Hall Jazz Band, Maynard Ferguson, Art Blakey, Woody Herman, John Scofield, Stan Getz, Count Basie, Sarah Vaughan, Jan Garbarek, Pharoah Sanders, Annie Ross, Betty Carter, Oregon, Flora Purim and Airto Moreira, the World Saxophone Quartet, Branford Marsalis, and J. J. Johnson.

——. **Half Note Club.** Divisidero Street. It flourished during the 1960s when it specialized in the presentation of bop.

——. **Hangover Club.** See Club Hangover.

——. **Hungry i.** Jackson Street. It was an important venue for bop in the 1950s and 1960s. Among the musicians who played there was Vince Guaraldi.

——. **Jack's Tavern.** Sutter Street, between Fillmore Street and Webster Street. It flourished in the 1940s and was an early venue for bop in the city. Pony Poindexter, who was to be closely connected with a number of San Francisco clubs, played an engagement there early in his career.

——. **Jazz Cellar.** It was known familiarly to musicians as The Cellar. One of its founders (in the 1950s) was the drummer Willy Carson and it became known for the performance of bop. The house band was led by Leo Wright until 1959 (when he joined Dizzy Gillespie) and then by Pony Poindexter, who later moved on to the Coffee Gallery (see above). Like many clubs in the city, its fortunes waned in the 1960s when rock music diverted the attention of audiences away from jazz.

——. **Jazz Workshop.** Broadway, near Grant Street. One of the principal jazz venues on the West Coast, it engaged the most important bop and free-jazz musicians in the 1950s and 1960s. Among those who played there were Cannonball Adderley, who recorded *The Cannonball Adderley Quintet in San Francisco* (Riv. 311) at the club in 1959, Ornette Coleman (1960, 1967), John Coltrane (with his quartet in 1961 and his quintet in July–August 1966), and Charles Mingus (1964), whose performance was recorded and issued as *Right Now* (Fan. 86017). Other notable performances were given by Brew Moore, Wes Montgomery, Jackie McLean, Kenny Dorham, and Roland Kirk.

——. **Jimbo's Bop City.** Post Street at Buchanan Street. An after-hours club owned by Jimbo Edwards, it was an important venue for jam sessions, in which many leading bop musicians took part. Between 1949 and 1953 Dexter Gordon, Sonny Criss, Hampton Hawes, Roy Porter, and Pony Poindexter were regularly heard there.

——. **Keystone Korner.** Vallejo Street at Stockton Street. Situated on the northeast corner of the intersection, the club was opened around 1972 and its activities were directed by Todd Barkan. In the 1970s and early 1980s it was one of the most important jazz venues in the USA. Aided by its fine acoustics, comfortable performing conditions, and appreciative audiences, it attracted internationally renowned bop musicians. A number of recordings were made there, including *In this Korner* (1978, Conc. 68) by Art Blakey and his Jazz Messengers and Tete Montoliu's *Live at Keystone Corner* (1979, Tim. 138). National Public Radio broadcast performances from the club every year on New Year's Eve as part of a coast-to-coast celebration. It closed in the 1980s.

——. **Kimball's.** 300 Grove Street. It was active as a venue for jazz performance during the mid-1980s. Among the notable players in various styles who have appeared there are Cedar Walton, Bireli Lagrene, George Coleman, Jimmy Heath, Dewey Redman, Art Farmer, Eddie Harris, Johnny Griffin, Charlie Rouse, Toshiko Akiyoshi, JoAnne Brackeen, Chet Baker, Freddie Hubbard, Joe Henderson, Anita O'Day, Paquito D'Rivera, the Timeless All-Stars, and Stan Getz.

——. **Mark Hopkins Hotel.** See Top of the Mark.

——. **El Matador.** Another of the city's many venues specializing in bop in the 1950s and early 1960s, it presented performances by such prominent musicians as Eddie Duran, Kenny Burrell, and Cal Tjader.

——. **Milestones.** 376 5th Street. It flourished from the mid-1980s, when the proprietor was Sonny Buxton. Performances have been given there by Teddy Edwards, John Handy, Harold Land, Johnny Coles, and Freddie Hubbard.

——. **On the Levee.** This nightclub was owned and managed by Kid Ory from at least the mid-1950s. His band was the resident ensemble from 1954 to 1961; others who led groups there included Joe Sullivan (1961) and Muggsy Spanier (early 1960s).

——. **Pergola Dancing Pavilion.** 949 Market Street. Dance hall. Among the bands to have been resident at this venue was King Oliver's Creole Jazz Band, which performed there from 12 June 1921.

——. **Pier 23.** Nightclub. It was in operation as a jazz venue from at least the early 1950s. Burt Bales performed a long residency there from 1954 to 1966.

——. **Top of the Mark.** Mark Hopkins Hotel, Nob Hill, at California Street and Jones Street. From at least the mid-1970s solo and small-group jazz has been played for the entertainment of patrons in the revolving restaurant and bar on the top floor of the hotel.

——. **Tropics Club.** It operated as a venue for jazz from the 1950s at least. Brew Moore performed there in 1958.

——. **Venus Club.** It was active in the late 1940s under the direction of its Greek proprietor. Among the resident bands at that period was Kid Ory's (including Joe Darensbourg and Bob Scobey), which appeared there in 1948.

For other venues in the San Francisco Bay area see El Cerrito and Oakland.

BIBLIOGRAPHY

San Francisco

J. Lind: "When Jazz was King," *North Beach Magazine*, i/2 (1985), 6

SANTA MONICA, CA. See Los Angeles (metropolitan area).

SEATTLE. **Black and Tan.** 12th Avenue and Jackson. Around the turn of the 1920s to the 1930s it was owned by Noodles Smith and was one of Seattle's top nightclubs. Among the jazz musicians who were resident at this club were the pianist Phil Moore (1931) and Eubie Blake (1934). It was also on the touring circuit for the big bands of the swing era and many important musicians played one-night engagements there.

——. **Elks Club.** It was active from at least the mid-1940s. Around 1946 Ray Charles played his first engagement in Seattle as the leader of a trio at the Elks.

——. **The Entertainers.** 12th Avenue and Jackson. It was a small upstairs venue in premises next door to the Black and Tan, and was also owned by Noodles Smith; its activities were managed by George Moore. Among the jazz musicians who performed there in the early 1930s were Joe Darensbourg and Bumps Myers.

SILVER SPRING, MD. **Showboat Lounge.** Active at least by the 1970s, it was directed at that time by Pete Lambrose. In 1976 a performance given there by Phil Woods's sextet was recorded and released as *"Live" from the Showboat* (1976, RCA BGL2-2202), which confirmed Woods's reputation as one of the finest mainstream saxophonists.

SOMERVILLE, MA. **The Willow.** This nightclub, in the metropolitan area of Boston, opened in the early 1980s. Among the jazz musicians to have appeared there are John Scofield, Charles McPherson, Steve Turré, Freddie Redd, James Williams, Mal Waldron and Chico Freeman, Horace Tapscott, Andrew Hill, and Sonny Fortune.

SPRINGFIELD, IL. **Club Rio.** West Grand Avenue. Restaurant. It was owned by Vito Impastato and featured jazz from at least the 1940s. Among the musicians who performed at this venue were the Brown Cats led by the guitarist Adam Lambert (1942), Paul Barbarin's band (from September to December 1943), Sidney Bechet (two residencies in 1944), and Punch Miller (early autumn 1944).

SQUAW VALLEY, CA. **Squaw Valley Lodge.** Situated high in the Californian Sierras, around 200 miles northeast of San Francisco, Squaw Valley was the site of the Winter Olympics in 1959–60. Alex Cushing, the owner of the lodge, engaged Ralph Sutton to perform there for four winter seasons from 1958 to 1961.

WASHINGTON. **Blues Alley.** Blues Alley, Georgetown. It opened in 1965 under the direction of Tommy Gwaltney, who also led the house band, and has flourished into the 1980s. Its repertory is mainstream jazz and many renowned performers have appeared there.

——. **Constitution Hall.** 18th Street, between C Street and D Street. The hall was opened and originally run by the Daughters of the American Revolution. It has long been used for jazz concerts and in the 1980s was one of the most important auditoriums in the city for large events of this kind.

——. **Crystal Cavern.** Jazz was played there from at least the mid-1920s, when Claude Hopkins and his band played an extended engagement. Around the turn of the decade Elmer Calloway led a group (which included Jimmy Mundy) there.

BIBLIOGRAPHY

USA

J. Durante and J. Kofoed: *Nightclubs* (New York, London, and Toronto, 1931)

G. Fernett: *Swing Out: Great Negro Jazz Bands* (Midland, MI, 1970)

R. Russell: *Jazz Style in Kansas City and the Southwest* (Berkeley, CA, Los Angeles, and London, 1971/*R*1983, rev. 2/1973)

R. M. Sudhalter, P. R. Evans, and W. Dean-Myatt: *Bix: Man and Legend* (New Rochelle, NY, and London, 1974)

J. Darensbourg: *Telling it Like it is*, ed. P. Vacher (London, 1987; Baton Rouge, LA, 1987, as *Jazz Odyssey: the Autobiography of Joe Darensbourg*)

GENERAL BIBLIOGRAPHY

P. E. Miller, ed.: *Esquire's Jazz Book* (New York, 1944–6) [three vols., pubd annually; abridged P. Miller and R. Venables (London, 1947)]

O. Keepnews and B. Grauer, Jr.: *A Pictorial History of Jazz: People and Places from New Orleans to Modern Jazz* (New York, 1956, rev. 2/1966)

A. McCarthy: *Big Band Jazz* (New York and London, 1974)

D. Morgenstern: *Jazz People* (New York, 1976) [with photographs by O. Brask]

E. Townley: *Tell your Story: a Dictionary of Jazz and Blues Recordings* (Chigwell, England, 1976–87)

C. Goddard: *Jazz away from Home* (London and New York, 1979)

M. Berger, E. Berger, and J. Patrick: *Benny Carter: a Life in American Music* (Metuchen, NJ, and London, 1982)

F. Driggs and H. Lewine: *Black Beauty, White Heat: a Pictorial History of Classic Jazz, 1920–1950* (New York, 1982)

M. Zwerin: *La tristesse de Saint Louis: Swing under the Nazis* (London, 1985)

P. Clayton and P. Gammond: *Jazz: A–Z* (Enfield, nr London, 1986)

C. Sheridan: *Count Basie: a Bio-discography* (Westport, CT, and London, 1986)

J. Chilton: *Sidney Bechet: the Wizard of Jazz* (London, 1987)

INDEX

A

T

Ta-Ba-Ris Club: Argentina, Buenos Aires
Tabaris (Dancing): Netherlands, The Hague
Taj Mahal Hotel: India, Bombay
Talk of the Town: GB, London (Hippodrome)
Tango Gardens: USA, New York
Tango Palace: USA, New York (Tango Gardens)
Tap Room: USA, New York (Adrian's Tap Room)
Tejar's Slipper Lounge: USA, Chicago
Tempo Club: France, Paris
Ten Gallons: France, Paris
Théâtre des Galeries: Belgium, Brussels
1369 Club: USA, Cambridge
Three Deuces: USA, Chicago, New York
Three Sixes: USA, Detroit
331 Club: USA, Los Angeles
Tic-Toc Club: USA, Boston
Tiffany Club: USA, Los Angeles
Tina's Lounge: USA, Milwaukee
Tin Palace: USA, New York
Tin Roof Café [Tin Roof Dance Hall]: USA, New Orleans
Tipitina's: USA, New Orleans
Tip Toe Inn: USA, Los Angeles
Tip Top Inn: USA, Dallas
Tivoli Terrace: USA, Denver
Tivoli Theatre: Australia, Adelaide
Toit de Paris, le: France, Paris
Tokyo Gardens: USA, New Orleans
Tom Anderson's Annex: USA, New Orleans (Anderson's Annex)
Tom Anderson's New Cabaret and Restaurant [Tom Anderson's Saloon]: USA, New Orleans
Toodlum's Bar: USA, New Orleans
Top of the Gate: USA, New York (Village Gate)
Top of the Mark: USA, San Francisco
Torreon Ballroom, el: USA, Kansas City
Town Hall: USA, New York
Town Tavern: Canada, Toronto
Tralfamadore Café: USA, Buffalo
Tranchina's Restaurant: USA, New Orleans
Trastienda, la: Argentina, Buenos Aires (La Oreja)
Tre Musketerer, de: Denmark, Copenhagen
Trianon Ballroom: USA, Chicago, Los Angeles
Trocadero: USA, Los Angeles
Trocadero Ballroom: USA, Denver
Trois Mailletz [Maillets], les: France, Paris
Tropics Club: USA, San Francisco
Tudor Inn: USA, Los Angeles
Tune Town Ballroom: USA, St. Louis (Arcadia Ballroom)
Tuxedo Dance Hall: USA, New Orleans
25, the: USA, New Orleans (Big 25)
Two Saints: USA, New York (Five Spot)
Tyler's: USA, New Orleans

U

Ubangi Club: USA, New York
Uptown Club: Australia, Melbourne
Uptown Lowdown Club: USA, New York (Harlem Uproar House)

V

Vanity Fair Hotel: Australia, Sydney
Vendome Hotel: USA, Buffalo
Vendome Theater: USA, Chicago
Venetian Room: USA, Chicago
Venus Club: USA, San Francisco
Victoria Café: USA, New York
Victory Club: USA, Chicago
Vida Dance Hall, la: USA, New Orleans
Viennese Roof Room: USA, New York (St. Regis Hotel)
Vieux Colombier, le: France, Juan-les-Pins, Paris
Villa Café [Villa Cabaret]: USA, New Orleans
Villa d'Este: France, Paris
Village Fair: USA, New York (Village Vanguard)
Village Gate: USA, New York
Village Vanguard: USA, New York
Village West: USA, New York
Vincennes Hotel: USA, Chicago (Platinum Lounge)
Vostok: USSR, Leningrad
V Wandy Warskiej: Poland, Warsaw

W

Waldorf Astoria: USA, New York
Waldorf Cellar: USA, Los Angeles
Wally's Paradise: USA, Boston
Watusi Club: USA, Philadelphia
Weinberg Bar: Austria, Vienna
West Boondock: USA, New York
West End: USA, New York
West End Hotel: USA, Detroit
Whippoorwill: USA, New York
White City Ballroom: USA, Chicago
White House Restaurant: USA, Minneapolis
White's Emporium: USA, Chicago
Widder-Bar: Switzerland, Zurich
Wiener Metropol: Austria, Vienna
Willow, the: USA, Somerville
Wilson's Café: USA, Philadelphia
Wisconsin Theater: USA, Milwaukee (Roof Ballroom)
Wolsey's: GB, London
World Stage: USA, Detroit

Y

Yacht Club: USA, New York
Yardbird Suite: Canada, Edmonton
Yeah Man: USA, New York
Yellow Front Cafe: USA, Kansas City
Ye Old Nest: USA, New York
Yoshi's (Night Spot): USA, Oakland

Z

Zanderzaal: Netherlands, Haarlem
Zanzibar [Club Zanzibar, Café Zanzibar]: USA, New York
Zanzibar Club: USA, Los Angeles
Zardi's (Jazzland): USA, Los Angeles (Sardi's)
Zelli's: France, Paris
Zeppelin Inn: USA, Chicago
Zinno's: USA, New York
Zombie: USA, New York

Nighthawk Orchestra. Shortened form of the name Coon–Sanders Original Nighthawk Orchestra, taken in 1924 by the band led by Carleton Coon and JOE SANDERS; the band was established (with fewer members) as the Coon–Sanders Novelty Orchestra in 1920 and became known as the Nighthawks as a result of playing on late-night radio programs from 1922.

Night Hawks. Name used by the CRUSADERS in the late 1950s.

Nilson, Gunnar [Siljabloo] (*b* Luleå, Sweden, 2 Sept 1925). Swedish clarinetist and singer. He played in amateur bands in northern Sweden before moving in the 1940s to Stockholm, where he belonged to a professional singing group, the Flickery Flies (1947–51). From 1952 to 1955 he was associated with Carl-Henrik Norin's band at the Nalen in Stockholm (recording in 1953–4); he later worked for many years as a freelance and made several fine recordings. Nilson is one of few male jazz singers to have emerged in Sweden; he is effective both at bop improvisation and at more conventional singing of standards. He is well represented as a singer on *If you Could See me Now* (1979, Odeon EO62-35147), recorded with a trio led by the pianist Åke Johansson. ("På omslaget" [On the cover], *Orkester journalen*, xxii/1 (1954), 4)

Oral history material in *SSsv*.

ERIK KJELLBERG

Nilva. Record label established in Geneva by ALVIN QUEEN around 1980. Issues have featured Queen and his associates in a wide range of contexts.

Nimitz, Jack (Jerome) (*b* Washington, 11 Jan 1930). Baritone saxophonist. He learned clarinet at the age of 13 and later played alto saxophone in local bands. He continued to play in Washington for a time, but in late 1953 he became Woody Herman's baritone saxophonist. After leaving Herman in mid-1955 he joined Stan Kenton (1956), with whom he recorded and made a European tour. As a freelance in 1957–8 he recorded with Herbie Mann (1957), then in 1959 he re-joined Kenton to record and make appearances at several important jazz festivals. In the 1960s he worked in films (Johnny Mandel and David Amram were among the composers with whom he collaborated), but he also played with Terry Gibbs and Gerald Wilson and again with Kenton. In Los Angeles in 1964 he led a quintet with Bill Hood, which was made up of various combinations of saxophones and clarinets (besides his principal instrument Nimitz plays other saxophones, soprano and bass clarinets, and flute). He continued to work as a studio musician in the 1970s and played on the soundtrack to the film *Lady Sings the Blues* (1972). One of the founders of Supersax, he toured and recorded with the group from 1972. He was also associated with the big bands of Oliver Nelson (recording in 1966–7), Bill Berry (recording in 1974 and 1976), and Gerald Wilson (recording in 1981). Nimitz is best known for the secure foundation he provides in big-band performances, but he is a capable instrumentalist in all the styles and settings in which he plays.

SELECTED RECORDINGS

As sideman: S. Kenton: *Stan Kenton in Hi-Fi* (1956, Cap. W724), incl. The Peanut Vendor; H. Mann: *Sultry Serenade* (1957, Riv. 234); Supersax: *Supersax Plays Bird* (1972, Cap. ST11177)

BIBLIOGRAPHY

FeatherE; *Feather '60s*; *Feather–Gitler '70s*

LAWRENCE KOCH

Nimmons, Phil(ip Rista) (*b* Kamloops, Canada, 3 June 1923). Canadian composer and clarinetist. He played in dance bands and on radio broadcasts in Vancouver, Canada (1940–45), attended the Juilliard School, and worked for the CBC in Toronto as a bandleader and composer of incidental music (1950). In 1957 he formed the group Nimmons 'n' Nine (from 1965 Nimmons 'n' Nine Plus Six), which performed on broadcasts of the CBC for more than 20 years and made several albums, including *Take 10* (1963, RCA LCPS1066) and a recording of Nimmons's composition *The Atlantic Suite* (1975, Sack. 2008). Nimmons has taught at the Advanced School of Contemporary Music (Toronto), the Banff Jazz Workshop, and the University of Toronto.

BIBLIOGRAPHY

J. Batten: "Anybody wanta Pay Attention!," *The Canadian* (23 June 1979)
M. Miller: "Nimmons, Phil," *Encyclopedia of Music in Canada*, ed. H. Kallmann, G. Potvin, and K. Winters (Toronto, Buffalo, and London, 1981) [incl. discography]
——: "Phil Nimmons," *Boogie, Pete & the Senator: Canadian Musicians in Jazz: the Eighties* (Toronto, 1987), 181

MARK MILLER

Niosi, Bert [Bartolo] (*b* London, Canada, 10 Feb 1909; *d* Toronto, 3 Aug 1987). Canadian clarinetist, alto saxophonist, and bandleader. In 1931 he formed a nine-piece dance band in Toronto and the following year it began a long engagement (which lasted until 1950) at the Palais Royale; Niosi continued to lead similar bands from time to time through the 1970s. He also worked for CBC radio as a composer, arranger, conductor, and music director, and from 1952 to 1959 played with the Happy Gang on its daily program. He made recordings with a small jazz group in 1947 and with a large studio orchestra in 1963; he also recorded soundtracks for films made for the National Film Board. Two of Niosi's brothers were also jazz musicians: Joe (*b* London, 26 May 1906; *d* Toronto, 14 May 1977) played double bass with Trump Davidson and others, and Johnnie (*b* London, 26 Sept 1914; *d* Toronto, 21 Nov 1965) was a drummer.

BIBLIOGRAPHY

M. Miller and H. McNamara: "Niosi, Bert," *Encyclopedia of Music in Canada*, ed. H. Kallmann, G. Potvin, and K. Winters (Toronto, Buffalo, and London, 1981)

JACK LITCHFIELD

Nistico, Sal (i). *See* NESTICO, SAMMY.

Nistico, Sal(vatore) (ii) (*b* Syracuse, NY, 12 April 1940). Tenor saxophonist. He first played alto saxophone in 1949, then changed to the tenor instrument in 1956 and spent three years playing with local rhythm-and-blues bands. He first gained recognition in 1959–61 as a member of the Jazz Brothers, a group led by Chuck and Gap Mangione, with which he made his first recordings. In 1962–5 he played with Woody Herman, and he has maintained this association intermittently into the 1980s; Nistico's driving solos and virile sound have made him an important asset to Herman's groups. After playing with Count Basie for five months in 1965 he lived in Sweden, then in 1966 returned to Herman's band for a tour of Africa. A further period with Basie (1967) was followed by two more engagements with Herman (1968–70 and 1971), between which Nistico worked in Los Angeles, briefly with Don Ellis, and in Boston. From 1972 he lived in New York, apart from a tour of Europe with Slide Hampton. His work as a freelance has included periods with Buddy Rich's band in 1974 and the National Jazz Ensemble under Chuck Israels in the mid- and late 1970s; he has also led his own groups. In 1981–2 he performed and recorded again with Herman. Nistico fuses elements of the styles of Charlie Parker, Sonny Stitt, Gene Ammons, and Sonny Rollins into a powerful bop idiom of his own, which is best displayed on Herman's *Northwest Passage* (1965).

SELECTED RECORDINGS

As leader: *Heavyweights* (1961, Jlnd 966); *Neo/Nistico* (1978, BH 7006)
As sideman with W. Herman: *Woody Herman, 1963* (1962, Phi. 600065); *Encore, 1963* (1963, Phi. 600092); *Woody's Winners* (1965, Col. CS9236), incl. Northwest Passage
As sideman with others: Jazz Brothers: *Hey Baby!* (1961, Riv. 9371); B. Rich: *The Buddy Rich Septet* (1974, GM 3301); C. Israels: *National Jazz Ensemble* (1975, Chi. 140)

BIBLIOGRAPHY

Feather '60s; *Feather–Gitler '70s*
L. Tompkins: "Personally Speaking: Sal Nistico," *Crescendo*, iii/6 (1965), 27 [interview]
——: "Sal Nistico," *CI*, xiii/5 (1974), 12

SCOTT YANOW

NJF. *See* NORSK JAZZFORBUND.

NJSO. *See* NATIONAL JAZZ SERVICE ORGANIZATION.

Noble, Ray(mond Stanley) (*b* Brighton, England, 17 Dec 1903; *d* London, 2 April 1978). English bandleader, arranger, and composer. He studied classical piano but became interested in dance music, serving as house conductor for HMV records from 1929 and attracting attention with the recordings of his New Mayfair Dance Orchestra (1930–34), particularly those with the singer Al Bowlly. He moved to the USA to direct his own orchestra at the Rainbow Room in New York (1935–7), then went to Los Angeles and worked as a bandleader and radio personality into the 1950s. In the jazz field Noble's significance was as a catalyst rather than as a performer. His own arrangements and performances were generally of "sweet" dance music, and his major compositions were highly successful romantic ballads such as *Goodnight, sweetheart* (1931), *Love is the sweetest thing* (1932), *The very thought of you* (1934), *The touch of your lips* (1936), and *I hadn't anyone till you* (1938). However, his New York band, assembled by Glenn Miller (who also provided its more jazz-oriented arrangements, and thereby discovered his own distinctive way of writing), included such musicians as Pee Wee Erwin, Charlie Spivak, Sterling Bose, Johnny Mince, Bud Freeman, Will Bradley, and Claude Thornhill. Noble's instrumental composition *Cherokee* became the theme tune of Charlie Barnet's band (1938, Bruns. 8247); as a familiar test piece for jazz musicians in the early bop style, it was also associated with Charlie Parker.

BIBLIOGRAPHY

FeatherE

G. T. Simon: *The Big Bands* (New York, 1967, rev. and enlarged 2/1971, rev. 3/1974, 4/1981)

J. H. Klee: "Noble American, 1935–37," *MR*, iv/1 (1976), 1

ANDREW LAMB

Nock, Mike [Michael Anthony] (*b* Christchurch, New Zealand, 27 Sept 1940). New Zealand keyboard player. He began taking piano lessons at the age of 11, and became a professional musician four years later. When he was 18 he moved to Australia, where he formed a hard-bop trio; it traveled to England in 1961, but Nock left, and went to the USA to attend the Berklee College of Music. A year later he left the college to become the house pianist at a club in Boston. After touring with Yusef Lateef (1953–5) he formed a trio in New York. He worked with Art Blakey, then moved to San Francisco, where, in 1968, he established the Fourth Way, a jazz-rock group. This disbanded in 1970 and Nock composed and recorded film soundtracks on synthesizer for a time, before returning to New York in 1975 to work as a studio musician. Early in 1985 he went back to Australia, where he composed, and taught improvisation at New South Wales State Conservatorium in Sydney. Nock plays in many styles and contexts, and is a technically accomplished and gifted improviser and composer.

SELECTED RECORDINGS

As unaccompanied soloist: *Piano Solos* (1978, Tim. 134); *Talisman* (1978, Enja 3071)

As leader: *Almanac* (1967, ImA 373851); *Magic Mansions* (1977, Laurie 6001); *Ondas* (1981, ECM 1220)

As sideman: Y. Lateef: *Live at Pep's* (1964, Imp. 69); J. Handy: *Projections* (1968, Col. CS9689)

BIBLIOGRAPHY

M. Rozek: "Profile: Mike Nock," *DB*, xliv/7 (1977), 35

P. Hinely: Liner notes, *In, Out, and Around* (Tim. 119, 1978)

B. Blumenthal: Liner notes, *Climbing* (Tomato 8009, 1979)

L. Means and B. Primack: "Mike Nock, Journeyman Keyboardist Rediscovers Acoustic Jazz," *Keyboard*, v/9 (1979), 18 [incl. discography]

BOB DOERSCHUK

Nocturne. Record company and label. The company was established around 1953 in Los Angeles by Roy Harte and Harry Babasin. It was devoted to West Coast jazz, and its catalogue included recordings by Bud Shank, Babasin, and Bob Gordon (all 1954), but it was only short-lived.

BIBLIOGRAPHY

R. Gordon: *Jazz West Coast: the Los Angeles Jazz Scene of the 1950s* (London and New York, 1986), 98

A. Morgun: "The Nocturne Label," *DF*, no.1 (1960), 13

NOJC. *See* NEW ORLEANS JAZZ CLUB.

NOJCC [NOJCOC]. *See* NEW ORLEANS JAZZ CLUB OF CALIFORNIA.

Noone, Jimmie [Jimmy] (*b* Cut Off, nr New Orleans, 23 April 1895; *d* Los Angeles, 19 April 1944). Clarinetist and bandleader. After playing guitar as a youth he took up clarinet at the age of 15 and studied with Lorenzo Tio, Jr., and possibly also with Sidney Bechet (who was two years his junior). In 1913–14 he substituted for and then replaced Bechet in Freddie Keppard's band; later, with Buddy Petit, he led the Young Olympia Band (1916). Noone left New Orleans for Chicago in 1917 and toured the Midwest with Keppard's Creole Band until it broke up in spring 1918. After returning briefly to New Orleans he left the city permanently in autumn 1918, traveling with King Oliver to Chicago where they joined the band led by Bill Johnson (i) at the Royal Gardens. Noone left the Royal Gardens in 1920 to join Doc Cook's Dreamland Orchestra, with which he played until 1926. During this period he recorded 20 sides for Gennett, Okeh, and Columbia.

Noone's most important and influential period began after he left Cook in autumn 1926 to take up residence at the Apex Club in Chicago. Here he led his own group, Jimmie Noone's Apex Club Orchestra, which eventually included Joe Poston (alto saxophone), Earl Hines (piano), Bud Scott (banjo), and Johnny Wells (drums). With this group he made a classic series of recordings for Vocalion in spring and summer of 1928. During the 1930s, except for engagements in New York in 1931 and 1935, Noone remained in Chicago leading small groups at various clubs. In the early 1940s he was taken up by the New Orleans revival movement and joined Kid Ory, Zutty Singleton, Jack Teagarden, and others in club jobs and recording sessions in San Francisco and Los Angeles. Shortly before his death he joined an all-star revival band organized for Orson Welles's CBS variety show.

Noone, along with Bechet and Johnny Dodds, was one of the most significant New Orleans reed players, and a vital link between the older New Orleans style of clarinet playing and the Chicago swing manner. His musical style was influenced by his teachers and colleagues in New Orleans, especially Bechet. Later, in Chicago, his formal study with Franz Schoepp, a classically trained clarinetist, helped give him a secure command of all three clarinet registers. His expressive performance of blue notes and solo breaks is nowhere better illustrated than in his four recordings with Oliver's band from October 1923. His later Apex Club recordings of *I Know that you Know*, *Four or Five Times*, and *Apex Blues* set a new standard for post-New Orleans ensemble playing. These recordings use the New Orleans ensemble style with a revised orchestration: alto saxophone as lead instrument, clarinet providing embellishments, and a three-piece rhythm section, with Hines often supplying a third independent line with his "trumpet-style" right hand. Noone's manner influenced many of his contemporaries as well as subsequent generations of jazz musicians, including the clarinetists Buster Bailey, Barney Bigard, Joe Marsala, Omer Simeon, and, in particular, Benny Goodman; saxophonists as varied as Bud Freeman and Eric Dolphy also admitted to being influenced by Noone.

Noone's son, Jimmie Noone, Jr. (*b* Chicago, 1938), is also a clarinetist. After spending much of his career in obscurity in San Diego, in the 1980s he commenced an active recording and international touring schedule.

See also BLUES, §2; for illustrations *see* CLARINET, fig.3, and DRUM SET, fig.4.

SELECTED RECORDINGS

As leader: I know that you know (1928, Voc. 1184); Four or Five Times (1928, Voc. 1185); Apex Blues (1928, Voc. 1207); The blues jumped a rabbit (1936, Parl. 2303)

As sideman: Ollie Powers: Play that thing (1923, Para. 12059); K. Oliver: Chattanooga Stomp/New Orleans Stomp (1923, Col. 13003D); Camp Meeting Blues (1923, Col. 14003D); Capitol Jazzmen: Clambake in B Flat (1943, Cap. 10009)

BIBLIOGRAPHY

ChiltonW
"Discography of Jimmie Noone," *Jazz Information*, ii (8 Nov 1940), 15
"Jimmie Noone," *Jazz Information*, ii (21 March 1940), 10; (4 Oct 1940), 6
A. J. McCarthy: "Jimmy Noone," *Hot Notes*, ii/3 (1947), 13
J. G. Jepsen: "Discographie de Jimmie Noone," *Cahiers du jazz*, no.8 (1963), 93
A. J. McCarthy: "Jimmie Noone," *JM*, x/4 (1964), 10
M. Williams: *Jazz Masters of New Orleans* (New York and London, 1967/ *R*1978)
G. Schuller: *Early Jazz: its Roots and Musical Development* (New York, 1968)
B. McRae: "A B Basics, no.36: Jimmie Noone," *JJ*, xxii/12 (1969), 16
V. McHugh: "The Blues for Jimmie," *Selections from the Gutter: Jazz Portraits from "The Jazz Record"*, ed. A. Hodes and C. Hansen (Berkeley, CA, Los Angeles, and London, 1977), 105
J. Simmen: "Jimmy Noone Junior," *BHcF*, no.320 (1984), 9
S. Dance: "Jimmie Noone Junior," *JJI*, xxxviii/7 (1985), 18 [interview]
J. Simmen: "About Jimmy Noone, Jr.," *Jimmy Remembers Jimmie* (Stomp Off 1121, 1985) [liner notes]
——: "Jimmy Noone," *BHcF*, no.329 (1985), 1
——: "A Note on Jimmy Noone," *Sv*, no.127 (1986), 19

RICHARD WANG

Noordijk, Piet (*b* Rotterdam, Netherlands, 25 May 1932). Dutch alto saxophonist and clarinetist. He attended the Rotterdam Conservatory (1950–54) and taught himself to play alto and soprano saxophones. From 1957 to 1962 he led a group with his brother, the tenor saxophonist Kees Noordijk, and worked on radio with Pia Beck, the pianist Ger van Leeuwen, and the violinist Frans Poptie. With Misha Mengelberg he led a quartet from 1964 to 1967 that appeared at the Newport Jazz Festival in 1966; later he performed on radio broadcasts with the Skymasters, the Ramblers, the accordionist and bandleader Malando, and the pianists Tony Nolte and Ruud Bos. Noordijk is a versatile alto saxophonist who has played dixieland with the Storktown Dixie Kids, Latin jazz with Malando and the guitarist Tom Kelling, bop with a big band led by the pianist Boy Edgar, and free jazz with Mengelberg and Willem Breuker. His playing can be heard to advantage on his album *Loverman* (1980, VR 22112).

WIM VAN EYLE

Nordskog. Record company and label. The company was established in 1921 in Santa Monica, California, by Andrae Nordskog. Its records were at first pressed by Arto in New Jersey, and the two companies issued pressings of each other's masters. Nordskog is particularly notable for having been the first company to make recordings of a black band from New Orleans; three titles by Kid Ory's band were issued on the Nordskog label under the pseudonym Spikes' Seven Pods of Pepper, and were also released on SUNSHINE.

BIBLIOGRAPHY

J. Bentley and R. W. Miller: "Andrae Nordskog," *JM*, v/3 (1959), 8
C. Kendziora: "Behind the Cobwebs: Nordskog," *Record Research*, no.91 (1968), 6
F. Owen: "A Glimpse of the Past, 12: Sunshine and Nordskog," *Sv*, no.21 (1969), 94

Norgran. Record label. It was founded in Los Angeles in 1953 by Norman Granz. On it were issued new recordings by swing and bop musicians, as well as a considerable amount of material that had previously been put out on CLEF. With the latter label it was absorbed in 1956 into Granz's new company, VERVE. (M. Ruppli: *The Clef/Verve Labels*, Westport, CT, 1986)

Norin, Carl-Henrik (*b* Västerås, Sweden, 27 March 1920; *d* Stockholm, 23 May 1967). Swedish tenor saxophonist, bandleader, composer, and arranger. He made recordings in 1941–7 and joined the band of Thore Ehrling, for which he also wrote compositions and arrangements. At the Nalen in Stockholm he led a group from 1948 which played a wide repertory of standards and of newer material by several arrangers. The group made several recordings (1949–62) before taking a largely commercial orientation in the 1960s; he also played at the Paris Jazz Fair (1949) and recorded with many Swedish and foreign musicians, including Peanuts Holland (1948), Roy Eldridge (1951), and Lars Gullin (1953). Norin is well represented as soloist, arranger, and bandleader on *Blue and Sentimental* (1958, HMV 7EGS89).

BIBLIOGRAPHY

"Svenskt stjärnalbum" [Swedish star-album], *Orkester journalen*, x/9 (1942), 5
"På omslaget" [On the cover], *Orkester journalen*, xxiii/11 (1955), 4
C.-E. Lindgren: Untitled article, *Estrad*, xxiv/1 (1962), 4
Obituary, R. Dahlgren, *Orkester journalen*, xxxv/6 (1967), 5
E. Kjellberg: *Svensk jazzhistoria: en översikt* [Swedish jazz history: an overview] (Stockholm, 1985)

ERIK KJELLBERG

Norman, Charlie [Karl-Erik Albert] (*b* Ludvika, Sweden, 4 Oct 1910). Swedish pianist and entertainer. He worked professionally from the mid-1930s, belonged to Håkan von Eichwald's big band, and played in Seymour Österwall's orchestra (1939–41); he also played boogie-woogie as an unaccompanied soloist. During World War II he worked with Alice Babs and from 1943 led his own groups, with which he made many recordings (including *AFN-boogie*, 1946, Col. DS1610, DS1687). He also performed in Paris (1947) and Germany (1949). In the 1950s he was a popular disc jockey and at the same time worked in Sweden and abroad as the leader of a quartet; he continued his career as an entertainer into the 1980s. Norman's autobiography, *Musikant med brutet gehör* (Musician with broken ear), was published in Stockholm in 1980.

BIBLIOGRAPHY

"Svenskt stjärnalbum" [Swedish star-album], *Orkester journalen*, ix/4 (1941), 3
E. Kjellberg: *Svensk jazzhistoria: en översikt* [Swedish jazz history: an overview] (Stockholm, 1985)

ERIK KJELLBERG

Norman, Fred (*b* Leesburg, FL, 5 Oct 1910). Arranger. He joined Claude Hopkins's orchestra in 1932 as a trombonist and singer, and also occasionally wrote arrangements; he may be heard as a trombone soloist on a recording of one of his own compositions, *Church Street Sobbin' Blues* (Decca 1286), made by Hopkins in 1937. After leaving Hopkins he worked full-time as an arranger for Benny Goodman (for whom he wrote *Smoke House Rhythm*, 1938, Vic. 26107), Gene Krupa (1938–40), Lionel Hampton, Teddy Powell, and Jack Teagarden (all 1939), Artie Shaw (1941), and others, including Bunny Berigan and Tommy Dorsey. From 1940 to 1943 he was a staff arranger for Gene Krupa; he worked with Tommy Dorsey in 1945, and later with Charlie Spivak. In the 1950s he was employed by record companies as a music director for such musicians as Sarah Vaughan and Dinah Washington. He continued to write arrangements into the 1970s.

BIBLIOGRAPHY
ChiltonW; *FeatherE*
J. Simmen: "Fred Norman," *BHcF*, no.181 (1968), 6 [interview]
S. Dance: *The World of Swing* (New York, 1974) [colln of previously pubd interviews], 232

Normann, Robert (*b* Sarpsborg, Norway, 27 June 1916). Norwegian guitarist. He played accordion and tenor saxophone before taking up the guitar and played swing from 1937. He worked with Freddie Valier (1938), the group String Swing (1939–42), and Gunnar Due (1939–41); he also led a quartet and from 1945 belonged to a big band led by the drummer Pete Brown. In the 1950s he worked with the violinist Frank Ottersen and the pianist Willy Andresen; he was seldom active after 1955. A leading performer in Europe, Normann was little known elsewhere owing largely to his avoidance of publicity. A good example of his work is String Swing's recording *Farewell Blues/ Swingtime in the Rockies* (1940, Col. GN5067).

Oral history material in *NOnj*.

BIBLIOGRAPHY
K. Sandregen and others: *Boken om jazz* (Oslo, 1954)
O. Angell, J. E. Vold, and E. Økland: *Jazz i Norge* (Oslo, 1975)
J. Evensmo: *The Guitars of Charlie Christian, Robert Normann, Oscar Aleman (in Europe)* (n.p. [Oslo], n.d. [?1976]) [discography]
K. Michelsen, ed.: *Cappelens musikkleksikon* (Oslo, 1978)

VIDAR VANBERG

Norris, Al(bert) (*b* Kane, PA, 4 Sept 1908; *d* 26 Dec 1974). Guitarist. He played banjo with territory bands in Buffalo from 1927, and in 1932 joined Jimmie Lunceford as a banjoist; he changed to the guitar in 1933 and also occasionally played violin (for illustration *see* LUNCEFORD, JIMMIE). He took solos on several of Lunceford's recordings, including *Organ Grinder's Swing* (1936, Decca 908). Apart from a period in the army during World War II, Norris remained with Lunceford's band until it broke up in 1949. He then played and recorded with Eddie Wilcox in 1949–50 before ceasing to work as a musician. (*ChiltonW*; *FeatherE*)

Norris, Ray (*b* Saskatoon, Canada, 1916; *d* Toronto, 21 Dec 1958). Canadian guitarist and leader. In the 1930s he played on radio and in theater and grandstand bands. He formed a quintet in Vancouver, which played in clubs and theaters for many years. After a period in Toronto from 1949, he went back to Vancouver, where he presented his own television program; his only two recording sessions took place around this time – one with a quintet in Toronto (*c*1949) and the other with a sextet in Vancouver (1951). He returned to Toronto in 1958 and played with the Rhythm Pals and Rudy Toth's orchestra.

JACK LITCHFIELD

Norris, Walter (*b* Little Rock, AR, 27 Dec 1931). Pianist. He studied piano as a child and attended the Manhattan School of Music (1965–70). He worked in Little Rock with Howard Williams (1944–50), in Houston with the saxophonist Jimmy Ford (1952–3), and in Las Vegas with his own trio (1953–4). In 1954 he moved to Los Angeles, where he recorded with Jack Sheldon (1954), Frank Rosolino (1955), Herb Geller (1958), and Ornette Coleman (1958), and from 1963 to 1970 he worked in New York as the music director of the Playboy Club. He joined the Thad Jones–Mel Lewis Orchestra in 1974, with which he played at the Village Vanguard in New York and toured Europe (where he also recorded with Klaus Weiss, 1974, and Pepper Adams, 1975) and Japan (where he also recorded with Frank Foster, 1975). After leaving the orchestra in 1976 he played for seven months in Scandinavia with Red Mitchell and the quartets of Dexter Gordon and Red Rodney, and in the autumn of 1976 returned to New York, where he worked for a brief period in Charles Mingus's quintet. In Berlin from 1977 he belonged to the orchestra of Sender Freies Berlin (to 1980) and in 1984 joined the faculty of the Hochschule, where he has taught piano improvisation; at the same time he has performed throughout Europe with Aladár Pege and made annual visits to the USA. Norris is proficient in many styles, including bop, cool jazz, and free jazz; he has been influenced not only by the jazz pianists Art Tatum and Bud Powell but also by such classical composers as Chopin, Debussy, and Bartók. He has recorded several of his own compositions, including *Space Maker*, *Drifting*, *Stepping on Cracks*, and *Synchronicity*.

SELECTED RECORDINGS

Duos: with G. Mraz: *Drifting* (1974, Enja 2044), incl. Drifting, Space Maker; with A. Pege: *Synchronicity* (1978, Enja 3035); with Phillip Wilson: *Live at the Berklee Performance Center* (1985, Shiah 117)
As leader: *Stepping on Cracks* (1978, Prog. 7039)
As sideman with O. Coleman: *Something Else!!!! The Music of Ornette Coleman* (1958, Cont. 3551)

BIBLIOGRAPHY
FeatherE; *Feather–Gitler '70s*
J. S. Wilson: "And Now, Walter Norris," *Hi Fidelity/Musical America*, xxv/5 (1975), 64
C. J. Safane: Review of *Synchronicity* (1978), *DB*, xlvii/9 (1980), 39
F. Bouchard: "Waxing On: Triology," *DB*, l/12 (1983), 45 [review of *Stepping on Cracks* (1978)]
W. Balliett: "Herr Professor," *New Yorker*, lxii (12 Jan 1987), 88

GREGORY E. SMITH

Norsk Jazzarkiv. Archive founded in Oslo in 1981; *see* LIBRARIES AND ARCHIVES, §2.

Norsk Jazzforbund [Norwegian Jazz Federation, NJF]. Norwegian national jazz organization founded in 1953 in Trondheim. Its objectives are to promote interest in and knowledge of jazz in Norway, to support amateur activity and local clubs, and to establish national and international contacts with other organizations. From 1960 it published the journal *Jazznytt* (Jazz News) and in 1967 produced its first LP, which was also Jan Garbarek's first recording; in 1981 it set up the Odin record company. NJF is a member of the International Jazz Federation and has links with the other Nordic countries through Nordjazz (established in 1974). From 1978 it received a small amount of funding from the Norwegian government, and the following year it participated in the formation of the Foreningen Norske Jazzmusikere (Association of Norwegian Jazz Musicians); it is also associated with the Norsk Jazzarkiv (Norwegian Jazz Archive), established in 1981. (*The Norwegian Jazz Scene*, Paris, 1985)

North Sea Jazz Festival. Festival held annually from 1976 in The Hague. It was founded by Paul Acket, who continued as its director into the late 1980s, and has been sponsored by the Dutch ministry of culture (1976–82), the Japanese Victor Corporation (from 1986), and the British American Tobacco Company (from 1987). The festival takes place over three days in July at the Congresgebouw and offers simultaneous performances at 12 venues, as well as showings of jazz films and videos. This extreme concentration of activity makes it unique among jazz festivals; in 1986 800 musicians performed before a combined audience of 40,000. The styles represented range from dixieland to free jazz. Buddy Rich has appeared at the festival, as have Chris Barber, Anthony Braxton, Art Blakey, Benny Carter, Miles Davis, Lionel Hampton, Herbie Hancock, the Preservation Hall Jazz Band, Steps Ahead, Sun Ra, Clark Terry, Weather Report, and Phil Woods. (R. D'Rozario: *North Sea Jazz Festival, 1976–1985*, The Hague, 1985 [photographs])

PAUL R. LAIRD

Norvo, Red [Norville, Kenneth] (*b* Beardstown, IL, 31 March 1908). Xylophonist and vibraphonist. He took up marimba at about the age of 14, and later learned to play xylophone. After touring with a marimba band in the late 1920s he joined Paul Whiteman's orchestra; Mildred Bailey, the singer in the band, became his first wife (see illustration). In New York from 1933 he worked as a freelance; he also led a sextet with Charlie Barnet on 52nd Street (1935–6) and a small orchestra with Bailey (1936–9). He continued to lead big bands and then smaller groups before joining Benny Goodman's sextet (1944), at which time he changed permanently to the vibraphone. Given carte blanche for a recording session in 1945, Norvo organized an unusual swing and bop octet which included Charlie Parker, Dizzy Gillespie, and Teddy Wilson. He was a soloist with Woody Herman's First Herd (1946), and he toured with Billie Holiday. During the 1950s he led trios with guitar and double bass, one of which was an outstanding West Coast jazz ensemble with Tal Farlow and Charles Mingus (1950–51; for illustration *see* MINGUS, CHARLES). In 1959 he toured Europe with Goodman. He rejoined Goodman briefly in 1961 and, after a serious ear operation, toured Europe as a soloist (1968) and with George Wein's Newport All Stars (1969), but during the 1960s and 1970s he worked mainly in Nevada and California. Several albums with famous swing musicians in the mid- to late 1970s announced his return to the international arena. In the 1980s he has toured Europe with regularity, re-formed a trio with Farlow, and joined Benny Carter, Louie Bellson, and others for an acclaimed swing concert in New York (1985).

In the early 1930s, with Whiteman and later with his own ensembles, Norvo proved himself an exceptional improviser on the xylophone, a previously neglected instrument in jazz. He has usually played the vibraphone without vibrato, almost like a xylophone. His improvising, strongly influenced by Teddy Wilson's piano style, suffers an occasional rhythmic stiffness at fast tempos, but is outstanding on such jazz ballads as *Ghost of a Chance* (1945), recorded during a concert at Town Hall in New York. As a bandleader Norvo prefers delicate sounds. In the 1930s he led a drummerless sextet (trumpet, tenor saxophone, clarinet, xylophone, guitar, double bass) and an orchestra noted for its subtle approach to swing. In 1936–7 this orchestra specialized in the performance of highly praised arrangements by Eddie Sauter, particularly *Remember*, which has an outstanding solo by Norvo. Subsequently bringing his concern for clarity and restraint to the trio with Farlow and Mingus, Norvo was, among leading musicians of the swing era, unusually successful in making a transition to the bop style.

Red Norvo and Mildred Bailey, New York, 1935

Oral history material in *NjR* (JOHP).

SELECTED RECORDINGS

As leader: Knockin' on Wood/Hole in the Wall (1933, Bruns. 6562); Bughouse (1935, Col. 3079D); Remember (1937, Bruns. 7896); Hallelujah (1945, Dial 1045); Ghost of a Chance (1945, Baronet 47103); September Song (1950, Dis. 147); Move (1950, Dis. 145); *Red Norvo Trio* (1953, Fan. 3–12); *Vibes a la Red* (1974–5, FaD 105); with R. Tompkins: *Red and Ross* (1979, Conc. 90)

As sideman: B. Goodman: Slipped Disc (1945, Col. 36817); W. Herman: Igor/Nero's Conception (1946, Col. 37228); G. Wein: *Newport All Stars* (1969, Atl. 1533); [no leader]: *Swing Reunion* (1985, Book-of-the-Month 717627)

BIBLIOGRAPHY

L. Feather: "The Vibraharp," *The Book of Jazz: a Guide to the Entire Field* (New York, 1957, rev. 2/1965)

G. T. Simon: *The Big Bands* (New York, 1967, rev. and enlarged 2/1971, rev. 3/1974, 4/1981)

Arnold Shaw: *The Street that Never Slept: New York's Fabled 52nd Street* (New York, 1971/*R*1977 as *52nd Street: the Street of Jazz*)

W. Balliett: "The Music is More Important," *Ecstasy at the Onion* (New York and Indianapolis, 1971), 194; repr. in *Improvising: Sixteen Jazz Musicians and their Art* (New York, 1977), 113

R. Stewart: "Red Norvo: a Tale of a Pioneer," *Jazz Masters of the Thirties* (New York and London, n.d. [?1972]), 71

S. Woolley: "Red Norvo: Interview," *Cadence*, ii/1 (1976), 3

J. McDonough: "Red Norvo: a Man for All Eras," *DB*, xliv/18 (1977), 16

D. H. Kraner: "The Red Norvo Trio with Tal Farlow and Charlie Mingus," *Journal of Jazz Discography*, no.2 (1977), 6

S. Klett: "Red Norvo: Interview," *Cadence*, v/7 (1979), 5

L. Tomkins: "Happy Again with the Trio: Red Norvo," *CI*, xx/4 (1981), 22

BARRY KERNFELD

Norwegian Jazz Federation. *See* NORSK JAZZFORBUND.

Nose flute. Any kind of flute that is sounded by nasal breath; of non-Western origin, nose flutes are occasionally used by jazz musicians whose work includes elements of so-called world music. Roland Kirk also played nose flutes. *See* FLUTE, §6.

Nosov, Konstantin (Georgyevich) (*b* Leningrad, 24 July 1938; *d* Sofia, 29 June 1984). Russian trumpeter and composer. He studied trumpet at the N. A. Rimsky-Korsakov music school in Leningrad (graduated 1956), belonged to a group led by the alto saxophonist Orest Kandat, and played at the Leningrad Jazz Club from 1958. He gained considerable recognition while playing under the bandleader Josef Vainstein (1959–66), and with Gennady Gol'shteyn he led a quintet composed of members of Vainstein's orchestra. Later he toured with Ady Rosner and belonged to the Kontsertny estradny orkestr Tsentral'novo TV i Vsesoyuznovo Radio (Concert variety orchestra of the central TV and all-union radio) in 1968, to the big band of the restaurant Vecherny arbat in Moscow in 1969–73, and to the ensemble Melodiya; he also took part in concerts with Oleg Lundstrem's orchestra. In 1980 he settled in Sofia, where he played in the groups Sofia and Dinamit Brass Band. Nosov never recorded as a leader, but he can be heard as a guest soloist on about a dozen albums, including Georgy Garanyan's

Labirint (1974, Mel. C60052778), on which he plays his composition *Ognennaya reka* (Fiery river); among his other compositions is *Skoree k Dul'sinee Tobosskoy* (Faster to Dulcinea of Toboso). (S. F. Starr: *Red and Hot: the Fate of Jazz in the Soviet Union, 1917–1980* (New York, and Oxford, England, 1983), 254)

WALTER OJAKÄÄR

Notation. Any means, graphic or (more loosely) verbal, of representing musical sounds, either by symbolizing them or by giving instructions for producing them. This article deals with notations used in jazz, some of which originated in and remain specific to jazz, while others are borrowed from or shared with other musical traditions.

1. Introduction. 2. Notation for performance. 3. Notation for teaching and learning. 4. Notation for transcription. 5. Notational symbols: (i) Introduction (ii) Pitch and melody (iii) Harmony (iv) Rhythm, duration, and tempo (v) Timbre and articulation.

1. Introduction. Aural tradition and improvisation are central to the practice of jazz, and their importance has given rise to the common misconception that jazz is an unwritten music. It is true that notation plays no part in many great jazz performances, and that a number of prominent jazz musicians, being unable to read music, learned their art entirely from recordings and through performance with others. But throughout its history much jazz has been notated and most of its practitioners have been musically literate, at least to some degree.

The association of musical notation and jazz falls into three main categories: prescriptive notation for performance; prescriptive notation for the teaching and learning of jazz; and descriptive notation for transcription and analysis. (A subcategory, which overlaps with the first and last of these, is notation for the purpose of preserving copyright in music not originally written down.) The problems and conventions of notation in each area are to some extent peculiar to it, and each is therefore treated somewhat separately in the following discussion.

By and large, composers, arrangers, performers, teachers, and scholars of jazz use conventional Western staff notation, supplemented by symbols and usages to convey information not adequately expressed by the standard means. Western staff notation efficiently transmits equal-tempered pitch, rational subdivisions of individual beats, and local or large-scale changes in tempo and dynamics; but the essence of jazz lies precisely in the characteristics that standard notation cannot easily show, such as subtle and intricate rhythmic play, expressive nuances of accent and timbre, and pitches and pitch complexes outside equal temperament. Many and various attempts have been made to capture such elements in notation, but no standard solutions to the problems they pose have been reached.

2. Notation for performance. Notated versions of jazz pieces for the purpose of performance may take any form from the sketchiest of cue sheets to a fully written-out composition or arrangement. The term "chart," which in jazz parlance means a score, part, or any item of written music, accurately indicates the relationship of most notated instructions for jazz performance to the performance itself; the notation is only a map to guide musicians while playing, and many essential elements of the music are prescribed only vaguely, if at all. (Although this is true for most kinds of music that employ notation, the extent to which the written source and its realization differ seems particularly marked in jazz.)

The notational vehicle most favored in small-group jazz is the "lead sheet." A lead sheet typically presents only the melody of a composition, written in the treble clef, the lyrics if any, and the essential harmonic changes, shown by chord symbols (see §5(iii) below) placed above or below the staff. Additional information, such as cues for essential accompanimental figures (fills, ostinatos, inner lines, etc.) and elements of the arrangement, may also be included (ex.1). This format is ubiquitous in the manuscript and (often illegally) printed tune books known as fake books (*see* Fake book), which are widely used by jazz musicians.

Somewhat more elaborate than the lead sheet is the "master rhythm part," which is often produced as the result of a sketchy

Ex.1 Excerpt from O. Nelson: *111-44*, in lead-sheet format

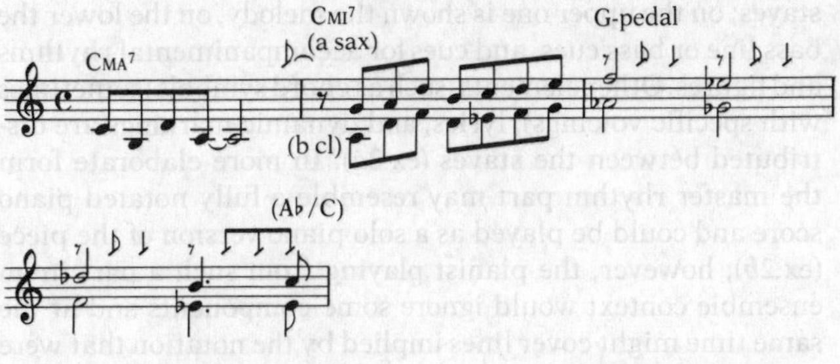

Ex.2

(a) Excerpt from the master rhythm part for M. Tyner: *In Search of my Heart*

(b) Excerpt from the master rhythm part for H. Silver: *Ecaroh*

transcription from a recording. It is typically written on two staves; on the upper one is shown the melody, on the lower the bass line or bass cues, and cues for accompanimental rhythms and figures. Other elements, such as chord symbols (sometimes with specific voicings), lyrics, and dynamic markings are distributed between the staves (ex.2*a*). In more elaborate form the master rhythm part may resemble a fully notated piano score and could be played as a solo piano version of the piece (ex.2*b*); however, the pianist playing from such a part in an ensemble context would ignore some components and at the same time might cover lines implied by the notation that were not being taken by other members of the group.

Jazz musicians also occasionally use the sheet music for a popular song as the source for a performance based on it. In this form, songs are normally printed on three staves; the uppermost shows the melody, lyrics, and chord symbols (often with guitar or ukulele tablature), while the lower two are occupied by a fully written-out piano arrangement (ex.3). The

Ex.3 Excerpt from the sheet music for *Detour Ahead!*, by John Frigo, Lou Carter, and Herb Ellis

* chord symbols for guitar, tablature for ukulele tuned *g′–c′–e′–a′*

notated piano parts and tablature in sheet music are generally unidiomatic to jazz and are therefore ignored by jazz musicians, who treat the sheet music as if it were a lead sheet and indeed may well transcribe the music into lead-sheet form rather than play from the printed copy (this not only eliminates superfluous piano and guitar parts but also allows the musician to reposition awkward page turns and enlarge chord symbols that are too small to be easily read).

Where lead sheets, master rhythm parts, or sheet music are used, all the musicians usually work from identical parts, extracting what they need from the notation and relying on their experience, custom and usage, their own creativity, and visual cues for the other ingredients of the performance. Occasionally in such a situation some musicians may have parts of their own that differ from those used by the other members of the ensemble: the players of transposing instruments sometimes use parts written out at the relevant pitch (though a professional player is usually expected to play from an untransposed part); the drummer may be given, or may be required to create, a more elaborate part than the others, including cues for specific events which he must accompany and written instructions for the deployment of the various elements of the drum set.

In the majority of cases the overall form, structure, and organization of the performance are not specified in scores of the types discussed above. The order, number, and length of choruses and improvised solos, the presence or absence of an introduction, coda, and interludes, and often changes in instrumentation, texture, and dynamics, are decided on during rehearsal, or established during the performance itself by means of various visual or aural cues. The notation gives only the form and structure of the tune upon which the performance is to be based.

A more detailed form of notation is used by many big bands, and also by ensembles of medium size (such as Miles Davis's nonet, which recorded the sessions later issued as *Birth of the Cool*), ensembles playing third-stream music, some groups that use arranged themes and interludes (such as Horace Silver's quintet), and even some free-jazz groups (particularly those, such as Anthony Braxton's, that employ elements of the European classical tradition). Large segments of a piece may be fully written out as individual parts. The rhythm section generally plays from less formally notated parts, but these may still contain cues for specific rhythmic events. In pieces of this level of elaboration the overall form may be fully indicated; nevertheless some flexibility as regards the order, number, nature, and length of improvised sections is generally retained.

In all but the most fully composed works (see below) room is allowed for improvisation. While accompanimental figures in these passages may be fully notated for wind instruments (often with cues showing specific events in other voices), for the soloists only the harmonic basis and duration of the improvisation are notated (in the form of a lead sheet). Exceptionally, in performances of extremely famous pieces, the soloist may have both a lead sheet and a transcription of an existing solo and may choose whether to improvise something fresh or recreate the famous original version.

Fully notated pieces that leave no opportunity at all for improvisation, such as Ellington's *Ko-Ko* (1940), occur much more rarely. But even in this instance the rhythm parts would probably take the form of a lead sheet; Ellington himself usually improvised the piano rhythm part, adding obbligato figures in the background. It should be noted that until perhaps the 1960s it was not always customary to make full scores even for pieces notated to this degree of precision, and composers and arrangers sometimes learned and practiced their craft using only individual parts. Benny Carter, for example, began by studying and writing in this manner, and only later discovered how to use stock arrangements and full scores. Furthermore, the individual parts are often unavailable to any but the musicians who use them, being (except for stock arrangements) largely unpublished; in the case of *Ko-Ko*, for instance, neither the original score (if it exists) nor the original parts are published, and any version of the piece is attainable only through transcription from the recording (this is true of the extract from a full score printed in ELLINGTON, DUKE, ex.1, as well as of the full score and parts transcribed by Dave Berger and Alan Campbell for performance by the National Jazz Ensemble and then published around 1980 by United Artists Music). From the 1960s the advent of the third-stream and jazz education movements brought greater ties with the publishing traditions of Western art music, and scores (in either full or short form) by such composers as John La Barbera, Sammy Nestico, Hank Levy, Thad Jones, Toshiko Akiyoshi, and Oliver Nelson became widely available. In the 1970s and 1980s a large amount of excellent band music from the swing era has become accessible, not through publication, but through the donation of manuscripts formerly in private hands to public collections; for important holdings of such material *see* LIBRARIES AND ARCHIVES.

See also ARRANGEMENT.

3. NOTATION FOR TEACHING AND LEARNING. Notation for pedagogical purposes, such as may be found in method books and arrangements for student ensembles, is frequently more detailed than that intended for professional performers. Because they assume a certain level of familiarity with the conventions of jazz, parts for professionals are largely unencumbered with detailed instructions for phrasing, articulation, and ornamentation, whereas those for student players are deemed to need prescriptions of this kind. Jazz method books, which have appeared in increasing numbers since the 1960s, have their origins in the banjo and ragtime tutors of the 19th century and exhibit a variety of notational techniques. Pedagogical texts on jazz theory differ widely in their approach to the notation of harmony, variously using chord symbols, figured-bass notation, and roman-numeral notation, and defining chordal and scalar relationships in terms of modes. Likewise method and exercise books for specific instruments often include ad hoc notations that show optimum fingerings, systems of counting for rhythms, and other elements. All these differences underline the lack of standard practice in the notation of jazz, particularly in the field of education.

4. NOTATION FOR TRANSCRIPTION. In that they are used to explain to the performers what should be played and in what way, the notations discussed above are prescriptive. Notations used in jazz research and scholarship, by contrast, are descriptive, and aim to represent and document existing recorded performances by rendering them in written form. The systems used for this purpose tend to be more complex and detailed than those used by teachers, and more complex still than those used by performers. (This is not to say, however, that teachers and performers do not on occasion use the descriptive transcriptions made by researchers; indeed, such material has become an important resource in the teaching of the intricacies of jazz practice to aspiring musicians.) To represent on paper the nuances of jazz in sufficient detail to make meaningful study possible, a large collection of notational symbols is required in addition to the repertory of the Western staff system; some of these are discussed and illustrated in §5 below.

Certain mechanical, electrical, or electronic devices have been invented for, or adapted to, the task of transcription. Each of these produces its own machine-generated notation which must be learned before the information thus presented can be properly comprehended. One of the earliest mechanical transcription devices, the melograph model C, was devised to assist ethnomusicologists, but has been applied to recorded jazz with interesting results. With advances in computer and synthesizer technologies it has become possible to obtain a computer-generated transcription of material played on a suitably equipped synthesizer. This is a valuable means of recording the working practices of living musicians. Data created by such methods is most efficient as a descriptive notation, however, and can rarely be used for prescriptive purposes. (For the principles, history, and methodology of written versions of recorded jazz, *see* TRANSCRIPTION (i).)

5. NOTATIONAL SYMBOLS.

(i) Introduction. The basis of jazz notation is the standard Western system with its symbols for elements such as dynamics, phrasing, accentuation, attack, etc. Those signs and symbols used in jazz with their established meanings are not dealt with extensively here. Instead the discussion focuses on signs from the standard system that have acquired peculiar meanings in jazz, and on new symbols and usages devised by jazz notators (or borrowed from ethnomusicology) to indicate aspects of the performance. As well as symbols, verbal instructions are often added to musicians' parts: for example, to indicate to a trumpeter that a certain mute should be used an arranger may simply name the mute in the part; in a drum part the word "fill" indicates that the drummer should insert a fill at that point.

Composers, arrangers, teachers, and transcribers have all devised their own ways of representing the sounds of jazz; although there have been attempts at standardization (particularly in the field of education by such groups as the National Association of Jazz Educators) there exists no agreed practice in the use of notational symbols nor has any systematic survey been made of the many and disparate methods adopted. The following discussion offers selected examples of the many symbols employed to notate various elements of the music.

(ii) Pitch and melody. While standard notation is easily adapted to represent melody in jazz, it has only limited ability to convey such deviations from standard pitch as vibrato, blue notes, bends, and various other microtonal and intonational nuances. Often such effects go unnotated since musicians may be expected to inflect notes, according to convention and personal style, without being specifically instructed to do so. Where the microtonal alteration of a pitch must be indicated, an arrow is sometimes placed above the note head, pointing upwards if the note is to be raised, downwards if it is to be lowered; the degree of adjustment may be indicated by the number of arrow heads. Verbal instructions are also sometimes used, keyed by means of asterisks or crosses to the notes to be inflected; the cross, particularly, is employed to indicate a blue note.

Symbols for the various types of GLISS vary according to context; many scribes simply write "gliss" (or one of the names denoting a specific type of gliss) above the note or between the notes concerned. Graphic marks, placed above or beside the note or notes, take the form of straight or curved, thin or thick,

Ex.4 Symbols for various types of gliss

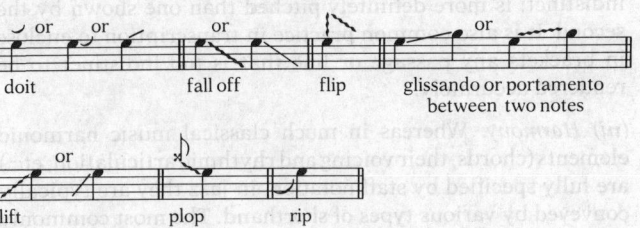

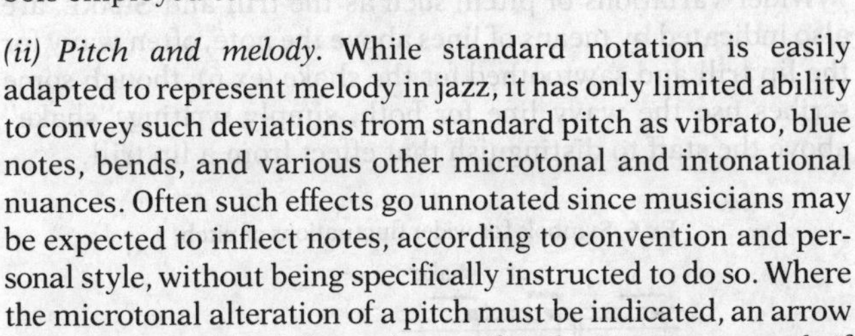

wavy or sawtoothed lines. These may or may not indicate the extent of the deviation from the given pitch, but they do generally prescribe its direction (inferred from the angle of the line) and show whether the gliss precedes or follows the note. Some examples of the many markings used to notate glisses are shown in ex.4.

In parts for wind players OVERBLOWING and MULTIPHONICS are requested by means of verbal instructions. Brass parts carry the instruction HALF-VALVE or the symbol ∅ above or below the staff when that technique is required.

Vibrato may be indicated verbally, or by means of a wavy line placed above the note or beside it on the staff (ex.5*a*, 5*b*); the dip is shown by a U-shaped symbol above the staff (ex.5*c*).

Ex.5 Symbols for various types of vibrato

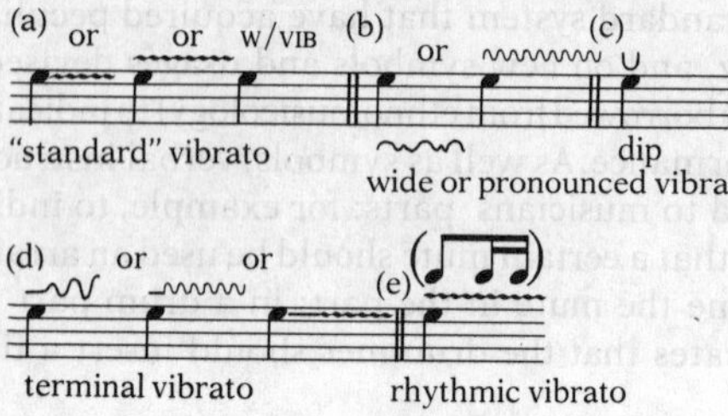

Although the degree of pitch fluctuation is rarely specified, certain transcribers (notably André Hodeir) have devised symbols that indicate approximately the point during the note at which the vibrato begins. The gradual introduction of vibrato into a note (*see* TERMINAL VIBRATO) is indicated by the symbols shown in ex.5*d*; the notation sometimes used for vibrato executed with a certain rhythm is shown in ex.5*e*.

Wider variations of pitch, such as the trill and SHAKE, are also indicated by means of lines above the note, often wavy for the lip trill and sawtoothed for the shake (ex.6), though some scribes use the wavy line for both, simply writing "shake" above the staff to distinguish that effect from a lip trill.

Ex.6 Symbols for wider fluctuations of pitch

Vague or indeterminate pitches such as the GHOST NOTE are indicated variously by placing the note head in parentheses, using a cross-shaped note head, or combining both symbols (ex.7); some transcribers employ both parentheses and cross-shaped note heads, using the first to indicate a note that, though

Ex.7 Symbols for the ghost note

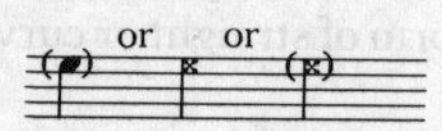

indistinct, is more definitely pitched than one shown by the second. It is also common practice in transcription to enclose in brackets any passage or line that is too indistinct to be rendered accurately.

(iii) Harmony. Whereas in much classical music harmonic elements (chords, their voicing and rhythmic articulation, etc.) are fully specified by staff notation, in jazz they are typically conveyed by various types of shorthand. The most commonly used and universally applicable of these is the system of chord symbols based on the letter names of the notes. These symbols designate the root and, either implicitly or explicitly, the other members of a chord, but generally leave other factors (inversion, range, voicing, and rhythmic articulation) to the discretion of the player. As well as providing information for the rhythm section, chord symbols indicate to soloists the harmonic structure to keep in mind while improvising. (It should be noted that whereas performers and practitioners always use chord-symbol notation, analysts and transcribers often use roman numerals to define chords in their harmonic relationships to one another.)

The chord-symbol system is by no means a standardized notational language, but certain conventions pertain. The following discussion presents symbols and abbreviations in general use: those given in parentheses are less common.
See also HARMONY (i), esp. §1(v) (a).

(a) Triads. The root of a chord is shown by a capital letter. The quality of a chord is indicated by letters, symbols, or numerals (or combinations of these), which follow the root designation.

A major triad is most often indicated by a capital letter standing alone. The major triad is seen to be the most common chord; thus an unmodified root symbol is taken, by default, to mean the major triad. Abbreviations for the word "major" may be added.

C (CMA Cma Cmaj)

There is also a symbol for the major triad that instructs the performer (who might otherwise expand the chord by enriching the harmony) to play only the notes of the triad itself:

C△

The minor triad is notated by any of the following symbols:

CMI Cm C− (Cmi Cmin)

The minus sign may also be used to inflect an individual element of a chord (see §(c) below). Although this is a potential cause of ambiguity, performers generally infer what is intended by drawing on prior knowledge, custom, and convention.

The augmented triad is generally indicated by a plus sign, more rarely by other means:

C+ (CAUG $C^{(\sharp 5)}$ $C^{5\sharp}$ $C^{(+5)}$)

The sharp and plus signs (as in the last three symbols above) may also be used to inflect other elements of a chord (see §(c) below).

The diminished triad is a special case, interpreted according to jazz convention rather than traditional systems. It is commonly indicated by the symbols:

C° CDIM

Strictly these simply indicate a diminished triad with pitches a minor 3rd and a diminished 5th from the root. In practice, however, jazz musicians render this triad as a tetrad, adding a diminished seventh above the root, for which strictly the symbols would be:

$C^{\circ 7}$ CDIM^{7}

Thus the symbols ° and DIM apparently serve a double function, indicating that both the triad and the added seventh are diminished. Should the diminished triad without the seventh be required the triad is notated as an inflected minor triad (see also §(c) below):

CMI$^{(\flat 5)}$

The half-diminished chord, that is a diminished triad with an added minor seventh, is indicated by an adaptation of the symbol for the diminished chord, though in this case the seventh is specified:

C^{ø7}

This chord is also commonly referred to as a minor seventh chord with a flatted fifth:

CMI$^{\substack{7\\ \flat 5}}$

The commonly occurring chord in which the fourth is substituted for the third (generally called in jazz, misleadingly, a suspension, whether or not it is technically suspended from the preceding chord or ultimately resolves to the third) is shown by the following symbol:

Csus

(b) Extended chords. To indicate more complex chords, numerals are appended to the root designation. These are understood to indicate diatonic degrees added to a major triad treated as though it were built on the dominant of the key: the upper elements therefore produce the following intervals from the root: minor 7th, major 9th, perfect 11th, and major 13th. Thus it is understood that the addition of the figure 7 to a chord symbol indicates that the pitch a minor 7th from the root is to be added to the triad in question, whether or not that interval results in a diatonic scale degree. This applies equally to the major, minor, and augmented triads (ex.8*a*). Should the pitch

Ex.8

(a) (b)

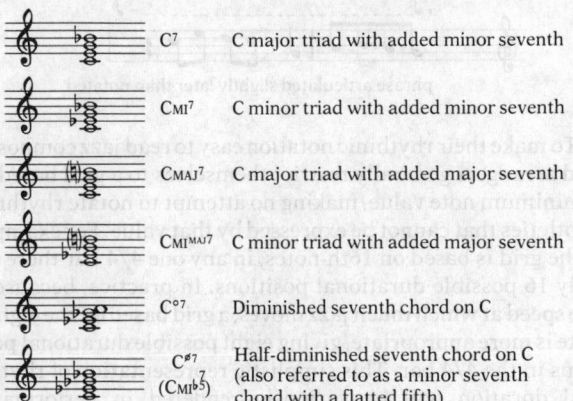

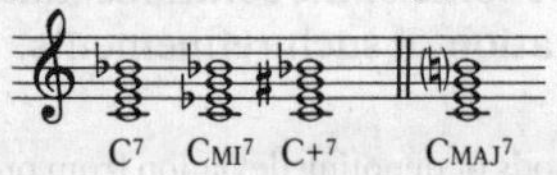

a major 7th from the root be required it is indicated by the figure 7 preceded by the abbreviation for "major" (ex.8*b*). The chord symbols for common forms of the seventh chord, together with the intervals they indicate, are shown in Table 1.

Chords of the ninth, 11th, and 13th are similarly indicated. In expressing chords made up entirely of diatonic elements, it is common to indicate only the uppermost extension, the presence of the intermediate elements being assumed. For example,

TABLE 1: Chord symbols for seventh chords

	C^{7}	C major triad with added minor seventh
	CMI^{7}	C minor triad with added minor seventh
	CMAJ^{7}	C major triad with added major seventh
	CMI$^{\text{MAJ}7}$	C minor triad with added major seventh
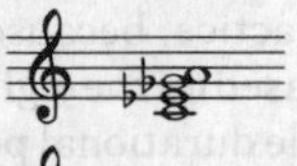	C$^{\circ 7}$	Diminished seventh chord on C
	C^{ø7} (CMI$^{\substack{7\\ \flat 5}}$)	Half-diminished seventh chord on C (also referred to as a minor seventh chord with a flatted fifth)

the chord of the ninth is expected also to include the seventh and the figure 7 need not appear; similarly the chord of the 11th is assumed to include the seventh and ninth. In practice musicians voice these chords according to taste and custom and may omit certain elements or rearrange them. For example, certain conventions apply to the chord of the 11th. The symbol

C^{11}

indicates the chord shown in ex.9*a* but generally a jazz musician would omit the third degree of this chord, as in ex.9*b*, to

Ex.9

(a) implied (b) sounded

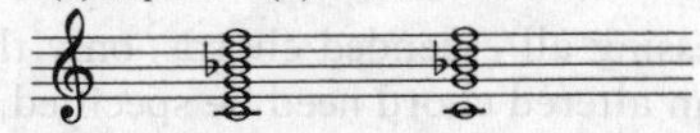

eliminate the interval of a minor 9th between it and the top note. Another such omission is standard when the major dominant chord of the 13th is indicated: instead of the full chord (ex.10*a*) a jazz player would generally omit the 11th (to avoid

Ex.10 (a) implied chord (b) notes sounded (c) idiomatic voicings

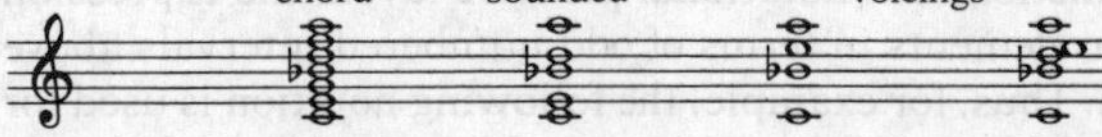

the minor 9th between it and the third) and often the fifth as well (ex.10*b*). The most characteristic voicings of the chord of the 13th in jazz are shown in ex.10*c*. Musicians realize the symbol in this manner according to unwritten "rules," which they absorb as they learn jazz; indeed, it has all but lost its function as an index to the elements of the chord and has come instead to represent a particular aggregate.

(c) Altered chords. Chromatic alterations to the upper elements of a chord are indicated by sharps and flats (or plus and minus signs), which precede the arabic numerals. Where more than one element is designated, the numerals are stacked (or may be placed one after the other to the right of the capital letter), and altered elements are sometimes placed in parentheses (ex.11). An exception to the use of sharps and flats to inflect

Ex.11

the elements of a chord is often made in the case of the seventh; as shown in Table 1 the note a major 7th above the root is normally inflected by means of the abbreviation "MAJ" (or "MA") and not by the sharp sign. The chord comprising the pitches C E G B is expressed as:

CMAJ^{7} (C△^{7} C^{⑦})

The chord comprising the pitches C E♭ G B D is expressed as:

CMI$^{\substack{9\\ (\text{MAJ}\,7)}}$

The convention of using sharp and flat signs to specify inflected chord elements is also applied to the fifth, so that the diminished and augmented triads may be indicated respectively by the symbols ♭5 and ♯5 added to the root (as shown in §(a) above).

Complex chords are expressed by combining the principles for notating extensions and alterations. For example, should the chord shown in ex.12 be required, the scribe would simply build up a symbol showing altered extensions as necessary, using the sign for an augmented chord on C with an added (minor) seventh, raised ninth, and raised 11th.

Ex.12

$C+\begin{smallmatrix}\sharp 11\\ \sharp 9\\ 7\end{smallmatrix}$

As in expressing all extended chords, only the uppermost extension of an altered chord need be specified, provided the intervening elements are unaltered. All altered elements must, however, be specified. Some scribes use a notational shorthand for extended altered chords on the dominant. The symbols

C^{7}(ALT) CALT

indicate (among others) the chord given in ex. 12.

Chords are usually spelled according to their context and tonal function. But notational practice favors the expression of upper elements in terms of odd-numbered intervals above the root. Thus, for example, the following notation is used for a chord of the seventh based on C to which a raised ninth degree is to be added:

$C^{\sharp 9}_{7}$

This obscures harmonic and tonal function, since the uppermost note is equivalent to a flatted 10th (which clashes with the major third of the chord, creating the effect of a blue note). In jazz that scale degree is notated as a raised ninth so as to preserve the odd-numbered naming of the degrees.

(d) Omission and addition of individual notes. If an individual pitch is to be left out of a chord a specific instruction to this effect may be given, usually in parentheses:

C^{7} (omit 3)

If an individual pitch is to be added, the verbal instruction "add" followed by the relevant numeral is used, indicating that this pitch alone, and not all the other partials otherwise implied by the numeral, be included in the chord:

C (add 9)

(e) Other chordal symbols and annotations. Should two chords be required simultaneously they are set above and below a horizontal line, showing the upper and lower sonorities:

C	C△	C triad
F♯	F♯△	F♯ triad

The triangles, denoting that unmodified triads are required, and the annotation "triad" are sometimes used to prevent confusion with the similar symbol shown below, in which the slash (solidus) indicates that the triad (shown to the left) should be played over a "foreign" bass note (shown to the right). Further clarification in this case may be achieved by the addition of the word "bass" to the bass note.

C/F♯ (C/F♯ bass)

The notation using a slash is also used to express inversions of simple chords: for example, a second inversion of the chord of C major could be indicated thus:

C/G (C/G bass)

If the harmonic accompaniment is to be discontinued during a certain passage various written indications are used: "NC" (no chord), "harmony tacet," or "break." A line of dashes above the staff normally indicates the duration of the passage, though this may also be shown by the symbol for a full bar's rest annotated with the requisite number of bars.

(f) Conclusion. Theoretically chord-symbol notation is capable of expressing precisely almost any vertical aggregate. However, most arrangers, composers, and music copyists use symbols that specify only the bare essentials of the chordal progression, assuming that individual players will enrich the harmony and voice the chords according to context, usage, and their own preference. Many of the refined notational details described above have been evolved for the purposes of teaching jazz or making descriptive transcriptions, and would not normally be found in parts for professional musicians.

(iv) Rhythm, duration, and tempo. Rhythm is one of the most elusive elements of jazz to represent in notated form, because, by its very nature, jazz relies on rhythmic subtleties and complexities not accurately shown by standard notation. The principal rhythmic subtleties characteristic of jazz are the largely undefinable element of swing (*see* SWING (i)) and the highly refined and complex rhythmic play achieved by manipulation of the placement of the BEAT. The jazz composer and arranger use standard durational signs and expect the performer to introduce his own rhythmic adjustments. Many transcribers, however, being concerned with the accurate representation of a particular performance, have devised methods of indicating very precisely the nuances of rhythmic and durational variation. Ex.13 shows some of the solutions that transcribers have found for the notation of such refinements.

Ex.13 Methods of denoting deviation from prevailing pulse

(a)

← = note slightly anticipated
→ = note slightly delayed

(b)

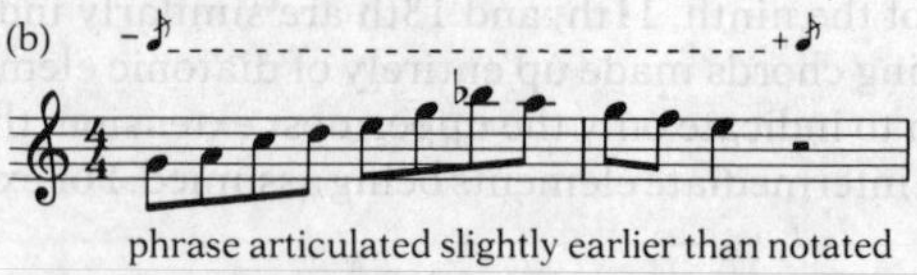

phrase articulated slightly earlier than notated

phrase articulated slightly later than notated

To make their rhythmic notation easy to read jazz composers and arrangers generally restrict themselves to a grid based on a minimum note value, making no attempt to notate rhythmic subtleties that cannot be expressed by that value. For example, if the grid is based on 16th-notes, in any one 4/4 bar there are only 16 possible durational positions. In practice, because of the speed at which much jazz moves, a grid based on the eighth-note is more appropriate, giving eight possible durational positions in the 4/4 bar. This simplistic representation of rhythm and duration will be variously rendered in performance depending on the tempo of the piece and the "time feel" of the players. At extremely slow or fast tempos and in certain styles of jazz (such as LATIN JAZZ and JAZZ-ROCK) the notated rhythms are usually rendered much as they are written; but in the broad range of more moderate tempos the notated rhythms are freely and inventively manipulated.

The most prevalent aspect of jazz rhythm is the triplet lilt known as "swing," which varies in degree according to context. By common consent most composers and arrangers and even transcribers assume that in jazz that swings rhythms notated as regular duple subdivisions of the beat are performed as if they were based on a triple subdivision (ex.14); any player who

Ex.14

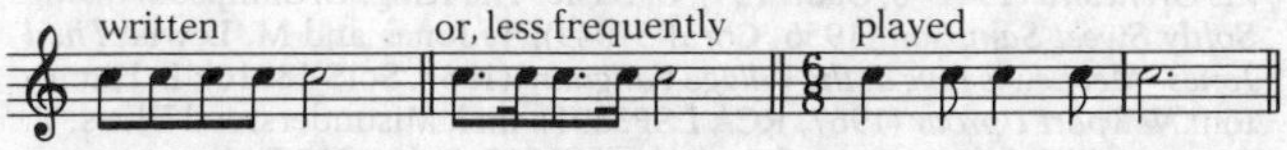

rendered them as written would be guilty of a performance that lacked one of the most basic attributes of jazz. A number of scribes have attempted a more accurate representation of swing rhythms as they are performed, using dotted notes or compound meter (the use of compound meter for the notation of jazz was advocated by Hoke Roberts as early as 1939); generally, however, only the most scholarly transcriptions attempt to present swing rhythms as they are actually played.

Tempo indications are normally given (if at all) in English and are placed at the head of the piece in the conventional way. These range from simple indications of speed (e.g., "medium fast,") to descriptions of the style of music (e.g., "fast funk" or "slow ballad").

Arrangers and composers commonly observe certain conventions when notating rhythm-section parts. If a certain rhythmic articulation is required it is indicated on a staff by means of slash marks, and, if necessary, rests. The slashes for quarter-note pulses do not take stems, and indicate simply that the performer should maintain the pulse, though not necessarily by articulating every quarter-note. Diamond-shaped note heads are used for half-notes and longer values; slashes with stems, tails, and beams are used to show shorter durations (ex.15). The symbol commonly used in classical music to specify that a bar should be repeated is also used in jazz, as shown in the fourth bar of ex.15.

Ex.15

Drum and percussion parts are generally shown on the standard five-line staff, and use the slash-mark notation shown above. Different styles and patterns, instructions as to which components of the drum set or which sticks should be used, and cues may be indicated verbally (e.g., "Latin," "two beat," "cym.," "brushes"), rather than by special symbols. More fully notated parts, with written-out lines for each component of the drum set, are less common, but by no means unknown. Under one convention (shown in ex.16) the individual components of the set are notated on a single staff with a bass clef: the bass drum part is notated in the lowest space, that for the snare drum in the third space up, and those for hi-hat and other cymbals in the top space; the top space is also used for the tom-tom and miscellaneous instruments. Where precise notation of a more elaborate instrumentarium is needed the third

Ex.16

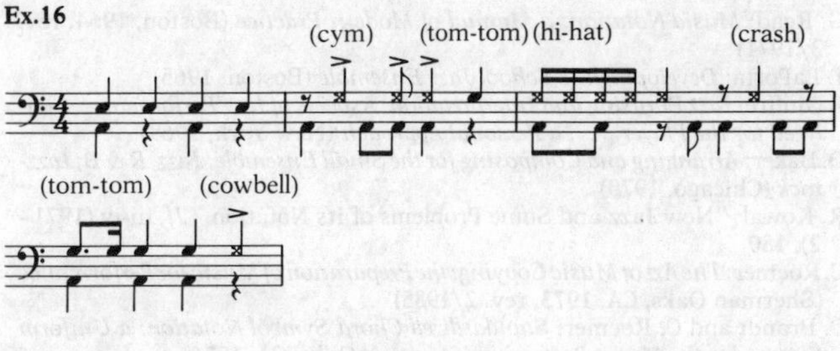

and fourth spaces and the space above the staff may be used to indicate parts for three differently pitched independent instruments. Similar notations have been devised to aid the programming of drum machines.

(v) Timbre and articulation. In jazz as in most other types of music, timbre and articulation (attack and release) lend themselves least easily to representation by notation. Customarily they are not meticulously prescribed by jazz composers and arrangers: they are held to be elements of a player's individual style, or of a collective style transmitted by aural (and oral) tradition, or they are regarded as matters to be decided by discussion during rehearsal. Nevertheless some symbols have gained wide currency.

Among the most important standard signs, which are applicable to many instruments, are those that mean "closed" (i.e., choked, stopped, damped, muted) and "open" (i.e., sounding freely, unmuted, etc.) (ex.17). These symbols may be used to

Ex.17 Symbols for "open" and "closed"

indicate the DU WAH on brass instruments; stopped and open strings; closed and open hi-hat; or, even more generally, the application or removal of a mute (though these instructions are more commonly given verbally, the particular kind of mute normally being specified).

More specific signs are used for different instrumental groups: the most common of these are for wind and brass. Thomas Owens uses phonetic syllables to denote different types of tonguing on wind instruments: "TA" for a sharp attack, "DA" and "TH" for softer ones, and, for the HONK, the symbol shown

Ex.18 Symbol for the honk

in ex.18. FALSE FINGERING is most often denoted by the placement of a written direction, sometimes specifying that a side key should be used. Timbral or articulatory directions specific to brass instruments include the symbol used by Gunther Schuller in *Early Jazz* for the GROWL, shown in ex.19.

Ex.19 Symbol for the growl

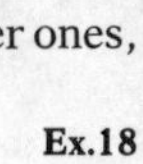

Generally symbols for accents have been borrowed from the Western classical tradition, as have dynamic markings where they are needed.

BIBLIOGRAPHY

H. Roberts: "Jazz Should be Written in Six-eight Time," *DB*, vi/6 (1939), 9
J. Coker: *Improvising Jazz* (Englewood Cliffs, NJ, 1964)

G. Read: *Music Notation: a Manual of Modern Practice* (Boston, 1964, rev. 3/1971)
J. LaPorta: *Developing the School Jazz Ensemble* (Boston, 1965)
J. Giuffre: *Jazz Phrasing and Interpretation: Aspects of Jazz Performance, Analyzed for the Player . . . a Personal Approach* (New York, 1969)
D. Baker: *Arranging and Composing for the Small Ensemble: Jazz, R & B, Jazz-rock* (Chicago, 1970)
R. Kowal: "New Jazz and Some Problems of its Notation," *Jf*, iii-iv (1971–2), 180
C. Roemer: *The Art of Music Copying: the Preparation of Music for Performance* (Sherman Oaks, CA, 1973, rev. 2/1985)
C. Brandt and C. Roemer: *Standardized Chord Symbol Notation: a Uniform System for the Music Profession* (Sherman Oaks, CA, 1976)
K. Stone: *Music Notation in the Twentieth Century: a Practical Guidebook* (New York, London, and Toronto, 1980)

ROBERT WITMER

Notes. Nickname of RICHARD WILLIAMS.

Noto, Sam (*b* Buffalo, 17 April 1930). Trumpeter and flugelhorn player. His first important associations were with Stan Kenton (1955–8, 1960), Louie Bellson (1959), and Count Basie (1964–5, 1967). After leaving Basie he formed a quintet in Buffalo with Joe Romano, then from 1969 to 1975 he worked as a freelance in Las Vegas. He was recommended to the producer Don Schlitten by Red Rodney, with whom he made his first recording (1974). Schlitten produced several recordings for Noto, most of which were released on the former's label, Xanadu. In 1975 Noto moved to Toronto and worked in studios and at clubs; until the early 1980s he played and composed for Rob McConnell's group Boss Brass, which recorded about 20 of his pieces. He also recorded in 1978 with Blue Mitchell, Al Cohn, and Dexter Gordon in an all-star group at the Montreux International Jazz Festival. In the early 1980s he operated the Renaissance II club in Buffalo. Around 1983 he began playing frequently with show bands in Toronto, where he has continued to work as a freelance. Noto is recognized for his assertive, virtuoso style of improvisation; his playing reflects the influence of Clifford Brown and Dizzy Gillespie, but he also draws on other sources.

SELECTED RECORDINGS

As leader: *Entrance!* (1975, Xan. 103); *Act One* (1975, Xan. 127); *Notes to You* (1977, Xan. 144); *Noto-riety* (1978, Xan. 168)
As sideman: R. Rodney: *Superbop* (1974, Muse 5046); R. McConnell: *The Jazz Album* (1976, Attic 1015); *Again!* (1978, Umbrella 1-12)

BIBLIOGRAPHY

FeatherE; *Feather '60s*; *Feather–Gitler '70s*

ROBERT DICKOW

Notte, Flavius (*b* Martinique, ?1890s; ? *d* Paris, after 1931). Martinique drummer and bandleader. He performed with Bertin Salnave's band in France in 1925 and during the 1930s he worked in Paris, notably at the club La Coupole. In 1931 he made recordings as a leader for Ultraphone with such Caribbean musicians as Salnave and the trumpeter Abel Beauregard (including *'Tain't no Sin*, AP121, and *I've found a wonderful girl*, AP144). (A. Boulanger: Liner notes, *Jazz and Hot Dance in Martinique*, Harl. 2018, 1985)

RAINER E. LOTZ

Nottingham, Jimmy [James Edward, Jr.; Sir James] (*b* New York, 15 Dec 1925; *d* New York, 16 Nov 1978). Trumpeter and flugelhorn player. His professional career began in 1943 when he performed in Brooklyn with Cecil Payne. After serving in Willie Smith's navy band (1944–5) he gained a reputation as a high-note player while he was with Lionel Hampton (1945–7). Always in demand, he spent periods with Charlie Barnet and Lucky Millinder (both 1947), Count Basie (1948–50), and Herbie Fields (1951); he then played with several Latin bands (1951–3). In 1954 he joined the staff of CBS, and worked with the company for 20 years, dividing his time between jazz and popular music. He also led a group with Budd Johnson (1962) and performed as a sideman with many orchestras, including those of Dizzy Gillespie (with whom he played in France in 1962), Oliver Nelson, Quincy Jones, Ray Charles, Benny Goodman, Thad Jones and Mel Lewis (1966–70), and Clark Terry (1974–5). A versatile lead trumpeter and an expert with the plunger mute, Nottingham was a player of great taste and sensitivity.

SELECTED RECORDINGS

As sideman: on L. Hampton: *Rarities* (c1946, MCA 1351), Cobb's Idea (1946); first issued on [no leader]: *Wardell Gray, Featuring Stan Hasselgard and his Orchestra* (1947–8, Spot. 134), C. Basie: The King; E. Sampson: *Swing Softly Sweet Sampson* (1956, Coral 57049); T. Jones and M. Lewis: *Thad Jones–Mel Lewis Live at the Village Vanguard* (1967, SolS 18016); L. Hampton: *Newport Uproar* (1967, RCA LSP3891), incl. Misunderstood Blues; T. Jones and M. Lewis: *Central Park North* (1969, SolS 18058)

BIBLIOGRAPHY

FeatherE; *Feather–Gitler '70s*
R. Horricks: *Count Basie and his Orchestra: its Music and its Musicians* (London and New York, 1957), 165
Obituary, *DB*, xlvi/1 (1979), 10

SCOTT YANOW

Novi Singers. Polish vocal group. It was formed around 1965 by Bernard Kawka with the singers Alexander Głuch, Janusz Mych, Waldemar Parzyński, and Ewa Wanat. Originally it was a quintet but when Głuch left the group around 1968 it continued as a quartet. Kawka went to the USA in 1974, and the ensemble performed briefly as a trio; later Kawka's place was taken by the pianist and singer Tomasz Ochalski. In the tradition of such groups as Lambert, Hendricks, and Ross and the Double Six, it sang closely arranged music with little opportunity for individual improvisation; in later years elements of rock music were incorporated into performances. In the early 1970s its album of vocal arrangements of compositions by Chopin, *Novi Sings Chopin* (1971, Muza 0755), became a popular hit. The group was accompanied by many notable Polish jazz musicians, including Adam Makowicz, Michal Urbaniak, Zbigniew Namysłowski, and Tomasz Stańko.

BIBLIOGRAPHY

J. Byrczek: "Eurojazz Personalities: Poland," *JF* [intl edn], no.17 (1972), 85
J. Fest: "Whatever Happened to Bernard Kawka?," *JF* [intl edn], no.37 (1975), 40
——: "Ad lib with the Novi Singers," *JF* [intl edn], no.39 (1976), 42

WOLFRAM KNAUER

Nucleus. Group founded in 1969 by IAN CARR.

Nugetre. Pseudonym of AHMET ERTEGUN.

Nuñez, Alcide "Yellow" (*b* New Orleans, 17 March 1884; *d* New Orleans, 2 Sept 1934). Clarinetist. He began playing professionally as a guitarist, but from 1902 concentrated entirely on the clarinet and played in many New Orleans groups, including Papa Jack Laine's Reliance Brass Band and Tom Brown's band. He was also a member of a trio at the 101 Ranch in Storyville. After journeying to Chicago in March 1916 with Johnny Stein's group, Nuñez and three other band members (Nick LaRocca, Eddie Edwards, and Henry Ragas) formed a group that later became the Original Dixieland Jazz Band. Disagreements between Nuñez and LaRocca, however, caused the clarinetist to leave the group at the end of October. He toured briefly on the vaudeville circuit, then joined Anton

Lada's LOUISIANA FIVE (1918–19), with whom he made his most representative recordings. In the mid-1920s he toured with his own quartet, but after 1927 worked for various leaders in New Orleans.

Nuñez's tone was harsh and brittle and he was skilled in the production of "barnyard" effects. Although he had a talent for improvisation, his vaudevillian approach to the music sometimes detracted from his performances.

SELECTED RECORDINGS

As sideman: Louisiana Five: I ain't-en got-en no time to have the blues (1919, Col. A2775); Ringtail Blues/ Blues my naughty sweetie gives to me (1919, Emerson 1083)

BIBLIOGRAPHY

ChiltonW

H. O. Brunn: *The Story of the Original Dixieland Jazz Band* (Baton Rouge, LA, 1960/*R*1977)

S. B. Charters and L. Kunstadt: *Jazz: a History of the New York Scene* (Garden City, NY, 1962/*R*1981)

F. Ramsey, Jr.: Liner notes, *Jazz Odyssey*, i: *The Sound of New Orleans (1917–1947)* (Col. C3L30, *c*1964)

G. Schuller: *Early Jazz: its Roots and Musical Development* (New York, 1968)

LAWRENCE KOCH

Nussbaum, Adam (*b* New York, 29 Nov 1955). Drummer. He studied drumming with Charli Persip, and from 1975 played at clubs in New York with Monty Waters, Al Dailey, and the pianist Nina Sheldon, and in Washington with Dave Liebman. From 1978 to 1981 he worked with John Scofield, performing and recording with him in Europe (1978–9) and playing in sessions led by Hal Galper (1979). Nussbaum and Scofield also worked with Liebman (1980) and toured and made recordings (including the album *Shinola*, 1981, Enja 4004) in a trio with Steve Swallow (1980–81). From the early 1980s Nussbaum has worked with Gil Evans's orchestra, touring Europe and Japan in 1985. He has also recorded with Bill Evans (iii) (1983) and Bobby Watson and Art Farmer (both 1984), and worked briefly with Eddie Gomez (1984) and Gary Burton. (J. Woodard: "Adam Nussbaum: New York Blues," *MD*, x/6 (1986), 22)

NYJRC. *See* NEW YORK JAZZ REPERTORY COMPANY.

NYRL. *See* NEW YORK RECORDING LABORATORIES.

O

Obendorfer, Jenő. *See* Chappy.

Oboe. A double-reed woodwind instrument of narrow, conoidal bore, terminating in a moderately flared bell. Its basic scale begins on *c'* and its compass generally extends from *b♭* to about *a'''*. There are several larger versions of the Western orchestral instrument, of which the english horn (or cor anglais), the tenor member of the family, is pitched in F (a 5th below the oboe) and has a distinguishing feature in its bulb-shaped bell. Jazz musicians have also been drawn increasingly to the numerous types of non-Western oboe, notably the *nāgasvaram* of south India and the *zūrnā* of the Arab world (which has many derivatives elsewhere).

The oboe is quite rare in jazz. It first appeared in the 1920s, when it was included, for the sake of its tone-color, in the reed section of the band; its use was prompted by the influence of symphonic jazz. Don Redman played oboe in his arrangement of *Shanghai Shuffle*, recorded by Fletcher Henderson in 1924 (PAct 036157), and oboe parts were also written for Paul Whiteman's orchestra. In these contexts the oboist was a section member, playing from written parts, and had the opportunity neither to improvise nor to play solos. The oboe continued to be used in this way: Alec Wilder wrote for the instrument in a series of light, jazzlike octets composed in 1939, and from that year Mitch Miller played oboe and english horn in Wilder's orchestra accompanying Mildred Bailey on several recordings of Wilder's songs; Miller also performed as a member of a group (otherwise consisting mostly of string players) that accompanied Charlie Parker on a recording in 1949; and George Barnes's octet recorded chamber pieces with a jazz flavor that included oboe.

The oboe was first used as a solo instrument and for improvisations during the 1950s when jazz musicians began to explore orchestral instrumentation and classical compositional forms. Several examples of the use of oboe and english horn in cool jazz and West Coast jazz include the work of Bob Cooper (principally a tenor saxophonist), who played both instruments on several of his recordings. In the later 1950s Yusef Lateef began to play oboe (as well as other wind instruments), adopting a soulful, bluesy style and a rich tone; an example of his playing may be heard on the track *In the Evening* from the album *The Complete Yusef Lateef* (1967, Atl. 1499). Marshall Allen plays a solo on oboe on *Thither and Yon* from Sun Ra's album *Cosmic Tones for Mental Therapy* (1963, Sat. 408). Paul McCandless, who came to prominence as a member of the group Oregon (formed 1970), is most highly regarded for his extraordinary playing of jazz oboe and english horn, though he also plays soprano saxophone and other wind instruments; Oregon's repertory incorporates elements of ethnic music and is not always identified with jazz, but McCandless's solos (well represented by the album *Together*, 1976, Van. 79377) clearly draw on the tradition of John Coltrane's soprano saxophone playing and reveal the influence of the *nāgasvaram*, which Coltrane also admired. Another musician to synthesize the style of Coltrane with ethnic traditions is Charlie Mariano, who studied the *nāgasvaram* in South Asia and has been deeply influenced by Carnatic music. Use of the oboe in jazz-rock includes the work of Andrew White, who plays a solo on english horn on the track *Unknown Soldier* (1971) from Weather Report's album *I Sing the Body Electric* (1971–2, Col. KC31352). The oboe has also occasionally been used by the Art Ensemble of Chicago. Dewey Redman plays an instrument related to the oboe, which he calls the Musette.

BIBLIOGRAPHY

P. A. T. Bate: *The Oboe* (London, 1956, rev. 2/1962, 3/1975)
P. Bate and N. O'Loughlin: "Oboe," *GroveI*

LEWIS PORTER

O'Brien, Floyd (W.) (*b* Chicago, 7 May 1904; *d* Chicago, ?26 Nov 1968). Trombonist. He first played professionally in the early 1920s with local bands in Chicago and with many of the Austin High School Gang. After working in a pit band in Des Moines, Iowa (1930–31), he returned to Chicago and performed with a number of bandleaders, including Floyd Town (1932), Joe Venuti, and Mal Hallett. In New York he played with Mike Durso (1933–4) and recorded with Fats Waller (1934). He was in demand for recording dates, and his warm playing, inspired by the great New Orleans musicians, may be heard on *Tennessee Twilight* recorded with Eddie Condon (1933) and *Old Fashioned Love* recorded with Mezz Mezzrow (1934). O'Brien then worked with the drummer and singer Phil Harris (1935–9), Gene Krupa (1939–40), and Bob Crosby (1940–42); *Tin Roof Blues* recorded with Crosby in 1942 shows O'Brien in a robust mood. In Los Angeles he played with Eddie Miller (1943) and as a freelance musician, and recorded with Bunk Johnson (1944). He returned in 1948 to Chicago, where he worked with Bud Freeman and recorded with Art Hodes (1954), Danny Alvin (1958), and the trumpeter Smokey Stover (1959–60). He was also active as a brass teacher and piano tuner. In 1965 he appeared with members of the Austin High School Gang in a festival organized by *Down Beat*.

SELECTED RECORDINGS

As sideman: B. Freeman: Can't help lovin' dat man (1928, OK 41168); E. Condon: Tennessee Twilight (1933, Bruns. 01690); M. Mezzrow: Old Fashioned Love (1934, Vic. 25202); G. Wettling: I wish I could shimmy like my sister Kate (1940, Decca 18044); B. Crosby: Tin Roof Blues (1942, Bruns. 04003); C. LaVere: Baby won't you please come home (1944, Jump 1); A. Nicholas: *All Star Stompers* (1959, Del. 209)

BIBLIOGRAPHY

ChiltonW; *FeatherE*; *Feather–Gitler '70s*
G. Avakian: "Why Bury O'Brien," *Jazz Information*, ii/3 (1940), 12
W. H. Miller: "Floyd O'Brien," *Three Brass*, v (Melbourne, Australia, 1945)
M. Mezzrow and B. Wolfe: *Really the Blues* (New York, 1946/*R*1972), 268, 345
A. Shaw: *The Trouble with Cinderella: an Outline of Identity* (New York, 1952/*R*1979), 146

BRIAN PEERLESS

O'Bryant, Jimmy [Jimmie] (*b* Arkansas, *c*1896; *d* Chicago, 24 June 1928). Clarinetist and alto saxophonist. He toured with a vaudeville troupe, the Tennessee Ten (*c*1920–1921), and in early 1923 was a member of the short-lived band led by Jelly Roll Morton and W. C. Handy in Chicago. During the same year he began recording for Paramount, working as the regular clarinetist with the studio's house band, Lovie Austin's Blues Serenaders (1923–6). After playing briefly with King Oliver (1924) he made a number of recordings under his own name with the Washboard Band (1925–6). In 1927 he was a member of Paul Stuart's Wee Hours Serenaders in Terre Haute, Indiana, but early the following year he returned to Chicago.

O'Bryant's tone was sweet and plaintive in the upper register (notably when he accompanied singers), though his fast vibrato and characteristic edge caused his playing to stand out in ensemble work. In the chalumeau register of the instrument his tone was full-bodied and warm, and he often made judicious use of feather tonguing for dramatic effect – a legacy of his years on the vaudeville circuit. During his brief career at Paramount O'Bryant made more recordings than any other Chicago jazz clarinetist; a tribute to the quality of these performances is that his playing has often been mistaken for that of Johnny Dodds or Junie Cobb.

SELECTED RECORDINGS

As leader: Georgia Break Down (1925, Para. 12277); Three J Blues/Steppin' on the Gas (1925, Para. 12294); The Joys/Switch it, Miss Mitchell (1925, Para. 12297)
As sideman: I. Cox: Graveyard Dream Blues/Weary Way Blues (1923, Para. 12044); L. Austin: Peepin' Blues (1925, Para. 12277)

BIBLIOGRAPHY

C. Hillman: "Paramount Serenaders, 1923–1926," *Sv*, no.67 (1976), 8; no.70 (1977), 149; no.72 (1977), 226 [incl. discography]
D. M. Bakker: "Jimmie O'Bryant, 1923–26," *Micrography*, no.44 (1977), 14

MICHAEL TOVEY

Octave divider. An electronic device that takes as input a pitch played on an instrument and adds to it a replica one or more octaves lower. The result is an instrumental line in parallel octaves; often some modification of the original timbre also takes place. Commercially available effects units that exploit this principle include the Multivider, the Octivider, and the Varitone. The device has been used by several jazz musicians, most notably Eddie Harris.

Octobans. A set of eight single-headed drums; *see* DRUM SET, §I, 4.

October Revolution in Jazz. A series of free-jazz concerts organized in 1964 by BILL DIXON.

O'Day, Anita [Colton, Anita Belle] (*b* Kansas City, MO, 18 Oct 1919). Singer. She took the stage name O'Day while working as a contestant in dance marathons, and at about the age of 19 sang professionally in nightclubs in Chicago. From 1941 to 1943 she was a member of Gene Krupa's big band (see illustration), with which she recorded her biggest hit, *Let me off uptown*. After singing in Stan Kenton's band (1944–5) and again with Krupa (1945–6) she embarked on a solo career that was

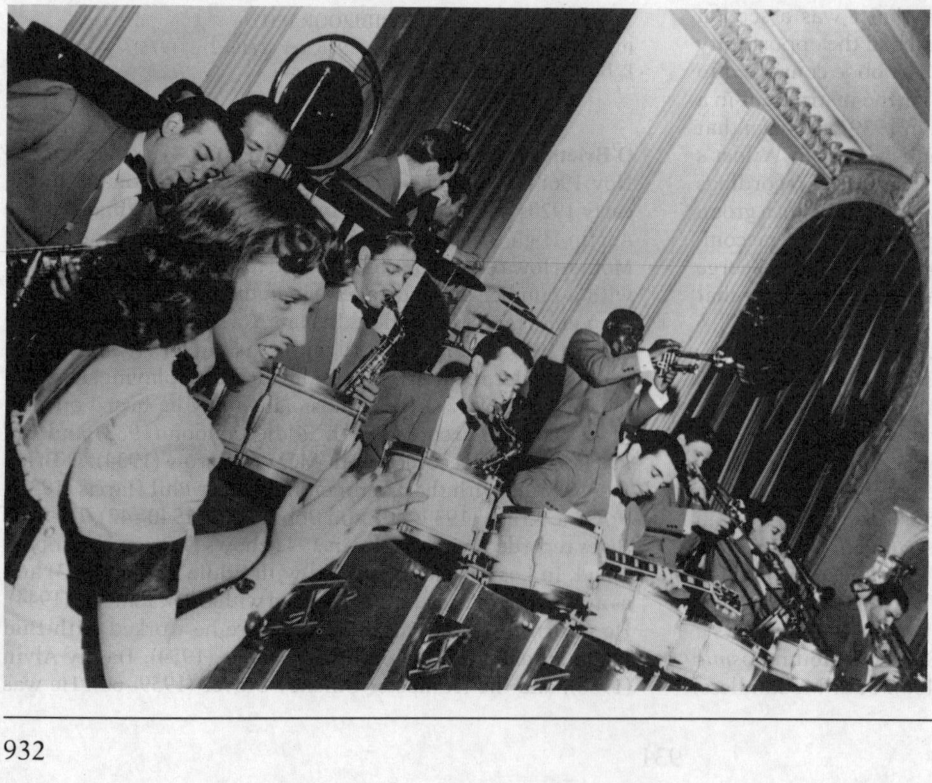

Anita O'Day (front) with Gene Krupa's big band at the Hotel Pennsylvania, New York, 1941; the trumpet soloist (standing) is Roy Eldridge and the guitarist is Ray Biondi

interrupted periodically by problems stemming from heroin addiction. In the mid-1950s O'Day recorded several albums for Verve which were very well received. She made a sensational appearance at the Newport Jazz Festival in 1958 (captured in the film *Jazz on a Summer's Day*), and thereafter worked regularly in clubs both in the USA and elsewhere. In 1964 she made the first of several tours of Japan, and in 1972 she established Anita O'Day (later Emily) Records. She gave a concert at Carnegie Hall in 1985 to celebrate her fiftieth year in jazz. O'Day excels at improvisation; whether scat singing or skillfully interpreting a song text she allows herself all the liberties of instrumental jazz performance in refashioning a popular song.

SELECTED RECORDINGS

As leader: *Anita* (1955, Verve 2000); *Pick Yourself Up* (1956, Verve 2043); *Anita O'Day Sings the Winners* (1958, Verve 8283); *Cool Heat* (1959, Verve 8312); *All the Sad Young Men* (1961, Verve 68442); *Live at Mingos* (1976, Emily 11579); *Mello'Day* (1979, GNP 2126); *Live at the City* (1979, Emily 102479); *A Song for You* (*c*1984, Emily 83084)

As sideman with G. Krupa: Let me off uptown (1941, OK 6210)

BIBLIOGRAPHY

D. Cerulli: "Anita's Back," *DB*, xxiii/18 (1956), 13

A. Surpin: "Dawn of a New O'Day," *DB*, xxxvi/23 (1969), 16

H. Howard: "Anita O'Day," *JP*, xxx/6 (1980), 4

A. O'Day and G. Eells: *High Times, Hard Times* (New York, 1981) [autobiography]

A. Duncan: "Anita O'Day Can Still Command a Band – and an Audience," *Christian Science Monitor* (18 June 1985), 29

W. Friedwald: "Anita O'Day: What a Difference a Day Makes," *The Wire*, no.23 (1986), 28

BARRY KERNFELD

Odeon. Record label. Named after a theater in Paris, it was established for issue in France and Germany by the International Talking Machine Co., then acquired in 1910 by Carl Lindström. From the early 1920s Odeon was used to release much important jazz (drawn mostly from Okeh) in France, Belgium, Germany, Spain, Italy, Scandinavia, and parts of South America; this role was maintained after 1925, when Lindström sold his interests to Columbia International, Ltd., and after 1931, when the latter company merged with the Gramophone Co. to form EMI. Odeon's most notable material included two recordings by Carroll Dickerson on which Louis Armstrong played; these were released in Argentina, though never put out by Okeh in the USA. The Odeon Swing Music Series, first issued on German Odeon in 1937–9 and later sold throughout occupied Europe during World War II, ran to 92 discs and contained much fine jazz. There was also a designated swing series on Italian Odeon. After 1945 the label remained in use for jazz reissues in France, Japan, and Germany; these included a scheme set up in 1978 to rerelease material from the Swing Music Series.

In the USA the label name was used by the General Phonograph Corp., at first for classical music, then, in 1929, for a series intended for sale on the West Coast. This contained material by many of Okeh's most important musicians (including the Casa Loma Orchestra), often in versions specially recorded without the vocal part; these were presumably aimed at the Spanish-speaking community.

BIBLIOGRAPHY

H. Sagawe: "A Glimpse of the Past, 14: the German Odeon Swing Series, 1937–39," *Sv*, no.25 (1969), 14

B. Rust: *The American Record Label Book* (New Rochelle, NY, 1978), 210

Odin. Record company and label. It was established in May 1981 by the NORSK JAZZFORBUND to produce recordings of Norwegian jazz, in particular music that would not be issued by a commercial record company.

O'Farrill, Chico [Arturo] (*b* Havana, 28 Oct 1921). Cuban composer, arranger, and trumpeter. He studied composition in Havana, and in the mid-1940s played with a band led by Armando Romeu and with his own group. In 1948 he moved to New York, where he wrote music for Benny Goodman, Stan Kenton, Machito and Charlie Parker, and Dizzy Gillespie; in the early 1950s he formed his own band, which played at Birdland, toured the USA, and recorded as a leader the album *Jazz* (1951–2, Clef 132). Towards the end of the decade he moved to Mexico, and in 1962–3 he gave concerts in Mexico City. After returning to the USA in 1965 he settled in New York and worked as an arranger and music director for CBS on the television program "Festival of the Lively Arts"; among the musicians who took part were Count Basie, Gillespie, Gerry Mulligan, and Stan Getz. In 1965–6 O'Farrill wrote arrangements of pop songs for albums by Basie. From the 1970s he was less active in jazz, but he wrote pieces for Gato Barbieri and Kenton (both 1974), and a band led by Gillespie and Machito (1975).

RECORDED COMPOSITIONS

(all arranged by O'Farrill)

Recorded by others: B. Goodman: Undercurrent Blues (1949, Cap. 15409); S. Kenton: Cuban Episode (1950, Cap. 28000); Machito: *Afro-Cuban Jazz Suite* (1950, Clef 505); on D. Gillespie: *Afro* (1954, Norg. 1003), Manteca Suite; on D. Gillespie and Machito: *Afro-Cuban Jazz Moods* (1975, Pablo 2310771), Oro, incienso y mirra

BIBLIOGRAPHY

FeatherE; *Feather '60s*; *Feather–Gitler '70s*

S. Woolley: "The Spanish Tinge," *JJI*, xxxviii/7 (1985), 8

CRISTÓBAL DÍAZ AYALA

Offbeat. Any beat of the bar other than the first or downbeat; *see* BEAT, esp. §4(i).

Off-note. A note played slightly out of tune (usually flat) for expressive effect; the term is sometimes used as a synonym for "blue note" (*see* BLUE NOTE (i)).

Oganesyan [Khovanesyan], **Tatevik** (*b* Yerevan, Armenian SSR, 3 June 1955). Armenian singer. She began singing jazz as a child and when she was 13 made her first recording, a version of Harold Arlen's *It's only a paper moon*, for Armenian radio. She studied choral conducting at the Melikyan Music School in Yerevan (graduated 1974) and sang with the Armenian State Variety Orchestra under the bandleader Konstantin Orbelyan (1974–7); later she worked with groups led by Igor Bril, Vladimir Chekasin, Aleksey Kuznetsov, Lembit Saarsalu, and Tiit Paulus. Oganesyan has performed at many concerts and festivals in the USSR and at festivals in Belgrade (1978) and Debrecen, Hungary (1985). Her singing can be heard to advantage on her recording *Dnevnïe mechtï* (Day dream; 1986, Mel. C6023665000).

WALTER OJAKÄÄR

Ogerman, Claus [Ogermann, Klaus] (*b* Ratibor, Germany [now Racibórz, Poland], 29 April 1930). German composer, conductor, and pianist. After studying classical piano in Nuremberg he played with Kurt Edelhagen (1952) and performed and recorded with Max Greger (1952–7). In 1955 he began to write arrangements for recordings. Ogerman went to the USA in 1959 and established himself as a successful commercial arranger who also composed classical music. He earned some critical acclaim for his work on jazz albums, notably those with Antonio Carlos Jobim (1963), Bill Evans (ii) (1965), Oscar Peterson (1969), and Mike Brecker (1982). He formed two music publishing companies and also produced albums for such popular performers as Caterina Valente. In the 1970s Ogerman turned away from commercial writing and began to compose more classical and jazz music, including *Symbiosis* for jazz piano and orchestra (1975). A collection of his complete printed works is in the music division of the Deutsche Bibliothek in Berlin; *see* LIBRARIES AND ARCHIVES, §2.

SELECTED ARRANGEMENTS

Recorded by others: A. C. Jobim: *Antonio Carlos Jobim, the Composer of "Desafinado," Plays* (1963, Verve 68547); B. Evans: *Bill Evans Trio with the Symphony Orchestra* (1965, Verve 68640); O. Peterson: *Motions and Emotions* (1969, MPS 15251); M. Brecker: *Cityscape* (1982, WB 23698)

BIBLIOGRAPHY

Feather '60s; *Feather–Gitler '70s*
G. Lees: "The Real Claus Ogerman Stands up," *High Fidelity/Musical America*, xxv/10 (1975), 19

STEVEN STRUNK

Ogun. Record company and label. The company was established in London in 1973 by HARRY MILLER, his wife Hazel Miller, and Keith Beal. By 1987 it had issued more than 30 albums. The repertory consists mainly of free jazz and improvised music. Much of the material is by musicians resident in England, including Trevor Watts, Evan Parker, and SOS, and several expatriate South Africans, notably members of Brotherhood of Breath, but the company has also recorded the work of some European players (including Irène Schweizer) and Americans. In 1977 Ogun released the only album Miller made as the leader of his own group Isipingo; this included the playing of Louis Moholo and Keith Tippett.

SIMON ADAMS

Ohno [Ono], **Shunzo** (*b* Gifu, Japan, 22 March 1949). Japanese trumpeter. After moving to Tokyo he played with the alto saxophonist Keiichiro Ebihara and his Lobsters (from 1968) and the groups Sound Limited and Soul Media; he then belonged to a quintet led by the drummer George Otsuka and in 1973 moved to New York. He played with Roy Haynes and Norman Connors, recorded as a leader (1975, 1979–80), and with Machito recorded two albums (1982) and performed at the North Sea Festival in The Hague; later he played with Gil Evans and in 1985 performed frequently in Japan. Ohno has a rich, warm, brilliant tone; he is perhaps best known for his recording of his own composition *Bubbles*.

SELECTED RECORDINGS

Something's Coming (1975, EW 7011); *Bubbles* (1975, EW 8028); *Quarter Moon* (1979, EB SKS8008); *Anteress* (1980, EB K28P-6013); *Manhattan Blue* (1986, EB K32Y-6168)

YOZO IWANAMI

Okeh. Record company and label. The label was established by the General Phonograph Corp., an enterprise set up in New York in 1916 (as the Otto Heinemann Phonograph Corp.) to manage the American operations of Carl Lindström's German company; it was launched in September 1918. Jazz recordings commenced around two months later with items by the New Orleans Jazz Band; these discs were vertically cut. Issue of laterally cut records began in February 1920; in the same month Perry Bradford persuaded Okeh's agent for artists and repertory, Fred Hagar, to organize sessions by Mamie Smith. The resulting recordings established Okeh's primacy in the field, which was reinforced in summer 1921 by the setting up of a specific race series, the 8000s (until 1923 called the Colored Catalog). With Clarence Williams supervising artists and repertory in New York, and Richard M. Jones in Chicago, this became an extremely important jazz catalogue, and included material by Williams himself (from 1921, notably many important recordings with the Blue Five from 1923), King Oliver

Label for "Cake-walking Babies from Home," recorded by Clarence Williams's Blue Five for Okeh (1925)

(1923), Louis Armstrong's Hot Five and Hot Seven (1925–9), Lonnie Johnson (1925–32), and many others. Searches for talent in other cities brought to the label such ensembles as Bennie Moten's band, which recorded several times for Okeh between 1923 and 1925. Discs by Frankie Trumbauer, Bix Beiderbecke, and Eddie Lang were issued in a general popular series. The company's activities were little affected when it was taken over by Columbia in 1926; Heinemann ran Okeh as a new subsidiary, the Okeh Phonograph Corp., and maintained a largely independent program of recording. Thereafter control ultimately passed to ARC–BRC in August 1934. Later that year the 8000 series was discontinued; of the many race series inaugurated in the 1920s this was one of the most prolific and the longest lasting, having run to almost a thousand issues. ARC–BRC dropped the name Okeh, but CBS, which acquired the company in 1938, revived it, and continued the numerical series of the Vocalion label, pressing early issues anew with Okeh labels. In the early 1950s, when artists and repertory were directed by Danny Kessler, the label became CBS's main outlet for rhythm-and-blues, and maintained a jazz catalogue that included work by Wild Bill Davis and Red Saunders.

BIBLIOGRAPHY

Okeh Race Records (New York, n.d. [?1924]/*R*1976) [*R*1976 is a facs. of Clarence Williams's annotated copy]
Okeh Race Records: the Blue Book of Blues (New York, n.d. [?1927]/*R*)
J. Godrich and R. M. W. Dixon: *Blues & Gospel Records, 1902–1942* (Hatch End, nr London, 1964, rev. 2/1969, rev. and enlarged 3/1982 as R. M. W. Dixon and J. Godrich: *Blues & Gospel Records, 1902–1943*), 18
R. M. W. Dixon and J. Godrich: *Recording the Blues* (London, 1970)
R. D. Kinkle: "Okeh Numerical List," "Vocalion–Okeh Numerical List," *The Complete Encyclopedia of Popular Music and Jazz, 1900–1950* (New Rochelle, NY, and Westport, CT, 1974), iv, 2123, 2255
B. Rust: *The American Record Label Book* (New Rochelle, NY, 1978), 212
A. Shaw: "Groove 20: Danny Kessler and Okeh Records," *Honkers and Shouters: the Golden Years of Rhythm and Blues* (New York, 1978), 445

Okoshi, Tiger [Toru] (*b* Ashita, Japan, 21 March 1950). Japanese trumpeter and synthesizer player. From 1972 he has been resident in the USA and has worked with Gary Burton, among others; his playing may be heard to advantage on Burton's album *Times Square* (1978, ECM 1111). Okoshi has led several of his own bands and has recorded in Rhode Island for the Japanese label JVC (1980–81). In 1983 he performed and recorded with Bob Moses. His style, which he refers to as "Baku music," has gained much inspiration from the early jazz-rock work of Miles Davis, and has led to his being recognized as the leading Japanese jazz-rock musician of the 1980s.

Old and New Dreams. Quartet formed in 1976 by Don Cherry (trumpet), Dewey Redman (tenor saxophone), Charlie Haden (double bass), and Ed Blackwell (drums).

Oliva, Hernán (*b* Valparaíso, Chile, 4 July 1913). Chilean violinist. A self-taught musician, he played popular music in Chile before moving in 1935 to Argentina. While a member of René Cóspito's orchestra (1935–40) he studied violin with Jascha Bergosky (1937); during the following years he worked with Enrique Villegas (1940), Oscar Alemán (recording to 1943), and Ray Ventura's orchestra (1944). In 1945 he performed and recorded in a group led by Louis Vola that was modeled after the Quintette du Hot Club de France. Later he worked as a sideman (to 1955), as a leader (to 1967), and as a member of a swing quintet that made several recordings in the 1970s (including *El paso del tigre*, 1975, Redondel 10510, and *El violin del jazz*, 1978, Redondel 10523). He has continued to perform into the late 1980s.

LAUREANO FERNÁNDEZ, OMAR GARCÍA BRUNELLI

Oliver, King [Joe] (*b* in or nr New Orleans, 11 May 1885; *d* Savannah, GA, 8 or 10 April 1938). Cornetist and bandleader. He is said to have begun to study music as a trombonist, and from about 1907 he played in brass bands, dance bands, and in various small groups in New Orleans bars and cabarets. In 1918 he moved to Chicago (at which time he may have acquired his nickname), and in 1920 he began to lead his own band. After taking it to California (chiefly San Francisco and Oakland) in 1921, he returned to Chicago and, with some of the same musicians, started an engagement at Lincoln Gardens as King Oliver's Creole Jazz Band (June 1922). This group was joined a month later by the 22-year-old Louis Armstrong as second cornetist. With two cornets (Oliver and Armstrong), clarinet (Johnny Dodds), trombone (Honore Dutrey), piano (Lil Hardin), drums (Baby Dodds), and double bass and banjo (Bill Johnson (i)), Oliver began recording in April 1923 (see illustration). Many young white jazz musicians had the opportunity to hear him then, either on recordings or live at Lincoln Gardens.

By late 1924, after a tour of the Midwest and Pennsylvania, the completely reorganized band included two or three saxophones, and played in Chicago as the DIXIE SYNCOPATORS (February 1925 to March 1927); the most distinguished of the saxophonists who played with this band were Barney Bigard and Albert Nicholas. Soon after a brief but successful engagement at the Savoy Ballroom in New York (from May 1927) the members began to disperse and by autumn the group had disbanded, but Oliver stayed in New York, recording frequently with ad hoc orchestras. From 1930 to 1936 he toured widely, chiefly in the Midwest and upper South, with various ten- to 12-piece bands; he himself seldom performed during this period, and he made no further recordings after April 1931. He spent the final months of his life in Savannah retired from music.

Oliver is generally considered one of the most important musicians in the New Orleans style. Like other early New Orleans cornetists, he played in a relatively foursquare rhythm and clipped melodic style (contrasting with the deliberate irregularity of the younger Armstrong and his imitators) and had a repertory of expressive deviations of rhythm and pitch, some verging on theatrical novelty effects and others derived from blues vocal style (*see* BLUES, §2). He frequently used timbre

King Oliver's Creole Jazz Band, Chicago, 1923: (back, left to right) Honore Dutrey (trombone), Baby Dodds (drums), Oliver (cornet), and Bill Johnson (i) (banjo); (front) Louis Armstrong (soprano trombone; also known as the slide cornet), Lil Hardin (piano) and Johnny Dodds (clarinet)

modifiers of various sorts, and was especially renowned for his wa-wa effects, as in his famous three-chorus solo on *Dipper Mouth Blues* (1923), which was learned by rote by many trumpeters of the 1920s and 1930s and which, as *Sugar Foot Stomp*, became a jazz standard. (For a partial transcription of *Dipper Mouth Blues see* HARMONY (i), ex.19.) As a soloist he may best be heard in a number of blues accompaniments, notably with Sippie Wallace.

In contrast to his near-contemporaries Freddie Keppard and Bunk Johnson, Oliver integrated his playing superbly with his ensemble, and was an excellent leader; the Creole Jazz Band may have been successful largely because of the discipline he imposed on his musicians. Indeed, of the earlier New Orleans cornetists, only Oliver was extensively recorded in the 1920s with an outstanding ensemble, and the revival of New Orleans style, which began shortly after his death, owed much to the rediscovery of his early three dozen Creole Band recordings, which were internationally known by the 1940s. After 1924 the quality of his recordings declined, partly because of recurrent tooth and gum ailments and partly because his style was at odds with that of his younger sidemen; but with a good orchestra he was capable of coherent and energetic playing even as late as 1930. Almost all of his recorded performances have been reissued.

Oliver's influence is difficult to assess: his playing during his New Orleans period (his best years, according to Souchon) was not recorded, and by 1925 his style had largely been superseded by Armstrong's. He had an obvious formative impact on Ellington's sideman Bubber Miley, and perhaps on such white musicians as Muggsy Spanier; his mute tricks were copied by Johnny Dunn; and trumpeters such as Natty Dominique and Tommy Ladnier, who remained apart from Armstrong's influence, may have derived their styles in part from Oliver. The extent of Oliver's influence on Armstrong himself, though clearly audible and significant, has yet to be examined properly. Oliver is credited with many melodies on record labels and in copyright registrations; it is not known how many of these he actually composed.

See also TRUMPET, §3.

SELECTED RECORDINGS

Duos with J. R. Morton: King Porter/Tom Cat (1924, Aut. 617)

As leader of the Creole Jazz Band: Canal Street Blues (1923, Gen. 5133); Mandy Lee Blues/I'm going away to wear you off my mind (1923, Gen. 5134); Chimes Blues (1923, Gen. 5135); Weather Bird Rag/Dipper Mouth Blues (1923, Gen. 5132); Snake Rag/High Society Rag (1923, OK 4933); Zulu's Ball/ Working Man's Blues (1923, Gen. 5275); Chattanooga Stomp/ New Orleans Stomp (1923, Col. 13003D); London Cafe Blues/Camp Meeting Blues (1923, Col. 14003D)

As leader of other groups: Deep Henderson/Jackass Blues (1926, Voc. 1014); Someday, Sweetheart/Dead Man Blues (1926, Voc. 1059); Call of the Freaks/ The Trumpet's Prayer (1929, Vic. 38039); St. James Infirmary/When you're smiling (1930, Vic. 22298)

As sideman: S. Wallace: Morning Dove Blues/Every dog has his day (1925, OK 8205); Devil Dance Blues (1925, OK 8206); V. Spivey: My Handy Man/ Organ Grinder Blues (1928, OK 8615); Texas Alexander: 'Frisco Train Blues (1928, OK 8658)

BIBLIOGRAPHY

ChartersJ
P. Jackson: "King Oliver: Daddy of the Trumpet," *Hot News*, i (1935), no.2, p.5; no.3, p.3
F. Ramsey, Jr.: "King Oliver," *Jazzmen*, ed. F. Ramsey, Jr., and C. E. Smith (New York, 1939/*R*1977)
R. Blesh: *Shining Trumpets: a History of Jazz* (New York, 1946, rev. and enlarged 2/1958/*R*1975)
W. C. Allen and B. A. L. Rust: *King Joe Oliver* (Belleville, NJ, 1955)
E. Souchon: "King Oliver: a Very Personal Memoir," *JR*, iii/4 (1960), 6; repr. in *Jazz Panorama*, ed. M. Williams (New York and London, 1962/*R*1979)
M. Williams: *King Oliver* (London, 1960); repr. in *Kings of Jazz*, ed. S. Green (South Brunswick, NJ, and New York, 1978)
K. Kramer: "MCA Booked Oliver in 1924," *SL*, xi/11–12 (1961), 13
L. Gushee: "King Oliver," *Jazz Panorama*, ed. M. Williams (New York and London, 1962/*R*1979) [colln of previously pubd articles]
G. Schuller: *Early Jazz: its Roots and Musical Development* (New York, 1968)
"Ladies and Gentlemen . . .: the King," *Sv*, no.46 (1973), 136
L. O. Koch: "Structural Aspects of King Oliver's 1923 Okeh Recordings," *JJS*, iii/2 (1976), 36
W. Balliett: "For the Comfort of the People," *Improvising: Sixteen Jazz Musicians and their Art* (New York, 1977) [colln of previously pubd articles], 21
J. L. Collier: *Louis Armstrong: an American Genius* (New York, 1983, London, 1984 as *Louis Armstrong: a Biography*)
B. Bigard: *With Louis and the Duke*, ed. B. Martyn (London, 1985)
H. S. Kaye: "Some Observations on King Oliver's Death," *IAJRCJ*, xix/4 (1986), 18
L. Wright and others: *Walter C. Allen & Brian A. L. Rust's "King" Oliver* (Chigwell, England, 1987) [completely rev. version of Allen and Rust: *King Joe Oliver* (Belleville, NJ, 1955)]

LAWRENCE GUSHEE

Oliver, Paul (Hereford) (*b* Nottingham, England, 25 May 1927). English writer. He first wrote about jazz in the early 1950s. In the following decades he wrote articles and reviews for *Jazz Journal* (1952–*c*1960), *Music Mirror* (1954–9), and *Jazz Monthly* (1956–70), columns for *Jazz Beat* (in the 1960s) and *Hi-fi News and Record Review* (from the 1960s to 1980), and many liner notes, and became particularly well known for his writings on early jazz and the blues; he also gave broadcasts over the BBC (from 1954). Oliver successfully brought the techniques of ethnomusicology to the study of blues; he made field visits to Africa and the American South, and challenged many of the assumptions of such earlier writers on jazz as Rudi Blesh by finding a stronger kinship with the blues and early jazz in the music of the savannahs than in that of West Africa. He has also conducted important research into the influence of the songster and sermon traditions on race records. In addition to his work as a writer he has given lectures on jazz at Cambridge University, and his drawings of jazz and blues musicians have appeared in *Jazz Journal* and *Radio Times*. He is also well known as an architectural historian and critic, having written many books and articles on the subject and taught architecture and design at universities in England, the USA, and Africa.

WRITINGS
(selective list)

Bessie Smith (London, 1959); repr. in *Kings of Jazz*, ed. S. Green (South Brunswick, NJ, and New York, 1978)
Blues Fell this Morning: the Meaning of the Blues (London, 1960, New York, 1961, repr. 1963 as *The Meaning of the Blues*; Fr. trans. as *Le monde du blues*, Paris, 1962)
Conversation with the Blues (London, 1965)
Screening the Blues (London, 1968, New York, 1970, as *Aspects of the Blues Tradition*)
The Story of the Blues (London, 1969)
Savannah Syncopators: African Retentions in the Blues (London, 1970)
"Blues," "Gospel Music," §II, *Grove6*; rev. and enlarged in P. Oliver, M. Harrison, and W. Bolcom: *The New Grove Gospel, Blues and Jazz* (London and New York, 1986)
Blues off the Record: Thirty Years of Blues Commentary (New York, and Tunbridge Wells, England, 1984) [colln of previously pubd items]
Songsters and Saints: Vocal Traditions on Race Records (Cambridge, England, and elsewhere, 1984)

BIBLIOGRAPHY

T. Mazzolini: "A Conversation with Paul Oliver," *Living Blues*, no.84 (1982), 24

ROBERT GANNON

Oliver, Sy [Melvin James] (*b* Battle Creek, MI, 17 Dec 1910; *d* New York, 28 May 1988). Arranger and trumpeter. He was brought up in Zanesville, Ohio, where he learned trumpet and performed in local bands. He played with and wrote arrangements for Zack Whyte's Chocolate Beau Brummels (1927–30) and spent a short period with Alphonso Trent. He then settled in Columbus, Ohio, and worked as a teacher and freelance arranger. In 1933 he joined Jimmie Lunceford's orchestra, for which he wrote arrangements and compositions, played, and occasionally sang (*see* LUNCEFORD, JIMMIE). From 1934 until 1939 he regularly wrote arrangements for Benny Goodman. He remained with Lunceford until 1939, when he ceased performing on trumpet and became a member of Tommy Dorsey's orchestra as an arranger and singer; after army service he again worked as a freelance arranger and received regular commissions from Dorsey. In 1946 he briefly led his own band in New York, and thereafter worked as a music director and supervisor for various record companies, often recording with his own bands. He toured frequently during the 1960s and 1970s. After directing a band in Paris (1968–9) he resumed playing trumpet and led a nonet, which was resident at several clubs in New York; among his sidemen were Money Johnson, Britt Woodman, Cliff Smalls, Bobby Jones, Haywood Henry, Mousey Alexander, and Chris Woods. This group, which played Oliver's well-known arrangements for big band, newly orchestrated for a smaller ensemble, continued to perform into the 1980s.

Oliver achieved widespread fame during his association with Lunceford, mainly because of his arrangements, but also on account of his fine trumpet playing and pleasant singing. His scores for Lunceford invariably inspired the band to swing; they combine surface charm and simplicity with an inner variety and richness. Manuscript scores of his works are in the holdings of the BMI Archives in New York.

Oral history material in *LNT*.

See also ARRANGEMENT, §3, Table 4, and ex.2.

RECORDED COMPOSITIONS

(selective list; recorded by J. Lunceford with Oliver as sideman)

For Dancers Only (1937, Decca 1340); Le jazz hot (1939, Voc./OK 4595)

SELECTED ARRANGEMENTS

* – with Oliver as singer

† – with Oliver as singer and trumpeter

As leader: †*Yes, Indeed* (1973, BB 33048)

Recorded by J. Lunceford: Stomp it off/My Blue Heaven (1934, 1935, Decca 712); Organ Grinder's Swing (1936, Decca 908); *On the Beach at Bali-Bali (1936, Decca 915); Slumming on Park Avenue (1937, Decca 1128); Margie (1938, Decca 1617); 'Tain't what you do (it's the way that you do it) (1939, Voc./OK 4582)

Recorded by T. Dorsey: On the Sunny Side of the Street (1944, Vic. 201648)

BIBLIOGRAPHY

B. Coss: "Triple Play," *Metronome*, lxxvii/11 (1960), 40 [interview]
S. Dance: "The Return of Sy Oliver," *JJ*, xxiii/9 (1970), 2; repr. in *The World of Swing* (New York, 1974), 125
C. Carrière: "Welcome, Sy Oliver," *Jh*, no.294 (1973), 16
L. Verdeaux and D. Brigaud: "Sy Oliver," *BHcF*, no.229 (1973), 7 [interview]
B. Priestley: "Sy Oliver," *Into Jazz*, i/7 (1974), 11 [interview]
Z. Knauss: *Conversations with Jazz Musicians* (Detroit, 1977), 150
D. J. Travis: *An Autobiography of Black Jazz* (Chicago, 1983), 435 [incl. interviews]
M. Jones: *Talking Jazz* (London, 1987) [colln of previously pubd interviews], 170

EDDIE LAMBERT

Olu Dara [Jones, Charles, III] (*b* Louisville, MS, 12 Jan 1941). Trumpeter and bandleader. He was brought up in Natchez, Mississippi. After navy service, in 1963 he moved to New York, where he adopted his Yoruba name in 1969. In addition to modern trumpet, he plays cornet, a wooden African sideblown trumpet, and harmonica. With his Natchezsippi Band and Okra Orchestra, he cultivates an entertainment-oriented style which emphasizes dance rhythms but incorporates elements of West African music, the blues, marches by John Philip Sousa, and soul ballads; improvisation is lyrical but energetic and sometimes stark in character. Olu Dara frequently drawls sexually suggestive monologues over a vamp; his solos are highly melodic and cover a wide dynamic range (he often uses mutes). He has not recorded under his own name, but as a sideman he has worked with Art Blakey's Jazz Messengers, various reed players belonging to the Black Artists Group (such as Oliver Lake), David Murray, Henry Threadgill, the bass player Bill Laswell, and others.

SELECTED RECORDINGS

As sideman: O. Lake: *Heavy Spirits* (1975, Ari. 1008); H. Bluiett: *Endangered Species* (1976, IndN 1025); D. Murray: *Home* (1981, BS 0055); H. Threadgill: *Just the Facts and Pass the Bucket* (c1983, About Time 1005); D. Murray: *Live at Sweet Basil* (1984, BS 0085, 0095); J. Newton: *The African Flower* (1985, BN 85109); D. Pullen: *The Sixth Sense* (1985, BS 0088)

BIBLIOGRAPHY

R. Woessner: "Profile: Olu Dara," *DB*, xlix/8 (1982), 52
S. McElfresh: "A Taste of Okra Every Day," *Ear: Magazine of New Music*, xi/2 (1986)

HOWARD MANDEL

Olympia. Theater in Paris; *see* NIGHTCLUBS AND OTHER VENUES.

Olympia Brass Band. New Orleans group founded in 1958 by Harold Dejan. It has performed and recorded frequently in New Orleans with a typical instrumentation of three trumpets, two trombones, two saxophones, tuba, snare drum, and bass drum, although it toured and made recordings in Europe (including *Dejan's Olympia Brass Band in Europe*, 1968, 77 LEU31) as a smaller ensemble. Its regular sidemen have included the trumpeters Andy Anderson (i), Milton Batiste, and Kid Sheik Colar, the trombonists Paul Crawford and Gerald Joseph, the tenor saxophonist Emanuel Paul, the snare drummer Andrew Jefferson, and the bass drummers John Smith, Henry "Booker T" Glass, and Glass's son Nowell "Papa" Glass. The Olympia Brass Band has become closely associated with Preservation Hall: some of its members play there on Sundays, while until his death in 1987 the hall's owner, Allan Jaffe, appeared regularly as the group's sousaphone or helicon player. Among the band's later recordings is the album *Here Come da Great Olympia Band* (c1978, VPS 4).

BIBLIOGRAPHY

J. Roberts: "Talking to Harold Dejan," *JB*, ii/7 (1965), 19
B. Martyn: Liner notes, *Dejan's Olympia Brass Band in Europe* (77 LEU31, 1969)
G. Valentin: "Harold 'Duke' Dejan," *Fn*, vi/5 (1975), 4

WILLIAM J. SCHAFER

Olympia Orchestra. New Orleans dance band active from about 1906 to 1914. It was formed by Freddie Keppard and consisted of between five and seven musicians, a typical instrumentation being cornet, trombone, clarinet, guitar or banjo, piano, double bass or tuba, and drums. As leader of the group Keppard gained a reputation as one of the finest early jazz cornetists; when he left in 1912 the leadership of the orchestra passed to A. J. Piron, who replaced Keppard with King Oliver. Among the sidemen at various times under Keppard were Joseph Petit, Alphonse Picou, Sidney Bechet, Louis Keppard, and the drummer Ernest Trepagnier, while those under Piron included Zue Robertson, Clarence Williams, Billy Marrero, John Lindsay, and Louis Cottrell, Sr.

WILLIAM J. SCHAFER

Omer, Jean (*b* Nivelles, Belgium, 9 Sept 1912). Belgian clarinetist and alto saxophonist. He first played violin in an amateur orchestra and began his professional career with a band in Strasbourg, France. After performing in Brussels he returned to France for a six-month engagement with the bandleader Billy Smith. Omer then replaced André Ekyan in the Golden Stars and played in a group led by René Compère. Later he toured Europe as a soloist with the Carolina Stomp Chasers, but as a result of problems with his work permit was forced to return to Belgium. In Brussels he attempted to establish his own band and worked with Robert De Kers in the orchestra accompanying Josephine Baker (until 1936), then toured as a member of the quartet the Four Notes, which included Ernst van 't Hoff. Thereafter he played in Brussels at the Cotton Club and performed regularly at le Boeuf sur le Toit, where he continued to lead his own band until the early 1960s. Omer recorded with Gus Deloof (1931), Rudy Bruder (1941), and as a leader (1937, 1940–43, 1951, and 1958).

ROBERT PERNET

101 Ranch. Dance hall in New Orleans; *see* NIGHTCLUBS AND OTHER VENUES.

100 Club. One of the several venues to have occupied premises at 100 Oxford Street, London; *see* NIGHTCLUBS AND OTHER VENUES.

Ones. Single bars, as in the expression "to trade ones"; *see* FORMS, §1(ii).

Ono, Shunzo. *See* OHNO, SHUNZO.

Onward Brass Band (i). New Orleans group active from 1885 to 1930. It was led from 1903 by Manuel Perez and became closely identified with his dignified and classical style of playing; the group was considered by important contemporary jazz musicians to be the most consistent and exciting of the early brass bands. It comprised ten to 12 players, with an instrumentation of three cornets (trumpets), two trombones, two clarinets, alto horn, baritone horn, tuba, snare drum, and bass drum. Members of the band at various times included Isidore Barbarin, the trombonist George Filhe, Lorenzo Tio, Jr., Peter Bocage and, occasionally, George Baquet and King Oliver.

For illustration *see* BRASS BAND, fig.1.

WILLIAM J. SCHAFER

Onward Brass Band (ii). New Orleans group active from 1960 to 1978. Modeled on its predecessor the Onward Brass Band (i), it was founded and led until 1969 by Paul Barbarin, and directed thereafter by Louis Cottrell, Jr.; it has also made a few appearances since Cottrell's death in 1978 led by the snare drummer Placide Adams. The group consisted of eight to ten players and had a typical instrumentation of two trumpets, two trombones, clarinet, tuba, snare drum, and bass drum. It toured widely in the late 1960s, presenting early brass-band practices in an authoritative manner. Among the sidemen who recorded with the band were Cag Cagnolatti, Kid Howard, Andrew Morgan, Joe Thomas (i), and Louis Barbarin (all 1965), and Alvin Alcorn, Cagnolatti, Danny Barker, and Freddie Kohlman (all 1968).

BIBLIOGRAPHY

C. Bolton: "Summer Concerts Begin: Onward Band Jazzes it up," *SL*, xx/7–8 (1968), 77

J. V. Buerkle and D. Barker: *Bourbon Street Black: the New Orleans Black Jazzman* (New York, 1973)

WILLIAM J. SCHAFER

Onyx (i). Nightclub in New York; *see* NIGHTCLUBS AND OTHER VENUES.

Onyx (ii). Record company and label. The company was established in 1973 by Don Schlitten (the organization's president) and Joe Fields. The label was devoted to reissues, and to the release of material that had previously been confined to archives (including items taken from the collection of Jerry Newman, who made recordings at clubs in Harlem during the early 1940s). Schlitten and Fields collected much valuable and obscure music that had never before been available on LPs; items were issued by, among others, Art Tatum, Coleman Hawkins, Louis Armstrong, Johnny Hodges, Hot Lips Page, Charlie Shavers, Teddy Edwards, Wardell Gray, and Charlie Parker. Not two years after its inception, however, Onyx was placed in receivership; from that time the catalogue and some 18 albums issued by the owners' other company, Muse (*see* MUSE (ii)), have been the subject of litigation which has continued into the late 1980s.

MARK GARDNER

Open. Unstopped or unmuted. The word is used in jazz principally of the trumpet and trombone to distinguish the full tone produced when a mute is not used from the muffled sound of the muted instrument (*see also* MUTE and DU WAH). It is also applied to the hi-hat, the two cymbals of which stand apart until the controlling pedal is fully depressed (when they are brought into contact and thus stop each other) (*see* DRUM SET, §I, 5). The symbol commonly used for open in these cases is shown in NOTATION, ex.17.

Orange Blossoms. Name by which the CASA LOMA ORCHESTRA was originally known.

Orchard, Frank [Francis H.] (*b* Chicago, IL, 21 Sept 1914; *d* New York, 27 Dec 1983). Trombonist. He studied at the Institute of Musical Art, New York (1932–3), then worked as a salesman until 1941, when he joined Jimmy McPartland. After playing with Bobby Hackett (1942) he performed and recorded with Max Kaminsky, Wingy Manone, and Joe Marsala (all 1944). As a freelance he appeared with dixieland groups in New York until the mid-1950s; he then moved to Dayton, Ohio, and later to St. Louis, where he occasionally organized jam sessions. Having returned to New York in the 1960s, he performed with Billy Butterfield (1969), and in 1970–71 often played informally at Jimmy Ryan's. A typical example of his playing may be heard on *Muskrat Ramble/Bugle Call Rag* (Black & White 24), which he recorded with Kaminsky's band (under the name the Lion's Band) in 1944. (*ChiltonW*; *FeatherE*)

Orchestra U.S.A. Large ensemble that combined the instrumentation of a big band with orchestral woodwind and string sections. It was formed in the autumn of 1962 by John Lewis, and led by Lewis, Gunther Schuller, and the percussionist Harold Farberman. It included jazz and classical musicians and devoted its performances largely to third-stream works; among those who wrote compositions for the orchestra were Lewis, Schuller, Gary McFarland, Miljenko Prohaska, Hall Overton, Jimmy Giuffre, Teo Macero, and Benny Golson. Although the quality of the orchestra's repertory was uneven, its performances were of a high standard; Eric Dolphy, Phil Woods, Jim Hall, and Richard Davis were regular members, and Golson, Gerry Mulligan, and Ornette Coleman appeared occasionally as guest soloists. Although the orchestra disbanded in 1965 six of its members recorded another album the following year. During its brief existence the group played an influential role in the development of third stream music.

SELECTED RECORDINGS

Orchestra U.S.A.: *Debut* (1963, Colpix 448); *Jazz Journey* (1964, Col. CS9047); *Sonorities* (1965, Col. CS9195)

Sextet of Orchestra U.S.A.: *Mack the Knife* (1966, RCA LSP3498)

BIBLIOGRAPHY

B. Coss: "John Lewis and the Orchestra," *DB*, xxx/4 (1963), 20

G. Lees: "View of the Third Stream," *DB*, xxxi/4 (1964), 16

WOLFRAM KNAUER

Ore, John (Thomas) (*b* Philadelphia, 17 Dec 1933). Double bass player. After studying cello at the New School of Music, Philadelphia (1943–6), then double bass at the Juilliard School (1952), he played with Tiny Grimes (1953), George Wallington and Lester Young (both 1954), Ben Webster, Coleman Hawkins, and Elmo Hope (all 1955), and Bud Powell (1955, 1957). In 1958 he led his own group, and for the next two years worked as a freelance in and around New York. Ore joined Thelonious Monk's quartet in 1960, and remained with the group until 1963, making two tours of Europe. After performing in Canada with the Double Six (1964) he worked in the trios led by Bud Powell and Teddy Wilson (1964–5). He recorded with Earl Hines in 1977. Ore is noted for his rhythmic precision and the fullness of his tone.

SELECTED RECORDINGS

As sideman: L. Young: *Somebody Loves Me* (1954, Norg. 1022); E. Hope: *Meditations* (1955, Prst. 7010); T. Monk: *Monk's Dream* (1962, Col. CS8765); *Criss Cross* (1963, Col. CS8838); E. Hope: *Last Sessions* (1966, IC 1018, 1037); E. Hines: *Jazz is his Old Lady and my Old Man* (1977, Cat. 7622)

BIBLIOGRAPHY

FeatherE; *Feather '60s*

J. L. Ginibre and P. Carles: "Dictionnaire de la contrebasse," *Jm*, no.166 (1969), 51

DIANNA RHYAN

Oregon. Jazz chamber ensemble. Its original members, Paul McCandless (oboe, english horn, bass clarinet), Glen Moore (double bass, violin, piano, flute), Ralph Towner (acoustic guitar, piano, french horn, trumpet, flugelhorn), and Collin Walcott (tablā, sitar, clarinet, percussion), all played in the Paul Winter Consort before forming their own group in 1970; Walcott died in 1984 and was replaced by Trilok Gurtu. Oregon's eclectic but integrated style combines elements of classical music, modern jazz, and ethnic music, and reveals the influence of composers and musicians as diverse as John Dowland, Bach, Stravinsky, Bartók, the serialists, John Coltrane, Bill Evans (ii), and Scott LaFaro. The sensitive interaction of the players in performance allows them to improvise collectively without assuming rigidly defined roles. Their recordings include pieces based upon complex harmonies, such as *Yellow Bell*, and others based on a drone or totally free improvisation. While the soaring oboe in *Icarus* is characteristic, the fact that the musicians play 60 to 80 different instruments gives the group a wide palette of sounds.

SELECTED RECORDINGS

Our First Record (1970, Van. 79432); *Together* (1976, Van. 79377); *Friends* (1977, Van. 79370); *Violin* (1978, Van. 79397); *Out of the Woods* (1978, Elek. 154), incl. Yellow Bell; *Oregon in Performance* (1979, Elek. 304), incl. Icarus; *Oregon* (1983, ECM 1258)

BIBLIOGRAPHY

M. Bourne: "The Natural Timbre of Oregon," *DB*, xli/16 (1974), 14

C. Mitchell: "Ralph Towner: a Chorus of Inner Voices," *DB*, xlii/12 (1975), 16

R. Henschen: "The Musical Worlds Meet in Oregon," *Music Journal*, xxxvii/2 (1979), 5

M. Zipkin: "Oregon: Out of the Woods, Into the World," *DB*, xlvi/5 (1979), 13

L. Lyons: "Goodbye Oregon," *Musician*, no.29 (1981), 56

S. Larson: *Some Aspects of the Album "Out of the Woods" by the Chamber Ensemble "Oregon"* (thesis, U. of Oregon, 1981)

——: "Yellow Bell and a Jazz Paradigm," *In Theory Only*, vi/2 (1982), 31

H. U. Werner and K. Bettermann: "Oregon: Acoustic State of Music: eine dokumentarisch-analytische Annäherung," *Jf*, xviii (1986), 87

J. Diliberto: "Oregon: Beauty, and the Beat," *DB*, lv/2 (1988), 24 [incl. discography and interviews]

STEVE LARSON

Orendorff, George (Robert) (*b* Atlanta, 18 March 1906; *d* California, 1984). Trumpeter. He learned cornet and after working in Chicago (from 1923) he traveled to Los Angeles in a show band (1925). He performed and recorded on trumpet with Paul Howard (1925–30) and as a member of Les Hite's band (1930–39), which also made recordings with Louis Armstrong (1930–31) and performed in several films, including *Sing, Sinner, Sing* (1933). He played with the guitarist Ceele Burke until 1943 and again in 1945 after military service. Although he ceased full-time performing from the mid-1940s, he continued to play regularly and recorded with such musicians as Maxwell Davis; in 1959 he appeared in the film *Imitation of Life*. Orendorff's big-band playing is well represented by Howard's *Quality Shout* (1929, Vic. 38122), while his style of blues accompaniment may be heard on *Born to be no good* (1947, Cap. 70025), which he recorded with the singer and guitarist T-Bone Walker.

BIBLIOGRAPHY

B. Wood: "George Orendorff: Quality Serenader," *JJ*, x (1957), no.1, p.4; no.2, p.4

J. Simmen: "Carnet de notes, 9: Un trompette-poète: George Orendorff," *BHcF*, no.172 (1967), 8

A. McCarthy: *Big Band Jazz* (New York and London, 1974)

based on *ChiltonW*

Organ. A keyboard instrument, which in jazz is commonly one of two types: a pipe organ or an electric (or electronic) organ. The former consists of one or more scale-like rows of individual pipes, which are made to sound by air under pressure from a wind-raising device and admitted to the pipes by means of valves operated by the keyboard. In the latter, sounds emulating those of the pipe organ are generated electronically. The Reed organ has also been used in jazz.

1. The pipe organ. 2. The electronic organ.

1. The pipe organ. By the early part of the 20th century two distinct types of pipe organ were available to jazzmen: neither was portable, and both were governed by their location. The first type was the church or concert organ, which in the 1920s generally had two or three manuals (keyboards), operating, in effect, three separate organs – great, choir, and swell; each of these could also be brought into action by a pedalboard (which sometimes governed an additional set of pipes of its own). The individual organs each contained several sets or "ranks" of pipes, and by selecting particular combinations or "registrations" of these by means of "stops," an extremely large range of tone colors and timbres was available. Since organ keyboards are not touch sensitive, and open or close valves to the pipes by means of mechanical, electric, or hydraulic linkage, the only means of regulating the volume is to change the number of pipes sounding at any one time; on the swell organ, however, the pipes are enclosed in a case with shutters, which may be used to control volume.

The second type of organ used in jazz was the theater organ, which was a greatly expanded version of the church or concert instrument introduced at the beginning of the 20th century by the Wurlitzer company of Chicago. It was developed by Robert Hope-Jones (1859–1914) to provide the perfect accompaniment to silent films, and had a wide range of stops designed to imitate various instruments. Theater organs were installed in movie houses and theaters throughout the USA and in many parts of Europe. An innovation of Hope-Jones's, fitted to many of these instruments, was "second touch" – additional ranks of pipes which could be brought into action by pressing the keys beyond their normal resting point.

The first significant jazz organist was Fats Waller, whose experience playing the church instrument and as organist at the Lincoln and Lafayette theaters in New York gave him a unique command of the expressive possibilities of the pipe organ. He performed on the instrument with all sizes of ensemble: in duos with singers, in trios, quartets, and his swing sextet, and in Fletcher Henderson's orchestra. In all contexts he showed mastery of the possibilities of registration afforded by the organ to vary the timbre of a performance, and of the number of strategies designed to overcome the difficulty of making what was often a cumbersome instrument conform to the rhythmic needs of jazz.

Waller's recordings were made largely on two instruments: the modified Estey church organ in the Victor studios in Camden, New Jersey, and the Compton theater organ at the HMV studios in London. He adopted the same technique on both organs, achieving momentum by employing pedal-operated notes on the first and third beats of the bar, playing sustained chords or comping gently with his left hand, and providing melodic and rhythmic impetus (using a great variety of registration) with his right. In his analysis of the musician's organ work (1985), Machlin suggests that Waller used changes in registration as a deliberate extension of the possibilities available to him for improvisation, and argues that his choice of stops in his performance on *Rusty Pail* (1927, Vic. 20492) was based on the compositional framework of the piece.

In ensemble work, Waller frequently relied on the other instrumentalists to provide rhythmic impetus (the very reverse of his technique on piano), and used the organ for tonal and melodic effects. This is evident on his recordings with the Louisiana Sugar Babes (1929), on which he allows the rhythmic momentum to be furnished by James P. Johnson on piano, Jabbo Smith on cornet, or Garvin Bushell on reed instruments. He also used this technique with Henderson's group on *The Chant* (1926, Col. 817D), where he plays sustained chords on the organ against the movement of the whole big band.

The scarcity of church and theater organs in the venues where jazz was usually performed restricted their use, though a small number of organists came to prominence in New York; in addition to Waller, such musicians as Milt Herth and Count Basie played in the theaters of Broadway and Harlem. Basie's recording activity was limited to the availability of suitably equipped studios. Like Waller (his tutor on the organ), he employed changes in registration to highlight parts of his solos and to shade the accompaniment to other soloists in the band, and used the pedals to emphasize the first and third beats of the bar. His recording of *Live and love tonight* (on the album *Count Basie in Discographical Order*, v, 1939, Ajax 150), made with a reduced version of his band on the organ at United Studios in Chicago – an instrument which had not been in use for some time – demonstrates another drawback of the pipe organ in jazz: mechanical noise almost drowns Basie's right-hand trills on a 4′ flute stop, which initially caused the takes to be rejected.

The pipe organ has not been widely employed as a jazz instrument since the 1940s. Isolated experiments in its use have continued, however, in particular during the 1960s in the work of Michael Garrick, who followed an exploration of the integration of jazz and the spoken word with a series of devotional pieces. On *Jazz Praises at St. Paul's* (1968, Airborne 0021), for full choir and bop jazz ensemble, he plays the organ of St. Paul's Cathedral, London. Garrick's settings from the mass and of other texts, including Psalm 73, integrate formal composed passages for choir with sections in which organ and ensemble improvise. He exploits the reverberation and echo effects of the building as an integral part of his compositions, contrasting the sharp rhythms from bass and drums with sustained chords from the choir and organ.

1. Count Basie playing the pipe organ at radio station WHAS, Louisville, KY, February 1947

In 1979 Fred Van Hove recorded in a free-jazz style on pipe organ (*Church Organ*, FMP SAJ25), and in the 1970s and 1980s Dick Hyman has performed and recorded on Wurlitzer theater organs (notably in a duo with the cornetist Ruby Braff on the album *Fats Waller's Heavenly Jive*, 1976, Chi. 162), using the immense tonal possibilities of the instrument to complement his own eclectic style, which draws on many periods of jazz.

2. THE ELECTRONIC ORGAN. The first electronic organ to be widely used in jazz was the Hammond organ (manufactured from 1935), the relative portability of which led to its adoption on a much wider scale than the pipe organ. On the earliest models the sound was generated by a system of rotating steel "tone wheels" and an electromagnetic pickup, but developments from about 1960 led to a considerable degree of sophistication and the introduction of frequency division and crystal oscillators in the sound generation process, which eventually supplanted the use of tone wheels. It was not possible for players to control the attack of notes on the tone-wheel models, and in order to overcome this rhythmic shortcoming they developed a some-

what staccato style. The innovation of the "percussion" stop greatly increased the definition of attack, and this, together with the use of the rotating LESLIE speaker, which produces a tremulant effect, characterized the sound of the Hammond organ (compared with that of other types of electric organ) and made it particularly suitable for jazz as well as for gospel and soul music.

The Hammond organ was immediately adopted by Waller, who recorded a series of spirituals in 1939; these contrast directly with his recordings of the same pieces on pipe organ the previous year. Since the electronic instrument was capable of more rhythmic definition than the pipe organ, he tended to return to a style more akin to that of his piano playing, and made fewer changes in registration. Waller took a Hammond organ with him on tour in the late 1930s, and made more frequent use of it in performance than his relatively few recordings on the instrument would suggest.

The recordings made in 1939 by Glenn Hardman with a contingent from Basie's orchestra are some of the earliest to include the Hammond organ in an ensemble context. On *Upright Organ Blues* (1939, Col. 35263) Hardman comps firmly on the beat; there is little evidence of the use of pedals, and only in his solo does his right hand escape the attempt to define the tempo in an emulation of a swing trumpet or saxophone solo. On the faster *Who?* (1939, Voc. 4971), from the same session, he relies on Freddie Green on guitar and Jo Jones on drums to maintain the beat; he then uses the organ to play riff patterns behind the soloists and to punctuate the ensemble passages with occasional, but effective, chords, while sustaining root harmonies in his left hand. In this, Hardman's technique is the precursor of that adopted in the late 1940s by Wild Bill Davis and from 1952 by Milt Buckner.

2. Members of Bill Doggett's band during a recording session for Columbia, New York, February 1962: (left to right) Wilmer Snakesnider and Clifford Davis (tenor saxophones), Les Taylor (baritone saxophone), and Doggett (Hammond B3 electronic organ; the lever on the left below the keyboards operates the Leslie speaker)

Jimmy Smith formed his first trio in 1955, having taken up Hammond organ in 1951. He brought together a unification of the pipe-organ style of Waller and Basie and the more bop and rhythm-and-blues oriented style of Davis and Buckner, and quickly became one of the most significant figures in jazz. He also introduced to the secular bop idiom elements of the style associated with the Hammond organ in sacred black gospel music (which was developing as a consequence of the widespread adoption of the instrument in black churches during the early 1950s). His mature improvisational style, combining these three features, was coupled with a prodigious technique, which in itself would have made him worthy of critical attention. Smith developed his skill on pedals to a point where he played full walking bass lines with his feet, together with chordal accompaniment with his left hand, and everything from fast bop lines to stabbing punctuating chords with his right. A good example of his work is the album *New Sounds on the Organ* (1956, BN 1514). Since Smith's style allowed him to take on most of the work of a conventional rhythm section, the sidemen in his trios tended to be a drummer and a saxophonist. Smith influenced a number of other musicians who specialized on Hammond organ, notably Brother Jack McDuff, Jimmy McGriff, Groove Holmes, and Shirley Scott. In England the trio format was also employed by Mike Carr, particularly in his work with Ronnie Scott.

The Hammond organ, through its promotion by Smith and its assimilation into rock music (in the work of Billy Preston and others), made a vital contribution to the development of jazz in the 1960s and 1970s. In the mid-1960s Jacques Loussier extended his experiments on piano with the trio Play Bach to the organ, using a Hammond instrument set to replicate the sound of a Baroque church organ. On *Play Bach*, iv (1963, Lon. 3365), Loussier may be heard on organ and piano simultaneously, an effect achieved by means of double tracking, and within the self-imposed limitations of his genre the results add tonal variety to his work.

In the late 1960s Wild Bill Davis joined Duke Ellington's orchestra, adding yet another texture to those available to Ellington for his compositions. On *Blues for New Orleans*, from *New Orleans Suite* (1970, Atl. 1580), Davis and Ellington tackle the same problems of integrating the organ into the big band that Waller and Henderson faced 44 years previously. For Davis's solo, Ellington adopts the solution of reinforcing the organist's sustained chords with a rhythmic piano accompaniment, just as Waller relied for this support on the playing of James P. Johnson.

In the 1970s Larry Young brought the improvisational language of modal free jazz to the Hammond organ, but by the end of the decade the proliferation of other electronic keyboard instruments began to turn the attention of players away from the organ (*see also* SYNTHESIZER).

BIBLIOGRAPHY

J.-E. Berendt: *Das Jazzbuch: Entwicklung und Bedeutung der Jazzmusik* (Frankfurt am Main, Germany, 1953, rev. 2/1959 as *Das neue Jazzbuch*, Eng. trans., New York, 1962; rev. and enlarged 5/1981 as *Das grosse Jazzbuch: von New Orleans bis Jazz Rock*, Eng. trans. as *The Jazz Book: from New Orleans to Fusion and Beyond*, Westport, CT, 1982)

M. Brooks: Liner notes, *Superchief: Count Basie, 1936–1942* (CBS M67205, 1972)

H. Davies: "Hammond organ," *GroveI*

P. Williams and B. Owen: "Organ," *GroveI*
C. Basie and A. Murray: *Good Morning Blues: the Autobiography of Count Basie* (New York, 1985)
P. S. Machlin: *Stride: the Music of Fats Waller* (Boston and London, 1985), 41
H. C. Boyer: "Gospel music, §II," *GroveAM*

ALYN SHIPTON

Original Creole Band [Original Creole Orchestra, Original Creole Jass Band]. Early jazz band. The band grew from a trio formed by the double bass player BILL JOHNSON (i) to tour the Southwest around 1908; the other members of the original group were the cornetist Ernest Coycault and the trombonist H. Pattio or Paddio. When the tour was over the musicians settled in Los Angeles. The name Original Creole Band may have been used from around 1912 and was certainly in use from the time, in 1913, when the pianist and drummer Dink Johnson, the guitarist Norwood Williams (*b c*1880), and the violinist Jimmy Palao (*c*1885–*c*1925), all of whom had been working in New Orleans, joined the ensemble. When in 1914 the band was invited to play at sports events and to tour, Johnson sent to New Orleans for the cornetist Freddie Keppard, the clarinetist George Baquet, and the trombonist Eddie Vincent (Venson; *b c*1885). The band toured on the Pantages, Loew, and Orpheum circuits (without Dink Johnson, who decided to remain in Los Angeles), and during the next three years played long-term engagements in Chicago and New York. It disbanded in Boston in the spring of 1917, but re-formed in New York in the autumn of that year, when Baquet was replaced by Big Eye Louis Nelson; the clarinetist Jimmie Noone and the trombonist George Filhe (1872–1954) worked with the band in Chicago before it finally broke up in April 1918.

A photograph of the band taken around 1914 shows the name Original Creole Orchestra on the bass drum, and after Keppard left it (*c*1916) it appeared on the East Coast as the Original Creole Jass Band. It was also billed as "the Famous Creole Band from New Orleans" and was sometimes known simply as the Creole Band, Creole Orchestra, or Creole Jass Band; it may have been Johnson's band that recorded under the last name for Victor in 1918.

BIBLIOGRAPHY

S. B. Charters and L. Kunstadt: *Jazz: a History of the New York Scene* (Garden City, NY, 1962/*R*1981), 55
A. Rose and E. Souchon: *New Orleans Jazz: a Family Album* (Baton Rouge, LA, 1967, rev. 2/1978, rev. and enlarged 3/1984)
A. Barrell: "B is for . . . Baquet," *Fn*, xvii/3 (1986), 4

MIKE HAZELDINE

Original Dixieland Jazz [Jass] **Band** [ODJB]. Five-piece jazz band. Its original members, all from New Orleans, were Nick LaRocca (leader and cornet), Larry Shields (clarinet), Eddie Edwards (trombone), Tony Sbarbaro (drums), and Henry Ragas (who was replaced by J. Russel Robinson, piano). After playing in Chicago in 1916, the five musicians moved to New York where they enjoyed sensational receptions during their residency at Reisenweber's Restaurant from January 1917. During the same year, the group became the first jazz band to make phonograph recordings, and in doing so the musicians achieved a degree of eminence that was out of proportion to their musical skills. During the mid-1920s, when the vogue for jazz dancing temporarily subsided, the group disbanded; it re-formed again in 1936, but the reunion was brief and only moderately successful.

No member of the Original Dixieland Jazz Band was particularly talented as an improviser, and the group's phrasing was rhythmically stilted; but even so, its collective vigor had an infectious spirit. When black jazz bands began to record regularly it soon became apparent that many of them were more adept at jazz improvising and phrasing than was the

The Original Dixieland Jazz Band, New York, 1917: (left to right) Tony Sbarbaro (drums), Eddie Edwards (trombone), Nick LaRocca (cornet), Larry Shields (clarinet), and Henry Ragas (piano)

Original Dixieland Jazz Band. Detractors of the band maintain that it merely simplified the music of black New Orleans groups, and cite specific antecedents for its compositions *Tiger Rag* and *Sensation Rag*. Casual listeners were intrigued by its repertory, however, which was unlike anything else then on record. The group presented a new sound rather than a new music; this sound, and the rhythms in which it was couched, appealed to young dancers, who were eager to break away from the rigidly formal dance steps of the era.

The most passionate advocate of the Original Dixieland Jazz Band's importance to jazz history was LaRocca himself, who never ceased claiming that his band had played a vital role in the "invention" of jazz in New Orleans during the early years of the 20th century. The fact that there is no evidence to support LaRocca's contention has caused many jazz devotees to ignore the merits of the band's music. But it is indisputable that the group played a major part in popularizing the dixieland style of jazz throughout the USA and Europe.

SELECTED RECORDINGS

(all recorded for Victor)

Livery Stable Blues (1917, 18255); Tiger Rag (1918, 18472); Sensation Rag (1918, 18483); Clarinet Marmalade Blues (1918, 18513); Jazz me Blues (1921, 18722); Royal Garden Blues (1921, 18798); Skeleton Jangle/Tiger Rag (1936, 25524)

BIBLIOGRAPHY

SL, vi/9–10 (1955) [special issue]

H. H. Lange: *The Fabulous Fives* (Lübbecke, Germany, 1959, rev. 2/1978 by R. Jewson, D. Hamilton-Smith, and R. Webb) [discography]

——: *Nick LaRocca: ein Porträt* (Wetzlar, Germany, 1960)

H. O. Brunn: *The Story of the Original Dixieland Jazz Band* (Baton Rouge, LA, 1960/*R*1977)

R. Blesh: Liner notes, *The Original Dixieland Jazz Band* (RCA LPV547, 1967)

B. Rust: "Grateful for the Warning," *Sv*, no.9 (1967), 24

D. Morgenstern: Liner notes, *The Original Dixieland Jazz Band* (GHB 100, 1983)

JOHN CHILTON

Original Memphis Five. Dixieland quintet. Its formation in 1917 is credited variously to the trumpeter Phil Napoleon (who became its leader) and the pianist Frank Signorelli. The other regular members of the group were the clarinetist Jimmy Lytell (1922–5), the drummer Jack Roth, and one or other of the trombonists Miff Mole and Charlie Panelli. Numerous other players recorded with it occasionally, including many of the best session and dance-band musicians of the period. Between 1921 and 1931 it made hundreds of recordings for almost every label in the USA and also regularly appeared at the Balconades, a club on Broadway.

The repertory of the Original Memphis Five included much contemporary popular music, but consisted mainly of New Orleans and dixieland standards, blues, and original pieces. The group's performance routine was fairly inflexible: pieces were made up of opening and closing ensemble choruses and a series of solos for the members of the front line and sometimes the piano. The soloists played with energy and power, though their style has something of the jerkiness of ragtime. Lytell's solos are lyrical, making expressive use of the chalumeau register, while Mole plays ruggedly but with splendid control and melodic flair. Napoleon, often criticized for a preoccupation with technique, gives a firm lead. On the early recordings, made before the development of electric techniques in 1925, the drums were often silenced and the quintet had to rely on the piano alone for rhythmic support, thereby forfeiting some depth and immediacy. In the 1940s and 1950s the name Original Memphis Five was used again by both Napoleon and Signorelli for occasional performances and recordings.

SELECTED RECORDINGS

My Honey's Lovin' Arms (1922, Arto 9140); I Wish I Could Shimmy Like my Sister Kate (1922, Para. 20161); Aggravatin' Poppa (1923, Voc. 14506); Sweet Lovin' Mama (1923, PAct 020921); Great White Way Blues/Shufflin' Mose (1923, Edison 51204); Jazz me Blues (1931, Col. 2588D)

BIBLIOGRAPHY

R. Harris and B. Rust: *Recorded Jazz: a Critical Guide* (Harmondsworth, England, 1958), 161

H. H. Lange: *The Fabulous Fives* (Lübbecke, Germany, 1959, rev. 2/1978 by R. Jewson, D. Hamilton-Smith, and R. Webb) [discography]

KEN RATTENBURY

Original New Orleans Jazz Band (i). New Orleans jazz band. It was active from around 1916 in Chicago under the leadership of the cornetist and trombonist Merritt Brunies. Besides Brunies, members of the Chicago band included the trombonist and cornetist Emile Christian, the clarinetist Johnny Fischer, the pianist Freddie Rose, and the drummer Freddie Williams. The band did not record, and it ceased to be active in 1918. (A. Rose and E. Souchon: *New Orleans Jazz: a Family Album*, Baton Rouge, LA, 1967, rev. 2/1978, rev. and enlarged 3/1984)

MIKE HAZELDINE

Original New Orleans Jazz Band (ii). New Orleans jazz band. It was formed as the New Orleans Jazz Band in New York in 1918 by the comedian and pianist Jimmy Durante, who modeled it on the Original Dixieland Jazz Band, which he had heard at Reisenweber's Restaurant; the other members were Frank Christian (cornet), Achille Baquet (clarinet), Frank L'Hotak (trombone), and Johnny Stein (drums). Stein was replaced later in 1918 by Arnold Loyacano, but returned by 1920. As the Original New Orleans Jazz Band the group recorded *Ole Miss/Ja-da* (1918, OK 1156) and *Ja-da/He's had no lovin' for a long, long time* (1919, Gen. 4508). In 1920 it performed and recorded as Jimmy Durante's Jazz Band.

BIBLIOGRAPHY

A. Rose and E. Souchon: *New Orleans Jazz: a Family Album* (Baton Rouge, LA, 1967, rev. 2/1978, rev. and enlarged 3/1984)

H. R. Rookmaaker: Liner notes, *New Orleans Boys, 1918–1927* (Riv. 8818, 1966)

MIKE HAZELDINE

Original Nighthawk Orchestra. Shortened form of the name Coon–Sanders Original Nighthawk Orchestra, taken in 1924 by the band led by Carleton Coon and JOE SANDERS.

Original Teddies [International Teddies, Teddies]. Swiss swing band. It was led by TEDDY STAUFFER from 1929 and was re-formed by him in 1939; when he left in 1941 the leadership was assumed by the former sideman EDDIE BRUNNER. Among the group's principal soloists were Kurt Hohenberger, Ernst Höllerhagen, Walter Dobschinski, and Brunner.

Original Tuxedo Orchestra [Tuxedo Brass Band, Tuxedo Jazz Orchestra]. New Orleans group active as a brass band and a dance orchestra. Although Papa Celestin's group, which played at the Tuxedo Dance Hall from 1910, was sometimes known as the Tuxedo Brass Band, the Original Tuxedo Orchestra was founded in 1917 by Celestin and the trombonist William "Baba" Ridgley. It served as an important training ground for several musicians and included such players as Mutt Carey, Willie Pajeaud, Louis Armstrong, Alphonse Picou, Sam Dutrey, Sr., Isidore Barbarin, and Louis Keppard. In 1925 divisions within the ensemble led to a breakup of the group, with Ridgley taking many of the sidemen and keeping the original name, and Celestin forming a new band called the Tuxedo Jazz Orchestra. Celestin made a number of recordings with his new group (1926–7).

See also CELESTIN, PAPA; for illustration *see* BANJO.

WILLIAM J. SCHAFER

Oriole (i). Record label. It was established by McCrory's stores in 1921, and at first drew its catalogue from those of Emerson and Grey Gull. From the mid-1920s the label belonged to the Plaza group, and is of interest in that it occasionally issued takes of recordings that were not put out on Plaza's other labels; these included items by Clarence Williams's groups. The label was continued after the formation of the AMERICAN RECORD COMPANY, becoming one of that organization's "dime-store" labels with its own important race series. It was discontinued after ARC–BRC was taken over by CBS in 1938.

BIBLIOGRAPHY

J. Godrich and R. M. W. Dixon: *Blues & Gospel Records, 1902–1942* (Hatch End, nr London, 1964, rev. 2/1969, rev. and enlarged 3/1982 as R. M. W. Dixon and J. Godrich: *Blues & Gospel Records, 1902–1943)*

R. M. W. Dixon and J. Godrich: *Recording the Blues* (London, 1970)

B. Rust: *The American Record Label Book* (New Rochelle, NY, 1978), 220

Oriole (ii). Record label. It was owned by Levy's of London, and made issues only intermittently. The 1000 series, which contained 13 discs released from 1927, is commonly known as Oriole's race series, because all but one of its titles were drawn from Vocalion's race repertory. In 1931 issue began of the P100 series, which consisted of recordings made in Britain, including some by Adelaide Hall accompanied by the pianists Francis Carter and Joe Turner (i). The LV100 series of 1934 drew its repertory from the French label Ultraphon, and contained discs by the Quintette du Hot Club de France and an excellent item by the trumpeter Freddy Taylor and his group. Levy's revived the label again in 1950, taking material from several American labels, most notably Mercury. In the early 1960s a related company, Oriole Records Ltd., embarked on a major program of reissues of jazz LPs from Savoy, which they released on the Realm label. After 1965 Realm was maintained by CBS.

BIBLIOGRAPHY

L. Wright: "A Glimpse into the Past, 5: the Oriole 1000 Series," *Sv*, i/6 (1966), 26

R. Jewson, D. Smith, and R. Webb: "Arthur Gainsbury's Guide to Junkshoppers: Oriole," *Sv*, no.34 (1971), 148

B. Rust: *The American Record Label Book* (New Rochelle, NY, 1978), 221

H. Rye: "Visiting Firemen, 10(a): Adelaide Hall, Joe Turner, and Francis J. Carter," *Sv*, no.114 (1984), 211

Orlay, Jenő [Orlay-Obendorfer, Chappy]. *See* CHAPPY.

Orquesta Cubana de Música Moderna. Cuban group. It was founded in 1967 by the alto saxophonist Paquito D'Rivera, the trumpeter Arturo Sandoval, and the pianist Chucho Valdés; its name was intended to disguise the fact that it played jazz, which was not officially tolerated by the Cuban government in the 1960s and 1970s. Around 1973 the three founders and other members of the group formed IRAKERE.

Ørsted Pedersen, Niels-Henning [NHOP] (*b* Osted, Denmark, 27 May 1946). Danish double bass player. He played piano as a child and took up double bass when in his teens. By 1962, having mastered the bass in an astonishingly brief time, he had recorded with Bud Powell and Brew Moore and joined the house band at the Montmartre Jazzhus in Copenhagen. He refused offers to join Count Basie's orchestra in the USA in order to finish his studies, but in the early 1960s toured Europe with Bill Evans (ii). He then performed and recorded with Don Byas, Roland Kirk, Kenny Dorham, Sahib Shihab, Kenny Drew, Ben Webster, Johnny Griffin, Karin Krog, and, most notably, Dexter Gordon, with whom he was associated until 1976. In the 1970s and early 1980s he toured and recorded with Oscar Peterson (see illustration), and also worked frequently with Joe Pass and Drew. Later in the decade he performed in a trio with Palle Mikkelborg and the keyboard player Kenneth Knudsen.

Niels-Henning Ørsted Pedersen (double bass) and Oscar Peterson (piano) at the BBC television studios, London, c1982

Although Ørsted Pedersen has performed in swing and free-jazz ensembles, he is at his best as a sideman in bop groups. His perfect sense of rhythm, compelling walking bass lines, and deep, roaring timbre are particularly evident on the album *Catalonian Fire* (1974), recorded with Tete Montoliu. He is especially talented in the manipulation of rapid solo lines in the higher register of the instrument and at playing pizzicato with three or four fingers of his right hand; he is also accomplished in the use of the bow.

SELECTED RECORDINGS

Duos: with K. Drew: *Duo* (1973, Ste. 1002); with J. Pass: *Chops* (1978, Pablo 2310830); with A. Shepp: *Looking at Bird* (1980, Ste. 1149)

As sideman: D. Byas: *Anthropology* (1963, Debut 142); D. Gordon: *One Flight Up* (1964, BN 84176); T. Montoliu: *Catalonian Fire* (1974, Ste. 1017); O. Peterson: *Oscar Peterson at the Montreux Jazz Festival 1975* (1975, Pablo 2310747); *The Paris Concert* (1978, PL 2620112); C. Basie: *Kansas City Six* (1981, Pablo 2310871)

BIBLIOGRAPHY

J. Lind: "Danish Modern: Niels-Henning Ørsted Pedersen," *DB*, xxxii/12 (1965), 18

D. C. Hunt: "Definitive Bass Artistry: Niels-Henning Ørsted Pedersen and Charles 'Buster' Williams," *J&P*, ix/10 (1970), 43

I. S. Petersen: "N. H. O. P.," *Jh*, no.316 (1975), 16; Eng. trans. in *Coda*, xii/6 (1975), 2

J. Solothurnman: "The Life and Experiences of Niels-Henning Oersted Pedersen," *JF* [intl edn], no.39 (1976), 34

BARRY KERNFELD

Ortega, Tony [Anthony Robert; Batman] (*b* Los Angeles, 7 June 1928). Alto and tenor saxophonist, clarinetist, and flutist. His early professional work included performances and recordings with the bandleader Earle Spencer (1947). After two years in the army (1948–50) he joined Lionel Hampton's big band, and recorded with Hampton, Gigi Gryce, and Art Farmer in Paris (1953). He played briefly with Milt Buckner, then formed his own group in Los Angeles. In 1955 he moved to New York, where he worked with Nat Pierce from 1956 to 1958. He then returned to Los Angeles and played with Paul Bley, the Lighthouse All Stars, and Claude Williamson; he also recorded the album *Jazz for Young Moderns* with Jimmy Cleveland and other former members of Hampton's band. This received extremely unfavorable reviews and Ortega had difficulty finding significant work during the next few years; he played in hotels, theaters, and desert nightclubs in California and Nevada. In 1965, however, he was engaged by Don Ellis and Gerald Wilson, and the following year he began to perform and record once more as a leader. During the 1970s he played flute and alto saxophone for Wilson. Although he is essentially a bop musician, Ortega began in the 1960s to incorporate some of the stylistic innovations of Ornette Coleman into his playing.

SELECTED RECORDINGS

As leader: Blues for Ortega/I can't get started (1954, Musica 9006); *Jazz for Young Moderns* (1958–9, Beth. 79); *New Dance!* (1966–7, Rev. 3); *Rain Dance* (1978, Dis. 788)

As sideman: M. Ferguson: *Boy with Lots of Brass* (1957, EmA 36114); N. Pierce: *Chamber Music for Moderns* (1957, Coral 57128); M. Wofford: *Mike Wofford Plays Jerome Kern* (c1980, Dis. 808)

BIBLIOGRAPHY

FeatherE

J. Delmas: "Comment Anthony Ortega fait sa musique avec un jugement circonstancié sur la relation Konitz/Ortega/Braxton," *Jh*, no.311 (1974), 14

F. Billard and M. Gourgues: "Quand le silence est d'Ortega," *Jm*, no.304 (1982), 20

BRENDA PENNELL

Ory, Kid [Edward] (*b* La Place, LA, 25 Dec *c*1890; *d* Honolulu, 23 Jan 1973). Trombonist and bandleader. Between 1912 and 1919 he led one of the most prominent bands in New Orleans. He then moved to California, where he led a group known first as Kid Ory's Brownskinned Babies and later as Kid Ory's Original Creole Jazz Band, or, occasionally, Sunshine Orchestra; in Los Angeles in 1922, as SPIKES' SEVEN PODS OF PEPPER, it became the first of the black New Orleans style jazz bands to issue a recording, *Ory's Creole Trombone/Society Blues*. In 1925 he went to Chicago, where he participated in some of the period's most important jazz recording sessions, with Louis Armstrong's Hot Five (for illustration *see* ARMSTRONG, LOUIS, fig.1), Jelly Roll Morton's Red Hot Peppers, the NEW ORLEANS WANDERERS, and King Oliver's Dixie Syncopators. Ory returned to Los Angeles in 1930 and in 1933 abandoned music to work on a poultry farm and in a railroad office; he resumed playing in 1942, however, regaining prominence through his performances on Orson Welles's radio broadcasts in 1944. He then toured extensively with his band until 1966, when he retired to Hawaii. Ory's playing was highly rhythmic; he made full use of slurs and glissandos in the early tailgate trombone style, of which he was the most famous exponent, and was also notable for his use of mutes (*see* MUTE, §3). He composed the well-known *Muskrat Ramble*.

Oral history material in *LNT*.

SELECTED RECORDINGS

As leader: of Spikes' Seven Pods of Pepper: Ory's Creole Trombone/Society Blues (1922, Nordskog 3009); *Kid Ory's Creole Jazz Band, 1954* (1954, GTJ 12004)

As sideman: L. Armstrong: Muskrat Ramble (1926, OK 8300); New Orleans Wanderers: Gate Mouth (1926, Col. 698D); J. R. Morton: Doctor Jazz (1926, Vic. 20415); K. Oliver: Every Tub (1927, Voc. 1114); L. Armstrong: Ory's Creole Trombone (1927, Col. 35838)

BIBLIOGRAPHY

R. Blesh: "Listen to What Ory Says," *Jazz Record*, no.37 (1945), 8

K. Ory: "What Did Ory Say?," *Record Changer*, vi/9 (1947), 5

J. G. Jepsen: *Kid Ory* (Copenhagen, 1957) [discography]

Giltrap and Dixon: *Kid Ory* (London, n.d. [?1958])

T. Standish: "Ory & Co.," *JJ*, xii/12 (1959), 3

G. Marne: "The Kid Ory Story," *IM*, lxii/6 (1964), 18

E. Lambert: "Quality Jazz, no.4: Kid Ory," *JJ*, xviii/11 (1965), 19

J. Lucas: "Kid StOry," *JJ*, xviii/1 (1965), 6

M. Williams: "The Kid," *Jazz Masters of New Orleans* (New York and London, 1967/R1978), 205

M. Jones: "The New Orleans Kid," *MM* (3 Feb 1973), 18

H. Panassié: "Kid Ory," *BHcF*, no.225 (1973), 3

A. Hubner: "Kid Ory," *Selections from the Gutter: Jazz Portraits from "The Jazz Record"*, ed. A. Hodes and C. Hansen (Berkeley, CA, Los Angeles, and London, 1977), 112

J. Darensbourg: *Telling it Like it is*, ed. P. Vacher (London, 1987; Baton Rouge, LA, 1987, as *Jazz Odyssey: the Autobiography of Joe Darensbourg*)

JOSÉ HOSIASSON

Osborne, Mary (*b* Minot, ND, 17 July 1921). Guitarist and singer. She first worked professionally for radio station KDKA, Pittsburgh, in the late 1930s, and around 1941 she performed with Joe Venuti. In 1945 she moved to New York. She recorded with Mary Lou Williams (1945), Coleman Hawkins, Mercer Ellington, and Beryl Booker (all 1946), and led her own swing groups in several recordings (1945–8). She played with Elliot Lawrence's quartet on Jack Sterling's radio program on CBS (1952–63), then recorded with Tyree Glenn (1957–8) and again as a leader (1959). After moving to Bakersfield, California, in 1968, she operated the Osborne Guitar Co. with her husband, the trumpeter Ralph Scaffidi, taught music, and performed locally and in Los Angeles. She appeared at the Kool Jazz Festival in New York (1981) and recorded tracks that were issued, with others recorded earlier, on the album *Now and Then* (1959, ?1981, Stash 215).

BIBLIOGRAPHY

L. Ferris: "Mary Osborne – a Unique Roll in Jazz Guitar History," *GP*, viii/2 (1974), 10

S. Placksin: *American Women in Jazz, 1900 to the Present: their Words, Lives, and Music* (New York, 1982), 184

L. Dahl: *Stormy Weather: the Music and Lives of a Century of Jazzwomen* (London, Melbourne, Australia, and New York, 1984), 259 [interview]

Osborne, Mike [Michael Evans; Ossie] (*b* Hereford, England, 28 Sept 1941). English alto saxophonist and clarinetist. After moving to London in 1959 to study clarinet, piano, and harmony at the Guildhall School of Music and Drama he quickly developed associations with leading bop musicians. He worked with Mike Westbrook (1959–63, 1967–71), Chris McGregor (1961–75), Stan Tracey (1972, 1975–80), SOS (a trio with Alan Skidmore and John Surman, 1973–5), and Keith Tippett (1980). Between 1961 and 1977 he led his own trios (including one in the mid-1970s with Harry Miller and Louis Moholo), and from 1970 he made several recordings as a leader, including *Marcel's Muse* (1977, Ogun 810). He ceased to perform in public in 1982.

BIBLIOGRAPHY

R. Williams: "Mike: Underrated but Undefeated," *MM* (3 Jan 1970), 8

M. Walters: "Fresh Music from Osborne," *Sounds* (6 Feb 1971), 12

C. Fox and V. Wilmer: *The Jazz Scene* (London, 1972), 40

R. Cotterell, ed.: *Jazz Now: the Jazz Centre Society Guide* (London, 1976)

MARK GILBERT

Osterwald, Hazy [Osterwälder, Rolf] (*b* Berne, 18 Feb 1922). Swiss trumpeter, vibraphonist, and bandleader. He studied piano in Berne. At the age of 17 he wrote an arrangement of

Rosetta for a recording by Fred Böhler, on which it was coupled with his own composition *Fred's Jump* (1939, Col. ZZ1006). He performed as a trumpeter with Böhler (1941), Edmond Cohanier, Philippe Brun, and Teddy Stauffer's Original Teddies. In 1944 he formed his own band, with which he made a large number of recordings (1946–78); among his soloists were Ernst Höllerhagen and Werner Dies. He also recorded as a sideman with the bandleader Bob Huber (1942), the Original Teddies under Eddie Brunner (1944), and Gil Cuppini (1949). Osterwald performed and recorded on vibraphone at the Paris Jazz Fair (1949) with various American musicians, including Sidney Bechet and Charlie Parker, and he toured Europe, Latin America, Israel, and the USA. His band's recordings of modern jazz are well represented by *Boppin' at the Dodge* (1950, Musica 3135), while it may be heard playing swing on *Tired Cats* (1955, Col. ESFD1181). Osterwald's life was the subject of the film *Musik ist Trumpf (Die Hazy Osterwald Story)* (1961).

BIBLIOGRAPHY

ReclamsJ
W. Grieder: *Hazy Osterwald Story: Musik ist Trumpf* (Zurich, 1961)
J.-R. Hippenmeyer: *Le jazz en Suisse, 1930–1970* (Yverdon, Switzerland, 1971)

RAINER E. LOTZ

Österwall, Seymour (*b* Stockholm 20 Feb 1908; *d* Stockholm, 3 Aug 1981). Swedish bandleader and tenor saxophonist. He first played banjo, then changed to tenor saxophone. He was the leader of the Astoria band, which appeared regularly at the Nalen in Stockholm from 1935 to 1948; later he continued to lead the group, now known as Seymour Österwall's Orchestra, until it disbanded in 1959. Österwall established a repertory that included both jazz and popular music, and he achieved popularity as a leader in the 1940s; his recordings include *Margie* (1941, Son. 3783). A sister, Irmgard, a singer, and a brother, Arthur, a double bass player, were also well-known to Swedish audiences.

BIBLIOGRAPHY

"Svenskt stjärnalbum" [Swedish star-album], *Orkester journalen*, xi/11 (1943), 5
R. Dahlgren: Obituary, *Orkester journalen*, xlix/9 (1981), 6

ERIK KJELLBERG

Ostinato. An accompanimental pattern, usually of one, two, or four bars, repeated continuously beneath precomposed or improvised lines; *see* FORMS, §§1(i)(e) and 7.

Ottersen, Frank (*b* Oslo, 14 March 1921; *d* Kolding, Denmark, 22 May 1971). Norwegian violinist and saxophonist. He played violin from the age of ten and studied with Arvid Fladmo before beginning his career in jazz in Oslo in 1938. He led orchestras at the Chat Noir and the Grand Hotel, toured Norway, and made recordings as a leader (1942–5, including *Ding dong dang/ Skumring* (Twilight), 1942, Odeon N3893), with Alf Søgaard's big band, and with the accordionist Rolf Syversen (1945); later he worked in Denmark with Stuff Smith. Ottersen's style as a violinist was influenced by that of Stephane Grappelli and Svend Asmussen.

BIBLIOGRAPHY

K. Sandegren and others: *Boken om jazz* (Oslo, 1954)
O. Angell, J. E. Vold, and E. Økland: *Jazz i Norge* (Oslo, 1975)
K. Michelsen, ed.: *Cappelens musikkleksikon* (Oslo, 1978)

VIDAR VANBERG

Ousley, Harold (Lomax) (*b* Chicago, 23 Jan 1929). Tenor saxophonist and composer. He began playing professionally in the 1940s, and once accompanied Billie Holiday. From 1949 to 1956 he performed with circus bands, and in King Kolax's band with Gene Ammons, who strongly influenced his playing. He then joined a rock-and-roll group that traveled to New York (1957). A performance with Dinah Washington at the Newport Jazz Festival (1958) led to his first recording engagement. In 1959 he went to Paris with a song revue; after returning to the USA he played with Clark Terry, Howard McGhee, Joe Newman, Machito, Lionel Hampton (1970), and Count Basie (1973–4), and from the 1960s led groups of his own. In his later career Ousley became known chiefly as a performer of soul jazz; he made recordings with Brother Jack McDuff (1966) and as a leader (including *The People's Groove*, 1972, Cob. 9017). (P. Brodowski: "Harold Ousley: Jazz Crusader," *JF* [intl edn], no.61 (1979), 24 [interview])

Out chorus. The final chorus of a piece (*see* FORMS, §2). The term is used generally to mean the repetition of the theme (or "head") at the end of a piece; it is applied more specifically to early styles of jazz where it is used of the final, collectively improvised chorus of a lively piece, played in a loud spirited manner.

Outside [out]. To play "outside" or "out" is to depart, in improvisation, from the harmonic structure of the theme. The term came into use in the early 1960s, in conjunction with its antonym, "inside," to describe the playing of musicians who brought into performances of hard bop and modal jazz some of the harmonic license of free jazz; the outstanding exponent of playing outside was Eric Dolphy. The term is cleverly used in the title of Yusef Lateef's album *The Doctor is In . . . and Out* (1976, Atl. 1685).

Ouwerx, John [Jean] (*b* Nivelles, Belgium, 8 March 1903; *d* Brussels, 1983). Belgian pianist. A classically trained musician, he moved in August 1925 to New York and for about four months played organ at the Strand Palace. On his return to Belgium he gave the first Belgian performance of George Gershwin's *Rhapsody in Blue* (18 Nov 1927), worked with the group Bistrouille A.D.O., and lectured on jazz. From 1928 he toured the Netherlands, Switzerland, Italy, and Egypt, and, as a member of the band of the violinist Marek Weber, Hungary, Switzerland, and Germany; he also arranged film music. After making his first recording (with Gus Deloof, 1931) he worked in 1934 with Robert De Kers in Antwerp and in the same year performed with Stan Brenders. While playing from 1936 to 1944 in Brenders's big band he toured in 1941 with Jean Omer. In the following years he took part in concerts of music for two pianos and four pianos (with, among others, Johnny Jack and Egide Van Gils), worked with Fud Candrix (1945), and played at the Continental in Brussels. He then opened a piano bar on the Belgian coast, played for eight years in the Belgian Congo (now Zaïre), and then returned to Brussels for the World's Fair of 1958; he later ran a piano bar in Brussels for 14 years.

ROBERT PERNET

Overblowing. A term applied to the technique by means of which the player of a wind instrument produces the octave, 12th, 15th, and further partials above the fundamental in place of the fundamental itself. The technique involves increasing the air pressure and making minute adjustments to the embouchure. Overblowing is a basic facet of wind technique, providing as it does the principal ranges of brass instruments (on some of which the fundamentals or pedal notes are too low to be much used) and the higher octaves in the ranges of woodwinds. Woodwind instruments are often said to "overblow" at a certain interval (the flute and saxophone at the octave, for example, the clarinet at the 12th).

In jazz overblowing is used not only to produce the normal instrumental range, but also to create particular effects. Using FALSE FINGERING and adjusting the embouchure as required a player overblows to produce pitches above the instrument's normal range and unusual timbres. The exponents in jazz of such unconventional forms of overblowing are principally saxophonists, including Coleman Hawkins, Illinois Jacquet, John Coltrane, Albert Ayler, John Gilmore, Pharoah Sanders, Richie Cole, Joseph Jarman, Roscoe Mitchell, and Anthony Braxton, but such techniques are also practiced by the bass clarinetist Eric Dolphy (from the 1960s), the clarinetist John Carter, and the flutist James Newton.

Overton, Hall (F.) (*b* Bangor, MI, 23 Feb 1920; *d* New York, 24 Nov 1972). Composer and pianist. He began composing while still in high school and later studied at the Juilliard School (1947–51) and took private lessons with Wallingford Riegger and Darius Milhaud. While serving in the army (1942–5) he developed great skill as a jazz improviser, and later played with such musicians as Stan Getz, Oscar Pettiford, Teddy Charles, and Jimmy Raney. He also wrote arrangements for Thelonious Monk's orchestra (*The Thelonious Monk Orchestra at Town Hall*, 1959, Riv. 1138) and contributed articles to *Down Beat* and *Jazz Today*. His own music was deeply influenced by jazz, but without his trying to make jazz "respectable" through the unnatural imposition of classical forms or materials.

OLIVER DANIEL/R

Owens, Charles [Brown, Charles M.] (*b* Phoenix, AZ, 4 May 1939). Saxophonist. He began to learn saxophone while a student at the University of San Diego, and after military service attended the Berklee College of Music, where he studied alto saxophone with Joe Viola. In 1967–8 he was a member of Buddy Rich's band (he arranged *Ode to Billy Joe* for Rich's LP *Mercy, Mercy*); he then played in Mongo Santamaria's group for two years. During the 1970s he played principally tenor saxophone, though he also worked on the soprano instrument. After appearances with Bobby Bryant, Paul Humphrey, and the group accompanying the pop and soul singer Diana Ross, he toured with the blues-rock musician John Mayall (1971) and with Frank Zappa (1972), and recorded with Bryant (1971) and the bass player Henry Franklin (1971, 1974). Later he worked with Patrice Rushen and Gerald Wilson on the West Coast. In 1978 and 1980 he made recordings as a leader, including compositions of his own such as *Night Cry*. He also recorded with Lorez Alexandria (1978), James Newton (1979, 1985), and John Carter (1982), from the late 1970s doubling frequently on oboe, english horn, and flute. In the 1980s Owens has worked with Horace Tapscott, with whose band he toured Europe in 1987, and held the baritone saxophone chair in Mercer Ellington's orchestra. He is the leader of the Jazz Winds, a group made up of four wind players.

SELECTED RECORDINGS

As leader: *The Two Quartets* (1978, Dis. 787), incl. Night Cry; *Charles Owens Plays the Music of Harry Warren* (1980, Dis. 811)

As sideman: B. Rich: *Mercy, Mercy* (1968, PJ 20133), incl. Ode to Billy Joe; H. Franklin: *The Skipper* (1971, Black Jazz 7); *The Skipper at Home* (1974, Black Jazz 17); L. Alexandria: *How will I Remember You?* (1978, Dis. 782)

BIBLIOGRAPHY

Feather–Gitler '70s

J. A. Simon: "Charles Owens: the Two Quartets," *DB*, xlvi/6 (1979), 24 [record review]

DAVID WILD

Owens, Jimmy [James Robert] (*b* New York, 9 Dec 1943). Trumpeter, flugelhorn player, and composer. He played informally with Miles Davis's band in 1958, and studied trumpet with Donald Byrd; in 1959–60 he was a member of Marshall Brown's Newport Youth Band. Later he performed with Slide Hampton (1962–3), Lionel Hampton (1963–4), Maynard Ferguson, Gerry Mulligan (both 1964), Charles Mingus, Hank Crawford (both 1964–5), Herbie Mann (1965–6), and Max Roach. He was a founding member of the Thad Jones–Mel Lewis Orchestra (1966), then played with the New York Jazz Sextet (1966–8) and Clark Terry's big band; he also performed in a band led by Billy Taylor (ii) on the "David Frost Show." In 1968 he toured Europe with Dizzy Gillespie; the following year he performed and recorded with Duke Ellington, and he later worked with Count Basie. Owens has been involved in education and business administration; in 1969 he was one of the founders of Collective Black Artists, an organization dedicated to teaching and performing jazz, and he has taught and played with Jazzmobile. From 1969 into the mid-1970s he toured and recorded with his own group, the Jimmy Owens Quartet Plus One; during this period he also toured Europe with the Young Giants of Jazz (1973), worked with radio orchestras in Germany and Holland, and played with Chuck Israels's National Jazz Ensemble. Later he recorded with Mingus Dynasty (1979) and the pianist Errol Parker (1980). He is at his best when improvising fast, deftly articulated hard-bop melodies. His compositions include *Complicity* and *Milan is Love*.

SELECTED RECORDINGS

As leader: with K. Barron: *You had Better Listen* (1967, Atl. 1491); *No Escaping it!* (1970, Pol. 2425031), incl. Complicity, Milan is Love; *Young Man on the Move* (1976, A&M Hor. 712)

As sideman: H. Mann: *Herbie Mann Today* (1965, Atl. 1454); J. Byard: *On the Spot* (1965, 1967, Prst. 7524); on Newport in New York '72: *The Jam Sessions* (1972, Cob. 9025), Lo-slo-bluze; Mingus Dynasty: *Chair in the Sky* (1979, Elek. 248)

BIBLIOGRAPHY

Feather–Gitler '70s

G. Hoefer: "Marshall Brown's Talent Incubator," *DB*, xxxiv/19 (1967), 19

I. Gitler: "Jimmy Owens: Going up," *DB*, xxxv/2 (1968), 20

L. Underwood: "Creating the Business Legacy," *DB*, xlv/17 (1978), 15

E. Jost: *Jazzmusiker: Materialen zur Soziologie der afro-amerikanischen Musik* (Frankfurt am Main, Germany, Berlin, and Vienna, 1982), 97

M. Richards: "Jimmy Owens," *JJI*, xxxix/8 (1986), 6

FREDERICK A. BECK

Owl. Record company and label. The company was founded in 1975 in Paris by Jean-Jacques Pussiau. It has remained in operation into the mid-1980s, and has issued new recordings by French and American instrumentalists in styles as diverse as swing, bop, modal jazz, free jazz, and third stream.

BIBLIOGRAPHY

S. Loupien: "Deux stratégies phonographiques en France: Owl par Jean-Jacques Pussiau," *Jm*, nos.266–7 (1978), 25

B. McRae: "The Wise Owl," *JJI*, xxxiii/6 (1980), 26

Oxley, Tony [Oxo] (*b* Sheffield, England, 15 June 1938). English drummer and percussionist. After playing in military bands and collaborating with Derek Bailey and the double bass player Gavin Bryars, he moved in 1967 to London, where he came to public attention as a resident drummer at Ronnie Scott's club. He accompanied numerous American visitors, and in 1968 won a readers' poll in *Melody Maker*; as a result he was invited to record, and his first album, *The Baptised Traveller* (1969), illustrated his growing commitment to free improvisation. In 1971 he began experimenting with amplified percussion and helped to found Incus, an English record company devoted to the promotion of music of limited commercial appeal. He joined the London Jazz Composers Orchestra, and in 1978 formed the trio SOH with Alan Skidmore and Ali Haurand. During the 1970s his music was more readily accepted on the Continent than in Britain, and in 1979 he settled in Germany. In the mid-1980s he concentrated on working with his Celebration Orchestra, a group that confirms his fascination with a peculiarly European jazz language. Although he has never completely rejected the notion of the drummer as timekeeper Oxley has always championed rhythmic freedom; his achievements in the field of free jazz have made him one of the most respected contemporary percussionists.

SELECTED RECORDINGS

As leader: *The Baptised Traveller* (1969, CBS 52664); *Four Compositions for Sextet* (1970, CBS 64071); *Ichnos* (1971, RCA SF8215); *February Papers* (1977, Incus 18); of SOH (with A. Haurand and A. Skidmore): *SOH* (1981, View 0018); *Tomorrow is Here* (1985, Dossier 7507)

As sideman with J. McLaughlin: *Extrapolation* (1969, Marmalade 608007)

BIBLIOGRAPHY

D. Bailey: *Improvisation: its Nature and Practice in Music* (Ashbourne, England, 1980), 102

B. Noglik: "Tony Oxley," *Jazzwerkstatt international* (Berlin, 1981), 447 [incl. interview, discography]

B. Priestley: "A Drum Celebration," *The Wire*, no.32 (1986), 22

I. Carr: "Oxley, Tony," in I. Carr, D. Fairweather and B. Priestley: *Jazz: the Essential Companion* (London, 1987)

MARK GILBERT

Ozone. Record label established by BORIS ROSE in the early 1970s.

Ozone, Makoto (*b* Kōbe, Japan, 25 March 1961). Japanese pianist. The son of a jazz pianist, he began teaching himself to play at the age of five; his formal studies began when he was 12. He was influenced first by Jimmy Smith, then by Oscar Peterson, some of whose solos he transcribed. From 1980 he attended the Berklee College of Music, where he quickly assimilated new ideas through his work with Gary Burton and from the playing of such musicians as Chick Corea. After graduating Ozone joined Burton's band and also began to give solo performances. In 1984 with Burton and Eddie Gomez he recorded the album *Makoto Ozone* (Col. FC39624), which demonstrates the versatility and skill that led by the mid-1980s to his being recognized, despite his youth, as an important jazz musician.

BIBLIOGRAPHY

F. Bouchard: "Profile: Makoto Ozone," *DB*, liii/9 (1985), 48

R. Hershon and B. Doerschuk: "The Future of Jazz Piano Rests Secure in the Hands of Makoto Ozone," *Keyboard*, xi/11 (1985), 22

BOB DOERSCHUK

P

Paakkunainen, Seppo [Baron, Paroni] (*b* Tuusula, nr Kerava, Finland, 24 Oct 1943). Finnish baritone saxophonist, flutist, and composer. He studied flute at the Sibelius Academy (1962–6) and composition at the Berklee College of Music (1975–6). Paakkunainen is a versatile studio musician, but is best known for his unusual fusions of jazz with ethnic music. In the 1970s his group Karelia successfully combined jazz and Finnish folk music, and his Conjunto Baron introduced Latin jazz in Finland. With the Lapp singer Nils-Aslak Valkeapää he forged an amalgam of jazz and traditional *joiku* singing. His style is well illustrated by his album *Nunnu* (1971, Blue Master 301). Paakkunainen has also written film and theater music.

BIBLIOGRAPHY

A. Granholm: *Finnish Jazz* (Helsinki, 1974, rev. and enlarged by M. Konttinen 2/1982, rev. and enlarged by J.-P. Vuorela 3/1986), 27

J. Sermila: "Seppo Paakkunainen: Baron's Beat," *JF* [intl edn], no.36 (1975), 42 [incl. discography]

PEKKA GRONOW

Pablo. Record company and label. The company was established in Los Angeles in 1973 by NORMAN GRANZ, and named after the artist Pablo Picasso. It rapidly became extremely successful, continuing the rather conservative recording policies that Granz had pursued during his association with Verve. Material by such well-known performers as Oscar Peterson, Count Basie, Joe Pass, and Ella Fitzgerald predominates in the catalogue. Granz also set up two subsidiary labels. One of these, Pablo Live, established in 1977, has been used to issue recordings of concert performances. The first 14 albums were made at the Montreux International Jazz Festival of 1977; later recordings have been taken at various venues throughout the world. On the other, Pablo Today (founded in 1979), albums are released in much the same styles as those on Pablo itself. By the late 1980s the three labels had been used to issue hundreds of albums, some by previously existing groups, others by all-star ensembles specially organized for the occasion by Granz. The company issues mainly new recordings, but the catalogue also includes reissues of material Granz produced for his earlier labels Clef, Norgran, and Verve; a few albums by Jazz at the Philharmonic groups; and an LP recorded by John Coltrane in 1963. In 1987 Granz sold Pablo to Fantasy.

BIBLIOGRAPHY

E. Tiegel: "Granz Gamble: Veteran Producer Says Plenty Material Exists for Two Labels," *Billboard*, lxxxix (15 Jan 1977), 29

M. Jones: "Granz: the Prolific Patron," *MM* (30 Dec 1978), 11 [interview]

E. Tiegel: "Granz will Introduce New Label," *Billboard*, xci (21 April 1979), 3

Pace, Sal(vatore) (*b* White Plains, NY, 10 Aug 1910). Clarinetist and saxophonist. He studied clarinet from 1918. He played traditional jazz with the Crescent City Five in New York from 1924 to 1928. During the 1930s he performed in Joe Haymes's swing band (1936); he then played with Al Donahue (1940), Bunny Berigan (1941), and Charlie Spivak (1942–5). At the height of the dixieland revival Pace was performing traditional jazz again. He joined Phil Napoleon in 1949, then worked with Billy Butterfield, Yank Lawson, and Jimmy McPartland (1951–3). He recorded three albums with Pee Wee Erwin (1953, 1955, 1956) and one with Billy Maxted (1955–6). He also played with Maxted at Nick's in New York. The track *After You've Gone* from Erwin's album *Dixieland at the Grandview Inn* (1956, Cadence 1011) exemplifies Pace's style. (*FeatherE*)

Pacific Jazz. Record company and label. The company was founded in Los Angeles in 1952 by Richard Bock and the drummer Roy Harte; Bock later became the sole owner. Its most important early recordings were of the quartet led by Gerry Mulligan and Chet Baker, which were extremely successful and contributed to the formation of the West Coast jazz style. Under Bock's astute artistic direction Pacific Jazz became one of the most dynamic independent companies on the West Coast in the 1950s, building an impressive catalogue that included the work of some of the most famous instrumentalists in California. Though many later signed contracts with larger organizations, the company captured the finest early work of several musicians, including Chet Baker, Clare Fischer, Jim Hall, Groove Holmes, Les McCann, Art Pepper, Wes Montgomery, Chico Hamilton, Curtis Amy, Joe Pass, and Don Ellis, all of whom recorded their first sessions as leaders for the label. Bock said that he felt this documentation to have been his most satisfying achievement.

In 1958 Bock first recorded the work of the Indian sitarist Ravi Shankar. Feeling that Pacific Jazz was an inappropriate label for this music, he founded a subsidiary, World Pacific, to issue Shankar's recordings. This was used to issue several different kinds of music, including some jazz, but was only short-lived. Disillusioned by trends in jazz of the 1960s Bock sold the enterprise to Liberty in 1965; he continued nevertheless to work in an advisory capacity until 1970, when he became a film producer. Control of Pacific Jazz ultimately passed to Capitol, but in the late 1980s comprehensive reissue of the catalogue was undertaken by Mosaic (ii); material was also put out on compact disc under leasing arrangements with Japanese companies.

MARK GARDNER

Packay, Peter [Paquet, Pierre] (*b* Brussels, 8 Aug 1904; *d* Westende, Belgium, 26 Dec 1965). Belgian trumpeter, composer, and arranger. With his family he moved at an early age to China, where he first studied music. He returned in 1912 to Brussels, and despite an accident that left him without the use of one arm took up the trumpet in 1924. In the following years he belonged to the Varsity Ramblers and with David Bee to the group Bistrouille A.D.O., as a member of which he wrote such compositions as *Alabama Mamma, The Blue Duke,* and *Dixie Melody*; the last named was recorded by the band in 1930 (Col. DF319). After Bee's departure from the group early in 1927 Packay became its leader and devoted greater attention to composing. With several members of Bistrouille A.D.O. he later formed a band called Packay's Swing Academy, which accompanied Coleman Hawkins in Brussels; he also wrote arrangements for the American bandleader Billy Arnold. He recorded his piece *Lullaby for a Mexican Alligator* with his own group in 1939 (Jazz Club 4200), but after World War II he abandoned the trumpet and worked exclusively as a composer and arranger.

ROBERT PERNET

Page, Hot Lips [Oran Thaddeus] (*b* Dallas, 27 Jan 1908; *d* New York, 5 Nov 1954). Trumpeter and singer. He worked as a professional musician in his home state of Texas during the 1920s, and maintained that he learned to play authentic blues by listening to the local performers there. He was a member of the band that accompanied Ma Rainey and also toured on the TOBA circuit, accompanying such singers as Bessie Smith and Ida Cox. He played with Walter Page's Blue Devils from 1928 to 1931, then joined Bennie Moten's band in Kansas City (for illustration *see* MOTEN, BENNIE). In 1936 he was briefly with Count Basie as a principal soloist, but left at the behest of Louis Armstrong's manager Joe Glaser to become a solo artist (a move generally regarded as having crippled a potentially illustrious career). He led his own bands in New York from 1937, but also spent a period in Artie Shaw's band (1941–2), during which time he attracted much publicity. From 1943 to 1949 he concentrated on playing in smaller groups, and during the 1950s he appeared mainly as a soloist.

Page made many fine recordings under his own name (1938–54), often leading bands made up of some of the finest swing musicians, including Earl Bostic, Don Byas, J. C. Higginbotham, and Ben Webster. His purposeful, exciting trumpet playing and his deeply felt blues singing were probably too rugged to gain widespread favor, however. Throughout his career he thrived on the atmosphere of impromptu jam sessions, in which his searing tone, dramatic phrasing, and improvised blues lyrics were a source of considerable inspiration to his fellow musicians.

SELECTED RECORDINGS

As leader: Skull Duggery (1938, Bb 7583); Pagin' Mr. Page (1944, Savoy 520); The Sheik of Araby (1944, V-disc 418); St. James Infirmary (1947, Har. 1069)

As sideman: B. Moten: Milenberg Joys (1932, Vic. 24381); A. Shaw: St. James Infirmary (1941, Vic. 27895); E. Condon: Uncle Sam Blues (1944, V-disc 191)

BIBLIOGRAPHY

E. Anderson: "Lips the Hard-luck Man," *MM*, xxx (20 Nov 1954), 7
H. Panassié: "Lips Page," *BHcF*, no.93 (1959), 3
J. G. Jepsen and K. Mohr: *Hot Lips Page* (Basle, Switzerland, 1961) [discography]
D. Morgenstern and others: "Hot Lips Page on Record," *JJ*, xv (1962), no.11, p.13; no.12, p.17
G. Murphy: "The Forgotten Ones: Hot Lips Page," *JJI*, xxxiv/8 (1981), 12
N. W. Pearson, Jr.: *Goin' to Kansas City* (Urbana, IL, and London, 1988)

JOHN CHILTON

Page, Walter (Sylvester) (*b* Gallatin, MO, 9 Feb 1900; *d* New York, 20 Dec 1957). Double bass player and bandleader. He played occasionally with Bennie Moten's band in the early 1920s, and in 1925 founded his own band, the Blue Devils, in Oklahoma City. At various times this group included Hot Lips Page, Buster Smith, Count Basie, Jimmy Rushing, Lester Young, and other leading figures in the Southwest style, making the Blue Devils, along with Moten's group, the most influential jazz band in the area. In 1931 Page was forced for financial reasons to give up leadership of the Blue Devils, and he joined Moten until 1934. After playing briefly with Basie and then with the Jeter–Pillars Orchestra in St. Louis, he began a fruitful association with Basie's band (1936–42, 1946–9; *see* BASIE, COUNT, §2). He was a mainstay of Basie's celebrated rhythm section (for illustrations *see* FILMS, fig.3, and JONES, JO), where the solidity and swing of his playing enabled the leader to dispense with stride left-hand patterns and Jo Jones to transfer the pulse to the hi-hat cymbals. *Pagin' the Devil,* recorded with the Kansas City Six, a unit from Basie's band, includes one of the earliest jazz solos on double bass. These and other performances established Page as the leading jazz bass player of the late 1930s, and a creator of the walking bass style. Later, apart from his second period with Basie from 1946 to 1949, Page played mainly on a freelance basis with various swing and dixieland groups in New York.

SELECTED RECORDINGS

As leader: Blue Devil Blues/Squabblin' (1929, Voc. 1463)

As sideman: Kansas City Six: Pagin' the Devil (1938, Com. 512); C. Basie: Oh! Red/Fare thee honey, fare thee well (1939, Decca 2780)

BIBLIOGRAPHY

W. Page: "About my Life in Music," *JR*, i/1 (1958), 12
G. Schuller: *Early Jazz: its Roots and Musical Development* (New York, 1968), 293
R. Russell: *Jazz Style in Kansas City and the Southwest* (Berkeley, CA, Los Angeles, and London, 1971/*R*1983, rev. 2/1973)
N. W. Pearson, Jr.: *Goin' to Kansas City* (Urbana, IL, and London, 1988)

J. BRADFORD ROBINSON

Paich, Marty [Martin Louis] (*b* Oakland, CA, 23 Jan 1925). Arranger, composer, pianist, and bandleader. He began playing and writing arrangements in Oakland at the age of 16, and from 1943 to 1946 served as arranger for the US Army Air Force Band. He then studied composition with Mario Castelnuovo-Tedesco (1946–50) and gained bachelor's and master's degrees from the Los Angeles Conservatory of Music. After touring with Jerry Gray (1951) he provided a repertory of compositions for Dan Terry's orchestra (1952), played with Shelly Manne, worked as pianist and conductor for Peggy Lee (1953), and performed with Shorty Rogers's Giants (1954). He became well known in the 1950s for his arrangements for Mel Tormé (which he recorded with his own group, the Marty Paich Dek-tette), as well as work for the Dave Pell Octet (1957) and for Art Pepper (1959). He has written music for several other artists, including Ella Fitzgerald, Anita O'Day, Chet Baker, Ray Brown, Buddy Rich, and Stan Kenton, as well as for films and television.

SELECTED ARRANGEMENTS

(all recorded by others with Paich as sideman)

M. Tormé: *Mel Tormé with the Marty Paich Dek-tette* (1956, Beth. 52); A. O'Day: *Anita O'Day Sings the Winners* (1958, Verve 8283); A. Pepper: *Art Pepper + Eleven* (1959, Cont. 3568); E. Fitzgerald: *Whisper Not* (1966, Verve 64071)

BIBLIOGRAPHY

FeatherE
J. Tynan: "Marty Paich," *DB*, xxv/18 (1958), 18
P. Gowers: "Modern Jazz," *Musical Times*, ciii (1962), 389
M. Jones: "Marty Paich," *MM* (8 July 1967), 6

STEVEN STRUNK

Pairing. *See* COUPLING.

Palmer, Earl (C., Sr.) (*b* New Orleans, 25 Oct 1924). Drummer. He performed in vaudeville for several years, then moved to Los Angeles in 1957. He formed several rock-and-roll bands that recorded for Capitol, Aladdin, and other labels (1957–61). As a studio musician, he recorded swing and pop (with Neal Hefti and Frank Sinatra) and blues (with Joe Turner (ii)); his playing is well represented by *Honeysuckle Rose* on Earl Bostic's *Hits of the Swing Age* (1957, King 571). He also played with Red Callender (1959) and Buddy Collette, and recorded with Carter and at the Monterey Jazz Festival with Dizzy Gillespie; he toured the Middle East with Carter in 1975–6. Palmer performs occasionally with his own band and continues to work regularly as a studio musician, playing in various popular styles of the 1980s. In 1983 he served as secretary of the musicians' union in Los Angeles.

BIBLIOGRAPHY

J. Broven: "Earl Palmer," *Blues Unlimited*, no.115 (1975), 4
R. Flans: "Earl Palmer," *MD*, vii/5 (1983), 8

Palmer, Robert (*b* Little Rock, AR, 19 June 1945). Writer. As a youth he played reed instruments with rock, country, and soul bands, and later performed as a member of an eclectic group called the Insect Trust, with which he recorded two albums. He was a co-founder of the Memphis Blues Festival in 1966, and the following year graduated from the University of Arkansas. In New York thereafter he became a widely published freelance writer on jazz, rock, and the avant garde. From 1975 he was a regular reviewer for the *New York Times* and in 1981 he was appointed to its staff of jazz and pop critics; he resigned this post in 1988. Palmer has written four books, the most important of which is a study of the Delta blues (*Deep Blues*, New York and London, 1981). He has held teaching positions at Bowdoin College, the University of Mississippi, Memphis State University, Brooklyn College, CUNY, and Yale University. He has also collaborated musically on informal projects with Ornette Coleman, among others. Palmer is rare among jazz writers in maintaining an unembarrassed interest in a range of music that extends far beyond the traditional boundaries of jazz.

JOHN ROCKWELL

Palmer, Roy (*b* New Orleans, 2 April 1892; *d* Chicago, 22 Dec 1963). Trombonist. He first played guitar and worked in New Orleans in the Rozele Orchestra (1906). After taking up trombone he played with Richard M. Jones, Freddie Keppard (1911), Willie Hightower (*c*1914–15), and the Tuxedo and Onward brass bands (1915–16). He toured in 1917, then settled in Chicago, where he played with Lawrence Duhé, King Oliver, and Keppard. He also made recordings with Jelly Roll Morton, including *Fish Tail Blues/High Society* (1924, Autograph 606). After 1932 he worked mostly in factories, but also taught music; among his pupils were Preston Jackson and Albert Wynn.

BIBLIOGRAPHY

W. C. Allen: "Trombone Giants, 1: Roy Palmer," *Hot Notes*, no.13 (n.d. [1948]), 2
P. Van Vorst: "Roy Palmer's Story," *MR*, v/5 (1978), 1

BILL RUSSELL

Palmer, Singleton [William] (*b* St. Louis, 13 Nov 1912). Double bass and tuba player. He performed and recorded on tuba with the cornetist and singer Oliver Cobb (1929–31) and on double bass with the pianist Eddie Johnson (1931–?1934). He then worked with Dewey Jackson (?1934–1941) and George Hudson (1942–8), recorded with Clark Terry (1947), and played with Jimmy Forrest (1948), before joining Count Basie. He left Basie in 1950 to form his own group, the Dixieland Band, which worked regularly in St. Louis into the 1980s. A good example of his playing may be heard on *I can't believe that you're in love with me* on the album *At the Opera House* (1961, Norman 206).

Oral history material in *MoU-St.*

BIBLIOGRAPHY

ChiltonW
B. Rusch: "Singleton Palmer," *Cadence*, xiii/2 (1987), 5

FRANK DRIGGS

Palmier(i), Remo (*b* New York, 29 March 1923). Guitarist. His first professional work was with the Nat Jaffe Trio in New York (1942). He then played with Coleman Hawkins (1943) and Red Norvo (1944) and recorded with Barney Bigard (1944) and, with Charlie Parker, in Dizzy Gillespie's sextet (1945). Although Palmier's primary influences were Django Reinhardt and Charlie Christian, he later adopted the melodic and harmonic concepts of Hawkins and Parker. In 1945 he received the "new star" award from *Esquire* magazine and began a 27-year period as guitarist for the "Arthur Godfrey Show" on television. He performed in California at the Concord Jazz Festival's "Guitar Explosion" with Herb Ellis, Emily Remler, Howard Roberts, Tal Farlow, and Barney Kessel in 1975, and during the 1970s also played with Benny Goodman and Dick Hyman. In 1985 he appeared with Red Norvo, Louie Bellson, Teddy Wilson, and others at an acclaimed concert in New York.

SELECTED RECORDINGS

As leader: with H. Ellis: *Wildflower* (1978, Conc. 56); *Remo Palmier* (1978, Conc. 76)

As sideman: D. Gillespie: Groovin' High (1945, Guild 1001); All the things you are (1945, Musi. 488); [no leader]: *Swing Reunion* (1985, Book-of-the-Month 717627)

BIBLIOGRAPHY

FeatherE
A. Berle and J. Obrecht: "Remo Palmieri: from Jamming with Jazz Greats on 52nd Street to 27 Years with CBS," *GP*, xii/8 (1978), 38

JIM FERGUSON

Palo Alto. Record company and label. The company was founded in Palo Alto, California, in 1981 by Jim (James) Benham (*b* Joliet, IL, 24 Nov 1935), chairman of the Benham Capital Management Group and a big-band trumpeter. Until 1985 it operated in Palo Alto under the artistic direction of its executive director, Herb Wong, who was well respected in the San Francisco Bay area as a jazz educator and disc jockey. At first it concentrated on issuing new bop recordings, but after a shift in its emphasis towards insubstantial jazz-rock, Wong left the company and the office in Palo Alto closed. The organization later moved to Studio City, California.

BIBLIOGRAPHY

L. Feather: "Jim Benham: He Has Full Faith in his Jazz and Business Credits," *San Francisco Chronicle Datebook* (6 Jan 1985), 18
M. Langton: "Jazz Label Closes Bay Area Office, Fires Executive," *San Francisco Examiner* (10 Oct 1985), §C, p.5

Palomar Ballroom. Ballroom in Los Angeles; *see* NIGHTCLUBS AND OTHER VENUES.

Panachord. Record label. It was established in 1931 by Warner Bros. as a British counterpart to American Brunswick's subsidiary Melotone. After 1932 it was administered by Decca, and issue continued until 1939; the jazz catalogue was drawn first from Brunswick, then from the American Record Company, and later from Decca. Dutch Decca also used a Panachord label to release cheap recordings in the Netherlands, including important items by such Americans resident in Europe as Coleman Hawkins. The label was revived in the 1980s (by the company Stichting Granny's Records) for a series of reissues on LP of these and of contemporary Dutch jazz recordings.

BIBLIOGRAPHY

J. Hayes: "Date that Disc!, no.4: Panachord 25000 Series," *Gunn Report* (June 1972), 42
B. Rust: *The American Record Label Book* (New Rochelle, NY, 1978), 224

Panassié, Hugues (*b* Paris, 27 Feb 1912; *d* Montauban, France, 8 Dec 1974). French writer. After studying saxophone he first wrote about jazz at the age of 18. He was one of the founders (in 1932) and then president of the HOT CLUB DE FRANCE, and from 1935 to 1946 he was the editor of the journal *Jazz hot*. With his unrivaled enthusiasm for communication, Panassié wrote hundreds of articles for this and other periodicals and was the author of several books, notably *Le jazz hot* (1934), an important study that was among the first to treat jazz seriously. In 1938 Count Basie dedicated to him and recorded a composition called *Panassié Stomp*. The same year, in New York, Panassié organized a series of small-group recording sessions with Mezz Mezzrow which also included (at various times) Tommy Ladnier and Sidney Bechet; these were highly influential and contributed considerably to the New Orleans revival movement. In 1939 he recorded a swing septet under the leadership of Frankie Newton. However, Panassié's reputation as an articulate advocate of jazz has to some extent been tarnished by his extreme conservatism: from the mid-1940s he expressed the opinion that bop was not jazz, thus denying the evolution of the genre. His private collection is now in the Discothèque Municipale at Villefranche-de-Rouergue (*see* LIBRARIES AND ARCHIVES, §2).

For illustration *see* MEZZROW, MEZZ.

WRITINGS
(selective list)

Le jazz hot (Paris, 1934; Eng. trans., rev. Panassié, London and New York, 1936/*R*1970; Sp. trans., Santiago, 1939)
The Real Jazz (New York and Toronto, 1942 [in Eng. trans.], rev. and enlarged by Panassié 2/1960; Fr. orig. pubd as *La véritable musique de jazz*, Paris, 1945, rev. and enlarged 2/1952)
La musique de jazz et le swing (Paris, 1943, [2]/1945)
Douze années de jazz (1927–1938): souvenirs (Paris, 1946)
Cinq mois à New-York (Paris, 1947)
Louis Armstrong (Paris, 1947)
Jazz panorama (Paris, 1950)
with M. Gautier: *Dictionnaire du jazz* (Paris, 1954, rev. and enlarged 2/1971, enlarged 3/1980, rev. and enlarged [4]/1987; Eng. trans., London, 1956, rev. A. A. Gurwitch as *Guide to Jazz*, Boston, 1956)
Petit guide pour une discothèque de jazz (Paris, 1955)
Discographie critique des meilleurs disques de jazz (Paris, 1958)
Histoire du vrai jazz (Paris, 1959)
La bataille du jazz (Paris, 1965)
The Panassié Sessions (RCA RD7887, 1967) [liner notes]
Louis Armstrong (Paris, 1969; Eng. trans., New York, 1971)
Monsieur Jazz (Paris, 1975)

ANDRÉ CLERGEAT

Papa Bue [Jensen, Arne Bue] (*b* Copenhagen, 8 May 1930). Danish trombonist and bandleader. In the mid-1950s he performed and recorded with the Bonanza Jazz Band, Chris Barber, the pianist Adrian Bentzon, and the clarinetist Henrik Johansen. From 1956 he led the New Orleans Jazz Band, a septet based in Copenhagen, which he renamed the Viking Jazz Band in 1958. The band remained in existence, with only infrequent changes of personnel, into the 1980s; among those who recorded with it were George Lewis (i) (1959), the pianist Champion Jack Dupree (1962), Art Hodes (1970), and Wild Bill Davison (1970, 1974). Papa Bue's playing is well represented on his albums *Papa Bue's Viking Jazz Band with Wingy Manone and Edmond Hall* (1966, Sto. 192) and *On Stage* (1982, Tim. 511).

BIBLIOGRAPHY

Reclams J
O. Bendix: *Papa Bue* (Copenhagen, 1962)

Pâques, Jean (*b* Liège, Belgium, 16 Sept 1901; *d* Liège, 19 April 1974). Belgian pianist and composer. From the end of World War I he worked as an unaccompanied soloist and in small groups, and in 1923–6 he led the Five Merry Kids, which played mainly in Liège. He performed in the Netherlands and Germany in the Russian North Star Orchestra (recording in 1928), a dixieland septet led by the reed player Grégoire Nakchounian, and worked with Sid Phillips in England, where he also made more than 200 recordings as the house pianist of the Edison Bell Co. He made five tours of Italy with the singer Lydia Johnson and in Belgium played at the Carlton in Blankenberge and the Barclay in Liège. After World War II he worked mostly in piano bars and made many recordings in a distinctive "sweet" style. A good example of his work is his recording of his own composition *Hot Piano* (1928, EBR 804).

ROBERT PERNET

Paquet, Pierre. *See* PACKAY, PETER.

Paquinet, André (*b* Arcueil, France, 1 Oct 1926). French trombonist, son of Guy Paquinet. He played first with his father (1944), then with the saxophonist Tony Proteau (1946–8), under the bandleader Jacques Hélian (1951–2), again with Proteau (1953), and with Claude Bolling (1954–7), Michel Legrand (1956–7), and Fred Gerard (1957). From 1958 for a short time he played and made recordings with the trombonist Benny Vasseur (including *The Man I Love*, *Mood Indigo*, and *Sonny Boy*, *c*1959, Festival 2183). He also played with the vibraphonist Dany Doriz (1966), André Hodeir (1963, 1966), the trumpeter Jean-Claude Naude (1967, 1971, 1975), the trombonist François Guin's group Four Bones (1968), Slide Hampton, the trumpeter Ivan Jullien (1970–71), and Roy Eldridge (1970), and under Paul Kuntz in Berlin (1973–7). At the height of his career Paquinet's playing was remarkable for his breath control and his production of a good sound over the full compass of the instrument.

MICHEL LAPLACE

Paquinet, Guy [Patrick] (*b* Tours, France, 13 Aug 1903; *d* Selles-sur-le-Bied, France, 5 Jan 1981). French trombonist. He played with a military band, the group Melody Six, Paul Gason's band

(1925, 1928), Lud Gluskin (1926, 1932), the bandleader and percussionist Fred Mélé (1926–8), the alto saxophonist Don Parker, and Gregor (1930). From 1934 to 1936, using the pseudonym Patrick, he led an orchestra in performances and recordings; he then played with Ray Ventura (1937–40), Django Reinhardt (1940), and Alix Combelle (1940), and again with Ventura (1945–9). He led his own groups from time to time in the 1940s, in one of which (1944) his son André Paquinet, also a trombonist, gained his first professional experience; from 1949 to 1951 he was leader of a seven-piece orchestra. In the latter part of his career he played with the saxophonist Tony Proteau, Dizzy Gillespie, and Sidney Bechet (1953). Paquinet was a pioneer of jazz trombone in France; his playing is well represented on recordings made by the group Jazz Dixit in 1940 (*Strictement pour les persans/Saut d'une heure,* Col. DF2819). (M. Laplace: *Portraits of French Jazz Musicians* (Menden, Germany, 1985), 14)

MICHEL LAPLACE

Paradiddle. One of the drumstrokes collectively known as RUDIMENTS.

Paradox. Record label. It was launched in September 1948 by Globe Industries of New York, and managed by Dante Bolletino. The catalogue consisted mainly of recordings by such traditional-jazz performers as Ray Burke and Knocky Parker. Both 78 r.p.m. discs and LPs were issued. Operations ceased in February 1952 at the same time as those of Bolletino's label British Rhythm Society. The catalogue was acquired by Chimes Music Shop, which reissued the material on the label Pax from 1952. This arrangement ceased in 1956; Paradox's repertory was later made available to Jazztone. (D. Mahony and others: "The Dante Bolletino Labels," *Matrix,* no.58 (1965), 3)

Paramount. Record label. The main label of the New York Recording Laboratories of Port Washington, Wisconsin, it was established in 1916. The first issues were of $9\frac{1}{2}$-inch vertical-cut discs; lateral-cut discs were first put out in 1919. A race series, the 12000s, commenced in August 1922, and proved extremely successful; it ran into the 13000s, and by the time it was discontinued in 1932 more than 1100 releases had been made. The work of singers predominated, including that of Ma Rainey (the label's most famous musician), Ida Cox, and Alberta Hunter. Many discs in the race catalogue are now acknowledged to be classics, including recordings by King Oliver and Freddie Keppard and longer series by such small groups based in Chicago as Lovie Austin's Blues Serenaders and Jimmy O'Bryant's Original Washboard Band. Artists and repertory were directed by Art Satherley (who later worked for the American Record Company), and by J. Mayo Williams, who supervised the race series until 1927. Williams also managed an associated music publisher, Chicago Music, which published many of the compositions released on the label. Paramount's General Series, the 20000s, contained a smaller proportion of jazz, but included some discs by Fletcher Henderson and the Original Memphis Five, and a considerable amount of hot dance music.

For much of its history Paramount's activities were linked with those of other companies. During the early 1920s it was closely associated with the Bridgeport Die & Machine Co., and also exchanged many masters with Plaza (later part of ARC). As well as its own recording studios in New York, which closed in 1926, Paramount used the recording facilities of Marsh Laboratories in Chicago in 1924–7 and of the Starr Piano Co. (owners of Gennett) at Richmond, Indiana, in 1929. That year it transferred its business, which was steadily declining, to Grafton, Wisconsin. Operations ceased in 1932. Thereafter, however, a small number of race issues appeared (under circumstances not yet fully understood) in a Paramount 9000 series produced by ARC. The collector John Steiner revived the label in the late 1940s, putting out in a 14000 series both reissues dubbed from early Paramount discs, and also new material. LPs of the latter were released until the early 1950s.

BIBLIOGRAPHY

M. Wyler: *A Glimpse of the Past: an Illustrated History of some Early Record Companies that Made Jazz History* (West Moors, England, 1957)
J. Godrich and R. M. W. Dixon: *Blues & Gospel Records, 1902–1942* (Hatch End, nr London, 1964, rev. 2/1969, rev. and enlarged 3/1982 as R. M. W. Dixon and J. Godrich: *Blues & Gospel Records, 1902–1943*), 24
R. M. W. Dixon and J. Godrich: *Recording the Blues* (London, 1970)
M. E. Vreede: *Paramount 12/13000 Series* (London, 1971) [discography]
C. Hillman: "Paramount Serenaders 1923–1926," *Sv,* no.67 (1976), 8; no.68 (1976), 52; no.69 (1977), 91; no.70 (1977), 149; no.72 (1977), 226; no.73 (1977), 29; no.74 (1977), 67; no.75 (1978), 84 [incl. discography]
B. Rust: *The American Record Label Book* (New Rochelle, NY, 1978), 226
D. M. Bakker: "Duke Ellington and the Paramount Re-issue Series," *Names & Numbers,* no.3 (1986), 10

Paramountorkestern. Swedish band. Formed in 1926 by the violinist Folke "Göken" Andersson (1902–76), it had from six to nine members at various times. Among those who belonged to the band were the trumpeters Gösta "Smyget" Redlig, Gösta "Chicken" Törnblad, and Ragge Läth; the saxophonists Sam Jacobsson, Tony Mason, and Olle Henricson; the pianists Nils Lind and Nils Soderman; the banjoists Curt Ljunggren and Jean Paban; and the drummer Anders Soldén. The Paramountorkestern was the first important jazz band in Sweden; it gave many performances on radio and made about 100 recordings (including *Tambou,* 1928, Col. 8629), most of which had a commercial orientation. The group disbanded about 1930.

BIBLIOGRAPHY

B. Englund: "Paramountorkestern: Sveriges första egentliga jazzorkester" [Paramountorkestern: Sweden's first real jazz orchestra], *Orkester journalen,* xxxvi/12 (1968), 8

ERIK KJELLBERG

Paraphernalia. British jazz-rock group formed by BARBARA THOMPSON around 1972.

Parenti, Tony [Anthony] (*b* New Orleans, 6 Aug 1900; *d* New York, 17 April 1972). Clarinetist and saxophonist. He first played jazz in 1914 in a band led by Alfred "Baby" Laine, and by the age of 15 he was working frequently at the Pup Cabaret. From 1917 he led his own band in New Orleans, with which he recorded in 1925–6 and 1928. In 1927 Parenti went to New York, where he often deputized for Benny Goodman in Ben Pollack's band. He joined the staff orchestra at CBS in 1930, and also led a saxophone quartet for radio broadcasts; he then played for four years with the orchestra at Radio City Music Hall. From 1939 until summer 1945 he traveled with Ted Lewis's orchestra. On his return to New York he performed with Eddie Condon and Georg Brunis, and later led his own band. After working in Chicago with Muggsy Spanier (1947) and Miff Mole (1948–9) he moved to Miami (1950), where he played briefly with the Dukes of Dixieland (1952). He also led his own group before returning in 1954 to New York, where he led house bands at Condon's (1962–3) and Ryan's (1963–9).

Parenti was a master of ragtime and dixieland jazz, and was also comfortable in classical ensembles. Although he greatly admired the playing of Leon Roppolo, he developed his own distinctive, swinging style.

Oral history material in *LNT*.

SELECTED RECORDINGS

As leader: That's a Plenty/Cabaret Echoes (1925, OK 40308); Old Man Rhythm (1929, Ban. 0580); Crawfish Crawl/Lily Rag (1949, Cir. [USA] 1056); Blues for Faz/Bugle Call Rag (1949, Jlgy 2); *Jazz, that's all* (1955, Jzt. 1215), incl. City of the Blues, Vieux Carré

As sideman: Preacher Rollo: Ostrich Walk (1951, MGM 30446)

BIBLIOGRAPHY

ChiltonW
B. Aurthur: "That's a Parenti," *Jazz Record*, no.49 (1946), 7
B. Rust: "A Study of Anthony Parenti," *Hot Notes*, ii/4 (1947), 15
T. Parenti: "Early Years in New Orleans," *SL*, ii (1951), no.9, p.6; no.10, p.7; no.11, p.5
N. Shapiro and N. Hentoff, eds.: *Hear me Talkin' to ya: the Story of Jazz by the Men who Made it* (New York and London, 1955/R1966)
Obituary, T. Piazza, *DB*, xxxix/11 (1972), 10

RAYMOND J. GARIGLIO

Parham, Tiny [Hartzell Strathdene] (*b* Winnipeg, Canada, 25 Feb 1900; *d* Milwaukee, 4 April 1943). Pianist, bandleader, and organist. He grew up in Kansas City, where he played in a theater in 1923. He toured the Southwest with a big band (1925), then moved to Chicago and led a group with the violinist Leroy Pickett (1926–7). From 1926 to 1930 he made more than 30 recordings, mainly accompanying blues singers, but also with the Paramount Pickers and Johnny Dodds; a fine example of his skill as an accompanist is *19th Street Blues*, recorded with Dodds in 1927 (Para. 12483). He also led his own groups, which at times included Punch Miller, on recordings such as *Cuckoo Blues* (1928, Vic. 21553). After leading big bands until 1936, Parham worked as a solo organist until his death. He recorded again in 1940 as a leader of a quintet that included Darnell Howard.

BIBLIOGRAPHY

ChiltonW
Obituary, *Chicago Defender* (24 April 1943)
A. McCarthy: *Big Band Jazz* (New York and London, 1974), 29
C. Strachwitz: Liner notes, *Tiny Parham and his Musicians* (Folklyric 9028, c1981)

Parham, Truck [Charles Valdez] (*b* Chicago, 25 Jan 1911). Double bass player. He was a professional football player and boxer in the early 1930s, and began his musical career as a tuba player and singer with Zack Whyte (1932–4). He studied double bass with Walter Page and with Nathan Gangursky of the Chicago SO. At the Three Deuces in Chicago he played with Zutty Singleton (1935), Art Tatum (1935–6), and Roy Eldridge (1936–8). He also recorded with Mildred Bailey (1937). From 1940 to 1942 Parham was a member of Earl Hines's orchestra, providing the rhythmic impetus for such recordings as *Jelly Jelly* (1940). With Hines, and later with Jimmie Lunceford (1942–7), he developed the powerful yet buoyant swing style that had been established by Page. Later he performed and recorded with Muggsy Spanier (1950–55), Louie Bellson (1957–9), and Art Hodes (intermittently, 1957–68). He has continued to work into the mid-1980s, performing frequently at Andy's, Chicago (from 1980).

Oral history material in *ICU*.

SELECTED RECORDINGS

Duos with A. Hodes: *Plain Old Blues* (1962, EmA 26005), incl. Buddy Bolden's Blues

As sideman: M. Bailey: You're laughin' at me (1937, Voc. 3456); R. Eldridge: Heckler's Hop (1937, Voc. 3577); E. Hines: Jelly Jelly (1940, Bb 11065); J. Lunceford: *Dance Date* (1942–3, Swing Classics 1); M. Spanier: Dixie Flyer/Lazy Piano Man (1950, Mer. 5424); L. Bellson: *Louis Bellson at the Flamingo* (1957, Verve 8256); A Hodes: *Hodes' Art* (1968, Del. 213)

BIBLIOGRAPHY

ChiltonW; *FeatherE*
B. Rusch: "Truck Parham," *Cadence*, xiii (1987), no.11, p.17; no.12, p.19

JOHN CURRY

Paris, Jackie (*b* Nutley, NJ, 20 Sept 1926). Singer. He played guitar in New York with Nick Jerret during the early 1940s. After serving in the army (1944–6) he returned to New York to perform, principally as a singer, with groups on 52nd Street. As a leader he recorded intermittently from 1947 to 1962 (he is best known for his recording of *Skylark*, 1947, MGM 10114), and he sang, but did not record, with Lionel Hampton (1949–50). Although he was named "best new male vocalist" by *Down Beat* in 1953, he had difficulty securing steady work as a jazz musician; nevertheless he performed at nightclubs and resorts in the 1950s and 1960s, sometimes accompanying his wife, the singer Anne Marie Moss. A recording made with Donald Byrd and Gigi Gryce (*Modern Jazz Perspective*, 1957, Col. CL1058) features his scat singing in swing and bop styles. He also recorded with Charles Mingus in 1974 (*Duke Ellington's Sound of Love*, on the LP *Changes Two*, Atl. 1678).

Parker, Charlie [Charles, Jr.; Bird; Chan, Charlie; Yardbird] (*b* Kansas City, KS, 29 Aug 1920; *d* New York, 12 March 1955). Alto saxophonist. He was one of the most important and influential improvising soloists in jazz, and a central figure in the development of bop in the 1940s. A legendary figure in his own

1. Charlie Parker at Dial's recording studios, Los Angeles, February 1947

lifetime, he was idolized by those who worked with him, and he inspired a generation of jazz performers and composers.

1. Life. 2. Style. 3. Influence.

1. Life. He was the only child of Charles and Addie Parker. In 1927 the family moved to Kansas City, Missouri, an important center of black-American music in the 1920s and 1930s. Parker had his first music lessons in the local public schools; he began playing alto saxophone in 1933 and worked occasionally in semiprofessional groups before leaving school in 1935 to become a full-time musician. From 1935 to 1939 he worked mainly in Kansas City with a wide variety of local blues and jazz groups. Like most jazz musicians of his time, he developed his craft largely through practical experience: listening to older local jazz masters, acquiring a traditional repertory, and learning through the process of trial and error in the competitive Kansas City bands and jam sessions.

In 1939 Parker first visited New York (then the principal center of jazz musical and business activity), staying for nearly a year. Although he worked only sporadically as a professional musician, he often participated in jam sessions. By his own later account (see Levin and Wilson), he was bored with the stereotyped changes that were being used then: "I kept thinking there's bound to be something else . . . I could hear it sometimes, but I couldn't play it." While working over *Cherokee* in a jam session with the guitarist Biddy Fleet, Parker suddenly found that by using the higher intervals of a chord as a melody line and backing them with appropriately related changes, he could play what he had been "hearing." Yet it was not until 1944–5 that his conceptions of rhythm and phrasing had evolved sufficiently to form his mature style.

Parker's name first appeared in the music press in 1940; from this date his career is more fully documented. From 1940 to 1942 he played in Jay McShann's band, with which he toured the Southwest, Chicago, and New York, and took part in his first recording sessions in Dallas (1941). These recordings, and several made for broadcasting from the same period, document his early, swing-based style, and at the same time reveal his extraordinary gift for improvisation. In December 1942 he joined Earl Hines's big band, which then included several other young modernists such as Dizzy Gillespie. By May 1944 they, with Parker, formed the nucleus of Billy Eckstine's band.

During these years Parker regularly participated in after-hours jam sessions at Minton's Playhouse and Monroe's Uptown House in New York, where the informal atmosphere and small groups favored the development of his personal style, and of the new bop music generally. Unfortunately a strike by the American Federation of Musicians silenced most of the recording industry from August 1942, causing this crucial stage in Parker's musical evolution to remain virtually undocumented (there are some obscure acetate recordings of him playing tenor saxophone dating from early 1943). When the recording ban ended, Parker recorded as a sideman (from 15 September 1944) and as a leader (from 26 November 1945), which introduced his music to a wider public and to other musicians.

The year 1945 marked a turning-point in Parker's career: in New York he led his own group for the first time and worked extensively with Gillespie in small ensembles. In December 1945 he and Gillespie took the new jazz style to Hollywood, where they fulfilled a six-week nightclub engagement. Parker continued to work in Los Angeles, recording and performing in concerts and nightclubs, until 29 June 1946, when a nervous breakdown and addiction to heroin and alcohol caused his confinement at the Camarillo State Hospital. He was released in January 1947 and resumed work in Los Angeles.

Parker returned to New York in April 1947. He formed a quintet (with Miles Davis, Duke Jordan, Tommy Potter, and Max Roach), which recorded many of his most famous pieces. The years from 1947 to 1951 were Parker's most fertile period. He worked in a wide variety of settings (nightclubs, concerts, radio, and recording studios) with his own small ensembles, a string group, and Afro-Cuban bands, and as a guest soloist with local musicians when traveling without his own group. He visited Europe (1949 and 1950) and recorded slightly over half his surviving work. Though still beset by problems associated with drugs and alcohol, he attracted a very large following in the jazz world, and enjoyed a measure of financial success.

In July 1951 Parker's New York cabaret license was revoked at the request of the narcotics squad: this banned him from nightclub employment in the city and forced him to adopt a more peripatetic life until the license was reinstated (probably in autumn 1953). Sporadically employed, badly in debt, and in failing physical and mental health, he twice attempted suicide in 1954 and voluntarily committed himself to Bellevue Hospital, New York. His last public engagement was on 5 March 1955 at Birdland, a New York nightclub named in his honor. He died seven days later in the Manhattan apartment of his friend the Baroness Pannonica de Koenigswarter, sister of Lord Rothschild.

2. Style. Parker was among the supremely creative improvisers in jazz, one whose performances, like Armstrong's before him, changed the nature of the music. The force and originality of his style was such that many listeners rejected his music as no longer part of the jazz tradition, and as other jazz musicians took up and elaborated his innovations the music sank to what was then its lowest ebb in popular acceptance. Only decades after his death did Parker shed the élite aura attached to him by fellow musicians and admiring jazz fans and begin to assume a classical status in the popular imagination.

Although Parker was an innovator, his music is rooted firmly in tradition. Like the Kansas City music he heard when young, Parker's repertory was built on a very limited number of models: the 12-bar blues, a number of popular songs, several jazz standards, and newly invented jazz melodies using the underlying harmonies of popular songs. This last-named category and blues account for about half of the pieces he recorded. Although the device of composing new melodic themes to borrowed chord progressions was not new to jazz, bop musicians of the 1940s employed this technique much more extensively, partly for financial reasons (to avoid paying copyright royalties) and partly to frighten the uninitiated (who could not always recognize the underlying chord patterns), but also to invent themes that were more consistent with the new jazz style than the original melodies. Thus, by restricting himself to a few harmonic sources, Parker was able to improvise over a few familiar patterns, against which he constantly tested his ingenuity and powers of imagination. A number of Parker's newly composed melodic themes (based on existing harmonic and metric structures) themselves became jazz standards, among them *Anthropology* (based on the chord progressions of George Gershwin's *I got rhythm*, and written in collaboration with Gillespie), *Now's the Time* (blues), *Ornithology* (based on Morgan Lewis's *How High the Moon*, probably written in collaboration with Little Benny Harris, and incorporating a melodic phrase improvised by Parker on Jay McShann's *Jumpin' the Blues* in 1942), and *Scrapple from the Apple* (the *a* section from *I got rhythm* and the bridge from Fats Waller's *Honeysuckle Rose*).

Parker's outstanding achievement was not his composition but his brilliant improvisation. His improvised line combined drive and a complex organization of pitch and rhythm with a clarity rarely achieved by earlier soloists. In contrast to the rich timbres of Johnny Hodges and Benny Carter, the two most important predecessors on his instrument, Parker developed a penetrating tone with a slow, narrow vibrato. This suited the aggressive nature of the new music, and allowed him to concentrate on line and rhythm. Parker's improvisations usually ignore the original melody, being based instead on its harmonic structure. Melodic ornamentation or paraphrase occasionally occurs, but characteristically these are reserved for thematic statements of popular melodies in the opening or closing chorus (ex.1). However, his use of rhythm and pitch is sometimes subtly linked to the pulse and the chord progressions of the original. In *Groovin' High* (ex.2, opposite) Parker maintained the prominent descending 3rds of Dizzy Gillespie's theme, but distorted them by inversion and elision (bar 1), compression (bar 5), and displacement (bar 10), the last two being ornamented as well. Other portions of the solo (bars 4, 7–8, 11–15) likewise follow the theme in pitch and contour, with bar 12 reducing the corresponding bar of the theme at the same time that it foreshadows the broken chords of the succeeding bar. In contrast to Gillespie's theme, Parker's solo breaks the quarter-note pulse, steadfastly maintained by the accompanying double bass, into a succession of varied and discontinuous subdivisions; this rhythmic variety is one of the foremost features of his style. The pulse, meter, and harmonic rhythm are further obscured by syncopation and the persistently contrasting accents and phrase lengths.

Ex.1 Parker's opening thematic statement on *Out of Nowhere* (1948, Le Jazz Cool 102); transcr. J. Patrick

Ex.3 *Klactoveedsedstene* (1947, Dial 1040); transcr. J. Patrick

Parker's line typically includes pitches outside the given harmony: in addition to those produced by passing notes, suspensions, and other familiar devices, these result from free use of chord extensions beyond the 7th (particularly the flatted 9th and raised 11th), chromatic interpolations suggesting passing chords, the interchange of triads with others on the same root, and the anticipation or prolongation of chords within the given progression. Despite this harmonic complexity, Parker's best work has a clear and coherent line. Sometimes this is achieved by motivic development, as in the first ten bars of his solo on *Klactoveedsedstene* (ex.3), based on the chord progressions of Juan Tizol's *Perdido*. This passage is constructed almost entirely of three very short ideas, developed and combined (bars 4 and 8), with silences of subtly varied length throughout.

Parker most often used a technique of improvisation known in musicology as the *cento* (or patchwork) method, where the performer draws from a corpus of formulae and arranges them into ever-new patterns. This aspect of Parker's art has been exhaustively investigated by Owens (*Charlie Parker*, 1974), who codified Parker's improvisational work according to about 100 formulae. Many of these are specific to certain keys (where they may be easier to finger) or to particular pieces. Some occur in earlier swing music, particularly in the work of Lester Young, but others originated with Parker himself, and later became common property among musicians working in the bop style. Ex.4 shows a few of Parker's favorite and most characteristic formulae. Although it is based on a limited number of such formulae, Parker's work is neither haphazard nor "formulaic" in a restricted sense: the arrangement of the formulae was subject to constant variation and redisposition, and his performances of a piece were never identical. The overriding criterion was always the coherence and expressiveness of the musical line.

Ex.4 Some characteristic Parker formulae

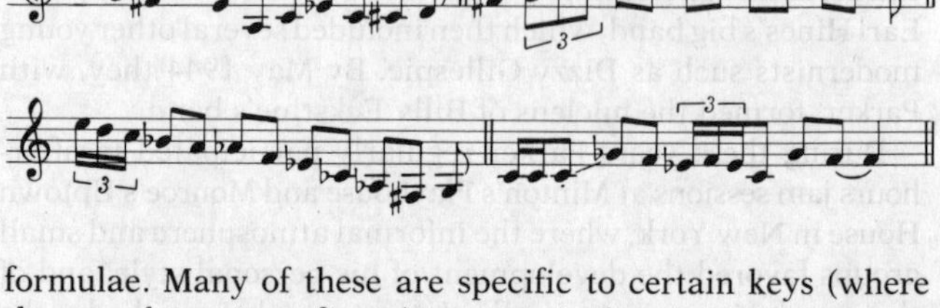

Closely related to this "formulaic" approach is Parker's use of musical quotations. Probably no jazz musician before him was as fond of this device, or as wide-ranging in his choice of material, as Parker, particularly in private performances in a relaxed atmosphere. His improvisations contain snatches of melody from Wagner, Bizet, and Stravinsky; from popular songs and light classics; from earlier jazz performances such as Armstrong's *West End Blues;* and even quotations from his own jazz compositions. He retained this device throughout his career, and it is another measure of his authority in jazz that witty quotations became characteristic of the bop style as a whole.

3. INFLUENCE. Although Parker was not solely responsible for the development of the bop style, he was its most important representative and a source of inspiration to all musicians who took part in its early growth. His influence was not limited to performers on his own instrument: his lines, rhythmic devices, and favorite motifs were transferred to instruments other than reeds, such as the trombone, vibraphone, piano, and guitar, and many innovations of bop drummers were made in response to the increased rhythmic complexity of his music.

Parker's influence was immediate and intense. His most famous early solos were learned note-for-note by thousands of aspiring young bop musicians on all instruments; as early as 1948 published transcriptions of them were available for study purposes. Some were even given texts by bop singers and performed as independent pieces. Parker's impact was naturally strongest on alto saxophonists such as Sonny Stitt, Cannonball Adderley, Phil Woods, and many others; only Lee Konitz and West Coast musicians such as Paul Desmond managed to create viable independent styles on alto saxophone. Despite the differences in timbre and mobility of the lower-pitched, bulkier instrument, many tenor saxophonists also came under Parker's sway, most notably Sonny Rollins and John Coltrane. Only in the early 1960s did Parker's influence gradually wane as the modal style led to the abandonment of bop's formulaic approach and the smoothing out of its erratic rhythms, and the free-jazz style dispensed with preset harmonic patterns; nor did Parker's music play a role in the emergence of jazz-rock in the early 1970s. Nevertheless, his work remained available on disc in more or less complete reissue series, and recordings of his performances were discovered on private tapes, matrices, or radio recordings, and issued posthumously.

With the revival of bop in the mid-1970s Parker's music once again became a vital force in the evolution and teaching of jazz. The Fine Arts Library at the University of Texas, Austin, holds the world's largest collection of recordings by Parker, and hundreds of his solos are now available to the student in published transcriptions. The group Supersax, based in Los Angeles, achieved some popular success playing Parker's solos in harmonized arrangements for saxophone chorus. His work has been the subject of several university dissertations. Although the evanescent, hieratic, and emotionally disturbing nature of Parker's music precludes popularity on a par with that of Armstrong or Ellington, his place alongside them as a creative force in jazz history is assured.

Oral history material in *TxU*.

See also BLUES, §11; IMPROVISATION, §§4(iii), 5(ii), and ex.2; JAZZ (i), §§V, 2, 3, and fig.5; and SAXOPHONE, esp. §3.

SELECTED RECORDINGS

EARLY STYLE

As sideman with J. McShann: on C. Parker: *First Recordings!* (1940–45, Onyx 221), Lady be Good (1940); Swingmatism (1941, Decca 8570); The Jumpin' Blues (1942, Decca 4418); Sepian Bounce (1942, Decca 4387)

Others: on C. Parker: *First Recordings!* (1940–45, Onyx 221), [no leader]: Cherokee (1942 or 1943); first issued on *Birth of the Bebop* (Stash 260), Boogie Woogie, Embraceable You, Indiana, Sweet Georgia Brown, Three Guesses (1943)

MATURE STYLE

As sideman: T. Grimes: Tiny's Tempo (1944, Savoy 526); Red Cross (1944, Savoy 532); D. Gillespie: Groovin' High (1945, Guild 1001); Dizzy Atmosphere (1945, Musi. 488); Shaw 'Nuff (1945, Guild 1002); Salt Peanuts/Hot House (1945, Guild 1003); R. Norvo: Slam Slam Blues (1945, Dial 1045); C. Thompson: 20th-century Blues/The Street Beat (1945, Apollo 759)

As leader (all recorded for Savoy): Billie's Bounce/Now's the Time (1945, 573); Thriving from a Riff (1945, 903); Koko (1945, 597); Donna Lee (1947, 652); Chasin' the Bird (1947, 977); Cheryl (1947, 952); Bluebird (1948, 961); Klaunstance (1948, 967); Barbados (1948, 936); Ah-leu-cha (1948, 939); Parker's Mood (1948, 936); Perhaps (1948, 938)

As leader (all recorded for Dial): Moose the Mooche/Yardbird Suite (1946, 1003); Ornithology/A Night in Tunisia (1946, 1002); Lover Man (1946, 1007); Cool Blues (1947, 1015); Relaxin' at Camarillo (1947, 1012); Carvin' the Bird (1947, 1013); Dexterity (1947, 1032); Embraceable you (1947, 1024); Klactoveedsedstene (1947, 1040); Scrapple from the Apple (1947, 1021); Crazeology (1947, 1034)

As leader (all recorded for Mercury/Clef unless otherwise indicated): The Closer (1949, Mer. 35013); Bloomdido (1950, 11058); An Oscar for Treadwell (1950, 10082); Relaxin' with Lee (1950, 11076); Au Privave (1951, 11087); Charlie Parker (1951–3, Clef 287) [EP], incl. Blues for Alice (1951); Swedish Schnapps (1951, 11103); Chi Chi (1953, Clef 89138)

Others: first issued on *Charlie Parker in Historical Recordings,* ii (1948–50, Le Jazz Cool 102), Out of Nowhere (1948); on *Charlie Parker and the Swedish*

Ex.2 Parker's improvisation on D. Gillespie, *Groovin' High* (1945, Guild 1001); transcr. J. Patrick

2. Charlie Parker and Dizzy Gillespie at Birdland, New York, 1951: (left to right) Tommy Potter (double bass), Parker (alto saxophone), Gillespie (trumpet), and John Coltrane (tenor saxophone)

All Stars (1950, Sonet 27), Anthropology; Jazz at Massey Hall: *Quintet of the Year* (1953, Debut 2, 4), incl. All the Things you Are, Perdido, Salt Peanuts

TRANSCRIPTIONS

[M. Feldman, ed.]: *Charles Parker's Bebop for Alto Sax: 4 Solos* (New York, 1948)

P. Pinkerton, ed.: *Charlie Parker: Nine Solos Transcribed from Historic Recordings* (New York, 1961)

W. D. Stuart: *Famous Transcribed Recorded Jazz Solos: Charlie "Bird" Parker* (New York, 1961)

Charlie Parker: Sketch Orks, Designed for Small Groups (New York, 1967)

T. Owens: *Charlie Parker: Techniques of Improvisation*, ii (diss., UCLA, 1974) [190 pieces]

S. Watanabe, ed.: *Jazz Improvisation: Transcriptions of Charlie Parker's Great Alto Solos* (Tokyo, *c*1975) [25 pieces]

J. Aebersbold and K. Slone, eds.: *Charlie Parker Omnibook* (New York, 1978) [60 pieces]

A. White, ed.: *The Charlie Parker Collection: 308 Transcribed Alto Saxophone and Tenor Saxophone Solos* (Washington, 1978–9)

BIBLIOGRAPHY

DOCUMENTS AND SOURCES

N. Hentoff and R. Sanjek: *Charlie Parker* (New York, 1960) [list of compositions]

R. Reisner: *Bird: the Legend of Charlie Parker* (New York, 1962/*R*1975)

J. G. Jepsen: *A Discography of Charlie Parker* (Copenhagen, 1968)

T. Williams: "Charlie Parker Discography," *Discographical Forum* (Sept 1968–Sept 1970)

G. R. Davies: "Charlie Parker Chronology," *Discographical Forum*, nos.17–26 (1970–71)

D. Morgenstern and others: *Bird and Diz: a Bibliography* (New York, 1973)

P. Koster and D. M. Bakker: *Charlie Parker*, i: *1940–1947* (Alphen aan de Rijn, Netherlands, 1974); ii: *1948–1950* (Alphen aan de Rijn, 1975); iii: *1951–1954* (Alphen aan de Rijn, 1975); iv: *1940–1955* (Alphen aan de Rijn, 1976) [addns and corrections] [discography]

C. Parker and F. Paudras: *To Bird with Love* (Antigny, France, 1981) [photographs]

BIOGRAPHICAL STUDIES

L. Feather: *Inside Be-bop* (New York, 1949/*R*1977 as *Inside Jazz*), 11

M. Levin and J. S. Wilson: "'No Bop Roots in Jazz': Parker," *DB*, xvi/17 (1949), 1; rev. as "The Chili Parlor Interview," *DB*, xxxii/6 (1965), 13

N. Shapiro and N. Hentoff, eds.: *Hear me Talkin' to ya: the Story of Jazz by the Men who Made it* (New York and London, 1955/*R*1966), esp. 312

M. Harrison: *Charlie Parker* (London, 1960); repr. in *Kings of Jazz*, ed. S. Green (New York, 1978)

R. G. Reisner: "Charlie Parker: a Biography in Interviews," *JR*, iii (1960), no.8, p.6; no.9, p.8; iv/1 (1961), 12

I. Gitler: "Charlie Parker and the Alto and Baritone Saxophonists," *Jazz Masters of the Forties* (New York, 1966/*R*1983 with discography)

J. Burns: "Bird in California," *JJ*, xxii/7 (1969), 10

D. Amram: "Bird in Washington," *JJ*, xxiii/8 (1970), 4

M. Williams: *The Jazz Tradition* (New York, 1970, rev. 2/1983)

R. Russell: *Jazz Style in Kansas City and the Southwest* (Berkeley, CA, Los Angeles, and London, 1971/*R*1983, rev. 2/1973)

——: *Bird Lives: the High Life and Hard Times of Charlie "Yardbird" Parker* (New York, 1973; Ger. trans., Vienna, 1985)

——: "West Coast Bop," *J&B*, iii/2 (1973), 9

N. T. Davis: *Charlie Parker's Kansas City Environment and its Effects on his Later Life* (diss., Wesleyan U., 1974)

J. Patrick: "Al Tinney, Monroe's Uptown House, and the Emergence of Modern Jazz in Harlem," *ARJS*, ii (1983), 150

B. Priestley: *Charlie Parker* (Tunbridge Wells, England, and New York, 1984) [incl. discography]

I. Gitler: *Swing to Bop: an Oral History of the Transition in Jazz in the 1940s* (New York, and Oxford, England, 1985)

G. Giddins: *Celebrating Bird: the Triumph of Charlie Parker* (New York, 1987)

ANALYTICAL STUDIES

A. Hodeir: *Hommes et problèmes du jazz, suivi de La religion du jazz* (Paris, 1954; Eng. trans., rev. Hodeir, as *Jazz: its Evolution and Essence*, New York, 1956/*R*1975), 99

A. Morgan: "Charlie Parker: the Dial Recordings," *JM*, i/7 (1955), 7

L. Feather: *The Book of Jazz: A Guide to the Entire Field* (New York, 1957, rev. 2/1965), 231

R. Russell: "The Evolutionary Position of Bop," *The Art of Jazz: Essays on the Nature and Development of Jazz*, ed. M. Williams (New York, 1959/*R*1979), 195

M. James: *Ten Modern Jazzmen: an Appraisal of the Recorded Work of Ten Modern Jazzmen* (London, 1960), 111

J. F. Mehegan: *Jazz Improvisation*, ii (New York, 1962), 101

D. Heckman: "Bird in Flight: Parker the Improviser," *DB*, xxxii/6 (1965), 22

J. Siddons: "Parker's Mood," *DB*, xxxii/6 (1965), 25

F. Tirro: "The Silent Theme Tradition in Jazz," *Musical Quarterly*, lii (1967), 313

D. Baker: "Charlie Parker's 'Now's the Time' Solo," *DB*, xxxviii/19 (1971), 32

O. Peterson: "Early Bird," *JJ*, xxiv/4 (1971), 34

R. Wang: "Jazz Circa 1945: a Confluence of Styles," *Musical Quarterly*, lix (1973), 531
T. Owens: "Applying the Melograph to 'Parker's Mood'," *Selected Reports in Ethnomusicology*, ii/1 (1974), 167
——: *Charlie Parker: Techniques of Improvisation* (diss., UCLA, 1974)
L. Koch: "Ornithology: a Study of Charlie Parker's Music," *JJS*, ii/1 (1974), 61; ii/12 (1975), 61
——: "A Numerical Listing of Charlie Parker's Recordings," *JJS*, ii/2 (1975), 86
J. Patrick: "Charlie Parker and Harmonic Sources of Bebop Composition: Thoughts on the Repertory of New Jazz in the 1940's," *JJS*, ii/2 (1975), 3
——: Liner notes, *Charlie Parker: the Complete Savoy Studio Recordings* (Savoy 5501, 1978)
T. Hirschmann: *Untersuchungen zu den Kompositionen von Charlie Parker* (diss., U. of Mainz, Germany, 1982)

OTHER STUDIES

DB, xxxii/6 (1965) [Parker issue]
J. Patrick: "The Uses of Jazz Discography," *Notes*, xxix (1972–3), 17
——: "Discography as a Tool for Musical Research and Vice Versa," *JJS*, i/1 (1973), 65
——: "Musical Sources for the History of Jazz," *Black Perspective in Music*, iv (1976), 46
Coda, no.181 (1981) [Parker issue]
B. Priestley and others: "Charlie Parker: Thirty 'Bird' Years Away," *The Wire*, no.13 (1985), 25

JAMES PATRICK

Parker, Erik (*b* Århus, Denmark, 13 July 1918). Danish trumpeter. He grew up in Copenhagen and became a leading jazz soloist, playing with Svend Asmussen (1938) and Leo Mathisen (1939–45); he made many recordings with Mathisen (including *I don't want to walk without you, baby*, 1944, Tono Z18014) and others. Later he worked as a club manager, as an actor (1945–51), and as a trumpet teacher and restaurant manager in the Los Angeles area (from 1953).

ERIK WIEDEMANN

Parker, Evan (Shaw) (*b* Bristol, England, 5 April 1944). English tenor and soprano saxophonist. In the early 1960s he played in Birmingham with a quartet inspired by the work of John Coltrane. After moving to London in 1965 he became involved with the free-jazz movement, working with the Spontaneous Music Ensemble (1967–9). While with this group he met Derek Bailey, with whom he formed the Music Improvisation Company in 1968; he played with the group until 1971. From the late 1960s Parker was a member of Tony Oxley's Sextet. Like many of his colleagues, he found a sympathetic response to his playing in continental Europe, where he worked with Alex Schlippenbach's trio and quartet and the Globe Unity Orchestra (both from 1970). With Bailey and Oxley he founded Incus Records in 1970, which he and Bailey have continued to run into the 1980s. During the 1970s he worked with Chris McGregor's Brotherhood of Breath, Company (for illustration *see* Jazz (i), fig.9), and other ensembles with Bailey, and in duets with John Stevens and the drummer Paul Lytton (1971–6). He also began working as an unaccompanied soloist, and has continued to play in this way in the 1980s, developing an idiosyncratic style in which he strives for complete spontaneity.

Although conventional scalar material forms the basis of Parker's vocabulary, his frequent and fluent use of such techniques as false fingering, multiphonics, and circular breathing identifies him as one of the most innovative and virtuoso saxophonists in Europe.

SELECTED RECORDINGS

(recorded for Incus unless otherwise indicated)

As unaccompanied soloist: *Saxophone Solos* (1975, 19); *Monoceros* (1978, 27); *Six of One* (1980, 39)
Duos: with P. Lytton: *Collective Calls (Urban)* (1972, 5); with D. Bailey: *The London Concert* (1975, 16)
As sideman: Spontaneous Music Ensemble: *Karyöbin* (1968, Isl. 9079); T. Oxley: *The Baptised Traveller* (1969, CBS 52664); Music Improvisation Company: *The Music Improvisation Company 1968–71* (1969–70, 17); D. Bailey: *Company 1* (1976, 21); C. McGregor: *Procession* (1977, Ogun 524); Globe Unity Orchestra: *Intergalactic Blow* (1982, Japo 60039); A. Schlippenbach: *Anticlockwise* (1982, FMP 1020)

BIBLIOGRAPHY

I. Carr: "Evan Parker," *Music Outside: Contemporary Jazz in Britain* (London, 1973), 68
P. Riley: "Incus Records," *Coda*, no.167 (1979), 3
B. Rusch: "Evan Parker: Interview," *Cadence*, v/4 (1979), 8
D. Bailey: *Improvisation: its Nature and Practice in Music* (Ashbourne, England, 1980)
T. Johnson: "Evan Parker's Free Sax," *VV* (19 Nov 1980), 82
G. Rouy: "Evan Parker: le message des anches," *Jm*, no.282 (1980), 22; contd as "Evan Parker d'une musique à l'autre," no.284 (1980), 32
G. Cerutti and R. Bergerone: *Discographie: Evan Parker* (Sierre, Switzerland, n.d. [?1981]; rev. and enlarged 2/n.d. [?1985] as *Evan Parker Discography (on Records and Cassettes), 1968–1983*)
B. Noglik: "Evan Parker," *Jazzwerkstatt international* (Berlin, 1981), 9 [incl. interview, discography]
B. McRae: "Evan Parker: Moving Forward with Tradition," *JJI*, xxxviii/1 (1985), 10
P. Keegan: "Evan Parker: the Breath and Breadth of the Saxophone," *DB*, liv/4 (1987), 26 [incl. discography]

MARK GILBERT

Parker, Frank (*b* New Orleans, 18 Aug 1919). Drummer. He first played in the band led by the trumpeter Kid Clayton, then in 1941 moved to the West Coast and worked with, among others, Horace Henderson. By 1948 he was back in New Orleans, where he played with the rhythm-and-blues singer and pianist Fats Domino and the trumpeter Joe Phillips. In the 1950s Parker performed with several rhythm-and-blues groups, and in 1958 he toured with Ray Charles. He spent a further period in California from 1959 to 1970, but thereafter he worked in his home town with such musicians as the trumpeters Wallace Davenport, Thomas Jefferson, and Kid Sheik Colar; he also played with his wife, the pianist and singer Lavergne Smith (1975–9). From 1980 he has worked regularly at Preservation Hall and has made several tours of the USA and Europe with the band under the leadership of Percy Humphrey. Parker is a solid drummer who is capable of playing traditional music as well as in more modern styles; in 1981 he recorded an album, *Shake it & Break it* (Nola 22), with the clarinetist Michael White.

BIBLIOGRAPHY

M. Joly: "Frank Parker: Beating my Way through the World," *Fn*, xv/1 (1983), 15
D. Dudine: "Portraits: Preservation Hall's Frank Parker," *MD*, x/12 (1986), 34

MARCEL JOLY

Parker, Johnny [John] (*b* Beckenham, England, 6 Nov 1929). English pianist. He was largely self-taught, and worked with Mick Mulligan in 1950–51 before joining Humphrey Lyttelton's band. With this ensemble he performed, broadcast, made recordings (including *Bad Penny Blues*, 1956, Parl. R4184), and accompanied Sidney Bechet and Eddie Condon; he also played in the supporting band to Louis Armstrong's All Stars (1956). After leaving Lyttelton he played with the trombonist Graham Stewart, recording in Denmark in 1958. During the following decade Parker was active only intermittently as a musician, but worked occasionally with Monty Sunshine, Alexis Korner (1962–3), and others. In 1968 he joined Kenny Ball's Jazzmen, initially on a temporary basis, and remained with the group for ten years. Thereafter he worked as a freelance and led his own bands. His performances with such American musicians as Wild Bill Davison and Buddy Tate in the 1980s have confirmed his reputation as one of Britain's leading stride pianists.

He has written several pieces for piano, one of which, *Feline Stomp*, he recorded in 1958 (Sto. 366 [EP]). (G. Bielderman: *Johnny Parker Discography*, Zwolle, Netherlands, 1987)

SALLY-ANN WORSFOLD

Parker, Knocky [John W., Jr.] (*b* Palmer, TX, 8 Aug 1918; *d* Los Angeles, 3 Sept 1986). Pianist. He began his career playing in Texas with western swing bands, including the Wanderers (with whom he played and recorded in 1935) and the Light Crust Doughboys (1937–9). After his military service in World War II Parker worked with Zutty Singleton and Albert Nicholas. He gained a PhD in American studies from the University of Kentucky, and thereafter he taught at Kentucky Wesleyan College and the University of South Florida. During the same period he performed and recorded with Omer Simeon, Doc Evans (intermittently, 1954–65), Tony Parenti, the singer Carol Leigh, and others. In addition to piano, Parker played harpsichord and celeste. He made the first recordings of the majority of the piano rags of Scott Joplin and James Scott; with these he helped to familiarize specialist audiences with much little-known music. In 1986 a recording he made with Joe Turner (ii) was nominated for a Grammy Award.

Oral history material in *LNT*.

SELECTED RECORDINGS

As unaccompanied soloist: *The Complete Piano Works of Scott Joplin* (c1960, Audiophile 71-2); *The Complete Piano Works of James Scott* (c1962, Audiophile 76-7); *Golden Treasury of Ragtime* (c1968, Audiophile 89-92); *Complete Piano Works of Jelly Roll Morton* (c1970, Audiophile 102-5)

As sideman: *Big Joe Turner with Knocky Parker and his Houserockers* (1983, Slnd 13)

BIBLIOGRAPHY

ChiltonW; *FeatherE*

T. Cundall: "'The Strenuous Life': Knocky Parker," *JJ*, v/9 (1952), 1

J. Daugherty: "Ragtime Revival Makes Sense to Knocky," *St. Petersburg Times* (6 Nov 1974)

Obituary, R. Rhodes and T. Wyndham, *MR*, xiii/12 (1986), 5

D. Phillips and L. Phillips: "Knocky Parker, Professor of Blues Piano," *Grit* (22 June 1986), 3

JOHN EDWARD HASSE

Parker, Leo (*b* Washington, 18 April 1925; *d* New York, 11 Feb 1962). Baritone saxophonist. He first recorded on alto saxophone with Coleman Hawkins in 1944. He changed to baritone saxophone during his tenure with Billy Eckstine's orchestra (1944–5, 1946) and became known as one of the finest performers in the bop style on that instrument, modeling his playing on that of Charlie Parker. He worked on 52nd Street with a small group led by Dizzy Gillespie in 1946, and performed briefly in Gillespie's big band. His recording with Sir Charles Thompson of *Mad Lad* (1947), which gained him wider public attention, demonstrates a style of improvisation combining elements of bop with an extroverted rhythm-and-blues idiom. In 1947 Parker joined the group led by Illinois Jacquet and worked intermittently with Jacquet into the 1950s. He recorded two albums as a leader shortly before his death.

SELECTED RECORDINGS

As leader: Wee Dot (1947, Savoy 950); *Leo Parker's All Stars* (1948, Savoy 9009), incl. Sweet Talkin' Leo; *Let me Tell you 'bout it* (1961, BN 84087)

As sideman: C. Hawkins: Woody 'n You (1944, Apollo 751); I. Jacquet: Jivin' with Jack the Bellboy (1947, Ala. 179); F. Navarro: Fat Girl (1947, Savoy 906); I. Jacquet: Robbins' Nest (1947, Apollo 769); C. Thompson: Mad Lad (1947, Apollo 773); D. Gordon: Settin' the Pace (1947, Savoy 913)

BIBLIOGRAPHY

L. Feather: *Inside Be-bop* (New York, 1949/R1977 as *Inside Jazz*)

J. Burns: "Leo Parker," *JJ*, xviii/4 (1965), 16

I. Gitler: *Jazz Masters of the Forties* (New York, n.d. [?1966]/R1983 with discography), 38

D. Stewart: "The Forgotten Ones: Leo Parker," *JJI*, xxxviii/3 (1985), 12

SCOTT DeVEAUX

Parlan, Horace (Louis) (*b* Pittsburgh, 19 Jan 1931). Pianist. He studied piano from the age of 12 and after suffering from polio developed a strong left-hand technique. He played in Pittsburgh (1952–7) and briefly with Sonny Stitt in Washington, then performed and recorded with Charles Mingus's Jazz Workshop (1957–9), Lou Donaldson (1959–60), the Playhouse Four with Booker Ervin, George Tucker, and Al Harewood (1960–61), a quintet led by Eddie "Lockjaw" Davis and Johnny Griffin (1961–2), and Roland Kirk (1963–6). In 1973 he moved to Copenhagen, where he recorded regularly for Steeplechase with Dexter Gordon (1975), Red Mitchell (1976), Frank Foster (1982), and Michal Urbaniak (1984), and as a leader. Parlan cites Ahmad Jamal, Bud Powell, and James Miller as having most strongly influenced his style, and emphasizes the importance of his association with Mingus.

SELECTED RECORDINGS

As unaccompanied soloist: *Musically yours* (1979, Ste. 1141)

Duos with A. Shepp: *Trouble in Mind* (1980, Ste. 1139)

As leader: *Us Three* (1960, BN 4037); *Arrival* (1973, Ste. 1012); *No Blues* (1975, Ste. 1056); *Frank-ly Speaking* (1977, Ste. 1076)

As sideman: C. Mingus: *Mingus Ah Um* (1959, Col. CL1370); B. Ervin: *That's it!* (1961, Can. 9014); S. Turrentine: *Up at Minton's* (1961, BN 4069-70); D. Gordon: *Doin' Allright* (1961, BN 84077); R. Kirk: *I Talk to the Spirits* (1964, Lml. 86008); D. Gordon: *Stable Mable* (1975, Ste. 1040)

BIBLIOGRAPHY

FeatherE; *Feather '60s*

D. Morgenstern: "Horace Parlan," *Jazz*, ii/4 (New York, 1963), 7

H. E. Philip and I. S. Petersen: "Horace Parlan," *Coda*, xi/3 (1973), 6

J. Jeremy: "Parlan: a Happy Exile," *MM*, xlix (27 April 1974), 24

PAUL RINZLER

Parlato, David (Charles) (*b* Los Angeles, 31 Oct 1945). Bass player. He performed and recorded with Don Ellis while attending Valley City (North Dakota) State College (1966–8). He was associated for several years with Paul Horn (1968–71) and the saxophonist Gil Melle (1969–74), but also played and recorded during this period with Warne Marsh and Frank Strazzeri (both 1969) and John Klemmer (1972–4), and played with Frank Zappa (1972), in a quintet with sitar, tablā, vibraphone, and keyboards (1973), and with Gábor Szabó (1974–5). His playing is heard to advantage on Ellis's *Electric Bath* (1967, Col. CS9585). (*Feather–Gitler '70s*)

Parlophone. Record company and label. The company was established in Britain after World War I as a subsidiary of the German company Lindström. The label became the British outlet for the catalogue of jazz and race recordings produced by Lindström's American affiliate Okeh; it retained this role after Lindström's company was acquired by Columbia International, Ltd., in October 1925, and also after Columbia's merger into EMI in March 1931. Parlophone's artists and repertory were supervised by Ted Sommerfield, and issues of jazz were initially made as part of the company's general popular-music catalogues. In November 1929, however, the New Rhythm Style Series was launched, specifically for jazz; this was superseded in May 1932 by the Second New Rhythm Style Series. From 1934 issue took place annually in a Super Rhythm Style Series; this continued into the 1950s. Although these discs bore catalogue numbers taken from the main sequence, they were distinguished by series numbers on the labels. At first repertory was drawn from Okeh, and after 1934 also from the American

Record Company and Brunswick, until rights to this material were lost in the 1950s.

From the mid-1930s Parlophone also became important for its British recordings, both of American expatriates such as Coleman Hawkins (1934) and Valaida Snow (1935–7), and of such British musicians as Harry Parry and Humphrey Lyttelton. EMI also used the label Parlophone (or, where linguistically more appropriate, Parlophon) in other territories, including Australia, Switzerland, Scandinavia, and Germany, issuing similar material in each country. In 1929 the Spanish company Parlophon made notable recordings of Sam Wooding and his Chocolate Kiddies when the group visited Barcelona. A Parlophone label was also used briefly in the USA (1929–32) to issue pseudonymously on the West Coast some 200 items drawn from Okeh's catalogue; these included versions without voice of songs previously issued with a vocal part.

In the 1950s Parlophone was used in Britain to put out recordings made by the American company King, but its importance as a jazz label declined from the mid-1960s. Nevertheless from that time an important series of chronological reissues was made on LPs of material made for Okeh before 1931, the rights to which EMI held until the copyrights expired.

BIBLIOGRAPHY

E. Jackson: *The Parlophone "Rhythm-Style" Series: the Complete List of Records up to and Including December, 1935, Arranged Alphabetically and Numerically Together with the Personnels of the Orchestras and Index to Artistes* (London, n.d. [?1936], rev. and enlarged 2/n.d. [1941], rev. and enlarged 3/n.d. [1942], rev. and enlarged 4/n.d. [1944], rev. and enlarged 5/n.d. [1946], rev. and enlarged 6/n.d. [1948], with various titles)

H. H. Lange: *Die Deutsche Jazz-Discographie: eine Geschichte des Jazz auf Schallplatten von 1902 bis 1955* (Berlin, 1955), 26

C. Ellis: "The Programming of Re-issue LPs," *Sv*, no.32 (1970), 44

B. Englund: "Sam Wooding's Parlophons," *Sv*, no.49 (1973), 13

B. Rust: *The American Record Label Book* (New Rochelle, NY, 1978), 212

P. Pelletier: "The Columbia and Parlophone Labels," *Record Information*, no.5 (1985), 6

B. Englund: "A Glimpse into the Past: Parlophon B12500 Series," *Sv*, no.124 (1986), 132

Parnell, Jack (*b* London, 6 Aug 1923). English drummer. He studied piano as a child and took up drums at the age of 14. He played and recorded with Buddy Featherstonhaugh in the RAF (1943–4), led a group with Vic Lewis (1944–5), and recorded with Kenny Baker (1946–7). From 1944 to 1951 he worked with Ted Heath's orchestra, then until 1955 led his own band, which at various times included Jimmy Deuchar, Ronnie Scott, Phil Seamen, Hank Shaw, and Joe Temperley; he may be heard to good effect in a drum duet with Seamen on *The Champ* (1952, Parl. R3607). After studying conducting (1956) Parnell led the Associated Television staff orchestra for more than 20 years. From the mid-1970s he played in the Best of British Jazz with Baker, the trombonist Don Lusher, and Betty Smith, and in the 1980s he worked at the Pizza Express in London, playing with, among others, Ruby Braff.

BIBLIOGRAPHY

FeatherE; *Feather–Gitler '70s*

J. Parnell: "I'm really only a mildly frustrated drummer," *Crescendo*, i/1 (1962), 16

L. Tomkins: "Looking back, and forward with Jack Parnell," *CI*, xiv/11 (1976), 20

NEVIL SKRIMSHIRE

Parrish, Avery (*b* Birmingham, AL, 24 Jan 1917; *d* New York, 10 Dec 1959). Pianist. He attended Alabama State Teachers College and was a member of the 'Bama State Collegians, which was directed by Erskine Hawkins. After the band performed in New York in 1934 Parrish chose to stay there to work professionally with Hawkins; among the recordings he made with the group was one of his own compositions, the blues solo *After Hours* (1940, Bb 10879), which became extremely popular. After leaving Hawkins in 1941 Parrish worked in California until the following year, when injuries sustained in a fight left him partly paralyzed. (*ChiltonW*; *FeatherE*)

Parry, Harry (*b* Bangor, Wales, 1912; *d* London, 12 Oct 1956). Welsh clarinetist and bandleader. He was playing cornet and tenor horn in a brass band by the age of ten; thereafter he tried drums and violin before taking up clarinet and alto saxophone in 1927. Five years later he moved to London, where he worked with dance bands led by the pianist Percival Mackey and others before forming his own sextet. A residency at the St. Regis Hotel in 1940 led to his being selected by the BBC as the resident leader for a series of radio programs, "Radio Rhythm Club." With his sextet, which included George Shearing and the singer Doreen Villiers, he later made more than a hundred recordings for Parlophone, including *Blues for Eight/Thrust and Parry* (1942, R2832). After World War II he began working in television and radio as a compère and disc jockey. Parry's fluent, technically proficient playing was often likened to that of Benny Goodman in the 1940s.

CLARRIE HENLEY

Pasquall, Jerome Don (*b* Fulton, KY, 20 Sept 1902; *d* 18 Oct 1971). Saxophonist and clarinetist. In 1903 his family moved to St. Louis. He played mellophone in brass bands as a child and in his teens, before changing to clarinet. He worked with Ed Allen (around 1919) then in 1921 played with Charlie Creath and with Fate Marable on the Mississippi riverboats; later that year he began studying at the American Conservatory in Chicago, where he played and recorded with Doc Cook's Dreamland Orchestra for two years, mainly on tenor saxophone. He studied at the New England Conservatory (to 1927), then worked as the lead alto saxophonist with Fletcher Henderson (1927–8). His solo soprano saxophone playing may be heard on *There's a rickety rackety shack* (1927, Ban. 6129). He led his own band in Chicago (after 1928) and worked with Freddie Keppard, Dave Peyton (1930), Jabbo Smith (1931), Tiny Parham (1931–2), Fess Williams, and Eddie South. He re-joined Henderson in 1936 and spent several years with Noble Sissle (1937–44) before settling in New York, where he continued to work as a freelance musician.

BIBLIOGRAPHY

F. Driggs and T. Hagert: "Jerome Don Pasquall," *JJ*, xvii (1964), no.4, p.22; no.5, p.19

W. C. Allen: *Hendersonia: the Music of Fletcher Henderson and his Musicians: a Bio-discography* (Highland Park, NJ, 1973)

T. J. Hennessey: "The Black Chicago Establishment 1919–1930," *JJS*, ii/1 (1974), 15–45

based on *ChiltonW*

Pass, Joe [Passalaqua, Joseph Anthony Jacobi] (*b* New Brunswick, NJ, 13 Jan 1929). Guitarist. Soon after beginning his career he began to take drugs and spent many years in prisons, hospitals, and halfway houses. In 1961, together with other jazz musicians in Synanon, a self-help organization for drug addicts, he issued a collective album which attracted some critical attention to his easy-going manner and astounding technical prowess. He then worked for several years in studios in Los Angeles but remained more or less in obscurity until 1973, when he was retained for the Pablo label and recorded his first solo album, *Virtuoso*. The success of this album catapulted him to fame and he immediately began to dominate jazz popularity polls for his instrument. From that time on he was greatly in demand for concerts, festivals, and recording sessions, notably as an accompanist to Ella Fitzgerald and Sarah Vaughan, and as a member of Oscar Peterson's groups. By the 1980s he was probably the most widely recorded jazz guitarist, making many albums as an unaccompanied soloist, in duos, and as a sideman in Count Basie's reconstituted "Kansas City" ensembles.

Pass is one of the few jazz guitarists to have mastered the technique of finger picking, which allows him to give fully satisfying performances as an unaccompanied soloist. Like Art Tatum, with whom he is often compared because of his comprehensive grasp of instrumental technique, Pass is heard to best advantage in his elaborate solo paraphrases of popular songs, where he reveals a refined sense of harmony and an uncommonly wide array of accompaniment textures. The published collections of transcriptions of his performances include *Intercontinental* (Brookline, MA, 1979; 10 pieces), *Portraits of Duke Ellington* (Brookline, 1981; 9 pieces), and *Virtuoso* (Brookline, 1981; 12 pieces).

SELECTED RECORDINGS

(all recorded for Pablo unless otherwise indicated)

As unaccompanied soloist: *Virtuoso* (1973, 2310708); *At the Montreux Jazz Festival* (1975, 2310752); *Virtuoso*, ii (1976, 2310788); *Virtuoso*, iii (1977, 2310805); *I Remember Charlie Parker* (1979, PT 2312109)

Duos: with E. Fitzgerald: *Take Love Easy* (1973, 2310702); with O. Peterson: *Porgy & Bess* (1976, 2310779); with N.-H. Ørsted Pedersen: *Chops* (1978, 2310830); with Z. Sims: *Blues for Two* (1982, 2310879)

As leader: *Eximious* (1982, 2310877); *Whitestone* (1985, 2310912)

As sideman: Sounds of Synanon: *Sounds of Synanon* (1961, PJ 48); C. Basie: *Kansas City Six* (1981, 2310871)

BIBLIOGRAPHY

J. Tynan: "Joe Pass: Building a New Life," *DB*, xxx/17 (1963), 18

"Joe Pass Discography," *SJ*, xxix/6 (1975), 238

L. Underwood: "Joe Pass: Life on the Far Side of the Hour Glass," *DB*, xlii/5 (1975), 14

B. James: "Joe Pass: Interview," *JJ*, xxix (1976), no.5, p.12; no.6, p.24

J. Sievert: "Joe Pass," *The Guitar Player Book* (Saratoga, CA, and New York, 1978, 2/1979) [colln of previously pubd articles]

L. Underwood: "Joe Pass: Virtuoso Revisited," *DB*, xlv/7 (1978), 16

J. Ferguson: "Joe Pass: Reflections of a Jazz Virtuoso," *GP*, xviii/9 (1984), 51 [incl. discography]

T. Schneckloth: "Joe Pass on Guitar," *DB*, li/3 (1984), 21

J. Pass: "One on One with Joe Pass: Learn Solo Jazz from the Master," *GP*, xx/8 (1986), 78 [incl. discography]

J. BRADFORD ROBINSON

Jaco Pastorius playing at the Grande Parade du Jazz, Nice, France, 1983

Passport. German group, formed in 1970 by Klaus Doldinger; it was known as Passport from 1971. Its principal members in the mid-1970s were Doldinger, the keyboard player Kristian Schulze, the electric bass guitarist Wolfgang Schmid, and the drummer Curt Cress. The group was the first jazz-rock ensemble in Germany and in the 1970s its recordings had considerable success. In the middle of the decade it made annual tours of the USA and also toured South America. It reached a still larger audience in the 1980s by emphasizing simple melodies and dance rhythms rather than improvisation.

For recordings and bibliography *see* DOLDINGER, KLAUS.

WOLFRAM KNAUER

Pastor, Tony [Pestritto, Antonio] (*b* Middletown, CT, 26 Oct 1907; *d* Old Lyme, CT, 31 Oct 1969). Bandleader, singer, and saxophonist. He began his career as a sideman in the orchestras of John Cavallaro, Irving Aaronson, and Vincent Lopez, and was a tenor saxophone soloist and singer in that of Artie Shaw from 1936 until it disbanded in 1940. He then formed his own band, which included some of Shaw's former sidemen. Many of the arrangements played by this group were written by the guitarist Al Avola; others were contributed by Budd Johnson, Walter Fuller, and Ralph Flanagan. In the late 1940s he performed with Rosemary Clooney and her sister Betty. He disbanded his orchestra in 1959 and, with his two sons, formed a small group with which he performed at nightclubs until his retirement in 1968. Pastor acknowledged the strong influence of Louis Armstrong's vocal style on his own, which was throaty and somewhat gruff; a good example of his singing may be heard on Shaw's recording of *Indian Love Call* (1938).

SELECTED RECORDINGS

(recorded for Bluebird unless otherwise indicated)

As leader: Dance with a Dolly with a Hole in her Stocking (1940, B10582); Let's Do it (1940, B10902); Confessin' (1940, B11105); I Wonder, I Wonder, I Wonder (1947, Col. 37353)

As sideman with A. Shaw: Indian Love Call (1938, B7746); Rosalie (1939, B10126)

BIBLIOGRAPHY

G. T. Simon: *The Big Bands* (New York, 1967, rev. and enlarged 2/1971, rev. 3/1974, 4/1981)

C. Garrod: *Tony Pastor and his Orchestra* (Zephyrhills, FL, 1973, rev. 2/1986) [discography]

L. Walker: *The Big Band Almanac* (Hollywood, CA, 1978), 335

MARK TUCKER

Pastorius, Jaco [John Francis] (*b* Norristown, PA, 1 Dec 1951; *d* Fort Lauderdale, FL, 21 Sept 1987). Electric bass guitarist. He grew up in Fort Lauderdale, where he accompanied visiting rhythm-and-blues and pop musicians while still a teenager. By 1975 he had come to the attention of jazz musicians such as Pat Metheny, and in the following year he attracted widespread notice with his performances on the album *Heavy Weather* by Weather Report, with whom he had a long association (for illustration *see* ZAWINUL, JOE). From that time he was much in demand as a bass player and producer in a wide variety of settings. Unlike many jazz and rock bass guitarists, Pastorius used a fretless instrument, and played with immaculate intonation. Although sometimes faulted for his flamboyant stage personality and eclecticism, he won the admiration of jazz and rock bass players for his fleet technique and the imaginative fusion of styles in his solos. From 1980 to about 1983 he toured with his own group, Word of Mouth, with which he recorded in 1980 (together with many leading jazz musicians) and 1982 (as a big band). In 1983–4 he recorded an album with the drummer Brian Melvin. He died as a result of injuries sustained during a brawl at the Midnight Club in Fort Lauderdale.

SELECTED RECORDINGS

As leader: *Jaco Pastorius* (*c*1975, Epic 33949); *Word of Mouth* (1980, WB 3535); *Invitation* (1982, WB 3876)

As sideman: P. Metheny: *Bright Size Life* (1975, ECM 1073); Weather Report: *Heavy Weather* (1976, Col. PC34418); A. Mangelsdorff: *Trilogue* (1976, Pausa 7055); Joni Mitchell: *Hejira* (1976, Asy. 7E1087); Weather Report: *Night Passage* (*c*1980, Col. JC36793)

BIBLIOGRAPHY

J. E. Berendt: "Jaco Pastorius: the Human Sound on the Bass Guitar," *JF* [intl edn], no.48 (1977), 35

N. Tesser: "Jaco Pastorius: the Florida Flash," *DB*, xliv/2 (1977), 12

D. Roerich: "Jaco Pastorius: the Musician Interviewed," *Musician*, no.26 (1980), 38

C. Silvert: "Jaco Pastorius: the Word is Out," *DB*, xlviii/12 (1981), 17

B. Milkowski: "Jaco Pastorius: Bass Revolutionary," *GP*, xviii/8 (1984), 58 [incl. discography]

J. BRADFORD ROBINSON

Pathé(–Frères–Pathéphone). Recording company and record label. The company was established by the brothers Charles and Emile Pathé in France in 1894. Shortly thereafter it began manufacturing cylinders, and by 1906, when it started issuing vertical-cut discs (in various sizes up to 20 inches in diameter, and playing at 90 r.p.m.) it also had branches in Britain, Italy, and Russia. Cylinders were discontinued in 1914, but the discs (albeit by this time in standard sizes and playing at 80 r.p.m.) were manufactured into the 1920s, and remained extremely popular in France. Recordings made in Paris by Mitchell's Jazz Kings (1921–3) were issued in this form; lateral-cut records were not released in France until the mid-1920s.

In 1914 the company established an American branch, managed by Russell Hunting, which made notable recordings in New York of early jazz by the bands of Noble Sissle (1917–20) and James Reese Europe (1919). Lateral-cut discs, at first bearing the label Actuelle, later Pathé Actuelle, were introduced in the USA in September 1920 and in Britain twelve months later. A parallel series of vertical-cut issues was maintained until November 1925 in the USA, and later in some other territories. A subsidiary label, PERFECT, was established in 1922 to issue cheaper records in the USA. All the company's discs were made in a unique manner whereby the music was recorded onto vast master cylinders, then dubbed onto records of the required size and format.

Though not notable for the quantity of jazz it recorded, Pathé issued some items of excellent quality. These included material by Fletcher Henderson, and a series of recordings by white musicians based in New York; the series included important discs by the Original Memphis Five, and the Redheads, a group led by Red Nichols. The 7500 race series, which began in 1926, included most prominently the work of Rosa Henderson, Buddy Christian, the Dixie Jassers Washboard Band, and early material by Duke Ellington. The company also exchanged masters with Ajax and various members of the Plaza group.

In 1928, the American branch, by that time called the Pathé Phonograph and Record Corp., merged with the Cameo Record Corp.; the two companies pooled their repertory and maintained their labels. The following year the new organization merged with Plaza to form the AMERICAN RECORD COMPANY, and the label Pathé was dropped in March 1930. The European sections of the company, and Pathé Orient, Ltd., which traded in the Far East, were purchased in 1928 by Columbia International, Ltd. The label was terminated in Britain, but continued in France (where Sam Wooding's band was recorded in 1929) and elsewhere. Thereafter issue was sporadic, but remained widespread; jazz items were released on Pathé in China in the 1930s. From 1960 the French branch of EMI, trading as Pathé–Marconi–EMI, has used the label Pathé for reissues of early jazz.

BIBLIOGRAPHY

J. Godrich and R. M. W. Dixon: *Blues & Gospel Records, 1902–1942* (Hatch End, nr London, 1964, rev. 2/1969, rev. and enlarged 3/1982 as R. M. W. Dixon and J. Godrich: *Blues & Gospel Records, 1902–1943*), 22

R. M. W. Dixon and J. Godrich: *Recording the Blues* (London, 1970), 10, 67

B. Rust: *The American Record Label Book* (New Rochelle, NY, 1978), 236

A. Badrock: *English Pathé Perfect: a Catalogue and History* (Hayes, England, 1983)

Patrick. Pseudonym of GUY PAQUINET.

Patrick, Pat [Laurdine] (*b* Nov 1929). Saxophonist. As a child he studied piano and drums and took trumpet lessons from his father and Clark Terry; he met John Gilmore, Clifford Jordan, and Richard Davis at Du Sable High School in Chicago. He played with Sun Ra at intervals from 1954 into the 1980s, and with James Moody, John Coltrane, Cootie Williams, and Duke Ellington; in 1970 he was a member of Thelonious Monk's quartet and later he played with the Jazz Composer's Orchestra under Clifford Thornton and Grachan Moncur III. Patrick is a well-schooled, versatile soloist and ensemble player and made an important contribution to Sun Ra's music. Besides his principal instrument, which is baritone saxophone, he plays flutes, bass, and percussion.

Oral history material in *NjR*.

SELECTED RECORDINGS

As sideman with Sun Ra: *Super Sonic Sounds* (1956, Saturn 216); *Atlantis* (1960, Saturn 507); *Live at Montreux* (1976, IC 1039)

As sideman with others: J. Coltrane: *Africa/Brass* (1961, Imp. 6); C. Thornton: *The Gardens of Harlem* (1974, JCOA 1008); G. Moncur III: *Echoes of Prayer* (1974, JCOA 1009)

BIBLIOGRAPHY

T. Fiofori: "Pat's Rhythm Thing," *MM*, xlvi (10 April 1971), 28

M. Cullaz: "Pat Patrick," *Jh*, no.330 (1976), 34

V. Wilmer: *As Serious as your Life: the Story of the New Jazz* (London, 1977, rev. 1980)

P. Schaap: "Pat Patrick," *Jm*, no.306 (1982), 18

ED HAZELL

Patterson, Don(ald B.) [Duck] (*b* Columbus, OH, 22 July 1936; *d* Philadelphia, 10 Feb 1988). Organist. He played piano as a youth, but decided to change to Hammond organ after hearing Jimmy Smith, and made his professional début as an organist in 1959. From that date he performed with such musicians as Sonny Stitt (at intervals, 1962–9), Eddie "Lockjaw" Davis (1963), Gene Ammons, and Wes Montgomery, and recorded with Ammons (1962), Stitt (1964–5, 1968, 1971), and Eric Kloss (1965–6). During the 1960s he played frequently in a duo with Billy James, and in the 1960s and 1970s made a number of recordings as a leader. In 1981 he first played with Al Grey, with whom he formed a lasting association. Patterson's style is highly individual, and his early training as a pianist profoundly influenced his approach to the organ.

SELECTED RECORDINGS

As leader: *Four Dimensions* (1967, Prst. 7533); *The Return of Don Patterson* (1972, Muse 5005); *Why Not?* (1978, Muse 5148)

As sideman: E. Kloss: *Introducing Eric Kloss* (1965, Prst. 7442)

BIBLIOGRAPHY

Feather '60s

PAUL RINZLER

Patterson, (Anna-)Ottilie (*b* Comber, Ireland, 31 Jan 1932). Irish singer. She began singing the blues during her early teens, and worked with local bands before moving to England in 1955. Thereafter she performed, recorded, and participated in broadcasts with Chris Barber, who was then her husband, for some 15 years (for illustration *see* BARBER, CHRIS). Her early style may be heard to advantage on *I hate a man like you/Reckless Blues* (1955, Decca DFE6303), and her later work is well represented by *Squeeze me* and *Too Many Drivers* from the album *Chris Barber at the London Palladium* (1961, Col. 33SX1436). Patterson began incorporating Irish folk songs into her repertory in the late 1950s, and has also written the music to texts by Shakespeare and the poet Louis MacNeice. Illness forced her to retire in the 1970s, but she has resumed performing with Barber on a part-time basis in the 1980s.

BIBLIOGRAPHY

FeatherE

B. Matthew: *Trad Mad* (London, 1962)

SALLY-ANN WORSFOLD

Patton, Big John (*b* Kansas City, MO, 12 July 1935). Organist. He played piano from 1948 and at the start of his career toured with the rock-and-roll singer Lloyd Price (1954–9). He then took up the Hammond organ and made his first recordings, with Lou Donaldson (1962–4), Johnny Griffin and Harold Vick (both 1963), Grant Green (1963, 1967), and Clifford Jordan (1966). From 1963 to 1969 he led his own soul-jazz trio, which included, among others, Clifford Jarvis and James "Blood" Ulmer; the group recorded with such guest soloists as Vick, Junior Cook, Bobby Hutcherson, Blue Mitchell, and Richard Williams. Patton's playing is well represented by *The Way I Feel* (1964, BN 84174). He later recorded with Johnny Lytle (1977) and again as a leader, making the album *Soul Connection* (Nilva 3406) with a quintet in 1983.

BIBLIOGRAPHY

Feather '60s

B. Priestley: "Patton, 'Big' John," in I. Carr, D. Fairweather, and B. Priestley: *Jazz: the Essential Companion* (London, 1987)

Pauer, Fritz (*b* Vienna, 14 Oct 1943). Austrian pianist, composer, and leader. He played with Hans Koller from 1960 to 1962, and then, leading his own groups, accompanied Dexter Gordon, Don Byas, Booker Ervin, Art Farmer, and other American jazzmen in clubs in Berlin (1962–8). In 1966 he recorded with Friedrich Gulda in Vienna and with Annie Ross in Frankfurt am Main, Germany. He taught jazz at the conservatory in Vienna in 1968; two years later he joined the dance orchestra of Österreichischer Rundfunk, with which he recorded in 1973 and 1979. He made recordings as a leader (from 1970, including *Fritz Pauer Trio*, 1970, MPS 15268), again with Gulda (1971), and with Klaus Weiss (1971–2), Peter Herbolzheimer (1979), and Koller (1980), as well as accompanying Farmer on four albums (1970–81). After spending a year in Peru (1985–6) he settled in Switzerland and resumed playing.

BIBLIOGRAPHY

Feather–Gitler '70s

H. Weber: "Plattentest mit Fritz Pauer," *JP*, xxvii/6 (1978), 12

Paul, Emanuel (*b* New Orleans, 2 Feb 1904; *d* New Orleans, 23 May 1988). Tenor saxophonist. He first played violin when he was 18, then, after working as a banjoist in the 1920s, took up saxophone. From 1940 he played with the Eureka Brass Band (for illustration *see* BRASS BAND, fig.2), and was largely responsible for initiating the role of the tenor saxophone in place of the baritone horn in such ensembles. His brass-band style was arpeggio based; he often moved in octaves with the brass bass and broke into eighth-notes on final choruses. This is exemplified by *Jazz at Preservation Hall*, i: *The Eureka Brass Band of New Orleans* (1962, Atl. 1408). Around 1942 Paul began an association with Kid Thomas that continued into the 1980s and produced many notable recordings; he is heard to advantage on *New Orleans Today: a Jazz Document* (1957, 77 LP11), recorded with Thomas. Paul modified his ensemble and solo style little over the years, as is demonstrated on *Kid Thomas Valentine and his Algiers Stompers in Lugano* (1983, Picayune KID1). He also recorded with Papa Celestin (1953), Emanuel Sayles (1961), and as a member of Harold Dejan's Olympia Brass Band (1966–71), with which he made two tours of Europe (1967, 1968).

BIBLIOGRAPHY

ChartersJ

D. Fairweather: "Paul, Emmanuel [*sic*]," in I. Carr, D. Fairweather, and B. Priestley: *Jazz: the Essential Companion* (London, 1987)

Pauls, Raimond (*b* Riga, Latvian SSR, 12 Jan 1936). Latvian pianist, composer, and bandleader. He attended the Latvian SSR Y. Vitol State Conservatory in Riga (graduated 1958) and studied composition (1962–5). From 1964 to 1971 he led the Rīgas Estrādes Orkestris (REO; Riga variety orchestra), in which he also played piano and with which he made recordings (including *REO džeza ritmā* (REO in jazz rhythm), 1970, Mel. CM020456). In 1973 he formed the jazz-rock group Modo; he played with the group until 1978, when he became the music director and conductor of the Latvian television and radio orchestra. Pauls's compositions include many jazz pieces, a ballet, two musicals, television and film scores, and more than 300 popular songs. He was named a People's Artist of the USSR in 1985.

WALTER OJAKÄÄR

Paulus, Tiit (*b* Tallinn, Estonian SSR, 14 June 1945). Estonian guitarist and composer. A self-taught musician, he played in dance bands and jazz groups from the age of 16, in the Estonian Philharmonic Society from 1966, and in the dance orchestra of the Estonian Television and Radio from 1974. He has performed at concerts and festivals in the USSR, Europe, Cuba, Syria, Iraq, Lebanon, and Sudan and recorded several albums, including *Tiit Paulus ja sõbrad* (Tiit Paulus and friends; 1981, Mel. C60154578). Paulus's compositions include *Sunday*, *Melanhoolne valss* (Melancholy waltz), *Simmanilugu* (Tune from a village party), and the well-known *Bluus kahele* (Blues for two), which he has recorded in a duo with the tenor saxophonist Arvo Pilliroog.

WALTER OJAKÄÄR

Pavageau, Alcide "Slow Drag" [Drag] (*b* New Orleans, 7 March 1888; *d* New Orleans, 19 Jan 1969). Double bass player. He taught himself to play guitar at an early age, and then became celebrated as a dancer, taking his sobriquet "Slow Drag" from the dance of that name. About 1927 he learned to play a homemade three-string double bass, and in the following years performed with Buddy Petit, Herb Morand, and Emile Barnes. In 1943 he was engaged by George Lewis (i), with whom he remained identified for the rest of his career. Pavageau recorded extensively with Lewis in 1944–5, both in a trio (with Lawrence Marrero) and as a member of Bunk Johnson's band; he was also with Johnson's group in New York in 1945–6. He continued to work with Lewis in New Orleans in the late 1940s and early 1950s at Manny's Tavern and El Morocco, and during the late 1950s and early 1960s at Preservation Hall. In later years he was active as a grand marshal with brass bands.

Pavageau was a key member of Lewis's band, commonly providing a consistent and heavy 4/4 beat and outlining the fundamental notes of each chord. Although he could play lightly under intimate circumstances, his characteristic timbre was, like that of Pops Foster, intensely percussive; he made use of a very low string action and employed a slapping technique to great effect, especially in final choruses.

Oral history material in *LNT*.

For illustrations *see* HUMPHREY and JOHNSON, BUNK.

SELECTED RECORDINGS

As sideman: B. Johnson: Tiger Rag/See See Rider (1944, AM 251); G. Lewis: *American Music by George Lewis* (1944–5, AM 639), incl. Burgundy Street Blues; *Jazz at Vespers* (1954, Riv. 230); on *George Lewis & Turk Murphy at Newport* (1957, Verve 8232), That's a plenty

BIBLIOGRAPHY

ChartersJ; *ChiltonW*
L. Borenstein and B. Russell: *Preservation Hall Portraits* (Baton Rouge, LA, 1968) [pictures by N. Rockmore]
G. Russell: "Magee String Band," *Sv*, no.49 (1973), 14 [interview]
A. Shipton: "Styles of New Orleans Bass Playing," *Fn*, vii/1 (1976), 18

ALDEN ASHFORTH

Payne, Bennie [Benjamin E.] (*b* Philadelphia, 18 June 1907; *d* Los Angeles, 2 Sept 1986). Pianist and singer. His professional career began in 1926 and he worked with various groups before joining Wilbur Sweatman (1928). He studied with Fats Waller, then (1929–30) played in revues in Europe and New York; he also worked as an accompanist for singers and recorded with Waller (in a duo, 1929) and Duke Ellington (1930–31). His principal association was with Cab Calloway's band (1931–43; for illustration *see* CALLOWAY, CAB; 1946) but he seldom played solos for Calloway and may be heard to greater advantage on Chu Berry's *Ebb Tide* (1937, Var. 657), one of the few recordings he made in a small group; the other number on this disc, *My Secret Love Affair*, provides an example of Payne's singing. After leaving Calloway he worked with Pearl Bailey and led his own trio, and from 1950 he accompanied the singer Billy Daniels. (Obituary, J. Simmen, *BHcF*, no.348 (1987), 29)

based on *ChiltonW*

Payne, Cecil (McKenzie) (*b* New York, 14 Dec 1922). Baritone saxophonist. He learned guitar, then alto saxophone, and played clarinet in army bands (1943–6). He first played baritone saxophone in 1946 in Clarence Briggs's band, and his last recorded work on the alto instrument was in a bop session with J. J. Johnson later the same year. He worked briefly with Roy Eldridge, but established his reputation as a great bop saxophonist with a weighty timbre while a member of Dizzy Gillespie's big band (1946–9); his inventive solos on *Ow!* and *Stay on it* are good examples of his playing. He worked in New York for James Moody and Tadd Dameron, then as a freelance (1949–52), before touring with Illinois Jacquet (1952–4). Despite the many fine recordings Payne made during the mid-1950s, notably those with Duke Jordan and Randy Weston, he left music temporarily. With Kenny Drew he acted in and composed songs for Jack Gelber's play *The Connection* (1961–2). He was a soloist with Machito's Afro-Cubans (1963–4) and a member of Lucky Thompson's octet, and toured Europe with Lionel Hampton (1964), but then left music again. Later he worked with Weston (1966), Woody Herman (1966–7), and Gillespie (1968); by these years his approach had softened, and he produced a lighter, more breathy sound. He then worked with Count Basie (1969–71) and led a quartet. He continued to play into the 1980s, recording with Nick Brignola in 1979 and performing with Bill Hardman in Richard Wyand's trio in San Francisco in 1986.

Oral history material in *GBLnsa*, *NjR*.

SELECTED RECORDINGS

As leader: *Cecil Payne and his Quartet/Quintet* (1956, Signal 1203); *Patterns of Jazz* (1957, Signal 1204); *Charlie Parker Music* (1961, CP 801); *The Connection* (1962, CP 806); *Bird Gets the Worm* (1976, Muse 5061); *Bright Moments* (1979, Spot. 21)

As sideman: J. J. Johnson: Coppin' the Bop/Jay Jay (1946, Savoy 615); D. Gillespie: Ow! (1947, Vic. 202480); Stay on it (1947, Vic. 202603); K. Dorham: *Afro Cuban* (1955, BN 1535); D. Jordan: *Duke Jordan Trio and Quintet* (1955, Signal 1202); R. Weston: *Jazz à la Bohemia* (1956, Riv. 232); on D. Jordan, S. Hakim: *East and West of Jazz* (1962, CP 805), D. Jordan: Yes, he's Gone

BIBLIOGRAPHY

B. Coss: "Cecil Payne: Baritonist by Choice," *DB*, xxx/13 (1963), 22
M. Gardner: "Discography: Cecil Payne," *JM*, x (1964), no.3, p.5; no.4, p.5; no.5, p.7
"Payne: One of the Few," *MM*, xli (12 Nov 1966), 6
S. Woolley: "Cecil Payne: Interview," *Cadence*, iii/8 (1977), 14

BARRY KERNFELD

Payne, Don(ald Ray) (*b* Wellington, TX, 7 Jan 1933). Bass player. From 1955 to 1958 he played with Art Pepper, Joe Maini, the composer and pianist Calvin Jackson, Georgie Auld, and Maynard Ferguson in California. He also played on Ornette Coleman's first album (*Something Else!!!! The Music of Ornette Coleman*, 1958, Cont. 3551). He then moved to New York (1958) and worked with Mundell Lowe, Chris Connor, and Tony Bennett (1959). He joined Herbie Mann in 1959 and toured Africa with him in 1960. He toured South America and Japan with Astrud Gilberto in 1961 and recorded bossa nova albums with Gilberto and Stan Getz (1963); during the same period he led a trio in New York, the other members of which at different times included Gene Bertoncini, Mike Abene, and Joe Beck. In 1964 he took up the electric bass guitar and began to play jazz-rock, rhythm-and-blues, and pop. From 1966 he was a studio musician in New York, though he continued to tour occasionally with jazz players and appear at festivals; he also recorded with Ferguson (1967) and Bobby Hackett (1968), and on electric bass guitar with Jackie Cain and Roy Kral (1966).

BIBLIOGRAPHY

FeatherE; *Feather '60s*
R. Gordon: *Jazz West Coast: the Los Angeles Jazz Scene of the 1950s* (London and New York, 1986)

Payne, Sonny [Percival] (*b* New York, 4 May 1926; *d* Los Angeles, 29 Jan 1979). Drummer, son of Chris Columbus. He studied with Vic Berton in 1936. After playing with the band led by Dud and Paul Bascomb and that of Hot Lips Page (both 1944) he worked with Earl Bostic (1945–7) and performed and recorded with Tiny Grimes (1947, 1949–50) and Erskine Hawkins (1950–53). From 1953 to 1955 he led his own band, then early in 1955 joined Count Basie's orchestra as a replacement for Gus Johnson. A forceful generator of swing rhythms, Payne provided the band with an exciting impetus; this is evident on the album *Count Basie Swings, Joe Williams Sings*, which also includes *In the Evening*, an example of his softer, more sensitive playing. He remained with Basie until 1965, when he formed his own trio and also worked as an accompanist to Frank Sinatra. Payne then played with Harry James's orchestra (1966–*c*1973) before spending another period with Basie (1973–4). He toured and recorded in Europe with Illinois Jacquet and Milt Buckner in 1976, and performed again with James shortly before his death.

SELECTED RECORDINGS

As leader: on *More Drums on Fire* (1959, WP 1261), Clap hands, here comes Charlie

As sideman: C. Basie: *Count Basie Swings, Joe Williams Sings* (1955, Clef 678), incl. In the Evening; P. Quinichette: *The Kid from Denver* (1956, Dawn 1109); Lambert, Hendricks, and Ross: *The Swingers* (1959, WP 1264); C. Basie: *Breakfast Dance and Barbecue* (1959, Roul. 52028); *The Count Basie Story* (1960, Roul. 1); *Basie at Birdland* (1961, Roul. 52065)

BIBLIOGRAPHY

FeatherE; Feather '60s; Feather–Gitler '70s
J. Tynan: "Sonny Payne: Count Basie's Swinger," *DB*, xxiii/13 (1956), 14
M. Laverdure: "L'explosif Sonny Payne," *Jm*, no.186 (1971), 18
S. Payne: "You've got to Study All Forms of Music," *CI*, ix/12 (1971), 15
Obituary, *DB*, xlvi/6 (1979), 9

LEROY OSTRANSKY

Paz. English group. It was formed in 1972 by the vibraphonist and composer Dick Crouch; other members have included the alto saxophonist and flutist Ray Warleigh, the keyboard player Geoff Castle, the electric bass guitarist Ron Mathewson, the guitarists Phil Lee and Jim Mullen, and the percussionists Simon Morton and Chris Fletcher. The group's music exhibits the influences of jazz, rock, and funk, and classical, folk, and ethnic music; its style is characterized by the extensive use of Brazilian percussion instruments. Exciting Latin American rhythms, skillful jazz solos, and imaginative writing have won the group both popular and critical acclaim, and it has recorded five albums, among them *Look Inside* (1983, Paladin 001), which included the disco hit *AC/DC*. (R. Tee: "Paz Jazz," *Blues and Soul*, no.398 (1984), 16)

MARK GILBERT

Peacock, Gary (*b* Burley, ID, 12 May 1935). Double bass player. He played piano and drums from the age of 13 and took up the double bass around 1956 while serving in the US Army in Germany, where he remained after his discharge and played with such musicians as Bud Shank, Bob Cooper, Albert Mangelsdorff, Hans Koller, Attila Zoller, and Tony Scott. After moving in 1958 to Los Angeles he performed and recorded with Barney Kessel, Clare Fischer, and Don Ellis and played with Paul Bley; in the early 1960s he settled in New York, from 1962 to 1963 belonged to the trio of Bill Evans (ii), and worked again with Bley and with Jimmy Giuffre and George Russell. He toured with Miles Davis and Albert Ayler in 1964 and with Ayler made the first of several adventurous recordings in the same year; he also toured Europe with Ayler and Don Cherry, worked again briefly with Davis in the late 1960s, and recorded with Paul Bley (1967, 1970). These performances established him as one of the most accomplished double bass players in jazz. In the mid-1960s he studied Eastern philosophy and medicine and in 1969 moved to Japan, where he recorded with Sadao Watanabe, Masabumi Kikuchi, and several visiting Americans. After two and a half years he returned to the USA (1972) and studied biology at the University of Washington (1972–6); in the summer of 1976 he returned to Japan for a tour with Bley and Barry Altschul and from 1977 made several recordings as a leader, for which he also wrote compositions. From the late 1970s into the late 1980s he performed and recorded in a trio with Keith Jarrett and Jack DeJohnette; he also taught in the mid-1980s at the Cornish Institute of the Allied Arts in Seattle.

SELECTED RECORDINGS

(recorded for ECM unless otherwise indicated)

As leader: *Tales of Another* (1977, 1101); *Shift in the Wind* (1980, 1165); *Voice from the Past* (1981, 1210)

As sideman: B. Evans: *Trio '64* (1963, Verve 68578); A. Ayler: *New York Eye and Ear Control* (1964, ESP 1016); P. Bley: *Ballads* (1967, 1010); *Paul Bley with Gary Peacock* (1970, 1003); K. Jarrett: *Standards*, i (1983, 1255); *Changes* (1983, 1276); *Standards*, ii (1983, 1289)

BIBLIOGRAPHY

M. Williams: "Gary Peacock: the Beauties of Intuition," *DB*, xxx/13 (1963), 16
M. Solomon: "Bassist Peacock into Zen, Est and ECM," *DB*, xlvi/10 (1979), 9
G. Endress: *Jazz Podium: Musiker über sich selbst* (Stuttgart, Germany, 1980), 196

MICHAEL ULLMAN

Peacock's Progressive Jazz. Record label. It was founded in 1958 by Peacock, a long-established record company based in Houston that specialized in rhythm-and-blues and country music. The jazz division existed for less than twelve months, and the catalogue contained only a few items; nevertheless the repertory included notable LPs by Sonny Criss and Betty Carter, and it remained in Peacock's catalogues for many years. In the 1980s it was reissued in the UK.

MARK GARDNER

Pearson, Duke [Columbus Calvin, Jr.] (*b* Atlanta, 17 Aug 1932; *d* Atlanta, 4 Aug 1980). Pianist, composer, and arranger. He was nicknamed by an uncle who admired Duke Ellington's music. As a youth he studied piano and several brass instruments, but dental problems prevented his becoming a professional trumpeter. He worked as a pianist in Florida and Georgia (1954–9), then moved to New York, where he played most often with Pepper Adams and Donald Byrd (Byrd recorded his best-known compositions, *Jeannine* and *Cristo Redentor*). He also joined the Jazztet briefly (1960) and toured internationally as the accompanist to Nancy Wilson (1961). From 1963 to 1970 Pearson worked as a producer for Blue Note records. During this period he formed a big band, initially led also by Byrd; as the Duke Pearson Band (1967–70), it rivaled the Thad Jones–Mel Lewis Orchestra, which also shared some of the same personnel. Its soloists included Adams, Frank Foster, Jerry Dodgion, Lew Tabackin, Randy Brecker, the trumpeter Joe Shepley, and Garnett Brown. The ensemble provided a forum for the performance of Pearson's lyrical, swing-oriented compositions. In 1971 Pearson taught at Clark College, and the following year re-formed his band with virtually the same musicians as before. He toured with Carmen McRae and Joe Williams from 1972 to 1973; in the late 1970s his ability to play was impaired by the onset of multiple sclerosis.

SELECTED RECORDINGS

As leader: *Wahoo!* (1964, BN 84191); *Honeybuns* (1965, Atl. 3002); *Sweet Honey Bee* (1966, BN 84252); *Introducing Duke Pearson's Big Band* (1967, BN 84276); *Now Hear This* (1968, BN 84308); *It Could only Happen to you* (1970, BN LA317)

As sideman: D. Byrd: *Byrd in Flight* (1960, BN 4048); *Donald Byrd at the Half Note Cafe* (1960, BN 84061), incl. Jeannine; *A New Perspective* (1963, BN 84124), incl. Cristo Redentor; J. Coles: *Little Johnny C.* (1963, BN 84144)

BIBLIOGRAPHY

M. Gardner: "Duke Pearson," *JM*, xiii/8 (1967), 11
I. Gitler: "The Other Duchy: Duke Pearson's New Big Band," *DB*, xxxv/8 (1968), 25
M. Gardner: "Discography: Duke Pearson," *JM*, no.175 (1969), 29 [incl. list of compositions]
B. Rusch: "Duke Pearson: Interview," *Cadence*, vi/9 (1980), 12

BARRY KERNFELD

Peck, Nat (*b* New York, 13 Jan 1925). Trombonist. He first played with Glenn Miller (1943–5) and Don Redman (1947). From 1947 to 1951 he lived in France; he performed and recorded with Coleman Hawkins (1949), James Moody (1949–50), Roy Eldridge, Don Byas, and Kenny Clarke (1950), and studied at the Paris Conservatoire (1949–51). He returned to New York in 1951 to work in television but continued to appear intermittently in Paris; his work in the 1950s is well represented by recordings with Dizzy Gillespie made on the Vogue label (22 February 1953). By the early 1960s he had again settled in France, where he played and recorded with Michel Legrand, André Hodeir (1963), and Duke Ellington. He also lived in England and in Germany, where he was a staff musician at Sender Freies Berlin, played with Quincy Jones, and recorded with the Clarke–Boland Big Band (he played on all their recordings between 1963 and 1969 and may be heard as a soloist on *Bei mir war es immer so schön* on the album *More Smiles*, 1968, MPS 746) and the Norddeutscher Rundfunk Jazz Workshop (1964). From 1965 he was based in London, working as a studio musician; he played on the soundtracks of more than 100 films and was also active in television. In the 1970s he recorded with Benny Goodman (1970–72) and Peter Herbolzheimer (1979).

BIBLIOGRAPHY

Feather '60s
B. Dawson: "New Trombone Man in Town: Nat Peck," *Crescendo*, v/3 (1966), 23

Peck horn. A colloquial American term for the E♭ alto or tenor horn; *see* SAXHORN.

Pecora(ro), Santo (Joseph) [Mr. Tailgate] (*b* New Orleans, 31 March 1902; *d* New Orleans, 29 May 1984). Trombonist. He first studied french horn but changed to trombone for commercial work when in his teens. He was a member of the New Orleans Rhythm Kings (1924–5), and his recordings with the group, including versions of his own compositions *I never knew what a gal could do* and *She's Crying for me Blues*, show him to have been a strong exponent of the tailgate ensemble style. During the late 1920s he worked in theaters in Chicago. Pecora was a good reader and spent the early 1930s in big bands, including those of Buddy Rogers, Will Osborne, and Ben Pollack, but returned to small groups with Paul Mares (1935), Sharkey Bonano (1936), and Wingy Manone (1938). He then became a studio musician in Hollywood and appeared in the films *Rhythm on the River* (1940, with Manone) and *Blues in the Night* (1941). After returning to New Orleans he led his own group and worked again with Bonano (1948–late 1950s). He took his band to Chicago (1959), and from 1960 to the mid-1970s played at the Famous Door and the Dream Room in New Orleans.

Pecora's nephew Santo Pecoraro (*b* 1906) was a drummer who worked frequently with Johnny Wiggs.

Oral history material in *LNT*.

SELECTED RECORDINGS

As leader: Rose of the Rio Grande/Canal Street Stomp (1950, Clef 8914); *Dixieland Mardi Gras* (1956, Vik 1081)
As sideman: New Orleans Rhythm Kings: I never knew what a gal could do (1925, OK 40422); She's Crying for me Blues (1925, OK 40327); P. Mares: Reincarnation/The Land of Dreams (1935, OK 41575); S. Bonano: Mudhole Blues/Swing in, swing out (1936, Voc. 3353)

BIBLIOGRAPHY

ChiltonW; *FeatherE*
Obituary, *MR*, xi/9 (1984), 4

LAWRENCE KOCH

Pedersen, Guy (*b* Grand-Fort-Philippe, nr Dunkerque, France, 10 June 1930). French double bass player. After studying at the Conservatoire in Roubaix he moved in 1952 to Paris, where he worked with Henri Renaud, Sacha Distel, and Jean-Louis Viale at the clubs Tabou and Ringside (1954). He played for one year in a commercially oriented band led by Jacques Hélian and at the same time worked in studios. He belonged to Michel Legrand's big band, with which he appeared in Moscow, to André Hodeir's Jazz Groupe de Paris, and to Stephane Grappelli's quintet. From 1960 to 1965 he worked with Martial Solal; he also played with Roland Kirk and in 1963 toured with Dexter Gordon. For the next three years he toured the world with the Swingle Singers; after returning to France he recorded with Grappelli (at intervals, 1972–6), played in Baden Powell's group (from around 1974 to around 1977), and recorded with Noah Howard (1977).

SELECTED RECORDINGS

As sideman: J. Archey: *Jimmy Archey et l'orchestre Michel Attenoux* (1955, Barclay 84001); L. Hampton: *Hamp and his French New Sound* (1955, Barclay 84004–5); S. Grappelli: *Django* (1962, Barclay 84089); M. Solal: *Suite pour une frise* (1962, Col. ESDF1430); *Jazz à Gaveau* (1963, Col. FPX221, FPX253); J.-L. Ponty: on *Jazz Long Playing* (1964, Phi. 77810), Manoir de mes rêves; C. Bolling: *Toot Suite* (1981, CBS 73999)

BIBLIOGRAPHY

J.-L. Ginibre: "Le troisième homme," *Jm*, no.115 (1965), 16

ANDRÉ CLERGEAT

Peer, Beverly (*b* New York, 7 Oct 1912). Double bass player. He began working as a pianist, but later changed to double bass. In 1936 he joined Chick Webb's orchestra (for illustration *see* WEBB, CHICK); it often accompanied Ella Fitzgerald and she assumed its leadership after Webb's death in 1939. Peer made many recordings with the band, including *Undecided* (1939, Decca 2323). After leaving in 1942 he played with Taft Jordan (1942) and Sabby Lewis (1944) and in the 1950s and 1960s he worked briefly with Harry Dial, Barbara Carroll, and Sarah Vaughan. Among the jazz musicians with whom he recorded were Mildred Bailey (1946–7), Chris Connor (1954), and Ellis Larkins (*c*1955, 1956). In the 1970s he performed with the singer and pianist Bobby Short, with whom he also recorded (1968–73).

based on *ChiltonW*

Pege, Aladár (*b* Budapest, 8 Oct 1939). Hungarian double bass player. He took up double bass at the age of 15, and studied classical music at the Béla Bartók Musical Training College. He worked in dance orchestras, then in 1963 formed a jazz quartet, which performed in Yugoslavia at the Bled Jazz Festival. While attending the Franz Liszt Academy he worked in commercial recording studios, and after his graduation (1969) remained to teach double bass. He then re-formed his jazz quartet, which appeared at the Montreux International Jazz Festival (1970); Pege's prodigious technique greatly impressed audiences there. From 1975 to 1978 he lived in Berlin, where he found greater opportunities to play bop and free jazz, but he later returned to his teaching post and commercial work in Budapest. His talents became more widely known through recordings with Walter Norris (1978, 1980) and concerts with Mingus Dynasty; the latter included a performance at the Jazzyatra in Bombay (1980), which moved Mingus's widow to give Pege one of her husband's instruments. In 1982 Pege played at the Kool Jazz Festival in New York with Herbie Hancock and Tony Williams. He often includes arrangements of Hungarian folksongs in his performances.

SELECTED RECORDINGS

Duos with W. Norris: *Synchronicity* (1978, Enja 3035); *Winter Rose* (1980, Enja 3067)
As leader: *Montreux Inventions* (1970, Hungaroton 17418); *Live* (1981–2, Krém 17742)
As sideman with Mingus Dynasty: *Live at Montreux* (1980, Atl. 16031)

BIBLIOGRAPHY

G. Noel and M. Noel: "Aladár Pege," *Jh*, no.266 (1970), 25

B. Noglik: "Aladár Pege," *Jazzwerkstatt international* (Berlin, 1981), 212 [incl. interview, discography]

L. Jeske: "Profile: Aladár Pege," *DB*, l/1 (1983), 47

BARRY KERNFELD

Peiffer, Bernard (*b* Epinal, France, 23 Oct 1922; *d* Philadelphia, 7 Sept 1976). French pianist. He studied classical piano at conservatories in Marseilles and Paris and began to play jazz at the age of 17. He performed with Django Reinhardt, Hubert Rostaing, and André Ekyan, and recorded in Basle with Rex Stewart (1948) and in Paris with Bill Coleman, Don Byas, Sidney Bechet, and James Moody (all 1949). During this period he was best known for his playing and recording in Paris as a soloist and the leader of a trio; his elaborately ornamented, swinging performances earned him strong support from the American writers Barry Ulanov and Leonard Feather. He went to the USA in 1954 and first worked in New York in 1955, but his career suffered, perhaps because he was frequently compared with Art Tatum. After settling in Philadelphia he recorded in New York (1956–60), made several concert tours of universities (1959–65), and played in France (1966), but he worked mainly in clubs in Philadelphia, making his last appearances in 1974.

SELECTED RECORDINGS

As unaccompanied soloist: Jealousy/Caravan (1952, BStar 260)

As leader: Jeepers Creepers/Slow Burn (1952, BStar 263); *Bernie's Tunes* (1956, EmA 36080); *Modern Jazz for People who Like Original Music* (1960, Laurie 1006)

As sideman: R. Stewart: Jug Blues/Vernon's Story (1948, Elite 8192)

BIBLIOGRAPHY

L. Feather: "Bernard Peiffer Proves to be France's Loss, America's Gain," *DB*, xxii/15 (1955), 36

F. Manskleid: "Un musicien français peut-il réussir en Amérique?" *Jh*, no.164 (1961), 22

J.-L. Ginibre: "Antibes 007: Bernard Peiffer," *Jm*, no.134 (1966), 40

BARRY KERNFELD

Pell, Dave [David] (*b* New York, 26 Feb 1925). Tenor and baritone saxophonist and bandleader. He toured with Tony Pastor (1944–5) and then settled on the West Coast, where he played and recorded with Bob Crosby (1946) and Les Brown (1947–55). From 1953 he led his own groups (often an octet), which he organized from former members of Brown's band. His recordings became increasingly commercial (for example, *Dave Pell Plays Berlin*, 1953, Trend 1003), but he employed such sidemen as Pepper Adams, Benny Carter, Don Fagerquist, Mel Lewis, Red Mitchell, Marty Paich, Art Pepper, and Ray Sims. Pell also recorded with Shorty Rogers (1953), John Graas (1955–6), Pete Rugolo (1956, 1958), Benny Goodman (1958), and Gene Krupa (1959). In 1984 he made a further recording as leader, *The Dave Pell Octet Plays Again* (Fresh Sound 101); the group included Mel Flory, Buddy Clark, and Frank Capp, who had played with Pell in the 1950s. He also worked as a producer for Tops Records (from 1955), Liberty Records (from 1961), Uni Records (from 1966), and again for Liberty Records (from 1967). (*FeatherE*)

Pelzer, Jacques (*b* Liège, Belgium, 24 June 1924). Belgian alto saxophonist, flutist, and composer. As a member of the Bob Shots he played in France, the Netherlands, and Czechoslovakia (1945–6), and occasionally during the following years in Belgium and at festivals in Nice and Paris. After the group disbanded he worked with René Thomas in Liège and at monthly intervals in Paris, and made 14 visits to the Belgian Congo (now Zaïre). In 1959 he met Chet Baker, with whom he performed in Italy, at clubs in the USA, and at Carnegie Hall in New York. Later he played briefly in the Open Sky Unit, a jazz-rock group, and remained active throughout Europe into the late 1980s.

ROBERT PERNET

Pemberton, Bill [William McLane] (*b* New York, 5 March 1918; *d* New York, 13 Dec 1984). Double bass player. After studying violin as a youth he changed to double bass and worked in New York with Frankie Newton (1941–5), Herman "Ivory" Chittison (1945–7), Mercer Ellington and Eddie Barefield (both 1946), and Billy Kyle (1948). He later performed and recorded with Art Tatum (1956) and recorded with Rex Stewart in the Fletcher Henderson reunion band (1957–8), although he had never worked with Henderson. His association with Earl Hines (1966–9) included a tour of Russia (1966). In 1967 he toured Europe with Buck Clayton's group Jazz from a Swinging Era. He was a member of the JPJ Quartet with Budd Johnson, Oliver Jackson, and Dill Jones from 1969 to 1975; in 1972 this ensemble undertook a tour of high schools in 24 cities as part of the educational project New Communications in Jazz. During this period Pemberton also worked with Ruby Braff (1972), Max Kaminsky (1973), and Vic Dickenson, with whom he recorded in New York (1974) and France (1975). From 1979 to 1983 Pemberton worked with Panama Francis and the Savoy Sultans; his recordings with this ensemble demonstrate the continuing vitality of traditional jazz double bass playing, and display his powerful sense of rhythm, warmth of expression, and straightforward swing style. His final association was with Doc Cheatham, with whom he recorded in 1984.

SELECTED RECORDINGS

As leader of JPJ Quartet (with O. Jackson, B. Johnson, and D. Jones): *Montreux '71* (1971, MJR 8111)

As sideman: M. Ellington: Metronome All Out/Pass me by (1946, Musi. 379); R. Stewart: *The Big Reunion* (1957, Jzt. 1285); P. Francis: *Gettin' in the Groove* (1979, BB 33320–21); D. Cheatham: *The Fabulous Doc Cheatham* (1984, Parkwood 104)

BIBLIOGRAPHY

ChiltonW; *FeatherE*; *Feather '60s*

Battestini: "Bill Pemberton," *BHcF*, no.279 (1980), 8 [interview]

Obituary, *DB*, lii/4 (1985), 14

JOHN CURRY

Peña, Ralph (Raymond) (*b* Jarbidge, NV, 24 Feb 1927; *d* Mexico City, 20 May 1969). Double bass player. He studied baritone horn and tuba as a child and worked professionally from the age of 15. After attending college in San Francisco he played West Coast jazz with Art Pepper, Cal Tjader, Barney Kessel, and Stan Getz and belonged to the big bands of Billy May (recording in 1953) and Charlie Barnet (1954). In the following years he made recordings with Shorty Rogers (1955–8) and Jimmy Giuffre (1955, 1956) and in a duo with Pete Jolly (1959), and sometimes played with all three musicians in the same group. Later he worked with Frank Sinatra (touring the world in 1962), Ben Webster (1960), and George Shearing (touring Europe in 1962); in 1963 he performed and recorded with Joe Pass. He also worked occasionally as the leader of a group that played his own compositions and recorded with Nancy Wilson, Ella Fitzgerald, and Anita O'Day. Peña's playing was marked by a rich sound in the lower register of his instrument and a strong drive; his style is particularly well represented by his recordings with Jolly and as a member of Giuffre's trio. He was adept in his use of the bow, as may be heard on the track *Slow Freight* from the album *Bob Brookmeyer* (1957).

SELECTED RECORDINGS

Duos with P. Jolly: *Impossible* (1959, Metro. 1014)

As sideman: J. Giuffre: *Tangents in Jazz* (1955, Cap. T634); on *The Jimmy Giuffre Clarinet* (1956, Atl. 1238), Quiet Cook; *The Jimmy Giuffre 3* (1956, Atl. 1254); B. Brookmeyer: on *Bob Brookmeyer* (1957, Crown 5318), Brook's Blues, Slow Freight

BIBLIOGRAPHY

FeatherE; *Feather '60s*; *Feather–Gitler '70s*

LAWRENCE KOCH

Pepper, Art(hur Edward, Jr.) (*b* Gardena, CA, 1 Sept 1925; *d* Panorama, CA, 1 June 1982). Alto saxophonist. In 1943 he played in the big bands of Benny Carter and Stan Kenton. After serving in the US Army he toured with Kenton as the band's outstanding soloist (1946–51; see illustration) and also performed as a freelance in Los Angeles. Thereafter his career was hampered by a series of jail terms for drug abuse. He attempted several times to resume playing, joining a quintet with Jack Montrose (1956), issuing several acclaimed recordings for the Contemporary label (1957–60), and performing with Howard Rumsey's Lighthouse All-Stars (1960). In 1964 he adopted the tenor saxophone and began to play free jazz, then in 1968 returned to mainstream jazz by joining Buddy Rich's band; serious ailments forced his departure in the following year, however. Pepper spent three years in a rehabilitation center and worked as a bookkeeper before returning to music as a demonstrator for Buffet instruments (1973) and as a saxophonist in Don Ellis's orchestra (1975). From 1977 until his sudden death he gave a series of sensational bop performances in Japan and also in New York at the Newport Jazz Festival and the Village Vanguard, which brought him increasing recognition and popularity. He made some notable contributions to film soundtracks, notably those of *The Enforcer* (1976) and *Heart Beat* (1979), and was the subject of a documentary, *Art Pepper: Notes from a Jazz Survivor* (1982).

Soloists with Stan Kenton's band, ?Los Angeles, December 1947: (left to right) Conte Candoli (trumpet), Art Pepper (alto saxophone), and Bob Cooper (tenor saxophone)

Pepper was a leading figure in WEST COAST JAZZ, a movement with which he was associated not only because of his choice of location and musical colleagues but also because of his light, clear, precise sound on alto saxophone; he took part in the earliest recordings in this style under the leadership of Shorty Rogers in 1951. However, Pepper was a stronger, more fiery improviser than his fellow West Coast musicians, as is amply demonstrated by his recordings in 1957 and 1960 with Miles Davis's rhythm section. His album *Art Pepper + Eleven* (1959), with Marty Paich's harmonized recastings of solos by Charlie Parker, foreshadowed by 15 years the popular recordings of the Los Angeles group Supersax. In the mid-1960s, under the overwhelming influence of John Coltrane, he took up tenor saxophone, on which his playing stressed intense and expressive noise elements. Eventually, returning to the alto instrument, he combined the two approaches in performances such as *Cherokee* (1977), in which traditional bop lines erupt at explosive moments into squeals, growls, and flurries of notes.

Oral history material in *NjR*.

SELECTED RECORDINGS

As leader: *The Early Show* (1952, Xan. 108); *Art Pepper Meets the Rhythm Section* (1957, Cont. 3532); *Art Pepper + Eleven* (1959, Cont. 3568); *Gettin' Together* (1960, Cont. 3573); *Smack Up* (1960, Cont. 7602); *Living Legend* (1975, Cont. 7633); *Saturday Night at the Village Vanguard* (1977, Cont. 7644), incl. Cherokee; *Straight Life* (1979, Gal. 5127); *Roadgame* (1981, Gal. 5142)

As sideman: S. Kenton: Art Pepper (1950, Cap. 28008); Jump for Joe (1951, Cap. 1704); Street of Dreams (1951, Cap. 1823); S. Rogers: Over the Rainbow (1951, Cap. 15764); B. Rich: *Mercy, Mercy* (1968, PJ 20133)

BIBLIOGRAPHY

J. McKinney: "Art Pepper: Profile of a Comeback," *Metronome*, lxxvii (1960), Sept, 26

J. Tynan: "The Return of Art Pepper," *DB*, xxvii/8 (1960), 17

——: "End of the Road," *DB*, xxvii/25 (1960), 13

——: "Art Pepper's not the Same," *DB*, xxxi/22 (1964), 18

C. Marra: "Art Pepper: 'I'm Here to Stay!'," *DB*, xl/4 (1973), 16

L. Underwood: "Pepper's Painful Road to Pure Art," *DB*, xlii/11 (1975), 16

A. Pepper and L. Pepper: *Straight Life: the Story of Art Pepper* (New York and London, 1979) [incl. discography by T. Selbert]

P. Welding: "Art Pepper: Rewards of the Straight Life," *DB*, xlvi/18 (1979), 16 [incl. discography]

"Art Pepper," *SJ*, xxxiv/1 (1980), 162 [discography]

D. N. Pepperell: "Art Pepper: I Want to Play so Bad," *The Wire*, no.28 (1986), 26

BARRY KERNFELD

Peraza, Armando (*b* Havana, 30 May 1924). Cuban percussionist. After moving to the USA while working with Mongo Santamaria in 1948, he played and recorded with Machito. He performed on the West Coast with Slim Gaillard (1950) and then played with Cal Tjader, the bandleader Perez Prado, and Dave Brubeck. From 1953 to 1962 he was a soloist in George Shearing's quintet, making a number of recordings. He also worked with Stan Kenton and Wes Montgomery. He performed and recorded with Tjader (1964–70) and in 1970, after touring and recording with Santamaria, he worked with the Latin-rock group Azteca in San Francisco. In 1971 he joined Carlos Santana, whose group plays in a style that blends elements of jazz, rock, and Latin American music, and in the 1970s he also recorded with rock groups. In 1988 he was a member of the band led by Santana and Wayne Shorter. Peraza's principal percussion instruments are bongos and congas.

SELECTED RECORDINGS

As sideman: Machito: Cu-bop City (1949, Roost 502); G. Shearing and the Montgomery Brothers: *Love Walked in* (1961, Jlnd 955); C. Tjader: *Along Comes Cal* (1967, Verve 68671)

BIBLIOGRAPHY
FeatherE; *Feather '60s*; *Feather–Gitler '70s*
R. Tolleson: "Santana's Percussion: a Profile in Latin Artistry," *MD*, vi/7 (1982), 12

RICK MATTINGLY

Perciful, Jack (T.) (*b* Moscow, ID, 26 Nov 1925). Pianist. He played with an army band in Japan (1945–6), and with bands in Los Angeles and Las Vegas during the early 1950s. In 1958 he joined Harry James and recorded and toured widely with him, performing at jazz festivals on several occasions; his playing may be heard on a recording he made as a member of the Harry James Septet (1964, MGM 4274). He also recorded with Charlie Barnet (1959) and Corky Corcoran (1972). After leaving James in 1974 he played with Red Kelly in Tumwater, Washington, in 1975.

BIBLIOGRAPHY
FeatherE; *Feather '60s*; *Feather–Gitler '70s*
J. Perciful: "A Sideman's Story," *CI*, x/3 (1971), 14

Percussion. In jazz, the term is used to refer to the equipment of the drummer (*see* DRUM SET) and a number of additional instruments (*see* BONGOS, CONGA, CUÍCA, MARIMBA, STEEL DRUM, TABLĀ, TIMBALES, VIBRAPHONE, and XYLOPHONE).

Perez, Manuel [(Emile) Emanuel] (*b* New Orleans, 28 Dec 1871; *d* New Orleans, 1946). Cornetist and bandleader. A cigar maker by trade, he was active in brass and dance bands in New Orleans. He joined the Onward Brass Band (*see* ONWARD BRASS BAND (i)) in 1900 and led it from 1903 until it disbanded in 1930; he was also the leader of the IMPERIAL ORCHESTRA (1901–8). In 1915 he played in Chicago with the trombonist George Filhe and Charlie Elgar (he re-joined Elgar there in 1928). After returning to New Orleans he performed on the SS *Capitol* and from the 1920s led dance orchestras in clubs and dance halls in the city.

Perez was regarded as one of the finest parade cornetists; he played wide-ranging melodies with a sharp, clear attack and beautiful tone. He believed that playing in a brass band tested a musician's sight-reading skill and technical execution and was generally more demanding than playing jazz; he prided himself on the ability of the members of his brass bands to play from written arrangements, though when such bands began to include improvisation in their work he was prepared to engage good improvisers, including the young Joe (later King) Oliver. As a dance-band musician he proved that he too could improvise competently.

BIBLIOGRAPHY
ChiltonW
D. Barker: *A Life in Jazz*, ed. A. Shipton (London and New York, 1986)
J. de Donder: "Emanuel Perez," *Fn*, xvii/6 (1986), 4

KARL KOENIG

Perfect. Record label. It was established in June 1922 by American Pathé and was used to issue cheap records, most of which were also released at full price on Pathé. A race series, the Perfect 100s, equivalent to Pathé's 7500s, was started in 1926. There was also a British label Perfect, which ran for a year from December 1927, and was used mostly to issue items first put out on American Perfect and Pathé; these, however, are of little jazz interest. American Perfect survived the incorporation of its parent into the AMERICAN RECORD COMPANY, and became one of the new organization's "dime-store" labels. The race series was continued until around July 1935; its issues were also put out on the other dime-store labels. From September 1935 Perfect's numerical sequence was aligned with ARC's; a popular series was maintained in addition to the race material. With the other "dime-store" labels Perfect was discontinued by CBS after it acquired ARC–BRC.

BIBLIOGRAPHY
C. Kendziora, Jr., and P. Armagnac: "Perfect Dance-series and Race-series Catalog, 1922–1930," *Record Research*, nos.51–2 (1963), 13
J. Godrich and R. M. W. Dixon: *Blues & Gospel Records, 1902–1942* (Hatch End, nr London, 1964, rev. 2/1969, rev. and enlarged 3/1982 as R. M. W. Dixon and J. Godrich: *Blues and Gospel Records, 1902–1943*)
R. M. W. Dixon and J. Godrich: *Recording the Blues* (London, 1970)
R. D. Kinkle: "Perfect Numerical List," *The Complete Encyclopedia of Popular Music and Jazz* (New Rochelle, NY, and Westport, CT, 1974), iv, 2236
B. Rust: *The American Record Label Book* (New Rochelle, NY, 1978), 236
A. Badrock: *English Pathe Perfect: a Catalogue and History* (Hayes, England, 1983)

Perkins, Bill [William Reese] (*b* San Francisco, 22 July 1924). Tenor and baritone saxophonist, flutist, and clarinetist. He grew up in Chile, then in Santa Barbara, California; after serving in the armed forces during World War II he studied music and engineering in California, belonged to the big band of the clarinetist Jerry Wald (1950–51), and worked with Woody Herman (1951–3). While playing with Stan Kenton (1953–4, 1955–9) and again with Herman (1954) he figured prominently as a soloist. He recorded in 1956 with John Lewis, and in the same year recorded an album as a leader with Richie Kamuca and Art Pepper, for which he also wrote arrangements and a blues; in the 1960s he worked in studios both as a performer and as a recording engineer, and from 1968 played occasionally in the orchestra of the "Tonight Show." From 1974 to 1977 he performed and recorded (usually as a baritone saxophonist) with the Toshiko Akiyoshi–Lew Tabackin Big Band. In the mid-1980s he performed in England in a quartet with Tommy Whittle. In his early career Perkins favored a light style of playing influenced by Lester Young, which is well represented by his work on John Lewis's album *Two Degrees East, Three Degrees West* (1956). His later style is exemplified by his own recording *Journey to the East* (1984), which displays the influence of John Coltrane (on the track *From the Hip*) and Sonny Rollins (on *I'm an Old Cowhand*), as well as Perkins's fine sense of structure.

For illustration *see* MULLIGAN, GERRY.

SELECTED RECORDINGS

As leader: *On Stage: the Bill Perkins Octet* (1956, PJ 1221); with R. Kamuca and A. Pepper: *Just Friends* (1956, PJ 401); *Journey to the East* (1984, Cont. 14011), incl. From the Hip, I'm an Old Cowhand

As sideman: S. Kenton: *Music of Bill Russo and Bill Holman* (1954, Cap. H526), incl. King Fish; W. Herman: *The Woody Herman Band!* (1954, Cap. T560), incl. Autobahn Blues, Hittin' the Bottle, Sleep, Wild Apple Honey; S. Kenton: Opus in Chartreuse (1955, Cap. 3243); J. Lewis: *Two Degrees East, Three Degrees West* (1956, PJ 1217)

BIBLIOGRAPHY
B. Korall: "Bill Perkins," *Metronome*, lxxii/ (1956), 21
J. Tynan: "From Slipstick to Jazz Horn," *DB*, xxiii/9 (1956), 13
——: "Two Tenor Conversation," *DB*, xxv/10 (1958), 14
A. Morgan: "Woody's Tenors," *JM*, vi (1960–61), no.7, p.4; no.8, p.13; no.12, p.9
S. Voce: "Bill Perkins," *JJI*, xxxix (1986), no.2, p.16; no.3, p.8
L. Tomkins: "I'd Never Trade what I've Done . . .: Bill Perkins," *CI*, xxiv/6 (1987), 20; contd as "Bill Perkins is Given a New Pulsation," xxiv/7 (1987), 22

MICHAEL ULLMAN

Perkins, Carl (*b* Indianapolis, 16 Aug 1928; *d* Los Angeles, 17 March 1958). Pianist. He played rhythm-and-blues with Big Jay McNeely (1948–9) in California, where he settled in 1949. He performed with Miles Davis in 1950 and recorded with Illinois Jacquet in 1951. After serving in the US Army (1951–

3) he rejoined Davis and performed and recorded with Oscar Moore (1953–4). From the mid-1950s he worked with bop groups, playing with Jim Hall, Teddy Edwards, and Red Mitchell, and recording with Clifford Brown and Max Roach (1954), Dexter Gordon (1955), Chet Baker (1956), Pepper Adams, Buddy DeFranco, and Victor Feldman (all 1957), Art Pepper (1958), and others. He was a member of Curtis Counce's band from 1956 to 1958; he also led his own bop trios and recorded two albums as a leader (1956, 1957, including *Introducing Carl Perkins*, 1956, Dootone 211).

BIBLIOGRAPHY

L. Grigson and A. Morgan: "Carl Perkins," *JM*, viii/5 (1962), 11 [incl. discography]
R. Gordon: *Jazz West Coast: the Los Angeles Jazz Scene of the 1950s* (London and New York, 1986)

Perkins, Walter (*b* Chicago, 10 Feb 1932). Drummer. He performed around Chicago with Ahmad Jamal (1956–7) and with Coleman Hawkins at the Playboy Jazz Festival (1959), and formed the group MJT + 3, with which he moved to New York in 1960. After the group disbanded in 1962 he remained in New York, where he performed with Carmen McRae (1961–3), Sonny Rollins (1962), Art Farmer (1963), and Teddy Wilson (1964) and made many recordings, including albums with George Shearing, McRae, Gene Ammons (1961, 1962), Billy Taylor (ii) (1962), Booker Ervin, Farmer, and Charles Mingus (all 1963), Clark Terry and Jaki Byard (both 1964), and Lucky Thompson. Later he recorded with Pat Martino (1967), Harold Mabern (1968), and Charles Earland (1977). Perkins's drumming is notable for its drive and swing; he plays to support the soloist rather than to display his own technique.

SELECTED RECORDINGS

As leader: *MJT + 3* (1959, VJ 1013)
As sideman: A. Jamal: *Count 'em 88* (1956, Argo 610); G. Shearing and Montgomery Brothers: *Love Walked in* (1961, Jlnd 955); C. Mingus: *Mingus, Mingus, Mingus, Mingus, Mingus* (1963, Imp. 54); B. Ervin: *Exultation!* (1963, Prst. 7293); J. Byard: *Out Front* (1964, Prst. 7397); L. Thompson: *Happy Days are Here Again* (1965, Prst. 7394)

BIBLIOGRAPHY

Feather '60s

J. KENT WILLIAMS

Perla, Gene (August) (*b* Hackensack, NJ, 1 March 1940). Bass player. He attended the Berklee College of Music, where he recorded as a pianist with the college band, and the Boston Conservatory of Music. Having changed to double bass, in the late 1960s he played in lofts in New York and performed with Woody Herman (1969–70), Sarah Vaughan (1970), Elvin Jones (1971–3), and Sonny Rollins (1974–5); he recorded with Herman and Jones. Around 1971 he often played with the Thad Jones–Mel Lewis Orchestra and Quartet. As a studio artist he recorded with Jeremy Steig (1970–71), Dave Liebman and Frank Foster (both 1974), Steve Grossman (1973–6), Jones (1975), and Charlie Mariano (1979). In 1975 he formed the Stone Alliance with Grossman and Don Alias; the group's recordings include *Stone Alliance* (1975–6, PM 013). Perla owns a music publishing company (Perla Music Co.) and two record companies (PM Records and Plug Records); he writes compositions and arrangements and also teaches music.

BIBLIOGRAPHY

Feather–Gitler '70s
P. Brodowski: "Gene Perla: a Musician with a Business Sense," *JF* [intl edn], no.24 (1973), 37
B. Rusch: "Gene Perla: Interview," *Cadence*, vii/6 (1982), 10

Perrin, Mimi (Jeannine) (*b* Paris, 2 Feb 1926). French pianist, singer, and arranger. She began her career as the leader of a trio and in 1956 recorded as a pianist and singer. Around the same year she joined the Blue Stars, of which she remained a member until 1958; she also recorded with the pianist Christian Chevallier (1959). She is best known for having led the DOUBLE SIX (1959–66), with which she made recordings (including *Dizzy Gillespie et les Double Six*, 1963, Phi. 200106); she also appeared in Martin Ritt's film *Paris Blues* (1961) and from 1968 lived in the USA. Perrin's style was strongly influenced by the work of King Pleasure and Lambert, Hendricks, and Ross.

BIBLIOGRAPHY

Feather '60s
M. Cullaz: "Mimi Perrin," *Jh*, no.346 (1978), 53

MICHEL LAPLACE

Perry, Ray (*b* Boston, 25 Feb 1915; *d* New York, 1950). Violinist and alto saxophonist. He began performing on violin and became known for singing in unison with his playing; from 1935 he also worked as an alto saxophonist. In 1940 he spent several months with Blanche Calloway before joining Lionel Hampton, with whom he remained until 1943. He made a number of recordings with Hampton, including *Fiddle-dee-dee* (1940, Vic. 27364), which was designed as a vehicle for his solo violin playing. He also recorded with Sabby Lewis (1944), Ethel Waters (as a member of J. C. Heard's orchestra in 1946), and Illinois Jacquet (1946, 1947); he later played again with Lewis (1948) and Jacquet (1950). Perry briefly led his own bands in 1946, 1947, and 1948.

based on *ChiltonW*

Persiany, André [Persiani, André Paul Stephane] (*b* Paris, 19 Nov 1927). French pianist. He led his own group from 1946 and recorded as a sideman with Bill Coleman (1949, 1955–6), Buck Clayton (1949, 1953), Mezz Mezzrow (1951), and Lionel Hampton (1953). In New York he worked with various leaders from 1956 to 1957; from 1961 to 1969 he was a member of Jonah Jones's quartet. After returning to France he performed with Charlie Shavers (1970) and recorded with Milt Buckner (1973, 1975) and Cat Anderson (1978). Persiany is an able swing player, influenced by Buckner, who employs block chords in his playing; his style is well represented by his album *Swinging Here and There* (1956–8, Pathé 05411721). Besides his work as a performer he has written several arrangements.

BIBLIOGRAPHY

FeatherE
H. Panassié and M. Gautier: *Dictionnaire du jazz* (Paris, 1954, rev. and enlarged 2/1971, enlarged 3/1980; Eng. trans., London, 1956, rev. A. A. Gurwitch as *Guide to Jazz*, Boston, 1956)
A. Clergeat: *Dictionnaire du jazz* (Paris, 1966)

MICHEL LAPLACE

Persip, Charli(e) [Charles Lawrence] (*b* Morristown, NJ, 26 July 1929). Drummer. After playing with Tadd Dameron (1953), he toured and recorded with Dizzy Gillespie (1953–8). He joined Harry Edison's quintet and (briefly) the Harry James Orchestra before forming his own group, the Jazz Statesmen, with Freddie Hubbard and Ron Carter in 1960. At around this time he also recorded with many leading swing and bop musicians, including Lee Morgan (1956–7), Dinah Washington (1957), Kenny Dorham and Zoot Sims (both 1958), Red Garland (1958, 1960–61), Gil Evans (1960), Don Ellis (1960–61), Carter and Eric Dolphy (1961), Roland Kirk (1961), and Gene Ammons (1962). He toured for several years as a drummer and conductor with Billy Eckstine (1966–*c*1973). From 1974 he was the principal drum instructor for Jazzmobile in New York, though he continued to perform and record, with Kirk (1976), Archie Shepp (1977), and Frank Foster (1977–8). He led a big band, Superband, with the trumpeter Gary La Furn, which recorded in New York in 1980, and in 1984 played in a trio with Jack DeJohnette and Eddie Gomez and recorded with his own group Superband (II).

Persip is one of the foremost bop big-band drummers and prefers the big-band setting to that of the small group; however, his work is heard to greater advantage on *We Free Kings*, made by Kirk's quartet in 1961, on which the drums are prominently recorded. He displays his command of a wide variety of modern styles on *How Time Passes*, which he recorded as a member of Ellis's quartet (1960).

SELECTED RECORDINGS

As leader: *The Jazz Statesmen* (1960, Beth. 6046); with G. La Furn: *Charli Persip and Gary La Furn's 17-Piece Superband* (1980, Stash 209); *In Case you Missed it* (1984, SN 1079)

As sideman: D. Gillespie: *World Statesman* (1956, Norg. 1084): *Dizzy Gillespie with Sonny Rollins and Sonny Stitt* (1957, Verve 8260); D. Ellis; *How Time Passes* (1960, Can. 9004); G. Evans: *Out of the Cool* (1960, Imp. 4); R. Carter: *Where?* (1961, NewJ 8265); R. Kirk: *We Free Kings* (1961, Mer. 60679)

BIBLIOGRAPHY

M. Jones: "Persip: All the Way from Dizzy to Eckstine," *MM* (16 Dec 1967), 6

J. B. Litweiler: "Profile: Charlie Persip," *DB*, xlii/3 (1975), 28

B. Primack: "Blindfold Test: Charli Persip," *DB*, xlvi/16 (1979), 61

BARRY KERNFELD

Person, Houston (*b* Florence, SC, 10 Nov 1934). Tenor saxophonist. Although he was taught piano by his mother as a child, he took little interest in music until he began collecting jazz recordings and playing tenor saxophone at the age of 17. During his military service in Germany he played in groups that included Eddie Harris, Lanny Morgan, Leo Wright, Cedar Walton, and Lex Humphries. He attended the Hartt School of Music and then toured with Johnny Hammond; from that time he showed a liking for working with organists. After leaving Hammond he formed his own group, which, with changing personnel, has made a number of recordings. He performed intermittently with Etta Jones from 1968 and from 1973 they worked together regularly, making nightclub and concert appearances. Besides his recordings as a leader, Person has taken part in sessions as a sideman with Groove Holmes's quintet and Charles Earland, and in a duo with Ran Blake. In 1984 he performed at the Grande Parade du Jazz, Nice, France. The influence of rhythm-and-blues is evident in Person's direct, swinging style and full-toned sound; he performs blues and ballads with particular skill.

SELECTED RECORDINGS

As leader: *The Nearness of You* (1977, Muse 5178); *Wild Flower* (1977, Muse 5161)

As sideman: E. Jones: *Love me with All your Heart* (1983, Muse 5262)

BIBLIOGRAPHY

Feather–Gitler '70s

E. Cook: "'I Just Like People who Swing': Houston Person," *JJI*, xxxviii/1 (1985), 13

EDDIE COOK

Persson, Åke (*b* Hässleholm, Sweden, 25 Feb 1932; *d* Stockholm, 5 Feb 1975). Swedish trombonist. He worked with Simon Brehm (1951–2, recording in 1951–4), Arne Domnérus (1952–3, recording at intervals from 1952 to 1960), and Hacke Björksten (recording in 1955–7, performing in 1957) and belonged to Harry Arnold's Radio Band (1956–9, recording in 1956–61); he also recorded with Lars Gullin (1951–7), George Wallington (1953), Roy Haynes (1954), and Benny Bailey and the drummer Joe Harris (*The Golden Touch*, 1959, Met. 15030). After playing in Quincy Jones's orchestra he joined the band of RIAS, Berlin, in 1961, with which he remained until 1975; at the same time he played in the Clarke–Boland Big Band (recording in 1963 and 1967–71) and appeared with Count Basie (recording in 1962), Duke Ellington, and Dizzy Gillespie.

BIBLIOGRAPHY

FeatherE; *Feather–Gitler '70s*

R. Dahlgren: Obituary, *Orkester journalen*, xliii (1975), March, 5

C.-E. Lindgren: "Mannen med unikaboxen" [The man with the lunch-box], *Orkester journalen*, xliii (1975), April, 10

ERIK KJELLBERG

Persson, Bent (*b* Blekinge, Sweden, 6 Sept 1947). Swedish cornetist. In the 1970s he played traditional jazz with Maggie's Blue Five and the Weatherbird Jazzband. He worked in the 1980s as the leader of Bent's Blue Rhythm Band. He is best known for his recording *Louis Armstrong's 50 Hot Choruses for Cornet* (1979, Kenneth 2044-5), on which he performs recreations of solos by Armstrong. (E. Kjellberg: *Svensk jazzhistoria: en översikt* [Swedish jazz history: an overview] (Stockholm, 1985), 248)

PEKKA GRONOW

Peterson, Chuck [Charles] (*b* Detroit, 1915; *d* Michigan, 21 Jan 1978). Trumpeter. He played horn and trombone in his high school band, then changed to trumpet and played with several local ensembles before joining a band led by Hank Biagini. In 1937 he became a member of Artie Shaw's band, and made several recordings with it (including *One Foot in the Groove*, 1939, Bb 10202); after leaving Shaw he played and recorded with Tony Pastor (1939–41), Tommy Dorsey (1939–42; for illustration *see* DORSEY, TOMMY), and Woody Herman (1941–2). He served in the army then returned to live and work in Detroit, though he recorded with Herman's First Herd in Chicago (1946) and possibly with Benny Carter in Los Angeles (1949).

based on *ChiltonW*

Peterson, Hannibal (Marvin) [Marvin (Charles); Hannibal] (*b* Smithville, TX, 11 Nov 1948). Trumpeter and composer. He learned drums and cornet in his youth and while studying at North Texas State University (1967–9) played trumpet in a college band. In 1970 he moved to New York and made a tour of the East Coast with Roland Kirk. The following year he began playing with the Gil Evans Orchestra, an association that continued into the 1980s. He performed and recorded with Pharoah Sanders (1971), Roy Haynes (*c*1972), and Elvin Jones (1973), then formed his own band to present his composition *Children of the Fire* (1974). From that time he has played trumpet and koto as leader of the Sunrise Orchestra (a quintet or sextet with the cellist Diedre Murray and a conventional rhythm section) and other small ensembles, including a free-jazz group with Enrico Rava, Roswell Rudd, Ken McIntyre, and Pat Patrick (1976). As a trumpet soloist, Peterson sometimes interrupts carefully articulated bop melodies with piercing sweeps through the upper register of the instrument. His preference for combining aspects of bop and free jazz extends also to his choice of repertory and sidemen: on the album *Naima*, for example (recorded with Kenny Barron, Cecil McBee, Billy Hart, and David Murray), the musicians improvise in a bop manner on the standard *In a Sentimental Mood*, whereas the title track involves them in freer playing.

SELECTED RECORDINGS

As leader: *Children of the Fire* (1974, Sunrise 1944); *Hannibal* (1975, MPS 68061); *Naima* (1978, EMI 98004); *The Angels of Atlanta* (1981, Enja 3085)

As sideman: P. Sanders: *Black Unity* (1971, Imp. 9219); R. Davis: *Epistrophy and Now's the Time* (1972, Muse 5002); R. Haynes: *Senyah* (*c*1972, Mstr. 351)

BIBLIOGRAPHY

L. Goddet: "Interview: Hannibal," *Jh*, no.304 (1974), 11

B. J. Primack: "Hannibal," *DB*, xliv/15 (1977), 24

BARRY KERNFELD

Peterson, Oscar (Emmanuel) (*b* Montreal, 15 Aug 1925). Canadian pianist. He studied classical piano from the age of six, and when he was 14 won a local talent contest. During his late teens he played on a weekly Montreal radio show and throughout the mid-1940s was heard with Canada's well-known Johnny Holmes Orchestra, playing in a style that blended elements from the styles of Teddy Wilson, Art Tatum, Nat "King" Cole, Erroll Garner, and others. Norman Granz invited him to appear at Carnegie Hall in 1949 in a Jazz at the Philharmonic concert, and from that time onwards managed Peterson's career. Peterson toured regularly with Jazz at the Philharmonic during the early 1950s and formed his own trio using the combination of piano, guitar, and double bass popularized by Cole. His most popular trio, the other members of which were Herb Ellis (guitar) and Ray Brown (double bass), remained together from 1953 until 1958 (see illustration), when the guitarist was eventually replaced by a drummer, Ed Thigpen. In this form the group, considered by many to have been the ideal vehicle for Peterson's unique talents, remained intact from 1959 until 1965. In 1960, with Brown, Thigpen, and Phil Nimmons, Peterson established the Advanced School of Contemporary Music in Toronto, which he ran for three years. He sang for the first time since the mid-1950s on the album *With Respect to Nat* (1965), dedicated to Cole.

In the early 1970s Peterson began concentrating on solo performances, proving incontestably that he was one of the greatest solo pianists in the history of jazz. Since the mid-1970s he has played with symphony orchestras throughout North America and has joined established jazz musicians such as Dizzy Gillespie, Clark Terry, Joe Pass, and Niels-Henning Ørsted Pedersen for a number of memorable duo performances (for illustration *see* ØRSTED PEDERSEN, NIELS-HENNING), many of them recorded by Granz for Pablo Records.

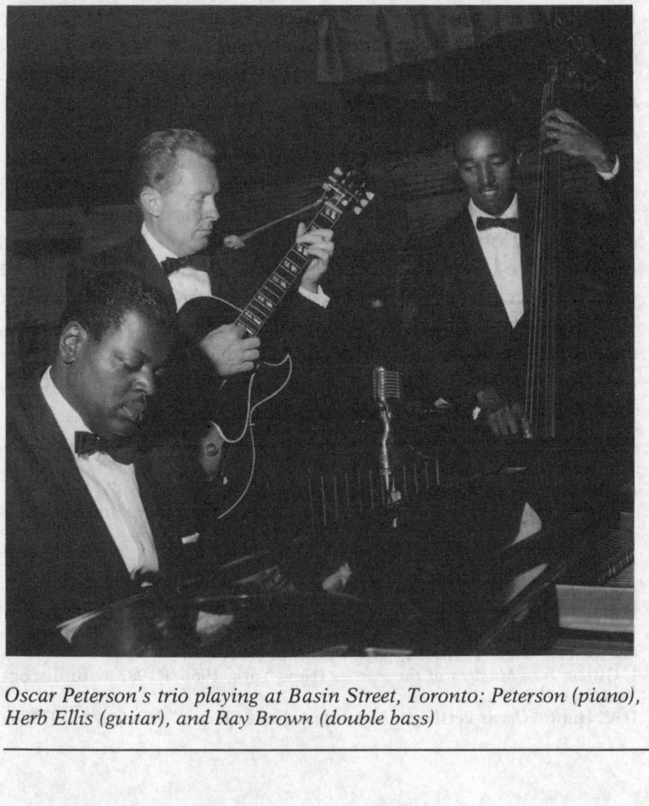

Oscar Peterson's trio playing at Basin Street, Toronto: Peterson (piano), Herb Ellis (guitar), and Ray Brown (double bass)

Peterson is a prolific recording artist, having issued as many as five or six albums a year. He has also been active as a jazz composer (his *Canadiana Suite* was nominated by the National Academy of Recording Arts and Sciences as one of the best jazz compositions of 1965). Because of his extraordinary technique and his comprehensive grasp of jazz piano history, Peterson is often compared with Art Tatum, with whom he shares an exceptional gift for inspiring awe from musicians, critics, and listeners alike.

SELECTED RECORDINGS

As unaccompanied soloist: *My Favorite Instrument* (1980, MPS 68076)

Duos with D. Gillespie: *Oscar Peterson and Dizzy Gillespie* (1974, Pablo 2310740)

As leader: *Affinity* (1962, Verve 68516); *The Oscar Peterson Trio Plus One: Clark Terry* (1964, Mer. 60975); *With Respect to Nat* (1965, Lml. 86029); *Oscar Peterson in Russia* (1974, Pablo 2625711); *The Way I Really Play* (1980, MPS 68075)

BIBLIOGRAPHY

B. James: "Oscar Peterson," *Essays on Jazz* (London, 1961/*R*1985), 134

A. Johnson and L. Tomkins: "Oscar Peterson: my Approach to Playing," *Crescendo*, ii/9 (1964), 10 [interview]

R. Palmer: "Oscar Peterson," *JJ*, xxi/3 (1968), 4

L. Feather: *From Satchmo to Miles* (New York, 1972), 187

L. Lyons: "Oscar Peterson: Piano Worship," *DB*, xlii/21 (1975), 12

S. Quaver: "Oscar Peterson: the History of an Artist," *CI*, xiii (1975), no.8, p.17; no.9, p.17; no.10, p.16

L. Feather: "Piano Giants of Jazz: Oscar Peterson," *CK*, iv/7 (1978), 53

L. Lyons: "Oscar Peterson," *CK*, iv/3 (1978), 30

M. Miller: "Oscar Peterson," *Encyclopedia of Music in Canada*, ed. H. Kallmann, G. Potvin, and K. Winters (Toronto, Buffalo, and London, 1981), 748

R. Palmer: "Oscar Peterson: Genesis and Revelation," *JJI*, xxxiv (1981), no.7, p.8; no.8, p.6; no.10, p.6

J. Litchfield: *The Canadian Jazz Discography, 1916–1980* (Toronto, Buffalo, and London, 1982), 552–640

G. Armbruster: "Oscar Peterson: a Jazz Piano Giant Talks about his Synthesizer Debut," *Keyboard*, ix/10 (1983), 56 [incl. discography]

L. Lyons: *The Great Jazz Pianists, Speaking of their Lives and Music* (New York, 1983), 130

Richard Palmer: *Oscar Peterson* (Tunbridge Wells, England, 1984) [incl. discography]

BILL DOBBINS

Pethman, Esa (*b* Kouvola, Finland, 17 May 1938). Finnish tenor saxophonist, flutist, and composer. He played with Erkki Melakoski's band (1959–63), and in 1962 formed a quartet with his brother, the drummer Anssi Pethman, and the pianist Heikki Sarmanto. He performed at the Landskrona (1963) and Montreux (1967) jazz festivals. Pethman combines a flowing style of playing with an ability to create original jazz compositions, using unusual forms and instrumental colors. His work is well represented by the album *The Modern Sound of Finland* (1964, RCA LSP10040).

PEKKA GRONOW

Petit, Buddy [Buddie; Crawford, Joseph] (*b* White Castle, LA, *c*1897; *d* New Orleans, 4 July 1931). Trumpeter and bandleader. He began attracting favorable attention with his trumpet playing in New Orleans while he was still a teenager. After working in the Young Olympia Band, he became joint leader of a group with Jimmie Noone (whose place was later taken by Albert Nicholas). In 1917 he played briefly in California with Jelly Roll Morton; he then returned to New Orleans and formed his own band which, for the next ten years, had long-term engagements in several Louisiana towns, including Mandeville and Covington. The band also worked regularly in New Orleans and occasionally in Florida. Petit himself paid another short visit to California around 1922 as a member of Frankie Dusen's band. By the late 1920s he was working aboard the SS *Madison*.

There are no recorded examples of Petit's playing, which over the years has taken on legendary qualities. There can be no doubt that he was an exceptional musician, remembered even more for his tone and expressive ideal than for his range. Several New Orleans trumpeters, including Punch Miller, Herb Morand, and Wingy Manone, cited Petit as an influence.

For illustration *see* BANDS, fig.2.

BIBLIOGRAPHY

J. D. Donder: "My Buddy," *Fn*, xiv/3 (1983), 24; xiv/4 (1983), 4

JOHN CHILTON

Petit, Joseph (*b* New Orleans, 1873; *d* New Orleans, 1946). Trombonist, stepfather of Buddy Petit. Before World War I he led the Security and Terminal brass bands, then in the early 1920s worked with Wooden Joe Nicholas's Camellia Orchestra and Brass Band. He recorded, with Nicholas, as a member of the Original Creole Stompers for the American Music label in 1945. (*ChartersJ*)

MARCEL JOLY

Petrowsky, Ernst-Ludwig (*b* Gustrow, Germany, 10 Dec 1933). German reed player and flutist. He first played jazz in a small group and a big band, both led by the pianist Eberhard Weise (1955–60). In 1962 he formed the Manfred Ludwig Sextet with the reed player Manfred Schulze and in 1966 the ensemble Studio IV, which performed on radio; in the 1960s he also played with Joachim Kühn. He worked with the big band of Berlin radio (1970–79), Ulrich Gumpert's group SOK, and big bands led by Klaus Lenz. He also played in the cooperative group Synopsis (formed 1973, re-formed 1984 as the Zentral-Quartett) and performed with the Ulrich Gumpert Workshop Band. From 1972 he led trios (with the double bass player Klaus Koch and Günter Sommer, with Koch and the flugelhorn player Heinz Becker, and with Koch and the guitarist Helmut "Joe" Sachse) and worked in a duo with the singer Uschi Brüning. In the early 1980s he joined George Gruntz's Concert Jazz Band, began working with the Globe Unity Orchestra, and toured with the Bergisch-Brandenburgisches Quartett. Petrowsky's saxophone playing can be heard to advantage on *Selbdritt* (1980, FMP 0890), recorded with Koch and Becker, and an album of duos made with Brüning (*Das neue Usel*, 1986, FMP S18). (B. Noglik: "Ernst-Ludwig Petrowsky, Günter Sommer," *Jazzwerkstatt international* (Berlin, 1981), 315–45 [incl. interview, discography])

BERT NOGLIK

Petrucciani, Michel (*b* Orange, France, 28 Dec 1962). French pianist. The son of a jazz guitarist, he studied classical piano for seven years and gave his first concert at the age of 13; two years later he played with Kenny Clarke and Clark Terry. At the age of 17 he moved to Paris, where he recorded his first album. Around this time he began working with Lee Konitz. In 1982 he traveled to California and became associated with Charles Lloyd; their performance at the Montreux International Jazz Festival won the Prix d'excellence in 1982. Petrucciani began receiving acclaim in the USA after his performance at Carnegie Recital Hall in 1983 as part of the Kool Jazz Festival. He has worked with such musicians as John Abercrombie, Jim Hall, and Jack DeJohnette. His style combines the lyricism and thoughtful harmonic approach of Bill Evans (ii) with a technical assurance comparable with that of Oscar Peterson. During performances Petrucciani often extemporizes medleys of standards and his own compositions linked by freely improvised transitional passages.

SELECTED RECORDINGS

As unaccompanied soloist: *Oracle's Destiny* (1983, Owl 032); *100 Hearts* (1984, Conc. 3001)

Duos with L. Konitz: *Toot Sweet* (1982, Owl 028)

As leader: *Michel Petrucciani Trio* (1981, Owl 925); *Pianism* (1985, BN 85124); *Power of Three* (1986, BN 75133)

As sideman: C. Lloyd: *Montreux '82* (1982, Elek. Mus. 960220)

BIBLIOGRAPHY

L. Gourse: "Profile: Michel Petrucciani," *DB*, li/1 (1984), 49
B. Doerschuk: "Michel Petrucciani," *Keyboard*, xii/11 (1986), 34 [incl. discography]
W. Goode: Liner notes, *Pianism* (BN 85124, 1986)

BOB DOERSCHUK

Pettiford, Oscar (*b* Okmulgee, OK, 30 Sept 1922; *d* Copenhagen, 8 Sept 1960). Double bass player, cellist, and bandleader. Of mixed black and American Indian extraction, he was born into a large, musical family and learned many instruments in the family's touring band, which was based in Minneapolis. In 1943 he was engaged as a double bass player for Charlie Barnet's band (see illustration), with which he traveled to New York in the same year. After working with a quintet led by Roy Eldridge (1943) he found a place in the emerging bop scene, and, with Dizzy Gillespie, led a group at the Onyx Club (winter 1943–4). Personal differences caused this pioneering group to disband, but one year later he and Gillespie recorded together. From 1944 Pettiford played in numerous small bop ensembles and in various big bands, notably those of Duke Ellington (1945–8) and Woody Herman (1949). In the mid-1950s he led his own big band which, though highly regarded for its inventive arrangements and instrumentation, suffered from instability of personnel, owing in part to Pettiford's difficult temperament. He emigrated to Europe in 1958, and in his final years was based in Copenhagen.

Pettiford was the first jazz bass player to adapt and elaborate the innovations of Jimmy Blanton within a bop context, and his ideas and discoveries had a lasting influence on the bop style as a whole. His earliest recorded solos, such as *The man I love* (1943), were learned by rote by many aspiring bop bass players, though few could approach his penetrating tone and clear projection of ideas. Later, from about 1950, he transferred his solo style to amplified cello, which he played in a bouncy, dexterous style, reminiscent of Charlie Christian. Together with Ray Brown and Charles Mingus, who owed much to his influence, Pettiford was influential in establishing the double bass as a jazz solo instrument equal in importance to the winds.

SELECTED RECORDINGS

As leader: *Basically Duke* (1954, Beth. 1019); *The Oscar Pettiford Orchestra in Hi-fi* (1956–7, ABC-Para. 135, 227)

As sideman: C. Hawkins: The man I love (1943, Sig. 9001); D. Ellington: Swamp Fire (1946, Vic. 201992); L. Thompson: *Lucky Thompson Featuring Oscar Pettiford* (1956, ABC-Para. 111, 171)

BIBLIOGRAPHY

FeatherE
P. Harris: "Oscar Pettiford now on Cello Kick," *DB*, xvii/26 (1950), 20
N. Hentoff: "An Oscar," *DB*, xxiv/6 (1957), 17
G. Hoefer: "Oscar Pettiford," *DB*, xxxiii/11 (1966), 25
I. Gitler: *Jazz Masters of the Forties* (New York, 1966/*R*1983 with discography), 150
D. C. Hunt: "Oscar Pettiford: Absolute Artistic Clarity," *JJ*, xxvi/8 (1973), 6

Members of Charlie Barnet's band, summer 1943: (left to right) Howard McGhee (trumpet), Trummy Young (trombone), Oscar Pettiford (double bass), Peanuts Holland (trumpet) and Barnet (leader)

C. Carrère: "Pitter Panther Patter: les bassistes de Duke Ellington," *Jh*, no.316 (1975), 10

J. E. Berendt: "Thank you, Oscar Pettiford," *Ein Fenster aus Jazz: Essays, Portraits, Reflexionen* (Frankfurt am Main, Germany, 1977), 135

J. BRADFORD ROBINSON

Pettis, Jack (*b* Danville, IL, 1902). Saxophonist, clarinetist, and bandleader. He taught himself to play C-melody saxophone at the age of 16 and worked in Chicago with Elmer Schoebel and Paul Mares (1919). He was a member of Mares's Friars Society Orchestra, which first recorded in 1922 and was later renamed the NEW ORLEANS RHYTHM KINGS (1923). He moved to New York and in 1924 joined the violinist Ben Bernie's orchestra, in which he played tenor and C-melody saxophone and clarinet. From 1926 he made a number of recordings as a leader, some of which were issued under pseudonyms. His bands contained many well-known musicians, including Jack Teagarden and Benny Goodman. Pettis played with a distinctive tone in the hot style; he continued performing into the 1930s.

SELECTED RECORDINGS

As leader: Dry Martini/Hot Heels (1928, Voc. 15703); Spanish Dream/Doin' the New Low Down (1928, Vic. 21559); Freshman Hop/Sweetest Melody (1929, OK 41411)

As sideman: I. Mills: St. Louis Blues (1929, Ban. 32701); I wonder what my gal is doin'?/What a Night! (1929, 1930, Bruns. 4998); Crazy 'bout my Gal/Railroad Man (1930, Bruns. 4838)

BIBLIOGRAPHY

W. W. Vaché, Sr.: "The Piquant Puzzle of Jack Pettis," *MR*, xiii/2 (1985), 7 [incl. discography]

WARREN VACHÉ, SR.

Peyton, Benny [Benton E.] (*b c*1890; *d* New York, 24 Jan 1965). Drummer. After traveling to Europe as a member of Will Marion Cook's Southern Syncopated Orchestra (1919), he formed his own group from members of the band and led the Jazz Kings in London. It made two recordings for Columbia (1920), neither of which was issued, and was resident at the Hammersmith Palais (1921). In the 1920s and 1930s he continued to perform with his own band throughout Europe; among his sidemen were Tommy Ladnier and June Cole (both 1929). He also toured the USSR with the trombonist Frank Withers and Sidney Bechet (1926) and with Joe Turner (i) accompanied Adelaide Hall in Zurich (1935). In 1939 Peyton returned to New York and became closely involved in the AFM (Local 802); during the 1950s he played regularly as a percussionist.

BIBLIOGRAPHY

A. McCarthy: *Big Band Jazz* (New York and London, 1974), 309

F. Driggs and H. Lewine: *Black Beauty, White Heat: a Pictorial History of Classic Jazz, 1920–1950* (New York, 1982)

based on *ChiltonW*

Peyton, Dave (*b c*1885; *d* Chicago, 1956). Bandleader and pianist. After playing in Wilbur Sweatman's trio in Chicago from around 1908 to 1912, he led his own band there; in the late 1920s his sidemen included Charlie Allen, George Mitchell, Bob Shoffner, Reuben Reeves, Kid Ory, Bud Scott, Jasper Taylor, Jimmy Bertrand, and Baby Dodds, and in the early 1930s Preston Jackson, Darnell Howard, Jerome Don Pasquall, and Lee Collins. Peyton also worked as a band contractor and supplied musicians for other engagements. In the mid-1930s his orchestra was resident at the Regal Theatre, after which he performed mainly as a soloist until the late 1940s. Peyton was best known for his abilities as a leader and organizer; he made only one recording (*Baby o' Mine*, 1935, Decca 7115), with Richard M. Jones. From 10 October 1925 to 24 August 1929 he wrote a weekly column on music for the *Chicago Defender*.

BIBLIOGRAPHY

T. J. Hennessey: "The Black Chicago Establishment 1919–1930," *JJS*, ii/1 (1974), 15–45

A. McCarthy: *Big Band Jazz* (New York and London, 1974), 36

based on *ChiltonW*

Phase shifter. An electronic device that transforms the timbre of an instrument or a voice by superimposing on the original sound a copy of it, the phase patterns of which are altered. It is closely akin to a FLANGER, and can produce a similar effect.

Philburn, (Michael) Al(oysius) (*b* Newark, NJ, 24 Aug 1902; *d* Glen Cove, NY, 29 Feb 1972). Trombonist. He learned trombone from the age of 14 and first performed locally. He played and recorded in the orchestras of Paul Specht (1925–7) and Cass Hagen (1927–8), and performed frequently with the singer Ed Kirkeby (1927–30), with whom, as a member of the California Ramblers, he made several recordings (1927). After playing with Bert Lown's orchestra for some years (from 1929) he worked in studios, recording with many musicians, among them Chick Bullock (1933), Adrian Rollini (1933, 1934), and Red McKenzie and Bob Howard (both 1936); he may be heard as a soloist on Louis Armstrong's *Yes! Yes! My! My!* (1936, Decca 698). Philburn was a staff musician at radio station WNGW and NBC (1936–48) and in the 1950s he concentrated on session work. After a brief period with Tony Parenti (1962) he led his own dixieland band (until 1964). He continued performing until the late 1960s.

based on *ChiltonW*

Phillips, Barre (*b* San Francisco, 27 Oct 1934). Double bass player. He began playing at the age of 13, first in school orchestras, then in dixieland and bop groups. He met Ornette Coleman and in 1962 moved to New York, where he played free jazz with Don Heckman and Don Ellis (1962), and with Archie Shepp, Bill Dixon, and Paul Bley (1963). He performed in the première of Larry Austin's *Improvisations for Orchestra and Jazz Soloists* with the New York PO under Leonard Bernstein in 1962. He was a member of Jimmy Giuffre's trio for two years (1963–5), and in 1964 toured Europe with George Russell's big band. In 1965 he began playing with the pianist Peter Nero's trio, recorded with Bob James, and appeared with Shepp at the Newport Jazz Festival. Having found European audiences more receptive to his playing than American ones he moved to London, where by 1967 he was playing with John Stevens and Evan Parker; he performed in France with Marion Brown and in Germany with Gunter Hampel. In 1968 he recorded a solo album, *Journal violone,* which was the first LP to consist entirely of improvised music for unaccompanied double bass. After working in a trio with John Surman and the drummer Stu Martin (1969–71, 1976–7) he formed the sextet Music By (1979). In 1984 he was musician-in-residence at the Music Gallery in Toronto. He has continued to play frequently in Europe.

SELECTED RECORDINGS

As unaccompanied soloist: *Journal violone* (1968, Music Man 601)
Duos with D. Holland: *Music for Two Basses* (1971, ECM 1011)
As leader: *Journal violone*, ii (1979, ECM 1149); *Music By* (1980, ECM 1178)
As sideman: B. James: *Explosions* (1965, ESP 1009); L. Austin: *Improvisations for Orchestra and Jazz Soloists* (1967, Col. MS6733); G. Hampel: *Jubilation* (1983, Birth 0038)

BIBLIOGRAPHY

G. Schoukroun: "Phillips à la barre," *Jm*, no.296 (1981), 26
B. Smith: "Barre Phillips," *Coda*, no.198 (1984), 19

JOHN VOIGT

Phillips, Flip [Filipelli, Joseph Edward] (*b* New York, 26 March 1915). Tenor saxophonist. After playing clarinet in a restaurant band in Brooklyn (1934–9) and with Frankie Newton (1940–41) he replaced Vido Musso as tenor saxophonist in Woody Herman's First Herd (1944; for illustration *see* HERMAN, WOODY, fig.1*a*). While with Herman (1944–6), and later, on tours with Jazz at the Philharmonic (1946–57), he acquired a reputation for his energetic improvisations (notably on *Perdido*); despite his rather tasteless, honking tone, these performances were popular with audiences, but unfortunately tended to overshadow his sumptuous ballad playing (as on *Sweet and Lovely*) and the many swinging, melodic solos he recorded as the leader of small groups. After touring Europe with Benny Goodman (late 1959) Phillips settled in Pompano Beach, Florida, where he played part-time and managed an apartment building. He appeared at the Colorado Jazz Party (1970) and with Herman at the Newport Jazz Festival (1972), and resumed full-time playing in 1975. His later recordings exhibit the control, imagination, and warmth of his playing. He made a tour of Europe in 1982 and continued to perform into the late 1980s.

SELECTED RECORDINGS

As leader: *Flip Phillips Quintet* (1954, Clef 260–62); *Phillips' Head* (1975, Choice 1013); *Flipenstein* (1981, Prog. 7063)
As sideman: R. Norvo: Slim Slam Blues (1945, Dial 1045); W. Herman: Apple Honey (1945, Col. 36803); Sweet and Lovely (1946, MGM 30602); Jazz at the Philharmonic: Perdido (1947, Mer./Clef 11000–02); The Opener (1949, Mer./Clef 11054–6); Jam Session: *Jam Session no.2* (1952, Clef 4002), incl. Funky Blues, What is this thing called love?

BIBLIOGRAPHY

A. Morgan: "Woody's Tenors," *JM*, vi/8 (1960), 13
J. Burns: "Swing Tenors," *JJ*, xix/12 (1966), 13
B. Rusch and S. Miller: "Flip Phillips," *Cadence*, ii/12 (1977), 6 [interview]
M. L. Hester: "Flip: Past and Present," *MR*, xv/4 (1988), 1

BARRY KERNFELD

Phillips, Sid [Simon] (*b* London, 14 June 1907; *d* Chertsey, England, 23 May 1973). English clarinetist and arranger. He studied violin and piano as a child and taught himself theory and harmony. In his late teens he began playing saxophone and clarinet and performed with his brothers' band in Europe. He worked as staff arranger for a music publisher and as music director for the Edison–Bell Gramophone Co. From 1930 he wrote arrangements for Bert Ambrose and led his own quintet. Later he joined Ambrose's band (1933), with which he recorded on clarinet and alto and baritone saxophones (1933–7). In 1937 Phillips visited the USA, where he broadcast and recorded with American musicians. After serving in the RAF he formed another quintet (1946) and composed several classical works for the BBC SO. From 1949 until his death he led his own dixieland band; among his sidemen were George Shearing, Colin Bailey, Tommy Whittle, and Kenny Ball. Phillips made several recordings as a leader from 1928 into the 1970s.

BIBLIOGRAPHY

J. Godbolt: *A History of Jazz in Britain, 1919–50* (London, Melbourne, Australia, and New York, 1984)
D. Fairweather: "Phillips, Sid," in I. Carr, D. Fairweather, and B. Priestley: *Jazz: the Essential Companion* (London, 1987)
E. S. Walker: "Sid Phillips: the Early Years," *Sv*, no.130 (1987), 143

NEVIL SKRIMSHIRE

Phillips, Sonny (*b* Mobile, AL, 7 Dec 1936). Organist and pianist. He grew up in a musical family, though he did not concentrate on studying music until 1959, when he took some lessons on piano with Ahmad Jamal. He soon changed to organ after hearing Jimmy Smith, and, listening to Thelonious Monk, Bud Powell, and Oscar Peterson, developed an individual style in the blues tradition. In the 1960s and 1970s he traveled in the Northeast with Eddie Harris, Gene Ammons, and Lou Donaldson. After settling in New York in 1967 Phillips converted to Islam (which he had studied since 1959) and, with the Congolese drummer Titos Sompa, began to operate the Tanawa Art Center. From 1969 to 1970, and again from 1974, he played and recorded with, and also wrote arrangements for, Houston Person's group. Illness curtailed his activities in 1980, but the following year he moved to Los Angeles, where he has performed as a pianist and organist and worked as a teacher.

SELECTED RECORDINGS

As leader: *My Black Flower* (1976, Muse 5118); *I Concentrate on You* (1977, Muse 5157)

As sideman: H. Person: *Wild Flower* (1977, Muse 5161)

BIBLIOGRAPHY

S. Freedman: "Profile: Sonny Phillips," *DB*, xlvi/14 (1979), 46

STEVEN STRUNK

Phoemipol Aduldej. *See* BHUMIBOL ADULYADEJ.

Phoenix Jazz. Record company and label. The company was established by Bob Porter in Kingston, New Jersey, in 1972; its policy was to reissue historic jazz. The first album in the catalogue was a collection of all the material recorded by Cootie Williams with Bud Powell for Hit and Majestic. Later releases presented small-group and big-band material by Dizzy Gillespie and rare items by Nat "King" Cole, Charlie Ventura, Coleman Hawkins, Roy Eldridge, Billie Holiday, and Sabby Lewis. Perhaps the most important issues, however, were two LPs that contained recordings made in 1953–4 (for broadcasting purposes) of performances given by Charlie Parker in Boston. To celebrate the fifth anniversary of its formation, the company issued in 1977 a compilation of obscure but enlightening material by Gillespie, Hawkins, Benny Golson, and Bill Harris (i). Thereafter its activities declined, but the company has remained in existence into the late 1980s.

MARK GARDNER

Piano [pianoforte]. A keyboard instrument distinguished by the fact that its strings are struck by rebounding hammers. From the end of the 18th century it has been the principal domestic keyboard instrument in Europe and the USA. The modern piano has a range of a little over seven octaves, from *A''* to *c'''''*; the player can sound a large number of notes simultaneously and vary their loudness by changing the force with which the keys are struck. The present article covers the history and use of the piano in jazz.

1. Development of early jazz piano. 2. The stride school and Art Tatum. 3. Swing and boogie-woogie. 4. The transition to bop. 5. After 1950: the acoustic piano. 6. After 1950: the electric and electronic piano.

1. DEVELOPMENT OF EARLY JAZZ PIANO. The piano, both as a solo instrument and in ensembles of various sizes, was important in the development of early jazz. During the first two decades of the 20th century (before the arrival of radio and television) piano playing was a major form of domestic entertainment. Player pianos, which reproduced performances mechanically from punched paper rolls, served to disseminate RAGTIME (the immediate predecessor of jazz) to a wide public, and during the same period pianists in New Orleans, as well as those in other southern cities, developed the playing and harmonization of the BLUES.

The piano was the major performance medium for ragtime, the percussive nature of the instrument being perfect for the clipped syncopations of the music; in addition it was possible for the piano to imitate an entire group. While the player's left hand kept strict time, alternating pedal notes with chords in the "oompah" manner of the marching band, the right hand played syncopated "raggy" figures, often derived from chordal hand positions, in the treble. The general left-hand approach, with its repeated leap from bass note to chord, formed the basis of the later jazz style known as stride (see §2 below). Scott Joplin's *Maple Leaf Rag* was one of the best known and most typical examples of the characteristics of ragtime piano (ex.1).

Ex.1 From Scott Joplin's *Maple Leaf Rag*, as recorded on a piano roll in 1916; transcr. L. Koch

In the development from ragtime to jazz the major transforming element was an increased sense of freedom, in which the left hand gradually took on more linear aspects – walking 10ths and octaves and melodic runs – as well as a greater feeling of movement. At the same time the right hand was liberated from a literal reading of composed ragtime melodies by several distinct innovations: a growing use of swinging eighth-notes; a freer approach to rhythm by playing ahead of or behind the beat set up by the left hand; and a more liberal treatment of the melody in a tendency towards paraphrase and a gradual increase in other, freer, procedures of improvisation. Joplin's *Maple Leaf Rag* played as composed (as on the piano roll made in 1916 from which ex.1 was transcribed) compares strikingly with the recording made by Jelly Roll Morton for the Library of Congress (1938, Circle [USA] 22), which was a conscious attempt to re-create the innovations of early jazz performers (ex.2). Not only does Morton illustrate some of the points already mentioned, he also injects a true jazz rhythmic feeling into his playing with four beats to the bar, completely obliterating the stiff, march-like rhythms of ragtime.

Ex.2 From Jelly Roll Morton's version of *Maple Leaf Rag* (1938, Circle [USA] 22); transcr. L. Koch

An investigation of Morton's solo piano recordings from 1923–4 reveals many elements of early jazz piano techniques, some of them within the fashion for using the piano in "orchestral imitation." Among these was the "Spanish tinge," an early instance of Latin jazz, in which the left hand created a tango-influenced rhythm within the basic stride style; good examples may be heard on *New Orleans Joys* (1923, Gen. 5486) and *Mamanita* (1924, Gen. 5632).

The early jazz piano style was developed to its full potential by Earl Hines, who displayed great originality both as an unaccompanied soloist and as a band pianist. His solo on *Save it, pretty mama* (1928, OK 8657), with Louis Armstrong's Savoy Ballroom Five, illustrates strings of walking 10ths, a suspension of the stride rhythm at climactic points, and a melodic use of eighth-notes in the left hand; and in the right, virtuoso 16th-notes runs and arpeggios which genuinely further his musical ideas rather than being solely decorative. The overall performance gives a sense of unbridled swing coupled with stark originality.

In ensembles, however, the early jazz pianist changed roles to suit the varying needs of the group. The percussive nature of the piano made it an ideal accompanying instrument, along with the banjo and drums, for wind and brass players, but the pianist could be freer than the other instrumentalists in the rhythm section and add embellishments to the ensemble sound. Because of its ability to maintain a strongly rhythmic bass line, the piano was sometimes employed as a solo instrument to provide contrast to the group sound; it was also occasionally used in a lone capacity to accompany an improvised solo. Lil Hardin provides a good example of the latter in her own composition *Sweet Lovin' Man* (1923, OK 4906), recorded with King Oliver's Creole Jazz Band, in which she alone accompanies Johnny Dodds's blues improvisations, using tasteful ornamental figures; during the rest of the piece, however, she plays in a strict ensemble style, even being charged with keeping a firm bass. Along the same lines, but with stronger emphasis on musical interchange and on the piano and pianistic techniques, is the classic duet between Earl Hines and Louis Armstrong, *Weather Bird* (1928, OK 41454). While maintaining a relentless drive, Hines varies his approaches to accompaniment. In general Hines and other early pianists adopted such devices as dividing the stride bass pattern between the hands, playing four chords to a bar, and adding right-hand embellishments over a stride left hand. Hines's performance on *Weather Bird* also gives ample evidence of his "trumpet" style, in which he played octaves instead of full chords in the right hand; his octave attack was sharp, like that of a brass instrument, and he used tremolos on long notes to simulate vibrato and/or a breath crescendo.

A similar variety of approaches to accompaniment and to solo playing within an ensemble may be heard on almost any of the recordings made by Morton with his Red Hot Peppers for Victor between 15 September 1926 and 11 June 1928. *Cannonball Blues* (1926, Vic. 20431) offers some excellent examples of his use of embellishment, such as the passages in double-time over each phrase-ending of a low guitar solo; he also plays a beautiful piano solo, using treble notes only, over the sustained chords of the brass and wind instruments.

2. The stride school and Art Tatum. The style most directly associated with ragtime, and which grew out of it by way of the so-called East Coast ragtimers, was that of the Harlem stride piano school, which had its origins around the time of World War I. Its main practitioners were Luckey Roberts, Willie "the Lion" Smith, and James P. Johnson. When playing as soloists, Count Basie and Duke Ellington were also formidable exponents of stride. The distinctive "stride bass" (ex.3), adapted from left-hand patterns of ragtime, represents only one of

Ex.3 A typical stride bass

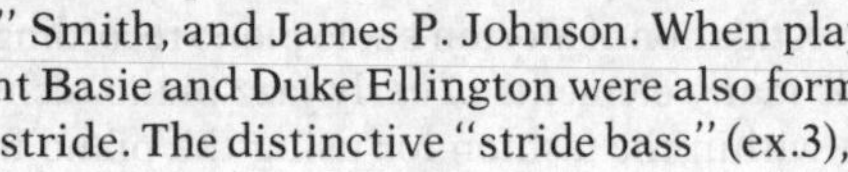

the increased virtuoso demands of the style, which in general called for fast tempos, a full use of the piano's range, and a wide array of pianistic devices – some from the classical repertory in which many of the Harlem pianists were trained. While the pieces performed by the stride pianists were fully composed (Johnson's *Carolina Shout* (1921, OK 4495) is per-

1. Art Tatum, c1942

2. Teddy Wilson, 1942

haps the most famous early example), they were nevertheless seen as a basis for improvisation. Paul Machlin's analysis of the music of Johnson's pupil, Fats Waller, discusses at length the latter's improvisational approach, notably in an examination of different takes of some of his solo recordings made in 1929.

The culmination of stride piano is probably the work of Art Tatum, where dazzling ornamental runs and arpeggios and a sophisticated harmonic vocabulary are fused to the basic style. The approaches that influenced Tatum, and the growth of the stride style, may be heard in such recordings as Hines's *Save it, pretty mama,* Waller's *Numb Fumblin'* (1929, Vic. 38508), and Johnson's *You've got to be modernistic* (1930, Bruns. 4762). Later, Tatum's prodigious technique, use of advanced harmonies, and sympathy for popular-song material resulted in some refinement of the style, but his individual approach was a direct development of stride. His recordings set a standard for solo jazz piano in terms of virtuosity: *Tiger Rag* (1940, Decca 18051), in particular, demonstrates both his debt to the true stride style and his personal refinement of it.

3. Swing and boogie-woogie. Generally speaking the solo piano style became more refined during the swing period. In order for players to deal with the faster tempos they made more use of single bass notes and simple chords (sometimes merely broken 10ths or seventh chords used in an "oompah" fashion), thus lightening the left-hand part; walking 10ths remained an important device for connecting chord progressions. The right-hand part was treated in a similar fashion, so that it often carried only single notes. Teddy Wilson's recording of *Between the devil and the deep blue sea* (1937, Bruns. 8025) exemplifies these qualities (ex.4).

Ex.4 From the fourth chorus of Teddy Wilson: *Between the Devil and the Deep Blue Sea* (1937, Bruns. 8025); transcr. H. Martin (Martin, 1986)

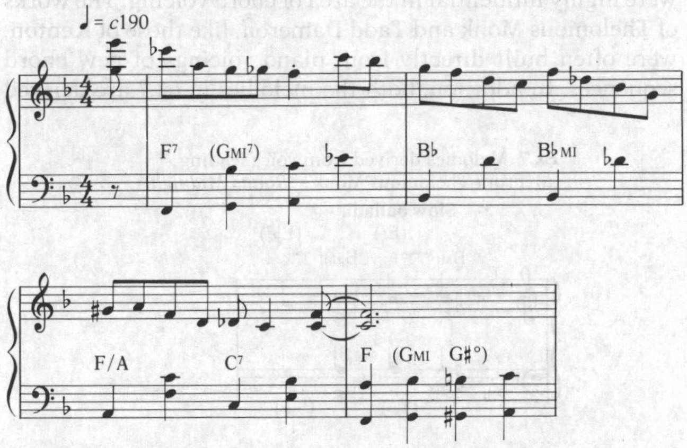

Wilson carried his lightness of touch into his group playing, as may be heard on *China Boy* (1936, Vic. 25333) and many other titles he recorded between 1935 and 1938 as a member of Benny Goodman's small groups.

Perhaps the varied approaches to the use of the piano as an ensemble instrument in the swing period are best illustrated by the four tunes with which Count Basie began his recording career in 1936. *Shoe Shine Boy* (Voc. 3441) has an introduction of pure stride piano and passages of "oom-pah" comping; the embellished accompaniment to the melody instruments on *Evenin'* (also Voc. 3441) is light and swinging; on *Boogie Woogie* (Voc. 3459) Basie comps in a rhythmically free manner behind the soloists, placing isolated chords in the manner echoed later by bop pianists; and *Lady Be Good* (also Voc. 3459) offers an example of a spare solo introduction in the right hand and quietly jabbed random left-hand chords (there are also moments when Basie's four-beat accompaniment of Lester Young's solo resembles the playing of a guitar). Basie employed the same techniques when playing in larger ensembles, and his recordings of the late 1930s provide good examples of band piano.

There was an important exception to the move towards refinement, however, in the resurgence during the late 1930s and early 1940s of the more earthy blues style known as Boogie-woogie, which had developed in the 1920s and is typified by Pine Top Smith's *Pine Top's Boogie Woogie* (1928, Voc. 1245). Its reappearance resulted in a renewed interest in the work of such pianists as Pete Johnson, Meade "Lux" Lewis, and Jimmy Yancey. Boogie-woogie is characterized by a repetitive pounding bass pattern, usually in eighth-notes, on a simple 12-bar blues progression, and examples of widely used patterns are shown in ex.5. Johnson's *Lone Star Blues* (1939, first issued on *Riverside History of Classic Jazz,* 1924–39, Riv. 114; ex.5*a*) shows a typical walking line with a rocking motion; this type of bass generally became more even as the tempo of the piece increased. Memphis Slim's pattern on *44 Blues* (from the album *The Real Boogie Woogie,* 1959, FW 3524; ex.5*b*) is also common, either in straight eighth-notes or in the more rocking fashion created by triplets. The term "honky-tonk" became associated with the figure (and its variants) in Lewis's *Honky Tonk Train Blues* (1927, Para. 12896; ex.5*c*); Bill Doggett's rhythm-and-blues hit *Honky Tonk* (1956, King 4950) gained its name from this type of accompaniment. Yancey's bass line in *Yancey Stomp* (1939, Vic. 26589; ex.5*d*) is an interesting pattern sometimes referred to as "the fives," and is best played keeping the eighth-notes slightly uneven (a tenuto mark has been used in the transcription to indicate this). The final example, from Johnson's *Let 'em jump* (1939, Solo Art 12005; ex.5*e*), shows the honky-tonk pattern with an even subdivision of the beat (usually played at a faster tempo than the figures in ex.5*a–d*). The blues improvisations played in the right-hand above these ostinatos could

Ex.5 Typical left-hand boogie patterns

contain riff-like passages in the high treble, tremolos, single-line melodies, and punctuated chords. Often interesting cross-rhythms were created. Lewis contributes a characteristic "bluesy" flavor to *Honky Tonk Train Blues* by striking adjacent pitches to produce the effect of blue notes and makes deliberate use of dissonance.

4. The transition to bop. The 1940s was a decade in which jazz pianists began to liberate the left hand from the tyranny of timekeeping. This was at first a subtle movement, but later, with the advent of bop, it became more blatant. On *Fly Right* (*Epistrophy*) (1942, first issued on *Jazz Odyssey,* iii: *The Sound*

of Harlem, Col. C3L33), recorded with Cootie Williams's big band, Kenny Kersey plays the first half of his solo in a "swing stride" style, after the manner of Teddy Wilson; at the bridge, however, he strikes a low pedal note, breaks the stride, and proceeds in a more "modern" fashion, with no steady left-hand pulse. There are short passages of block chords, unison playing with a single note in each hand, as well as angular uses of rhythm.

Examples of another technique of the period – comping – may be heard on recordings made by Kersey and Thelonious Monk in jam sessions in 1941. Kersey's approach seems to be governed by the harmony of the piece; on *Kerouac* (*Exactly Like You*) and *Stardust* (on the album *The Harlem Jazz Scene,* 1941, Eso. 4), both with Dizzy Gillespie, he freely plays two-handed chord voicings at times. Monk, however, shows a greater concern with rhythm: on *Swing to Bop* (*Topsy;* on the album *Jazz Immortal,* 1941, Eso. 1), with Charlie Christian, he jabs chords in between, and sometimes with, Kenny Clarke's drum kicks.

The new concepts of harmony and rhythm that were developed by these musicians during informal jam sessions in the early 1940s were the main elements that transformed the jazz piano style. Because of a dispute between the musicians' union and the recording industry, however, no commercial recordings were made between August 1942 and late 1943, and an important formative year in the development of bop remains undocumented.

Two pieces recorded by Stan Kenton's orchestra just after the ban was lifted in 1943 illustrate the influence of this group on the development of jazz piano, particularly with regard to chord voicing for comping and in the use of orchestral imitation. *Artistry in Rhythm* (first issued as *Production on Theme*) and *Eager Beaver* (both Cap. 159) have melodies that are derived from a right-hand distribution of a chord – just as were many ragtime melodies. In these examples, however, the right-hand structures emphasize higher partials of chords: sixths, sevenths, and ninths (ex.6). It would appear that Kenton worked these voicings out at the piano and then transferred them to the format of the big band. His orchestra's early popularity (despite, or because of, controversy) ensured that his music was heard throughout the USA, and many pianists began to transfer his voicings back to the keyboard.

Ex.6

(a) Opening of Stan Kenton: *Artistry in Rhythm* (first issued as *Production on Theme,* 1943, Cap. 159); transcr. L. Koch

* = basic chord from which melody is derived

(b) Opening of Kenton: *Eager Beaver* (1943, Cap. 159); transcr. L. Koch

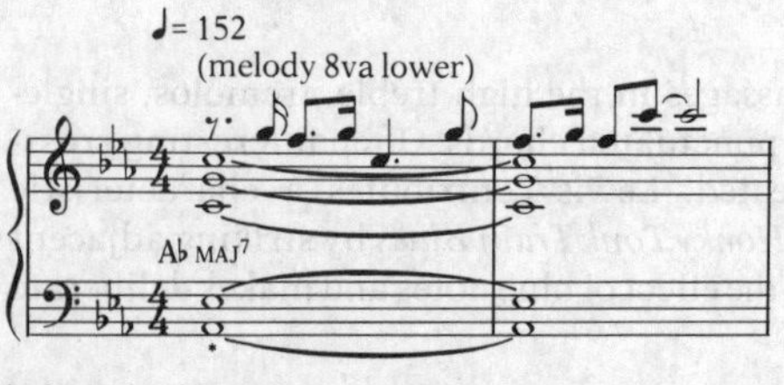

* = basic chord from which melody is derived

A comparison between ex.6*b* and ex.1 shows how both compositions are pianistically related: Joplin's melody is derived from the position of the chord of A♭, with C as the pivotal note; Kenton's has its origins in the right-hand part of a two-handed band voicing of an A♭ major seventh chord, where the major seventh (G) is the pivot. (Morton's jazz version of Joplin's piece (ex.2) also contains the major seventh.)

Both Kenton's works illustrate (at the end of the *a* section) the distinct chromaticism often apparent in band voicing which helped shape the melody. Further examples of influential features are the chord voicings in the bridge of the opening theme of *Eager Beaver,* where each phrase ends on a diminished fifth (later a bop trademark), and the rubato statement of the melody by the piano in *Artistry in Rhythm.*

Jazz musicians whose major instrument is other than the piano have always used the keyboard as a self-teaching tool, to formulate interesting voicings and to understand harmonic principles for the creation of solos on their main instrument. (As early as 1927 Bix Beiderbecke was using his piano composition *In a Mist* (*Bixology*) (1927, OK 40916) to explore impressionistic seventh chords (incorporating diminished fifths) combined with a bluesy stride style.) During the 1940s, when harmony was the basis of so many new concepts in jazz, an ability to play the piano at a fairly basic level was almost a prerequisite for any instrumentalist. An example of a figure better known for his work on another instrument is Milt Jackson, whose piano accompaniments with the Boptet led by Howard McGhee and Fats Navarro may be heard on *The Skunk/Boperation* (1948, BN 558); Jackson's style also gives an insight into the rhythmic nature of comping.

Similarly, two pianists who could more correctly be defined as composers used the piano in an experimental fashion and were highly influential in the area of chord voicing. The works of Thelonious Monk and Tadd Dameron, like those of Kenton, were often built directly from piano voicings of new chord sequences. In addition, both the melodies in ex.7 are derived from the principle of voice leading: in Monk's *'Round Midnight,* for example, the 7th of one chord resolves onto the 3rd of the next – A (7th of Bm7) to A♭ (enharmonic 3rd of E); A♭ (7th of

Ex.7 Melodies derived from voice leading

(a) From Thelonious Monk's *'Round Midnight*

(b) From Tadd Dameron's *If you could see me now*

B♭m7) to G (3rd of E♭7). Monk's approach to the piano – a jagged use of 2nds, 7ths, and other dissonant intervals and much feeling of space – is a study in itself. When playing unaccompanied he often employed a disjointed stride style, and his pieces usually involved unpredictable rhythmic displacement.

Indeed, rhythm was also a strong factor in the development of bop piano, and much stylistic modification arose through the changing function of the rhythm section. With the coming of amplification, the guitar began to be used as a solo instrument, and its new-found power often upset the delicate balance of the section. The recordings issued on the album *The Harlem Jazz Scene* also illustrate this aspect: the new rhythmic feel and the accents played by Monk may be heard quite well during Christian's solos, but are obliterated when the latter strums an accompaniment. A performance by Tiny Grimes of Charlie Parker's *Red Cross* (1944, Savoy 532) is also instructive: the guitarist is effective when doubling the melody with Parker, taking a solo, or playing background licks, but he impedes the rhythm when he strums squarely on all four beats. The pianist, Clyde Hart, had already mastered the new comping style and sounds comfortable; his solo, however, is still of the swing type. On a further recording by the same group, *Tiny's Tempo* (1944, Savoy 526), Grimes strums a four-beat rhythm almost throughout, and Hart, unsure where to place his chords so as not to cause conflict, plays in the high treble register after the manner of Count Basie.

A comparison of this last performance with one made by Gillespie and Parker only eight months later – Gillespie's *Salt Peanuts* (1945, Guild 1003) – shows in the later recording the complete transition of the jazz piano style and the new role of the instrument in the rhythm section. There is no guitar, and the pianist, Al Haig, provides perfect examples of pure bop comping, complete with extended chord voicings jabbed in a rhythmically free manner during gaps in the melodic lines. Haig's improvised solo is also pure bop: his right hand plays running figures in imitation of Gillespie and Parker, and his left performs the comping function exactly as in his role as accompanist, but with spare chords or intervals (often only a root and a 7th) so as not to limit his choice of notes in the melodic line.

Pure bop piano reached its apotheosis in the work of Bud Powell. The statement of the theme in his trio performance of *All God's Chillun Got Rhythm* (1949, Mer./Clef 11046) provides excellent examples of bop chord voicings. His linear right-hand improvisation shows supreme creativity and technique, and his left hand also exhibits a number of interesting devices: ostinato octave leaps on the dominant against tonic harmony; spare intervals such as 10ths and 7ths; and occasional single notes in the bass moving in half-notes (mostly when the chord progression follows a succession of fifths). Powell's hammer-like approach to the piano lent great drive to his performances, and such solos as that on Parker's *Ornithology* (1950; on the album *Charlie Parker in Historical Recordings*, i, 1948, 1950, Le Jazz Cool 101) had a great influence on other bop pianists.

In his solo work Powell treated the instrument in a similar fashion, simply allowing the feeling of a rhythm section to be implied. In *Hallucinations* (1951) on the album *Bud Powell Moods* (1950–51, Clef 610) (ex.8) he derives his melody from successive hand positions of ninth chords played alternately up and down in an arpeggiated manner, while his left hand shows the use of spare intervals and single notes.

Even as many bop pianists were relieving the emphasis on the left hand and lightening the instrument's role in the rhythm section, an alternative approach was being developed by Erroll

Ex.8 From the second improvised chorus of Bud Powell: *Hallucinations*, (1951), from the album *Bud Powell Moods* (1950–51, Clef 610); transcr. L. Feather (Feather, 1957)

Garner. Garner sometimes created the effect of continuous strumming in his left hand, articulated by occasional accents in the lower register, thus recalling the impression of a swing rhythm section. His right-hand playing, with its use of treble chords and/or octaves, also drew on earlier styles, but Garner's harmonic vocabulary was close to that of bop musicians. His playing is most effective when unaccompanied, though it is also successful in trios and in solos within an ensemble. On the slowest take of Parker's *Cool Blues* (1947, Dial 1015), for instance, Garner plays a full chorus before the closing theme in this manner; in all other solos in the piece, however, he adopts a blend of swing and bop elements. Garner's mature style is well represented by the album *Concert by the Sea* (1955, Col. CL883).

Certain elements of swing era big-band music were also transformed and carried over into bop piano. One of these was the "locked hands" block-chord style, which derived from the voicing of big-band saxophone sections. The pianist harmonized each note of the melody with a four-note chord in the right hand, while the left hand doubled the melody an octave lower (*see* HARMONY (i), §1(iv)). Phil Moore is credited with developing this style as early as 1939 and Milt Buckner made use of it in Lionel Hampton's band during the early 1940s. Lennie Tristano, on *Blue Boy* (*Fine and Dandy*) (1947, Key. 681), shows a strong understanding of its potential, using block chords when comping, in solo passages, and in simultaneous improvisation with the guitarist Billy Bauer. But the true popularizer of the technique was George Shearing (ex.9); Shearing added vibraphone to the upper melody line of the piano and guitar to the lower, creating a distinctive ensemble sound that brought him much commercial success.

Ex.9 Beginning of the bridge section in the first chorus of George Shearing: *Bop, Look, and Listen* (1949, MGM 10426); transcr. L. Koch

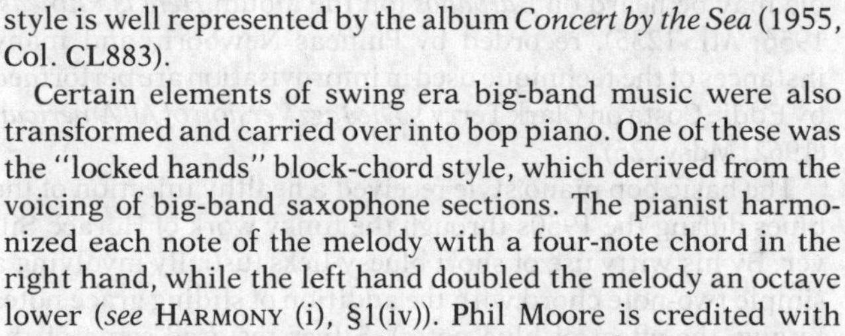

The nature of the locked hands style generates nonharmonic tones in every voice, producing in effect "passing chords" and "neighbor chords" within the basic progression. Although very effective in a group setting, this approach was generally not satisfactory in solo playing unless it was interspersed with other styles; the lack of steady rhythm and bass roots was too difficult to overcome by implication. Furthermore, the use of such a block-chord texture can tend to become monotonous. Shearing usually played his improvisations in a single-line manner and reserved the locked hands style mainly for melody statements, which created a balanced performance.

Later pianists who made exemplary use of block chords in improvisation include Dick Hyman (for example, Charlie Parker's *Hot House* (1952) on the album *New Bird*, ii, 1951–4, Phoenix 12); Lennie Tristano (*Ghost of a Chance* on *Lennie Tristano*, 1955, Atl. 1224); Bill Evans (ii) (*Green Dolphin Street* (1959) on *Peace Piece and other Pieces*, 1959, 1962, Mlst. 47024); and Oscar Peterson (*Give me the simple life* on *Tracks*, 1970, MPS 879).

5. AFTER 1950: THE ACOUSTIC PIANO. During the 1950s a number of pianists expanded the block-chord style by adopting a two-handed full-chord approach, imitating more closely the orchestral sound of a big-band brass section. The effect created also bore some resemblance to the voicings (though not, of course, the rhythms) used in Afro-Cuban jazz in the late 1940s. An early use of expanded block chords may be heard played by Red Garland with the Miles Davis Quintet on *Bye Bye Blackbird* (on the album *'Round about Midnight*, 1955–6, Col. CL949).

Another approach, which derived, more or less, from the Latin style, was that of playing a single-note melody simultaneously in both hands, one or more octaves apart. An example may be heard on *Barbados* (on the album *Here is Phineas*, 1956, Atl. 1235), recorded by Phineas Newborn, and many instances of the technique used in improvisation are performed by Eddie Costa on Clark Terry's *The Jazz Version of All American* (1962, Mdsv. 26).

The basic bop piano style received a healthy injection of the blues during the 1950s through the funky work of Horace Silver. By his witty use of short bluesy licks (usually involving a simple two-note chord with the addition of sliding grace notes to give the effect of blue notes), Silver restored some of the earthiness which the bop musicians had deliberately destroyed. His approach is well represented by *Doodlin'* (on the album *Horace Silver and the Jazz Messengers*, 1954, BN 5058) (ex.10) and *The Preacher* (on *Horace Silver and the Jazz Messengers*, 1955, BN 5062).

Ex.10 Bars 10–11 of the first improvised chorus of Horace Silver: *Doodlin'*, from the album *Horace Silver and the Jazz Messengers* (1954, BN 5058); transcr. L. Koch

An interesting comparison can be made by examining the work of John Lewis in the early 1950s (for example, any of his recordings with the Modern Jazz Quartet between 1952 and 1957) and that of Wynton Kelly at the beginning of the next decade (in particular his recordings with Miles Davis in 1961). Both pianists follow in the footsteps of Bud Powell, but Lewis's spare style was strongly influenced by the cool-jazz movement, while Kelly's more funky approach exhibits the use of expanded block chords and a number of impressionistic touches.

The impressionistic aspect of jazz piano was unveiled in the late 1950s by Bill Evans (ii), who used in his left hand rootless voicings which implied chord roots (sometimes a choice of several); an effect of unabated tension was created by the progression of ambiguous chords that never seemed to resolve (ex.11). This method resulted in a new sound for the pianist

Ex.11 From Bill Evans (ii): *Blue in Green*, on the album *Portrait in Jazz* (1959, Riv. 1162); transcr. L. Koch

and gave much freedom of choice to the double bass player. In *Blue in Green* (on the album *Portrait in Jazz*, 1959, Riv. 1162), when he reaches a climactic point in his solo, Evans makes use of this type of voicing in rhythm with his right-hand ideas; this produces the same feeling as the older block-chord technique, but, since the left-hand voicing does not move with the melody, gives a more hammer-like effect. For comping within an ensemble, the rootless voicings could be used in the left hand while the right hand played contrasting chords, sometimes setting up dual harmonic implications; they could also be transferred to the right hand so that the left could provide a bass line. For a solo performance, however, this style is usually best when modified with the addition of some bass notes and an injection of rhythmic vitality, and/or melded with earlier jazz styles, as in Evans's performance in *Alone* (1969, Verve 68792).

Other pianists also began using rootless voicings in a more blues-based manner, sometimes employing fuller chords. With the advent of modal and free jazz at the end of the 1950s, the left hand soon became preoccupied with voicings in fourths in order to accommodate the nonharmonic nature of the music. In the modal style pianists often played improvisatory patterns in the right hand against the fourths, using the pentatonic or other modal scales, or, particularly when comping, added to the structure by playing block chords; the same approach was used in freer performances, but more random tonalities were employed. Another technique of modal jazz was to derive a melodic improvisation from the position of fourths in the right hand (just as the bop pianists had done with right-hand chord voicings – see ex.8).

In the 1960s pianists had to adjust to nonharmonic thinking. Before that time, most melodies (both composed and improvised) were harmonically derived. The best examples as to how this adjustment was achieved may be found in the work of McCoy Tyner, a pianist of equivalent standing in a more modern era to that of Bud Powell in the bop period. Tyner's recorded performances are infused with an underlying blues feeling and jazz vitality whatever approach he chooses to take – bop, modal, or freer style. On *Village Blues* (on the album *Coltrane Jazz*, 1959–60, Atl. 1354), an early recording with Coltrane, he shows a bluesy type of voicing used by Evans, in which chords seem to be built from the elements of mixolydian scales; at several points in his improvisations on *Blue Monk* (ex.12*a*) (on his own LP *Nights of Ballads and Blues*, 1963, Imp. 39) he combines this type of voicing (in which chords derive from a C mixolydian

3. Cecil Taylor at Ronnie Scott's in London, 1985

scale – C–D–E–F–G–A–B♭) with chords voiced in fourths. On *Tunji* (on the album *Coltrane*, 1962, Imp. 21) Tyner accompanies Coltrane with one open chord in a repeated pattern (ex.12*b*), but for his solo he reverts to the blues form, using rootless structures in seventh-chord mixolydian voicings (ex. 12*c*). *The night has a thousand eyes* (on his own LP *Song for my Lady*, 1972, Mlst. 9044) gives (in the right hand) countless examples of phrases derived from pentatonic scales (ex. 12*d*), while the

Ex.12 Some elements of McCoy Tyner's style: (a) and (d) transcr. P. Rinzler (Rinzler, 1983); (b) and (c) transcr. L. Koch

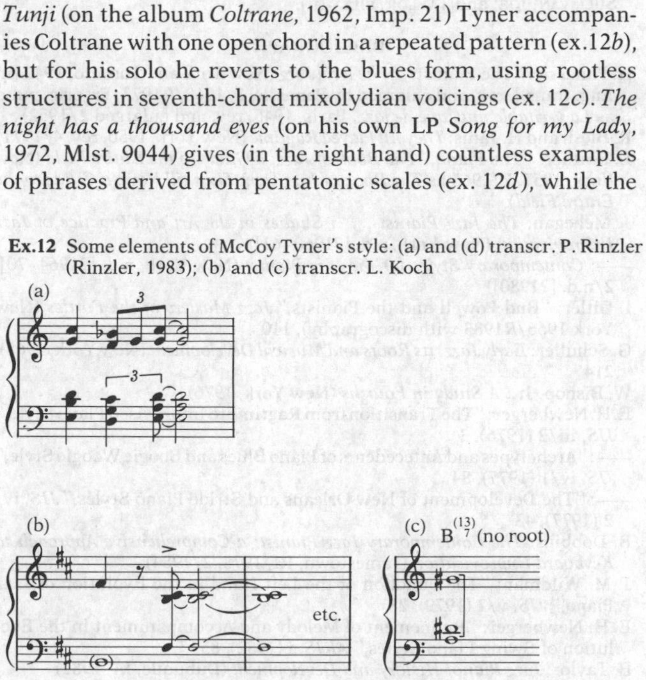

album *Expansions* (1968, BN 84338) includes a modern approach to ballad form; Tyner exhibits a surprisingly gentle though crystal clear touch on *I thought I'd let you know* and engages in a "free" exchange with the drummer on *Smitty's Place*.

Other pianists departed more radically from the bop style, applying such free-jazz techniques as "gesture-derived" figures (i.e., passages originating through a physical gesture), tone clusters, atonal motivic development, and unusual attacks (with the palm or fist, etc.), and ignoring a steady rhythmic pulse. Lennie Tristano experimented with atonal music, mostly in a linear fashion, in the late 1940s (notably on *Intuition*, 1949, Cap. 1224), but the most exemplary musician in this style is Cecil Taylor, who began recording in 1956. *Enter Evening* (on the album *Unit Structures*, 1966, BN 84237) (ex.13) shows the use of gesture-derived figures, fourths, and a final tone cluster.

Ex.13 "Gesture-derived" figures from Cecil Taylor: *Enter Evening* on the album *Unit Structures* (1966, BN 84237); transcr. H. Martin (Martin, 1986)

In the 1970s free-jazz procedures were ingeniously fused with diatonic harmonies and a lyrical approach to the piano in the work of Keith Jarrett, as may be heard on his album *Eyes of the Heart* (1976, ECM 1150), while the synthesis of "modern" and bop techniques that has evolved in the 1980s is exemplified by the playing of Michel Petrucciani, notably on the album *Pianism* (1985, BN 85124).

A healthy eclecticism may be seen most clearly in the evolution of the piano as a solo instrument. In the hands of a technician such as Oscar Peterson, a variety of styles and approaches are evident on a single album (*Tracks*, 1970, MPS 879). The development from the 1950s of a single-note walking bass or rock ostinato in the left hand to imitate a bass player gave new scope to the solo pianist. Dave McKenna adopted a "rolling" approach to a walking bass on his album *Dancing in the Dark and other Music of Arthur Schwartz* (1985, Conc. 292), while on *Have you Met Miss Jones* (on the LP *Music for Perla*, 1974, Ste. 1021), Tete Montoliu exhibits a driving use of the technique at a fast tempo. Roland Hanna's album *Sir Elf* (1973, Choice 1003) shows various left-hand formulas, including some derived from Erroll Garner's personal style, a humorous stride after Thelonious Monk, and a rock-influenced line. A good example of a pianist assimilating new techniques into an older jazz style in a creative manner is Earl Hines (*Hines Does Hoagy*, *c*1973, Audiophile 113), and a masterful approach to the piano as a lone accompanying instrument is demonstrated by Jimmie Rowles in his duets with Stan Getz on the album *The Peacocks* (1977, Col. JC34873). A fine overview may be gained from the album *A Jazz Piano Anthology* (Col. KG32355), on which the featured pianists range from Eubie Blake to Cecil Taylor (details of dates and supporting players may be found in a review by Dan Morgenstern in *Down Beat*, xli/1, 1974).

6. After 1950: the electric and electronic piano. With the advent of electronically amplified instruments, many musicians felt that the volume of the acoustic piano was not ade-

quate. (More practically, there was a need for a portable instrument which could be taken to venues that had either no piano or, more commonly, a piano that was out of tune and ill cared for.) As early as 1940 Earl Hines recorded two titles, *Body and Soul/Child of a Disordered Brain* (Bb 10642), on the Storytone piano, which relied on vacuum tubes and sounded like a fuzz-toned harpsichord. Hines also took the instrument on tour until its unwieldiness (it weighed one and a half tons) became overwhelming.

The earliest electric piano used to any extent in jazz, however, was developed in 1954 by Benjamin F. Miessner (whose early patent was also responsible for the manufacture of the Storytone) and marketed by Wurlitzer. Miessner's instrument was based on struck tuned reeds of steel, with individual electronic pickups for amplification affixed near each reed. Many musicians used this piano for practical purposes (it weighed only about 75 pounds), but most were disgruntled because of the touch and sound. A pianist's touch is a mark of individuality, and one which the use of an electric or electronic instrument, where the sound is not generated purely by the striking power of the player, threatened to obliterate. The later models of Miessner's piano, however, made with a plastic case, were more touch sensitive than the metal prototype. Some pianists, such as Joe Zawinul, found the tone of the instrument extremely pleasing: he played it when touring with Ray Charles in 1959 and again in the 1960s, as a member of Cannonball Adderley's group. Sun Ra recorded with it on *Medicine for a Nightmare* and *A Call for all Demons* (on the album *Angels and Demons at Play*, 1955–7, Saturn 407).

The electric piano that eventually found favor in the eyes of jazz musicians was that designed by Harold Rhodes and Leo Fender (who invented the electric bass guitar) and manufactured from 1965. It has lengths of tunable thin steel wire which are struck by rubber hammers; the wire forms one tine of a structure resembling a tuning-fork, the other tine of which is a longer, flat "tone bar" tuned to reinforce and sustain the vibrations of the wire. The sound of the Fender-Rhodes piano is more bell-like than that of the acoustic piano, and certain voicings tend to blur more than others. Pianists therefore had to revise their approach to playing when using the instrument (Bill Evans, for instance, never found it very satisfactory), and it took well over a decade of experimentation before musicians ascertained that the Fender-Rhodes piano was an instrument in its own right and not just a replacement for the acoustic piano.

The Fender-Rhodes piano was very effective in jazz-rock groups during the 1970s, when triadic voicings were formulated and pianists began to use it in a guitar-like manner. Herbie Hancock, who at the urging of Miles Davis played it on *Miles in the Sky* (1968, Col. CS9628), went on to employ the instrument to great artistic and commercial success on his album *Headhunters* (1973, Col. KC32731). Zawinul may be heard playing a creative solo on *American Tango* on Weather Report's album *Mysterious Traveler* (*c*1974, Col. KC32494).

The perfect union of artist and instrument, however, and one which has set the standard for performance on the Fender-Rhodes piano, is probably that demonstrated by Chick Corea. Whether it is the balance between volume setting and finger force, the regulation of volume, or his general sensitivity to the instrument that allows penetration of Corea's personality remains unknown, but nevertheless he plays with true expression. His long, clean right-hand lines (often derived from pentatonic scales) ring out over clipped figures comped in the left hand; he gives the impression that each note is being treated to a different level of force. Surprisingly, Corea (who, like Hancock, was introduced to the Fender-Rhodes piano by Davis) claims that at first he disliked the feel of the instrument, and he had many adjustments to make to it. The fruits of these adjustments may readily be heard on the album *Light as a Feather* (1973, Pol. 5525), recorded with his band Return to Forever, which shows a highly effective use of the piano in a jazz context. Corea's solo on the title track is particularly well suited to the instrument; there is a passage in *Five Hundred Miles High* where he plays a repeated note with rapid changes of fingering, the execution of which shows his intuitive knowledge of its capabilities; and his use of rubato in the introduction to *Spain* demonstrates its lyrical quality.

Many musicians have found problems with the electric piano when using it for comping to back acoustic instruments, and have had to take account of different soloists when making volume adjustments. Bob James, for example, almost buries Paul Desmond with his accompaniment on *Autumn Leaves* and *Tangerine* on Chet Baker's album *She Was Too Good to Me* (1975, CTI 6050); moreover, the instrument seems constantly to intrude on Desmond's ideas – although it sounds effective behind Baker's solos. Corea achieves a perfect balance, however, in his accompaniment of Stan Getz on the title track of the latter's LP *Captain Marvel* (1972, Col. KC32706).

Future advances in the development of electric and electronic technology will doubtless result in the manufacture of further new instruments, as makers aspire to produce the equivalent of the acoustic piano. One of these is the Yamaha CP70, an electric grand piano that sounds much like an acoustic instrument with pickups attached to it, and which is admired by many jazz pianists for its touch and sound.

For further illustrations *see* BASIE, COUNT; EVANS, BILL (ii); HERMAN, WOODY, fig. 1*a*; JAZZ (i), fig.8; JONES, fig.1*a*; MONK, THELONIOUS; SHEARING, GEORGE; SULLIVAN, JOE; and TAYLOR, BILLY (ii).

BIBLIOGRAPHY

H. Panassié: "The Pianists," *The Real Jazz* (New York and Toronto, 1942 [in Eng. trans.], rev. and enlarged by Panassié, 2/1960/*R*1973; Fr. orig. pubd as *La veritable musique de jazz*, Paris, 1945, rev. and enlarged 2/1952)
R. Blesh and H. Janis: *They All Played Ragtime* (New York, 1950, rev. 4/1971)
L. Feather: "The Piano," *The Book of Jazz: a Guide to the Entire Field* (New York, 1957, 2/1965 as *The Book of Jazz from Then till Now: a Guide to the Entire Field*)
J. Mehegan: *The Jazz Pianist . . .: Studies in the Art and Practice of Jazz Improvisation* (New York, n.d. [?1960–61])
——: *Contemporary Styles for the Jazz Pianist* (New York, n.d. [?1964–70], 2/n.d. [?1980])
I. Gitler: "Bud Powell and the Pianists," *Jazz Masters of the Forties* (New York 1966/*R*1983 with discography), 110
G. Schuller: *Early Jazz: its Roots and Musical Development* (New York, 1968), 214
W. Bishop, Jr.: *A Study in Fourths* (New York, 1976)
E. H. Newberger: "The Transition from Ragtime to Improvised Piano Style," *JJS*, iii/2 (1976), 3
——: "Archetypes and Antecedents of Piano Blues and Boogie Woogie Style," *JJS*, iv/1 (1977), 84
——: "The Development of New Orleans and Stride Piano Styles," *JJS*, iv/2 (1977), 43
B. Dobbins: *The Contemporary Jazz Pianist: a Comprehensive Approach to Keyboard Improvisation* (Jamestown, RI, 1978, 2/1984)
J. M. Wildman: "The Function of the Left Hand in the Evolution of Jazz Piano," *JJS*, v/2 (1979), 23
E. H. Newberger: "Refinement of Melody and Accompaniment in the Evolution of Swing Piano Styles," *ARJS*, i (1982), 85
B. Taylor: *Jazz Piano: History and Development* (Dubuque, IA, 1982)
M. Weiss: *Jazz Styles and Analysis: Piano* (Chicago, *c*1982)
L. Koch: "Thelonious Monk: Compositional Techniques," *ARJS*, ii (1983), 67
P. Rintzler: "McCoy Tyner: Style and Syntax," *ARJS*, ii (1983), 109–49
M. Williams: "Jelly Roll Morton," "Art Tatum," "Thelonious Monk," *The Jazz Tradition* (New York, rev. 2/1983), 16–46, 92, 154

J. Jeckovich: "The Forms and Orchestration of Five Jelly Roll Morton Piano Solos," *ARJS*, iii (1985), 1
P. S. Machlin: *Stride: the Music of Fats Waller* (Boston and London, 1985)
T. Rhea: "The Electric Piano," *The Art Of Electronic Music*, ed. T. Dorter and G. Armbruster (New York, 1985), 16
H. Martin: "Piano Styles," *Enjoying Jazz* (New York, 1986), 156

LAWRENCE KOCH

Piano(la) roll. A roll, usually of paper, on which music is preserved in the form of perforations; it is recorded and played back mechanically on a player piano or pianola. *See* RECORDING, §I, 1(ii).

Picard, John (Francis) (*b* London, 17 May 1934). English trombonist. He studied piano from the age of six but was self-taught on trombone. After his military service he performed and recorded with Cy Laurie (1953–4), then with Humphrey Lyttelton (1954–61), Bruce Turner and Sandy Brown (both 1960–62), and Tony Coe (with whom he led a quintet, 1962–5); he also recorded as a leader (1955). His playing may be heard to advantage on Lyttelton's *Triple Exposure* (1959, Parl. PMC1110). During the 1970s and 1980s the style of his work became more catholic. He recorded with Brian Lemon (1970), wrote for and played with the London Jazz Big Band (1975–83), and worked with the group Rocket 88 with the pianist Ian Stewart and the rock drummer Charlie Watts (1978–), and the Charlie Watts Big Band (1985–). In addition, from the late 1960s he led several progressive small groups, which have, at various times, included Coe, Kathy Stobart, the trumpeter Colin Smith, Art Themen, and Trevor Tompkins. Picard's son, Simon Picard, plays tenor saxophone in several small groups. (R. Cotterrell, ed.: *Jazz Now: the Jazz Centre Society Guide*, London, 1976)

DIGBY FAIRWEATHER

Piccolo. The highest-pitched member of the orchestral flute family, sounding an octave higher than the flute itself; *see* FLUTE, §§1 and 3.

Piccolo bass. A small DOUBLE BASS with sloping shoulders (like those of a viol) and four strings tuned in 4ths (usually *E–A–d–g*); it should not be confused with the half- and three-quarter-size double basses, which have the characteristics of the full-size instrument. The piccolo bass was developed for double bass players who wished to extend the solo opportunities offered by the cello to an instrument constructed and played like a double bass. The cello has several advantages over the double bass as a solo instrument: its higher range enables it to be better heard when pitted against an accompanying rhythm section, and the closer spacing of the fingerings means that shifts in position of the left hand are necessary less often and are smaller than on the double bass, so that greater mobility and speed of execution are possible. A few double bass players took up the cello, among them Oscar Pettiford and Ray Brown, who both developed a pizzicato technique for solo work on the instrument. But many players who might have wished to double on the cello did not do so because the instrument was tuned in 5ths instead of 4ths, and because it had tuning pegs instead of machine heads, making quick retuning difficult.

In 1960, in collaboration with the Kay Company of Chicago, Ray Brown developed a hybrid instrument combining features of the cello and the double bass; it had machine-head tuning and a modified bridge, which, together with its thin, flexible strings, made the instrument peculiarly suitable for solo pizzicato playing. In time this was developed into the piccolo bass. The instrument is not widely used, but Ron Carter regularly doubles on it, and in the early 1970s had made for him a piccolo bass tuned *A–d–g–c'*. (Frederick Lyman, who has built instruments for Carter, is the principal maker of piccolo basses.) The first albums on which Carter played piccolo bass were those he made for the label CTI in 1973–6; on *Piccolo* (1977, Mlst. 55004) and *Parfait* (1980, Mlst. 9107) he plays only piccolo bass, accompanied by a rhythm section.

BIBLIOGRAPHY

M. Jones: "Down the Poll: Ray Brown," *MM*, xl (25 March 1961), 12
L. Tomkins: "The Bass in the Foreground: Ron Carter," *CI*, xix/10 (1981), 6

ALYN SHIPTON

Pichon, Fats [Walter] (*b* New Orleans, 1906; *d* Chicago, 26 Feb 1967). Pianist, singer, and arranger. He began playing piano as a child, moved to New York when he was in his teens, and later studied in Boston at the New England Conservatory. During the 1920s he returned intermittently to New Orleans, where he performed in the Tulane Orchestra, led his own band at the Pelican Cafe, and worked with Sidney Desvigne on the SS *Island Queen* (on riverboat jobs he sometimes played calliope). Also in the 1920s he toured Mexico and Texas, worked in New York for various bands, including that of Luis Russell, and recorded as the leader of a trio with Henry "Red" Allen and Teddy Bunn (*Doggin' that Thing/Yo Yo*, 1929, Vic. 38544). After returning to New Orleans in the early 1930s Pichon was again associated with Desvigne, played in A. J. Piron's big band, and led his own band on the SS *Capitol*; throughout the 1940s and 1950s he worked regularly as a soloist, while continuing to tour outside New Orleans. Although troubled by failing eyesight, he continued to play intermittently in the 1960s.

BIBLIOGRAPHY

ChiltonW; *FeatherE*
Obituary, *SL*, xviii (1967), 40
A. Rose and E. Souchon: *New Orleans Jazz: a Family Album* (Baton Rouge, LA, 1967, rev. 2/1978, rev. and enlarged 3/1984), 100

ALDEN ASHFORTH

Pickering, Tom [Thomas Mansergh] (*b* Burra, Australia, 8 Aug 1921). Australian clarinetist, tenor saxophonist, bandleader, and composer. He grew up in Hobart, Tasmania, where he played clarinet from 1936 and helped to form a dixieland group, the Barrelhouse Four. Following wartime dance-band work he reconstituted the Barrelhouse Four (1945), which played at the first Australian Jazz Convention (Melbourne, 1946). From 1949 until the late 1950s Pickering led a group which held important residencies at the 7HT Theatrette and the Town Hall in Hobart. The release of his first recording on the Swaggie label (1970) revitalized his jazz activity and, except in 1979 when he was traveling on a Churchill Fellowship, he continued to lead his own group; he is heard to advantage on the album *Red Hot & Blue* (1983, Candle 122), which he recorded as joint leader with Ian Pearce. In 1982 he was made a Member of the Order of Australia.

BIBLIOGRAPHY

A. Bisset: *Black Roots, White Flowers: a History of Jazz in Australia* (Sydney, 1976), 117
B. Johnson: "Pickering, Thomas Mansergh (Tom)," *The Oxford Companion to Australian Jazz* (Melbourne, Australia, 1987)

BRUCE JOHNSON

Pickup group. A group assembled for a particular engagement, consisting of musicians who do not normally play together.

Picou, Alphonse (Floristan) (*b* New Orleans, 19 Oct 1878; *d* New Orleans, 4 Feb 1961). Clarinetist. From the age of 16 he played regularly with "reading" bands and orchestras in New Orleans, including the Excelsior Brass Band, but his improvising skills also allowed him to work successfully with smaller jazz groups. He often played in the Tuxedo Brass Band, on B♭ and E♭ clarinets, and while with this ensemble is said to have developed a solo on *High Society* which has since become a traditional part of the tune's performance. In 1932 Picou reduced his musical activities and devoted more time to his occupation as a tinsmith; but, with the revival of interest in traditional jazz, he re-emerged to record with Kid Rena in 1940. He worked with Papa Celestin in the late 1940s, and led his own small group at The Paddock in the early 1950s. Picou became a doyen of New Orleans music, playing fairly regularly until just before his death. His recorded work lacks the fire and the passionate flow of the great New Orleans clarinetists, but his tone and graceful articulation won him admirers.

Oral history material in *LNT*.

SELECTED RECORDINGS

As sideman: K. Rena: Low Down Blues (1940, Delta 803); High Society Rag (1940, Delta 804); Weary Blues (1940, Delta 806); Ricard Alexis: Clarinet Marmalade (1951, Palm 3020); Paddock Jazz Band: *Paddock Jazz Band, 1953* (1953, Center 10), incl. Eh la bas

BIBLIOGRAPHY

G. Hoefer: "The Hot Box," *DB*, xvii/19 (1950), 6
K. G. Mills: "Discography of Alphonse Picou," *Jazz Report*," i/8 (1961), 3
Obituary, *SL*, xi/3–4 (1961), 3
W. J. Schafer: "Breaking into 'High Society': Musical Metamorphoses in Early Jazz," *JJS*, ii/2 (1975), 53
P. Haby: "Alphonse Picou: New Orleans Creole," *Fn*, xi/5 (1980), 4

JOHN CHILTON

Pierce, Bill(y) [William] (*b* Hampton, VA, 25 Sept 1948). Tenor and soprano saxophonist. He began playing professionally around 1970 in Boston, where he performed in the bands at various clubs, accompanying visiting soul musicians such as Marvin Gaye and Stevie Wonder. He later played and recorded with James Williams (1979–80, 1984–5). From 1980 to 1982 he toured the USA and Europe with Art Blakey, with whom he made several recordings on tenor saxophone, including *Album of the Year* (1981, Tim. 155). After returning to Boston in 1982, he continued to perform and also taught privately. He recorded the album *William the Conqueror* (Sunnyside 1013) as a leader in 1985. (S. Vandermark: "Bill Pierce: Interview," *Cadence*, xi/11 (1985), 5)

Pierce, De De [Joseph De Lacrois [De Lacroix]] (*b* New Orleans, 18 Feb 1904; *d* New Orleans, 23 Nov 1973). Cornetist and singer. He was largely self-taught. Although he worked principally as a brick mason, he played with several dance bands in New Orleans (including that of Arnold De Pass in 1924) and was in demand as a member of brass bands for parades. During the 1930s he worked in riverfront honky-tonks. In 1935 he married the pianist and blues singer Billie Pierce (née Wilhelmina Goodson) (*b* Marianna, FL, 8 June 1907; *d* New Orleans, 29 Sept 1974), who had arrived in New Orleans in 1929 to replace her older sister Sadie Goodson in Buddy Petit's band. Billie had grown up in a musical family and, at the age of 15, had accompanied Bessie Smith for two weeks. After their marriage the two usually worked together, mostly in obscure neighborhood dance halls. De De's sight failed in the 1950s and he retired from music, but by 1965 he had revived his career and thereafter made a number of recordings with his wife. He also became well known as one of the leaders of the Preservation Hall band, which toured the USA and Europe. De De was recognized as the leading interpreter of songs in Creole patois, while Billie was a forceful and energetic pianist.

Oral history material in *LNT*.

SELECTED RECORDINGS

New Orleans Jazz (1959, Folk Lyric 110); *Blues in the Classic Tradition* (1961, Riv. 9370); *Jazz at Preservation Hall* (1962, Atl. 1409); *Billie and De De* (1966, Preservation Hall 3)

BIBLIOGRAPHY

ChartersJ
C. Strachwitz: Liner notes, *Billie and De De* (Arhoolie 2016, *c*1971)
D. Dawson: "De De Pierce: Romance and Reality," *Fn*, v/1 (1973), 4
S. Harris: *Blues Who's Who: a Biographical Dictionary of Blues Singers* (New Rochelle, NY, 1979)
J. De Donder: "Billie and De De," *MR*, viii (1981), no.7, p.1; no.8, p.7

BILL RUSSELL

Pierce, Nat(haniel) (*b* Somerville, MA, 16 July 1925). Pianist, arranger, and bandleader. He worked professionally from 1943, mainly with bands in Boston, including one led by Shorty Sherock. After playing with Larry Clinton (1948) and others he joined Woody Herman's band (1951), and worked at various times as its pianist (1951–5, 1961–6), arranger, and road manager (1960s). During the same period he led a group with Dick Collins (1954), directed his own band, and worked as an arranger for Count Basie, Ella Fitzgerald, Quincy Jones, and others, and took part in many recording sessions. He also wrote all the arrangements for the television show "The Sound of Jazz" (1957), including that of his own composition, *Open all Night*, which was performed as the program's opening number by an all-star band under Basie's direction. Pierce settled in Los Angeles in 1971 and remained active as an arranger, working for Anita O'Day, Carmen McRae, Earl Hines, and others. He also undertook much freelance work, including tours and recordings with Louie Bellson and reunions with Herman (both intermittently into the 1980s). In 1975, with Frank Capp, he formed the Capp–Pierce Orchestra (later known as the Capp–Pierce Juggernaut), and the following year he toured with Basie's band during the latter's illness. In the 1970s and 1980s he has been a regular sideman for recordings on the Concord label, including several by Scott Hamilton.

Pierce is a talented swing pianist who has often attenuated his own musical personality to imitate Basie, notably in his association with Capp. His ability to propel a rhythm section is particularly evident on his recordings for Concord.

SELECTED RECORDINGS

As leader: with D. Collins: *Herdsman* (1954, Fan. 3-14); *Kansas City Memories* (1956, Coral 57091); with F. Capp: *Juggernaut* (1977, Conc. 40); *Live at the Century Plaza* (1978, Conc. 72); *Juggernaut Strikes Again* (1981, Conc. 183)
As sideman with W. Herman: Beau Jazz (1953, Mars 900); *Swing Low, Sweet Clarinet* (1962, Phi. 600004); *Woody's Winners* (1965, Col. CS9236)
As sideman with others: Lambert, Hendricks, and Ross: *Sing a Song of Basie* (1958, ABC-Para. 223); B. Brookmeyer: *Kansas City Revisited* (1958, UA 4008); R. Eldridge: *The Nifty Cat* (1970, MJR 8110); J. Hanna: *Kansas City Express* (1976, Conc. 22)

SELECTED ARRANGEMENTS

As leader with F. Capp: on *Juggernaut* (1977, CJ 40), Dickie's Dream
Recorded by others: C. Basie: New Basie Blues (1952, Clef 8964); W. Herman: Blue Lou (1953, Mars 700); Opus de funk, on Herman: *Road Band* (1955, Cap. T658)

BIBLIOGRAPHY

FeatherE; *Feather '60s*; *Feather–Gitler '70s*
L. Tomkins: "The Nat Pierce Story," *Crescendo*, iv (1966), no.10, p.16; no.11, p.35

"The Benefits of Maturity: Nat Pierce," *CI*, xviii/6 (1980), 20
S. Dance: *The World of Count Basie* (New York and London, 1980) [colln of previously pubd interviews], 236
S. Voce: "In Deep with Nat Pierce," *JJI*, xxxiv/10 (1981), 19
C. Deffaa: "Profile: Jazz Veteran Nat Pierce Grooves on the Music not on the Business," *Keyboard*, xii/6 (1986), 19

SCOTT YANOW

Pike, Dave [David Samuel] (*b* Detroit, 23 March 1938). Vibraphonist. He played drums from the age of eight and taught himself to play vibraphone; he was influenced from an early age by the work of Milt Jackson and Lionel Hampton. After moving with his family to Los Angeles in 1953 he worked professionally from the following year and soon after played hard bop with Curtis Counce, Harold Land, Elmo Hope, and Dexter Gordon. He also worked for two years with Paul Bley (recording in 1958) and for a brief period led a quartet that played in the San Francisco area in 1959; by this time he had begun to play marimba in addition to his principal instrument. He moved in 1960 to New York and began to use amplification in his performances; from 1961 to 1965 he toured with Herbie Mann's group, as a member of which he played a repertory consisting largely of bossa nova. In 1968 he gave a performance at the Berliner Jazztage that was well-received. He remained in Europe and formed the Dave Pike Set, a quartet that included Volker Kriegel and J. A. Rettenbacher; this group performed at clubs and festivals during the next five years. Pike also recorded with the Clarke–Boland Big Band (1968). Later he returned to the USA and settled in southern California, where he formed a group that from the mid-1970s played regularly at Hungry Joe's Club in Huntington Beach.

SELECTED RECORDINGS

As leader: *It's Time for Dave Pike* (1961, Riv. 9360); *Times Out of Mind* (1975, Muse 5092); *Let the Minstrels Play On* (1979, Muse 5203); *Moon Bird* (1981, Muse 5261); *Pike's Groove* (1986, Criss Cross 1021)
As sideman with H. Mann: *Live at Newport* (1963, Atl. 1413)

BIBLIOGRAPHY

FeatherE; *Feather '60s*; *Feather–Gitler '70s*
M. Barker: "Dave Pike," *Crescendo*, ii/3 (1963), 18

GARY THEROUX

Pillars, Hayes (*b* North Little Rock, AR, 30 April 1906). Tenor saxophonist and bandleader. After playing with bands based in Little Rock, Arkansas, and Jackson, Tennessee, he worked with Alphonso Trent's orchestra (1927–8), then became a leader of the JETER–PILLARS ORCHESTRA. He continued to perform in the St. Louis area from the 1950s into the mid-1980s. (B. Rusch: "Hayes Pillars," *Cadence*, xii/12 1986), 17)

Oral history material in *NjR* (JOHP).

Pilz, Michel (*b* Bad Neustadt an der Saale, Germany, 28 Oct 1945). German bass clarinetist. After studying classical clarinet at the Conservatoire of the city of Luxembourg he belonged to Manfred Schoof's quintet from 1968 into the 1980s. At the same time he played with the German All Stars (1971), in the trio of Alex Schlippenbach, and until 1982 in Schlippenbach's Globe Unity Orchestra. He worked as a leader from 1972 and from 1978 played occasionally with the trumpeter Itaru Oki, with whom he toured Japan in 1979. Pilz's style is more lyrical and less intellectual than that of other European free-jazz players; one can discern in his playing the influence of Eric Dolphy as well as of Eastern music, with which he became familiar while touring Asia.

SELECTED RECORDINGS

As leader: *Carpathes* (1975, FMP 0250); with I. Oki and R. Hübner: *One Year: Afternoon & Evening* (1978, FMP 0720)
As sideman: M. Schoof: *Scales* (1976, Japo 60013); Globe Unity Orchestra: *Improvisations* (1977, Japo 60021); M. Schoof: *Light Lines* (1977, Japo 60019); Globe Unity Orchestra: *Compositions* (1979, Japo 60027)

WOLFRAM KNAUER

Pine, Courtney (*b* London, 18 March 1964). English tenor and soprano saxophonist and bass clarinetist. He first played clarinet and later took up saxophone. In his teens he formed a hard-bop group, Dwarf Steps, then worked with various reggae and funk bands; from the early 1980s, however, he has played jazz exclusively. After taking part in John Stevens's workshops he occasionally performed with the latter's group Freebop, and in 1984 he formed Abibi Jazz Arts; this organization, intended to promote interest in jazz among black British musicians, gave rise in 1985 to the all-black big band Jazz Warriors, which fused jazz with other styles of black music. In 1985 Pine began to lead his own small groups, including the World's First Saxophone Posse (a saxophone quartet). His playing is well represented on *Journey to the Urge Within* (Isl. 9846), which he recorded as a leader in 1986. He has also worked with Grand Union and with Art Blakey's Jazz Messengers (at the Camden Festival, London, in 1986), and has toured with Elvin Jones, George Russell, and a big band led by the rock drummer Charlie Watts.

BIBLIOGRAPHY

B. Case: "A Cool Blast of Pine," *Sunday Times Magazine* (3 Aug 1986)
S. Nicholson: "Young Turks: Courtney Pine," *The Wire*, no.25 (1986), 31

SIMON ADAMS

Pinkett, (William) Ward (*b* Newport News, VA, 29 April 1906; *d* New York, 15 March 1937). Trumpeter. He grew up in a musical family, and in 1926 moved to New York, where he played with several musicians, including Jelly Roll Morton (1928, 1930) and Chick Webb (1929); he may be heard to advantage on Morton's *Shoe Shiner's Drag* (1928, Vic. 21658). He also recorded with King Oliver (1929–31), Bubber Miley and Clarence Williams (both 1930), and James P. Johnson (1931); from 1933 he performed with Rex Stewart, Teddy Hill, Albert Nicholas, Bernard Addison, and Louis Metcalf. Later he replaced Freddie Jenkins in a quartet led by Nicholas that played at Adrian's Tap Room, New York; this group, augmented to a sextet and using the name the Little Ramblers, recorded six tracks in 1935. By this time, however, Pinkett's chronic alcoholism was beginning to impair his playing.

BIBLIOGRAPHY

ChiltonW
A. J. McCarthy: "Ward Pinkett," *JF* [intl edn], no.2 (1946), 24; repr. in *Jazz Reprints*, no.2 (1963), 39
M. Boujut: "Un certain Ward Pinkett: portrait," *Jm*, no.136 (1966), 62
D. Barker: *A Life in Jazz*, ed. A. Shipton (London and New York, 1986)
E. Townley: "The Forgotten Ones: Ward Pinkett," *JJI*, xl/1 (1987), 15

Piron, A(rmand) J(ohn) (*b* New Orleans, 16 Aug 1888; *d* New Orleans, 17 Feb 1943). Violinist and composer. He received a strict training in music from his father, a professional teacher, whose dance orchestra he joined after 1900. Later he became a member of the Bloom Philharmonia Orchestra (1903) and the Peerless Orchestra (*c*1910). From 1912 to 1914 he was the leader of the Olympia Orchestra (succeeding Freddie Keppard), which included Clarence Williams. The Piron and Williams Publishing Company, established in New Orleans in 1915, published many of Piron's compositions, including his highly successful song *I wish I could shimmy like my sister Kate*. In

1918, with Peter Bocage, Piron formed the Piron Orchestra, a "sweet" society band, to play regularly at Tranchina's restaurant at Spanish Fort on Lake Pontchartrain (for illustration *see* BANDS, fig.1); among the orchestra's personnel were Lorenzo Tio, Jr., and the gifted pianist Steve Lewis, with whom Piron wrote his theme song, *The Purple Rose of Cairo.* The band performed in New York in 1923 at the Cotton Club and the following year at the Roseland Ballroom, and also made a number of recordings for Victor, Columbia, and Okeh. After returning to New Orleans it continued to play at Tranchina's until it disbanded in 1928. Thereafter Piron led the Moonlight Serenaders aboard the SS *Pelican,* and he continued to work on river steamers until his death.

SELECTED RECORDINGS

Bouncing Around/Kiss me sweet (1923, OK 40021); New Orleans Wiggle/Mama's gone, goodbye (19233, Vic. 19233); Sud Bustin' Blues/West Indies Blues (1923, Col. 14007D)

BIBLIOGRAPHY

ChartersJ; *ChiltonW*
E. S[ouchon]: "Armand J. Piron," *SL*, iii/1 (1952), 4 [incl. discography and list of compositions]
F. Driggs and H. Lewine: *Black Beauty, White Heat: a Pictorial History of Classic Jazz, 1920–1950* (New York, 1982), 24

ALDEN ASHFORTH

Pisano, John (*b* New York, 2 June 1931). Guitarist. He studied piano as a child and started playing guitar at the age of 14. After touring with an air force band (1952–5) he played in Chico Hamilton's quintet (1956–8), with which he appeared in the film *The Sweet Smell of Success* (1957). He then settled in Los Angeles, where he played with Buddy DeFranco and Jimmy Giuffre and recorded some excellent duets with Billy Bean; he also recorded with Fred Katz and Joe Pass, among others. From 1960 to 1969 he worked as an accompanist for the singer Peggy Lee, and from 1965 to 1969 he toured the world as a member of Herb Alpert's band, the Tijuana Brass. Pisano collaborated with the songwriter Burt Bacharach and wrote some material for Sergio Mendes's group Brazil '66. In the early 1970s he performed with the guitarists Lee Ritenour and Tony Rizzi in Los Angeles. Pisano's agile playing is influenced by the styles of Chuck Wayne, Jimmy Raney, and Tal Farlow, but is laced with the more assertive timbre and rhythmic vitality of jazz-rock.

SELECTED RECORDINGS

As leader with B. Bean: *Makin' it* (1958, Decca 9206); *Take your Pick* (1958, Decca 9212)
As sideman: C. Hamilton: *The Chico Hamilton Quintet* (1956, PJ 1225); F. Katz: *Fred Katz and his Jammers* (1958, Decca 9217); J. Pass: *For Django* (1964, PJ 85)

BIBLIOGRAPHY

Feather '60s
F. R. Nemko: "John Pisano," *GP*, viii/11 (1974), 18

NORMAN MONGAN

Pitman, Booker (T.) (*b* Fairmont Heights, MD, 3 Oct 1909; *d* São Paulo, 13 Oct 1969). Alto saxophonist and clarinetist. His name is sometimes misspelled Pittman. He probably made his professional début in Philadelphia with Blanche Calloway, with whom he recorded in 1931; he also played as a sideman with the bandleaders Bennie Moten and Jap Allen. After a short time as the leader of his own group, the Blue Moon Chasers, he joined the orchestras of Count Basie (Kansas City, Missouri) and Ralph Cooper (Chicago). In 1933 he toured Europe as a member of Lucky Millinder's band; while in Europe he worked with the Brazilian bandleader Romeu Silva and later toured with him in Brazil (1935). For the next 15 years Pitman worked in South America, where in the late 1940s he recorded with the Cotton Pickers led by the Turkish guitarist Ahmed Ratip. In 1950 Pitman retired from music, but in 1959 made his first recordings as a leader, working with trios, quartets, big bands, and the São Paulo Dixielanders; he also accompanied his daughter, the singer Eliana Pitman. During the 1950s and 1960s he again toured Latin America. His playing during this period may be heard to advantage on *Booker Pitman Plays Again,* (1959, RCA BBL1028) and *The Fabulous Booker Pitman,* (1959, Hi-Fi Jazz 111). Pitman's preferred instrument was the alto saxophone, on which he was strongly influenced by the swing style of Johnny Hodges; he also occasionally played in bop and dixieland styles.

BIBLIOGRAPHY

S. Fonseca: Liner notes, *The Fabulous Booker Pitman* (Hi-Fi Jazz 111, 1959)
J. Guinle, L. Rangel, and N. R. Ortíz Oderigo: Liner notes, *Booker Pitman Plays Again* (RCA BBL1028, 1959)

RAINER E. LOTZ

Pizza Express. Two restaurants in London belonging to this chain regularly offer performances of jazz; *see* NIGHTCLUBS AND OTHER VENUES.

Pizza Man. Nickname of RAY PIZZI.

Pizzarelli, Bucky [John (Paul, Sr.)] (*b* Paterson, NJ, 9 Jan 1926). Guitarist, father of John Pizzarelli. He learned to play banjo and guitar when he was young. At the age of 17 he toured with Vaughn Monroe's dance band, which he re-joined (after military service) in 1946; he made recordings with the band for RCA and also played on radio. In 1952 he joined the staff of NBC. After touring for two years (1956–7) with the Three Suns trio, he returned to New York to work in recording studios and as a freelance. He played and toured with Benny Goodman, forming an association with him that lasted until Goodman's death; he also led his own trio and recorded duos with Zoot Sims (1976), Bud Freeman (?1975), Stephane Grappelli (1979), and his son John (from around 1981). Pizzarelli plays a seven-string electric guitar; the extra string (tuned to *A'*) allows him to play a bass line to his own solos. He is known not only for his exceptional solo performances on the electric instrument, but also for his proficiency as a classical guitarist.

SELECTED RECORDINGS

As leader: *Bix Beiderbecke Arrangements by Bill Challis* (1974, MonE 7066); *Bucky's Bunch* (1975, MonE 7082); *Nightwings* (1975, FD 1120); *The Café Pierre Trio* (1982, MonE 7093)
As sideman: J. Venuti: *Blue Four* (1974, Chi. 134)

BIBLIOGRAPHY

Feather–Gitler '70s
L. Tomkins: "'Some of my Best Things are Duos,' Says Bucky Pizzarelli," *CI*, xviii/4 (1979), 18
C. Deffaa: "Bucky and John Pizzarelli: Like Father, Like Son," *MR*, xi/12 (1984), 1

WARREN VACHÉ, SR.

Pizzarelli, John (Paul, Jr.) (*b* Paterson, NJ, 6 April 1960). Electric guitarist, son of Bucky Pizzarelli. In 1980 he began to play and sing in a duo with his father, with whom he made recordings. He joined Tony Monte's trio in 1986 and performed with it on radio station WNEW in New York. He has also performed and recorded as a leader; his secure technique on the seven-string electric guitar is displayed on his album *I'm Hip* (1983, Stash 226). (C. Deffaa: "Bucky and John Pizzarelli: Like Father, Like Son," *MR*, xi/12 (1984), 1)

WARREN VACHÉ, SR.

Pizzi, Ray(mond Michael) [Pizza Man] (*b* Everett, MA, 19 Jan 1943). Tenor and soprano saxophonist, bassoonist, and flutist. He began clarinet lessons as a child and from 1960 to 1966 he studied at the Boston Conservatory and the Berklee School of Music. He taught for five years in the public schools of Randolph, Massachusetts (1964–9), during which period he also toured with Woody Herman (*c*1966). In 1969 he moved to California. Pizzi has worked with a wide variety of groups and musicians, including the Thad Jones–Mel Lewis Orchestra, Frank Zappa (1977), Shelly Manne (1978), Willie Bobo (1979), Nancy Wilson (1982), and Milcho Leviev (1986). He has recorded with a number of these leaders and with the baritone saxophonist Moacir Santos (*c*1972–5), Mark Levine (1975), and Dizzy Gillespie (1976); the last session was organized by Gillespie after he heard Pizzi play in the band of the "Dinah Shore Show." Pizzi has also made recordings as a leader (from 1975), some of which have included his own compositions. His work draws on a range of contemporary musical styles; he has been influenced by guitarists as well as saxophonists and this has led to his exploring vibrato, bends, slides, and glisses in his playing. He is one of the few reed players in jazz to feature the bassoon as a main instrument.

SELECTED RECORDINGS

As leader: *Appassionato* (1975, P.Z. 333); *Conception* (1976, Pablo 2310795); *The Love Letter* (1979, Dis. 801); *Expressivo* (1981, Dis. 853)
As sideman: M. Santos: *Maestro* (*c*1972, BN LA007F); D. Gillespie: *Dizzy's Party* (1976, Pablo 2310784)

BIBLIOGRAPHY

F. R. Nemko: "Profile: Ray Pizzi," *DB*, xliii/8 (1976), 38
L. Underwood: "Ray Pizzi: West Coast Breakthrough," *DB*, xliv/17 (1977), 18 [incl. discography]
A. J. Liska: "Versatile Jazzman, and Not a Bad Actor Either," *Los Angeles Times* (15 April 1986), 2

PAUL RINZLER

Plantation. The name of several venues, notably ones in Chicago, Los Angeles, and New York; *see* NIGHTCLUBS AND OTHER VENUES.

Plater, Bobby [Robert] (*b* Newark, NJ, 13 May 1914; *d* Lake Tahoe, NV, 20 Nov 1982). Alto saxophonist and flutist. After taking up the alto saxophone at the age of 12 he played with the pianist Don Lambert while in his early teens and worked professionally from 1937, when he joined the Savoy Dictators. He played with Tiny Bradshaw (1940), served in the armed forces (1942–5), and worked briefly with Cootie Williams. In 1946 he joined the band of Lionel Hampton, in which two years later he became a principal soloist; he also wrote arrangements for the band, most of which were intended specifically for the singer Sonny Parker. In 1964 he left Hampton's band to replace Frank Wess in Count Basie's orchestra; he became the principal alto saxophonist in this group in 1970 and eventually Basie's music director. Although he seldom took solos on recordings he did so frequently in concert, usually on such ballads as *Soft as Velvet*. Plater had a rich, mellifluous style that was influenced first by Earle Warren and Willie Smith and later by Benny Carter and Johnny Hodges. A fine example of his work as an arranger is his version of *Lonesome Nights*, recorded in 1960 (*The Many Sides of Lionel Hampton*, Gladhamp 1001).

SELECTED RECORDINGS

As sideman: Savoy Dictators: Rhythm & Bugs/Tricks (1939, Savoy 100); L. Hampton: *Apollo Hall Concert, 1954* (1954, Phi. 10157), incl. The Nearness of you; *Hamp's Big Band* (1959, Audio-Fidelity 1913), incl. Elaine and Daffy, Red Top; C. Basie: *Basie Big Band* (1975, Pablo 2310756), incl. Soft as Velvet; *Farmers Market Barbecue* (1982, Pablo 2310874), incl. Blues for the Barbecue, Lester Leaps In

BIBLIOGRAPHY

ChiltonW; *FeatherE*; *Feather '60s*
J. Morgantini: "Bobby Plater: musicien trop méconnu," *BHcF*, no.54 (1956), 3
J. Dawson: "Bobby Plater: Basie's Right-hand Man," *MM* (23 Dec 1972), 42
S. Dance: *The World of Count Basie* (New York and London, 1980) [colln of previously pubd interviews], 223

CHRIS SHERIDAN

Plaxico, Lonnie (Luvell) (*b* Chicago, 4 Sept 1960). Double bass player. After working with Junior Cook, Sonny Stitt, and Chet Baker, he joined Wynton Marsalis's group in 1982. In 1983 he played with Dexter Gordon and Hank Jones, then became a member of Art Blakey's Jazz Messengers, playing not only with the regular group, but also with an all-star ensemble of the same name which performed and recorded in Japan that year; Blakey disbanded this version of the Jazz Messengers in 1986. Plaxico has recorded albums with Dizzy Gillespie and David Murray (both 1984) and with Blakey (notably *Blue Night*, 1985, Tim. 217), and has also played with Blakey's sidemen Terence Blanchard and Donald Harrison in the group New York Second Line. (I. Gitler: Liner notes, A. Blakey: *Art Blakey Live at Sweet Basil*, 1985, PW 6357)

Plaza Music Company. Record company. It established the label Banner in January 1922, and at the end of the same year opened its own recording studios. During the mid- and late 1920s the company either founded or supplied with discs the labels Regal, Domino, Oriole, Conqueror, Jewel, and Homestead; in August 1929 it joined Cameo and Pathé to form the AMERICAN RECORD COMPANY. The matrix series started by Plaza in 1922 was continued by ARC and survived to become CBS's main numerical sequence for material recorded in New York; the same matrix series was used in the 1950s and 1960s for 45 r.p.m. singles taken from tape masters.

BIBLIOGRAPHY

J. Godrich and R. M. W. Dixon: *Blues & Gospel Records, 1902–1942* (Hatch End, nr London, 1964, rev. 2/1969, rev. and enlarged 3/1982 as R. M. W. Dixon and J. Godrich: *Blues & Gospel Records, 1902–1943*), 22
W. Allen, P. Armagnac, and C. Kendziora: "Plaza–A. R. C.: a Clarification," *Matrix*, no.70 (1967), 3
B. Rust: *The American Record Label Book* (New Rochelle, NY, 1978)

Pleasure, King [Beeks, Clarence] (*b* Oakdale, nr Harriman, TN, 24 March 1922; *d* Los Angeles, 21 March 1981). Singer. He grew up in Cincinnati, and became inspired to write original lyrics to famous instrumental solos after hearing Lester Young's recording of *DB Blues* (1945). He moved to Hartford, Connecticut; later he won a talent contest at the Apollo Theatre, New York, singing Eddie Jefferson's lyrics to James Moody's *I'm in the mood for love* (1949). This success resulted in a contract with Prestige, and his version of the song, *Moody's Mood for Love*, became a substantial hit in 1952. The following year he achieved some success with *Parker's Mood*, but thereafter, apart from occasionally taking part in recording sessions, he receded into obscurity. He spent much of his later life in California. Pleasure was responsible for popularizing Jefferson's invention, vocalese; as such he instigated a trend for this style that boosted the career of the group Lambert, Hendricks, and Ross. Other singers and ensembles such as Al Jarreau and Manhattan Transfer, owe much to his innovations.

SELECTED RECORDINGS

Moody's Mood for Love (1952, Prst. 924); Parker's Mood (1953, Prst. 880); *Golden Days* (1960, HiFi 425)

BIBLIOGRAPHY

FeatherE
D. Halperin: Liner notes, *Golden Days* (Vogue LAE12258, 1961)
K. Pleasure: Liner notes, *Golden Days* (HiFi 425, 1961)
I. Gitler: Liner notes, *Original Moody's Mood* (Prst. 7586, 1968)
R. Russell: *Bird Lives: the High Life and Hard Times of Charlie (Yardbird) Parker* (New York, 1973), 322

MARK GARDNER

Pletcher, Stew(art F.) (*b* 1907; *d* 29 Nov 1978). Trumpeter. He studied at Yale University and played trumpet and sang with the Yale Collegians. In the early to mid-1930s he led his own band and recorded as a leader (1930, 1936) and with Ben Pollack (1934). He is best known for his association with Red Norvo (1936–7), with whom he made several recordings (including *Remember*, 1937, Bruns. 7896). Pletcher also worked with Tony Pastor (1939) and Jack Teagarden (1945, 1955) and in 1949 he performed and recorded with Nappy Lamare. His son Tom Pletcher is a cornetist.

based on *ChiltonW*

Plop. A rapid GLISS falling to the beginning of a note; the gliss precedes the beat.

Plunger (mute). *See* MUTE, §2(i).

Pocket cornet. A miniature CORNET with closely coiled tubing, having a range equivalent to the cornet of usual size. Don Cherry plays a pocket cornet, which he terms a pocket trumpet.

Pocket trumpet. Name used by Don Cherry for the pocket cornet he plays (*see* CHERRY, DON); pitched in B♭, the instrument was built in the first half of the century by the French company Besson.

Poindexter, Pony [Norwood] (*b* New Orleans, 8 Feb 1926; *d* Oakland, CA, 14 April 1988). Alto saxophonist. He studied clarinet in elementary school, and began playing alto saxophone at the age of 12 and the soprano instrument four years later. He worked with local musicians in Oakland, California, before his military service; after being discharged in 1946, he performed briefly with Jack McVea then toured with Billy Eckstine. In 1951–2 Poindexter worked with Lionel Hampton; he then led his own groups in San Francisco, and in 1961 joined the group that accompanied Lambert, Hendricks, and Ross (later Lambert, Hendricks, and Bavan), remaining until 1963. From 1964 to 1979 he lived and worked in Europe; he then returned to the USA and settled in Oakland. After an illness in 1979 forced him to cease playing saxophone he began performing as a singer. Although Poindexter's early work favored the styles of Jimmy Dorsey and Johnny Hodges, his recordings show clearly that the principal influence upon his playing was that of Charlie Parker.

SELECTED RECORDINGS

As leader: *Pony's Express* (1962, Epic 17035); *Gumbo!* (1962, Prst. 16001)
As sideman: J. Hendricks: *A Good Git Together* (1959, WP 1283); Lambert, Hendricks, and Bavan: *Lambert, Hendricks, and Bavan at Basin Street East* (1962, RCA LSP2635)

BIBLIOGRAPHY

J. Howard: "Pony Poindexter: the European Circuit," *Radio Free Jazz*, xvii/2 (1976), 7
M. Hennessey: "Europajazz," *JT* (1985), Aug, 8
N. Poindexter: *The Pony Express: Memoirs of a Jazz Musician* (Frankfurt am Main, Germany, 1985)

THOMAS OWENS

Polcer, Ed(ward Joseph) (*b* Paterson, NJ, 10 Feb 1937). Cornetist. He studied from the age of eight and in his teens formed a dixieland group. He played with local groups while studying at Princeton University (1954–8). From 1958 to 1969 he played traditional jazz at Ryan's and other clubs in and around New York, at the same time pursuing a career in business. In 1969 he joined Red Balaban's group, with which he worked intermittently until 1985 (as joint leader from 1975). He toured North America with Benny Goodman (1972), and made recordings with swing groups led by Jane Harvey and Dick Wellstood (for example, *You Fats . . . me Jane*, 1975, CJ 15) and the singer Cathy Chamberlain (1976). From 1970 he led sextets and quintets, which accompanied many prominent jazz musicians, and from 1983 to 1985 his group Midtown North played at Eddie Condon's club in New York. (*Feather–Gitler '70s*)

Polish Jazz Society. *See* POLSKIE STOWARZYSZENIE JAZZOWE.

Pollack, Ben (*b* Chicago, 22 June 1903; *d* Palm Springs, CA, 7 June 1971). Drummer and bandleader. By 1923 he was playing with the NEW ORLEANS RHYTHM KINGS, where he established himself as the leading drummer in the early Chicago style of white jazz, particularly on account of his innovative cymbal technique. In 1926 he founded the first of several jazz-oriented dance bands for which he is largely remembered today. Although commercially only moderately successful, these bands were highly regarded by contemporary jazz musicians, and provided valuable exposure early in their careers for such important players as Benny Goodman, Glenn Miller, Bud Freeman, Jack Teagarden, Harry James, and Muggsy Spanier. In 1934 Pollack's band broke up in California, and most of its members subsequently formed the nucleus of Bob Crosby's band. From the 1940s Pollack occasionally organized groups in California in the dixieland revival style, but was chiefly active as a restaurateur.

SELECTED RECORDINGS

As leader: 'Deed I do (1926, Vic. 20408); My Kinda Love (1929, Vic. 21944); Two Tickets to Georgia (1933, Vic. 24284); Song of the Islands (1937, Decca 1424)
As sideman with New Orleans Rhythm Kings: Sweet Lovin' Man (1923, Gen. 5104); Shimmeshawabble (1923, Gen. 5106); Tin Roof Blues (1923, Gen. 5105)

BIBLIOGRAPHY

S. B. Charters and L. Kunstadt: *Jazz: a History of the New York Scene* (Garden City, NY, 1962/*R*1981), chap.13
A. Napoleon and J. R. T. Davies: "A Discography," *Sv*, no.36 (1971), 222
A. Napoleon: "May it Please you: Thoughts on Ben Pollack," *JJ*, xxiv/9 (1971), 10
A. McCarthy: *Big Band Jazz* (New York and London, 1974), 182
T. D. Brown: *A History and Analysis of Jazz Drumming to 1942* (diss., U. of Michigan, 1976), 282, 560
J. Chilton: *Stomp Off, Let's Go! The Story of Bob Crosby's Bob Cats & Big Band* (London, 1983)

J. BRADFORD ROBINSON

Pollard, Terry (Jean) (*b* Detroit, 15 Aug 1931). Pianist and vibraphonist. She performed and recorded in Detroit with Thad and Elvin Jones in Billy Mitchell's quintet (1952–3), playing both piano and vibraphone. From 1953 to 1957 she toured and made recordings as the pianist and second vibraphonist in Terry Gibbs's groups (including *Terry Gibbs Quartet*, 1953, Bruns. BL58055); she also recorded with her own quintet in Los Angeles and with Dick Garcia in New York (1955). In 1957 she returned to Detroit, where she played piano in clubs and took part in recording sessions with Yusef Lateef (1958–9). She recorded with Dorothy Ashby in 1961. (*FeatherE*)

Ben Pollack's band outside the MGM studios in Culver City, CA, summer 1927: (left to right) Larry Binyon (tenor saxophone), Benny Goodman (clarinet), Gil Rodin (alto saxophone), Al Lasker (tuba), Pollack (drums, leader), Al Gifford (banjo), Wayne Allen (piano, arranger), Al Harris and Harry Greenberg (trumpets), and Glenn Miller (trombone)

Polo, Danny (*b* Toluca, IL, 22 Dec 1901; *d* Chicago, 11 July 1949). Clarinetist and saxophonist. He grew up in Clinton, Indiana, and played clarinet in a local marching band. His first professional engagements were with Elmer Schoebel in Chicago (*c*1923) and Merritt Brunies. During the winter of 1926–7 he deputized for Don Murray in Jean Goldkette's orchestra and the following summer he toured Europe with Dave Tough. He also worked with the banjoist George Carhart throughout Europe, recording with his New Yorkers in Berlin (*see* NEW YORKERS (i)) before leading his own band in Paris. He remained in France until 1929, playing with Arthur Briggs, Lud Gluskin, and Ray Ventura, then moved to London, where he performed and recorded with Bert Ambrose's orchestra (intermittently, 1929–35); he worked again with Gluskin in 1932. After a period in the USA (1935–8) Polo returned to Europe and played with Ambrose in London and Ventura in Paris. He resettled in the USA in 1939 and played with Joe Sullivan at Café Society, New York, before spending two years with Jack Teagarden. In 1942 he joined Claude Thornhill's band, and in the mid-1940s led his own groups; he re-joined Thornhill shortly before his death. Polo was often credited with popularizing jazz in Britain. His playing was smooth, gentle, and restrained.

SELECTED RECORDINGS

As leader: Stratton Street Strut/More than Somewhat (1937, Decca F6518); Money for Jam/Mr. Polo Takes a Solo (1937, Decca F6578)

As sideman: J. Goldkette: My Pretty Girl (1927, Vic. 20588); Clementine (1927, Vic. 20994); Rhythmic Eight: Kansas City Kitty/Louise (1929, Zonophone 5437); B. Ambrose: Cotton Pickers' Congregation/Caravan (1937, Decca F6458); Varsity Seven: It's Tight Like that/Easy Rider (1939, Vars. 8147); C. Thornhill: Robbin's Nest (1947, Col. 38136)

BIBLIOGRAPHY

ChiltonW
J. Burns: "The Forgotten Boppers," *J&B*, ii/3 (1972), 4
D. Schiedt: *The Jazz State of Indiana* (Pittsboro, IN, 1977)
J. Godbolt: *A History of Jazz in Britain, 1919–50* (London, Melbourne, Australia, and New York, 1984)

RAYMOND J. GARIGLIO

Polskie Stowarzyszenie Jazzowe [Polish Jazz Society]. A Polish jazz organization which sponsors and arranges concerts and festivals, and issues records and periodicals. It evolved from the Federacja Polskich Klubów Jazzowych (Federation of Polish Jazz Clubs), formed in 1956 by Jan Byrczek, Roman Waschko, and others. After this organization disbanded the Polska Federacja Jazzowa (Polish Jazz Federation) was formed in March 1963; this became the Polskie Stowarzyszenie Jazzowe by 1967 and was led by Byrczek until December 1975, when Zbigniew Namysłowski became the society's president and Byrczek and Jan Wróblewski its vice-presidents. Andrezej Jaroszewski succeeded Namysłowski in December 1977, and Tomasz Tluczkiewicz became president in 1980.

The society has sponsored and organized a piano competition and workshop in Kalisz; workshops in Radost (near Warsaw) and Chodziez; and a festival, the Pomorian Jazz Autumn, in Toruń and Bydgoszcz. It also founded the journal *Jazz Forum* and in 1972 became affiliated with the record label Poljazz. It played an important role in establishing the International Jazz Federation. In 1982 it established a jazz archive; *see* LIBRARIES AND ARCHIVES, §2.

Pomeroy, (Irving) Herb(ert, III) (*b* Gloucester, MA, 15 April 1930). Bandleader, trumpeter, and teacher. After studying at the Berklee College of Music (1950–52) he toured as a trumpeter with Lionel Hampton (1953–4) and Stan Kenton (1954). He then returned to Boston, and in 1955 began teaching at Berklee. He led a 16-piece swing and bop ensemble that performed regularly at The Stables (1956–60); among its sidemen were Joe Gordon, Jaki Byard (who was then playing tenor saxophone), Boots Mussulli, and later, Charlie Mariano and Bill Berry. From 1960 to 1962 he was the leader of another band, which played some of his own arrangements; its 13 members included Dusko Goykovich, Michael Gibbs, Sam Rivers, Hal Galper, and Alan Dawson. Pomeroy has directed jazz bands at the Massachusetts Institute of Technology from 1963. In 1975 he organized a third group, bringing together students, members of his original band, and such well-known jazzmen as John LaPorta and Phil Wilson.

SELECTED RECORDINGS

As leader: *Jazz in a Stable* (1955, Tran. 1); *Band in Boston* (1958, UA 4015); *Pramlatta's Hips* (*c*1980, Shiah 1)

As sideman: C. Mariano: *Boston All Stars* (1953, Prst. 153); S. Chaloff: *The Fable of Mable* (1954, Sto. 317)

BIBLIOGRAPHY

FeatherE; *Feather '60s*
L. Feather: "Herb Pomeroy Orchestra," *DB*, xxiv/13 (1957), 35
"The New Herb Pomeroy," *DB*, xxvii/11 (1960), 14
K. C. Sulkin: "Herb Pomeroy," *DB*, xliv/17 (1977), 32

BARRY KERNFELD

Ponder, Jimmy [James Willis] (*b* Pittsburgh, 10 May 1946). Electric guitarist. In 1966 he began an association with Charles Earland that continued into the late 1970s, and from 1969 to 1972 he performed in a group led by Joe Thomas (v). After leading a band, Final Edition, with the drummer Grassella Oliphant (1975) he continued to lead his own ensembles, and also performed and recorded with other musicians, notably Stanley Turrentine. Ponder's playing combines aggressive rhythm-and-blues figurations with swift and lucid bop lines. His choice of material is influenced by a keen ear for chromaticism, which gives his performances an emotionally volatile yet distanced, astringent quality.

SELECTED RECORDINGS

As sideman: C. Earland: *Soul Crib* (1969, Choice 520); *Infant Eyes* (1979, Muse 5181); S. Turrentine: *Straight Ahead* (1985, BN 85105)

BIBLIOGRAPHY

Feather–Gitler '70s

ANDREW WAGGONER

Ponomarev, Valery (*b* Moscow, 20 Jan 1943). Russian trumpeter. He studied music in Moscow and became interested in jazz after hearing a recording by Clifford Brown. He performed at the Youth Club in Moscow (1965–9) and at jazz festivals in the USSR, and recorded for the Melodiya label with a hard-bop group led by the pianist Vadim Sakun. After defecting to the West in the mid-1970s, in 1977 Ponomarev joined Art Blakey's Jazz Messengers; he toured Europe, Brazil, and Japan with the group and took part in a number of recordings, including *In my Prime* (1977–8, Tim. 114, 118). In 1980 he organized his own band, Universal Language.

BIBLIOGRAPHY

Feather–Gitler '70s
L. Birnbaum: "Profile: Valery Ponomarev," *DB*, xlvi/12 (1979), 46
B. Rusch: "Valery Ponomarev: Interview," *Cadence*, xi/2 (1985), 10

Ponty, Jean-Luc (*b* Avranches, France, 29 Sept 1942). French violinist. His father was a violin teacher and the director of the school of music in Avranches, and his mother taught piano. He played violin and piano from the age of five and clarinet from the age of 11. At 13 he left school to concentrate on becoming a concert violinist; he studied for two years at the Paris Conservatoire, winning the *premier prix* when he was 17. He then played with the Concerts Lamoureux orchestra for three years, during which time he was introduced to jazz; he first played jazz as an amateur clarinetist and tenor saxophonist, but by 1962 he was performing and recording on violin with Jef Gilson, with whom he continued to be associated for some time.

After his military service (1962–4) Ponty devoted himself exclusively to jazz. He led a quartet with René Urtreger and in 1964 performed at the Antibes–Juan-les-Pins Jazz Festival. He then played and recorded in quartets and trios with Eddy Louiss and Daniel Humair (1964–7) and as the leader of a quartet with Wolfgang Dauner, Niels-Henning Ørsted Pedersen, and Humair (1967). He made his first visit to the USA in 1967 to play in a violin workshop at the Monterey Jazz Festival. His quartet first played in England in February 1969, and in March he went to Los Angeles, where he played and recorded with Frank Zappa and made an album that included some of Zappa's compositions (*King Kong*); in the same year he joined George Duke's trio. After returning to France he led a free-jazz group, the Jean-Luc Ponty Experience (*c*1970–72). He settled in the USA in 1973 and toured with Zappa's Mothers of Invention, then with the second Mahavishnu Orchestra (1974–5). From 1975 he led jazz-rock bands, touring extensively and reaching a large audience with his recordings.

Jean-Luc Ponty playing at the Newport Jazz Saratoga Festival, 1978

By developing a range of new sounds, grounded in electronic effects, Ponty has made a place for the violin in modern jazz styles. At first he simply amplified his acoustic violin in order to be heard, but from 1969 he used mainly electric violin and violectra (an electric instrument tuned an octave below the violin), which he played through distortion, Echoplex, phase shifter, and wa-wa devices, sometimes combining these with the conventional mute. In 1977 he replaced the two instruments with a five-string electric violin, the lowest string on which (tuned to *c*) offered part of the violectra's range. With his own bands he also plays synthesizer and in the 1980s he has often reverted from electric to acoustic violin, using the synthesizer to create electronic effects. The broad spectrum of sounds he produces and the contrast between them and conventional jazz timbres may be heard on the swing album *Violin Summit* (1966), recorded with Svend Asmussen, Stephane Grappelli, and Stuff Smith, and the jazz-rock album *Jean-Luc Ponty – Stephane Grappelli* (1973).

Ponty's versatility is rare among jazzmen: he is equally at home in swing, bop, modal jazz, free jazz, and jazz-rock and plays distinguished improvisations in every style. One of the most creative European jazz musicians, he is a supreme exponent of jazz-rock. *Upon the Wings of Music* (1975) marked his move away from the raucous styles of Zappa and the Mahavishnu Orchestra; instead he developed a style in which his imaginative themes and improvisations – at times soaring and lyrical, at times bluesy, biting, and rhythmically complex – are accompanied by rich, highly polished ostinatos based on soul and rock rhythms.

See also IMPROVISATION, §§4(iii), 4(vi), and ex.6.

SELECTED RECORDINGS

As leader: *Jazz Long Playing* (1964, Phi. B77810L); with S. Asmussen, S. Grappelli, and S. Smith: *Violin Summit* (1966, Saba 15099); *Sunday Walk* (1967, Saba 15139); *King Kong* (1969, PJ 20172); *Jean-Luc Ponty–Stephane Grappelli* (1973, Amer. 6139); *Upon the Wings of Music* (1975, Atl. 18138); *Imaginary Voyage* (1976, Atl. 19136); *Individual Choice* (*c*1983, Atl. 80098)

As sideman: J. Gilson: *Enfin!* (1962–3, Club de l'échiquier 30J1002); *Oeil vision* (1962, 1965, Club de l'échiquier AF1); W. Dauner: *Free Action* (1967, Saba 15095); Mahavishnu Orchestra: *Visions of the Emerald Beyond* (1974, Col. PC33411)

BIBLIOGRAPHY

J. Tronchot: "Jean-Luc Ponty: de Jef Gilson à la gloire," *Jh*, no.198 (1964), 8

M. Hennessey: "French Cookin': Jean-Luc Ponty," *DB*, xxxiii/22 (1966), 24

M. Gardner: "Jean-Luc Ponty: Violin Virtuoso," *JJ*, xxii/3 (1969), 5 [incl. discography]

P. Senoff: "Jean-Luc Ponty," *J&P*, ix/3 (1970), 26

R. Palmer: "Soaring with the Frenchman Jean-Luc Ponty," *DB*, xlii/20 (1975), 17 [incl. discography]

L. Magee and E. F. von Bergen: "The Jazz-rock Violin of Jean-Luc Ponty," *The Instrumentalist*, xxx/6 (1976), 62

T. Schneckloth: "Jean-Luc Ponty: Synthesis for the Strings," *DB*, xliv/20 (1977), 12 [incl. discography]

M. Glaser and S. Grappelli: *Jazz Violin* (New York and elsewhere, 1981) [incl. transcrs.]

M. Mandel: "Jean-Luc Ponty's Electronic Muse," *DB*, li/1 (1984), 20 [incl. discography]

BARRY KERNFELD

Pope, Odeon (*b* Ninety Six, SC, 24 Oct 1938). Trumpeter and bandleader. He grew up in Philadelphia, where he learned saxophone and studied harmony with Ray Bryant. After he was introduced by Jymie Merritt to Max Roach he toured Europe (1967–8) with Roach's quartet, accompanying Vi Redd in a recording session in London (1967). In 1971 he formed the cooperative group Catalyst, which recorded four albums between 1972 and 1975, and in 1977 he organized the Saxophone Choir. Pope led this band, made up of eight saxophones and a rhythm section, until 1979, when he joined Roach for another tour of Europe; he also made further recordings with Roach's group, including *Chattahoochee Red* (1980, Col. FC37367). In the early 1980s he recorded with his own trio and continued to lead the Saxophone Choir, which recorded in 1985. (R. Woessner: "Profile: Odeon Pope," *DB*, 1/3 (1983), 46)

Popular song form. A term applied to the forms common in the refrains of popular songs and therefore in the jazz pieces based on them; *see* FORMS, esp. §1(i)(a).

Porcino, Al (*b* New York, 14 May 1925). Trumpeter. After studying in New York with Charles Colin he played from 1943 with Georgie Auld, Louis Prima, Tommy Dorsey, and Gene Krupa, and later with Stan Kenton (1947–8), Chubby Jackson (1949), and Woody Herman (1949–50). During the 1950s he rejoined Herman (to tour Europe in 1954) and Kenton (1954–5), and also played with Pete Rugolo, Elliot Lawrence, and Charlie Barnet. In 1957 he settled in Los Angeles, where he formed the Jazz Wave Orchestra with Med Flory; it performed and made recordings until 1959. He spent the next three years working with Terry Gibbs, with whom he also recorded. He played in big bands at the Monterey Jazz Festival in 1958, 1959, and 1962. In the 1960s he toured with popular singers, worked in studios, and played with Buddy Rich in London (1968) and the Thad Jones–Mel Lewis Orchestra (1969–70). He then worked with Chuck Mangione (1970–72), playing in the premières of three of his compositions, and again toured with Herman (1972). He formed his own big band in 1974, which accompanied various popular singers, among them Mel Tormé. Porcino is an experienced big-band lead trumpeter, well known for the brilliance and forcefulness of his sound.

SELECTED DISCOGRAPHY

As leader: with M. Flory: *Jazz Wave Orchestra* (1957, Jub. 1066); *In Oblivion* (1986, Jazz Mark 106)

As sideman: T. Gibbs: *The Exciting Big Band of Terry Gibbs* (1961, Verve 62151); W. Herman: *The Raven Speaks* (1972, Fan. 9416); C. Mangione: *Together* (1973, Mer. 2-7501); M. Tormé: *Live at the Maisonette* (1974, Atl. 18129); T. Jones and A. Rully: *Thad and Aura* (1977, Four Leaf Clover 5020)

BIBLIOGRAPHY

R. Williams: "Al Porcino," *MM* (22 Nov 1969), 18

W. Whiteworth: "Al Porcino: the Art of Playing Lead," *DB*, xxxix/8 (1972), 14

T. Baron: "The Peripatetic Al Porcino," *Cadence*, ii/5 (1977), 8

FREDERICK A. BECK

Pori (International) Jazz (Festival). Festival held annually from 1966 in Pori, Finland. It takes place in July at several venues, particularly on outdoor stages along the banks of the River Kokemaenjoki and in the Kirjurinluoto Concert Park; its duration was changed in 1985 from an extended weekend to nine days. Pori Jazz is among Europe's oldest jazz festivals and one of the most diverse in its programming; all styles of jazz are offered, as well as blues and rock. The performances draw a combined audience of more than 40,000 at 12 separate venues. In the 1980s the festival's director was Jyrki Kangas. Soviet musicians appeared at the festival for the first time in 1982, and Benny Goodman performed in the same year. Other participants have included the Dirty Dozen Brass Band, Steps Ahead, and groups led by Lou Donaldson, Bob Moses, and Flora Purim and Airto Moreira.

PAUL R. LAIRD

Portal, Michel (*b* Bayonne, France, 27 Nov 1935). French saxophonist and clarinetist. After studying clarinet, he played under the bandleaders Henri Rossotti and (in Spain in 1958) Perez

Prado, and with the drummer Benny Bennett (1960), Aimé Barelli, Don Cherry, Jef Gilson (1963, 1965), Nathan Davis (1965), André Hodeir (1966), the Paris Jazz All Stars (1966), Enrico Rava, Sunny Murray (1968), Anthony Braxton, Alan Silva (1969–70), Joachim Kühn (1969), Kenny Wheeler, and John Surman (1970). He recorded as a leader in 1969–71, then in 1972 formed the group Portal Unit; his playing is well represented on the album *Alors!* (1970, Futura 12). He also played with Derek Bailey (1974) and Eddy Louiss (1979), in a trio with Pierre Favre and the bass player Leon Francioli (1980), and with Albert Mangelsdorff (1981), Steve Lacy (1981), George Lewis (ii) (1984), and Mino Cinelu (1985). In addition to his work in jazz, he has played classical clarinet and written film scores.

BIBLIOGRAPHY

P. L. Rossi: "Michel polyvalent Portal," *Jm*, no.142 (1967), 24
P. Carles and F. Marmande: "Michel Portal ou la parole au présent," *Jm*, no.210 (1973), 10
D. Soutif: "Michel Portal: le prix de la musique," *Jm*, no.329 (1984), 51

MICHEL LAPLACE

Portamento. A continuous slide in pitch over a given interval without the sounding of discrete intermediate steps. In jazz no distinction in terminology is made between the portamento and the glissando (a slide in which intermediate steps may be heard): *see* GLISS.

Porteña Jazz Band. Argentine band. Formed in 1964 under the leadership of the pianist Ignacio Romero, its other original members were the cornetist Norberto Gandini, the trombonist Sergio Tamburri, the saxophonists Horacio Schere and Alfredo Espinosa, the clarinetist Ernesto Carrizo, the banjoists Alfredo Carozzi and Ricardo Scarremberg, the tuba player Carlos Balmaceda, the double bass player Alberto Mazza, and the drummer Daniel Passero. The band made several recordings during the following decades and in 1985–6 toured the USSR, Germany, the Netherlands, and Belgium. It is among the best-known traditional-jazz bands in Argentina, and may be heard to advantage on the album *Porteña Jazz Band* (1972–3, Trova 80073).

LAUREANO FERNÁNDEZ, OMAR GARCÍA BRUNELLI

Porter, Gene [Eugene] (*b* Pocahontas, nr Jackson, MS, 7 June 1910). Saxophonist and clarinetist. He began his career as an alto saxophonist, then studied clarinet with Omer Simeon (*c*1929). He worked in New Orleans and on Mississippi riverboats with various musicians, including Papa Celestin, Joseph Robichaux (1933, with whom he recorded), and Sidney Desvigne (1935). In 1935 he joined the Jeter–Pillars Orchestra, but he left in 1937 to work with Don Redman; his tenor saxophone playing is well represented on Redman's *Swingin' with the Fat Man* (1937, first issued on the album *Don Redman*, 1932–7, CBS 52539). He again played with the Jeter–Pillars Orchestra (1937–42) and, after spending some months with Jimmie Lunceford (1942), performed, recorded, and made several films with Benny Carter (1942–4), whose assistant leader he became. After army service (1944–5) he re-joined Carter and also recorded with Dinah Washington (1945), Charles Mingus (1946), and Lloyd Glenn (1947), among others. He played with Walter Fuller (1948–60) then led his own small group. Besides reeds, Porter also played flute and sang. (K. Gert zur Heide: "Eugene Porter," *Fn*, vii (1976), no.5, p.11; no.6, p.17)

based on *ChiltonW*

Porter, Roy (*b* Walsenburg, CO, 30 July 1923). Drummer and bandleader. He toured briefly with Milt Larkin (1943), then after military service moved to Los Angeles and worked with Teddy Bunn's Spirits of Rhythm (1944) and Howard McGhee (1945–7). Porter also participated in Charlie Parker's first sessions for Dial (1946), and may be heard to advantage on *Ornithology/A Night in Tunisia* (Dial 1002). Thereafter he performed and recorded with Teddy Edwards (1947) and Dexter Gordon (1947–8), working with Gordon in New York. He then led a big band that included Eric Dolphy, Art and Addison Farmer, Jimmy Knepper, and Chet Baker. After this disbanded in 1949, Porter played at clubs in San Francisco, notably Bop City, with Sonny Criss, Hampton Hawes, Edwards, Gordon, and others. Back in Los Angeles he worked with Earl Bostic, Louis Jordan, and Perez Prado (all 1957). During the 1960s he was active as a session musician outside jazz, but in 1970 he organized and led his own group. He recorded several times as a leader and a sideman before illness caused him to cease drumming in 1978.

BIBLIOGRAPHY

M. Gardner: "Roy Porter," *J&B*, i (1971), no.4, p.10; no.5, p.26 [interview]
G. Mack and H. Mansfield, Jr.: "Roy Porter," *Be-bop and Beyond*, iii (1985), no.4, p.10; no.5, p.17
S. Klett: "Roy Porter: Interview," *Cadence*, xii (1986), no.9, p.5; no.10, p.5

Porter, Yank [Allen] (*b* Norfolk, VA, *c*1895; *d* New York, 22 March 1944). Drummer. After settling in New York in 1926 he worked mainly with Cliff Jackson until 1930. Later he played in a band led by the pianist and arranger Charlie Matson (1932), and worked with Louis Armstrong and Bud Harris (both 1933) and James P. Johnson (1934). He then performed and recorded with Fats Waller (1935–6), and worked with the pianist Dave Martin (1936). After playing with Johnson again (1939) and with Joe Sullivan at Café Society (1940) he was a member of Teddy Wilson's small band and recorded as a freelance with Benny Carter (1940) and Art Tatum (1941). Porter's mature style was highly discreet, and is well represented on Waller's *Oooh! look-a there, ain't she pretty?* (1936, Vic. 25255); his earlier, more assertive, work may be heard on Armstrong's *Basin Street Blues* (1933, Vic. 24351).

based on *ChiltonW*

Poston, Joe [Doc; Joseph E.] (*b* Alexandria, LA, *c*1895; *d* Illinois, May 1942). After working with Doc Cook (1922–4) he played with Fate Marable on riverboats. In 1927 he returned briefly to Cook's band, then from 1928 to 1930 he performed and made recordings with Jimmie Noone (including *Four or Five Times*, 1928, Voc. 1185). He spent a further period with Cook before illness forced him to retire.

based on *ChiltonW*

Potter, Tommy [Charles Thomas] (*b* Philadelphia, 21 Sept 1918; *d* March 1988). Double bass player. He first studied piano and guitar, and did not take up double bass until 1940. After early associations with John Malachi and Trummy Young he played with Billy Eckstine's big band (1944–5). He is best known for his work from 1947 to 1950 when he was a member of Charlie Parker's quintet; the recordings he made with Parker for Savoy and Dial demonstrate his clear tone and ability to create varied and interesting lines while maintaining a strong, reliable pulse, even at extreme tempos. As a result of his association with Parker, Potter was, after Oscar Pettiford, one of the best-respected double bass players of the bop era. In the late 1940s he recorded prolifically with such musicians as Fats Navarro, Wardell Gray, and Bud Powell. He continued to be in great demand during the 1950s and early 1960s and for club dates and recordings, working with musicians as diverse as Stan Getz, Eckstine, Earl Hines, Artie Shaw, Powell, Tyree Glenn, and Harry Edison. He went into semiretirement in the mid-1960s.

For illustration *see* PARKER, CHARLIE, fig.2.

SELECTED RECORDINGS

As sideman with C. Parker (all recorded in 1947): Donna Lee/Buzzy (Savoy 652); Cheryl/Bird Gets the Worm (Savoy 952); Bongo Bop/Embraceable You (Dial 1024); The Hymn/Drifting on a Reed (Dial 1056)

As sideman with others: B. Eckstine: Blowin' the Blues Away (1944, De Luxe 2001); B. Powell: Bouncing with Bud/Wail (1949, BN 1567); D. Lanphere: Wailing Wall (1949, NewJ 819); Go (1949, NewJ 812); W. Gray: Twisted (1949, NewJ 817); M. Davis: Conception (1951, Prst. 868); S. Rollins: *Sonny Rollins Quartet* (1954, Prst. 190); H. Edison: *Patented by Edison* (1960, Roul. 52041)

BIBLIOGRAPHY

FeatherE; *Feather '60s*; *Feather–Gitler '70s*

M. Jones: "Tommy Potter, a Baby Bass Checker," *MM*, xxxix (31 Oct 1964), 6

SCOTT DeVEAUX

Potts, Bill [William Orie] (*b* Arlington, VA, 3 April 1928). Arranger, pianist, and conductor. In his youth he played Hawaiian guitar, then accordion. During his army service in Washington (1949–54) he played in military ensembles and from 1951 wrote arrangements for the Orchestra (the radio band of the broadcaster Willis Conover). In 1954–5 he also provided arrangements for Tony Pastor, Stan Kenton, and Woody Herman. His work as a pianist in Washington included performances with Lester Young (1956), which were recorded and later released as *Lester Young in Washington, DC* (PL 2308219, 2308225, 2308228, 2308230). After touring with Herman (1957–9) Potts arranged and conducted *The Jazz Soul of Porgy and Bess* (1959, UA 4032), an acclaimed interpretation of Gershwin's opera that included solos by Zoot Sims, Al Cohn, Bob Brookmeyer, Art Farmer, and Harry Edison. He recorded with his own studio band in 1963 and again in 1967, when he also worked as an arranger for Buddy Rich. From the early 1970s he taught arranging at Montgomery College.

BIBLIOGRAPHY

FeatherE

A. Scott: "Jazz Composer Calls the Tunes in Washington," *Metronome*, lxxv/10 (1958), 16

Povel, Ferdinand (*b* Haarlem, Netherlands, 13 Feb 1947). Dutch tenor saxophonist and flutist. He is self-taught as a musician. He played with Dusko Goykovich, Kurt Edelhagen, Kenny Clarke, Francy Boland, Slide Hampton, Maynard Ferguson, and Peter Herbolzheimer and recorded with the pianist Martin Haak (1964), Goykovich (1970–71), Ferguson (1973), Herbolzheimer (from 1973), Hampton (1974), and many Dutch radio bands; he also appeared at several festivals. In addition to his principal instruments he is an adept player of the soprano and alto saxophones.

SELECTED RECORDINGS

As leader: *Beboppin'* (1983, Limetree 198403)

As sideman: D. Goykovich: *Live at the Domicile* (1970, Session 102851-6); *It's About Blues Time* (1971, Ensayo 48); D. Raney: *Meeting the Tenors* (1983, Criss Cross 1006)

WIM VAN EYLE

Powell, Baden. *See* BADEN POWELL.

Powell, Benny [Benjamin Gordon] (*b* New Orleans, 1 March 1930). Trombonist. He studied music with local teachers, and played trombone from the age of 12; he made his professional début on New Year's Day 1944. After playing with the 'Bama State Collegians and various bands in Texas and Oklahoma in the mid-1940s he toured with Lionel Hampton (1948–51). In October 1951 he joined Count Basie's band, and some months later began to share the trombone solo work with Henry Coker; in 1956 he won the critic's poll in *Down Beat*. During the 1950s he also recorded frequently with smaller ensembles, and in 1963 he left Basie to lead his own groups in New York. While playing for Merv Griffin's television show and working as an administrator for Billy Taylor (ii) and Jazzmobile, he performed and recorded with the Thad Jones–Mel Lewis Orchestra (1966–70) and Duke Pearson's big band (1967–70). In 1970 he moved to Los Angeles, where he played with Bill Holman (1974) and performed and recorded with Bill Berry (*c*1974–1976). In 1986 he played at a memorial concert for Louis Armstrong in New York. Powell's style owes much to the influence of J. J. Johnson; he has a fluent technique, the ability to enunciate rapid notes clearly, and a strong sense of melodic line.

SELECTED RECORDINGS

As sideman: C. Basie: *Dance Session no.1* (1953, Clef 626); B. Clayton: on *How High the Fi* (1953, Col. CL567), Moten Swing, Sentimental Journey; F. Wess: *Frank Wess Quintet* (1964, Com. 20031), incl. Basie ain't Here, You're my Thrill; *North, South, East . . . Wess* (1956, Savoy 12072); C. Basie: *Basie–Eckstine, Inc.* (1959, Roul. 52029); L. Hampton: *Newport Uproar!* (1967, RCA LSP3891); *Newport '78* (1978, Tim. 142)

BIBLIOGRAPHY

FeatherE; *Feather '60s*; *Feather–Gitler '70s*

L. Feather: "More Gen on Basie's Men," *MM*, xxx (3 April 1954), 13

R. Horricks: *Count Basie and his Orchestra: its Music and its Musicians* (London and New York, 1957), 268

S. Voce: "Benny Powell and the Count Basie Trombone Team," *JJ*, x/11 (1957), 1

H. Siders: "Spendour in the Brass," *DB*, xl/2 (1973), 13

LEROY OSTRANSKY

Powell, Bud [Earl] (*b* New York, 27 Sept 1924; *d* New York, 1 Aug 1966). Pianist, brother of Richie Powell. From 1940 he took part in informal jam sessions at Minton's Playhouse, New York, where he came under the tutelage and protection of Thelonious Monk and contributed to the emerging bop style. By 1942–4, when he played in the band of his guardian Cootie Williams, he had already developed his individual style in most of its essentials. After sustaining a head injury during a racial incident in 1945, he suffered the first of many nervous collapses, which were to confine him to sanatoriums for much of his adult life. Thereafter, in the late 1940s and early 1950s, he appeared intermittently in New York clubs with leading bop musicians or in his own trio. From the mid-1950s, as his mental health and musical powers deteriorated, he gradually restricted his public appearances. He moved in 1959 to Paris, where he led a trio (1959–62) with Kenny Clarke, the third member of which was usually Pierre Michelot, and enjoyed a certain celebrity status. After returning to the USA in August 1964, he made a disastrous appearance at Carnegie Hall (1965), and soon was obliged to abandon music altogether.

Powell was the most important pianist in the early bop style, and his innovations transformed the jazz pianism of his time. A prodigious technician, he was able at will to reproduce the demanding styles of Art Tatum and Teddy Wilson, echoes of which can sometimes be heard in his ballad performances. At fast and medium tempos, however, he preferred the spare manner that he devised in the early 1940s: rapid melodic lines in the right hand punctuated by irregularly spaced, dissonant chords in the left. This almost antipianistic style (which was adopted by most bop pianists of the time) left him free to pursue linear melody in the manner of bop wind players, and it was

LEROY OSTRANSKY

Bud Powell, 1965

as a melodist that Powell stood apart from his many imitators. At its best, Powell's playing was sustained by a free unfolding of rapid and unpredictable melodic invention, to which he brought a brittle, precise touch and great creative intensity. Except in his later years, when his virtuosity flagged and he selfconsciously adopted a primitivism resembling Monk's, Powell never altered this basic approach, but worked ceaselessly within it to devise new melodic ideas, harmonies, and ways of coupling the hands. He greatly extended the range of jazz harmony by reducing his chordal underpinning to compounds of 2nds and 7ths, and achieved an extraordinary variety in his phrase lengths, which range from brief flurries to seemingly inexhaustible lines that ignore the structure of the original.

Although most at ease in a trio setting, Powell was stimulated to his best work in competition with other leading bop soloists such as Charlie Parker, Dizzy Gillespie, J. J. Johnson, Sonny Stitt, and especially Fats Navarro. Powell also composed a number of excellent jazz tunes, among them *Hallucinations* (recorded by Miles Davis as *Budo*), *Dance of the Infidels*, *Tempus Fugue-it*, and *Bouncing with Bud*, as well as the remarkable *The Glass Enclosure*, a musical impression of his experiences in mental asylums, which points to a talent for composition that was unfortunately left undeveloped. Transcriptions of six of his solos have been published by C. J. Safane (*Bud Powell*, New York, 1978).

See also Jazz (i), §V, 4; and Piano, §4.

SELECTED RECORDINGS

As leader: Bud's Bubble (1947, Roost 509); Tempus Fugue-it (1949, Clef 11045); All God's chillun got rhythm (1949, Clef 11046); Bouncing with Bud (1949, BN 1567); Dance of the Infidels (1949, BN 1568); Hallucinations (1950, Clef 610); Un poco loco (1951, BN 1577); The Glass Enclosure (1953, BN 1628)

As sideman: C. Williams: Floogie Boo (1944, Hit 8089); J. J. Johnson: Jay Bird (1946, Savoy 975); Bebop Boys: Webb City (1946, Savoy 585); S. Stitt: Fine and Dandy (1950, Prst. 706); Jazz at Massey Hall: *Quintet of the Year* (1953, Debut 2, 4), incl. All the things you are, Perdido, Salt Peanuts

BIBLIOGRAPHY

S. Pease: "Bud Powell's Style," *DB*, xviii/12 (1951), 16

L. Feather: *The Book of Jazz: a Guide to the Entire Field* (New York, 1957, rev. 2/1965), 238

M. James: *Ten Modern Jazzmen: an Appraisal of the Recorded Work of Ten Modern Jazzmen* (London, 1960), 125

M. Harrison: "Bud Powell," *Jazz Era: the 'Forties*, ed. S. Dance and others (London, 1961/*R*1985), 200

I. Gitler: *Jazz Masters of the Forties* (New York, 1966/*R*1983 with discography), 110

J. G. Jepsen: *A Discography of Thelonious Monk & Bud Powell* (Copenhagen, 1969)

R. Johnson: "Bud Powell on Blue Note," *JM*, no.188 (1970), 8

"Bud Powell," *SJ*, xxxi/13 (1977), 298 [discography]

J. Réda: "La force de Bud Powell," *L'improviste: une lecture de jazz* (Paris, 1980), 158

C. Schlouch: *Once upon a Time: Bud Powell: a Discography* (Marseille, France, 1983)

B. Doerschuk: "Bud Powell," *Keyboard*, x/6 (1984), 26 [incl. discography]

F. Paudras: *La danse des infidèles: Bud Powell* (Paris, 1986)

A. Groves: *Bud Powell* (Tunbridge Wells, England, in preparation) [incl. discography]

J. BRADFORD ROBINSON

Powell, Jimmie [James Theodore] (*b* New York, 24 Oct 1914). Alto saxophonist. He worked with Frankie Newton (1931) and other bandleaders in New York during the mid-1930s, and between 1938 and 1941 played with Edgar Hayes and Sidney Bechet, recorded with Gene Sedric and Hot Lips Page, and performed and recorded with Benny Carter and Fats Waller. From 1943 to 1946 he was a member of Count Basie's band (for illustration *see* Films, fig.3), with which he made a number of recordings, including *Taps Miller* (1944, Col. 36831). He also performed with Don Redman, Eddie Heywood, Sid Catlett, and Page, recorded with Lester Young (1944), and worked with Lucky Millinder (1952) and Lucky Thompson (1953). Powell toured Latin America with Dizzy Gillespie (1956) and Machito (1958), then in the 1960s and early 1970s worked with rhythm-and-blues and soul musicians. He resumed playing swing when he joined Sy Oliver's band in 1975.

BIBLIOGRAPHY

ChiltonW; *FeatherE*

C. Battestini and J.-P. Battestini: "Jimmy Powell," *BHcF*, no.270 (1979), 3

Powell, Mel [Epstein, Melvin] (*b* New York, 12 Feb 1923). Pianist and arranger. He worked in New York with Bobby Hackett, Georg Brunis, Zutty Singleton (1939), and Muggsy Spanier (1940). In 1941 he played and recorded with Wingy Manone and wrote arrangements for Earl Hines. At this time he changed his name, and as Mel Powell worked and recorded as a pianist and arranger for Benny Goodman (1941–2); Goodman's *The Earl* (1941, OK 6474) is typical of his arrangements. He then became a member of the CBS orchestra under Raymond Scott (1942). During his military service he toured and recorded with Glenn Miller's band (1943) and recorded in Paris with the Jazz Club American Hot Band (1944, 1945), which included Django Reinhardt, with Ray McKinley and as an unaccompanied soloist (both 1945). After being discharged he recorded with Goodman in New York (1945), then went to Los Angeles where he worked for studios and recorded with Jazz at the Philharmonic (1946), intermittently with Goodman (1946–7), and as a leader (1947, 1949). He studied composition at Yale (BM 1952) with the composer Paul Hindemith, and from that time pursued a career as a classical composer in the serial tradition and as a teacher. His activities as a jazz musician largely ceased but from 1953 to 1955 he worked again with Goodman and recorded as a leader; the tracks *Gone with the Wind* and *Pennies from Heaven* on his own LP *Out on a Limb* (1955, Van. 8506) provide good examples of his playing. He performed again as a jazz soloist in 1986, when he played with all-star swing and bop groups on the cruise ship *Norway*.

BIBLIOGRAPHY

FeatherE; *Feather–Gitler '70s*

L. Feather: "Mel Powell, the Rip Van Winkle of Jazz," *San Francisco Chronicle* (16 Nov 1986)

R. Swift: "Powell, Mel," *GroveAM*

W. Balliett: "Profiles: What Ever Happened to Mel Powell?" *New Yorker*, lxiii (25 May 1987), 37

Powell, Richie [Richard] (*b* New York, 5 Sept 1931; *d* Pennsylvania, 26 June 1956). Pianist, brother of Bud Powell. He studied music at City College, New York, and learned to improvise while practicing at the home of Mary Lou Williams in New York, where musicians often met. He played with the saxophonists Paul Williams (1951–2) and Johnny Hodges (1952–4) and was the pianist and arranger for Clifford Brown's and Max Roach's group (1954–6).

SELECTED RECORDINGS

As sideman: on J. Hodges: *More of Johnny Hodges* (1951–4, Norg. 1009), Autumn in New York (1954); C. Brown and M. Roach: *Clifford Brown with Max Roach* (1954–5, EmA 36036); *Study in Brown* (1955, EmA 36037); S. Rollins: *Sonny Rollins plus Four* (1956, Prst. 7038)

BIBLIOGRAPHY

FeatherE

PAUL RINZLER

Powell, Rudy [Everard Stephen, Sr.; Root; Karweem, Musheed] (*b* New York, 28 Oct 1907; *d* New York, 30 Oct 1976). Clarinetist and alto saxophonist. He played from 1928 to 1930 at the Lenox Club in New York with Cliff Jackson and then worked with Elmer Snowden, Dave Nelson, and Rex Stewart (1933). Although best known for his work with Fats Waller (at intervals, 1935–7) he also had a successful career as a member of bands led by Claude Hopkins (1938–9), Teddy Wilson (1939), Andy Kirk (1940–41), Fletcher Henderson (1941–2), Eddie South (1942–3), and Don Redman (1943); he also toured Europe with Edgar Hayes in 1937. Later he played in the bands of Cab Calloway (1945–8), Lucky Millinder (1949–51), Jimmy Rushing (1951–2), Buddy Tate (1953), Ray Charles (1960–62), and Buddy Johnson, and in 1960 recorded with Al Casey, who had also worked as a sideman with Waller. From 1965 to 1969 he belonged to the Saints and Sinners, with whom he toured internationally; although he played less frequently from 1969 owing to illness he continued to work occasionally around New York until his death. Powell played conventional swing alto saxophone, but his clarinet work (particularly with Waller) was more distinctive; Lyttelton characterizes it as having "a persistently rasping tone . . . geared, like his restless, angular phrasing, to generating heat."

SELECTED RECORDINGS

As sideman: F. Waller: Louisiana Fairy Tale (1935, Vic. 24898); 12th Street Rag/Sweet Sue (1935, Vic. 25087); Truckin' (1935, Vic. 25116); Henry "Red" Allen: When did you Leave Heaven?/Algiers Stomp (1936, Voc. 3302); E. Hayes: Blue Skies/Sweetheart (1937, Decca 1684); Saints and Sinners: *Saints and Sinners in Europe* (1968, Saba 15174)

BIBLIOGRAPHY

ChiltonW; *FeatherE*; *Feather '60s*

D. Hague: "Rudy Powell and Jimmy Rushing," *JJ*, x/7 (1957), 3

E. Smith: "Saga of a Sideman," *Record Research*, no.20 (1958), 3 [interview]

A. Lawrie: "The Big Names: Rudy Powell Reminisces," *Toronto Globe and Mail* (11 Nov 1967)

F. Owens: "Rudy Powell," *JJ*, xxiii/6 (1970), 20

H. Lyttelton: *The Best of Jazz*, ii: *Enter the Giants* (London, 1981), 57

WARREN VACHÉ, SR.

Powell, Seldon (*b* Lawrenceville, VA, 15 Nov 1928). Tenor saxophonist and flutist. He received classical music training in New York and in 1949 he worked briefly with Tab Smith before joining Lucky Millinder, with whom he recorded in 1950. During his military service (1951–2) he continued his playing career, and after receiving his discharge established himself in New York as a freelance and studio musician; at this time he formed associations with Sy Oliver and Erskine Hawkins, and recorded as a leader and with Neal Hefti (1955), Louie Bellson (1955), Friedrich Gulda (1956), Johnny Richards (1957–8), and the composer Billy Ver Planck (1957–8). He also studied at the Juilliard School. In 1958 he traveled to Europe with Benny Goodman's band and he then played briefly with Woody Herman. In the 1960s he worked chiefly for ABC TV but he also played and recorded with Buddy Rich (1960), Bellson (1962–4), Clark Terry (1963), and Ahmed Abdul-Malik (1964). His numerous recordings as a studio musician include many made in the late 1960s and early 1970s with soul and soul-jazz musicians, including Groove Holmes (*c*1973), and sessions in the big bands that accompanied Gato Barbieri (1974) and Anthony Braxton and Dizzy Gillespie (both 1976). He performed as a principal soloist in Gerry Mulligan's 16-piece orchestra at the JVC Jazz Festival, New York, in 1987.

SELECTED RECORDINGS

As leader: *Seldon Powell Plays* (1955, Roost 2205); *Seldon Powell Sextet* (1956, Roost 2220); on *We Paid our Dues* (1961, Epic 17018), Bowl of Soul, For Lester, Two for One

As sideman: on L. Bellson: *The Driving Louis Bellson* (1955, Norg. 1020), All right jump it man, Basie, Charlie-o, Greetings; B. Ver Planck: *Jazz for Play Girls* (1957, Savoy 12121)

BIBLIOGRAPHY

FeatherE; *Feather '60s*

B. Ulanov: Untitled review, *DB*, xxii/21 (1955), 14

LAWRENCE KOCH

Powell, Specs [Gordon] (*b* New York, 5 June 1922). Drummer. After achieving recognition in the late 1930s as a pianist and drummer with his own small group he played drums exclusively for the rest of his career, principally with swing groups. He played with Edgar Hayes (1939), Eddie South (1939–40), John Kirby (1941–2), Benny Carter (1942), and Ben Webster (in New York in the early 1940s), then worked at CBS with Raymond Scott; as a staff musician at CBS (from 1943) he played both popular and symphonic works. During the following years he performed and recorded with Benny Goodman (1944) and Red Norvo (1944–5) and also recorded with Sidney and Wilbur De Paris (1944), Joe Bushkin (1944), Mildred Bailey (1944–6), Clyde Hart (1945), and Billie Holiday (1945); later he made recordings with Erroll Garner (1956), with Gerry Mulligan and Teddy Wilson at the Newport Jazz Festival (1957), and as a member of Monday Night at Birdland (1958), an all-star group that also included Lee Morgan, Curtis Fuller, and Hank Mobley.

SELECTED RECORDINGS

As leader: *Movin' In with Specs Powell* (1957, Roul. 52004)

As sideman: E. South: Oh! Lady be Good (1941, Col. 36193); S. Benskin: Cherry/When all the World is Waiting for the Sunrise (1945, BN 522); E. Garner: *The Most Happy Piano* (1956, Col. CL939); B. Butler: *Guitar Soul* (1969, Prst. 7734)

BIBLIOGRAPHY

FeatherE
J. M. Doran: *Erroll Garner: the Most Happy Piano* (Metuchen, NJ, and London, 1985), 80 [incl. discography]

EDDIE LAMBERT

Pöyry, Pekka (*b* Pori, Finland, 10 Dec 1939; *d* Helsinki, 4 Aug 1980). Finnish saxophonist and flutist. He studied law but his admiration for Charlie Parker led him to take up a career in jazz. He joined Juhani Vilkki's sextet in the mid-1960s and was soon a leading soloist in Finnish jazz. Of a retiring disposition, Pöyry shunned the responsibilities of a bandleader and played with a number of different groups. In the early 1970s he was a member, with Jukka Tolonen, of the jazz-rock group Tasavallan presidentti, and in the mid- and late 1970s performed and recorded with the Uuden Musiikin Orkesteri, a big band. He also recorded with Eero Koivistoinen, Erik Lindström, Seppo Paakkunainen, Esa Pethman, Heikki Sarmanto, and Dexter Gordon. Pöyry may be heard to advantage on the album *Sunweb* (Love 156), which he recorded with Mike Koskinen in 1975. (A. Granholm: *Finnish Jazz* (Helsinki, 1974, rev. and enlarged by M. Konttinen 2/1982, rev. and enlarged by J.-P. Vuorela 3/1986), 32)

PEKKA GRONOW

Pozo, Chano [Pozo y Gonzales, Luciano] (*b* Havana, 7 Jan 1915; *d* New York, 2 Dec 1948). Cuban drummer, singer, and dancer. His drumming and singing were rooted in the Cuban *lucumí* faith, derived from West African rituals. On 29 September 1947 he and the bongo player Chiquitico performed in a concert at Carnegie Hall with Dizzy Gillespie — this was the first time an attempt had been made to fuse elements of jazz and Latin music at a serious artistic level. Pozo was murdered before he could fully develop his ideas with Gillespie, but during his brief career in the USA he provided the starting point for much popular music of the late 1940s and the 1950s. The collaboration between the two men supplied the initiative for American musicians, and some of the listening public, to appreciate fully the tradition of Latin music. Pozo was a cousin of Chino Pozo.

For illustration *see* GILLESPIE, DIZZY.

SELECTED RECORDINGS

As sideman with D. Gillespie: *Dizzy Goes to College* (1947, Jazz Showcase 5000, 5002); Algo bueno/Minor Walk (1947, Vic. 203186); Cool Breeze/Cubana Be/Cubana Bop (1947, Vic. 203145); Manteca (1947, Vic. 203023); Good Bait/Ool-ya-koo (1947, Vic. 202878); *Afro-Cuban Suite* (1948, Swing 33301); *Melodic Revolution* (1948, Alto 703)
As sideman with others: M. Jackson: Boppin' with Robin (1948, Sensation 19); T. Dameron: Jahbero (1948, BN 559)

BIBLIOGRAPHY

D. Gillespie and A. Fraser: *To be, or not . . . to Bop: Memoirs* (Garden City, NY, 1979)
J. S. Roberts: *The Latin Tinge: the Impact of Latin American Music on the United States* (New York, and Oxford, England, 1979)

JOHN STORM ROBERTS/R

Pozo, Chino [Francisco] (*b* Havana, 4 Oct 1915; *d* New York, *c*1980). Cuban percussionist. He taught himself to play piano and double bass. After moving to the USA in 1937 he worked with Machito (1941–3) and accompanied a dance troupe (1943–9). In 1948 he performed with Tadd Dameron and Fats Navarro, recording the single *Jahbero* (Gazell 2019) with Dameron's sextet (of which Navarro was also a member). While working in various Latin groups he recorded with Dizzy Gillespie and with Machito and Charlie Parker (both 1950). Thereafter he toured with Peggy Lee (1954–5), performed with Stan Kenton (1955) and Herbie Mann (1956), and recorded with Illinois Jacquet (1954), Phineas Newborn (1957), Billy Taylor (ii) (1959), and Gábor Szabó (1965). From the 1960s he worked as percussionist for the singer Paul Anka. Pozo was a cousin of Chano Pozo. (*FeatherE*)

Practice mute. *See* MUTE, §1.

Preacher. Nickname of WARDELL JONES.

Pres. Nickname of LESTER YOUNG.

Preservation Hall. Venue in New Orleans; *see* NIGHTCLUBS AND OTHER VENUES.

Preservation Hall Jazz Band. New Orleans jazz band. In the 1950s the art dealer Larry Borenstein engaged veteran jazz musicians to play at his art gallery on St. Peter Street, New Orleans, and from 1961 the performances took place in part of an adjacent building, which Borenstein opened as Preservation Hall. The tuba player Allan Jaffe and his wife, Sandra, took over the administration of the hall and began to organize tours for the musicians who regularly played there, calling the group the Preservation Hall Jazz Band. In early 1963 Kid Thomas and George Lewis (i) led the band on a tour of the USA; then, under Lewis's leadership, Punch Miller (trumpet), Louis Nelson (trombone), Joseph Robichaux (piano), Emanuel Sayles (banjo), John Joseph (double bass), and Joe Watkins (drums) toured Japan, where the band returned in 1964 and 1965. For a tour of Europe in 1967, the members of the band were De De Pierce (trumpet), Nelson, Willie Humphrey (clarinet), Billie Pierce (piano), Chester Zardis (double bass), and Cié Frazier (drums); a similar group performed at the Newport Jazz Festival (1970). For a tour of Japan, Australia, Canada, and Europe in 1971 the band was made up of Nelson, Emanuel Paul (saxophone), Albert Burbank (clarinet), Charlie Hamilton (piano), Joseph Butler (double bass), and Alonzo Stewart (drums), with Kid Thomas again acting as leader. From the mid-1970s Percy Humphrey led the main touring band, the personnel of which consisted of Humphrey himself (occasionally replaced by Thomas), Willie Humphrey, Jim Robinson (trombone; replaced after his death by Frank Demond), Sing Miller (piano), Narvin Kimball (banjo), Allan Jaffe (until his death in 1987; tuba), and Frank Parker (drums). Another group often toured with Kid Sheik Colar as its leader. Despite the advanced age of its members the band continues to tour worldwide.

For illustration *see* HUMPHREY.

SELECTED RECORDINGS

Billie and De De Pierce and their Preservation Hall Jazz Band (1966, Preservation Hall 3); *New Orleans* (1977, 1981, 1983, Col. M34549, FM37780, FM38650)

BIBLIOGRAPHY

T. Dash: "Kid Thomas in Europe," *Fn*, iii/2 (1971), 16
B. Byler: "Dancing in the Aisles," *MR*, iv/10 (1977), 1
N. Thimmesch: "Jazzmen Deserve a Medal," *Philadelphia Inquirer* (2 Aug 1979), §A, p.11
"Veterans Unleashed," *MM*, lv (20 Sept 1980), 24

MIKE HAZELDINE

Pressing. The process whereby a recording in its original form is converted into a marketable commodity in the shape of a disc (*see* RECORDING, §I, 1(i)), hence a synonym for a commercial disc.

Press roll. A type of roll, one of the drumstrokes collectively known as RUDIMENTS.

Prestige. Record company and label. The company was established in 1949 in New York by Bob Weinstock, and quickly embarked upon an ambitious program of recording many famous young musicians of the day. The catalogue included mainstream jazz, bop, cool jazz, and hard bop by such musicians as Gene Ammons, Wardell Gray, Miles Davis, Thelonious Monk, Sonny Rollins, Stan Getz, John Coltrane, and many others; some recordings were issued on a subsidiary label, New Jazz. In the 1950s many sessions were recorded by Rudy Van Gelder at his studio in Hackensack (later in Englewood Cliffs),

Label for "Strike up the Band," recorded by the quartet led by Sonny Stitt and Bud Powell for Prestige (New York, 26 January 1950)

New Jersey. In 1960 the company began to diversify, setting up new labels: Swingville (to put out material from a growing catalogue of mainstream jazz by older musicians); Moodsville (to release muted, atmospheric recordings by swing and bop musicians); and Bluesville (a blues label). Artists and repertory were supervised by Weinstock, though others, including Chris Albertson, Ozzie Cadena, Ira Gitler, Bob Porter, and Don Schlitten, were also involved with the catalogue at various times. From the late 1950s until the late 1970s Prestige was chiefly associated with soul jazz, issuing recordings by Brother Jack McDuff, Groove Holmes, Shirley Scott, and Johnny Hammond with various tenor saxophonists. In 1967 the company transferred its headquarters to Bergenfield, New Jersey; in May 1971 it was acquired by Fantasy, which ran the catalogue and label from its base in Berkeley, California.

BIBLIOGRAPHY

A. Morgan: "The Prestige–Swingville Series," *JM*, xiii (1967), no.1, p.19; no.2, p.15; no.3, p.17; [no.7], p.21

M. Ruppli: *Prestige Jazz Records, 1949–1969 [recte 1971]: a Discography* (n.p. [Copenhagen], 1972; rev. and enlarged, Westport, CT, and London, 2/1980, with B. Porter, as *The Prestige Label: a Discography*)

Preston, Don(ald Ward) (*b* Flint, MI, 21 Sept 1932). Synthesizer player. He studied and played piano with Herbie Mann while in the army; after being discharged in the early 1950s he worked in Detroit with Tommy Flanagan and Elvin Jones, and in Los Angeles with Carla Bley (1957–8) and Charlie Haden (1959). An interest in experimental music and theatrical performance prompted him to establish the mixed-media group Aha! (1963) and other similar ensembles. Preston joined Frank Zappa and the Mothers of Invention in 1967, and worked intermittently with the group until 1974. During this time he also toured and recorded with Gil Evans and organized an ensemble with Buell Neidlinger (both 1971); he later recorded with Neidlinger (1973). In 1985 he recorded the album *Alien* (Watt 15) in a duo with Mike Mantler.

BIBLIOGRAPHY

Feather–Gitler '70s

L. Underwood: "Profile: Buell Neidlinger & Don Preston," *DB*, xlii/7 (1975), 28

J. Woodward: "Don Preston: Synthesizer from Apocalypse Now to Zappa," *DB*, liv/8 (1987), 25 [incl. discography]

Preston, Eddie [Edward L.] (*b* Dallas, 5 Sept 1928). Trumpeter. He gained early experience in big bands (from 1945) and then joined Lionel Hampton, with whom he recorded in Los Angeles (1955) and toured Europe, recording in Paris and Madrid (1956). After touring with Ray Charles (1959) and Louis Jordan (1960–61) he briefly played and recorded in New York with Duke Ellington (1962) and Count Basie (1963). He first worked with Charles Mingus in the mid-1960s, performing at the Village Gate in New York and recording (both 1963) and playing with his group in 1964 and 1965; he renewed this association in the 1970s, when he toured Europe (1970) and Japan (1971) and took part in recording sessions (1971–2). Preston's playing is well represented by *Blue Bird* (1970, Amer. 6110), recorded at a concert in Paris. He also recorded with Sonny Stitt (1966), played with Frank Foster, and toured and recorded in the USA and Europe with Ellington (1971). In 1973 he formed his own quintet which took part in Jazzmobile's work and performed in young people's concerts into the 1980s; his sidemen included Walter Perkins. In the late 1970s he recorded with Roland Kirk (1977) and toured with Archie Shepp (1979).

BIBLIOGRAPHY

V. Wilmer: "Eddie: a Chance to be Heard," *MM*, xlv (21 Nov 1970), 10

M. Jones: "Preston: a Leading Question," *MM*, xlvi (6 Nov 1971), 24

B. Priestley: *Mingus: a Critical Biography* (London, Melbourne, Australia, and New York, 1982)

Previn, André (George) [Priwin, Andreas Ludwig] (*b* Berlin, 6 April 1929). Pianist, conductor, and composer, of Russian descent. He studied piano as a child at the Berlin Hochschule für Musik; in 1938 his family moved to Paris, where he studied at the Conservatoire, and the following year they emigrated to the USA and settled in Los Angeles; he continued his musical training there, studying piano, theory, and composition. He became an American citizen in 1943. Influenced by Art Tatum, he worked professionally as a jazz pianist and as an arranger for MGM while he was still in high school. In 1945 he made his first recording, for the Sunset label; his early recordings for RCA (1947) were substantial hits and earned him considerable success. Although he was not immediately sympathetic to bop when he first heard it in 1950 he eventually embraced the style. After his army service (during which he studied conducting in San Francisco with Pierre Monteux) he settled in Los Angeles and became extremely active as a pianist. He played with the acclaimed Jazz at the Philharmonic All-Stars in Los Angeles (1952), and his collaboration with Shelly Manne, *My Fair Lady* (1956), started a fashion for jazz albums based on Broadway musicals and continued to be popular for many years. He worked with such musicians as Benny Goodman,

Herb Ellis, Shorty Rogers, Pete Rugolo, Jackie Cain and Roy Kral, and Ella Fitzgerald. In 1961 he received a Grammy Award for the album *André Previn Plays Harold Arlen.* During the 1960s and 1970s Previn devoted his time to conducting and composing classical and popular music, and did not play jazz again until the early 1980s. Although he is not an innovator, Previn is a technically fluent and musical jazz pianist.

For illustration *see* MULLIGAN, GERRY.

SELECTED RECORDINGS

(recorded for Contemporary unless otherwise indicated)

As leader: *André Previn All-Stars* (1946, Monarch 203); *André Previn* (1947, Vic. 20-3040, 20-3041, 20-3042, 20-3043) [album of 78 r.p.m. discs]; with R. Freeman: *Double Play!* (1957, 3537); *André Previn Plays Vernon Duke* (1958, 3558); *Like Previn!* (1960, 7575); *André Previn Plays Harold Arlen* (1960, 7586); *A Different Kind of Blues* (1980, HMV ASD3965)

As sideman: S. Manne: *My Fair Lady* (1956, 3527); on B. Goodman: *Happy Session* (1958, Col. CL1324), You'd be so nice to come home to

BIBLIOGRAPHY

FeatherE; Feather '60s; Feather–Gitler '70s

E. Greenfield: *André Previn* (London, 1973)

M. Bookspan and R. Yockey: *André Previn: a Biography* (Garden City, NY, 1981)

H. D. Ruttencutter: *Previn* (New York, 1985)

PAUL RINZLER

Prévost, Eddie [Edwin] (*b* Hitchin, England, 22 June 1942). English drummer. In 1965 he founded the free-jazz group AMM with Lou Gare and the guitarist Keith Rowe; it made its first recording in 1966, toured Europe in the late 1960s, visited the USA in 1968 and 1971, and disbanded in 1972. Later he recorded in a duo with Gare, AMM II (1972, 1974), then in the mid-1970s began leading groups that employed the same principles of collective improvisation, though not necessarily the same harmonic format or instrumentation, as New Orleans jazz. From 1975 he and Rowe also worked in a duo, AMM III; their album *It had been an Ordinary Enough Day in Pueblo, Colorado* (1979, Japo 60031) received considerable acclaim. In the 1980s Prévost has worked with another version of AMM, with his own quartet, and with a trio, Resound.

BIBLIOGRAPHY

K. Gann: "AMM's Continual Quest for Failure," *Chicago Reader* (25 May 1984), 7

K. Ansell: "AMM: the Sound as Music," *The Wire*, no.11 (1985), 21

MARK GILBERT

Prez. Nickname of LESTER YOUNG.

Price, Jesse (*b* Memphis, 1 May 1909; *d* Los Angeles, 19 April 1974). Drummer, bandleader, and singer. He took up drums at the age of 14 and later performed in the pit orchestra at the Palace Theater, Memphis, and toured extensively with major blues singers. In 1934 he moved to Kansas City, where he played with territory bands and with Count Basie (1936). After leading his own big band in the late 1930s Price worked with Harlan Leonard (1939–41) and performed and recorded in Los Angeles with Ella Fitzgerald (1941). He remained on the West Coast and led his own groups (often supporting blues singers), though he also worked with Louis Armstrong (1943), Basie (1944), and Benny Carter (1948). Price helped to develop the smooth, understated, but always swinging, style of playing that was particularly characteristic of Basie's drummers, and which is well illustrated by his performance on Leonard's *Rock and Ride* (1940, Bb 10883).

Oral history material in *TxU*.

BIBLIOGRAPHY

ChiltonW

R. Russell: "Master Drummer: Jesse Price," *J&B*, iii/4 (1973), 14

BOB WEIR

Price, Ray (*b* Sydney, 20 Nov 1921). Australian bandleader, banjoist, and guitarist. He gained early experience playing with his family's band, then worked at the Booker T. Washington Club in Sydney during his army service (1940–43). From at least 1947 he played intermittently with the Port Jackson Jazz Band, a dixieland band of which he was the leader in 1955–62. In 1949 he began to play double bass and he later belonged to orchestras of the Australian Broadcasting Company and to the Sydney SO (from which he was dismissed in 1956 because of his jazz activities). He led a series of groups which toured for the Arts Council of Australia and from the mid-1950s to 1980 presented jazz education programs in schools. Among the numerous Australian jazz musicians who have played in his groups are John Sangster, Bob Barnard, and Dick Hughes. He made many recordings as a leader, including *Jazz Part no.1* (1975, Dixie RPQ001). He retired in 1982 but from 1985 occasionally played at reunions of the Port Jackson Jazz Band. (B. Johnson: "Price, Ray," *The Oxford Companion to Australian Jazz*, Melbourne, Australia, 1987)

BRUCE JOHNSON

Price, Sammy [Sam, Samuel Blythe] (*b* Honey Grove, TX, 6 Oct 1908). Pianist and singer. He toured as a dancer with Alphonso Trent's band, then led a band in Athens, Texas. Later he formed a big band in Dallas and played with theater bands and touring revues. In 1929 he made radio broadcasts in Oklahoma City, Oklahoma, with Lem Johnson and the trumpeter Leonard Chadwick, and made his first recordings in Dallas, where he was active until 1933. Later he worked in Chicago and Detroit (1934–7). In 1937 he became a staff musician for Decca in New York, accompanying many well-known blues and gospel singers, including Blue Lu Barker. He also led his own group, the Texas Blusicians, which included at various times Lester Young, Emmett Berry, Ike Quebec, J. C. Heard, and Sid Catlett. During the 1940s Price worked mainly as a soloist at clubs in New York. He recorded an influential series of solo boogie-woogie performances for Mezz Mezzrow's King Jazz label (1945), and also recorded with Mezzrow and Sidney Bechet (1945, 1947). In 1948 he played at the Nice Jazz Festival, and toured France. In the early 1950s he lived in Dallas, where he owned two clubs. Thereafter he returned to New York, then toured Europe as the leader of the Blusicians (1955–6); he worked at the Metropole with Henry "Red" Allen (late 1950s and early 1960s) and Tony Parenti (at Eddie Condon's, 1962–3). From that time he has visited Europe frequently; as well as undertaking several tours he has performed at the festivals in Antibes, France (1963), and Lugano, Switzerland (1986).

Oral history material in *MoKmh, NjR* (JOHP), and *NjR*.

SELECTED RECORDINGS

As leader: Do you dig my jive? (1941, Decca 8575); Harlem Gin Blues (1941, Decca 8609); *The Price is Right* (1956, Jzt. 1260); with D. Cheatham: *Black Beauty: a Salute to Black American Songwriters* (1979, Sack. 3029)

As sideman: Cow Cow Davenport: The Mess is Here (1938, Decca 7813); B. L. Barker: That made him mad (1938, Decca 7538); S. Bechet: *Sidney Bechet with Sammy Price's Blusicians* (1956, Swing 30041)

BIBLIOGRAPHY

ChiltonW

M. Jones: "Call it Sam's Song," *MM* (20 Dec 1969), 12

J. Simmen: "Samuel B. Price," *BHcF*, no.196 (1970), 3; no.197 (1970), 6; no.198 (1970), 5

B. Rusch: "Sammy Price: Oral History," *Cadence*, ii/10–11 (1977), 3

V. Montgomery: "Texas Bluesician Sammy Price," *JJI*, xxxv (1982), no.10, p.9; no.11, p.6 [incl. discography]
D. Kochakian: "The Legacy of Sam Price," *Whiskey, Women, and . . .*, nos.12–13 (1983), 8 [incl. discography]
B. Osgood: "Sam Price," *MR*, x/9 (1983), 6 [interview]
S. Price and C. Richmond: *What do they Want? A Jazz Autobiography* (in preparation) [incl. discography by B. Weir]

MICHAEL TOVEY

Priester, Julian (Anthony) [Mtoto, Pepo] (*b* Chicago, 29 June 1935). Trombonist. He studied piano as a child, took up the euphonium while in his teens, and changed to trombone two years later. He played blues with Muddy Waters and rhythm-and-blues with Bo Diddley, then joined Sun Ra's ensemble in 1954, which he left after two years to tour with Lionel Hampton. After working for a year with Dinah Washington he moved to New York, and in 1958 joined a group led by Max Roach that at various times included Booker Little, Clifford Jordan, and Eric Dolphy; he also recorded with Abbey Lincoln. He left Roach's group to work as a freelance in recording studios and pit orchestras in New York, then belonged to Duke Ellington's orchestra for six months (1969–70) and to Herbie Hancock's sextet (1970–73); while a member of Hancock's group he took the Swahili name Pepo Mtoto. Later he worked in the San Francisco area, where he made recordings with Stanley Cowell (1977–8) and Red Garland's quintet (1979); in the 1980s he recorded with Dave Holland (1983, 1984) and George Gruntz's big band (1983).

SELECTED RECORDINGS

As leader: *Spiritsville* (1958, Jlnd 25); *Polarization* (1977, ECM 1098)
As sideman: Sun Ra: *Super Sonic Jazz* (*c*1955, Sat. 216); M. Roach: *Percussion Bitter Sweet* (1961, Imp. 8); H. Hancock: *Mwandishi* (*c*1970, WB 1898); B. Harper: *Capra-black* (1973, SE 19739); R. Garland: *Strike up the Band* (1979, Gal. 5135)

BIBLIOGRAPHY

E. Chadbourne: "Wandering Spirit Song: Pepo's Interview," *Coda*, xii/2 (1974), 2
M. Crooks: "Julian Priester: Interview," *Cadence*, iv/1 (1978), 12

DAVID WILD

Priestley, Brian (*b* Manchester, England, 10 July 1946). English pianist and writer. After private piano tuition he led college groups at Leeds University and played in a big band led by the drummer Tony Faulkner (1971–3). With the saxophonist Dave Gelly and the drummer Ken Hyder he led Stylus (1979–80), then with Don Rendell formed a group that was variously a sextet or a septet (1980). In 1971 he began an association with Alan Cohen, which continued intermittently into the 1980s. With Cohen he recorded the first complete transcription of Duke Ellington's composition *Black, Brown, and Beige* (1972, Argo 159). Priestley has made many transcriptions of the works of Ellington, including *In the Beginning, God* (1982), and *Cottontail, C-jam Blues*, and *Caravan* (all 1984). He is a frequent broadcaster and from 1971 presented the weekly program "All that Jazz" for BBC Radio London. He writes prolifically and besides publishing several books has contributed regularly to the journals *Down Beat*, *Jazz Journal International*, *Jazz Express*, and *The Wire*.

WRITINGS
(selective list)

Mingus: a Critical Biography (London, Melbourne, Australia, and New York, 1982)
Charlie Parker (Tunbridge Wells, England, and New York, 1984) [incl. discography]
John Coltrane (London, 1987) [incl. discography]
with I. Carr and D. Fairweather: *Jazz: the Essential Companion* (London, 1987)

DIGBY FAIRWEATHER

Prima, Leon (*b* New Orleans, 28 July 1907). Trumpeter, brother of Louis Prima. He began studying piano but later learned trumpet. After working with Leon Roppolo, Ray Bauduc, and Jack Teagarden, he joined Peck Kelley's Bad Boys in Texas (1925), then returned to New Orleans, where he led the Melody Masters with Sharkey Bonano (*c*1928–1930). He played with his brother's orchestra in New York (1940–46) and led his own small band in New Orleans until 1955, when he ceased full-time performing. His recordings as a leader include *Leon Prima and his New Orleans Jazz Band* (1954, Slnd 210). (*FeatherE*)

MIKE HAZELDINE

Prima, Louis [Loui, Louie] (*b* New Orleans, 7 Dec 1911; *d* New Orleans, 24 Aug 1978). Trumpeter and singer, brother of Leon Prima. He studied violin from 1918 and after teaching himself trumpet (1925) he performed in New Orleans. He remained in New Orleans until 1935 except for brief spells with Red Nichols in Cleveland (*c*1932) and in New York (1934), where he made a number of recordings for Brunswick. His residency at the Famous Door, New York, in 1935 was followed by long-term engagements in Chicago and Los Angeles. In the 1940s he led a big band, and in the 1950s and 1960s he again worked with small bands. He was married for a time (1952–61) to Keely Smith, and together they achieved great commercial success with recordings in a popular style. Prima also appeared in many films, including *The Benny Goodman Story* (1955), and played long engagements in Las Vegas. Prima's hoarse singing and extrovert trumpet playing were influenced by Louis Armstrong, but both his diction and his fingering technique displayed a more flashy approach. After 1940 his style became overtly commercialized and closer to cabaret than to jazz; except for those made for Brunswick in the 1930s, his recordings are not generally representative of his qualities as a performer.

SELECTED RECORDINGS
(all recorded for Brunswick)

Let's Have a Jubilee (1934, 7394); It's the Rhythm in me (1934, 7471); Dinah (1936, 7666); Let's Get Together and Swing (1936, 7740)

BIBLIOGRAPHY

ChiltonW
"Backstage with Louis Prima and Keely Smith," *DB*, xxvi/4 (1959), 14
Arnold Shaw: *The Street that Never Slept: New York's Fabled 52nd Street* (New York, 1971/*R*1977 as *52nd Street: the Street of Jazz*)

MIKE HAZELDINE

Prime Time. Band formed in 1975 by ORNETTE COLEMAN.

Prince, Roland (Don Matthew) (*b* St. John's, Antigua, 27 Aug 1946). Antiguan guitarist. He lived in Toronto in the mid-1960s and played with local musicians, then in 1969 moved to New York, where he performed with Brother Jack McDuff (1969–70), Billy Mitchell (from 1970), Wynton Kelly, Art Blakey (1971), Stanley Turrentine, and Jimmy Smith (1974). He also led his own trio. He toured Europe and made recordings with Elvin Jones (1974–6, including *New Agenda*, 1975, Van. 79362), and took part in sessions with Roy Haynes (*c*1972), James Moody (1975), Frank Foster (1976), and Don Pullen (1976–7). (*Feather–Gitler '70s*)

Prince of Darkness. Nickname of MILES DAVIS.

Privin, Bernie [Bernard] (*b* New York, 12 Feb 1919). Trumpeter. He was self-taught, and performed locally from the age of 16. In 1937 he joined Harry Reser; thereafter he played with

Bunny Berigan and Tommy Dorsey. He worked in 1938–9 with Artie Shaw, who gave him considerable prominence. In 1940–41 he was a member of Charlie Barnet's band, which he rejoined in 1943 after working with the clarinetist Mal Hallett (1941) and Benny Goodman (1941–42). During his military service Privin was the trumpet soloist in Glenn Miller's Army Air Force Band (1943–6), with which he worked in Europe. After being discharged he returned to Goodman's band, worked for NBC, then spent 22 years as a staff musician for CBS. During this period he also took part in many sessions, mostly with big bands, including those of Sy Oliver (1949–51), and Goodman (intermittently 1951–61); he also recorded as a soloist with the guitarist Al Caiola (1955). In the 1960s he achieved popularity in Sweden, where he performed several times; during the following decade he worked as a freelance, touring Europe with the Tommy Dorsey Orchestra under Warren Covington, and with Pee Wee Erwin (both 1974), and visiting Russia with the New York Jazz Repertory Company (1975). Privin has remained active into the late 1980s.

SELECTED RECORDINGS

As leader: When did you leave heaven?/East of the Sun (1969, 7BD-268)
As sideman: A. Shaw: *In the Blue Room/In the Cafe Rouge* (1938–9, RCA LPT6000); C. Barnet: Lois (1941, Bb 11265); G. Miller: I can't give you anything but love (1944, V-disc 482); Jazz Club Mystery Hot Band: If Dreams Come True (1944, JCF 121); M. Powell: Avalon (1946, Com. 1522); V. Giordano: *New Orleans Night Hawks* (1980, GHB 98)

BIBLIOGRAPHY

ChiltonW; FeatherE
L. Karlsson: "Bernie Privin," *JJ*, xxvii/4 (1974), 4
L. Tomkins: "The Bernie Privin Story," *CI*, xii/12 (1974), 9
B. Korall: Liner notes, A. Shaw: *The Complete Artie Shaw*, ii: *1939* (RCA AXM2-5533, 1977)
G. Butcher: *Next to a Letter from Home* (Edinburgh, 1986)

BRIAN PEERLESS

Probert, George (Arthur, Jr.) (*b* Los Angeles, 5 March 1927). Soprano saxophonist, clarinetist, and bandleader. He played and made recordings with Bob Scobey (1950–53) and with Kid Ory (including *Creole Jazz Band 1954*, 1954, GTJ 12004). From 1954 to 1969 he played and recorded with the FIREHOUSE FIVE PLUS TWO, a traditional-jazz band formed from among employees of the Walt Disney studio, and in 1955 he became music director of the studio. He also recorded with Georg Brunis (1957, 1968). From 1973 he led bands that performed traditional jazz on the West Coast and in Europe: he has performed frequently in the Netherlands at the Breda Oude Stijl Jazz Festival and he recorded at the Manassas (Virginia) Jazz Festival (1973) and in Budapest with the Benko Dixieland Band (1978).

BIBLIOGRAPHY

R. Cremer: "George Probert and his Happy Riff Machine," *6e internationale Oude Štijl Jazz Festival: Breda, 27–30 May 1976* (Breda, Netherlands, 1976), 34 [program book]

Procope, Russell (*b* New York, 11 Aug 1908; *d* New York, 21 Jan 1981). Alto saxophonist and clarinetist. He studied violin for eight years before taking up clarinet and alto saxophone as a teenager. He performed and recorded as a clarinetist with Jelly Roll Morton (1928), then played alto saxophone and clarinet in the big bands of Benny Carter (1929), Chick Webb (1929–31), Fletcher Henderson (1931–4), Tiny Bradshaw (1934–5), and Teddy Hill (1935–7), with the last of whom he toured Europe. From 1938 to 1943 he was the alto saxophonist in John Kirby's sextet. During his army service he was stationed in New York, where he continued to play, mainly in shows. He re-joined Kirby for a brief period (1945) before becoming a member of Duke Ellington's orchestra in 1946; he remained with Ellington until 1974, except for a spell with Wilbur De Paris in 1961. After Ellington's death he played in New York with Brooks Kerr, in the musical *Ain't Misbehavin'*, and as the leader of the group Ellingtonia. Although he recorded as a soloist with Morton, Henderson, Hill, and Kirby, early in his career Procope was not an innovative improviser and was valued chiefly as a reliable section player. His reading of *Mood Indigo* (1950) established his later reputation as a bluesy, warm-toned clarinetist.

Oral history material in *CtY, NjR, NjR* (JOHP).

For illustrations *see* BAILEY, BUSTER, ELLINGTON, DUKE, fig.2, HENDERSON, FLETCHER, and KIRBY, JOHN.

SELECTED RECORDINGS

As sideman: J. R. Morton: Red Hot Pepper/Deep Creek (1928, Vic. 38055); F. Henderson: I'm crazy 'bout my baby (1931, Mlt. 12145); Blue Rhythm (1931, Crown 3180); T. Hill: Blue Rhythm Fantasy (1936, Voc. 3247); The Harlem Twister (1937, Bb 6908); J. Kirby: It's only a Paper Moon/Fifi's Rhapsody (1941, Vic. 27598); D. Ellington: *Masterpieces* (1950, Col. ML4418), incl. Mood Indigo; The Mooche (1952, Col. B1629); C. Anderson: *Cat Anderson Plays at 4 a.m.* (1958, Col. FPX116); D. Ellington: *Duke Ellington's Seventieth Birthday Concert* (1969, SolS 19000), incl. 4.30 Blues

BIBLIOGRAPHY

ChiltonW
J. Armitage: "Russell Procope," *Jazz Music Mirror*, v/7 (1958), 5
S. Dance: "Russell Procope," *JJ*, xvi (1963), no.1, p.14; no.2, p.4
R. Procope: "Wonderful, Wonderful Jazz," *JJ*, xx/5 (1967), 6
S. Dance: *The World of Duke Ellington* (London and New York, 1970/*R* 1981) [colln of previously pubd articles and interviews]
G. Colombe: "Russell Procope," *JJI*, xxxiv/4 (1981), 10
J. Armitage: "Russell Procope," *BHcF*, no.331 (1985), 7

BARRY KERNFELD

Profit, Clarence (*b* New York, 26 June 1912; *d* New York, 22 Oct 1944). Pianist and leader. He began playing at the age of three and during his teens he performed with local dance bands, broadcast with Edgar Sampson, and held a number of engagements in New York as the leader of his own ten-piece band. In 1930–31 he was a member of Teddy Bunn's Washboard Serenaders. After visiting Antigua, West Indies, he led an octet there and also worked in Bermuda and St. Kitts. In 1936 he returned to New York and formed his own trio, which was resident at several well-known clubs, including Kelly's Stable (1940–43). By the time he made his first recordings Profit was already an able and energetic stride pianist, as may be heard on the Washboard Serenaders' *Teddy's Blues/Tappin' the Time Away* (1930, Vic. V38610). In his maturity he achieved a greater delicacy of touch and originality of melodic and harmonic ideas (evident on his own trio's *Times Square Blues/Hot and Bothered*, 1940, Decca 8503); his playing was widely influential and he became a favorite opponent of Art Tatum's in cutting contests.

BIBLIOGRAPHY

ChiltonW; FeatherE
J. Simmen: "Clarence Profit," *JM*, no.180 (1970), 14; Fr. version, as "Un grand pianiste peu remarqué: Clarence Profit," *BHcF*, no.204 (1971), 7

HOWARD RYE

Progressive. Record company and label. The company was established in New York in 1950 by Gus Statiras, but it has functioned only sporadically from that time. Its first session was by Al Cohn, who later recorded twice more for the label (1953, 1954); the catalogue also included two albums by George Wallington (1951, 1955). Thereafter, however, operations declined for several years, and much of the material was later sold to and reissued by Savoy. In 1970 a session recorded by Cohn for Progressive in 1954, but never released, was issued on Prestige. The company became active again in the late 1970s, cooperating with the Japanese company Baybridge to reissue the excellent album *George Wallington Quartet at Cafe Bohemia* (1955) in a new format that included some previously unreleased material. This was followed by newly recorded albums by J. R. Monterose, Al Haig, and Tommy Flanagan, among others; the sessions were supervised by Statiras, who also took photographs and wrote notes for the liners. All new material was issued with facsimiles of the label of the 1950s.

MARK GARDNER

Progressive jazz. A term applied, mainly in the 1940s and 1950s, to continuations and extensions of the jazz orchestral tradition. It is associated chiefly with the more ambitious parts of the output of Stan Kenton's large band, though it is also applied to shorter-lived ensembles of Boyd Raeburn and, less importantly, Earle Spencer; it is used, too, in connection with a few bands whose main activity lay elsewhere, for example, the group with which Charlie Barnet recorded some excellent pieces for Capitol in 1949, such as *Cu-ba* (Cap. 15417).

The music of these bands grew directly out of that of the big swing groups of the 1930s and early 1940s – Kenton's *Intermission Riff* (1946, Cap. 298), for instance, using the same theme as Jimmie Lunceford's *Yard Dog Mazurka* (1941, Decca 4032). In pieces such as *Chorale for Brass, Piano and Bongos* (1947, Cap. 10183) and *Fugue for Rhythm Section* (1947, Cap. 10127), however, Kenton and, more particularly, Pete Rugolo (Kenton's chief composer and arranger during this period) arrived at a significant further development of orchestral jazz. This was consolidated by later recordings by Kenton, such as Bill Holman's *Invention for Guitar and Trumpet* (1952, Cap. EAP2-383). In partial contrast, Bob Graettinger's music for the Kenton band made additional use of a medium-sized string section and a considerably more dissonant harmonic vocabulary, and conveyed a dark emotional turbulence that almost invoked the Second Viennese School. An example is the four-movement *City of Glass* (1951, Cap. 28062-3).

Boyd Raeburn's output during the same period was also self-consciously modernistic, as is suggested by titles such as *Boyd meets Stravinsky* (1946, Jwl 10002). Yet the scores, by George Handy (a pupil of Aaron Copland), Ed Finckel and others, retain their interest; their characteristically complex textures and dissonant harmony were qualified by the exhilaratingly full-throated power of the band's performance. Raeburn also performed works in a quieter, pastel-toned vein, exemplified by Handy's and Hal McKusick's *Yerxa* (1945, 10001).

In the late 1950s the term "progressive jazz" was also used as a synonym for "modern jazz."

See also FORMS, §4, and JAZZ (i), §V, 6.

BIBLIOGRAPHY

A. Jackson: "Boyd Raeburn," *JM*, xii/11 (1966), 5
M. Sparke, P. Venudor, and J. Hartley: *Kenton on Capitol: a Discography* (Hounslow, England, 1966, 2/1967)
A. Morgan: "The Progressives," *Jazz on Record: a Critical Guide to the First 50 Years: 1917–1967*, ed. A. McCarthy and others (London, 1968), 361
M. Harrison: "Stan Kenton: the 'Innovations' Band," *JJI*, xxxii (1979), no.4, p.4; no.5, p.18.
W. F. Lee: *Stan Kenton: Artistry in Rhythm* (Los Angeles, 1980) [incl. discography]

MAX HARRISON

Pruitt, Carl (B.) (*b* Birmingham, AL, 3 June 1918). Bass player. From 1944 to 1951 he performed and made recordings with Cootie Williams, Roy Eldridge, the Jeter–Pillars Orchestra, Lucky Millinder, and Mary Lou Williams (including *Piano Panorama*, 1951, Atl. 114). He played intermittently in concerts and sessions with Earl Hines from 1953, and performed briefly with the Sauter–Finegan Orchestra in 1955. His principal work was as a studio musician, however, and he recorded with Sahib Shihab, Roland Kirk (both 1956), Eddie "Lockjaw" Davis (1957), Shorty Baker, George Shearing (both 1958), and many blues and rhythm-and-blues musicians. Pruitt became less active after 1960, but he recorded at the Monterey (California) Jazz Festival with Woody Herman (1967), in New York with Ray Nance (1969), and in Paris with Sam Price (*c*1970) and Doc Cheatham (1975).

BIBLIOGRAPHY

FeatherE
S. Dance: "Earl's Four," *JJ*, xiii/7 (1960), 9

Ptaszyn [Ptak]. Nickname of JAN WRÓBLEWSKI.

Puertas, Josep (*b* Spain, *c*1910; *d* after 1947). Spanish trumpeter and violinist. After the Spanish Civil War he played with many important big bands in Barcelona, and also led his own groups, sometimes with his sister Cecilia Melé, a singer. During the 1940s he recorded prolifically, although his output was predominantly highly commercialized music. In 1947 he took part in a session with Don Byas and George Johnson that was organized in Barcelona under the auspices of the jazz magazine *Ritmo e melodia*; Puertas's trumpet playing may be heard to advantage on *Janine/Byas Jump* (Gramophone 738). His style as a trumpeter was in the tradition of Louis Armstrong, and his violin playing had a ferocity reminiscent of Stuff Smith's work.

ALFREDO PAPO

Pugh, Jim [James Edward] (*b* Butler, PA, 12 Nov 1950). Trombonist. He studied at the Eastman School (1968–72), where he played in the jazz ensemble under Chuck Mangione. In 1972 he joined Woody Herman's band, with which he toured Europe and the USA and recorded several albums (including *Giant Steps*, 1973, Fan. 9432) as the lead trombonist and as a soloist. He performed at a concert with Chick Corea and Return to Forever in New York in 1977, and in 1983 he recorded with Marvin Stamm's big band.

BIBLIOGRAPHY

Feather–Gitler '70s
J. Pugh: "I've Settled into the Suitcase Lifestyle," *CI*, xiv/9 (1976), 19

Pukwana, Dudu [Mtutuzel] (*b* Port Elizabeth, South Africa, 18 July 1938). South African alto saxophonist. He played piano in Port Elizabeth in the late 1950s, then alto saxophone with the Jazz Giants and Chris McGregor's Blue Notes; with the latter group he moved to London in 1965. He formed the group Spear in 1973 and recorded the albums *In the Townships* (1973, Caroline 1504) and *Flute Music* (1974, Caroline 1512); at the same time he played with and wrote compositions for McGregor's big band Brotherhood of Breath. He recorded *Thunder in our Hearts* with Julian Bahula in 1977, then made the first of a series of tours with the band Zila, which he formed in 1978. Pukwana, a seasoned session musician, has been influenced by the music of the South African townships, the melodies of Ben Webster, and the free forms of Ornette Coleman. His vibrant playing may be heard to advantage on Hugh Masekela's recording *Home is where the Music is* (1972, Chisa 6003) and on Johnny Dyani's *Song for Biko* (1978, Ste. 1109).

BIBLIOGRAPHY

R. Cotterrell, ed.: *Jazz Now: the Jazz Centre Society Guide* (London, 1976)
R. Latxaque: "Dudu: change de cap," *Jm*, no.319 (1983), 30 [incl. discography]
C. de Ledesma: "Afro Jazz: Evolution and Revolution," *The Wire*, no.12 (1985), 26, esp. 30f

CHARLES DE LEDESMA

Pullen, Don (Gabriel) (*b* Roanoke, VA, 25 Dec 1941). Pianist. He gained his first experience by playing gospel music in church and rhythm-and-blues in local groups. In his late teens he became interested in jazz, initially in the work of Art Tatum, and then that of Eric Dolphy and Ornette Coleman. His important early associations were with Muhal Richard Abrams's Experimental Band in Chicago (*c*1964) and Giuseppi Logan's quartet in New York (1964–5). But work in free-jazz ensembles was scarce, and Pullen supported himself by accompanying rhythm-and-blues singers, such as Big Maybelle, Ruth Brown, and Arthur Prysock, and by playing organ in soul-jazz groups. Between 1965 and 1972 he led such a group, sometimes of three, sometimes of four members; he played organ and his sidemen included Roland Prince, Tina Brooks, and Al Dreares. He also played in a duo with Milford Graves (1966). From 1973 to 1975 he worked with Charles Mingus, whose eclectic approach enabled Pullen to exploit the diverse styles in which he practiced. He first recorded as a soloist in 1975. He also recorded frequently with free-jazz musicians, including Sam Rivers (1975), David Murray, Hamiet Bluiett (1977), and members of the Art Ensemble of Chicago (1978–9). He performed intermittently as a leader with Beaver Harris of 360 Degree Music Experience; in 1979 he recorded with this ensemble and with Mingus Dynasty, and began leading small groups with George Adams. Pullen's playing draws on his varied musical experience: melodic lines in the style of bop are underpinned by rhythms and harmonies characteristic of soul jazz and decorated with devices often associated with free jazz, such as glissandos and tone clusters.

SELECTED RECORDINGS

As unaccompanied soloist: *Solo Piano Album* (1975, Sack. 3008); *Healing Force* (1976, BS 0010); *Evidence of Things Unseen* (1983, BS 0080)
Duos with M. Graves: *Nommo* (1966, SRP 290)
As leader: with S. Rivers: *Capricorn Rising* (1975, BS 0004); with D. Moye: *Milano Strut* (1978, BS 0028); with G. Adams: *Don't Lose Control* (1979, SN 1004), *Melodic Excursions* (1982, Tim. 166)
As sideman: G. Logan: *The Giuseppi Logan Quartet* (1964, ESP 1007); C. Mingus: *Mingus Moves* (1973, Atl. 1653); Mingus Dynasty: *Chair in the Sky* (1979, Elek. 248)

BIBLIOGRAPHY

V. Frazer: "Don Pullen: an Interview," *Coda*, no.151 (1976), 2
L. Goddet: "Free Blues: Don Pullen," *Jh*, no.331 (1976), 15
A. J. Smith: "Don Pullen," *DB*, xliv/13 (1977), 17
P. Gamble: "Don Pullen," *JJI*, xxxiii/6 (1980), 28

BARRY KERNFELD

Puma, Joe [Joseph J.] (*b* New York, 13 Aug 1927). Electric guitarist. He came from a family of guitarists. He began his professional career performing and recording with Joe Roland (1949–50, 1953) and Louie Bellson, Don Elliott, and Artie Shaw (all 1954). He then recorded with Eddie Bert and Dick Garcia (both 1955), Herbie Mann (1955, 1957), Mat Mathews, Bernard Peiffer, and Chris Connor (all 1956), Candido Camero (1956–8), and Paul Quinichette (1957), and as a leader. After playing with Lee Konitz and Dick Hyman (1958), Puma accompanied Morgana King for two years. During the 1960s he recorded with Sir Charles Thompson (1961), Bobby Hackett (1963), Gary Burton (1964), and Carmen McRae (1965). Puma formed a duo with Chuck Wayne in 1972, which appeared at the Newport Jazz Festival in New York in 1973; when the duo broke up after five years Puma led his own trio. He also taught at Housatonic College in Bridgeport, Connecticut. A versatile guitarist, Puma has a light, restrained sound and a jaunty playing style.

SELECTED RECORDINGS

Duos with C. Wayne: *Interactions* (1973, Choice 1004)
As leader: *Joe Puma Quintet* (1954, Beth. 1012); *Like Tweet* (1961, Col. CS8418)
As sideman: H. Mann and S. Most: *Herbie Mann–Sam Most Quintet* (1955, Beth. 40); H. Mann: *Salute to the Flute* (1957, Epic 3395); G. Burton: *Groove Sound* (1964, RCA LSP3360)

BIBLIOGRAPHY

Feather '60s; *Feather–Gitler '70s*
R. Gogerty: "Chuck Wayne/Joe Puma: a Magical Jazz Duo," *GP*, viii/3 (1974), 20

GARY CARNER

Purbrook, Colin (Thomas) (*b* Seaford, England, 26 Feb 1936). English pianist. He worked with Sandy Brown (1957–60), Kenny Ball and Ronnie Scott (1960), Tubby Hayes (1961), and Kenny Baker, among others. He led a group with Tony Coe (1961–3) and recorded under Coe's leadership (1962, 1966). He also broadcast on radio with his own trio and octet, performed on television and in the film *All Night Long* (1961), and played double bass in Dudley Moore's trio in the revue *Beyond the Fringe*. In the 1970s and 1980s he accompanied such visiting American musicians as Benny Carter, Dexter Gordon, Chet Baker, Art Farmer, Barney Kessel, Eddie "Lockjaw" Davis, and Buddy Tate. He performed and recorded with Humphrey Lyttelton (1972) and was music director for the shows *Bubbling Brown Sugar* (1977), and *One Mo' Time* (1981). In the 1980s he continued to lead his own small groups; he performed in the London production of *Lady Day* with Dee Dee Bridgewater. Purbrook's playing may be heard to advantage on the album *Shades of Blue* (1964, Col. SX1733), which he recorded in a sextet led by Don Rendell and Ian Carr.

NEVIL SKRIMSHIRE

Purdie, Bernard [Pretty] (*b* Elkton, MD, 11 June 1939). Drummer. After moving to New York in 1960, he worked as a studio musician, recording with the soul singer James Brown, King Curtis, and others. As the drummer for the recording company CTI (1968–74) he recorded with various musicians, including Grover Washington, Jr. In 1970 he toured with Curtis and the soul singer Aretha Franklin; he was Franklin's music director during the next five years. He continued to work in studios in the 1970s and recorded with a number of jazz performers, among them Louis Armstrong (1970) and Gato Barbieri (1971, *c*1973), and many rock and pop musicians. In 1980 he recorded at the Montreux International Jazz Festival with Dizzy Gillespie, with whom he toured in 1982–3. He made three recordings with Hank Crawford (1983–5). Purdie is best known for his work with soul musicians in the 1960s and as an innovator in the funk style of drumming in the 1970s. His playing is characterized by a reliance on precise, syncopated ostinatos rather than busy technique.

SELECTED RECORDINGS

As leader: *Soul is . . . Pretty Purdie* (1972, FD 10154)
As sideman: J. Brown: It's a man's, man's, man's world (1966, King 6035); K. Curtis: *King Curtis Live at the Fillmore West* (1971, Atco 359); A. Franklin: *Aretha Franklin Live at the Fillmore West* (1971, Atl. SD7205); D. Gillespie: *Dizzy Gillespie at Montreux, 1980* (1980, PL 2308226); H. Crawford: *Roadhouse Symphony* (1985, Mlst. 9140)

BIBLIOGRAPHY

Feather–Gitler '70s
G. Gray: "Bernard Purdie: Soul Beat Mavin," *DB*, xxxviii/2 (1971), 18
B. Niquet: "Bernard Purdie," *Pj*, no.7 (1972), 4 [incl. discography]

C. Iero: "Bernard Purdie," *MD*, iii/3 (1979), 20
M. Weinberg: "Pretty Purdie," *The Big Beat* (Chicago, 1984), 60
C. Fisher: "Pretty Purdie," *MD*, ix/11 (1985), 8

RICK MATTINGLY

Puretone. Record label. It was established by the Bridgeport Die & Machine Co. after the latter ceased to issue records on its label Puritan. Many issues first made on Puritan were repressed with Puretone labels, and the catalogue drew on the same sources as that of its predecessor. The repertory included recordings by Jelly Roll Morton (drawn from Paramount) and a reissue of one side of Duke Ellington's first recording (originally put out on Blu-disc). Production ceased in mid-1925.

BIBLIOGRAPHY

B. Rust: *The American Record Label Book* (New Rochelle, NY, 1978), 255
M. E. Vreede: "Puritanism in Discography," *Sv*, no.89 (1980), 178

Purim, Flora (*b* Rio de Janeiro, 6 March 1942). Brazilian singer. The daughter of professional musicians, she studied piano and guitar. She performed in São Paulo and Rio de Janeiro with AIRTO MOREIRA (*c*1966–1967), whom she later married (1972). After moving to Los Angeles and then to New York she joined Stan Getz's Latin jazz group in 1968. She recorded with Duke Pearson (1969–70) and Moreira (from 1971), worked with Gil Evans (1971), and gained considerable renown as a member of Chick Corea's quintet RETURN TO FOREVER (with Moreira, Stanley Clarke, and Joe Farrell, 1971–3). Purim's high-pitched voice and soft, airy tone may be heard to advantage on Corea's recording of *Five Hundred Miles High*, on which she sings dreamy lyrics in English with a strong Portuguese accent; *Spain* provides an example of her deft skill as a scat singer. Purim and Moreira left Corea in 1973 to form their own group, but from 1974 to 1975 Purim was imprisoned for possessing cocaine. After her release from prison she continued to work as a jazz singer, but aimed at more commercial markets on her recordings as a leader (1976–8). In 1978 she formed another group, but without Moreira, as the two had begun to attract different audiences. In the mid-1980s she resumed working with Moreira, touring internationally.

SELECTED RECORDINGS

As leader: *Butterfly Dreams* (1973, Mlst. 9052); *500 Miles High at Montreux* (1974, Mlst. 9070); *That's What she Said* (1976, Mlst. 9081); *Nothing Will Be as it Was . . . Tomorrow* (*c*1976, WB 2985)

As sideman: D. Pearson: *It Could only Happen to you* (1970, BN LA317); C. Corea: *Light as a Feather* (1972, Pol. 5525), incl. Five Hundred Miles High, Spain; *Return to Forever* (1973, ECM 1022)

BIBLIOGRAPHY

J. E. Berendt: "Flora Purim: eine Stimme der Freiheit," *Ein Fenster aus Jazz: Essays, Portraits, Reflexionen* (Frankfurt am Main, Germany, 1977), 89
H. Nolan: "Flora Purim: Flying High on Freedom," *DB*, xlv/16 (1978), 23
L. Underwood: "Airto and his Incredible Gong Show," *DB*, xlv/8 (1978), 15
J. Williams: "New Music and Direction for Flora Purim," *Billboard*, xc (27 May 1978), 46

BARRY KERNFELD

Puritan. Record label. It was established before 1920, and was used to issue discs produced by three different companies – the United Phonographs Corp., the New York Recording Laboratories (both subsidiaries of the Wisconsin Chair Co.), and the Bridgeport Die & Machine Co. The organizations pooled their masters for this purpose, though the most important jazz material (including items by King Oliver and Jelly Roll Morton) came from NYRL and was often also issued on Paramount; the catalogue also contained recordings by the Original Memphis Five and the California Ramblers. Each company manufactured and distributed the discs in its own territory (UPC and NYRL in the Midwest, BD&M in the North); until 1923 the catalogue numbers in each company's series were the same. Thereafter, however, the sequences began to diverge, and BD&M left the scheme and established the label Puretone. NYRL continued to issue discs on Puritan until 1927, using both its own repertory and material leased from Plaza.

BIBLIOGRAPHY

B. Rust: *The American Record Label Book* (New Rochelle, NY, 1978), 256
M. E. Vreede: "Puritanism in Discography," *Sv*, no.89 (1980), 178

Purnell, Alton (*b* New Orleans, 16 April 1911; *d* Inglewood, CA, 14 Jan 1987). Pianist and singer. After studying piano with Burnell Santiago and Walter Pichon he worked from around 1928 at the Pelican Annex. He toured in the mid-1930s with Isaiah Morgan, belonged to Sidney Desvigne's big band, and in the early 1940s performed at the Famous Door with the singer Cousin Joe. In 1945 he moved to New York to join Bunk Johnson's band, with which he remained when the group's leadership was assumed by George Lewis (i). He moved in 1957 to California, where he worked as a soloist and with Teddy Buckner, the Young Men from New Orleans, and Kid Ory's last band. He toured the world as a guest soloist from 1964 and later as a member of the LEGENDS OF JAZZ. Purnell's driving style made him the most influential traditional-jazz pianist of the postwar era. His brother was the reed player Theodore Purnell (1908–74).

Oral history material in *LNT*.

SELECTED RECORDINGS

As leader: *Alton Purnell Quartet* (1958, WB 1228)

As sideman: B. Johnson: One Sweet Letter from you/Franklin Street Blues (1945, Vic. 40-0129); G. Lewis: *New Orleans Stompers* (1955, BN 7207–8); New Orleans All Stars: *New Orleans All Stars* (1966, GHB 35); *It's the Talk of the Town* (1972, 77 SEU44); Legends of Jazz: [untitled album] (1973, Crescent 1); K. Thomas: *Kid Thomas* (1975, Smoky Mary 1975T)

BIBLIOGRAPHY

ChiltonW
G. Boatfield: Liner notes, *Live with Keith Smith's Climax Jazz Band* (77 LEU13, 1965)
T. Stagg: Liner notes, *It's the Talk of the Town* (77 SEU44, 1972)
J. Darensbourg: *Telling it Like it is*, ed. P. Vacher (London, 1987; Baton Rouge, LA, 1987, as *Jazz Odyssey: the Autobiography of Joe Darensbourg*)
Obituary, F. Levin, *Fn*, xviii/4 (1987), 4

MARCEL JOLY

Purnell, Keg [William] (*b* Charleston, WV, 7 Jan 1915; *d* New York, 25 June 1965). Drummer. He played with the Campus Revellers, led by the pianist Chappie Willett, while attending West Virginia State College (1932–4), and then worked with King Oliver (1934–5). In addition to leading his own trio in the late 1930s, he played with Thelonious Monk (1939), Benny Carter (1939–40, recording in 1940), and Claude Hopkins (1941–2). Between 1942 and 1952 his principal association was with Eddie Heywood, with whom he had recorded in the Quintones in 1940; he also recorded with Rex Stewart (1945), Teddy Wilson (1947), and Willie "the Lion" Smith (1953). From 1957 he worked with Snub Mosley at the Sands Beach Hotel in Howard Beach, New York.

SELECTED RECORDINGS

As sideman: B. Carter: Shufflebug Shuffle/More than you Know (1939, Voc./OK 5508); Sleep/Slow Freight (1940, Voc./OK 5399); Quintones: Honey Bunny Boo/Harmony in Harlem (1940, Voc. 5596); E. Heywood: Blue Lou/Please don't talk about me when I'm gone (1944, Decca 23427); on S. Mosley: *Cascade of Quartets*, i (1959, Col. 33SX1191), So Sad Blues

BIBLIOGRAPHY

ChiltonW; *FeatherE*; *Feather '60s*

AL VOLLMER

Purtill, Moe [Maurice] (*b* Huntington, NY, 4 May 1916). Drummer. He worked with lesser-known bandleaders in New York during the mid-1930s, then performed and made recordings with Red Norvo (including *I got rhythm*, 1936, Decca 779), Mildred Bailey (1936–7), Glenn Miller (1937, 1939–42), and Tommy Dorsey (1938–9). After navy service he was briefly a member of the memorial Glenn Miller Orchestra under Tex Beneke, then worked mostly as a session musician in New York. He also recorded as a sideman with Billy Maxted (*c*1958).

For illustrations *see* MILLER, GLENN, and MUTE, fig.3.

BIBLIOGRAPHY

ChiltonW
G. T. Simon: *Glenn Miller and his Orchestra* (New York, n.d. [?1974])

Purvis, Jack (*b* Kokomo, IN, 11 Dec 1906; San Francisco, 30 March 1962). Trumpeter and trombonist. After playing in Lexington, Kentucky, with the Original Kentucky Night Hawks he worked as a freelance trumpeter and arranger (1926) and played briefly in Europe (1928). He joined Hal Kemp's band as a trombonist in 1929, then changed to trumpet before leaving the band the following year. During this period he also made recordings with his own band, including *Down Georgia Way* (1929, OK 8782). In 1930 he played with the California Ramblers in New York. Later he worked in radio orchestras, and also recorded as a freelance with the Dorsey Brothers and other bands. Occasionally he served as the fourth trumpeter with Fletcher Henderson, and in 1933 he played briefly with Charlie Barnet. After a short period in California as an arranger in film studios, Purvis led his own quartet in New York and recorded with Frank Froeba (1935). He then toured briefly with Joe Haymes, but thereafter played only sporadically.

BIBLIOGRAPHY

P. Kelley: "Poor Jack Purvis," *JJ*, xx/10 (1967), 17 [incl. discography]
P. A. Larson: "Final Curtain," *Sv*, no.39 (1972), 83
S. A. Worsfold: "The Forgotten Ones: Jack Purvis," *JJI*, xxxv/3 (1982), 20

based on *ChiltonW*

Pyne, (Norman) Chris(topher) (*b* Bridlington, England, 14 Feb 1939). English trombonist, brother of Mick Pyne. He was taught piano as a child but later changed to trombone. He worked with the drummer Fat John Cox (1963) and Alexis Korner's Blues Incorporated (1964–5). During his association with Humphrey Lyttelton (1966–70) he also recorded with John Dankworth (1967) and Ronnie Scott (1968) and performed with Tubby Hayes. Thereafter he played with Maynard Ferguson (1970) and toured with Frank Sinatra. As a studio musician, he accompanied Ella Fitzgerald and Tony Bennett and recorded with Michael Gibbs and John Surman, among others. In the mid-1980s he worked with Stan Tracey and in the orchestra led by the drummer Charlie Watts.

BIBLIOGRAPHY

R. Cotterrell, ed.: *Jazz Now: the Jazz Centre Society Guide* (London, 1976)
I. Carr: "Pyne, Chris," in I. Carr, D. Fairweather, and B. Priestley: *Jazz: the Essential Companion* (London, 1987)

NEVIL SKRIMSHIRE

Pyne, Mick [Michael John] (*b* Thornton Dale, England, 2 Sept 1940). English pianist, brother of Chris Pyne. He was taught piano from the age of three; he later learned violin and when he was 13 he began playing cornet. Around 1957 he formed a band with his brother, and in 1961 he moved to London, where he worked with Tony Kinsey for two years and Alexis Korner (1965). He made many recordings during his associations with Tubby Hayes (1966–73) and Humphrey Lyttelton (1973–85); he also recorded in duos with Lyttelton (*Once in a While*, 1974, 1976, BL 12149) and John Eardley (1977) and in Cecil Payne's quintet (1979). After 1985 he performed with the rhythm-and-blues singer Georgie Fame, the group Hefty Jazz, led by Keith Smith, and the drummer Charlie Watts, and accompanied visiting American musicians in London and Europe. Pyne's piano and cornet playing may be heard to advantage on his recording as a soloist *Alone Together* (1977, Spot. 506).

BIBLIOGRAPHY

R. Cotterell, ed.: *Jazz Now: the Jazz Centre Society Guide* (London, 1976)
I. Carr: "Pyne, Mike," in I. Carr, D. Fairweather, and B. Priestley: *Jazz: the Essential Companion* (London, 1987)

NEVIL SKRIMSHIRE

Q

Q (i). Nickname of HISAO ISHIKAWA.

Q (ii). Nickname of QUINCY JONES.

QRS. Manufacturer of piano rolls. The company was established in Chicago before 1916 by Melville Clark, the inventor of the "marking piano." This machine made possible the cutting of piano rolls that accurately captured performances. Involved at an early stage in the recording of ragtime, QRS soon also turned to jazz, especially after Max Kortlander joined its staff and it transferred its premises to New York around 1921. Among the notable musicians who cut rolls for the company were James P. Johnson (1921–7) and Fats Waller (1923–43); in 1926 some eleven million rolls were cut.

The company also established a record label of the same name, on which it put out three series of discs. The first of these, during the early 1920s, was of items previously put out on Gennett. The second, the 7000 race series of 1928–9, was more notable: it included recordings made especially for the company under the supervision of Arthur E. Satherley, who had earlier worked in Paramount's artists and repertory department. In 1929, shortly after QRS merged with a film company, the DeVry Corp., a third series of records appeared, made by the Cova Record Corp. of New York. This continued until mid-1930, but contained very little important jazz.

By this time the market for piano rolls had severely declined, and in 1931 Kortlander bought the company. For many years its existence was frequently precarious, and its employees often worked only part-time. These included the stride pianist J. Lawrence Cook, who made many rolls, some under the pseudonym Sid Laney. By the 1950s production had dropped to around 20,000 rolls per year, although thereafter interest revived among collectors. Kortlander died in 1961, and the company was acquired by Ramsi P. Tick, who moved production to Buffalo in 1966. Earl Hines cut some rolls for QRS in the 1970s, and operations continued into the mid-1980s. The meaning of the acronym is unknown; the initials have been interpreted as standing for "Quality Reigns Supreme," and "Quality, Reliability, Service."

BIBLIOGRAPHY

M. Wyler and B. Kumm: "QRS Past and Present," *Sv*, ii/7 (1966), 19 [incl. discography]

B. Kumm: "Mr. Piano Roll: J. Lawrence Cook," *Sv*, no.10 (1967), 14

R. M. W. Dixon and J. Godrich: *Recording the Blues* (London, 1970), 58

T. Magnusson: "The Piano Rolls by Thomas Waller and by 'Fats' Waller," *Matrix*, no.106 (1975), 3

B. Rust: *The American Record Label Book* (New Rochelle, NY, 1978), 259

M. Montgomery: "James P. Johnson Rollography," in F. H. Trolle: *James P. Johnson, Father of the Stride Piano* (Alphen aan de Rijn, 1981), 25

L. Wright: "QRS," *Sv*, no.114 (1984), 218

Quealey, Chelsea (*b* Hartford, CT, 1905; *d* Las Vegas, NV, 6 May 1950). Trumpeter. He first played saxophone, then took up trumpet and worked with the bandleader Jan Garber (*c*1925) and the California Ramblers (1926–7). In 1927 he sailed to England, where he performed and made recordings (including *Singapore Sorrows*, 1929, Parl. R1201) with Fred Elizalde, until illness forced him to return to the USA in 1929. After working again with the California Ramblers he played briefly with Paul Whiteman, then joined Ben Pollack in Chicago and traveled with him to California. In 1935–6 he was a member of Isham Jones's band, then returned to the East Coast, where he undertook a residency with Red McKenzie and Joe Marsala (1936) and played with Frankie Trumbauer (1937). Thereafter he worked as a freelance and performed with Bob Zurke's big band (1939–40). In the early 1940s he played regularly at Nick's, New York, with Georg Brunis, Brad Gowans, Miff Mole, and others before returning to California around 1946.

based on *ChiltonW*

Quebec, Ike (Abrams) (*b* Newark, NJ, 17 Aug 1918; *d* New York, 16 Jan 1963). Tenor saxophonist. He began his career as a pianist and dancer, but in 1940 he changed to tenor saxophone and played with the Barons of Rhythm. During the early 1940s he performed with various small bands in the New York area, including those led by Benny Carter, Kenny Clarke, Roy Eldridge, Coleman Hawkins, Frankie Newton, Hot Lips Page, and Trummy Young. He was a member of Cab Calloway's orchestra from 1944 to 1951 and he also played in the Cab Jivers, Calloway's small group within the band. Quebec served as artists and repertory agent for Blue Note records during the late 1940s and took an active part in promoting bop recordings. He led his own small band until the late 1950s, when he ceased working as a full-time musician. He performed again in the early 1960s, however, and achieved some success, but soon after he became seriously ill and he died of lung cancer in 1963. Quebec's style was modeled after that of Hawkins, though he was also influenced by Herschel Evans and Joe Thomas (iii).

A strong and direct performer, he was particularly impressive when playing slow blues.

SELECTED RECORDINGS

As leader: Blue Harlem (1944, BN 37); Mad about you (1944, BN 42); I. Q. Blues (1945, Savoy 570); *It Might as Well be Spring* (1961, BN 84105)

As sideman with C. Calloway: Cruisin' with Cab (1944), Dawn Time (1945), We the cats (1945), first issued on *Cab Calloway 1943–1946* (1943–6, Spot. 148)

BIBLIOGRAPHY

FeatherE

C. Schlouch: *In Memory of Ike Quebec: a Discography* (Marseille, France, 1983)

M. Cuscuna: "Ike Quebec," *The Complete Blue Note Recordings of Ike Quebec and John Hardee* (Mosaic 107, 1984) [liner notes]

EDDIE LAMBERT

Queen, Alvin (*b* New York, 16 Aug 1950). Drummer. He worked with George Benson and Stanley Turrentine, then traveled to Europe with Charles Tolliver's quartet. In 1979 he settled in Switzerland, where he estabished his own record label, Nilva. From that time he has worked mainly in Switzerland and France. In 1982 he toured France with Plas Johnson and Harry Edison and recorded with John Collins (*The Incredible John Collins*, Nilva NQ3412) and Junior Mance (*Glidin' and Stridin'*, Nilva NQ3403). He later worked in Zurich with Wild Bill Davis's trio (1983). *Lenox and Seventh* (1985, BB 33178), recorded by a trio led by Queen and Lonnie Smith, perfectly captures Queen's commitment to a powerful and varied swing style.

BIBLIOGRAPHY

J. Simmen: "Jazz au Widder-Bar," *BHcF*, no.306 (1983), 9

H. Panassié and M. Gautier: *Dictionnaire du jazz* (Paris, rev. and enlarged by A. Vasset and J. Pescheux 3/1987), 379

J. Simmen: "Trois disques avec Alvin Queen," *BHcF*, no.345 (1987), 24

HOWARD RYE

Queener, Charlie [Charles Conant] (*b* Pineville, KY, 27 July 1923). Pianist. Early in his career he played and made recordings with Muggsy Spanier (1942), Harry James (1944), Glen Gray (*c*1944), Joe Marsala (1944–5, including *Southern Comfort/Gotta be this or that*, 1945, Musi. 328), and Benny Goodman (1945–6). From 1946 he worked for four years at Nick's in New York, and then, after a brief return to his home town, as a freelance, playing swing and traditional jazz with Billy Butterfield, Jimmy McPartland, Max Kaminsky, Bobby Hackett, Ruby Braff, Pee Wee Erwin, and others; his longest-lasting association was with Clarence Hutchenrider, with whom he played from 1958 to 1973. In 1963–4 he led a trio with Carl Kress and Bob Wilber. He recorded with Hackett (1948), Jerry Gray (1951), Wingy Manone (1954–60), Wild Bill Davison (*c*1958), Sidney De Paris (1962), and the drummer Merrill Morris (1970). From the mid-1960s, having studied with Paul Creston, he composed orchestral works. He continued to be active as a performer in the late 1980s.

BIBLIOGRAPHY

FeatherE

W. W. Vaché, Sr.: "Quiet Queener," *MR*, xiv/5 (1988), 18

Quersin, Benoit (*b* Brussels, 24 July 1927). Belgian double bass player. He studied classical piano from the age of six and first played jazz with Toots Thielemans when he was 16. He then took up double bass as a member of the Big John Trio and played with Francis Coppieters at the Versailles in Brussels; with Thielemans he performed at the first Paris Jazz Fair. He belonged for a year to the Jump College (1950–51) and worked for eight years in Paris, during which time he accompanied French musicians and visiting soloists and made many recordings. After returning in 1957 to Belgium he spent three months in Africa before moving back to Brussels, where he wrote four film scores and opened the Blue Note Club. In 1961 he joined the staff of Belgian Radio, where he formed a jazz department. During the following decades he made several trips to Africa, wrote articles for various periodicals, and worked as the director of the Art Museum of Central Africa, Kinshasa, Zaïre. Quersin has made recordings in Belgium, France, and Italy with Thielemans, the Jump College, and many other musicians, including Chet Baker (notably *Chet is Back*, 1962, RCA LPM10307), Sidney Bechet, Billy Byers, Jay Cameron, Blossom Dearie, the pianist Jack Dieval, Stephane Grappelli, Lionel Hampton, Bobby Jaspar, Jonah Jones, Helen Merrill, Jack Pelzer, André Persiany, Jack Sels, Zoot Sims, Martial Solal, René Thomas, Lucky Thompson, René Urtreger, and Maurice Vander.

ROBERT PERNET

Quíca. *See* CUÍCA.

Quicksell, Howdy [Howard] (*b*1901; *d* Pontiac, MI, 30 Oct 1953). Banjoist. From 1922 to 1927 he was a member of Jean Goldkette's orchestra (for illustration *see* BEIDERBECKE, BIX), though he also recorded with Bix Beiderbecke (1925) and Frankie Trumbauer. The former made a recording of *Sorry* (1927, OK 41001), which Quicksell composed and arranged. He ceased to work as a musician in the 1930s.

BIBLIOGRAPHY

O. G. Dwight: "Bix's Pal Howdy," *Des Moines Register and Tribune* (24 April 1952); repr. in *SL*, vii/9–10 (1956), 1

R. M. Sudhalter, P. R. Evans, and W. Dean-Myatt: *Bix: Man & Legend* (New Rochelle, NY, and London, 1974)

based on *ChiltonW*

Quill, Gene [Daniel Eugene] (*b* Atlantic City, NJ, 15 Dec 1927). Alto saxophonist and clarinetist. He started playing saxophone as a child and began working professionally at the age of 13. For many years his activities centered on big bands; in the 1950s and early 1960s he performed and recorded in the dance and jazz bands of Buddy DeFranco, Claude Thornhill, Gene Krupa, Quincy Jones, Johnny Richards, Manny Albam, Johnny Carisi, Bill Potts, Gerry Mulligan (1960–62), and others. He also played in the small groups of Mundell Lowe and Jimmy Knepper, and led his own ensembles. He is best known for his association with Phil Woods in the late 1950s. He later worked as a session musician, but his career was cut short in the late 1970s by partial paralysis following brain damage.

In the 1950s Quill was among the best of Charlie Parker's imitators, but in the following decade, influenced perhaps by Lee Konitz or Paul Desmond, he tempered his fluent style with a mellower tone quality and more relaxed rhythms.

SELECTED RECORDINGS

As leader: *Jazzville '56* (1955, Dawn 1101); *Three Bones and a Quill* (1958, Roost 2229)

As sideman with P. Woods: *Pairing Off* (1956, Prst. 7046); *Phil Talks with Quill* (1957, Epic 3521)

BIBLIOGRAPHY

FeatherE; *Feather '60s*

I. Gitler: Liner notes, *Pairing Off* (Prst. 7046, 1957)

M. Goode: Liner notes, *Phil Talks with Quill* (Odyssey PC36806, 1980)

THOMAS OWENS

Quinichette, Paul (*b* Denver, 17 May 1916; *d* New York, 25 May 1983). Tenor saxophonist. He was taught clarinet and alto saxophone as a child, but later changed to tenor saxophone.

He played with local bands, then toured with Nat Towles and the trumpeter Lloyd Hunter, and in the late 1930s worked with Shorty Sherock. In the early 1940s he played with Ernie Fields (1942), Jay McShann (1942–3), the rhythm-and-blues drummer Johnny Otis, Benny Carter, and Sid Catlett. He moved to New York in the late 1940s and performed there with several musicians, including Louis Jordan, Lucky Millinder, J. C. Heard, Henry "Red" Allen, Eddie Wilcox, Dinah Washington, and Hot Lips Page. At the time of his association with Count Basie (1951–3) Quinichette was nicknamed the Vice Pres because his playing was very similar to that of Lester Young. With the success of some recordings made under his own name he left Basie to lead his own groups; he also played with Benny Goodman and Nat Pierce (both 1955), John Coltrane (1957), and Billie Holiday. In the 1960s he worked as an electrical engineer, and although he performed again in the 1970s his activities were restricted by ill-health. Quinichette's style displayed a sense of swing unequaled among those musicians who followed Young.

SELECTED RECORDINGS

As leader: *The Vice Pres* (1952–3, EmA 26022); with J. Coltrane: *Cattin' with John Coltrane and Paul Quinichette* (1957, Prst. 7158); *For Basie* (1957, Prst. 7127)

As sideman: D. Washington: Cold, Cold Heart (1951, Mer. 5728); New Blowtop Blues (1951, Mer. 8269); C. Basie: New Basie Blues/Sure Thing (1952, Clef 8964)

BIBLIOGRAPHY

ChiltonW

Len: "'More like Pres than Pres himself': Meet Mr. Quinichette," *DB*, xix/18 (1952), 7

B. Rusch: "Paul Quinichette, Jazz Master," *Cadence*, i/4 (1976), 3

S. Dance: *The World of Count Basie* (New York and London, 1980) [colln of previously pubd interviews], 298

EDDIE LAMBERT

Quintette du Hot Club de France. French quintet. It was formed in Paris in 1934 in connection with the HOT CLUB DE FRANCE, founded two years earlier. It grew out of informal sessions in which the guitarists Django Reinhardt and Roger Chaput, the violinist Stephane Grappelli, and the double bass player Louis Vola, all members of Vola's band, played together backstage during breaks in their performances at the Hôtel Claridge. After a third guitarist, Joseph Reinhardt, was added, the quintet gave its first concert at the Ecole Normale de Musique on 2 December 1934. Soon afterwards it made its first recordings, which were highly acclaimed: the public was immediately drawn by the unfamiliar style of the music, and by the mixture of seductiveness and exuberance that Grappelli and Django Reinhardt brought to the group's playing. Between 1934 and 1939 Chaput was replaced successively by Pierre Ferret, Marcel Bianchi, and Eugene Vees, and Vola's place was taken by Lucien Simoens, Roger Grasset, and Emmanuel Soudieux. The group performed widely in the late 1930s and soon became established as a major force in French jazz. Grappelli moved to England during World War II and was replaced by the clarinetist Hubert Rostaing; at the same time the drummer Pierre Fouad was substituted for the third guitarist. On Grappelli's return to France in 1946 the group was re-formed with its original members, but it disbanded in 1949. The original quintet recorded almost 200 titles, which continue to fascinate listeners by Grappelli's weaving of delicate traceries around the improvised guitar lines of great genius produced by Reinhardt.

See also STRING BAND; for illustrations *see* GUITAR, fig.1, and JAZZ (i), fig.4.

SELECTED RECORDINGS

Dinah (1934, Ultraphone 1422); Djangology (1935, Ultraphone 1548); Sweet Chorus (1936, HMV K7843); Minor Swing (1937, Swing 23); My Sweet (1938, Decca F6769); Hungaria (1939, Decca F7198); Swing 39 (1939, Decca F7027); Echoes of France (1946, Swing 229)

BIBLIOGRAPHY

C. Delaunay: *Django Reinhardt: souvenirs* (Paris, 1954; Eng. trans., London, 1961/*R*1981, 1982, rev. 2/1981)

——: *Django, mon frère* (Paris, 1968)

ANDRÉ CLERGEAT

R

Rabbit (i). Nickname of GEORGE HUNT.

Rabbit (ii). Nickname of JOHNNY HODGES.

Race, Steve [Stephen Russell] (*b* Lincoln, England, 1 April 1921). English pianist and broadcaster. After studying at the Royal Academy of Music, London, he worked as an arranger for Ted Heath in the early 1940s and recorded with his own bop group in 1949. During the early 1950s he worked as a freelance and began to develop a reputation as a propagandist for jazz. From 1955 to 1960 he was the adviser on light music to the television company Associated–Rediffusion; later he presented the BBC radio program "Jazz Record Requests." His abilities as a pianist and arranger may be heard on the album *Take One* (World Record Club 453), which he recorded with a big band in 1965.

BIBLIOGRAPHY

FeatherE
S. Race: *Musician at Large: an Autobiography* (London, 1979)
J. Godbolt: *A History of Jazz in Britain, 1919–50* (London, Melbourne, Australia, and New York, 1984)

MARK GILBERT

Race record. A term applied between 1921 and 1942 to phonograph recordings made especially for black listeners. It was coined by Ralph Peer of Okeh, the first company to have a "race series"; he adapted the generic term "the Race," which was employed at that time in the black press. Okeh commenced its 8000 series in 1921; other race series included, from 1922, the Paramount 12000s; from 1923, Columbia's 14000s; from 1926, Vocalion's 1000s; and from 1927, the Victor 21000s and 38000s (among others). Many smaller companies had race series and by 1927 some 500 race records were being issued each year. Sales declined with the Depression and many concerns closed. But in 1933 Victor's Bluebird subsidiary commenced issuing race records to compete with the issues of the American Record Corporation labels, and the English Decca company started its successful American Decca 7000 race series in 1934.

Although a number of instrumental jazz recordings were issued in the race series, jazz titles were often circulated on general lists that did not differentiate between black and white performers. The appeal of jazz was broader than that of blues or gospel, and the large number of white jazz bands made any distinction on grounds of color invalid. While instrumental jazz recordings were, and are, often loosely categorized in the race series proper as race records, vocal recordings predominated. Between 1921 and 1925 these were mainly by professional "classic" blues singers and spiritual and gospel quartets. Self-accompanied blues singers became popular in 1926, and field trips to record new talent in the South were undertaken by several companies. Recordings by preachers, either as soloists or accompanied by their congregations (and sometimes musicians), sold well, but were less popular after 1930. By that time performances by "classic" blues singers and vocal duets were also losing their popularity, but quartets became increasingly sophisticated, and small groups accompanied blues singers to boost sales of their recordings in the 1930s.

After World War II the term "race records" was dropped and "rhythm-and-blues" used in its stead, until the latter assumed a more specific stylistic meaning. To collectors, "race record" is applied generally to 78 r.p.m. discs intended for the black market; with their increasing rarity many such records are much prized.

See also RECORDING, §II, 2.

BIBLIOGRAPHY

D. Mahony: *The Columbia 13/14000-D Series* (Stanhope, NJ, 1961)
R. C. Foreman, Jr.: *Jazz and Race Records, 1920–1932: their Origins and their Significance for the Record Industry and Society* (diss., U. of Illinois, 1968)
R. M. W. Dixon and J. Godrich: *Recording the Blues* (London, 1970)
M. E. Vreede: *Paramount 12/13000* (London, 1971)
P. Oliver: *Songsters and Saints: Vocal Traditions on Race Records* (Cambridge, England, and elsewhere, 1984)

PAUL OLIVER

Rader, Don(ald Arthur) (*b* Rochester, PA, 21 Oct 1935). Trumpeter, teacher, arranger, and composer. He began playing at the age of five, studying with his father. He played with Woody Herman (1959–61), Maynard Ferguson (1961–3), and Count Basie (1963–4) and wrote arrangements for all three bands. He also performed with Louie Bellson, Harry James, Terry Gibbs (with whom he recorded in 1965), and Frank Foster's quintet. In the period 1967–72 he played with Les Brown on three world tours. As a member of Stan Kenton's band he appeared as a principal soloist in a special program on PBS television in 1969; he also taught in Kenton's jazz workshops (1968–70). In 1972 he formed his own quintet, with which he gave numerous concerts and classes throughout the country; he also worked as a freelance musician in and around Los Angeles. Rader has been active in the field of jazz education, performing and adjudicating at many college jazz festivals; he has written a number of articles for the *Jazz Educators Journal*. His compositions include *Polluted Tears*, which he recorded with his own band.

SELECTED RECORDINGS

As leader: *Polluted Tears* (1972, DRM 3236); *Wallflower* (1978, Dis. 796)
As sideman: M. Ferguson: *Maynard '62* (1962, Roul. 52083); E. Fitzgerald: *Ella and Basie* (1963, Verve 64061); W. Herman: *Woody's Winners* (1965, Col. CS9236); T. Gibbs: *Terry Gibbs Quartet* (1965, Dot 3683); D. Menza: *Burnin'* (1980, RT 301)

SELECTED ARRANGEMENTS

* – with Rader as sideman

Recorded by M. Ferguson: *Sin Blues, on *Maynard '63* (1963, Roul. 52090)
Recorded by W. Herman: Greasy Sack Blues, *My Funny Valentine, *Poor Butterfly, on *Woody's Winners* (1965, Col. CS9236)

BIBLIOGRAPHY

Feather '60s; *Feather–Gitler '70s*

FREDERICK A. BECK

Radiobandet. Group led from 1956 to 1965 by HARRY ARNOLD.

Radioens Big Band [Danish Radio Big Band]. Danish big band. Formed in 1964 in affiliation with Danmarks radio, it was known during its first three years as the Ny Radiodanseorkester and led during this period by Ib Glindemann, who was influenced chiefly by Stan Kenton. From 1968 its repertory was more diverse, and several European and American musicians worked with the band as guest soloists and leaders; among the band's full-time leaders were the saxophonist Ray Pitts, Palle Mikkelborg, Ole Kock Hansen, and from 1977 to 1978 Thad Jones, who may be heard leading the band on the album *By Jones, I Think we've Got it* (1978, Met. 15629), recorded in concert. The band continued to perform into the 1980s. ("Reaching other Parts: the Danish Radio Big Band," *CI*, xxiv/2 (1987), 6)

ERIK WIEDEMANN

Radiojazzgruppen [Danish Radio Jazz Group] **(i).** Danish big band. It was formed in 1961 as a nine-piece workshop group and later acquired additional members. The group was led from its inception by Erik Moseholm (who may be heard as its leader on the album *The Radio Jazz Group*, 1965, Debut 1145), then by the saxophonist Ray Pitts (1966–7) and Palle Mikkelborg (1967–72), under whose direction it was known by the name Opportunity. In 1973 the group reverted to its original name and from this time had several leaders, including the trumpeter Lars Togeby, under whom it also performed as the Crème Fraîche Big Band in the 1970s. After a period of relative inactivity the group was formally disbanded in 1986. Most members of the Radioens Big Band played first in the Radiojazzgruppen, which was less closely associated with Danmarks radio and had a more adventurous programming policy.

ERIK WIEDEMANN

Radiojazzgruppen [Swedish Radio Jazz Group] **(ii).** Swedish group. Formed in 1967 as a studio ensemble, its leaders have been Arne Domnérus (1967–78) and Lennart Åberg (from 1978); its regular members have included Jan Johansson, Bengt Hallberg, and Georg Riedel. The group has performed works by George Russell, Carla Bley, Anthony Braxton, Gil Evans, Thad Jones, and several Swedish jazz composers, and made about 15 recordings of compositions by Russell (1977), Jones (*Greetings and Salutations*, 1975, Four Leaf Clover 5001), and others. After a reorganization in the early 1980s the group comprised a smaller number of permanent members whose ranks were supplemented by visiting soloists.

PEKKA GRONOW

Rae, Johnny [John; Pompeo, John Anthony] (*b* Boston, 11 Aug 1934). Drummer, vibraphonist, and percussionist. He studied piano at the New England Conservatory, timpani at the Boston

Boyd Raeburn's band at the Virginia Polytechnic Institute, Blacksburg, Virginia, 12 April 1947: (back row, left to right) Ray Rossi (piano), Joe Burriece (double bass), Irv Kluger (drums), Wes Hensel, Pete Candoli, Bernie Glow, and Gordon Boswell (trumpets); (middle row, left to right) Steve Jordan (guitar), Leon Cox, Dick Noel, and Hal Smith (trombones); (front row, left to right) Jay Johnson and Ginnie Powell (voice), Lloyd Otto and Vince DeMino (french horns), Sam Spumberg (clarinet), Shirley Thompson (tenor saxophone), Raeburn (bass saxophone), Buddy DeFranco (clarinet), Jerry Sanfino (alto saxophone), Frank Socolow (tenor saxophone), and Hy Mandel (baritone saxophone)

Conservatory, and drums at Berklee College. After performing in Boston with such leaders as the pianist Al Vega (1953), Herb Pomeroy (1953–4), and Jay Migliori (1954) he moved to New York (1955), where he worked as a vibraphonist with George Shearing (1955–6), Johnny Smith (1956–7), Ralph Sharon (1957), Cozy Cole (1956), Herbie Mann (1959–60, with whom he toured Africa in 1960), and Peter Appleyard (1960–1). He played drums with Cal Tjader in San Francisco for five years from 1961, during which time he also recorded with Stan Getz (1962). Rae led his own group in Aspen, Colorado, then worked with Gábor Szabó, first as a drummer and later as a vibraphonist, and performed and recorded with Vince Guaraldi. During his second association with Tjader (1968–70) he worked as a freelance with Guaraldi, Herb Ellis, and Joe Pass. From 1973 to 1975 he played with Charlie Byrd and was a member of Great Guitars, and thereafter he began performing in show bands and concentrated on playing Latin jazz. He has written two books, *Jazz Phrasing for Mallets, Vibes, Marimba, Xylophone* (New York, 1961) and *Latin Guide for Jazz Drummers* (late 1960s).

SELECTED RECORDINGS

As leader: *Opus de jazz*, ii (1960, Savoy 12156); *Afro-Jazz Septet* (1961–2, UA 4042)

As sideman: G. Shearing: *The Shearing Spell* (1955, Cap. T648); C. Tjader: *Cal Tjader Plugs In* (1969, Skye 10); Great Guitars (C. Byrd, H. Ellis, and B. Kessel): *Three Guitars* (1974, Conc. 4)

BIBLIOGRAPHY

FeatherE; *Feather '60s*; *Feather–Gitler '70s*

C. M. Bernstein: "John Rae: Total Musicality," *MD*, ix/3 (1985), 25

RICK MATTINGLY

Raeburn [Raden], **Boyd(e Albert)** (*b* Faith, SD, 27 Oct 1913; *d* Lafayette, LA, 2 Aug 1966). Bandleader and tenor and bass saxophonist. He led various types of commercial dance band from 1933 but is most important for his jazz groups of 1944–8, which played advanced arrangements influenced by both bop and European concert music. Raeburn's bands included at various times major bop musicians, among them Dizzy Gillespie, Little Benny Harris, Sonny Berman, Don Lamond, and Buddy DeFranco. Initially a tenor saxophonist, Raeburn began to play baritone saxophone in 1945, then from 1946 concentrated on the bass instrument. His arrangements were commissioned from important modernists of the day, including Gillespie, Johnny Mandel, and George Handy. The music was characterized by harmonic ideas drawn from the French impressionist composers and, especially, Stravinsky (*see* PROGRESSIVE JAZZ). Although Raeburn's bands were greatly admired by musicians, the music puzzled ordinary dance-band enthusiasts. By 1950 Raeburn had returned to more commercial styles and finally left music altogether.

SELECTED RECORDINGS

Night in Tunisia (1945, Guild 107); March of the Boyds (1945, Guild 111); Tonsillectomy (1945, Jwl 10000); Yerxa (1945, Jwl 10001); Boyd Meets Stravinsky (1946, Jwl 10002)

BIBLIOGRAPHY

G. Hoefer: "Boyd Raeburn," *DB*, xxix/9 (1962), 24

A. Jackson: "Boyd Raeburn: 'the Successful Failure'," *JM*, xii/9 (1966), 5

G. Hall: *Boyd Raeburn and his Orchestra: a Complete Discography* (Laurel, MD, 1972)

S. Woolley: "The Forgotten Ones: Boyd Raeburn," *JJI*, xxxvii/2 (1984), 18

C. Garrod and B. Korst: *Boyd Raeburn and his Orchestra plus Johnny Bothwell and George Handy* (n.p. [Zephyrhills, FL], 1985) [discography]

JAMES LINCOLN COLLIER

Ragas, Henry (W.) (*b* New Orleans, 1891; *d* New York, 18 Feb 1919). Pianist. After working as a solo pianist from 1910 to 1913, he joined Johnny Stein's band and moved with it to Chicago in 1916. A few months later Ragas, Nick LaRocca, and Eddie Edwards left Stein to form the Original Dixieland Jass Band; in 1917 it began playing at Reisenweber's Restaurant in New York and made the first recordings of jazz (*see* ORIGINAL DIXIELAND JAZZ BAND). Ragas composed *Bluin' the Blues*, which was recorded by the band in 1918 (Vic. 18483).

BIBLIOGRAPHY

"Henry Ragas," *SL*, vi/9–10 (1955), 29

H. O. Brunn: *The Story of the Original Dixieland Jazz Band* (Baton Rouge, LA, 1960/*R*1977)

MIKE HAZELDINE

Raglin, Junior [Alvin Redrick] (*b* Omaha, NE, 16 March 1917; *d* Boston, 10 Nov 1955). Double bass player. From 1938 to 1941 he played with Eugene Coy's Happy Black Aces, a territory band based in Amarillo, Texas. In Los Angeles he deputized for Jimmy Blanton in Duke Ellington's orchestra and became a full-time member of the band in 1941 when Blanton became seriously ill; he remained with the band until 1945. Blanton's influence had caused Ellington to expand the role of the double bass in his arrangements to include demanding ensemble parts and solo passages, with which Raglin coped admirably; his playing is particularly prominent on *Emancipation Celebration* from the suite *Black, Brown and Beige* (1943) and *Carnegie Blues* (1945). He also worked with Ray Nance's quartet (1943–4), and recorded with Edmond Hall (1944), Rex Stewart (1945), Ella Fitzgerald (1946), and Al Hibbler (1947). In 1946 he won the "new star" award from *Down Beat* and re-joined Ellington, but he left the band again the following year and thereafter fell into obscurity.

SELECTED RECORDINGS

As sideman with D. Ellington: *Carnegie Hall Concert*, (1943, Jazz Panorama 1), incl. Emancipation Celebration; Carnegie Blues (1945, Vic. 201644); Diminuendo and Crescendo in Blue (1945, V-disc 534)

As sideman with others: E. Hall: Big City Blues (1944, BN 36); R. Stewart: Dutch Treat/Rexercise (1945, Cap. 10035); E. Fitzgerald: I'm a Lucky So and So (1946, Decca 18814)

BIBLIOGRAPHY

ChiltonW

Obituary, *DB*, xxiii/1 (1956), 9

C. Carrière: "Pitter Panther Patter: les bassistes de Duke Ellington," *Jh*, no.316 (1975), 10

JOHN CURRY

Ragtime. A style of American popular music that flourished from about 1890 to World War I.

1. Definition and origins. 2. Piano ragtime. 3. Band and orchestral ragtime.

1. DEFINITION AND ORIGINS. The term "ragged time" came to be used in the late 19th century to describe the idiomatic syncopation characteristic of a style of popular music, predominantly for the piano, that emanated from the South and Midwest. The word "ragtime" was a corruption of this; the practice of syncopation was described as "ragging," and typical pieces, in which an internally syncopated melodic line was set against a rhythmically straightforward bass, as "rags." Although ragtime was primarily a written genre, ragtime tunes and performance practices were influential in shaping the direction of solo and collective improvisation in early jazz. In the early decades of the 20th century the term "ragtime" was used synonymously with "jazz" by many performers, particularly in New Orleans (*see* NEW ORLEANS JAZZ), and, even later, jazz musicians referred to the characteristic syncopation of a melody as "ragging a tune." Whereas it began as a style for solo piano, ragtime subsequently encompassed popular songs, and, towards

the end of the era, broadened to include band and orchestral repertory.

2. Piano ragtime. During the 1890s itinerant black pianists such as Scott Joplin, Tom Turpin, James Scott, and Artie Matthews composed and notated works that formalized practices hitherto improvisatory and irregular. Early published rags resembled cakewalks but adopted the work "rag" in their titles – for example, William H. Krell's *Mississippi Rag* (1897). In 1899 Joplin's *Original Rags* and *Maple Leaf Rag* appeared, the latter achieving nationwide success.

Piano ragtime as conceived by midwestern pianist-composers was a multithematic form with three or four discrete 16-bar strains (*see* Forms, esp. §1(d)). The music was melodically inventive and rhythmically lively, built on a bright, steady duple pulse and making use of strong tonal progressions. The multithematic structure of ragtime compositions became incorporated into many early jazz pieces, both for solo piano and for ensemble, but while in ragtime performances the themes were repeated literally as written, in jazz improvised variations were introduced. Solo pianists began to make use of more sophisticated rhythms, and, in particular, introduced syncopation in the duple subdivision of the beats in the left hand.

As the term "ragtime" came to be applied indiscriminately to many forms of popular music, and indeed to the age itself, availability of piano scores and player-piano rolls disseminated the music widely to middle-class Americans, and as the repertory expanded, so too did the variety of more jazz-oriented performance styles associated with it. "Novelty" piano pieces and rags less identifiable as "classic," such as Charles Johnson's *Dill Pickles Rag* (1906), George Botsford's *Black and White Rag* (1908), Adeline Shepherd's *Pickles and Peppers* (1908), and Henry Lodge's *Temptation Rag* (1909), were widely performed by parlor pianists. Meanwhile the more jazz-oriented aspects of ragtime were incorporated in the compositions of Eubie Blake and Jelly Roll Morton. Ragtime subsequently formed the basis of the stride piano style (*see* Piano, §2), whose exponents possessed a consummate technical command of the keyboard, made more extensive use of improvisation, and employed a much broader range of expressive devices. Composers such as James P. Johnson, Fats Waller, Willie "the Lion" Smith, and Luckey Roberts used the multithematic forms of ragtime as the foundation for their works.

From the late 1940s there has been a revival of piano ragtime. Performers such as Max Morath and Ralph Sutton have integrated elements of stride piano with the purer ragtime style, whilst the musicologist Joshua Rifkin has endeavored, in his recordings and concert appearances, to preserve a relatively unsyncopated form of the music, adhering more closely to the notated scores.

3. Band and orchestral ragtime. From the late 1890s, when the first ragtime pieces were published, arrangements of the more popular pieces were made available for dance or theater orchestras, whose instrumentation predated that of the earliest jazz bands. Accompanying or rhythmic parts were taken by piano, guitar, double bass, and drums, and the melodic parts were assigned to one or two violins, one or two cornets or trumpets, flute, clarinet, trombone, and cello. Composers added tonal color to the repetition of each strain of the music by making use of alternate combinations of strings, brass, or woodwind. An early collection of orchestral pieces for such forces, *The Red Back Book of Rags* (*c*1915), which consisted principally of works by Joplin (notably *Maple Leaf Rag* and the more accomplished *Sugar Cane Rag*), set the standard for orchestration, although string bands and spasm bands in New Orleans and elsewhere in the South performed ragtime tunes on a variety of instruments, usually including mandolins and guitars. The multithematic element of most of the compositions in *The Red Back Book* also influenced early jazz, and pieces such as *High Society* and W. H. Tyer's *Panama* were adopted as staple items in the jazz repertory. Ragtime was later transcribed for the large concert bands of John Philip Sousa and Arthur Pryor, but the instrumentation of earlier arrangements was preserved by the society orchestras of New Orleans, such as that led by A. J. Piron, that flourished in the early 1920s.

In the late 1940s some musicians, notably Tony Parenti's Ragtimers and Mutt Carey's New Yorkers (both 1947), attempted to re-create the sound of early ragtime orchestras. Perhaps the most influential recordings of the period, however, have been those collectively issued as *The Last Testament of Bunk Johnson* (1947, Col. GL520), on which the New Orleans trumpeter plays with a group of New York session musicians. Later ensembles dedicated to the music have included the Love–Jiles Ragtime Orchestra of New Orleans, which endeavored to reproduce the orchestral sound of works from *The Red Back Book*, and the more formal New Orleans Ragtime Orchestra and the New England Conservatory group led by Gunther Schuller. Schuller attempts, in his arrangements of compositions from *The Red Back Book*, to convey in notated form some of the likely variety of tone color and texture of the early performances.

BIBLIOGRAPHY

R. Blesh and H. Janis: *They all Played Ragtime* (New York, 1950, rev. 4/1971)
R. J. Carew: "Reminiscing in Ragtime," *JJ*, xvii/11 (1964), 8
D. A. Jasen: "Ragtime: a Re-evaluation," *JJ*, xxi/4 (1968), 22
G. Schuller: *Early Jazz: its Roots and Musical Development* (New York, 1968)
B. Rust: "Ragtime on Records," *Sv*, no.27 (1970), 110
D. Flowitt: "Ragtime in Retrospect," *Sv*, no.36 (1971), 203
D. A. Jasen: "Ragtime Explained," *Sv*, no.37 (1971), 4
——: *Recorded Ragtime, 1897–1958* (Hamden, CT, 1973) [incl. 78 r.p.m. recordings of jazz versions of ragtime pieces]
W. J. Schafer and J. Riedel: *The Art of Ragtime* (Baton Rouge, LA, 1973)
T. Waldo: *This is Ragtime* (New York, 1976) [incl. discography]
D. A. Jasen and T. J. Tichenor: *Rags and Ragtime: a Musical History* (New York, 1978)
E. A. Berlin: *Ragtime: a Musical and Cultural History* (Berkeley, CA, Los Angeles, and London, 1980/*R*1984 with addns)
E. S. Walker: "The Spread of Ragtime in England," *Sv*, no.88 (1980), 123
J. E. Hasse, ed.: *Ragtime: its History, Composers, and Music* (New York and London, 1985)
R. E. Lotz: *German Ragtime and the Prehistory of Jazz*, i: *The Sound Documents* (Chigwell, England, 1985)

WILLIAM J. SCHAFER

Ragtime Reinhold. Name used for recording purposes by Reinhold Svensson.

Rainey, Chuck [Charles W., III] (*b* Youngstown, OH, 17 June 1940). Electric bass guitarist. As a youth he studied violin, piano, and trumpet. At the age of 21 he moved to Cleveland, where he played electric guitar and electric bass guitar with rhythm-and-blues groups. Later he joined King Curtis's group in New York (1964). From this time he took part in hundreds of recording sessions with soul, pop, and jazz musicians, including Jerome Richardson (1967), Grady Tate (1968), and Mose Allison, Gato Barbieri, and Gene Ammons (all 1971). He also performed with Eddie "Cleanhead" Vinson at the Montreux International Jazz Festival (1971) and toured and recorded with the soul singer Aretha Franklin. After moving to Los Angeles he performed with the Crusaders (1972–3) and Hampton Hawes (1974–5), and recorded with Donald Byrd (1973–

5), Sonny Rollins (1975), and John Handy (1976). Later he recorded with Hiroshi Fukumura in Japan (1978). Rainey's versatility and professionalism are highly regarded by critics and musicians alike.

SELECTED RECORDINGS

The Chuck Rainey Coalition (c1971, Cob. 9008); *Born Again* (1981, Hammer n' Nails 1949)

BIBLIOGRAPHY

M. Cuscuna: "Dreams," *J&P*, x/3 (1971), 32
M. Cullaz: "Chuck Rainey et Cornell Dupree," *Jh*, no.293 (1973), 12
R. Williams: "King Bass," *MM* (3 Feb 1973), 37

BILL MILKOWSKI

Rainey, Ma [Pridgett, Gertrude] (*b* Columbus, GA, 26 April 1886; *d* Rome, GA, 22 Dec 1939). Singer. Her career began in a talent show in Columbus when she was 12, and soon afterwards she appeared as a cabaret singer. She married Will "Pa" Rainey in 1904, and toured with him in F. S. Wolcott's Rabbit Foot Minstrels and other shows until 1916, when they formed their own company. By the time she first recorded (1923) she had become famous throughout the South. In five years she made more than 100 recordings. These did little justice to her vocal powers, but a majestic phrasing and "moaning" style close to folk tradition are evident from two of her first titles (and most celebrated compositions), *Bo-weavil Blues* and *Moonshine Blues*. She also recorded with Louis Armstrong and with her Georgia Jazz Band, which at various times included Tommy Ladnier, Joe Smith, and Coleman Hawkins. Although she recorded under the name of Ma Rainey, she was known as "Madame" on tour with the Georgia Jazz Band during the 1920s, when she played to large audiences throughout the South and in Mexico and established a lasting reputation as the most significant early female blues singer (for illustration *see* BLUES, fig.1). Her rumbustious disposition is rarely evident in her recordings, and *Ma Rainey's Black Bottom* is one of the few to demonstrate her humor. In the early 1930s Rainey was still touring, sometimes as a featured entertainer. Her attempts to recapture her popularity were unsuccessful, however, and in 1935 she retired to Columbus, where she was active in the Baptist church.

SELECTED RECORDINGS
(all recorded for Paramount)

Bo-weavil Blues (1923, 12080); Moonshine Blues (1923, 12083); See See Rider (1924, 12252); Jelly Bean Blues (1924, 12238); Yonder come the blues (1926, 12357); Soon this morning (1927, 12438); Ma Rainey's Black Bottom (1927, 12590)

BIBLIOGRAPHY

D. Stewart-Baxter: *Ma Rainey and the Classic Blues Singers* (New York and London, 1970)
S. Harris: *Blues Who's Who: a Biographical Dictionary of Blues Singers* (New Rochelle, NY, 1979)
S. R. Lieb: *Mother of the Blues: a Study of Ma Rainey* (Amherst, MA, 1981) [incl. discography]

PAUL OLIVER

Ramblers. Dutch big band, formed in September 1926 by Theo Uden Masman. It achieved great popularity in the Netherlands with a repertory of jazz, popular tunes, and nonsense songs and acquired an international following after recording with Coleman Hawkins (1935, 1937), Benny Carter (1937), and Freddy Johnson (1937–8); it was sometimes known as the Ramblers Dance Orchestra. The group continued to be led by Masman until 1964, when it changed its name to the VARA Dance Orchestra (after the Verenigde Arbeiders Radio, on which it played) and its repertory to one consisting entirely of popular music. In the mid-1980s it was led by Marcel Thielemans, who had played trombone under Masman. Among the Ramblers' representative recordings are *The Ramblers, 1936–1940* (1936–40, Panachord 2002) and *Zuiderzee Blues* (1938–9, Panachord 2013). (J. Bulterman: *The Ramblers Story*, Bussum, Netherlands, 1973)

WIM VAN EYLE

Ramey, Gene [Eugene Glasco] (*b* Austin, TX, 4 April 1913; *d* Austin, 8 Dec 1984). Double bass player. After performing on trumpet in his college band he took up sousaphone, which he played professionally for some years. He moved to Kansas City in 1932 and changed to double bass, taking lessons from Walter Page. In the early 1930s he led his own band and performed with other local groups. From 1938 to 1943 he worked with Jay McShann. When the latter joined the army Ramey traveled to New York, where he worked as a freelance with many of the most important musicians, including Ben Webster, Coleman Hawkins, Charlie Parker, Eddie "Lockjaw" Davis, Miles Davis, and Lester Young. In 1954 he played with Art Blakey. Thereafter he continued to perform and record extensively on a freelance basis with Buck Clayton (including tours of Europe, 1959, 1961), Muggsy Spanier (1962), and Teddy Wilson (1963), as well as playing on occasions with McShann (1969, 1979). He returned to Texas in 1976 and continued to work regularly into the early 1980s. Ramey's playing was indebted to Page and the rhythmic propulsiveness of the Kansas City style.

Oral history material in *MoKmh* and *NjR* (JOHP).

SELECTED RECORDINGS

As sideman: J. McShann: Swingmatism (1941, Decca 8570); Red River Blues (1941, Decca 8595); C. Basie: *The Count Basie Sextet* (1952, Clef 146); L. Young: *Pres and Teddy* (1956, Verve 8205)

BIBLIOGRAPHY

ChiltonW
G. Reisner: *Bird: the Legend of Charlie Parker* (New York, 1962/R1975)
A. Hope: "You Can Bank on Gene," *MM* (6 May 1972), 50
R. Morris: "Kansas City Man on Bass," *MR*, iii/10 (1976), 1
S. Dance: *The World of Count Basie* (New York and London, 1980) [colln of previously pubd interviews]

Ramirez, Ram [Roger] (*b* Puerto Rico, 15 Sept 1913). Pianist, organist, and composer. He grew up in New York and was a child prodigy as a pianist. At the age of 13 he joined the musicians' union, and his first engagements followed in the early 1930s with the Louisiana Stompers, an amateur band. He accompanied Monette Moore in 1933, and in the summer of that year performed with Rex Stewart and Sid Catlett at the Empire Ballroom in New York. In 1934 he joined the Spirits of Rhythm and early in 1935 became a member of Willie Bryant's band; he traveled to Europe with Bobby Martin in June 1937. After returning to the USA in 1940 he led his own groups in Asbury Park, New Jersey, then played with Ella Fitzgerald and Frankie Newton (1940–42), with Charlie Barnet (1942), again with Newton (1943), and for two years with John Kirby's sextet. He performed with Catlett at the Downbeat club in New York (1945) and from 1945 to 1953 worked as a freelance, both as a soloist and in a trio. While fulfilling an engagement at the Senator Hotel in Atlantic City, New Jersey (1953), he was inspired by the example of Wild Bill Davis to take up the electronic organ, which he played at several clubs in New York. He toured Europe with the blues singer and guitarist T-Bone Walker (1968) and in the summers of 1979 and 1980 played piano in the Harlem Blues and Jazz Band, with which he appeared at the 10th Anniversary Dixieland Festival in Dresden, Germany (the band was the first American ensemble to be invited to this event). Later he worked again as a freelance pianist and in 1987 rejoined the Harlem Blues and Jazz Band for a cruise of the Caribbean. As a pianist and organist Ramirez has an exceptional sense of time, swing, and melody. Among his compositions is the ballad *Lover Man*, which has become a jazz standard; the best-known of many recordings of the song is by Billie Holiday (1944, Decca 23391).

Oral history material in *NjR* (JOHP).

SELECTED RECORDINGS

As unaccompanied soloist: *Rampant Ram* (1973–4, MJR 8122)
As leader: *Lover Man* (1966–7, RCA LPM3616)
As sideman: R. Stewart: Stingaree/Baby, ain't you Satisfied? (1934, Voc. 2880); W. Bryant: Is it True what they Say about Dixie?/Moonrise on the Lowlands (1936, Bb 6362); B. Martin: Crazy Rhythm/Let's Dance (1938, Bruns. 81578); E. Fitzgerald: If it weren't for you/Sing Song Swing (1940, Decca 3126); Harlem Blues and Jazz Band: *Harlem Blues & Jazz, 1973–1980* (1973–80, Barron 403)

BIBLIOGRAPHY

ChiltonW
P. LaFargue: Liner notes, *Lover Man* (RCA PM42419, c1967)
S. Dance: *The World of Swing* (New York, 1974) [colln of previously pubd interviews], 325

ALBERT VOLLMER

Rampart. Record label. It was operated by Harry Crawford between 1948 and 1950. The catalogue included some of the first recordings by Bob Wilber and Dick Wellstood, and also contained American issues of material by European and Australian traditional-jazz bands. The records remained available until 1952. Crawford also managed another label, Mouldie Fygge (1947–9), dedicated to reissuing jazz of the 1920s. (D. Mahony: "The Mouldie Fygge and Rampart Labels," *Matrix*, no.40 (1962), 17)

Ramsey, (Charles) Fred(eric, Jr.) (*b* Pittsburgh, 29 Jan 1915). Writer and record producer. He attended Princeton University (BA 1936), then worked as an editor for the publisher Harcourt, Brace (1936–9) and a writer for the US Department of Agriculture (1941–2) and the Voice of America (from 1942); at the same time, with Charles Edward Smith, he edited the anthology *Jazzmen: the Story of Hot Jazz Told in the Lives of the Men who Created it* (1939), an influential early study of jazz that includes a moving account by Ramsey of King Oliver's career. In 1953 and 1955 he made visits to the South sponsored by Guggenheim fellowships, during which he made field recordings of musical performances and interviews; he later used these recordings to produce a series of commercial discs issued by Folkways, *Music from the South* (1954), and a television documentary of the same name (1957). For Folkways he also produced a series of recordings entitled *Jazz*, a historical anthology of recordings made in the 1920s and 1930s. His published writings include *Been Here and Gone* (1960), a treatment of traditional black music of the South that combines photographs and oral history. In 1970 Ramsey became a consultant on educational programs to the Institute of Jazz Studies, Rutgers, which in the same year published his book *Where the Music Started: a Photographic Essay*. Later he undertook research into the life and music of Buddy Bolden with grants from the National Endowment for the Humanities (1974–5) and the Ford Foundation (1975–6). In 1987 he presented a series of five interviews on early jazz entitled "Been Here and Gone" for National Public Radio.

WRITINGS
(selective list)

ed. with C. E. Smith: *Jazzmen: the Story of Hot Jazz Told in the Lives of the Men who Created it* (New York, 1939/*R*1977)
with C. E. Smith and others: *The Jazz Record Book* (New York, 1942/*R*1978) [listeners' guide with discography]
Chicago Documentary: Portrait of a Jazz Era (London, 1944)
A Guide to Longplay Jazz Records (New York, n.d. [1954]/*R*1977) [listeners' guide]
Been Here and Gone (New Brunswick, NJ, and London, 1960)
Where the Music Started: a Photographic Essay (New Brunswick, NJ, 1970)

DANIEL ZAGER

Rand, Odell (*b c*1905; *d* Chicago, 22 June 1960). Clarinetist. During the late 1930s he played E♭ clarinet on recordings by the Harlem Hamfats, including *It was Red/Jam Jamboree* (1937, Decca 7312). He also made recordings with the blues singer Big Bill Broonzy (notably *Just Wondering*, 1939, Voc. 05043). Thereafter he led his own band, the Ebonites, for many years, playing several residencies in Chicago. Rand later worked with Baby Dodds (1957) and Lil Armstrong (1959).

See also CLARINET, §2.

based on *ChiltonW*

Randall, Freddy [Frederick James] (*b* Buckhurst Hill [now in London], England, 6 May 1921). English trumpeter and cornetist. He played trumpet from 1937, formed the St. Louis Four (1939) and a dixieland band (1943), and from 1944 played traditional jazz with the Garbage Men, led by the drummer Freddy Mirfield. After performing on the radio series "BBC Jazz Club" and working again as a leader he performed as a guest soloist with such British musicians as Ted Heath, Henry Hall, Harry Parry, and Bert Ambrose, and such visitors from the USA as Pee Wee Russell, Wild Bill Davison, Bud Freeman, Teddy Wilson, Sidney Bechet, Bill Coleman, and Jimmy and Marian McPartland. He performed in New Orleans and toured the southern USA in 1956. Owing to a lung ailment he retired from music in 1958; he resumed playing part-time in 1963. In 1971 he recorded with the clarinetist Dave Shepherd, and from the following year belonged with Shepherd to Britain's Greatest Jazz Band, which became known as the Randall–Shepherd All Stars; it broadcast on radio and television and gave a successful performance at the Montreux Jazz Festival in 1973. Randall is a technically accomplished musician who is capable both of singing lyricism and of boisterous playing in the style of Bix Beiderbecke and Billy Butterfield.

SELECTED RECORDINGS

As leader: Hurry On Down/Cook's Ferry Parade (1948, Cleveland 5–6); That's a-plenty/Since my Best Gal Turned me Down (1951, Parl. R3382); I'm Coming Virginia/Professor Jazz (1953, Parl. R3709); with W. B. Davison: *Wild Bill Davison with Freddy Randall's Band* (1965, BL 30187), incl. Ghost of a Chance, Memories of you; with D. Shepherd: *"Live" at Montreux Jazz Festival* (1973, BL 214)
As sideman with F. Mirfield: Good Old Wagon Blues/Miss Annabelle Blues (1944, Decca F8526)

BIBLIOGRAPHY

FeatherE
B. Dawbarn: "Randall," *MM*, xxxi (14 April 1956), 3
——: "Of Course Trad isn't Dead!, Says Freddy Randall," *MM*, xxxviii (11 May 1963), 5
E. Lambert: "Wild Bill Davison with Freddy Randall's Band," *JJ*, xviii/3 (1965), 24
B. Turner: *Hot Air, Cool Music* (London, Melbourne, Australia, and New York, 1984)
G. Bielderman and R. Stansby: *Freddy Randall Discography* (Zwolle, Netherlands, and Hornchurch, England, 1987)
D. Fairweather: "Randall, Freddy," in I. Carr, D. Fairweather, and B. Priestley: *Jazz: the Essential Companion* (London, 1987)

KEN RATTENBURY

Randolph, Irving "Mouse" (*b* St. Louis, 22 Jan 1909). Trumpeter. He began playing in the bands of Walt Farrington (1923–4), Willie Austin (1925–6), Art Sims and Norman Mason (both 1926), Fate Marable (1927), Floyd Campbell (1927–8), Alphonso Trent (1928), and J. Frank Terry (1929–30). After working with Andy Kirk (1931–4) he performed in big bands under Fletcher Henderson, Benny Carter (both 1934), Luis Russell (1934–5), Cab Calloway (1935–9), Ella Fitzgerald (1939–42), and Don Redman (1943), recording as a soloist with all but Russell and Fitzgerald. From 1944 to 1947 he was a member of Edmond Hall's sextet, after which he played with Eddie Barefield (1950). During the 1950s he toured with Marcellino Guerra's Latin American Orchestra, and from 1958 into the 1970s he worked regularly with Chick Morrison in New York. Initially, Randolph's playing resembled that of Henry "Red" Allen, but he later settled into a simpler and more individual style: he had a big tone and his solo lines tended to follow the melody.

SELECTED RECORDINGS

As sideman: F. Henderson: Shanghai Shuffle (1934, Decca 158); B. Carter: Shoot the works (1934, Voc. 2898); C. Calloway: Are you in love with me again? (1936, Bruns. 7685); T. Wilson: Tea for Two (1936, Bruns. 7816)

BIBLIOGRAPHY

ChiltonW
J. Evensmo: *The Trumpets of Dizzy Gillespie, 1937–43, Irving Randolph, Joe Thomas* (n.p. [Oslo], n.d. [?1982]) [discography]

FRANK DRIGGS

Randolph, Zilner T(renton) (*b* Dermott, AR, 28 Jan 1899). Trumpeter and arranger. He played at clubs in St. Louis in the early 1920s and from 1927 to 1930 performed in Milwaukee with a band led by the trumpeter Bernie Young. After moving to Chicago in 1931 he worked with Louis Armstrong as a trumpeter and arranger, touring and recording with him intermittently until 1935; he arranged and played on *Swing you Cats* (1933, Bb 10225) and his composition *Old Man Mose* was recorded by Armstrong in 1935 (Decca 622). During this period he also worked with Carroll Dickerson (1934), and in 1936 he formed his own big band. In the late 1930s he was a staff arranger for Woody Herman and wrote arrangements for Earl Hines, Duke Ellington, Fletcher Henderson, and Blanche Calloway. During the 1940s he led his own quartet, taught, and played in a musical act with his children. He continued to teach into the 1970s.
Oral history material in *NjR* (JOHP).

BIBLIOGRAPHY

ChiltonW; *FeatherE*
P. Van Vorst: "Z. T. & Old Man Mose," *MR*, ii/6 (1975), 1
J. L. Collier: *Louis Armstrong: an American Genius* (New York, 1983, London, 1984, as *Louis Armstrong: a Biography*)

Raney, Doug (*b c*1957). Electric guitarist, son of Jimmy Raney. He made his first recording with his father and Al Haig (1975) and worked in a duo with his father from 1977. For Steeplechase he made recordings as a leader (1977–85, including *Lazy Bird*, 1985, 1200), as a leader and in a duo with his father (1979, 1983), and as a sideman with Horace Parlan (1978), Chet Baker (1979), and Bernt Rosengren (1983); he also recorded with his father for Criss Cross (1981) and as a leader for Criss Cross and Hot Club (1983). In the 1980s he lived in Copenhagen. (D. Morgenstern: Liner notes, *Stolen Moments*, Ste. 1118, 1979)

Raney, Jimmy [James Elbert] (*b* Louisville, KY, 20 Aug 1927). Guitarist, father of Doug Raney. His mother played guitar, and he studied with the guitarist Hayden Causey, whom he replaced in the band led by Jerry Wald. In 1944 he moved to Chicago, where he worked with Lou Levy. In 1948 he joined Woody Herman's orchestra and recorded with Stan Getz. After leaving Herman he played with Al Haig, Buddy DeFranco, Artie Shaw (1949–50), and Terry Gibbs, then joined Getz's quintet; he became internationally known for his playing on several of Getz's important albums (1951–3). He worked with Red Norvo (1953–4) and the trumpeter Les Elgart, and played for several years (1955–60) at the Blue Angel, New York, in a trio led by the pianist Jimmy Lyon. He re-joined Getz in 1962 but remained with him only until the following year; in the mid-1960s he was active in New York as a studio musician in radio and television. He returned to Louisville in 1968. He later played at clubs in New York (1972), gave a recital at Carnegie Hall with Al Haig (1974), and toured internationally with Haig and with his son Doug Raney, with whom he also recorded guitar duos. In the 1980s he performed and recorded as the leader of his own groups, which included his son.

Raney was first influenced by Charlie Christian, but adapted his style to accommodate elements of bop; his flawless technique enabled him successfully to transfer the bop vocabulary to the guitar. As a soloist he emphasized lines inspired by those of Lester Young. He compensated for the emotional coolness of his improvisations by employing long melodic lines, cleanly articulated. One of the true innovators on his instrument, Raney exercised a profound influence upon guitarists of the 1950s.

SELECTED RECORDINGS

Duos with D. Raney: *Duets* (1979, Ste. 1134)
As leader: *Jimmy Raney Quintet* (1955, Prst. 199); with A. Haig: *Special Brew* (1974, Spot. 8)
As sideman: S. Getz: *Jazz at Storyville* (1951, Roost 407, 411); R. Norvo: *Red Norvo Trio* (1953, Fan. 3-12)

BIBLIOGRAPHY

I. Gitler: "Jimmy Raney," *DB*, xxviii/15 (1961), 19
A. Morgan: "Jimmy Raney," *JM*, ix/8 (1963), 16
J. Gourley: "Jimmy Raney," *Jh*, no.283 (1972), 26
A. Berle: "Jimmy Raney: a Legend in Jazz Guitar," *GP*, xi/3 (1977), 29
L. Tomkins: "The Jimmy Raney Story," *CI*, xv/11 (1977), 14

NORMAN MONGAN

Ranger, Claude (*b* Montreal, 3 Feb 1941). Canadian drummer. He belonged to show bands in Montreal and played jazz with the saxophonist Lee Gagnon, the trumpeter Ron Proby, the pianist Pierre Leduc, and the saxophonist Brian Barley before moving to Toronto in 1972. There he worked as a sideman with Canadian musicians (including Sonny Greenwich, Moe Koffman, and Don Thompson) and with visiting Americans (including James Moody and Phil Woods); he also recorded with Greenwich, Thompson, and Lenny Breau. Though less active in the 1980s he did lead several small free-jazz ensembles (which included many important young Canadian sidemen), both in Toronto and in Vancouver, where he moved in 1987. Ranger's playing may be heard to advantage on the album *Dreams* (1975, PM 007), which he recorded in a quartet led by the keyboard player Doug Riley.
Oral history material in *CaQMG*.

BIBLIOGRAPHY

M. Miller: "Claude Ranger," *DB*, xxxxv/16 (1978), 48
——: "Ranger, Claude," *Encyclopedia of Music in Canada*, ed. H. Kallmann, G. Potvin, and K. Winters (Toronto, Buffalo, and London, 1981)
——: "Crazy," *Jazz in Canada: Fourteen Lives* (Toronto, Buffalo, and London, 1982), 166
——: "Claude Ranger," *Boogie, Pete & the Senator: Canadian Musicians in Jazz: the Eighties* (Toronto, 1987), 226

MARK MILLER

Rank, Bill [William C.] (*b* Lafayette, IN, 8 June 1904; *d* Cincinnati, 20 May 1979). Trombonist. He worked in Florida and Indiana, then played with Jean Goldkette's band in Detroit from 1923 to 1927; during this period he recorded frequently with his colleague Bix Beiderbecke. In 1927 he played with

Adrian Rollini and worked as a freelance before joining Paul Whiteman's band, with which he played until 1938; he may be heard to advantage on *Walkin' the Dog* (OK 41344), which he recorded with Eddie Lang and a group drawn from Whiteman's orchestra in 1929. After working as a studio musician in Hollywood in the late 1930s and early 1940s he moved to Cincinnati, where he led a ten-piece band through the decade. Although he ceased to play full-time he worked steadily until shortly before his death, performing (1968, 1969) and recording (1968) in Europe, playing with Gene Mayl (1971), recording as a leader in Vancouver (1973), and appearing at numerous jazz festivals. (L. Wright: "Bill Rank," *Sv*, no.19 (1968), 18; no.20 (1968–9), 44)

based on *ChiltonW*

Rappolo, Leon. Name by which LEON ROPPOLO has often (and incorrectly) been identified.

Rare Silk. Vocal group. It was formed in Boulder, Colorado, in 1979, and consists of four singers: Gaile Gillespie (*b* San Fernando, CA, 22 Aug 1949); Marylynn Gillespie (*b* San Fernando, 1 Feb 1951); Todd Buffa (*b* Beloit, WI, 27 Nov 1952); and Barbara Reeves. Rather than concentrating, like many vocal groups, on vocalese, it has forged a style that employs a wide variety of complex and sophisticated textures. Among its recordings are songs as diverse as *Up from the Skies* by the rock guitarist Jimi Hendrix, Thelonious Monk's *'Round Midnight*, and Spyro Gyra's *Hello*. Most of the group's vocal arrangements are written by Buffa.

SELECTED RECORDINGS

New Weave (1983, Pol. 810028–1); *American Eyes* (1985, PAlt 8086), incl. Hello, 'Round Midnight, Up from the Skies; *Black and Blue* (1986, PAlt-TBA 214)

BIBLIOGRAPHY

R. Robbins: "Rare Silk: New Weave," *CI*, xxii/2 (1984), 28
S. Yanow: "Hodgepodge and Shorties," *Cadence*, xi/7 (1985), 29

PAUL RINZLER

Raskin, Milt(on William) (*b* Boston, 27 Jan 1916; *d* Los Angeles, 16 Oct 1977). Pianist. He studied at the New England Conservatory in the early 1930s, and by 1937 had moved to New York, where he performed with Wingy Manone and recorded with Ziggy Elman, whose *Love is the sweetest thing* (1939, Bb 10741) is a good example of his early style. He played in the big bands of Gene Krupa (1938–9, 1941–2), Teddy Powell (1939–40), Alvino Rey (1940), and Tommy Dorsey (1942–4), recording with all but Rey; he may be heard to advantage as a soloist on Dorsey's *Well, Git it* (1942, Vic. 27887). Raskin then moved to Los Angeles, where he recorded with Artie Shaw and Billie Holiday (both 1946), Woody Herman and Manone (both 1947), Sarah Vaughan (1951), Georgie Auld (1952), B. B. King (1959), Stan Kenton (1963, 1965), and others. He also worked as a music director, conductor, and arranger for studio orchestras and occasionally wrote lyrics for pop songs. (*ChiltonW*; *FeatherE*; *Feather '60s*)

Rasmussen, Peter (Christian Hans) (*b* Hørsholm, Denmark, 16 Dec 1906). Danish trombonist and bandleader. He played with Valdemar Eiberg (1925–6) and Kai Ewans (1927–8), then was a principal soloist with Bernard Etté in Germany (1928–31). After returning to Denmark he was a prominent member of the bands of Kai Julian (1931–2), Erik Tuxen (1932–6), and Ewans (1936–43). In 1943 he assumed leadership of Svend Asmussen's group and until the early 1950s led small groups that played in a style influenced partly by bop; his work is represented on several recordings (including *Fine and Dandy*, 1951, Odeon DK1128). He led big bands in the mid- and late 1950s, then worked for several years as a freelance radio producer.

ERIK WIEDEMANN

Ratamacue. One of the drumstrokes collectively known as RUDIMENTS.

Ratip, Ahmed [Mike; Muhiddin, Ahmed] (*b* Constantinople [now Istanbul], 24 Sept 1905). Argentine bandleader, banjoist, guitarist, and singer of Turkish birth. While attending the University of Michigan he played banjo under the name Ahmed Muhiddin in student bands (1924–31) and in an orchestra led by Jean Goldkette (1927). He worked as a newspaper correspondent in Uruguay and at the same time played in and around Montevideo in a trio led by the pianist Luis Rolero, with which he later moved to Buenos Aires; after this group disbanded in 1934 he joined the Dixie Pals, led by the violinist Paul Wyer, with which he recorded several tracks for Victor, including a version of his own composition *Africa* (1934, 37642). From 1936 to the early 1940s he played with the pianist Rene Cospito and his Orquesta argentina de jazz, with the drummer Mario D'Alo's Rhythm Kings, and in a group modeled after the Quintette du Hot Club de France that included Hernán Oliva (violin), Dave Washington (second guitar), and Louis Vola (double bass). He studied harmony in the late 1930s with the bandleader Russ Goudy; by this time he had taken the name Ahmed Ratip. Early in 1943 he formed the Cotton Pickers, as the leader of which he made several recordings between 1946 and 1952 for Victor (including *El boogie de los platillos*, 1950, 60-1857), and performed at clubs, at concerts, and on radio in Argentina, Chile, Brazil, and Uruguay until his retirement in 1960; he also operated a nightclub from 1944. He should not be confused with the pianist Arman Ratip (*b* Cyprus), who has worked as a journalist in London (where in 1970 he recorded two albums, the second with Marc Charig and Harry Miller) and played with Maggie Nichols and Mongezi Feza. (G. Olliver: Liner notes, *Jazz and Hot Dance in Argentina*, Harl. 2010, 1984)

GUILLERMO I. OLLIVER, RAINER E. LOTZ

Raubiško, Raymond (*b* Riga, Latvian SSR, 28 May 1939). Latvian tenor saxophonist and composer. He began his career in an orchestra led by the pianist Ivan Mazur and in 1964 became a principal soloist in the Rīgas Estrādes Orkestris (Riga variety orchestra) under Raimond Pauls. After studying clarinet at the Latvian SSR Y. Vitol State Conservatory in Riga (graduated 1968) he performed at the International Jazz Festival Prague (1970) under the bandleader Václav Zahradník. From 1974 he belonged to the dance orchestra of the Riga Radio and Television, led his own groups, and worked as a freelance in concerts and in studios. His first recording, *Kartinï drevnevo Egipta* (Pictures of ancient Egypt; 1984, Mel. C6020651000), features a cycle of four pieces of his own composition.

WALTER OJAKÄÄR

Rava, Enrico (*b* Trieste, Italy, 20 Aug 1943). Italian trumpeter. He was brought up in Turin. He played New Orleans jazz on trombone from the age of 16, and at 18, inspired by Miles Davis, he taught himself trumpet. He played in Rome, first working with Gato Barbieri (*c*1965) and Mal Waldron, and then toured and recorded in Europe and the Americas with Lee Konitz and as a freelance (1966–9). Having visited New York with Steve

Lacy in 1967, he returned in 1969 to work with Roswell Rudd, with whom he subsequently recorded (from 1973) and toured (1977–8). He settled in the city but began in 1972 to tour and record regularly as a leader in Europe and South America; in 1975 he performed as a guest soloist with the Globe Unity Orchestra, of which he later became a member. By the mid-1980s he had returned to Italy, where he led two quartets, one of which included Tony Oxley; this group, with the addition of the berimbau player Nana Vasconcelos, recorded in 1984 as the Rava String Band. Rava continued to tour widely and in 1985 recorded as a sideman with Archie Shepp.

Rava's work with Lacy in the late 1960s familiarized him with free jazz, elements of which have persisted in his style, although from the 1970s he preferred to play and compose lyrical melodies; a free-jazz gesture he often employs is to bring an improvisation to a climax with rapid, blurred, sweeping lines of imprecise pitch. His timbre, warm and clear in the trumpet's middle register, becomes nasal in the high register, and at this extreme his attack becomes noticeably coarse; these qualities suggest similarities between Rava's playing and that of Davis.

SELECTED RECORDINGS

As leader: *Quotation Marks* (1973–4, Japo 60010); *The Plot* (1976, ECM 1078); *Enrico Rava Quartet* (1978, ECM 1122); *Opening Night* (1981, ECM 1224); *Rava String Band* (1984, SN 1114)

As sideman: S. Lacy: *The Forest and the Zoo* (1966, ESP 1060); M. Schoof: *European Echoes* (1969, FMP 0010); G. Hampel: *Angel* (1972, Birth 009); R. Rudd: *Inside Job* (1976, Ari. 1029); Globe Unity Orchestra: *Pearls* (1977, FMP 0380)

BIBLIOGRAPHY

G. Rouy: "Enrico Rava," *Jm*, no.215 (1973), 44 [incl. discography]
M. Cuscuna: "Enrico Rava," *DB*, xli/7 (1974), 15
D. Soutif: "Enrico Rava entre New York et l'Italie," *Jm*, no.252 (1977), 14 [incl. discography]
H. Mandel: "Enrico Rava: Italian on the Upswing," *DB*, xlv/3 (1978), 16 [incl. discography]
L. Jeske: "Free Jazz Players from Many Lands Form Globe Unity Orchestra," *DB*, xlvii/9 (1980), 28
E. Jost: *Jazzmusiker: Materialen zur Soziologie der afro-amerikanischen Musik* (Frankfurt am Main, Germany, Berlin, and Vienna, 1981), 155
K. Brodacti: "Enrico Rava Update," *JF* [intl edn], no.92 (1985), 41

BARRY KERNFELD

RCA Victor. Name by which VICTOR gradually became known after it was taken over by RCA (Radio Corporation of America) in 1929.

Reardon, Casper [Glissandi, Arpeggio] (*b* Little Falls, NY, 15 April 1907; *d* New York, 9 March 1941). Harpist. He belonged to the Philadelphia Orchestra and while the principal harpist of the Cincinnati SO played jazz on the radio under the pseudonym Arpeggio Glissandi. He made recordings with Jack Teagarden (including *Junk Man*, 1934, Bruns. 7652) and Paul Whiteman, worked in Hollywood, and led his own small groups in New York and Chicago. (H. Mückenberger: *Meet me Where they Play the Blues: Jack Teagarden und seine Musik* (Gauting, Germany, 1986), 97)

Rebillot, Pat(rick Earl) (*b* Louisville, OH, 21 April 1935). Keyboard player. He was classically trained, and was a church organist during his teens. In 1957 he graduated from Cincinnati College-Conservatory with a degree in music education. During military service (1958–60) he performed with a variety of musicians and entertainers. After being discharged Rebillot worked as a freelance in New York, playing jazz and commercially-oriented music. His better-known associations at this time were with Jeremy Steig, Benny Goodman, Paul Winter (with whom he toured Brazil in 1965), Sarah Vaughan, Zoot Sims, and Roy Eldridge. Thereafter he was a member of groups led by Gary Burton (1971–2) and Herbie Mann (1972–6). In the 1980s, as well as working with Mann intermittently, Rebillot has continued to play jazz, Latin-American music, and pop.

SELECTED RECORDINGS

As leader: *Free Fall* (1973, Atl. 1663)

As sideman: F. Foster: *Soul Outing* (1966, Prst. 7479); C. O'Farrill: *Nine Flags* (1966, Imp. 9175); P. Desmond: *Crystal Illusions* (1969, A&M 3024); H. Mann: *Hold on, I'm Comin'* (1972, Atl. 1632); M. Murphy: *Bridging a Gap* (1972, Muse MR5009); D. Newman: *Newmanism* (1973, Atl. 1662); David Friedman: *Futures Passed* (1976, Enja 2068); J. Klemmer: *Arabesque* (1977, ABC 1068); H. Mann: *Brazil, Once Again* (1978, Atl. 19169)

BIBLIOGRAPHY

Feather–Gitler '70s

SCOTT YANOW

Rebop. *See* BOP.

Recording. A term applied to any of the various means by which sound and visual images are stored, and to the storage medium. This article concerns the general developments in sound-recording technology and their applications in jazz; for a discussion of recordings involving visual images with sound, *see* FILMS. The systematic study of sound recordings as documents and as physical objects is the subject of the article DISCOGRAPHY.

I. Technological developments. II. History of jazz recording.

I. Technological developments.

1. The acoustical era: 1877–1925: (i) Cylinders and discs (ii) Piano rolls. 2. The electrical era: 1925–47. 3. New techniques of recording and playback after 1947: (i) Magnetic tape (ii) Microgroove discs (iii) Stereophonic sound on tape and disc (iv) Other developments. 4. The digital era.

1. THE ACOUSTICAL ERA: 1877–1925.

(i) Cylinders and discs. The earliest methods of sound recording are described as "acoustical" and employ only mechanical means for both recording and playback. The sounds to be preserved are directed into a large horn, which at its tapered end is connected to a cutting stylus. In response to the vibrations of air in the horn, the stylus cuts a spiral groove in the thick wax coating of a cylinder or disc, rotated steadily by means of a crank. The cutting process creates variations in the groove analogous to the varying frequency and amplitude of the vibrations; the stylus moves up and down in "hill-and-dale" or "vertical cut" recording and from side to side in "lateral cut" recording.

To convert a disc from its original form into a marketable commodity, a process known as "pressing" is employed. It involves several stages during which alternately negative and positive images are made of the master version. The procedure as it is described here in terms of disc recording remained essentially unchanged until the advent of digital technology in the 1980s, though an additional stage was added once master recordings began to be made on magnetic tape instead of disc (see §3(i) below). The grooved master disc (sometimes called a wax (*see* WAX (i)) in the early recording era, later sometimes a "lacquer" – in both cases owing to the material with which it is coated) is electroplated; from this is formed a ridged negative (also called a master), which is stronger than the original positive; a further, sturdy positive, the "mother" (also known as the "matrix"), is made from the second master, and a metal negative stamper from the mother; from the stamper (which can withstand heat) the final discs are pressed. Roughly 1000 to 1500 discs can be made before the stamper wears out, and a new one must be made. A "master pressing" is one made from a master cut directly from a microphone or recording horn; the term thus applies to all recordings made before the introduction of magnetic tape recording (and also to those made in the 1970s by the direct-to-disc method, see §3(iv) below). A "dub pressing" is one made from a master cut from a preexisting pressing, a process adopted when all master material is lost or otherwise unavailable.

Mechanical playback of acoustical recordings involves a reversal of the recording process: a stylus tracks along the groove, following its contours, the variations of which are converted into analogous vibrations of the air inside the horn. (Acoustical recordings may also be played back on electrical equipment; see §2 below.)

The principal deficiencies of the acoustical recording process were the limitations and variability of its "fidelity." (Fidelity is the accuracy with which the original sound is reproduced by recording and playback, and depends on the range of frequencies reproduced and on the degree of distortion caused by the recording, pressing, and playback processes.) Acoustical recording never yielded high fidelity, its dynamic range was limited, and because of the sensitivity of the technology, it required a high degree of skill in the recording engineer. The quality of acoustical recordings varied greatly, depending on the equipment used and on the ability of the engineer to position the performers correctly in relation to the horn. The quality of the equipment and the technical expertise available to some companies was so low that they were unable to use standard instrumentation; bass instruments were particularly problematical (see §II, 2, below).

The first sound-recording mechanism practical for commercial use was invented in 1877 by Thomas Edison (1847–1931) as an adjunct to his experiments with a telegraphic repeater. Edison's "phonograph" used a wax cylinder about five to six inches long and utilized the hill-and-dale recording technique. In the first decade after the invention of the phonograph, other important inventors in the USA received patents for recording devices; they included Alexander Graham Bell (1847–1922), who shared a patent with his cousin Chichester A. Bell and Charles S. Tainter in 1886 for a flat recording disc of wax-coated cardboard, and Emile Berliner (1851–1929), who received a patent for a disc phonograph in 1888. The duration of both cylinder and disc recordings was typically two to four minutes. Berliner's machine employed lateral cut recording, which became the standard method of commercial disc recording until the introduction of stereophonic recording in the 1950s (see §3(iii) below).

The principal uses that Edison and other early inventors envisioned for recording included communications, business stenography, telegraphy, and to some extent entertainment; Berliner appears to have been the first to look upon recording primarily as an entertainment and cultural medium. Venture capital was obtained for the manufacture of sound recorders from investors who were attracted by the apparent security of the patents and the likelihood of substantial returns. In spite of continuing patent litigation, the financial rewards of the recording industry on the whole justified their confidence. In 1889 the first playback device was produced for sale by a German toy factory, Kammerer & Reinhardt of Waltershausen, and in 1893 machines of the same kind became available in the USA.

Other developments in the late 19th century were also of great importance to the future of sound recording. Patents for recording sound in synchronization with moving film were established by Georges Demeny in 1892 and Edison in 1894, and a patent for the "telegraphone," a magnetic recording device, was issued in 1898 to Valdemar Poulsen (1869–1942). A number of patents for "wireless" devices for radio broadcasting were secured by Guglielmo Marconi (1874–1937), beginning in 1896, and other radio equipment was under development by the international firms of Marconi (1897) and Telefunken (1899).

By the turn of the century several companies had been set up to manufacture recordings and playback equipment based on the patents of Edison, the Bells and Tainter, and Berliner and his associate Eldridge Johnson. The phonograph and gramophone industry expanded rapidly in the USA, England, and Europe; among the important firms were American Graphophone, Berliner Gramophone, and Columbia Phonograph. Patent-pool agreements in 1902 between Columbia and the Victor Talking Machine Company (which had grown out of the Berliner firm and taken over its patents) helped to establish the dominance of these two companies in the USA during the first half of the 20th century. Between 1900 and the outbreak of World War I the cultural and entertainment applications of recording came to surpass other uses in commercial significance.

In 1914 several basic patents expired, which led to a diversification in the manufacture of records and record-playing equipment by new companies such as Brunswick–Balke–Collender. In the same year the American Society of Composers, Authors and Publishers (ASCAP) was organized to collect fees for the use of published music, and General Electric began the manufacture of vacuum tubes for electronic amplification (Lee de Forest's patent on this process had been granted in 1907).

By this time flat discs were the predominant medium for sound recording. (Although Edison continued to manufacture recorded cylinders until 1929, and blank cylinders continued

1. The Gramophone Co.'s H.M.V. Model 125 table gramophone, 1922

to be used for business stenography and portable recording equipment, it was, by 1930, many years since any repertory had been recorded only on cylinders.) In the early period of sound recording the characteristics of discs varied from one manufacturer to another. Until the mid-1930s sizes varied greatly: discs of diameters of between 5 and 20 inches were made and though the standard sizes became 10 and 12 inches, 8-inch discs continued to be produced in large numbers into the 1930s. The playing time of the standard disc was between three and four minutes per side. Recording and playing speeds ranged from 72 to 86 r.p.m., the standard settling at 78 (though Columbia, for example, issued 80 r.p.m. discs for some time after 1920). The materials of which discs were made and with which they were coated were also various; shellac eventually became the commonest material. By around 1920 lateral cut recording was the norm; a less exacting technique than vertical cut, it produced a level of fidelity adequate to the standard of the equipment the general public could afford to buy.

(ii) Piano rolls. Another mechanical recording medium was developed during the acoustical era – the piano (or pianola) roll. This is a roll, usually of paper, on which music is encoded in the form of perforations. The roll is marked mechanically as a player performs the piece on a recording piano; the marks are then cut by hand by an operator. The recording is played back on a mechanical instrument known as a player piano or pianola, by means of a pneumatic system that automatically operates the keys of the instrument in response to the perforations in the roll.

Player-piano devices were first developed in the 1890s, in the form of separate cabinets that were moved up to the keyboard and played it mechanically; they gave a range of 65 notes at first, later the full 88. Around the turn of the century the apparatus was built into the piano itself. The first instruments to record faithfully all the nuances of a performance were built in Germany, by Edwin Welte in Freiburg in 1904 and by the firm Hupfeld of Leipzig in 1905. By 1913 two American reproducing player-piano mechanisms had been developed, the Duo-Art, made by the Aeolian Co., and the Ampico, made by the American Piano Co. (which became the Ampico Corporation in 1915). At their best, reproducing player pianos could recreate the style of the original artist to a remarkably accurate degree.

2. The electrical era: 1925–47. In electrical recording the sounds to be preserved are gathered by a transducer (a microphone) and the vibrations converted into an analogously varying electrical signal, which is amplified and applied to another transducer (a stylus), which cuts a spiral groove in a waxed or (later) lacquered disc; the deviations of the incised groove from the regular path correspond to the variations in the electrical signal. In playback the process is reversed, the signal being converted through a phonograph cartridge, an amplifier, and a loudspeaker into sound. The term "electrical recording" is normally used in contradistinction to "acoustical recording" (in the preceding era) and "magnetic tape recording" and "microgroove recording" (in the succeeding era); even though the process described here continued, broadly, to be standard until the advent of digital recording in the 1980s, and electricity, of course, has remained essential to recording and playback processes of all kinds, the term "electrical recording" is not customarily used after the introduction of magnetic tape in 1947.

The first electrical recording was issued in 1925 and from that time electronic amplification became the principal technological factor in the development of recording. The physical format of electrical recordings remained the same as that of the many acoustical ones utilizing the lateral cut technique; thus acoustical and electrical recordings were usually compatible and could be played on the same equipment. Electronic amplification made possible a dramatic improvement in fidelity. Other developments of importance to the recording industry during this period were the growth of commercial radio broadcasting, the standardization of synchronized sound-film recording, and the invention of the coin-operated jukebox; connected with the increase in the number of radio stations was the making and marketing of recordings designed specifically for broadcasting, so-called broadcast transcriptions (*see* Transcription (iii)), which employed a technology superior to that of commercially available recordings, based on a 16-inch disc that played at 33⅓ r.p.m. and offered about 15 minutes of playing time.

3. New techniques of recording and playback after 1947.

(i) Magnetic tape. The process of recording on magnetic tape involves the conversion of sound signals, by means of a transducer (a microphone), into electrical impulses, which are recorded analogously as variations of magnetic flux along the tape. To make discs from tape masters the recording is first cut on a master disc before the normal series of operations that constitute the pressing process can begin.

Although Poulsen's magnetic recording patent was granted in 1898, it was not until the advent of electronic amplification that the musical potential of the technique could be realized. And because of complex economic and political factors a practical method of recording music magnetically, which required a reliable and inexpensive medium, was not arrived at until around 1950.

Poulsen's magnetic recorder used steel wire, and solid steel tape was used for magnetic recorders developed in Europe by both Kurt Stille and Ludwig Blattner in the 1920s, and by S. J. Begun and C. Lorenz in 1935. Work on paper and plastic recording tape coated with magnetic oxides was carried out in the 1930s by BASF in Germany and TDK in Japan, and by 1936 these companies were producing a limited amount of coated paper and plastic tape. The German company AEG demonstrated its Magnetophon tape recorder in 1935. In the USA magnetic recording techniques were being developed by such firms as Bell Laboratories (1937) and Brush Soundmirror (1938). Development (by Brush and the Webster–Chicago Corporation) of magnetic wire recorders for American military applications continued throughout World War II on a limited basis, but major work took place in Germany between 1935 and 1945. In September 1944 an improved version of the AEG Magnetophon was obtained by American forces as war booty from Radio Luxembourg, which had been occupied by the Germans. That machine provided the model for the first high-quality magnetic recorder for studio use in the USA, produced by the Ampex Corporation in 1947; the Brush and Magnecord companies also had tape recorders in production by 1947. By that time, too, oxide-coated recording tape with a paper or plastic base, which had been under development in the USA by the Minnesota Mining and Manufacturing Company (3M) from 1944, was available commercially.

After 1947 the recording, broadcasting, and film industries in the USA achieved general agreement on standards for magnetic recording. The main advantages of tape over the disc were the relative ease of editing and the substantially lower cost. Magnetic tape was also reusable and seemingly less fragile. (In some cases, though, it has proved disastrously fragile: in the 1980s it has been discovered that after 20 or 30 years some types of adhesive used to bind the oxide to the plastic base, notably that produced by 3M for the recording industry's standard tape in the 1950s and 1960s, have disintegrated, transforming irreplaceable master recordings into useless boxes of blank tape and magnetic dust.) By 1950 magnetic tape had become the predominant medium for making sound recordings.

(ii) Microgroove discs. Changes of parallel importance took place in the area of disc recording in the postwar period; these arose principally from the development of polyester plastics, called polyvinyl chloride (PVC) or "vinyl," a comparatively unbreakable material, with a smaller grain structure than shellac (of which 78 r.p.m. discs were commonly made) and thus capable of receiving more refined impressions. The introduction of vinyl discs made possible a new standard "pitch" (or groove spacing) of around 100 grooves to the centimeter (superseding the old standard on shellac and other discs of fewer than 40); these "microgroove" discs allowed the recording of a broader range of frequencies and dynamics than their predecessors and suffered considerably less from surface noise. An incidental advantage of vinyl was its ready availability: since it is made from petroleum it could be obtained from sources within the USA, whereas shellac had to be imported (principally from India and Southeast Asia).

The advent of the microgroove disc led to the fixing of new standard speeds for recording and playback, longer playing times, and new physical formats for records. The $33\frac{1}{3}$ r.p.m. "long-playing" disc, introduced by Columbia in 1948, eventually allowed for about 25 minutes of music per side (although its duration was initially limited, for technical reasons, to that of a broadcast transcription – about 15 minutes); though by no means the first disc of its kind (there were experiments with long-playing discs in the 1920s and 1930s, see §II, 3, below), the 12-inch (less often 10-inch or 7-inch) $33\frac{1}{3}$ r.p.m. disc quickly became standard, replacing multiple-disc albums of 78s. The 45 r.p.m., 7-inch "single," first marketed by RCA Victor in 1949, ultimately replaced the single 78 r.p.m. disc (having a similar playing time of three to four minutes per side) and has continued to account for many new issues. In due course two notable variants of the 45 r.p.m. disc were devised: the 7-inch EP (extended-play disc), which normally has two tracks on each side and runs for twice as long as a single, and the 12-inch single, which normally runs for up to 12 minutes per side.

A combination of factors accounts for the volatile expansion of the recording industry after 1950. The new discs gave better fidelity and were less fragile than their predecessors; a decrease in the cost of materials, manufacturing, and distribution also made them more affordable than recordings had been in the past. The use of easily edited magnetic tape improved the efficiency of the record companies' operations, and this, together with the favorable economic conditions of the 1950s, encouraged new companies to compete with established larger firms. Finally the record-buying public was larger, more affluent, and, as a result of wartime travel and radio broadcasting, more catholic in its musical taste than it had ever been.

(iii) Stereophonic sound on tape and disc. The technique of stereophonic (or stereo) recording and playback produces the effect of sound coming from different directions in three-dimensional space. It is achieved by means of two channels, recorded and played back independently, and relied for its development on the invention of two-track magnetic tape. The principal manifestation of the technique is the stereophonic,

2. Disc-cutting lathe on which the signals from the master tape are transcribed as a microgroove spiral on the disc

long-playing, microgroove disc made from two-track master tapes (later from multitrack master tapes mixed down to two channels, see below). (Other formats in which stereophonic recordings are issued are the cassette tape and the compact disc, see respectively §(iv) and §4 below.) On a microgroove disc the two channels are recorded as independent variations in the left and right walls of a V-shaped groove (the stylus moving vertically and laterally at the same time). The introduction of stereophonic sound thus gives higher fidelity than a process involving only lateral cutting. Although stereo recordings were made as early as the 1930s, it was only with the advent of high-fidelity microgroove discs that the technique gained importance.

Spurred on by the use of stereophonic sound in both broadcasting and films, the recording industry introduced stereophonic discs in 1957. Stereo recordings rapidly supplanted monophonic ones in the 1960s, and for newly made recordings this represented a significant improvement in every way. But the market forces set in motion by the introduction of the new technology proved disastrous in the area of reissues of recordings made earlier. Monophonic recordings were quickly relegated to a separate section of standard record listings, such as Schwann's *Long Playing Record Catalog*, and then disappeared entirely. In order to continue selling established material, record companies needed to adapt it so that it qualified for inclusion in the catalogues and satisfied public demand for stereo sound. Many (not all) companies added a false and muddled second track to monophonic recordings, marketing them as "enhanced for stereo effect" or "simulated stereo." Unfortunately such "improvements" were commercially successful. Only in the 1970s and 1980s have there appeared substantial collections of classic monophonic recordings issued in their original form, with identical signals recorded on each channel.

Two-track tape was the first step in what became known as "multitrack recording," which made possible not only stereophonic sound but also new and complex editing techniques in the recording studio; introduced in the late 1950s, it was standard practice by 1970. Multitrack recording involves the synchronized recording, either simultaneously or consecutively, of multiple tracks (each normally carrying a single voice or line), which are then mixed and remixed until the desired result is obtained; up to 24 tracks may be recorded on tape up to two inches wide. (Some analogue studios can offer extended facilities by linking two 24-track consoles. This technique is commonly referred to as "48-track" recording, though in fact only 46 are available because, to enable the two recorders to be synchronized, a time pulse is recorded onto one track of each console. Techniques using digital technology – also referred to as "multitrack recording" – follow related procedures, but there are fewer limitations as to the track capacity; see §4 below.)

(iv) Other developments. A number of other experiments with recording formats and techniques were made possible by the technological advances of the postwar era; some produced results that proved short-lived, others were commercially highly successful.

In the early 1960s an attempt was made to introduce long-playing discs recorded at $16\frac{2}{3}$ r.p.m., but by that time the $33\frac{1}{3}$ and 45 r.p.m. discs were well established and the slower speed attracted little interest. A decade later a similar failure attended quadraphonic sound, which extended the stereo principle to the use of four channels. In the mid-1970s direct-to-disc recording enjoyed a brief vogue. This technique combines the high fidelity made possible by contemporary equipment with the simplicity of the electrical recording process, whereby the signal is recorded directly onto the disc; although it gives higher fidelity than conventional tape-transfer methods (in which a subtle loss of quality results from the transference of the signal from tape to disc), the direct-to-disc process means that recordings cannot be edited, since each sound is irrevocably etched on the disc as the performance proceeds.

The commercial exploitation of magnetic tape was revolutionized by the introduction by Philips in 1966 of the stereophonic compact cassette (a sealed case containing a miniature reel-to-reel tape), and the machine on which it could be used. By 1980 the cassette had become competitive with the disc, and albums were usually issued in both forms. Cassette recorders have the additonal advantage of portability. From 1965 electronic devices for reducing unwanted noise were developed and applied by the recording industry for studio use, and later included in domestic equipment; one of these, Dolby-B (1970), markedly improved the sound quality of cassette tapes and contributed substantially to their success. The level of fidelity on cassettes was further improved by Dolby-C and the studio system DBX, as well as variations in the materials used for tape coating – cobalt, chrome, and combinations of these with iron.

4. THE DIGITAL ERA. Digital technology had been in use in computers for a quarter of a century before it began to be employed by the recording industry. Until the mid-1970s most advances in recording technology were refinements or extensions of basic analogue principles established in the 19th century.

So-called digital recording techniques use digital technology either in combination with or in place of the analogue techniques based on the continuously varying signals that characterize electrical and stereophonic recording. In 1976 the process of "digital mastering," which combines digital and analogue techniques, was introduced. It involves the initial preservation of sound on magnetic tape by encoding the continuously varying characteristics of sound waves as a sequence of discrete numbers, stored in the form of magnetic pulses; the digital master tapes are then decoded to produce analogue discs (sometimes described, misleadingly, as "digital recordings"). An important application of such hybrid techniques, particularly in jazz, is the potential they offer for subtle manipulation of the recorded sound: using "digital remastering" – that is, the making of a new digital master on magnetic tape – recordings of the acoustical and electrical eras can be re-recorded while in digitally encoded form for the purpose of improving clarity and balance and minimizing undesired noise.

In the early 1980s a medium based entirely on digital recording and playback technology – the compact disc – was introduced. The fidelity of discs recorded by analogue methods is affected by the inability of the medium to reproduce the sound signal in its entirety with sufficient accuracy at the extremes of the frequency range, and by the surface noise produced in playback by the physical contact between the stylus and the disc. Digital methods of recording and playback solve both these difficulties. A digital recorder "samples" the sound signal more than 40,000 times per second, and assigns each sample a binary number, thus creating multimillion-character streams of numbers. This digital representation of the sound is encoded by a process known as pulse-code manipulation (PCM) and recorded optically as a sequence of microscopic pits in the surface of a plastic disc (approximately eight billion pits are needed to record the hour or so of music that can be carried by the 5-inch disc). The stored signal never loses its original quality and can be copied many times with no audible change. A small semiconductor laser is used to play back the recording from the disc so that there is no loss of definition in the sound and no surface noise; compact discs revolve at a constant linear speed rather than at a constant angular speed, as do conventional discs.

The first applications of digital technology in recording appeared in the late 1970s in the form of electronic equipment used in the studio in multitrack recording; the public first encountered its results in the sound-modification devices used in rock and electroacoustic music. At the turn of the decade the more affluent recording companies installed expensive digital magnetic tape recorders for making master tapes. By the mid-1980s marketing decisions about the format in which recorded music was issued suggested that the compact disc might supersede the 12-inch microgroove album, just as the album superseded the 78 r.p.m. single.

Other developments in digital recording were taking place during the late 1980s, notably a system on magnetic tape called "DAT." One implementation of DAT, known as RDAT, followed standards of compatibility reached by international agreement. The RDAT system uses a special cassette to hold the recording medium and, in contrast to the compact disc, enables digital recordings to be copied. The RDAT format can record both stereophonic and quadraphonic music, as well as computer data; it may become a significant commercial factor in the last decade of the 20th century.

II. History of jazz recording.

1. Introduction. 2. Early recordings. 3. Major companies and the big bands. 4. Developments outside the USA. 5. The war years and the AFM recording ban. 6. The re-emergence of independent labels. 7. The effects of technological change. 8. Non-American companies and labels, and reissues.

1. Introduction. The relationship between jazz and sound recording is of paramount importance. In the case of many other genres, whether musical or not, the recording effectively immortalizes a completed, even perfected, statement; such statements remain essentially the same whenever they are recorded or performed. Most jazz, however, has the property of spontaneity, its creativity being concentrated in the act of improvisation – a form of impromptu composition. As a result, any recording of improvised or partly improvised jazz acts as a snapshot, freezing a single creative moment which can never be repeated without subconscious change. Because it is impossible for such a performance to be repeated exactly, each recording acquires a unique value, and it is this that has made the recording of jazz so vitally important: no other genre rivals jazz in its preoccupation with issues of alternative and multiple takes of individual titles.

In addition, jazz – to a greater extent than any other musical genre – quickly came to rely for its geographical expansion, and hence its continued existence, on documentation by means of recordings. An improvised music, played for uneducated audiences, it spread locally by aural experience; its dissemination beyond the immediate locality of its origins was achieved through demonstrations given by itinerant musicians plying their trade. Economically generated migrations carried it further afield, but it was the advent of sound recordings that transmitted it fastest and gave rise to further musical development.

2. Early recordings. Initially the paths of jazz and recording did not cross, even though they originated in the same period. Nothing more frivolous than telegraphy and communications was at first seen as the object of the fledgling technology, so it is unsurprising that the musical movement then growing up in New Orleans and elsewhere, at that time also in its infancy, went largely undocumented. No recorded evidence survives of the manner in which jazz developed from its roots in blues, spirituals, folk music, African rhythm and harmony, marches, dance music, and creole music. A persistent but unsubstantiated claim exists that Buddy Bolden, who is generally credited with taking important steps in the shaping of the music, was recorded on cylinder in 1894 improvising the instrumental blues *Make me a pallet on the floor.*

While Bolden's cylinder remains part of the music's colorful mythology, there is a surprisingly large number of extant recordings of ragtime, one of the principal roots of early jazz. They serve to highlight a major problem of early recording techniques: although ragtime was essentially piano music, it proved difficult to register the sound of the piano on recordings, so banjo and small ensembles were often substituted for it. The characteristics of ragtime were diluted by the use of saxophone, accordion, and trombone (by Arthur Pryor, among others), and xylophone, the piano appearing only rarely before World War I; Charles H. H. Booth's unaccompanied piano solo *Creole Belles* (1901, Vic. 1079) is a notable exception.

Because of these technical difficulties almost all early piano recordings, especially those by the composers themselves, including Scott Joplin, were made on piano rolls. The crucial drawback of this medium was that the rolls could very easily be "doctored" by the cutting of additional holes, and this has caused the accuracy of some surviving recordings to be questioned. The piano roll, the most important producer of which was QRS, flourished into the 1920s and has survived into the 1980s. It provides an essential source for early recordings of the Harlem stride pianists, such as James P. Johnson (who made nearly 60 piano rolls as a freelance player in 1917–18 and exclusively for QRS from 1921 to 1927) and Fats Waller. In the 1970s QRS made many recordings on piano roll of the work of Earl Hines.

It was not until 1917 that the first jazz records were made and released – ironically by several different companies; after ignoring the music for 30 years, record companies began to compete for jazz, and the race commenced, albeit with a stuttering start. The immense popularity of ragtime, boosted by sheet-music sales and spurred on by early recordings, provided the commercial bedrock for the infant recording industry. It is hardly surprising, then, that late in 1916 two leading companies, Columbia and Victor (both founded at the turn of the century), began casting about for a fresh novelty. Early the following year that need was satisfied when the Original Dixieland Jazz Band opened at the chic Reisenweber's Restaurant in New York. By mid-January the group had become a sensation and on the penultimate day of the month it recorded for Columbia the tunes *Darktown Strutters' Ball* and *Indiana*. Columbia was slow to issue its recordings, however, and as the ODJB's phenomenal success at Reisenweber's continued, Victor stepped in. On 26 February 1917 the group recorded *Livery Stable Blues* and *Dixie Jass Band One-step*, and Victor rushed the first pressing into the shops a week later, on Monday 5 March. The first jazz release was numbered 18255, cost 75c, and sold more than a million copies.

Despite this commercial success, recording companies' interest in jazz remained low. A number of lesser-known bands modeled on the Original Dixieland Jazz Band, including the Louisiana Five, recorded between 1917 and 1920. But on the whole, before 1920 the companies grossly underestimated the possible market for jazz, especially among the black population, none of whom, it was erroneously believed, could afford the equipment to play back records. Even when this view was modified, the companies still failed to grasp the extent of the jazz market.

Their second chance to exploit the untapped resources of the record-buying public – which again they failed spectacularly to realize – arose with the arrival in New York in 1919 of the black songwriter Perry Bradford, a shrewd southern businessman, who had identified the possibilities offered by the market. After unsuccessful attempts to interest the prominent Columbia and Victor companies in his work, Bradford eventually persuaded Fred Hager, a director of the General Phonograph Corporation, to record two of his songs in February 1920, using Mamie Smith. Issued on the General Phonograph Corporation's label Okeh, the pairing *That Thing Called Love* and *You can't keep a good man down* (OK 4119), though not a resounding success, sold well enough to justify a further venture. *Crazy Blues* and *It's right here for you* (OK 4169) were recorded on 10 August 1920 and 100,000 copies were sold in the last month of summer, sparking off interest in the neglected black market.

Thus so-called race records were born. At this time of the Harlem renaissance, with its emphasis on black virtues, the word "race" was not regarded as pejorative. The term RACE RECORD was subsequently assigned to many (though by no means all) recordings by black artists, and it indicates a segregationist attitude that led to what has been perceived as the second great mistake made by many record companies. Assuming that white buyers would have no interest in blues, gospel, and, later, some jazz, companies issued black music in special series, often on separate labels (Victor even scratched the word "colored" in the record's wax). In the populous North, race records were advertised only in the black media and distributed only to black areas; in the rural South they were marketed by mail order, which accounts for the extensive race catalogues maintained by Sears Roebuck and Montgomery Ward.

Now, swept along in the wake of a tide of classic blues recordings by such singers as Ma Rainey, Clara Smith, Mamie Smith, and, most notably, Bessie Smith – who often included among their accompanists distinguished jazzmen such as Fletcher Henderson, Charlie Green, Louis Armstrong, and Jabbo Smith – and with not a little commercial impetus from the hyperbole of such musicians as Paul Whiteman, the record companies discovered jazz. Their activities baptized the "jazz age."

The development of jazz through recording was initially, and has continued to be, fostered not only by the major recording companies but also (except during the 1930s) by numerous independent labels. Among the earliest and most important of the latter were Gennett, Paramount, and Okeh.

Gennett not only established the noteworthy claim of being the first recording concern west of the Allegheny Mountains, but also served as a model for similar companies. Formed by the famous Starr Piano Co. in 1917, the recording side of the business was named after the Starr directors, Harry, Fred, and Clarence Gennett. Gennett operated two studios, one in New York, the other in Richmond, Indiana (see fig.3); the latter especially carved a niche in jazz history for turning out important early recordings, yet the company entered the jazz field almost by accident. As the result of a chance call at the neighboring Friar's Inn, Fred Wiggens, the manager of Starr's Chicago music store, strongly recommended the resident band to the Gennett executives. The success of the recordings made in 1922 by the New Orleans Rhythm Kings (under the name Friars Society Orchestra) gained for Wiggens a free hand in deciding whom the label would record. His musical judgment, allied with his liberal attitude towards jazzmen, white or black, enabled Gennett to attract many of the seminal artists and bands of early jazz. Besides the New Orleans Rhythm Kings, these included King Oliver's Creole Jazz Band, Bix Beiderbecke and the Wolverines, Jelly Roll Morton, and Alphonso Trent.

However, recording jazz in the acoustic era was a taxing

3. The Wolverines at Gennett's recording studio in Richmond, Indiana, 18 February 1924: (left to right) Min Leibrook (sousaphone), Jimmy Hartwell (clarinet), George Johnson (tenor saxophone), Bob Gillette (banjo), Vic Moore (drums), Dick Voynow (piano), Bix Beiderbecke (cornet), and Al Gandee (trombone)

business. Gennett's Richmond studio was especially notorious, consisting of a wood-paneled room, capable of squeezing in eight musicians; they were asked to play into (or at) two large horns suspended on the wall at one end. Interruptions were frequent: if cold weather did not cause grease to clog the recording machinery, then steam locomotives clanked past on the line running alongside the studio. Even playing caused problems. Georg Brunis, the trombonist on Gennett's first recordings by the Friars Society Orchestra, recalled being made to face the side wall of the studio because when he played directly into the horn the cutting needle jumped about on the wax master disc. George Wettling, a white Chicagoan drummer, noted that the first great percussionist in jazz, Baby Dodds playing with King Oliver, was confined by the limitations of early recording technology to playing on woodblocks and the rims of snare and bass drums, and struck the cymbals only sparingly. The records therefore obscured more than they revealed of his work. If a bass instrument was used, similar problems of balance and audibility meant that it was more often a tuba or bass saxophone, or the pianist's left hand, than a double bass.

Compared with the major companies, Gennett undoubtedly produced low-fidelity recordings, but at least the documentation of jazz was under way. Other race-music specialists included Paramount, which began recording jazz, hillbilly music, and foreign-language discs as an adjunct to the manufacture of phonograph cabinets. Centered in Chicago, Paramount built the foundations of its catalogue with classic blues recordings by singers such as Ma Rainey and Ida Cox, but also recorded important instrumentalists, including Johnny Dodds. In 1924 it reached a leasing agreement with the first, and for a time the only, black recording company, Black Swan.

Other important small labels included Banner, Brunswick, Columbia's subsidiary Harmony, and Okeh, which swiftly outpaced Gennett in the astute ability to select fine musicians. Okeh contracted such luminaries of jazz as Oliver, Beiderbecke, the duo of Joe Venuti and Eddie Lang, James P. Johnson, Clarence Williams, and most notably Louis Armstrong, whose Hot Five and Hot Seven recordings for the company would prove to be among the most influential and enduring of all jazz.

The series of sessions Armstrong led for Okeh (1925–8) straddled the next great step forward in recording techniques, the first electrical recording, issued in 1925. Electronic amplification dramatically improved the fidelity of recordings, but it was a measure of the low status of jazz and the relative poverty of the smaller labels that the breakthrough, patented by the company Western Electric, did not have an impact on jazz for another two years. When it finally arrived, electrical recording emancipated drummers, pianists, and double bass players from the shadowy position imposed on them by more primitive recording techniques. It also facilitated the carriage of recording equipment into the field, though some acoustic recordings had already been made in temporary studios on location: Okeh recorded Bennie Moten's orchestra in St. Louis (1923–4) and Kansas City (1925), and Papa Celestin in New Orleans (1925). But electrical recording increasingly opened up these fresh areas of development to listeners, notably the territory bands, which were a barometer of the burgeoning of jazz in Kansas City and the Southwest. Recordists also moved properly into the birthplace of jazz, New Orleans, and captured elements of the music's prehistory through distinguished recordings made *en locale*; Papa Celestin (1926) and Sam Morgan (1927) recorded for Columbia, the cornetist Louis Dumaine's Jazzola Eight (1927) and the Jones and Collins Astoria Hot Eight (1929) for Victor.

3. Major companies and the big bands. Other significant technical advances – the growth of radio and sound films – began to affect jazz in the 1930s. Allied with the economic depression, radio, films, and later the jukebox had far-reaching effects on the recording industry and the music profession as a whole. During the 1920s many musicians, including those in jazz, had been regularly employed in performing for silent films, but moving pictures with synchronized sound removed some of their job opportunities. Musicians who worked in cafés, taverns, and clubs were similarly replaced by jukeboxes. Radio became a popular diversion, rivaling phonograph recordings; from the late 1920s and especially from 1935 until the late 1940s many broadcasting organizations installed land lines to clubs and ballrooms to allow them to make remote broadcasts of performances.

Of greater immediate consequence was the onset of the Depression following the 1929 Wall Street crash. Between 1927 and 1932 annual sales of records in the USA dropped from a flood to a trickle – from nearly 100 million to 6 million – and annual sales of phonographs fell from nearly 1 million to 40,000. This caused a sharp cut in recording activity and wiped out almost all of the independent labels. Most disappeared altogether. Gennett stopped making commercial discs, but continued in business as a custom-recording concern. Paramount went bankrupt. Others of the best, such as Brunswick, Okeh, and Vocalion, were taken over by major companies. Furthermore the major companies realigned. Symptomatic of the growing symbiotic relationship between radio and recording was the merger in 1929 of RCA (Radio Corporation of America), which had been formed from the Marconi Company in 1919, and Victor. Other important changes included the mergers of the Plaza Music Company, Pathé Phonograph and Radio Corporation, and Cameo Record Corporation with the American Record Company (ARC) in 1929, the further merger of ARC with the Brunswick Record Corporation (BRC) in 1931, and the acquisition by the Columbia Broadcasting System (CBS) of American Columbia and ARC–BRC in 1938.

1932 may have marked the recording industry's nadir in one respect; in another it saw a technical advance – stereo recording – the earliest examples of which were to remain, paradoxically, a secret for 55 years. Why these first examples were made is uncertain; it may have been simply a matter of chance. At that time jazz was becoming increasingly constrained by the three-minute time limit imposed on recordings by 78 technology. In informal clubs and jam sessions musicians were improvising quite lengthy performances (Kansas City was noted for jam sessions that continued all night on a single tune), and the formal theaters, where big bands would evolve the swing style, also required elaborate, extended performances.

Chief among those trying to break out of the straitjacket of the three-minute piece was the music's principal composer, Duke Ellington, who had already produced his first formally extended work, *Creole Rhapsody* (1931), which spread over two sides of a 78. At this time Ellington was recording largely (but not exclusively) for Victor, who in 1931–2 began to experiment with recording at a speed of $33\frac{1}{3}$ r.p.m. as a means of extending the playing time of a record. The process was expensive, and it is thought that, to avoid any possibility of failure, two cutting turntables, each with its own microphone, were used; the result was a pair of masters, which, played simultaneously, reproduced a performance in true stereo. But this was not discovered until 1981, when a collector in California obtained a pair of masters of one of the two recordings now known to have been made – full-length versions of *Black and Tan Fantasy* and *Creole Love Call*. Whether Victor's stereo recordings were simply a lucky by-product of an experiment directed towards other ends or a deliberate attempt to obtain stereo sound remains open to conjecture. In either case their discovery has sparked off speculation that many other stereo recordings were made, and the hunt for them is on.

But the Victor experiment fizzled out and Ellington was left to create extended works that divided in a way that coincided with the duration of the 78, notably *Reminiscing in Tempo* (1935), which spreads over four sides. These extended works were exceptions in an output that sublimated the three-minute form.

By now jazz had also begun to be seen and heard on film. The work of a handful of makers of "shorts" has become justly celebrated, whereas Hollywood's attitude from the beginning was largely patronizing and has remained so. An interesting sidelight on the sound film (which is discussed at length in FILMS) is that although optical track recording allowed extended playing time, this was rarely taken up. In addition it is worth noting that, apart from a few flimsily plotted musicals and generally embarrassing biographical features, the genre's one concession to the commercial success of swing was the series of so-called soundies recorded in the early 1940s (*see* FILMS, §II, 2). These productions – by RCM (Roosevelt, Coslow & Mills) – were three-minute films of a single performance for replay on a kind of jukebox in bars and clubs, each play costing 14c; they featured such musicians as Count Basie, Cab Calloway, Duke Ellington, and Lucky Millinder.

More significant for jazz was the continuing growth of radio broadcasting, which in the 1930s gradually took over as the leading source of entertainment for the family; by 1935 the radio set was a standard item of furniture in most homes. Once that had happened the broadcasting of jazz provided another source of unique performances for recording.

The swing era at its height saw a battle fought by the major record companies, involving price cutting and the taking of large stakes in the infant broadcasting industry with its potential for promoting their recorded product. At the same time radio itself was a voracious user of material, broadcasting nightly for hours at a time from a succession of ballroom venues where the big bands played. However, the most popular bands were not always booked by the most accessible venues, so their popularity boosted another recorded product, the broadcast transcription (*see* TRANSCRIPTION (iii)), a type of recording made exclusively for the purposes of broadcasting. Transcriptions were usually on 16-inch discs which allowed up to 15 minutes of playing time, but once again few bands or musicians took advantage of it, though the arrangements used in ballrooms and dance halls regularly included more instrumental parts and solo opportunities than commercial releases.

Independent of this burgeoning business were the activities of devoted amateur recordists, ever mindful that every jazz performance is unique. Using disc cutters and, later, wire recorders, they made recordings for their own pleasure on location or from radio broadcasts (the latter are known as "air checks" or "air shots"), capturing much material that would otherwise not have survived; although the sound quality was predictably inferior to that of recordings made in the studio with professional equipment, they provided material for an explosion of unofficial issues when copyrights began to expire in the 1970s.

4. DEVELOPMENTS OUTSIDE THE USA. Throughout the 78 r.p.m. era, and even later in some areas (for example, Japan), non-Americans learned about jazz primarily by listening to recordings and to radio broadcasts (usually themselves consisting of recordings, rather than of live transmissions). The simple reason for this is that the early history of jazz is dominated by musicians who usually performed and recorded in the USA. Certainly there were many instances of Americans touring and even living abroad (*see* JAZZ (i), esp. §IV, 5), but all such events and circumstances taken together were comparatively insignificant beside the activity going on in the USA, particularly in the matter of stylistic innovation.

In the early decades of jazz, therefore, non-American record companies were important for rather different reasons from their American counterparts. Their significant contributions were, first, to issue recordings made in the USA, an activity (pursued by labels such as Brunswick, Odeon, and Panachord) that formed the bedrock of the dissemination of jazz in Europe and the rest of the world; second to document the development of the music in their own countries; and only third to make important new recordings by performers of the first rank.

Although they may have been comparatively few, noteworthy recordings of major figures were nevertheless made by European countries. Columbia recorded the Original Dixieland Jazz Band in London in 1919–20. Deutsche Grammophon recorded Arthur Briggs in Berlin in 1927–8. During his residency in Europe in the mid-1930s Benny Carter recorded for Vocalion and in the same period Coleman Hawkins, also living for a time in Europe, recorded for Parlophone. Carter and Hawkins also recorded for Decca, as did Duke Ellington, Stephane Grappelli, and Django Reinhardt; the Quintette du Hot Club de France for Ultraphone; Carter, Hawkins, Bill Coleman, and the Quintette du Hot Club de France for His Master's Voice; and Hawkins for Panachord. Perhaps the most important of the European organizations was the small label Swing, established in Paris in 1937 by Charles Delaunay and Hugues Panassié, which produced fine sessions by the Quintette du Hot Club de France, Carter, Hawkins, Coleman, Rex Stewart, Dicky Wells, and Teddy Weatherford. Weatherford also later recorded for Columbia in Calcutta (1942–3).

5. THE WAR YEARS AND THE AFM RECORDING BAN. As the 1940s began, little at first sight seemed likely to affect the enormous boom being enjoyed by those guiding the progress of the swing era. But events were combining that would forever change the face of jazz and the way it was documented on disc. The crucial event was the war. Its immediate effects on the American treasury led to several significant fiscal and other measures. Driving for pleasure was banned to save gasoline; a cabaret tax of 30% (later reduced to 20%) was imposed, making smaller, cheaper bands a more attractive booking proposition; and for a time a midnight curfew was introduced. In addition, the stresses of wartime, as though echoing those of the Depression, increased popular demand for the sentimental and the reassuring; this in turn boosted the standing of vocalists, who very soon began to see their names appearing in headlines at the top of the bill, before the bands' names.

At the same time the loss of employment opportunities for musicians, which the AFM put down to the new popularity of radio, caused a backlash against broadcasting. Because musicians were losing jobs as places of public entertainment closed – partly as a result of potential patrons having a ready-made source of entertainment at home in the form of broadcasting, partly because of wartime measures – the AFM called for a royalty payment to be made to the union by record companies for each commercial disc sold. When no progress was made in talks, the union demand was backed by a ban on instrumental recording from 1 August 1942, which lasted roughly two years. Decca came to an agreement with the AFM in September 1943 and Blue Note in November, but Columbia and Victor did not settle the dispute until November 1944, when they agreed to pay into a union fund a percentage of their income, amounting to between 0.25c and 5c for each disc sold. In the meantime singers, who were not members of the AFM, continued to be able to record, and the prominence this gave them put another nail in the coffin of the big-band business.

The strike, coupled with the dispersal of vast numbers of people into branches of wartime service, led to a need to organize the entertainment industry in new ways. Major network radio series and wholly new ones were transcribed for the Armed Forces Radio Service on 16-inch discs, which were freighted to service personnel all over the world for replay at their bases. And, in the absence of commercial record issues, the US War Department authorized the special series called V-discs exclusively for military personnel. Culled from commercial recordings, broadcasts, and transcriptions, as well as specially organized sessions, some eight million V-discs were distributed between 1943 and 1949, on 12-inch 78s that could carry up to $6\frac{1}{2}$ minutes of sound. The AFM, having banned commercial recordings, permitted musicians to take part in the V-disc sessions on condition that the discs would be treated as army surplus at the end of hostilities and destroyed; many were, but it is believed that few, if any, titles were lost altogether.

Thus V-discs, together with the broadcast transcription products of AFRS, Associated, Lang–Worth, Standard, Thesaurus (of NBC), and World Transcriptions, form a jazz archive covering an immensely important period, which (except for "soundies") is otherwise undocumented because of the AFM ban. However, instead of providing a view of the music's continual development in the mid-1940s, these recordings effectively present a picture of jazz frozen as it was at the beginning of the decade, thus obscuring the major changes that emerged suddenly, as though they were revolutionary, when recording began again in 1944–5.

6. The re-emergence of independent labels. After the demise of many independent companies during the Depression, a certain recovery had already begun before the AFM ban. Towards the end of the 1930s, as a reaction to the commercial excesses of the swing era, a fresh group of companies emerged to record "pure" styles that their proprietors felt were being neglected.

Among the first was Milt Gabler's label Commodore, named for his record store in New York. Although it was formed to record the greatly neglected music of the white Chicago school of the 1920s led by Eddie Condon, its short existence (to the mid-1940s) resulted in highly influential recordings by small swing bands, featuring such musicians as Lester Young, Coleman Hawkins, Chu Berry and Roy Eldridge, Eddie Durham (who made some of the first recordings on electric guitar), Hot Lips Page, Don Byas, and many others. Commodore was also one of the first record companies to encourage longer performances by issuing them on 12-inch 78 r.p.m. discs, a format avoided by the major companies, who were locked in a price war and regarded 12-inch discs as uneconomic, reserving them for classical music.

Varsity was established in 1939 by Eli Oberstein, formerly a recording manager at Victor. Although it was short-lived, the label preserved important performances by Roy Eldridge, Benny Carter, and Coleman Hawkins (each as a principal soloist in a single group), Stuff Smith, and John Kirby's sextet (under Buster Bailey's name), which together with Fats Waller and his Rhythm (on Victor and Bluebird) was the most commercially successful small group of the era. Other notable documenters of small-group swing and the transition to bop

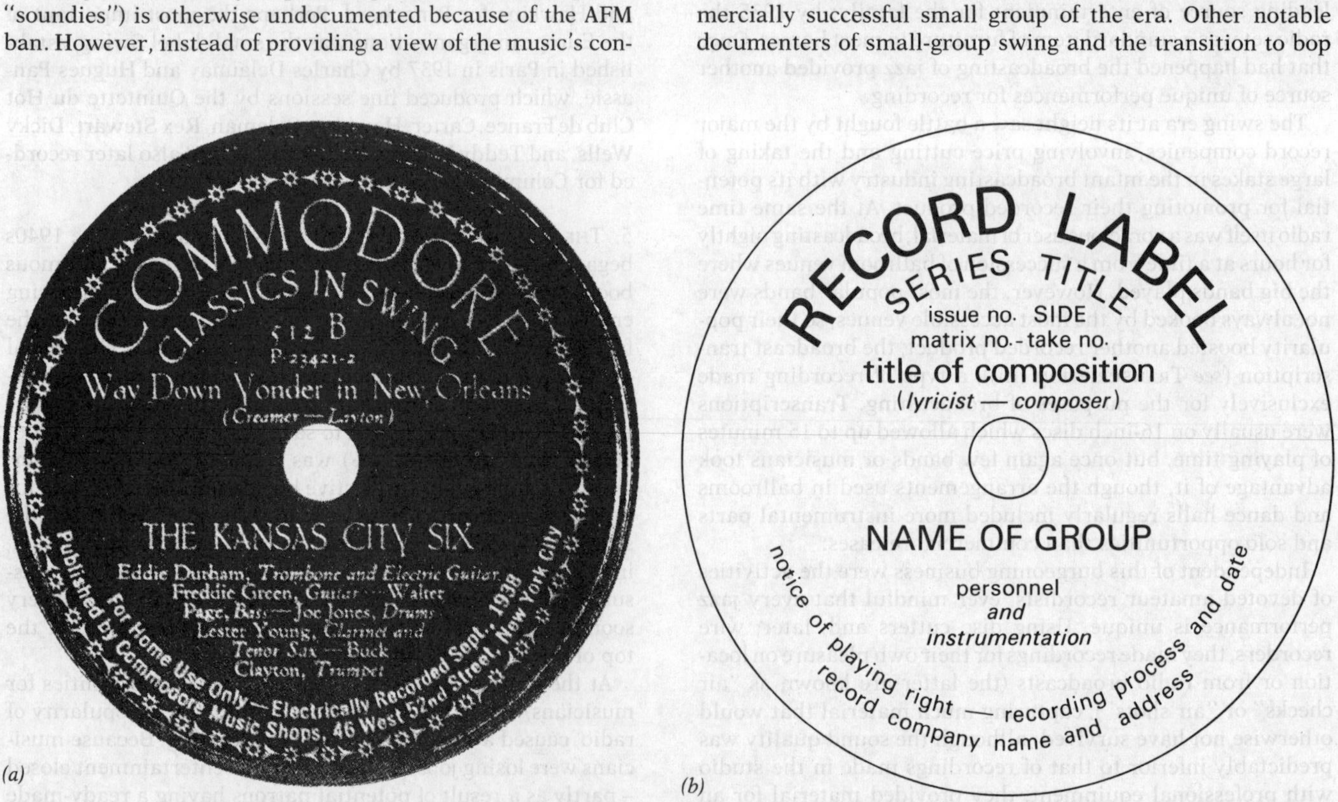

4. (a) Label for "Way Down Yonder in New Orleans," recorded by the Kansas City Six for Commodore (1938); (b) key, identifying the types of information that may appear on a label (the matrix number is always inscribed on the disc itself close to or beneath the label)

5. *Gerry Mulligan's quartet during a recording session for Columbia, December 1958 or January 1959; (left to right) Dave Bailey (drums), Mulligan (baritone saxophone), Bill Crow (double bass), and Art Farmer (trumpet)*

included Black & White, Continental, Musicraft, and the vital label Keynote, run by Harry Lim (who later, in 1972, established the company and label Famous Door).

Alongside these, another group of entrepreneurs was allowing the public to rediscover New Orleans styles through recordings for Jazz Man, Climax, and, most important, American Music, on which players such as Bunk Johnson, George Lewis (i), Wooden Joe Nicholas, and Baby Dodds provided a glimpse of the music's prehistory. Another label, King Jazz, partly owned by Mezz Mezzrow, recorded 56 masters in its brief existence (1945–8), the most important being quintet and septet titles featuring Sidney Bechet.

Such enterprises ensured that the past remained in the present and from this time on the development and documentation of jazz would lie almost completely in the hands of the independent labels. The major companies, whose interest in jazz declined sharply with the disintegration of the big-band era, henceforth confined their jazz activities to styles and musicians of proven commercial worth or prospect.

The first major new style to be nurtured by the independents was bop, which had been rapidly developing in clubs along New York's 52nd Street during the difficult years of the war and the AFM recording ban. An avant-garde movement, its documentation was left almost exclusively to the custody of small, independent, specialist labels such as Guild, Manor, and Ross Russell's Dial, and three that were destined to become giants – Clef, Savoy, and Blue Note.

Clef, under the direction of Norman Granz, arose from the documentation of the rousing and often rowdy jam sessions given as part of his Jazz at the Philharmonic series. It grew to encompass both new and old styles and became perhaps the most important label in defining the jazz mainstream. Absorbed into Verve in 1956, it was sold to MGM late in 1960. Clef was also one of the few labels before the LP era (another was Gene Norman Presents) to break away from the restriction of commercial issues to a duration of three or four minutes: many of the jam session recordings preserve performances of between 10 and 25 minutes, and in their original form were therefore issued on three to seven sides of a set of 78 r.p.m. discs.

Savoy, founded in 1942 by Herman Lubinsky, owed its musical success to its artists and repertory men, including Ozzie Cadena, Buck Ram, and Teddy Reig. But its economic survival was due to its activities in the area of rhythm-and-blues and gospel music, though it recorded many important bop sessions, including one by Charlie Parker's quintet in 1945.

Blue Note more than any other label gained cult status among listeners, not through following fashions but simply because of the quality of its recordings. It was founded in 1939 by Alfred Lion to provide a practical means of expressing his enthusiasm for the boogie-woogie pianists Albert Ammons and Meade "Lux" Lewis, who had impressed him at John Hammond's first "Spirituals to Swing" concert in Carnegie Hall in 1938. 50 pressings each of the five performances could hardly secure a future for the new label but a single performance from the next, greatly contrasting, session did: Sidney Bechet's profound interpretation of *Summertime* (1939, BN 6).

Although they suspended recording activities during the war, Lion and his partner Francis Wolff continued to sell existing recordings; Wolff noted that wartime and the AFM ban sharpened demand and allowed Blue Note to build financial reserves for its next phase of recording. This began in November 1943 and documented the first aspect of the postwar changes in jazz – the rapid growth of small swing groups that split away from the disintegrating big bands. Some of these were led by Ike Quebec, who became the talent scout for Blue Note, leading Lion and Wolff to bop and enabling them to make classic recordings by Thelonious Monk, Bud Powell, Fats Navarro, and others. In the 1950s Blue Note groomed the talents of such musicians as Art Blakey, Horace Silver, Hank Mobley, and Kenny Dorham, dominating the scene against powerful competition by means of carefully planned sessions, always preceded by sufficient rehearsal time to allow challenging material to be played with the greatest creativity.

In the middle of this period there was a second recording ban, less effective than the first. By October 1947 the AFM had announced that a strike would begin on 1 January 1948. The warning gave companies several months in which to accumulate new recordings, which they did with the cooperation of their musicians; they then issued these recordings through the period of the ban, which ended early in 1949. The ban seems to have pushed forward somewhat the demise of the big bands – even Benny Goodman concentrated on leading small groups – but it was no more than a minor factor in their decline.

In general this was a great age for jazz, witnessing the simultaneous flowering of traditional and mainstream as well as modern styles, all assiduously catered for by independent producers. Blue Note documented the entire period, stamping on it a distinctive sound so beloved of collectors that the label was able to make a comeback from 1985 under the guidance of Michael Cuscuna.

But it had important competitors, notably Bob Weinstock's labels Prestige and New Jazz, established after the ban ended in 1949, and the Riverside label of Orrin Keepnews and Bill Grauer, established in 1953, and its subsidiary Jazzland, set up in 1960. Both enterprises discovered important new stars and rediscovered important old ones: Miles Davis and John Coltrane recorded for Prestige, Monk, Bill Evans (ii), and Wes Montgomery for Riverside. As was often the case, however, these two companies lost musicians, once their reputations were firmly established, to the major companies, which tended to acquire rather than develop talent: Columbia took Davis in 1955 and Monk in 1962, Verve took Evans in 1963 and Montgomery in 1964. This was not necessarily detrimental, since Columbia recorded many of Davis's finest albums, as well as some of Charles Mingus's best work, and Verve found a proper setting for Jimmy Smith after his less notable sessions for Blue Note.

During the 1950s, with the advent of the long-playing disc, musicians finally began regularly to record extended performances. The decade also saw the rise of West Coast jazz, documented by labels of high quality such as Richard Bock's Pacific Jazz, Lester Koenig's Contemporary, and Atlantic (particularly

6. Members of the Count Basie Orchestra in the control room at Power Station studio, New York, during the recording of "Long Live the Chief," June 1986: (back row, left to right) Frank Foster (tenor saxophone), Freddie Green (guitar), Dennis Wilson (trombone), Lynn Seaton (bass), and John Williams (baritone saxophone); (front row) Ralph Petersen, Jr., and Malcolm Pollack (engineer)

the sectors of the catalogue supervised by Nesuhi Ertegun). In New York, Vanguard established its series Jazz Showcase under the direction of John Hammond, which presented Count Basie, Buck Clayton, Vic Dickenson, and other leading swing musicians. In the mid-decade Atlantic turned its attention to jazz, recording diverse styles and mounting sessions by Wilbur De Paris and his New New Orleans Jazz, the Modern Jazz Sextet, and Mingus; at the turn of the decade it recorded John Coltrane and Ornette Coleman, and in 1962, as part of a series called Jazz at Preservation Hall, it recorded the first technically well-made album of a New Orleans brass band, the Eureka.

In 1960 the company Impulse! was formed, which became one of the most important new labels of the decade, above all for Coltrane's modal-jazz and free-jazz recordings. Ironically Coltrane's extended improvisations on individual titles, in a number of instances covering one or both sides of a long-playing disc, caused a curious reversal in critics' attitudes: those who disliked Coltrane now lamented the demise of the three-minute performance, which obliged a soloist to be concise.

7. The effects of technological change. From the late 1940s, when magnetic tape became the principal recording medium, the possibility existed of editing (cutting and splicing) recordings; the development of multitrack recording a decade later allowed the isolation and separate manipulation of individual components and voices of a recording. These advances exaggerated the distinction between performance and recording, and meant that, in theory at least, recordings could no longer be regarded as the documentation of a spontaneous act of creation. However, the facility for "improving" on a recorded performance by editing was, on the whole, used less in jazz than, for instance, in classical music, and musicians and listeners alike continued to value the indefinable effect of the element of risk that had hitherto characterized all recordings.

At first editing was used simply to remove blatant mistakes and to retrieve fine passages from otherwise flawed performances. Thus, for example, Keepnews explains that Monk's composition *Brilliant Corners* was so difficult that even such formidable players as Sonny Rollins and Oscar Pettiford were unable to make their way through a completely satisfactory take at a session on 23 December 1956; the issued track is therefore a composite, in which the final statement of the theme is part of a different take from the remainder of the performance. Similar work was done on recordings by Mingus; he was notorious for producing brand-new material at a recording session, and as a result he was obliged to rely on studio editing to eliminate mistakes.

It was only after rock musicians led the way in the mid-1960s that jazz musicians turned to editing as a means of exploring new sounds. The first important examples were the fruits of the collaboration between Miles Davis and his producer at Columbia, Teo Macero. In their work from 1968 into the 1980s the recording session itself was only the first part of making a recording: tapes of hours of improvisation provided the raw material from which they created the structure and content of an issued track. In effect Davis's producer became as important a member of his group as any individual sideman.

The technical innovations of the 1970s had, on the whole, little impact on jazz. Cassette tapes became generally available, but they have never replaced the LP for jazz listeners. There are several possible reasons for this: even with sophisticated recorders, equipped with music sensor devices, it is difficult to locate individual tracks on tape; few listeners possess the expensive equipment needed to produce a sound that rivals a good (not even a great) phonograph; and the extensive liner notes and handsome photographs and artwork that have become an essential part of the presentation of a jazz recording cannot be successfully reduced to the tiny size of a cassette tape box. Direct-to-disc recording had small importance for jazz. Retakes were expensive and editing impossible. The discs themselves were also costly and most companies trying the process risked it only on lightweight forms of jazz. The high fidelity proved to be insufficient compensation for these shortcomings and no label attempted more than a few direct-to-disc recordings.

The digital techniques that have come to prominence in the 1980s are a different matter altogether. The industry has wholeheartedly embraced the technology, and seems likely in time to replace the 12-inch long-playing album with the compact digital disc for all new recordings. In the area of reissues the picture is less clear. The compact disc has become established in the middle of a period of unprecedented success for LP reissues of earlier recordings (see §8 below), one important aspect of which is the popularity of facsimiles. It seems possible, therefore, that for reissues at least, the conventional LP will hold its own against the compact disc, unless the latter takes advantage of its longer playing time to provide comprehensive collections of old recordings.

8. Non-American companies and labels, and reissues. Between the end of World War II and the late 1950s there emerged in Europe and elsewhere a number of new companies, recording bop and the revived traditional styles played by touring Americans and by new, important non-American players. These enterprises included Esquire and Tempo in England, Barclay, Blue Star, and Vogue in France, Cupol, Metronome, Sonet, and Storyville in Scandinavia, Supraphon in Czechoslovakia, Muza in Poland, and Swaggie in Australia.

From the late 1960s numerous European companies came to prominence, several in the recording of new styles of jazz – a significant development in consideration of the earlier role of the European companies as followers of the American lead. Among the most important were Black and Blue (1968–) in France; MPS (1968–), ECM and FMP (both 1969–), and Enja (1971–) in Germany; Incus (1970–), Ogun (1973–), and Leo (ii) (1980–) in England; Steeplechase (1972–) in Denmark; Hat Hut (1974–) in Switzerland; Black Saint (1975–) and Soul Note (1979–) in Italy; Timeless (1975–) and Criss Cross Jazz (1981–) in the Netherlands; and Leo (i) (*c*1978–) in Finland. Black Saint, FMP, Hat Hut, and Incus, as well as portions of the catalogues of ECM, Enja, the Leos, and Ogun, are devoted to free jazz, in interesting contrast to the more conservative repertory of swing and bop offered by the principal new labels established in the USA in the same period, which included Master Jazz Recordings (1967–), Chiaroscuro (1970–), Muse (ii) (1972–), Concord (1973–), Pablo (1977–), and Palo Alto (1981–).

Concurrently reissues flourished. Noteworthy anthologies included a Time–Life series of boxed sets, each one consisting of three albums devoted to leading early jazz and swing soloists, a monumental and stylistically comprehensive series of 100 albums issued by the Franklin Mint in Philadelphia, and scholarly collections put together by the Smithsonian Institution in Washington. Fantasy issued double (and in a few cases triple) albums drawn from the catalogues of Prestige and Riverside, RCA revived the Bluebird catalogue on a series of double albums, Mosaic (ii) offered boxed sets of the complete recordings of a number of musicians for Blue Note, Pacific Jazz, and

Black Lion, and first Arista then (from around 1985) Muse (ii) reissued the Savoy catalogue. An important development was the revival in 1985 of the Blue Note label, both for reissues and new recordings.

By the 1980s several Japanese labels had introduced the concept of facsimile reproductions of acclaimed albums. This idea was taken up by French Verve, then, more importantly, by Fantasy, which in 1983 set up the Original Jazz Classics label, offering facsimiles of hundreds of albums from the catalogues of Contemporary, Debut, Fantasy, Jazz Workshop, Prestige, and Riverside. An even larger collection of this kind was concurrently developed by the Spanish company Fresh Sounds, which drew material from RCA Victor, Pacific Jazz, Bethlehem, Roulette, Columbia, and other labels, both American and European.

Digital remastering techniques (see §I, 4, above) have had a profound, and also controversial, effect on reissues. The most notable engineer in this field is the Australian Robert Parker, whose work was broadcast and issued on tape, disc, and compact disc as the result of a collaborative venture by the Australian Broadcasting Company and the BBC. While Parker's techniques of filtering and clarifying acoustical recordings have produced some remarkable results, at the time of their first appearance (in the mid-1980s) a critical storm arose about their faithfulness to the original performances in comparison with the best monaural analogue transfers of the 1960s; Parker's addition of echo effects and attempts to simulate stereophonic sound were particularly criticized.

The following record companies and labels have entries in this dictionary:

Ace of Hearts, Actuelle, Affinity, AFRS, Ajax, Alto (ii), American Music, American Record Company, Arc, ARC–BRC, Arco, Argo, Arista, Artists House, Arto, Atco, Atlantic, Audiophile, Aurora, Autograph, Ava

Bakton, Banner, Bee Hive, Bet-Car, Bethlehem, Birth, Black and Blue, Black & White, Black Jazz, Black Lion, Black Patti, Black Saint, Black Swan, Blu-disc, Bluebird, Blue Note (ii), Blue Star, Bosco, Bridgeport Die & Machine Co., Broadway, Brunswick, Buddy

Cadet, Cadillac (ii), Cameo, Candid, Capitol, Cardinal, Catalyst, CBS, Champion, Charlie Parker Records, Chiaroscuro, Choice, Circle (i), Circle (iii), Classic Jazz, Claxtonola, Clef, Climax, Cobblestone, Collectors Items, Columbia, Commodore, Concord, Conqueror, Contact, Contemporary, Continental, Creole, Crescent, Criss Cross Jazz, Crown, Cupol

Daffodil, Dauntless, Davis & Schwegler, Decca, Delmark, Delta, De Luxe, Derby (ii), Deutsche Grammophon, Dial, Dire, Discovery, Diva, Domino

East: West, East Wind (i), East Wind (ii), ECM, Edison, Edison-Bell, Electrola, Elektra Musician, EmArcy, Emerson, EMI, Emily, Enja, Epic, ESP-disk, Esquire, Everybody's, Exclusive

Famous, Famous Door (ii), Fantasy, Felsted, Flying Dutchman, Flyright, FMP, Freedom, Fresh Sounds

Galaxy, Gazell, General, Gennett, GHB, Gilt-edge, GNP, Good Time Jazz, Gramavision, Gramophone Co., Grey Gull, Groove, GRP, Guardsman, Guild

Handy Record Company, Harlequin, Harmograph, Harmony (ii), Hat Hut, Hep, Herwin (i), Herwin (ii), Hifijazz, His Master's Voice, Hit of the Week, Hollywood, Horizon, Hot Record Society

IAJRC (i), Imperial, Impulse!, Incus, Inner City, Interstate Music

Jaro, Jazz (ii), Jazzland, Jazzline, Jazzology, Jazz Record, Jazz Society (i), Jazz Society (ii), Jazztime, Jazztone, Jazz West, Jewel, Judson

Keynote, King, King Jazz, Klacto, Krazy Kat

Landmark, Lang–Worth, Legend, Leo (i), Leo (ii), Liberty Music Shop, Limelight, Lincoln, Lindström, London

Magpie, Manor, Marathon, Marsh Laboratories, Master (ii), Master Jazz Recordings, Medallion, Melotone, Mercury, Meritt (i), Meritt (ii), Metrojazz, Metronome, Milestone, Modern, Moers Music, Mole, Montgomery Ward, Moodsville, Mosaic (i), Mosaic (ii), MPS, Muse (i), Muse (ii), Musicraft

National (i), National (ii), National (iii), Nessa, New Jazz, New York Recording Laboratories, Nilva, Nocturne, Nordskog, Norgran

Odeon, Ogun, Okeh, Onyx (ii), Oriole (i), Oriole (ii), Owl, Ozone

Pablo, Pacific Jazz, Palo Alto, Panachord, Paradox, Paramount, Parlophone, Pathé, Peacock's Progressive Jazz, Perfect, Phoenix Jazz, Plaza Music Company, Prestige, Progressive, Puretone, Puritan

QRS

Rampart, RCA Victor, Regal (i), Regal (ii), Regal (iii), Regal–Zonophone, Regina, Regis, Reprise, Retrieval, Revelation, Rex, Rialto, Ring, Ristic, Riverside, Romeo, Roulette, Royal Roost (ii)

Saba, Sackville, Savoy (i), Savoy (ii), Scala, Scepter, SESAC, Session (ii), Session Disc, 77, Signal, Silvertone, Sittin' in With, Solid State, Solo Art, Sonet, Sonora, Soul Note, Spotlite (ii), Starr, Stateside, Steam, Steeplechase, Storyville (ii), Storyville (iii), Strata-East, Sun (i), Sun (ii), Sunnyside, Sunrise, Sunset, Sunshine, Super Disc, Superior, Supertone (i), Supertone (ii), Supertone (iii), Supreme, Swaggie, Swing (ii), Swingville, Symphonola

Teddy Wilson School for Pianists, Tempo (ii), Theresa, Time (ii), Timeless, Timely Tunes, Transition, Triangle, Trip

UHCA, United, United Artists, United Phonographs Corp.

Vanguard, Variety (i), Variety (ii), Varsity, Vault, V-disc, Verve, Victor, Vocalion, Vogue, V.S.O.P. (ii)

Warwick, Wave, Wax (ii), World Pacific, World Wide

Xanadu

Zonophone

BIBLIOGRAPHY

R. D. Darrell: *The Gramophone Shop Encyclopedia of Recorded Music* (New York, 1936, rev. and enlarged 3/1948/*R*1970)

F. F. Clough and G. J. Cuming, eds.: *The World's Encyclopedia of Recorded Music* (London, 1952/*R*1970; suppls. 1953, 1957)

R. Gelatt: *The Fabulous Phonograph* (New York, 1954, 3/1977)

H. Lyttelton: "Introducing the Tape Surgeon," *Second Chorus* (London, 1958), 38

O. Read and W. L. Welch: *From Tin Foil to Stereo* (Indianapolis and New York, 1959/*R*1971, rev. 2/1976)

V. K. Chew: *Talking Machines, 1877–1914: some Aspects of the Early History of the Gramophone* (London, 1967, rev. 2/1973)

J. Bornoff and L. Salter: *Music and the Twentieth Century Media* (Florence, Italy, 1972)

C. Hamm: "Technology and Music: the Effect of the Phonograph," in C. Hamm, B. Nettl, and R. Byrnside: *Contemporary Music and Music Cultures* (Englewood Cliffs, NJ, 1975), 253

B. Lane: "75 Years of Magnetic Recording," *Wireless World*, lxxxi (1975), 102, 161, 222, 283, 341

E. B. Moogk: *Roll Back the Years: History of Canadian Recorded Sound and its Legacy: Genesis to 1930* (Ottawa, 1975)

R. Angus: "The History of Recording," *Modern Recording*, i (1975–6), no.1, p.22; no.2, p.18; no.3, p.22; no.4, p.22; no.5, p.28; no.6, p.26

W. R. Isom, ed.: "The Phonograph and Sound Recording after 100 Years," *Journal of the Audio Engineering Society*, xxv/10–11 (1977) [complete issue]

H. Lindsay: "Magnetic Recording," *DB: the Sound Engineering Magazine*, xi/12 (1977), 38; xii/1 (1978), 40

J. B. Smart and J. W. Newsom: *A Wonderful Invention* (Washington, 1977) [catalogue of Library of Congress exhibition on the centennial of the phonograph]

H. W. Hitchcock, ed.: *The Phonograph and our Musical Life*, Institute for Studies in American Music Monographs, xiv (New York, 1980)

M. Berger, E. Berger, and J. Patrick: *Benny Carter: a Life in American Music* (Metuchen, NJ, and London, 1982)

I. Carr: *Miles Davis: a Critical Biography* (London and New York, 1982; Ger. trans., Baden-Baden, Germany, 1985) [incl. discography by B. Priestley]

C. Hamm: "Changing Patterns in Society and Music: the U.S. since World War II," *Music in the New World* (New York, 1983), 35–70

P. Oliver: *Songsters and Saints: Vocal Traditions on Race Records* (Cambridge, England, and elsewhere, 1984)

GORDON MUMMA/R (I)
CHRIS SHERIDAN (II, 1–3, 5–6)
BARRY KERNFELD (II, 4, 7–8)

Record label. (1) The paper disc glued to the center of a record on which details of the recorded performance and various other items of information are shown; *see* RECORDING, fig.4.

(2) The name under which a record company issues recordings; recordings are thus spoken of as appearing "on a label." The name of the company and the label may be but need not be the same; many companies own more than one label, often using a different name for each of their catalogues of recordings (the catalogues normally cover different styles or may be intended for different markets); any one catalogue may be subdivided into titled series (for example, the Parlophone label issued a number of series named New Rhythm Style Series, Super Rhythm Style Series, etc.). Record labels are often identified in printed form (notably on the paper disc glued to the center of a record, see (1) above) by distinctive typography or by a trademark or logo; perhaps the most famous of these is the image, used by His Master's Voice, of the dog with his ear cocked to the horn of an old-fashioned phonograph. A list of

the record labels on which entries appear in this dictionary is given at the end of RECORDING.

Red, Sonny [Kyner, Sylvester] (*b* Detroit, 17 Dec 1932; *d* Detroit, 20 March 1981). Alto saxophonist and bandleader. He first worked with Barry Harris (1949–52). In 1954 he played tenor saxophone with Frank Rosolino but returned to the alto instrument when he joined Art Blakey later the same year. He went with Curtis Fuller to New York in 1957, and settled there in 1959; he recorded with Paul Quinichette and Fuller (both 1957) and made albums under his own name (1958–62), including *Out of the Blue* (1959–60, BN 4032). During the 1960s and 1970s Red worked as a freelance in hard-bop groups, playing with Donald Byrd (early 1960s) and Kenny Dorham (1966), and recording with Clifford Jordan (1961), Pony Poindexter (1962), Byrd (1966, 1967), Yusef Lateef (1968), and Howard McGhee (1978).

BIBLIOGRAPHY

FeatherE; *Feather '60s*
Obituary, *DB*, xlviii/8 (1981), 13

Redd, Freddie (*b* New York, 29 May 1928). Pianist and composer. He received some instruction in music as a child but is largely self-taught as a pianist. After serving in the army (to 1949) he worked at clubs in New York and Syracuse, New York, in a small group led by the drummer Johnny Mills, and in 1951 recorded with Tiny Grimes and toured the South in Cootie Williams's sextet. In 1952 he returned to New York, where in the following year he worked briefly with Oscar Pettiford and Charles Mingus. He belonged to the Jive Bombers with the saxophonist Earl Johnson, the double bass player Clarence Palmer, and the singer and guitarist Pee Wee Tinney (1954), recorded with Art Farmer's and Gigi Gryce's quintet and Gene Ammons's All Stars (1955), and with Ernestine Anderson and Rolf Ericson toured Sweden in the summer of 1956, where he also recorded with Ericson and Tommy Potter and as the leader of a trio. On returning to the USA he moved to San Francisco, where he played for a brief period with Mingus at the Black Hawk and worked as the house pianist at Bop City. He wrote the music for Jack Gelber's play *The Connection*, in performances of which he took part in New York (1959–60) and London and Paris (1961); he also performed on the soundtrack to a filmed version of the play. From the early 1960s he lived and performed in Paris, Denmark, and the Netherlands. After returning to the USA in 1974 he settled in Los Angeles and became progressively less active in music, although he did record an album as the leader of a trio in 1977. Redd's playing has been described as a barrelhouse equivalent of that of Bud Powell.

SELECTED RECORDINGS

As leader: *Freddie Redd Trio* (1955, Prst. 197); *San Francisco Suite* (1957, Riv. 250); *Music from "The Connection"* (1960, BN 84027); *Under Paris Skies* (1971, Futura Swing 03); *Straight Ahead!* (1977, Inter. 7715)
As sideman with A. Farmer: *Art Farmer Quintet* (1955, Prst. 209)

BIBLIOGRAPHY

FeatherE; *Feather '60s*
V. Wilmer: "Freddie Redd," *JJ*, xiv/4 (1961), 3
F. Postif: "Freddie Redd," *Jh*, no.269 (1971), 15
J. Barr: Liner notes, *Straight Ahead!* (Inter. 7715, 1977)
W. F. Lee: "Freddie Redd," *People in Jazz: Jazz Keyboard Improvisors of the 19th and 20th Centuries* (Hialeah, FL, 1984)

GREGORY E. SMITH

Redd, Vi [Elvira] (*b* Los Angeles, 20 Sept 1928). Alto and soprano saxophonist, and singer. She grew up in a musical family; her father, Alton Redd, played drums with Les Hite and Kid Ory. She played in Las Vegas (1962) and toured with Earl Hines (1964), then in 1965–6 led a bop quartet in San Francisco with her husband, the drummer Richie Goldberg. In the late 1960s she played at Ronnie Scott's in London (1967), with Max Roach in Copenhagen, and at clubs in the USA; in 1968 she joined Dizzy Gillespie and toured Africa and Europe with Count Basie. She returned to Los Angeles the following year to teach. She was a guest performer with Roland Kirk at UCLA (1974), and later appeared at Marian McPartland's jazz festival in Rochester, New York (1977). Redd's performances are emotionally charged and highly personal; she employs an unusual voice in the service of a strong, deeply felt blues style, which may be heard to advantage on *Dinah*, recorded in 1965 with Al Grey. As an alto saxophonist she was influenced chiefly by Charlie Parker. She remained active in the late 1980s.

SELECTED RECORDINGS

As leader: *Bird Call* (1962, UA 15016)
As sideman: on A. Grey: *Shades of Grey* (1965, Tangerine 1504), Dinah, Put it on Mellow; G. Ammons and D. Gordon: *The Chase!* (1973, Prst. 10010); M. McPartland: *Now's the Time!* (1977, Hal. 115)

BIBLIOGRAPHY

L. Feather: "Focus on Alto Saxophonist, Soprano Saxophonist, Vocalist Vi Redd," *DB*, xxix/24 (1962), 23
P. Carles and L. Feather: "Vi Redd ou le saxe fort," *Jm*, no.148 (1967), 29
S. Nurullah: "Vi Redd: Interview," *Cadence*, iii/9 (1978), 3
S. Placksin: *American Women in Jazz, 1900 to the Present: their Words, Lives and Music* (New York, 1982), 259

LEROY OSTRANSKY

Red Heads. Recording group led in the late 1920s by RED NICHOLS.

Red Hot Peppers. Recording group led by JELLY ROLL MORTON in Chicago from 1926. It was formed to make recordings for Victor, and consisted at any one time of seven or eight of the best freelance players available: among them were the cornetist George Mitchell, the trombonist Kid Ory, the clarinetists Omer Simeon and Johnny Dodds, the banjoists Johnny St. Cyr and Bud Scott, the double bass player John Lindsay, and the drummers Andrew Hilaire and Baby Dodds. *Black Bottom Stomp*, *Smoke-House Blues*, *The Chant*, and *Doctor Jazz* (1926) set a standard for arranged jazz for small groups that has never been surpassed. After Morton moved to New York in 1928 he began to use members of his regular band for recordings under the name Red Hot Peppers, and occasionally also borrowed players from other orchestras; only the trumpeter Ward Pinkett played on every session in 1930, after which the name ceased to be used. (L. Wright: *Mr Jelly Lord*, Chigwell, England, 1980)

For recordings, further bibliography, and illustration *see* MORTON, JELLY ROLL.

MIKE HAZELDINE

Rediske, Johannes (*b* Berlin, 11 Aug 1926; *d* Berlin, 22 Jan 1975). German electric guitarist. He was the founder of the group Berlin Swingsters (1947), which performed at American clubs and on broadcasts of the AFN. He led a swing quartet (from 1948) and a swing quintet (from 1949), both of which performed on radio and television and from 1951 to 1959 made recordings (including *Moonlight in Vermont*, 1957, Amiga 550036 [EP]). From 1954 he appeared at festivals in Germany and accompanied visiting American musicians; he wrote the score to the film *Begrenztes Wochenende* in 1959.

BIBLIOGRAPHY

FeatherE; *Feather–Gitler '70s*; *ReclamsJ*
Untitled item, *JP*, viii/4 (1959), 84

HEIDI BOULTON

Redland, Charles [Nilsson, Carl Gustaf Mauritz] (*b* Södertälje, Sweden, 7 July 1911). Swedish saxophonist, composer, arranger, and bandleader. His father, John, was a musician, and from an early age he studied several wind, percussion, and string instruments. In the 1930s he belonged to many bands, in which he played clarinet and alto saxophone most often and trumpet, trombone, and other instruments occasionally. As a leader he performed from the mid-1930s and made a number of recordings (including *Atlantic Stomp*, 1935, Sonora 3079, and *Blue Evening*, 1941, Sonora 3738); in 1936 he recorded as a clarinetist with Benny Carter in Sweden. He also became highly sought after as a composer and arranger of jazz, popular music, and film scores. Scores used by his band are in the Svenskt Visarkiv, Stockholm; *see* LIBRARIES AND ARCHIVES, §2.
Oral history material in *SSsv*.

BIBLIOGRAPHY

"Svenskt stjärnalbum" [Swedish star-album], *Orkester journalen*, iv/12 (1936), 3
"Våra arrangörer" [Our arrangers], *Estrad*, iii/12 (1942), 8
"Mannen bakom orkestern" [The man behind the orchestra], *Estrad*, v/9 (1944), 11
J. Bruér and B. Nyquist: "Charles Redland: Jazzmusiker, jag?" [Charles Redland: jazz musician, me?], Liner notes, *Svensk jazzhistoria*, iii (Cap. 2014, 1984), 6 [interview]
E. Kjellberg: *Svensk jazzhistoria: en översikt* [Swedish jazz history: an overview] (Stockholm, 1985)

ERIK KJELLBERG

Redman, (Walter) Dewey (*b* Fort Worth, 17 May 1931). Tenor saxophonist and musette player. He studied clarinet from the age of 13, later taking up alto saxophone, and finally changing to the tenor instrument at Prairie View Agricultural and Mechanical University (BS 1953). From 1956 to 1960 he worked as a high-school teacher and also played professionally while attending North Texas State University (MA 1959). His commitment to a career in jazz was marked by a move to San Francisco, where he played with Donald Garrett. From late 1967 to late 1974 Redman was a member of Ornette Coleman's group in New York, although he also played in Charlie Haden's Liberation Music Orchestra (1969) and Keith Jarrett's group (1971–6), and led his own bands; Eddie Moore was one of his most frequent sidemen. During this period Redman adopted a startling manner of vocalizing through, and together with, his saxophone, and took up musette as his second instrument. In 1976, with Don Cherry, Haden, and Ed Blackwell (his former associates in Coleman's band), he formed the group Old and New Dreams, with which he toured and recorded into the 1980s. He has continued to lead his own small groups in the mid-1980s, performing (as, for example, on the album *The Struggle Continues*) a repertory of blues, bop, and free jazz, which testifies to his versatility and wide-ranging interests.

SELECTED RECORDINGS

Duos with E. Blackwell: *Redman and Blackwell in Willisau* (1980, BS 0093)
As leader: *Look for the Black Star* (1966, Fon. 881311); *Ear of the Behearer* (1973, Imp. 9250); *Coincide* (1974, Imp. 9300); of Old and New Dreams (with D. Cherry, C. Haden, and E. Blackwell): *Old and New Dreams* (1976, BS 0013); *Soundsigns* (1978, Gal. 5130); of Old and New Dreams: *Old and New Dreams* (1979, ECM 1154); *The Struggle Continues* (1982, ECM 1225)
As sideman: O. Coleman: *New York is Now* (1968, BN 84287); C. Haden: *Liberation Music Orchestra* (1969, Imp. 9183); K. Jarrett: *El juicio* (1971, Atl. 1673); P. Metheny: *80/81* (1980, ECM 1180–81)

BIBLIOGRAPHY

J. Litweiler: "Dewey Redman: Coincidentals," *DB*, xlii/18 (1975), 14
R. Riggins: "Dewey Redman," *Coda*, no.171 (1980), 28
C. Silvert: "Old and New Dreams," *DB*, xlvii/6 (1980), 16
H. Mandel: "Dewey Redman: Nobody's Foil," *DB*, l/2 (1983), 18
S. Crouch: Untitled article, *VV*, xxx (13 Aug 1985), 31

BARRY KERNFELD

Don Redman, c1932

Redman, Don(ald Matthew) (*b* Piedmont, WV, 29 July 1900; *d* New York, 30 Nov 1964). Composer, arranger, bandleader, and alto saxophonist. He was a child prodigy from a musical family, and learned to play most conventional instruments. By the end of his years in high school he had already begun writing arrangements. At the age of 20 he graduated from Storer College in Harper's Ferry, West Virginia, with a degree in music. After working professionally for about a year in Piedmont he joined Billy Paige's Broadway Syncopators, a band based in Pittsburgh. Here he played clarinet and saxophones, and also wrote some arrangements. While on tour with Paige's band Redman met FLETCHER HENDERSON in New York, and joined him in several recording sessions. When Henderson formed an orchestra shortly afterwards Redman was one of the members (for illustration *see* JAZZ (i), fig.2); besides writing the band's arrangements he played clarinet, saxophones, and occasionally other instruments. The addition of Louis Armstrong in 1924–5 as jazz specialist had a deep impact on all the players and also on Redman's arrangements; the band turned increasingly from dance music to jazz, and by the mid-1920s it was the most prominent black jazz orchestra in the country.

Redman left Henderson in 1927 to become music director of MCKINNEY'S COTTON PICKERS, and in a few months he transformed this group from a little-known novelty ensemble into one of the major jazz orchestras of the period. The Cotton Pickers focused less attention on its soloists than Henderson's band had done and concentrated more on Redman's arrangements, which were played with precision and control. Redman's writing became more elaborate, especially in harmony and rhythm; his new sophistication is apparent in his outstanding arrangement of *Rocky Road*. Besides playing as a soloist (principally on alto saxophone) and in the reed section, Redman began to appear as a singer, performing in a high pitched, half-spoken style. He also composed his best-known popular songs with the Cotton Pickers: *Cherry* and *Gee, ain't I good to you?*.

In October 1931 Redman formed his own band with Benny Morton, Harlan Lattimore, and others. In that year he composed *Chant of the Weed*, perhaps his most masterly work. Although the success of his band waned in later years, it broadcast regularly on radio and made numerous recordings for Brunswick, Victor, and other labels before breaking up in 1940.

Redman spent most of the 1940s composing and writing arrangements for radio, television, and many big bands, including those of Count Basie and Jimmy Dorsey. He organized a big band to tour Europe shortly after World War II, and in 1951 became music director for Pearl Bailey, an association which lasted throughout the 1950s. At the end of the decade he once again issued a few jazz recordings. He seldom performed during his final years, but spent his time writing several extended works (which have never been performed in public).

Redman was an outstanding jazz arranger and the first master of jazz orchestration; several of his innovations have since become standard features of jazz arranging. His influence was greatest during his early years as chief arranger for Henderson. His early arrangements integrated solo improvisations with passages for ensemble in the style of improvised jazz, and he also incorporated certain aspects of collectively improvised jazz, such as breaks, chases, and call-and-response patterns, into his scores. His versions of *Copenhagen*, *Sugar Foot Stomp*, *Go 'long mule*, and *Shanghai Shuffle* for Henderson are important landmarks in the evolution of ensemble jazz.

See also ARRANGEMENT, §2.

SELECTED ARRANGEMENTS

• – composed by Redman

As leader: •Chant of the Weed/•Shakin' the African (1931, Bruns. 6211); Got the jitters (1934, Bruns. 6745); Sweet Sue (1937, Var. 605)

Recorded by F. Henderson with Redman as sideman: Go 'long mule (1924, Col. 228D); Shanghai Shuffle (1924, PAct 036157); Copenhagen (1924, Voc. 14926); Sugar Foot Stomp (1925, Col. 395D); The Henderson Stomp (1926, Col. 817D)

Recorded by McKinney's Cotton Pickers with Redman as sideman: •Cherry (1928, Vic. 21730); Shim-me-sha-wabble (1928, Vic. 21611); •Gee, ain't I good to you? (1929, Vic. 38097); Rocky Road (1930, Vic. 22932)

Recorded by L. Armstrong with Redman as sideman: Save it, pretty mama (1928, OK 8657)

BIBLIOGRAPHY

B. Ulanov: "Thanks, Mr. Redman, for Modern Style," *Metronome*, lvii/6 (1941), 20

H. Panassié: "An Evening with Don Redman," *Hot Notes*, no.12 (1948)

F. Driggs: "Don Redman, Composer-arranger," *JR*, ii/10 (1959), 6; repr. as "Don Redman: Jazz Composer-arranger," in *Jazz Panorama*, ed. M. Williams (New York and London, 1962/R1979), 91

C. Fox: "The Big Band Era: Don Redman," *JM*, viii/2 (1962), 8

M. Mezzrow: "Sur Don Redman," *BHcF*, no.145 (1965), 3

D. Ives: "A View of Don Redman," *JJ*, xxi/7 (1968), 14

G. Schuller: *Early Jazz: its Roots and Musical Development* (New York, 1968), 256

W. C. Allen: *Hendersonia: the Music of Fletcher Henderson and his Musicians: a Bio-discography* (Highland Park, NJ, 1973)

J. Chilton: *McKinney's Music: a Bio-discography of McKinney's Cotton Pickers* (London, 1978)

M. Berger, E. Berger, and J. Patrick: *Benny Carter: a Life in American Music* (Metuchen, NJ, and London, 1982), 74

ROBERT KENSELAAR

Red Onion. Nightclub in New Orleans; *see* NIGHTCLUBS AND OTHER VENUES.

Red Onion Jazz Babies. Recording group assembled for Gennett in 1924. It was based on the members of the Clarence Williams Blue Five, which had recorded for Okeh, and consisted of Louis Armstrong (cornet), Buster Bailey or Sidney Bechet (clarinet and soprano saxophone), Aaron Thompson or Charlie Irvis (trombone), Buddy Christian (banjo), and Lil Armstrong (piano). In the course of four sessions the group recorded four instrumental numbers and five titles accompanying Alberta Hunter (who, because she was contracted to Paramount, used the pseudonym Josephine Beatty for these releases). The recordings were later issued collectively as *Louis Armstrong with the Red Onion Jazz Babies* (1924, Fountain 107).

BIBLIOGRAPHY

T. Lord: *Clarence Williams* (Chigwell, England, 1976), 113, 442

J. L. Collier: *Louis Armstrong: an American Genius* (New York, 1983, London, 1984, as *Louis Armstrong: a Biography*), 141

MIKE HAZELDINE

Reece, Dizzy [Alphonso Son] (*b* Kingston, Jamaica, 5 Jan 1931). Jamaican trumpeter. Born into a musical family, he studied baritone horn from the age of 11 and trumpet from the age of 14; among his classmates were Joe Harriott and Wilton "Bogey" Gaynair. After working in Jamaica with Jack Brown's swing band in 1947, he moved in the following year to London, then to Paris, where he played with Jay Cameron and Don Byas. From 1950 he worked in the Netherlands, Germany, and Italy with Wallace Bishop, the pianist Rob Pronk, and the double bass player Buddy Banks; in 1954 he returned to London, where he worked with Kathy Stobart, Terry Shannon, and Kenny Graham's Afro-Cubists (1954) and made recordings as a leader (1955–7). He also belonged for a brief period to Tony Crombie's big band (1955) and in 1956 performed in Paris with Martial Solal, again with Byas, and with members of the Modern Jazz Quartet. After recording in London with groups led by Victor Feldman (1956–7), which included Tubby Hayes, Ronnie Scott, and Jimmy Deuchar as sidemen, he moved in 1959 to New York, where in the following year he led a group at the Village Vanguard. Later he worked as a freelance sideman and occasionally as a leader; in 1978 he recorded as the leader of an all-star sextet that included Clifford Jordan and Roy Haynes. Reece is an inventive, disciplined soloist in the bop idiom who extemporizes in extended, thoughtfully developed, and melodically constructed phrases.

SELECTED RECORDINGS

As leader: O Moon/Bang! (1955, Tempo A115); Chorus/Basie Line (1956, Tempo A140); *Progress Report* (1956, Tempo TAP9), incl. Out of Nowhere, Scrapple from the Apple; Nowhere to Go (1958, Tempo EXA86) [EP], incl. Main Title, The Search; *Star Bright* (1959, BN 4023), incl. Groovesville, The Rake; *Soundin' Off* (1960, BN 4033); *Manhattan Project* (1978, BH 7001)

As sideman: V. Feldman: on *Victor Feldman in London* (1956, Tempo TAP8), Wilbert's Tune; P. J. Jones: *'Round Midnite* (1966, Passport 11-115), incl. 'Round Midnite

BIBLOGRAPHY

FeatherE; *Feather '60s*

J. Cooke: "Dizzy Reece: an Introduction," *JM*, v/8 (1959), 25 [incl. discography]

M. James: "Out of the Bag, Number Six: Dizzy Reece," *JM*, ix/7 (1963), 14

T. Hall: Liner notes, *Progress Report* (Jasmine 2013, 1982)

KEN RATTENBURY

Reed, Waymon (*b* Fayetteville, NC, 10 Jan 1940; *d* Nashville, 25 Nov 1983). Trumpeter. He grew up in Nashville, and played trumpet in school bands. Later he attended the Eastman School of Music for a year. After touring with carnival and rhythm-and-blues bands he settled in Miami, where he played in bands with Ira Sullivan and Pee Wee Ellis and led his own group. From 1965 to 1969 he was a member of James Brown's soul band. He then worked briefly as a freelance in New York before playing in Count Basie's orchestra (1969–73). He recorded with the big bands led by Frank Foster (1975), Thad Jones and Mel Lewis (1975–6), and Basie (1977–8), as well as with his own bop quintet (1977). From 1978 to 1980 he toured with his wife, Sarah Vaughan, as the principal soloist in her quartet and director of her orchestra.

SELECTED RECORDINGS

As leader: *46th and 8th* (1977, AH 10)

As sideman: E. Jefferson: *Still on the Planet* (1976, Muse 5063); C. Basie: *Count Basie Big Band, Montreux '77* (1977, Pablo 2308207); S. Vaughan: *Duke Ellington Song Book* (1979, PT 2312111, 2312116)

BIBLIOGRAPHY

S. Dance: Liner notes, *46th and 8th* (AH 10, 1978)

BARRY KERNFELD

Reed organ. A generic term for those keyboard instruments whose sound is produced by freely vibrating reed tongues and activated by air under pressure or suction. Common names for such instruments include harmonium (generally used in Europe), melodeon, vocalion, seraphine, *orgue expressif*, cabinet organ, and American organ; the last of these is also a European term, used to distinguish suction from pressure instruments. Reed organs vary in size from compact single-manual instruments powered by one or two foot treadles to large models with two manuals and pedals and several sets of reeds which are operated by a separate blowing lever or electric motor. Other members of the reed-organ family include the accordion and concertina.

The reed organ is comparatively rare in jazz, and recorded examples of its use date in general from the early period. Probably the best-known instance of an early appearance of the instrument is in accompaniments to jazz-oriented songs written and orchestrated by Kurt Weill, particularly in the period 1925–9. In the USA it was sometimes employed to accompany blues and vaudeville singers; a notable example may be heard on Bessie Smith's *The St. Louis Blues* (1925, Col. 14064D) and *Reckless Blues* (1925, Col. 14056D), where the singer is accompanied by Fred Longshaw (and also Louis Armstrong). It is possible that the instrument played by Fats Waller with Fletcher Henderson's band on *The Chant* (1926, Col. 817D) is a reed organ. Some avant-garde musicians have made use of the unusual tone-color of the instrument, but for practical purposes it has been supplanted by the electric or electronic organ (*see* ORGAN, §2).

ALYN SHIPTON

Reed section. A term applied to the reed instruments (i.e., saxophones and clarinets, and, occasionally, flutes) within a big band; *see* BANDS, §§2, 4.

Reeves, Reuben [Red] (*b* Evansville, IN, 25 Oct 1905; *d* New York, Sept 1975). Trumpeter. He traveled in 1924 to New York, where he played at Smalls' Paradise. The following year he moved to Chicago and worked with Erskine Tate (1926, 1927–8) and Dave Peyton (1927, 1928–30); he also gained a master's degree from the American Conservatory and led his own groups for recordings (including *Papa Skag Stomp*, 1929, Voc. 1297). After playing with the pianist and organist Jerome Carrington (1931) he joined Cab Calloway in New York, then returned to Chicago, where he led his own band (1933–5). From the late 1930s until the end of World War II Reeves played with and led army bands, then after demobilization worked with Harry Dial. In 1952 he ceased to work as a full-time musician, but he continued to perform occasionally with Dial and other leaders.

BIBLIOGRAPHY

F. S. Driggs: "Reuben 'Red' Reeves," *JJ*, xii/7 (1959), 6
H. Dial: *All that Jazz about Jazz: the Autobiography of Harry Dial* (Chigwell, England, 1984)
D. Barker: *A Life in Jazz*, ed. A. Shipton (London, 1986), 129

based on *ChiltonW*

Reeves, Talcott (*b* Little Rock, AR, 15 June 1904). Banjoist and guitarist. He began playing banjo at the age of 20 and studied at Wilberforce College, Ohio, where in 1925 he joined Horace Henderson. He performed regularly with Henderson until 1930 and worked with Benny Carter (1928–9). In the 1930s and early 1940s he played intermittently with Don Redman, with whom he made several recordings (including *Chant of the Weed*, 1931, Bruns. 6211). He ceased full-time performing after 1943 but continued to work as a freelance musician.

based on *ChiltonW*

Regal (i). Record label. Issue began in spring 1921, and at first most of the catalogue was drawn from Emerson. By 1923, however, the Plaza Music Co. was the source; most of the material was also put out on Banner and other labels connected with Plaza, though different takes were sometimes used. The label was discontinued by the American Record Co. in the summer of 1931. (B. Rust: *The American Record Label Book*, New Rochelle, NY, 1978), 263)

Regal (ii). Record label. It was established by the British branch of Columbia, and issue began in April 1914; it was used for cheap recordings. The label name was also used by Australian Columbia after its formation in 1926. American material was drawn from Columbia and Harmony, and included a considerable amount of jazz. The label was maintained after British Columbia merged with the Gramophone Co. to form EMI in March 1931, but around the beginning of 1933 Regal was merged with the Gramophone Co.'s label Zonophone to form REGAL–ZONOPHONE, which was used both in Britain and Australia. The name Regal was later used by EMI for issues in territories where its other labels were not available. Thus albums of recordings by Duke Ellington were issued on Regal in Spain that were put out elsewhere on Columbia; an important series of jazz reissues (on LPs) of the 1970s was released under the name Regal.

BIBLIOGRAPHY

P. Burgis: "Discs from Down Under," *Sv.* no.11 (1967), 4
B. Rust: *The American Record Label Book* (New Rochelle, NY, 1978), 264

Regal (iii). Record company and label. The company was established in July 1949 by the four Braun brothers after the termination of the arrangement whereby they operated their earlier label De Luxe as an autonomous subsidiary of King. Regal was based at Linden, New Jersey, and recorded the work of such musicians as Alberta Hunter and Cab Calloway. The last recording sessions were organized in May 1951; the company ceased to exist around six months later. (B. Daniels: "Regal Records 1949–1951," *Whiskey, Women, and . . .*, no.10 (1982), 12)

Regal Theater. Theater in Chicago; see NIGHTCLUBS AND OTHER VENUES.

Regal–Zonophone. Record label. It was formed by EMI in both Britain and Australia by the merger of Columbia's label Regal with the Gramophone Co.'s cheap label Zonophone. The Regal numerical series were continued, but some Zonophone issues were re-pressed with the new label. American repertory was drawn from Bluebird, including work by such jazz musicians as Wingy Manone and Hot Lips Page. After 1939 the label's importance waned, and it was finally discontinued in 1949.

BIBLIOGRAPHY

R. Jewson, D. Smith, and R. Webb: "Arthur Gainsbury's Guide to Junkshoppers: Regal," *Sv*, no.42 (1972), 211

B. Rust: *The American Record Label Book* (New Rochelle, NY, 1978), 265

Regina. Record company and label. The company was established in New York in the early 1960s; the catalogue included albums by Charlie Mariano, Roger Kellaway, Eddie Thompson, and the pianist Dorothy Donegan.

MARK GARDNER

Regis. Record label. It was launched in 1943 by the Regis Record Co. of Newark, New Jersey; the proprietor was Irving Berman. At first the catalogue consisted only of gospel music, but it was soon expanded to include the work of Tiny Bradshaw, Tab Smith, and other jazz musicians. Operations ceased at the end of 1944, and the artists and repertory were transferred to Berman's new label, Manor, which maintained Regis's matrix series. ("Regis–Manor–Arco," *Blues Research*, no.15 (n.d. [?1966]), 2)

Regoli, Enrique [Soler, Enrique Llácer] (*b* Alcoy, Spain, 20 June 1934). Spanish drummer, percussionist, and composer. He taught himself to play drums, then undertook further conservatory training in Valencia and Madrid. In 1952 he began playing jazz in Barcelona, then moved to Madrid, where he worked mostly at the Whisky Jazz Club and played with many visiting American bop soloists, including Gerry Mulligan, Slide Hampton, and Pony Poindexter. In 1972 he began performing as a percussionist with the National SO and became a professor of percussion at the conservatory in Madrid. Regoli has written many compositions in various styles. Among his most celebrated jazz pieces are *Blues for David* (dedicated to the double bass player David Thomas), *Spiritual*, and *Regoli's Blues*. He is one of the most versatile drummers in Spain, and has continued to perform and make recordings as a leader (including the album *Fundamentos del ritmo*, 1983, Phi. 412262I) into the 1980s.

ALFREDO PAPO

Rehak, Frank (James) (*b* New York, 7 July 1926; *d* Badger, CA, 26 June 1987). Trombonist. He studied piano, cello, and baritone horn. While in the navy during World War II he took up trombone, and played in a swing sextet in Hawaii. In 1949 he joined Gene Krupa's band, forming with Frank Rosolino and Urbie Green an outstanding trombone section. Rehak became addicted to heroin while touring as a principal soloist with Jimmy Dorsey's orchestra (1950–52); he found some commercial studio work in New York, but in 1955 left music and became a plumber. The following year he toured the Near East and South America with Dizzy Gillespie's big band, then resumed studio work, notably as a member of the Gil Evans–Miles Davis Orchestra (1957–62), and began to make a name as a bop soloist. In the early 1960s, however, he once more became dependent on heroin, which brought an end to his career. In 1969 he entered Synanon's drug rehabilitation center in Los Angeles, where in 1973 he established a music department. Thereafter he became the director of Synanon in Houston.

SELECTED RECORDINGS

As sideman: A. Cohn: *Be Loose* (1956, Dawn 1110); on *Down Beat* Critic Poll Winners: *Winner's Choice* (1957, Beth. 6024), If I'm Lucky, Love and the Weather; on Prestige All Stars: *Roots* (1957, NewJ 8202), Roots; G. Quill: *3 Bones and a Quill* (1958, Roost 2229)

BIBLIOGRAPHY

M. Hohman: "Frank Rehak," *DB*, xliv/9 (1977), 36

J. Kafalos and T. Everett: "Frank Rehak: Interview," *Cadence*, x (1984), no.8, p.5; no.9, p.16

BARRY KERNFELD

Reichenbach, Bill [William Frank] **(i)** (*b* Washington, 18 Dec 1923). Drummer, father of Bill Reichenbach (ii). He played in dance bands while in the armed forces during World War II, then worked in Tommy Dorsey's orchestra (1951). He accompanied the singer Georgia Gibbs (1958–9). From 1962 to 1973 he was a member of Charlie Byrd's trio, and he played with Byrd and Stan Getz on the album *Jazz Samba* (1962, Verve 68432). He worked from 1976 as a freelance with Teddy Wilson, Hank Jones, Urbie Green, and Eddie "Lockjaw" Davis, and in 1984 performed in New Zealand with his son. (*Feather '60s*)

Reichenbach, Bill [William Frank] **(ii)** (*b* Takoma Park, MD, 30 Nov 1949). Trombonist, son of Bill Reichenbach (i). After studying at the Eastman School (BMus 1971), he recorded as a sideman in big bands led by Buddy Rich (1972), Toshiko Akiyoshi and Lew Tabackin (1976–7), Tom Scott (1983), and others, and in Don Menza's septet (1979). He led his own bop quartet on the album *Quartet* (1984, Silver Seven 701) and in 1982–5 made annual tours of New Zealand. A resident of California, he has worked extensively in television and films as well as playing for popular groups and commercial artists. He also plays euphonium and bass trombone.

Reid, Rufus (L.) (*b* Sacramento, CA, 10 Feb 1944). Double bass player. He first played trumpet, then took up double bass while serving in the US Air Force. He played with Buddy Montgomery in Sacramento, then studied music in Seattle and in Chicago (1969–1971), where he played hard bop with Sonny Stitt, James Moody, Milt Jackson, Curtis Fuller, and Dizzy Gillespie. He also performed and recorded in Chicago with Kenny Dorham, Dexter Gordon, Lee Konitz, and Howard McGhee (all 1970). From the early 1970s he made a number of international tours, with Bobby Hutcherson's and Harold Land's quintet (1971), Freddie Hubbard and Nancy Wilson (1971), Eddie Harris (1971–4), and Gordon (1977–9). In 1976 he moved to New York, where he played and recorded with the quartet led by Thad Jones and Mel Lewis (1976–7), and from 1979 he taught at William Paterson College in Wayne, New Jersey (he is the author of two double bass tutors). He made recordings with most of the leaders with whom he played in the 1970s and also with Konitz (1976), Ricky Ford (1981), and Jack DeJohnette's group Special Edition (1982, 1984), in a duo with Kenny Burrell (1983), with a quintet led by Frank Foster and Frank Wess (1983–4), and with Art Farmer (1984) and Jimmy Heath (1985). As a leader he made an album, *Perpetual Stroll* (1980, The. 111), with Gordon's former rhythm section. (L. Gourse: "Rufus Reid, the Evolving Bassist," *JT* (June 1986), 15)

Reilly, Dean (Edwin) (*b* Auburn, WA, 30 June 1926). Double bass player. He played swing and bop in San Francisco with Georgie Auld, Sonny Criss, and Jackie Cain and Roy Kral, performed and made recordings with Earl Hines (including the album *Earl "Fatha" Hines Plays "Fats" Waller*, 1955–6, Fan. 3217), Vince Guaraldi (1956–7), and Eddie Duran (1957), and also recorded with Mel Lewis (1956). After a lengthy association with the folk group the Kingston Trio, Reilly resumed playing jazz and recorded with George Barnes (1977), Duran (1979), Cal Tjader (1981), and the singer Dee Bell (as a member of the orchestra led by Duran and Stan Getz, 1982, 1984). (*FeatherE*)

Reinhardt, Django [Jean Baptiste] (*b* Liberchies, nr Luttre, Belgium, 23 Jan 1910; *d* Fontainebleau, France, 16 May 1953). French guitarist, brother of Joseph Reinhardt. The son of a traveling entertainer, he grew up in a gypsy settlement outside Paris. He first played violin and later took up guitar, and began working professionally in 1922 with the accordionist Guérino. In 1928 he was badly burned in a caravan fire; the resulting mutilation of his left hand, which deprived him of the use of two fingers, led him to devise a unique fingering method to overcome his handicap. After a period of convalescence he worked in cafés in Paris and in a duo with the singer Jean Sablon. In 1934 he was a founding member, with Stephane Grappelli, of the ensemble that became known as the QUINTETTE DU HOT CLUB DE FRANCE; in the years before World War II the group gained considerable renown through its numerous recordings, and Reinhardt became an international celebrity. He appeared throughout Europe and recorded with many important American musicians who visited the Continent. During the war, while Grappelli lived in Britain, Reinhardt remained in France. He led a big band, then achieved considerable success as the leader of a new quintet in which the clarinetist Hubert Rostaing took Grappelli's place; he also became interested in composition and, with André Hodeir, arranged the music for the film *Le village de la colère* (1946). In 1946 he visited England and Switzerland, toured the USA as a soloist with Duke Ellington's band (playing an amplified guitar for the first time), and worked in New York. After his return to France he lived in Samois and toured and recorded with his quintet, which sometimes again included Grappelli.

Reinhardt's grasp of harmony, remarkable technique, and trenchant rhythmic sense made him an excellent accompanist; his incisive support is heard to advantage on *Stardust* (1935), recorded with Coleman Hawkins. He later developed into a soloist of unique character, creating a deeply personal style

Django Reinhardt with the clarinetist Maurice Meunier, Bad Nauheim, Germany, 27 July 1947

out of his own cultural patrimony. By 1937, when he recorded *Chicago* with the Quintette, he was established as the first outstanding European jazz musician, a stylist with great melodic resourcefulness and a mastery of inflection. He was a gifted composer of short evocative pieces and had a flair for pacing a performance so that the maximum variety could be wrung from it without compromising its homogeneity; an excellent example is *St. Louis Blues* (1937). Endowed with remarkable sensitivity, he could work with visiting American performers without forsaking his own essentially romantic style. In the 1940s he changed to the electric guitar, but without coarsening his playing as he used its power with discretion. The rhythmic content of his work became more varied, as in *Minor Swing* (1947), and his improvised lines more flexible. The asymmetrical, occasionally violent, playing heard in some later performances shows the continual widening of his expressive scope. A documentary film, *Django Reinhardt* (1958), was made after his death by the director Paul Paviot; it includes an introduction by Jean Cocteau, and music performed by Grappelli, Rostaing, and Joseph Reinhardt.

Django's two sons, Lousson and Babik, were both fine guitarists, and after their father's death Babik established a reputation in his own right.

See also GUITAR, §2, and fig.1; JAZZ (i), fig.4; and STRING BAND.

SELECTED RECORDINGS

As unaccompanied soloist: Improvisation (1937, HMV B8587)

As leader with S. Grappelli of the Quintette du Hot Club de France: Lady be Good (1934, Ultraphone 1422); Confessin' (1935, Ultraphone 1443); Djangology (1935, Ultraphone 1548); Limehouse Blues (1936, HMV K7706); Tears (1937, HMV B8718); Chicago (1937, Swing 2); The Sheik of Araby (1937, HMV B8737); Nuages (1940, Swing 88)

As leader of other groups: St. Louis Blues (1937, Swing 7); Eclats de Cuivres (1942, Rythme 5024); For Sentimental Reasons (1947, BStar 30); September Song (1947, BStar 46); Nuages (1947, Swing 438); Minor Swing/Douce ambiance (1947, Swing 439); *Django Reinhardt et ses rythmes* (1953, BStar 6830), incl. Insensiblement, Manoir de mes rêves; I Cover the Waterfront (1953, Decca MF36166)

As sideman: C. Hawkins: Stardust (1935, HMV K7527); Honeysuckle Rose/Crazy Rhythm (1937, Swing 1); S. Grappelli: Sugar (1937, Swing 69); R. Stewart: Montmartre (1939, Swing 56)

BIBLIOGRAPHY

C. Delaunay: *Django Reinhardt: souvenirs* (Paris, 1954; Eng. trans., London, 1961/*R*1981, 1982, rev. 2/1981) [incl. discography]
G. S. McKean: "Django Reinhardt," *Jam Session: an Anthology of Jazz*, ed. R. J. Gleason (New York and London, 1958), 111
M.-C. Jalard: "Django et l'école tsigane du jazz," *Cahiers du jazz*, no.1 (1959), 54
D. Schulz-Köhn: *Django Reinhardt: ein Porträt* (Wetzlar, Germany, 1960)
A. Hodeir: *Toward Jazz* (New York, 1962/*R*1976), 186
G. Hoefer: "The Magnificent Gypsy," *DB*, xxxiii/14 (1966), 21
C. Delaunay: *Django, mon frère* (Paris, 1968)
C. Evans: "Django Reinhardt," *JM*, no.162 (1968), 30; no.163 (1968), 31
A. Morgan: "Django Reinhardt," in A. McCarthy and others: *Jazz on Record: a Critical Guide to the First 50 Years: 1917–1967* (London, 1968), 241
——: "Collectors' Notes: Django Reinhardt," *JM*, no.171 (1969), 26; no.178 (1969), 28; no.180 (1970), 29
"'Django and I Had the First Three-guitar Group – without Electricity!,' Says Jazz Violin Virtuoso Stephane Grappelli," *CI*, ix/4 (1970), 26
C. N. Cooper: "Djangologie: an Examination of a Monument to a Jazz Master," *JJ*, xxiv/6 (1971), 10
M. Abrams: *The Book of Django* (Los Angeles, 1973) [bio-discography]
D. E. Hensley: "Remembering Django Reinhardt," *DB*, xliii/4 (1976), 15
M. Abrams: "Django Reinhardt: the Jazz Gypsy," *Sv*, no.77 (1978), 163
I. Cruickshank: *The Guitar Style of Django Reinhardt and the Gypsies* (Woodcote, nr Reading, England, 1982, rev. and enlarged 2/1985)
R. Spautz: *Django Reinhardt: Mythos und Realität* (Luxembourg, 1983; Fr. trans., Paris, 1984) [incl. discography]
A. Doutart: "Django Reinhardt, mythes ou réalité?," *BHcF*, no.322 (1984), 8
A. Schmitz and P. Maier: *Django Reinhardt: sein Leben, seine Musik, seine Schallplatten* (Gauting, Germany, 1985)
M. Zwerin: *La Tristesse de Saint Louis: Swing under the Nazis* (London, Melbourne, Australia, and New York, 1985)

MICHAEL JAMES

Reinhardt, Joseph [Nin Nin] (*b* Paris, 1 March 1912; *d* Paris, late February 1982). French guitarist, brother of Django Reinhardt. As a member of the Quintette du Hot Club de France he accompanied his brother and made many recordings, but never recorded a solo. After his brother's death in 1953 he led a quintet and made several recordings, including *Joseph Reinhardt joue pour Django* (1966–7, Simm 192). He appeared in the films *Mon pote, le gitan* (dir. François Gir, 1958), *Django Reinhardt* (Paul Paviot, 1958), and *Paris Blues* (Martin Ritt, 1961). (M.-C. Jalard: "Django et l'école tsigane du jazz," *Cahiers du jazz*, no.1 (1959), 54)

For illustrations *see* GUITAR, fig.1, and JAZZ (i), fig.4.

ANDRÉ CLERGEAT

Reis Leite, Tania Maria. *See* MARIA, TANIA.

Release. The penultimate section in the refrain of a popular song, leading to the final repeat of the opening section (section *b* in the form *aaba*); it provides a contrast, often tonal as well as harmonic and melodic, with the opening section. *See* FORMS, esp. §1(i)(a).

Reliance Brass Band. New Orleans group formed during the 1890s by PAPA JACK LAINE.

Remler, Emily (*b* New York, 18 Sept 1957). Guitarist. She played guitar from the age of ten and was inspired first by the work of the rock guitarists Jimi Hendrix and Johnny Winter and later while attending the Berklee College of Music by that of the jazz guitarists Wes Montgomery, Pat Martino, and Charlie Christian. She moved to New Orleans, where as the house guitarist at the Fairmont Hotel she accompanied Nancy Wilson, Michel Legrand, and the popular singer Robert Goulet. Her career was aided by Herb Ellis, who introduced her at the Concord (California) Jazz Festival in 1978. During the following years she played with Astrud Gilberto (for three years in the early 1980s) and recorded an album of duos with Larry Coryell (1985); she has also appeared with the group Great Guitars (which includes Ellis, Barney Kessel, and Charlie Byrd) and in a quartet with Eddie Gomez, Bob Moses, and the trumpeter John D'Earth. Remler is equally adept at playing with and without a pick in such diverse styles as bop, jazz-rock, and Latin music; her playing incorporates fluid eighth-note passages, doublings at the octave in the manner of Montgomery, and blues phrasing.

SELECTED RECORDINGS

(all recorded for Concord)

Duos with L. Coryell: *Together* (1985, 289)
As leader: *The Firefly* (1981, 162); *Transitions* (1983, 236)

BIBLIOGRAPHY

A. Berle: "A Jazz Guitarist's Promising Debut," *GP*, xv/9 (1981), 100
A. J. Liska: "Profile: Emily Remler," *DB*, xlix/5 (1982), 49
J. Coryell: "Emily Remler: Life after Wes," *DB*, lii/5 (1985), 23 [incl. discography]

JIM FERGUSON

Remue, Chas [Charles] (*b* Brussels, 15 Oct 1903; *d* Brussels, 5 Feb 1971). Belgian alto saxophonist and clarinetist. A classically trained musician, he played in 1924 with Red Mill's Jazz and with the Bing Boys. He belonged to the White Diamonds, led by the drummer Billy Smith, and to the Royal Dance Orchestra (1926–7), then formed a band that recorded several tracks in London as the New Stompers Orchestra (June 1927); these were the first jazz recordings made by a group consisting entirely of Belgian musicians. At the suggestion of Frank Guarente Remue joined the Savoy Orpheans (December 1927), then formed his own big band (recording in 1929) and worked with Bernard Etté. He joined the orchestra of Stan Brenders in 1936 and continued to work with various groups until his death.

ROBERT PERNET

Remus, Alfredo (*b* Buenos Aires, 9 Nov 1938). Argentine double bass player. He made recordings with Lalo Schifrin (1957, 1970) and Enrique Villegas (1968), as a leader (1968, 1970, 1972), with Jorge López Ruiz (1971), and in the swing and bop big band of the pianist Bubby Lavecchia (1977). From 1984 he belonged to the TRÍO ARGENTINA; he also recorded with Jorge Navarro (1984–5). The album *Trauma* (Ten 100), which he recorded as a leader in 1968, offers good examples of his work.

LAUREANO FERNÁNDEZ, OMAR GARCÍA BRUNELLI

Rena, Joseph (*b* New Orleans, 11 March 1897; *d* New Orleans, 26 Dec 1973). Drummer, brother of Kid Rena. In 1920 he was a member of the Liberty Bell Orchestra led by the trumpeter Wesley Don. Thereafter he worked in bands with his brother, recording for the Delta label in 1940. He retired from music in 1945 to become a preacher.

MARCEL JOLY

Rena, Kid [René, Henry; Little Turk] (*b* New Orleans, 30 Aug 1898; *d* New Orleans, 25 April 1949). Trumpeter, brother of Joseph Rena. He was taught in about 1912, along with Louis Armstrong, at Joseph Jones's Colored Waif's Home, and later studied with Manuel Perez. In 1919 he succeeded Armstrong in Kid Ory's band, remaining until Ory left for California, and in 1921 he founded his own Dixieland Jazz Band, which included Joseph Rena and often George Lewis (i). During the 1920s he also played with the Tuxedo Brass Band, then in the 1930s he formed the Pacific Brass Band. Thereafter Rena led various groups in New Orleans until illness forced his retirement in 1947.

Rena took part in only one recording session, in 1940, but reports of his performances in the 1920s suggest he had a particularly strong tone and an ability to play in the upper register of the instrument for long periods; he is reputed to have developed a remarkable high obbligato for the final strain of *High Society*, later adapted by Sharkey Bonano. By the 1930s he played more in the middle register, but retained a characteristic warm tone and considerable melodic grace. Unfortunately, by the time he recorded (with a band that included Big Eye Nelson, Alphonse Picou, and Jim Robinson), his playing had been reduced by ill-health to a cautious straightforward lead, and exhibited only a few remnants of his former individuality.

Oral history material in *LNT*.

RECORDINGS

(all recorded in 1940 for Delta)

Panama/High Society Rag (800, 804); Milenberg Joys/Clarinet Marmalade (802, 805); Gettysburg March/Lowdown Blues (801, 803); Weary Blues/ Get it right (806–7)

BIBLIOGRAPHY

Charters J
M. Jones: "Those Kid Rena Records," *MM*, xxviii (9 Feb 1952), 9
A. Rose and E. Souchon: *New Orleans Jazz: a Family Album* (Baton Rouge, LA, 1967, rev. 2/1978, rev. and enlarged 3/1984)

ALDEN ASHFORTH

Rena Rama. Swedish quartet, formed in 1971. Its original members were the saxophonist Lennart Åberg, the pianist Bobo Stenson, the double bass player Palle Danielsson, and the drummer Bengt Berger; Danielsson was later replaced by Anders Jormin and Berger by Anders Kjellberg. The group's style is a fusion of modal jazz and other genres, including the folk music of India and Africa. It appeared at festivals in India (Jazzyatra, 1978, 1980) and several European countries and made a number of recordings, including *Inside-Outside* (1979, Caprice 1182).

BIBLIOGRAPHY

L. Westin: "Rena Rama," *Inside-Outside* (Caprice 1182, 1979) [liner notes]
E. Kjellberg: "Rena Rama and Lisa's Piano: an Essay in Jazz Analysis," *Studia musicologica upsaliensa* (Uppsala, Sweden, 1985), 323

ERIK KJELLBERG

Renaud, Henri (*b* Villedieu-sur-Indre, France, 20 April 1925). French pianist and leader. He studied violin from the age of five and piano from the age of eight; in 1946 he moved to Paris. As a member of a group led by the tenor saxophonist Jean-Claude Fohrenbach he accompanied such American musicians as Don Byas, James Moody, and Roy Eldridge. In 1952 he formed a group that played regularly at the Tabou in Paris, where it accompanied Lester Young, Sarah Vaughan, and Clifford Brown; he produced important recordings by Brown in 1953. Around the same time he produced and played piano on recordings by many other musicians, including Milt Jackson, Al Cohn, Oscar Pettiford, Max Roach, and J. J. Johnson (1953) and Pettiford, Frank Foster, Bob Brookmeyer, and Roy Haynes (1954). He led a small group in France that worked with June Richmond (recording in 1957), then moved to New York, where he appeared at Birdland with Philly Joe Jones; on his return to Paris he played at the Blue Note with Kenny Clarke and at Les Trois Mailletz with Buck Clayton. In 1964 he ceased working full-time as a performer to become the head of the jazz division of the CBS label in France and to produce radio and television programs. As a pianist Renaud has a refined, economical style that is well suited to accompaniment. In addition to his work as a performer and producer he has contributed to *Jazz hot* and *Jazz magazine* and been a music consultant for Bertrand Tavernier's film *Round Midnight* (1986).

SELECTED RECORDINGS

As leader: *Henri Renaud–Al Cohn Quartet* (1954, Swing 33332); *Henri Renaud All Stars* (1954, Swing 33320–21); *Henri Renaud Trio* (1957, Ducretet-Thomson 052)

As sideman: L. Konitz: *Lee Konitz Plays* (1953, Vogue 169); C. Brown: *Clifford Brown Quartet* (1953, Vogue 179); Z. Sims: *Zoot Sims Sextet* (1953, Vogue 170); O. Pettiford: *Oscar Pettiford Sextet* (1954, Swing 33326); L. Thompson: *Lucky Thompson* (1956, Ducretet-Thomson 024)

BIBLIOGRAPHY

N. Hentoff: "French Jazz Fans, Musicians Come out of Basin Street, Pick up on Moderns," *DB*, xxi/12 (1954), 12
A. Morgun and N. Renaud: "Henri Renaud Discography," *JM*, iv (1958), no.2, p.23; no.3, p.26; no.6, p.32
L. Malson: "Henri Renaud ou l'épreuve de la réflexion," *Jm*, no.69 (1961), 34
H. Renaud: "Bebop Highlights," *Jh*, no.305 (1974), 18
P. Carles: "Quand Renaud revient," *Jm*, no.284 (1980), 34

ANDRÉ CLERGEAT

Rendell, Don(ald Percy) (*b* Plymouth, England, 4 March 1926). English tenor saxophonist. After early experience in bands led by the trumpeter Duncan Whyte, the saxophonist George Evans, and the violinist Oscar Rabin, he played with John Dankworth's septet (1950–53), one of the most important bop-influenced British groups of the period. In 1954 he formed a sextet, and the following year he led a band that accompanied Billie Holiday in Manchester. After working briefly in Ted Heath's band (1955) Rendell undertook a European tour with the Stan Kenton Orchestra (1956); he continued to demonstrate an aptitude for the West Coast style both in the bands he led in the late 1950s and during a tour of Europe as a member of Woody Herman's Anglo-American Herd in 1959. Rendell was early influenced by the work of Lester Young, but by the late 1950s he had begun to incorporate elements of John Coltrane's style into his playing; the results may be heard on *Roarin'* (1961). In the mid-1960s he led a quintet with Ian Carr which received considerable acclaim before it disbanded in 1969. From that time Rendell has led a number of small groups, and worked with such musicians as Barbara Thompson, Neil Ardley, and Stan Tracey; he has also earned a considerable reputation as a teacher through his work in London at the Royal Academy of Music (1974–7) and the Guildhall School of Music and Drama (from 1984).

Oral history material in *GBLnsa*.

SELECTED RECORDINGS

As leader: *Meet Don Rendell* (1955, Tempo 1); *Playtime* (1958, Decca 4265); *Roarin'* (1961, Jlnd 951); with I. Carr: *Shades of Blue* (1964, Col. SX1733), *Live* (1968, Col. SCX6316), *Change is* (1969, Col. SCX6368); *Spacewalk* (1971, Col. SCX6491); *Earth Music* (1979, Spot. 515)

As sideman: J. Dankworth: Get Happy (1950, Esquire 10103); Leon Bismarck (1951, Esquire 10173); S. Tracey: *The Latin American Caper* (1968, Col. SCX6358); N. Ardley: *Greek Variations* (1969, Col. SCX6414)

BIBLIOGRAPHY

P. J. Sullivan: "Rendell/Carr," *JJ*, xxi/6 (1968), 21 [incl. discography]
M. C. King: "British Jazzmen, 1: Don Rendell," *JJ*, xxiii/7 (1970), 7 [incl. discography]
C. Fox and V. Wilmer: *The Jazz Scene* (London, 1972)
I. Carr: *Music Outside: Contemporary Jazz in Britain* (London, 1973)
R. Cotterrell, ed.: *Jazz Now: the Jazz Centre Society Guide* (London, 1976)

MARK GILBERT

Reno Club. Nightclub in Kansas City; *see* NIGHTCLUBS AND OTHER VENUES.

Reprise. Record company and label. The company was established by Frank Sinatra in Burbank, California, in 1961, after he ceased to record for Capitol. It immediately embarked on an extensive program of jazz recordings, encouraged partly by Sinatra's interest in jazz. The catalogue included eight albums recorded during the 1960s by Duke Ellington (who also supervised sessions for the company in Paris), and material by Count Basie, Bud Powell, Dizzy Gillespie, Ben Webster, Frank Rosolino, Barney Kessel, Chico Hamilton, Shorty Rogers, Jimmy Witherspoon, Don Ellis, Erroll Garner, Jack Sheldon, Calvin Jackson, and Al Hibbler. Sinatra himself recorded many albums for the company; on three of these he was accompanied by Basie's band, on another by Antonio Carlos Jobim.

MARK GARDNER

Reser, Harry (F.) (*b* Piqua, OH, 17 Jan 1896; *d* New York, 27 Sept 1965). Banjoist and bandleader. He performed and recorded with Paul Whiteman (1923), and his prolific studio work included sessions as an accompanist to Bessie Smith (1924), and as the leader of his own bands, which sometimes included Red Nichols and Joe Venuti. His importance to jazz lies in his work as an organizer of studio bands in the 1920s, in which capacity he engaged many white jazz musicians. As a player Reser was essentially a virtuoso popular instrumentalist, but he may be heard in a jazz setting on Bessie Smith's *Easy Come, Easy Go Blues* (1924, Col. 14005D), where he provides a sympathetic (though hardly swinging) banjo accompaniment. He also composed novelty ragtime tunes and wrote methods for banjo, ukulele, and guitar.

BIBLIOGRAPHY

ReclamsJ
W. W. Triggs: *The Great Harry Reser* (London, 1978)

Retrieval. Record label established by JOHN R. T. DAVIES in 1972.

Rettenbacher, J(ohannes) A(nton) [Hans] (*b* Vienna, ?*c*1935). Austrian double bass player. He studied double bass and musicology in Austria, then attended the Berklee College of Music. He worked with Gerd Dudek and Manfred Schoof in Germany (1958), toured Scandinavia with Stan Getz (1960), and played in small groups and big bands with Friedrich Gulda. After studying at the Advanced School of Contemporary Music in Toronto (1963) he played with Eric Dolphy and Fatty George (1964), Joe Nay (1965), and Rolf Kühn, Erwin Lehn, and Don Ellis (1967). He recorded with Oscar Klein (1964), Gulda (1969–70), Milt Buckner (1970), Eugen Cicero (*Balkan Rhapsodie*, 1970, MPS 2120754), and Kühn (*c*1971). From 1968 to 1971 he performed and recorded as a member of the Dave Pike Set. (*ReclamsJ*)

WOLFRAM KNAUER

Return to Forever. Jazz-rock group, formed in late 1971 by CHICK COREA; its other original members were Stanley Clarke (electric bass guitarist), Joe Farrell (reed player), Flora Purim (singer), and Airto Moreira (percussionist). The group toured and made two recordings, which exhibited the influence of Latin music and were notable for the clarity of the individual lines; the album *Light as a Feather* (1972) best exemplifies this early style. In 1973 Corea re-formed the ensemble, which from this time included Corea, Clarke, the electric guitarist Bill Connors (replaced for a tour in 1974 by Earl Klugh), and the drummer Lenny White. The group adopted an amplified style, reminiscent of the work of John McLaughlin, that was strongly oriented towards rock and marked by Corea's use of the Fender-Rhodes electric piano, Hohner Clavinet, Yamaha organ, Minimoog and ARP Odyssey synthesizers, and various electronic gadgets and pedals. It found a wide, young audience and became still more popular after Al Di Meola replaced Connors in 1974. By late 1975 the group's playing had begun to lose its vitality; nevertheless its album *Romantic Warrior* (1976) became its most popular recording. In the late 1970s Corea formed a third group under the name Return to Forever; this 13-piece ensemble, the instrumentation of which resembled that of a chamber orchestra and made less use of electronics, included Corea, Clarke, Farrell, the singer and keyboard player Gail Moran, and string and brass sections; it trod an uncomfortable stylistic line between third stream jazz and light pop music and met with little favor from the critics. Between 1972 and 1979 Corea produced recordings both under the name Return to Forever and under his own name, on all of which members of the ensemble played; he then continued to use the name for various projects. In 1983 he joined Clarke, Di Meola, and White for a tour of the USA.

SELECTED RECORDINGS

Light as a Feather (1972, Pol. 5525); *Return to Forever* (1973, ECM 1022); *Where Have I Known you Before?* (1974, Pol. 6509); *Romantic Warrior* (1976, Col. PC34076); *Live: the Complete Concert* (1977, Col. C4X34350)

BIBLIOGRAPHY

C. Berg: "Professor C. C. and his Amazing Perpetual Communication Company," *DB*, xliii/6 (1976), 12 [interview; incl. discography]

PATRICK T. WILL

Reuss, Allan (*b* New York, 15 June 1915). Guitarist. He studied with George Van Eps, whom he replaced in Benny Goodman's band in 1935. He toured with Goodman until 1938, then played with Paul Whiteman, Jack Teagarden (1939–40), and Jimmy Dorsey (1942). After working for NBC (1942–3) he spent a second period with Goodman (1943–4) and performed with Harry James (1944–5). Reuss was also in demand for studio recording sessions during the late 1930s and early 1940s, and worked with such artists as Teddy Wilson and Billie Holiday (1936–8), Lionel Hampton (1937–9), Glenn Miller (1939), Coleman Hawkins (1945), and Corky Corcoran (1946). Although he continued to play as a freelance, in later years he concentrated on teaching. Reuss was an excellent big-band rhythm guitarist and was known for his sophisticated chordal melodies, which are often compared with those of his mentor Van Eps; he recorded notable solos with Teagarden (*Pickin' for Patsy*, 1939) and Dorsey (*Sorghum Switch*, 1942).

SELECTED RECORDINGS

As sideman: J. Teagarden: Pickin' for Patsy (1939, Bruns. 8401); J. Dorsey: Sorghum Switch (1942, Decca 18372); C. Corcoran: Minor Blues (1946, Key. 621)

BIBLIOGRAPHY

ChiltonW
B. Kessel: "Allan Reuss and Oscar Moore," *GP*, xi/7 (1977), 10
M. J. Summerfield: *The Jazz Guitar: its Evolution and its Players* (Gateshead, England, 1978), 175

JIM FERGUSON

Revelation. Record company and label. The company was established in 1965 in Los Angeles by John William Hardy and Jon Horwich. The first release was an album by Dennis Budimir; among the musicians who recorded regularly for the label were Clare Fischer, Gary Foster, Warne Marsh, Tony Ortega, and Joe Albany. In the late 1970s the premises were transferred to Gainesville, Florida; from that time the repertory has included albums by such leaders as Jerry Coker and Carmell Jones. By 1984 the company had issued 45 albums, most of which have remained in the catalogue. Revelation is most notable for having helped to revive interest in the work of neglected players like Marsh and Albany, and for having given vital exposure to Fischer, Foster, and Budimir when they were little known outside California.

MARK GARDNER

Reverberation unit. An electroacoustic or electronic device that produces a variety of delay effects, including a simulation of natural room reverberation.

Revolutionary Ensemble. Trio. It was formed in 1971 by the violinist Leroy Jenkins, the double bass player Sirone, and the drummer Frank Clayton; all three men also sang and performed on various percussion instruments, and Jerome Cooper, who replaced Clayton in September 1971, played piano, bugle, and flute as well as drums. Each player contributed equally to the trio's wide-ranging improvisations. Years of rehearsal allowed the members to respond immediately to one another and meant that, although they played free jazz, their music was extremely well organized. But their uncompromising music never reached a substantial audience. Occasionally they performed in concert at colleges and museums, and they appeared once at the Ann Arbor Blues and Jazz Festival (1973) and made a farewell tour of Europe. The group disbanded in 1977.

SELECTED RECORDINGS

Vietnam (1972, ESP 3007); *Manhattan Cycles* (1972, IndN 1023); *The People's Republic* (1975, A&M Hor. 708); *Revolutionary Ensemble* (1977, Enja 3003)

BIBLIOGRAPHY

R. Riggins: "The Revolutionary Ensemble," *DB*, xl/19 (1973), 15
B. McRae: "Avant Courier no.32: Manhattan Cycles," *JJ*, xxviii/1 (1975), 8

BARRY KERNFELD

Rex. Record label. It was established in England in 1937 by the record company Crystalate. Its catalogue included commercially oriented jazz drawn from the American Record Company. After British Decca acquired the parent company in 1937 it maintained Rex for the issue of similar material recorded by American Decca. Both owners also used the label to release items recorded in England; these included a disc by the singer and bandleader Jack Payne (1935) on which Garland Wilson performed. There were also Rex labels in other countries; Indian Rex, for example, was used to issue a notable recording made in Bombay in 1936 by Crickett Smith and his Symphonians. Rex was discontinued in 1947.

BIBLIOGRAPHY

B. Rust: *The American Record Label Book* (New Rochelle, NY, 1978), 268
J. A. Payne: "Can't We Talk it Over," *Sv*, no.102 (1982), 204

Reynolds, Jimmy [James Russel] (*b* c1907; *d* New York, 16 Feb 1963). Pianist. In the 1930s and 1940s he led a band at the Hollywood Cafe in New York and worked with other leaders, including Kaiser Marshall (1935). Reynolds made recordings with Henry "Red" Allen (including *Nothing's Blue but the Sky* (1936, Voc. 3245), on which he is heard as both a soloist and a sensitive obbligato player), Jabbo Smith (1938), Hot Lips Page (1938–40), Bill Dillard (1947), and the singer Larry Darnell (1952). In the 1960s he worked with Harry Dial and Lester Boone.

based on *ChiltonW*

Reys, Rita [Maria Everdina] (*b* Rotterdam, Netherlands, 21 Dec 1924). Dutch singer. She sang with a Hawaiian band (from 1940), a theater orchestra led by her father (1942), the guitarist Lex Van Spall (1942–4), the double bass player Ted Powder (1945, touring Belgium and Luxembourg), and the tenor saxophonist Piet Van Dijk (1947–50, touring Spain and North Africa). In 1945 she married Wessel Ilcken, with whom she led a sextet that toured Europe and often performed on the radio stations of the American Forces Network. On tours of the USA she sang with Mat Mathews and Art Blakey in 1956 and with Chico Hamilton and Jimmy Smith the following year; in 1958 she worked with Kurt Edelhagen and Bengt Hallberg in Germany and Sweden. After the death of Ilcken (1957) she married Pim Jacobs in 1960 and embarked on a career as a soloist, appearing often at festivals and making many recordings. She received an Edison award from the Dutch Recording Industries in 1961.

SELECTED RECORDINGS

Our Favorite Songs (1973, CBS 65620); *That Old Feeling* (1979, CBS 83981); *Memories of you* (1983, Utopia 814273-1)

BIBLIOGRAPHY

FeatherE

WIM VAN EYLE

Rhodes, Todd (Washington) (*b* Hopkinsville, KY, 31 Aug 1900; *d* Flint, MI, 1965). Pianist and arranger. He studied at the Springfield (Ohio) School of Music (1915–17) and the Erie (Pennsylvania) Conservatory (1919–c1921) before joining William McKinney's Synco Jazz Band; this group was renamed McKinney's Cotton Pickers and Rhodes remained a member until 1934 (for illustration *see* MCKINNEY'S COTTON PICKERS), apart from a brief period in 1932–3. He then settled in Detroit, where he played with local bands until the early 1940s. In 1946 he organized his own rhythm-and-blues group, which recorded under his name between 1947 and 1953 and with the trumpeter and singer Dave Bartholomew (1951) and the singer Wynonie Harris (1951–2); Rhodes may be heard to advantage playing with his septet on *Red Boy at the Mardi Gras* (1949, Sensation 15), which he composed and probably arranged.

BIBLIOGRAPHY

ChiltonW; *FeatherE*
J. Chilton: *McKinney's Music: a Bio-discography of McKinney's Cotton Pickers* (London, 1978)

Rhumboogie Club. Nightclub in Chicago; *see* NIGHTCLUBS AND OTHER VENUES.

Rhythm. The grouping of musical sounds, principally by means of duration and stress; for a discussion of rhythm in jazz as it depends on beat, meter, and accent *see* BEAT.

Rhythmakers. Recording group. Its output, produced during four sessions in 1932, represents some of the most exciting small-group jazz ever recorded, and its existence did much to further the cause of racially mixed groups. The nine titles resulting from the first two sessions (18 April and 23 May) were issued under Billy Banks's name. The exuberant playing of Henry "Red" Allen (trumpet) found a perfect foil in Pee Wee Russell (clarinet and tenor saxophone), while Eddie Condon (banjo), Jack Bland (guitar), and Zutty Singleton (who took over from Gene Krupa on drums after the first session) formed the basis of a fine rhythm section. Joe Sullivan (piano) and Al Morgan (double bass) were replaced in the third session (26 July) by Fats Waller and Pops Foster, and Jimmy Lord (clarinet) also joined the group to record a further four outstanding numbers. For the final session (8 October) Lord, Waller, and Banks were succeeded by Happy Caldwell (tenor saxophone), Frank Froeba, and Chick Bullock, and Tommy Dorsey (trombone) was added; the four titles produced by this ensemble were recorded under Bland's leadership. The group's recordings were later reissued under a variety of names, including the Chicago Rhythm Kings.

SELECTED RECORDINGS

Margie/Oh, Peter (1932, Ban. 32462); Mean Old Bed Bug Blues/Yellow Dog Blues (1932, Ban. 32502); Who stole the lock/Someone stole Gabriel's horn (1932, Ban. 32605)

BIBLIOGRAPHY

M. Doyle: "The Rhythmakers," *Discographical Forum*, no.19 (1970)
B. Rust: Liner notes, *The Rhythmakers* (VJM 53, 1983)

MIKE HAZELDINE

Rhythm Club. The name of several nightclubs, notably one in New York; *see* NIGHTCLUBS AND OTHER VENUES.

Rhythm section. A term applied to the rhythm, or accompanying, instruments (i.e., piano, guitar or banjo, tuba or double bass (later electric bass guitar), and drums) within a band; *see* BANDS, §§2, 4.

Rialto. Record label. It was owned by the Rialto Music House of Chicago; the discs were produced by Marsh Laboratories, Inc. Only one issue is known; one side of this is the only release believed to have been made of Jelly Roll Morton's solo recording of *London Blues* (1924). It is probable that the records were intended for demonstration purposes in the parent company's several stores.

BIBLIOGRAPHY

B. Rust: *The American Record Label Book* (New Rochelle, NY, 1978), 270
L. Wright: *Mr Jelly Lord* (Chigwell, England, 1980), 26

Ricci, Paul (J.) (*b* New York, 6 April 1914). Clarinetist and saxophonist. He began playing at the age of 12; he worked in New York in taxi dance halls and then in the early 1930s with Lud Gluskin, Red McKenzie, Adrian Rollini, Joe Venuti, Red Nichols, Joe Haymes, and others. As a studio musician he was on the staff of various record companies, NBC (from 1940), and Paramount and Universal (1950–66); he later settled in Miami, where he continued to work in studios. Ricci's numerous recordings were made mainly with big bands, such as those of Benny Goodman (1954) and Dizzy Gillespie (1960), but he also recorded with small groups, among them the trio Three's a Crowd (1938) and Carl Kress's quintet (1947). His relaxed and fluent clarinet playing may be heard on Bob Howard's *If Love is Blind* (1936, Decca 862).

based on *ChiltonW*

Rich, Buddy [Bernard] (*b* New York, 30 Sept 1917; *d* Los Angeles, 2 April 1987). Drummer and singer. He appeared on stage in his parents' vaudeville act before his second birthday, played drums and tap-danced on Broadway at four, and from the age of six toured the USA and Australia, leading his own stage band when he was 11. He joined Joe Marsala's band in 1937 and then played briefly with Bunny Berigan, Harry James, Artie Shaw, and Benny Carter, and for somewhat longer with Tommy Dorsey (1939–42; for illustration *see* DORSEY, TOMMY). After serving with the US Marines he worked again with Dorsey in 1944–5, then led his own band intermittently until 1951, while also playing with Norman Granz's Jazz at the Philharmonic, Les Brown, and Charlie Ventura's Big Four. From 1953 to 1966 Rich was with Harry James's group apart from spells with Dorsey (1954–5) and with his own small group (1957–61), when he also performed as a singer in a style resembling that of Frank Sinatra. In 1966 he organized a second big band, and achieved remarkable international success with it until its dissolution in 1974. Thereafter he played mainly in New York with a small group in his own club, Buddy's Place. In the 1980s he began to tour again, with a big band of young musicians.

Rich's playing was characterized by phenomenal speed and dexterity. He was an extrovert performer who produced complex patterns with metronomic clarity and simpler lines with an exquisite precision.

Oral history material in *GBLnsa*.

SELECTED RECORDINGS

As leader: with Lester Young: I found a new baby (1946, Clef 11048); with L. Hampton and A. Tatum: *The Lionel Hampton–Art Tatum–Buddy Rich Trio* (1955, Clef 709); *Buddy Rich vs Max Roach* (1959, Mer. 20448); *Swingin' New Big Band* (1966, PJ 20113); *Lionel Hampton Presents Buddy Rich* (1977, Who's Who in Jazz 21006)

As sideman: A. Shaw: Serenade to a Savage (1939, Bb 10385); T. Dorsey: The Minor Goes Muggin' (1945, Vic. 45-0002); C. Parker: Bloomdido (1950, Mer./Clef 11058)

BIBLIOGRAPHY

G. Hoefer: "Buddy Rich: Portrait of a Man in Conflict," *DB*, xxvii (1960), no.12, p.17; no.13, p.20
R. Kettle: "Roach vs Rich: a Notated Analysis of Two Significant Modern Jazz Drumming Styles," *DB*, xxxiii/6 (1966), 20
J. Burns: "Lesser Known Bands of the 40s: Buddy Rich and Johnny Bothwell," *JM*, no.175 (1969), 6
S. Dance: *The World of Swing* (New York, 1974) [colln of previously pubd interviews]
D. Meriwether, Jr.: *The Buddy Rich Orchestra and Small Groups* (Spotswood, NJ, 1974, rev. 2/1984 as *We Don't Play Requests: a Musical Biography/Discography of Buddy Rich*)
S. Woolley: "Buddy Rich: Drummer, Bandleader and Wit," *JJ*, xxvii/11 (1974), 4
W. Balliett: "Super Drummer," *Improvising: Sixteen Jazz Musicians and their Art* (New York, 1977) [colln of previously pubd articles], 151
"Rich + Tormé = Wild Repartee," *DB*, xlv (1978), no.3, p.13; no.4, p.20
K. Strateman: *Buddy Rich and Gene Krupa: a Filmo-discography* (Lübbecke, Germany, 1980)
C. Iero: "Buddy Rich: Revisited," *MD*, iv/6 (1980), 12
E. Tiegel: "Rich Raps," *DB*, xlix/3 (1982), 17
J. Nesbitt: *Inside Buddy Rich: a Study of the Master Drummer's Style and Technique* (Delevan, NY, 1984)
R. Mattingly: "Buddy Rich," *MD*, x/1 (1986), 15
B. Korall: "Buddy Remembered," *MD*, xi/7 (1987), 22
J. MacSweeney: "Buddy's Classic RadioKings," *MD*, xi/7 (1987), 29

JOSÉ HOSIASSON

Rich, Fred (*b* Warsaw, 3 Jan 1898; *d* California, 8 Sept 1956). Pianist and bandleader. In the 1920s he led commercial big bands, touring Europe (1925–6, 1927–8) and performing in New York. Among the jazz musicians who played under him in studio bands were Bunny Berigan, Benny Goodman, the Dorsey brothers, Tony Parenti, and Joe Venuti. In the late 1930s he was a music director in radio, and in 1942 he joined the staff of United Artists; although partly paralyzed in 1945, he continued to work in studios into the 1950s. Rich made numerous recordings between 1925 and 1940, few of which can be classified as jazz; among them, however, is *Till we Meet Again* (1940, Voc. 5507), arranged by Benny Carter and including solos by Carter and Roy Eldridge.

based on *ChiltonW*

Richards, (Margaret) Ann (Borden) (*b* San Diego, 1 Oct 1935; *d* Hollywood Hills, CA, on or before 1 April 1982). Singer. After performing with local groups in San Francisco and Oakland and working briefly with Charlie Barnet, she joined Stan Kenton's band in early 1955. She toured and recorded with the band that year, and married Kenton in October. From this time she limited her performances to occasional engagements at clubs in Los Angeles, but undertook some recording sessions both as a leader and with Kenton. The two were divorced in 1961, and during the 1960s Richards continued to perform at clubs in Los Angeles; she may be heard to advantage on the album *Ann, Man!* (1961, Atco 136), where she is accompanied by Jack Sheldon, Barney Kessel, Red Callender, and Larry Bunker.

BIBLIOGRAPHY

FeatherE; *Feather '60s*
D. Hague: "Stan Kenton," *JJ*, ix/10 (1956), 11

Richards, Emil [Radocchia, Emilio Joseph] (*b* Hartford, CT, 2 Sept 1932). Vibraphonist and percussionist. He studied xylophone from the age of six; he attended the Hartford School of Music (1949–52) and played percussion in several local symphony orchestras (1950–54). During his military service he played in an army band in Japan (1954–5), where he worked with Toshiko Akiyoshi; after being discharged he became a studio musician in Los Angeles (1956). He performed and recorded with George Shearing (1956–8) and Paul Horn (1960–64), played with Don Ellis (1964–9), and led his own group, the Microtonal Blues Band (1967). He became interested in ethnic music and assembled a collection of unusual percussion instruments, and in 1969 he went to India to study meditation. After returning to the USA he played with Roger Kellaway and worked with the composer and inventor of instruments Harry

Partch; he also performed with popular musicians and recorded film music. In 1983 he published a book of exercises for advanced players of the vibraphone and marimba. As a vibraphonist Richards plays in a swing style that resembles the work of Lionel Hampton and Milt Jackson. In the 1970s and 1980s he has used exotic percussion instruments, such as crotales, cuíca, windchimes, and waterphone, on recordings of jazz in several different styles.

SELECTED RECORDINGS

As sideman: P. Horn: *Something Blue* (1960, HiFi 615); G. Duke: *Liberated Fantasies* (1974, MPS 68026), incl. I can hear that; Walfredo de los Reyes and L. Bellson: *Ecue ritmos cubanos* (1977, Pablo 2310807); L. Bellson: *Prime Time* (1977, Conc. 64); Shadowfax: *Shadowfax* (1982, Windham Hill 1022)

BIBLIOGRAPHY

Feather–Gitler '70s

L. Tomkins: "James Blades of London Meets Emil Richards of Los Angeles," *CI*, xiv/12 (1976), 20

S. Bradley: "Emil Richards," *DB*, xliv/15 (1977), 46

D. Levine: "Show and Studio: Emil Richards," *MD*, vi/1 (1982), 50

LEROY OSTRANSKY

Richards, Johnny [Cascales, John] (*b* Querétaro State, Mexico, 2 Nov 1911; *d* New York, 7 Oct 1968). Composer, arranger, and bandleader. He grew up in Schenectady, New York, and learned piano, violin, banjo, and trumpet as a child; by the age of 17 he was saxophonist and house orchestrator at the Mastbaum Theater, Philadelphia. After attending Syracuse University he composed film scores, first in London for Gaumont (1932-3), then in Hollywood as Victor Young's assistant at Paramount (1933–40). While there he studied with the composer Arnold Schoenberg and received a master's degree from the University of Southern California. He led a big band from 1940 to 1945, then returned to Hollywood to write arrangements for Boyd Raeburn (1946–7), Charlie Barnet, and others. In 1952 he joined Stan Kenton, for whom he composed many successful pieces. Later he moved to New York and from 1956 to 1960 led a second band, whose recordings and performances received much critical acclaim; he organized a third group in 1964–5. One of Richards's most popular compositions is *Young at Heart*, which was a hit for Frank Sinatra in 1954; he also wrote many classical works and some pieces for theater band. He is best known, however, through his writing for Kenton and his own bands; a pioneer of progressive jazz, he never compromised his standards in order to cater to commercial interests.

RECORDED COMPOSITIONS

As leader: *The Rites of Diabolo* (1958, Roul. 52008); *Aqui se habla Espanol* (1966, Roul. 25351)

Recorded by S. Kenton: Prologue: this is an Orchestra! (1952, Cap. 15966-7); *Cuban Fire!* (1956, Cap. T731); *Adventures in Time* (1962, Cap. ST1844)

BIBLIOGRAPHY

B. Coss: "The Johnny Richards Orchestra," *Metronome*, lxxiv/12 (1957), 18

J. C. Thomas: "Johnny Richards: Man with a Passion," *DB*, xxxv/4 (1968), 22

Obituary, *New York Times* (9 Oct 1968)

STEVEN STRUNK

Richards, Red [Charles Coleridge] (*b* New York, 19 Oct 1912). Pianist. He learned piano from the age of ten and played classical music for six years, before changing to jazz when he heard Fats Waller. He worked with Tab Smith at the Savoy Ballroom, New York (1945–9), and with Sidney Bechet and Bob Wilber in Boston (both 1951). In 1953 he toured Italy and France and recorded several albums as a member of Mezz Mezzrow's band, which included Buck Clayton and Big Chief Moore. Later in the year he accompanied Frank Sinatra on tour. He played with Muggsy Spanier (1953–7, 1959), as a soloist in Columbus, Ohio (1958), and with Wild Bill Davison (1958–9). In October 1960 he and Vic Dickenson formed a sextet called the SAINTS AND SINNERS, which they led together until it disbanded in 1970; it toured Europe twice and made several recordings. He worked as an intermission pianist at Eddie Condon's, New York (1975–7), and held two engagements with his own trio (1977–8). From 1979 he toured internationally as a soloist and in Panama Francis's Savoy Sultans; he performed in Spain and Japan (1986) and Australia (1987).

SELECTED RECORDINGS

As unaccompanied soloist: *Soft Buns* (1978, West 54 8000)

As leader: *In a Mellow Tone* (1979, West 54 8005)

BIBLIOGRAPHY

C. Richards: "Charles 'Red' Richards," *BHcF*, no.26 (1953), 4

H. McNamara: "Jazz," *The Telegram* (Toronto, 26 Jan 1967), 68

P. Scott: "The Handwriting on a Wailing Wall," *Toronto Daily Star* (3 June 1967), 62

B. Rusch: "Red Richards: Interview," *Cadence*, i/5 (1976), 7

C. Battestini and J.-P. Battestini: "Red Richards," *BHcF*, no.279 (1980), 6 [interview]

S. Dance: "Red Richards," *JJI*, xxxiii/1 (1980), 18

E. Townley: "Gentleman of Swing: an Interview with Charles 'Red' Richards," *Sv*, no.88 (1980), 149

JAMES M. DORAN

Richardson, Jerome (C.) (*b* Sealy, TX, 15 Nov 1920). Reed player. He grew up in California, began playing alto saxophone when he was eight, and studied at San Francisco State College. After making his professional début at the age of 14 he worked with local dance bands until 1941. Before joining the navy he served briefly as a replacement for Willie Smith in Jimmie Lunceford's band; during military service (1942–5) he played in a dance band directed by Marshall Royal. After being discharged he toured with Lionel Hampton (1949–51) and Earl Hines (1952–3). He moved in 1953 to New York, where he led his own group at Minton's Playhouse and played with Oscar Pettiford in 1956–7. During the 1950s he also worked with Lucky Millinder, Cootie Williams, Chico Hamilton, Johnny Richards, Gerry Mulligan, and Gerald Wilson. In 1959–60 he was a member of Quincy Jones's orchestra, which toured Europe and performed in the show *Free and Easy* in Paris. He maintained his association with Jones, but also worked with several jazz and popular singers, including Peggy Lee, Billy Eckstine, Brook Benton, and Julie London; Richardson himself has also worked as a singer. In December 1965 he was a founding member of the Thad Jones–Mel Lewis Orchestra, serving as its lead alto saxophonist until 1970. After moving to Hollywood in 1971 he became active as a session musician and resumed his collaboration with Quincy Jones, touring Japan three times. In 1980 he toured Europe with Nat Adderley. Richardson's prolific work in studios has tended to overshadow his highly competent work as a soloist, but he is extremely versatile and adaptable, and particularly effective on tenor saxophone and flute.

SELECTED RECORDINGS

As leader: *Jerome Richardson Sextet* (1958, NewJ 8205); *Roamin' with Jerome Richardson* (1959, NewJ 8226); *Going to the Movies* (1962, UA 15006)

As sideman: O. Pettiford: *Oscar Pettiford Orchestra in Hi-fi* (1956, ABC-Para. 135); *Oscar Pettiford and his Birdland Band* (1957, Spot. 153); Q. Jones: *The Great Wide World of Quincy Jones* (1959, Mer. 60221); *The Quintessence of Quincy Jones* (1961, Imp. 11); T. Jones and M. Lewis: *Monday Night* (1968, SolS 18048); *Central Park North* (1969, SolS 18058)

BIBLIOGRAPHY

FeatherE; *Feather '60s*; *Feather–Gitler '70s*

B. Messinger: Liner notes, *Going to the Movies* (UA 15006, 1963)

"Jerome Richardson Talking," *CI*, ix/7 (1971), 13

L. Tomkins: "Go to New York, Young Man, Advises Jerome Richardson," *CI*, xix/7 (1981), 16
B. Rusch: "Jerome Richardson," *Cadence*, xiii/12 (1987), 5 [interview]

MARK GARDNER

Richardson, Rodney (V.) (*b* New Orleans, 1917). Double bass player. He first worked with territory bands in Tennessee during the 1930s, playing double bass and guitar with the Georgia Boys in Chattanooga and guitar with the Royal Knights in Nashville. In 1943 he traveled to California with Harlan Leonard, worked with the tenor saxophonist "Big Six" Reeves in Hollywood, played informally with Art Tatum, and joined Count Basie's band. From 1943 to 1947 he toured and recorded with Basie, and also made swing recordings in New York with the Kansas City Seven (including *Lester Leaps Again*, Key. 1302), Herbie Fields, and Earle Warren (all 1944), Lester Young (1944, 1947), Lucky Thompson (1945), and Roy Eldridge (1946). He worked with Tiny Grimes, and later with Erroll Garner, and played with Duke Burrell's Louisiana Shakers, touring Europe in 1975. After settling in California he continued to play occasionally with local pianists. (P. Vacher: "Rodney Richardson's Story," *MR*, viii/1 (1980), 5)

Richman, Boomie [Abraham Samuel] (*b* Brockton, MA, 2 April 1921). Tenor saxophonist and clarinetist. He played at clubs in Boston before moving in 1942 to New York, where he played and recorded with the clarinetist Jerry Wald (1942), Muggsy Spanier (1944), Tommy Dorsey (1945–51), and Benny Goodman (1951–5); he may be heard to advantage on Goodman's album *B. G. in Hi-fi* (1954, Cap. W565). During the 1950s he was active as a freelance: he worked in radio and television and made recordings with the Sauter–Finegan Orchestra (1952), Neal Hefti and Spanier (both 1954), Ruby Braff (1955), Al Cohn (1956), Red Allen and Urbie Green (both 1957), and Cootie Williams (1958). He worked as a studio musician in New York in the 1960s, no longer playing jazz. (*FeatherE*)

Richmond, Dannie [Charles D.] (*b* New York, 15 Dec 1935; *d* New York, 16 March 1988). Drummer. He played rhythm-and-blues tenor saxophone while in his teens before taking up drums. From 1956 to 1970 he was Charles Mingus's regular drummer and played on many of his albums; he then played jazz-rock for three years with the group Mark–Almond, accompanied the rock singer Joe Cocker, and toured with the rock singer and pianist Elton John. He played for a brief period with Chet Baker, then rejoined Mingus in 1974; after Mingus's death in 1979 he played with Mingus Dynasty and led a quartet. With George Adams and Don Pullen, who also had been sidemen with Mingus, he began a collaboration in 1979 that led to several outstanding albums.

While Richmond employed the freer elements from jazz of the 1960s, his playing was rooted in a deep understanding of swing and bop, and was occasionally further enlivened with the forcefulness of rhythm-and-blues. His drumming was emotional and unpredictable, and he could play explosively or with considerable restraint; his ability to shift from one extreme to the other is displayed to advantage on the track *Double Arc Jake* from George Adams's and Don Pullen's album *Don't Lose Control* (1979).

SELECTED RECORDINGS

As leader: *Ode to Mingus* (1979, SN 1005); *Dannie Richmond Plays Charles Mingus* (1980, Tim. 148); with G. Adams: *Gentlemen's Agreement* (1983, SN 1057)

As sideman with C. Mingus: *Mingus ah um* (1958, Col. CL1370); *Town Hall Concert* (1962, UA 15024); *The Great Concert of Charles Mingus* (1964, Amer. 003–5); *Changes Two* (1974, Atl. 1678); *Three or Four Shades of Blues* (1977, Atl. 1700)

As sideman with others: Mark–Almond: *Mark–Almond 2* (1972, Blue Thumb 32); D. Pullen: *Jazz a confronto 21* (1975, Horo 101–21); G. Adams and D. Pullen: *Don't Lose Control* (1979, SN 1004), incl. Double Arc Jake

BIBLIOGRAPHY

D. Morgenstern: "Mingus' Man Dannie Richmond," *DB*, xxxiii/6 (1966), 18
M. Plummer: "Danny: from Mingus to Mark–Almond," *MM* (13 Nov 1971), 30
P. Senoff: "New Bands: Mark–Almond," *J&P*, x/6 (1971), 18
B. Primack: "The Gospel According to Mingus: Disciples Carry the Tune," *DB*, xlv/20 (1978), 12
B. Shoemaker: "Danny Richmond," *Coda*, no.179 (1981), 4
B. Priestley: *Mingus: a Critical Biography* (London, Melbourne, Australia, and New York, 1982)
Obituary, S. Voce, *The Independent* (30 March 1988)

JEFF POTTER

Richmond, June (*b* Chicago, 9 July 1915; *d* Göteborg, Sweden, 14 Aug 1962). Singer. After performing with Les Hite in California, she joined Jimmy Dorsey's band (1938). She made recordings with Cab Calloway (1938) and Andy Kirk (1939–42, including *Hey Lawdy Mama*, 1942, Decca 4405). From 1948 she worked in Europe, recording as a leader in Stockholm in 1951 and with Quincy Jones's orchestra in Paris in 1957.

based on *ChiltonW*

Richmond, Mike [Michael] (*b* Philadelphia, 26 Feb 1948). Bass player. After attending Temple University he taught high school in Philadelphia and performed in local orchestras. In the early 1970s, while playing with Chico Hamilton, he began an association with Arnie Lawrence, with whom he later appeared at the Berliner Jazztage (1977). He also toured and recorded with Stan Getz, Jack DeJohnette, Horace Silver, Hubert Laws, and, intermittently from 1973 to 1979, Gil Evans. In 1980 his interest in Indian music took him to Bombay, where he performed with the sitar player Ravi Shankar. He has also recorded with Franco Ambrosetti (1978, 1981), Dannie Richmond (1979), and George Adams and Richmond (1980, 1983). From 1980 to 1985 he was music director of Mingus Dynasty and in 1980 played with the group at the Montreux International Jazz Festival. He has written a tutor, *Modern Walking Bass Technique* (Englewood, NJ, 1983).

Oral history material in *GBLnsa*.

SELECTED RECORDINGS

As leader: *Dreamwaves* (1977, IC 1065)

As sideman: J. DeJohnette: *Untitled* (1976, ECM 1074); S. Getz: *Another World* (1977, Col. JG35513); Mingus Dynasty: *Live at Montreux* (1980, Atl. 16031); A. Lawrence: *Renewal* (1981, PAlt 8033)

BIBLIOGRAPHY

A. J. Smith: "Profile: Mike Richmond," *DB*, xlv/13 (1978), 42

WILLIAM S. BROCKMAN

Ricotti, Frank (*b* London, 31 Jan 1949). English vibraphonist. A member of the National Youth Jazz Orchestra in his teens, he studied at Trinity College of Music, London (1967–70), and played with Neil Ardley (recording in 1968, 1969, and 1971) and the tenor saxophonist Dave Gelly. He formed his own quartet in the early 1970s, but also worked with Graham Collier, Mike Gibbs (recording in 1969–72), Stan Tracey (recording in 1970), and Gordon Beck's Gyroscope (1973–4). In the 1980s Ricotti has played with Chris Laurence and John Taylor in Paragonne, recording the LP *Aspects of Paragonne* (1985, MMC 010). Latterly, however, he has concentrated on studio work, playing and composing music for television and other media.

(R. Cotterrell, ed.: *Jazz Now: the Jazz Centre Society Guide*, London, 1976)

SIMON ADAMS

Riddle, Nelson (*b* Oradell, NJ, 1 June 1921; *d* Los Angeles, 6 Oct 1985). Composer, arranger, and leader. In the 1940s he worked as a trombonist and arranger for big bands, including those of Jerry Wald, Tommy Dorsey (from May 1944), Bob Crosby, and Charlie Spivak. Later he wrote arrangements and led backup orchestras for such jazz and popular singers as Peggy Lee, Judy Garland, Nat "King" Cole, Sarah Vaughan, and Ella Fitzgerald, with whom he collaborated on the album *Ella Fitzgerald Sings the Jerome Kern Songbook* (1963, Verve 84060). He is best known for his association with Frank Sinatra, whose success in the late 1950s owed much to Riddle's arrangements; some of these were slow and introspective, others vigorous and swinging. He also worked occasionally as a leader and around 1957 recorded the album *Hey, Let yourself Go* (Cap. T814). During the 1960s and 1970s he was most active in films and television; among his last work was a series of three albums of popular songs from the 1920s and 1930s that he recorded with the singer Linda Ronstadt.

BIBLIOGRAPHY

"Nelson Riddle Talking," *CI*, vi/1 (1967), 10

N. Riddle: "Branching Out from the Sound," *CI*, vi/2 (1967), 20

H. Siders: "Nelson Riddle: Arranger, Composer, Conductor," *IM*, lxxi/12 (1973), 9

L. Tomkins: "Nelson Riddle Today," *CI*, xx/1 (1981), 20; contd as "Nelson Riddle & the Standards of Sinatra," xx/2 (1981), 24 [interview]

MARK TUCKER

Ride. To improvise, or an IMPROVISATION; the word, which was current in early jazz and the swing era, carries connotations, variously, of inventiveness, freedom of delivery, and swinging rhythmic momentum. A good example of its usage occurs in the title of a recording by the Mills Blue Rhythm Band – *Ride, Red, Ride* (1935, Col. 3087D) – on which Henry "Red" Allen plays an extended solo. "To take a ride" is to improvise a solo and a "ride man" is an improvising soloist. (*See also* RIDE-OUT.)

Ride cymbal [top cymbal]. A large cymbal used from the late 1930s to carry the regular beat; *see* DRUM SET, §§I, 5; II, 5, 6.

Ride-out. The final chorus of a lively piece, collectively improvised in a loud, spirited manner (*see* FORMS, §2); the term is associated with early styles of jazz.

Ridley, Larry [Laurence Howard, II] (*b* Indianapolis, 3 Sept 1937). Double bass player. He learned to play violin as a child, then, after hearing Ray Brown, took up double bass. He often played in Indianapolis with Freddie Hubbard, who was a childhood friend, but his first job, at the age of 16, was with Wes Montgomery. He entered Indiana University to study violin, but soon changed to double bass. After receiving instruction from Percy Heath at the Lenox (Massachusetts) School of Jazz (1959) he played briefly in New York with Hubbard, then toured with Slide Hampton (1960). He performed throughout the 1960s with such hard-bop musicians as Max Roach, Philly Joe Jones, Roy Haynes, and Horace Silver, and in 1969 recorded in Europe with veteran swing musicians as a member of George Wein's Newport All-Stars. The following year he toured Japan with Thelonious Monk, and remained a member of his group for three years. In 1971 Ridley obtained a degree in music education from New York University, and subsequently became head of the jazz program and chairman of the music department at Livingston College (Rutgers), Piscataway, New Jersey. He played in Jones's group Dameronia (1981–5) and has served on the executive committee of the National Jazz Service Organization (from 1984). Ridley's driving hard-bop style may be heard to advantage on *Anthropology*, which he recorded with James Moody (1973).

For illustration *see* MANGELSDORFF, ALBERT.

SELECTED RECORDINGS

As leader: *Sum of the Parts* (1975, SE 19759)

As sideman: S. Hampton: *Somethin' Sanctified* (1960, Atl. 1362); R. Haynes: *Cracklin'* (1963, NewJ 8286); L. Morgan: *Cornbread* (1965, BN 84222); H. Silver: *The Jody Grind* (1966, BN 84250); S. Grappelli and J. Venuti: *Venupelli Blues* (1969, BYG 529122); J. Moody: *Feelin' it Together* (1973, Muse 5020), incl. Anthropology; T. Edwards: *The Inimitable Teddy Edwards* (1976, Xan. 134)

BIBLIOGRAPHY

E. Meadow: "Spotlight on Larry Ridley," *DB*, xxxviii/4 (1971), 16

S. Freedman: "Larry Ridley has a Bass for Jazz Studies, Thanks to Grants, Gifts, Nearby New York," *DB*, xlvi/7 (1979), 12

BARRY KERNFELD

Riedel, Georg (*b* Karlovy Vary, Czechoslovakia, 8 Nov 1934). Swedish double bass player and composer of Czechoslovakian birth. He was classically trained as a double bass player and made his professional début in 1953 as a member of Lars Gullin's quintet (recording in 1953–6). He performed and recorded from 1955 into the 1980s with Arne Domnérus, and also worked with Jan Johansson, recording the LPs *M* (1965–7, Megafon 24–5) and *300.000* (1967–8, Megafon 18). In the 1980s he formed the Trio con Tromba with Bengt Hallberg and Jan Allan. He was among the first in Sweden to write jazz compositions for large forces; in such works as *Riedaglia* (1967, Sveriges Radio 1051) and *Rainbow Sketches* (1974, CAM 5906) he reveals a gift for orchestration and a strong sense of form. He has composed music for many films.

BIBLIOGRAPHY

FeatherE; *Feather–Gitler '70s*

E. Kjellberg: "Riedel, Georg," *Sohlmans musiklexikon*, ed. G. Morin, C.-A. Moberg, and E. Sundström (Stockholm, 1948–52, rev. and enlarged 2/1975–9 ed. H. Åstrand)

C.-E. Lindgren: "På omslaget" [On the cover], *Orkester journalen*, xxiii/1 (1955), 4

E. Kjellberg: *Svensk jazzhistoria: en översikt* [Swedish jazz history: an overview] (Stockholm, 1985)

L. Westin: "Jazzen är basen för Georg Riedel" [Jazz is the bass for Georg Riedel], *Orkester journalen*, lv/12 (1987), 15 [interview]

ERIK KJELLBERG

Riel, Alex (Poul) (*b* Copenhagen, 13 Sept 1940). Danish drummer. He played with various traditional groups (1957–60), and as the house drummer at the Montmartre Jazzhus in Copenhagen (1963–5) accompanied many American soloists. He belonged to Erik Moseholm's trio (1964–7) and the Danish Radiojazzgruppen (1965–8), and with Palle Mikkelborg led a quintet (which performed at the Montreux and Newport festivals in 1968) and the octet V8 (1970–75); he also played with the rock group Savage Rose (1968–72) and later worked with Six Winds and other groups. Riel made many recordings with American musicians, including Dexter Gordon, Jackie McLean, Sahib Shihab, Stuff Smith, and Ben Webster, and in 1965 recorded the album *Alex Riel Trio* (Fona PWS111) with Kenny Drew and Niels-Henning Ørsted Pedersen; this includes the track *In a Way*, on which Riel plays an unaccompanied drum solo. (D. Samuels: "Drums Around the World: Denmark's Alex Riel," *MD*, vii/10 (1983), 25)

ERIK WIEDEMANN

Riff. A short melodic ostinato, usually two or four bars long, which may either be repeated intact (strict riff) or varied to accommodate an underlying harmonic pattern. The riff is thought to derive from the repetitive call-and-response patterns of West African music, and appeared prominently in black-American music from the earliest times. It was an important element in New Orleans marching band music (where the word "riff" apparently originated), and from there entered jazz, where by the mid-1920s it was firmly established in background ensemble playing and as the basis for solo improvisation. Riffs also appeared in the accompaniments of many early blues, being particularly suited to their repeating structure. The conflict between an unvaried riff pattern and the changing harmonies of the blues progression became one of the most distinctive features of the blues and its derivatives.

The riff came to the fore in the early 1930s in the Southwest tradition of orchestral jazz, where the influence of rural blues musicians was notably strong. Among the innovations of these groups was the "double" or "compound" riff, in which the brass and reed sections played separate riffs in counterpoint. As exploited by Bennie Moten and, from 1936, by Count Basie's band, riffs of this sort came to dominate large-ensemble jazz, either as the accompaniment to solo improvisation or as self-sufficient sections within a score. An outstanding example of a compound riff occurs at the end of Basie's theme song *One o'Clock Jump*, where the trumpet, trombone, and saxophone sections play contrasting riffs in three distinct rhythms (ex.1).

Ex.1 Riffs from C. Basie: *One o'Clock Jump* (air-shot recording, first issued on *Shout and Feel It*, 1937, Alamac 2412); transcr. J. B. Robinson

Especially sensitive use of the riff may be found in Duke Ellington's orchestral scores from this period (e.g., *Harlem Air-shaft*, 1940, Vic. 26731). Another development of the swing era was the "riff tune," in which riff patterns were fashioned into melodies; Glenn Miller's hit *In the Mood* (1939, Bb 10416A, adapted from a stock jazz riff at least as old as Wingy Manone's *Tar Paper Stomp*, 1930, Champion 16153) is perhaps the best known, but superior examples may be found in Charlie Christian's many compositions for Benny Goodman's small groups (e.g., *Good Enough to Keep*, 1941, Col. 36099).

By the 1940s the riff had become a jazz cliché. It was taken over into rhythm-and-blues, where it became a favorite accompaniment device, and eventually entered rock-and-roll, rock, and other offshoots of rhythm-and-blues. Postwar urban blues, however, drew on a more primitive form of the riff from the rural blues tradition, a notable example being Bo Diddley's *I'm a Man* (1955, Checker 814), which consists of a simple four-note riff repeated over a tonic drone. In postwar jazz the riff was used more sparingly: bop musicians were fond of riff themes (Dizzy Gillespie's *Salt Peanuts*, 1945, Manor 5000, and *Oop-pop-a-dah*, 1947, Vic. 202480, are typical) but avoided riffs in their improvisations. By the 1950s the riff could be exploited for its latent nostalgia (as in Miles Davis's *All Blues*, on the album *Kind of Blue*, 1959, Col. CL1355), its comic potential (Shorty Rogers's *Martians go home*, on *The Swinging Mr. Rogers*, 1955, Atl. 1212), or its earthy connotations (for example, in the primitivist pieces of Charles Mingus). Many overlapping riffs may be heard on Ornette Coleman's avant-garde album *Free Jazz* (1960, Atl. 1364), and riffs often appear in the works of composers interested in jazz techniques, from Darius Milhaud's *La création du monde* (1923) to Leonard Bernstein's *Prelude, Fugue and Riffs* (1949). Jazz composers have continued to combine the riff with the 12-bar blues in new ways (e.g., Carla Bley's *Floater*, on the album *Social Studies*, 1980, Watt 11), and the riff still flourishes in the big-band tradition, in which composers and arrangers are constantly inventing new variants of this time-honored device.

J. BRADFORD ROBINSON

Riley, Ben(jamin A.) (*b* Savannah, GA, 17 July 1933). Drummer. Between 1956 and 1965 he played with Randy Weston, Sonny Stitt, Stan Getz, Woody Herman, Junior Mance, Kenny Burrell, Eddie "Lockjaw" Davis and Johnny Griffin (1960–62), Paul Winter, Jeremy Steig, Ahmad Jamal, Roland Hanna, Billy Taylor (ii), Walter Bishop, Jr., Kai Winding, and Ray Bryant, and recorded with Mance (1961), Winter (1963), Steig (1963), and Bryant (1964). He became best known for his work as Thelonious Monk's drummer from 1964 to 1967, during which time he traveled extensively. He recorded with Alice Coltrane (1968–75) and performed with her from 1971; the same year he joined the NEW YORK JAZZ QUARTET, with which he played at intervals into the 1980s. He also performed in the USSR with Toots Thielemans, Milt Jackson, and Bob James, and played with Ron Carter's quartet (1975), with which he later recorded (1977), and for a brief period in 1981 with Jim Hall's trio. Later he formed the group SPHERE with Charlie Rouse, Buster Williams, and Kenny Barron, and from 1984 played with Abdullah Ibrahim, with whom he toured the USA and Africa. Riley is known for his sense of swing, his command of coloristic effects, and his attention to theme and structure.

SELECTED RECORDINGS

As leader of Sphere (with C. Rouse, B. Williams, and K. Barron): *Four in One* (1982, Elek. Mus. 60166); *Flight Path* (1983, Elek. Mus. 60313)

As sideman with T. Monk: *It's Monk's Time* (1964, Col. CS8984); *Monk* (1964, Col. CS9091); *Live at the It Club* (1964, Col. C2-38030); *Live at the Jazz Workshop* (1964, Col. C2-38269); *Underground* (1967, Col. CS9632)

As sideman with others: A. Ibrahim: *Ekaya* (1983, Ekapa 005); M. Muldaur: *Transblucency* (1984–5, Upt. 2725)

BIBLIOGRAPHY

Feather '60s; *Feather–Gitler '70s*

J. Pareles: "The Thelonious Monk Tradition, and then Some," *New York Times* (27 Aug 1982), §C, p.12

P. Watrous: "Riffs: 'Round Sphere," *VV*, xxix (31 Jan 1984), 74

J. Potter: "Ben Riley: Making History," *MD*, x/9 (1986), 26

JEFF POTTER

Riley, Herman (*b* New Orleans, 31 Aug 1940). Tenor saxophonist. He played with swing and blues bands in New Orleans and in an army band (1953–5). After his military service he moved (1957) to California, where he attended San Diego City College (until 1963), and played in Los Angeles with Bobby Bryant, Count Basie, Shelly Manne, Quincy Jones, Benny Carter, Joe Williams, and Donald Byrd; he recorded with Bryant (1967, 1969, 1971), and performed with him at the Monterey Jazz Festival in 1969. He also recorded with Gene Ammons (1972) and Blue Mitchell (1972–3). In 1973 he performed at the Concord Jazz Festival with Jones and the following year he toured South Africa with Monk Montgomery's band. He later recorded with the Capp–Pierce Juggernaut (1978), Lorez Alexandria (1980), Lionel Hampton (1980–81), Paul Humphrey

(1981), and the trumpeter Stacy Rowles (1984), and as a leader (*Herman*, *c*1983, JAM 017). (*Feather–Gitler '70s*)

Riley, (John) Howard (*b* Huddersfield, England, 16 Feb 1943). English pianist and composer. He played piano from the age of six and took an interest in jazz by the age of 13. He studied from 1961 at the University of Wales (BA 1964, MA 1966), from 1966 at Indiana University (MMus 1967), where he was a pupil of Dave Baker, and from 1967 at York University in England (MPhil 1970). After belonging briefly to Evan Parker's quartet (1966) he led a trio from 1967 to 1976 that included Barry Guy and the drummers Alan Jackson, Jon Hiseman, and Tony Oxley, with which he toured widely; he also worked in a duo with John McLaughlin (1968), in the London Jazz Composers Orchestra (from 1970 into the 1980s), and in Oxley's group (1972–81). From 1976 into the 1980s he played in a trio with Guy and the violinist Phil Wachsmann, and as an unaccompanied soloist in Europe, the USA, and Canada. Later he worked in a quartet with Guy, Trevor Watts, and John Stevens (1978–81), in duos with Keith Tippett (from 1981), Jaki Byard (from 1982), and Elton Dean (from 1984), and in a trio with the double bass player Jeff Clyne and the drummer Tony Levin (from 1985). He has taught in London at the Guildhall School of Music and Drama (from 1969) and Goldsmiths' College (from 1975). Riley's recordings invariably feature his own compositions; in addition to works for jazz ensemble he has written orchestral pieces (such as *Angle* and *Overview*), duos for flute and piano, string quartets, and piano music.

SELECTED RECORDINGS

As unaccompanied soloist: *Intertwine* (1975, Mosaic 771); *Toronto Concert* (1976, Vinyl 112)

As leader: *The Howard Riley Trio* (1967, Opportunity 2499); *The Day Will Come* (1970, Col. 564077); *Flight* (1971, Turtle 301); *Synopsis* (1973, Incus 13); with J. Byard: *Live at the Royal Festival Hall* (1984, Leo 133)

As sideman: B. Guy: *Ode for Jazz Orchestra* (1972, Incus 6–7); London Jazz Composers Orchestra: *Stringer* (1980, FMP SAJ41)

BIBLIOGRAPHY

R. Williams: "Riley, Oxley, and the New Music," *MM* (29 Nov 1969), 10
M. Barry: "Howard Riley and 'Non-jazz'," *Contact*, no.14 (1976), 12
S. Lake: "Life of Riley," *MM*, li (16 Oct 1976), 48
A. J. Smith: "Profile: Howard Riley," *DB*, xliv/3 (1977), 33
B. Case: "Confrontation with the Insidious Forces of Industry," *New Musical Express* (25 Feb 1978), 42
K. Ansell: "Howard Riley and his Music," *JJI*, xxxiii/10 (1980), 20
D. Ilic: "Howard Riley," *The Wire*, no.5 (1983), 7

ED HAZELL

Rimington, Sammy [Samuel] (*b* London, 29 April 1942). English clarinetist and alto saxophonist. He began his professional career in 1959 with Barry Martyn and from 1960 to 1965 performed with Ken Colyer; he also played guitar and mandolin in Colyer's skiffle group. From 1965 he worked in the USA, after initially touring and recording in 1964 with the International Jazz Band, which also included Kid Thomas. After returning to Europe he played in Belgium with Martyn and led his own band in England (1969); later he experimented with jazz-rock as the leader of the group Armada (1971). From the mid-1970s he played with George Webb (1973), Martyn's Legends of Jazz (1974), Duke Burrell's Louisiana Shakers and his own trio (both 1974–5), and his own quintet and Chris Barber (both 1977–9). Rimington has performed and recorded with many important New Orleans jazz musicians and has continued to lead his own bands in Europe. He was strongly influenced by George Lewis (i) and Capt. John Handy, and is widely regarded as one of the foremost European exponents of traditional New Orleans jazz. His playing may be heard on *The December Band* (1965, Jazz Crusade JC2007–8), a recording made by Thomas and Handy.

BIBLIOGRAPHY

D. Griffiths: "World Shakers," *MR*, ii/6 (1975), 13
G. Bielderman: *Sammy Rimington Discography, 1959–82* (Zwolle, Netherlands, 1982)
M. Harrison, C. Fox, and E. Thacker: *The Essential Jazz Records*, i: *Ragtime to Swing* (London, and Westport, CT, 1984), 62
D. Fairweather: "Rimington, Sammy (Samuel)," in I. Carr, D. Fairweather, and B. Priestley: *Jazz: the Essential Companion* (London, 1987), 420

DEREK COLLER

Rim shot. The action of striking simultaneously the rim and head of a snare drum, or of striking one stick against the other while it is resting on the drumhead.

Ring. Record label, used before the late 1970s by Moers Music Verlag; *see* MOERS MUSIC.

Rip. A loud, violent GLISS rising to the beginning of a note.

Ristic. Record label. It was established by JOHN R. T. DAVIES in Burnham, England; issue began in 1950. At first 10-inch 78 r.p.m. discs were used, later 10-inch EPs; the bulk of the catalogue, however, was put out on 10-inch LPs. Throughout the label's life the repertory consisted of dubbed reissues of classic early jazz from American labels no longer in operation, recordings of traditional jazz by bands resident in the UK, and unusual items from various sources. Regular issue ceased in the 1970s, though Davies's masters have been put out in several reissue series throughout the world.

Ritenour, Lee (Mack) [Captain Fingers] (*b* Hollywood, CA, 11 Jan 1952). Guitarist. He studied guitar at the University of Southern California and also took private lessons with Joe Pass and Howard Roberts. After touring Japan with Sergio Mendes's band Brasil '77 (1973) he found regular work as a studio guitarist in Los Angeles, recording with rock, disco, and jazz groups. From 1977 he recorded in Japan with Sadao Watanabe and also as the leader of his own jazz-funk ensembles. The following year he began touring with one of these bands under the name Friendship, and by the early 1980s spent most of his time performing with the group. Although Ritenour was influenced initially by Wes Montgomery, he feels his playing limited both rhythmically and harmonically by the bop style; he has a liking for dance rhythms and electronic effects. His album *Rit* reached a wide audience in 1982, when it appeared simultaneously on jazz and several pop charts.

SELECTED RECORDINGS

As leader: *First Course* (*c*1976, Epic 33947); *Gentle Thoughts* (1977, JVC 1); *Rit* (*c*1982, Elek. 6E-331)

As sideman: P. Da Costa: *Agora* (1976, Pablo 2310785); S. Rollins: *The Way I Feel* (1976, Mlst. 9074); S. Watanabe: *Autumn Blow* (1977, FDisk 6006)

BIBLIOGRAPHY

J. Levine: "Profile: Lee Ritenour," *DB*, xlii/5 (1975), 34
J. Sievert: "Lee Ritenour: Poll-winning Studio Guitarist, Dazzling Jazz-rock Soloist," *GP*, xiii/2 (1979), 58 [incl. discography]
R. Palmer: "This Guitar's for Hire," *RS*, no.321 (10 July 1980), 43 [interview]
Z. Stewart: "True Rit: the Outspoken Lee Ritenour," *DB*, li/4 (1984), 24 [incl. discography]
T. Mulhern: "Allan Holdsworth, Lee Ritenour: SynthAxe," *GP*, xx/6 (1986), 109

BARRY KERNFELD

Rivers, Sam(uel Carthorne) (*b* El Reno, OK, 25 Sept 1930). Saxophonist, pianist, and composer. He studied piano, reed instruments, and viola in Little Rock, Arkansas, and Chicago, and attended the Boston Conservatory of Music (1947–52). He performed regularly in the Boston area until the mid-1960s, during which time he went to great lengths to develop a personal approach, shunning imitation and creating his own exercises and practice regimen. Rivers first achieved critical notice as the saxophonist with the Miles Davis Quintet in 1964, when he left Boston for New York; during the same year he performed and recorded with the group in Japan. In the late 1960s he worked with Cecil Taylor, whom he also joined as artist in residence at the Fondation Maeght, St. Paul de Vence, France. In 1970, with his wife Bea, Rivers established Studio Rivbea in SoHo, an important forum for new music. From that time he has toured and recorded with his own groups (playing piano more frequently since the late 1970s), and has continued to develop a highly individual musical personality, particularly in totally improvised music. His work with Dave Holland, in quartet, trio, and duo settings, has been especially influential.

SELECTED RECORDINGS

Duos with D. Holland: *Sam Rivers/Dave Holland* (1976, ImA 373843, 373848)
As leader: *Fuchsia Swing Song* (1964, BN 84184); *Hues* (1971–3, Imp. 9302)
As sideman: M. Davis: *Miles in Tokyo* (1964, CBS Sony SOPL162); D. Holland: *Conference of the Birds* (1972, ECM 1027)

BIBLIOGRAPHY

B. Palmer: "Sam Rivers: an Artist on an Empty Stage," *DB*, xlii/3 (1975), 12
R. Jacchetti: "Discografia Sam Rivers," *Musica jazz*, xxxii (1976), Aug–Sept, 46
W. A. Brower: "Sam Rivers: Warlord of the Lofts," *DB*, xlv/19 (1978), 21
D. Johnson: "Play it again, Sam!," *JJI*, xxxi/12 (1978), 6
L. Lyons: "Sam Rivers: Avant-garde Jazz Pianist and Multi-instrumentalist," *CK*, iv/6 (1978), 16
M. Ullman: *Jazz Lives: Portraits in Words and Pictures* (Washington, 1980)
M. Turner: "Sam Rivers," *Coda*, no.185 (1982), 4

BILL DOBBINS

Riverside. Record company and label. The company was established in New York in 1953 by Bill Grauer(, Jr.) and Orrin Keepnews. Initially it issued famous early jazz recordings drawn principally from the catalogues of Paramount, but also derived material from Champion, the American label Circle, Gennett, Hot Record Society, QRS, and others. In 1954, beginning with two 10-inch albums by Randy Weston, the company started recording modern jazz; it soon became, after Blue Note and Prestige, the most important organization of its era. Most of the new sessions were produced by Keepnews; among the musicians best represented were Thelonious Monk (1955–61), Bill Evans (ii) (1956–62), Cannonball Adderley, Johnny Griffin (both 1958–63), Wes Montgomery (1959–63), and Barry Harris (1960–62). The items by Monk rival his earlier material for Blue Note and later work for Columbia, while the sessions by Evans, Adderley, and Montgomery produced each musician's finest recordings. Riverside established the subsidiary labels Judson (late 1950s) and Jazzland (1960). The company also undertook new recordings of older styles of jazz. Many of these were issued in the series Living Legends, which was recorded in New Orleans and Chicago in the early 1960s and included the work of Earl Hines, Al Wynn, Peter Bocage, and Kid Thomas. Grauer died in December 1963, and the company went bankrupt the following year. From the mid-1970s, however, Riverside's catalogue has figured prominently in reissues on Fantasy's labels Milestone and Original Jazz Classics. (S. Furusho: *Riverside Jazz Records*, Chiba, Japan, 1984)

Roach, Max(well) (*b* New Land, NC, 10 Jan 1924). Drummer and composer. His mother was a gospel singer and he first played drums at the age of ten in gospel bands; this early involvement with black religious music had a significant influence on his musical development, though he also studied formally at the Manhattan School of Music. In 1942 he became associated with Charlie Parker, Dizzy Gillespie and others and, as the house drummer at Monroe's Uptown House, participated in the jam sessions there and at Minton's Playhouse that led to the development of the bop style. From the 1940s Roach played and recorded frequently with bop groups in New York, notably as a member of quintets led by Gillespie (1944) and Charlie Parker (1945, 1947–9, and intermittently, 1951–3). During the same period, however, he also performed with musicians as dissimilar as Louis Jordan, Henry "Red" Allen, and Coleman Hawkins (with whom he made his first recordings, 1943), and took part in sessions with Miles Davis (1948–50), some of the results of which were issued as *Birth of the Cool*.

Max Roach at Massey Hall, Toronto, 1953

From 1954 to 1956, with Clifford Brown, Roach led an important quintet; this group produced a number of seminal recordings, including *Study in Brown* and *At Basin Street*, that epitomized the style of jazz known as hard bop. During the late 1950s and early 1960s Roach made a series of recordings that prefigured developments associated with free jazz; on *Max Roach Plus 4 at Newport* and *Deeds Not Words* (both 1958) he occasionally omitted the piano from his ensembles; on *We Insist! Freedom Now Suite* (1960) he utilized a wide variety of open formal structures instead of the more usual theme and variation format; and on *Drums Unlimited* (1966) he drew on his earlier innovatory concept of performing solo drum improvisations as independent pieces (*Drum Conversation*, 1953).

In the 1960s Roach became an articulate spokesman and

activist in the black-American cultural arts movement, and the titles of many of his compositions and albums from that period – notably *We Insist! Freedom Now Suite*, on which he collaborated with Oscar Brown, Jr. – reflect his awareness of and involvement in the struggle for racial equality. Much of his work was undertaken in conjunction with the singer Abbey Lincoln, his wife at the time, and made use of solo voices and chorus as well as jazz ensemble. From that time he has also composed music for Broadway musicals, films, television, and symphony orchestra. Roach has continued to work regularly with his own groups; in 1970 he organized M' BOOM RE: PERCUSSION, an ensemble of ten percussionists that performs and records works written specifically for percussion instruments. He has also made recordings with such artists as Abdullah Ibrahim (1977), Anthony Braxton (1978–9), Archie Shepp (1979), and Cecil Taylor (1979), and as a soloist with a string quartet (*Survivors*, 1984). He has been an active lecturer on jazz and has held positions at the Lenox (Massachusetts) School of Jazz and the University of Massachusetts at Amherst.

Roach holds a significant position in the history of jazz. With Kenny Clarke, he was particularly important in establishing the practice of setting the fixed pulse on the ride cymbal instead of the bass drum; this enabled more flexible use to be made of the other parts of the drum set and allowed for greater polyrhythmic texture. His imaginative performances as a soloist and his mature technique of improvisation, which is based on the use of deft interaction of pitch and timbral variety, subtleties of silence and sound, rhythmic and metrical contrast, and a refreshingly flexible approach to the fixed pulse, establish him as one of the most outstanding and innovative drummers of his time.

See also BLUES PROGRESSION.

Oral history material in *CtY*.

SELECTED RECORDINGS

As unaccompanied soloist: Drum Conversation (1953, Debut 107); on *Drums Unlimited* (1965–6, Atl. 1467), Drums Unlimited (1966)

Duos with A. Braxton: *Birth and Rebirth* (1978, BS 0024)

As leader: Maxology (1949, Prst. 702) [J. Moody orig. credited as leader]; with C. Brown: *Study in Brown* (1955, EmA 36037), *At Basin Street* (1956, EmA 36070); *Max Roach Plus 4 at Newport* (1958, EmA 80010); *Deeds Not Words* (1958, Riv. 1122); *We Insist! Freedom Now Suite* (1960, Can. 9002), incl. Driva' Man, Freedom Day, Tears for Johannesburg; *Percussion Bitter Sweet* (1961, Imp. 8), incl. Garvey's Ghost; *It's Time* (1962, Imp. 16); *Drums Unlimited* (1965–6, Atl. 1467); *Lift Every Voice and Sing* (1971, Atl. 1587); *Collage* (1984, SN 1059); *Survivors* (1984, SN 1093); *Easy Winners* (1985, SN 1109)

As sideman: C. Hawkins: on *Tenor Sax Stylings* (1943, Bruns. 58030), Blues Changes, Lover come back to me; C. Parker: Ko-Ko (1945, Savoy 597); M. Davis: Move/Budo (1949, Cap. 15404); B. Rich: *Buddy Rich vs Max Roach* (1959, Mer. 20448)

BIBLIOGRAPHY

"Stravinsky, Bird, Vibes Gas Roach," *DB*, xvi/10 (1949), 6

J. Cooke: "We Insist! The Max Roach Group Today and the Freedom Now Suite," *JM*, viii/5 (1962), 3

J. Goldberg: *Jazz Masters of the Fifties* (New York and London, 1965/*R*1980)

G. Hoefer: "Hot Box: Max Roach," *DB*, xxxii/7 (1965), 18

R. Kettle: "Max Roach vs Buddy Rich: a Notated Analysis of Two Significant Modern Jazz Drumming Styles," *DB*, xxxiii/6 (1966), 19

I. Gitler: *Jazz Masters of the Forties* (New York, 1966/*R*1983 with discography)

M. Roach: "What Jazz Means to me," *Black Scholar*, iii/2 (1972), 3

C. A. Parks: "Self-determination and the Black Aesthetic," *Black World*, xxiii (1973), Nov, 62

"Max Roach," *SJ*, xxxi/11 (1977), 288 [discography]

B. Primack: "Max Roach: There's no Stoppin' the Professor from Boppin'," *DB*, xlv/18 (1978), 20

D. Gillespie and A. Fraser: *To Be, or not . . . to Bop: Memoirs* (Garden City, NY, 1979)

H. Howland: "Max Roach: Back on the Bandstand," *MD*, iii/1 (1979), 12

B. Rusch: "Max Roach: Interview," *Cadence*, v/6 (1979), 3

G. Endress: *Jazz Podium: Musiker über sich selbst* (Stuttgart, Germany, 1980), 104

N. Richmond: "Max Roach: an Interview," *Coda*, no.172 (1980), 4

J. Runcie: "Max Roach: Militant Black Artist," *JJI*, xxxiii/5 (1980), 20

S. K. Fish: "Max Roach," *MD*, vi/4 (1982), 8

S. Laszlo: "Behind the Beat of a Different Drummer," *The Wire*, no.1 (1982), 22

C. Fox: "Sit Down and Listen: the Story of Max Roach," *Repercussions: a Celebration of African American Music*, ed. G. Haydon and D. Marks (London, 1985), 80

K. Whitehead: "Max Roach: Drum Architect," *DB*, lii/10 (1985), 16

OLLY WILSON

Roane, Kenneth (A.) (*b* Hartford, CT, *c*1902; *d* New York, 3 March 1984). Trumpeter and arranger. He moved to New York in 1923, by which time he was playing trumpet, clarinet, saxophones, and oboe (he was one of the first musicians to play the oboe in a jazz context). He worked with various musicians, including Jelly Roll Morton and Cecil Scott, and recorded with the drummer Lloyd Scott (1927) and Fess Williams (1927, 1929), for whom he also wrote arrangements. He led his own band in the 1930s and performed regularly with Charlie Johnson and Sam Wooding. In 1939 he recorded on trumpet a selection of Creole and Haitian tunes of marginal jazz significance with Sidney Bechet and Willie "the Lion" Smith in a quintet called the Haitian Orchestra. Roane performed with Cecil Scott (1943), Louis Jordan, Buddy Johnson, Claude Hopkins (1944), and Fats Waller, among others, and continued working and teaching until his death; he was also for many years an official of the AFM. His trumpet playing may be heard on Lloyd Scott's *Harlem Shuffle* (1927, Vic. 21491), one of his own compositions and arrangements.

based on *ChiltonW*

Robert, Jean (*b* Brussels, 25 June 1908; *d* Hilversum, Netherlands, 28 Feb 1981). Belgian tenor saxophonist. He studied piano, then played saxophone with various small groups in Brussels. He worked in 1928 with Peter Packay in London (taking part in recordings issued under the name of the Red Robins) and in the following year belonged to Gus Deloof's first professional group and performed and recorded with Chas Remue's big band. In 1930–31 he played with Deloof and with Albert Sykes in Egypt and Oostende, Belgium; during the following years he led his own band at the Atlanta in Brussels (1933), played in the Netherlands with the drummer Freddie Beerman and in Belgium with Robert de Kers (1935), and led a quartet at the Cotton Club in Brussels and in Switzerland. In 1937 he met Coleman Hawkins, Benny Carter, and Freddy Johnson; he played at the Cotton Club in Johnson's trio (February 1938), and substituted for Hawkins at the Negro Palace in Amsterdam. He also worked in the Netherlands with the reed player Jascha Trabsky and others. On his return to Brussels he joined a group led by Jean Omer, with which he also played at the Salle Pleyel in Paris; around 1943 he performed with Lutz Templin in Germany. Later he appeared with Omer at le Boeuf sur le Toit in Brussels (until 1962) and then moved to Hilversum, where he worked principally as a composer and arranger.

ROBERT PERNET

Roberts, Howard (Mancel) (*b* Phoenix, AZ, 2 Oct 1929). Guitarist. He studied music privately and received some formal instruction in the concepts of the theorist Joseph Schillinger. In 1950 he moved to Los Angeles, where he quickly established himself as an active and versatile studio musician; by the early 1970s he had made thousands of jazz, rock, and pop recordings. He also led his own group and worked with other West Coast bands, including those of Buddy DeFranco, Shorty Rogers, Paul Horn, and Bud Shank. In the early 1970s he began teaching, writing (including a monthly instructional column for *Guitar Player* magazine), and giving seminars, and in 1976 was a co-founder of the Guitar Institute of Technology (now the Musician's Institute) in Hollywood. Roberts's interest in 20th-century classical music and composition is reflected in his sophisticated approach to bop and fusion. This may be heard on his first recording, *Mr. Roberts Plays Guitar*, on which he made use of a string quartet, and throughout his work in his uncommonly advanced view of harmony and melody.

SELECTED RECORDINGS

Mr. Roberts Plays Guitar (1956–7, Verve 8192); *Good Pickin's* (1957, Verve 8305); *H. R. is a Dirty Guitar Player* (1963, Cap. ST1961); *The Real Howard Roberts* (1977, Conc. 53)

BIBLIOGRAPHY

D. Menn: "Howard Roberts," *GP*, xiii/6 (1979), 54
L. Tomkins: "Howard Roberts," *CI*, xxii/6 (1985), 22
H. Roberts: "When I had to Put Stardom Aside," *CI*, xxiv/10 (1987), 8

JIM FERGUSON

Roberts, Luckey [Charles Luckey(e)th] (*b* Philadelphia, 7 Aug 1887; *d* New York, 5 Feb 1968). Pianist and composer. He was a child acrobat, and studied piano from around 1900. By about 1910 he had settled in New York, where in 1911 his first musical comedy, *My People*, was produced, and in 1913 his first published composition, *Junk Man Rag*, appeared. 13 further musical comedies followed in the next two decades. From the 1920s he was a popular bandleader at exclusive social functions on the East Coast; he performed at Carnegie Hall in 1939, and from 1940 to 1954 owned the Rendezvous, a Harlem bar.

By reputation Roberts was the most technically gifted member of the post-ragtime stride school, although he left the least trace of his work. He recorded a number of piano rolls in 1923, but made few phonograph recordings, and those late in his career. Among his compositions are *Pork and Beans* (1913), *Music Box Rag* (1914), *Ripples of the Nile* (popularized by Glenn Miller as *Moonlight Cocktail* in 1941), and works for piano and orchestra.

SELECTED RECORDINGS

Railroad Blues (1946, Cir. [USA] 1026); Pork and Beans (1946, Cir. [USA] 1027); Ripples of the Nile/Shy and Sly (1946, Cir. [USA] 1028); *Harlem Piano Solos* (1958, GTJ 12035), incl. Nothin'

BIBLIOGRAPHY

ChiltonW
R. Blesh and H. Janis: *They All Played Ragtime* (New York, 1950, rev. 4/1971)
L. Feather: *The New Yearbook of Jazz* (New York, 1958), 145
M. Montgomery: "Luckey Roberts Rollography," *Record Research*, no.30 (1960), 2
G. Hoefer: "Luckey Roberts," *JJ*, xvi/3 (1963), 7
"Dill Jones in New York," *JB*, ii/9 (1965), 14
B. Kumm: "Charles Luckeyeth Roberts: Discovery of a Disc," *Sv*, no.14 (1967–8), 30
J. Bradley: "Luckey Roberts," *BHcF*, no.176 (1968), 4
Obituary, B. Kumm, *Sv*, no.17 (1968), 1
T. Vinding: "Forgotten People," *SL*, xxiii (1970), May–June, 329
W. J. Schafer: "Fizz Water: Ragtime by Eubie Blake, Luckey Roberts and James P. Johnson," *MR*, iii/2 (1975), 1

J. R. TAYLOR/R

Robertson, Dick (*b* New York, 3 July 1903). Singer. He began performing as a soloist but from 1928 he recorded prolifically with various leaders, including Ben Pollack (1928), Red Nichols (1929–32), Duke Ellington, Irving Mills, and Andy Kirk (all 1930), Eubie Blake, Benny Goodman, and Fletcher Henderson (all 1931), and Clarence Williams (1934). He also made recordings as the leader of studio bands; among his sidemen were Nichols and Glenn Miller (both 1929), Red Norvo (1936), and Bobby Hackett (1937). From the mid-1940s he concentrated on composing and no longer worked as a full-time performer. Robertson's singing can be heard on Eubie Blake's *Thumpin' and Bumpin'* (1931, Vic. 22737). (C. Morgan: "Dick Robertson Discography," *JJ*, xxi/8 (1968), 20)

based on *ChiltonW*

Robertson, Zue [C. Alvin] (*b* New Orleans, 7 March 1891; *d* Los Angeles, 1943). Trombonist. After learning piano he took up the trombone at the age of 13. He spent much of his career in circus and show bands. He was a member of the Olympia Band (*c*1914) and played trombone with Manuel Perez, Richard M. Jones, and John Robichaux. He moved to Chicago in 1917 to work at the De Luxe Café, and by the mid-1920s was playing with leaders of the stature of Jelly Roll Morton, with whom he recorded *Some Day Sweetheart/London Blues* (1923, OK 8105), and King Oliver (1924). He toured extensively with W. C. Handy before returning to Chicago to join Dave Peyton at the Grand Theatre. From spring 1929 he lived in New York, where he played mainly piano and organ, giving up trombone entirely in 1930. After moving to California he worked on piano and double bass throughout the 1930s. (L. Wright: "Who's Zue?," *Sv*, no.1 (1965), 18)

based on *ChiltonW*

Robeson [Roberson], **Orlando** (*b* Tulsa, OK, 4 March 1909). Singer. He recorded two items with Fats Waller in 1929. His most important association was with Claude Hopkins, with whom he worked at intervals between 1933 and 1940, making a number of recordings (including *Marie*, 1934, Col. 2904D). He also performed briefly with Louis Metcalf in New York (1936), as a co-leader with Clarence Love (1936–7), and as the leader of his own band in Birmingham, Alabama. In 1943 he sang with an army group in Phoenix, Arizona, and after leaving the army he moved to the West Coast.

based on *ChiltonW*

Robichaux, John (*b* Thibodaux, LA, 16 Jan 1886; *d* New Orleans, 1939). Bandleader, drummer, and violinist, uncle of Joseph Robichaux. After moving to New Orleans in 1891, he played bass drum with the Excelsior Brass Band from 1892 to 1903. Mainly as a violinist, he led various bands from 1893 until his death, including a 36-piece orchestra, formed in 1913; his ensembles, which played mainly at sight, included many of the city's best musicians. He made a large number of orchestral arrangements (now housed in the William Ransom Hogan Jazz Archive at Tulane University in New Orleans; *see* LIBRARIES AND ARCHIVES, §2) and composed over 350 songs. Robichaux should not be confused with his nephew John Robichaux (*b* New Orleans, *c*1915), also a drummer, who was active mainly in Louisiana; he joined the New Orleans Ragtime Orchestra in 1971 and toured widely with this and with the musical show *One Mo' Time*. (*ChartersJ*)

MIKE HAZELDINE

Robichaux, Joseph [Joe] (*b* New Orleans, 8 March 1900; *d* New Orleans, 17 Jan 1965). Pianist, nephew of John Robichaux. He was taught piano by Steve Lewis and after playing as a soloist in New Orleans went to Chicago with the trumpeter Tig Chambers (1918). He returned to New Orleans, where he worked with Papa Celestin, the saxophonist David Jones, and Lee Collins. He toured with the Black Eagles in 1922–3 and around 1928 worked in the JONES AND COLLINS ASTORIA HOT EIGHT, with which he also recorded (1929). He played briefly with Willie O'Connell and Kid Rena and in 1931 formed the New Orleans Rhythm Boys, which made recordings in New York (1933);

among its sidemen were Gene Porter, Sidney Desvigne, and Sam Dutrey, Jr. After the group, by then 15 pieces, disbanded in 1939, Robichaux again worked as a solo pianist in New Orleans during the 1940s, and in the early 1950s he accompanied Lizzie Miles in California. From 1957 to 1964 he was a member of the band of George Lewis (i), which toured Europe and Japan. Robichaux' extrovert style and stage manner masked his sensitive, shy personality.

Oral history material in *LNT*.

SELECTED RECORDINGS

As leader: Every Tub (1933, Voc. 2827); The Riff (1933, Voc. 2592)

As sideman: Jones–Collins Astoria Hot Eight: Astoria Strut/Duet Stomp (1929, Vic. 38576); Damp Weather/Tip Easy Blues (1929, Bb 10952); G. Lewis: *The Perennial George Lewis* (1958, Verve 8277)

BIBLIOGRAPHY

ChiltonW

T. Standish: "Joseph Robichaux: Those Early Days," *JJ*, xii/4 (1959), 10

M. Simpson: "Joe Robichaux, New Orleans Piano: a Biography," *Jazz Reprints*, i/3 (1963), 3

K. Gert zur Heide: "Eugene Porter," *Fn*, vii/6 (1976), 17

MIKE HAZELDINE

Robinson, Banjo. *See* ROBINSON, IKEY.

Robinson, Bill [Luther; Bojangles] (*b* Richmond, VA, 25 May 1878; *d* New York, 25 Nov 1949). Dancer. As a child he appeared in restaurants and vaudeville as a "pickaninny," the term applied to a black child entertainer with traveling troupes. He toured on the TOBA circuit and later was one of the few black dancers to become a star attraction on the Keith circuit. During his routines he gave his feet anthropomorphic characteristics and commented humorously on them, and told anecdotes. He did not perform in a Broadway show until he was almost 50, when he danced and sang *Doin' the new low down* in *Blackbirds of 1928*. A good example of Robinson's recorded work may be heard on *Doin' the new low down* (1929, Bruns. 4535), made by Irving Mills and his Hotsy Totsy Gang. He appeared in several black revues and musicals, including *Hot Mikado* (1939), and *Memphis Bound* (1945), a "swing" version of *H.M.S. Pinafore*. During the 1930s he also appeared in films with the child actress Shirley Temple, often performing his best-known routine, tap-dancing up and down a staircase; he took a major part in both *Hooray for Love!* (1935) and *Stormy Weather* (1943). Two clips from films made by Robinson can be seen in *No Maps on my Taps* (1978). Although not as original as other vernacular dancers, Robinson perfected several dances and pioneered tap-dancing on the toes (as opposed to the flat-footed style of his predecessors). (M. Stearns and J. Stearns: *Jazz Dance: the Story of American Vernacular Dance*, New York and London, 1968)

SAMUEL S. BRYLAWSKI/R

Robinson, Eli [Mr. Eli] (*b* Greenville, nr Woodbury, GA, 23 June 1908; *d* New York, 24 Dec 1972). Trombonist and arranger. He was brought up in Charleston, West Virginia, and took up trombone in 1925. From 1930 he worked in Cincinnati with various musicians, including Speed Webb, Zack Whyte, McKinney's Cotton Pickers, and Blanche Calloway, with whom he made his first recordings (1935). In early 1936 he settled in New York, where he performed with Willie Bryant, Teddy Hill, and the Mills Blue Rhythm Band under Lucky Millinder; he also played briefly with Roy Eldridge in Chicago (1939). From 1941 to 1947 he was a member of Count Basie's band (for illustration *see* FILMS, fig.3), after which he again worked with various leaders, including Millinder. Robinson played regularly with Buddy Tate's Celebrity Club Orchestra from 1954, and his work as a soloist and arranger may be heard on Tate's *Swinging Like Tate* (1958, Fel. SJA2004).

BIBLIOGRAPHY

ChiltonW

S. Dance: "Skip Hall and Eli Robinson," *JM*, iv/7 (1958), 27

Robinson, Fred(erick L.) (*b* Memphis, 20 Feb 1901; *d* New York, 11 April 1984). Trombonist. He began playing while at high school in Memphis, then studied music in Warren, Ohio. In 1927 he moved to Chicago where he joined Carroll Dickerson's band at the Savoy Ballroom; he played in the band with Louis Armstrong (who returned to it, after an absence, in March 1928) and took part in Armstrong's Hot Five recordings in June to December 1928. In May 1929 Robinson traveled to New York with Dickerson's band under Armstrong's leadership and remained with it until later that year, when he joined Edgar Hayes at the Alhambra Theater. During the 1930s he worked in the bands of Marion Hardy (1931) and Charlie Turner (which often toured with Fats Waller until 1937), and for short periods with Fletcher Henderson (1935, 1938, 1939, 1941). During this time he also performed and recorded with Don Redman (1931–3), Benny Carter (1933), and Andy Kirk (1939–40). He then played with George James (1943) and Cab Calloway (1944–5), recorded with Sy Oliver (1946–50), worked as a freelance musician in New York, and played with Noble Sissle (1950–51). He ceased to work as a full-time musician in 1954 but continued to perform during the 1960s. Although he was a superb trombonist in a big-band context, he is best remembered for his recordings of *West End Blues* in small groups led by Louis Armstrong (1928, OK 8597) and Jelly Roll Morton (1939, Bb 10442). (*ChiltonW*; *FeatherE*)

MIKE HAZELDINE

Robinson, Ikey (L.) [Robinson, Banjo [Ike]; Banjo Ike(y); Banjo Joe] (*b* Dublin, nr Radford, VA, 28 July 1904). Banjoist and guitarist. He led his own band from 1918 and began playing professionally with other leaders in 1922. After moving to Chicago (1926) he performed with Jelly Roll Morton and Clarence Moore (1928–9); he also recorded as a leader and with Jabbo Smith (1929), among others. In 1930 he traveled to New York, where he worked with Wilbur Sweatman and Noble Sissle, played and sang on a number of recordings with Clarence Williams (1930, 1933), and led two groups. He returned to Chicago in 1934 and performed with Carroll Dickerson and Erskine Tate, before forming his own band the following year; he worked as a leader of small groups (1940s) and in a duo with Mike McKendrick (until 1960). He then played in the Original Jass All Stars, led by Franz Jackson (1960s), and toured Europe (early 1970s); from the late 1970s he worked mainly in Chicago. Robinson's singing and guitar playing may be heard on *My Four Reasons* (1933, Voc. 25011), a duet he recorded with Herman "Ivory" Chittison.

See also BANJO.

BIBLIOGRAPHY

B. Englund: "Ikey Robinson: an Introduction and Discography," *JM*, viii/10 (1962), 10

B. Rusch: "Ikey Robinson: Interview," *Cadence*, v/4 (1979), 12

P. Van Vorst: "Banjo Ikey," *MR*, xi/9 (1984), 5

based on *ChiltonW*

Robinson, Janice (*b* Clairton, PA, 1951). Trombonist. As a teenager she played trombone in the comedian Bill Cosby's nationally broadcast television program. She graduated from the

Eastman School in 1973 and then moved to New York, where the following year she joined Clark Terry's big band. She visited Japan while playing with the Thad Jones–Mel Lewis Orchestra (1975–6), toured Europe with Gil Evans (1976), and returned to Japan while a member of Frank Foster's big band (1977–8). Shortly afterwards she performed with Slide Hampton (*c*1979). Robinson has also worked in jazz repertory companies and free-jazz ensembles: she recorded with the Jazz Composer's Orchestra in 1974 and appeared with Sam Rivers at the Newport Jazz Festival New York in 1976. After leading, with the pianist Sharon Freeman, a bop quintet that appeared at the first Kansas City Women's Jazz Festival (1978) she formed her own quintet, which included Buster Williams and Kenny Kirkland.

SELECTED RECORDINGS

As sideman: on T. Jones and M. Lewis: *Suite for Pops* (1975, A&M Hor. 701), The Farewell; *New Life* (1975–6, A&M Hor. 707); F. Foster: *Twelve Shades of Black: for All Intents and Purposes* (1978, Leo 007)

BIBLIOGRAPHY

"Janice Robinson," *Newsletter of the International Trombone Association*, viii/3 (1981), 7
Y. A. Salaam: "Profile: Janice Robinson," *DB*, xlviii/4 (1981), 48
S. Placksin: *American Women in Jazz, 1900 to the Present: their Words, Lives, and Music* (New York, 1982; London, 1985, as *Jazzwomen, 1900 to the Present: their Words, Lives, and Music*), 285

BARRY KERNFELD

Robinson, Jim [Nathan; Big Jim, Jim Crow] (*b* Deer Range, LA, 25 Dec 1892; *d* New Orleans, 4 May 1976). Trombonist. He took up guitar as a youngster, when he became known as "Jim Crow," reportedly on account of his American Indian facial features. He began playing trombone in 1917 while stationed in France during army service, and received some instruction from Willie Foster; later he took lessons with the trombonist Charles "Sunny" Henry. Robinson first worked professionally in New Orleans in 1919, with Kid Rena, and with Lee Collins in the Golden Leaf Band (led by the banjoist Jesse Jackson). In 1923 he joined the Morgan Band, and worked first under the leadership of Isaiah and then of Sam Morgan, recording with the group in 1927 and performing in Chicago in 1929. During the mid- and late 1930s he played with Capt. John Handy and Kid Howard. He recorded with Kid Rena in 1940 and with Bunk Johnson and George Lewis (i) from 1942 to 1946; his version of *Ice Cream* (1944), in which he leads the band without a trumpeter, is justly celebrated. Later Robinson played regularly with Lewis in New Orleans and toured with him in the USA (1952–4) and Europe (1959). After 1960 he performed at Preservation Hall with Lewis and other leaders (notably Percy Humphrey), and continued to tour and record frequently.

Robinson's highly individual style was characterized by an ebullient shouting tone and frequent employment of tongued staccato articulation, glottal ghost notes, and pedal notes; he also made judicious use of glissandos. His sense of melodic inventiveness never allowed him to neglect the fundamental role of the bass line in an ensemble, and he was a leading exponent of the New Orleans tailgate style.

Oral history material in *LNT*, *NjR*.

For illustrations *see* HUMPHREY and JOHNSON, BUNK.

SELECTED RECORDINGS

As leader: Ice Cream (1944, AM 254); *Robinson's Jacinto Ballroom Orchestra* (1964, GHB 28)

As sideman: S. Morgan: Short Dress Gal/Bogalusa Strut (1927, Col. 14351D); K. Rena: Weary Blues/Get it right (1940, Delta 806-7); B. Johnson: Careless Love Blues/Weary Blues (1944, AM 258); G. Lewis: *George Lewis at the San Jacinto Hall* (1964, San Jacinto 2); P. Humphrey: *Climax Rag* (1965, Pearl 3)

BIBLIOGRAPHY

ChiltonW
J. Robinson: "New Orleans Trombone," *Jazz Record*, no.38 (1945); repr. in *Selections from the Gutter: Jazz Portraits from "The Jazz Record"*, ed. A. Hodes and C. Hansen (Berkeley, CA, Los Angeles, and London, 1977), 124
M. Jones: "New Orleans Brassmen," *MM*, xxxiv (10 Jan 1959), 11
A. Barrell: "Jim Robinson," *Fn*, vii/2 (1975–6), 4 [incl. discography]
D. Donahoe: "Jim Robinson: a Tribute," *Fn*, vii/5 (1976), 29
K. Koenig: "Nathan 'Big Jim' Robinson: Jazz Trombonist," *SL*, xxxv (win. 1983), 24

ALDEN ASHFORTH

Robinson, J(oseph) Russel (*b* Indianapolis, 8 July 1892; *d* Palmdale, CA, 30 Sept 1963). Songwriter and pianist. He was principally self-taught as a pianist, and began his career accompanying silent films in Indianapolis when he was a teenager. Since he was crippled in his right arm by polio, he developed a distinctive left-hand style incorporating gymnastic and unorthodox passages. His playing was particularly popular with piano-roll companies, and he recorded dozens of rolls for Imperial and the United States Music Company in Chicago (1917–18) before moving under exclusive contract to the QRS company in New York to record blues songs (1918–21). From 1919 to 1921 Robinson was pianist for the ORIGINAL DIXIELAND JAZZ BAND, with which he toured England, and also managed W. C. Handy's music publishing firm. He had a number of hits with his own popular songs, beginning with *Margie* (1920). Between 1923 and 1926 he accompanied a number of jazz and blues singers (including Lizzie Miles), and during the 1930s he played on radio. Later he settled in southern California, where he continued to compose songs, but with diminishing success.

Robinson broke with social tradition by collaborating extensively with black musicians, including Handy, Noble Sissle, and Spencer Williams; the last named once praised him as "the white man with the colored fingers," and his accompaniments to blues singers reveal his mastery of that Afro-American idiom. Robinson excelled both in the performance and composition of blues- and jazz-influenced material, and his *That Eccentric Rag* (1912) became a staple of the traditional jazz repertory (as *Eccentric*, rev. 1923). Other well-known songs include *Singin' the blues (til my daddy comes home)* (1920), made famous in a recording by Bix Beiderbecke with Frankie Trumbauer's orchestra (1927, OK 40772), *Aggravatin' papa (don't you try to two-time me)* and *Beale Street Mama*, recorded by Bessie Smith (1923, Col. A3877), and *A Portrait of Jennie*, recorded by, among others, Donald Byrd (on the album *At the Half Note Cafe*, 1960, BN 84060).

SELECTED RECORDINGS

Duos with L. Hegamin: Down Hearted Blues/Wanna go South Again Blues (1923, Cameo 381)

As sideman: Original Dixieland Jazz Band: Ostrich Walk/Sensation Rag (1919, Col. 736); Al Bernard: Memphis Blues/Hesitation Blues (1927, Bruns. 3553); Original Dixieland Five: Barnyard Blues/Original Dixieland One-step (1938, Vic. 25502)

BIBLIOGRAPHY

J. R. Robinson: "Dixieland Piano," *Record Changer* (1947), Aug, 7
J. E. Hasse: *The Creation and Dissemination of Indianapolis Ragtime, 1897–1930* (diss., Indiana U., 1981), 159

JOHN EDWARD HASSE

Robinson, Perry (Morris) (*b* New York, 17 Aug 1938). Clarinetist. His father, the songwriter Earl Robinson, was responsible for much of his musical background. He first studied piano, but changed to clarinet at the age of nine. He attended the High School of Music and Art (1952–6) and the Manhattan School of Music (1958); after meeting Ornette Coleman in 1959 while studying at the Lenox School of Jazz he became interested in free jazz. He played with Chuck Israels, and later with Tete Montoliu in Spain (1960), then with Don Friedman, Archie Shepp, and Bill Dixon elsewhere in Europe. He formed a group with Bill Folwell and Tom Price while playing in a band in the US Navy; later he worked with Sunny Murray, Roswell Rudd, Charlie Haden, and the Jazz Composers Guild in New York. He recorded with Henry Grimes (1965), took part in the recording of Carla Bley's *Escalator over the Hill* (1968–71), and in the early 1970s played with the keyboard player Darius Brubeck and with Gunter Hampel in the Galaxie Dream Band, of which he remained a member into the 1980s. He also led several groups with unusual instrumentation, including Pipe Dreams, the other members of which were two singers and a guitarist.

SELECTED RECORDINGS

As leader: *Kundalini* (1978, IA 373856); *Licorice Factory* (1985, Jazzmania 41206)

As sideman: H. Grimes: *Henry Grimes Trio* (1965, ESP 1026); C. Bley: *Escalator over the Hill* (1968–71, JCOA EOTH); G. Hampel: *Jubilation* (1983, Birth 0038)

BIBLIOGRAPHY

G. Endress: "Der Magier der Klarinette," *JP*, xxi/7 (1972), 228

B. Palmer: "Perry Robinson: Clarinet Energy," *DB*, xxxix/16 (1972), 16

A. Kreye: "Aktiv mit drei Formationen: Perry Robinson," *JP*, xxxiii/8 (1984), 24

DAVID WILD

Robinson, Prince (*b* Portsmouth, VA, 7 June 1902; *d* New York, 23 July 1960). Clarinetist and tenor saxophonist. At the age of 14 he taught himself to play clarinet, and performed with local bands for three years before going to New York in 1923. There he worked with Lionel Howard's Musical Aces, Elmer Snowden, June Clark, Duke Ellington, and the saxophonist Billy Fowler. In 1927 he toured South America with Leon Abbey, then joined McKinney's Cotton Pickers (for illustration *see* MCKINNEY'S COTTON PICKERS). After leaving the group he played with Blanche Calloway (1935–7), Willie Bryant (1937–8), Roy Eldridge (1938–40), Louis Armstrong (1940–42), Lucky Millinder (1942–3), Benny Morton (1944), Claude Hopkins (1945–52), Henry "Red" Allen (1954), and Freddie Washington (1955–9). He also led his own band briefly in 1953.

Robinson was one of the few reed players in jazz who regularly played solos on both clarinet and saxophone in a single tune; he preferred clarinet, but his playing of the tenor saxophone in the late 1920s and early 1930s, when he was recording with McKinney's Cotton Pickers, rivaled that of Coleman Hawkins. Thereafter, although he continued to be well regarded by his fellow musicians, he did not attain widespread recognition.

SELECTED RECORDINGS

As sideman: McKinney's Cotton Pickers: Four or Five Times (1928, Vic. 21583); I want a little girl (1930, Vic. 23000); B. Calloway: Line-a-jive (1935, Voc. 3113); T. Wilson: My Last Affair (1937, Bruns. 7840); R. Eldridge: *Roy Eldridge at the Arcadia Ballroom, August/September 1939* (1939, Jazz Archives 14), incl. Arcadia Shuffle

BIBLIOGRAPHY

ChiltonW

J. Chilton: *McKinney's Music: a Bio-discography of McKinney's Cotton Pickers* (London, 1978)

FRANK DRIGGS

Roccisano, Joe(y) [Joseph Lucian] (*b* Springfield, MA, 15 Oct 1939). Alto saxophonist, bandleader, and arranger. He studied music education at SUNY, Potsdam (BS 1963). He toured with Tommy Dorsey's orchestra under Sam Donahue (1964), and in the mid-1960s he settled in Los Angeles, where he played and recorded with Don Ellis (1966–8), with whom he also appeared at the Monterey and Newport jazz festivals, and worked with Ray Charles (1967–8). As a freelance he played with Louie Bellson, Terry Gibbs, Don Menza, and Bill Holman, and recorded with Don Rader (*c*1973). From 1976 he led a 15-piece band, Rocbop. He wrote arrangements for several jazz musicians, including Bellson, Ellis, Doc Severinsen, and Woody Herman; his score for *Green Earrings* on Herman's album *Chick, Donald, Walter, and Woodrow* (1978, Cen. 1110) was nominated for a Grammy Award, and the album *Apogee* (1978, WB 3236) by Pete Christlieb and Warne Marsh, for which he wrote the arrangements, also includes his composition *Tenors of the Time*. In 1981 Roccisano recorded with the Capp–Pierce Juggernaut.

BIBLIOGRAPHY

Feather–Gitler '70s

L. Underwood: "Joe Roccisano," *DB*, xliii/9 (1976), 37

——: "Caught!: Joey Roccisano's Rocbop," *DB*, xlvi/8 (1979), 35

Roche, Betty [Mary Elizabeth] (*b* Wilmington, DE, 9 Jan 1920). Singer. She won an amateur contest at the Apollo Theatre in Harlem and later sang with the Savoy Sultans (1941–2) and with Hot Lips Page and Lester Young. She joined Duke Ellington in 1943. Although she made no studio recordings with Ellington, she was the first to sing the *Blues* sequence of his *Black, Brown and Beige*, performed at Carnegie Hall in January 1943. She worked and recorded with Earl Hines (1944), then spent a period in relative obscurity before rejoining Ellington in 1952, when she recorded an acclaimed version of *Take the "A" Train*. After a period of semiretirement she recorded three solo albums (1956, 1960, 1961). Roche performed mostly blues and ballads in the 1940s, and her warm, personal style was well suited to Ellington's band. Her early work is superior to her bop singing of the 1950s.

SELECTED RECORDINGS

As leader: *Take the "A" Train* (1956, Beth. 64); *Singin' and Swingin'* (1960, Prst. 7187); *Lightly and Politely* (1961, Prst. 7198)

As sideman: D. Ellington: on *Carnegie Hall Concert: January 1943* (1943, Prst. 34004), Black, Brown and Beige; E. Hines: Blues on my Weary Mind/I'll get by (1944, Apollo 358); D. Ellington: Take the "A" Train (1952, Col. B1566)

BIBLIOGRAPHY

B. Ulanov: *Duke Ellington* (New York, 1946/R1975), 249

G. T. Simon: *The Big Bands* (New York, 1967, rev. and enlarged 2/1971, rev. 4/1981)

D. Ellington: *Music is my Mistress* (Garden City, NY, 1973), 222

REG COOPER

Rockets. Big band formed by HARLAN LEONARD after the Kansas City Rockets disbanded in 1937.

Roda, Ricard (*b* Barcelona, 13 Nov 1931). Spanish alto saxophonist. He studied music at the conservatory in Barcelona, and began playing jazz in 1947, participating in the jam sessions organized at the Hot Club de Barcelona. While working at the Jamboree Club he played with such visiting soloists as Tony Scott, Art Farmer, Tete Montoliu, Guy Lafitte, and Lucky Thompson and established a reputation as one of the finest Spanish saxophonists. In 1968 he participated in the cooperative recording *Nuits de jazz at Jamboree* (Edigsa 221). Around this time he also worked with the commercial orchestras led by Xavier Cugat and Frank Pourcel. Thereafter he concentrated on teaching and playing for television.

ALFREDO PAPO

Rodgers, Gene [Eugene R., Jr.] (*b* New York, 5 March 1910; *d* New York, 23 Oct 1987). Pianist and arranger. He began playing in 1924 and worked in New York from 1928 as a leader and in various bands, including that of Chick Webb; he also recorded with Clarence Williams and King Oliver. After performing with Kaiser Marshall and Teddy Hill he formed a variety act, which toured the USA, Great Britain, and Australia; while on tour he recorded as a soloist and with Benny Carter in London (1936). He wrote arrangements for Coleman Hawkins (with whom he also recorded, 1939–40) and Fats Waller, was a member of Zutty Singleton's trio (1940), and played with Erskine Hawkins (1943). From 1943 he performed as a soloist in California and appeared in several films (1944–5). He worked again in New York (1945–6, 1948, late 1950s) and traveled widely in the USA and Canada (early 1950s). Rodgers continued to perform and record during the 1960s and 1970s, and in 1981–2 he worked with the Harlem Blues and Jazz Band. His playing as a soloist is well represented by *G. R. Blues* (1945, Joe Davis 8889) and he is heard to advantage in the setting of a small group on *Gene Rodgers/Slam Stewart/Jo Jones* (1972, BB 33047). (J. Godrich: "Margin Notes, no.33," *Vintage Jazz Mart* (1970), April, 3)

based on *ChiltonW*

Rodin, Gil(bert A.) (*b* Russia, 9 Dec 1906; *d* Palm Springs, CA, 17 June 1974). Saxophonist and clarinetist. After working in a dance band in Chicago in the mid-1920s he moved to California, where he played briefly with Harry Bastin's orchestra, then in 1927 joined Ben Pollack's band; he also recorded as a leader with some of Pollack's sidemen (1930–31). When Pollack's group disbanded in 1934 Rodin organized a new band that recorded under the name of the singer Clark Randall in 1935; Bob Crosby assumed leadership of the group later that year. Rodin worked for Crosby as president, music director, and business manager and as a sideman until he was drafted in 1942. After military service he led a band with Ray Bauduc (1944–5), though in the late 1940s he worked again with Crosby. During the 1950s and 1960s he was a producer for radio and television.

Rodin composed *Boogie Woogie Maxixe*, which was popularized by Crosby's band in 1939. His playing was influenced by the work of Eddie Miller, Matty Matlock, Benny Goodman, and Irving Fazola, but he preferred to work as a section player and rarely took solos.

For illustrations *see* CROSBY, BOB, and POLLACK, BEN.

SELECTED RECORDINGS

As leader: Beale Street Blues (1930, Crown 3017); Ninety-nine out of a hundred wanna be loved (1931, Crown 3045)

As sideman: B. Pollack: He's the last word (1926, Vic. 20425); Memphis Blues (1927, Vic. 21184); Night on the Desert/Sleepy Head (1934, Col. 2929D); C. Randall: Jitter Bug/If you're looking for someone to love (1935, Bruns. 7466); B. Crosby: Boogie Woogie Maxixe (1939, Decca 2848)

BIBLIOGRAPHY

G. T. Simon: *The Big Bands* (New York, 1967, rev. and enlarged 2/1971, rev. 3/1974, 4/1981), 131

J. Chilton: "Gil Rodin," *Stomp Off, Let's Go! The Story of Bob Crosby's Bob Cats & Big Band* (London, 1983), 173

RAYMOND J. GARIGLIO

Rodney, Red [Chudnick, Robert] (*b* Philadelphia, 27 Sept 1927). Trumpeter. He began playing at the age of 13 and went on tour only two years later in a big band led by the clarinetist Jerry Wald. He then spent short periods with Jimmy Dorsey, Elliot Lawrence (1945), Benny Goodman, and Les Brown. Although he was originally a swing player influenced by Harry James, Rodney modernized his style after hearing Dizzy Gillespie and Charlie Parker. During associations with Gene Krupa (1946), Claude Thornhill (1947), and Woody Herman (1948–9), he gained recognition as one of the finest young bop trumpeters. The peak of his early career was his work in Charlie Parker's quintet (1949–51); the recording of the group's concert at Carnegie Hall demonstrates his mastery of the harmonic vocabulary of bop. Rodney spent a brief period with Charlie Ventura before drug addiction interrupted his career during the 1950s. After playing with local dance bands and working as a booking agent in Philadelphia he settled in Las Vegas in 1960 and played in show bands. In 1972 he returned to jazz and gradually regained his former prominence. A chance meeting with Ira Sullivan while he was touring in 1980 led the two men to form a group; its new material (much of it written by the pianist Garry Dial) was a challenge to Rodney, and revitalized his playing. During the 1980s his solos have been as creative as they were in the 1940s; a volume containing 11 transcriptions of his performances, *Red Rodney Jazz Transcriptions*, was published in New York in 1983.

SELECTED RECORDINGS

As leader: first issued on [no leader]: *Advance Guard of the '40s* (1945–9, EmA 36016), All God's Children Got Rhythm, The Goof and I (both 1947); Honeysuckle Rose/Buckle my Shoe (1952, OK 6922); *Modern Music from Chicago* (1955, Fan. 3208); *Red Rodney, 1957* (1957, Signal 1206); *Superbop* (1974, Muse 5046); *The Three R's* (1979, Muse 5290)

As leader with I. Sullivan: *Live at the Village Vanguard* (1980, Muse 5209); *Night and Day* (1981, Muse 5274); *Sprint* (1982, Elek. Mus. 60261)

As sideman with C. Parker: *Live at Carnegie Hall* (1949, CP 2); on Charlie Parker (1951–3, Clef 287) [EP], Blues for Alice (1951); Si si/Swedish Schnapps (1951, Mer./Clef 11103); Back Home Blues (1951, Mer./Clef 11095)

BIBLIOGRAPHY

M. Gardner: "Red Rodney Talks," *JM*, no.182 (1970), 2 [interview]

M. James: "Red Rodney on Record," *JM*, no.187 (1970), 4

R. Baggenaes: "Red Rodney," *Coda*, no.144 (1976), 13 [interview]

M. Smith: "Red Rodney," *Cadence*, vi (1980), no.7, p.5; no.9, p.5 [interview]

L. Birnbaum: "Red Rodney: his Bite is Back," *DB*, xlviii/2 (1981), 20

G. Giddins: *Riding on a Blue Note: Jazz and American Pop* (New York, and Oxford, England, 1981) [colln of previously pubd interviews], 228

D. Long: "Red Rodney," *Cadence*, xii/12 (1986), 5 [interview]

SCOTT YANOW

Rodriguez, Rod [Nicholas Goodwin] (*b* Havana, 10 Sept 1906). Pianist. He worked as an ensemble pianist with Jelly Roll Morton in 1929–30. He performed and recorded with Benny Carter (1932–3) and Don Redman (1938–43), recorded with Spike Hughes (1933), and appeared with Alberto Socarras (1939). After accompanying the singer Frances Brock on an overseas tour (1945–6), he joined the drummer Herbert Cowens (1946). In the 1950s and 1960s he taught piano and played with Johnny Coles (1953), Louis Armstrong (1961), and Doc Cheatham (mid-1960s). *How come you do me like you do?* (1933, Decca F3972), one of the recordings Rodriguez made with a small group drawn from Spike Hughes's orchestra, provides a typical example of his solo style.

based on *ChiltonW*

Roger Henrichsen, Børge (*b* Copenhagen, 4 Oct 1915). Danish pianist, bandleader, composer, and trumpeter. He studied classical piano and played jazz with Svend Asmussen and others from 1937. He made many recordings of his own compositions (including *Dream Melody* (1938, HMV X6053) as the leader of a trio, and *Prelude in C* (1942, HMV DX6877) in a duo with Niels Foss) and led a quintet from 1940 to 1946. From 1950 he was director of jazz programs for Statsradiofonien (from 1959 Danmarks Radio), a position he held until 1980; he also published several volumes of jazz studies for piano, and wrote *Noget om jazz* (Something about jazz; Copenhagen, 1961), an introductory text published in conjunction with a radio series. (B. Jørgensen: *Børge Roger Henrichsen*, Copenhagen, 1963)

ERIK WIEDEMANN

Rogers, Shorty [Rajonsky, Milton M.] (*b* Great Barrington, MA, 14 April 1924). Trumpeter, composer, arranger, and bandleader. He studied at the High School of Music and Art, New York, and played professionally with Will Bradley and Red Norvo while still a teenager. After military service he was a member of Woody Herman's band (1945–50; for illustration *see* HERMAN, WOODY, fig.1*b*), where he attracted attention as an arranger of adventurous big-band scores. Later he contributed a number of important scores to the library of Stan Kenton's band (1950–51). Rogers then settled in Los Angeles, where he studied classical composition privately and led a series of outstanding big bands and groups with former Kenton sidemen: Bud Shank, Bob Cooper, Jimmy Giuffre, Maynard Ferguson, Conte Candoli, Shelly Manne, Stan Levey, Mel Lewis, and, most notably, Art Pepper. He supervised such early jazz film scores as *The Wild One* (1953, composed by Leith Stevens) and *The Man with the Golden Arm* (1955, composed by Elmer Bernstein), and also served as an artistic director for Atlantic Records (1955) and RCA Victor (from 1954). From the 1960s he became less active in jazz as he turned increasingly to Hollywood studios, where he was in steady demand as a composer of expertly crafted film scores and as supervisor of soundtrack recording sessions.

Rogers was a leading figure in the West Coast style of jazz in the early 1950s, not only as an instrumentalist, composer, and arranger, but also as an organizer of concerts and teacher of young talent. His big-band scores were among the most inventive of their day, whether exploring irregular ostinatos (*Tale of an African Lobster*), bitonality (*I'm gonna go fishin'*), or increasing timbral densities (*Infinity Promenade*). In his own groups, and in those of Jimmy Giuffre and Teddy Charles, Rogers attempted to broaden the theoretical foundations of jazz, dispensing at times with chord progressions, improvising on modes, and, in *Three on a Row* (1954), pioneering the use in jazz of the 12-tone technique. His arrangements for small group are remarkable for their unusual variety of instrumental textures, *Martians Go Home* (1955) being a particularly intriguing and influential example. Rogers was also among the earliest jazz musicians to take up flugelhorn (see illustration) which, like the trumpet, he played in a subdued manner indebted to Miles Davis's early style and well described in Stravinsky's *Conversations*, where the composer points to Rogers as a possible influence on his use of that instrument in *Threni*. Some of his best solo playing may be heard on Teddy Charles's album *New Directions* (1953, Prst. 164), Shelly Manne's recording *The Three*, and his own *The Swinging Mr. Rogers*.

RECORDED COMPOSITIONS

(selective list)

As leader: *Cool and Crazy* (1953, RCA LPM3138), incl. Boar-jibu, Contours, Infinity Promenade, The Sweetheart of Sigmund Freud, Tale of an African Lobster; on *The Swinging Mr. Rogers* (1955, Atl. 1212), Martians go home; on *Jazz Waltz* (1962, Rep. 96060), I'm gonna go fishin', Jazz Waltz

Recorded by others: W. Herman: Keeper of the Flame (1948, Cap. 57616); S. Kenton: Art Pepper (1950, Cap. 28008); Maynard Ferguson (1950, Cap. 28009); on S. Manne: *The Three* (1954, Cont. 2516), Three on a Row

SELECTED ARRANGEMENTS

Recorded by W. Herman: That's Right (1948, Cap. 15427); Lemon Drop (1948, Cap. 15365); More Moon (1949, Cap. 15844); Lollypop (1949), on *Classics in Jazz* (1948–50, Cap. H324)

Recorded by S. Kenton: Jolly Rogers (1950, Cap. 1043); Viva Prado (1950, Cap. 1279); Round Robin (1950, Cap. 15848)

BIBLIOGRAPHY

N. Shapiro and N. Hentoff, eds.: *Hear me Talkin' to ya: the Story of Jazz by the Men who Made it* (New York and London, 1955/R1966), 350

I. Stravinsky and R. Craft: *Conversations with Igor Stravinsky* (London, 1959), 116

H. Lucraft: "The Gentle Giant," *JJI*, xxxii/2 (1979), 4

S. Voce: "Cool and Crazy," *JJI*, xxxv/10 (1982), 14

C. Hofmann and E. M. Bakker: *Shorty Rogers: a Discography* (Amsterdam, 1983)

L. Tomkins: "The Shorty Rogers Story," *CI*, xxi (1983), no.5, p.20; no.7, p.12

J. BRADFORD ROBINSON

Rohde, Bryce (Benno) (*b* Hobart, Australia, 12 Sept 1923). Australian pianist and composer. He was a leading modern jazz player in Adelaide before moving to Canada in 1953; with other Australian musicians there he founded the Australian Jazz Quartet, which played at many important venues, including Birdland and Carnegie Hall, New York, and recorded seven albums; latterly it worked as a quintet. After a tour of Australia in 1958 the group disbanded; Rohde then led several quartets in Australia during the next six years, and was also influential in the dissemination of the theories from George Russell's book *The Lydian Chromatic Concept of Tonal Organization* (1953) in Australia. Rohde's mature compositional style may be heard on his albums *Corners* (1963, CBS BP233046) and *Just Bryce* (1965, CBS BP233196). From 1965 he has lived in California, but has been active professionally only intermittently.

BIBLIOGRAPHY

A. Bisset: *Black Roots, White Flowers: a History of Jazz in Australia* (Sydney, 1979)

B. Johnson and others: *The Oxford Companion to Australian Jazz* (Melbourne, Australia, 1987)

JEFF PRESSING (with JOHN WHITEOAK)

Roidinger, Adelhard (*b* Windischgarsten, Austria, 28 Nov 1941). Austrian double bass player and composer. In Austria he studied piano, violin, guitar, and double bass, then classical double bass at the Hochschule in Graz (1966–72); at the same time he studied jazz composition with Janosz Gregorz and ensemble playing with Eje Thelin. He played with Thelin and Joachim Kühn (1970–72), Hans Koller (1971–5), and Wolfgang Dauner (1972–8), and occasionally with Attila Zoller, Karl Berger, Yosuke Yamashita (with whom he recorded in 1977), Alan Skidmore, George Russell, Dusko Goykovich, Kenny Clarke, Mal Waldron, and Woody Shaw. Roidinger's style was at first strongly influenced by the music of the Bill Evans Trio; he became interested in free jazz in 1968 and from 1983 experimented with compositions that use elements of electroacoustic and computer music. His published writings include *Der Kontrabass im Jazz* (Vienna, 1980), *Der Elektrobass im Jazz* (Vienna, 1981), and *Jazzimprovisation und Pentatonik* (Rottenburg, Baden-Württemberg, Germany, 1984).

SELECTED RECORDINGS

As leader: *Schattseite* (1981, ECM 1221); *Computer & Jazz Program !* (1984, Thein 100384)

Duos with Y. Yamashita: *Inner Space* (1977, Enja 3001)

As sideman: E. Thelin: *Acoustic Space* (1970, Odeon EO6234180); H. Koller: *Phoenix* (1972, MPS 2121293–9); *Kunstkopfindianer* (1974, MPS 2122019–2)

BIBLIOGRAPHY

W. Panke: "Adelhard Roidingers neuer Weg der Musikerziehung," *JP*, xxii/11 (1973), 10

WOLFRAM KNAUER

Roker, Mickey [Granville William] (*b* Miami, 3 Sept 1932). Drummer. While growing up in Philadelphia he worked with Jimmy Heath and in various rhythm-and-blues groups, and took part in jam sessions with local friends Lee Morgan, Reggie Workman, Kenny Barron, and McCoy Tyner. In 1959 he went to New York, where he played with Gigi Gryce at the Five Spot;

Shorty Rogers playing flugelhorn, August 1958

he recorded with Gryce the following year, and later worked with Ray Bryant (1961–3), Joe Williams (1963–5), Duke Pearson (intermittently, 1964–9), Nancy Wilson (1965–7), and Morgan (1969–71). His freelance engagements during this period included performances with Art Farmer (1967), Clifford Jordan, and Mary Lou Williams; he also recorded with Sonny Rollins (1964–5), and worked as a studio musician for Blue Note. From 1971 to 1979 Roker was a member of Dizzy Gillespie's band, and became especially adept at playing Latin jazz. After a tour of Europe with Ella Fitzgerald in 1980 he worked as a freelance with Oscar Peterson, Zoot Sims, Sam Jones, and others. In the 1980s he has continued an association with Milt Jackson that began in the mid-1960s, and has also played regularly with Ray Brown's trio, with which he toured Europe in 1985. Although Roker's drumming is in the swing style it draws upon the inherent impetus of the blues.

SELECTED RECORDINGS

(all recorded for Pablo unless otherwise indicated)

As sideman with D. Gillespie: *Dizzy Gillespie's Big 4* (1974, 2310719); *Jazz Maturity . . . Where it's Coming from* (1975, 2310816); *Bahiana* (1975, 2625708); *Dizzy's Party* (1976, 2310784)

As sideman with others: G. Gryce: *The Rat Race Blues* (1960, NewJ 8262); D. Pearson: *Wahoo!* (1964, BN 84191); S. Turrentine: *Rough 'n' Tumble* (1966, BN 84240); H. Hancock: *Speak like a Child* (1968, BN 84279); L. Morgan: *Live at the Lighthouse* (1970, BN 89906); H. Silver: *United States of Mind: Phase II* (1971, BN 84368); Machito: *Afro-Cuban Jazz Moods* (1975, 2310771); R. Bryant: *Potpourri* (1980, 2310860)

BIBLIOGRAPHY

"Mickey Roker," *Jm*, no.247 (1976), 24

L. Tomkins: "Mickey Roker Tells his Story," *CI*, xvii/10 (1979), 12

J. Potter: "Mickey Roker: the Natural," *MD*, ix/10 (1985), 18

JEFF POTTER

Roland, Gene (*b* Dallas, 15 Sept 1921; *d* New York, 11 Aug 1982). Composer, arranger, and multi-instrumentalist. He first worked for Stan Kenton, composing songs for June Christy and playing his own new fifth trumpet parts (1944). After brief periods with Lionel Hampton and Lucky Millinder he rejoined Kenton as an arranger and trombonist, again on a new fifth part (1945). He began writing arrangements for four tenor saxophones while in New York in 1946, and continued his experiments in Los Angeles (where he played piano with Stan Getz, Jimmy Giuffre, Herbie Steward, and Zoot Sims); this innovation later led to the distinctive grouping of the Four Brothers within the Woody Herman Orchestra. In the late 1940s Roland played trombone with Georgie Auld and trumpet with Count Basie, Charlie Barnet, and Millinder; he also wrote arrangements for Claude Thornhill and Artie Shaw. In 1950 he led a 26-piece big band which included Dizzy Gillespie, Charlie Parker, and other prominent bop musicians, but it was unsuccessful and he resumed work as an arranger for Kenton (from 1951) and Herman (1956–8). In writing for four mellophoniums he introduced a new sound to Kenton's band; he also played as a soloist on mellophonium and soprano saxophone in his compositions for Kenton's album *Adventures in Blues* (1961). Roland visited Copenhagen in 1967 to compose for and conduct the Radiohus Orchestra. He toured with Kenton again in 1973, but thereafter worked in New York, playing piano, tenor saxophone, and trumpet, and writing arrangements for his own big bands. A fine example of his trumpet playing and an unusual instance of his singing may be heard on Jimmy Knepper's *Gee baby, ain't I good to you* on the album *A Swinging Introduction to Jimmy Knepper* (1957, Beth. 77).

RECORDED COMPOSITIONS

(selective list; recorded by S. Kenton with Roland as sideman)

Ain't no misery in me (1946, Cap. 289); *Adventures in Blues* (1961, Cap. ST1985)

SELECTED ARRANGEMENTS

(recorded by others with Roland as sideman)

S. Kenton: Tampico (1945, Cap. 202); [no leader]: *Swingin' Friends!* (1963, Bruns. 754114)

BIBLIOGRAPHY

B. Coss: "Gene Roland: the Untold Story," *DB*, xxx/24 (1963), 17

D. Nelson: "Gene Roland," *BMI: the Many Worlds of Music* (1971), Oct, 17

W. F. Lee: *Stan Kenton: Artistry in Rhythm* (Los Angeles, 1980) [incl. discography]

S. Woolley: "Gene Roland," *JJI*, xxxv/11 (1982), 16

BARRY KERNFELD

Roland, Joe [Joseph Alfred] (*b* New York, 17 May 1920). Vibraphonist and bandleader. He began his career as a clarinetist, studying at the Institute of Musical Art, New York (1937–9), and leading his own groups; in 1940 he began to play xylophone as well. After the war he bought a vibraphone and worked as a freelance in New York. He organized his own bop group, which recorded in 1949 and 1950, and played and recorded with Oscar Pettiford (1951). From 1951 to 1953 he was a member of George Shearing's quintet; after leaving Shearing he led a group with Howard McGhee. He then toured and made recordings with Artie Shaw's Gramercy Five (including *Sunny Side Up*, on the album *Artie Shaw and his Gramercy Five*, 1953–4, Clef MGC159-60) and also made recordings under his own name (including *Easy Living*, 1955, Beth. 17). After resuming freelance work he recorded with Mat Mathews and Aaron Sachs (both 1956).

BIBLIOGRAPHY

FeatherE
J. Burns: "Good Vibes," *J&B*, ii/5 (1972), 7

Roll. One of the drumstrokes collectively known as RUDIMENTS.

Rollini, Adrian (*b* New York, 28 June 1904; *d* Homestead, FL, 15 May 1956). Bass saxophonist, brother of Art Rollini. He originally played piano and xylophone, and led his first band at the age of 14. In the early 1920s he worked with the California Ramblers, and while with the group made hundreds of recordings; during this time he took up bass saxophone, and specialized on that instrument throughout the 1920s and early 1930s. He also provoked admiring astonishment among fellow musicians by playing jazz on novelty instruments such as the "hot fountain pen" (*see* CLARINET, §5) and the GOOFUS, and recorded frequently as the leader of the Goofus Five. Rollini spent a period in London performing with Fred Elizalde (1927–9), then on his return to New York worked principally as a freelance musician. In 1934 he organized his own club, Adrian's Tap Room, at the President Hotel, and continued throughout the 1930s and 1940s to lead small groups for long residencies at various hotels. He moved in the early 1950s to Florida, where for the last years of his life he undertook engagements that were mainly commercial.

Rollini was one of the first outstanding white jazz musicians; his adept improvisations on the unusually cumbersome bass saxophone were melodically inventive and possessed a rhythmic vitality that made him one of the first saxophonists to swing. He is best remembered for his series of recordings with Bix Beiderbecke, wherein he displays considerable adroitness, both in the improvised ensembles and in his solos. During the 1930s he began to concentrate on playing vibraphone; he never rose above competence on that instrument, however, whereas in his by then rare performances on bass saxophone he still showed mastery.

SELECTED RECORDINGS

As leader: Bouncin' in Rhythm (1935, Vic. 25208); Tap Room Swing (1936, Decca 787)

As sideman: M. Mole: Feelin' no Pain (1927, OK 40890); B. Beiderbecke: At the Jazz Band Ball (1927, OK 40923); J. Venuti: Jig Saw Puzzle Blues (1933, Col. 2782D)

BIBLIOGRAPHY

H. Taylor: "Adrian Rollini," *MM*, xiii (6 Nov 1937), 10
Obituary, *DB*, xxiii/13 (1956), 9
A. Napoleon: "The Bass Sax in Jazz," *Sv*, no.8 (1966), 15; no.9 (1967), 18
T. Shoppee: "Adrian Rollini," *JJ*, xxiii (1970), no.8, p.20; no.10, p.7
J. Altman: "Adrian Rollini," *CI*, xiv/11 (1976), 22
S.-A. Worsfold: "The Forgotten Ones: Adrian Rollini," *JJI*, xxxiv/6 (1981), 21
Art Rollini: *Thirty Years with the Big Bands* (London, Urbana, IL, and Chicago, 1987) [autobiography]

JOHN CHILTON

Rollini, Art(hur Francis) [Mousie, Schneeze] (*b* New York, 13 Feb 1912). Tenor saxophonist, brother of Adrian Rollini. He began playing professionally in the late 1920s, occasionally with the California Ramblers. In March 1929 he joined his brother in London to play with Fred Elizalde's orchestra at the Savoy Hotel. After returning to New York in December that year he began working as a freelance, playing with the reformed California Ramblers and with Paul Whiteman. He contributed elegant, often exciting solos to many of his brother's recordings, and in 1934 he joined Benny Goodman's band. His solos from this period (such as that on *I've found a new baby*) display an appealing sense of light swing derived in part from the work of Bud Freeman. After 1936 Goodman allocated most solos to his other tenor saxophonists, and Rollini left the band in 1939. That year he participated in the first all-star recording session to be organized under the auspices of the magazine *Metronome*. During the 1940s he worked as a freelance, played with the bandleaders Richard Himber (1940–41) and Will Bradley (1941–2), then joined the staff of ABC. From the 1960s he played only infrequently, but ran a rehearsal studio. Rollini was a superb musician, but he was frequently overshadowed by other players.

SELECTED RECORDINGS

As sideman: Adrian Rollini: Blue Prelude/Happy as the Day is Long (1933, Col. 2785D); B. Goodman: Nitwit Serenade/Bugle Call Rag (1934, Col. 2958D); Sometimes I'm Happy (1935, Vic. 25090); I've found a new baby (1936, Vic. 25355); B. Gowans: *Brad Gowans and his New York Nine* (1946, RCA LJM3000), incl. Jazz me Blues, Singin' the Blues

BIBLIOGRAPHY

ChiltonW; FeatherE
D. R. Connor: *BG off the Record: a Bio-discography of Benny Goodman* (Fairless Hills, PA, 1958, rev. and enlarged [2]/1969 as *BG on the Record: a Bio-discography of Benny Goodman*, rev. and enlarged [3]/1984 as *The Record of a Legend: a Bio-discography of Benny Goodman*)
A. Rollini: *Thirty Years with the Big Bands* (London, Urbana, IL, and Chicago, 1987) [autobiography]

RICHARD SUDHALTER

Rollins, Sonny [Theodore Walter; Newk] (*b* New York, 9 Sept 1930). Tenor saxophonist.

1. Life. 2. Style.

1. LIFE. He first learned piano, studied alto saxophone from about the age of 11, and took up the tenor instrument in 1946. In high school he led a group with Jackie McLean, Kenny Drew, and Art Taylor. He rehearsed with Thelonious Monk for several months in 1948, and from 1949 to 1954 recorded intermittently with a number of leading bop musicians and groups, including J. J. Johnson, Charlie Parker, Fats Navarro, Bud Powell, Max Roach, Art Blakey, Monk, and the Modern Jazz Quartet. His most frequent associate during these early years was Miles Davis, with whom he performed in clubs from 1949 and recorded from 1951. In one of these recording sessions with Davis, in 1954, he introduced three compositions of his own which later became jazz standards: *Airegin*, *Doxy*, and *Oleo*. In 1955, while overcoming his dependence on drugs, he worked in Chicago and, in December, joined the Clifford Brown–Max Roach Quintet. He remained with Roach until May 1957, then performed briefly in Davis's quintet; thereafter, however, he has led his own groups.

In 1956 came the first of a series of landmark recordings issued under Rollins's own name: *Valse hot* introduced the practice, now common, of playing bop in 3/4 meter; *St. Thomas* initiated his explorations of calypso patterns; and *Blue 7* was hailed by Gunther Schuller as demonstrating a new manner

Sonny Rollins, 1962

of "thematic improvisation," in which the soloist develops motifs extracted from his theme. *Way Out West* (1957), Rollins's first album using a trio of saxophone, double bass, and drums, offered a solution to his longstanding difficulties with incompatible pianists, and exemplified his witty ability to improvise on hackneyed material (*Wagon Wheels*, *I'm an old cowhand*). *It could happen to you* (also 1957) was the first in a long series of unaccompanied solo recordings, and *The Freedom Suite* (1958) foreshadowed the political stances taken in jazz in the 1960s. During the years 1956 to 1958 Rollins was widely regarded as the most talented and innovative tenor saxophonist in jazz. Nevertheless, he was discontented: he could not find compatible sidemen, saw shortcomings in his own playing, and suffered from poor health. For these reasons he voluntarily withdrew from public life from August 1959 to November 1961. During this period of retirement his habit of practicing on the Williamsburg Bridge in New York became legendary.

On resuming his career Rollins had improved his already prodigious skills, but his style was now considered conservative. In an effort to rejoin the vanguard of jazz fashion he began, in mid-1962, collaborating with Don Cherry, Billy Higgins, and other musicians playing free jazz; *East Broadway Run Down* (1966) illustrates the furthest extent to which he incorporated noise elements into his playing. During these years, as Rollins continued to struggle with changing personnel and instrumentation, he focused increasingly on unaccompanied playing, and by the end of the decade he had become famous for his extended, "stream-of-consciousness" extemporizations on traditional tunes and on his own calypso songs.

In 1965 Rollins wrote the film score for *Alfie* (apart from the title song, which is by Burt Bacharach). He pursued spiritual interests in India for five months in 1968, and abandoned music altogether from September 1969 to November 1971. From 1972, when he resumed playing once more, he has led various groups of young, lesser-known musicians, performing in a commercial vein and making use of electronic instruments and black-American dance rhythms; a film made the following year, *Sonny Rollins Live*, captures the exuberance of a concert performance. Rollins has continued to experiment, recording on soprano saxophone in 1972 and on lyricon in 1979. However, touring the USA in 1978 as a member of the Milestone Jazzstars (with McCoy Tyner, Ron Carter, and Al Foster), he demonstrated that, as an individual, he remained essentially true to the bop tradition, an aspect of his playing that was again especially apparent in an acclaimed solo performance at the Museum of Modern Art, New York, in 1985. Except for a six-month hiatus in 1983, after he collapsed from exhaustion, Rollins has remained active through the late 1980s, touring the USA, Europe, and Japan, and recording a fusion of bop and soul music with his quintet.

2. STYLE. Rollins established himself as the outstanding jazz saxophonist between Charlie Parker and John Coltrane and a leading figure in the hard-bop style (*see* SAXOPHONE, esp. §3). The prevailing interpretation of his method of improvisation derives from Schuller's "thematic analysis" of Rollins's celebrated solo on *Blue 7* (1956); other writers, accepting and expanding on Schuller's insights, have even declared thematic improvisation to be Rollins's greatest contribution to jazz. This view demands reconsideration: Schuller's analysis accounts for only part of Rollins's solo, and several of the motifs in that part do not derive from the theme but occur elsewhere in Rollins's earlier work (most obviously in *Vierd Blues*, which he recorded with Davis). Rollins, like most bop musicians of the period, paid little attention to composed melodies, preferring instead to improvise athematic, "formulaic" responses to underlying chord progressions. In slow ballads, of course, he often paraphrased the theme, and he occasionally developed motifs from his own calypso themes (as in ex.1, where the first two notes of the theme, inverted and rhythmically displaced, alternate with formulaic bop runs), but he rarely applied this

Ex.1 From *St. Thomas*, on *Saxophone Colossus* (1956, Prst. 7079); transcr. C. Blancq

technique to blues or popular songs. Similarly, he seldom used fragments from familiar tunes to anchor long stretches of newly improvised material; *Wagon Wheels* (1957) provides the clearest example of this technique. In essence Rollins has adhered to the bop practice of varying and elaborating a large repertory of formulas and, in a wide range of material, shows a rhythmic imagination, harmonic subtlety, and freedom of design that have perhaps been surpassed only by Charlie Parker.

SELECTED RECORDINGS

AS LEADER

Sonny Rollins Quartet (1954, Prst. 190); *Worktime* (1955, Prst. 7020); *Sonny Rollins Plus 4* (1956, Prst. 7038), incl. Valse hot; *Tenor Madness* (1956, Prst. 7047); *Saxophone Colossus* (1956, Prst. 7079), incl. Blue 7, St. Thomas; *Way Out West* (1957, Cont. 3530), incl. I'm an old cowhand, Wagon Wheels; *Sonny Rollins*, ii (1957, BN 1558); *The Sound of Sonny* (1957, Riv. 241), incl. It could happen to you [unaccompanied solo]; *A Night at the Village Vanguard* (1957, BN 1581); *The Freedom Suite* (1958, Riv. 258); *Newk's Time* (1958, BN 4001); *The Bridge* (1962, RCA LSP2527); *Our Man in Jazz* (1962, RCA LSP2612); *Sonny Rollins on Impulse!* (1965, Imp. 91)

Alfie (1966, Imp. 9111); *East Broadway Run Down* (1966, Imp. 9121); *Sonny Rollins' Next Album* (1972, Mlst. 9042); *Horn Culture* (1973, Mlst. 9051); *The Cutting Edge* (1974, Mlst. 9059); *Easy Living* (1977, Mlst. 9080); *No Problem* (1981, Mlst. 9104); *Reel Life* (1982, Mlst. 9108); *Sunny Days, Starry Nights* (1984, Mlst. 9122)

AS SIDEMAN

J. J. Johnson: Bee Jay (1949, Savoy 949); B. Powell: 52nd Street Theme (1949, BN 1568); M. Davis: Morpheus/Blue Room (1951, Prst. 734); *Miles Davis Quintet* (1954, Prst. 187), incl. Airegin, Doxy, Oleo; *Collector's Items* (1953, 1956, Prst. 7044), incl. Vierd Blues (1956); C. Brown and M. Roach: *At Basin Street* (1956, EmA 36070); T. Monk: *Brilliant Corners* (1956, Riv. 226); M. Roach: *Jazz in Three-quarter Time* (1956–7, EmA 36108); Milestone Jazzstars: *Milestone Jazzstars in Concert* (1978, Mlst. 55006)

BIBLIOGRAPHY

N. Hentoff: "Sonny Rollins," *DB*, xxiii/23 (1956), 15

D. Cerulli: "Theodore Walter Rollins," *DB*, xxv/14 (1958), 16

G. Schuller: "Sonny Rollins and the Challenge of Thematic Improvisation," *JR*, i/1 (1958), 6

M. James: "Sonny Rollins on Record: 1949–1954," *JM*, v/8 (1959), 7

W. Balliett: *Dinosaurs in the Morning* (Philadelphia, 1962/R1978) [colln of previously pubd articles and reviews]

B. Coss: "The Return of Sonny Rollins," *DB*, xxix/1 (1962), 13

J. Goldberg: "The Further Adventures of Sonny Rollins," *DB*, xxxii/18 (1965), 19

B. McRae: "Sonny Rollins," *JJ*, xviii/3 (1965), 6

I. Gitler: "Sonny Rollins: Music is an Open Sky," *DB*, xxxvi/10 (1969), 18

M. Williams: *The Jazz Tradition* (New York, 1970, rev. 2/1983)

T. Fiofori: "Re-entry: the New Orbit of Sonny Rollins," *DB*, xxxviii/17 (1971), 14

J. Delmas: "Traditions et contradictions de Theodore Walter 'Sonny' Rollins," *Jh*, no.307 (1974), 14

C. Berg: "Sonny Rollins: the Way Newk Feels," *DB*, xliv/7 (1977), 13 [incl. discography]

C. Blancq: *Melodic Improvisation in American Jazz: the Style of Theodore "Sonny" Rollins, 1951–1962* (diss., Tulane U., 1977); rev. as *Sonny Rollins: the Journey of a Jazzman* (Boston, 1983)

M. Ullman: "Sonny Rollins," *New Republic*, clxxviii (1 April 1978), 25

B. Blumenthal: "The Bridge: Sonny Rollins is a Tenor for All Times," *RS*, no.295 (12 July 1979), 56

"Sonny Rollins," *SJ*, xxxiii/1 (1979), 220 [discography]

D. Baker: *The Jazz Style of Sonny Rollins: a Musical and Historical Perspective* (Lebanon, IN, 1980) [incl. transcrs.]

G. Endress: *Jazz Podium: Musiker über sich selbst* (Stuttgart, Germany, 1980), 136

D. Forte: "Sonny Rollins: Tenor Titan," *Musicians' Industry*, ii/2 (1980), 52

E. Meadow: "Rollins Reflects," *JJI*, xxxiii/6 (1980), 11

B. Blumenthal: "Sonny Rollins," *DB*, xlix/5 (1982), 15 [incl. discography]

C. Cioe: "Backbeat: Sonny Rollins: 'I'm Still Reaching' . . . and Still Surprising his Audiences," *Hi Fidelity*, xxxiii/5 (1983), 76 [incl. discography]

M. Isherwood: "Sonny Rollins," *JJI*, xxxvi/4 (1983), 8

T. Sjøgren: *The Sonny Rollins Discography* (Copenhagen, 1983)

R. Cook: "Sonny Rollins: Return of the Colossus," *The Wire*, no.18 (1985), 28

F. Davis: *In the Moment: Jazz in the 1980s* (New York, and Oxford, England, 1986) [colln of previously pubd articles], 117

BARRY KERNFELD

Rollography. A type of DISCOGRAPHY listing piano rolls, usually those recorded by a particular performer.

Roman New Orleans Jazz Band. Italian traditional jazz band. It was formed in Rome in April 1949 and given its name by Louis Armstrong. The group's original members were the trumpeter Giovanni Borghi, the trombonist Luciano Fineschi, the clarinetist Marcello Riccio, the saxophonist Ivan Vandor, the pianist Franco Nebbia (soon replaced by Giorgio Zinzi), the banjoist Bruno Perris, the bass tuba player Pino Liberati, and the drummer Peppino d'Intino. In October 1949 the band took part in a jam session with Armstrong, Jack Teagarden, and Earl Hines, and from March of the following year made recordings (including *At the Jazz Band Ball*, 1951, HMV HN2947). The group continued to perform and record into the late 1980s.

ADRIANO MAZZOLETTI

Romano, Aldo (*b* Belluno, Italy, 16 Jan 1941). Italian drummer. He moved to France while a child, studied guitar, then taught himself the drums (from 1961). He performed in clubs in Paris with Barney Wilen, Michel Portal, and Jean-Luc Ponty, and with such visiting Americans as Jackie McLean and Don Cherry (1965). From 1965 he specialized in playing free jazz, recording with Cherry (1965), Steve Lacy (1965–6), Lacy and Carla Bley in Jazz Realities (1966), Giorgio Gaslini (1966), Gato Barbieri (1967), Rolf Kühn (1967), Joachim Kühn (1969), Karin Krog (1970), and Robin Kenyatta (1972). In the 1970s he led his own rock group (1971–3), worked with Philip Catherine, Charlie Mariano, and Jasper van 't Hof in the band Pork Pie (1973–5), and recorded with François Jeanneau (1976–7), Enrico Rava (1978, 1981), and as a leader (from 1978). In the early 1980s Romano adopted a more classical drumming style and worked with Michel Petrucciani.

SELECTED RECORDINGS

As leader: with J.-F. Jenny-Clark: *Divieto di Santificazione* (1977, Horo 07); *Alma Latina* (1983, Owl 031)

BIBLIOGRAPHY

"7 noms, 7 têtes: voici les nouveau-nés du jazz français: Aldo Romano," *Jm*, no.117 (1965), 28

P. Carles and V. Delubac: "Aldo Romano: une valeur en hausse," *Jm*, no.155 (1968), 16

ANDRÉ CLERGEAT

Romano, Joe [Joseph] (*b* Rochester, NY, 17 April 1932). Tenor and alto saxophonist. He played and recorded sporadically with Woody Herman from 1956, and performed with the band at the Monterey Jazz Festival in 1967 and the Newport and Kansas City festivals in the 1970s. He also recorded with the baritone horn player Gus Mancuso (1957), and worked in Rochester with Chuck Mangione (early 1960s) and in Buffalo with Sam Noto (1966–7). In California he performed and recorded intermittently with Buddy Rich (1968–74) and played with Les Brown (1970–72) and Louie Bellson. Romano later returned to New York, where he worked with Chuck Israels's National Jazz Ensemble (1976), recorded as a soloist with Noto's bop quintet on the album *Act One* (1975, Xan. 127), performed occasionally with the Thad Jones–Mel Lewis Orchestra, and toured and recorded with Bellson (1978, 1980). (*Feather–Gitler '70s*)

Romao, Dom Um (*b* Rio de Janeiro, 3 Aug 1925). Brazilian percussionist. During the 1960s he worked regularly with the keyboard player Sergio Mendes; he was a member of Mendes's Bossa Rio sextet, and recorded with Mendes and Cannonball Adderley in 1962. He moved to the USA and played with Oscar Brown, Jr., in Chicago (1965). From the mid-1960s he worked in Los Angeles and in 1967 he toured with Mendes. After the departure of Airto Moreira from Weather Report, Romao joined the group in 1971, and played with it until 1974; his playing may be heard to advantage on *I Sing the Body Electric* (1971–2, Col. KC31352). He established a rehearsal studio in New York, where he had settled in the early 1970s. After recording in Zurich with George Gruntz (1976), he worked regularly with the Swiss group Om from 1977; in that year he also recorded with Collin Walcott and as a member of Percussion Profiles, with Jack DeJohnette, Gruntz, Pierre Favre, Fredy Studer, and David Friedman. He performed and recorded at the Donaueschingen Musiktage für Zeitgenössische Tonkunst as a member of the group World Music, which combines jazz wind and rhythm instruments with Indian, Caribbean, and Brazilian instruments.

Romeo. Record label. It was a subsidiary of the Cameo Record Corp., and was established in July 1926; the records were sold through the chain of stores of S. H. Kress. The repertory was drawn from Cameo's catalogue; items were generally released under pseudonyms. The label was maintained after the formation of the AMERICAN RECORD COMPANY. It became one of that company's "dime-store" labels and its catalogue numbers were aligned with those of the others from September 1935. Issues under ARC's ownership included an important series by the Washboard Rhythm Boys (1933) and major race series. Romeo was discontinued by CBS after it acquired ARC–BRC in 1938.

BIBLIOGRAPHY

J. Godrich and R. M. W. Dixon: *Blues & Gospel Records, 1902–1942* (Hatch End, nr London, 1964, rev. and enlarged 3/1982 as R. M. W. Dixon and J. Godrich: *Blues & Gospel Records, 1902–1943*), 20
R. M. W. Dixon and J. Godrich: *Recording the Blues* (London, 1970), 67, 78
B. Rust: *The American Record Label Book* (New Rochelle, NY, 1978), 272

Ronnie Scott's. Nightclub in London; *see* NIGHTCLUBS AND OTHER VENUES.

Roost. Name used on liners by the record company Royal Roost; *see* ROYAL ROOST (ii).

Root. Nickname of RUDY POWELL.

Root, Billy [William] (*b* Philadelphia, 6 March 1934). Tenor and baritone saxophonist. He played with Roy Eldridge (1951), changed to alto saxophone temporarily when he joined Hal McIntyre (1952), and worked briefly with Red Rodney. After performing and recording with Bennie Green (1953–4) he toured and recorded with Stan Kenton (1956, 1959). He also recorded with Clifford Brown (1956), Dizzy Gillespie's big band (1957), and the septet Dizzy Atmosphere with, among others, Lee Morgan (1957). In 1958 Root performed and recorded at Birdland, New York, in a hard-bop sextet that included Hank Mobley, Morgan, and Curtis Fuller; he also recorded with Green and with Rodney (*Red Rodney Returns*, 1958, Argo 643), and formed his own group, which played in New York and Philadelphia. He was with Rodney again from 1959 to 1960, and later he worked with Dakota Staton, appearing with her at the Newport Jazz Festival in 1963. (*FeatherE*)

Roppolo, (Joseph) Leon (*b* Lutcher, LA, 16 March 1902; *d* Louisiana, 5 Oct 1943). Clarinetist and composer. His name is often misspelled Rappolo. He was taught to play clarinet by his father, and also learned guitar, which he played occasionally throughout his career. After working with Georg Brunis and Paul Mares (*c*1916) and Eddie Shields and Santo Pecora (*c*1917) he toured in the New Orleans area and played on Mississippi riverboats. He traveled to Chicago with Brunis and Mares and around 1921 joined Mares's Friars Society Orchestra, remaining with the group when it became known as the NEW ORLEANS RHYTHM KINGS. Roppolo went with Mares to New York in 1923 and the following year worked with Peck Kelley in Texas, then returned to New Orleans. He joined Abbie Brunies's Halfway House Orchestra and played with Mares's re-formed New Orleans Rhythm Kings (1925), but thereafter suffered a mental breakdown. He spent most of the remainder of his life in a sanitorium, where he organized a band and continued to play, mainly on tenor saxophone.

Despite his short career, Roppolo was one of the most influential jazz clarinetists. He was a superb ensemble player but also, which was rare at that time, a highly imaginative soloist. He made use of subtle tonal inflections (as in *Tin Roof Blues*), and the dynamic contrast he achieved between the plaintive tone of the high register of the instrument and the full-bodied sound of its low register (*Wolverine Blues*) lent his playing an emotional quality that set him apart from his contemporaries. Among the compositions he wrote with others are such standards as *Farewell Blues*, *Milenberg Joys* (*Golden Leaf Strut*), *Sugar Babe*, and *Tin Roof Blues*.

SELECTED RECORDINGS

As sideman: New Orleans Rhythm Kings: Farewell Blues (1922, Gen. 4966); That's a Plenty/Tin Roof Blues (1923, Gen. 5105); Weary Blues/Wolverine Blues (1923, Gen. 5102); London Blues/Mad (1923, Gen. 5221); Halfway House Orchestra: Pussy Cat Rag/Barataria (1925, OK 40318); New Orleans Rhythm Kings: She's Crying for me Blues/Golden Leaf Strut (1925, OK 40327)

BIBLIOGRAPHY

ChiltonW
D. Dexter: "Immortals of Jazz: Leon Rappolo," *DB*, vii/20 (1940), 10
P. Mares: "Leon Rappolo as I Knew him," *Jazz Quarterly*, ii (1944), 3
M. Williams: "N. O. R. K.," *Jazz Masters of New Orleans* (New York and London, 1967/*R*1978), 121
S.-A. Worsfold: "The Forgotten Ones: Leon Roppolo," *JJI*, xxxiii/2 (1980), 21
G. W. Kay: "Joe Mares and his New Orleans Memories," *MR*, viii/3 (1981), 8

MICHAEL TOVEY

Rose, Boris (*b* New York, 4 Jan 1918). Record company executive. He attended CUNY (degree in chemical engineering) and began collecting records around 1938 while working during vacations in a record shop. He later formed several dozen record labels (the most important of which were Alto, Ozone, and Session (iii)), under which he issued about 400 LPs; these included acetate dubs of previously issued records, and transcriptions of broadcast performances from the period 1936–61. The records feature performances by leading swing and bop musicians from the late 1940s and early 1950s (such as Miles Davis, Charlie Parker, Stan Getz, and Lester Young) and broadcasts from Birdland by Charles Mingus, Art Blakey, John Coltrane, and Thelonious Monk; a recording of a broadcast by Davis's jazz-rock group was issued on Session. (B. Minor: "Sub Rosa Stuff," *Jazz Digest*, ii (1973), 263)

Rose, Denis (*b* London, *c*1922; *d* London, 22 Nov 1984). Pianist and trumpeter. He was chiefly active at pubs and clubs in London. In the mid-1940s he was a member of a band led by the trumpeter Johnny Claes; during World War II his activities were restricted because he evaded conscription and found it necessary to avoid being apprehended by the authorities. He organized various informal sessions with other young British musicians, including Ronnie Scott, and was responsible for important events at Club Eleven. Rose was one of the first

English players to grasp the essentials of the bop style, which he passed on to Scott and others. He participated in only two recording sessions: the second of these, led by Scott, included *Scrapple from the Apple* (1949, Esquire 10038), on which he played trumpet; this demonstrates just how well Rose had assimilated the bop vocabulary. He remained interested in musical developments both in London and abroad, and continued to perform into the late 1960s.

BIBLIOGRAPHY

P. Grammond, ed.: *The Decca Book of Jazz* (London, 1958)
V. Schonfield: "Denis Rose," *JJ*, xiv/10 (1961), 16
D. Fairweather: "Taking Things as they Come: the Saga of Denis Rose," *J&B*, ii/1 (1972), 20

STAN BRITT

Rose, Wally [Walter L.] (*b* Oakland, CA, 2 Oct 1913). Pianist. In 1939 he met Lu Watters and joined the Yerba Buena Jazz Band (*see* WATTERS, LU). He introduced a ragtime piano solo to the band's dance sets, and in its first recording session (19 December 1941) played, with an accompaniment of banjo, double bass, and drums, *Black and White Rag*, which became very popular in radio broadcasts. After the breakup of the Yerba Buena Jazz Band in 1950, Rose joined Bob Scobey the following year and then worked with Turk Murphy's band until late 1954. Thereafter he has performed as a solo pianist at clubs throughout the San Francisco Bay area, including the Shadow Box, the Gold Street, the Palace Hotel, and the Cirque Room of the Fairmont Hotel. With the Yerba Buena Jazz Band, Rose was directly responsible for instigating the revival of instrumental ragtime and many early jazz pieces. His playing is characterized by a percussive touch, a loping rhythmic style, and a steady though never monotonous pulse. In his rags Rose generally gives a rather literal reading of the music, but often adds variety by doubling certain notes at the octave.

SELECTED RECORDINGS

As unaccompanied soloist: *Ragtime Piano Masterpieces* (1953, Col. CL6260); *Wally Rose on Piano* (1970, Blackbird 12007)
As leader: *Wally Rose and the Yerba Buena Jazz Band Live from the Dawn Club* (1946, Fairmont 102)
As sideman with L. Watters: Maple Leaf Rag/Black and White Rag (1941, Jazz Man 1)

BIBLIOGRAPHY

FeatherE
T. Waldo: *This is Ragtime* (New York, 1976)
P. Martin: "Wally Rose & the West Coast Revival," *MR*, viii/1 (1980), 1 [incl. discography]
R. Stein: "Wally Rose: the Friendliest Piano Player in Town," *San Francisco Chronicle* (19 March 1980), 34
J. Goggin: *Turk Murphy: Just for the Record* (San Leandro, CA, 1982) [incl. discography]

JOHN EDWARD HASSE

Roseland Ballroom. Ballroom in New York named after a successful venue in Philadelphia; *see* NIGHTCLUBS AND OTHER VENUES.

Rosengarden, Bobby [Robert Marshall] (*b* Elgin, IL, 23 April 1924). Drummer and percussionist. He was given a drum set as a child, and began to play seriously at the age of 12. After taking up a music scholarship at the University of Michigan he performed with army and air force bands during his military service (1944–5). His first important association was with the trumpeter Henry Busse (1945–6), after which he played in New York with the tenor saxophonist Alvy West (1946–8). Thereafter he worked as a studio musician, recording as a percussionist with, among others, Duke Ellington (1959), Miles Davis and the orchestra led by Gil Evans (1961), and Benny Goodman's band conducted by the composer Igor Stravinsky (1965); his association with Goodman continued intermittently into the 1980s. Rosengarden also played in ensembles at the NBC television studios (1949–68) before leading a band at ABC for Dick Cavett's show (1969–74). He achieved wider attention as a member of the World's Greatest Jazz Band (1974–8). A spirited and insistent drummer, his playing also proved ideal for such groups as Soprano Summit (1975–8) and the Blue Three (with Kenny Davern and Dick Wellstood, 1981–3). His versatility also made him much in demand for performances with the New York Jazz Repertory Company (from 1974) and Gerry Mulligan's sextet (from 1976). Rosengarden continues to maintain a rigorous schedule, performing at festivals and regularly leading a band, notably at the Rainbow Room, New York.

SELECTED RECORDINGS

As leader with M. Hinton and Hank Jones: *The Trio* (1977, Chi. 188)
As sideman: B. Wilber and K. Davern: *Soprano Summit* (1973, World Jazz 5); D. Hyman: *Satchmo Remembered* (1974, Atl. 1671); World's Greatest Jazz Band: *The World's Greatest Jazz Band of Yank Lawson and Bob Haggart on Tour* (1975, World Jazz 8); D. Smith: *Love for Sale* (1976, Prog. 7002); K. Davern and F. Phillips: *John and Joe* (1977, Chi. 199); Blue Three: *At Hanratty's* (1981, Chaz Jazz 109)

BIBLIOGRAPHY

Feather–Gitler '70s
S. Traill: "Drums Double Bill," *JJI*, xxxi/4 (1978), 26
R. D. Johnson: "It's Fun, not Work!," *MR*, vii/3 (1980), 10
J. Buerger: "Show and Studio: Bobby Rosengarden," *MD*, v/8 (1981), 92

BRIAN PEERLESS

Rosengren, Bernt (Åke) (*b* Stockholm, 24 Dec 1937). Swedish tenor saxophonist, flutist, arranger, composer, and bandleader. He came to prominence in the 1950s through his performances in the Swedish hard-bop group Jazz Club '57, his membership of Marshall Brown's International Youth Band (1958), and his work in Poland (where he played with Krzysztof Komeda, 1961, and performed as a soloist on the soundtrack to Roman Polanski's film *Knife in the Water*, 1962) and in other European countries. During the following years he worked with George Russell (performing in 1965–7, recording in 1967 and 1977), Don Cherry (recording in 1968 and 1973), and Lars Gullin (recording in 1969–70 and 1973–6); he also made recordings from 1959 as the leader of small groups (including *Live in Stockholm*, 1974–5, Amigo 815, 818) and occasionally as the leader of a big band (including *Big Band*, 1979, Caprice 1214). From 1978 he recorded as a member of Doug Raney's bop groups. Rosengren is among the finest Swedish saxophonists; he has a true command of the vocabulary of bop and associated styles. His compositions and arrangements are straightforward, yet lucid and inventive.

BIBLIOGRAPHY

FeatherE
B. Sundin: "Unga jazzmusiker," *Orkester journalen*, xxviii/9 (1960), 10
K. Knox: "Bernt Rosengren: en ovanlig musiker" [Bernt Rosengren: an unusual musician], *Musiktidningen*, ii/1 (1974), 25
R. Cotterrell: "Bernt Rosengren," *JF* [intl edn], no.43 (1976), 24 [incl. discography]
A. von Konow: "Bernt!," *Orkester journalen*, liii/2 (1985), 9

ERIK KJELLBERG

Rosner, Ady [Jack; Rozner, Adolf] (*b* Berlin, 26 May 1910; *d* Berlin, 8 Aug 1976). German trumpeter, bandleader, and violinist. After studying music at the Berlin Hochschule für Musik, he turned to jazz and dance music in 1928. He played with Willi Rosé-Petösy (1929) and performed and recorded with the Weintraub Syncopators (1930–33). He left Germany for the Netherlands (1933) and toured Belgium (1934–5), before settling in Poland and leading his own band in Kraków (1935–

6). While on tour in Europe (1938–9) he made a number of recordings in Paris (including *Midnight in Harlem* (1938, Col. DF2404), which is a good example of his trumpet playing). On the invasion of Poland in 1939 he fled to the USSR, where he entertained troops, toured, and made recordings (including *St. Louis Blues*, 1944, SSSR 12215). He spent nine years in a labor camp (1946–55); after his release he formed a symphony orchestra, which he continued to lead until his return to Berlin in 1973. (H. J. P. Bergmeier: *The Weintraub Story Incorporating the Ady Rosner Story* (Menden, Germany, 1982) [incl. discography])

RAINER E. LOTZ

Rosolino, Frank (*b* Detroit, 20 Aug 1926; *d* Los Angeles, 26 Nov 1978). Trombonist. He began playing guitar when he was ten, and took up trombone as a teenager. At the age of 18 he began military service, and performed with army bands in the USA and the Philippines. After being discharged he played in the big bands of the tenor saxophonist Bob Chester (1946–7), Glen Gray (1947), Gene Krupa (1948–9), Tony Pastor (1949), Herbie Fields (1950), and Georgie Auld (1951). Thereafter he led his own group in Detroit (1952) before working with Stan Kenton (1952–4). Most of his later career was spent in California. After playing with Howard Rumsey's Lighthouse All Stars (1954–60) he served as a member of Donn Trenner's band on Steve Allen's television program (1962–4). He was also active as a studio musician in Hollywood. In 1973–5 he worked at intervals in Europe with Conte Candoli, and in 1974 he toured the USA with Benny Carter. He also worked with Supersax, and performed in Japan with Quincy Jones, who also frequently employed him for recording sessions and film soundtracks.

Rosolino also sang, specializing in comic material, but it is as one of the most technically adroit trombonists of the bop era that he will be remembered. His large tone and staccato attack marked him as a true individual, but he was also an excellent section player.

Oral history material in *NjR*.

SELECTED RECORDINGS

As leader: Frank Rosolino Quartet (1952, DeeGee 4012) [EP]; *Stan Kenton Presents: Frank Rosolino Sextet* (1954, Cap. T6507); *I Play Trombone* (1956, Beth. 26); *Turn me Loose!* (1961, Rep. 96016); *Thinking about you* (1976, Sack. 2014)

As sideman: G. Auld: *Georgie Auld Quintet* (1951, Roost 403); on S. Kenton: *New Concepts of Artistry in Rhythm* (1952, Cap. H383), Frank Speaking, Twenty-three Degrees North, Eighty-two Degrees West; S. Levey: *This Time the Drum's on me* (1955, Beth. 37); H. Rumsey: *Music for Lighthouse-keeping* (1956, Cont. 3528); S. Levey: *Grand Stan* (1956, Beth. 71); G. Auld: *Georgie Auld Plays the Winners* (1963, Phi. 600096)

BIBLIOGRAPHY

J. Burns: "Bopping Bones," *J&B*, ii/7 (1972), 16

L. Tomkins: "Frank Rosolino," *CI*, xii/1 (1973), 6; contd as "Frank Rosolino: Life in Hollywood," xii/2 (1973), 24; contd as "Frank Rosolino: My Approach to Playing," xii/7 (1974), 14 [interview]

L. Underwood: "Frank Rosolino: Conversation with the Master," *DB*, xliv/19 (1977), 18 [incl. discography]

Obituary, M. Hennessey, *JJI*, xxxii/2 (1979), 22

A. Astrup: "Frank Rosolino," *Coda*, no.187 (1982), 9

MARK GARDNER

Ross, Annie [Lynch [née Short], Annabelle] (*b* Mitcham, England, 25 July 1930). English singer. She was taken to Los Angeles in 1933 by her aunt Ella Logan, a band and cabaret singer. She had early success there as a child film actress, then traveled to Europe in 1947 and sang in cabaret and with bands. After returning to the USA in 1950 she created a sensation with her vocalese on *Twisted* and *Farmer's Market* (both 1952) and *Jackie* (1953). The highlight of another visit to Europe was her enormous success in the revue *Cranks*, in which she also performed in New York in 1956. She then joined Dave Lambert and Jon Hendricks to record the multitracked *Sing a Song of Basie*, in which the trio sang all the section parts and instrumental solos with only a rhythm section for support. Successful but strenuous tours and recordings with the trio proved too much for Ross, however, and she retreated to England in 1962 to recuperate. She continued to record as a soloist and also ran her own club, Annie's Room (October 1964 to autumn 1965). She began to undertake film work, recording theme songs and dubbing dialogue, and by the 1970s was appearing on stage (in, among other things, her own show, *An Evening with Annie Ross*, 1976) and television. She also took acting roles in the films *Yanks* (1979) and *Superman III* (1983). In 1985 she returned to the USA, where she again worked as a singer.

Ross is considered one of the finest British jazz singers. She has a superb technique and is adept at performing in many styles, from ballads, such as *Skylark*, to cabaret songs and sophisticated vocalese. Although initially her range was wide, by the early 1960s her voice had deepened to a warm contralto.

See also LAMBERT, HENDRICKS, AND ROSS.

SELECTED RECORDINGS

As leader: Twisted (1952, Prst. 794); Farmer's Market (1952, Prst. 839); Jackie (1953, Met. 647); *Cranks* (1956, HMV 1082); *Annie by Candlelight* (1956, Pye 0316), incl. Skylark

As leader of Lambert, Hendricks, and Ross: *Sing a Song of Basie* (1957, ABC-Para. 223); *Sing a Song with Mulligan* (1958, WP 1253); *The Swingers* (1958, WP 1264); *A Gasser* (1959, WP 1285); *Loguerhythms* (1962, Transatlantic 107)

As leader with others: P. Poindexter: *German Jazz Festival* (1966, Saba/MPS 15082); C. Laine and J. Dankworth: *Façade* (1967, Fon. 5449); Georgie Fame: *In Hoagland '81* (1981, Baldeagle 181)

As sideman with C. Basie: *Sing along with Basie* (1958, Roul. 52018)

BIBLIOGRAPHY

M. Jones: "Annie Ross: a Clear Case of Talent," *MM*, xxxi (21 April 1956), 13

L. Keating: "The Dave Lambert Singers," *JJ*, xv/4 (1962), 2

R. Cooper: "The Art of Annie Ross," *JJI*, xxxii/7 (1979), 9

R. Cooper and D. Tarrant: "Annie Ross Discography," *Journal of Jazz Discography* (1979), no.4; p.9; no.5, p.1

L. Gourse: *Louis' Children: American Jazz Singers* (New York, 1984), 283

REG COOPER

Ross, Arnold (*b* Boston, MA, 29 Jan 1921). Pianist. He played violin, clarinet, and trumpet, and began learning piano at the age of 12. After playing on a cruise ship that visited the West Indies and South America (1937–8), he moved to New York (1938), where he performed and recorded with Jack Jenney (1939) and worked with the bandleader and singer Vaughn Monroe (1940–42) and Glenn Miller (1943–4). He recorded as a member of Harry James's band (1944–7) and with Harry Edison and Charlie Ventura (both 1945), Jazz at the Philharmonic (1946), and Charlie Parker (1947). He worked as a freelance in California and in 1947–8 he accompanied the popular singer Lena Horne, with whom he later toured Europe (1952). In the early 1950s Ross recorded with several leaders, among them Dizzy Gillespie. He performed, conducted, and wrote arrangements for Bob Crosby's television show (1954–6), accompanied Billy Eckstine (1956), and led his own trio in California (late 1950s). From 1968 to 1976 he worked with Nelson Riddle in radio and television; he continued performing into the 1980s.

SELECTED RECORDINGS

As leader: Stairway to the Stars/Bye bye Blues (1946, Key. 648)

As sideman: H. James: When your lover has gone/I'm Confessin' (1944, Col. 36773); C. Ventura: I don't stand a ghost of a chance/Tea for Two (1945, Sunset 10051); H. Edison: September in the Rain/Pennies from Heaven (1953, PJ 612)

BIBLIOGRAPHY

FeatherE; *Feather '60s*; *Feather–Gitler '70s*
S. Pease: "Arnold Ross Busy with James & Wax," *DB*, xiii/21 (1946), 12

JAMES M. DORAN

Ross, Ronnie [Albert Ronald] (*b* Calcutta, 2 Oct 1933). Scottish baritone saxophonist. He settled in the UK in 1946, and began his career as a tenor saxophonist, but changed to the baritone instrument at the request of Don Rendell, with whom he played in the mid-1950s. After working with such musicians as Lars Gullin, Tony Crombie, and Ted Heath, in 1958 he represented the UK at the Newport Jazz Festival as a member of Marshall Brown's International Youth Band. He also recorded (1958) and toured Europe (1959) with the Modern Jazz Quartet. In 1959 he toured and recorded in the USA with the Jazz Makers, a band he led with Allan Ganley, and performed in England with Woody Herman's Anglo-American Herd. From the 1960s Ross participated in several recording sessions of popular and commercial music, an example of his work being the well-known solo on *Walk on the Wild Side* by the rock singer Lou Reed. He continued to play jazz, however, leading his own groups, including a quartet with Bill Le Sage (1961–5), and working as a sideman with a variety of musicians; he recorded with John Dankworth (1961–4), the Clarke–Boland Big Band (1965–6), Friedrich Gulda (1966), Tony Kinsey (1974), and Clark Terry (1977). He toured the UK in 1986 with his own quartet.

SELECTED RECORDINGS

As leader: *The Ronnie Ross Quintet* (1958, Parl. 1079); of the Jazz Makers (with A. Ganley): *Swinging Sounds of the Jazz Makers* (1959, Atl. 1333); *Cleopatra's Needle* (1968, Fon. 915)

As sideman: D. Rendell: *Meet Don Rendell* (1955, Tempo TAP1); John Lewis: *European Windows* (1958, RCA LPM1742); J. Dankworth: *The Zodiac Variations* (1964, Fon. 5229); L. Reed: Walk on the Wild Side (RCA 0887, 1972)

BIBLIOGRAPHY

FeatherE; *Feather '60s*; *Feather–Gitler '70s*
P. Sullivan: "Ronnie Ross: Honest to Goodness Jazz," *JF* [intl edn], no.76 (1982), 46

MARK GILBERT

Rossi, Aldo (*b* Milan, 1911; *d* c1980). Italian clarinetist, alto saxophonist, and leader. From the mid-1930s he played with Kramer Gorni and recorded with his orchestra; he also worked in small groups with Gorni, Cosimo Di Ceglie, and the pianist Enzo Ceragioli. After World War II he formed a big band, the Orchestra del momento; from 1947 this was led alternately by Kramer and by Rossi, who led the orchestra on several recordings made for Fonit, including *Rhumboogie/Cow Cow Boogie* (12220), *9:20 Special* (12218), and *Diggin' for Dex/Undecided* (12219) in 1945, and *Cement Mixer* (12459) in 1947. Among Rossi's sidemen was Giorgio Gaslini.

ADRIANO MAZZOLETTI

Rostaing, Hubert (*b* Lyons, France, 17 Sept 1918). French tenor saxophonist, clarinetist, and bandleader. He performed with the Red Hotters in Algiers and in 1939 moved to Paris, where he performed at the Mimi Pinson club. He played and recorded as a member of the Quintette du Hot Club de France (1940–48) and from 1940 to 1962 made many recordings as a leader, including *To be bop or not to be bop* (1947, BStar 118). He also played with the bandleader and saxophonist Raymond Legrand, Aimé Barelli (recording 1940–43), Harry Cooper, Jacques Hélian's band, and Rex Stewart. Rostaing pursued a career outside jazz as a composer of film scores and a clarinetist; the composer Jean Barraqué dedicated a clarinet concerto to Rostaing, the first performance of which he gave in London in 1969.

BIBLIOGRAPHY

A. Hodeir: "Panorama du jazz français," *BHcF*, 1st ser., no.1 (1945), 9
B. Vian: "Hubert Rostaing," *Jh*, no.7 (1946), 11

MICHEL LAPLACE

Rotondo, Nunzio (*b* Palestrina, Italy, 1924). Italian trumpeter, composer, and leader. As a child he studied piano, then trumpet. In 1948–9 he formed the sextet of the Hot Club di Roma and played in Rome with Louis Armstrong. In 1951 he took part in jam sessions with Bill Coleman, Flavio Ambrosetti, Roy Eldridge, Zoot Sims, Toots Thielemans, and Duke Ellington; during the following decade he performed and recorded as the leader of bop groups that included Gil Cuppini (from 1952), Roberto Nicolosi (1954), and Romano Mussolini (from 1954). In the 1960s he gave only two concerts – one in a big band with Albert Mangelsdorff, Martial Solal, and Niels-Henning Ørsted Pedersen (1965), the other in a quintet with Mussolini (1966) – but he performed often on radio with, among others, Gato Barbieri, Franco D'Andrea, Mal Waldron, and Pierre Favre. He led a quintet with D'Andrea from 1970 to 1973, was inactive for several years, then resumed playing publicly in 1980–81. Rotondo's playing is most effective in lyrical, sentimental tunes of his own composition; a good example of his style is his recording *Ten Men Blowin'* on the album *IIIrd Festival del Jazz del San Remo* (1958, Carish 15301). Among his original works are *Garineipaulus*, *Suoni lunghi*, and *Suoni flautati*. (*FeatherE*)

ADRIANO MAZZOLETTI

Roto-toms. A set of shallow tunable single-headed frame drums; *see* DRUM SET, §I, 4.

Roulette. Record company and label. The company was founded in New York in 1957 by a group of directors headed by Morris Levy. It produced a wide variety of material, chiefly in commercially-oriented styles, but also established the Birdland Series, which was devoted to jazz. This included, most importantly, new recordings by Count Basie (1957–62), as well as material by Joe Williams (1957–62), Maynard Ferguson (1958–64), Harry Edison (1958, 1960), Jack Teagarden (1959, 1961), Randy Weston (1960), and Sarah Vaughan (1960–64). Although much of the back catalogue is no longer available, Roulette has continued to exist into the late 1980s, occasionally organizing new sessions by such musicians as Betty Carter (1969, 1976), Lee Konitz (1976) and Art Blakey (1976–7), and keeping most of Basie's albums in print.

Rouse, Charlie [Charles] (*b* Washington, 6 April 1924). Tenor saxophonist. He studied clarinet before taking up tenor saxophone. He played in the bop big bands of Billy Eckstine (1944) and Dizzy Gillespie (1945), but made his first recordings as a soloist only in 1947, with Tadd Dameron and Fats Navarro. After playing rhythm-and-blues in Washington and New York, he was a member of the Duke Ellington Orchestra (1949–50) and Count Basie's octet (1950). He took part in Clifford Brown's first recordings in 1953, then worked with Bennie Green (1955) and played in Oscar Pettiford's sextet (c1955); with JULIUS WATKINS, also one of Pettiford's sidemen, he led Les Modes (later the Jazz Modes), a bop quintet (1956–9). He joined Buddy Rich briefly before playing in Thelonious Monk's quartet (1959–70), the association for which he is best known. During the 1970s he worked as a freelance, and recorded three albums as a leader. In the early 1980s he was a member and joint leader of the quartet SPHERE, which was dedicated to the performance of Monk's music; he performed in Wynton Marsalis's group at the Concord Jazz Festival (California) in 1987 and the following year recorded compositions by Monk in San Francisco with Carmen McRae. In the 1960s Rouse adapted his style to Monk's work, improvising with greater deliberation than most bop tenor saxophonists, and restating melodies often. His distinctive solo playing with Monk may be heard on *Shuffle Boil* (1964), in which he alternates reiterations of the principal thematic motif with formulaic bop runs.

SELECTED RECORDINGS

As leader: with J. Watkins: *The Most Happy Fella* (1957, Atl. 1280); *Takin' Care of Business* (1960, Jlnd 919); *Moment's Notice* (1977, Sto. 4079); of Sphere (with K. Barron, Buster Williams, and B. Riley): *Four in One* (1982, Elek. Mus. 60166)

As sideman: T. Dameron: The Squirrel/Our Delight (1947, BN 540); C. Brown: *New Star on the Horizon* (1953, BN 5032); D. Byrd: *Byrd in Hand* (1959, BN 4019); T. Monk: *5 by Monk by 5* (1959, Riv. 1150); Benny Carter: *Further Definitions* (1961, Imp. 12); T. Monk: *Monk Misterioso* (1963–5, Col. CS9216); on Monk: *It's Monk's Time* (1964, Col. CS8984), Shuffle Boil; D. Jordan: *Duke's Delight* (1975, Ste. 1046)

BIBLIOGRAPHY

D. Morgenstern: "Charlie Rouse and the Long Road to Recognition," *Metronome*, lxxvii/9 (1960), 20
D. DeMicheal: "Charlie Rouse: Artistry and Originality," *DB*, xxviii/11 (1961), 17
J.-P. Binchet: "Portrait: monsieur passe-partout," *Jm*, no.92 (1963), 24 [incl. discography]
J.-L. Ginibre: "La longue marche de Charlie," *Jm*, no.105 (1964), 20
P. Danson: "Charlie Rouse," *Coda*, no.187 (1982), 4
A. D. Franklin: "Charlie Rouse," *Cadence*, xiii/6 (1987), 5

BARRY KERNFELD

Rovère, Gilbert [Bibi] (*b* Toulon, France, 29 Aug 1939). French double bass player. From 1957 to 1959 he performed and recorded in Paris with hard-bop groups led by Barney Wilen. As a sideman at the Blue Note (1962–3) he played with Kenny Drew, Johnny Griffin, Dexter Gordon, and Kenny Clarke. He performed and recorded with Bud Powell (1963) and Duke Ellington (1963–4), and recorded with Lou Bennett (1963, 1969), Jean-Luc Ponty (1964), and Jef Gilson (1964, 1966). After working with the pianist Art Simmons in 1964–5 he joined Martial Solal in 1965. While with Solal's trio he also recorded with Ivan Jullien (1966) and René Urtreger (1970). He has played at numerous Continental jazz festivals. In 1974 he recorded the album *Invitation* (1974, Spot. 4) as a sideman with Al Haig's bop trio.

BIBLIOGRAPHY

Feather '60s
J.-L. Ginibre: "Les secrets de Gilbert: entretien à coeur ouvert," *Jm*, no.106 (1964), 20

Rowles, Jimmie [Jimmy; Hunter, James George] (*b* Spokane, WA, 19 Aug 1918). Pianist. He took the name Rowles from his stepfather. He was largely self-taught, though he received lessons in jazz piano, developing a taste for the style of Teddy Wilson. He played in bands in Seattle while studying at the University of Washington, then moved to Los Angeles, where he joined Lester Young's group in 1942. During the 1940s he played with various musicians, including Benny Goodman and Woody Herman, but it was as an accompanist to singers, particularly Billie Holiday and Peggy Lee, that he became best known. In the late 1950s he played on film soundtracks and worked as a studio musician. After performing at the Newport Jazz Festival in 1973 he settled in New York, where he worked in clubs, mainly in duos with Zoot Sims, George Mraz, and Buster Williams. He toured for more than two years in the early 1980s as Ella Fitzgerald's accompanist. He returned to southern California and in 1986 was honored in Los Angeles by the declaration of 14 September as "Jimmie Rowles Day." Rowles is a sensitive player with a swinging, mainstream style, who shows a particular liking for Duke Ellington's music. He has composed many memorable tunes, one of which, *The Peacocks*, was included in the soundtrack to the film *Round Midnight* (1986).

Oral history material in *NjR* (JOHP).

SELECTED RECORDINGS

As unaccompanied soloist: *Jazz is a Fleeting Moment* (1974, Jazzz 103)

Duos: with Rusty Gilder: *The Special Magic of Jimmy Rowles* (1974, Hal. 110); with G. Mraz: *Music's the Only Thing that's on my Mind* (1976, Prog. 7009); with A. Cohn: *Heavy Love* (1977, Xan. 145)

As leader: *Rare – but Well Done* (1954, Lib. 3003); *Grandpaws* (1976, Choice 1014)

As sideman: B. Holiday: *Music for Torching* (1955, Clef 669); C. McRae: *Great American Songbook* (1971, Atl. 2-904); S. Vaughan: *Sarah Vaughan and the Jimmy Rowles Quintet* (1972, Mstr. 404); Z. Sims: *Zoot Sims Party* (1974, Choice 1006); S. Getz: *The Peacocks* (1977, Col. JC34873)

BIBLIOGRAPHY

W. Balliett: "Dancing on the Carpet," *New Yorker*, l (1 April 1974), 43
L. Feather: "Piano Giants of Jazz: Jimmy Rowles," *CK*, iv/11 (1978), 93 [incl. transcr.]
L. Lyons: "Jimmy Rowles: Noted New York Jazz Pianist and Accompanist," *CK*, iv/7 (1978), 14; repr. in *The Great Jazz Pianists, Speaking of their Lives and Music* (New York, 1983), 151
L. Tomkins: "Jimmie Rowles," *CI*, xviii (1979), no.2, p.22; no.3, p.16

BOB DOERSCHUK

Rowser, Jimmy [James Edward] (*b* Philadelphia, 18 April 1926). Double bass player. From 1954 to 1956 he was a member of the house band at the Blue Note in Philadelphia. Thereafter he played with Dinah Washington (1956–7, 1959–60) and performed and recorded with Maynard Ferguson (1957–9) and Red Garland and Lee Morgan (both 1959). During the 1960s he worked as a freelance in New York, recording with Junior Mance (*Big Chief*, 1961, Jlnd 953), Ray Bryant (at intervals, 1961–9), and Illinois Jacquet and Herb Ellis (both 1962). He toured Mexico and recorded with Benny Goodman in 1963 and performed and recorded in Argentina with Friedrich Gulda the following year. After playing with Al Cohn and Zoot Sims, Rowser joined Les McCann (1969), and worked with him through the 1970s, performing in the film *Soul to Soul* (1971) and at the Monterey Jazz Festival (1972). He rejoined Bryant for a recording session in 1980. (*FeatherE*; *Feather '60s*; *Feather–Gitler '70s*)

Roy, Badal (*b* East Pakistan [now Bangladesh], *c*1945). Pakistani tablā player. He moved to the USA in 1968 to study. He played jazz-rock in clubs in New York, often with John McLaughlin, with whom he recorded in 1970. He then toured and recorded with Miles Davis (1972–*c*1974), and also recorded with Pharoah Sanders (1972) and Lonnie Liston Smith (1973). Between 1973 and 1976 he was a member of Dave Liebman's group Lookout Farm, with which he toured Europe, India, and Japan and made a number of recordings (including the album *Sweet Hands*, 1975, A&M Hor. 702); he also performed and recorded with the bass player Frank Tusa (1975) and recorded with Ryo Kawasaki (1977).

BIBLIOGRAPHY

B. Henschen: "Tabla Talk: Badal Roy," *MD*, i/4 (1977), 8
D. Liebman and others: *Lookout Farm: a Case Study of Improvisation for Small Jazz Group* (n.p., 1978)

Roy, Harry (*b* London, 12 Jan 1900; *d* London, 1 Feb 1971). English bandleader, clarinetist, singer, and composer. From 1919 he organized dance bands with his brother Syd, including Syd Roy's Lyricals; they performed in London at Oddenino's,

Rector's, the Hammersmith Palais, and the Café de Paris, and at Rector's in Paris. In 1928 the brothers toured South Africa and Australia, then returned to England to play in vaudeville theaters before touring Germany. In 1931 Harry formed his own band and, after touring (1933), held residencies at the Café Anglais and the Mayfair Hotel in London. He continued to tour extensively in theaters until 1939 and throughout World War II but after 1945 never regained his former status in London's clubland. Roy was essentially a show-band leader – an energetic front man, a light, sometimes comic, singer, and a clarinetist in the style of Ted Lewis. Although hardly a jazz musician himself he employed as sidemen a number of players who later became prominent in jazz. His signature tune, *Bugle Call Rag* (1933), set the style for his own compositions such as *Hurricane Harry* (1933) and *The Roy Rag* (1934). Another composition, *Sarawaki* (1938), was dedicated to his first wife Elizabeth Brooke (known as Princess Pearl), the daughter of the Rajah of Sarawak.

SELECTED RECORDINGS

* – composed by Roy

Bugle Call Rag/Stormy Weather (1933, Parl. R1526); *Hurricane Harry/Somebody Stole my Gal (1933, Parl. R1553); *The Roy Rag (1934, Parl. R1896); *Sarawaki (1938, Parl. F1178)

BIBLIOGRAPHY

A. McCarthy: *The Dance Band Era: the Dancing Decades from Ragtime to Swing, 1910–1950* (London, 1971/R1982)

S. Colin: *And the Bands Played On* (London, 1980)

KEN RATTENBURY

Roy, Teddy [Theodore Gerald] (*b* Du Quoin, IL, 9 April 1905; *d* New York, 31 Aug 1966). Pianist. He played cornet for seven years before taking up piano. He made race records in Chicago, and played with the Coon–Sanders Nighthawk Orchestra, Jean Goldkette, and Frankie Trumbauer. He worked in Boston with Bobby Hackett and Pee Wee Russell (both 1933), then led his own band at Cape Cod, Massachusetts (1934). After the war he played with Max Kaminsky (1945–6), and made recordings (including *Shake it and Break it/When you and I were Young, Maggie*, 1946, Com. 612) with the revived Original Dixieland Jazz Band, led by Eddie Edwards, of which Kaminsky and Wild Bill Davison were also members. From 1946 to 1959 he worked as a freelance in New York and on Long Island, playing with Russell (1951), Miff Mole, Kaminsky, and Wingy Manone (1958–9), and as an unaccompanied soloist. (*ChiltonW*; *FeatherE*; *Feather–Gitler '70s*)

Royal, Ernie [Ernest Andrew] (*b* Los Angeles, 6 Feb 1921; *d* New York, 16 March 1983). Trumpeter, brother of Marshall Royal. He played with Les Hite (1937–8) and Lionel Hampton (1940–42), then after serving in the US Navy (1942–5) worked with Count Basie (1946) and was a member of Woody Herman's Second Herd (1947–9; for illustration *see* HERMAN, WOODY, fig.1*b*). In summer 1950 he toured Europe with Duke Ellington; later that year he returned to France, where he worked with the bandleader Jacques Hélian. After leading a band in Hollywood with Wardell Gray (1952) he toured the USA with Stan Kenton (1953) and worked as a freelance in New York; from 1957 to 1972 he was a staff musician for ABC radio and television. He performed and recorded with Gil Evans intermittently from 1957 (touring Europe in 1978), and recorded prolifically under such leaders as Quincy Jones (1955–64), Oliver Nelson (1961–7), and Friedrich Gulda (1966). Royal specialized in playing high notes, and was an imaginative improviser, capable of producing fine melodic lines.

SELECTED RECORDINGS

As leader: *Accent on Trumpet* (c1954, Urania 1203)

As sideman: S. Rollins: *Brass/Trio* (1958, Metro. 1002); Q. Jones: *The Birth of a Band!* (1959, Mer. 20444); C. Adderley: *African Waltz* (1961, Riv. 9377); on G. Evans: *Blues in Orbit* (1969, 1971, Ampex 10102), Blues in Orbit, Thoroughbred

BIBLIOGRAPHY

FeatherE; *Feather–Gitler '70s*

L. Tomkins: "Ernie Royal," *CI*, xvi (1978), no.10, p.22; no.12, p.14

LEROY OSTRANSKY

Royal, Marshall (Walton) (*b* Sapulpa, OK, 12 May 1912). Alto saxophonist and clarinetist, brother of Ernie Royal. He learned violin and guitar as well as reed instruments as a child, and gave his first professional performance at the age of 13. During most of the 1930s he played with Les Hite, and from 1940 to 1942 he was with Lionel Hampton. After serving in a navy band he performed in New York with Eddie Heywood (1946), then moved to the West Coast, where he worked as a studio musician. In 1951 he joined Count Basie's septet, and soon helped Basie to organize a new big band; as well as playing lead alto saxophone Royal also took solos. He remained with the band for 20 years as its music director, and, although his responsibility for disciplining the musicians to play as a precise ensemble led to some friction, his success as a rehearsal leader was acknowledged by the other members of the group. In 1970 Royal left Basie and settled in Los Angeles, where he performed and recorded with Bill Berry's big band and the Capp–Pierce Juggernaut and recorded as a soloist with small groups under such leaders as Dave Frishberg (1977) and Warren Vaché (1978). He also recorded as the leader of a band with Snooky Young (1978) and with his own groups (1978, 1980). Royal has a clear, crisp tone, reminiscent of Benny Carter's; his playing remains firmly rooted in the swing style, and is both harmonically and rhythmically solid.

Oral history material in *NjR* (JOHP).

SELECTED RECORDINGS

As leader: with S. Young: *Snooky and Marshall's Album* (1978, Conc. 55); *Royal Blue* (1980, Conc. 125)

As sideman: C. Basie: *Basie* (1957, Roul. 52003), incl. Fantail; *The Count Basie Story* (1960, Roul. 1); *Back to Basie* (1962, Roul. 52113); *Basie in Sweden* (1962, Roul. 52099); D. Frishberg: *Getting Some Fun out of Life* (1977, Conc. 37); Concord All Stars: *Festival Time* (1979, Conc. 117)

BIBLIOGRAPHY

ChiltonW; *FeatherE*; *Feather–Gitler '70s*

S. Dance: "Marshall Royal," *JJ*, xv/3 (1962), 2 [interview]

P. Hughes: "Anglo-American Exchange: the Basie Band's Marshall Royal," *Crescendo*, ii/7 (1962), 22

C. Battestini and J.-P. Battestini: "Marshall Royal: allons à l'essential," *BHcF*, no.284 (1980), 10 [interview]

S. Dance: *The World of Count Basie* (New York and London, 1980) [colln of previously pubd interviews], 164

L. D. Holmes and J. W. Thomson: *Jazz Greats: Getting Better with Age* (New York, 1986) [colln of interviews]

Karrah: "Marshall Royal," *Cadence*, xiv/3 (1988) 20 [interview]

LEROY OSTRANSKY

Royal Gardens. Ballroom in Chicago; *see* NIGHTCLUBS AND OTHER VENUES.

Royal Roost (i). Nightclub in New York; *see* NIGHTCLUBS AND OTHER VENUES.

Royal Roost [Roost] **(ii).** Record company and label. The company was established by Teddy Reig in New York around 1950. Named after the nightclub in New York, it used the full name on the discs themselves, but only the word "Roost" on liners. It organized important sessions by Stan Getz in 1950–51 and reissued many of the tracks recorded by Charlie Parker for Dial in 1947. The company's principal artists were Johnny Smith (1952–62) and Sonny Stitt (1952–*c*1965). The catalogue also included material by Bud Powell (made for De Luxe in 1947 but not issued), Coleman Hawkins (1950), Billy Taylor (ii) (1951–2), Seldon Powell (1955–6), and Gene Quill (1958). From the late 1950s the catalogue was distributed by Roulette and it soon became a division of that company, which continued to market albums under the name Roost until 1971.

Rozenbergs, Gunārs (*b* Riga, Latvian SSR, 23 March 1947). Latvian trumpeter, composer, and arranger. He played jazz from 1965 and in 1967 led a quartet at the festival in Tallinn. During the following years he continued to lead small groups, as well as a big band that performed in Riga, Tallinn, and Moscow. In 1984 he became the conductor of the orchestra of the Latvian TV and Radio and in 1986 graduated from the Latvian SSR Yazep Vitol State Conservatory in Riga with a degree in trumpet. Rozenbergs's trumpet playing is well illustrated by his album *Laura* (1979, Mel. C601122930). His best-known composition is *Limping Blues*, which is in 11/8 time (i.e., 3/8 + 3/8 + 3/8 + 2/8). He has written many arrangements of pieces by Latvian composers, especially Raimond Pauls.

WALTER OJAKÄÄR

Rudd, Roswell (Hopkins, Jr.) (*b* Sharon, CT, 17 Nov 1935). Trombonist. He studied horn from the age of 11 and taught himself to play trombone while in his teens. While attending Yale University he belonged to Eli's Chosen Six (to 1958), a dixieland band. He worked with Herbie Nichols (1960–62), belonged to a quartet with Steve Lacy and Dennis Charles that for some time played exclusively the music of Thelonious Monk (1961–3), and in early 1962 joined Bill Dixon's free-jazz group, of which Archie Shepp and Charles were also members. In the summer of 1964 he was a founding member with John Tchicai and Milford Graves of the New York Art Quartet, for which he also wrote compositions and arrangements, and later that year he took part in the October Revolution in Jazz. He joined Shepp's group in the winter of 1965, with which he played in London and at the Donaueschingen Musiktage in 1967. With Robin Kenyatta, Karl Berger, and Lee Konitz he formed the Primordial Quartet early in 1968, the size and membership of which varied considerably during the next few years. In 1969 he worked with Charlie Haden's Liberation Music Orchestra, then joined a group led by Gato Barbieri that included Haden, Beaver Harris, and Lonnie Liston Smith as sidemen; he later recorded with the group. After disbanding the Primordial Quartet in March 1970 he wrote compositions for the Jazz Composer's Orchestra (these may be heard on his album *Numatik Swing Band*, 1973) and performed and recorded as a leader into the 1980s. Rudd has brought to free jazz many of the qualities more often associated with the early jazz trombone; these include a large, warm tone, an earthy vocal sound punctuated by growls, and a deeply felt sense of rhythm.

SELECTED RECORDINGS

As leader: *Roswell Rudd* (1965, Amer. 6114); *Everywhere* (1966, Imp. 9126); *Numatik Swing Band* (1973, JCOA 1007); *Flexible Flyer* (1974, Ari. 1006); *Maine* (1976, BVHaast 011); *The Definitive* (1979, Horo 12); *Regeneration* (1982, SN 1054)

As sideman: S. Lacy: *Schooldays* (1963, Emanem 3316); A. Shepp: *Archie Shepp Live in San Francisco* (1966, Imp. 9118)

BIBLIOGRAPHY

Feather '60s; *Feather–Gitler '70s*

D. Heckman: "Roswell Rudd," *DB*, xxxi/3 (1964), 14

B. McRae: "Avant Courier: Roswell Rudd: All the Way from Dixie," *JJI*, xxviii/5 (1975), 20

M. Luzzi: *Uomini e avanguardie jazz* (Milan, 1980)

M. Zwerin: *Close Enough for Jazz* (London, 1983) [autobiography]

G. Giddins: "Technicolor Repertory," *Rhythm-a-ning: Jazz Tradition and Innovation in the '80s* (New York, and Oxford, England, 1985) [colln of previously pubd articles], 168

LEE JESKE/R

Rudiments. Patterns of strokes used by percussion players. Evidence of rudimental drumming patterns dates from 15th-century Swiss military ordinances, and similar patterns were used by European drummers and brought to the USA in the 18th and 19th centuries during the numerous wars waged in North America. In 1932 the National Association of Rudimental Drummers (NARD) codified the most popular of these military patterns into 26 standard rudiments, many of which have mnemonic names; since most sticking figures may be analyzed as belonging to one or more rudimental patterns, it is difficult to strike a drum without playing one rudiment or another. The earliest jazz drummers also invented patterns to which they applied mnemonic names (*see* DRUM SET, §II, 1), using them in much the same way as did their military counterparts – as a teaching device and to accompany particular melodic figures or specific dance arrangements; this practice has continued throughout the history of jazz drumming (for example, in the employment of ragtime rat-tat-tats, shuffle rhythm, and fatback rhythm, which involves a strong backbeat). The term rudimental drumming is often applied to the playing of Gene Krupa and several other swing and dixieland drummers of the 1930s and 1940s. At times it has been used derisively to describe the work of drummers who do not play with a jazz-like feel, but a number of well-known musicians, including Cozy Cole, Buddy Rich, Sonny Payne, Joe Morello, and Steve Gadd, have incorporated various rudiments into their playing with startling results. Rudimental patterns have also been used by other percussionists in jazz, notably the timbales player Willie Bobo and Lionel Hampton, who initially worked as a drummer and subsequently adapted his technique to the vibraphone. The patterns played on conga drum in Afro-Cuban jazz and the intricate rhythmic formulas performed on tablā in Indian music also have their basis in rudimental systems.

Ex.1 Some of the most popular rudiments used in jazz drumming

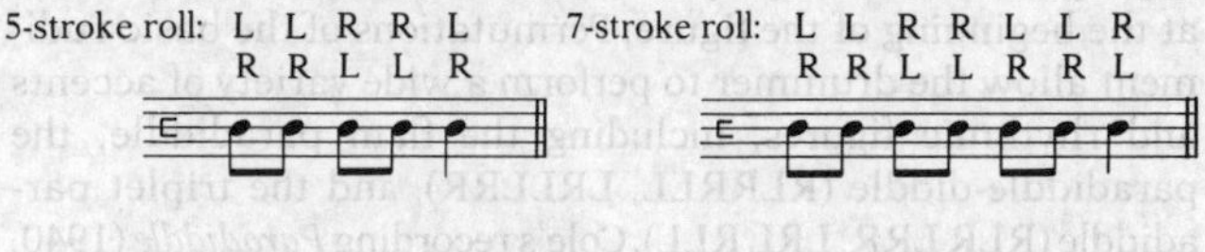

Jazz drummers use rudiments almost exclusively during solos, fills, and kicks, some of the most popular being the following:

(a) The roll. The roll produces a sustained sound and is achieved either by striking the sticks alternately on the drumhead in an even manner (a single-stroke roll) or by bouncing alternate sticks (a double-stroke, closed, or buzz roll). The single-stroke

roll is extremely difficult to play fast, and it is commonly believed that Rich is the performer par excellence of this rudiment. The double-stroke roll and the closed or buzz roll, played at various lengths (5, 7, 9, 11, and 15 strokes) and ending with a single tap, have been used from the earliest days of jazz in patterns suited to fit the music. The most common accompaniment figure during the 1920s and 1930s is shown in ex.2; it has since been replaced by cymbal accompaniment patterns, although the sound still remains in the swish of the brushes. Another type of roll, the press roll, consists of a succession of double-stroke rolls of varying lengths played in march or syncopated march rhythms.

Ex.2 The accompanimental figure most commonly used during the 1920s and 1930s

(b) The flam. The flam is a two-note pattern consisting of a principal note preceded by a grace note. Like most rudiments, flams may be played alternately or successively. Jazz drummers have executed them in a variety of ways, from the open flam (played by delaying the principal note) to the flat flam (played by striking both sticks almost simultaneously).

(c) The ruff. There are two types of ruff. The double-stroke ruff is played with one stick and consists of a principal note preceded by two grace notes, while the four-stroke ruff is played with alternate sticks and consists of a principal note preceded by three grace notes. Jazz drummers often execute a ruff before a kick.

(d) The drag. The term is used as a synonym for a double-stroke ruff and is also applied to a ruff played at a slow tempo.

(e) The ratamacue. The ratamacue is played by following a double-stroke ruff with a triplet, and may be lengthened by additional ruffs to form double ratamacues and triple ratamacues. These are well illustrated in Cole's solo *Ratamacue* (1939, Voc. 4700), recorded with Cab Calloway's band.

(f) The paradiddle. The paradiddle consists of four even notes, first starting with the right hand and then the left; double and triple paradiddles are played by adding alternate single strokes at the beginning of the figure. Permutations of the basic rudiment allow the drummer to perform a wide variety of accents and rhythmic figures, including the flam paradiddle, the paradiddle-diddle (RLRRLL, LRLLRR), and the triplet paradiddle (RLR LRR, LRL RLL). Cole's recording *Paradiddle* (1940, Voc./OK 5467), also with Calloway, provides a good example of this technique.

T. DENNIS BROWN

Rüegg, Mathias (*b* 1952). Swiss pianist, composer, and arranger. He was the founder in 1977 of the VIENNA ART ORCHESTRA.

Ruff. One of the drumstrokes collectively known as RUDIMENTS.

Ruff, Willie (Henry, Jr.) (*b* Sheffield, AL, 1 Sept 1931). Double bass and french horn player, and teacher. He learned french horn in the army, and played in bands at the Lockbourne (Ohio) Air Force Base, where in 1947 he met Dwike Mitchell. Ruff continued to study orchestral horn, and was also a pupil of the composer Paul Hindemith at Yale University (MA 1954). He then joined Lionel Hampton's band, with which Mitchell was already playing, and the two musicians formed a duo in 1955. They have lectured and performed throughout the USA, and in 1959, on tour with the Yale Russian Chorus, they were the first Western jazz musicians to perform in the USSR after World War II. In 1966 they accompanied President Lyndon Johnson to Mexico, and the following year they made a film in Brazil which traced the African roots of Brazilian music. As a professor of music at Yale, Ruff inaugurated the Duke Ellington Fellowship Program in 1972. In 1979, with the scientist John Rodgers, he recorded a realization of *Harmonices mundi*, a treatise by the German mathematician and music theorist Johannes Kepler. The duo played in China in 1981, and Ruff recorded as an unaccompanied soloist in St. Mark's basilica, Venice, in 1983. He is fluent in eight languages, and his unusual talents as both a performer and a teacher have helped to make jazz accessible to audiences throughout the world.

Oral history material in *CtY*.

SELECTED RECORDINGS

As unaccompanied soloist: *Willie Ruff at Saint Mark's* (1983, Kepler 1931)
Duos with D. Mitchell: *Mitchell–Ruff Duo* (1955, Epic 3221); *Appearing Nightly* (1957, Roul. 52002); *Jazz Mission to Moscow* (1959, Roul. 52034); *Strayhorn* (1969, Mstr. 335); *Virtuoso Elegance in Jazz* (1984, Kepler 1234)
As leader: with D. Mitchell: *Ruff–Mitchell Duo Plus Strings and Brass* (1958, Roul. 52013); with D. Mitchell and Charlie Smith: *Catbird Suite* (1961, Atl. 1374); with D. Mitchell and Elcio Melito: *Brazilian Trip* (1966, Epic 26360); with D. Mitchell and D. Gillespie: *Dizzy Gillespie and the Mitchell–Ruff Duo in Concert* (1971, Mstr. 325), *Dizzy Gillespie Live with the Mitchell–Ruff Duo* (1970, 1979–80, Book-of-the-Month 516517)

BIBLIOGRAPHY

"Willie Ruff Translates Russ Tour," *Variety*, ccxvi (7 Oct 1959), 63
"Johnson Takes Jazz on Mexico Trip," *DB*, xxxiii/11 (1966), 12
J. Blanksteen: "Computer Synthesizes 'Music of the Spheres'," *New York Times* (24 April 1979), §C, p.1
H. Schonberg: "The Planets are not Candidates for the Hit Parade," *New York Times* (24 April 1979), §C, p.1
R. Sudhalter: "Mitchell and Ruff are Well-traveled Musicians," *New York Post* (6 June 1980), 40
W. Zinsser: *Willie and Dwike: an American Profile* (New York and Toronto, 1984) [biographies of Willie Ruff and Dwike Mitchell]

PHILIP GREENE

Rugolo, Pete(r) (*b* San Piero, Sicily, 25 Dec 1915). Arranger and composer. He was one of the generation of jazz composers and arrangers who studied under Darius Milhaud. While still a serviceman he sold his arrangement *Opus a Dollar Three Eighty* to Stan Kenton, and became Kenton's full-time collaborator during the band's period of greatest success (1945–9). The large number of Rugolo's compositions recorded by Kenton includes items in all the genres associated with the band, but little that was memorable outside the hothouse atmosphere of Kenton's organization. As a record producer Rugolo had the distinction of commissioning Miles Davis's famous nonet sessions of 1949–50, but the recordings with his own band in 1954 and subsequent albums under his name showed a tendency to turn attractive ideas about orchestration into gimmickry. In the 1950s, earlier than most of his jazz-influenced colleagues, Rugolo found a niche writing background music for films and for television series such as "The Thin Man" and "Dr. Kildare."

SELECTED ARRANGEMENTS

As leader: You stepped out of a dream/Bazaar (1954, Col. 40223); *Music for Hi-fi Bugs* (1956, EmA 36082); *Out on a Limb* (1956, EmA 36115)
Recorded by S. Kenton: Opus a Dollar Three Eighty (1944, AFRS DB87); Artistry in Percussion (1946, Cap. 289); Machito (1947, Cap. 408); Chorale for Brass, Piano and Bongo (1947, Cap. 10183); Abstraction (1947, Cap. 10184)

BIBLIOGRAPHY

"Rugged Rugolo," *Metronome*, lxiii/4 (1947), 27
W. F. Lee: *Stan Kenton: Artistry in Rhythm* (Los Angeles, 1980) [incl. discography]

BRIAN PRIESTLEY

Ruiz, Hilton (*b* New York, 29 May 1952). Pianist. He was classically trained, and played at Carnegie Recital Hall at the age of eight. As a teenager he worked in Latin bands, and his first major association as a jazz musician was with Frank Foster (1970). He was a pupil of Mary Lou Williams (from 1971), and thereafter played with Joe Newman, Cal Massey's big band (1971–2), Freddie Hubbard and Joe Henderson (both 1972), Clark Terry, Jackie McLean, Charles Mingus (briefly, 1973), Roland Kirk (intermittently, 1973–7), Betty Carter, Archie Shepp, and Chico Freeman. A highly versatile musician, Ruiz may be heard at his best on the albums he has recorded as a leader, particularly *Cross Currents*.

SELECTED RECORDINGS

As leader: *Piano Man* (1975, Ste. 1036); *Excition* (1977, Ste. 1078); *New York Hilton* (1977, Ste. 1094); *Cross Currents* (1984, Stash 248)
As sideman: R. Kirk: *Return of the 5000 lb Man* (1976, WB 2918); *Kirkatron* (1976, WB 2982); C. Freeman: *Beyond the Rain* (1977, Cont. 7640)

BIBLIOGRAPHY

Feather–Gitler '70s
L. Birnbaum: "Hilton Ruiz," *DB*, liv/9 (1987), 15

SCOTT YANOW

Rully [née Urziceanu], **Aura** (*b* Bucharest, 14 Dec 1946). Romanian singer. She studied violin and voice, attending the Bucharest Conservatory in 1965–7; in 1965 she toured the USSR, Poland, and Israel with Janos Kőrössi's trio. From 1966 to 1969 she performed with the Bucharest Jazz Quintet and recorded as its leader in 1971; she married the group's drummer Ron Rully and moved with him to Canada. She performed with Duke Ellington at the Newport Jazz Festival in 1972, then worked in Europe with Art Farmer and Slide Hampton; she made further recordings as a leader around 1973–4. After working in Canada with Gene DiNovi (1974) and touring the USA and Japan with Quincy Jones she performed with the Thad Jones–Mel Lewis Orchestra; in 1977 she recorded the album *Thad and Aura* (1977, Four Leaf Clover 5020) with Jones in Sweden. Rully has a pure, full tone, which rises to piercing intensity when she is scat singing.

BIBLIOGRAPHY

Feather–Gitler '70s
J. Byrczek and H. Matuszewska: "Eurojazz Personalities," *JF* [intl edn], no.37 (1975), 69
R. Flohil: "Ron and Aura Rully: Powerhouse Percussion and Stunning Singing," *Canadian Composer*, no.105 (1975), 12

KIMBERLY McCORD

Rumsey, Howard (*b* Brawley, CA, 7 Nov 1917). Double bass player. As a youth he played drums, and changed to double bass while at college. His first important engagement was with Vido Musso's band in the late 1930s. When the band's pianist, Stan Kenton, formed his own ensemble in 1941 Rumsey joined it as the double bass player. From 1942 he worked as a freelance in southern California before forming a group in 1949 that became resident at the Lighthouse Cafe, Hermosa Beach, near Los Angeles. He remained associated with the club for nearly 20 years, and eventually became its manager and joint owner. During this period the Lighthouse became an important center for innovative jazz on the West Coast. From 1951 to 1960 Rumsey's group, known as the Lighthouse All Stars, regularly included such distinguished sidemen as Jimmy Giuffre, Shorty Rogers, Max Roach, and Stan Levey. Rumsey's excellent ensemble playing provided a discreet but solid foundation for even the most unusual textures. In the early 1960s the group was gradually replaced by others, and by 1968 Rumsey had ceased playing. In 1972 he opened a new club, Concerts by the Sea, in Redondo Beach, California.

See also NIGHTCLUBS AND OTHER VENUES (Los Angeles).

SELECTED RECORDINGS

As leader: *Music for Lighthousekeeping* (1956, Cont. 3528)
As sideman: S. Kenton: Concerto for Doghouse (1942, Decca 4254); C. Barnet: Skyliner (1944, Decca 18659); J. Giuffre: Big Boy (1952, Tampa 114); M. Roach: *Drummin' the Blues* (1957, Lib. 3064)

BIBLIOGRAPHY

FeatherE; *Feather '60s*; *Feather–Gitler '70s*
L. Feather: *The Passion for Jazz* (New York, 1980), 167
L. D. Holmes and J. W. Thomson: *Jazz Greats: Getting Better with Age* (New York, 1986)

SCOTT DeVEAUX

Ruppli, Michel (*b* Coulommiers, France, 3 July 1934). French discographer. He attended the University of Paris and the Ecole Normale Supérieure des Télécommunications and from 1960 worked as an electronics engineer. At the same time he compiled important discographies of several jazz labels of the postwar era (sometimes in collaboration with Bill Daniels and Bob Porter) based on his research into the record companies' ledgers and files; these contain detailed information on thousands of recording sessions and are far more complete and accurate than earlier discographies. In addition to those already published, discographies of Blue Note, Capitol, and other labels were in preparation in the late 1980s. Ruppli has also contributed discographies of individual musicians to *Jazz hot*.

WRITINGS
(selective list)

Prestige Jazz Records, 1949–1969 [*recte 1971*]: *a Discography* (n.p. [Copenhagen], 1972; rev. and enlarged, Westport, CT, and London, 2/1980, with B. Porter, as *The Prestige Label: a Discography*)
Atlantic Records: a Discography (Westport, CT, and London, 1979)
with B. Porter: *The Savoy Label: a Discography* (Westport, CT, and London, 1980)
The Chess Labels: a Discography (Westport, CT, and London, 1983) [incl. listings for Argo and Cadet]
with B. Daniels: *The King Labels: a Discography* (Westport, CT, and London, 1985) [incl. listings for Bethlehem]
with B. Porter: *The Clef/Verve Labels: a Discography* (New York, Westport, CT, and London, 1986)

Rusch, Bob [Robert (D.)] (*b* New York, *c*1945). Writer. He studied clarinet and drums, played drums in workshops with Jaki Byard (1968–71) and Cedar Walton (1972), and in the 1960s and 1970s wrote for American and European periodicals, including *Down Beat*, *Jazz Journal*, and *Jazz Forum*. In 1975 he began publishing the monthly magazine *Cadence*, which in the following years printed many wide-ranging interviews with jazz and blues musicians and reviews of recordings. He later formed Cadence Jazz Records (1980), which in its first six years issued more than 30 recordings by such musicians as Bill Dixon, Chet Baker, and Beaver Harris, and North Country Record Distribution (1983), which distributes jazz and blues recordings of about 550 small independent labels. He has donated his extensive indexed collection of books and journals, covering jazz and blues literature in the English language, to the Schomburg Center for Research in Black Culture of the New York Public Library; *see* LIBRARIES AND ARCHIVES, §2. Rusch is a knowledgeable, perceptive, and accurate interviewer who is adept at eliciting useful information from his subjects. Several of his interviews are included in the collection *Jazz Talk: the Cadence Interviews* (Secaucus, NJ, 1984).

DANIEL ZAGER

Rushen, Patrice (Louise) (*b* Los Angeles, 30 Sept 1954). Keyboard player and singer. She studied classical piano from the age of three before turning to jazz while in her teens. After leading a group that won an award for young musicians at the Monterey Jazz Festival (1972) she played with Melba Liston, Abbey Lincoln, Gerald Wilson, Donald Byrd, and Benny Golson and recorded with Jean-Luc Ponty (1975), Stanley Turrentine (1975), and Sonny Rollins (1976). She played piano and electronic keyboards in Lee Ritenour's group (1977), which she left to devote more attention to singing. Rushen's first album as a leader (1974) showed the influence of bop, but she later abandoned improvisation, at which she had evinced considerable skill, in favor of a fusion of jazz and rhythm-and-blues; in the late 1970s she acquired a large following among pop audiences by performing a bland style of pop-soul. In 1988 she belonged to the group led by Carlos Santana and Wayne Shorter.

SELECTED RECORDINGS

As leader: *Prelusion* (1974, Prst. 10089); *Before the Dawn* (1975, Prst. 10098)
As leader with others: J.-L. Ponty: *Upon the Wings of Music* (1975, Atl. 18138); S. Rollins: *The Way I Feel* (1976, Mlst. 9074); L. Ritenour: *Sugarloaf Express* (1977, JVC 2)

BIBLIOGRAPHY

Feather–Gitler '70s
L. Lyons: "Profile: Patrice Rushen," *DB*, xliii/2 (1976), 30
F. Nemko: "Patrice Rushen: a New Jazz Talent Talks about her Music," *CK*, ii/6 (1976), 8
M. Zipkin: "Patrice Rushen: Rushen to the Top," *DB*, xlv/5 (1978), 16

BARRY KERNFELD

Rushing, Jimmy [James Andrew; Mr. Five by Five] (*b* Oklahoma City, OK, 26 Aug 1903; *d* New York, 8 June 1972). Singer. He was born into a musical family and learned violin, piano, and singing. He appeared in the Midwest, in California, and in a touring show, before singing with Walter Page's Blue Devils (1927–9) and Bennie Moten's Kansas City Orchestra (1929–35). With these important bands he developed a mature singing style derived from the blues and completely idiomatic to the rhythms of jazz, an uncommon accomplishment even for experienced black singers in the late 1920s. He first achieved renown with Count Basie's band from 1935, his excellent intonation and robust yet sensitive manner perfectly complementing the group and helping to shape its identity. He remained with Basie until 1950, and thereafter worked with his own group and as a soloist, making foreign tours with several bands, including those of Basie, Buck Clayton, Eddie Condon, and Benny Goodman, and playing in New York with Zoot Sims (1971–2).

See also BLUES, §9; for illustrations *see* BLUES, fig.3, and MOTEN, BENNIE.

SELECTED RECORDINGS

As leader: *Listen to the Blues* (1955, Van. 8505)
As sideman: B. Moten: Liza Lee/Get Goin' (1930, Vic. 23023); C. Basie: Good Morning Blues (1937, Decca 1446); Georgianna (1938, Decca 1682); The blues I like to hear (1938, Decca 2284); I'm gonna move to the outskirts of town (1942, Col. 36601)

BIBLIOGRAPHY

J. Armitage: "It's Blues Time, Folks, with Jimmy Rushing," *Music Mirror*, iv/8 (1957), 6
D. Hague: "Jimmy Rushing," *JJ*, x/9 (1957), 1 [interview]
N. Hentoff: "Jimmy Rushing," *DB*, xxiv/5 (1957), 20 [interview]
P. Oliver: "Jimmy Rushing: the Formative Years," *JM*, iii/10 (1957), 2
——: "Rushing in Retrospect," *Music Mirror*, iv/10 (1957), 17
R. Ellison: "Remembering Jimmy," *JJ*, xi/11 (1958), 10
H. McNamara: "The Odyssey of Jimmy Rushing," *DB*, xxxii/8 (1965), 22
C. Albertson: "Jimmy Rushing: a Sturdy Branch of the Learning Tree," *DB*, xxxvi/23 (1969), 17
B. McRae: "A B Basics, no.50: Jimmy Rushing," *JJ*, xxiv/2 (1971), 32
H. Lyttelton: "Rushing," *JJ*, xxv/8 (1972), 4
S. Dance: *The World of Count Basie* (New York and London, 1980) [colln of previously pubd interviews], 17
L. Gourse: *Louis' Children: American Jazz Singers* (New York, 1984), 71
J. Armitage: "Souvenirs personnels de Jimmy Rushing," *BHcF*, no.329 (1985), 20
C. Basie and A. Murray: *Good Morning Blues: the Autobiography of Count Basie* (New York, 1985)
T. Burke and D. Penny: "Stand up and Shout the Blues: Jimmy Rushing," *Blues & Rhythm*, no.13 (1985), 4; no.14 (1985), 4 [incl. discography]
B. Clayton and N. M. Elliott: *Buck Clayton's Jazz World* (London, 1986)

JAMES DAPOGNY

Rushton, Joe [Joseph Augustine, Jr.] (*b* Evanston, IL, 1 Nov 1907; *d* San Francisco, 2 March 1964). Bass saxophonist. He took up bass saxophone in 1928, after having played drums, clarinet, and other saxophones. He led his own band in Chicago until 1932, then played there with other bandleaders for the rest of the decade. In the early 1940s he worked with Jimmy McPartland and Bud Freeman, then went to California with Benny Goodman (1942–3), with whom he played on the soundtrack to the film *The Gang's All Here* (1943). After settling in California he played with the pianist and bandleader Horace Heidt (1944–5), and made recordings as a leader (1945, 1947) and with others; his playing is well represented by *Carolina in the Morning* (1945, Jump 4), recorded by Floyd O'Brien's State Street Seven. Rushton then worked with Red Nichols (1947–63), recording, touring Europe, and playing in the film *The Five Pennies* (1958). He also recorded during this period with Louis Armstrong (1947), and with Matty Matlock, Eddie Miller, and others in the Rampart Street Paraders (1954).

BIBLIOGRAPHY

ChiltonW; *FeatherE*; *Feather '60s*
A. Napoleon: "The Bass Sax in Jazz," *Sv*, no.8 (1966–7), 15; no.9 (1967), 18
R. J. Hopf: "I Wonder what's Become of Joe?," *Jazzfreund*, xxii/3 (1980), 4

Russell, Bill [William; Wagner, Russell William] (*b* Canton, MO, 26 Feb 1905). Jazz historian, record producer, violinist, and composer. He played violin from the age of ten, and later studied music in Chicago (1924). After private violin tuition in New York (1927) he attended Columbia University Teachers College (1929), where he took up composition. While touring with the Red Gate Shadow Players (1934–40) he began collecting early jazz records, reselling many through the Hot Record Exchange that he ran from 1935 with the painter Steve Smith. He contributed articles to the magazine *Jazz hot* and wrote three chapters of *Jazzmen: the Story of Hot Jazz Told in the Lives of the Men who Created it* (ed. F. Ramsey, Jr., and C. E. Smith, New York, 1939/*R*1977). Russell played an important role in rediscovering Bunk Johnson, first recording him in 1942. From 1944 to 1957 he undertook a historic series of recordings for his AMERICAN MUSIC label, visiting Los Angeles, New Orleans, and New York to record such musicians as Baby Dodds, Bunk Johnson, Dink Johnson, George Lewis (i), Wooden Joe Nicholas, and Jim Robinson; the recordings continue to retain an influence on playing styles in Europe and Japan.

Russell was curator of the jazz archive at Tulane University, New Orleans, from 1958 to 1965, and, with Richard B. Allen, interviewed dozens of veteran musicians for its oral history project. From 1967 he has played in the New Orleans Ragtime Orchestra, recorded extensively, appeared at festivals, and toured Europe (1975, 1987). His vast knowledge and generous nature make him much sought after by jazz researchers and he remains an inspiration to all. In 1987 he was preparing books on Jelly Roll Morton and New Orleans playing styles. A collection of his published and unpublished writings and other materials is in the William Ransom Hogan Jazz Archive at Tulane University in New Orleans; *see* LIBRARIES AND ARCHIVES, §2.

Oral history material in *LNT*.

BIBLIOGRAPHY
R. A. Tiug: "Shopping at Bill's," *SL*, xv/1–2 (1964), 9
T. Bethell: *George Lewis: a Jazzman from New Orleans* (Berkeley, CA, and London, 1977)

MIKE HAZELDINE

Russell, Curly [Dillon] (*b* New York, 19 March 1917; *d* New York, 3 July 1986). Double bass player. He gained his early professional experience in the big bands of Don Redman (1941) and Benny Carter (1942–3). On returning to New York after touring he played in small groups at clubs on 52nd Street; at about this time Dizzy Gillespie and Charlie Parker were developing the musical ideas that led to the creation of bop, and in 1945 Russell joined their quintet at the Three Deuces. For the rest of the decade and into the 1950s Russell worked as a freelance with such musicians as Parker, Coleman Hawkins, Miles Davis, Bud Powell, and Thelonious Monk; during a period when the responsibility for maintaining cohesion in the rhythm section rested primarily with the bass player, Russell's consistent time-keeping and penetrating tone were greatly valued. By the late 1950s Russell had drifted away from jazz and was playing mainly with rhythm-and-blues groups.

Oral history material in *NjR*.

For illustration *see* Jazz (i), fig.5.

SELECTED RECORDINGS

As sideman: D. Gillespie: Salt Peanuts/Hot House (1945, Guild 1003); C. Parker: Billie's Bounce/Now's the Time (1945, Savoy 573); D. Gordon: Long Tall Dexter (1946, Savoy 603); C. Hawkins: Bean and the Boys (1946, Son. 3024); B. Powell: I'll Remember April/Off Minor (1947, Roost 513); C. Parker: Ah-leu-cha (1948, Savoy 939); B. Powell: Un poco loco (1951, BN 1577); T. Monk: *Thelonious Monk Quintet* (1954, Prst. 180), incl. Smoke gets in your eyes

BIBLIOGRAPHY
FeatherE
"Annuaire biographique de la contrebasse," *Jm*, no.94 (1963), 28
H. Renard: "Témoinages: la chasse aux souvenirs," *Jm*, no.94 (1963), 37

SCOTT DeVEAUX

Russell, George (Allan) (*b* Cincinnati, 23 June 1923). Composer and theorist. He played drums in local clubs while a student at Wilberforce University High School. During a long illness in 1945–6 he formulated the basis of his "Lydian concept," a system of composition based on grading intervals by the distance of their pitches from a central note. After his recovery he wrote scores for Dizzy Gillespie, including *Cubana Be/Cubana Bop* (one of the earliest works to combine jazz and Latin influences), and for Buddy DeFranco (*A Bird in Igor's Yard*) and Lee Konitz (*Ezz-thetic* and *Odjenar*); meanwhile he also studied composition with Stefan Wolpe. From 1950 he consolidated and refined his ideas on music theory, publishing them in book form as *The Lydian Chromatic Concept of Tonal Organization* (1953, 2/1959), which was immediately received as the first major contribution by a jazz musician to the field of music theory. Works followed on an increasingly large scale, establishing Russell, along with Gil Evans, as a leading postwar jazz composer; he combined advanced jazz idioms with an unusually rigorous concern for structure, harmony, and the balance between composition and improvisation. In 1958–9 he taught at the Lenox (Massachusetts) School of Jazz, and about the same time he took up piano, which he played in his own jazz sextet (1960–61); among the group's sidemen at various times were Don Ellis, Eric Dolphy, Chuck Israels, and Steve Swallow. In 1963 Russell moved to Europe and taught at Lund University in Sweden and the Vaskilde Summer School in Denmark, then in 1969 returned to the USA to join the faculty of the New England Conservatory. During the mid-1970s he ceased to compose and worked on a second volume of *The Lydian Chromatic Concept*. Russell made several recordings of his compositions in the late 1970s and early 1980s, including an album as the leader of the Swedish Radiojazzgruppen (1977) and two with his own big bands in New York (1982–3). Among his many honors are composer awards from the magazines *Metronome* and *Down Beat*, the Oscar du Disque de Jazz, two Guggenheim fellowships, three NEA grants, and the National Music Award.

RECORDED COMPOSITIONS
(selective list)

As leader: *The Jazz Workshop* (1956, RCA LPM1372), incl. The Ballad of Hix Blewitt, Concerto for Billy the Kid, Ezz-thetic, Knights of the Steamtable, Ye Hypocrite, Ye Beelzebub; *Jazz in the Space Age* (1960, Decca 79219); *Stratusphunk* (1960, Riv. 9341), incl. Stratusphunk; *The Essence of George Russell* (1965, 1971, Sonet 1411–12), incl. Now and Then; *The George Russell Sextet at Beethoven Hall* (1965, Saba 15059-60), incl. Takin' Lydia Home; *Listen to the Silence* (c1971, Concept 002)

Recorded by others: D. Gillespie: Cubana Be/Cubana Bop (1947, Vic. 203145); B. DeFranco: A Bird in Igor's Yard, on L. Tristano: *Crosscurrents* (1949, Cap. 11060); L. Konitz: Odjenar (1951, Prst. 753); Ezz-thetic (1951, Prst. 743); Lydian M-1, on T. Charles: *The Teddy Charles Tentet* (1956, Atl. 1229); The Day John Brown was Hanged, on H. McKusick: *Jazz Workshop* (1956, RCA LPM1366); All about Rosie, on Brandeis Jazz Festival: *Modern Jazz Concert* (1957, Col. WL127); Bill Evans (ii): *Living Time* (1972, Col. KC31490)

BIBLIOGRAPHY
D. Cerulli: "George Russell," *DB*, xxv/11 (1958), 15
L. Gottlieb: "Brandeis Festival Album," *Jazz: a Quarterly of American Music*, no.2 (1959), 151
J. B. Brooks: "George Russell," *JR*, iii/2 (1960), 38
M. Harrison: "George Russell: 'Jazz Workshop'," *JR*, iii/9 (1960), 28
G. Russell: "Where do we go from here?," *The Jazz Word*, ed. D. Cerulli, B. Korall, and M. Nasatir (New York, 1960) [incl. previously pubd articles]
B. Korall: "Who is George Russell?," *DB*, xxviii/4 (1961), 14
M. Harrison: "George Russell," *Jazz on Record: a Critical Guide to the First 50 Years: 1917–1967*, ed. A. McCarthy and others (London, 1968), 251
G. Crane: *Jazz Elements and Formal Compositional Techniques in Third Stream Music* (diss., Indiana U., 1970) [incl. detailed analysis of *All about Rosie*]
P. Wilson: "George Russell's Constant Quest," *DB*, xxxix/8 (1972), 15
O. Jones: "A New Theory for Jazz," *Black Perspective in Music*, ii (1974), 63
B. Rusch: "George Russell: Interview," *Cadence*, iii/7–8 (1977), 3
D. N. Baker, L. M. Belt, and H. C. Hudson, eds.: *The Black Composer Speaks* (Metuchen, NJ, and London, 1978) [incl. list of works, discography, bibliography]
B. Blumenthal: "George Russell: Stratus Seeker," *DB*, l/10 (1983), 24
M. Harrison: "George Russell: Rational Anthems," *The Wire*, no.3 (1983), 30
F. Davis: *In the Moment: Jazz in the 1980s* (New York, and Oxford, England, 1986) [colln of previously pubd articles], 167
S. Woolley: "George Russell," *JJI*, xxxix/10 (1986), 8 [incl. discography]

JAMES G. ROY, JR./CARMAN MOORE/R

Russell, Johnny [John W.] (*b* Charlotte, NC, 4 June 1909). Tenor saxophonist. He was taught violin from 1918 and later learned tenor saxophone; he played both instruments with Jimmy Campbell in 1926. He moved to New York, where he worked with Harry White, Benny Carter (1933–4), and Willie Bryant (1935–6), among others; he recorded as a tenor saxophonist with Carter and Bryant. He played several solos on the soundtrack of Erich von Stroheim's film *L'alibi* (1936). He toured Europe with Bobby Martin's orchestra until 1938 and then joined Willie Lewis (1939), with whom he made several recordings on tenor saxophone and clarinet (including *Happy Feet*, 1941, ES 4067). After returning to the USA in 1941 he played with Garvin Bushell (1942), various army bands (until 1945), and Cecil Scott (1945). He ceased full-time playing in the late 1940s. (J. Evensmo: *The Tenor Saxophones of Henry Bridges, Robert Carroll, Herschal [sic] Evans, Johnny Russell*, n.p. [Oslo], n.d. [?1976] [discography])

based on *ChiltonW*

Russell, Luis (Carl) (*b* Careening Cay, nr Bocas del Toro, Panama, 6 Aug 1902; *d* New York, 11 Dec 1963). Bandleader, arranger, and pianist. His first significant employment was with King Oliver in Chicago (1925–7). After moving to New York he took over George Howe's band, and several long engagements followed. It was during this period, especially 1929–30, that Russell's most representative recordings were made. Having accompanied Louis Armstrong for several months in 1929, the band provided his backing from 1935 to 1943, although by then it had lost most of its character. Russell then formed another band and worked around New York, without distinction, until 1948, when he abandoned music to become a chauffeur and shopkeeper.

Although an unexceptional pianist, Russell was an important jazz bandleader of the 1920s. He attempted to adapt the New Orleans ensemble style to make his group more integrated, but the band's freshness and vigor continued to derive from its solo improvisations. Some of Henry "Red" Allen's most characteristic early trumpet work is found in recordings with Russell, and Albert Nicholas's clarinet improvisations around the closing ensembles of such pieces as *Panama* resemble Barney Bigard's later work with Duke Ellington's band; other important soloists were J. C. Higginbotham and Charlie Holmes.

SELECTED RECORDINGS

Savoy Shout (1929, OK 8760); The New Call of the Freaks (1929, OK 8734); Saratoga Shout/Song of the Swanee (1930, OK 8780); Muggin' Lightly (1930, OK 8830); Panama/High Tension (1930, OK 8849)

BIBLIOGRAPHY

F. Manskleid: "Luis Russell Revisited," *JM*, iii/2 (1957), 11
A. McCarthy: "Luis Russell," *JM*, vi/6 (1960), 9
G. Hoefer: "Luis Russell," *DB*, xxix/28 (1962), 43
H. Grut: "Luis Russell," *JJ*, xvii/3 (1964), 19
P. Munnery: "Luis Russell Orchestra, 1929–1931," *Jazz Times*, iii (1966), no.6, p.7; no.7, p.7
D. Ives: "Luis Russell 1902–1963," *JJ*, xx/6 (1967), 4
E. Lambert: "Luis Russell," *JJ*, xxii/9 (1969), 6
A. McCarthy: *Big Band Jazz* (New York and London, 1974), 25
H. Lyttelton: "Luis Russell," *The Best of Jazz*, i: *Basin Street to Harlem: Jazz Masters and Masterpieces, 1917–1930* (London, 1978), 185
B. Bigard: *With Louis and the Duke*, ed. B. Martyn (London, 1985)

MAX HARRISON

Russell, Pee Wee [Charles Ellsworth] (*b* St. Louis, 27 March 1906; *d* Alexandria, VA, 15 Feb 1969). Clarinetist. After studying several instruments he took up clarinet and in the early 1920s played in Texas with Jack Teagarden and in St. Louis with Bix Beiderbecke. In 1927 he moved permanently to New York, where he played and recorded first with Red Nichols, and later with a wide variety of important jazz musicians, including Louis Prima (1935–7). From 1937 he played intermittently for three decades with Eddie Condon, frequently in dixieland clubs in New York, and later on tour (1964, 1967). When not with Condon, he continued to work with leading dixieland musicians, though late in life he experimented with new styles, for example appearing with Thelonious Monk at the Newport Jazz Festival in 1963. From the late 1950s he also toured with dixieland groups led by George Wein.

Russell's unique, complex style involved seemingly effortless variation of intentionally unorthodox timbres, growls alternating with hard attacks, and softly articulated notes held with a slow, almost sour, vibrato. He often played lines composed of greatly contrasting rhythmic values (unlike the successions of eighth-notes preferred by contemporary clarinetists) and unusual choices of pitch; by playing imperceptibly behind the beat he often gave a weighty quality to individual notes. His playing encompassed and was conditioned by the

Pee Wee Russell, c1939

popular music of the 1930s, and is heard to best advantage on his highly individual performances of that repertory.

SELECTED RECORDINGS

As leader: Baby won't you please come home?/Dinah (1938, HRS 1000); *Portrait of PeeWee Russell* (1958, Counterpoint 562)

As sideman: R. Nichols: Feelin' no Pain (1927, Vic. 21183); E. Condon: The Eel/Home Cooking (1933, Bruns. 6743); B. Hackett: A Ghost of a Chance (1938, Voc./OK 4565)

BIBLIOGRAPHY

ChiltonW
B. Coss: "Pee Wee Russell: the Gambling Kind," *DB*, xxx/14 (1963), 16
T. Gwaltney: "Pee Wee's Last Days," *DB*, xxxvi/12 (1969), 20
W. Balliett: "Even his Feet Look Sad," *Improvising: Sixteen Jazz Musicians and their Art* (New York, 1977) [colln of previously pubd articles], 81

JAMES DAPOGNY/R

Russell, Ross (*b* Los Angeles, *c*1920). Record store owner who founded the record company Dial in 1946. He also served as Charlie Parker's personal manager (1946–7), and has been active as a lecturer and writer on jazz. He has contributed articles to *Down Beat*, *Jazz hot*, *Orkester journalen*, and the *Jazz Review*, and his books include *Jazz Style in Kansas City and the Southwest* (Berkeley, CA, Los Angeles, and London, 1971) and *Bird Lives: the High Life and Hard Times of Charlie "Yardbird" Parker* (New York, 1973). During the 1960s and 1970s he taught courses on Afro-American music at the University of California and Palomar College. Russell's collection was purchased in January 1981 by the University of Texas, and is held at Austin; see Libraries and archives, §2. (R. G. Reisner: "Ross Russell," *Bird: the Legend of Charlie Parker*, New York, 1962/*R*1975)

Russin, Babe [Irving] (*b* Pittsburgh, 18 June 1911; *d* Los Angeles, 4 Aug 1984). Tenor saxophonist. His first professional engagements were with the California Ramblers (1926); after touring Europe (1928) he traveled to New York, where he worked with Red Nichols and others. In 1930 he played with Ben Pollack, then rejoined Nichols, with whom he remained until 1932. In the mid-1930s he was a staff musician for CBS. After three months with Benny Goodman (late 1937 – early 1938) and a longer period with Tommy Dorsey he led his own band (1940–41), which undertook residencies in New York and Florida. Later he was a member of Jimmy Dorsey's band (1942–4; for illustration *see* JAZZ (i), fig.3), played in an AFRS band during military service (1944–6), then worked sporadically with Goodman from the late 1940s. He also appeared in several films, including *The Glenn Miller Story* (1953) and *The Benny Goodman Story* (1955). The latter years of his career were spent as a studio musician in California; he continued to perform in reunions of Goodman's band. Russin is notable for his warm, full tone, and for having kept pace with the growth and development of jazz; his early style was heavily influenced by Coleman Hawkins and Bud Freeman, but his later work reflected further stylistic innovations. He may be heard to advantage on *You Hit the Spot* (1936, Decca 689), which he recorded with Bunny Berigan's band under the leadership of the singer Bob Howard. Russin's brother Jack was a pianist who sometimes also worked with Nichols; his sister, known as Sunny, also played piano professionally. (*ChiltonW*; *FeatherE*)

Russo, Bill [William Joseph, Jr.] (*b* Chicago, 25 June 1928). Composer and arranger. He attended high school with Lee Konitz and as a teenager studied with Lennie Tristano (1943–7) and played trombone in several jazz bands. From 1947 to 1950 he led a rehearsal orchestra, Experiment in Jazz, and from 1950 to 1954 was associated with Stan Kenton's orchestra as a trombonist, composer, and arranger. He also studied composition privately in Chicago (1953–7); some of his arrangements were later published in *Down Beat* (intermittently, 1957–9). Russo toured Europe as the leader of a quintet in 1955. In 1958 he won a grant from the Koussevitzky Foundation and moved to New York, where he formed and conducted the Russo Orchestra, a large jazz ensemble with cellos, and taught at the Lenox (Massachusetts) School of Jazz (1957–60) and the Manhattan School of Music (1959–61). After traveling to Rome in 1961 he lived in London and conducted the London Jazz Orchestra (1962–5) and worked for the BBC. Russo returned to Chicago in 1965 and directed the Center for New Music at Columbia College (1965–75). He was composer-in-residence for the city and county of San Francisco in 1975–6, then took up work in film studios. In 1979 he resumed teaching at Columbia College.

Russo composed much of Kenton's most experimental material in the 1950s and distinguished himself as a composer and arranger early in his career. His third-stream music, much of which was written in the late 1950s for the Russo Orchestra, is informed by jazz-influenced rhythms; his writing shows a sure sense of form and transition and also exploits the contrasts between disparate styles. He is the author of two texts on arranging, *Composing for the Jazz Orchestra* (Chicago and London, 1961) and *Jazz Composition and Orchestration* (Chicago and London, 1968, rev. 2/1975).

SELECTED RECORDINGS

The World of Alcina (1955, Atl. 1241); *The Seven Deadly Sins* (1960, Roul. 52063)

RECORDED COMPOSITIONS

(selective list; all recorded by S. Kenton)

Hall of Brass (1950, Cap. 28010); Bill's Blues (1952, Cap. EOX569)[EP]; on *New Concepts of Artistry in Rhythm* (1952, Cap. H383), Frank Speaking, Portrait of a Count, Twenty-three degrees north, eighty-two degrees west

SELECTED ARRANGEMENTS

(recorded by S. Kenton)

Portraits on Standards (1953–4, Cap. H462); Don't Worry 'bout me (1955), first issued on *Some Women I've Known* (1944–63, CW 1029)

BIBLIOGRAPHY

L. Feather: "Russo: Young Man with a Mind," *MM*, xxxi (18 June 1955), 2

L. Tomkins: "In my Opinion: Bill Russo," *Crescendo*, i/3 (1962), 26

M. Sparke, ed.: *The Great Kenton Arrangers* (Whittier, CA, 1968) [incl. discography]

J. D. Dilts: "William Russo: Iconoclast in Orbit," *DB*, xxxvi/24 (1969), 15

W. F. Lee: *Stan Kenton: Artistry in Rhythm* (Los Angeles, 1980) [incl. discography]

J. Balleras: "William Russo," *DB*, xlix/5 (1982), 26

GENEVIEVE VAUGHN/R

Russo, Sonny [Santo] (*b* New York, 20 March 1929). Trombonist. He was principally a sideman and soloist in big bands. He first worked with Buddy Morrow (1947), Lee Castle (1948), and Sam Donahue (1949), and played and recorded with Artie Shaw (1949–50). He was a member of Buddy Rich's orchestra (1951–2) and played and recorded with the clarinetist Jerry Wald (1951–2), the Sauter–Finegan Orchestra (1953–5), and Tommy Dorsey (1955–6); he also took part in sessions with Neal Hefti (1954–5), John LaPorta (1955), and the drummer Mickey Sheen (*Have Swing Will Travel*, 1955, Herald 0105). In 1956 he began to work in Broadway shows, but he continued to record, with Sauter and Finegan (1956–*c*1961), Louie Bellson and Dinah Washington (both 1957), Toots Thielemans and Rex Stewart (both 1958), Lionel Hampton (1960), Bobby Hackett (1964), Dorothy Ashby and Benny Goodman (both 1965), and Grover Washington, Jr. (1973), and with such ensembles as Trombone Scene (1956), Urbie Green and 21 Trombones (1968), and All Star Trombone Spectacular (1977). (*FeatherE*)

Rust, Brian (Arthur Lovell) (*b* London, 19 March 1922). English discographer. He began collecting records at the age of five and from 1945 to 1960 worked in the gramophone library at the BBC, where he supervised the selection of recordings for broadcast. At the same time he wrote reviews of recordings for *The Gramophone* (1948–70) and from 1960 worked as a freelance writer of articles, liner notes, and discographies, all on early jazz; he was the host from 1973 to 1984 of the program "Mardi Gras" for Capital Radio in London. His *Jazz Records* (1961) is the definitive discography of early jazz.

WRITINGS

(selective list)

with W. C. Allen: *King Joe Oliver* (Belleville, NJ, 1955) [completely rev. version by L. Wright (Chigwell, England, 1987)]

with R. Harris: *Recorded Jazz: a Critical Guide* (Harmondsworth, England, 1958) [listeners' guide]

Jazz Records, i: *1897–1931* (Hatch End, nr London, 1961, 2/1962 with index by R. Grandorge); ii: *1932–1942* (Hatch End, 1965); i, ii, as *Jazz Records, A-Z, 1897–1942* (London, rev. [3]/1969, rev. and enlarged 4/1978, rev. 5/n.d. [1983]) [discography]

The Victor Master Book, ii: *1925–1936* (Stanhope, NJ, 1970) [discography; projected vol.i: 1903–25, and vol.iii: 1936–42, not pubd]

The Dance Bands (London, 1972)

with A. G. Debus: *The Complete Entertainment Discography, from the mid-1890s to 1942* (New Rochelle, NY, 1973)

The American Dance Band Discography, 1917–1942 (New Rochelle, NY, 1975)

The H.M.V. Studio House Bands, 1912–1939 (Chigwell, England, 1976)

The American Record Label Book (New Rochelle, NY, 1978)

Discography of Historical Records on Cylinders and 78s (Westport, CT, and London, 1979)

Brian Rust's Guide to Discography (Westport, CT, and London, 1980)

BIBLIOGRAPHY

M. Wyler: "Collector's Profiles, 4: Brian Rust," *JM*, ii/8 (1956), 29

J. Godbolt: "Brian Rust: King of the Zulus," *Jazz Circle News*, no.7 (1978), 18

ROBERT GANNON

Ruther, Wyatt (Robert) [Bull] (*b* Pittsburgh, 5 Feb 1923). Double bass player. He played trombone in high school, then took up the double bass; he studied both instruments at the San Francisco Conservatory of Music (1949) and the Pittsburgh Musical Institute (1950). Based in New York in the early 1950s he played and recorded with Dave Brubeck (1951–2) and intermittently with Erroll Garner (1951–5), toured with the singer Lena Horne (1953), and recorded with Toshiko Akiyoshi (1956). He then moved to Canada where he studied at the Royal Conservatory of Music, Toronto (1956), played with the Canadian Jazz Quartet (1956–7) and Peter Appleyard (1957), and taught in Hull, Ottawa, and Toronto (1956–7). During this period he returned to New York to record with Ray Bryant and a quintet led by Zoot Sims and Bob Brookmeyer (both 1956); he also recorded with Chico Hamilton in Los Angeles (1958), played with Gerry Mulligan (1962), and toured and recorded with George Shearing (1959), Buddy Rich (1960–61), and Count Basie (1964–5). From 1969 to 1980 Ruther worked as a freelance musician in and around Vancouver. In the mid-1970s he joined a trio led by Fraser MacPherson, with which he toured Canada and the Soviet Union and recorded (to 1979). In 1984 he returned to the San Francisco Bay area where he led his own trio and taught privately. Ruther is known for his firm tone and ebullient sense of swing; his solo on *Bull in a China Shop* (1955) displays a proficient technique and the influence of Jimmy Blanton on his phrasing and melodic ideas.

For illustrations *see* DOLPHY, ERIC, and GARNER, ERROLL.

SELECTED RECORDINGS

As leader with M. Hinton and W. Marshall: *Basses Loaded* (1955, RCA LPM1107), incl. Bull in a China Shop, Begin the Beguine, Crazy she Calls me, I poured my Heart into a Song

As sideman: D. Brubeck: *Modern Complex Dialogues* (1951, Alto 711); E. Garner: *Caravan* (1953, Col. CL535); *Contrasts* (1954, EmA 36001); C. Hamilton: *Gongs East* (1958, WB 1271); F. MacPherson: *Live at the Planetarium* (1975, Conc. 92)

BIBLIOGRAPHY

Feather '60s

J. M. Doran: *Erroll Garner: the Most Happy Piano* (Metuchen, NJ, 1985), 75

JOHN CURRY

Rutherford, Paul (William) (*b* London, 29 Feb 1940). English trombonist. After service in the RAF (1958–63), he studied trombone, piano, and composition at the Guildhall School of Music and Drama, London (1964–8). During this time he played with Neil Ardley's New Jazz Orchestra (1964–6) and with John Stevens and Trevor Watts ran the Little Theatre Club, London, presenting freely improvised music (1965–8). He was a founding member of the Spontaneous Music Ensemble in 1965, of Watts's Amalgam in 1967 and of the London Jazz Composers Orchestra in 1970. Also in 1970 he formed, with Barry Guy and Derek Bailey, the group Iskra 1903, an improvising ensemble of electric and electronic instruments; this was re-formed in 1980 with Guy and the violinist Phil Wachsmann. Rutherford also played with Mike Westbrook's bands (1967–78) and the Globe Unity Orchestra (1973–81) and in groups led by Tony Oxley (1969–74), Peter Kowald (1972–6), Stevens (1982–4), and Watts (1984–5). In 1983 he formed a trio with the double bass player Paul Rogers and the drummer Nigel Morris. An accomplished solo improviser, Rutherford has worked in a wide variety of contexts, his often lyrical and mellifluous free playing sometimes aided by electronics; he has created new sonorities on the trombone by speaking into the instrument. In some of his work he has also played euphonium, notably in duos with Paul Lovens (1976–7), on an unaccompanied solo album (1978), and with Stevens (1984).

SELECTED RECORDINGS

As unaccompanied soloist: *The Gentle Harm of the Bourgeoisie* (1974, Emanem 3305); *Old Moers Almanac* (1976, Ring 01014); *Neuph* (1978, Sweet Folk & Country 092)

Duos with P. Lovens: *And When I Say Slowly . . .* (1976–7, Po Torch 3)

As leader: *Iskra 1903* (1970–72, Incus 3–4)

As sideman: Globe Unity Orchestra: *Live in Wuppertal* (1973, FMP 0160); Improvisors' Symposium: *Pisa 1980* (1980, Incus 37); J. Stevens: *Folkus: the Life of Riley* (1984, Affinity 130)

BIBLIOGRAPHY

R. Brown: "Paul Rutherford," *JJ*, xxvi/3 (1973), 4 [interview]

R. Cotterrell, ed.: *Jazz Now: the Jazz Centre Society Guide* (London, 1976)

P. Carles: "Paul Rutherford," *Jm*, no.273 (1979), 30 [incl. discography]

D. Ilic: "Paul Rutherford," *The Wire*, no.3 (1980), 6

B. Noglik: "Paul Rutherford," *Jazzwerkstatt international* (Berlin, 1981), 346 [incl. interview, discography]

D. Bailey: "Soundcheck: Derek Bailey Discusses the Improvising of Paul Rutherford," *The Wire*, no.36 (1987), 43

SIMON ADAMS

Rutherford, Rudy [Elman] (*b* Detroit, 1912). Baritone and alto saxophonist and clarinetist. He played baritone saxophone in Lionel Hampton's big band (for a brief period in 1943), then in Count Basie's orchestra, which he joined as Jack Washington's replacement; when Washington rejoined the orchestra in 1946 Rutherford changed to alto saxophone. In the spring of 1947 he left Basie's group to join that of Teddy Buckner, and in 1951 he made recordings as a member of Basie's octet; his performances on these recordings are usually attributed, mistakenly, to Serge Chaloff. Later he performed and recorded with Wilbur De Paris (1959), the rock-and-roll singer and guitarist Chuck Berry (in the film *Jazz on a Summer's Day*, made at the Newport Jazz Festival in 1958), Buddy Tate (1960, 1964), and Earl Hines (1973–6). Although best known for his work as a member of saxophone sections, he took most of his solos on the clarinet.

SELECTED RECORDINGS

(recorded for V-disc unless otherwise indicated)

As sideman: C. Basie: Kansas City Stride (1944, 258B); Gee, baby, ain't I good to you? (1944, 289B); Playhouse no.2 Stomp (1945, 493A); High Tide (1945, 483B); on W. De Paris: *Over and Over Again* (1959–60, Atl. 1552), Would you Care (1959); E. Hines: *Swingin' Away* (1973, Black Lion 30190)

CHRIS SHERIDAN

Ryan's. Nightclub in New York, properly known as Jimmy Ryan's; *see* NIGHTCLUBS AND OTHER VENUES.

Rypdal, Terje (*b* Oslo, 23 Aug 1947). Norwegian electric guitarist and composer. He studied classical piano and taught himself to play guitar. At Oslo University he studied composition with Finn Mortensen and the Lydian chromatic concept of tonal organization with its originator, George Russell, in whose sextet and big band he also played. He worked with Jan Garbarek from the late 1960s and first achieved recognition outside Norway at the New Jazz Meeting, Baden-Baden, Germany (1969), at which he also presented some of his own compositions. In 1972 he formed the group Odyssey, with which he visited London and the USA, recorded, and performed (with Palle Mikkelborg as a guest soloist) at the Festspill in Bergen, Norway, in 1978. From 1984 he led a trio that included the drummer Audun Kleive and the bass player Bjørn Kjellemyr; with this group he appeared at festivals in Molde, Norway (1985), and Eastern Europe and toured the Continent and

England. In 1986 he performed in a duo with Mikkelborg in Molde.

Rypdal is widely regarded as one of the most important electric guitarists in European jazz; his style incorporates elements of rock and modern concert music, and such novel sonorities as note clusters produced by playing the electric guitar with a violin bow. He is also one of Norway's most important young composers; his works, which owe something to the music of the composer Krzysztof Penderecki, include *Eternal Circulation* for symphony orchestra and jazz ensemble (1972), *Somehow it's Making me Smile Inside* for guitar (1975), *Imagi* for dancers and big band (1984), and orchestral and chamber music. He received the Buddy Award from the Norwegian Jazz Federation in 1985.

SELECTED RECORDINGS

(all recorded for ECM)

As unaccompanied soloist: *After the Rain* (1976, 1083)

As leader: *What Comes After* (1973, 1031); *Whenever I seem to be Far Away* (1974, 1045); *Odyssey* (1975, 1067–8); *Waves* (1977, 1110); *Descendre* (1979, 1144); with J. DeJohnette and M. Vitous: *To be Continued* (1981, 1192); *Chaser* (1985, 1303)

BIBLIOGRAPHY

R. Williams: "Song of Norway," *MM* (8 April 1972), 20

R. Hultin: "Terje Rypdal: a Great Musical Personality," *JF* [intl edn], no.27 (1974), 48

S. Lake: "Song of Norway," *MM*, lii (12 Feb 1977), 48

J. Sievert: "Terje Rypdal: Norwegian Composer/Guitarist," *GP*, xi/5 (1977), 30 [incl. discography]

J. Diliberto: "Profile: Terje Rypdal," *DB*, xlvii/11 (1980), 52

RANDI HULTIN

S

Saarsalu, Lembit (*b* Roosna-Alliku, nr Paide, Estonian SSR, 8 July 1948). Estonian saxophonist and composer. He made his début at the jazz festival in Tallinn, Estonian SSR, in 1965 and the same year began an association with the Estonian Philharmonic Society, playing first in its dance orchestra and later in its groups Viru and Laine. After studying clarinet and brass-band conducting at the Tallinn Music School (graduated 1975) he worked as a leader from 1978 and in 1984 formed a duo with the pianist Leonid Vintskevich. Saarsalu has performed in East Africa, the Near East, Cuba, Hungary (where he appeared at festivals in Nagykanizsa, 1980, and Debrecen, 1981), Bulgaria, and Belgium; in 1986 he played in Berlin and The Hague and worked with the jazz-rock group Radar at the Bratislava Jazz Days. A good example of his playing is the album *Džässkvartett "Tallinn"* (1983, Mel. C6019783007); his compositions, which include *2 × labajalg* (2 × rustic waltz) and *Ringtants* (Round dance), incorporate elements of Estonian folk music. He is the subject of *Old Melody*, a film made for television in 1981.

WALTER OJAKÄÄR

Saba. Record label. It was owned by the company of the same name that manufactured radio receivers and tape recorders in Villingen–Schwenningen, Germany. The label was established by Hans Georg Brunner-Schwer (grandson of the company's founder); its initial purpose was to provide recordings for use on a car tape player (the Sabamobil) first marketed in 1963. An important catalogue of jazz quickly developed; by 1967 it contained 35 albums, including fine recordings by Oscar Peterson, the Clarke–Boland Big Band, and the group Violin Summit. During that year Saba also acquired the distribution rights to 32 albums from Prestige. But in 1968 the parent company was taken over by an American firm that did not wish to continue the recording operation. Brunner-Schwer therefore retained the rights to the catalogue (which by this time also included, among other items, an important album by the quintet led by Ben Webster and Don Byas) and founded a new record company, MPS. ("The MPS Decade 1968–1978," *JJI*, xxxi/5 (1978), suppl.)

Sachs, Aaron (*b* New York, 4 July 1923). Tenor saxophonist and clarinetist. He first played clarinet and alto saxophone, but had changed to tenor saxophone by the end of the 1940s. He worked with Babe Russin (1941) and the pianist Van Alexander (1942–3), and performed and recorded with Red Norvo (intermittently, 1941–5) and Benny Goodman (1945). During the 1940s Sachs also made recordings with Eddie Heywood (including *How High the Moon/Sarcastic Lady*, Sig. 40002), Flip Phillips, and Sarah Vaughan (all 1944), Horace Henderson (1945), and Buddy Rich and Charlie Ventura (both 1946). In 1947 he recorded as the leader of a bop quintet that included Terry Gibbs and Gene DiNovi. Later he toured and recorded with Earl Hines (1952–3), recorded as a leader (1954, 1956) and with Gene Krupa (1956), and was active as a freelance, performing at clubs in New York. He worked sporadically with the percussionist Tito Rodriquez for several years, then toured and recorded with Louie Bellson (1959). In the early and mid-1950s he was married to Helen Merrill.

BIBLIOGRAPHY

FeatherE
J. Burns: "The Forgotten Boppers," *J&B*, ii/3 (1972), 4

Sackville. Record company and label. The company was established in Toronto in 1968 by John Norris and Bill Smith, respectively the publisher and editor of the magazine *Coda.* The label has been used to issue material in various styles, most of it newly recorded in Canada. The catalogue contains over 50 albums, including the work of Frank Rosolino, Buddy Tate, Doc Cheatham, Archie Shepp, and Humphrey Lyttelton. Sackville has been particularly active recording pianists, notably Ralph Sutton, Sir Charles Thompson, Sammy Price, Jay McShann, Dollar Brand, Don Pullen, Junior Mance, Art Hodes, Willie "the Lion" Smith, and Don Ewell. A few important reissues have also been made, among them an LP recorded in 1957 by Bill Holman's big band.

MARK GARDNER

Sacramento Dixieland Jubilee. Festival held annually from 1974 in Sacramento, California. It was first organized by Bill Borcher, who continued as its executive director into the 1980s. The festival is sponsored by the Sacramento Traditional Jazz Society and has also received funds from city, county, and state governments. It takes place over four days in September at various venues in Sacramento; bands that take part are chosen through taped auditions. Among the groups that have performed at the festival are the Sveriges Jazz Band from Stockholm and the Jazz Band Ball Orchestra from Kraków, Poland; in 1987 the group Leningrad Dixieland made its first visit to the USA to take part. The jubilee is the largest traditional-jazz festival in the world. In 1985 101 bands from 16 countries performed at 51 venues before a combined audience of 250,000. (B. Knowles: "Jazz on the Coast: Sacto: the Chief Speaks," *MR*, xii/9 (1985), 12)

PAUL R. LAIRD

Sadi, Fats [Lallemand, Sadi "Fats"; Lallemand, Sadi Pol] (*b* Andenne, Belgium, 23 Oct 1927). Belgian vibraphonist. He formed Sadi's Hot Five in Namur (1945), worked with the reed player Raoul Faisant and René Thomas (in Brussels) and with Faisant and Gus Deloof (in Liège), and appeared at the Cotton Club in Brussels. After working with the Bob Shots (recording in Paris, 1949) and in Germany with Vicky Thunus he lived from 1950 to 1961 in Paris, where he worked regularly with Bobby Jaspar; he also sang as an original member of the Blue Stars and recorded with Django Reinhardt (1953) and Don Byas (1955). After his return to Belgium he belonged to the orchestra of the Belgische Radio en Televisie/Radiodiffusion-télévision Belge, led a quartet, and performed throughout Belgium and the Netherlands, often as a member of the Clarke–Boland Big Band. He also toured the USA and South America with the singer Caterina Valente. (*FeatherE*; *Feather–Gitler '70s*; *ReclamsJ*)

ROBERT PERNET

Sadowski, Krzysztof (*b* Warsaw, 15 Dec 1936). Polish pianist and organist. He studied piano for eleven years while at school and after graduating from the Warsaw Institute of Technology took up a career in jazz (1957). In the early 1960s he played and recorded with Zbigniew Namysłowski's Jazz Rockers and Jan Wróblewski's Jazz Outsiders (both 1961–2), and worked with Andrzej Kurylewicz and the Swingtet led by the alto saxophonist Jerzy Matuszkiewicz. He achieved considerable success with his own group Bossa Nova Combo (from 1963), with which he toured the USSR (1965) and Scandinavia (1967). In 1967, influenced by Jimmy Smith, he took up the Hammond organ and formed a hard-bop ensemble, the Organ Group. He also toured and recorded with his wife, the pop singer and flutist Liliana Urbańska. Sadowski has composed many popular hits in Poland, as well as music for films, theater, radio, and television, and two suites, *On the Cosmodrome* (recorded on *Na Kosmodromie*, 1972, Muza 7048) and *Our Common World*.

BIBLIOGRAPHY

J. Byrczek: "Eurojazz Personalities: Poland," *JF* [intl edn], no.18 (1972), 87
"Krzysztof Sadowski: Hammond Man," *JF* [intl edn], no.32 (1974), 19

WOLFRAM KNAUER

Safranski, Eddie [Edward] (*b* Pittsburgh, 25 Dec 1918; *d* Los Angeles, 10 Jan 1974). Double bass player. He studied violin as a boy, then played double bass in high school. In 1941 he joined Hal McIntyre, with whom he played until 1945 and for whom he also wrote a number of arrangements; he then worked with Miff Mole (1945), Stan Kenton (1945–8), and Charlie Barnet (1948–9). While he was with Kenton he became better known and he moved to New York to seek work in radio and television; he was a staff musician at NBC and also played with Benny Goodman (1951–2). He continued to undertake studio work until the late 1960s, when he became a representative for a double bass manufacturer, running workshops and masterclasses; from that time he also played traditional and modern jazz with various groups in Los Angeles. Safranski was essentially a swing musician. As a member of a rhythm section he provided a steady, dependable beat and played with a forthright clarity and precision; his solos for Kenton were based on solid rhythms and a robust sense of the swing style.

SELECTED RECORDINGS

As leader: Spellbound/Lem me Go (1946, Savoy 601); Sa-frantic/Bass Mood (1947, Atl. 851)
As sideman with S. Kenton: Painted Rhythm (1945, Cap. 250); Safranski (Artistry in Bass) (1946, Cap. 288); Concerto to End all Concertos (1946, Cap. 382); Lover (1947, Cap. 904)
As sideman with others: D. Byas: Little White Lies/You Came Along (1945, Jamboree 902); B. Goodman: East of the Sun (1952, Col. EPB1845) [EP]; Johnny Smith: Where or When (1952, Roost 558)

BIBLIOGRAPHY

FeatherE
Obituary, *IM*, lxxii/11 (1974), 14
W. M. Lee: *Stan Kenton: Artistry in Rhythm* (Los Angeles, 1980) [incl. discography]

LEROY OSTRANSKY

St. Clair, Cyrus (*b* Cambridge, MD, 1890; *d* New York, 1955). Sousaphone player. He began playing cornet in a local band, but later changed to sousaphone. Around 1925 he moved to New York, where he worked with Wilbur De Paris and Charlie Johnson, with whom he made a number of recordings (including *The Boy in the Boat*, 1928, Vic. 21712). He recorded with Clarence Williams's orchestra from 1926 to 1929, during which time the band accompanied several singers, among them Bessie Smith (1929). He played with Cozy Cole's Hot Cinders in 1930 and in the mid-1930s he again made recordings with Williams. He ceased working for some time, but in 1947 took part in Rudi Blesh's radio series "This is Jazz" (also playing double bass) and recorded with Tony Parenti's Ragtimers.

based on *ChiltonW*

St. Cyr, Johnny [John Alexander] (*b* New Orleans, 17 April 1890; *d* Los Angeles, 17 June 1966). Guitarist and banjoist. He taught himself to play on a homemade guitar, and from 1905 to 1908 led his own trio. After playing in bands led by Manuel Gabriel and A. J. Piron (1908–9) he worked with the Superior, Olympia, and Tuxedo bands (1910–14) and the Kid Ory–King Oliver band (1915–17). For most of his work after this time St. Cyr played on a six-string "guitar banjo" that he had constructed himself from a banjo head and a guitar neck and fingerboard; in his later years, however, he returned to playing a regular guitar, and in the 1940s also used an electric guitar. He joined Fate Marable's riverboat band in 1918 and in 1923 went to Chicago, where he recorded with Oliver, Louis Armstrong (1925–7) and Jelly Roll Morton (1926). The unusual sound St. Cyr obtained from his hybrid instrument may be heard on Armstrong's *Gut Bucket Blues*, where he plays a low single-string solo with a few accompanying chords. He was a member of Doc Cook's Dreamland Orchestra from 1924 to 1929. The following year he returned to New Orleans and worked principally as a plasterer, but continued to play with Paul Barbarin, Alphonse Picou, and others. He moved to Los Angeles in 1955 and led his own band, the Young Men from New Orleans, at Disneyland from 1961 until his death.

In ensemble work St. Cyr played in the relaxed, four-beat chordal manner associated with New Orleans jazz, though he used a variety of styles in his solo work, sometimes even playing high tremolos.

Oral history material in *LNT*.

See also BANJO; for illustrations *see* ARMSTRONG, LOUIS, fig.1, and NIGHTCLUBS AND OTHER VENUES, fig.3.

SELECTED RECORDINGS

As leader: *J. St. Cyr and his Hot Five* (1954, Slnd 212)
As sideman: L. Armstrong: Yes, I'm in the barrel/Gut Bucket Blues (1925, OK 8261); Oriental Strut/You're next (1926, OK 8299); D. Cook: Messin'

Around (1926, OK 8390); J. R. Morton: Black Bottom Stomp/The Chant (1926, Vic. 20221); Smoke House Blues/Steamboat Stomp (1926, Vic. 20296); L. Armstrong: Jazz Lips/Skid-dat-de-dat (1926, OK 8436); Wildman Blues/Gully Low Blues (1927, OK 8474)

BIBLIOGRAPHY

ChiltonW
J. St. Cyr: "Jazz as I Remember it," *JJ*, xix (1966), no.9, p.6; no.10, p.22; no.11, p.6; xx (1967), no.1, p.14
Obituary, *SL*, xvii (1966), Sept–Oct, 107
B. Rust: "Johnny St. Cyr," *Sv*, no.51 (1974), 100

BILL RUSSELL

Saints and Sinners. Sextet formed in 1960 by Red Richards and Vic Dickenson. It was initially a pickup band, but rapidly developed into a first-class mainstream dixieland group with polished routines and an extensive repertory unparalleled during the time for its quality and durability. The Saints and Sinners received regular bookings in Cleveland, Columbus (Ohio), Pittsburgh, and Toronto. Before the group disbanded in 1970 it also made two highly acclaimed tours of Europe (1968, 1969), recording the album *Saints and Sinners in Europe* (Saba 15174) during its first trip. Among the group's sidemen were Herman Autrey, Buster Bailey, Rudy Powell, Buddy Tate, Truck Parham, Barrett Deems, and the drummer George Foster. (S. Dance: "The Saints and Sinners Go Marching on," *DB*, xxxv/12 (1968), 24)

BOB WEIR

Sakata, Akira (*b* Hiroshima, Japan, 21 Feb 1945). Japanese alto saxophonist. He played clarinet in a high-school brass band and alto saxophone in a college band. After moving to Tokyo in 1969 he performed in several clubs and played free jazz in Japan and Europe as a member of Yosuke Yamashita's trio from 1972 to 1979. With his own group he toured Germany and France and appeared at the Newport Jazz Festival in New York in 1979. Sakata's performances display considerable virtuosity and an engaging sense of humor.

SELECTED RECORDINGS

Counter Clockwise Trip (1975, Frasco 7001); *Dekin* (1977, Frasco 7023); *4 o' Clock* (1981, Better Days YF7026); *Dance* (1981, Enja 4002); *Da-da-da* (1985, VariBori BM32–2002)

YOZO IWANAMI

Salle Pleyel. Concert hall in Paris; *see* NIGHTCLUBS AND OTHER VENUES.

Salmi, Klaus (*b* Helsinki, 3 Dec 1908). Finnish trombonist and bandleader. He played with Fred Pell's Novelty Buddians (1928–9), and in 1930 formed his own group, the Ramblers, which played English and American arrangements of dance tunes; the Finnish-American alto saxophonist Wilfred "Tommy" Tuomikoski, who is regarded as having introduced jazz improvisation in Finland in 1926, played with the group in the early 1930s. The Ramblers made a large number of recordings, but only two, *Muistan sua, Elaine* (1931, Homocord 23141) and *You can't stop me from dreaming* (1938, Col. DY172), display the band's talent for jazz. After World War II Salmi worked principally as a record producer.

BIBLIOGRAPHY

O. Häme: *Rytmin voittokulku* [The triumph of rhythm] (Helsinki, 1949), 148
P. Jalkanen: *Ravintola: ja tanssiorkesterilaitoksen murros Helsingissä 1920-luvulla* [Changes in the dance orchestra in Helsinki in the 1920s] (diss., U. of Helsinki, 1975), 118

PEKKA GRONOW

Salnave, Bertin (Depestre) (*b* Port-au-Prince, Haiti, 5 Sept 1892; *d* ? Port-au-Prince, 1970s). Haitian flutist and saxophonist. He taught himself flute as a child and in 1913 he moved to France, where he studied classical music in Paris and Montpellier. He first worked professionally with a tango band in Paris in 1918, then the following year joined Will Marion Cook's Southern Syncopated Orchestra in London. After taking up the saxophone (1920), he performed in Scandinavia with the pianist George Clapham (1921), in Belgium and Austria with Arthur Briggs, and in Spain with Crickett Smith (1925). He formed his own band in the late 1920s and made recordings as a sideman and leader (1931, including *Brown Love,* Ultraphone SU5002). He played with Benny Peyton in France in 1937–8 and toured Switzerland and Romania with Leon Abbey until 1939, when he returned to Haiti and ceased full-time performing. (B. Demeusy: "The Bertin Depestre Salnave Musical Story," *Sv*, no.78 (1978), 207)

RAINER E. LOTZ

Saluzzi, Dino [Timoteo] (*b* Campo Santo, Argentina, 20 May 1935). Argentine bandoneon player. After moving in 1952 to Buenos Aires he belonged to tango orchestras in which he played the bandoneon, a type of button accordion or concertina often used in South America. He studied composition with Jacobo Ficher, belonged again to tango orchestras and to folk groups, and from 1970 worked with such musicians as Gato Barbieri in a style of jazz that incorporated elements of Argentine folk music. In 1979 he formed a quartet, with which he toured Europe in 1983; the same year he performed with George Gruntz at the Jazzfest Berlin, and made recordings as an unaccompanied soloist and with Gruntz. In Argentina in 1984 he recorded as a leader two albums bearing the title *Vivencias* (RCA TLP 50162, 50361); the following year he recorded in Europe with Palle Mikkelborg, Charlie Haden, and Pierre Favre. In 1986 he worked in a duo with Haden in Los Angeles and toured Europe with Mikkelborg, Enrico Rava, and Eddie Gomez.

LAUREANO FERNÁNDEZ, OMAR GARCÍA BRUNELLI

Salvador, Sal (*b* Monson, MA, 21 Nov 1925). Guitarist. He became interested in jazz when, at the age of 15, he heard recordings by Charlie Christian. From 1945 he played in and around Springfield, Massachusetts; after moving to New York in 1949 he played with Terry Gibbs and Mundell Lowe. In summer 1952 he joined Stan Kenton's orchestra, with which he remained through 1953. From December of that year he worked as a freelance and led bop groups that included Eddie Costa and Phil Woods; he performed in the film *Jazz on a Summer's Day* (1958) and led a big band (1958–63). In the 1970s he played in a guitar duo with Allen Hanlon. He resumed recording as a leader in 1978 and re-formed his big band in the 1980s. He was named head of the guitar department at the University of Bridgeport. Salvador has written several guitar methods, including *Sal Salvador's Complete Chord Method for Guitar* (New York, n.d. [?1956]) and *Sal Salvador's Single String Studies for Guitar* (New York, n.d. [?1961]).

SELECTED RECORDINGS

As leader: *Starfingers* (1978, BH 7002); *Juicy Lucy* (1978, BH 7009)
As sideman with S. Kenton: *New Concepts of Artistry in Rhythm* (1952, Cap. H383), incl. Invention for Guitar and Trumpet

BIBLIOGRAPHY

FeatherE
R. Alberto: "Sal Salvador: a Jazz Great for Thirty Years," *GP*, viii/7 (1974), 14

R. D. Kinkle: *The Complete Encyclopedia of Popular Music and Jazz, 1900–1950* (New Rochelle, NY, and Westport, CT, 1974)
W. F. Lee: *Stan Kenton: Artistry in Rhythm* (Los Angeles, 1980) [incl. discography]

WILLIAM F. LEE III

Samba. A dance of Brazilian and African origin. The word is also used by extension for the accompanying music, and for any music in that style, which is in duple meter, lively in tempo, and characterized by many interlocking, syncopated lines in the melody and accompaniment (ex.1). The samba first became known in the USA in the 1930s and 1940s when Vincent Youmans's *Carioca* (1933), Ary Barroso's *Brazil* (1939), and Zequinha Abreu's *Tico tico* (1943) became hits; the dance itself was introduced to the USA in 1939 at the New York World's Fair, and was popularized by the films of the singer and dancer Carmen Miranda in the next two decades. However, the idiom was not adopted on a large scale by American jazz musicians until the 1950s, when growing interest in it was reflected by such recordings as Charlie Parker's *Tico tico* (1951, Mer./Clef 11091), Kenton's *Baia* (1953, Cap. 2511), Laurindo Almeida's album *The Laurindo Almeida Quartet, Featuring Bud Shank* (1954, PJ 7, 13), and Oscar Peterson's *Carioca*, from his LP *Warren and Youmans* (1959, Verve 62059). In some cases the conventional jazz rhythm section was augmented by a percussionist playing Brazilian instruments; otherwise the guitarist, drummer, and double bass player provided the rhythmic impetus (ex.2).

Ex.1 From *Cetulio Marinho: Caboclo do matto* (1940s, Col. 36504); transcr. T. Owens

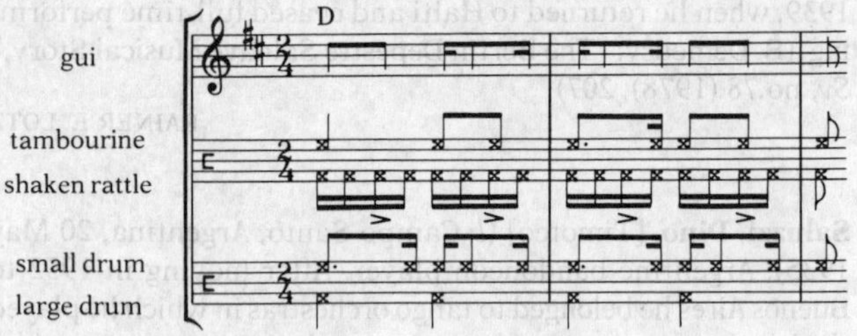

Ex.2 From *Carioca Hills*, on L.A. Four: *The L.A. Four Scores!* (1975, Conc. 8); transcr. T. Owens

In the late 1950s Brazilian musicians began to play in a style known as Bossa nova, which was slower and more sedate than the music customarily used to accompany the samba, employing longer themes and more elaborate, jazz-influenced harmonies. In the USA the brief craze for this style, in part instigated by the album *Jazz Samba* (1962, Verve 68432) by Stan Getz and Charlie Byrd, prompted many bop musicians to incorporate Brazilian rhythms and melodies into their music. It also encouraged many Brazilians to travel to the USA to perform and record. Although the influence of samba and bossa nova became less marked from the late 1960s the idioms have remained sources of inspiration for jazz musicians. (*See also* Latin jazz.)

BIBLIOGRAPHY

G. Duran: *Recordings of Latin American Songs and Dances: an Annotated Selected List of Popular and Folk Music* (Washington, 1942, rev. and enlarged ed. G. Chase 2/1950), 29 [incl. discography]
O. Alvarenga: *Música popular brasileña* (Buenos Aires, 1947)
C. Perry: "The Samba," *IM*, li/12 (1959), 24
J. Tynan: "The Real Story of the Bossa Nova," *DB*, xxix/28 (1962), 21
J. S. Roberts: *Black Music of Two Worlds* (New York, Washington, and London, 1972)
G. Behague: "Bossa and Bossas: Recent Changes in Brazilian Urban Popular Music," *Ethnomusicology*, xvii (1973), 209
J. S. Roberts: *The Latin Tinge: the Impact of Latin American Music on the United States* (New York, and Oxford, England, 1979)
N. Goldberg: "South of the Border: the Samba," *MD*, vii/12 (1983), 106

THOMAS OWENS

Sample, Joe [Joseph Leslie] (*b* Houston, 1 Feb 1939). Pianist. In his early teens he was a founding member of the group that eventually became known as the Crusaders, and his career remained associated with that of the band for more than 30 years. He studied at Texas Southern University and in 1958 moved to Los Angeles. Although at first he played only piano, on the Crusaders' early soul-jazz albums (from 1961 the Jazz Crusaders), he recorded on organ, then experimented with the Wurlitzer electric piano (*c*1962–1963), and the Fender–Rhodes electric piano, on which he developed a hard, percussive, bluesy approach. From the late 1960s Sample also worked independently of the Crusaders: he accompanied pop artists such as Diana Ross and the Jackson Five, played in the bop quintet led by Harold Land and Bobby Hutcherson (1967–8, *c*1971), and was a member of Tom Scott's quartet which, as the L.A. Express, toured and recorded with Joni Mitchell (1973–4). The last-named association led to his taking part in studio sessions with rock and folk artists. Sample continued to play both jazz and soul in the early 1980s.

SELECTED RECORDINGS

As leader: *Fancy Dance* (1969, Sonet 611); with R. Brown and S. Manne: *The Three* (1975, EW 10001); *Rainbow Seeker* (*c*1977, ABC 1050); *The Hunter* (c1982, MCA 5397)
As sideman: B. Hutcherson: *San Francisco* (*c*1971, BN 84362); T. Scott: *Tom Scott and the L.A. Express* (1973, Ode 77021); R. Laws: *Pressure Sensitive* (*c*1975, BN LA452)

BIBLIOGRAPHY

E. Kriss: "Backstage with Joe Sample," *CK*, i/1 (1975), 41
L. Feather: "Piano Giants of Jazz: Joe Sample," *CK*, v/5 (1979), 61
B. Doerschuk: "Joe Sample: Branching out after 25 Years with the Crusaders," *CK*, v/8 (1979), 44
A. J. Liska: "The Lone Crusaders," *DB*, l/11 (1983), 20
G. Armbruster: "Joe Sample: Painter in Sound and Time," *Keyboard*, x/4 (1984), 44

BARRY KERNFELD

Sampson, Edgar (Melvin) [The Lamb] (*b* New York, 31 Aug 1907; *d* Englewood, NJ, 16 Jan 1973). Saxophonist, violinist, composer, and arranger. He began playing violin as a child and took up alto saxophone as a teenager. His first engagement was with the pianist Joe Coleman (1924), after which he worked with Duke Ellington (1925), Bingie Madison and the saxophonist Billy Fowler (both 1926), the pianist Arthur Gibbs (1927–8), Charlie Johnson (1928–30), and the bass saxophonist Alex Jackson (1930). He then played with Fletcher Henderson (1931–2; for illustration *see* Henderson, fletcher), recording as solo violinist on *The House of David Blues* (1931). Sampson began writing arrangements while working with Rex Stewart (1933);

during his time as a member of Chick Webb's orchestra (1933–6) he composed many tunes, such as *Stomping at the Savoy* and *Don't be that way*, which are among the best-known standards of the swing era. He then became a freelance arranger, working for Webb, Benny Goodman, Artie Shaw, Red Norvo, and Teddy Wilson. Sampson resumed playing as music director for Ella Fitzgerald (1939) and as alto and baritone saxophonist for Al Sears (1943), and also led his own band (1949–51). During the early 1950s he performed with and wrote arrangements for the Latin bands of Marcellino Guerra, Tito Puente, and Tito Rodriguez, and in the late 1950s and early 1960s he led his own small groups.

SELECTED RECORDINGS

As leader: *Swing Softly Sweet Sampson* (1956, Coral 57049)
As sideman with F. Henderson: The House of David Blues (1931, Ban. 32733)

RECORDED COMPOSITIONS

(selective list; all recorded by C. Webb with Sampson as sideman)

If dreams come true (1934, Col. CB754); Let's get together (1934, Col. CB741); Stomping at the Savoy (1934, Col. 2926D); Blue Minor (1934, OK 41572); Don't be that way (1934, Decca 483); Blue Lou (1934, Decca 1065); Facts and Figures (1935, Decca 830)

BIBLIOGRAPHY

ChiltonW

FRANK DRIGGS

Samuels, Dave (*b* Waukegan, IL, 9 Oct 1948). Vibraphonist. He studied with Gary Burton, then taught percussion and jazz improvisation at the Berklee College of Music. After moving to New York (1974) he toured internationally and recorded with Gerry Mulligan (1974–7); during this period he also performed and recorded with Carla Bley (1975) and Gerry Niewood (1977). In 1975 he formed a duo with Dave Friedman in which both men played vibraphone and marimba; they made recordings with Harvie Swartz and Hubert Laws under Friedman's name in 1975 and with Michael Di Pasqua and Swartz as Double Image in 1977–80 (including *Double Image*, 1977, Enja 2096), toured Europe, and taught in workshops and at the Manhattan School of Music. Later, while continuing to work with Double Image (recording again in *c*1985), he played in the cooperative group Gallery (from 1980) and recorded with Spyro Gyra (from *c*1979); he toured with Spyro Gyra from 1983 and became a full member by 1986. Samuels also recorded with Paul McCandless (1979), Art Lande (1981), Anthony Davis (1983), and Bobby McFerrin (1984), and as an unaccompanied soloist (1981). He played the marimba solo on Spyro Gyra's *Morning Dance*, from the album of the same name (1979, Infinity 9004).

BIBLIOGRAPHY

H. Nolan: "Dave Friedman and Dave Samuels: Two Man Percussion Crusade," *DB*, xliii/20 (1976), 12
J. Peterscak: "Musically Speaking," *Percussive Notes*, xiv/3 (1976), 18
S. K. Fish: "Introducing Dave Samuels," *MD*, v/2 (1981), 74

Sanborn, David (William) [Dave] (*b* Tampa, FL, 30 July 1945). Alto saxophonist. He played alto saxophone briefly at about the age of eight and again to strengthen his lungs while he was recovering from polio. He was strongly influenced by Hank Crawford, and he played rhythm-and-blues professionally from the age of 14, working in St. Louis with the singer and electric guitarist Albert King. After studying music at Northwestern University (1963–4) and the University of Iowa (1965–7) he toured and recorded with Paul Butterfield's blues band (1967–71), the soul singer Stevie Wonder (1971–3), and the rock singer David Bowie (1974); he also recorded with other soul, pop, and rock musicians. He was a soloist with Gil Evans's orchestra (at intervals from 1973 to the mid-1980s) and the Brecker Brothers (1975) and from 1976 toured and recorded as a leader; his album *Voyeur* (*c*1980) won a Grammy Award for "best rhythm-and-blues instrumental" in 1981. Sanborn is a cautious soloist, whose immaculate playing shows complete control of the traditional formulas of gospel preaching and blues; his remarkable tone is full-bodied, intense, and often heart wrenching.

SELECTED RECORDINGS

(all recorded for Warner Bros.)

Heart to Heart (*c*1978, 3189); *Hideaway* (*c*1979, 3379); *Voyeur* (*c*1980, 3546); *As we Speak* (*c*1981, 23650); *Backstreet* (*c*1982, 23906)

BIBLIOGRAPHY

C. Berg: "Dave Sanborn's Alto Spectrum," *DB*, xliii/2 (1976), 11
L. Tomkins: "Dave Sanborn," *CI*, xvi/9 (1978), 23
S. Sutherland: "Crossing the R & B Bridge to Melodic Jazz," *Billboard*, xciii (2 May 1981), 35
R. Tolleson: "David Sanborn Interview: the Voice of Emotion," *DB*, 1/3 (1983), 15 [incl. discography]
"David Sanborn," *SJ*, xxxviii/2 (1984), 217 [discography]
G. Kalbacher: "R & B Altology: David Sanborn," *DB*, liii/8 (1986), 16 [incl. discography]

BARRY KERNFELD

Sanchez Reinoso, Raúl (Armando) (*b* Buenos Aires, 18 Dec 1908; *d* Buenos Aires, 7 Sept 1957). Argentine guitarist, banjoist, and bandleader. He formed the SANTA PAULA SERENADERS in 1933 and led the group until it disbanded in 1948.

LAUREANO FERNÁNDEZ, OMAR GARCÍA BRUNELLI

Sanders, Joe [Joseph L.] (*b* Thayer, KS, 15 Oct 1896; *d* Kansas City, MO, 14 May 1965). Pianist, singer, and bandleader. With the drummer Carleton (A.) Coon(, Sr.) (*b* Rochester, MN, 5 Feb 1894; *d* Chicago, 4 May 1932) he led the Coon–Sanders Novelty Orchestra, a small band which they formed in Kansas City in 1920. It made its first broadcast in 1921 and from December 1922 played on late-night programs, earning the nickname the Nighthawks. With additional members it began performing and recording in Chicago in 1924 as the Coon–Sanders Original Nighthawk Orchestra or the Coon–Sanders Nighthawks; Sanders's solo playing may be heard on *Deep Henderson* (1926, Vic. 20081). The band was resident at the Blackhawk, Chicago, from 1926 and toured widely during the summer. After Coon's death Sanders continued to lead it, as the Joe Sanders Original Nighthawks, until the end of the 1930s. In the 1940s he worked in Hollywood studios and led a band that occasionally returned to Chicago to perform at the Blackhawk. He sang regularly with the Kansas City Opera during the 1950s.

BIBLIOGRAPHY

P. F. Karberg: "Commercial Swing Bands, no.1: Joe Sanders and his Nighthawks," *Swing Music*, ii/3 (1936), 57
B. Colton and L. Kunstadt: "Encore: the Story of Coon–Sanders," *Record Research*, no.13 (1957), 3
H. Schultz: "The Dancing World of Coon–Sanders," *Saturday Review*, xlix (14 May 1966), 57 [see also R. P. Hopkins, 24 June 1966, 58]
D. A. Johnson: "The Happy-go-lucky Sounds of Coon–Sanders Nighthawks," *MR*, i/3 (1974), 7

based on *ChiltonW*

Sanders, Pharoah [Farrell] (*b* Little Rock, AR, 13 Oct 1940). Tenor saxophonist. He started playing professionally while in high school, trying numerous instruments before adopting tenor saxophone, and after graduating in 1959 he played rhythm-and-blues and avant-garde jazz in the San Francisco Bay area. In 1962 he moved to New York, where he worked with Billy Higgins, Don Cherry, and, unofficially, in John Coltrane's group (1965–7; for illustration *see* COLTRANE, JOHN). Here he made his mark with harsh, shrieking improvisations that combined multiphonics and sweeping runs of indefinite pitch. Remarkable examples may be heard on Coltrane's album *Live at the Village Vanguard Again* and on *Preview*, which Sanders recorded in 1968 as a principal soloist with the Jazz Composer's Orchestra. After Coltrane's death in 1967 Sanders remained briefly with Alice Coltrane, then from 1969 to 1970 he led a group with Leone Thomas. In such performances as *The Creator Has a Master Plan*, Sanders's intense sounds were juxtaposed with tuneful melodies, usually played over serene, hypnotic vamps. His groups of the mid-1970s merely imitated his first successes, and his popularity declined accordingly, but after an unsuccessful flirtation with disco music (1977–8) his career revived considerably. In the 1980s both his repertory and his playing style have covered a wide range, embracing not only the energetic free jazz and calm modal jazz of his earlier periods, but also swing, rhythm-and-blues, and, especially, bop, as may be heard on several acclaimed albums recorded for the Theresa label in 1981–2. Sanders performs most frequently as the leader of a quartet whose members have included Idris Muhammad and the pianist John Hicks.

SELECTED RECORDINGS

As leader: *Karma* (1969, Imp. 9181), incl. The Creator Has a Master Plan; *Jewels of Thought* (1969, Imp. 9190); *Summun Bukmun Umyun* (1970, Imp. 9199); *Rejoice* (1981, The. 112–13); *Heart is a Melody* (1982, The. 118); *Pharoah Sanders Live* (1982, The. 116)

As sideman: J. Coltrane: *Ascension* (1965, Imp. 95); *Live at the Village Vanguard Again* (1966, Imp. 9124); D. Cherry: *Symphony for Improvisors* (1966, BN 84247); on Jazz Composer's Orchestra: *The Jazz Composer's Orchestra* (1968, JCOA 1001-02), Preview

BIBLIOGRAPHY

M. Williams: "Pharoah's Tale," *DB*, xxxv/10 (1968), 21
E. Raben: *A Discography of Free Jazz* (Copenhagen, 1969)
B. Palmer: Pharoah Sanders," *RS*, no.57 (30 April 1970), 44
"Pharoah Sanders," *J&P*, ix/2 (1970), 3; repr. in *Black Giants*, ed. P. Rivelli and R. Levin (New York and Cleveland, 1970/*R*1980 as *Giants of Black Music*)
S. Randolph: "A Good Look at Pharoah Sanders," *JM*, no.181 (1970), 2
J. Welch: "Pharoah Sanders: 'I Play for the Creator'," *DB*, xxxviii/10 (1971), 15
E. Jost: *Free Jazz* (Graz, Austria, 1974)
G. Giddins: "Pharoah Sanders Goes Secular," *VV*, xxi (11 April 1977), 53
P. Kemper: "Pharoah Sanders: zwischen Mythos und Logos," *JP*, xxviii/12 (1979), 6
G. Tate: "The Son Bobs some Brand New Funk," *VV*, xxvi (29 July 1981), 49

BARRY KERNFELD

Sandoval, Arturo (*b* Artemisa, Cuba, 6 Nov 1949). Cuban trumpeter, pianist, and composer. He was one of the founding members of the Orquesta Cubana de Música Moderna, which around 1973 grew into the group Irakere. With other members of the group he recorded with David Amram in 1977. After leaving Irakere in 1981 he toured internationally with his own group, and recorded with it in Cuba. He is a protégé of Dizzy Gillespie, and has played with him in Cuba, the USA, Puerto Rico, and England; the two men recorded the album *To a Finland Station* (Pablo 2310889) as the leaders of a quintet in Finland in 1982.

BIBLIOGRAPHY

J. Brody: "Version latine: trompettiste à Cuba," *Jm*, no.329 (1984), 50
S. Steward: "Cubana be, cubana bop," *The Wire*, no.21 (1985), 26

CRISTÓBAL DÍAZ AYALA

Sands, Bobby (*b* New York, 28 Jan 1907). Tenor saxophonist. He played in New York with the saxophonist Billy Fowler (*c*1927) and in a band led by Charlie Skeete (1929). During the 1930s he worked with Claude Hopkins, with whom he made several recordings (including *Mush Mouth*, 1932, Col. 2674D). He ceased full-time performing in the 1940s.

based on *ChiltonW*

Sandström, Nisse [Nils] (*b* Katrineholm, Sweden, 13 March 1942). Swedish tenor saxophonist. He studied music from the mid-1950s and won an amateur contest on television in 1958. In the 1960s he led free-jazz groups; he then adopted a bop style and recorded the album *The Painter* (1972, Odeon 062-34659), which was awarded a Gold Disc by *Orkester journalen* in 1972. He performed and recorded with Red Mitchell's Swedish group Communication (from ?1973), appeared in the USA and Sweden with Mitchell and Tommy Flanagan in the late 1970s, and in the 1980s worked as a leader and as a teacher. Sandström is a versatile soloist with a wide-ranging knowledge of jazz and a strong sense of harmony.

BIBLIOGRAPHY

L. Westin: "Nils Sandström," *Orkester journalen*, xli/2 (1973), 6

ERIK KJELLBERG

Sangster, John (Grant) (*b* Melbourne, Australia, 17 Nov 1928). Australian drummer and composer. He first played trombone, and by 1948 was a respected trumpeter in the traditional style. In 1950, however, he learned drumming for an overseas tour with Graeme Bell; after this he concentrated on percussion, and his approach became increasingly progressive. From 1961 to 1967 he led a quartet at El Rocco, Sydney; in 1967 this group recorded the album *Conjurman* (CBS BP233450). He also worked with Don Burrows, performing with him at Expo 67 in Montreal and Expo 70 in Osaka, Japan. His many albums of original compositions include *Lord of the Rings* (1974, EMI EMC2525-6). In 1977 he recorded on vibraphone with Alan Lee. Sangster's works, which are widely performed, often draw inspiration from the Australian environment; they contain elements of both traditional and modern jazz, and display his concern for color and swing. Some of his pieces in this vein may be heard on the album *Australia and All that Jazz* (1971, CPS 1008).

BIBLIOGRAPHY

Jazz, Catalogues of Australian Compositions (Sydney, 1978) [incl. discography, list of compositions; pubn of Australia Music Centre]
A. Bisset: *Black Roots, White Flowers: a History of Australian Jazz* (Sydney, 1979)
M. Williams: *The Australian Jazz Explosion* (London and elsewhere, 1981), 53
B. Johnson and others: *The Oxford Companion to Australian Jazz* (Melbourne, Australia, 1987)
J. Sangster: *Seeing the Rafters* (in preparation)

JEFF PRESSING (with JOHN WHITEOAK)

San Jacinto Hall. Venue in New Orleans; *see* Nightclubs and other venues.

Santamaria, Mongo [Ramon] (*b* Havana, 7 April 1922). Cuban conga player and bandleader. He was born in a poor district of Havana which was known for its Afro-Cuban culture. He traveled to the USA via Mexico as a young man in 1950, and performed and recorded with Cal Tjader (1957–60). His composition *Afro-blue* became a jazz standard and was recorded by Tjader, John Coltrane, Dizzy Gillespie, and others. He formed a group based on the classic Latin *charanga* format of flute and violin, but added to it jazz-oriented brass and saxophone players. In the 1960s Santamaria recorded and toured as the leader of a series of diverse bands that combined elements of jazz with Latin and black popular music, and at various times included such musicians as Hubert Laws and Chick Corea. These bands, which played both Latin jazz and Latin soul, were enormously influential on the next generation of black-American musicians – especially percussionists – and were in a large part responsible for the gradual absorption of Latin rhythms into black music. However, Santamaria always retained contact with his musical roots in recordings that ranged from early Afro-Cuban percussion performances to classic salsa in the late 1970s. He has also remained associated with jazz musicians, and recorded with Dizzy Gillespie in 1980.

SELECTED RECORDINGS

As leader: *Yambu* (1958, Fan. 3267); *Mongo* (1959, Fan. 3291); *Go, Mongo!* (1962, Riv. 9423); *Watermelon Man* (1962–3, Battle 96120); *Mongo at the Village Gate* (1963, Battle 96129)

As sideman: C. Tjader: *Cal Tjader Goes Latin* (1959, Fan. 8030); *Concert by the Sea* (1959, Fan. 8038), incl. Afro-blue; D. Gillespie: *Summertime* (1980, Pablo Live 2308229), incl. Afro-blue

BIBLIOGRAPHY

M. Santamaria: "Mongo Makes some Points," ed. L. Tomkins, *CI*, x/1 (1971), 16

A. J. Smith: "Mongo Santamaria: Cuban King of Congas," *DB*, xliv/8 (1977), 19

J. S. Roberts: *The Latin Tinge: the Impact of Latin American Music on the United States* (New York, and Oxford, England, 1979)

JOHN STORM ROBERTS/R

Santana, (Devadip) Carlos (*b* Tijuana, Mexico, 20 July 1947). Guitarist. He came to attention in San Francisco during the late 1960s, when psychedelic rock was the dominant form in popular music. His first album, *Santana* (1969, Col. PC9781), established his group's style – a form of improvised rock influenced by Latin-American rhythms. Santana is the leading and most commercially successful proponent of this style. His lyrical guitar solos are backed by a rhythm section combining Cuban and salsa percussion and jazz or blues keyboard playing; his singing style has varied, but often has a strong rhythm-and-blues tinge. Santana's recordings have moved between this fairly earthy style and a somewhat ethereal jazz-rock, typified by his album *Caravanserai* (1972, Col. PC31610). In the early 1970s he began working with John McLaughlin, with whom he made the highly experimental album *Love, Devotion, Surrender* (*c*1973, Col. KC32034); this received critical acclaim as one of the first successful fusions of jazz and rock. *Amigos* (1976, Col. PC33576) signaled an abrupt and exhilarating return to the blend of rock and Latin music on which his original success was based. In the late 1970s Santana and his group adopted a more concise and accessible style that owed little to jazz, resulting in such hit singles as *She's not there* (1977) and *Winning* (1981). In 1988, with Wayne Shorter, he led a Latin jazz-rock group which toured internationally.

BIBLIOGRAPHY

M. Brooks: "Carlos Santana: Still Evolving," *GP*, viii/11 (1974), 22

H. Mandel: "Devadip Carlos Santana: Ethnic Evolution," *DB*, xliv/8 (1977), 17

J. Coryell and L. Friedman: *Jazz-rock Fusion: the People, the Music* (New York and London, 1978)

D. Forte: "Carlos Santana," *GP*, xii/6 (1978), 42

L. Stewart: "Carlos Santana," *GP*, xiii/10 (1979), 144

JOHN STORM ROBERTS

Santa Paula Serenaders. Argentine big band. Formed in 1933 as a sextet by Raúl Sanchez Reinoso, who led the group throughout its existence, it later included four saxophones, two trumpets, a trombone, two violins, an accordion, two pianos, a guitar or banjo, a double bass, drums, and one or two singers. It played jazz standards and Argentine dances (such as the *paso doble*, a two-step generally in 6/8 rhythm, and the *guaracha*, an Afro-Cuban form based on the *habanera* rhythm), and displayed in the work of some of its soloists the influence of Coleman Hawkins and Joe Venuti. Apart from a tour of Brazil in 1936 the band performed exclusively in Argentina. It recorded about 200 tracks (including *Tiger Rag/Santa Paula Stomp*, 1935, Parl. E1130) before disbanding in 1948.

LAUREANO FERNÁNDEZ, OMAR GARCÍA BRUNELLI

Sardaby, Michel (*b* Fort-de-France, Martinique, 4 Sept 1935). Martinique pianist. After leading his own 18-piece band in the Caribbean he traveled to Paris, where he studied music and began around 1956 to perform in clubs. He played swing with Benny Waters (1957), and bop with Don Byas, J. J. Johnson, and Kenny Clarke (all 1961), Sonny Criss, Clark Terry (1965–6), Johnny Griffin, Dexter Gordon, and Art Taylor (all 1967), and Hal Singer (*c*1970); he also played and recorded with the blues singers Sonny Boy Williamson (1963) and T-Bone Walker (1968). Among his recordings is the album *Mike Sardaby in New York* (1972, Debs 540), on which he was accompanied by Ray Barretto, Billy Cobham, and Richard Davis; he also recorded in a trio with Percy Heath and Connie Kay (1970), and in a quartet that included Davis and Billy Hart (1975).

BIBLIOGRAPHY

Feather–Gitler '70s

D. Constant: "Jazz informations: Sardaby story," *Jm*, no.218 (1974), 5

M. Zwerin: "Michel Sardaby: Lucid, World-class Improviser," *International Herald Tribune* (9 Jan 1987), 7

Sarmanto, Heikki (*b* Helsinki, 22 June 1939). Finnish pianist, keyboard player, and composer, brother of Pekka Sarmanto. He studied at the Sibelius Academy, Helsinki (1962–4), and at the Berklee College of Music (1968–9, 1970–71). From 1962 he played with Esa Pethman, Christian Schwindt, and his own small jazz groups, and appeared at the Montreux (1971) and Newport (New York; 1979) jazz festivals. He made recordings with Pethman, Schwindt, Eero Koivistoinen, and Seppo Paakkunainen, and as a soloist (including *Flowers in the Water*, 1969, Col. 5E062-34044), and toured Europe and the USA. In addition to jazz compositions he has written vocal, orchestral, and theatrical works. (A. Granholm: *Finnish Jazz* (Helsinki, 1974, rev. and enlarged by M. Konttinen 2/1982, rev. and enlarged by J.-P. Vuorela 3/1986), 36)

PEKKA GRONOW

Sarmanto, Pekka (*b* Helsinki, 15 Feb 1945). Finnish double bass player, brother of Heikki Sarmanto. He studied violin and double bass at the Sibelius Academy in Helsinki and joined his brother's band in 1965. He made recordings with Eero Koivistoinen (from 1967), Edward Vesala (1969, 1983), Ted Curson (1970), his brother (from 1971), and Charlie Mariano and Juhani Aaltonen (1974), and in a quintet led by Dizzy Gillespie and Arturo Sandoval (*To a Finland Station*, 1982, Pablo 2310889). (A. Granholm: *Finnish Jazz* (Helsinki, 1974, rev. and enlarged by M. Konttinen 2/1982, rev. and enlarged by J.-P. Vuorela 3/1986), 37)

PEKKA GRONOW

Sarrusophone. A brass instrument of conical bore played with a double reed. A family of such instruments, ranging from the sopranino to the contrabass, was designed in the mid-19th century to substitute for the double-reed woodwind instruments (oboes and bassoons) in military bands; they continued to be played in military, brass, and wind bands, and made isolated appearances in classical scores but were largely obsolete by the mid-20th century. The sarrusophones resemble the saxophones in compass, keywork and fingering, and tone. They are rarely used in jazz: Sidney Bechet plays one (the bass in B♭) on *Mandy, make up your mind* (OK 40260), recorded by Clarence Williams's Blue Five in 1924.

Sassy. Nickname of SARAH VAUGHAN.

Satchmo [Satchelmouth]. Nickname of LOUIS ARMSTRONG.

Sato, Masahiko (*b* Tokyo, 6 Oct 1941). Japanese pianist, composer, and arranger. He studied violin and piano from the age of five, attended Keio University in Tokyo, and belonged to George Kawaguchi's group Big Four (known during his membership as Big Four Plus One). He studied at the Berklee College of Music from 1966 until 1968, when he returned to Tokyo. He then formed a trio and recorded his first album, *Palladium* (1969), which was critically acclaimed. Between 1971 and 1973 he won readers' polls sponsored by *Swing Journal* for his work as a pianist, as a composer, and as an arranger; at the same time he recorded in Tokyo with Charles Mingus and Helen Merrill (1971) and in Germany as a leader (1971) and with Attila Zoller (1971), Karl Berger (1971), and Albert Mangelsdorff (1973). Sato's best-known compositions include *Samardhi, Fairy Rings, Fall Out* (1972), *Yamataifu* (1972, played by Toshiyuki Miyama's New Herd), *Sosho* (1973), *Yun* (1976), *Kamjizai* (1976), and *Escape Velocity* (1986, played by Sato, Eddie Gomez, and Steve Gadd). He has written arrangements for many recordings, including *Maiden Voyage* (1983, Interface 7073), recorded by Art Farmer's quartet and a string section, on which Sato also plays piano.

SELECTED RECORDINGS

As leader: *Palladium* (1969, TE 8004); with G. Peacock: *Samardhi: Masahiko Meets Gary Peacock* (1971, TE 9003); *Kanzigai* (1976, Col. YX7501); *Brink* (1983, Cntl HL5027)

BIBLIOGRAPHY

Feather–Gitler '70s
M. Gourges: "Masahiko Sato," *Jm*, no.233 (1975), 37

YOZO IWANAMI

Saunders, Red [Theodore] (*b* Memphis, 2 March 1912; *d* Chicago, 5 March 1981). Drummer and bandleader. He was brought up in Milwaukee and began his career there as a drummer. He moved to Chicago, where he worked with the pianist Stomp King at the Annex and other clubs, and with Tiny Parham at the Savoy Ballroom (*c*1934), before joining the house band at the Club DeLisa; from 1937 until the club closed in the late 1950s he led his own group there. He also led the house bands at Roberts' Show Lounge (1959) and the Regal Theater (1960–67). He made recordings as the leader of a sextet (1945–6) and a big band (1949–54), including *Mistreatin' Woman Blues/Hey Bartender* (1951, OK 7061), on which the singer is Joe Williams. Saunders continued to work into the 1970s, performing with Art Hodes (1968) and Little Brother Montgomery (1969), and leading his own big band (1970).

Oral history material in *NjR* (JOHP), *NNC*.

BIBLIOGRAPHY

ChiltonW; FeatherE
A. Hodes: "Sittin' in: Looking at Red," *DB*, xxxiv/16 (1967), 18
H. Rye: "Red Saunders Columbia and Okeh Sessions," *Journal of Jazz Discography*, no.5 (1979), 9
D. J. Travis: *An Autobiography of Black Jazz* (Chicago, 1983) [incl. interviews], 123

Saury, Maxim (*b* Enghien-les-Bains, France, 27 Feb 1928). French clarinetist. He studied violin from the age of 12, then changed to clarinet after hearing Hubert Rostaing play with Django Reinhardt. After working with amateur groups in Paris he played with Claude Bolling from 1947 to 1952 (recording in 1948–50), apart from a period in 1949 during which he led his own trio. Later he formed a big band, the New Orleans Sound, which he led for 15 years in Paris and at many festivals in Europe. Saury's fluid style, which is reminiscent of that of Barney Bigard, is well represented by his album *Rendez-vous à la Nouvelle-Orléans* (1960–61, Pathé 1133-4).

BIBLIOGRAPHY

FeatherE
L. Malson: "Maxim Saury ou le sens de l'équilibre," *Jm*, no.59 (1960), 28

ANDRÉ CLERGEAT

Sauter, Eddie [Edward Ernest] (*b* New York, 2 Dec 1914; *d* Nyack, NY, 21 April 1981). Arranger and composer. After studying at the Juilliard School he became a member of Red Norvo's trumpet section in late 1935, and shortly afterwards, by mutual consent, the full-time arranger for Norvo's band. From 1939 he worked as a freelance, writing arrangements for such bandleaders as Benny Goodman (for whom he did his most notable work) and Artie Shaw, and established a strong reputation among musicians. His only period of public recognition (in the mid-1950s) stemmed from the success of a band assembled, initially for recording purposes only, by Sauter and BILL FINEGAN, formerly an arranger for Tommy Dorsey and Glenn Miller. Sauter continued as a freelance writer for stage, film, and television, but also produced occasional pieces of "absolute" music, such as *Q.T.* for the New York Saxophone Quartet.

Sauter's arrangements of popular song material for Norvo displayed a wealth of invention, and his deft handling of dynamics and unstilted counterpoint suggest an acquaintance with the methods of Duke Ellington. These elements were fully developed in his original works for Goodman, such as *Benny Rides Again* (1940) and *Clarinet à la King* (1941). The lightweight character of the most popular recordings by the Sauter–Finegan Orchestra, such as *Doodletown Fifers* or *Midnight Sleigh Ride* (both on the album *The Sauter–Finegan Orchestra*, 1952, RCA LPM3115, the latter an adaptation of the "Troika" from Prokofiev's *Lieutenant Kijé*), should not obscure those orchestral and contrapuntal touches that foreshadowed the explorations of Gil Evans. If some of Sauter's work seems superficial, the best is a vindication of his versatility and sensitivity; in particular, his writing for chamber string ensemble on Stan Getz's album *Focus* (1961) represents one of the most convincing fusions of jazz and nonjazz elements. Further collaborations with Getz included the film soundtrack of Arthur Penn's *Mickey One* (1965) and the *Tanglewood Concerto* (1966).

Oral history material in *NjR* (JOHP).

RECORDED COMPOSITIONS
(selective list)

Recorded by B. Goodman: Benny Rides Again (1940, Col. 55001); Superman (1940, Col. 55002); Clarinet à la King (1941, OK 6544)
Recorded by others: S. Getz: *Focus* (1961, Verve 68412); on *Stan Getz & Arthur Fiedler at Tanglewood* (1966, RCA LSC2925), Tanglewood Concerto; on New York Saxophone Quartet: *The New York Saxophone Quartet* (1980, Stash 210), Q.T.

SELECTED ARRANGEMENTS

Recorded by R. Norvo: A Porter's Love Song to a Chambermaid/I know that you know (1936, Bruns. 7744); Remember (1937, Bruns. 7896)
Recorded by B. Goodman: How High the Moon (1940, Col. 35391); My Old Flame (1941, Col. 36754)
Recorded by A. Shaw: Summertime (1945, Vic. 28-0406)

BIBLIOGRAPHY

L. Feather: "Men Behind the Bands: Eddie Sauter," *DB*, vii/5 (1940), 17
"Coda: Eddie Sauter," *JF* [intl edn], no.71 (1981), 59

BRIAN PRIESTLEY

Savannah Syncopators. Name used on some recordings made by King Oliver and the DIXIE SYNCOPATORS.

Savery, Finn (*b* Gentofte, Denmark, 24 July 1933). Danish pianist and composer. From the early 1950s he was active in both jazz and classical music. As a jazz musician he led trios (from 1955), made several recordings, and played in a trio led by Erik Moseholm (1960–61). His works include musicals (such as *Teenagerlove*, 1962) and third-stream compositions. Savery's playing may be heard to advantage on his album *Many Moments* (1982, Met. 15818), which includes the track *Streams*.

ERIK WIEDEMANN

Savoy (i). Record label. It was established around 1931 in Chicago by the company Melrose and Montgomery. The five issues of jazz and race material were derived from Gennett. ("Afterthoughts 468," *Sv*, no.102 (1982), 240)

Savoy (ii). Record company and label. The company was founded late in 1942 in Newark, New Jersey, by Herman Lubinsky; among the label's first issues were items recorded in 1939 by the Savoy Dictators. These inaugurated a substantial catalogue of jazz which made Savoy one of the most important independent labels of the 1940s. From 1945 to 1952 artists and repertory were directed by Teddy Reig, who was responsible for introducing to the label, despite Lubinsky's initial doubts, several musicians of the emerging bop school. Savoy organized sessions by Charlie Parker (1945, 1947–8), Dexter Gordon and Fats Navarro (both 1946–7), J. J. Johnson (1946–7, 1949), and Serge Chaloff and Miles Davis (both 1947), the results of which are now among the most highly prized recordings of the style. Nevertheless the most successful parts of the catalogue were recordings of swing, and of jazz with a strong beat and blues feeling that later came to be categorized as rhythm-and-blues. An office was opened on the West Coast in 1948; in charge of artists and repertory was Ralph Bass, who was responsible for bringing Erroll Garner to the label.

Savoy began purchasing other enterprises in 1948. The first of these was Fred Mendelsohn's label Regent; those of particular jazz interest were National, Bop, and Discovery, all of which had extensive jazz catalogues. In addition the company leased a large amount of important jazz from small organizations, including traditional material by Mutt Carey and Punch Miller first issued by Century, and Fletcher Henderson's recordings for Crown. Savoy also reissued the catalogue of the Jewell label, best known for its recordings by Boyd Raeburn of 1945–6.

Reig's successor, Lee Magid, altered the emphasis of the company's recording policy, concentrating on more commercially oriented types of Afro-American music, but jazz remained important under the supervision of Ozzie Cadena, who controlled artists and repertory from 1954 to 1959. Cadena instigated reissues on LP of major recordings of the 1940s, and also organized important bop sessions by Kenny Clarke (1954–6), Cannonball Adderley (1955), and Yusef Lateef (1957, 1959). Lubinsky established a subsidiary label, WORLD WIDE, in 1958. After working for other organizations Mendelsohn returned to the company in 1960, and was responsible for its development of the largest catalogue of black gospel music; from this time jazz and other secular music began to figure less prominently. Surprisingly, the company nevertheless recorded isolated free-jazz sessions by Sun Ra (1961) and Bill Dixon and Archie Shepp (both 1964). Lubinsky died in 1974; the following year Savoy's entire catalogue was purchased by Arista, which began a systematic program of reissues. This was continued by the company Muse, which acquired the repertory around 1985. Reissues have also been made in Europe by RCA, and under the Savoy name in Japan.

BIBLIOGRAPHY

"Savoy Stomp Off with 28 Doubles," *Jazz Circle News*, no.11 (1978), 12
A. Shaw: "Savoy Records of Newark, New Jersey" *Honkers and Shouters: the Golden Years of Rhythm and Blues* (New York, 1978), 343
M. Ruppli: *The Savoy Label: a Discography* (Westport, CT, and London, 1980)
C. Sheridan: "Savoy Records: the Hidden Treasures," *JJI*, xxxiii (1980), no.10, p. 17; no.12, p.18

Savoy Ballroom. The name of several ballrooms, notably ones in Chicago and New York; *see* NIGHTCLUBS AND OTHER VENUES.

Savoy Sultans (i). Swing band. Led by Al Cooper, it was formed from a group for which Willie Bryant and John Hammond arranged an audition at the Savoy Ballroom, New York, where it became resident as the Savoy Sultans in September 1937. It comprised two trumpets, three reed instruments, and a rhythm section that occasionally included a guitar. The principal soloists were Rudy Williams (alto saxophone), Sam Massenberg (trumpet), Cyril Haynes (piano), and George Kelly (tenor saxophone), while Cooper sometimes performed clarinet solos. The band, which was extremely popular with dancers at the Savoy Ballroom and was also much admired by other musicians, made several recordings between 1938 and 1941 and continued performing until around 1946. It played simple, straightforward written arrangements in the powerful swing style that came to be known as jump.

SELECTED RECORDINGS

(all issued under A. Cooper's name)

The Thing/Gettin' in the Groove (1938, Decca 7525); Jumpin' at the Savoy/We'd rather jump than swing (1939, Decca 2526); Jumpin' the Blues/When I grow too old to dream (1939, Decca 2930); Wishing and crying for you/Sophisticated Jump (1940, Decca 3274); Second Balcony Jump/Jackie Boy (1941, Decca 8545)

BIBLIOGRAPHY

A. McCarthy: *Big Band Jazz* (New York and London, 1974), 277
S. Dance: Liner notes, *Jumpin' at the Savoy* (MCA 1345, 1982)

JOHNNY SIMMEN

Savoy Sultans (ii). Jazz and dance band. It was formed by Panama Francis to play at a concert in New York in 1974 and began performing regularly in 1979. It consists of two trumpets, three reed instruments, and a rhythm section (including guitar). Among the members are Irvin Stokes, Franc Williams, George Kelly (who had also worked with Al Cooper's Savoy Sultans), John Smith, Red Richards, and Bill Pemberton. The group has toured and recorded under various leaders in Europe and played occasionally at the Rainbow Room, New York. Although it does not always re-create the performances of the first Savoy Sultans exactly, it plays in the same spirit, emphasizing the strong relationship between jazz and dancing, and it has become one of the best swing and dance bands of its time. Its repertory includes compositions by Kelly and other members of the group.

SELECTED RECORDINGS

G. Kelly: *George Kelly in Cimiez* (1979, BB 33161); J. Witherspoon: *Jimmy Witherspoon* (1980, BB 33177); P. Francis: *Grooving* (?1982, Stash 218); *Everything Swings* (1984, Stash 233)

BIBLIOGRAPHY

G. Giddins: *Rhythm-a-ning: Jazz Tradition and Innovation in the '80s* (New York, and Oxford, England, 1985) [colln of previously pubd articles], 12

For further recordings and bibliography *see* FRANCIS, PANAMA.

JOHNNY SIMMEN

Saxello. A variant of the B♭ soprano saxophone; *see* SAXOPHONE, §6(v).

Saxhorn. A family of valved brass instruments, designed by Adolphe Sax and first manufactured between 1843 and 1855, having a tapering bore, a bell of moderate flare (usually facing upwards), a deep cup-shaped mouthpiece, and usually three piston valves. The TUBA and related instruments are sometimes referred to as members of the saxhorn family; organologically, both families of instruments are classified as valved bugle horns.

Of the entire range of saxhorns (from soprano to contrabass, pitched alternately in B♭ and E♭), those most commonly found in jazz are the B♭ baritone and the E♭ alto or tenor (known in colloquial American usage as the "peck horn"); they are normally referred to as "horns" rather than "saxhorns." The name "baritone horn" is commonly applied indifferently to the baritone saxhorn and the euphonium in the USA, where makers have minimized the structural differences between the two; indeed "baritone" has become the normal term for the valved instrument pitched in B♭ and makers simply offer a range of instruments of different bores, sometimes designating the largest "euphoniums."

Saxhorns were originally intended for use in military music and found their way thence into brass and other wind bands, and from there into early jazz parade bands. The first Onward Brass Band, formed in 1885, was typical of New Orleans brass bands in including alto and baritone horns, and Feather records Eubie Blake's recollection of the use of these instruments in early jazz. They are found as late as 1946 on recordings made by the re-created Original Zenith Brass Band, on which Harrison Barnes played euphonium or baritone horn, Isidore Barbarin alto horn and mellophone, and Joe Howard tuba. Later use of saxhorns in jazz has been rare. The alto horn has been played by Dick Cary (on Bobby Hackett's *Gotham Jazz Scene*, 1957, Cap. T857) and Kate Westbrook (on Mike Westbrook's *On Duke's Birthday*, 1984, HA 2012). Paul Rutherford has played euphonium, recording duos with Paul Lovens (1976–7) and an unaccompanied solo album *Neuph* (1978, Sweet Folk & Country 092).

BIBLIOGRAPHY

L. Feather: *The Book of Jazz: a Guide to the Entire Field* (New York, 1955, 2/1965 as *The Book of Jazz from Then till Now: a Guide to the Entire Field*)

CLIFFORD BEVAN

Saxophone [sax]. A single-reed instrument invented by Adolphe Sax around 1840. Although it has remained a peripheral instrument in the classical music tradition, the saxophone has played a leading role in jazz, and it is here that its technical and expressive potential has been most fully explored.

This article deals with the members of the saxophone family in order of their importance in jazz. Reference is made to specific recordings only to exemplify unusual or particularly important uses of the instruments or to illustrate the use of rare types of saxophone; for numerous recorded examples of saxophone playing see the lists following entries on individual saxophonists.

1. The saxophone family: (i) Structure and compass (ii) General history. 2. The tenor saxophone. 3. The alto saxophone. 4. The soprano saxophone. 5. The baritone saxophone. 6. Other saxophones: (i) The C-melody saxophone (ii) The bass saxophone (iii) The sopranino saxophone (iv) The contrabass saxophone (v) The saxello (vi) The manzello (vii) The stritch (viii) The slide saxophone.

1. THE SAXOPHONE FAMILY.

(i) Structure and compass. All members of the saxophone family have a conical tube of wide bore, made of metal, and a single reed; this combination of characteristics puts them in an instrumental category of their own. They overblow at the octave to yield the second register. The body of the saxophone is made of thin metal, commonly brass, flaring slightly at the bell. It has between 18 and 21 tone-holes controlled by keys (some that open holes and some that close holes), and two small "octave" or speaker keys at the mouthpiece end, which facilitate the production of notes in the high register. The fingering is based on that of the simple-system oboe combined with the Boehm system for the right hand, but a number of modifications have been made to the basic system by different instrument builders.

The larger saxophones, because of the length of their tubes, have a U-bend (usually in the region of the third lowest tone-hole), a forward-tilting bell, and a detachable crook for the section above the main tone-holes. Even the soprano and sopranino instruments have sometimes been made in this configuration for the sake of uniformity, though a straight design without a crook, similar to that of the clarinet, is more characteristic.

The saxophone mouthpiece, originally made of wood but now commonly of ebonite or hard rubber (and sometimes of metal, glass, or plastic), is similar to that of the clarinet, though it has different relative proportions and interior shape. It slides over the top of the mouthpipe, which is lapped with a thin cork sheet to make an airtight joint, and the position of the mouthpiece may be minutely adjusted to allow for a certain degree of fine tuning. The variety of mouthpiece and ligature designs available, the style and hardness of the reed selected, and the relatively loose embouchure required (which gives greater flexibility of timbre, intonation, and vibrato than any other wind instrument) allow the player to shape a thoroughly individual sound; in many instances an innovative jazz saxophonist has been able to develop his own instantly recognizable style of playing, which his followers have then imitated.

The saxophone family as patented was of 14 instruments, from sopranino to contrabass, pitched alternately in F and C or E♭ and B♭; the written compass of the entire family is the same – normally *b*♭ to *f*‴, though some instruments have *a* as the lowest note and some players can extend the range to *d*⁗ or even *f*⁗ – and all but the orchestral soprano in C require transposition. The basic sounding ranges of the principal instruments discussed in this article are: sopranino in E♭, *d*♭′–*a*♭‴; soprano in B♭, *a*♭–*e*♭‴; alto in E♭, *d*♭–*a*♭″; tenor in C (C-melody saxophone), *B*♭-*f*″; tenor in B♭, *A*♭–*e*♭″; baritone in E♭, *C*–*a*♭′; bass in B♭, *A*♭′–*e*♭′; contrabass in E♭, *D*♭′–*a*♭.

There have been few technical developments to the saxophone in the 20th century that have affected the playing of jazz musicians. A general improvement in the mechanism has allowed smoother, faster playing, especially in the extreme low and high registers, and the addition of a high F♯ key on many models from the 1970s has extended the upper range. On the whole, however, the instrument is the same as it was in the 1920s. A brief vogue for plastic instruments did not lead to their general adoption.

From the 1960s a variety of electronic and electric attachments have been devised to modify the sound of the saxophone, but they have had short-lived success; most saxophonists content themselves with amplifying the instrument in the usual way. A few players, among them Wayne Shorter, Sonny Rol-

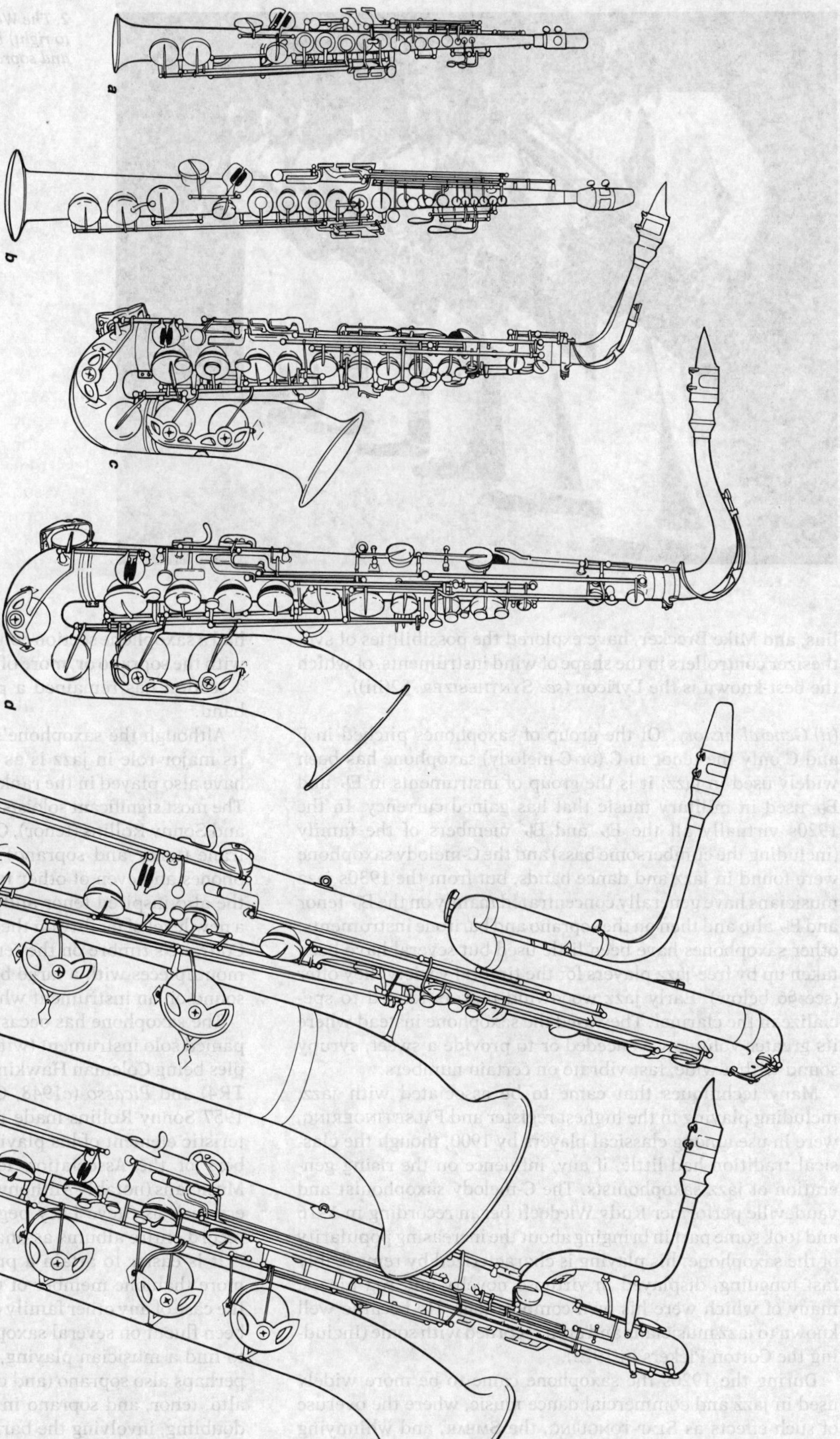

1. Saxophones: (a) sopranino in E♭; (b) soprano in B♭; (c) alto in E♭; (d) tenor in B♭; (e) baritone in E♭; (f) bass in B♭; (b)–(d) have top F♯ keys; (e) has a low A key

2. The Weintraub Syncopators in 1933 with (left to right) bass, baritone, two tenor, two alto, and soprano saxophones

lins, and Mike Brecker, have explored the possibilities of synthesizer controllers in the shape of wind instruments, of which the best-known is the Lyricon (*see* SYNTHESIZER, §2(iii)).

(ii) General history. Of the group of saxophones pitched in F and C only the tenor in C (or C-melody) saxophone has been widely used in jazz; it is the group of instruments in E♭ and B♭ used in military music that has gained currency. In the 1920s virtually all the E♭ and B♭ members of the family (including the cumbersome bass) and the C-melody saxophone were found in jazz and dance bands, but from the 1930s jazz musicians have generally concentrated mainly on the B♭ tenor and E♭ alto and then on the soprano and baritone instruments; other saxophones have been little used but several have been taken up by free-jazz players for the timbral variety they offer (see §6 below). Early jazz woodwind players tended to specialize in the clarinet. They used the saxophone instead where its greater volume was needed or to provide a sweet, syrupy sound with a wide, fast vibrato on certain numbers.

Many techniques that came to be associated with jazz, including playing in the highest register and FALSE FINGERING, were in use among classical players by 1900, though the classical tradition had little, if any, influence on the rising generation of jazz saxophonists. The C-melody saxophonist and vaudeville performer Rudy Wiedoeft began recording in 1916 and took some part in bringing about the increasing popularity of the saxophone; his playing is characterized by remarkably fast tonguing, displayed in virtuoso novelty and rag pieces, many of which were his own compositions. He became well known to jazz musicians and even recorded with some (including the Cotton Pickers in 1923).

During the 1920s the saxophone came to be more widely used in jazz and commercial dance music, where the overuse of such effects as SLAP-TONGUING, the SMEAR, and whinnying sounds marred the playing of many bands; although jazz musicians at first imitated these effects, within a decade they were far less frequently used. By 1930 the saxophone had become an established member of jazz ensembles, and any large group had a saxophone section consisting of alto, tenor, and baritone, with the soprano or, more often, the clarinet to give color. Such a section has remained a permanent feature of the jazz big band.

Although the saxophone's ensemble position is important, its major role in jazz is as a solo instrument (many soloists have also played in the ranks of large ensembles or big bands). The most significant soloists – Coleman Hawkins, Lester Young, and Sonny Rollins (tenor), Charlie Parker (alto), and John Coltrane (tenor and soprano) – influenced players of all saxophones and even of other instruments. Parker's virtuosity on the alto inspired tenor and baritone saxophonists to attempt a new level of facility on their more cumbersome instruments; Coltrane's timbre on the tenor led alto saxophonists to adopt mouthpieces with a large bore in an effort to capture his full sound on an instrument whose tone is naturally thinner.

The saxophone has occasionally been used as an unaccompanied solo instrument (without rhythm section), early examples being Coleman Hawkins's *Hawk Variation* (1945, Baronet TR4) and *Picasso* (*c*1948, Clef [unnumbered].) Beginning in 1957 Sonny Rollins made the unaccompanied solo a characteristic element of his playing, and from the late 1960s members of the Association for the Advancement of Creative Musicians (notably Anthony Braxton) and other free-jazz players such as Steve Lacy began to give entire concerts and to record entire albums as unaccompanied soloists.

It is easier to attain a professional level of proficiency on more than one member of the saxophone family than it is in the case of any other family of instruments. Many players have been fluent on several saxophones, and it is not at all unusual to find a musician playing, for example, alto and tenor, and perhaps also soprano (and certainly clarinet), in early jazz, or alto, tenor, and soprano in a modern combo. Other types of doubling, involving the baritone and bass instruments, occur as well, though less commonly. For this reason, as well as because of the wide influence of important players, there has been considerable sharing of techniques and imitating of sound among saxophonists. A logical development from this trend was the formation of ensembles made up principally (though not exclusively) of saxophones, in which harmony and bass lines were usually played on saxophones, not on the instruments that conventionally play those lines in other ensembles. A vaudeville group, the Six Brown Brothers, made recordings in ragtime and early jazz styles between 1914 and 1920, but of greatest interest are the English trio SOS (1973–5) and the World Saxophone Quartet (1976–).

2. THE TENOR SAXOPHONE. In ensembles the role of the tenor saxophone, when not playing a solo, has generally been that of a supporting voice, playing, for example, a line beneath the lead alto saxophone in a big band, or doubling a trumpet melody an octave lower in rendering a bop theme. But far more important is its solo role. The tenor saxophone is the principal solo voice, not only within its own section of a big band but within the band as a whole; from the swing era onwards it has often figured equally prominently in small groups. It is perhaps rivalled only by the trumpet as the most important instrument in jazz.

Coleman Hawkins is generally regarded as the first major jazz improviser on the saxophone (though he denied this himself, mentioning Prince Robinson, Happy Caldwell, and Stump Evans). The importance of Hawkins's achievement lies in his developing an original style designed specifically for the saxophone, rather than adapting the style of the clarinet (which like many saxophonists he played early in his career). Hawkins's playing is identifiable by its powerful emotion and drive, and the huge sound he produced. His highly original technical patterns for the most part display great harmonic awareness and are not designed merely to show off speed of fingering or

3. John Coltrane playing tenor saxophone

tonguing. His arpeggiated lines obviously owe something to clarinet styles of the day, but the tenor saxophone was always his specialty and after 1924 he was rarely heard on any other instrument. He favored a wide vibrato and large, dark tone. During the 1920s he became technically more accomplished and progressed from a heavy to a smoother articulation, abandoning the occasional use of such devices as slap-tonguing. He extended his command of the upper range, as his famous recording of *Body and Soul* (1939, Bb 10523) demonstrates (it ascends to *g‴*, sounding *f″*).

By the end of the 1920s Hawkins had become the model for most jazz tenor saxophonists. Many players developed their own styles, but the influence of Hawkins is apparent in the basic approach of Charlie Barnet, Tex Beneke, Chu Berry, Herschel Evans, Vido Musso, and Ben Webster (who was also indebted to the alto saxophonist Johnny Hodges), and a later generation, including Arnett Cobb, Illinois Jacquet (who was also influenced by Lester Young), Flip Phillips, Ike Quebec, Al Sears, Buddy Tate, and the important modern stylist Don Byas. Bud Freeman began as a disciple of Hawkins but soon went his own way and is often mistakenly referred to as an influence on Lester Young, who became the next important figure in the development of the tenor saxophone in jazz.

Young was born only five years after Hawkins, but his influence was not widely apparent until the late 1930s, because until he made his first recording in 1936 he was little known outside Minneapolis and the Midwest. His style was soon adopted by younger players as an alternative to that of Hawkins. In important matters – tone, phrasing, melody, rhythm – Young's playing differed strikingly from Hawkins's, showing the influence of the C-melody saxophonist Frankie Trumbauer and the alto saxophonist Jimmy Dorsey. The essence of Young's tenor style was a smooth, singing tone of great beauty, in strong contrast to Hawkins's aggressive sound; Young achieved this originally using a metal mouthpiece but later changed to a hard rubber one made by Brilhart, which gave a darker effect. Instead of Hawkins's constant wide vibrato, Young's vibrato was very varied and fitted each phrase: many phrases had no vibrato at all, certain notes had a light, narrow vibrato, and some passages were highlighted by a wide vibrato close to Hawkins's style. Young was relatively unconcerned with the kind of technical and harmonic exploration that interested Hawkins and concentrated instead on the shaping of the melodic line, though his melodies always express a sophisticated understanding of the harmonic substructure.

Young's concepts of melody and phrasing were so persuasive that their influence extended far beyond saxophonists to jazz performance on many instruments. From about 1940 his authority is felt in the playing of his contemporary Budd Johnson (who earlier in his career was closer to Hawkins) and in that of the next two generations of saxophonists; these included Dexter Gordon and Charlie Parker (who also admired Hawkins's technical approach), and, during the mid-1940s, Gene Ammons, Al Cohn, John Coltrane, Allan Eager, Stan Getz (at first closer to Hawkins), Wardell Gray, Lee Konitz, Jackie McLean, Warne Marsh, James Moody, Art Pepper, Sonny Rollins (who, with Coltrane, studied the playing of Hawkins, and also Parker), Zoot Sims, Sonny Stitt, and countless others. The nature of the influence Young exercised on these players is, however, far more subtle than that of Hawkins on his followers: in the work of Cohn, Eager, Getz, Gray, Konitz, Marsh, and Pepper, Young's conception of tone shows clearly, yet by the mid-1940s Parker's bop playing on alto saxophone was perhaps a more powerful influence than Young's tenor style. And while

Hawkins's influence remained strong for the first 20 years during which he recorded, Young's lasted at its height no more than ten.

After World War II Sonny Rollins combined the virtuosity, rhythmic complexity, and forceful wit of the alto saxophonist Charlie Parker with a gruff Hawkins-like sound and a Youngian sense of phrasing and structure. His authoritative personality has left its mark on most tenor saxophonists since the mid-1950s, including Joe Henderson, Roland Kirk, Yusef Lateef (known for his interest in Eastern traditional music), Barney Wilen, and many others.

John Coltrane was also influenced by Parker, but he soon began to move in different directions. Coltrane's sound (usually produced using a metal mouthpiece) had a biting quality and a fierce emotional cry. He liberally employed OVERBLOWING, the high register, and MULTIPHONICS. There is hardly a saxophonist in the late 20th century whose playing does not reflect the influence of Coltrane's sound and an awareness, at least, of his typical melodic formulas. Such players include Bob Berg, Mike Brecker, George Coleman, Dave Liebman, Joe Farrell, Sonny Fortune, Steve Grossman, Charles Lloyd, and Branford Marsalis. The highly original work of Coltrane's younger contemporary Wayne Shorter, a brilliant improviser and composer, seems to fall somewhere between Coltrane's and Rollins's.

Many free-jazz tenor saxophonists derive their style from Coltrane or the alto player Ornette Coleman or both, but also influential is Albert Ayler, whose extreme and unique vocalistic sounds have been taken up most strikingly by David Murray. Other important free-jazz musicians to exploit such sounds are Pharoah Sanders and Archie Shepp (both of whom also play soprano saxophone), Gato Barbieri, Willem Breuker, Peter Brötzmann, and Jan Garbarek.

3. THE ALTO SAXOPHONE. In big bands the role of the alto saxophone has generally been to lead the saxophone section. From the early period of jazz a number of players became recognized as much for their abilities as section leaders as for their prowess as soloists; these include Johnny Hodges (with Duke Ellington), Charlie Holmes (with Luis Russell), and Earle Warren (with Count Basie).

The solo tradition for the alto saxophone was established in the mid-1920s and the two principal innovators were Jimmy Dorsey and Frankie Trumbauer. Dorsey was a showy player who utilized multiphonics and false fingerings as early as 1926 on two versions of *That's no Bargain* recorded with Red Nichols (Bruns. 3407, PAct 36576). He owed some of his approach to Rudy Wiedoeft, and occasionally developed technical display pieces in a similar way – for example, the version of *I'm just wild about Harry* recorded in 1930 (Decca F1876), the second chorus of which involves a prepared virtuoso passage of triple-tonguing, perfectly executed. Trumbauer, who specialized in alto and tenor C-melody saxophones (see §6(i) below), introduced a new lightness and poise into saxophone playing; his clear tone and delicate, cantabile phrasing were as influential on alto as on tenor players.

Johnny Hodges joined Duke Ellington in 1928 and his creamy, elegant style soon became a trademark of Ellington's music. A pupil of Sidney Bechet, Hodges brought to his alto saxophone solos a mixture of Bechet's formulaic set-piece constructions (evolved for the soprano) and a singing blues style recognizable by the way in which he held and bent the pitch of long notes. Other leading alto saxophone soloists of the 1930s included Hilton Jefferson, Willie Smith, and the brilliant and stylish Benny Carter (who was equally proficient as a trumpeter).

Charlie Parker was the leading figure in the development of bop on the saxophone. His first recordings, from 1940, suggest the strong influence of Lester Young, but also individual qualities – an unprecedented technical virtuosity, lightness, wit (including the clever interpolation of humorous quotations), long lines, and passing dissonances – all of which were to be further explored as he matured. Parker's sound had a bite to it which offended many critics, but those who called his tone thin missed its body and carrying power, as well as its unique color and personality; to achieve it Parker generally used a hard rubber mouthpiece and a hard reed. His influence extended to the saxophonists Cannonball Adderley, Ornette Coleman, Eric Dolphy, Arne Domnérus, Lou Donaldson, Jackie McLean, Charles McPherson, Charlie Mariano, Sonny Stitt, and Phil Woods, and virtually all jazz players who came to maturity during the 1950s.

An alternative to Parker's approach for the alto instrument came indirectly from the tenor playing of Young, as adapted by Lee Konitz (on alto) and Warne Marsh (on tenor). Through working with their teacher Lennie Tristano both men found that softer reeds and a smoother melodic style gave a different method of approaching bop. Art Pepper and Paul Desmond also found similar individual new directions.

Ornette Coleman's saxophone playing has been highly controversial, but he has affected musicians of many persuasions, even Coltrane and Rollins. When he came to prominence in the late 1950s he was playing a plastic saxophone with a rubber mouthpiece; by the 1970s he had adopted an instrument made by Selmer with a metal mouthpiece and a medium-soft reed. His basic sound, which has a singing, folklike quality, and his style remain unmistakable, but these have more to do with his conception of improvised melody than with any particular characteristic of the alto saxophone.

Eric Dolphy pursued Parker's style in a different direction. His rhythms and phrasing clearly derive from Parker but his choice of pitches is highly dissonant and unpredictable. He is widely admired, even among critics with whom free jazz generally finds little favor, for his technical achievements, which include an astounding ability to leap fluently between registers.

Among the followers of Coleman are John Tchicai, Marion Brown, Gennady Gol'shteyn, and Vladimir Chekasin. Jimmy Lyons retained an individual approach to free jazz, based on Parker with some touches of influence from Dolphy. Gary Bartz and Sonny Fortune both found highly individual adaptations of Coltrane's style for soprano and alto saxophones.

4. THE SOPRANO SAXOPHONE. The soprano saxophone is made in two designs, one straight, the other with an outward curve at the bell; it has a clear and somewhat strident sound, though the curved instrument is noticeably less strident than the straight one. It is notoriously difficult to pitch accurately. Played without vibrato it can sound remarkably similar to the oboe, but with the right combination of reed and "lay" of the mouthpiece and with vibrato it can emulate aspects of all the other saxophones.

The first important exponent of the soprano saxophone was Sidney Bechet, who achieved a high level of virtuosity and improvisational inventiveness on the instrument well before 1923 when he made his first recordings. Bechet saw the soprano saxophone as complementary to the clarinet, which at first was his main instrument, and never developed a serious interest in the other saxophones. Nevertheless he influenced Johnny Hodges and other players, such as Don Redman, Woody Herman, and Charlie Barnet, all of whom played soprano and other saxophones. In the 1930s few saxophonists specialized on soprano, with the notable exception of Emmett Mathews, and during the 1940s and 1950s it became extremely rare.

The instrument was taken up again by the iconoclastic musician Steve Lacy and by others, including the Danish player Max Bruel, but it regained its popularity only after 1960 when John Coltrane (perhaps under Lacy's influence) began to play it: virtually every musician listed above as a follower of Coltrane plays the soprano as well as the tenor saxophone. Older players who had established their reputations on alto or tenor also took up the soprano, including Dexter Gordon, Budd Johnson, Oliver Nelson, Jerome Richardson, Sam Rivers, Lucky Thompson, and even (briefly) Cannonball Adderley and Sonny Rollins. Bob Wilber, perhaps the most accomplished of Bechet's pupils, with his band Soprano Summit (led jointly with Kenny Davern), did much to popularize the instrument among traditional and mainstream jazz players; Bechet himself, through his postwar residence in France, fueled an important (though imitative) school of European soprano players, among them Jean-Pierre Bonnel and Claude Luter, and the Englishman Wally Fawkes, all of whom have played the instrument regularly in the 1970s and 1980s. It has been exploited in free jazz by Lacy and, as a result of Lacy's influence, by Evan Parker; during the 1970s Wayne Shorter came to prominence as a player of the soprano, and more recently still Jane Ira Bloom has joined the small ranks of soprano specialists, developing an individual style that centers on a powerful tone.

5. The baritone saxophone. Despite its comparatively low range, the baritone saxophone functions far more often as a melodic instrument or an inner voice within a chordal texture than as a bass instrument. Exceptions to this occur, most frequently in Latin jazz, where the stinging crispness of its tone effectively carries ostinato bass lines, as for example at the beginning of Dizzy Gillespie's *Manteca* (1947, Vic. 203023). The baritone saxophone has mainly been used in larger ensembles, notably in the saxophone sections of big bands. The rich color of Harry Carney's baritone playing was a staple of Duke Ellington's band sound for 50 years and Jack Washington played an analogous role in Count Basie's orchestra. Both men were capable, though rarely used, soloists and in their way influential. It was not until the 1950s, with the emergence of Gerry Mulligan and Lars Gullin, that a clearly defined solo school of baritone playing emerged. Other baritone players of some importance include Serge Chaloff, Leo Parker, Cecil Payne, and Ronnie Ross. Pepper Adams was admired by many musicians on account of his hard-edged sound, virtuosity, and wit. During the 1960s Coltrane's influence came through in the baritone playing of Charles Davis, John Surman, and others. Later, Hamiet Bluiett became one of the few avant-garde musicians to specialize on baritone saxophone, using such radical virtuoso techniques as overblowing in the highest register. The instrument has also found some use in dixieland and mainstream ensembles from the 1960s; a notable soloist is John Barnes, who has played with Alex Welsh and Humphrey Lyttelton.

6. Other saxophones.

(i) The C-melody saxophone. This tenor saxophone survived in jazz well into the 1920s, when Frankie Trumbauer was its principal exponent. Although he played solo pieces in the virtuoso style of Rudy Wiedoeft he was mainly an improvising jazz musician. He developed a singing tone and legato style on the instrument, making ample use of portamento and other expressive devices; his improvisations employ a natural, vocalistic articulation and a dry wit, expressed in surprising pauses and unusual phrase lengths. Many players (both black and white) modeled elements of their style on his: Budd Johnson, Eddie Barefield, and Lester Young have all testified to the respect Trumbauer inspired as a jazz player.

Other musicians to use the instrument in the 1920s were Stump Evans (with King Oliver), Jack Pettis, and Spencer Clark (with the California Ramblers). In the 1980s it was used infrequently by the revivalists Bob Wilber and Kenny Davern.

(ii) The bass saxophone. The unwieldy bass saxophone was made largely redundant in the big-band saxophone section by the addition to the baritone saxophone of keywork that extended its range downwards. The instrument has occasionally been used as a substitute for the tuba or double bass. Its first, and most significant, solo exponent was Adrian Rollini, who developed a role for it as a novelty instrument, and acquired a considerable degree of facility on it; he used slap-tonguing to achieve the effect of the tuba in playing a bass line, but in his solos emerged from the ensemble and played predominantly in the upper register, effectively within the range of the baritone. Other significant players of the instrument include Charlie Jackson (with King Oliver), Billy Fowler (in Fletcher Henderson's orchestra), Spencer Clark, and, later, Joe Rushton and Vince Giordano.

After World War II the bass saxophone was still used occasionally by Boyd Raeburn, Rushton (with Red Nichols in the 1950s), and Charlie Ventura. It was also the main instrument of the bandleader Harry Gold. In free jazz Anthony Braxton has used it, as have Roscoe Mitchell and Joseph Jarman of the Art Ensemble of Chicago and Vinny Golia. In 1986 the BBC made an influential film about the use of the instrument in jazz, *The Lowest of the Low*.

(iii) The sopranino saxophone. The highest-pitched of the saxophone family, the sopranino has a range about an octave above that of the alto. It has been adopted as a doubling instrument by Joseph Jarman (from around 1969) and Anthony Braxton (from around 1973), who both use it regularly (together with many other wind instruments) to supply timbral contrast in their improvisations. Braxton plays the sopranino intermittently on his album *The Montreux–Berlin Concerts* (1975–6, Ari. 5002); on the track *29 M 36* it contrasts sharply with the sound of the contrabass.

(iv) The contrabass saxophone. Its range is about an octave below that of the baritone instrument and like the sopranino it has been used by Braxton (from around 1976) for purposes of timbral variety; he plays it on *73°S Kelvin* on the anthology *Wildflowers 2: the New York Loft Jazz Sessions* (1976, Douglas 7046).

(v) The saxello. A variant of the B♭ soprano saxophone, it was manufactured by King from the 1920s, and the name was the company's trademark. It has a gentle curve in the neck, and the bell faces outwards. It is a relatively rare instrument but has been used by Bennie Maupin and Elton Dean.

(vi) The manzello. A modified version of the saxello, it was used (and named) by Roland Kirk. It has a larger bell than the saxello, which gives it a broader sound. Kirk is its sole exponent; on the track *Parisian Thoroughfare* on Jaki Byard's album *The Jaki Byard Experience* (1968, Prst. 7615) he changes between several wind instruments during the raucous introduction, then

4. Roland Kirk playing the stritch

plays manzello followed by tenor saxophone in the statement of the theme, and then improvises a fine bop solo on the same two saxophones.

(vii) The stritch. The stritch is Roland Kirk's modified version of the straight E♭ alto saxophone manufactured by Buescher in the late 1920s. His adaptations to the original instrument include the addition of extra keywork to allow one-handed playing. Kirk may be heard playing a solo on the instrument on *Skater's Waltz* from his album *Kirk's Work* (1961, Prst. 7210).

(viii) The slide saxophone. Although examples of various types of slide saxophone were made in France during the 1920s, the only instrument to have been adopted in jazz is a variant of the B♭ soprano, developed and played by Snub Mosley. It has a conventional saxophone mouthpiece and crook, which is attached to the head of a straight tube, held vertically, with a longitudinal opening instead of tone-holes. A slide runs inside the tube and is manipulated by the player's right hand; as the slide is pushed in, it progressively closes the longitudinal opening on the instrument's body so that the air column is restricted within the body and slide. The problem of pitching notes accurately made it a difficult instrument to master and even Mosley (who used it mostly for ballads) was capable of performances that were badly out of tune.

For further illustrations *see* BYAS, DON; COLTRANE, JOHN; DOMNÉRUS, ARNE; FOSTER, POPS; GARBAREK, JAN; GIUFFRE, JIMMY; GORDON, DEXTER; LACY, STEVE; MULLIGAN, GERRY; PEPPER, ART; ROLLINS, SONNY; SHORTER, WAYNE; SIMS, ZOOT; WILLIAMS, MARY LOU; and YOUNG, LESTER.

BIBLIOGRAPHY

J.-E. Berendt: *Das Jazzbuch: Entwicklung und Bedeutung der Jazzmusik* (Frankfurt am Main, Germany, 1953, rev. 2/1959 as *Das neue Jazzbuch*, Eng. trans., New York, 1962; rev. and enlarged 5/1981 as *Das grosse Jazzbuch: von New Orleans bis Jazz Rock*, Eng. trans. as *The Jazz Book: from New Orleans to Fusion and Beyond*, Westport, CT, 1982)
L. Feather: *The Book of Jazz: a Guide to the Entire Field* (New York, 1957, 2/1965 as *The Book of Jazz from Then till Now: a Guide to the Entire Field*)
H. Miedema: *Jazz Styles and Analysis: Alto Sax* (Chicago, 1975) [125 transcrs. of solos by 103 players]
J. Viera: *Das Saxophon im Jazz* (Vienna, 1977)
M. Cuscuna: Liner notes, R. Kirk: *Pre-Rahsaan* (Prst. 24080, 1978)
D. Sickler: *The Artistry of John Coltrane* (New York, 1979)
P. Cohen: "The Saga of the F Alto Saxophone," *Saxophone Journal*, v/1 (1980), 10
P. Bate and J. B. Robinson: "Saxophone," *GroveI*
P. Cohen: "Vintage Saxophones Revisited," *Saxophone Journal*, x/2 (1985), 4; x/3 (1985), 4
H. R. Gee: *Saxophone Soloists and their Music, 1844–1985* (Bloomington, IN, 1986)

LEWIS PORTER

Sayles, Emanuel (René) [Manny] (*b* Donaldsonville, LA, 31 Jan 1907; *d* New Orleans, 5 Oct 1986). Banjoist and guitarist, son of George Sayles. He taught himself banjo and guitar and after moving to New Orleans worked with Fate Marable on the SS *Capitol* (1928). His banjo playing may be heard on *Astoria Strut* (Vic. 38576), which he recorded with the JONES AND COLLINS ASTORIA HOT EIGHT in 1929. He performed as a leader and under many musicians in Chicago (1939–49) and again in New Orleans (from 1949); he also recorded as a leader (1961–3). Sayles was equally accomplished as a guitarist, displaying a light chordal style in ensembles and a formidable single-string solo technique on the acoustic instrument. His work is especially well demonstrated on an album recorded by Louis Cottrell, Jr., *Bourbon Street Parade* (1961, Riv. 9385), and particularly on the track *Sayles' Broken String Blues*. He traveled to Japan with George Lewis (i) (1963–4) and also toured with Sweet Emma Barrett (1964). He worked again in Chicago (1965–8) then regularly at Preservation Hall, New Orleans (1968); in 1969 Sayles performed as a soloist in Britain. During the 1970s and 1980s he continued to play, mainly in New Orleans, though he also toured with the Preservation Hall Jazz Band (1971, 1979) and others. Among the many leaders with whom he recorded were Peter Bocage (1961–2, 1964), Barrett (1961, 1963–4), Punch Miller (1962), Lewis (1962, 1963), Kid Thomas (1971, *c*1974, 1975, 1981, 1983), and Earl Hines (1975).

See also BANJO; for illustration *see* HUMPHREY.

BIBLIOGRAPHY

H. Friedwald: Liner notes, L. Cottrell: *Bourbon Street Parade* (Riv. 9385, 1961)
B. Turnock: "Emanuel Sayles Reminiscing," *Fn*, xi/4 (1980), 4
Obituary, L. Whittaker, *Fn*, xviii/2 (1986–7), 17

based on *ChiltonW*

Sayles, George (*b* New Orleans, *c*1880; *d* after 1930). Guitarist, father of Emanuel Sayles. He was a member of the Silver Leaf Orchestra from about 1898 until it disbanded in 1918, and thereafter retired, playing only occasionally during the early 1920s.

MARCEL JOLY

Sbarbaro, Tony [Antonio; Spargo, Tony] (*b* New Orleans, 27 June 1897; *d* New York 30 Oct 1969). Drummer. He began playing in New Orleans with the Frayle Brothers' Band (1911) and later with Papa Jack Laine's Reliance Band, Merritt Brunies, and the pianist Carl Randall. In 1916 he moved to Chicago to join the ORIGINAL DIXIELAND JAZZ BAND. He was the only original member of the group to remain with it until its final dissolution in 1956. Sbarbaro also played in New York with several dixieland musicians, including Miff Mole, Phil Napoleon, Big Chief Moore, Pee Wee Erwin, Jimmy Lytell, Tony Parenti, Eddie Condon, and the pianist Mike Loscalzo, with some of whom he recorded. He ceased performing in the early 1960s.

Sbarbaro's early playing contrasts sharply with that of his New Orleans contemporaries Baby Dodds and Zutty Singleton. His showy technique and exuberant improvisatory style are rooted in the ragtime playing of such drummers as James Lent, Buddy Gilmore, and John Lucas. His earliest recordings, notably *Indiana, Dixie Jass Band One-step*, and *Tiger Rag* (all 1917), belie the idea that the equipment and playing techniques of drummers were restricted in early recording studios. His cymbal, woodblock, cowbells, snare drum, and bass drum (played by double-drumming) are clearly heard on these tracks.

Oral history material in *LNT*.

SELECTED RECORDINGS

As sideman: Original Dixieland Jazz Band: Indiana (1917, Col. A2297); Dixie Jass Band One-step (1917, Vic. 18255); Tiger Rag (1917, Aeolian Voc. 1206); Crazy Blues (1921, Vic. 18729); Fidgety Feet (1936, Vic. 25668); Original Dixieland One-step (1936, Vic. 25502); E. Condon: Mandy Make up your Mind (1943, Com. 604)

BIBLIOGRAPHY

ChiltonW
F. Manskleid: "Sixty Years of Tony Sbarbaro," *JM*, iv/9 (1958), 24
H. O. Brunn: *The Story of the Original Dixieland Jazz Band* (Baton Rouge, LA, 1960/*R*1977)
T. D. Brown: *A History and Analysis of Jazz Drumming to 1942* (diss., U. of Michigan, 1976)

T. DENNIS BROWN

Scala. Record label. It was established in England in 1911; at first the catalogue consisted of German recordings pressed in Germany. When production resumed after World War I the repertory was expanded, drawing on American material taken from Gennett and Vocalion, including a few jazz items issued under pseudonyms. Among items recorded in London were the first made by a racially integrated jazz band, a group of British and expatriate Afro-American musicians who recorded under the leadership of Victor Vorzanger in mid-1922. The label was discontinued late in 1927. (B. Rust: *The American Record Label Book* (New Rochelle, NY, 1978), 275)

Scat singing. A technique of jazz SINGING in which onomatopoeic or nonsense syllables are sung to improvised melodies. Some writers have traced scat singing back to the practice, common in West African musics, of translating percussion patterns into vocal lines by assigning syllables to characteristic rhythms. However, since this allows little scope for melodic improvisation and the earliest recorded examples of jazz scat singing involved the free invention of rhythm, melody, and syllables, it is more likely that the technique began in the USA as singers imitated the sounds of jazz instrumentalists.

Scat singing was one of the "novelty" devices of early New Orleans jazz; it can also be heard in undeveloped form on some early blues and washboard-band recordings. The most celebrated early instances are by Louis Armstrong, whose highly successful recording *Heebie Jeebies* (1926, OK 8300) established his reputation as a jazz singer; his early scat solos rival his trumpet improvisations in virtuosity, range of feeling, and variety of attacks and timbres (see ex.1, which illustrates his

Ex.1 From L. Armstrong: *Hotter than that* (1927, OK 8535); transcr. J. B. Robinson

clear imitation of a trumpet rip). Armstrong started a vogue for scat singing, and it was soon popularized by singers such as Cab Calloway, whose many scat solos in the 1930s served as a model for the "citified" black music of Sportin' Life in Gershwin's *Porgy and Bess.*

As jazz improvisation grew increasingly complex, scat singing followed suit, with the result that later scat singers could improvise effortlessly in the complex bop idiom. Ella Fitzgerald in particular made a specialty of imitating various jazz instruments and even particular soloists, thereby greatly expanding the range of timbres and attacks in scat singing (ex.2). Other important scat singers in the bop style included

Ex.2 From E. Fitzgerald: *Flying Home* (1945, Decca 23956); transcr. J. B. Robinson

Eddie Jefferson, Betty Carter, Anita O'Day, Joe "Bebop" Carroll, Sarah Vaughan, Carmen McRae, Jon Hendricks, Babs Gonzales, and Dizzy Gillespie. Like other jazz musicians, each scat singer adopted a unique, immediately recognizable, timbre and delivery and developed a personal stock of syllables and vocal devices; Clark Terry's distinctive "mumbling" technique and Gillespie's imitations of trumpet smears are extreme but not untypical examples. Bop scat singing was also vitiated and popularized, mainly by Ward Swingle and the Swingle Singers, whose application of scat techniques to the classical repertory arose originally from a desire to find new solfège exercises for classically trained singers. In addition, the usefulness of bop scat singing for teaching jazz was discovered, notably by Lennie Tristano, and accounts for the relatively large number of scat singing manuals that are in fact primers in jazz improvisation and ear training.

The 1960s saw a vast expansion of the timbres and resources available to scat singers, and the international spread of scat singing to other types of music. Leone Thomas incorporated pygmy yodeling techniques of Central Africa into his singing, while many scat singers (including Karin Krog from Norway, Urszula Dudziak from Poland, and Flora Purim from Brazil) came to jazz from other musical cultures. The extension of vocal improvisation to include sounds formerly regarded as nonmusical, such as cries, screams, sobbing, and laughter, was one of the principal innovations of this period, and at times brought jazz singing close to avant-garde art music; this is apparent, for example, in the work of Cleo Laine or, later, Lauren Newton. Dudziak in particular explored the possibilities of electronic manipulation and distortion of the voice.

With the bop revival in the mid-1970s there was also a revival of interest in bop scat singing, leading to comebacks for singers such as Betty Carter and Eddie Jefferson who had previously worked in obscurity. Many young scat singers regarded themselves as belonging to the classic bop tradition; among the best of these are Al Jarreau, who is particularly adept at creating vocal equivalents of complex jazz-rock rhythms, and Bobby McFerrin, whose extraordinarily wide range and mobility are evident in his unaccompanied solo performances. Contemporary scat singers have shown that this vocal art can strike out in directions of its own, independent of developments in instrumental jazz or avant-garde music.

BIBLIOGRAPHY

L. Feather: "An Explanation of Vocalese," *Jazz: a Quarterly of American Music*, no.3 (1959), 261

P. Coker and D. Baker: *Vocal Improvisation: an Instrumental Approach* (Lebanon, IN, 1981) [incl. discography]

K. Henriques: "Scatting and Bopping," *The Wire*, no.1 (1982), 14

J. BRADFORD ROBINSON

Scepter. Record company and label. The company was established in New York in 1964. It recorded several excellent albums by Art Farmer and James Moody, and by the New York Jazz Sextet, which included Farmer, Moody, and Tom McIntosh; the last also produced several recordings for the company. Within two years of its foundation, however, Scepter had ceased to operate.

MARK GARDNER

Schenkelbach, Fülöp. *See* FILU.

Schertzer, Hymie. *See* SHERTZER, HYMIE.

Schifrin, Lalo (Boris) (*b* Buenos Aires, 21 June 1932). Argentine composer and pianist. He learned piano as a child and later won a scholarship to the Paris Conservatoire, where he was supervised by Charles Koechlin and studied with Olivier Messiaen. While in Paris he played with local jazz artists and in 1955 represented Argentina in the third International Jazz Festival. On his return home he established himself as a composer, arranger, conductor, and pianist who was equally at ease in popular, jazz, and art-music circles; he also formed the first Argentine big band in the Basie–Gillespie tradition. In 1958 Schifrin moved to New York, where he gained recognition as the pianist in Gillespie's jazz quintet (1960–62) and recorded with other well-known jazz musicians. From 1962 he has concentrated on writing, and has become a major composer of film music; his *Jazz Suite on the Mass Texts* (1965) is highly regarded.

SELECTED RECORDINGS

As leader: *Lalo Schifrin* (1962, Roul. 52088)

As sideman with D. Gillespie: *An Electrifying Evening with the Dizzy Gillespie Quintet* (1961, Verve 68401); *New Wave!* (1962, Phi. 600070)

RECORDED COMPOSITIONS
(selective list)

Recorded by others: D. Gillespie: *Gillespiana* (1960, Verve 68394); *New Continent* (1962, Lml. 86022); P. Horn: *Jazz Suite on the Mass Texts* (1965, RCA LSP3414)

SELECTED ARRANGEMENTS

Recorded by others: S. Getz: *Reflections* (1963, Verve 68554); Jimmy Smith: *The Cat* (1964, Verve 68587)

BIBLIOGRAPHY

G. Lees: "Lalo = Brilliance," *DB*, xxix/8 (1962), 18

J. Tynan: "Lalo Schifrin," *BMI: the Many Worlds of Music* (1965), Nov, 11

H. Siders: "Keeping Score on Schifrin: Lalo Schifrin and the Art of Film Music," *DB*, xxxvi/5 (1969), 16

L. Tomkins: "Lalo Schifrin: My Approaches to the Film Score," *CI*, xv (1976), no.2, p.8; no.3, p.15

T. Darter and B. Doerschuk: "Lalo Schifrin: Piano Roots of a Master Film Composer," *CK*, ix/2 (1983), 8 [incl. discography]

R. Palmer: "Reel Job," *JJI*, xxxix/2 (1986), 19 [incl. discography]

MICHAEL J. BUDDS/R

Schildkraut, Dave(y) [David] (*b* New York, 7 Jan 1925). Alto saxophonist. He gained his first professional experience with Louis Prima (1941), and then played with Buddy Rich (intermittently from 1947) and Anita O'Day (1947). After touring Europe and recording with Stan Kenton (1953–4) he played and recorded with Pete Rugolo (1954) and George Handy (1955); he was a soloist on the album *Miles Davis Quintet* (1954, Prst. 185), from which the track *Solar* well represents his playing. He also recorded with Oscar Pettiford (1954), Ralph Burns and Eddie Bert (both 1955), Tito Puente and Chuck Wayne (both 1956), and Sam Most (1957). After working again with Kenton in 1959, he led his own quartet at clubs in New York and worked as a freelance. Schildkraut was a fluent bop musician whose playing was occasionally mistaken for that of Charlie Parker.

BIBLIOGRAPHY

FeatherE

R. Reisner: *Bird: the Legend of Charlie Parker* (New York, 1962/*R*1975), 206

Schilperoort, Peter [Bronx, Pat] (*b* The Hague, 4 Nov 1919). Dutch clarinetist and saxophonist. He is self-taught as a musician. He began his career with the Bouncers (1938–9) and the Swing Papa's (1939–43) and played under the bandleader Klaas van Beeck (1943). With the pianist Frans Vink he formed the Dutch Swing College, a school for jazz, in 1944 and the DUTCH SWING COLLEGE BAND the following year; he succeeded Vink as the leader in 1946. He left the Dutch Swing College in September 1955 to work in the aircraft industry and to lead a quartet and a quintet from 1956 until 1959, when he again assumed leadership of the band, a position he retained into the 1980s. A good example of his work is the album *Quartet and Quintet* (Dureco 51022), recorded in 1957–8. (*FeatherE*)

WIM VAN EYLE

Schlinger, Sol (*b* New York, 6 Sept 1926). Baritone saxophonist. He first played tenor saxophone in dance bands (1940–43), then took up the baritone instrument and played with Buddy Rich (1943). After working alternately with Tommy Dorsey (?1943–4, 1949–51) and Jimmy Dorsey (1947, 1951), he played briefly with Charlie Barnet, Jerry Gray, Herbie Fields, Louis Jordan, and the Latin dance-band leader Perez Prado. As a tenor saxophonist he toured (1952) and performed in New York (1956) with Benny Goodman; playing the baritone instrument he recorded with Neal Hefti (1952), the Sauter–Finegan Orchestra (1952–3), Goodman (1954–8), Al Cohn (1954, 1956), Manny Albam (1955–7), Teddy Charles, Coleman Hawkins, Phil Woods, Don Elliott, and Bob Brookmeyer (all 1956), Urbie Green (1956, 1958, 1961), Chuck Wayne (1957), Bill Potts (1959), Benny Golson and Mundell Lowe (both 1961), and Dave Frishberg (1968). His work is well represented by Cohn's albums *Mr. Music* (1954, RCA LPM1024) and *The Sax Section* (1956, Epic 3278). Schlinger performed and recorded with Goodman's big band at Carnegie Hall (1978), and in 1983 recorded a re-creation of music by Glenn Miller. (*FeatherE*)

Schlippenbach, Alex(ander von) (*b* Berlin, 7 April 1938). German pianist, composer, and bandleader. He took piano lessons from the age of eight and studied at the Staatliche Hochschule für Musik, Cologne, with the composers Bernd Alois Zimmermann and Rudolf Petzold. He played from 1963 with Gunter Hampel and in 1964–7 was a member of Manfred Schoof's quintet. His composition *Globe Unity* (1966) was performed to considerable acclaim by the GLOBE UNITY ORCHESTRA at the Berliner Jazztage, and his association with the orchestra continued, interrupted only in 1971–2, into the 1980s. From 1967 he led a number of small groups, including a trio with Evan Parker and Paul Lovens (formed 1970), with which Alan Silva performed occasionally, and a duo with the drummer and singer Sven-Åke Johansson (formed 1976); he also performed and recorded as a soloist. Schlippenbach's music combines elements of free jazz and avant-garde classical music; his performances on such recordings as Hampel's *Heartplants* (1965) and the Manfred Schoof Quintet's *Voices* (1966) were influential in the development of free jazz in Europe.

SELECTED RECORDINGS

As unaccompanied soloist: *Piano Solo* (1977, FMP 430)
Duos with S.-Å. Johansson: *Drive* (1979, FMP 0810); *Kalfaktor A. Falke und andere Lieder* (1982, FMP 0970)
As leader of small groups: *Pakistani Pomade* (1972, FMP 0110); *The Hidden Peak* (1977, FMP 410); *Detta fra di noi* (1981, Po Torch 10, 11)
As leader of Globe Unity Orchestra: *Globe Unity* (1966, Saba 15109); *Improvisations* (1977, Japo 60021); *Intergalactic Blow* (1982, Japo 60039)
As sideman: G. Hampel: *Heartplants* (1965, MPS 15026); M. Schoof: *Voices* (1966, CBS 62621)

BIBLIOGRAPHY

Feather–Gitler '70s
L. Jeske: "Free Players from many Lands Form Globe Unity Orchestra," *DB*, xlvii/9 (1980), 28 [incl. interview]
B. Noglik: "Alexander von Schlippenbach," *Jazzwerkstatt international* (Berlin, 1981), 97–127 [incl. interview, discography]

BERT NOGLIK

Schlitten, Don (*b* 1932). Record producer who in 1975 founded the record company and label XANADU; *see also* MUSE (ii), ONYX (ii), and SIGNAL.

Schlüter, Wolfgang (*b* Berlin, 12 Nov 1933). German vibraphonist. He studied piano as a child and percussion and timpani in 1950–55, during which time he also played in dance bands. He belonged to Michael Naura's quintet and played with Rolf Kühn (1956), Horst Jankowski (1961), and the German All Stars (1963); from the early 1960s into the 1980s he was a member of the dance orchestra of the Norddeutscher Rundfunk in Hamburg. He also worked with Volker Kriegel (1978) and in the 1980s led a small swing group. He recorded albums of duos with Michael Naura (*Country Children*, 1977, ECM 5803) and the pianist Christoph Spendel (*Orange Town*, 1981, MRC 06664599), and played in a small band with Dick Wellstood. In addition to his activities as a performer he has worked as a composer and arranger of jazz and dance music. (*FeatherE*; *ReclamsJ*)

WOLFRAM KNAUER

Schmidli, Peter (*b* Basle, Switzerland, 20 Sept 1937). Banjoist and guitarist. He played as an amateur with local dixieland bands in the 1950s and 1960s and recorded with Oscar Klein (1969, 1971, 1973). In the early 1970s he joined the Tremble Kids, with whom he recorded in 1971–7; at the same time he led the P. S. Corporation (to 1981), which played jazz and popular music on radio and television broadcasts and on several recordings. He has belonged for several years to the group Buddha's Gamblers, with which he recorded the album *Swinging with Buddha's Gamblers* (Swiss Jazz 6336) in 1982.

PETER SCHWALM

Schneeze. Nickname of ART ROLLINI.

Schnitter, David (Bertram) (*b* Newark, NJ, 19 March 1948). Tenor saxophonist. He studied clarinet as a child but changed to tenor saxophone at the age of 15. He began his professional career playing at weddings and as a member of various rock bands. In 1972 Schnitter formed his own group in New York. After playing with Ted Dunbar (1973) he began his most important association, with Art Blakey (1974–9). He worked with Freddie Hubbard from 1979, recording with him in 1980 and 1981; he also played with Frank Foster, Charles Earland, Groove Holmes, and Johnny Lytle. Schnitter's style is based firmly on hard bop; his sound has been compared in particular with Dexter Gordon's, though the influences of Sonny Rollins and John Coltrane are also detectable.

SELECTED RECORDINGS

As leader (all recorded for Muse): *Invitation* (1976, 5108); *Goliath* (1977, 5153); *Thundering* (1978, 5197); *Glowing* (1979, 5222)
As sideman: S. Stitt: *In Walked Sonny* (1975, Sonet 691); A. Blakey: *Backgammon* (1976, Roul. 5003); *In my Prime* (1977–8, Tim. 114, 118); *In this Korner* (1978, Conc. 68)

BIBLIOGRAPHY

Feather–Gitler '70s
C. Delaunay: "Nice Plus . . . Dave Schnitter," *Jh*, no.330 (1976), 20
A. Lange: Review of *Thundering* (1978), *DB*, xlvii/4 (1980), 44
J. Howard: "A Message from Today," *JF* [intl edn], no.70 (1981), 38

PAUL RINZLER

Schoebel, Elmer (*b* East St. Louis, IL, 8 Sept 1896; *d* St. Petersburg, FL, 14 Dec 1970). Arranger, composer, and pianist. He first played piano for silent films and vaudeville shows, then moved to Chicago. In 1922–3 he played and wrote arrangements for the New Orleans Rhythm Kings. He then led his own band at the Midway Gardens, and worked as an arranger for the Melrose Brothers Music Co. Later he became a staff arranger for Warner Bros. in New York, and remained with this company until the 1940s. Thereafter he resumed playing and continued to perform until shortly before his death. Scarcely audible as a pianist on most of his recordings, Schoebel was most important as an arranger and composer. He arranged for publication many early jazz pieces, notably those of Jelly Roll Morton, and his work displays a development from his early, rather naive, scores to later, more sophisticated ones. His compositions include many popular songs and jazz standards, including *Bugle Call Rag* (his arrangement of which was later recorded as *Bugle Call Blues*), *Farewell Blues*, and *Prince of Wails*.

SELECTED RECORDINGS

As leader: Copenhagen/Prince of Wails (1929, Bruns. 4652)
As sideman with New Orleans Rhythm Kings: Discontented Blues/Bugle Call Blues (1922, Gen. 4967)

BIBLIOGRAPHY

ChiltonW
M. Williams: "N. O. R. K.," *Jazz Masters of New Orleans* (New York and London, 1967/*R*1978), 82

JAMES DAPOGNY

Schoof, Manfred (*b* Magdeburg, Germany, 6 April 1936). German trumpeter. He attended the Musikakademie in Kassel (1955–8) and studied composition (with Bernd Alois Zimmermann), trumpet, and piano at the Hochschule in Cologne (1958–61); he wrote arrangements for a school band while he was a student and for orchestras led by Kurt Edelhagen and Harald Banter soon after. He belonged to Gunter Hampel's quartet (1963–5), led a quintet, with Gerd Dudek, Alex Schlippenbach, Buschi Niebergall, and the drummer Jaki Liebezeit as his sidemen, that was one of the first free-jazz groups in Europe (1965–8), and worked with the Globe Unity Orchestra from 1966 into the 1980s. In 1969 he led a free-jazz orchestra on the recording *European Echoes* and formed the New Jazz Trio with Cees See and Peter Trunk, which incorporated into its playing elements of ethnic music; he also belonged to George Russell's orchestra (1969–71) and the Clarke–Boland Big Band (1969–72). Later he led a jazz-rock quintet and sextet with Michel Pilz (1974–9), worked with Mal Waldron (1974–80), formed his own orchestra (1980), and wrote compositions and arrangements for big band (1983).

SELECTED RECORDINGS

As leader: *The Early Quintet* (1966, FMP 0450); *European Echoes* (1969, FMP 0010); of New Jazz Trio (with P. Trunk and C. See): *Page One* (1970, MPS 15276); *Horizons* (1979, Japo 60030); *Reflections* (1983, Mood 42)
As sideman with M. Waldron: *Hard Talk* (1974, Enja 2050)

BIBLIOGRAPHY

Feather–Gitler '70s; *ReclamsJ*
R. Williams: "Schoof: Apostle of the New Music," *MM* (14 March 1970), 12
R. Reichelt: "Manfred Schoof: Beyond Free Jazz," *JF* [intl edn], no.61 (1979), 41

ROBERT J. IANNAPOLLO

Schroeder, Gene [Eugene Charles] (*b* Madison, WI, 5 Feb 1915; *d* Madison, 16 Feb 1975). Pianist. His mother played piano and his father performed on trumpet with his own band. Schroeder studied piano (1924–7) and played clarinet at high school; he studied music for a year at the University of Wisconsin (1932). In 1939 he moved to New York, where he led his own group at the Town Topics club. He worked with Joe Marsala (1940) and Marty Marsala (1941), and with Wild Bill Davison in Chicago, Boston, and New York (1942–3). In 1943 he was resident at Nick's, New York, initially in Miff Mole's group, and shortly afterwards he joined Eddie Condon (*c*1943), with whom he remained for 17 years, playing at his club in Greenwich Village (for illustration *see* NIGHTCLUBS AND OTHER VENUES, fig.5). He also studied with the composer Paul Creston (1948–50). From 1961 to 1964 Schroeder was a member of the Dukes of Dixieland and in the late 1960s he worked with Tony Parenti.

SELECTED RECORDINGS

As leader: Liza/I ain't got nobody (1944, Black & White 33); Sweet Georgia Brown/Tea for Two (1944, Black & White 5)
As sideman: W. B. Davison: Riverboat Shuffle/Muskrat Ramble (1943, Com. 618); E. Condon: Maple Leaf Rag/Jazz me Blues (1950, Decca 27035)

BIBLIOGRAPHY

ChiltonW
E. Condon and H. O'Neal: *The Eddie Condon Scrapbook of Jazz* (New York, 1973)
O. Coyle: "Quiet Mastery," *MR*, ix/3 (1982), 1

JAMES M. DORAN

Schuller, Gunther (Alexander) (*b* New York, 22 Nov 1925). Composer, conductor, and writer. The son of a violinist with the New York PO, he studied theory, flute, and horn privately and played horn professionally with the American Ballet Theatre (1943), the Cincinnati SO (1943–5), and the Metropolitan Opera in New York (1945–59); he began his career in jazz by recording as a horn player with Miles Davis (1949–50). While lecturing at Brandeis University in 1957 he coined the term "third stream" to describe music that combined elements of Western art music and jazz; during the following decades he became an enthusiastic advocate of this style and wrote many works according to its principles, including *Transformation* (1957), for jazz ensemble, Concertino (1959), for jazz quartet and orchestra (one of the movements of which, *Progression in Tempo*, has sometimes been performed separately), *Abstraction* (1959), for nine instruments, and Variants on a Theme of Thelonious Monk (1960), for 13 instruments, which was recorded by Ornette Coleman, Eric Dolphy, and Bill Evans (ii). For some time he was associated with John Lewis; this led to the performance and recording by the Modern Jazz Quartet of several of Schuller's works, including *Conversation* (on *Third Stream Music*, 1957, 1959, 1960, Atl. 1345) and the Concertino. With Lewis and Harold Farberman he led the big band ORCHESTRA U.S.A. from 1962 to 1965. He also oversaw the programming and performance of third stream works at concerts and festivals (such as one at Brandeis University, 1957), and with Lewis and others formed the Lenox School of Jazz in Massachusetts. From 1967 to 1977 he was the president of the New England Conservatory; at the same time he promoted the music of Scott Joplin, Jelly Roll Morton, Duke Ellington, and Paul Whiteman by preparing editions, making transcriptions, and giving performances of their works; his recordings of music by Joplin include the opera *Treemonisha* and selections from *The Red Back Book*, a collection of orchestrated ragtime compositions. He formed the firms Margun Music in 1975 and Gunmar Music four years later, which publish jazz and third stream works by Charles Mingus, George Russell, Johnny Carisi, Ran Blake, and Jimmy Giuffre, as well as his own editions of music by Joplin, Joseph Lamb, and Eubie Blake; in 1980 he formed GM Recordings. Of his published writings the most influential have been his contributions to the *Jazz Review* (1958–60) and his book *Early Jazz: its Roots and Musical Development* (1968).

Oral history material in *NjR*.

WORKS

(selective list)

Orch: Symphonic Tribute to Duke Ellington, 1955; Concertino, jazz qt, orch, 1959, Passacaglia arr. jazz qt, band, Progression in Tempo pubd separately; Journey into Jazz (Schuller, N. Hentoff), nar, jazz qnt, orch, 1962; numerous arrs. and transcrs. for orch and other inst ens of works by E. Blake, J. P. Johnson, S. Joplin, J. Lamb, and others
Chamber: Jumpin' in the Future (Atonal Jazz Study), 12 insts, 1948; Twelve by Eleven, jazz nonet, 1955; Transformation, jazz ens, 1957; Abstraction, 9 insts, 1959; Conversations, jazz qt, str qt, 1959; Variants on a Theme of John Lewis, 11 insts, 1960; Variants on a Theme of Thelonious Monk, 13 insts, 1960

SELECTED RECORDINGS

As leader: *Three Little Feelings* (1956, Col. CL941); *Jazz Abstractions* (1960, Atl. 1365), incl. Abstraction, Variants on a Theme of Thelonious Monk; *Vintage Dolphy* (1986, GMR 3005)
As sideman: M. Davis: *Classics in Jazz* (1949–50, Cap. H459), incl. Deception, Moon Dreams, Rocker; Darn that Dream (1950, Cap. 1221); Brandeis Jazz Festival: *Modern Jazz Concert* (1957, Col. WL127), incl. Transformation; M. Davis: *Porgy and Bess* (1958, Col. CL1274)

WRITINGS

(selective list)

"Sonny Rollins and the Challenge of Thematic Improvisation," *JR*, i/1 (1958), 6; repr. in *Jazz Panorama*, ed. M. Williams (New York and London, 1962/*R*1979), 239
"Thelonious Monk," *JR*, i/1 (1958), 22; iii/6 (1960), 26; repr. in *Jazz Panorama*, ed. M. Williams (New York and London, 1962/*R*1979), 216
"Jazz and Classical Music," in L. Feather: *The Encyclopedia of Jazz* (New York, rev. and enlarged 2/1960), 497
"Third Stream Redefined," *Saturday Review*, xliv (13 May 1961), 54
Horn Technique (London, New York, and Toronto, 1962)
"The Future of Form in Jazz," *The American Composer Speaks: a Historical Anthology, 1770–1965*, ed. G. Chase (n.p. [Baton Rouge, LA], 1966), 216
Early Jazz: its Roots and Musical Development (New York, 1968)
Musings: the Musical Worlds of Gunther Schuller (New York, and Oxford, England, 1986)

BIBLIOGRAPHY

G. Chase, ed.: *The American Composer Speaks: a Historical Anthology, 1770–1965* (n. p. [Baton Rouge, LA], 1966)
S. Mitchell: "Third Stream Visitation: a Talk with Gunther Schuller," *DB*, xxxv/4 (1968), 20
B. Persia: *Two Works for Jazz Quartet and Ensemble by Gunther Schuller* (diss., Eastman School, 1973) [on *Conversations* and *Concertino*]
R. Palmer: "Gunther Schuller: on the American Musical Melting Pot," *DB*, xliii/3 (1976), 12
D. Baker: "A Talk with Gunther Schuller," *MR*, vi/9 (1979), 5
J. Hasse: "An Interview with Gunther Schuller," *ARJS*, i (1982), 39
D. Reffkin: "The Ragtime Machine," *MR*, xi/1 (1983), 8

MARK TUCKER

Schutt, Arthur (*b* Reading, PA, 21 Nov 1902; *d* San Francisco, 28 Jan 1965). Pianist, arranger, and composer. He was pianist and arranger for Paul Specht's orchestra from 1918 to 1924. He early established himself in New York, contributing to the emerging novelty piano idiom and recording with many dance bands and such jazz groups as the Georgians (1922–4), led by Frank Guarente, and the Charleston Chasers (1925, 1927, 1929). During the 1920s he was closely associated with Rube Bloom and frequently alternated with him in local bands. Schutt worked with some of the most important jazz artists of the 1920s and 1930s, including Red Nichols (1926–9, 1931), the Dorsey Brothers' orchestra (1928–31), and Benny Goodman (1931, 1934); he also recorded as a soloist and leader and in the Chicago Loopers with Bix Beiderbecke and Frankie Trumbauer. In the 1940s and 1950s he was employed by film studios in Hollywood. Among his important works for piano is *Bluin' the Black Keys* (1926).

SELECTED RECORDINGS

As sideman: Georgians: I wish I could shimmy like my sister Kate (1922, Col. A3775); Charleston Chasers: Farewell Blues (1927, Col. 1539D)

RECORDED COMPOSITIONS

(selective list; all recorded by Schutt as unaccompanied soloist)

The Ghost of the Piano (1923, Regal G8032); Teasin' the Ivories (1923, Regal G8046); Rambling in Rhythm (1928, Har. 860H); Piano Puzzle (1929, OK 41243)

BIBLIOGRAPHY

ChiltonW
D. A. Jasen: *Recorded Ragtime, 1897–1958* (Hamden, CT, 1973) [incl. 78 r.p.m. recordings of jazz versions of ragtime pieces]
D. A. Jasen and T. J. Tichenor: *Rags and Ragtime: a Musical History* (New York, 1978)

DAVID THOMAS ROBERTS

Schwab, Sigi [Siegfried] (*b* Ludwigshafen, Germany, 5 Aug 1940). German guitarist. He belonged to blues, folk, and jazz groups while studying classical guitar and double bass at the Musikhochschule in Mannheim. In 1965 he worked for RIAS in Berlin and for the next 15 years was active mainly as a studio musician, recording with Svend Asmussen (1974), George Shearing (1974), and Benny Bailey (1976); at the same time he wrote music for films. In the 1980s he played in a duo with Chris Hinze (recording the album *Live at the Northsea Jazz Festival*, 1980, Kt. 705) and from 1983 with the jazz-rock and Latin group Percussion Academia (recording the album *Rondo a tre*, 1983, Melos 703). He has produced two series of guitar workshops for German television and has also worked as a classical guitarist.

WOLFRAM KNAUER

Schwaller, Roman (*b* Frauenfeld, Switzerland, 18 Jan 1957). Swiss tenor saxophonist. He studied classical clarinet from the age of 14 and changed to jazz alto saxophone when he was 17; he took up the tenor saxophone while attending the Swiss Jazz School in Berne. After moving to Munich in 1977 he performed and toured as a member of Klaus Weiss's quintet, with which he recorded the album *Density* (1980, MRC 06646195); in 1979 he worked in New York and made his first recording as a leader. He performed and recorded with the Vienna Art Orchestra from 1980; he also toured, performed on radio and television, and appeared at festivals in Europe.

PETER SCHWALM

Schweizer, Irène (*b* Schaffhausen, Switzerland, 2 June 1941). Swiss pianist. She taught herself piano from the age of 12, and played in bands from the age of 15. In 1963 she formed a trio with Uli Trepte (double bass) and Mani Neumeier (drums); around 1966–7 this became one of the first European groups to play free jazz. Between 1968 and 1970 Schweizer worked in trios and quartets with Pierre Favre, sometimes with Peter Kowald. From that time she has played with such prominent European improvisers as Peter Brötzmann, Evan Parker, John Tchicai, Han Bennink, Paul Lovens, and the Swedish drummer Sven-Åke Johansson; she began to work with the bass clarinetist and tenor saxophonist Rüdiger Carl in various settings in 1973. Schweizer was a founding member of the Feminist Improvising Group (in the late 1970s) and later of the European Women Improvising Group. Among her many recordings are two solo LPs as well as albums of duos with such drummers as Louis Moholo and Günter Sommer.

SELECTED RECORDINGS

As unaccompanied soloist: *Hexensabbat* (1977, FMP 0500)
Duos with R. Carl: *The Very Centre of Middle Europe* (1978, HH X)
As leader: *Early Tapes* (1967, FMP 0590); *Irène Schweizer Live at Taklos* (1984, Intakt 001)

BIBLIOGRAPHY

G. Rouy: "Irène Schweizer," *Jm*, no.235 (1975), 16 [incl. discography]
B. Noglik: "Irène Schweizer: Uncompromising Continuity," *JF* [intl edn], no.65 (1980), 34
——: "Irène Schweizer," *Jazzwerkstatt international* (Berlin, 1981), 298 [incl. discography]

BERT NOGLIK

Schwindt, Christian [Chrisse] (*b* Helsinki, 14 March 1940). Finnish drummer. He played in dance bands while he was in high school. In the 1960s he recorded as a leader (1963–4) and as the leader with Otto Donner of a quintet (*For Friends and Relatives*, 1965, RCA LSP10070). He was a founder and director of Love Records (1966–76), which issued many Finnish jazz albums. After the company failed, Schwindt worked mostly with entertainers but played briefly with various jazz groups; in 1972 and 1979 he recorded with Hacke Björksten. Schwindt is regarded as the most influential Finnish drummer of the 1960s.

PEKKA GRONOW

Scobey, Bob [Robert Alexander, Jr.] (*b* Tucumcari, NM, 9 Dec 1916; *d* Montreal, 12 June 1963). Trumpeter. He spent much of his life in California, and grew up in Stockton. After moving to Berkeley he played commercial music in San Francisco. From 1940 to 1950 Scobey performed with Lu Watters and the Yerba Buena Jazz Band (for illustration *see* WATTERS, LU). During his military service (1942–6) he was a member of an army band. In the 1950s he led his own Frisco Jazz Band and in the early 1960s he lived in Chicago. With Watters and Turk Murphy, Scobey was a key figure in the "West Coast" or San Francisco revival of traditional jazz, in which the importance of the whole band was emphasized rather than the role of individual soloists; several new compositions inspired by New Orleans jazz were added to the older repertory. Scobey recorded as a leader from 1947 to 1961; among his sidemen at various times were Clancy Hayes (1950–59), Jesse Crump (1956), Matty Matlock and Ralph Sutton (both 1956–7), the trumpeter Rich Matteson (1958–9), and Art Hodes (1959). He recorded as a sideman with Sidney Bechet (1953) and Bing Crosby (1957).

SELECTED RECORDINGS

As leader: *The Great Bob Scobey and his Frisco Band* (1956, Jansco 6250, 6252)

As sideman: L. Watters: Working Man Blues/Big Bear Stomp (1946, West Coast 104); Chattanooga Stomp/Creole Belles (1946, West Coast 102); New Orleans Joys/Panama (1946, West Coast 115); B. Crosby: *Bing with a Beat* (1957, RCA LPM1473)

BIBLIOGRAPHY

FeatherE
B. Nicholls: "The West Coast Revival," *Music Mirror*, iii/2 (1956), 6
Obituary, *SL*, xiv/7–8 (1963), 17
J. Scobey: *He Rambled! 'Til Cancer Cut Him Down* (Northridge, CA, 1976)
J. Darensbourg: *Telling it Like it is*, ed. P. Vacher (London, 1987; Baton Rouge, LA, 1987, as *Jazz Odyssey: the Autobiography of Joe Darensbourg*)

JOHN EDWARD HASSE

Scofield, John (*b* Dayton, OH, 26 Dec 1951). Electric guitarist. He became attracted to rhythm-and-blues, urban blues, and rock-and-roll at an early age, particularly the playing of the guitarists B. B. King, Albert King, and Chuck Berry. From 1970 to 1973 he attended the Berklee College of Music, where he studied with Gary Burton and Mick Goodrick. In 1974 the latter recommended him for a reunion concert at Carnegie Hall of the band led by Gerry Mulligan and Chet Baker. Shortly thereafter Scofield was invited to join the jazz-rock group led by Billy Cobham and George Duke; he remained with this ensemble for two years. Later he played with Burton for a year, and also performed and recorded with such musicians as Charles Mingus (1977), Jay McShann (1977–8), Ron Carter, and Lee Konitz. In 1977 he formed his own band, with Richard Beirach, George Mraz, and Joe LaBarbera, with which he toured Europe and recorded *John Scofield Live*, his first album as a leader. He recorded again the following year, and in 1980 formed a trio with Adam Nussbaum and Steve Swallow which made three highly acclaimed albums. At the end of 1982 he joined Miles Davis's band, which had two guitarists until Mike Stern left in 1983. After leaving Davis he continued to record as a leader; his recordings for Gramavision display his blend of blues and country styles with the harmonic sophistication of bop. Scofield is also a member of the band Bass Desires with Peter Erskine and Bill Frisell. He has composed many pieces for his own albums.

SELECTED RECORDINGS

* – composed by Scofield

As leader: *John Scofield Live* (1977, Enja 3013), incl. *Gray and Visceral; *Rough House* (1978, Enja 3033); *Who's Who* (1979, AN 3018); *Bar Talk* (1980, AN 3022), incl. *Fat Dancer, *New Strings Attached; **Shinola* (1981, Enja 4004); *Out Like a Light* (1981, Enja 4038); *Electric Outlet* (1984, Gram. 8405); *Still Warm* (1985, Gram. 8508); *Blue Matter* (1986, Gram. 8702); *Loud Jazz* (?1987, Gram. 188801)
As sideman with M. Davis: *Star People* (1982–3, Col. FC38657); *Decoy* (1983–4, Col. FC38991); *You're under Arrest* (?1984, Col. FC40023)

BIBLIOGRAPHY

L. Jeske: "Profile: John Scofield," *DB*, xlvii/2 (1980), 51
S. Freedman: "John Scofield: Music for the Connoisseur," *DB*, xlix/9 (1982), 18 [incl. discography]
J. Ferguson: "John Scofield: Bebop Expressionist," *GP*, xvii/2 (1983), 30 [incl. discography]
M. Gilbert: "John Scofield," *JJI*, xxxvi/8 (1983), 6
J. Ferguson: "John Scofield on Recording with Miles Davis: the new 'Decoy' LP," *GP*, xviii/9 (1984), 45 [incl. discography]
B. Milkowski: "John Scofield: All Shades of Blue," *DB*, liv/1 (1987), 16 [incl. discography]

BILL MILKOWSKI

Scoop. On wind instruments, a GLISS rising to the beginning of a note, achieved entirely with the embouchure.

Scott, Bud [Arthur, Jr.] (*b* New Orleans, 11 Jan ?1890; *d* Los Angeles, 2 July 1949). Guitarist, banjoist, and singer. He played violin and guitar from his childhood, and in the years around 1905 played with John Robichaux and, briefly, Freddie Keppard. He left New Orleans in 1913 and performed on the southern vaudeville circuit, then in 1915 went to New York and worked as a nightclub singer and violinist in theater orchestras. He also studied at the Institute of Musical Art and, while working in Baltimore (1917), at the Peabody Conservatory. During the 1920s he played intermittently in Chicago with King Oliver (it is his voice that shouts "Oh play that thing!" on Oliver's second recording (1923) of *Dipper Mouth Blues*) and on the West Coast with Kid Ory and the drummer Curtis Mosby's Blue Blowers. After leaving Oliver finally in 1926 Scott worked in Chicago with Erskine Tate, Dave Peyton, and Jimmie Noone, while also acting as manager of the Café de Paris. In 1927 he recorded with Johnny Dodds and took part in some of Jelly Roll Morton's finest ensemble sessions; Scott was well known for his sophisticated knowledge of harmony, and Morton referred to him as "the great guitarist" (Lomax). In 1929 Scott moved to California, where he played with Mutt Carey's Jeffersonians in the early 1930s and led his own trio for several years. He was again a member of Ory's band (1944–8) and appeared with Louis Armstrong in the film *New Orleans* (1947).

SELECTED RECORDINGS

As sideman: K. Oliver: Dipper Mouth Blues (1923, OK 4918); J. Dodds: Oh! Lizzie/The New St. Louis Blues (1927, Bruns. 3585); J. R. Morton: Wild Man Blues/Jungle Blues (1927, Bb 10256); J. Noone: I know that you know (1928, Voc. 1184); Blues my naughty sweetie gives to me (1928, Voc. 1215); K. Ory: Muskrat Ramble/The girls go crazy (1945, Decca 25133); L. Armstrong: Where the blues were born in New Orleans/Mahogany Hall Stomp (1946, Vic. 202088)

BIBLIOGRAPHY

ChiltonW
C. Chain: "Bud Scott," *Musica jazz*, iii/3 (1948); repr. in *Jazz Reprints*, i/3 (1963), 35
A. Lomax: *Mister Jelly Roll: the Fortunes of Jelly Roll Morton, New Orleans Creole and "Inventor of Jazz"* (New York, 1950, 2/1973)
J. Vincent: "The Banjo in Jazz," *JJ*, xxx/3 (1977), 20
D. M. Marquis: *In Search of Buddy Bolden, First Man of Jazz* (Baton Rouge, LA, and London, 1978)
J. Darensbourg: *Telling it Like it is*, ed. P. Vacher (London, 1987; Baton Rouge, LA, 1987, as *Jazz Odyssey: the Autobiography of Joe Darensbourg*)

DAVID FLANAGAN

Scott, Cecil (Xavier) (*b* Springfield, OH, 22 Nov 1905; *d* New York, 5 Jan 1964). Clarinetist and tenor and baritone saxophonist. He formed a trio during his teens with his brother Lloyd (*b* Springfield, OH, 21 Aug 1902), who played drums, and Don Frye. From 1922 to 1929 he led a band with Lloyd in Ohio, Pittsburgh, and New York, where, from 1927, it was resident at the Savoy Ballroom. It made recordings under both Lloyd's name (1927) and Cecil's (1929). Among the group's regular sidemen were Dicky Wells, Frankie Newton, and Bill Coleman; Joe Thomas (iv), Roy Eldridge, Johnny Hodges, and Chu Berry also performed with the ensemble. Cecil became sole leader in 1929 and the band toured and continued to play in clubs in New York. In the early 1930s he ceased playing temporarily because of a serious accident. Thereafter he worked with the double bass player Ellsworth Reynolds (1932–3), Teddy Hill (1936–7), and Alberto Socarras (until 1942) and made several recordings with Clarence Williams, Willie "the Lion" Smith, and Henry "Red" Allen. In 1942 he formed his own big band and during the rest of the decade he led a trio and played with such musicians as Hot Lips Page and Art Hodes. From 1950 he worked for various leaders, including Jimmy McPartland, and continued to lead his own small groups. Scott recorded mainly on clarinet and tenor saxophone. He played with much drive and zest and his style was characterized by quirky, idiosyncratic effects.

SELECTED RECORDINGS

As leader: Springfield Stomp (1929, Vic. 38117); *Chris Barber Presents Harlem Washboard: Cecil Scott and his Washboard Band* (1959, Col. 33SX1232)

As sideman: C. Williams: Chizzlin' Sam (1933, Col. 2829D); W. Smith: Echo of Spring (1935, Decca 7040); H. Allen: Roll along, prairie moon (1935, Voc. 2997)

BIBLIOGRAPHY

ChiltonW; FeatherE

H. B. Mackey: "Everybody Loves Cecil: a Special Interview," *Jazz Record*, no.56 (1947), 8; repr. in *Selections from the Gutter: Jazz Portraits from "The Jazz Record"*, ed. A. Hodes and C. Hansen (Berkeley, CA, and London, 1977), 215

T. Grove and M. Grove: "Cecil Scott and his Bright Boys," *JJ*, vi/12 (1953), 29; vii/1 (1954), 3

A. McCarthy: *Big Band Jazz* (New York and London, 1974), 43

J. Evensmo: *The Tenor Saxophones of Budd Johnson, Cecil Scott, Elmer Williams, Dick Wilson, 1927–1942* (n.p. [Oslo], n.d. [?1977]) [discography]

EDDIE LAMBERT

Scott, Hazel (Dorothy) (*b* Port of Spain, Trinidad, 11 June 1920; *d* New York, 2 Oct 1981). Pianist and singer. She studied classical piano at the Juilliard School from the age of eight and played jazz in nightclubs and on the radio; from 1939 to 1943 she was a leading attraction at both the downtown and uptown branches of Café Society. In the 1940s she appeared in five films (including *Rhapsody in Blue*, 1945) and during the following decades performed as the leader of various groups, among them a trio that included Bill English and the double bass player Martin Rivera; she continued to play occasionally in nightclubs until the year of her death. Scott was best-known for her jazz improvisations on familiar classical pieces, which continued a practice favored by earlier stride and ragtime pianists.

SELECTED RECORDINGS
(all recorded for Decca)

Hungarian Rhapsody no.2 (Liszt)/Valse in D Flat Major (Chopin, op.64 no.1) (1940, 18129); Hazel's Boogie Woogie (1942, 18340); Embraceable you (1942, 18341); Hallelujah (1942, 18342)

BIBLIOGRAPHY

"Scott, Hazel," *CBY 1943*

A. Taylor: "Hazel Scott," *Notes and Tones: Musician-to-musician Interviews* (Liège, Belgium, 1977/*R*1982), 254

Obituary, J. McAfee, Jr., *JSN*, ii/4 (1982), 19

MARK TUCKER

Scott, Lloyd (*b* 1902). Drummer, brother of CECIL SCOTT.

Scott, Raymond [Warnow, Harry] (*b* New York, 10 Sept 1910). Bandleader and pianist. After studying at the Institute of Musical Art in New York he joined CBS as a staff pianist and composer in 1934. He recorded novelty pieces as the leader of a studio quintet (1936–8), wrote film scores, and also worked as an actor. Between 1939 and 1942 he toured and recorded with his own big band, but this had neither strong soloists nor a good sense of swing. In 1942 he returned to CBS as a music director, and organized a studio sextet that included Emmett Berry, Jerry Jerome, and Cozy Cole. By 1944 Scott had expanded this ensemble to include Charlie Shavers, Ben Webster, Benny Morton, Johnny Guarnieri, George Johnson, Israel Crosby, and Specs Powell. During the 1950s and 1960s he worked in popular music as a composer, arranger, recording engineer, and conductor. He settled in California in the early 1970s. A collection of Scott's scores and other materials is held in the American Heritage Center of the University of Wyoming in Laramie; *see* LIBRARIES AND ARCHIVES, §2.

BIBLIOGRAPHY

ChiltonW; FeatherE

G. T. Simon: *The Big Bands* (New York, 1967, rev. and enlarged 2/1971, rev. 3/1974, 4/1981)

Scott, Ronnie [Schatt, Ronald] (*b* London, 28 Jan 1927). English tenor saxophonist and bandleader. He first played soprano saxophone, and took up the tenor instrument at the age of 15; his early style reflected the influence of Coleman Hawkins. After touring with the trumpeter Johnny Claes (1944–5), Ted Heath (1946), and others he became one of a number of British players who worked on transatlantic liners solely to travel to the USA to hear the new jazz being played by such musicians as Dizzy Gillespie, Charlie Parker, and Bud Powell (1946–8). He was a founding member of the Club Eleven in 1948. Scott then worked briefly with Jack Parnell in 1952 before forming his own nine-piece band in 1953; this group was notable for the quality of its music and for its talented young British players, who included Jimmy Deuchar, the alto saxophonist Derek Humble, Victor Feldman, and Phil Seamen. From 1957 to 1959, with Tubby Hayes, he was the leader of the Jazz Couriers, then from 1960 to 1967, in his own club (established in Gerrard Street, London, in 1959), he led a quartet that featured Stan Tracey. While a member of the Clarke–Boland Big Band (1962–73), Scott continued to lead his own groups – an eight-piece band including Kenny Wheeler (1968–9) and a trio in which Mike Carr played Hammond organ (1971–5). From 1975 he has worked with a quartet or quintet, frequently with the trumpeter Dick Pearce.

After a period in which his playing tended to reflect changing fashions in American jazz, Scott settled down to improvising fluidly in a manner identifiably his own, injecting standard harmonic progressions with an individual muscularity and quirkiness. In Ronnie Scott's Club (which moved to larger premises in Frith Street in 1967) he has specialized in presenting American jazz soloists in informal surroundings, and the establishment soon became recognized internationally as London's major center for modern jazz. In 1981 Scott was awarded the OBE.

For illustration *see* NIGHTCLUBS AND OTHER VENUES, fig.2.

SELECTED RECORDINGS
(all recorded for Esquire unless otherwise indicated)

As leader: Wee Dot (1949, 10036); Too marvellous for words/Have you met Miss Jones? (1951, 10131); Chasing the Bird/Little Willie Leaps (1951, 10141); Close your eyes/I didn't know what time it was (1951, 10185); *Ronnie Scott Jazz Group* (1952, 32001), incl. The Champ; Tangerine (1953, 10311); Double or Nothing (1953, 10331); *Ronnie Scott Jazz Group* (1954, 32006), incl. Fuller Bop Man; Seaman's Mission (1954, 31) [EP]; This Heart of Mine (1955, 10462); Bang (1955, 10466); with T. Hayes: *The Jazz Couriers in Concert* (1958, Tempo TAP22), incl. Some of my best friends are blues, *The Last Word* (1959, Tempo TAP26); *The Night is Scott and You're so Swingable* (1965, Fon. 5332), incl. Baubles, Bangles and Beads; *Live at Ronnie's* (1968, CBS 52661), incl. Lord of the Ready River

As sideman: K. Clarke and F. Boland: *Sax No End* (1967, Saba 15138), incl. Milkshake; Pablo All Star Jam: *Montreux '77* (1977, PL 2308210)

BIBLIOGRAPHY

Feather E; Feather '60s; Feather–Gitler '70s

L. Tomkins: "Ronnie Scott's Opinions," *CI*, x/12 (1972), 22; xi/1 (1972), 14

R. Cotterell, ed.: *Jazz Now: the Jazz Centre Society Guide* (London, 1976)

S. Woolley: "Ronnie Scott: Interview," *Cadence*, iv/2–3 (1978), 11

K. Grime: *Jazz at Ronnie Scott's* (London, 1979)

R. Scott: "The First Twenty Years," *JJI*, xxxii/10 (1979), 7

L. Tomkins: "The Club and I," *CI*, xvii (1979), no.10, p.6; no.11, p.20; no.12, p.12; xviii/1 (1979), 12 [interview]

A. Bausch: *Jazz in Europa* (Echternach, Luxembourg, 1985) [colln of interviews]

J. Fordham: *Let's Join Hands and Contact the Living: Ronnie Scott and his Club* (London, 1986)

CHARLES FOX/DIGBY FAIRWEATHER

Scott, Shirley (*b* Philadelphia, 14 March 1934). Organist. She studied piano as a child and took up trumpet in high school. When, through the playing of Jimmy Smith, the Hammond organ became popular in jazz, a club owner in Philadelphia rented an instrument for her (*c*1955), and she quickly became one of the finest jazz organists. She played and recorded frequently in trios (with drums) led by Eddie "Lockjaw" Davis (*c*1955–1960) and Stanley Turrentine (1960–71), whom she married in 1961. After her marriage ended in 1971 Scott made a number of commercial recordings for the Chess label, then from 1974 led a bop trio with Harold Vick. She later recorded with Jimmy Forrest (1978) and Dexter Gordon (1982). Scott takes advantage of the special characteristics of the Hammond organ, playing with a biting, percussive attack, and using the instrument's full, fast, mechanical vibrato. A masterful improviser, she combines complex bop lines with a repertory of simple, soulful melodic formulas derived from blues and gospel music.

SELECTED RECORDINGS

As leader: *Great Scott!* (1958, Prst. 7143); *Happy Talk* (1962, Prst. 7262); *One for Me* (1974, SE 7430)

As sideman: E. Davis: *The Eddie Lockjaw Davis Cookbook* (1958, Prst. 7141, 7161); S. Turrentine: *Dearly Beloved* (1961, BN 84081); *A Chip off the Old Block* (1963, BN 84150)

BIBLIOGRAPHY

B. Gardner: "Shirley Scott: a Woman First," *DB*, xxix/27 (1962), 20
M. Jones: "Shirl's her own Girl," *MM*, l (23 Aug 1975), 27
S. Scott and L. Tomkins: "My Approach to the Organ, and to Music," *CI*, xiv/2 (1975), 8

BARRY KERNFELD

Scott, Tom [Thomas Wright] (*b* Los Angeles, 19 May 1948). Tenor saxophonist, composer, and leader. He studied clarinet and soprano and alto saxophone before settling on the tenor instrument. By the age of 19 he had played with the orchestras of Oliver Nelson and Don Ellis and in groups led by Howard Roberts and Roger Kellaway; he had also been in demand as a studio musician and composed music for films. On his first recording as a leader (1967) he made use of rock rhythms and electronic effects; he also included one of his best-known compositions, *Blues for Hari*. Scott turned firmly to jazz-rock in 1973 with his group the L.A. Express, a fusion quartet (later a quintet) which toured and recorded with the singer Joni Mitchell. Its performances were hybrid, combining Mitchell's poetic folk lyrics with jazz improvisation and rock accompaniment. Max Bennett and John Guerin provided the rhythmic underpinning; other members were Joe Sample and Larry Carlton (who were replaced by Kellaway and Robben Ford in 1974). Scott was the principal soloist on Carole King's hit recording *Jazzman* (*c*1974). Having previously studied Indian music he toured as music director and soloist with the sitar player Ravi Shankar and the rock musician George Harrison in 1975; thereafter he briefly re-formed the L.A. Express with Bennett, Guerin, Ford, and the keyboard player Larry Nash. From the late 1970s he toured occasionally, but concentrated on studio work in Los Angeles. In the early 1980s he played saxophone and lyricon in groups that blended elements of jazz and soul music.

SELECTED RECORDINGS

As leader: *The Honeysuckle Breeze* (1967, Imp. 9163), incl. Blues for Hari; *Rural Still Life* (1967, Imp. 9171); *Paint your Wagon* (1970, FD 114); *Great Scott* (*c*1973, A&M 4330); *Tom Scott and the L.A. Express* (1973, Ode 77021); *Apple Juice* (*c*1981, Col. FC37419)

As sideman: R. Kellaway: *Spirit Feel* (1967, PJ 20122); J. Mitchell: *Court and Spark* (*c*1974, Asy. 1001); C. King: Jazzman (*c*1974, Ode 66101); V. Feldman: *Your Smile* (*c*1974, Choice 1005)

BIBLIOGRAPHY

B. Libby: "Tom Scott: Groovy Californian," *J&P*, vi/11 (1967), 13
D. Rensin: "Tom Scott: Joni's Spark," *RS*, no.166 (1 Aug 1974), 28
L. Underwood: "Playback on Scott: Studio Brat Turned Monster," *DB*, xlii/1 (1975), 16
A. J. Liska: "Tom Scott," *DB*, xlviii/7 (1981), 28

BARRY KERNFELD

Scott, Tony [Sciacca, Anthony] (*b* Morristown, NJ, 17 June 1921). Clarinetist. While studying at the Institute of Musical Art he took part in jam sessions at Minton's Playhouse (from 1941) and became skilled as a player in the emerging bop style, which, however, offered little work for clarinetists. From 1942 to 1945 he served in the US Army in the New York area, playing alto saxophone in big bands, tenor saxophone in dixieland bands, and clarinet and piano in small swing groups. He performed on his preferred instrument in numerous short-lived groups, including those of Ben Webster (1943), Sid Catlett, Trummy Young, and Earl Bostic, and led his own quartets intermittently until 1956 (the last of which numbered Bill Evans (ii) among its sidemen). Scott also worked frequently as a saxophonist in big bands (with Buddy Rich, 1946; Tommy Dorsey; Claude Thornhill, 1949; and, most notably, Duke Ellington, early 1953), an arranger (for Billie Holiday, Sarah Vaughan, and others), a pianist, and a music director (for the singer Harry Belafonte, 1955) – activities that only furthered his appetite for bop jam sessions. After a successful tour of Europe in 1957 he traveled extensively from 1959 to 1965 throughout the Far East, where his performances drew on Indonesian, oriental, and Indian musics. Thereafter Scott returned to the USA briefly to work in nightclubs, but from the 1970s he has lived in Italy and appeared principally in Europe. He played and recorded in Stockholm (1972–3) and later, after an extended break from recording, made an album in England (1981) and Italy (1984).

SELECTED RECORDINGS

I cover the waterfront/Goodbye (1953, Bruns. 80242); *A Touch of Tony Scott* (1956, RCA LPM1353); *The Modern Art of Jazz* (1957, Secco 425); *South Pacific Jazz* (1958, ABC-Para. 235); *52nd Street Scene* (1958, Coral 57239); *Music for Zen Meditation* (1964, Verve 68634); *Music for Yoga Meditation and other Joys* (1967, Verve 68742); *Tony Scott* (*c*1969, Verve 68788); *African Bird: Come Back! Mother Africa* (1981, 1984, SN 1083)

BIBLIOGRAPHY

N. Hentoff: "Scott Free," *DB*, xxiii/21 (1956), 11
L. Feather: "A Pied Piper?," *DB*, xxiv/23 (1957), 19
D. Morgenstern: "The Long-awaited Return of Tony Scott," *DB*, xxxii/25 (1965), 19
W. Balliett: "Musical Events," *New Yorker*, xliii (3 Aug 1967), 80
J. Burns: "The Forgotten Boppers," *J&B*, ii/3 (1972), 4
A. Morgan: "Ten Lessons with Tony," *J&B*, iii/1 (1973), 14
G. Endress: *Jazz Podium: Musiker über sich selbst* (Stuttgart, Germany, 1980), 160

BARRY KERNFELD

Scott-Heron, Gil (*b* Chicago, 1 April 1949). Singer and songwriter. He moved to New York at the age of 13, and later attended Lincoln University in Philadelphia. His first novel, *The Vulture*, was published when he was 19; in 1970 he recorded an album of jazz and poetry. In the 1970s he collaborated with the pianist Brian Jackson on a number of recordings containing spoken verse and protest songs; among these were *Pieces of a Man* (1971), which included the song *The Revolution will not be Televised*, *Free Will* (1972), and *Winter in America* (1973). His album *The First Minute of a New Day* (1974) was the first recording on which he was accompanied by the Midnight Band, a proficient backup ensemble. On this and the albums that followed it, Scott-Heron and his group developed a terse, concise blend of jazz and the popular style funk, over which he recited monologues or sang in a deep, mellow voice. In an era when funk and disco recordings often contained facile or meaningless lyrics and monotonously repetitive accompaniments, Scott-Heron constructed songs that combined perceptive social and political comment with the exuberance of dance music and the improvisatory fluidity of jazz. Many of these are stern reprimands to the public about the misuse of drugs or alcohol (*The Bottle*), or warnings about apartheid (*Johannesburg*), but he never resorts to mere preaching. *B-movie*, for example, is a sardonic attack on conservative politics with a long, humorous spoken introduction, and *Storm Music* is a passionate, hopeful rhythm-and-blues song which predicts justice for all oppressed peoples. On *Is that Jazz?* Scott-Heron traces the history of the music in terms of black consciousness.

SELECTED RECORDINGS

As leader: *Pieces of a Man* (1971, FD 10143), incl. The Revolution will not be Televised; *Free Will* (1972, FD 10153); *Reflections* (*c*1981, Ari. 9566), incl. B-movie, Is that Jazz?, Storm Music; *Moving Target* (1982, Ari. 9606)

As leader with B. Jackson: *Winter in America* (1973, SE 19742), incl. The Bottle; *The First Minute of a New Day* (1974, Ari. 4030), incl. We beg your pardon, America; *From South Africa to South Carolina* (*c*1975, Ari. 4044), incl. Johannesburg; *It's Your World* (1976, Ari. 5001), incl. Bicentennial Blues; *Secrets* (1978, Ari. 4189)

BIBLIOGRAPHY

R. Townley: "El Jefe's Manifesto," *DB*, xlii/8 (1975), 13

Seamen, Phil(lip William) (*b* Burton on Trent, England, 28 Aug 1926; *d* London, 13 Oct 1972). English drummer. He played in bands led by the trumpeter Ken Turner, Nat Gonella (1946–7), and Joe Loss, and performed and recorded with Jack Parnell (1952–4), Ronnie Scott (1954–7), Kenny Baker (1956–8), the Jazz Couriers (1959), Tubby Hayes (1959), and Joe Harriott (1953–5, 1960–62, 1967). During the early 1960s Seamen became involved with the blues movement in England, working with the singers Georgie Fame (from 1962) and Alexis Korner (1963). Thereafter he was employed as the resident drummer at Ronnie Scott's (1964–8), played, toured, and recorded with Air Force (led by his pupil the drummer Ginger Baker, 1969–70), and worked as a freelance musician (1970–72).

Seamen was a technically accomplished and highly perceptive musician. Throughout his working life he maintained a brilliant, though occasionally anarchic, career, performing in theaters, working as a session musician, and frequently leading small groups in London clubs and pubs. A master of most styles from swing to rock, his catholic taste did not confine him to the bop style with which he was most closely associated.

SELECTED RECORDINGS

As leader: on *Third Festival of British Jazz* (1956, Decca LK4180), Manteca Suite; *Now! . . . Live!* (1968, Vogue SVLP9220), incl. Who's afraid of the big bad wolf; *Phil on Drums!* (1971, 77 SEU53), incl. Allen's Alley

As sideman with S. Tracey: *Little Klunk* (1959, Vogue 160155)

BIBLIOGRAPHY

Feather '60s; *Feather–Gitler '70s*

B. Blain: "I Remember Phil . . .," *Jazz Now: the Jazz Centre Society Guide*, ed. R. Cotterell (London, 1976), 25

A. Korner and others: "Phil," *The Wire*, no.2 (1983–4), 22

S. Goodwin: "From the Past: England's Phil Seamen," *MD*, xii/1 (1988), 44

DIGBY FAIRWEATHER

Séance de boeuf (Fr.). JAM SESSION.

Sears, Al(bert Omega) (*b* Macomb, IL, 21 Feb 1910). Tenor saxophonist. He first played professionally with Chick Webb (1928), Zack Whyte (1929), and Elmer Snowden (1931–2), then led his own groups during the 1930s. After working with Andy Kirk (1941–2) he joined Duke Ellington's band (1944), succeeding Ben Webster as one of its principal tenor saxophonists. Sears's flamboyant and emotionally direct style is prominent on many of Ellington's recordings. After leaving the band (1949) he played in a small group led by Johnny Hodges (1951–2). When the recording by Hodges of Sears's composition *Castle Rock* became a commercial success he formed a music publishing company, Sylvia Music Inc., and later concentrated on rhythm-and-blues. From the late 1950s he performed only infrequently, but he has continued to play at reunions of Ellington's former sidemen.

SELECTED RECORDINGS

As leader: *Swing's the Thing* (1960, Swingville 2018)

As sideman with D. Ellington: I ain't got nothing but the blues (1944, Vic. 201623); The Blues (1944, Vic. 280400); Carnegie Blues (1945, Vic. 201644); It don't mean a thing (1945, Vic. 270054); Hiawatha (1946, Musi. 464); *Liberian Suite* (1947, Col. CL6073)

As sideman with others: Z. Whyte: It's tight like that/West End Blues (1929, Gen. 6798); J. Hodges: Castle Rock (1951, Clef 8944); Swingville All-Stars: *Swingville All-Stars* (1960, Swingville 2010)

BIBLIOGRAPHY

ChiltonW; *FeatherE*

L. Feather: *The Book of Jazz: a Guide to the Entire Field* (New York, 1957, rev. 2/1965 as *The Book of Jazz from Then till Now: a Guide to the Entire Field*)

P. Turley: "Three Forgotten Men," *JM*, iv/12 (1959), 29

V. Wilmer: " 'Big' Al Sears Talks," *JM*, ix/7 (1963), 12

G. E. Lambert: "The Ellingtonians, 2: Al Sears," *JM*, xi/4 (1965), 19

B. Niquet: "Deux précurseurs: Red Prysock, Al Sears," *Soul Bag*, no.65 (1978), 7 [incl. discography by K. Mohr]

O. Peterson: "Al Sears," *JJI*, xl/3 (1987), 16

SCOTT DeVEAUX

Sebesky, Don(ald J.) (*b* Perth Amboy, NJ, 10 Dec 1937). Composer, arranger, and trombonist. While studying at the Manhattan School of Music he worked with Kai Winding, Claude Thornhill, and Tommy Dorsey. He played trombone and wrote arrangements for Maynard Ferguson (1958–9) and Stan Kenton (1959–60), but in 1960 he ceased playing trombone; he then devoted his time to composing and making arrangements, working as a leader and for Wes Montgomery (1965, 1967–8), Buddy Rich (1968–9), Paul Desmond (1969), Freddie Hubbard (1971, 1974), and Sonny Stitt (1973). As an arranger Sebesky is noted for paying scrupulous attention to the capabilities and limitations of the instruments for which and the players for whom he writes; his compositions, which include scores for film and television, combine elements of jazz, classical music, and rock. He is the author of *The Contemporary Arranger* (Port Washington, NY, 1975).

SELECTED RECORDINGS

As leader: *Giant Box* (1973, CTI 6031–2); *Full Cycle* (1984, Crescendo 2164); of Contemporary Arrangers Workshop: *Moving Lines* (1984, Doctor Jazz 40155)

As sideman with M. Ferguson: *A Message from Newport* (1958, Roul. 52012)

SELECTED ARRANGEMENTS

Recorded by W. Montgomery: *Bumpin'* (1965, Verve 68625)

Recorded by P. Desmond: *Bridge over Troubled Water* (1969, A&M 3032)

Recorded by F. Hubbard: *First Light* (1971, CTI 6013)

BIBLIOGRAPHY

FeatherE; *Feather '60s*; *Feather–Gitler '70s*

A. Smith: "Date with Sebesky," *DB*, xli/19 (1974), 16 [incl. discography]

PATRICK T. WILL

Section. A group of homogeneous instruments within a band; *see* BANDS, §§2, 4.

Sedergreen, Bob [Robert Alexander] (*b* 'Akko, Palestine [now in Israel], 24 Aug 1943). Australian pianist. As a child he lived in England, where he first studied piano. His family moved to Melbourne, Australia, in 1950 and during the 1960s he gained experience with various ensembles there. He played and recorded with the drummer Ted Vining (from 1969), Alan Lee (1972–3), and Brian Brown (from 1974), and accompanied such visiting Americans as Dizzy Gillespie, David Baker, Phil Woods, Jimmy Witherspoon, Milt Jackson, and Lee Konitz; he toured Scandinavia with Brown in 1978. In 1984 he formed the group Blues on the Boil, which was influenced by the blues styles of Chicago and the Mississippi Delta; he also plays with Onaje, a group led by the drummer Allan Browne. He is on the faculty of the Victorian College of the Arts in Melbourne, where he teaches jazz. The rhythmic buoyancy and drive of Sedergreen's playing and his ability to build solos to a peak of intensity may be heard to particular advantage on *Impressions*, from the album *The Ted Vining Trio Live at PBS-FM* (1981, Jazznote 029).

BIBLIOGRAPHY

A. Bisset: *Black Roots, White Flowers: a History of Jazz in Australia* (Sydney, 1979)

A. Jackson: "Bob Sedergreen," *Jazz: the Australasian Contemporary Music Magazine*, i/6 (1981), 23

B. Johnson and others: *The Oxford Companion to Australian Jazz* (Melbourne, Australia, 1987)

TONY GOULD

Sedric, Gene [Eugene Hall; Honey Bear] (*b* St. Louis, 17 June 1907; *d* New York, 3 April 1963). Tenor saxophonist and clarinetist. His father was the ragtime pianist Paul "Can Can" Sedric. He worked in St. Louis with Charlie Creath and on riverboats with Fate Marable and Dewey Jackson. In the early 1920s he toured with Jimmy Cooper's Black and White Revue and traveled with it to New York; there he joined Sam Wooding's orchestra, with which he performed at the Nest Club in Harlem and at the Club Alabam (where the orchestra replaced that of Fletcher Henderson) and in 1925 toured Europe. After returning in 1931 to the USA he worked briefly with Fletcher Henderson in 1934 and performed and recorded with Alex Hill; later that year he joined Fats Waller's group, of which he remained a member (except for an occasional absence) until 1942 (for illustration *see* WALLER, FATS). For a period in 1939 he played with Don Redman. He worked as a leader in New York, in 1944 joined a quartet led by the pianist Phil Moore, and late in the following year toured with Hazel Scott. In 1946 and 1947 he performed with a group of Waller's former sidemen under the leadership of the pianist Pat Flower. He then worked again as a leader and played with Jimmy McPartland (recording in 1950) and Bobby Hackett (1951). In 1953 he toured Europe with Mezz Mezzrow and recorded in Paris with Mezzrow and Buck Clayton; later that year he began a long association with the trombonist Conrad Janis. He worked as a freelance from the late 1950s but, after playing and recording with Dick Wellstood in 1961, retired owing to ill health.

SELECTED RECORDINGS

As leader (all recorded in 1938 for Vocalion): The Joint is Jumpin'/Off Time (4576); Choo Choo/The Wail of the Scromph (4552)

As sideman with F. Waller: Something Tells me/Don't Try to Cry your Way Back to me (1938, Vic. 25817); You Out-smarted yourself/Hold Tight (1939, Bb 10116); The Darktown Strutters' Ball/I can't Give you Anything But Love (1939, Bb 10573)

BIBLIOGRAPHY

ChiltonW; *FeatherE*; *Feather '60s*

G. Sedric: "Gene 'Honeybear' Sedric," *BHcF*, no.26 (1953), 4

G. Hoefer: "The Hot Box," *DB*, xxi/5 (1954), 8

J. Bradley: "'Honeybear': Gene Sedric, 1907–1963," *Coda*, v/10 (1963), 21

L. Kunstadt: "Eugene Sedric: Gentleman Musician," *Record Research*, no.55 (1963), 3

C. Albertson: Liner notes, S. Wooding: *Sam Wooding and his Chocolate Dandies* (Biograph 12025, *c*1970)

G. Sedric: "Trouping with Fats Waller," *Selections from the Gutter: Jazz Portraits from "The Jazz Record"*, ed. A. Hodes and C. Hansen (Berkeley, CA, Los Angeles, and London, 1977), 223

WARREN VACHÉ, SR.

See, Cees (*b* Amsterdam, 5 Jan 1934; *d* The Hague, 9 Dec 1985). Dutch drummer. A self-taught musician, he played with the double bass player Freddy Logan (1955–6), the tenor saxophonist Jack Sels (1956–60), the Millers (1956–7, 1960), Rolf Kühn (1962), Pim Jacobs's trio (1964–6), the quartet of the clarinetist and saxophonist Herman Schoonderwalt (1965), Teddy Wilson (1965–9), and Klaus Doldinger (1965–9). During the following years he worked in a group led by Dusko Goykovich and Nathan Davis (1969–72) and with Jan Hammer (1968) and Volker Kriegel (1968, 1971–3); with Manfred Schoof and Peter Trunk he belonged to the New Jazz Trio (1970–71), which made recordings (including *Page One*, 1970, MPS 15276). At around the same time he worked with Wolfgang Dauner (1971) and as a percussionist with Chris Hinze (1971–2). He also gave concerts and appeared at festivals with Schoof, Cannonball Adderley, Kenny Drew, Donald Byrd, Yusef Lateef, Dexter Gordon, Don Byas, Rita Reys, Art Farmer, Tete Montoliu, Jean-Luc Ponty, and Benny Bailey. See was proficient in many styles, notably bop, hard bop, and free jazz. (*ReclamsJ*)

WIM VAN EYLE

Segal, Jerry [Gerald] (*b* Philadelphia, 16 Feb 1931). Drummer. He was mainly active in styles derived from bop. He performed and recorded with Bennie Green and Pete Rugolo (both 1954), and then (after playing at clubs in Philadelphia for a time) with Johnny Smith and Terry Gibbs (both 1955–6), Teddy Charles (1955, 1957), and Stan Getz (1957). During this period he also worked with the composer Edgard Varèse and in the late 1950s with Charles Mingus, Herbie Mann, and Lennie Tristano. He recorded with Bob Dorough (1956), Teo Macero (1957), Curtis Fuller and Hampton Hawes (1957), and Dick Cary's dixieland octet (1957), as a member of the Prestige Jazz Quartet (1957, with Mal Waldron, Teddy Charles, and Addison Farmer), and with Green (1958), Mose Allison (1959–60), and Dave McKenna (1960). From 1958 to 1960 he performed and recorded with Bernard Peiffer. (*FeatherE*)

Segure, Roger (*b* New York, 22 May 1905). Arranger. He was largely self-taught. He first worked as a pianist with Midge Williams, touring the USA and the Far East, then in the late 1930s wrote arrangements for Louis Armstrong, Andy Kirk, and John Kirby. From 1940 to 1944 he was Jimmie Lunceford's arranger; examples of his work for Lunceford include *Blue Afterglow* (1940, Col. 35919) and the film score for *Blues in the Night* (1941), in which the band played. After settling in Los Angeles in the late 1940s Segure was music director for a television show and a dance orchestra; he then worked as a teacher. (*FeatherE*)

Sehring, Rudi (*b* Langen, Hessen, Germany, 13 June 1930). German drummer. He began his career in the late 1940s as a member of the Joe Klimm Combo and in 1953 joined Hans Koller's group, with which he played at intervals until 1959; he also recorded as the leader of a trio (*Long John/Just you, Just me*, 1955, Modern 06021). He toured Italy and Scandinavia, worked with Bill Russo, Lee Konitz, and Zoot Sims, and from

1957 played in the jazz ensemble of the Hessischer Rundfunk, Frankfurt am Main, and worked with Albert Mangelsdorff and Emil Mangelsdorff. In 1960 he joined the dance orchestra of the Hessischer Rundfunk and became less active in jazz. (*ReclamsJ*)

WOLFRAM KNAUER

Seifert, Zbigniew [Zbiggy] (*b* Kraków, Poland, 6 June 1946; *d* Munich, 15 Feb 1979). Polish violinist and alto saxophonist. He studied violin from the age of six and alto saxophone while in his teens. From 1965 he led a quartet in which he played saxophone in a style modeled after that of John Coltrane; he again took up the violin while playing free jazz with Tomasz Stańko's quintet (1969–73) and by 1971 ceased playing saxophone. After moving to Germany in 1973 he belonged to Hans Koller's group Free Sound (1974–5) and worked as a freelance with Volker Kriegel, Joachim Kühn, Jasper van 't Hof, and others. In the USA he performed at the Monterey Jazz Festival with John Lewis (1976) and recorded with Oregon (*c*1977). On his acclaimed album *Man of the Light* (1976) he plays with a rhythm section (consisting of Kühn, Cecil McBee, and Billy Hart) that recalls that of Coltrane; the album also includes a ballad recorded in a duo with van 't Hof. Seifert's recordings of jazz-rock and classical music were less successful.

SELECTED RECORDINGS

As unaccompanied soloist: *Solo Violin* (1976, MRC 06645088)
As leader: *Man of the Light* (1976, MPS 68163); *Passion* (1977, Cap. ST11923)
As sideman: T. Stańko: *Purple Sun* (1973, Calig 30610); V. Kriegel: *Lift* (1973, MPS 68035); Oregon: *Violin* (*c*1977, Van. 79397)

BIBLIOGRAPHY

"Seifert, Zbigniew," *JF* [intl edn], no.18 (1972), 89
R. Kowal: "Zbigniew Seifert: Rapid Ascent," *JF* [intl edn], no.34 (1975), 53
J.-E. Berendt: "Profile: Zbigniew Seifert," *DB*, xliv/17 (1977), 32
R. Kowal: "Zbigniew Seifert: a Musical Legacy," *JF* [intl edn], no.59 (1979), 42 [incl. discography]

BARRY KERNFELD

Selden, Fred (Laurence) (*b* Los Angeles, 22 Jan 1945). Alto saxophonist. He studied music at UCLA (BA 1966) and took private lessons in composition and arrangement with Shorty Rogers, film scoring with Lalo Schifrin, and alto saxophone with Bud Shank. He led a quintet (1968–78) and played and recorded as the lead alto saxophonist of Don Ellis's orchestra (1969–74). His fluid approach and singing tone may be heard on the album *Live at Fillmore* (1970, Col. G30243), recorded with Ellis; this album includes *The Magic Bus Ate my Donut*, an acclaimed example of his work as a composer and arranger. He worked with the big bands of Louie Bellson and Bill Holman (mid-1970s), then led a quintet (1979–81) and a trio (1982–4) with Milcho Leviev. He also plays flute, clarinet, and tenor and soprano saxophone, and is highly regarded as a studio musician. He has composed music for television shows and films in addition to writing jazz and classical works and has published several books of arrangements for flute.

BIBLIOGRAPHY

Feather–Gitler '70s
J. Burger and J. Rona: "Fred Selden: a Studio Reed Player Goes Electronic," *Keyboard*, xiii/7 (1987), 54

Sels, Jack [Jean Jaques] (*b* Antwerp, Belgium, 29 Jan 1922; *d* Antwerp, 21 March 1970). Belgian tenor saxophonist. He studied piano in Belgium and England, played saxophone with the trombonist Mickey Bunner at the Cascade in Antwerp, and also appeared in Antwerp at the GI Club and the 13th Port. In 1947 he worked at the Exi Club and toured France, and in the following year he played in an army big band. He performed in Antwerp, Knokke, Belgium, and Amsterdam as the leader of Jack's All Star Bop Orchestra, worked in radio, and from 1950 again led a group. Later he played with Dizzy Gillespie in a concert of Jazz at the Philharmonic (1952) and performed at various clubs in Germany (1953). He made several recordings as a leader and also recorded rock-and-roll (1955) and film music.

ROBERT PERNET

Semple, Archie [Archibald Stuart Nisbet] (*b* Edinburgh, 31 March 1928; *d* London, 26 Jan 1974). Scottish clarinetist. He first worked semiprofessionally in Edinburgh, often with his brother John, a trumpeter. He led several groups before starting work as a full-time musician in 1952, when he joined Mick Mulligan's band in London. After touring and recording with Freddy Randall (1953–5) he worked with Alex Welsh (1955–62), becoming an important member of the latter's band; the originality and inventiveness of his playing made a considerable impact. Semple also recorded frequently as a leader (1952, 1957–63) before illness forced him to retire. He led a quartet in 1957 for recordings that were first released on an untitled 10-inch album, 77 LP10, and later issued with quintet recordings from 1958 on the album *The Clarinet of Archie Semple* (77 LEU6). Although he was influenced by Pee Wee Russell and Edmond Hall, he found a highly personal voice that was not bound by convention. His playing made particularly effective use of the clarinet's low register and variety of timbre.

BIBLIOGRAPHY

FeatherE
R. Harris: *Jazz* (London, 1952, 5/1957), 244
D. Fairweather: "Semple, Archie (Archibald)," in I. Carr, D. Fairweather, and B. Priestley: *Jazz: the Essential Companion* (London, 1987)

Senior, Milton (E.) (*b* Springfield, OH, *c*1900; *d c*1948). Saxophonist and clarinetist. He was one of the founding members of the Synco Septet in 1921; William McKinney assumed its leadership and the band was known as the Synco Jazz Band before it became McKinney's Cotton Pickers in 1926. Senior made a number of recordings as a member of the reed section. He left McKinney in 1928 and in the early 1930s he led his own band, which included Art Tatum and Teddy Wilson. (J. Chilton: *McKinney's Music: a Bio-discography of McKinney's Cotton Pickers*, London, 1978)

based on *ChiltonW*

SESAC. Record label. It was established in the late 1950s by the music licensing agency SESAC Inc. (founded in 1931 as the Society of European Stage Authors and Composers). Devoted to broadcast transcriptions, the jazz catalogue included material by such musicians as Count Basie, Woody Herman, Coleman Hawkins, and Charlie Shavers. The repertory consisted only of compositions licensed by the organization and material in the public domain, because the recordings were made under an arrangement that forbade the use of material owned by members of ASCAP or BMI. (S. Voce and B. Priestley: "SESAC: Discography of a Transcription Label," *J&B*, ii (1972), no.2, p.16; no.3, p.22)

Session (i). A term most commonly used in jazz of a continuous period in a recording studio, but also (in the standard sense) of any period during which musicians play together, as in the expression JAM SESSION. A player who works exclusively in recording studios, whether as a freelance or as the employee of a recording or film company, is described as a "session musician" (*see also* BANDS, §3(e)) or "studio musician."

Session (ii). Record company and label. The company was established in 1943 by Phil Featheringill and D. W. Bell, and was operational for about a year. It is best remembered for its recordings of unaccompanied blues and boogie-woogie piano solos by Jimmy Yancey, Alonzo Yancey, and Cripple Clarence Lofton, and of traditional jazz sessions by Punch Miller and others and swing by Trummy Young. 31 discs were issued. The masters were later purchased by Dante Bolletino who issued recordings on his label Pax. Later reissues were made on Jazztone in the USA, on Vogue and Storyville in Europe, and on various private labels. ("Session: a Label Listing," *Matrix*, no.70 (1967), 10)

Session (iii). Record label established by BORIS ROSE in the early 1970s.

Set. A group of pieces played one after the other in a public performance, and therefore a segment of a performance during which musicians are continuously on stage. A performance is normally divided into two or more "sets," each lasting from 45 minutes to an hour, between which the musicians rest; during the intermission there may be no live music, or another band or (more often) an unaccompanied soloist may play. Less commonly the term is used of shorter periods (20–30 minutes) in a continuous presentation during which the musicians never leave the stage; in this case the sets are separated by breaks of a few minutes to allow the musicians to decide on the next group of pieces to be played or to put their music in order. (*GoldJL*)

Sete, Bola [De Andrade, Djalma] (*b* Rio de Janeiro, 16 July 1923; *d* Greenbrae, nr San Rafael, CA, 14 Feb 1987). Brazilian guitarist. He grew up in a musical family, and studied at the National School of Music in Rio de Janeiro (MusM, 1949). His early work with local samba groups was followed by further study in Rio at the conservatory, and he became interested in jazz after hearing Barney Kessel. After a period as a staff guitarist with radio stations he moved in 1959 to the USA. He performed in various hotels until he was discovered by Dizzy Gillespie, with whom he played at the Monterey Jazz Festival and recorded in 1962 at the start of the craze for bossa nova. He worked with Vince Guaraldi (1963–6), led his own Brazilian group (1966–71), then performed mostly as a soloist, playing both guitar and lutar (a lute-shaped guitar of his own design). Sete was a highly distinctive guitarist whose classical technique was inspired by Andrés Segovia, although his work on the electric instrument was related stylistically to that of George Van Eps, Kessel, and Tal Farlow. His playing combined harmonic ideas influenced by jazz with the rhythmic vitality of the samba.

SELECTED RECORDINGS

As unaccompanied soloist: *Ocean* (1972, Takoma 1049)
As leader: *Bossa nova* (1962–3, Fan. 3349); *Bola Sete Live at the Monterey Jazz Festival* (1966, Verve 68689)
As sideman: on D. Gillespie: *New Wave!* (1962, Phi. 600070), Chega de saudade; V. Guaraldi: *At El Matador* (1966, Fan. 8371)

BIBLIOGRAPHY

Feather '60s; *Feather–Gitler '70s*
D. McCarthy: "Bola Sete," *GP*, i/4 (1967), 8
B. Sete: "Pro's Reply," *GP*, viii/7 (1974), 6 [incl. discography]
Obituary, *San Francisco Examiner* (15 Feb 1987)

NORMAN MONGAN

78 (r.p.m. disc). Generally a shellac disc of 10- or 12-inch diameter, recorded and played back at 78 r.p.m., and having a playing time of three to four minutes per side; *see* RECORDING, §I, 1(i).

77. Record company and label. The company was established in 1957 by Doug Dobell (*b* London, 1918; *d* Nice, France, 10 July 1987), the owner of a record store in London. The first discs to be released were 10-inch EPs; these were put out in limited quantities. Later the catalogue was expanded to include 12-inch LPs; by the mid-1970s the company had issued more than 50 albums, mostly of traditional and mainstream jazz. The catalogue included albums made by such English musicians as Tubby Hayes, Bruce Turner, Dick Morrissey, Keith Smith, Kenny Baker, and Tony Coe, and items by visiting Americans, among them Bud Freeman, Eddie Miller, Buck Clayton, Albert Nicholas, and George Lewis (i). In 1962 the company sponsored and issued the results of Jack McVea's first session as a leader in 15 years. Much of the repertory was produced by Dobell, who, as a pianist himself, was responsible for recording albums by Dick Wellstood, Dill Jones, Brian Lemon, Don Ewell, Dick Katz, Joe Turner (i), and Ralph Sutton. In addition 77 issued some albums first put out by Delmark and other small American labels.

After 1979 the company made no new recordings, although much of the repertory remained available for some years. In the early 1980s, however, Dobell began to dispose of the catalogue to other companies, selling many of the masters to Harlequin, and others (particularly of traditional jazz) to American organizations. By 1984 the company had ceased to function.

BIBLIOGRAPHY

"Record Dealer Starts New Jazz Disc Company," *Jazz News* (March 1957), 8
F. Owen: "The Sound of Dobell's," *Sv*, i/4 (1966), 20

MARK GARDNER

Severinsen, Doc [Carl Hilding] (*b* Arlington, OR, 7 July 1927). Trumpeter and bandleader. He played trumpet in the big bands of Charlie Barnet (intermittently, 1947–9), Tommy Dorsey (1949–*c*1951), and Benny Goodman (for a brief period). In 1949 he joined NBC and from that time worked almost continuously in television. He became the assistant leader in 1962 of Skitch Henderson's orchestra on the "Tonight Show" and in 1967 replaced Henderson as the orchestra's leader and as the program's music director; he became well-known to television audiences for his virtuoso playing and quick wit. In addition to his work in television he has led workshops for young brass players, conducted the Phoenix (Arizona) Pops and performed as a soloist with other symphony orchestras, and led his own groups, including Xebron, a jazz-rock quintet formed in 1981. A good example of his work is the album *The Tonight Show Orchestra with Doc Severinsen* (1986, Amherst 3311).

BIBLIOGRAPHY

B. Willis: "Meet the Doc," *CI*, vi/9 (1968), 24
N. Dunlap: "Doc Severinsen: Ideal Model," *DB*, xxxvi/1 (1969), 16
G. Lees: "Tonight with Doc Severinsen," *HiFi/MusAm*, xx/4 (1970), 122
L. Underwood: "Doc Takes Issue," *DB*, xli/20 (1974), 12
Z. Stewart: "Doc Severinsen: Tonight's the Night," *DB*, lii/11 (1985), 16

MARK TUCKER

Shake. An effect produced on a brass instrument by shaking it against the lips while playing. It resembles a trill or an exaggerated vibrato, but usually covers a wider interval – often a 3rd or a 5th, but sometimes as much as an octave. It is notated by the normal symbol for the trill accompanied by the word "shake" (*see* NOTATION, §5 (ii), and ex.6). A succession of slow shakes occurs at the beginning of the third blues chorus of Clark Terry's solo on *Feedin' the Bean* from Coleman Hawkins's *Back in Bean's Bag* (1962, Col. CS8791). Although the shake is essentially a brass technique it may be imitated on woodwind instruments by rapidly lipping pitches up and down (*see* LIP). On the title track of the album *Two for the Blues* (1983, Pablo 2310905) the tenor saxophonists Frank Foster and Frank Wess imitate the sound of the brass and wind sections of a big band; an element in the imitation is the execution of a shake on a held note (*see* HONK, ex.1).

BIBLIOGRAPHY

G. Schuller: *Early Jazz: its Roots and Musical Development* (New York, 1968)

A. Napoleon: "The Music Goes Down and Around: (a Case of Mistaken Identity)," *Sv*, no.37 (1971), 18

A. Blatter: *Instrumentation/Orchestration* (New York and London, 1980)

M. Laplace: "La trompette et le cornet dans le jazz et la musique populaire," pt vi, *Brass Bulletin*, no.47 (1984), 39

BARRY KERNFELD

Shakti. Fusion group. It was formed in the USA in 1973 as a trio by JOHN MCLAUGHLIN, the South Indian violinist Lakshminarayana Shankar (brother of L. Subramaniam), and the North Indian tablā player Zakir Hussein; to suit the character of the other instruments, McLaughlin played a specially designed acoustic guitar based on the Indian *vīṇā*. After giving concerts before small audiences on the East Coast, the group recorded *Shakti* (1975, Col. PC34162), in which the original members were joined by the percussionists Vikku Vinayakaram (whose main instrument was the *ghaṭam*, a clay pot drum) and R. Raghavan (*mṛdaṅgam*, a wooden, double-headed barrel drum). As a quartet (without Raghavan) Shakti recorded *A Handful of Beauty* (1976, Col. PC34372), then in 1977 toured Europe and made another recording, before disbanding later in the year. The name Shakti, meaning "together," refers to the union of jazz guitar improvisation with North and South Indian rhythms. The group favored fast tempos in complex meters, but its use of repetitive patterns and simple harmonies suggested links with jazz-rock.

BIBLIOGRAPHY

M. Jackowski: "Lakshminarayana Shankar, the Indian Wizard of the Fiddle," *JF* [intl edn], no.48 (1977), 28

J. Szprot: "Shakti and Afterthoughts," *JF* [intl edn], no.48 (1977), 32

C. Welch: "Pot Luck," *MM*, lii (21 May 1977), 9

C. Berg: "John McLaughlin: Evolution of a Master," *DB*, xlv/12 (1978), 12

Shank, Bud [Clifford Everett, Jr.] (*b* Dayton, OH, 27 May 1926). Alto saxophonist and flutist. He studied clarinet, alto and tenor saxophones, and flute, and attended the University of North Carolina (1944–6). He abandoned the tenor saxophone for the alto while playing with Charlie Barnet (1947–8), and played flute and alto saxophone with Stan Kenton (1950–51). In the 1950s he was an important figure in West Coast jazz; he performed and recorded with Howard Rumsey's Lighthouse All Stars, recorded with Laurindo Almeida in a style that combined bop and Brazilian music, and toured with Bob Cooper. In the early 1960s he performed at festivals and concerts in Europe and South America with such bossa nova musicians as Sergio Mendes. From the mid-1960s he worked principally as a studio musician but during the bop revival of the mid-1970s appeared occasionally with his own quintet in Los Angeles. In 1974 he formed the L. A. FOUR with Almeida, Ray Brown, and Chuck Flores (replaced by Shelly Manne, who was in turn replaced by Jeff Hamilton); later he toured with Shorty Rogers (from 1983) and in a duo with Almeida. By the mid-1980s Shank had abandoned his work as a studio musician and had left the L. A. Four. He stopped playing flute around 1986 to concentrate on performing bop as an alto saxophonist.

SELECTED RECORDINGS

As leader: with S. Rogers: *Shorty Rogers Compositions* (1954, Nocturne 2); *Bud Shank Quartet* (1956, PJ 1215): of L. A. Four (with L. Almeida, R. Brown, and S. Manne): *The L. A. Four Scores!* (1975, Conc. 8); S. Rogers: *Yesterday, Today, and Forever* (1983, Conc. 223)

As sideman: on S. Kenton: [untitled EP] (1947–51, Cap. EAP1-508), Theme for Alto (1951); L. Almeida: *Laurindo Almeida Quartet Featuring Bud Shank* (1954, PJ 7, 13)

BIBLIOGRAPHY

FeatherE; *Feather–Gitler '70s*

L. Tomkins: "Bud Shank," *CI*, xviii (1979–80), no.2, p.14; no.3, p.22; no.8, p.20; no.11, p.23; xix/6 (1981), 23

W. F. Lee: *Stan Kenton: Artistry in Rhythm* (Los Angeles, 1980) [incl. discography]

L. Tomkins: "Bud Shank: Enjoying a more Interesting Life," *CI*, xxii/4 (1984), 8

B. Korall: "That Old New Feeling: Bud Shank," *DB*, liii/9 (1986), 23 [incl. discography]

L. Tomkins: "Back on the Road Again: Bud Shank," *CI*, xxiv/4 (1987), 8

——: "Bud Shank is Given Food for Thought," *CI*, xxiv/7 (1987), 20; contd as "Improvisation: Can it be Learned?," xxiv/8 (1987), 8

L. Hildebrand: "Studio Saxophonist Bebops Back into Jazz," *San Francisco Chronicle Datebook* (14 Feb 1988)

WILLIAM F. LEE III

Shannon, Terry [Terence] (*b* London, 5 Nov 1929). English pianist. A self-taught musician, he played piano from the age of seven. He performed and recorded with Victor Feldman and Wilton "Bogey" Gaynair (1956–9) and regularly toured and recorded with the Jazz Couriers led by Tubby Hayes and Ronnie Scott (1957–9). He continued to work with Hayes, as a member both of his big band and various small groups, throughout the 1960s; his playing may be heard on *Blues Flues* (on the album *A Tribute to Tubbs*, 1963, Spot. SPJ902). Shannon also recorded with Dizzy Reece (in London, 1956, and in Paris with Donald Byrd, 1958), Jimmy Deuchar, and Paul Gonsalves and Ray Nance (1965). He remained active in the late 1980s. (*FeatherE*)

SALLY-ANN WORSFOLD

Shapiro, Artie [Arthur] (*b* Denver, 15 Jan 1916). Double bass player. He grew up in New York, playing trumpet from the age of 13 and double bass from the age of 18. He worked with Gil Rodin (1933–4) and played and recorded with Wingy Manone (1934–6) before living briefly in Washington. He returned to New York, where he played and recorded with Manone, Joe Marsala, and Tommy Dorsey (all 1937–8). From the mid-1930s he worked as a studio musician, recording with Frank Froeba and Sharkey Bonano (both 1936), Red McKenzie (1937), the Original Dixieland Jazz Band, Bud Freeman, and Chu Berry (all 1938), and Eddie Condon (1938–41). He was a member of Paul Whiteman's band (1938–40) and performed at Nick's in New York with Bobby Hackett (1939), then briefly re-joined Marsala (1940) and Whiteman (1941) before moving to Hollywood (1941); there he was again active as a freelance musician, recording with Jack Teagarden (1943), Charlie LaVere (1944–5), Charlie Ventura and Joe Sullivan (both 1945), Artie Shaw (1946), and Benny Goodman (1947). From 1949 to 1959 he worked for MGM, and until 1962 he continued to record, with popular singers such as Bing Crosby and Frank Sinatra.

SELECTED RECORDINGS

As sideman: C. Berry: Sittin' in/Forty-six West Fifty-two (1938, Com. 516): E. Condon: Sunday/California, Here I Come (1938, Com. 515); B. Goodman: That's a Plenty/Henderson Stomp (1947, Cap. 15766); J. Stacy: *A Tribute to Benny Goodman* (1954–5, Atl. 1225)

BIBLIOGRAPHY

ChiltonW
"Metronome's Hall of Fame: Artie Shapiro," *Metronome*, lvii/7 (1941), 24

Shapiro, Nat(haniel M.) (*b* New York, 27 Sept 1922; *d* New York, 15 Dec 1983). Writer and record producer. After attending Brooklyn College he worked as a national director of promotion for Mercury Records (1948–50), as a public-relations representative for BMI (1954–5), and as the director of international artists and repertory for Columbia Records (1956–66). He produced about 100 albums for Columbia, Philips, Vanguard, Epic, RCA, and other labels, including recordings by Miles Davis and Michel Legrand. With Nat Hentoff, he edited *Hear me Talkin' to ya: the Story of Jazz by the Men who Made it* (1955) and *The Jazz Makers* (1957). In addition to his work in jazz he compiled (and until 1979 continued to revise) an important work entitled *Popular Music: an Annotated Index of American Popular Songs* (New York, 1964–7).

WRITINGS
(*selective list*)

ed. with N. Hentoff: *Hear me Talkin' to ya: the Story of Jazz by the Men who Made it* (New York and London, 1955/*R*1966; Ger. trans. as *Jazz erzählt*, Munich, 1959/*R*1984)

ed. with N. Hentoff: *The Jazz Makers* (New York, 1957/*R*1975, 1979 as *The Jazz Makers: Essays on the Greats of Jazz*)

DANIEL ZAGER

Sharkey. *See* BONANO, SHARKEY.

Sharon, Ralph (*b* London, 17 Sept 1923). Pianist, arranger, and bandleader. He performed and recorded with Ted Heath (from 1946) and recorded with Ronnie Scott in the Esquire Five (1948) and Melody Maker's All Stars (1951–2). Thereafter he played and recorded in London as the leader of a sextet that included Victor Feldman. He moved to the USA in 1953 and became an American citizen in 1958. In New York he continued to work as a leader, recording with such distinguished swing and bop sidemen as Teddy Charles, Charles Mingus, Kenny Clarke, Milt Hinton, Jo Jones, Lucky Thompson, and Oscar Pettiford; he is heard to advantage on *The Ralph Sharon Trio* (1956, Beth. 41). He was music director and accompanist to Tony Bennett (1954–65, and from 1979), writing many arrangements for him, including those for his sessions with Count Basie in 1958; he also worked with Bennett in collaboration with Duke Ellington, Woody Herman, and Buddy Rich. He recorded with Chris Connor (1955–9), and Johnny Hartman and Mel Tormé (both 1956), and worked as accompanist to Rosemary Clooney. He recorded under his own name in the 1960s and again with Bennett in 1987. (*FeatherE*)

Sharps and Flats. Big band led from 1952 by NOBUO HARA.

Sharrock, Sonny [Warren Harding] (*b* Ossining, NY, 27 Aug 1940). Electric guitarist. He sang rock-and-roll with a doo-wop group, the Echoes (1954–8), and from 1959 played guitar, which he learned largely by teaching himself. After attending the Berklee College of Music for one semester (1961) he moved in 1965 to New York, where he played free jazz with Byard Lancaster, Pharoah Sanders, and the tenor saxophonist Marzette Watts. He belonged to Herbie Mann's group at intervals from 1967 to 1974, and at the same time played as a sideman with Don Cherry, Wayne Shorter, and Milford Graves; from 1969 he worked as a leader, often with his wife, the singer Linda Sharrock. From 1975 he worked only occasionally as a sideman, but in the early 1980s he became more prominent, owing in part to the influence that his early work had exerted on avant-garde rock musicians in New York; in 1982 he recorded with the art-rock group Material. Later he performed with the group Last Exit (1986), which also included Peter Brötzmann, Ronald Shannon Jackson, and the electric bass guitarist Bill Laswell, and formed two groups, one a quartet that consisted in addition to Sharrock of an electric bass guitarist and two drummers, the other an ensemble that included the trumpeter Ted Daniel and made use of synthesizers. Sharrock was among the first jazz guitarists to employ the slide and electronic distortion, and he has ignored the standard jazz technique based on linear solos and chordal comping; he has also used drones that are suggestive of Indian music.

SELECTED RECORDINGS

As unaccompanied soloist: *Guitar* (1986, Enemy 102)

As leader: *Black Woman* (1969, Vortex 2014); with L. Sharrock: *Paradise* (1975, Atco 36-121); of Last Exit (with P. Brötzmann, R. S. Jackson, and B. Laswell): *Last Exit* (1986, Enemy 101)

As sideman: P. Sanders: *Tauhid* (1966, Imp. 9138); H. Mann: *Memphis Underground* (1968, Atl. 1522); D. Cherry: *Eternal Rhythm* (1968, Saba 15204); W. Shorter: *Super Nova* (1969, BN 84332); Material: *Memory Serves* (1982, Elek. Mus. E1-60042)

BIBLIOGRAPHY

G. Endress: "So erregend wie Bläser: Gitarrist Sharrock," *JP*, xviii (1969), 10; repr. as "Sonny Sharrock," *Jh*, no.247 (1969), 28
J. Bisceglia and J.-L. Ginibre: "Sharrock: la dent dure et les dents longues," *Jm*, no.180 (1970), 34
M. Bourne: "Sonny Sharrock's Story," *DB*, xxxvii/12 (1970), 16
"Like No Other Guitarist Ever Born," *MM* (27 June 1970), 24

ROBERT J. IANNAPOLLO

Shaughnessy, Ed(win Thomas) (*b* Jersey City, NJ, 29 Jan 1929). Drummer and composer. He played with Jack Teagarden (1946), George Shearing (1948), and Charlie Ventura (1948–50), and in a band led by the trumpeter Randy Brooks. After touring Europe as a member of Benny Goodman's sextet (1950) he played for a brief period with Lucky Millinder and with Tommy Dorsey, performed and recorded with Teddy Charles (from 1952), and became a staff drummer for CBS television. He worked as a studio musician from 1954 and as a freelance with Charles Mingus and Duke Ellington, then left CBS in the late 1950s, led the Jazz Four for two years with Teddy Charles, and joined the orchestra of the "Tonight Show" in 1964, with which he moved to Los Angeles in 1972; he also recorded five albums with Count Basie in 1966–7. In Los Angeles he has led a big band, Energy Force (formed 1974), and led drumming workshops. Shaughnessy's specialty is strong, driving big-band drumming. His compositions, which are in a big-band style, include *Blues detambour* and *Nigerian Walk*. Some of his earlier pieces have been recorded by Teddy Charles and Clare Fischer; his later works have been played by his own ensemble.

SELECTED RECORDINGS

As sideman: T. Charles: *A Word from Bird* (1956, Atl. 1274); C. Basie: *Broadway Basie's Way* (1966, Command 905); on O. Nelson: *Happenings* (1966, Imp. 9132), Jazztime U.S.A.

BIBLIOGRAPHY

J. Szantor: "Eddie Shaughnessy: 'Play like you mean it'," *DB*, xl/7 (1973), 16
R. Cook: "Ed Shaughnessy: Swinger on Staff," *MD*, ii/3 (1978), 6
L. Tomkins: "Ed Shaughnessy Talks Drums," *CI*, xviii/6 (1980), 6

T. Smith: "Driver's Seat: Ed Shaughnessy on the Road," *MD*, viii/3 (1984), 60
R. Flans: "Ed Shaughnessy," *MD*, x/4 (1986), 17

JEFF POTTER

Shavers, Charlie [Charles James] (*b* New York, 3 Aug 1917; *d* New York, 8 July 1971). Trumpeter and arranger. After working with Tiny Bradshaw and Lucky Millinder he made a sensational impact on the New York jazz scene at the age of 19 when he joined John Kirby's sextet (1937; for illustration *see* KIRBY, JOHN). During his time with the group he also became its principal arranger and wrote several deft compositions, including *Undecided*. Shavers left Kirby in 1944 and the following year began working in Tommy Dorsey's big band, where he was featured in spectacular arrangements that displayed his bravura approach and his talents as a jazz musician; he also sang. For the next 11 years he performed intermittently with Dorsey and in a wide variety of studio bands, but spent the latter part of his life playing mainly in small groups, where he continued to display an astonishing versatility. In 1950 he was the leader, with Louie Bellson and Terry Gibbs, of a sextet, and during the 1960s he regularly led his own quartet. He also made a number of overseas tours with Frank Sinatra (from 1965), and visited Europe as a soloist (1969, 1970).

Shavers was originally influenced by Roy Eldridge, but he soon developed a bold individualism that radiated confidence and good humor. He was a well-schooled musician who displayed remarkable technical fluency, and was able to harness this skill in agile improvisations that were particularly noteworthy for their wide dynamic range. He was one of the first jazz trumpeters to improvise long lines in the altissimo register of the instrument with complete control; however, these high-note excursions did not diminish his flexibility or the warmth of his low notes.

See also TRUMPET, §4.

SELECTED RECORDINGS

As leader: Stardust (1944, Key. 1305)
As sideman: J. Kirby: Undecided (1938, Decca 2216); Opus Five (1939, Voc./OK 5048); S. Bechet: Mood Indigo (1941, HMV JK2718); All Stars: *Session at Riverside* (1956, Cap. T761), incl. Broadway; H. Singer: *Blue Stompin'* (1959, Prst. 7153), incl. Fancy Pants

BIBLIOGRAPHY

T. Hassell: "Charlie Shavers," *JM*, x/1 (1964), 6
S. Voce: "What'd I Say? Jug and Trumpet," *JJ*, xvii/3 (1964), 12
H. Panassié: "Charlie Shavers," *BHcF*, no.177 (1968), 3
S. Traill: "Charlie Shavers," *JJ*, xxiii/5 (1970), 8
L. Tomkins: "Playing Soft for the Fun of it," *CI*, viii/11 (1970), 12
O. Bryce: "Charlie Shavers: an Appreciation," *JJI*, xxxii/11 (1979), 16
R. Horricks: "The Man they Called Firecracker: Charlie Shavers," *CI*, xxi/6 (1983), 23

JOHN CHILTON

Shaw, Arnold (*b* New York, 28 June 1909). Writer. He studied English literature at the City College of New York (BS 1929) and Columbia University (MA 1931) and American literature at New York University. From 1950 to 1966 he held administrative positions with a number of popular music publishers, and in 1981 he joined the faculty of the University of Nevada, Las Vegas. He is a prolific author in the areas of black and contemporary music and jazz, and in addition to his more than 150 articles, reviews, and liner notes, has written several books. He won ASCAP–Deems Taylor awards in 1968 and 1979.

WRITINGS
(*selective list*)

Sinatra: Twentieth-century Romantic (New York, 1965)
The Street that Never Slept: New York's Fabled 52nd Street (New York, 1971/R1977 as *52nd Street: the Street of Jazz*)
Honkers and Shouters: the Golden Years of Rhythm and Blues (New York, 1978)
The Jazz Age: Popular Music in the 1920s (New York, and Oxford, England, 1987)

PAULA MORGAN

Shaw, Artie [Arshawsky, Arthur Jacob] (*b* New York, 23 May 1910). Clarinetist, bandleader, composer, and arranger. He grew up in New Haven, Connecticut, where in summer 1925 he joined Johnny Cavallaro's dance band as an alto saxophonist. While touring with Cavallaro the following year he took up the clarinet, which later became his principal instrument. From 1926 to 1929 he worked in Cleveland and established a lasting reputation as music director and arranger for an orchestra led by the violinist Austin Wylie. He then toured as a tenor saxophonist with Irving Aaronson's band, and while in Chicago in 1929 played in jam sessions with several local musicians. At the same time he discovered the music of Debussy and Stravinsky; both influences were important in his musical development.

Later that year Shaw traveled with Aaronson to New York, where he played in Harlem jam sessions and came under the influence and tutelage of Willie "the Lion" Smith. From 1931 to 1935 he worked as a freelance studio musician and in 1936 he formed his first group, for a concert at the Imperial Theater. Shaw's unorthodox band, consisting of a string quartet, three rhythm instruments, and clarinet, created a sensation by performing his chamber composition *Interlude in B♭*. Adding two trumpets, trombone, saxophone, and a singer, he signed a recording contract with Brunswick and led a band at New York's Lexington Hotel. However, the public remained indifferent to the group's unusual style and instrumentation, and Shaw was forced to disband in March 1937.

One month later Shaw formed a conventional swing band with a new library of music by Jerry Gray, the trombonist Harry Rogers, and himself, later adding pieces by the best popular-song composers of the day. With this group, which briefly included Billie Holiday, he recorded his first big hit – Cole Porter's *Begin the Beguine* (1938). This marked his breakthrough to public fame and established him as a rival to Benny Goodman. Constitutionally and emotionally unequal to his role as a matinée idol, however, Shaw withdrew from public view in November 1939, a move which served only to provoke the publicity he sought to avoid.

In early 1940 Shaw worked in Hollywood on the film *Second Chorus* and recorded his next big hit, *Frenesi*, using a studio orchestra with a large string section. The success of this recording forced him on tour again with a big band augmented by nine strings. From within this group Shaw organized the GRAMERCY FIVE, including Johnny Guarnieri (harpsichord) and Billy Butterfield (trumpet), and recorded one of his best-known compositions, *Summit Ridge Drive* (1940). Despite high critical acclaim, Shaw again dissolved his band a few months later, settling in New York to record with studio groups and to study orchestration. His last prewar band, organized in September 1941, included Hot Lips Page, Max Kaminsky, Georgie Auld, and Guarnieri.

After enlisting in the US Navy in January 1942 Shaw was asked to form a band which he then led throughout the Pacific war zone in 1943. Following his discharge and convalescence he organized a new group in 1944, which was by all accounts his best jazz-oriented band; one of its recordings, *Little Jazz* (1945) with Roy Eldridge, became a classic. He also continued to perform and record with a small group, drawn from the

Artie Shaw's Gramercy Five at the Strand Theatre, New York, 1945: (left to right) Dodo Marmarosa (piano), Roy Eldridge (trumpet), Shaw (clarinet), Barney Kessel (guitar), and Morris Rayman (double bass)

members of the big band, under the name Gramercy Five (see illustration). During the next decade Shaw organized two more big bands, appeared at Carnegie Hall, and issued recordings on several labels. He assembled his last Gramercy Five in October 1953, and after recording with the group in February and March 1954 he went into retirement. In 1983, however, he was persuaded to reorganize his band, which he has continued to conduct occasionally; it mainly performs under the leadership of Dick Johnson, who also plays clarinet.

Shaw was a leading musician of the swing period, and a public figure whose handsome features and eight marriages made him a darling of gossip columnists. His clarinet playing has often been compared with that of his rival Benny Goodman; though less hot than Goodman, he demonstrated superb technical facility in his recordings of fast and lively numbers and a genuine sense of jazz phrasing in ballads. The full range of his gifts is displayed in his recording *Concerto for Clarinet* (1940). Like Goodman, Shaw was an energetic spokesman for racial equality in jazz, hiring and recording black musicians such as Holiday, Page, and Eldridge. His autobiography (1952) sets him apart from many of his jazz colleagues by its intelligent and lucid writing. His collection of scores and other materials is now in the library of Boston University; *see* LIBRARIES AND ARCHIVES, §2.

SELECTED RECORDINGS

Begin the Beguine (1938, Bb 7746); Any Old Time (1938, Bb 7759); Nightmare (1938, Bb 7875); Frenesi (1940, Vic. 26542); Summit Ridge Drive (1940, Vic. 26763); Star Dust (1940, Vic. 27230); The Blues (1940, Vic. 27411); Concerto for Clarinet (1940, Vic. 36383); Moon Glow (1941, Vic. 27405); Little Jazz (1945, Vic. 201668)

BIBLIOGRAPHY

Artie Shaw: "I Finally Know what I Want to Do," *DB*, xviii/13 (1951), 1

——: *The Trouble with Cinderella: an Outline of Identity* (New York, 1952/*R*1979)

J. Burns: "Artie Shaw," *JM*, xiii/9 (1967), 2

F. Jacobs: "Non-stop Flight: Re-appraisal of the Music of Artie Shaw," *JJ*, xx/3 (1967), 8

G. T. Simon: *The Big Bands* (New York, 1967, rev. and enlarged 2/1971, rev. 3/1974, 4/1981)

O. Peterson: "Artie Shaw," *JJ*, xxii (1969), no.9, p.15; no.10, p.14

"Recreating my Sound," *CI*, vii/12 (1969), 30 [interview]

J. McDonough: "Artie Shaw: Nonstop Flight from 1938," *DB*, xxxvii/2 (1970), 12

G. T. Simon: *Simon Says: the Sights and Sounds of the Swing Era, 1935–1955* (New Rochelle, NY, 1971)

V. Simosko: "Artie Shaw and his Gramercy Fives," *JJS*, i/1 (1973), 34

E. L. Blandford: *Artie Shaw* (Hastings, England, 1974) [bio-discography]

B. Korst and C. Garrod: *Artie Shaw and his Orchestra* (Spotswood, NJ, and Zephyrhills, FL, 1974, rev. 2/1986) [discography]

A. McCarthy: *Big Band Jazz* (New York and London, 1974)

J. McDonough: "Clarinet King Artie Shaw is back with a New Instrument: his Band," *Chicago Tribune* (22 April 1984), 8

C. Deffaa: "Artie Shaw is back with the Big Band at 75," *MR*, xiii/2 (1985), 1

J. McDonough: "Artie Shaw's Big Band Obsession," *DB*, liii/2 (1986), 26

R. Soar: "Artie Shaw: Update," *JJI*, xl/11 (1987), 6

RICHARD WANG

Shaw, Arvell (*b* St. Louis, 15 Sept 1923). Double bass player. He was taught trombone and tuba at high school and learned double bass while playing with Fate Marable on Mississippi riverboats in 1942. After serving in navy bands he toured with Louis Armstrong's big band; his association with Armstrong's All Stars (1945–53) was interrupted in 1951, when he studied harmony and composition in Geneva. He played with Armstrong intermittently until 1957, regularly from 1963 to 1965, and again intermittently until Armstrong's death. In 1958 Shaw toured Europe with Benny Goodman and performed and recorded with Sidney Bechet, Teddy Buckner, and Sammy Price. He played in Teddy Wilson's trio from the late 1950s to the early 1960s, recording with it in 1959. In 1974 he performed and made recordings in France with Barney Bigard, Earl Hines, and Claude Hopkins, and in an all-star sextet that included Hopkins, Vic Dickenson, and Buddy Tate. In the 1980s Shaw worked as a freelance in New York and in show bands on Broadway; he also toured in "The Wonderful World of Louis Armstrong" under Keith Smith.

SELECTED RECORDINGS

As sideman: L. Armstrong: *Louis Armstrong Plays W. C. Handy* (1954, Col. CL6334-5); A. Persiany: Concerto du blues/If it weren't for you (1956, Col. ESDF 1140) [EP]; D. Donegan: *The Many Faces of Dorothy Donegan* (1975, Mahogany 558101)

BIBLIOGRAPHY

Feather '60s; *Feather–Gitler '70s*

E. Cook: "The Wonderful World of Louis Armstrong," *JJI*, xxxiv/9 (1981), 9

P. Vacher: "Arvell Shaw," *JJI*, xxxvi/10 (1983), 12

JOHNNY SIMMEN

Shaw, Charles "Bobo" (*b* Pope, MS, 5 Sept 1947). Drummer and leader. He studied drums with Ben Thigpen and others, and also briefly played trombone and double bass. In the late 1960s he was one of the founders of the Black Artists Group in St. Louis; he went to Europe with members of that organization, and played free jazz for a year in Paris with Anthony Braxton, Steve Lacy, Frank Wright, Alan Silva, and Michel Portal. In 1971 he recorded in St. Louis with Oliver Lake, and during the 1970s made several recordings, notably *Streets of St. Louis* (1974, Moers 02020), as the leader of the Human Arts Ensemble with Lake, Lester and Joseph Bowie, Julius Hemphill, and others. He also recorded with Lester Bowie (1974, 1975, 1977), Frank Lowe and Lake (both 1975), and Hamiet Bluiett (1976). After touring and recording in Europe with the Human Arts Ensemble (1977–8) he returned to the USA, and later recorded with Billy Bang (1984). (V. Wilmer: *As Serious as your Life: the Story of the New Jazz*, London, 1977, rev. 1980)

Shaw, Hank [Henry; Shalofsky, Henry] (*b* London, 23 June 1926). English trumpeter. A self-taught musician, he first performed professionally with the trumpeter Teddy Foster (1942) and the bandleader Oscar Rabin (1944–5). After playing informally with Maynard Ferguson and Oscar Peterson in Canada (1947) he was a founding member of Club Eleven, London (1948), and also worked with Vic Lewis (1948–50). He then played in dance bands led by Roy Fox and Harry Roy before joining Jack Parnell, with whom he recorded in 1953–4; he later worked with Ronnie Scott (1954–6) and Joe Harriott (1959–60). In the 1960s Shaw recorded with Harry South (1966), Kenny Wheeler (1968), and Stan Tracey and Jon Hendricks (both 1969). He was a member of Bill Le Sage's Bebop Preservation Society from 1971 to 1983, during which period he also recorded with John Dankworth (1972–4), Tony Kinsey (1974, 1976), and others. In the mid-1980s he has led his own quartet. Examples of his playing may be heard on Le Sage's *Bebop Preservation Society* (1971, Dawn 3027) and on Red Rodney's *Red Rodney with the Bebop Preservation Society* (1975, Spot. 7).

BIBLIOGRAPHY

FeatherE

R. Cotterell, ed.: *Jazz Now: the Jazz Centre Society Guide* (London, 1976)

NEVIL SKRIMSHIRE

Shaw, Woody (Herman, II) (*b* Laurinburg, NC, 24 Dec 1944). Trumpeter. He grew up in Newark, New Jersey, and began to play trumpet at the age of 11. In 1963, after many local professional jobs, he worked for Willie Bobo (with Chick Corea) and also performed and recorded as a sideman with Eric Dolphy. The following year Dolphy invited Shaw to join him in Paris; Dolphy died shortly before Shaw's departure, but he decided to make the trip nonetheless, and found steady work in Paris with Nathan Davis and such veteran expatriate American musicians as Bud Powell, Kenny Clarke, Johnny Griffin, and Art Taylor. He performed in Paris, Berlin, and London with a group that included Larry Young (recording in Germany under Davis's name), then played in Horace Silver's quintet (1965–6) and recorded with Corea (1966), Jackie McLean (1967), McCoy Tyner (1968), and Andrew Hill (1969). In 1968–9 he worked intermittently with Max Roach, with whom he appeared at a festival in Iran, and during the same period he began to work as a studio musician and in pit orchestras for Broadway musicals. Thereafter he formed a quintet with Joe Henderson (1970) and held an important engagement with Art Blakey's Jazz Messengers (1971–2) before settling in San Francisco, where he led a group with Bobby Hutcherson.

Shaw was again in New York in 1975 as a member of the Louis Hayes–Junior Cook Quintet, which after Cook's departure became the Woody Shaw–Louis Hayes Quintet. Cook was soon replaced by Rene McLean, and then by Dexter Gordon, who adopted the band for his acclaimed homecoming performances in 1976. By 1977 Shaw was working regularly as the sole leader of small groups whose style was oriented towards hard bop, but also incorporated elements of modal jazz and some of the harmonic freedom associated with free jazz. Among his regular sidemen during the 1970s were the saxophonist Carter Jefferson, Onaje Allen Gumbs, Stafford James, and the drummer Victor Lewis, and from 1980 to 1983 his quintet included Steve Turré, the pianist Mulgrew Miller, James, and the drummer Tony Reedus. After touring and recording with a group of constantly changing personnel, in 1986 Shaw formed a new quintet with Larry Willis (also his sideman in 1979–80), David Williams, and the drummer Teri Lynne Carrington.

An accomplished soloist, Shaw improvises rapid, precise, subtle melodies in the tradition of Clifford Brown while maintaining a round, sweet tone. His consistently imaginative playing may be heard to advantage on all his recordings as a leader.

Oral history material in *GBLnsa*.

SELECTED RECORDINGS

As leader: *Blackstone Legacy* (1970, Cont. 7627-8); *The Moontrane* (1974, Muse 5058); *The Ironmen* (1977, Muse 5160); *United* (1981, Col. FC37390); *Lotus Flower* (1982, Enja 4018); *Master of the Art* (1982, Elek. Mus. 60131); *Time is Right* (1982, Red 168); *Setting Standards* (1983, Muse 5318)

As sideman: E. Dolphy: *Iron Man* (1963, Douglas 785); H. Silver: *The Cape Verdean Blues* (1965, BN 84220); *The Jody Grind* (1966, BN 84250); C. Corea: *Tones for Joan's Bones* (1966, Vortex 2004); A. Blakey: *Buhaina* (1973, Prst. 10067); *Anthenagin* (1973, Prst. 10076); L. Hayes and J. Cook: *Ichi-ban* (1976, Tim. 102); D. Gordon: *Homecoming* (1976, Col. PG34650)

BIBLIOGRAPHY

E. Chadbourne: "Woody Shaw," *Coda*, no.144 (1976), 10

S. Lake: "The Intimidator," *MM*, li (2 Oct 1976), 48

L. Tomkins: "Keeping Jazz Alive . . . Our Way: Louis Hayes and Woody Shaw," *CI*, xv/3 (1976), 20

W. Shaw: "My Approach to the Trumpet, and to Jazz," *CI*, xv/8 (1977), 14

C. Berg: "Woody Shaw," *DB*, xlv/14 (1978), 22

A. Baraka: Liner notes, *Woody III* (Col. JC35977, 1979)

"Woody Shaw," *JF* [intl edn], no.57 (1979), 19

B. Rusch: "Woody Shaw: Interview," *Cadence*, vii/1 (1981), 12

"Woody Shaw," *SJ*, xxxvi/14 (1982), 242 [discography]

L. Reitman: "Woody Shaw: Linked to a Legacy," *DB*, l/1 (1983), 18 [incl. discography]

BARRY KERNFELD

Shearer, Dick [Richard Bruce] (*b* Indianapolis, 21 Sept 1940). Trombonist. He grew up in California and played there with Si Zentner (1960–61) and Billy May (1961). After performing with various groups in Los Angeles he worked briefly with Tex Beneke (1964), the pop singers the Righteous Brothers (1964–5), and Louie Bellson (1965). From 1967 to 1978 he was the lead trombonist and a soloist in Stan Kenton's band, with which he toured, recorded, and taught at workshops; he sometimes also substituted for Kenton as the band's director. His solo on *Chiapas*, from the album *Stan Kenton Live at Redlands University* (1970, CW 1015), is a good example of his playing. In the 1980s he has led his own band, performed in the Detroit SO, and worked as a freelance.

BIBLIOGRAPHY
Feather–Gitler '70s
D. Shearer: "Growing up with the Kenton Band," *CI*, xi/10 (1973), 6
W. F. Lee: *Stan Kenton: Artistry in Rhythm* (Los Angeles, 1980) [incl. discography], 337

Shearing, George (Albert) (*b* London, 13 Aug 1919). Pianist. Blind from birth, he began playing piano at the age of three, but his only formal training in music was at the Linden Lodge School for the Blind, which he attended from the ages of 12 to 16. By 1936 he was listening to recordings of Earl Hines, Fats Waller, Teddy Wilson, Meade "Lux" Lewis, and Art Tatum. He absorbed the musical vocabulary of jazz so quickly and convincingly that the *Melody Maker* poll voted him the top British pianist for seven consecutive years. In 1947 he emigrated to the USA and settled in New York, where he was strongly influenced by the bop style – particularly the aggressive rhythmic playing of Bud Powell.

The historic "Shearing sound" originated in recordings for Discovery in 1949, made with a quintet of piano, vibraphone, guitar, double bass, and drums. Using the piano as the leading instrument, Shearing played in the block chord style known as "locked hands," which he developed from Milt Buckner's earlier model, and from the chordal playing of Glenn Miller's saxophone section. In this style, each note of the melody is harmonized with a three-note chord in the right hand, the left hand doubling the melody an octave below (*see* PIANO, ex.9). In Shearing's quintet the upper melody note was then doubled by the vibraphone, and the lower one by the guitar (see ex.1). By popularizing this particular ensemble sound Shearing achieved commercial success on a scale rarely known in the jazz world. Among the many important sidemen who played in his quintet are Cal Tjader, Gary Burton, Toots Thielemans, Joe Pass, Israel Crosby, and Vernel Fournier. As well as piano, Shearing also played accordion, notably on *Cherokee/Four Bars Short*.

During the late 1950s Shearing began performing classical concertos with symphony orchestras in concerts which sometimes included orchestral arrangements featuring his quintet. From the early 1970s he has performed more extensively as a soloist and in duos, which best display the full range of his abilities as a pianist and improviser. His best-known composition, *Lullaby of Birdland*, was written in 1952 as a theme for the legendary jazz club and its radio shows. A volume of tran-

Ex.1 From *Sorry, Wrong Rhumba* (1949, Dis. 106); transcr. B. Dobbins
(♩ = 144)

George Shearing's quintet, New York, 1949: Shearing (piano), John Levy (double bass), Margie Hyams (vibraphone), Chuck Wayne (guitar), and Denzil Best (drums)

scriptions, *The Genius of George Shearing*, was published in 1984.

See also PIANO, §4.

SELECTED RECORDINGS

As unaccompanied soloist: *My Ship* (1974, BASF 2022369)
Duos: with B. Torff: *Blues Alley & Jazz* (1979, Conc. 110); with M. McPartland: *Alone Together* (1981, Conc. 171)
As leader: So Rare (1947, Savoy 689); Bop's your Uncle/Sophisticated Lady (1947, Savoy 718); Cherokee/Four Bars Short (1949, Dis. 107); Sorry, Wrong Rhumba (1949, Dis. 106); Lullaby of Birdland (1952, MGM 11354); *Latin Escapade* (1956, Cap. T737); *San Francisco Scene* (1960, Cap. T1715); *Jazz Concert* (1963, Cap. T1992)

BIBLIOGRAPHY

L. Tomkins: "George Shearing: How I Found the Sound," *Crescendo*, v/3 (1966), 15 [interview]
H. Frost: "Cheers for Shearing," *DB*, xxxiv/21 (1967), 21
S. Quaver: "So Now we'll be Hearing more from George Shearing," *CI*, xiii/4 (1974), 26
L. Lyons: "George Shearing: Sophisticated Jazz Piano," *CK*, ii/4 (1976), 10
L. Feather: "Piano Giants of Jazz: George Shearing," *CK*, iii/8 (1977), 39
"George Shearing," *SJ*, xxxii/3 (1978), 294 [discography]
L. Lyons: *The Great Jazz Pianists, Speaking of their Lives and Music* (New York, 1983), 93
G. Shearing: "Good Times and Good Time," *CI*, xxii/2 (1984), 22
K. Kevorkian: "George Shearing: Tips for Jazz Apprentices from an Old Master," *Keyboard*, xiii/2 (1987), 46

BILL DOBBINS

Sheba. Record company and label established in 1969 by George Shearing. Both ceased activity in 1973, and the following year Shearing began an association with MPS.

Sheet music. A term applied to a single item of published music, typically a piano piece or a popular song in "short score" (i.e., a version in which the accompaniment is reduced to a piano part and usually also to chord symbols or tablature so that it may be realized on plucked string instruments). For the way in which sheet music is adapted by jazz musicians for their use *see* NOTATION, §2.

Sheets of sound. A term coined by Ira Gitler ("Trane on the Track," *DB*, xxv/21 (1958), 16) to describe the rapid, sweeping lines, in which individual pitches are indistinguishable, played by JOHN COLTRANE from the late 1950s.

Sheik, Kid. *See* COLAR, KID SHEIK.

Sheldon, Jack (*b* Jacksonville, FL, 30 Nov 1931). Trumpeter. He studied trumpet in Detroit from the age of 12 and first worked professionally a year later. In 1947 he moved to Los Angeles, where for two years he attended Los Angeles City College. While serving in the air force he belonged to military bands in Texas and California; after his discharge in 1952 he played West Coast jazz with his own quintet and with groups led by Jimmy Giuffre (recording in 1955), Curtis Counce (1956–8), Art Pepper (recording in 1956, 1958, and 1960), Dave Pell (recording in 1957), Herb Geller, Wardell Gray, Stan Kenton (1958), and Benny Goodman, with whom he toured Europe (1959). In the 1960s he became well-known as an actor and comedian, and in 1964–5 portrayed a jazz trumpeter on a television series; he also recorded with Gary Burton (1963). Later he played regularly on television (on the "Merv Griffin Show"), performed and recorded with big bands led by Bill Berry (1976) and Goodman (1978), recorded with June Christy (1977) and Woody Herman (1983), and led a small group in the Los Angeles area. Sheldon's trumpet style is reminiscent of that of Miles Davis.

SELECTED RECORDINGS

As leader: *Jack's Groove* (1957, 1959, GNP 60); *Jazz Profile of Ray Charles* (1961, Rep. 2004); *Stand By for the Jack Sheldon Quartet* (1983, Conc. 229)
As sideman: C. Counce: *The Curtis Counce Group* (1956, Cont. 3526); B. Goodman: *The Sound of Music* (1959, MGM 3810); A. Pepper: *Smack Up* (1960, Cont. 7602)

BIBLIOGRAPHY

FeatherE; *Feather '60s*; *Feather–Gitler '70s*

GARY THEROUX

Shepard, Ernie [Ernest, Jr.] (*b* Beaumont, TX, 19 July 1916; *d* Hamburg, Germany, 23 Nov 1965). Double bass player and singer. He worked in Texas during the 1930s, then played in California with Gerald Wilson and the pianist Phil Moore. In 1945 he worked briefly with the quintet led by Charlie Parker and Dizzy Gillespie, and recorded as a singer with Lem Davis; he recorded on double bass with Eddie Heywood in 1945–6. In New York he performed and recorded as a singer and double bass player with Slim Gaillard (1951), Gene Ammons (1951–2, 1955), Sonny Stitt (1952), and Johnny Hodges (*c*1955). After spending some time out of work in Los Angeles, in 1962 he joined Duke Ellington, with whom he toured Europe and recorded. He recorded on double bass and as a scat singer with Paul Gonsalves (*Tell it the Way it is*, 1963, Imp. 55), and on double bass with Johnny Hodges (1964). He left Ellington in 1964 and settled in Germany, where he undertook session work, including engagements for radio and television.

BIBLIOGRAPHY

Feather '60s; *ReclamsJ*
D. Ellington: *Music is my Mistress* (Garden City, NY, 1973), 230

Shepherd, Shep [Berisford] (*b* Honduras, 19 Jan 1917). Drummer and arranger. He grew up in Philadelphia and was conservatory trained. From 1932 to 1941 he worked with the bandleader Jimmy Gorham in and around Philadelphia, and in 1941–2 he played with Benny Carter. He also recorded with Artie Shaw in June 1941. After military service (1943–6) he worked extensively as an arranger, undertook a short tour with Cab Calloway (1946), played with Buck Clayton (1947), and spent three years with Earl Bostic. Shepherd was in Philadelphia from 1950 to 1952, arranging and copying for music publishers and playing for local recording sessions. From 1952 to 1959 he was a member of Bill Doggett's group; with Doggett he composed *Honky Tonk* (1956, King 4950), which became a hit. Thereafter he performed and recorded prolifically as a freelance; he played for many shows on Broadway, took part in sessions with Sy Oliver, and worked occasionally with Erskine Hawkins. In the mid-1960s he settled in San Francisco, where he continued to work as a freelance.

based on *ChiltonW*

Shepp, Archie (Vernon) (*b* Fort Lauderdale, FL, 24 May 1937). Saxophonist, playwright, and teacher. He grew up in Philadelphia, and studied dramatic literature at Goddard College (BA 1959). While seeking theatrical work in New York he played alto saxophone in dance bands, but under the influence of John Coltrane he took up the tenor instrument and performed in avant-garde groups. He was a member of Cecil Taylor's quartet (1960–62) and served as co-leader of a quartet with Bill Dixon (1962–3) and of the New York Contemporary Five with Don Cherry and John Tchicai (1963–4). Thereafter he led his own groups, which included such distinguished sidemen as Roswell Rudd (1964, 1966), Bobby Hutcherson (1965), Beaver Harris (1966–8, 1971, 1975), and Grachan Moncur III (1966–9). Shepp became an eloquent spokesman and apologist for free jazz, which he interpreted as a medium for political expression. He also wrote a play, *Junebug Graduates Tonight!*, which ran briefly in early 1967. From 1969 to 1974 he was a member of the faculty of black studies at SUNY, Buffalo, and in 1974 he transferred to the University of Massachusetts, where four years later he was named an associate professor. He remains active in the 1980s and has made regular tours of Europe, where he has recorded the majority of his albums, including a series of duos with Max Roach, Horace Parlan, Niels-Henning Ørsted Pedersen, and Jasper van 't Hof.

Shepp has continually developed and expanded his style. His early recordings abound in such elements of free jazz as collective improvisation, atonality, and harsh fragments of melody. From the mid-1960s he began to make use of powerful poems evocative of life in the black ghettos (*Malcolm, Malcolm, semper Malcolm*) and African percussion, and to play marches, slow blues, and sentimental ballads (*Prelude to a Kiss, In a Sentimental Mood*); his tone became correspondingly full-bodied, and he employed old-fashioned growls and bends and wide vibrato. He simplified his style radically in the early 1970s, however, as he embraced rhythm-and-blues (*Attica Blues*), and later his academic historical pursuits prompted him to incorporate into his repertory bop (*Looking at Bird*), early blues (*Trouble in Mind*), and electronic music (*Mama Rose*).

SELECTED RECORDINGS

Duos: with M. Roach: *The Long March* (1979, HH 13); with H. Parlan: *Trouble in Mind* (1980, Ste. 1139); with N.-H. Ørsted Pedersen: *Looking at Bird* (1980, Ste. 1149); with J. van 't Hof: *Mama Rose* (1982, Ste. 1169)

As leader: with B. Dixon: *Archie Shepp–Bill Dixon Quartet* (1962, Savoy 12178); with D. Cherry and J. Tchicai: *Archie Shepp and the New York Contemporary Five* (1963, Sonet 36); *Four for Trane* (1964, Imp. 71); *Fire Music* (1965, Imp. 86), incl. Malcolm, Malcolm, semper Malcolm, Prelude to a Kiss; *On this Night* (1965, Imp. 97), incl. In a Sentimental Mood; *Archie Shepp Live in San Francisco* (1966, Imp. 9118), incl. In a Sentimental Mood; *Mama too Tight* (1966, Imp. 9134); *The Way Ahead* (1968, Imp. 9170); *Attica Blues* (1972, Imp. 9222); *Steam* (1976, Enja 2076); *I Know about the Life* (1981, Sack. 3026); *My Man* (1981, Impro 06); *African Moods* (1984, Cir. [G] 29)

As sideman: G. Evans: *Into the Hot* (1961, Imp. 9); J. Coltrane: *Ascension* (1965, Imp. 95)

BIBLIOGRAPHY

L. Jones: "Voices from the Avant Garde: Archie Shepp," *DB*, xxxii/1 (1965), 18

D. Heckman: "Archie Shepp," *BMI: the Many Worlds of Music* (1967), May, 22

N. Hentoff: "Archie Shepp: the Way Ahead," *J&P*, vii/6 (1968); repr. in *Black Giants*, ed. P. Rivelli and R. Levin (New York and Cleveland, 1970/*R*1980 as *Giants of Black Music*), 118

E. Raben: *A Discography of Free Jazz* (Copenhagen, 1969)

V. Wilmer: *Jazz People* (London, Indianapolis, and New York, 1970/*R*1985)

E. Jost: *Free Jazz* (Graz, Austria, 1974), 105

J. B. Litweiler: "Shepp: an Old Schoolmaster in Brown Suit," *DB*, xli/18 (1974), 15 [incl. discography]

B. McRae: "Avant Courier: Things Have Got to Change," *JJ*, xxvii/2 (1974), 26

——: "Avant Courier: the Traditionalism of Archie Shepp," *JJ*, xxviii/9 (1975), 14

"Discographie: Archie Shepp," *Jh*, no.325 (1976), 24

D. N. Baker, L. M. Belt, and H. C. Hudson, eds.: *The Black Composer Speaks* (Metuchen, NJ, and London, 1978)

G. Giddins: "Archie Shepp without Rhetoric," *VV*, xxiii (27 Nov 1978), 88

B. Primack: "Archie Shepp: Back to Schooldays," *DB*, xlv/21 (1978), 27

J. Runcie: "Archie Shepp," *JJI*, xxxiii (1980), no.3, p.26; no.4, p.28

G. Cerutti and G. Maertens: *Discographie Archie Shepp, 1960–1980* (Sierre, Switzerland, 1982)

S. Crouch: "Archie Shepp's Neoclassicist Dilemma," *VV*, xxvii (3 Feb 1982), 63

S. Freedman: "Archie Shepp: Embracing the Jazz Ritual," *DB*, xlix/4 (1982), 22 [incl. discography]

R. Sanderson: "Archie Shepp," *The Wire*, no.3 (1983), 16

B. Smith: "Archie Shepp: Four for Trane," *Coda*, no.204 (1985), 20

G. Putschögl: "Zur Schlüsselfunktion der Musik in der Afro-Amerikanischen Kultur: Archie Shepp über die Musiktradition der schwarzen Amerikaner," *Jf*, xviii (1986), 67

BARRY KERNFELD

Sheriff, the. Nickname of CLIFF LEEMAN.

Sherman, Herman (Edward, Sr.) (*b* New Orleans, 28 June 1923; *d* New Orleans, 10 Sept 1984). Saxophonist and bandleader. He learned clarinet at high school and later took up alto and tenor saxophone. By 1941 he had begun to work with various brass bands in New Orleans, and soon became a specialist in this type of music, playing with the Eureka, Onward, and Young Tuxedo bands. In 1971 he became leader of the Young Tuxedo Brass Band, with which he toured widely in the USA and also visited Berlin (1980). Although Sherman occasionally undertook dance-band engagements, he concentrated on his work with the Young Tuxedo band, which may be heard under his leadership on the album *Jazz Continues* (1983, 504 Records 10). (M. Joly: "New Orleans, 1984," *Fn*, xv/6 (1984), 28)

ALYN SHIPTON

Sherman, Jimmy [James Benjamin] (*b* Williamsport, PA, 17 Aug 1908; *d* Philadelphia, 11 Oct 1975). Pianist and arranger. He first played at local dances and worked occasionally with Jimmy Gorham's band in and around Philadelphia. His first professional engagement was with Alphonso Trent on the Great Lakes steamboats (1930); later he worked with Peanuts Holland (1931), Al Sears (1932), Stuff Smith (1933–4, 1936), and Lil Armstrong (1935, 1937). He also made recordings in 1936–7 with Putney Dandridge, Mildred Bailey, and Billie Holiday (including *A Sailboat in the Moonlight*, 1937, Voc. 3605). From 1938 to 1952 Sherman worked as an accompanist and arranger for a vocal group, the Charioteers, with which he toured Europe in 1948. He then returned to Pennsylvania, where he continued to play regularly into the 1970s.

based on *ChiltonW*

Sherock, Shorty [Cherock, Clarence Francis] (*b* Minneapolis, 17 Nov 1915; *d* Northridge, CA, 19 Feb 1980). Trumpeter. He took up cornet as a child and played locally while he was in high school at Gary, Indiana. He first attracted attention as a soloist with Ben Pollack's band (1936), and then worked as a sideman with Jimmy Dorsey (1937–9), Bob Crosby (1939–40), Gene Krupa (1940–41), and Tommy Dorsey (1941), before forming a series of less important associations with Raymond Scott, Bud Freeman, and others (to 1945); he played several excellent solos at the first Jazz at the Philharmonic concert in 1944. He led his own orchestra from 1945 to 1948, then during the 1950s and 1960s worked in studios in Los Angeles, playing in many different styles and contexts; a highly respected and much sought-after musician, he continued to be active as a freelance until autumn 1979. Sherock was principally a swing trumpeter, whose playing was influenced by that of Roy Eldridge, but he was also at home in the dixieland and bop styles. Although in his later years he played few solos he continued to inject a spirit of excitement into many recordings in which he took part.

SELECTED RECORDINGS

As leader: Meandering/It's the Talk of the Town (1946, Sig. 28113); Snafu/The Willies (1946, Sig. 28118)

As sideman: G. Krupa: Alreet (1941, OK 6118); Slow Down (1941, OK 6154); Jazz at the Philharmonic: Rosetta (1944, Disc 6027); I've found a new baby (1944, Clef 106); M. Matlock: *And they Called it Dixieland* (1958, WB 1262); Benny Carter: *BBB & Co.* (1962, Swingville 203)

BIBLIOGRAPHY

ChiltonW; *FeatherE*

W. H. Miller: "Shorty Cherock," *Jazz Session* (1946), July, 24

"The Survey in Detail," *Brass Bulletin*, no.4 (1973), 39

Obituary, *DB*, xlvii/6 (1980), 12

SCOTT YANOW

Sherrill (Guilmenot), Joya (*b* Bayonne, NJ, 20 Aug 1927). Singer. She worked with Duke Ellington for a short spell in 1942 and, after writing the lyrics to *Take the "A" Train*, joined his band in 1944. She married Richard Guilmenot in 1946. After four years with Ellington she became a solo singer but returned to the band to perform in the television program "A Drum is a Woman" (1956). Sherrill toured the USA in 1959, appearing in nightclubs and at army bases, then took an acting role in a Broadway play. She went to the USSR with Benny Goodman (1962), performed and recorded with Ellington in Chicago (1963), and also recorded two albums as a leader (*c*1960, 1965). Ellington had a high regard for Sherrill, whose diction and articulation he considered excellent.

Oral history material in *CtY*.

SELECTED RECORDINGS

As leader: *Sugar and Spice* (*c*1960, Col. CS8207); *Joya Sherrill Sings Ellington* (1965, 20CF 4070)

As sideman with D. Ellington: I'm beginning to see the light (1944, Vic. 20-1618); The Blues (1944, Vic. 28-0400); on *A Drum is a Woman* (1956, Col. CL951), Carribee Joe, Zajj's Dream; on *My People* (1963, Contact 1), The Blues Ain't

BIBLIOGRAPHY

FeatherE

B. Ulanov: *Duke Ellington* (New York, 1946/*R*1975)

G. T. Simon: *The Big Bands* (New York, 1967, rev. 4/1981)

D. Ellington: *Music is my Mistress* (Garden City, NY, 1973), 216

REG COOPER

Shertzer [Schertzer], **Hymie** [Schertzer, Herman] (*b* New York, 2 April 1909; *d* New York, 22 March 1977). Alto saxophonist. In 1934 he worked with the alto saxophonist Gene Kardos at Birdland, New York, then recorded with Benny Goodman and became the lead alto saxophonist in his band. After leaving Goodman (1938) he performed and recorded with Tommy Dorsey (1938–40), then worked alternately with Dorsey and Goodman for two years; he eventually re-joined Goodman, with whom he toured and recorded from 1942 to around 1945. He also recorded with Bunny Berigan (1937), Lionel Hampton (1937, 1939), and Billie Holiday (1941, 1944). In the mid-1940s he became a staff musician at NBC. As a studio player he recorded in big bands led by Ella Fitzgerald (1947, 1951, 1955), Sarah Vaughan (1949), Sy Oliver (1949, 1950), Louis Armstrong (1949–53), Artie Shaw (1950, 1953), and Goodman (1951–8); around 1957 he recorded the album *Hymie Shertzer* (Disneyland 3017), which contained tunes that were made famous by Goodman's orchestra. He continued to work in studios until shortly before his death.

BIBLIOGRAPHY

FeatherE

Obituary, *DB*, xliv/10 (1977), 10

Shew, Bobby [Joratz, Robert] (*b* Albuquerque, NM, 4 March 1941). Trumpeter and flugelhorn player. He first worked professionally at the age of 13 as a trumpeter at local dances; he decided to make music his career after performing in bands during his military service. He was briefly a member of the Tommy Dorsey Orchestra under Sam Donahue (1964–5), and played with Woody Herman (1965) and Buddy Rich (1966–7, for a time as Rich's lead trumpeter). He then lived for nine years in Las Vegas, accompanying popular singers, playing in show bands, and working in films and television. In 1973 he moved to Los Angeles, where he continued to be active as a studio musician and resumed his career in jazz. In the late 1970s he received critical acclaim as a sideman in the Toshiko Akiyoshi–Lew Tabackin Big Band, and also enlivened the playing of the orchestras led by Don Menza, Frank Capp and Nat Pierce, and Louie Bellson. He ceased to play in big-band settings in the 1980s, and instead worked with many small groups; he performed and recorded as the leader of a quintet (with Bill Mays, Dick Berk, Bob Magnusson, and the saxophonist Gordon Brisker), and played with groups led by Art Pepper and Bud Shank. He also performed and taught at workshops in the USA, the Far East, Europe, and Australia. Although Shew's tone is soft, it is easily identifiable in a big band, and he has a flawless technique.

SELECTED RECORDINGS

As leader: *Outstanding in his Field* (1978–9, IC 1077); *Breakfast Wine* (1983, Pausa 7171)

As sideman: T. Akiyoshi and L. Tabackin: *Kogun* (1974, RCA JPL1-0236); *Tales of a Courtesan* (1975, RCA JPL1-0723); *Insights* (1976, RCA AFL1-2678); L. Bellson: *Dynamite!* (1979, Conc. 105); *London Scene* (1980, Conc. 157)

BIBLIOGRAPHY

L. Tomkins: "Bobby Shew," *CI*, xviii/6 (1980), 16; xix (1981), no.6, p.12; no.8, p.14

SCOTT YANOW

Shields. Family of musicians. The four Shields brothers rank with members of the Brunies and Laine families as among those most influential in the development of the early New Orleans style as it was taken up by white musicians. The oldest member of the family was the guitarist Pat Shields (*b* New Orleans, *c*1891). From 1904 to 1908 he played in a band led by the violinist Alex "King" Watzke; he also worked at various times with his younger brothers (see 1–3 below).

(1) Larry [Lawrence] **Shields** (*b* New Orleans, 13 Sept 1893; *d* Los Angeles, 21 Nov 1953). Clarinetist. He took up clarinet at the age of 14, and less than a year later joined Nick LaRocca's first band. After working around New Orleans he moved in 1915 to Chicago, where he played with Bert Kelly; later that year he joined a band led by Tom Brown which played in New York. The following year he joined LaRocca and Eddie Edwards in the Original Dixieland Jazz Band. Although reticent by nature, he was widely considered to be the most accomplished member of the band and as influential as the more flamboyant LaRocca. With the latter he wrote such staples of the ensemble's repertory as *At the Jazz Band Ball*, *Fidgety Feet*, and *Livery Stable Blues*. He toured the UK with the group in 1919–20, and remained with it until 1921. Thereafter he worked briefly with Paul Whiteman and moved to California, where he remained for the rest of the decade. During the 1930s he was active again in New Orleans, and later performed and recorded with re-creations of the Original Dixieland Jazz Band. He then returned to California, where he played only infrequently.

SELECTED RECORDINGS

(all recorded for Victor unless otherwise indicated)

As sideman with Original Dixieland Jazz Band: Livery Stable Blues/Dixie Jass Band One-step (1917, 18255); Skeleton Jangle/Tiger Rag (1918, 18472); Fidgety Feet/Lazy Daddy (1918, 18564); Mournin' Blues/Clarinet Marmalade Blues (1918, 18513); Skeleton Jangle/Tiger Rag (1936, 25524); Clarinet Marmalade/Bluin' the Blues (1936, 25525); Barnyard Blues/Original Dixieland One-step (1936, 25502); Drop a Nickel in the Slot/Jezebel (1938, Bb 7454)

BIBLIOGRAPHY

ChiltonW; *FeatherE*

Obituary, *Record Changer*, xiii (1954), Feb, 4

H. O. Brunn: *The Story of the Original Dixieland Jazz Band* (Baton Rouge, LA, 1960/*R*1977)

A. Rose and E. Souchon: *New Orleans Jazz: a Family Album* (Baton Rouge, LA, 1967, rev. 2/1978, rev. and enlarged 3/1984)

(2) Eddie Shields (*b* New Orleans, ?1896; *d* New Orleans, 1936). Pianist. He was one of the group of white musicians active in New Orleans in the early 1910s, and for long engagements at Toro's Cabaret led a band which included at various times Santo Pecora and Leon Roppolo. Thereafter he joined the band of Alcide "Yellow" Nuñez, which played an unsuccessful engagement at Vernon's Café in Chicago. Nick LaRocca invited Shields to replace Henry Ragas in the Original Dixieland Jazz Band in New York after the latter's death in 1919, but the association proved unfruitful and Shields returned to New Orleans.

(3) Harry Shields (*b* New Orleans, 30 June 1899; *d* New Orleans, 18 Jan 1971). Clarinetist and baritone saxophonist. He spent most of his life in New Orleans, where he worked with the trumpeter Johnny Bayersdorffer, and made his first recordings (*Peculiar/Dirty Rag*, OK 40337) with the pianist Norman Brownlee in 1925. Later he worked with Johnny Wiggs (1950) and the Dukes of Dixieland (1952); he was also active as a recording musician, participating in sessions with Papa Jack Laine (1951), Monk Hazel and Tom Brown (both 1954), Al Hirt (1955), and Emile Christian and Armand Hug (both 1958).

Oral history material in *LNT*.

BIBLIOGRAPHY

FeatherE

A. Rose and E. Souchon: *New Orleans Jazz: a Family Album* (Baton Rouge, LA, 1967, rev. 2/1978, rev. and enlarged 3/1984)

A. Rose: "Wolf in Sheep's Clothing," *SL*, xviii (1967), Jan–Feb, 13

RICHARD SUDHALTER

Shihab, Sahib [Gregory, Edmund] (*b* Savannah, GA, 23 June 1925). Alto and baritone saxophonist, and flutist. He studied with Elmer Snowden, and first worked professionally in a band led by the pianist Luther Henderson (1938). After attending Boston Conservatory (1941–2) he was the lead alto saxophonist in Fletcher Henderson's band (1944–6); he then became a Muslim and adopted the name Shihab. From 1947 he worked with some of the most prominent modern jazz bandleaders, including Tadd Dameron, Thelonious Monk, Art Blakey, Dizzy Gillespie, and Illinois Jacquet, and in 1959 he traveled to Europe with Quincy Jones in Harold Arlen's show *Free and Easy*. Apart from an extended stay in Los Angeles (1973–6) Shihab remained in Europe into the mid 1980s. In 1963 he settled in Copenhagen, where he worked with the Clarke–Boland Big Band (1963–72), the Danish Radiojazzgruppen, Ernie Wilkins's Almost Big Band, and other ensembles; he has also been active as a soloist. In 1965 he composed the score for a jazz ballet based on the folk tale *The Red Shoes* by Hans Christian Andersen. He returned to the USA in 1986.

Shihab was one of the first bop musicians to make use of the flute, but his playing on baritone saxophone, which combines a delicate tone with an inventive flow of ideas, is held by many to be his best work.

SELECTED RECORDINGS

As leader: *Jazz-Sahib* (1957, Savoy 12124); *Sentiments* (1971, Sto. 1008); with J. Steig, J. Moody, and C. Hinze: *Flute Summit* (1973, Atl. 50027)

As sideman: T. Monk: In walked Bud (1947, BN 548); 'Round about Midnight (1947, BN 543); Monk's Mood/Who Knows? (1947, BN 1565); Four in One/Straight no Chaser (1951, BN 1589); Ask me now (1951, BN 1591); J. Coltrane: *Coltrane* (1957, Prst. 7105); E. Wilkins: *Montreux* (1983, Ste. 1190)

BIBLIOGRAPHY

J. Lind: "Sahib Shihab's Expatriate Life," *DB*, xxx/7 (1963), 17

F. Postif: "Sahib Shihab," *Jh*, no.259 (1970), 22

R. Baggenaes: "Sahib Shihab," *Coda*, no.204 (1985), 6

D. Salemann, D. Hartmann, and M. Vogler: *Edmund Gregory, Sahib Shihab: Solography, Discography, Band Routes, Engagements, in Chronological Order* (Basle, Switzerland, 1986)

ROLAND BAGGENAES

Shimizu, Jun (*b* Kobe, Japan, 27 Feb 1928). Japanese drummer. He attended Kansai University in Osaka until shortly after World War II, then began working professionally as a drummer and moved to Tokyo in 1946. He played with the Red Hot Boys, the Gramercy Five, and the CB Nine, one of the first bop groups in Japan. After a period of relative inactivity in the 1960s he led trios and quartets in the 1970s. Shimizu is highly regarded in Japan for his sensitive, energetic, and melodic style of playing.

SELECTED RECORDINGS

As leader with Ō. Sampei: *Swing on Birdland*, ii (1977, Canyon 2005)

As sideman: S. Moriyasu: *The Historic Mocambo Session '54* (1954, Pol. 2490–1); S. Yuzuru: *Sera Yuzuru Live at Birdland* (1975, Vic. 859)

YOZO IWANAMI

Shirley, Jimmy [James Arthur] (*b* Union, SC, 31 May 1913). Guitarist. His father was a musician who worked in Cleveland. Shirley first played with bands in Cincinnati (1934–6). After leading his own quartet in Cleveland he was a member of Clarence Profit's trio in New York (1937–41), then spent two years as an accompanist to Ella Fitzgerald. In 1944 he joined Herman "Ivory" Chittison's trio, with which he played intermittently for ten years; during this period he also led his own group for residencies at the Onyx Club (1946) and elsewhere in New York. In the 1960s he also played electric bass guitar with George James and Buddy Tate. Later he recorded as a leader in Paris (1975) and with Johnny Guarnieri (1975) and Stephane Grappelli (1978).

Shirley used a tremolo arm on his guitar during the 1940s which gave his playing a characteristic Hawaiian sound. Inspired by the work of Al Casey and Teddy Bunn, he articulates his sober, blues-tinged lines with the hard, percussive attack commonly used by players who have made the transition from the acoustic to the electric instrument.

SELECTED RECORDINGS

As leader: *China Boy* (1975, BB 33081)

As sideman: C. Profit: Times Square Blues/Hot and Bothered (1940, Decca 8503); H. Chittison: The Song is Ended/How High the Moon (1944, Musi. 315); S. De Paris: Who's Sorry Now (1944, BN 41); S. Grappelli: *Steff and Slam* (1978, BB 33076)

BIBLIOGRAPHY

ChiltonW; *FeatherE*

H. Panassié and M. Gautier: *Dictionnaire du jazz* (Paris, 1954, rev. and enlarged 2/1971, enlarged 3/1980; Eng. trans., London, 1956, rev. A. A. Gurwitch as *Guide to Jazz*, Boston, 1956)

NORMAN MONGAN

Shoemake, Charlie [Charles Edward] (*b* Houston, 27 July 1937). Vibraphonist and bandleader. He studied piano at Southern Methodist University in Dallas for a year, then from 1959 to 1963 played in Los Angeles, with Charles Lloyd, Art Pepper, and Howard Rumsey's Lighthouse All Stars, among others. After taking up the vibraphone in 1965 he worked as a studio musician, recording with Lalo Schifrin, Quincy Jones, Nelson Riddle, and Johnny Mandel. From 1966 to 1973 he played with George Shearing's quintet, recording, touring the USA, and performing at jazz festivals. He then taught, and played at clubs with his own groups; among his sidemen have been Tom Harrell, Hank Jones, and Paul Motian. His recordings as a leader (1978–81, 1984–5) include *Away from the Crowd* (1980–81, Dis. 856). (*Feather–Gitler '70s*)

Shoffner, Bob [Robert Lee] (*b* Bessie, TN, 4 April 1900; *d* Chicago, 5 March 1983). Trumpeter. He was brought up in St. Louis, where he performed on trumpet in dance bands and also played ragtime piano. He first worked in a jazz band and began to improvise when he joined Charlie Creath (1919). After moving to Chicago in 1921 he performed with Freddie Keppard, and in 1924 he became a member of Honore Dutrey's band. He twice worked for King Oliver as second trumpeter, replacing Louis Armstrong (1924) and then Tommy Ladnier (1925–7), but he is perhaps best known as Ladnier's successor in Lovie Austin's Blues Serenaders, in which he recorded regularly for the Paramount label with Austin and Jimmy O'Bryant (1925–6). Shoffner also recorded as a soloist with a septet led by Luis Russell (1926). Thereafter he played with Charlie Elgar (1928), Erskine Tate and McKinney's Cotton Pickers (both 1931–2), and Frankie "Half Pint" Jaxon (1932–3), and worked as a freelance in New York and Chicago. In 1940 he left full-time music, but later resumed playing and joined Franz Jackson's traditional band, with which he recorded from 1957 to 1965.

Oral history material in *LNT*.

SELECTED RECORDINGS

As sideman: J. O'Bryant: Everybody Pile/Charleston Fever (1925, Para. 12312); I. Cox: How can I miss you when I've got dead aim/I ain't got nobody (1925, Para. 12334); L. Russell: Plantation Joys/Please don't turn me down (1926, OK 8424); F. Jackson: *A Night at the Red Arrow* (1961, Pinnacle 104)

BIBLIOGRAPHY

G. M. Erskine: "Ever-fresh Bob Shoffner," *DB*, xxix/2 (1962), 18
C. -U. Durr: "Bob Shoffner (in the 1920s)," *Record Research*, no.64 (1964), 3 [incl. discography]
C. Hillman: "Paramount Serenaders, 1923–1926," *Sv* (1976), no.67, p.8; no.68, p.52; (1977), no.69, p.91; no.70, p.149; no.72, p.227; no.73, p.29; no.74, p.67; (1978), no.75, p.84 [incl. discography]

BARRY KERNFELD

Short, Bob [Robert E.] (*b* 26 Aug 1911; *d* Shellville, CA, 4 April 1976). Tuba player. He worked with Jack Teagarden (1945), then performed and recorded in Portland, Oregon, with the Castle Jazz Band (1946–50). In San Francisco he played traditional jazz with Turk Murphy (1951–4), occasionally performing on cornet or trumpet; a good example of his style is Murphy's recording *Dancing Jazz* (1954, Col. CL650). After working with Bob Scobey (1956–8) he was again a member of Murphy's group (1958–61), and he also made further recordings with the Castle Jazz Band (1957, 1959). Later Short recorded with Clancy Hayes (1963) and Murphy and Lu Watters (both 1964).

BIBLIOGRAPHY

FeatherE
J. Goggin: *Turk Murphy: Just for the Record* (San Leandro, CA, 1982), 56

Shorter, Wayne (*b* Newark, NJ, 25 Aug 1933). Tenor and soprano saxophonist and composer. He began playing clarinet at the age of 16, then changed to tenor saxophone. From 1952 he studied music at New York University (BME 1956) and played in a local band. He performed briefly with Horace Silver in 1956 before being drafted, and in 1958 he joined Maynard Ferguson's group, in which he first met Joe Zawinul. Shorter then began an important association with Art Blakey's Jazz Messengers (1959–63), ultimately serving as the band's music director. After a brief period of rest and work on his own recordings he joined Miles Davis's quintet in September 1964. He remained with the group until 1970, taking up soprano saxophone in late 1968 as Davis experimented with electronic instruments and new ensembles, though during the same period he recorded regularly as a leader. Late in 1970, with Zawinul, he founded WEATHER REPORT, which the two men continued to lead into the 1980s (for illustration *see* ZAWINUL, JOE). Shorter also recorded an acclaimed album presenting Milton Nascimento (1974) and toured and recorded with V.S.O.P. (1976–7; *see* V.S.O.P. (i)). From the mid-1970s he has devoted his time equally to playing tenor and soprano saxophones. In 1985 he greatly reduced his activities with Weather Report, concentrating instead on recording, making international tours with his new group, and appearing in reunion concerts with many of his colleagues from the 1960s. He also performed in the film *Round Midnight* (1986). In 1988, with Carlos Santana, he led a Latin jazz-rock group which made a number of international tours.

Wayne Shorter playing at the Newport Jazz Saratoga Festival, 1987

Shorter is a leading figure in hard bop and jazz-rock, both as an instrumentalist and as a composer of jazz tunes. In the early 1960s his tone and ideas strongly resembled those of John Coltrane, with whom he had practiced after leaving the army. As his personal style emerged he developed varied approaches on the tenor and soprano instruments that had in common a certain terseness. Typically he plays subdued bop runs or Coltrane-like flourishes, liberally interspersed with periods of silence and sometimes with fragments of thematic material, especially as signposts in unconventional compositions. From soul music he has adopted a funky style (the simplicity of which suits his sense of economy), combining a biting attack and bluesy, syncopated dance phrases with an often esoteric selection of pitches. On the soprano saxophone he produces a remarkably beautiful tone.

Shorter's jazz compositions are highly original. One type is illustrated by *E.S.P.* (1965) (historically significant as the title track of the album that marked Davis's turn towards a new repertory) and by *Pinocchio* (1967). Here Shorter's point of departure is the bop tradition: walking bass lines, complex swinging drum patterns, and a structure in which solos are interspersed among statements of the theme. His jittery melodies are set to successions of nonfunctional and dense harmonies that at times are grouped in asymmetrical phrases; improvisations are virtually pantonal. Another type, which provided the inspiration for Weather Report, is represented by *Nefertiti* (1967) and *Sanctuary* (1969). Here the "accompanists" improvise while the "soloists" reiterate strange, slow-moving melodies. Much of Shorter's writing for Weather Report is based on simple dance ostinatos and lyrical melodies. The rapidly changing textures of his *Surucucú* (on the group's album *I Sing the Body Electric*, 1971–2, Col. KC31352), on the other hand, probably resulted from Weather Report's collective improvisation rather than from the composer's design.

SELECTED RECORDINGS

* – composed by Shorter

AS LEADER

Night Dreamer (1964, BN 84173), incl. *Armageddon, *Black Nile, *Night Dreamer, *Virgo; *Juju* (1964, BN 84182), incl. *Deluge, *House of Jade, *Juju, *Mahjong, *Yes or No; *Speak no Evil* (1964, BN 84194), incl. *Fee-fi-fo-fum, *Speak no Evil, *Wild Flower, *Witch Hunt; *The Soothsayer* (*c*1964, BN LT988), incl. *Lady Day, *The Soothsayer; *The All Seeing Eye* (1965, BN 84219), incl. *The All Seeing Eye, *Chaos, *Face of the Deep, *Genesis; *Adam's Apple* (1966, BN 84232), incl. *Adam's Apple, *El gaucho, *502 Blues; *Schizophrenia* (1967, BN 84297), incl. *Go, *Miyako, *Schizophrenia, *Tom Thumb

Super Nova (1969, BN 84332); *Odyssey of Iska* (1970, BN 84363), incl. *De pois do amor, o vazio; *Moto grosso feio* (*c*1971, BN LA014G); *Native Dancer* (1974, Col. PC33418), incl. *Ana Maria, *Beauty and the Beast; *Atlantis* (1985, Col. FC40055)

AS SIDEMAN

With A. Blakey: *The Big Beat* (1960, BN 84029), incl. *Lester left town; *Meet you at the Jazz Corner of the World* (1960, BN 84054-5); *The Freedom Rider* (1961, BN 84156); *Caravan* (1962, Riv. 9438); *Ugetsu* (1963, Riv. 9464); *Free for All* (1964, BN 84170)

With M. Davis: *E.S.P.* (1965, Col. CS9150), incl. *E.S.P., *Iris; *Live at the Plugged Nickel* (1965, CBS Sony 25AP291); *Miles Smiles* (1966, Col. CS9401), incl. *Dolores, *Footprints; *Sorcerer* (1967, Col. CS9532), incl. *Prince of Darkness; *Nefertiti* (1967, Col. CS9594), incl. *Fall, *Nefertiti, *Pinocchio; *In a Silent Way* (1969, Col. CS9875); *Bitches Brew* (1969, Col. GP26), incl. *Sanctuary

With H. Hancock: *V.S.O.P.* (1976, Col. PG34688)

For further recordings *see* WEATHER REPORT.

BIBLIOGRAPHY

L. Jones: "Introducing Wayne Shorter," *JR*, ii/10 (1959), 22

B. Page: "Shorter View," *DB*, xxvii/25 (1960), 15

R. Atkins: "Wayne Shorter," *JM*, ix/10 (1963), 14

N. Hentoff: "The Long Future of Wayne Shorter," *IM*, lxiii/9 (1965), 20

T. Logan: "Wayne Shorter: Double Take," *DB*, xli/12 (1974), 16

C. Silvert: "Wayne Shorter: Imagination Unlimited," *DB*, xliv/13 (1977), 15

M. C. Gridley: *Jazz Styles* (Englewood Cliffs, NJ, 1978, rev. 2/1985 as *Jazz Styles: History and Analysis*, with suppl. *Instructor's Manual and Discography*)

A. Liska: "Wayne Shorter: Coming Home," *DB*, xlix/7 (1982), 18 [incl. discography]

R. Cook: "Wayne Shorter," *The Wire*, no.11 (1985), 31

M. Gilbert: "Wayne Shorter," *JJI*, xxxix/4 (1986), 8

S. Yanow: "The Wayne Shorter Interview," *DB*, liii/4 (1986), 17 [incl. discography]

B. Witherden: "Wayne Shorter: the Phantom Speaks," *The Wire*, no.38 (1987), 14

BARRY KERNFELD

Shout. In jazz the word has three main applications, all having to do with a style or manner of performance.

(1) An energetic piece performed by a stride pianist. The most famous example is James P. Johnson's composition *Carolina Shout* (1921; this title refers to a black-American religious dance, the ring shout). By extension a shout pianist is one who plays in this style and manner. (*See* PIANO, §2.)

(2) A "blues shouter" is a rough-voiced male performer, who shouts rather than sings the lyrics of the blues. The term is associated especially with singers from the Southwest, such as Jimmy Rushing and Joe Turner (ii) (*see* BLUES, §9).

(3) A "shout chorus" is a loud, spirited, climactic chorus in a performance by a big band, in which the brass section leads the whole ensemble.

SHQ. Group led by KAREL VELEBNÝ from the mid-1960s. It succeeded the S & H Quintet, which in turn succeeded the S & H Quartet (formed 1961).

Shu, Eddie [Shulman, Edward] (*b* New York, 18 Aug 1918; *d* Tampa, FL, 4 July 1986). Reed player, trumpeter, and singer. He learned violin and guitar as a child, then played harmonica and tenor saxophone in vaudeville shows from the age of 17. During military service he played trumpet and clarinet, and also developed an act as a ventriloquist; after leaving the army he continued to work as an entertainer, then performed and recorded with the bands of Tadd Dameron (1947), George Shearing (1948), Buddy Rich, Lionel Hampton (1949–50), and Charlie Barnet (on the West Coast, 1950). He played with Chubby Jackson in 1952, and from 1953 to 1958 he was a member of Gene Krupa's trio, in which his versatility was fully exploited. Thereafter he worked in Cuba until the revolution, when he moved to Miami and again led his own group. In the early 1960s Shu performed as a freelance in Los Angeles before playing clarinet in Louis Armstrong's All Stars (1964–5). He rejoined Hampton briefly in 1966, but left to resume freelance work in New York. During the early 1980s he performed and taught in the Virgin Islands, then in 1985 settled in Florida. Shu was an extremely talented performer on each of the instruments he played.

SELECTED RECORDINGS

As leader: *I only Have Eyes for Shu* (1954, Beth. 1013)

As sideman: K. Winding: *Dixieland vs Birdland* (1953, MGM 231); G. Krupa: *The Rocking Mr. Krupa: Sing, Sing, Sing* (1953, Clef 627), incl. Harmonica Shu Boogie; *Drummer Man* (1956, Verve 2008); *Hey! Here's Gene Krupa* (1957, Verve 8300); L. Armstrong: *The Best Live Concert* (1965, Festival 200)

BIBLIOGRAPHY

ChiltonW; *FeatherE*; *Feather '60s*

BRIAN PEERLESS

Shuffle. (1) A dance step of indefinite southern black-American origin, perhaps dating from the 18th century, in which the feet are moved rhythmically across the floor without being lifted.

(2) A rhythm derived from the dance step. The term is onomatopoeic, "sh" describing its characteristic smoothness (and especially its sound when played on the snare drum). The alternation of long and short syllables (shuf-fle, shuf-fle, . . .) evokes its distinguishing rhythm (ex.1), a subdivision of the

Ex.1 A typical shuffle rhythm

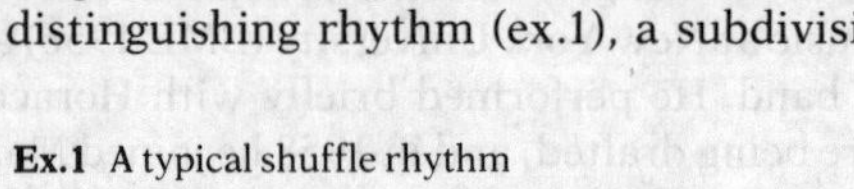

beat into uneven triplets which is more specific than the fundamental swing or boogie-woogie rhythm only in that it is usually played legato and at a relaxed tempo. The shuffle rhythm is generally confined to earlier styles of jazz, up to and including swing; however it is not unknown in later styles, and may be heard, for example, on a version of *Birdland* recorded in concert by Weather Report and included on the album *8:30* (*c*1979, Col. PC2-36030). Although the rhythm is most often executed on the snare drum using brushes, some drummers, notably Paul Barbarin, were adept at producing it with sticks.

(3) A term used in the titles of jazz pieces, principally in the late 1920s and the 1930s; although the shuffle rhythm was widely used during this period, such pieces are not necessarily associated with the dance step or the rhythm. The term was introduced after the success of the revue *Shuffle Along* (1921) by Noble Sissle and Eubie Blake, a work which included, but was by no means restricted to, the shuffle dance step. Later titles confuse the rhythmic meaning of the term: no clear rhythmic thread ties together such a diverse body of pieces as King Oliver's *Showboat Shuffle* (1927, Voc. 1114), Frankie Trumbauer's *Riverboat Shuffle* (1927, OK 40822), Duke Ellington's *Syncopated Shuffle* (1929, OK 8746) and *Showboat Shuffle* (1935, Bruns. 7461), and Jan Savitt's *Futuristic Shuffle* (1938, Bb 7733). A late and unusual example, in the hard-bop style, is Charles Mingus's *Boogie Stop Shuffle* (on his album *Mingus Ah Um*, 1959, Col. CL1370), which calls attention to the relationship of shuffle to boogie-woogie; Mingus presents the shuffle rhythm most clearly in the tune's opening melody rather than as an underlying motif, and the tempo is far too fast for a characteristic shuffle.

Shulman, Joe [Joseph] (*b* New York, 12 Sept 1923; *d* New York, 2 Aug 1957). Double bass player. He worked briefly with Les Brown (1942), then toured the USA and Europe with Glenn Miller's Army Air Force Band (1943–4); while in Paris he recorded with Django Reinhardt (1944) and Mel Powell (1945). After returning to New York he performed and recorded with Buddy Rich (1946) and Claude Thornhill (1947), and toured with Dave Barbour and the singer Peggy Lee (1948, 1950). In 1949 Shulman worked again with Thornhill, participated in Miles Davis's famous "Birth of the Cool" recording sessions (for illustration *see* JAZZ (i), fig.6), and played with Lennie Tristano at Carnegie Hall. After recording in a trio with Duke Ellington and Billy Strayhorn, and with Lester Young's quartet (both 1950), he joined Barbara Carroll's trio (1951); he married Carroll in 1954 and continued to work with the trio until his death. (*FeatherE*)

Side. In recording parlance, one face of a disc. During the 78 r.p.m. era the word was used, by extension, to mean the musical number recorded on one side of a disc, and hence, in the most general way, the recording itself. The use of "side" to mean a musical number became inappropriate with the introduction of long-playing discs (each side of which usually contains several numbers) and in this sense the word was superseded by "track."

Sideman. Any member of a band other than the leader.

Signal. Record company and label. The company was established in New York in 1955 by Jules Colomby, Harold Goldberg, and Don Schlitten. It developed a reputation for well prepared, perfectly engineered recordings which were issued in attractive liners. The catalogue included albums by Duke Jordan, Cecil Payne, Red Rodney, and Gigi Gryce, as well as an LP by an all-star sextet recorded at the Five Spot, New York, as a tribute to Charlie Parker. Signal also introduced the Jazz Laboratory series, in which each album contained music by a quartet (saxophone and rhythm section) on one side, and the same music without the saxophone on the other. These proved extremely useful as an aid to practicing improvisation. Part of Signal's catalogue was sold to Savoy, which later reissued various items, including the albums by Payne and Gryce and the tribute to Parker.

MARK GARDNER

Signorelli, Frank (*b* New York, 24 May 1901; *d* New York, 9 Dec 1975). Pianist and composer. After studying piano with a cousin, Pasquale Signorelli, he played with the ORIGINAL MEMPHIS FIVE (1917), the Original Dixieland Jazz Band (1921), and again with the Original Memphis Five (to 1926, recording to 1931). He worked with Joe Venuti (September 1926), belonged to Adrian Rollini's New Yorker Band, and recorded with Venuti (1927–31), in a duo with Eddie Lang (1927–8), and with Frankie Trumbauer and Bix Beiderbecke (1927); he also performed with the Original Dixieland Jazz Band after its re-formation (1936–8) and with Paul Whiteman (1938). He recorded in 1946 as a leader and sideman with Phil Napoleon and appeared at Nick's in New York with Napoleon (in the late 1940s) and Bobby Hackett (1947). In the late 1950s he re-formed the Original Memphis Five and performed occasionally with the group on radio and television; at the same time he performed as an unaccompanied soloist in Greenwich Village and recorded with Connee Boswell (1956) and Miff Mole (1958). Signorelli's compositions include *I'll Never be the Same* (recorded by Billie Holiday and Teddy Wilson, 1937), *Stairway to the Stars* (recorded by Ella Fitzgerald, 1939), and *A Blues Serenade* (recorded by Johnny Hodges, 1938).

SELECTED RECORDINGS

As leader: St. Louis Hop/A Blues Serenade (1926, PAct 36535); Margie/Jingling the Bells (1946, Davis 9001)

As sideman (all recorded for Okeh): B. Beiderbecke: Royal Garden Blues/Goose Pimples (1927, 8544); T. Dorsey: Daddy, Change your Mind/You can't Cheat a Cheater (1929, 41422); J. Venuti: Little Buttercup (I'll Never be the Same) (1931, 41506)

BIBLIOGRAPHY

ChiltonW; *FeatherE*

R. M. Sudhalter, P. R. Evans, and W. Dean-Myatt: *Bix: Man and Legend* (New Rochelle, NY, and London, 1974)

JAMES M. DORAN

Silva, Alan (Treadwell) (*b* Bermuda, 22 Jan 1939). Double bass player and leader. He grew up in Brooklyn, New York, where he studied piano and violin from the age of ten and trumpet for three years with Donald Byrd; he later attended the New York College of Music and took up the double bass around 1962. Having taken an interest in free jazz he worked in the Free Form Improvisation Ensemble with Burton Greene and took part in the October Revolution in Jazz. He played with Cecil Taylor (1965–9), Sun Ra (1965–70), Albert Ayler (1966–70), Sunny Murray (1969), and Archie Shepp (1969), then settled in France, where he formed the Celestrial Communication Orchestra, a free-jazz group of varying membership, and belonged to trios and quartets with Frank Wright, the pianist Bobby Few, and the drummer Muhammad Ali. From the mid-1970s he lived and taught in both New York and Paris; he recorded with, among others, Taylor, Bill Dixon, and Andrew Hill (all 1980) and the Globe Unity Orchestra (1982).

SELECTED RECORDINGS

As leader: *Luna Surface* (1969, BYG 529312); *Seasons* (1970, BYG 529342–4); with B. Few and F. Wright: *Solos, Duets* (1975, Sun 102–3)

As sideman: C. Taylor: *Unit Structures* (1966, BN 84237); *Conquistador!* (1966, BN 84260); *Great Paris Concert* (1966, Fre. 147309–10); A. Ayler: *Albert Ayler in Greenwich Village* (1966–7, Imp. 9155); on Jazz Composer's Orchestra: *The Jazz Composer's Orchestra* (1968, JCOA 1001–2), Communications no.11; S. Murray: *Big Chief* (1969, Pathé-Marconi 10096); *Hommage to Africa* (1969, BYG 529303)

BIBLIOGRAPHY

D. Caux and M. Chiari: "Alan Silva: de la contrebasse au violon," *Jh*, no.247 (1969), 21 [incl. discography]

J. Bisceglia: "Alan Silva: un sideman et ses leaders," *Jm*, no.182 (1970), 32

V. Wilmer: "Silva: Making History," *MM*, l (5 April 1975), 41

P. Carles: "Alan Silva ou le triangle des Bermudes," *Jm*, no.280 (1979), 38 [incl. discography]

P. Carles and S. Loupien: "Les écoles d'Alan Silva," *Jm*, no.278 (1979), 50

ANDRÉ CLERGEAT

Silva, Michael (*b* New York, 12 Nov 1925). Drummer. After military service (1943–5) he worked for the Norman Diller Dancers, Hot Lips Page, Cyril Haynes, and the entertainer Sammy Davis, Jr. (1958–68). In 1971 he settled in France, where he performed and recorded with many visiting and expatriate Afro-American musicians, including the blues singer and guitarist Clarence "Gatemouth" Brown (1972), and Arnett Cobb, Milt Buckner, Candy Johnson, Al Casey, Helen Humes, Sy Oliver, and the pianist Sonny Thompson (all 1973); he also worked with Claude Bolling's big band. His group accompanied the tap-dancer Jimmy Slyde on the album *Special Tap Dance* (1974, BB 33066). Silva has toured France, and has continued to perform in Paris, where he has led a quartet (1979), played in duos with the pianists Bob Vatel (1981) and Red Richards (1983), and again accompanied Slyde (1985). (J.-P. Battestini: "Michael Silva," *BHcF*, no.218 (1972), 10)

HOWARD RYE

Silver [Silva], **Horace (Ward Martin Tavares)** (*b* Norwalk, CT, 2 Sept 1928). Pianist, bandleader, and composer. As a child he was exposed to Cape Verdean folk music performed by his father, who was of Portuguese descent. He began studying saxophone and piano in high school, when his influences were blues singers such as Memphis Slim, and boogie-woogie and bop pianists, especially Bud Powell and Thelonious Monk. In 1950 Stan Getz made a guest appearance in Hartford, Connecticut, with Silver's piano trio, and subsequently engaged the group to tour regularly with him. Silver remained with Getz for a year, during which time three of his compositions, *Penny*, *Potter's Luck* (written for Tommy Potter), and *Split Kick*, were recorded.

By 1951 Silver had developed sufficient confidence to move to New York, where he performed as a freelance with such established professionals as Coleman Hawkins, Lester Young, Oscar Pettiford, and Art Blakey. In 1952 he was engaged by Lou Donaldson for a recording session with Blue Note; this led to his own first recordings as a leader and to an exclusive relationship with Blue Note for the next 28 years. From 1953 to 1955 he played in a cooperative band called the Jazz Messengers which he led with Blakey. By 1956, however, he was performing and recording solely as the leader of his own quintet, while Blakey continued as leader of the Jazz Messengers.

Silver's music was a major force in modern jazz on at least four counts. He was the first important pioneer of the style known as HARD BOP, which combined elements of rhythm-and-blues and gospel music with jazz, influencing pianists such as Bobby Timmons, Les McCann, and Ramsey Lewis. Second, the instrumentation of his quintet (trumpet, tenor saxophone, piano, double bass, and drums) served as a model for small jazz groups from the mid-1950s until the late 1960s. Further, Silver's ensembles provided an important training ground for young players, many of whom (such as Donald Byrd, Art Farmer, Blue Mitchell, Woody Shaw, Benny Golson, and Joe Henderson) later led similar groups of their own. Finally, Silver refined the art of composing and arranging for his chosen instrumentation to a level of craftsmanship as yet unsurpassed in jazz. He is a prolific composer, and one of very few jazz musicians to record almost exclusively original material; his work consistently combines simplicity and profundity in a rhythmically infectious style which, despite its sophistication, sounds completely natural. Several of his compositions have become jazz standards, including *The Preacher*, *Doodlin'*, *Opus de Funk*, *Señor Blues*, *Nica's Dream*, *Sister Sadie*, and *Song for my Father*.

Horace Silver, 1956

From the mid-1960s Silver has written lyrics as well as music for a series of three quintet recordings, *The United States of Mind*, and recorded a number of albums featuring the quintet with ensembles of brass, woodwind, percussion, voices, and strings. His quintet continues to tour regularly in the 1980s, performing a wide range of material from his impressive and influential library of original works.

Oral history material in *GBLnsa*.

See also PIANO, §5.

SELECTED RECORDINGS

(all recorded for Blue Note unless otherwise indicated)

As leader: Opus de Funk (1953, 1625); *Horace Silver and the Jazz Messengers* (1954, 5058), incl. Doodlin'; *Horace Silver and the Jazz Messengers* (1955, 5062), incl. The Preacher; *Six Pieces of Silver* (1956, 1539), incl. Señor Blues; *Blowin' the Blues Away* (1959, 4017), incl. Sister Sadie; *Horace-scope* (1960, 84042), incl. Nica's Dream; *Song for my Father* (1964, 84185), incl. Song for my Father; *The Cape Verdean Blues* (1965, 84220); *That Healin' Feelin' (The United States of Mind, Phase I)* (1970, 84352); *Total Response (Phase II)* (*c*1971, 84368); *All (Phase III)* (*c*1973, 84420); *Silver 'n' Brass* (1975, LA406); *Silver 'n' Wood* (1976, LA581); *Silver 'n' Voices* (1977, LA708); *Silver 'n' Percussion* (1977, LA853); *Silver 'n' Strings Play the Music of the Spheres* (1978–9, LWB 1033)

As sideman: S. Getz: Penny (1950, Roost 556); Potter's Luck (1950, Roost 538); Split Kick (1950, Roost 526); A. Blakey: *A Night at Birdland* (1954, 5037–9); *The Jazz Messengers at the Café Bohemia* (1955, 1507–8)

BIBLIOGRAPHY

N. Hentoff: "Even Mynheers Turn to Silver," *DB*, xxiii/22 (1956), 17
"Horace Silver: the Rumors and the Facts," *DB*, xxvii/14 (1960), 18
B. Gardner: "Inside the Horace Silver Quintet," *DB*, xxx/14 (1963), 20
B. McRae: "Horace Silver," *JB*, iii/10 (1966), 14
M. Williams: *The Jazz Tradition* (New York, 1970, rev. 2/1983)
J. H. Klee: "Horace Silver's United States of Mind," *DB*, xxxviii/7 (1971), 16
V. Wilmer: "Horace Silver," *J&B*, i/11 (1972), 14 [interview]
H. Nolan: "In Pursuit: Horace Silver," *DB*, xl/15 (1973), 16
L. Lyons: "Horace Silver: Father of Funk," *CK*, ii/1 (1976), 18
J. R. Taylor: "Horace Silver Discography," *Radio Free Jazz*, xviii (1977), March, 21
L. Feather: "Piano Giants of Jazz: Horace Silver," *CK*, v/9 (1979), 68
M. Cuscuna: "Horace Silver's Blue Note Swan Song," *DB*, xlvii/11 (1980), 16
F. Foster: "On Horace Silver: Take a Deeper Look," *JSN*, ii/1 (1980), 8
M. Ullman: *Jazz Lives: Portraits in Words and Pictures* (Washington, 1980)
L. Lyons: *The Great Jazz Pianists, Speaking of their Lives and Music* (New York, 1983), 120
E. S. Meadows: "Prolegomenon to the Music of Horace Silver," *Jf*, xviii (1986), 123

BILL DOBBINS

Silvertone. Record label. It was the main label of the mail-order organization Sears–Roebuck and was established shortly before World War I. During the 1920s it was used to issue material from many companies. Most of the material of jazz interest was derived from Gennett and Paramount, often from their race series. Issues from these labels were invariably made under pseudonyms and often with alternative tune titles; this has created many problems for discographers. Pseudonyms were also often used for items from other companies. The label appears to have been discontinued at the end of 1930, but it was briefly revived in 1940 for the release of recordings from Columbia and Okeh, including items by Benny Goodman.

BIBLIOGRAPHY

J. Godrich and J. McKenzie: "Silvertone 3500 Series," *Matrix*, no.56 (1964), 3
R. M. W. Dixon and J. Godrich: *Recording the Blues* (London, 1970), 54
B. Rust: *The American Record Label Book* (New Rochelle, NY, 1978), 277

Šima, Jan (*b* Prague, 17 Oct 1911). Bohemian bandleader. In 1934 he joined the Harry Harden Orchestra, for which he wrote arrangements and in which he may have played piano. From 1935 to 1937 he led the Gramoklub Orchestra, which gave the first jazz concert in Prague and afforded to such young soloists as Kamil Behounek the opportunity to perform. Joe Turner (i) recorded two tracks with the orchestra in 1936 (*Joe Turner Stomp/Joe Turner Blues*, Ultraphon A11400).

GERHARD CONRAD

Simeon, Omer (Victor) (*b* New Orleans, 21 July 1902; *d* New York, 17 Sept 1959). Clarinetist. He began to play clarinet after he moved with his family to Chicago in 1914, and took lessons from Lorenzo Tio, Jr. (1918–20). He played in the band of his brother Al Simeon, a violinist, then worked with Charlie Elgar's Creole Orchestra in Chicago and Milwaukee (1923–7). He recorded with Jelly Roll Morton in 1926 and immediately became one of Morton's favorite clarinetists. His playing on *Black Bottom Stomp* is typical of his fluent and imaginative style; passages in which he displays the warm beauty of the instrument's low register are contrasted with others of biting intensity. In 1927 Simeon joined King Oliver and toured with him to St. Louis and New York, where he also played with Luis Russell and recorded again with Morton (1928). After returning to Chicago he worked with Erskine Tate (1928–30), Earl Hines (1931–7; for illustration *see* HINES, EARL), Horace Henderson (1938), Walter Fuller (1940), and Coleman Hawkins (1941), then became a member of Jimmie Lunceford's orchestra (1942). While with the band Simeon also recorded with Kid Ory in Hollywood (1944–5). After Lunceford's death in 1947 Simeon remained with the group until 1950 under the leadership of Eddie Wilcox. He spent the rest of his life working in New York, where he performed and recorded regularly with Wilbur De Paris (1951–9).

Oral history material in *LNT*.

SELECTED RECORDINGS

As leader: Smoke House Blues/Beaukoo Jack (1929, Bruns. 7109)
As sideman with J. R. Morton: Black Bottom Stomp/The Chant (1926, Vic. 20221); Shoe Shiner's Drag/Shreveport [Stomp] (1928, Vic. 21658); Georgia Swing/Mournful Serenade (1928, Vic. 38024)
As sideman with others: K. Ory: Blues for Jimmie Noone/Get out of here (1944, Crescent 2); W. De Paris: *Rampart St. Ramblers* (1952, Atl. 141, 143)

BIBLIOGRAPHY

ChiltonW
H. Rosenberg and E. Williams: "Omer Simeon," *Jazz Information*, ii/1 (1940), 7
E. Keartland: "Discography of Omer Simeon," *Hot Notes*, ii/5 (1947), 14
H. Panassié: "Omer Simeon," *BHcF*, no.92 (1959), 3
J. R. T. Davies: "The Curious Case of the Forgotten Years," *Sv*, i/1 (1965), 8
H. Openeer, Jr.: "Omer Simeon," *Doctor jazz*, no.42 (1970), 6; no.43 (1970), 4
O. Simeon: "Mostly about Morton," *Selections from the Gutter: Jazz Portraits from 'The Jazz Record'*, ed. A. Hodes and C. Hansen (Berkeley, CA, Los Angeles, and London, 1977), 92
W. J. Schafer: "Clarinet Kings," *MR*, x/11 (1983), 1

BILL RUSSELL

Simmen, Johnny [Hans Georg] (*b* Brugg, Switzerland, 7 April 1918). Swiss writer. His numerous articles have appeared in magazines published in Belgium, France, Germany, Switzerland, the UK, and Canada, and he has given lectures on jazz in several countries. One of the most knowledgeable jazz writers, he specializes in musicians of the pre-bop era and writes with a deep understanding of the improviser's craft; his biographical features clearly indicate the trust and confidence that his subjects, who are usually veteran musicians, place in him. Although Simmen studied piano for seven years he never played professionally, but his knowledge of keyboard technique makes his articles on jazz pianists particularly incisive. His extraordinarily acute musical ear allows him to recognize jazz soloists with ease, and his lectures on individual musicians are models of learned enthusiasm.

WRITINGS

(selective list)

"Carnet de notes, xvii: Mrs. Emily Kraft-Banga and Mr. Kaiser Marshall," *BHcF*, no.208 (1971), 4; no.209 (1971), 7; rev. Eng. trans. in *Sv*, no.41 (1972), 176
"Kenneth J. Hollon: Portrait of an Unsung Musician," *Coda*, xi/9 (1974), 2
"Crystal Clear," *Coda*, xii/3 (1975), 25 [on Bill Coleman]
"Sandy Williams," *BHcF* (1984), no.315; p.3; no.316, p.2; no.317, p.4; no.318, p.7; no.319, p.1; Eng. trans., abbreviated, in *Sv*, no.116 (1984–5), 48 [incl. discography]
"Joe Turner," *Sv*, no.123 (1986), 97

JOHN CHILTON

Simmons, John (Jacob) (*b* Haskell, OK, 14 June 1918; *d* Los Angeles, 19 Sept 1979). Double bass player. He first played trumpet, then took up double bass. He worked with Nat "King" Cole and recorded in Los Angeles with Teddy Wilson's quintet (1937), then moved to Chicago, where he played in the bands of Johnny Letman (1940), Roy Eldridge (1940–41), Benny

Goodman (1941), and Cootie Williams and Louis Armstrong (both 1942). He worked in CBS radio orchestras, performed briefly with Duke Ellington (1943), appeared in the acclaimed film *Jammin' the Blues* (1944), then played with Eddie Heywood in Los Angeles and Illinois Jacquet in New York (both 1945). Between 1944 and 1946 he also recorded with James P. Johnson, Hot Lips Page, Sid Catlett, Ben Webster, Billie Holiday, the Kansas City Six, Heywood, Sidney De Paris, Erroll Garner, Al Casey, Coleman Hawkins, Don Byas, Benny Carter, and Bill De Arango. Later he recorded with Ella Fitzgerald (1947), Sir Charles Thompson (1947–8), and Thelonious Monk (1948) and played in Garner's trio in New York (1949–52). In 1955 he performed with Harry Edison and in Scandinavia with the quintet led by Rolf Ericson and Duke Jordan; the following year he recorded with Tadd Dameron. Illness prevented Simmons from working steadily thereafter but he recorded with Edison in 1958 and played with Phineas Newborn in 1959–60. He was equally at home working with mainstream and bop groups; his round tone and sensitive, solid playing is heard to advantage on the recordings he made with Catlett.

Oral history material in *NjR* (JOHP).

SELECTED RECORDINGS

As sideman: T. Wilson: Ain't Misbehavin' (1937, Bruns. 7964); Just a Mood (1937, Bruns. 7973); H. L. Page: My gal's gone/The blues jumped a rabbit (1944, Com. 593); S. Catlett: Sleep/Linger awhile (1944, Com. 546); Memories of You/Just a Riff (1944, Com. 1515); I never knew/Love for Sale (1945, Cap. 10032); R. Ericson: Flight to Jordan (1956, Met. 192) [EP]; This time the dream's on me (1956, Met. 193) [EP]; P. Newborn: *Piano Portraits* (1959, Roul. 52031), incl. Star Eyes; *I Love a Piano* (1959, Roul. 52043), incl. Real Gone Guy

BIBLIOGRAPHY

ChiltonW; *FeatherE*; *Feather–Gitler '70s*
Obituary, *DB*, xlvi/18 (1979), 13
J. Doran: *Erroll Garner: the Most Happy Piano* (Metuchen, NJ, and London, 1985) [incl. discography]

JOHNNY SIMMEN

Simmons, (Sarney) Norman (*b* Chicago, 6 Oct 1929). Pianist, arranger, and teacher. He studied piano at the Chicago School of Music with Max Sinzheimer (1945–9), performed with Clifford Jordan (1946), and belonged to Paul Bascomb's group (1953). After working as the house pianist at the Bee Hive (1953–6) he formed a trio with Vernel Fournier and Victor Sproles (with which he recorded under Wardell Gray's leadership), led a band at the C & C Lounge in Chicago (1957–9), and accompanied Dakota Staton (1958, recording in 1961–3) and Ernestine Anderson (1959). After moving in 1959 to New York he wrote arrangements for recordings issued by Riverside (including Johnny Griffin's *The Big Soul Band*, 1960, 1179), performed and recorded in a quintet with Griffin and Eddie "Lockjaw" Davis, and accompanied Carmen McRae (1960–69); he also accompanied Betty Carter (1969–71), with whom he made several recordings (one of which was recorded in concert, 1969), and, in the 1970s, Anita O'Day, Helen Humes, and Joe Williams. Later he recorded with Roy Eldridge (1976) and a group led by Scott Hamilton and Warren Vaché (1978, 1979); he led a trio and continued to write arrangements into the 1980s. Simmons began teaching piano and ensemble for the Jazzmobile in 1974 and joined the faculty of Paterson State College in 1982. He is the composer of the well-known tune *Jan* (1953).

SELECTED RECORDINGS

As leader: *Norman Simmons Trio* (1956, Argo 607); *Ramira the Dancer* (1976, Spot. 13); *13th Moon* (1986, Milljac 1003)

As sideman: R. Rodney: *Modern Music from Chicago* (1955, Fan. 3208); E. Davis: *Battle Stations* (1960, Prst. 7282)

BIBLIOGRAPHY

Feather '60s
M. Gardner: "Norman Simmons," *JM*, no.188 (1970), 4; no.189 (1970), 2; no.190 (1970), 14; no.191 (1971), 6
J. Olsson: "Norman Simmons," *Orkester journalen*, xlvii/12 (1979), 9 [discography]
S. Troup: "His Excellence Keeps him Scarce," *Newsday* (29 Nov 1985), 7

JAMES M. DORAN

Simmons, Sonny [Huey] (*b* Sicily Island, LA, 4 Aug 1933). Alto saxophonist. After moving with his family in the early 1940s to Oakland, California, he began teaching himself to play saxophone in 1950. In 1954 he met Prince Lasha, with whom he performed and recorded in the 1960s; later he performed on the East and West coasts in groups that included his wife, Barbara Donald, and in the late 1960s moved to Woodstock, New York. After returning to the West Coast in 1970 he performed in the San Francisco area with Lasha and Bobby Hutcherson before retiring from music in the early 1970s. In addition to his principal instrument Simmons played tenor saxophone, heckelphone, oboe, and english horn.

SELECTED RECORDINGS

As leader: *Staying on the Watch* (1966, ESP 1030); with P. Lasha: *Firebirds* (1967, Cont. 7617); *Music from the Spheres* (1968, ESP 1043); *Manhattan Egos* (1969, Arhoolie 8003); *Rumasuma* (1970, Cont. 7623); *Burning Spirits* (1971, Cont. 7625–6)

As sideman: P. Lasha: *The Cry!* (1962, Cont. 7610); Elvin Jones and J. Garrison: *Illumination* (1963, Imp. 49)

BIBLIOGRAPHY

J. Tynan: "Take Five," *DB*, xxx/9 (1963), 40
L. Feather: "Blindfold Test: Sonny Simmons," *DB*, xxxv/10 (1968), 33
R. Russell: "Sonny Simmons," *Jh*, no.267 (1970), 16
D. C. Hunt: "Sonny Simmons," *J&P*, x/5 (1971), 20

DAVID WILD

Simon, George T(homas) (*b* New York, 9 May 1912). Writer and record producer. He played drums in his own band while attending Harvard University (BA 1934) and later for a brief period in Glenn Miller's orchestra (1937), which he had also helped to organize. After working as an associate editor of *Metronome* (1935–9) he served as its editor-in-chief (1939–55), and changed the magazine's orientation away from articles on instrument making and publishing towards items on recording and the work of such big-band leaders as Bunny Berigan, Benny Goodman, and the Dorsey brothers; he wrote much of the material in *Metronome* himself (under pseudonyms) before engaging Barry Ulanov and others as staff writers. Later he supervised artists and repertory for the record company Jazztone, serving as the program director of the Jazztone Society (1956–7), a mail-order scheme. He was also a writer, producer, and consultant for several television programs (including the "Timex All Time Jazz" series), and the president of Bouree Productions (1958–60), a record production company. From 1961 to 1972 Simon was the executive director of the National Academy of Recording Arts & Sciences. He also produced jazz recordings for Capitol, Columbia, Victor, and Warner Bros., and wrote about jazz in the *New York Herald Tribune* (1961–4) and the *New York Post* (1980–81). He won the ASCAP–Deems Taylor Award in 1968 for his book *The Big Bands* (1967) and a Grammy Award in 1978 for his liner notes to the album *Bing Crosby: a Legendary Performer* (RCA CPL1-2086(e), 1977).

WRITINGS

(selective list)

The Feeling of Jazz (New York, 1961)
The Big Bands (New York, 1967, rev. and enlarged 2/1971, rev. 3/1974, 4/1981)

Simon Says: the Sights and Sounds of the Swing Era, 1935–1955 (New Rochelle, NY, 1971)
Glenn Miller and his Orchestra (New York, 1974)
with others: *The Best of the Music Makers* (Garden City, NY, 1979)

DANIEL ZAGER

Simon, Maurice (James) (*b* Houston, 26 March 1929). Saxophonist. He worked in Texas with Russell Jacquet (1943–4), then moved to Los Angeles (*c*1945), where he played and recorded on tenor saxophone with Jacquet and Gerald Wilson; he recorded on baritone saxophone with Wilson's big band accompanying Dinah Washington (1946), and with Maxwell Davis (1949). He performed and recorded with Illinois Jacquet (1949–50), then led a group (1950–53) with his brother Freddie, a trumpeter. After playing briefly with Count Basie (1953), he worked in New York with Cootie Williams, and performed and recorded with Cab Calloway and Wild Bill Davis (both 1958). During the 1960s he led groups that accompanied singers in Las Vegas and Los Angeles, recorded with Jimmy Witherspoon (1961), and worked with Ray Charles (1967). He later played tenor, alto, and baritone saxophones with the Duke Ellington Orchestra under Mercer Ellington (1974–5). A robust and earthy player in swing and rhythm-and-blues styles, Simon may be heard to advantage playing the baritone instrument on Helen Humes's *You Played on my Piano* (1952, Decca 48282). (*FeatherE*; *Feather–Gitler '70s*)

Simpkins, Andy [Andrew] (*b* Richmond, IN, 29 April 1932). Double bass player. His first instruments were clarinet and piano; he began to play double bass while in the army (1953). In 1956 he was a founding member of the Four Sounds, which the following year became the THREE SOUNDS. He remained with the group until 1968; it played swing and bop tinged with the blues, and was highly successful. Simpkins also recorded film soundtracks during this period: one of his notable performances is an eerie duet with Ray Brown for *In Cold Blood* (1967). From 1968 to 1974 he toured and recorded with George Shearing; he also performed with Carmen McRae and Joe Williams, and recorded with Clare Fischer (1971), Stephane Grappelli and Shearing (1976), Dave Mackay (*c*1977), Monty Alexander (1977–8), and Don Menza and Buddy DeFranco (both 1981). From 1979 he has been a member of the trio that accompanies Sarah Vaughan, and from the early 1980s he has recorded as a leader. Simpkins is an energetic, creative soloist with a keen sense of rhythm.

SELECTED RECORDINGS

As leader: of the Three Sounds (with B. Dowdy and G. Harris): *Bottoms Up* (1959, BN 4014), *Moods* (1960, BN 84044); with D. Mackay: *Happying* (*c*1977, Studio 7403); *Love Will Win* (*c*1982, Dis. 883); *Summer Strut* (*c*1983, Dis. 892)
As sideman: G. Shearing: *The George Shearing Trio* (1971, Sheba 103); S. Vaughan: *Crazy and Mixed Up* (1982, PT 2312137)

BIBLIOGRAPHY

FeatherE; *Feather '60s*; *Feather–Gitler '70s*
J. L. Ginibre and P. Carles: "Dictionnaire de la contrebasse," *Jm*, no.166 (1969), 56

DIANNA RHYAN

Simpson, Cassino (Wendell) (*b* Chicago, or Venice, Italy, 22 July 1909; *d* Elgin, IL, 27 March 1952). Pianist. He was given lessons by Zinky Cohn. He recorded in Chicago with the trumpeter Bernie Young (1923) and worked with Arthur Simm's orchestra; from around 1926 it was led by Young, with whom he remained until 1930. He performed and made several recordings with Jabbo Smith, among them *Little Willie Blues* (1929, Bruns. 7058), on which he plays a particularly fine solo, and *Ace of Rhythm* (1929, Bruns. 7071). He worked with Erskine Tate and recorded as a freelance, and from around 1931 to 1933 he led his own bands, which included Smith and Milt Hinton. He then accompanied Frankie "Half Pint" Jaxon, but the association ended abruptly when Simpson was charged with attempting to kill Jaxon. Shortly afterwards (1935) he was admitted to a mental hospital, where he continued performing and recorded piano solos (early 1940s). The few readily available recordings of his work confirm the view of his contemporaries that Simpson was an exceptional pianist, whose playing became increasingly impressive towards the end of his short career.

BIBLIOGRAPHY

J. S. Shipman: "Cassino Simpson," *JJ*, viii/11 (1955), 1
J. Simmen: "Cassino Simpson," *Sv*, no.28 (1970), 123, rev. and enlarged in *BHcF*, no.206 (1971), 6
A. McCarthy: *Big Band Jazz* (New York and London, 1974), 37
A. Vollmer: "Rhythm Aces," *Sv*, no.86 (1979–80), 70

based on *ChiltonW*

Sims, Ray (C.) (*b* Wichita, KS, 18 Jan 1921). Trombonist, brother of Zoot Sims. After experience in dance bands, in 1947 he recorded with Anita O'Day and worked briefly with Benny Goodman; he recorded *How High the Moon* (Cap. 20127) as a member of Goodman's septet. From 1947 to 1957 he played trombone and sang ballads with Les Brown; he also played with Dave Pell's octet (1953–7), the members of which were drawn from Brown's band. While working and recording with Harry James (1957–69) he made occasional recordings with other leaders (Bill Holman, 1957–8; Red Norvo, 1958; Charlie Barnet, 1959). Later he recorded again with James (1973), as a singer with Corky Corcoran (1973), and as a trombonist and singer in his brother's quintet on the album *The Swinger* (1979–80, Pablo 2310861).

BIBLIOGRAPHY

FeatherE; *Feather '60s*
R. D. Kinkle: *The Complete Encyclopedia of Popular Music and Jazz, 1900–1950* (New Rochelle, NY, and Westport, CT, 1974) [incl. discography]

Sims, Zoot [John Haley] (*b* Inglewood, CA, 29 Oct 1925; *d* New York, 23 March 1985). Tenor saxophonist and leader, brother of Ray Sims. He grew up in a family of vaudeville artists and played drums and clarinet as a child; he took up tenor saxophone when he was 13. He worked as a professional musician from the age of 15, touring in dance bands, and in 1943 began the first of several engagements with Benny Goodman, which later included trips to Europe (1950, 1958, 1972), the USSR (1962), and Australia (1973). In 1944 Sims played in New York at Café Society (Uptown) with Bill Harris (i) and recorded with this group under the nominal leadership of Joe Bushkin, then performed in California with Sid Catlett. After serving in army bands he worked again with Goodman (1946–7) and also with Gene Roland. From 1947 to 1949 he was a member of Woody Herman's big band, where Roland's writing for four tenor saxophones led to the establishment of the famous saxophone section known as the Four Brothers (for illustration *see* HERMAN, WOODY, fig.1*b*); Sims is the second soloist (following Stan Getz) to be heard on Herman's recording of *Keen and Peachy* and the first on *Four Brothers* (both 1947). Sims then played briefly with Buddy Rich, replaced Wardell Gray in Goodman's bop group (1950), and worked with Chubby Jackson (1950) and

Elliot Lawrence (1951), but performed and recorded principally as a freelance. After a brief period in Stan Kenton's band (1953) he toured Europe and recorded as a sideman with Gerry Mulligan's groups (1954–6) and played as a soloist in Mulligan's Concert Jazz Band (1960). From 1957 to the early 1980s Sims regularly led bop quintets with Al Cohn (see illustration); his appearances with these groups included tours of Scandinavia (1974) and Japan (1978). He also toured England (1967) and Europe (1975) with Jazz at the Philharmonic, and performed at the Grande Parade du Jazz in Nice with ensembles that played in styles ranging from dixieland to bop.

Sims was traditional in his outlook and preferred to improvise with a conventional rhythm section comprising piano, double bass, and drums, a format he retained when working with local musicians in major cities from the late 1960s until his death. He was a tireless performer whose exuberant, driving sense of swing may be heard on a series of excellent recordings made in the 1970s.

Oral history material in *GBLnsa*.

SELECTED RECORDINGS

As leader: Don't worry about me (1950, Vogue 5054); Tangerine/Zootcase (1952, Prst. 1348) [EP]; with A. Cohn: *You 'n' Me* (1960, Mer. 60606), *Body and Soul* (1973, Muse 5016); *Zoot at Ease* (1973, FaD 2000); *Nirvana* (1974, GM 533); *Zoot Sims and Friend* (1975, CJ 21)

As sideman: W. Herman: Keen and Peachy (1947, Col. 38213); Four Brothers (1947, Col. 38304); G. Mulligan: *Concert Jazz Band* (1960, Verve 68388); P. Adams: *Encounter* (1968, Prst. 7677); C. Basie: *Basie and Zoot* (1975, Pablo 2310745)

BIBLIOGRAPHY

B. Hodgkins: "Zoot," *Metronome*, lxvi/12 (1950), 16
I. Gitler: "The Colorful World of Zoot Sims," *DB*, xxviii/8 (1961), 20
A. Entwhistle: "Zoot Sims: Fratricidal Enigma," *JM*, no.164 (1968), 10
M. Bourne: "Zoot Sims: Elemental Elegance," *DB*, xliii/20 (1976), 13
C. Carrière and A. Tercinet: "Zoot Sims," *Jh*, nos.339–40 (1977), 24
A. Astrup: *The John Haley Sims Discography* (Lyngby, Denmark, 1980; suppl. 1983)
G. Endress: *Jazz Podium: Musiker über sich selbst* (Stuttgart, Germany, 1980), 122
D. Long: "Zoot Sims: Interview," *Cadence*, ix/5 (1983), 5
B. Rusch: "Zoot Sims: Interview," *Cadence*, x/11 (1984), 5; xi/1 (1985), 5
Obituary, J.S. Wilson, *New York Times* (24 March 1985)
W. Balliett: "Zoot and Louise," *American Musicians: Fifty-six Portraits in Jazz* (New York, and Oxford, England, 1986), 273

BARRY KERNFELD

Sinatra, Frank [Francis Albert] (*b* Hoboken, NJ, 12 Dec 1915). Singer. His parents were Italian immigrants from whom he inherited an inborn predilection for the bel canto style of singing. He first attracted widespread attention while singing on radio programs in New York, and was engaged as a big-band vocalist with Harry James in 1939. This was followed by a three-year period with Tommy Dorsey (1940–42; for illustration *see* DORSEY, TOMMY), during which he became a celebrity among young people on a scale matched only by Benny Goodman before him and later by Elvis Presley and the Beatles. After leaving Dorsey he was constantly in demand as a soloist, singing as many as 100 songs daily on a tight touring and recording schedule. Inevitably this overexposure began to tell on Sinatra's voice and popularity, and from 1947 his career entered a noticeable decline. He continued to make recordings for Columbia, generally of ballads, but failed to match his former success, and by 1952 he was without a recording contract.

The following year, however, Sinatra re-established himself in the public eye through a nonsinging role in the film *From Here to Eternity*, and signed a new recording contract with Capitol which placed him in a more congenial, jazz-oriented context. There followed a long series of best-selling recordings

Zoot Sims (right) and Al Cohn in Toronto, 1960

using arrangements by Billy May, Gordon Jenkins and, most notably, Nelson Riddle, whose expert handling of big band and strings drew out the many facets of Sinatra's musical personality to excellent advantage. From this point Sinatra projected an image as a "swinger" rather than a balladeer, though he continued to excel in ballad performances as well. Once again he began to dominate the popularity polls for male vocalists. Other important film roles followed, both in musicals such as *Guys and Dolls* (1955), *High Society* (1956), and *Can-can* (1960) and in nonsinging roles, particularly in *The Man with the Golden Arm* (1955; *see* FILMS, §I, 4(iv)). The years around 1960 probably represented the crest of his popularity. He ceased to record for Capitol, and founded his own record company and label, REPRISE, in 1961. For this organization he recorded with Count Basie (1962–6) and Duke Ellington (1967). He announced his retirement in 1971, but this proved impossible for a man so quintessentially a public performer, and from 1973 he resumed his career with national and international tours, television spectaculars, and recordings. He received the Presidential Medal of Freedom in 1985.

Sinatra is best known as a popular singer, but he is nevertheless highly respected in jazz circles, above all for his relaxed and subtle sense of swing. Although improvisation is not one of the main characteristics of his style, whenever he departs radically from the given material, he always does so with excellent taste and to expressive purpose. From Dorsey he adopted certain key aspects of jazz phrasing, particularly regarding breathing; later he expressed a debt to Billie Holiday. But the crucial innovations in Sinatra's approach were based (unwittingly) on the Italian bel canto tradition, particularly his legato attack (known to his detractors as "mooing"), his handling of portamento and rubato, and his sensitive modulation of vowel sounds. Like Crosby, he made full use of the microphone, but with a new awareness of its potential as an "instrument" for achieving a wide range of dynamics and for magnifying the expressive effects of singing at medium volume. His lightness of breath and "forward" vocal production permitted an extraordinarily clear enunciation and allowed him to concentrate on shading and nuance. Though Sinatra spawned countless imitators – few popular singers outside the rock tradition entirely escaped his influence – none was able to match the note of almost autobiographical sincerity in his singing, the result of a unique fusion of a turbulent and controversial public career and an intuitive penetration and projection of the meaning of a song and its lyric.

SELECTED RECORDINGS

As leader with C. Basie: *An Historical Music First* (1962, Rep. 1008); *It Might as Well be Spring* (1964, Rep. 1012); *Frank Sinatra/Count Basie at the Sands* (1966, Rep. 1019)

As sideman with T. Dorsey: Without a Song (1941, Vic. 36396); Everything happens to me (1941, Vic. 27359)

BIBLIOGRAPHY

E. J. Kahn: *The Voice* (New York, 1947)
A. Shaw: *Sinatra: Twentieth-century Romantic* (New York, 1965)
H. Pleasants: "Frank Sinatra – a Great Vocalist Retires," *Stereo Review*, xxvii/5 (1971), 59 [incl. discography]
——: *The Great American Popular Singers* (New York, 1974)
E. Wilson: *Sinatra: an Unauthorized Biography* (New York, 1976)
J. Ridgway: *The Sinatra File* (Birmingham, England, 1977–80)
J. Rockwell: *Sinatra: an American Classic* (New York, 1984)

HENRY PLEASANTS/R

Singer, Hal [Harold; Cornbread] (*b* Tulsa, OK, 8 Oct 1919). Tenor saxophonist and bandleader. He first learned violin, but played clarinet and alto saxophone from 1933. After changing to tenor saxophone he worked with the bandleader Ernie Fields (1938), the trumpeter Lloyd Hunter, Nat Towles (1939), and Tommy Douglas (1939–41). He then moved to New York with Jay McShann and performed there with Hot Lips Page (1943), Roy Eldridge (1944), Don Byas (1945), Henry "Red" Allen and Sid Catlett (both 1946–7), and Lucky Millinder and Duke Ellington (both 1948). He gained his nickname from one of his first recordings as a leader (*Corn Bread*, 1948, Savoy 671). He toured with his own band for a decade (1949–58) and was then a house musician at the Metropole, New York (1958–61). In the early 1960s he toured with a trio and led a band in New York. He settled in Paris in 1965 and continued to perform and record into the 1980s. His playing is well represented by his album *Blue Stompin'* (1959, Prst. 7153).

BIBLIOGRAPHY

ChiltonW; *FeatherE*; *Feather–Gitler '70s*
A. McCarthy: "The Hal Singer Story," *JM*, iv/11 (1959), 11
C. Roby: "Blue Stomping at the Trois Mailletz," *JB*, ii/11 (1965), 4
J. Elliott: "All Tenor Players Owe Something to Hawkins," *CI*, iv/12 (1966), 10
J. Pescheux: "Hal Singer," *BHcF*, no.155 (1966), 7

Singing.

1. General: (i) The place of singing and singers in jazz (ii) Jazz vocal techniques and styles. 2. The precursors of jazz singing. 3. The influence of the blues. 4. Early jazz singers. 5. The swing era. 6. New singers and styles of the 1940s and 1950s. 7. After 1960.

1. General.

(i) The place of singing and singers in jazz. Jazz has developed its own tradition of singing and has evolved a number of distinctive techniques and styles. Both historically and stylistically it is closely allied to other forms of popular music and its connection with classical music is remote. Few jazz singers (or vocalists, as they are normally called in jazz) have a classical training or bring to their performance classical techniques of breathing, voice production, and vibrato (a notable exception is Sarah Vaughan). Similarly the traditional naming of the voices according to range, though it is sometimes found in writing on jazz, is not altogether appropriate: singers whose voices fall into the alto (or contralto), tenor, and baritone ranges are far more often found than are sopranos and basses, but many singers anyway employ techniques (such as falsetto and scat yodeling, see below) that carry the voice out of the basic range.

Jazz singing arises from and overlaps with two other traditions – the blues and popular song. The definition of a singer as a blues, jazz, or popular singer is often controversial, especially as there is no clear distinction in terms of repertory. Particularly in the earlier periods of jazz, the numbers a singer was called upon to perform consisted almost entirely of items from the blues and popular repertories; the distinction in these periods lies rather in the character of the accompaniment, the way in which the singer interacts with the instruments in the group, and the style of delivery and expression. The first of these considerations is often the most important: for example, a blues singer whose personal style differs in no significant way from that of other singers in the genre might be regarded as a jazz singer because he or she was singing with a jazz band.

The importance of the singer in jazz has varied according to style and period. In early jazz, performances of the blues and vaudeville numbers often involved singers (usually women), but performances of marches and ragtime pieces were always instrumental. Once popular songs began to enter and indeed dominate the repertory (from the 1920s) the singer found a regular place in jazz performance. The singing of popular songs reached its zenith during the swing era, when jazz and popular music effectively merged and every big band had at least one singer. It continued through the bop era (alongside new styles of jazz singing) and into Latin jazz, especially that in bossa nova style. Nevertheless, the prominence of the popular song did not eclipse the blues, which has continued to form part of the jazz repertory.

At periods when instrumentalists were almost always male, singing was an important route by which women entered jazz. While a large proportion of leading male singers have been first and foremost instrumentalists (Louis Armstrong, Jack Teagarden, and Clark Terry, for example), most female singers have tended to concentrate on singing alone. All of the greatest jazz singers have been American: although there are fine European and Latin American singers, including Alice Babs, Annie Ross, and Urszula Dudziak, none has been nearly so influential as such non-American instrumentalists as Django Reinhardt, Stephane Grappelli, Jean-Luc Ponty, Albert Mangelsdorff, Toots Thielemans, and Airto Moreira. The reasons for this are not altogether clear, though they may have to do with the importance of the English language in the jazz singing repertory and the centrality of the black-American musical heritage, with its characteristic timbres and modes of expression and delivery.

The place of the singer in jazz is different from that of any other member of the jazz ensemble for several reasons. In a band the singer almost always performs as a soloist even when he or she is technically a sideman. In those rare instances where the singer's line is integrated into an instrumental ensemble passage (as with the wordless vocalizing of Kay Davis in some of Duke Ellington's numbers) the voice still does not blend thoroughly with the instrumental sound. Singers have often been bandleaders (among them Bessie Smith, Cab Calloway, and Billy Eckstine) but neither this role nor that of a sideman in another leader's band signifies the same degree of success for a singer as it does for an instrumentalist. The most important landmark in the careers of some jazz singers is not the joining or leading of a band but the graduation from affiliation with an ensemble to work as a solo artist, touring and recording in varied settings, as did, for example, Ella Fitzgerald; in jazz and popular music such a singer is said to be working as a "single." The finest singers sometimes collaborate with one another, though less often than is the case with leading instrumentalists. Important examples include Louis Armstrong with Jack Teagarden and a number of vocal ensembles, notably the duo of Jackie Cain and Roy Kral, the trios Lambert, Hendricks, and Ross and the Boswell Sisters, and the quartets the Mills Brothers, the Novi Singers, and Manhattan Transfer. The Swingle Singers, whose scat versions of classical music are of questionable taste and peripheral importance to jazz, the Double Six, and the Vienna Art Choir are among the few large vocal ensembles.

(ii) Jazz vocal techniques and styles. Despite its derivation from and connection with blues and popular song, jazz has developed its own vocal techniques and practices, not all of which fall into the category of conventional singing.

SCAT SINGING, in which the voice is used as a surrogate instrument and the singer employs nonsense syllables rather than words, was a regular element in early jazz and swing; it gained greater importance in bop, and was later also adapted to fusions of jazz and soul music. Scat singing and some other styles of jazz singing often involve the use by male singers of the falsetto range and by low-voiced female singers of an equivalent high range. Many kinds of wordless vocalizing are exploited by jazz singers, from expressive growls and screeches to gentle humming, from vocal sounds that are close to speech (notably Clark Terry's mumbling) to convincing imitations of the timbres of particular instruments. A unique technique is Leone Thomas's scat yodeling. A form of vocal practice that is, in a way, the converse of scat singing is VOCALESE, an instrumental melody reproduced vocally with added text.

Besides these exceptional practices, jazz singers have adopted a great variety of approaches to the delivery of lyrics, ranging from careful interpretation to distortion in the interests of other aspects of the performance (line, vocal inflection, timbre, etc.). A controversial figure is Sarah Vaughan, who has been criticized for concentrating on instrumental sound rather than on meaning, and consequently destroying the sense of the words she sings. It should be said in her defense that the lyrics of popular songs of the 1920s to the 1940s are often trite and sentimental, if not sometimes nonsensical, and a lack of clarity is therefore small loss compared with the gain in the quality of the vocal sound. Among those who have evolved alternative approaches to such lyrics are Fats Waller, whose treatments ranged from serious to satirical (see Berger), and Billie Holiday, who developed an ability to infuse them with depth and meaning.

The use of vocal sounds in jazz is by no means confined to singers: many instrumentalists vocalize while playing. A number of performers provide a vocal accompaniment to their improvised instrumental lines, most often in unison or at the octave above or below, but sometimes at other intervals; exponents include Ray Perry (violin), Slam Stewart and Major Holley (double bass), George Benson (electric guitar), Tania Maria (piano), and Roland Kirk (flute). The important technique of humming or singing through the instrument is used in the production of MULTIPHONICS and the GROWL and is intrinsic to playing the KAZOO; performers sometimes incorporate the same practice in their improvisations – Dewey Redman, for example, has developed a unique manner of humming through the tenor saxophone. Vocal sounds and effects, often of a less "musical" kind, are employed in some free jazz, notably by the members of the Art Ensemble of Chicago, and many of the instrumental gestures associated with the style have an inherently vocal character. (It is interesting, given these aspects of the music, that there have been no singers of great significance in free jazz.)

An unusual form of vocal production used occasionally in jazz is whistling. The notable exponents are Toots Thielemans and the bop whistler Ron McCroby. It must be said, however, that the rather smooth and saccharine sound of whistling does not generally meld well with the characteristic timbres of jazz.

In the mid-1920s the introduction of the microphone revolutionized the practice of popular singing, allowing singers to explore a much broader range of dynamic variation than had previously been possible, and leading to a new, intimate style of delivery, which in some cases involved whispering, speaking, or half-speaking the lyrics of songs. Singers used the microphone not only to amplify volume but also to project notes in extreme registers and of subtle timbres. With the widespread availability from the 1970s of electronic sound-modifying devices of a more varied and complex kind, the range of sound effects available to performers increased enormously. The singer to have exploited the possibilities offered by electronics most creatively is Urszula Dudziak.

2. THE PRECURSORS OF JAZZ SINGING. The roots of jazz singing are to some extent more clearly traceable than those of instrumental jazz and in many respects predate them. During the late 19th century such forms as the work song and the spiritual presaged the birth of vocal jazz and by the turn of the century the BLUES was becoming established as a song form. All these styles were cultivated exclusively by Blacks. The work song, sung to pace the execution of manual labor, often followed a CALL-AND-RESPONSE pattern, while the spiritual, a kind of sacred folksong performed in church or less formally in the fields, had a more song-like structure. The opinions of musicians and scholars differ as to whether the blues grew out of the work song or the spiritual. Early groups, such as the Jubilee Singers of Fisk University, who from the 1870s transferred the spiritual to the concert hall, employed the bent notes and other inflections that characterize the blues, though these nuances were often eliminated in performances for white (particularly European) audiences.

3. THE INFLUENCE OF THE BLUES. The way in which the blues developed into a vocal form can only be guessed, since the transition took place before the era of the phonograph and in a stratum of society about which written documentation is scarce. The nature of early blues is perhaps best represented by the recordings of primitive country blues made in the 1920s by Blind Lemon Jefferson and in the 1920s and 1930s by Leadbelly (Huddie Ledbetter). These songs were based on the 12-bar BLUES PROGRESSION. They often followed what became the traditional lyric pattern, one similar to that of classical English verse and familiar through the works of Shakespeare, which made use of the iambic pentameter:

> I love to hear my baby call my name
> She calls so sweet and calls so doggone plain.

Both men accompanied themselves on guitar and made extensive use of BLUE NOTES (usually the flatted third and seventh). Jefferson developed a plaintive, moaning vocal style, suited to the melancholy cast of his lyrics, while Leadbelly had a more varied, robust approach, with a full, rough tone and a harsh vibrato. Leadbelly moved, late in his career, to New York, where he became popular in nightclubs and the concert hall.

A separate tradition of blues singing was established by a group of women, who were the first to record the blues, in the early 1920s. Several of them grew up in vaudeville and were thus accustomed to a performing tradition much closer to jazz than were street musicians such as Jefferson and Leadbelly. They sang with powerful emotion, full voices, and a wide range of expression, and are regarded as contributing important elements to the development of jazz singing style. They were usually accompanied by pianists or small groups: Fletcher Henderson's orchestra, Clarence Williams's small ensembles, and Lovie Austin's Blues Serenaders were among the bands that supplied accompanists. Some female blues singers had their own groups – Mamie Smith's Jazz Hounds was the group in which Coleman Hawkins began his career – and they sometimes worked with soloists of the first rank, most notably Louis Armstrong.

Ma Rainey, the first of the classic female blues singers, recorded some 90 songs in the 1920s, but the blues became known to a black audience mainly through the work of Mamie Smith (fig.1), whose *Crazy Blues* (1920, OK 4160), the first highly successful RACE RECORD, set a vital precedent. It was the passionate, rasping sound and strong personality of Bessie Smith that did most to create the legendary status of the female blues singers and their songs alike. She recorded predominantly for race record series, toured the TOBA circuit, and starred in the all-black film *St. Louis Blues* (1929). The success of her first recording, *Down-hearted Blues* (1923, Col. A3844), written by another early blues artist, Alberta Hunter, and her many other records through the rest of the decade established her as an imperiously individual stylist. However, by the time Smith made her last recording in 1933 the blues as a pure vocal form had lost much of its popularity, and jazz singing was no longer confined to the blues.

1. Mamie Smith, 1922

4. EARLY JAZZ SINGERS. In contrast to the blues, born out of slavery in the American South, other vocal traditions developed in other parts of the USA. Midwestern ragtime had scarce significance for jazz singing, its manifestation in jazz being exclusively instrumental, but in New York the emergence from similar roots of popular songwriting under the broad banner of Tin Pan Alley was of great importance. The origins of Tin Pan Alley go back to the 1880s and the publication of various forms of vaudeville music, including so-called ragtime songs. This tradition entered jazz after World War I, when individual popular songs and songs written for the musical theater were taken up by jazz musicians. (For numerous examples *see* FORMS, §1(i)(a)).

Ethel Waters was the first singer to move away from a strong association with the blues into a broader-based style that encompassed popular songs of the day. By comparison with the blues singers her voice had more of the characteristics generally considered typical of popular singing: her timbre was cleaner, her phrasing more relaxed, and her personality both more conventional and more positive. These qualities may be heard on her many recordings, such as the highly successful *Dinah* (1925, Col. 487D).

Louis Armstrong, whose early performances included blues which he both sang and played, was also able to break away into new stylistic areas. He was the first important exponent of the technique of scat singing; a good example (and one of the earliest) is provided by *Heebie Jeebies* (1926, OK 8300), recorded with the Hot Five. In due course scat singing became an important element in jazz singing, particularly in the bop period, though some of the great singers, including Billie Holiday, never employed it. Armstrong's contribution transcended such novelties. He brought to jazz the ability to imbue even the most trivial popular song with a gruff emotional integrity, which established him in vocal jazz as firmly as his playing had in instrumental jazz. On recordings of popular songs such as *I can't give you anything but love* (1929, OK 8669) he drastically alters the melodic line to suit his own concept of the song. While saxophones offer in the background a staid, literal rendering of the melody, Armstrong centers large parts of his new melody on repeated pitches, introduces fragments of scat singing to fill spaces between phrases, and delivers brief excerpts from the original line, almost always placing all these elements well ahead of or behind the beat, rarely on it (ex.1, p.458). Although he remained a masterful blues singer, he gradually enlarged his scope until he could successfully interpret anything from a nonsense song to a ballad in a beguiling vocal performance.

Armstrong's rejection of the orthodox approach to singing inspired numerous imitators. Some of these were, like him, trumpeters – Henry "Red" Allen, Roy Eldridge, Wingy Manone, and Louis Prima, for instance, not only imitated Armstrong's trumpet playing but also translated his melodic style of wind improvisation into vocal terms. However, it has rightly been said that every singer, male or female, whether an instrumentalist or not, has come under the influence of the unique impact of Armstrong's work in the 1920s and 1930s. Even Waters copied Armstrong in her own rendition of *I can't give you anything but love* (1932, Bruns. 6517).

5. THE SWING ERA. The big band, which developed from the mid-1920s, came to great prominence in the 1930s, when for

Ex.1 Louis Armstrong's reworking of the melody of *I can't give you anything but love* (1929, OK 8669; original song by Dorothy Fields and Jimmy McHugh): transcr. B. Kernfeld

the first time jazz merged with popular music, producing the style known as swing. Every big band included a singer, if indeed it was not led by one, and many featured two (a man and a woman) to present the hit songs of the day. Some singers were integrated into ensembles in a memorable fashion, as was the case with Kay Davis, Adelaide Hall, Ivie Anderson, Betty Roche, Joya Sherrill, and Alice Babs in Duke Ellington's orchestra; they performed not only popular songs (many newly composed by Ellington), but blues, and works by Ellington that involved a semiclassical style of singing. Also of great importance was the work of forceful blues singers in Count Basie's orchestra (see below). In other settings singers were merely accessories to a more important instrumental ensemble; strikingly there is no vocal part in almost any of the greatest hits made by Benny Goodman's orchestra (one of the most popular bands of the time), even though the ensemble gave countless performances with singers.

The most creative and influential singers of the swing era did a considerable amount of work outside the big bands. Despite the attempts of Sophie Tucker and other white singers to imitate black styles, no important white jazz singers emerged until 1929–30, when Mildred Bailey and Jack Teagarden, both of whom moved with ease between small groups and big bands, made their first recordings. Bailey brought an effortless vocal production, a light timbre, and swinging vitality to her performances of popular songs, some of them influenced by the blues and spirituals but most quite conventional products of Tin Pan Alley. Hoagy Carmichael's *Rockin' Chair* became the theme song of her numerous radio broadcasts in the 1930s; among her several recordings of this song is a representative version made in 1937 (Voc. 3553).

Jack Teagarden was exposed as a youth to the sound of black spirituals sung at revivalist meetings. He became a master of the trombone and a singer who brought his rich, warm tone to songs in many different styles from genuine blues to such popular numbers as *I've got a right to sing the blues*, which became the theme song of his big band in the 1940s. Teagarden later entered into a close association with Armstrong, and (under Armstrong's leadership) they recorded vocal duets together, including the pairing *Back o' Town Blues/St. James Infirmary* (1947, Vic. 404006); they occasionally sang in harmony but for the most part alternated phrases or choruses, responding to and building upon each other's improvised paraphrasing of a familiar melody or lyric. Teagarden's lazy, relaxed sound established him as the only white male jazz singer of consequence of the time.

Lee Wiley, who sang with Paul Whiteman, Eddie Condon, Willard Robison, and other prominent bandleaders in the 1930s and 1940s, was another white jazz singer to develop a distinctive style. Her huskily erotic interpretations of songs by Gershwin and Cole Porter were marked by a wide vibrato and a sensitive understanding of lyrics. Many of her best-known recordings were made with dixieland bands.

In the mid-1930s two singers came to prominence, Billie Holiday and Ella Fitzgerald, whose influence on the development of jazz singing was to be decisive. Holiday made two attempts at affiliations with big bands, but she was at her most effective in small and medium-sized groups, perhaps because her inventive, irrepressible gift for improvisation was confined by big-band arrangements. Her sound, rugged and rasping, owed something to the influence of both Armstrong and Bessie Smith, though most of her best work involved standard popular songs rather than the blues; she also contributed to the composition of several songs that she performed superlatively, including *God bless the child* (1941, OK 6720) and a poignant piece about a lynching, *Strange Fruit* (1939, Com. 526). Like many jazz singers, Holiday mostly had to work with inferior material; a number of songs are remembered only because she gave them immortality (on recordings made in the 1930s and 1940s) by improvising memorably on their melodies and investing their trite lyrics with a profound depth. Although her voice deteriorated in later years, the emotional impact of her performances was without parallel. Her influence has been felt by every other singer from Frank Sinatra onwards.

Ella Fitzgerald, by contrast, moved freely during this period between Chick Webb's orchestra and her own recording octet. Her voice, with its clear, bell-like tone, was the antithesis of Holiday's. Delightful recordings with Webb, including *Sing me a Swing Song* (1936, Decca 830), established her as a leading vocalist of the swing era. In the 1940s, unlike Holiday, she ventured into the bop style and became one of the first successful modern scat singers, as for example on her version of *How High the Moon* (1947, Decca 24387). But her most significant work was a series of albums of the compositions of Duke Ellington (often with Ellington's orchestra), Irving Berlin, Cole Porter, and others, recorded in the 1950s for Norman Granz's labels. Her rhythmic versatility, wide compass, and full, appealing tone have proved adaptable to many different styles in the course of her long career, during which she has continued to broaden her range.

Alongside the synthesis of popular music and jazz that is the chief characteristic of big-band style, the blues continued to be cultivated by male singers, who came to be known as "blues shouters." Working initially in the Southwest, they sang the blues in a raw, raucous style. First and foremost in this line of modern blues singers was Jimmy Rushing, a member of Walter Page's Blue Devils, Bennie Moten's orchestra, and, most importantly, Count Basie's orchestra. Later notable exponents were Joe Turner (ii), who worked as a soloist or in a duo with the boogie-woogie pianist Pete Johnson, Jimmy Witherspoon with Jay McShann's orchestra, and Joe Williams with Count Basie. Rushing, whose talent for blues singing may be heard on Basie's *Boogie Woogie* (1936, Voc. 3459), also performed popular songs, and some of his early recordings with Moten (1930) were in a heavy-handed vaudeville style. Williams eventually became accepted not only as a pre-eminent blues performer but also as a consummate interpreter of rhythmic popular songs and ballads.

Among leading male singers of the swing era, Cab Calloway and Billy Eckstine offered a contrast to the gruff approaches established separately by Armstrong and the blues shouters. It is not coincidence that both were from the northern states. They favored clarity of sound, and they enunciated in a manner closer to conventional American English than to black-American speech. Calloway's piercing timbre and humorous, mock-Hebrew scat singing may be heard on his *Minnie the Moocher* (1931, Bruns. 6074), Eckstine's creamy baritone on Earl Hines's *Jelly Jelly* (1940, Bb 11065).

While most singers during the swing era were associated with current popular songs, standards, or the blues, one young musician broke out of the mold in 1937. Maxine Sullivan, with her recording of the Scottish folksong *Loch Lomond* (Voc./OK 3654), established the possibility of bringing together traditional music and jazz, adapting the original song by making subtle variations to the melody and setting it against a jazz-oriented accompaniment. This famous performance, however, had no immediate successors. The idea emerged again, independently and much later, with the explosion of non-American jazz in the 1960s and 1970s: Astrud Gilberto introduced authentic bossa nova singing into jazz, sometimes performing songs with Portuguese lyrics, and Urszula Dudziak created jazz-rock versions of Polish folksongs in her work with Michal Urbaniak's group Fusion.

6. NEW SINGERS AND STYLES OF THE 1940S AND 1950S. With the emergence of bop in the 1940s and of succeeding styles such as cool jazz, progressive jazz, and third stream, the fortunes of the singer in jazz underwent a dramatic change. From a situation in which there was at least one singer in almost every big band and the leading ensembles were almost all big bands, there developed one in which the most important and innovative ensembles were small groups, concentrating overwhelmingly on instrumental music and having no place for a singer as a permanent member. While there were many prominent singers such as Sarah Vaughan who maintained groups of their own or worked successfully as soloists, and while singers continued to occupy their old position in bands that pursued existing styles of jazz, the major groups at the forefront

of change – those, for example, of Charlie Parker, Charles Mingus, Thelonious Monk, Miles Davis, John Coltrane, Art Blakey, Horace Silver, Tadd Dameron, Fats Navarro, and many others – though they might from time to time work and record with singers, did not regularly include a singer among their personnel. (A notable exception is Dizzy Gillespie's bop big band, of which the singer Joe "Bebop" Carroll was a member from 1949.)

Despite a certain curtailment of opportunities for singers, the bop era saw a blossoming of jazz vocal techniques, notably scat singing. The impetus for this came from the new style itself: singers wishing to explore bop improvisation, to imitate with the voice the playing of soloists such as Parker and Gillespie, found scat an appropriate vehicle. The technique developed and broadened (as did other aspects of vocal production such as range, timbre, and special effects) into a well-established virtuoso practice, as convincing in its way as the parallel instrumental one. The 1940s also saw the development by Eddie Jefferson of vocalese, though the technique was not widely used until the 1950s, when King Pleasure and Lambert, Hendricks, and Ross took it up.

Among the singers who maintained the tradition of the big-band vocalist in the bop era was Anita O'Day, who came to prominence as a member of Gene Krupa's and Stan Kenton's orchestras. She became a symbol of the so-called hip singer of the 1940s, with a loose, casual style involving musicianly extemporizing. Despite occasional flaws of intonation, her highly individual, husky voice gained her popularity and inspired others, notably June Christy and Chris Connor, both of whom later followed her into Kenton's orchestra.

A high level of musicianship marked out several influential singers whose careers were launched in the 1940s and 1950s. Dinah Washington, Sarah Vaughan, and Carmen McRae, for example, were all not only superb singers but also competent pianists. Washington, who toured with Lionel Hampton's orchestra, had a tart, vinegary sound, which was superbly suited to the blues; but after making a series of blues hits (including *Evil Gal Blues*, 1943, Key. 605) she achieved even greater acceptance as a singer of popular songs, often with fine jazz accompanists. Vaughan made her recording début as a leader with a group that included Dizzy Gillespie, an association that indicates her close allegiance to the bop movement; her acute ear for chord changes enabled her to bring new and vivid life to such old songs as *East of the Sun* (1944, Contl 6031). But her involvement with bop was more important for the affiliations she established – with bands led by Gillespie and Parker – than for her singing style. Over the years her range and repertory expanded continuously. Many observers felt that she could have been a successful opera singer and she has gone some way in that direction in numerous semiclassical performances in the 1970s and 1980s.

Carmen McRae, though four years older than Vaughan and Washington, was all but unknown until the early 1950s; at the start of her career she spent some years as an intermission pianist at a Harlem club, but her talents as a singer gradually emerged and the influence of Billie Holiday (who was a close friend) became apparent. Later she developed a more personal, occasionally sardonic, style, and her work became greatly respected among her fellow singers.

An even more accomplished musician than these three is Mel Tormé, who was still in his teens when he formed a highly acclaimed vocal group, the Mel-Tones; the group's recordings with Artie Shaw's orchestra continued to be available into the 1980s. Tormé is an extraordinarily versatile and authoritative performer, one of the few jazz singers to seem equally at home in a pop song and a wordless bop number. Like Joe Williams and McRae he is widely esteemed by other singers.

Eddie Jefferson is believed to have been the first singer and lyricist to devise texted versions of instrumental improvisations. Although solos such as Coleman Hawkins's famous *Body*

2. Lambert, Hendricks, and Ross at the Newport Jazz Festival, 1960

and Soul made intricate and demanding vocal vehicles, vocalese was taken up by other singers in the 1950s, notably King Pleasure, Jon Hendricks, and Annie Ross (who recorded her own words to solos by Wardell Gray and Art Farmer). Towards the end of the decade Hendricks and Ross joined Dave Lambert (already established as a bop singer) to form the trio Lambert, Hendricks, and Ross (fig.2). They recorded two albums of vocalese on orchestral numbers by Count Basie's band, mostly with lyrics by Hendricks; the first, *Sing a Song of Basie* (1957, ABC-Para. 223), promptly established them as the most innovative new vocal group. Hendricks has continued to perform vocalese, leading a group with his wife and two daughters into the 1980s.

7. After 1960. The new styles of jazz that evolved after 1960 have in general called still less often for singers than those of the preceding period. Free jazz finds almost no regular place for singing, and one of the principal characteristics that distinguishes jazz-rock from rock music itself is the absence of vocal parts. However, other forms of fusion, those of jazz with bossa nova, soul music, and pop music, have provided more scope for singers (such as Astrud Gilberto and Flora Purim besides those discussed separately below), and a number of singers have explored various individual and eclectic styles that combine the extended techniques of avant-garde art music with different elements of jazz (among notable figures here are Bobby McFerrin (see below), Urszula Dudziak, and Karin Krog).

It is by no means the case, though, that because singers are not always at the spearhead of the newest styles in jazz their art has declined. Alongside the innovatory developments, former styles continue to flourish, maintained both by the performers who created them and by new adherents. Thus opportunities for singers are plentiful in types of jazz that have now entered the mainstream, from blues in the style of Bessie Smith to bop vocalese and scat singing.

Betty Carter, though she had worked with Lionel Hampton's orchestra between 1948 and 1951, came to the attention of most jazz fans and critics somewhat belatedly. Her style, always jazz-oriented, and marked by great melodic freedom and (as with Anita O'Day) more individual flair than accurate substance, brought her acclaim and popularity during the 1960s and 1970s. Also a late beginner was Sheila Jordan, who made her recording début in 1963 but failed to gain more than a minimal following until much later; her buoyant, sensitive singing and sometimes poignant way with ballads took many years to persuade audiences and critics alike. In the 1980s she has been heard most often in an unusual setting, accompanied solely by the double bass player Harvie Swartz, and creating provocative routines within this limited context.

The most original new jazz singer to emerge in the 1970s was Bobby McFerrin, who developed a unique manner of equipping his mostly wordless and usually unaccompanied performances with a variety of sound effects. Among his formidable arsenal of vocal techniques are rapid leaps of register (giving the impression of his singing both melody line and accompaniment), bitonality, chest thumping for percussive effects, and an enormous range of "nonmusical" sounds such as shrieks and grunts.

More popular than McFerrin with general audiences, though less creative, are Al Jarreau (fig.3), a virtuoso scat singer who has also performed in a more pop-oriented style with groups of that character, and the electric guitarist George Benson, who, like Nat "King" Cole in the 1940s, has sacrificed what might have been a triumphant career as a jazz musician to pursue a commercial success in popular music. In 1986 Diane Schuur became a major recording artist with the help of such sponsors as Stan Getz and Dave Grusin. Capable of compelling work on ballads, she showed the influence of Dinah Washington, whom she had heard as a child.

3. Al Jarreau, New York, 1977

In the late 1980s jazz singing has suffered the loss of several performers who might have made significant contributions to jazz but for whom popularity and commercial success seem more important and who have therefore moved away from jazz into pop and rock music. Among vocal groups only Manhattan Transfer, whose splendid album *Vocalese* (1985, Atl. 81266) was recorded in collaboration with Hendricks, has made any measurable strides in the last decade. But the arrival of McFerrin is a promising sign that a strong tradition of jazz singing will continue.

BIBLIOGRAPHY

J.-E. Berendt: *Das Jazzbuch: Entwicklung und Bedeutung der Jazzmusik* (Frankfurt am Main, Germany, 1953, rev. 2/1959 as *Das neue Jazzbuch*, Eng. trans., New York, 1962; rev. and enlarged 5/1981 as *Das grosse Jazzbuch: von New Orleans biz Jazz Rock*, Eng. trans. as *The Jazz Book: from New Orleans to Fusion and Beyond*, Westport, CT, 1982)

L. Feather: *The Book of Jazz: a Guide to the Entire Field* (New York, 1957, 2/1965 as *The Book of Jazz from Then till Now: a Guide to the Entire Field*)

——: "An Explanation of Vocalese," *Jazz: a Quarterly of American Music*, no.3 (1959), 261

M. Berger: "Fats Waller: the Inside Outsider," *JJS*, i/1 (1973), 3

H. Pleasants: "Bel Canto in Jazz and Pop Singing," *Music Educators Journal*, lix/9 (1973), 54

——: *The Great American Popular Singers* (New York, 1974)

D. Bogle: *Brown Sugar: Eighty Years of America's Black Female Superstars* (New York, 1980)
S. Placksin: *American Women in Jazz, 1900 to the Present: their Words, Lives, and Music* (New York, 1982; London, 1985, as *Jazzwomen, 1900 to the Present: their Words, Lives, and Music*)
K. Grime: *Jazz Voices* (London, 1983) [incl. interviews]
L. Dahl: *Stormy Weather: the Music and Lives of a Century of Jazzwomen* (London, Melbourne, Australia, and New York, 1984)
L. Gourse: *Louis' Children: American Jazz Singers* (New York, 1984)
B. Crowther and M. Pinfold: *The Jazz Singers: from Ragtime to the New Wave* (Poole, England, 1986)
V. Lupo: *Vocal Groups in Modern Jazz, Vocalese: storia, discografia, biografie* (Ferrara, Italy, 1986)

LEONARD FEATHER (with BARRY KERNFELD)

Single (i). In jazz parlance a performer who pursues a career as a soloist; the word is often applied to singers, who are backed by a pianist or a small group, or pianists, who play as unaccompanied soloists.

Single (ii). In popular-music usage, a disc having a single musical number on each side (or occasionally a complete piece covering both sides). The term is mostly applied to the 7-inch 45 r.p.m. disc that has a playing time normally of $3\frac{1}{2}$–4 minutes per side, but from the late 1970s it has also been used of the 12-inch single that can run for up to about 12 minutes per side. (It is not customarily used of the 78 r.p.m. disc.) *See* RECORDING, §I, 3(ii).

Singleton, Zutty [Arthur James] (*b* Bunkie, LA, 14 May 1898; *d* New York, 14 July 1975). Drummer. He played drums in several important New Orleans bands, such as those of Papa Celestin and Luis Russell, and from 1921 to 1923 worked in Fate Marable's riverboat groups, with which he made his first recordings in 1924. The following year he recorded with Charlie Creath in St. Louis, and by 1927 had moved to Chicago, where after playing with Doc Cook and Jimmie Noone he joined the band led by the pianist Clarence Jones. His recordings with Louis Armstrong in 1928 and in a trio with Jelly Roll Morton and Barney Bigard in 1929 made Singleton well known in the jazz world. His style was sufficiently flexible and progressive to keep him active during the swing period of the 1930s, sometimes as the leader of his own group and at other times accompanying performers such as Sidney Bechet and Roy Eldridge. In later years he worked mainly as a freelance in New York, either leading his own dixieland bands or working with such traditional and mainstream musicians as Slim Gaillard, Eddie Condon, Bobby Hackett, and Wilbur De Paris. He toured Europe in 1951–3, and worked variously with Mezz Mezzrow, Hot Lips Page, and Bill Coleman. Singleton held a long residency at Ryan's in New York from 1963 until he was incapacitated in 1970 by a stroke.

Singleton's career and musical development closely resemble those of Baby Dodds, with whom he is often, and sometimes unfavorably, compared. Unlike Dodds, however, he incorporated the innovations of 1920s Chicago drummers into his playing, thereby forming a link from the New Orleans style to later swing drummers, notably Sid Catlett. He was among the first drummers to use the sock cymbals (a forerunner of the hi-hat) and wire brushes, both of which appear on his recordings with Armstrong (1928); and he was particularly innovative on his recordings with Morton and Victoria Spivey (1929), where he may be heard playing rim shots, ride patterns on the top cymbal, unchoked cymbal crashes, and offbeat accents on the bass drum, all of which later became familiar features of jazz drumming. Although Singleton played solo choruses at least from the mid-1920s, and was famous for his imaginative breaks and

Zutty Singleton at Jimmy Ryan's in New York, 1941

fills (transcriptions by G. Wettling in *DB*, vii/19, 1940), he is known primarily as an expert and highly musical accompanist, as is attested by the many important musicians of several generations who sought him out for recording sessions.

Oral history material in *LNT*, *NjR* (JOHP), *NjR*.

SELECTED RECORDINGS

As leader: *Zutty and the Clarinet Kings* (1967, Fat Cat's Jazz 100–101)
As sideman: F. Marable: Frankie and Johnny (1924, OK 40113); L. Armstrong: Muggles (1928, OK 8703); V. Spivey: Funny Feathers (1929, OK 8713); J. R. Morton: My Little Dixie Home/That's like it ought to be (1929, Vic. 38601); Climax Rag (1939, Bb 10442); F. Waller: Moppin' and Boppin' (1943, Vic. 404003); S. Gaillard: Dizzy Boogie (1945, Beltone 753); Flat Foot Floogie (1945, Beltone 758)

BIBLIOGRAPHY

H. Panassié: "Zutty Singleton, le plus grand drummer du monde, est arrivé en France," *BHcF*, no.12 (1951), 3
M. Williams: "Zutty Singleton, the Pioneer Jazz Forgot," *DB*, xxx/30 (1963), 18
W. Balliett: "Zutty," *Such Sweet Thunder* (Indianapolis, 1966) [colln of previously pubd articles and reviews]
M. Williams: "Zutty," *Jazz Masters of New Orleans* (New York and London, 1967/*R*1978), 178
M. Jones: "Satchmo's Master Drummer," *MM*, 1 (26 July 1975), 29
T. D. Brown: *A History and Analysis of Jazz Drumming to 1942* (diss., U. of Michigan, 1976), 245

J. BRADFORD ROBINSON

Siobud, André (*b* Guadeloupe, *c*1915). Guadeloupe tenor saxophonist and clarinetist. In the 1940s he recorded with many bands and musicians in Paris, among them the drummer Fredy Jumbo, the guitarist Jean Ferret, the Ensemble Swing du Hot Club Colonial (*c*1943), and Harry Cooper (1943). He performed in the antillean style, and on his recordings as a clarinetist (including Ferret's *Swing Guitars*, 1943, Pathé 2187) he uses the vibrato characteristic of Creole music in his jazz improvisations. His name is given as Sylvio Siobud in some sources. (A. Boulanger: Liner notes, *Jazz and Hot Dance in Martinique*, Harl. 2018, 1985)

RAINER E. LOTZ

Sirone [Jones, Norris] (*b* Atlanta, 28 Sept 1940). Double bass player. He played in Atlanta with The Group (1957–61), a cooperative ensemble that included George Adams. After moving to New York in 1965 he helped to form the free-jazz group Untraditional Jazz Improvisational Team with Dave Burrell, and played and made recordings with Marion Brown (1966), Gato Barbieri (1967), and Pharoah Sanders, Noah Howard, and Sonny Sharrock (all 1969). During this period he also worked with Sunny Murray, Albert Ayler, Archie Shepp, Sun Ra, Bill Dixon, Rashied Ali, Don Cherry, and Jackie McLean. From 1971 to 1977 he worked with the REVOLUTIONARY ENSEMBLE, which he formed with Leroy Jenkins and Frank Clayton (Clayton was soon replaced by Jerome Cooper); he also made recordings with Clifford Thornton (1972), Roswell Rudd (1973), Dewey Redman (1973–4, including *The Ear of the Behearer*, 1973, Imp. 9250), Cecil Taylor (1973, 1978), and Walt Dickerson (1982).

BIBLIOGRAPHY

Feather–Gitler '70s
V. Wilmer: "Sirone is One Hell of a Dirty Bass Player," *MM* (15 July 1972), 44
R. Riggins: "The Revolutionary Ensemble," *DB*, xl/19 (1973), 15
V. Wilmer: *As Serious as your Life: the Story of the New Jazz* (London, 1977, rev. 1980)

Sissle, Noble (Lee) (*b* Indianapolis, 10 July 1889; *d* Tampa, FL, 17 Dec 1975). Singer, composer, and bandleader. He achieved much success as a singer and songwriter in vaudeville and on Broadway with Eubie Blake (for illustration *see* BLAKE, EUBIE), with whom he produced the show *Shuffle Along* (1921) and performed in London (1925–6). In 1927 he returned alone to Europe to perform in France, and the following year he was persuaded by Cole Porter to form a 12-piece band for a residency at Les Ambassadeurs in Paris. The band, which became known as the Orchestra O Belgium, performed in France, Belgium, and Britain; among Sissle's sidemen were Sidney Bechet, Arthur Briggs, Johnny Dunn, Otto Hardwick, Demas Dean, Tommy Ladnier, Buster Bailey, and Russell Smith. After returning to the USA in 1930 Sissle and his orchestra played in New York and broadcast on CBS. He again led a band in Paris, briefly, in the summer of 1931. In 1935 he organized a new band called the International Orchestra, with Lena Horne as the singer, which performed throughout the USA and was resident at Billy Rose's Diamond Horseshoe in New York from 1938 to 1942 and again from 1945 until the mid-1950s; during World War II Sissle toured for the USO. From the 1960s he managed his own publishing company and worked occasionally as a leader.

Although he is best known as a composer and lyricist, with Blake and others, Sissle's importance in jazz was chiefly as a bandleader and singer. He made recordings throughout his career as a singer under other leaders, including several with James Reese Europe and various studio orchestras before 1920 and with studio bands in Britain in the 1920s; he also recorded many sides with Blake as his accompanist. The most important jazz recordings that carry his name are those made in 1937–8 with a small group, the Swingsters, drawn mainly from his band, though Sissle himself took little part in them; his activities as a leader are perhaps more accurately represented by *Basement Blues* (1931, Bruns. 6129).

BIBLIOGRAPHY

ChiltonW
J. R. T. Davies: "Blake and Noble Sissle," *Sv*, ii/7 (1966), 7
R. Kimball and W. Bolcom: *Reminiscing with Sissle and Blake* (New York, 1973)
A. McCarthy: *Big Band Jazz* (New York and London, 1974), 296
H. Rye: "Visiting Firemen, 7: Eubie Blake and Noble Sissle," *Sv*, no.105 (1983), 88
J. Chilton: *Sidney Bechet: the Wizard of Jazz* (London and New York, 1987), 79

JOHN GRAZIANO

Sitar. A large, plucked, fretted string instrument used chiefly in the classical repertory of the South Asian subcontinent. It became familiar to Western audiences in the late 1960s when it was used by several rock musicians, and was introduced to jazz soon after; Miles Davis recorded in 1969 with a group that included a sitar. In the same year Collin Walcott played sitar on the title track of Tony Scott's album *Homage to Lord Krishna* (Verve 68788), and he later came to be regarded as the most important sitarist in jazz; he played the instrument regularly in the groups Oregon and Codona. A fine example of jazz sitar playing is Walcott's solo on the track *Witchi-tai-to* from Oregon's album *Out of the Woods* (1978, Elek. 154).

BARRY KERNFELD

Sit in. To play with a band of which one is not a member, either by advance invitation or on the spur of the moment; an outsider is said to sit in when, for example, he plays for one engagement or set, or participates in a jam session.

Sittin' in With. Record label. It was operated by Bob Shad for about three years from 1948. Its catalogue contained notable recordings by John Hardee, Julian Dash, Wardell Gray, and other musicians of the late swing period. The label was also used to put out a small number of bop recordings, though the latter style was better represented on Shad's label Jax (1951–2). Shad later became the owner of Mainstream, which also had a considerable jazz catalogue.

BIBLIOGRAPHY

"The Shad Labels," *Blues Research*, no.16 (n.d. [?1966]), 2
A. Shaw: *Honkers and Shouters: the Golden Years of Rhythm and Blues* (New York, 1978), 140

Six, Jack (*b* Danville, IL, 26 July 1930). Double bass player. He studied trumpet from 1945 to 1947, worked in Chicago, Los Angeles, and New York (1948–55), and studied composition for a year at the Juilliard School. In New York he played double bass as a freelance with Claude Thornhill (1958) and Woody Herman (1959–60) and studied with Wendell Marshall. He belonged to the Dukes of Dixieland (recording in 1963) and to a small group led by Herbie Mann (recording in 1964) and worked with Don Elliott and Jimmy Raney. From 1968 he belonged with Gerry Mulligan to Dave Brubeck's quartet, and he remained with the group for two years after Mulligan's departure in 1972; he also recorded with Tal Farlow (1969), Illinois Jacquet (1974), and Jay McShann (1978), worked as a freelance in New York in the 1970s, and in the following decade worked both as a musician and as a music director in Atlantic City, New Jersey. Six's playing is well represented by his albums with Brubeck, such as *Compadres* (1968, Col. CS9704), which includes the track *Amapola*, and *All the Things we are* (1973–4, Atl. SD1684), on which he plays a well-constructed solo entitled *Here's that Rainy Day*. In addition to his work in jazz he has written several classical compositions. (*Feather–Gitler '70s*)

LAWRENCE KOCH

Sizzle cymbal. A cymbal with holes drilled around its edge in which rivets are loosely fastened; these sustain its sound and alter its timbre (*see* DRUM SET, §I, 5). A similar effect is achieved by suspending a light chain on the surface of a cymbal.

Sjösten, Lars (*b* Oskarshamn, Sweden, 7 May 1941). Swedish pianist and leader. He worked in Stockholm in the early 1960s with Eje Thelin, then recorded with Idrees Sulieman (1964) and performed and recorded with Lars Gullin (1964) and Bernt Rosengren (1965). Principally a bop soloist, he worked as the house pianist at the Gyllene Cirkeln, where he played with Dexter Gordon, Art Farmer, Sonny Stitt, and Steve Lacy. Later he recorded (1967) and studied with George Russell. During the late 1960s he undertook radio and studio work and toured Sweden with Rolf Ericson and Czechoslovakia with Rosengren. Sjösten worked as a leader from the early 1970s, recording with his own group several times (1971, 1972, 1977, 1980); especially representative is his LP *Select Notes* (1980, Caprice 1216). He also recorded with Putte Wickman (1970), Ericson and Brew Moore (both 1971), Gunnar Nilson (1971, 1972), Gordon (1977), and Lee Konitz (1983). (*Feather–Gitler '70s*)

Oral history material in *SSsv*.

Skidmore, Alan (Richard James) (*b* London, 21 April 1942). English tenor saxophonist, son of Jimmy Skidmore. In the early 1960s he worked with Alexis Korner, the drummer Eric Delaney, and Ronnie Scott (1965) before collaborating with such visiting American musicians as Chick Corea and Herbie Hancock. His performance at the Montreux International Jazz Festival in 1969 earned him a scholarship to the Berklee College of Music, which he declined. From 1970 to 1980 he toured at intervals with the rhythm-and-blues singer Georgie Fame. In 1973 Skidmore formed the trio SOS with Mike Osborne and John Surman. After this disbanded (1975) he toured with the George Gruntz Concert Jazz Band (1976–82). In 1977 he formed the EUROPEAN JAZZ QUINTET, with which he worked until it disbanded in 1982. He established the trio SOH with Tony Oxley and Ali Haurand in 1978, and performed with it for several years. Skidmore toured extensively in 1985 as a member of the quartet Tenor Tonic, and the following year he performed with Elvin Jones at Ronnie Scott's, London. Strongly influenced by the work of John Coltrane, he is among the most fluent British players of his generation. His work with trios perhaps best displays his passionate but controlled solos.

SELECTED RECORDINGS

As leader: *Once Upon a Time* (1969, Deram 11); *TCB* (1970, Phi. 6308041); of SOS (with M. Osborne and J. Surman): *SOS* (1975, Ogun 400); of SOH (with T. Oxley and A. Haurand): *SOH* (1979, Ego 4011)

As sideman: Eric Delaney and L. Bellson: *Repercussion* (1963, EMI 169)

BIBLIOGRAPHY

L. Evans: "Reed Clinic," *Crescendo*, iv/10 (1966), 24

L. Henshaw: "Alan Follows in Dad's Footsteps," *MM*, xliv (15 March 1969), 11

I. Carr: "Notes on Some Virtuosi," *Music Outside: Contemporary Jazz in Britain* (London, 1973), 12

B. Case: "In the Tradition," *Jazz Now: the Jazz Centre Society Guide*, ed. R. Cotterrell (London, 1976), 73

C. J. Gans: "Alan Skidmore: All in the Family," *JF* [intl edn], no.76 (1982), 35

MARK GILBERT

Skidmore, Jimmy [James Richard] (*b* London, 8 Feb 1916). English tenor saxophonist, father of Alan Skidmore. A self-taught musician, he first worked with Harry Parry's sextet (1942–4), then performed and recorded with the Spirits of Rhythm led by the guitarist Frank Deniz (1944), played with George Shearing, and worked in London clubs with Carlo Krahmer and others. He recorded with George Chisholm (1944), Vic Lewis (1945, 1947), Ralph Sharon (1950–52), and Kenny Baker (1951, 1955, 1956), and was a member of the bands led by Eric Delaney (1954–6) and Humphrey Lyttelton (1956–60), with whom he toured the USA; he is heard to advantage on *Humphrey Lyttelton Plays Standards* (1960, Col. 33SX1305). He continued to play during the 1970s and 1980s, often as the leader of small groups with sidemen such as Kathy Stobart and Tommy Whittle.

BIBLIOGRAPHY

FeatherE

R. Cotterrell, ed.: *Jazz Now: the Jazz Centre Society Guide* (London, 1976)

D. Fairweather: "Skidmore, Jimmy," in I. Carr, D. Fairweather, and B. Priestley: *Jazz: the Essential Companion* (London, 1987)

NEVIL SKRIMSHIRE

Skiffle. A hybrid style of popular music that has affinities with jazz and country blues. The term "skiffle" appears originally to have been applied in the USA during the 1930s to entertainment provided at rent parties, which encompassed blues, barrelhouse, boogie-woogie, and other styles of black popular music. This music was revived in the 1950s, mostly by Whites, who learned the repertory from touring black performers and from recordings. Skiffle bands played in a style loosely based on that of the spasm bands from New Orleans and such groups as the Mound City Blue Blowers led by Red McKenzie. They often included acoustic guitar, harmonica, kazoo, jug, washtub bass, and washboard or drums, and the chordal and melodic instruments provided a simple three- or four-chord accompaniment to a vocal part.

While the skiffle revival of the 1950s embraced the USA and Germany, it gained most ground in Great Britain. The earliest recordings by Chris Barber (1951) and Ken Colyer (1954), made with skiffle groups drawn from their jazz bands, exemplified the style of such ensembles, but the best-known recording of the period was *Rock Island Line* (1954, Decca F10647) by Lonnie Donegan with Barber's group. Donegan's work was modeled on that of the blues singer and guitarist Leadbelly (Huddie Ledbetter). Donegan and his imitators enjoyed considerable popularity until about 1959, when skiffle gave way, both in the USA and Europe, to "beat" music and rock-and-roll.

See also JUG BAND, SPASM BAND, and WASHBOARD BAND.

BIBLIOGRAPHY

D. Boulton: *Jazz in Britain* (London, 1958), 126

G. Melly: *Revolt into Style: the Pop Arts in Britain* (London, 1970), 28

Skins. Slang term for drums; *see* DRUM SET.

Skjoldborg, Anker (*b* Copenhagen, 11 Dec 1903; *d* Los Angeles, 3 April 1986). Danish tenor saxophonist and bandleader. He began his career as the first Danish jazz drummer, then took up the saxophone; he played both instruments with Valdemar Eiberg (1923–5) and Kai Ewans (1927), and in the group We Three with Otto Lington and Leo Mathisen (1927–8). He then worked exclusively as a saxophonist with Lington (1928–9), with Bernard Etté and others in Germany (1929–31), with Kai Julian in Denmark (1932–3), and with bands in Italy (1933–4). From 1935 to 1939 he led a fine band in Denmark which made several recordings, including *Rug Cutters Swing* (1936, Odeon D759). He emigrated to the USA in 1939 and later worked as a draftsman in the Los Angeles area.

ERIK WIEDEMANN

Slack, Freddie [Frederic Charles] (*b* nr Westby, WI, 7 Aug 1910; *d* Hollywood, CA, 10 Aug 1965). Pianist and leader. After playing piano in Johnny Tobin's band in Chicago he moved to Los Angeles in 1931. He toured and recorded with Ben Pollack (1934–6), then worked with Jimmy Dorsey (1936–9). Between 1939 and 1941 he was a soloist in the band led by Will Bradley and Ray McKinley, and became well known for his boogie-woogie playing on such recordings as *Beat me daddy, eight to the bar* (1940, Col. 35530). In 1941–2 he recorded with Joe Turner (ii), whose versions of *Rocks in my Bed* and *Goin' to Chicago* (1941, Decca 4093) demonstrate Slack's ability to perform in a blues idiom far removed from the boogie-woogie style. Slack formed his own band in 1942, and had a hit with his recording of *Cow Cow Boogie* (1942, Cap. 102). He continued to record as a leader during the 1940s, and played at clubs in California during the 1950s.

BIBLIOGRAPHY

ChiltonW; FeatherE; Feather '60s
G. T. Simon: *The Big Bands* (New York, 1967, rev. and enlarged 2/1971, rev. 3/1974, 4/1981), 93
C. Garrod and B. Korst: *Will Bradley, Freddie Slack* (Zephyrhills, FL, 1986) [discography]

Slap-bass [slap]. An effect produced on the double bass by means of an exaggerated pizzicato technique: the string is drawn away from, or across, the fingerboard at high tension and then released suddenly so that the resulting note is accompanied by a percussive click or slapping sound as the string hits the fingerboard. Slap-bass was first used in New Orleans jazz; an early recorded example occurs in John Lindsay's accompaniment to the clarinet and banjo solos in Jelly Roll Morton's *Black Bottom Stomp* (1926, Vic. 20221). It was taken up by double bass players in the big bands of the 1930s, notably Pops Foster, who interchanged it with bowing and conventional pizzicato on many of his recordings with Luis Russell and with Louis Armstrong, for example, on *Swing that Music* (1936, Decca 866). During the swing era the technique ceased to be widely used, but it re-emerged during the New Orleans revival in the 1940s, through the playing of Alcide "Slow Drag" Pavageau (with Bunk Johnson and George Lewis (i)) and Ed "Montudi" Garland (with Kid Ory). Traditional and revival bands continue to use the effect occasionally. In other styles of jazz slap-bass is normally employed for comic purposes or as a conscious archaism, as on Charles Mingus's recording *Cocktails for Two* on *My Favorite Quintet* (1965, Charles Mingus 009). It has become one of the arsenal of unusual effects in the playing of avant-garde musicians such as Barry Guy. A similar effect, often known simply as slapping, is used on the ELECTRIC BASS GUITAR.
(A. Shipton: "Styles of New Orleans Bass Playing," *Fn*, vii/1 (1976), 18)

ALYN SHIPTON

Slap-tonguing. A technique used in playing single-reed wind instruments. Using the length of the tongue, slightly arched, the player presses hard against the reed, at the same time sucking so as to create a vacuum between reed and tongue; he then draws the tongue sharply away so that the vacuum is broken and the reed is released, producing a dull slapping sound. The technique may be used alone, in which case the pitch of the note being fingered is only faintly heard (this is particularly effective in a low register), or to give a loud percussive attack to notes blown in the usual way.

Slap-tonguing has been employed chiefly on the clarinet, notably by Joe Darensbourg, whose use of the technique may be heard on Kid Ory's *Yaaka hula hickey dula* (1950, Col. CL845). Although it has been adopted on most saxophones it is especially successful on the bass, and is heard to advantage in traditional and swing ensembles, in which players such as Adrian Rollini played bass saxophone in place of tuba or double bass. Because its execution is physically awkward slap-tonguing may lead to a disjointed style of playing which is the antithesis of swing; Coleman Hawkins employed it as a melodic device in early improvisations, but he quickly discarded it in favor of a smoother approach to articulation.

ALYN SHIPTON

Slide (i). In such instruments as the TROMBONE, a telescopic joint used to extend or reduce the sounding length of the instrument's tubing and thus to alter the fundamental.

Slide (ii). In jazz parlance a synonym for GLISS.

Slide cornet [slide trumpet]. Name used colloquially to refer to the soprano trombone; *see* TROMBONE, §1.

Slide saxophone. A saxophone fitted with a slide instead of tone-holes; the only instruments of the type used in jazz were one designed and played by Snub Mosley, and one played by Roland Kirk. *See* SAXOPHONE, §6(viii).

Slim and Slam. Duo formed in the late 1930s by SLIM GAILLARD and SLAM STEWART.

Slow drag [drag]. A social dance of the late 19th and early 20th centuries performed by couples to a slow blues with leisurely, sensuous rhythms; by association, any piece in that style or tempo. It is so called because the musical rhythms drag behind the beat (*see* BEAT, §2), reflecting the smooth, voluptuous movements of the dance. Alcide "Slow Drag" Pavageau received his nickname from his expertise at this dance.

Smack. Nickname of FLETCHER HENDERSON.

Smalls, Cliff [Clifton Arnold] (*b* Charleston, SC, 3 March 1918). Pianist. He first toured with the Carolina Cotton Pickers (1935–42), then worked with Earl Hines, playing trombone and second piano (1942–6). After a period with Billy Eckstine he was a member of Earl Bostic's popular small group (1950–51). A road accident forced his temporary retirement, but he returned to work with Al Sears (1953) and Bennie Green (1953–6). He then played alto and baritone saxophone in rhythm-and-blues groups and backed such singers as Clyde McPhatter, Brook Benton (for seven years), and Smokey Robinson. Later he resumed playing jazz, working with Sy Oliver (from 1968); he also recorded with Eddie Barefield and a quintet led by Paul Gonsalves and Roy Eldridge (both 1973), Buddy Tate (1975), Milt Hinton (1976), and Oliver Jackson (1977, 1982), and as a leader. Smalls plays in a personal style that combines harmonic subtlety with a flexibility and drive reminiscent of Hines.

SELECTED RECORDINGS

As leader: *Swing and Things* (1976, MJR 8131); *Cliff Smalls* (1978, BB 33134)
As sideman: S. Oliver: *Yes, Indeed* (1973, BB 33048); B. Tate: *The Texas Twister* (1975, MJR 8128); O. Jackson and H. Henry: *Real Jazz Express* (1977, BB 33126); O. Jackson: *Le Quartet* (1982, BB 33180)

BIBLIOGRAPHY

ChiltonW; Feather–Gitler '70s
S. Dance: *The World of Earl Hines* (New York, 1977) [interviews], 261
A. Balalas: "Cliff Smalls," *BHcF*, no.271 (1979), 5

PETER VACHER

Smalls' Paradise. Nightclub in New York; *see* NIGHTCLUBS AND OTHER VENUES.

Smear. An exaggerated BEND of a semitone or a tone down and then up again, executed with a harsh or "dirty" tone; it is most often associated with brass instruments in jazz. An example may be heard in bar 23 of Louis Armstrong's solo on *Wolverine Blues* (1940, Decca 3105). (M. Laplace: "La trompette et le cornet dans le jazz et la musique populaire," pt vi, *Brass Bulletin*, no.47 (1984), 39)

Smetaček, Pavel (*b* Prague, 4 Jan 1940). Czechoslovak clarinetist, saxophonist, and bandleader. He studied clarinet at the Prague Conservatory from 1957 and the same year founded the Traditional Jazz Studio, with which he recorded regularly from 1959. Through his association with the studio he worked with such musicians as Albert Nicholas, Benny Waters (with whom he recorded in 1976), and Tony Scott, and toured internationally. In 1977 he took part in the New Orleans Jazz and Heritage Festival. Smetaček's work is well represented on the recording *Traditional Jazz Studio, 1959–1979* (1959–79, Sup. 1115 2606H). (G. Conrad: "Pavel Smetaček und das Traditional Jazz Studio," *Der Jazzfreund*, no.94 (1979), 4)

GERHARD CONRAD

Smietana, Jarosław (*b* Kraków, Poland, 29 March 1951). Polish guitarist, composer, and leader. Trained in the jazz department of the Academy of Music at Katowice (graduating in 1974), he made his professional début with Klaus Lenz's big band at the International Jazz Jamboree, Warsaw, in 1972. In 1974 he founded (with the pianist Władysław Sendecki) Extra Ball, which became Poland's leading jazz-rock group and won many prizes; Smietana himself won the award for the best soloist at the festival Jazz on the Odra at Wrocław in 1974. During international tours he performed at major European events such as the North Sea Jazz Festival (The Hague) and Jazz Ost-West (Nuremberg); he also appeared with Extra Ball and the Katowice Big Band at American festivals in Reno, Nevada, and Berkeley, California (1978), and later made a coast-to-coast tour of the USA with Extra Ball (1980). He disbanded this group in 1984 and two years later formed the Jarosław Smietana Sounds, which plays contemporary jazz in a straight-ahead manner with Latin and rock elements. In the early 1980s he also led a successful big band, the Symphonic Sounds Orchestra. A virtuoso player and a prolific composer, Smietana has been voted the most popular guitarist in several *Jazz Forum* readers' polls. He has recorded ten albums as a leader, and has worked with all of Poland's foremost jazz musicians, including Zbigniew Namysłowski, Janusz Muniak, Zbigniew Seifert, and Jan Wróblewski.

SELECTED RECORDINGS

As leader: *Birthday* (1976, Muza SX1414); *Go Ahead* (1979, Muza SX1795); *Mosquito* (1981, Poljazz PSJ104); *Talking Guitar* (1983, Muza SX2197); *From One to Four* (1987, Poljazz PSJ191); *Sound Colors* (1987, Muza SX2537)
As sideman: Z. Seifert: *Kilimanjaro* (1978, Poljazz PSJ101–2)

BIBLIOGRAPHY

K. Czyz: "Jarosław Smietana: Rolling Straight Ahead," *JF* [intl edn], no.73 (1981), 44

PAWEL BRODOWSKI

Smith, Ben(jamin J.) (*b* Memphis, 1 March 1905). Alto saxophonist and clarinetist. After playing with lesser-known ensembles in Tennessee and Texas he led his own band, the Blue Syncopators (1927–9). He worked briefly in Omaha, Nebraska, and led a group in Kansas City before playing with George E. Lee (1930) and others. In 1932 he led the White Hut Orchestra in Pittsburgh and Philadelphia. Thereafter he worked with Blanche Calloway and Charlie Gaines, and directed and played in sessions by the Washboard Rhythm Kings. Around 1934 he moved to New York, where he played with Fess Williams, Claude Hopkins (*c*1936) and Jabbo Smith (1938). He then performed and made recordings with Hot Lips Page; his warm-toned clarinet playing may be heard on *He's Pulling his Whiskers* (1938, Decca 7451). During the 1940s Smith worked with Lucky Millinder, Andy Kirk, and Snub Mosley, but was mainly active leading his own groups. As well as continuing to lead bands in the 1950s he organized his own business as an arranger and copyist, and owned a record company.

BIBLIOGRAPHY

F. Driggs: "Ben Smith," *Record Research*, no.29 (1960) [interview]
O. Flückiger: "Biography and Discography of Ben Smith," *Jazz Statistics*, no.21 (1961), 9
T. Zwicky: "I'm Gonna Beat me Some Washboard: the Washboard Rhythm Kings and Affiliated Groups (1930–35)," *Sv*, no.19 (1968), 3; no.20 (1968–9), 47; no.22 (1969), 148 [incl. discography]

based on *ChiltonW*

Smith, Bessie (*b* Chattanooga, TN, 15 April 1894; *d* Clarksdale, MS, 26 Sept 1937). Singer. She began her professional career in 1912 by singing in the same show as Ma Rainey, and subsequently performed in various touring minstrel shows and cabarets. By the 1920s she was a leading artist in black shows, on the TOBA circuit and at the 81 Theatre in Atlanta. After further tours she was sought out by Clarence Williams to record in New York. Her first recording, *Down-hearted Blues*, established her as the most successful black performing artist of her time; she recorded regularly until 1928 with important early

Bessie Smith, c1923

jazz instrumentalists such as Williams, James P. Johnson, and various members of Fletcher Henderson's band, including Louis Armstrong, Charlie Green, Joe Smith, and Tommy Ladnier. During this period she also toured throughout the South and North, performing to large audiences. In 1929 she appeared in the film *St. Louis Blues* (*see* FILMS, §I, 1, and fig.1). By then, however, alcoholism had severely damaged her career, as did the Depression, which affected the recording and entertainment industries. A recording session, her last, was arranged in 1933 by John Hammond for the increasing European jazz audience; it featured among others Jack Teagarden and Benny Goodman. By 1936 Smith was again performing in shows and clubs, but she died, following an automobile accident, before her next recording session had been arranged.

Smith was unquestionably the greatest of the vaudeville blues singers, and brought the emotional intensity, personal involvement, and expression of blues singing into the jazz repertory with unexcelled artistry. *Baby Doll* and *After you've gone*, both made with Joe Smith, and *Nobody knows you when you're down and out*, with Ed Allen on cornet, illustrate her capacity for sensitive interpretation of popular songs. Her broad phrasing, fine intonation, blue-note inflections, and wide, expressive range made hers the measure of jazz-blues singing in the 1920s (for further discussion of her vocal technique *see* GROWL). She made almost 200 recordings, of which her remarkable duets with Armstrong are among her best. Although she excelled in the performance of slow blues, she also recorded vigorous versions of jazz standards. Joe Smith was her preferred accompanist, but possibly her finest recording (and certainly the best-known in her day) was *Back Water Blues*, with James P. Johnson. Her voice had coarsened by the time of her last session, but few jazz artists have been as consistently outstanding as she.

See also BLUES, §3.

SELECTED RECORDINGS

(all recorded for Columbia unless otherwise indicated)

Duo with C. Williams: Down-hearted Blues (1923, A3844)

As leader: The St. Louis Blues (1925, 14064D); Cake Walkin' Babies (from Home) (1925, 35673); J. C. Holmes Blues (1925, 14095D); Baby Doll (1926, 14147D); Back Water Blues (1927, 14195D); After you've gone (1927, 14197D); Alexander's Ragtime Band (1927, 14219D); Nobody knows you when you're down and out (1929, 14451D); Gimme a pigfoot (1933, OK 8949)

BIBLIOGRAPHY

B. Rust: "On Bessie Smith," *Hot Notes*, ii/2 (1947), 6

P. Oliver: *Bessie Smith* (London, 1959); repr. in *Kings of Jazz*, ed. S. Green (South Brunswick, NJ, and New York, 1978)

G. Schuller: *Early Jazz: its Roots and Musical Development* (New York, 1968), 226

C. Albertson: *Bessie: Empress of the Blues* (New York, 1972)

S. Harris: *Blues Who's Who: a Biographical Dictionary of Blues Singers* (New Rochelle, NY, 1979)

E. Brooks: *The Bessie Smith Companion: a Critical and Detailed Appreciation of the Recordings* (Wheathampstead, nr Harpenden, England, and New York, 1982)

PAUL OLIVER

Smith, Betty (*b* Sileby, nr Leicester, England, 6 July 1929). English tenor saxophonist. She studied piano and saxophone from an early age and began to play jazz while a teenager. She toured the Middle East with the pianist Billy Penrose (1948) and played and toured (together with her husband, the double bass player Jack Peberdy) in Freddy Randall's band (1953–6, recording in 1953–5). She led her own quintet (1957–64) and played and sang in Ted Heath's orchestra, then worked as a guest soloist on radio and television programs and had her own program on Radio Luxembourg. From the mid-1970s she performed in the Best of British Jazz with Kenny Baker, the trombonist Don Lusher, and Jack Parnell; her playing is well represented on this group's recording *Exactly Like You* (1981, ASV ALM4001). (D. Fairweather: "Smith, Betty," in I. Carr, D. Fairweather, and B. Priestley: *Jazz: the Essential Companion*, London, 1987)

NEVIL SKRIMSHIRE

Smith, Bill [William O(verton)] (*b* Sacramento, CA, 22 Sept 1926). Clarinetist and composer. He studied at the Juilliard School, and with the composer Darius Milhaud at Mills College (MA 1951); with his fellow student Dave Brubeck he led an octet which performed and recorded between 1947 and 1951. While teaching at the University of Southern California he recorded in Los Angeles with Red Norvo (1957) and Shelly Manne (1957, 1958) and on three occasions with Brubeck's quartet (1959–61) as a replacement for Paul Desmond; he also composed for Brubeck. In 1960 he won a Guggenheim Fellowship for composition and he spent the next six years based in Italy; during this period he organized a bop quartet, the American Jazz Ensemble, with which he toured and recorded in Europe and the USA. From 1966 he directed the Contemporary Music Group at the University of Washington, Seattle. In 1981 he recorded with the Italian pianist Enrico Pieranunzi and in 1981–4 he toured and made recordings with Brubeck; his playing is well represented by *Take Five* on the album *Concord on a Summer Night* (1982, Conc. 198). Using the name William O. Smith he has composed and performed many classical works, some of which contain elements of jazz.

BIBLIOGRAPHY

Feather '60s

L. Tomkins: "Bill Smith," *CI*, xxi (1983), no.5, p.6; no.6, p.16

Smith, Brian (*b* Wellington, New Zealand, 3 Jan 1939). New Zealand saxophonist and flutist. After playing in local rock, jazz, and dance bands he moved to England in 1964, and the following year he joined Alexis Korner's Blues Incorporated. He then played at Ronnie Scott's (1966–7) and worked as a member of big bands led by Maynard Ferguson and Tubby Hayes (both 1969). Smith later recorded with Ferguson (1970–74) and played for his tours of Japan and the USA (1972, 1974). In 1969 he joined the group Nucleus, with which he worked extensively until 1982; his playing is well represented on the album *Roots* (1973, Vertigo 6360100). He has also performed with Gordon Beck's group Gyroscope (*c*1968), Annie Ross, and Graham Collier (early 1970s), and has played and recorded with Mike Westbrook (1969), Mike Gibbs (1970), the Spontaneous Music Ensemble (1970, 1971), and Keith Tippett's group Centipede (1971). In 1978 Smith appeared at the first Jazzyatra in India. He returned to New Zealand in 1982, where he formed his own quartet; in 1984 its album *Southern Excursions*, recorded on the New Zealand label Ode, was voted Australian Jazz Record of the Year.

Smith should not be confused with the American free-jazz double bass player Brian Smith, who recorded with Barry Altschul and Fred Anderson (both 1978), Muhal Richard Abrams (1980), Henry Threadgill (1982), and the World Bass Violin Ensemble (1982–3).

BIBLIOGRAPHY

R. Cotterrell, ed.: *Jazz Now: the Jazz Centre Society Guide* (London, 1976), 167

I. Carr: "Smith, Brian," in I. Carr, D. Fairweather, and B. Priestley: *Jazz: the Essential Companion* (London, 1987)

DIGBY FAIRWEATHER

Smith, Buster [Henry] (*b* Alfdorf, nr Ennis, TX, 24 Aug 1904). Alto saxophonist, clarinetist, and arranger. He taught himself to play clarinet and worked with local groups in Dallas from around 1923; he took up the alto saxophone by 1925, when he joined Walter Page's Blue Devils, a territory band based in Oklahoma that performed in Kansas City and the Southwest. By 1928 the band's other members included Hot Lips Page, Jimmy Rushing, Count Basie, and Eddie Durham, all of whom later left to play with Bennie Moten. In 1931 Smith assumed leadership of the band, which now included Lester Young and which later became known as the 13 Original Blue Devils. After the group disbanded late in 1933 he settled in Kansas City, where he too joined Moten's group; this disbanded after the death in 1935 of its leader. Smith joined a band led by Basie, which included other musicians who had worked with Moten, and which performed in Kansas City at the Reno Club; when Basie moved to New York he remained in Kansas City, played with Claude Hopkins and Andy Kirk, and wrote arrangements for Nat Towles. In 1937 he formed his own group, which included Jay McShann, Fred Beckett, and Charlie Parker, who was then 17 years old; a year later he moved with the band to New York, where, unable to secure engagements as a leader, he worked instead as an arranger for Basie, Benny Carter, and Snub Mosley and as a sideman with Don Redman. He moved in late 1942 to Dallas and led small groups at clubs and hotels; although he ceased playing saxophone in 1959 he continued to play piano, double bass, and guitar until his retirement around 1980.

Smith's importance lies in his work as an arranger and above all in his having been a mentor of Parker. His few recordings (including *Cherry Red*, 1939; *I ain't got nobody*, 1940; and *Moten's Swing*, 1940) reveal a style close to that of Parker's early work, and sometimes that of his mature work. It is not to diminish Parker's importance as the originator, with Gillespie, of a completely new language of jazz to note that several elements of his style – his tone and attack, certain turns of phrase, and his basically linear conception – may be traced to Smith's buoyant, fluent playing and his warm sound.

Oral history material in *NjR* (JOHP).

SELECTED RECORDINGS

As leader: *The Legendary Buster Smith* (1959, Atl. 1323)

As sideman: W. Page: Blue Devil Blues/Squabblin' (1929, Voc. 1463); D. Redman: Chew, Chew, Chew (1939, Vic. 26258); Ain't I Good to you? (1939, Vic. 26266); Pete Johnson: Cherry Red/Baby, Look at you (1939, Voc./OK 4997); H. L. Page: I ain't got nobody/Gone with the Gin (1940, Decca 7714); E. Durham: I Want a Little Girl/Moten's Swing (1940, Decca 18126)

SELECTED ARRANGEMENTS

Recorded by C. Basie: Smarty (1937, Decca 1379); One o'Clock Jump (1937, Decca 1363); The Blues I Like to Hear (1938, Decca 2284)

Recorded by H. L. Page: Gone with the Gin (1940, Decca 7714)

BIBLIOGRAPHY

D. Gazzaway: "Conversations with Buster Smith," *JR*, ii/11 (1959), 18; iii/1 (1960), 11; contd as "Buster and Bird: Conversations with Buster Smith," iii/2 (1960), 12 [incl. discography]

——: "Before Bird: Buster," *JM*, vii/11 (1962), 4

B. Rusch: "Buster Smith: Interview," *Cadence*, iv/4 (1978), 14

GUNTHER SCHULLER

Smith, Carl [Tatti] (*b* Marshall, TX, *c*1908). Trumpeter. After working with Terrence Holder's band in Kansas City, Missouri (1931), he played mainly on the West Coast with the bandleader Gene Coy (1931–4). He then returned to Kansas City, where he worked with Count Basie; in Chicago he made recordings (including *Shoe Shine Boy*, 1936, Voc. 3441) with Jones–Smith, Inc., a sextet led by Basie. Smith left Basie in 1937 and until 1940 worked mainly with the Gentlemen of Swing, a group led by the clarinetist and saxophonist Skeets Tolbert; he also performed with Hot Lips Page in 1939. Later he played occasionally with Leon Abbey and Benny Carter, and in 1944 he was a member of Chris Columbus's band. After World War II Smith moved to South America, where he continued to play into the 1950s.

based on *ChiltonW*

Smith, Carrie (*b* Fort Gaines, GA, 25 Aug 1941). Singer. She was brought up in Newark, New Jersey, and sang in a local church choir, with which she made recordings at the Newport Jazz Festival in 1957. She performed only occasionally until 1970, when she toured with the band led by the pianist and singer Big Tiny Little (1970–72). After working with Tyree Glenn (1973) she joined the New York Jazz Repertory Company, with which she visited the USSR in 1975. Smith sang at the Grande Parade du Jazz, Nice, in 1979 and then toured Europe. She has continued to perform in the USA and has frequently returned to Europe, where she recorded *When You're Down and Out* (1977, BB 33119) with George Kelly and Ram Ramirez. In 1987 she toured Europe with Yank Lawson's band and appeared at the Guinness Jazz Festival in Cork, Ireland.

BIBLIOGRAPHY

E. Townley: "The Carrie Smith Story," *JJ*, xxix/11 (1976), 4

M. Cullaz: "A Touch of Gospel," *Jh*, nos.351–2 (1978), 50

G. Endress: "Stimme aus Gospel und Blues: Carrie Smith," *JP*, xxvii/10 (1978), 8

S. Harris: *Blues Who's Who: a Biographical Dictionary of Blues Singers* (New Rochelle, NY, 1979)

HOWARD RYE

Smith, Carson (Raymond) (*b* San Francisco, 9 Jan 1931). Double bass player. He played and recorded West Coast jazz in Los Angeles with Gerry Mulligan (1952–3), Chet Baker (1953–5), Russ Freeman (1955–6), and Chico Hamilton (1955–7); he also recorded with Clifford Brown and Dick Twardzik (both 1954), and with Billie Holiday in a concert at Carnegie Hall (1956). During the late 1950s he worked as a freelance in Los Angeles, toured and recorded with Stan Kenton (1959), and recorded with Hamilton (1959) and Charlie Barnet (1960). After moving to Las Vegas he performed and recorded with Charlie Teagarden (1962) and recorded in a sextet led by Teagarden and Lionel Hampton (1963). In 1964 he toured Japan with Georgie Auld and played with Mulligan at the Hollywood Bowl. He recorded with Buddy Rich in 1966.

BIBLIOGRAPHY

FeatherE; *Feather '60s*

R. Gordon: *Jazz West Coast: the Los Angeles Jazz Scene of the 1950s* (London and New York, 1986)

Smith, Charles Edward (*b* Thomaston, CT, 8 June 1904; *d* New York, 16 Dec 1970). Writer. In the mid-1930s he wrote scripts for "Saturday Night Swing Session," the first series of jazz programs to be broadcast live on network radio. With Fred Ramsey, he collaborated on the writing of scripts for "Jazz in America" (1942–3), a series of radio programs produced by the Office of War Information, and on the writing of *Jazzmen: the Story of Hot Jazz Told in the Lives of the Men who Created it* (1939), an important early anthology for which he also wrote essays; he wrote *The Jazz Record Book* (1942) with Ramsey and others, as well as many reviews, articles, and liner notes. In 1959 he received the "Silver Medal" award from *Down Beat*. Smith was a founder of the Institute of Jazz Studies, where his personal papers are now held.

WRITINGS

(selective list)

ed. with F. Ramsey, Jr.: *Jazzmen: the Story of Hot Jazz Told in the Lives of the Men who Created it* (New York, 1939/*R*1977)

with others: *The Jazz Record Book* (New York, 1942/R1978) [listeners' guide with discography]
"Jack Teagarden," "Pee Wee Russell," "Billie Holiday," *The Jazz Makers: Essays on the Greats of Jazz*, ed. N. Shapiro and N. Hentoff (New York, 1957/R1975,1979), 59, 103, 276

DANIEL ZAGER

Smith, Charlie [Charles] (*b* New York, 15 April 1927; *d* New Haven, CT, 15 Jan 1966). Drummer. He first played professionally with various groups in New York in 1947, and the following year he joined Ella Fitzgerald. He then performed and recorded with such artists as Hot Lips Page, Erroll Garner, Benny Goodman, Slim Gaillard, Oscar Peterson, Artie Shaw, Joe Bushkin, Slam Stewart, and Duke Ellington. In 1952 he appeared in a television show with Charlie Parker and Dizzy Gillespie. During the 1950s Smith worked with Billy Taylor (ii) (1952–4) and Aaron Bell (1954–6, 1958) and performed as a freelance. He then moved to New Haven, where he played in a trio with Dwike Mitchell and Willie Ruff (recording in 1961). Towards the end of his life he worked as a composer and teacher. A proficient drummer in both bop and swing styles, he was known especially for his brush playing.

SELECTED RECORDINGS

As leader: on *Jazzville*, iii (1956, Dawn 1114), Blues for Sale, Flying Home
As sideman: E. Garner: *Piano Selections* (1949, Atl. 109); S. Gaillard: Yip Roc Heresy/The Hip Cowboy (1951, Clef 8956); B. Taylor: *Billy Taylor Trio* (1954, Prst. 184); H. Renaud: *Henri Renaud All Stars* (1954, Swing 33320–21); H. Mann: *Sultry Serenade* (1957, Riv. 234)

BIBLIOGRAPHY

FeatherE

RICK MATTINGLY

Smith, Clara (*b* Spartanburg, SC, 1894; *d* Detroit, 2 Feb 1935). Singer. She began working in vaudeville around 1910, and by 1918 was a principal performer on the TOBA circuit. For the next five years she toured, mainly in the South, before traveling in 1923 to New York, where she sang at clubs in Harlem and made her first recordings; thereafter, until her last sessions in 1932, she worked in studios with such distinguished musicians as Fletcher Henderson, Don Redman, Coleman Hawkins, Louis Armstrong, Charlie Green, and Joe Smith. In 1924 she opened a theatrical club in New York, but continued to tour extensively, working as far afield as the West Coast (1924–5). She appeared frequently in revues in Harlem from 1928 to 1931; in the early 1930s she worked with Paul Barbarin in New York, and also performed in Detroit and Cleveland.

Smith recorded exclusively for Columbia, whose catalogue also included the work of Bessie Smith; the fame of the latter has undoubtedly distracted audiences from Clara Smith's work. She was often known as the "Queen of the Moaners" – this facet of her style may be heard on *Awful Moanin' Blues* – but actually had a lighter tone than her contemporary. During the early part of her career she displayed a penchant for very slow tempos; from about 1925 she developed a richer sound and a greater emotional range that mark her as one of the most important vaudeville blues singers.

SELECTED RECORDINGS

(all recorded for Columbia)

Duos: with F. Henderson: I never miss the sunshine/Awful Moanin' Blues (1923, A4000); with Lemuel Fowler: Whip it to a Jelly (1926, 14150D)
As leader: Death Letter Blues/Prescription for the Blues (1924, 14045D); Shipwrecked Blues/My John Blues (1925, 14077D); with B. Smith: My Man Blues (1925, 14098D); It's tight like that (1929, 14398D); Papa I don't need you now (1929, 14398D)

BIBLIOGRAPHY

ChiltonW
H. Panassié and M. Gautier: *Dictionnaire du jazz* (Paris, 1954, rev. and enlarged 1971, enlarged 2/1980, rev. and enlarged by A. Vasset and J. Pescheux 3/1987; Eng. trans., London, 1956, rev. A. A. Gurwitch as *Guide to Jazz*, Boston, 1956), 285
P. Oliver: "Clara Voce: a Study in Neglect," *JM*, iv/2 (1958), 8
S. Harris: *Blues Who's Who: a Biographical Dictionary of Blues Singers* (New Rochelle, NY, 1979), 466
G. Herzhaft: *Encyclopédie du blues* (Lyons, France, 1979), 81
E. Brooks: *The Bessie Smith Companion: a Critical and Detailed Appreciation of the Recordings* (Wheathampstead, nr St. Albans, England, and New York, 1982), 31, 93
D. Seroff: "Blues Itineraries: Clara Smith on the Road," *Whiskey, Women, and . . .*, nos.12–13 (1983), 58
E. Townley: "The Forgotten Ones: Clara Smith," *JJI*, xxxviii/7 (1985), 16

HOWARD RYE

Smith, Crickett [William Cricket] (*b* Nashville, 15 Aug 1883; *d* ?New York, ? late 1947). Cornetist and trumpeter. He toured in vaudeville shows as a youth, then played and recorded in New York with James Reese Europe's Clef Club Society Orchestra (1913–14) and Ford Dabney (1917–19), and in Europe with Louis Mitchell's Jazz Kings (1919–24); he took over the leadership of Mitchell's group in 1923, renaming it the Real Jazz Kings. He led his own group in Spain (1925, 1931–3), worked in Paris (1928–31), then was associated with Herb Flemming (1933–4), Leon Abbey (1936–7), Teddy Weatherford (1937–8), and others, playing in Ceylon, Java, and India. He returned to the USA probably in 1943. Smith was past his prime when sound recording became established, and recorded only one solo, *Taj Mahal* (in Bombay; 1936, Rex 7994), as leader of his own group, the Symphonians.

For illustration *see* NIGHTCLUBS AND OTHER VENUES, fig.1.

BIBLIOGRAPHY

R. Gulliver: "Crickett Smith," *IAJRC Journal*, xii/3 (1979), 3
P. Darke: "The Mystery of Crickett Smith," *Sv*, no.111 (1984), 90

RAINER E. LOTZ

Smith, Derek (Geoffrey) (*b* London, 17 August 1931). English pianist. He played with Kenny Graham in the early 1950s, then performed and recorded with John Dankworth's big band (1954–5), and with his own groups (1954–7); he also recorded with Vic Ash (1954, 1956), and Kenny Baker, Jimmy Skidmore, and Bertie King (all 1956), and worked as a studio musician for the BBC. After emigrating to the USA he recorded as the leader of a trio (1957), the other members of which were Connie Kay and Percy Heath, and played with Benny Goodman; around 1960 he led a trio that included John Drew and which recorded in 1961 as the British Jazz Trio. From 1967 to 1974 he was the pianist in the big band that played for Johnny Carson's television show. Among the leaders with whom he recorded in the 1970s and 1980s were Goodman (1971), the singer Marlena Shaw (1972, 1973), Bill Watrous (1975), Buddy DeFranco and Nick Brignola (both 1977), Sal Salvador and Dick Meldonian (both 1978), and Arnett Cobb (1978, 1980); he also made several recordings as a leader, including *The Man I Love* (1978, Prog. 7035). In 1983 he toured Japan with Benny Carter. (*FeatherE*)

Smith, Floyd [Wonderful] (*b* St. Louis, 25 Jan 1917; *d* Indianapolis, 29 March 1982). Guitarist. He played ukulele from 1932, working locally with Dewey Jackson and Charlie Creath, and performed on acoustic guitar with the pianist Eddie Johnson's Crackerjacks from 1934 to 1936. He first recorded on electric guitar as a member of the Jeter–Pillars Orchestra (1937–8). He then played with Andy Kirk (1939–42, 1945–6), with whom he recorded his showpiece *Floyd's Guitar Blues* (1939, Decca 2483), one of the first notable recordings of a blues solo by an electric guitarist. After leading his own trio in Chicago Smith worked with Horace Henderson and Wild Bill Davis (*c*1952–1957). Later he played with various groups in St. Louis and with Bill Doggett in New York (1959–64). In 1964 he formed another group, with which he later moved to Indianapolis. While visiting Europe with Davis in 1972 he recorded in France as a leader and with Davis, Buddy Tate, and Al Grey.

BIBLIOGRAPHY

ChiltonW; *FeatherE*

J. Obrecht: "Pro's Reply: Floyd Smith," *GP*, xiii/11 (1979), 8

Obituary, J. McAfee, Jr., *JSN*, ii/4 (1982), 20

Smith, Frank [Francis Percival] (*b* Sydney, 30 July 1927; *d* Melbourne, Australia, 18 Feb 1974). Australian reed player and teacher. After first performing in a group led by his father he played extensively during the 1940s and 1950s with dance bands in Sydney, including those led by Frank Coughlan and the trombonist Ralph Mallen. He studied at the New South Wales Conservatorium of Music and became an important and influential teacher; many of his pupils later became prominent jazz musicians. In the late 1950s he moved to Melbourne, where he worked as a studio musician and composed for radio and television. He also acted as the music director for many visiting musicians, including the singers Billy Eckstine and Andy Williams. In 1959–60 he led his own group at the Embers in Melbourne. His playing is well represented on *Ockeration* from the album *Music Maker 1957 All Stars* (*c*1957, Parl. AuPMD07511).

BIBLIOGRAPHY

A. Bisset: *Black Roots, White Flowers: a History of Jazz in Australia* (Sydney, 1979), 93, 105

B. Johnson and others: *The Oxford Companion to Australian Jazz* (Melbourne, Australia, 1987)

TONY GOULD

Smith, Howard [Harold] (*b* Ardmore, OK, 19 Oct 1910). Pianist. He lived with his family in Montreal from 1919, then moved in 1933 to New York, where he played briefly with Benny Goodman at Billy Rose's Music Hall and recorded with Adrian Rollini (both 1934). In 1935 he played with Ray Noble, then performed and recorded alongside Woody Herman in Isham Jones's Juniors (1935–6); he also recorded with Red Norvo (1936) and Glenn Miller (1937). From 1937 to 1940 he toured and recorded with Tommy Dorsey; he may be heard playing a solo on Dorsey's *Boogie Woogie* (1938, Vic. 26054). He later worked as a studio musician. (*FeatherE*; *ChiltonW*)

Smith, Jabbo [Cladys] (*b* Pembroke, GA, 24 Dec 1908). Trumpeter and singer. He was one of many youngsters who learned their musical skills at Jenkins' Orphanage in Charleston, South Carolina. By the age of 16 he was a professional musician, and from 1925 to 1928 worked with Charlie Johnson's band. In 1927 he took part in a recording session with Duke Ellington's orchestra that produced a brilliant version of *Black and Tan Fantasy*. After touring with James P. Johnson in the revue *Keep Shufflin'* (1928) Smith worked in Chicago during the late 1920s and the 1930s with various leaders, including Carroll Dickerson, Earl Hines, Erskine Tate, Charlie Elgar, Tiny Parham, and Fess Williams; he also led his own bands in Chicago and Milwaukee. From 1936 to 1938 he was a member of Claude Hopkins's band, but for most of the 1940s he led his own groups in Milwaukee. Thereafter he played only part-time, but after his appearances in the successful show *One Mo' Time* in 1978 he enjoyed widespread acclaim. Despite a period of ill-health in the early 1980s Smith continued to perform as a singer; he appeared at festivals in Europe in 1983 and, with Don Cherry, at the Jazzfest Berlin in 1986.

Like several other brilliant jazz trumpeters of the 1920s and 1930s, Smith lived in the shadow of Louis Armstrong. His technique, range, and instrumental flexibility were highly impressive, and his vocal style had great charm. However, owing partly to circumstances, but partly also to a lack of striking originality, for most of his life his fame has been restricted to jazz aficionados. Besides his principal instrument he also played trombone and piano.

Oral history material in *CtY*, *LNT*, *NjR* (JOHP), and *NjR*.

See also TRUMPET, §4.

SELECTED RECORDINGS

As leader: Jazz Battle (1929, Bruns. 4244); Sweet and Low Blues (1929, Bruns. 7061); Till times get better (1929, Bruns. 7078)

As sideman: D. Ellington: Black and Tan Fantasy (1927, OK 40955); C. Johnson: Charleston is the best dance after all (1928, Vic. 21491)

BIBLIOGRAPHY

D. DeMicheal: "Focus on Jabbo Smith," *DB*, xxviii/17 (1961), 22

H. Pekar: "Jabbo Smith," *JJ*, xviii/7 (1965), 8

G. Schuller: *Early Jazz: its Roots and Musical Development* (New York, 1968), 207

L. Terjanian: "The Legendary Cladys 'Jabbo' Smith," *Pj*, no.7 (1972), 32

O. Coyle: "Jabbo Smith: his Horn is Hot again," *MR*, iii/9 (1976), 1

A. Vollmer: "Rhythm Aces," *Sv*, no.86 (1979–80), 70

J. Chilton: *A Jazz Nursery: the Story of the Jenkins' Orphanage Bands of Charleston, South Carolina* (London, 1980), 27

W. Balliett: "Starting at the Top," *Jelly Roll, Jabbo and Fats* (New York, and Oxford, England, 1983) [colln of previously pubd articles], 63

E. Cook: "Jabbo Smith," *JJI*, xxxvii/4 (1984), 6

J. Reldy: "Gabbin' with Jabbo," *BHcF*, no.319 (1984), 7

M. Laplace: "Jabbo Smith: Le méconnu," *Brass Bulletin*, no.49 (1985), 47

A. Shipton: "Jabbo Smith: Hidden Treasure," *Fn*, xviii/3 (1987), 15

JOHN CHILTON

Smith, Jimmie [James Howard] (*b* Newark, NJ, 27 Jan 1938). Drummer and arranger. After studying at the Al Germansky School for Drummers in Newark (1951–4) and the Juilliard School (1959–60) he recorded in the New York area with Jimmy Forrest (1960) and Larry Young (1960, 1962), and in 1963 with Pony Poindexter, Jimmy Witherspoon, and Gildo Mahones. He performed and recorded with Lambert, Hendricks, and Ross (1962–3, appearing at the Newport Jazz Festival in 1963), toured and recorded with Erroll Garner (1967–74), and after settling in California in the mid-1970s performed with Benny Carter (1975, 1978). He performed and recorded with Bill Henderson (1975), Hank Jones (1976), and Harry Edison (1976–8, recording in groups led by Edison and Eddie "Lockjaw" Davis, and Edison and Zoot Sims), at the Montreux International Jazz Festival in 1977 (with Carter, Davis, Milt Jackson, Dizzy Gillespie, and Count Basie), and with Terry Gibbs (1978). He also made recordings with Sonny Criss (*Out of Nowhere*, 1975, Muse 5089), Lorez Alexandria (1977–8), and Great Guitars (1980), and in 1981 with Barney Kessel, Herb Ellis, and a group led by Gibbs and Buddy DeFranco. Smith has been much sought after as a sideman owing to his clear, crisp sound and his reliable sense of swing.

BIBLIOGRAPHY

Feather–Gitler '70s

J. M. Doran: *Erroll Garner: the Most Happy Piano* (Metuchen, NJ, 1985), 106

CHRIS SHERIDAN

Smith, Jimmy [James Oscar] (*b* Norristown, PA, 8 Dec 1925). Organist. He first learned piano, largely from his parents and through self-instruction, although in Philadelphia he attended the Hamilton School of Music (1948) and the Ornstein School of Music (1949–50). He took up the Hammond organ in 1951, and acquired a formidable reputation in the Philadelphia area before making his extremely successful début in New York at the Café Bohemia in 1956. An appearance at Birdland and a

Jimmy Smith playing a Hammond organ

highly acclaimed performance at the Newport Jazz Festival in 1957 launched his international career as the first important jazz player on his instrument. Although the organ had been played previously in jazz (for example, by Fats Waller and Count Basie), it was usually treated as a novelty instrument. Smith spent the next 20 years touring, visiting Israel in 1974 and Europe in 1975. He then settled in Los Angeles, where, with his wife Lola, he opened his own club, Jimmy Smith's Jazz Supper Club. He resumed touring in the early 1980s, and performed in New York in 1982 and 1983.

Smith was the first player to make the organ effectively serve as a group (minus drums), providing walking bass lines with his feet, chordal accompaniment in his left hand, and a solo line in his right. His powerful style, which combined rhythm-and-blues elements with the more sophisticated bop vocabulary, has influenced virtually every subsequent jazz organist, including Don Patterson, Brother Jack McDuff, Jimmy McGriff, Groove Holmes, and Larry Young.

See also ORGAN, §2.

SELECTED RECORDINGS

The Sermon (1957–8, BN 4011); *Midnight Special* (1960, BN 84078); *The Unpredictable Jimmy Smith: Bashin'* (1962, Verve 68474); *The Cat* (1964, Verve 68587); with W. Montgomery: *The Dynamic Duo* (1966, Verve 68678); *Off the Top* (1982, Elek. 52418)

BIBLIOGRAPHY

J. Cooke: "The Electric Organ in Jazz: Jimmy Smith and some Others," *JM*, vii/11 (1962), 11
B. Gardner: "Jimmy Smith: Reaching the People," *DB*, xxix/14 (1962), 17
H. Siders: "Jimmy Smith: a New Deal for the Boss," *DB*, xxxvii/20 (1970), 14
L. Birnbaum: "Jimmy Smith: Sermonizing in the '70s," *DB*, xliv/21 (1977), 22
B. Doerschuk: "Jimmy Smith," *CK*, iv/8 (1978), 26
G. Giddins: "Return of the Organ Grinder," *Rhythm-a-ning: Jazz Tradition and Innovation in the '80s* (New York, and Oxford, England, 1985) [colln of previously pubd articles], 166

BILL DOBBINS/R

Smith, Joe [Joseph C.] (*b* Ripley, OH, 28 June 1902; *d* New York, 2 Dec 1937). Trumpeter, brother of Russell Smith. In the early 1920s he worked as a freelance in New York and also toured and recorded with Ethel Waters and Mamie Smith. He was a member of Fletcher Henderson's orchestra from 1925 to 1928, during which time he recorded with many blues singers, notably Bessie Smith. After working with McKinney's Cotton Pickers (1929–30, 1931–2) he settled in Kansas City, Missouri, but ill-health prevented him from performing regularly. He attempted to play with Henderson's band in Detroit, but shortly afterwards entered a sanatorium in New York.

For a brief period in the 1920s Smith was considered to be the chief rival of Louis Armstrong, who, like Smith, had also played as a soloist with Henderson. However, the style of the two men was entirely different, Smith relying mainly on a mellow tone, subtle inflections, and lyrical playing in the middle register of the instrument. Viewed in retrospect, his work has considerable period charm, but little of Armstrong's invention, versatility, and durability. Smith was particularly adept with the plunger mute, producing a touching, vocal sound which enhanced several of the recordings he made with Bessie Smith.

SELECTED RECORDINGS

As sideman: B. Smith: Money Blues (1926, Col. 14137D); Baby Doll (1926, Col. 14147D); F. Henderson: Rocky Mountain Blues (1927, Col. 970D); Fidgety Feet (1927, Voc. 1092); McKinney's Cotton Pickers: Gee, ain't I good to you? (1929, Vic. 38097)

BIBLIOGRAPHY

B. Houghton: "Joe Smith: a Biography and Appreciation," *JJ*, xviii/12 (1965), 18
W. C. Allen: "Addenda: Joe Smith," *JJ*, xx/8 (1967), 6
H. Panassié: "Il y a 30 ans, le 1er décembre 1937 [*sic*], mourait Joe Smith," *BHcF*, no.173 (1967), 4
G. Schuller: *Early Jazz: its Roots and Musical Development* (New York, 1968), 234
J. Chilton: *McKinney's Music: a Bio-discography of McKinney's Cotton Pickers* (London, 1978), 27
C. Sheridan: "The Forgotten Ones: Joe Smith," *JJI*, xxxiv/12 (1981), 12

JOHN CHILTON

Smith, John (William) (*b* Atlanta, 27 Nov 1908). Guitarist. In Atlanta he played banjo with the pianist J. Neal Montgomery in the late 1920s; in New York he studied guitar with Edwin Colts in the early 1930s while playing in Otto Hardwick's band and working as a freelance. As a member of Teddy Hill's band (1932–9) he toured Europe in 1937. He played in both the big band and the small group of Fats Waller (1939–40), then toured with the popular singers the Mills Brothers until late in 1942, when he joined Benny Carter's orchestra. After working briefly in Dizzy Gillespie's big band he played with Cab Calloway (1946–8, and at intervals to 1951), performed as a solo singer and guitarist for a number of years, and played banjo and guitar with Wilbur De Paris (1958–66). He retired from music before resuming his career as a guitarist with Panama Francis and his Savoy Sultans from the late 1970s into the 1980s.

SELECTED RECORDINGS

As sideman: F. Waller: first issued on [album of unknown title] (1939, Vic. RD7552), Honeysuckle Rose; P. Francis: *Grooving* (?1982, Stash 218)

BIBLIOGRAPHY

ChiltonW
Battestini: "John Smith," *BHcF*, no.279 (1980), 10
E. Townley: "From Down in Atlanta, GA: an Interview with John Smith," *Sv*, no.99 (1982), 91
D. Barker: *A Life in Jazz*, ed. A. Shipton (London and New York, 1986), 176

EDDIE LAMBERT

Smith, Johnny [John Henry, Jr.] (*b* Birmingham, AL, 25 June 1922). Guitarist and leader. Self-taught, he played trumpet, violin, and viola before specializing in electric guitar. From 1947 to 1953 he worked as a studio musician for NBC in New York, playing trumpet and guitar. In 1952 he organized his own group and recorded *Moonlight in Vermont* (Roost 542), which *Down Beat* named "jazz record of the year." Under the pseudonym Sir Jonathan Gasser he played on the album *Jazz Studio* (1953, Decca 8058) with an all-star group that included Bennie Green, Hank Jones, and Kenny Clarke. During the 1950s he recorded prolifically as a leader and led groups at Birdland, New York. After moving to Colorado in the 1960s he opened a music store and performed and taught; he continued to record in New York until 1968. In the late 1970s he toured England with Bing Crosby.

BIBLIOGRAPHY

FeatherE; *Feather '60s*
L. Henshaw: "Smith to a D," *MM*, liv (18 Feb 1979), 47
R. Yellin: "Johnny Smith," *GP*, xvi/1 (1982), 36 [interview; incl. discography]

Smith, Johnny Hammond. *See* HAMMOND, JOHNNY.

Smith, (Dorothy Jacqueline) Keely (*b* Norfolk, VA, 9 March 1932). Singer. She first worked as a singer and comedienne with local bands in Norfolk, then in 1948 joined Louis Prima, whom she married in 1953. They performed and wrote songs together, made recordings of popular jazz, and appeared in the film *Hey Boy, Hey Girl* (1959). After their divorce in 1961 Smith had only limited success as a soloist, but in 1985 she recorded the album *I'm in Love Again* (Fan. 9639), accompanied by a West Coast jazz septet of varying personnel that included Bud Shank, Bill Perkins, Bob Cooper, Monty Budwig, and Jeff Hamilton.

BIBLIOGRAPHY

FeatherE
"Backstage with Louis Prima and Keely Smith," *DB*, xxvi/4 (1959), 14
R. D. Kinkle: *The Complete Encyclopedia of Popular Music and Jazz, 1900–1950* (New Rochelle, NY, and Westport, CT, 1974) [incl. discography]

Smith, Keith (John) (*b* London, 19 March 1940). English trumpeter. He began playing locally and worked with the San Jacinto Jazz Band (1958) and the double bass player Mickey Ashman, before forming his own Climax Jazz Band. While touring the USA he recorded with George Lewis (i) in New Orleans (1965). In 1966 he performed in Europe as a member of the New Orleans All Stars, which included Jimmy Archey, Darnell Howard, Alton Purnell, Pops Foster, and Cié Frazier, and he then moved to the USA, where he made a recording with Capt. John Handy (1966). He led his own band and ran a record company in England (after 1969) and performed and recorded in Denmark with Papa Bue's Viking Jazz Band (1972–5). After returning to England (1975) he formed the band Hefty Jazz and promoted a record label of the same name; his recordings as the group's leader include *Up Jumped the Blues* (1978, Hefty Jazz 105). In 1981 he began performing on tour with such presentations as "The Wonderful World of Louis Armstrong" and "100 Years of Dixieland Jazz."

BIBLIOGRAPHY

K. Smith: "In my Opinion," *JJ*, xxii/8 (1969), 13
R. Laing: "I'm only Interested in Music which Works!," *JJI*, xxxii/5 (1979), 7
E. Cook: "The Wonderful World of Louis Armstrong," *JJI*, xxxiv/9 (1981), 6
T. Dash: "Profile on Keith Smith," *Fn*, xvi/6 (1985), 4
"Keith Smith's Hefty Jazz," *Jazz Express*, no. 92 (1988), 8

DEREK COLLER

Smith, Leo (*b* Leland, MS, 18 Dec 1941). Trumpeter and flugelhorn player. He played mellophone and french horn before taking up trumpet. After high school he worked in rhythm-and-blues and army bands, then in 1967 became a member of the ASSOCIATION FOR THE ADVANCEMENT OF CREATIVE MUSICIANS (AACM). With Leroy Jenkins and Anthony Braxton, he was leader of the Creative Construction Company (1967–70), which performed in Europe (1969–70) and, with other AACM members, recorded in New York (1970). In 1970 Smith made the documentary film *See the Music* with Marion Brown. Later that year, in New Haven, Connecticut, he formed New Dalta Ahkri, a two- to five-piece group whose members have included Henry Threadgill, Anthony Davis, the double bass player Wes Brown, Bobby Naughton, Oliver Lake, and the reed player Dwight Andrews. In 1971 Smith established his own record label, Kabell. Shortly after publishing a pamphlet explaining his musical philosophy (*Notes (8 Pieces) Source a New World, Music: Creative Music*, 1973), he studied ethnomusicology at Wesleyan University (1974–5). He then worked with Braxton again (1976) and with Derek Bailey's group Company in London (1977), and led a trio with Peter Kowald and Günter Sommer. Smith's preference for music that displays lyricism, pleasing timbres, and sustained calmness sets him apart from many of his colleagues in free jazz. He also plays flute, percussion, and non-Western instruments.

For illustrations *see* JAZZ (i), fig.9, and LACY, STEVE.

SELECTED RECORDINGS

As unaccompanied soloist: *Creative Music* (1971, Kabell 1); *Solo Music Ahkreanvention* (*c*1981, Kabell 4)
As leader: *Reflectativity* (1974, Kabell 2); *The Mass on the World* (1978, Moers 01060); *Divine Love* (1978, ECM 1143); *Spirit Catcher* (1979, Nessa 19); *Rastafari* (1983, Sack. 3030)
As sideman: A. Braxton: *Three Compositions of New Jazz* (1968, Del. 415); *Silence* (1969, Freedom 40123); Creative Construction Company: *Creative Construction Company* (1970, Muse 5071, 5097); A. Davis: *Hemispheres* (1983, Gram. 8303)

BIBLIOGRAPHY

B. Smith: "Leo Smith," *Coda*, no.143 (1975), 2 [incl. discography]
B. Ness: "Profile: Leo Smith," *DB*, xliii/16 (1976), 36
V. Wilmer: *As Serious as your Life: the Story of the New Jazz* (London, 1977, rev. 1980)
G. Rouy: "L'esthétique noire selon Leo Smith," *Jm*, no.277 (1979), 30
——: "Leo Smith pour la musique créative," *Jm*, no.278 (1979), 80 [incl. discography]
B. Smith: "Leo Smith: Rastafari," *Coda*, no.192 (1983), 4

BARRY KERNFELD

Smith, Lonnie Liston(, Jr.) (*b* Richmond, VA, 28 Dec 1940). Keyboard player. His father sang and played with a gospel group, the Harmonizing Four. After graduating in music education from Morgan State University (1961) Smith went to New York, where he worked with Betty Carter (1963–4), Roland Kirk (1964–5), Art Blakey (1966–7), Joe Williams (1967–8), Pharoah Sanders (1969–71), Gato Barbieri (1971–3), and Miles Davis (1972–*c*1973). In the last three groups he tended to supply harmonic drones by reiterating shimmering or rhythmic chordal patterns. In 1974, with one of his brothers, the singer Donald Smith, he formed the Cosmic Echoes. Although the group was soundly criticized in jazz record reviews for its use of predictable improvisations, bland funk vamps, and sugary lyrics, its album *Expansions* (1975) reached high positions on the jazz, pop, and soul charts. During the late 1970s the Cosmic Echoes achieved considerable popularity through its performances on the club circuit.

SELECTED RECORDINGS

As leader: *Expansions* (*c*1975, FD 10934); *Renaissance* (*c*1977, RCA APL1-1822)

As sideman: P. Sanders: *Karma* (1969, Imp. 9181); on S. Turrentine: *Sugar* (1970, CTI 6005), Sugar; G. Barbieri: *Fenix* (1971, FD 10144); M. Davis: *Big Fun* (1972, Col. PG32866)

BIBLIOGRAPHY

M. Cullaz: "Lonnie Liston Smith J° a beaucoup de choses à raconter," *Jh*, no.282 (1972), 14
E. Chadbourne: "Astral Travelling," *Coda*, xi/4 (1973), 2 [interview]
A. J. Smith: "Lonnie Liston Smith: Cosmic Head on Electronic Neck," *DB*, xliii/1 (1976), 12 [incl. discography]
R. Palmer: "Lonnie Liston Smith's Power for the People," *RS*, no.279 (30 Nov 1978), 35

BARRY KERNFELD

Smith, (Edward) Louis (*b* Memphis, 20 May 1931). Trumpeter and leader. He studied music at Tennessee State University and toured with the Tennessee State Collegians, performing in New York at Carnegie Hall. After playing with an army band (1954–5) he taught at a high school in Atlanta. In 1958 Smith traveled to New York to fulfil a contract with Blue Note; he recorded two albums (including *Smithville*, 1958, BN 1594) as the leader of hard-bop quintets with such distinguished sidemen as Tommy Flanagan, Duke Jordan, Cannonball Adderley (who used the pseudonym Buckshot la Funke), Charlie Rouse, Paul Chambers, and Art Taylor. In the same year he also recorded with Kenny Burrell and toured briefly with Horace Silver. He then returned to teaching, but in 1960 recorded in New York with the Young Men from Memphis, a group that included Booker Little, Phineas and Calvin Newborn, and George Coleman. Smith later led a quartet in Louisville, Kentucky (1967), and made recordings as a leader in New York (including *Just Friends*, 1978, Ste. 1096, with Coleman again among his sidemen).

BIBLIOGRAPHY

FeatherE
M. Gardner: "Wilber Harden and Louis Smith: Forgotten Faces of the Fifties," *JJ*, xxi/5 (1968), 19 [incl. discography]

Smith [née Robinson], **Mamie** (*b* Cincinnati, 26 May 1883; *d* New York, ?30 Oct 1946). Singer and entertainer. She toured as a dancer with Tutt-Whitney's Smart Set Company when in her early teens, and gained a reputation as a singer in Harlem clubs and theaters before World War I. In 1920 she became the first black jazz-blues singer to record when she took part in a session in place of Sophie Tucker. Shortly afterwards she had a huge success with *Crazy Blues*, which made a fortune both for the singer and her promoter Perry Bradford; it was also important in that it opened the way for the subsequent recording of other black singers. Following this, Smith had many engagements, touring as far as New Orleans and Dallas and appearing as the featured singer in her own shows. She also made several films, both short subjects and full-length features, notably with Lucky Millinder's band in *Paradise in Harlem* (1939). She possessed a lively stage personality, was extremely attractive, and had a strong voice. Many of her best recordings were made with her Jazz Hounds, a group that included Johnny Dunn and, sometimes, Bubber Miley on cornet. *Jenny's Ball* gives a good indication of her appeal as a singer. Smith was a vaudeville performer rather than a blues singer and, unlike Bessie Smith, seldom used the blues form or blues inflections.

For illustration *see* SINGING, fig.1.

SELECTED RECORDINGS

That thing called love (1920, OK/Phonola 4113); Crazy Blues (1920, OK/Phonola 4169); I ain't gonna give nobody none o' this jelly-roll (1922, OK 4752); The Darktown Flappers' Ball (1922, OK 4767); Jenny's Ball (1931, OK 8915)

BIBLIOGRAPHY

S. B. Charters and L. Kunstadt: *Jazz: a History of the New York Scene* (Garden City, NY, 1962/*R*1981)
P. Bradford: *Born with the Blues: . . . the True Story of the Pioneering Blues Singers and Musicians in the Early Days of Jazz* (New York, 1963)
R. C. Foreman, Jr.: *Jazz and Race Records, 1920–32: their Origins and their Significance for the Record Industry and Society* (diss., U. of Illinois, 1968)
S. Harris: *Blues Who's Who: a Biographical Dictionary of Blues Singers* (New Rochelle, NY, 1979)
S. Placksin: *American Women in Jazz, 1900 to the Present: their Words, Lives, and Music* (New York, 1982; London, 1985, as *Jazzwomen, 1900 to the Present: their Words, Lives, and Music*), 21

PAUL OLIVER

Smith, Marvin "Smitty" [Smith, Marvin (O., II); Smitty] (*b* Waukegan, IL, 24 June 1961). Drummer. After studying at the Berklee College of Music he played in New York for two years with Jon Hendricks's group (from December 1980) and with John Hicks, Bobby Watson, and Slide Hampton. He then worked as a freelance musician, recording with Archie Shepp (1982, 1984), recording (1983–4) and performing in a quintet led by Frank Foster and Frank Wess, and recording with Hamiet Bluiett, Kevin Eubanks, and David Murray (all 1984). He also played with Ray Brown, Ron Carter, Dave Holland, Hank Jones, and the Jazztet. In 1987 Smith recorded with Sonny Rollins and Donald Byrd and made his first album as a leader; later in the year he played in the touring band of the rock musician Sting.

SELECTED RECORDINGS

As leader: *Keeper of the Drums* (1987, Conc. 325)
As sideman: D. Holland: *Seeds of Time* (1984, ECM 1292); Steve Coleman: *Motherland Pulse* (1985, JMT 850001); Jazztet: *Back to the City* (1986, Cont. 14020); B. Montgomery: *Ties of Love* (1986, Landmark 1512)

BIBLIOGRAPHY

C. Stern: "Marvin 'Smitty' Smith: Drum History in Transition," *MD*, x/3 (1986), 22

RICK MATTINGLY

Smith, Michael (Joseph) (*b* Tiline, KY, 13 Aug 1938). Keyboard player, composer, and leader. He studied privately with Ran Blake and David Baker, at the New England Conservatory, and at the Juilliard School. He worked with the Paul Bley Synthesizer Show and recorded as a leader in Copenhagen (1972). After moving to Paris in 1973 he performed and recorded as an unaccompanied soloist and with Steve Lacy and Noah Howard (all 1974). He settled in Sweden in 1975 and the following year recorded free jazz with Anthony Braxton in New York, in a duo with Lacy in Oslo, and as a leader (*Austin Stream*, FMP SAJ09). Further recordings made with Lacy in 1978 were not issued. His compositions, which include *Symphony for Geomusic* (*c*1973), gained several Swedish awards in the late 1970s and early 1980s.

BIBLIOGRAPHY

Feather–Gitler '70s
S. Traill: "Meet Michael Smith," *JJ*, xxiv/4 (1971), 10

Smith, Paul (Thatcher) (*b* San Diego, 17 April 1922). Pianist and leader. He played with Johnny Richards (1941) and, during his military service (1943–5), with Ziggy Elman. After working with the guitarist Les Paul (1946–7) he toured and recorded with Tommy Dorsey (1947–9), then moved to Los Angeles, where he was active in radio and television and as a session musician. From 1949 into the 1980s he performed and recorded as an unaccompanied soloist and with his own small groups; his sidemen included Alvin Stoller (early 1950s) and Fred Middlebrooks (from 1963). His playing as an unaccompanied soloist and in the setting of a trio is well represented on his album

The Big Men (1959, Verve 62130). Among the many leaders with whom he recorded were Dizzy Gillespie (1950), Ray Anthony (1953–*c*1958), Billy May (1954–6), Ella Fitzgerald (intermittently 1956–78), Anita O'Day (1956), Buddy Rich and Buddy DeFranco (both 1957), Louie Bellson (1961, 1978), Stan Kenton (1961), and Chet Baker (1969).

BIBLIOGRAPHY

FeatherE
B. Doerschuk: "Backstage with Paul Smith," *CK*, iv/1 (1978), 6

BARRY KERNFELD

Smith, Pine Top [Clarence] (*b* Troy, AL, 11 June 1904; *d* Chicago, 15 March 1929). Singer and pianist. From about 1920 he toured as a pianist and tap-dancer in various revues, including that of Ma Rainey, before being discovered by the pianist Charles "Cow Cow" Davenport. In 1928–9 he made a number of recordings in Chicago, of which eight were released. Among these was the remarkably successful *Pine Top's Boogie Woogie*, probably the most influential and widely imitated of all blues recordings; a re-creation of a rent-party dance or "boogie," it at once established and popularized the blues piano style known as BOOGIE-WOOGIE. Most of his recordings were novelty pieces or comic monologues; only *Pine Top's Blues*, which he sang in a high, even petulant and childlike, voice, was in the traditional blues vein. He greatly influenced Albert Ammons, who used the "powerhouse" rhythm of left-hand walking bass figures, but his own playing had a light, rolling quality also evident in the playing of his contemporaries Cripple Clarence Lofton, Charles Avery, and Romeo Nelson. He was accidently shot during a brawl in the masonic lodge where he was performing.

SELECTED RECORDINGS

Pine Top's Boogie Woogie/Pine Top's Blues (1928, Voc. 1245); I'm sober now (1929, Voc. 1266); Now I ain't got nothin' at all (1929, Voc. 1298)

BIBLIOGRAPHY

W. Russell: "Boogie Woogie," *Jazzmen: the Story of Hot Jazz Told in the Lives of the Men who Created it*, ed. F. Ramsey, Jr., and C. E. Smith (New York, 1939/R1977), 187
B. Hall and R. Noblett: "The Birth of the Boogie," *Blues Unlimited*, no.133 (1979), 10
F. Smith: "I Saw Pine Top Spit Blood, or How Pine Top Smith Didn't Die," *Blues Unlimited*, no.139 (1980), 34

PAUL OLIVER

Smith, Russell (T.) [Pops] (*b* Ripley, OH, 1890; *d* Los Angeles, 27 March 1966). Trumpeter, brother of Joe Smith. He began playing professionally in 1906 or 1907, and around 1910 he settled in New York. He served in army bands for many years and then performed in revues. In 1925 he joined Fletcher Henderson, with whom he played first trumpet until 1941 (for illustration *see* HENDERSON, FLETCHER); during this period he also worked with Horace Henderson (1933), Claude Hopkins (1935–6), and Benny Carter (1934, 1939–40). Thereafter he was a member of Cab Calloway's band (1941–6) and performed with Noble Sissle (until around 1950). In the 1950s he settled in California, where he played occasionally and worked as a teacher. Smith's assured technique and flawless reading of lead trumpet parts was much admired by other musicians, but writers often criticized his stiff staccato playing on the recordings he made with Fletcher Henderson up to about 1932. He had been performing for many years before Louis Armstrong's influence began to transform jazz in the mid-1920s, and he took some time to adapt to the flexible, legato phrasing of the new style. His impeccable and exemplary work as a lead trumpeter in the 1940s and 1950s did not always receive due recognition.

SELECTED RECORDINGS

As sideman: H. Henderson: Happy Feet (1933, Parl. R1792); Rhythm Crazy (1933, Parl. R1743); F. Henderson: Big John's Special (1934, Decca 214); Down South Camp Meetin' (1934, Decca 213); B. Carter: Everybody Shuffle (1934, Voc. 2870); Pom pom (1940, Decca 3262); Cuddle up, huddle up (1941, Bb 11197)

BIBLIOGRAPHY

A. Judd: "A Portrait of Russell Smith," *JJ*, xx/4 (1967), 5
W. C. Allen: *Hendersonia: the Music of Fletcher Henderson and his Musicians: a Bio-discography* (Highland Park, NJ, 1973)

JOHNNY SIMMEN

Smith, Stuff [Hezekiah Leroy Gordon] (*b* Portsmouth, OH, 14 Aug 1909; *d* Munich, 25 Sept 1967). Violinist. After early study with his father and performances with his family's band he won a scholarship to Johnson C. Smith University, but at the age of 15 joined a touring revue. He performed with Alphonso Trent (1926–8) and briefly with Jelly Roll Morton, but left the latter because he felt that his playing could not be heard, and returned to Trent's band until 1930. He then spent several years in Buffalo, and moved in 1936 to New York, where he led a quintet at the Onyx club that included Jonah Jones and Cozy Cole; here he began using an amplified violin. Smith was chosen to lead Fats Waller's band after the pianist's death in 1943. A lull in his career was followed by a series of excellent recordings for Norman Granz in 1957. He began touring more extensively in the 1960s, and in 1965 he settled in Copenhagen, where he remained quite popular until his death.

Smith was an innovative musician. He played violin in a raucous style and with a sense of swing that was of unequaled intensity. Harmonically his work was extremely adventurous, and he evolved radical techniques to accommodate his wildly inventive ideas. Wide vibrato, hoarse tone, expressive intonation, and rhythmic creativity are all hallmarks of his style. Dizzy Gillespie has cited Smith as a profound influence upon his playing.

For illustration *see* FILMS, fig.5.

SELECTED RECORDINGS

As leader: I'se a Muggin' (1936, Voc. 3169); After you've Gone (1936, Voc. 3201); Upstairs (1937, Decca 1287); Save all your honey for me/Is, is (1944, Savoy 528); *Have Violin, Will Swing* (1957, Verve 8282); *Soft Winds* (1957, Verve 8206); with S. Grappelli: *Violins no End* (1957, Pablo 2310907); with S. Asmussen, S. Grappelli, and J.-L. Ponty: *Violin Summit* (1966, Saba 15099); *Black Violin* (1967, Saba 15147)

BIBLIOGRAPHY

ChiltonW
J. Pescheux: "Stuff Smith," *BHcF*, no.150 (1965), 3
V. Wilmer: "Stuff Smith: the Genius of Jazz Violin," *JB*, ii/6 (1965), 16 [interview]
Obituary, *DB*, xxiv/23 (1967), 13
D. Morgenstern: "Jazz Fiddle," *DB*, xxxiv/3 (1967), 16
S. Dance: *The World of Swing* (New York, 1974) [colln of previously pubd interviews], 176
P. Shelasky: Liner notes, *Hot Swing Fiddle Classics* (Folklyric 9025, 1979)
M. Glaser and S. Grappelli: *Jazz Violin* (New York and elsewhere, 1981) [incl. transcrs.]
M. L. Hester: "Hot Stuff!," *MR*, xi/6 (1984), 8

MATT GLASER

Smith, Tab [Talmadge] (*b* Kinston, NC, 11 Jan 1909; *d* St. Louis, 17 Aug 1971). Alto and soprano saxophonist, arranger, and bandleader. He began his musical studies on piano, and played C-melody saxophone before taking up the alto and soprano instruments. From 1927 to 1929 he led the Carolina Stompers, after which he spent a brief period with Ike Dixon in Baltimore. He then played with Eddie Johnson's Crackerjacks (1933–4), Fate Marable (1934), Lucky Millinder and the Mills Blue Rhythm Band (1936–7), and Frankie Newton (1938–9). In 1940 he worked briefly with Teddy Wilson, Count Basie,

Millinder, and Eddie Durham, and at the end of the year rejoined Basie, with whom he remained until 1942. He was with Millinder's band again from 1942 to 1944, but thereafter directed his own groups.

Smith was highly regarded as a soloist on both alto and soprano saxophone. He achieved great success in the 1940s and 1950s, particularly at the Savoy Ballroom in New York, playing in a style that later became associated with rhythm-and-blues. Among his best-known arrangements are *Barrel House* and *Tab's Blues*.

SELECTED RECORDINGS

As leader: Tab steps out (1944, Regis 7000); Granny Dodging at the Savoy (1945, 20C 20-45)

As sideman: Mills Blue Rhythm Band: Barrel House (1936, Col. 3156D); F. Newton: Tab's Blues (1939, Voc. 4821)

BIBLIOGRAPHY

ChiltonW

R. Horricks: *Count Basie and his Orchestra: its Music and its Musicians* (London and New York, 1957), 175

M. Pinfold: "The Forgotten Ones: Tab Smith," *JJI*, xxxv/10 (1982), 8

FRANK DRIGGS

Smith, Teddy [Theodore] (*b* Washington, 22 Jan 1932). Double bass player. He worked with Betty Carter (1960), then performed and recorded with Clifford Jordan and Kenny Dorham (both 1961–2); he played on Dorham's album *El matador* (1962, UA 15007). After working with Jackie McLean and Slide Hampton (1962–3) he joined Horace Silver's hard-bop quintet, with which he recorded *Song for my Father* (1964, BN 84185) and performed at the Paris, Antibes–Juan-les-Pins, and Montreux jazz festivals (all 1964). He also recorded with Sonny Rollins (1964–5) and Sonny Simmons's free-jazz group (1966). (*Feather '60s*)

Smith, Trixie (*b* Atlanta, 1895; *d* New York, 21 Sept 1943). Singer. After studying at Selma University she moved to New York (*c*1915). She worked on the TOBA circuit from around 1918 and in the early 1920s began regularly to make recordings. Between 1920 and 1933 she performed frequently in New York's black theaters, both as a singer and an actor. She performed on Broadway and recorded for Silvertone under the pseudonym Bessie Lee. Smith recorded prolifically throughout her career as a leader (1921–5), as a sideman with Jimmy Blythe (1926), and as the leader of various all-star groups (1938–9); among the bands that accompanied her in recording sessions were groups led by James P. Johnson (1921) and Fletcher Henderson (1922, 1924–5). Her style is well represented in *The world's jazz crazy and so am I/Railroad Blues* (1925, Para. 12262) and *My Daddy Rocks me*, pt ii/*No Good Man* (1938, 1939, Decca 7617).

BIBLIOGRAPHY

S. Harris: *Blues Who's Who: a Biographical Dictionary of Blues Singers* (New Rochelle, NY, 1979)

D. Fairweather: "Smith, Trixie," in I. Carr, D. Fairweather, and B. Priestley: *Jazz: the Essential Companion* (London, 1987)

Smith, Warren (Doyle) [Smitty] **(i)** (*b* Middlebourne, WV, 17 May 1908; *d* Santa Barbara, CA, 28 Aug 1975). Trombonist. He moved with his family in 1920 to Dallas, where he first worked as a saxophonist. After taking up the trombone he played in Chicago with the drummer Abe Lyman (1928–35) and toured and recorded with Bob Crosby (1936–40; for illustration *see* CROSBY, BOB); he may be heard to advantage on Crosby's *Till we Meet Again* (1939, Decca 2825). Between 1940 and 1945 he performed in and around Chicago with Wingy Manone and others. He then moved to California, where he worked and recorded with Crosby (1945), the cornetist Pete Dailey (1947–9), and Lu Watters (1949–50), and played with Jess Stacy (1950) and Nappy Lamare (1951). Although he was mainly associated with dixieland bands, he also played briefly in New York with Duke Ellington in 1955. He later recorded with Bob Scobey (1956, 1957), played and recorded with Joe Darensbourg (1957–60), and worked with Wild Bill Davison and Ben Pollack. In the early 1960s he joined Red Nichols, and in 1964 toured Japan with him. He continued to play in California until 1975. (*ChiltonW*; *FeatherE*; *Feather–Gitler '70s*)

Smith, Warren(, Jr.) (ii) (*b* Chicago, 4 May 1932). Percussionist. He studied saxophone and clarinet with his father from the age of three and took up drumming when he was six. After attending the University of Illinois (BS in music education, 1957) and the Manhattan School of Music (MM in percussion, 1958) he worked in pit orchestras in New York and formed the Composer's Workshop Ensemble (1961); he also toured with Nat "King" Cole (1964), performed and recorded with Sam Rivers (1964–76), and recorded with the soul singer Aretha Franklin in the 1960s. In 1968 he established Studio WIS, a percussion studio at which M'BOOM RE: PERCUSSION, of which he was a founding member, rehearsed from 1970; at the same time he played in Gil Evans's orchestra (1968–76), for which he also wrote compositions, and belonged to the New York Jazz Repertory Company (1968–70) and Collective Black Artists. He was a founder with Ken McIntyre and others of the Afro-American program at SUNY, Old Westbury (1971), where he taught into the 1980s. With Andrew White he led a tribute to John Coltrane in 1976; later he made recordings as a leader (1977, 1982) and as a sideman with Julius Hemphill (1980) and Muhal Richard Abrams (1983).

SELECTED RECORDINGS

Duos with Hidefumi Toki: Warren Smith and Toki (1977, RCA [Japan] RVL8501) [EP]

As leader of Composer's Workshop Ensemble: *Cricket Poem Song* (1982, Miff 1006)

As sideman: G. Evans: *Montreux Festival '74* (1974, Phi. 6043); S. Rivers: *Essence* (1976, Cir. [G] 1); M. Roach: *M'Boom Re: Percussion* (1979, Col. IC36247); J. Hemphill: *Flat Out Jump Suite* (1980, BS 0040); M. R. Abrams: *Rejoicing with the Light* (1983, BS 0071)

BIBLIOGRAPHY

Feather–Gitler '70s

A. J. Smith: "Profile: Warren Smith," *DB*, xlii/11 (1975), 30

E. Hazell: "Warren Smith," *Coda*, no.211 (1986), 18

B. Rusch: "Warren Smith," *Cadence*, xiv/3 (1988), 5 [interview]

ED HAZELL

Smith, William O(verton). *See* SMITH, BILL.

Smith, Willie [William McLeish] (*b* Charleston, SC, 25 Nov 1910; *d* Los Angeles, 7 March 1967). Alto saxophonist. He attended Fisk University in Nashville, where he came to the attention of Jimmie Lunceford, and from 1929 to 1942 he played in Lunceford's well-known swing band (for illustration *see* LUNCEFORD, JIMMIE), establishing a reputation as a highly competent section leader and superior soloist; he also wrote some characteristic early arrangements for the group (*Sophisticated Lady*, *Rose Room*) and occasionally sang. After leaving Lunceford to work with Charlie Spivak (1942–3) Smith played mainly in Harry James's band (1944–51, 1954–64), with interruptions to replace Johnny Hodges briefly in the Duke Ellington Orchestra (1951–2), to tour with Jazz at the Philharmonic, and to lead his own small jazz and rhythm-and-blues groups in Los Angeles. Along with Hodges and Benny Carter, Smith was the oustanding soloist on his instrument during the swing period. He played in a driving, broken-chord style and had a distinctive manner of slipping momentarily out of the background harmonies to create bitonal effects.

SELECTED RECORDINGS

As sideman: J. Lunceford: Sophisticated Lady (1934, Decca 129); Rose Room (1934, Decca 131); Blue Blazes (1939, Voc./OK 4667); Uptown Blues (1939, Voc./OK 5362); H. James: Who's sorry now? (1945, Col. 36973); Moten's Swing (1946, Col. 37351); D. Ellington: Caravan/Indian Summer (1951, Mercer 1968)

BIBLIOGRAPHY

ChiltonW
"Willie Smith," *Ebony* (1949), June, 41
S. Dance: *The World of Swing* (New York, 1974) [colln of previously pubd interviews], 93

J. BRADFORD ROBINSON

Smith, Willie "the Lion" [William Henry Joseph Bonaparte Bertholoff] (*b* Goshen, NY, 25 Nov 1897; *d* New York, 18 April 1973). Pianist and composer. Born of Jewish and black parentage (according to his own assertions he served as a cantor for a time during the 1940s), he grew up in Newark, New Jersey, where his mother's keyboard playing in church sparked his early interest in music. He started playing piano at the age of six. After a largely informal music education he began to work professionally while still in his teens, and soon became one of the most illustrious and influential proponents of the stride or Harlem ragtime style. He earned his nickname "the Lion" during World War I through his heroism at the front. On his discharge from the army in 1919 he established himself in the forefront of New York's stride pianists. The friendship and mutual admiration he enjoyed with Duke Ellington during these early years were musically documented in Ellington's *Portrait of the Lion* (1939) and Smith's *Portrait of the Duke* (1957).

Willie "the Lion" Smith at the RCA Victor recording studios, New York, 1960s

Smith remained virtually unknown to the general public until 1935, when Decca issued a series of his recordings with groups. His solo recordings for Commodore in 1939, however, best illustrate the full maturity of his style. The eight original pieces recorded during this session clearly reveal his acknowledged interest in classical music and stand as masterpieces of stride piano literature, comparable with earlier works by James P. Johnson and Fats Waller. Of particular interest are the counterpoint in *Passionette* and the impressionistic qualities in *Echoes of Spring*, inspired by images of clouds, trees, and morning in a New York park.

During the 1940s Smith's popularity grew as Artie Shaw and Tommy Dorsey performed arrangements of his compositions, and the success of a tour of Europe in 1949 was representative of the increased recognition and respect that he enjoyed in his final years. In the 1950s he played regularly at the Central Plaza, and in 1954 he appeared in the film *Jazz Dance*. He continued to perform at festivals during the 1960s and the early 1970s, and also made two further tours of Europe (1965, 1966). As an entertainer, Smith's flamboyant behavior and dashing appearance, with derby hat and fat cigar, became almost legendary. As a pianist and composer, his blending of ragtime, impressionism, and counterpoint, coupled with an ability to contrast delicate and subtle melodic lines with passages of intense swing, constituted a unique contribution to the jazz tradition.

Oral history material in *NjR*.

SELECTED RECORDINGS

As unaccompanied soloist: Echoes of Spring/Fading Star (1939, Com. 521); Rippling Waters/Finger Buster (1939, Com. 522); Morning Air/Passionette (1939, Com. 523); Concentrating/Sneakaway (1939, Com. 524); *Reminiscing the Piano Greats* (1950, Vogue LD008) [oral history]; *Memoirs* (1967, RCA LSP6016) [oral history]
As leader: *The Lion Roars* (1957, Dot 3094), incl. Portrait of the Duke

BIBLIOGRAPHY

W. Smith and G. Hoefer: *Music on my Mind: the Memoirs of an American Pianist* (Garden City, NY, 1964/*R*1975)
H. Panassié: "Willie Smith 'le Lion'," *BHcF*, no.152 (1965), 3
J. Simmen: "Some Piano Compositions of Willie 'the Lion' Smith Played by other Musicians," *Sv*, no.44 (1972–3), 44; no.45 (1973), 98
L. Feather: "Piano Giants of Jazz: Willie 'the Lion' Smith," *CK*, iii/10 (1977), 55
M. G[autier] P[anassié]: "Une visite au Lion," *BHcF*, no.289 (1981), 3
J. Collinson: "Willie 'the Lion' Smith," *Sv*, no.132 (1987), 211 [incl. discography]

BILL DOBBINS/R

Smitty. Nickname of WARREN SMITH (i).

Smythe, Pat(rick) (*b* Edinburgh, 2 May 1923; *d* London, 6 May 1983). Scottish pianist. After working as a lawyer, he moved to London in the late 1950s and played in clubs with musicians such as Dizzy Reece. He played and recorded with Joe Harriott's quintet (which included Shake Keane, Coleridge Goode, and Phil Seamen) from 1960 to 1964; during this period he also recorded with Keane (1961) and Paul Gonsalves (1963) as well as under his own name (1962). He stayed with Harriott in 1965–7 as a member of the free-jazz group Indo-jazz Fusions (led by Harriott and the violinist John Mayer); his playing may be heard to advantage on *Abstract Doodle* from the group's *Personal Portrait* (1967, Col. SCX6249). During the 1970s Smythe played in Kenny Wheeler's groups and worked (sometimes as a leader) with Dave Holland, John McLaughlin, and others.

BIBLIOGRAPHY

Feather '60s

R. Cotterrell, ed.: *Jazz Now: the Jazz Centre Society Guide* (London, 1976)

B. Priestley: "Pat Smythe: a Sad Loss," *The Wire*, no.4 (1983), 17 [obituary]

NEVIL SKRIMSHIRE

Snaer, Albert (Joseph) (*b* New Orleans, 29 Jan 1902; *d* California, *c*1962). Trumpeter. After playing locally with the Excelsior Brass Band he worked for several years on riverboats. In 1925–6 he performed and made recordings with Dewey Jackson, including *She's crying for me* (1926, Voc. 1040), on which he is the soloist playing without a mute. Thereafter Snaer worked with his own band and with Fate Marable (1928), then moved to New York (*c*1930), where he played briefly with Andy Kirk and others. From 1932 to 1941 he worked intermittently with Claude Hopkins. Later he ceased to work as a full-time musician but continued to play occasionally, with Sidney Bechet (1949), Frank "Big Boy" Goudie (early 1960s), and others. He moved to the West Coast in the late 1950s. (J. De Donder: "Reminiscing with Mary Sayles: Some Notes on Albert Snaer," *Fn*, xii/4 (1981), 25)

based on *ChiltonW*

Snare drum. The principal drum in the jazz drum set. *See* DRUM SET, esp. §§I, 3; II, 1–4; *see also* BRASS BAND.

Snow, Valaida (*b* Chattanooga, TN, 2 June ?1903; *d* New York, 30 May 1956). Trumpeter, singer, and dancer. Her mother taught her to play several instruments and her sisters Alvaida, Hattie, and Lavaida (*b* 1914) also became professional entertainers. She toured the USA in various revues during the 1920s and early 1930s. From 1926 to 1928 she and Lavaida, a singer, performed in the Far East with Jack Carter (Lavaida later married Carter's brother Herman); Lavaida also recorded with Noble Sissle (1934) and under her own name (1936). Valaida toured and recorded extensively in Europe with her own groups (1935–40) and with other leaders; she also took part in a session in New York with Earl Hines (1933). Good examples of her playing may be heard on *I got rhythm* (1937, Parl. F1048), recorded with her own group, and *My heart belongs to daddy* (1939, Sonora 3557), recorded under Lulle Ellboj. She was imprisoned in Denmark from 1940 to 1942 on charges of theft and misuse of drugs, but continued to work as a singer and trumpeter in the USA until her death. She also appeared in films.

BIBLIOGRAPHY

ChiltonW

H. Stonor: "Can't we Talk it over," *Sv*, no.66 (1976), 213

H. T. Sampson: *Blacks in Blackface: a Source Book on Early Black Musical Shows* (Metuchen, NJ, 1980)

S. Placksin: *American Women in Jazz, 1900 to the Present: their Words, Lives, and Music* (New York, 1982)

L. Dahl: *Stormy Weather; the Music and Lives of a Century of Jazzwomen* (London, Melbourne, Australia, and New York, 1984)

G. Huygens: "Valaida Snow: reine noire de la trompette," *Pj*, no.20 (1986), 14

RAINER E. LOTZ

Snowden, Elmer (Chester) [Pops] (*b* Baltimore, 9 Oct 1900; *d* Philadelphia, 14 May 1973). Bandleader and banjoist. He played in Baltimore with Eubie Blake (1915) and worked in Washington as a member of Duke Ellington's trio (1919–20) before leading his own bands throughout the 1920s and early 1930s. He employed a number of excellent musicians as sidemen, and his first groups, in Washington and Atlantic City, New Jersey, included Otto Hardwick and Artie Whetsol (1921–3). These two traveled with Snowden to New York and were joined by Sonny Greer and Ellington (1923); with Bubber Miley (replacing Whetsol) and Charlie Irvis, this group became known as the WASHINGTONIANS (and later, without Snowden, as the Duke Ellington Orchestra). Snowden's later big bands in New York included Miley, Jimmie Lunceford, Count Basie (replaced by Claude Hopkins), and Tricky Sam Nanton (*c*1926); Rex Stewart, Jimmy Harrison, Prince Robinson, Fats Waller, and Chick Webb (1927–8); and Roy Eldridge, Al Sears, Dicky Wells, and Sid Catlett (1930–33). The last named, all members of his Smalls' Paradise Orchestra, participated in the short film *Smash your Baggage* (1932). After settling in Philadelphia (1933) Snowden taught banjo, mandolin, and saxophone. He led small groups in the Northeast and in Canada (1941–63), then moved to Berkeley, California. He was well received at the Monterey Jazz Festival (1963), where he led an unusual quartet with Darnell Howard, Pops Foster, and the young bop drummer Tony Williams. He also taught and played with Turk Murphy, and in 1967 made a tour of Europe.

For illustration *see* WASHINGTONIANS.

SELECTED RECORDINGS

As leader: *Harlem Banjo* (1960, Riv. 9348)

As sideman: Viola McCoy: West Indies Blues (1924, Voc. 14801); Bessie Smith: I ain't got nobody (1925, Col. 14095D); Te Roy Williams: Oh Malinda/Lindbergh Hop (1927, Har. 439); Lonnie Johnson: *Blues and Ballads* (1960, Bluesville 1011)

BIBLIOGRAPHY

B. Demeusy: "Elmer Snowden Discography," *JJ*, xvi/4 (1963), 15

D. Ives: "Elmer Snowden," *JJ*, xvi/1 (1963), 26

"Elmer Snowden: the Bandleader who Fired Basie!," *CI*, vi/5 (1967), 16

L. Muscutt: "Discovering Elmer," *Sv*, (1968), no.16, p.3; no.17, p.4; no.18, p.4

S. Dance: *The World of Swing* (New York, 1974) [colln of previously pubd interviews], 45

BARRY KERNFELD

Socarras, Alberto (*b* Manzanillo, Cuba, 19 Sept 1908). Reed player, flutist, and bandleader. After playing with local orchestras he moved to the USA, where he recorded with Clarence Williams and others in the late 1920s. He was the first important jazz flutist, and his playing may be heard to advantage on Lizzie Miles's *You're such a cruel papa to me* (1928, Col. 14335D). From 1928 to 1933 he worked in orchestras for revues, during which time he made a tour of Europe. He continued to record occasionally; his clarinet and alto saxophone playing on *Big Ben* (1930, Col. 14557D) by Bennett's Swamplanders is an example of his more emotive work. From the 1930s Socarras led his own bands with such sidemen as Prince Robinson, Cecil Scott, Edgar Sampson, Cab Calloway, and Mongo Santamaria. He also worked with Benny Carter (1933), Sam Wooding (1935), and Erskine Hawkins (1937). For many years he played classical music, and in 1945 he performed as a soloist at Carnegie Hall. He continued to be active as a teacher into the 1970s.

Oral history material in *NjR* (JOHP).

BIBLIOGRAPHY

H. Friedwald: "The Alberto Socarras Story," *Sv*, no.90 (1980), 220 [interview]

based on *ChiltonW*

Society band. A type of dance band active in the early years of the 20th century; *see* BANDS, §4(i).

Sock. A hard blow, hence in jazz argot a strong accent, or to play with heavy accentuation, loudly and propulsively; "sock rhythm" or "sock style" is used of a style of playing characterized by heavy off-beat accents. A "sock chorus" is the final chorus of a lively piece, played in a hardhitting, emphatic manner (*see* FORMS, §2); the term is used chiefly of early jazz.

Sock cymbal. Name originally applied to the Charleston cymbal and used to describe a pair of pedal-operated cymbals on a low stand; later it was also applied to the hi-hat (*see* DRUM SET, §I, 5).

Socolow, Frank (*b* New York, 18 Sept 1923; *d* New York, 30 April 1981). Tenor saxophonist. In the early 1940s he played in big bands, including that led by Georgie Auld (1942). He toured and recorded with Boyd Raeburn's orchestra (1944–5), Chubby Jackson (1947–9), and Artie Shaw (1949–50); in some recordings, notably Jackson's *Tiny's Blues* (1949, Col. 38623), he played alto saxophone. Socolow continued to be associated intermittently with Raeburn (for illustration *see* RAEBURN, BOYD), recording with him again in 1948 and 1956–7. During the 1940s he also recorded with Sid Catlett (1944) and Johnny Bothwell (1945), as the leader of a bop quintet that included Freddie Webster and Bud Powell among its members (1945), and with Buddy DeFranco and Charlie Ventura (1949). From 1950 he worked as a freelance in New York, recording with Charlie Parker (1950), Sal Salvador (1953), Terry Gibbs (1955, 1956), Cecil Payne (*Patterns of Jazz*, 1957, Signal 1204), Manny Albam (1957–62), Gene Krupa (1958), Teddy Charles (1959), and Joe Morello (1961); he also recorded as a leader (*Sounds by Socolow*, 1956, Beth. 70) and played and recorded with Johnny Richards (1957–9).

Oral history material in *NjR*.

BIBLIOGRAPHY

FeatherE
Obituary, *DB*, xlviii/10 (1981), 13

Soft Machine. English jazz-rock group. It was formed in Canterbury in 1966 by the keyboard player Mike Ratledge, the drummer Robert Wyatt, the electric bass guitarist Kevin Ayers, and the electric guitarist Daevid Allen. After working in London and France the group toured the USA as a support act to Jimi Hendrix and recorded its first album in New York. Its next recording was more jazz oriented, and its third album, *Third* (1970, CBS 66246), recorded with members – including Elton Dean – of Keith Tippett's band Centipede, confirmed this new direction. Frequent changes of personnel often radically altered the character of its music, but Soft Machine was one of the most adventurous, influential, and enduring of English fusion groups. Although the early recordings are generally regarded as the group's most inventive work, it made several more albums before disbanding in 1981.

BIBLIOGRAPHY

M. Watts: "The Softs Blow Hot and Cold in Holland," *MM* (31 Oct 1970), 24
"The Soft Machine File," *MM* (9 Dec 1972), 51 [incl. individual biographies]
K. Dallas: "Soft Machine," *MM*, l (5 April 1975), 18 [incl. individual biographies]
R. Williams: "The Softs Parade," *MM*, lii (30 July 1977), 35

MARK GILBERT

SOH. Trio formed in 1978 by the tenor saxophonist Alan Skidmore, the drummer Tony Oxley, and the double bass player Ali Haurand.

Solal, Martial (*b* Algiers, 23 Aug 1927). French pianist. He studied piano with his mother, an opera singer, from the age of seven. After working locally in Algiers from 1942, he settled in 1950 in Paris, where he played with Django Reinhardt and Don Byas (recording with both in 1953), Lucky Thompson (recording in 1956, 1959, and 1961), and Kenny Clarke (recording in 1956 and 1957), and led a quartet with Sidney Bechet (recording in 1957). In 1968 he recorded with Lee Konitz in Italy and later performed with him at the Antibes–Juan-les-Pins Jazz Festival (1974), the Berliner Jazztage (1980), and the Grande Parade du Jazz (1980–81). From 1974 into the 1980s Solal and Konitz have played and recorded together as a duo and in small groups, and broadcast throughout Europe.

Solal has the rare ability to accommodate his playing to widely varying styles. He was a member of a trio with two double basses (1969–71), and has occasionally worked as leader of a big band, making several recordings (1956, 1957, 1962, 1981), broadcasting in Paris (1980), and performing at the Montreux International Jazz Festival (1984). His best music, however, has been made in a conventional trio of piano, double bass, and drums, and shows a grasp of form uncommon among improvisers; *Jordu* (from *Jazz à Gaveau*), for example, develops entirely from seemingly unimportant melodic, harmonic, and rhythmic alterations to the theme, and *Gavotte à Gaveau* (from the same LP) gradually integrates dissimilar fragments into a tight structure. Solal has also composed music for more than 20 films.

SELECTED RECORDINGS

As unaccompanied soloist: *Nothing but Piano* (1975, MPS 2022680-8); *Bluesine* (1983, SN 1060)
Duos with L. Konitz: *Duplicity* (1977, Horo 17–18)
As leader: *Martial Solal Live* (1959–85, Stefanotis Flat and Sharp 1963); *Jazz à Gaveau* (1960, Col. FPX221), incl. Jordu, Gavotte à Gaveau; *Martial Solal at Newport* (1963, RCA LSP2777); *Suite for Trio* (1978, MPS 15497); *Martial Solal Big Band* (1981, Gaumont Musique 753804)
As sideman with L. Konitz: *Impressive Rome* (1968, Campi 12003); *Jazz à Juan* (1974, Ste. 1072)

BIBLIOGRAPHY

FeatherE; *Feather '60s*; *Feather–Gitler '70s*
J.-L. Ginibre: "Autopsie dans un miroir," *Jm*, no.83 (1962), 20
M. Harrison: "Two from Solal," *JM*, no.152 (1967), 7
B. Priestley: "Postwar Pianists," in A. McCarthy and others: *Jazz on Record: a Critical Guide to the First 50 Years: 1917–1967* (London, 1968), 351
M. Williams: *Jazz Masters in Transition, 1957–69* (New York and London, 1970/R1980) [colln of previously pubd reviews], 119
J.-C. Levinson: "Quelques réflexions sur Martial Solal," *Jh*, no.287 (1972), 18
A. Dutilh: "Martial Solal," *Jh*, no.306 (1974), 16 [interview]
R. Palmer: "Pianos in the Background," *JJI*, xxxvii/11 (1984), 16

MAX HARRISON/R (text, bibliography)
ANDRÉ CLERGEAT (recording-list)

Solid State. Record label, founded around 1966 as a subsidiary of UNITED ARTISTS.

Solo Art. Record company and label. The company was established by Dan Qualey, and in 1939–40 the label was used to issue recordings of piano solos. Apart from one disc by Art Hodes these were all of boogie-woogie, including material by Meade "Lux" Lewis, Albert Ammons, Pete Johnson, Jimmy Yancey, and Cripple Clarence Lofton. 15 78 r.p.m. records were issued before the label ceased to operate; recordings by Yancey and Lofton not issued by Solo Art were made available by Riverside in the 1950s. (B. Rust: *The American Record Label Book* (New Rochelle, NY, 1978), 279)

Soloff, Lew(is Michael) (*b* New York, 20 Feb 1944). Trumpeter. He studied at the Eastman and Juilliard schools of music and played in New York with Tony Scott, Machito, Gil Evans, and the percussionist Tito Puente. In 1968 he joined Blood, Sweat and Tears, making international tours and recording with the group until 1973; he also performed with Clark Terry (at Carnegie Hall, 1970), recorded with Mongo Santamaria (1970, 1972), and played and recorded in the Thad Jones–Mel Lewis Orchestra (intermittently, 1968–76). Soloff toured and recorded with Evans from 1973 into the 1980s; in 1974 he recorded with both Robin Kenyatta and Stanley Clarke, and the following year he organized a quintet with Jon Faddis. Later he recorded the album *Stomp Off, Let's Go* with Sonny Stitt (1976, FD 1538), and also made recordings with Stanley Turrentine (1976–7), George Russell (1978, 1980), Spyro Gyra and Teo Macero (both 1983), and Franco Ambrosetti and Bill Evans (iii) (both 1985). In 1987, in a concert entitled "Ornette Coleman Celebration" at Weill Recital Hall, Carnegie Hall, he performed as the soloist in *The Sacred Mind of Johnny Dolphin*. Soloff is a highly accomplished player and has a firm, bright tone.

BIBLIOGRAPHY

J. H. Klee: "The Uses of Adversity: Lew Soloff," *DB*, xl/3 (1973), 18
M. Jones: "Solo Soloff Minus Tears," *MM*, l (11 Oct 1975), 48
A. J. Smith: "Lew Soloff: Seeking the Right Sound," *DB*, xliv/3 (1977), 14
M. Bourne: "Lew Soloff: Big Band Brass Man," *DB*, liv/9 (1987), 24 [incl. discography]

Solography. A type of Discography listing solos recorded by an individual performer.

Soloist. Any musician who plays or sings a solo. *See* Bands, §3(c); *see also* Improvisation, §2.

Solomon, Reuben (*b* Rangoon, Burma, 1918). British clarinetist. While at college in Burma in the late 1930s he organized a cooperative group, the Jive Boys. After the Japanese invaded Burma in 1942 he was evacuated to India and played as a freelance before joining Teddy Weatherford at the Grand Hotel, Calcutta; among the recordings he made with a small group from the band is *One Dozen Roses* (1942, Col. FB40231). Solomon left Weatherford at the end of 1944 and formed a new Jive Boys group, which recorded extensively, then after Weatherford's death (1945) he took some of the former's members and augmented his own group to 14 pieces. He also wrote arrangements for this new band. He emigrated to Australia after World War II and worked initially as a musician in Sydney.

BIBLIOGRAPHY

K. P. Darke: "Teddy Weatherford's Indian Recording Sessions 1941–45," *Matrix*, nos.107–8 (1975), 3
P. Darke and R. Gulliver: "Teddy Weatherford," *Sv*, no.65 (1976), 175
——: "Roy Butler's Story," *Sv*, no.71 (1977), 178

PETER DARKE

Solo-tone mute. A name under which the double mute has been manufactured; *see* Mute, §2(b).

Sommer, Günter [Baby] (*b* Dresden, Germany, 15 Aug 1943). German drummer and percussionist. He studied at the conservatory in Dresden and in 1963–70 played in bands led by the trumpeter Klaus Lenz. While playing in a trio with the reed player Friedhelm Schönfeld (1967–74) he became increasingly involved in free improvisation. In 1971–3 he played with the group SOK and in 1972 became a member of Ulrich Gumpert's Jazz-Werkstatt Orchester (later the Ulrich Gumpert Workshop Band). In 1973 he formed a duo with Gumpert and joined the cooperative quartet Synopsis which included Ernst-Ludwig Petrowsky, with whom he continued to play and record in small groups. He worked as a soloist from 1973 and also played with the organist Hans-Günther Wauer. In 1979 he formed a trio with Leo Smith and Peter Kowald and from the early 1980s worked with various groups, including ML DD 4 with Fred van Hove, Marc Charig, and the violinist Phil Wachsmann. In 1984 Sommer instigated the re-formation of Synopsis as Zentral-Quartett. He may be heard as an unaccompanied soloist on his album *Hörmusik* (1979, FMP 0790).

BIBLIOGRAPHY

R. Reichelt: "Günter Sommer: Baby Comes of Age," *JF* [intl edn], no.67 (1980), 47
B. Noglik: "Ernst-Ludwig Petrowsky, Günter Sommer," *Jazzwerkstatt international* (Berlin, 1981), 315–45 [incl. interview, discography]

BERT NOGLIK

Sonet. Record company. It was founded in 1956 by Sven Lindholm and Gunnar Bergström, who have remained its managers into the late 1980s. Another executive, Dag Haeggqvist, joined the organization in 1960; Gazell, the label he had established in 1950, became incorporated into Sonet. The company quickly expanded, setting up a subsidiary of the same name in Denmark; this in turn acquired the Danish firm Storyville, which had been active recording traditional jazz in Copenhagen from the early 1950s. The organization later established branches in England, Finland, and France, as well as publishing houses in England and Scandinavia, a film and video production company, and a fine-art division.

Sonet's catalogue offers a wide variety of music, in most styles of jazz. The company has issued albums by many notable musicians, including (on Gazell) Zoot Sims and Toots Thielemans (both 1950), Svend Asmussen (1969), Arne Domnérus (1969–70), and Rolf Ericson (1971); (on Storyville) Chris Barber (1953-4), Papa Bue (1956–77), Sahib Shihab (1971), and the quintet led by Lee Konitz and Warne Marsh (1975); (on Danish Sonet) Archie Shepp and the New York Contemporary Five (1963) and Asmussen (1978); (on Norwegian Sonet) Karin Krog (1970); (on Swedish Sonet) Lars Gullin (1953, 1958), Bengt Hallberg (1968), Thielemans (1972), Domnérus (1972–9), and Al Cohn and Zoot Sims (both 1974). The repertory also contains material reissued from many sources; this includes recordings made in Finland by Jukka Tolonen and items from the catalogues of Chiaroscuro and Roulette. In the 1980s Sonet has issued particularly important sessions by Zoot Sims (1984), and Chet Baker and Benny Carter (both 1985).

ERIK KJELLBERG

Song form. A term applied to the forms common in the refrains of popular songs and therefore in the jazz pieces based on them; *see* Forms, esp. §1(i)(a).

Sonora. Record company and label. The label was established in Sweden in 1932, and its catalogue included two swing series. The first was issued from January 1937 to December 1941 and consisted of items put out as part of the company's main series but given a distinctive label and number; the second, inaugurated in August 1940, was a separately numbered series which ran until 1948. Both were devoted mainly to the work of local musicians, but also included items recorded during visits to Sweden by Valaida Snow and Peanuts Holland. Sonora also released recordings made in Sweden by Benny Carter in 1936.

BIBLIOGRAPHY

B. Englund: *Sonora II: Swing-series* (Stockholm, 1974)
——: Liner notes, *Jubileumsskivan Sonora 50 år* (Son. 6363062, 1982)

Sønstevold, Gunnar (*b* Elverum, Norway, 26 Nov 1912). Norwegian pianist. He belonged to the Funny Boys with Kalle Engstrøm, Øivind Bergh (later replaced by the guitarist and saxophonist Finn Westbye), and the saxophonist and drummer Svein Øvergaard; with the quartet he toured Europe and made one recording in 1938 before the group disbanded in the following year. He led small groups in Norway and during World War II moved to Sweden, where he recorded with Gösta Törner and Thore Jederby. After 1945 he was largely inactive in jazz; he studied music in Vienna in 1960–67 and later became well-known in Norway as a composer of symphonic works and of music for films and the theater. Sønstevold's playing is exemplified by his recording *You got me woodooed/It Happened in Kaloha* (1940, Col. DS1219).

Oral history material in *NOnj.*

BIBLIOGRAPHY

O. Angell, J. E. Vold, and E. Økland: *Jazz i Norge* (Oslo, 1975)
K. Michelsen, ed.: *Cappelens musikkleksikon* (Oslo, 1978)

VIDAR VANBERG

Soph, Ed(ward B.) (*b* Coronado, CA, 21 March 1945). Drummer. He studied drumming in Houston, where he played informally with Arnett Cobb. While at North Texas State University (1963–8) he worked for summer seasons with Ray McKinley and Stan Kenton (1965). He toured and recorded with Woody Herman (1968–*c*1971), then returned briefly to university for graduate study. After moving to New York in 1971 he worked as a freelance, playing on Herman's album *Giant Steps* (1973, Fan. 9432), and recording with Bill Watrous (1974) and Clark Terry (1974–5). Later he recorded with Joe Henderson (1977), and in Australia with Dave Liebman and at the Monterey Jazz Festival with Herman (both 1979). From the late 1970s he has taught both privately and at colleges and workshops; he has also contributed articles about drumming to several magazines.

BIBLIOGRAPHY

Feather–Gitler '70s
M. Rozek: "Profile: Ed Soph," *DB*, xliii/11 (1976), 3
S. K. Fish: "Ed Soph: Idealist," *MD*, ix/11 (1985), 18

Sopranino clarinet. The highest member of the clarinet family in common use, normally pitched in E♭; *see* CLARINET, §§1 and 2.

Sopranino saxophone. The highest instrument of the saxophone family, normally pitched in E♭; *see* SAXOPHONE, §6(iii).

Soprano. In general musical terminology the highest vocal part or range; the word is also used as a qualifying adjective to distinguish those members of certain families of instruments (especially wind) that are pitched in that range (e.g., "soprano clarinet" is the full name of the principal member of the CLARINET family, though the qualifying adjective is not normally used in this case). In jazz argot "soprano" is used alone to mean the soprano saxophone (*see* SAXOPHONE).

Soprano clarinet. The principal member of the clarinet family, pitched in B♭, A, or C; *see* CLARINET, §§1 and 3.

Soprano saxophone. The soprano instrument of the saxophone family, normally pitched in B♭; *see* SAXOPHONE, §4.

Soprano Summit. Group led by Bob Wilber and Kenny Davern. The two musicians first played together at the Colorado Jazz Party of 1972, and worked together at intervals before forming a full-time partnership in 1974. Soprano Summit was established shortly thereafter with the addition of a rhythm section, including the guitarist Marty Grosz. The original concept of the front-line musicians was to re-create the soprano saxophone and clarinet duos of Sidney Bechet and Mezz Mezzrow, but they drew on a wider instrumentation when subsequently Wilber played alto saxophone and Davern took up the C-melody instrument. The group toured the USA and Europe; it was also the first jazz ensemble to play in South Africa to nonsegregated audiences. It made a number of recordings, including *Soprano Summit* (1973, World Jazz 5), before disbanding in 1979.

BIBLIOGRAPHY

"Soprano Summit" *Full Swing*, i/3 (1976), 3
D. Coller and B. Whyatt: "Soprano Summit Discography," *JJI*, xxxv (1982), no.4, p.22; no.5, p.43

DEREK WEBSTER

SOS. Trio formed in 1973 by the saxophonists Alan Skidmore, Mike Osborne, and John Surman.

Souchon, Edmond(, II) [Doc] (*b* New Orleans, 25 Oct 1897; *d* New Orleans, 24 Aug 1968). Guitarist and writer. He trained as a physician in Chicago, and was largely self-taught as a guitarist. He was a founding member of the Six and Seven Eighths Band, a string nonet which enjoyed considerable popularity between about 1911 and the early 1920s. In 1945 he helped to revive this group as a quartet, and made some recordings (1949, 1959) of the early repertory for string band, including *High Society* (1949, New Orleans 1000); the group continued to perform until the 1960s. Souchon often played and recorded with such prominent New Orleans musicians as Johnny Wiggs (1950, 1954–7, 1958), Sherwood Mangiapane, Papa Jack Laine (1951), Raymond Burke (1952), and Paul Barbarin (1956); he also recorded as a leader (1955, 1958, 1959).

Although not a founder of the New Orleans Jazz Club, he was an early president of the organization. He produced its weekly radio program on WWL for several years, and was the editor of its journal, *Second Line*, from 1951 until his death, contributing frequently to it under the pseudonym R. A. Tuig. He also wrote articles for periodicals such as *Jazz* and *Jazz Report* and, with Al Rose, compiled *New Orleans Jazz: a Family Album* (Baton Rouge, LA, 1967, rev. 2/1978, rev. and enlarged 3/1984). Souchon assisted in the establishment of the National Jazz Foundation in 1942 and of the New Orleans Jazz Museum in the 1950s. He owned 2000 recordings of early New Orleans jazz, which he donated to the New Orleans Public Library; his collection of materials relating to folk music and jazz is now in the William Ransom Hogan Jazz Archive at Tulane University in New Orleans (*see* LIBRARIES AND ARCHIVES, §2). ("Biographical Data on Dr. Edmond Souchon, II," *SL*, xx (1968), 97)

Soul jazz [funk, funky jazz]. A type of HARD BOP dating from the mid-1950s. Played most often in small groups led by a tenor or alto saxophonist, a pianist, or a Hammond organist, it is characterized by simple, tuneful themes and improvisations, modeled on the speech inflections of black preachers in the sanctified churches. Themes are sometimes 16 (rather than 12 or 32) bars long and are occasionally in 6/8 meter. Harmonic progressions and riffs often emphasize the subdominant, and the plagal cadence (IV–I) long associated in church music with the singing of the word "amen." In most respects, however, the definable differences between soul jazz, hard bop, and the parent style, Bop – the instrumentation, structures of tunes, melody, harmony, rhythm, and techniques of improvisation – are negligible, and the stylistic labels connote feeling and atmosphere rather than distinctive musical characteristics.

The words "soul" and "funk" describe the essential qualities of the style, which were perceived as distinguishing it from the cold, intellectualized West Coast jazz of the period. "Funk" (a black American dialect word used of the odor of the female genitalia, hence to mean "dirt") is the older term, implying earthiness; an early occurrence of the word in this sense is found in the title of a piece recorded by Horace Silver in 1953 – *Opus de Funk*. "Soul" evokes the emotional and spiritual depth of black American culture and in particular suggests links with the gospel church; "soul" was also used in titles during the 1950s, but the term "soul jazz" achieved widespread currency only from 1960, when Cannonball Adderley's quintet began to be promoted as a soul-jazz group on the Riverside label.

Other exponents of the style, which has persisted virtually unchanged into the 1980s, include Gene Ammons (late in his career), Charles Earland, Groove Holmes, Willis "Gator" Jackson, Les McCann, Brother Jack McDuff, Jimmy McGriff, Charles Mingus (in those of his performances influenced by gospel music), Harold Ousley, Don Patterson, Houston Person, Shirley Scott, Johnny Hammond, Bobby Timmons, Stanley Turrentine, and Harold Vick.

The terms "funk" and "soul" later became more widely known in connection with styles of popular music; the former was used for the hard, percussive dance rhythm invented by the singer and bandleader James Brown, and the latter for the style that blended elements of gospel and rhythm-and-blues. Once established these genres were in turn combined with jazz when fusions of jazz with other styles became fashionable. Hybrids of jazz and soul music, and of jazz and the popular style funk, however, have little in common with soul jazz.

BIBLIOGRAPHY

D. Heckman: "Soul jazz and the Need for Roots," *JM*, viii/1 (1962), 5
P. Tamony: "Funk," *Americanisms: Content and Continuum* (San Francisco, c1969)

BARRY KERNFELD

Soul Note. Record label. It was founded in 1979 in Milan by Giovanni Bonandrini as a companion to his label Black Saint. By the mid-1980s it had become extremely important; on it are issued recordings by such renowned hard-bop and free-jazz musicians as George Adams, Billy Bang, Bill Dixon, Art Farmer, and George Russell. (F. Davis: *In the Moment: Jazz in the 1980s* (New York, and Oxford, England, 1986) [colln of previously pubd articles], 206)

Sound recording. *See* Recording.

Sousaphone. A type of bass Tuba named for the American bandmaster John Philip Sousa and built in the circular shape of the helicon.

South, Eddie (*b* Louisiana, MO, 27 Nov 1904; *d* Chicago, 25 April 1962). Violinist. After extensive study of music, including a period at Chicago Musical College, he became the music director of Jimmy Wade's Syncopators in 1924. He traveled in 1928 to Europe, where he toured, and studied in Paris and Budapest. In 1931 he returned to Chicago and organized a band with Everett Barksdale and Milt Hinton that recorded for Victor. South went back to Paris in 1937, and the historic recordings he made with Django Reinhardt and Stephane Grappelli during this visit represent the peak of his output. Later he played residencies in New York, Chicago, and Los Angeles (1939), and he continued to lead his own groups during the next two decades. He performed several times on radio and television, working for WMGM in New York in 1945. He spent his last years in Chicago.

South was one of the finest classically trained violinists ever to play jazz. He had a dark tone, powerful bowing attack, and immaculate left-hand technique. At fast tempos he achieved a considerable sense of swing, whereas in slower pieces he employed a more rhapsodic style, inspired by gypsy music.

SELECTED RECORDINGS

My! Oh My!/Gotta Go! (1933, Vic. 24343); Eddie's Blues/Sweet Georgia Brown (1937, Swing 8); Dinah (1937, Swing 12); Interpretation sur le premier mouvement du Concerto en re mineur de Jean-Sebastien Bach (1937, Swing 18); *The Dark Angel of the Fiddle* (1958, Trip 5803)

BIBLIOGRAPHY

L. Feather: "Back Comes Eddie South: and he's Still a Virtuoso," *MM*, xxviii (15 Nov 1952), 3
D. Morgenstern: "Jazz Fiddle," *DB*, xxxiv/3 (1967), 16
J. Brown: Liner notes, *The Dark Angel of the Fiddle* (Trip 5803, late 1970s)
M. Glaser and S. Grappelli: *Jazz Violin* (New York and elsewhere, 1981) [incl. transcrs.]
B. Crowther: "The Forgotten Ones: Eddie South," *JJI*, xxxvi/8 (1983), 12 [incl. discography]
H. Rye: "Visiting Firemen, 8: Eddie South," *Sv*, no.108 (1983), 207

MATT GLASER

South, Harry [Henry P.] (*b* London, 7 Sept 1929). English pianist, arranger, and composer. He wrote material for Ronnie Scott's band (1954–5) and performed with Tony Crombie, Tubby Hayes, Joe Harriott, and Dizzy Reece in the mid- and late 1950s. In 1959 he formed an all-star big band and in 1960–61 worked for one year with Dick Morrissey in India; on his return to England he formed a quartet with Morrissey. He was associated for some time with the rhythm-and-blues singer Georgie Fame, with whom he recorded the album *Sound Venture* (1966, EMI SX6076) and toured (as Fame's pianist and music director), notably for two weeks with Count Basie's band; he also recorded as a leader the album *Presenting the Harry South Big Band* (1966, Mer. 20081). Later he worked as a music director for Annie Ross and wrote arrangements for Sarah Vaughan, Buddy Rich, and Jimmy Witherspoon. Thereafter South concentrated on writing music for films and television, and achieved considerable success in this field in the 1970s and 1980s.

BIBLIOGRAPHY

FeatherE
P. Gammond, ed.: *The Decca Book of Jazz* (London, 1958), 238
R. Cotterell, ed.: *Jazz Now: the Jazz Centre Society Guide* (London, 1976)

DIGBY FAIRWEATHER

Southall, Henry (Branch) (*b* Richmond, VA, 25 Aug 1931). Trombonist. After playing informally while a student he worked with Stan Kenton in 1958. He then toured and recorded from 1962 to 1966 with Woody Herman; among the recordings he made with the group is the album *My Kind of Broadway* (1965, Col. CS9157). (*Feather '60s*)

Southwest jazz. *See* Kansas City jazz.

Spanier, Muggsy [Francis Joseph] (*b* Chicago, 9 Nov 1906; *d* Sausalito, CA, 12 Feb 1967). Cornetist. He played cornet from

Members of Muggsy Spanier's Ragtime Band at the Panther Room, Hotel Sherman, Chicago, 1939: (left to right) Bob Casey (double bass), Marty Greenberg (drums), Spanier (cornet), Georg Brunis (trombone), and Rod Cless (clarinet)

the age of 13, and began his professional career in 1921 with Elmer Schoebel's band. He was first recorded in 1924, and performed with several Chicago dance bands until 1929, when he became an important member of Ted Lewis's orchestra, with which he performed in two films (1929, 1935). In 1936 he joined Ben Pollack's group, but serious illness, partly the effect of alcoholism, forced him to leave in 1938. On his recovery the following year he organized his Ragtime Band (see illustration), an eight-instrument dixieland group that included Georg Brunis and Rod Cless, with which he made a series of 16 recordings that contributed substantially to the New Orleans revival of the 1940s. The group performed in Chicago and New York but was forced to disband through lack of commercial success. Spanier briefly rejoined Lewis, led a recording group with Sidney Bechet called the BIG FOUR (1940), and played in Bob Crosby's dixieland big band (1940–41); for a short time he led his own big band, modeled on Crosby's (1941–3), but thereafter he played and recorded almost exclusively in small dixieland groups, usually as their leader and often with Earl Hines (1950s). He toured Europe in 1960 and retired in 1964.

Spanier played in a clipped middle-register style that was closer to King Oliver's than Louis Armstrong's and unusual for his generation. He was not a virtuoso soloist, but his strong, simple lead parts in the New Orleans style ideally suited the music he favored from 1939, and his recordings in that year with his Ragtime Band remain models for reinterpretive traditional jazz.

Oral history material in *LNT*.

See also BLUES, §8.

SELECTED RECORDINGS

As leader: of Bucktown Five: Mobile Blues/Someday, Sweetheart (1924, Gen. 5405); Big Butter and Egg Man (1939, Bb 10417); At the Jazz Band Ball/Livery Stable Blues (1939, Bb 10518); Relaxin' at the Touro (1939, Bb 10532); *Spanier in Chicago* (1958, VJM LC2)

BIBLIOGRAPHY

G. Hoefer: "Muggsy Still a Driving, Communicative Jazzman," *DB*, xviii/9 (1951), 2
N. Shapiro and N. Hentoff, eds.: *Hear me Talkin' to ya: the Story of Jazz by the Men who Made it* (New York and London, 1955/*R*1966), 115
L. Gushee: "Muggsy Spanier," *JR*, i/2 (1958), 40
M. Harrison: "Backlog, 15: Muggsy Spannier [sic]," *JM*, x/2 (1964), 6
R. Hadlock: *Jazz Masters of the Twenties* (New York, 1965/*R*1985)
E. Ward: "Muggsy Spanier Discography," *Jazz Register*, i–ii (1965–6)
W. Esposito: "The Spanier Big Band," *JJ*, xx/10 (1967), 10
I. Crosbie: "The Big Band Muggsy Spanier," *Coda*, xii/2 (1974), 8
A. McCarthy: *Big Band Jazz* (New York and London, 1974), 218
D. Curran: "Hear that Ragtime Band," *Selections from the Gutter: Jazz Portraits from "The Jazz Record"*, ed. A. Hodes and C. Hansen (Berkeley, CA, Los Angeles, and London, 1977), 182
A. Hubner: "Muggsy Spanier," *Selections from the Gutter: Jazz Portraits from "The Jazz Record"*, ed. A. Hodes and C. Hansen (Berkeley, CA, Los Angeles, and London, 1977), 1

J. R. TAYLOR/R

Spann, Les(lie L., Jr.) (*b* Pine Bluff, AR, 23 May 1932). Electric guitarist and flutist. While studying music education and flute at Tennessee State University (1950–57) he played with local bands. Although he is principally a guitarist, he has frequently played flute. He performed and recorded with Phineas Newborn (1957), played briefly with Ronnell Bright, then worked with Dizzy Gillespie (1958–9); in 1959 he took part in a recording session with Gillespie that produced two albums, *The Ebullient Mr. Gillespie* (Verve 6068) and *Have Trumpet, Will Excite* (Verve 6047). From 1959 to 1961 he toured Europe and recorded with Quincy Jones, and during the same period recorded with Abbey Lincoln, Ben Webster, Duke Ellington, and Johnny Hodges. Playing flute, Spann recorded in 1960 as the leader of a hard-bop quintet that included Julius Watkins and Tommy Flanagan; he also made recordings with Nat Adderley, Benny Bailey, and Randy Weston. Later he played in sessions for Curtis Fuller and Charlie Shavers (both 1961), Red Garland, Jerome Richardson, Wild Bill Davis, and Charles Mingus (all

1962), Duke Pearson (1965), Sonny Stitt and Eddie "Lockjaw" Davis (both 1966), and Hodges (1967).

BIBLIOGRAPHY

FeatherE
M. C. J.: "Les Spann," *Jm*, no.61 (1960), 29 [incl. discography]

Spargo, Tony. *See* SBARBARO, TONY.

Sparks, Ernie. Pseudonym of DAVID BEE.

Spasm band. An ensemble consisting largely of homemade instruments. Spasm bands were active in New Orleans during the first three decades of the 20th century, and performed a repertory of blues, ragtime, and the popular songs of the day. They generally included a chord-playing instrument, such as a ukulele or guitar, a kazoo or comb-and-paper, and various percussion instruments – for example, washboard or tambourine. Some instruments associated with the "second line" of marching bands (the popular following that accompanied street parades) were also used, notably the boom-bam, a broom handle on which metal bottle-tops are nailed to give an effect similar to that of the metal discs in the shell of a tambourine. (D. Barker: *A Life in Jazz*, ed. A. Shipton, London and New York, 1986)

Spaulding, James (Ralph, Jr.) [Jimmy] (*b* Indianapolis, 30 July 1937). Alto saxophonist and flutist. He studied music from 1957 in Chicago, where he also performed and recorded with Sun Ra. From 1962 he worked in New York with his own group, and also with Freddie Hubbard (with whom he recorded, 1963–9), Max Roach, Randy Weston, Art Blakey, and others. Spaulding has been active mainly as a sideman from 1970, playing with a variety of musicians, among them Horace Silver, Bobby Hutcherson, Budd Johnson, Milt Jackson, and Bob Wilber, but he has performed occasionally as the leader of his own small ensembles. In 1975 he received a BA from Livingston College, Rutgers. Spaulding is a highly creative hard-bop soloist, and has a fiery, driving style on alto saxophone; his flute playing is light and lyrical. From 1976 he has recorded only rarely, but the album *Ashanti* (1981) by the drummer Alvin Queen includes some particularly good examples of his playing.

SELECTED RECORDINGS

As leader: *James Spaulding Plays the Legacy of Duke Ellington* (1976, Sto. 1019)
As sideman: F. Hubbard: *Breaking Point* (1964, BN 84172); *Backlash* (1966, Atl. 1477); H. Mobley: *A Slice of the Top* (1966, BN LT995); W. Shaw: *Woody III* (1978, Col. JC35977); A. Queen: *Ashanti* (1981, Nilva 3402)

BIBLIOGRAPHY

Feather '60s; *Feather–Gitler '70s*
D. C. Hunt: "James Spaulding: for Spee's Sake," *J&P*, no.12 (1968), 23
D. Wallace: "James Spaulding," *JJ*, xxiii/4 (1970), 6

ROLAND BAGGENAES

Speers, Stewie [Speer, Stewart] (*b* Melbourne, Australia, 26 June 1928; *d* Sydney, 16 Sept 1986). Australian drummer. In the late 1950s he became known for his abilities in several styles; he played traditional jazz with Roger Bell, Bob Barnard, Frank Traynor, and others as well as performing in a more modern idiom with Brian Brown at Jazz Center 44 in Melbourne. Later, in Sydney, he worked at El Rocco with groups led by John Sangster, Judy Bailey, the pianist Col Nolan, Don Burrows, and others. In 1967 he joined a rock group, Max Merritt and the Meteors, and toured the UK, where he later performed with Alexis Korner. He returned in 1980 to Sydney, where he remained active, playing with several important musicians.

BIBLIOGRAPHY

A. Bisset: *Black Roots, White Flowers: a History of Australian Jazz* (Sydney, 1979)
B. Johnson and others: *The Oxford Companion to Australian Jazz* (Melbourne, Australia, 1987)

JEFF PRESSING (with JOHN WHITEOAK)

Spencer, O'Neill [William] (*b* Cedarville, OH, 25 Nov 1909; *d* New York, 24 July 1944). Drummer. He first performed with Al Sears in Buffalo (1930), and then worked with several well-known jazz bands and leaders, including the Mills Blue Rhythm Band (1931–6), Henry "Red" Allen (recording 1935 and 1936), John Kirby's sextet (1937–41), and Mildred Bailey (recording 1938–42); he played washboard and drums on several recordings with Johnny Dodds and his Chicago Boys in 1938. Later in the same year he recorded with his own trio, which included Buster Bailey (clarinet) and Billy Kyle (piano). He also worked as a singer during this period, making recordings with Kirby, Dodds, Jimmie Noone (1937), the organist Milt Herth (1937–9), and Andy Kirk and Noble Sissle (both 1938), as well as with his own trio. Towards the end of his career he played briefly with Louis Armstrong's big band (1941) and again with Kirby (1942). Spencer's drumming style was accurate and disciplined, especially in his work with large groups, where his fills were subtle and imaginative.

For illustrations *see* KIRBY, JOHN, and MILLS BLUE RHYTHM BAND.

SELECTED RECORDINGS

As leader: Afternoon in Africa (1938, Decca 1873); Baby, won't you please come home (1938, Decca 1941)
As sideman: Mills Blue Rhythm Band: Ridin' in Rhythm (1933, Col. CB734); M. Herth: The Dippsy Doodle/That's a Plenty (1937, Decca 1553); J. Dodds: Wild Man Blues (1938, Decca 2111); J. Kirby: Close Shave (1941, Vic. 27568)

BIBLIOGRAPHY

ChiltonW; *FeatherE*

T. DENNIS BROWN

Sperling, Jack (*b* Trenton, NJ, 17 Aug 1922). Drummer. He performed and recorded in New York with Bunny Berigan (1941–2), and during military service played in a navy band led by Tex Beneke (1943–5); he continued to tour and record with Beneke until 1949. He then played in and around Los Angeles with Les Brown (1949–53), Bob Crosby (1954–7, 1960), Dave Pell's octet (1953, 1955, 1957) and Pete Fountain (1959–63); his work may be heard to advantage on Crosby's album *The Bob Cats in Hi Fi* (1957, Coral 57170) and *I Had the Craziest Dream* (1955–7, Cap. T925), recorded with Pell. Sperling also recorded with Eddie Miller (*c*1957), Benny Goodman (1960), Charlie Barnet (1962, 1966), Bob Florence (*c*1968), and again with Brown (1963, 1974, and at the Aurex Jazz Festival, Tokyo, 1983).

BIBLIOGRAPHY

FeatherE
T. Borst: "Portraits: Jack Sperling," *MD*, vii/3 (1983), 68

Sphere. Bop quartet. It was organized in the early 1980s by the tenor saxophonist Charlie Rouse, the pianist Kenny Barron, the double bass player Buster Williams, and the drummer Ben Riley. Its activities were intended to commemorate the work of Thelonious (Sphere) Monk, and its first album, *Four in One* (1982, Elek. Mus. 60166), was devoted entirely to Monk's music. Thereafter the members added their own compositions to the group's repertory. Sphere recorded again in 1983, 1985, and 1987 (for further details *see* WILLIAMS, BUSTER); the 1985 album is a recording of a concert the group gave in Italy. (J. Levenson: "Sphere: Monk and Beyond," *DB*, li/1 (1984), 22)

Spikes' Seven Pods of Pepper. Recording group. In spring 1922, under the direction of the Spikes Brothers agency and using the name Spikes' Seven Pods of Pepper, Kid Ory's Original Creole Jazz Band became the first black jazz band to record commercially. Ory's group had been active on the West Coast (first as Kid Ory's Brownskinned Babies) from 1919. The personnel for the recording band consisted of Ory (trombone), Mutt Carey (cornet), Freddie Washington (piano), Ed "Montudi" Garland (double bass), Ben Borders (drums), and Dink Johnson, a pianist and drummer who had recently taken up clarinet and replaced Ory's usual clarinetist, Wade Whaley. The sextet recorded only two titles, *Ory's Creole Trombone* and *Society Blues* (1922, Nordskog 3009), but during the same session, as Ory's Sunshine Orchestra, it made a further four as the accompanying band for the singers Roberta Dudley and Ruth Lee.

BIBLIOGRAPHY

R. MacNic: "Reb Spikes: Music Maker," *Sv*, no.21 (1969), 100
P. Vacher: Liner notes, D. Johnson: *Dink's Good Time Music* (Nola 12, 1977)

MIKE HAZELDINE

Spill. A GLISS falling from the end of a note.

Spirits of Rhythm. String band. It grew out of a group known variously as the Sepia Nephews, Ben Bernie's Nephews, and the Five Cousins, which included the tiple players Wilbur and Douglas Daniels, and (from 1929) the singer and tiple player LEO WATSON. After the ensemble was augmented in 1932 by the addition of the guitarist Teddy Bunn it changed its name to the Spirits of Rhythm, and first recorded under this title the following year; a fifth member, Virgil Scoggins, played various homemade percussion instruments. The band worked successfully on 52nd Street, New York, in Hollywood, and on tours, becoming one of the most influential string bands of the decade (*see* STRING BAND); it was noted for its driving rhythmic style and good-humored songs (often with comic or nonsensical lyrics), and may be heard to advantage on such recordings as *I got rhythm/Rhythm* (1933, Bruns. 01715). The Spirits of Rhythm remained active until 1946; at various times it included Wellman Braud, Marlowe Morris, and Zutty Singleton. In 1934 it made recordings accompanying Red McKenzie. (M. Jones: "Teddy Bunn, the Spirit of Rhythm," *The Spirits of Rhythm, 1933–34* (JSP 1088, 1985) [liner notes])

See also TIPLE.

FRANK DRIGGS

Spivak, Charlie [Charles] (*b* Kiev, Ukraine, 17 Feb 1907; *d* Greenville, SC, 1 March 1982). Trumpeter and bandleader. He arrived in the USA as a small child and grew up in New Haven, Connecticut, where he began to learn trumpet at the age of 10. Between 1924 and 1931 he worked mostly with an orchestra led by the violinist Paul Specht. Although he was not a jazz musician, Spivak was in great demand among jazz bandleaders during the 1930s for his sweet tone and wide range, and his playing enlivened the trumpet sections of Ben Pollack (1931–4), the Dorsey Brothers (1934), Ray Noble (1935), Bob Crosby (1937–8), Tommy Dorsey (1938–9), and Jack Teagarden (1939); in 1936–7 he was the highest-paid studio musician in New York. In November 1939 Glenn Miller financed Spivak's first orchestra; this soon disbanded, but his second group, which included such sidemen as Dave Tough (1941–2) and Willie Smith (1943), prospered until 1959, when it broke up. Spivak, who was billed as "the sweetest horn in the world," enjoyed great popularity as the result of his band's success. After working in Florida, Las Vegas, and South Carolina he led a new orchestra on a tour of the South in the late 1970s.

SELECTED RECORDINGS

As leader: Let's Go Home (1941, OK 6366); Autumn Nocturne (1941, OK 6476); Star Dreams (1941, OK 6546); *The Uncollected Charlie Spivak* (1943–6, Hindsight 105)

As sideman: G. Miller: Time on my Hands (1937, Bruns. 7915); B. Crosby: South Rampart Street Parade (1937, Decca 15038)

BIBLIOGRAPHY

ChiltonW
G. T. Simon: *The Big Bands* (New York, 1967, rev. and enlarged 2/1971, 4/1981), 426
C. Garrod: *Charlie Spivak and his Orchestra* (Spotswood, NJ, and Zephyrhills, FL, 1974, rev. 2/1986) [discography]
Z. Knauss: *Conversations with Jazz Musicians* (Detroit, 1977), 178
G. Buck: "Charlie Spivak," *Jazzology Newsletter*, viii/3 (1982), 2

SCOTT YANOW

Spivey, Victoria (Regina) (*b* Houston, 15 Oct 1906; *d* New York, 3 Oct 1976). Singer and pianist. The daughter of the leader of a string band, she learned piano as a child and by the age of 12 was performing at the Lincoln Theatre in Dallas. After working with local artists, including the blues singer and guitarist Blind Lemon Jefferson, she commenced her recording career in St. Louis; *Black Snake Blues*, to her own piano accompaniment, was an instant success. Her voice was lean and nasal and she made much use of moaned syllables. A partnership in the late 1920s with Lonnie Johnson produced many notable titles. In 1929 Spivey appeared in *Hallelujah!*, an all-black film directed by King Vidor, and also recorded several titles with Henry "Red" Allen's New York Orchestra. She toured with her husband, the dancer Billy Adams, in the 1930s; she also worked with Louis Armstrong, and occasionally made recordings – often of a mildly risqué nature – such as *Good Cabbage*. In the 1940s she settled in New York, where she continued to perform in jazz clubs. In 1962 she formed her own Spivey record company and recorded a number of well-known singers as well as her own works, reviving an old partnership with Johnson on *Somebody's got to go*. Her voice remained strong and her vivacious stage personality undiminished even in her last years.

SELECTED RECORDINGS

As leader: Black Snake Blues (1926, OK 8338); T. B. Blues (1927, OK 8494); Murder in the First Degree (1927, OK 8581); Moaning the Blues (1929, Vic. 38546); Good Cabbage (1937, Voc. 03639); *The Queen and her Knights* (1965, Spivey 1006), incl. Somebody's got to go

As sideman with H. Allen: Funny Feathers Blues (1929, Vic. 38088)

BIBLIOGRAPHY

"Blues Elpees on the Spivey Label," *JM*, xi/7 (1965), 25
P. Garon and A. O'Neal: "Victoria Spivey, 1906–1976," *Living Blues*, no.29 (1976), 5
S. Harris: *Blues Who's Who: a Biographical Dictionary of Blues Singers* (New Rochelle, NY, 1979)
D.D. Harrison: *Black Pearls: Blues Queens of the 1920s* (New Brunswick, NJ, 1988)

PAUL OLIVER

Splash cymbal. A small cymbal used for special and novelty effects; *see* DRUM SET, §I, 5.

Spontaneous Music Ensemble. British free-jazz group. It was founded as a cooperative band in 1965 at the Little Theatre Club, London, by the drummer John Stevens and the saxophonist Trevor Watts. Stevens has worked consistently with the group into the 1980s, providing a connecting thread through its many changes in personnel. Watts left temporarily in 1967; singers were first included in 1969, but the group was pared down to a duo (Stevens and Watts) in 1973, and later worked for a time as the 20-piece Spontaneous Music Orchestra (from 1975). Among its members have been the guitarist Derek Bailey, the trumpeters Ian Carr and Kenny Wheeler, the double bass players Barry Guy and Dave Holland, the saxophonist Evan Parker, the trombonist Paul Rutherford, and the singers Maggie Nicols, Julie Tippetts, and Norma Winstone. One of the finest free-jazz bands, the Spontaneous Music Ensemble performs its group improvisations in a nonlinear, often abstract, style, frequently involving intimate dialogues between the musicians, as may be heard on its album *Karyöbin* (1968, Isl. 9079). (M. Harrison: "The Spontaneous Music Ensemble," *J&B*, ii/12 (1973), 8)

For further bibliography *see* STEVENS, JOHN.

SIMON ADAMS

Spotlite (i). The name of several nightclubs, notably one in New York; *see* NIGHTCLUBS AND OTHER VENUES.

Spotlite (ii). Record company and label. The company was established by Tony Williams (who should not be confused with the drummer of the same name) in 1968. Though originally based in London, in 1974 it moved to Sawbridgeworth, Hertfordshire. Its first release (in a limited pressing of 99 copies) was of broadcasts by Billy Eckstine's orchestra; this was followed by the comprehensive reissue (on six LPs) of all the available material recorded by Charlie Parker for Dial. Eventually the company rereleased Dial's entire catalogue, and made further contributions to the collecting and organizing of Parker's material when it compiled sets of his recordings made in Sweden, France, and the USA. A great deal of broadcast material from the 1940s and 1950s has been issued in a well-received series, Jazz off the Air. In 1973 Spotlite began making new recordings; the first of these was an album made in London by Pepper Adams. During the 1970s the company was largely responsible for rekindling interest in such bop musicians as Joe Albany, Al Haig, and Red Rodney; it has also provided an important outlet for the work of such English musicians as Peter King and Don Rendell. Some of the company's sessions have been sponsored by the Arts Council of Great Britain. By 1987 Spotlite had issued more than a hundred LPs (most of which remain in the catalogue), and had become one of the most successful enterprises of its kind.

MARK GARDNER

Spring, Bryan (*b* London, 24 Aug 1945). English drummer. He was largely self-taught, though he later studied with Philly Joe Jones. In the early 1960s he worked as a freelance musician in London, then joined Stan Tracey, with whom he played and recorded between 1965 and 1977; he can be heard to advantage on Tracey's album *Bracknell Connection* (1976, Steam 103). During the same period he performed and recorded with Frank Ricotti (1967–9), Joe Harriott (1969), the Bebop Preservation Society led by Bill Le Sage (1971), Klaus Doldinger's Passport (1972), and Nucleus (1974). From 1975 he worked again as a freelance and led his own bands; he also toured with Hannibal Peterson, and, in 1979, became joint leader with the tenor saxophonist Don Weller of the Weller–Spring Quartet, with which he recorded the same year. Spring has performed with such musicians as Jean-Luc Ponty, Tubby Hayes, Joe Williams, Charlie Shavers, George Coleman, and Charlie Rouse. (R. Cotterell, ed.: *Jazz Now: the Jazz Centre Society Guide* (London, 1976), 169)

DIGBY FAIRWEATHER

Springer, Joe [Joseph] (*b* New York, 22 May 1916). Pianist. He first played professionally in 1931 in Coney Island, New York. In 1935 he worked with Wingy Manone, and in 1940 he played at the Hickory House with Louis Prima, with whom he made his recording début. He then joined Buddy Rich and performed and made recordings (including *That Drummer's Band*, 1942, Col. 36819) with Gene Krupa (1942–3). Thereafter he worked with Oscar Pettiford, Tiny Grimes, Ben Webster, Charlie Barnet, Jimmy McPartland, and others; in the mid-1940s he was also a regular accompanist for Billie Holiday. In 1952 Springer played briefly with Rich, and during the 1960s he worked as a freelance in New York before moving to Florida.

based on *ChiltonW*

Sproles, Victor (*b* Chicago, 18 Nov 1927). Double bass player. After private musical study, followed by army service, he worked as house double bass player at the French Poodle, Chicago. He then took up a residency at the Bee Hive, where as a member of Norman Simmons's trio (with Vernel Fournier) he played with such visiting performers as Charlie Parker and Wardell Gray (both 1955), Sonny Stitt, Lester Young, and Dexter Gordon. After the club closed in 1956 he recorded with Stan Getz (1958) and toured and recorded with Johnny Griffin and Eddie "Lockjaw" Davis (both 1960). He then toured Europe and Japan with Carmen McRae (recording in 1963–4); Simmons was also one of McRae's sidemen during this time. For two periods between 1964 and 1968 Sproles worked with Art Blakey's Jazz Messengers, again touring Europe and Japan; he also recorded with Lee Morgan (1965, 1967) and Andrew Hill (1968). In 1969 he began a long association with Clark Terry, with whom he performed at the Montreal Expo and toured Europe in 1975. He played with Simmons again in 1981 at the Chicago Kool Jazz Festival, and, with other musicians who had formerly worked at the Bee Hive (including Clifford Jordan), the two men recorded the album *Hyde Park after Dark* in celebration of the club's heyday.

SELECTED RECORDINGS

As sideman: R. Rodney: *Modern Music from Chicago* (1955, Fan. 3208); I. Sullivan: *Nicky's Tune* (1958, Del. 422); L. Morgan: *The Rumproller* (1965, BN 84199); C. Terry: *Ain't Misbehavin'* (1979, PT 2312105); Hyde Park after Dark: *Hyde Park after Dark* (1981, BH 7014)

BIBLIOGRAPHY

Feather–Gitler '70s

J. L. Ginibre and P. Carles: "Dictionnaire de la contrebasse," *Jm*, no.166 (1969), 56

J. Litweiler: Liner notes, *Hyde Park after Dark* (BH 7014, 1983)

WILLIAM S. BROCKMAN

Spyro Gyra. Jazz-rock group, formed in 1975 by the soprano and alto saxophonist Jay Beckenstein and the pianist Jeremy Wall. From the following year the group also included the electric guitarist Chet Catallo, the electric bass guitarist David Wolford, the drummer Eli Konikoff, and the percussionist Gerardo Velez; Wall was soon replaced by the keyboard player Tom Schuman, but he continued to work with the group as a producer, composer, arranger, and studio pianist. Other studio musicians have also played with the group on its recordings, notably Dave Samuels, who by 1986 had become a full member. Spyro Gyra acquired a loyal following in Buffalo soon after the group was formed, and its first recording, issued on an independent label, achieved considerable commercial success.

Its second album, *Morning Dance* (1979), became popular with rock audiences, but the group's emphasis on instrumental music rather than songs prevented it from achieving widespread exposure on radio. Much of the ensemble's popularity, therefore, was generated by means of performances. During the 1970s Spyro Gyra undertook several long, demanding tours of small clubs across the USA; by the end of the decade it had gained enough of an audience to fill the major concert halls. During the 1980s the group toured the world, performed at the Kool and JVC festivals in New York, among others, and continued to record with substantial success. Beckenstein's mellifluous playing and Wall's production have consistently helped to define Spyro Gyra's sound, which is characterized by funk and Latin rhythms, and structures derived from those of popular songs.

SELECTED RECORDINGS

(recorded for MCA unless otherwise indicated)

Spyro Gyra (1976, Amherst 1014); *Morning Dance* (1979, Infinity 9004); *Catching the Sun* (1980, 5108); *Carnaval* (1980, 5149); *Freetime* (1981, 5238); *Incognito* (1982, 5368); *City Kids* (1983, 5431); *Access All Areas* (1983, 6893); *Alternating Currents* (1986, 5606); *Breakout* (1986, 5753); *Stories with Words* (1987, 42046)

BIBLIOGRAPHY

J. H. Hunt: "Spyro Gyra," *DB*, xlvi/8 (1979), 33
J. Aikin: "Tom Schuman and Jeremy Wall: Synthesizers and Smokebombs with Spyro Gyra," *Keyboard*, vii/8 (1981), 16
P. Rothbart: "Spyro Gyra: Relaxin' at 30,000 Volts," *DB*, xlviii/10 (1981), 14 [incl. discography]
G. Santoro: "The Spyro Gyra Interview," *DB*, liii/9 (1986), 20 [incl. discography]

PATRICK T. WILL

Squadronaires. English dance band. It was formed in 1940 as the principal dance orchestra of the RAF and comprised musicians from leading English dance bands. Among its original personnel were George Chisholm, Tommy McQuater, the saxophonist Andy McDevitt, the pianist Ronnie Aldrich, and the drummer Jock Cummings. It broadcast regularly on radio and made recordings for Decca (e.g., *That's a Plenty*, 1941, Decca F8127); its repertory included a number of big-band versions of well-known dixieland numbers. By 1947 the Squadronaires had become a civilian orchestra; it continued performing and recording under the leadership of Aldrich until it disbanded in 1964.

Oral history material in *GBLnsa* ("Miller, Jimmy").

BIBLIOGRAPHY

"There's Something in the Air," *Fanfare*, iv/6 (1946), 4
A. McCarthy: *The Dance Band Era: the Dancing Decades from Ragtime to Swing, 1910–1950* (London, 1971), 142
T. Middleton: *The Squadronaires R. A. F. Dance Orchestra: an Exploratory Discography, 1940–1945* (London, 1976)

NEVIL SKRIMSHIRE

Squires, Bruce (W.) (*b* Berkeley, CA, 21 Jan 1910; *d* North Hollywood, CA, 8 May 1981). Trombonist. He first played in the early 1930s with lesser-known bands. From 1935 to 1937 he was with Ben Pollack; among the recordings he made with the group are *Spreadin' knowledge around/Zoom zoom zoom* (1936, Voc. 3342), issued under the name the Dean and his Kids. Thereafter Squires played with Jimmy Dorsey (1937–8), Gene Krupa (1938–9), Benny Goodman (1939), Harry James (1939–40), Freddie Slack (1940–41), and Bob Crosby (1942). After World War II he worked mainly as a studio musician, and continued to perform into the 1970s.

based on *ChiltonW*

Stabulas, Nick [Nicholas] (*b* New York, 18 Dec 1929; *d* nr Great Neck, NY, 6 Feb 1973). Drummer. After working as a commercial musician he performed and recorded in New York with Phil Woods (1954–7); good examples of his solo playing may be heard on the tracks *Be my love*, *Woodlore*, *Get Happy*, and *On a slow boat to China* on Woods's album *Woodlore* (1955, Prst. 7018). He also took part in a number of sessions with such musicians as Jon Eardley (1955–6), Jimmy Raney (1955, 1957), Eddie Costa, Friedrich Gulda (both 1956), George Wallington (1956–7), Al Cohn (1956–7, 1960), Zoot Sims, Gil Evans (both 1957), Mose Allison (1957–8), and Carmen McRae and Don Elliott (both 1958). Later he worked with Chet Baker, Kenny Drew, and Bill Evans (ii), and in 1964 participated in a concert led by Lennie Tristano at the Half Note that was recorded and broadcast. Stabulas continued to work into the 1970s, but was killed in an automobile accident. (*FeatherE*; *Feather–Gitler '70s*)

Stacy, Jess (Alexandria) (*b* Bird's Point, MO, 11 Aug 1904). Pianist. He was largely self-taught, gaining his first professional experience on riverboats during the early 1920s. He moved in the mid-1920s to Chicago, where he worked sporadically with such established musicians as Muggsy Spanier and Frank Teschemacher. He was most influential as the pianist with Benny Goodman's orchestra (1935–9). His highly personal style was technically precise and rhythmically incisive, containing elements derived from the playing of both Earl Hines and Teddy Wilson. His first solo recordings, made in 1935, include the earliest recorded versions of Bix Beiderbecke's *Flashes* and *In the Dark*. Stacy continued working and recording with popular big bands throughout the 1940s, including those led by Bob Crosby, Horace Heidt, Tommy Dorsey, and Goodman. He moved to California in 1947 and played mostly in bars, where the work was unrewarding, until the late 1950s when he ceased to be a professional musician. However, since his reappearance at the 1974 Newport Jazz Festival New York, where he was highly acclaimed, he has continued to perform in public occasionally. A volume of transcriptions of his work, *Piano Solos*, was published in 1944.

Oral history material in *LNT*, *NjR*.

SELECTED RECORDINGS

As unaccompanied soloist: In the Dark/Flashes (1935, Para. 2233); Candlelights/Ain't goin' nowhere (1939, Com. 517); *Stacy Still Swings* (1974, Chi. 133)

As sideman with B. Goodman: *Carnegie Hall Concert* (1938, Col. SL160), incl. Sing, sing, sing

BIBLIOGRAPHY

"Is Jess Stacy the Greatest White Pianist?," *Music and Rhythm*, ii/6 (1941), 84
R. Hadlock: "The Chicagoans," *Jazz Masters of the Twenties* (New York, 1965/R1985), 106
W. Balliett: "Back from Valhalla," *Improvising: Sixteen Jazz Musicians and their Art* (New York, 1977) [colln of previously pubd articles], 97
L. Feather: "Piano Giants of Jazz: Jess Stacy," *CK*, v/3 (1979), 68
D. Coller: "Jess Stacy: the Recent Past," *MR*, xi/9 (1984), 16
B. Rusch and K. D. Rusch: "Jess Stacy: Interview," *Cadence*, xii/5 (1986), 8
L. D. Holmes and J. W. Thomson: *Jazz Greats: Getting Better with Age* (New York, 1986) [colln of interviews]

BILL DOBBINS

Stafford, George (*b* c1898; *d* New York, spring 1936). Drummer. After performing with Sam Wooding in Atlantic City, New Jersey, he moved to New York, where he accompanied his sister, the singer Mary Stafford. Around 1920 he joined Charlie Johnson's band in Atlantic City; he played regularly with Johnson until shortly before he died and made several recordings with him (1925–9, including *Walk that Thing*, 1928, Vic. 21712).

He also recorded with Eddie Condon (1929), Henry "Red" Allen (1935), and Mezz Mezzrow (1936), among others. (E. Condon and T. Sugrue: *We Called it Music: a Generation of Jazz* (New York, 1947/*R*1985), 186)

based on *ChiltonW*

Stage band. A term used in American schools as a synonym for "big band"; *see* BANDS, esp. §§4(ii) and (iii).

Stahl, David (*b* Reading, PA, 23 Jan 1949). Trumpeter. After receiving a BS in music education from the Pennsylvania State University (1970) he played in an army band in Washington. Between 1973 and 1975 he toured and recorded as a lead trumpeter with Woody Herman; he is heard to advantage on the tracks *Superstar* and *Montevideo* on Herman's *The Herd at Montreux* (1974, Fan. 9470). Later he worked with Count Basie (1975, 1980) and recorded as a leader the LP *Anaconda* (1987, Abeecake 1001), including *Scream Machine*, in which he plays in a full-bodied, high-pitched melodic style after the manner of Maynard Ferguson. (*Feather–Gitler '70s*)

Stamm, Marvin (Louis) (*b* Memphis, 23 May 1939). Trumpeter and flugelhorn player. He began to learn trumpet formally at the age of 12 and later studied at North Texas State University (BMus 1961); in his final year at college he also worked briefly with Buddy Morrow and Stan Kenton. In spring 1961 he joined Kenton's Mellophonium Orchestra, and his concise, tightly muted trumpet tone may be heard to great effect on many of the band's finest recordings from the early 1960s. He remained with Kenton for two years and later worked with Woody Herman (1965–6). Stamm then embarked on a career as a studio musician in New York, playing as a member of the Thad Jones–Mel Lewis Orchestra (1966–72) and with Duke Pearson (1967–70). He recorded mainly with studio big bands, but in 1968 he made several recordings with smaller groups, including a sextet led by Frank Foster; he also played in a sextet called Jazz for a Sunday Afternoon which included Chick Corea, Richard Davis, and Elvin Jones. Stamm led his own quartet intermittently during the 1970s, and from autumn 1974 to mid-1975 he worked with Benny Goodman. Although from the mid-1960s he has been most active as a session musician, he has retained an enthusiasm for jazz performance. He was a founding member of the American Jazz Orchestra in 1986, and the following year he toured as a soloist with George Gruntz's Concert Jazz Band.

SELECTED RECORDINGS

As leader: *Machinations* (1968, Verve 68759); *Stammpede* (1982, PAlt 8022)
As sideman: S. Kenton: *Sophisticated Approach* (1961, Cap. ST1674); *Adventures in Blues* (1961, Cap. ST1985); *Adventures in Time* (1962, Cap. ST1844); W. Herman: *Jazz Hoot* (1966, Col. CS9352)

BIBLIOGRAPHY

Feather '60s; *Feather–Gitler '70s*
B. Houston: "Marvin Stamm: Not Just an Up-tempo Specialist," *MM* (19 March 1966), 8
M. Rozek: "Marvin Stamm: Technical Magic/Subtle Persuasion," *DB*, xliii/8 (1976), 19
G. Kalbacher: "Trumpetman Marvin Stamm: Business before Pleasure," *DB*, li/2 (1984), 29 [incl. discography]

STAN WOOLLEY

Standard. A composition, usually a popular song, that becomes an established item in the repertory; by extension, therefore, a song that a professional musician may be expected to know. Standards in jazz include popular songs from the late 19th century (e.g., *When the saints go marching in*), songs from Broadway musicals and Hollywood films by composers such as George Gershwin, Jerome Kern, Harold Arlen, Irving Berlin, Cole Porter, and Richard Rogers, and tunes newly composed by jazz musicians (e.g., Thelonious Monk's *Round Midnight*, Dizzy Gillespie's *A Night in Tunisia*, and John Coltrane's *Giant Steps*). Jazz musicians themselves, however, distinguish further between these categories, referring to the first as comprising dixieland standards, the second as unqualified or mainstream standards, and the last as jazz standards; it is the consensus that the essential repertory of standards is comprehended within the mainstream category. Many jazz performances are based on standards, taking not only the melody but also the harmonies of the entire piece, or more often the refrain only, as the theme (*see* FORMS, esp. §1); part of the impact of a performance based on a standard derives from its being familiar to the listeners, who are the better able to appreciate skillful arrangement and inventive improvisation because they know the original work.

ROBERT WITMER

Stańko, Tomasz (*b* Rzesźow, Poland, 11 July 1942). Polish trumpeter. He formed the quartet Jazz Darings in 1962 with Adam Makowicz (later replaced by Janusz Muniak); this was one of the first European groups to be influenced by Ornette Coleman. He played with Krzysztof Komeda (1963–7) and Andrzej Trzaskowski (mid-1960s), then led the Tomasz Stańko Quintet (1968–73), which included Muniak and Zbigniew Seifert and received considerable critical acclaim. In 1970 he performed with the Globe Unity Orchestra; later he worked with Michal Urbaniak. From 1974 to 1978 he played in a quartet with Edward Vesala; thereafter he performed again as a leader, and in 1980 recorded as an unaccompanied soloist in India at the Taj Mahal and the Karla Caves temple. In addition to occasional solo engagements (from 1978) he played in the group Heavy Life with Chico Freeman, James Spaulding, and others (1980), performed with Jack DeJohnette and Rufus Reid (both 1983), belonged to Cecil Taylor's big band (1984), and formed his own group Freelectronic (1985). Technically Stańko is highly accomplished; he plays a form of free jazz that displays both European and American influences.

SELECTED RECORDINGS

As unaccompanied soloist: *Music from Taj Mahal and Karla Caves* (1980, Leo 011)
As leader: *Music for K* (1970, Muza 0607); *Balladyna* (1975, ECM 1071)
As sideman: K. Komeda: *Astigmatic* (1965, Muza 0298); G. Peacock: *Voice from the Past* (1981, ECM 1210)

BIBLIOGRAPHY

Feather–Gitler '70s
K. Czyz: "Tomasz Stańko: Hat-trick," *JF* [intl edn], no.33 (1975), 41 [incl. discography]

BERT NOGLIK

Stapleton, Bill [William John] (*b* Blue Island, IL, 4 May 1945; *d* 1984). Trumpeter and arranger. He studied music at North Texas State University (1963–7, 1971), where he was a member of a student band. From 1972 to 1974 he worked with Woody Herman, playing trumpet and flugelhorn, and his style is well represented on *The Raven Speaks* (1972, Bellaphon 19132); he also arranged five pieces for the album *Giant Steps* (1973, Fan. 9432), including the title track. Stapleton later worked with Neal Nefti (1974) and Bill Holman (1974–5), and performed with Herman at the Concord Jazz Festival (1981). (*Feather–Gitler '70s*)

Stark, Bobby [Bobbie; Robert Victor] (*b* New York, 6 Jan 1906; *d* New York, 29 Dec 1945). Trumpeter. He studied alto horn, piano, and reed instruments before taking up trumpet. He played with Chick Webb intermittently (1926–7), then worked with Fletcher Henderson (November 1927 to early 1934; for illustration *see* HENDERSON, FLETCHER), though in 1932 he spent a brief period with Elmer Snowden; he was Henderson's principal trumpet soloist for about a year until Rex Stewart joined the band. After a brief period with Charlie Turner's Arcadians he returned to Webb (July 1934; for illustration *see* WEBB, CHICK), and remained with the band under Ella Fitzgerald (1939–40). He served in the army, then worked with Garvin Bushell and, in September 1944, joined Benny Morton's sextet.

Stark's early playing was craggy and full of bravura, marked by a staccato attack and daring melismas, which, though they were often unsuccessful musically, were somewhat redeemed by deft turns of phrase. The spectacular work he produced in 1928 was very similar to that of Jabbo Smith during the same period. From the early 1930s his solos had a lissome smoothness that was sometimes reminiscent of Bill Coleman's playing; there was more intensity in his work which, along with his phrasing and figuration (of, for example, *King Porter's Stomp*, 1933), influenced Roy Eldridge, especially in his early work with Henderson. Long lines spun from a motif were characteristic of Stark's playing and his invention became more artfully dazzling as time went on; a good example of his improvisation is provided by *Squeeze me* (1937). In the late 1930s he used smears and heightened rubato and his low register gained an attractive sibilant resonance. His late work resembled Harry Edison's in style.

SELECTED RECORDINGS

As sideman: Chocolate Dandies: Bugle Call Rag/Dee Blues (1930, Col. 2543D); F. Henderson: My sweet tooth says I wanna (1931, Vic. 22786); Honeysuckle Rose (1932, Col. 2732D); King Porter's Stomp (1933, Voc. 2527); H. Henderson: Rhythm Crazy (1933, Parl. R1743); C. Webb: Clap hands! Here comes Charley (1937, Decca 1220); Squeeze me (1937, Decca 1716); Spinnin' the Webb (1938, Decca 2021); Liza (1938, Decca 1840)

BIBLIOGRAPHY

ChiltonW
W. C. Allen: *Hendersonia: the Music of Fletcher Henderson and his Musicians: a Bio-discography* (Highland Park, NJ, 1973)
A. McCarthy: *Big Band Jazz* (New York and London, 1974), 267

BOB ZIEFF

Starr. Record label. It was established by the Starr Piano Co. of Richmond, Indiana, which was the parent company of the label GENNETT. The company's first records were issued using the Starr label in 1915. The name was maintained by the Starr Co. of Canada, originally a record distributing business, which in mid-1919 began issue on its own label Starr; these records were pressed in Canada by Compo. A considerable quantity of jazz from Gennett's catalogue was issued on Canadian Starr, with a heavy emphasis on more popular styles. Issues were also made of material from other American labels, but the link with Gennett ended late in 1925 when Canadian Starr was purchased by Compo, which transferred the operation from London, Ontario, to Toronto.

BIBLIOGRAPHY

J. Kidd: "Canadiana: the Starr–Gennett Story," *Matrix*, no.59 (1965), 13; no.61 (1965), 9
B. Rust: *The American Record Label Book* (New Rochelle, NY, 1978), 282
A. Robertson: "Canadian Gennett and Starr–Gennett 9000 Numerical," *Record Research*, nos.195–6 (1983), 1; nos.197–8 (1983), 7; nos.199–200 (1983), 10; nos.201–2 (1983), 10; nos.203–4 (1983), 8

Starr, Kay [Starks, Kathryn La Verne] (*b* Dougherty, nr Sulphur, OK, 21 July 1922). Singer. She joined Joe Venuti at the age of 13 and remained with his band until 1939, when she sang briefly with Glenn Miller and Bob Crosby. She was known initially for her deep-voiced blues style. Between 1943 and 1945 she performed and recorded with Charlie Barnet; she also recorded with Wingy Manone (1944) and made the track *If I Could Be with You* (1945, Cap. 10031) with the Capitol Jazzmen (an all-star group that included Bill Coleman, Buster Bailey, Benny Carter, Max Roach, Coleman Hawkins, and Nat "King" Cole). Starr achieved great popularity from the mid-1940s, and performed on her own television show. She recorded as a leader accompanied by Venuti, Barney Bigard (both 1946), Red Norvo (1947), Red Nichols (1947, 1949), Ben Webster (1961), and Count Basie (1968). After working only occasionally for several years she performed with small swing groups in London (1983) and New York (1985).

BIBLIOGRAPHY

FeatherE
G. Giddins: "A Starr is Reborn," *VV*, xxx (12 Nov 1985), 48

Stateside. Record label, operated from 1962 to 1974 by EMI; it was used specifically to issue in the UK material first put out in the USA by American independent companies. It was revived in 1986.

State Street Ramblers. Name used by several informally organized bands that recorded for the Gennett label. Their repertory reflected the music played at rent parties on Chicago's South Side. The bands were formed by the pianist Jimmy Blythe, who took part in all their recording sessions: one in August 1927 with the drummer Baby Dodds, the clarinetist Johnny Dodds, and the cornetist Natty Dominique, during which three tracks were recorded; two in February and April of 1928 with the alto saxophonist Joe Walker and the washboard player W. E. "Buddy" Burton; two in July 1928 with the clarinetist Angelo "Alvin" Fernandez, the alto saxophonist Baldy McDonald, the double bass player Bill Johnson, and the drummer Clifford "Snags" Johnson, during which 16 tracks were recorded (these were probably influenced by the recordings that Doc Poston made with Jimmie Noone); and two on 17 and 20 March 1931 with the trombonist Roy Palmer, the drummer Jasper Taylor, the kazoo player Alfred Bell, the clarinetist Darnell Howard, and the banjoist Ed Hudson, during which 17 tracks were recorded. Blythe frequently used the same groups, or much the same ones, to record for rival companies: thus sessions by the Dixieland Thumpers (for Paramount, 1927), the CHICAGO FOOTWARMERS (for Okeh, 1927), and J. C. Cobb's Grains of Corn (for Vocalion, 1928) often took place within weeks of those of the State Street Ramblers; sometimes these groups even recorded the same material. Little Brother Montgomery also led a band called the State Street Ramblers in the mid-1970s.

SELECTED RECORDINGS

The Weary Way Blues/Cootie Stomp (1927, Gen. 6232); My Baby/Pleasure Mad (1928, Gen. 6454); Barrel House Stomp/Kentucky Blues (1931, Champion 16320)

BIBLIOGRAPHY

C. Hillman and M. Tovey: "Chicago South Side, 1927–1932," *Sv*, no.124 (1986), 14; no.130 (1987), 124

MIKE HAZELDINE

Staton, Dakota [Rabia, Aliyah] (*b* Pittsburgh, 3 June 1932). Singer. After performing in clubs in the USA and Canada she began recording in 1954. She achieved critical success and popular acclaim for her album *The Late, Late Show* (1957, Cap. T876), on which she performed standards and scat solos accompanied by a swing sextet that included Jonah Jones and Hank Jones. She also recorded with George Shearing (1957), performed at Town Hall, New York (1959), toured with Benny Goodman (*c*1960), and recorded at the Newport Jazz Festival (1963). Staton moved to England in 1965 and sang with Kurt Edelhagen's big band at the Deutsches Jazz Festival, Frankfurt am Main, in 1968. In the 1970s she returned to the USA, where she recorded two soul-jazz and gospel-oriented albums (*c*1972, 1973). She has continued to perform into the 1980s.

BIBLIOGRAPHY

FeatherE; *Feather-Gitler'70s*
J. Olsson: "Man måste vara trogen sin publik: Dakota Staton," [One must truly love one's public: Dakota Staton], *Orkester journalen*, xlv/11 (1977), 6
L. Dahl: *Stormy Weather: the Music and Lives of a Century of Jazzwomen* (London, Melbourne, Australia, and New York, 1984), 155

Stauffer, Teddy [Stauffifere, Ernest Henry] (*b* Morat am Murtensee, Switzerland, 2 May 1909). Swiss bandleader. He played saxophone and violin in and around Berne in 1927, and in 1929 he began performing in Germany with his own band under the name Teddy and his Band; the group was first billed as the Original Teddies in June 1929. In the early 1930s Stauffer led the band on transatlantic steamships and he rose to prominence in 1936 through its performances in Berlin and its highly successful recording *Goody Goody* (1936, Tel. 478). They toured Germany and Switzerland and recorded prolifically until the outbreak of World War II, when Stauffer settled in Zurich. In 1939 he formed a new group under the name the Original Teddies (also known as the Teddies and the International Teddies), which he led in performances and on a large number of recordings (including *Stop, It's Wonderful*, 1940, ES 4007) until 1941. He then moved to Acapulco de Juárez, Mexico, where he became a nightclub owner; although he ceased full-time performing he recorded in Mexico (1944, 1950), Los Angeles (1946), and Zurich (1947). In the 1960s and 1970s he worked in radio and television studios in London and Berlin.

BIBLIOGRAPHY

T. Stauffer: *Es war und ist ein herrliches Leben* (Berlin, Frankfurt am Main, Germany, and Vienna, 1968)
O. Flückiger: "Zur Geschichte der Schweizer Jazz- und Hot-Dancebands," *Jazz + Classic* (Muttenz, Switzerland), v/6 (1978), 14; vi/4 (1979), 13
J. Schütte and A. Stöcklin: *Teddy Stauffer: Discographie der Original Teddies (Teddy Stauffer und Eddie Brunner) und der kleinen Formationen mit Musikern der Teddies* (Menden, Germany, 1983)
W. J. Stock: "Teddy Stauffer: Swing ist ein guter Rhythmus," *JP*, xxxii/2 (1983), 16

RAINER E. LOTZ

Steam. Record label established in 1965 by STAN TRACEY.

Stearns, Marshall W(inslow) (*b* Cambridge, MA, 18 Oct 1908; *d* Key West, FL, 18 Dec 1966). Writer. He learned to play drums before attending Harvard University as an undergraduate (BS 1931) and law student (1932–4), then studied medieval English literature at Yale University (PhD 1942) and began contributing articles to *Down Beat*; during the following decades he taught English literature at several universities while continuing to write about jazz. In 1950 he received a Guggenheim Fellowship to begin work on *The Story of Jazz* (1956), a historical survey that became widely used. Stearns founded the INSTITUTE OF JAZZ STUDIES in 1952 and later became its first executive director; he also taught music at the New School for Social Research (1954–66) and was a consultant in the 1950s to the US State Department and the Voice of America. In 1956 he accompanied Dizzy Gillespie's band on a tour of the Middle East sponsored by the State Department.

See also LIBRARIES AND ARCHIVES, §2.

WRITINGS

(selective list)

The Story of Jazz (New York, 1956, rev. and enlarged 2/1958, enlarged 1970; Ger. trans., Munich, 1959; Dan. trans., Copenhagen, 1962; Port. trans., São Paulo, 1964)
with J. Stearns: *Jazz Dance: the Story of American Vernacular Dance* (New York and London, 1968/*R*1979)

DANIEL ZAGER

Steckar, Marc (*b* Cherbourg, France, 1 June 1935). French bass trombonist and tuba player. After studying music he played with the drummer Benny Bennett (1958), Aimé Barelli (1959), the Dixieland Stompers led by the trumpeter Jack Jay (1961), the trombonist Raymond Fonsèque, the pianist Jacques Denjean (1962), the trumpeter Sonny Grey (1967, 1980), Slide Hampton, and the trumpeter Ivan Jullien (from 1970). He recorded a solo tuba album in 1978, and played with Martial Solal, the Caratini–Fosset Onztet (1980–83), the double bass player Bob Quibel (1981–5), the pianist Patricio Villaroel (1982), Michel Portal (1983), and a brass quintet led by the trumpeter Bernard Marchais (1984). He has formed tuba ensembles, including Tubapack (1981), which enjoyed considerable success; his playing is well represented on the album *En concert: turbanisation* (*c*1984, Ida 001). (F. Billard: "Les voix graves de Marc Steckar," *Jm*, no.305 (1982), 36)

MICHEL LAPLACE

Steel drum. A tuned percussion instrument, usually made from an oil drum, that developed in Trinidad during the 1930s and 1940s. The head of a steel drum contains several depressions, each of which produces a different pitch; the instrument is played with rubber-headed sticks. The steel drum came to be used occasionally in jazz in the late 1970s; its best-known exponent has been Andy Narell, who usually plays steel drum solos over Latin jazz and jazz-rock ostinatos, and who sometimes also uses the instrument in highly chromatic bop passages, such as those that occur in Victor Feldman's *Seven Steps to Heaven*, recorded by Narell on his first album, *Hidden Treasure* (1979, IC 1053).

BARRY KERNFELD

Steele, Joe [Joseph A.] (*b c*1900; *d* New York, 5 Feb 1964). Pianist. After studying at the New England Conservatory, he performed and recorded with the Savoy Bearcats (1926). He worked with the banjoist Henri Saparo at the Bamboo Inn, New York (1927), and led his own band there in the late 1920s; among his sidemen were Ward Pinkett, Langston Curl, Jimmy Archey, Charlie Holmes, Joe Garland, and Frank Smith. He made a number of recordings as a leader, including *Top and Bottom* (1929, Vic. 38066). As a member of the trumpeter Pike Davis's orchestra he toured with the show *Rhapsody in Black* (1931–2). He later performed mainly with Chick Webb (1932–6), with whom he also recorded (1933–4). (A. McCarthy: *Big Band Jazz*, New York and London, 1974)

based on *ChiltonW*

Steeplechase. Record company and label. The company was established by Nils Winther in Copenhagen in 1972, and that year issued its first LP, recorded by Jackie McLean at the Montmartre Jazzhus. From that time Winther developed one of the leading European bop-oriented catalogues. Its main series, by

1987 numbering well over 200 albums, contains material recorded in both Copenhagen and New York; especially well represented are Dexter Gordon, Walt Dickerson, Tete Montoliu, Clifford Jordan, Duke Jordan, Kenny Drew, and Niels-Henning Ørsted Pedersen. The catalogue includes several other brief series, which consist of reissues or first issues of material recorded (chiefly by Gordon and Bud Powell) between 1959 and 1965; an isolated session recorded in 1946 under Don Redman's leadership; three albums recorded direct-to-disc; and several blues recordings. To facilitate sales in the USA, Winther established the company Steeplechase Productions in Chicago in 1978. Within Denmark, Steeplechase has also served as a distributor for other important European labels, including ECM, Enja, Circle (iii), and Black Saint. (G. Rouy: "Nils Winther: Steeplechase ou sept ans de production," *Jm*, no.286 (1980), 28)

Stefański, Janusz (*b* Kraków, Poland, 14 June 1946). Polish drummer. He studied percussion at the Fryderyck Chopin school of music and at the High School of Music in Kraków (graduating in 1972). He first performed with Zbigniew Seifert, the pianist and trombonist Jan Jarczyk (1965), and Tomasz Stańko (1967). From 1969 he worked in the orchestra of the Polish Radio Jazz Studio under Jan Wróblewski (recording in 1969); he also performed and recorded with Stańko (1970–73), Hans Koller's Free Sound (1973–6), Seifert's Various Spheres (1975–6), and Zbigniew Namysłowski (1976–8). In 1978 Stefański formed the cooperative group The Quartet with Tomasz Szükalski (tenor and soprano saxophone), and Namysłowski's former sidemen Slawomir Kulpowicz (piano) and Pawel Jarzebski (double bass); he is heard to advantage on its album *Loaded* (1979, Leo 010). During the late 1970s and early 1980s he worked in Austria, playing and recording with Koller (1979–80) and the Vienna Art Orchestra (1981), and occasionally touring with Leszek Zadlo's Polski Jazz Ensemble (1983, 1985).

BIBLIOGRAPHY

J. Byrczek: "Eurojazz Personalities: Poland," *JF* [intl edn], no.18 (1972), 87
K. Brodacki: "Janusz Stefanski: 'I Envy Horn Players'," *JF* [intl edn], no.66 (1980), 42 [incl. discography]

WOLFRAM KNAUER

Stegmeyer, Bill [William John] (*b* Detroit, 8 Oct 1916; *d* Long Island, NY, 19 Aug 1968). Clarinetist. After playing and working as a staff arranger for the dance-band leader Austin Wylie (1937) he played alto saxophone and clarinet with Glenn Miller (1938), did radio work in Detroit, and performed and recorded with Bob Crosby (1939–40). From 1942 he was in New York, where he worked as an arranger and played and recorded with Billy Butterfield (1944–7) and Yank Lawson (1944–5). He also made recordings with Bobby Hackett (1943, 1946), Una Mae Carlisle (1944), as a leader (*Sentimental Journey/Frantic Rhapsody*, 1945, Sig.15014), and with Pearl Bailey and Billie Holiday (both 1945–7). From 1948 to 1950 he was staff arranger for a radio station in Detroit, and from 1950 to 1958 he arranged popular music for the television show "Hit Parade" in New York. During the same period Stegmeyer played clarinet in a band led by Lawson and Bob Haggart (1951–4, 1959–60, 1965); he may be heard playing a duet feature with Peanuts Hucko on *Lover* on the group's album *All Star Jazz Concert* (1954, Decca 8151-2). He also recorded with Jimmy McPartland (1953, 1955–7), Will Bradley (1953), and Ruby Braff (1956). During the 1960s he worked as a staff conductor at CBS. (*ChiltonW*; *FeatherE*)

Steig, Jeremy (*b* New York, 23 Sept 1943). Flutist. He began playing recorder at the age of six, studied flute from the age of 11, and started playing professionally when he was 15. His career was interrupted in 1962 by a motorcycle accident, but he made his recording début (as a leader) the following year, and in 1966 played with the popular singer Tim Hardin. From 1967, when he formed Jeremy and the Satyrs (one of the first bands consistently to play jazz-rock), he has led groups of his own; he has also collaborated frequently with Eddie Gomez.

Steig has turned gradually from playing harmonically sophisticated standards, such as *Willow weep for me*, to a style of melodic improvisation that is modally oriented. His desire to encompass a variety of sounds has led him to play all the instruments in the flute family, to exploit a wide range of performance techniques, and to make use of such electronic devices as the ring modulator and the wa-wa pedal.

SELECTED RECORDINGS

Duos with E. Gomez: *Outlaws* (1976, Enja 2098)
As leader: *Flute Fever* (1963, Col. CS8964), incl. Willow weep for me; *Jeremy and the Satyrs* (1967, Rep. 6282); *Monium* (1974, Col. KC32579); *Firefly* (1977, CTI 7075); with E. Gomez: *Rain Forest* (1980, CMP 12)

BIBLIOGRAPHY

A. Heineman: "Jeremy and the Satyrs: Potential Unlimited," *DB*, xxxv/12 (1968), 17
W. Diehans: "Jeremy Steig," *JP*, xxviii/5 (1979), 14

DAVID FLANAGAN

Stein, Johnny [John (Hountha); Hountha, Philip John, Jr.] (*b* New Orleans, 15 June 1891 or 1895; *d* New Orleans, 30 Sept 1962). Drummer. In 1915 he formed a band in New Orleans, the other members of which were Alcide "Yellow" Nuñez, Eddie Edwards, Henry Ragas, and Nick LaRocca, and in March 1916 took it to Chicago to play a long engagement at the Schiller Café. Edwards, Ragas, and LaRocca left him to form the Original Dixieland Jazz Band in May that year; afterwards Stein claimed that the credit for their success belonged to him because he had brought the nucleus of the group together. After their departure he organized a new band to fulfill his contract at the Schiller Café. He then moved to New York to join the pianist Jimmy Durante's Original New Orleans Jazz Band, with which he played during 1918–19; he returned to the band (by now known as Jimmy Durante's Jazz Band) in 1920, and took part in its recording *Why Cry Blues* (1920, Gen. 9045). He continued to perform as a leader and with other bands in New York and Chicago before returning to New Orleans in 1961.

BIBLIOGRAPHY

H. O. Brunn: *The Story of the Original Dixieland Jazz Band* (Baton Rouge, LA, 1960/*R*1977)
Obituary, *SL*, xiv/3–4 (1963), 9

KARL KOENIG

Stein, Lou(is) (*b* Philadelphia, 22 April 1922). Pianist. He played informally with Buddy DeFranco, Charlie Ventura, and Bill Harris (i) before joining Ray McKinley's band in 1942. In the mid-1940s he played with Glenn Miller's Army Air Force Band in the USA, but did not tour abroad with the group. After rejoining McKinley and recording with him (1946–7) he worked with Ventura, with whom he recorded his composition *East of Suez* (1947, Nat. 9048). During the 1950s he played in a variety of styles, including dixieland, bop, and popular music; he performed and recorded with Yank Lawson and Bob Haggart (1951–60) and Billy Butterfield (1954), and made recordings with Kai Winding (1951–2), Benny Goodman and Sarah Vaughan (both 1952), the Sauter–Finegan Orchestra (1952–3, 1958), Neal Hefti (1952–4), Joe Newman (1954), Louie Bellson (1955–6), Edgar

Sampson (1956), Peanuts Hucko (1956–7), Henry "Red" Allen and Coleman Hawkins (both 1957), and Lester Young (1958). He also recorded several times as a leader (1954–6). A good example of his solo playing may be heard on the album *Session at Riverside* (1956, Cap. T761), recorded with an all-star group. Although Stein played little jazz during much of the 1960s, he later recorded and toured Europe with Joe Venuti (1969, 1971–2), and recorded as a leader (from 1971), as an unaccompanied soloist (from 1976), in a duo with McKinley (1981), and with Flip Phillips (1981), Nick Fatool (1987), and Lawson and Haggart (1987). (*FeatherE*)

Stellio, Alexandre [Alexandre, Fructueux Stellio] (*b* L'Anse du Four, nr Les Trois-Ilets, Martinique, 16 April 1885; *d* Paris, 24 July 1939). Martinique clarinetist and bandleader. He moved with his orchestra to Paris in May 1929 and that year recorded six sides for Odeon (including *Sêpent maigre*, Odeon 165794). A pioneer of Creole music, he continued to work as a leader and made more than 100 recordings with such soloists as the trombonist Archange St. Hilaire and Ernest Léardée. Although Stellio's clarinet playing has been compared with that of Johnny Dodds, his style remained deeply rooted in the Creole traditions of the French Antilles. He was also active as a composer.

BIBLIOGRAPHY

A. Boulanger: Liner notes, *Jazz and Hot Dance in Martinique* (Harl. 2018, 1985)

"Fructueux Stellio Alexandre dit Alexandre Stellio: une liste exploratoire de ses compositions," *La Gidouille/CMH-info*, no.1 (1987), 6; no.2 (1987), 12

RAINER E. LOTZ

Stenson, Bobo [Bo Gustav] (*b* Västerås, Sweden, 4 Aug 1944). Swedish pianist and composer. After beginning his career in jazz with the Swedish tenor saxophonist Börje Fredriksson (recording in 1966–7) he toured Africa with Stan Getz (1968) and played with Red Mitchell (1968–71, recording in 1969) and Jan Garbarek (1973–6, recording as a leader with Garbarek the album *Dansere*, 1975, ECM 1075). With Palle Danielsson he formed Rena rama in 1971; this was among the first jazz groups in Europe to incorporate into its playing elements of folk music, in particular that of Bulgaria and India. In the 1970s he formed the group Oriental Wind with the Turkish drummer Okay Temiz, which performed at the Jazzyatra festival in Bombay in 1980. Later he recorded an album with the Karnataki College of Percussion that combined jazz with the classical music of south India.

BIBLIOGRAPHY

A. Westin: "Bobo Stenson," *Orkester journalen*, xliv/1 (1976), 10

J. Scherwin: "Bobo Stenson," *Dagens nyheter* (8 March 1984), 9

E. Kjellberg: *Svensk jazzhistoria: en översikt* [Swedish jazz history: an overview] (Stockholm, 1985), 249

PEKKA GRONOW

Steps Ahead. Group formed under the name Steps in 1979 by the vibraphonist Mike Mainieri. It grew from informal associations among studio musicians in New York, who had toured together and played in jam sessions; the other original members were the tenor saxophonist Mike Brecker, the keyboard player Don Grolnick, the double bass player Eddie Gomez, and the drummer Peter Erskine. The group toured Japan and recorded three albums there. In 1983 Grolnick was replaced by the pianist Eliane Elias, who performed with the group, now known as Steps Ahead, on its album of the same name (the first it made in the USA). Elias was in turn replaced in 1984 by the keyboard player Warren Bernhardt, whose expert synthesizer playing defined to a large degree the sound of the group's successful album *Modern Times* (1984). Gomez and Bernhardt left the group later the next year; they were replaced by various studio musicians, who performed on the album *Magnetic* (1986), a commercially oriented recording. By late 1986 Brecker was co-leader of the quintet, which included Mike Stern (electric guitar), Darryl Jones (electric bass guitar), and Steve Smith (drums). Steps Ahead's repertory is characterized by a spare texture that shows to advantage the virtuoso playing of the group's members.

SELECTED RECORDINGS

Smokin' in the Pit (1979, Better Days YB7010–11); *Step by Step* (1980, Better Days YF7020); *Steps Ahead* (1983, Elek. Mus. 60168); *Modern Times* (1984, Elek. Mus. 60351); *Magnetic* (1986, Elek. 960441-1)

BIBLIOGRAPHY

H. Mandel: "Steps Ahead," *DB*, l/8 (1983), 18 [incl. discography]

M. Gilbert: "Mike Mainieri," *JJI*, xxxvii/12 (1984), 10 [interview]

PATRICK T. WILL

Stereo(phonic) recording. A term applied to techniques of sound recording (and playback) that produce the effect of sound coming from different directions in three-dimensional space; *see* Recording, esp. §I, 3(iii).

Stern, Mike [Michael] (*b* Boston, *c*1954). Electric guitarist. He listened to rock and blues as a youth, and was influenced by the guitarists B. B. King, Jimi Hendrix, and Eric Clapton. While attending the Berklee College of Music, where he was a pupil of Pat Metheny and Mick Goodrick, he became interested in jazz. In 1976 Metheny recommended him for a vacancy with Blood, Sweat and Tears, and Stern remained with this group for two years. Later he worked with Billy Cobham (1978), then joined Miles Davis's new band (1981). After leaving Davis in 1983 Stern played with Jaco Pastorius's group Word of Mouth. Around this time he made his first recordings as a leader, and in 1985 he toured again with Davis. He has also worked with Steps Ahead and in bands led by Harvie Swartz and Mike Brecker.

See also Blues, §13.

SELECTED RECORDINGS

As leader: *Upside Downside* (*c*1985, Atl. 81656)

As sideman: M. Davis: *The Man with the Horn* (1980–81, Col. FC36790); *We want Miles* (1981, Col. C2-38005); *Star People* (1982–3, Col. FC38657); H. Swartz: *Urban Earth* (1985, Gram. 8503); *Smart Moves* (1986, Gram. 8607)

BIBLIOGRAPHY

H. Mandel: "Profile: Bill Evans, Mike Stern, and Mino Cinelu," *DB*, xlviii/11 (1981), 52

B. Milkowski: "Mike Stern: Bebop Rocker with Miles Davis," *GP*, xvi/11 (1982), 113

J. Chambers: *Milestones*, ii: *The Music of Miles Davis since 1960* (Toronto, Buffalo, and London, 1985)

J. Ferguson: "Mike Stern: the Jazz Voice of the Late '80s?," *GP*, xxi/3 (1987), 56 [incl. discography]

B. Milkowski: "Mike Stern's New Lease on Life," *DB*, liv/8 (1987), 28 [incl. discography]

BILL MILKOWSKI

Stevens, John (William) (*b* Brentford, England, 10 June 1940). English drummer. He played drums from the age of 17, belonged to an orchestra in the RAF with Trevor Watts and Paul Rutherford (1958–63), and from 1963 worked in London. With Watts he formed the Spontaneous music ensemble late in 1965, which from January 1966 performed regularly in London, undergoing many changes in size and membership; among those who worked with the ensemble were Rutherford, Derek Bailey, Evan Parker, Kenny Wheeler, Julie Tippetts, and the double bass players

John Ryan and Jeff Clyne. He also belonged to Watts's group Amalgam and worked with Stan Tracey, Dudu Pukwana, John Tchicai, and such rock musicians as John Lennon and Yoko Ono. In the mid-1970s he formed a jazz-rock band, Away, and in the mid-1980s led Freebop, a 12-piece band that included Bobby Bradford, Evan Parker, and Peter King as sidemen.

SELECTED RECORDINGS

As leader: of Spontaneous Music Ensemble (with others): *Challenge* (1966, Eyemark 1002), *Karyöbin* (1968, Isl. 9079), *So, what do you Think?* (1971, Tangent 118); of Amalgam: *Amalgam Plays Blackwell and Higgins* (1972, A Records 002); of Away: *Integration* (1978, RR 009)

BIBLIOGRAPHY

V. Schonfield: "Rule Brittania?," *DB*, xxxv/14 (1968), 24
R. Williams: "Total Honesty is John's Motivation," *MM* (27 March 1971), 12
——: "Stevens: Getting in a Jam," *MM* (22 July 1972), 14
I. Carr: *Music Outside: Contemporary Jazz in Britain* (London, 1973), 39
A. Turner: "John Stevens: Spontaneous Music," *The Wire*, no.1 (1982), 30; no.2 (1982), 30
I. Carr: "Stevens, John William," in I. Carr, D. Fairweather, and B. Priestley: *Jazz: the Essential Companion* (London, 1987)

ED HAZELL

Stevenson, George (Edward) (*b* Baltimore, 20 June 1906; *d* New York, 21 Sept 1970). Trombonist. He studied saxophone and trombone and performed locally with his Baltimore Melody Boys. In 1928 he moved to New York, where he played trombone with many musicians, including Charlie Johnson (1932–3), Rex Stewart (1934), Fletcher Henderson (1935), Claude Hopkins (1936), Ovie Alston (1937), and Lucky Millinder (1939–43). In the mid- to late 1940s he worked with Cootie Williams and Roy Eldridge (both 1944), and Cat Anderson (1947). As a freelance (from 1948) he performed with such players as Tony Parenti, Chris Columbus, Don Redman, and Sy Oliver. His playing is particularly well represented by *Trombone Blues* (on *The Price is Right*, 1956, Jzt. 1260), which he recorded while on tour in Europe with Sammy Price's Blusicians (1955–6). After returning to the USA Stevenson made recordings with Willie "the Lion" Smith (1957) and Stewart (1958) and led his own band in Wantagh, New York (late 1950s). In the 1960s he performed with Joe Thomas (iv), Lem Johnson, Max Kaminsky, and others. (*ChiltonW*; *FeatherE*)

Stevenson, Tommy [Steve] (*b c*1914; *d* New York, Oct 1944). Trumpeter. In 1933 he joined Jimmie Lunceford, with whom he made a number of recordings (1933–4). After leaving Lunceford in 1935 he performed and recorded with Blanche Calloway (1935–6) and Don Redman (1939–40). He worked with Slim Gaillard's small group and Coleman Hawkins's big band (from 1940) and later worked with Lucky Millinder and Cootie Williams. His playing may be heard on Lunceford's *Stomp it Off* (1934, Decca 712). (A. McCarthy: *Big Band Jazz*, New York and London, 1974)

based on *ChiltonW*

Steward, Herbie [Herbert] (*b* Los Angeles, 7 May 1926). Tenor and alto saxophonist. Early in his career he recorded with Barney Kessel (1945) and performed and recorded in the big bands of Artie Shaw (1944–6) and Alvino Rey (1946). He was an original member of Woody Herman's Second Herd (formed 1947) and played one of the solos on the first recording of *Four Brothers* (1947). After leaving Herman in 1948 he worked as a freelance, then played with Shaw (1949), and with the orchestras of Tommy Dorsey, Elliot Lawrence (1950–51), and Harry James (1951–4). In the mid-1950s he moved to Las Vegas, where he worked in orchestras accompanying shows; he later played film music in Hollywood. From that period he performed and recorded jazz only occasionally: he played on the album *Four Brothers Together Again* (1957) with three other former sidemen of Herman's and recorded again with Kessel. Steward is renowned for his versatility and exceptional sight-reading; his playing is cool and restrained and his phrasing is notable for its clarity and simplicity.

SELECTED RECORDINGS

As leader: *Passport to Pimlico* (1950, Roost 515); with S. Chaloff, A. Cohn, and Z. Sims: *Four Brothers Together Again* (1957, Vik 1096)
As sideman: W. Herman: Four Brothers (1947, Col. 38304); B. Kessel: *Barney Plays Kessel* (1975, Conc. 9)

BIBLIOGRAPHY

FeatherE; *Feather '60s*
A. Morgan: "Woody's Tenors," *JM*, vi (1960), no.7, p.4; no.8, p.13; (1961), no.12, p.9
J. A. Treichel: *Woody Herman and the Second Herd, 1947–1949* (n. p., 1978), 13 [discography]

DAVE GELLY

Stewart, Bob (*b* Sioux Falls, SD, 3 Feb 1945). Tuba player. He played trumpet from the age of ten and studied trumpet, then tuba, at the Philadelphia College of the Performing Arts (1962–6). After teaching in public schools he played traditional jazz at Your Father's Moustache in Philadelphia and in 1968 moved to New York; the same year he became an original member of the tuba ensemble Gravity. He worked with Carla Bley (from 1968), Frank Foster's Loud Minority (from 1968), the orchestras of Sam Rivers and Gil Evans (from 1968), small groups led by Arthur Blythe (from 1973), the Globe Unity Orchestra (from 1978), David Murray's big band (from 1983), and Lester Bowie's Brass Fantasy (from 1984), and he continued all these associations into the late 1980s; he also played with Charles Mingus (1971), McCoy Tyner (1973), and Henry Threadgill's orchestra (1986). Stewart has an unusual command of the tuba throughout the instrument's range; he constructs bass lines of great rhythmic and melodic complexity.

SELECTED RECORDINGS

As sideman: Jazz Composer's Orchestra: *The Jazz Composer's Orchestra* (1968, JCOA 1001–2); A. Blythe: *The Grip* (1977, IndN 1029); C. Bley: *European Tour 1977* (1977, Watt 8); A. Blythe: *Bush Baby* (1977, Adelphi 5008); G. Evans: *Gil Evans Live at the Royal Festival Hall* (1978, RCA PL25209); Globe Unity Orchestra: *Intergalactic Blow* (1982, Japo 60039)

BIBLIOGRAPHY

L. Jeske: "Profile: Bob Stewart," *DB*, xlvii/12 (1980), 48
B. Case: "Jazz: Tuba or Not Tuba," *MM*, lvii (9 Jan 1982), 23

ED HAZELL

Stewart, Buddy (*b* Derry, NH, 1922; *d* New Mexico, 1 Feb 1950). Singer. As a child he had a successful career in vaudeville. He later worked in a vocal trio and, after moving to New York, in a duo with Martha Wayne, whom he married; in the early 1940s they both sang in the vocal groups associated with the bands of Glenn Miller and Claude Thornhill. With Dave Lambert and Gene Krupa's band Stewart made the first vocal recording in the bop style – *What's this?* (1945). He continued to be associated with Lambert and two other fellow sidemen in Krupa's group, Charlie Ventura and Red Rodney: in 1946, under Rodney's leadership, Stewart and Lambert recorded *Wahoo*, a wordless variant on the tune *Perdido*, and in 1947 Stewart was a principal soloist with Ventura's ensemble (he was also voted "leading band vocalist" by *Down Beat*). The following year Kai Winding left Ventura to form his own group and Stewart went with him; in 1949 he sang with Charlie Barnet's band and performed again with Lambert and Winding. He was killed in an automobile accident. Although Stewart was known for his warm interpretation of ballads, his major contribution to jazz lies in his pioneering efforts in bop vocalese, both alone and with Lambert.

SELECTED RECORDINGS

As leader: If Love is Trouble/Hee haw (1948, SiW 515); Laughing Boy/Shawn (1948, SiW 512)

As sideman: G. Krupa: What's this? (1945, Col. 36819); A tender word will mend it (1945, Col. 36846); D. Lambert: Perdido (Wahoo) (1946, Key. 657); C. Ventura: Synthesis (1947, Nat. 9036); Pennies from Heaven (1947, Nat. 9077); first issued on C. Parker: *What's this?* (1949, SCAM 3), Deedle, What's This?; C. Barnet: Bebop Spoken Here (1949, Cap. 640)

BIBLIOGRAPHY

FeatherE

LAWRENCE KOCH

Stewart, Louis (*b* Waterford, Ireland, 5 Jan 1944). Irish electric guitarist. A visit to New York in 1961 with a showband led by the clarinetist Jim Doherty stimulated his passion for jazz, and on his return to Ireland he studied intensively before playing with a trio led by the pianist Noel Kelehan. After winning an award as the outstanding European soloist at the Montreux International Jazz Festival, where he played with Doherty's quartet (1968), he worked with Tubby Hayes (1968), toured three times with Benny Goodman (1969–71), was a member of Ronnie Scott's quartet (1975–9), and performed with George Shearing (1977–80). In the early 1980s Stewart worked as a freelance in the UK and abroad; he also developed associations with Scandinavian musicians which led to his recording the album *Good News* (1986, Villa 001) with a Norwegian quartet.

BIBLIOGRAPHY

L. Henshaw: "The Source of Stewart," *MM*, liii (15 April 1978), 59
S. Britt: "Louis Stewart," *The Jazz Guitarists* (Poole, England, 1984), 116

MARK GILBERT

Stewart, Rex (William, Jr.) (*b* Philadelphia, 22 Feb 1907; *d* Los Angeles, 7 Sept 1967). Cornetist. He played in minor New York groups from 1921 before becoming a cornetist in Fletcher Henderson's band in 1926. Feeling unequal to this position, which Louis Armstrong had previously filled, he soon left to join Horace Henderson's Wilberforce College group, but by 1928 he had returned to Fletcher Henderson, with whom he remained (with interruptions) until 1933, contributing many solos in a forceful, good-humored style, indebted equally to Armstrong, Bubber Miley, and Bix Beiderbecke. In 1934 Stewart joined the Duke Ellington Orchestra, beginning his most creative period. During his 11 years with the band he created a distinctive element in Ellington's ensemble sound, particularly with his mock-conversational "talking" style and the novel HALF-VALVE effects which he explored from 1937. Stewart was co-composer of several of Ellington's pieces (including *Boy Meets Horn* and *Morning Glory*), and also led excellent small-group recording sessions using other members of Ellington's band. After leaving Ellington he joined Jazz at the Philharmonic (1945) and made a long tour of Europe (1947–51), during which he lectured on jazz at the Paris Conservatoire (1948). He entered semiretirement in the early 1950s, but led the Fletcher Henderson reunion band in 1957 and 1958. In his later years he became well known as a writer of urbane, anecdotal pieces on jazz, several of which were reprinted posthumously as *Jazz Masters of the Thirties* (New York and London, n.d. [?1972]).

Oral history material in *NjR*.

For illustrations *see* BANDS, fig.3, and HENDERSON, FLETCHER.

SELECTED RECORDINGS

As leader: Rexatious/Lazy Man's Shuffle (1936, Var. 517); Fat Stuff Serenade (1939, Voc./OK 5448); with D. Wells: *Chatter Jazz* (1959, RCA LSP2024)

As sideman: F. Henderson: The Stampede (1926, Col. 654D); Singin' the Blues (1931, Col. 2565D); D. Ellington: Trumpet in Spades (Rex's Concerto) (1936, Bruns. 7752); Braggin' in Brass (1938, Bruns. 8099); Boy Meets Horn (1938, Bruns. 8306); Morning Glory (1940, Vic. 26536); Take the "A" Train (1941, Vic. 27380); Main Stem (1942, Vic. 201556)

BIBLIOGRAPHY

G. E. Lambert: "Rex Stewart," *JM*, iii/11 (1958), 2
B. Houghton: "Rex in Perspective," *JJ*, xix/5 (1966), 18
J. Postgate: "Rex Stewart," *JM*, xii/3 (1966), 3
S. Voce and A. Judd: "Rexatious," *JJ*, xxi (1968), no.2, p.14; no.3, p.12; no.4, p.12
G. Conrad: "Rex Stewart in Berlin," *JJ*, xxiv/3 (1971), 13
F. Thorne: "Rex William Stewart, Jr.," *Jazz Masters of the Thirties*, ed. R. Stewart (New York and London, n.d. [?1972]), 209
G. M. Colombé: "Rex Stewart in Europe, 1966," *JJ*, xxvi/8 (1973), 22
J. Simmen: "Crystal Clear," *Coda*, xii/1 (1974), 25

J. BRADFORD ROBINSON

Stewart, Slam [Leroy Elliott] (*b* Englewood, NJ, 21 Sept 1914; *d* Binghamton, NY, 10 Dec 1987). Double bass player. He studied at the Boston Conservatory, and first attracted attention in 1938 in a novelty duo called "Slim and Slam" with the guitarist Slim Gaillard; their riff tune *The Flat Foot Floogie* became extremely popular. Later Stewart worked as a freelance with a number of important swing and mainstream musicians, including Red Norvo and Benny Goodman, but most notably as a member of Art Tatum's trios (intermittently from 1943 to the early 1950s; for illustration *see* TATUM, ART). He played with Roy Eldridge's quartet (1953), Beryl Booker (1955–7), and the singer and pianist Rose Murphy (late 1950s and 1960s). From 1971 he taught music at SUNY, Binghamton, but continued to perform, touring with Goodman (1973–5) and forming in 1978 a partnership with Bucky Pizzarelli. Although best known for his unique solo style, in which he bowed and hummed the melody simultaneously at the interval of an octave, Stewart was also a fleet accompanist, as is evident from his early bop recordings with Dizzy Gillespie, and especially his remarkable saxophone and bass duos with Don Byas (1945). In 1984 he was awarded an honorary doctorate by SUNY, Binghamton.

Oral history material in *CtY*, *NjR* (JOHP).

SELECTED RECORDINGS

Duos with D. Byas: Indiana (1945, Jazz Star 47101); I got rhythm (1945, Jazz Star 47102)

As sideman: S. Gaillard: The Flat Foot Floogie (1938, Voc. 4021); J. Guarnieri: Bowing Singing Slam (1944, Savoy 530); A. Tatum: Topsy (1944, Asch 4522); D. Gillespie: Groovin' High (1945, Guild 1001); A. Tatum: *Art Tatum Trio* (1952, Cap. H408)

BIBLIOGRAPHY

J. Burns: "Slim & Slam," *JJ*, xxi/9 (1968), 4
F. Borromeo: "Slam Stewart Discography," *DF*, no.21 (1970) – no.31 (1972); contd in no.36 (1976), 1
L. Tomkins: "How my Bass Started Singing," *CI*, xiii/4 (1974), 17 [interview]
D. Long: "Slam Stewart," *Cadence*, viii (1982), no.9, p.8; no.11, p.8
J. M. Doran: *Erroll Garner: the Most Happy Piano* (Metuchen, NJ, and London, 1985), 59

J. BRADFORD ROBINSON

Stichting Jazz en Geïmproviseerde Muziek in Nederland. Organization formed in August 1965 as the Stichting Jazz in Nederland (SJIN) to foster an interest in jazz in the Netherlands and to administer the annual award of the Wessel Ilcken Prize (later known as the Boy Edgar Prize, then as the Dutch National Jazz Prize). The organization first included musicians on its managing board in November 1970 and worked with the Beroepsvereniging van Improviserende Musici (Professional association of improvising musicians) from its formation in November 1971. The organization also advises the Dutch government on the granting of subsidies for performance to jazz musicians. Its headquarters are in Amsterdam.

WIM VAN EYLE

Stichting National Jazz Archief. Dutch foundation formed in 1980 to run the National Jazz Archief in Amsterdam; *see* LIBRARIES AND ARCHIVES, §2.

Stick. The standard beater used by the jazz drummer; *see* DRUM SET, §I, 8.

Stief, Bo (*b* Copenhagen, 15 Oct 1946). Danish bass player. He began his career as a freelance. He played at the Montmartre Jazzhus (1963), worked with Dollar Brand in 1964, toured with Don Cherry (1966), and belonged to a quintet led by Alex Riel and Palle Mikkelborg (1967–8) and to the octet V8 (1970–75); later he played in Mikkelborg's group Entrance (1975–85), with which he recorded (*Cream*, 1977, Met. 15612). Stief has also worked as a leader and recorded with such American musicians as Jackie McLean and Ben Webster.

ERIK WIEDEMANN

Stinson, Albert (Forrest, Jr.) (*b* Cleveland, 2 Aug 1944; *d* Boston, 2 June 1969). Bass player. He played piano, trombone, and tuba as a child and double bass from the age of 14. He worked with Terry Gibbs (from 1961), Chico Hamilton (1962–5), and Charles Lloyd's quartet (from late 1965), then worked as a freelance in California from 1966; he also toured with John Handy (1967) and Larry Coryell (1969). Stinson had reliable intonation, a virtuoso technique, and a clear, sharp attack that recalled the playing of Charles Mingus; his solos were notable for the elegance of their structure.

SELECTED RECORDINGS

As sideman: C. Hamilton: *Passin' thru* (1962, Imp. 29); *A Different Journey* (1963, Rep. 96078); *Man from 2 Worlds* (1963, Imp. 59); D. Budimir: *The Session with Albert* (1964, Rev. 14); C. Hamilton: *El Chico* (1965, Imp. 9102)

BIBLIOGRAPHY

J. W. Hardy: "Caught in the Act," *DB*, xxxiii/5 (1966), 34
M. Hennessey: "Albert and the New Breed of Bass Players," *MM* (2 Sept 1967), 6
D. C. Hunt: "Al Stinson: Exciting New Bass Face," *J&P*, vii/8 (1968), 40
Obituary, *DB*, xxxvi/15 (1969), 7

JOHN VOIGT

Stitt, Sonny [Edward] (*b* Boston, 2 Feb 1924; *d* Washington, 22 July 1982). Saxophonist. He played alto saxophone in Tiny Bradshaw's big band in the early 1940s, then in 1945 joined Billy Eckstine's big band, which included such young bop players as Fats Navarro, Dexter Gordon, Gene Ammons, and Art Blakey. His association with the leaders of the new bop movement continued in Dizzy Gillespie's sextet and big band of 1946. During 1949–51 he began playing tenor and baritone saxophones as well as alto, often in a septet that he led with Ammons. Throughout much of the rest of his career he led a variety of small groups, often assembling them ad hoc for each new engagement as he traveled from city to city. However, he rejoined Gillespie for a time in the late 1950s, replaced John Coltrane in the Miles Davis Quintet in 1960, played with Ammons again in the early 1960s, and from time to time worked during short tours with various all-star groups such as the Giants of Jazz (1971–2, with Gillespie, Kai Winding, Thelonious Monk, Al McKibbon, and Blakey). His last performance took place in Japan just a few days before his death.

Stitt's early recorded solos show clearly that he was a disciple of Charlie Parker; he used Parker's favorite melodic formulas and imitated his tone quality and vibrato. Only small details of phrasing and articulation – an occasional slight hesitation in connecting notes in a Parkeresque phrase, or a subtly different way of tonguing – betray the imitator. Over the years he gradually added a number of individual melodic formulas to his vocabulary, but Parker's influence always dominated his solos on the alto saxophone, even when he used the Varitone, an electronic sound-modifying attachment which he adopted soon after its appearance on the market in 1966. He probably turned initially to the tenor and baritone saxophones in an effort to escape his image as Parker's follower; the baritone instrument proved to be but a temporary diversion, but the tenor opened up new lines of musical thought for him. He made his most distinctive statements on this instrument, which he played frequently from 1950.

Sonny Stitt

SELECTED RECORDINGS

As leader: Imagination (1950, Prst. 733); *Sonny Stitt Sits in with the Oscar Peterson Trio* (1959, Verve 8344); *Stitt Plays Bird* (1963, Atl. 1418); *What's New!!! Sonny Stitt Plays the Varitone* (1966, Roul. 25343); *Constellation* (1972, Cob. 9021)

As sideman: D. Gillespie: Oop bop sh-bam/That's Earl, brother (1946, Musi. 383); Bebop Boys: Boppin' a Riff (1946, Savoy 588); Fat Boy (1946, Savoy 587); Giants of Jazz: *The Giants of Jazz* (1971, Atl. 2-905)

BIBLIOGRAPHY

D. B. Bittan: "Don't Call me Bird," *DB*, xxvi/10 (1959), 19
M. Jones: "Stitt, Parker, and the Question of Influence," *JM*, v/11 (1960), 9
M. Williams: "Sonny Stitt in the Studio," *JJ*, xvi/8 (1963), 12
B. McRae: *The Jazz Cataclysm* (London, South Brunswick, NJ, and New York, 1967/*R*1985), 20
J. Burns: "Early Stitt," *JJ*, xxii/10 (1969), 6
Obituaries: *Los Angeles Times* (23 July 1982); *New York Times* (24 July 1982)
"Sonny Stitt," *SJ*, xxxvi/3 (1982), 240 [discography]
D. Salemann, D. Hartmann, and M. Vogler: *Sonny Stitt: Solography, Discography, Band Routes, Engagements, in Chronological Order* (Basle, Switzerland, 1986)

THOMAS OWENS

Stitzel, Mel(ville J.) (*b* Germany, 9 Jan 1902; *d* Chicago, 31 Dec 1952). Pianist and arranger. He was brought up in Chicago. In 1923 he made several recordings as a member of the New Orleans Rhythm Kings (for illustration *see* New Orleans Rhythm Kings), among them *Maple Leaf Rag* (Gen. 5104) and – credited in some sources as his own composition – *Tin Roof Blues* (Gen. 5105). He also recorded with Muggsy Spanier in the Bucktown Five (1924) and Stomp Six (1925) and in a trio with Benny Goodman (1928). From 1925 he played and wrote arrangements for a large number of bands in Chicago and he continued performing regularly in the 1930s. He later led his own band (1940s) and worked with Danny Alvin (early 1950s).

based on *ChiltonW*

Stivín, Jiří (*b* Prague, 23 Nov 1942). Czechoslovak flutist, alto and tenor saxophonist, and composer. He studied classical flute and taught himself to play saxophone, which he played in rock bands (1961). He led the group Jazz Q with the keyboard player Martin Kratochvíl and belonged to Karel Velebný's group SHQ (1967–9). In London he attended John Dankworth's classes at the Royal Academy of Music and played in the Scratch Orchestra, an experimental group led by the avant-garde composer Cornelius Cardew. He led a free-jazz group, Stivín and Co. Jazz System, which recorded as a sextet that included Rudolf Dašek, Barre Phillips, and Zbigniew Seifert (*Five Hits in a Row*, 1972, Sup. 1151229), and he played and recorded with Dašek in the duo Tandem (1971–5, re-formed 1985). With the keyboard player Gabriel Jonáš, the Kühn Chorus, and the Talich String Quartet he recorded an album of his own compositions in 1976 (*Zodiak*, Sup. 1152015); he also recorded in a trio with Dašek and Tony Scott (1978) and in a duo with Pierre Favre (1979). In the 1980s he often performed as a soloist and with the percussionist Alan Vitous. In addition to his work in jazz Stivín has recorded concertos for recorder by Georg Philipp Telemann and Antonio Vivaldi. (*Feather–Gitler '70s*)

BERT NOGLIK

Stobart, Kathy [Florence Kathleen] (*b* South Shields, England, 1 April 1925). English tenor saxophonist. She grew up in a musical family, and studied piano then saxophone. At the age of 14 she joined a band in Newcastle, and in 1942 she moved to London, where she played with various informal groups. After World War II she worked briefly in a band led by the Canadian pianist Art Thompson, who was at that time her husband. In 1949 she toured and recorded with Vic Lewis's band; later she formed her own ensemble, which recorded in 1951 but disbanded soon afterwards. She renewed her association with Lewis and later went into semiretirement while she brought up her family. During this period she worked as a session musician and deputized briefly for Jimmy Skidmore in Humphrey Lyttelton's band (1957). She worked with this ensemble again for some eight years from 1969. From the mid-1970s she has led her own groups, which have included Harry Beckett, John Burch, and the vibraphonist Lennie Best; her recordings as a leader include *Arbeia* (1978, Spot. 509). She also plays alto, soprano, and baritone saxophones, and has been active as a teacher.

BIBLIOGRAPHY

Feather '60s
L. Tomkins: "The Kathy Stobart Story," *CI*, xii/8 (1974), 14
R. Cotterell, ed.: *Jazz Now: the Jazz Centre Society Guide* (London, 1976)
V. Wilmer: "Kathy Stobart: Music in my Blood," *JF* [intl edn], no.76 (1982), 43
S. Worsfold: "Kathy Stobart: Interview," *Turntable* (July 1986)

SALLY-ANN WORSFOLD

Stock arrangement. A simplified, strictly practical arrangement in a conventional style, usually commercially available in published form; *see* Arrangement, §1.

Stokes, Irvin (*b* Greensboro, NC, 11 Nov 1926). Trumpeter. In 1947 he moved to New York, where he recorded in a sextet led by the alto saxophonist Charlie Singleton (1949). During the 1950s he worked mainly in big bands, including those of Tiny Bradshaw, Andy Kirk, Jimmie Lunceford, Erskine Hawkins, Duke Ellington, and Buddy Johnson (1956–8). He then played with the sextet led by the guitarist Austin Powell (1959–60) and recorded with Bobby Donaldson (1960). From 1979 Stokes performed regularly with Panama Francis's Savoy Sultans, and his playing is well represented on the group's recordings; he also recorded with George Kelly (1982). He toured Europe with Illinois Jacquet in 1982 and with Oliver Jackson in 1984; as joint leaders Stokes and Jackson recorded the album *Broadway* (1984, BB 33151). (J. Simmen: "Irvin Stokes: une voix importante sur la scène d'aujourd'hui," *BHcF*, no.327 (1985), 3)

HOWARD RYE

Stoller, Alvin (*b* New York, 7 Oct 1925). Drummer. His first professional engagement, with the pianist Van Alexander, was quickly followed by work with the bandleaders Raymond Scott and Teddy Powell. He later played with many of the foremost bands of the time, including those of Benny Goodman (1942), Charlie Spivak (1943–5), Tommy Dorsey (1945–7), Georgie Auld (1949), Harry James (1950, 1951), Jerry Gray (1950–52), Billy May (1951–7), Charlie Barnet (1954, 1956), Maynard Ferguson (1955–6), Claude Thornhill, and Bob Crosby. By the 1950s he was active as a studio musician, but he also took part in many recordings with small groups, most of which were produced by Norman Granz: they included sessions with Erroll Garner (1949), Billie Holiday (1952, 1956–7), Roy Eldridge (1953), Harry Edison (1953, 1956–7), Ben Webster (1953, 1957), Art Tatum (1955), Herb Ellis (1955–6), Ella Fitzgerald (1956, 1957), Buddy DeFranco (1957), Coleman Hawkins (1957), and Benny Carter (1966).

SELECTED RECORDINGS

As sideman: E. Garner: I Surrender, Dear/Love Walked In (1949, Savoy 701); H. Edison: *Sweets at the Haig* (1953, PJ 4); A. Tatum: *The Art Tatum–Roy Eldridge–Alvin Stoller–John Simmons Quartet* (1955, Clef 679); M. Ferguson: *Around the Horn with Maynard Ferguson* (1955–6, EmA 36076); H. Ellis: *Ellis in Wonderland* (1955–6, Norg. 1081); C. Hawkins: *The Genius of Coleman Hawkins* (1957, Verve 8261); B. Carter: *Additions to Further Definitions* (1966, Imp. 9116)

BIBLIOGRAPHY

FeatherE

SCOTT YANOW

Stomp. A term variously applied in early jazz to rhythmic swing or, as in blues, to a heavy, strongly marked beat. It is undoubtedly derived from "stamp" and its use in jazz arises from the dances associated with ragtime and early blues forms, which were characterized by stamping steps. The word was frequently used in titles such as Jelly Roll Morton's *King Porter Stomp* (1906) and *Black Bottom Stomp* (1925) and Edgar Sampson's *Stompin' at the Savoy* (1934).

A "stomp chorus" is the final chorus of a lively piece, played in a loud, spirited manner (*see* Forms, §2); the term is used mostly of early jazz. A bandleader "stomps (or kicks) off" by striking the beat of a piece with his heel on the floor; this marks the tempo and gives a signal to the musicians so that they begin playing in time and together.

GUNTHER SCHULLER

Stone, Fred(die) (*b* Toronto, 9 Sept 1935; *d* Toronto, 10 Dec 1986). Canadian trumpeter, composer, and conductor. He studied music from the age of 12 and made his professional début as a trumpeter with the Casino Theatre orchestra in Toronto. During the 1950s and 1960s he played with a number of symphony orchestras, and for a period was principal trumpeter of the CBC SO. His work with jazz musicians included associations with Ron Collier (1960–73), Phil Nimmons (1965–70), and Rob McConnell (1968–70). In 1970–71 he toured with Duke Ellington's orchestra, and a good example of his playing may be heard on *Aristocracy à la Jean Lafitte* (on the album *New Orleans Suite*, 1970, Atl. 1580). Thereafter he led his own bands in Toronto. Stone also composed a number of works for jazz orchestra and for his own small groups.

BIBLIOGRAPHY

Feather–Gitler '70s
M. Miller: "Stone, Fred," *Encyclopedia of Music in Canada*, ed. H. Kallmann, G. Potvin, and K. Winters (Toronto, Buffalo, and London, 1981)
——: "Fred Stone," *Boogie, Pete & the Senator: Canadian Musicians in Jazz: the Eighties* (Toronto, 1987), 241

EDDIE LAMBERT

Stone, Jesse (*b* Atchison, KS, 1901). Pianist and arranger. He was brought up in St. Joseph and Kansas City, Missouri, and from about 1920 to 1928 he led the Blues Serenaders, recording with the band in 1927. After leading the Blue Moon Chasers in and around Dallas he joined George E. Lee and helped Terrence Holder form a new band (1929). He then worked as Lee's music director and arranger (1930–31) and directed the KANSAS CITY ROCKETS with Thamon Hayes (1932–4). From 1935 he led the Cyclones (with such sidemen as Jabbo Smith and Budd Johnson) in Chicago, and in 1937 he made two recordings with another orchestra (including *Snaky Feeling*, Var. 521). Stone continued working as a leader in the 1940s and performed overseas on a tour sponsored by the US State Department; from the early 1950s he worked as an artists and repertory agent.

Oral history material in *NjR* (JOHP).

BIBLIOGRAPHY

F. S. Driggs: "Kansas City and the Southwest," *Jazz: New Perspectives on the History of Jazz*, ed. N. Hentoff and A. J. McCarthy (New York, 1959/*R*1974), 189
R. Russell: *Jazz Style in Kansas City and the Southwest* (Berkeley, CA, Los Angeles, and London, 1971/*R*1983, rev. 2/1973), 117
A. McCarthy: *Big Band Jazz* (New York and London, 1974), 139
N. W. Pearson, Jr.: *Goin' to Kansas City* (Urbana, IL, and London, 1988)

based on *ChiltonW*

Stop-time. A technique used to focus attention on a singer or an instrumental soloist. An ensemble or pianist repeats in rhythmic unison a simple one- or two-bar pattern consisting of sharp accents and rests, while the soloist takes command. Meter and tempo remain intact; only the texture of the accompaniment changes. An unusual instance in ragtime may be found in Scott Joplin's *Ragtime Dance* (1906). The technique is common in jazz; famous examples occur during Johnny Dodds's clarinet solos on King Oliver's two recorded versions of *Dipper Mouth Blues* (1923, Gen. 5132; OK 4918) and Louis Armstrong's trumpet solo on *Potato Head Blues* (1927, OK 8503). A more recent type of stop-time occurs in urban blues and related popular genres where, in the four opening tonic bars of the 12-bar blues progression, the group places a heavy accent on the downbeat of each bar and then gives way to the singer.

BIBLIOGRAPHY

G. Schuller: *Early Jazz: its Roots and Musical Development* (New York, 1968)
E. A. Berlin: *Ragtime: a Musical and Cultural History* (Berkeley, CA, Los Angeles, and London, 1980/*R*1984 with addns)

BARRY KERNFELD

Story, Nat(haniel Edward) (*b* Oak Station, nr East Paducah, KY, 8 Aug 1904; *d* Evansville, IN, 21 Nov 1968). Trombonist. He worked on the Mississippi riverboats with Fate Marable in the 1920s, and in the early 1930s he moved to New York, where he played with Luis Russell (with whom he recorded) and Sam Wooding (both 1934), among others. He joined Chick Webb in 1936 (for illustration *see* WEBB, CHICK) and stayed to work under Ella Fitzgerald's leadership after Webb died (1939). He made a number of recordings with both leaders and he may be heard as a soloist on Webb's *Pack up your sins and go to the devil* (1938, Decca 1894). He left the band in 1940 and after playing with Andy Kirk and Lucky Millinder he ceased to work full-time as a musician, though he continued to perform into the 1960s.

BIBLIOGRAPHY

J. Simmen: "Carnet de notes, 15: Nat Story 'Mr Pinch-Penny'," *BHcF*, no.189 (1969), 10
F. Driggs: "Story's Story," *Sv*, no.79 (1978), 24

based on *ChiltonW*

Storyville (i). The name of the brothel district of New Orleans around the turn of the century. It has been adopted for various purposes in jazz: as the name of a number of nightclubs (*see* NIGHTCLUBS AND OTHER VENUES), at least two record labels (*see* STORYVILLE (ii) and STORYVILLE (iii)), and a notable journal (see Appendix 1: Bibliography (Periodicals)).

Storyville (ii). Record company and label. The company was formed by George Wein in Boston in 1951; it evolved from the club of the same name that he had opened the previous year. The catalogue contained recordings made both at the club and in studios; it included albums by Lee Konitz, Serge Chaloff, Toshiko Akiyoshi, Ruby Braff, Vic Dickenson, Ellis Larkins, Sidney Bechet, Johnny Windhurst, Joe Newman, Zoot Sims, and Jo Jones. Several singers also made recordings for the label, among them Lee Wiley, Jackie Cain, and Roy Kral.

The company also leased some material from other companies, including the results of a session recorded by Buck Clayton in Paris. It was at its most active in 1953–5, but thereafter Wein's increasing involvement with the Newport Jazz Festival and associated activities began to demand most of his time. The label had virtually been discontinued by the late 1950s. Parts of the catalogue were issued contemporaneously on Vogue in the UK and France, and a few albums have been rereleased in Japan, but there has been no comprehensive reissue program.

MARK GARDNER

Storyville (iii). Record company and label; the company began recording traditional jazz in Copenhagen in the early 1950s and shortly thereafter was taken over by SONET.

Stovall, Don(ald) [Donnie] (*b* St. Louis, 12 Dec 1913; *d* New York, 20 Nov 1970). Alto saxophonist. He first played with Dewey Jackson (1930–31) and Fate Marable (1932–3), then worked with Lil Armstrong (1936) and Peanuts Holland (1936–8). After moving to New York he recorded with Armstrong, Pete Johnson (*627 Stomp*, 1940, Decca 18121), the trumpeter

Joe Brown and Sammy Price (both 1940–41), and Snub Mosley (1941). He also played with Eddie Durham, Mercer Ellington, and Cootie Williams. From 1942 to 1949 he was a member of Henry "Red" Allen's sextet, with which he also made a number of recordings, including his own composition *Count me out* (1946, Vic. 201956). Stovall ceased to play in 1951, when he took a job with a telephone company.

BIBLIOGRAPHY

ChiltonW

J. Simmen: "Don Stovall: an Appreciation," *Coda*, x/2 (1971), 31

——: "Un des grands swingmen du saxophone: Don Stovall," *BHcF*, no.207 (1971), 11

FRANK DRIGGS

Straight ahead. A term describing a conventional, simple, or straightforward approach to playing in the bop style and its derivatives; in some contexts it also carries connotations of a positive, forceful manner. It may be applied to the playing of a soloist or a group, or to the style of a piece.

Straight mute. *See* MUTE, §2(a).

Strata-East. Record company and label founded in 1971 by CHARLES TOLLIVER and Stanley Cowell.

Strayhorn, Billy [William; Swee' Pea] (*b* Dayton, OH, 19 Nov 1915; *d* New York, 31 May 1967). Composer, arranger, and pianist. As a youth in Hillsborough, North Carolina, and Pittsburgh, he received an extensive training in music. In December 1938 he submitted a composition to Duke Ellington, who was so impressed by the young man's talent that three months later he recorded Strayhorn's *Something to live for* with the composer as pianist. Four more of Strayhorn's pieces were recorded during 1939 – *I'm checkin' out, goo'm bye* and *Grievin'* by Ellington, and *Barney goin' easy* and *Lost in Two Flats* by Barney Bigard – as well as a work by Ellington written as a tribute, *Weely (a Portrait of Billy Strayhorn)*. After serving briefly as a pianist in Mercer Ellington's orchestra, Strayhorn joined Duke Ellington's band as associate arranger and second pianist, and for nearly three decades worked in close collaboration with the leader. The two men were so attuned to one another musically, and Strayhorn's work was such a perfect complement to Ellington's, that it is now impossible to establish the exact extent of the former's contribution to Ellington's oeuvre. Their relationship was described in flattering terms by Ellington in his autobiography (1973). Strayhorn collaborated on more than 200 items in Ellington's repertory, including such standards as *Take the "A" Train* (one of the band's theme tunes) and *Satin Doll*. His ballads, including *Lush Life*, *Something to live for*, *Day Dream*, *After all*, *Passion Flower*, *Chelsea Bridge*, *Lotus Blossom*, and *Blood Count*, are harmonically and structurally among the most sophisticated in jazz. Strayhorn was a technically fluent pianist, and made a notable contribution to several small-group recordings by various of Ellington's sidemen, including Cootie Williams (1939), Bigard (1939–40), Johnny Hodges (1939, 1947, 1956–8), the Ellingtonians (1950), the Coronets (1950–51), Louie Bellson (1952), Ben Webster (1954), and Clark Terry (1957); he also recorded a number of titles in a trio with Ellington and either Wendell Marshall or Joe Shulman, which were issued on an album under his own name (*Billy Strayhorn Trio*, 1950, Mercer 1001).

RECORDED COMPOSITIONS
(selective list)
* – with Strayhorn as sideman

Recorded by D. Ellington: *(I want) Something to live for (1939, Bruns. 8365); I'm checkin' out, goo'm bye (1939, Col. 35208); Grievin' (1939, Col. 35310); Take the "A" Train (1941, Vic. 27380); *After all (1941, Vic. 27434); *Chelsea Bridge (1941, Vic. 27740); Raincheck (1941, Vic. 27880); *Johnny come lately (1942, Vic. 201556); Midriff (1946, Swing 230); Satin Doll (1953, Cap. 2458); Upper Manhattan Medical Center, on *Historically Speaking: the Duke* (1956, Beth. 60); Such Sweet Thunder (1957), on *Such Sweet Thunder* (1956–7, Col. CL1033); *Far East Suite* (1966, RCA LSP3782); Blood Count, on "*. . . and his Mother Called him Bill*" (1967, RCA LSP3906)

Recorded by others: B. Bigard: Barney goin' easy (1939, Voc./OK 5378); *Lost in Two Flats (1939, Voc./OK 5422); J. Hodges: Day Dream (1940, Bb 11021); Passion Flower (1941, Bb 300817); Charlotte russe (Lotus Blossom), on *Johnny Hodges* (1947, Mercer 1000); Lush Life, on J. Coltrane: *Lush Life* (1957–8, Prst. 7188); A. Farmer: *Something to Live for: the Music of Billy Strayhorn* (1987, Cont. 14029)

BIBLIOGRAPHY

B. Coss: "Ellington & Strayhorn, Inc.," *DB*, xxix/12 (1962), 22

S. Dance: *The World of Duke Ellington* (London and New York, 1970/*R*1981) [colln of previously pubd articles and interviews]

D. Ellington: *Music is my Mistress* (Garden City, NY, 1973)

D. Jewell: *Duke: a Portrait of Duke Ellington* (London and New York, 1977, 2/1978)

J. L. Collier: *Duke Ellington* (New York and London, 1987)

JOSÉ HOSIASSON

Strazzeri, Frank (John) (*b* Rochester, NY, 24 April 1930). Pianist. He began playing tenor saxophone and clarinet in 1942, then changed to piano, which he studied at the Eastman School. In 1952 he accompanied visiting jazz musicians (including Roy Eldridge, J. J. Johnson, and Billie Holiday) as the house pianist at a club in Rochester. Two years later he moved to New Orleans, where he performed with Sharkey Bonano and Al Hirt. After playing with Charlie Ventura (1957–8) he performed in Las Vegas, then joined Woody Herman's band in 1959. He settled in Los Angeles the following year and worked as a studio musician for Pacific Jazz, Verve, and Atlantic, recording with Herb Ellis, Terry Gibbs, Carmell Jones, and Red Mitchell during this period. He also toured with Joe Williams, Maynard Ferguson, and Howard Rumsey's Lighthouse All Stars. After three years with Les Brown's band he joined Cal Tjader's quintet in 1974. From 1975 he has led his own groups and undertaken session work; he has made recordings with Louie Bellson (in London, 1980, 1982), and Tal Farlow (1984). Strazzeri's generally conservative playing reflects the relaxed approach and technical competence of the finest keyboard players in Los Angeles.

SELECTED RECORDINGS

As unaccompanied soloist: *Relaxin'* (1982, Seabreeze 1007)

As leader: *After the Rain* (1976, Cat. 7607); *Straz* (1977, Cat. 7623)

As sideman: C. Tjader: *Last Night when we were Young* (1975, Fan. 9482); D. Menza: *Hip Pocket* (1981, PAlt 8010); B. Perkins: *Journey to the East* (1984, Cont. 14011)

BIBLIOGRAPHY

H. Wong: "Profile: Frank Strazzeri," *DB*, xliii/1 (1976), 32

BOB DOERSCHUK

Stretch out. To improvise for an extended period, sufficiently long to allow a thorough working out of the possibilities offered by a theme. The term implies an unexpectedly lengthy, inventive, even self-indulgent solo in a context in which a short improvisation would be normal, and presumably derives from the consequent "stretching out" or extension of the piece as a whole. A renowned example of such a solo is Paul Gonsalves's 27-chorus improvisation on Duke Ellington's *Diminuendo and*

Crescendo in Blue at the Newport Jazz Festival in 1956 (the recording of which was issued on the album *Ellington at Newport*, Col. CL934).

Stride. A style of solo jazz piano; *see* PIANO, §2.

String band. Any ensemble consisting largely or wholly of string instruments. The string-band tradition is an independent one that has developed in parallel with jazz, and the characteristic types of ensemble have their roots in blues, ragtime, and society music from the turn of the century. Later influences have been elements of gypsy and eastern European music.

In his interviews with Alan Lomax for the Library of Congress, Jelly Roll Morton recalled the repertory of waltzes, schottisches and quadrilles played by the string groups of New Orleans in the early 1900s. No recordings from this period exist, but Edmond Souchon recorded with a typical ensemble, the Six and Seven Eighths Band, in 1949. Its instrumentation consisted of mandolin, steel guitar, guitar, and double bass and it performed in a style that was to some extent a precursor of skiffle, as may be heard on *High Society* (1949, New Orleans 1000).

Similar string ensembles (the members of which possessed a considerable degree of virtuosity) performed ragtime music. The principal instrument used in these ragtime bands was the banjo, and the recordings of Fred Van Eps, Sr. (for example, *Florida Rag*, 1912, Vic. 17308), made with a trio of two banjos and piano, illustrate the early style. Ragtime later came to be performed on guitar (notably by the Rev. Gary Davis and his protégé Stefan Grossman) and flourished predominantly as a solo tradition; banjo-based ensembles therefore became less common until the ragtime revival of the 1970s.

A more enduring style was that of the blues-based ensembles, such as those led by Lonnie Johnson. Johnson made many blues recordings with his brother James "Steady Roll" Johnson in string bands consisting of guitar, banjo, and violin; the brothers were each adept at playing all three instruments. Johnson commanded a formidable guitar technique, and his solo work (best demonstrated on his remarkable tour de force *To do this you gotta know how*, 1926, OK 40695), together with a series of guitar duets recorded with Eddie Lang (including *Bull Frog Moan/A Handful of Riffs*, 1929, OK 8695), set the pattern for string-band jazz of the late 1920s. With Joe Venuti, Lang had previously recorded duets which combined the rhythmic, chordal work of the guitar with a swinging and melodic violin line; *Stringing the Blues* (1926, Col. 914D) is one of the earliest recorded duets for violin and guitar, and was as influential as Lang's work with Johnson.

Lang's recordings (under his own name and under the pseudonym Blind Willie Dunn) coupled the musical language of blues and early jazz with a string technique as dextrous as that of the best ragtime players. His style reached its high point in his duets with Carl Kress, notably *Pickin' my Way* (*Guitar Mania*, pt i) (1932, Bruns. 6254). As early as 1927 Lang was involved in another series of string-band recordings that influenced many string and vocal groups of the 1930s. These were with Red McKenzie, whose skiffle or spasm-band style involved the use of homemade and string instruments as accompaniment to popular or simple blues singing.

McKenzie recorded in the mid-1930s with the most influential American string band of the decade, the Spirits of Rhythm. This ensemble was renowned for its driving rhythmic pulse, obtained by chordal work on tiples (played by Leo Watson and the brothers Wilbur and Douglas Daniels) and guitar (Teddy Bunn); other instruments were double bass and homemade percussion. The group's repertory of songs with nonsense or scat lyrics, often incorporating Harlem slang or "jive" talk (for example, *My Old Man*, 1933, Bruns. 6728), became particularly associated with American string bands; it also formed the basis for the work of Slim and Slam (Slim Gaillard and Slam Stewart), whose most important recording, *The Flat Foot Floogie* (1938, Voc. 4021), was made with guitar, bowed double bass, piano, and drums.

During the mid-1930s there were parallel developments in Europe in the work of the Quintette du Hot Club de France, an instrumental band consisting of three guitars, double bass, and violin. The principal members of the quintet, Stephane Grappelli and Django Reinhardt, emulated the approach of Venuti and Lang, allowing the melodic lines to pass from the violin to the guitar; Reinhardt played a combination of single-string, chordal, and tremolo solos (the last accomplished by rapid strumming with the right hand) against a solid 4/4 pulse in the rhythm guitars and bass. But the quintet also made use of the harmonic vocabulary of Romany music and the central European guitar tradition. Reinhardt employed the conventional guitar keys of E, A, and B in many of his compositions and made free use of augmented chords and whole-tone scales. The temperament of these sharp keys proved a strong contrast to those more usual in jazz (such keys as F, B♭, and E♭ allowing brass and woodwind instruments to play together with ease), and gave a characteristic edge to the group's performances. (Johnson and Lang, however, had already demonstrated the flexibility of string ensembles in respect of keys in *Have to change keys to play these blues*, 1928, OK 8637.)

After World War II the universal adoption of the electric guitar led to the virtual discontinuation of the string-band tradition. From 1939 Reinhardt added clarinet or saxophone and drums to the instrumentation of the quintet, and he began to meld his own style with the bop approach of Charlie Christian. Grappelli continued to work sporadically with string-band accompaniment, and in the 1970s and 1980s returned to a formula similar to that of the quintet when he played with a trio of two guitars and double bass, generally led by the English guitarists Diz Disley or Martin Taylor.

Other Romany players, including Reinhardt's brother Joseph, Paul Ferret, and Bireli Lagrene, kept alive the style of the Quintette du Hot Club de France, though Lagrene later abandoned the acoustic guitar and played in various fusion styles. Generally speaking, the string-band tradition has not been continued by bop ensembles involving several guitarists (such as Great Guitars), or by musicians performing in duo or trio formats (Kenny Burrell, John McLaughlin, Larry Coryell, Philip Catherine, and Al Di Meola). The only significant attempt to meld the string-band style with bop was made by the French guitarists Boulu and Elios Ferré.

BIBLIOGRAPHY

C. Delaunay: "The Founding of the String Quintet," *Django Reinhardt: souvenirs* (Paris, 1954; Eng. trans., London, 1961/*R*1981, 1982, rev. 2/1981)

I. Cruickshank: *The Guitar Style of Django Reinhardt and the Gypsies* (Woodcote, nr Reading, England, 1982, rev. and enlarged 2/1985)

M. Jones: "Teddy Bunn, the Spirit of Rhythm," *The Spirits of Rhythm, 1933–34* (JSP 1088, 1985) [liner notes]

ALYN SHIPTON

String bass. *See* DOUBLE BASS.

String Trio of New York. Trio formed in 1977 by BILLY BANG.

Stritch. A modified version of the straight E♭ alto saxophone, used and named by Roland Kirk; *see* SAXOPHONE, §6(vii).

Stroll. *See* LAY OUT.

Strong, Jimmy (*b* 29 Aug 1906; *d* after 1940). Clarinetist and tenor saxophonist. He performed with the Nighthawks, led by the pianist Lottie E. Hightower, in Chicago in the early 1920s and after touring with a show (1925) he played with several bands in California. He returned to Chicago and worked with the clarinetist Clifford King's big band (1928) and Carroll Dickerson (1927–9). He is best known for the recordings he made as a member of Louis Armstrong's Hot Five and Savoy Ballroom Five in 1928 and 1929, among them *Fireworks* (1928, OK 8597). In the 1930s he led his own group and joined Zinky Cohn (1937) and Jimmie Noone's big band (1939); he then moved to Jersey City, New Jersey, where he again worked as a leader (from 1940). Although Strong's clarinet playing was rather harsh and brittle, and less attractive than his tone on tenor saxophone, he was known and recorded mainly as a clarinetist. (A. McCarthy: *Big Band Jazz*, London and New York, 1974)

based on *ChiltonW*

Strozier, Frank (R.) (*b* Memphis, 13 June 1937). Alto saxophonist, flutist, and clarinetist. He began learning piano while at school in Memphis; after moving to Chicago (1954) he worked with other Memphis musicians such as Harold Mabern, George Coleman, and Booker Little, and also played with Walter Perkins's group MJT + 3 (recording in 1959–60). In 1959 he moved to New York, where he appeared with Miles Davis for a brief period in 1963 (alongside Mabern and Coleman) and with Roy Haynes's quartet. After six years in Los Angeles, during which he performed with Chet Baker (recording in 1965) and groups led by Shelly Manne (1965–*c*1967) and Don Ellis (1968), he returned to New York in 1971; he joined the Jazz Contemporaries, led by the drummer Keno Duke (recording in 1974), and the New York Jazz Repertory Company. He recorded as a leader in 1976–7, and also played with Horace Parlan (1977). Strozier is a dynamic and committed performer with a blues-based style that enlivens any context in which he appears. His tone and phrasing have a biting edge reminiscent of Jackie McLean's playing.

SELECTED RECORDINGS

As leader: *Waltz of the Demons* (1960, VJ 1007); *What's Goin' On* (1977, Ste. 17001)

As sideman: R. Haynes: *Cymbalism* (1963, NewJ 8287)

BIBLIOGRAPHY

Feather '60s; *Feather–Gitler '70s*

BRIAN PRIESTLEY

Stuart, Kirk [Kincheloe, Charles] (*b* Charleston, WV, 13 April 1934; *d* 17 Dec 1982). Pianist. After conservatory training he worked as an accompanist to Billie Holiday (1956), then toured and recorded as a pianist, arranger, and conductor for the singers Della Reese (1957–9) and Sarah Vaughan (1961–3); he may be heard to advantage on Vaughan's album *Sassy Swings the Tivoli* (1963, Mer. 60831), which was recorded in Copenhagen. He later led his own group in Los Angeles, and recorded with Al Grey (1965), and again with Reese (1967). Thereafter he taught at Howard University for several years, led his own group at clubs in Las Vegas, and accompanied Joe Williams in Los Angeles.

BIBLIOGRAPHY

Feather '60s
Obituary, *JT* (March 1983), 8

Stubblefield, John(ny, IV) (*b* Little Rock, AR, 4 Feb 1945). Tenor and soprano saxophonist. After moving to Chicago he joined the Association for the Advancement of Creative Musicians, studied with Muhal Richard Abrams and George Coleman, and recorded with Joseph Jarman (1968). In 1971 he went to New York, where he played with the Collective Black Artists' big band and with Mary Lou Williams. He also worked with Charles Mingus, the Thad Jones–Mel Lewis Orchestra, and the percussionist Tito Puente, and in 1972 performed and recorded at Town Hall, New York, with Anthony Braxton; as a free jazz player he is well represented on Braxton's album *Town Hall 1972* (1972, Trio 3008–9). The following year he recorded in Europe with Abdullah Ibrahim and worked with Miles Davis. In 1974 Stubblefield recorded with McCoy Tyner (playing oboe and flute), Gil Evans (at the Montreux International Jazz Festival), and Lester Bowie. Later he made recordings with Nat Adderley (1976), Sonny Phillips (1977), Kenny Barron (1980, 1986, 1987), and Teo Macero (1983). He recorded as a leader (1976, 1984, 1986) and is heard to advantage playing bop on *Confessin'* (1984, SN 1095). He has also been active as a teacher, working with the Jazzmobile, and lecturing, leading seminars, and organizing workshops at several universities and colleges.

BIBLIOGRAPHY

G. Urban: "Jazzmobile Introduced Fine New Musicians to Area," *Times Record* (Albany, NY, 5 Aug 1975), 24
A. J. Smith: "Profile: John Stubblefield," *DB*, xliii/2 (1976), 30
V. Wilmer: *As Serious as your Life: the Story of the New Jazz* (London, 1977, rev. 1980)
I. Leymarie: "John Stubblefield: 'l'A.A.C.M. m'a sauvé la vie'," *Jm*, no.346 (1986), 34

Stubø, Thorgeir (*b* Narvik, Norway, 12 Nov 1943; *d* Narvik, 22 Oct 1986). Norwegian electric guitarist. He played in northern Norway with the pianist Terje Bjorklund, the tenor saxophonist Henning Gravrok, and others. His recording of his own compositions, *Notice* (1981, Odin 1), was the first made on the Norwegian Jazz Federation's own label and won an award. He made further bop recordings with Doug Raney (1983), in a quintet with Bernt Rosengren, Egil Kapstad, Egil Johansen, and the double bass player Terje Venaas (1984), in a group with Alex Riel (1985), and with Raney and Art Farmer (1986). He named Tal Farlow as the principal influence on his style.

RANDI HULTIN

Studer, Fredy (*b* Lucerne, Switzerland, 16 June 1948). Swiss drummer and percussionist. A self-taught musician, he played drums from the age of 16. In 1970 he moved to Rome, where he worked as a member of the electric jazz quartet Om (1972–82) and in a trio with the pianist Rainer Brüninghaus and the trumpeter Markus Stockhausen (1981–4). He also played with Joe Henderson, Joachim Kühn, Albert Mangelsdorff, Enrico Rava, Tomasz Stańko, Miroslav Vitous, Eberhard Weber, and Kenny Wheeler, and recorded with John Tchicai (1971), in a rhythm section with Wolfgang Dauner, Pierre Favre, and others in the group String Summit (1980), and in Favre's percussion quartet Singing Drums, which also included Paul Motian and Nana Vasconcelos; his playing with this ensemble may be heard on the album *Singing Drums* (1984, ECM 1274). In the late 1980s he worked in the band led by Charlie Mariano and Jasper van 't Hof. Studer has made tours of the USA, Central and South America, the Caribbean, North Africa, and Japan. (I. Carr: "Studer, Fredy," in I. Carr, D. Fairweather, and B. Priestley: *Jazz: the Essential Companion*, London, 1987)

Studio musician. A musician who works exclusively in recording studios, whether as a freelance or as the employee of a recording or film company, or of a television or radio station; *see also* SESSION (i).

Stuyvesant Casino. Ballroom in New York; *See* NIGHTCLUBS AND OTHER VENUES.

Subramaniam, L(akshminarayana) (*b* Madras, India, 23 July 1947). Indian violinist and leader. He learned violin and performed in classical concerts in his youth. He later studied medicine, but then traveled to the USA for graduate study in Western music, receiving an MFA from California Institute for the Arts. In 1973–4 he toured the USA and Europe with the rock guitarist George Harrison and the sitar player Ravi Shankar, playing a fusion of Indian music and rock. He composed for and recorded with Stu Goldberg in 1978, and the same year recorded a series of duos with Larry Coryell and his first album as a leader. Later he recorded the album *Fantasy without Limit* (1979, Trend 524) as a member of the group Rainbow with John Handy and the sarod player Ali Akbar Khan, as the leader of a quartet comprising Coryell, George Duke, and Tom Scott (*c*1982), and as a leader with Stephane Grappelli (1984). His brother Lakshminarayana Shankar, also a violinist, was a member of John McLaughlin's group Shakti. (L. Underwood: "L. Subramaniam," *DB*, xlvii/11 (1980), 53)

Substitute [sub]. A musician employed on an occasional or short-term basis; *see* BANDS, §3.

Substitute chord. A chord used to replace one in a given harmonic progression; *see* HARMONY (i), §1(v)(b).

Substitute fingering. *See* FALSE FINGERING.

Subtone. A soft, caressing, breathy tone, produced in the lowest range of the saxophone or clarinet by carefully controlled suppression of the higher partials of a note. Subtone is produced by means of a small, slow, but steady stream of air, projected through a tight embouchure; the player must blow firmly to prevent the sound from breaking or fading altogether, but gently so that the upper partials of the note are not produced. On the saxophone, especially the tenor, the effect contrasts with the HONK, a loud low-pitched sound in which the high partials are prominent.

Subtone occurs most often in ballads. Ben Webster used it freely, as for example on Sid Catlett's *Memories of you* (1944, Com. 1515), notably in bar 7 of his opening statement of the theme. Another characteristic use is in bossa nova melodies, following the example of Stan Getz in the theme of *Desafinado* on his album *Jazz Samba* (1962, Verve 68432). John Coltrane's recording of *Alabama* on *Live at Birdland* (1963, Imp. 50) offers a clear example of the contrast between subtone, heard on the lowest pitches of the descending phrase of the theme at every statement throughout the performance, and Coltrane's normal penetrating tone.

BARRY KERNFELD

Suchanek, Bronisław (*b* Bielsko-Biała, Poland, 30 Aug 1948). Polish double bass player. He studied double bass at the Higher School of Music in Katowice (1967–72) and during that time played with the Silesian Jazz Quartet (late 1960s), Jan Wróblewski (1970), the pianist Mieczyslaw Kosz (1971), and Tomasz Stańko (1969–72); he is heard to advantage on *Jazz Message from Poland* (1972, JG 030), recorded with Stańko. From 1969 Suchanek worked regularly with the orchestra of the Polish Radio Jazz Studio, then in the mid-1970s he moved to Scandinavia, where he performed and recorded with the tenor saxophonist Urban Hansson (1976) and the Swedish Radiojazzgruppen under the leadership of George Russell (1977). In 1983 he played in the group G.A.P., based in Austria, and in 1983 and 1985 toured with Leszek Zadlo's Polski Jazz Ensemble. (J. Byrczek:"Eurojazz Personalities: Poland," *JF* [intl edn], no.18 (1972), 87)

WOLFRAM KNAUER

Sulieman, Idrees (Dawud ibn) (*b* St. Petersburg, FL, 7 Aug 1923). Trumpeter. After playing for four years with the Carolina Cotton Pickers he recorded with Thelonious Monk in 1947 and became a member of Cab Calloway's band the following year. Later he worked with many other big bands, including those of Count Basie, Lionel Hampton, and Dizzy Gillespie. In 1956 he played in Friedrich Gulda's ensemble of American musicians, and in 1958–9 he worked with Randy Weston. He toured Europe in the late 1950s with a group led by the pianist Oscar Dennard, and in 1961 he settled in Stockholm, where he began playing alto saxophone. From the mid-1960s to 1973 Sulieman was a member of the Clarke–Boland Big Band. In 1964 he moved to Copenhagen, and from that time has played mainly in Denmark; he has worked with the Radioens Big Band from the early 1970s. Sulieman's playing is rooted in the bop tradition; indeed, it has been said that he was one of the first musicians to adopt the bop style.

SELECTED RECORDINGS

As leader: *Now is the Time* (1976, Ste. 1052); *Bird's Grass* (1976, Ste. 1202)

As sideman: T. Monk: Humph (1947, BN 560); Evonce (1947, BN 547); Suburban Eyes/Thelonious (1947, BN 542); M. Waldron: *Mal 1* (1956, Prst. 7090); on *Mal 2* (1957, Prst. 7111), From this moment on, One by one, The way you look tonight; H. Parlan: *Arrival* (1973, Ste. 1012); Radioens Big Band: *By Jones, I Think we've Got it* (1978, Met. 15629), incl. New York City, Tip Toe

BIBLIOGRAPHY

J. G. Jepsen: "Idrees Sulieman diskografi," *Orkester journalen*, xxxii (1964), no.12, p.46; xxxiii (1965), no.1, p.30; no.2, p.27

M. Gardner: Liner notes, *Now is the Time* (Ste. 1052, 1976)

G. Henderson: "Idrees Sulieman: Interview," *Cadence*, v/9 (1979), 3

ROLAND BAGGENAES

Sulieman, Jamil. *See* NASSER, JAMIL.

Sullivan, Charles (Henry) (*b* New York, 8 Nov 1944). Trumpeter, flugelhorn player, and bandleader. He studied at the Manhattan School of Music (BA 1967), and from 1965 worked intermittently for off-Broadway theater productions. After playing with Lionel Hampton (1968) and Roy Haynes's Hip Ensemble (1969) he toured briefly as lead trumpeter with Count Basie (1970) and worked with Lonnie Liston Smith (1971), Sy Oliver (1972), and Norman Connors (1973). In 1973 he toured Europe and recorded with Abdullah Ibrahim, then worked intermittently with Sonny Fortune, recording in 1974–5 and touring the USA in 1978. He also recorded with Carlos Garnett, Bennie Maupin, and as a leader (all 1974), with Kenny Barron and Charles Greenlee (both 1975), with Ricky Ford, Eddie Jefferson, and Walter Davis (all 1977), and with Woody Shaw (1978–9). His playing may be heard to advantage on Ford's album *Loxodonta Africana* (1977, New World 204). From 1978 Sullivan led his own small group and a big band, Black Legacy. Despite his abilities as a soloist and section player, he remains an underrated musician.

BIBLIOGRAPHY

Feather–Gitler '70s

L. A. Emenari III: "Profile: Charles Sullivan," *DB*, xlvii/10 (1980), 50

Sullivan, Ira (Brevard, Jr.) (*b* Washington, 1 May 1931). Trumpeter and saxophonist. He grew up in a musical family and at the age of four began to learn trumpet and saxophone with his parents. Although he concentrated on the trumpet, when he began to play engagements during his high-school years it was more often as a tenor saxophonist than as a trumpeter. During the 1950s he was based in Chicago except for a brief period with Art Blakey in New York (1956). His skill on both his instruments (and soon on alto and baritone saxophones as well) and his mastery of the bop style became widely known and he played with many prominent musicians. Always reluctant to travel, having settled in Florida in the early 1960s he had fewer opportunities to play with major jazzmen, though he appeared regularly in Miami and Fort Lauderdale; except for playing occasionally in recording sessions he was seldom heard outside Florida until 1980. During the 1960s he tired of bop and evolved a freer style, at the same time taking up soprano saxophone and flutes. Through contact with younger players at the University of Miami (including Pat Metheny and Jaco Pastorius) he began to teach. In 1980 he formed a quintet with his friend Red Rodney. On Sullivan's insistence it played new compositions rather than bop standards and as a consequence its music was among the most creative and stimulating of the 1980s. It also formed a favorable setting for Sullivan's playing, and enabled him to demonstrate his remarkable ability to create an individual and original style on each of his instruments.

Joe Sullivan at Café Society, New York, 1941

SELECTED RECORDINGS

As leader: *Nicky's Tune* (1958, Del. 422); *Bird Lives!* (1962, VJ 3033); *Horizons* (1967, Atl. 1476); *Ira Sullivan* (1975–6, A&M Hor. 706); *Peace* (1978, Gal. 5114); *Multimedia* (1978, Gal. 5137); with R. Rodney: *Live at the Village Vanguard* (1980, Muse 5209); *Ira Sullivan Does it All* (1981, Muse 5242); with R. Rodney: *Night and Day* (1981, Muse 5274), *Sprint* (1982, Elek. Mus. 60261)

As sideman: R. Rodney: *Red Rodney: 1957* (1957, Signal 1206); R. Kirk: *Introducing Roland Kirk* (1960, Argo 669)

BIBLIOGRAPHY

FeatherE; *Feather–Gitler '70s*

D. DeMicheal: "Ira Sullivan: Legend in the Making," *DB*, xxvii/19 (1960), 18

D. D. Spitzer: "Ira Sullivan: Living Legend," *DB*, xxxix/3 (1972), 14 [incl. discography]

G. Rouy: "Ira Sullivan," *Jm*, no.290 (1980), 38; no.291 (1980), 36; no.292 (1980), 44 [incl. discography]

N. Tesser: "Ira Sullivan: Multi Mystique," *DB*, xlviii/2 (1981), 21 [incl. discography]

SCOTT YANOW

Sullivan, Joe [Joseph Michael] (*b* Chicago, 4 Nov 1906; *d* San Francisco, 13 Oct 1971). Pianist and composer. He studied for two years at the Chicago Conservatory and played on the vaudeville circuit before obtaining regular work in Chicago, where he appeared with many bandleaders and performed on radio. He made a memorable recording début in December 1927 with Red McKenzie and Eddie Condon's Chicagoans, playing a powerful, driving solo on *China Boy*. During an engagement with Bob Crosby's orchestra in 1936 he became ill with tuberculosis, but after his recovery resumed working as a soloist and with ensembles. He rejoined Crosby's band briefly (1939), then led one of the earliest racially integrated ensembles in New York at Café Society (see illustration) and the Famous Door (1940). For some years thereafter he traveled frequently between the East and West coasts, fulfilling short-lived engagements and recording sporadically; among his notable achievements were his solo on *After you've gone* (1951) and his recording of eight unpublished compositions by Fats Waller (1952). In 1955 Sullivan became intermission pianist at the Club Hangover, San Francisco. He continued to work into the early 1960s, and in 1963 appeared at the Monterey Jazz Festival and began playing at the Trident in San Francisco, but he was taken ill at the Newport Jazz Festival the following year and thereafter performed only infrequently. He appeared in several films in the 1930s; he also led a sextet in a jazz sequence in the documentary *The Fight for Life* (1940) and improvised music for a film about blind children, *Who's Enchanted?* (1963).

Sullivan was strongly influenced by the blues and the stride piano style of Waller; he also drew inspiration from Earl Hines, Jimmie Noone, and Louis Armstrong. He typically exploited the resources of his instrument with the bravura of a concert pianist, improvising with tremendous animation and ferocity of attack. A strong rhythmic pulse of four beats to the bar was usually present in his playing, and at times broke through even the poignant lyricism with which he interpreted slow or medium-tempo ballads such as *I cover the waterfront*. Among his best-known compositions are *Gin Mill Blues*, *Little Rock Getaway*, and *Farewell to Riverside*.

SELECTED RECORDINGS

As unaccompanied soloist: Gin Mill Blues (1933, Col. 2876D); Little Rock Getaway/Just Strolling (1935, Decca 600); *Fats Waller First Editions* (1952,

Epic 1003); *New Solos by an Old Master* (1953, Riv. 202), incl. I cover the waterfront, Farewell to Riverside; *Mr. Piano Man* (1955, Down Home 2), incl. In the middle of a kiss; *Joe Sullivan* (1963, Pumpkin 112)

As sideman: McKenzie and Condon's Chicagoans: China Boy (1927, OK 41011); Chicago Rhythm Kings: I've found a new baby (1928, Bruns. 4001); E. Condon: Indiana (1928, Parl. R2932); R. Nichols: Shim-me-sha-wabble (1930, Bruns. 80005); E. Condon: There'll be some changes made (1939, Decca 18041); B. Crosby: Till we meet again (1939, Decca 2825); G. Wettling: *George Wettling's Dixielanders* (1951, Col. CL6189), incl. After you've gone; E. Condon: *Chicago and all that Jazz* (1961, Verve 68441), incl. China Boy

BIBLIOGRAPHY

D. Biggar: "Gin Mill Joe," *Piano Jazz*, no.1 (1945), 22
R. Hadlock: *Jazz Masters of the Twenties* (New York, 1965/*R*1985)
K. Gallacher: "Joe Sullivan: a Study in Neglect," *JJ*, xx/4 (1967), 2
R. Hadlock: "Joe Sullivan: the Last Days," *J&B*, iii/3 (1973), 6
N. P. Gentieu: "Notes for a Bio-discography of Joe Sullivan," *JJS*, iv/2 (1977), 33; *ARJS*, i (1982), 128; ii (1983), 81; iii (1985), 11
R. Hadlock: Liner notes, *Joe Sullivan* (TL 27, 1982)

NORMAN P. GENTIEU

Sullivan, Maxine [Williams, Marietta] (*b* Homestead, PA, 13 May 1911; *d* New York, 7 April 1987). Singer. She first attracted attention in 1937 in Claude Thornhill's band, particularly with her successful recording *Loch Lomond*, which typecast her as a singer of folk and light-classical material for the rest of her career. In the following year she appeared in two Hollywood film musicals, *Going Places* (opposite Louis Armstrong) and *St. Louis Blues*, and in the Broadway show *Swingin' the Dream* (again with Armstrong). Until 1942 she sang frequently in the ensemble led by her husband John Kirby, where her gentle delivery, pristine enunciation, and light sense of swing perfectly complemented the group's concept of chamber jazz. Thereafter Sullivan embarked upon a solo career, occasionally performing on valve trombone and flugelhorn. In the mid-1950s she trained as a nurse, and then became active in community services in New York, appearing infrequently at clubs and festivals with jazz musicians such as Bobby Hackett, Charlie Shavers, Earl Hines, and Bob Wilber. In the 1970s she sang regularly with the World's Greatest Jazz Band of Bob Haggart and Yank Lawson, and she continued to perform and record in the 1980s with all her former prowess. Her album *The Great Songs from the Cotton Club* was nominated for a Grammy Award in 1986.

Oral history material in *NjR* (JOHP), *NjR*.

For illustration *see* FILMS, fig.5.

SELECTED RECORDINGS

Loch Lomond (1937, Voc./OK 3654); Nice work if you can get it (1937, Voc./OK 3848); St. Louis Blues (1938, Vic. 25895); When your lover has gone/My Ideal (1942, Decca 18555); *The Complete Charlie Shavers with Maxine Sullivan* (1956, Period 1113); *The Queen* (1981–5, Kenneth 2052–5); *The Great Songs from the Cotton Club by Harold Arlen and Ted Koehler* (1984, Milan 270); *Uptown* (1985, Conc. 288)

BIBLIOGRAPHY

Arnold Shaw: *The Street that Never Slept: New York's Fabled 52nd Street* (New York, 1971/*R*1977 as *52nd Street: the Street of Jazz*)
R. Johnson: "Maxine Sullivan," *Coda*, xi/6 (1974), 26
S. Traill: "Maxine Sullivan," *JJ*, xxviii/11 (1975), 6
B. Rusch: "A Talk with Maxine Sullivan," *Cadence*, i/10 (1976), 4
D. J. Travis: *An Autobiography of Black Jazz* (Chicago, 1983) [incl. interviews], 451
C. Deffaa: "Still Gently Swinging," *MR*, xii/10 (1985), 10
J. S. Wilson: "Maxine Sullivan: 50 years a Singer and Still Growing," *New York Times* (15 Dec 1985), §II, 29
Obituary, L. Feather, *Jazz Express*, no.84 (1987), 7

J. BRADFORD ROBINSON

Summa cum Laude Orchestra. Octet formed in 1939 by BUD FREEMAN.

Sun (i). Record label. It was established in Canada in the very early 1920s, and drew its repertory from Okeh's catalogue. The issues include some of Mamie Smith's earliest recordings. (B. Rust: *The American Record Label Book* (New Rochelle, NY, 1978), 284)

Sun (ii). Record company and label. The company was established in 1973 in Paris by Sébastien Bernard and flourished during the mid-1970s. It concentrated on recording American free-jazz musicians who were resident in France, including Frank Wright and Noah Howard. (S. Loupien: "Deux stratégies phonographiques en France: Sun par Sébastien Bernard," *Jm*, nos.266–7 (1978), 26)

Sunnyside. Record company and label. It was established in New York in 1982 by François Zalacain and Christine Berthe. At first it recorded mostly unaccompanied pianists and ensembles without drums, but later expanded its repertory to include the work of more standard groups. Among its most important musicians are Kirk Lightsey, Lee Konitz, Rufus Reid, James Williams, Bill Pierce, and the pianist Harold Danko. Its catalogue is distributed in the USA by Muse.

Sun Ra [Blount, Herman ("Sonny"); Bourke, Sonny; Le Sony'r Ra] (*b* Birmingham, AL, May 1914). Composer, bandleader, and keyboard player. He played piano in Fletcher Henderson's orchestra in 1946–7 (using the names Herman "Sonny" Blount and Le Sony'r Ra), and first attracted attention as an arranger. Later he led his own group in Chicago. During the mid-1950s his Myth-Science (or Solar) Arkestra became significant in Chicago's avant-garde jazz movement and began to issue recordings; it also played in the film documentary *The Cry of Jazz* (1959), for which Sun Ra composed the score. He moved to New York in 1960, by which time he had begun to develop a unique and highly inventive ensemble style that was to attract a considerable following, particularly among European jazz enthusiasts. In the 1970s Sun Ra and the Arkestra settled in Philadelphia. They reached large audiences by touring and lecturing at American colleges and universities, by performing in Europe, and above all by appearing on the nationally broadcast television program "Saturday Night Live" (1976). A documentary film, *Sun Ra: a Joyful Noise*, was made in 1980, directed by Robert Mugge. Although over the years he has often had little work, Sun Ra has kept his band together; inspired by their leader's intense devotion to his music, the players rehearse constantly. Sidemen in the group have included Marshall Allen, Ronnie Boykins, Craig Harris, Lex Humphries, Clifford Jarvis, Pat Patrick, Julian Priester, and, most notably, John Gilmore. The band continued to tour and record into the late 1980s.

Along with Cecil Taylor and Ornette Coleman, Sun Ra significantly influenced the new jazz styles of the 1960s. Much of his earlier work derived from the popular and commercial jazz of the time; *Reflections in Blue* (1957) is in a conventional bop style, also incorporating blues patterns and common formal designs. But if the accepted recording dates for the album *Angels and Demons at Play* – 1955 to 1957 – are correct, then by this time Sun Ra had already anticipated elements of the free-jazz style. For example, his composition *A Call for All Demons* from this album presents a wonderfully humorous combination of atonal improvising and Latin dance rhythms: the piece might best be described as a free-jazz mambo. Within ten years works such as *Cosmic Chaos* showed a radical, complex, often frenetic idiom, and an obsession with percussion instruments. Sun Ra

Sun Ra with members of his Arkestra, Central Park, New York, 1987

employs freely improvised solos in busy combinations with microtonal melodies and electronic effects, often juxtaposing standard jazz tunes with aleatory solo work on such instruments as piccolo, violin, and synthesizer in addition to saxophones and trumpets. (For observations on the complexity of collective improvisation in so large a group *see* BANDS, §1.) These musical innovations are combined with novel mixed-media techniques loosely based on astronomical and ancient Egyptian imagery; the band's performances commonly include slide and light shows and modern dance.

Sun Ra's importance as a keyboard player lies in his use of new instruments to explore new timbres. He is a capable pianist, but has made notable recordings on electric piano (from 1956), clavioline (from 1963), and Moog synthesizer (from 1969). He has also performed on other conventional and unusual keyboard instruments, including celesta, organ, and rocksichord – an electric keyboard that combines the sharp attack of a harpsichord with the glossy, sustained sound of an electric piano.

See also BLUES, §12, and JAZZ (i), §VI, 3.

RECORDED COMPOSITIONS
(selective list)

Angels and Demons at Play (1955–7, Saturn 407), incl. A Call for All Demons; *Jazz by Sun Ra* (1956, Tran. 10); *Sound of Joy* (1957, Del. 414), incl. Reflections in Blue; *The Futuristic Sounds of Sun Ra* (1961, Savoy 12169); *When the Sun Comes Out* (1962–3, Saturn 402); *The Magic City* (?1965, Saturn 403); *The Heliocentric Worlds of Sun Ra* (1965, ESP 1014, 1017), incl. Cosmic Chaos; *Nothing Is* (1966, ESP 1045); *The Solar Myth Approach* (1970–71, Actuel 40); *Live at Montreux* (1976, IC 1039); *Visions* (1978, Ste. 1126); *The Other Side of the Sun* (1978–9, Sweet Earth 1003)

BIBLIOGRAPHY

B. McRae: "Sun Ra," *JJ*, xix/8 (1966), 15
L. Jones: *Black Music* (New York, 1967/R1980)
T. Fiofari: "The Music of Sun Ra: Space Age Music," *Negro Digest*, xix/3 (1970), 23
R. Townley: "Sun Ra," *DB*, xl/21 (1973), 18
E. Jost: *Free Jazz* (Graz, Austria, 1974)
B. McRae: "Avant Courier: Another Look at Sun Ra," *JJ*, xxviii/12 (1975), 14
H. Pekar: "Sun Ra," *Coda*, no.139 (1975), 2
J. E. Berendt: "Sun Ra und sein schwarzer Kosmos," *Ein Fenster aus Jazz: Essays, Portraits, Reflexionen* (Frankfurt am Main, Germany, 1977), 109
V. Wilmer: *As Serious as your Life: the Story of the New Jazz* (London, 1977, rev. 1980)
B. Primack: "Captain Angelic: Sun Ra," *DB*, xlv/9 (1978), 14 [interview]
J. Buzelin and A. R. Hardy: "Disco Sun Ra," *Jh*, no.361 (1979), 15; no.362 (1979), 23
H. Geerken: *Chronological Discography of the Acoustic Works of Sun Ra, 1956–1981* (Athens, 1982)
L. Lyons: *The Great Jazz Pianists, Speaking of their Lives and Music* (New York, 1983), 83
T. Stahl: *Sun Ra Materialen/Sun Ra Materials* (Freudenberg, nr Siegen, Germany, 1983, rev. and enlarged 2/1987) [Ger. and Eng. texts; incl. discography]
J. Litweiler: *The Freedom Principle: Jazz after 1958* (New York, 1984), 129

ROBERT DICKOW/R

Sunrise. Record label. A subsidiary of RCA, it was operational for about a year from August 1933. Its catalogue included a fair proportion of jazz recordings; all items issued on Sunrise were also put out on Bluebird. (B. Rust: "A Glimpse of the Past: Sunrise and Timely Tunes," *Sv*, no.16 (1968), 17)

Sunset. Record label. It existed in California from 1922 to 1926; on it were issued some of the earliest recordings made on the West Coast of Afro-American jazz. These included particularly important items by the California Poppies (1923) and the Stompin' Six (1925), which were both groups associated with the pianist Sonny Clay.

BIBLIOGRAPHY

B. Rust: *The American Record Label Book* (New Rochelle, NY, 1978), 286
H. Rye: "West Coast Recordings 1922–1935," *Collectors Items*, no.40 (1987), 14

Sunset Cafe. Nightclub in Chicago; *see* NIGHTCLUBS AND OTHER VENUES.

Sunset Crystal Palace. Nightclub in Kansas City; *see* NIGHTCLUBS AND OTHER VENUES.

Sunshine. Record label. It was established by John C. Spikes and Benjamin "Reb" Spikes in Los Angeles in 1922. Its catalogue contained only three items, but these are notable in that they were the first recordings made by a black band from New Orleans, Ory's Sunshine Orchestra. These were recorded by NORDSKOG, and were also issued on that company's label. (F. Owen: "A Glimpse of the Past, 12: Sunshine & Nordskog," *Sv*, no.21 (1969), 94).

Sunshine, Monty (*b* London, 8 April 1928). English clarinetist. Self-taught, he was a founding member of the Crane River Jazz Band, with which he performed and recorded from 1949 to 1953. He then joined Ken Colyer's Jazzmen. In 1954 the personnel of Colyer's group formed a new band, which was led by Chris Barber (for illustration *see* BARBER, CHRIS). After leaving Barber in 1960, Sunshine began to work as a leader; his sidemen have included Johnny Parker, the trumpeter Rod Mason, and the trombonist Geoff Sowden. Good examples of his solo playing may be heard on Barber's recordings of *Wild Cat Blues* (1953, Sto. KB206) and *Hushabye* (1956, Nixa NJ2011). Later he again recorded with the Crane River Jazz Band (which was reunited in 1972 and 1973) and also with Barber (1975). In the 1980s, while continuing to play and record with his own band, Sunshine performed in a touring show with Lonnie Donegan.

BIBLIOGRAPHY

R. Harris: *Jazz* (London, 1952, 5/1957)
D. Boulton: *Jazz in Britain* (London, 1958)
D. Fairweather: "Sunshine, Monty," in I. Carr, D. Fairweather, and B. Priestley: *Jazz: the Essential Companion* (London, 1987)

NEVIL SKRIMSHIRE

Suomen Jazzliitto [Finnish Jazz Federation, FJF]. Organization formed in 1966 by Pekka Gronow and others to promote jazz in Finland. It organizes and sponsors jazz performances, lectures, tours, and workshops, as well as the Finnish National Jazz Days, held each November in various cities. The federation issued the periodical *Rytmi* from 1967 to 1981 and has also published several books on jazz in Finland, including Åke Granholm's *Finnish Jazz* (Helsinki, 1974, rev. and enlarged by M. Konttinen 2/1982, rev. and enlarged by J.-P. Vuorela 3/1986) and Hans Westerberg's *Suomolaiset jazzlevytysket, 1932–1976/a Finnish Jazz Discography, 1932–1976* (Helsinki, 1977). It has 26 affiliates in Finland and belongs in turn to the International Jazz Federation and Nordjazz. In 1987 the federation's president was Jaakko Tahkolahti and its executive director was Timo Vähäsilta.

Superbone. A hybrid trombone with both slide and valves, designed and used by Maynard Ferguson; *see* TROMBONE.

Super Disc. Record label. It existed from 1945 to 1947; the proprietors were Irvin Feld, Israel Feld, and Viola Marsham. The catalogue was devoted to race records, and included important material by Don Byas, Sid Catlett, and others. ("Super Disc," *Blues Research*, no.16 (n. d. [?1966]), 12)

Superior. Record label. It was established by the Starr Piano Co. after that organization discontinued Gennett; the discs were apparently sold in chain stores. 339 issues were made between December 1930 and June 1932, including many race and jazz items.

BIBLIOGRAPHY

G. W. Kay: "The Superior Catalog," *Record Research*, no.37 (1961), 1; no.38 (1961), 10; no.39 (1961), 19; no.41 (1962), 11; no.42 (1962), 11; no.43 (1962), 19; no.47 (1962), 19; no.48 (1963), 10
R. M. W. Dixon and J. Godrich: *Recording the Blues* (London, 1970)
B. Rust: *The American Record Label Book* (New Rochelle, NY, 1978), 287

Supersax. Ensemble of studio musicians. It was founded in Los Angeles in 1972, and was dedicated mainly to performing arrangements of the improvised solos of Charlie Parker. At first it was led by Buddy Clark and Med Flory, and consisted of Flory and Bill Perkins (alto saxophones), Warne Marsh and Jay Migliori (tenor saxophones), Jack Nimitz (baritone saxophone), Conte Candoli (trumpet), Ronnell Bright (piano), Clark (double bass), and Jake Hanna (drums). Clark left the group in 1975; although there have also been other changes of personnel, Flory has remained the group's leader and chief arranger into the 1980s. In 1981 it made a video recording, *Let the Bird Fly*.

A typical arrangement by Supersax begins with the theme, followed by a reproduction of Parker's solo; both of these are accompanied by block harmonies, and the melody is doubled at the lower octave by the baritone saxophonist. After solos by one or more players the piece ends with a further block harmonization of the theme. In the late 1970s Flory began adding to the group's repertory arrangements of solos by Bud Powell and John Coltrane, as well as of his own solos in the style of Charlie Parker.

SELECTED RECORDINGS

Supersax Plays Bird (1972, Cap. ST11177); *Supersax Plays Bird*, ii: *Salt Peanuts* (*c*1973, Cap. ST11271); *Chasin' the Bird* (1977, MPS 68160); *Dynamite!* (1978, MPS 68210); *Supersax & L. A. Voices*, iii: *Straighten up & Fly Right* (1986, Col. FC40547)

BIBLIOGRAPHY

H. Siders: "Caught in the Act: Supersax Plays Bird," *DB*, xl/3 (1973), 30
M. Morgan: "Caught in the Act: Supersax," *DB*, xlv/5 (1978), 39

THOMAS OWENS

Supertone (i). Record label. It was used in 1924 by the mail-order company Sears–Roebuck to issue material drawn from Olympic and Paramount. The company later revived the name for the issue in 1928–30 of repertory first issued on Gennett; this included a considerable number of race records.

Supertone (ii). Record label. It was established in the 1920s by Straus and Schram, a company that owned a store in Chicago. The catalogue was drawn from Grey Gull, Columbia, Paramount, and Pathé.

Supertone (iii). Record label. A subsidiary of Brunswick, it was used in 1930–31 to issue under pseudonyms recordings made by the parent company of such musicians as Benny Goodman and Red Nichols. The S2000 series included a sequence of race recordings.

Supreme. Record label. It was established on the West Coast late in 1947 by Al Patrick, and was devoted to race records. Jimmy Witherspoon was the most important musician in the catalogue, which also included Buddy Tate and Jay McShann. The label was also used to issue Fletcher Henderson's last commercial recording. Trading ceased in December 1950, after a ruinous lawsuit against Decca over an alleged cover version of a rhythm-and-blues recording; the masters were acquired by Swing Time. Supreme should not be confused with the earlier label of the same name, a subsidiary of Grey Gull from 1926 to 1929. (G. A. Moonoogian: "Supreme," *Whiskey, Women, and . . .*, no.16 (1987), 24)

Surman, John (Douglas) (*b* Tavistock, England, 30 Aug 1944). English baritone and soprano saxophonist. While still at school he played in jazz workshops organized by Mike Westbrook (1958–62), then studied at the London College of Music (1962–5) and London University Institute of Education (1965–6). He continued to play with Westbrook until 1968 and to record with him until 1975, and while performing in his group at the 1968 Montreux International Jazz Festival won an award as best soloist. During the late 1960s he also played with Graham Collier, Mike Gibbs, Dave Holland, Chris McGregor, and John McLaughlin, and in 1970 he toured Europe with Francy Boland's big band.

Surman formed the first of his own groups in 1968 and recorded as a leader the same year. From 1969 to 1972 he toured internationally with Barre Phillips and the drummer Stu Martin as The Trio (the group re-formed in 1977 as Mumps with the addition of Albert Mangelsdorff), and from 1973 to 1975 he played with Mike Osborne and Alan Skidmore in the saxophone trio SOS. Thereafter he collaborated with the Carolyn Carlson dance company at the Paris Opéra (1974–9), recorded duos with Karin Krog (1977) and Stan Tracey (1978), and worked with Miroslav Vitous (1979–82) and Azimuth. In the 1980s he has been active with an ensemble of 11 brass and rhythm players known as the Brass Project (from 1981), and with Graham Collier's big band Hoarded Dreams and Gil Evans's British Orchestra (both 1983). He toured again with Evans in 1986 and 1987.

Surman's prodigious talent was first noticed during his time as a soloist with Westbrook. He is remarkable for having transferred John Coltrane's characteristic phrasing to the baritone saxophone, a feat requiring considerable technical powers. He has also utilized for the first time the extreme upper register of the baritone by his mastery of its harmonics, thus expanding its versatility as a solo instrument. As a member of The Trio, his incredible range and wide tonal coloration brought him international acclaim, establishing him as one of the world's finest baritone saxophonists since Harry Carney, whom Surman acknowledges as a major influence. With SOS he employed synthesizers and electronic techniques, pre-programming synthesizer parts over which the three saxophones improvised in performance; he further developed this aspect of his work throughout the 1970s. Surman's personal style is one of stunning dexterity, technical mastery, and emotional depth, his playing mixing a harsh, forceful delivery with softer lyricism. The fluency and range he achieved early in his career on both baritone and soprano saxophones may be heard on the innovative jazz-rock album *Extrapolation* (1969), recorded with McLaughlin. Soon after making this recording he turned to more personal methods of expression and his solos on *Westering Home* (1972), using bass clarinet and a variety of other instruments in addition to the two saxophones, explore folk-related themes, at the same time making effective use of multiple recording techniques. His intensely personal music is often evocative and atmospheric, and draws heavily on his knowledge and experience of English and European folk, brass-band, classical, and church music. He has won jazz polls for both his performing and his recorded work, and as a composer has received commissions for church music and ballet scores. His work with the Brass Project in collaboration with John Warren demonstrates his often neglected strengths as a composer and arranger.

SELECTED RECORDINGS

As unaccompanied soloist: *Westering Home* (1972, Isl. 10); *Upon Reflection* (1979, ECM 1148); *Withholding Pattern* (1984, ECM 1295)

Duos with S. Tracey: *Sonatinas* (1978, Steam 106)

As leader: *John Surman* (1968, Deram 1030); *How Many Clouds Can You See?* (1969, Deram 1045); of The Trio (with B. Phillips and S. Martin): *The Trio* (1970, Dawn 3006), *Conflagration* (1971, Dawn 3022); *Morning Glory* (1973, Isl. 9237); of SOS (with M. Osborne and A. Skidmore): *SOS* (1975, Ogun 400); with J. DeJohnette: *The Amazing Adventures of Simon Simon* (1981, ECM 1193); *Such Winters of Memory* (1982, ECM 1254)

As sideman: J. McLaughlin: *Extrapolation* (1969, Marmalade 608007); *Where Fortune Smiles* (1970, Dawn 3018); M. Westbrook: *Citadel/Room 315* (1975, RCA SF8433); K. Krog: *Cloud Line Blue* (1977, Pol. 2382093); M. Vitous: *Journey's End* (1982, ECM 1242); G. Evans: *The British Orchestra* (1983, Mole 8)

BIBLIOGRAPHY

V. Schonfield: "World Class Baritone from West Country," *MM* (12 Aug 1967), 6

L. Henshaw: "Now Surman Joins the British Jazz Brain Drain," *MM* (14 June 1969), 10

R. Williams: "Surman: the Happy Wanderer," *MM* (14 March 1970), 8

M. Paton: "Surman on the Mount," *MM*, liii (22 April 1978), 52

L. Tomkins: "John Surman and Albert Mangelsdorff," *CI*, xvi (1978), no.6, p.23; no.7, p.14

R. Cotterrell: "John Surman: Perpetual Motion," *JF* [intl edn], no.76 (1982), 25

P. Danson: "John Surman," *Coda*, no.189 (1983), 12

G. Lock: "Save the Wail," *The Wire*, no.14 (1985), 35

SIMON ADAMS

Sutton, Mynie [Myron Pierman] (*b* Niagara Falls, Canada, 9 Oct 1903; *d* Niagara Falls, 17 June 1982). Canadian alto saxophonist and bandleader. He played with dance bands in the northern USA from 1924 to 1931, when he formed the Canadian Ambassadors with other black musicians, including Lou Hooper. The band played in and around Montreal, but in 1938 the members drifted apart owing to lack of work. Sutton returned to his home town, where he led a dance band and small groups. A number of his performances are preserved on amateur recordings from the 1930s, 1940s, and 1970s; his arrangement of a tune based on *Honeysuckle Rose* (recorded *c*1947) was issued on the anthology *Jazz and Hot Dance in Canada, 1916–1949* (Harl. 2023, 1986; with liner notes and discography by J. Litchfield). His collection of photographs and other materials is now in the archives of Concordia University, Montreal; *see* LIBRARIES AND ARCHIVES, §2.

Oral history material in *CaQMG*.

JACK LITCHFIELD

Sutton, Ralph (Earl) (*b* Hamburg, nr St. Louis, 4 Nov 1922). Pianist. He played in and around St. Louis in the late 1930s before joining Jack Teagarden's band in 1941. In 1947 he appeared on the weekly radio show "This is Jazz," then worked as the intermission pianist at Eddie Condon's club in New York (1948–56). He was a founding member of the World's Greatest Jazz Band in 1968, and played regularly with the group until 1974. From that time he has performed at clubs and jazz festivals and recorded both as a soloist and as an ensemble player. In the early 1980s he made a series of duo recordings with various musicians; he appeared at the Kool Jazz Festival, New York, in 1983 and performed at Dick Gibson's Colorado Jazz Party in Denver in 1985.

Sutton's playing is in the Harlem stride tradition of Fats Waller, James P. Johnson, and Willie "the Lion" Smith; it is characterized by a robust but tastefully controlled technique, an impeccably precise sense of rhythm, and an ebullient dancing quality. He performs works such as Bix Beiderbecke's *In a Mist* and Meade "Lux" Lewis's *Honky Tonk Train* in their original form; jazz standards, popular songs, and rags, however, are metamorphosed and enriched with melodic innovations of remarkably expressive power and vitality, including arabesque-like figures and riffs ingeniously adapted from traditional jazz motifs. In the late 1980s he was playing with undiminished drive, verve, and virtuosity, his repertory broader than before, and his basic style enhanced by a sparkling, melodious treble and subtle polyrhythms.

SELECTED RECORDINGS

As unaccompanied soloist: Dill Pickles/St. Louis Blues (1949, Cir. [USA] 1053); Whitewash Man/Carolina in the Morning (1949, Cir. [USA] 1052); In a Mist (1950, Com. 1525); *Ragtime* (*c*1962–3, Roul. 25232), incl. Honky Tonk Train; *The Other Side of Ralph Sutton* (1980, Chaz Jazz 107)

Duos: with G. Wettling: *Ralph Sutton at the Piano* (1952, Cir. [USA] 413), incl. Fascination, Drop me off in Harlem, Bee's Knees; with R. Braff: *Ralph Sutton & Ruby Braff* (1980, Chaz Jazz 101–2); with J. McShann: *Ralph Sutton & Jay McShann* (1980, Chaz Jazz 103–4); with K. Davern: *Ralph Sutton & Kenny Davern* (1980, Chaz Jazz 105–6); with E. Miller: *We've Got Rhythm* (1982, Chaz Jazz 110); with J. Lesberg: *Live at Hanratty's* (1982, Chaz Jazz 111); with P. Hucko: *Big Noise from Wayzata* (1982, Chaz Jazz 112); with V. Dickenson: *Blowin' Bubbles* (1982, Chaz Jazz 114)

As leader: with W. B. Davison: *Together Again!* (1977, Sto. 4027); *The Jazzband* (1982, Chaz Jazz 113)

BIBLIOGRAPHY

R. Johnson: "Ralph Sutton," *Coda*, xii/5 (1975), 9
J. D. Shacter: *Piano Man: the Story of Ralph Sutton* (Chicago, 1975) [incl. discography]
"Caught in the Act," *MM*, liv (23 June 1979), 61; lv (21 June 1980), 24
G. Endress: "Ralph Sutton," *JP*, xxix/11 (1980), 6
J. De Muth: "Ralph Sutton: on the Road with a Jazz Piano Veteran," *Keyboard*, vii/12 (1981), 30

NORMAN P. GENTIEU

Suzuki, Isao [Hisao] (*b* Tokyo, 2 Jan 1946). Japanese double bass player. He recorded with the pianist Shotaro Mariyasu (1954), played with Sleepy Matsumoto (1961–4) and Sadao Watanabe (1964–5), and led a bop group in Tokyo (1965–9); he also recorded with Hampton Hawes (1968). After working in New York with Art Blakey (1969–70) he returned to Japan, where he worked again as a leader. He plays double bass and cello on four albums recorded between 1973 and 1975 (including *Blow up*, 1973, Three Blind Mice 15), and piccolo bass on an album recorded in 1978, on which he is accompanied by Hank Jones, Ron Carter, Roy Haynes, and a string quartet. (*Feather–Gitler '70s*)

BARRY KERNFELD

Suzuki, Yoshio (*b* Nagano, Japan, 21 March 1946). Japanese double bass player and pianist. He studied piano and violin at an early age and guitar in his teens, and played piano in a band at Waseda University in Tokyo. At the suggestion of Sadao Watanabe he took up double bass, then played with Watanabe's quartet from 1969 and Masabumi Kikuchi's sextet from 1971. After moving to New York in 1973 he played with Stan Getz and with Art Blakey and the Jazz Messengers; in 1984 he returned to Tokyo to compose and to perform his own music. He formed a group in 1985 and performed at Sogetsu Kaikan in Tokyo in April 1986.

SELECTED RECORDINGS

As leader: *Matsuri* (1979, CBS–Sony 25AP1611); *Wings* (1981, Trio PAP25013); *Morning Picture* (1984, JVC JMI28005); *Fairy Tale* (1987, JVC VDJ1078)

As sideman with A. Blakey: *Backgammon* (1976, Roul. 5003)

YOZO IWANAMI

Svenska Hotkvintetten. Swedish recording quintet, formed in 1939. Its instrumentation was modeled after that of the Quintette du Hot Club de France, which had visited Sweden in the spring of 1939; the group's members were the violinist Emil Iwring, the guitarists Sven Stiberg, Kalle Löhr, and Folke Eriksberg, and the double bass player Roland Bengtsson. Among those who performed and recorded with the quintet as guest soloists were Thore Jederby and the clarinetist John "Joppla" Björling. The Svenska Hotkvintetten may be heard to advantage on two recordings made for Columbia in 1940, *Opus 5* (1210) and *Honest and Truly/Wham* (1199); the group disbanded in 1942.

ERIK KJELLBERG

Svensson, Reinhold [Ragtime Reinhold] (*b* Husum, nr Örnsköldsvik, Sweden, 20 Dec 1920; *d* Stockholm, 23 Nov 1968). Swedish pianist, composer, and arranger. Almost blind from birth, he made his professional début recording some solo piano works (1941–2), then played in a quintet led by the violinist Hasse Kahn (1942–8). He quickly made his name as a swing pianist, though he also used bop idioms; in 1949 he performed successfully at the Paris Jazz Fair. He took part in many recording sessions, and his quintet recordings in the style of George Shearing (for example, *Tasty Pastry*, 1952, Met. J245) brought him fame in the USA and elsewhere; he also recorded as the leader of a trio and, as Ragtime Reinhold, on the Hammond organ. From 1948 to 1960 Svensson played regularly in Putte Wickman's sextet; he made many well-worked arrangements for the group, and contributed compositions of his own such as *Lobster's Delight* (1955, Odeon SD5851) and *Impressions* (1957, Odeon GEOS64 [EP]).

BIBLIOGRAPHY

"Svenskt stjärnalbum" [Swedish star album], *Orkester journalen*, xii/6 (1944), 5
"På omslaget" [On the cover], *Orkester journalen*, xxiv/5 (1956), 4
R. Dahlgren: "Reinhold Svensson," *Orkester journalen*, xxxvii/1 (1969), 8
E. Kjellberg: *Svensk jazzhistoria: en översikt* [Swedish jazz history: an overview] (Stockholm, 1985)

ERIK KJELLBERG

Swaggie. Record company and label. The company was established in Australia in 1949 by Graeme Bell. During its first decade it was devoted mainly to the documentation of Australian jazz, especially of the traditional revival; it has retained this role into the 1980s. However, the label became more widely known internationally in the early 1960s, when it was used for an extensive series of reissues, on 7-inch LPs, of vintage jazz; the material was drawn from all the major American companies, obtained by leasing agreements with their Australian branches and agents. This series was succeeded in the 1970s by a similar sequence of 12-inch LPs which drew mainly on American Decca and (through Australian EMI) on Okeh and the French label Swing. In the 1980s an additional series, Vintage Jazz Archives, has been devoted to the definitively programmed chronological reissue (using dubbings of the highest quality) of early jazz. Swaggie is managed by Nevill Sherburn.

BIBLIOGRAPHY

N. Sherburn and G. Hulme: "The Swaggie Label," *Matrix*, no.23 (1959), 3; no.24 (1959), 11; no.27 (1960), 3; nos.29–30 (1960), 37; nos.35–6 (1961), 29
"Reissue Listing: Swaggie," *JM*, no.169 (1969), 26
N. Sherburn: "Swaggie Jazz Collector Series," *Matrix*, nos.81–8 (1969–70) [series of suppls.]

Swallow, Steve [Stephen W.] (*b* Fair Lawn, NJ, 4 Oct 1940). Bass player. He played professionally with visiting jazz musicians while a student at Yale. In 1960 he began an apprenticeship with Paul Bley; later he mastered an advanced bop style in groups with Art Farmer and, from 1965, with Stan Getz. In Getz's group he also began his long and productive association with Gary Burton, whose quartet he joined in 1967. Shortly thereafter he took up electric bass guitar, which quickly became his principal instrument. Swallow was a key figure in working out a jazz vocabulary for the electric bass. Unlike rock bass players he uses no distorting devices, concentrating instead on facility and precision of attack, and on new melodic patterns suitable to a jazz context. In the mid-1970s he taught at the Berklee College of Music in Boston, but left teaching to return to performing. He has toured widely with Burton, Carla Bley (both into the mid-1980s), and John Scofield, and has directed his attention increasingly to composing, most notably in *Home* (1979), a setting of poems by Robert Creeley.

SELECTED RECORDINGS

As leader: with G. Burton: *Hotel Hello* (1974, ECM 1055); *Home* (1979, ECM 1160)

As sideman: G. Russell: *Ezz-thetics* (1961, Riv. 9375); P. Bley: *Footloose* (1962–3, Savoy 12182); G. Burton: *A Genuine Tong Funeral* (1967, RCA LSP3988); C. Bley: *Social Studies* (1980, Watt 11); J. Scofield: *Shinola* (1981, Enja 4004); C. Bley: *Night-glo* (1985, Watt 16)

BIBLIOGRAPHY

M. Williams: "Steve Swallow," *DB*, xxx/27 (1963), 22

J. Rosenbaum: "Steve Swallow: Renegade Jazz Bassist," *GP*, xv/12 (1981), 60

H. Mandel: "Steve Swallow: Bass in Progress," *DB*, xlix/11 (1982), 21

W. P. Hinely: "The Strings of Change," *JF* [intl edn], no.80 (1983), 36; no.81 (1983), 34

J. BRADFORD ROBINSON

Swan. Nickname of HOWARD JOHNSON (i).

Swanerud, Thore (*b* Stockholm, 18 June 1919). Swedish pianist, vibraphonist, and composer. He performed and recorded from the late 1930s and belonged to a trio from 1947 to 1949, with which he also recorded. He led a sextet from 1949 to 1951, recorded with James Moody (1949) and Ernestine Anderson (1956), and worked with Gösta Theselius. He made recordings as a leader into the 1980s (including *Star Dust*, 1984, Dra. 100); among his best-known compositions is the lyrical *Södermalm*. Although he commenced his career playing in the swing tradition, Swanerud was later influenced by modern trends and won a reputation as a fine soloist and accompanist.

Oral history material in *SSsv*.

BIBLIOGRAPHY

"Svenskt stjärnalbum" [Swedish star-album], *Orkester journalen*, ix/3 (1941), 5

ERIK KJELLBERG

Swartz, Harvie (*b* Chelsea, MA, 6 Dec 1948). Double bass player. He took up double bass in 1967 and played in Boston with Mose Allison, Chris Connor, and Al Cohn and Zoot Sims. In 1972 he moved to New York, where, with Mike Abene, he accompanied such singers as Connor, Jackie Cain and Roy Kral (recording in 1973), and Jackie Paris; he later played with Thad Jones and Mel Lewis and with Gil Evans. He worked regularly in the mid-1970s at Richard's Lounge in Lakewood, New Jersey, accompanying (among others) Lee Konitz, Jan Hammer, and John Abercrombie, and from 1974 to at least 1976 was a member of Barry Miles's Silverlight, in which he doubled as an electric bass guitarist. He played with various of David Friedman's groups (recording between 1975 and 1981), notably a trio with Eddie Daniels (1976) and Double Image (co-led by Dave Samuels). He also performed with Dave Matthews's big band (1976) and recorded with Steve Kuhn (1977–81). In the 1980s Swartz has experimented with unusual instrumental combinations: his album *Underneath it All*, for instance, features an ensemble of double bass, piano, flugelhorn, cello, percussion, and drums. In 1982–3 he led the Harvie Swartz String Ensemble, which included Terry King (violin) and Erik Friedlander (cello), and in the mid-1980s he worked frequently in a duo with Sheila Jordan.

SELECTED RECORDINGS

As leader: *Underneath it All* (1980, Gram. 8202); *Urban Earth* (1985, Gram. 8503); *Smart Moves* (1986, Gram. 8607)

As sideman: B. Miles: *Barry Miles and Silverlight* (1974, Lon. 651); D. Friedman: *Futures Passed* (1976, Enja 2068); S. Kuhn: *Last Year's Waltz* (1981, ECM 1213)

BIBLIOGRAPHY

Feather–Gitler '70s

A. J. Smith: "Profile: Harvie Swartz," *DB*, xliii/5 (1976), 32

WILLIAM S. BROCKMAN

Swayze, Edwin [King] (*b* Marshall, TX, 13 June 1906; *d* New York, 31 Jan 1935). Trumpeter. He played with Alex Hill and in 1924 joined Alphonso Trent, with whom he performed intermittently until 1928. In 1925–6 he toured and made several recordings with the singer Sammy Lewis (including *Hateful Papa Blues*, 1926, Voc. 1029, on which he plays an excellent muted solo). He also toured with Jelly Roll Morton and made two recordings with him in New York (1928). In 1929 he worked with Chick Webb and traveled to Europe, where in 1930 he joined Herb Flemming's International Rhythm Aces and led the Plantation Band. After returning to New York, Swayze recorded regularly with Cab Calloway (from July 1931), performed with Webb and Sam Wooding, and played and arranged for the bandleader Eugene Kennedy (1932); he then joined Calloway's band, with which he played until his death. Because of its pronunciation, Swayze's name has consistently been misspelled Swayzee.

BIBLIOGRAPHY

A. McCarthy: *Big Band Jazz* (New York and London, 1974)

D. Raichelson: Liner notes, *Jazz in Harlem, 1926–1931* (Arcadia 2008, 1976)

based on *ChiltonW*

Sweatman, Wilbur (C.) (*b* Brunswick, MO, 7 Feb 1882; *d* New York, 9 March 1961). Clarinetist, bandleader, and composer. His first professional work was in the late 1890s with circus bands. In 1902 he formed his own large quasi-symphonic orchestra, with which he toured and held residencies in Chicago; he moved to New York in 1913. Duke Ellington played in his Rag Time and Jazz Band for one week in 1923. From the 1930s Sweatman also ran a booking agency and became involved in music publishing and publicity work. He is best known, however, for his ability to play three clarinets simultaneously, and as the composer of *Down Home Rag*.

BIBLIOGRAPHY

L. Kunstadt and B. Cotton: "Daddy of the Clarinet: Wilbur Sweatman," *Record Research*, no.24 (1959), 3

A. McCarthy: *Big Band Jazz* (New York and London, 1974), 13

EDDIE LAMBERT

Swedish Radio Big Band. Group led from 1956 to 1965 by HARRY ARNOLD.

Swedish Radio Jazz Group. *See* RADIOJAZZGRUPPEN (ii).

Swee' Pea. Nickname of BILLY STRAYHORN.

Sweethearts of Rhythm. Name given to various bands led in the 1950s by the singer Anna Mae Winburn after the INTERNATIONAL SWEETHEARTS OF RHYTHM disbanded.

Sweets. Nickname of HARRY EDISON.

Swing (i). (1) A quality attributed to jazz performance. Although basic to the perception and performance of jazz, swing has resisted concise definition or description. Most attempts at such refer to it as primarily a rhythmic phenomenon, resulting from the conflict between a fixed pulse and the wide variety of actual durations and accents that a jazz performer plays against that pulse (*see* BEAT, esp. §3). However, such a conflict alone does not necessarily produce swing, and a rhythm section may even play a simple fixed pulse with varied amounts or types of swing. Clearly other properties are also involved, of which one is probably the forward propulsion imparted to each note by a jazz player through manipulation of timbre, attack, vibrato, intonation, or other means; this combines with the proper rhythmic placement of each note to produce swing in a great variety of ways.

(2) The name given to a jazz style and to a related phase of popular music which originated around 1930 when New Orleans jazz was in decline; it is characterized by a greater emphasis on solo improvisation, larger ensembles, a repertory based largely on Tin Pan Alley songs, and above all the more equal weight given to the four beats of the bar (hence the term "four-beat jazz" occasionally applied to this style). This important change in jazz rhythm took place gradually between 1930 and 1935 as the tuba was superseded by the double bass (played in the walking bass style) and the banjo by the rhythm guitar, and the basic pulse was transferred from the snare drum to the hi-hat or ride cymbal. The harmonic rhythm in swing was generally much faster than in New Orleans jazz, sometimes changing as often as twice a bar, and soloists were expected to improvise melodies freely over these "changes." There was a notable increase in instrumental virtuosity among soloists in this period; some of the most prominent were Henry "Red" Allen, Roy Eldridge, Coleman Hawkins, Chu Berry, Benny Goodman, Johnny Hodges, and Lester Young. At the same time instruments not previously regarded as suitable for solo work began to be given solo roles, including the drums (Gene Krupa and Chick Webb), double bass (Jimmy Blanton), vibraphone (Lionel Hampton and Red Norvo), and guitar (Django Reinhardt and Charlie Christian). The development of swing coincided with the emergence by 1932 of the 13-piece dance band (consisting of 3 trumpets, 2 trombones, 4 reed instruments, piano, guitar, double bass, and drum set); the music was thus most often played in "big bands" such as those led by Duke Ellington, Fletcher Henderson, Count Basie, Jimmie Lunceford, Benny Goodman, Artie Shaw, and Earl Hines (*see* BANDS, §4 (iii); *see also* BATTLE OF BANDS). However, the musicians often preferred to work in smaller groups, which allowed more scope for solo improvisation and extended their repertory beyond the confines of dance music. Important small groups working in this style included Goodman's groups, the Brunswick recording bands led by Teddy Wilson, the John Kirby Sextet, Fats Waller and his Rhythm, and various ad hoc recording groups drawn from the Ellington and Basie bands (*see also* BANDS, §4 (iv)). The swing rhythm section became an important element in rhythm-and-blues and hence in early rock-and-roll, and was also used by some traditional jazz groups from the early 1940s. A simple relaxed style of swing, played chiefly by small groups, developed in the late 1930s and became known as JUMP; this also influenced early rhythm-and-blues. Although in the late 1940s the swing style ceased to be the dominant movement in jazz, it continued to attract excellent young players such as Ruby Braff, Rolf Kühn, Claude Bolling, and Scott Hamilton, and remained commercially viable in the 1980s.

See also FORMS, §3, and JAZZ (i), §IV, 1, 2.

BIBLIOGRAPHY

A. Hodeir: *Hommes et problèmes du jazz, suivi de La religion du jazz* (Paris, 1954; Eng. trans., rev. Hodeir, as *Jazz: its Evolution and Essence*, New York, 1956/*R*1975)

G. Schuller: *Early Jazz: its Roots and Musical Development* (New York, 1968), 6ff

M. C. Gridley: *Jazz Styles* (Englewood Cliffs, NJ, 1978, rev. 2/1985 as *Jazz Styles: History and Analysis*, with suppl. *Instructor's Manual and Discography*)

C. Bohländer: *Die Anatomie des Swing* (Frankfurt am Main, Germany, 1986)

J. BRADFORD ROBINSON

Swing (ii). Record label. It was established in Paris in 1937; artists and repertory were directed by Charles Delaunay and Hugues Panassié, and the recordings were made and marketed by the French branch of EMI. As well as the recordings of the Quintette du Hot Club de France, the catalogue included extensive documentation of the work of such American visitors to France as Benny Carter, Coleman Hawkins, Dicky Wells, and Garland Wilson. From 1940 to 1944, though jazz was forbidden in France by the occupying Nazi regime, demand for the music increased and the label's operations flourished. Items were issued during this period by local and Antillean musicians, and by Americans who had escaped internment, such as Harry Cooper. After the war Swing's management commissioned several recordings that were made in the USA specifically for issue in France. In 1948, however, control of the label passed to Vogue, which Delaunay joined as manager of artists and repertory. Swing's back catalogue remained the property of EMI. Vogue continued to issue discs, some of them LPs, on Swing throughout the 1950s; these included items leased from such small American enterprises as Dial, Pacific Jazz, and Fantasy, as well as recordings made in France. The name has been used in the 1980s by the American company DRG for an important series of reissues of early jazz and swing, including material originally issued in France on Swing before 1948. (I. Frésart: "Swing: a Numerical Listing of the 78 r.p.m. Issues," *Matrix*, nos.62–79 (1965–8) [series of suppls.])

Swingle, Ward (Lamar) (*b* Mobile, AL, 21 Sept 1927). Singer and leader. From 1943 to 1945 he played alto saxophone and sang with the big band of the songwriter Ted Fio Rito. After receiving a master's degree from the Cincinnati Conservatory he studied piano on a Fulbright scholarship in Paris (1951), where he settled in 1956. He worked with the Blue Stars (1957–61), performed and recorded with the Double Six (1959–61), and with Christiane Legrand formed the Swingle Singers, a vocal ensemble, in 1962. This group became well-known for singing scat jazz versions of pieces from the classical repertory, in particular those of J. S. Bach; as its leader, Swingle toured the USA and Europe and recorded with the Modern Jazz Quartet (1966), Stan Getz (1971), and André Hodeir (1972). After the group disbanded in 1973 he formed Swingle II, which sang conventionally in addition to scat singing and which acquired a large repertory including madrigals, ragtime, popular songs, and rock; under the name the Swingle Singers this group recorded in 1979 and performed into the late 1980s.

BIBLIOGRAPHY
Feather '60s
M. Kerner: "Ward Swingle has New Four-four Ensemble," *Christian Science Monitor* (2 June 1978), 23

Swingle Singers. French vocal group. The eight academically trained singers were brought together in Paris in 1962 by Ward Swingle and Christiane Legrand to improve their sight-singing and musicianship. They developed a distinctive style, performing scat arrangements of Baroque and classical instrumental music, in which they added a jazz bass and percussion as accompaniment, embellished rhythmic sections, and improvised solos. They toured Europe and the USA, and made several successful recordings. In summer 1973 the group disbanded and Swingle formed a new, English, group, Swingle II. Making less use of scat singing, it performed a wider repertory, including madrigals, early jazz, and pop songs, and introduced new music by such composers as Luciano Berio.

RAYMONDE S. KRAMLICH

Swingsters. Name used by the CRUSADERS in the early 1950s.

Swingville. Record label founded in 1960 as a subsidiary of PRESTIGE.

Swope, Earl (Bowman) (*b* Hagerstown, MD, 4 Aug 1922; *d* Washington, 3 Jan 1968). Trombonist, brother of Rob Swope. His parents, a sister, and two other brothers were also musicians. He began his professional career at the age of 20 with Sonny Dunham's orchestra, before playing with Boyd Raeburn (1943–4), Georgie Auld (1945), and Buddy Rich (1945–7); when he joined Woody Herman's Second Herd he was replaced in Rich's band by his brother Rob. He was one of the few trombonists in the 1940s to develop a style that was not influenced by J. J. Johnson; he played in a modern barrelhouse style, which is clearly heard on the recordings he made with small groups led by Serge Chaloff and Stan Getz during the period he was with Herman (1947–9). In the 1950s he played with Elliot Lawrence (1950–51) and was a freelance player for some time in New York and Washington; then he again worked regularly in bands, playing in Jimmy Dorsey's last orchestra (1957) and with Louie Bellson (1959), with whom he recorded in Los Angeles. He spent the 1960s as a freelance in Washington, playing jazz of a commercialized type.

SELECTED RECORDINGS

As sideman: B. Rich: Dateless Brown/It Couldn't be True (*c*1945, Mer. 3001); S. Chaloff: Gabardine and Serge (1947, Savoy 978); A Bar a Second (1947, Savoy 906); W. Herman: *Classics in Jazz* (1948–50, Cap. T324), incl. Lollypop (1949); That's Right (1948, Cap. 15427); Lemon Drop (1948, Cap. 15365); S. Getz: Stan Gets Along (1949, Savoy 966); Fast (1949, Savoy 947); Not Really the Blues (1949, Cap. 57–837)

BIBLIOGRAPHY
FeatherE; Feather–Gitler '70s
I. Gitler: *Jazz Masters of the Forties* (New York, n.d. [?1966]/*R*1983 with discography)
J. Burns: "Bopping Bones," *J&B*, ii/7 (1972), 16

LAWRENCE KOCH

Swope, (George) Rob(ert) [Bob] (*b* Washington, 2 Dec 1926; *d* Washington, 9 Jan 1967). Trombonist, brother of Earl Swope. He performed and recorded with Buddy Rich (1947) and Chubby Jackson (from 1948 to early 1949), recorded with the clarinetist Jerry Wald (1947), and performed and recorded with Gene Krupa (1949–50) and Elliot Lawrence (1950–51). During the 1950s he led a trio in Washington, where he also belonged to the Orchestra, a big band that accompanied Charlie Parker (1953) and Dizzy Gillespie (1955). In New York he performed and recorded with the trumpeter Larry Sonn (1957) and worked briefly with Boyd Raeburn, Claude Thornhill, Jimmy Dorsey, and Louie Bellson. Later he returned to Washington and worked again as a leader. As a soloist, he is heard to advantage on *Godchild* (1949, Col. 38451), recorded with Jackson. (*FeatherE*)

Syeed, Luquman Abdul. *See* DAVIS, STEVE.

Symonds, Nelson (*b* Halifax, Canada, or Hammonds Plains, near Halifax, 24 Sept 1933). Canadian guitarist. He toured Canada and the USA with a carnival (1955–8), then settled in Montreal, where from the mid-1960s he worked as a sideman with visiting Americans (including Art Farmer, Benny Golson, Jimmy Heath, and Booker Ervin) and as a leader. He acquired a considerable reputation in Montreal in the 1980s but seldom toured and never recorded jazz. Symonds's style of playing is intense and roughly virtuoso.

Oral history material in *CaQMG*.

BIBLIOGRAPHY
M. Miller: "Symonds, Nelson," *Encyclopedia of Music in Canada*, ed. H. Kallmann, G. Potvin, and K. Winters (Toronto, Buffalo, and London, 1981)
——: "My Head will Never get Big," *Jazz in Canada: Fourteen Lives* (Toronto, Buffalo, and London, 1982), 146
——: "Nelson Symonds," *Boogie, Pete & the Senator: Canadian Musicians in Jazz: the Eighties* (Toronto, 1987), 250

MARK MILLER

Symphonic jazz. A term coined in the 1920s partly in connection with attempts, some of them sponsored by Paul Whiteman, to fuse jazz with classical forms, and therefore a predecessor of the term THIRD STREAM. The tendency emerged before jazz was identified as such, and there are a number of works such as Frederick Delius's *Appalachia* (1896, rev. 1903), subtitled "Variations on an old Slave Song," which reveal a keen perception of specifically American song and dance idioms.

Perhaps symphonic jazz may be said to have begun with George Gershwin's one-act opera *Blue Monday* (1922), although a variety of comparable works appeared during the same period from both the classical and jazz camps, among them two ballets – Darius Milhaud's *La création du monde* (1923) and Cole Porter's *Within the Quota* (1923, revived as *Times Past*, 1970). It was *Blue Monday*, however, that led Whiteman to commission *Rhapsody in Blue* (1924), undoubtedly the most famous piece of symphonic jazz. Other pieces by Gershwin followed, such as the Piano Concerto (1925) and the folk opera *Porgy and Bess* 1935), which may be considered the movement's peak.

Whiteman meanwhile obtained a considerable number of other pieces from both classical and jazz composers, such as George Antheil's Jazz Symphony (1925, rev. 1955) and Ferde Grofé's *Metropolis* (*c*1928). These in turn were a stimulus for a variety of other works, notably in England. Indeed, though associated primarily with the 1920s, the tendencies embodied in symphonic jazz remained until the arrival in the late 1950s of third stream music. Later commissions by Whiteman included *The Blue Belles of Harlem* from Duke Ellington (1942) and *Scherzo à la russe* from Igor Stravinsky (1944).

Ellington had always been aware of the endeavors of his predecessors, and began to step outside the normal time limits and functional purposes of much early jazz with such multi-sectional works as *Creole Rhapsody* (1931, two versions, *see* FORMS, §3), *Reminiscing in Tempo* (1935), and a number of other pieces. Classical music continues to be affected by jazz, notable instances being Stefan Wolpe's Quartet for trumpet, tenor saxophone, piano and percussion (1950) and Michael Tippett's Symphony no.3 (1970–72). Jazz likewise remains influenced by the large forms of classical music, examples including Carla Bley's opera *Escalator over the Hill* (1968–71), a latter-day *Porgy and Bess*, and Charlie Haden's *Ballad of the Fallen* (1982). None of this later music should be described as symphonic jazz, yet it would have been considerably different without that movement's earlier examples of cross-fertilization.

For further discussion *see* BANDS, §4, esp. (ii), and JAZZ (i), §III,4.

BIBLIOGRAPHY

P. Whiteman and M. M. McBride: *Jazz* (New York, 1926)

J. Sypniewski: *Ein Problem der Gegenwartsmusik: Jazz, unter besonderer Berücksichtigung des symphonisches Jazz (George Gershwin)* (diss., U. of Zurich, 1949)

M. Harrison: *A Jazz Retrospect* (Newton Abbot, England, 1976, rev. 2/1977)

MAX HARRISON

Symphonola. Record label. It was owned by the Larkin Co. of Buffalo, and was used to issue items produced by Emerson in 1918 and 1919. The catalogue included some of Emerson's recordings of the Louisiana Five. (B. Rust: *The American Record Label Book* (New Rochelle, NY, 1978), 291)

Synco Jazz band. Big band formed from the Synco Septet by William McKinney; in 1926 it became known as MCKINNEY'S COTTON PICKERS.

Syncopation. In measured music an effect of rhythmic displacement created by articulating weaker beats or metrical positions that do not fall on any of the main beats of the bar, while stronger beats are not articulated; *see* BEAT, §4(iii).

Synthesizer. An electronic instrument capable of generating and processing a wide variety of sounds. Synthesizers were first used as tools for composition in electronic music studios, but they have come to play an increasingly important role in performance, and have been used extensively by jazz musicians.

1. Technological development. 2. Use: (i) Introduction (ii) Keyboard synthesizers (iii) Other control devices (iv) Role of the synthesizer.

1. TECHNOLOGICAL DEVELOPMENT. The earliest instruments that employed the principles of synthesis were constructed around 1950, but it was not until 1964 that synthesizers were manufactured on a commercial basis. From that time the many types that have been produced have differed considerably in their capabilities, manner of operation, size, and appearance. The instruments are customarily divided on the basis of their methods of sound production into two types, analogue and digital. In principle, an analogue synthesizer is one that uses continuously varying voltages to model sound waves; a digital synthesizer employs discrete units of information that when combined in very rapid succession create an identical effect.

The first instruments to become commercially available in the mid-1960s employed the principle of analogue synthesis, and were composed of specially designed forms of the discrete devices found in electronic music studios – sound sources (oscillators) and sound processors (filters, modulators, envelope shapers, and mixers) – presented as standardized "modules," that is, separate items that could be connected in many configurations. The individual elements were linked by an important innovation, the voltage control system, by means of which a varying voltage could be made to affect certain aspects of the operation of any of these devices in a manner that had previously been possible only by the manual operation of an external control, such as a knob, slider, or switch. Such effects can be imitated by digital processes, and in the early 1980s many manufacturers began to include on their instruments at least one small microprocessor, which enabled the user of the digital synthesizer to store in its memory the data for creating timbres (thus facilitating the instant recall of sounds previously programmed), and, in some cases, to digitize external sound (by the technique known as sampling) which can then be played from the keyboard, and to set up complex patterns of repetition (by the technique known as sequencing). To further expand their capabilities many digital synthesizers can also be linked to small computers, usually by means of the Musical Instrument Digital Interface (MIDI), a system of standard code signals that was introduced in 1983. By the middle of the decade the use of MIDI had become so widespread that in performance several instruments could be controlled by a single keyboard on stage, enabling the synthesizers to be concealed elsewhere. In the late 1970s hybrid instruments began to appear that combined both analogue and digital elements. The distinctions between analogue and digital techniques are not always reflected in the selection and type of controls provided for the performer.

The earliest synthesizers were monophonic (that is, capable of playing only one note at a time); the first commercially available polyphonic instruments appeared in 1974. Although at this stage the state of the technology meant that the number of voices available at any one time was limited (for example, to four, six, or eight), polyphonic synthesizers made possible the playing of chords, which could be voiced in timbres not available on other instruments. The polyphonic synthesizer should not be confused with the string synthesizer, string ensemble, or polyphonic ensemble, hybrid polyphonic instruments that first became available in the late 1960s and combine some of the timbral capabilities of the synthesizer with the fixed registration options of the electronic organ, but do not have the flexibility or potential for tonal variation of the polyphonic synthesizer proper.

Even though on some early synthesizers manufacturers explored other methods of controlling pitch – such as touch-plates and ribbons – the most common controller has been the standard chromatic keyboard. By the mid-1980s, however, other systems had been considerably improved, and controllers resembling (and requiring similar performance techniques to) wind instruments, the electric guitar, and, especially, drums, became quite common. The drum machine, a dedicated digital synthesizer which is pre-programmed and plays sequences of preset drum sounds, has also been used, chiefly by jazz-rock musicians.

2. USE.

(i) Introduction. During the late 1960s the modular synthesizer was in regular use in both rock and avant-garde art music, and its currency in these styles undoubtedly contributed to its adoption by jazz musicians. By 1970 many pianists had taken up electric piano in addition to (or sometimes instead of) the acoustic instrument, and several also doubled on electronic organ; for these players the synthesizer represented a logical extension of the means at their disposal. Small monophonic keyboard synthesizers like the Minimoog, unlike any other keyboard instruments used in jazz, allowed the musician to play a melody line in any of a multitude of timbres, to inflect it with pitch bends and portamento (which are extremely idiomatic to jazz), and to vary the sustaining properties of notes; in general it provided a versatility of expression otherwise unavail-

able. Polyphonic synthesizers further expanded this facility, and gave the player the opportunity to voice chords in previously unobtainable colorations. The centrality of timbral manipulation to the concept of synthesis has led to the instrument's adoption in styles where exploration of new sounds is prevalent, such as free jazz and jazz-rock. Accordingly, most musicians in older styles with long-established conventions, such as swing and mainstream jazz, have been slower to accept the instrument.

(ii) Keyboard synthesizers. Although experiments combining jazz and taped electronic music took place as early as 1951, and the use of home-made electronic instruments and investigation of the potential of signal processors began in the mid-1960s (most notably by the saxophonist Gil Mellé), the synthesizer itself was not adopted in jazz on a widespread basis until after 1968, when manufacture of Moog's modular system began on a larger scale. Early users of the modular Moog included Sun Ra (who played the instrument on his album *My Brother, the Wind*, i, 1969, Saturn 521), Emil Richards, Oliver Nelson, Dick Hyman, Richard Teitelbaum of Musica Elettronica Viva, and Paul Bley (working with Annette Peacock in the Bley–Peacock Synthesizer Show); though designed for studio use it was employed in concerts by some of these musicians, as well as by other players. Bley also used the ARP 2500 modular system (which may be heard to advantage on his album *Revenge: the Bigger the Love the Greater the Hate*, 1969, Pol. 244046) for about four years before abandoning electronic instruments. Of the two other synthesizers to be produced on a commercial basis before 1970, the Buchla and the Synket, only the latter found favor with improvising musicians (notably Bill Smith and the Gruppo di Improvvisazione Nuova Consonanza), and then only on a limited scale.

The first portable keyboard synthesizer, Moog's Minimoog, appeared in 1970; it remained a firm favorite with musicians for many years. Indeed, many have continued to play it into the late 1980s, despite the vast technological superiority of later models, because it has a particularly rich timbre not matched by other instruments; it may be heard on Sun Ra's album *It's After the End of the World* (1970, MPS 2120748). The Minimoog and two similar synthesizers introduced the following year by ARP, the Odyssey and the 2600, were only monophonic, but they offered a wide range of sounds and resources in a single small unit, and also introduced a pitch-bend controller. Operated by the left hand, this normally takes the form of a wheel – as on the Minimoog – which the player moves forwards or backwards from a central position (to which it returns when released), providing an average compass of pitch variation of a minor 3rd (in some instruments up to an octave) upwards and downwards.

The development of jazz-rock by Miles Davis's group from the late 1960s, and by several of his former colleagues from 1971 (in such ensembles as Weather Report, Return to Forever, and the Mahavishnu Orchestra) was closely linked with the proliferation of electronic instruments. From playing the electric piano with Davis, Herbie Hancock, Chick Corea, and Joe Zawinul soon turned to synthesizers (though another of Davis's sidemen, Keith Jarrett, did not). For example, Hancock used the ARP Odyssey for the bass line at the beginning of *Chameleon*, from the album *Headhunters* (1973, Col. KC32731); Corea played particularly interesting Minimoog solos on the tracks *Nite Sprite* and *Lenore* from the album *The Leprechaun* (1975, Pol. 6062); and Zawinul made use of the ARP 2600 to simulate a trombone on *River People*, from Weather Report's album *Mr. Gone* (c1978, Col. JC35358). (In addition, musicians who had worked with Davis who were not keyboard players, including Wayne Shorter, John McLaughlin, and Billy Cobham, explored synthesizer controllers in other forms (see (iii) below).) Other musicians who early adopted the Minimoog were Sun Ra, George Duke, and Jan Hammer, who used it as a solo instrument on such recordings as the Mahavishnu Orchestra's *Birds of Fire* (1972, Col. KC31996).

From the late 1960s other companies began to manufacture synthesizers in Europe, Japan, and the USA. In 1974 the American company Oberheim produced the first commercially available polyphonic instruments, the Four-, Six-, and Eight-voice models. Among the first jazz musicians to use these were Corea, Zawinul (who played an Oberheim on the title track of Weather Report's album *Black Market*, c1976, Col. PC34099), Lyle Mays, and Hammer. Hammer controlled the synthesizer by means of the Probe, a four-octave portable keyboard which is suspended from the shoulder like a guitar, and played with the right hand, while the left operates the pitch-bend and other controls; the resulting texture was primarily melodic, with occasional chordal passages. This and other similar keyboard controllers (including the Clavitar, played by Hancock and Duke) permit the musician to move around on stage while performing, and to step forward to take solos.

Gil Evans introduced parts for the synthesizer into his scores from 1971, and from the mid-1970s Quincy Jones frequently employed the instrument. By 1975 it had been adopted by Bob James. Free-jazz musicians such as Michael Waisvisz (working with Steve Lacy and Willem Breuker) and Wolfgang Dauner also began to explore its possibilities. In the second half of the decade it became more widely accepted, particularly (but by no means exclusively) by jazz-rock musicians, many of whom assembled substantial arrays of keyboards that surrounded them in performance on three sides. But increasing use of electronic instruments has not meant that the piano has been abandoned. Indeed several keyboard players have avoided the synthesizer for long periods of their careers, such as Hancock and Corea (who took up the instrument again after many years in 1985). Outside jazz-rock a number of musicians, particularly in Europe, adopted the synthesizer; these included Neil Ardley (who has played various makes), Alvin Curran (who uses the EMS Putney and the Serge), Gordon Beck, George Gruntz, Jasper van 't Hof, various successive members of the group Nucleus (playing the Putney), Stan Tracey, and John Taylor.

In 1976 the first fully polyphonic instruments appeared, beginning with the Polymoog (for some time Teitelbaum's main instrument); this was followed by Sequential Circuits' Prophet 5 and several models each from Korg, Oberheim, Roland, and Yamaha. All of these enabled the user to create a huge variety of sounds; most of them also offered some form of programmability, a storage facility which can memorize timbres which can then instantly be recalled as required (on non-programmable synthesizers sounds are lost as soon as the setting is changed). Around this time new companies began manufacturing larger, computer-based instruments, including the PPG Wave Computer, the Fairlight CMI, and the Synclavier. Largely because of their cost, these highly sophisticated digital systems have been used in jazz only relatively rarely, though van 't Hof and Oscar Peterson have used the PPG, and Hancock and Hammer the Fairlight. Those who have performed on the Synclavier include Corea, Duke, Peterson, Jean-Luc Ponty, and Mays, who played the instrument on the title track of Pat Metheny's album *Offramp* (1980, ECM 1190). Cheaper digital synthesizers began to appear in the early 1980s; Yamaha's DX7 model, which was first manufactured in 1983, rapidly became the best selling synthesizer ever produced. An extremely versatile, fully programmable instrument, it can imitate many other instruments with remarkable fidelity, and has found favor with established jazz musicians (it is the only synthesizer played in the mid-1980s by Sun Ra, and has been used by Davis, John Surman, Django Bates and many others). Unlike most other commodities, digital equipment becomes cheaper as the technology develops. Thus whereas analogue synthesizers were available in the 1970s only to the more successful musicians, digital instruments can be afforded by those less affluent. An important consequence of this is the widespread adoption of the instruments by professional and amateur alike.

(iii) Other control devices. Because the earliest synthesizers were manufactured with chromatic keyboards, they were first played mostly by pianists and organists, but several other control systems have been developed that make the facilities of the equipment available to other musicians. Special drums or drum pads may be used to trigger percussion sounds (which are either synthesized or – on later equipment – sampled). These include the Moog drum (a special drum controlling a Minimoog), first manufactured in the early 1970s and used by Billy Cobham from 1973, and played by Joe Gallivan in Gil Evans's orchestra in 1975. The most popular drum synthesizer system among jazz musicians is the Simmons set, which is played (often in conjunction with an acoustic set, as an extension to the timbral possibilities of the conventional instrumentarium) by Cobham, Jon Hiseman, Bill Bruford, Steve Smith (in Steps Ahead), and Tony Williams. Cobham was also one of the first jazz musicians to explore the potential of the electronic drum machine, and although the rhythmic rigidity of the device has discouraged its widespread adoption, it has been employed to good effect by certain jazz-rock musicians, notably Hancock and Bill Evans (iii); Miles Davis has praised the machine's steady and constantly accurate pulse. Models by Linn, Oberheim, and Roland are among the most popular. A controller for pitched percussion, Simmons's Silicon Mallet, resembles a vibraphone; it was introduced in 1987, and has been played by such musicians as Orphy Robinson in Courtney Pine's Jazz Warriors.

Two controllers in the form of wind instruments were developed in the mid-1970s. The Lyricon was played for a time by Wayne Shorter (on *Black Market* and other recordings), Sonny Rollins (on such pieces as *Tai-chi*, from his album *Don't Ask*, 1979, Mlst. 9090), Michal Urbaniak, Bennie Maupin, and Klaus Doldinger; and the Electronic Valve Instrument (EVI), invented by Nyle Steiner (and sometimes known as the Steinerphone) was played by several members of Sun Ra's Arkestra. In 1987 the Japanese company Akai began production of a new model of the EVI, and a related controller, the Electronic Wind Instrument (EWI); the latter has been used by such musicians as Mike Brecker (on his album *Michael Brecker*, 1987, MCA/Imp. 5980) and Phil Todd of Nucleus. The introduction in the same year of a new model by Yamaha, the WX7, indicates continued interest in the potential of wind controllers.

Controllers in the form of guitars (known as guitar synthesizers) were introduced by Roland in 1977, and ARP's Avatar appeared the following year; these have been played by Pat Metheny (who uses such an instrument to control a Synclavier on the title track of *Offramp*, and has also played the Roland GR300), John Abercrombie, Bill Frisell (Roland GR300), Terje Rypdal, David Torn, Mike Stern (in Steps Ahead), and John McLaughlin. Lee Ritenour and Allan Holdsworth use the computerized SynthAxe.

(iv) Role of the synthesizer. During the late 1960s use of the synthesizer was largely restricted to the recording studio (because the equipment was bulky and difficult to transport), and it remains crucial to the recording techniques of many musicians. Indeed several jazz recordings of the 1980s have depended very heavily on synthesizers, drum machines, and sophisticated digital effects. The best-known of these is Miles Davis's album *Tutu* (1986, WB 254904), on which the majority of the instrumental sounds, other than the trumpet, are synthetic; recordings by Don Cherry, Eddie Harris, Bill Evans (iii), and Jamaaladeen Tacuma also make considerable use of the instruments. (It is often difficult to reproduce such complex effects in concerts; nevertheless digitization, and MIDI in particular, has made this possible to some degree.) Some pianists who do not use the synthesizer in performance have adopted it in the studio, often as a tool for composition. These include Oscar Peterson (who has played Korg, Roland, and Moog instruments from the late 1970s, and in the 1980s the Synclavier and the Rhodes Chroma) and Ray Charles.

Other musicians, not principally keyboard players, occasionally play synthesizers both in the studio and on stage; among these are Davis (Yamaha DX7 and Oberheim OB-Xa), Ralph Towner (Prophet 5), Ponty (who used the ARP Odyssey in a synthesizer quartet, the other members of which played the ARP Omni, 2600, and Avatar; he has also played the Prophet 5 and the Synclavier), and John Surman (DX7 and Putney VCS-3). Particularly interesting is Surman's technique of setting the instrument to play repetitive patterns and slowly changing textures, over which he then plays saxophone solos; this may be heard to advantage on the track *Sunday Morning*, from the album *Such Winters of Memory* (1982, ECM 1254). George Lewis (ii) has developed a sophisticated computer program that enables a computer to respond to a soloist's playing by instantly composing an appropriate accompaniment in a free-jazz style; this is then put out, via MIDI, on a synthesizer. Many ensembles now use at least one instrument – Django Bates of Loose Tubes uses a DX7, an Ensoniq Mirage, and a Prophet 5, and Vyacheslav Ganelin plays models by Roland and Casio. *Muta in . . .*, from Ganelin's LP *Con amore* (1986, Leo 147), includes excellent examples of his work on the instrument. Several groups comprehend two or more synthesizer players, notably Steps Ahead (which, as well as keyboard instruments, contains the drum and guitar controllers mentioned above) and the jazz-rock groups Casiopea (Japan) and Mezzoforte (Iceland). Others who by the mid-1980s had begun using the synthesizer include Graham Collier, Ramsey Lewis, Patrice Rushen, Joachim Kühn, Muhal Richard Abrams, Jimmy McGriff, and Chris Barber. That musicians so diverse should adopt the instrument is perhaps indication of its versatility and flexibility, as well as its continuing and increasing popularity.

BIBLIOGRAPHY

C. Harman: "Music Moves into the Future," *BMI: the Many Worlds of Music* (sum. 1970), 10

D. Rubinstein: Liner notes, H. Hancock: *Treasure Chest* (WB 2807, 1974)

R. Townley: "Hancock Plugs in," *DB*, xli/17 (1974), 13

T. Darter: "Chick Corea: Multi-keyboardist Giant," *CK*, i/1 (1975), 20

H. Nolan: "Jan Hammer: Saved by the Synthesizer," *DB*, xliii/5 (1976), 17

L. Underwood: "Chick Corea: Soldering the Elements, Determining the Future," *DB*, xliii/17 (1976), 13

D. Milano and others: "Herbie Hancock," *CK*, iii/11 (1977), 26

D. Milano: "An Introduction to Polyphonic Synthesizers," *CK*, iv/4 (1978), 10

——: "Jan Hammer," *CK*, iv/10 (1978), 20

C. Silvert: "Joe Zawinul: Wayfaring Genius," *DB*, xlv (1978), no.11, p.13; no.12, p.21

M. Davis: "Lyle Mays," *CK*, vi/10 (1980), 12

J.-E. Berendt: *Das Grosse Jazzbuch: von New Orleans bis Jazz Rock* (Frankfurt am Main, Germany, 51981; Eng. trans. as *The Jazz Book: from New Orleans to Fusion and Beyond*, Westport, CT, 1982)
D. Forte: "Pat Metheny," *GP*, xv/12 (1981), 90
G. Armbruster: "Oscar Peterson: a Jazz Piano Giant Talks about his Synthesizer Debut," *Keyboard*, ix/10 (1983), 56
J. Diliberto and K. Haas: "Lyle Mays: Straight Talk on Synths," *DB*, 1/7 (1983), 25
L. Lyons: "Chick Corea," "Herbie Hancock," "Joe Zawinul," *The Great Jazz Pianists, Speaking of their Lives and Music* (New York, 1983)
H. Davies: "Electronic Instruments," *GroveI*
H. Mandel: "Jean-Luc Ponty's Electronic Muse," *DB*, li/1 (1984), 18
D. Roberts and H. Davies: "Synthesizer," *GroveI*
B. Milkowski: "Allan Holdsworth's New Horizons," *DB*, lii/11 (1985), 19
T. Mulhern: "Allan Holdsworth, Lee Ritenour: SynthAxe," *GP*, xx/6 (1986), 109
R. Valentino: "Le altre elettroniche," *Nuova Atlantide: il continente della musica elettronica 1900–1986* (Venice, Italy, 1986) [exhibition catalogue; incl. discography]
B. Doerschuk and others: "Miles Davis: the Picasso of Invisible Art," *Keyboard*, xiii/10 (1987), 64

HUGH DAVIES

Szabados, György (*b* Budapest, 13 July 1939). Hungarian pianist, composer, and arranger. He formed a band in 1955, and in 1963 presented a program of his compositions at the Dália club in Budapest. He performed mostly as a soloist and with small groups, and from the late 1960s was regarded as Hungary's leading exponent of avant-garde jazz; in 1972 he led a quintet in a performance of his *Psalm of the Axe* at the festival in San Sebastián, Spain, and won first prize in the free-jazz category. He has written works for chamber orchestra and ballets, and has recorded several of his own compositions, including *B–A–C–H Impressions* (1964, Qual. 7279–80), *The Wedding* (1974, Hungaroton 17475), and *Adyton* (1982, Krém 17724). From 1982 he performed occasionally with Anthony Braxton, with whom he recorded an album of duos in 1984 (*Szabraxtondos*, Krém 17909) and in the mid-1980s formed a duo with the saxophonist Mihály Dresch. Szabados developed his style of free jazz evidently without knowing of parallel trends in the USA. He has been influenced by folk music and by the works of such composers as Béla Bartók. (B. Noglik: "György Szabados Forgotten Songs," *Jazz* (Basle, Switzerland), no.6 (1985))

GÉZA GÁBOR SIMON, RAINER E. LOTZ (with BERT NOGLIK)

Szabo, Frank (J.) (*b* Budapest, 16 Sept 1952). Trumpeter. After studying in Los Angeles with Tom Scott (1962–9) he played in Las Vegas and toured with Harry James (1970–71); he also performed, recorded, and toured in Europe, Japan, and the USA with Ray Charles (1971). From 1972 to 1974 he worked with Louie Bellson, and from 1974 to 1975 toured and recorded with Count Basie. Later Szabo played with Chuck Mangione and Harry Edison, performed and recorded with the Capp–Pierce Juggernaut (1978), and toured England and recorded with Bellson (1980); he also made further recordings with Frank Capp and Nat Pierce (1981) and Basie (1981, 1983). He joined Woody Herman's orchestra in 1983; in the mid-1980s he has been active as a freelance in and around Los Angeles. (*Feather–Gitler '70s*)

Szabó, Gábor (*b* Budapest, 8 March 1936; *d* Budapest, 26 Feb 1982). Guitarist. He left Hungary after the failed revolution of 1956 and while attending the Berklee College of Music belonged to Marshall Brown's International Youth Band. He played West Coast jazz as a member of Chico Hamilton's quintet (1962–5) and in 1964 was named "best new jazz guitarist" by *Down Beat*. In 1965 he made his first recording as a leader and arranged Hamilton's score to Roman Polanski's film *Repulsion*; he also toured with Charles Lloyd and the singer Lena Horne. From 1969 his playing became strongly influenced by blues and rock; after settling in Los Angeles he worked in television.

SELECTED RECORDINGS

As leader: *Jazz Raga* (1966, Imp. 9128); *More Sorcery* (1967, Imp. 9167)
As sideman with C. Hamilton: *Drumfusion* (1962, Col. CS8607)

BIBLIOGRAPHY

FeatherE; *Feather–Gitler '70s*
P. Rivelli: "Gabor Szabo," *Jazz*, v/8 (New York, 1966), 8
D. DeMicheal: "Gabor Szabo: Jazz and the Changing Times," *DB*, xxxiv/20 (1967), 17
P. Senoff: "Gabor Szabo Interview," *J&P*, ix/9 (1970), 37
M. Summerfield: "Gabor Szabo," *The Jazz Guitar: its Evolution and its Players* (Gateshead, England, 1978), 197
L. Tomkins: "Gabor Szabo," *CI*, xviii/4 (1979), 20
H. Wong: Obituary, *DB*, xlix/6 (1982), 14

FRANK A. DIBUSSOLO

Szukalski, Tomasz [Szakal] (*b* Warsaw, 8 Jan 1948). Polish tenor and soprano saxophonist, and bass clarinetist. He played piano from the age of five, and later studied clarinet at school and at the State Higher School of Music in Warsaw (from 1968). In 1964 he began to play tenor saxophone in amateur dixieland bands. By 1970 he had established a national reputation, and thereafter performed and recorded with Zbigniew Namysłowski (1971–5) and Tomasz Stańko (intermittently from 1973). He played regularly with the orchestra of the Polish Radio Jazz Studio and in 1978 joined The Quartet, with which he recorded *Loaded* (1979, Leo 010). This group started a trend in Poland back towards acoustic jazz after the popularity of electric instruments during the 1970s. Szukalski is experienced in many different styles but acknowledges in particular the influence of Jan Garbarek's quartet of the 1970s.

BIBLIOGRAPHY

J. Byrczek: "Eurojazz Personalities: Poland," *JF* [intl edn], no.18 (1972), 87
R. Kowal: "Tomasz Szukalski: 'Music Must Pack a Punch'," *JF* [intl edn], no.41 (1976), 51 [incl. discography]

WOLFRAM KNAUER

T

Tabackin, Lew(is Barry) (*b* Philadelphia, 26 March 1940). Saxophonist and flutist. He first learned flute, and took up tenor saxophone in high school. He attended the Philadelphia Conservatory of Music (BM 1962), though his studies outside this institution, notably with the composer Vincent Persichetti, had more impact on his development. Towards the end of a period of army service (1962–5) he played in New Jersey with Tal Farlow and Don Friedman, among others. Tabackin then moved to New York, where he worked with big bands led by Les and Larry Elgart, Cab Calloway (briefly in 1965), Buddy Morrow, Maynard Ferguson (recording about 1966), Thad Jones and Mel Lewis, Clark Terry, Duke Pearson (recording in 1967–8), Chuck Israels, and Joe Henderson. He led a trio at La Boheme, Philadelphia, in 1968–9, and played in other small groups with Elvin Jones, Donald Byrd, Attila Zoller, and Roland Hanna.

Lew Tabackin (right) and Toshiko Akiyoshi, June 1979

After performing with Bobby Rosengarden in 1969, he worked with Doc Severinsen and with the studio band for Dick Cavett's television show; in the same year he appeared as a soloist in Europe with the Hamburg Jazz Workshop and the Danish Radiojazzgruppen, and in the International Jazz Quartet (with Daniel Humair, George Gruntz, and Israels). In 1970, with Toshiko Akiyoshi (whom he married), he formed a quartet which toured Japan and appeared at the Expo '70 jazz festival. The couple jointly led a big band in Los Angeles from 1973, which continued to perform, with Tabackin as a principal soloist, until around 1984 (*see* AKIYOSHI, TOSHIKO); in 1983 they moved back to New York. Tabackin has also played in a variety of other contexts, notably in recording sessions with the big bands of Louie Bellson (1977) and Bill Berry (1978).

Tabackin's flute playing combines a classical approach with an oriental flavor that is often enhanced by the style of Akiyoshi's distinctive arrangements. His work on tenor saxophone, by contrast, is based firmly in the jazz tradition; its idiom and timbre display an individual blend of influences from many of the performers active before John Coltrane.

SELECTED RECORDINGS

As leader: with T. Akiyoshi: *Kogun* (1974, RCA JPL1-0236); *Tabackin* (1974, RCA RVP6271); *Black and Tan Fantasy* (1979, JAM 5005); with T. Akiyoshi: *Farewell to Mingus* (1980, JAM 003); *Lew Tabackin Quartet* (1983, Ewd 90025)

As sideman: D. Byrd: *Electric Byrd* (1970, BN 84349); S. Manne: *Essence* (1977, Gal. 5101)

BIBLIOGRAPHY

Feather–Gitler '70s
L. Feather: "Lew Tabackin: Tabackin Road," *DB*, xlv/2 (1978), 14
Liner notes, *Tabackin* (IC 1038, 1978)
G. Endress: *Jazz Podium: Musiker über sich selbst* (Stuttgart, Germany, 1980), 174
L. Feather: *The Passion for Jazz* (New York, 1980), 109
C. Kuhl: "Akiyoshi & Tabackin: Interview," *Cadence*, viii/7 (1982), 8
H. Hill: "Lew Tabackin: Tenor Gladness," *Coda*, no.197 (1984), 4

For further recordings and bibliography *see* AKIYOSHI, TOSHIKO.

DAVID WILD

Tabányi, Mihály (*b* Pilis, Hungary, 1 Feb 1921). Hungarian accordionist. He became well known when he won first prize in an accordion competition in Budapest in 1940. He first recorded as a swing soloist in 1942 and he then led several recording bands (1942–9); he also toured Europe and the Lebanon as a leader. Among his sidemen were Elek Bacsik and the tenor saxophonist Rudolf Wirth. He made further recordings as a leader from 1954 to 1963 and also as a sideman with Aladár Pege, Andor Kovács, and Gyula Kovács. His playing may be heard on *Suzy* (1949, Tonalit C307), one of his own arrangements.

GÉZA GÁBOR SIMON, RAINER E. LOTZ

Tablā. A pair of small kettledrums played with the hands and used chiefly in the classical repertory of the South Asian subcontinent. The instrument became well-known to audiences in the West in the late 1960s when several rock musicians incorporated into their work South Asian musical elements and instruments, and in the following years it came to be used in jazz as well. The tablā player Zakir Hussain undertook a collaboration with John Handy that resulted in a surprisingly effective fusion of bop, modal jazz, and Indian classical music; this may be heard to advantage on Handy's album *Karuna Supreme* (1975, MPS 2022791). Hussain later worked in the group Shakti with John McLaughlin. A number of tablā players have played in jazz-rock groups; the best-known of these is Badal Roy, who has played with McLaughlin, Dave Liebman (on, for example, Liebman's album *Lookout Farm*, 1973, ECM 1039), and Miles Davis. The tablā has also been used in groups that draw on diverse styles of jazz (including free jazz and jazz-rock), classical music, and folk music of various cultures. Collin Walcott played tablā in several groups of this kind, including Oregon (as a member of which he recorded an unaccompanied tablā solo on the track *Story Telling* from the album *Out of the Woods*, 1978, Elek. 154) and Codona.

In the hands of musicians schooled in the traditional techniques of playing the instrument, the tablā has enriched jazz: it has brought to the music many complex rhythms that are entirely independent of the African sources from which most jazz rhythms are drawn. The tablā has also been used by jazz musicians who have sought to exploit its timbre while replacing the rhythms that are indigenous to the instrument with conventional jazz rhythms, or with new ones; in these cases the results have been consistently disappointing.

BARRY KERNFELD

Tacuma, Jamaaladeen [McDaniel, Rudy] (*b* Hempstead, NY, 11 June 1956). Electric bass guitarist. He grew up in Philadelphia, and sang in a doo-wop group as a teenager. At the age of 13 he took up double bass and began playing in local bands. His first major engagement was with Charles Earland; thereafter he played with the soul singer Edwin Birdsong. In 1975 he joined Ornette Coleman's electric band Prime Time, with which he recorded in Paris. During his stay there he converted to Islam and took a Muslim name. After leaving Prime Time Tacuma began recording as a leader for Gramavision. His first album, *Show Stopper*, combined the HARMOLODIC THEORY of Coleman with a funky dance style derived from rhythm-and-blues. *Music World* was recorded with musicians from all over the world at studios in the USA, Europe, and Asia. Tacuma has also worked as a sideman with Jeff Beck, James "Blood" Ulmer, and many others, and in the mid-1980s has performed and recorded again with Prime Time. He also leads Cosmetic, a group based in Philadelphia that plays dance music. Tacuma is a highly innovative musician; he achieves the melodic agility of a soloist without neglecting his instrument's rhythmic role.

SELECTED RECORDINGS

As leader: *Show Stopper* (1982–3, Gram. 8301); *Renaissance Man* (1983–4, Gram. 8308); *Music World* (1985, Gram. 8613)

As sideman: O. Coleman: *Dancing in your Head* (1975, A&M Hor. 722); *Body Meta* (1975, AH 1); J. Ulmer: *Tales of Captain Black* (1978, AH 7); O. Coleman: *Of Human Feelings* (1979, Ant. 2001); *Ornette and Prime Time: Opening the Caravan of Dreams* (1985, Caravan of Dreams 85001); *In All Languages* (1987, Caravan of Dreams 85008)

BIBLIOGRAPHY

C. Tinder: "Jamaaladeen Tacuma: Electric Bass in the Harmolodic Pocket," *DB*, xlix/4 (1982), 19 [incl. discography]

C. J. Gans: "Jamaaladeen Tacuma: 21st Century Electrical Bass Guitarist," *JF* [intl edn], no.80 (1983), 51

B. Milkowski and C. Stern: "Jamaaladeen Tacuma: Breaking Bass Barriers," *GP*, xvii/5 (1983), 76 [incl. discography]

S. Lake: "A Renaissance Man for All Seasons," *The Wire*, no.21 (1985), 18

BILL MILKOWSKI

Tag. A phrase (usually of a few bars, sometimes no more than a motif) added to the end of a theme, chorus, or (most often) an entire piece. It may or may not be related thematically to the rest of the piece; a frequent practice is to repeat (once or twice) the last two bars of the final chorus. *See* FORMS.

Tailgate. The style of trombone playing used in New Orleans jazz. In about 1900 the slide trombone replaced the valve trombone in popularity because of its ability to play portamentos, or "slurs." The portamento (*see* GLISS) became modish just as jazz was developing, and as a consequence became part of the New Orleans style. Early bands frequently played on advertising wagons, and it was supposed that the trombonist must stand on the wagon's "tailgate" so that he would have room to play. The tailgate style was derived mainly from trombone patterns in marches. The trombone, usually carrying an inner voice, supplies connecting links between the main phrases of the song in the middle or low register, frequently moving between harmony notes of successive chords by scalar or chromatic movement, or portamentos. The trombone may also undergird the melody with a pedal point, usually on the tonic or fifth.

JAMES LINCOLN COLLIER

Takahashi, Tatsuya (*b* Yamagata, Japan, 24 Dec 1931). Japanese bandleader and tenor saxophonist. He played professionally from 1951 and worked at American military bases near Sendai, Honshu, before moving to Tokyo in the late 1950s; his early style was influenced by that of Hidehiko Matsumoto. In 1961 he joined the alto saxophonist Ebihara Keiichiro and his Lobsters and from 1966 led Tokyo Union, a big band that won the Japan Jazz Prize in 1977 for its recording *Scandinavian Suite*. From 1980 he won readers' polls sponsored by *Swing Journal*; he also appeared at festivals in Monterey (California) and Montreux (Switzerland). Takahashi's saxophone playing owes much to the work of Sonny Rollins and the style of his band is strongly rhythmic. He has commissioned arrangements by, among others, Slide Hampton, Ueda Chikara, and Toshiyuki Honda.

SELECTED RECORDINGS

As leader: *Maiden Voyage* (1976, TBM 3001); *Scandinavian Suite* (1977, TBM 1005); *Funpico with Ueda Chikara* (1978, WB 8004); *Black Pearl* (1980, Vic.–Zen Zen 5001); *Chasin' the Duke* (1983, Carnival RJL8063); *Beauties* (1984, TDK T28P1007)

As sideman with N. Naoki: *Straight No Chaser* (1981, Full House PAP25001)

YOZO IWANAMI

Take. In recording (both sound recording and film) the recorded result of a single uninterrupted performance, whether complete or partial. The word is usually applied in sound recording to each of the attempts made at a single session to record any one piece, and these different versions are designated "first take," "second take," etc. In sound recording during the 78 r.p.m. era, each take was assigned a "take number," usually a numeral or a letter, which is a component of the MATRIX NUMBER, usually its last element. The takes might be numbered in chronological order of successful attempts; this was the usual practice in the 1920s. But by the 1930s many companies evaluated all takes, then assigned take numbers in order of preferred performance, the best version being called the "first take"; for example, most original issues on Decca 78s are take "A." Procedures were by no means standardized. A third practice may be found, for example, in sessions recorded by Dial, which numbered takes chronologically, including incomplete takes (some less than 30 seconds in duration) interspersed among complete ones.

The concept of a take lost some of its meaning with the advent of mastering on magnetic tape, because of the possibilities inherent in editing on tape. Nonetheless, a considerable amount of jazz, especially improvised jazz, continues to be recorded without significant alteration of tapes through editing. Moreover, a spoiled or abridged take might include within it, for example, a fine unissued improvisation, and if interest in an artist proves sufficient, a record company may decide to issue this material, just as companies have released different takes from the 78 r.p.m. era. Examples abound in late (and sometimes posthumous) issues of material recorded by John Coltrane and Charles Mingus: such issues may consist of alternative takes of titles previously issued, rejected takes (i.e., previously unissued titles), or full takes (i.e., titles previously issued only in edited or abridged versions).

Correspondingly, although the take number has lost much of its significance in the modern era of recording, some companies have continued to assign such numbers to sections of a master tape; as before, the take number forms a component of a number that identifies the attempts at a single title. In this case the take number has no relationship to the various types of numbers (for example, issue numbers or pressing numbers) that may appear on an album, except in those instances where an entire album comprises a single take: apart from listening, one may distinguish between the two takes of Coltrane's album-long performance of *Ascension* (both issued under the same cover as Imp. 95) only by finding which of the two numbers is etched onto the space between the centermost groove and the label.

Tanner, Paul (O. W.) (*b* Skunk Hollow, nr Newport, KY, 15 Oct 1917). Trombonist. He performed and recorded as a member of Glenn Miller's second orchestra from its formation in 1938 until it disbanded in 1942 (for illustrations *see* MILLER, GLENN, and MUTE, fig.3), then worked with Les Brown and Charlie Spivak and toured and recorded with Tex Beneke (1946–51). From 1952 to 1968 he belonged to the music staff of ABC in Los Angeles and at the same time attended UCLA (BA 1958, MA 1962, PhD 1978), where from 1958 to 1981 he taught jazz history. He also worked in film, television, and recording studios and in symphony orchestras, performed as a sideman with Henry Mancini, Nelson Riddle, Neal Hefti, and Pete Rugolo and as a soloist, and in 1975 was a founder of the World Jazz Association. He has written compositions and arrangements for trombone and piano, arrangements for big band, trombone methods, and, with Maurice Gerow, the text *A Study of Jazz* (Dubuque, IA, 1964, rev.5/1983, rev.6/1987 with D. W. Megill).

BIBLIOGRAPHY

Feather '60s; *Feather–Gitler '70s*
C. Miller: "Musician Travels Far from Skunk Hollow," *San Diego Union* (15 May 1986), 1

Tapscott, Horace (*b* Houston, 4 or 6 April 1934). Pianist and leader. He moved with his family to Los Angeles in 1945 and began his career as a trombonist. He played with Eric Dolphy and Don Cherry in a school band (1948–52) and with Gerald Wilson (1950–51), and while a member of an air force band (1953–7) also took up the piano. After working as a leader (1958) and touring with Lionel Hampton (1959–61) the piano became his principal instrument in the early 1960s owing to injuries that he had suffered in an automobile accident. He settled in Los Angeles, where from 1961 he led the Pan Afrikan Peoples Arkestra, which at various times included Arthur Blythe, Azar Lawrence, and Jimmy Woods as sidemen. He also recorded with Lou Blackburn (1963), played with Leone Thomas, Lorez Alexandria, and Charles Lloyd, and composed the music for Sonny Criss's album *Sonny's Dream* (1968, Prst. 7576); in 1969 he recorded as a leader with Blythe. Later he made recordings (principally for his own label, Nimbus) as the leader of the Arkestra (1978; *The Call*, 1979, Nimbus 246), as an unaccompanied soloist (1978, 1982–3), as the leader of a trio in New York (1979) and at the Lobero Festival in Italy (1981), and in a duo with the drummer Everett Brown, Jr. (1980).

BIBLIOGRAPHY

Feather–Gitler '70s
D. Keller: "Horace Tapscott," *JT* (1982), Oct, 8
J. Weiss and C. Gauffre: "Horace Tapscott: l'autre West Coast," *Jm*, no.321 (1983), 28 [incl. discography]
E. Cohen: "Horace Tapscott Talking: 'A Legacy to Pass on'," *Cadence*, x (1984), no.7, p.8; no.8, p.12 [incl. discography]
R. Mitchell: "Horace Tapscott," *DB*, lv/1 (1988), 13

Tarasov, Vladimir (Petrovich) (*b* Arkhangel'sk, Russian SFSR, 29 June 1947). Russian drummer. He is largely self-taught as a musician. He played drums from 1961, worked with the saxophonist Vladimir Rezitski in 1967–8, then moved to Vilnius, where in 1969 he formed a duo with Vyacheslav Ganelin; this became the Ganelin Trio (later known as the G–T–Ch Trio) when they were joined by Vladimir Chekasin in 1971. Tarasov has made recordings with the trio, in a duo with Ganelin, and as a soloist (*Atto*, 1984, Mel. C6023565004). In addition to his work in jazz he plays percussion in the Lithuanian State SO.

BIBLIOGRAPHY

B. Noglik: "Wjatscheslaw Ganelin, Wladimir Tschekassin, Wladimir Tarassow," *Jazzwerkstatt international* (Berlin, 1981), 29 [incl. interview, discography]
F. Maino: "Ganelin, Tarasov, and Chekasin: Interview," *Cadence*, ix/1 (1983), 19
A. Duncan: "Soviet Trio Takes Daring Liberties with Familiar Jazz Styles," *Christian Science Monitor* (30 June 1986), 29

WALTER OJAKÄÄR

Tarto, Joe [Tortoriello, Vincent Joseph] (*b* Newark, NJ, 22 Feb 1902; *d* Morristown, NJ, 24 Aug 1986). Tuba and double bass player and arranger. He performed with several lesser-known bandleaders in the early 1920s, then played with Red Nichols, Miff Mole, the Dorsey Brothers, Eddie Lang, Phil Napoleon, Bix Beiderbecke, and others. As an arranger Tarto worked with a number of bandleaders, including Fletcher Henderson and Chick Webb; he composed and arranged *Black Horse Stomp*, which Henderson recorded in 1926 (Har. 153). *I must have that man*, recorded by Joe Venuti, is an excellent example of his skill as an arranger, and includes one of his better solos. Tarto recorded with such singers as Ethel Waters, Sophie Tucker, Bing Crosby, and the Boswell Sisters. After 1930 he played jazz only occasionally, and worked mostly with radio, theater, pit, and symphony orchestras. He also played with Nichols (1935–6), and was associated intermittently for some 25 years with

Paul Whiteman. During the late 1940s he performed at Nick's, New York. Thereafter he led a band, the New Jersey Dixieland Brass Quintet, periodically into the 1980s, and also worked with other traditional jazz musicians. In 1984 he was a guest soloist at the Oude Stijl Jazz Festival at Breda in the Netherlands.

SELECTED RECORDINGS

As sideman: R. Nichols and M. Mole: Black Bottom Stomp (1926, Edison 51878); M. Mole: The Darktown Strutters' Ball (1927, OK 40784); J. Venuti: I must have that man (1928, OK 41133); E. Waters: Am I Blue? (1929, Col. 1837D); E. Lang: Freeze and Melt (1929, OK 8696)

BIBLIOGRAPHY

W. Miller: "Joe Tarto," *Australian Jazz Quarterly*, no.7 (1948), 3
J. Tarto and H. Openeer: "A Joe Tarto Story," *Doctor jazz*, no.33 (1968), 5
W. Vaché, Sr.: "Joe Tarto: a Tribute," *Jersey Jazz*, v/3 (1977), 4; repr. in *Jersey Jazz*, x/3 (1982), 9
S. Hester: Liner notes, *Joe Tarto, Titan of the Tuba* (Broadway Intermission 108, 1981)
C. Deffaa: "Joe Tarto: Last of the Five Pennies," *MR*, xii/4 (1985), 1

CHIP DEFFAA

Tate, Buddy [George Holmes] (*b* Sherman, TX, 22 Feb 1915). Tenor saxophonist. He began his professional career in 1927 and worked with Terrence Holder (1930–33), Count Basie (1934), and Andy Kirk (1934–5). He played with Nat Towles until 1939 when he replaced Herschel Evans in Basie's band, with which he remained for ten years (for illustration *see* FILMS, fig.3). He then performed with Hot Lips Page, Lucky Millinder, and Jimmy Rushing (1950–52), and in 1953 he formed his own band, which was resident at the Celebrity Club, New York, for over 20 years. During this time he also played with other leaders and occasionally again with Basie. He toured Europe with Buck Clayton (1959, 1961), as a leader (1967–8), and with the Saints and Sinners; he made particularly fine recordings in France in a trio with Milt Buckner (organ) and Wallace Bishop (drums) in 1967 and 1968. He led a band with Paul Quinichette at the West End Café, New York (1975), and later performed and recorded with Jay McShann and Jim Galloway in Canada. In the 1980s he toured with the Texas Tenors, led by Illinois Jacquet, and played at jazz festivals in Newport (1980) and Cork (1983, 1985) and regularly at the Grande Parade du Jazz, Nice. Tate has a big tone and an exceptional command of the harmonics in the upper register, which he uses as an extension of the tenor saxophone's normal range.

Oral history material in *MoKmh*, *NjR* (JOHP).

SELECTED RECORDINGS

As leader: *Buddy Tate and his Orchestra* (c1955, Halo 50322), incl. Skip it; *Buddy Tate Featuring Milt Buckner* (1967, BB 33014), incl. When I'm Blue; with E. Warren: *The Count's Men* (1973, RCA LPL1-5034); *The Texas Twister* (1975, Master Jazz 8128)

As sideman: C. Basie: Rock-a-bye Basie (1939, Voc. 4747)

BIBLIOGRAPHY

ChiltonW
H. Panassié: "Buddy Tate," *BHcF*, no.61 (1956), 3
B. Tate and F. Driggs: "My Story," *JR*, i/2 (1958), 18
F. Driggs: "The Buddy Tate Story," *JM*, v/2 (1959), 2
J. Mansion: "Dig . . . Dingue . . . Dong . . ., iii: The Swinging Gentleman," *BHcF*, no.116 (1962), 6
J. R. Haddon: "Buddy Tate," *JM*, xii/6 (1966), 9
J. Poinsot, L. Verdeaux, and P. Walter: "Quelques propos de Buddy Tate," *BHcF*, no.181 (1968), 10
B. Esposito: "Tate the Tenor," *JJ*, xxv/2 (1972), 14
L. Verdeaux: "Buddy Tate vous parle," *BHcF*, no.240 (1974), 10 [interview]
J. Simmen: "Crystal Clear," *Coda*, no.144 (1976), 29
S. Woolley: "Tate à tete," *JJ*, xxx/2 (1977), 6
J. Pescheux and J.-P. Battestini: "Buddy Tate en Europe," *BHcF*, no.271 (1979), 3
S. Dance: *The World of Count Basie* (New York and London, 1980) [colln of previously pubd interviews], 111
S. Klett: "Buddy Tate: Interview," *Cadence*, vi/5 (1980), 15
M. L. Hester: "Tate on Tenor," *MR*, xiv/8 (1987), 14
D. Kochakian: "Buddy Tate," *Whisky, Women, and . . .*, no.16 (1987), 32 [incl. discography by D. Penny]

EDDIE COOK

Tate, Erskine (*b* Memphis, 19 Dec 1895; *d* Chicago, 17 Dec 1978). Bandleader. He grew up in a musical family and moved as a teenager to Chicago. He studied at the American Conservatory of Music, and in 1912 he began playing violin professionally. From 1919 to 1928 he led an orchestra that was resident at the Vendome Theater and made the recordings *Cutie Blues/Chinaman Blues* (1923, OK 4907) and *Static Strut/Stomp off, let's go* (1926, Voc. 1027). Thereafter this ensemble played at various theaters before working regularly at the Savoy Ballroom (1931–8) and the Cotton Club. As the leader of the most prominent theater orchestra in Chicago, Tate provided invaluable training for young musicians. These included Louis Armstrong, Boyd Atkins, Buster Bailey, Jimmy Bertrand, Earl Hines, Milt Hinton, Darnell Howard, Guy Kelly, Freddie Keppard, Omer Simeon, Jabbo Smith, and Teddy Weatherford. Around 1945 Tate retired from performing to concentrate on teaching; he continued to work in this capacity into the mid-1970s. Although mainly a violinist, he played and taught most orchestral instruments.

BIBLIOGRAPHY

ChiltonW
T. J. Hennessey: "The Black Chicago Establishment 1919–1930," *JJS*, ii/1 (1974), 15–45
A. McCarthy: *Big Band Jazz* (New York and London, 1974), 21
S. Dance: *The World of Earl Hines* (New York, 1977) [interviews]
P. van Vorst: "Erskine Tate," *MR*, vi/6 (1979), 6

MICHAEL TOVEY

Tate, Grady (*b* Durham, NC, 14 Jan 1932). Drummer and singer. He played drums from the age of five and was at first self-taught; he learned jazz drumming while serving in the air force (1951–5). On his discharge he returned to Durham, where he studied theater, literature, and psychology at North Carolina College and worked part-time as a musician. He then moved to Washington (1959), played with Wild Bill Davis, and in 1963 moved to New York to work with Jerome Richardson and in Quincy Jones's big band. Later he played with Duke Ellington, Count Basie, Jimmy Smith, Wes Montgomery, Roland Kirk, Stan Getz, Kenny Burrell, Bill Evans (ii), Oscar Peterson, Lalo Schifrin, Oliver Nelson, J. J. Johnson, Kai Winding, Billy Taylor (ii), and Zoot Sims. He also accompanied several jazz and popular singers, including Peggy Lee, Sarah Vaughan, Ella Fitzgerald, Astrud Gilberto, Chris Connor, Ray Charles, Blossom Dearie, and Lena Horne, recorded albums as a singer in a quasi-popular idiom, and worked as an actor. He has remained active as a freelance into the 1980s, recording with both Ray Brown and Monty Alexander in 1985. As a drummer Tate is highly regarded for his forceful, driving playing and for his ability to adapt to a wide range of musical styles.

SELECTED RECORDINGS

As leader (all as singer): *Feeling Life* (1969, Skye 7); *After the Long Ride Home* (1969, Skye 17); *Master Grady Tate* (c1977, Imp. 9930)

As sideman (all as drummer): O. Nelson: *More Blues and the Abstract Truth* (1964, Imp. 75); J. Smith and W. Montgomery: *The Dynamic Duo* (1966, Verve 68678); S. Getz: *Sweet Rain* (1967, Verve 68693); R. Kirk: *Now Please don't you Cry Beautiful Edith* (1967, Verve 68709); Q. Jones: *Walking in Space* (1969, A&M Hor. 3023); Z. Sims: *Zoot Sims and the Gershwin Brothers* (1975, Pablo 2310744); New York Jazz Quartet: *Blues for Sarka* (1978, Enja 3025); O. Peterson: *Silent Partner* (1979, Pablo 2312103); R. Rodney: *The 3 R's* (1979, Muse 5290); R. Brown: *Don't Forget the Blues* (1985, Conc. 293)

BIBLIOGRAPHY

R. Palmer: "Grady Tate," *JJ*, xxiii/11 (1970), 18
E. Meadow: "Grady Tate: he'd Rather Sing," *DB*, xxxviii/10 (1971), 18

C. Iero: "Grady Tate," *MD*, iii/3 (1979), 22
B. Korall: "Exploring the Versatility of Grady Tate," *IM*, lxxxiii/1 (1984), 6

J. KENT WILLIAMS

Tatum, Art(hur, Jr.) (*b* Toledo, OH, 13 Oct 1909; *d* Los Angeles, 5 Nov 1956). Pianist.

1. Life. 2. Musical style.

1. LIFE. Despite seriously impaired vision (he was blind in one eye and had only partial sight in the other), he received some formal piano training as a teenager at the Toledo School of Music, and learned to read sheet music with the aid of glasses as well as by the Braille method. Otherwise he was self-taught, learning from piano rolls, phonograph recordings, radio broadcasts, and various musicians whom he encountered as a young man in the area around Toledo and Cleveland. Tatum acknowledged Fats Waller as his primary inspiration, with the popular radio pianist Lee Sims, whose interpretations contained many interesting harmonies, as an important secondary influence. He was playing professionally in Toledo by 1926, and performed on radio in 1929–30. In 1932 he traveled to New York as the accompanist for Adelaide Hall. There, in March 1933, he made his first solo recordings, for Brunswick. After leaving Hall he worked in Cleveland (1934–5) and led a group in Chicago (1935–6). His reputation as the outstanding pianist in jazz was consolidated in 1937 with his performances in various New York clubs and on radio shows. He toured England the following year, and appeared regularly in New York and Los Angeles in the late 1930s and early 1940s. Taking Nat "King" Cole's successful jazz trio as a model, Tatum founded his own influential trio with Slam Stewart (double bass) and Tiny Grimes (electric guitar) in 1943 (see illustration). Grimes left the following year, but Tatum continually returned to this format, using in particular Everett Barksdale.

In 1944 Tatum played in a jazz concert at the Metropolitan Opera House, and in 1947 he made a cameo appearance in the film *The Fabulous Dorseys*. Although he was regularly active in nightclubs, radio shows, and recording studios, and was lionized by jazz musicians and critics, during this period he did not acquire a large popular following and he was bypassed in jazz popularity polls. In 1953 he began an association with the record producer Norman Granz that led to a number of outstanding small-group recordings with such mainstream musicians as Benny Carter, Roy Eldridge, and Ben Webster. More importantly, he was recorded in a long series of solo performances which indicated both the extent of his repertory and his extraordinary imagination. Tatum remained active until shortly before his death, constantly improving his art.

2. MUSICAL STYLE. Tatum transported the art of jazz piano improvisation beyond the real and imagined confines of his day. His first professional solo recordings in 1933 were seen as a challenge to his own and future generations of jazz and popular pianists. His technical abilities, lightness of touch, and control of the full range of the instrument were unprecedented among popular pianists; he had an unerring sense of rhythm and swing, a seemingly unlimited capacity to expand and enrich a melody, and a profound and continually evolving grasp of substitute harmonies. Throughout his career Tatum retained the original melody and harmonies of a tune as starting points for his improvisations. Most often he chose models from the standard popular repertory, though he also interpreted the blues and sometimes performed parodies on light classical pieces. Only occasionally did he play original works. He was often described as having two distinct musical personalities:

Art Tatum (piano) with Slam Stewart (double bass) and Tiny Grimes (guitar) at the Three Deuces, New York, 1944

in his professional appearances he was thoroughly business-like, obliging audiences with almost literal repetitions of his recorded performances, seldom taking encores, and, in a studio, rarely recording more than one take of a performance. Among friends he was inclined to play (and sing) the blues, to improvise for hours on given chord sequences, and to depart radically and dramatically from the original tune. He made more than 600 recordings (as unaccompanied soloist, with his trios, and with other small and large ensembles), which provide ample evidence of his uncommonly creative genius as an improviser.

Tatum integrated the practices and characteristic gestures of the stride and swing keyboard traditions, at the same time transforming them through his virtuosity. Simple decorative techniques became complex harmonic sweeps of color; traditional repetitive patterns became areas of unpredictable and ever-changing shifts of rhythm. Later generations of jazz musicians were particularly impressed by his intensification of the original harmonies of a tune (ex.1 shows his celebrated recasting of the simple tonic 7th of the blues), particularly his interpolation of passing harmonies, and the textural variety of his

Ex.1 *Aunt Hagar's Blues* (1949, Cap. 15520); transcr. J. Mehegan

work, which frequently led to contrapuntal relationships among lines in different registers. Also important were his ability to apply different variation techniques simultaneously and his astonishing rhythmic sleight of hand. His influence on later jazz pianists was enormous: even musicians of radically different outlook, such as Bud Powell, Lennie Tristano, and Herbie Hancock, learned key Tatum performances by rote, though few could compass his technical range or re-create his inimitable, plush tone. Other musicians, among them Charlie Parker, were inspired by Tatum's technical accomplishments to bring a similar virtuosity to their own instruments.

See also PIANO, §2, and fig.1.

SELECTED RECORDINGS

AS UNACCOMPANIED SOLOIST

Tea for Two (1933, Bruns. 6553); Tiger Rag (1933, Bruns. 6543); Gone with the Wind/Stormy Weather (1937, Decca 1603); Elegie (1940, Decca 18049); Sweet Lorraine/Get Happy (1940, Decca 18050); St. Louis Blues (1940, Decca 8550); Rosetta (1940, Decca 8502); Hallelujah/Memories of You (1945, American Recording Artists 4501); Yesterdays (1949, Just Jazz 69); Willow Weep for me/Aunt Hagar's Blues (1949, Cap. 15520); Nice work if you can get it (1949, Cap. 15519)

Piano Music (1949, Cap. H216), incl. Blue Skies; *Art Tatum Piano Discoveries* (1950, 1955, 20CF 3033), incl. Mr. Freddie Blues (1950), I cover the waterfront (1955); *The Genius of Art Tatum*, ii (1953, Clef 613), incl. Makin' Whoopee; *The Genius of Art Tatum*, vi (1953, Clef 657), incl. Jitterbug Waltz; *The Genius of Art Tatum*, v (1953, Clef 618), incl. Stompin' at the Savoy; *The Genius of Art Tatum*, x (1953, Clef 661), incl. Too marvelous for words; *The Genius of Art Tatum*, viii (1953, Clef 659), incl. Ain't misbehavin'

AS LEADER

Body and Soul (1937, Decca 1197); *Pieces of Eight* (1939–55, Smithsonian 029), incl. Exactly like you; Wee Baby Blues/Battery Bounce (1941, Decca 8526); Stompin' at the Savoy/Last Goodbye Blues (1941, Decca 8536); Corinne, Corinna (1941, Decca 8563); I got rhythm/I ain't got nobody (1944, World Jam Session 32); Body and Soul (1944, Comet 2); Flying Home (1944, Comet 3); Boogie (1944, Asch 4521); with B. Carter and L. Bellson: *The Art Tatum–Benny Carter–Louis Bellson Trio* (1954, Clef 643), incl. Idaho

with L. Hampton and B. Rich: *The Lionel Hampton–Art Tatum–Buddy Rich Trio* (1955, Clef 709), incl. More than you know; *The Art Tatum Trio* (1956, Verve 8118), incl. Trio Blues; with B. Webster: *The Art Tatum–Ben Webster Quartet* (1956, Verve 8220), incl. All the things you are, Night and Day, Where or When

AS SIDEMAN

L. Feather: Esquire Bounce/ Esquire Blues (1943, Com. 547); My Ideal (1943, Com. 548); B. Bigard: Please don't talk about me when I'm gone (1945, Black & White 14); Blues for Art's Sake (1945, Black & White 13); L. Hampton: *Lionel Hampton and his Giants* (1955, Norg. 1080), incl. Verve Blues

BIBLIOGRAPHY

W. Balliett: "Art and Tatum," *Saturday Review*, xxxvii (24 Oct 1955), 44

A. Hodeir: "Art Tatum: a French Critic Evaluates the Music of a Great Pianist," *DB*, xxii/17 (1955), 9

O. Keepnews: "Art Tatum," *The Jazz Makers*, ed. N. Shapiro and N. Hentoff (New York, 1957/*R*1979 as *The Jazz Makers: Essays on the Greats of Jazz*), 156

M. Gibson: "The Paradox of Art Tatum," *JJ*, xiii/10 (1960), 3

J. Mehegan: *Jazz Improvisation*, ii: *Jazz Rhythm and the Improvised Line* (New York, 1962)

D. Katz: "Art Tatum," *Jazz Panorama*, ed. M. Williams (New York and London, 1962/*R*1979) [colln of previously pubd articles]

J. Mehegan: *Jazz Improvisation*, iii: *Swing and Early Progressive Piano Styles* (New York, 1964)

R. Spencer: "Art Tatum Discography," *JJ*, xix/10 (1966), 13

——: "The Tatum Story," *JJ*, xix/8 (1966), 6

——: "The Tatum Style," *JJ*, xix/9 (1966), 11

W. Balliett: "One Man Band," *New Yorker*, xliv (7 Sept 1968); repr. in *Ecstasy at the Onion* (New York and Indianapolis, 1971), 111

S. Rothman: "The Art of Tatum," *The Blade Sunday Magazine* (Toledo, OH, 14 June 1970), 4

J. A. Howard: *The Improvisational Techniques of Art Tatum* (diss., Case Western Reserve U., 1978)

D. C. Brigaud: *Art Tatum: essai pour une discographie des enregistrements hors commerce* (Paris, 1980) [incl. listings of radio broadcasts, film music, and V-discs]

Keyboard, vii/10 (1981) [special issue]

J. Distler: *Art Tatum* (New York, 1981)

A. Bridgers: "Art Tatum," *Jazzophone* (1982)

A. Laubich and R. Spencer: *Art Tatum: a Guide to his Recorded Music* (Metuchen, NJ, 1982) [bio-discography]

A. Balalas: "Art Tatum," *BHcF*, no.304 (1983), 3

F. A. Howlett: *An Introduction to Art Tatum's Performance Approaches: Composition, Improvisation, and Melodic Variation* (diss., Cornell U., 1983)

M. Williams: "Art Tatum: not for the Left Hand Alone," *American Music*, i/1 (1983), 36

FELICITY HOWLETT, J. BRADFORD ROBINSON

Taylor, Art(hur S., Jr.) (*b* New York, 6 April 1929). Drummer. He played in a church in Harlem with Sonny Rollins and Jackie McLean and worked with Howard McGhee in 1948. He performed and recorded with Coleman Hawkins (1950–51), Buddy DeFranco (1952), Bud Powell (1952–4 and at intervals to the mid-1960s), Art Farmer (1954–5, recording in 1955), George Wallington (1954–6), and Miles Davis (1955–7, recording in 1955 and 1956). In New York he led the group Taylor's Wailers at The Pad, a club in Greenwich Village, until 1956; he also made several trips to Europe, the first of which was with Donald Byrd and Bobby Jaspar (1958), and played with Thelonious Monk (1959). While living in France (from 1963) and Belgium (from 1970) he played frequently with Johnny Griffin and toured the USA. A collection of his interviews with other jazz musicians was published as *Notes and Tones: Musician-to-musician Interviews* (Liège, Belgium, 1977) and after returning to New York in 1984 he was the host of an interview program on radio station WKCR. Taylor recorded prolifically (especially in the late 1950s) and may be heard on nearly 300 recordings, including John Coltrane's *Giant Steps* (1959), the title track of which well illustrates Taylor's bop style.

SELECTED RECORDINGS
(recorded for Prestige unless otherwise indicated)

As leader: *Taylor's Wailers* (1957, 7117); *A. T.'s Delight* (1960, BN 4047)
As sideman with J. Coltrane: *Dakar* (1957, 7280); *Soultrane* (1958, 7142); *Black Pearls* (1958, 7316); *Giant Steps* (1959, Atl. 1311)
As sideman with others: M. Waldron: *Mal 2* (1957, 7111); R. Garland: *Soul Junction* (1957, 7181); *Dig it* (1957–8, 7229); G. Ammons: *Groove Blues* (1958, 7201); D. Gordon: *A Day in Copenhagen* (1969, MPS 15230)

BIBLIOGRAPHY

I. Gitler: "Art Taylor," *DB*, xxvii/21 (1960), 23
M. Gibson: "Art Taylor," *JJ*, xv/3 (1962), 17
N. Hentoff: "Soundings: Art Taylor," *J&P*, ix/8 (1970), 9
V. Wilmer: "Taylor's New Tricks," *MM* (18 April 1970), 8
S. Crouch: "Drumming up a Book," *VV*, xxvii (19 Oct 1982), 36

JEFF POTTER

Billy Taylor (ii), New York, 1946

Taylor, Billy [William, Sr.] **(i)** (*b* Washington, 3 April 1906; *d* Fairfax, VA, 2 Sept 1986). Double bass and tuba player. He began playing tuba in his teens. After moving to New York (1924) he worked with Elmer Snowden (1925) and Charlie Johnson (1927–9) and, as a member of Duke Ellington's orchestra, recorded with the singer Ozie Ware (1928). He recorded with McKinney's Cotton Pickers in 1929, and toured with the group from 1931 until it disbanded the following year, when he returned to New York and again worked with Johnson (1932–3). In 1934 he performed and recorded with Fats Waller and his Rhythm and briefly joined Fletcher Henderson. Taylor came to prominence as a double bass player with Ellington (1935–40), when he shared bass duties first with Hayes Alvis and later with Jimmy Blanton. He also recorded with other members of Ellington's band, including Barney Bigard (1936–9), Cootie Williams (1937–9), and Johnny Hodges (1938–9). In the 1940s he was associated with Coleman Hawkins (1940), Henry "Red" Allen (1940–41), Joe Sullivan (1942), Williams (1944), Bigard (1944–5), and Benny Morton (1945, with whom he had previously made a recording of his composition *Taylor Made*); he also recorded with many other leaders at this time. From 1945 he worked as a freelance in New York (with such musicians as Cozy Cole, 1945, 1949), and in Washington. His son Billy, Jr. (*d* Washington, 15 Nov 1977), was also a double bass player.

Oral history material in *CtY*.

SELECTED RECORDINGS

As leader: Carney-val in Rhythm/Night Wind (1944, Key. 615); Taylor Made/ Flight of the Be-bop (1947, HRS 1045)
As sideman: O. Ware: Santa Claus, bring my man back to me/I Done Caught you Blues (1928, Vic. 21777); Bessie Smith: Gimme a pigfoot (1933, OK 8949); B. Morton: Taylor Made (1934, Col. 2924D); D. Ellington: Tough Truckin'/Indigo Echoes (1935, Col. 37297); J. Guarnieri: These Foolish Things/Salute to Fats (1944, Savoy 511)

BIBLIOGRAPHY

ChiltonW; *FeatherE*
C. Carrère: "Pitter Panther Patter: les bassistes de Duke Ellington," *Jh*, no.316 (1975), 10
J. Simmen: "Les Billy Taylor," *BHcF*, no.351 (1987), 1

LAWRENCE KOCH

Taylor, Billy [William] **(ii)** (*b* Greenville, NC, 24 July 1921). Pianist and educator. He studied music at Virginia State College (BMus 1942), then moved to New York. His first major engagement was with Ben Webster, and during the 1940s he played with several important musicians, including Dizzy Gillespie, Eddie South, Stuff Smith, Cozy Cole, Machito, Slam Stewart, Don Redman, and Charlie Parker. In 1951 he became house pianist at Birdland, where he supported such players as Roy Eldridge, Lee Konitz, and Oscar Pettiford, but from 1952 he has performed principally as the leader of his own trio; among his sidemen have been Ed Thigpen and Earl May (1950s) and Vic Gaskin and Freddie Waits (1980s). Taylor led an 11-piece band for the "David Frost Show" on television from 1969 to 1972, and was later the founder and director of the radio program "Jazz Alive!." From 1981 he has presented interviews and reports and played on CBS television, making regular appearances on Charles Kuralt's show "Sunday Morning."

Taylor's interest in jazz education was first manifested in four brief primers on jazz piano styles. At the University of Massachusetts he earned a DME in 1975 for his dissertation *The History and Development of Jazz Piano: a New Perspective for Educators*; he published a further work, *Jazz Piano: History and Development*, in 1982. Through his involvement in workshops and JAZZMOBILE, which he helped establish in 1965, he has become an articulate and respected spokesman for the arts in general and jazz in particular. Despite his commitments to education he has continued to develop as a pianist, displaying a light, fluid, and inventive bop style. He has composed a number of works, including the Suite for Jazz Piano and Orchestra (1973).

Oral history material in *NjR*.

SELECTED RECORDINGS

As unaccompanied soloist: The Very Thought of You (1946, Swing 234)
As leader: *Piano Panorama* (1951, Atl. 113); *Jazz at Storyville* (1952, Roost 406); *A Touch of Taylor* (1955, Prst. 7001); *One for Fun* (1959, Atl. 1329); *Sleeping Bee* (1969, MPS 15234); *Where've You Been?* (1980, Conc. 145)

BIBLIOGRAPHY

S. A. Pease: "Taylor: One of the Creators among the Progressives," *DB*, xvii/16 (1950), 12
A. Hodeir: "Critic's Reply to Billy Taylor," *DB*, xxii/22 (1955), 34
B. Taylor: "Progressive Jazz," *DB*, xxiii/5 (1956), 11
D. Gold: "Billy Taylor," *DB*, xxv/1 (1958), 16
F. H. Mitchell: "A Matter of Ego," *DB*, xxviii/22 (1961), 22

D. Morgenstern: "Taylor-made Frostings," *DB*, xxxviii/5 (1971), 18
Arnold Shaw: *The Street that Never Slept: New York's Fabled 52nd Street* (New York, 1971/*R*1977 as *52nd Street: the Street of Jazz*)
W. Fowler: "How to Complete the Spectrum of your Music Education," *DB*, xli/7 (1974), 36
L. Lyons: "Billy Taylor: Jazz Pianist, PhD," *CK*, ii/6 (1976), 18
Z. Knauss: *Conversations with Jazz Musicians* (Detroit, 1977), 202
A. J. Smith: "Jazzmobile: Billy Taylor and Dave Bailey, Magnetizing the Arts," *DB*, xliv/20 (1977), 14 [interview]
W. A. Brower: "Jazz Alive!: Ad-free Radio Taylored for you," *DB*, xlvi/9 (1979), 18
B. Parker-Sparrow: "Billy Taylor Presents America's Classical Music," *DB*, xlvii/5 (1980), 24 [interview]
L. P. Bass: "Marathon Man of Jazz Education," *Music Educators Journal*, lxviii/5 (1982), 31 [interview]
L. Lyons: *The Great Jazz Pianists, Speaking of their Lives and Music* (New York, 1983), 176
J. Roberts: "Billy Taylor: Primarily Piano," *DB*, lii/3 (1985), 26 [interview]
J. Simmen: "Les Billy Taylor," *BHcF*, no.351 (1987), 1

BILL BENNETT/R

Taylor, Cecil (Percival) (*b* New York, 15 March 1929). Pianist and composer. He grew up on Long Island, where his mother, a highly cultured woman who played the piano, encouraged him to begin piano lessons at the age of five. Later he also studied percussion with a timpanist, probably influencing his percussive approach to the keyboard. In 1952 he entered the New England Conservatory, where he studied piano and theory; however, he soon detected a lack of appreciation in the academic world for the aesthetic values of black culture. After exploring the music of Dave Brubeck, Lennie Tristano, and Igor Stravinsky, he came under the decisive influence of Duke Ellington, Thelonious Monk, and Horace Silver. In 1956 he made his first important recording, *Jazz Advance*, in a quartet with Steve Lacy, Buell Neidlinger, and Dennis Charles. In the same year he began an extended engagement at the Five Spot in New York, which virtually established that club as a major forum for new jazz; he also made an appearance at the Newport Jazz Festival which won him considerable prestige. Neither of these achievements captured a large audience for his music or secured him further work, however, and by 1962, when he was given the *Down Beat* "new star" award for pianists, he was, ironically, unemployed. In winter 1962–3 he made a fairly successful tour of Scandinavia in a trio with Jimmy Lyons (who became a regular member of his groups) and Sunny Murray.

Throughout the following decade Taylor faced a baffling combination of high critical acclaim and little or no work. He made perhaps one major concert appearance each year, but otherwise worked sporadically in nightclubs for modest to low pay. These difficulties undoubtedly stemmed from the unrelenting demands posed by his music on the listener. Taylor himself said of his piano style that he tries "to imitate on the piano the leaps in space a dancer makes." Although in the 1950s and early 1960s he frequently incorporated single-note melodies and conventional rhythms in his playing, by the late 1960s he was concentrating on clusters and glissandos produced with open palms, fists, elbows, and forearms, and making use of dense, aperiodic rhythms that seemed to bear little resemblance to those traditionally associated with jazz. Indeed, Taylor's later work is more akin to the European avant garde than the jazz of his predecessors.

After a brief and unsatisfying venture into college teaching during the early 1970s Taylor's professional career began to gather momentum, and from 1973 he toured fairly regularly either as a solo pianist or as the leader of his own group; in 1987 he led a quintet which included Leroy Jenkins, Thurman Barker (playing marimba), and Freddie Waits. He remains totally uncompromising as an artist and, after 30 years in jazz, is still a controversial figure.

Oral history material in *NjR*.

See also Improvisation, §3; Jazz (i), §VI, 1; and Piano, §5, and fig.3.

SELECTED RECORDINGS

As unaccompanied soloist: *Silent Tongues* (1974, Ari. 1005)
As leader: *Jazz Advance* (1956, Tran. 19); *Looking Ahead!* (1958, Cont. 3562); *Unit Structures* (1966, BN 84237); *Conquistador!* (1966, BN 84260); *Dark to Themselves* (1976, Enja 2084); *Three Phasis* (1978, New World 303)
As sideman: G. Evans: *Into the Hot* (1961, Imp. 9); on Jazz Composer's Orchestra: *The Jazz Composer's Orchestra* (1968, JCOA 1001-2), Communications no.11

BIBLIOGRAPHY

G. Schuller: "Reviews: Recordings," *JR*, ii/1 (1959), 28
J. Goldberg: *Jazz Masters of the Fifties* (New York and London, 1965/*R*1980)
N. Hentoff: "The Persistent Challenge of Cecil Taylor," *DB*, xxxii/5 (1965), 17
A. B. Spellman: "Cecil Taylor," *Four Lives in the Bebop Business* (New York, 1966/*R*1970 as *Black Music: Four Lives*), 1–76
E. Raben: *A Discography of Free Jazz* (Copenhagen, 1969)
E. Jost: *Free Jazz* (Graz, Austria, 1974)
J. B. Figi: "Cecil Taylor: African Code, Black Methodology," *DB*, xlii/7 (1975), 12
B. Smith: "Unit Structures," *Coda*, xii/4 (1975), 2 [interview]
B. Rusch: "Cecil Taylor: Interview," *Cadence*, iv/1 (1978), 3
G. Cerutti: "Discographie de Cecil Taylor," *Jazz 360*, no.22 (1979), 9
P. Rothbart: "Orchestrating the Collective Consciousness," *DB*, xlvii/4 (1980), 17
T. Darter: "Piano Giants of Jazz: Cecil Taylor," *CK*, vii/5 (1981), 56
M. Hames: *Albert Ayler, Sunny Murray, Cecil Taylor, Byard Lancaster & Kenneth Terroade on Disc and Tape* (Ferndown, England, 1983)
L. Lyons: *The Great Jazz Pianists, Speaking of their Lives and Music* (New York, 1983), 301
M. Buholzer and U. Breger: "Cecil Taylor: Interview," *Cadence*, x/12 (1984), 5
B. Doerschuk: "Cecil Taylor: in the Eye of the Hurricane," *Keyboard*, xi/1 (1985), 38 [incl. discography]
G. Giddins: "Pick a Card, any Card," *Rhythm-a-ning: Jazz Tradition and Innovation in the '80s* (New York, and Oxford, England, 1985) [colln of previously pubd articles], 7
K. Lynch: "Cecil Taylor and the Poetics of Living," *DB*, liii/11 (1986), 22 [incl. discography]

BILL DOBBINS

Taylor, Eva [Gibbons, Irene] (*b* St. Louis, 22 Jan 1895; *d* Mineola, NY, 31 Oct 1977). Singer. As a child she worked in traveling shows and toured Australia and New Zealand (1900, 1914) and Europe (1906). In 1921 she moved to New York and married Clarence Williams. From 1922 (when she assumed the stage name Eva Taylor) she worked on radio and in stage shows and revues, and recorded as a soloist and sideman. She made a large number of recordings with Williams's group (1924–41), one of the finest of which is *Cake-walking Babies from Home* (1925, OK 40321). She ceased full-time performing in the 1940s and sang only occasionally in the 1950s and early 1960s, but from the mid-1960s she worked in England, New York, Copenhagen, and Sweden.

BIBLIOGRAPHY

"Looking Back with Eva," *Sv*, no.14 (1967–8), 17; no.15 (1968), 18; no.16 (1968), 19
A. Napoleon: "The Return of Eva Taylor," *JJ*, xxi/1 (1968), 30
S. Harris: *Blues Who's Who: a Biographical Dictionary of Blues Singers* (New Rochelle, NY, 1979)

based on *ChiltonW*

Taylor, Gene [Calvin Eugene] (*b* Toledo, OH, 19 March 1929). Double bass player. He lived in Detroit from 1936 and played sousaphone and for a brief period piano before taking up double bass. He achieved prominence as a member of Horace Silver's quintet (1958–64), and performed and recorded with another member of the group, Blue Mitchell. From 1966 to 1968 he worked with the popular singer Nina Simone, for whom he wrote the song *Why? (The King of Love is Dead)*, a tribute to Martin Luther King, Jr.; he also accompanied the folksinger Judy Collins (1968–76). In the 1970s he played in New York in duos and trios led by Duke Jordan, Barry Harris, and Cedar Walton, and toured with Buddy Rich, Philly Joe Jones, Louie Bellson, Charli Persip, Junior Mance, and Billy Taylor (ii); in 1980 he appeared at Carnegie Hall. He began teaching music in the New York public schools in 1985. Taylor has a relaxed, confident manner, and a style marked by short, percussive notes played with a swinging intensity.

SELECTED RECORDINGS

As sideman: H. Silver: *Finger Poppin'* (1959, BN 4008); *Blowin' the Blues Away* (1959, BN 4017); *Horace-Scope* (1960, BN 84042); B. Mitchell: *The Cup Bearers* (1963, Riv. 9439); E. Jefferson: *Come Along with me* (1969, Prst. 7698); B. Harris: *Barry Harris Plays Tadd Dameron* (1975, Xan. 113)

BIBLIOGRAPHY

FeatherE; *Feather '60s*; *Feather–Gitler '70s*

JOHN VOIGT

Taylor, Jasper (*b* Texarkana, TX, 1 Jan 1894; *d* Chicago, 7 Nov 1964). Drummer, washboard player, and percussionist. He moved in 1913 to Memphis, where he worked in theaters and performed with Jelly Roll Morton. During an association with W. C. Handy that began in 1913 Taylor first experimented with playing rhythms on a washboard. In 1917 he moved to Chicago, where he recorded with Handy. During World War I he served with a military band in France. Thereafter he played with Will Marion Cook and Handy in New York before returning to Chicago in 1922. Playing variously drums, washboard, and percussion he participated in many recordings, notably with Morton (1923), Jimmy O'Bryant's Washboard Band (1924–5), Clarence Williams, Jimmy Blythe, and Freddie Keppard (all 1926), and Fess Williams (1927–8). He also recorded on washboard as a leader (1927, 1928) and, as a drummer, took part in a classic series of recordings by Reuben Reeves (1929). Taylor left music for some years in the 1930s, but later worked with such musicians as Punch Miller (1945), Natty Dominique (1952), and Lil Armstrong (1959–60), and led his own band (1962). Although he is remembered mainly for having introduced the washboard as a musical instrument, he was also a versatile percussionist. The rhythmic accuracy and sophisticated accentuation of his work with Reeves fully support his reputation as one of the finest drummers of his generation.

Oral history material in *LNT*.

SELECTED RECORDINGS

As leader: Stomp Time Blues/It must be the blues (1927, Para. 12409); Jasper Taylor Blues/Geechie River Blues (1928, Voc. 1196)

As sideman: J. O'Bryant: Washboard/Brand New Charleston (1925, Para. 12265); Dixie Washboard Band: Boodle am/I've found a new baby (1926, Ban. 1781); F. Keppard: Stock Yards Strut/Salty Dog (1926, Para. 12399); R. Reeves: Papa Skag Stomp/Bugle Call Blues (1929, Voc. 1297); Blue Sweets/Texas Special Blues (1929, Voc. 1411)

BIBLIOGRAPHY

ChiltonW

MICHAEL TOVEY

Taylor, John (*b* Manchester, England, 25 Sept 1942). English pianist. He had no formal musical education, but drew instinctively on the influences of Oscar Peterson, Bill Evans (ii), and, later, Herbie Hancock. After early professional experience in dance bands he moved to London (1964), where he worked frequently in a trio accompanying singers; his first important engagement was with Tommy Whittle at the Hopvine. Later he was associated with Alan Skidmore (recording in 1969 and 1971), John Surman, John Dankworth and Cleo Laine (1970–73), and especially Norma Winstone, whom he married in 1972. He also recorded with Harry Beckett (1970–71) and Volker Kriegel (1971–3). In the 1970s Taylor led a sextet, which included Kenny Wheeler, for six years; he also played in Ronnie Scott's band for six months (1977) and accompanied leading American bop musicians at Scott's club. From 1977 he has become best known for his work as a performer and composer for the trio Azimuth with Winstone and Wheeler; his dynamic, romantic style combines with Winstone's singing and Wheeler's plangent flugelhorn playing to produce strikingly individual results. Taylor has also recorded as a sideman with Jon Eardley (1977), Arild Andersen (1981), Miroslav Vitous (1982), and Wheeler (1983), and has toured and recorded with Jan Garbarek (1977–8).

SELECTED RECORDINGS

As leader: *Decipher* (1973, MPS 2121290); of Azimuth (with K. Wheeler and N. Winstone): *Azimuth* (1977, ECM 1099), *Azimuth '85* (1985, ECM 1298)

As sideman: J. Surman: *How Many Clouds can you See?* (1969, Deram 1045); J. Dankworth: *Full Circle* (1972, Phi. 6308122); J. Surman: *Morning Glory* (1973, Isl. 9237); R. Scott: *Serious Gold* (1977, Pye 18542); J. Eardley: *Namely Me* (1977, Spot. 17)

BIBLIOGRAPHY

R. Cotterell, ed.: *Jazz Now: the Jazz Centre Society Guide* (London, 1976)

A. Macintosh: "John Taylor & Norma Winstone: a Jazz Partnership," *JF* [intl edn], no.59 (1979), 38

CHRIS SHERIDAN

Taylor, Mike [Michael] (*b* London, 1938; *d* 1969). English pianist, composer, and arranger. He learned piano as a child, and played clarinet briefly. After military service he led various groups, ranging from quartets to octets, which included such musicians as Jack Bruce, Jon Hiseman, the drummer Ginger Baker, the trumpeter Frank Powell, the trombonist John Mumford, and the tenor saxophonist Dave Gelly. In 1966 he recorded the album *The Mike Taylor Trio* (1966, Col. SX6137); this includes the track *Abena*, which offers a particularly fine example of his work. As well as composing for his own ensembles (his style is well represented by the tracks *Half Blue* and *Black and White Raga* from the album *Pendulum*, 1965, Col. SX6042) Taylor wrote arrangements and pieces for the New Jazz Orchestra, Norma Winstone, and the rock group Cream. He is believed to have committed suicide; his body was found on the beach near Leigh-on-Sea, Essex.

SALLY-ANN WORSFOLD

Taylor, Sam "the Man" [Samuel L.] (*b* Lexington, TN, 12 July 1916). Tenor and baritone saxophonist, and clarinetist. After working with the singer Scat Man Crothers (1937–8) and the Sunset Royal Orchestra (1939–41), he performed and recorded with Cootie Williams (1941–3, 1944–6) and Lucky Millinder (1943–4). During his association with Cab Calloway (1946–52) he toured South America and the Caribbean (1951–2). As a session musician (after 1952) Taylor made a large number of recordings, many of them in a style oriented towards rhythm-and-blues; he recorded as a leader and with Ella Fitzgerald and Ray Charles (both 1953), Buddy Johnson (1955), Louis Jordan (1956), Joe Turner (ii) (1957), and Sy Oliver (1958), among others. He led his own bands into the 1960s and toured Japan in 1963. *Birmingham Special/Old Fashioned Blues* (1952, MGM 11409), recorded in a quintet called the Blues Chasers that included Taft Jordan, Milt Hinton, and Panama Francis, displays the driving swing that characterized his playing.

BIBLIOGRAPHY

FeatherE

H. Panassié and M. Gautier: *Dictionnaire du jazz* (Paris, 1954, rev. and enlarged 2/1971, enlarged 3/1980; Eng. trans., London, 1956, rev. A. A. Gurwitch as *Guide to Jazz*, Boston, 1956), 310

Tchicai, John (Martin) (*b* Copenhagen, 28 April 1936). Danish saxophonist and bandleader. His father was Congolese, his mother Danish. He grew up in Århus, where he played violin from the age of ten and clarinet and alto saxophone from the age of 16; he studied alto saxophone for three years at the Royal Conservatory in Copenhagen. In 1962 he appeared at festivals in Helsinki, where he met Archie Shepp, and Warsaw, where he made his first recording (as the leader of a quintet). After moving to New York he played with Shepp and Don Cherry in the New York Contemporary Five (1963) and with Roswell Rudd and Milford Graves in the New York Art Quartet (1964–5); with both groups he toured Europe and made recordings. He also recorded as a member of the Jazz Composers Guild and with Shepp, John Coltrane, and Albert Ayler. In 1966 he returned to Denmark, where he led the workshop ensemble Cadentia nova danica (1967–71), with which he performed in London in 1968. For several years (from 1972) he performed less frequently and worked principally as a teacher; he resumed playing full-time in 1977 and joined Pierre Dørge's New Jungle Orchestra, with which he appeared at the Chicago Jazz Festival (1986). In his early career Tchicai favored a staccato attack and a dry tone that recalled the work of Lee Konitz; after changing from alto to soprano saxophone around 1983 he employed a fuller sound and a style of phrasing that displayed the influence of the work of Sonny Rollins. In addition to his principal instrument he plays bass clarinet proficiently.

SELECTED RECORDINGS

As unaccompanied soloist: *Solo* (1977, FMP SAJ12)

Duos with P. Dørge: *Ball at Louisiana Museum of Art* (1981, Ste. 1174)

As leader: with D. Cherry and A. Shepp: *Archie Shepp and the New York Contemporary Five* (1963, Sonet 36); of New York Art Quartet (with R. Rudd): *The New York Art Quartet* (1964, ESP 1004); of Cadentia nova danica: *Afrodisiaca* (1969, MPS 15249); *Real Tchicai* (1977, Ste. 1075); *John Tchicai & the Strange Brothers* (1977, FMP SAJ15)

As sideman: A. Ayler: *New York Eye and Ear Control* (1964, ESP 1016); A. Shepp: *Four for Trane* (1964, Imp. 71); on Jazz Composers Guild Orchestra: *Communication* (1964, Fon. 881011), Roast; J. Coltrane: *Ascension* (1965, Imp. 95); J. Dyani: *Witchdoctor's Son* (1978, Ste. 1098); P. Dørge: *Ballad Round the Left Corner* (1979, Ste. 1132); *Pierre Dørge and the New Jungle Orchestra* (1982, Ste. 1162); *Brikama* (1984, Ste. 1188); C. Taylor: *Winged Serpent* (1984, SN 1089); J. Dyani: *Angolian Cry* (1985, Ste. 1209); P. Dørge: *Very Hot: Even the Moon is Dancing* (1985, Ste. 1208)

BIBLIOGRAPHY

J.-L. Comolli: "Tchicai sans chique," *Jm*, no.137 (1966), 28

D. Morgenstern: "John Tchicai: a Calm Member of the Avant-garde," *DB*, xxxiii/3 (1966), 20

A. Barnett: "John Tchicai: of Three Continents," *JM*, no.164 (1968), 2

"Je m'appelle John Tchicai," *Jh*, no.272 (1971), 9 [incl. discography]

E. Jost: *Free Jazz* (Graz, Austria, 1974), 109

M. Hames: *John Tchicai on Disc and Tape* (Ferndown, England, 1979) [discography]

G. Cerutti: *Discographie de John Tchicai* (Sierre, Switzerland, n.d. [?1979]; rev. and enlarged 2/n.d. [?1982], rev. and enlarged 3/n.d. [?1986] as *John Tchicai Discography (on Records), 1962–1985*)

G. Rouy: "John Tchicai: jours tranquilles à Copenhague," *Jm*, no.286 (1980), 26

B. Noglik: "John Tchicai," *Jazzwerkstatt international* (Berlin, 1981), 399 [incl. interview, discography]

K. Yianoulopoulos: "'Die eigene spirituelle Erfahrung spüren lassen': John Tchicai," *JP*, xxxi/4 (1982), 4 [incl. discography]

C. Irgens-Møller: "Tchicai: et begreb" [Tchicai: a notion], *Dansk musik tidsskrift*, lxi/3 (1986–7), 111

OLE MATTHIESSEN/ERIK WIEDEMANN

Teagarden. Family of musicians.

(1) Helen Teagarden [née Geingar] (*b c*1890; *d* 1982). Pianist. She taught piano in Chappel, Nebraska, and later (around 1920) in Oklahoma City, and was largely responsible for the musical education of her children. She was not particularly a jazz-oriented player, but did appear at the Monterey Jazz Festival in 1963 in a band that was led by (2) Jack Teagarden and also included (3) Norma and (4) Charlie Teagarden. (J. D. Smith and L. Guttridge: *Jack Teagarden: the Story of a Jazz Maverick*, London, 1960)

(2) Jack [Weldon Leo] **Teagarden** [Big T] (*b* Vernon, TX, 29 Aug 1905; *d* New Orleans, 15 Jan 1964). Trombonist and singer. He started learning piano with his mother (1) Helen Teagarden when he was five, then turned to baritone horn, and took up trombone at the age of ten. He began playing professionally as a teenager, working mainly in the Southwest with local bands, including Peck Kelley's Bad Boys (1921–3, 1924), the Original Southern Trumpeters (1924), and Doc Ross's Jazz Bandits (1924–7). He then went to New York, where he played briefly with Wingy Manone. After working as a freelance for a while he joined Ben Pollack's band in 1928, though he continued to play and record with other musicians such as Red Nichols, Louis Armstrong, and Eddie Condon. In December 1933 he became a member of Paul Whiteman's band. For one month in 1936 he played after hours at the Hickory House on 52nd Street in New York with his fellow Whiteman sidemen Frankie Trumbauer and his brother (4) Charlie Teagarden in a group known as the Three T's. Teagarden remained as a star soloist and singer with Whiteman until December 1938. He then set up his own big band, a venture which was successful musically but financially unrewarding, as it ended with his being declared bankrupt in 1946. He led a sextet from late 1946 until he joined the first Louis Armstrong All Stars in 1947 (see illustration), then formed his own dixieland group, also known as the All Stars, in 1951. He continued to lead small groups, which included such musicians as Don Ewell, Max Kaminsky, Dick Wellstood, and his brother Charlie, until his death.

Teagarden is considered by many critics to be the finest of all jazz trombonists, but his style was so personal that he had few followers, and founded no school. Significantly, he grew

Jack Teagarden (trombone) with Louis Armstrong (trumpet) and Bobby Hackett during a rehearsal for a concert by Armstrong's All Stars at Town Hall, New York, May 1947

up in rough southwestern towns containing large black populations, and was far more familiar than most early white jazz players with black spirituals, work songs, and the blues, having experienced them first-hand from earliest childhood. As a consequence he was one of the first white jazz musicians to master the blues, and probably the first to make use of blue notes. He usually detached his solo line markedly from the ground beat, weaving lazy arabesques of melody. He tended to play in the upper register of the instrument, and his cloudy tone, at first relatively rough, grew smoother in his later years. Because of his deceptively simple style, few listeners realized how technically adroit he was; he was particularly skilled in playing lip trills, which became a prominent feature of his style. Teagarden is also considered one of the finest jazz singers. His style was much simpler than that of his highly decorative playing, but characterized by a similar lazy quality, and his husky voice was particularly suitable for the blues (*see* BLUES, §4). Teagarden's recorded output is very consistent, but especially fine are his performances on *Knockin' a Jug* (1929), *Jack hits the road* (1940), and *Makin' Friends* (1928), the last named including an eccentric solo played with the bell of the trombone removed.

Oral history material in *LNT*.

SELECTED RECORDINGS

As leader: A Hundred Years from Today (1933, Bruns. 6716); What did I do to be so black and blue? (1941, Decca 3844); Blues after Hours (1947, Vic. 202458); A Jam Session at Victor (1947, Vic. 400138); *The Swingin' Gate* (1960–63, Giants of Jazz 1026); *Jack Teagarden Sextet in Person* (1963, Fanfare LP32-132)

As sideman: Roger Wolfe Kahn: She's a great great girl (1928, Vic. 21326); E. Condon: Makin' Friends (1928, OK 41142); B. Pollack: My Kinda Love (1929, Vic. 21944); L. Armstrong: Knockin' a Jug (1929, OK 8703); R. Nichols: The Sheik of Araby (1930, Bruns. 4885); J. Venuti and E. Lang: Beale Street Blues (1931, Voc. 15864); E. Condon: Serenade to a Shylock (1938, Com. 1501); B. Freeman: Jack hits the road (1940, Col. 35854); L. Armstrong: Rockin' Chair (1947, Vic. 40-4004); St. James Infirmary (1947, Vic. 40-4006)

BIBLIOGRAPHY

W. Scholl: "The New Vocal Sensation: Jack Teagarden," *MM*, x (26 May 1934)
C. Wilford: "An Anatomy of Teagarden," *Jazz Music*, no.6 (1943); repr. in *Jazz Reprints*, i/1 (1962), 12
L. Feather: *The Book of Jazz: a Guide to the Entire Field* (New York, 1957, 2/1965 as *The Book of Jazz from Then till Now: a Guide to the Entire Field*)
C. E. Smith: "Big Gate," *JM*, iii/8 (1957), 2
J. Tynan: "Teagarden Talks," *DB*, xxiv/5 (1957), 19
G. Hoefer: "The Change in Big T," *DB*, xxvi/24 (1959), 18
J. D. Smith and L. Guttridge: *Jack Teagarden: the Story of a Jazz Maverick* (London, 1960)
H. J. Waters, Jr.: *Jack Teagarden's Music: his Career and Recordings* (Stanhope, NJ, 1960)
W. Balliett: "Slow Sleeper," *Dinosaurs in the Morning* (Philadelphia, 1962) [colln of previously pubd articles and reviews], 207
B. James: "Blues for Jack Teagarden," *JJ*, xvii/3 (1964), 2
R. Hadlock: *Jazz Masters of the Twenties* (New York, 1965/*R*1985)
H. Woodfin: "Say it Simple: the Art of Jack Teagarden," *JM*, xii/9 (1966), 10
M. Williams: "In Praise of Jack Teagarden," *JJ*, xxi/6 (1968), 4
——: *Jazz Masters in Transition, 1957–69* (New York and London, 1970/*R*1980) [colln of previously pubd reviews]
R. Blesh: "Big T," *Combo, USA: Eight Lives in Jazz* (Philadelphia and London, 1971), 58
R. Russell: "Jack Teagarden and the Texas School," *Jazz Style in Kansas City and the Southwest* (Berkeley, CA, Los Angeles, and London, 1971/*R*1983, rev. 2/1973)
H. Lyttelton: *The Best of Jazz*, ii: *Enter the Giants, 1931–1944* (London, 1981), 92
W. Balliett: "Profiles: Jack Teagarden," *New Yorker*, lx (2 April 1984), 47
H. Mückenberger: *Meet me Where they Play the Blues: Jack Teagarden und seine Musik* (Gauting, Germany, 1986)

(3) Norma (Louise) Teagarden (*b* Vernon, TX, 29 April 1911). Pianist. She was taught by her mother, (1) Helen Teagarden, and began playing as a solo pianist in dance halls and clubs in 1926 to supplement her income as a telephone switchboard operator. After working in Oklahoma City and New Mexico she moved in 1941 to California, and the following year joined the big band led by her brother (2) Jack Teagarden. From 1946 to 1949 she was the leader of her own band, then took up teaching. Teagarden performed with a variety of bands, notably those of Ben Pollack and Ada Leonard, and in 1953–4 was a member of Jack's small group. She made recordings with Jack and (4) Charlie Teagarden at the Monterey Jazz Festival in 1963, including *Basin St. Blues* (first issued on J. Teagarden: *The Swingin' Gate*, Giants of Jazz 1026). In 1983, at the Sacramento Dixieland Jubilee, she was elected "Empress of Jazz," and she continued to work on the West Coast in bands and as a soloist in the mid-1980s.

BIBLIOGRAPHY

FeatherE
S. Placksin: *American Women in Jazz, 1900 to the Present: their Words, Lives, and Music* (New York, 1982)
B. Doerschuk: "Norma Teagarden: Queen of Stride Piano," *Keyboard*, x/5 (1984), 28
C. McFadden: "Miss Norma," *San Francisco Examiner* (14 Nov 1985)
A. C. Williams: "The Enduring Grace of Norma Teagarden," *MR*, xiv/3 (1987), 1

(4) Charlie [Charles] **Teagarden** [Little T] (*b* Vernon, TX, 19 July 1913; *d* Las Vegas, NV, 10 Dec 1984). Trumpeter. After first working with bands in Oklahoma he joined Ben Pollack in New York in 1929. He recorded there with various bands, notably those of Red Nichols (1931) and Roger Wolfe Kahn (1932), before following his brother (2) Jack Teagarden into Paul Whiteman's orchestra (1933). While he was with Whiteman (1933–40) he made club appearances with Jack and Frankie Trumbauer in the Three T's, and also recorded with a larger group of the same name (*I'se a muggin'*, 1936, Vic. 25273). In September 1940 Teagarden joined Jack's big band, with which he performed intermittently throughout the decade, although he also led his own band briefly in 1942. Thereafter he spent a number of periods with Jack's small groups, while also playing with Jimmy Dorsey (1948–50), Pollack (1950–51), and Bob Crosby (1954–8). After moving to Las Vegas in 1959 Teagarden gradually withdrew from performing in favor of a career in the musicians' union, for which he worked throughout the 1970s. He also led his own quartet, however, which recorded the album *Big Horn* in 1962 (Coral 757410). (*ChiltonW*; *FeatherE*; *Feather '60s*)

(5) Cub [Clois Lee] **Teagarden** (*b* Vernon, TX, 16 Dec 1915; *d* ?Riverton, NY, 1969). Drummer. In 1929 he joined Frank Williams's Oklahomans as drummer and singer, and during the 1930s played with various groups. He was a member of the band led by his brother (2) Jack Teagarden from 1939 to 1940, but his tenure was relatively unsuccessful, and he was soon replaced by Dave Tough. He then performed with the Oklahoma SO and briefly led his own band before moving to California, where he worked as a freelance. He virtually ceased to play in 1948. (*FeatherE*)

ALYN SHIPTON (1, 3–5)
JAMES LINCOLN COLLIER (2)

Teague, Thurman (*b* Illinois, 1910). Double bass player. He first performed on banjo and guitar in Chicago, then played regularly with the guitarist Jack Goss in the early 1930s. After changing to double bass he worked with Ben Pollack and later with the pianist and bandleader Vincent Lopez and others. His solid, rhythmic playing may be heard to advantage on *I never knew what a gal could do* (1937, Col. 36159), by Santo Pecora and his Back Room Boys. From 1939 to 1944 Teague played with Harry James. Thereafter he worked with Red Nichols (1945–6), then became active as a studio musician on the West Coast.

based on *ChiltonW*

Teddies. *See* ORIGINAL TEDDIES.

Teddy Wilson School for Pianists. Record label. Its material was recorded in 1938–9 by the American Record Company, and made available for sale by the school, which was based in New York. Five 78 r.p.m. discs were released, all unaccompanied solos by Wilson; the discs were issued with scores and analytical texts. (J. Callanan: Liner notes, *Teddy Wilson: the Complete 'School for Pianists' Recordings, 1938–1939*, Meritt 23, 1984)

Tee, Richard (Edward) (*b* New York, 24 Nov 1943). Keyboard player. He first became active as a sideman during the period when the dance rhythms of black popular music were fashionable in jazz: he recorded with Shirley Scott and Les McCann (both 1969), Gary Burton (1969–70), Hank Crawford (1969–75), Herbie Mann, King Curtis, and Snooky Young (all 1971), Stanley Turrentine (1971, 1973), Grover Washington, Jr. (1971–3), Roland Kirk (1971, 1975), David "Fathead" Newman (1972), Ron Carter (1973, 1975), Hubert Laws (1974, 1980), Jimmy Witherspoon (1975), and Carla Bley (1976). From 1974 to 1984 he led his own funk group, Stuff, which included the guitarists Eric Gale and Cornell Dupree, the electric bass guitarist Gordon Edwards, and at various times the drummers Steve Gadd and Chris Parker. During the same period he worked with many popular entertainers and commercial groups and recorded film soundtracks. Tee later recorded with Gadd and Sadao Watanabe (both 1984) and Ronnie Cuber (1985), and issued the album *The Bottom Line* (1985, EB 6364) under his own name.

BIBLIOGRAPHY

J. Stix: "Richard Tee: from New York Session Work to 'Stuff'," *CK*, iii/11 (1977), 16 [incl. discography]
J. Coryell and L. Friedman: *Jazz-rock Fusion* (New York and London, 1978)

Teitelbaum, Richard (Lowe) (*b* New York, 19 May 1939). Composer and synthesizer player. He studied music at Yale University (MM 1964), then traveled to Italy on a Fulbright fellowship. While there, with other composers based in Rome, he formed Musica Elettronica Viva for the performance of live electronic music; the group continued to perform and record collaborative improvisations, mainly in Europe, until 1970, during which time it was joined by Steve Lacy and the trombonist Garrett List. Teitelbaum then returned to the USA for further study, and at Wesleyan University formed the World Band with musicians from the Middle and Far East who shared his interest in collective improvisation. He has performed with Anthony Braxton (1974–1980s), with whom he has made such recordings as the duo albums *Time Zones* (1976, Freedom 41037) and *Open Aspects* (1982, HA 1995–6). He has also recorded in a quartet with George Lewis (ii) (*Homage to Charles Parker*, 1979, BS 0029).

JOAN LA BARBARA/R

Temperance Seven. English traditional jazz band. It was formed in 1956 to perform dance music of the 1920s. Its original members were the trumpeter and euphonium player Cephas Howard, the banjoist John Gieves-Watson, the drummer Brian Innes, the singer Paul McDowell, the reed players Alan Cooper and Ray Whittam, and the pianist and music director Colin Bowles. Clifford Bevan was the tuba player from 1957 until 1959, when his place was taken by Martin Fry; Bevan later replaced Bowles as director. John R. T. Davies, who wrote arrangements and played trombone, trumpet, and alto saxophone, joined in 1959. The musicians' adoption of fanciful nicknames was characteristic of their humorous approach. The band made several recordings, including *The Temperance Seven, 1961* (1961, Parl. PMC1152); the most successful were *You're driving me crazy* and *Pasadena*, which reached the top of the popular-music charts in the UK in 1961. It also appeared in *Take me Over* (1962) and other films. It disbanded in 1968, but in the early 1970s some of the players formed the New Temperance Seven. The name was later used for various bands by the multi-instrumentalist Bobby Mickleburgh.

BIBLIOGRAPHY

"The Temperance Seven: Personal Appearance," *Jazz News*, v/28 (1961), 16
I. Berg, I. Yeomans, and N. Brittan: *Trad: an A to Z Who's Who of the British Traditional Jazz Scene* (London and elsewhere, 1962), 70
B. Matthew: *Trad Mad* (London, 1962)
G. Martin and J. Hornsby: *All you Need is Ears* (London, 1979)

DEREK COLLER

Temperley, Joe [Joseph] (*b* Cowdenbeath, Scotland, 20 Sept 1929). Scottish baritone saxophonist. He first learned alto saxophone, but recorded on the tenor instrument with Harry Parry (1949), Jack Parnell (1953), and Tony Crombie (1954), and on baritone with the tenor saxophonist Tommy Whittle (1955–6). He first achieved national prominence as a member of Humphrey Lyttelton's band (1958–65), with which he played tenor and then baritone saxophone; he made several important recordings with the group and toured the USA (1959). In 1965 he settled in New York, where he worked with Woody Herman (1966–7), Buddy Rich, Joe Henderson, Duke Pearson, and the Jazz Composer's Orchestra, and recorded with the Thad Jones–Mel Lewis Orchestra (1969), Clark Terry (1970), and Eumir Deodato (1973). In October 1974, as Harry Carney's replacement, Temperley toured and recorded with Duke Ellington's orchestra (at that time led by Mercer Ellington). He then resumed his freelance activities, which include regular tours as a soloist in England. The broad base of Temperley's style has won him praise from such diverse players as Charles Mingus and Warren Vaché; that he took the place of a musician of Carney's caliber in Ellington's orchestra was a colossal achievement and shows him to be a player of high standing.

SELECTED RECORDINGS

As leader with J. Knepper: *Just Friends* (1978, Hep 2003)
As sideman: H. Lyttelton: *Humph Plays Standards* (1960, Beth. 6063), incl. Prelude to a Kiss; B. Clayton: *Le vrai Buck Clayton* (1964, 77 LEU11); M. Ellington: *Continuum* (1974–5, Fan. 9481)

BIBLIOGRAPHY

FeatherE; *Feather–Gitler '70s*

DIGBY FAIRWEATHER

Temple block. A spherical wooden slit-drum used in jazz from the 1920s to produce novelty effects; *see* DRUM SET, §I, 7(ii).

Templin, Lutz [Ludwig] (*b* Düsseldorf, Germany, 18 June 1901; *d* nr Stuttgart, Germany, 7 March 1973). German bandleader. He studied violin and composition and during the 1930s he worked as a tenor saxophonist and arranger for various dance bands. In 1941 he formed his own big band, which worked in radio and recording studios (1941–9); its swing recordings include *Immer wieder tanzen/Rhythmus in Dosen* (1942, Grammophon 47705). Under the name Charlie and his Orchestra his band made recordings of arrangements by American jazz musicians; these were broadcast on radio by the German authorities with added texts that purveyed propaganda against the Allies. Because of the bombardment of Berlin, Templin's orchestra was evacuated in 1943 to Stuttgart, where it performed until 1944. Templin continued to work in and around Stuttgart and for a short time he was music director of the dance orchestra of Süddeutscher Rundfunk.

BIBLIOGRAPHY

R. E. Lotz: Liner notes, *Charlie and his Orchestra: Propaganda Swing* (Discophilia 13UTC1–2, 1975)

H. H. Lange: Liner notes, *Die grossen Tanzorchester, 1930–1950: Lutz Templin* (Pol. 2437629–30, ?1978)

RAINER E. LOTZ

Tempo (i) (It.). The "time" of a piece of music, hence the speed at which the performance proceeds; for a discussion of tempos in jazz *see* BEAT, esp. §2.

Tempo (ii). Record label. It was established by the Tempo Record Society of London, and issue began in September 1946. The catalogue contained two series. The A- sequence was used to issue new recordings by British bands, mostly of traditional jazz; the R- series contained reissues of early jazz from American labels no longer in operation. The last issues were made in October 1952; early the following year the operation was taken over by British Vogue, which immediately discontinued the reissue series. No further issues in the A- series were made until 1955, when British Decca, which had absorbed Vogue, used the label to release new material by such bop artists as Ronnie Scott, Tubby Hayes, Don Rendell, Victor Feldman, Dizzy Reece, and Jimmy Deuchar. (G. Hulme and B. Holland: "Tempo," *Matrix*, no.44 (1962), 3; no.45 (1963), 11; no.46 (1963), 15; no.47 (1963), 21)

Tenor. In general musical terminology the vocal part or range lying below the alto and above the baritone; the word is also used as a qualifying adjective to distinguish those members of certain families of instruments (especially wind) that play in that range (e.g., tenor horn; *see* SAXHORN). In jazz argot "tenor" is used alone to mean the tenor saxophone (*see* SAXOPHONE); "tenor man" (also sometimes "tenor") is used of the player of that instrument.

Tenor cor. *See* MELLOPHONE.

Tenor [alto] **horn.** The alto instrument of the SAXHORN family, pitched in E♭; it normally plays the alto part, occasionally the tenor.

Tenor saxophone. The tenor instrument of the saxophone family, normally pitched in B♭; it was formerly found also in C (the C-melody saxophone). *See* SAXOPHONE, §2.

Terminal vibrato. A vibrato of increasing breadth introduced in the course of a note; a sustained note begins without vibrato, then gradually develops a pitch oscillation which becomes broader or quicker or both towards the end of the note. The effect often occurs at the end of a phrase. Hodeir coined the term to describe a characteristic of Dicky Wells's playing and referred to Louis Armstrong's use of the effect; Hodeir gave two instances of it in Wells's playing, including his solo on Count Basie's *Panassié Stomp* (1938; ex.1). Schuller discussed

Ex.1 Opening phrase of D. Wells's solo on C. Basie: *Panassié Stomp* (1938, Decca 2224); transcr. B. Kernfeld

many examples in Armstrong's music, noting that Armstrong sometimes ended a terminal vibrato with a SHAKE. The effect is notated by a representational symbol (see ex.1).

BIBLIOGRAPHY

A. Hodeir: *Hommes et problèmes du jazz, suivi de La religion du jazz* (Paris, 1954; Eng. trans., rev. Hodeir, as *Jazz: its Evolution and Essence*, New York, 1956/*R*1975)

G. Schuller: *Early Jazz: its Roots and Musical Development* (New York, 1968)

BARRY KERNFELD

Terrell, Pha (Elmer) (*b* Kansas City, MO, 25 May 1910; *d* Los Angeles, 14 Oct 1945). Singer. In the early 1930s he sang, danced, and worked as a compère at the 18th Street Club, Kansas City. He was recruited in 1933 by Andy Kirk, with whom he performed and made recordings (including *Blue Illusion*, 1936, Decca 772) until 1941. Thereafter he worked in Indianapolis with the bandleader Clarence Love and toured and performed on the West Coast as a soloist. (L. Gourse: *Louis' Children: American Jazz Singers* (New York, 1984), 77)

based on *ChiltonW*

Territory band. A term applied to dance bands of the 1920s and early 1930s that worked in a very large area bordered roughly by St. Louis on the east and Denver on the west, and extending from Texas to Nebraska. It is normally used of bands that were based in small regional capitals and made extended tours of the outlying area, playing in local dance halls. Because of the lack of recording opportunities the work of territory bands is poorly documented, and the contribution of individual bands to the formation of KANSAS CITY JAZZ is difficult to trace. From the mid-1920s there were more than 100 active territory bands, among the most important being those of Alphonso Trent (Dallas), Doc Ross (El Paso and Oklahoma City), Troy Floyd (San Antonio), Walter Page (Oklahoma City), and Jesse Stone (Missouri and Kansas).

See also BLUES, §6.

BIBLIOGRAPHY

G. Schuller: *Early Jazz: its Roots and Musical Development* (New York, 1968)

R. Russell: *Jazz Style in Kansas City and the Southwest* (Berkeley, CA, Los Angeles, and London, 1971/*R*1983, rev. 2/1973)

N. W. Pearson, Jr.: *Goin' to Kansas City* (Urbana, IL, and London, 1988)

J. BRADFORD ROBINSON

Terry, Clark [Mumbles] (*b* St. Louis, 14 Dec 1920). Trumpeter and flugelhorn player. He performed with Charlie Barnet (1947) and in Count Basie's big band and small groups (1948–51) before beginning an important affiliation with Duke Ellington, which lasted from 1951 to 1959. During this period Terry took part in many of Ellington's suites and acquired a lasting reputation for his wide range of styles (from swing to hard bop), technical proficiency, and infectious good humor. After leaving Ellington he became a frequent performer in New York studios and a staff member of NBC; he appeared regularly on the "Tonight Show," where his unique "mumbling" scat singing became famous. He also continued to play jazz with musicians such as J. J. Johnson and Oscar Peterson, and led a group with Bob Brookmeyer which achieved some popularity in the early 1960s. In the 1970s Terry began to concentrate increasingly on the flugelhorn, from which he obtains a remarkably full, ringing tone. In addition to his studio work and teaching at jazz workshops, Terry toured regularly in the 1980s with small groups (including Peterson's) and as the leader of his Big B-A-D Band (formed *c*1970). His humor and command of jazz trumpet styles are nowhere more apparent than in his "dialogues" with himself, either on different instruments or on the same instrument, muted and unmuted.

Oral history material in *CtY*, *NjR*, and *TNF*.

SELECTED RECORDINGS

Duos with R. Mitchell: *Clark Terry–Red Mitchell* (1986, Enja 5011)
As leader: *Introducing Clark Terry* (1955, EmA 36007), incl. Kitten, Swahili; *Serenade to a Bus Seat* (1957, Riv. 237); *The Happy Horns of Clark Terry* (1964, Imp. 64); *Big B-A-D Band* (1970, Etoile IA); *Memories of Duke* (1980, PT 2312118)
As leader with B. Brookmeyer: *Tonight* (1964, Mstr. 6043); *The Power of Positive Swinging* (1964, Mstr. 6054); *Mumbles* (1965, Mstr. 6066); *Gingerbread Man* (1966, Mstr. 6086)
As sideman: D. Ellington: *A Drum is a Woman* (1956, Col. CL951); J. Hodges: *The Big Sound* (1957, Verve 8271); O. Peterson: *The Oscar Peterson Trio Plus One – Clark Terry* (1964, Mer. 60975)

BIBLIOGRAPHY

M. Walker: "Clark Terry Discography (1947–1960)," *JM*, vii/10 (1961), 18; vii/11 (1962), 18
D. Morgenstern: "Why is this Man so Happy?," *DB*, xxxiv/11 (1967), 16
S. Dance: *The World of Duke Ellington* (London and New York, 1970/*R*1981) [colln of previously pubd articles and reviews], 182
V. Wilmer: "The Sweet Smell of Success," *Jazz People* (London, Indianapolis, and New York, 1970/*R*1985), 103
E. Wilkins: "My Friend Clark Terry," *DB*, xl/2 (1973), 17
A. J. Smith: "Clark Terry: Jazz Ed, Mumbles Style," *DB*, xliii/19 (1976), 12
B. Rusch: "Clark Terry: Interview," *Cadence*, iii/6 (1977), 3
A. Morgan: "Clark Terry: Jazz Ambassador," *JJI*, xxxi/5 (1978), 6
L. Birnbaum: "Clark Terry: Big B-A-D Brassman," *DB*, xlviii/9 (1981), 22
C. Terry: "Clark Terry and his Jolly Giants: the African Safari, 1979," *JSN*, ii/4 (1982), 137
D. J. Travis: *An Autobiography of Black Jazz* (Chicago, 1983) [incl. interviews], 457
S. Voce: "Clark Terry," *JJI*, xxxix/12 (1986), 10; xl/1 (1987), 16

J. BRADFORD ROBINSON

Teschemacher, Frank [Tesch] (*b* Kansas City, MO, 13 March 1906; *d* Chicago, 13 March 1932). Clarinetist, alto saxophonist, and violinist. He spent his childhood in Chicago, where he studied various instruments. Around 1922 he was one of the so-called Austin High School Gang of young Chicago jazz musicians (see illustration); he played with Jimmy McPartland and other members of this group in various bands. From 1926 he performed mainly in commercial dance orchestras in Chicago, though he continued to record in small jazz groups. In summer 1928 he played with Red Nichols in New York. Teschemacher's importance rests primarily on his performing style as a clarinetist, though he played that instrument regularly only from 1925 to about 1930. He was strongly influenced by Bix Beiderbecke, and his best work makes telling use of the distinctive articulation and accented ninths and elevenths of Beiderbecke's cornet style. His dirty tone resembles (and may have influenced) that of PeeWee Russell and the young Benny Goodman. Teschemacher's low-register solo on *Darktown Strutters Ball* was frequently copied, but poor intonation and insecure technique mar many of his recordings, of which he made about three dozen before his early death in an automobile accident.

SELECTED RECORDINGS

As sideman: McKenzie–Condon Chicagoans: Sugar/China Boy (1927, OK 41011); Nobody's Sweetheart/Liza (1927, OK 40971); Jungle Kings: Friars Point Shuffle/Darktown Strutters Ball (1928, Para. 12654)

BIBLIOGRAPHY

N. Shapiro and N. Hentoff, eds.: *Hear me Talkin' to ya: the Story of Jazz by the Men who Made it* (New York and London, 1955/*R*1966), 118
R. Hadlock: *Jazz Masters of the Twenties* (New York, 1965/*R*1985), 106
B. Esposito: "Jazz Juxtaposition: Bix . . . Tesch," *JJ*, xxv/10 (1972), 4
V. Simosko: "Frank Teschemacher: a Reappraisal," *JJS*, iii/1 (1975), 28
T. Tolley: "Teschemacher and the Chicagoans in New York: an Investigation," *Sv*, no.111 (1984), 84
B. Whyatt: "Tesch and the Chicagoans: More Ideas and Thoughts," *Sv*, no.114 (1984), 204

J. R. TAYLOR/R

Four members of the Austin High School Gang, Chicago, c1927: (left to right) Frank Teschemacher, Jimmy McPartland, Dick McPartland, and Bud Freeman, with Freeman's brother Arnie Freeman

Tevelian, Meg(uerditsch) (*b* ?Turkey, 1902; *d* Vienna, 23 Oct 1976). Armenian guitarist. He fled Turkey in 1921 owing to the persecution of the Armenian people and settled in Berlin, where, by the 1930s, he was highly sought after for concert, dance, and studio work. Among the bandleaders with whom he played and recorded are Michael Jary (1939–40), Willy Berking (1939–42), Kutte Widmann (1940–41), Horst Winter, Helmuth Zacharias (both 1941–2), Benny de Weille (1941–3), and Primo Angeli and Willy Stech (both 1942–3). His most significant recordings were made as a leader in 1941 with personnel from the bands of Ernst van 't Hoff and Jean Omer, and include his own arrangement *Lieselott* (Pallas 1205). Tevelian moved to Vienna in 1943 and later left music to work for an oil company. (K. Schulz: "Sehen Sie, ich lebe weiter: die Meg Tevelian-Story," *Der Jazzfreund: Mitteilungsblatt für Jazzfreunde in Ost und West*, xii/4 (1970), 4)

RAINER E. LOTZ

Tharpe, Sister Rosetta [Nubin, Rosetta] (*b* Cotton Plant, AR, 20 March 1915; *d* Philadelphia, 9 Oct 1973). Singer and guitarist. She was brought up in Chicago, where she was influenced by her mother's singing of spirituals and was attracted to blues guitar techniques and to the ecstatic religion of the Sanctified Church. She gained a reputation as a singer-evangelist in Chicago and then moved to New York, where she became known for her compositions and her electrifying performances. In 1938 she appeared in the "From Spirituals to Swing" concert at Carnegie Hall and sang with Cab Calloway; she also performed at the Cotton Club, at Café Society downtown, and with Benny Goodman. Her first recording was a lively and rhythmical version of *Hide me in thy bosom* with the secularized title *Rock me*, which she performed both in theaters and churches, altering the lyrics to suit the location. Later she sang in Lucky Millinder's big band, making a number of recordings. She had a hit with *Strange things happening every day*, recorded with Sammy Price's trio, and she recorded several outstanding vocal duets with her mother, Katie Bell Nubin (1880–1969), and with Sister Marie Knight, playing guitar in a vivid style recalling that of Big Bill Broonzy. On later, religious, recordings, she used choirs and accompanying groups that tended to cloud the bright sound of her voice and the brilliance of her guitar playing, which she offset by using an electric instrument. She made two European tours, performing in Great Britain with Chris Barber's Jazz Band.

SELECTED RECORDINGS

As leader: Rock me (1938, Decca 2243); Strange things happening every day (1944, Decca 18669)

As sideman with L. Millinder: Rock Daniel (1941, Decca 3956); I want a tall skinny papa (1942, Decca 18386)

BIBLIOGRAPHY

T. Heilbut: *The Gospel Sound: Good News and Bad Times* (New York, 1971, rev. 2/1985)

C. Hayes: *A Discography of Gospel Records, 1937–1971* (n.p. [Copenhagen], 1973) [covers 14 musicians and groups]

H. Panassié: "Rosetta Tharpe," *BHcF*, no.232 (1973), 3

Obituary, *Black Perspective in Music*, ii (1974), 227

PAUL OLIVER

Theater Owners' Booking Association [TOBA]. An organization formed by Sherman Dudley in 1920 in order to manage vaudeville bookings for black performers efficiently. Originally there were 32 theaters belonging to the TOBA circuit around which the artists traveled, but eventually the association extended to more than 80 houses in most of the major cities and several smaller towns in the South, Southwest, and Midwest. The acts booked into the theaters were primarily abbreviated versions of musical comedies (tabloid shows); solo singers, comedy teams, song-and-dance duos, and specialty acts (jugglers, acrobats, etc.) also appeared. Although notorious for its demanding schedules and low pay, the organization enabled many Blacks to appear before black audiences and created steady employment for such performers as Ma Rainey, Bessie Smith, and Ethel Waters. A number of early jazz musicians, including Bennie Moten and Count Basie, also started their careers on the circuit. By 1932, however, the Depression, competition from the film industry, and personal conflicts among theater owners led to the demise of the organization, and nearly all its houses were converted to motion picture theaters.

BIBLIOGRAPHY

L. Hughes and M. Meltzer: *Black Magic: a Pictorial History of the Negro in American Entertainment* (Englewood Cliffs, NJ, 1967), 66

M. Stearns and J. Stearns: *Jazz Dance: the Story of American Vernacular Dance* (New York, 1968)

H. T. Sampson: *Blacks in Blackface: a Source Book on Early Black Musical Shows* (Metuchen, NJ, 1980)

T. Riis: *Black Musical Theatre in New York, 1890–1915* (diss., U. of Michigan, 1981)

THOMAS RIIS

Thelin, Eje (Eilert) (*b* Jönköping, Sweden, 9 June 1938). Swedish trombonist. He worked with dixieland groups while in his early teens, played bop in Sweden with the drummer Joe Harris (1958–9) and Putte Wickman (1959–60), and from 1961 to 1965 led a quintet that won acclaim in Europe. He played with George Russell and led a quartet with Barney Wilen in the mid-1960s, then joined the faculty of the Musikakademie in Graz, Austria (1967); at the same time he performed and recorded with many European free-jazz musicians, notably Joachim Kühn, with whom he led groups. In 1970 he was named "new star" on the trombone by *Down Beat*. After returning to Sweden in 1972 he continued to work as a leader. In 1973–4 he played with John Surman. In his early career Thelin developed a fluent style that owed something to the work of J. J. Johnson. He turned to free jazz in the mid-1960s, and later became known for his ensemble leadership; his playing shows a sensitive contrasting of melodies of different shapes, rhythmic statements, and lush textures.

SELECTED RECORDINGS

So Far (1963, Col. SSX1005); *At the German Jazz Festival* (1964, Met. 15158); *Acoustic Space* (1970, Odeon E062-34180); *Eje Thelin Group* (1974, Caprice 1091); *Live -76* (1976, Caprice 2007); *Bits & Pieces* (1980, Phono Suecia 9)

BIBLIOGRAPHY

B. Sundin: "Unga jazzmusiker: Eje Thelin" [Young jazz musician: Eje Thelin], *Orkester journalen*, xxviii/11 (1960), 14

L. Hansson: "Eje Thelin diskografi," *Orkester journalen*, xxxv/12 (1967), 48

L. Westin: "Eje Thelin," *Orkester journalen*, xli/1 (1973), 9 [incl. discography]

——: "Trials and Tribulations of a Swedish Trombonist," *DB*, xliii/16 (1976), 18

——: "Vill ha debatt och solidaritet: Eje Thelin" [Wants to have debate and solidarity: Eje Thelin], *Orkester journalen*, xliv/3 (1976), 10

ERIK KJELLBERG

Theme. In jazz a harmonized melody, often 16 or 32 bars long, or in some cases (notably the blues progression) simply a series of harmonies, used as the basis for a piece or section of a piece; *see* FORMS.

Themen, Art(hur Edward George) (*b* Manchester, England, 26 Nov 1939). English tenor saxophonist. He was a self-taught musician. While studying medicine at Cambridge he played with the university's jazz group (1959–62). After moving to London he worked with the blues musicians Jack Bruce (from 1962) and Alexis Korner (1963). In 1965 he was a member of the international Peter Stuyvesant Jazz Orchestra at the jazz festival in Zurich. Thereafter he performed with the rock singers Rod Stewart and Joe Cocker, the drummer Charlie Watts (1965–7), Graham Collier, and Michael Garrick (*c*1968–1971). In 1974 Themen began an association with Stan Tracey, working as a member of various of his groups, ranging from duo to octet; his playing may be heard to advantage on *Stan Tracey's Hexad Live at Ronnie Scott's* (1985, Steam 113). He toured extensively with Tracey, visiting India, South America, and Indonesia, as well as performing throughout the UK. Themen has also toured and recorded with American musicians, including Al Haig and Sal Nistico (ii), and has performed with Nat Adderley, George Coleman, and Billy Mitchell.

BIBLIOGRAPHY

R. Cotterrell, ed.: *Jazz Now: the Jazz Centre Society Guide* (London, 1976)

D. Gelly: "The Best of British, no.1: Art Themen," *JJI*, xxxi/1–2 (1978), 6

DIGBY FAIRWEATHER

Theresa. Record company and label. The company was founded by Allen Pittman in El Cerrito, California, in 1980. By the middle of the decade it had established an important catalogue, including, most notably, material by Pharoah Sanders, John Hicks, and George Coleman.

Theselius, Gösta (*b* Stockholm, 9 June 1922; *d* Stockholm, 24 Jan 1976). Swedish tenor saxophonist, pianist, composer, and arranger. He first worked as a tenor saxophonist in recordings with Thore Jederby (1940, 1941) and thereafter played with big bands led by Håkan von Eichwald (1940–41), Sam Samson (1941–3), Lulle Ellboj (1943–6), and Thore Ehrling (recording in 1944, 1951, and 1953), gaining a reputation as a fine soloist in the style of Chu Berry. Theselius was also well known as a fluent and versatile arranger; his arrangements and compositions represent some of the best-integrated Swedish jazz writing of the 1940s and 1950s, and show the influence of Duke Ellington, Pete Rugolo, Claude Thornhill, and Lennie Tristano. As a pianist he played and recorded with such musicians as James Moody (1949), Arne Domnérus (1949–50), Charlie Parker (1950), and Benny Bailey (1959).

RECORDED COMPOSITIONS
(selective list)

As leader: Siesta (1949, Met. J101); Three Without a Key (1951, RCA S52) [EP]

Recorded by others: S. Samson: Express (1942, Bruns. A83007); L. Ellboj: Hot Gravy (1945, Col. DS1600); Jazzkritikerorkestern: *Cream of the Crop* (1951, Cupol 9007); H. Arnold: *This is Harry Arnold and the Mystery Band* (1957, Met. MLP15006), incl. Six-ten

BIBLIOGRAPHY

"Svenskt stjärnalbum," *Orkester journalen*, x/1 (1942), 5
"Våra arrangörer" [Our arrangers], *Estrad*, iv/2 (1942), 7
"Årets musiker" [Musician of the year], *Estrad*, xiv/1 (1952), 5
"På omslaget" [On the cover], *Orkester journalen*, xxi/5 (1953), 4
R. Dahlgren: "Gösta Theselius in memoriam," *Orkester journalen*, xliv/3 (1976), 6
E. Kjellberg: *Svensk jazzhistoria: en översikt* [Swedish jazz history: an overview] (Stockholm, 1985)

ERIK KJELLBERG

Thielemans, Toots [Jean Baptiste] (*b* Brussels, 29 April 1922). Belgian harmonica player, guitarist, and whistler. He played the accordion at the age of three, and took up chromatic harmonica when he was 17. In the early 1940s, under the influence of Django Reinhardt, he taught himself to play guitar. He toured Europe in 1950 with an all-star group under the leadership of Benny Goodman, and the following year emigrated to the USA. From 1953 to 1959 he was a member of George Shearing's quintet. He then worked as a freelance, traveling between the USA and Sweden; he first recorded his best-known composition, *Bluesette*, on which he played the guitar and whistled, in Stockholm in 1961. From the 1960s Thielemans obtained regular work as an instrumentalist and whistler in American recording studios, and he was often featured as a soloist with Quincy Jones's orchestra. From the early 1970s he made annual trips to Brussels and began to appear more frequently in public as a leader of swing and bop quartets. He also recorded at the Montreux International Jazz Festival as a sideman with Oscar Peterson (1975) and Dizzy Gillespie (1980), as well as with Paquito D'Rivera (1984). Thielemans's whistling is excessively sweet and cute. His guitar playing, although completely professional, is not exceptional. But his harmonica playing is rivaled only by that of Larry Adler and Stevie Wonder in popular genres, and is unrivaled in jazz. His lush timbre is revealed in such pretty songs as *Brown Ballad*, and he improvises on the harmonica with the dexterity expected of an accomplished bop saxophonist.

SELECTED RECORDINGS

As leader: *Man Bites Harmonica* (1957, Riv. 257); *Time Out* (1958, Decca 9204); *Toots Thielemans* (1961–2, ABC-Para. 482), incl. Bluesette; *Toots Thielemans Captured Alive* (1974, Choice 1007); *Live in the Netherlands* (1980, PL 2308233)

As sideman: G. Shearing: Body and Soul (1953, MGM 11493); *On Stage!* (1958, Cap. T1187); on Q. Jones: *Smackwater Jack* (1971, A&M 3037), Brown Ballad; O. Peterson: *The Oscar Peterson Big Six at Montreux* (1975, Pablo 2310747); D. Gillespie: *Dizzy Gillespie at Montreux, 1980* (1980, PL 2308226)

BIBLIOGRAPHY

D. Morgenstern: "Triple Threat Toots Thielemans," *DB*, xxxviii/20 (1971), 11
R. Cotterrell: "Toots Thielemans: a Traveling Man," *JF* [intl edn], no.55 (1978), 33
B. Primack: "Toots Thielemans: Miracle Harmonica Man," *DB*, xlv/14 (1978), 25
L. Tomkins: "Toots Thielemans," *CI*, xvi (1978), no.8, p.20; no.9, p.8
A. Berle: "Toots Thielemans," *GP*, xiii/1 (1979), 34
D. Francfort and G. Rouy: "Tout tout Toots sur Thielemans," *Jm*, no.309 (1982), 54

BARRY KERNFELD

Thigpen, Ben(jamin F.) (*b* Laurel, MS, 16 Nov 1908; *d* St. Louis, 5 Oct 1971). Drummer, father of Ed Thigpen. At the age of 15 he joined Bobby Boswell's band in South Bend, Indiana. He accompanied a dance team, then settled in Chicago and studied with Jimmy Bertrand. He played throughout the Midwest with Albert Wynn, Doc Cheatham, Charlie Elgar, Eli Rice, and J. Frank Terry. For 17 years from 1930 he played with Andy Kirk's Clouds of Joy (for illustration *see* WILLIAMS, MARY LOU), during which time he earned the respect of his colleagues for his steady, swinging beat; occasionally he sang with the band. After leaving the Clouds of Joy in 1947 he settled in St. Louis, where he led groups and performed with the Singleton Palmer Orchestra through the 1960s.

SELECTED RECORDINGS
(all recorded for Decca)

As sideman with A. Kirk: Walkin' and Swingin' (1936, 809); Lotta Sax Appeal/ Bearcat Shuffle (1936, 1046); Git (1936, 931); Jump Jack Jump/Ghost of Love (1938, 2226); Honey/Mary's Idea (1938, 2326)

As sideman with M. L. Williams: Corny Rhythm/Isabelle (1936, 1021); Baby Dear/Harmony Blues (1940, 18122)

BIBLIOGRAPHY

ChiltonW
Obituary, *DB*, xxxviii/20 (1971), 9

J. KENT WILLIAMS

Thigpen, Ed(mund Leonard) (*b* Chicago, 28 Dec 1930). Drummer and jazz educator, son of Ben Thigpen. He began his career during the 1950s with Cootie Williams, Dinah Washington, Johnny Hodges, Lennie Tristano, Bud Powell, Jutta Hipp, and Billy Taylor (ii). From 1959 to 1965 he worked with Ray Brown in a trio led by Oscar Peterson, who had earlier used a guitarist in place of a drummer; the group toured widely and made many recordings, and was highly acclaimed. He joined Ella Fitzgerald's backup group in 1966, moved to Los Angeles in the following year to work as a freelance, and worked again with Fitzgerald (1968–72). After moving in 1972 to Copenhagen he taught at the Malmö Conservatory in Sweden and performed with his group Action-re-action. Thigpen is respected for his energetic, swinging style, his sensitivity to timbre and dynamics, and his facility with sticks and brushes. He frequently uses his hands and timpani mallets on the drum set, and has explored diverse percussion instruments and styles, both Western and non-Western, in his performances. He is the author of *Talking Drums* (Toronto, 1965), *Rhythm Analysis and Basic Coordination* (Copenhagen, 1977), and *The Sound of Brushes* (Copenhagen, 1981), and has led workshops in Europe and North America.

SELECTED RECORDINGS

As leader: *Out of the Storm* (1966, Verve 68663); *Action-re-action* (1974, GNP 2098)

As sideman with O. Peterson: *Fiorello!* (1959, Verve 8366); *The Trio: Live from Chicago* (1961, Verve 68420); *West Side Story* (1962, Verve 68454)
As sideman with others: D. Ashby: *The Jazz Harpist* (1956, Reg. 6039); J. Coltrane and P. Quinichette: *Cattin'* (1957, Prst. 7158); J. Griffin: *Blues for Harvey* (1973, Ste. 1004); A. Farmer: *Manhattan* (1981, SN 1026); K. Parker: *Havin' myself a Time* (1981, SN 1033)

BIBLIOGRAPHY

D. DeMicheal: "Edmund Thigpen: Gentleman and Jazzman," *DB*, xxviii/18 (1961), 17
L. Tomkins: "The Ed Thigpen Story," *Crescendo*, iv/1 (1965), 14
H. McNamara: "Ed Thigpen: on the Move," *DB*, xxxiv/6 (1967), 18
L. Tomkins: "There's Action, Reaction, and Interaction in Europe Says Ed Thigpen," *CI*, xiv/5 (1975), 6
M. Hurley: "Ed Thigpen: Intercontinental Swinger," *MD*, vi/7 (1982), 16
E. Soph: "Drum Set Forum: Ed Thigpen," *Percussive Notes*, xxiii/2 (1985), 22

J. KENT WILLIAMS

Thilo, Jesper (*b* Copenhagen, 28 Nov 1941). Danish alto and tenor saxophonist and clarinetist. He studied clarinet, worked with mainstream bands from 1960, and belonged to the Radioens Big Band from 1966; he also played mainstream jazz as a leader and as a sideman. Thilo is a versatile soloist who has been influenced by musicians ranging from Ben Webster to Charlie Parker and Dexter Gordon. His style is well represented by the album *Jesper Thilo Quintet Featuring Harry Edison* (1986, Sto. 4120), which includes the track *What's New*.

ERIK WIEDEMANN

Third stream. A term coined by Gunther Schuller, in a lecture at Brandeis University in 1957, for a type of music which, through improvisation or written composition or both, synthesizes the essential characteristics and techniques of contemporary Western art music and various ethnic or vernacular musics. At the heart of this concept is the notion that any music stands to profit from a confrontation with another; thus composers of Western art music can learn a great deal from the rhythmic vitality and swing of jazz, while jazz musicians can find new avenues of development in the large-scale forms and complex tonal systems of classical music.

The term was originally applied to a style in which attempts were made to fuse basic elements of jazz and Western art music – the two mainstreams joining to form a "third stream." This style had been in existence for some years, and is exemplified by such pieces as Red Norvo's *Dance of the Octopus* (1933, Bruns. 6906), Ralph Burns's *Summer Sequence* (recorded by Woody Herman's band, 1946, Col. 38365-7), George Handy's *The Bloos* (1946, Jazz Scene [unnumbered]), Robert Graetinger's *City of Glass* (recorded by Stan Kenton's orchestra, 1951, Cap. 28062-3), Alec Wilder's *Jazz Suite* (1951, Col. 39727), and Rolf Liebermann's *Concerto for Jazz Band and Orchestra* (recorded by the Sauter–Finegan Orchestra, ?1956, Vic. LPM1888). Since the late 1950s the application of the term has broadened, notably through the work of Ran Blake, to encompass fusions of classical music with elements drawn not only from Afro-American sources but also from other ethnic musics, such as Greek folk and popular music, and Sephardic, Armenian, Japanese, and Hindu traditional music.

The third-stream movement attracted much controversy and has often erroneously been allied with the SYMPHONIC JAZZ movement of the 1920s; symphonic jazz, however, lacked the essential element of improvisation. Other critics have seen the movement as an inevitable outcome of postwar eclecticism and stylistic and technical synthesis. Third stream, like all musical syntheses, courts the danger of exploiting a superficial overlay of stylistic exotica on an established musical idiom, but genuine cross-fertilization has occurred in the work of musicians deeply rooted in dual traditions.

Composers and performers associated with the third-stream movement include J. J. Johnson (*Poem for Brass*, 1956, Col. CL941); André Hodeir (*On a Blues*, on the album *American Jazzmen Play André Hodeir's Essais*, 1957, Savoy 12104); Milton Babbitt (*All Set*, on the Brandeis Jazz Festival album *Modern Jazz Concert*, 1957, Col. WL127); Bill Russo (*An Image of Man*, on the album *An Image: Lee Konitz with Strings*, 1958, Verve 8286); Gunther Schuller (*Concertino for Jazz Quartet and Orchestra*, on the Modern Jazz Quartet's album *Modern Jazz Quartet and Orchestra*, 1960, Atl. 1359); Don Ellis (*Improvisational Suite no.1*, on the album *How Time Passes*, 1960, Can. 9004); Bill Smith (*Concerto for Jazz Soloist and Orchestra*, 1962, CRI 320); Jimmy Giuffre (*Three We*, on the album *Free Fall*, 1962, Col. CS8764); Larry Austin (*Improvisations for Orchestra and Jazz Soloists*, 1967, Col. MS6733); Mike Mantler (*13*, on the album *13-3/4* (recorded with Carla Bley), 1975, Watt 3); Ran Blake (*Jim Crow*, *Silver Fox*, both on the album *Wende*, 1976, Owl 05; *Portfolio of Dr. Mabuse*, 1977, Owl 29); Anthony Braxton (*Composition 82*, on the album *For Four Orchestras*, 1978, Ari. 8900); Leo Smith (*The Burning of Stones*, on the album *Spirit Catcher*, 1979, Nessa 19); and Steve Lacy (*Worms*, on the Globe Unity Orchestra's album *Compositions*, 1979, Japo 60027). A large number of third-stream works have been published by Margun Music; others have been issued by such publishers as MJQ Music, C. F. Peters, and Cireco Music.

See also FORMS, §4.

BIBLIOGRAPHY

G. Schuller: "Jazz and Classical Music," *FeatherE*
——: "'Third Stream' Redefined," *Saturday Review*, xliv (13 May 1961), 54
——: "The Future of Form in Jazz," *The American Composer Speaks: a Historical Anthology, 1770–1965*, ed. G. Chase (n.p. [Baton Rouge, LA], 1966), 216
G. Crane: *Jazz Elements and Formal Compositional Techniques in Third Stream Music* (thesis, Indiana U., 1970)
C. J. Stuessy, Jr.: *The Confluence of Jazz and Classical Music from 1950 to 1970* (diss., Eastman School, 1970)
M. Harrison: *A Jazz Retrospect* (Newton Abbot, England, 1976, rev. 2/1977)
R. Blake: "Teaching Third Stream," *Music Educators Journal*, lxiii/4 (1976), 30
L. Lyons: "Ran Blake: Pianist and Teacher from the Third Stream," *CK*, iv/10 (1978), 16
A. Lange: "Ran Blake's Third Stream Visions," *DB*, xlvii/2 (1980), 24
E. Santosuosso: "Third Stream: a Label for an 'Anti-label' Music," *Boston Globe* (19 July 1980), §A, p.9
G. Schuller: "The Avant-garde and Third Stream," *Mirage* (New World 216, 1985) [liner notes]
M. Williams: "Third Stream Problems," *Jazz Heritage* (New York, and Oxford, England, 1985) [colln of previously pubd reviews]
G. Schuller: "Third Stream Revisited," *Musings: the Musical Worlds of Gunther Schuller* (New York, and Oxford, England, 1986)

GUNTHER SCHULLER

Thomas, Fathead [George] (*b* Charleston, WV, *c*1903; *d* New Haven, CT, Nov 1930). Singer. From 1925 until his death he was the featured singer with McKinney's Cotton Pickers (for illustration *see* MCKINNEY'S COTTON PICKERS), and his remarkable tenor voice may be heard to advantage on *Baby won't you please come home?* (1930, Vic. 22511). In addition, he played saxophone with this group, but was not prominent as a soloist. Thomas also recorded with Duke Ellington (1926). He was killed in an automobile accident. (J. Chilton: *McKinney's Music: a Bio-discography of McKinney's Cotton Pickers*, London, 1978)

based on *ChiltonW*

Thomas, Foots [Walter Purl] (*b* Muskogee, OK, 10 Feb 1907; *d* Englewood, NJ, 26 Aug 1981). Reed player and arranger, brother of Joe Thomas (ii). He grew up in Topeka, Kansas, and began his career as a musician while attending college. After moving to New York in 1927 he worked with Jelly Roll Morton, Luis Russell, and the pianist Joe Steele, and in 1929 joined the Missourians; he remained a member of this band after Cab Calloway assumed its leadership (for illustration *see* CALLOWAY, CAB), and he contributed many arrangements to its repertory, including *Minnie the Moocher*, recorded in 1931 (Bruns. 6074). He left the band in 1943, played for a brief period with Don Redman, and in 1944 worked as a leader. In 1948 he ceased playing to pursue a successful career as an agent, manager, and music publisher. Thomas played alto, tenor, and baritone saxophones, clarinet, and flute; he may be heard as a soloist on early recordings by the Missourians and Calloway, but in his later years he worked chiefly as a section player and arranger.

Oral history material in *NjR* (JOHP).

SELECTED RECORDINGS

As leader: Every Man for himself (1944, Joe Davis 8128); Bird Brain (1945), first issued on *The Walter "Foots" Thomas All Stars* (1944–5, Prst. 7584)

As sideman: J. R. Morton: Crazy Chords (1930, Vic. 23307); C. Calloway: Bugle Call Rag (1931, Bruns. 6196)

BIBLIOGRAPHY

ChiltonW; *FeatherE*

L. D. Holmes and J. W. Thomson: *Jazz Greats: Getting Better with Age* (New York, 1986) [colln of interviews]

EDDIE LAMBERT

Thomas, Joe [Brother Cornbread] **(i)** (*b* New Orleans, 3 Dec 1902; *d* New Orleans, 18 Feb 1981). Clarinetist. In 1923, having bought an Albert system clarinet for $5.00, he began his career playing with the trombonist Joe Harris. Later he worked with the trombonist Jack Carey, Kid Rena, and Chris Kelly. From the early 1940s he led a band at the H & J Tavern for several years. He joined Papa Celestin's band in 1951, and continued to play with the group under the leadership both of the trombonist Eddie Pierson and the banjoist Albert French; his work may be heard on the album *A Night at Dixieland Hall* (1963, Nobility 702). In 1975 he took Joe Darensbourg's place in the Legends of Jazz, with which he toured until 1978. Thomas was well known for his singing and his sense of humor.

Oral history material in *LNT*.

BIBLIOGRAPHY

M. MacMurray: "Joseph 'Brother Cornbread' Thomas," *SL*, xxxi (spr. 1979), 16

M. Tovey: "Brother Cornbread Thomas," *Fn*, xii/6 (1981), 28

BILL RUSSELL

Thomas, Joe [Joseph, Jr.] **(ii)** (*b* Muskogee, OK, 23 Dec 1908). Tenor and alto saxophonist, brother of Foots Thomas. After performing with the Virginia Ravens (1927) he toured Pennsylvania and Ohio with Jelly Roll Morton's band, with which he recorded in New York (1929–30). From 1930 he played with Cozy Cole (1930), Blanche Calloway, the bandleader Vernon Andrade (1934), and the pianist Dave Martin (early 1940s). He ceased full-time performing in 1949 and worked as a vocal coach and in the artists and repertory departments of Decca (1949–50) and Victor (1950–51). No discography adequately distinguishes him from Joe Thomas (iii). Besides the sessions with Morton (on which he and Foots Thomas may not always be securely identified) the only recordings on which he is reasonably certain to have played are those of 1951 with Big John Greer (for Victor) and Howard Biggs's orchestra led by Titus Turner (for Okeh); he may have been the player on recordings with Barney Bigard (1945) and Billie Holiday (1947, 1949), but since he rarely performed after 1950 he is unlikely to be the Joe Thomas who took part in many sessions from 1956 into the 1970s.

BIBLIOGRAPHY

FeatherE

L. Wright: *Mr Jelly Lord* (Chigwell, England, 1980), 62

Thomas, Joe [Joseph Vankert] **(iii)** (*b* Uniontown, PA, 19 June 1909; *d* Kansas City, 3 Aug 1986). Tenor saxophonist. He began playing on alto saxophone with Earl Hood and Horace Henderson (1930–31), then changed to tenor saxophone and worked with Stuff Smith (1932) and the drummer Guy Jackson (1933). From 1933 to 1947 he was with Jimmie Lunceford, and his ebullient personality as both singer and saxophone soloist played a major role in establishing the band's success (for illustration *see* LUNCEFORD, JIMMIE). After Lunceford's death Thomas became leader of the band with Eddie Wilcox, but left to form his own group, which he led until the early 1950s. He then joined his family's undertaking firm, but continued to play occasionally; he appeared at the Newport Jazz Festival in 1970 and recorded as the leader of a quartet with Jimmie Rowles in 1979. Thomas was inspired by Coleman Hawkins and Chu Berry, and when playing solos tended to remain close to the melody and concentrate on the tune's rhythmical aspects. His huge and occasionally grainy tone influenced an entire generation of saxophonists in the 1940s.

SELECTED RECORDINGS

As leader: Don't blame me (1945, Melodisc 113); *Raw Meat* (1979, Upt. 2701)

As sideman with J. Lunceford: Black and Tan Fantasy (1934, Decca 453); Posin' (1937, Decca 1355); Le jazz hot (1939, Voc./OK 4595); Baby won't you please come home? (1939, Voc./OK 4667); I'm alone with you (1939, Col. 35484); *Jimmy Lunceford* (1940, Alamac QSR2422), incl. Stardust; *Jimmie Lunceford and his Orchestra 1940* (1940, Cir. [USA] 11), incl. Annie Laurie; What's your story, morning glory? (1940, Col. 35510); Moonbeams (1948, Manor 1111)

BIBLIOGRAPHY

ChiltonW; *FeatherE*

"Le saxo ténor Joe Thomas," *BHcF*, no.76 (1958), 3

B. Niquet: "Les Joe Thomas," *Pj*, no.8 (1973), 76 [incl. discography]

FRANK DRIGGS

Thomas, Joe [Joseph Lewis] **(iv)** (*b* Webster Groves, MO, 24 July 1909; *d* New York, 6 Aug 1984). Trumpeter. He first played in the lesser-known bands of Cecil Scott (1928), the pianist Darrel Harris (1929), the saxophonist Eli Rice (1930–32), Shuffle Abernathy (1932–3), the drummer Harold Flood (1933), Ira Coffey (1933–4), and Ferman Tapp (1934). He then joined Charlie Turner's Arcadians (1934) before working with Fletcher Henderson (1934, 1935–6), Baron Lee (1934–5), Willie Bryant (1937), Claude Hopkins (1938–9), and Benny Carter (1939–40). After briefly leading his own band he played with James P. Johnson, Joe Sullivan (1940–41), Teddy Wilson (1942–3), and Barney Bigard (1944–5). From the late 1940s he worked extensively as a freelance, notably with Cozy Cole (1948), Bud Freeman (1949), and Hopkins (1966), though he occasionally led his own groups. Ill-health curtailed his activities during the 1970s. Thomas was a great admirer of Louis Armstrong. He was noted for his superb, big tone and his understated style of playing staccato, which was heard to best advantage at slow and medium tempos.

Oral history material in *NjR* (JOHP).

SELECTED RECORDINGS

As leader: Black Butterfly (1946, Key. 642)

As sideman: Lil Armstrong: Bluer than Blue (1937, Decca 1299); on [no leader]: *Jazz Odyssey*, iii: *The Sounds of Harlem* (1920s–1940s, Col. C3L33), B. Carter: When lights are low; C. Cole: Thru' for the Night (1944, Key. 1301); R. Norvo: Russian Lullaby (1944, Key. 1310)

BIBLIOGRAPHY

ChiltonW

A. J. McCarthy: "Joe Thomas," *JM*, ix/6 (1963), 12

J. Postgate: "The St. Louis Sound," *JM*, no.158 (1968), 2

B. Niquet: "Les Joe Thomas," *Pj*, no.8 (1973), 76 [incl. discography]

J. Evensmo: *The Trumpets of Dizzy Gillespie, 1937–1943, Irving Randolph, Joe Thomas* (n.p. [Oslo], n.d. [?1982]) [discography]

J. Simmen: "Joseph Lewis 'Joe' Thomas," *BHcF* (1985), no.324, p.21; no.325, p.16

FRANK DRIGGS

Thomas, Joe (v) (*b* Newark, NJ, 16 June 1933). Flutist and tenor saxophonist. He studied music before moving in 1949 to Canada, where he worked with the singer Dee Dee Ford. After returning to Newark he led a quintet with the drummer Bill Elliott that recorded in 1963. In the following years he made several recordings as a leader, on which his sidemen included Jimmy Ponder (1969, 1972) and Ernie Royal, Garnett Brown, and Seldon Powell (1972); he is heard to advantage on *Joy of Cookin'* (*c*1972, GM 504). He also recorded an album of compositions with a big band led by Chico O'Farrill (1971). (B. Niquet: "Les Joe Thomas," *Pj*, no.8 (1973), 76 [incl. discography])

Thomas, John (L.) (*b* Louisville, KY, 18 Sept 1902; *d* Chicago, 7 Nov 1971). Trombonist. He was brought up in Chicago, where his first professional work was with the orchestra led by the saxophonist Clarence Miller (1923). Later he played with Erskine Tate (1927–8), Dave Peyton, Fess Williams, and Jerome Pasquall (all 1928), and toured with Freddie Keppard. While in California he worked with Speed Webb and others; he then returned to Chicago (*c*1930), where he performed with Tate, Cassino Simpson (1931), and Reuben Reeves (1933). After playing briefly with McKinney's Cotton Pickers in Detroit and Buffalo (late 1934) he worked with Zack Whyte. In spring 1937 Thomas toured with Nat "King" Cole's band in the revue *Shuffle Along*. He performed again with Tate (*c*1940) and spent a short period with the guitarist Walter Dysett (1944), then abandoned performing for ten years. In late 1960 he joined Franz Jackson's band the Original Jass All-Stars with which he performed regularly until summer 1965. References to Thomas's presence at recording sessions early in his career are open to doubt, but it is generally accepted that he is the trombonist on Louis Armstrong's *Melancholy Blues* (1927, OK 8496); his playing may be heard to advantage on Jackson's album *Franz Jackson and the Original Jass All-Stars* (1961, Riv. 9406). (B. Demeusey: "The Musical Career of John Thomas," *JJ*, xx/1 (1967), 23)

based on *ChiltonW*

Thomas, Kid [Valentine, Kid Thomas; Valentine, Thomas] (*b* Reserve, LA, 3 Feb 1896; *d* New Orleans, 16 June 1987). Trumpeter and bandleader. He began playing at the age of ten. When he was 14 he joined the Pickwick Brass Band, of which his father was a member, and four years later formed a band with Edmond Hall and other members of Hall's family. In 1922 he moved to New Orleans, where from the early 1930s he led his own band. He became associated with the dance-hall proprietor Specks Rodriguez in the late 1930s, playing for him at various venues in Louisiana – notably at the Moulin Rouge in Marrero (from World War II into the 1950s). Thomas made his first recordings in 1951. He began working at Preservation Hall when it opened in 1961 and in the mid-1980s continued to lead his band the Algiers Stompers, sometimes under the name of the PRESERVATION HALL JAZZ BAND; he also toured overseas with the group on numerous occasions.

Thomas developed an individual style that was allusive, elliptical, impressionistic, and, above all, rhythmic. A superb lead trumpeter, he would state the melody sparsely but in a forthright manner, before exploding into a progression of little rhythmic clusters of white-hot notes, jabbing through the ensemble with his wide vibrato and searing tone. His use of various mutes was a strong characteristic of his playing; on *Panama*, for example, he generally employed a plunger mute in a performance that was both electrifying and highly comical, then changed to a metal derby to build to the climax of the piece. Occasionally, on slower numbers such as *Just a closer walk with thee*, he could be heard taking a solo; using a harmon mute he played softly and with great poignancy.

Oral history material in *LNT*.

SELECTED RECORDINGS

As leader: *Kid Thomas' Algiers Stompers* (1951, AM 642); *Kid Thomas at Moulin Rouge* (1956, Center 14); *Kid Thomas Valentine's Creole Jazz Band* (1959, 77 LA9), incl. Panama; *Kid Thomas at Kohlman's Tavern* (1968, La Croix 4–5); on *Original Jass Band and Kid Thomas' Jazz Band in Scandinavia* (1964, 1971, Rarities 16), Just a closer walk with thee (1971); *Kid Thomas 1981* (1981, Lulu White's Black Label 033)

As sideman with J. Robinson: *Jim Robinson and his New Orleans Band* (1964, Center 8)

BIBLIOGRAPHY

H. Souchon: "Speck's Moulin Rouge," *SL*, vii/2 (1956), 7

T. Bethell: "Kid Thomas: his Recordings," *Jazz Times*, iv (1967), no.6, p.7; no.7, p.9; no.8, p.27; no.9, p.9

R. B. Allen: Liner notes, *Thomas Valentine at Kohlman's Tavern* (New Orleans 7201, 1972)

C. De Vore: "The True New Orleans Sound of Kid Thomas Valentine," *MR*, i/4 (1974), 1

D. M. Marquis: "The King of Old-time Jazz," *Passages: the Magazine of Northwest Orient Airlines*, ix/2 (1978), 10

B. Martyn: "The People Pleaser from Algiers," *Fn*, xi/1 (1979), 14

M. Tovey: "Kid Thomas Valentine: his Musical Background and Early Years," *Fn*, xi/1 (1979), 4

Almost Slim [J. Hannusch]: "Kid Thomas," *Wavelength*, i/6 (1981), 12

B. Martyn: "Rattle of a Simple Man," *Fn*, xviii/6 (1987), 21

P. Van Vorst: "A New Orleans Original: Kid Thomas Valentine (1896–1987)," *MR*, xiv/10 (1987), 1 [incl. discography]

MICHAEL TOVEY

Thomas, Leone [Thomas, (Amos) Leon(, Jr.)] (*b* East St. Louis, IL, 4 Oct 1937). Singer. While studying music at Tennessee State University he played in a local group with Hank Crawford. After moving in 1958 to New York he performed at the Apollo Theatre, where he took part in a show that later toured the black theater circuit. He worked with Count Basie (briefly in 1961 and again in 1964–5), Mary Lou Williams, Randy Weston, Joe Newman, Roland Kirk, Benny Powell, Oliver Nelson, and Tony Scott; while performing and recording in the late 1960s with Pharoah Sanders he gained considerable attention for his virtuosity. Later he performed and recorded as a leader, and as a sideman with Carlos Santana, Louis Armstrong (1970), and Freddie Hubbard (1979); he changed his forename from Leon to Leone in 1976. Thomas's work is characterized by a unique, glottal approach to scat singing and a style of yodeling that is strongly suggestive of African pygmy music.

SELECTED RECORDINGS
(all recorded for Flying Dutchman)

As leader: *Spirits Known and Unknown* (1969, 10115); *The Leon Thomas Album* (1970, 10132); *Blues and the Soulful Truth* (*c*1972, 10155); *Full Circle* (1973, 10167)

As sideman with P. Sanders: *Karma* (1969, Imp. 9181); on *Shukuru* (?1983, The. 121), Mas in Brooklyn, Sun Song

BIBLIOGRAPHY

Feather–Gitler '70s

N. Hentoff: "Spirits Known and Unknown," *Black Giants*, ed. P. Rivelli and R. Levin (New York and Cleveland, 1970/*R*1980 as *Giants of Black Music*)

J. H. Klee: "Leon Thomas: Avant-garde with Roots," *DB*, xxxvii/25 (1970), 18

D. Stewart-Baxter: "Blues & Views," *JJ*, xxiii/12 (1970), 25; xxiv/1 (1971), 29
A. Taylor: *Notes and Tones: Musician-to-Musician Interviews* (Liège, Belgium, 1977/*R*1982)

LEE JESKE/R

Thomas, Millard G. (*b* USA, ?1880s; *d* after 1930). Pianist, composer, and bandleader. He lived in Montreal, where from at least 1920 to 1927 he led the Chicago Novelty Orchestra, a five-piece black jazz band; the principal instruments were winds and piano, though several of the members played more than one instrument. The band performed in theaters, hotels, and dance halls and, in 1923, on radio station CKAC in Montreal. Thomas recorded eight items with his band (1924), two as a soloist (1924), and four as accompanist to the clarinetist Theador West (1925). He also wrote the lyrics for a Broadway musical, *Brown Buddies*, and traveled to New York in 1930, where he recorded with a studio orchestra.

JACK LITCHFIELD

Thomas, René (*b* Liège, Belgium, 25 Feb 1927; *d* Santander, Spain, 3 Jan 1975). Belgian guitarist. He was essentially self-taught, but was early influenced by Django Reinhardt. He first worked as a freelance with various Belgian and French musicians, most notably Bobby Jaspar and Jacques Pelzer. In the mid-1950s he became one of Jimmy Raney's most ardent disciples in Europe, and his first important engagements were with visiting Americans in Paris, among them Chet Baker (1955). In 1958 he moved to Canada, then visited New York, where he played and recorded with Sonny Rollins and with Toshiko Akiyoshi. He returned to Paris in 1963 and played with Kenny Clarke at the Blue Note, then toured throughout Europe with Eddy Louiss and with Stan Getz (1969–72), with whom he also played in Mexico. Thomas's playing combined the precise approach of Raney with the adventurous spirit of Reinhardt to form an innovative style, and his influence among guitarists in Europe was widespread.

SELECTED RECORDINGS

As leader: *Guitar Groove* (1960, Jlnd 27); *Meeting Mr. Thomas* (1963, Barclay 84091); with K. Clarke and E. Louiss: *Eddy Louiss–Kenny Clarke–René Thomas* (?1974, RCA CY3004)
As sideman: S. Rollins: *Brass/Trio* (1958, Metro. 1002); S. Getz: *Dynasty* (1971, Verve 68802)

BIBLIOGRAPHY

FeatherE; *Feather–Gitler '70s*
J.-L. Ginibre: "L'homme aux lunettes d'écaille," *Jm*, no.86 (1962), 33

NORMAN MONGAN

Thomas, Walter. *See* THOMAS, FOOTS.

Thompkins, Eddie [Edward] (*b* Kansas City, MO, 1908; *d* Tennessee, 17 April 1943). Trumpeter and singer. He played with Terrence Holder, the bandleader Eli Rice, Jesse Stone, and the clarinetist Grant Moore before entering the University of Iowa in 1926. While a student he worked with George E. Lee and others. Thereafter he rejoined Moore, then played with Holder, Benny Moten, Tommy Douglas, and Rice (1931). Later he joined Jimmie Lunceford, with whom he performed and made recordings (including *Black & Tan Fantasy*, 1934, Decca 453), until 1939. He died in a shooting accident during military service.

based on *ChiltonW*

Thompson, Barbara (Gracey) (*b* Oxford, England, 27 July 1944). English saxophonist and flutist. She studied flute, clarinet, piano, and composition at the Royal College of Music in London for three years, and also learned saxophone privately. In 1964 she joined Neil Ardley's New Jazz Orchestra, and made recordings with it intermittently until 1978; while a member of this ensemble she met Jon Hiseman, whom she later married. During the same period she played with other jazz and rock musicians, including John Dankworth, Don Rendell, and Cleo Laine. Around 1972 she formed the jazz-rock group Paraphernalia, which established an identity about three years later when the keyboard player Colin Dudman joined it; her other sidemen have included Hiseman, Pete Lemer, and Roy Babbington. She has continued to tour and make recordings with the group (including *Barbara Thompson's Paraphernalia*, 1978, MCA 2852, and *Live in Concert*, 1980, MCA 309) into the mid-1980s. From 1973 to 1980 she also led a Latin-jazz nonet, Jubiaba. She has performed and recorded with the United Jazz and Rock Ensemble (from 1975), and composed for films and television.

BIBLIOGRAPHY

B. van Rooyen: "Barbara Thompson: Woman in Jazz," *JF* [intl edn], no.48 (1977), 39
M. Hennessey: "Barbara Thompson," *JJI*, xxxiii/3 (1980), 27

STAN BRITT

Thompson, Butch [Richard Enos] (*b* Marine, MN, 28 Nov 1943). Pianist and clarinetist. After playing with local bands he moved to Minneapolis and St. Paul, where he joined the Hall brothers' New Orleans Jazz Band in 1962; the group worked for more than 20 years at the Mendota Emporium, playing frequently with well-known guest artists such as George Lewis (i), Kid Thomas, Pops Foster, Manuel Manetta, Ray Burke, Art Hodes, and Eubie Blake. Thompson also led his own trio, which in 1974 began a 12-year engagement with Garrison Keillor's radio show "A Prairie Home Companion"; this became the USA's most popular radio program, and Thompson was heard (on both piano and clarinet) by millions of listeners each week. He toured extensively both as a soloist and with the trio, appearing in Europe, the Far East, and South America as well as in the USA, and also toured with the Black Eagle Jazz Band of Boston (recording in 1975–6) and the New Orleans Ragtime Orchestra (1977). In the 1980s he frequently led his King Oliver Centennial Band in Europe, notably at the Festa New Orleans Music, Ascona.

SELECTED RECORDINGS

As unaccompanied soloist [pf]: *A'Solas* (1981, Stomp Off 1037), incl. Creepy Feeling
As sideman with K. Thomas [cl]: *Kid Thomas at San Jacinto Hall* (1965, San Jacinto 4), incl. Merry Christmas Blues

BIBLIOGRAPHY

"Talking Ragtime," *Fn*, xvi/4 (1985), 15 [interview]

BILL RUSSELL

Thompson, Chuck [Charles Edmund] (*b* New York, 4 June 1926). Drummer. In Los Angeles he played with the trumpeter Charlie Echols (1943) and in New York briefly played and recorded with Charlie Parker's bop quintet (1946), the other members of which included Joe Albany and Miles Davis. In 1947 he worked with Howard McGhee and Benny Carter, recorded with Gerald Wilson, and performed and recorded with the quintet of Dexter Gordon and Wardell Gray; in 1949 he made recordings as a member of the Kenton All Stars (other members of which included Art Pepper and Hampton Hawes), in concert with Erroll Garner, and with Sonny Criss. After recording again with Gray (1950) and Gordon (1952, 1955) he was associated from 1955 to 1956 with Hawes; the two recorded in a trio with Red Mitchell (1955–6) and in 1955 as sidemen with Barney Kessel and Mitchell. Thompson recorded again with Criss in Los Angeles in 1956, worked in San Francisco as a freelance, and belonged to a quartet at the Cellar in the Cellar in San Francisco (1959). Good examples of his playing are Gordon's *Bikini* (1947, Dial 1022) and Mitchell's album *Jam for your Bread* (1955, Beth. 38).

BIBLIOGRAPHY

FeatherE
R. Gordon: *Jazz West Coast: the Los Angeles Jazz Scene of the 1950s* (London and New York, 1986)

Thompson, Don(ald Winston) (*b* Powell River, Canada, 18 Jan 1940). Canadian double bass player and pianist. He worked in Vancouver, Canada, with the pianist Chris Gage and others (1960–65), moved to San Francisco, and toured as a double bass player in John Handy's quintet (1965–7). In 1969 he settled in Toronto, but thereafter he continued to tour frequently, playing double bass with Paul Desmond (1975–6), and double bass and piano with Jim Hall (1975–82) and in a duo with George Shearing (1982–7). He made recordings as a leader from 1969 (including *A Country Place*, 1975, PM 008, and *A Beautiful Friendship*, 1984, Conc. 243), which often feature his own compositions; he also recorded as a sideman with Sonny Greenwich (1969–78), Jay McShann (1972), Desmond (1975), Ed Bickert (1975–8), Hall (1975–81), Frank Rosolino (1976), Shearing (from 1983), and Dave Liebman (1984).

BIBLIOGRAPHY

M. Miller: "Don Thompson: Sideman in the Spotlight," *JF* [intl edn], no.58 (1979), 34 [incl. discography]
——: "Thompson, Don," *Encyclopedia of Music in Canada*, ed. H. Kallman, G. Potvin, and K. Winters (Toronto, Buffalo, and London, 1981) [incl. discography]
B. Smith and D. Lee: "Don Thompson," *Coda*, no.190 (1983), 4 [incl. discography]
L. Tomkins: "Don Thompson," *CI*, xxii/3 (1984), 20
M. Miller: "Don Thompson," *Boogie, Pete & the Senator: Canadian Musicians in Jazz: the Eighties* (Toronto, 1987), 262

MARK MILLER

Thompson, Eddie [Edgar Charles] (*b* London, 31 May 1925; *d* London, 6 Nov 1986). English pianist. He was born blind and learned piano as a child. Around 1946 he began working in clubs in London with Carlo Krahmer. In the 1950s he worked with dance bands and in radio studios, and made recordings as a leader of small groups (1954–9) and with Vic Ash and Freddy Randall (1955). During the ten years he spent in the USA (1962–72) he was resident for some time at the Hickory House, New York; he also performed at various clubs and recorded as a leader (1963, 1970) and soloist (1970). After returning to Great Britain Thompson toured as a soloist, in a duo with Roger Kellaway, and with his trio, visiting the USA, Australia, New Zealand, and Europe. He also made further recordings (1978, 1980, including *When Lights are Low*, 1980, Hep 2007), and performed on television and radio. He played frequently at various clubs in London, and worked with Kellaway in New York (1985). A brilliant pianist, Thompson was also well known for the dry wit and occasionally anarchic sense of humor he brought to his performances. (R. Cotterrell, ed.: *Jazz Now: the Jazz Centre Society Guide*, London, 1976)

Oral history material in *GBLnsa*.

DIGBY FAIRWEATHER

Thompson, Leslie (Anthony Joseph) (*b* Kingston, Jamaica, 17 Oct 1901; *d* London, 26 Dec 1987). Jamaican trumpeter. He trained with the band of the West India Regiment, and played in cinemas and performed in recitals before moving to London in 1929. The following year he joined Spike Hughes's group, with which he played trumpet and trombone until 1932; he may also be heard playing double bass on the band's recording of *Sirocco* (1932, Decca F2844). After touring France, Italy, and Switzerland with Louis Armstrong (1934–5) Thompson formed a band with the encouragement of Ken Johnson. The latter danced with the group in 1936, and the following year assumed leadership of it. Thompson recorded with Armstrong in Paris (1934) and with Benny Carter in London (1936–7), and a good example of his playing may be heard on *Organ Grinder's Swing* (1936, Crown 275) by Billy Merrin's Commanders. From 1937 until his military service Thompson played in a band led by Edmundo Ros; after World War II he performed at clubs and dance halls in London, but he ceased to work as a professional musician in 1954.

BIBLIOGRAPHY

O. Wright and K. Wright: "My Face is my Fortune," *Sv*, no.83 (1979), 196; no.84 (1979), 215
J. Green: "Leslie Thompson," *Black Perspective in Music*, xii (1984), 98
L. Thompson and J. P. Green: *An Autobiography* (Crawley, England, 1985)

JEFFREY P. GREEN

Thompson, Lucky [Eli] (*b* Columbia, SC, 16 June 1924). Tenor and soprano saxophonist. He toured with the 'Bama State Collegians, then moved to New York in 1943. After six months with Lionel Hampton he became a member of Billy Eckstine's bop orchestra in 1944 and spent a year with Count Basie (1944–5). He then moved to Los Angeles, where he was in great demand as a studio musician. He played on more than 100 recordings in two years, both as a leader (he later cited as a personal favorite the magnificent version of *Just one more Chance* recorded in 1947) and as a sideman; in 1946 he participated in sessions with Charlie Parker and Dizzy Gillespie.

After returning to New York (1948) Thompson led his own band at the Savoy (1951–3) and in 1954 made a major contribution to the session in which Miles Davis recorded *Walkin'*. In 1956 he made a number of recordings as a leader in Paris, and then toured Europe and the USA with Stan Kenton. From 1957 to 1962 he lived in France; during this period he mastered the soprano saxophone and he worked steadily throughout Europe. After a period of comparative inactivity he lived again in France (1968–71). In 1973–4 he taught at Dartmouth College, and then, disillusioned with the music business, he retired.

Thompson was an important player whose style drew on the work of Coleman Hawkins and Don Byas, tempered by the lighter tone of Lester Young and his own creative approach. He was one of the first of the modern group of soprano saxophonists.

SELECTED RECORDINGS

As leader: Just one more Chance/Boppin' the Blues (1947, Vic. 202504); From Dixieland to Bop (1947, Vic. 203142); *Lucky Thompson Featuring Oscar Pettiford* (1956, ABC–Para. 111); *Lucky Strikes* (1964, Prst. 7365); *Body and Soul* (1970, Ensayo 35); *I Offer you* (1973, GM 517)

As sideman: C. Basie: Taps Miller (1944, Col. 36831); I didn't know about you (1944, Col. 36766); D. Washington: My Lovin' Papa (1945, Apollo 371); My voot is really vout/Blues for a Day (1945, Apollo 388); D. Marmarosa: How High the Moon (1946, Atomic 225); M. Davis: *Miles Davis* (1954, Prst. 182), incl. Blue and Boogie, Walkin'

BIBLIOGRAPHY

L. Feather: *Inside Be-bop* (New York, 1949/R1977 as *Inside Jazz*), 98
N. Hentoff: "Lucky Thompson," *DB*, xxiii/7 (1956), 9; contd as "Call him Lucky(?)," xxiii/9 (1956), 14
R. Horricks: "Lucky Thompson: a Jazz Musician without a School," *JM*, i/11 (1956), 6
——: *Count Basie and his Orchestra: its Music and its Musicians* (London, 1957), 180
V. Wilmer: "Lucky Thompson," *JM*, viii/7 (1962), 12

T. Williams: *Lucky Thompson Discography and Biography*, i: *1944–51* (London, *c*1967)
C. Kuhl: "Lucky Thompson: Interview," *Cadence*, viii (1982), no.1, p.10; no.2, p.8
H. A. Mims: "E. L. "Lucky" Thompson: in Search of what the Creator Intended for him," *JSN*, ii/4 (1982), 102
M. Jones: *Talking Jazz* (London, 1987) [colln of previously pubd interviews], 72

SCOTT YANOW

Thompson, Sir Charles [Charles Phillip] (*b* Springfield, OH, 12 March 1918). Pianist, organist, and composer. He first studied violin, but took up piano as a teenager. He began his professional career in the late 1930s playing with midwestern territory bands, including the Nat Towles Orchestra (1937–9). He joined Lionel Hampton's band in 1940, but left to work in small groups, such as that led by Lee and Lester Young at Café Society in New York; through a number of engagements on 52nd Street in the mid-1940s he became familiar with the emerging bop style. In 1945 he worked with Howard McGhee in the band that Coleman Hawkins took to California; his solo on Hawkins's *Stuffy* is a characteristically witty and concise single line that makes effective use of silences. On his return to New York later the same year Thompson performed and recorded with Charlie Parker, and from 1947 to 1948 he played in the group led by Illinois Jacquet, who recorded his most popular composition, *Robbins' Nest*. During the 1950s Thompson worked as a freelance, performing mostly as an organist. He continued to lead small groups during the 1960s and 1970s.

Oral history material in *NjR* (JOHP).

SELECTED RECORDINGS

As leader: Twentieth-century Blues (1945, Apollo 759); Mad Lad (1947, Apollo 773); *Bop This* (1953, Van. 8003); *Sir Charles Thompson with Coleman Hawkins* (1954, Van. 8009); *Rockin' Rhythm* (1961, Col. CS8463); *Hey, there!* (1974, BB 33071)

As sideman: C. Hawkins: Ladies Lullaby (1945, Asch 3552); Stuffy (1945, Cap. 15254); I. Jacquet: Robbins' Nest (1947, Apollo 769)

BIBLIOGRAPHY

ChiltonW
K. Gallacher and B. Fairweather: "Sir Charles Thompson," *JJ*, xv/3 (1962), 11
S. Dance: *The World of Count Basie* (New York and London, 1980) [colln of previously pubd interviews], 333

SCOTT DeVEAUX

Thornhill, Claude (*b* Terre Haute, IN, 10 Aug 1909; *d* New York, 1 July 1965). Bandleader, composer, and pianist. After studying piano and composition at the Cincinnati Conservatory and the Curtis Institute he recorded with Bud Freeman (1935), Chick Bullock (1935–7), and Billie Holiday (1938) and performed and recorded with Benny Goodman (1934–5), Ray Noble (1935), and Maxine Sullivan (1937–8); he also wrote arrangements for radio orchestras and for jazz bands, including those of Goodman and Skinnay Ennis. In 1937 he recorded as a leader and from 1940 to 1942 led a band that he re-formed in 1946. With his arrangers Bill Borden and Gil Evans, and such leading members of his ensemble as Lee Konitz and Gerry Mulligan, he developed a strikingly original big-band sound that emphasized static textures, without vibrato, in the lower registers and depended for coloristic effect on several instruments usually associated with classical music, including the horn, tuba, and bass clarinet. Evans's arrangement of *Anthropology* (1947) provides a particularly noteworthy example of Thornhill's style, which influenced Miles Davis's recordings in 1949 for Capitol and many musicians who followed. Thornhill led a number of less successful bands in the 1950s and early 1960s.

SELECTED RECORDINGS

Gone with the Wind (1937, Voc. 3595); Snowfall/Where or when (1941, Col. 36268); Autumn Nocturne (1941, Col. 36435); There's a Small Hotel (1942, Col. 36725); A Sunday Kind of Love (1946, Col. 37219); Anthropology (1947, Col. 38224); Polkadots and Moonbeams (1947, Col. 38437); *Claude on a Cloud* (1958, Decca 8722)

BIBLIOGRAPHY

M. W. Stearns: *The Story of Jazz* (New York, 1956, rev. and enlarged 2/1958, enlarged 1970)
N. Hentoff: "The Birth of the Cool," *DB*, xxiv (1957), no.9, p.15; no.10, p.16
E. Edwards, Jr.: "A Claude Thornhill Discography," *JM*, viii/11 (1963), 13; ix/1 (1963), 16
A. Morgan: "Claude Thornhill," *JM*, viii/11 (1963), 11
G. T. Simon: *The Big Bands* (New York, 1967, rev. and enlarged 2/1971, rev. 3/1974, 4/1981)
I. Crosbie: "Prophet without Honor," *JJ*, xxiv (1971), no.3, p.6; no.4, p.28
C. Garrod: *Claude Thornhill and his Orchestra* (Spotswood, NJ, and Zephyrhills, FL, 1971, rev. 2/1975) [discography]
I. Crosbie: "Claude Thornhill," *Coda*, no.142 (1975), 2

RONALD M. RADANO

Thornton, Argonne (Dense). *See* HAKIM, SADIK.

Thornton, Clifford (Edward, III) (*b* Philadelphia, 6 Sept 1936). Cornetist and trumpeter. After attending Temple University (1954–6) he worked with Ray Draper (1956–7), studied with Donald Byrd (1957), and toured Korea and Japan with an army band (1958–61). In New York he performed and recorded with Sun Ra, worked with Pharoah Sanders (1963–7), recorded with the saxophonist Marzette Watts (*c*1964), and played with John Tchicai (1966). He formed the New Arts Ensemble, a free-jazz group with which he recorded as a leader in 1967, then appeared at the festival in Amougies, Belgium (1969), and performed and recorded in Paris with Dave Burrell and Sunny Murray (1969) and with Archie Shepp and his own band (1969–70); he also recorded with Shepp at the Antibes–Juan-les-Pins Jazz Festival (*Archie Shepp Live in Antibes*, 1970, BYG 529338–9). While a member of the faculty at Wesleyan University (1969–75) he recorded again with Shepp (1972), wrote compositions, and led groups in performances and recordings (1971, 1972, 1974). In 1976 he became an educational counselor at the African American Institute, an organization supported by UNESCO.

BIBLIOGRAPHY

Feather–Gitler '70s
V. Wilmer: Interview, *J&B*, ii/2 (1972), 12
P. Carles: "Clifford Thornton: pour l'exemple," *Jm*, no.208 (1973), 14 [incl. discography]
V. Wilmer: *As Serious as your Life: the Story of the New Jazz* (London, 1977, rev. 1980)
D. Constant: "Clifford Thornton," *Jm* (1978), no.262, p.40; no.263, p.34 [incl. discography]

Threadgill, Henry (Luther) (*b* Chicago, 15 Feb 1944). Alto saxophonist and composer. As a child he played percussion in street marching bands; he later took up baritone saxophone, and began clarinet in high school. In the early 1960s he played hard bop and free jazz in a sextet with Joseph Jarman and Roscoe Mitchell, and also performed with Muhal Richard Abrams's Experimental Band and Phil Cohran's Heritage Ensemble. Later in the decade he became a member of the Association for the Advancement of Creative Musicians and toured with the gospel singer Jo Jo Morris (1965–7). After a period of military service (during which he played in an army rock band) he worked in the house band at a blues club in Chicago and recorded with Abrams. Threadgill then studied flute, piano, and composition at the American Conservatory of Music (gaining the BM) and at Governors State University. In 1971 he formed the cooperative trio Reflection with Steve McCall and Fred Hopkins; after the group reassembled as AIR in 1975 he toured and recorded regularly with it, also composing most of its repertory. In the mid-1970s he moved to New York, where he became the leader of a sextet (which in fact has seven members – Threadgill regards the two drummers as one element of the ensemble), the Windstring Ensemble, and the Society Situation Orchestra. He also worked as a sideman with Mitchell, Olu Dara, and David Murray (recording in 1980–82).

Threadgill constructs his solos around fragmentary motifs; although his improvisations are well thought out, his playing, with its dry but urgent tone, remains exciting. His compositions, which incorporate improvised elements, have become increasingly complex in the 1980s. Those recorded by his sextet (1982–7) reflect a concern with death and employ unpredictable voicings and rhythms that are determinedly askew.

SELECTED RECORDINGS

(most tracks recorded as leader composed by Threadgill)

As leader: *X-75 Volume 1* (1979, AN 3013); *When was That?* (1982, About Time 1004); *Just the Facts and Pass the Bucket* (c1983, About Time 1005); *Subject to Change* (1986, About Time 1007); *You Know the Number* (c1986, RCA Novus 3013-1-N); *Easily Slip into Another World* (1987, RCA Novus 3025-1-N)

As leader of Air (with S. McCall and F. Hopkins): *Air Song* (1975, Why Not 7123); *Air Time* (1977, Nessa 12); *Air Lore* (1979, AN 3014), incl. Buddy Bolden's Blues, King Porter Stomp, The Ragtime Dance, Weeping Willow Rag; *Air Mail* (1980, BS 0049); *80° Below '82* (1982, Ant. 1007); of New Air (with P. Ak Laff and F. Hopkins): *Air Show no.1* (1986, BS 0099)

As sideman: on M. R. Abrams: *Young at Heart, Wise in Time* (1969, Del. 423), Wise in Time; on R. Mitchell: *Nonaah* (1976–7, Nessa 9–10), Nonaah (1977); M. R. Abrams: *1-0QA+19* (1977, BS 017); on R. Mitchell: *L-R-G, The Maze, S II Examples* (1978, Nessa 14–15), The Maze

BIBLIOGRAPHY

J. Blum: "Henry Threadgill," *JT* (Sept 1983), 10
G. Giddins: *Rhythm-a-ning: Jazz Tradition and Innovation in the '80s* (New York, and Oxford, England, 1985) [colln of previously pubd articles], 185
H. Mandel: "Henry Threadgill: Music to Make the Sun Come Up," *DB*, lii/7 (1985), 26 [incl. discography]
S. Buchanan: "Henry Threadgill," *Be-bop and Beyond*, iv/2 (1986), 21 [interview]
F. Davis: *In the Moment: Jazz in the 1980s* (New York, and Oxford, England, 1986) [colln of previously pubd articles], 217

HOWARD MANDEL

Three Deuces. The name of several nightclubs, notably ones in Chicago and New York; *see* NIGHTCLUBS AND OTHER VENUES.

360 Degree Music Experience. Cooperative group formed in 1968 by BEAVER HARRIS with Grachan Moncur III and Dave Burrell.

Three Sounds. Instrumental trio. In 1956 the drummer Bill Dowdy formed a quartet, the Four Sounds. The following year this group became a trio, the Three Sounds; the other members were the pianist GENE HARRIS and the double bass player Andy Simpkins. In 1958 the ensemble traveled to New York, where it began making recordings and achieved considerable popularity, particularly among patrons of supper clubs. It specialized in playing standards, employing a swing style enlivened with occasional bop figures and hints of the blues. Among its best recordings are *Willow, weep for me* (which may be heard on the album *Introducing the Three Sounds*, 1958, BN 1600), and *Summertime* and *Poinciana* (from *Here we Come*, 1960, BN 84088). It also recorded with the guest leaders Nat Adderley (1958), Lou Donaldson (1959), Stanley Turrentine (1960), and Anita O'Day (1962). Dowdy left the group in 1966, as did Simpkins two years later; Harris led larger ensembles called the Three Sounds, which played jazz-rock, until 1974. (*Feather '60s*)

LEROY OSTRANSKY

Three T's. Group formed in 1936 by Jack and Charlie Teagarden and Frankie Trumbauer; *see* TEAGARDEN family, (2) JACK.

Thumb piano. *See* LAMELLAPHONE.

Tiberi, Frank (*b* Camden, NJ, 4 Dec 1928). Tenor saxophonist. He taught himself to play saxophone and flute. He played with the bandleader Bob Chester (1948–9), Benny Goodman's quintet (1954–5), Urbie Green, and Dizzy Gillespie. During the 1960s he worked as a freelance musician on the East Coast, and in film and television studios. He studied bassoon with Sol Schoenbach of the Philadelphia SO. In 1969 he joined Woody Herman's band as lead tenor saxophonist, though he also played bassoon and flute. In the 1970s and 1980s he toured Europe with Herman, and recorded and performed at jazz festivals in Monterey (1970, 1979) and Japan (1982). He is heard to advantage on Herman's album *Thundering Herd* (1974, Fan. 9452). One of Herman's longest-serving sidemen, Tiberi led the band during Herman's absences (1977, 1986, 1987) and after his death, and has written arrangements for it.

See also BASSOON.

BIBLIOGRAPHY

Feather–Gitler '70s
S. Woolley: "The Reign of Tiberi," *MM*, lii (5 Nov 1977), 48

Timbales. A pair of cylindrical, single-headed drums used in Latin American dance music, and in fusions of this music with rock and soul. The instrument has also been used in Afro-Cuban jazz: Machito included timbales among the many percussion instruments in his orchestras from the 1940s to the 1980s, and the percussionist Willie Bobo often played the instrument (on, for example, his album *Bobo's Beat*, 1963, Roul. 52097).

Time (i). A word loosely used for meter and sometimes also applied in other contexts to do with rhythm and tempo; *see* BEAT.

Time (ii). Record company and label. The company was established in New York in 1960; until operations ceased around 1966 it produced a series of excellent albums under the artistic direction of Bob Shad. The catalogue included material by Max Roach, Kenny Dorham, Booker Little, Sonny Clark, Tommy Turrentine, Stanley Turrentine, Terry Gibbs, Marian McPartland, and Bennie Green. A few of the discs were also released by Oriole in the UK. Time's masters were comprehensively reissued (in replicas of the original liners) in Japan in the 1980s.

MARK GARDNER

Timeless. Record company and label. The company was founded in 1975 in Wageningen, the Netherlands, by Wim Wigt. Although it has recorded the work of ensembles as diverse as Lionel Hampton's swing orchestra and Machito's salsa band, the company's principal series of issues is devoted to bop, especially hard bop, and offers important recordings by artists including Cedar Walton, Art Blakey, and George Adams. A second, smaller series consists of traditional jazz and swing recordings led by such musicians as Chris Barber, Papa Bue, and Peanuts Hucko. The company also sponsors the Timeless All-Stars, a sextet formed by Wigt around 1981. Its members are Harold Land, Curtis Fuller, Bobby Hutcherson, Walton, Buster Williams, and Billy Higgins. The group has recorded two albums (1982–3), and tours Europe regularly, but it seldom performs in the USA.

BIBLIOGRAPHY
P. Carles: "Deux faces du disque: Timeless, Hat Hut," *Jm*, no.338 (1985), 42
J. Hamlin: "The Timeless All-Stars: Famed Jazzmen Set for a Rare Gig," *San Francisco Chronicle Datebook* (13 April 1986), 20

BARRY KERNFELD

Timely Tunes. Record label. It was a subsidiary of RCA Victor, and was operational between April and July 1931. Among its 41 issues were recordings by Dave Nelson and Blanche Calloway that were made specifically for Timely Tunes and not put out on any other labels in the Victor group. (B. Rust: "A Glimpse of the Past: Sunrise and Timely Tunes," *Sv*, no.16 (1968), 17)

Timmons, Bobby [Robert Henry] (*b* Philadelphia, 19 Dec 1935; *d* New York, 1 March 1974). Pianist and composer. He studied piano from the age of six. After moving to New York (1954) he played bop with Kenny Dorham's Jazz Prophets (1956), Chet Baker (1956–7), Sonny Stitt (1957), and Maynard Ferguson (1957–8). While a member of Art Blakey's Jazz Messengers (1958–9), with whom he toured Europe, he became well known for his composition *Moanin'*, a funky, gospel-oriented tune. From 1959 to 1960 Timmons worked with Cannonball Adderley and recorded two further soul-jazz compositions that became hits, *This here* (also called *Dis here*) and *Dat dere*. He rejoined Blakey briefly in 1960, but thereafter his career declined rapidly because of alcoholism, possibly brought on by artistic frustration. Timmons was a sophisticated and versatile pianist, but he became stereotyped and inhibited by the success of his simple compositions.

SELECTED RECORDINGS

As leader: *This Here is Bobby Timmons* (1960, Riv. 317); *Easy Does It* (1961, Riv. 9363)

As sideman: K. Dorham: *'Round about Midnight at the Cafe Bohemia* (1956, BN 1524); Lee Morgan: *The Cooker* (1957, BN 1578); A. Blakey: *With the Jazz Messengers* (1958, BN 4003), incl. Moanin'; *At the Jazz Corner of the World* (1959, BN 4015–6); C. Adderley: *The Cannonball Adderley Quintet in San Francisco* (1959, Riv. 311), incl. This here; *Them Dirty Blues* (1960, Riv. 1170), incl. Dat dere

BIBLIOGRAPHY
P. Keepnews: "Remember Bobby," *Moanin'* (Mlst. 47031, 1975) [liner notes]
L. Feather: "Bobby Timmons," *CK*, vi/8 (1980), 48

BARRY KERNFELD

Timpani. Kettledrums which are capable of producing notes of definite pitch; these may be altered by tightening or slackening the drumhead by means of screws or other mechanisms. Timpani have occasionally been used in jazz; *see* DRUM SET, §I, 9.

Tinney, Al(len) (*b* Ansonia, CO, 28 May 1921). Pianist. As a child performer he appeared in the original production of Gershwin's *Porgy and Bess* in 1935. From 1939 to 1943 he led the house band at Monroe's Uptown House in New York, where he was in the forefront of the modernist movement that crystallized in the bop idiom. Though his work was seldom recorded, his harmonically advanced, flowing, and lightly percussive style mark him as an important forerunner of such early modern pianists as Bud Powell, George Wallington, Al Haig, and Duke Jordan. Repelled by the influence of drugs in jazz, from 1946 he turned increasingly to commercial music. In 1968 he settled in Buffalo, New York, where he has performed and taught at SUNY.

BIBLIOGRAPHY
L. Feather: *Inside Be-bop* (New York, 1949/*R*1977 as *Inside Jazz*), 15
D. Gillespie and A. Frazer: *To be, or not . . . to Bop: Memoirs* (Garden City, NY, 1979), 205
J. Patrick: "Al Tinney, Monroe's Uptown House, and the Emergence of Modern Jazz in Harlem," *ARJS*, ii (1983), 150
I. Gitler: *Swing to Bop: an Oral History of the Transition in Jazz in the 1940s* (New York, and Oxford, England, 1985), 77

JAMES PATRICK

Tio. Family of musicians active in New Orleans.

(1) Papa (Luis) Tio (*b* Mexico, Jan 1863; *d* New Orleans, 1927). Clarinetist. His parents were born in Louisiana and, as "free persons of color," were probably able to emigrate to Mexico (possibly to Tampico) around 1860. He received training in classical music before the family returned to New Orleans around 1878. In 1887 he made a national tour with the Georgia Minstrels, and in the 1890s was a member of the Excelsior Brass Band and the Lyre Club Symphony. He also played in dance bands led by A. J. Piron and John Robichaux, and later worked with Manuel Manetta and Peter Bocage. By 1910 Tio had adapted to the emerging jazz idiom, and was successful as a teacher of the "split-time" style; among his pupils was Barney Bigard.

Oral history material in *LNT*.

BIBLIOGRAPHY
ChartersJ

(2) Lorenzo Tio, Sr. (*b* Mexico, Aug 1866; *d* Jackson, MS, *c*1920). Clarinetist, brother of (1) Papa Tio. He received formal training in music before his family returned to New Orleans around 1878, and was also taught by his brother. He performed with the Lyre Club Symphony (founded in 1889) and the Excelsior Brass Band (in which he played E♭ clarinet), and around 1900 toured with a minstrel company. He was noted in the Creole musical community for his purity of tone, excellence of musicianship, and influence as a teacher. After moving to Jackson, Mississippi, in 1906, Tio ceased to be active as a musician.

Oral history material in *LNT*.

BIBLIOGRAPHY
ChartersJ

(3) Lorenzo Tio, Jr. (*b* New Orleans, 21 April 1893; *d* New York, 24 Dec 1933). Clarinetist, son of (2) Lorenzo Tio, Sr. He was brought up in Bay St. Louis, Mississippi, but returned to his birthplace in New Orleans during late childhood. By the time he was nine he was playing in parade bands and from about 1910 performed regularly in the Onward and Excelsior brass bands. He spent a year in Chicago (1917) working with Charlie Elgar and Manuel Perez, then returned to New Orleans and joined Papa Celestin. From 1918 Tio was a member of A. J. Piron's orchestra, with which he also played in New York; his recordings with this group reveal his instrumental brilliance. In 1930 he decided to settle in New York, where during the last few months of his life he held a residency at the Nest Club. Tio's most lasting influence came through the success of his many pupils, who included Paul Barnes, Barney Bigard, and Louis Cottrell, Jr. It is also said that he supplied Duke Ellington with several compositions.

Oral history material in *LNT*.

For illustrations *see* BANDS, fig.1, and BRASS BAND, fig.1.

SELECTED RECORDINGS

(all as sideman with A. J. Piron)

Bouncing Around (1923, OK 40021); New Orleans Wiggle (1923, Vic. 19233); Bright Star Blues (1924, Col. 99D); Lou'siana Swing (1924, OK 40189); Red Man Blues (1925, Vic. 19646)

BIBLIOGRAPHY
ChartersJ
B. Bigard: *With Louis and the Duke*, ed. B. Martyn (London, 1985)

ALDEN ASHFORTH (1, 2)
JOHN CHILTON (3)

Tiple [tipple] (Sp.: treble, soprano). A small guitar of Spain, Colombia, Guatemala, Puerto Rico, and Venezuela. Although the tiple's size and tuning are not standard, the instrument usually has four metal strings (or four courses, each consisting of two or three strings), which are tuned to the same pitches as the four upper strings of the guitar. The most important tiple players in jazz were three members of the Spirits of Rhythm, Leo Watson and the brothers Wilbur Daniels and Douglas Daniels, who played tiples with courses of multiple strings; like the group's guitarist, Teddy Bunn, they did not use a plectrum, even when one string alone was used to play a solo. The tiples provided the group with a chordal backing that was lighter than that afforded by guitars in other string bands; the instrument was also well-suited to the playing of incisive solos, which tonally were reminiscent of those played on the mandolin, but which had a somewhat deeper timbre. The Spirits' recording of *I'll be ready when the great day comes* (1933, Bruns. 6728), on which solos are taken alternately on tiple and guitar, demonstrates clearly the contrasting sound of the two instruments. The tiple was seldom used in jazz after the late 1930s, though it was revived briefly in the early 1970s by the English blues singer and guitarist Alexis Korner.

BIBLIOGRAPHY

R. Brown: "Jazz at the Docks," *JJ*, xxv/4 (1972), 28
M. Jones: "Teddy Bunn, the Spirit of Rhythm," *The Spirits of Rhythm, 1933–34* (JSP 1088, 1985) [liner notes]

ALYN SHIPTON

Tippett, Keith (Graham) (*b* Bristol, England, 25 Aug 1947). English pianist and composer. After playing traditional jazz and bop in Bristol he moved to London in 1967; he later recorded twice with his own group (1968, 1969), and also led recordings by the 50-piece ensemble Centipede (1971), the small group Ovary Lodge (1972, 1973, 1975), and the 22-piece band Ark. During the 1970s he played with Stan Tracey in a duo, T 'n' T, recording in 1974; he also recorded with Trevor Watts's Amalgam (1974), Elton Dean (1976–80), Dudu Pukwana (1977), Harry Miller (1977, 1978), Louis Moholo (1978), and Howard Riley (1979–81). In the 1980s he has worked increasingly in duos and alone, adopting a meditative approach very different from the boisterousness of his earlier large ensembles. His unaccompanied solo style, which mixes the phrasing of jazz with elements of ethnic music and freely improvised material, may be heard to advantage on the album *Mujician* (1981, FMP SAJ37).

BIBLIOGRAPHY

R. Cotterrell, ed.: *Jazz Now: the Jazz Centre Society Guide* (London, 1976), 174
K. Ansell: "No Gossip from the Mujician," *The Wire*, no.2 (1982), 10

MARK GILBERT

Tippetts [née Driscoll], **Julie (Dawn)** (*b* London, 8 June 1947). English singer. Encouraged by her father, the trumpeter Reg Driscoll, she sang in London coffee bars from 1959, and she performed with his band in 1963. After singing with Brian Auger in the rhythm-and-blues band Steampacket (1964–6), she became a member of the Brian Auger Trinity in 1966, when the singers Rod Stewart and Long John Baldry left; she enjoyed international success with the group's version of Bob Dylan's *This Wheel's on Fire* (1968). She left the group after an American tour in 1968 and returned to England, where she released her first solo album in the following year. In 1970 she married the pianist Keith Tippett; she collaborated with him in Centipede (1970–75), Ovary Lodge (from 1973), and Ark (1975–8), and also performed in a duo with him, occasionally contributing lyrics. In 1975–6 she sang with her own group, Butterfly, and in 1976 she formed the vocal quartet Voice with Maggie Nicols, Brian Ely, and Phil Minton; she also worked with the Spontaneous Music Ensemble (1971), Derek Bailey and Company (1982), and Working Week (1984–5). In the mid-1980s she performed and recorded in a trio with Tippett, the third member of which was at different times Nicols, the drummer Willi Kellers, or Louis Moholo. From the 1970s Tippetts moved away from the blues and rock style of her early work and began to favor wordless, free improvisation, creating contrapuntal interplay with other members of the ensemble; her performances are remarkable for their inventive lines and the intensity of her delivery.

SELECTED RECORDINGS

Duos with M. Nicols: *Sweet and S'ours* (1978, FMP SAJ38)
As leader: *1969* (1969, Pol. 2383077); *Sunset Glow* (1975, Utopia 601)

SIMON ADAMS

Tizol, Juan [Vincente Martinez] (*b* San Juan, 22 Jan 1900; *d* Inglewood, CA, 23 April 1984). Valve trombonist and composer. After working in a municipal concert orchestra in San Juan he moved to the USA in 1920 and worked for a long period at the Howard Theatre in Washington, where he met Duke Ellington. He played briefly with Bobby Lee's Cotton Pickers and the White Brothers Band, then joined Ellington in September 1929. He left to join Harry James in 1944 and thereafter spent most of his time alternating between the two bands, interspersed among periods working with other leading artists, such as Louie Bellson and Pearl Bailey, and as a studio musician. He was with Ellington from 1951 to 1953 and again in 1960 and 1961. He retired to California and later lived in Las Vegas.

Tizol was rarely heard playing solos with Ellington's orchestra, but his large, yet unassertive, tone and great mobility made him a key voice in the ensemble. He contributed a number of compositions to the band, such as *Moonlight Fiesta*, *Pyramid*, *Caravan*, and *Perdido*, many of which, including the latter two, have become standards. These works, with their Latin-American melodies and rhythms, reflect Tizol's Puerto Rican background, and his thematic statements on such numbers as *Caravan* and *Moonlight Fiesta* delineate their exotic mood perfectly.

Oral history material in *CtY*, *NjR* (JOHP).

For illustrations *see* BANDS, fig.3; TROMBONE; and TRUMPET.

SELECTED RECORDINGS

As sideman: D. Ellington: Twelfth Street Rag (1931, Bruns. 6038); Caravan (1937, Master 131); Lost in Meditation (1938, Bruns. 8083); Pyramid (1938, Bruns. 8168); Battle of Swing (1938, Bruns. 8923); Raincheck (1941, Vic. 27880); *Duke Ellington and his Orchestra* (1941, Temple 550), incl. Perdido; The Coronets: Moonlight Fiesta (1951, Mercer 1967)

BIBLIOGRAPHY

S. Dance: *The World of Duke Ellington* (London and New York, 1970) [colln of previously pubd articles and interviews)
D. Ellington: *Music is my Mistress* (Garden City, NY, 1973)

EDDIE LAMBERT

Tjader, Cal(len Radcliffe, Jr.) (*b* St. Louis, 16 July 1925; *d* Manila, 5 May 1982). Vibraphonist. He studied music at San Francisco State University. From 1949 to 1951 he played drums with Dave Brubeck's trio; thereafter he worked with Alvino Rey and later led his own group until 1953, when he joined George Shearing's highly successful quintet, playing both vibraphone and percussion. His bongo playing may be heard to advantage on Shearing's *Wrap your Troubles in Drums* (1953). During this period he became interested in Latin music. After leaving Shearing in 1954, Tjader formed his own quintet, which played a blend of Latin and Afro-Cuban music and jazz; among his sidemen were Willie Bobo and Mongo Santamaria. By the end of the decade he had achieved great popularity. Although he remained based on the West Coast he made a tour of the East late in 1959, and during the 1960s and 1970s appeared frequently in New York. Tjader's recordings range from almost pure salsa (with the vibraphonist Tito Puente and the pianist Eddie Palmieri) to jam sessions (with such musicians as Luis Gasca and the saxophonist José "Chombo" Silva). Ironically, the album *La onda va bien* (1979), which won a Grammy Award, was recorded with relatively unknown musicians.

SELECTED RECORDINGS

As leader: *Cal Tjader: Vibist* (1953, Savoy 9036); *Cal Tjader Plays Afro-Cuban* (1954, Fan. 3-17); *Cal Tjader Plays Tjazz* (1955, Fan. 3211); *Mas ritmo caliente* (1957, Fan. 3262); with S. Getz: *Cal Tjader–Stan Getz Sextet* (1958, Fan. 3266); *Concert by the Sea* (1959, Fan. 8038); *West Side Story* (1960, Fan. 8054); *Warm Wave* (1964, Verve 68585); *Soul Sauce* (1964, Verve 68614); *Breathe Easy* (1977, Gal. 5107); *La onda va bien* (1979, Conc. 113); *The Shining Sea* (1981, Conc. 159); *A fuego vivo* (1981, Conc. 176)

As sideman: D. Brubeck: *Dave Brubeck Trio* (1950, Fan. 3-1, 3-2, 3-4); G. Shearing: Mood for Milt (1953, MGM 11677); Wrap your Troubles in Drums/ Easy to Love (1953, MGM 11600)

BIBLIOGRAPHY

J. Tynan: "Cal Tjader: not that he's Tjaded with Concerts, but he Prefers his Tjazz in Saloons," *DB*, xxiv/17 (1957), 17
D. A. Ramsey: "Cal Tjader," *JM*, viii/9 (1962), 7
R. Carr: "Bossa Nova? It's Beautiful," *Crescendo*, ii/7 (1964), 18 [interview]
H. Siders: "The Latinization of Cal Tjader," *DB*, xxxiii/18 (1966), 21
J. S. Roberts: *The Latin Tinge: the Impact of Latin American Music on the United States* (New York, and Oxford, England, 1979)
Obituary, *New York Times* (6 May 1982)

JOHN STORM ROBERTS/R

TOBA. *See* THEATER OWNERS' BOOKING ASSOCIATION.

Togashi, Masahiko (*b* Tokyo, 22 March 1940). Japanese drummer, percussionist, and composer. He studied violin at an early age, took up drums, and made his début when he was 14. After playing with Sadao Watanabe and his Cozy Quartet he formed the group Jazz Academy in 1961 with Masabumi Kikuchi and the guitarist Masayuki Takayanagi, then worked as a leader from 1965. An accident in 1969 that left him unable to play drums led him from the following year to devote himself exclusively to playing percussion and writing compositions, which show a strong oriental influence.

SELECTED RECORDINGS

Duos with S. Lacy: *Eternal Duo* (1981, PW K28P6219)

As leader: *Song for myself* (1974, EW 7006); *Rings* (1975, EW 900127); *Spiritual Nature* (1975, EW 8013); *Essence* (1976, Denon YX7513); *Sketch* (1977, Denon YX7516); *Al-alarf: Improvisation Jazz Orchestra* (1980, PW K22P602122); *Flame up* (1981, PW K28P6205); *Follow the Dream* (1984, PW K25P632829); *Scene* (1987, Cornelius CCD701)

As leader with others: I Suzuki: *A Day of the Sun* (1979, PW K35Y6003); M. Kikuchi: *Poesy* (1981, Phi. HS6507); S. Lacy: *Spiritual Moments* (1981, PW K28P6138)

YOZO IWANAMI

Tokyo Union. Big band led from 1966 by TATSUYA TAKAHASHI.

Tolliver, Charles (*b* Jacksonville, FL, 6 March 1942). Trumpeter. He grew up in New York. He spent three years in Washington at Howard University, then returned to New York, where he performed and recorded with Jackie McLean (1964). This was the first of several brief associations that Tolliver formed with leading bop musicians, including Art Blakey and Sonny Rollins. Later he played in Gerald Wilson's big band in California (1966–7) and in Max Roach's quintet (1967–9). In 1969 he formed Music, Inc., a cooperative bop quartet that occasionally expanded to become a big band. Members of the group's rhythm section included the pianists Stanley Cowell and John Hicks, the double bass players Cecil McBee, Reggie Workman, and Clint Houston, and the drummers Jimmy Hopps and Clifford Barbaro. In 1971 Tolliver and Cowell founded Strata-East Records, an innovative company that allowed participating jazz musicians to control the rights to their own recordings. Music, Inc. performed and recorded until the late 1970s, and in the early 1980s Tolliver led a quartet in Europe. Tolliver is a sensitive, swinging, consistently inventive hard-bop trumpeter who plays with a bright, but rounded, timbre. He has recorded a number of his own compositions, including the fine bop waltz *Peace with Myself*.

SELECTED RECORDINGS

As leader: *Paper Man* (1968, Arista 1002), incl. Peace with Myself; *Live at Slugs* (1970, SE 1972, 19720); *Music Inc. Big Band* (1971, Pol. 2383138); *Live in Tokyo* (1973, SE 19745); *Impact* (1975, SE 19757)

As sideman: J. McLean: *It's Time* (1964, BN 84179); R. Ayers: *Virgo Vibes* (1967, Atl. 1488); H. Silver: *Serenade to a Soul Sister* (1968, BN 84277); M. Roach: *Members Don't Git Weary* (1968, Atl. 1510)

BIBLIOGRAPHY

V. Wilmer: "What Charles Tolliver Can Use," *DB*, xxxvi/4 (1969), 16
——: "Making it Alone," *MM*, xlv (10 Oct 1970), 18
R. Williams: "Tolliver's Travels," *MM*, xlvii (2 Sept 1972), 18
E. Chadbourne: "Strata East," *Coda*, xii/3 (1975), 7
A. Taylor: *Notes and Tones: Musician-to-Musician Interviews* (Liège, Belgium, 1977/*R*1982), 76

BARRY KERNFELD

Tolonen, Jukka (*b* Helsinki, 16 April 1952). Finnish guitarist. He founded the jazz-rock group Tasavallan presidentti with Pekka Pöyry and others; this was active from 1969 to 1974. He later pursued a career as a soloist with his own groups and with the Swedish guitarist Coste Apetrea, and toured Central Europe. A brilliant solo player on both acoustic and electric instruments in jazz and rock styles, he has made many recordings as a leader (1971–8, including *The Hook*, 1974, Love 113) and with others, such as Charlie Mariano (1974) and Eero Koivistoinen (1970, 1973, 1976). (A. Granholm: *Finnish Jazz* (Helsinki, 1974, rev. and enlarged by M. Konttinen 2/1982, rev. and enlarged by J.-P. Vuorela 3/1986), 44)

PEKKA GRONOW

Tom Anderson's. Nightclub in New Orleans; *see* NIGHTCLUBS AND OTHER VENUES.

Tomkins, Les(lie Charles) (*b* London, 31 Oct 1930). English writer. In 1950 he ran a jazz club near London in which a number of well-known British bop musicians performed, and from 1957 to 1960 he was secretary of an informal group known as the Contemporary Jazz Society. To broaden the society's activities he began to interview musicians, including Americans visiting England; some of these interviews were later published in *Melody Maker* (1959–60). In 1961–2 he was a freelance contributor to *Jazz News* and in 1962 he began an association with *Crescendo* which continued into the 1980s; he was its editor and art editor from 1966 to 1967 and has served as a freelance editor, contributor, and art director from 1970. Throughout his association with *Crescendo* Tomkins has published three or four interviews with jazz musicians each month; this collection of interviews now represents a major archive of source material for the study of jazz. He has also written liner notes, program notes, and reviews.

Tompkins, Eddie. *See* THOMPKINS, EDDIE.

Tompkins, Ross (*b* Detroit, 13 May 1938). Pianist. He studied at the New England Conservatory. In New York he performed and recorded at intervals with Kai Winding (1960–67); he also played briefly with Eric Dolphy (1964), Wes Montgomery (1966), Bob Brookmeyer's and Clark Terry's quintet (1966), and Benny Goodman (1968). He performed frequently with Bobby Hackett (1965–70) and the quintet led by Al Cohn and Zoot Sims (1968–72). In 1971 he moved to Los Angeles, where he played in Louie Bellson's big band and in the orchestra of the "Tonight Show" under Doc Severinsen. From 1975 he recorded often for Concord.

SELECTED RECORDINGS

As unaccompanied soloist: *Scrimshaw* (1976, Conc. 28)
Duos with H. Ellis: *A Pair to Draw to* (1975, Conc. 17)
As leader: with J. Venuti: *Live at Concord '77* (1977, Conc. 51); with R. Norvo: *Red and Ross* (1979, Conc. 90); *Symphony* (c1984, FaD 146)
As sideman: L. Bellson: *Prime Time* (1977, Conc. 64); Concord All Stars: *Festival Time* (1979, Conc. 117)

BIBLIOGRAPHY

Feather–Gitler '70s
J. Balleras: Review of *Scrimshaw* (1976), *DB*, xliv/10 (1977), 35
L. Jeske: Review of *Red and Ross* (1979), *DB*, xlvii/11 (1980), 32
S. Traill: "Ross Tompkins," *JJI*, xxxiii/10 (1980), 41

PAUL RINZLER

Tompkins, Trevor (*b* London, 12 May 1941). English drummer. He began listening to jazz at the age of 13 on Voice of America broadcasts. After playing trombone he took up drumming; at first he played mostly commercially-oriented music, and worked with jazz groups only informally. He also studied harmony, theory, and orchestral percussion. Later he became a full-time jazz musician when he joined the quintet led by Ian Carr and Don Rendell (1963). He may be heard to advantage with this ensemble on *Tan san fu*, from the album *Dusk Fire* (1966, Col. ESX6064). In the mid-1960s he worked in the USA, and from 1969 to the mid-1970s he performed and recorded with Michael Garrick. Thereafter he worked with Dick Morrissey, Barbara Thompson, and Mike Westbrook in the late 1970s. He has also been associated with such visiting American musicians as Ben Webster, Tal Farlow, Joe Newman, and Spike Robinson. Tompkins has played many times at Ronnie Scott's club and has also participated in several broadcasts and recording sessions. (R. Cotterrell, ed.: *Jazz Now: the Jazz Centre Society Guide* (London, 1976), 175)

SALLY-ANN WORSFOLD

Tom Terrific. Nickname of ALAN TURNBULL.

Tom-tom. Double-headed rod-tensioned drum. Mounted on the bass drum, or free-standing, two or more of them have generally been used in the drum set from the 1940s onwards; *see* DRUM SET, esp. §§I, 4; II, 4, 5.

Top cymbal. Name by which the ride cymbal is also known; *see* DRUM SET, §§I, 5; II, 5, 6.

Top of the beat, on. Expression used to describe the performance of a player or singer who (deliberately or unintentionally) places notes slightly before or too precisely on the beat as it is articulated by the rhythm section or implied by the playing of the rest of the ensemble; *see* BEAT, §2.

Torff, Brian (*b* Hinsdale, IL, 16 March 1954). Double bass player. After studying at the Berklee College of Music and the Manhattan School of Music he toured with Cleo Laine (1974) and briefly with Erroll Garner (February 1975). In New York he played with David Amram and Laine, and performed and recorded at the Cookery in a duo with Mary Lou Williams (1975). With Stephane Grappelli he toured and in 1978 recorded at Carnegie Hall; he also performed and recorded with Marian McPartland (1978, 1979). He played in a duo with George Shearing (1979, 1980) that recorded an album of swing and bop tunes (*Blues Alley & Jazz*, 1979, Conc. 110), and recorded with Jackie Cain and Roy Kral (1979, 1980), Eiji Kitamura (1980), and Shearing and Mel Tormé (1982).

BIBLIOGRAPHY

A. J. Smith: "Profile: Brian Torff," *DB*, xliii/12 (1976), 34
J. M. Doran: *Erroll Garner: the Most Happy Piano* (Metuchen, NJ, 1985), 114

Tormé [Torme], **Mel(vin Howard)** (b Chicago, 13 Sept 1925). Singer and songwriter. He studied piano and drums and while still in his teens toured as singer, arranger, and drummer with a band led by the comedian Chico Marx (1942–3), appeared in the film *Higher and Higher* (1943), led a vocal swing group, the Mel-Tones, and made his first recordings. After his discharge from the army in 1946 he became known as a first-rate arranger. His reputation as one of the finest pop and jazz singers of his generation is based on his versatility; his repertory has included sentimental ballads, swing numbers with big bands, and popular songs in jazz arrangements that involve scat singing. Early in his career his high, husky voice caused him to be nicknamed "the Velvet Fog," but in time it deepened into a well-controlled baritone. Although the sophistication and jazz orientation of his best singing precluded widespread appeal, Tormé achieved periodic success in nightclubs, on television, and through recordings, and is widely admired by fellow musicians. From the 1960s he produced television shows and developed his career as an actor and writer. He has composed around 300 popular songs, notably *The Christmas Song* (1946). In the 1980s he continued to perform and record regularly in groups and in a duo with George Shearing.

SELECTED RECORDINGS

As leader: *Live at the Crescendo* (1957, Beth. 6020); *I Dig the Count, I Dig the Duke* (1960–61, Verve 68491); *Live at the Maisonette* (1974, Atl. 18129); with G. Shearing: *An Evening with George Shearing & Mel Tormé* (1982, Conc. 190); with R. McConnell: *Mel Tormé, Rob McConnell and the Boss Brass* (1986, Conc. 306)
As sideman with Artie Shaw: What is this thing called love? (1946, Musi. 390); Get out of town (1946, Musi. 389)

BIBLIOGRAPHY

J. McDonough: "The Velvet Fog in Mellow Pose: Mel Torme," *DB*, xliii/9 (1976), 16
M. R. Pitts and L. H. Harrison: *Hollywood on Record: the Film Stars' Discography* (Metuchen, NJ, 1978)
W. Balliett: "Profiles: a Vast Minority," *New Yorker*, lvii (16 March 1981), 49
"Tormé, Mel," *CBY 1983*

MICHAEL J. BUDDS/R

Törner, Gösta (*b* Stockholm, 27 Oct 1912; *d* Stockholm, 11 Nov 1982). Swedish trumpeter and bandleader. Active as a professional musician from the late 1920s, he became one of Sweden's earliest and most consistent hot jazz improvisers and one of her finest trumpeters. Between 1936 and 1938 he made several recordings in small-band jam sessions with the Sonora Swing Swingers under the leadership of Thore Jederby, among them *Louisiana* and *Easy Swing*; these were the first of their kind in Sweden and were influenced by Bix Beiderbecke, Louis Armstrong, and Roy Eldridge. Törner worked with a large number of Swedish bands of the 1930s and 1940s – notably those led by the double bass player Sune Lundwall (1933–5), Arne Hülphers (1937–40), the drummer Sven Fors (1940–42), and Thore Ehrling (1941–50) – and also led his own group (1943–7). After the war he recorded with various small ensembles, and led another band from 1958 to 1964. Scores used by his band are in the Svenskt Visarkiv, Stockholm; *see* LIBRARIES AND ARCHIVES, §2.

Oral history material in *SSsv*.

SELECTED RECORDINGS

As leader: I found a new baby (1943, Tel. A5369); Queen Street Blues (1944, Tel. A5388); with B. Laine: Blues Cupol/Ain't Misbehavin' (1947, Cupol 4011); At the Jazz Band Ball (1949, Artist B3008); *Living Legend* (1964, Phon. NOST7607), incl. Lazy River

As sideman with T. Jederby: Louisiana (1936, Son. 3217); Easy Swing (1936, Son. 3218)

BIBLIOGRAPHY

"Svenskt stjärnalbum" [Swedish star-album], *Orkester journalen*, iv/11 (1936), 3

"Mannen bakom orkestern" [The man behind the orchestra], *Estrad*, vi/6 (1944), 11

B. Nyquist: "Gösta: vår första stora jazzartist" [Gösta: our first great jazz artist], *Orkester journalen*, l/11 (1982), 33

E. Kjellberg: *Svensk jazzhistoria: en översikt* [Swedish jazz history: an overview] (Stockholm, 1985)

ERIK KJELLBERG

Toshiko. *See* AKIYOSHI, TOSHIKO.

Totah, Nobby [Nabil (Marshall)] (*b* Ramallah, Transjordan [now Jordan], 5 April 1930). Double bass player. His nickname is often misspelled Knobby. He emigrated to the USA in 1944 to attend school in Providence, Rhode Island, studied political science at Haverford College (graduated 1952), and took up double bass in 1953. While serving in the US Army he belonged to a military band and played in Japan with Hampton Hawes and Toshiko Akiyoshi (1953–4). In 1954 he worked briefly with Charlie Parker and the following year he first played with Gene Krupa and Johnny Smith, with both of whom his association continued for many years; he also performed with Les Elgart (1955) and Cy Coleman (1955–7), performed and recorded with Zoot Sims (at intervals, 1956–9), and worked with Eddie Costa (1957), Herbie Mann (1958–61), Bobby Hackett (*c*1960), Sol Yaged (1961), and Teddy Wilson (1960–64). In the 1970s he played with Max Kaminsky and Benny Goodman (both 1976) and Hazel Scott (1978–80) and recorded with Lee Konitz (1977). He was a member of Peter Duchin's band in New York in the 1980s. From 1972 he led small groups of his own; among his sidemen have been Horace Parlan, Mike Longo, Attila Zoller, and Pepper Adams. Totah's style is that of an accompanist: he plays simple bass lines behind the beat, which support the soloist rather than display his own virtuosity.

SELECTED RECORDINGS

As sideman: Z. Sims: *Zoot* (1956, Argo 608); B. Jaspar: *Bobby Jaspar Quartet* (1956, Col. FPX123); G. Wallington: *Jazz at Hotchkiss* (1957, Savoy 12122); T. Farlow: *This is Tal Farlow* (1958, Verve 8289); H. Mann: *Family of Mann* (1961, Atl. SD1371)

BIBLIOGRAPHY

FeatherE; *Feather '60s*

J. Bany: "Double Double-Bass," *International Society of Bassists*, xiii/1 (1986), 25

JOHN VOIGT

Touff, Cy(ril James) (*b* Chicago, 4 March 1927). Bass trumpeter. From the age of six he played piano, C-melody saxophone, xylophone, then trumpet. After playing trombone in an army band with Conte Candoli and Red Mitchell (1944–6) he returned to Chicago, where he studied with Lennie Tristano and worked with Bill Russo, Charlie Ventura, Ray McKinley, and Boyd Raeburn. He took up the bass trumpet in the late 1940s, performed, recorded, and toured the USA and Europe with Woody Herman (1953–6), and in 1954 recorded in Paris as a member of the Herdsmen (a group of Herman's sidemen) and as a soloist on several tracks of the album *The Woody Herman Band!* (Cap. T560); he also recorded with Nat Pierce's and Dick Collins's nonet (1954) and as a leader of West Coast jazz groups (1955). He then worked as a freelance in Chicago, played in dance bands, and recorded as the leader of a dixieland sextet (*c*1956) and a hard-bop quintet (1958) and in 1957 as a sideman with Chubby Jackson and Lorez Alexandria. Later he recorded in Chicago with the drummer Fred Wacker (1965) and the sextet Hyde Park after Dark (1981), of which Clifford Jordan and Von Freeman were also members; in the early 1980s he also worked in studios and with local groups.

BIBLIOGRAPHY

FeatherE

J. Tracy: "Meet Cy Touff; the Man who Brought Bass Trumpet to Prominence," *DB*, xxii/25 (1955), 14

E. Jost: *Jazzmusiker: Materialen zur Soziologie der afro-amerikanischen Musik* (Frankfurt am Main, Germany, Berlin, and Vienna, 1981), 223

R. Gordon: *Jazz West Coast: the Los Angeles Jazz Scene of the 1950s* (London and New York, 1986)

Tough, Dave [David Jaffray] (*b* Oak Park, IL, 26 April 1907; *d* Newark, NJ, 9 Dec 1948). Drummer. As a member of the Austin High School Gang in the mid-1920s he had a formative influence on the Chicago style of white jazz. In the late 1920s he toured Europe, where he made his first recordings (in Berlin, 1927), and took part in numerous recording sessions in New York with Eddie Condon, Red Nichols, and others. He was incapacitated by illness from 1932 to 1935, but thereafter played in Tommy Dorsey's big band (1936–7), replaced Gene Krupa in the Benny Goodman Orchestra (1938), then rejoined Dorsey (1938–9). Tough was a leading drummer of the swing period: two prominent features of his playing with Dorsey – his ride patterns on Chinese cymbal (and later on large Turkish cymbal) and his irregular bass drum figures – were far in advance of their time, becoming widespread only in the bop style of the 1940s. He also adapted to the progressive big-band style as a member of Woody Herman's Herd (1944–5; for illustration *see* HERMAN, WOODY, fig.1*a*). An unusually versatile drummer, he was comfortable in any group. His final years, when not interrupted by ill-health or the effects of alcoholism, were spent in settings as varied as the group led by Charlie Ventura and Bill Harris (i) and the traditional bands of Muggsy Spanier.

SELECTED RECORDINGS

As sideman: New Yorkers: Hoosier Sweetheart (1927, Homokord 42420); T. Dorsey: Marie/Song of India (1937, Vic. 25523); B. Goodman: The Blues in your Flat/The Blues in my Flat (1938, Vic. 26044); B. Freeman: Prince of Wails (1940, Col. 35853); W. Herman: Caldonia (1945, Col. 36789)

BIBLIOGRAPHY

L. Feather: "Dave," *Eddie Condon's Treasury of Jazz*, ed. E. Condon and R. Gehman (New York, 1956/*R*1975), 162

J. Lucas: "Tough Stuff," *JJ*, xii/6 (1959), 5

R. Hadlock: "The Chicagoans," *Jazz Masters of the Twenties* (New York, 1965/*R*1985), 106–44

W. Balliett: "Jazz: Little Davy Tough," *New Yorker*, lxi (18 Nov 1985), 160; repr. in *American Musicians: Fifty-six Portraits in Jazz* (New York, and Oxford, England, 1986), 121

S. Voce: *Woody Herman* (London, 1986)

J. BRADFORD ROBINSON

Toussaint, Jean (*b* Aruba, Lesser Antilles, 27 July 1957). Antillean tenor saxophonist. Brought up in St. Thomas in the Virgin Islands, he played in Boston and studied at the Berklee College of Music (1978–82). From 1982 to 1986 he was a member of Art Blakey's Jazz Messengers, with which he toured internationally; typical of his recordings with the group is the album *Blue Night* (1985, Tim. 217). (I. Gitler: Liner notes, A. Blakey: *Art Blakey Live at Sweet Basil*, 1985, PW 6357)

Towles, Nat (*b* New Orleans, 10 Aug 1905; *d* Berkeley, CA, Jan 1963). Bandleader and double bass player. He first learned guitar and violin, and after changing to double bass worked with the Melody Jazz Band (1922) and Buddy Petit and Henry "Red" Allen (both 1923). In 1923 he formed the Creole Harmony Kings, which played in New Orleans and toured Oklahoma, Texas, and New Mexico (1923–7). During this period he also worked briefly with Fate Marable (*c*1925). He left New Orleans in 1929 as a member of the banjoist Thomas Benton's Seven Black Aces. Thereafter he led his own band in Jackson, Mississippi (1930–33). He assumed leadership in 1935 of a student band at Wiley College, Austin, Texas, with which he performed in Dallas. It held a very successful engagement in Omaha, Nebraska (1936–7), and toured the Southwest; among its members were Money Johnson, Fred Beckett, Henry Coker, Sir Charles Thompson, and Buddy Tate. Although most of his sidemen joined Horace Henderson in 1940, Towles continued to work as a leader; his few recordings include *There you are/Strictly Swing* (1943, Tower 1257). He ceased performing after moving to California in 1959.

BIBLIOGRAPHY

F. S. Driggs: "Kansas City and the Southwest," *Jazz: New Perspectives on the History of Jazz*, ed. N. Hentoff and A. J. McCarthy (New York, 1959/*R*1974), 189

"The (Incomplete) Story of Nat Towles Orchestra," *Jazz Statistics*, no.10 (1959), 8

A. McCarthy: "The Nat Towles Story," *JM*, no.168 (1969), 2

R. Russell: *Jazz Style in Kansas City and the Southwest* (Berkeley, CA, Los Angeles, and London, 1971/*R*1983, rev. 2/1973), 69

A. McCarthy: *Big Band Jazz* (New York and London, 1974), 131

based on *ChiltonW*

Towner, Ralph (N.) (*b* Chehalis, WA, 1 March 1940). Acoustic guitarist. Born into a musical family, he studied trumpet, taught himself piano, and later received a BA in composition from the University of Oregon (1963). He then took up guitar, studying classical technique with Karl Scheit in Vienna in 1963 and again in 1967. After his return to the USA he worked in small jazz groups in New York, mainly as a pianist, before rising to prominence with a notable solo for 12-string guitar issued on Weather Report's *I Sing the Body Electric* (1971). Towner was one of the founders, in 1971, of the group OREGON, with which he has explored a highly individual mixture of classical, rock, jazz, and Indian musics. He is one of the few postwar jazz guitarists to specialize in the acoustic guitar, which he plays with a "pianistic" approach, drawing on the instrument's full range and often carrying on several processes simultaneously in different registers. Although his work is only tenuously connected with jazz, he performs well in duos with jazz musicians. His solo performances, almost always based on his own compositions, unite a wide range of material, from impressionism to folk music, with unusual coherence.

SELECTED RECORDINGS

As unaccompanied soloist: *Diary* (1973, ECM 1032); *Solo Concert* (1979, ECM 1173); *Blue Sun* (1982, ECM 1250)

Duos with G. Burton: *Matchbook* (1974, ECM 1056); *Slide Show* (1985, ECM 1306)

Duos with J. Abercrombie: *Sargasso Sea* (1976, ECM 1080); *Five Years Later* (1981, ECM 1207)

As leader: of Oregon (with P. McCandless, G. Moore, and C. Walcott): *Music of Another Present Era* (1972, Van. 79326); *Solstice* (1974, ECM 1060); of Oregon: *Roots in the Sky* (1979, Elek. 6E224)

As sideman: on Weather Report: *I Sing the Body Electric* (1971–2, Col. KC31352), The Moors

BIBLIOGRAPHY

L. Lyons: "Ralph Towner: Oregon's Classical/Jazz Master," *GP*, ix/12 (1975), 10

C. Mitchell: "Ralph Towner: a Chorus of Inner Voices," *DB*, xlii/12 (1975), 16

J. Reese: "La guitare pianistique de Ralph Towner," *Jh*, no.378 (1980), 10

L. Nowakowski: "Ralph Towner: Acoustic Eclectic," *DB*, 1/5 (1983), 14

J. BRADFORD ROBINSON

Town Hall. Concert hall in New York, which was used frequently for performances of jazz; *see* NIGHTCLUBS AND OTHER VENUES.

Tracey, Stan(ley William) (*b* London, 30 Dec 1926). English pianist and composer. He was largely self-taught, and first worked as a professional musician at the age of 16. During the 1950s he played in various bands, including those led by Kenny Baker, Tony Crombie, Ronnie Scott, and Ted Heath (1957–9). As house pianist at Ronnie Scott's club from 1960 to 1967 he worked with a large number of visiting American soloists, notably Zoot Sims, Sonny Rollins, and Ben Webster. Up to the mid-1960s Tracey had performed as a pianist (and occasionally as a vibraphonist), apparently influenced by the work of Thelonious Monk and Duke Ellington, but at this point it became apparent that he was not only a remarkable soloist, his style pungent, percussive, and harmonically daring, but also an exceptionally original composer. In 1964 he established a quartet which included Bobby Wellins, and the following year, with this ensemble, he recorded his suite based on Dylan Thomas's *Under Milk Wood*, a work generally considered a masterpiece of British jazz. Thereafter Tracey wrote a number of suites for big band, notably *Alice in Jazzland* (1966), *Seven Ages of Man* (1969), and *Genesis* (1987), many of which he recorded on his own label, Steam (established in 1965). He also made arrangements of some of Ellington's compositions (recorded on the album *We Love You Madly*, 1968, Col. SX6320). For much of

Stan Tracey (right) and Gil Evans in London during an interview at Radio London's studios, February 1978

the early 1970s he composed for and played in small groups, and during a short period improvised in the free-jazz manner, although his work retained its highly individual harmonic character. From 1976 to 1985 Tracey led an octet, and in 1979 he formed a sextet, later known as Hexad; he has also worked regularly in duos with such musicians as Tony Coe, Alan Skidmore, Mike Osborne, Keith Tippett, and John Surman, with his quartet (which from 1978 has comprised Art Themen, Roy Babbington, and Tracey's son, the drummer Clark Tracey), and with his orchestra. He has taught at Goldsmiths' College and the Guildhall School of Music. In 1986 he was awarded the OBE.

Oral history material in *GBLnsa*.

RECORDED COMPOSITIONS
(selective list)

As unaccompanied soloist: on *Stan Tracey . . . in Person* (1966, Col. SX6124), Let them crevulate

As leader: on *Little Klunk* (1959, Vogue 160155), Little Klunk; *Under Milk Wood* (1965, Col. 33SX1774), incl. Cockle Row, No good boyo, Under Milk Wood; *Alice in Jazzland* (1966, Col. SX6051), incl. Afro-Charlie meets the white rabbit; *Seven Ages of Man* (1969, Col. SCX6413); *Salisbury Suite* (1977, Steam 105); *Crompton Suite* (1981, Steam 109); *The Poets' Suite* (1984, Steam 111); *Genesis* (1987, Steam 114)

BIBLIOGRAPHY

Feather '60s; *Feather–Gitler '70s*

M. Jones: "Tracey: So Busy Doing Nothing," *MM* (15 Oct 1966), 8

S. Tracey: "Freedom is Nothing without Self-discipline," *CI*, xiv/1 (1975), 24

R. Cotterrell, ed.: *Jazz Now: the Jazz Centre Society Guide* (London, 1976)

J. Solothurnmann: "Stan Tracey," *JF* [intl edn], no.46 (1977), 44 [incl. discography]

CHARLES FOX/DIGBY FAIRWEATHER

Track. (1) The groove in a phonograph disc; *see* Recording, §1.

(2) One of two or more discrete musical items on a single side of a disc, hence by extension such items on an EP (*see* Recording, §I, 3(ii)) or any form of Album. On microgroove discs the items are normally but not always marked off by narrow bands that carry an unmodulated spiral groove.

(3) One of two or more paths on magnetic recording tape receiving information from a single input channel; hence by extension the single voice or line recorded, whether on tape or by digital means. *See* Recording, §I, 3.

Trad. A style of traditional jazz current in Britain between the mid-1950s and the early 1960s. The term was applied to a particularly commercial and simplified form of revivalist jazz which was modeled on the serious attempts of Ken Colyer and Chris Barber to re-create New Orleans styles. Trad bands followed the instrumentation of New Orleans groups (trumpet, trombone, clarinet, banjo, double bass, and drums); the principal and most influential were those of Barber, Acker Bilk, and Kenny Ball. Their repertory was bland, ranging from jazz interpretations of popular songs and nursery rhymes (such as Barber's *Bobby Shaftoe*, 1954, Decca F10492) to cloying, sentimental clarinet solos, notably those of Monty Sunshine (with Barber) and Bilk, whose greatest hit was his theme music for the television series "Stranger on the Shore." The brief vogue for trad resulted in part from shrewd marketing techniques, which featured such anachronistic touches as the association of Bilk's band with bowler hats and Victorian waistcoats.

A number of bands were formed to exploit the commercial potential of trad, but they proved short-lived, and after riots at the Beaulieu Festival in 1961 and the rift between supporters of traditional and modern styles of jazz, the repertory lost popularity. Some elements of the style have remained in use in continental Europe (notably in West Germany and the Netherlands), but trad in its strict sense was a spent force by 1965.

BIBLIOGRAPHY

R. Harris: *Jazz* (London, 1952, 5/1957)

——: *Enjoying Jazz* (London, 1961)

I. Berg, I. Yeomans, and N. Brittan: *Trad: an A to Z Who's Who of the British Traditional Jazz Scene* (London and elsewhere, 1962)

B. Matthew: *Trad Mad* (London, 1962)

G. Melly: *Revolt into Style: the Pop Arts in Britain* (London, 1970)

ALYN SHIPTON

Trade. In jazz to divide a chorus between or among solo players, so that each takes a phrase in turn. The length of phrases traded is usually four bars, but eight-bar and two-bar phrases and even single bars are also treated in this way; the players are said to "trade fours" ("eights," "twos," "ones"). *See* Forms, §1(ii); *see also* Chase.

Traditional jazz. A term that arose in polemical writings of the late 1930s to distinguish New orleans jazz of the 1920s from the swing style of the 1930s; it was later applied to the music of New Orleans revival groups, and is now used almost exclusively in that sense. Beginning in 1938, four forces led to a revival of a supposedly authentic New Orleans style: first, several nationally prominent black jazz musicians (Sidney Bechet, Jelly Roll Morton, and Jimmie Noone) were recorded playing a purportedly traditional repertory using traditional instrumentation; second, a significant number of white musicians, both in the USA (Turk Murphy and Lu Watters in San Francisco) and elsewhere, turned to recordings of New Orleans jazz of the 1920s for models (during the 1980s, in an attempt to re-create earlier performance practice, some groups using instruments of the period played exact transcriptions of recordings); third, a number of older black New Orleans musicians who had never or rarely played outside Louisiana were recorded by white aficionados; finally, older Dixieland jazz musicians, many of whom had retired to New Orleans, were recorded from the mid-1950s, often under the auspices of the New Orleans Jazz Club. The music of the third group (beginning with the recordings made under Kid Rena's leadership in 1940 and continuing with those of Bunk Johnson and George Lewis (i)) has come to be regarded as the authentic bearer of the New Orleans tradition of jazz, which is thought to continue in the music still played at Preservation Hall, New Orleans. However, this revival style, often excellent in its own right, was a locally evolved idiom that responded to market forces (an appetite for folklore, nostalgia, and primitivism), rather than a resurrection of a type of music that was originally more cosmopolitan and technically demanding. Whatever the case, the traditional jazz movement has a very large and devoted audience and many active performers, especially outside the USA, with an eclectic repertory and performing style.

See also Jazz (i), §§IV, 7, V, 10.

BIBLIOGRAPHY

Second Line (1948–)

W. L. Grossman and J. W. Farrell: *The Heart of Jazz* (New York, 1956/*R*1976)

A. J. McCarthy: "The Re-emergence of Traditional Jazz," *Jazz: New Perspectives on the History of Jazz*, ed. N. Hentoff and A. J. McCarthy (New York, 1959/*R*1974), 303

Footnote (1969–)

Mississippi Rag (1973–)

T. Stagg and C. Crump: *New Orleans, the Revival: a Tape and Discography of Negro Traditional Jazz Recorded in New Orleans or by New Orleans Bands, 1937–1972* (n.p. [London], 1973)

T. Ikegami: *New Orleans Renaissance on Record* (Tokyo, 1980) [discography]

LAWRENCE GUSHEE

Traill, (Eric) Sinclair [Sinc] (*b* Camborne, England, Dec 1904; *d* Brighton, England, 10 Jan 1981). English writer and editor. After a brief career in banking he began to write about jazz, and with Bill Elliott he developed the feature "Collector's Corner" for *Melody Maker*. During World War II he served with the RAF in India, where he produced a program for the radio network of the armed forces, then moved to London, where from 1946 to 1947 he published the magazine *Pick Up*. He is best known for having edited *Jazz Journal* (from 1977 known as *Jazz Journal International*) from May 1948 until his death. As an editor Traill won respect for his taste, tact, fairness, humor, and considerable flamboyance.

WRITINGS
(selective list)

ed.: *Play that Music: a Guide to Playing Jazz* (London, 1956)
ed.: *Concerning Jazz* (London, 1957)
ed. with G. Lascelles: *Just Jazz* (London, 1957–60) [four annual vols.: D. Coller and E. Townley: *Jazz Discography, 1956* [–*1957*]; F. Dutton and E. Townley: *Jazz Discography, 1958*; G. Cherrington: *Jazz Discography, 1959/60*]
with E. Kirkeby and D. P. Schiedt: *Ain't Misbehavin': the Story of Fats Waller* (London and New York, 1966)

BIBLIOGRAPHY

Obituary, R. Laing and others, *JJI*, xxxiv/3 (1981), 4

ROBERT GANNON

Tram. Nickname of FRANKIE TRUMBAUER.

Transcription (i). In jazz the act of fixing in notated form music that is entirely or partly improvised, or for which no written score exists; also the resulting notated version itself. The term is also applied to the traditional practice of memorizing and reproducing a recorded improvisation without necessarily notating it. It should not be confused with TRANSCRIPTION (ii), the process of copying sound from one source to another, or TRANSCRIPTION (iii), a type of sound recording. This article deals with the principles, purposes, techniques, and history of transcription and discusses its value as a means of disseminating jazz and as a tool for studying it. For a discussion of the ways in which transcribers have adapted the symbols of standard Western notation to jazz *see* NOTATION, §4.

1. Introduction. 2. Techniques and applications. 3. History.

1. INTRODUCTION. As with other forms of music transmitted by oral tradition, there was little need initially for jazz to be notated. Much of it was improvised or relied on certain musical conventions – melodic patterns, chord progressions, rhythmic devices – known to and shared by players and learned through imitation. Although musicians might glean similar principles of melodic, harmonic, and rhythmic transformation from published compositions (e.g., theme and variations, arrangements of popular songs), they could absorb the distinctive sounds of jazz and the specific techniques of jazz improvisation only through listening to the music.

The first musicians who wished to learn jazz had to find ways to translate the music they heard into something they could play. Most commonly they achieved this by developing their aural memory – by learning something in one context and attempting to re-create it later in another; by imitating phrases played by teachers or colleagues; and by copying parts directly from recordings or piano rolls, often by slowing down the speed at which these were being played and repeating passages many times. Many musicians who engaged in such activities had no need of notation, but some found it a useful bridge between the acts of listening and performing; by notating a solo, a player might come to understand the basic principles of improvisation and thereby generate fresh, original statements. Thus transcriptions facilitated analysis as well as performance.

2. TECHNIQUES AND APPLICATIONS. Transcription as practiced by jazz musicians is usually a self-taught skill. There are no fixed rules for transcribing jazz, nor is there a standard set of symbols used to indicate pitch inflection, articulation, rhythmic deviation, and other expressive devices. Transcription is merely an extension of the technique, learned by every music student, of taking aural dictation, in which it is necessary to listen accurately, to construe analytically, and to notate. Repetition is an integral part of the process; accordingly, tape recorders are generally easier to work with than record players, and reel-to-reel machines offer more flexibility than do cassette players. Variable speed settings and a graphic equalizer may assist the transcriber to perceive rapid passages and cloudy textures.

Transcription becomes considerably more complicated for those wishing to study jazz. Unlike performing musicians, who may adopt an attitude of practical efficiency towards transcription, scholars have been concerned to bring a high level of detail and scientific rigor to the task. These different approaches roughly follow Charles Seeger's categories of "prescriptive" and "descriptive" notation (described in his article in *Musical Quarterly*, 1958), and also reflect the different philosophies behind performing and study editions. Whereas the player might intuitively know how to interpret or adjust notated rhythms to make them sound like the rhythms in a recorded performance, the scholar is interested in describing them as precisely as possible; in an effort to give a faithful graphic representation of an aural document, scholarly transcriptions therefore tend to exhibit a plethora of signs and symbols. Yet ironically, the more the transcriber travels in the direction of accuracy and precision, the more he or she departs from a score that may actually have been used in performance or one that can easily be read and interpreted in the future.

Western notation is weak in its ability to represent the rhythms and timbres of jazz. Thomas Owens (1974) made a preliminary attempt to analyze a solo by Charlie Parker using a melograph model C (an electronic instrument that produces graphic representation of a melody), but his results were inconclusive. Owens found that the machine (which was designed by Seeger) could reveal valuable information concerning pitch phrasing, duration of note-values, and vibrato; however, it was unable to measure timbre and, owing to the "extreme rhythmic complexity of Parker's improvised melody," revealed a high margin of error in reading pitches.

Milton Stewart and Richmond Browne, building on the hand graph method described by Bruno Nettl in *Theory and Method in Ethnomusicology* (New York, 1964), proposed a "grid" notation to help show more clearly the rhythmic displacement in an improvised solo. This makes use of vertical lines of different lengths within bars to indicate subdivisions of the beat, and then positions the pitches of a solo in relation to the lines. Stewart also added superscript symbols designed to give "a clear visual representation of articulation patterns and the resultant structures" (1982). But the resulting transcriptions, while in theory more accurate, are difficult to use. Neither the melograph nor the grid notation system has been widely adopted by transcribers of jazz; it is possible, however, that computer-aided transcription will yield a greater degree of precision in measuring the parameters of the music.

Yet no matter how much transcribers aim for accuracy, consistent notational practice, and expressive detail in their scores, the goal of capturing the essential element of jazz on paper may ultimately remain elusive; somehow it is a process at odds with the aesthetic values of the music and the creative spirit of its practitioners. Lee Castle acknowledged this problem and spoke for all transcribers in his preface to *Louis Armstrong's Immortal Trumpet Solos* (New York, 1947) when he wrote, "I have tried to compile what I think to be typical Louis. It wasn't easy, for black dots on white paper just can't express what's in his soul." And in many instances players have found it impossible to reproduce their own solos: James Moody, for example, on examining a transcription of his recording of *Cherokee*, exclaimed good-humoredly, "I don't even know how to play all those things" (1973).

3. History. While many professional jazz musicians regard transcription as an integral part of their own education, few have discussed the transcribing process in any detail (though Andrew White presents an account of his approach to the subject in *A Treatise on Transcription*, 1978); writers on jazz have also largely passed over the subject. As a result the history of jazz transcription still awaits fuller documentation and can be suggested only in broad outline. The informal process of transcribing jazz – copying solos or individual parts from recordings – probably began as soon as the latter became available, in the late 1910s. Even earlier, players had engaged in the same activity as they strove to emulate what they heard others perform in clubs, cabarets, and dance halls, at parades, and on riverboats. Recordings, however, made it easier for musicians to absorb other ideas and techniques, and at least one major figure, Freddie Keppard, supposedly resisted making them for fear that rivals would steal his tricks.

From the 1920s professional jazz musicians have used the transcribing process to learn from other professionals. When Charlie Parker, at the age of 16, worked in the band led by George E. Lee, he reportedly played solos taken from recordings made by Lester Young. (David Baker, at Indiana University, and other contemporary jazz educators maintain the tradition when they require students to memorize improvisations by Young, Parker, Armstrong, and other outstanding soloists.)

Another application of the technique has been common in big bands, in which musicians have been obliged to re-create solos they or others have played in earlier performances: Tommy Dorsey, for example, required Buddy DeFranco constantly to reproduce the first solo he had improvised on *Opus no.1*, and Thad Jones cited the onus of repeating his original solo on *April in Paris* (with its interpolation of *Pop Goes the Weasel*) as a reason for his leaving Count Basie's orchestra. New members of bands with a long history of recording – such as that led by Duke Ellington – were often expected to know important solos played by their predecessors and to reproduce them as an act of homage; this was also an acknowledgment that such solos helped define the identity of the piece in question as well as the ensemble itself. Several trumpeters in bands led by Fletcher Henderson, Benny Goodman, and others paid lip service to King Oliver's solo on *Dippermouth Blues* when they performed *Sugar Foot Stomp*. The same respect for instrumentalists has been shown by singers, among them Eddie Jefferson, King Pleasure, and Jon Hendricks, who have set lyrics to notable recorded solos, and by groups such as Supersax, which has specialized in performing arrangements of Parker's improvisations.

It is not possible to define precisely the moment when transcriptions were first notated. A signal event, however, was the appearance in 1927 of two collections of Louis Armstrong's improvisations, *50 Hot Choruses for Cornet* and *125 Jazz Breaks for Cornet*, published by Melrose Brothers of Chicago. The former publication claimed in its foreword that it differed from others of its type: "The solos in this book depart in principle of production from any solos on the market. They are genuine improvisations obtained, not by the old method of the artist writing down his solos one note at a time, but from actual recordings." Armstrong supposedly recorded his improvisations in the Melrose offices, where presumably a staff member notated them. Although no copy of these recordings has been traced, the "hot choruses" in the collection do bear a resemblance to the work of Armstrong in the late 1920s, so perhaps the publisher's claim may be believed. The foreword also made clear the practical application of the solos: "All that is necessary is to place this book on the music stand next to the orchestration – then when the orchestration reaches the cornet strain read your book instead of the orchestration." In the same way, *125 Jazz Breaks for Cornet* offered the jazz soloist solutions that Armstrong himself had employed, or might employ, in the relevant context.

In 1927 Melrose also advertised collections of solo breaks by Benny Goodman and Glenn Miller and arrangements of solos by Frankie Trumbauer, Ted Lewis, Jelly Roll Morton, Goodman, Miller, and Armstrong. Some of these publications may have involved the use of transcription, but it is difficult to determine how much; the arrangers employed by Melrose, and other publishers, may have been working from lead sheets, orchestrations, actual recordings, their own imagination, or any combination of these. Indeed, when staff arrangers produced sheet music or orchestrated versions of jazz pieces that had already been recorded, they sometimes incorporated solos taken from the recording. Examples of this may be found in sheet-music versions of Duke Ellington's *The Creeper* and *Birmingham Breakdown* published by Gotham Music Service in 1927.

In the 1930s transcriptions began to appear in periodicals aimed at jazz musicians, such as *Metronome* and *Down Beat*; Armstrong's *West End Blues* was the first transcribed solo to be published in the latter, in 1936. As writers turned their attention to jazz subjects they sometimes used transcriptions to illustrate their points. An early instance of this may be found in Roger Pryor Dodge's article "Jazz Trumpets and Harpsichords" (*Hound and Horn*, 1934), in which the author transcribed several versions of Bubber Miley's trumpet solo on different recordings of Ellington's *Black and Tan Fantasy*. Many transcribed music examples appeared in Winthrop Sargeant's *Jazz, Hot & Hybrid* (1938), and the composer Lou Harrison helped with notation in Rudi Blesh's history of jazz *Shining Trumpets* (1946).

The early 1940s saw the publication of a number of folios of transcriptions (or what were advertised as transcriptions). Like the volumes published in the 1920s, these were intended for players who wished to imitate their musical idol, or at least to perform in a style that was strongly identified with a particular soloist. The Robbins Music Corporation issued a series devoted to pianists, among them Teddy Wilson, Earl Hines, Bob Zurke, Fats Waller, Mary Lou Williams, Willie "the Lion" Smith, and Art Tatum. Some of these folios included the word "transcription" in their titles, while others used "arrangement" or a similar euphemism (for example, *Teddy Wilson Piano Patterns*, *Rube Bloom Piano Impressions*). Again, the question of whether these publications contained actual transcriptions or merely arrangements in the style of major figures has yet to be fully answered. The uniform length of most of the solos raises doubts about authenticity; whereas the average recorded or live performance would be fairly extended, the published versions often end tidily after one or two choruses.

Other publishing firms that issued folios of transcriptions were M. M. Cole in Chicago and Harms and Leeds in New York. Leeds published a major series of solos by boogie-woogie and blues pianists and also collections of "warm-up exercises" by such artists as Rex Stewart and J. C. Higginbotham; the volume by the last named was said to contain "exact transcriptions from original recordings made by J. C. Higginbotham." The practice of identifying the soloist as the transcriber was unusual, and frequently the identity of the transcriber (or arranger) was not revealed; when in 1947 Leeds issued *Louis Armstrong's Immortal Trumpet Solos*, however, the transcriber was a well-known trumpeter and admirer of Armstrong, Lee Castle, who also wrote a preface to the collection.

As jazz education burgeoned in the 1960s and 1970s, there was a corresponding growth in the publication of transcriptions. The second of John Mehegan's four volumes on jazz improvisation, *Jazz Rhythm and the Improvised Line* (1962), consists largely of transcribed solos by artists ranging from Bessie Smith to Oscar Peterson. Some enterprising transcribers, such as Jamie Aebersold and Andrew White, started their own mail-order distribution services, while others, including Don Sickler, Dave Berger, and Alan Campbell, have had their transcriptions issued by major publishing firms; many more, however, work in isolation and do not circulate their scores beyond a limited geographical area.

While in the 1980s transcriptions continue to serve a practical pedagogical function, their use has broadened through the jazz repertory movement and also through the gradually awakening interest in jazz shown by musicologists and music theorists. Transcriptions are essential for musicians active in jazz repertory groups, which aim to re-create past styles and recorded performances, since in many cases the original scores (or any other kind of written parts the players may have used) are unavailable or have been lost. The accuracy of such transcriptions, as well as their faithfulness to the original recordings and flexibility of interpretation, varies considerably, depending on the musicians involved and the context in which they are performing. Among the major figures who have been involved in jazz repertory are Gunther Schuller (who has transcribed and performed compositions by Morton, Ellington, and others), Chuck Israels (leader of the National Jazz Ensemble), Martin Williams (who organized the Smithsonian Jazz Repertory Ensemble), Gary Giddins and John Lewis (who formed the American Jazz Orchestra), and Doug Richards and Andrew Homzy (both of whom have established successful repertory ensembles in colleges).

Transcriptions intended for the purpose of study rather than performance may be found in musicological and theoretical dissertations on jazz; among these are works by Thomas Owens on Charlie Parker, Charles Blancq on Sonny Rollins, Lewis Porter on John Coltrane, Franz Kerschbaumer on Miles Davis, Barry Kernfeld on Cannonball Adderley, Coltrane, and Davis, Scott DeVeaux on Coleman Hawkins and Howard McGhee, Ron Radano on Anthony Braxton, Mark Tucker on Duke Ellington, Felicity Howlett on Art Tatum, Steve Larsen on versions of Thelonious Monk's *'Round Midnight*, and Greg Smith on Bill Evans (ii). Some published works are also notable for their inclusion of transcriptions – for example, Schuller's *Early Jazz* (1968), Brian Priestley's *Mingus: a Critical Biography* (1982), and *Benny Carter: a Life in American Music* (1982) by M. Berger, E. Berger, and J. Patrick – as are such periodicals as the *Annual Review of Jazz Studies*, the *Journal of Jazz Studies*, and *Jazzforschung*.

In the mid-1980s only one major scholarly edition of transcriptions had appeared – James Dapogny's *Ferdinand "Jelly Roll" Morton: the Collected Piano Music* (1982). This volume represents a landmark in the history of jazz transcription and is exemplary in its thoroughness, attention to detail, and high editorial standards; it is a source intended for both study and performance, and thus accommodates the aims of scholars as well as those involved with repertory.

BIBLIOGRAPHY

C. Seeger: "Prescriptive and Descriptive Music Writing," *Musical Quarterly*, xliv/2 (1958), 184

"James Moody's solo 'Cherokee'," *DB*, xl/15 (1973), 38

T. Owens: "Applying the Melograph to 'Parker's Mood'," *Selected Reports in Ethnomusicology*, ii/1 (1974), 167

A. N. White, III: *A Treatise on Transcription* (Washington, 1978)

M. L. Stewart: "Grid Notation: a Notation System for Jazz Transcription," *ARJS*, i (1982), 3

T. S. Koger: "Fifty Years of *Downbeat* Solo Jazz Transcriptions: a Register," *Black Music Research Journal* (1985), 43

D. Morgenstern: "Comments on Fifty Years of *Downbeat* Solo Jazz Transcriptions," *Black Music Research Journal* (1986), 23

MARK TUCKER

Transcription (ii). The process of copying sound from one source to another; also the result of such a process; in some cases the term is synonymous with "dubbing" (and "dub"). It is applied to a number of types of recording: for example, to one made from the radio (*see* AIR CHECK); to one made from a performance that is broadcast – in which case the recording is made simultaneously with the broadcast but not from the radio (and may or may not be used as a transcription in the sense described in TRANSCRIPTION (iii)); and to the converting of a recording made by analogue means (e.g., a multitrack magnetic tape recording) into a digital recording.

Transcription [broadcast transcription] **(iii).** A recording (on disc or tape) produced for sale or distribution to radio stations for broadcasting. The term is commonly applied only to discs. Almost all such "transcriptions" are recorded specially in the studio (as, for example, in the case of sessions by Fats Waller and Clarence Williams for Lang–Worth and by Roy Eldridge and Louis Jordan for World), but some derive from performances broadcast live and simultaneously recorded, and a few (chiefly those made by AFRS) from commercially available recordings. In the 1930s and 1940s broadcast transcriptions were recorded on 16-inch discs that played at $33\frac{1}{3}$ r.p.m., allowing up to 15 minutes of playing time; some were recorded from the center outwards (a technique known as "center start"), rather than from the rim inwards (the conventional "rim-start" technique); and many were cut vertically at a time when commercial discs were cut laterally. These characteristics together had the incidental advantage that the recordings could not be played except on equipment available in radio stations. However, the advantages of exclusivity were quickly sacrificed by transcription companies once microgroove recordings, which offered superior reproduction, became available.

For a short period in the early years of sound films, before the development of optical methods of recording sound on film, transcription technology (i.e., the 16-inch disc recorded at $33\frac{1}{3}$ r.p.m.) was used to provide synchronized soundtracks. Thus in a few cases soundtracks are preserved independently of the films to which they belong; an example is Duke Ellington's *Black and Tan Fantasy* (1929), the soundtrack of which is preserved on an RKO transcription disc.

The term "transcription turntable" is sometimes applied to a turntable used for playing microgroove recordings, which shares certain technical characteristics with the turntables used by radio stations to play broadcast transcriptions in the 1930s and 1940s.

See also RECORDING, esp. §II, 3.

Transition. Record company and label. The company was established by Tom Wilson in Cambridge, Massachusetts, in 1955. Though it remained in existence only for about two years it established an important reputation by enabling Donald Byrd, Cecil Taylor, Herb Pomeroy, Jay Migliori, Doug Watkins, and Sun Ra to make their first recordings as leaders. Around 20 albums were issued, including three by Byrd and one by Johnny Windhurst, as well as Curtis Fuller's studio début. The company also sponsored sessions by Fuller that included John Coltrane, but only issued one of the four tracks that resulted; the remaining material was later issued by Blue Note under Coltrane's name. Rather than liner notes, the albums were accompanied by booklets that contained information about the music. Transition's catalogue was acquired around 1958 by United Artists, for whom Wilson was by that time working as a producer. Some of the repertory was issued in different formats by Esquire in England; other items were put out by Delmark. From 1979 several of Transition's albums were released in Japan in replicas of the original packages.

MARK GARDNER

Trappier, Art(hur Benjamin) [Traps] (*b* Georgetown, SC, 28 May 1910; *d* New York, 17 May 1975). Drummer. He first played professionally in New York with the pianist Charlie Skeete (1928), and worked there in the 1930s with Tiny Bradshaw, Blanche Calloway, and Buddy Johnson. He first recorded in 1939 with the clarinetist and alto saxophonist Skeets Tolbert. After extensive work with Fats Waller in 1941–2 (for illustration *see* WALLER, FATS), he performed and recorded with a number of other traditional and swing musicians, among them Wilbur De Paris and James P. Johnson (both 1944), Edmond Hall (1944–5), Louis Armstrong (1945), Sy Oliver and Albert Nicholas (both 1947), Ralph Sutton (1948, 1950), Tony Parenti and Wingy Manone (both 1949), Hot Lips Page and Sidney Bechet (both 1950–51), and Willie "the Lion" Smith (1957). During the 1950s and 1960s Trappier also played with various dixieland bands, including his own; he continued as a freelance player in the New York area until his death. His recordings demonstrate his unobtrusive, subtle style.

SELECTED RECORDINGS

Duos with R. Sutton: *Bix Beiderbecke Suite* (1950, Com. 30001)

As sideman: F. Waller: We Need a Little Love/The Jitterbug Waltz (1942, Bb 11518); Swing Out to Victory (1942, Bb 11569)

BIBLIOGRAPHY

ChiltonW; *FeatherE*

T. DENNIS BROWN

Trap set. *See* DRUM SET.

Travis, Nick [Travascio, Nicholas Anthony] (*b* Philadelphia, 16 Nov 1925; *d* New York, 7 Oct 1964). Trumpeter. After playing with Vido Musso (1942) and Woody Herman (intermittently, 1942–4) he performed in Paris during his military service. He then worked with Ray McKinley (intermittently, 1946–50), Benny Goodman (1948–9), Gene Krupa and Ina Ray Hutton (both late 1940s), Tommy Dorsey and Tex Beneke (both 1950), Herman (1950–51), Jerry Gray, Bob Chester, and Elliot Lawrence (all 1951), and Jimmy Dorsey (1952–3). He was a principal soloist in the Sauter–Finegan Orchestra from 1953 to 1956; the following year he became a member of the NBC staff in New York, and he was active into the 1960s as a studio musician. From 1960 to 1962 he toured and recorded with Gerry Mulligan's Concert Jazz Orchestra, and in 1963 he played with a ten-piece band led by Thelonious Monk at Lincoln Center and Carnegie Hall. Travis was considered an excellent and versatile trumpeter with a strong, clear tone; he spent most of his career playing in big bands, but may be heard as a bop soloist on recordings with the quintets led by Al Cohn and Zoot Sims and also as the leader of his own quintet.

SELECTED RECORDINGS

As leader: *The Panic is On* (1954, RCA LPM1010)

As sideman: A. Cohn: *Al Cohn with Nick Travis, Horace Silver, Curley Russell, and Max Roach* (1953, Prog. 3004); E. Sauter and B. Finegan: *Inside Sauter–Finegan* (1953, RCA LPM1003); E. Lawrence: *Swinging at the Steel Pier* (1956, Fan. 3236); Z. Sims: *Zoot!* (1956, Riv. 228); M. Albam: *The Jazz Giants of our Time* (1957, Coral 57173); W. Herman: *The Herd Rides Again* (1958, Ev. 5003)

BIBLIOGRAPHY

FeatherE

Obituary, *DB*, xxxi/30 (1964), 10

FREDERICK A. BECK

Travo, Manuel. Pseudonym of DAVID BEE.

Traxler, Gene [Eugene F.] (*b* Chambersburg, PA, 28 June 1913). Double bass player. After leading his own seven-piece band in high school he worked with local groups in the early 1930s and played in Baltimore and Buffalo. He recorded with Joe Venuti in 1934, and then worked with Joe Haymes; from 1935 to 1940 he played and sang with Tommy Dorsey's band. Thereafter he performed in New York at the Hickory House with Joe Marsala, with whom he made recordings (including *Three o'Clock Jump/Reunion in Harlem*, 1940, General 3001). He also worked as a studio musician for NBC (*c*1942–5) and recorded with Benny Goodman (1944). From 1945 to 1972 Traxler played in the band for the "Arthur Godfrey Show" on CBS; in 1956 he recorded with Connee Boswell. He performed with a show band in Florida from 1972 to 1978, when he retired. (H. Sanford: *Tommy and Jimmy: the Dorsey Years*, New Rochelle, NY, 1972)

Traynor, Frank [Thomas Francis] (*b* Melbourne, Australia, 8 Aug 1927; *d* Melbourne, 22 Feb 1985). Australian trombonist. After making his début as a jazz musician on piano (1944) he changed to trombone, and performed and recorded with Len Barnard (1949–55). In 1956 he formed the Jazz Preachers, which he led until his death. The band toured regularly, and made many recordings of traditional jazz, some of which were issued in Europe and North America as well as Australia; the most commercially successful of these was the single *Sweet Patootie* (1962, W&G 1524), which was a hit in Australia. In 1961 he opened Frank Traynor's, a folk and jazz club in Melbourne, which became known internationally. He was an important figure in the revival of traditional jazz in the 1950s and 1960s, organizing concerts and festivals, and teaching, as well as performing and recording.

BIBLIOGRAPHY

A. Bisset: *Black Roots, White Flowers: a History of Jazz in Australia* (Sydney, 1979)

B. Johnson and others: *The Oxford Companion to Australian Jazz* (Melbourne, Australia, 1987)

TONY GOULD

Treadwell, George (McKinley) (*b* New Rochelle, NY, 21 Dec 1919; *d* New York, 14 May 1967). Trumpeter. After performing in the house band at Monroe's Uptown House, New York (1941–2), he joined Benny Carter's orchestra on the West Coast (late

1942). He then worked with the pianist Ace Harris and the Sunset Royals and Tiny Bradshaw and performed and made several recordings with Cootie Williams (1943–6). In 1946–7, while a member of J. C. Heard's group, he met Sarah Vaughan, whom he married in 1947; during this period he recorded with Heard (notably *The Walk/Heard but not Seen*, 1946, Contl 6022), and also with Dicky Wells and Ethel Waters (both 1946) and Vaughan (1946, 1947). He ceased playing trumpet to become Vaughan's manager, a role which he retained after their divorce. In the 1950s he also managed such rhythm-and-blues musicians as the Drifters and Ruth Brown, worked as an artists and repertory agent, and wrote songs (from 1959). (*ChiltonW*; *FeatherE*)

Trenner, Donn [Donald R.] (*b* New Haven, CT, 10 March 1927). Pianist. He studied classical piano, played in the big band of the songwriter Ted Fiorito (1943–5), and led a military band (1946). With his wife, the singer Helen Carr, he worked in Buddy Morrow's orchestra (1947), led a trio in San Francisco (1948), and performed and recorded with Charlie Barnet (1950–51). From 1952 to 1953 he played with Jerry Gray, Stan Getz, Georgie Auld, and Charlie Parker; his excellent solo playing may be heard in a live performance with Parker (*On the Coast*, 1952, Jazz Showcase 5007). He also recorded with Auld (1952). Trenner performed and recorded with Les Brown at intervals from 1953 to 1960; at the same time he recorded with Dave Pell (1954, 1955), his wife (1955), and Howard McGhee and Betty Roche (1956), worked briefly in New York with Oscar Pettiford and Anita O'Day (1957), and recorded with Frank Capp (1960) and Ben Webster (1961). He was the music director and pianist for Steve Allen's television program (1962–4) and the producer and conductor on Allen's recordings; his sidemen included Conte Candoli, Herb Ellis, and Frank Rosolino. Trenner's composition *Leave it to me*, used by Allen as his commercial-break theme in the 1960s, was recorded on the album *Anita O'Day and the Three Sounds* (1962, Verve 68514). He also recorded as a pianist with Herb Ellis (1963) and as the leader of his own band, which accompanied Nancy Wilson (1968). In the 1970s he was active as a bandleader and music director, and in 1983 played with Gerry Mulligan at a jazz festival in Stockholm. (*FeatherE*; *Feather '60s*)

Trent, Alphonso [Alphonse] **(E.)** (*b* Fort Smith, AR, 24 Aug 1905; *d* Fort Smith, 14 Oct 1959). Bandleader and pianist. He performed in Arkansas and Oklahoma before taking over a small territory band in 1923, which shortly afterwards began a long tenure at the Adolphus Hotel, Dallas. The group's performances, radio broadcasts, and tours made it the most successful and respected of the early southwestern jazz bands. Its recordings of 1928 show a polished ensemble style as advanced as those of Duke Ellington or Fletcher Henderson at that time, and include excellent improvised solos by Stuff Smith, Snub Mosley, and a trumpeter thought to be Peanuts Holland. The group played in New York around 1930 with notable success, but Trent refused further offers to work on the East Coast; he remained based in the Southwest and filled engagements on steamboat lines, a decision which greatly restricted his opportunities to record and the fame that his group might otherwise have attained. The second of two recording sessions, in 1930 and 1933, shows a remarkable ensemble precision and swing, which influenced Jimmie Lunceford later in the decade. Trent's group then disbanded, and from 1934 he led various lesser ensembles in the Southwest, including one in 1938 that featured Charlie Christian.

Advertisement for an appearance of Alphonso Trent and his orchestra at the Showboat, New Lebanon, NY, September 1931

SELECTED RECORDINGS

Louder and Funnier/Gilded Kisses (1928, Gen. 6664); Black and Blue Rhapsody/Nightmare (1928, Gen. 6710); After you've gone/St. James Infirmary (1930, Gen. 7161); Clementine/I've found a new baby (1933, Champion 16587)

BIBLIOGRAPHY

F. Driggs: "Kansas City and the South West," *Jazz: New Perspectives on the History of Jazz*, ed. N. Hentoff and A. J. McCarthy (New York, 1959/*R*1974), 189–231

G. Schuller: *Early Jazz: its Roots and Musical Development* (New York, 1968), 299

R. Russell: *Jazz Style in Kansas City and the Southwest* (Berkeley, CA, Los Angeles, and London, 1971/*R*1983, rev. 2/1973)

A. McCarthy: *Big Band Jazz* (New York and London, 1974), 21

N. W. Pearson, Jr.: *Goin' to Kansas City* (Urbana, IL, and London, 1988)

J. BRADFORD ROBINSON

Triangle. Record label. The catalogue was issued between 1922 and 1925 by the Bridgeport Die & Machine Co. The repertory was mostly derived from the New York Recording Laboratories and included items by Jelly Roll Morton, Fletcher Henderson, and the Original Memphis Five that had previously been put out on Paramount. Some recordings from Emerson's catalogue, and one of Duke Ellington's first recordings as a leader (originally made for Blu-disc) were also released on Triangle.

BIBLIOGRAPHY

C. Kendziora: "Behind the Cobwebs: Triangle," *Record Research*, no.93 (1968), 93

B. Rust: *The American Record Label Book* (New Rochelle, NY, 1978), 295

Trío Argentina. Argentine trio. It was formed in 1984 by the pianist Jorge Navarro, the double bass player Alfredo Remus, and the drummer Pocho Lapouble. The group recorded the albums *Pasando* (1984, EMP 3003) and *Carlitos* (1985, Amadeo 829447-1) with the Austrian saxophonist Karlheinz Miklin, performed regularly in Buenos Aires, and toured Austria and Germany.

LAUREANO FERNÁNDEZ, OMAR GARCÍA BRUNELLI

Trip. Record company and label. The company was established by the producer Fred Norsworthy in Rahway, New Jersey, in 1974. It developed mainly from a licensing agreement with Polydor whereby it reissued material that had originally been put out on EmArcy, Limelight, and Mercury. It also ran a subsidiary label, Up Front. Operations ceased in 1979.

Trippel, Fritz [Little Fritz] (*b* Chur, Switzerland, 10 Dec 1937). Swiss pianist. He studied with Joe Turner (i) in 1954–6 and from 1957 toured Austria, France, Switzerland, the Netherlands, and Germany with such musicians as Albert Nicholas (who gave him the nickname Little Fritz) and Don Byas. After belonging to the Swiss dixieland group the Tremble Kids (1960–61) he joined the orchestra of the vibraphonist and trombonist Kurt Weil (1962) and from 1963 to 1968 toured and recorded as a soloist and in a trio with Wallace Bishop. Later he played in the Far East and Southeast Asia (at intervals from 1969 to 1977); in Chur he has worked not only as a pianist but also as a concert promoter, record producer, and journalist. A good example of Trippel's playing is his recording *Whisky Time* (1964, Phi. 625101).

PETER SCHWALM

Tristano, Lennie [Leonard Joseph] (*b* Chicago, 19 March 1919; *d* New York, 18 Nov 1978). Pianist and teacher. He first studied with his mother, an amateur pianist and opera singer, and later at a school for the blind, where from 1928 to 1938 he learned piano and several wind instruments and received a thorough grounding in music theory. He then entered the American Conservatory in Chicago, graduating with a BMus in 1943. During these years he played piano and wind instruments semiprofessionally in a wide variety of jazz settings and began teaching jazz privately in Chicago. By 1945 he had attracted his first important pupils – Billy Bauer, Lee Konitz, and Bill Russo – and was drawing critical attention with his performances in Chicago clubs. His earliest solo and trio recordings, though not issued until 1977, were made at this time.

In 1946 Tristano moved to New York, where he immediately attracted a cult following. He performed with Charlie Parker and Dizzy Gillespie in concerts and broadcasts, issued his first album as a leader, and was named *Metronome* magazine's "musician of the year" for 1947. (He contributed two articles on bop to the magazine during that year.) In 1948 he acquired an important new pupil in Warne Marsh, and when Konitz and Bauer rejoined him shortly thereafter he had the basis of his now famous sextet. The recordings of this group in 1949 are representative of Tristano's powers as an improviser and group leader at the highest level, but they caused controversy among musicians and sold poorly.

Having by then attracted a large number of private students, in 1951 Tristano founded a school of jazz in New York, the first significant institution of its kind. For his teaching staff he used his most important pupils, including Konitz, Marsh, Bauer, and Sal Mosca. From this point he increasingly withdrew from public life, appearing rarely and issuing only a few experimental recordings as an adjunct to his teaching. He gradually lost his staff as his pupil-disciples embarked on their own careers, and in 1956 he dissolved his school to live in semiseclusion as a private teacher on Long Island. He performed occasionally at the Half Note (between 1958 and 1965) and also toured Europe in 1965, but made his last public appearance in the USA in 1968. In 1973 French television broadcast an hour-long documentary interview on his life and work. After his death many of his recordings were reissued and a number of private tapes made by his students became commercially available.

Tristano's music stands apart from the main tradition of modern jazz, representing an alternative to bop which poses severe demands of ensemble precision, intellectual rigor, and instrumental virtuosity. Rather than the irregular cross-accents of bop, Tristano preferred an even rhythmic background against which to concentrate on line and focus his complex changes of time signature. Typically, his solos consisted of extraordinarily long, angular strings of almost even eighth-notes provided with subtle rhythmic deviations and abrasive polytonal effects. He was particularly adept in his use of different levels of double time and was a master of the block-chord style of George Shearing, Dave Brubeck, and others, carefully gauging the accumulation of dissonance. His experiments in multitrack recording and overdubbing, beginning in 1951 with *Ju-Ju* (not issued until 1971), inspired similar performances by Bill Evans (ii) and others in the 1960s. With his groups he also explored free collective improvisation, most notably in *Intuition* and *Digression* (1949). Although he was accused at the time of being willfully experimental, "free" performances of this sort were in fact part of Tristano's teaching practice (many were taped privately by Bauer) and pointed the way to similar experiments by Charles Mingus and Ornette Coleman in the late 1950s.

Tristano excelled as a teacher, demanding and receiving firm loyalty from his pupils, many of whom sacrificed more lucra-

Lennie Tristano (piano) with Lee Konitz (alto saxophone) and Warne Marsh (tenor saxophone) at the Isis Theater, Indianapolis, September 1959

tive careers to continue their work with him. His method stressed advanced ear training and a close analysis of the work of several seminal jazz improvisers, including Louis Armstrong, Earl Hines, Roy Eldridge, Charlie Parker, and Bud Powell. Because of his knowledge of several instruments and broadminded approach Tristano attracted players of different instruments and schools, among them such established musicians as Bud Freeman, Art Pepper, and Mary Lou Williams. Perhaps more than in his own scant recordings, Tristano's influence is felt most strongly in the work of his best pupils – many of whom also became outstanding teachers – and in his example of high-mindedness and perfectionism, characteristics which presupposed for jazz the highest standards of music as art.

See also PIANO, §§4 and 5.

SELECTED RECORDINGS

Yesterdays (1946, Jazz Guild 1008); Out on a Limb (1946, Key. 647); I surrender dear/Coolin' off with Ulanov (1947, Key. 680); A Ghost of a Chance (1947, Vic. 27-0145); Abstraction (1947, Cupol 9003); Dissonance (1947, Selmer Y7154); Progression/Retrospection (1949, NewJ 832); Subconscious-Lee/Judy (1949, NewJ 80001); Wow/Crosscurrent (1949, Cap. 60003); Yesterdays /Intuition (1949, Cap. 1224); Digression (1949, Cap. EAP1-491); Ju-Ju/Passtime (1951, Jazz 101); *Lennie Tristano* (1955, Atl. 1224); *New York Improvisations* (1955–6, Elek. 96-0264-1); *The New Tristano* (1960–62, Atl. 1357)

BIBLIOGRAPHY

B. Ulanov: "Master in the Making," *Metronome*, lxv/8 (1949), 14
H. Pekar: "Lennie Tristano," *JR*, ii/6 (1960), 13
——: "Lennie Tristano," *JM*, viii/4 (1962), 6
B. Coss: "Lennie Tristano Speaks Out," *DB*, xxix/24 (1962), 19
G. Endress: "Lennie Tristano," *JM*, xi/12 (1966), 21 [interview]
I. Gitler: *Jazz Masters of the Forties* (New York, 1966/R1983 with discography), 226–61
J. Delmas: "Tristano et ses fils," *Jh*, no.325 (1976), 6; no.326 (1976), 6
J. F. McKinney: *The Pedagogy of Lennie Tristano* (diss., Fairleigh Dickinson U., 1978)
C. Sheridan: "Lennie Tristano," *JP*, xxviii/2 (1979), 12
L. Feather: "Piano Giants of Jazz: Lennie Tristano," *CK*, vi/1 (1980), 60
H. Hollenstein: *Lennie Tristano on LPs [sic] Records* (Sierre, Switzerland, 1984) [discography]
R. Beirach: "Lennie Tristano's 'Line Up': the Essence of Bebop from a Neglected Pioneer of Jazz Piano Overdubbing," *Keyboard*, xi/7 (1985), 44
H. Hellhund: *Cool Jazz: Grundzüge seiner Entstehung und Entwicklung* (Mainz, Germany, 1985), 36–148
J. W. Susat: *Discography of the "Uncompromising Lennie Tristano"* (Menden, Germany, 1986)

J. BRADFORD ROBINSON

Trombar, Frank. Pseudonym of FRANKIE TRUMBAUER.

Trombone. A brass instrument of mainly cylindrical bore, with a cup-shaped mouthpiece. It is usually considered the tenor–baritone counterpart of the trumpet.

1. The trombone family. 2. Use.

1. THE TROMBONE FAMILY. In its most familiar form the trombone has a U-shaped telescopic tube known as a slide, by means of which the player alters the sounding length of the instrument's tubing, hence changing the pitch; this form of the instrument is known as the slide trombone. By the 17th century there existed a complete family of soprano, alto, tenor, and bass trombones. The upper and lower limits of the trombone's range are dependent on the player's ability to control his embouchure. The tenor in B♭ became, and has remained (especially in jazz), the most widely used; it has a complete chromatic compass from *E* to around *f''* and, in addition, seven pedal notes – *E'* to *B♭'*. Some players prefer the B♭/F tenor–bass trombone, which has a thumb-operated valve (also known as a "trigger" or "plug") that lowers the pitch of the instrument by a perfect 4th and adds the chromatic pitches between *C* and *E♭* to the compass. The B♭/F/E bass trombone has a second valve that allows a *B♮'* to be played; this second valve also facilitates the playing of fast passages in the lower register. Both the B♭/F and B♭/F/E instruments, when built with a wide bore, may be considered bass trombones. The true bass trombone is larger than the tenor and is capable of producing a more robust, sonorous tone. The lowest pitch regularly used by players of the B♭/F/E tenor–bass trombone and the bass trombone is *C'*, but pitches below *F'* are mainly used only as

held notes. A soprano trombone (often described as a slide cornet) has also been used in jazz very occasionally, principally as a novelty doubling instrument, though more often for photographic poses (for example by Freddie Keppard, *c*1911, for illustration *see* NELSON, BIG EYE LOUIS; and Louis Armstrong, 1923, for illustration *see* OLIVER, KING) than in performance. It is limited by having a slide that moves through only six positions (as opposed to seven on the other members of the trombone family), and its tone compares unfavorably with that of the cornet and trumpet.

The valve trombone (generally a tenor instrument in B♭) was invented in the early 19th century and has a system of valves instead of a slide. The advantages of compactness, and for some purposes a greater technical facility, must be set against the disadvantages of a constant need to correct intonation by changes in embouchure and the greater difficulty of producing a sensitive legato. These intonation problems are compounded on some instruments by the addition of a fourth valve that lowers the compass by a 4th.

Some attempts have been made to produce hybrid instruments with both a slide and valves (as in the trombone duplex made by G. A. Besson, Paris, in the 1840s). These combine the versatility and expressive capabilities of the slide trombone with the technical facility of the valve instrument. On the valide, adopted by Brad Gowans, the slide, though generally locked, can be brought into operation when needed for glissandos and other effects. The superbone, invented by Maynard Ferguson in the 1970s, is a tenor trombone with a large bore that has valves played with the right hand and a slide controlled by the left.

2. USE. While the slide trombone may appear clumsy and the manipulation of the slide cumbersome, the inherent freedom from the fixed pitches of a tonal scale which this allows adapts the instrument well for use in any and all styles of jazz. The ease with which bends, blue notes, and glisses (*see* BEND, BLUE NOTE (i), and GLISS) may be produced on the slide trombone, simply by exploiting its basic technique, contrasts with the difficulty of executing those effects on many other instruments used in jazz. These factors go some way towards explaining the pre-eminence in jazz of the slide trombone over the valve trombone, which though more agile is perhaps less well suited to most styles of jazz. The valve instrument was often used in parade bands, which influenced early jazz, but it had declined in popularity by around 1900 and was not used again widely until the 1940s, when players were faced with the technical demands of bop. An important aspect of jazz trombone playing is the use of different types of mute to produce not only a quieter sound but also a variety of special effects (*see* MUTE, §3).

The trombone, like most instruments in jazz, has both an ensemble and a solo function. In the earliest jazz groups it played a bass line in the polyphonic texture collectively improvised by the melody instruments. In later styles a single trombone in an ensemble usually plays an inner line or doubles the melody played by another instrument (perhaps at the lower octave); a trombone section forms the foundation for the brass grouping.

In the 1920s brass sections usually consisted of two trumpets and one trombone until Henderson (1927) and Ellington (1929) added a second trombone, thus introducing the potential for four-part brass harmony. In the 1930s Ellington's band expanded to include a six-piece brass section (three trumpets and three trombones). Kenton's use of four trombones (with five trumpets) in the 1940s yielded a practical and long-lasting pattern for the big band. This section of four instruments (usually three tenors and one bass) may be used to play a riff in unison; to play as a four-voice unit in combination with the rhythm section, in which case the first or lead tenor trombone would normally play the melody; or to carry inner voices within passages for all the brass and reeds. Even the bass trombone, despite its name, rarely plays bass lines; in a big band the double bass (or electric bass guitar) usually provides the bass line while the bass trombone plays a low-pitched inner voice.

In early jazz and swing styles the trombone was often used as a solo instrument. In later contexts it has sometimes been overshadowed by other instruments, but nonetheless has found a place as a distinctive solo voice in bop and free jazz, and also (though less prominently) in jazz-rock.

The various playing styles of jazz trombonists, whose technical capabilities have possibly improved more markedly over the course of jazz history than those of any other instrumentalists, are connected by clear lines of descent. Blesh observed that the trombone inherited the functions of the baritone and alto horns (*see* SAXHORN) in the early jazz band. As its deeper notes could serve both contrapuntal and rhythmic purposes, the trombone forged an important link between the melody instruments (trumpet and clarinet) and the rhythm section. Syncopated impetus could be achieved with considerable economy of means: Ike Rodgers, who recorded in Chicago (1929–34), is described by Keepnews and Grauer as "a crude trombonist (said to be able to play 'only two notes')." Jim Robinson, who recorded with Sam Morgan in 1927 and later played with the bands of Bunk Johnson and George Lewis (i), demonstrated on *Tishomingo Blues* (1945, Decca 25131), recorded with Johnson, that only a very few more notes were necessary to fulfill the instrument's function in the ensemble – an occasional staccato accent in the appropriate part of the bar was sufficient. Other trombonists, however, gave more prominence to the type of contrapuntal tenor part heard in American military bands of the Civil War period; these more proficient players included Georg Brunis and, in particular, Kid Ory, who exploited the portamento and vibrato effects that form an intrinsic part of the trombone's TAILGATE style. Ory's use of such effects may be heard on his showpiece *Ory's Creole Trombone* (1927, Col. 35838), recorded with Louis Armstrong's Hot Seven, as well as on later recordings such as *Snag it* (1947, Cir. [USA] 12001), recorded with his own band.

Miff Mole is usually considered the first jazz trombonist fully to have mastered the instrument. During his association with Red Nichols (1925–8) he demonstrated both a trumpet-like clarity of attack and an ability to produce a sweet, legato, controlled sound; he is heard to advantage on *Nothing does-does like it used to do-do-do* (1927, PAct 36707), recorded with Nichols's Red Heads. Mole is an acknowledged influence on the trombonists and bandleaders Jack Teagarden, Tommy Dorsey, and Glenn Miller; classical orchestral musicians were also influenced by his technique. Trummy Young, however, felt that Mole displayed a virtuoso command of the instrument at the expense of the jazz content of his playing. Jimmy Harrison, a member of Fletcher Henderson's band from 1926 to 1931, also made a lasting effect on other players; his sonorous tone, bold ideas, and flexible technique led to his being called "the father of swing trombone."

Tricky Sam Nanton, who worked with Ellington from 1926, developed the "growl and plunger" technique to contribute to the "jungle" sound of Ellington's early recordings (*see* JUNGLE MUSIC). When Ellington added a second trombone to his orchestra in 1929 he chose the valve trombonist Juan Tizol, whose tone blended equally well with trumpets and reeds. The duet by Nanton and Tizol on the 1931 version of Ellington's *Creole Rhapsody* (Bruns. 6093) is one of the first recorded trombone duets. Ellington's orchestra demonstrated the range of approaches to the trombone current in jazz when Nanton and Tizol were joined in 1932 by a third distinctive soloist, Lawrence Brown (see illustration), whose playing explored the lyrical and legato possibilities of the slide trombone. Tizol was one of few players to employ the valve trombone before the bop era. Others were the trumpeter Jabbo Smith, who played the valve instrument on his recording of *Lina Blues* (1929, Bruns. 7087), and the cornetist Wild Bill Davison, who between 1933 and 1941 also performed on valve trombone.

Throughout the swing era a variety of styles of trombone playing flourished. Tommy Dorsey was known for his sumptuous interpretations of sentimental ballads; Vic Dickenson was a noted blues player, with a husky tone; J.C. Higginbotham had a rich, powerful, raucous sound, reminiscent of the earlier GUTBUCKET style; and Benny Morton was noted for his controlled vibrato and imaginative improvisations. Louis Armstrong's favorite trombonist was Jack Teagarden, who had an outstanding technique and a strongly personal blues style; his recordings with Armstrong include *Some Day* (1947, Vic. 202530). An element of humor is associated with the styles of many trombonists, including Trummy Young and Dicky Wells; the latter was also known for his legato playing.

While the revival of traditional jazz during the late 1930s and early 1940s embraced a renewed interest in the tailgate style and related approaches to playing, concurrently the bop style evolved from swing, and trombonists took on the new challenge of executing fast-moving bop melodies. Between 1944 and 1950 Bill Harris (i) demonstrated a wide expressive range with a precisely controlled vibrato and almost veiled tone in slow numbers, as well as a new rhythmic vigor in faster ones. The most important trombonist of the period was J. J. Johnson, who showed that fast-moving bop melodies could be played on the slide trombone at a time when the technical demands of the style had resulted in the valve trombone coming back into popular use. He developed a fluid technical facility similar to that of bop saxophonists and comparable with Dizzy Gillespie's mastery of the trumpet. From 1954 to 1956 Johnson performed in a duo with Kai Winding that influenced a whole generation of players; a good example of their playing is *This could be the start of something* from the album *The Great Kai and JJ* (1960, Imp. 1). While players such as Frank Rosolino, Carl Fontana, and Bill Watrous followed their example, the influence of Morton and Teagarden could still be heard in the playing of Bennie Green and Lou McGarity respectively.

Harris and Johnson, and a number of lesser players, occasionally played the valve trombone as well as the slide trombone. Some trombonists, though, concentrated on the valve instrument to the exclusion of the slide trombone. The most notable of these was the West Coast musician Bob Brookmeyer, whose playing is well represented on the album *Stan Getz at the Shrine Auditorium* (1954, Norg. 2000). A notable exponent of the bass trombone in this period was George Roberts, who performed and recorded with the big bands of Gene Krupa (1950) and Stan Kenton (1951–7).

The playing of Slide Hampton, who has used the technique of circular breathing, and of the brilliant Jimmy Knepper, who is best known for his work with Charles Mingus, provided a link between bop and the free-jazz styles of the 1960s. During that decade several European free-jazz musicians, notably Eje Thelin, Paul Rutherford, and Albert Mangelsdorff, came to prominence alongside the American Roswell Rudd. These players, among others, have explored the expressive potential of the trombone by the use of MULTIPHONICS, achieved through adjustments of the embouchure in combination with humming into the instrument. Mangelsdorff has recorded both as an unaccompanied soloist and as a leader; his playing in this

Duke Ellington's trombone section, 1933: (left to right) Tricky Sam Nanton, Juan Tizol, and Lawrence Brown; Tizol is playing a valve trombone

manner is well represented by *Mahusale* from the album *Albert Mangelsdorff Live in Tokyo* (1971, Enja 2006). Thelin has also experimented with electronic effects, attaching a pickup to his instrument. Rutherford (an admirer of Robinson), Mangelsdorff, and Rudd, together with such younger players as Ray Anderson and George Lewis (ii), have adopted and exaggerated techniques and sounds from early jazz playing, which are well suited to the expressiveness of free jazz – a raw, brassy tone, distorted pitches, "splatting," and exuberant portamentos. Lewis has also explored a new context for trombone playing by improvising together with a computer-programmed synthesizer.

The trombone is of little importance in jazz-rock and other fusions. Such medium-sized groups as Chicago, Tower of Power, and Blood, Sweat and Tears (all closer to rock music than to jazz), have included a trombone within a three- to five-piece wind section, playing both boppish lines and simple riffs in the style of rock or soul music. Many modern big bands, such as those of Gil Evans, Thad Jones and Mel Lewis, Toshiko Akiyoshi and Lew Tabackin, and Maynard Ferguson, have regularly performed tunes based on rock rhythms and harmonies. Trombonists have taken solos in this context but no innovatory players of great significance have emerged; solos usually consist of lines in the bop style superimposed on a rock accompaniment, or distorted gesturing in a manner reminiscent of some electric guitarists. Among the few players to make notable original contributions in fusion styles are Wayne Henderson, heard in the 1970s as one of the principal melodic voices of the Crusaders, and Bill Watrous, who for a time was the leader of a jazz-rock group. Ferguson has performed and recorded regularly on his superbone; a fine example of his playing style is the improvised exchange with the baritone saxophonist Bruce Johnstone on the track *Superbone Meets the Bad Man* from Ferguson's album *Chameleon* (1974, Col. KC33007).

For further illustrations *see* JOHNSON, J. J.; MANGELSDORFF, ALBERT; MILLER, GLENN; and TEAGARDEN.

BIBLIOGRAPHY

R. Blesh: *Shining Trumpets: a History of Jazz* (New York, 1946, rev. and enlarged 2/1958/R1975)
J.-E. Berendt: *Das Jazzbuch: Entwicklung und Bedeutung der Jazzmusik* (Frankfurt am Main, Germany, 1953, rev. 2/1959 as *Das neue Jazzbuch*: Eng. trans., New York, 1962; rev. and enlarged 5/1981 as *Das grosse Jazzbuch: von New Orleans bis Jazz Rock*, Eng. trans. as *The Jazz Book: from New Orleans to Fusion and Beyond*, Westport, CT, 1982)
O. Keepnews and B. Grauer, Jr.: *A Pictorial History of Jazz: People and Places from New Orleans to Modern Jazz* (New York, 1956, rev. 2/1966/R1981)
D. Heckman: "Jazz Trombone: Five Views," *DB*, xxxii/2 (1965), 17 [incl. transcrs.]
G. Schuller: *Early Jazz: its Roots and Musical Development* (New York, 1968)
D. Baker: *Jazz Styles & Analysis: Trombone: a History of the Jazz Trombone via Recorded Solos, Transcribed and Annotated* (Chicago, 1973)
A. C. Baines: "Trombone," *GroveI*
M. Laplace: "Le trombone dans le jazz et la musique populaire," *Brass Bulletin*, (1985), no.50, p.36; no.51, p.40; no.52, p.20

CLIFFORD BEVAN

Trotman, Lloyd (Nelson) (*b* Boston, 25 May 1923). Double bass player. After studying at the New England Conservatory he began performing in Boston and toured with Blanche Calloway (1941). In 1945 he moved to New York, where he played with Eddie Heywood, Hazel Scott, Duke Ellington, Pete Brown, Edmond Hall, and Wilbur De Paris (all 1945), Boyd Raeburn (1948–9), and Johnny Hodges (1951–2). From the late 1940s he worked mainly as a studio musician, notably for King, Atlantic, and Groove, recording with Lucky Millinder (1952), Ray Charles (1953), Joe Turner (ii) (1956–8), and many other musicians whose styles were strongly influenced by rhythm-and-blues. He also recorded with Oscar Pettiford (1950), in a trio with Bud Powell and Art Blakey (1955), and with Henry "Red" Allen (1957), with whom he later performed at the Newport Jazz Festival (1959). His playing may be heard on Hodges's *Sideways/A Pound of Blues* (1952, Clef 8961).

BIBLIOGRAPHY

FeatherE
D. Kochakian: "Bey Perry," *Whiskey, Women, and . . .*, no.15 (1985), 48
——: "Charlie Cox," *Whiskey, Women, and . . ., no.15 (1985), 44*

Trovajoli, Armando (*b* Rome, 2 Sept 1917). Italian pianist and composer. He formed a group modeled after the Benny Goodman Sextet in 1944 and studied piano at the conservatory in Rome, from which he graduated in 1949; the same year he performed at the Paris Jazz Fair in a trio with Kramer Gorni and Gil Cuppini. In 1950 he recorded as the leader of trios with Franco Cerri and the drummer Paolo Tagliaferri, and with Cuppini and Roberto Nicolosi; he also recorded with Django Reinhardt, Stephane Grappelli, Toots Thielemans, and Flavio Ambrosetti. From 1956 to 1958 he led an orchestra for RAI that played arrangements by, among others, Bill Russo and Bill Holman; his sidemen included Cuppini and Oscar Valdambrini. Trovajoli recorded as the leader of a quartet, a sextet, and a big band (1956–8); his playing may be heard to advantage on *Pick Yourself up* (1959, RCA LPM10019). He wrote film scores from 1952, and musical comedies from the 1960s. Trovajoli's importance lies in his work as a pianist, and in his having formed one of the first big bands in Italy and introduced jazz to a large audience through his film and television scores.

ADRIANO MAZZOLETTI

Trueheart, John (*b* Baltimore, *c*1900; *d* New York, 1949). Guitarist and banjoist. He worked in Baltimore, then New York, with his close friend Chick Webb, performing and making recordings (including *Blue Minor*, 1934, Decca 172) from the early 1930s. In 1937 illness interrupted his career, but two years later he rejoined Webb. After the latter's death Trueheart remained with the band under Ella Fitzgerald's leadership until 1940. Thereafter he played with Art Hodes (1943) and others before illness forced him to retire.

based on *ChiltonW*

Trujillo, Bill [William Lee] (*b* Los Angeles, 7 July 1930). Tenor saxophonist. He studied at Westlake Music College in Los Angeles. While in his teens he performed in local dance bands and in 1950–51 he played with the guitarist Alvino Rey. In 1953–4 he performed and recorded with Woody Herman's New Third Herd, and he took a brief solo on the band's recording *The Moon is Blue* (1953, Mars 1002). After leading his own quartet at the Key Club in Chicago in 1955, he toured Europe with Bill Russo (1955) and worked with Charlie Barnet (1956–7) and Jerry Gray (1958); he made recordings with all three leaders. He then toured and recorded with Stan Kenton (1958–9), before moving to Las Vegas in 1960, where he has played with numerous visiting jazz musicians. Besides his principal instrument he plays other saxophones, clarinets, and flute.

BIBLIOGRAPHY

FeatherE
A. Morgan: "Woody's Tenors," *JM*, vi (1960–61), no.7, p.4; no.8, p.13; no.12, p.9

Trumbauer, Frankie [Frank; Trombar, Frank; Tram] (*b* Carbondale, IL, 30 May 1901; *d* Kansas City, MO, 11 June 1956). Alto and C-melody saxophonist. After serving in the US Navy during World War I he became a professional musician, working first in local bands before moving to Chicago to play (and record) with the Benson Orchestra and Ray Miller. In 1925–6 he led a band in St. Louis with Bix Beiderbecke, who became his close associate. The two men later worked together in orchestras led by Jean Goldkette (1926), Adrian Rollini (1927), and Paul Whiteman (from 1927). By this time Trumbauer's originality was easily discernible, and in 1927 he gained his own recording contract with Okeh, leading to the creation of some of the most important recordings of the era by white jazz musicians. These performances reveal Trumbauer and Beiderbecke, together with Eddie Lang, at the peak of their inspiration. In 1934, while still with Whiteman, Trumbauer led his own recording band, which included several young "swing" stars, such as Bunny Berigan. After a brief spell in 1936 as a member of the Three T's with Jack and Charlie Teagarden he moved to California. As Frank Trombar he occasionally led his own big band, but was more occupied with studio work. He was a test pilot during World War II; thereafter he played briefly in studio groups (1945–7) before leaving music altogether to work in aeronautics.

Trumbauer played most members of the saxophone family but specialized on alto and C-melody saxophones; he was the only successful jazz specialist on the C-melody instrument. His graceful, light-toned improvisations were extremely individual. They were acknowledged to have influenced the tenor saxophone style of Lester Young, who was greatly impressed by the recording of *Singin' the Blues* (1927) which Trumbauer made in the company of Beiderbecke. Trumbauer introduced delicacy into the art of jazz saxophone playing; he was a model of musical poise when improvising, and his long, singing phrases were beautifully constructed and delivered in a restrained but attractive tone. His individuality was effectively displayed on many of his recordings with Paul Whiteman's orchestra, where his pithy sense of understatement and dry, delicate tone stood out against the lush backgrounds. Later he had difficulty adjusting to the new swing style, and in his recordings from the mid-1930s his timing often appeared stiff and uneasy and his phrasing anachronistic.

SELECTED RECORDINGS

As leader: Trumbology (1927, OK 40871); Clarinet Marmalade/Singin' the Blues (1927, OK 40772); I'm coming, Virginia/'Way down yonder in New Orleans (1927, OK 40843)

As sideman: P. Whiteman: You took advantage of me (1928, Vic. 21398)

BIBLIOGRAPHY

M. Brian: "America's Public Swing Star Number One," *MM*, xiv (10 Sept 1938), 10

"Frank Trumbauer Quits Jazz," *DB*, vii/13 (1940), 13

D. Dexter: "Giants of Jazz," *DB*, vii/21 (1940), 10

F. Trumbauer: "The Good Old Days," *DB*, ix/8 (1942), 6

R. M. Sudhalter, P. R. Evans, and W. Dean-Myatt: *Bix: Man & Legend* (New Rochelle, NY, and London, 1974)

JOHN CHILTON

Trumpet. A brass instrument made in a range of pitches from sopranino to bass.

1. Technical aspects. 2. The importance of jazz trumpet playing. 3. The trumpet in early jazz. 4. The swing era. 5. Bop and traditional jazz. 6. Free jazz, jazz-rock, and the continuation of established styles.

1. Technical aspects. The trumpet generally has three valves and tubing of a mainly cylindrical profile; the tubing is "folded" through several reversals, so that it lies parallel in a horizontal plane, with the bell pointing forwards. The mouthpiece of the modern trumpet is cup-shaped and relatively shallow. The written compass of the trumpet in B♭ (the principal member of the modern trumpet family) is *f♯–c'''* (sounding *e–b♭''*), though many players add a further octave to the upper limit of the range, and some another octave still.

Jazz musicians almost all play the standard trumpet in B♭. Dizzy Gillespie adopted an instrument (first patented in 1866 by the Schreiber Cornet Manufacturing Company of New York) in which the familiar outline of the trumpet is modified so that the bell points upwards at an angle of 45°. A few players have used other members of the trumpet family: those who have taken up the bass trumpet in B♭ include Cy Touff (as a soloist within Woody Herman's trombone section), Johnny Mandel (in several bands during the 1950s), and Ray Premru (in the 1960s in Kenny Baker's group); Don Cherry specializes in a pocket instrument, also in B♭ (for illustration *see* Cherry, Don); and Don Ellis, under the influence of the Czech player Jaromír Hnilička, has played the four-valve "quarter-tone" trumpet. In the early 1970s Maynard Ferguson invented a combination valve and slide trumpet known as the Firebird; the slide mechanism, operated by the left hand, allows the player effortlessly to produce such effects as blue notes and glisses. Ellis and Al Hirt occasionally used the instrument and Ferguson may be heard playing it on his album *Hollywood* (1982, Col. FC37713).

2. The importance of jazz trumpet playing. The general approach to trumpet playing in the 20th century has been influenced significantly by jazz musicians. In Western art music, while the trumpet was prominent as a concertante instrument in the Baroque era, for the following two centuries it held at best a secondary position within the orchestra. In the military tradition, although the trumpet was always considered the principal melodic instrument, the demands made by the music on players were not extreme. From the late 19th century, however, with the ad hoc experimentation within brass bands in the southern USA (particularly those in New Orleans) and, later, with the evolution of jazz (and notably the innovations of Louis Armstrong), the concept of how the trumpet might be played was brought to a level far higher than had previously been imagined.

Among the developments brought about by these musicians, all later carried over into other genres, were an extension of the upper range (to *e♭'''*); a potpourri of personal approaches to the use of vibrato (including Terminal vibrato) of varying amplitude and speed, produced by the chin, the diaphragm, or the motion of the right hand; the ability to execute smoothly various kinds of Gliss (including the rip, the doit, and the fall off); a number of manipulations of the embouchure and fingers to achieve such effects as the Growl, the Half-valve, and the Smear; the production of an airy tone by tightening the lips more than usual and blowing with force so that part of the lip tissue does not vibrate; the playing of Multiphonics by tightening or relaxing the lips unduly and blowing between the partials or by the act of simultaneously playing and singing, which results in various tones and beats being created (best workable in the low register); the invention of new mutes to achieve an array of new timbres (*see* Mute); and the achievement of a technical facility previously unknown, not merely in scale passages, but also in the negotiation of difficult chromatic intervallic leaps which are not idiomatic to the instrument.

3. The trumpet in early jazz. For historical and sociological reasons the soprano brass instrument in early jazz bands was the Cornet. However, the word "cornet" was used in the USA in the 19th century to refer to any soprano brass instrument that played the melodic part, a usage that implied a somewhat interchangeable nature between trumpet and cornet; since many players who began on cornet later took up trumpet as well as

or instead of the former, the history of the two instruments in jazz is best considered as a single continuous tradition.

In New Orleans the leader of brass and jazz bands, and of related groups, was most frequently a cornetist, who would take the most prominent role by playing the melody; as well as being the player with the most volume, he was generally the finest musician in the ensemble. There are numerous accounts among jazz brass players of musicians beginning in their youth as drummers and gradually working their way from the lower brass instruments to the higher, with the position of cornetist being the coveted goal. Universally credited as being the first accomplished cornetist was the legendary Buddy Bolden, who was renowned for his authoritative style. Among those influenced by Bolden were Manuel Perez, Buddy Petit, and, notably, Freddie Keppard; Keppard used his powerful tone over a much wider compass than hitherto, as may be heard on *Stock Yards Strut* (1926, Para. 12399), and exhibited a new delight in exploiting the instrument's technical possibilities.

The typically brusque melodic style and four-square rhythmic approach of New Orleans cornetists was characteristic of King Oliver's playing when he moved from that city to Chicago in 1918, yet his performance of blues numbers was distinctively vocal. Oliver was a good leader and his bands were notable for their integrated teamwork. He was also a considerable influence on other musicians – particularly Mutt Carey, a reliable lead player renowned (like Oliver) for his muted effects, and Tommy Ladnier, a fluent improviser whose relaxed yet controlling phrasing had implicit swing without explicit syncopation. Oliver's Creole Jazz Band was augmented after only a month in Chicago by the arrival of Louis Armstrong, which brought into existence a team of two cornets. This was the first of many such pairings: among Oliver's later partners were Bob Shoffner, Louis Metcalf, and Dave Nelson, while George Mitchell and Natty Dominique appeared together in recording bands led by Johnny Dodds, contributing to the distinctive sound heard, for example, on *Come on and stomp, stomp, stomp* (1927, Bruns. 3568).

Armstrong first recorded on trumpet on 28 May 1926, and soon jettisoned many earlier attitudes, contributing a new approach not only to trumpet playing but also to the wider field of jazz. Using a technique that was basically conventional, his tone was remarkable for its clarity and often sheer beauty, particularly in the control of sustained notes and apposite use of vibrato. He developed a range of three octaves and was one of the first to include chords of the minor and diminished seventh in his improvisations. Most importantly, he created the idea of the featured soloist within the integrated New Orleans sound. His overall gift was that of communication, which he achieved through the exquisite simplicity of his ideas, his subtle use of syncopation and rubato, and the undisputed authority of his playing; a good example of a performance displaying these characteristics is *Sweethearts on Parade* (1930, Col. 2688D).

In the late 1920s most cornet players found it advisable to take up trumpet. A notable exception was Bix Beiderbecke, who nevertheless had a considerable influence over the course of jazz trumpet development. His restrained, elegant, and sensitive playing, improvising close to the melody, indicated the possibilities of the "cool" approach 20 years before its time. Unlike Armstrong, who modified his tone as the situation seemed to demand, Beiderbecke rarely altered his, which was for the most part straight, with only a slight vibrato at the end of certain notes and phrases.

The matter of tone assumed increasing importance during the 1920s. Bubber Miley, the foremost soloist in Duke Ellington's orchestra from 1923 to 1929, had a great melodic gift, but is remembered more for establishing the band's "jungle" sound, typified on *East St. Louis Toodle-oo* (1927, Vic. 21703). Miley was influenced by Oliver's use of mutes, and his growl and wa-wa techniques were subsequently adopted by other

Part of Duke Ellington's brass section at a recording session for BBC Radio, London, 1933: (left to right) Freddie Jenkins (trumpet), Lawrence Brown (trombone), Cootie Williams (trumpet), and Juan Tizol (valve trombone)

sidemen in Ellington's band – Cootie Williams, Rex Stewart, Ray Nance, and Clark Terry.

Big bands began to emerge from the mid-1920s, and consequently trumpeters began to work in trumpet sections or, more generally, with trombonists in brass sections. The size of trumpet sections gradually increased, from Oliver's two instruments in 1922 to Fletcher Henderson's three in 1924. Paul Whiteman foreshadowed a development of the 1930s by including a section of four players in his band in 1928, and by 1951 the trumpets in Stan Kenton's orchestra numbered five; four, however, remained the norm.

4. THE SWING ERA. By the late 1920s the primacy of the soprano brass instrument – now generally the trumpet rather than the cornet – was being challenged by the saxophone, and aspects of saxophone performance began to affect the way in which trumpeters played. Armstrong's influence, which extended far beyond other trumpeters, was felt especially in the playing of such leading figures as Jabbo Smith and Henry "Red" Allen, but his emphasis on relaxed melody was beginning to give way to an exploration of dexterity. Smith, who in 1928 succeeded Armstrong in Carroll Dickerson's band, introduced the fast fingering techniques and frequent use of the high register that later became characteristic of bop trumpeters. He also suffered the major drawback of such a style: a thin tone, resulting from the speed of the air through the instrument not allowing full resonance. This may be clearly heard on *Jazz Battle* (1929, Bruns. 4244). There was an even closer approach to bop in Allen's inclination to obscure the joins between phrases. He too included fast-moving passages as an integral part of his style, but unlike Smith, who showed considerable skill in obtaining high notes, Allen tended to use force, often introducing smears and rips into his playing. His vibrato, however, was generally more restricted than was usual for the time.

Of those influenced by Allen, Roy Eldridge was arguably the most important, yet his playing in the high register perhaps owed more to Smith's control than Allen's force. His rhythmic drive has been compared with that of Armstrong, and his virtuoso technique allowed him to use saxophone-like phrasing, as may be heard on Chu Berry's *Forty-six West Fifty-two* (1938, Com. 516).

A smoother and more gentle trumpeter than Eldridge, Buck Clayton employed a wider vibrato, often resorting to the use of a cup mute and showing a preference for traditional harmonies. Charlie Shavers also owed a debt to Allen. He had a strong technique and a remarkable range that allowed him to obtain extreme high and low notes in close proximity; while his style was often very syncopated, his playing at slower tempos is sometimes considered sentimental.

A wider use of the trumpet's high register, possibly stemming from Armstrong's inclination to build up to a climax literally through increasingly higher notes, became noticeable during the 1930s and 1940s. Cat Anderson was the most celebrated high-note specialist in Ellington's orchestra, but Maynard Ferguson, in Kenton's bands of the 1940s and later in his own groups, was most consistently impressive in the high tessitura up to and including *e♭''''*; a good example of his playing may be heard on *MacArthur Park* on the album *M. F. Horn* (1970, Col. C30466).

5. BOP AND TRADITIONAL JAZZ. By the 1940s the saxophone was the most important instrument in jazz, and as a result the most significant development in brass playing (first for the trumpet and later for the trombone, french horn, and tuba) was the acquisition of a nonidiomatic technical facility that would enable players to rival the facility of bop saxophonists. This was achieved first by Dizzy Gillespie, the most innovative trumpeter after Armstrong. Gillespie's contribution, like Armstrong's, marked a stylistic turning point. Through a remarkable technique he was able to give full vent to his fluent skill for improvisation, utilizing a harmonic rather than a melodic basis. He had scant use for vibrato, but for the most part the notes came so fast that tone was of little importance. In 1947, with *Cubana Be/Cubana Bop* (Vic. 203145) and *Manteca* (Vic. 203023), he introduced a new element: Afro-Cuban jazz.

Fats Navarro and Clifford Brown were virtuoso players and remarkable improvisers, playing difficult and sophisticated bop solos, yet maintaining a warm, beautiful, velvety tone. They were the precursors of the hard-bop trumpeters that emerged during the 1950s, such as Donald Byrd, Lee Morgan, Freddie Hubbard, and, later, Woody Shaw.

Unable and unwilling to play so high, so fast, or with such precision as Gillespie, Navarro, and Brown, Miles Davis became a strong influence on trumpet players of the 1950s. His introverted, cool style involved even less vibrato than Gillespie's, and at times his notes seemed to be implied rather than stated. While over three decades he led his groups through several landmarks in the evolution of jazz styles, Davis's own playing changed little, though he took up the stemless harmon mute in 1954 to produce a brooding sound so striking that subsequent users of the effect may be said to be only imitating Davis.

Concurrent with developments in bop and related styles was a renewed interest in early cornet and trumpet playing, beginning with the rediscovery in New Orleans of Bunk Johnson and leading to the widespread popularity of traditional jazz and trad bands. While this movement had no great consequences for the development of trumpet styles, it did allow the instrument, among a wide circle of musicians, to re-establish its principal role within the jazz ensemble.

6. FREE JAZZ, JAZZ-ROCK, AND THE CONTINUATION OF ESTABLISHED STYLES. There have been only a small number of important trumpeters in free jazz – notably Don Cherry (playing a pocket instrument), Bill Dixon, Don Ellis, Lester Bowie, Mike Mantler, and Leo Smith – and fewer in jazz-rock, the most important being Davis, Ferguson, and Chuck Mangione (who later took up flugelhorn). Significant developments in the 1960s and 1970s in the role and capabilities of the trumpet are rare, contrasting sharply with the changes affecting, for example, the saxophone and the instruments of the rhythm section. Dixon and Bowie differentiated themselves from others not by developing new effects, but by bringing heavy emphasis to the special effects that had been developed in early jazz and swing. Ellis's work with the quarter-tone trumpet has had little influence. Ferguson adapted his playing to jazz-rock with no change whatsoever in his high-pitched melodic style. Ellis and Davis both explored electronic devices, Ellis working, for example, with a ring modulator, Davis with a fuzz box and a wa-wa pedal (as may be heard on his album *Live-Evil*, 1970, Col. G30954), but their experiments had more to do with synthesized sound than with trumpet playing; in Davis's case it served only to make the instrument sound more like a cheap electric guitar than a trumpet.

Thus, after the unprecedented early achievements of jazz trumpeters in mainstream and bop styles, the trumpet seems to have reached a halt in its development. Perhaps the emergence of musicians such as Wynton Marsalis, classically trained and equally at home performing a trumpet concerto with a symphony orchestra or working with Art Blakey and Herbie

Hancock, may give some clue as to the part to be played by a straight, clear tone, faultless technique, and lively imagination.

For further illustrations *see* Allen, henry "red"; Bowie, lester; Davis, Miles, fig.2; Eldridge, roy; Ellis, don; Hubbard, freddie; Marsalis, wynton; Mezzrow, mezz; Napoleon, fig.1*a*; and Teagarden.

BIBLIOGRAPHY

R. Blesh: *Shining Trumpets: a History of Jazz* (New York, 1946, rev. and enlarged 2/1958/*R*1975)
I. Lang: *Jazz in Perspective: the Background of the Blues* (London and elsewhere, 1947/*R*1976)
R. Harris: *Jazz* (London, 1952, 5/1957)
J.-E. Berendt: *Das Jazzbuch: Entwicklung und Bedeutung der Jazzmusik* (Frankfurt am Main, Germany, 1953, rev. 2/1959 as *Das neue Jazzbuch: Entwicklung und Bedeutung*, It. trans., Florence, Italy, 1959, Eng. trans., New York, 1962, Sp. trans., Mexico City, *c*1962; rev. and enlarged 5/1981 as *Das grosse Jazzbuch: von New Orleans bis Jazz Rock*, Eng. trans. as *The Jazz Book: from New Orleans to Fusion and Beyond*, Westport, CT, 1982)
O. Keepnews and B. Grauer, Jr.: *A Pictorial History of Jazz: People and Places from New Orleans to Modern Jazz* (New York, 1956, rev. 2/1966/*R*1981)
L. Feather: *The Book of Jazz: a Guide to the Entire Field* (New York, 1957, 2/1965 as *The Book of Jazz from Then till Now: a Guide to the Entire Field*)
B. Ulanov: *A Handbook of Jazz* (New York, n.d. [?1957]/*R*1975)
N. Hentoff and A. J. McCarthy, eds.: *Jazz: New Perspectives on the History of Jazz by Twelve of the World's Foremost Jazz Critics and Scholars* (New York and Toronto, 1959/*R*1974)
J. Goldberg: *Jazz Masters of the Fifties* (New York and London, 1965/*R*1980)
G. Schuller: *Early Jazz: its Roots and Musical Development* (New York, 1968)
M. Williams: *The Jazz Tradition* (New York, 1970, rev. 2/1983)
G. Collier: *Inside Jazz* (London, 1973)
A. J. Smith: "Maynard Ferguson: Conquistador of Double High C," *DB*, xliv/16 (1977), 14
M. Laplace: "La trompette et le cornet dans le jazz et la musique populaire," *Brass Bulletin*, nos.42–4 (1983); nos.45–7 (1984)

CLIFFORD BEVAN

Trunk, Peter (*b* Frankfurt am Main, Germany, 17 May 1936; *d* New York, 31 Dec 1973). German double bass player. After participating in concerts and broadcasts in Germany with Kenny Clarke, Zoot Sims (both 1957), and Stan Getz (1958) he performed and recorded with Albert Mangelsdorff (1958–61). He also recorded with Sims, the dixieland group the Two Beat Stompers (both 1958), and Hans Koller (1958–9). Thereafter he performed and recorded with Klaus Doldinger (1963–7) and Dusko Goykovich (1965, 1966), and recorded with Tete Montoliu (1962, 1968), Benny Bailey (1964), Don Byas, Ben Webster (1968), and Volker Kriegel (1968, 1971); he is heard to advantage on *Ben Webster Meets Don Byas in Black Forest* (1968, Saba 15159). Trunk worked with Manfred Schoof in 1969, recording with him as a member of the New Jazz Trio in 1970–71, and with Kurt Edelhagen in 1972. He died in an automobile accident.

BIBLIOGRAPHY

FeatherE; *ReclamsJ*
J. E. Berendt: "In memoriam Peter Trunk," *Ein Fenster aus Jazz: Essays, Portraits, Reflexionen* (Frankfurt am Main, Germany, 1977), 159

Trzaskowski, Andrzej (*b* Kraków, Poland, 23 March 1933). Polish pianist and composer. He played the piano as a child and later studied musicology at university in Kraków (to 1957); he also took private lessons in composition and contemporary music theory and was active at the experimental studio of Polish radio. In 1951 he helped to form Melomani, one of the first Polish swing and bop groups. During 1958 he played and recorded with the Jazz Believers, a quintet that included Wojciech Karolak and Jan Wróblewski, and worked with another quintet, led by Jerzy Matuszkiewicz. The following year he formed his own hard-bop group, the Wreckers, with which he toured the USA in 1962; as the leader of small groups he performed and recorded with American musicians visiting Poland, such as Stan Getz (1960) and Ted Curson (1965–6). Many leading Polish musicians, including Zbigniew Namysłowski, Tomasz Stańko, and Michal Urbaniak, played with his groups early in their careers. Trzaskowski began to incorporate avant-garde techniques in his work from 1964. In the late 1960s he worked regularly for Norddeutscher Rundfunk in Hamburg, West Germany, writing more than 20 compositions and participating in workshops, then from 1975 he led an orchestra for Polish radio and television. Although an excellent pianist, from the early 1970s he has concentrated more on composition. He has written music for films and theater, two jazz ballets, and *Nihil novi*, a third-stream work performed by Don Ellis at the International Jazz Jamboree in Warsaw (1962).

SELECTED RECORDINGS

The Wreckers (1960, Muza 0133); *The Andrzej Trzaskowski Quintet* (1965, Muza 0258); *Andrzej Trzaskowski Sextet Featuring Ted Curson* (1966, Muza 0378)

BIBLIOGRAPHY

Feather–Gitler '70s
J. Byrczek: "Eurojazz Personalities: Poland," *JF* [intl edn], no.18 (1972), 87

WOLFRAM KNAUER

Tsfasman, Aleksandr (Naumovich) (*b* Zaporozh'ye, Ukraine, 14 Dec 1906; *d* Moscow, 20 Feb 1971). Russian bandleader, pianist, and composer. In 1926 he formed the orchestra AMA-Jazz (the jazz ensemble of the Assotsiyatsia Moskovskikh avtorov (Association of Moscow authors)), which became the first jazz band in the USSR to broadcast on radio (1928) and the first to make a recording (*Hallelujah*, 1929). While leading the band he studied piano with Felix Blumenfeld at the Moscow P. I. Tchaikovsky State Conservatory, from which he graduated in 1930; the same year AMA-Jazz disbanded. He led other bands from the mid-1930s, then the jazz orchestra of the Vsesoyuznoe radio (All-union radio) from 1939 to 1946, and made many recordings. Tsfasman was the first improvising virtuoso in soviet jazz. His compositions include jazz pieces, two piano concertos, film scores, music for the stage, and popular songs. The album *Aleksandr Tsfasman: Kompozitor, pianist, dirizher* (Mel. 33M603658992) includes several previously unissued tracks that he recorded in the 1930s and 1940s. He was named a Merited Artist of the Russian SFSR in 1957. (S. F. Starr: *Red and Hot: the Fate of Jazz in the Soviet Union, 1917–1980* (New York, and Oxford, England, 1983), 134)

WALTER OJAKÄÄR

Tuba. A valved brass instrument of wide conical bore. The tubing is usually coiled into an elliptical shape and terminates in a wide bell (usually pointing upwards) and a deep, cup-shaped mouthpiece. The instrument has an open fundamental of 8′ *C* (or lower) and is equipped with three to six (usually four, rarely seven) valves to alter the length of the tubing and hence the pitch. It is generally used in jazz as the bass or contrabass member of the band.

A group of related instruments, in various shapes and sizes, may be said to constitute a tuba family; its members are known generically as brass bass. The most important are the euphonium (sometimes referred to, especially in the USA, as the baritone horn, *see* Saxhorn), which is essentially a tenor tuba in B♭; and the helicon and sousaphone, which are both types of bass tuba distinguished from the rest of the family by their circular shape. The lower members of the saxhorn group are also sometimes regarded as forming part of the tuba group. The sousaphone, named after the composer and bandmaster John Philip Sousa, is used mainly in marching bands. Like the helicon (now almost obsolete), it encircles the player, resting on the left shoulder and passing under the right arm, with the bell pointing forwards above the player's head; this form was devised to facilitate carrying the instruments while marching. Some upright tubas have been made with the bell facing forwards; this "recording" bell was introduced during the 1920s, when the tuba often substituted for the double bass in recording studios.

As an important military instrument the tuba was commonly found in early marching bands, though by the early 1900s the double bass was normally preferred in jazz bands. (This might not have been the case had more tuba players of the caliber of Cyrus St. Clair been available.) During the 1920s the sousaphone was used to provide the crisp attack necessary to the fulfilling of the primarily rhythmic function of the bass instruments; Paul Whiteman's orchestra, for example, included two. Driven from the dance band by the double bass when swing became the predominant style in jazz, the tuba reappeared during the dixieland revival of the 1940s; in dixieland it is often found in conjunction with the banjo (just as the double bass is usually paired with the guitar).

In the later 1940s the tuba began to be used in a different role in such bands as those of Claude Thornhill and Miles Davis, where it was valued because it offered a deep brass sound combined with considerable agility. It left the rhythm section to join the brass section, in which, since its timbre was similar, it was frequently linked with the orchestral horn. Gil Evans has used the instrument in a consistently imaginative way; among the first to play tuba in his arrangements was Bill Barber, who as a member of Miles Davis's nonet took part in the recordings (1949–50) that were later issued collectively as *The Birth of the Cool*. Don Butterfield, playing in groups led by Sonny Rollins, Cannonball Adderley, Charles Mingus, and others in the 1950s and 1960s, became known for the exceptional agility and virtuosity of his solos. Howard Johnson (ii), who played tuba in the bands of Archie Shepp and Evans (he may be heard as a soloist on *Thoroughbred* from Evans's *Svengali*, 1973, Atl. 1643), led his own tuba band in the 1970s and remains the leading jazz tuba player. The euphonium also enjoyed a revival in postwar jazz: the orchestra assembled in London in 1964 for Benny Golson included a euphonium alongside its four orchestral horns, and the instrument was played by Bernard McKinney and occasionally by Maynard Ferguson.

For illustration *see* Jazz (i), figs.2 and 6.

BIBLIOGRAPHY

O. Keepnews and B. Grauer, Jr.: *A Pictorial History of Jazz: People and Places from New Orleans to Modern Jazz* (New York, 1956, rev. 2/1966)
C. J. Bevan: *The Tuba Family* (London and New York, 1978)
M. Laplace: "Les tubas dans le jazz et les musiques populaires," *Brass Bulletin*, no.56 (1986), 18; no.57 (1987), 84

CLIFFORD BEVAN

Tubs. Slang term for drums; *see* Drum set.

Tucker, Ben(jamin Mayer) (*b* Nashville, 13 Dec 1930). Double bass player. He studied music at Tennessee State University and played at clubs in Nashville. After military service he performed and recorded in Los Angeles in the West Coast jazz groups of Warne Marsh and Bill Perkins (both 1956), Art Pepper (1956–7, 1958), and Chico Hamilton (1958). He then moved to New York, where in 1959 he performed and recorded with Kenny Burrell and Roland Hanna and toured with Chris Connor. In 1961 Tucker performed and recorded in Rio de Janeiro as a member of an all-star bop group that included Kenny Dorham, Al Cohn, and Zoot Sims. In the early 1960s he was associated with Herbie Mann and Billy Taylor (ii); he is heard to advantage on *Comin' Home Baby* from *Standing Ovation at Newport* (1965, Atl. 1445), recorded with Mann. His extensive work as a studio musician included sessions with Yusef Lateef (1960), Lou Donaldson (1960, 1961), Marian McPartland (1960, 1963), Dave Bailey, Connor (both 1961), Gerry Mulligan, Vi Redd (both 1962), Illinois Jacquet (1963, 1968), Mose Allison, Dave Burrell (both 1964), Eddie "Lockjaw" Davis (1967), Pat Martino (1967–8), Taylor (1967, 1969), and Harold Vick (1975).

Oral history material in *TNF*.

BIBLIOGRAPHY

FeatherE; *Feather '60s*
R. Gordon: *Jazz West Coast: the Los Angeles Jazz Scene of the 1950s* (London and New York, 1986)

Tucker, Bobby [Robert Nathaniel, Jr.] (*b* Morristown, NJ, 8 Jan 1923). Pianist. He began performing at the age of 14 and later studied in New York at the Institute of Musical Art. In 1946 he became accompanist first to Mildred Bailey and then to Billie Holiday, with whom he remained until 1949; he also played in clubs on 52nd Street with Lucky Thompson and Stuff Smith. Tucker continued to make recordings with Holiday in the 1950s (1951, 1954, 1955, including *I thought about you*, 1954, Clef 89150). In 1949 he joined Billy Eckstine, with whom he toured the USA, Europe, Australia, and Japan into the 1980s; he began writing arrangements for Eckstine in the 1960s.

BIBLIOGRAPHY

ChiltonW; *FeatherE*
J. Chilton: *Billie's Blues: a Survey of Billie Holiday's Career, 1933–1959* (London, 1975)
E. Southern: "'Mr. B' of Ballad and Bop," *Black Perspective in Music*, viii (1980), 64 [interview, incl. biography of Tucker]

Tucker, George (Andrew) (*b* Palatka, FL, 10 Dec 1927; *d* New York, 10 Oct 1965). Double bass player. He studied double bass at the New York Conservatory of Modern Music (1948), and his early performing experience included engagements with Earl Bostic, John Coltrane, and Jackie McLean. In the 1950s Tucker was a member of the house bands at the Continental Lounge, Minton's Playhouse, and The Playhouse, where he also appeared with Horace Parlan and Booker Ervin. After playing with Jerome Richardson and Junior Mance he toured with Lambert, Hendricks, and Bavan (1962–3); he also recorded frequently with Ervin, Parlan, Stanley Turrentine, and Shirley Scott (all 1960–61). He was well known for his sensitivity as an accompanist and the precision of his playing.

SELECTED RECORDINGS

As sideman: C. Jordan: *Cliff Craft* (1957, BN 1582); E. Dolphy: *Outward Bound* (1960, NewJ 8236); H. Parlan: *Us Three* (1960, BN 4037); D. Gordon: *Doin' Allright* (1961, BN 84077); Lambert, Hendricks, and Bavan: *At Newport '63* (1963, RCA LSP2747); C. Hawkins: *Coleman Hawkins with the Earl Hines Trio* (1965, Pumpkin 105); J. Byard: *Live at Lennie's* (1965, Prst. 7419, 7477)

BIBLIOGRAPHY

Obituary, *DB*, xxxii/24 (1965), 12
D. C. Hunt: "Unforgettable," *JM*, no.162 (1968), 14
P. S. Friedman: "Discography: George Tucker," *JM*, no.163 (1968), 24; no.166 (1968), 30; no.167 (1969), 30

BRENDA PENNELL

Tucker, Mickey [Michael B.] (*b* Durham, NC, 28 April 1941). Pianist. He studied piano from the age of six and first worked with the singer Damita Jo (1965); he was then a sideman for the comedian Timmie Rogers (1966–7) and the pop group Little Anthony and the Imperials (1967–8). He played bop with James Moody (1969–72), the Thad Jones–Mel Lewis Orchestra (briefly in 1973), Roy Brooks (1973–5), and the group Final Edition (1975); he also recorded as an organist with Roland

Kirk (1971) and as a pianist with Eric Kloss (1973, 1976) and Eddie Jefferson (1974, 1976). In 1976 he toured Europe and North Africa with Art Blakey. Later he recorded in New York with Philly Joe Jones, Billy Harper, and Junior Cook (1977), toured Europe and recorded with Frank Foster (1977–9), and recorded with Art Farmer's and Benny Golson's Jazztet (1983).

SELECTED RECORDINGS

(recorded for Muse unless otherwise indicated)

As leader: *Triplicity* (1975, Xan. 128); *Mister Mysterious* (1978, 5174); *The Crawl* (1979, 5223)

As sideman: J. Moody: *Never Again* (1972, 5001); E. Kloss: *Essence* (1973, 5038); E. Jefferson: *Things are Getting Better* (1974, 5043)

BIBLIOGRAPHY

Feather–Gitler '70s
C. Berg: Review of *Triplicity* (1975), *DB*, xliv/2 (1977), 41
M. Shera: Review of *The Crawl* (1979), *JJI*, xxiv/4 (1981), 43

PAUL RINZLER

Turnaround [turnback]. A chord pattern at the end of the final phrase of a chorus, which leads back to the beginning of the theme; *see* HARMONY (i), §1(v)(b).

Turnbull, Alan (Lawrence) [Tom Terrific] (*b* Melbourne, Australia, 23 Nov 1943). Australian drummer. He began playing professionally at the age of 14, and was influenced by Stewie Speers and Graham Morgan. In 1961 he worked with Frank Smith at a club in Melbourne, the Embers, and in 1965 he moved to Sydney where he worked regularly with John Sangster, Don Burrows, and others. In 1972 he played with Burrows's quartet at the Montreux and Newport jazz festivals; he may be heard to advantage on the album *Live at Montreux* (CPRS 1010). The following year he performed in Don Banks's *Nexus* with the Sydney SO. He has maintained his association with Burrows into the 1980s, and continues to perform and record as a sideman; he has worked with Gary Burton, Milt Jackson, Sonny Stitt, Phil Woods and Joe Henderson (both 1981), and George Cables (1985).

BIBLIOGRAPHY

A. Bisset: *Black Roots, White Flowers: a History of Jazz in Australia* (Sydney, 1979)
J. Shand: "Alan Turnbull," *Jazz: the Australasian Contemporary Music Magazine*, ii/9 (1982), 22
B. Johnson and others: *The Oxford Companion to Australian Jazz* (Melbourne, Australia, 1987)

JEFF PRESSING (with JOHN WHITEOAK)

Turner, Bruce (*b* Saltburn, England, 5 July 1922). English alto and soprano saxophonist and clarinetist. He taught himself clarinet at school and took up alto saxophone while in the RAF (1943). After a short spell with a bop group (1946) he played dixieland with Freddy Randall (1948–50). He was leader of a quartet with Dill Jones and Peter Ind on board the *Queen Mary*, and, while visiting New York, studied with Lee Konitz. Turner worked again with Randall (1951–3), then with Humphrey Lyttelton (1953–7), and from 1957 to 1965 led the Jump Band; this group was featured in Jack Gold's film *Living Jazz* (1961), for which Turner arranged the music. He was a member of Acker Bilk's band from 1966 to 1970, and in 1972 rejoined Lyttelton, with whom he has continued to work into the mid-1980s.

Turner's style on alto saxophone is highly individual, reflecting the early influence of Pete Brown as well as that of Charlie Parker and Konitz, whereas his playing on soprano saxophone shows an affinity with that of Bob Wilber. His performances on clarinet are flexible and vary in style. He is extremely self-critical and continually analyzes his own performances.

SELECTED RECORDINGS

As leader: with W. Fawkes: The Sheik of Araby/Fishmouth/Exactly like you/Oh Baby (1954, Decca 6193) [EP]; *Accent on Swing* (1959, International Jazz Club 4)

As sideman: F. Randall: Tight Lines/Baby won't you please come home? (1951, Parl. 3494); H. Lyttelton: *Live at the Royal Festival Hall* (1954, Parl. 1032); *Midnight at Nixa* (1956, Nixa 3); K. Smith: *Up Jumped the Blues* (1978, Hefty Jazz 105); D. Green: *Fingers Remembers Mingus* (1979, Spot. 521)

BIBLIOGRAPHY

FeatherE
H. Lyttelton: *I Play as I Please: the Memoirs of an Old Etonian Trumpeter* (London, 1954)
——: *Second Chorus* (London, 1958)
D. Oliver: *B. Turner Jump Bands* (Summerhill, Suffolk, England, 1968)
S.-A. Worsfold: "Bruce Turner: Confessions of a Jazz Maverick," *JJI*, xxx (1977), no.5, p.6; no.6, p.22
B. Turner: *Hot Air, Cool Music* (London, 1984) [incl. discography]

REG COOPER

Turner, Charlie [Fat Man] (*b* early 20th century; *d* 27 Oct 1964). Tuba and double bass player and bandleader. He played with Doc Cheatham (1926), then recorded with Richard M. Jones's Jazz Wizards (1927), and his imaginative tuba playing may be heard to advantage on *Boar Hog Blues* (1927, Vic. 21203). After touring with Jelly Roll Morton he moved to New York as a member of Marion Hardy's Alabamians (1929). By 1933 he was leading his own band, which, under the name Turner's Arcadians, was resident at the Arcadia Ballroom in 1934. Between November 1934 and around May 1935 this group was used by Fletcher Henderson for various engagements, and from 1935 to 1938 some of its members, including Turner himself, formed the nucleus of Fats Waller's touring band. Turner also recorded with Waller's Rhythm and with Emmett Mathews; *You came to my rescue* (1936, Voc. 3332), recorded with the latter, provides a good example of Turner's double bass playing. Thereafter he worked in a backup group for Ethel Waters (1938–9) and later played again with Waller (1941–2).

BIBLIOGRAPHY

W. C. Allen: *Hendersonia: the Music of Fletcher Henderson and his Musicians: a Bio-discography* (Highland Park, NJ, 1973), 572
H. Dial: *All that Jazz about Jazz: the Autobiography of Harry Dial* (Chigwell, England, 1984)

HOWARD RYE

Turner, (J.) Danny (*b* Farrell, PA, *c* late 1920s). Alto saxophonist. Brought up in Niagara Falls, New York, he played his first engagements in the Buffalo area at the age of 18. After moving to Philadelphia in 1948 he toured briefly with the vocal group Four Kings and a Queen and, in the early 1950s, with Gerald Wilson's band, accompanying Billie Holiday. He played in Milt Buckner's trio for about four years from 1954 and is heard to advantage on *Rockin' with Milt* (1955, Cap. T642). In the 1960s he played intermittently with Machito and recorded with Dakota Staton (1963), Brother Jack McDuff (1963, 1966–7), Ray Charles (1964), Jimmy Witherspoon and Pat Martino (both 1967), and Jimmy McGriff (1968–9). He worked as a substitute in Count Basie's band from 1971 to 1975, when he became a full-time member, first on tenor saxophone, then as lead alto saxophonist (1983). He also plays clarinet and flute.

BIBLIOGRAPHY

P. Vacher: "Counting the Score," *MM*, li (3 Jan 1976), 27
D. J. Gibson: "Count Basie Saxophone Section Celebrates 50th Anniversary," *Saxophone Journal*, xi/3 (1986), 40; xi/4 (1987), 39 [interview]

Turner, Henry (B.) (*b* Quincy, FL, 28 June 1904; *d* New York, 26 July 1980). Double bass player. He first performed in Tuskegee, Alabama, then in Hartford, Connecticut (1925), playing tuba and trombone. Later he worked in New York with the bandleader Charlie Skeete before joining Claude Hopkins at the Venetian Gardens (1929). Illness interrupted his career in 1936. After his recovery he joined Snub Mosley (1937), then played with Sidney Bechet (1938) and Joe Sullivan (1939–40). Sullivan's *Low Down Dirty Shame* (1940, Voc. 5531) offers a good example of Turner's dependable, swinging rhythm work. Thereafter he worked with Louis Jordan (1940–41), George James (1942–3), Garvin Bushell (1944), Lem Johnson (1945, *c*1947), Herman "Ivory" Chittison (1946), Bobby Sands (1947–8), Harry Dial (1949–52), and Wilbur De Paris (1957). He then worked as a freelance, performing and recording regularly, and played for radio and television.

based on *ChiltonW*

Turner, Joe [Joseph H.] **(i)** (*b* Baltimore, 3 Nov 1907). Pianist. He was first taught piano by his mother when he was five. He moved to New York around 1925 and enjoyed much popularity among musicians in Harlem, working with June Clark (1927–8), Benny Carter (1929), and Louis Armstrong (1930). He accompanied the singer Adelaide Hall in a piano duo with Alex Hill and then with Francis Carter; he and Carter toured Europe with Hall in 1931. Turner performed as a soloist throughout Europe until 1939, and then in the USA. After working as a member of an army band led by Sy Oliver (1944–5) and with Rex Stewart (1946) he returned to Europe and played in Hungary (1948) and Switzerland (1949–62). He then settled in Paris, where from 1962 he has held a residency at La Calvados; he has also performed in Great Britain, Switzerland, and the USA. Turner was influenced mainly by James P. Johnson, Fats Waller, Art Tatum, and Erroll Garner. A true stride pianist, he performs test pieces of the genre with faultless phrasing, a brilliant technique, and a strong sense of swing. His playing is well represented on *Harlem Strut* (1974).

SELECTED RECORDINGS

As unaccompanied soloist: *Stridin' in Paris* (1952, Vogue 047); *Joe's Back in Town* (1974, BB 33064), incl. Harlem Strut; *Another Epoch: Stride Piano* (1975–6, Pablo 2310763)

Duos with P. Francis: *Effervescent* (1976, BB 33102)

BIBLIOGRAPHY

M. Jones: "Joe Turner Strides out," *MM* (17 June 1972), 26

B. Rusch: "A Talk with Joe 'Stride' Turner," *Cadence*, ii/2 (1976), 7

H. Rye: "Visiting Firemen, 10(a): Adelaide Hall, Joe Turner, and Francis J. Carter," *Sv*, no.114 (1984), 211

J. Simmen: "Joe Turner," *Sv*, no.123 (1986), 97

——: "A Personal Survey of the Recordings of Joe Turner," *Sv*, no.124 (1986), 140

JOHNNY SIMMEN

Turner, (Big) Joe [Joseph Vernon] **(ii)** (*b* Kansas City, MO, 18 May 1911; *d* Inglewood, CA, 24 Nov 1985). Singer. He began working as a barman and cook at the age of 14 in various clubs in Kansas City. There he became known as "the singing bartender" and attracted the attention of such bandleaders as Bennie Moten, Andy Kirk, and Count Basie, with whom he subsequently toured. From the mid-1930s he was frequently accompanied by Pete Johnson, with whom he appeared at the "From Spirituals to Swing" concert at Carnegie Hall in 1938 shortly before recording his first titles. *Roll 'em, Pete*, with spectacular piano playing by Johnson, is an example of Turner's forceful, half-shouted vocal style; tension is built up towards the close of the piece by his use of repeated phrases. Although he was best known as a "blues shouter," Turner had a musical voice and was a sensitive singer on slow blues (*see* BLUES, §9). Throughout the 1940s and 1950s he toured extensively with bands and solo pianists. With his relaxed singing style and the hot tone, strength, and subtle inflections of his voice, he soon became recognized as a model for other jazz-blues singers. His recording of *Shake Rattle and Roll* precipitated a revolution in popular music, though it was Bill Haley and his Comets who made a reputation out of the rock-and-roll theme. In spite of his many popular hits, Turner remained at his best in jazz-blues performances, and in his 60s was much in demand for concerts, films, and television appearances.

Oral history material in *NjR* (JOHP), *NjR*.

Duo with P. Johnson: Roll 'em, Pete (1938, Voc. 4607)

As leader: Old Piney Brown is gone (1948, Swingtime 154); Shake Rattle and Roll (1954, Atl. 1026); *Joe Turner Sings Kansas City Jazz* (1956, Atl. 1234), incl. You're driving me crazy

As sideman with A. Tatum: Lucille (1941, Decca 8577)

Joe Turner (ii) (far right) with (from left) Harold Blacksheer, Lionel Hampton, Jack McVea, and Pete Johnson, Los Angeles, c1947

BIBLIOGRAPHY

P. H. Oliver: "Boss of the Blues," *Jazz Music Mirror*, v/5 (1958), 4
V. Wilmer: "Blues for Mr. Turner," *JB*, ii/7 (1965), 4 [interview]
P. Clinco: "Joe Turner," *Living Blues*, no.10 (1972), 20 [interview]
S. Harris: *Blues Who's Who: a Biographical Dictionary of Blues Singers* (New Rochelle, NY, 1979)
D. Pomus: "Joe Turner," *Whiskey, Women, and . . .*, no.11 (1983), 3
T. Burke and D. Penny: "Big Joe Turner," *Blues & Rhythm: the Gospel Truth*, no.11 (1985), 4; no.12 (1985), 4
D. Garçon: "Bad Luck Blues," *Soul Bag*, no.105 (1986), 34

PAUL OLIVER

Turney, Norris (William) (*b* Wilmington, OH, 8 Sept 1921). Alto saxophonist. After working in Ohio with the tenor saxophonist A. B. Townsend he toured with the Jeter–Pillars Orchestra and in 1945 played with Tiny Bradshaw in Chicago. He performed and recorded with Billy Eckstine in New York (1945–6), returned to Ohio, then worked in Philadelphia with Elmer Snowden (1951); in 1967 he toured Australasia with Ray Charles. He substituted for Johnny Hodges in Duke Ellington's band (1969), then became a regular member of the band until 1973; during the following decade he worked in pit orchestras in New York. In the 1980s he resumed his career in jazz as a member of Panama Francis's Savoy Sultans and of George Wein's Newport All Stars, with which he has toured internationally. A versatile musician, Turney is among the most lyrical of alto saxophonists, as well as an adept player of flute and clarinet.

Oral history material in *CtY*.

SELECTED RECORDINGS

As leader: *I Let a Song* (1979, BB 33140)
As sideman: D. Ellington: *The Seventieth Birthday Concert* (1969, SolS 19000); *Toga brava Suite* (1971, UA 92); R. Eldridge: *What it's All About* (1976, Pablo 2310766); P. Francis: *Gettin' in the Groove* (1979, BB 33320–21)

BIBLIOGRAPHY

Feather–Gitler '70s
B. Rusch: "Norris Turney: Interview," *Cadence*, v/2 (1979), 18
M. Richards: "Norris Turney," *JJI*, xxxix/6 (1986), 12

MARTIN RICHARDS

Turn the rhythm [beat, time] **around.** Accidentally or deliberately to redefine meter over a long period by the displacement of normal accents or the disturbance of phrase structures; *see* Beat, §4(iii).

Turré, Steve (*b* Omaha, NE, 12 Sept 1948). Trombonist. He grew up in California, and studied music at North Texas State University (1968–9). In San Francisco he recorded with the Latin rock group Santana (1970) and from 1968 played sporadically with Roland Kirk. After touring with Ray Charles (1972) he worked briefly with Woody Shaw, then traveled to New York with Art Blakey's Jazz Messengers and toured Europe with the Thad Jones–Mel Lewis Orchestra (both 1973). Turré performed and recorded on trombone and electric bass guitar with Chico Hamilton (1974–6). At the same time he played trombone with Shaw (1974–5); his solos are particularly prominent on the album *Moontrane* (1974, Muse 5058). After working again with Kirk (*c*1976–1977) he was a member of and wrote arrangements for Slide Hampton's World of Trombones; he also worked as a composer and arranger for Max Roach, led his own quartet, and toured with Cedar Walton. In 1980 he returned to Shaw's band, with which he made a number of recordings (including *Master of the Art*, 1982, Elek. Mus. 60131).

BIBLIOGRAPHY

Feather–Gitler '70s
T. Nuccio: "Steve Turré," *DB*, xlix/9 (1982), 53
D. Pagani: "Steve Turré: Interview," *Cadence*, xi/4 (1985), 5
M. Bourne: "Steve Turré: Trombone Straight from the Hip," *DB*, liv/12 (1987), 24 [incl. discography]

Turrentine, Stanley (William) (*b* Pittsburgh, 5 April 1934). Tenor saxophonist, brother of Tommy Turrentine. After touring in rhythm-and-blues bands with Ray Charles and others he replaced John Coltrane in Earl Bostic's group (1953), and later played with Max Roach (1959–60). He achieved his reputation in the 1960s, when he made a number of recordings for Blue Note, both as a leader and as a sideman, notably with Jimmy Smith and Shirley Scott (who was at that time Turrentine's wife). Influenced by Don Byas, Coleman Hawkins, and Sonny Rollins, he played in an earthy blues style characterized by brief moans and wails. From 1965 Turrentine began to record with larger ensembles, producing work that appealed to a large popular market; *Sugar*, for which he composed the title track, was the first of a number of albums that appeared on the charts. Turrentine has maintained a popularity unusual by jazz standards.

SELECTED RECORDINGS

As leader: *Stan "the Man" Turrentine* (*c*1959–60, Time 52086); *A Chip off the Old Block* (1963, BN 84150); *Sugar* (1970, CTI 6005); *Pieces of Dreams* (1974, Fan. 9465); *Soothsayer* (*c*1979, Elek. 217); *Tender Togetherness* (*c*1981, Elek. 534)
As sideman: M. Roach: *Quiet as it's Kept* (1960, Mer. 20491); J. Smith: *Midnight Special* (1960, BN 84078); S. Scott: *Everybody Loves a Lover* (1964, Imp. 73)

BIBLIOGRAPHY

M. James: "Introducing Stanley Turrentine," *JM*, vii/5 (1961), 7
H. Nolan: "Dues on Top of Dues: Stanley Turrentine," *DB*, xlii/18 (1975), 12
B. Primack: "Stanley Turrentine: We're in the Marketplace Now!," *DB*, xlv/17 (1978), 13 [interview]
L. Tomkins: "Tenor Integrity for the People: Stanley Turrentine," *CI*, xix (1981), no.9, p.6; no.10, p.12 [interview]
G. Kalbacher: "The Blue Notes of Mr. T.," *DB*, lii/5 (1985), 16 [incl. discography]

MARK C. GRIDLEY/R

Turrentine, Tommy [Thomas Walter, Jr.] (*b* Pittsburgh, 22 April 1928). Trumpeter, brother of Stanley Turrentine. His father played tenor saxophone with Al Cooper's Savoy Sultans, and Tommy began learning trumpet in his early teens. He played with Benny Carter (1946), Earl Bostic (1952–5), Charles Mingus (1956), and Max Roach (1959–60); he also performed in the big bands of Billy Eckstine, Dizzy Gillespie, and Count Basie. In the early 1960s he worked as a freelance in New York, and his best recordings, made with such leaders as his brother, Horace Parlan, Jackie McLean, Sonny Clark, and Lou Donaldson, date from this period. He has been largely inactive in the 1970s and 1980s. Turrentine's lyrical, full-toned playing is stylistically related to that of Gillespie and Fats Navarro, and his crisp, long-breathed solos invariably display a fine sense of balance and structure. He has unfortunately recorded only one album as a leader.

SELECTED RECORDINGS

(all recorded for Blue Note unless otherwise indicated)

As leader: *T. Turrentine* (1960, Time 70008)
As sideman: H. Parlan: *Speakin' my Piece* (1960, 4043); *On the Spur of the Moment* (1961, 4074); J. McLean: *A Fickle Sonance* (1961, 84089); S. Clark: *Leapin' and Lopin'* (1961, 84091); S. Turrentine: *Jubilee Shouts* (1961–2, LA883J2); L. Donaldson: *The Natural Soul* (1962, 84108)

BIBLIOGRAPHY
FeatherE
N. Hentoff: Liner notes, *T. Turrentine* (Time 70008, 1960)
——: Liner notes, H. Parlan: *Speakin' my Piece* (BN 84043, 1961)

MARK GARDNER

Tusa, Frank (*b* New York, 1 April 1947). Double bass player. He performed and recorded with Paul Bley (1970–71), then worked in the trio Open Sky with Dave Liebman and Bob Moses (1972–4); he also played with Dave Holland and Collin Walcott and taught at workshops. From 1973 to 1976 he performed, recorded, and toured Europe as a member of Liebman's group Lookout Farm with Badal Roy and Richard Beirach; around this time he also worked as a freelance with Barry Miles, Booker Ervin, Don Cherry, Freddie Hubbard, Lee Konitz, and Harold Mabern. Tusa recorded on electric bass guitar with Dom Um Romao (1973), and also made albums with Beirach (1974) and as a leader (*Father Time*, 1975, Enja 2056). Later he played a fusion of Indian ragas and jazz-rock with Roy, joined Beirach in the trio Eon, and played as a freelance with Art Blakey (all 1977). From 1983 he has played in the San Francisco Bay area with the group Bebop and Beyond.

BIBLIOGRAPHY
C. Berg: "Frank Tusa: Triple Threat Bassman," *DB*, xliv/15 (1977), 20
D. Liebman and others: *Lookout Farm: a Case Study of Improvisation for Small Jazz Group* (n.p., 1978)

Tuxedo Brass Band. *See* ORIGINAL TUXEDO ORCHESTRA.

Tuxen, Erik (*b* Mannheim, Germany, 4 July 1902; *d* Copenhagen, 28 Aug 1957). Danish bandleader. He was trained as a classical musician and conducted theater orchestras for several years. From 1932 to 1936 he led an important big band, which included Kai Ewans, Leo Mathisen, and Peter Rasmussen among its members and made several outstanding recordings, among them two for Polyphon in 1933, *New York* (XS50204) and *Københavner-rhapsodie* (XS50201). From 1936 until his death he was the conductor of the Danish RO.

ERIK WIEDEMANN

Twardzik, Dick [Richard] (*b* Danvers, MA, 1931; *d* Paris, 21 Oct 1955). Pianist. In 1951 he played bop in Boston with Serge Chaloff and participated in a broadcast with Charlie Parker. He worked with Charlie Mariano (1951–2) and toured with Lionel Hampton. After recording with Chaloff and as a leader (both 1954) he joined Chet Baker for a European tour (1955). His playing may be heard to advantage on Baker's acclaimed album *Rondette* (1955, Barclay 84009), which was recorded shortly before Twardzik died of a drug overdose.

BIBLIOGRAPHY
FeatherE
A. Morgan: "Dick Twardzik," *JM*, ix/9 (1963), 27 [discography]
R. Williams: "Chet Baker," *MM*, li (7 Aug 1976), 13

Twelve Clouds of Joy. Name sometimes used by the Kansas City jazz band led by ANDY KIRK from 1929 to 1948.

Two-beat. A term applied to music in which the first and third beats of a bar in 4/4 meter are accented. It is pertinent to the marches and rags on which early jazz drew, and therefore to some pieces from the jazz repertory; slow ballads may also be performed with two-beat accentuation. *See* BEAT, §4(ii).

Twofer. In popular parlance a double ALBUM (albums containing three discs are also usually categorized for convenience as twofers). The term derives from the phrase "two for the price of one"; originally some record companies did indeed market two discs at the price of one, though often the playing time of the two together might scarcely exceed that of a single disc. Latterly the double album has come to cost nearly as much as two separate LPs.

Twos. Two-bar phrases, as in the expression "to trade twos"; *see* FORMS, §1(ii).

Tyler, Charles (Lacy) (*b* Cadiz, KY, 20 July 1941). Baritone and alto saxophonist, and teacher. He studied clarinet and alto saxophone as a youth and played baritone saxophone in an army band. He moved in 1960 to Cleveland, where he performed with Albert Ayler, then to New York, where he became involved in free jazz and performed and recorded with Ayler, and then to California, where for four years he taught music at Merritt College. He returned to New York in 1976 to lead his own groups. He has also performed with Dave Baker, Dewey Redman, Frank Lowe, David Murray, the drummer Steve Reid, and Cecil Taylor, and recorded as a member of the Billy Bang Quintet (1981–2). Tyler has been influenced by Ayler, by bop saxophonists, and by folk and blues musicians.

SELECTED RECORDINGS
As leader: *Live in Europe* (1975, Akba 1010); *Saga of the Outlaws* (1976, Nessa 16); *Definite* (1981, Sto. 4098–9)
As sideman: A. Ayler: *Spirits Rejoice* (1965, ESP 1020)

BIBLIOGRAPHY
C. Flicker: "Charles Tyler," *Jm*, no.255 (1977), 18
E. Jost: *Jazzmusiker: Materialen zur Soziologie der afro-amerikanischen Musik* (Frankfurt am Main, Germany, Berlin, and Vienna, 1981), 123
J. Litweiler: "Charles Tyler," *DB*, li/5 (1984), 56

DAVID G. SUCH

Tyner, (Alfred) McCoy [Saud, Sulaimon] (*b* Philadelphia, 11 Dec 1938). Pianist. He began to study piano formally at the age of 13, and later took theory lessons at the Granoff School of Music. His early influences included Richie and Bud Powell, Art Tatum, and Thelonious Monk. His first important professional engagement was in 1959 when he joined the Benny Golson–Art Farmer Jazztet, but he achieved international acclaim as the pianist in John Coltrane's quartet from 1960 to 1965. During the same period he also made a series of influential recordings under his own name for the Impulse and Blue Note labels. After a brief lull in his career during the late 1960s he began to record with Milestone in 1972, and his subsequent albums have gained him a large popular following. He toured and recorded with the Milestone Jazzstars in 1978, and in the mid-1980s led a quintet that included Gary Bartz and the violinist John Blake. Tyner's music has been a major influence in the adoption in jazz of quartal and quintal harmonies, modes and pentatonic scales, and African rhythmic elements. A volume of transcriptions, *Inception to Now*, was published in 1983. *See also* PIANO, §5.

SELECTED RECORDINGS
As leader: *Inception* (1962, Imp. 18); *The Real McCoy* (1967, BN 84264); *Sahara* (1972, Mlst. 9039); *Supertrio* (1977, Mlst. 55003); *Four Times Four* (1980, Mlst. 55007)

As sideman with J. Coltrane: *Impressions* (1961, 1963, Imp. 42); *Selflessness* (1963–5, Imp. 9161); *A Love Supreme* (1964, Imp. 77)

BIBLIOGRAPHY

M. Bourne: "McCoy Tyner," *DB*, xl/20 (1973), 14
M. Luzzi: "Discographia McCoy Tyner," *Musica jazz*, xxxi/12 (1975), 45; xxxii (1976), no.1, p.47; no.2, p.47; no.3, p.46; xxxiii/3 (1977), 48
L. Underwood: "McCoy Tyner: Savant of the Astral Latitudes," *DB*, xlii/15 (1975), 12
J. E. Berendt: "McCoy Tyner: Echoes of a Friend," *Ein Fenster aus Jazz: Essays, Portraits, Reflexionen* (Frankfurt am Main, Germany, 1977), 75
D. Clark: "Milestone Jazzstars on Tour," *DB*, xlv/19 (1978), 16
L. Feather: "Piano Giants of Jazz: McCoy Tyner," *CK*, iv/8 (1978), 54
B. Doerschuk: "McCoy Tyner," *CK*, vii/8 (1981), 28
H. Rock: "Profiling McCoy Tyner," *JSN*, ii/3 (1981), 10
L. Lyons: *The Great Jazz Pianists, Speaking of their Lives and Music* (New York, 1983), 235
P. Rinzler: "McCoy Tyner: Style and Syntax," *ARJS*, ii (1983), 109–49
J. Diliberto: "McCoy Tyner: Piano Visionary," *DB*, li/2 (1984), 20
B. Rusch: "McCoy Tyner: Interview," *Cadence*, x/1 (1984), 5

BILL DOBBINS

U

UDJ. *See* UNION DEUTSCHER JAZZMUSIKER.

UHCA [United Hot Clubs of America]. Record label. It was established in 1936 by Milt Gabler, who ran the enterprise from his Commodore Music Shop in New York. Its catalogue included items leased from many of the most important companies of the 1920s and 1930s; in many cases UHCA's recordings were pressed directly from original masters. At first the records were sold only by means of a subscription scheme; later they became more widely available.

BIBLIOGRAPHY

G. Millstein: "For Kicks," *New Yorker*, xxii (9 March 1946), 40; xxii (16 March 1946), 34; repr. as "The Commodore Shop and Milt Gabler," *Eddie Condon's Treasury of Jazz*, ed. E. Condon and R. Gehman (New York, 1956/R1975), 98

B. Rust: *The American Record Label Book* (New Rochelle, NY, 1978), 297

Ukulele [ukelele]. A small instrument resembling a guitar, usually associated with the music of Hawaii. It has four plucked strings that are generally tuned *a'–d'–f♯'–b'* or *g'–c'–e'–a'*. The instrument's best-known exponent in jazz is Ike Edwards (also known as Ukulele Ike), who recorded in a duo with Adrian Rollini (*That's all there is*, 1925, PAct 025132) and later made recordings as a leader with such sidemen as Red Nichols, Miff Mole, and Jimmy Dorsey (until 1935); he used the instrument both to play solo melodies and to provide rhythmic, chordal accompaniment. The ukulele playing of Roy Smeck, which relied to a greater extent than that of Edwards on pyrotechnics and perhaps as a result gained a larger following, was seldom as musically rewarding. Other jazz ukulele players, such as Frank Crumit and the singer Annette Hanshaw, used the instrument only to provide chordal accompaniment.

JULIAN F. V. VINCENT, DAVID C. PHILLIPS

Ukulele banjo. *See* BANJULELE.

Ulmer, James "Blood" (*b* St. Matthews, SC, 2 Feb 1942). Electric guitarist, singer, and composer. At home he learned guitar and sang in a gospel group. He began his professional career playing with funk groups in Pittsburgh (1959–64) and around Columbus, Ohio (1964–7). After rehearsing for four years in Detroit he went to New York with his band in 1971; he performed for nine months at Minton's Playhouse, where he was able to introduce many of his new dance tunes. He joined Art Blakey briefly, then in 1973 began to study and perform with Ornette Coleman, which brought about a dramatic change in his career. He embraced Coleman's HARMOLODIC THEORY, according to which all the instruments in an ensemble are regarded as equally important and engage in harmonically free improvisation. In the late 1970s Ulmer led a group that presented daring new blends of funk, avant-garde jazz, and hard rock, but his originality gradually diminished as he sought greater precision. His tendency to abandon jazz elements and rely on increasingly rigid structures culminated in an album appropriately entitled *Black Rock* (1982). From around 1983 he has led Odyssey, a trio consisting of violin, electric guitar, and drums. George Adams performed on tenor saxophone with Ulmer's more conventional trio of electric guitar, electric bass guitar, and drums for a concert in England in 1985.

SELECTED RECORDINGS

As leader: *Tales of Captain Black* (1978, AH 7); *Are You Glad to Be in America?* (1980, Rough Trade 16); of Music Revelation Ensemble (with D. Murray, Amin Eli, and R. S. Jackson): *No Wave* (1980, Moers 01072); *Freelancing* (1981, Col. ARC37493); *Black Rock* (1982, Col. ARC38285)

As sideman: R. Ali: *Rashied Ali Quintet* (c1973, Survival 102); A. Blythe: *Lenox Avenue Breakdown* (1978, Col. JC35638)

BIBLIOGRAPHY

G. Giddins: "Jazz-funk," *VV*, xxiv (25 June 1979), 53

R. Palmer: "The Futuristic Jazz-funk of James Ulmer," *RS*, no.319 (12 June 1980), 23

C. J. Safane: "The Harmolodic Diatonic Funk of James 'Blood' Ulmer," *DB*, xlvii/10 (1980), 22

B. Loupias: "James Blood Ulmer: un sang nouveau pour nos sillons?," *Jm*, no.294 (1981), 34 [incl. discography]

G. Giddins: "Harmolodic Hoedown," *VV*, xxix (27 March 1984), 38

S. Lake: "Blood: off the Tracks," *The Wire*, no.22 (1985), 24

BARRY KERNFELD

Union Deutscher Jazzmusiker [UDJ]. German professional organization. It was established in Marburg in 1973 to promote the interests of jazz musicians in the Federal Republic of Germany. Aiming to enhance the music's reputation, and to gain wider recognition for it, the UDJ has made many efforts to represent the case for jazz to state bodies and other organizations. It also sponsors the Deutsches Jazz Forum, a program of concerts, seminars, and discussions held for two days each November, and encourages the teaching of jazz in German schools. From 1985 the organization has supported the German–French Jazz Ensemble, led by Albert Mangelsdorff and Jean-François Jenny-Clark. The UDJ is a member of the Deutscher Musikrat (German Music Council), and of the International Jazz Federation. In 1987 it had about 500 members and was led by Mangelsdorff and Peter Ortmann; its offices in Wendeburg-Ersehof, near Hannover, were managed by Otto Wolters.

BERT NOGLIK

United. Record company and label. The company was established in Chicago in 1951 by Lew Simpkins (who had formerly been responsible for artists and repertory with Miracle and Premium) and Leonard Allen. The label and its subsidiary, States (launched in 1952), were used to issue a wide range of Afro-American music. The best-remembered jazz recordings were by Tab Smith, Paul Bascomb, and Jimmy Forrest, whose *Night Train* (1951, United 110) became a hit throughout the USA. Simpkins died in May 1953, but Allen continued the company until 1957. United's masters were purchased in 1975 by Delmark, which embarked on a program of important reissues, and also put out some items from the repertory that had not previously been released.

BIBLIOGRAPHY

B. Koester: "The United/States Masters," *Blues Unlimited*, no.123 (1977), 14; no.124 (1977), 11
R. Pruter: "Obituary: Leonard Allen," *Living Blues*, no.67 (1986), 39

United Artists. Record company and label. The company was established in New York in 1958 as a subsidiary of the film company of the same name. It quickly assembled a remarkably comprehensive catalogue that contained a wide variety of mainstream and modern jazz. Among its most notable recordings were the excellent album *Money Jungle* by Duke Ellington, Charles Mingus, and Max Roach, and the only recording made jointly by John Coltrane and Cecil Taylor. In addition the company released albums by Art Blakey, Roy Ayers, Count Basie, Billie Holiday, Bill Potts, Art Farmer, Curtis Fuller, Thad Jones, Mose Allison, Ruby Braff, Gerry Mulligan, the Modern Jazz Quartet, Betty Carter, Dave Lambert, Rex Stewart, Oliver Nelson, Benny Golson, Herb Pomeroy, Booker Little, Milt Jackson, Howard McGhee, Bud Freeman, Teddy Charles, Kenny Dorham, Zoot Sims, and Billy Strayhorn. This extensive repertory was produced by Tom Wilson, Jack Lewis, Alan Douglas, and George Wein. Around 1966 United Artists established an offshoot, Solid State, which achieved considerable artistic and commercial success, and is best known for a long series of albums by the Thad Jones–Mel Lewis Orchestra. By the 1980s the company had been taken over by a subsidiary of EMI, Manhattan, which reissued much of the catalogue. When *Money Jungle* was reissued in 1987 it included four previously unreleased tracks; this suggests that there is a considerable amount of unissued material in the United Artists archive.

MARK GARDNER

United Hot Clubs of America. *See* UHCA.

United Jazz and Rock Ensemble. International group based in West Germany. It was organized by Wolfgang Dauner in 1975 for a television series in Stuttgart, and its members are Ack van Rooyen, Ian Carr, and Kenny Wheeler (trumpets), Albert Mangelsdorff (trombone), Charlie Mariano (alto and soprano saxophone and *nāgasvaram)*, Barbara Thompson (tenor and soprano saxophone), Volker Kriegel (guitar), Dauner (keyboards), Eberhard Weber (double bass and electric bass guitar), and Jon Hiseman (drums); Wheeler joined in 1978, but otherwise the membership of the ensemble has remained constant since its formation. After their first public appearance (July 1976) the musicians met about once a year to tour and record. They also established their own record label, Mood, which was at first used exclusively by the ensemble but later made available for recordings by others in various musical styles. The group's fusion of rock and jazz elements has proved highly successful; *Live im Schützenhaus* (1977, Mood 28-600), its first LP, became the best-selling jazz album produced in Germany.

BIBLIOGRAPHY

V. Kriegel: "Jazz & Rock," *Jazzrock: Tendenzen einer modernen Musik*, ed. B. König (Reinbek, Germany, 1983), 35–77
A. Höll: "The United Jazz & Rock Ensemble," *JP*, xxxiv/12 (1985), 32
H. Kumpf: "10 Jahre United Jazz & Rock Ensemble," *JP*, xxxiv/5 (1985), 27

WOLFRAM KNAUER

United Phonographs Corp. [UPC]. Record company. It was established by the Wisconsin Chair Co. at Sheboygan, Wisconsin, and in the early 1920s issued recordings on Puritan and Paramount.

Upbeat. The beat or subdivision of the beat that immediately precedes the first beat of the bar or downbeat; *see* BEAT, §4(i).

Upchurch, Phil (*b* Chicago, 19 July 1941). Electric guitarist. He first worked with rhythm-and-blues groups (1958–62) and as a session musician in Chicago, then played at clubs in Europe while in the army (1965). After returning to the USA he recorded as a leader (1967, 1969), and with Jimmy Smith (1968), Woody Herman, Brother Jack McDuff, and John Klemmer (all 1968–9), and Dizzy Gillespie (1969). From 1969 to 1970 he was a member of Ramsey Lewis's quartet, then worked with Quincy Jones in California and toured Japan with him in 1972. During the 1970s Upchurch made several recordings as a leader, including *Phil Upchurch* (*c*1978, Marlin 798). He also recorded with Jones, Cannonball Adderley, and Grover Washington, Jr. (all 1974), the Crusaders (1980), and Mose Allison (1982), toured and recorded with George Benson (1974, 1976–9), led a quintet, and continued to play rhythm-and-blues. He is best known for his tasteful, articulate rhythm guitar playing.

BIBLIOGRAPHY

Feather–Gitler '70s
D. Morgenstern: "Phil Upchurch: Studio Soul," *DB*, xxxvi/13 (1969), 13
J. Sievert: "Sharing Leads with George," *GP*, xiii/7 (1979), 87 [incl. discography]
J. Ferguson: "Phil Upchurch: from '50s R & B to '80s Pop: Fusing Blues, Funk, and Jazz," *GP*, xix/2 (1985), 56 [incl. discography]

Up tempo. Fast.

Urbaniak, Michal [Michał] (*b* Warsaw, 22 Jan 1943). Polish violinist, tenor saxophonist, and bandleader. He studied violin (from the age of six), soprano saxophone, then tenor saxophone, and briefly played dixieland and swing before settling into the bop style. He played tenor saxophone with Zbigniew Namysłowski (1961), Andrzej Trzaskowski (1962–4), and Krzysztof Komeda (1962–5) and at the same time worked as a classical violinist. From 1965 he led a group in Scandinavia with Urszula Dudziak, whom he married in 1967, and after returning to Poland in 1969 he formed the eclectic group Constellation with Dudziak, Adam Makowicz, Czesław Bartkowski, and Pawel Jarzebski (replaced by Roman Dylag in 1972–3). By 1974 he had moved to New York, where he formed the jazz-rock group Fusion, which he led until 1977; the group's playing exploited the unusual scat singing of Dudziak, and some of the pieces in its repertory, such as *New York Batsa*

(1974), used the melodies and irregular meters of Polish folk music. Later he performed and recorded with Larry Coryell (1982–3) and Dudziak and as a leader; he also worked as a sideman with Archie Shepp. Like Jean-Luc Ponty, Urbaniak played the electric violin and the violectra (an electronic bowed string instrument that sounds an octave lower than the violin) before taking up a five-string hybrid instrument (the lowest string on which was tuned to *c*) and later a six-string instrument (with the addition of a string tuned to *F*); he uses electronic pedals to alter his instrument's timbre.

SELECTED RECORDINGS

Duos with L. Coryell: *The Larry Coryell–Michal Urbaniak Duo* (1982, Key. 716)

As leader: *Super Constellation* (*c*1973, CBS 65744); *Constellation in Concert* (1973, Muza 1010); *Atma* (1974, Col. KC33184), incl. New York Batsa; *Fusion III* (*c*1975, Col. PC33542); *Urbaniak* (1977, IC 1036); *Music for Violin and Jazz Quartet* (1980, JAM 001); *Take Good Care of my Heart* (1984, Ste. 1195)

As sideman: R. Kühn: *Solarius* (1964, Amiga 850046); [no leader:] *Jazz Workshop East–West* (1965, Col. SMC83875); *New Violin Summit* (1971, MPS 3321285)

BIBLIOGRAPHY

J. Byrczek: "Eurojazz Personalities: Poland," *JF* [intl edn], no.18 (1972), 93
R. Townley: "Profile: Michal Urbaniak," *DB*, xli/17 (1974), 38
L. Jeske: "Michal Urbaniak: Stranger in a Strange Land," *DB*, xlix/5 (1982), 22 [incl. discography]

BARRY KERNFELD

Urso, Phil(ip) (*b* Jersey City, NJ, 2 Oct 1925). Tenor saxophonist. He played clarinet at the age of 13, then studied tenor saxophone at high school in Denver. After moving to New York in 1947 he played and recorded with Elliot Lawrence (1948–50) and Woody Herman (1950–51); he was the principal soloist on Herman's *By George* (1951, MGM 10975). In the 1950s he was associated with a number of leaders, including Jimmy Dorsey (1951) and Miles Davis (1952), and recorded with Don Elliott (1952), Terry Gibbs (1952), and Oscar Pettiford (1953), and as the leader of small groups (1953, 1954, 1956, 1958); on one of these sessions (1954) he and Bob Brookmeyer led a quintet in which the sidemen were Horace Silver, Kenny Clarke, and Percy Heath. After working as a freelance musician he joined Chet Baker (1955), with whom he played and recorded (on alto as well as tenor saxophone) in Los Angeles (1956); he recorded again with Baker in 1965. He moved back to Denver in the late 1950s, though he worked with Ernie Ross in Las Vegas in 1959–60. He continued to play in Denver in the late 1970s. Urso is one of the many tenor saxophonists of the 1950s to be strongly influenced by Lester Young; he is heard to advantage on *Little Pres* and *Three Little Words*, both from the EP *New Trends of Music*, xii (1953, Savoy 8059).

For illustration *see* JACKSON, MILT.

BIBLIOGRAPHY

FeatherE
A. Morgan: "Woody's Tenors," *JM*, vi (1960–61), no.7, p.4; no.8, p.13; no.12, p.9
I. Gitler: Liner notes, B. Moore and others: *Brothers and Other Mothers*, ii (Savoy 2236, 1979)

Urtreger, René (*b* Paris, 16 July 1934). French pianist. From the age of four he studied classical piano with such well-known teachers as Marguerite Long. He played jazz from the age of 17, belonged to a student band, and after winning an amateur contest in 1953 worked professionally with Buck Clayton and Don Byas. After serving in the army (to 1957) he worked regularly at the Club Saint-Germain in Paris, where he accompanied many American soloists, including Miles Davis, Lester Young, Lionel Hampton, Stan Getz, Chet Baker (recording in 1955), Johnny Griffin, Milt Jackson, Dexter Gordon, and Stuff Smith and Stephane Grappelli (recording in 1965). He interrupted his career in jazz for several years, during which he worked principally as an accompanist for French popular singers; after 1977 he worked again as a jazz musician, both as an unaccompanied soloist and as a leader of small groups, one of which toured France with Sonny Stitt in 1982. He was awarded the Prix Django Reinhardt by the Académie du jazz in 1960. Although Urtreger's playing is frequently likened to that of Bud Powell, he apparently developed his style before becoming familiar with Powell's music.

SELECTED RECORDINGS

As leader: *Trio* (1955, Barclay 84003); with D. Humair and P. Michelot: *HUM* (1960, Vega 837); *Jazzman* (1985, Carlyne 010)

As sideman: M. Davis: *Ascenseur pour l'échafaud* (1957, Fon. 460603); L. Young: *Lester Young in Paris* (1959, Verve 8378)

BIBLIOGRAPHY

H. Olier: "René Urtreger," *Jh*, no.93 (1954), 14 [interview]
R. Mouly: "René ou le blues pour Marianne," *Jm*, no.63 (1960), 20
J. Chesnel: "Le roi René," *Jh*, no.358 (1979), 32 [interview]
Y. Lucas: "Urtreger renaît," *Jm*, no.293 (1981), 22

ANDRÉ CLERGEAT

Urziceanu, Aura. *See* RULLY, AURA.

Usselton, Billy [William Hugh] (*b* New Castle, PA, 2 July 1926). Tenor saxophonist. He performed and recorded in swing bands led by Sonny Dunham (1946–8), Ray Anthony (1948–50, 1951–3), and Tommy Dorsey (1950), and during the second period with Anthony also led a group with Bill Harris (i). From 1954 to 1960 he was the principal tenor saxophonist with Les Brown's band, with which he performed, recorded, and toured Europe, North Africa, and the Far East. In 1956 Usselton made his first recording as a leader, *His First Album* (Kapp 1051), and in 1960 he recorded with Frank Capp. (*FeatherE*)

Utyosov, Leonid (Osipovich) (*b* Odessa, Ukraine, 21 March 1895; *d* Moscow, 10 March 1982). Russian singer and bandleader. He studied violin as a child, worked in theaters from 1911, and sang roles in operettas. He staged shows in which he sang, danced, played violin, and conducted an orchestra and a choir, and in 1929 formed a jazz theater orchestra, which he led until 1975. The orchestra included several capable jazz musicians and acquired a large following; it gave thousands of concerts, recorded many tracks (of which seven, dating from 1932 to 1934, are included on *Perviė shagi* (The first step; Mel. M6045827006), the first album in the series Anthology of Soviet Jazz), and appeared in a film comedy, *Veseliė rebyata* (Merry fellows; 1934). Utyosov was named a People's Artist of the USSR in 1965. (S. F. Starr: *Red and Hot: the Fate of Jazz in the Soviet Union, 1917–1980* (New York, and Oxford, England, 1983), 144)

WALTER OJAKÄÄR

V

Vaché, Warren(, Jr.) (*b* Rahway, NJ, 21 Feb 1951). Cornetist. He began his career playing traditional jazz with his father, a double bass player, and studied trumpet with Pee Wee Erwin (1970–80). He first earned critical acclaim for a performance with the New York Jazz Repertory Company at Carnegie Hall in 1975, at which he re-created solos by Bix Beiderbecke. He worked with Benny Goodman (intermittently, 1975–85) and was a member of the house band at Eddie Condon's club (1976–9). In 1976 he began playing with Scott Hamilton, forming an association which continued fruitfully into the mid-1980s. They have recorded more than 15 albums, and have played together under the leadership of Benny Goodman and Woody Herman, in the Concord Super Band (1979–82), and with the Newport Jazz Festival All-Stars (from 1984). Vaché has also played with Hamilton's quintet, and in 1985 he appeared in a film, *The Gig*.

Vaché has become a leading exponent of swing in the 1980s. He is the first major player since Ruby Braff to be inspired by the work of Louis Armstrong (whose influence can clearly be heard on *Cadillac Taxi*, for example), but he has also taken elements from the playing of other musicians (notably Clifford Brown) and formed them into a style that is immediately recognizable as his own. Both Vaché and Hamilton are expanding upon the swing tradition, and together they tend to establish the character of any group they play with.

SELECTED RECORDINGS

(recorded for Concord unless otherwise indicated)

As leader: *First Time Out* (1976, MonE 7081); *Jersey Jazz at Midnight* (1978, Jersey Jazz 1002); *Polished Brass* (1979, 98); *Iridescence* (1981, 153), incl. Sweet and Slow; *Midtown Jazz* (1982, 203)

As leader with S. Hamilton: *In New York City* (1978, 70); *Skyscrapers* (1979, 111), incl. Cadillac Taxi

As sideman: B. Goodman: *Fortieth Anniversary Concert* (1978, Lon. 2PS918–9); D. Hyman: *Music of Jelly Roll Morton* (1978, Smithsonian 006); Concord Super Band: *In Tokyo* (1979, 80); *Concord Super Band II* (1979, 120); W. Herman: *A Concord Jam* (1980, 142); Newport Jazz Festival All-Stars: *The Newport Jazz Festival All-Stars* (1984, 260)

BIBLIOGRAPHY

S. Klett: "Warren Vaché Jr.: Interview," *Cadence*, vi/1 (1980), 11
J. Wilson: "Cornet Player who Turned Away from Dixieland," *New York Times* (19 Nov 1982), §C, p.6
D. Morgenstern: "Warren Vaché: Classic Cornet," *DB*, l/2 (1983), 24 [incl. discography]
C. Deffaa: "A Profile of Warren," *MR*, xii/5 (1985), 7

CHIP DEFFAA

Valdambrini, Oscar (*b* Turin, Italy, 11 May 1924). Italian trumpeter and composer. He studied violin and trumpet as a child and took part in a jam session with Rex Stewart (1948). With Gianni Basso he led a quintet that recorded in 1952, and performed and recorded with the Sestetto Italiano (1955–7). In 1955 the two men formed the Basso–Valdambrini Quintet, for many years the best-known group in modern Italian jazz, which from 1962, with the addition of the trombonist Dino Piana, worked frequently as a sextet. Valdambrini worked with Armando Trovajoli as a trumpeter and arranger (1957–8) and played in orchestras led by Gil Cuppini (1964–71), Giorgio Gaslini (1968–9), Duke Ellington (1968–9), and Maynard Ferguson (1970–71). He formed another sextet with Basso in 1972; on Basso's departure in 1974 he led the group as a quintet, then as a sextet that remained active into the 1980s and performed with Dusko Goykovich and Kai Winding. From 1972 he worked with the Television Orchestra of Rome, in which capacity he played with Frank Rosolino, Conte Candoli, Freddie Hubbard, Franco Ambrosetti, Ernie Wilkins, and Mel Lewis. As a trumpeter Valdambrini favors a bop style and is most convincing in slow, lyrical compositions; his best-known original works include *Gin Blues* (1952), *Lo struzzo Oscar*, and *Lotar* (1959).

SELECTED RECORDINGS

As leader with G. Basso: Gin Blues (1952, Col. CJ1002); *Basso–Valdambrini Quintet* (1959, Music 2079), incl. Lotar, Lo Struzzo Oscar; *The Best Modern Jazz in Italy* (1962, RCA PML10326)

As leader with D. Piana: *Afrodite* (1976, Vedette 8337)

BIBLIOGRAPHY

FeatherE; *Feather–Gitler '70s*

ADRIANO MAZZOLETTI

Valdés, Chucho (*b* Quivicán, nr San Antonio de los Baños, Cuba, 9 Oct 1941). Cuban keyboard player, composer, and bandleader. As a teenager he directed a band led by his father, Bebo Valdés. In 1967, with Arturo Sandoval and Paquito D'Rivera, he formed the Orquesta Cubana de Música Moderna, then around 1973 he and other members of this group established IRAKERE; Valdés became its music director the following year. He has recorded with Irakere, as an unaccompanied soloist, and as the leader of a trio. His compositions include *100 años de juventud* (1979).

BIBLIOGRAPHY

J. Brody: "Chucho, le piano d'Irakere," *Jm*, no.334 (1984), 10
S. Steward: "Cubana be, cubana bop," *The Wire*, no.21 (1985), 26

CRISTÓBAL DÍAZ AYALA

Valdez, Carlos "Potato" (*b* Havana, 4 Nov 1926). Cuban conga player and percussionist. He moved in 1953 to the USA, where he played with the Latin bands of Machito and Tito Puente. From 1959 to 1972 he played with Herbie Mann, with whom he toured Africa in 1960 and made several recordings (including *Live at Newport*, 1963, Atl. 1413). He also recorded with Kenny Dorham (1955), Art Blakey (1957), Dizzy Gillespie (1959, 1971), Art Taylor (1960), Max Roach (1961), Duke Pearson (1968), Dave Liebman (1974), and the pianist Jorge Dalto (1985), and made recordings demonstrating Latin percussion techniques (1974–80). His nickname has also been spelled "Patato."

BIBLIOGRAPHY

FeatherE; *Feather '60s*
J. Brody: "Carlos Patato Valdes," *Jm*, no.340 (1985), 28

CATHERINE COLLINS

Valentine, Jerry [Gerald] (*b* Chicago, 14 Sept 1914). Arranger and trombonist. Although he studied piano, composition, and harmony as a youth, he was self-taught on trombone. He first joined Earl Hines as a composer and arranger, and among his arrangements for the group were *The Jitney Man* (1941, Bb 11535) and *Second Balcony Jump* (1942, Bb 11567). From 1944 to 1947 he performed and recorded with Billy Eckstine, for whom he arranged *Blowin' the Blues Away* (1944, DeLuxe 2001) and *I'll wait and pray* (1944, DeLuxe 2002); the latter was Sarah Vaughan's first recording with Eckstine's band. Valentine later worked as an artists and repertory adviser for National Records (1950–52) and wrote arrangements for sessions by the Prestige Blues Swingers, an all-star group that included Art Farmer, Pepper Adams, and Coleman Hawkins (1958, 1959).

BIBLIOGRAPHY

FeatherE
I. Gitler: *Jazz Masters of the Forties* (New York, 1966/*R*1983 with discography), 277

Valentine, Kid Thomas. *See* THOMAS, KID.

Valide. A hybrid trombone with both slide and valves used in jazz by Brad Gowans; *see* TROMBONE, §1.

Vamp. A short passage, which is simple in rhythm and harmony, played in preparation for the entry of a soloist; it is usually repeated ad libitum until the soloist is ready, hence the rubric "vamp till ready." The term is applied to the technique of playing ostinatos before or between solos, and, by extension, during or after solos. For example, on Miles Davis's recording of *Someday my prince will come* (on the album of the same title, 1961, Col. CS8456), Wynton Kelly improvises a delicate piano ostinato until Davis enters with the melody, and the band repeats the vamp at the end of the piece. Although the term "vamp" may be almost synonymous with "ostinato," it carries the additional idea that duration is at the discretion of a soloist. In jazz-rock, Latin jazz, and other fusions of jazz and popular music, and especially in modal jazz, an entire piece may be based on a succession of open-ended vamps. (B. D. Kernfeld: *Adderley, Coltrane, and Davis at the Twilight of Bebop: the Search for Melodic Coherence (1958–59)* (diss., Cornell U., 1981), 158)

DEANE L. ROOT/R

Van Breedam, Camiel (*b* Boom, Belgium, 29 June 1936). Belgian trombonist. He studied piano (1948–54), in 1966 took up the tuba, which he played in a local brass band, and in 1969 changed to trombone and traditional jazz. With his brother Johnny, a trumpeter and the leader of the Red Roses Brass Band, he opened the Jazzclub het Veerhuis in Willebroek in 1970 (*see* NIGHTCLUBS AND OTHER VENUES); the following year they formed the Fondy Riverside Bullet Band, with which he later recorded (*Red Roses for a Blue Lady*, 1982, Fondy 7775). He made frequent visits to New Orleans, performed at festivals in Europe, and recorded several albums with such musicians as Alvin Alcorn and the pianist Jeannette Kimball. Van Breedam plays a style of traditional jazz influenced by the work of Jim Robinson. (P. Chielens and J. Gerber: "Het dubbeltalent van Camiel Van Breedam," *'t pebbeltje*, no.17 (1986), 8)

MARCEL JOLY

Vance, Dick [Richard Thomas] (*b* Mayfield, KY, 28 Nov 1915; *d* New York, July or August 1985). Trumpeter and arranger. He grew up in Cleveland, where he studied violin before taking up the trumpet. After touring with the trombonist and bandleader Frank Terry (1932–4) and working for brief periods with Lil Armstrong (1934–5), Kaiser Marshall, and Willie Bryant, he became the lead trumpeter with Fletcher Henderson's band (1936–8), in which he also occasionally sang. He then joined Chick Webb as a trumpeter and arranger (1939) and he remained in the group under Ella Fitzgerald's leadership (1939–41). During the 1940s he wrote arrangements for several bands, including those of Glen Gray, Cab Calloway, Don Redman, Billy Eckstine, and Harry James; he also performed with Redman, Barnet, Eddie Heywood (1944–5), and many others. He was a member of the trumpet section in Duke Ellington's band during 1951–2 and arranged most of the items on the album *Ellington '55* (1953–4, Cap. W521). He then worked as a freelance and in the 1970s played with Eddie Barefield. Vance's playing is not well represented on recordings, but he may be heard at his best with Henderson's group on *Sextet* (1950); his warm tone and lyrical swing style on this album suggest the reasons for his popularity during his prime.

SELECTED RECORDINGS

As sideman: M. L. Williams: Stardust (1944, Asch 5521); F. Henderson: *Sextet* (1950, Alamac 2444); on R. Stewart: *The Big Reunion* (1957, Jzt. 1285), Honeysuckle Rose

BIBLIOGRAPHY

ChiltonW; *FeatherE*; *Feather–Gitler '70s*
W. C. Allen: *Hendersonia: the Music of Fletcher Henderson and his Musicians: a Bio-discography* (Highland Park, NJ, 1973)
C. Battestini and J.-P. Battestini: "Dick Vance," *BHcF*, no.296 (1982), 8 [interview]

SCOTT YANOW

Vander(schueren), Maurice (*b* Paris, 11 June 1929). French pianist. He performed and recorded with Don Byas (1951, 1955), Django Reinhardt (1952–3), Bobby Jaspar (1952, 1954, 1955), Jimmy Raney (1954), Stephane Grappelli (at intervals, 1955–7), Chet Baker (1956, 1977), and Kenny Clarke (1957, 1959, 1980). From 1965 he accompanied the singer Claude Nougaro; at the same time he worked as a leader (recording occasionally from 1955), took part with several pianists in the recording of *Piano Puzzle* (1970, Saravah 10011, 10015), and performed as a sideman with Johnny Griffin (1975), Billy Cobham (1977), and Richie Cole (1980). He is highly regarded for his sense of swing and for his inspired bop style, which bears some resemblance to that of Bud Powell. (A. Clergeat: *Dictionnaire du jazz*, Paris, 1966)

MICHEL LAPLACE

Van Dijk, Louis (*b* Amsterdam, 27 Nov 1941). Dutch pianist. He studied piano and organ at the Sweelinck Conservatory in

Amsterdam and from 1960 to 1964 led a quartet with the vibraphonist Carl Schulze; he also won the first prize at the jazz competition in Loosdrecht, near Hilversum, in 1961. With John Engels and the double bass player Jacques Schols he formed a trio in 1964 that remained in existence until the late 1970s and made several recordings, including *Triology* (1975, CBS 80527). In 1981 he recorded as an unaccompanied soloist. In addition to his activity in jazz van Dijk is a classical pianist who specializes in the works of J. S. Bach.

WIM VAN EYLE

Van Eps, George (Abel) (*b* Plainfield, NJ, 7 Aug 1913). Guitarist. He was brought up in a musical family; his mother played piano and his father Fred, Sr., was an internationally known ragtime banjoist (*see* BANJO). George taught himself banjo and by the age of 11 was playing professionally; two years later, influenced by Eddie Lang, he took up guitar, and by the time he was 15 was active as a teacher. He played with Smith Ballew (1929–31, working for a six-month period alongside Lang), and with Freddy Martin (1931–3), Benny Goodman (1934–5), and Ray Noble (1935–6). He then worked as a freelance studio musician in Hollywood (1936–40), where he wrote a definitive text on guitar playing and designed a seven-string guitar which enabled him to play his own bass lines. After a further period with Noble (1940–41) he worked in his father's sound recording laboratory (1941–3), then returned to the West Coast to continue as a freelance; he took part in the film *Pete Kelly's Blues* (1955) and the subsequent television series of the same name (1959). Despite illness Van Eps continued to play at festivals in the 1960s and 1970s, and in 1986 performed in Europe with Peanuts Hucko. His unique sound and innovative harmonic mastery are well represented by *Lover* and *The Blue Room* from the album *Soliloquy*.

Van Eps had three brothers, all of whom were professional musicians: Bobby (Robert), a pianist, worked with Red Nichols (1928, 1958), Smith Ballew (1929–30), Freddy Martin (1933), the Dorsey brothers (1934–5), Jimmy Dorsey (1935–7), and Kid Ory (1961); Freddy (Fred, Jr.), a trumpeter, played with the California Ramblers (1928–31) and worked as an arranger for Jack Teagarden's orchestra (1939); John(ny), a tenor saxophonist, recorded with Tommy Dorsey and Joe Haymes (both 1935), Ray Noble (1936), Larry Clinton (1938–9), Jack Teagarden (1939), and Will Bradley (1941).

SELECTED RECORDINGS

As unaccompanied soloist: *Soliloquy* (1968 or 1969, Cap. ST267), incl. The Blue Room, Lover

Duos with Frank Flynn: *My Guitar* (1966, Cap. ST2533)

As leader: I wrote it for Jo/Kay's Fantasy (1949, Jump JA1); *Mellow Guitar* (1956, Col. CL929); *George Van Eps' Seven-string Guitar* (1967, Cap. ST2783)

As sideman: A. Rollini: Somebody Loves Me (1934, Decca 359); R. Norvo: Bughouse (1935, Col. 3079D); R. Noble: Dinah (1935, Vic. 25223); E. Miller: Back Home/It's easy to remember (1946, Jump 16); J. Stacy: Indiana (1951, Bruns. 80172); M. Matlock: *Pete Kelly's Blues* (1955, Col. CL690); W. B. Davison: *Wild Bill Davison Plays the Greatest of the Greats* (1958, Dixieland Jubilee 508)

BIBLIOGRAPHY

ChiltonW; *FeatherE*; *Feather '60s*; *Feather-Gitler '70s*

J. Tynan: "George Van Eps: a Master Guitarist's Reflections and Comments," *DB*, xxxi/21 (1964), 16

M. J. Summerfield: *The Jazz Guitar: its Evolution and its Players* (Gateshead, England, 1978), 205

M. Grosz and L. Cohn: Liner notes, *Giants of Jazz: the Guitarists* (TL 12, 1980), 23

T. Greene: "George Van Eps: Harmonically Speaking, the Greatest Ever," *GP*, xv/8 (1981), 78 [incl. discography]

I. Mairants: "George Van Eps: Living Legend and Guitarist Extraordinary," *Classical Guitar*, v/11 (1987), 18

BRIAN PEERLESS

Vanguard. Record company and label. The company was established in New York in 1950 by Maynard Solomon and Seymour Solomon. Although devoted mainly to classical music it also made important contributions to the jazz repertory. The label Vanguard Jazz Showcase was used between 1953 and 1959 to issue recordings produced by John Hammond. These were put out under the sponsorship of the magazine *Down Beat* (the logo of which also appeared on the record labels) and included, most importantly, the first issues of recordings made in 1938–9 at concerts in Hammond's series Spirituals to Swing. Other repertory, newly recorded for the label between 1953 and 1957, included albums by Vic Dickenson, Sir Charles Thompson, Buck Clayton, Urbie Green, Mel Powell, Jimmy Rushing, Ruby Braff, Don Elliott, Count Basie (in the first recordings made for commercial purposes of performances at the Apollo Theatre, New York), and Rolf Kühn. Though its jazz activities decreased in the 1960s, during the following decade the company made recordings of jazz-rock and other types of fusion, most importantly by Larry Coryell and Oregon. The company was purchased by the Welk Music Group of Santa Monica, California, in 1986.

Van Ha Trio. Belgian rhythm section. Formed in 1965, its original members were the double bass player Roger Van Haverbeke (*b* Oostende, Belgium, 1930), the drummer Freddy Rottier, and the pianist Tony Bauwens (later replaced by Johan Clément). It has accompanied many leading American soloists, including Clark Terry, Johnny Griffin, Art Farmer, Joe Newman, and Jerome Richardson.

ROBERT PERNET

Van Hove, Fred (*b* Antwerp, Belgium, 19 Feb 1937). Belgian pianist. He studied classical piano from the age of ten, became interested in bop in the early 1950s, and by 1962 developed a modal style of playing that showed the influence of John Coltrane. After meeting Peter Brötzmann at a festival in Comblain-la-Tour, Belgium, he joined his quartet and later belonged to a trio with Brötzmann and Han Bennink (*c*1969–*c*1976); he also worked as an unaccompanied soloist from the early 1970s and in a duo with the saxophonist Cel Overbeghe from 1972 to 1974. In 1978 he formed the free-jazz group MLA (Musica Libera Antwerpen); later he performed and recorded with Lol Coxhill (1979, 1983) and from 1980 with Phil Wachsmann and with Günter Sommer. Besides his work in jazz van Hove has written music for films and the theater; as an organist he has recorded (1979), performed at festivals in Sinzig, Germany (1980, 1982), and Lille, France (1982), and toured Germany (1985).

SELECTED RECORDINGS

As unaccompanied soloist: *Live at the University* (1974, Vogel 004); *Verloren maandag* (1977, FMP SAJ11); *Church Organ* (1979, FMP SAJ25)

As leader: with P. Brötzmann and H. Bennink: *Outspan nr.2* (1974, FMP 0200);

BIBLIOGRAPHY

G. Rouy: "Belgique: Fred Van Hove," *Jm*, no.220 (1974), 24 [incl. discography]

——: "Fred van Hove: une force s'est manifestée parmi nous," *Jm*, no.262 (1978), 35

B. Noglik: "Fred van Hove," *Jazzwerkstatt international* (Berlin, 1981), 47 [incl. interview, discography]

B. Shoemaker: "Fred van Hove: Belgium," *Coda*, no.180 (1981), 12 [incl. discography]

G. Cerutti: *Fred van Hove Discography, 1968–1983 (on Records)* (Sierre, Switzerland, 1984)

ROBERT J. IANNAPOLLO

Van Lake, Turk [Hovsepian, Vanig] (*b* Boston, 15 June 1918). Guitarist and composer. He was first associated with big bands, and wrote arrangements for Chick Webb (1937) and performed and recorded with Charlie Spivak and Teddy Powell (both 1941). After working with Georgie Auld (1941–2) he played with Sam Donahue (1942) and performed and recorded with Charlie Barnet (1943–4); a second period with Auld (1944–5) was followed by work as an arranger for Count Basie, Lionel Hampton, Buddy Rich, and Benny Goodman (1945–8). Later Van Lake recorded with Terry Gibbs (1953, 1955, 1956), Sarah Vaughan (1955), and Eddie "Cleanhead" Vinson (1957), led his own quartet, performed and recorded with the trumpeter Les Elgart (1954–8), and toured and recorded with Goodman (1958–9); he is heard to advantage on *Cheerful Little Earful/Lollypop* (1953, Bruns. 80219), recorded with Gibbs. During the 1960s he accompanied various singers, including Nancy Wilson. In 1962 he toured the USSR with Goodman, and in 1965 he recorded with Herbie Mann. (*FeatherE*; *Feather '60s*)

Van Rooyen, Ack (*b* The Hague, 1 Jan 1930). Dutch trumpeter and flugelhorn player. He attended the Royal Conservatory in The Hague (1947–50) and played with Ernst van 't Hoff (1951), in a sextet led by his brother, the trumpeter Gerry van Rooyen (1954), and with the Ramblers (1955–7). He worked in France with Aimé Barelli (1957–60), Kenny Clarke, and others, and in Germany for Sender Freies Berlin (1960–67); he also played with Erwin Lehn (1967). Later he worked as a freelance in Germany and the Netherlands, made recordings with big bands led by Peter Herbolzheimer (from around 1970), Charlie Antolini (1972–80), Gustav Brom (1976), and Hans Koller (1977, 1980), joined the United Jazz and Rock Ensemble (1975) and recorded with the quartet of the guitarist Stephan Dietz (1978); at the same time he worked as an arranger for radio orchestras. He toured with Clark Terry, Gil Evans, and others in 1979; thereafter he settled in the Netherlands, where he continues to work as a freelance; he has also been active as a teacher at conservatories. A good example of his work is his recording *Didn't we* (1970, RCA LSP10299).

WIM VAN EYLE

Van 't Hof, Jasper (*b* Enschede, Netherlands, 30 June 1947). Dutch keyboard player. He formed a quartet with the guitarist Toto Blanke that won a second prize at the jazz competition in Loosdrecht, near Hilversum, in 1970. He played in Association PC (1970–72), led by Pierre Courbois, and with Chris Hinze (1973, recording in 1974), the group Piano Conclave (1974), and Archie Shepp (1974). In the mid-1970s he led the group Pork Pie with Charlie Mariano and Philip Catherine; other members of this group included Jean-Luc Ponty (1975–7) and Manfred Schoof (recording in 1976–7, performing in 1977). During this period he also played with Zbigniew Seifert. Later he recorded several times as a leader (from 1973), as an unaccompanied soloist (1977, 1981), in a duo with Shepp (1982), and in the trio Total Music with Chris Hinze and Sigi Schwab (1982). In 1987 he recorded again with Shepp.

SELECTED RECORDINGS

My World of Music (1981, Kt. 3-100); *Balloons* (1982, MPS 0068292); *Pili pili* (1984, Kt. 731)

BIBLIOGRAPHY

P. Carles: "Pays-bas: Jasper Van't Hoff [*sic*]," *Jm*, no.220 (1974), 31 [incl. discography]

R. Reichelt: "Jasper van 't Hof: 'I just want to play with everyone who is able to communicate'," *JF* [intl edn], no.43 (1976), 27 [interview]

WIM VAN EYLE

Van 't Hoff, Ernst (*b* ? Netherlands, *c*1900; *d* Brussels, 17 May 1955). Dutch bandleader and pianist. He played piano on the radio (1937–40) and in his own band. In 1940 he formed a big band under orders from the Germans during their occupation of the Netherlands; this group performed principally in Germany and to a lesser degree in the Netherlands and Belgium, and played jazz clandestinely although forbidden to do so. In 1944 van 't Hoff led the band, which now had 36 members, in performances for the American troops in Europe; it disbanded around 1946, then was re-formed for a brief period in 1951. A good example of van 't Hoff's work is the recording *Ernst van 't Hoff Orkest* (1941–2, Pol. 2664213).

WIM VAN EYLE

Van Vliet, Toon (*b* Rotterdam, Netherlands, 1922; *d* Zandvoort, Netherlands, 5 Nov 1975). Dutch tenor saxophonist. He studied clarinet, and after changing to tenor saxophone in 1945 he entertained the American troops in Europe. He worked with the Pacific Boptet and Ernst van 't Hoff (1951), a group led by Wessel Ilcken and Rita Reys (1952–3), the pianist Boy Edgar (1960–64), and the Vara dance band (1960–70); among those with whom he recorded were Ilcken (1955–7), the Rhythme All Stars (1958–60), Reys (1962), and Edgar (1965–75). Van Vliet modeled his style of playing after those of Sonny Rollins and Al Cohn; his playing is well represented by his recording *Toon Van Vliet* (1959, BVHaast 059).

WIM VAN EYLE

Vapirov, Anatoly (Petrovich) (*b* Berdyansk, Ukrainian SSR, 24 Nov 1947). Russian saxophonist, clarinetist, and composer. He played in the Leningrad Jazz Club from 1965 and in 1966–7 belonged to the student quintet of the Leningrad N. A. Rimsky-Korsakov State Conservatory, from which he graduated as a clarinetist in 1971. From 1967 to 1976 he played tenor saxophone (occasionally as a soloist) in the orchestra of the Leningradsky Myuzik-kholl and in 1974 first worked as a leader. He returned to the Leningrad Conservatory to teach saxopone (1976–82), gain a graduate degree in saxophone (1979), and lead the student jazz band (1981–2). He also recorded in Sofia and made the first of five annual appearances at the jazz festival in Slanchev Bryag (near Burgas, Bulgaria, 1978). In 1983 he formed the ensemble Zolotïe Godï Dzhaza (which consisted of musicians from Riga, Latvian SSR, Donetsk, Ukrainian SSR, and Novosibirsk, Russian SFSR) and the Trio Sovremennovo Kamernovo Dzhaza and began conducting the dance ensemble of the Buryat (Russian SFSR) Philharmonic Society, in which capacity he remained until the following year. Vapirov's work can be heard to advantage on *Misteriya* (1980, Mel. C60135756), a recording of his own composition for jazz soloist and symphony orchestra. He has also written a saxophone concerto, a saxophone quartet, and *Macbeth*, a set of ten jazz scenes.

WALTER OJAKÄÄR

Variety (i). Record label. It was established in 1927, and was used to issue, under pseudonyms, items from Cameo's catalogue. It is not known who owned the label, nor for how long it existed, but it had apparently ceased to operate before the formation of the American Record Company. (B. Rust: *The American Record Label Book* (New Rochelle, NY, 1978), 299)

Variety (ii). Record label. It was established in February 1937 by Irving Mills as a low-price counterpart to his label Master. Artists and repertory were supervised by Helen Oakley (later Helen Oakley Dance); 171 discs were issued between 1 April and 15 October 1937. These included records by Cab Calloway and by small groups made up of members of Duke Ellington's orchestra, and much other important jazz. Recording and manufacture were undertaken by the American Record Company; by the end of the year the musicians' contracts and Variety's catalogue had been transferred to ARC's label Vocalion.

BIBLIOGRAPHY

H. Dance: Liner notes, J. Hodges: *Hodge Podge* (CBS 52587, 1969)
B. Whyatt: "Discography: Master and Variety," *Vintage Jazz Monthly* (April 1970), 2
B. Rust: *The American Record Label Book* (New Rochelle, NY, 1978), 299
S. Placksin: *American Women in Jazz, 1900 to the Present: their Words, Lives, and Music* (New York, 1982), 122

Varsity. Record label. The principal label of the United States Record Corporation, it was founded in 1939 by Eli Oberstein, formerly an executive of Victor, to issue records more cheaply than major companies. The popular 8000 series included some of the more commercially-oriented jazz of the period, while the 6000 race series was used mainly to reissue older material from Paramount, Crown, and Gennett. The parent company ceased to operate late in 1940, but its masters were purchased by Musicraft and were later made available on several labels, many associated with Oberstein.

BIBLIOGRAPHY

R. Wile: "The United States Record Corporation and its Successors: Some Afterthoughts," *Record Research*, i/4 (1955), 8
F. Dutton, J. Godrich, M. Wyler, and J. McKenzie: "The Varsity 6000 Race Series," *Matrix*, no.32 (1961), 3 [corrections in no.40 (1962), 17]
J. Godrich and R. M. W. Dixon: *Blues & Gospel Records, 1902–1942* (Hatch End, nr London, 1964, rev. 2/1969, rev. and enlarged 3/1982 as R. M. W. Dixon and J. Godrich: *Blues & Gospel Records, 1902–1943*), 25
R. M. W. Dixon and J. Godrich: *Recording the Blues* (London, 1970), 100
B. Rust: *The American Record Label Book* (New Rochelle, NY, 1978), 300

Vasconcelos, Nana (*b* Recife, Brazil, *c*1945). Brazilian percussionist. At the age of 12 he played bongos and maracas in a band led by his father, a professional guitarist. He worked as a drummer in Rio de Janeiro in the mid-1960s, and while performing with Milton Nascimento learned to play several indigenous instruments, including the berimbau. Later he was taken by Gato Barbieri to Argentina, the USA (1971), and Europe. He lived for two years in Paris, where he worked with handicapped children, and played occasionally in Sweden with Don Cherry. From 1976 to 1977 he toured and recorded with Egberto Gismonti, then in 1978, with Cherry and Collin Walcott, he founded the trio Codona, which performed a style of jazz that incorporated characteristics of African, Asian, and South American music; when Codona disbanded after Walcott's death in 1984 Vasconcelos played with Cherry's group Nu. He was also a member of Pat Metheny's jazz-rock group (1980–83). Like Airto Moreira, Vasconcelos is a master of unconventional percussion: the subtle melodies and rhythms he creates on berimbau and cuíca transform these instruments into strikingly original solo voices.

SELECTED RECORDINGS

As leader: *Saudades* (1979, ECM 1147); of Codona (with D. Cherry and C. Walcott): *Codona*, ii (1980, ECM 1177); *Codona*, iii (1982, ECM 1243)
As sideman: E. Gismonti: *Danca des cabecas* (1976, ECM 1089); C. Walcott: *Codona* (1978, ECM 1132); P. Metheny: *Offramp* (1981, ECM 1216)

BIBLIOGRAPHY

L. Jeske: "Profile: Nana Vasconcelos," *DB*, xlix/2 (1982), 52

BARRY KERNFELD

Vauchant(-Arnaud), Léo [Arnaud, Noël Léon Marius] (*b* Cauzan, France, 24 July 1904). French trombonist. He studied cello but later changed to trombone (his father was a trombonist). In 1917 he moved to Paris, where he led a group of his own (1924) and studied orchestration with the composer Maurice Ravel (1924–7), in consideration of which he gave advice on the notation of trombone solos in two of Ravel's works. He played with the Chicago Hot Spots (1924), Paul Gason's band (1925), the bandleader and percussionist Fred Mélé, Irving Aaronson (1927), Lud Gluskin (1927–8), Jack Hylton (in England and Germany, 1928–30), and Gregor (1930). Having appeared as a guest with Ray Ventura and the Collegians from 1929 he made recordings with them in 1931, including *The girl friend of a boy friend of mine* (Virginia 221D). He also played in the USA with Fred Waring's band (1931–6), the Casa Loma Orchestra, the singer Russ Columbo (1932), Roger Wolfe Kahn's band, and the drummer Abe Lyman. Later he arranged film music in Hollywood. Vauchant-Arnaud's playing showed control and flexibility over a wide range of the instrument; he was the first French jazz trombonist to become well known.

BIBLIOGRAPHY

L.-V. Maily: "Le légendaire Léo Vauchant, *Jh*, no.256 (1969), 26
——. "Léo Vauchant vous parle," *Jh*, no.257 (1970), 23
M. Laplace: *Portraits of French Jazz Musicians* (Menden, Germany, 1985), 13

MICHEL LAPLACE

Vaughan, Sarah (Lois) [Sassy] (*b* Newark, NJ, 27 March 1924). Singer. She sang in the choir of Mount Zion Baptist Church, Newark, as a child, where at the age of 12 she became organist. In October 1942 she won an amateur contest at the Apollo Theatre; shortly afterwards, in April 1943, she joined Earl Hines's big band as second pianist and singer to Hines and Billy Eckstine. Eckstine formed his own bop-oriented big band early in 1944, and Vaughan joined him a few months later, making her first recording with his orchestra on 31 December. She left Eckstine after about a year, and thereafter, except for a brief stay in John Kirby's group in winter 1945–6, she worked only as a soloist. After George Treadwell (her manager and first husband) refashioned her stage appearance and repertory she achieved considerable success on television, in recordings from the late 1940s, and in international performances from the early 1950s. Although she began to perform predominantly slow, popular ballads with heavy vibrato to the accompaniment of "easy listening" orchestras, her early associations with bop musicians (especially Dizzy Gillespie and Charlie Parker, with whom she recorded *Lover Man* in 1945) established her lasting reputation as a jazz singer. This reputation endured in part because of her tendency to treat her voice more as a jazz instrument than as a vehicle for lyrics: she negotiated wide leaps within her full-bodied contralto range, improvised subtle melodic and rhythmic embellishments, and made fluid alterations of timbre – from a bell-like clarity to a bluesy growl.

During the five-year contract with Columbia that marked her rise to stardom (1949–54), she recorded often with studio orchestras and only once in a jazz context (with Miles Davis in 1950). A new contract with Mercury (1954–9) allowed her to pursue a dual career: for Mercury she made commercial discs, including her hit *Broken-hearted Melody* (1958), while for EmArcy, Mercury's jazz subsidiary, she recorded with Clifford Brown, Cannonball Adderley, the sidemen of Count Basie's orchestra, and other jazz musicians. She combined these activities under later contracts with Roulette, Mercury, and Columbia (1960–67). In 1971, after a five-year absence from recording, she began once again to make popular albums, occasionally employing a jazz-flavored accompaniment, as on her album with Oscar Peterson, Joe Pass, Ray Brown, and Louie Bellson in 1978. In public performances Vaughan is accompanied by a trio of piano, double bass, and drums, either alone or as

Sarah Vaughan singing with Joe Benjamin (double bass) and Roy Haynes (drums) at Birdland, New York, c1954

the nucleus of a big band or symphony orchestra. Among the distinguished members of her group have been Jimmy Jones (1947–52; 1954–8), Roy Haynes (1953–8), Richard Davis (late 1950s–early 1960s), Roland Hanna (early 1960s), Bob James (1965–8), Jan Hammer (1970–71), Jimmy Cobb (1970–78), Andy Simpkins (from 1979), and Harold Jones (from 1980). From 1978 to 1980 the trio became a quartet under the leadership of Vaughan's then manager, conductor, and husband, Waymon Reed. In 1987 Vaughan recorded an album of Latin-jazz songs.

SELECTED RECORDINGS

As leader: Body and Soul (1946, Musi. 494); I Cover the Waterfront (1947, Musi. 503); It's Magic (1947, Musi. 557); Mean to Me (1950, Col. 38899); Lullaby of Birdland (1954, EmA 6099); *In the Land of Hi-fi* (1955, EmA 36058); *Sassy* (1956, EmA 36089); Broken-hearted Melody (1958, Mer. 71477); *No Count Sarah* (1958, Mer. 20441); *After Hours* (1961, Roul. 52070); *Sarah + 2* (1964, Roul. 52118); *Sassy Swings Again* (1967, Mer. 21116); *Sarah Vaughan–Michel Legrand* (1972, Mstr. 361); *Live in Japan* (1973, Mstr. 401); *How Long Has This Been Going On?* (1978, Pablo 2310821); *Crazy and Mixed Up* (1982, PT 2312137); *Brazilian Romance* (1987, Col. FM42519)

As sideman: B. Eckstine: I'll wait and pray (1944, DeLuxe 2002); on *Billy Eckstine* (1945, Alamac 2415), Mean to Me; D. Gillespie: Lover Man (1945, Guild 1002); J. Kirby: It might as well be spring (1946, Crown 108)

BIBLIOGRAPHY

P. Leslie: "They Call her the Musical Miracle," *MM*, xxix (24 Jan 1953), 3
D. Gold: "Soulful Sarah," *DB*, xxiv/11 (1957), 13
B. Gardner: "Sarah," *DB*, xxviii/5 (1961), 18
R. Leydi: *Sarah Vaughan* (Milan, 1961)
G. Kopelowicz: "Tendre et divine Sarah," *Jm*, no.96 (1963), 25
G. Hoefer: "The First Big Bop Band," *DB*, xxxii/16 (1965), 23
B. Quinn: "Sassy '67," *DB*, xxxiv/15 (1967), 20
M. Williams: "Sarah Vaughan: Some Notes on a Singer before it's too Late," *JJ*, xxi/7 (1968), 36
L. Robinson: "The Divine Sarah," *Ebony*, xxx/6 (1975), 94
M. Jones: "Symphonies for Sarah," *MM*, li (14 Aug 1976), 47
W. Balliett: "New York Notes," *New Yorker*, liii (18 July 1977), 80
A. J. Smith: "Sarah Vaughan: Never Ending Melody," *DB*, xliv/9 (1977), 16 [incl. discography]
"Sarah Vaughan," *SJ*, xxxiv/4 (1980), 178 [discography]
J. Liska: "Sarah Vaughan: I'm Not a Jazz Singer," *DB*, xlix/5 (1982), 19 [incl. discography]
M. Williams: *The Jazz Tradition* (New York, rev. 2/1983), 214

BARRY KERNFELD

Vault. Record company and label. The company was established by Jack Lewerke in Los Angeles in 1965. Its first release was an album by Jack Wilson, who later recorded a second LP for the label. The organization remained in operation into the 1970s; the catalogue included two albums by Hampton Hawes, a collection of material by Charlie Barnet, and a splendid LP recorded by Larry Bunker's quartet with Gary Burton at Shelly's Manne Hole.

MARK GARDNER

V-disc. Record label. It was established in October 1943 for the issue of records to the US Armed Services; the term is also used, by extension, for the discs themselves.

The operation was run by the Music Section of the Special Services Division, under the management of Captain Robert Vincent. Artists and repertory were supervised by Steve Scholes and Walt Heebner (both previously employees of RCA Victor), Morty Palitz (previously with Decca), and Tony Janak (previously with Columbia); Palitz was replaced by George T. Simon in 1944. At first the records were intended only for the army, but from July 1944 until September 1945 there was also a V-disc program for the navy, in which material was issued under different catalogue numbers. There was also a brief series of discs issued for the Marine Corps. The records were distributed to military personnel around the world, and to posts in the USA for use on public address systems; they were also used on short-wave broadcasts by the Office of War Information and the Office of Inter-American Affairs.

The catalogue contained recordings made for commercial purposes (including both reissues and items or versions not previously issued); broadcasts; and the results of sessions specially organized by the management. The repertory forms a treasury of jazz, and includes notable work by many of the most important musicians of the day, in all styles then current. The program was established in the middle of a long recording ban by the American Federation of Musicians (July 1942 to November 1944), and was, to some extent, a result of it, in that V-disc's administration developed the scheme partly because no new material was being recorded at the time. The AFM agreed that its members could participate in the project provided that the records were not sold, and that the masters were ultimately destroyed. The nonprofit basis of the scheme enabled the management to organize sessions by groups of musicians who under other circumstances might never have recorded together because they were each under contract to different record companies; among the most notable examples of this are the recordings of concerts given (under the sponsorship of the magazine *Esquire*) by an ensemble led by Louis Armstrong, Coleman Hawkins, and Art Tatum.

The operation was maintained after World War II under Janak's direction, but it ceased in 1949. The circumstances under which the discs were produced has meant that an official program of reissues has been impossible. However, because the material put out on V-discs is historically so important, and often of such high quality, demand for it has been great, and extensive unofficial reissue schemes have been undertaken by several companies, chiefly in Italy and Japan.

See also RECORDING, §II, 5.

BIBLIOGRAPHY

S. Wante and W. DeBlock: *V-disc Catalogue*, i (Antwerp, Belgium, 1954)
K. Teubig: *V-disc Catalogue*, ii (Berlin, 1976)
R. S. Sears: *V-discs: a History and Discography* (Westport, CT, and London, 1980; suppl., 1986)

Velebný, Karel (*b* Prague, 17 March 1931). Czechoslovak vibraphonist, bass clarinetist, tenor saxophonist, pianist, arranger, and composer. He studied at the Prague Conservatory and played under V. Bradač and J. Šubert. He performed and from 1959 to 1961 recorded with Karel Krautgartner and Kamil Hala; at the same time he was a member of Studio 5 with Ludek Hulan. In 1961 he formed the S & H Quartet (later the S & H Quintet, then SHQ), which played cool jazz and hard bop; with the group he played at festivals in Landskrona, Sweden (1963), Bled, Yugoslavia (1964), and Berlin (1964), toured many European countries, and made recordings in 1962–6 and 1971 (including *SHQ a přátele* (SHQ and friends), 1965, Sup. SV9004). Velebný's best-known compositions include *Family Chronicle*, *Atila*, *Vernisáž* (Varnishing-day), and *Vycházka s neurotickým psem* (Walk with a neurotic dog). (*ReclamsJ*)

GERHARD CONRAD

Velvetone [velvet-tone]. An alternative name for the bucket mute; *see* MUTE, §2(g).

Velvet Tone. Record label. It was established by Columbia in 1929. At first the catalogue was the same as that of another subsidiary, Harmony (*see* HARMONY (ii)), but in 1930 the label was used to issue a separate race series, the 7000V sequence.

Venable, Lucius. Name under which LUCKY MILLINDER was known early in his career.

Vendome Theater. Movie theater in Chicago; *see* NIGHTCLUBS AND OTHER VENUES.

Ventura, Charlie [Venturo, Charles] (*b* Philadelphia, 2 Dec 1916). Tenor saxophonist. He first learned to play C-melody saxophone, and took up the alto instrument before finally settling on tenor saxophone. He played with Gene Krupa (1942–3) and Teddy Powell (1943–4), then worked as principal soloist in Krupa's new trio and big band (1944–6). In 1946 he launched his own big band, but found more regular work as leader of a sextet, which included at various times Bill Harris (i), Kai Winding, Buddy Stewart, Jackie Cain, and Roy Kral. In 1948 Ventura formed a new big band, which included his younger brothers the baritone saxophonist Ben (Benjamin), the tenor saxophonist Ernie (Ernest), and the trumpeter Pete (Peter), but soon reduced it to an octet, retaining Ben Ventura, Kral, Cain, and Bennie Green. In autumn 1948 the group took up the slogan "Bop for the People," and presented numerous clever arrangements in which voices and instruments performed bop themes in unison. Ventura, who also played baritone saxophone, was the principal soloist, although his driving improvisations were more firmly rooted in the swing era than the intricate bop style. During 1949 the octet's personnel changed frequently, and by the year's end Ventura realized that his efforts to popularize bop had failed. He led another big band (1950–51), formed the Big Four (a quartet with Marty Napoleon, Chubby Jackson, and Buddy Rich, 1951), and performed again with Krupa (1952–3) and Cain and Kral (1953). Despite long bouts of illness he continued to work with Krupa intermittently until the end of the 1960s, and also led his own small groups in Minneapolis, Las Vegas, and Denver. From 1978 he has played regularly in Windsor, Connecticut.

SELECTED RECORDINGS

As leader: C. V. Jump (1946, Sunset 10054); How High the Moon (1946, Nat. 7015); East of Suez (1947, Nat. 9048); Baby, baby all the time/I'm forever blowing bubbles (1947–8, Nat. 9057); Euphoria (1948, Nat. 9055); Pina Colada (1948, Nat. 9066); Boptura (1949, Vic. 203552); *Chazz 1977* (1977, FaD 115)

As sideman with G. Krupa: Dark Eyes (1945, Col. 36802); Stompin' at the Savoy/Body and Soul (1945, Col. 38214)

BIBLIOGRAPHY

J. Egan: "How Ventura Unit Got, Stays that Way," *DB*, xvi/5 (1949), 13
G. Hoefer: "Charlie Ventura," *IM*, lxiii (1964), July, 12
J. Burns: "Swing Tenors," *JJ*, xix/12 (1966), 13
R. Cotterell: "A Personal View of Charlie Ventura," *JM*, no.147 (1967), 4
J. Burns: "Charlie Ventura and Chubby Jackson," *JM*, no.163 (1968), 14
V. Schonfeld: "Charlie Ventura Reconsidered," *J&B*, i/1 (1971), 37
S. Woolley: "Charlie Ventura," *JJI*, xxxix/3 (1986), 14

BARRY KERNFELD

Ventura, Ray(mond) (*b* Paris, 16 April 1908; *d* Palma de Mallorca, Spain, 30 March 1979). French bandleader. From 1924 he played piano in an amateur band that became known as the Collegiate Five in 1925 and recorded for Columbia as the Collegians from late 1928. In January 1929 he became the leader of the group, which two years later became a professional show band (a versatile type of dance orchestra, the instrumentation of which was modeled on that of a big band); it made several recordings, including *St. Louis Blues/St. James Infirmary* (1932, Decca F2851). Ventura remained popular in France until 1939 (among those who performed with him as sidemen were Philippe Brun, Alix Combelle, and Guy Paquinet). He then led big bands in South America (1942–4) and again in France (1945–9); he also made a number of films. Ventura played an important role in introducing jazz to a large audience in France. (M. Laplace: "Ray Ventura Discography," *Jazz Press*, no.49 (1978), 10)

MICHEL LAPLACE

Venuti, Joe [Giuseppe] (*b* Philadelphia, 16 Sept 1903; *d* Seattle, 14 Aug 1978). Violinist. He grew up in Philadelphia, where he formed a longstanding musical partnership with Eddie Lang (see illustration, p.576). After moving to New York in 1925, he and Lang played with most of the leading white jazz musicians of the period, including Red Nichols, Frankie Trumbauer, Benny Goodman, and Jack Teagarden. Their recordings, especially an outstanding set of violin and guitar duos (1926–8), were highly influential in Europe, serving as a model for the quintet led by Django Reinhardt and Stephane Grappelli in Paris. Venuti led a moderately successful big band from 1935 to 1943, then returned to a small-group format, touring frequently. An acclaimed performance at the Newport Jazz Festival in 1968 marked the beginning of his return from several decades of relative obscurity. His many recordings during the 1970s with such important jazz musicians as Zoot Sims, Marian McPartland, and Earl Hines demonstrate that he had retained his prowess even at an advanced age. Venuti is considered the

Joe Venuti (right) with Eddie Lang, New York, c1929

most important violinist in early jazz, with a full tone, a jocular style, and a strong sense of rhythm.

See also VIOLIN.

SELECTED RECORDINGS

Duos: with E. Lang: Black and Blue Bottom/Stringing the Blues (1926, Col. 914D); Wild Cat/Sunshine (1927, OK 40762); Doin' Things/Goin' Places (1927, OK 40825); Doin' Things/Wild Cat (1928, Vic. 21561); with M. McPartland: *The Maestro and Friend* (1974, Hal. 112); with E. Hines: *Hot Sonatas* (1975, Chi. 145); with D. McKenna: *Alone at the Palace* (1977, Chi. 160)

As leader: Runnin' Ragged/Apple Blossoms (1929, OK 41361); Beale Street Blues/After you've gone (1931, Voc. 15864); Farewell Blues/Someday Sweetheart (1931, Voc. 15858); The Jazz me Blues/In de Ruff (1933, Col. 686); with Z. Sims: *Joe and Zoot* (1974, Chi. 128); with G. Barnes: *Live at the Concord Summer Festival* (1976, Conc. 30)

BIBLIOGRAPHY

D. M. Bakker: "Venuti–Lang and Friends," *Micrography*, no.5 (1969), 3

B. Englund: "Joe Venuti in Scandinavia in 1934," *Sv*, no.58 (1975), 138

J. H. Klee: "Hear the One about Joe Venuti?," *MR*, ii/10 (1975), 4

L. Tomkins: "Octogenarian Giant of Jazz: Joe Venuti," *CI*, xvi/2 (1977), 14 [interview]

M. Ullman: *Jazz Lives: Portraits in Words and Pictures* (Washington, 1980)

G. Giddins: "A Penchant for Mayhem," *Riding on a Blue Note: Jazz and American Pop* (New York, and Oxford, England, 1981) [colln of previously pubd articles], 79

M. Glaser and S. Grappelli: *Jazz Violin* (New York and elsewhere, 1981) [incl. transcrs.]

Jazz String Newsletter, ii/1 (1983) [complete issue]

D. Hyman: "Bix Beiderbecke and Joe Venuti," *Keyboard*, xi/6 (1985), 76 [incl. transcr.]

J. BRADFORD ROBINSON

Venuto, Joe [Joseph] (*b* New York, 20 June 1929). Vibraphonist and leader. He received a masters degree from the Manhattan School of Music, and after playing in clubs and dance bands in New York during the late 1940s he led his own quartet (1950–52). From 1953 to 1956 he was a percussionist with the Sauter–Finegan Orchestra; he continued to record with the band into the 1960s. After a brief association with Benny Goodman (1956) Venuto worked as a percussionist in the orchestra at Radio City Music Hall (1956–8), performed and recorded with Johnny Richards (1958–9), and took part in studio sessions. He recorded on vibraphone with Jack Teagarden (1958), on marimba with Rex Stewart (1959), and on both instruments as a leader (1959). He is heard to advantage on *Redhead* (1959, Design 1047), recorded with Stewart, and on his own album *Sounds Different* (1959, Ev. 5053). Later he made recordings with Budd Johnson and Shirley Scott (both 1963), Joe Mooney (1964), and Oliver Nelson, Gunther Schuller, and Johnny Hodges (all 1966). (*FeatherE*)

Verse. In popular music that section of a song in which the tune remains constant but the text changes with each repetition; for the use of the melodies of song verses in jazz pieces, *see* FORMS, esp. §1(i)(a).

Vertical cut recording. A term applied to a sound-recording technique that utilizes variations in the depth of the spiral groove on a cylinder or disc; *see* RECORDING, esp. §I, 1(i).

Verve. Record company and label. The company was established in Los Angeles in 1956 by NORMAN GRANZ around the time he became Ella Fitzgerald's manager, and at first issued new recordings that Granz had supervised in December the previous year. Its policy reflected his interests; of the major companies recording swing and bop musicians, Verve was the most conservative. Despite this, and despite Granz's propensity for creating all-star groups of musicians who did not play well together, the company issued material from hundreds of important new sessions. Granz's earlier labels, CLEF and Norgran, were absorbed into the new company; Verve reissued many items from the catalogues of both. Late in 1960 MGM bought the company from Granz, but it continued to issue new recordings, most notably those directed by Creed Taylor between 1961 and 1967. Much material from Verve's catalogue appeared in Europe and Japan under the same name, but the company also entered into agreements whereby numerous sessions were issued on the labels Columbia and HMV in England and on Barclay and Blue Star in France. In 1967 Polydor purchased Verve, and the following year the company ceased to operate. However, its catalogue has continued to be rereleased in the 1970s and 1980s by affiliated companies in the USA, England,

France, Germany, and Japan; the most ambitious reissue project has been undertaken by Polygram, using the Verve label, on which it has also begun to put out new albums. In addition, Granz retained the rights to Verve's extensive collection of recordings by Art Tatum and later released them on his new label, PABLO.

BIBLIOGRAPHY

A. Morgan: "The Verve History of Jazz," *JJI*, xxxi/4 (1978), 18
M. Ruppli and B. Porter: *The Clef/Verve Labels: a Discography* (New York, Westport, CT, and London, 1986)

BARRY KERNFELD

Vesala, Edward [Martti] (*b* Mäntyharju, Finland, 15 Feb 1945). Finnish drummer, percussionist, and composer. He studied percussion at the Sibelius Academy, Helsinki (1965–7), and played with Seppo Paakkunainen and others in the late 1960s; he made the first of a number of recordings as a leader in 1969. In the early 1970s he played with Jan Garbarek and toured Central Europe, and in 1974 he began working with Tomasz Stańko. From 1984 he led Sound and Fury, a workshop ensemble for young Finnish musicians. Vesala's playing, at first influenced chiefly by the free jazz of the 1970s, became increasingly colored by ethnic music as a result of his travels in India, Indonesia, and China. His compositions, which include jazz and vocal works, combine elements of free jazz, ethnic music, and avant-garde concert music. In the late 1970s Vesala founded his own record label, Leo (*see* LEO (ii)).

SELECTED RECORDINGS

As leader: *Nan Madol* (1974, ECM 1077); *Satu* (1976, ECM 1088); *Heavy Life* (1980, Leo 009); *Mau-Mau* (1982, Johanna 2071)
As sideman with J. Garbarek: *Triptykon* (1972, ECM 1029)

BIBLIOGRAPHY

A. Granholm: *Finnish Jazz* (Helsinki, 1974, rev. and enlarged by M. Konttinen 2/1982, rev. and enlarged by J.-P. Vuorela 3/1986), 46
T. Vähäsilta: "Edward Vesala: a Drummer from the North," *JF* [intl edn], no.92 (1985), 30

PEKKA GRONOW

Viale, Jean-Louis (*b* Neuilly-sur-Seine, France, 22 Jan 1933; *d* Paris, 10 May 1984). French drummer. He played as an amateur with Sacha Distel and René Urtreger (1951) and as a professional at Le Tabou in Paris with Henri Renaud, Bobby Jaspar (with whom he recorded in 1953–5), and Jimmy Gourley. In Paris he belonged to a band formed by Gigi Gryce that recorded with Clifford Brown (1953), and he also played regularly at the Club Saint-Germain. He interrupted his career in jazz for several years to accompany Distel, who was by that time working as a popular singer; from around 1956 he worked again in jazz, performing at the Blue Note with Zoot Sims, Lester Young, Stan Getz, and Martial Solal. He led a group for a brief period at the Club Saint-Germain and worked frequently in studios; from the mid-1970s he became progressively less active. Viale was highly regarded by soloists for his vitality as a drummer and his steady beat.

SELECTED RECORDINGS

As sideman: D. Reinhardt: [untitled EP] (1953, BStar 6830); G. Wallington: *A Day in Paris* (1953, Vogue 171); G. Gryce and C. Brown: *Gigi Gryce–Clifford Brown Sextet* (1953, Vogue 175); H. Renaud: *Henri Renaud Plays Gigi Gryce* (1953, Vogue 174); Z. Sims: *Zoot Sims Sextet* (1953, Vogue 170); F. Foster: *Frank Foster Quartet* (1954, Vogue 209); R. Urtreger: *Trio* (1955, Barclay 84003); B. Kessel: *Limehouse Blues* (1969, Black Lion 173)

BIBLIOGRAPHY

J.-L. Ginibre: "Test: pièges pour Jean-Louis," *Jm*, no.114 (1965), 30

ANDRÉ CLERGEAT

Vibraphone [vibraharp, vibes]. A tuned percussion instrument consisting of a set of metal bars arranged like a piano keyboard; in contrast with the two ranks of a xylophone, all the bars are mounted on one level, facilitating the use of three or four mallets and the playing of chords. Each bar is suspended over a tube resonator containing a revolving vane or metal disc; the rotation of the vane causes a repeated opening and closing of the resonator, producing a vibrato. The speed of rotation, and thus of the vibrato, is controlled by an electric motor. When no vibrato is desired, the motor is switched off and the vanes rest in a vertical position, leaving the resonators fully open. The vibraphone has a compass of three octaves ascending from *f* and is usually played with rubber-tipped or yarn-wound rubber mallets. It has a foot-controlled sustaining device that operates in a similar way to the sustaining pedal of a piano.

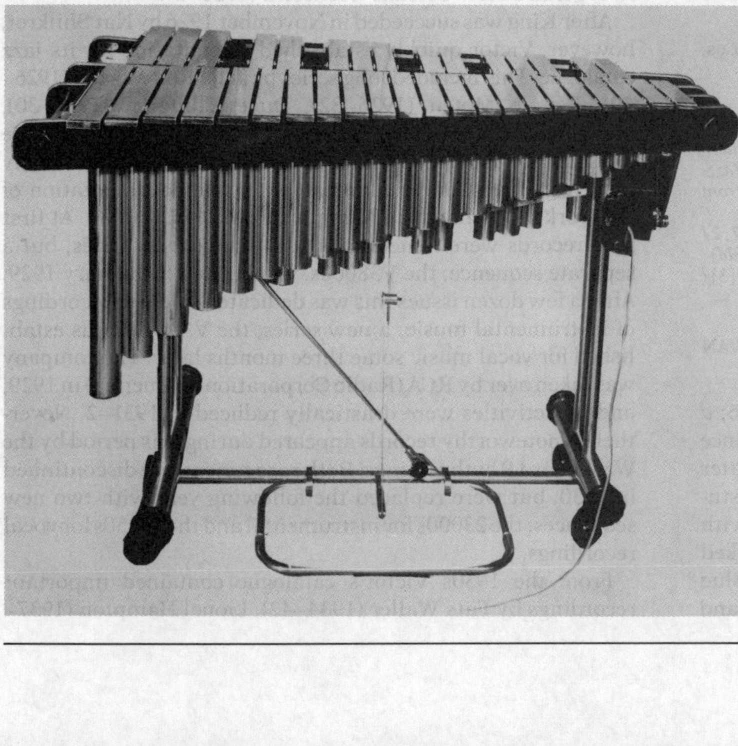

(a)

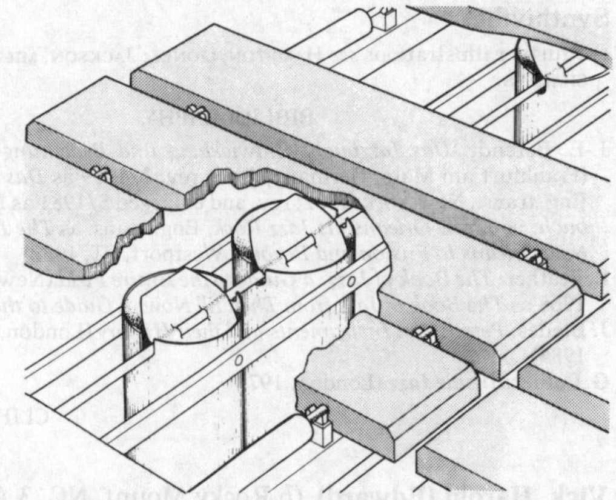

(b)

1. *(a) Vibraphone; (b) diagram to show position of vanes in vibraphone resonators*

The vibraphone was introduced in the USA in 1916 as a "steel marimba" and became popular as a jazz instrument in the early 1930s. Adrian Rollini used the vibraphone as a doubling instrument, and Lionel Hampton, who began his career as a drummer, played vibraphone in a short, improvised introduction to Louis Armstrong's *Confessin'* (OK 41448), which he recorded in July 1930 with Les Hite's band; Hampton later became the first outstanding vibraphone soloist, first as a sideman with Benny Goodman in the mid-1930s, then as the leader of his own band from 1940. His use of a fast vibrato and the crisp, brilliant articulation which reveals his background as a drummer may be heard to advantage on his album *Hamp in Harlem* (1979, Tim. 133). Red Norvo took up the vibraphone in 1944 and played it like the xylophone (which had earlier been his principal instrument), in that he did not use vibrato; his playing is well represented by his recording *Hallelujah/Slam Slam Blues* (1945, Dial 1045). Milt Jackson, who played with Dizzy Gillespie from 1945 and with the Modern Jazz Quartet from 1951 into the 1980s, did much to make the vibraphone popular as a jazz instrument; his use of a slow vibrato and of soft mallets of his own invention helped to define his distinctive, flowing style, which is exemplified by his recording *Plenty, Plenty Soul* (1957, Atl. 1269). Other important players have included Margie Hyams, a member of George Shearing's quartet, Teddy Charles, who in the 1950s prefigured some aspects of avant-garde jazz, Bill Le Sage, Bobby Hutcherson, and Terry Gibbs, whose playing in the 1950s displayed great virtuosity. In the 1960s the vibraphone was used as a doubling instrument by Victor Feldman and Tubby Hayes.

Vibraphone technique was brought to a new level of virtuosity by Gary Burton, who from the early 1960s has played with two mallets in each hand. He has also devised a method of "bending," or slightly lowering, pitches by holding a hard-headed beater against a bar at its nodal point (the point at which the bar is suspended by a cord) and then striking the bar with a soft-headed beater and pulling away the other beater instantly. A good example of Burton's innovative playing is provided by his album *In the Public Interest* (1973, Pol. 6503), and in particular by its track *Dance*. The vibraphone has been used as a free-jazz instrument by Walt Dickerson, Gunter Hampel, Karl Berger, and Jay Hoggard. In the 1970s the jazz-rock player Mike Mainieri invented an electronic vibraphone, the Synthivibe.

For further illustrations *see* HAMPTON, LIONEL; JACKSON, MILT; and MINGUS, CHARLES.

BIBLIOGRAPHY

J.-E. Berendt: *Das Jazzbuch: Entwicklung und Bedeutung der Jazzmusik* (Frankfurt am Main, Germany, 1953, rev. 2/1959 as *Das neue Jazzbuch*, Eng. trans., New York, 1962; rev. and enlarged 5/1981 as *Das grosse Jazzbuch: von New Orleans bis Jazz Rock*, Eng. trans. as *The Jazz Book: from New Orleans to Fusion and Beyond*, Westport, CT, 1982)

L. Feather: *The Book of Jazz: a Guide to the Entire Field* (New York, 1957, 2/1965 as *The Book of Jazz from Then till Now: a Guide to the Entire Field*)

J. Blades: *Percussion Instruments and their History* (London, 1970, rev. [3]/1984)

G. Collier: *Inside Jazz* (London, 1973)

CLIFFORD BEVAN

Vick, Harold (Edward) (*b* Rocky Mount, NC, 3 April 1936; *d* New York, 13 Nov 1987). Tenor saxophonist. His uncle Prince Robinson gave him a clarinet when he was 13; three years later he began playing tenor saxophone. He performed while a student of psychology at Howard University, playing mainly with rhythm-and-blues bands. In the early and mid-1960s he worked with soul-jazz organists, making several recordings for Blue Note and Prestige with Jimmy McGriff, Big John Patton, and others; his involvement with soul jazz continued when he recorded with Shirley Scott in the mid-1970s, and again with McGriff in 1980–81. In 1966 he made his first album as a leader, *Steppin' Out*, which displayed his penchant for the blues. In 1972 he recorded with Jack DeJohnette's group Compost, which played a blend of jazz, rock, and highly chromatic or atonal music. With this ensemble Vick's blues style was a galvanizing force, as appropriate in this context as it was on soul-jazz recordings.

SELECTED RECORDINGS

As leader: *Steppin' Out* (1963, BN 84138); *Caribbean Suite* (1966, RCA LSP3677); *Straight Up* (1966, RCA LSP3761); *Don't Look Back* (1974, SE 7431); *Commitment* (1975, Muse 5054)

As sideman: J. Patton: *Along Came John* (1963, BN 84130); J. DeJohnette: *Compost* (1972, Col. 31176); S. Scott: *One for Me* (1974, SE 7430)

BIBLIOGRAPHY

Feather–Gitler '70s

Liner notes, *Steppin' Out* (BN 84138, 1964)

M. Gardner: "Harold Vick," *JM*, no.171 (1969), 4 [incl. discography]

L. Tomkins: "Harold Vick," *CI*, xiv/3 (1975), 14

M. Gardner: "Harold Vick," *Coda*, no.148 (1976), 8

ANDREW WAGGONER

Victor. Record company and label. The company was established (as the Victor Talking Machine Co.) by Eldridge R. Johnson in Camden, New Jersey, in 1901. From its inception it was closely associated with Emile Berliner's Gramophone Co., with which it shared the rights to use equipment patented by Berliner; it also used the "dog and gramophone" logo that later became the trademark of His Master's Voice. The company issued some of the earliest recordings connected with jazz, those made in 1913–14 by James Reese Europe's Society Orchestra, and put out the first discs by the Original Dixieland Jazz Band. This early involvement was not sustained, however, and the label was not noted for jazz in the early 1920s when artists and repertory were directed by Edward T. King. The company was slow to record for the growing race market; it abandoned auditions for a race series in 1921, and discontinued a further attempt (though it included discs by Lizzie Miles and Rosa Henderson) after only a few issues. Most jazz recorded during this period was of the more polite type, notably the work of Paul Whiteman (with Victor from 1920 to 1928) and A. J. Piron's New Orleans Orchestra (1923–5).

After King was succeeded in November 1926 by Nat Shilkret, however, Victor quickly established a reputation for its jazz catalogue. This included long series by Jelly Roll Morton (1926–30), Bennie Moten (1926–32), Duke Ellington (1927–30), McKinney's Cotton Pickers (1928–31), and King Oliver and the Missourians (both 1929–30). The company also made many field recordings, undertaking an extensive documentation of the work of jug bands in Memphis from 1927 to 1930. At first race records were issued as part of the general series, but a separate sequence, the V38000s, was started in January 1929. After a few dozen issues this was dedicated solely to recordings of instrumental music; a new series, the V38500s, was established for vocal music some three months later. The company was taken over by RCA (Radio Corporation of America) in 1929, and its activities were drastically reduced in 1931–2. Nevertheless noteworthy records appeared during this period by the Washboard Rhythm Kings. Both race series were discontinued in 1930, but were replaced the following year with two new sequences: the 23000s for instrumental and the 23250s for vocal recordings.

From the 1930s Victor's catalogue contained important recordings by Fats Waller (1934–42), Lionel Hampton (1937–

40), and Benny Goodman's big band and small groups (1935–9). The company also made several attempts to establish a subsidiary label to issue cheap discs, starting in April 1931 with TIMELY TUNES; this was quickly succeeded by the short-lived Elektradisk, and later by SUNRISE and BLUEBIRD. In September 1931 Victor launched a series of experimental long-playing discs; these Program Transcriptions (so called, it is thought, because they looked like broadcast transcriptions and needed to be played on similar equipment) included material recorded specifically for the series by Louis Armstrong and Duke Ellington. It was discovered in the early 1980s that at many of Victor's sessions of this period (including those that produced Ellington's Program Transcriptions) two recordings of the same performance were taken, one each from two spatially separated microphones. Although only one from each pair of recordings was issued, in several cases a test pressing of the other has survived; when played simultaneously the two versions produce a perfect stereophonic sound (*see* RECORDING, §II, 3).

Many of Victor's recordings of the 1940s, especially those of Sidney Bechet (1940–41) and Ellington (1940–46), have come to be regarded as classics. The company started pressing discs out of vinyl in October 1946, and in February 1949 issued the first 45 r.p.m. single. Around this time it began to be known as RCA Victor, and used this name on labels; it has remained one of the most important jazz record companies into the 1980s, issuing new work by such musicians as Sonny Rollins (1962–4), Joe Williams (1962–5), J. J. Johnson (1964–6), and Phil Woods (1975–6), and rereleasing large sections of the back catalogue. In the early 1950s it established a subsidiary label, X, which it used for the systematic reissue of early jazz; this was one of the first schemes of its kind. RCA Victor terminated its arrangements with His Master's Voice in 1959. Thereafter, in territories formerly covered by that contract, it issued much of its material (including the highly regarded Vintage Series of the 1960s and 1970s) either by agreement with other companies (such as British Decca, 1959–71), or, later, by establishing autonomous subsidiaries. French RCA has been particularly notable for its reissue schemes Treasury of Jazz (1960s), Black & White (1970s; probably the largest single reissue program ever undertaken, and not to be confused with the label of the same name of the 1940s) and Jazz Tribune (1980s). RCA has also made use throughout the world of the label Camden, established in the 1950s for the issue of cheap records; the catalogue has included important jazz. By 1976 the albums on the Flying Dutchman label were manufactured and distributed by RCA Victor. In the late 1980s RCA revived Arista's Novus label.

For illustration *see* FILMS, fig.4.

BIBLIOGRAPHY

H. Panassié: *144 hot jazz Bluebird and Victor Records* (Camden, NJ, 1939)
J. Godrich and R. M. W. Dixon: *Blues & Gospel Records, 1902–1942* (Hatch End, nr London, 1964, rev. 2/1969, rev. and enlarged 3/1982 as R. M. W. Dixon and J. Godrich: *Blues & Gospel Records, 1902–1943*), 16
D. Mahony: "Notes on Victor Master Numbers," *Matrix*, no.68 (1966), 3
A. J. McCarthy: "German RCA 'Jazz Star Series'," *JM*, xiii (1967), no.4, p.13; no.6, p.15
"Reissue Series, 1: French Treasury of Jazz," *JM*, xii (1967), no.11, p.29; no.12, p.23
"Reissue Listing: RCA 'Vintage' Series," *JM*, no.156 (1968), 30
R. M. W. Dixon and J. Godrich: *Recording the Blues* (London, 1970)
"International Record Scene," *J&B*, i (1971), no.5, p.29; no.8, p.34; ii/2 (1972), 28
T. Russell: "Rock and Romance," *J&B*, ii/4 (1972), 14
R. D. Kinkle: "Victor Numerical List," *The Complete Encyclopedia of Popular Music and Jazz, 1900–1950* (New Rochelle, NY, and Westport, CT, 1974), iv, 2044
B. Rust: *The American Record Label Book* (New Rochelle, NY, 1978), 303
B. Kay: Liner notes, D. Ellington: *Reflections in Ellington: the 1932 Band in True Stereo* (Everybody's 3005, 1985)
B. Korst: *RCA Victor Record Listing, 20-1500 thru 20-7300*, ed. C. Garrod (Zephyrhills, FL, 1986)

Vienna Art Orchestra. Austrian big band formed in Vienna in 1977 by the Swiss pianist, composer, and arranger Mathias Rüegg. He modified the normal instrumentation of a big band by using fewer trumpets, trombones, and saxophones and adding tuba and vibraphone. The orchestra's wide-ranging repertory includes the music of Scott Joplin, Lennie Tristano, Anthony Braxton, Hans Koller, and the French composer Erik Satie. Among the soloists with whom the band played are John Surman, George Lewis (ii), Karin Krog, and Art Farmer. It made several recordings from 1979 (including *From No Time to Rag Time*, 1982, HA 1999–2000) and from 1980 it toured in Europe and performed at various jazz festivals; it visited the USA in 1984. In 1983 Rüegg formed the Vienna Art Choir, which consisted of about 12 singers; it recorded with members of the orchestra in the same year.

BIBLIOGRAPHY

J. Solothurnmann: "Mathias Rüegg & Vienna Art Orchestra," *JF* [intl edn], no.79 (1982), 30
K. Ansell: "Vienna Art Orchestra," *The Wire*, no.24 (1986), 24
F. Davis: "Variations on a Big Band Theme (Mathias Rüegg)," *In the Moment: Jazz in the 1980s* (New York, and Oxford, England, 1986) [colln of previously pubd articles], 75

KLAUS SCHULZ

Viking Jazz Band. Name by which a septet led by PAPA BUE was known from 1958.

Village Gate. Nightclub in New York; *see* NIGHTCLUBS AND OTHER VENUES.

Village Vanguard. Nightclub in New York; *see* NIGHTCLUBS AND OTHER VENUES.

Villegas, Enrique [Mono] (*b* Buenos Aires, 3 Aug 1913; *d* Buenos Aires, 10 July 1986). Argentine pianist. He studied with Alberto Williams at the Conservatorio Nacional (graduated 1932) and began his career as a classical pianist, giving the first performances in Argentina of Ravel's Concerto in G and in 1934 of Gershwin's *Rhapsody in Blue*. After working from 1943 to 1944 as a leader of jazz groups he settled in New York (1955), recorded with Milt Hinton and Cozy Cole (1955–7), and in 1964 returned to Buenos Aires, where he recorded two albums in a trio (*Cuerpo y alma*, 1965, Trova 1, and *Tributo a Monk*, 1967, Trova 12), as an unaccompanied soloist (1967, 1968), in a duo with Jorge López Ruiz (1968), and with Paul Gonsalves (1968). He moved again to New York in 1970 and remained there for one year. Later he recorded in a trio (1973) and a free-jazz quartet (1975) and performed at the Teatro Colón (1975); he made his last recording in 1977.

LAUREANO FERNÁNDEZ, OMAR GARCÍA BRUNELLI

Vinding, Mads (*b* Copenhagen, 7 Dec 1948). Danish double bass player. A self-taught musician, he began playing professionally in the mid-1960s, and from the early 1970s accompanied many visiting soloists. In 1974 he recorded under his own name the album *Danish Design* (Sonet 2560). He was a member of the Radioens Big Band from 1978 and of Ernie Wilkins's Almost Big Band from 1980 (recording in 1980 and 1983) as well as playing in groups led by Kenny Drew (recording in 1981), Svend Asmussen, the pianist Finn Savery, and others. He has also recorded with Duke Jordan (1973, 1975), Johnny Griffin (1973, 1976), Art Farmer (1981), and Dexter Gordon (1985). (J. Arntzen: "Jesper Lundgaard: Mads Vinding," *MM: tidskrift for rytmisk music m.m.*, xiv/4 (1982), 8)

ERIK WIEDEMANN

Vinnegar, Leroy (*b* Indianapolis, 13 July 1928). Double bass player. A self-taught musician, he first worked in Chicago (1952–3), principally as house double bass player at the Beehive. After moving to Los Angeles in 1954 he achieved a considerable reputation, and from 1955 to 1957 recorded with, among others, Stan Getz, Shorty Rogers, Herb Geller, Chet Baker, and Serge Chaloff. He was also a member, with Shelly Manne and André Previn, of the trio that recorded the best-selling jazz album *My Fair Lady* (1956). In 1957 he made his first recordings as a leader, on which he made a feature of his virile walking bass lines and played only pieces with titles that pertained to the act of walking. His second album (1962–3) included his compositions *For Carl* and *Hard to Find*. From 1959 Vinnegar collaborated frequently with Joe Castro and Teddy Edwards, sharing leadership duties with them on several occasions; their group also made a tour of Europe. Thereafter Vinnegar worked as a freelance with both jazz and semicommercial ensembles, recording with Les McCann and Eddie Harris (1969), and the quintet led by Howard McGhee and Edwards (1979). He made several appearances on television in the early 1980s as a member of the Panama Hats, a group that accompanied the actor and banjoist George Segal. Vinnegar is best known for his walking bass lines, but occasionally plays melodic solos, employing short, riff-like phrases and strong rhythmic punctuation; he has a keen sense of swing.

SELECTED RECORDINGS

As leader: *Leroy Walks* (1957, Cont. 3542); *Leroy Walks Again* (1962–3, Cont. 3608), incl. For Carl, Hard to Find

As sideman: S. Chaloff: *Blue Serge* (1956, Cap. T742), incl. All the things you are, The Goof and I, A Handful of Stars, I've got the world on a string, Susie's Blues; S. Manne: *My Fair Lady* (1956, Cont. 3527), incl. Wouldn't it be loverly?; T. Edwards: *Sonny Rollins at Music Inn/Teddy Edwards at Falcon's Lair* (1959, Metro. 1011), incl. Billie's Bounce

BIBLIOGRAPHY

FeatherE; *Feather '60s*; *Feather–Gitler '70s*

L. Koenig: Liner notes, *My Fair Lady* (Cont. 3527, 1956)

LAWRENCE KOCH

Vinson, Eddie "Cleanhead" (*b* Houston, 18 Dec 1917; *d* Los Angeles, 2 July 1988). Alto saxophonist and singer. He took up alto saxophone in 1934 and by the following year had joined Arnett Cobb and Illinois Jacquet in Chester Boone's big band, in which he played saxophone and sang the blues; he remained in the band under the leadership of Milt Larkin (1936–40) and Floyd Ray (1940–41). Vinson then toured the South with the blues musicians Big Bill Broonzy and Lil Green (*c*1941) before working in New York with Cootie Williams (1942–5). The hit recording of *Cherry Red Blues* that he made with Williams in 1944 marked his emergence as a popular singer. He then led a big band (1946–7) and a septet which included John Coltrane, Red Garland, and Johnny Coles (*c*1948). Thereafter his popularity waned, but he continued to work steadily, if in obscurity. In 1969 his career received new impetus after he made a tour of Europe with Jay McShann, during which he recorded *Wee Baby Blues*, an album that received much critical acclaim. From the early 1970s he performed and recorded regularly in Europe and the USA in ensembles led by swing and rhythm-and-blues musicians, including Count Basie and Johnny Otis.

Vinson was a sophisticated, forceful bop saxophonist who played with searing intensity. His blues singing was characterized by an intentionally broken falsetto with which he punctuated line endings, and he performed his earthy, humorous lyrics in a deliberately understated manner. He was also the composer of the bop standards *Tune-up* and *Four*, both of which were popularized by Miles Davis.

SELECTED RECORDINGS

As leader: Cleanhead Blues (1946, Mer. 8023); Kidney Stew Blues (1946, Mer. 8028); Alimony Blues (1947, Mer. 8076); Person to Person (1952, King 4582); *Wee Baby Blues* (1969, BB 33021); *Eddie Vinson and the Muse All-Stars Live at Sandy's* (1978, Muse 5208); *Mr. Cleanhead's Back in Town* (1980, JSP 1046)

As sideman: C. Williams: Cherry Red Blues (1944, Hit 7084); Juice Head Baby (1944, Cap. 237); C. Terry: *Yes, the Blues* (1981, Pablo 2312127); C. Basie: *Kansas City Six* (1981, Pablo 2310871)

BIBLIOGRAPHY

S. Dance: "Eddie Vinson of Houston," *Jazz*, vi/7 (1967), 13

C. Gillett: "Eddie 'Cleanhead' Vinson," *J&B*, i/11 (1972), 4

N. Hess: "They Call me Mr. Cleanhead," *Blues Unlimited*, no.114 (1975), 4

H. Nolan: "Just Call me Cleanhead," *DB*, xlii/9 (1975), 16 [incl. discography]

L. Tomkins: "Eddie Vinson," *CI*, xx/5 (1981), 21

L. Birnbaum: "Eddie Cleanhead Vinson," *DB*, xlix/10 (1982), 28 [incl. discography]

D. Penny and T. Burke: "Eddie 'Cleanhead' Vinson," *Blues & Rhythm, the Gospel Truth*, no.20 (1986), 4

BARRY KERNFELD

Viola, Al(fred) (*b* New York, 16 June 1919). Electric guitarist. After playing in an army band with Jimmie Rowles, Gil Evans, and Joe Mondragon (1942–5) he moved to California (1946), where he recorded with André Previn (1947) and toured with a trio led by the pianist Page Cavanaugh (1946–9). This group performed and recorded with Frank Sinatra in 1946–7, and Viola's association with Sinatra continued intermittently until 1980, including a world tour in 1962. From 1949 he worked as a studio musician, playing with the pianist Bobby Troup (1950–54), Ray Anthony (1955–6), Harry James (1957, 1962) and Marty Paich (late 1950s); he also worked occasionally with Buddy Collette and Les Brown. He is heard to advantage on *Buddy's Best* (1957, Dooto 245) recorded with Collette. Thereafter he recorded with Jimmy Witherspoon (1959, 1961), Helen Humes (1961), and June Christy (1963), and worked with Ray Anthony, Stan Kenton, Nelson Riddle, Pete Rugolo and Gerald Wilson. During the 1960s he was a staff musician for television programs; he also played mandolin on the soundtrack for the film *The Godfather*. In the late 1960s and 1970s Viola recorded several times, as an unaccompanied soloist (on acoustic guitar), as a leader, and as a sideman with Lionel Hampton and others. In the 1980s he worked with Collette, Terry Gibbs, and Ray Pizzi.

BIBLIOGRAPHY

Feather–Gitler '70s

F. Nemko: "Al Viola," *GP*, xi/4 (1977), 24 [incl. discography]

L. Tomkins: "Al Viola," *CI*, xv (1977); no.10, p.20; no.12, p.8

L. Underwood: "Profile: Al Viola," *DB*, xlvi/7 (1979), 36

Violin. The soprano member of the family of string instruments that includes the viola and cello. It was in existence in a three-stringed form by the 1520s, and by the early 17th century had become the backbone of the Western orchestra. The modern violin has four strings tuned *g–d'–a'–e''*, and in jazz it is usually played with the bow (arco) rather than plucked with the fingers (pizzicato). The instrument is held under the player's chin; the strings are stopped with the left hand and are bowed or plucked with the right hand.

The earliest use of the violin in a jazz-related context was as a solo instrument in the ragtime orchestras of the early 20th century. Most orchestral arrangements of ragtime – for example, those that appear in *The Red Back Book of Rags* (*c*1915) – included parts for violin (sometimes, indeed, parts for two violins), which were of equal melodic and structural importance to that of the clarinet or trumpet. The nature of the instrument's role may be heard in the recordings of the New Orleans Ragtime Orchestra (notably *The New Orleans Ragtime Orchestra*, 1971, Arhoolie 1058), a group that endeavors to recreate the sound of an early ragtime ensemble.

The violin was used in a similar manner at first in the society orchestras of New Orleans, but it gradually became subservient to the brass and woodwind instruments in the ensemble. A recording such as A. J. Piron's *Lou'siana Swing* (1924, OK 40189) provides a late example of the violin being employed as a full and equal member of the front line. Ironically, Piron's trumpeter, Peter Bocage, was an accomplished violinist (he played the instrument in Bunk Johnson's Superior Band), but he largely forsook the violin in favor of the trumpet on account of the latter's greater potential for jazz.

Territory bands, such as those led by Andy Kirk and Alphonso Trent, often included a violin in their instrumentation; a notable soloist who played in both groups was Claude Williams, who later took up guitar and worked in Count Basie's orchestra. Some big bands of the mid-1920s incorporated violin sections, the principal example being that of Paul Whiteman, where the section was led by Matty Malneck. Leaders of other ensembles, notably Erskine Tate (whose orchestra was resident at the Vendome Theatre in Chicago), played violin in addition to directing their bands.

Gradually the violin reasserted its position as a solo instrument. This was particularly owing to the work of three musicians – Joe Venuti, Stephane Grappelli, and Stuff Smith. Venuti established his reputation through his duet recordings with the guitarist Eddie Lang (beginning with *Stringing the Blues*, 1926, Col. 914D), and the two men developed one of the most significant partnerships of the early swing era. Similarly, Grappelli formed an association with the guitarist Django Reinhardt; in the Quintette du Hot Club de France they produced some of the most enduring, sophisticated, and swinging jazz ever recorded, with the metallic sound of Reinhardt's guitar perfectly complementing the mellow, sustained line of Grappelli's violin. Smith played an important role as a soloist in many small swing groups.

Other significant violinists of the swing era were Svend Asmussen, Eddie South, and Ray Nance. South, a classically trained musician with a fine technique, was influenced by gypsy music (he recorded with Reinhardt and Grappelli). Nance's best work was as a member of Duke Ellington's orchestra, though his solo ventures in collaboration with the tenor saxophonist Paul Gonsalves (for example, *Just-a-Sittin' and a-Rockin'*, 1970, BL 191), were also notable.

Different approaches to violin technique have led to a wide range of styles among jazz players: some have drawn on the techniques of classical and folk players, while others have invented original methods. Grappelli, retaining the tonal aesthetic of the classical violin tradition, explored the potential for flowing melodic lines, as may be heard on *Sweet Sue* (on the album *Homage à Django Reinhardt*, 1972, Festival 120). Venuti and Asmussen made more use of the instrument's harmonic resources and employed the bow in a percussive manner; Asmussen's technique is well represented by *Some of these Days* (1940, Odeon D408). Smith revolutionized the vocabulary of jazz violinists with his wild, biting attack, wide vibrato, unorthodox fingerings, and expressive intonation; a good example of his attack is recorded on *After you've gone* (1936, Voc. 3201). A particularly novel bowing technique was devised by Venuti to allow the player to sustain chords of three or four notes: this involved removing the pin from the frog of the bow, wrapping the bow hair around all four strings, and holding the stick of the bow underneath the body of the violin. The results may be heard on *Almost like being in love* on the album *Joe Venuti and his Violin* (*c*1955, Jazz Man 336).

The acoustical and musical demands of many types of modern jazz and rock have led to modifications in the way in which the violin is played. Jazz musicians have always found that the relatively quiet sound of the instrument has placed them at a disadvantage. Augustus Stroh attempted to overcome this problem at the beginning of the 20th century when he invented a type of violin that incorporated elements of the gramophone. In the late 1930s Smith was among the earliest players to amplify his instrument electronically. The majority of jazz violinists in the 1980s rely on amplification, making use of a microphone, a transducer, or an electric violin (in which the transducer is built into the body of the instrument). The thinness of sound produced by an amplified violin, however, has led to the adoption of electronic devices to enhance the instrument's timbre. These include time-delay, echo, and reverberation units, equalizers, and wa-wa pedal.

Creative players have shown that the violin is an instrument of great flexibility in jazz. Zbigniew Seifert, for example, executed fast trills as a substitute for vibrato, while Jean-Luc Ponty has chosen to abandon vibrato altogether. Others have experimented with non-Western tonal systems or have made extensive use of sliding pitch. John Blake, for example, studied Carnatic (south Indian) music for a number of years, and incorporates elements of that vocabulary into his playing; in the 1980s he has recorded in styles ranging from bop to free jazz, both as a leader and as a soloist with Cecil McBee, Wynton Marsalis, James Newton, and McCoy Tyner.

Other notable free-jazz violinists include Leroy Jenkins and Billy Bang, both of whom consistently play outside the equal-tempered system. Jenkins brings to the idiom a virtuoso classical technique: on his recording *For Players Only* (1975, JCOA 1010) he incorporates at different points effects associated with 20th-century art music (for example, playing sul ponticello, with and without a mute) and produces singing sustained tones in the high register of the instrument; the album also offers an example of a solo played through a wa-wa pedal. Another interesting exponent, who plays the instrument left-handed, is Ornette Coleman. He performs in an intense, percussive manner, using unorthodox fingerings and bowing positions (a good example of his playing may be heard on *Falling Stars* on the album *The Ornette Coleman Trio at the Golden Circle*, 1965, BN 84224-5). However, Coleman uses the violin less as an independent instrument than as one of two coloristic alternatives (with the trumpet) to his principal instrument, the alto saxophone.

Some musicians have sought ways of expanding the range of the violin downwards. Ponty and Michal Urbaniak played the violectra, an electric instrument sounding an octave below the conventional violin; both men later took up a five-string electric violin (the lowest string on which was tuned to *c*) and Urbaniak performs on a six-string model (with the addition of a string tuned to *F*). The tenor violin, which has a range between that of the viola and the cello, has been used in jazz by Asmussen and the studio orchestra concertmaster Harry Lookofsky. Lakshminarayana Shankar plays a ten-string violin with two necks, an instrument that he designed himself.

For illustrations *see* Asmussen, Svend; Grappelli, Stephane; and Ponty, Jean-Luc.

BIBLIOGRAPHY

J.-E. Berendt: *Das Jazzbuch: Entwicklung und Bedeutung der Jazzmusik* (Frankfurt am Main, Germany, 1953, rev. and enlarged 5/1981 as *Das grosse Jazzbuch: von New Orleans bis Jazz Rock*, Eng. trans. as *The Jazz Book: from New Orleans to Fusion and Beyond*, Westport, CT, 1982), 288

D. Morgenstern: "Jazz Fiddle," *DB*, xxxiv/3 (1967), 16

E. Jost: *Free Jazz* (Graz, Austria, 1974)

M. Glaser and S. Grappelli: *Jazz Violin* (New York and elsewhere, 1981) [incl. transcrs.]

MATT GLASER, ALYN SHIPTON

Violoncello [cello]. The bass instrument of the violin family. It has four strings, normally tuned *C–G–d–a*, which are sounded either with a bow (arco) or by plucking (pizzicato).

The cello had little importance in early jazz, though a cellist was among the members of Erskine Tate's Vendome Orchestra photographed in 1925. It was first used with any frequency during the bop era, when some double bass players employed it as a second instrument; Harry Babasin, for example, recorded pizzicato cello solos with Dodo Marmarosa in 1947, and Oscar Pettiford played the instrument in the early to mid-1950s. Because the cello is smaller than the double bass and therefore fewer changes of hand position are required to play a given line, double bass players found that they could execute fast bop melodies more easily on the cello than on their own instrument; moreover, the cello's higher register enabled it to be heard more easily than the bass above accompaniments. Ray Brown, Doug Watkins, Peter Warren, and Ron Carter also occasionally doubled on the cello, but this practice among double bass players lost its impetus with Carter's introduction of the Piccolo bass. Eberhard Weber doubled as a cellist during the early 1970s but he abandoned the instrument after 1976, as his six-string double bass allowed him to play comfortably in the cello's range.

In its own right the cello became more important in jazz between 1955 and 1962, when Fred Katz and Nat Gershman were, in succession, members of Chico Hamilton's quintet, which played West Coast jazz. In the late 1960s it began to be used as a solo instrument in styles derived from bop, in fusions of jazz improvisation with ethnic and classical music, and particularly in free jazz. Exponents include Irène Aebi (with Steve Lacy), Jean-Charles Capon, David Baker, Diedre Murray (with Hannibal Peterson), David Darling (with Ralph Towner and Terje Rypdal), David Eyges (with Byard Lancaster and Cecil McBee), the group Directions in Jazz (led by Bill Le Sage), and most notably Abdul Wadud.

For illustration *see* Dolphy, Eric.

BIBLIOGRAPHY

J.-E. Berendt: *Das Jazzbuch: Entwicklung und Bedeutung der Jazzmusik* (Frankfurt am Main, Germany, 1953, rev. and enlarged 5/1981 as *Das grosse Jazzbuch: von New Orleans bis Jazz Rock*, Eng. trans. as *The Jazz Book: from New Orleans to Fusion and Beyond*, Westport, CT, 1982), 259, 296

BARRY KERNFELD

Viseur, Gus(tave) (*b* Lessines, Belgium, ? 15 May 1915; *d* ?Le Havre, France, 25 Aug 1974). Belgian accordionist. He met Django Reinhardt in Paris (1934) and belonged to Boris Sarbeck's orchestra, then worked in France and Belgium with Philippe Brun, Joseph Reinhardt, and his own quintet. After touring the USA in 1963 he interrupted his career as a performer to open a record shop in Le Havre, but resumed playing around 1970. Viseur made several recordings as a leader, using such sidemen as Eddie Brunner, Oscar Alemán, Brun, Joseph Reinhardt, and Roger Guérin.

ROBERT PERNET

Vitous, Miroslav (Ladislav) (*b* Prague, 6 Dec 1947). Czechoslovak double bass player. He learned violin and piano before taking up double bass and, while studying at the Prague Conservatory, won a scholarship to the Berklee College of Music (1966). In 1967 he moved to New York, where he played with Art Farmer, Freddie Hubbard, the quintet led by Bob Brookmeyer and Clark Terry, and Miles Davis, then worked with Herbie Mann (1968–70); he also recorded with Donald Byrd (1967), Chick Corea, Jack DeJohnette (both 1968), Wayne Shorter (1969), and Larry Coryell (1970). In 1970 he toured with Stan Getz, rejoined Mann, and, with Shorter and Joe Zawinul, was a founding member of Weather Report. Vitous left the group in 1973 and spent several years experimenting with electric guitars. After he resumed playing double bass he joined the faculty of the New England Conservatory (1979), later becoming head of the jazz department there (1983). He has remained active as a performer, leading a quartet with John Surman, Kenny Kirkland or John Taylor, and Jon Christensen (1979–82), and, with Roy Haynes, playing in Chick Corea's Trio Music (from 1981). Vitous is best known for his work with Weather Report, in which he applied to jazz-rock the approach developed by Scott La Faro of treating the double bass as a lyrical, melodic instrument rather than as a timekeeper; his virtuoso use of the bow was also unusual. With his quartet and other musicians (notably Corea), he moved to bop and other styles of playing, which were better suited to these innovations. His arco playing may be heard to advantage on *Silver Lake* from his album *First Meeting* (1979).

SELECTED RECORDINGS

As unaccompanied soloist: *Emergence* (1985, ECM 1312)

As leader: *Infinite Search* (1969, Embryo 524); *First Meeting* (1979, ECM 1145), incl. Silver Lake; *Miroslav Vitous Group* (1980, ECM 1185); *Journey's End* (1982, ECM 1242)

As leader with T. Rypdal and J. DeJohnette: *Terje Rypdal–Miroslav Vitous–Jack DeJohnette* (1978, ECM 1125); *To Be Continued* (1981, ECM 1192)

As sideman with C. Corea: *Trio Music* (1981, ECM 1232-3); *Trio Music, Live in Europe* (1984, ECM 1310)

BIBLIOGRAPHY

M. Bateson: "Avant Courier: Miroslav Vitous," *JJI*, xxxvi/3 (1983), 16

F. Bouchard: "Miroslav Vitous: Both Sides of the Bass," *DB*, li/9 (1984), 18

BARRY KERNFELD

Vlach, Karel (*b* Prague, 8 Oct 1911; *d* Prague, 26 Feb 1986). Bohemian bandleader. He worked with an amateur orchestra in Prague in 1938 and became a professional musician in 1941, leading a big band which from 1945 included such musicians as Karel Krautgartner and the tenor saxophonist Milan Ulrich. From 1947 he worked in the theater, television, radio, and films, while continuing to lead his own swing band, which until the mid-1950s was the foremost group of its kind in Czechoslovakia. Vlach gave many concerts at home and abroad, and between 1942 and the mid-1960s made more than 1000 recordings; his work as a bandleader is well represented by the album *Let us Dance* (1953–8, Sup. 13169).

GERHARD CONRAD

Vocalese. A term for the practice of jazz Singing in which texts (newly invented) are set to recorded jazz improvisations. The word is a pun on the term "vocalise," combining the ideas of a jazz "vocal" and a private language (indicated by the suffix "-ese"). Eddie Jefferson performed vocalese from the 1940s, but the best-known early recordings were made by King Pleasure, including his version of Jefferson's *Moody's Mood for Love* (1952, Prst. 924), based on a saxophone solo by James Moody, and his own setting of *Parker's Mood* (1953, Prst. 880), using

Charlie Parker's blues improvisation of that title. Other important practitioners of vocalese were Dave Lambert, Annie Ross, and above all Jon Hendricks, who was extremely inventive in creating texts to capture the feeling of the original solos. In 1957 Lambert, Hendricks, and Ross (later Yolande Bavan) formed a vocal trio which attained some commercial success with their vocalese; it disbanded in 1964, but Hendricks continued to create and perform such pieces into the 1980s with a group comprising members of his family. Although the singing of vocalese is most closely associated with the bop style, it was also practiced later by such popular singers as the Pointer Sisters and, notably, Joni Mitchell in her version of Charles Mingus's *Goodbye Pork Pie Hat* (on the album *Mingus*, 1978, Asy. 5E505); the vocal quartet Manhattan Transfer recorded the album *Vocalese* in 1985 (Atl. 81266). (L. Feather: "An Explanation of Vocalese," *Jazz: a Quarterly of American Music*, no.3 (1959), 261)

J. BRADFORD ROBINSON/R

Vocalion. Record company and label. The company was a division of the Aeolian Co., a firm of piano manufacturers based in New York; it began issuing vertical-cut records in 1916; these included a now famous series by the Original Dixieland Jazz Band (1917). In January 1920 it issued its first lateral-cut discs. At first the records bore the name Aeolian Vocalion; the first word was dropped shortly before the company was sold around 1924 to Brunswick–Balke–Callender, which owned the label BRUNSWICK. Thereafter the new administration operated the two enterprises separately, but there was considerable interchange of artists and repertory, and their histories are interconnected. Although Vocalion had made race records before its purchase by Brunswick, only in 1926 was a race series formally established. The Vocalion 1000s, recorded under the supervision of Jack Kapp, and later of J. Mayo Williams, is well remembered for its issue of material by King Oliver, Jimmie Noone, and Duke Ellington.

In December 1920 a British subsidiary was established which recorded its own repertory and also provided material for several other labels, among them Coliseum and Guardsman; some of these were also used to issue American recordings, often under pseudonyms, that had been leased to British Vocalion. Rights to the label's name in the UK were later acquired for use by an autonomous English organization, the Vocalion Record Co., of Hayes, which drew its American repertory from Gennett. British Vocalion remained in existence but no longer used the label name, and issued material on such labels as Broadcast. Its affiliate in Australia continued to use the label name Vocalion for issue of material from Gennett and American Brunswick. For a few months in 1927 records were also issued on a Vocalion label by the British branch of Brunswick, using material from Gennett and American Brunswick.

In the USA Vocalion was taken over in 1930 (with the rest of Brunswick–Balke–Collender) by Warner Bros., and then sold in December 1931 to Consolidated Film Industries, which already owned the AMERICAN RECORD COMPANY. The new management discontinued the 1000 series in July 1933, but recommenced race issues in September 1933 in a 25000 series; the catalogue numbers were later changed to an 02500 series. Numbers in this sequence ran parallel with the general series; the prefix zero was used to denote race records. In several instances, however, the same issue number was used (once with, and once without, the prefix) for two different items; this practice has caused discographers much confusion. Among the important jazz issued on Vocalion in the 1930s were recordings by Billie Holiday (see illustration) and by Duke Ellington's small groups. Though ARC and Brunswick were taken over by CBS in 1938, issue continued on Vocalion until 1940, when the name was phased out in favor of the name Okeh. The numerical series, however, was maintained, and many early Vocalion recordings were reissued on Okeh with their original numbers.

Label for "Trav'lin' All Alone," recorded by Billie Holiday for Vocalion (New York, 13 September 1937)

In England the Vocalion Record Co. was purchased by Crystalate in 1932; the label name was revived in 1936, most notably for issue of a swing series drawn from ARC and Brunswick. Decca purchased Crystalate in March 1937, and continued the Swing Series until 1940; this eventually ran to 247 issues and is now considered a particularly important catalogue. The label was later used again by British Decca in October 1951 for the issue of its series Origins of Jazz. This ceased in 1954 after 41 items. Vocalion then remained dormant until 1962, when British Decca adopted the name for its subsidiary label Vogue after rights to the latter trademark reverted to the French parent company. The name Vocalion was dropped in 1968, but used again in 1976 for a short series (also put out in France) of reissues of early jazz and popular music taken from Brunswick's pre-1932 catalogue.

BIBLIOGRAPHY

E. Jackson and L. Hibbs: *Decca, Brunswick, Vocalion Encyclopedia of Swing* (London, 1941)

J. Godrich and R. M. W. Dixon: *Blues & Gospel Records, 1902–1942* (Hatch End, nr London, 1964, rev. 2/1969, rev. and enlarged 3/1982 as R. M. W. Dixon and J. Godrich: *Blues & Gospel Records, 1902–1943*), 20

A. G. Cox: "Discography of the Vocalion Swing Series, 1936–1940," *JJ*, xix (1966), no.3, p.22; no.4, p.17; no.5, p.25; no.6, p.38; no.8, p.38

P. Burgis: "Discs from Down Under," *Sv*, no.11 (1967), 4

R. M. W. Dixon and J. Godrich: *Recording the Blues* (London, 1970)

R. D. Kinkle: "Vocalion Numerical List," "Vocalion–Okeh Numerical List," *The Complete Encyclopedia of Popular Music and Jazz, 1900–1950* (New Rochelle, NY, and Westport, CT, 1974), iv, 2245, 2255

F. Dutton: "Numbers Runners Blues," *Sv*, no.79 (1978), 8

B. Rust: *The American Record Label Book* (New Rochelle, NY, 1978), 318

F. Dutton: "Numbers Runners Blues, 2," *Sv*, no.106 (1983), 125

P. Pelletier: "The Vogue–Vocalion Label," *Record Information*, no.1 (1983), 24

Vogel, Vic(tor Stéphane) (*b* Montreal, 3 Aug 1935). Canadian pianist and bandleader. He toured Quebec with the Double Six (1961) and from the late 1960s led several big bands. The last of these, formed in 1978, has a spirited, spontaneous style reminiscent of the orchestras of Duke Ellington; it performed in the 1980s at the Festival International de Jazz de Montréal, and in 1982 recorded the album *The Vic Vogel Band* (Spectra Scene 1706) and toured Europe. Among those who have appeared with the band as guest soloists are Phil Woods, Zoot Sims, Dizzy Gillespie, and Mel Tormé. Vogel has also worked as a leader and an arranger in studios, and in 1976 composed and conducted music for the Olympic Games in Montreal; he is a colorful, exacting leader.

Oral history material in *CaQMG*.

BIBLIOGRAPHY

S. Thomas: "Vogel, Vic," *Encyclopedia of Music in Canada*, ed. H. Kallmann, G. Potvin, and K. Winters (Toronto, Buffalo, and London, 1981)

M. Miller: "Vic Vogel Gives 'em Hell," *The Globe and Mail* (Toronto, 29 Jan 1982), 11

——: "Vic Vogel," *Boogie, Pete & the Senator: Canadian Musicians in Jazz: the Eighties* (Toronto, 1987), 276

MARK MILLER

Vogue. Record company and label. The company was established in France in 1948; artists and repertory were directed by Charles Delaunay. The extensive jazz catalogue included recordings by such native musicians as Henri Renaud, American expatriates (most notably Sidney Bechet), and visitors from the USA, including Clifford Brown, Bobby Jaspar, Jimmy Raney, and Art Farmer, as well as reissues of American material. The company also held licenses to distribute in France recordings made by small American companies; among those with important jazz catalogues were King, Coral, Contemporary, Good Time Jazz, Hot Record Society, Blue Note, and Fantasy (some of this material was issued on the label Jazz Selection, which Vogue administered).

A subsidiary was established in England in 1951 that was taken over by British Decca five years later. It retained its autonomy, however, until 1962, when the Vogue trademark reverted to the parent company. After using the name Vocalion for this catalogue for a brief period, Decca absorbed the label into its general operations. Vogue set up a new British subsidiary within the group of companies controlled by Pye. The French company has remained important for jazz into the 1980s; its catalogue includes a noteworthy reissue series, Jazz Legacy, as well as new recordings by Gérard Badini and Claude Luter. (P. M. Pelletier: "The Vogue–Vocalion Label," *Record Information*, no.1 (1983), 24)

Voicing. A term applied in jazz to the particular sonority of a chord, which depends on the vertical ordering, spacing, and instrumental distribution of its component notes; *see* HARMONY (i), §1(iv).

Volonté, Eraldo (*b* Milan, 5 Feb 1918). Italian tenor saxophonist and composer. He played violin in dance bands, then took up the tenor saxophone in 1936. In the 1940s he played in orchestras led by Enzo Ceragioli, Bruno Martelli, Kramer Gorni, and Aldo Rossi. He performed and recorded bop with big bands and small groups, both as a leader (1947–76) and as a sideman with Gil Cuppini (1948–74); he also worked with Glauco Masetti's Sestetto jazz moderno (1956–8). He recorded with an octet led by the pianist Piero Umiliani (1958), with big bands led by Umiliani (1963, 1966), Giorgio Gaslini (1968), and the double bass player Giorgio Azzolini (1971–2), and in a small group led by the double bass player Giorgio Buratti (1970). Volonté's playing may be heard to advantage on his recording *Zoot* on the album *IIIrd Festival del Jazz del San Remo* (1958, Carish 15301); among his compositions are *Eclypso* (1966) and *Dedicated to Duke Ellington* (1975).

ADRIANO MAZZOLETTI

Von Eichwald, Håkan (*b* Turku, Finland, 2 April 1908; *d* Stockholm, 1 April 1964). Swedish bandleader of Finnish birth. He studied piano and conducting and from 1930 to 1932 led a big band at the dance restaurant Kaos in Stockholm. In the 1930s he continued to work as a leader; his orchestra, which was the first in Sweden of any permanence, toured Europe and made recordings in Sweden and Germany (including *Rhythm*, 1932, Tel. A1228). Among those who performed and recorded under von Eichwald as sidemen was Thore Ehrling.

BIBLIOGRAPHY

B. Englund: "Håkan von Eichwald: han hade flera vitt skilda karriärer" [Håkan von Eichwald: he had several widely differing careers], *Orkester journalen*, xliii/12 (1975), 12 [incl. discography]; xliv/1 (1976), 12

ERIK KJELLBERG

Von Essen, Reimer. *See* ESSEN, REIMER VON.

Von Ohlen, John [Baron] (*b* Indianapolis, 13 May 1941). Drummer. He toured with Billy Maxted's Manhattan Jazz Band (1967–8), and recorded with Woody Herman at the Monterey Jazz Festival (1967); later he worked with Herman for a year (1969). After touring the USA and recording with Stan Kenton from 1970 to 1972 he organized and led a 17-piece band in Indiana. In 1973 he recorded the album *The Baron* (CW 3001) as the leader of a quartet.

BIBLIOGRAPHY

Feather–Gitler '70s

J. Von Ohlen: "John Von Ohlen," *CI*, x/8 (1972), 24

S. Fish: "John Von Ohlen: Natural Style," *MD*, ix/3 (1985), 16

Voynow, Dick [Richard F.] (*b* 1900; *d* Los Angeles, 15 Sept 1944). Pianist. He replaced the pianist Dud Mecum with the Wolverines during the band's first residency at the Stockton Club, Hamilton, Ohio. Later he became its business manager and nominal leader, and continued in this role after most of the original members had left. The band toured regularly until 1926, and sporadically thereafter, and performed on one occasion with Smith Ballew. Voynow can be heard to advantage on *Riverboat Shuffle* (1924, Gen. 5454) and *Royal Garden Blues* (1924, Gen. 20062), both recorded with the Wolverines. From the late 1920s he worked as an executive for recording companies. (R. M. Sudhalter, P. R. Evans, and W. Dean-Myatt: *Bix: Man & Legend*, New Rochelle, NY, and London, 1974)

For illustrations *see* RECORDING, fig.3, and WOLVERINES.

based on *ChiltonW*

V.S.O.P. (i). Group led by Herbie Hancock. Its name derived from the title of the album (Col. PG34688) documenting a retrospective concert of Hancock's music given at the Newport Jazz Festival in New York in 1976, where three groups performed: a quintet consisting of Hancock, the trumpeter Freddie Hubbard, the saxophonist Wayne Shorter, the double bass player Ron Carter, and the drummer Tony Williams; Hancock's sextet as it had been in 1971–3; and his jazz-rock group. The appearance of these diverse ensembles in the same program was deemed to constitute a "Very Special One-time-only Performance." In 1977 the initials of this phrase were used to name the quintet (all the members of which, with the exception of Hubbard, had been members of Miles Davis's famous quintet of the mid-1960s) when it toured the USA and performed in Tokyo and London; during the same year the ensemble, also known simply as the Quintet, recorded the album *V.S.O.P.: the Quintet* (Col. C2-34976). The group was reunited in 1979 and gave a concert in Japan, and a second version of the quintet, V.S.O.P. II (consisting of Hancock, Carter, Williams, and Wynton and Branford Marsalis), toured in 1983 (for illustration *see* HANCOCK, HERBIE).

BIBLIOGRAPHY

P. Keepnews: "Notes: Hancock," *Jazz Magazine*, ii/1 (1977), 24
L. Lyons: "Herbie Hancock: V.S.O.P., New Musical Directions," *CK*, iii/11 (1977), 28
R. Palmer: "Hancock's All-star Reunion," *RS*, no.249 (6 Oct 1977), 28
H. Saal and A. Kuflik: "Jazz Comes Back!," *Newsweek*, xc (8 Aug 1977), 51
I. Gitler: "Jazz Fests Italian Style," *JT* (Aug 1983), 5
H. Mandel: "Herbie Hancock: Keeping his Ears and Options Open," *JT* (Aug 1983), 10
K. Silsbee: "The Playboy Jazz Fest," *JT* (Aug 1983), 5

THOMAS OWENS

V.S.O.P. (ii). Record label. It was established in the early 1980s by CBS to issue several collections of recordings by Louis Armstrong. The initials stand for "Very Special Old Phonography."

W

Wachsmann, Phil(ipp John Paul) (*b* Kampala, Uganda, 5 Aug 1944). British violinist. He studied music in England, the USA, and Paris (1963–9) then taught at Durham University (1969–70). In 1971 he formed the group Chamberpot, which drew on many musical sources, including the music of Anton Webern, and from that time concentrated on free improvisation, developing the use of electronics as an integrated extension of the technical capabilities of the violin. Among the jazz musicians and groups with whom he has worked are Derek Bailey (1973–) and Bailey's group Company (1982–6), a trio with the drummer Paul Lytton and the trombonist Radu Malfatti (1974–5), Tony Oxley (1977–), the London Jazz Composers Orchestra (1979–), Fred van Hove (1979–84), Barry Guy and Paul Rutherford in Iskra 1903 (1980–), the Electric String Trio (1981–), and the King Übü Orchestrü (1984–). Among his compositions are *Colour Energy Reaction* (1981) for film and orchestra, as well as other mixed-media works that have been written in collaboration with dancers and artists. He was one of the founders in 1975 of the record label Bead. Wachsmann's playing may be heard to advantage on his solo album *Writing on Water* (1984, Bead 23).

BIBLIOGRAPHY

R. Cotterrell, ed.: *Jazz Now: the Jazz Centre Society Guide* (London, 1976)
I. Carr: "Wachsmann, Phil (Philipp John Paul)," in I. Carr, D. Fairweather, and B. Priestley: *Jazz: the Essential Companion* (London, 1987)

SIMON ADAMS

Wade, Jimmy [James F.] (*b* Jacksonville, IL, *c*1895; *d* Chicago, Feb 1957). Trumpeter, pianist, and bandleader. After leading his own band at Queen's Hall, Chicago (*c*1916), he spent several years as the music director of the band that accompanied Lucille Hegamin, working in Seattle and New York. He left in the early 1920s and returned to Chicago, where he played with Doc Cook. Later he formed his own band, which included Eddie South and Teddy Weatherford. It played many residencies in Chicago and also performed in New York at the Savoy Ballroom (1926) and the Club Alabam (1927). Its recordings include *Someday Sweetheart/Mobile Blues* (1923, Para. 20295); the latter song offers a particularly good example of Wade's solo trumpet playing. South acted as a leader with this band during the mid-1920s. Later in the decade Wade occasionally worked as a sideman with other leaders. During the 1930s he was active mainly with his own ensembles.

BIBLIOGRAPHY

T. J. Hennessey: "The Black Chicago Establishment 1919–1930," *JJS*, ii/1 (1974), 15–45
A. McCarthy: *Big Band Jazz* (New York and London, 1974)
R. Gulliver: "Jimmy Wade," *Sv*, no.56 (1974–5), 55 [incl. discography]

based on *ChiltonW*

Wadud, Abdul (Khabir) [DeVaughn, Ronald] (*b* Cleveland, 30 April 1947). Cellist. He learned cello from the age of nine. He studied at Youngstown State University (1966–7) and Oberlin College Conservatory (1968–70), where he played in the Black Unity Trio and met Julius Hemphill, with whom he has worked fruitfully into the 1980s; he took his Muslim name during this period. In 1970–77 he was a member of the New Jersey SO, and in 1972 gained a master's degree in performance at SUNY, Stony Brook. He first worked with Arthur Blythe, another long-time associate, in 1976; in the 1970s he also played and recorded with Frank Lowe (1975), George Lewis (ii) (1977), Oliver Lake (1978), Leroy Jenkins (in a duo, 1979), Sam Rivers, Cecil Taylor, David Murray, Chico Freeman, and others. From 1980 he worked with Anthony Davis in various settings, including a trio with James Newton (1982–4) and the octet Episteme. Through his sophisticated use of bowing and plucking techniques Wadud has expanded the cello's role in jazz as an accompanying and a solo instrument.

SELECTED RECORDINGS

As unaccompanied soloist: *By Myself* (1977, Bishara Music BR101)
As leader with A. Davis and J. Newton: *I've Known Rivers* (1982, Gram. 8201)
As sideman: J. Hemphill: *Dogon, A. D.* (1972, Mbari 5001); A. Blythe: *The Grip* (1977, IndN 1029); J. Hemphill: *Raw Materials and Residuals* (1977, BS 0015); A. Blythe: *Illusions* (1980, Col. JC36583)

BIBLIOGRAPHY

D. Lee: "Abdul Wadud," *Coda*, no.176 (1980), 8
L. Jeske: "Abdul Wadud: Profile," *DB*, xlix/11 (1982), 52

ED HAZELL

Wah-wah. *See* Wa-wa.

Waits, Freddie [Frederick Douglas; Dahoud] (*b* Jackson, MS, 27 April 1943). Drummer. He first played drums for blues singers such as Memphis Slim and John Lee Hooker. In the early 1960s he toured and recorded with soul singers associated with the Motown label before settling in New York, where he performed in styles ranging from swing to free jazz. Among the many musicians with whom he recorded are Ray Bryant (1966), Johnny Hodges (1968), Andrew Hill (1968–9, 1980), McCoy Tyner (1968–70), Richard Davis (1972), Ella Fitzgerald (1973), Bennie Maupin (1974), Mercer Ellington (1975), Teddy Edwards (1976), Curtis Fuller (1978), and Bill Dixon (1980). His work with Max Roach's ensemble M' BOOM RE: PERCUSSION (from 1971) has demonstrated his command of a wide array of percussion instruments. With Horacee Arnold and Billy Hart, Waits formed Colloquium III, a group that first performed in early 1979, and he played in 1987 in a quintet led by Cecil Taylor. He has also taught music in public schools in New York and has been a member of the faculty at Rutgers.

SELECTED RECORDINGS

As sideman: A. Hill: *Grass Roots* (1968, BN 84303); M. Tyner: *Expansions* (1968, BN 84338); R. Davis: *Epistrophy and Now's the Time* (1972, Muse 5002); M. Roach: *M' Boom Re: Percussion* (1979, Col. IC36247); B. Dixon: *Bill Dixon in Italy* (1980, SN 1008, 1011)

BIBLIOGRAPHY

Feather–Gitler '70s
B. Primack: "Drummers Colloquium III: Multiple Percussionists," *DB*, xlvi/17 (1979), 25
C. Iero: "Colloquium III: Freddie Waits, Horacee Arnold, Billy Hart," *MD*, iv/1 (1980), 12

BARRY KERNFELD

Waits, Tom (*b* Pomona, CA, 7 Dec 1949). Songwriter and composer. From 1972 he worked as a storyteller-pianist and guitarist, accompanied, whenever finances allowed, by his group the Nocturnal Emissions (tenor saxophone, double bass, and drums). His subjects were crude and vulgar, concerning life in greasy diners, striptease clubs, urban bus stations, and smoky bars, and his language was a slang of the 1940s and 1950s; his humor, however, was intellectually perceptive. His tales, funny at first, became increasingly morbid during the 1970s, and his already gravelly voice began to be affected by an excess of cigarettes and alcohol. He made a number of recordings for Asylum records, the finest of which was probably *Nighthawks at the Diner* (1975), a live performance which demonstrated his witty, improvisatory style. During the early 1980s Waits labored over the music for Francis Ford Coppola's film *One from the Heart* (1982). With the recording *Swordfishtrombones* (1983) he ceased to focus on lyrics and began to explore a broad spectrum of instrumental sounds, making use of synthesizers, bagpipes, and exotic percussion in addition to conventional jazz instruments. In 1983 he moved from Los Angeles to New York, where he has concentrated on a new career as an actor. He made a tour of Europe with a sextet in 1985.

SELECTED RECORDINGS

Closing Time (1972, Asy. 5061); *The Heart of Saturday Night* (1974, Asy. 7E-1015); *Nighthawks at the Diner* (1975, Asy. 7E-2008); *Small Change* (1976, Asy. 7E-1078); *Foreign Affairs* (1977, Asy. 7E-1117); *Blue Valentine* (1978, Asy. 6E-162); *Heartattack and Vine* (1980, Asy. 6E-295); *Swordfishtrombones* (1983, Isl. 90095-1); *Rain Dogs* (1985, Isl. 90299)

BIBLIOGRAPHY

S. Lake: "Waits: the Great White Hope," *MM*, l (4 Oct 1975), 16
M. Hohman: "Bitin' the Green Shiboda with Tom Waits," *DB*, xliii/12 (1976), 14
D. McGee: "Tom Waits," *RS*, no.231 (27 Jan 1977), 11
J. A. Scott: "On the Way to Burma Shave: Tom Waits and Ballad Form," *Popular Music and Society*, vii/2 (1980), 103 [analysis of lyrics]
P. Keepnews: "Singer Shuns 'Popularity Contest': Waits not Waiting for a Hit," *Billboard*, xcix (16 Nov 1985), 49
E. Murphy: "Tom Waits: the Drifter Finds a Home," *RS*, no.466 (30 Jan 1986), 20

BARRY KERNFELD

Walcott, Collin (*b* New York, 24 April 1945; *d* Magdeburg, Germany, 8 Nov 1984). Sitar and tablā player and percussionist. He learned to play violin, snare drum, and timpani, and during his teens was resident percussionist at the Yale Summer School of Music in Norfolk, Connecticut. In 1966 he graduated from Indiana University, where his major subject was percussion, then went to Los Angeles and studied sitar with Ravi Shankar and tablā with Alla Rakha. After moving to New York he performed and recorded a blend of bop and oriental music with Tony Scott (1967–9); he also recorded on sitar with Miles Davis (1972). Thereafter Walcott was a member of three groups devoted to combining jazz improvisation and instrumentation with elements of a wide range of classical and ethnic music: the Paul Winter Consort (1970–71); OREGON (with Ralph Towner, Paul McCandless, and Glen Moore, all former members of the Winter Consort, 1970–84); and Codona, a cooperative trio with Don Cherry and Nana Vasconcelos (1978–84).

SELECTED RECORDINGS

As leader: *Cloud Dance* (1975, ECM 1062); *Grazing Dreams* (1977, ECM 1096); *Codona* (1978, ECM 1132)

As sideman: T. Scott: *Music for Yoga Meditation and other Joys* (*c*1967, Verve 68742); P. Winter: *Icarus* (*c*1972, Epic 31643); M. Davis: *On the Corner* (1972, Col. KC31906); E. Gismonti: *Sol do meio dia* (1977, ECM 1116)

BIBLIOGRAPHY

M. Bourne: "The Natural Timbre of Oregon," *DB*, xli/16 (1974), 14
M. Zipkin: "Oregon: out of the Woods, into the World," *DB*, xlvi/5 (1979), 13
H. Howland: "Master Percussionist: Oregon's Collin Walcott," *MD*, v/4 (1981), 24
Freff: "Book-ends: Oregon's Collin Walcott and Glen Moore," *Musician*, no.70 (1984), 68 [interview]

BARRY KERNFELD

Waldron, Mal(colm Earl) (*b* New York, 16 Aug 1926). Pianist. He first aspired to become a classical pianist, and played jazz on alto saxophone, changing to piano only when he was a student at Queens College, CUNY (where he gained the BA in composition). After graduating he worked with various bands around New York, and he made his first recording in 1950 with Ike Quebec. He joined Charles Mingus (1954) and played with his Jazz Workshop at the Newport Jazz Festival (1955, 1956). He formed his own quintet, which included Gigi Gryce and Idrees Sulieman, late in 1956, and from 1956 to 1958 he recorded frequently as a leader and a sideman for the Prestige label. He was Billie Holiday's accompanist from April 1957 until her death in 1959, after which he worked with Abbey Lincoln and continued his activities as a studio musician. During the early 1960s he played in New York with a quintet led by Eric Dolphy and Booker Little. After suffering a nervous breakdown in 1963 Waldron had to relearn the fundamentals of playing, which he did partly by studying his own recordings. He moved to Europe in 1965 and in 1967 settled in Munich. He has performed frequently with expatriate and visiting musicians, including Steve Lacy and Archie Shepp, and has also become popular in Japan, where he first appeared in 1970; he began making return visits to the USA in 1975.

As a player and composer Waldron draws heavily upon Thelonious Monk's spare, angular style; his improvisations are based on motivic repetition with a minimum of development, or on strict mathematical structures. As well as jazz pieces, Waldron has written several film and ballet scores.

SELECTED RECORDINGS

As unaccompanied soloist: *Mingus Lives* (1979, Enja 3075)

Duos with S. Lacy: *Herbe de l'oubli* (1981, Hat Music 3515)

As leader: *Impressions* (1959, NewJ 8242); *Free at Last* (1969, ECM 1001); with G. Peacock: *First Encounter* (1970, Cat. 7906); *One Entrance, Many Exits* (1982, PAlt 8014); *Encounters* (1984, Muse 5305)

As sideman: C. Mingus: *Moods of Mingus* (1955, Savoy 15050); *Pithecanthropus erectus* (1956, Atl. 1237); [no leader]: *Interplay for Two Trumpets*

& Two Tenors (1957, Prst. 7112); B. Holiday: *Lady in Satin* (1958, Col. CL1157); E. Dolphy: *Eric Dolphy at the Five Spot* (1961, NewJ 8260); M. Roach: *Percussion Bitter Sweet* (1961, Imp. 8)

BIBLIOGRAPHY

I. Gitler: "Content on the Continent," *Radio Free Jazz*, xvii/10 (1976), 5
"Mal Waldron," *SJ*, xxxii/11 (1978), 286 [discography]
K. Whitehead: "Mal Waldron: Interview," *Cadence*, vi/10 (1980), 5
N. Mackey and H. Gray: "Notes from an Expatriate," *JSN*, ii/2 (1980–81), 18
B. Blumenthal: "Mal Waldron," *DB*, xlviii/4 (1981), 28 [incl. discography]
B. Doerschuk: "Mal Waldron: Life on the Borderline," *Keyboard*, x/7 (1984), 42 [incl. discography]

BOB DOERSCHUK

Walking bass. (1) In jazz, a line played pizzicato on a double bass in regular crotchets in 4/4 meter, the notes usually moving stepwise or in intervallic patterns not necessarily restricted to the main pitches of the harmony. The style arose as the use of stride piano patterns declined, and its first master was Walter Page in the late 1920s and early 1930s; it has since become *lingua franca* for jazz bass players, allowing them to contribute pulse, harmony and countermelody simultaneously.

(2) In boogie-woogie piano style, a repeating left-hand pattern of broken octaves. *See* BOOGIE-WOOGIE, ex.2.

GUNTHER SCHULLER

Wallace, Bennie (Lee, Jr.) (*b* Chattanooga, TN, 18 Nov 1946). Tenor saxophonist and clarinetist. He played clarinet from the age of 12 and later changed to tenor saxophone. He studied music at the University of Tennessee (BA 1968) and then played in small groups at various local after-hours clubs. While working in Denver, Colorado, he met Gary Burton, who encouraged him to move to New York. In 1971 he made his professional début with Monty Alexander. Thereafter he became involved with the loft-jazz movement and worked with many significant avant-garde musicians, including Sheila Jordan (1976). Wallace has led his own trio, which has comprised Eddie Gomez and the drummers Eddie Moore (1977–9) and Dannie Richmond or Alvin Queen (1979–82). During the 1980s he has been a member of a quartet that has worked in the USA, Europe, and Japan; this group sometimes included Ray Anderson, with whom Wallace had played intermittently from 1976. In addition to the work of Sonny Rollins, which has been the main influence on his playing, Eddie "Lockjaw" Davis and the rhythm-and-blues tenor saxophonist Red Prysock have contributed greatly to Wallace's energetic and highly charged style.

SELECTED RECORDINGS

Bennie Wallace plays Monk (1981, Enja 3091); *The Bennie Wallace Trio and Chick Corea* (1982, Enja 4028); *Big Jim's Tango* (1982, Enja 4046); *Twilight Time* (1985, BN 85107)

BIBLIOGRAPHY

A. D. Franklin: "Benny Wallace Inside and Out," *JT* (Nov 1982), 5
——: "Bennie Wallace: Interview," *Cadence*, ix/4 (1983), 5
C. Kuhn: "Bennie Wallace: Interview," *Cadence*, ix/5 (1983), 8

STAN WOOLLEY

Wallace, Cedric (*b* Miami, 3 Aug 1909; *d* ?New York, 19 Aug 1985). Double bass player. After moving to New York he worked with Reggie Johnson at the Saratoga Club (1932) and also played with Jimmie Lunceford. From 1938 to 1942 he performed and made recordings with Fats Waller (for illustration *see* WALLER, FATS); *Pantin' in the Panther Room* (1941, Bb 11175) offers an excellent example of Wallace's style. Later he worked with Gene Sedric, Garland Wilson, and others before forming his own band, which played residencies at several clubs in New York during the 1940s. He continued to work into the 1970s.

based on *ChiltonW*

Wallace, Sippie [née Thomas, Beulah Belle] (*b* Houston, 1 Nov 1898; *d* Detroit, 1 Nov 1986). Singer, songwriter, and pianist. Several members of her family were musicians, and she began performing at an early age. In 1923 she made her first recordings, singing in a blues style; later she was accompanied by King Oliver, Louis Armstrong, Sidney Bechet, and other important musicians. In her earliest work she attempted to project a vocal weightiness similar to that of Ma Rainey. Later she sang in a manner better suited to the lighter, prettier qualities of her voice, which may be heard to advantage on *I'm a mighty tight woman*. From the mid-1930s her repertoire was mainly gospel music, but in 1965 she began singing jazz and blues once more. From that date she performed throughout the USA and Europe, and in 1979 she began an association with James Dapogny which continued into the mid-1980s. In 1983 her album *Sippie* was nominated for a Grammy Award. Wallace composed most of her own songs, which are notable for the shapeliness and dignity of their melodies. *Special Delivery Blues* is a fine example of her work.

Oral history material in *NjR* (JOHP).

SELECTED RECORDINGS

Duos: with C. Williams: Caldonia Blues (1924, OK 8144); with L. B. Montgomery and R. Sykes: *Sippie Wallace Sings the Blues* (1966, Sto. 198)
As leader: Special Delivery Blues (1926, OK 8328); The Flood Blues (1927, OK 8470); I'm a mighty tight woman (1929, Vic. 38502); Bedroom Blues (1945, Mer. 2010); *Sippie* (1982, Atl. 19350)

BIBLIOGRAPHY

R. P. Harwood: "'Mighty Tight Woman': the Thomas Family and Classic Blues," *Sv*, no.17 (1968), 16
B. Rusch: "Sippie Wallace: Interview," *Cadence*, iv/10 (1978), 14
E. Townley: "The Texas Nightingale," *Sv*, no.108 (1983), 227
Obituary, J. Simmen, *BHcF*, no.348 (1987), 26

JAMES DAPOGNY

Waller, Fats [Thomas Wright] (*b* New York, 21 May 1904; *d* Kansas City, MO, 15 Dec 1943). Pianist, organist, singer, bandleader, and composer.

1. Life. 2. Works and style.

1. LIFE. His father Edward Waller, a baptist lay preacher, conducted open air religious services in Harlem, at which as a child Fats Waller played reed organ. He played piano at his public school and at the age of 15 became organist at the Lincoln Theatre on 135th Street. His father hoped that Waller would follow a religious calling rather than a career in jazz, but after the death of his mother Adeline Waller in 1920 he moved in with the family of the pianist Russell Brooks. Through Brooks, Waller met James P. Johnson, under whose tutelage he developed as a pianist, and through whose influence he came to make piano rolls, starting in 1922 with *Got to cool my doggies now*. There is some evidence to support Waller's claims that during his formative years as a pianist he studied with Leopold Godowsky, and also that he studied composition with Carl Bohm at the Juilliard School.

In October 1922 Waller made his recording début as a soloist for Okeh with *Muscle Shoals Blues* and *Birmingham Blues*. He began a series of recordings the same year as accompanist for several blues singers including Sara Martin, Alberta Hunter, and Maude Mills. In 1923 a collaboration with Clarence Williams led to the publication of Waller's *Wild Cat Blues*, which Williams recorded with his Blue Five, including Sidney Bechet (July 1923). Another composition, *Squeeze Me*, was published the same year, and these began to establish Waller's reputation as a composer of material performed and recorded by other artists. 1923 also saw his broadcasting début for a Newark local station, followed by regular appearances on WHN, New

Fats Waller and his Rhythm with the Deep River Boys at a recording session for Victor, New York, July 1942: (left to right) Gene Sedric (tenor saxophone), Cedric Wallace (double bass), Al Casey (guitar), John "Bugs" Hamilton (trumpet), the Deep River Boys (vocal quartet), Art Trappier (drums), and Waller (piano)

York. Waller continued to broadcast as a singer and soloist throughout his life, including the long-running "Fats Waller's Rhythm Club" and "Moon River" (on which he played organ). During the early 1920s he continued as organist at the Lincoln and Lafayette theaters, New York.

In 1927 Waller recorded his own composition *Whiteman Stomp* with Fletcher Henderson's orchestra; Henderson also made use of other works by Waller, including *Crazy 'bout my baby* and *Stealin' Apples*. Waller's other work as a composer with the lyricists Edgar Dowell, J. C. Johnson, Andy Razaf, and Spencer Williams produced such songs as *Honeysuckle Rose* and *Black and Blue*. With Razaf he worked on much of the music for the all-black Broadway musical *Keep Shufflin'* (1928). Their later collaborations for the stage included the shows *Load of Coal* and *Hot Chocolates* (which opened in May 1929 and transferred on to Broadway on 20 June and incorporated the song *Ain't Misbehavin'* as a vehicle first for Cab Calloway and later Louis Armstrong). Waller's Carnegie Hall début was on 27 April 1928, when he was piano soloist in a version of Johnson's fantasy *Yamekraw* for piano and orchestra.

In 1926 Waller began his recording association with Victor, his principal record company for the rest of his life, with the organ solos *St. Louis Blues* and his own *Lenox Avenue Blues*. Although he recorded with various groups, including Morris's Hot Babes (1927), Fats Waller's Buddies (1929) (one of the earliest interracial groups to record), and McKinney's Cotton Pickers (1929), his most important contribution to the Harlem stride piano tradition was a series of solo recordings of his own compositions: *Handful of Keys*, *Smashing Thirds*, *Numb Fumblin'*, and *Valentine Stomp* (1929). After sessions with Ted Lewis (1930), Jack Teagarden (1931), and Billy Banks's Rhythmakers (1932), he began in May 1934 the voluminous series of recordings with a small band known as Fats Waller and his Rhythm. This six-piece group usually included Herman Autrey (sometimes replaced by Bill Coleman or John "Bugs" Hamilton), Gene Sedric or Rudy Powell, and Al Casey.

In the mid-1930s Waller worked on the West Coast with Les Hite's band at Frank Sebastian's New Cotton Club. He also appeared in two films while in Hollywood in 1935: *Hooray for Love!* and *King of Burlesque* (*see* FILMS, §II, 1). For tours and recordings Waller often led his own big band. This began as an expanded version of the band led by his bass player (Charlie Turner's Arcadians), and in 1935, with most members of the Rhythm (as well as Don Redman, among others), it made its first recording. The group's version of *I got rhythm* includes a "cutting contest" of alternating piano solos by Waller and Hank Duncan.

In 1938 Waller undertook a European tour, recording in London with his Continental Rhythm as well as making solo pipe-organ recordings for HMV. His second European tour in 1939 was terminated by the outbreak of war, but whilst in Britain he recorded his *London Suite*, an extended series of six related pieces for solo piano: "Piccadilly," "Chelsea," "Soho," "Bond Street," "Limehouse," and "Whitechapel." It is Waller's longest composition and represents something of his aspirations to be a serious composer rather than just the author of a string of hit songs.

The last few years of Waller's life involved frequent recordings and extensive tours of the USA. In early 1943 he returned to Hollywood to make the film *Stormy Weather* with Lena Horne and Bill Robinson, in which he led an all-star band which included Benny Carter and Zutty Singleton. He undertook an exceptionally heavy touring load in that year, as well as collaborating with the lyricist George Marion, Jr., on the score for the stage show *Early to Bed* (which opened in Boston on 24 May 1943). The touring, constant abuse of his system through overeating and overdrinking, and the nervous strain of many years of legal trouble over alimony payments all took their toll and his health began to break down. He was taken ill during a return visit to the West Coast as solo pianist at the Zanzibar Room, Hollywood, and died of pneumonia while traveling back to New York by train with his manager Ed Kirkeby.

2. WORKS AND STYLE. Waller's greatest importance lies in his several contributions to jazz piano. His original stride pieces in the Johnson tradition (*Handful of Keys*, *Smashing Thirds*,

Numb Fumblin', *Valentine Stomp*, *Viper's Drag*, *Alligator Crawl*, and *Clothes Line Ballet*), composed and recorded between 1929 and 1934, clearly illustrate his imaginative and broadly expressive style. The fullness and variety of his tone are still unsurpassed, and he used a wide dynamic range to great expressive and dramatic effect. Harmonically, he sometimes added inner pitches to the customary octaves or 10ths in the left hand, producing richly voiced three-note chords; his chromatic alterations and passing tones undoubtedly influenced Art Tatum. His melodies were perhaps even more tuneful than those of his mentor Johnson, though in this he was not as consistently inventive as Earl Hines. Waller's use of rhythm is in the classic stride tradition, its characteristics including occasional three-beat cross-rhythms in the left hand. All of these features were present in his playing by 1929, as is made clear by *My feelin's are hurt* (ex.1), which was recorded in that year. With his group Fats Waller and his Rhythm he produced many musically rewarding sessions for Victor during the 1930s. Performances such as *Swingin' them jingle bells* (1936) reveal a remarkably tight ensemble and memorable solos by his sidemen.

Ex.1 *My feelin's are hurt* (1929, Vic. 38613); transcr. B. Dobbins

Waller was the first significant jazz organist (for a discussion of his style *see* ORGAN). During the mid-1930s he was one of the first musicians to employ the CELESTA in jazz and frequently played the instrument in combination with the piano.

Waller's successful popular songs *Ain't Misbehavin'* (1928) and *Honeysuckle Rose* (1929) are typical of a long series of such works that were responsible for his fame as a satirical entertainer and songwriter, and brought him a following rivaling that of Louis Armstrong. Because of this the serious side of his musical personality was little appreciated during his lifetime and remained largely underdeveloped. As a singer he could give creditable jazz renditions of songs which he considered to have real musical merit. His vocal style, clearly in the tradition established by Armstrong, showed a tasteful and highly personal use of vibrato. On his own novelty songs, such as *Your feet's too big*, his use of comic effects and spoken or shouted asides showed at times a genuine sense of comedy; more often, however, he used his wit to draw subtle but unmistakable attention to the vapidity of the material he was expected to record. Unfortunately, Waller's public often demanded more of his exaggerated stage personality than of his unique creative gifts.

Oral history material in *LNT*.

SELECTED RECORDINGS

(all recorded for Victor unless otherwise indicated)

Fats Waller Memorial, i–v (RCA 730570–74); *Fats Waller Memorial no.2*, i–v (RCA 731054–8); *Fats Waller Hitherto Unpublished Piano, Vocal and Conversation*, i–ii (RCA 730659–60); *Fats Waller Complete Recordings*, i–xxiii (RCA 741052, 741062, 741076, 741086, 741094, 741112, 741113, FPM17001, FPM17008, FPM17025, FPM17048, FXM17074, FXM17093, FXM17123, FXM17166, FXM17198, FXM17282, FXM17316, PM42027, PM42037, PM42391, PM42396, PM42416); *Fats Plus* (RCA PM43261) [collected reissue]

AS SOLOIST

Piano: Got to cool my doggies now (1922, QRS 2149) [piano roll]; Muscle Shoals Blues/Birmingham Blues (1922, OK 4757); Handful of Keys/Numb Fumblin' (1929, 38508); Ain't Misbehavin' (1929, 22092); Sweet Savannah Sue (1929, 22108); Valentine Stomp (1929, 38554); My feelin's are hurt/Smashing Thirds (1929, 38613); African Ripples/Alligator Crawl (1934, 24830); Clothes Line Ballet/Viper's Drag (1934, 25015); I ain't got nobody (1937, 25631); Piccadilly/Chelsea (1939, HMV B10059); Soho/Bond Street (1939, HMV B10060); Limehouse/Whitechapel (1939, HMV B10061); Carolina Shout (1941, 27563); Honeysuckle Rose (1941, 20-1580)

Organ: St. Louis Blues/Lenox Avenue Blues (1926, 20357); Lonesome Road (1938, HMV B8845); *Fats Waller at the Organ* (1939, Riv. 1021), incl. Go down Moses, Hallelujah! I'm a bum, Hand me down my walkin' cane, Swing low, sweet chariot [Hammond organ]

AS LEADER

Small group: The Minor Drag (1929, 38050); Honeysuckle Rose (1934, 24826); It's a sin to tell a lie (1936, 25342); Fractious Fingering (1936, 25652); Swingin' them jingle bells (1936, 25483); Yacht Club Swing (1938, Bb 10035); Squeeze Me (1939, Bb 10405); Your feet's too big (1939, Bb 10500)

Big band: I got rhythm (1935, HMV HE2902); In the gloaming (1938, 25847); Let's break the good news (1938, 25830); Chant of the Groove (1941, Bb 11262); The Jitterbug Waltz (1942, Bb 11518)

AS SIDEMAN

F. Henderson: Whiteman Stomp (1927, Col. 1059D); McKinney's Cotton Pickers: Plain Dirt/Gee, ain't I good to you (1929, 38097); T. Lewis: Dallas Blues/Royal Garden Blues (1931, Col. 2527D); J. Teagarden: You rascal, you (1931, Col. 2558D); B. Banks: Mean Old Bed Bug Blues (1932, Ban. 32502)

BIBLIOGRAPHY

D. E. Dexter: "Immortals of Jazz," *DB*, viii/2 (1941), 10

——: "Thomas Waller of Concert Stage isn't the Mellow Fats of Backroom Jazz," *DB*, ix/3 (1942), 3

K. Bright and I. Cavanaugh: "That Harmful Little Armful: Fats Waller in his Formative Years," *The Crisis*, li (1944), 109

R. Cooke: "The Genius of Thomas 'Fats' Waller," *JJ*, v/5 (1952), 13

M. Mezzrow: "Fats Waller," *BHcF*, no.18 (1952), 3

J. R. T. Davies: *The Music of Thomas "Fats" Waller* (London, 1953); rev. in *Sv*, nos.2–12 (1965–7) [discography]

G. Sedric: "Sedric vous parle de Fats Waller," *BHcF*, no.28 (1953), 3

N. Shapiro and N. Hentoff, eds.: *The Jazz Makers* (New York, 1957/R1975, 1979 as *The Jazz Makers: Essays on the Greats of Jazz*)

C. Fox: *Fats Waller* (London, 1960); repr. in *Kings of Jazz*, ed. S. Green (South Brunswick, NJ, and New York, 1978)

S. B. Charters and L. Kunstadt: *Jazz: a History of the New York Scene* (Garden City, NY, 1962/R1981)

R. Hadlock: *Jazz Masters of the Twenties* (New York, 1965/R1985)

M. Harrison: "Fats Waller," *JM*, xi/10 (1965), 21

B. Kumm: "Reflections on Fats," *Sv*, i/2 (1965), 2; i/6 (1966), 4

E. Kirkeby, D. P. Schiedt, and S. Traill: *Ain't Misbehavin': the Story of Fats Waller* (London and New York, 1966; Ger. trans., Ravensburg, Germany, 1981) [incl. rev. version of discography in *Sv*]

H. Panassié: "Destruction of a Theme: an Analysis of some Fats Waller Piano Solos," *JJ*, xix/7 (1966), 27

M. Williams: "The Comic Mask of Fats Waller," *JJ*, xix/6 (1966), 5

B. Kumm: "Further Facets of Fats," *Sv*, no.23 (1969), 179

H. Panassié: "Fats Waller in Paris," *Sv*, no.40 (1972), 140

M. Berger: "Fats Waller: the Outside Insider," *JJS*, i/1 (1973), 3

T. Magnusson: "Fats Waller with Gene Austin on the Record," *JJS*, iv/1 (1976), 75

L. Feather: "Piano Giants of Jazz: Fats Waller," *CK*, iii/2 (1977), 41

J. Vance: *Fats Waller: his Life and Times* (Chicago, 1977)

M. Waller and A. Calabrese: *Fats Waller* (New York and London, 1977) [incl. discography and list of compositions]

W. Balliett: "Jazz: Fats," *New Yorker*, liv (10 April 1978), 110

H. Rye: "Fats Waller in Britain: Some Native Reactions," *Sv*, no.81 (1979), 83

H. Rye and J. Beaton: "Fats Waller's British Diary," *Sv*, no.81 (1979), 85

M. Gautier-Panassié: "Fats Waller," *BHcF*, no.286 (1981), 3; no.287 (1981), 3

H. Lyttelton: *The Best of Jazz*, ii: *Enter the Giants, 1931–1944* (London, 1981), 30

W. Balliett: "Fats," *Jelly Roll, Jabbo and Fats* (New York, and Oxford, England, 1983) [colln of previously pubd reviews], 85

H. Dial: *All this Jazz about Jazz* (Chigwell, England, 1984), 55

P. S. Machlin: *Stride: the Music of Fats Waller* (Boston and London, 1985)
P. Malham: "Fats Waller: the Broadcasts," *Collectors Items*, no.33 (1985), 12
J. Simmen: "Herman Autrey [suite] une parenthèse: les autres trompettes de Fats," *BHcF*, no.336 (1986), 8
A. Shipton: *Fats Waller* (Tunbridge Wells, England, in preparation)

ALYN SHIPTON (1), BILL DOBBINS (2)

Wallin, Bengt-Arne (*b* Linköping, Sweden, 13 July 1926). Swedish trumpeter, arranger, and composer. After playing in Linköping and with Malte Johnson's big band in Göteborg (1948–50) he went to Stockholm, where he made a reputation as an excellent trumpeter in the swing and modern mainstream styles. He was a member of Seymour Österwall's band (1951–2), then played and recorded with Arne Domnérus's orchestra (1953–65) and in Harry Arnold's Radiobandet (1955–65). He also became well known as a composer and arranger, notably with Domnérus's orchestra; his album *Old Folklore in Swedish Modern* (1962, Dux 1700), which he recorded as the leader of a studio band, represents the earliest large-scale attempt to fuse jazz with Swedish folk melodies. Wallin has also composed several scores for films and the theater, and his writing for orchestra shows great skill and invention. Other recordings which he has made as a leader include *Varmluft* (1970, Sonet 2528), on which Clark Terry is the featured soloist, and *Miles from Duke* (1986, Phono Suecia 28). In the 1970s and 1980s he has taught at the Musikhögskolan, Stockholm.

BIBLIOGRAPHY

FeatherE; *Feather–Gitler '70s*
"På omslaget" [On the cover], *Orkester journalen*, xxii/11 (1954), 4
E. Kjellberg: *Svensk jazzhistoria: en översikt* [Swedish jazz history: an overview] (Stockholm, 1985)

ERIK KJELLBERG

Wallington, George [Figlia, Giacinto] (*b* Palermo, Sicily, 27 Oct 1924). Pianist and composer. His family emigrated to the USA in 1925. During the early 1940s he played in New York in jam sessions with Charlie Parker, Max Roach, and others, and, with Dizzy Gillespie, Don Byas, Oscar Pettiford, and Roach, was a member of the first bop group on 52nd Street (winter 1943–1944). After playing swing in Joe Marsala's quartet for a year he performed and recorded bop with groups led by Parker (1946), Serge Chaloff, Allan Eager (both 1947), Kai Winding (1949–*c*1951), Terry Gibbs, Brew Moore (both 1949), Al Cohn (1950), Gerry Mulligan (1951), and Zoot Sims and Red Rodney (both 1952). In summer 1953 he made a brief tour of Europe with Lionel Hampton – his only appearance in a big band. From 1954 to 1960 Wallington regularly led groups in New York; Donald Byrd and Phil Woods were among his sidemen. He then left music to work in his family's air-conditioning business, but resumed playing professionally in the early 1980s, and recorded an album as a soloist in 1984.

Wallington improvises clean, rapid, single-note lines in the manner of Bud Powell (though he met Powell only after having joined Gillespie's quintet in 1943). Despite his talent as a performer, however, his reputation rests more on his compositions: *Lemon Drop* was recorded by Woody Herman (1948), Gene Krupa (1949), and Woods (1957), and *Godchild* by Winding and Miles Davis (1949); both were performed frequently.

SELECTED RECORDINGS

As unaccompanied soloist: on Metronome All Stars: *Metronome All Stars, 1956* (1956, Verve 8030), Lady Fair; *Virtuoso* (1984, Interface 7092)
As leader: *George Wallington Trio* (1951, Prog. 3001); *George Wallington Trio* (1952, Prst. 136), incl. Tenderly [unaccompanied solo]; *The Workshop of the George Wallington Trio* (1954, Norg. 24); *Jazz for the Carriage Trade* (1956, Prst. 7032); *Knight Music* (1956, Atl. 1275), incl. Godchild
As sideman: S. Chaloff: Gabardine and Serge (1947, Savoy 978); K. Winding: Wallington's Godchild (1949, Roost 500); B. Jaspar: *Bobby Jaspar with George Wallington* (1957, Riv. 240); P. Woods: *Phil Woods Sextet* (1957, Mode 127), incl. Lemon Drop

BIBLIOGRAPHY

L. Feather: "Pen Portrait: George Wallington," *MM*, xxviii (8 March 1952), 4
J. Burns: "George Wallington," *JJ*, xviii/1 (1965), 24
J. Goodwin: "George Wallington: a Discography of Known Recordings," *JJ*, xxvii/2 (1974), 56 [incl. listing of compositions]
M. Gardner: "Piano Peer: the Legendary 'Lord' George Wallington," *JJI*, xxxviii/5 (1985), 10 [interview]

BARRY KERNFELD

Walrath, Jack (Arthur) (*b* Stuart, FL, 5 May 1946). Trumpeter. He was brought up in Montana, and began playing trumpet in 1955. In 1964–8 he studied at the Berklee College of Music; while in Boston he performed with other students and in backup groups for rhythm-and-blues singers. After moving to the West Coast in 1969, he worked as joint leader of the groups Change (with Gary Peacock) and Revival (with Glenn Ferris), and toured for a year with Ray Charles's band. In 1973 he moved to New York, where he played with Latin bands; he then worked with Charles Mingus (1974–8), contributing orchestrations to his last recordings. In the 1980s he has led his own groups and toured Europe with Dannie Richmond and with the British band Spirit Level. Walrath's playing is fluent and exciting, and reflects the impact of bop and later styles. He is also active as an arranger.

SELECTED RECORDINGS

As leader: *Revenge of the Fat People* (1981, Stash 221); *Killer Bunnies* (1986, Spot. 25)
As sideman: C. Mingus: *Changes One, Changes Two* (1974, Atl. 1677–8)

BIBLIOGRAPHY

Feather–Gitler '70s
A. J. Smith: "Profile: Jack Walrath," *DB*, xlv/6 (1978), 32
"Chords and Discords: Jack Walrath on me, myself an Eye," *DB*, xlvi/12 (1979), 11
B. Priestley: *Mingus: a Critical Biography* (London, Melbourne, Australia, and New York, 1982), 202

BRIAN PRIESTLEY

Walton, Cedar (Anthony, Jr.) (*b* Dallas, 17 Jan 1934). Pianist. He was taught piano by his mother and studied music at the University of Denver (1951–4). In 1955 he went to New York to play jazz but was drafted into the army, and, in Germany, played with Leo Wright, Don Ellis, and Eddie Harris. After returning to New York he recorded with Kenny Dorham (1958), then played in J. J. Johnson's group (1958–60) and the Jazztet (1960–61). Later he recorded with Farmer (1965, 1975–7). From 1961 to 1964 he was a member of Art Blakey's Jazz Messengers with Wayne Shorter and Freddie Hubbard. After a period as accompanist to Abbey Lincoln (1965–6) he recorded frequently with Lee Morgan (1966–8) and worked as house pianist for Prestige (1967–9), then re-joined Blakey for a tour of Japan (1973). From the mid-1960s Walton has performed frequently as the leader of a traditional bop quartet with Clifford Jordan, George Coleman, or Bob Berg, and Sam Jones and Billy Higgins; in 1975 it took the name Eastern Rebellion. As leader of the group Soundscapes in the mid-1970s he experimented with funk rhythms and the electric piano. He later toured the USA, Europe, and Japan as the leader of a trio, which often included Higgins. Walton has also performed as a soloist, in duos with various double bass players, and from around 1981 as a member of the Timeless All Stars.

SELECTED RECORDINGS

As unaccompanied soloist: *Piano Solos* (c1981, Clean Cuts 704)
As leader: *Spectrum* (1968, Prst. 7591); with H. Mobley: *Breakthrough* (1972, Cob. 9011); *A Night at Boomer's* (1973, Muse 5010, 5022); *Eastern Rebellion* (1975, Tim. 101); *Animation* (c1978, Col. JC35572); *Cedar Walton* (1985, Tim. 223)
As sideman: K. Dorham: *This is the Moment* (1958, Riv. 275); A. Farmer and B. Golson: *Big City Sounds* (1960, Argo 672); A. Blakey: *Caravan* (1962, Riv. 9438); L. Morgan: *Caramba* (1968, BN 84289); C. Jordan: *On Stage* (1975, Ste. 1071); Timeless All Stars: *It's Timeless* (1982, Tim. 178)

BIBLIOGRAPHY

G. Giddins: Liner notes, *A Night at Boomer's* (Muse 5010, 1973)
L. Tomkins: "Cedar Walton," *CI*, xiv (1976), no.7, p.20; no.8, p.6
L. Lyons: "Cedar Walton," *CK*, iii/2 (1977), 12
B. Case: "Cedar Walton: Earning the Steinway," *MM* (3 Feb 1979), 25
A. Moorhead: "Cedar Walton's Major League Play," *DB*, xlviii/1 (1981), 26 [incl. discography]
D. Lund: "Cedar Walton," *CI*, xxii/1 (1982), 22
L. Hildebrand: "The Cedar Walton Trio: Jazz Pianist Runs Free in his 'Briar Patch'," *San Francisco Chronicle Datebook* (11 Jan 1987), 40

BARRY KERNFELD

Walton, Greely (*b* Mobile, AL, 4 Oct 1904). Tenor saxophonist. He first played violin, and studied music at the University of Pittsburgh. After taking up tenor saxophone he worked with Elmer Snowden (1926), Benny Carter (1929), and others, then joined Luis Russell's band (1930). He performed and made recordings (including *Ease on Down*, 1930, Voc. 1579) with this ensemble until 1937, remaining with it under Louis Armstrong's leadership. Thereafter he worked with the bandleader Vernon Andrade (from 1938), Horace Henderson (1941), Cootie Williams (on baritone saxophone, 1942–3), and Cab Calloway (1943–5). He was music director for the popular vocal group the Ink Spots from 1945 to 1947. Later he played in an Afro-Cuban band (1947–8), during which time he also performed with Noble Sissle. From 1948 he worked mostly with Sy Oliver, playing for radio and television shows. He taught flute in the early 1950s and ceased playing in 1955. (D. Griffiths: "Greely Walton's Life Story," *Sv*, no.107 (1983), 165)

based on *ChiltonW*

Wanzo, Mel(vin) (*b* Cleveland, 22 Nov 1930). Trombonist. After playing with Joe Turner (ii), the singer Ruth Brown, and other rhythm-and-blues musicians in the 1950s he worked principally in big bands. He toured and recorded with the Glenn Miller Orchestra (under Ray McKinley's direction, 1965–8) and Woody Herman (1966–8) and from 1969 to 1980 belonged to Count Basie's orchestra; he also recorded with the Capp–Pierce Juggernaut (1981). After Basie's death in 1984 he rejoined Basie's orchestra, then led by Thad Jones. While principally a section player Wanzo may be heard as a soloist on the track *The Left-hand Corner* from the album *Count Basie Live in Japan '78* (1978, Pablo 28MJ3473). (*Feather–Gitler '70s*)

DANIEL ZAGER

Ward, Carlos (Nathaniel) (*b* Ancon, Panama Canal Zone, 1 May 1940). Saxophonist. After moving to the Seattle area in 1953 he took up clarinet, then changed to saxophone in 1955 and played in local rock-and-roll groups. While in the US Army he joined a military band (1961) and was sent to Germany; after being discharged he remained in Europe and performed with Dollar Brand (who later took the name Abdullah Ibrahim), Don Cherry, and Karl Berger. In April 1965 he returned to Seattle, where in October he played with John Coltrane at The Penthouse. He then moved to New York, where he played with Coltrane, Sunny Murray, and Sam Rivers. In 1967 he went west with Murray and settled in San Francisco; for some time he played only on weekends. He returned to New York in 1969, played and recorded with the funk group B. T. Express, performed with Murray (at the Newport Jazz Festival) and Rashied Ali's quartet, and joined the Jazz Composer's Orchestra Association; he also belonged to a group led by David Izenzon that included Berger, Gato Barbieri, and Barry Altschul. He worked with groups led by Carla Bley, Ibrahim, and Cherry into the 1980s.

SELECTED RECORDINGS

Duos with A. Ibrahim: *Live at Sweet Basil*, i (1983, Ekapa 004)
As sideman: K. Berger: *Karl Berger Quartet* (1966, ESP 1041); D. Brand: *Underground* (?1972, Trio PAP9018); D. Cherry: *Relativity Suite* (1973, JCOA 1006); R. Rudd: *Numatik Swing Band* (1973, JCOA 1007); R. Ali: *New Directions in Modern Music* (1973, Survival 103); C. Bley: *Dinner Music* (1976, Watt 6); A. Ibrahim: *Ekaya* (1983, Ekapa 005)

BIBLIOGRAPHY

L. Gabel: "Carlos Ward: Expressway to Creative Truth," *DB*, xlii/13 (1975), 17 [incl. discography]
I. Vroedindewey: "De stille gebeden van Carlos Ward" [The silent prayers of Carlos Ward], *Jazz nu*, no.77 (1985), 236; repr. as "Carlos Ward: a Love Supreme," *Coda*, no.202 (1985), 24 [interview; incl. discography]

DAVID WILD

Ward, Helen (*b* New York, 19 Sept 1916). Singer. She was taught piano as a child and began singing in her teens. After performing on radio station WOR in New York (1933) she became a staff musician at NBC and sang with Benny Goodman on the radio show "Let's Dance." From 1934 to 1936 she toured and made several recordings with Goodman (including *Goody-goody* (1936, Vic. 25245), which displays her exuberant, swinging style). During the period 1937–42 she sang only on recordings, accompanied by various musicians, among them Gene Krupa (1936–8), Teddy Wilson (1936–7, 1940, 1942), Bob Crosby (1939), Joe Sullivan (1940), and Harry James (1941). After 1942 she performed with Hal McIntyre, recorded with Red Norvo (1943), James (*c*1944), Wild Bill Davison (1952), and Peanuts Hucko (1956–7), and toured and recorded (1953, 1957, 1958) with Goodman. After a long period of inactivity, in 1979 she resumed performing and recording; she made the album *The Helen Ward Song Book* (Lyricon 1001) in 1981.

BIBLIOGRAPHY

R. D. Kinkle: *The Complete Encyclopedia of Popular Music and Jazz, 1900–1950* (New Rochelle, NY, and Westport, CT, 1974) [incl. discography]
L. Dahl: *Stormy Weather: the Music and Lives of a Century of Jazzwomen* (London, Melbourne, Australia, and New York, 1984), 132

SCOTT FREDRICKSON

Ware, David (S(pencer)) (*b* Plainfield, NJ, 7 Nov 1949). Tenor saxophonist. In his teens he played successively the baritone, alto, and tenor saxophones and from 1967 to around 1969 attended the Berklee College of Music. He formed the group Apogee around 1970, which performed in Boston until its members moved together to New York in 1973, then played in Cecil Taylor's orchestra in Carnegie Hall (1974). He performed and recorded with Andrew Cyrille (1974–6), worked in a trio with the trumpeter Raphe Malik in the mid-1970s, and toured Europe and recorded with Taylor (1976–7). Later he recorded as a leader, in 1977 belonged to a group led by Barry Harris, with whom he also recorded in a duo the same year, and resumed his association with Cyrille, recording with him in Milan (1978, 1980). Ware's style is a raucous, dissonant brand of free jazz that relies heavily on overblowing and multiphonics; it is exemplified by his playing on Cyrille's LP *Metamusicians' Stomp*

(1978, BS 0025). (B. Rusch: "David Ware: Interview," *Cadence*, vi/1 (1980), 5)

Ware, Leonard [L. W.] (*b* Richmond, VA, 28 Dec 1909). Guitarist and composer. He studied at Tuskegee Institute, where he played oboe in the band. In the early 1930s he changed to guitar and formed a trio that held various engagements in New York until the late 1940s, when he ceased full-time performing. In 1938 he recorded *Hold Tight* (*Want some sea food, mama*)/*Jungle Drums* (Voc. 4537) with Sidney Bechet; the first of these tracks was his own composition. He also made recordings with Buddy Johnson (1941), Joe Turner (ii) (1941, 1945), and the blues singer Albinia Jones (1944, 1945), and as a leader (1947).

BIBLIOGRAPHY

ChiltonW; *FeatherE*
H. Panassié and M. Gautier: *Dictionnaire du jazz* (Paris, 1954, rev. and enlarged 2/1971, enlarged 3/1980; Eng. trans., London, 1956, rev. A. A. Gurwitch as *Guide to Jazz*, Boston, 1956), 331

Ware, Munn [Winfred Nettleton] (*b* Quincy, MA, 1909; *d* Daytona Beach, FL, 9 Aug 1970). Trombonist. During the late 1940s he worked regularly with the band led by the clarinetist Bill Reinhardt at Jazz Ltd., Chicago. At this time he also recorded with Sidney Bechet, Muggsy Spanier, and Doc Evans. His playing may be heard to advantage on Bechet's *Maryland my Maryland*/*Careless Love* (1949, Jazz Limited 201). After playing with dixieland ensembles during the early 1950s he moved in 1952 to Florida, where he was active as a freelance.

BIBLIOGRAPHY

"Munn Ware," *SL*, xvii (1966), 59
K. L. Kramer: "Munn Ware: a Personal Memoir," *SL*, xxiii (1969–70), 429
J. Chilton: *Sidney Bechet: the Wizard of Jazz* (London and New York, 1987)

based on *ChiltonW*

Ware, Wilbur (Bernard) (*b* Chicago, 8 Sept 1932; *d* Philadelphia, 9 Sept 1979). Double bass player. He was early associated with Roy Eldridge and Sonny Stitt in Milwaukee (1946). Later, as a member of the house band at the Flame Lounge in Chicago, he worked with Joe Williams (1953), and Junior Mance and Eddie "Cleanhead" Vinson (both 1954). He also recorded with Johnny Griffin (1954) and played with Thelonious Monk. In June 1956 he joined Art Blakey's Jazz Messengers and moved to New York, where he became the house double bass player for Riverside. In this capacity he recorded with many important musicians and also led his own groups. He played with John Coltrane in Monk's quartet at the Five Spot (1957), and in Sonny Rollins's trio at the Village Vanguard. Illness forced Ware to return to Chicago in 1963, and he played infrequently until 1968 when he joined Archie Shepp's group. He performed and recorded sporadically with Shepp into the early 1970s, and also worked with Clifford Jordan, Blue Mitchell, Elvin Jones, and Sonny Rollins (all 1969), and Sun Ra (1973). Ware's heavy tone, percussive yet buoyant attack, and short notes were reminiscent of the styles of Wellman Braud and Walter Page, but his harmonic inventiveness, apparent for example on *Blues for Tomorrow*, was wholly modern. Unlike many of his contemporaries, who played legato solos, Ware developed his solos (such as that on *Softly, as in a Morning Sunrise*) rhythmically and motivically. In this way he anticipated the free-jazz style.
Oral history material in *NjR* (JOHP).

SELECTED RECORDINGS

As leader: *The Chicago Sound* (1957, Riv. 252)
As sideman: J. Griffin: *The Johnny Griffin Quartet* (1954, Argo 624); Z. Sims: *Zoot!* (1956, Riv. 228); on *Blues for Tomorrow* (1957, Riv. 243), [no leader]: Blues for Tomorrow; T. Monk: *Monk's Music* (1957, Riv. 242); *Thelonious Monk with John Coltrane* (1957, Jlnd 946); *Mulligan Meets Monk* (1957, Riv. 247); E. Henry: *Seven Standards and a Blues* (1957, Riv. 248); S. Rollins: *A Night at the Village Vanguard* (1957, BN 1581), incl. Softly, as in a Morning Sunrise; C. Jordan: *Starting Time* (1961, Jlnd 952); A. Shepp: *For Losers* (1969, Imp. 9188)

BIBLIOGRAPHY

B. Crow: "Introducing Wilbur Ware," *JR*, ii/11 (1959), 14
G. Kopel: "Au tableau d'honneur des pinceurs de cordes: Wilbur Ware et Scott La Faro," *Jm*, no.54 (1959), 16
H. Pekar: "The Development of the Modern Bass," *DB*, xxix/26 (1962), 20
V. Wilmer: "Ware on the Bass," *MM* (12 June 1971), 14
J. Litweiler: "Remembering Wilbur Ware," *DB*, xlvi/18 (1979), 27 [incl. discography]

JOHN CURRY

Warleigh, Ray(mond Kenneth) (*b* Sydney, 28 Sept 1938). Australian alto saxophonist and flutist. He learned music as a youth, and was inspired to take up saxophone after hearing Paul Desmond. In 1959 he began performing professionally. The following year he moved to England, where he worked at first with Alexis Korner, and later performed and recorded with such diverse musicians as Mike Gibbs, Tubby Hayes, Humphrey Lyttelton, Mick Pyne, Ronnie Scott, Kenny Wheeler, and Mike Westbrook. In 1968 he made his first recording as a leader (*Ray Warleigh's First Album*, Phi. 7881), which involved both a jazz band and an orchestra. He was associated in the late 1960s and early 1970s with various groups led by John Stevens, including the Spontaneous Music Ensemble. Thereafter he worked with Paz, Allan Holdsworth, and the drummer Tommy Chase; he recorded two new albums under his own name (1977, 1978), the latter as a leader with Chase. In the early 1980s he was a member of the radio band at Westdeutscher Rundfunk in Cologne, Germany, with which he accompanied such visiting Americans as Freddie Hubbard, Dizzy Gillespie, and Max Roach; he has also played in the big band led by the drummer Charlie Watts. Warleigh is a versatile musician, comfortable in many different styles; in addition to alto saxophone he also plays the soprano, tenor, and baritone instruments, and clarinet.

BIBLIOGRAPHY

"How Some of Today's Top Men Started," *MM* (29 Oct 1966), 17
R. Cotterrell, ed.: *Jazz Now: the Jazz Centre Society Guide* (London, 1976), 178
B. Sivyer: "Ray Warleigh: Sydney Sax Player Blows his Trumpet," *TNT Magazine*, no.178 (1987), 17

SIMON ADAMS

Warlop, Michel (*b* Douai, France, 23 Jan 1911; *d* Bagnères-de-Bigorre, France, 20 March 1947). French violinist. He studied music for some years. He played with Gregor (1932–4), then led a big band that backed such popular singers as Maurice Chevalier and Germaine Sablon (1934–5); he also worked with the group Jazz du Poste Parisien and in 1935 with the accordionist Louis Richardet. He recorded as a leader and sideman with Stephane Grappelli and Django Reinhardt (1934–7), in a violin trio with Grappelli and Eddie South (accompanied by a rhythm section, 1937), and in a duo with Garland Wilson (1938). In the 1940s he played with an orchestra led by the saxophonist and bandleader Raymond Legrand (1940–43), led a string septet (1941–3), and conducted the Orchestre Symphonique de Paris in a performance of his composition *Noël du prisonnier* (1942). Warlop's playing is exemplified by his recording *Tempête sur les cordes* (1941, Swing 115). (A. Hodeir: "Panorama du jazz français," *BHcF*, 1st ser., no.1 (1945), 9)

MICHEL LAPLACE

Warren, Butch [Edward Rudolph] (*b* Washington, 8 Sept 1939). Double bass player. He started his career at the age of 14 in a band led by his father, then played in and around Washington with Gene Ammons and Stuff Smith (*c*1956–7). He moved to New York to work with Kenny Dorham (1958–60), and as a house musician at Blue Note Records recorded with Jackie McLean (1961–2), Donald Byrd (1961, 1963), Herbie Hancock and Stanley Turrentine (both 1962), and Joe Henderson (1963). He also played in New York clubs and recorded with Sonny Clark (1961–2) and Dexter Gordon (1962). He was the regular double bass player in Thelonious Monk's quartet in 1963–4, touring Europe and Japan and making several recordings. After returning to the Washington area he performed on a local television show (1965–6) and backed touring pop groups such as the Platters (1966). Owing to illness he ceased to be active during the late 1960s and early 1970s, but he resumed playing in the mid-1970s – with Howard McGhee and Richie Cole (both 1975) – and continued to perform part-time.

Warren's style is notable for his ability to create swinging accompaniments, through a combination of well-phrased quarter-note lines and nicely placed accents with articulation marked by short decay. His solos, though limited in range, are effective, using walking lines and short phrases based on the blues.

SELECTED RECORDINGS

As sideman with T. Monk: *Miles and Monk at Newport* (1963, Col. CS8978); *Big Band and Quartet in Concert* (1963, Col. CS8964); *It's Monk's Time* (1964, Col. CS8984)

As sideman with others: K. Dorham: *The Arrival* (1958, Jaro 5007); S. Clark: *Leapin' and Lopin'* (1961, BN 84091); D. Byrd: *Free Form* (1961, BN 84118); H. Hancock: *Takin' Off* (1962, BN 84109); D. Gordon: *Go!* (1962, BN 84112); J. Henderson: *Page One* (1963, BN 84140)

BIBLIOGRAPHY

Feather '60s
P. Lattes: "Ornette et les autres je sais qu'ils savent ce qu'ils font," *Jh*, no.197 (1964), 26

JOHN CURRY

Warren, Earle [Earl Ronald] (*b* Springfield, OH, 1 July 1914). Alto saxophonist. He played piano, banjo, and ukulele in a family band before taking up C-melody, tenor, and finally alto saxophone. From 1930, when he began working professionally, he added an "e" to his name to distinguish himself from Hines and other jazz musicians named Earl. He led his own groups and toured around the Midwest with various bands, both black and white, before joining the Count Basie Orchestra in 1937 (for illustrations *see* BASIE, COUNT, and FILMS, fig.3). At first he shared baritone and lead alto saxophone duties with Jack Washington, then from 1938 to 1945 assumed the lead alto position; he also played clarinet and sang ballads. During the late 1940s he led his own bands and worked intermittently with Basie, and during the 1950s he became a manager of rhythm-and-blues and pop groups. From 1957 Warren made a number of tours and recordings with Buck Clayton, and in 1967 he toured Europe as a soloist. He performed in *Born to Swing* (1972), a film about former sidemen of Basie's band, and in 1973 he formed the Countsmen, a group that played regularly at the West End club in New York throughout the 1970s. He settled in Geneva in the early 1980s and has continued to play at international festivals. Although he rarely played as a soloist with Basie, Warren provided the melodic lead for many of the band's greatest recordings. Later in his career, however, he proved himself an able, energetic, and extrovert swing soloist.

Oral history material in *NjR* (JOHP), *NjR*.

SELECTED RECORDINGS

As leader: Circus in Rhythm (1944, Savoy 508); *The Countsmen* (1973, RCA LFL1-5034); *Earle Warren* (1974, RCA LFL1-5066), incl. Blues in my Heart

As sideman: C. Basie: Out the Window (1937, Decca 1581); Jumpin' at the Woodside (1938, Decca 2212); B. Clayton: *One for Buck* (1961, Col. 33SX1390); *Jazz from a Swinging Era* (1967, Fon. 200); *Buck Clayton Jam Session* (1974–6, Chi. 132, 143, 152)

BIBLIOGRAPHY

V. Wilmer: "Earl Warren's Story," *JJ*, xiii/8 (1960), 11
P. J. Sullivan: "Earle Warren," *JJ*, xx/11 (1967), 10
A. J. McCarthy: *Earle Warren* (RCA LFL1-5066, 1974) [liner notes]
S. Dance: *The World of Count Basie* (New York and London, 1980) [colln of previously pubd interviews], 71
B. Rusch: "Earle Warren: Interview," *Cadence*, vi (1980), no.7, p.15; no.9, p.9
E. Warren: "Meine Liebe: das Altsaxophon und Basie," *JP*, xxix/4 (1980), 4
J. Simmen: "Earle Warren, 1982," *BHcF*, no.303 (1983), 7

BARRY KERNFELD

Warren, John (*b* Montreal, 23 Sept 1938). Canadian baritone saxophonist and composer. He taught himself music before studying at McGill University Conservatory in 1959–61. From 1968 he led his own band in England, which at times included John Surman, Kenny Wheeler, John Taylor, Henry Lowther, Malcolm Griffiths, Alan Skidmore, and Ray Warleigh. In addition he played and recorded with Mike Westbrook's bands (1967–76), Bob Downes (1969), and Alan Cohen, and toured with the London Jazz Composers Orchestra (1972). He recorded his composition *Tales of the Algonquin* with John Surman in 1971 (Deram 1094), and later composed for and directed Surman's Brass Project (1982). His other principal works include *Solent Suite* (1979), *Six Tributes for 13 Players* (1985), and *Plus Four and Four More* (1986). He teaches regularly at summer schools, including those at Dartington, Devon, and Barry, Wales. (R. Cotterell, ed.: *Jazz Now: the Jazz Centre Society Guide*, London, 1976)

DIGBY FAIRWEATHER

Warren, Peter (*b* Hempstead, NY, 21 Nov 1935). Double bass player. As a youth he played cello, making his début at Carnegie Recital Hall, New York, at the age of 17 and then attending the Juilliard School; he later performed with the Atlanta SO. He took up double bass in Las Vegas, and studied with Chuck Israels in New York. From 1965 to 1967 he toured with the pop singer Dionne Warwick. He then settled in New York and became a member (with David Izenzon) of the New York Bass Revolution, which featured ten double bass players. During a period in Europe (from 1970) he collaborated in Belgium with three other double bass players on the album *Bass Is*, recorded for the new label Enja, and also worked with Rolf Kühn (recording in 1970), Jean-Luc Ponty, Don Cherry, and Terumasa Hino (recording in 1971), and Anthony Braxton, among others. After his return to the USA (1974) Warren joined Jack DeJohnette and was later awarded a grant by the NEA to compose and perform cello music (1976). He played in a group with John Scofield and Mike Stern in New York in 1982.

SELECTED RECORDINGS

As leader: with D. Holland, Jamie Faunt, and G. Moore: *Bass Is* (1970, Enja 2018); *Solidarity* (1981, Japo 60034)

As sideman: M. Sato: *Trinity* (1971, Enja 2008); A. Mangelsdorff: *Spontaneous* (1971, Enja 2064); J. DeJohnette: *Cosmic Chicken* (1975, Prst. 10094); *Tin Can Alley* (1980, ECM 1189)

BIBLIOGRAPHY

Feather–Gitler '70s
L. Jeske: "Profile: Peter Warren," *DB*, xlix/9 (1982), 52

WILLIAM S. BROCKMAN

Warwick. Record company and label. The company was founded by Morty Craft in New York in 1960; for a brief period it made jazz recordings. These included four important LPs produced by Teddy Charles: one of a concert given by his quartet at the Museum of Modern Art, New York; one by Curtis Fuller; an album led by Pepper Adams and Donald Byrd, on which Herbie Hancock made his studio début; and *The Soul of Jazz Percussion*, which contained the work of such musicians as Booker Little, Curtis Fuller, Bill Evans (ii), Mal Waldron, Byrd, and Adams. Warwick also released an album by Ralph Burns; thereafter, however, the company ceased to be involved with jazz.

MARK GARDNER

Warwick, (William) Carl [Bama] (*b* Birmingham, AL, 27 Oct 1917). Trumpeter. In the late 1930s he performed and recorded with the Mills Blue Rhythm Band (1937), Don Redman (1938), and Bunny Berigan (1939), and also played with Tiny Bradshaw and Teddy Hill. During military service he was the music director of an army band. Thereafter he worked with Woody Herman (1944–6), Buddy Rich (1946, 1947), and various commercial bands. In the early 1950s Warwick had his own group in California, played briefly with Lucky Millinder (1953), and led a group with Brew Moore in San Francisco (1954–5). After touring and recording with Dizzy Gillespie (1956–7) he worked as a freelance and as a leader; he recorded with Gillespie again in 1961. From 1966 he served as music director for the New York City Correctional Institute, and in 1973 he played with Benny Carter at the Newport Jazz Festival New York. Warwick worked mainly as a section player in big bands and rarely took solos. (*ChiltonW*; *FeatherE*; *Feather–Gitler '70s*)

Washboard band. An instrumental group that employs the common washboard as a rhythm instrument. The board is played by drawing a nail, fork, or thimbles over the corrugations to produce a loud, staccato rhythm. Cowbells, woodblocks, and improvised metallophones were often attached to add tonal variety. Early washboard bands also included string instruments and were frequently augmented by other improvised instruments such as a washtub bass or kazoo, as well as a harmonica. They are closely related to the children's "spasm bands" of New Orleans. The group of white musicians led by Stalebread Lacoume in 1897 is the best documented but it may not have included a washboard player. Washboards were frequently used to accompany blues singers, at least one of whom, Washboard Sam (Robert Brown), played a washboard while taking vocal parts. Almost alone among folk instruments the washboard was sometimes used by jazz bands, examples being Floyd Casey's crisp and forceful rhythms on numerous recordings by Clarence Williams, including *Beer Garden Blues* (1933, Voc. 2541), and Jimmy Bertrand's driving accompaniments to Louis Armstrong with Erskine Tate's Vendome Orchestra on *Stomp off, let's go* (1926, Voc. 1027) (*see also* DRUM SET, §I, 10). In the early 1930s the related groups of the Washboard Rhythm Kings and Washboard Serenaders recorded extensively; on the former's version of *Shoot 'em* (1931, Vic. 22814) the washboard is played by the drummer Jimmy Spencer, who also provides the vocal part. Sometimes a band included two trumpets and three reed instruments, but as the novelty appeal of the instrument declined the washboard returned to the folk idiom of blues. In the postwar years zydeco bands (black cajun groups in Louisiana and Texas) frequently used washboards. The most recent development has been the wearing of a corrugated metal vest, played with thimbles.

BIBLIOGRAPHY

B. Rust: Liner notes, *Clarence Williams Jug and Washboard Band* (Phi. 13653 A-JL, 1962)
P. Oliver: "Jug and Washboard Bands," *Jazz on Record: a Critical Guide to the First 50 Years: 1917–1967*, ed. A. McCarthy and others (London, 1968), 332
T. Zwicky: "I'm Gonna Beat me some Washboard: the Washboard Rhythm Kings and Affiliated Groups, 1930–35," *Sv*, no.19 (1968), 3; no.20 (1968–9), 47; no.22 (1969), 148
J. Broven: *South to Louisiana: The Music of the Cajun Bayous* (Gretna, LA, 1983)

PAUL OLIVER

Washboard Rhythm Kings. Recording group. It had no fixed personnel and usually consisted of local musicians from the areas around Camden, New Jersey, and Philadelphia. Regular members were Ben Smith and Cal Wade (saxophones), Eddie Miller or Clarence Profit (piano), Taft Jordan (trumpet), and Teddy Bunn (guitar). As musicians often played several instruments during a session, exact identification is impossible to determine. Jake Fenderson and Leo Watson were among the many singers who recorded with the group. After recording 12 titles for Vocalion as the Alabama Washboard Stompers in 1930–31, the group recorded 20 titles for Victor in 1931 as the Washboard Rhythm Kings. During 1932 an enlarged band recorded 24 titles for Victor and 21 for Vocalion; the following year it recorded for Columbia, Bluebird, and Vocalion, and in 1934–5 it recorded as the Georgia Washboard Stompers for Decca. The large number of the band's recordings made in the years of the Depression reflect changing tastes in music. These were issued under a variety of names, including the Rhythm Kings, the Washboard Rhythm Band, and the Washboard Rhythm Boys. The Washboard Rhythm Kings that recorded for Bluebird in Chicago in November 1935 had no connection with the group.

SELECTED RECORDINGS

(all recorded for Victor)

Pepper Steak (1932, 22958); Tiger Rag (1932, 24059); Sloppy Drunk Blues (1932, 23380)

BIBLIOGRAPHY

T. Zwicky: "I'm gonna beat me some washboard: the Washboard Rhythm Kings and Affiliated Groups, 1930–35," *Sv*, no.19 (1968), 3; no.20 (1968–9), 47; no.22 (1969), 148

MIKE HAZELDINE

Washington, Buck [Ford Lee] (*b* Louisville, KY, 16 Oct 1903; *d* New York, 31 Jan 1955). Pianist, singer, and trumpeter. From around 1912 he worked with John W. Sublett (who took the name John Bubbles) in the comedy and dance act Buck and Bubbles. They performed in shows on Broadway, visited England (1930), toured Europe (1936), and appeared in several films, among them *Cabin in the Sky* (1942). Washington also recorded with Louis Armstrong (the duet *Dear Old Southland*, 1930, OK 41454) and Coleman Hawkins (1934), led the band that accompanied Bessie Smith in her last recording session (1933), and recorded as a piano soloist (*Old-fashioned Love*, 1934, Col. 2925D). His only recordings as a trumpeter are those he made privately in 1944 (first issued on untitled album, Ristic SAG). Washington ceased to perform with Bubbles in 1953 and worked with the singer Timmie Rogers in a group led by Jonah Jones (1953–4).

BIBLIOGRAPHY

ChiltonW; *FeatherE*
L. Feather: "Mr. Washington of Buck & Bubbles," *MM*, xii (14 Oct 1936), 2
M. Mezzrow: "Ford Lee 'Buck' Washington," *BHcF*, no.48 (1955), 3

M. Stearns and J. Stearns: *Jazz Dance: the Story of American Vernacular Dance* (New York and London, 1968), 212
H. Rye: "Visiting Firemen, 10: Buck Washington (Buck & Bubbles)," *Sv*, no.114 (1984), 213

HOWARD RYE

Washington, Dinah [Jones, Ruth (Lee)] (*b* Tuscaloosa, AL, 29 Aug 1924; *d* Detroit, 14 Dec 1963). Singer. She grew up in Chicago, where she played piano for and directed her church choir. From the age of 15 she performed alternately in nightclubs as a singer and pianist and in Sallie Martin's gospel choir. She was given the name Dinah Washington by the manager of the Garrick Stage Bar, where she was heard by Lionel Hampton, and subsequently she worked as a member of Hampton's band (1943–6). Having recorded several blues hits in 1943, she enjoyed a successful solo career from 1946. Washington's singing was characterized by high-pitched, penetrating sounds, precise enunciation, contrasts between tender understatement and gospel-inspired intensity, and an entrancing languor. Like Ray Charles, she could rework any type of material. From 1949 to 1955 her rhythm-and-blues, classic blues, pop, and country recordings consistently reached the top ten on the rhythm-and-blues chart in the USA. *What a difference a day makes* (1959) marked her breakthrough into the general pop market where she obtained several other gold records, some in duet with the singer Brook Benton, before her early death from an accidental overdose of sleeping pills.

SELECTED RECORDINGS

As leader: Evil Gal Blues (1943, Key. 605); Trouble in Mind (1951, Mer. 8269); *The Swingin' Miss "D"* (1956, EmA 36104); What a difference a day makes (1959, Mer. 71435); with B. Benton: Baby (you got what it takes) (1959, Mer. 71565); *Dinah '62* (1962, Roul. 25170)
As sideman with L. Hampton: Blowtop Blues (1945, Decca 23792)

BIBLIOGRAPHY

L. Feather: "Feather's Nest," *DB*, xix/10 (1952), 16
B. Niquet: "Queen Dinah," *Jh*, no.266 (1970), 20 [discography]
A. Shaw: *Honkers and Shouters: the Golden Years of Rhythm and Blues* (New York, 1978)
S. Harris: *Blues Who's Who: a Biographical Dictionary of Blues Singers* (New Rochelle, NY, 1979)
G. Endress: *Jazz Podium: Musiker über sich selbst* (Stuttgart, Germany, 1980)
J. Haskins: *Queen of the Blues: a Biography of Dinah Washington* (New York, 1987) [incl. discography]

BARRY KERNFELD

Washington, Freddie (*b* Houston, *c*1900). Pianist. After moving to California around 1918 he joined Kid Ory in Oakland in 1921 and recorded with him the following year. During the 1920s and 1930s he led his own band, and also played with Ed "Montudi" Garland and Paul Howard. In 1944 he made recordings (including *Barney's Bounce/Lulu's Mood*, Cap. 10022) with Zutty Singleton. He remained active into the 1960s.

based on *ChiltonW*

Washington, George (*b* Brunswick, GA, 18 Oct 1907). Trombonist and arranger. His first important associations were with Luckey Roberts and Charlie Johnson in New York during the mid- and late 1920s. He worked with Don Redman in 1931, and the following year became associated with Benny Carter. Thereafter he played with and wrote arrangements for the Mills Blue Rhythm Band (intermittently to 1936; for illustration *see* MILLS BLUE RHYTHM BAND), worked as a staff arranger for Irving Mills, and made recordings (including *We're gonna have smooth sailing*, 1935, Ban. 33355) with Henry "Red" Allen. Later he played with Fletcher Henderson (1936–7) and Louis Armstrong (1937–43) and moved to the West Coast, where he worked with Horace Henderson (1945) and Carter. After recording in 1947 with Count Basie he led a band for many years in California and Las Vegas, then played with the drummer Johnny Otis. He recorded with Joe Darensbourg in 1960, and thereafter worked as a freelance studio musician and arranger. (W. C. Allen: *Hendersonia: the Music of Fletcher Henderson and his Musicians: a Bio-discography*, Highland Park, NJ, 1973)

based on *ChiltonW*

Washington, Grover, Jr. (*b* Buffalo, 12 Dec 1943). Saxophonist. At the age of 16 he toured with a rhythm-and-blues group. He played tenor saxophone and electric bass guitar in organ trios (1963–5) and performed in army bands (1965–7), then moved to Philadelphia, where he worked mostly with organists. His fine playing on tenor saxophone for Charles Earland led to a series of soul-jazz recordings for several leaders on the Prestige label (1970–71). Washington was engaged to record as a tenor saxophonist with Hank Crawford in 1971 but, after the latter failed to arrive for the session, he was given the opportunity to make his first recording as a leader; *Inner City Blues*, on which he played alto saxophone, was a huge success. Shortly afterwards he formed a touring band, the personnel of which has changed frequently over the years; during the mid-1970s he was also obliged by his recording company to use studio sidemen. *Mister Magic*, which reached no.1 on several charts (1975), was the first of his many albums to win gold or platinum records. Washington's repertory includes jazz standards of the 1920s to the 1960s, but his strength lies in a blend of jazz and soul music, where he improvises clipped, bluesy melodies over precise, highly syncopated ostinato accompaniments. From the late 1970s he also played flute.

SELECTED RECORDINGS

As leader: *Inner City Blues* (1971, Kudu 03); *Mister Magic* (1974, Kudu 20); *Live at the Bijou* (c1977, Kudu 36–7); *Skylarkin'* (c1980, Motown 7-933R1); with K. Burrell: *Togethering* (1984, BN 85106)
As sideman: C. Earland: *Living Black!* (1970, Prst. 10009); Johnny Hammond: *What's Goin' On?* (1971, Prst. 10015)

BIBLIOGRAPHY

H. Mandel: "Grover Washington, Jr.: No Tricks to Mister Magic's Music," *DB*, xlii/13 (1975), 14
S. Bloom: "Grover Washington, Jr.: Class Act of Commercial Jazz," *DB*, xlvi/8 (1979), 12 [incl. discography]
"Grover Washington, Jr.: Evolution of an Artist," *Radio Free Jazz*, xx (1979), July, 10
A. J. Liska: "Grover Washington, Jr.: the Midas Touch," *DB*, l/4 (1983), 14 [incl. discography]

BARRY KERNFELD

Washington, Jack [Ronald] (*b* Kansas City, KS, 17 July 1910; *d* Oklahoma City, OK, 28 Nov 1964). Baritone and alto saxophonist. He began his professional career with the pianist Paul Banks in 1926 and made his first recordings the following year with Jesse Stone. He then worked with Bennie Moten (1927–35), Buster Moten (1935), the pianist and tuba player Leslie Sheffield (1935–6), and Count Basie (1936–43). After army service (1943–6) Washington rejoined Basie, and remained in the band until 1950. Thereafter he took various day jobs, but during the 1950s continued to play regularly with Bobby Knott's band in Oklahoma City.

Although Washington's opportunities as a soloist were limited, particularly in Basie's orchestra (with its emphasis – both in arrangements and recordings – on two tenor saxophonists), he was an exceptionally gifted player. He progressed from emulating Harry Carney to a more fluid and highly expressive style of his own; this is especially noticeable in his recordings with smaller groups, such as Basie's sextet accompanying Jimmy Rushing on *Somebody stole my gal.*

For illustrations *see* BASIE, COUNT, FILMS, fig.3, and MOTEN, BENNIE.

SELECTED RECORDINGS

As sideman: B. Moten: New Vine Street Blues (1929, Vic. 23007); C. Basie: Topsy (1937, Decca 1770); *Count Basie at the Famous Door* (1938–9, Jazz Archives 41), incl. Doggin' Around, Indiana; Jive at Five (1939, Decca 2922); Somebody stole my gal (1940, Col. 35500); *Count Basie* (1947–50, RCA LPM1112), incl. Lopin'

BIBLIOGRAPHY

ChiltonW; *FeatherE*

R. Horricks: *Count Basie and his Orchestra: its Music and its Musicians* (London and New York, 1957), 183

FRANK DRIGGS

Washington, Kenny (*b* New York, 29 May 1958). Drummer. He performed and recorded in various groups led by Lee Konitz (1977–8), then played with Betty Carter (1978–9) and the quartets led by Johnny Griffin (from 1980). In the late 1970s he also began working as a freelance musician in New York, playing and recording with Kenny Burrell, Ron Carter, Frank Wess, Milt Jackson, George Coleman, Cedar Walton, and others. A hard-bop revivalist, Washington has distilled and combined the best elements from the work of earlier drummers and innovators to form his own style, which is characterized by the taste and clarity of his execution. He may be heard to advantage on the album *Call it Whachawana* (1983, Gal. 5146), recorded with Griffin.

CHUCK BRAMAN

Washington, Mack [William; McWashington, Willie] (*b* Kansas City, MO, 1908; *d* Kansas City, 1 Oct 1938). From 1926 he performed and made recordings (including *Toby*, 1932, Vic. 23384) with Bennie Moten (for illustration *see* MOTEN, BENNIE). He joined Count Basie at the Reno Club, Kansas City, in 1936. After being replaced by Jo Jones he worked with Buster Smith.

based on *ChiltonW*

Washington, Steve (*b* Philadelphia, *c*1900; *d* Boston, *c* Jan 1936). Banjoist and singer. From 1931 he worked with several bands in Pennsylvania. In the early 1930s he recorded as a banjoist, singer, guitarist, and mandolin player with the Washboard Rhythm Kings (1931–3); his singing may be heard on *Say it isn't so* (1932, Vic. 23364). After working as a soloist in cabarets he recorded as a leader (1933), accompanied by Benny Goodman, Joe Venuti, and others, and with the Georgia Washboard Stompers (1934, 1935). From 1934 he was a principal soloist with the pianist Ace Harris's Sunset Royal Orchestra.

based on *ChiltonW*

Washingtonians. Group formed in 1923 by Elmer Snowden. Led by Duke Ellington from the winter of the following year, its members included the trumpeter Bubber Miley, the trombonist Charlie Irvis (later replaced by Tricky Sam Nanton), the saxophonist Otto Hardwick, the banjoist Fred Guy, and the drummer Sonny Greer. From 1923 to 1927 the group was based at the Hollywood Club (renamed the Kentucky Club in 1924), and from 4 December 1927, when Ellington enlarged the band for appearances at the Cotton Club, the name Washingtonians was for the most part abandoned, though it continued to appear until 1929 on recordings the orchestra made for Brunswick, Cameo, and Harmony. (M. Tucker: *The Early Years of Edward Kennedy "Duke" Ellington, 1899–1927*, diss., U. of Michigan, 1986)

For recordings *see* ELLINGTON, DUKE.

MARK TUCKER

Waso. Belgian gypsy string band. It was formed in the early 1970s from a larger gypsy ensemble led by the multi-instrumentalist Piotto (Limberger), whose son Vivi Limberger became the group's rhythm guitarist; the other members were the double bass player Michel Verstraeten and the virtuoso guitarist Fapy Lafertin. In the late 1970s the leadership was taken over by Koen de Cauter, who played clarinet, saxophone, and solo acoustic guitar; he began to concentrate on guitar in 1981, and Lafertin's place was taken by the British saxophonist Bill Greenow. The group's playing is an engaging blend of string band music in the style of the Quintette du Hot Club de France

Duke Ellington's Washingtonians, New York, 1925: (left to right) Sonny Greer (drums), Charlie Irvis (trombone), Bubber Miley (trumpet), Elmer Snowden (banjo), Otto Hardwick (saxophone), and Ellington (piano)

and Hungarian and Romany folk idioms. A typical recording is *Waso Live in Laren* (1980, Pol. 2925111). (I. Cruickshank: *The Guitar Style of Django Reinhardt and the Gypsies*, Woodcote, nr Reading, England, 1982, rev. and enlarged 2/1985)

ALYN SHIPTON

Watanabe, Kazumi (*b* Tokyo, 14 Oct 1953). Japanese guitarist. He studied guitar at the Yamaha Music School in Tokyo with Sadanori Nakamure and performed and recorded professionally while still in his teens. He played jazz-rock from the mid-1970s and formed the group Kylyn in 1979. In 1983 he formed the Mobo Band with the saxophonist Mitsuru Sawamura, the pianist Ichiko Hashimoto, the electric bass guitarist Gregg Lee, the drummer Shuichi Murakami, and the percussionist Koyohiko Senba; with the band he played with several American musicians and often performed in New York.

SELECTED RECORDINGS

Infinite (1971, TE ETJ60001); *Endless Way* (1975, Col. YQ7511); *Milky Shade* (1976, Tei.–Union GU5003); *Olives Step* (1977, Col.–Better Days YX7580); *Kylyn* (1979, Col.–Better Days YX7595); *Tochika* (1980, Col. YX7265); *Dogatana* (1981, Col.–Better Days YF7037); *Mobo* (1983, Trio–Domo AW 20008–7); *Mobo Splash* (1985, Pol.–Domo H33P20050); *Spice of Life* (1987, Pol.–Domo H33P+20145)

BIBLIOGRAPHY

Feather–Gitler '70s
J. Ferguson: "Fusion Virtuoso: Kazumi Watanabe," *GP*, xx/4 (1986), 12 [incl. discography]

YOZO IWANAMI

Watanabe, Sadao (*b* Utsunomiya, Japan, 1 Feb 1933). Japanese alto and soprano saxophonist, flutist, and teacher. His father was a professional musician who played the biwa and sang. Watanabe was attracted to jazz at an early age and learned to play clarinet and alto saxophone in high school. In 1951 he moved to Tokyo and in 1953 began flute studies with Ririko Hayashi of the Tokyo PO. He also joined Toshiko Akiyoshi's bop quartet, taking over leadership of the group in 1956 when Akiyoshi went to the USA. From 1962 to 1965 he attended the Berklee College of Music and played and wrote arrangements for the school's Jazz in the Classroom series. While in the USA he worked with Gary McFarland, Chico Hamilton, and Gábor Szabó (1965). After returning to Tokyo, Watanabe was appointed director of the new Yamaha Institute of Popular Music, whose curriculum and teaching methods were modeled after those of Berklee. From 1966 he has presented concerts in Tokyo and toured internationally with his own quartet, which performs a repertory of bop, jazz-rock, soul, and pop music. He recorded in New York with Chick Corea (1970) and in Tokyo with the Galaxy All Stars (1978); he has also made more than 60 albums as a leader. In 1976 he became the first jazz musician to receive the annual Grand Prix Award from his government's cultural agency. Watanabe plays with a round, polished timbre, and adds growls for expressive effect.

SELECTED RECORDINGS

As leader: with C. Corea: *Round Trip* (1970, Van. 79344); *My Dear Life* (1977, FDisk 6001); *Bird of Paradise* (1977, FDisk 6017); *Rendezvous* (c1983, Col. FC37433)

As sideman: on C. Hamilton: *El Chico* (1965, Imp. 9201), Strange; on Galaxy All Stars: *Live Under the Sky* (1978, Gal. 95001), Confirmation, I'll remember April

BIBLIOGRAPHY

M. E. Lash: "Japan's First Jazz School," *DB*, xxxvi/10 (1969), 40
L. Feather: "Profile: Sadao Watanabe," *DB*, xliv/10 (1977), 39
G. Kalbacher: "Sadao Watanabe's Bop/Pop Chops," *DB*, liv/1 (1987), 19 [incl. discography]

BARRY KERNFELD

Waters, Benny [Benjamin] (*b* Brighton, MD, 23 Jan 1902). Tenor, soprano, and alto saxophonist, clarinetist, and arranger. He played piano and reed instruments as a child and first worked with Charlie Miller (1918–21). He studied at the New England Conservatory and subsequently became a teacher; among his pupils was Harry Carney. While playing and writing arrangements for Charlie Johnson (1926–31) he recorded with King Oliver and Clarence Williams. Despite his claim to have played for three years with Fletcher Henderson, he left the group in 1935 after about six months and rejoined Johnson (1936–7). He then worked with Hot Lips Page (1938, 1941), Claude Hopkins (1940–41), and Jimmie Lunceford (1942), recording with Hopkins and Lunceford. After leading his own band for four years he joined Roy Milton's rhythm-and-blues group. He played New Orleans jazz with Jimmy Archey from 1949, and when the group toured Europe he decided to stay; he settled eventually in Paris, where, until the end of the 1960s, he worked at the club La Cigale. He toured extensively in Europe in the 1970s and 1980s, playing at many festivals as well as recording, and also worked in New York during several brief visits early in the 1980s.

Although Waters performs as a soloist on alto saxophone, he is principally a tenor saxophonist and has a big tone reminiscent of that of Coleman Hawkins. He is a fine blues clarinetist and also an excellent singer.

Oral history material in *NjR* (JOHP), *NjR*.

SELECTED RECORDINGS

As leader: *Benny Waters and Traditional Jazz Studio, Prague* (1976, I giganti del jazz 9); *When You're Smiling* (1980, Hep 2010); *On the Sunny Side of the Street* (1981, JSP 1027)

As sideman: H. L. Page: If I were you/Small Fry (1938, Bb 7684); R. Milton: Groovy Blues/R. M. Blues (1946, Roy Milton 105); Great Traditionalists in Europe: *The Great Traditionalists in Europe* (1969, MPS 15228)

BIBLIOGRAPHY

P. Vacher: "La Cigale 1963," *JM*, ix/11 (1964), 10
——: "Benny Waters," *JM*, no.169 (1969), 5
R. Baggenaes: "Benny Waters," *Coda*, no.151 (1976), 8
D. Tarrant and R. Cooper: "Benny Waters Discography," *Journal of Jazz Discography*, no.2 (1977), 11; no.3 (1978), 2
B. Osgood: "Benny Waters: the First 80 Years," *MR*, x/2 (1982), 6
B. Waters: *The Key to a Jazzy Life* (n.p. [Toulouse], n.d. [1985])

REG COOPER

Waters [née Howard], **Ethel** (*b* Chester, PA, 31 Oct 1896; *d* Chatsworth, CA, 1 Sept 1977). Singer. She grew up in the Philadelphia area, where she came more strongly under the influence of white vaudeville singers, such as Nora Bayes and Fanny Brice, than did her southern contemporaries. Early in her career she sang "coon" songs, and became an outstanding example of the group of black singers known as "cake-walking babies" to distinguish them from southern classic blues singers such as Ma Rainey and Bessie Smith. Some of her performances from the mid-1920s (she began recording in 1921) foreshadow the scat-singing devices later developed by Louis Armstrong and Ella Fitzgerald. Later, in the 1930s, Waters found the mainstream of popular music, including jazz, congenial, and brought to it a combination of tragedy (in Harold Arlen's *Stormy Weather*, 1933) and comedy (in H. I. Marshall's *You can't stop me from loving you*, 1931) which, in its range, was unsurpassed by any other popular singer. Among the fine jazz instrumentalists who accompanied her in recording sessions were Fletcher Henderson (1921–6), Joe Smith (1922, 1924–7), Coleman Hawkins (1925), James P. Johnson and Clarence Williams (both 1928), Duke Ellington (1932), and Benny Carter (1939). From the late 1930s she began appearing on the stage, and her acting career eventually eclipsed her accomplishments as a singer in the public eye (for illustration *see* FILMS, fig.3).

Waters was the first black entertainer to move successfully from the vaudeville and nightclub circuits to what Blacks called "the white time" (the West Indian Bert Williams had done this earlier in the *Ziegfield Follies,* but in blackface). Her vocal resources were adequate though unexceptional, but this shortcoming was mitigated by an innate theatrical flair that enabled her to project the character and situation of every song she performed. The early recordings of Mildred Bailey, Lee Wiley, and Connee Boswell clearly reflect a debt to Waters, and most other popular singers of the time came under her influence to some degree. From 1960 to 1975 Waters toured with the evangelist Billy Graham, singing with less vocal prowess than before but with an undiminished ability to characterize her material.

SELECTED RECORDINGS

Kind Lovin' Blues (1922, Black Swan 14117); Go back where you stayed last night (1925, Col. 14093D); Tell 'em 'bout me/I've found a new baby (1925–6, Col. 561D); I can't give you anything but love (1932, Bruns. 6517); Stormy Weather (1933, Bruns. 6564); Dinah (1934, Decca 234); Stop myself from worryin' over you (1939, Bb 11284)

BIBLIOGRAPHY

E. Waters and C. Samuels: *His Eye is on the Sparrow* (New York and London, 1951) [autobiography]
C. Ellis: "Ethel Waters: Jazz Singer," *Sv,* no.22 (1969), 128
H. Panassié: "Ethel Waters," *BHcF,* no.207 (1971), 3
E. Waters [and C. Samuels]: *To me it's Wonderful* (New York and elsewhere, 1972) [autobiography]
H. Pleasants: *The Great American Popular Singers* (New York 1974)
——: "Happy Birthday, Ethel Waters," *Stereo Review,* xxxvii/4 (1976), 119
S. Harris: *Blues Who's Who: a Biographical Dictionary of Blues Singers* (New Rochelle, NY, 1979)

HENRY PLEASANTS/R

Waters, Monty [Monville Charles] (*b* Modesto, CA, 14 April 1938). Alto saxophonist. He led his own band in San Francisco, then worked with Jon Hendricks in 1965–8, also playing with King Pleasure and Miles Davis. After going to New York with Hendricks in 1968, he played with Elvin Jones, Joe Lee Wilson, Philly Joe Jones, George Coleman, Woody Shaw, and others. He recorded with Wilson (1975), the pianist Errol Parker (1976–80), Billy Higgins (1979), and Charli Persip (1980, 1984); a good example of his playing may be heard on Higgins's LP *The Soldier* (1979, Tim. 145). (*Feather–Gitler '70s*)

Watkins, Doug(las) (*b* Detroit, 2 March 1934; *d* nr Holbrook, AZ, 5 Feb 1962). Double bass player. He first left Detroit to tour with James Moody (1953), then returned to play with Barry Harris's trio (1954); this association enabled him to accompany such visiting musicians as Stan Getz, Charlie Parker, and Coleman Hawkins. In 1954 he performed in New York with Kenny Dorham and Hank Mobley, worked at Minton's Playhouse, and joined the Jazz Messengers; he left the group in 1956 to play with Horace Silver's quintet. His prolific work as a freelance for Prestige included recordings with Gene Ammons (1956–61), Sonny Rollins, Phil Woods, Mobley, Art Farmer, Donald Byrd (all 1956), and Kenny Burrell (1957). Thereafter Watkins took part in performances and recordings by Charles Mingus's Jazz Workshop when Mingus was playing piano (1960–61). He died in an automobile accident.

SELECTED RECORDINGS

As leader: *Watkins at Large* (1956, Tran. 20); *Soulnik* (1960, NewJ 8238)
As sideman: H. Silver: *Horace Silver and the Jazz Messengers* (1954, BN 5058); A. Blakey: *The Jazz Messengers at the Cafe Bohemia* (1955, BN 1507–8); S. Rollins: *Saxophone Colossus* (1956, Prst. 7079); H. Silver: *Six Pieces of Silver* (1956, BN 1539); G. Ammons: *Boss Tenor* (1960, Prst. 7180)

BIBLIOGRAPHY

FeatherE; *Feather '60s*
Obituaries: *IM,* lx/10 (1962), 33; *DB,* xxix/6 (1962), 15
J. L. Ginibre and P. Carles: "Dictionnaire de la contrebasse," *Jm,* no.166 (1969), 59

DIANNA RHYAN

Watkins, Earl (Thomas, Jr.) (*b* San Francisco, 29 Jan 1920). Drummer. After playing with a navy band (1942–5) he led his own bands in the San Francisco Bay area, and also recorded with Wilbert Baranco (1946). He later worked as a sideman in various groups, and in the 1950s played with Flip Phillips (1952) and the bands of Muggsy Spanier (mid-1950s) and Bob Scobey (1954–5, 1956). From 1955 to 1961 Watkins was a member of Earl Hines's group, which was resident at the Club Hangover and other venues in San Francisco. While in Chicago in 1961 this ensemble recorded for Riverside, and Watkins's varied playing may be heard to advantage on the album *A Monday Date* (Riv. RLP9398). He also made recordings as a freelance, and with Kid Ory (1957, 1959, ?1960). (*Feather '60s*)

Watkins, Joe [Watson, Mitchell] (*b* New Orleans, 24 Oct 1900; *d* New Orleans, 13 Sept 1969). Drummer. He first studied piano, though his chief interest was always drums, and about 1918 he taught himself to play. He worked with Kid Howard, Isaiah Morgan, Herb Morand, and Punch Miller, but is best known for his long tenure with George Lewis (i), which began in 1946. Later he toured Europe and Japan with the band, and his playing and singing may be heard to advantage on *George Lewis in Japan* (1963, GHB 16). Owing to ill-health he played irregularly after 1966. (T. Dash: "An Afternoon with Joe Watkins," *Fn,* i (1970), no.4, p.6; no.5, p.4)

Oral history material in *LNT.*

BILL RUSSELL

Watkins, Julius (*b* Detroit, 10 Oct 1921; *d* Short Hills, NJ, 4 April 1977). French horn player. He took up french horn at the age of nine, but in order to earn his living played trumpet with the big bands of Ernie Fields (1943–6) and Milt Buckner (1949–50). Thereafter he performed exclusively on french horn, on which he was the first to improvise fluently in the bop style. He studied at the Manhattan School of Music for three years, then recorded with Thelonious Monk and Sonny Rollins (1953), toured with Pete Rugolo (1954), and, with Charlie Rouse, joined Oscar Pettiford's sextet. In 1956 he and Rouse, with Gildo Mahones, Pettiford, and Ron Jefferson, formed Les Modes (later the Jazz Modes), a bop quintet; at times the group was enlarged to include the singer Eileen Gilbert and additional instrumentalists, such as Sahib Shihab and Chino Pozo. When it disbanded for lack of work, Watkins played with George Shearing (1959) and Quincy Jones (1961). Thereafter he worked as a freelance orchestral player in Broadway shows and as a session musician, recording with John Coltrane (1961), Tadd Dameron (1962), Milt Jackson (1963), Freddie Hubbard (1963), the Jazz Composer's Orchestra (1969), and, most frequently, Gil Evans (1958–64, 1969).

SELECTED RECORDINGS

As leader of Jazz Modes (with C. Rouse): *Jazzville* (1956, Dawn 1101); *The Jazz Modes* (1958, Atl. 1306)
As sideman: M. Buckner: Yesterdays (1949, MGM 10632); T. Monk: Let's call this/Think of one (1953, Prst. 1352); O. Pettiford: *Bass by Oscar Pettiford* (*c*1956, Beth. 6); J. Heath: *The Quota* (1961, Riv. 9372); P. Sanders: *Karma* (1969, Imp. 9181)

BIBLIOGRAPHY

J. S. Wilson: "The Horn that Nobody Wants," *DB*, xxvi/19 (1959), 15
J. Agrell: "Jazz and the Horn: Julius Watkins," *Brass Bulletin*, no.41 (1983), 20

BARRY KERNFELD

Watrous, Bill [William Russell, II] (*b* Middletown, CT, 8 June 1939). Trombonist. He was introduced to music by his father, the trombonist Ralph Waltrous; although he took music lessons in high school he was largely self-taught, and he gained early experience by playing in local dixieland bands. During his military service he studied with Herbie Nichols. He first played professionally with Billy Butterfield, and in 1962–7 was a member of Kai Winding's various groups, which included from two to five trombones. At the same time he worked as a freelance musician with many studio groups and big bands, including those led by Quincy Jones and Maynard Ferguson (recording with both in 1964), Johnny Richards, and Woody Herman (recording in 1967), and played in the orchestra on Merv Griffin's television show (1965–8). He was a staff musician at CBS in 1967–9, then in 1971 became a member of the jazz-rock group Ten Wheel Drive. Watrous came to prominence as the leader of the big band Manhattan Wildflower Refuge, which lasted from 1973 to 1977; among his sidemen were Joe Beck, Dick Hyman, Ed Soph, Ed Xiques, and the trumpeter Danny Stiles. In the late 1970s he moved to Los Angeles, where he continued to record frequently (often with Stiles), to lead a big band occasionally, and to work in studios. He gave a series of concerts in Germany in 1980 with Winding and Albert Mangelsdorff in Trombone Summit, a group formed especially for the purpose; in 1982 he performed and recorded in London. His effortless virtuosity and fluid solo style have had a significant influence on other trombonists.

SELECTED RECORDINGS

As leader: *'Bone Straight Ahead* (1972–3, FaD 101); *Manhattan Wildlife Refuge* (1974, Col. KG33090); *The Tiger of San Pedro* (1975, Col. PC33701); *I'll Play for you* (1980, FaD 134); *Coronary Trombossa* (1982, FaD 136); *Roarin' Back into New York, New York* (1982, FaD 144); *Someplace Else* (1986, Soundwings 2100); *Reflections* (1987, Soundwings 2104)

As sideman: J. Witherspoon: *Blues for Easy Livers* (1965–6, Prst. 7475); W. Herman: *Woody Live: East and West* (1965, 1967, Col. CS9493); D. Stiles: *In Tandem* (1974, FaD 103)

BIBLIOGRAPHY

Feather–Gitler '70s
S. Marks: "Bill Watrous: Swinging Refuge in the Wilds of Manhattan," *DB*, xlii/11 (1975), 14
S. Britt: "Bill Watrous," *JJI*, xxxv/11 (1982), 10
L. Tomkins: "The Most Musical Trombone of Bill Watrous," *CI*, xx/10 (1982), 20; contd as "Me and my Big Bands: Bill Watrous," xx/11 (1982), 6; contd as "Button up your Overtones, Advises Bill Watrous," xx/12 (1982), 16
R. Hepola: "The Complete Bill Watrous Jazz and Solo Discography," *ITA* [International Trombone Association] *Journal*, xiv/4 (1986), 42

SCOTT YANOW

Watson, Bobby [Robert Michael, Jr.] (*b* Lawrence, KS, 23 Aug 1953). Alto saxophonist. After receiving a degree in theory and composition from the University of Miami he traveled to New York. From 1977 to 1981 he performed, recorded, and toured with Art Blakey's Jazz Messengers, and may be heard to advantage on *Album of the Year* (1981, Tim. 155). He also served as Blakey's music director for two years during this period, and composed and arranged several pieces for the band, including *Time will Tell* (1978) on the album *In my Prime* (1977–8, Tim. 114, 118). Thereafter he played with George Coleman (1981) and Louis Hayes (1982), and recorded with Ricky Ford and Sam Rivers (both 1982). In 1983, with the double bass player Curtis Lundy and another business partner, Watson formed the record company New Notes, for which he recorded as a leader. Later he toured Europe and recorded as the leader of hard-bop groups (1983–5), played, recorded, and wrote arrangements for the 29th Street Saxophone Quartet (from 1983), and recorded with Charli Persip (1984). In 1987 he played at the Bass Clef club, London.

BIBLIOGRAPHY

R. Watson: "Pro Session: Arranging and Composing for the Jazz Messengers," *DB*, xlvi/17 (1979), 90
B. Rusch: "Bob Watson: Interview," *Cadence*, vii/12 (1981), 5
J. Giscard and D. Piatkowski: "Bobby Watson," *Coda*, no.210 (1986), 10 [incl. discography]
P. Bloom: "29th Street Saxophone Quartet," *DB*, liv/2 (1987), 26 [incl. discography]

Watson, Gilbert (*b c*1898; *d* Peterborough, Canada, 12 Aug 1959). Canadian pianist. He studied piano in Toronto and played at the Allen Theatre there. In 1925 he formed a dance orchestra, which played at Sunnyside and Gin's pavilions, the Prince George Hotel, and the Old Mill, and made radio broadcasts. The ten numbers it recorded in 1924–5 are among the earliest jazz recordings made by a Canadian band. Watson dissolved the orchestra in the late 1930s and retired from music.

BIBLIOGRAPHY

M. Miller: "Watson, Gilbert," *Encyclopedia of Music in Canada*, ed. H. Kallmann, G. Potvin, and K. Winters (Toronto, Buffalo, and London, 1981)

JACK LITCHFIELD

Watson, Leo (*b* Kansas City, MO, 27 Feb 1898; *d* Los Angeles, 2 May 1950). Singer. He began his career as a soloist, but from 1929 he performed as a singer and tiple player in a novelty act called Ben Bernie's Nephews. After changing its name to the SPIRITS OF RHYTHM (1932), the five-man group recorded (1933), held several successful engagements, and toured. In 1937 Watson left to join John Kirby at the Onyx Club, New York; as well as singing, he occasionally played drums and trombone. He worked with Artie Shaw (1937–8) and Gene Krupa (1938), before re-joining the Spirits of Rhythm in 1939; in that year he also played briefly with Jimmy Mundy and made four recordings as a leader. After appearing at the New York World's Fair (1940) the group moved to California, where it continued to play intermittently until about 1945. In spite of ill health Watson then again worked on his own as a drummer and singer, and made further recordings. His highly individual "stream-of-consciousness" style of scat singing was so original for his time that it is surprising Watson is not better known. His recordings are both entertaining and impressive.

SELECTED RECORDINGS

As leader: The Man with the Mandolin/Utt da zay (1939, Decca 2750); Ja da/It's the tune that counts (1939, Decca 2959); Sunny Boy/Tight and Gay (1946, Sig. 1007); Snake Pit/Jingle Bells (1946, Sig. 1004)

As sideman: Spirits of Rhythm: I got rhythm/Rhythm (1933, Bruns. 01715); A. Shaw: Fee fi fo fum (1937, Bruns. 7952); L. Feather: For he's a jolly good fellow (1938, Com. 528); G. Krupa: Nagasaki (1938, Bruns. 8188); Tutti Frutti (1938, Bruns. 8211)

BIBLIOGRAPHY

ChiltonW; *FeatherE*
M. Davidson: "Leo Watson: a Giant Lost in Time," *J&B*, iii/2 (1973), 14
M. Davison: "Leo Watson Discography," *DF*, no.33 (1974), 17; no.34 (1976), 15; no.36 (1976), 1 [addns and corrections]
L. Gourse: *Louis' Children: American Jazz Singers* (New York, 1984), 149

LAWRENCE KOCH

Watters, Lu(cious) (*b* Santa Cruz, CA, 19 Dec 1911). Bandleader, trumpeter, and arranger. He directed a swing band in Oakland, California, from which, in 1940, he extracted a small unit, the Yerba Buena Jazz Band (see illustration), to revive the New Orleans small-band style of King Oliver. Although

Lu Watters's Yerba Buena Jazz Band at the Dawn Club, San Francisco, 1946: (left to right) Harry Mordecai (banjo), Turk Murphy (trombone), Watters (trumpet), Bill Dart (drums), Bob Scobey (trumpet), Bob Helm (clarinet), Wally Rose (piano), and Dick Lammi (tuba)

other small dixieland bands existed at this time, notably those led by Muggsy Spanier and Bob Crosby, the element of authenticity projected by Watters's group set it apart and stimulated a large-scale revival of New Orleans and Chicago jazz throughout the world. Of the many revivalist bands formed during this period, two of the most successful were led by former sidemen in Watters's group, Bob Scobey and Turk Murphy. Watters also provided his band with a number of arrangements and original compositions, such as *Big Bear Stomp* and *Emperor Norton's Hunch*. He retired from music in 1957 to study geology and later to work as a chef in various California restaurants.

See also ROSE, WALLY.

SELECTED RECORDINGS

Maple Leaf Rag (1941, Jazz Man 1); London Blues/Sunset Cafe Stomp (1942, Jazz Man 14); Riverside Blues/Cake Walkin' Babies (1942, Jazz Man 5); Working Man Blues/Big Bear Stomp (1946, West Coast 104); Emperor Norton's Hunch (1946, West Coast 107)

BIBLIOGRAPHY

B. Colburn and G. Williams: "That Frisco Jazz Band," *Jazz*, i/3 (1942), 10
E. Bayley, Jr., and B. Kinnell: "Reincarnation: the First of Two Articles on the Yerba Buena Band," *American Jazz* (n.d. [1945]), 11
C. Shain: "Lu Watters Yerba Buena Jazz Band," *Jazz Session* (1946), July, 24
B. Nicholls: "The West Coast Revival," *Music Mirror*, ii/11 (1955), 10
M. W. Stearns: *The Story of Jazz* (New York, 1956, rev. and enlarged 2/1958, enlarged 1970)
G. Hulme: "Lu Watters: a Discography," *Matrix*, no.24 (1959), suppl. pp.i–xiii; nos.35–6 (1961), 35
D. Dexter, Jr.: *The Jazz Story: from the 90's to the 60's* (Englewood Cliffs, NJ, 1964)
P. Martin: "Lu Watters: the Legend, the Man," *MR*, xii/7 (1985), 1

WILLIAM H. TALLMADGE

Watts, Ernie [Ernest James] (*b* Norfolk, VA, 23 Oct 1945). Saxophonist and leader. After attending the Berklee College of Music he toured and recorded with Buddy Rich from 1966 to 1968, when he moved to Los Angeles. He then worked as a studio musician and as a staff musician for NBC, playing in the orchestra for the "Tonight Show" (1972). He also played with Gerald Wilson, performed and recorded with Bobby Bryant (1969), toured Africa with Oliver Nelson, and recorded with Jean-Luc Ponty (1969), Cannonball Adderley (1972), and Leonard Feather (*The Night Blooming Jazzmen*, c1975, Mstr. 348). From 1977 he was a member of Lee Ritenour's jazz-rock group. He recorded with Sadao Watanabe (1977, 1978), Anita O'Day (1978), J. J. Johnson (1980), and Wilson (1981), and received a Grammy Award in 1982 for his performance on the soundtrack to the film *Chariots of Fire*. Thereafter Watts recorded with Tom Scott and Stanley Clarke (both 1983) and Ritenour (1983, 1984), and continued to work in studios; he was a soloist with Charlie Haden's Liberation Music Orchestra, and has also led his own jazz-rock quartet.

BIBLIOGRAPHY

Feather–Gitler '70s
S. Y. Bradley: "Ernie Watts," *DB*, xlvi/9 (1979), 35
Z. Stewart: "Ernie Watts: Watts Happening," *DB*, li/11 (1984), 26 [incl. discography]

Watts, Grady (*b* Texarkana, TX, 30 June 1908). Trumpeter. He studied at the University of Oklahoma and began his professional career in Louisiana. After working with several bandleaders (1929–30) he was a soloist in the Casa Loma Orchestra (1931–42; for illustration *see* CASA LOMA ORCHESTRA); his solo playing may be heard on *No Name Jive* (1940, Decca 3089), one of many recordings he made with the band. He ceased full-time performing in 1945.

based on *ChiltonW*

Watts, Trevor (Charles) (*b* London, 26 Feb 1939). English alto and soprano saxophonist. He first played the saxophone during service in the RAF (1959–63). He became a founding member of the New Jazz Orchestra in 1963, and also played with various blues and rock musicians, including Long John Baldry, the singer Rod Stewart, and the singer and harmonica player Sonny Boy Williamson (1963–4). In 1965, after setting up the Little Theatre Club in London with Paul Rutherford and John Stevens to promote improvised music, he formed with Stevens the SPONTANEOUS MUSIC ENSEMBLE, a seminal free-improvisation group. He left the Spontaneous Music Ensemble in 1967 (though he worked with it again in the 1970s) and with Barry Guy and Rutherford formed Amalgam, whose style mixes elements of jazz, improvised music, folk, and rock; members have included Stevens, Bobby Bradford, Harry Miller, the electric bass guitarist Colin McKenzie, the electric guitarist Keith Rowe, Keith Tippett, and Stan Tracey, and in the mid-1980s the rock drummer Liam Genocky and the folk violinist Peter Knight. Watts also formed the String Ensemble (1976), the Universal Music Group (1978), the Drum Orchestra (1982), and Moiré Music (1982), which has worked as a band of six, 10 or 14 players. Besides leading these groups, he played in the London Jazz Composers Orchestra (1970–81) and Open Circle (with Danny Thompson and John Stevens, 1973–4), and with Don Cherry (1966), Steve Lacy (1966–74), Rashied Ali (with Amalgam, 1967), Bobby Bradford (1973), Stan Tracey (1973–4), Stevens's Dance Orchestra (1979–82), Keith Tippett (1978–80), and Archie Shepp (1981). He formed his own record label, Arc, in 1983.

One of the few musicians in Britain to have mastered the innovations of Ornette Coleman, Watts has consistently broken new ground in his music, and contributed significantly to the establishment of an indigenous jazz-related music in Britain. His distinctive style combines rugged intensity with lyricism and a strong melodic line. In Moiré Music the rhythmic drive and layering of themes that he first explored with the String Ensemble come together successfully; the group's style echoes African and other musics and shows parallels with the structures and momentum of minimalist music.

SELECTED RECORDINGS

As leader: of Amalgam: *Wipe Out* (1979, Impetus 47901), *Over the Rainbow* (1983, Arc 01); of Moiré Music: *Trevor Watts' Moiré Music* (1986, Arc 02)
As sideman: Spontaneous Music Ensemble: *Birds of a Feather* (1971, BYG 529023); B. Bradford: *Love's Dream* (1973, Emanem 302); S. Lacy: *Saxophone Special* (1974, Emanem 3310)

BIBLIOGRAPHY

Feather–Gitler '70s
I. Carr: *Music Outside: Contemporary Jazz in Britain* (London, 1973), 39
R. Cotterrell, ed.: *Jazz Now: the Jazz Centre Society Guide* (London, 1976)
K. Ansell: "Beyond the Mainstream: Closer to the Music of Trevor Watts," *JJI*, xxxiii/7 (1980), 30
M. Johnston: "Trevor Watts," *Coda*, no.185 (1982), 12
K. Ansell: "In Phase with Trevor Watts' Moiré Music," *The Wire*, no.9 (1984), 36

SIMON ADAMS

Wave. Record company and label. Established in New York in 1961, the company developed from the activities of two recording studios (one in Queens, one in Manhattan) owned by PETER IND, at which he recorded the work of many of his colleagues and friends (including Lee Konitz, Warne Marsh, Ronnie Ball, Joe Puma, Sheila Jordan, and Al Levitt). In addition, at the establishment in Manhattan Ind engineered sessions for Bethlehem. The first album on the label, also released in England by Esquire, was issued under Ind's name, and included items he had recorded with Ball, Sal Mosca, Jordan, and others. Thereafter the company's activities declined until Ind, English by birth, returned in the late 1960s to London, where he revived Wave and issued from his archives material by Mosca, Marsh, and Konitz. He also recorded a series of new albums with his quartet and sextet, as well as two LPs of double bass solos and various other discs. Among items by others released on Wave at this time were a reunion recording made in London by Konitz and Marsh, a collection by the New Paul Whiteman Orchestra of re-creations of the sound of Whiteman's original band, and albums by Buddy DeFranco and Martial Solal. After a further period during which operations were suspended, Ind reactivated the company in the late 1980s, releasing much of the back catalogue and planning new projects.

MARK GARDNER

Wa-wa [wah-wah]. The ululating sound achieved by regularly bringing into play and cutting out treble frequencies in the course of a note; the term is onomatopoeic. On brass instruments the wa-wa is created by means of muting (*see* MUTE), notably with the harmon mute, on woodwind instruments (saxophones, clarinets, and flutes) by FALSE FINGERING. A signal-processing device, generally operated by a pedal, can apply the wa-wa effect to notes played on any electrified instrument; it is associated especially with the electric guitar but has also been widely used with electric piano (for example, by Herbie Hancock and Joe Zawinul), violin (by Jean-Luc Ponty and Michal Urbaniak), and trumpet (by Miles Davis). A good example of the electronic wa-wa may be heard on Ponty's *Imaginary Voyage* on the album of the same name (1976, Atl. 19136), beginning shortly after the introduction to the second part of the piece.

Wax (i). The material in which sound recordings were cut until the early 1940s (*see* RECORDING, §I, 1 and 2), hence figuratively the shellac-based material of which most 78 r.p.m. discs are made; also, in jazz argot, to record.

Wax (ii). Record label established by AL HALL in the late 1940s.

Wayland, Hank [Frederic Gregson] (*b* Fall River, MA, 21 Jan 1906). Double bass player. He was taught to read music by his father and played in a band at high school. After moving to New York (1926) he worked in several theater and studio orchestras, and in 1934 he performed and recorded with Benny Goodman. He made recordings as a studio musician with such leaders as Red Norvo (1934), Artie Shaw (1936), Bunny Berigan (1937–9, including *Jazz me Blues*, 1939, Vic. 26244), and Larry Clinton (1939–41). In 1941–2 he was a member of Bob Chester's band and he then settled on the West Coast (1943). He played briefly with Eddie Miller's big band, again worked in studios, and performed with various leaders, among them Wingy Manone.

based on *ChiltonW*

Wayne, Chuck [Jagelka, Charles] (*b* New York, 27 Feb 1923). Guitarist. He first played mandolin, then changed to guitar and played with Clarence Profit (1941). After military service (1942–4) he worked on 52nd Street with Joe Marsala. During the mid-1940s he became involved with the bop movement and played on several important early recordings with Dizzy Gillespie and Benny Harris. He performed and recorded with Woody Herman's orchestra in 1946–7, and from 1949 to 1952 he was a regular member of George Shearing's quintet (for illustration *see* SHEARING, GEORGE). For most of the 1950s he worked as a freelance in New York, and from 1954 to 1957 he toured with Tony Bennett. He also wrote and performed the music for a production on Broadway of the play *Orpheus Descending* by Tennessee Williams (1957). Thereafter he joined the staff of CBS (1959), and from that time he has appeared frequently on television and continued to play occasionally at clubs. From 1972 to 1976 he performed and recorded with Joe Puma, and in the mid-1980s he was active as a teacher at Westchester Conservatory of Music, White Plains, New York. Wayne's playing has a mellow tone and he displays unusual technical facility; his style of improvising remains firmly rooted in bop.

SELECTED RECORDINGS

Duos with J. Puma: *Interactions* (1973, Choice 1004)
As leader: *Tapestry* (1963, Focus 333); *Morning Mist* (1964, Prst. 7367); *Traveling* (1976, Prog. 7008)

As sideman: C. Hart: Dee Dee's Dance/Little Benny (1944, Savoy 598); D. Gillespie: Groovin' High/Blue 'n' Boogie (1945, Guild 1001); C. Hawkins: Half Step Down Please/Jumpin' for Jane (1947, Vic. 203143); G. Shearing: Sorry, Wrong Rhumba/Cottontop (1949, Dis. 106)

BIBLIOGRAPHY

FeatherE; *Feather '60s*; *Feather–Gitler '70s*
B. Hodgins: "Chuck," *Metronome*, lxvii/4 (1951), 15
L. Feather: *The Book of Jazz: a Guide to the Entire Field* (New York, 1957, 2/1965 as *The Book of Jazz from Then till Now: a Guide to the Entire Field*)
D. Cerulli: "Chuck Wayne," *DB*, xxv/7 (1958), 19 [interview]

SCOTT DeVEAUX

Wayne, Frances (Claire) [Bertucci, Chiarina Francesca] (*b* Boston, 26 Aug 1924; *d* Boston, 6 Feb 1978). Singer and leader. After traveling to New York with a group led by her brother, the tenor saxophonist Nick Jerret, she worked with Charlie Barnet, with whom she recorded *That Old Black Magic* (1942, Decca 18541). During a period with Woody Herman (1943–6) she married Neal Hefti and made her first recording as a leader (1945). She later moved to California, where she recorded under her own name accompanied by Hefti's orchestra (1947) and worked as a soloist in clubs before going into semiretirement. During the early 1950s she again worked with Hefti, recording with him several times in New York. She also made a number of recordings as a leader, including the album *The Warm Sound* (1957, Atl. 1263), which was made up from several small-group sessions with such swing and bop musicians as Jerome Richardson, Milt Hinton, Al Cohn, and Hank Jones. In the mid-1970s Wayne performed occasionally as a soloist accompanied by such sidemen as Richie Kamuca and Frank Capp; she also sang with Hefti's orchestra in 1975.

BIBLIOGRAPHY

FeatherE; *Feather–Gitler '70s*
H. Webman: "Hefti's Band Full of Surprises: May be Eastern Crew of '52," *DB*, xix/12 (1952), 8
L. Feather: "Frances Wayne," *MM*, xlix (30 Nov 1974), 26

Weatherford, Teddy (*b* Pocahontas, VA, 11 Oct 1903; *d* Calcutta, 25 April 1945). Pianist. He moved to New Orleans at the age of 12 and began learning piano two years later. He was in Chicago from 1922, where he played at the Moulin Rouge Café with Jimmy Wade (1923–5), at the Vendome Theater with Erskine Tate (1925–6), and briefly as a soloist at the Dreamland; during this period he was Earl Hines's chief rival in Chicago. He sailed to the Far East in 1926 with an orchestra led by the drummer Jack Carter and he led his own band in Singapore, Manila, and Shanghai; in 1934 he returned to the USA, where he recruited Buck Clayton's big band for a residency at the Candidrome Ballroom in Shanghai. Weatherford played at the Taj Mahal Hotel in Bombay from 1936 to 1940, during which period he also recorded in Paris (1937) and played in Colombo, Ceylon, at the Galle Face Hotel (1939); after his contract in Bombay expired he took up an engagement at the Galle Face for a year (1940–41) then returned to India, where the band played at the Grand Hotel in Calcutta.

SELECTED RECORDINGS

As unaccompanied soloist: Tea for Two/Weather Beaten Blues (1937, Swing 5); Weather Blues/Maple Leaf Rag (1937, Swing 315)
As sideman: J. Wade: Someday Sweetheart/Mobile Blues (1923, Para. 20295); E. Tate: Static Strut/Stomp Off, Let's Go (1926, Voc. 1027)

BIBLIOGRAPHY

J. H. Wareing: "Some Reminiscences of Teddy Weatherford," *Jazz Forum*, no.4 (Fordingbridge, England, 1947), 10
K. P. Darke: "Teddy Weatherford's Indian Recording Sessions, 1941–45," *Matrix*, nos.107–8 (1975), 3
P. Darke and R. Gulliver: "Teddy Weatherford," *Sv*, no.65 (1976), 175

JAMES M. DORAN

Weather Report. Jazz-rock group. It was founded in December 1970, the original members being Joe Zawinul (keyboards), Wayne Shorter (soprano and tenor saxophone), Miroslav Vitous (double bass), Alphonse Mouzon (drums), and Airto Moreira (additional percussion). Over the years the group has undergone many personnel changes, with Zawinul and, until 1985, Shorter serving as the only constant members. Important subsequent players in the group include the percussionists Dom Um Romao (1971–4) and Alex Acuña (1975–7), the electric bass guitarist Alphonso Johnson (1974–6), the drummer Peter Erskine (1978–82), and particularly the electric bass guitarist Jaco Pastorius (1976–81). From 1982 Weather Report comprised Shorter, Zawinul, the electric bass guitarist Victor Bailey, the drummer Omar Hakim, and the percussionist José Rossy. Its membership has continued to change, however. The percussionist Mino Cinélu joined in 1984, and Erskine left Steps Ahead to rejoin the group around 1985, replacing Hakim. After fulfilling several outstanding commitments in 1985, Shorter took extended leave from the group; with Zawinul as sole leader and Steve Khan as Shorter's replacement, the quintet has performed from 1986 under a new name, Weather Update. Other instrumentalists and singers have contributed to individual recordings.

Weather Report's first albums provided several remarkable instances of unconventional collective playing, though their music remained accessible to a large audience. Discarding the traditional jazz roles of soloist and accompanist, the players took the lead by turn and created textures that were continuously changing; they elided tonal ostinato themes with improvisations, and alternated unmetered passages with others underpinned by rock or latin rhythms. Excellent examples of this novel approach to ensemble improvisation are *Seventh Arrow* and *Umbrellas* (1971), or *Crystal* and *Surucucú* (1971–2). By 1972 Zawinul dominated the group, which had moved towards rock. He had a preference for dance rhythms and fixed arrangements featuring complex electronic effects. His striving for commercial success precipitated the many personnel changes in the group, but also led to its resounding hit *Birdland* (1976). *Havona* (also 1976) demonstrated Jaco Pastorius's unusual command of the electric bass guitar, as well as the group's continuing ties to jazz improvisation.

See also HARMONY (i), §2, and exx.25 and 26; for illustration *see* ZAWINUL, JOE.

SELECTED RECORDINGS

(all recorded for Columbia)

Weather Report (1971, KC30661), incl. Seventh Arrow, Umbrellas; *I Sing the Body Electric* (1971–2, KC31352), incl. Crystal, Surucucú; *Sweetnighter* (*c*1973, KC32210); *Mysterious Traveller* (*c*1974, KC32494); *Tale Spinnin'* (*c*1975, PC33417); *Black Market* (*c*1976, PC34099); *Heavy Weather* (1976, PC34418), incl. Birdland, Havona; *Mr. Gone* (*c*1978, JC35358); *8:30* (*c*1979, PC2-36030); *Night Passage* (*c*1980, JC36793); *Weather Report* (*c*1981, FC37616); *Domino Theory* (1983, FC39147); *Sportin' Life* (*c*1985, FC39908)

BIBLIOGRAPHY

D. Morgenstern: "Weather Report: Outlook Bright and Sunny," *DB*, xxxviii/11 (1971), 14
L. Goddet: "Weather Report," *Jh*, no.317 (1975), 20
B. McRae: "Weather Report," *JJ*, xxix/6 (1976), 10
K. Dallas: "Weather Report," *MM*, lii (29 Oct 1977), 56
M. C. Gridley: *Jazz Styles* (Englewood Cliffs, NJ, 1978, rev. 2/1985 as *Jazz Styles: History and Analysis*, with suppl. *Instructor's Manual and Discography*)
L. Lyons: "This Year's Weather Report," *Hi-Fi/MusAm*, xxviii/9 (1978), 115
C. Silvert: "Joe Zawinul: Wayfaring Genius," *DB*, xlv (1978), no.11, p.13; no.12, p.21
L. Birnbaum: "Weather Report Answers its Critics," *DB*, xlvi/3 (1979), 14
L. Blumenthal: "Weather Report," *DB*, xlviii/2 (1981), 14
A. Liska: "On the Road with Weather Report," *DB*, xlix/10 (1982), 21

C. Murray: "Weather Report," *The Wire*, no.3 (1983), 4
P. Davis: "Weather Report: Fine and Warm," *CI*, xxii/4 (1984), 12
J. Zawinul and G. Armbruster: "The Evolution of Weather Report," *Keyboard*, x/3 (1984), 49

BARRY KERNFELD

Webb, Chick [William Henry] (*b* Baltimore, 10 Feb 1909; *d* Baltimore, 16 June 1939). Drummer and bandleader. He moved to New York around 1925 and from January 1927 led a group at the Savoy Ballroom that later became one of the outstanding bands of the swing period. Although the group did not include any prominent soloists during its years of prolific recording activity (Benny Carter, Jimmy Harrison, and Johnny Hodges had played with the band early on), it developed a distinctive style thanks in part to the compositions and arrangements provided by Edgar Sampson (e.g., *Blue Lou, Stomping at the Savoy*, and *Let's get together*) and especially to Webb's forceful drumming. In 1934 Ella Fitzgerald was engaged as the band's singer, and it soon achieved popular success with performances of such tunes as *A-tisket, A-tasket* (1938). Webb's band remained at the Savoy intermittently during the late 1920s and held long residencies there in the 1930s (see illustration), regularly defeating rival bands in the ballroom's famous cutting contests. After Webb's early death, Fitzgerald led the group until 1942, when it disbanded.

Webb, a diminutive hunchback, was universally admired by drummers for his forceful sense of swing, accurate technique, control of dynamics, and imaginative breaks and fills. Although he was unable to read music, he committed to memory the arrangements played by the band and directed performances from a raised platform in the center of the ensemble, giving cues with his drumming. Using specially constructed bass-drum pedals and cymbal holders, he could range effortlessly over a large drum set that offered a wide selection of colors. Unlike drummers of the 1920s, he used the woodblocks and cowbell only for momentary effects, and varied his playing with rim shots, temple-block work, and cymbal crashes. In his celebrated two- to four-bar fills, he abandoned earlier jazz drumming formulae for varied mixtures of duple- and triple-meter patterns. Webb was seldom given to long solos, but his style is well represented on *Liza* (1938), a superior response to Gene Krupa's solo performance with Benny Goodman's band on *Sing, sing, sing*.

SELECTED RECORDINGS

Let's get together (1934, Col. 741); Stomping at the Savoy (1934, Col. CB741); Blue Lou (1934, Decca 1065); Clap Hands! Here comes Charley (1937, Decca 1220); I got rhythm (1937, Decca 1759); Harlem Congo (1937, Decca 1681); Midnite in a Madhouse (1937, Decca 1587); A-tisket, A-tasket/Liza (1938, Decca 1840)

BIBLIOGRAPHY

S. B. Charters and L. Kunstadt: *Jazz: a History of the New York Scene* (Garden City, NY, 1962/R1981)
J. P. Noonan: "The Secrets of Chick Webb's Drumming Technique," *DB*, xxxix/13 (1972), 26
D. M. Bakker: "Chick Webb, 1928–1939," *Micrography*, no.31 (1974), 4
A. McCarthy: *Big Band Jazz* (New York and London, 1974), 265
T. D. Brown: *A History and Analysis of Jazz Drumming to 1942* (diss., U. of Michigan, 1976), 424
G. Murphy: "Chick Webb: the Mighty Atom Remembered by Greg Murphy," *JJI*, xxxix/4 (1986), 10
B. Korall: "Chick Webb: the Total Experience on Drums," *MD*, xii/1 (1988), 26

J. BRADFORD ROBINSON

Webb, George (Horace) (*b* London, 8 Oct 1917). English pianist and bandleader. In 1942 he formed a band which shortly afterwards became known as George Webb's Dixielanders; its members included Wally Fawkes and Eddie Harvey. It began by performing once a week at the Red Barn in Barnehurst, Kent (*see* NIGHTCLUBS AND OTHER VENUES), then through its recordings (including *South*, 1946, Decca F8735) and performances on radio and in clubs the group stimulated the jazz band movement that came to be known as "trad." After the Dixielanders disbanded in 1948 Webb joined his former sideman Humphrey Lyttelton, with whom he performed until 1951 when he ceased full-time playing. He ran several jazz clubs and worked in jazz

Chick Webb and his band at the Apollo Theatre, New York, in the late 1930s: (left to right) Mario Bauzá (trumpet), Beverly Peer (double bass), Bobby Stark (trumpet), Nat Story and Sandy Williams (trombones), Bardu Ali (conductor), Webb (drums), Ella Fitzgerald (voice), George Matthews (trombone), Tommy Fulford (piano), Teddy McRae and Wayman Carver (tenor saxophones), Hilton Jefferson (alto saxophone), Taft Jordan (trumpet), Garvin Bushell (alto saxophone, clarinet, flute), and ? Bobby Johnson (guitar)

promotion and as a booking agent. He again led his own band in 1972–4 and he has continued to perform occasionally.

Oral history material in *GBLnsa.*

BIBLIOGRAPHY

H. Lyttelton: *I Play as I Please: the Memoirs of an Old Etonian Trumpeter* (London, 1954), 116
D. Boulton: *Jazz in Britain* (London, 1958)
J. Godbolt: *A History of Jazz in Britain, 1919–50* (London, Melbourne, Australia, and New York, 1984), 200
D. Fairweather: "Webb, George," in I. Carr, D. Fairweather, and B. Priestley: *Jazz: the Essential Companion* (London, 1987)

DEREK COLLER

Webb, Speed [Lawrence Arthur] (*b* Peru, IN, 18 July 1906). Bandleader and drummer. He began by learning violin and mellophone, but changed to drums. After performing locally in 1923, he helped to form a cooperative band, the Hoosier Melody Lads, in 1925; he later assumed leadership of the band and in 1926 led it in a recording session for Gennett (though the results were not issued). It moved to California (1926), where it was resident at various clubs and appeared in several films (1928–9), the soundtracks of which, however, seem to have been recorded by studio orchestras (*see* FILMS, §I, 2). From 1929 Webb led a number of bands, mostly conducting them but occasionally playing drums and singing; among his sidemen were Roy Eldridge, Teddy Buckner, Vic Dickenson, Teddy Wilson, and Art Tatum. He ceased full-time performing in 1938.

BIBLIOGRAPHY

ChiltonW
D. Schiedt: "Speed Webb," *JM*, no.165 (1968), 2
G. Fernett: *Swing Out: Great Negro Dance Bands* (Midland, MI, 1970), 57
A. McCarthy: *Big Band Jazz* (New York and London, 1974), 122
K. Stratemann: *Negro Bands on Film*, i: *Big Bands, 1928–1950: an Exploratory Filmo-discography* (Lübbecke, Germany, 1981)

EDDIE LAMBERT

Weber, Eberhard (*b* Stuttgart, Germany, 22 Jan 1940). German double bass player, leader, and composer. He was taught by his father to play cello from the age of six, but took up double bass as his main instrument in 1956 and played in school orchestras, dance bands, and local jazz groups. As a participant in the Düsseldorf Amateur Jazz Festival (1961–3) he met Wolfgang Dauner, with whom he played over the next eight years, first in a duo and later in the group Et Cetera. From 1972 Weber used an electric double bass with an extra string at the top, and in 1976 he added another string above that; this greatly increased the potential of the double bass as a solo instrument by extending its range and making its sound more penetrating, and thereafter Weber ceased to perform on cello. After working with Dave Pike (1972), he led the group Spectrum with Volker Kriegel (1973–4). He won international renown with the recording *The Colours of Chloe* (1973), which well represents his playing: Weber has rejected Afro-American influences in favor of an inspirational aesthetic that emphasizes the importance of melody, and compositional techniques, borrowed from the composer Steve Reich, that use contrasting ostinato patterns in different voices. In 1974 he formed the group Colours, which became highly successful; it toured the USA in 1976, 1978, and 1979, and continued performing until 1981. From 1975 he played with the United Jazz and Rock Ensemble and from 1981 with Jan Garbarek; in the early 1980s he wrote film music and gave solo concerts.

SELECTED RECORDINGS

As leader: *The Colours of Chloe* (1973, ECM 1042); *Fluid Rustle* (1979, ECM 1137); *Chorus* (1984, ECM 1288)

As sideman: Baden Powell: *Poema on Guitar* (1967, Saba 15150); S. Grappelli: *Afternoon in Paris* (1971, MPS 15066); V. Kriegel: *Mild Maniac* (1974, MPS 2122020); R. Towner: *Solstice* (1974, ECM 1060); United Jazz and Rock Ensemble: *Live im Schützenhaus* (1977, Mood 28-600); K. Bush: *The Dreaming* (1982, Elec. 64589)

BIBLIOGRAPHY

Feather–Gitler '70s
M. Henkels: "An Interview with Eberhard Weber," *JF* [intl edn], no.40 (1976), 54
T. Schnabel: "Eberhard Weber: Interview," *Cadence*, iii/1–2 (1977), 6
L. Tomkins: "Eberhard Weber," *CI*, xvi (1977–8), no.7, p.6; no.8, p.14
U. J. Messerschmidt: "Einige Anmerkungen zum Werdegang des Jazz-Bassisten Eberhard Weber," *Jf*, no.19 (1987), 9–39 [incl. transcrs. and discography]
M. Tucker: "Eberhard Weber," *JJI*, xl/1 (1987), 12 [incl. discography]

GÜNTHER HUESMANN

Webster, Ben(jamin Francis) (*b* Kansas City, MO, 27 March 1909; *d* Amsterdam, 20 Sept 1973). Tenor saxophonist. He studied at Wilberforce University and worked as a professional jazz pianist before turning to saxophone around 1930. Despite this relatively late start he was a leading figure on the instrument, playing in such important southwestern bands as those of Bennie Moten (1931–3) and Andy Kirk (intermittently during the early 1930s). In 1934 he moved to New York, where he was retained for Fletcher Henderson's band. After playing in many swing groups, including Duke Ellington's orchestra (for two brief periods in 1935–6), Webster was offered a permanent engagement in 1940 with Ellington's band, which until that time had lacked an important soloist on tenor saxophone. Under Ellington's influence Webster's style matured remarkably: his

Eberhard Weber playing at the Roundhouse Arts Centre, London, during the Camden Jazz Week, 1980

striking, slightly unfocused tone, great rhythmic momentum, and distinctive rasping timbre at moments of tension played a key role in many of Ellington's masterpieces of the period, and he soon became established, with Chu Berry and Herschel Evans, as a leading exponent of the style fashioned by Coleman Hawkins. After leaving Ellington in 1943 Webster worked mainly as a freelance and with his own groups, excelling in warm renditions of popular ballads. He worked with Ellington again in 1948–9, toured with Jazz at the Philharmonic in the 1950s, and made numerous recordings as a studio musician, particularly as an accompanist to such singers as Billie Holiday, Ella Fitzgerald, and Carmen McRae. From 1964 he was based in Copenhagen, and played frequently in Europe in clubs and at festivals with local and expatriate American musicians.

For illustrations *see* BANDS, fig.3, and CARTER, BENNY.

SELECTED RECORDINGS

AS LEADER

Honeysuckle Rose/Blue Skies (1944, Savoy 553); *The Consummate Artistry of Ben Webster* (1953, Norg. 1001); *Music for Loving* (1953–4, Norg. 1018), incl. My Funny Valentine, Sophisticated Lady; *Ben Webster Plays Music with Feeling* (1954–5, Norg. 1039), incl. Blue Moon, Chelsea Bridge; with A. Tatum: *Art Tatum–Ben Webster Quartet* (1956, Verve 8220); *Coleman Hawkins Encounters Ben Webster* (1957, Verve 8327); *Ben Webster Meets Oscar Peterson* (1959, Verve 8349); with H. Edison: *Ben Webster and Sweets Edison* (1962, Col. CS8691); *See You at the Fair* (1964, Imp. 65); *Duke's in Bed* (1965, BL 190); with D. Byas: *Ben Webster Meets Don Byas in the Black Forest* (1968, Saba 15159)

AS SIDEMAN

With B. Moten: Toby (1932, Vic. 23384); The Blue Room/Milenberg Joys (1932, Vic. 24381); New Orleans (1932, Vic. 24216)

With D. Ellington: Conga brava (1940, Vic. 26577); Cotton Tail (1940, Vic. 26610); All too Soon (1940, Vic. 27247); Blue Serge (1941, Vic. 27356); Main Stem (1942, Vic. 201556)

With others: F. Henderson: Limehouse Blues (1934, Decca 157); B. Carter: Dream Lullaby (1934, Voc. 2898); T. Wilson: I'll see you in my dreams (1936, Bruns. 7816); F. Henderson: Sing you sinners (1937, Voc. 4125); J. Teagarden: St. James Infirmary/Shine (1940, HRS 2006); The world is waiting for the sunrise/Big Eight Blues (1940, HRS 2007); S. Gaillard: Ra-da-da-da (1942), first issued on B. Webster: *Giants of Jazz: Ben Webster* (1932–62, TL 21); S. Catlett: Sleep (1944, Com. 546); Memories of You (1944, Com. 1515); B. Morton: Conversing in Blue (1945, BN 46); B. Carter: Time out for the blues (1949, Modern 858); J. Witherspoon: *Roots* (1962, Rep. 96057)

BIBLIOGRAPHY

"Ben Webster Plays that Big Tenor," *DB*, xxii/20 (1955), 12
D. Cerulli: "Ben Webster," *DB*, xxv/13 (1958), 16
B. Houghton: "Ben Webster: a Biography and Appreciation," *JJ*, xv/12 (1962), 10
L. Tomkins: "Ben Webster Speaking," *Crescendo*, iii/7 (1965), 22
V. Wilmer: "Warm and Websterish," *JB*, ii/2 (1965), 19
S. Dance: *The World of Duke Ellington* (London and New York, 1970/*R*1981) [colln of previously pubd articles and interviews], 125
R. Stewart: *Jazz Masters of the Thirties* (New York and London, n.d. [?1972]), 120
J. Shaw: "Ben Webster," *JJ*, xxvi/11 (1973), 2
J. Evensmo: *The Tenor Saxophone of Ben Webster, 1931–1943* (n.p. [Oslo], n.d. [?1978]) [discography]
G. Matzorkis and J. Chilton: "Ben Webster," *Giants of Jazz: Ben Webster* (TL 21, 1981) [liner notes]
Y. Delmarche and I. Fresart: *A Discography of Ben Webster, 1931–1973* (n.p. [Surhout, Belgium], n.d. [1983])
L. Tomkins: "The Classic Interview: Ben Webster," *CI*, xxiv/9 (1987), 16

J. BRADFORD ROBINSON

Webster, Freddie (*b* Cleveland, 1916; *d* Chicago, 1 April 1947). Trumpeter. After leading his own band as a teenager and playing with Earl Hines and Erskine Tate (both 1938), he moved to New York, where he spent short periods with various orchestras. He played with Benny Carter (?1939–1940, 1943), Eddie Durham (1940), Lucky Millinder (1941–2, 1944), Jimmie Lunceford (1942–3), Cab Calloway (spring 1945), John Kirby's sextet (late 1945), Dizzy Gillespie's big band (1946), and Sonny Stitt (1947). Very few of his solos were recorded; he may be heard at his best on *I fell for you* (1945) by "Miss Rhapsody" (Viola Wells) and also plays outstandingly on Sarah Vaughan's *You're not the kind* (1946). (It is unaccountable that he is best known for his playing on Vaughan's *If you could see me now* (1946) for he can be heard on only eight bars of the song.) Webster was a harmonically adventurous trumpeter, and an early influence on Miles Davis. He has become something of a legendary figure. Gillespie said of him: "Freddie Webster probably had the best sound on a trumpet since it was invented."

SELECTED RECORDINGS

As sideman with L. Millinder: on *Lucky Millinder, 1941–3* (1941–3, Alamac 2425), Sweet Georgia Brown (1941); Savoy (1942, Decca 18353); Hurry Hurry (1944, Decca 18609)

As sideman with others: F. Socolow: The Man I Love/Reverse the Changes (1945, Duke 112); Miss Rhapsody: He may be your man/I fell for you (1945, Savoy 5532); S. Vaughan: If you could see me now/You're not the kind (1946, Musi. 380)

BIBLIOGRAPHY

ChiltonW
G. Hoefer: "The Hot Box: Freddy [*sic*] Webster," *DB*, xxviii/25 (1961), 48; xxix/1 (1962), 42 [incl. discography]
H. Pekar: "Freddie Webster," *JM*, viii/8 (1962), 12
I. Gitler: *Jazz Masters of the Forties* (New York, 1966/*R*1983 with discography), 89
D. Gillespie and A. Fraser: *To be, or not . . . to Bop: Memoirs* (Garden City, NY, 1979), 227

SCOTT YANOW

Webster, Paul (Francis) (*b* Kansas City, MO, 24 Aug 1909; *d* New York, 6 May 1966). Trumpeter. He played on a part-time basis before becoming a professional musician around 1927. He worked with George E. Lee, Bennie Moten (1927–8), the tuba and double bass player Jap Allen (*c*1930), Jimmie Lunceford (1931), Tommy Douglas (*c*1931), and the singer Eli Rice (1933–4). After he re-joined Lunceford (1935; for illustration *see* LUNCEFORD, JIMMIE) he began to specialize in playing in the high register; some of his best work was done with Lunceford and his playing is well represented on *For Dancers Only* (1937, Decca 1340). In 1944 he left Lunceford for Cab Calloway, with whom he played at intervals into the 1950s. Webster also worked under other bandleaders, including Charlie Barnet (1946–7, 1952–3), Sy Oliver (1947), Eddie Wilcox, and Count Basie (1950). He ceased full-time playing in 1953, but continued to perform into the 1960s.

BIBLIOGRAPHY

ChiltonW
J. Simmen: "Carnet de notes, 2: un LP où l'on entend beaucoup Paul Webster," *BHcF*, no.159 (1966), 3

EDDIE LAMBERT

Weersma, Melle (*b* Harlingen, Netherlands, 22 Jan 1908). Dutch bandleader and arranger. He studied piano and played with the Electorians (1926–8), under the bandleader Juan Llossas (in Germany, 1931–2), and with the drummer Bobby 't Sas (1933). In 1934 he formed a big band, the Red, White and Blue Aces, that played in a musically adventurous style and achieved little success; the following year he moved to London in February to write arrangements for Jack Hylton and to Chicago in October to write arrangements for Benny Goodman and the conductor André Kostelanetz. He moved to Argentina in 1938, then returned to the Netherlands after ending his career as a musician. Weersma is the composer of the well-known song *Penny Serenade*, recorded by, among others, Nat Gonella (1938). Weersma can be heard leading a trio and his big band on the album *Swing van Nederlandsch Fabrikaat* (1934–43, Panachord 2009).

WIM VAN EYLE

Wehner, Heinz (*b* Menden, Germany, *c*1910; *d* *c*1944). German bandleader, violinist, trumpeter, and singer. He studied at the Hanover Conservatory at the age of 12; after moving to Berlin around 1930, he formed a trio and then led a sextet. At the beginning of 1935 he formed a dance band which played in a style similar to that of the Casa Loma Orchestra; the players varied in number from 10 to 15 and included Willy Berking. The band, which earned a reputation for the refinement of its playing, made numerous recordings for Telefunken from 1935 to 1942; *White Jazz* (1935, M6118) and *Bugle Call Rag* (1936, A2007) are particularly fine recorded examples of German swing. Wehner was killed in action during World War II.

GÜNTHER HUESMANN

Wein, George (Theodore) (*b* Boston, 3 Oct 1925). Pianist, singer, and impresario. He studied classical piano from the age of seven with Margaret Chaloff (the mother of Serge Chaloff) and also took lessons from Sam Saxe (1935–45) and Teddy Wilson. As a youth he formed a 13-piece dance band, with which he played until 1941, and he appeared at nightclubs in Boston while still in his teens. He played with Max Kaminsky (1946), Edmond Hall (1949), and Wild Bill Davison (1949), and in 1950 graduated from Boston University, organized groups for the Savoy in Boston, and opened his own club, Storyville, for which he engaged well-known dixieland and swing players; the following year he established a record company of the same name (*see* STORYVILLE (ii)). Wein also played with Bobby Hackett (1950–54), recorded with Davison (at Storyville, 1951) and Ruby Braff (1954–69), and worked with Jo Jones (recording at Storyville around 1953), Pee Wee Russell, Vic Dickenson (recording around 1953 and around 1956), and Jimmy McPartland. He opened a second club, Mahogany Hall, which specialized in dixieland, and in 1953 he recorded with the Mahogany All Stars, which included Dickenson and Doc Cheatham.

Wein is best known as the founder of the Newport Jazz Festival, which he organized in February 1954 with financial support from Louis and Elaine Lorillard. At the same time he continued to work as a performer: from the late 1950s he toured internationally as the leader of the Newport Festival All-Stars, which included Dickenson, Russell, Braff, Buck Clayton, Bud Freeman, Red Norvo, and Barney Kessel, and in 1969 he recorded in Paris with Stephane Grappelli and Joe Venuti. He founded the Boston Globe Jazz & Heritage Festival in 1966, and by the 1970s he was involved in the organization of several international festivals, such as the Grande Parade du Jazz in Nice (from 1974), and had formed a company, Festival Productions Inc. in New York, to manage this area of his activities. He also formed the New York Jazz Repertory Company (1974) and continued to play with the Newport Jazz Festival All-Stars (from 1982 its other members were Scott Hamilton, Oliver Jackson, Harold Ashby, Slam Stewart, Norris Turney, and Warren Vaché); with the group he performed widely in the USA and in 1986 appeared at the Madarao festival in Japan and toured Europe. In addition to his work as a performer and promoter Wein has taught jazz history at Boston University (from 1954).

See also FESTIVALS and NIGHTCLUBS AND OTHER VENUES.

SELECTED RECORDINGS

As leader: *George Wein and the Newport All-Stars* (1962, Imp. 31); *The Newport Jazz Festival All-Stars* (1984, Conc. 260)

As sideman with S. Grappelli and J. Venuti: *Venupelli Blues* (1969, BYG 529122)

BIBLIOGRAPHY

FeatherE; *Feather '60s*; *Feather–Gitler '70s*

N. Hentoff: "Self Promotion: it Pays," *DB*, xxiv/11 (1957), 15

J. H. Klee: "Jazz from J to Z," *MR*, iii/9 (1976), 5

S. Traill: "From Newport to Nice to New Orleans," *JJI*, xxxi/7 (1978), 22

L. Tomkins: "George Wein," *CI*, xvii (1979), no.11, p.6; no.12, p.16

M. Brown: "The Man who Keeps Jazz in our Blood," *Sunday Times* (6 July 1986), 44

JAMES M. DORAN

Weintraub Syncopators. German band. It was founded as an amateur group in Berlin in 1924 by the pianist Stefan Weintraub (*b* Breslau, Germany (now Wrocław, Poland), 14 Aug 1897; *d* Sydney, 10 Sept 1981) and the clarinetist and alto saxophonist Horst Graff. The pianist and arranger Friedrich Holländer (*b* London, 18 Oct 1896; *d* Munich, Jan 1976) assumed the leadership in 1927 when Weintraub began to play drums. By 1928 the band was playing a more extreme style of hot jazz than any band in Germany and was highly successful. In that year it made the first of many recordings of hot dance music (*Up and at 'em/Jackass Blues*, Odeon O2353), and in 1930 appeared in the film *Der blaue Engel* with Marlene Dietrich and recorded with her. The band made concert tours and worked in radio and the theater in Germany until 1933, then toured Italy (1934), Scandinavia, the USSR (1935), Japan (1936–7), China (1937), and Australia (1937), where it disbanded around 1938. (H. J. P. Bergmeier: *The Weintraub Story Incorporating the Ady Rosner Story* (Menden, Germany, 1982) [incl. discography])

For illustration *see* SAXOPHONE, fig. 2.

GÜNTHER HUESMANN

Weiss, Klaus (*b* Gevelsberg, Germany, 17 Feb 1942). German drummer. He studied drumming from the age of ten; although largely self-taught he took lessons briefly from Kurt Edelhagen at the Musikhochschule, Cologne (1959–60). As a member of the Jazzopaters (from 1958) he accompanied Nelson Williams and the singer Inez Cavanaugh, and later worked with Klaus Doldinger (1962–5). In Paris he played with a group that included Johnny Griffin and Kenny Drew and also Bud Powell (1963), then formed a trio in 1966 and belonged to Erwin Lehn's big band (1967–8). After taking up residence near Munich in 1968 he played with Friedrich Gulda (1969–70) and performed and recorded as the leader of various groups, including a quartet, which recorded the album *Mythologie* (1971, BASF 2021111), and a group consisting of members of the Thad Jones–Mel Lewis Orchestra, which recorded the album *The Git Go* (1974, BASF 20224066). He also worked as a sideman with such visiting American musicians as Eddie "Lockjaw" Davis, Mal Waldron, Clifford Jordan, Don Byas, and Booker Ervin. Weiss has been influenced by, among others, Sid Catlett, Buddy Rich, Philly Joe Jones, and Art Blakey.

WOLFRAM KNAUER

Weiss, René (*b* Geneva, 1900; *d* Geneva, 28 Aug 1984). Swiss trombonist. After studying music, he played with the Illarez Orchestra (1922) and the bandleader and pianist Jean Yatov (1924). He then moved to Berlin, where he played with the violinist Marek Weber, Béla Dajos's band, Ben Berlin (1928), the double bass player Teddy Sinclair (1929), and Lud Gluskin (1930), to whom he returned in 1932 to make recordings. In France he played with Ray Ventura (1931–6), Guy Paquinet (1934–5), the orchestra of the Paramount theater (1937–8), and Fred Adison's band (1938). In 1939 Weiss left France for

Switzerland, where he played with Teddy Stauffer and led a group that made recordings in 1942–3 (among them *Boogie woogie* (1943, Col. ZZ1086), which well represents his style of playing).

MICHEL LAPLACE

Weiss, Sammy [Samuel] (*b* New York, 1 Sept 1910; *d* Encino, CA, 18 Dec 1977). Drummer and bandleader. From 1931 he performed and recorded in New York with the alto saxophonist and singer Gene Kardos (1931–8), Benny Goodman (1934), Tommy Dorsey (1935–6), Louis Prima (1935, 1937), and Artie Shaw (1936). He also worked with Paul Whiteman and made numerous recordings as a freelance with such musicians as Adrian Rollini (1935), Wingy Manone (1935, 1936), Miff Mole (1937), Louis Armstrong and Lil Armstrong (both 1938), and the pianist and singer Erskine Butterfield (1940, 1942), and in a trio with Johnny Guarnieri (1944). After moving to California (1945) he formed his own orchestra, which became very successful; he continued to work as a leader through the 1960s. Weiss's playing may be heard on Butterfield's *Tuxedo Junction* (1940, Decca 3042). Although he was principally a drummer he also played vibraphone.

based on *ChiltonW*

Weiss, Sid (*b* Schenectady, NY, 30 April 1914). Double bass player. He played violin, clarinet, and tuba before changing to double bass in his teens. He began performing in New York in 1931 and worked with Louis Prima (1934), Wingy Manone (1935–6), Charlie Barnet (1936), Artie Shaw (1936, 1937–9), Joe Marsala (1939), and Tommy Dorsey (1940–41; for illustration *see* DORSEY, TOMMY). From 1941 to 1945 he recorded frequently with Benny Goodman. After an overseas tour with Hal McIntyre (1945) he played mainly in studios, recording with such musicians as Muggsy Spanier, Pee Wee Russell, and Cozy Cole (all 1944), Duke Ellington and Bud Freeman (both 1945), and Wild Bill Davison (1947); he also played with Eddie Condon and Joe Bushkin. In 1954 he moved to Los Angeles, where he ceased full-time performing, though he continued to work occasionally as a freelance. His playing may be heard to advantage with Adrian Rollini and his Tap Room Gang on *Nagasaki* (1935, Vic. 25085).

based on *ChiltonW*

Wellins, Bobby [Robert Coull] (*b* Glasgow, 24 Jan 1936). Scottish tenor saxophonist. He was taught alto saxophone and harmony by his father and later studied keyboard harmony. In the mid-1950s he moved to London, where he worked as a tenor saxophonist with Buddy Featherstonhaugh (recording in 1956), Tony Crombie (recording in 1960–61), and Vic Lewis. In 1961 he gave a memorable concert performance of his composition *Culloden Moor*. As a member of Stan Tracey's quartet in the mid-1960s he took a prominent role on Tracey's successful recording *Under Milk Wood* (1965, Col. 33SX1774). Wellins was inactive for some years, but in 1977 he began to perform and record again as the leader of small groups; he also worked as a teacher. Wellins's playing is notable for its combination of passion and intelligence, which distinguishes, in particular, the albums *Jubilation* (1978, Vortex 1) and *Dreams are Free* (1979, Vortex 2); both these recordings demonstrate the reconciliation of keen spontaneity with a structured approach to collective improvisation, in the finest tradition of such music.

BIBLIOGRAPHY

Feather '60s

M. James: Review of *Jubilation* (1978) and *Dreams are Free* (1979), *JF* [intl edn], no.76 (1982), 54

MICHAEL JAMES

Wells, Dicky [Dickie; William] (*b* Centerville, TN, 10 June 1907; *d* New York, 12 Nov 1985). Trombonist. He grew up in Louisville, Kentucky, where he played in local bands as a teenager and encountered the playing of Jimmy Harrison. After moving to New York in 1926 he began working in better-known black bands, including those of Benny Carter (1932–3), Fletcher Henderson (from 1933), where he first made a name for himself, and Teddy Hill (1934–7). In 1938 he joined Count Basie's highly influential big band, where he formed a famous trombone team with Benny Morton. He remained in Basie's band, with minor interruptions, until 1950 (for illustration *see* FILMS, fig.3), after which time he worked briefly with other leaders until settling in New York as a freelance musician. He toured Europe with Buck Clayton in 1959 and 1961, and during the 1960s performed for brief periods with Ray Charles and the blues singer and guitarist B. B. King. In 1967 he took a day job, but he continued to play, and for several years worked with the group of veteran musicians known as the Countsmen.

Wells was one of a group of trombonists in the 1930s who developed further the legato style of Jimmy Harrison. He played in a rich, flamboyant style filled with portamentos, smears, and growls. He has many excellent brief solos on Basie's record-

Dicky Wells, 1935

ings, but his best-known performances are as the leader of a group recorded in Paris in 1937, some of which include Django Reinhardt. He should not be confused with Dickie Wells, owner of the Ebony and Dickie Wells's Shim Sham Club, New York.

SELECTED RECORDINGS

As leader: Lady Be Good/Dicky Wells Blues (1937, Swing 10)

As sideman: F. Henderson: King Porter's Stomp (1933, Voc. 2527); C. Basie: Texas Shuffle (1938, Decca 2030); Dickie's Dream (1939, Voc. 5118); E. Berry: *Beauty and the Blues* (1959, Col. 33SX1246)

BIBLIOGRAPHY

A. Hodeir: *Hommes et problèmes du jazz, suivi de La religion du jazz* (Paris, 1954; Eng. trans., rev. Hodeir, as *Jazz: its Evolution and Essence*, New York, 1956/*R*1975)

D. Wells and S. Dance: *The Night People: Reminiscences of a Jazzman* (Boston and London, 1971)

G. Colombe: "How do they Age so Well? Lawrence, Dicky and Vic," *JJ*, xxix/8 (1976), 4

L. Jeske: "The Return of Dicky Wells," *JJI*, xxxi/8 (1978), 6

S. Dance: *The World of Count Basie* (New York and London, 1980) [colln of previously pubd interviews], 88

J. Evensmo: *The Flute of Wayman Carver, the Trombone of Dickie Wells, 1927–1942, the Tenor Saxophone of Illinois Jacquet* (n.p. [Oslo], n.d. [?1983]) [discography]

JAMES LINCOLN COLLIER

Wells, Henry (James) (*b* Dallas, 1906). Trombonist and singer. He studied music at Fisk University and Cincinnati Conservatory and began playing professionally in 1926. He worked with Jimmie Lunceford (1929–35), with whom he made several recordings (1933–4, including *Jazznocracy*, 1934, Vic. 24522), Claude Hopkins (1932), and Cab Calloway. His association with Andy Kirk (1936–9, 1940–41, 1946) was interrupted by a period in which he led his own big band and worked with Gene Krupa and Teddy Hill, and another when he served in the army. He frequently recorded with Kirk and sang as his principal soloist (from 1940). He worked with Rex Stewart (1946) and Sy Oliver (1946–8) and in the 1960s he performed in California. (A. McCarthy: *Big Band Jazz*, New York and London, 1974)

based on *ChiltonW*

Wells, Johnny (*b* Kentucky, *c*1905; *d* New York, 25 Nov 1965). Drummer. After performing as a singer, comedian, and dancer at the Apex Club, Chicago, he joined Jimmie Noone's band which was resident there at that time; he made several recordings with the group, including *I know that you know* (1928, Voc. 1184). He continued working with Noone into the 1930s and then moved to New York, where he performed and recorded with Joe Sullivan (1939–40).

based on *ChiltonW*

Wellstood, Dick [Richard McQueen] (*b* Greenwich, CT, 25 Nov 1927; *d* Palo Alto, CA, 24 July 1987). Pianist. He learned to play boogie-woogie and stride during the mid-1940s. From 1946 to 1950 he performed in amateur and professional dixieland groups with Bob Wilber, and during the same period also worked under the leadership of Sidney Bechet, with whom he recorded in 1947 and 1949. When Jimmy Archey left Wilber, Wellstood joined the former's group (1950), which later toured Europe (1952). From 1953, while studying law, he played intermittently with Roy Eldridge and Conrad Janis's Tailgate Five; a brilliant scholar, fluent in Latin, he soon qualified as a lawyer, but did not practice until the mid-1980s. Until the mid-1960s he played in New York as a soloist or as an accompanist to a large number of swing and dixieland musicians, including Henry "Red" Allen, Ben Webster, Coleman Hawkins, Wild Bill Davison, Vic Dickenson, and Buster Bailey. He then joined Gene Krupa's quartet, with which he toured South America (1965) and Israel (1966). From 1966 to 1968 he performed in Brielle, New Jersey, but opportunities for band work diminished as rock became increasingly popular; in the 1970s he played with Paul Hoffman's society orchestra, but concentrated principally on developing a career as a solo pianist. He recorded many albums demonstrating his strengths, stride and ragtime, though his command of harmony allowed him to include in his repertory bop tunes, such as *Giant Steps*, that involve difficult chord progressions.

SELECTED RECORDINGS

As unaccompanied soloist: *Alone* (1970–71, Jlgy JCE73); *From Ragtime On* (1971, Chi. 109); *At the Cookery* (1975, Chi. 139); on *Piano Giants* (1980, Swingtime 8202), Giant Steps

As leader: *From Dixie to Swing* (*c*1972, Classic Editions 10); with P. Ind: *Some Hefty Cats!* (1977, Hefty Jazz 100)

As sideman: S. Bechet: Polka Dot Stomp/Kansas City Man Blues (1947, Col. 38319); R. Eldridge: *Swing Goes Dixie* (1956, Verve 1010); J. Venuti and Z. Sims: *Joe and Zoot* (1974, Chi. 128)

BIBLIOGRAPHY

D. Morgenstern: "The Life-flight of a Surrealistic Bent Eagle," *DB*, xxxiv/7 (1967), 22

M. Jones: "Wellstood: Barroom Blues," *MM*, xlix (2 Feb 1974), 51

J. Simmen: "Crystal Clear," *Coda*, no.146 (1976), 25

L. Tomkins: "Dick Wellstood," *CI*, xvi (1978), no.6, p.10; no.8, p.6

W. Balliett: "Easier than Working," *Jelly Roll, Jabbo and Fats* (New York, and Oxford, England, 1983) [colln of previously pubd articles], 97

BARRY KERNFELD

Welsh, Alex (*b* Edinburgh, 9 July 1929; *d* London, 25 June 1982). Scottish trumpeter, singer, and bandleader. He first played cornet, and formed his own group after moving to London in 1954. Within a year it had played several times at the Royal Festival Hall, made its first broadcasts and recordings, and established a reputation for its dedication to the dixieland style and the excellence of its playing. From 1955 it made several tours overseas, and in 1968 it played to great acclaim at the Newport Jazz Festival. The band accompanied many American soloists, including Wild Bill Davison and Earl Hines. In 1957 Welsh was invited to join Jack Teagarden, but did not accept. Although Welsh's ensemble was noted for its few personnel changes, by 1966 the trombonist Roy Crimmins had been replaced by Roy Williams and the clarinetist Archie Semple by John Barnes and Al Gay, who between them played seven different reed instruments. This gave the band a greater tonal variety and, although it retained its early ideals, it also began to approach other forms of jazz and became highly regarded for its versatility. Welsh continued to work as a leader until shortly before his death.

SELECTED RECORDINGS

The Melrose Folio (1958, Nixa 516); *Echoes of Chicago* (1962, Col. 33SX1429); *Strike One* (1966, Strike One 102); *Vintage '69* (1969, Col. SCX6333)

BIBLIOGRAPHY

Feather '60s; *Feather–Gitler '70s*

G. A. L. Smith: "Out of the Wilderness: the Alex Welsh Band," *JM*, vii/11 (1962), 14

R. Cotterell, ed.: *Jazz Now: the Jazz Centre Society Guide* (London, 1976), 179

Obituary, R. Crimmins, D. Fairweather, H. Gold, and M. Jones, *JJI*, xxxv/8 (1982), 24

D. Fairweather: "Welsh, Alex," in I. Carr, D. Fairweather, and B. Priestley: *Jazz: the Essential Companion* (London, 1987)

CLARRIE HENLEY

Werner, Lasse [Lars (Olof)] (*b* Malmö, Sweden, 22 May 1934). Swedish pianist, leader, and writer. He was influenced by bop musicians early in his career and in the 1950s made recordings in a trio. In the 1960s he worked regularly with the alto saxophonist Christer Boustedt and others in the group Lasse Werner och Hans Vänner, which gave performances that combined bop, free jazz, and improvised, burlesque, theatrical episodes. He also took part in the Swedish production of Jack Gelber's play *The Connection* in Stockholm in 1963 and has been an influential writer on jazz. Among his recordings are *Därför dricker jag* (That's why I'm drinking; 1967, Dra. 20) and *Helf me* (1975, Odeon 06235239).

Oral history material in *SSsv.*

BIBLIOGRAPHY

L. Kleberg: "Man saltar i pianot bara en gång" [You must salt the piano only once], *Orkester journalen,* xxxii/7–8 (1964), 18

L. Westin: "Lars Werner," *Orkester journalen,* xlii/6 (1974), 6

E. Kjellberg: *Svensk jazzhistoria: en översikt* [Swedish jazz history: an overview] (Stockholm, 1985)

ERIK KJELLBERG

Wess, Frank (Wellington) (*b* Kansas City, MO, 4 Jan 1922). Flutist and tenor and alto saxophonist. He grew up in Sapulpa, Oklahoma, and Washington. He first learned to play alto saxophone but, under the strong influence of Lester Young, changed to the tenor instrument. He worked with Blanche Calloway and during World War II served in army bands, then played briefly with Billy Eckstine (for illustration *see* ECKSTINE, BILLY), Eddie Heywood, Lucky Millinder, and the saxophonist Bull Moose Jackson before returning to Washington. He took up flute in 1949. From June 1953 to August 1964 he was a member of Count Basie's big band, in which, at first, he played tenor saxophone; his smooth, light tone provided a contrast to the rougher and larger sound produced by Frank Foster. Later, at Basie's request, he performed on alto saxophone (1957–64). Most importantly, Wess established the flute as an appropriate instrument for jazz; his swinging improvisations were played with a pleasing classical timbre, and he avoided many of the special effects that later became frequent in jazz flute playing. From 1964 he has recorded advertising jingles, performed in pit bands for Broadway shows, and played in studio bands for television. He became a member of the NEW YORK JAZZ QUARTET in 1974, worked with Dameronia from around 1981 to 1985, and in 1985 played in Woody Herman's band. With Foster he has performed and recorded in the 1980s as the leader of a quintet.

SELECTED RECORDINGS

As leader: *Frank Wess Quintet* (1954, Com. 20031); *North, South, East . . . Wess* (1956, Savoy 12072); *Frank Wess Quartet* (1960, Mdsv. 8); *Yo Ho!* (1963, Prst. 7231); with F. Foster: *Two for the Blues* (1983, Pablo 2310905), *Frankly Speaking* (1984, Conc. 276)

As sideman with C. Basie: Basie Goes Wess (1953, Clef 89112); *April in Paris* (1955–6, Verve 8012), incl. The Midgets; *Basie* (1957, Roul. 52003), incl. Fantail; *Chairman of the Board* (1959, Roul. 52032)

As sideman with the New York Jazz Quartet: *The New York Jazz Quartet in Concert in Japan* (1975, Salvation 703); *Oasis* (1981, Enja 3083)

BIBLIOGRAPHY

L. Feather: "Who's Who in the Basie Band," *MM,* xxx (27 March 1954), 9

S. Dance: "Wess Points," *DB,* xxxii/12 (1965), 28

M. Roman: "Frank Wess: the Modest Master," *JT* (Dec 1983), 7

BARRY KERNFELD

West, Cedric (Herbert) (*b* Rangoon, Burma, 9 Dec 1918). British guitarist and trombonist. He started playing guitar in the late 1930s with a college band in Burma. Following the Japanese invasion of Burma in 1942 he was evacuated to India and played guitar and, later, trombone with Teddy Weatherford's band at the Grand Hotel, Calcutta (1942–5). After Weatherford's death he was a featured soloist with Reuben Solomon's Jive Boys, with whom he also made some recordings (including *My Gal Sal,* 1942, Col. FB40231), but later in 1945 he returned to Burma with his own band. He went to England in 1947, led several bands, and played and recorded with many others. From 1968 until his retirement in 1984 he concentrated on radio and television work.

BIBLIOGRAPHY

K. P. Darke: "Teddy Weatherford's Indian Recording Sessions 1941–45," *Matrix,* nos.107–8 (1975), 3

P. Darke and R. Gulliver: "Teddy Weatherford," *Sv,* no.65 (1976), 175

——: "Roy Butler's Story," *Sv,* no.71 (1977), 178

P. Darke and B. White: "Cedric West: the Jazzman from Burma," *Sv,* no.109 (1983), 20; addns and corrns to discography in *Sv,* no.115 (1984), 6

PETER DARKE

West, Doc [Hal, Harold] (*b* Wolford, ND, 12 Aug 1915; *d* Cleveland, 4 May 1951). Drummer. He first played piano and cello, then changed to drums. He worked with Tiny Parham (1932), in Chicago with Erskine Tate and Roy Eldridge, and deputized for Chick Webb during the Webb orchestra's tour of Texas (1938). He worked intermittently with Hot Lips Page (1939–41), played in jam sessions at Minton's Playhouse, New York, and in the early 1940s deputized for Jo Jones in Count Basie's orchestra. By the middle of the decade he was in demand for recordings with small groups, playing in both swing and bop styles; he recorded with Sammy Price and Una Mae Carlisle (both 1941), Roy Eldridge (1943), Slam Stewart and Joe Turner (ii) (both 1945), and Leo Watson and Wardell Gray (both 1946). He is chiefly remembered for his playing on a session led by Tiny Grimes, which included Charlie Parker (1944), and on several excellent recordings with Erroll Garner's trio (1945, 1950). He died while on tour with Roy Eldridge.

For illustration *see* JAZZ (i), fig.5.

SELECTED RECORDINGS

As sideman: B. Holiday: Ghost of Yesterday/Falling in Love Again (1940, Voc./OK 5609); T. Grimes: Tiny's Tempo/I'll Always Love you Just the Same (1944, Savoy 526); Romance without Finance/Red Cross (1944, Savoy 532); D. Byas: Three o'Clock in the Morning/One o'Clock Jump (1945, Super Disc 1006); E. Garner: Tippin' out with Erroll/Lazy River (1950, Roost 614)

BIBLIOGRAPHY

ChiltonW; FeatherE

SCOTT YANOW

Westbrook, Mike [Michael John David] (*b* High Wycombe, England, 21 March 1936). English composer, pianist, and bandleader. After working in an accountant's office and studying painting he took up music professionally; he was largely self-taught and has an empirical approach to composition. Around 1960 he organized a jazz workshop in Plymouth, where he wrote for a small ensemble that included John Surman, then in 1962 he moved to London. From that time he has written pieces for a number of his own ensembles: the Mike Westbrook Band (1962–72), the Mike Westbrook Concert Band (1967–71), the multi-media group Cosmic Circus (1970–72), the jazz-rock band Solid Gold Cadillac (1971–4), the Mike Westbrook Brass Band (established in 1973 to perform in the theater and on television), the Mike Westbrook Orchestra (formed in 1974), A Little Westbrook Music (formed in 1982), and the Dance Band (formed in 1986).

Westbrook is particularly adept at providing jazz improvisers with stimulating themes and settings and then enfolding their contributions within a wider context. He draws his inspiration from a wide variety of styles, and his work (often written in collaboration with his wife, the singer Kate Westbrook) consists of highly personalized statements. Like Duke Ellington before him, he generally writes for specific musicians in his bands, notably the trumpeter Phil Minton and the saxophonist Chris Biscoe; this results in highly colored music that is subject to few of the clichés of jazz composition. Among his best-known pieces are *Marching Song* (1969), *Metropolis* (1971), *Citadel/Room 315* (1975), and *The Cortege* (1982). Westbrook has worked with other groups and also with a number of theater companies, notably the National Theatre (1971), the Foco Novo Theatre Company (1985), and the Extemporary Dance Theatre (1986). In addition he has toured widely, appeared at numerous festivals, and recorded extensively. He founded the record company Cadillac with John Jack in 1973 (*see* CADILLAC (ii)), and from 1985 he has issued a quarterly newsletter, the *Smith's Academy Informer*. He was made an OBE in 1988.

Oral history material in *GBLnsa*.

RECORDED COMPOSITIONS

(selective list)

Marching Song (1969, Deram 1047–8); *Metropolis* (1971, RCA SF8396); *Citadel/Room 315* (1975, RCA SF8433); *Mama Chicago* (1979, RCA PL25252); *The Cortege* (1982, Original 309); *On Duke's Birthday* (1984, HA 2012)

BIBLIOGRAPHY

Feather '60s; *Feather–Gitler '70s*
M. Shera: "Mike Westbrook and his Orchestra," *JJ*, xix/1 (1966), 10
L. Tomkins: "Mike Westbrook," *CI*, viii/1 (1969), 8
I. Carr: *Music Outside: Contemporary Jazz in Britain* (London, 1973), 15
K. Dallas: "Westbrook: Discipline of the 'Citadel'," *MM*, l (19 July 1975), 42
R. Cotterrell: "Mike Westbrook: Taking Music to the People," *JF* [intl edn], no.39 (1976), 38
B. Case: "Warehouse of the Western World," *MM*, liv (17 Feb 1979), 24
K. Dallas: "Jazz: Present Use of the Past Tense," *MM*, lvi (13 June 1981), 28
G. Lock: "Sweet Thunder," *The Wire*, no.14 (1985), 10

CHARLES FOX/DIGBY FAIRWEATHER

West Coast jazz. A style of jazz, developed by musicians based in Los Angeles in the 1950s and related aesthetically to the COOL JAZZ movement. Much of it was played by professional studio musicians as an avocation. Their public performances centered on the Lighthouse club at Hermosa Beach and the Haig in Los Angeles, but a good deal of their work took place in studios, their recordings displaying technical sophistication, exploration of resources new to jazz, and high executive skill. Prominent among this group, both as performers and composers, were Shorty Rogers, Art Pepper, John Graas, Bud Shank, Shelly Manne, Herb Geller, Jimmy Giuffre, Carl Perkins, and Lou Levy. Although some exceptionally spirited big-band music was produced, particularly by Rogers, the musicians worked mainly in small, experimental ensembles, emphasizing fairly elaborate, often contrapuntal, scores, yet leaving much scope for improvisation, which they sought to link closely to the written sections of their works. Their music was initially influenced by Miles Davis's recordings of 1949–50, later issued collectively as *The Birth of the Cool*, as is shown by such early West Coast performances as Rogers's *Didi* (1951, Cap. 15765) and *Westwood Walk* by Gerry Mulligan (on the album *Gerry Mulligan and his Ten-tette*, 1953, Cap. H439), but soon discovered directions of its own. Thus the West Coast players explored the jazz potential of serial technique, as in Rogers's *Three on a Row*, recorded on the album *The Three* (1954, Cont. 2516) by Manne, Rogers, and Giuffre; such works as *Abstract no.1* (also on *The Three*), and *Free Form*, on the album *The Chico Hamilton Quintet with Buddy Collette* (1955, PJ 1209), initiated the post-harmonic, collectively improvised music later associated with Ornette Coleman.

See also JAZZ (i), §V, 6.

BIBLIOGRAPHY

W. Claxton: *Jazz West Coast: a Portfolio of Photographs* (Hollywood, CA, 1954)
N. Shapiro and N. Hentoff, eds.: *Hear me Talkin' to ya: the Story of Jazz by the Men who Made it* (New York and London, 1955/*R*1966)
R. Gordon: *Jazz West Coast: the Los Angeles Jazz Scene of the 1950s* (London and New York, 1986)

MAX HARRISON/R

West End. Nightclub in New York; *see* NIGHTCLUBS AND OTHER VENUES.

Western swing. A style of music originating largely in the fiddle and guitar bands in Texas during the 1920s. Such groups regularly played traditional frontier dance music at country dances, but they were more innovative than country bands in the Southeast; they were eclectic in their repertory and improvised like jazz bands, from whom they borrowed freely. An early group, the Light Crust Doughboys of Fort Worth, was of the fiddle and guitar tradition but also performed current popular songs, blues, and jazz. After 1934 two former members popularized western swing. The singer Milton Brown led one of the most popular country string bands in the Southwest, the Musical Brownies of Fort Worth. Bob Wills formed the Texas Playboys, which performed in Tulsa (1934–42) and later in California and elsewhere; he was a traditional country fiddler, but receptive to innovative and jazz-oriented musicians. The Playboys began as a fiddle-dominated string band, but soon added drums, piano, electric guitars, and wind instruments, and became very similar to the big popular swing bands of the 1930s.

The term "western swing" was not used widely until after World War II, when the bandleader Spade Cooley billed himself as the "King of Western Swing." Similar bands led by a former singer with Cooley's band, Tex Williams (*b* 1917), Hank Penny (*b* 1918), and to a lesser extent Ray Whitley (*b* 1901) made California the new center of the style in the 1940s. The western swing bands there, and elsewhere in the USA, influenced the mainstream of country music in the use of drums, walking bass patterns, and electric instruments. Western swing experienced a revival in the early 1970s, largely through the performances of such musicians as Merle Haggard, Red Steagall and his Coleman County Cowboys, and, above all, the bands Asleep at the Wheel (led by the guitarist Ray Benson) and Alvin Crow and the Pleasant Valley Boys.

BIBLIOGRAPHY

B. C. Malone: *Country Music, U.S.A.: a Fifty-year History* (Austin, TX, 1968, rev. and enlarged 2/1985 as *Country Music, U.S.A.*)
J. Zolten: "Western Swingtime Music: a Cool Breeze in the American Desert," *Sing Out!*, xxiii/2 (1972), 2
C. Wolfe: "Making Western Swing: an Interview with Johnnie Lee Wills," *Old Time Music*, no.15 (1974–5), 11
C. R. Townsend: *San Antonio Rose: the Life and Music of Bob Wills* (Urbana, IL, Chicago, and London, 1976)
G. Hunkel: *Western Swing & Country Jazz: eine Einführung mit Kurzporträts über Bob Wills und Milton Brown* (Menden, Germany, 1983)

BILL C. MALONE

Weston, Randy [Randolph E.] (*b* New York, 6 April 1926). Pianist and composer. In the late 1940s he received informal tuition from Thelonious Monk by visiting the latter's apartment to hear him play. He first worked with rhythm-and-blues bands and then in bop groups with Kenny Dorham and Cecil Payne. In 1954 he became the first modern-jazz soloist to record for the Riverside label, and thereafter worked as a leader, often with his boyhood friends Ahmed Abdul-Malik, Ray Copeland,

and Payne, as well as with Booker Ervin and Melba Liston. He performed in Lagos, Nigeria (1961, 1963), toured Africa with a sextet (1967), and then settled in Rabat, Morocco, where he led a trio and ran a nightclub (1968–72). From 1972 he traveled extensively, and from 1974, when he appeared at a highly successful concert at the Montreux International Jazz Festival, has worked frequently as a soloist.

Weston is one of the few major pianists to borrow directly from the style of Monk: *Sweet Sue* (1955) and the simple but dissonant thematic riff of *Kucheza Blues* (1960) provide clear examples. His interests extend far beyond Monk's, however, and such recordings as the suite *Uhuru Africa!* (which makes use of lyrics by Langston Hughes and arrangements by Liston) and the popular jazz-funk album *Blue Moses* (1972) embrace African rhythms and romantic songs. Many of Weston's compositions, including *Little Niles* and *Hi-fly*, have become jazz standards.

Weston's son Azzedin (Niles) Weston performed and recorded as a jazz percussionist in the mid-1970s.

Oral history material in *CtY*, *NjR*.

SELECTED RECORDINGS

As unaccompanied soloist: *Informal Solo Piano* (1974, Hi-Fly 101); *African Nite* (1975, Owl 01)

As leader: *The Randy Weston Trio* (1955, Riv. 2515), incl. Sweet Sue; *With These Hands* (1956, Riv. 214), incl. Little Niles; on *New Faces at Newport* (1958, Metro. 1005), Hi-fly; *Uhuru Africa!* (1960, Roul. 65001), incl. Kucheza Blues; *Randy!* (1964, Bak. 1001); *Blue Moses* (1972, CTI 6016); *Tanjah* (1973, Pol. 5055)

BIBLIOGRAPHY

I. Gitler: "Randy Weston," *DB*, xxxi/6 (1964), 16

M. Gardner: "Randy Weston," *JM*, xii/11 (1967), 2 [incl. discography and list of compositions]

V. Wilmer: "Back to the African Heartbeat," *Jazz People* (London, Indianapolis, and New York, 1970/*R*1985), 75

M. Cullaz and L. Goddet: "Randy Weston," *Jh*, no.336 (1977), 11; Eng. trans. in *Coda*, no.159 (1978), 4

L. Birnbaum: "Randy Weston: African-rooted Rhythm," *DB*, xlvi/15 (1979), 18 [incl. discography]

L. Lyons: *The Great Jazz Pianists, Speaking of their Lives and Music* (New York, 1983), 210

BARRY KERNFELD

Wethington, (Arthur) Crawford (*b* Chicago, 26 Jan 1908). Saxophonist. He studied music in Chicago and after playing there with the pianist Lottie E. Hightower (*c*1925) he performed and recorded as an alto saxophonist in Carroll Dickerson's band (1928), with which he worked under Louis Armstrong's leadership in New York (1929). He made several recordings on clarinet and alto and baritone saxophones in the Mills Blue Rhythm Band (1930–36, including *Black and Tan Fantasy*, 1931, Ban. 32199) and in 1937 he recorded as a tenor saxophonist with Edgar Hayes. Wethington also taught music and although he ceased full-time performing after 1937 he continued to work as a teacher. (A. McCarthy: *Big Band Jazz*, New York and London, 1974)

For illustration *see* MILLS BLUE RHYTHM BAND.

based on *ChiltonW*

Wettling, George (Godfrey) (*b* Topeka, KS, 28 Nov 1907; *d* New York, 6 June 1968). Drummer. He worked in Chicago with a number of lesser-known bands (from 1924), played and recorded with Paul Mares (1935), toured with a band led in the USA by Jack Hylton, and performed with Wingy Manone in New York and Pittsburgh. After recording in Chicago with Jimmy McPartland (1936) and in New York with Manone, he worked with orchestras led by Artie Shaw (1936–7), Bunny Berigan (1937), Red Norvo (1938), and Paul Whiteman (1938–41). During the same time he was recording regularly as a freelance musician, often in dixieland groups with Eddie Condon. Thereafter he performed briefly with Bobby Hackett and Muggsy Spanier, then later with McPartland, Joe and Marty Marsala, the comedian Chico Marx, Benny Goodman (1943), and Miff Mole (1943–4). While working as a studio musician for ABC (1943–52) Wettling frequently appeared at Condon's club in New York. He also recorded with Yank Lawson (1943–4), Dick Cary, Billie Holiday, Pee Wee Russell, and Jack Teagarden (all 1944), Hackett (1944–5), Spanier (1944–6), Bud Freeman and Joe Sullivan (both 1945), Sidney Bechet (1949, 1950), and Ralph Sutton (1950, 1952). From 1953 he led his own dixieland bands in New York, but was associated intermittently with McPartland (1952–9), Condon (with whom he toured to England in 1957), Freeman (1955, 1957–60), and Spanier (1959–60). In the 1960s he continued to play with Condon, led a group at the Gaslight Club (from 1964), and worked with Clarence Hutchenrider. Wettling was influenced early in his career by Baby Dodds, but could adapt his playing to work in many different styles; he produced a crisp, clear sound and his inventive breaks make his recordings immediately identifiable. He also contributed as a writer to *Down Beat* magazine, and some of his work as an artist was used on album sleeves for recordings by Condon and Sullivan.

SELECTED RECORDINGS

Duos: with D. Cary: I thought about you/You took advantage of me (1944, Black and White 28); with R. Sutton: *Ralph Sutton at the Piano* (1952, Cir. [USA] 413)

As leader: Bugle Call Rag/I wish I could shimmy like my sister Kate (1940, Decca 18044); Home/Too marvelous for words (1944, Key. 1311); You brought a new kind of love to me/Somebody loves me (1944, Key. 1318); *George Wettling's High Fidelity Rhythms* (1954, Weathers Industries 5501)

As sideman: B. Freeman: The Blue Room/Exactly Like You (1938, Com. 513); E. Condon: *Tiger Rag & All That Jazz* (1958, WP 1292)

BIBLIOGRAPHY

ChiltonW; *FeatherE*; *Feather '60s*; *Feather–Gitler '70s*

M. Jones: "George Wettling at the Brushes," *JM*, iii/3 (1957), 10

J. Simmen: "George Wettling," *BHcF*, no.193 (1969), 5

B. Spinney: "From the Past: George Wettling," *MD*, vii/6 (1983), 44

JOHNNY SIMMEN

Wetzel [née Addleman], **Bonnie (Jean)** (*b* Vancouver, WA, 15 May 1926; *d* Vancouver, 12 Feb 1965). Double bass player. She received violin lessons, but taught herself double bass. In the mid-1940s she played for two years in the all-female band led by Ada Leonard and was a member of the trio led by the guitarist Marian Gange. She married Ray Wetzel in 1949, and worked with him in Tommy Dorsey's band in 1951. Thereafter she worked in New York with Charlie Shavers, Roy Eldridge, and Herb Ellis's trio Soft Winds. In 1953–4 she toured Europe with Beryl Booker's trio; the group recorded under its own name (*Beryl Booker with Bonnie Wetzel and Elaine Leighton*, 1953, Dis. 3021) and also with Don Byas (1954). Wetzel later worked as a freelance in New York.

BIBLIOGRAPHY

FeatherE; *Feather '60s*

R. Gordon: *Jazz West Coast: the Los Angeles Jazz Scene of the 1950s* (London and New York, 1986), 115

Wetzel, Ray (*b* Parkersburg, WV, 1924; *d* Sedgwick, CO, 17 Aug 1951). Trumpeter. He performed and recorded as the lead trumpeter in the bands of Woody Herman (1943–5) and Stan Kenton (1945–8), and also recorded with Vido Musso, Neal Hefti, and the Metronome All Stars (all 1947). He married Bonnie Addleman in 1949. After touring and recording with Charlie Barnet (1949–50) he worked in Los Angeles with Tommy Dorsey (1950) then rejoined Kenton briefly (1951); his solo playing is well represented on *Over the Rainbow* (1949, Cap. 744), recorded with Barnet. Thereafter he and his wife toured and recorded with Dorsey for several months. Wetzel was killed in an automobile accident. (*FeatherE*)

Wheeler, (E. B.) De Priest (*b* Kansas City, MO, 1 March 1903). Trombonist. After working in bands in Kansas City (from 1917) and St. Louis (1917), he performed with the saxophonist Dave Lewis and toured with a circus band (until 1922). In 1923 he joined the violinist Wilson Robinson's Syncopators, which toured the Pantages circuit, was resident as the Cotton Club Orchestra at the Cotton Club in New York (from 1925), and was called the Missourians before becoming Cab Calloway's orchestra. Wheeler played in the group until 1940, and made several recordings with it (1925, 1927, 1929–39); he may be heard on *Ozark Mountain Blues* (1929, Vic. 38071), issued under the Missourians' name. Although thereafter he ceased working as a full-time musician, Wheeler continued to perform occasionally. (A. McCarthy: *Big Band Jazz,* New York and London, 1974)

based on *ChiltonW*

Wheeler, Kenny [Kenneth Vincent John] (*b* Toronto, 14 Jan 1930). Canadian trumpeter and flugelhorn player. After studying harmony and trumpet at the Royal Conservatory in Toronto (1950–51) he moved in 1952 to London. He played in English dance bands, and while a member of John Dankworth's bop orchestra (1959–65) studied composition with Richard Rodney Bennett (1962–3) and Bill Russo (1963–4); with Dankworth's group he made a recording in 1968 of his own composition *Windmill Tilter,* a suite inspired by Cervantes's *Don Quixote.* He also played bop in small groups with Tubby Hayes (recording in 1966), Joe Harriott (recording in 1967), and Ronnie Scott (recording in 1968). Around this time he took an interest in free jazz, which he played with many important musicians and groups: the Spontaneous Music Ensemble (1966–70), Tony Oxley (1969–72), Anthony Braxton (at intervals from 1971 to 1973, regularly from 1974 to 1976), the Globe Unity Orchestra (from the early 1970s), the trio Azimuth (from 1976), which also included John Taylor and Norma Winstone, Dave Holland (from around 1983), and his own small group and big band. He also played jazz-rock, in particular on recordings with Mike Gibbs (1969–75) and Bill Bruford (1977), and as a member of the United Jazz and Rock Ensemble (from 1978). Although Wheeler devotes much attention to composition and writes all the material that he records as a leader, his work as a trumpeter and flugelhorn player is more important. His playing is well suited to what may be called the house style of the ECM record label; it is clear, relaxed, lyrical, and marked by a wide-ranging harmonic and rhythmic imagination.

Oral history material in *GBLnsa.*

SELECTED RECORDINGS

As leader: *Windmill Tilter* (1968, Fon. 5494); *Song for Someone* (1973, Incus 10); *Gnu High* (1975, ECM 1069); *Deer Wan* (1977, ECM 1102); of Azimuth (with J. Taylor and N. Winstone): *The Touchstone* (1978, ECM 1130); *Around 6* (1979, ECM 1156); *Double, Double you* (1983, ECM 1262)

As sideman: Spontaneous Music Ensemble: *Karyöbin* (1968, Isl. 9079); T. Oxley: *The Baptised Traveller* (1969, CBS 52664); A. Braxton: *New York, Fall 1974* (1974, Ari. 4032); *Five Pieces 1975* (1975, Ari. 4064); United Jazz and Rock Ensemble: *Live in Berlin* (1981, Mood 28628); D. Holland: *Jumpin' In* (1983, ECM 1269)

For further recordings *see* GLOBE UNITY ORCHESTRA.

BIBLIOGRAPHY

R. Cotterrell: "Kenny Wheeler: Speaking Softly but Carrying a Big Horn," *JF* [intl edn], no.57 (1979), 38
M. Miller: "Kenny Wheeler's Many Vehicles," *DB*, xlvii/4 (1980), 22 [incl. discography]
P. Husby: "Kenny Wheeler: Interview," *Cadence*, vii/5 (1981), 12
M. Miller: "Wheeler, Kenny," *Encyclopedia of Music in Canada*, ed. H. Kallmann, G. Potvin, and K. Winters (Toronto, Buffalo, and London, 1981)
B. Smith: "Kenny Wheeler: Windmill Tilter," *Coda*, no.207 (1986), 4
M. Miller: "Kenny Wheeler," *Boogie, Pete & the Senator: Canadian Musicians in Jazz: the Eighties* (Toronto), 1987), 290

BARRY KERNFELD

Whetsol, Artie [Arthur; Schiefe, Arthur Parker] (*b* Punta Gorda, FL, 1905; *d* New York, 5 Jan 1940). Trumpeter. He grew up in Washington, where he was a childhood friend of Duke Ellington and played in various local bands. In 1923, with Ellington, he moved to New York as a member of Elmer Snowden's band the Washingtonians, but returned to his home town the following year to study medicine at Howard University. He rejoined the band, by then under Ellington's leadership, in 1928, remaining until autumn 1936, when ill-health forced him to retire; despite repeated efforts, he was never able to resume full-time playing. Whetsol was an outstanding lead trumpeter and a distinctive soloist whose highly melodic style of performance was gentle and often wistful.

SELECTED RECORDINGS

(all as sideman with D. Ellington)

Black Beauty (1928, Vic. 21580); The Dicty Glide/Stevedore Stomp (1929, Vic. 38053); Jungle Jamboree (1929, OK 8720); Rocky Mountain Blues (1930, OK 8836); Mood Indigo (1930, Bruns. 4952); Black and Tan Fantasy, first issued on unnamed LP (1932, Vic. L16007)

BIBLIOGRAPHY

ChiltonW
H. Pekar: "Arthur Whetsol," *JJ*, xvi/7 (1963), 19
G. E. Lambert: "The Ellingtonians, 1: Arthur Whetsol," *JM*, x/2 (1964), 16

EDDIE LAMBERT

Whispa mute. *See* MUTE, §2(h).

White, Amos (Mordechai) (*b* Kingstree, SC, 6 Nov 1889). Cornetist. He entered Jenkins' Orphanage in Charleston, South Carolina, at the age of nine. After learning cornet he toured with the orphanage band, performed with circus and minstrel groups (1913–18), and led an army band in France. In 1919 he settled in New Orleans, where he performed as a part-time musician with such leaders as Papa Celestin and A. J. Piron and in the Excelsior Brass Band. After leading his own band he worked on the SS *Capitol* with Fate Marable, with whom he performed intermittently until 1924; his playing may be heard on Marable's *Frankie and Johnny* (1924, OK 40113), the only recording White made. From the mid-1920s he performed with several groups, toured with Mamie Smith (1927), and led the Georgia Minstrels (1928). He worked as a sideman and leader in Phoenix, Arizona (after 1928), and in 1934 he settled in Oakland, California; he ceased full-time performing, but continued to play occasionally into the 1960s.

Oral history material in *LNT.*

BIBLIOGRAPHY

ChartersJ
G. Mills: "Amos White and his New Orleans Ragtime Band," *Eureka*, i/5 (1960), 5
J. Chilton: *A Jazz Nursery: the Story of the Jenkins' Orphanage Bands of Charleston, South Carolina* (London, 1980)

based on *ChiltonW*

White, Andrew (Nathaniel, III) (*b* Washington, 6 Sept 1942). Tenor saxophonist. He played soprano saxophone as a child, then changed to alto saxophone and took up the oboe in his early teens. From 1960 he studied oboe and theory at Howard University (BM 1964) and from 1964 to 1968 he attended Dartmouth College, the Conservatoire in Paris, and SUNY, Buffalo. He was the principal oboist with the orchestra of the American Ballet Theatre in New York (1968–70) and an electric bass guitarist for the soul singer Stevie Wonder and the pop group the Fifth Dimension (1969–73); he also played electric bass guitar on recordings by Weather Report (1971–*c*1973) and took a solo on english horn on the track *Unknown Soldier* on the group's album *I Sing the Body Electric* (1971–2). In 1976 he arranged and conducted music for a big-band tribute to John Coltrane at the Newport Jazz Festival in New York. During the following decade he played alto and soprano saxophones as the leader of a quartet that included Mal Waldron and as a sideman with Elvin Jones (1980–81) and Beaver Harris (1983). In 1971 he formed Andrew's Music in Washington, which issues recordings of his own performances and publishes his own transcriptions of solos by Coltrane, Charlie Parker, and Eric Dolphy, books, and scores. He has written two books, *Hey Kid! Wanna Buy a Record? A Treatise on Self Production in the Music Business* (Washington, 1982) and *Andrew's X-rated Band Stories* (Washington, 1984).

SELECTED RECORDINGS

(all recorded for Andrew's Music)

Passion Flower (1974, 5); *Marathon '75*, iii (1975, 17); *Seven Giant Steps for Coltrane* (1976, 30); *Live in New York*, ii (1977, 31); *I Love Japan* (1979, 38)

BIBLIOGRAPHY

L. Goddet: "Interview: Andrew White," *Jh*, no.304 (1974), 14
B. Rusch: "Andrew White: Interview," *Cadence*, iv/4 (1978), 10
D. E. McGinty: "Conversation with Andrew White: 'Keeper of the Trane'," *Black Perspective in Music*, xii/1 (1984), 80

ED HAZELL

White, Bobby [Robert E.] (*b* Chicago, 28 June 1926). Drummer. He first worked in Los Angeles with the trombonist Earle Spencer (1947) and played with Harry James and Charlie Barnet. After performing and recording with Vido Musso (1951–2) and Art Pepper and Chet Baker (both 1953) he toured Europe with Buddy DeFranco's quartet (1954). He recorded in Oslo with a trio led by DeFranco's pianist Sonny Clark, and while in Paris recorded, with Clark, as a sideman in Jimmy Raney's quartet. White then returned to the West Coast, where he recorded with DeFranco (1954–6) and Cal Tjader (1955, 1957). He is heard to advantage on *In a Mellow Mood* (1954, Norg. 1079), recorded with DeFranco.

BIBLIOGRAPHY

FeatherE
R. Gordon: *Jazz West Coast: the Los Angeles Jazz Scene of the 1950s* (London and New York, 1986)

White, Chris(topher Westley) (*b* New York, 6 July 1936). Double bass player. He worked intermittently with Cecil Taylor (1955–9), then performed and recorded with Bernard Peiffer (1960) and the singer Nina Simone (1960–61). From 1962 to 1966 he was a member of Dizzy Gillespie's bop groups; his playing as a sideman with Gillespie is well represented by *The Day After* from the album *Something Old, Something New* (1963, Phi. 600091). He also recorded with Gillespie's saxophonist James Moody (1963). He then played with Billy Taylor (ii) (1966), worked as a freelance, taught, and studied at the Manhattan School of Music. He also played with Eubie Blake, Earl Hines, Moody, Teddy Wilson, and Willie "the Lion" Smith, and recorded with a quintet led by Owens and Kenny Barron (1967) and with Mary Lou Williams (*c*1969), and Owens once more (1970). From the mid-1960s White worked on numerous jazz education projects as a teacher, administrator, consultant, and writer; he was the director of the Institute of Jazz Studies at Rutgers until 1976. He performed and recorded with Andrew Hill (1974, 1975), Kenny Barron (1975), and Kalaparusha Maurice McIntyre (1976). In the 1980s he taught at Newark Community School of the Arts.

BIBLIOGRAPHY

Feather '60s; *Feather–Gitler '70s*
V. Wilmer: "The Advantages of Gregariousness," *DB*, xxxiv/15 (1967), 22

White, Harry (Alexander) [Father] (*b* Bethlehem, PA, 1 June 1898; *d* New York, 14 Aug 1962). Composer, arranger, and trombonist. He played drums in show bands while still in his teens, but after moving to Washington around 1919 he concentrated on trombone. He worked with Duke Ellington, Elmer Snowden, and Claude Hopkins, among others, before forming the White Brothers Orchestra in 1925 with members of his family; the group had a permanent engagement in Philadelphia and White traveled regularly to New York, where he played with June Clark, Snowden, and the drummer George Howe. He worked with Luis Russell in 1927–8 then formed another group of his own. In 1931 he and Edgar Hayes directed and wrote arrangements for the Mills Blue Rhythm Band, and the following year White joined Cab Calloway as an arranger, composer, and player. In 1935 he returned to Russell whose band was then accompanying Louis Armstrong. He ceased full-time playing in 1936 for two years, then played with and wrote arrangements for Manzie Johnson (with whom he sometimes played alto saxophone as well as trombone), Hot Lips Page, Hayes, and Bud Freeman. After a long illness he resumed part-time playing and writing in 1947.

RECORDED COMPOSITIONS

(selective list; all with White as sideman)

C. Calloway: Evenin' (1933, Vic. 24414); Zaz zuh zaz (1933, Vic. 24557); Chinese Rhythm (1933, Bruns. 6992)

SELECTED ARRANGEMENTS

(all with White as sideman)

Mills Blue Rhythm Band: Doin' the Shake/Wild Waves (1932, Ban. 32493); Rhythm Spasm (1932, Mlt. 12418); White Lightning (1932, Mlt. 12414); C. Calloway: Father's got his Glasses on (1933, Vic. 24451); H. L. Page: Skull Duggery (1938, Bb 7583)

BIBLIOGRAPHY

ChiltonW; *FeatherE*
A. McCarthy: *Big Band Jazz* (New York and London, 1974), 165
J. Simmen: "Father's Got his Glasses On," *Sv*, no.129 (1987), 83

LAWRENCE KOCH

White, Lenny [Leonard, III] (*b* New York, 19 Dec 1949). Drummer. He taught himself to play drums from the age of 14 and worked with Jackie McLean (1968). He recorded with Miles Davis (1969), Freddie Hubbard and Woody Shaw (1970), Gato Barbieri (1971), and Stanley Clarke (1972) and performed and recorded with Joe Henderson (1970–71) and Gil Evans (1971). After working with Stan Getz and the Latin rock group Azteca he toured as a member of RETURN TO FOREVER (1973–6), with which he played in an assertive style that incorporated elements of rock and Latin music. It was with this style that he became most closely identified, and he later led a group that was modeled after Return to Forever but that achieved far less critical success. White is also adept at playing hard bop, as he has shown in his performances and recordings with Hubbard, Henderson, Clarke, Chick Corea, and (at different times) the singers Chaka Khan and Nancy Wilson in a group known variously as Echoes of an Era, the Griffith Park Band, and the Griffith Park Collection (1981–2).

SELECTED RECORDINGS

As sideman: M. Davis: *Bitches Brew* (1969, Col. GP26); F. Hubbard: *Red Clay* (1970, CTI 6001); J. Henderson: *In Pursuit of Blackness* (1970–71, Mlst. 9034); C. Corea: *No Mystery* (1975, Pol. 6512); Echoes of an Era: *Echoes of an Era* (*c*1981, Elek. 60021)

BIBLIOGRAPHY

Feather–Gitler '70s
M. Rozek: "A Matter of Values: a Conversation with Lenny White," *DB*, xlii/8 (1975), 15
A. Wald: "Beyond Forever: MD Talks with Lenny White," *MD*, i/4 (1977), 4

BARRY KERNFELD

White, Michael (Walter) (i) (*b* Houston, 24 May 1933). Electric violinist and composer. He was brought up in Oakland, California, and first came to public attention at the Monterey Jazz Festival in 1965 as a member of John Handy's quintet. In the late 1960s he was a member of the jazz-rock group Fourth Way. He recorded with Pharoah Sanders (1970–73), McCoy Tyner (1973), and Joe Henderson (1973). From 1971 White has also led his own groups, with which he plays principally his own compositions: these include *The Sun and the Moon Have Come Together*; *Father Music, Mother Dance*; and the extended suite *The Land of Spirit and Light*.

White possesses a formidable technique and performs with considerable emotional intensity. His style has been influenced more by such musicians as John Coltrane and Eric Dolphy than by earlier violinists: for example, he makes liberal use of multiple stopping, and his rocking of the bow between two notes produces an effect comparable with that of a wide-interval tremolo played by Coltrane or Dolphy.

SELECTED RECORDINGS

As leader: *The Land of Spirit and Light* (1973, Imp. 9241); *Father Music, Mother Dance* (1974, Imp. 9268); *X Factor* (1978, Elek. 138)
As sideman: J. Handy: *Live at the Monterey Jazz Festival* (1965, Col. CS9262); Fourth Way: *The Sun and Moon Have Come Together* (1969, Harvest 423); P. Sanders: *Thembi* (1970, Imp. 9206); on M. Tyner: *Song for my Lady* (1972, Mlst. 9044), Native Song

BIBLIOGRAPHY

Feather '60s; *Feather–Gitler '70s*
R. Rouda: "The Fourth Way: Mike White," *Coda*, ix/12 (1971), 32
L. Feather: "Michael White: Blindfold Test," *DB*, xli/15 (1974), 31

DAVID FLANAGAN

White, Michael (ii) (*b* New Orleans, 29 Nov 1954). Clarinetist. He first played jazz with Doc Paulin's brass band (1975), then joined the Young Tuxedo Brass Band (1979). In 1980 he performed with the show *One Mo' Time*, and the following year he played at Preservation Hall with Kid Sheik Colar and formed his own trio and band; he is heard to advantage on his album *Shake it & break it* (1981, Nola 22). He has played with several jazz and brass bands, worked as a leader, and written and lectured on jazz history. White's full-bodied tone and imaginative improvisations reminiscent of Johnny Dodds have established his reputation as one of the most exciting young black musicians in New Orleans in the late 1980s. (M. Joly: "The Young Generation: Michael White," *SL*, xxxvii/4 (1985), 19)

MARCEL JOLY

White, Morris [Fruit] (*b* St. Louis, 17 Jan 1911). Guitarist and banjoist. He learned banjo as a child; by the 1920s he was doubling on guitar. He performed with Charlie Creath on the Mississippi riverboat *St. Paul* (1926), with Dewey Jackson in St. Louis (1927), and in a touring show with Ethel Waters. In 1928 he joined the Missourians (with which he recorded in 1929–30) and he remained with the band when Cab Calloway assumed its leadership in 1930. As Calloway's *Happy Feet* (1930, Ban. 0835) shows, White's banjo playing contributed a strong rhythmic drive to the orchestra's performances. He left Calloway in 1937 and after working briefly with Lionel Hampton (*c*1941) he ceased full-time performing. (A. McCarthy: *Big Band Jazz*, New York and London, 1974)

based on *ChiltonW*

White, Rocky [Quentin] (*b* San Mares, TX, 3 Nov 1952). Drummer. He studied music at Texas Southern University from 1971 to 1973, and then joined Duke Ellington's orchestra, remaining until the leader's death in April 1974. Among the recordings he made during this period was the album *Duke Ellington's Third Sacred Concert* (1973, RCA APL1-0785). He continued to play intermittently with the band under the direction of Mercer Ellington.

EDDIE LAMBERT

White, Sonny [Ellerton Oswald] (*b* Panamá, 11 Nov 1917; *d* New York, 28 April 1971). Pianist. From the mid-1930s he worked with Jesse Stone (1936–7), Willie Bryant (1937–8), and Teddy Hill (1938), and with Frankie Newton at the Café Society, New York (1939); he then performed and recorded with Billie Holiday (1939–40; for illustration *see* HOLIDAY, BILLIE). He played in Benny Carter's orchestra (1940) and with Artie Shaw (1941), and after his military service he re-joined Carter (1946) and worked with Hot Lips Page (1947). In 1947 he became a member of a band led by the trumpeter Harvey Davis, which was resident at the Cinderella Club, New York (1947–54), and at Jimmy Ryan's (1954). He performed and recorded with Wilbur De Paris (until the early 1960s), Louis Metcalf (1963–7), and Eddie Barefield's trio (1968). In 1969 he began playing with Jonah Jones, with whom he remained until his death.

SELECTED RECORDINGS

As sideman: M. Mezzrow: That's how I Feel Today (1937, Vic. 25636); Hot Club Stomp (1937, Vic. 25612); B. Holiday: Strange Fruit/Fine and Mellow (1939, Com. 526); B. Carter: Cocktails for Two/Takin' my Time (1940, Bb 10998)

BIBLIOGRAPHY

ChiltonW
J. Simmen: "Sonny White, 1917–1971," *BHcF*, no.212 (1971), 7
J. Chilton: *Billie's Blues: a Survey of Billie Holiday's Career, 1933–1959* (London, 1975)

JAMES M. DORAN

Whiteman, Paul (*b* Denver, 28 March 1890; *d* Doylestown, PA, 29 Dec 1967). Bandleader. He played viola in the Denver SO from 1907 and in the San Francisco SO from 1914. During World War I he led a 40-piece navy band, playing march tunes by day and show music by night. Sensing new dimensions for popular music in the transition from ragtime to jazz, he organized a dance band in San Francisco in 1918, later moving to Los Angeles and Atlantic City, New Jersey, before settling in New York in 1920. There he soon became the best-known American bandleader, particularly with his recording of *Whispering* and *Japanese Sandman* (1920), which sold more than a million

Paul Whiteman conducting his orchestra, 1938

copies. By the early 1920s his lush orchestral style was widely copied on countless bandstands at home and abroad. He toured the British Isles in 1923 and Europe in 1926.

For his first extended concert tour of the USA Whiteman commissioned George Gershwin to write *Rhapsody in Blue*, which, as part of Whiteman's concert called "An Experiment in Modern Music," was performed with the composer as soloist in Aeolian Hall, New York, in 1924. Favorable publicity prompted Whiteman to stage seven performances of this kind between 1925 and 1938, thereby obtaining wide exposure for such American composers as Victor Herbert, William Grant Still, and Duke Ellington (*see* SYMPHONIC JAZZ). Between 1928 and 1952 Whiteman's orchestras were featured on many network radio shows and took part in several films, beginning with *King of Jazz* (1930) (*see* FILMS, §I, 2). He provided music for six Broadway shows and produced more than 600 phonograph recordings. Later he served as music director for ABC.

Whiteman was a key figure in American popular music. While jazz purists accused him of diluting the character of early jazz for commercial purposes, less biased observers applauded the high polish and versatility of his orchestras, which had to be as comfortable in the concert hall as at a college dance. He employed a number of talented musicians: in the original arrangement of *Rhapsody in Blue* three of his reed players were required to play a total of 17 instruments. Although his dance music tended to be sedate, there were occasional jazz solos from musicians such as Bix Beiderbecke, Frankie Trumbauer, Eddie Lang, Bunny Berigan, and Jack Teagarden.

Whiteman's musical memorabilia, including his large library of more than 3000 arrangements, were bequeathed to Williams College in Williamstown, Massachusetts, where they now form the Whiteman Collection; *see* LIBRARIES AND ARCHIVES, §2.

See also JAZZ (i), §III, 4.

SELECTED RECORDINGS

Whispering/Japanese Sandman (1920, Vic. 18690); Whiteman Stomp (1927, Vic. 21119); Changes/Mary (1927, Vic. 21103); Concerto in F (Gershwin) (1928, Col. 50140D); Nobody's Sweetheart/After you've gone (1929, Col. 2098D); I'm coming Virginia/Aunt Hagar's Blues (1938, Decca 2145)

BIBLIOGRAPHY

P. Whiteman and M. M. McBride: *Jazz* (New York, 1926)
B. Rust: "Paul Whiteman: a Discography," *Recorded Sound*, no.27 (1967), 219; no.28 (1967), 255
M. Harrison: "Around Paul Whiteman," *JM*, no.185 (1970), 7
——: *A Jazz Retrospect* (Newton Abbot, England, 1976, rev. 2/1977), 184
C. Johnson: *Paul Whiteman: a Chronology* (Williamstown, MA, 1977, rev. 2/1979)
T. DeLong: *Pops: Paul Whiteman, King of Jazz* (Piscataway, nr New Brunswick, NJ, 1983)

CARL JOHNSON

Whitlock, Bob [Von Varlynn] (*b* Roosevelt, UT, 21 Jan 1931). Double bass player. During the 1950s he worked in Los Angeles, performing and recording with Gerry Mulligan (1952), Art Pepper and Chet Baker (both 1953), and Stan Getz (1954). He is heard to advantage on *Walkin' Shoes/Soft Shoe* (1952, PJ 606), recorded with Mulligan. He also played with Buddy DeFranco and recorded with Jack Sheldon (1956) and Joe Albany (1957). Later in the decade he led his own quartet and undertook graduate study at the University of California. During the 1960s he performed and recorded with Zoot Sims at the Blue Note in Paris (1961), recorded with Vi Redd and Curtis Amy (both 1962) and Victor Feldman (1962–3), and worked as a freelance. He toured with George Shearing in 1965–6, and recorded with him in 1968. Later he was a member of a trio led by Albany (1972).

BIBLIOGRAPHY

FeatherE; *Feather '60s*
R. Gordon: *Jazz West Coast: the Los Angeles Jazz Scene of the 1950s* (London and New York, 1986)

Whittle, Tommy [Thomas] (*b* Grangemouth, Scotland, 13 Oct 1926). Scottish tenor saxophonist. He played with the trumpeter Johnny Claes, the bandleader Lew Stone, and Carl Barriteau (all 1944–5), and performed and recorded with Harry Hayes (1944–6), Ted Heath (1946–52), and Tony Kinsey (1953–4). During the 1950s he worked in London with the BBC Show Band (1953–5), as the leader of his own quartet, which included Dill Jones, at the Flamingo club (1954), and as leader of a quintet, with Jones and Harry Klein, at Studio 51 (1955). He then led a touring octet with Kenny Wheeler, Keith Christie, and Joe Temperley (1955–6), played solo engagements, and performed in France and the USA with his quartet. Whittle has worked as a freelance musician from the late 1950s; he also led his own orchestra at the Dorchester Hotel, London (1959–61), and joined the ATV orchestra under Jack Parnell. His playing may be heard to advantage on the album *Jigsaw* (1977, Alamo 4501). Whittle, one of Britain's most highly respected saxophonists, is married to the singer Barbara Jay, with whom he recorded *The Nearness of You* (1982, TJ 101).

BIBLIOGRAPHY

Feather '60s
R. Cotterell, ed.: *Jazz Now: the Jazz Centre Society Guide* (London, 1976)
P. Vacher: "Best of British, No.5: Tommy Whittle, Jazz Refugee from the Mickey Mouse Bands," *JJI*, xxxi/7 (1978), 11
G. Copley: "Tommy Whittle," *JJI*, xxxviii/6 (1985), 16

DIGBY FAIRWEATHER

Whyte, Zack [Zach] (*b* Richmond, KY, 1898; *d* Kentucky, 10 March 1967). Bandleader and banjoist. He studied at Wilberforce College, Ohio, where he joined Horace Henderson's student band as an arranger and banjoist. He formed his own group around 1923 and in the late 1920s he began to lead the Chocolate Beau Brummels. Although the band was very successful it made only a small number of recordings, among them *Mandy* (1929, Gen. 6781; for illustration *see* GENNETT). His sidemen at various times included Herman "Ivory" Chittison, Vic Dickenson, Roy Eldridge, Quentin Jackson, Sy Oliver, and Al Sears. Whyte continued working as a leader into the 1930s.

BIBLIOGRAPHY

T. Zwicky: "Zack is the Name, Whyte that is!," *Sv*, no.24 (1969), 214
A. McCarthy: *Big Band Jazz* (New York and London, 1974), 160

based on *ChiltonW*

Wick, Joe [Josef] (*b* Siegburg, Germany, 19 March 1916). German bandleader. He studied violin, drums, and piano at the conservatory in Bonn. At the age of 22 he played drums in the dance orchestras of Will Glahé and Bernard Etté. He was appointed director of the Universum Film Aktiengesellschaft dance orchestra in 1942. He entertained German and British troops during and after the war and also broadcast on the BBC. He made a large number of recordings from 1948 (including *Blue Skies*, 1948, Bruns. 82341, and *Torpedo Junction*, 1949, Bruns. 82380), and appeared in three films. When he retired from music in 1964, most of his sidemen joined Kurt Edelhagen's big band. ("Auf den Spuren vertrauter Töne," *Magazin der Bundeshauptstadt Bonn*, iii/1 (1981), 42)

RAINER E. LOTZ

Wickman, Putte [Hans-Olof] (*b* Borlänge, Sweden, 10 Sept 1924). Swedish clarinetist and bandleader. He began his career around 1945 as a swing player, but later turned to more modern styles. After playing with Charlie Norman, Simon Brehm, and others, in 1948 he replaced the violinist Hasse Kahn as the leader of a group at the Nalen, Stockholm, and re-formed it as a sextet which featured Reinhold Svensson. Wickman recorded both with this group and with many other musicians, such as Jimmy Raney (1954) and Lars Gullin (1954, 1960), and in the 1960s led a large dance band. He later performed with Svend Asmussen, the pianist Leif Asp, and others; from the mid-1970s onwards he has worked mainly as a freelance soloist. Wickman's playing has always been of the highest order and has grown more personal and intense over the years. He is widely regarded as one of the outstanding soloists on his instrument.

SELECTED RECORDINGS

Happy New Year! (1973, Odeon E06234822); *Putte Wickman Quartet Live in Stockholm* (1977, Out 7710); *Mr. Clarinet* (1985, Four Leaf Clover 5083)

BIBLIOGRAPHY

FeatherE
"Svenskt stjärnalbum" [Swedish star album], *Orkester journalen*, xiii/12 (1945), 5
"På omslaget" [On the cover], *Orkester journalen*, xxi/1 (1953), 6
A. von Konow: "Det måste finnas en grund att stå på" [There must be ground to stand on], *Orkester journalen*, xxxvii/3 (1969), 10
L. Collin: "60-åriga Putte" [Putte at 60], *Orkester journalen*, lii/10 (1984), 13
E. Kjellberg: *Svensk jazzhistoria: en översikt* [Swedish jazz history: an overview] (Stockholm, 1985)

ERIK KJELLBERG

Widmann, Kutte [Kurt] (*b* Berlin, 2 March 1906; *d* Berlin, 27 Nov 1954). German bandleader. He began playing professionally with local bands in 1924. His own hot quintet was resident at the Imperator Diele in Berlin for ten years (1933–43). He made his first recordings of dance music and jazz as the leader of a big band in 1938. After military service (1943–4) he organized a new band and he was the first bandleader to resume recording commercially after the war (November 1946). On his numerous recordings (including *St. Louis Blues*, 1939, Tempo 4284, and *Hey-ba-ba-re-bop*, 1947, Odeon 31761) he occasionally plays drums, trombone, and accordion, and also sings. His life was the subject of a full-length film: *Die Kurt Widmann Story (Musik im Blut)* (1956).

RAINER E. LOTZ

Wiggins, Gerry [Gerald Foster, Sr.] (*b* New York, 12 May 1922). Pianist and arranger, father of J. J. Wiggins. He was first inspired by hearing Art Tatum play in New York. After touring with the comedian Stepin Fetchit he worked in Les Hite's orchestra (1942–3) and with Louis Armstrong and Benny Carter (1944). After moving to the West Coast he served as accompanist to the singer Lena Horne (1950–51), setting a pattern that has persisted for much of his career: he has also accompanied Kay Starr, Eartha Kitt, and Helen Humes. In the 1960s he worked as a music director and vocal coach in film studios and also led his own trios, with which he made several recordings. He continues to perform as a leader and with Gerald Wilson's orchestra, and his firm touch and all-round musicianship are evident whenever he plays.

SELECTED RECORDINGS

Duos with R. Callender: *Night Mist Blues* (1983, Hemisphere 1002)
As leader: *Wig is Here* (1974, BB 33069)
As sideman: H. Humes: *Muse All-Stars* (1979, Muse 5217); G. Wilson: *Love you Madly* (1982, Trend 531); Linda Hopkins: *How Blue Can You Get?* (1982, PAlt 8034), incl. Evil Gal Blues, Salty Papa Blues; Danny Turner: *First Time Out* (1983, Hemisphere 0001)

BIBLIOGRAPHY

FeatherE; *Feather '60s*; *Feather–Gitler '70s*
J. P. Battestini: "Gerald Wiggins," *BHcF*, no.237 (1974), 5 [interview]

PETER VACHER

Wiggins, J. J. [Gerald Foster, Jr.] (*b* Los Angeles, 15 April 1956). Double bass player, son of Gerry Wiggins. He made his professional début leading his own trio, and also played in a trio led by his father. From 1974 he worked with the Duke Ellington

Orchestra under the direction of Mercer Ellington; he made the album *Continuum* (1974–5, Fan. 9481) with the group.

EDDIE LAMBERT

Wiggs, Johnny [Hyman, John Wigginton] (*b* New Orleans, 25 July 1899; *d* New Orleans, 9 Oct 1977). Cornetist. He was inspired to become a musician after hearing King Oliver, and studied music at Loyola University. He began playing around 1920 with Earl Crumb, then worked with Norman Brownlee (1924–5) and Happy Schilling (1926). In 1927 he toured with a vaudeville troupe and recorded, as John Hyman, with his Bayou Stompers (*Ain't love grand/Alligator Blues*, Vic. 20593); the following year he performed and recorded with Tony Parenti. During the 1930s and 1940s Wiggs worked as a teacher, but then recommenced playing and, between 1948 and 1973, made several recordings with his own band. He continued to play until 1974.

Oral history material in *LNT*.

BIBLIOGRAPHY

A. Rose: "Both of Johnny Wiggs," *SL*, xi/9–10 (1961), 11
G. W. Kay: "The Johnny Wiggs Story," *JJ*, xxiii/6 (1970), 12
J. Wiggs: "Wiggs Self-explained," *SL*, xxix (1977), spring, 3
P. R. Haby: "Johnny Wiggs," *Fn*, ix/1 (1977), 4 [incl. discography]

BILL RUSSELL

Wilber, Bob [Robert Sage] (*b* New York, 15 March 1928). Clarinetist, soprano and alto saxophonist, arranger, and composer. In 1946–7 he studied with Sidney Bechet. With his first band, the Wildcats, he led the revival of traditional jazz on the East Coast after World War II. He played with Mezz Mezzrow at the Nice Jazz Festival in 1948. After army service (1952–4) he was a member of a cooperative group, the Six, which combined elements of modern and traditional jazz. Later he worked with many important musicians, including Bechet, Bobby Hackett (1957–8), Benny Goodman (with whom he toured in 1958 and 1959), Jack Teagarden, and Eddie Condon. He was a founding member of the World's Greatest Jazz Band in 1969, and from 1974 to 1979 led the group SOPRANO SUMMIT with Kenny Davern.

Many of Wilber's activities reflect his dedication to the preservation and dissemination of the traditions of jazz; in the late 1970s he began leading the Smithsonian Jazz Repertory Ensemble, and also founded his own record company, Bodeswell. From 1980 to 1983 he led the BECHET LEGACY, and in 1982 he became the director of jazz studies at Wilkes College. He arranged the music for the film *The Cotton Club*, for which he won a Grammy Award in 1986. His many compositions include *Ode to Bechet*. In spite of his association with Bechet, Wilber has developed a highly distinctive individual voice. His work is notable for its tastefulness and integrity.

Oral history material in *LNT*.

SELECTED RECORDINGS

As leader: Wild Cat Blues (1947, Com. 584); *The Music of Hoagy Carmichael* (1969, MonE 6917); with K. Davern: *Soprano Summit* (1973, World Jazz 5); *Original Wilber* (1978, Phon. 7519); *The Music of King Oliver* (1981, Bodeswell 107); *Ode to Bechet* (1982, Bodeswell 104), incl. Ode to Bechet; *Reflections* (1983, Bodeswell 106); *The Cotton Club* (1985, Geffen 70260)

As sideman: S. Bechet: I'm through, goodbye (1949, Cir. [USA] 1059); World's Greatest Jazz Band: *Extra* (1968, Project 5039); Pug Horton: *Don't go Away* (1979, Bodeswell 102)

BIBLIOGRAPHY

M. Williams: "Bob Wilber's Winnowed Ways," *DB*, xxxiii/25 (1966), 15
M. Jones: "Wilber: I Do my own Thing," *MM*, xlix (26 Jan 1974), 64
W. Balliett: "The Westchester Kids," *New Yorker*, liii (9 May 1977), 77; repr. in *Improvising: Sixteen Jazz Musicians and their Art* (New York, 1977) [colln of previously pubd interviews], 235
"Bob Wilber Today," *JJI*, xxxii/7 (1979), 7
E. Townley: "Specks and Spots and Other Things," *Sv*, no.81 (1979), 100 [interview]
G. Endress: *Jazz Podium: Musiker über sich selbst* (Stuttgart, Germany, 1980), 40
B. Korall: "Bob Wilber: Personalizing the Trad Repertoire," *DB*, xlvii/9 (1980), 20
E. Cook: "Keepers of the Flame," *JJI*, xxxiv/11 (1981), 16 [inteview]
J. Lucas: "The Jazz Baton: Bechet to Hodges to Wilber," *MR*, xii/3 (1985), 1
W. Royal Stokes: "Re-creating the Golden Age," *JT* (Nov 1985). 14
B. Rusch: "Bob Wilber: Interview," *Cadence*, xii/8 (1986), 5
M. Jones: *Talking Jazz* (London, 1987), 12
B. Wilber: *Music was not Enough*, ed. D. Webster (London and New York, 1987) [autobiography of Bob Wilber]

DEREK WEBSTER

Wilborn, Dave [David Buckley] (*b* Springfield, OH, 11 April 1904; *d* Detroit, 25 April 1982). Banjoist, guitarist, and singer. He played piano from the age of 12 and in 1922 began working with Cecil and Lloyd Scott. He then joined William McKinney's Synco Septet, which later became known as McKinney's Cotton Pickers. Wilborn performed with the group until 1937, making several recordings (1928–31); *Zonky* (1930, Vic. 38118) provides a fine example of his singing and rhythm banjo playing. He also recorded with Louis Armstrong (1928). Thereafter he played guitar with his own sextet until 1950, when he ceased full-time performing. From 1972 he was the featured singer with the New McKinney's Cotton Pickers; he recorded with the band (1972) as a leader at the Manassas Jazz Festival (1973).

For illustration *see* MCKINNEY'S COTTON PICKERS.

BIBLIOGRAPHY

T. Grove and M. Grove: "The Dave Wilbourne [*sic*] Story," *Music Mirror*, ii/6 (1955), 6
J. Chilton: *McKinney's Music: a Bio-discography of McKinney's Cotton Pickers* (London, 1978)
Obituary, J. Taylor, *MR*, ix/8 (1982), 7

based on *ChiltonW*

Wilcox, Eddie [Ed(win Felix)] (*b* Method, nr Raleigh, NC, 27 Dec 1907; *d* New York, 29 Sept 1968). Arranger and pianist. While studying at Fisk University (1925–7) he played in a band led by Jimmie Lunceford. He then performed in resorts in New Jersey (1927, 1928) and in June 1929 rejoined Lunceford. As an arranger he played an important part in developing the band's style; his work is well represented on *Flaming Reeds and Screaming Brass/While Love Lasts* (1933, first issued on *Lunceford Special*, Col. CS9515). When Lunceford died in 1947 Wilcox shared the leadership of the band with Joe Thomas (iii) for two years, and continued as sole leader into the 1950s. He then led small groups around New York, worked as a soloist and sideman, and formed a record company called Raecox with Teddy McRae. In 1968 he performed in Canada with Big Chief Moore.

BIBLIOGRAPHY

ChiltonW; *FeatherE*
I. Crosbie: "Jimmie Lunceford: Message from Memphis," *JJ*, xxv (1972), no.1, p.2; no.2, p.26
S. Dance: *The World of Swing* (New York, 1974) [colln of previously pubd interviews], 110

Wilder, Joe [Joseph Benjamin] (*b* Colwyn, nr Philadelphia, 22 Feb 1922). Trumpeter. The son of a bandleader, he studied music in Philadelphia, where his classmates included Red Rodney and Buddy DeFranco. He worked with Les Hite (from 1941) and Lionel Hampton (to 1946), led a marine band, and belonged to Dizzy Gillespie's orchestra. In the late 1940s he played with Jimmie Lunceford, Lucky Millinder, Sam Donahue, and Herbie Fields; while playing in pit orchestras on Broadway (to

1957) he worked for six months with Count Basie (1953–4) and took part in one session led by Ernie Wilkins. In 1957 he joined the music staff of ABC, with which he remained for 16 years; at the same time he toured the USSR with Benny Goodman and played on four occasions with the New York PO. From 1973 he worked as a freelance in television, films, and recording studios. He recorded with Benny Carter in 1985.

SELECTED RECORDINGS

As leader: *Wilder 'n' Wilder* (1956, Savoy 12063); with J. Newman: *Hangin' Out* (1984, Conc. 262)

As sideman: C. Basie: *Dance Session* (1953, Clef 626), incl. Softly with Feeling; P. Brown: *Peter the Great* (1954, Beth. 1011); E. Wilkins: *Top Brass* (1955, Savoy 12044), incl. Trick or Treat, Willow Weep for me; B. Carter: *A Gentleman and his Music* (1985, Conc. 285)

BIBLIOGRAPHY

FeatherE; *Feather '60s*; *Feather–Gitler '70s*

R. Horricks: *Count Basie and his Orchestra: its Music and its Musicians* (London and New York, 1957), 266

C. Deffaa: "Subtle Master," *MR*, xiii/10 (1986), 11

CHRIS SHERIDAN

Wilen, Barney [Bernard Jean] (*b* Nice, France, 4 March 1937). French tenor saxophonist. He grew up in the USA, recorded with Roy Haynes (1954), and around 1955 appeared at the Club St.-Germain in Paris with Kenny Clarke, J. J. Johnson, Benny Golson, and Bud Powell. After recording with John Lewis (1956) he worked again with Powell (1957, 1959), took part with Miles Davis in the recording of the soundtrack to the film *L'ascenseur pour l'échafaud* (1957), and recorded with Milt Jackson (1958) and Kenny Dorham (1959). As a member of Art Blakey's Jazz Messengers he worked on the soundtrack to the film *Les liaisons dangereuses 1960* (1959). In Europe he worked from 1967 as a leader in a style that incorporated elements of rock; in 1968 he recorded the album *Dear Prof. Leary* (MPS 15191). He lived in Africa from 1968 to 1973 and in 1977 returned to Nice. In 1982 he embraced jazz-rock and experimented with a fusion of jazz and African rhythms; in his later work he has favored a bop style that recalls his playing in the late 1950s.

BIBLIOGRAPHY

P. Carles and J.-L. Comolli: "Entretien avec Barney Wilen: portrait d'un fantôme," *Jm*, no.127 (1966), 30

M. LeBris: "Barney Wilen: ma direction c'est le rock," *Jh*, no.245 (1968), 28

M. Laplace: "Lexicon van Franse rietblazers," *Jazz Press*, no.12 (1977), 13

P. Lapijover: "Jazzman et Français," *Jh*, no.355 (1978), 30

"Wilen pour de vrai," *Jm*, no.357 (1987), 22

MICHEL LAPLACE

Wiley, Lee (*b* Fort Gibson, OK, 9 Oct 1915; *d* New York, 11 Dec 1975). Singer. She moved to New York around 1930 and soon began singing at the Central Park Casino. This led to regular exposure on radio, and she frequently took part in broadcasts with Paul Whiteman and Willard Robison, and was ultimately given her own program. In the early 1930s she began working with the arranger and composer Victor Young, with whom she wrote several songs, including *Got the South in my Soul* and *Any time, any day, anywhere*. In 1939–40, accompanied by small jazz groups, she made recordings of songs by George Gershwin, Cole Porter, Harold Arlen, and others, which proved highly successful. In the late 1930s Wiley became associated with Eddie Condon and his circle, and in 1943 she married Jess Stacy and toured with his short-lived big band. She performed in several of Condon's concerts at Town Hall, and continued to record periodically into the 1970s, producing several outstanding albums. The most notable of these was *Night in Manhattan* with Joe Bushkin and Bobby Hackett. With Mildred Bailey and Connee Boswell, Wiley was among the first white singers to build on the stylistic advances made by Ethel Waters. She had a husky, smoky contralto voice that was made more expressive by a pronounced vibrato; at times she also employed a higher head register.

SELECTED RECORDINGS

Lee Wiley on the Air, i (1932–6, Totem 1021); Hands across the Table/I'll follow my secret heart (1935, Decca 322); What is Love?/I've got you under my skin (1937, Decca 15034); I've got a crush on you (1939, LMS 282); A little birdie told me/You took advantage of me (1940, Gala/Rabson 3); *Lee Wiley on the Air*, ii (1944–5, Totem 1033); *Night in Manhattan* (1950, Col. CL6169), incl. Any time, any day, anywhere; *Lee Wiley Sings Rodgers and Hart* (1954, Sto. 312); *Back Home Again* (1971, MonE 7041)

BIBLIOGRAPHY

ChiltonW; *FeatherE*

G. Frazier: "Lee," *Eddie Condon's Treasury of Jazz*, ed. E. Condon and R. Gehman (New York, 1956/*R*1975), 143

G. Kuhlman: "Lee Wiley," *Coda*, xi/6 (1974), 8

M. Pinfold: "Dead, but not . . . Remembered," *JJI*, xxx/12 (1977), 12

C. Schlouch: *Lee Wiley, Love-Lee: a Discography* (Marseille, France, 1983)

L. Carr: Liner notes, *Lee Wiley Sings the Songs of George Gershwin and Cole Porter* (Audiophile AP1, 1985)

RICHARD SUDHALTER

Wilkins, Dave [David Livingstone] (*b* Barbados, 25 Sept 1914). Barbadian trumpeter. He learned to play in Salvation Army bands. He first heard jazz on American recordings in Barbados and St. Vincent, and through radio broadcasts in Trinidad, where he moved in 1935 to join the Blue Rhythm Orchestra, a band led by the double bass player John "Buddy" Williams. With three other musicians he traveled to London in 1937 to join Ken "Snake Hips" Johnson's West Indian Swing Band, with which he toured, recorded, and made radio broadcasts until Johnson's death in 1941. Wilkins then worked with English bandleaders, including Ted Heath, Harry Parry, and Joe Daniels; his playing may be heard to advantage on Parry's *I can't dance* (1942, Parl. R2851). He performed only sporadically for some years before ceasing to work in the 1970s.

BIBLIOGRAPHY

FeatherE

J. Green: "Bix in Barbados: Dave Wilkins, Trumpet," *Sv*, no.118 (1985), 136

JEFFREY P. GREEN

Wilkins, Ernie [Ernest Brooks] (*b* St. Louis, 20 July 1922). Composer, arranger, and saxophonist. He learned piano and violin, and later studied music at Wilberforce University; he first played jazz in his teens in and around St. Louis. During his military service he played in a band led by Willie Smith, after which he worked with the Jeter–Pillars Orchestra and Earl Hines's last big band (1948). Wilkins joined Count Basie in 1951, and played both alto and tenor saxophone; more importantly he gained widespread recognition as a composer. He performed in and provided arrangements for the band led by Dizzy Gillespie that toured the Middle East and South America in 1956, then wrote arrangements for Tommy Dorsey. From 1958 to 1960 he was a staff composer for Harry James's orchestra, and made several contributions to its repertory. During the 1960s he wrote for a band led by his brother the trombonist Jimmy Wilkins, and in 1968 he joined Clark Terry's Big B-A-D Band as its music director and principal composer. After appearing with Terry at the Montreux International Jazz Festival Wilkins assembled his own band. He wrote further compositions for Basie, then served as head of the artists and repertory department of Mainstream Records (1971–3). He toured Europe with Terry in the late 1970s, and in 1979 settled in Copenhagen, where he worked with both local and visiting musicians. In 1980 he organized his own group, the Almost Big Band.

SELECTED RECORDINGS

As leader: *Ernie Wilkins and the Almost Big Band* (1980, Sto. 4051); *Ernie Wilkins' Almost Big Band Live* (1981, Matrix 29203); *Montreux* (1983, Ste. 1190)

As sideman: C. Basie: *Dance Session* (1953, Clef 626); *Blues Backstage* (1954, Clef 666); C. Terry: *Live on 57th Street* (1970, Etoile 1); *Clark Terry Live at the Wichita Jazz Festival 1974* (1974, Van. 79355); *Clark Terry Live at Buddy's Place* (1976, Van. 79373)

RECORDED COMPOSITIONS

* – with Wilkins as sideman

Recorded by others: C. Basie: *Bread (1952, Clef 89085); *Sixteen Men Swingin' (1954), on Basie: *Dance Session*, ii (1952, 1954, Clef 647); on Q. Jones: *The Great Wide World of Quincy Jones* (1959, Mer. 20561), Everybody's Blues, Ghana; on H. James: *The Spectacular Sound of Harry James* (1961, MGM 3897), Connectin' the Bones, The Jazz Connoisseurs

BIBLIOGRAPHY

FeatherE; *Feather '60s*; *Feather–Gitler '70s*

R. Horricks: *Count Basie and his Orchestra: its Music and its Musicians* (London and New York, 1957), 247

L. Tomkins: "The Ernie Wilkins Story," *CI*, xiv (1975), no.2, p.23; no.4, p.6

B. Rusch: "Ernie Wilkins: Oral History," *Cadence*, ii/6–7 (1977), 3

STAN BRITT

Willebrandts, Dick (*b* 1911; *d* 1970). Dutch bandleader. He played piano with Kai Ewans in Copenhagen (1928), led a band with his brother, the pianist Philip Willebrandts (1929–34), and played with the bass player Jack de Vries (1935–8) and under the bandleader Klaas Van Beeck (1938–40). In 1942 he formed his own band, which made recordings (including *Dick Willebrandts*, 1943, HEP 10) and eventually had as many as 19 members (1944). His career suffered after World War II owing to a belief that he had collaborated with the Nazis. In the late 1950s he led a string orchestra, worked as a piano soloist on radio, and played briefly with a dixieland band and with the OK Wobblers, led by the trombonist Pi Scheffer; he ceased playing in 1963.

WIM VAN EYLE

William Ransom Hogan Jazz Archive. Archive founded as the Archives of New Orleans Jazz at Tulane University in New Orleans in 1957; *see* LIBRARIES AND ARCHIVES, §2.

Williams, Al(fred) (*b* Memphis, 17 Dec 1919). Pianist. He grew up in Chicago from 1922, studied piano from the age of seven, and worked professionally from the age of 16; in his late teens he studied classical piano and organ at the Lincoln Conservatory in Chicago with Blanche Smith Walton. He led a 12-piece orchestra that played at dance halls in Chicago (1936–8), in 1942 formed a trio, the Three Dudes, and joined Henry "Red" Allen's small group at the Down Beat Room, and then played with Jimmie Noone and Erskine Tate. In 1945 he married the singer Audrey Hobbs, and in 1948–9 the two performed together as Alfred and Audrey. He wrote arrangements for many bands in Chicago, worked in the early 1950s at the Savoy Ballroom, and played in New York with Sam "the Man" Taylor (1956–7) and in dixieland groups at the Metropole (1957). He toured Europe with Buck Clayton (1959) and Johnny Hodges (1961) and also played on Clayton's album *Copenhagen Concert* (1959, Ste. 6006–7). Later he recorded as the leader of a trio (1965), played piano for the satirical revue "The Establishment" (1968), and was the pianist, arranger, and music director for the Deep River Boys, led by Harry Douglas (1975). Williams's style is essentially that of a blues pianist, but also incorporates some elements of swing. He should not be confused with the New Orleans drummer Alfred Williams (1900–63).

Oral history material in *LNT*.

BIBLIOGRAPHY

FeatherE

A. J. McCarthy: "The Al Williams Story," *JM*, v/8 (1959), 12

JAMES M. DORAN

Williams, Bearcat. *See* WILLIAMS, JOHN (i).

Williams, Buster [Charles Anthony, Jr.] (*b* Camden, NJ, 17 April 1942). Double bass player. He was taught both double bass and drums by his father but chose to concentrate on the bass after hearing a recording of Oscar Pettiford's solo playing. He studied theory, harmony, and composition at Combs College of Music, Philadelphia (1959), then played with Jimmy Heath (1960), and toured and recorded with a quintet led by Gene Ammons and Sonny Stitt (1960–61). He played with Dakota Staton (1961–2) and Betty Carter (1962–3), and played and recorded with Sarah Vaughan (1963) and Nancy Wilson (1964–8). During his years with Wilson he moved to Los Angeles, where he played and recorded with the Jazz Crusaders (1967–9), performed with Miles Davis (1967), and recorded with Prince Lasha (1967) and a quintet led by Bobby Hutcherson and Harold Land (1967–8). In 1969 Williams moved to New York and joined Herbie Hancock, with whom he played until 1972, gaining recognition as a leading double bass player. He recorded with Dexter Gordon (1969, 1972), played and recorded with Mary Lou Williams (1973–5) and Ron Carter (1977–8), and made several recordings as a leader (1976–81). In the 1980s he played and recorded with Kenny Barron (1980–83), the Timeless All Stars (*see* TIMELESS), and SPHERE, whose repertory includes several of his own compositions. Williams has a dark, richly textured tone and uses a wide range of expressive techniques, including coarse slurring, articulate soloistic figures and a singing legato. His artistry as a soloist, characterized by excellent intonation and a consummate sense of swing, is well represented by *Bittersweet* on the album *Four for All* recorded with Sphere (1987).

SELECTED RECORDINGS

As leader: *Crystal Reflections* (1976, Muse 5101); *Heartbeat* (1978, Muse 5171); *Dreams Come True* (1981, Buddah 5728); of Sphere (with K. Barron, B. Riley, and C. Rouse): *Four in One* (1982, Elek. Mus. 60166), *Sphere on Tour* (1985, RR 191), *Four for All* (1987, Verve 831674), incl. Bittersweet

As sideman: G. Ammons and S. Stitt: *Boss Tenors* (1961, Verve 68426); S. Vaughan: *Sassy Swings the Tivoli* (1963, Mer. 60831); H. Hancock: *The Prisoner* (1969, BN 84321); M. L. Williams: *Free Spirits* (1975, Ste. 1043); R. Carter: *Piccolo* (1977, Mlst. 55004); L. Konitz: *Yes, Yes Nonet* (1979, Ste. 1119); James Williams: *The Arioso Touch* (1982, Conc. 192); F. Morgan: *Lament* (1986, Cont. 14021)

BIBLIOGRAPHY

Feather–Gitler '70s

D. C. Hunt: "Definitive Bass Artistry: Niels-Henning Ørsted Pedersen and Charles 'Buster' Williams," *J&P*, ix/10 (1970), 43

E. Meadow: "Buster Williams: About Time," *DB*, xxxvii/25 (1970), 20

R. Palmer: "Jazz Lives in New York," *RS*, no.248 (1977), 19

JOHN CURRY

Williams, Clarence (*b* Plaquemine, LA, 8 Oct ?1893; *d* New York, 6 Nov 1965). Pianist and composer. He moved to New Orleans in 1906 and traveled with a minstrel show as a singer and dancer in 1911. After returning to New Orleans he began a music publishing venture (*c*1915) with A. J. Piron. Later in the decade he moved briefly to Chicago and then permanently to New York, where he founded a music publishing firm and several music stores; he also organized many recording sessions, principally for Okeh (1923–30). The most important of Williams's groups was the Blue Five. Although noted more for its instrumental recordings made under Williams's name, this group was principally an accompanying band for such singers as Eva Taylor (Williams's wife from 1921), Sara Martin, and Sippie Wallace. It first recorded in 1923 with Thomas Morris (cornet), Charlie Irvis or John Mayfield (trombone), Sticky Elliott or Sidney Bechet (reeds), and Buddy Christian (banjo). From 1924 to 1925 the emerging genius of Louis Armstrong (who replaced Morris) rivaled Bechet's previous dominance in the group, and occasionally Buster Bailey, Aaron Thompson (replacing Bechet and Irvis), Coleman Hawkins, and Don Redman were added. This ensemble recorded a number of titles, including fine versions of *Mandy, make up your mind* and *Cake-walking Babies from Home*. After the departure of Armstrong and Bechet, the Blue Five, often including Bubber Miley, continued to record into 1927. Williams also made nearly one hundred recordings for Okeh (1927–30), Vocalion (1933–5), and Victor (1937–9) with his "washboard" bands, using such musicians as Ed Allen (cornet), Bailey or Cecil Scott (clarinet), and Floyd Casey (washboard).

Although he recorded more frequently than any other black musician of the 1920s (apart from Fletcher Henderson), Williams was a dependable rather than an exceptional pianist; his importance to early jazz lay instead in his gift for organization. He published and promoted the work of such composers as Fats Waller, James P. Johnson, Willie "the Lion" Smith, and most notably Spencer Williams. His many publications (in which he may have been involved as co-composer) include *Royal Garden Blues*, *Baby, won't you please come home*, *I ain't gonna give nobody none of my jelly roll*, *'Tain't nobody's business if I do*, and *Squeeze me*.

For illustrations *see* BECHET, SIDNEY, and OKEH.

SELECTED RECORDINGS

Duos with Bessie Smith: Down-hearted Blues (1923, Col. 3844); Baby Won't you Please Come Home Blues (1923, Col. 3888); 'Tain't nobody's business if I do (1923, Col. 3898)

As leader of Blue Five: Wild Cat Blues/Kansas City Man Blues (1923, OK 4925); Mandy, make up your mind (1924, OK 40260); Cake-walking Babies from Home (1925, OK 40321)

As leader of other groups: Nobody but my baby is getting my love/Candy Lips (1927, OK 8440); Walk that Broad/Have you ever felt that way? (1928, OK 8629)

As sideman with Bessie Smith: Nobody knows you when you're down and out (1929, Col. 14451D)

BIBLIOGRAPHY

L. Kunstadt and B. Colton: "Pioneer: Clarence Williams," *Record Research*, no.10 (1952), 8

S. B. Charters and L. Kunstadt: *Jazz: a History of the New York Scene* (Garden City, NY, 1962/*R*1981)

E. Taylor: "My Husband Clarence Williams," *Sv*, no.13 (1967), 22

B. Rust: "Clarence Williams: an Appreciation," *Sv*, no.13 (1967), 25

M. Williams: *Jazz Masters of New Orleans* (New York and London, 1967/*R*1978)

"Looking Back with Eva," *Sv*, no.14 (1967–8), 17; no.15 (1968), 18; no.16 (1968), 19

D. M. Bakker: *Clarence Williams on Microgroove* (Alphen aan de Rijn, Netherlands, 1976)

T. Lord: *Clarence Williams* (Chigwell, England, 1976)

J. R. TAYLOR/R (with MIKE HAZELDINE)

Williams, Claude [Fiddler] (*b* Muskogee, OK, 22 Feb 1908). Violinist. He played with a string band in local hotels, joined a road show, and worked in Oklahoma with the band of Oscar Pettiford and his brothers. In 1928 he joined Terrence Holder's important territory band, with which he remained after it became the Clouds of Joy under the leadership of Andy Kirk the following year. After working with Alphonso Trent (1932) he performed in Chicago with Nat "King" Cole and his brother, the double bass player Eddie Cole, and played guitar in Count Basie's orchestra from 1936 until March of the following year, when he was replaced by Freddie Green. During the following decades he worked in obscurity as a guitarist in Michigan (in the 1940s), as a member of the rhythm-and-blues band of Roy Milton (in the early 1950s), and in Kansas City (from the mid-1950s). A recording as a violinist and guitarist with Jay McShann in 1972 revived his career, and he toured with McShann in the 1970s and appeared as a soloist at jazz festivals into the 1980s. Williams's fluent style has been influenced chiefly by the work of Joe Venuti.

SELECTED RECORDINGS

As leader: *Call for the Fiddler* (1976, Ste. 1051)

As sideman: A. Kirk: Loose Ankles (1930, Bruns. 4803); C. Basie: St. Louis Blues, first issued on *The Count at the Chatterbox: 1937* (1937, Jazz Archives 16); J. McShann: *The Man from Muskogee* (1972, Sack. 3005)

BIBLIOGRAPHY

ChiltonW; *Feather–Gitler '70s*

B. Becker: "Claude Williams: Interview," *Cadence*, v (1979), no.9, p.8; no.10, p.19

CHRIS SHERIDAN

Williams, Cootie [Charles Melvin] (*b* Mobile, AL, 10 July 1911; *d* New York, 15 Sept 1985). Trumpeter and bandleader. He taught himself to play trumpet and toured with the Young Family band (which included Lester Young) when he was only 14. In 1928 he went to New York, where he made his first recordings (with James P. Johnson) and played briefly in the bands of Chick Webb and Fletcher Henderson. By February 1929 he had joined the Duke Ellington Orchestra as a replacement for Bubber Miley, beginning a long association which was to make him famous. In his first 11 years with Ellington his playing became an indispensable part of the band's sonority, and Ellington integrated solos for him into hundreds of compositions. Williams also took part in many excellent small-group recordings with Teddy Wilson, Billie Holiday, Lionel Hampton, Charlie Christian, and other leading jazz musicians of the swing period.

After leaving Ellington in November 1940, Williams played for a year in Benny Goodman's band and small groups, then formed his own successful big band, which was booked several times at the Savoy Ballroom, New York, and included some important aspiring bop musicians such as Charlie Parker and Bud Powell. Gradually, though still at the height of his powers, Williams faded from public view. Forced to reduce his band to a smaller ensemble in 1948, and finally to discontinue it altogether, he became active as a rhythm-and-blues musician in the 1950s and later led his own small jazz group, with which he took part in several important recording sessions with Rex Stewart in 1957–8. In 1962 he rejoined Ellington's band, where he remained, with brief interruptions, until the late 1970s.

Williams was a master of swing-style jazz trumpet playing, and achieved a range of tone and shading on his instrument that was unsurpassed in his day. Having quickly mastered the growl and plunger effects of Bubber Miley, his predecessor in Ellington's band, Williams extended these techniques to encompass an unprecedented variety of moods and timbres, from gentle nostalgia to searing vehemence. Although he remained supreme in the use of the growl and plunger mutes, Williams was equally adept on the open instrument, particularly as an accompanist to jazz singers and as an interpreter of the blues. His playing inspired Ellington to one of his greatest masterpieces, the *Concerto for Cootie* (1940), where Williams may be heard using straight mute, plunger mute, and open trumpet. In later years Williams's style lost some of its subtlety but none of its urgency and swing, as attested by his performance in the *New Concerto for Cootie* (1963), written by Ellington to celebrate his return to the band.

Cootie Williams (left) with Harry James (trumpet) and Benny Goodman (clarinet), 1941

Williams was also an effective if reluctant jazz singer, and collaborated with Ellington on several pieces, such as *Echoes of the Jungle,* as well as with Thelonious Monk on his well-known ballad *'Round about Midnight.*

Oral history material in *NjR* (JOHP).

For further illustration *see* TRUMPET.

SELECTED RECORDINGS

As leader: Diga diga doo (1937, Var. 555); West End Blues (1941, OK 6370); *Cootie in Hi-fi* (1958, RCA LPM1718)

As leader with R. Stewart: *The Big Challenge* (1957, Jazztone 1268); *Porgy and Bess Revisited* (1958, WB 1260)

As sideman with D. Ellington: Ring dem bells (1930, Vic. 22528); Echoes of the Jungle (1931, Vic. 22743); Echoes of Harlem (Cootie's Concerto) (1936, Bruns. 7650); The New East St. Louis Toodle-oo (1937, Master 101); Concerto for Cootie (1940, Vic. 26598); Harlem Air Shaft (1940, Vic. 26731); *Suite Thursday* (1963, Atl. 2-304), incl. New Concerto for Cootie

BIBLIOGRAPHY

A. Hodeir: *Hommes et problèmes du jazz, suivi de La religion du jazz* (Paris, 1954; Eng. trans., rev. Hodeir, as *Jazz: its Evolution and Essence,* New York, 1956/*R*1975)

H. P[anassié]: "Réflexions sur la récente tournée Cootie Williams," *BHcF,* no.86 (1959), 10

W. Balliett: *Such Sweet Thunder* (Indianapolis, 1966) [colln of previously pubd articles and reviews], 108

V. Wilmer: "Cootie Williams," *JM,* xiii/6 (1967), 2 [interview]

S. Dance: *The World of Duke Ellington* (London and New York, 1970/*R*1981) [colln of previously pubd articles and reviews], 102

E. Townley: "Reminiscing with Cootie Williams," *Sv,* no.71 (1977), 170

C. Battestini and J.-P Battestini: "Cootie Williams parle de son grand orchestre (1942–1947)," *BHcF,* no.283 (1980), 9

E. Lambert: "Regal Cootie," *JJI,* xxxiv/2 (1981), 18

T. Burke and D. Penny: "The Cootie Williams Orchestra, 1942–1950," *Blues & Rhythm: the Gospel Truth,* no.3 (1984), 12

J. BRADFORD ROBINSON

Williams, David [Happy] (*b* Trinidad, West Indies, 17 Sept 1946). Trinidadian double bass player. He worked in New York with Beaver Harris (1969) and studied with Ron Carter. After playing with Chuck Mangione in Rochester, New York (1969–70), he performed and recorded with the popular singer Roberta Flack (1970–72). Thereafter he worked with Ornette Coleman, Donald Byrd, Charles McPherson, and Billy Taylor (ii), performed and recorded with Duke Jordan (1973), and recorded with Charles Davis and Kenny Barron (1974, playing both double bass and electric bass guitar). In 1975 Williams toured Europe with Elvin Jones and recorded in Rome with Don Pullen, George Adams, and Archie Shepp. He is heard to advantage on *New Agenda* (1975, Van. 79362) recorded with Elvin Jones. After returning to the USA he continued to work with Jones (1975–6). Later he recorded with Sam Jones (1976), Art Pepper (1976, 1981), and Slide Hampton (1985), and performed and recorded with Cedar Walton (1983–5). In 1986 he became a member of Woody Shaw's quintet. (*Feather–Gitler '70s*)

Williams, Eddie [Edward] (*b* New York, *c*1910). Saxophonist. In the early 1930s he worked with Claude Hopkins and led his own band at the Savoy Ballroom, New York. He recorded on clarinet with Billy Kyle (1937), on tenor saxophone with the Mills Blue Rhythm Band, led by Lucky Millinder (1937) and Don Redman (1939), and on alto saxophone with Jelly Roll Morton (1940); his recordings with Morton include *Swinging the Elks* (General Tavern Tunes 1711), which displays his unusual, "slippery" tone. After re-joining Millinder he played with Ella Fitzgerald (1941), Henry "Red" Allen and Chris Columbus (1942), and the De Paris brothers, Redman, Cliff Jackson, and James P. Johnson (all 1943–4); he performed and recorded on tenor saxophone with Garvin Bushell (late 1944) on the West Coast. During his military service (1945–6) he played in Europe and from the late 1940s he led his own small band. He worked regularly with Happy Caldwell in the 1960s.

based on *ChiltonW*

Williams, Elmer (A.) [Tone] (*b* Red Bank, NJ, 1905; *d* Red Bank, June 1962). Tenor saxophonist and clarinetist. He worked with Claude Hopkins in 1926–7 and then joined Chick Webb, with whom he remained until 1934; he also played briefly with McKinney's Cotton Pickers in 1931. He made several recordings with Webb, and his tenor saxophone playing may be heard to advantage on *Stomping at the Savoy* (1934, Col. 2926D). Williams was a member of Fletcher Henderson's band from 1935 until 1939, when he joined Horace Henderson. He performed and recorded as a tenor saxophonist with Ella Fitzgerald (1941) and Lucky Millinder (1944–5) and also worked again with Hopkins (1946) and Fletcher Henderson (1950). In the late 1950s he played in Milan with the tenor saxophonist Freddy Mitchell.

BIBLIOGRAPHY

W. C. Allen: *Hendersonia: the Music of Fletcher Henderson and his Musicians: a Bio-discography* (Highland Park, NJ, 1973)

J. Evensmo: *The Tenor Saxophones of Budd Johnson, Cecil Scott, Elmer Williams, Dick Wilson, 1927–1942* (n.p. [Oslo], n.d. [?1977]) [discography]

based on *ChiltonW*

Williams, Fess [Stanley R.] (*b* Danville, KY, 10 April 1894; *d* New York, 17 Dec 1975). Bandleader, clarinetist, and alto saxophonist. He began playing violin, but after 1909 concentrated on clarinet. In 1914 he moved to Cincinnati, where he later worked as a leader (1919–23). After settling in New York (1924) he led his own Royal Flush Orchestra (from 1925), which was resident at the Savoy Ballroom (1926–8); he made a number of recordings with the band as a singer, clarinetist, and alto saxophonist (including *Make me know it*, 1926, OK 8322). In 1928 he acted as the leader of Dave Peyton's band in Chicago and after returning to New York (1929) he led his own bands there and on tour during the 1930s. Among his sidemen in the early 1930s were Bob Shoffner, Rex Stewart, Albert Nicholas, Garvin Bushell, and Jerome Don Pasquall. Williams ceased full-time playing, but continued to lead a small group in the 1940s. In the 1960s he performed occasionally and managed a vocal group.

BIBLIOGRAPHY

H. Smith: "The Fess Williams Story," *Record Research*, iii/3 (1957), 3
F. Driggs: "Good-bye Fess," *Sv*, no.67 (1976), 14

based on *ChiltonW*

Williams, Fiddler. *See* WILLIAMS, CLAUDE.

Williams, Franc(is) (*b* McConnell's Mills, PA, 20 Sept 1910; *d* Houston, PA, 2 Oct 1983). Trumpeter. He first performed with the Chicago Nightingales, led by the trombonist Frank Terry, in the 1930s, then in 1940 moved to New York and toured with the big band that Fats Waller directed for his stage shows. He continued to be associated with big bands, including those of Claude Hopkins, Edgar Hayes, Ella Fitzgerald (1941–2), Sabby Lewis (1943), and Machito (1944), before working with the Duke Ellington Orchestra (1945–9). An example of his solo playing may be heard on the third chorus of *Trumpet No End*, recorded with Ellington in 1946. During the 1950s and 1960s Williams played mainly with Latin bands and in theater orchestras, though he rejoined Ellington briefly in 1951. Thereafter he worked with Clyde Bernhardt, led his own quartet in New York, toured overseas as a solo artist, and performed in the Harlem Blues and Jazz Band. From the late 1970s he was a member of Panama Francis's Savoy Sultans.

Oral history material in *CtY*.

SELECTED RECORDINGS

As sideman: D. Ellington: Trumpet No End [Blue Skies] (1946, Musi. 484); P. Francis: *Grooving* (1982, Stash 218)

BIBLIOGRAPHY

ChiltonW
E. Townley: "Franc Williams," *Sv*, no.70 (1977), 124
"Francis Williams," *BHcF*, no.267 (1978), 4

EDDIE LAMBERT

Williams, Henry "Rubberlegs." *See* WILLIAMS, RUBBERLEGS.

Williams, James (*b* Memphis, 8 March 1951). Pianist. He began learning piano at the age of 13, and at first played gospel music and rhythm-and-blues; he did not become interested in jazz until he began attending Memphis State University. After graduating Williams moved to Boston, where he taught at the Berklee College of Music (1974–7) and worked with many groups in the area, including those of Alan Dawson, Joe Henderson, Woody Shaw, Milt Jackson, and Clark Terry. His most famous association was with Art Blakey's Jazz Messengers (1977–81), during which he matured as both a pianist and a composer. In the mid-1980s he has led his own groups and worked occasionally as a sideman with Sonny Stitt, Louis Hayes, and Slide Hampton, among others. Williams has recorded several times as a leader, often with groups that include lesser-known but talented players from Memphis. A pianist of great promise, he cites Red Garland, Wynton Kelly, Herbie Hancock, and Ahmad Jamal as influences upon his style.

SELECTED RECORDINGS

Duos with D. Irwin: *Focus* (1977, Red 132)
As leader: *Everything I Love* (1979, Conc. 104); *Images* (1980, Conc. 140); *The Arioso Touch* (1982, Conc. 192); *Alter ego* (1984, Sunnyside 1007); *Progress Report* (1985, Sunnyside 1012)
As sideman: A Blakey: *In my Prime* (1977–8, Tim. 114, 118); C. Fuller: *Four on the Outside* (1978, Tim. 124); A. Blakey: *In this Korner* (1978, Conc. 68); *Live at Bubba's* (1980, Who's Who in Jazz 21019); *Album of the Year* (1981, Tim. 155); *Straight Ahead* (1981, Conc. 168)

BIBLIOGRAPHY

F. Bouchard: "James Williams," *DB*, xlv/16 (1978), 48
J. Williams: "How to Write for the Jazz Messengers," *DB*, xlvi/17 (1979), 89
B. Rusch: "James Williams: Interview," *Cadence*, vii/4 (1981), 10
S. Vandermack: "James Williams," *Cadence*, x (1984), no.4, p.15; no.5, p.5

SCOTT YANOW

Williams, J. Mayo [Ink] (*b* Monmouth, IL, 1894; *d* Chicago, 2 Jan 1980). Record producer. After attending Brown University and working for a period as a professional football player, he became a producer and talent scout for Paramount's race series in Chicago around 1924; he also ran the associated publishing company Chicago Music. In March 1927 he left Paramount to establish his own Chicago Record Company, but its Black Patti label survived only until around September of that year. He worked for the Vocalion and Brunswick race series, and again managed a related publishing operation, which remained in existence after he became head of the race department of the newly formed Decca company (1934). As one of the very few Blacks employed in positions of responsibility in the recording business before World War II, he played an important role in recording many of the great jazz and blues musicians of the period. In the mid-1940s he worked as a freelance producer and ran a succession of small labels – Chicago, Southern, Harlem, and South Center – whose material was also leased to other companies, such as King and Decca. From the late 1940s his principal label was Ebony, on which he issued both newly recorded material and electronically modified reissues of prewar material. He retired owing to ill-health in the early 1970s.

BIBLIOGRAPHY

S. Dance: "Lightly and Politely 938: Back on the Scene," *JJ*, xvii/6 (1964), 24
R. M. W. Dixon and J. Godrich: *Recording the Blues* (London, 1970)
J. O'Neal and C. Baker: "Chicago Blues Label Guide," *Living Blues*, no.12 (1973), 8
Obituary, J. O'Neal, *Living Blues*, nos.45–6 (1980), 94

HOWARD RYE

Williams, Joe [Goreed, Joseph] (*b* Cordele, GA, 12 Dec 1918). Singer. He grew up in Chicago, where his primary musical influence was the gospel quartet in which he sang. He began performing professionally in 1937 and worked as a soloist in and around Chicago, occasionally singing with bands led by Jimmie Noone (1937), Coleman Hawkins (1941), Lionel Hampton (1943), Andy Kirk (1946), and Red Saunders (1950, 1951, 1953). From 1954 to 1961 he was a member of Count Basie's band, where his dramatic performance of ballads and powerful blues singing were an immediate success; among the many hit recordings he made with the group is *Every day I have the blues* (1955). Thereafter Williams maintained a career as a soloist, appearing in clubs, on television, and at festivals. He toured and recorded with such musicians as Harry Edison (1961–2), Junior Mance (1962–4), George Shearing (1971), and Cannonball Adderley (1973–5), and frequently rejoined Basie. He made a highly successful tour of the USA and Europe with the Count Basie Orchestra under the direction of Thad Jones in 1985.

With his rich bass-baritone voice and passionate style of delivery, Williams reshaped the role of the big-band singer and brought it up to date without sacrificing his innate taste and musical imagination.

SELECTED RECORDINGS

As leader: *Joe Williams Sings Everyday* (1950–51, Reg. 6002); *Together* (1961, Roul. 52069); *Joe Williams at Newport '63* (1963, RCA LSP2762); *Presenting Joe Williams* (1966, SolS 18008); *Joe Williams Live* (1973, Fan. 9441); with Prez Conference: *Prez and Joe* (1979, GNP Crescendo 2124)

As sideman: C. Basie: *Count Basie Swings & Joe Williams Sings* (1955, Clef MGC678), incl. Every day I have the blues; *Memories Ad-lib* (1958, Roul. 52021); on C. Bolling: *Jazz Gala 79* (1979, America 015-16), Blues in my Heart

BIBLIOGRAPHY

R. J. Gleason: "Every Day is a Good Day for Joe Williams," *DB*, xxiii/11 (1956), 11
R. Horricks: "Joe Williams," *JM*, ii/7 (1956), 7
L. Tomkins: "Frankly Speaking: Joe Williams," *Crescendo*, i/6 (1963), 10
B. Gardner: "Is Joe Williams Really Joe Williams?," *DB*, xxxi/32 (1964), 19
A. J. Smith: "Joe Williams: the Well Tempered Blaze of Vocal Excellence," *DB*, xliii/9 (1976), 11 [incl. discography]
S. Dance: *The World of Count Basie* (New York and London, 1980) [colln of previously pubd interviews], 198
J. E. Siegel: "Talking with Joe Williams," *Radio Free Jazz*, xxi (1980), Jan, 12
D. J. Travis: *An Autobiography of Black Jazz* (Chicago, 1983), 467
L. Gourse: *Every Day: the Story of Joe Williams* (London, Melbourne, Australia, and New York, 1985) [incl. discography]

BOB WEIR

Williams, John (Overton) [Bearcat] **(i)** (*b* Memphis, 13 April 1905). Saxophonist and clarinetist. He began performing in his teens. In 1923–8 he led his own band, with which he recorded (1927); during this time he married Mary Lou Scruggs, who was his pianist. In 1928 he joined Terrence Holder in Oklahoma City, and he remained with the band when Andy Kirk assumed its leadership the following year (for illustration *see* WILLIAMS, MARY LOU). His baritone saxophone playing may be heard on *Blue Clarinet Stomp* (1929, Bruns. 4694), one of many recordings he made with Kirk (1929–38). After leaving Kirk in 1939 he ceased playing until 1942, when he joined Cootie Williams's band as an alto and baritone saxophonist.

BIBLIOGRAPHY

M. L. Williams: "My Friends the Kings of Jazz," *MM*, xxx (3–17 April 1954)
A. McCarthy: *Big Band Jazz* (New York and London, 1974)

based on *ChiltonW*

Williams, John (ii) (*b* Windsor, VT, 28 Jan 1929). Pianist and leader. He played in Boston with a big band led by Mal Hallett (1945) and with Johnny Bothwell (1948) and Teddy Kotick before moving to New York (1949). After finishing military service in 1953 he played briefly with Charlie Barnet, then toured and recorded with Stan Getz. The following year he worked with Bob Brookmeyer, Nick Travis, and Bill De Arango, recorded as a leader, and rejoined Getz. He then led his own trio, and worked as a freelance, recording with Charlie Mariano, Cannonball Adderley, Jimmy Cleveland, and Phil Woods (all 1955), Al Cohn, Zoot Sims, and Jimmy Raney (all 1956), and the trombonist Lon Norman (*c*1957). He is heard to advantage on *Woodlore* (1955, Prst. 7018), recorded with Woods, and on his own album *John Williams Trio* (1955, EmA 36061).

BIBLIOGRAPHY

FeatherE
A. Morgan: "John Williams: the Pianist from Vermont," *JM*, viii (1962), no.8, p.3; no.9, p.13 [incl. discography]

Williams, John (Charles) (iii) (*b* London, 8 Feb 1941). English baritone saxophonist. His first professional work was as the leader of a resident big band at the Marquee Club, London (1961–3), where Neil Ardley and the electric guitarist Phil Lee were among his sidemen. He later formed an octet (1969) and big band (1973). In the 1980s the former has included the trumpeter Dick Pearce, the pianist Pete Saberton, and Trevor Tompkins; Williams's playing is well represented on *Snow Palace* from its LP *The Year of the Buffalo* (1985, Spot. 532). Among the other ensembles Williams has led are the saxophone quartet Changing Face (1976–8), the trio Spectrum (from 1985) and the Baritone Band (from 1985), which comprises four baritone saxophonists (including Ronnie Ross and Chris Biscoe) and a rhythm player; he has composed music for all his groups. He has also played and recorded with Keith Tippett (1970–75), Alan Cohen (1971–3), and Don Rendell (1979–81). He instituted an annual summer music festival at his home in Shropshire in 1981. (R. Cotterrell, ed.: *Jazz Now: the Jazz Centre Society Guide*, London, 1976)

NEVIL SKRIMSHIRE

Williams, John (B., Jr.) (iv) (*b* New York, 27 Feb 1941). Bass player. He first played drums, and took up double bass while in the army. After studying with Ron Carter for two years he performed, toured, and recorded with Horace Silver (1967–9) and worked with Kenny Burrell and Kai Winding (both 1969), Dizzy Gillespie and Hugh Masekela (both 1970), and Clark Terry and Zoot Sims. He recorded on double bass with Mose Allison (1970), on electric bass guitar with Count Basie (1970) and Leone Thomas (*c*1970), and on both instruments with Roy Ayers (1970–71) and as a member of the quintet led by Bobby Hutcherson and Harold Land (*c*1971). In 1972 he became a staff musician at NBC and played in the orchestra for the "Tonight Show." Later he performed and recorded with Billy Cobham, again playing electric bass guitar, and toured the Middle East as a member of Benny Carter's quintet (1975–6). Williams also recorded with Louie Bellson (1975, 1976, 1978), Carl Burnett (1980), Gerald Wilson and Paul Humphrey (both 1981), and Jon Hendricks and the Art Farmer–Benny Golson Quintet (both 1982). He is heard to advantage on his own album *Let's Have Fun Together* (1982, New York Jazz 004). (*Feather–Gitler '70s*)

Williams, Johnny [John, Jr.] (*b* Memphis, 13 March 1908). Double bass player. During the early 1930s he played tuba, then double bass, in southern territory bands. In 1936 he moved to New York, where he played with the Mills Blue Rhythm Band (1937–8), then worked briefly with Benny Carter. In 1939 he made the first of several recordings with Billie Holiday, played with Frankie Newton, and joined Coleman Hawkins. After leaving Hawkins the following year he played with Louis Armstrong until 1942 (he was also associated with Armstrong on a few later occasions). Thereafter he worked in small bands led by Teddy Wilson (1942–4; for illustration *see* WILSON, TEDDY) and Edmond Hall (1944–7) and played with Tab Smith (*c*1948–1952) and Johnny Hodges (*c*1952–1955). Williams then ceased working as a full-time musician, but in 1968 he traveled to France with Buddy Tate, and in the 1970s he worked frequently with Red Richards. He also toured with Bob Greene's concert troupe, the World of Jelly Roll Morton (1978–82), and with the Harlem Blues and Jazz Band (from 1978). He has continued to perform into the mid-1980s.

SELECTED RECORDINGS

As sideman: Mills Blue Rhythm Band: Blue Rhythm Fantasy (1937, Var. 503); B. Holiday: Strange Fruit (1939, Com. 526); C. Hawkins: Bouncing with Bean (1940, Bb 10693); L. Armstrong: Rockin' Chair, first issued on *Carnegie Hall Concert* (1947, Collectors' Rarities 520); J. Hodges: *Used to be Duke* (1954, Norg. 1060); D. Cheatham and H. Hall: *Fessor's Nighthawks* (1979, Met. 627)

BIBLIOGRAPHY

J. Poinsot and L. Verdeaux: "Johnny Williams," *BHcF*, no.245 (1975), 5 [interview]

J. Chilton: "Rhythm from Memphis," *Sv*, no.82 (1979), 132

P. Vacher: "Williams on Bass," *MR*, vii/12 (1980), 7

C. Deffaa: "Still Counting his Blessings," *MR*, xiii/3 (1986), 8

CHIP DEFFAA

Williams, Leroy (*b* Chicago, 3 Feb 1937). Drummer. He began playing drums at the age of 15 and was largely self-taught. He was a member of the trio led by the pianist Judy Roberts (1959–64) and then moved to New York, where he performed with Booker Ervin in 1967. In 1968 he played with Sonny Rollins and at the Newport Jazz Festival with Archie Shepp, and joined Clifford Jordan's ensemble. A year later he made the first of five albums with Barry Harris. After playing with Wilbur Ware, Williams worked with Hank Mobley (1970), Yusef Lateef (1971), and Ray Bryant (from 1971); while he was with Bryant he recorded two albums under Charles McPherson's leadership (1971–2). In 1973 he played with James Moody and Stan Getz. During the 1970s he recorded with Andrew Hill (1975), Sonny Stitt (1975), Al Cohn (1976), Rein de Graaff (1976–7), Earl Coleman (1977), Junior Cook (1977, 1979), and Buddy Tate and Bob Wilber (both 1978). He appeared with Pepper Adams at the Kansas City Jazz Festival in 1979 and the following year recorded with him and with Stitt. In the early 1980s he played (with Art Davis) in a rhythm section that accompanied Tommy Flanagan and Harris. A versatile drummer, Williams provides strong support for the ensemble and produces a clean, crisp sound.

SELECTED RECORDINGS

As sideman: B. Harris: *Magnificent* (1969, Prst. 7733); *Barry Harris Plays Tadd Dameron* (1975, Xan. 113); A. Cohn: *Al Cohn's America* (1976, Xan. 138); P. Adams: *The Master* (1980, Muse 5213)

BIBLIOGRAPHY

Feather–Gitler '70s

GARY CARNER

Williams, Martin (Tudor Hansford) (*b* Richmond, VA, 9 Aug 1924). Writer. After studying English literature at the University of Virginia (BA 1948), the University of Pennsylvania (MA 1950), and Columbia University, he held appointments as jazz critic for the *Saturday Review, Evergreen Review*, and the *New York Times*. With Nat Hentoff, he founded the *Jazz Review* in 1958, and served as editor until 1961. He has also contributed to *Down Beat* and other journals, and has written and edited several books. In 1970 Williams became director of the jazz and American culture programs in the division of performing arts of the Smithsonian Institution, and in 1983 was appointed editor of special projects in books and recordings at the Smithsonian Press. In this capacity, he regularly presents jazz concerts at the institution, and has selected and annotated recordings for the Smithsonian collections of Classic Jazz and (with Gunther Schuller) Big Band Jazz.

WRITINGS

(selective list)

ed.: *The Art of Jazz: Essays on the Nature and Development of Jazz* (New York, 1959/*R*1979)

King Oliver (London, 1960)

ed.: *Jazz Panorama* (New York and London, 1962/*R*1979)

Jelly Roll Morton (London, 1962)

Where's the Melody? A Listener's Introduction to Jazz (New York, 1966/*R*1983, rev. 2/1969)

Jazz Masters of New Orleans (New York and London, 1967/*R*1978)

Jazz Masters in Transition, 1957–69 (New York and London, 1970/*R*1980)

The Jazz Tradition (New York, 1970, rev. 2/1983)

Jazz Heritage (New York, and Oxford, England, 1985) [colln of previously pubd articles]

PAULA MORGAN/R

Williams, Mary Lou [née Scruggs, Mary Elfrieda] (*b* Atlanta, 8 May 1910; *d* Durham, NC, 28 May 1981). Pianist and composer. She grew up in Pittsburgh, where she played professionally from a very early age. Taking her stepfather's name, she performed as Mary Lou Burley. In 1925 she joined a group led by John Williams (i), whom she married. When in 1929 Andy Kirk took over Terrence Holder's band, of which John was a member, Mary Lou served the group as deputy pianist

Mary Lou Williams with Andy Kirk and the Twelve Clouds of Joy at the Trianon Ballroom, Cleveland, 1937: (back row, left to right) Earl Miller, John Williams (i), Dick Wilson, and John Harrington (saxophones), Ben Thigpen (drums); (middle row) Harry Lawson, Paul King, and Earl Thomson (trumpets), Ted Donnelly (trombone), Kirk (director), Booker Collins (double bass); (front) Williams (piano)

and arranger until April 1930, at which time she became a regular member (see illustration). The fame of Kirk's band in the 1930s was due largely to Williams's distinctive arrangements, compositions, and solo performances on piano; she also provided noteworthy swing-band scores for Benny Goodman, Earl Hines, Tommy Dorsey, and others. After leaving Kirk in 1942 Williams formed her own small group in New York with her second husband, Shorty Baker, as trumpeter. She briefly served as staff arranger for Duke Ellington, writing for him the well-known *Trumpet No End* in 1946. In the same year three movements from the *Zodiac Suite* were performed at Carnegie Hall by the New York PO, a very early instance of the recognition of jazz by a leading symphony orchestra.

By now Williams had become an important figure in New York bop, contributing scores to Dizzy Gillespie's big band and advancing the careers of many younger musicians. From 1952 to 1954 she was based in Europe. She retired from music in 1954 to pursue religious and charitable interests, but resumed her career in 1957. She remained active throughout the 1960s and 1970s, leading her own groups in New York clubs, composing sacred works for jazz orchestra and voices, and devoting much of her time to teaching. In 1970, as a solo pianist, and providing her own commentary, she recorded *The History of Jazz* (FW 2860). Towards the end of her life she received a number of honorary doctorates from American universities, and from 1977 taught on the staff of Duke University.

Williams was long regarded as the only significant female musician in jazz, both as an instrumentalist and as a composer, but her achievement is remarkable by any standards. She was an important swing pianist, with a lightly rocking, legato manner based on subtly varied stride and boogie-woogie bass patterns. Yet by constantly exploring and extending her style she retained the status of a modernist for most of her career. She adapted easily in the 1940s to the new bop idiom, and in the 1960s her playing attained a level of complexity and dissonance that rivaled avant-garde jazz pianism of the time, but without losing an underlying blues feeling. A similar breadth may be seen in her work as a composer and arranger, from her expert swing-band scores for Kirk (*Walkin' and Swingin'*, *Mary's Idea*) to the large-scale sacred works of the 1960s and 1970s. Her *Waltz Boogie* of 1946 was one of the earliest attempts to adapt jazz to non-duple meters. Among her sacred works are a cantata, *Black Christ of the Andes* (1963), and three masses, of which the third, *Mary Lou's Mass* (1970), became well known in a version choreographed by Alvin Ailey.

Oral history material in *CtY*, *GBLnsa*, *NjR* (JOHP), *NjR*.

SELECTED RECORDINGS

As leader: Little Joe from Chicago (1944, Asch 1002); Roll 'em (1944, Asch 1003); *Zodiac Suite* (1945, Asch 620–21); Waltz Boogie (1946, Vic. 202025); *In London* (1953, Vogue 22); *Black Christ of the Andes* (1963, Saba 15062); *Mary Lou Williams Presents* (1964, FW 32843); *From the Heart* (1970, Chi. 103); *Mary Lou's Mass* (1970–72, Mary 102); with C. Taylor: *Embraced* (1977, PL 2620108); *My Mama Pinned a Rose on Me* (1977, Pablo 2310819)

SELECTED ARRANGEMENTS

(all recorded by A. Kirk with Williams as sideman)

Mess-a-Stomp (1929, Bruns. 4694); Walkin' and Swingin' (1936, Decca 809); Froggy Bottom (1936, Decca 729); In the Groove (1937, Decca 1261); Mary's Idea (1938, Decca 2326)

BIBLIOGRAPHY

S. Pease: *Boogie-woogie Piano Styles* (Chicago, 1940, 1943) [incl. transcrs.]
M. Jones: "Mary Lou Williams: a Life Story," *MM*, xxx (3 April–12 June 1954)
M. McPartland: "Mary Lou," *DB*, xxiv/21 (1957), 12
L. Tomkins: "The Mary Lou Williams Story," *CI*, ix/12 (1971), 6; x/1 (1971), 25 [interview]
R. Baggenaes: "Mary Lou Williams: an Interview," *Coda*, xi/10 (1974), 2
A. McCarthy: *Big Band Jazz* (New York and London, 1974), 242
O. Coyle: "Mary Lou Williams & her Jazz Crusade," *MR*, iii/6 (1976), 5
W. Balliett: "Out Here Again," *Improvising: Sixteen Jazz Musicians and their Art* (New York, 1977) [colln of previously pubd articles], 59
C. Battestini and J.-P. Battestini: "Mary Lou Williams raconte sa vie," *BHcF*, no.266 (1978), 7
D. A. Handy: "First Lady of the Jazz Keyboard," *Black Perspective in Music*, viii (1980), 195
E. Townley: "An Interview with Mary Lou," *MR*, vii/3 (1980), 4
S. Britt: "The First Lady of Jazz: Mary Lou Williams," *JJI*, xxxiv/6 (1981), 10 [interview]
L. Lyons: *The Great Jazz Pianists, Speaking of their Lives and Music* (New York, 1983), 67
L. D. Holmes and J. W. Thomson: *Jazz Greats: Getting Better with Age* (New York, 1986) [colln of interviews]
M. McPartland: "Into the Sun: an Affectionate Sketch of Mary Lou Williams," *All in Good Time* (New York, and Oxford, England, 1987) [colln of previously pubd articles], 69

J. BRADFORD ROBINSON

Williams, Midge (*b* California, *c*1908; *d* ? after mid-1940s). Singer. She began singing professionally in 1927 and in the early 1930s she toured the Far East; she was resident at a club in Shanghai (1933) and then performed in Tokyo, where she recorded in Japanese. After returning to the USA (1934), she presented her own radio series in Los Angeles (1934–6) and toured for a time with Fats Waller. In the mid-1930s she recorded with Frank Froeba and Teddy Wilson (both 1936), and Miff Mole (1937), and in 1937–8 she made several recordings in Chicago as a leader (including *I was born to swing*, 1937, Voc. 3838); at others of these sessions she was accompanied by John Kirby's group. Williams sang with Louis Armstrong's big band for several years (1938–41) and recorded with Lil Armstrong (1940); after 1941 she worked as a solo singer.

based on *ChiltonW*

Williams, Nelson [Cadillac] (*b* Birmingham, AL, 26 Sept 1917; *d* Voorburg, Netherlands, late Nov 1973). Trumpeter. In the early 1930s he toured with the boogie-woogie pianist Cow Cow Davenport and with vaudeville shows. After working in Birmingham and Philadelphia he joined Tiny Bradshaw (1939), played in an army band for three years, and performed with Billy Eckstine, John Kirby, and Billy Kyle. From 1949 to 1951 he was a member of Duke Ellington's orchestra, with which he made several recordings, and in 1951 he moved to Paris. Williams remained in Europe, performing and recording swing and mainstream jazz as a trumpeter, singer, and leader; he also played with revivalist groups and rejoined Ellington's band on tour on several occasions (1956, 1958, 1969, 1970). By 1963 he had settled in Voorburg. Among his many recordings are *Casanova/Creole Love Call* (1951, Vogue 5108), which he made as the leader of a quintet including Don Byas and Zutty Singleton. (*ChiltonW*; *FeatherE*)

Williams, Pearlis (*b* Gloucester, MS, 14 May 1909). Drummer. His first job was with Albert Ammons. He then moved to Chicago, where he played and recorded with Herb Morand in the Harlem Hamfats from 1936 to 1938. Later, in St. Louis, he joined Cootie Williams, and toured with him to New York. Thereafter he settled in Kansas City, where in the early 1950s he played with Miles Davis. (P. Van Vorst: "The Harlem Hamfats," *MR*, iv/4 (1977), 5)

MICHAEL TOVEY

Williams, Richard (Gene) [Notes] (*b* Galveston, TX, 4 May 1931; *d* New York, 5 Nov 1985). Trumpeter. Having been inspired at an early age by the bop trumpet playing of Fats Navarro and the compositions of Charlie Parker, he took up the tenor saxophone, then the trumpet, while in his teens. He played in local bands on the Gulf coast of Texas, received a degree in music from Wiley College, and served for four years in the air force; on his discharge in September 1956 he joined Lionel Hampton's big band, with which he toured Europe as a principal trumpeter. After returning to the USA he received a master's degree from the Manhattan School of Music, then worked with Gigi Gryce (1959–62, recording in 1960–61), Charles Mingus (1959–64), Lou Donaldson (1960), Quincy Jones (1961), Slide Hampton (1961–3, performing and recording in Paris in 1962), Yusef Lateef (1963–4), Orchestra U. S. A. (1964), and Duke Ellington (1965, recording in 1965 and 1971). He toured Europe and Japan with the Thad Jones–Mel Lewis Orchestra (1966–9) and played with Gil Evans (1973), again with Lionel Hampton (1975), and in pit orchestras on Broadway. In the early 1970s in Europe he worked occasionally as a freelance with his own quartet; later he recorded with Duke Jordan (1975) and Sam Jones (1979) and as a member of Mingus Dynasty (1982).

SELECTED RECORDINGS

As leader: *New Horn in Town* (1960, Can. 9003)

As sideman: O. Nelson: *Screamin' the Blues* (1960, NewJ 8243); C. Mingus: *Mingus, Mingus, Mingus, Mingus, Mingus* (1963, Imp. 54); Y. Lateef: *Live at Pep's* (1964, Imp. 69); *Club Date* (1964, Imp. 9310); G. Evans: *Svengali* (1973, Atl. 1643); Mingus Dynasty: *Reincarnation* (1982, SN 1042)

BIBLIOGRAPHY

Feather '60s; *Feather–Gitler '70s*
N. Hentoff: Liner notes, *New Horn in Town* (Can. 9003, 1961)
H. Saunders: "Richard Williams: Graceful Notes," *JSN*, i/5 (1980), 34
B. Priestley: *Mingus: a Critical Biography* (London, Melbourne, Australia, and New York, 1982), 105

GARY THEROUX

Williams, Roy (*b* Salford, England, 7 March 1937). English trombonist. After military service he joined a band in London led by the trumpeter Mike Peters (1960), then performed and recorded with Terry Lightfoot (1961). With Alex Welsh's band, which he joined in 1965, he toured and recorded with such visiting American musicians as Bud Freeman, Wild Bill Davison, and Ruby Braff. At this time Williams gained widespread recognition for his forceful ensemble playing and fluent, imaginative solos. His work may be heard to advantage on *Tea for Two*, a duet which he recorded with George Chisholm accompanied by Welsh's rhythm section on the album *The Melody Maker Tribute to Louis Armstrong* (1970, Pol. 2460123-5). Shortly after leaving Welsh, in 1978 he joined Humphrey Lyttelton's band, with which he performed and recorded for four years. From 1983 he has worked as a freelance. During his periods with Welsh and Lyttelton, Williams became an excellent sight reader, capable of playing in a variety of settings. His warm-toned, accurate, high-register playing alternates with roaring tailgate or an emphatic swing style.

BIBLIOGRAPHY

E. Cook: "Roy Williams," *JJI*, xxxiii/10 (1980), 6
D. Fairweather: "Williams, Roy," in I. Carr, D. Fairweather, and B. Priestley: *Jazz: the Essential Companion* (London, 1987)

CLARRIE HENLEY

Williams, Rubberlegs [Henry] (*b* Atlanta, 14 July 1907; *d* New York, 17 Oct 1962). Singer and dancer. He began his career in Atlanta at an early age and first worked on the TOBA circuit in 1920. He toured the USA, performing in nightclubs and theaters for vaudeville and minstrel shows during the 1920s and 1930s, and became particularly well known for his song *Bring it on home*. He also appeared in several revues, notably *Blackbirds of 1933–4*. Williams's nickname "Rubberlegs" describes his "legomania" dancing, which combined high kicks, wriggles, shimmies, and other steps; the short film *Smash Your Baggage* (1933) clearly demonstrates his style of tap-dancing. Williams performed with Fletcher Henderson, Chick Webb, and Dicky Wells; he sang his own composition *That's the Blues* on a recording with Clyde Hart (1945, Contl 6013), and recorded under his own name accompanied by Herbie Fields's band (1945–6). From 1946 until his death he worked mainly away from the world of entertainment.

BIBLIOGRAPHY

M. Stearns and J. Stearns: *Jazz Dance: the story of American Vernacular Dance* (New York and London, 1968)
S. Harris: *Blues Who's Who: a Biographical Dictionary of Blues Singers* (New Rochelle, NY, 1979)

RAINER E. LOTZ

Williams, Rudy (*b* Newark, NJ, 1909; *d* Sept 1954). Saxophonist and clarinetist. He began playing saxophone at the age of 12; the alto saxophone became his chief instrument, though he also played tenor and baritone. He was a prominent member of Al Cooper's Savoy Sultans (1937–43), with which he made several recordings on alto saxophone, including *Little Sally Water* (1939, Decca 2819). In the early to mid-1940s he worked with Hot Lips Page, Luis Russell, and Chris Columbus (all 1943) and John Kirby (1945). He worked as a leader in 1944, 1945 (at Minton's Playhouse, New York), and 1948 (again in New York); after performing with Tadd Dameron at the Royal Roost, New York (1948), he led his own band in Boston (1949–50, 1951). In 1951 he played in California with Illinois Jacquet and Gene Ammons, then toured the Far East in a band led by Oscar Pettiford, of which J. J. Johnson was also a member and which recorded under Howard McGhee's name. After returning to the USA he led his own bands and worked as a freelance. Williams recorded with various musicians, among them Dud Bascomb and Don Byas (both 1944), Babs Gonzales (1947), Dameron and Eddie "Lockjaw" Davis (both 1948), Eddie "Cleanhead" Vinson (1950), Gene Ammons and Bennie Green (both 1951), and Johnny Hodges (1952). (D. Salemann, D. Hartmann, and M. Vogler: *Rudy Williams, 1936–1954: Solography, Discography, Band Routes, Engagements in Chronological Order*, Basle, Switzerland, 1987)

based on *ChiltonW*

Williams, Sandy [Alexander Balos] (*b* Summerville, SC, 24 Oct 1906). Trombonist. He grew up in Washington, and first studied tuba; his early work included jobs in theater bands. In 1929 he played with Claude Hopkins, then from 1929 to 1931 he worked with Horace Henderson, during which time he spent brief periods with Hopkins, Fletcher Henderson, and Cliff Jackson. After a longer spell with Fletcher Henderson (*c*January 1932–July 1933) he became a member of Chick Webb's band (1933), remaining with the group under Ella Fitzgerald's leadership (1939–40). He undertook further big-band engagements with Benny Carter (1940), Coleman Hawkins (1940–41), Lucky Millinder (1941), Fletcher Henderson (intermittently, 1941–2), and Cootie Williams (1942), then worked with Sidney Bechet, Wild Bill Davison, Mezz Mezzrow, and Pete Brown, successfully adapting his style to the needs of these small groups. Thereafter he played with Duke Ellington (summer 1943), Don Redman, Hot Lips Page, Roy Eldridge (summer 1944), Hopkins (1944–5), Rex Stewart (1946, and in Europe, 1947–8), and Art

Hodes (1946–7). Later he performed with various groups in New York at Ryan's (1949–50) and the Central Plaza (late 1950s).

Williams played within a fairly narrow compass and seldom ventured into the lower register of the instrument. He produced a full, bright, even overripe, open tone, to which he sometimes added a burr (on longer notes especially); he employed a loose yet pushing staccato. In solos he often paraphrased the melody or built on a succession of different riff passages, working on each one for four measures; he increased the interest with varied fills between repetitions of riffs, by adroitly fusing riffs and fills, or by referring to a riff used earlier in the solo.

Oral history material in *NjR*.

For illustrations *see* HENDERSON, FLETCHER, and WEBB, CHICK.

SELECTED RECORDINGS

As leader: Gee, baby, ain't I good to you (1946, HRS 1029)

As sideman: C. Webb: If dreams come true (1934, Col. CB754); Stompin' at the Savoy (1934, Col. 2926D); That Rhythm Man (1934, Decca 173); Blue Minor (1934, Decca 172); Gotham Stompers: My Honey's Lovin' Arms (1937, Var. 629); C. Hawkins: Rocky Comfort (1940, OK 6284); S. Bechet: I know that you know (1940, Vic. 27574); I ain't gonna give nobody none o' this jelly-roll (1940, Vic. 27447)

BIBLIOGRAPHY

ChiltonW

S. Dance, "Sandy Williams: Trombone," *The World of Swing* (New York, 1974) [colln of previously pubd interviews], 63

S. Traill and H. Whiston: "Sandy Williams: Confessions of a Trombonist," *JJ*, xxviii/2 (1975), 12

J. Simmen: "Sandy Williams," *BHcF* (1984), no.315, p.3; no.316, p.2; no.317, p.4; no.318, p.7; no.319, p.1; Eng. trans., abbreviated, in *Sv*, no.116 (1984–5), 48 [incl. discography]

BOB ZIEFF

Williams, Spencer (*b* New Orleans, 14 Oct *c*1889; *d* Flushing, NY, 14 July 1965). Composer and pianist. He grew up in Birmingham, Alabama, and played in Chicago before settling around 1916 in New York, where he worked with Clarence Williams and began to concentrate on composition. From the mid-1920s he worked mostly in Europe with Josephine Baker (1925–6, 1933), Fats Waller (1930–32, 1938), Lew Stone (1932), and several West Indian musicians. He gained his fame and income from his many compositions, including *Basin Street Blues*, *Mahogany Hall Stomp*, *Royal Garden Blues*, *I've found a new baby*, *Papa de da-da*, *Tishomingo Blues*, *Shim-me-sha Wobble*, and *Careless Love*. After returning briefly to the USA Williams lived in England from 1932; he moved to Stockholm in the 1950s. In his book *Black Manhattan* (New York, 1930/*R*1968), the writer and lyricist James Weldon Johnson named Williams as one of the best Afro-American writers of popular songs.

BIBLIOGRAPHY

ChiltonW

J. Green: "Spencer Williams: Composer," *Sv*, no.123 (1986), 88

JEFFREY P. GREEN

Williams, Tone. *See* WILLIAMS, ELMER.

Williams, Tony [Anthony] (*b* Chicago, 12 Dec 1945). Drummer. His family moved to the Boston area when Williams was about two years old. His father Tillmon Williams, a saxophonist, took him to sit in with musicians at various clubs, and by the age of 11 he was known well enough to visit the clubs on his own. He studied privately with Alan Dawson and, while still a child, played with Art Blakey and Max Roach; other influences were Philly Joe Jones, Jimmy Cobb, and Louis Hayes. By the time he was 15 he was active as a freelance musician in the Boston area.

In 1959–60 Williams began an important association with Sam Rivers, who became his informal mentor. In late 1962 he accompanied Jackie McLean, who invited him to join his group in New York. Here he was discovered by Miles Davis, and in May 1963 began to play in Davis's quintet. Williams stayed with Davis until mid-1969, earning an international reputation for the brilliance of his playing and for his interaction with other musicians. He frequently performed and recorded with other groups in New York and Boston, including those of Eric Dolphy, Herbie Hancock, and Rivers, and led his own studio groups. As Davis's quintet moved towards a fusion of jazz with rock, soul, and other elements, Williams became interested in forming a similar group of his own; the trio Lifetime, with Larry Young (organ) and John McLaughlin (electric guitar), issued its first recordings in 1969. But the group was not commercially successful, and its personnel changed over the next three years. From 1973 to 1975 Williams was inactive as a performer, and a new group founded in 1975 had to disband again a year later. Williams then returned to jazz, performing and touring with Hancock, Wayne Shorter, and other former associates under the name V.S.O.P. in 1976, 1977, 1979, and 1983 (*see also* V.S.O.P. (i)). From 1978 he has also appeared in jazz concerts and made recordings with Sonny Rollins, Hank Jones, Wynton Marsalis, and his own groups.

Williams is a highly innovative drummer and was a prime influence on jazz styles of the 1970s. From the 1960s he displayed astounding intuition in his accompaniment of soloists, often playing rhythmic figures together with the improviser. His own solos were dramatic essays composed of percussive effects without meter. Even at the fastest of tempos Williams's playing is characteristically delicate and light, and punctuated

Tony Williams

by surprising dynamic contrasts; he negotiates ritardandos and accelerandos with ease. He avoided the conventional accenting of alternate beats with the hi-hat, instead involving it in accents and drum patterns, and by 1966 he had introduced his trademark of closing the cymbal on every beat. His general approach to the drum set, in which he focused on the independence of the limbs, and his specific techniques with the hi-hat and other instruments were widely emulated by younger drummers. All recordings by Williams's own groups from 1969 contain heavily amplified guitar and driving rock rhythms, as well as experiments with dissonant sound effects. Williams played in a different style with these groups, using larger drums and thicker sticks. After his return to a jazz context in 1976, however, he played in a somewhat heavier manner than in his performances of the 1960s, but with equal brilliance and ingenuity.

SELECTED RECORDINGS

As leader: *Lifetime* (1964, BN 84180); *Spring* (1965, BN 84216); *Emergency* (1969, Pol. 24-4017-8)

As sideman with M. Davis: *Seven Steps to Heaven* (1963, Col. CS8851); *Miles Davis in Europe* (1963, Col. CS8983); *My Funny Valentine* (1964, Col. CS9106); *Miles in Tokyo* (1964, CBS SOPL162); *Miles in Berlin* (1964, CBS BPG62976); *Miles Smiles* (1966, Col. CS9401), incl. Freedom Jazz Dance; *Miles in the Sky* (1968, Col. CS9628), incl. Black Comedy

As sideman with others: H. Hancock: *My Point of View* (1963, BN 84126); J. McLean: *One Step Beyond* (1963, BN 84137); E. Dolphy: *Out to Lunch* (1964, BN 84163); S. Rivers: *Fuchsia Swing Song* (1964, BN 84184); H. Hancock: *Maiden Voyage* (1965, BN 84195); V.S.O.P.: *V.S.O.P.: The Quintet* (1977, Col. C2-34976); W. Marsalis: *Wynton Marsalis* (1981, Col. FC37574)

BIBLIOGRAPHY

D. DeMicheal: "Tony Williams: Miles' Man," *DB*, xxxii/7 (1965), 19
P. Cox: "Tony Williams: an Interview Scenario," *DB*, xxxvii/11 (1970), 14
S. Woods: "Tony Williams," *J&P*, ix/1 (1972), 16
C. D. Woodson: *Solo Jazz Drumming: an Analytical Study of the Improvisational Techniques of Anthony Williams* (thesis, UCLA, 1973)
V. Gibbs: "Tony Williams: Report on a Musical Lifetime," *DB*, xliii/2 (1976), 16
J.-E. Berendt: *Ein Fenster aus Jazz: Essays, Portraits, Reflexionen* (Frankfurt am Main, Germany, 1977), 101
"Discography of Ron Carter and Tony Williams," *SJ*, xxxi/12 (1977), 290
A. Taylor: *Notes and Tones: Musician-to-Musician Interviews* (Liège, Belgium, 1977/*R*1982)
S. Shaffer: "Tony Williams: Solo on 'Seven Steps to Heaven'," *MD*, iii/1 (1979), 48
L. Underwood: "Tony Williams: Aspiring to a Lifetime of Leadership," *DB*, xlvi/12 (1979), 20
P. de Barros: "Tony Williams: Two Decades of Drum Innovation," *DB*, l/11 (1983), 14
R. Mattingly: "Tony Williams," *MD*, viii/6 (1984), 8

LEWIS PORTER

Williamson, Claude (Berkeley) (*b* Brattleboro, VT, 18 Nov 1926). Pianist, brother of Stu Williamson. He was classically trained and studied at the New England Conservatory in Boston. His first important engagement was with Charlie Barnet (1947–9), though he worked briefly with Red Norvo in 1948. He led his own trio in the 1950s, then toured and recorded with Bud Shank (visiting Europe and North Africa, 1958). For the next two decades he worked sporadically in Hollywood, usually with a trio. His career took on a new impetus in the late 1970s, when he made a tour of Japan and recorded a series of fine albums for Japanese labels. Originally influenced by Teddy Wilson and Jess Stacy, Williamson was converted to a more modern approach, revising his style completely after hearing the work of Bud Powell. He brought to Powell's vocabulary a touch of elegance, and his playing has enlivened many West Coast recording sessions.

SELECTED RECORDINGS

As leader: *Keys West* (1955, Cap. T6511); *'Round Midnight* (1957, Beth. 69); *Williamson Mulls the Mulligan Scene* (1958, Criterion 601); *Claude Williamson in Italy* (1958, Broadway International 3001); *Tribute to Bud* (1981, Ewd 90009)

As sideman: C. Barnet: Cu-ba (1949, Cap. 15417); Claude Reigns (1949, Cap. 1222); T. Farlow: *The Interpretations of Tal Farlow* (1955, Norg. 1027); S. Williamson: *Pee-Jay* (1956, Beth. 55); B. Shank: *The Bud Shank Quartet* (1956, PJ 1215)

BIBLIOGRAPHY

FeatherE
"Claude Williamson," *SJ*, xxviii/7 (1974), 153 [discography]

MARK GARDNER

Williamson, Stu(art Lee) (*b* Brattleboro, VT, 14 May 1933). Trumpeter and trombonist, brother of Claude Williamson. He lived in Los Angeles from 1949 and worked as a sideman with Stan Kenton (1951, 1954–5), Woody Herman (1952–3), Billy May, Charlie Barnet, and Shelly Manne (at intervals, 1954–8); he also played in several studio orchestras led by Marty Paich. After taking up the valve trombone in 1954 he made many recordings of jazz (to 1968) and popular music. Although Williamson has often employed mutes his trumpet tone is consistently bright; this and his fluent valve trombone style make his playing strongly characteristic of West Coast jazz of the 1950s.

SELECTED RECORDINGS

As leader (all recorded for Bethlehem): *Sapphire* (1955, 1024); *Pee Jay* (1956, 55)

As sideman: W. Herman: Men from Mars (1953, Mars 800); S. Kenton: *Music of Bill Holman* (1954, Cap. H526), incl. King Fish; Z. Sims: *Zoot Sims Quintet* (1954, NewJ 1102); P. Adams: *Pepper Adams Quintet* (1957, Mode 112); M. Paich: *Broadway Bit* (1959, WB 1296)

BIBLIOGRAPHY

FeatherE
R. Gordon: *Jazz West Coast: the Los Angeles Jazz Scene of the 1950s* (London and New York, 1986)

SCOTT YANOW

Willis, Larry [Lawrence Elliott] (*b* New York, 20 Dec 1940). Pianist. After graduating from the Manhattan School of Music he played with Jackie McLean (1963) and Hugh Masekela (1964); he later recorded with McLean and Lee Morgan (both 1965). He is heard to advantage on McLean's album *Right Now!* (1965, BN 84215). He then worked with Kai Winding (1965–7) and Stan Getz (1969) and recorded with Robin Kenyatta (1969). From the 1970s he frequently played electric piano, and sometimes synthesizer, recording with Masekela (1970, 1972), Groove Holmes (*c*1972), and Joe Henderson (1973), and working with Cannonball Adderley (1971) and Earl May (1971–2). In 1972 Willis became a member of Blood, Sweat and Tears. He also recorded with Alphonse Mouzon (1972–3) and as a leader (*c*1973), and worked as a freelance in New York (1975). Later he recorded with Ryo Kawasaki (1977), Sonny Fortune (*c*1978), David "Fathead" Newman (1982) and Carla Bley (1985), and performed and recorded in San Francisco with Nat Adderley's hard-bop quintet (1982). He became a member of Woody Shaw's Quintet in 1986. (*Feather–Gitler '70s*)

Wills, Bob [James Robert] (*b* nr Kosse, TX, 6 March 1905; *d* Fort Worth, 13 May 1975). Fiddler, singer, and bandleader. In 1931 he became one of the founding members of the seminal western-swing band the Light Crust Doughboys (named after the flour company that sponsored it on Fort Worth radio). Three years later he assembled the Texas Playboys, who played on radio station KVOO in Tulsa from 1934 to 1942. The group became very popular in the Southwest through broadcasts, recordings, personal appearances, and nightly dances at Cain's Ballroom; during the 1940s it appeared in films, and throughout the 1950s and 1960s it toured and recorded extensively. As a fiddler Wills combined traditional hoedown music with blues inflections, but as a bandleader he was receptive to musicians who could play jazz or the hot dance tunes that he was incapable of playing. The Playboys consequently combined country-music string instruments with drums and wind instruments, and performed an eclectic repertory that included blues, jazz, popular standards, and country music. Along with Milton Brown, Wills was one of the chief popularizers of WESTERN SWING.

SELECTED RECORDINGS

Four or Five Times/St. Louis Blues (*c*1935, Voc. 03076); Steel Guitar Rag (1936, Voc. 03394); Rosetta (*c*1937, Voc. 03659); New San Antonio Rose (1940, OK 05694); Big Beaver (1940, OK 05905); *The Tiffany Transcriptions* (1945–8, Tishomingo 01)

BIBLIOGRAPHY

R. Sheldon: *Hubbin' it: the Life of Bob Wills* (Tulsa, OK, 1938)
C. R. Townsend: "Bob Wills," *Stars of Country Music*, ed. B. C. Malone and J. McCulloh (Urbana, IL, 1975), 157
——: *San Antonio Rose: the Life and Music of Bob Wills* (Urbana, IL, Chicago, and London, 1976) [incl. discography by B. Pinson]
R. Kienzle: Liner notes, *Bob Wills* (TL CW07, 1982)
G. Hunkel: *Western Swing & Country Jazz: eine Einführung mit Kurzporträts über Bob Wills und Milton Brown* (Menden, Germany, 1983)

BILL C. MALONE

Wilmer, Val(erie (Sybil)) (*b* Harrogate, England, 7 Dec 1941). English writer and photographer. She wrote about jazz from the age of 18 and in 1959–60 studied photography in London. During the following decades she contributed hundreds of articles to *Melody Maker* (from 1960 to the 1970s), *Down Beat* (of which she was the British correspondent from 1966 to 1970), *Jazz Journal*, *Jazz Monthly*, *Crescendo*, *Jazz magazine*, *Musica jazz*, *Swing Journal*, *Jazz Forum*, *The Wire*, and many other periodicals. She also provided the photographs used to illustrate several books (including *The Jazz Scene* (London, 1972), which she wrote with Charles Fox), as well as those used in John Jeremy's film *Jazz is our Religion* (1972). Her own writings include *Jazz People* (1970), an important collection of interviews with leading swing, bop, and free-jazz musicians, and *As Serious as your Life* (1977), a history of free jazz.

WRITINGS
(selective list)

Jazz People (London, Indianapolis, and New York, 1970/*R*1985)
The Face of Black Music (New York, 1976)
As Serious as your Life: the Story of the New Jazz (London, 1977, rev. 1980)

ROBERT GANNON

Wilson, Dennis (Edward) (*b* Greensboro, NC, 22 July 1952). Trombonist and arranger. He attended the Berklee College of Music (BM in music education 1974) and belonged to Lionel Hampton's orchestra (1973–5), for which he also worked for 18 months as music director. From 1974 he performed as a freelance with Stan Kenton, Clark Terry, and others, and in 1977 he joined Count Basie's orchestra, with which he made several recordings. He may be heard as the leader of Basie's orchestra on Manhattan Transfer's album *Vocalese* (1985, Atl. 81266), for which he also wrote arrangements.

For illustration *see* RECORDING, fig.6.

Wilson, Dick [Richard] (*b* Mount Vernon, IL, 11 Nov 1911; *d* New York, 24 Nov 1941). Tenor saxophonist. He was brought up in Seattle, where he was taught alto saxophone by Joe Darensbourg. After changing to tenor saxophone he joined Don Anderson in Portland, Oregon, in 1929, but returned to Seattle the following year to play with Darensbourg's band at the Jungle Temple Inn. He worked with Gene Coy's Happy Black Aces (1933–4), Zack Whyte (1934–5), and, finally, Andy Kirk's Clouds of Joy, with which he remained until his death (for illustration *see* WILLIAMS, MARY LOU).

Wilson developed a highly individual style on tenor saxophone which was influenced by Coleman Hawkins, Herschel Evans, and, possibly, Chu Berry, with a sinuous, slithery warmth of tone that suggests the later style of Paul Gonsalves. He is one of the rare musicians who is considered never to have recorded a bad solo.

SELECTED RECORDINGS
(all as sideman with A. Kirk)

Lotta Sax Appeal (1936, Decca 1046); Froggy Bottom/Christopher Columbus (1936, Decca 729); Wednesday Night Hop (1937, Decca 1303); In the Groove (1937, Decca 1261); Little Miss (1940, Decca 3491)

BIBLIOGRAPHY

ChiltonW
B. Niquet: "Dick Wilson," *BHcF*, no.62 (1956), 27
R. Russell: *Jazz Style in Kansas City and the Southwest* (Berkeley, CA, Los Angeles, and London, 1971/*R*1983)
A. McCarthy: *Big Band Jazz* (London and New York, 1974), 245
J. Evensmo: *The Tenor Saxophones of Budd Johnson, Cecil Scott, Elmer Williams, Dick Wilson, 1927–1942* (n.p. [Oslo], n.d. [?1977]) [discography]

FRANK DRIGGS

Wilson, Ed(ward John) [Milko] (*b* Sydney, 22 June 1944). Australian bandleader, trombonist, and arranger. He joined the Waratah Jazzmen (1959) and during the late 1960s worked with the Sydney SO and the dance band of the Australian Broadcasting Company, as well as in nightclubs. With Warren Daly he formed the Daly–Wilson Big Band, which was active in 1969–71 and 1973–83; its recording *The Daly–Wilson Big Band* (1975, Rep. 60-0023) provides a good example of his playing. He then moved to Murwillumbah in New South Wales where he formed another big band and small groups, and in 1986 became music director for the Jupiters casino in Gold Coast, Queensland. (B. Johnson and others: *The Oxford Companion to Australian Jazz*, Melbourne, Australia, 1987)

For further recordings and bibliography *see* DALY, WARREN.

BRUCE JOHNSON

Wilson, Garland (Lorenzo) (*b* Martinsburg, WV, 13 June 1909; *d* Paris, 31 May 1954). Pianist. He was resident at various clubs in Harlem, New York (1929–32), and first achieved acclaim through his recordings as a soloist in 1931–2. In 1932 he traveled to France as accompanist to the singer Nina Mae McKinney, with whom he recorded and toured Europe (1933–4). He then began a long association with Le Boeuf sur le Toit, Paris, which was interrupted by his tour of Great Britain with the bandleader Jack Payne (1935–6) and an engagement at the Shim Sham Club, London (1936). He recorded in Paris with the singer Jean Sablon (1936), as a soloist (1938), and with Danny Polo (1939). From 1939 he played in cabarets in Hollywood and New York, where he recorded with Cedric Wallace and performed with the singer Thelma Carpenter. He worked in London and Paris from 1951 until his death. He may be heard to advantage on *Blues en Si bémol* (1932, Bruns. A500220) and *Sweet Georgia Brown* (1951, HMV B10413).

BIBLIOGRAPHY

ChiltonW
M. Jones: "Garland Wilson: Self-portrait of a Jazz Pianist," *MM*, xxx (5 June 1954), 13
H. Rye: "Visiting Firemen, 11: Garland Wilson," *Sv*, no.119 (1985), 176

Wilson, Gerald (Stanley) (*b* Shelby, MS, 4 Sept 1918). Composer, arranger, bandleader, and trumpeter. When he was 14 his family moved to Detroit, and he studied music at high school. From 1939 to 1942 he worked with Jimmie Lunceford's band as a soloist, composer, and arranger (for illustration *see* LUNCEFORD, JIMMIE). He then moved to Los Angeles, where he performed with Les Hite (1942–3) and Benny Carter (1943). After playing with Clark Terry and Ernie Royal in Willie Smith's navy band he organized his first big band, which he led from 1944 to 1947; it included such musicians as Snooky Young and Melba Liston, and undertook a tour during which it played in New York. Wilson did not play jazz in the 1950s, but formed a new band in 1961 which recorded regularly until 1969 and gave many successful performances, most notably at the Monterey Jazz Festival in 1963. The orchestra was widely acclaimed, both for the caliber of its players (who included Harold Land, Teddy Edwards, Joe Pass, Carmell Jones, Tony Ortega, and Jack Wilson) and for the quality of Wilson's compositions. During the 1960s he also wrote music for films and television, and for such singers as Al Hibbler, Johnny Hartman, Sarah Vaughan, Nancy Wilson, and Ella Fitzgerald. He has taught jazz history at San Fernando Valley (California) State College, and at California State University, Northridge, and has led a new orchestra in the 1980s that includes such sidemen as Bobby Bryant, Land, Young, Oscar Brashear, and Ernie Watts.

SELECTED RECORDINGS

As leader: Moon Rise/Synthetic Joe (1945, Excelsior 122); *You Better Believe it!* (1961, PJ 34); *Portraits* (1963, PJ 80); *Jessica* (1982, Trend 531)
As sideman: L. Vinnegar: *Leroy Walks* (1957, Cont. 3542)

RECORDED COMPOSITIONS
(selective list)
* – with Wilson as sideman

As leader: *The Moment of Truth* (1962, PJ 61), incl. Josefina, The Moment of Truth, Nancy Jo, Viva tirado
Recorded by J. Lunceford: *Yard Dog Mazurka (1941, Decca 4032)

SELECTED ARRANGEMENTS

Recorded by others: on D. Ellington: *Piano in the Background* (1960, Col. CS8346), Perdido; N. Wilson: *Yesterday's Love Songs, Today's Blues* (1963, Cap. ST2012)

BIBLIOGRAPHY

FeatherE; *Feather '60s*; *Feather–Gitler '70s*
J. Tynan: "Facing Challenges: Gerald Wilson," *DB*, xxix/1 (1962), 18
L. Feather: "Gerald Wilson," *IM*, lxii/7 (1963), 18
L. Robinson: "Gerald Wilson," *Jazz*, iii/5 (1964), 12
J. Tynan: "Gerald Wilson," *BMI: the Many Worlds of Music* (1970), March, 20

FREDERICK A. BECK

Wilson, Jack(, Jr.) (*b* Chicago, 3 Aug 1936). Pianist. He studied music in Fort Wayne, Indiana, and began playing in local bands at the age of 14. After performing with James Moody (1953) he attended Indiana University for two years, then moved to Columbus, Ohio, where he played with Roland Kirk and led his own trio. In 1956–7 he worked with Dinah Washington; later he was active as a freelance in Chicago. He rejoined Washington in 1961 after military service, then the following year settled in Los Angeles. From that time he has worked with many important musicians and ensembles, including Roy Ayers (1963), Gerald Wilson, Harold Land, Shelly Manne, the quintet led by Clark Terry and Bill Brookmeyer, and Jimmy Witherspoon; he recorded with Terry in 1980. As well as working as a studio musician he has performed and recorded occasionally with his own groups. Wilson has long been underrated; he is an accomplished bop pianist, and can also play soul jazz after the manner of Horace Silver.

SELECTED RECORDINGS

As leader: *The Jack Wilson Quartet* (1963, Atl. 1406); *The Two Sides of Jack Wilson* (1963, Atl. 1427); *Something Personal* (1967, BN 84251); *Easterly Winds* (1967, BN 84270); *Innovations* (1977, Dis. 777)
As sideman: Earl Anderza: *Outa Sight* (1962, PJ 65); C. Amy: *Katanga* (1963, PJ 70); R. Ayers: *West Coast Vibes* (1963, UA 6325); G. Wilson: *The Golden Sword* (1966, PJ 20111); C. Barnet: *Big Band 1967* (1966, Vault 9004); I. Isaacs (i): *Ike Isaacs at Freddie Jett's Pied Piper* (1967, RGB 2000)

BIBLIOGRAPHY

Feather '60s; *Feather–Gitler '70s*
G. G. Vercelli: "Jack Wilson: Ivory Innovator," *DB*, xlv/5 (1978), 18 [incl. discography]

SCOTT YANOW

Wilson, Joe [Joseph] **Lee** (*b* Bristow, OK, 22 Dec 1935). Singer and leader. He studied classical singing, then attended Los Angeles City College, where he studied jazz. He began his career as a jazz singer in Santa Monica, California (1958), toured the West Coast and Mexico, and after moving to New York in 1962 worked with Sonny Rollins, Lee Morgan, Miles Davis, Pharoah Sanders, and Jackie McLean. From 1971 to 1972 he sang with Archie Shepp; his strong baritone voice may be heard to advantage on the title track of Shepp's album *Things have got to Change* (1971, Imp. 9212) and on the track *Steam* from Shepp's album *Attica Blues* (1972, Imp. 9222). He also worked with Sunny Murray and made recordings as a leader (1969, 1972, 1975), with the percussionist Mtume (*c*1972), and with the pianist Billy Gault (1974). From 1973 to 1978 he maintained a loft, the Ladies Fort; he also appeared at the Newport New York (1973) and Live Loft (1975) festivals and performed on radio and television. After recording in 1977 with Clifford Jordan he settled in England around 1978. Later he toured Europe, performed at clubs in London, and sang periodically in New York.

BIBLIOGRAPHY

Feather–Gitler '70s
V. Wilmer: "Joe Lee: 'Space' Singer," *MM*, li (28 Aug 1976), 28
D. Kastin: "Profile: Joe Lee Wilson," *DB*, xliv/4 (1977), 34
J. L. Wilson: "Joe Lee Wilson Travels Hopefully," *CI*, xvii/1 (1978), 15
P. Husby: "Joe Lee Wilson: Interview," *Cadence*, viii/3 (1982), 14

Wilson, Nancy (Sue) (*b* Chillicothe, OH, 20 Feb 1937). Singer. She gained early experience in nightclubs and on television shows in Columbus, Ohio, and on a tour of the Midwest and Canada with Rusty Bryant's band (1956–8). In 1959 she sang in Columbus with the quintet led by Cannonball Adderley, who encouraged her to go to New York. She obtained a recording contract with Capitol Records and soon received national recognition; her singing drew immediate accolades from established jazz musicians and she was hailed as a major new artist. She appeared in concert halls, nightclubs, and jazz clubs in the USA and Europe, and made several recordings, notably with Adderley and George Shearing. After concentrating on a career in popular music, in the early 1980s Wilson resumed her associations with leading jazz musicians, touring Japan and recording with Hank Jones's Great Jazz Trio (1981, 1982), and performing and recording in San Francisco with the Griffith Park Band (an all-star group including Joe Henderson and Chick Corea) and at the Playboy Jazz Festival with the quintet led by Art Farmer and Benny Golson (both 1982). Wilson is a remarkably versatile interpreter of popular music; her singing, with its wide range of musical and emotional intensity, reflects the influence of Dinah Washington, and her voice is noted for its subtle variations in timbre.

SELECTED RECORDINGS

As leader: with C. Adderley: *Nancy Wilson/Cannonball Adderley* (1962, Cap. ST1657); *Yesterday's Love Songs, Today's Blues* (1963, Cap. ST2012); *What's New* (1982, Ewd 90014)
As sideman with G. Shearing: *The Swingin's Mutual* (1960, Cap. ST1524)

BIBLIOGRAPHY

B. Gardner: "The Baby Grows up," *DB*, xxxi/30 (1964), 18
D. J. Travis: *An Autobiography of Black Jazz* (Chicago, 1983) [incl. interviews], 477

MICHAEL J. BUDDS/R

Wilson, Phil(lips Elder, Jr.) (*b* Belmont, MA, 19 Jan 1937). Trombonist, educator, and arranger. He first learned piano and later took up the trombone, which he studied at the New England Conservatory and later at the Navy School of Music. While in Boston he played in Herb Pomeroy's big band (1955–7); he played trombone and piano with Jimmy Dorsey intermittently in 1956–8, and in 1959 led his own band. During his military service he played trombone in the North American Air Defense Command Band (1962). He then became a regular soloist with Woody Herman, with whom he was associated from 1962 until 1965. The following year he was appointed to the faculty of the Berklee School of Music, where he became head of the trombone department and also taught theory and arrangement. Wilson wrote some arrangements for Buddy Rich (notably *Mercy, Mercy, Mercy*) during this period, and continued to make recordings sporadically (including the album *That's All* with Al Cohn), but by the 1980s he was known primarily as a teacher.

SELECTED RECORDINGS

As leader: *Prodigal Son* (1968, Freeform 101); with R. Matteson: *The Sound of the Wasp* (1975, ASI 203); *That's All* (1976, FaD 109); *Latin American Tour* (1985, Shiah 118)

As sideman with W. Herman: *Woody Herman, 1963* (1962, Phi. 600065), incl. It's a Lonesome Old Town; *Encore: 1963* (1963, Phi. 600092); on *The 40th Anniversary Carnegie Hall Concert* (1976, RCA BGL2-2203), Bijou

SELECTED ARRANGEMENTS

(recorded by B. Rich)

Basically Blues, on *Swingin' New Big Band* (1966, PJ 20113); Mercy, Mercy, Mercy, on *Mercy, Mercy* (1968, PJ 20133)

BIBLIOGRAPHY

Feather '60s; *Feather–Gitler '70s*

L. Tomkins: "My Search for Freedom, by Phil Wilson," *CI*, xxi/12 (1983), 20; contd as "Phil Wilson: the Dues Band is Good News for us All," xxii/1 (1983), 6

S. Voce: "Phil Wilson," *JJI*, xxxvii (1984), no.10, p.6; no.11, p.12 [interview]

L. Tomkins: "Talent Must be the Foundation, Insists Phil Wilson," *CI*, xxiv/4 (1987), 12

SCOTT YANOW

Wilson, Phillip (Sanford) (*b* St. Louis, 8 Sept 1941). Drummer. He took up the violin when he was eight years old and changed to drums when he was nine; from the age of ten to the age of 15 he played in drum and bugle corps, and when he was 16 he made his début as a professional with the organist Don James. With the organist Sam Lazar he worked as a sideman in the bands of Gene Ammons and Sonny Stitt in Chicago, and in 1960 he performed at Minton's Playhouse in New York. From 1960 to 1964 he traveled widely with many groups, including the rock-and-roll group the Drifters and Chocolate Campbell's big band, which accompanied such soul singers as Martha Reeves; he also played in St. Louis with John Coltrane (1962) and in a quartet that also included Lester Bowie and Julius Hemphill (1962–3). After moving to Chicago in 1965 he joined the Association for the Advancement of Creative Musicians and played free jazz with Roscoe Mitchell's Art Ensemble; he left Chicago in 1968 to play with the Paul Butterfield Blues Band (to 1970) and the rock group Mother Load (1971). He performed with Anthony Braxton at Town Hall, New York (1972), and in bands led by Bowie (from 1974 into the 1980s), and from 1975 to 1976 played soul and urban blues as a studio drummer for Stax Records in Memphis. After moving to New York in 1976 he worked principally in free jazz; he performed and recorded with David Murray (1976–7), played in Europe in a quartet that included Olu Dara and Frank Lowe (1978), and belonged to a trio with Johnny Dyani and Leo Smith.

SELECTED RECORDINGS

Duos with L. Bowie: *Duet* (1978, ImpA 373854)

As leader: *Philip Wilson Live at the Moers Festival* (1978, Moers 01062); *Fruits* (1978, Cir. [Ger.] 10)

As sideman with L. Bowie: *Fast Last* (1974, Muse 5055); *The Great Pretender* (1981, ECM 1209); *All the Magic* (1982, ECM 1246–7)

As sideman with others: R. Mitchell: *Old/Quartet* (1967, Nessa 5); A. Braxton: *Town Hall 1972* (1972, Trio 3008–9); D. Murray: *David Murray Live at the Lower Manhattan Ocean Club* (1977, IndN 1032, 1044)

BIBLIOGRAPHY

C. J. Safane: "Phillip Wilson," *DB*, xliv/15 (1977), 22

C. Stern: "Phillip Wilson: Beyond the Blues," *MD*, vii/10 (1983), 16

ED HAZELL

Wilson, Quinn (B.) (*b* Chicago, 26 Dec 1908; *d* Evanston, IL, 14 June 1978). Double bass and tuba player and arranger. He played violin as a child and later studied composition and arranging. He worked with various leaders from 1925, among them Tiny Parham (1927), Walter Barnes (1928), and Erskine Tate (1928–31), and as a freelance he recorded on tuba with Jelly Roll Morton (1927) and Richard M. Jones (1929). In the 1930s he played with Earl Hines (1931–9; for illustration *see* HINES, EARL), with whom he recorded on tuba and double bass and for whom he wrote a number of arrangements, including *That's a-plenty* (1934, Decca 182). During this time he also recorded on double bass with Jimmie Noone (1931, 1933) and Jimmy Mundy (1937). After leaving Hines he accompanied Walter Fuller (until 1942). In the 1940s and 1950s he was active as a freelance in Chicago (sometimes playing electric bass guitar), played for 11 years with a rhythm-and-blues group led by Lefty Bates, and recorded with many blues singers (1953–61). He worked with the clarinetist Bill Reinhardt in the 1960s and the trumpeter Joe Kelly in the 1970s.

Oral history material in *NjR* (JOHP).

BIBLIOGRAPHY

S. Dance: *The World of Earl Hines* (New York, 1977) [interviews], 171

D. Hill: "Quinn Wilson: Autobiographical Note," *Cadence*, xiii/4 (1987), 16

based on *ChiltonW*

Wilson, Shadow [Rossiere] (*b* Yonkers, NY, 25 Sept 1919; *d* New York, 11 July 1959). Drummer. From 1939 he worked with some of the leading big bands of the period; his most important engagements were with Lucky Millinder (1939), Benny Carter, Tiny Bradshaw (1940), Lionel Hampton (1940–41), Earl Hines (1941–3), Count Basie (1944–6, 1948), and Woody Herman (1949). He also played in small groups led by Illinois Jacquet (1946–7, 1949–50, 1952–4), Erroll Garner (1950–52), Ella Fitzgerald (1954–5), and Thelonious Monk (1957–8). During the 1950s he performed frequently with Sonny Stitt, and he recorded with a variety of leaders, including Basie, Joe Newman, Monk, and Lee Konitz. For the first decade of his career Wilson was noted as the driving rhythmic force behind large orchestras, and after 1950 he became highly regarded for his work in small groups. Equally proficient using sticks or brushes, he was one of the most flexible and accomplished drummers, and an unfailingly sensitive player.

SELECTED RECORDINGS

As sideman: C. Basie: Taps Miller (1944, Col. 36831); L. Young: Indiana (1944), first issued on *The Master's Touch* (1944–9, Savoy 12071); I. Jacquet: Jivin' with Jack the Bellboy (1947, Ala. 179); T. Dameron: *Fontainebleau* (1956, Prst. 7037), incl. Delirium; P. Woods and G. Quill: *Phil and Quill* (1956, RCA LPM1284); T. Monk: *Thelonious Monk with John Coltrane* (1957, Jlnd 946)

BIBLIOGRAPHY

FeatherE

I. Gitler: *Jazz Masters of the Forties* (New York, 1966/*R*1983 with discography), 190

MARK GARDNER

Teddy Wilson's sextet at Café Society, New York, June 1942: (left to right) Wilson (piano), Johnny Williams (double bass), Jack Parker (drums), Edmond Hall (clarinet), Emmett Berry (trumpet), and Benny Morton (trombone)

Wilson, Teddy [Theodore Shaw] (*b* Austin, TX, 24 Nov 1912; *d* New Britain, CT, 31 July 1986). Pianist. He grew up in Tuskegee, Alabama, and briefly studied music at Talladega College. After working in Chicago with Jimmie Noone, Louis Armstrong, and others he moved in 1933 to New York to join Benny Carter's band. He played informally with Benny Goodman in 1935 and officially joined Goodman's trio the following year, thereby becoming one of the first black musicians to appear prominently with white artists. Wilson remained with Goodman until 1939, playing on many of the latter's small-group recordings and also on recordings under his own name with other important swing musicians, above all Billie Holiday and Lester Young. After leaving Goodman he briefly led his own big band (1939–40), and thereafter worked primarily as a leader of small ensembles and as a soloist. Around 1950 he was an instructor at the Juilliard School in New York, an early instance of the recognition of jazz by an important conservatory. He frequently rejoined Goodman for reunions, most notably for a tour of the USSR (1962), an appearance at the Newport Festival (1973), and a concert at Carnegie Hall (1982).

Wilson was the most important pianist of the swing period. His early recordings reveal a percussive style, with single-note lines and bold staccatos, that was indebted to Earl Hines; but by the time of his first performances with Goodman he had fashioned a distinctive legato idiom that served him for the rest of his career. Wilson's style was based on the use of conjunct 10ths in the left hand; by emphasizing the tenor voice and frequently omitting the root of the chord until the end of the phrase he created great harmonic refinement and contrapuntal interest. For the right hand he adapted Hines's "trumpet" style, playing short melodic fragments in octaves, frequently separated by rests and varied with fleet, broken-chord passage-work. He used the full range of the piano, often changing register or texture to underscore formal divisions. His poised, restrained manner and transparent textures are especially evident on his solo recordings from the late 1930s, which served as models for countless pianists in the late swing period. From 1940 Wilson's playing became somewhat florid, with frequent pentatonic passage-work, but he retained his basic approach and prowess into the 1980s.

Oral history material in *ATaT* and *NjR* (JOHP).

See also IMPROVISATION, §4 (iii); and PIANO, §3, and fig.2.

SELECTED RECORDINGS

As unaccompanied soloist: Liza (1935, Bruns. 7563); Between the Devil and the Deep Blue Sea (1937, Bruns. 8025); I can't get started (1941, Col. 36633); *With Billie in Mind* (1972, Chi. 111); *Striding after Fats* (1974, BL 308); *Cole Porter Classics* (1977, BL 51505)

As leader: I wished on the moon (1935, Bruns. 7501); Mean to me (1937, Bruns. 7903); Just a Mood (1937, Bruns. 7973); What shall I say? (1939, Bruns. 8314); with L. Young: *Pres and Teddy* (1956, Verve 8205); *Three Little Words* (1976, BB 33094)

As sideman: B. Carter: Symphony in Riffs (1933, Col. 2898D); B. Goodman: Body and Soul (1935, Vic. 25115); Sweet Sue, Just You (1936, Vic. 25473); B. Holiday: Jim (1941, OK 6369)

BIBLIOGRAPHY

L. Feather: *The Book of Jazz: a Guide to the Entire Field* (New York, 1957, rev. 2/1965)

J. Mehegan: *Jazz Improvisation*, ii: *Jazz Rhythm and the Improvised Line* (New York, 1962), 80

——: *Jazz Improvisation*, iii: *Swing and Early Progressive Piano Styles* (New York, 1964), 15

J. Simmen: "Le grand orchestre de Teddy Wilson, 1939–1940," *BHcF*, no.201 (1970), 10; no.202 (1970), 10

D. M. Bakker: *Billie & Teddy on Microgroove, 1932–1944* (Alphen aan de Rijn, Netherlands, 1975)

S. Dance: *The World of Earl Hines* (New York, 1977) [interviews], 183

J. McDonough: "Teddy Wilson: History in the Flesh," *DB*, xliv/4 (1977), 17

D. Hyman: "Thinking about Teddy Wilson," *Keyboard*, viii/9 (1982), 59 [incl. transcr.]

L. Lyons: *The Great Jazz Pianists, Speaking of their Lives and Music* (New York, 1983), 59

Obituary, B. Doerschuk, *Keyboard*, xii/10 (1986), 29

J. BRADFORD ROBINSON

Windhurst, Johnny [John Henry] (*b* New York, 5 Nov 1926). Trumpeter. A self-taught musician who has never learned to read music, he made his professional début in 1944 and in the following year recorded with Sidney Bechet. He played with Art Hodes and James P. Johnson at the "Jazz at Town Hall" concert in September 1946, then worked in Chicago, with Edmond Hall in California (1947–8), and with Louis Armstrong and Nappy Lamare before leading his own band in Ohio and Boston. After working in 1950 with Eddie Condon and recording in the following year with Ruby Braff in one of the groups known as Jazz at Storyville in Boston he played at Condon's club in New York (1952–3) and made recordings in New York with the singer Barbara Lea (1955–7), Jack Teagarden (1955), and his own swing quartet (*Jazz at Columbus Avenue*, 1956, Tran. 2), which included Buell Neidlinger as a sideman. Later he played in a stage band (1956), worked again in Ohio and toured as a leader (1957–9), and performed again at Condon's club. (*FeatherE*)

Winding, Kai (Chresten) (*b* Århus, Denmark, 18 May 1922; *d* Yonkers, NY, 6 May 1983). Trombonist. He moved with his family to the USA when he was 12 and took up the trombone while in his teens; he was largely self-taught. He played in the big bands of Sonny Dunham and Alvino Rey and belonged for three years to a service band while he was a member of the US Coast Guard (from 1942); he also took part in early bop jam sessions at Minton's Playhouse and Monroe's Uptown House in New York, and was a member of big bands led by Benny Goodman (1945–6), Stan Kenton (1946–7), and Charlie Ventura (1947–8). He played bop with Charlie Parker and in 1954 formed a quintet with J. J. Johnson that was known as Jay and Kai; after the quintet disbanded in 1956 he toured briefly with Johnson in 1958 and led a septet consisting of four trombones and a rhythm section. In the 1960s he worked as a music director for the Playboy clubs in New York; he also toured with the Giants of Jazz (1971–2), and with Curtis Fuller led the group Giant Bones (1979–80). He moved to California in 1969 and to Spain in 1977; in 1982 he appeared at the Aurex Jazz Festival in Japan with Johnson and at the Kool Jazz Festival in New York.

Winding was one of the first bop trombonists and one of the most important. The distinct sound he brought to Kenton's trombone section was achieved partly by his persuading the players to produce a vibrato with the lip rather then with the slide (van Engelen). His solo work was characterized initially by a rough, exuberant, biting tone, recalling earlier trombone styles (a fine example may be heard on Kenton's recording of *Lover*, 1947), though a more restrained manner is evident in the brief solos he contributed to the first of Miles Davis's sessions that resulted in the *Birth of the Cool* (1949). On forming the group Jay and Kai, Winding began to produce a delicate sound; he improvised in a manner so close to that of Johnson that it is sometimes difficult to distinguish between the two musicians.

For illustrations *see* JAZZ (i), fig.6, and NAVARRO, FATS.

SELECTED RECORDINGS

As leader: Sid's Bounce/A Night on Bop Mountain (1949, NewJ 809); *Great Kai and J. J.* (1961, Imp. 1); *Incredible Trombones* (1961, Imp. 3); *The Kai Winding Trombones* (1963, Jazz Vault 107); *Danish Blue* (1977, Glendale 6003)

As leader with others: J. J. Johnson: *Jay and Kay: December 3, 1954* (1954, Prst. 195); Giants of Jazz: *Giants of Jazz* (1971, Atl. 2-905); C. Fuller: *Giant Bones at Nice* (1980, Ahead 757)

As sideman: S. Kenton: Ain't no misery in me/Artistry in Percussion (1946, Cap. 289); Willow weep for me (1946, Cap. 287); Machito (1947, Cap. 900); Lover (1947, Cap. 904); M. Davis: Godchild (1949, Cap. 60005); Budo (1949, Cap. 15404); Brew Moore: Mud Bug (1949, Savoy 968); Z. Sims: Tangerine/Zootcase (1952, Prst. 1348)[EP]

BIBLIOGRAPHY

FeatherE; *Feather '60s*; *Feather–Gitler '70s*

J. Burns: "Bopping Bones," *J&B*, ii/7 (1972), 16

K. Winding: "Still Multiplying the Trombones," *CI*, xi/5 (1972), 26

N. Catalano: "His Long and Winding Road," *DB*, xlv/15 (1978), 27

S. Woolley: "Meandering with Kai," *JJI*, xxxii/9 (1979), 14

"The Primary Purpose of Kai Winding," *CI*, xix/3 (1980), 12; contd as L. Tomkins: "Trombone Topics," xix/4 (1980), 23

P. van Engelen: *Where's the Music? The Discography of Kai Winding* (Amsterdam, 1985)

LEE JESKE/R

Winstone, Norma (*b* London, 23 Sept 1941). English singer. Trained as a pianist and organist, she began singing in the 1950s, and by the age of 17 was working semiprofessionally with a dance band led by Al Dukardo (who taught her voice control); she was especially influenced by the interpretations of jazz standards by such singers as Frank Sinatra, Lena Horne, and Ella Fitzgerald. In the early 1960s, however, she came under the influences of Miles Davis, Eric Dolphy, and John Coltrane. She met their challenge to find a greater freedom of performance with a singularly expressive brand of wordless improvisation; this instrumental style sprang from her work in Michael Garrick's sextet (from 1968), in which she replaced a saxophonist. During the 1960s Winstone was married to the drummer Ted Humphrey. She became internationally known as a partner of John Taylor (whom she married in 1972), most notably in the trio Azimuth (with Kenny Wheeler). She has also toured with John Dankworth's orchestra as a substitute for Cleo Laine (November–December 1972) and recorded with Mike Westbrook (1970), Eberhard Weber (1979), and others. In addition to using her voice instrumentally, she remains a fine interpreter of popular songs.

SELECTED RECORDINGS

As leader: *Edge of Time* (1971, Argo 148); of Azimuth (with J. Taylor and K. Wheeler): *Azimuth* (1977, ECM 1099), *Azimuth '85* (1985, ECM 1298); *Somewhere Called Home* (1987, ECM 1337)

As sideman: M. Westbrook: *Love Songs* (1970, Deram 1069); M. Garrick: *The Heart is a Lotus* (1970, Argo 135); *Home Stretch Blues* (1972, Argo 154)

BIBLIOGRAPHY

Feather–Gitler '70s

B. Dawbarn: "Norma: New Voice from the Pubs of London," *MM* (5 March 1966), 6

S. Woolley: "Norma Winstone," *JJ*, xxviii/7 (1975), 4

A. Macintosh: "John Taylor & Norma Winstone: a Jazz Partnership," *JF* [intl edn], no.59 (1979), 38

S. Gore-Humphries and P. Hanson: "Avant Courier: Norma Winstone," *JJI*, xxxvi/8 (1983), 10

G. Lock: "The Singing is the Song," *The Wire*, no.15 (1985), 40

CHRIS SHERIDAN

Winter, Horst (*b* Beuthen, Germany [now in Poland], 24 Sept 1914). Austrian clarinetist, singer, and bandleader. He began to play jazz in Berlin in the 1930s. During World War II he made recordings for the German record label Tempo with Willi Berking, Meg Tevelian, and others. He moved to Vienna in 1945 and became an Austrian citizen the following year. He formed the Wiener Tanz Orchester (1946), with which he made many recordings, including *Gin Fizzes* (1947, ES 8225). A gifted swing clarinetist, Winter played in the style of Artie Shaw; he ceased to perform jazz in the mid-1950s.

BIBLIOGRAPHY

D. H. Kraner and K. Schulz: *Jazz in Austria: historische Entwicklung und Diskographie des Jazz in Österreich* (Graz, Austria, 1972) [Eng., Ger. texts]

A. McCarthy: *Big Band Jazz* (New York and London, 1974)

KLAUS SCHULZ

Winter, Paul (Theodore, Jr.) (*b* Altoona, PA, 31 Aug 1939). Soprano and alto saxophonist and bandleader. While at Northwestern University he formed the Paul Winter Sextet, with which he played alto saxophone. In 1961 this group won the Intercollegiate Jazz Festival, at which the judges included Dizzy Gillespie and John Hammond; the latter engaged the group to record for Columbia. In the 1960s Winter's performances and recordings brought him to national and international prominence; in 1962, sponsored by the US State Department, he undertook an extensive tour of Latin America. At this time he considered establishing a group that departed from the conventional instrumentation of jazz; in 1967 he formed the Paul Winter Consort, which combined Latin American, African, and Western instruments. In the early 1970s the group included the guitarist Ralph Towner, the double bass player Glen Moore, the sitarist and percussionist Collin Walcott, the reed player Paul McCandless, and the cellist David Darling. *Icarus*, composed by Towner, became Winter's theme tune. During this period Winter became concerned with conservation and the problem of endangered species. He joined expeditions by the organization Greenpeace and, in often successful attempts to communicate with animals in the wild, played to whales off the Canadian coast and to wolves in the mountains of California and Minnesota. Tapes of these experiments formed the basis for the album *Common Ground* (1977). In 1980 he formed a nonprofit organization dedicated to fostering general participation in music and a new awareness of the potential of harmony and rhythm. Winter and his group continue to perform and record on the organization's behalf, often in natural environments such as the Grand Canyon.

SELECTED RECORDINGS

Jazz Premiere: Washington (1961–2, Col. CS8797); *Jazz Meets the Bossa Nova* (1962, Col. CS8725); *New Jazz on Campus* (1963, Col. CS8864); *Rio* (1964, Col. CS9115); *Something in the Wind* (1969, A&M 4207); *Icarus* (c1971, Epic 31643); *Earthdance* (1977, A&M 4653); *Common Ground* (1977, A&M 4698); *Callings* (1980, Living Music 0001); *Missa gaia/Earth Mass* (1982, Living Music 0002); *Concert for the Earth* (1985, Living Music 0005); *Canyon* (1985, Living Music 0006); *Whales Alive* (1987, Living Music 00013)

BIBLIOGRAPHY

Feather '60s; *Feather–Gitler '70s*
D. DeMicheal: "The Paul Winter Sextet from the Campus to the White House," *DB*, xxx/1 (1963), 17
M. Bourne: "Paul Winter: One World Music," *DB*, liii/5 (1986), 26 [incl. discography]

BILL MILKOWSKI

Winters, Tiny [Gittens, Frederick] (*b* London, 24 Jan 1909). English double bass player and singer. He began playing professionally in the 1930s and performed with the bandleaders Roy Fox and Bert Ambrose (both 1932) and Lew Stone (1932–7), took part in several recording sessions with Ray Noble (1932–4), and performed again with Ambrose (1937–40). He also made recordings with Coleman Hawkins (including *Lady Be Good*, 1934, Parl. R2007) and under his own name (*How many times/Frankie and Johnnie*, 1936, Decca F6031). After military service he played again for Stone, was resident at Hatchett's Club, London (1948–55), worked as a session musician, and played regularly in theater orchestras. From 1962 to 1972 Winters performed for the "Black and White Minstrel Show," and for three and a half years during this period was a member of George Chisholm's Jazzers. He retired briefly in the mid-1970s, but resumed working as a freelance and led his own trio and big band. From 1982 he has performed with Digby Fairweather and recorded regularly as a freelance.

DIGBY FAIRWEATHER

Witherspoon, Jimmy [James] (*b* Gurdon, AR, 8 Aug 1923). Singer. He sang in his local baptist church choir and listened to recordings by blues singers at an early age. While in the Merchant Marine (1941–3) he performed in Calcutta with Teddy Weatherford's band. From 1944 to 1948 he was a member of Jay McShann's group, then in 1949 he formed his own six-piece band. He soon became a leading singer, and in 1947 achieved great success on the rhythm-and-blues chart with his recording of *Ain't nobody's business*. The loss of his popularity after the advent of rock-and-roll, together with the bad management of his finances, resulted in Witherspoon being declared bankrupt in 1953, and he worked infrequently until 1958. But thereafter he began recording albums with major jazz musicians and established a flourishing career as a soloist. He made tours of Europe (with Buck Clayton, 1961) and Japan (with Count Basie, 1963) and appeared frequently on television and at festivals. Witherspoon was one of the first singers who managed to adapt his classic and extrovert style of blues shouting to the harmonic and rhythmic demands of modern jazz styles without sacrificing its essential qualities (*see* BLUES, §9).

Oral history material in *GBLnsa*.

SELECTED RECORDINGS

As leader: Ain't Nobody's Business (1947, Supreme 1506); *Jimmy Witherspoon at Monterey* (1959, HiFi 421); *Roots* (1962, Rep. 96057); *Spoonful* (1975, BN LA534G)

As sideman: with B. Clayton: *Olympia Concert* (1961, Vogue 546)

BIBLIOGRAPHY

P. Welding: "Spoon: an Informal Portrait," *DB*, xxix/29 (1962), 22
A. Rotante: "Jimmy Witherspoon Discography," *Record Research*, no.62 (1964), 5; no.63 (1964), 7; no.64 (1964), 4; no.65 (1964), 2; no.66 (1965), 8; no.67 (1965), 10; no.68 (1965), 7; no.71 (1965), 10
V. Wilmer: "Jimmy Witherspoon: There'll always be Blues," *DB*, xxxiv/14 (1967), 23
A. Shaw: *Honkers and Shouters: the Golden Years of Rhythm and Blues* (New York, 1978), 211
S. Dance: *The World of Count Basie* (New York and London, 1980) [colln of previously pubd interviews], 306

BOB WEIR

Wolff, Mike [Michael Blieden] (*b* Victorville, CA, 31 July 1952). Pianist and keyboard player. He grew up in Tennessee, then studied music at the University of California in Los Angeles and Berkeley (1970–71) and at the Manhattan School of Music. After working with Cal Tjader (1972–4) he was a member of Airto Moreira's group Fingers for several months (1974–5). In 1975 he worked briefly with Cannonball Adderley's quintet, recording the soul-jazz album *Phenix* (Fan. 79004). He subsequently recorded with Tom Harrell (1976, on piano and electric piano) and worked with Sonny Rollins (1976–8) and Nancy Wilson (1978–83), for whom he wrote a number of arrangements; from 1978 to 1980 he was also joint leader of the group Answering Service with the saxophonist Alex Foster. Wolff performed with Art Farmer and Benny Golson at the Playboy Jazz Festival in Los Angeles in 1982. From the mid-1980s he has worked as a jazz comedian.

BIBLIOGRAPHY

Feather–Gitler '70s
H. Wong: "Profile: Mike Wolff," *DB*, xli/21 (1974), 32

Wolverines [Wolverine Orchestra]. Band formed in 1923 in the Chicago area. After appearing later that year at the Stockton Club in Hamilton, Ohio, and early the following year at Doyle's Dance Hall in Cincinnati, it recorded in Richmond, Indiana, for Gennett (for illustration *see* RECORDING, fig.3) with the following members: Dick Voynow, pianist and leader; Bix Beiderbecke, cornetist; Al Gandee, trombonist; Jimmy Hartwell, clarinetist and alto saxophonist; George Johnson, tenor saxophonist; Bob Gillette, banjoist; Min Leibrook, brass bass player; and Vic Moore, drummer (later replaced temporarily by Vic Berton). After Gandee left the band it played on weekends with Hoagy Carmichael and during the week at the Rainbow Casino Gardens in Indianapolis, and in May 1924 again recorded for Gennett. After moving later that year to New York it performed at the Cinderella Ballroom and recorded several tracks (on some of which Georg Brunis was a guest trombonist and on others of which Jimmy McPartland replaced Beiderbecke), then disbanded. The Wolverines were most strongly influenced by the New Orleans Rhythm Kings.

SELECTED RECORDINGS
(all recorded in 1924 for Gennett)

Fidgety Feet/Jazz me Blues (5408); Oh Baby/Copenhagen (5453); Riverboat Shuffle/Susie (5454); Sensation/Lazy daddy (5542); When my Sugar Walks Down the Street/Prince of Wails (5620)

BIBLIOGRAPHY

G. Johnson: "The Wolverines and Bix," *Frontiers of Jazz*, ed. R. de Toledano (New York, 1947, rev.2/1962) [colln of previously pubd articles], 123
B. James: *Bix Beiderbecke* (London, 1959); repr. in *Kings of Jazz*, ed. S. Green (South Brunswick, NJ, and New York, 1978)
R. M. Sudhalter, P. R. Evans, and W. Dean-Myatt: *Bix: Man and Legend* (New Rochelle, NY, and London, 1974), 92–122

WARREN VACHÉ, SR.

Wood, Booty [Bootie, Mitchell W.] (*b* Dayton, OH, 27 Dec 1919; *d* Dayton, 10 June 1987). Trombonist. His professional career began in the late 1930s, and in the early 1940s he played with Tiny Bradshaw (1942–3) and Lionel Hampton (1943–4). During his navy service in World War II he performed in a band that included Clark Terry, Willie Smith, and Gerald Wilson. When he left the navy (1945) he again worked with Hampton before playing with Arnett Cobb's small band (1947–8), Erskine Hawkins (1948–50), and Count Basie (1951). He ceased performing for a time, but in 1959 he joined Duke Ellington, with whom he worked until 1960 and again briefly in 1963 and the early 1970s. He toured with Earl Hines in 1968 and continued to play with various leaders, among them Mercer Ellington (1970s), and Basie, with whom he performed and recorded from 1979 to the mid-1980s. During his time with Ellington, Wood became a skilled specialist in playing with the plunger mute; in his unmuted solos his style resembled that of Trummy Young.

SELECTED RECORDINGS

As sideman: A. Cobb: Cobb's Boogie (1947, Apollo 781); E. Hawkins: Beale Street Blues (1950, Vic. 20-3668); D. Ellington: *Blues in Orbit* (1959, Col. CS8241), incl. Sweet and Pungent; *Nutcracker Suite* (1960, Koala 14117), incl. Black and Tan Fantasy, Creole Love Call, The Mooche

BIBLIOGRAPHY

S. Dance: *The World of Duke Ellington* (London and New York, 1970/*R*1981) [colln of previously pubd articles and interviews], 199
B. Rusch: "Booty Wood," *Cadence*, x/9 (1984), 5

EDDIE LAMBERT

Woodblock. A wooden slit-drum with a resonant and penetrating tone; *see* DRUM SET, §I, 7(i).

Woode, Jimmy [James Bryant] (*b* Philadelphia, 23 Sept 1928). Double bass player. The son of a music teacher, he played baritone horn and studied piano and double bass. After serving

The Wolverines, 1924: (left to right) Vic Moore (drums), George Johnson (tenor saxophone), Jimmy Hartwell (clarinet and alto saxophone), Dick Voynow (piano, standing), Bix Beiderbecke (cornet), Al Gandee (trombone), Min Leibrook (sousaphone), and Bob Gillette (banjo)

in the US Navy he formed a trio (1946). He toured with Flip Phillips (1949), recorded with Zoot Sims and Toots Thielemans in Stockholm (both 1950), and also worked with Sarah Vaughan and Ella Fitzgerald (both 1950) and Nat Pierce (at intervals, 1951–2). For two years he was the house double bass player at Storyville in Boston, where he recorded with Sidney Bechet and Billie Holiday (both 1953) before playing in Duke Ellington's band from 1955 to 1959 (for illustration *see* ELLINGTON, DUKE, fig.2). During this period he also recorded as a leader (1957) and as a sideman with Johnny Hodges (1955–8), Clark Terry (1956–9), and others. In the 1960s he moved to Sweden, worked with the Clarke–Boland Big Band (with which he remained associated until it disbanded in 1973), and recorded with Eric Dolphy (1961). He then moved successively to Cologne, Germany (1964), where the Clarke–Boland Big Band was based and where he managed his own publishing firm, the Netherlands (1966), and Munich (by 1975). During this period he worked frequently in radio, television, and films, appeared at many festivals, and recorded with such musicians as Don Byas and Albert Nicholas (both 1963), Johnny Griffin (1964–8), Sahib Shihab (1964–8), the quartet led by Ted Curson and Booker Ervin (1966), Milt Buckner (1966–9), Benny Bailey (1968), with whom he also sang, Mal Waldron (1968–77), and Helen Humes (1974). In the 1980s he lived in Vienna while working occasionally with Nathan Davis's Paris Reunion Band.

SELECTED RECORDINGS

As leader: *The Colorful Strings of Jimmy Woode* (1957, Argo 630)

As sideman: C. Parker: *New Bird: Hi Hat Broadcasts, 1953* (1953, Phoenix Jazz 10), incl. Ornithology [side A]; J. Hodges: *Creamy* (1955, Norg. 1045); D. Ellington: *Such Sweet Thunder* (1956–7, Col. CL1033), incl. Sonnet in Search of a Moor; [no leader]: *Americans in Europe*, ii (1963, Imp. 37), incl. A. Nicholas: Why Daughter, how are you?; M. Waldron: *One-upmanship* (1977, Enja 2092)

BIBLIOGRAPHY

FeatherE; *Feather '60s*; *Feather–Gitler '70s*

J.-L. Ginibre: "Woode: de Duke à Klook," *Jm*, no.121 (1965), 26 [interview]

Wooding, Sam(uel David) (*b* Philadelphia, 17 June 1895; *d* New York, 1 Aug 1985). Pianist, arranger, and bandleader. He organized his first band, the Society Syncopators, in 1919 to work at Scott's Hotel in Atlantic City, New Jersey, and later played in clubs in New York, including the Club Alabam (1924–5). The band then accompanied the touring revue *Chocolate Kiddies* to Europe, where Wooding remained; he also toured South America with his all-star group, which included Tommy Ladnier, Herb Flemming, Garvin Bushell, and Gene Sedric. The orchestra presented a mixture of comedy routines and outstanding jazz performances, and achieved great eminence in Europe; it was unable, however, to duplicate its success in the USA on its return there in 1927, and the following year Wooding again traveled to Europe, taking additional soloists – Doc Cheatham, Albert Wynn, and Jerry Blake. He disbanded this group late in 1931 and organized another that played in the New York area until 1935. He then studied music at the University of Pennsylvania and later became a full-time music teacher. He led the Southland Spiritual Choir (1937–41) and then another vocal group (from the mid-1940s), and in the 1950s founded his own record label, Ding Dong. He made a world tour with the singer Rae Harrison in the 1960s. Wooding also wrote a number of arrangements, including *Shanghai Shuffle*.

Oral history material in *NjR* (JOHP).

SELECTED RECORDINGS

Shanghai Shuffle/Alabamy Bound (1925, Vox 01890); Carrie (1929, Parl. B25420); Downcast Blues (1929, Pathé X8684)

BIBLIOGRAPHY

ChiltonW

A. Napoleon: "A Pioneer Looks Back: Sam Wooding, 1967," *Sv* (1967), no.9, p.3; no.10, p.4

H. Flemming: "Old Sam: the Man who Brought Jazz to Europe," *JJ*, xxi/5 (1968), 8

M. Jones: "Sam Wooding: Bandleader from the Past," *MM* (7 Dec 1968), 8; (14 Dec 1968), 10

B. H. Behncke: "Sam Wooding and the Chocolate Kiddies at the Thalia-Theater in Hamburg, 28th July 1925 to 24th August 1925," *Sv*, no.60 (1974), 214

A. McCarthy: *Big Band Jazz* (London and New York, 1974), 310

H. J. P. Bergmeir: "Sam Wooding Recapitulated," *Sv*, no.74 (1977–8), 44

G. Bushell and M. Tucker: "On the Road with the Chocolate Kiddies in Europe and South America, 1925–1927," *Sv*, no.131 (1987), 182; no.132 (1987), 213

FRANK DRIGGS

Woodman, Britt (*b* Los Angeles, 4 June 1920). Trombonist. He was a boyhood friend and early musical associate of Charles Mingus. He played on the West Coast with the pianist Phil Moore and Les Hite, and after army service (1942–6) worked with Boyd Raeburn and Eddie Heywood, then joined Lionel Hampton in late 1946. Between 1948 and 1950 he studied music at Westlake College, Los Angeles, after which he replaced Lawrence Brown in Duke Ellington's band, where he played brilliantly as the leader of the trombone section. His performances as a soloist covered a wide range of styles, and Ellington captured an aspect of his musical personality in the miniature concerto *Sonnet to Hank Cinq* (from *Such Sweet Thunder*). In 1955 Woodman recorded, with Mingus, in a quintet led by Miles Davis; later he played in three sessions under Mingus's leadership (1960–63). After leaving Ellington in 1960 he worked in a number of Broadway shows. In 1970 he returned to California, where he performed as a freelance and recorded with his own octet (1977) and as a member of the Akiyoshi–Tabackin (1974–6), Bill Berry (1974–7), and Capp–Pierce (1976, 1978) big bands. He toured Japan twice with Benny Carter (1977–8), then returned to New York and continued to work intermittently in the 1980s with all-star swing and bop groups.

Oral history material in *CtY*.

SELECTED RECORDINGS

As leader: *In L.A.* (1977, Falcon 100)

As sideman with D. Ellington: *Seattle Concert* (1952, RCA LJM1002), incl. Sultry Serenade; *Dance to the Duke* (1953–4, Cap. T637), incl. Things ain't what they used to be; *Ellington Showcase* (1953–5, Cap. T679), incl. Theme for Trambeam; *Such Sweet Thunder* (1956–7, Col. CL1033), incl. Sonnet to Hank Cinq; *Jazz at the Plaza*, ii (1958, Col. C32471), incl. Red Garter

As sideman with others: C. Mingus: on *Mingus!* (1960, Can. 9021), MDM; B. Berry: *For Duke* (1977, RT 101), incl. Perdido

BIBLIOGRAPHY

R. Horricks: "An Interview with Britt Woodman," *JM*, v (1959), no.5, p.9; no.7, p.10; no.9, p.13; rev. as "From the Sidelines: Britt Woodman," *CI*, xxi (1983), no.8, p.24; no.9, p. 24

R. Sinclair: "Britt Woodman Today," *JJI*, xxxiii/3 (1980), 7 [incl. discography]

EDDIE LAMBERT

Woods, Chris(topher Columbus) (*b* Memphis, 25 Dec 1925; *d* New York, 4 July 1985). Alto saxophonist. He first played professionally in Memphis, then moved to St. Louis, where he worked with the Jeter–Pillars Orchestra and the trumpeter George Hudson and recorded as a leader (1952–62). He was also active as a composer, and his work is well represented by *Rhode Island Red*, recorded by Brew Moore on *Brew Moore* (1957, Fan. 3264). From 1962 Woods lived in New York and played, toured, and recorded with Dizzy Gillespie and Clark Terry. After performing with Sy Oliver from 1970 to 1973 he worked as a freelance musician before joining Count Basie in

1983. Besides his principal instrument he also played flute and baritone saxophone. Equally at home in small groups or big bands, Woods was a compelling soloist; his style was influenced by Charlie Parker but had a fierce edge derived from his own roots in rhythm-and-blues.

SELECTED RECORDINGS

As leader: *Somebody Done Stole my Blues* (1952, Del. 434); *Chris Meets Paris* (1973, Futura 2007); *Modus Operandi* (1978, Del. 437)

As sideman: T. Curson: *Cattin' Curson* (1973, Marge 01); S. Oliver: *Yes, Indeed* (1973, BB 33048), incl. Move, Pennies from Heaven, Rumble, Undecided; C. Terry: *Ain't Misbehavin'* (1979, PT 2312105); C. Basie: *Me and You* (1983, Pablo 2310891), incl. Bridge Work.

BIBLIOGRAPHY

Feather–Gitler '70s
K. Harris: "Chris Woods – TDWR," *JSN*, ii/1 (1980), 22
B. Rusch: "Chris Woods: Interview," *Cadence*, x/6 (1984), 5

PETER VACHER

Woods, Phil(ip Wells) (*b* Springfield, MA, 2 Nov 1931). Alto saxophonist and leader. He devoted himself to the saxophone from the age of 12. While completing his studies at the Juilliard School (where he was obliged to major in clarinet), he briefly played in Charlie Barnet's dance band. In 1955–6 he worked with George Wallington, Kenny Dorham, and Friedrich Gulda, and traveled to the Near East and South America with Dizzy Gillespie. For the next decade he led a number of small jazz groups, including a quintet with Gene Quill, Phil and Quill (intermittently, 1957–8). He also performed in Buddy Rich's band, toured Europe with Quincy Jones (1959–60) and the USSR with Benny Goodman (1962), and worked as a studio musician, playing various reed instruments for recording sessions, television, films, and advertising jingles. During the summers from 1964 to 1967 he taught at the Ramblerny performing arts camp in New Hope, Pennsylvania.

In March 1968 Woods moved to France, which marked his return to playing small-group jazz. In Paris that same year he formed a quartet called the European Rhythm Machine with the pianist George Gruntz (later Gordon Beck), the double bass player Henri Texier, and the drummer Daniel Humair. The group remained intact until 1972, when Woods organized an experimental electronic quartet in Los Angeles; this was given a cold reception and soon disbanded. Woods then moved to the East Coast, and in October 1973 formed an outstanding acoustic jazz group with Mike Melillo, Steve Gilmore, and Bill Goodwin. With this ensemble he won acclaim as the finest alto saxophonist in mainstream jazz, a reputation confirmed by his performances on *Images* (1975, with Michel Legrand), *Live from the Showboat* (1976, recorded with an expanded group including guitar and percussion), and *I love you just the way you are* (1977, with the popular singer Billy Joel), all of which received Grammy awards. With Hal Galper replacing Melillo (1981) and Tom Harrell added to the group (1983), Woods has continued to tour internationally and record into the late 1980s. He has begun to play clarinet on a regular basis, especially in combination with Harrell's muted trumpet.

Woods acknowledged a profound debt to Charlie Parker, and his effortless virtuosity, bright tone, witty quotations, gruff ballad style, and frequent references to the blues invited comparison between the two musicians, as did Woods's renditions of tunes associated with Parker (*Patterns of Jazz*, 1957). His melodic lines, however, like those of Cannonball Adderley, were more continuous and chromatic than Parker's (*Cottontail*, *Body and Soul*, 1961), and he often repeated ideas, sometimes displacing them within the meter or developing them sequentially (*A Bit of Blues*, 1956). In later years these features remained central to his style of improvisation. His repertory expanded to include not only bop (*Airegin*, 1974), but also, with the European Rhythm Machine, funk (*The Meeting*) and occasional passages of free jazz (*Riot*) (both 1970), and, with his new group, Latin jazz (*Brazilian Affair*, 1976). In the 1970s Woods began to make his instrument sound like a tenor saxophone, developing a larger and brighter tone and adding a carefully controlled, many-shaded growl reminiscent of Coleman Hawkins (*A Sleepin' Bee*, 1976). He has written large-scale suites such as

Phil Woods, New York, 1977

Rights of Swing (1961) and *I Remember* (1978) which, like his shorter jazz pieces, serve as vigorous frameworks for improvisation; a volume of transcriptions of his performances, *Phil Woods: Improvised Saxophone Solos*, has been published (Hialeah, FL, 1981). In 1984 he recorded an album with Chris Swansen on which the latter attempted to achieve the sound of a big band on a synthesizer, but it was poorly received. On his other, highly successful, recordings of the 1980s (above all the album *Integrity*), Woods has continued to play in an unamplified but fiery hard-bop style.

SELECTED RECORDINGS

AS LEADER

Woodlore (1955, Prst. 7018); with D. Byrd: *The Young Bloods* (1956, Prst. 7080); *Warm Woods* (1957, Epic 3436); *Rights of Swing* (1961, Can. 9016); *Greek Cooking* (c1966, Imp. 9143); *Round Trip* (1969, Verve 68791); *Phil Woods and his European Rhythm Machine at the Montreux Jazz Festival* (1970, MGM 4695), incl. Riot; *Phil Woods and his European Rhythm Machine at the Frankfurt Jazz Festival* (1970, Embryo 530), incl. The Meeting; *Musique du bois* (1974, Muse 5037), incl. Airegin; *"Live" from the Showboat* (1976, RCA BGL2-2202), incl. Brazilian Affair, A Sleepin' Bee; *Songs for Sisyphus* (1977, Gryphon 782); *I Remember* (1978, Gryphon 788); *Quartet* (1979, Clean Cuts 702); *Birds of a Feather* (1981, Ant. 1006); *At the Vanguard* (1982, Ant. 1013); with Budd Johnson: *The Ole Dude and the Fundance Kid* (1984, Upt. 2719); *Integrity* (1984, Red 177)

AS SIDEMAN

J. Raney: *Jimmy Raney Quartet* (1955, NewJ 1106); G. Wallington: *Jazz for the Carriage Trade* (1956, Prst. 7032); [no leader:] *The Birdland Stars on Tour* (1956, RCA LPM1327-8), incl. A Bit of Blues; C. Payne: *Patterns of Jazz* (1957, Signal 1204); T. Monk: *The Thelonious Monk Orchestra at Town Hall* (1959, Riv. 1138); Q. Jones: *Live at Newport '61* (1961, Mer. 60653); B. Carter: *Further Definitions* (1961, Imp. 12), incl. Body and Soul, Cottontail; T. Monk: *Big Band and Quartet in Concert* (1963, Col. CS8964); M. Legrand: *Images* (1975, RCA BGL1-1027); on B. Joel: *The Stranger* (1977, Col. PC34987), I love you just the way you are

BIBLIOGRAPHY

N. Hentoff: "Phil is Now out of the Woods," *DB*, xxiv/2 (1957), 13
I. Gitler: "This is Phil Woods," *DB*, xxviii/9 (1961), 20
M. Gardner: "Phil Woods," *JM*, no.184 (1970), 2; no.185 (1970), 2
A. J. Smith: "Out of the Forest into the Woods," *DB*, xlii/21 (1975), 22 [incl. discography]
Z. Knauss: *Conversations with Jazz Musicians* (Detroit, 1977), 226–61
J. DeMuth: "Phil Woods: Working More and Enjoying it no Less," *DB*, xlvi/1 (1979), 14
L. Tomkins: "Phil Woods Today," *CI*, xix (1981), no.6, p.20; no.7, p.12 [interview]
D. Morgenstern: "Phil Woods: Chief Alto of the Jazz Tribe," *DB*, xlix/1 (1982), 16 [incl. discography]
"Phil Woods," *SJ*, xxxvii/10 (1983), 212 [discography]
L. Tomkins: "Phil Woods: Update," *CI*, xxiv/3 (1987), 8

BARRY KERNFELD

Woodyard, Sam(uel) (*b* Elizabeth, NJ, 7 Jan 1925). Drummer. He was a self-taught musician. After playing with local groups in and around Newark, New Jersey, he joined Paul Gayten's rhythm-and-blues group (1950), then worked with the tenor saxophonist Joe Holiday (1951) and Roy Eldridge (1952) and performed and recorded with Milt Buckner's trio (1953–5). In July 1955 he joined the Duke Ellington Orchestra, with which he remained (with occasional breaks) until November 1966. Thereafter he became a member of the trio that accompanied Ella Fitzgerald, and settled in Los Angeles, but during the early 1970s he suffered from ill-health. Later Woodyard performed occasionally with Bill Berry and played conga with Ellington and Buddy Rich. From the late 1970s he worked in New York and toured in Europe, where he appeared with Claude Bolling's band and performed at many jazz festivals; in 1983 he recorded an album with Teddy Wilson, Buddy Tate, Slam Stewart, and others. Woodyard is a temperamental musician, but at his best is one of the greatest jazz drummers. His work with Ellington was frequently of the highest quality, combining an understanding of the leader's requirements with an individual, earthy kind of swing.

SELECTED RECORDINGS

As sideman with D. Ellington: *Ellington at Newport* (1956, Col. CL934); *Such Sweet Thunder* (1956–7, Col. CL1033); *Newport '58* (1958, Col. CL1245); *The Symphonic Ellington* (1963, Rep. 6097); *Duke Ellington's Jazz Violin Session* (1963, Atl. 1688); *Duke Ellington Plays Mary Poppins* (1964, Rep. 6141), incl. Step in Time; *Soul Call* (1966, Verve 68701), incl. La plus belle Africaine

As sideman with Great Eight: *Swingin' the Forties with the Great Eight* (1983, Tim. 185-6)

BIBLIOGRAPHY

"Interviews with the Men besides [*sic*] Duke Ellington: Sam Woodyard," *Jazz Statistics*, no.8 (1959), 9
S. Dance: *The World of Duke Ellington* (London and New York, 1970/*R*1981) [colln of previously pubd articles and interviews], 189
C. Carrière: "Jam with Sam," *Jh*, no.318 (1975), 17

EDDIE LAMBERT

Wooldridge, Gaby. *See* LINCOLN, ABBEY.

Wootten, Red [Lawrence Bernard] (*b* Social Circle, GA, 5 Nov 1921). Double bass player. After playing with Jan Savitt (1945) and Tony Pastor (1947) he performed and recorded in Los Angeles with Tommy Dorsey (1949), Woody Herman (1951), and Charlie Barnet (1956). In 1957 he worked in rhythm sections with Red Norvo on recordings by Harry Babasin's Jazzpickers and Jack Montrose; he is heard to advantage on *Command Performance* (1957, EmA 36123) recorded with the Jazzpickers. He performed and recorded with Norvo (1957–8) and in 1959 toured Europe with Benny Goodman. He recorded with Goodman in 1959 and 1960. Thereafter he became less active as a jazz musician, and concentrated instead on studio work; he also composed and arranged film scores. In the mid-1970s he recorded with Anita O'Day. His name has occasionally been spelled Wootton. (*FeatherE*)

Workman, Reggie [Reginald] (*b* Philadelphia, 26 June 1937). Double bass player. He played piano, tuba, and euphonium before taking up double bass with rhythm-and-blues groups in 1955. His first association as a jazz musician was with Gigi Gryce (1958); thereafter he worked with Red Garland and Roy Haynes (both 1959), John Coltrane (1961), James Moody (1962), Art Blakey's Jazz Messengers (1962–4), Albert Heath (1964), Yusef Lateef (1964–5), Herbie Mann (1966), and Thelonious Monk (1967). He also recorded with Freddie Hubbard (1962–3, 1969), Archie Shepp (1964, 1967), Lee Morgan (1964, 1968), and Cedar Walton (1969). In the late 1960s Workman became active in music education; he first taught at the New Muse Community Museum of Brooklyn, where in 1975 he was appointed director of the music workshop. He has also taught at several colleges and universities on the East Coast. During the 1970s he worked with Max Roach (1973–4) and recorded with Charles Tolliver (1972, 1975), Billy Harper (1973), Shepp (1977), Art Farmer (in Tokyo, 1979), and many others. He has continued to record in the 1980s, notably with Juhani Aaltonen (1981), and Mal Waldron and David Murray (both 1983).

Workman is one of several outstanding double bass players who came to prominence in the 1960s. He is equally comfortable with hard bop or free jazz, and his playing is strongly rhythmic and melodic. His unflagging bass lines and inventive solos were particularly appreciated by Coltrane and Blakey.

SELECTED RECORDINGS

As sideman: G. Gryce: *Sayin' Something* (1960, NewJ 8230); D. Jordan: *Flight to Jordan* (1960, BN 4046); J. Coltrane: *Africa/Brass* (1961, Imp. 6); *Olé Coltrane* (1961, Atl. 1373); *Live at the Village Vanguard* (1961, Imp. 10); A. Blakey: *Free for All* (1964, BN 84170); *Indestructible* (1964, BN 84193); W. Shorter: *Juju* (1964, BN 84182); Y. Lateef: *Psychicemotus* (1965, Imp. 92); B. Ervin: *The Trance* (1965, Prst. 7462); W. Shorter: *Adam's Apple* (1966, BN 84232); L. Morgan: *Taru* (1968, BN LT1031); D. Murray: *Morning Song* (1983, BS 0075)

BIBLIOGRAPHY

Feather '60s; *Feather–Gitler '70s*

MARK GARDNER

World Pacific. Record label founded by Richard Bock in 1958 as a subsidiary of his company PACIFIC JAZZ.

World Saxophone Quartet [WSQ]. It was founded in 1976 by David Murray (tenor saxophone) and three members of the Black Artists Group of St. Louis: Oliver Lake (alto), Julius Hemphill (alto), and Hamiet Bluiett (baritone). Although the players concentrate on saxophones, they also occasionally play flute, alto clarinet, and bass clarinet. Their style is fundamentally original, though they have drawn extensively on rhythmic, melodic, and timbral traditions of blues-flavored black-

American popular music, and the jazz approaches of Ornette Coleman and Albert Ayler. Their compositions sometimes recall the saxophone writing of Duke Ellington, Thad Jones, and Oliver Nelson. Although the quartet occasionally plays passages of free jazz, by deftly interweaving composed parts with improvised solos and ensembles, the musicians achieve a greater balance of contrasts than Coleman. Also significant are their broad spectrum of earthy tone-colors, their light-hearted manner, and their unique amalgam of compositional approaches, ranging from 20th-century concert music to rhythm-and-blues and free jazz. The World Saxophone Quartet has continued to tour regularly in the 1980s, and in 1986–7 devoted considerable attention to performing and recording each member's arrangements of songs by Duke Ellington and Billy Strayhorn.

SELECTED RECORDINGS

Point of No Return (1977, Moers 01034); *Steppin' with the World Saxophone Quartet* (1978, BS 0027); *World Saxophone Quartet* (1980, BS 0046); *Revue* (1980, BS 0056); *The World Saxophone Quartet Plays Duke Ellington* (1986, Nonesuch 79137-1)

BIBLIOGRAPHY

C. J. Safane: "The World Saxophone Quartet," *DB*, xlvi/16 (1979), 26
K. R. Bachmann: "World Saxophone Quartet," *JP*, xxxiv/5 (1985), 23
F. Davis: *In the Moment: Jazz in the 1980s* (New York, and Oxford, England, 1986) [colln of previously pubd articles], 243
P. Elwood: "Saxophone Quartet Digs Deep into Duke Ellington," *San Francisco Examiner* (8 Nov 1986)

MARK C. GRIDLEY

World's Greatest Jazz Band (of Yank Lawson and Bob Haggart). Ensemble founded in 1968 by the trumpeter Yank Lawson and the double bass player Bob Haggart. Its original sidemen were the trumpeter and flugelhorn player Billy Butterfield, the trombonists Lou McGarity and Carl Fontana, the clarinetist and soprano saxophonist Bob Wilber, the tenor saxophonist Bud Freeman, the pianist Ralph Sutton, the drummer Morey Feld, and the banjoist, guitarist, and singer Clancy Hayes. It grew from a band that played from the early 1960s at engagements organized by the businessman Dick Gibson and which worked from 1965 at the Trocadero Ballroom in Denver, using variously the names the Eight, Nine, or Ten Greats of Jazz. Gibson encouraged the members to work full-time in this ensemble; he also suggested its new name, under which it first performed in New York in November 1968. After this Hayes and Feld left, and the latter was replaced by Gus Johnson. With Maxine Sullivan, the group undertook several long residencies in New York. Haggart's arrangements of jazz classics and contemporary pop songs, spiced with the powerful solo work of the musicians, were an important aspect of the band's appeal to a younger audience. In 1971 Barker Hickox replaced Gibson as the group's impresario and organized its record label, World Jazz. By this time the trombonists were Ed Hubble and Vic Dickenson. Butterfield left in 1972; by 1975 the group had seven members, including Benny Morton as the sole trombonist, but it was augmented for special events. In 1978 Lawson and Haggart abandoned the band's title, but they have used it again on occasions in the mid-1980s.

SELECTED RECORDINGS

World's Greatest Jazz Band (1968, Project 5033), incl. Ode to Billy Joe, Up, up, and away; *Extra* (1969, Project 5039), incl. Alfie; *Jazz in the Troc* (1969, WCS 3330); *World's Greatest Jazz Band Live at the Roosevelt Grill* (1970, Atl. 1570); *What's New?* (1970, Atl. 1582); *Century Plaza* (1972, World Jazz 1); *World's Greatest Jazz Band in Concert*, ii: *At Carnegie Hall* (1973, World Jazz 4); *World's Greatest Jazz Band of Yank Lawson and Bob Haggart on Tour* (1975, World Jazz 8); *World's Greatest Jazz Band of Yank Lawson and Bob Haggart Plays Duke Ellington* (1976, World Jazz 9); *World's Greatest Jazz Band of Yank Lawson and Bob Haggart Plays George Gershwin* (1977, World Jazz 11)

BIBLIOGRAPHY

I. Gitler: "'Now is the Renaissance': the World's Greatest Jazz Band," *DB*, xxxvi/9 (1969), 16
G. W. Kay: "The World's Greatest (and Happiest) Jazz Band," *SL*, xxii (1969), Sept–Oct, 221
K. Gallacher: "The World's Greatest Jazz Band," *JM*, no.182 (1970), 9
J. S. Wilson: "The World's Greatest Jazz Band," *IM*, lxviii/12 (1970), 11
K. Gallacher: "The World's Greatest Jazz Band," *J&B*, i/8 (1971), 9
J. Klee: "The World's Greatest Jazz Band of Yank Lawson and Bob Haggart," *DB*, l/16 (1973), 18
B. Korall: *The World's Greatest Jazz Band of Yank Lawson and Bob Haggart* (n.p. [Phoenix, AZ], 1973)

BRIAN PEERLESS

World Wide. Record label. A subsidiary of Savoy (ii), it was established by Herman Lubinsky in Newark, New Jersey, in 1958. It was intended that the repertory should exploit to best advantage the innovations of stereo recording techniques, but only two albums were issued; both, by an all-star band that included Bobby Jaspar, Frank Rehak, Frank Wess, Bill Harris (i), Joe Wilder, and Pepper Adams, were produced by Ozzie Cadena.

MARK GARDNER

Wright. Family of musicians.

(1) Lammar Wright(, Sr.) (i) (*b* Texarkana, TX, 20 June 1907; *d* New York, 13 April 1973). Trumpeter. He grew up in Kansas City, and in 1923 became a member of Bennie Moten's band, which was playing at the Panama Club. In 1927 he went to New York to join the Missourians, remaining with the group when it was taken over by Cab Calloway; Wright, a high-note specialist and a soloist, worked as Calloway's lead trumpeter regularly until 1942 (for illustration *see* CALLOWAY, CAB), then intermittently for the rest of the decade. He also played with Don Redman (1943), Claude Hopkins (1944–6), Cootie Williams (1944), Lucky Millinder (periodically, 1946–52), Sy Oliver (1947), and Louis Armstrong. Occasionally Wright led his own band and, in the 1950s and 1960s, while also working as a teacher, he became active as a studio musician. He recorded with Arnett Cobb and Count Basie (both 1951) and the Sauter–Finegan Orchestra (1957), among others, and performed and recorded with George Shearing's big band (1959).

SELECTED RECORDINGS

As sideman: B. Moten: Elephant's Wobble (1923, OK 8100); Missourians: Market Street Stomp (1929, Vic. 38067); C. Calloway: Gotta darn good reason now (1930, Bruns. 4936); S. Oliver: Lammar's Boogie (1947, MGM 10133); G. Shearing: *Satin Brass* (1959, Cap. ST1326)

BIBLIOGRAPHY

ChiltonW; *FeatherE*
R. Russell: *Jazz Style in Kansas City and the Southwest* (Berkeley, CA, Los Angeles, and London, 1971/*R*1983, rev. 2/1973), 93
Obituary, *DB*, 1/11 (1973), 41
A. McCarthy: *Big Band Jazz* (New York and London, 1974)

(2) Lammar Wright(, Jr) (ii) (*b* Kansas City, MO, 28 Sept 1927; *d* ?Los Angeles, 8 July 1983). Trumpeter, son of (1) Lammar Wright. He played with Lionel Hampton (1943–6) and Dizzy Gillespie (1947), then worked as a principal soloist in Charlie Barnet's band (1948–9).

SELECTED RECORDINGS

As sideman: L. Hampton: Million Dollar Smile (1944, Decca 18719); D. Gillespie: Algo bueno (1947, Vic. 203186); C. Barnet: Redskin Rhumba (1948, Cap. 10174)

BIBLIOGRAPHY

FeatherE
Obituary, *Coda*, no.192 (1983), 35

(3) Elmon Wright (*b* Kansas City, MO, 27 Oct 1929; *d* 1984). Trumpeter, son of (1) Lammar Wright. He performed and recorded with Dizzy Gillespie (1946–50), and also worked with Roy Eldridge (1946) and toured with Earl Bostic (1954–5). Thereafter he became active as a freelance musician in New York and played with rhythm-and-blues groups at the Apollo Theatre and with rock-and-roll bands. In 1959 he performed with Buddy Rich and Earle Warren, and in 1963 he recorded with Milt Jackson.

SELECTED RECORDINGS

As sideman: D. Gillespie: One Bass Hit (1946, Musi. 404); R. Eldridge: Tippin' out (1946, Decca 23637); E. Bostic: Cocktails for Two (1955, King 4790)

BIBLIOGRAPHY

FeatherE
Obituary, *Orkester journalen*, lii/6 (1984), 26

FREDERICK A. BECK

Wright, Frank (*b* Grenada, MS, 9 July 1935). Tenor saxophonist and leader. While growing up he played electric bass guitar in rhythm-and-blues groups in Memphis and in Cleveland, where he met Albert Ayler; he was inspired by Ayler's example to take up the tenor saxophone. After moving to New York in the early 1960s he played free jazz with Larry Young, Noah Howard, and Sunny Murray, worked briefly with Cecil Taylor and John Coltrane, and recorded as a leader (1965, 1967); his playing is well represented by *No End* from his album *Your Prayer* (1967, ESP 1053). He moved in 1969 to France, where he led a quartet in which his sidemen were Howard (later replaced by Alan Silva), the pianist Bobby Few, and the drummer Muhammad Ali; with this group he made recordings in 1969 and 1970 before returning for a brief period to the USA (1971). After moving again to France he continued to lead the quartet (recording in 1972 and 1974) and toured Europe. In the mid-1980s he performed and recorded with Taylor.

BIBLIOGRAPHY

B. McRae: "Avant Courier: Frank Wright: Working On," *JJ*, xxviii/8 (1975), 12
J. Eigo: "Frank Wright," *Coda*, no.151 (1976), 33 [review]
V. Wilmer: *As Serious as your Life: the Story of the New Jazz* (London, 1977, rev. 1980)

Wright, Gene [Eugene Joseph] (*b* Chicago, 29 May 1923). Double bass player. He studied cornet in school, then took up double bass. He worked with his own group, the Dukes of Swing (1943–6), before performing and recording with Gene Ammons (1946–51), Count Basie (1948–9), Arnett Cobb (1951–2), Buddy DeFranco (1953–5), Red Norvo (1955–6), and Cal Tjader (1955–8). In 1958 he became a member of the Dave Brubeck Quartet, in which his solid timekeeping provided the foundation for Brubeck's experiments with polyrhythms. After the quartet disbanded in 1967 Wright presented concerts at colleges (1969–70) and played in Monty Alexander's trio (1971–4). From 1974 he became involved in television and film work and was active as a teacher and composer; for a time he served as chairman of the jazz department at the University of Cincinnati and as a member of the advisory board of the jazz division of the International Society of Bassists (1974–6). Wright has continued to play for reunions of Brubeck's quartet, notably at the Kool Jazz Festival in 1985.

See also BRUBECK, DAVE.

SELECTED RECORDINGS

As leader: *The Wright Groove* (1962, Phi. 8755)
As sideman: on G. Ammons: *"Jug" Sessions* (1947–9, EmA 2-400), Going for the okey doak (1947); B. DeFranco: *In a Mellow Mood* (1954, Norg. 1079); C. Tjader: *Jazz at the Blackhawk* (1957, Fan. 3241), incl. Thinking of you, MJQ: D. Brubeck: *Dave Brubeck in Europe* (1958, Col. CL1168); *Countdown Time in Outer Space* (1961–2, Col. CS8575), incl. Why Phillis; M. Alexander: *Here Comes the Sun* (1971, MPS 2120913)

BIBLIOGRAPHY

Feather–Gitler '70s
M. Jones: "This World of Jazz," *MM*, xxxiii (22 Feb 1958), 13
A. J. Smith: "A Quarter of a Century Young: the Dave Brubeck Quartet," *DB*, xliii/6 (1976), 18
E. Tiegel: "Eugene Wright: Acoustic Bassist Eager to Resume Brubeck Touring," *Billboard*, lxxxix (12 March 1977), 141

BRENDA PENNELL

Wright, Leo (Nash) (*b* Wichita Falls, TX, 14 Dec 1933). Alto saxophonist, flutist, and clarinetist. He studied saxophone with his father and John Hardee. He made his first recording with Dave Pike (1958) and performed with Charles Mingus at the Newport Jazz Festival in 1959. From 1959 to 1962 he played in Dizzy Gillespie's quintet and big band, appearing at the Monterey, Newport, and Antibes–Juan-les-Pins festivals and recording several albums. He also recorded with Richard Williams (1960) and Eldee Young (1961), and in New York as the leader of bop quartets and quintets (1960–63); his sidemen included Junior Mance, Art Davis, Charli Persip, Williams, Kenny Burrell, and Ron Carter. After leaving Gillespie, Wright recorded with Lalo Schifrin and Brother Jack McDuff (both 1962) and Antonio Carlos Jobim, Jimmy Witherspoon, and Johnny Coles (all 1963). In Europe he worked as a freelance and recorded with George Gruntz (1965) and with Lee Konitz in the all-star group Alto Summit (1968). After settling in Berlin he played with the studio band of Sender Freies Berlin and other groups, and appeared at jazz festivals in Germany, Switzerland, and Finland. He later lived in Vienna and retired from music for a period from 1979; he first played again in 1986, recording an album of duets with his wife and performing with Nat Adderley, Grachan Moncur III, and Kenny Drew in the Paris Reunion Band. A versatile instrumentalist, Wright was strongly influenced as a saxophone player by Johnny Hodges; his timbre on the alto instrument and the bluesy character of his solos show evidence of this. His flute sound, supported by a superb technique, is airy and resonant.

SELECTED RECORDINGS

As leader: *Blues Shout* (1960, Atl. 1358); *Modern Jazz Studio Nr.4* (1965, Amiga 855056); *It's All-Wright* (1972, MPS 21375)
As sideman: D. Gillespie: *A Musical Safari* (1961, Booman 1001); *New Wave* (1962, Phi. 600070); Alto Summit: *Alto Summit* (1968, Saba 675); R. Garland: *I Left my Heart* (1978, Muse 5311)

BIBLIOGRAPHY

FeatherE; *Feather '60s*; *Feather–Gitler '70s*

GARY CARNER

Wright, Specs [Charles] (*b* Philadelphia, 8 Sept 1927; *d* Philadelphia, 6 Feb 1963). Drummer. After belonging to a band in the US Army (to 1947) he played bop with Jimmy Heath, toured France and recorded with Howard McGhee (1948), and performed and recorded with Dizzy Gillespie (1949–51). He made recordings with Earl Bostic (1952), with whom he also toured, and Kenny Drew (1953) and at the same time worked as a freelance in Philadelphia (to 1955). During the following years he performed and recorded with Cannonball Adderley (1955–6) and Carmen McRae (1957–8) and also made recordings with Nat Adderley (1956), Art Blakey (1957), and Ray Bryant (1957). In 1958 he recorded with Monday Night at Birdland (an all-star bop group the other members of which included Hank Mobley, Curtis Fuller, and Lee Morgan), Sonny Rollins, and Betty Carter; later he played and recorded with Red Garland (1959) and worked with Lambert, Hendricks, and Ross (1960–61). He is heard to advantage on *Red Garland at the Prelude* (1959, Prst. 7170). (*FeatherE*; *Feather '60s*; *ReclamsJ*)

Wrightsman, Stan(ley) (*b* Gotebo, OK, 15 June 1910; *d* Palm Springs, CA, 17 Dec 1975). Pianist. He played at a hotel in Gulfport, Mississippi, in territory bands in Oklahoma, and in New Orleans under the bandleader Ray Miller (1930). He worked for a period in California, belonged to Ben Pollack's group in Chicago (1935–6), and after settling in Los Angeles recorded in Hollywood with Santo Pecora (1937). From the late 1930s he worked as a freelance and played frequently in film studios; he also recorded with Artie Shaw (1940), performed and recorded dixieland at intervals with Wingy Manone (1940–49) and Eddie Miller (1944–50), and played and recorded with Nappy Lamare (1945, 1946). In 1950–51 he played and recorded with Bob Crosby. During the following years he recorded with the Rampart Street Paraders (1953–7), Matty Matlock (1954–60), and Pete Fountain (1956); in 1958 he made recordings with Bob Scobey, Ray Bauduc, and Wild Bill Davison and played on the soundtrack to the film *The Five Pennies*. Later he performed and recorded again with Fountain (1959–67), recorded with Muggsy Spanier (1962), and worked in television and films. He is heard to advantage on *Pete Fountain on Tour* (1961, Coral 57337). *(ChiltonW; FeatherE; Feather–Gitler '70s)*

Wróblewski, Jan [Ptaszyn, Ptak] (*b* Kalisz, Poland, 27 March 1936). Polish tenor saxophonist and composer. He is known among his colleagues as Ptaszyn or Ptak (Bird). He played clarinet, tenor saxophone, and piano while studying agricultural mechanics at the polytechnic in Poznań, then took courses in music theory at the Higher School of Music in Kraków (from 1958). His professional début was in 1956, when he performed and recorded with Krzysztof Komeda at the first jazz festival in Sopot. He was chosen to play in Marshall Brown's International Youth Band at the Newport Jazz Festival in 1958 and thereafter was invited to play with many Polish groups. He led the Jazz Believers (1958–9), a quintet (1959–61), the Jazz Outsiders (1961–3), and the Polish Jazz Quartet (1963–6), and also played with Andrzej Kurylewicz (1962–3). In the second half of the 1960s he worked mainly as a freelance musician, then in 1968 he formed the orchestra of the Polish Radio Jazz Studio, which he led until 1977; most of the important Polish jazz musicians played in this group at one time or another. During the same period Wróblewski worked for radio and served as vice-president and later president of the Polish Jazz Society. In the 1970s he led Mainstream with Wojciech Karolak; Chałturnik, an orchestra that mainly played experimental works and musical persiflages; and a quartet, with which he toured the USA.

Wróblewski was one of the first Polish musicians to play in a free-jazz style and, although later he used a more traditional approach, he remained open to musical experimentation. Some of his compositions are influenced by Polish folk music, such as *Bandoska in Blue*; another major composition, *Wariant Warszawski* (*Warsaw variant*), was performed by his jazz quartet with a symphony orchestra in 1975.

SELECTED RECORDINGS

As leader: *Jazz Outsiders* (1962, Muza 0197); *Polish Jazz Quartet* (1964, Muza 0246); with W. Karolak: *Mainstream* (1973, Muza 1139); *S.P.P.T. Chałturnik* (early 1970s, Muza 1079)

As sideman with A. Kurylewicz: *Go Right* (1963, Muza 0186)

BIBLIOGRAPHY

Feather–Gitler '70s

J. Byrczek: "Eurojazz Personalities: Poland," *JF* [intl edn], no.18 (1972), 87

K. Czyz: "Jan Ptaszyn Wroblewski: the Sole Survivor," *JF* [intl edn], no.73 (1981), 24 [incl. discography]

WOLFRAM KNAUER

WSQ. *See* WORLD SAXOPHONE QUARTET.

Wyands, Richard (*b* Oakland, CA, 2 July 1928). Pianist. He began his professional career in 1944, working with local groups; later he accompanied many leading soloists as a member of a house band at a club in San Francisco. During the mid-1950s he worked with Ella Fitzgerald and Carmen McRae before moving in 1958 to New York, where he played with Roy Haynes, Charles Mingus (1959), Jerome Richardson (1959), and Gigi Gryce. Wyands was at his most prolific in 1960–61 when his tidy solos enlivened recordings by musicians as diverse as Gryce, Oliver Nelson, Etta Jones, Eddie "Lockjaw" Davis, the vibraphonist Lem Winchester, Gene Ammons, Willis Jackson, and Taft Jordan. From 1965 to 1974 he toured with Kenny Burrell's group, traveling to England in 1969 and Japan in 1971. He was also active as a freelance, and recorded with Freddie Hubbard in 1971. Wyands became a member of Budd Johnson's JPJ Quartet in 1974, and recorded with Benny Bailey in 1978 and Zoot Sims in 1982. He continues to be in demand as an accompanist and ensemble player, but his worth as a soloist has inexplicably been undervalued. His sensitive and effective playing of ballads is reminiscent of the work of Hank Jones.

SELECTED RECORDINGS

As leader: *Then Here and Now* (1978, Sto. 6)

As sideman: J. Richardson: *Roamin' with Jerome Richardson* (1959, NewJ 8226); G. Gryce: *Sayin' Something* (1960, NewJ 8230); O. Nelson: Screamin' the Blues (1960, NewJ 8243); E. Jones: *Don't Go to Strangers* (1960, Prst. 7186); R. Haynes: *Just us* (1960, NewJ 8245); G. Ammons: *Jug* (1961, Prst. 7192); K. Burrell: *The Tender Gender* (1966, Cadet 772); C. Payne: *Casbah* (1985, Empathy E–1005)

BIBLIOGRAPHY

FeatherE; *Feather–Gitler '70s*

MARK GARDNER

Wyble, Jimmy [James Otis] (b Port Arthur, TX, 25 Jan 1922). Guitarist. He worked in Houston with local bands, including that of Peck Kelley, and was a staff musician for a radio station (1941–2). After completing his military service he moved, around 1946, to Los Angeles as a member of Bob Wills's Texas Playboys. During the following years he worked in television and films, recorded with Shorty Rogers (1952) and Barney Kessel (1953), and performed and recorded with Red Norvo (1957–64); he is heard to advantage on *Hi-five* (1957, RCA LPM1420), recorded with Norvo. With Benny Goodman he toured abroad (1959, 1960, 1963) and performed and recorded in the USA (1960–61). In 1964 he toured in the backup group of Frank Sinatra, of which Norvo was also a member. Later he worked as a freelance musician in studios in Los Angeles (1965–75) and from the mid-1970s belonged to Tony Rizzi's Five Guitars, which performed five-part harmonizations of compositions by Charlie Christian. During the 1970s and 1980s he has incorporated elements of classical guitar style into his playing; this preoccupation and his activities as a teacher in Los Angeles have led him to publish several texts on guitar techniques.

BIBLIOGRAPHY

Feather E; *Feather–Gitler '70s*

F. R. Nemko: "Whether with Spade Cooley, Benny Goodman, or in L.A.'s Studios . . . he's Always been Jimmy Wyble," *GP*, xi/6 (1977), 22 [incl. discography]

Wynn, Al(bert (L.)) (*b* New Orleans, 29 July 1907; *d* Chicago, May 1973). Trombonist. He toured with Ma Rainey (for illustration *see* BLUES, fig.1), led his own band in Chicago (1926–8), and performed and recorded with Charlie Creath in St. Louis (1927); his style is particularly well represented on *Down* *by the Levee/Parkway Stomp* (1928, Voc. 1220). In 1928 he moved to Europe, where he became a freelance musician and then worked with Sam Wooding (from 1929) and the pianist Harry Flemming. After returning to the USA (1932) he played in New York with the New Orleans Feetwarmers and in Chicago with Jesse Stone, Jimmie Noone, Richard M. Jones, and Earl Hines. He performed with Fletcher Henderson (1937–9) and then joined Noone's big band. In the 1940s and early 1950s he played as a freelance in Chicago with various musicians, including the drummer Floyd Campbell, Baby Dodds, and Lil Armstrong. He worked with Franz Jackson (1956–60) and the Gold Coast Jazz Band (1960–64) and in 1961 he made recordings with Lil Armstrong and as a leader (including *Al Wynn's Gutbucket Seven*, Riv. RLP9426) as part of Riverside's Living Legends series. Ill-health restricted his musical activities from the mid-1960s.

Oral history material in *LNT*.

BIBLIOGRAPHY

ChiltonW; *FeatherE*
H. Panassié: "Albert Wynn," *Jazz Forum: Quarterly Review of Jazz and Literature*, no.3 (1947), 13

X

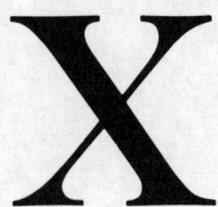

Xanadu. Record company and label. The company was founded in New York in 1975 by Don Schlitten (*b* New York, 4 March 1932), a record producer who had formerly been involved with Signal, Muse (ii), Onyx, Cobblestone, and several other companies. It quickly became a highly respected enterprise, and by 1987 it had issued more than 200 albums. The repertory is divided into two parts. The Silver Series contains newly made recordings by such leaders as Al Cohn, Barry Harris, Dolo Coker, Jimmy Raney, Sonny Criss, Dexter Gordon, Bob Mover, Frank Butler, and others, and a sequence of albums made at the Montreux International Jazz Festival of 1978. The Gold Series is devoted to reissues, chiefly of swing and bop. These included Billy Eckstine's first recordings, many historically important items from the early 1930s, and material produced by Bob Shad after World War II. As well as producing all new sessions himself, Schlitten designs the album liners, takes the photographs, and in some instances has written the accompanying notes. He has also been concerned to ensure that musicians or their families are paid the appropriate royalties for reissues. To mark the tenth anniversary of its inception the company issued a sampler of representative material from its catalogues.

In 1976 Xanadu sponsored several of its musicians to undertake a tour of Japan, where it holds leasing agreements. A similar visit was organized in 1980 to West Africa, where the company was one of the first to present American jazz and to record African jazz for distribution elsewhere. (M. Segell: "Once More, Jazz is Big Business," *RS*, no.282 (1978–9), 78)

MARK GARDNER

Xiques, Ed(ward F., Jr.) (*b* New York, 9 Oct 1939). Saxophonist. He worked with Jaki Byard and Herb Pomeroy while studying music at Boston University (BM 1962). After moving to New York he worked as a schoolteacher (1962–8), played as a freelance with Buddy Morrow, the trumpeter Les Elgart and the alto saxophonist Larry Elgart, and Duke Pearson, and toured briefly and recorded with Woody Herman (1970). From 1971 to the late 1970s he performed, recorded, and toured Europe with the Thad Jones–Mel Lewis Orchestra as a member of which he played flute and clarinet in addition to his principal instrument (for illustration *see* JONES, fig.1*b*). At the same time he worked as a freelance, performing and recording with Bill Watrous (1974, 1975), Frank Foster (in Tokyo, 1975), and McCoy Tyner (1977). He is heard to advantage on *The Tiger of San Pedro* (1975, Col. PC33701), recorded with Watrous. He later performed and recorded with Toshiko Akiyoshi (1983–6). (*Feather–Gitler '70s*)

Xylophone. A tuned percussion instrument probably of African or Asian origin, known in Europe from the early 16th century. The modern orchestral instrument consists of a set of wooden bars arranged in two ranks similar to a keyboard configuration, each bar suspended over a tube resonator. The xylophone has a compass of four octaves ascending from *c'* or three and a half octaves from *f'* or *g'*. When struck with hard-headed mallets it produces a bright, penetrating sound; softer mallets, giving a less distinct sound, are occasionally used. It has been used infrequently in jazz. Red Norvo began his career as a xylophone player and recorded on the instrument both as a leader (*Hole in the Wall*, 1933, Bruns. 6562) and as a sideman with Hoagy Carmichael (*Moon Country*, 1934, Vic. 24627); he continued to play xylophone regularly until 1944. The xylophone was the second instrument of the washboard player Jimmy Bertrand, who in 1928 played it during a recording session led by the blues singer Blind Blake, in which Johnny Dodds also took part.

BIBLIOGRAPHY

L. Feather: *The Book of Jazz: a Guide to the Entire Field* (New York, 1957, 2/1965 as *The Book of Jazz from Then till Now: a Guide to the Entire Field*)

J. Blades: *Percussion Instruments and their History* (London, 1970, rev. [3]/1984)

CLIFFORD BEVAN

Y

Yaged, Sol(omon) (*b* New York, 8 Dec 1922). Clarinetist. He was inspired to take up the clarinet by Benny Goodman's broadcasts for the National Biscuit Company (1935) and studied for several years with Simeon Bellison of the New York PO; he declined the offer of a chair in the Buffalo PO. He played at the Swing Club, New York, in 1942 and, after army service, worked at Jimmy Ryan's for a year beginning in 1945. He continued to work mainly in New York: after playing with various renowned musicians, notably Phil Napoleon's Memphis Five, from the mid-1950s he usually led his own trios, quartets, and quintets. He was technical adviser for the film *The Benny Goodman Story* (1956) and taught Steve Allen to play clarinet. Among the numerous clubs in New York at which he played were the Metropole (1954–61), the Gaslight (from 1966), and Jimmy Weston's (1970s); in 1977 he was said to be the city's busiest musician. Yaged established a reputation as Goodman's most fanatical admirer, and an unabashed imitator of the style that Goodman perfected in the 1930s and early 1940s; this reputation has tended to overshadow his own proficiency as a performer as well as his leaning towards a dixieland idiom. He is heard to advantage on his album *It Might as Well be Swing* (*c*1956, Herald 0103).

BIBLIOGRAPHY

FeatherE

L. Feather: "Meet Mr. Yaged: he's all for Benny Goodman, Body and Sol," *DB*, xxiii/3 (1956), 16

J. S. Wilson: "No.1 Benny Goodman Fan Takes his Work Seriously," *New York Times* (19 March 1972)

——: "Sol Yaged," *IM*, lxxi/4 (1972), 6

Z. Knauss: *Conversations with Jazz Musicians* (Detroit, 1977), 262

JEFFREY COOPER

Yagi, Masao (*b* Tokyo, 14 Nov 1932). Japanese pianist, composer, and arranger. He began his career playing Hawaiian music, then played jazz with the Ichiban Octet, led by the tenor saxophonist Shin Matsumoto, and as Toshiko Akiyoshi's replacement in Sadao Watanabe's Cozy Quartet. He formed a group in 1959 that in the following year recorded music by Thelonious Monk, in whose work he had taken a keen interest. In 1964 he recorded with Charlie Mariano and Hidehiko Matsumoto and began working as a composer and arranger; he also recorded with Helen Merrill (1969). Later he led a jazz-rock ensemble, continued to lead a bop group, and recorded as a leader (1976). Yagi's best-known composition is *Oniwa soto, fukuwa uchi;* his others include *Grow, Etude,* and *Jinku* (all 1964). He has written arrangements for Nobuo Hara's Sharps and Flats (*Little Giant* and *Flute Salad,* both 1969), the female singing group Eve, and the singer Yoshiko Goto.

SELECTED RECORDINGS

(all recorded for King)

As leader: *Masao Yagi Plays Thelonious Monk* (1960, 3014); *Inga* (1976, SKA3021)

As sideman: C. Mariano and H. Matsumoto: *Jazz Interaction* (1964, K20P6155); A. Miyazawa: *Round Midnight* (1985, K28P6358)

YOZO IWANAMI

Yamashita, Yosuke (*b* Tokyo, 26 Feb 1942). Japanese pianist. He worked professionally from the age of 17, attended the Kunitachi College of Music, Tokyo (1962–7), and belonged to quartets led by Masahiko Togashi and Sadao Watanabe. His early style, which owed something to the work of Bill Evans (ii), gave way to one considerably more adventurous around 1969, and he played free jazz as the leader of a trio and as a sideman with the tenor saxophonists Kazumi Takeda and Seiichi Nakamura and the reed player Akira Sakata. From 1974 he worked principally in Europe, and he recorded in Germany as the leader of a trio (1974–6), as a sideman with Manfred Schoof (1975), as an unaccompanied soloist (1975–6), and in a duo with Adelhard Roidinger (1977); he also appeared at festivals in Germany and Yugoslavia, and at the Newport Jazz Festival in New York. He made recordings in Japan into the 1980s.

SELECTED RECORDINGS

Concert in Jazz (1969, Union JUP4); *Frozen Days* (1974, Crown GGP6); *Clay* (1974, Enja 2052); *Chiasma* (1975, MPS 2022678–6); *Arashi* (1976, Frasco 7019–20); *First Time* (1979, Frasco 7029); *Jugenmu* (1981, Frasco 28PJ1005); *Live and then Picasso* (1982, Panja YF7070); *In Europe 1983* (1983, Panja YF7079); *Breath with Hozan Togashi* (1984, Denon YF7091); *Sentimental* (1985, Kitty H33K20018)

BIBLIOGRAPHY

Feather–Gitler '70s

A.-R. Hardy: "Le piano terrible de Yamashita," *Jm*, no.253 (1977), 18 [incl. discography]

B. Doerschuk: "Conflict and Harmony at the Fringes of Jazz: Avant-garde Pianist Yosuke Yamashita," *Keyboard*, xi/8 (1985), 42

YOZO IWANAMI

Yancey, Jimmy [James Edwards] (*b* Chicago, *c*1894; *d* Chicago, 17 Sept 1951). Pianist. From the age of six he toured the USA and Europe as a singer and tap-dancer in vaudeville shows. He gave this up in 1915 to settle in Chicago, where from 1925 until just before his death he was groundskeeper at Comiskey

Park for the Chicago White Sox baseball team. He played informally at clubs and rent parties, helping to establish the style known as BOOGIE-WOOGIE and influencing Meade "Lux" Lewis and Albert Ammons. He received some attention as a result of Lewis's recording of *Yancey Special* in 1936, and in 1939–40 issued a series of his own recordings, including many works composed by him years earlier. These highly regarded performances reveal a remarkable balance and expressivity despite Yancey's unassuming technique and limited harmonic and melodic resources. Unlike other boogie pianists, Yancey frequently altered his bass patterns in response to the right hand, producing shifting polyrhythms and varied bass lines. In later years he continued to record, sometimes accompanying his own singing or that of his wife Mama Yancey, with whom, in 1948, he appeared at Carnegie Hall. Transcriptions of his solos are included in the volume *Six Blues-root Pianists* by E. Kriss (New York and London, 1973).

See also PIANO, §3.

SELECTED RECORDINGS

Yancey Stomp/State Street Special (1939, Vic. 26589); Slow and Easy Blues/The Mellow Blues (1939, Vic. 26591); Cryin' in my Sleep/Death Letter Blues (1940, Bb 8630); Yancey's Bugle Call/35th and Dearborn (1940, Vic. 27238); At the Window (1943, Session 10-005)

BIBLIOGRAPHY

D. Stewart-Baxter: "Mama and Jimmy Yancey," *JJ*, viii/10 (1954), 3

M. Harrison: "Boogie-woogie," *Jazz: New Perspectives on the History of Jazz*, ed. N. Hentoff and A. J. McCarthy (New York and Toronto, 1959/*R*1974), 105–35

W. Russell: "Jimmy Yancey," *The Art of Jazz: Essays on the Nature and Development of Jazz*, ed. M. Williams (New York, 1959/*R*1979 as *The Art of Jazz: Ragtime to Bebop*), 98

M. Harrison: "*State Street Special*: an Analysis," *JR*, iii/3 (1960), 41

Y. Bruynoghe: "Jimmy Yancey," *Jazz Era: the 'Forties*, ed. S. Dance and others (London, 1961/*R*1985), 249

J. Holley: "Jimmy Yancey: a Discography," *Matrix*, no.95 (1971), 3

B. Rusch: "Mama Yancey: Interview," *Cadence*, iv/11 (1978), 3

J. BRADFORD ROBINSON

Yardbird. Nickname of CHARLIE PARKER.

Yaw, Ralph (Percy) (*b* Enosburg Falls, VT, 22 Oct 1898). Composer and arranger. After moving in 1919 to Los Angeles he played piano in bands that toured California and Arizona. From 1927 to 1934 he worked as a pianist and manager at the Coconut Grove in Bakersfield, California; during the following years he wrote arrangements for Eddie Barefield (1934–5) and Cab Calloway (1935–9) and occasionally for Chick Webb, Isham Jones, Count Basie, and Les Brown. For Stan Kenton in the early 1940s he wrote arrangements and about 40 original compositions, including *Two Moods* (recorded in 1940 and first issued on *The Kenton Era*, 1940–54, Cap. WDX569); he also wrote arrangements for Red Nichols and Johnny Richards. After ending his career in jazz in 1947 he played and wrote country music. (*FeatherE*)

Yerba Buena Jazz Band. Traditional jazz band formed in 1940 in Oakland, California, by LU WATTERS.

Yoder, Walt(er E.) (*b* Hutchinson, KS, 21 April 1914; *d* California, 2 Dec 1978). Double bass player. He began playing piano at the age of ten, but changed to double bass in his teens. After working with Joe Haymes and Tommy and Jimmy Dorsey he joined Isham Jones, with whom he also recorded (1934–6). When Jones's group disbanded Yoder became a member of the band Woody Herman formed from its members. A fine example of his playing may be heard on Herman's *Yardbird Shuffle* (1941, Decca 4353). He left Herman in 1942, but worked with him again in 1947–8, after moving to California. He performed regularly with Ben Pollack in the late 1940s and early 1950s and made three recordings with his group in 1949; he also worked with Bob Crosby and Russ Morgan and later recorded with Red Nichols (1963). In the 1970s Yoder settled in Studio City, California, where he worked as a freelance musician.

based on *ChiltonW*

Young, David A. [Dave] (*b* Nashville, 14 Jan 1912). Tenor saxophonist. As a child he moved with his family to Chicago, where he studied music. He played with various leaders from 1932, among them Frankie "Half Pint" Jaxon (1933), Carroll Dickerson (1936), and Roy Eldridge (1936–8). After working with Fletcher Henderson (1939) he joined Horace Henderson; his tenor saxophone playing may be heard on Horace Henderson's *Shufflin' Joe* (1940, Voc. 5518). He left Henderson in 1940 and in the early 1940s he played with Walter Fuller and Eldridge and recorded with Lucky Millinder and Sammy Price (1942). In 1944–5 he was a member of a navy band and after his military service he led his own band in Chicago; it recorded with Dinah Washington (1947) and accompanied her at the Ritz Lounge. Young then ceased full-time performing.

BIBLIOGRAPHY

W. C. Allen: *Hendersonia; the Music of Fletcher Henderson and his Musicians: a Bio-discography* (Highland Park, NJ, 1973)

D. J. Travis: *An Autobiography of Black Jazz* (Chicago, 1983) [incl. interviews], 486

based on *ChiltonW*

Young, Eldee (*b* Chicago, 7 Jan 1936). Bass player. He learned double bass at high school and later studied at the Chicago Conservatory. After working with the trumpeter King Kolax (1951) and with various blues singers, including Joe Turner (ii) and Joe Williams (mid-1950s), from 1956 he played cello and double bass in Ramsey Lewis's trio, which made many recordings for Argo. Young also recorded as a sideman with Lorez Alexandria (1957) and James Moody (*Hey! It's Moody*, 1959, Argo 666) and as a leader (1961). In 1966 he and Redd Holt (Lewis's drummer) left Lewis and formed the soul band Young–Holt Unlimited, with which Young played both double bass and electric bass guitar. (*FeatherE*; *Feather '60s*)

Young, Larry [Aziz, Khalid Yasin Abdul] (*b* Newark, NJ, 7 Oct 1940; *d* New York, 30 March 1978). Organist. Although his father was an organist Young never took formal organ instruction and instead studied piano. He began his career in 1957 in Elizabeth, New Jersey, as a member of rhythm-and-blues groups, and in 1960 he recorded with Jimmy Forrest and as a leader. After recording his first album (*Groove Street*, 1962) he played hard bop with Grant Green (recording in 1964–5), Joe Henderson, Lee Morgan, Donald Byrd, and Tommy Turrentine, and in 1964 toured Europe; in the following year he won critical recognition for his album *Into Somethin'*. He performed with John Coltrane, recorded in 1965 as the leader of a group that included Woody Shaw and Elvin Jones, and played jazz-rock with Miles Davis (1969), John McLaughlin (1970), and Tony Williams's Lifetime (1969–71). Young is best known for his free-jazz organ playing, of which he was the leading exponent; he modeled his style after the later work of Coltrane.

SELECTED RECORDINGS

As leader: *Groove Street* (1962, Prst. 7237); *Into Somethin'* (1964, BN 84187); *Unity* (1965, BN 84221); *Lawrence of Newark* (1973, Perception 34); *Spaceball* (1975, Ari. 4072)

As sideman: M. Davis: *Bitches Brew* (1969, Col. GP26); J. McLaughlin: *Devotion* (1970, Douglas 4); T. Williams: *Turn it Over* (1970, Pol. 4021); *Ego* (1971, Pol. 4065)

BIBLIOGRAPHY

Feather '60s; *Feather–Gitler '70s*
A. Frenier: "Portrait de Larry Y," *Jm*, no.178 (1970), 18
L. K. McMillan, Jr.: "Larry Young: a Sound Apart," *JF* [intl edn], no.25 (1973), 43

GARY THEROUX

Young, Lee [Leonidas Raymond] (*b* New Orleans, 7 March 1917). Drummer, brother of Lester Young. He moved to Minneapolis with his family in 1920 and studied soprano saxophone, trumpet, trombone, and piano before he took up drums. With his brother Lester and his sister Irma, he played in an orchestra led by his father, the pianist Willis Handy Young, performing on the TOBA circuit. After moving to Los Angeles he sang with the pianist Walter Johnson (1934) and played drums with Mutt Carey (1934), Buck Clayton (1936), Eddie Barefield (1936–7), and Fats Waller (at the Famous Door, 1937), with whom he also recorded. Young then worked for the Paramount and Metro–Goldwyn–Mayer studios and performed and recorded as a singer and drummer with Lionel Hampton (September 1940 to January 1941). In 1941 he recorded with Nat "King" Cole and, from May of that year, led a sextet with his brother Lester, which included Red Callender and played material written by Billy Strayhorn and Gerald Wilson; in September 1942 this group performed at Café Society, New York. Young was later employed by Columbia Pictures (1944–8) and made recordings with Dinah Washington (1945), Ivie Anderson (1946), and Mel Powell (1947), and performed and recorded with Jazz at the Philharmonic (1944, 1946), Hampton (1947), and Benny Goodman (1947–8). From 1953 to 1962 he was a member of Cole's trio. Thereafter he worked as a producer and executive for Vee-Jay Records (1964–5) and Motown Records (from 1979). Young's position in most of the bands with which he played was principally that of a time-keeper; he may be heard in this role on many albums, though most are unfortunately poorly recorded. His work is better represented on *Jazz at the Philharmonic*, ii, iii, xi (1946, Mer./Clef 35003, 35004, 35011).

Oral history material in *NjR* (JOHP).

BIBLIOGRAPHY

ChiltonW; *FeatherE*; *Feather '60s*
V. Wilmer: "The Lee Young Story," *JJ*, xiv/1 (1961), 3
L. Porter: *Lester Young* (Boston and London, 1985)

Young, Lester (Willis) [Pres, Prez] (*b* Woodville, MS, 27 Aug 1909; *d* New York, 15 March 1959). Tenor saxophonist, brother of Lee Young.

1. Life 2. Music.

1. Life. Young was the oldest of three children and grew up in the vicinity of New Orleans. By 1920 he had moved to Minneapolis with his father, Willis Handy Young, a versatile musician who taught all his children instruments and eventually formed a family band that toured with carnivals and other shows. Young studied violin, trumpet, and drums, settling on alto saxophone by about the age of 13. After one of many disputes with his father he left the family band at the end of 1927. He spent the following year touring with Art Bronson's Bostonians, where he took up tenor saxophone. He returned to his family in New Mexico during 1929, but stayed behind when they moved to California. In 1930 he played briefly with Walter Page's Blue Devils and again with Bronson, then settled in Minneapolis, where he played during 1931 with Eddie Barefield and various leaders at the Nest Club. Early in 1932 Young joined the Thirteen Original Blue Devils, and while on tour in Oklahoma City met Charlie Christian. When the Blue Devils disbanded in the middle of 1933, Young made Kansas City his base, and played with the Bennie Moten–George E. Lee Band, Clarence Love, King Oliver, and, on one night in December, Fletcher Henderson, then on tour with his star saxophonist, Coleman Hawkins.

Lester Young

Early in 1934 Young joined Count Basie, beginning an association that eventually led to national recognition. He left Basie at the end of March as a provisional replacement for Hawkins in Henderson's band. Henderson's musicians rejected Young's very different approach to the saxophone, however, and he left after a few months. He joined Andy Kirk en route back to Kansas City, then Boyd Atkins and Rook Ganz in Minnesota, and for the next year performed mostly in these two areas on a freelance basis. By 1936 Young had resumed his association with Basie. In November of that year, with a unit from Basie's band, he made his first recordings. His solos on *Lady be Good* and *Shoe Shine Boy* were immediately regarded by musicians, many of whom learned them note for note. During the next few years, as Basie's band became more famous, Young was prominently featured on its recordings and broadcasts. Although he received mixed reviews from the critical establishment, the younger generation of musicians, including Dexter Gordon, Illinois Jacquet, and others, were enthusiastic about his music. His small-group performances, particularly *Lester leaps in* (1939) and his many recordings with Billie Holiday, were especially influential.

Young left Basie in December 1940 to form his own small band, which performed at Kelly's Stable, New York, early in 1941. In May he moved to Los Angeles to lead a band with his brother Lee, which went to New York's Café Society in September 1942. This group disbanded early the following year, and Young played as a freelance in New York and on tour with a USO band before rejoining Basie in December 1943. It was during this second tenure with Basie that Young came to the notice of the general public. In 1944 he won first place in the *Down Beat* poll for tenor saxophonists, the first of many such honors. He also became the favorite of a new generation of jazz musicians, among them John Coltrane, Sonny Rollins, and Stan Getz. He was prominently featured in the film *Jammin' the Blues*.

On 30 September 1944 Young was drafted into the army, which he found a nightmarish experience. Cut off from his musical outlets, he was discovered using drugs and was court-martialed the following February. After serving several months in detention barracks in Georgia he was released at the end of 1945 and resumed recording and performing in Los Angeles. At his first recording session he produced a masterpiece, *These Foolish Things*.

Beginning in 1946 Young spent part of almost every year playing with Jazz at the Philharmonic, touring the rest of the time with his own small groups. From 1947 to 1949 his style showed the influence of some of the young bop musicians in his groups in the occasional use of double-time and in the selection of repertory. He continued to develop and modify his approach successfully except when he was drinking; by this time his reliance on alcohol was becoming a health problem. From about 1953 until his death his recordings were noticeably less consistent, yet he was still able to produce some of his best work on concert recordings such as *Prez in Europe* (1956). He made guest appearances with Basie's band in 1952–4 and again at the Newport Jazz Festival in 1957, but he never rejoined as a regular member. He became increasingly dependent on alcohol, and on several occasions he was hospitalized. In January 1959 he began an engagement at the Blue Note club in Paris. He made his last recordings there in March, then became severely ill and returned to New York, where he died shortly afterwards.

2. Music. Young was one of the most influential musicians in jazz. His style was viewed as revolutionary when he was first recorded during the late 1930s, and it was a primary force in the development of modern jazz in general and the music of Charlie Parker in particular (*see* Saxophone, §2). The only influences Young ever admitted to were two white saxophonists of the 1920s, Jimmy Dorsey and Frankie Trumbauer, especially the latter. Both possessed exceptional classical technique and a light, dry sound. Dorsey was fond of timbral effects achieved through low honks and alternative fingerings, and Young carried these further. From Trumbauer, Young adopted a strong sense of musical form, which was apparent even in his earliest recordings, such as *Lady be Good* (ex.1) with its short motivic and rhythmic constructions, each building upon its predecessor. Young's beautiful and delicate sound must be heard in order to appreciate fully the impact of this solo.

Young's work of the 1940s and 1950s was different in style from that of his early years, but not necessarily inferior, as many critics have claimed. His tone was much heavier and his vibrato wider. He was more overtly emotional and filled his solos with wails, honks, and blue notes. He drew more heavily

Ex.1 From *Lady be Good* (1936, Voc. 3459); transcr. L. Porter

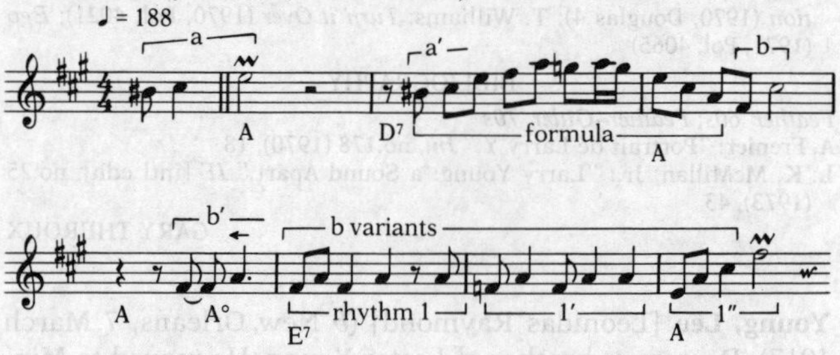

← = note slightly anticipated
ʌʌ = pronounced vibrato

on a small repertory of formulas, especially simple ones such as the arpeggiation of the tonic triad in first inversion at phrase endings. His solos also contained astonishing leaps and bold contrasts (ex.2), relying more on the alternation of repetition and surprise than on motivic development. Significantly, musicians have praised his recordings of the 1940s alongside his early ones, indicating a clear appreciation of their musical value.

Ex.2 From *After Theatre Jump* (1944, Key. 1302); transcr. L. Porter

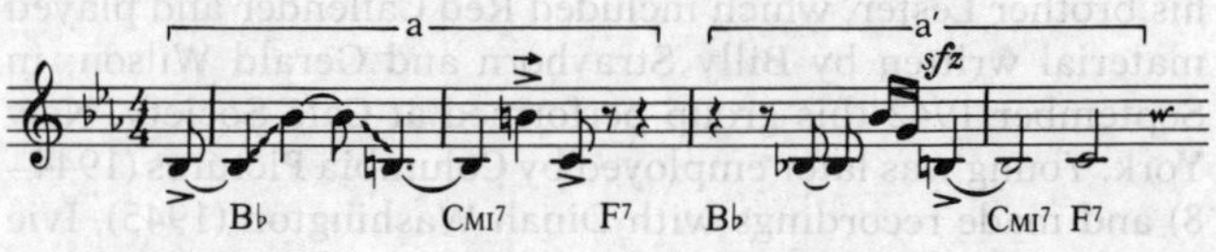

→ = note slightly delayed

Young's impact on the course of jazz was profound. His superb melodic gift and logical phrasing were the envy of musicians on all instruments, and his long, flowing lines set the standard for all modern jazz. His personal formulas are now the common property of all jazz musicians, and recur in countless jazz compositions and improvisations. Sadly, the public, while familiar with Young's name, has little awareness of his music and its role in jazz history. The feature film *Round Midnight* (1986), which was dedicated to Young and Bud Powell, was largely based on Young's life story.

Oral history material in *NjR*.

SELECTED RECORDINGS

AS LEADER

with N. Cole: Indiana/Body and Soul (1942, Philo 1000); Sometimes I'm Happy (1943, Key. 604); These Foolish Things (1945, Philo/Ala. 124); Jumpin' with Symphony Sid (1947, Ala. 163); *The Lester Young Story* (1949–56, Verve 8308), incl. [with T. Wilson:] Pres Returns; *Prez in Europe* (1956, Onyx 218), incl. Lester leaps in

AS SIDEMAN

Jones–Smith, Inc. [C. Basie]: Shoe Shine Boy (1936, Voc. 3441); Lady be Good (1936, Voc. 3459); C. Basie: *Count Basie and his Orchestra, 1938* (1938, Fanfare 18), incl. Flat Foot Floogie, Lady be Good; Jumpin' at the Woodside (1938, Decca 2212); Kansas City Six: Them There Eyes (1938, Com. 511); C. Basie: Taxi War Dance (1939, Voc. 4748); Clap hands, here comes Charlie (1939, Voc. 5085); Lester leaps in (1939, Voc. 5118); Tickle Toe (1940, Col. 35521); Easy does it (1940, Col. 35448)

B. Goodman: Ad-lib Blues, Lester's Dream (both 1940), first issued on C. Christian and L. Young: *Together Again* (1940–41, Jazz Archives 6); B. Holiday: All of me (1941, OK 6214); Kansas City Seven: After Theatre Jump (1944, Key. 1302)

BIBLIOGRAPHY

P. Harris: "Pres Talks about Himself, Copycats," *DB*, xvi/8 (1949), 15
L. Feather: "Here's Pres!," *MM*, xxvi (15 July 1950), 3
——: "Pres Digs Every Kind of Music," *DB*, xviii/22 (1951), 13
N. Hentoff: "Pres," *DB*, xxiii/5 (1956), 9
JM, ii/10 (1956) [special issue]

N. Hentoff: "Lester Young," in N. Shapiro and N. Hentoff, eds.: *The Jazz Makers* (New York, 1957/*R*1975, 1979 as *The Jazz Makers: Essays on the Greats of Jazz*), 243–75
D. Morgenstern: "Lester Leaps In," *JJ*, xi/8 (1958), 1
W. Burckhardt and J. Gerth: *Lester Young: ein Porträt* (Wetzlar, Germany, 1959)
L. Gottlieb: "Why so Sad, Pres?," *Jazz: a Quarterly of American Music*, no.3 (1959), 185
H. P[anassié]: "Lester Young," *BHcF*, no.87 (1959), 4
F. Postif: "Lester: Paris, 1959," *JR*, ii/8 (1959), 6; repr. in *Jazz Panorama*, ed. M. Williams (New York and London, 1962/*R*1979), 139; new transcr., *Jh*, no.362 (1979), 18; no.363 (1979), 34
V. Franchini: *Lester Young* (Milan, 1961)
D. Heckman: "Pres and Hawk: Saxophone Fountainheads," *DB*, xxx/1 (1963), 20
J. G. Jepsen: *A Discography of Lester Young* (Copenhagen, 1968)
M. Williams: *The Jazz Tradition* (New York, 1970, rev. 2/1983)
J. Burns: "Lester Young: the Postwar Years," *J&B*, i/4 (1971), 4
J. Hammond and H. Woodfin: "Two Views of Lester Young: Recollections and Analysis," *J&B*, iii/5 (1973), 8
G. Colombé: "Time and the Tenor: Lester Young in the Fifties," *Into Jazz*, i/3 (1974), 32
H. Schröder: [discography], *Micrography*, no.41 (1976), 21; no.42 (1976), 21; no.44 (1977), 19; no.48 (1977), 16
J. Evensmo: *The Tenor Saxophone and Clarinet of Lester Young, 1936–1942* (n.p. [Oslo], n.d. [?1977], rev. [2]/n.d. [?1983] as *The Tenor Saxophone and Clarinet of Lester Young, 1936–1949*) [discography]
S. Dance: *The World of Count Basie* (New York and London, 1980) [colln of previously pubd interviews]
J. McDonough: Liner notes, *Lester Young* (TL J13, 1980)
L. Gushee: "Lester Young's 'Shoeshine Boy,' " *IMSCR*, xii *Berkeley 1977*, ed. D. Heartz and B. Wade (Basle, 1981), 151
R. A. Luckey: *A Study of Lester Young and his Influence on his Contemporaries* (diss., U. of Pittsburgh, 1981)
L. Porter: "Lester Leaps In: the Early Style of Lester Young," *Black Perspective in Music*, ix (1981), 3
B. Cash: *An Analysis of the Improvisation Technique of Lester Willis Young, 1936–1942* (thesis, U. of Hull, England, 1982)
W. Balliett: "Pres," *Jelly Roll, Jabbo and Fats* (New York, and Oxford, England, 1983) [colln of previously pubd articles], 119
D. H. Daniels: "History, Racism, and Jazz: the Case of Lester Young," *Jf*, xvi (1984), 87
D. Gelly: *Lester Young* (Tunbridge Wells, England, 1984)
D. H. Daniels: "Lester Young: Master of Jive," *American Music*, iii (1985), 313
L. Porter: *Lester Young* (Boston and London, 1985)
D. H. Daniels: "Big Top Blues: Jazz-minstrel Bands and the Young Family Tradition," *Jf*, xviii (1986), 133

LEWIS PORTER

Young, Snooky [Snookie; Eugene Edward] (*b* Dayton, OH, 3 Feb 1919). Trumpeter. From 1939 to 1942 he was lead trumpeter and soloist in Jimmie Lunceford's orchestra (for illustration *see* LUNCEFORD, JIMMIE), and was featured with the band on the soundtrack for the film *Blues in the Night* (1941). He worked with Count Basie in Dayton (1942), then toured with Lionel Hampton (1942–3) and played in California with Les Hite and Benny Carter. In 1943 he spent another period with Basie before joining Gerald Wilson's big band, then returned to Hampton. He worked with Basie again from 1945 to 1947, and from 1957 to 1962, when with Wendell Culley and Thad Jones he was a member of a notable trumpet section; during the intervening years he led his own group in Dayton. In 1962 Young became a studio trumpeter for NBC. He was a founding member of the Thad Jones–Mel Lewis Orchestra in 1966, and remained with that band until 1972, when he moved to Los Angeles with the "Tonight Show" orchestra. He toured with the Basie Alumni in 1981. Although he has usually been employed as a lead trumpeter, Young is an accomplished improviser.

SELECTED RECORDINGS

As leader: on *The Boys from Dayton* (1971, MJR 8130), L'il Darlin', Hard Boiled Rock; with M. Royal: *Snooky's and Marshall's Album* (1978, Conc. 55); *Horn of Plenty* (1979, Conc. 91)

As sideman: J. Lunceford: Uptown Blues (1939, Voc./OK 5362); C. Basie: *Chairman of the Board* (1959, Roul. 52032), incl. Who Me?; R. Bryant: *Lonesome Traveler* (1966, Cadet 778)

BIBLIOGRAPHY

ChiltonW
S. Dance: *The World of Count Basie* (New York and London, 1980) [colln of previously pubd interviews], 137
E. Townley: "Horn of Plenty: Snooky Young," *JJI*, xxxv/11 (1982), 19
B. Rusch: "Snooky Young: Interview," *Cadence*, xii/7 (1986), 5

BARRY KERNFELD

Young, Trummy [James Osborne] (*b* Savannah, GA, 12 Jan 1912; *d* San Jose, CA, 10 Sept 1984). Trombonist and singer. He first played trumpet but soon took up trombone, and made his professional début in Washington, where he played from 1928 with Booker Coleman and his Hot Chocolates. He acquired his nickname while in a band led by the drummer Tommy Myles. In late 1933 he followed Myles's arranger Jimmy Mundy into Earl Hines's orchestra. Although he played on some 40 commercial recordings with Hines's band, Young contributed solos to only a small number; his style was in the process of formulation at this period, and his work displays an indication of his relaxed and individual approach to timing as well as his formidable command of the trombone's upper register. He developed his talents fully while a member of Jimmie Lunceford's orchestra (1937–43), and Lunceford's arranger, Sy Oliver, wrote several pieces to display his gifts as a soloist. He obtained a full and rounded tone throughout the range of the instrument and perfected his "trumpet style," which owed something to the influence of Jimmy Harrison and Louis Armstrong. Young was also one of the band's singers; he had a rather high-pitched and distinctive voice and was frequently called on to perform "jive" and somewhat comic songs, such as *Margie*.

After leaving Lunceford, Young led his own band, worked with Roy Eldridge and Claude Hopkins (both 1944) and Benny Goodman (1945), among others, toured with Jazz at the Philharmonic (1946, 1947), and then moved to Hawaii. In 1952 he joined Armstrong's All Stars, a step that was seen as controversial at the time, since the dixieland-oriented repertory of the group was regarded by some as too restrictive for his improvisational and harmonic ideas. Young used the affiliation as an opportunity to develop the role of the trombone in traditional jazz, and his range and power made him an ideal partner for Armstrong. His contribution to the ensemble (which represented a considerable simplification of his earlier style) was less of a solo line and more a modification of the tailgate style with a sophisticated harmonic and rhythmic content, and was far more balanced than that of his predecessor, Jack Teagarden. On opening statements of a theme Young often played in parallel harmony to Armstrong's melody, throwing the clarinet part into relief against the brass, before adopting a mobile contrapuntal line and syncopated eighth-notes for subsequent choruses. His own solos were characterized by a biting attack and great power as well as the use of vocal tones. Young left Armstrong on 1 January 1964 and returned to Hawaii, though he continued to tour as a soloist and work with a number of bandleaders in the last two decades of his life, notably with Chris Barber in Europe and, in the early 1980s, at the Grande Parade du Jazz in Nice, France.

Oral history material in *NjR* (JOHP).

For illustrations *see* LUNCEFORD, JIMMIE, and PETTIFORD, OSCAR.

SELECTED RECORDINGS

As sideman: J. Lunceford: Margie (1938, Decca 1617); Tain't what you do (1939, Voc./OK 4582); I got it (1940, Col. 35510); L. Armstrong: on *The Best of Louis Armstrong's All Stars in Concert* (1953, Rarities 18–19), Margie; *Louis Armstrong Plays W. C. Handy* (1954, Col. CL591); *Satch Plays Fats* (1955, Col. CL708); on *Louis Armstrong at Pasadena* (1956, GNP 11001), My bucket's got a hole in it; L. Armstrong and D. Ellington: *The Great Reunion* (1961, Roul. 52103), incl. The Beautiful Americans

BIBLIOGRAPHY

ChiltonW

A. J. McCarthy: "Trummy Young," *JM*, i/3 (1955), 10

M. Jones: "Young Man with an Axe," *MM*, xxxi (5 May 1956), 3; (12 May 1956), 6; (19 May 1956), 6

B. Esposito: "Trummy Young, Trombonist," *JJ*, xxiii/7 (1970), 20

S. Dance: *The World of Earl Hines* (New York, 1977) [interviews], 220

C. E. Martin: "Trummy Young: an Unfinished Story," *SL*, xxx (sum. 1978), 30

M. A. Bloom: "Trummy Young: Interview," *Cadence*, vii/5 (1981), 5

J. Reldy: "En bavardant avec Trummy," *BHcF*, no.288 (1981), 5 [interview]

M. L. Hester: "Trummy," *MR*, xv/2 (1987), 1

ALYN SHIPTON

Young Tuxedo Brass Band. New Orleans group. It was founded in 1938 by John Casimir, who served as leader until his death in 1963, and became one of the most important groups in the resuscitation of the brass-band tradition in New Orleans after World War II. Numbering between nine and 11 players, and consisting typically of two trumpets, two trombones, two reed players, sousaphone, snare drum, and bass drum, it recorded in 1958 (*New Orleans Joys*, Atl. 1297) with such musicians as the trumpeters Andy Anderson (i) and John Brunious, the trombonists Clement Tervalon, Eddie Pierson, and Jim Robinson, Herman Sherman, Andrew Morgan, Paul Barbarin, and the bass drummer Emile Knox. The band was revived by Sherman in 1972, remained active until his death in 1984, and was subsequently re-formed by the trumpeter Greg Stafford. (G. Giddins: *Rhythm-a-ning: Jazz Tradition and Innovation in the '80s* (New York, and Oxford, England, 1985) [colln of previously pubd articles], 183)

WILLIAM J. SCHAFER

Ysaguirre, Bob [Robert] (*b* Belize, British Honduras [now Belize City, Belize], 22 Feb 1897; *d* New York, 27 March 1982). Double bass and tuba player. He began playing tuba at the age of 18, and after performing in a military band (1917–19) he moved to New Orleans, where he played with Amos White (1922). He made a number of recordings as a tuba player with A. J. Piron's orchestra in New York (1923–5), then worked with Elmer Snowden (1925–6) and the Plantation Orchestra, led by the violinist Alex Jackson (1926–9). Ysaguirre also recorded with the trombonist Te Roy Williams (*Oh Malinda/Lindbergh Hop*, 1927, Har. 439) and performed briefly with Fletcher and Horace Henderson. In 1931 he began a long association with Don Redman, with whom he made many recordings on tuba and double bass; his double bass playing may be heard on *I got rhythm* (1932, Bruns. 6354). Ysaguirre left Redman in 1940 and continued to play in and around New York until the late 1960s. His strong sense of rhythm is clearly displayed in his performances on both instruments.

based on *ChiltonW*

Yukl, Joe [Joseph] (*b* New York, 5 March 1909; *d* Los Angeles, March 1981). Trombonist and leader. After moving to New York in 1927 he played with Red Nichols, worked as a staff musician for CBS, and recorded with the orchestra of Jimmy and Tommy Dorsey in 1930. He worked in Baltimore in the early 1930s before returning to New York to perform and record under the bandleader Joe Haymes (1934). In 1934–5 he performed and again recorded with the Dorseys, and after moving with Jimmy Dorsey to California in 1935 he performed and recorded with Dorsey (to 1937), worked with Louis Armstrong (1936), and made recordings with Bing Crosby (1935–7) and as a member of Ray McKinley's sextet (*New Orleans Parade*, 1936, Decca 1019); he also performed and recorded with Ben Pollack (1937–8) and worked with Frankie Trumbauer (1938) and the orchestra of the songwriter Ted Fio Rito (1939). Later he played and recorded as a freelance and worked in studios in Hollywood; he recorded dixieland with Wingy Manone (1944–6), with Charlie LaVere (1944, 1949), and as a leader (1945), acted and performed (in a dixieland band that also included Manone) in the film *Rhythm Inn* (1951), and played some of the trombone solos in *The Glenn Miller Story* (1953). (*ChiltonW*; *FeatherE*)

Z

Zadlo, Leszek (*b* Kraków, Poland, 1 April 1945). Polish tenor and soprano saxophonist, clarinetist, and flutist. He first played clarinet in local bands, then, after winning a scholarship in a competition in Vienna, moved to Austria to study at the Hochschule für Musik in Graz (1966). During his three years there he played with Eje Thelin before joining the newly formed big band of Österreichischer Rundfunk (1970), led from 1972 by Erich Kleinschuster. Later he played with Kleinschuster's sextet and from around 1970 also led his own groups. In 1974 he moved to Munich, and he soon became active in the German jazz scene. He performed with the European Jazz Quintet (1977–82), and recorded with Michael Naura and the poet Peter Rühmkorff (1978, 1987), and with Springtime, led by Günter Lenz (1979). In the 1980s he toured with George Russell and Elvin Jones, and recorded with Bireli Lagrene (1982). After martial law was declared in his home country he organized a touring band, the Polski Jazz Ensemble, which gave concerts in aid of the Polish trade union Solidarność (1983–6). He teaches in Munich and Würzburg and also composes music for films and the theater. He is heard to advantage on *Sting* (1980, Fusion 8001), recorded with his own quartet. (J. Borkowski: "Leszek Zadlo: Inner Silence," *JF* [intl edn], no.24 (1973), 41)

WOLFRAM KNAUER

Zappa, Frank [Francis Vincent, Jr.] (*b* Baltimore, 21 Dec 1940). Electric guitarist and composer. He moved with his family to California at the age of ten, began playing drums when he was 12, and took up the guitar soon after. He sang blues and rock while in his teens and for six months studied theory at Chaffey College, Alta Loma, California. Although he is best known as a rock songwriter and guitarist, his work has often included elements of jazz. His group the Mothers of Invention, which he led from the mid-1960s to the mid-1970s, included such jazz-rock musicians as the saxophonist Ian Underwood (on a regular basis), and George Duke and the trombonist Bruce Fowler (both periodically during the early 1970s). In 1969 Jean-Luc Ponty recorded an album of Zappa's compositions (*King Kong*, PJ 20172), and in 1972 Zappa led the Grand Wazoo, a jazz-rock big band that included Jay Migliori, Charles Owens, and David Parlato as sidemen. Always a highly eclectic musician, as a soloist Zappa incorporates blues, rock, raga, and jazz licks into his improvised lines. From the mid-1970s his work has been more often closely related to rock and to contemporary classical music than to jazz, but connections with the jazz aesthetic remain on, for example, the album *Jazz from Hell* (*c*1986, Barking Pumpkin 74205), which in 1988 won a Grammy Award for best rock instrumental.

BIBLIOGRAPHY

Feather–Gitler '70s

L. Kart: "Frank Zappa: the Mother of us All," *DB*, xxxvi/22 (1969), 14

H. Siders: "Meet the Grand Wazoo," *DB*, xxix/18 (1972), 13

D. Walley: *No Commercial Potential: the Saga of Frank Zappa and the Mothers of Invention* (New York, 1972, 2/1980) [incl. discography]

J. Schaffer: "The Perspective of Frank Zappa," *DB*, 1/15 (1973), 14

R. Denyer, I. Guillory, and A. M. Crawford: *The Guitar Handbook* (London and Sydney, 1982), 28

Zarchy, Zeke [Rubin] (*b* New York, 12 June 1915). Trumpeter. After recording under the bandleader Joe Haymes (1935–6) he toured and recorded with Benny Goodman (1936) and Artie Shaw (1936–7), by turns with Bob Crosby and Red Norvo (1937–9), and with Tommy Dorsey (1939–40) and Glenn Miller (1940); he continued to play in Miller's bands while working as a staff musician at NBC (recording in 1941 and 1942) and while serving in the US Army (touring and recording from 1942 to 1945). He settled in Los Angeles, where he worked in studios and as a freelance; he made recordings with Boyd Raeburn (1945), Goodman and Woody Herman (1947), Crosby (1950–51), Jerry Gray (1950, *c*1959), Sarah Vaughan (1951), Ray Anthony (1955), and Frank Capp (1960). Although he re-created solos by Louis Armstrong, Bix Beiderbecke, and others as a member of the Great Pacific Jazz Band in the early 1980s, Zarchy is not an improviser.

BIBLIOGRAPHY

FeatherE

R. Gulliver: "Zeke Zarchy," *JJI*, xxxvi/12 (1983), 14

J. Chilton: *Stomp Off, Let's Go! The Story of Bob Crosby's Bob Cats & Big Band* (London, 1983), 46

Zardis, Chester (*b* New Orleans, 27 May 1900). Double bass player. He learned double bass in 1916 and performed locally (*c*1919) and in California with Buddy Petit. In the 1920s he played in New Orleans with Chris Kelly, Kid Rena, and A. J. Piron, among others, and in the early 1930s on the Mississippi riverboats with Sidney Desvigne (on double bass and tuba) and Fats Pichon, with whom he also played in Memphis (1934–5). He worked with Harold Dejan (1936–7), Kid Howard (*c*1937), as a leader, and again with Pichon on the SS *Capitol* (1939); Zardis may be heard to advantage on Howard's *Sweet Georgia Brown/Song of the Wanderer* (*c*1937, first issued on *Dance New*

Weather Report playing at the Montreux International Jazz Festival, 1976: (left to right) Joe Zawinul (keyboards), Wayne Shorter (tenor saxophone), Manolo Badrena (percussion), Alex Acuña (drums), and Jaco Pastorius (electric bass guitar)

Orleans Style, 1937–41, MONO 12). He recorded with Bunk Johnson (1942) and George Lewis (i) (1943) and after military service he continued performing until 1954. He again worked as a musician in New Orleans from 1965; he played regularly at Preservation Hall and performed and recorded with the Preservation Hall Jazz Band in New Orleans (1966) and Europe (1967). In the 1980s he led his own band and performed with the Legends of Jazz (from 1983) and in Europe with Kid Thomas (1983).

Oral history material in *LNT*.

BIBLIOGRAPHY

B. Turnock: "'Little Bear' Chester Zardis," *Sv*, no.26 (1969), 60
A. Shipton: "Styles of New Orleans Bass Playing," *Fn*, vii/1 (1976), 18

based on *ChiltonW*

Zawadi, Kiane [McKinney, Bernard (Atwell) [Bernie]] (*b* Detroit, 26 Nov 1932). Euphonium player and trombonist. He played with Barry Harris and Sonny Stitt in the early 1950s and in 1954 joined Art Blakey's group in Philadelphia. After returning to Detroit he recorded with Donald Byrd (1955) and played with Yusef Lateef, then worked in New York with Illinois Jacquet (1959) and Slide Hampton (1959–60); he recorded with Pepper Adams (1958), Curtis Fuller (1959), and Hampton, and in 1961 with James Moody, Sun Ra, and Freddie Hubbard. He took the name Kiane Zawadi before recording again with Hubbard in 1965. Later he recorded in styles ranging from bop to free jazz in big bands led by Archie Shepp (1971), McCoy Tyner (1973), Dollar Brand (in Germany, 1973), Charles Tolliver and Carlos Garnett (1975), and Frank Foster (in Tokyo, 1977); he also recorded as a member of Harold Vick's octet (1974). In 1985 he took part in a tribute to Charlie Parker at Town Hall in New York. Zawadi is best known for his crisp bop solos on the euphonium; *Arietis*, on Hubbard's album *Ready, for Freddie* (1961, BN 84085), is a fine example of his work.
(*FeatherE* ("McKinney, Bernie"))

Zawinul, Joe [Josef Erich] (*b* Vienna, 7 July 1932). Keyboard player, composer, and bandleader. He played accordion as a child and later studied music at the Vienna Conservatory. In the early 1950s he performed with leading Austrian dance and radio orchestras and worked as house pianist for Polydor; he also played with Friedrich Gulda. In 1959 he emigrated to the USA. After touring with Maynard Ferguson (1959) and serving as accompanist to Dinah Washington (1959–61) he joined Cannonball Adderley (1961), with whom he performed and recorded until 1970. He also played with Miles Davis in the late 1960s and early 1970s. In December 1970, with Wayne Shorter, Zawinul founded WEATHER REPORT (see illustration), and led it until 1985. He toured Europe and the USA as a soloist in 1985.

Zawinul is one of the most original and prolific jazz composers and arrangers to have emerged in the 1970s: *Mercy, Mercy, Mercy* achieved considerable popular success in its recording by Adderley; *In a Silent Way* served as the title track of an album on which Davis made an early attempt, with strong impressionist overtones, to fuse jazz and rock; and *Birdland* became a disco hit in a recording by Weather Report as well as receiving much exposure in versions by Maynard Ferguson and Manhattan Transfer. Zawinul's performances in Adderley's group on Wurlitzer and Fender-Rhodes electric pianos influenced other jazz musicians to adopt these instruments in place of the standard piano, thus drastically altering the tone color of an entire branch of jazz music. His use of the Oberheim, ARP, and Prophet synthesizers and the ring modulator has also been masterful. In Weather Report, where the role of the individual soloists was subservient to that of the ensemble, which produced rich and varied tone colors and fresh and exotic rhythmic textures, he created one of the first musically successful vehicles for collective improvisation since the early New Orleans bands. Manuscript scores of his works are in the holdings of the BMI Archives in New York.

See also HARMONY (i), §2, and ex.25; and PIANO, §6.

SELECTED RECORDINGS

As leader: *Money in the Pocket* (1966, Atl. 3004); *The Rise and Fall of the Third Stream* (1967, Vortex 2002); *Zawinul* (1970, Atl. 1579)
As sideman: C. Adderley: *Nippon Soul* (1963, Riv. 9477); B. Webster: *Soul Mates* (1963, Riv. 9476); C. Adderley: *Mercy, Mercy, Mercy* (1966, Cap.

ST2663); *Country Preacher* (1969, Cap. SKAO404); M. Davis: *In a Silent Way* (1969, Col. CS9875); *Bitches Brew* (1969, Col. GP26)

For further recordings *see* WEATHER REPORT.

BIBLIOGRAPHY

P. Welding: "From Vienna with Love: Joe Zawinul," *DB*, xxxiii/23 (1966), 23
R. Townley: "The Mysterious Travellings of an Austrian Mogul," *DB*, xlii/2 (1975), 15
L. Lyons: "Josef Zawinul: Multiple Keyboard Magician," *CK*, iii/9 (1977), 26
J. Coryell and L. Friedman: *Jazz-rock Fusion* (New York and London, 1978)
M. C. Gridley: *Jazz Styles* (Englewood Cliffs, NJ, 1978, rev. 2/1985 as *Jazz Styles: History and Analysis*, with suppl. *Instructor's Manual and Discography*)
C. Silvert: "Joe Zawinul: Wayfaring Genius," *DB*, xlv (1978), no.11, p.13; no.12, p.21
L. Feather: "Piano Giants of Jazz: Joe Zawinul," *CK*, vi/5 (1980), 48
L. Lyons: *The Great Jazz Pianists, Speaking of their Lives and Music* (New York, 1983), 284
G. Armbruster: "Zawinul Continued Hot, Chance of Record Highs," *Keyboard*, x/3 (1984), 44 [incl. discography]
J. Diliberto: "The Siren Song of Synths: Zawinul," *DB*, li/8 (1984), 16
I. Carr: "Zawinul, Joe," in I. Carr, D. Fairweather, and B. Priestley: *Jazz: the Essential Companion* (London, 1987)

MARK C. GRIDLEY/R

Zeitlin, Denny [Dennis Jay] (*b* Chicago, 10 April 1938). Keyboard player. He grew up in a musical family and had extensive classical training, though he was always interested in improvisation. As a medical student at Johns Hopkins University he played frequently, concentrating on bop, and while studying at Columbia University in 1963 he played an audition for John Hammond, who subsequently produced four albums by Zeitlin's trio. Later in 1963 Zeitlin moved to the San Francisco area, where he pursued two careers – one in psychiatry and one as a jazz musician. He formed a trio, which from 1964 to 1967 included Charlie Haden. His experiments with prepared piano in the late 1960s led him to use electronic keyboard instruments. Although he has written some film scores (including that for Philip Kaufman's *Invasion of the Body Snatchers*, 1978), Zeitlin's main activity as a musician has been to give concerts as a soloist or with small ensembles; these display his thorough grasp of jazz theory, a sense of structure, and mastery of free improvisation.

SELECTED RECORDINGS

As unaccompanied soloist: *Soundings* (1978, 1750 Arch 1770); *Homecoming* (1986, Living Music 998)
Duos with C. Haden: *Time Remembers One Time Once* (1981, ECM 1239)
As leader: *Zeitgeist* (1966–7, Col. CS9548); *Expansion* (1973, Double Helix 1); *Syzygy* (1977, 1750 Arch 1759)

BIBLIOGRAPHY

R. B. Hadlock: "The Combined Careers of Denny Zeitlin: Analyst's Couch and Piano Bench," *DB*, xxxii/22 (1965), 14
S. Toomajian: "Body & Soul: the Total Experience of Denny Zeitlin," *DB*, xxxiv/21 (1967), 19
M. Zipkin: "Denny Zeitlin: Keyboard Patching for Body Snatching," *DB*, xlvi/10 (1979), 16
D. Milano: "The Psychology of Improvisation," *Keyboard*, viii/10 (1984), 25

BOB DOERSCHUK

Zentner, Si(mon H.) (*b* New York, 13 June 1917). Trombonist and bandleader. He played with Les Brown (1940–42), Harry James (1943), Jimmy Dorsey (1944), and various groups in Los Angeles (1944–9). He then worked as a studio musician for MGM from 1949 to 1957, when he formed his own band; in the early 1960s Zentner's was the only newly formed jazz-oriented big band to achieve success. *Up a Lazy River* (1960, Lib. 55374), an arrangement by Bob Florence of the standard by Hoagy Carmichael and Sidney Arodin, was Zentner's biggest hit. The group has toured the USA, accompanying such popular singers as Johnny Mathis and Nancy Wilson, and plays frequently in Las Vegas. Zentner is firmly committed to the concept of big bands and campaigns vigorously to promote them.

BIBLIOGRAPHY

FeatherE; *Feather '60s*
J. Tynan: "The Struggles of Si," *DB*, xxviii/9 (1961), 18
D. Cerulli: "Si Zentner: 'The Disappointments are Many, but so are the Discoveries'," *IM*, lxi/5 (1962), 13
J. Wölfer: *Si Zentner and his Orchestra, also Including Bob Florence and his Orchestra: a Discography* (Langenhagen, Germany, 1981)

WAYNE SCHNEIDER

Zetterlund, Monica (*b* Hagfors, Sweden, 20 Sept 1938). Swedish singer. In 1957 she sang with Ib Glindemann's band in Copenhagen and performed with Arne Domnérus's orchestra in Stockholm; she made several recordings with Domnérus (from 1958), and also recorded with studio bands of various sizes. She appeared in Great Britain and the USA in 1959–60. Notable among her recordings are *Waltz for Debby* (1964, Phi. 08222PL), made with a trio led by Bill Evans (ii); *Hej man* (1975, Odeon 06235171), recorded under her own name; and *It Only Happens Every Time* (1977, EMI 06235454), with Thad Jones as leader. Zetterlund's style is cool but sensitive, and shows a genuine sympathy with the jazz idiom, though her repertory includes Swedish classical songs and folksongs. She is also an actress, and has worked in both films and the theater.

Oral history material in *SSsv*.

BIBLIOGRAPHY

C.-E. Lindgren: "Babs är bäst!" [Babs is best!], *Estrad*, xix/4 (1958), 7
A. von Konow: "Monica Z. i våra hjärtan!" [Monica Z. in our hearts!], *Orkester journalen*, li/7–8 (1983), 11

ERIK KJELLBERG

Zgraja, Krzysztof (*b* Gliwice, Poland, 1950). Polish flutist and composer. He played violin and piano from the age of six, then studied flute and composition at the music academy in Katowice. Although he was educated in classical music, he was also interested in rock, and around 1970 started to play jazz; he began with experiments in free jazz, only later acquiring a knowledge of earlier styles. He formed a duo with the double bass player Czeslaw Gladowski and continued to explore this instrumental combination into the 1980s. He played and recorded with Barre Philips (1975) and with Jacek Bednarek (from 1976); he is heard to advantage on *La concha* (1981, JG 052), recorded with Bednarek. After the proclamation of martial law in Poland in 1981, both Zgraja and Bednarek settled in Hannover, Germany. (B. Noglik: "Krzysztof Zgraja," *Jazzwerkstatt international* (Berlin, 1981), 414 [incl. interview, discography])

WOLFRAM KNAUER

Zinger cymbal. A Turkish cymbal clamped to a bass drum and activated by a small striker attached to the bass-drum beater; *see* DRUM SET, §I, 5.

Zoller, Attila (Cornelius) (*b* Visegrad, nr Budapest, 13 June 1927). Hungarian guitarist. He first studied violin and trumpet, and changed to guitar when he decided to make music his career. He played with Tabanyi Pinoccio's jazz ensemble in Budapest (1946–8), then performed and recorded in Vienna with Vera Auer (1948–54). In Germany he played bop with Jutta Hipp (1954–5), Hans Koller (1956–9), and visiting American musicians, notably Oscar Pettiford (he occasionally played double bass while Pettiford played cello). In 1959 he was awarded a scholarship to the Lenox School of Jazz and moved to the

USA. After a short period with Chico Hamilton (1960) he played with Herbie Mann (1962–5), then became leader, with Don Friedman, of a modal-jazz quartet (1965–6). From the mid-1960s he worked regularly in the USA and Europe: he played swing with Red Norvo (1966) and Benny Goodman (1967), recorded in trios with Koller (1965, 1979) and as co-leader of a group with Lee Konitz and Albert Mangelsdorff (1968), and performed and recorded in a duo with Jimmy Raney (1979–80). Zoller also works as a designer of electronic instruments, and patented a bidirectional pickup for guitars in 1971.

SELECTED RECORDINGS

As unaccompanied soloist: *Conjunction* (1979, Enja 3051)
Duos with J. Raney: *Jim and I: Live in Frankfurt* (1980, L+R 40013)
As leader: with L. Konitz and A. Mangelsdorff: *Zo-ko-ma* (1968, MPS 15170); *Gypsy Cry* (1969, Embryo 523); *Dream Bells* (1976, Enja 2078)
As sideman: O. Pettiford: *Das Oscar Pettiford Quartet* (1959, DSC 24); H. Mann: *Live at Newport* (1963, Atl. 1413)

BIBLIOGRAPHY

FeatherE; *Feather '60s*; *Feather–Gitler '70s*
A. Berle: "Attila Zoller," *GP*, xiii/12 (1979), 61

DAVID FLANAGAN

Zonophone. Record label. It was founded in 1899 by Frank Seamon, and was continued by Victor after that company took over Seamon's National Gramophone Corp. After 1910, the name was not used in the USA, but it remained in use in Britain (and was later also adopted in Australia) as the Gramophone Co.'s cheap label. Much of the repertory was recorded in Britain, and includes some of the most highly regarded British hot dance music of the 1920s; the catalogue also contained American material recorded by Victor. After the formation of EMI, Zonophone was merged in January 1933 with Columbia's label Regal to form REGAL–ZONOPHONE. (B. Rust: *The American Record Label Book* (New Rochelle, NY, 1978), 332)

Zubov, Aleksey (Nikolayevich) (*b* Moscow, 15 Nov 1936). Russian saxophonist and composer. He is self-taught as a musician. He played clarinet in the brass band of the Moscow M. V. Lomonosov State University, where he studied physics (graduated 1958), and played tenor saxophone in the big band of the Tsentral'ny Dom Rabotnikov Iskusstva (Central house of artists; 1954–7). In 1956 he joined the octet Vosmoyrka, at that time the best jazz group in Moscow. Later he belonged to Oleg Lundstrem's orchestra (1960–65) and to the Kontsertny Estradny Orkestr Tsentral'novo TV i Vsesoyuznovo Radio (Concert variety orchestra of the central TV and all-union radio), led two groups in 1967–8 known by the name Crescendo (a quintet to which the vibraphonist Leonid Garin belonged in 1968 and a quartet), and played with the ensemble Melodiya (1974–9). In the 1980s he worked as a freelance and wrote film music, and from 1985 he lived in the USA. Zubov's playing is well represented by the album *Barometr* (Barometer; 1983, Mel. C6019675001). In addition to his principal instrument he plays flute and synthesizer. (S. F. Starr: *Red and Hot: the Fate of Jazz in the Soviet Union, 1917–1980*, New York, and Oxford, England, 1983)

WALTER OJAKÄÄR

Zuccheri, Luciano (*b* Spilimbergo, Italy, 1911; *d* Asti, Italy, *c*1977). Italian guitarist and leader. He played guitar from the age of six. In 1934 he recorded as an unaccompanied soloist and in 1938 formed a group that later became the Quintetto Ritmico di Milano; this was modeled after the Quintette du Hot club de France and included three guitars (of which Zuccheri played the lead), a violin (from 1947 a clarinet), and a double bass. Zuccheri's style is exemplified by the recording *Programma BBC* (1947, Fonit 12593).

ADRIANO MAZZOLETTI

Zudekoff, Moe. See MORROW, BUDDY.

Zurke, Bob [Robert Albert; Zukowski, Bogusław Albert] (*b* Detroit, 17 Jan 1912; *d* Los Angeles, 16 Feb 1944). Pianist and composer. At an early age he displayed a precocious talent for assertive, confident piano playing, influenced by the blues. He worked in Philadelphia with an orchestra led by the pianist Oliver Naylor, recording in 1925 and appearing at the Palace d'Or and the Orient restaurant in the late 1920s and early 1930s; he also played for a time with the Playboys led by the double bass player Thelma Terry (recording in 1928). After working with the singer Seymour Simons and at Smokey's Club in Detroit, he came to prominence as Joe Sullivan's replacement in Bob Crosby's band (late 1936). He remained with Crosby until mid-1939, gaining recognition as a leading exponent of the boogie-woogie style (he was named "best pianist" by *Down Beat* in 1939). At this time he also published transcriptions of music by Count Basie and others, and three of his own compositions, *Hobson Street Blues*, *Eye Opener*, and *Southern Exposure* (1939). After a brief and unsuccessful period as a bandleader (1939) he worked in Chicago, Detroit, and St. Paul as an unaccompanied soloist. From the summer of 1942 until his death he was resident at the Hangover Club in Los Angeles, and in January 1944 recorded the music for the cartoon film *Jungle Jive*.

SELECTED RECORDINGS

As sideman: B. Crosby: Fidgety Feet (1937, Decca 1593); Big Foot Jump (1938, Decca 2108); The Big Crash from China (1938, Decca 1756); All Star Band: Blue Lou/The Blues (1939, Vic. 26144)

BIBLIOGRAPHY

ChiltonW; *FeatherE*
P. Pitt: "Bob Zurke," *JJ*, xxii/2 (1969), 6

KEN RATTENBURY

Illustration Acknowledgments

We are grateful to those listed below, who have supplied illustrative material, or given permission for it to be reproduced, or both: where two or more names are given, separated by a spaced slash (/), the name given first is usually that of the supplier of the illustration, who may or may not be the copyright holder; names of photographers are given wherever possible, preceded by "photo." Every effort has been made to contact copyright holders and we apologize to anyone whose name may have been omitted from this list.

The majority of photographs have been supplied from his own collection by Frank Driggs (New York); only where the photographer of one of these is known is the item listed below, following the abbreviation FD /. Alan Forster prepared the drawings (except where otherwise stated).

Ali, Rashied FD / photo © Bill Smith, Toronto
Allen, Henry "Red" FD / photo © Popsie Randolph
Art Ensemble of Chicago photo David Redfern, London
Asmussen, Svend photo David Redfern, London
Ayler, Albert FD / photo © Bill Smith, Toronto

Bands *4* FD / photo © Charles B. Nadell, New York; *5* FD / photo © Popsie Randolph; *6* David Redfern Photography, London / photo David Ellis
Barnet, Charlie FD / photo Al Hauser, New York
Bechet, Sidney FD / photo Otto Hess
Bigard FD / photo Bill Deppe, Wilmington, NC
Bley, Carla photo David Redfern, London
Blues *2* FD / photo Otto Hess
Bowie, Lester photo David Redfern, London
Brass band *2* FD / photo Dr. Bernard M. Steinau, Las Cruces, NM
Braxton, Anthony FD / photo © Bill Smith, Toronto
Brown, Clifford Mike Hennessey, London

Calloway, Cab FD / photo Ray Rising, Chicago
Carter, Benny FD / photo © Danny Barker, New Orleans
Clarinet *1* Macmillan Publishers Ltd., London; *2* Brian and Constance Dear; *4* FD / photo © Duncan P. Schiedt, Pittsboro, IN
Clarke, Kenny FD / photo © Popsie Randolph
Cole, Nat "King" FD / photo © Metropolitan Photo Service, New York
Coltrane, John FD / photo © Bill Smith, Toronto
Corea, Chick photo David Redfern, London

Dankworth, John photo David Redfern, London
Davis, Miles *2* photo David Redfern, London
DeJohnette, Jack photo David Redfern, London
Dodds, Johnny FD / photo William Russell, New Orleans
Dolhpy, Eric FD / photo © Duncan P. Schiedt, Pittsboro, IN
Double bass *2* FD / photo © Bill Smith, Toronto
Drum set *1a* FD / photo Kaufman & Fabry, Chicago; *1b, 2, 3* Alan Forster, London; *4* FD / photo Sam Bowerman; *5* photo David Redfern, London

Eldridge, Roy FD / photo Otto Hess
Ellis, Don photo David Redfern, London
Evans, Bill (ii) photo © Chuck Stewart, Teaneck, NJ

False fingering *1, 2* Alan Forster, London
Farmer, Art photo © Chuck Stewart, Teaneck, NJ
Films *5* photo Nancy Miller Elliott, New York; *6* National Film Archive, London / courtesy of The Samuel Goldwyn Co., Los Angeles
Flute *1* Macmillan Publishers Ltd., London; *2* photo © Chuck Stewart, Teaneck, NJ
Foster, Pops FD / Don Peterson, Chevy Chase, MD / photo Charles Peterson

Garbarek, Jan photo David Redfern, London
Getz, Stan FD / photo Joe Alper
Gillespie, Dizzy FD / photo Greg Kerr, Ithaca, NY
Giuffre, Jimmy photo © Chuck Stewart, Teaneck, NJ
Gordon, Dexter photo David Redfern, London
Griffin, Johnny photo © Chuck Stewart, Teaneck, NJ
Guitar *2a* Brian and Constance Dear; *2b* Arbiter Musical Instruments Ltd., London; *3* photo David Redfern, London

Haig, Al FD / photo © Popsie Randolph
Hall FD / photo © Duncan P. Schiedt, Pittsboro, IN

Hancock, Herbie David Redfern Photography, London / photo Suzi Gibbons
Heath photo David Redfern, London
Henderson, Fletcher FD / photo Firestone Photo Service, Atlantic City, NJ
Herman, Woody *1a* FD / Columbia Records, New York; *1b* FD / photo © Popsie Randolph
Hines, Earl FD / photo Standard Photo Service, Philadelphia
Hodges, Johnny FD / photo Otto Hess
Holiday, Billie FD / photo Otto Hess
Hubbard, Freddie FD / photo © Popsie Randolph

Jackson, Milt FD / photo © Popsie Randolph
Jarrett, Keith FD / photo © Bill Smith, Toronto
Jazz (i) *2* FD / photo White Studio, New York; *5* FD / photo © Charles B. Nadell, New York; *6* FD / photo © Popsie Randolph; *7, 8* photo David Redfern, London; *9* Compatible Recording and Publishing (Promotions) Ltd. / photo Roberto Masotti
Johnson, Bunk FD / photo Octave Romaine, New York
Johnson, J. J. FD / photo © Popsie Randolph
Jones *1a* photo © Chuck Stewart, Teaneck, NJ; *1b* photo David Redfern, London; *1c* FD / photo © Popsie Randolph
Jones, Quincy photo © Chuck Stewart, Teaneck, NJ

Kenton, Stan FD / photo Fries, Philadelphia
Kirby, John FD / photo Ray Rising, Chicago
Kirk, Roland David Redfern Photography, London / photo Andrew Putler

Lacy, Steve FD / photo © Bill Smith, Toronto
Lang, Eddie FD / photo Apeda Studios, New York
Lateef, Yusef photo © Chuck Stewart, Teaneck, NJ
Lewis, John photo © Chuck Stewart, Teaneck, NJ

McLaughlin, John photo © Chuck Stewart, Teaneck, NJ
Mangelsdorff, Albert photo David Redfern, London
Marsalis, Wynton photo David Redfern, London
Mingus, Charles FD / photo John W. Miner, Oshkosh, WI
Mills Blue Rhythm Band FD / photo Achille Volpe, New York
Montgomery FD / photo © Duncan P. Schiedt, Pittsboro, IN
Morton, Jelly Roll FD / photo Bloom Studios, Chicago
Moten, Bennie FD / photo © Duncan P. Schiedt, Pittsboro, IN
Mute *1* Alan Forster, London

Napoleon *1b* FD / photo Bloom Studios, Chicago; *1c* FD / photo John W. Miner, Oshkosh, WI
Navarro, Fats FD / photo © Popsie Randolph
New Orleans Rhythm Kings FD / Bloom Studios, Chicago
Nightclubs and other venues *1* FD / photo Ruysdal, Paris; *2* photo David Redfern, London; *3* FD / photo A. P. Bedou, New Orleans; *4, 6* David Redfern Photography, London / photo William Gottlieb; *5* FD / photo © Popsie Randolph
Norvo, Red FD / photo © Timme Rosenkrantz

O'Day, Anita FD / photo © Leo Arsene
Oliver, King FD / photo Daguerre, Chicago
Organ *1* FD / photo Robert Steinau, Louisville, KY
Original Dixieland Jazz band FD / photo Apeda Studios, New York
Ørsted Pedersen, Niels-Henning photo David Redfern, London

Parker, Charlie *1* FD / photo Ray Whitten, Los Angeles
Pastorius, Jaco photo David Redfern, London
Peterson, Oscar photo © Chuck Stewart, Teaneck, NJ
Piano *3* David Redfern Photography, London / photo Andrew Putler
Ponty, Jean-Luc photo David Redfern, London
Powell, Bud FD / photo © Duncan P. Schiedt, Pittsboro, IN

Raeburn, Boyd FD / photo Rube Lewis, Chicago
Recording *1* Trustees of the Science Museum, London; *2* EMI Records Ltd., London; *4b* Alan Forster, London; *6* photo Nancy Miller Elliott, New York
Reinhardt, Django FD / photo Jack Albers, Bad Nauheim, Germany
Rogers, Shorty photo © Chuck Stewart, Teaneck, NJ
Rollins, Sonny photo © Chuck Stewart, Teaneck, NJ
Russell, Pee Wee FD / photo Otto Hess

Saxophone *1* Brian and Constance Dear; *2* Popperfoto, London; *3* FD / photo Joe Alper; *4* photo © Chuck Stewart, Teaneck, NJ
Shaw, Artie FD / photo © Leo Arsene
Shorter, Wayne photo David Redfern, London
Singing *1* Paul Oliver Collection, Woodstock, England
Singleton, Zutty FD / photo ZOG, New York
Smith, Bessie FD / photo Edward F. Elcha, New York
Smith, Jimmy photo © Chuck Stewart, Teaneck, NJ
Stitt, Sonny FD / photo © Popsie Randolph
Sullivan, Joe FD / photo Jack Masters
Sun Ra photo David Redfern, London

Tabackin, Lew photo © Chuck Stewart, Teaneck, NJ
Tatum, Art FD / photo © Dunc Butler
Taylor, Billy (ii) FD / photo © Charles Nadell
Tracey, Stan photo David Redfern, London
Tristano, Lennie FD / photo © Duncan P. Schiedt, Pittsboro, IN

Vaughan, Sarah FD / photo © Popsie Randolph
Vibraphone *1a* Macmillan Publishers Ltd., London; *1b* Brian and Constance Dear

Waller, Fats FD / photo Metropolitan Photo Service, New York
Watters, Lu FD / photo © Duncan P. Schiedt, Pittsboro, IN
Webb, Chick FD / photo Apeda Studios, New York
Weber, Eberhard photo David Redfern, London
Wells, Dicky FD / photo © Timme Rosenkrantz
Williams, Mary Lou FD / photo Gordon Conner Studio, Cleveland
Woods, Phil photo David Redfern, London

Young, Lester FD / Don Peterson, Chevy Chase, MD / photo Charles Peterson

Zawinul, Joe David Redfern Photography, London / photo Andrew Putler

Music Example Acknowledgments

We are grateful to music publishers, and others, as listed below, for permission to reproduce copyrighted material. Every effort has been made to trace copyright holders and we apologize to anyone whose name may have been omitted from this list.

Armstrong, Louis *3* reproduced by permission of EMI Music Publishing Ltd. and International Music Publications, London
Coltrane, John *1, 2* Andrew's Musical Enterprises, Inc., Washington, DC; *2* by permission of *Annual Review of Jazz Studies*, New Brunswick, NJ
Evans, Bill (ii) *1* © 1965 Acorn Music Corp., New York, used by permission
Fill *2* reproduced by permission of T. D. Brown
Ghost note The International Society for Jazz Research, Graz, Austria
Gliss *3* by permission of *Annual Review of Jazz Studies*, New Brunswick, NJ
Harmony (i) *2* © 1964, 1965 Acorn Music Corp., New York, used by permission; *3, 14* from *Schirmer Scores: a Repertory of Western Music*, © 1975 Schirmer Books, a division of Macmillan Inc., New York, reprinted by permission; *7, 8, 9, 11* by permission of *Down Beat*, Chicago
Improvisation *1* by permission of *Down Beat*, Chicago; *3* Andrew's Musical Enterprises Inc., Washington, DC
Konitz, Lee *1* © 1941, 1942, MCA Music Publishing, a division of MCA, Inc., New York, used by permission
Monk, Thelonious *1, 2* © Bocu Music Ltd., London
Notation *2a* Aisha Music Co., Alpine, NJ; *2b* by permission of Ecaroh, Inc., Malibu, CA; *3* Woodrow Music, Newington, CT
Piano *4* from H. Martin: *Enjoying Jazz*, © 1986 Schirmer Books, a division of Macmillan, Inc., New York, reprinted by permission; *13* © 1966 Unit Core (BM1), worldwide administration rights controlled by Celestial Harmonies, div. of Mayflower Music Corp.; *12a, 12d* by permission of *Annual Review of Jazz Studies*, New Brunswick, NJ, © Paul Rinzler; *8* by permission of Leonard Feather
Rollins, Sonny by permission of Twayne Publishers, a division of G. K. Hall & Co., Boston
Singing reproduced by permission of Columbia Pictures Publications, Miami, FL, and EMI Music Publishing Ltd. and International Music Publications, London
Young, Lester *1, 2* by permission of Twayne Publishers, a division of G. K. Hall & Co., Boston

Appendix 1

BIBLIOGRAPHY

This bibliography is based on items cited at the ends of individual articles in the dictionary; further items have been added to make a comprehensive (though not exhaustive) listing of resources on jazz. In general only items concerning jazz are cited, though some on related styles (such as ragtime and blues) have been included because they contain substantial amounts of relevant information. The following kinds of publication are not generally included here: the catalogues of libraries and sound archives (*see* the individual entries on such collections in the article LIBRARIES AND ARCHIVES), anthologies of transcriptions, pedagogical texts, and booklets published in conjunction with recordings. Exceptionally, a small number of important articles in journals are included.

The list is divided into the following categories: Bibliographies and reference materials; Discographies (General, Name discographies, Record label listings, Other listings); Other books; and Periodicals (bio-discographies are listed under "Other books"). Within each category, except the last, entries are ordered alphabetically by name(s) of author(s), then by title (ignoring the definite and indefinite articles). In the list of periodicals entries are ordered alphabetically by title; periodicals of the same name are ordered chronologically by date of first issue. Subtitled items follow items with the same title but no subtitle (this is pertinent chiefly to those periodicals named *Jazz* and *Jazz: . . .*). Cross-references are included throughout the list where they are helpful (from the names of second authors, and alternative titles of journals, for example); unless otherwise indicated these references should be understood to lead to entries within the same category or subcategory.

BIBLIOGRAPHIES AND REFERENCE MATERIALS

A. J. Agostinelli: *The Newport Jazz Festival, Rhode Island, 1954–1971: a Bibliography, Discography, and Filmography* (Providence, RI, 1977)

D. Allen: *Bibliography of Discographies*, ii: *Jazz* (New York and London, 1981)

W. C. Allen: *Allen's Poop Sheet* (Belleville, NJ, 1958–74) [catalogue of books on jazz, issued irregularly]

Australian Music Centre, see *Jazz: Australian Compositions*

R. J. Benford, see A. P. Merriam

C. Bohländer and K. H. Holler: *Reclams Jazzführer* (Stuttgart, Germany, 1970, rev. and enlarged 2/1977) [*ReclamsJ*]

M. W. Booth: *American Popular Music: a Reference Guide* (Westport, CT, and London, 1983)

J. Bradley, see D. Morgenstern

P. Carls [*sic*], see F. Ténot

I. Carr, D. Fairweather, and B. Priestley: *Jazz: the Essential Companion* (London, 1987)

S. B. Charters: *Jazz: New Orleans, 1885–1957: an Index to the Negro Musicians of New Orleans* (Belleville, NJ, 1958, rev. 2/1963/R1983 as *Jazz: New Orleans, 1885–1963: an Index to the Negro Musicians of New Orleans*) [*ChartersJ*]

J. Chilton: *Who's Who of Jazz: Storyville to Swing Street* (London, 1970, rev. and enlarged 4/1985) [*ChiltonW*]

C. Clark: *Jazz* (Penzance, England, 1982)

P. Clayton and P. Gammond: *Jazz: A–Z* (Enfield, nr London, 1986)

A. Clergeat: *Dictionnaire du jazz* (Paris, 1966)

D. E. Cooper: *International Bibliography of Discographies: Classical Music and Jazz & Blues, 1962–1972* (Littleton, CO, 1975)

R. Cotterrell, ed.: *Jazz Now: the Jazz Centre Society Guide* (London, 1976)

A. M. Dauer, see S. Longstreet

H.-G. Ehmke, see J. Jørgensen

K. O. Ekland: *Jazz West, 1945–1985: the A–Z Guide to West Coast Jazz Music* (Carmel, CA, 1986) [biographical dictionary]

A. Elings: *Bibliografie van de nederlandse jazz* (Nijmegen, Netherlands, 1966)

T. G. Everett: "An Annotated List of English-language Jazz Periodicals," *JJS*, iii/2 (1976), 47 [addns and corrections in *JJS*, iv/1 (1977), 110; iv/2 (1977), 94; v/2 (1978), 99; *ARJS*, i (1982), 167; *ARJS*, iii (1984), 205]

D. Fairweather, see I. Carr

L. Feather: *The Encyclopedia of Jazz* (New York, 1955, rev. and enlarged 2/1960/R1984) [*FeatherE*]

——: *The Encyclopedia of Jazz in the Sixties* (New York, 1966/R1986) [*Feather '60s*]

L. Feather and I. Gitler: *The Encyclopedia of Jazz in the Seventies* (New York, 1976/R1987) [*Feather–Gitler '70s*]

S. A. Floyd, Jr., and M. J. Reisser: *Black Music in the United States: an Annotated Bibliography of Selected Reference and Research Materials* (Millwood, nr Ossining, NY, 1983)

P. Gammond: *A Guide to Popular Music* (London, 1960)

P. Gammond, see also P. Clayton

J. Ganfield: *Books and Periodical Articles on Jazz in America from 1926–1932* (New York, 1933)

M. Gautier: *Jazz au cinéma* (Paris, 1961)

M. Gautier, see also H. Panassié

I. Gitler, see L. Feather; D. Morgenstern

R. S. Gold: *A Jazz Lexicon: an A–Z Directory of Jazz Terms* (New York, 1964, rev. 2/1975 as *Jazz Talk*) [*GoldJL*]

A. A. Gurwitch [*sic*], see H. Panassié

S. Harris: *Blues Who's Who: a Biographical Dictionary of Blues Singers* (New Rochelle, NY, 1979)

M. Hayes, R. Scribner, and P. Magee: *The Encyclopedia of Australian Jazz* (Brisbane, Australia, 1976)

A. Heerkens: *Jazz* (Alkmaar, Netherlands, n.d. [?1956]) [pictorial encyclopedia; parallel texts in Dutch, Fr., Eng., and Ger.]

B. Hefele: *Jazz Bibliography: International Literature on Jazz, Blues, Spirituals, Gospel and Ragtime Music with a Selected List of Works on the Social and Cultural Background from the Beginning to the Present/Jazz-Bibliographie: Verzeichnis des internationalen Schrifttums über Jazz, Blues, Spirituals, Gospel und Ragtime, mit einer Auswahlbibliographie über den sozialen und kulturellen Hintergrund von den Anfängen bis zur Gegenwart* (Munich and elsewhere, 1981) [texts in Eng. and Ger.]

G. Herzhaft: *Encyclopédie du blues* (Lyons, France, 1979)

J.-R. Hippenmeyer: *Jazz sur films, ou 55 années de rapports jazz-cinéma vus à travers plus de 800 films tournés entre 1917 et 1972: filmographie critique* (Yverdon, Switzerland, 1973)

K. H. Holler, see C. Bohländer

D. Horn: *The Literature of American Music in Books and Folk Music Collections: a Fully Annotated Bibliography* (Metuchen, NJ, 1977)

Jazz: Australian Compositions (Sydney, 1978) [pubn of Australian Music Centre]

B. Johnson and others: *The Oxford Companion to Australian Jazz* (Melbourne, Australia, 1987)
J. Jørgensen and E. Wiedemann, eds.: *Jazzens hvem-hvad-hvor* (Copenhagen, 1962; rev. Ger. trans. by H.-G. Ehmke as *Mosaik Jazzlexikon*, Hamburg, Germany, 1966)
H. Kallmann, G. Potvin, and K. Winters, eds.: *Encyclopedia of Music in Canada* (Toronto, Buffalo, and London, 1981)
R. Kane, see J. Voigt
D. Kennington: *The Literature of Jazz: a Critical Guide* (London, 1970, rev. 2/1980 with D. L. Read)
R. D. Kinkle: *The Complete Encyclopedia of Popular Music and Jazz, 1900–1950* (New Rochelle, NY, and Westport, CT, 1974) [incl. discography and full listings for a number of major labels during a portion of the 78 era]
P. R. Klotman: *Frame by Frame: a Black Filmography* (Bloomington, IN, and London, 1979)
Knaurs Jazz Lexikon, see S. Longstreet
W. Laade, W. Ziefle, and D. Zimmerle: *Jazz-Lexikon* (Stuttgart, Germany, and elsewhere, 1953)
D.-R. de Lerma: *Bibliography of Black Music* (Westport, CT, and London, 1981–)
S. Longstreet and A. M. Dauer: *Knaurs Jazz Lexikon* (Munich and Zurich, 1957)
P. Magee, see M. Hayes
C. Major: *Dictionary of Afro-American Slang* (New York, 1970, London, 1971, as *Black Slang: a Dictionary of Afro-American Talk*)
R. Markewich: *Bibliography of Jazz and Pop Tunes Sharing the Chord Progressions of Other Compositions* (New York, 1970, rev. 2/1974 [privately pubd])
E. S. Meadows: *Jazz Reference and Research Materials: a Bibliography* (New York and London, 1981)
C. G. Herzog zu Mecklenburg: *International Jazz Bibliography: Jazz Books from 1919 to 1968* (Strasbourg, France, and Baden-Baden, Germany, 1969; suppls. 1971, 1975)
C. G. Herzog zu Mecklenburg and N. Ruecker: *International Bibliography of Jazz Books*, i: *1921–1949* (Baden-Baden, Germany, 1983)
D. Meeker: *Jazz in the Movies: a Tentative Index to the Work of Jazz Musicians for the Cinema* (London, 1972)
——: *Jazz in the Movies: a Guide to Jazz Musicians, 1917–1977* (London, 1977, rev. 2/1981 as *Jazz in the Movies*)
A. P. Merriam and R. J. Benford: *A Bibliography of Jazz* (Philadelphia, 1954/*R*1970)
D. Morgenstern, I. Gitler, and J. Bradley: *Bird and Diz: a Bibliography* (New York, 1973)
H. Panassié and M. Gautier: *Dictionnaire du jazz* (Paris, 1954, rev. and enlarged 1971, enlarged 2/1980, rev. and enlarged 3/1987 by A. Vasset and J. Pescheux, rev. and enlarged [4]/1987; Eng. trans., London, 1956, rev. A. A. Gurwitch [*sic*] as *Guide to Jazz*, Boston, 1956)
J. Pescheux, see H. Panassié
G. Poole: *Enciclopedia de swing* (Buenos Aires, 1939)
G. Potvin, see H. Kallmann
B. Priestley, see I. Carr
D. L. Read, see D. Kennington
Reclams Jazzführer, see C. Bohländer
C. Reggentin-Scheidt, see N. Ruecker
R. G. Reisner: *The Literature of Jazz: a Preliminary Bibliography* (New York, 1954, rev. and enlarged 2/1959 as *The Literature of Jazz: a Selective Bibliography*)
M. J. Reisser, see S. A. Floyd, Jr.
A. Rose and E. Souchon: *New Orleans Jazz: a Family Album* (Baton Rouge, LA, 1967, rev. 2/1978, rev. and enlarged 3/1984)
N. Ruecker: *Jazz Literature* (Frankfurt am Main, Germany, 1981–4; Schmitten, Germany, 1985–) [nos.1, 2, untitled; nos.3–5 as *Jazz Blues Literature*; nos.7– as *Jazz Literature, Jazz Videos*] [annual catalogue, with annual suppl. from no.5]
N. Ruecker and C. Reggentin-Scheidt: *Jazz Index: Bibliographie unselbständiger Jazzliteratur/Bibliography of Jazz Literature in Periodicals* (Frankfurt am Main, Germany, 1977–87) [7 vols.]
N. Ruecker, see also C. G. Herzog zu Mecklenburg
B. Rust: *The American Record Label Book* (New Rochelle, NY, 1978)
H. R. Schleman: *Rhythm on Record: a Complete Survey and Register of all the Principal Recorded Dance Music from 1906 to 1936, and a Who's Who of the Artists Concerned in the Making* (London, 1936)
R. Scribner, see M. Hayes
G. G. Simon: *Benkó Dixieland Band: Bibliográfia és cikkgyűjtemény* [The Benkó Dixieland Band: bibliography and selected articles] (Budapest, 1988)
J. Skowronski: *Black Music in America: a Bibliography* (Metuchen, NJ, and London, 1981)
J. Slawe: *Wörterbuch zur Jazzmusik* (Zurich, 1953)
E. Souchon, see A. Rose
E. Southern: *Biographical Dictionary of Afro-American and African Musicians* (Westport, CT, 1982)
F. Ténot and P. Carls [*sic*]: *Dictionnaire du jazz* (Paris, 1967)
G. C. Testoni and others: *Enciclopedia del jazz* (Milan, 1953, rev. and enlarged 2/1954)
E. Townley: *Tell your Story: a Dictionary of Jazz and Blues Recordings, 1917–1950* (Chigwell, England, 1976)
——: *Tell your Story: a Dictionary of Mainstream Jazz and Blues Recordings*, ii: *1951–1975* (Chigwell, England, 1987)
D. Tudor and others, eds.: *Popular Music Periodicals Index, 1973[–6]* (Metuchen, NJ, 1974–7)
A. Vasset, see H. Panassié
J. Voigt and R. Kane: *Jazz Music in Print* (Winthrop, ME, 1975, rev. and enlarged 3/1982 as *Jazz Music in Print and Jazz Books in Print*)
M. White: *"You Must Remember This . . .": Popular Songwriters, 1900–1980* (London, 1983)
E. Wiedemann, see J. Jørgensen
S. D. Winick: *Rhythm: an Annotated Bibliography* (Metuchen, NJ, 1974)
K. Winters, see H. Kallmann
W. Ziefle, see W. Laade
D. Zimmerle, see W. Laade

DISCOGRAPHIES

General

A. J. Agostinelli, see BIBLIOGRAPHIES AND REFERENCE MATERIALS
G. Avakian, see C. Delaunay
J. Bergh, see OTHER BOOKS, B. Stendahl
Bielefelder Katalog, see M. Scheffner
O. Blackstone: *Index to Jazz* (Fairfax, VA, 1945–8)
R. Boretti: *Collector's Catalog* (Cosenza, 1969, rev. 2/1977) [see also PERIODICALS, *Collector*]
D. Brigaud: *Liste alphabétique des disques chroniqués dans Le bulletin du Hot Club de France (3ème série, no.1 à 243)* (Paris, 1979)
W. Bruyninckx: *50 Years of Recorded Jazz, 1917–1967* (n.p. [Mechelen, Belgium], n.d. [1968–?1975]; rev. and enlarged 2/n.d. [1978–80] as *60 Years of Recorded Jazz, 1917–1977*; suppls. 1985–)
——: *Modern Big Bands* (n.p. [Mechelen, Belgium], n.d. [1985–])
——: *Modern Jazz, Be-bop, Hard Bop & West Coast* (n.p. [Mechelen, Belgium], n.d. [1984–])
——: *Progressive Jazz, Free, Third Stream, Fusion* (n.p. [Mechelen, Belgium], n.d. [1984–])
——: *Swing, 1920–1985: Swing Dance Bands & Combos* (n.p. [Mechelen, Belgium], n.d. [1986–])
——: *Traditional Jazz, 1897–1985: Origins, New Orleans, Dixieland, Chicago Styles* (n.p. [Mechelen, Belgium], n.d. [1987–])
M. Cabanowski and H. Choliński: *Polska dyskografia jazzowa, 1955–1972* (Warsaw, 1974)
D. Carey and A. J. McCarthy: *The Directory of Recorded Jazz and Swing Music* [cover title *Jazz Directory*], i–iv (Fordingbridge, England, 1949–51, ii-iv rev. 2/1955–7); v, vi (London, 1954–7)
Catalogue des 33 Tours de Jazz de la Communaute Française de Belgique (Brussels, 1984)
G. Cherrington and others: *Jazz Catalogue 1960[–1971]*, i–viii (London, n.d.); ix–xi (Sevenoaks, England, n.d.) [periodical discography]
H. Choliński, see M. Cabanowski
G. Conrad: *Discographie der Jazz- und Semijazzaufnahmen im Bereich der heutigen Volksdemokratien* (Menden, Germany, n.d. [1983–])
C. Crump, see T. Stagg
W. R. Daniels: *The American 45 and 78 rpm Record Dating Guide, 1940–1959* (Westport, CT, and London, 1985)
A. G. Debus, see B. Rust
C. Delaunay: *Hot Discography* (Paris, 1936, rev. 4/1943 as *Hot discographie*, rev. and enlarged by W. E. Schaap and G. Avakian as *New Hot Discography: the Standard Directory of Recorded Jazz*, New York, 5/1948/*R*1982)
C. Delaunay and K. Mohr: *Hot discographie encyclopédique* (Paris, 1951) [inc., A–Hefti, Neal only]
R. M. W. Dixon, see J. Godrich
J. de Donder: *"On Tour": a Disco- and Tapeography of the Recordings Made by New Orleans Musicians with Local Bands* (Dilbeek, Belgium, 1983)
E. Edwards, Jr., G. Hall, and B. Korst: *Modern Jazz Piano* (Whittier, CA, 1965)
B. Englund, see H. Nicolausson
S. Forbes, see B. Rust
J. Godrich and R. M. W. Dixon: *Blues & Gospel Records, 1902–1942* (Hatch End, nr London, 1964, rev. 2/1969, rev. and enlarged 3/1982 as R. M. W. Dixon and J. Godrich: *Blues & Gospel Records, 1902–1943*)
U. Goeman, see OTHER BOOKS, P. Klaasse
R. Grandorge, see B. Rust
J. Grunnet Jepsen, see J. G. Jepsen
A. Gurwitsch, see A. Schwaninger
G. Hall, see E. Edwards, Jr.
S. Harris: *A Critical Guide to Jazz on Compact Disc* (in preparation)
L. H. Harrison, see M. R. Pitts
C. Hayes: *A Discography of Gospel Records, 1937–1971* (n.p. [Copenhagen], 1973) [covers 14 musicians and groups]
J.-R. Hippenmeyer: *Swiss Jazz Disco* (Yverdon, Switzerland, 1977)

IJS Jazz Register (Newark, NJ, 1979–) [incl. indexes; on microfiche; issued irregularly]
T. Ikegami: *New Orleans Renaissance on Record* (Tokyo, 1980)
D. A. Jasen: *Recorded Ragtime, 1897–1958* (Hamden, CT, 1973) [incl. listings of 78 r.p.m. recordings of jazz versions of ragtime pieces]
J. G. Jepsen: *Jazz Records, 1942–[1969]: a Discography*, v, vi (Copenhagen, 1963); vii, viii, i–*iva* (Holte, Denmark, 1964–8); iv*b–d* (Copenhagen, 1969–70)
B. Korst, see E. Edwards, Jr.
R. D. Laing and C. Sheridan: *Jazz Records: the Specialist Labels* (Copenhagen, 1981)
H. H. Lange: *Die deutsche "78er": Discographie der Jazz- und Hot-Dance-Musik, 1903–1958* (Berlin, 1966, rev. and enlarged 2/1978)
——: *Die deutsche Jazz-Discographie: eine Geschichte des Jazz auf Schallplatten von 1902 bis 1955* (Berlin, 1955)
M. Leadbitter and N. Slaven: *Blues Records, January, 1943 to December, 1966* (London, 1968, rev. and enlarged 2/1987)
——: *Blues Records, 1943–1970: a Selective Discography* (London, 1987–)
J. Leder: *Women in Jazz: a Discography of Instrumentalists, 1913–1968* (Westport, CT, 1985)
J. Litchfield: *The Canadian Jazz Discography, 1916–1980* (Toronto, Buffalo, and London, 1982)
——: *This is Jazz* (Montreal, 1985) [index to a radio program]
R. E. Lotz: *German Ragtime and the Prehistory of Jazz*, i: *The Sound Documents* (Chigwell, England, 1985) [lists discs, cylinders, piano rolls, music boxes, and films]
A. McCarthy: *Jazz Discography*, i: *An International Discography of Recorded Jazz, Including Blues, Gospel and Rhythm-and-blues for the Year January–December 1958* (London, 1960)
A. McCarthy, see also D. Carey
W. H. Miller, see J. Mitchell
J. Mitchell: *Australian Discography*, ed. W. H. Miller (Melbourne, Australia, 1950, 2/1960)
K. Mohr: *Discographie du jazz: tous les disques actuellement dans le commerce en Suisse* (Geneva, 1945)
K. Mohr, see also C. Delaunay
H. Nicolausson: *Svensk jazzdiskografi* (Stockholm, 1953, rev. and enlarged with B. Englund as *Swedish Jazz Discography* 2/1983)
K. Pensoneault and C. Sarles: *Jazz Discography Additions and Corrections* (Jackson Heights, NY, 1944)
G. Pétard: *The Black Female LPs Catalogue & Price Guide* (Boulogne, France, 1987)
M. R. Pitts and L. H. Harrison: *Hollywood on Record: the Film Stars' Discography* (Metuchen, NJ, 1978)
E. Raben: *A Discography of Free Jazz* (Copenhagen, 1969)
P. Renaud: *La discographie du jazz anglais* (Chaumont, France, 1985)
The Rigler and Deutsch Record Index: a National Union Catalog of Sound Recordings (Syracuse, NY, 1985) [pt i: 78 r.p.m. recordings in the holdings of members of the ARSC; in microform]
A. Rogers: *Dance Bands and Big Bands* (Tempe, AZ, 1986) [discography and price guide]
B. Rust: *The American Dance Band Discography, 1917–1942* (New Rochelle, NY, 1975)
——: *The HMV Studio House Bands, 1912–1939* (Chigwell, England, 1976)
——: *Jazz Records*, i: *1897–1931* (Hatch End, nr London, 1961, 2/1962 with index by R. Grandorge); ii: *1932–1942* (Hatch End, 1965); i, ii, as *Jazz Records: A–Z, 1897–1942* (London, rev. [3]/1969, rev. and enlarged 4/1978, rev. 5/n.d. [1983])
——: *The Zonophone Studio House Bands, 1924–1932* (Chigwell, England, 1976)
B. Rust and A. G. Debus: *The Complete Entertainment Discography, from the mid-1890s to 1942* (New Rochelle, NY, 1973)
B. Rust and E. S. Walker: *British Dance Bands, 1912–1939* (London, 1973, rev. and enlarged 2/1986 by Rust and S. Forbes as *British Dance Bands on Record, 1911–1945*)
C. Sarles, see K. Pensoneault
W. E. Schaap, see C. Delaunay
M. Scheffner, see OTHER BOOKS, C. G. Herzog zu Mecklenburg
M. Scheffner and others, eds.: *Katalog der Jazzschallplatten* [from 1974 *Bielefelder Katalog: Verzeichnis der Jazzschallplatten*, from 1981 *G. Braun – Bielefelder Katalog Jazz: Verzeichnis der Jazz-Schallplatten*, from 1984 *Bielefelder Katalog, Schallplatten, Compact Discs: Jazz*, from 1986 *Bielefelder Katalog, Schallplatten, Compact Discs, MusiCassetten: Jazz*] (Bielefeld, Germany, 1959–80; Karlsruhe, Germany, 1981–3; Stuttgart, Germany, 1984–) [periodical catalogue, yearly]
A. Schwaninger and A. Gurwitsch: *Swing discographie* (Geneva, 1945)
C. Sheridan, see R. D. Laing
G. G. Simon: *Magyar jazzlemezek/Hungarian Jazz Records, 1912–1984* (Pécs, Hungary, 1985)
N. Slaven, see M. Leadbitter
J. R. Smart: *Radio Broadcasts in the Library of Congress, 1924–1941: a Catalog of Recordings* (Washington, 1982)
T. Stagg and C. Crump: *New Orleans, the Revival: a Tape and Discography of Negro Traditional Jazz Recorded in New Orleans or by New Orleans Bands, 1937–1972* (n.p. [London], 1973)
K. Stratemann: *Jazz Ball & Feather on Jazz* (Menden, Germany, 1981) [index to two television programs]
——: *Negro Bands on Film*, i: *Big Bands, 1928–1950: an Exploratory Filmo-discography* (Lübbecke, Germany, 1981)
E. Towler: *British Dance Bands (1920–1949) on 12-inch Long-playing Records* (Harrow, England, 1985)
K. Tsuchiyama: *Blues Albums in Japan, 1960–1964, plus Supplement '85: a Guide to 25 Years of Blues LPs* (Tokyo, 1986)
W. van Eyle, see H. Zwartenkot
E. S. Walker, see B. Rust
H. Westerberg: *Suomalaiset jazzlevytykset, 1932–1976/A Finnish Jazz Discography, 1932–1976: 45 Americans, 92 Europeans, and Hundreds of Finns* (Helsinki, 1977)
H. Zwartenkot and others: *The Dutch Jazz and Blues Discography, 1916–1980*, ed. W. van Eyle (Amsterdam, 1981)

Name discographies

B. H. Aasland: *The "Wax Works" of Duke Ellington* (Stockholm, 1954); part rev. and enlarged as *The "Wax Works" of Duke Ellington*, i: *6 March 1940 –30 July 1942: RCA Victor Period* (Järfälla, nr Sollentuna, Sweden, 1978); ii: *31 July 1942 – 11 Nov 1944: the Recording Ban Period* (Järfälla, 1979) [contd in *DEMS* [Duke Ellington Music Society] *Bulletin*]
A. Astrup: *The John Haley Sims Discography* (Lyngby, Denmark, 1980; suppl. 1983)
——: *The Stan Getz Discography* (Texarkana, TX, 1978; rev. and enlarged 2/1984 as *The Revised Stan Getz Discography*)
D. M. Bakker: *Billie & Teddy on Microgroove, 1932–1944* (Alphen aan de Rijn, Netherlands, 1975) [Billie Holiday and Teddy Wilson]
——: *Clarence Williams on Microgroove* (Alphen aan de Rijn, Netherlands, 1976)
——: *Duke Ellington on Microgroove: 1923–February 1940* (Alphen aan de Rijn, Netherlands, 1972; rev. 2/1974 as *Duke Ellington on Microgroove, 1923–1942*; rev. 3/1977 as *Duke Ellington on Microgroove*, i: *1923–1936*)
D. M. Bakker, see also P. Koster
E. M. Bakker, see C. Hofmann
R. Bergerone: *Company, 1976–1983: Radio Broadcasts, Records, Concerts* (Sierre, Switzerland, 1983)
R. Bergerone, see also G. Cerutti
G. Bielderman: *Chris Barber Discography, 1949–1975* (Zwolle, Netherlands, 1976; looseleaf suppl. *c*1978)
——: *Cy Laurie, Eggy Ley: Discography* (Zwolle, Netherlands, 1986)
——: *Dutch Swing College Band* (Zwolle, Netherlands, 1984)
——: *Jan Morks Discography* (Zwolle, Netherlands, 1986)
——: *Johnny Parker Discography* (Zwolle, Netherlands, 1987)
——: *Ken Colyer Discography, Incorporating the Crane River Jazz Band* (Zwolle, Netherlands, 1983)
——: *Max Collie Discography* (Zwolle, Netherlands, 1987)
——: *Sammy Rimington Discography, Nov. 1959 – Jan. 1981* (Zwolle, Netherlands, 1981, enlarged 3/1982 as *Sammy Rimington Discography, 1959–1982*)
——: *Sandy Brown Discography* (Zwolle, Netherlands, 1985)
G. Bielderman and E. Elvers: *Oscar Klein Discography* (Zwolle, Netherlands, 1986)
G. Bielderman and R. Stansby: *Freddy Randall Discography* (Zwolle, Netherlands, and Hornchurch, England, 1987)
L. Bijl and F. Canté: *Monk on Records: a Discography of Thelonious Monk* (Amsterdam, 1982, enlarged 2/1985)
R. Boenzli: *Discography of Howard McGhee* (Basle, Switzerland, 1961)
P. Borthen, see J. Evensmo
D. C. Brigaud: *Art Tatum: essai pour une discographie des enregistrements hors commerce* (Paris, 1980) [incl. listings of radio broadcasts, film music, and V-discs]
E. Bryce, see M. Hill
J. Callis: *Charlie Christian, 1939–1941: a Discography* (London, 1958)
F. Canté, see L. Bijl
G. Cerutti: *Discographie de John Tchicai* (Sierre, Switzerland, n.d. [?1979]; rev. and enlarged 2/n.d. [?1982], rev. and enlarged 3/n.d. [?1986] as *John Tchicai Discography (on Records), 1962–1985*)
——: *Fred van Hove Discography, 1968–1983 (on Records)* (Sierre, Switzerland, 1984)
——: *Joe McPhee Discography* (Sierre, Switzerland, 1983)
G. Cerutti and R. Bergerone: *Discographie: Evan Parker* (Sierre, Switzerland, n.d. [?1981]; rev. and enlarged 2/n.d. [1985] as *Evan Parker Discography (on Records and Cassettes), 1968–1983*)
G. Cerutti and G. Maertens: *Discographie Archie Shepp, 1960–1980* (Sierre, Switzerland, 1982)
J. Chilton: *Bill Coleman on Record* (London, 1966)
M. N. Clutten: *A Bruce Turner Discography* (South Harrow and Leicester, England, n.d. [1972])
——: *A George Chisholm Discography* (Leicester, England, 1977; discographical suppl. i, 1980, discographical suppl. ii by S. R. Gallichan, 1984)

M. Clutten, see also OTHER BOOKS, B. Turner

H. de Craen and E. Janssens: *Anthony Braxton Discography* (Brussels, 1982)

——: *Marion Brown Discography* (Brussels, 1985)

H. de Craen, see also E. Janssens

M. Cuscuna, see D. Wild

J. R. T. Davies: *The Music of Thomas "Fats" Waller* (London, 1953); rev. in *Sv*, nos.2–12 (1965–7)

M. Davis, see R. Hunter

E. P. Deckers: *Booker Ervin Discography* (in preparation)

Y. Delmarche and I. Fresart: *A Discography of Ben Webster, 1931–1973* (n.p. [Surhout, Belgium], n.d. [1983])

——: *A Discography of Coleman Hawkins, 1922–1969* (n.p., n.d. [?1983])

E. Edwards, Jr.: *Bill Harris (Trombone): a Complete Discography* (n.p. [?Whittier, CA], 1966)

——: *Woody Herman and his Orchestra: a Discography*, i, ii (Brande, Denmark, 1961); iii: *1959–1965* (Whittier, CA, 1965)

E. Edwards, Jr., G. Hall, and B. Korst: *Charlie Barnet and his Orchestra* (Whittier, CA, 1965, rev. 2/1970)

——: *Jimmie Lunceford* (Whittier, CA, 1965)

——: *Jimmy Dorsey and his Orchestra* (Whittier, CA, 1966)

E. Elvers, see G. Bielderman

J. Evensmo: *The Flute of Wayman Carver, the Trombone of Dickie Wells, 1927–1942, the Tenor Saxophone of Illinois Jacquet* (n.p. [Oslo], n.d. [?1983])

——: *The Guitars of Charlie Christian, Robert Normann, Oscar Alemán (in Europe)* (n.p. [Oslo], n.d. [?1976])

——: *The Tenor Saxophone and Clarinet of Lester Young, 1936–1942* (n.p. [Oslo], n.d. [?1977], rev. [2]/n.d. [?1983] as *The Tenor Saxophone and Clarinet of Lester Young, 1936–1949*)

——: *The Tenor Saxophone of Ben Webster, 1931–1943* (n.p. [Oslo], n.d. [?1978])

——: *The Tenor Saxophone of Coleman Hawkins, 1929–1942* (n.p. [Oslo], n.d. [?1976])

——: *The Tenor Saxophone of Leon Chu Berry* (n.p. [Oslo], n.d. [?1976])

——: *The Tenor Saxophones of Budd Johnson, Cecil Scott, Elmer Williams, Dick Wilson, 1927–1942* (n.p. [Oslo], n.d. [?1977])

——: *The Tenor Saxophones of Henry Bridges, Robert Carroll, Herschal [sic] Evans, Johnny Russell* (n.p. [Oslo], n.d. [?1976])

——: *The Trumpet of Roy Eldridge, 1929–1944* (n.p. [Oslo], n.d. [?1979])

——: *The Trumpets of Bill Coleman, 1929–1945, Frankie Newton* (n.p. [Oslo], n.d. [?1978])

——: *The Trumpets of Dizzy Gillespie, 1937–1943, Irving Randolph, Joe Thomas* (n.p. [Oslo], n.d. [?1982])

J. Evensmo and P. Borthen: *The Trumpet and Vocal of Henry Red Allen, 1927–1942* (n.p. [Oslo], n.d. [?1977])

J. Evensmo, P. Borthen, and I. S. Thomsen: *The Alto Saxophone, Trumpet and Clarinet of Benny Carter, 1927–1946* (n.p. [Oslo], n.d. [?1982])

L. Fält and H. B. Håkånsson: *Hymn to George: George Lewis on Record and Tape* (n.p. [Malmö, Sweden, and Stockholm], 1985)

O. Flückiger: *Discography and Solography of Cab Calloway* (Reinach, nr Basle, Switzerland, 1960); repr. in *JJ*, xiv (1961), no.5, p.1; no.6, p.13; no.7, p.11

——: *Lionel Hampton: Selected Discography, 1966–1978* (Reinach, nr Basle, Switzerland, 1978, rev. and enlarged 2/1980 as *Lionel Hampton: Porträt mit Discography, 1966–79*)

I. Fresart, see Y. Delmarche

M. Frohne: *Subsconscious-Lee: 35 Years of Records and Tapes: the Lee Konitz Discography, 1947–1982* (Freiburg, Germany, 1983)

S. R. Gallichan, see M. N. Clutten

D. Garçon, see J. Lubin

C. Garrod: *Charlie Barnet and his Orchestra* (Spotswood, NJ, and Zephyrhills, FL, 1973, rev. 2/1984)

——: *Charlie Spivak and his Orchestra* (Spotswood, NJ, and Zephyrhills, FL, 1974, rev. 2/1986)

——: *Claude Thornhill and his Orchestra* (Spotswood, NJ, and Zephyrhills, FL, 1971, rev. 2/1975)

——: *Elliot Lawrence and his Orchestra* (Spotswood, NJ, and Zephyrhills, FL, 1974)

——: *Hal McIntyre and his Orchestra* (Spotswood, NJ, and Zephyrhills, FL, 1974)

——: *Jimmy Dorsey and his Orchestra* (Zephyrhills, FL, 1980)

——: *Les Brown and his Orchestra, 1936–1952* (Spotswood, NJ, 1974, rev. and enlarged 2/1986 as *Les Brown and his Orchestra, 1936–1960*)

——: *Stan Kenton and his Orchestra*, i: *1940–1951*; ii: *1952–1959* (Zephyrhills, FL, 1984)

——: *Tex Beneke and his Orchestra* (Spotswood, NJ, 1973, rev. 2/1986)

——: *Tony Pastor and his Orchestra* (Zephyrhills, FL, 1973, rev. 2/1986)

——: *Woody Herman and his Orchestra*, i: *1936–47* (Zephyrhills, FL, 1985); ii: *1948–57* (Zephyrhills, 1986)

C. Garrod and P. Johnston: *Harry James and his Orchestra*, i: *1937–1946*, ii: *1947–1954* (Zephyrhills, FL, 1975); iii: *1955–1982* (Zephyrhills, 1985)

C. Garrod and B. Korst: *Boyd Raeburn and his Orchestra plus Johnny Bothwell and George Handy* (Zephyrhills, FL, 1985)

——: *Gene Krupa and his Orchestra*, i: *1935–1946*; ii: *1947–1973* (Zephyrhills, FL, 1984)

——: *Nat "King" Cole: his Voice and his Piano* (Zephyrhills, FL, 1987)

——: *Will Bradley, Freddie Slack* (Zephryhills, FL, 1986)

C. Garrod, W. Scott, and F. Green: *Tommy Dorsey and his Orchestra* (Zephyrhills, FL, n.d. [?1980–1982])

C. Garrod, see also B. Korst

H. Geerken: *Chronological Discography of the Acoustic Works of Sun Ra, 1956–1981* (Athens, 1982)

J. Gicking: *Charlie Haden's Discography* (New York, 1979)

A. V. Gillet: *The European Recordings by Louis A. Mitchell* (Brussels, 1957, rev. 2/1957)

——: *The Mitchell's Jazz Kings (discographie critique)* (Brussels, 1957)

B. Goldberg: *WKCR Miles Davis Festival Handbook* (New York, 1979)

F. Green, see C. Garrod

J. Grunnet Jepsen, see J. G. Jepsen

H. B. Håkånsson, see L. Fält

G. Hall: *Boyd Raeburn and his Orchestra: a Complete Discography* (Laurel, MD, 1972)

——: *Harry James and his Orchestra* (Laurel, MD, 1971)

——: *Nat "King" Cole: a Jazz Discography* (Laurel, MD, 1965)

——: *The Ruby Braff Discography* (Laurel, MD, 1965)

G. Hall and S. Kramer: *Gene Krupa and his Orchestra* (Laurel, MD, 1975)

G. Hall, see also E. Edwards, Jr.

C. Hallstrom, see B. Scherman

M. Hames: *Albert Ayler, Sunny Murray, Cecil Taylor, Byard Lancaster, and Kenneth Terroade on Disc and Tape* (Ferndown, England, 1983)

——: *John Tchicai on Disc and Tape* (Ferndown, England, 1979)

M. Hames and R. Wilbraham: *Don Cherry on Disc and Tape* (Ferndown, England, 1980)

D. Hamilton-Smith, see H. H. Lange

E. Harkins: *Maynard Ferguson: a Discography* (n.p. [Solana Beach, nr Del Mar, CA], 1976)

J. Hartley, see M. Sparke

F. Hedman, K. Liliedahl, and L. Zackrisson: *Alice Babs* (Stockholm, 1973)

R. Hilbert, Jr., see OTHER BOOKS, S. E. Brown

M. Hill and E. Bryce: *Jelly Roll Morton: a Microgroove Discography and Musical Analysis* (Salisbury East, South Australia, 1977)

C. Hofmann: *Man of Many Parts: a Discography of Buddy Collette* (Amsterdam, 1985) [incl. interview and list of compositions]

C. Hofmann and E. M. Bakker: *Shorty Rogers: a Discography* (Amsterdam, 1983)

H. Hollenstein: *Lennie Tristano on LPs [sic] Records* (Sierre, Switzerland, 1984)

G. J. Hoogeveen: *Bob Gordon Discography* (in preparation)

R. Hunter and M. Davis: *Hampton Hawes Discography* (Manchester, England, 1986) [incl. biography and list of compositions]

E. Janssens and H. de Craen: *Art Ensemble of Chicago Discography: Unit and Members* (Brussels, 1983) [incl. list of compositions]

E. Janssens, see also H. de Craen

G. von Jena: *Discografie [sic] of Serge Chaloff* (Berlin, 1986)

J. G. Jepsen: *A Discography of Charlie Parker* (Copenhagen, 1968)

——: *A Discography of Dizzy Gillespie* (Copenhagen, 1969)

——: *A Discography of Fats Navarro, Clifford Brown* (Brande, Denmark, 1960)

——: *A Discography of Lester Young* (Copenhagen, 1968)

——: *A Discography of Louis Armstrong, 1923–1971* (Copenhagen, 1973)

——: *A Discography of Thelonious Monk & Bud Powell* (Copenhagen, 1969)

——: *Kid Ory* (Copenhagen, 1957)

J. G. Jepsen and K. Mohr: *Hot Lips Page* (Basle, Switzerland, 1961)

J. G. Jepsen, see also B. Scherman

R. Jewson, see H. H. Lange

P. Johnston, see C. Garrod

I. Kanth: *A Discography of Jimmy Blanton* (Stockholm, 1970)

D. Koechlin: *50 ans de jazz avec Barney Bigard* (n.p. [Darnetal, France], n.d. [1979])

——: *Liste des enregistrements réalisés avec Jay McShann* (n.p., n.d.)

B. Korst and C. Garrod: *Artie Shaw and his Orchestra* (Spotswood, NJ, and Zephyrhills, FL, 1974, rev. 2/1986)

B. Korst, see also E. Edwards, Jr.; C. Garrod

P. Koster and D. M. Bakker: *Charlie Parker*, i: *1940–1947* (Alphen aan de Rijn, Netherlands, 1974); ii: *1948–1950* (Alphen aan de Rijn, 1975); iii: *1951–1954* (Alphen aan de Rijn, 1975); iv: *1940–1955* (Alphen aan de Rijn, 1976) [addns and corrections]

P. Koster and C. Sellers: *Dizzy Gillespie*, i: *1937–1953* (Amsterdam, 1985)

S. Kramer, see G. Hall

D. H. Kraner: *Die Hans Koller Discographie, 1947–1966* (Graz, Austria, c1967)

H. H. Lange: *The Fabulous Fives* (Lübbecke, Germany, 1959, rev. 2/1978 by R. Jewson, D. Hamilton-Smith, and R. Webb) [Original Dixieland Jazz Band, Louisiana Five, New Orleans Jazz Band, Original Indiana Five, Original Georgia Five, Original Memphis Five]

——: *Stan Kenton: Discography* (Berlin, 1959) [bound with H. J. Dietzel: *Stan Kenton: Biography*, see OTHER BOOKS]

P. H. Larsen: *Turn on the Stars: Bill Evans, the Complete Discography* (Holte, Denmark, 1984)

H. H. Lerfeldt and T. Sjøgren: *Chet: the Discography of Chesney Henry Baker* (Copenhagen, 1985)

K. Liliedahl, see F. Hedman

H. L. Lindenmaier: *25 Years of Fish Horn Recording: the Steve Lacy Discography, 1954–1979* (Freiburg, Germany, 1982) [incl. list of compositions]
H. L. Lindenmaier and H. Salewski: *The Man who Never Sleeps: the Charles Mingus Discography, 1945–1978* (Freiburg, Germany, 1983)
K. Lohmann, see M. Selchow
G. Lombardi: *Eddie Condon on Record, 1927–1971* (Milan, 1987)
J. Lubin and D. Garçon: *Louis Jordan Discography, 1929–1974* (Levallois-Perret, France, 1987)
A. J. McCarthy, see OTHER BOOKS, B. Holiday
G. Maertens, see G. Cerutti
L. Massagli, L. Pusateri, and G. M. Volonté: *Duke Ellington's Story on Records* (Milan, 1966–83)
H. J. Mauerer: *A Discography of Sidney Bechet* (Copenhagen, 1969)
T. Middleton: *The Squadronaires R.A.F. Dance Orchestra: an Exploratory Discography, 1940–1945* (London, 1976)
——: *Vic Lewis: a Discography* (Amsterdam, 1985)
T. Middleton, see also OTHER BOOKS, R. Horricks
J. Millar: *Born to Sing: a Discography of Billie Holiday* (Copenhagen, n.d. [?1979])
K. Mohr, see J. G. Jepsen
M. Montgomery, see F. H. Trolle
P.-A. Monti: *Booker Little Discography* (Sierre, Switzerland, 1983)
——: *Discographie de Phineas Newborn* (Sierre, Switzerland, n.d. [?1980])
L. Moxhet: *A Discography of Earl Hines, 1923–1977* (Sannois, France, 1978)
P. Murphy: *Chick Bullock: a Discography of his Recordings* (Melbourne, Australia, 1983)
R. Nieus: *A Discography of Dexter Gordon* (n.p. [Jambes, Belgium], n.d. [1986])
C. Popa: *Jerry Gray and his Orchestra* (Zephyrhills, FL, 1984)
——: *Ray McKinley and his Orchestra* (Zephyrhills, FL, 1979)
J. Popa: *Cab Calloway and his Orchestra* (Zephyrhills, FL, 1976)
B. Priestley, see OTHER BOOKS, I. Carr
J. Purser, J. Wilyman, and P. Schwalm: *Humph: a Discography of Humphrey Lyttelton, 1945–1983* (Walton-on-Thames, England, 1985)
L. Pusateri, see L. Massagli
C. de Radzitsky: *A 1960–1967 Clark Terry Discography with Biographical Notes* (n.p. [Brasschaat, Belgium], 1968)
B. Räftegård: *The Kenny Dorham Discography* (Karlstad, Sweden, 1982)
U. Reichardt: *Like a Human Voice: the Eric Dolphy Discography* (Schmitten, Germany, 1986)
M. Ruppli: *Charles Mingus Discography* (Frankfurt am Main, Germany, 1982)
B. Rust, see OTHER BOOKS, P. Foster
H. Salewski, see H. L. Lindenmaier
L. Sanfilippo: *General Catalogue of Duke Ellington's Recorded Music* (Palermo, Sicily, 1964)
B. Scherman, C. Hallstrom, and J. G. Jepsen: *A Discography of Count Basie* (Copenhagen, 1969)
C. Schlouch: *Come Back! Hank Mobley: a Discography* (n.p. [Marseille, France], 1983)
——: *In Memory of Wardell Gray: a Discography* (Marseille, France, 1983)
——: *Lee Wiley, Love-Lee: a Discography* (Marseille, France, 1983)
——: *Once upon a Time: Bud Powell: a Discography* (Marseille, France, 1983)
J. Schütte and A. Stöcklin: *Teddy Stauffer: Discographie der Original Teddies (Teddy Stauffer und Eddie Brunner) und der kleinen Formationen mit Musikern der Teddies* (Menden, Germany, 1983)
P. Schwalm, see J. Purser
W. Scott, see C. Garrod
T. Selbert, see OTHER BOOKS, A. Pepper
M. Selchow and K. Lohmann: *Edmond Hall: a Discography* (Westoverledingen and Göttingen, Germany, 1981)
C. Sellers, see P. Koster
T. Shoppee, see OTHER BOOKS, S. Voce
G. G. Simon: *Lajos Martiny: a Discography* (in preparation)
R. Simonds: *King Curtis: a Discography* (Edgware, England, 1983, rev. 2/1984)
T. Sjøgren: *The Duke Jordan Discography* (Copenhagen, 1982, rev. and enlarged 2/1984)
——: *Long Tall Dexter: the Discography of Dexter Gordon* (Copenhagen, 1986)
——: *The Sonny Rollins Discography* (Copenhagen, 1983)
T. Sjøgren, see also H. H. Lerfeldt
I. Skovgaard and E. Traberg: *Some Clark Bars: Sonny Clark: a Discography* (Copenhagen and Madrid, 1984) [incl. biography]
M. Sparke, P. Venudor, and J. Hartley: *Kenton on Capitol: a Discography* (Hounslow, England, 1966, 2/1967)
R. Stansby, see G. Bielderman
A. Stöcklin, see J. Schütte
K. Stratemann: *Buddy Rich and Gene Krupa: a Filmo-discography* (Lübbecke, Germany, 1980)
J. W. Susat: *Discography of the "Uncompromising Lennie Tristano"* (Menden, Germany, 1986)
T. Tajiri: *Gil Evans Discography, 1941–1982* (Tokyo, 1983)
I. S. Thomsen, see J. Evensmo
E. Traberg, see I. Skovgaard
F. H. Trolle: *James P. Johnson: Father of the Stride Piano* (Alphen aan de Rijn, Netherlands, 1981) [incl. rollography by M. Montgomery]
J. Valburn: *The Directory of Duke Ellington's Recordings* (Hicksville, NY, 1986)
P. van Engelen: *Where's the Music? The Discography of Kai Winding* (Amsterdam, 1985)
W. F. van Eyle: *Don Byas Discography* (Zaandam, Netherlands, 1967)
R. Venables and C. White: *A Complete Discography of Red Nichols and his Five Pennies* (Melbourne, Australia, 1946, 2/1947)
P. Venudor, see M. Sparke
J.-F. Villetard: *Coleman Hawkins*, i: *1922–1944* (Amsterdam, 1984); ii: *1945–1957* (Amsterdam, 1985)
G. M. Volonté, see L. Massagli
H. Wachtmeister: *A Discography & Bibliography of Anthony Braxton* (Stocksund, nr Stockholm, 1982)
G. Wattiau: *Book's Book: a Discography of Booker Ervin* (Amsterdam, 1987)
R. Webb, see H. H. Lange
B. Weir: *Art Ford's TV Jazz Party 1958: TV & Radio Broadcasts* (Cardiff, 1987)
——: *Buck Clayton Discography* (Chigwell, England, in preparation)
——: *Clarence Gene Shaw Discography* (Cardiff, 1986, rev. and enlarged 2/1986)
——: *Clifford Brown Discography* (Cardiff, 1982, rev. and enlarged 2/1983, rev. and enlarged 3/1984, rev. and enlarged 3[*recte* 4]/1986)
——: *Dupree Bolton Discography* (Cardiff, 1986, rev. and enlarged 2/1986)
——: *Helen Merrill Discography* (Amsterdam, 1987)
——: *The L. A. Four Discography* (Cardiff, 1985, rev. and enlarged 2/1986)
B. Weir, see also OTHER BOOKS, B. Clayton; S. Price
R. Wernboe: *Lee Morgan Discography* (Saltsjöbaden, Sweden, 1985)
H. Westerberg: *Boy from New Orleans: Louis "Satchmo" Armstrong, on Records, Films, Radio and Television* (Copenhagen, 1981) [incl. discography]
B. White: *The Eddie Condon "Town Hall Broadcasts," 1944–1945: a Discography* (Oakland, CA, 1980)
C. White, see R. Venables
R. J. Wilbraham: *Jackie McLean: a Discography with Biography* (London, 1968)
——: *Milt Jackson: a Discography and Bibliography* (London, 1968)
R. Wilbraham, see also M. Hames
D. Wild: *The Recordings of John Coltrane* (Ann Arbor, MI, 1979)
D. Wild and M. Cuscuna: *Ornette Coleman, 1958–1979: a Discography* (Ann Arbor, MI, 1980)
J. Wilyman, see J. Purser
J. Wölfer: *Si Zentner and his Orchestra, also Including Bob Florence and his Orchestra: a Discography* (Langenhagen, Germany, 1981)
L. Zackrisson, see F. Hedman

Record label listings

AFR&TS Gold Label transcriptions catalogue, see R. E. Lotz
AFRS Jubilee transcriptions catalogue, see R. E. Lotz
F. Andrews: *Columbia 10" Records, 1904–30* (London, 1985) [pubn of City of London Phonograph and Gramophone Society]
Atlantic catalogues, see P. A. Grendysa; M. Ruppli
A. Badrock: *English Pathé Perfect: a Catalogue and History* (Hayes, England, 1983)
B. Bennett: *Capitol Record Listing 101–3031* (Zephyrhills, FL, 1987)
Bluebird catalogues, see H. Panassié; BIBLIOGRAPHIES AND REFERENCE MATERIALS, R. D. Kinkle
Brunswick catalogues, see J. G. Hayes; E. Jackson; *Jazz on LP's*; P. Pelletier; BIBLIOGRAPHIES AND REFERENCE MATERIALS, R. D. Kinkle
Capitol catalogues, see B. Bennett; *Jazz on LP's*; M. Montgomery; P. Pelletier
Challenge catalogue, see M. Montgomery
Chess catalogue, see M. Ruppli
Clef/Verve catalogue, see M. Ruppli
Columbia catalogues, see D. Mahony; M. Montgomery; P. Pelletier; *Other listings*, G. Avakian; BIBLIOGRAPHIES AND REFERENCE MATERIALS, R. D. Kinkle
Coral catalogues, see *Jazz on LP's*; P. Pelletier
Cupol catalogue, see B. Englund
B. Daniels, see M. Ruppli
W. DeBlock, see S. Wante
Decca catalogues, see J. G. Hayes; E. Jackson; *Jazz on LP's*; *Jazz on 78s*; P. Pelletier; BIBLIOGRAPHIES AND REFERENCE MATERIALS, R. D. Kinkle
R. Dethlefson, see R. R. Wile
Deutsche Grammophon catalogue, see J. Grundmann
Ducretet-Thompson catalogue, see *Jazz on LP's*
Durium catalogue, see *Jazz on LP's*
Edison catalogues, see R. R. Wile
Edison Bell Winner catalogue, see J. G. Hayes
B. Englund: *Jazz på Cupol* (Stockholm, 1982)
——: *Sonora II: Swing-serien* (Stockholm, 1974)
Felsted catalogues, see *Jazz on LP's*; P. Pelletier
S. Furusho: *Riverside Jazz Records* (Chiba, Japan, 1984)
C. Garrod, see B. Korst
P. A. Grendysa: *Atlantic Master Book #1* (Milwaukee, 1975)
J. Grundmann: *Jazz aus den Trummern: Discographie der Eigenaufnahmen der Deutschen Grammophon, 1945–48* (Menden, Germany, 1982)

J. G. Hayes: *Edison Bell Winner: the W1 Series, 1933–1935* (Liverpool, England, 1984)
——: *The F1000 Series, Decca, 1929–1934*, Disc Research England (Liverpool, England, 1970/R1984)
J. G. Hayes, B. Luxton, and D. Luxton: *English Brunswick 78/45 r.p.m. (0)1000 Series*, i: *Issues 1001 to 02000 (Dec 1930 to May 1935)*, Numerical Catalogue Listings, no.E1 (n.p., n.d.)
His Master's Voice catalogues, see E. Jackson; P. Pelletier
E. Jackson: *"His Master's Voice" Swing and Hot Rhythm Records* (Hayes, nr London, n.d. [?1941])
——: *The Parlophone "Rhythm-Style" Series: the Complete List of Records up to and Including December, 1935, Arranged Alphabetically and Numerically Together with the Personnels of the Orchestras and Index to Artistes* (London, n.d. [?1936], rev. and enlarged 2/n.d. [1941], rev. and enlarged 3/n.d. [1942], rev. and enlarged 4/n.d. [1944], rev. and enlarged 5/n.d. [1946], rev. and enlarged 6/n.d. [1948], with various titles)
E. Jackson and L. Hibbs: *Decca, Brunswick, Vocalion Encyclopedia of Swing* (London, 1941)
Jazz on LP's: a Collectors' Guide to Jazz on Decca, Brunswick, Capitol, London and Felsted Long Playing Records (London, 1955, rev. 2/1956 as *Jazz on LP's: a Collectors' Guide to Jazz on Decca, Brunswick, London, Felsted, Ducretet-Thompson, Vogue, Coral, Telefunken and Durium Long Playing Records*)
Jazz on 78s: a Guide to the Many Examples of Classic Jazz (London, 1954) [pubn of Decca Record Co.]
F. J. Karlin: *Edison Diamond Discs, 50001–52651, 1912–1929* (Santa Monica, CA, 1972)
King catalogue, see M. Ruppli
B. Korst: *RCA Victor Record Listing, 20-1500 thru 20-7300*, ed. C. Garrod (Zephyrhills, FL, 1986)
London catalogues, see *Jazz on LP's*; P. Pelletier
R. E. Lotz: *The AFR&TS (Gold Label) Transcription Library: a Label Listing* (Menden, Germany, 1978)
R. E. Lotz and U. Neuert: *The AFRS "Jubilee" Transcription Programs: an Exploratory Discography* (Frankfurt am Main, Germany, 1985)
B. Luxton and D. Luxton, see J. G. Hayes
D. Mahony: *The Columbia 13/14000-D Series: a Numerical Listing* (Stanhope, NJ, 1961, rev. 2/1966/R1973 with addns)
Melotone catalogue, see BIBLIOGRAPHIES AND REFERENCE MATERIALS, R. D. Kinkle
M. Montgomery: *Columbia, Capitol, Supertone, and Challenge Word Roll Catalog* (n.p. [Southfield, MI], n.d. [?1984])
U. Neuert, see R. E. Lotz
Okeh catalogue, see BIBLIOGRAPHIES AND REFERENCE MATERIALS, R. D. Kinkle
Okeh Race Records (New York, n.d. [?1924]/R1976) [R1976 is a facs. of Clarence Williams's annotated copy]
Okeh Race Records: the Blue Book of Blues (New York, n.d. [?1927]/R)
Palette catalogue, see P. Pelletier
H. Panassié: *144 Hot Jazz Bluebird and Victor Records* (Camden, NJ, 1939)
Paramount catalogue, see M. E. Vreede
Parlophone catalogue, see E. Jackson
Pathé catalogue, see A. Badrock
[P. Pelletier]: *British Brunswick Complete Singles Listing* (London, ?1977; suppl. 1980) [Record Information Services pubn]
——: *British Capitol Singles & E.P.s*, i: *1948–1955* (London, 1977) [Record Information Services pubn]
——: *British London Jazz Complete L.P. Listing* (London, 1976) [Record Information Services pubn]
——: *British London Label L.P./E.P. Listing* (London, 1974) [pt i of *British London Label Complete Listing*; Record Information Services pubn]
——: *British London Complete Listing, Part Two* (London, 1974) [Record Information Services pubn]
——: *London – American 78/45 r.p.m. Singles from 1949 to December 1974* (London, 1975) [pt iii of *British London Label Complete Listing*; Record Information Services pubn]
——: *British London Label Complete Listing, Part Four, plus Felsted & (Vogue-) Coral* (London, 1975) [Record Information Services pubn]
——: *British London, London Jazz E.P. Listing* (London, 1976) [Record Information Services pubn]
——: *British London Singles, Felsted Popular Singles & EPs Listing* (London, 1976) [Record Information Services pubn]
——: *British Sue Complete Singles, E.P.s & L.P.s Listing* (London, 1976) [Record Information Services pubn]
——: *British Top Rank, Stateside Long-play Listing* (London, 1975) [Record Information Services pubn]
——: *British Top Rank, Stateside, Triumph, Palette Singles/E.P. Listing* (London, 1975) [Record Information Services pubn]
P. M. Pelletier: *British Capitol 45 r.p.m. Singles Catalogue: 1954–1981* (Chessington, England, 1982) [Record Information Services pubn]
——: *Complete British Directory of Popular 78/45 r.p.m. Singles, 1950–1980*, i: *Columbia, Decca, H.M.V.* (London, 1986) [Record Information Services pubn]
——: *Decca 78 r.p.m. Ten-inch and 45 r.p.m. Seven-inch Complete Singles Catalogue, 1954–1983* (Chessington, England, 1984) [Record Information Services pubn]
——: *London 78 r.p.m. Ten-inch and 45 r.p.m. Seven-inch Complete Singles Catalogue: 1949–1982* (Chessington, England, 1982) [Record Information Services pubn]
Perfect catalogues, see A. Badrock; BIBLIOGRAPHIES AND REFERENCE MATERIALS, R. D. Kinkle
B. Porter, see M. Ruppli
Prestige catalogue, see M. Ruppli
RCA Victor catalogue, see B. Korst
Record Information Services, see P. Pelletier
Riverside catalogue, see S. Furusho
M. Ruppli: *Atlantic Records: a Discography* (Westport, CT, and London, 1979)
——: *The Chess Labels: a Discography* (Westport, CT, and London, 1983) [Chicago blues, some jazz]
——: *Prestige Jazz Records, 1949–1969 [recte 1971]: a Discography* (n.p. [Copenhagen], 1972; rev. and enlarged, Westport, CT, and London, 2/1980, with B. Porter, as *The Prestige Label: a Discography*)
M. Ruppli and B. Daniels: *The King Labels: a Discography* (Westport, CT, and London, 1985) [country music, rhythm-and-blues, some jazz]
M. Ruppli and B. Porter: *The Clef/Verve Labels: a Discography*, i: *The Norman Granz Era*; ii: *The MGM Era* (New York, Westport, CT, and London, 1986)
——: *The Savoy Label: a Discography* (Westport, CT, and London, 1980)
B. Rust: *The Victor Master Book*, ii: *1925–1936* (Stanhope, NJ, 1970) [projected vol. i: 1903–25, and vol. iii: 1936–42, not pubd]
Savoy catalogue, see M. Ruppli
R. S. Sears: *V-discs: a History and Discography* (Westport, CT, and London, 1980; suppl., 1986)
Sonora catalogue, see B. Englund
Stateside catalogues, see P. Pelletier
Sue catalogue, see P. Pelletier
Supertone catalogue, see M. Montgomery
Telefunken catalogue, see *Jazz on LP's*
K. Teubig: *V-disc Catalogue*, ii (Berlin, 1976)
Top Rank catalogues, see P. Pelletier
Triumph catalogue, see P. Pelletier
V-disc catalogues, see R. S. Sears; K. Teubig; S. Wante
Verve catalogue, see M. Ruppli
Victor catalogues, see B. Korst; H. Panassié; B. Rust; BIBLIOGRAPHIES AND REFERENCE MATERIALS, R. D. Kinkle
Vocalion catalogues, see E. Jackson; BIBLIOGRAPHIES AND REFERENCE MATERIALS, R. D. Kinkle
M. E. Vreede: *Paramount 12/13000 Series* (London, 1971)
Vogue catalogue, see *Jazz on LP's*
S. Wante and W. DeBlock: *V-disc Catalogue*, i (Antwerp, Belgium, 1954)
R. R. Wile: *Edison Disc Artists & Records, 1910–1929*, ed. R. Dethlefson (New York, 1985) [incl. dating guide]
——: *Edison Disc Recordings* (Philadelphia, 1977) [pubn of Eastern National Park and Monument Assn]

Other listings

Angelicum Santandrea catalogo generale, see *Santandrea catalogo generale*
G. Avakian: *Jazz from Columbia: a Complete Jazz Catalog* (New York, 1956) [listeners' guide]
Bielefelder Katalog, see *General*, M. Scheffner
Catalogo: discos – long play (Buenos Aires, 1962–?); annual cumulative indexes [periodical catalogue, quarterly]
G. Cherrington, see OTHER BOOKS, S. Traill
D. Coller, see OTHER BOOKS, S. Traill
Le courrier du disque microsillon (Paris, ?1952–1958), new ser. (Paris, 1959–?) [periodical catalogue, weekly, from nos.64–5 (6 Feb 1959) fortnightly]
M. Cullaz: *Guide des disques de jazz: les 1000 meilleurs disques de spirituals, gospel songs, blues, rhytm [sic] and blues, jazz, et leur histoire* (Paris, 1971)
Diapason: la revue du disque microsillon, new ser. (Angers, France, Oct–Dec 1955 – Nov 1956; Paris, Dec 1956–?); monthly suppl. *La discographie de la France* (1955–64), contd independently (see PERIODICALS) [periodical catalogue, 11 issues yearly]
La discographie française: revue bi-mensuelle du disque [by no.12 (15 May 1957) *La discographie française: la seule revue complète d'actualité du disque*; from no.121 (15 Sept 1962) *La discographie française et L'édition musicale française*] (Paris, 1 Dec 1956–) [periodical catalogue, fortnightly]
Discopop '77: tous les disques de pop, blues, folk, free-jazz, rock (Paris, 1977) [catalogue]
Disques de longue durée (Paris, aut. 1953 – ?); various suppls. [periodical catalogue, bimonthly, from no.12 (1957) yearly]
F. Dutton, see OTHER BOOKS, S. Traill
C. Ferguson and M. Johnson: *Mainstream Jazz Reference and Price Guide, 1949–1965* (Phoenix, AZ, 1984) [price guide]
Forty-fiver (New York, Sept 1951 – ? Dec 1957) [periodical catalogue, monthly]
C. Fox, P. Gammond, and A. Morgan: *Jazz on Record: a Critical Guide* (London, 1960) [listeners' guide]
C. Fox, see also M. Harrison

P. Gammond and R. Horricks: *Big Bands*, Music on Record, ii (Cambridge, England, 1981)
P. Gammond, see also C. Fox
P. Guralnick: *The Listener's Guide to the Blues* (Poole, England, 1982)
R. Harris and B. Rust: *Recorded Jazz: a Critical Guide* (Harmondsworth, England, 1958) [listeners' guide]
M. Harrison and others: *Modern Jazz: the Essential Records: a Critical Selection* (London, 1975) [listeners' guide]
M. Harrison, C. Fox, and E. Thacker: *The Essential Jazz Records*, i: *Ragtime to Swing* (London, and Westport, CT, 1984) [listeners' guide]
R. Horricks, see P. Gammond
A. Jackson, see E. Jackson
E. Jackson, A. McCarthy, A. Jackson, and R. Seeley, eds.: *The Gramophone Long Playing Popular Record Catalogue* [from July 1955 *The Gramophone Popular Record Catalogue*; from ?1973 *Gramophone Popular Catalogue*; from March 1985 *The Pop Cat*] (Harrow, nr London, July 1954 – Sept 1987); annual cumulative indexes (1955–84) [periodical catalogue, quarterly]
Jazz Catalogue, see *General*, G. Cherrington
Jazz 'n Pops: a Comprehensive Catalog of Jazz and Popular Longplay Records, see *The Long Player*
M. Johnson, see C. Ferguson
Morley Jones: *Jazz*, Simon and Schuster's Listener's Guides, ed. A. Rich (New York, 1980)
G. Lascelles, see OTHER BOOKS, S. Traill
The Long Player [from v/7 (July–Aug 1956) *The Long Player: a Complete Catalog of Long-playing Records*] (New York, 1952 – sum. 1959); separate catalogue of jazz and popular music as *The Long Player: a Complete Catalog of Popular & Jazz Longplay Records* (New York, Jan 1957 – sum. 1959) [from i/2 (March 1957) *Jazz 'n Pops: a Comprehensive Catalog of Jazz and Popular Longplay Records*] [periodical catalogue]
L. Lyons: *The 101 Best Jazz Albums: a History of Jazz on Records* (New York, 1980) [listeners' guide]
A. McCarthy and others: *Jazz on Record: a Critical Guide to the First 50 Years: 1917–1967* (London, 1968) [listeners' guide]
A. McCarthy, see also E. Jackson
D. Marsh, see J. Swenson
Micro surco: catálogo completo de discos larga duracion: $33\frac{1}{3}$ y 45 r.p.m. (Buenos Aires, 1955–?) [periodical catalogue]
A. Morgan, see C. Fox
Music Master [*1974*] [from 1984 *Music Master: the World's Greatest Record Catalogue*] (London, 1974–?1978; Hastings, England, ?1979–?) [periodical catalogue, yearly]
H. Panassié: *Petit guide pour une discotheque de jazz* (Paris, 1955)
——: *Discographie critique des meilleurs disques de jazz* (Paris, 1958)
F. Ramsey, Jr.: *A Guide to Longplay Jazz Records* (New York, n.d. [1954]/*R*1977) [listeners' guide]
Revista "Long-playing" (n.p., ?1957–1960; São Paulo, 1960–?) [periodical catalogue, bimonthly, from no.27 (Nov/Dec 1960) quarterly]
A. Rich, see Morley Jones
The Rolling Stone Jazz Record Guide, see J. Swenson
B. Rust, see R. Harris
Santandrea catalogo generale dischi microsolio $33\frac{1}{3}$ e 45 e.p. [from xv/2 (March/April 1968) *Angelicum Santandrea catalogo generale dischi microsolio $33\frac{1}{3}$ e 45 e.p.*] (Milan, Jan/Feb 1955–?) [periodical catalogue, bimonthly]
[W. Schwann]: *Long Playing Record Catalog* [from March 1953 *Schwann: Long Playing Record Catalog*, from Jan 1971 *Schwann Record & Tape Guide*, from Jan 1972 *Schwann-1: Record & Tape Guide*, from Dec 1983 *The New Schwann*, by 1987 *Schwann*] (Cambridge, MA, 1949–53; Boston, 1953–); half-yearly suppl. *The Schwann Catalog of Imported Records* [from 1966 *The Schwann Supplementary Catalog*, from 1971 *The Schwann Supplementary Record Guide*, from 1972 *Schwann-2: Record & Tape Guide*] (1964–83); monthly suppl. *Schwann Compact Disc* (1986–) [periodical catalogue, monthly]
R. Seeley, see E. Jackson
C. E. Smith and others: *The Jazz Record Book* (New York, 1942/*R*1978) [listeners' guide with discography]
J. Swenson, ed.: *The Rolling Stone Jazz Record Guide* (New York and Toronto, 1985) [listeners' guide; incl. material previously pubd in D. Marsh and J. Swenson, eds.: *The Rolling Stone Record Guide* (New York, 1979)]
E. Thacker, see M. Harrison
E. Townley, see OTHER BOOKS, S. Traill
S. Traill, see OTHER BOOKS
J. S. Wilson: *The Collector's Jazz: Modern* (Philadelphia, 1959) [listeners' guide]
——: *The Collector's Jazz: Traditional and Swing* (Philadelphia, 1958) [listeners' guide]
——: *Jazz: the Transition Years, 1940–1960* (New York, 1966) [listeners' guide]

OTHER BOOKS

M. Abrams: *The Book of Django* (Los Angeles, 1973) [bio-discography]
A. J. Agostinelli: *Don Ellis: a Man for our Time (1934–1978)* (Providence, RI, 1986) [bio-discography]
——: *Stan Kenton: the Many Musical Moods of his Orchestras* (Providence, RI, 1986) [bio-discography]
C. Albertson: *Bessie: Empress of the Blues* (New York, 1972)
R. B. Allen, see W. J. Schafer
W. C. Allen: *Hendersonia: the Music of Fletcher Henderson and his Musicians: a Bio-discography* (Highland Park, NJ, 1973)
W. C. Allen, ed.: *Studies in Jazz Discography*, i (New Brunswick, NJ, 1971) [proceedings of *Discographical Research*, i *New Brunswick, NJ, 1968*; *Discographical Research*, ii *New Brunswick, NJ, 1969*; *Preservation and Extension of the Jazz Heritage: New Brunswick, NJ, 1969*]
W. C. Allen and B. A. L. Rust: *King Joe Oliver* (Belleville, NJ, 1955) [completely rev. version by L. Wright (Chigwell, England, 1987)]
O. Alvarenga: *Música popular brasileña* (Buenos Aires, 1947)
R. Ambor: *Ella: ein Bildband* (Hamburg, Germany, 1961)
American Folklife Center, Library of Congress, see *Ethnic Recordings in America*
B. Amstell and R. T. Deal: *Don't Fuss, Mr. Ambrose: Memoirs of a Life Spent in Popular Music* (Tunbridge Wells, England, 1986) [autobiography of Billy Amstell]
E. Anderson, ed.: *Esquire's 1947 Jazz Book: Year Book of the Jazz Scene* (New York, 1947); see also P. E. Miller
J. Anderson: *This was Harlem: a Cultural Portrait, 1900–1950* (New York, 1982)
M. Anderson: *Music in the Mix: the Story of South African Popular Music* (Johannesburg, 1981)
U. Andresen: *Keith Jarrett: sein Leben, seine Musik, seine Schallplatten* (Gauting, Germany, n.d. [1985])
O. Angell, J. E. Vold, and G. Økland, eds.: *Jazz i Norge* (Oslo, 1975)
L. Armstrong: *Ma Nouvelle-Orléans* (Paris, 1952; Eng. orig. pubd as *Satchmo: my Life in New Orleans*, New York, 1954; Ger. trans., Zurich, 1977)
——: *Swing that Music* (London, New York, and Toronto, 1936) [incl. transcrs.]
[L. Armstrong] *Satchmo: Collector's Copy* (Hollywood, CA, 1971) [iconography]
L. M. G. Arntzenius: *Amerikaansche kunstindrukken* (Amsterdam, 1927)
H. Asbury: *The French Quarter: an Informal History of the New Orleans Underworld* (London, 1937)
D. Asher, see H. Hawes
J. Asman, see S. F. Dance
A. Asriel: *Jazz: Analysen und Aspekte* (Berlin, 1966)
M. Audibert: *Fletcher Henderson et son orchestre, 1924–1951: sa place dans l'histoire du jazz* (Bayonne, France, 1983)
M. Ausserbauer, see G. Filtgen
D. Bailey: *Improvisation: its Nature and Practice in Music* (Ashbourne, England, 1980; Englewood Cliffs, NJ, 1980, as *Musical Improvisation: its Nature and Practice in Music*; Ger. trans., Hofheim, Germany, 1986)
D. Baker: *Advanced Improvisation* (Chicago, 1971, rev. 1979)
——: *Arranging and Composing for the Small Ensemble: Jazz, R & B, Jazz-rock* (Chicago, 1970)
——: *Jazz Improvisation: a Comprehensive Method for all Players* (Chicago, 1969, rev. 2/1983)
——: *The Jazz Style of Cannonball Adderley: a Musical and Historical Perspective* (Lebanon, IN, 1980) [incl. transcrs.]
——: *The Jazz Style of Clifford Brown: a Musical and Historical Perspective* (Hialeah, FL, 1982) [incl. transcrs.]
——: *The Jazz Style of Fats Navarro: a Musical and Historical Perspective* (Hialeah, FL, 1982) [incl. transcrs.]
——: *The Jazz Style of John Coltrane: a Musical and Historical Perspective* (Lebanon, IN, 1980) [incl. transcrs.]
——: *The Jazz Style of Miles Davis: a Musical and Historical Perspective* (Lebanon, IN, 1980) [incl. transcrs.]
——: *The Jazz Style of Sonny Rollins: a Musical and Historical Perspective* (Lebanon, IN, 1980) [incl. transcrs.]
——: *Jazz Styles & Analysis: Trombone: a History of the Jazz Trombone via Recorded Solos, Transcribed and Annotated* (Chicago, 1973)
——: *J. J. Johnson, Trombone* (New York, 1979) [transcrs.; incl. discography and list of compositions]
D. N. Baker, L. M. Belt, and H. C. Hudson, eds.: *The Black Composer Speaks* (Metuchen, NJ, and London, 1978)
D. Baker, see also P. Coker
W. Balliett: *Alec Wilder and his Friends* (Boston, 1974) [colln of previously pubd articles]
——: *American Musicians: Fifty-six Portraits in Jazz* (New York, and Oxford, England, 1986)
——: *American Singers* (New York, 1979)
——: *Dinosaurs in the Morning* (Philadelphia, 1962/*R*1978) [colln of previously pubd articles and reviews]
——: *Ecstasy at the Onion* (New York and Indianapolis, 1971) [colln of previously pubd articles and reviews]
——: *Improvising: Sixteen Jazz Musicians and their Art* (New York, 1977) [colln of previously pubd articles]
——: *Jelly Roll, Jabbo and Fats* (New York, and Oxford, England, 1983) [colln of previously pubd articles]
——: *New York Notes: a Journal of Jazz, 1972–1975* (Boston, 1976) [colln of previously pubd reviews]
——: *Night Creature: a Journal of Jazz, 1975–1980* (New York, 1981) [colln of previously pubd reviews]

——: *The Sound of Surprise* (New York, 1959/*R*1978) [colln of previously pubd articles and reviews]
——: *Such Sweet Thunder* (Indianapolis, 1966) [colln of previously pubd articles and reviews]
Amiri Baraka: *The Autobiography of Leroi Jones* (New York, 1984)
Amiri Baraka and Amina Baraka: *The Music: Reflections on Jazz and Blues* (New York, 1987)
Amiri Baraka: other works listed under alternative name, L. Jones
A. Baresel: *Das Jazz-Buch: Anleitung zum Spielen, Improvisieren und Komponieren moderner Tanzstücke mit besonderer Berücksichtigung des Klaviers* (Leipzig, Germany, 1926, rev. ?2/1929 as *Das neue Jazzbuch: ein praktisches Handbuch für Musiker, Komponisten, Arrangeure, Tänzer und Freunde der Jazzmusik*)
D. Barker: *A Life in Jazz*, ed. A. Shipton (London and New York, 1986) [autobiography of Danny Barker; incl. discography]
D. Barker, see also J. V. Buerkle
C. Barnet and S. Dance: *Those Swinging Years: the Autobiography of Charlie Barnet* (Baton Rouge, LA, and London, 1984) [incl. discography]
S. C. Barr: *The (Almost) Complete 78 rpm Record Dating Guide* (Toronto, 1980)
T. Barrow, see V. Lewis
E. Bartsch: *Neger, Jazz und tiefer Süden* (Leipzig, Germany, 1956)
L. Bash, see J. Kuzmich, Jr.
C. Basie and A. Murray: *Good Morning Blues: the Autobiography of Count Basie* (New York, 1985)
A. Bausch: *Jazz in Europa* (Echternach, Luxembourg, 1985) [colln of interviews]
G. Beall: *Frontiers of Jazz* (New York, 1947, rev. 2/1962)
S. Bechet: *Treat it Gentle: an Autobiography*, ed. D. Flower (New York and London, 1960/*R*1975; Ger. trans. as *Alle Kinder Gottes tragen eine Krone: eine Autobiographie*, Zurich, 1961)
S. F. Bedwell: *A Glenn Miller Discography and Biography* (London, 1955)
R. Belcher: *Maynard Ferguson File* (Caversham, England, 1975–6) [colln of articles and printed ephemera]
L. M. Belt, see D. N. Baker
K. Benson, see J. Haskins
K. W. Benston: *Baraka: the Renegade and the Mask* (New Haven, CT, and London, 1976)
K. W. Benston, ed.: *Imamu Amiri Baraka (Leroi Jones): a Collection of Critical Essays* (Englewood Cliffs, NJ, 1978)
B. Benward and J. Wildman: *Jazz Improvisation in Theory and Practice* (Dubuque, IA, 1984)
J.-E. Berendt: *Ein Fenster aus Jazz: Essays, Portraits, Reflexionen* (Frankfurt am Main, Germany, 1977)
——: *Das Jazzbuch: Entwicklung und Bedeutung der Jazzmusik* (Frankfurt am Main, Germany, 1953, rev. 2/1959 as *Das neue Jazzbuch: Entwicklung und Bedeutung der Jazzmusik*, It. trans., Florence, Italy, 1959, Eng. trans., New York, 1962, Fr. trans. as *Le jazz*, Paris, 1962, Sp. trans., Mexico City, *c*1962; rev. and enlarged 5/1981 as *Das grosse Jazzbuch: von New Orleans bis Jazz Rock*, Eng. trans. as *The Jazz Book: from New Orleans to Fusion and Beyond*, Westport, CT, 1982)
——: *Der Jazz: eine zeitkritische Studie* (Stuttgart, Germany, 1950)
——: *Nada Brahma: die Welt ist Klang* (Frankfurt am Main, Germany, 1983)
——: *Photo-Story des Jazz* (Frankfurt am Main, Germany, 1978; Eng. trans., New York and London, 1979)
——: *Variationen über Jazz* (Munich, 1956)
I. Berg, I. Yeomans, and N. Brittan: *Trad: an A to Z Who's Who of the British Traditional Jazz Scene* (London and elsewhere, 1962)
D. Berger, see M. Hinton
E. Berger, see M. Berger; C. Nanry
M. Berger, E. Berger, and J. Patrick: *Benny Carter: a Life in American Music* (Metuchen, NJ, and London, 1982)
J. Bergh, see B. Stendahl
H. J. P. Bergmeier: *The Weintraub Story: Incorporating the Ady Rosner Story* (Menden, Germany, 1982) [incl. discography]
H. J. P. Bergmeier and R. E. Lotz: *Alex Hyde Bio-discography* (Menden, Germany, 1985)
E. A. Berlin: *Ragtime: a Musical and Cultural History* (Berkeley, CA, Los Angeles, and London, 1980/*R*1984 with addns)
E. Bernhard and J. de Vergnies: *Apologie du jazz* (Brussels, 1945)
P. Bernhard: *Jazz: eine musikalische Zeitfrage* (Munich, 1927)
C. E. B. Bernhardt and S. Harris: *I Remember: Eighty Years of Black Entertainment, Big Bands, and the Blues* (Philadelphia, 1986) [autobiography of Clyde Bernhardt; incl. discography]
J. Bernlef, see P. Klaasse
J. Berry, J. Foose, and T. Jones: *Up from the Cradle of Jazz: New Orleans Music since World War II* (Athens, GA, and London, 1986)
R. Berton: *Remembering Bix: a Memoir of the Jazz Age* (New York and elsewhere, 1974)
T. Bethell: *George Lewis: a Jazzman from New Orleans* (Berkeley, CA, and London, 1977)
E. Biagioni: *Herb Flemming: a Jazz Pioneer around the World* (Alphen aan de Rijn, Netherlands, n.d. [?1977])
G. Bielderman: *Beryl Bryden: Discography, Biography* (Zwolle, Netherlands, 1979, rev. and enlarged 4/1985)
B. Bigard: *With Louis and the Duke*, ed. B. Martyn (London, 1985) [autobiography of Barney Bigard]
J. Bisceglia: *Black & White Fantasy* (Troense, Denmark, 1984)
A. Bisset: *Black Roots, White Flowers: a History of Jazz in Australia* (Sydney, 1979)
D. C. Black: *Matrix Numbers, their Meaning and History* (Melbourne, Australia, n.d. [1940s])
J. Blades: *Percussion Instruments and their History* (London, 1970, rev. [3]/1984)
C. Blancq: *Melodic Improvisation in American Jazz: the Style of Theodore "Sonny" Rollins, 1951–1962* (diss., Tulane U., 1977); rev. as *Sonny Rollins: the Journey of a Jazzman* (Boston, 1983)
E. L. Blandford: *Artie Shaw* (Hastings, England, 1974) [bio-discography]
A. Blatter: *Instrumentation/Orchestration* (New York and London, 1980)
R. Blesh: *Combo, USA: Eight Lives in Jazz* (Philadelphia and London, 1971)
——: *Shining Trumpets: a History of Jazz* (New York, 1946, rev. and enlarged 2/1958/*R*1975)
R. Blesh and H. Janis: *They all Played Ragtime* (New York, 1950, rev. 4/1971)
D. Bogle: *Brown Sugar: Eighty Years of America's Black Female Superstars* (New York, 1980)
——: *Toms, Coons, Mulattoes, Mammies, and Bucks: an Interpretive History of Blacks in American Films* (New York, 1973)
C. Bohländer: *Die Anatomie des Swing* (Frankfurt am Main, Germany, 1986)
——: *Das Wesen der Jazzmusik* (Frankfurt am Main, Germany, 1954)
W. Bolcom, see R. Kimball; P. Oliver
A. Bontemps, see W. C. Handy
M. Bookspan and R. Yockey: *André Previn: a Biography* (Garden City, NY, 1981)
L. Borenstein and B. Russell: *Preservation Hall Portraits* (Baton Rouge, LA, 1968) [photographs by N. Rockmore]
E. Borneman: *A Critic Looks at Jazz* (London, 1946) [orig. pubd in *Record Changer*]
D. Boulton: *Jazz in Britain* (London, 1958)
L. G. Bourgois III: *Jazz Trombonist J. J. Johnson: a Comprehensive Discography and Study of the Early Evolution of his Style* (diss., Ohio State U., 1986)
M. Bouvier-Ajam: *Connaissance du jazz* (Paris, 1952)
P. Bradford: *Born with the Blues: . . . the True Story of the Pioneering Blues Singers and Musicians in the Early Days of Jazz* (New York, 1963)
A. G. Bragaglia: *Jazz Band* (Milan, 1929)
C. Brandt and C. Roemer: *Standardized Chord Symbol Notation: a Uniform System for the Music Profession* (Sherman Oaks, CA, 1976)
O. Brask, see D. Morgenstern
G. Braunschweig and others: *Jazz et photographie* (Paris, 1983) [exhibition catalogue of the Musée d'Art Moderne, Paris]
Bricktop and J. Haskins: *Bricktop* (New York, 1983) [autobiography of Bricktop (Ada Smith)]
R. Brinkmann, ed.: *Avantgarde, Jazz, Pop: Tendenzen zwischen Tonalität und Atonalität* (Mainz, Germany, and London, 1978)
S. Britt: *The Jazz Guitarists* (Poole, England, 1984)
N. Brittan, see I. Berg
E. Brooks: *The Bessie Smith Companion: a Critical and Detailed Appreciation of the Recordings* (Wheathampstead, nr St. Albans, England, and New York, 1982)
W. Broonzy and Y. Bruynoghe: *Big Bill: mes blues, ma guitare et moi* (Brussels, 1955, rev. and enlarged 2/1987 as *Big Bill Blues*; Eng. orig. pubd as *Big Bill Blues*, London, 1955) [autobiography of Big Bill Broonzy]
J. Broven: *South to Louisiana: the Music of the Cajun Bayous* (Gretna, LA, 1983) [incl. discography]
——: *Walking to New Orleans: the Story of New Orleans Rhythm and Blues* (Bexhill-on-Sea, England, 1974; Gretna, LA, 1983, as *Rhythm & Blues in New Orleans*) [incl. discography]
C. Brown, see R. Brown
L. W. Brown: *Amiri Baraka* (Boston, 1980)
M. Brown: *Recollections: Essays, Drawings, Miscellanea* (Frankfurt am Main, Germany, 1984)
R. Brown and C. Brown: *Georgia on my Mind: the Nat Gonella Story* (Horndean, England, 1985)
S. E. Brown: *A Case of Mistaken Identity: the Life and Music of James P. Johnson* (diss., Yale U., 1982); rev. and enlarged as *James P. Johnson: a Case of Mistaken Identity* (Metuchen, NJ, and London, 1986) [incl. R. Hilbert, Jr.: *A James P. Johnson Discography, 1917–1950*]
T. D. Brown: *A History and Analysis of Jazz Drumming to 1942* (diss., U. of Michigan, 1976)
[D. Brubeck] *Biography of Dave Brubeck* (New York, 1972)
H. Brubeck: *Dave Brubeck* (New York, 1961) [BMI pubn; incl. discography]
H. O. Brunn: *The Story of the Original Dixieland Jazz Band* (Baton Rouge, LA, 1960/*R*1977)
Y. Bruynoghe, see W. Broonzy
M. J. Budds: *Jazz in the Sixties: the Expansion of Musical Resources and Techniques* (Iowa City, IA, 1978)
J. V. Buerkle and D. Barker: *Bourbon Street Black: the New Orleans Black Jazzman* (New York, 1973)
J. Bulterman: *The Ramblers Story* (Bussum, Netherlands, 1973)

W. Burckhardt and J. Gerth: *Lester Young: ein Porträt* (Wetzlar, Germany, 1959)
G. Butcher: *Next to a Letter from Home: Major Glenn Miller's Wartime Band* (Edinburgh, 1986) [incl. discography]
R. Byrnside, see C. Hamm
A. Calabrese, see M. Waller
R. Callender and E. Cohen: *Unfinished Dream: the Musical World of Red Callender* (London, 1985) [autobiography of Red Callender]
C. Calloway and B. Rollins: *Of Minnie the Moocher and me* (New York, 1976) [autobiography of Cab Calloway]
D. B. Caplan: *In Township Tonight! South Africa's Black City Music and Theatre* (London and New York, 1985)
A. Caraceni: *Il jazz dalle origini ad oggi* (Milan, 1937, rev. 2/1945)
P. Carles and J.-L. Comolli: *Free Jazz, Black Power* (Paris, 1971)
P. Carles, see also F. Ténot
H. Carmichael: *The Stardust Road* (New York and Toronto, 1946/*R*1969, 1983) [autobiography]
[H. Carmichael] *An Exhibition Honoring the 75th Birthday of Hoagland Howard Carmichael, Ll.B., 1926, D.M., 1972, Indiana University* (Bloomington, IN, 1972) [catalogue]
H. Carmichael and S. Longstreet: *Sometimes I Wonder: the Story of Hoagy Carmichael* (New York, 1965/*R*1976)
I. Carr: *Miles Davis: a Critical Biography* (London and New York, 1982; Ger. trans., Baden-Baden, Germany, 1985) [incl. discography by B. Priestley]
——: *Music Outside: Contemporary Jazz in Britain* (London, 1973)
R. Carr, B. Case, and F. Dellar: *The Hip: Hipsters, Jazz and the Beat Generation* (London and Boston, 1986)
H. Carruth: *Sitting in: Selected Writings on Jazz, Blues, and Related Topics* (Iowa City, IA, 1986)
L. T. Carter: *Eubie Blake: Keys of Memory* (Detroit, 1979)
B. Case, see R. Carr
B. Cash: *An Analysis of the Improvisation Technique of Lester Willis Young, 1936–1942* (thesis, U. of Hull, England, 1982)
V. Castelli and others: *The Bix Bands: a Bix Beiderbecke Disco-biography* (Milan, 1972)
L. Cerri: *Antologia del jazz* (Pisa, Italy, 1955)
——: *Jazz: musica d'oggi* (Milan, 1948)
D. Cerulli, B. Korall, and M. Nasatir, eds.: *The Jazz Word* (New York, 1960) [incl. previously pubd articles]
D. Chamberlain and R. Wilson, eds.: *The Otis Ferguson Reader* (Highland Park, IL, 1982) [colln of previously pubd articles]
J. Chambers: *Milestones*, i: *The Music and Times of Miles Davis to 1960* (Toronto, Buffalo, and London, 1983); ii: *The Music and Times of Miles Davis since 1960* (Toronto, Buffalo, and London, 1985)
R. Charles and D. Ritz: *Brother Ray: Ray Charles' own Story* (New York, 1978)
S. B. Charters: *The Country Blues* (New York and Toronto, 1959)
——: *The Roots of the Blues: an African Search* (Boston and London, 1981)
S. B. Charters and L. Kunstadt: *Jazz: a History of the New York Scene* (Garden City, NY, 1962/*R*1981)
G. Chase, ed.: *The American Composer Speaks: a Historical Anthology, 1770–1965* (n.p. [Baton Rouge, LA], 1966)
G. Cherrington, see S. Traill
J. Chilton: *Billie's Blues: a Survey of Billie Holiday's Career, 1933–1959* (London, 1975) [incl. discography]
——: *Jazz* (Sevenoaks, England, 1979)
——: *A Jazz Nursery: the Story of the Jenkins' Orphanage Bands of Charleston, South Carolina* (London, 1980)
——: *McKinney's Music: a Bio-discography of McKinney's Cotton Pickers* (London, 1978)
——: *Sidney Bechet: the Wizard of Jazz* (London and New York, 1987)
——: *Stomp Off, Let's Go! The Story of Bob Crosby's Bob Cats & Big Band* (London, 1983)
J. Chilton, see also Max Jones
F. Chisenhall, see M. McKee
J. H. Clarke, ed.: *Harlem, U.S.A.* (Berlin, 1964)
W. Claxton: *Jazz West Coast: a Portfolio of Photographs* (Hollywood, CA, 1954)
B. Clayton and N. M. Elliott: *Buck Clayton's Jazz World* (London, 1986) [incl. discography by B. Weir]
P. Clayton, see P. Gammond
M. Clutten, see B. Turner
A. Coeuroy: *Histoire générale du jazz: strette, hot, swing* (Paris, 1942)
A. Coeuroy and A. Schaeffner: *Le jazz* (Paris, 1926)
E. Cohen, see R. Callender
J. Coker: *Improvising Jazz* (Englewood Cliffs, NJ, 1964)
——: *The Jazz Idiom* (Englewood Cliffs, NJ, and London, 1975)
J. Coker and others: *Patterns for Jazz* (Lebanon, IN, 1970)
P. Coker and D. Baker: *Vocal Improvisation: an Instrumental Approach* (Lebanon, IN, 1981) [incl. discography]
B. Coleman: *Trumpet Story: souvenirs d'un grand du jazz* (Paris, 1981 [in Fr. trans.]; Eng. orig., London, in preparation) [autobiography]
S. Colin: *And the Bands Played on* (London, 1980)
——: *Ella: the Life and Times of Ella Fitzgerald* (London, 1986)
D. Coller, see S. Traill
G. Collier: *Inside Jazz* (London, 1973)
——: *Jazz: a Student's and Teacher's Guide* (London, 1975; Ger. trans., Wilhelmshaven, Germany, 1982)
J. L. Collier: *Duke Ellington* (New York and London, 1987)
——: *Louis Armstrong: an American Genius* (New York, 1983, London, 1984, as *Louis Armstrong: a Biography*)
——: *The Making of Jazz: a Comprehensive History* (New York and London, 1978)
L. Collins (autobiography), see F. J. Gillis
S. Combe: *Anleitung zur Improvisation für Schlagzeug* (Mainz, Germany, 1974)
J.-L. Comolli, see P. Carles
E. Condon and R. Gehman, eds.: *Eddie Condon's Treasury of Jazz* (New York, 1956/*R*1975)
E. Condon and H. O'Neal: *The Eddie Condon Scrapbook of Jazz* (New York, 1973)
E. Condon and T. Sugrue: *We Called it Music: a Generation of Jazz* (New York, 1947/*R*1985)
D. R. Connor: *BG off the Record: a Bio-discography of Benny Goodman* (Fairless Hills, PA, 1958, rev. and enlarged [2]/1969 by Connor and W. W. Hicks as *BG on the Record: a Bio-discography of Benny Goodman*, rev. and enlarged [3]/1984 by Connor as *The Record of a Legend: a Bio-discography of Benny Goodman*)
G. Conrad: *Posaunen-Dob: kleine Biographie Walter Dobschinskis* (Menden, Germany, 1983)
C. Cons and G. Von Physter: *Destiny: a Sketch-book from the Lives of Swing Musicians* (Chicago, 1938)
B. Cook: *Listen to the Blues* (New York, 1973, New York and London, 1975) [3 vols.]
G. Cook, see F. C. Taylor
T. Coolman: *The Bass Tradition: Past, Present, Future* (New Albany, IN, 1987)
J. Coryell and L. Friedman: *Jazz-rock Fusion* (New York and London, 1978)
C. Cosmetto: *La vraie musique de jazz: les échos du jazz* (Lausanne, Switzerland, 1945)
R. Cotterrell, ed.: *Orbit: a Jazz Anthology of Articles and Features* (Leicester, England, 1973) [colln of previously pubd articles]
H. Courlander: *Negro Folk Music U.S.A.* (New York and London, 1963)
G. Crane: *Jazz Elements and Formal Compositional Techniques in Third Stream Music* (thesis, Indiana U., 1970)
A. M. Crawford, see R. Denyer
R. Crawford: *Music in the Street* (New Orleans, 1983) [exhibition catalogue]
B. Crosby [and P. Martin]: *Call me Lucky* (New York, 1953) [autobiography of Bing Crosby]
B. Crowther: *Gene Krupa* (Tunbridge Wells, England, and New York, 1987) [incl. discography]
——: *Benny Goodman* (London, 1988)
B. Crowther and M. Pinfold: *The Jazz Singers: from Ragtime to the New Wave* (Poole, England, 1986)
I. Cruickshank: *The Guitar Style of Django Reinhardt and the Gypsies* (Woodcote, nr Reading, England, 1982, rev. and enlarged 2/1985)
M. Cuney-Hare: *Negro Musicians and their Music* (Washington, 1936/*R*1974)
L. Dahl: *Stormy Weather: the Music and Lives of a Century of Jazzwomen* (London, Melbourne, Australia, and New York, 1984)
V. Danca: *Bunny: a Bio-discography of Jazz Trumpeter Bunny Berigan* (Rockford, IL, 1978)
S. Dance: *The World of Count Basie* (New York and London, 1980) [colln of previously pubd interviews]
——: *The World of Duke Ellington* (London and New York, 1970/*R*1981) [colln of previously pubd articles and interviews]
——: *The World of Earl Hines* (New York, 1977) [interviews]
——: *The World of Swing* (New York, 1974) [colln of previously pubd interviews]
S. Dance and others: *Jazz Era: the 'Forties* (London, 1961/*R*1985)
S. F. Dance, J. Asman, and B. Kinnell, eds.: *Jazz Notebook* (Chilwell, nr Newark-on-Trent, England, n.d. [?1945])
S. Dance, see also C. Barnet; M. Ellington; D. Wells
A. Dankworth: *Jazz: an Introduction to its Musical Basis* (London, New York, and Toronto, 1968)
M. Danzi and R. E. Lotz: *American Musician in Germany, 1924–1939* (Schmitten, Germany, 1986) [autobiography of Mike Danzi]
J. Darensbourg: *Telling it Like it is*, ed. P. Vacher (London, 1987; Baton Rouge, LA, 1987, as *Jazz Odyssey: the Autobiography of Joe Darensbourg*)
R. Daschkey, A. Erlewein, and P. E. Weisenborn, eds.: *1969–1984: 15 Jahre Jazz in Dortmund* (Dortmund, Germany, 1984)
A. M. Dauer: *Jazz, die magische Musik: ein Leitfaden durch den Jazz* (Bremen, Germany, 1961)
——: *Der Jazz: seine Ursprünge und seine Entwicklung* (Kassel, Germany, 1958, 3/1977)
——: *Tradition afrikanischer Blasorchester und Entstehung des Jazz* (Graz, Austria, 1985)
J. David: *Le jazz et les hommes d'aujourd'hui* (Brussels, 1946)
J. R. T. Davies and L. Wright: *Morton's Music* (London, 1968)
F. Davis: *In the Moment: Jazz in the 1980s* (New York, and Oxford, England, 1986) [colln of previously pubd articles]
N. Davis: *Writings in Jazz* (Dubuque, IA, 2/1978, 3/1985)

N. T. Davis: *Charlie Parker's Kansas City Environment and its Effects on his Later Life* (diss., Wesleyan U., 1974)
U. B. Davis: *The Afro-American Musician and Writer in Paris during the 1950s and 1960s: a Study of Kenny Clarke, Donald Byrd, Chester Himes, and James Baldwin* (diss., U. of Pittsburgh, 1983) [incl. oral history material]
D. D. Deakins: *Cylinder Records* (Bombay, 1956, 2/1958)
R. T. Deal, see B. Amstell
W. Dean-Myatt, see R. M. Sudhalter
C. Delaunay: *Delaunay's Dilemma: de la peinture au jazz* (Mâcon, France, 1985)
——: *De la vie et du jazz* (Lausanne, Switzerland, 1939, 2/1941)
——: *Django, mon frère* (Paris, 1968)
——: *Django Reinhardt: souvenirs* (Paris, 1954; Eng. trans., London, 1961/R1981, 1982, rev. 2/1981) [incl. discography]
——: *Hot Iconography* (Paris, 1939)
——: *Sidney Bechet* (Paris, 1963)
——: *Souvenirs* (Lausanne, Switzerland, 1954)
C. Delaunay and P. du Peuty: *Noirs au blanc: images de jazzmen* (Paris, 1986) [portraits]
T. S. DeLay, Jr.: *An Historical Study of the Armed Forces Radio Service to 1946* (diss., U. of Southern California, 1951)
F. Dellar, see R. Carr
T. DeLong: *Pops: Paul Whiteman, King of Jazz* (Piscataway, nr New Brunswick, NJ, 1983)
D. DeMicheal, see G. Lees
R. S. Demory, see D. D. Megill
R. Denyer, I. Guillory, and A. M. Crawford: *The Guitar Handbook* (London and Sydney, 1982)
S. Deveaux: *Jazz in Transition: Coleman Hawkins and Howard McGhee, 1935–1945* (diss., U. of California, Berkeley, 1985)
D. Dexter, Jr.: *Jazz Cavalcade: the Inside Story of Jazz* (New York, 1946/R1977)
——: *The Jazz Story: from the '90s to the '60s* (Englewood Cliffs, NJ, 1964)
H. Dial: *All this Jazz about Jazz: the Autobiography of Harry Dial* (Chigwell, England, 1984)
C. Díaz Ayala: *Musica cubana del areyto a la nueva trova* (San Juan, PR, 1981)
H. J. Dietzel and H. H. Lange: *Stan Kenton* (Berlin, 1959) [H. J. Dietzel: *Stan Kenton: Biography* and H. H. Lange: *Stan Kenton: Discography* bound together]
J. Distler: *Art Tatum* (New York, 1981)
Dixon, see Giltrap
B. Dixon: *L'opéra: a Collection of Letters, Writings, Musical Scores, Drawings, and Photographs*, i: *1967–1986* (in preparation)
R. M. W. Dixon and J. Godrich: *Recording the Blues* (London, 1970)
B. Dobbins: *The Contemporary Jazz Pianist: a Comprehensive Approach to Keyboard Improvisation* (Jamestown, RI, 1978, 2/1984)
W. Dodds and L. Gara: *The Baby Dodds Story* (Los Angeles, 1959)
R. Dollase, M. Rusenberg, and H. J. Stollenwerk: *Das Jazzpublikum: zur Sozialpsychologie einer kulturellen Minderheit* (Mainz, Germany, and London, 1978)
J. M. Doran: *Erroll Garner: the Most Happy Piano* (Metuchen, NJ, and London, 1985) [incl. discography]
M. Dorigné: *La guerre du jazz* (Paris, 1948)
——: *Jazz*, i: *Les origines du jazz: le style Nouvelle-Orléans et ses prolongements* (Paris, 1968)
——: *M.J.C. valise culturelle sur le jazz* (Paris, 1967) [pubn of Fédération des Maisons de Jeunes et de la Culture]
L. Dorůžka and I. Poledňák: *Československý jazz: minulost a přítomnost* [Czech jazz, past and present] (Prague, 1967) [with Eng. summary]
Down Beat Jazz Record Reviews, see G. Lees
Down Beat's Yearbook of Swing, see P. E. Miller
E. Dreyer, see L. Saxon
F. Driggs and H. Lewine: *Black Beauty, White Heat: a Pictorial History of Classic Jazz, 1920–1950* (New York, 1982)
R. D'Rozario: *North Sea Jazz Festival, 1976–1985* (The Hague, 1985) [photographs]
W. Dufty, see B. Holiday
J. Durante and J. Kofoed: *Nightclubs* (New York, London, and Toronto, 1931)
F. Dutton, see S. Traill
C. Easton: *Straight Ahead: the Story of Stan Kenton* (New York, 1973)
G. Eells, see A. O'Day
H. Eklund and L. Lindström: *Jazzen i Stockholm, 1920–1960* (Stockholm, 1983)
D. Ellington: *Music is my Mistress* (Garden City, NJ, 1973; index by H. F. Huon separately pubd, Melbourne, Australia, n.d. [?1977], rev. 2/1982) [autobiography of Duke Ellington]
M. Ellington and S. Dance: *Duke Ellington in Person: an Intimate Memoir* (Boston and London, 1978; Ger. trans., Stuttgart, Germany, and Vienna, 1980)
N. M. Elliott, see B. Clayton
R. Ellison: *Shadow and Act* (New York, 1964)
L. F. Emery: *Black Dance in the United States from 1619 to 1970* (Palo Alto, CA, 1972)
G. Endress: *Jazz Podium: Musiker über sich selbst* (Stuttgart, Germany, 1980)
A. Erlewein, see R. Daschkey
Esquire's Jazz Book, see E. Anderson; P. E. Miller
Esquire's World of Jazz, see J. Poling
Ethnic Recordings in America: a Neglected Heritage: Washington 1977 (Washington, 1982) [pubn of the American Folklife Center, Library of Congress]
P. R. Evans, see R. M. Sudhalter
D. Ewen: *All the Years of American Popular Music* (Englewood Cliffs, NJ, 1977)
R. Fark: *Die missachtete Botschaft: publizistische Aspekte des Jazz im soziokulturellen Wandel* (Berlin, 1971)
J. W. Farrell, see W. L. Grossman
L. Feather: *The Book of Jazz: a Guide to the Entire Field* (New York, 1957, 2/1965 as *The Book of Jazz from Then till Now: a Guide to the Entire Field*)
——: *The Encyclopedia Yearbook of Jazz* (New York, 1956)
——: *From Satchmo to Miles* (New York, 1972)
——: *Inside Be-bop* (New York, 1949/R1977 as *Inside Jazz*)
——: *The Jazz Years: Earwitness to an Era* (London and New York, 1986)
——: *Modern Jazz: an Exciting Story of the Past 20 Years* (Los Angeles, 1958)
——: *The New Yearbook of Jazz* (New York, 1958)
——: *The Passion for Jazz* (New York, 1980)
——: *The Pleasures of Jazz: Leading Performers on their Lives, their Music, their Contemporaries* (New York, 1976)
L. Feather and J. Tracy: *Laughter from the Hip* (New York, 1963/R1979 as *Laughter from the Hip: the Lighter Side of Jazz*)
L. Feather, see also Max Jones
L. Feigin, ed.: *Russian Jazz: New Identity* (London, 1985)
E. Ferand: *Die Improvisation in der Jazzmusik: eine entwicklungsgeschichtliche und psychologische Untersuchung* (Zurich, 1938)
O. Ferguson, see D. Chamberlain
G. Fernett: *Swing Out: Great Negro Jazz Bands* (Midland, MI, 1970)
G. Filtgen and M. Ausserbauer: *John Coltrane: sein Leben, seine Musik, seine Schallplatten* (Gauting, Germany, 1983)
G. Filtgen, see also H. Weber
S. W. Finkelstein: *Jazz: a People's Music* (New York, 1948/R1975)
T. Fitterling: *Thelonious Monk: sein Leben, seine Musik, seine Schallplatten* (Waakirchen, nr Bad Tölz, Germany, 1987)
T. Fletcher: *100 Years of the Negro in Show Business* (New York, 1954/R1984)
H. N. Flint, see M. A. Hood
D. Flower, see S. Bechet
J. Flower: *Moonlight Serenade: a Bio-discography of the Glenn Miller Civilian Band* (New Rochelle, NY, 1972)
O. Flückiger: *John Gordon, Trombone Master* (Reinach, nr Basle, Switzerland, 1982)
D. Fontaine: *Father Time: a Biography of Art Blakey* (in preparation)
J. Foose, see J. Berry
J. Fordham: *Let's Join Hands and Contact the Living: Ronnie Scott and his Club* (London, 1986)
R. C. Foreman, Jr.: *Jazz and Race Records, 1920–32: their Origins and their Significance for the Record Industry and Society* (diss., U. of Illinois, 1968)
P. Foster, T. Stoddard, and R. Russell: *Pops Foster: the Autobiography of a New Orleans Jazzman* (Berkeley, CA, Los Angeles, and London, 1971) [incl. discography by B. Rust]
P. Fountain and B. Neely: *A Closer Walk: the Pete Fountain Story* (Chicago, 1972)
C. Fox: *Fats Waller* (London, 1960); repr. in *Kings of Jazz*, ed. S. Green (South Brunswick, NJ, and New York, 1978)
——: *Jazz in Perspective* (London, 1969)
C. Fox and V. Wilmer: *The Jazz Scene* (London, 1972)
T. Fox: *Showtime at the Apollo* (New York, 1983)
V. Franchini: *Lester Young* (Milan, 1961)
A. Francis: *Jazz* (Paris, 1958; rev. Eng. trans. by Martin Williams, New York and London, 1960/R1976)
A. V. Frankenstein: *Syncopating Saxophones* (Chicago, 1925)
A. Fraser, see D. Gillespie
W. A. Fraser: *Jazzology: a Study of the Tradition in which Jazz Musicians Learn to Improvise* (diss., U. of Pennsylvania, 1983)
B. Freeman: *If you Know of a Better Life, Please Tell me* (Dublin, 1976) [autobiography of Bud Freeman]
——: *You don't Look like a Musician* (Detroit, 1974) [autobiography of Bud Freeman]
C. Friedman and G. Giddins: *A Moment's Notice: Portraits of American Jazz Musicians* (New York and London, 1983)
L. Friedman, see J. Coryell
P. Gammond: *Duke Ellington* (London, 1987) [incl. discography]
P. Gammond, ed.: *The Decca Book of Jazz* (London, 1958)
——: *Duke Ellington: his Life and Music* (London and New York, 1958/R1977)
P. Gammond and P. Clayton: *Fourteen Miles on a Clear Night* (London, 1966)
L. Gara, see W. Dodds
M. Gardner, see P. Klaasse
G. Garlick, see C. Wareing
H. R. Gee: *Saxophone Soloists and their Music, 1844–1985* (Bloomington, IN, 1986)
R. Gehman, see E. Condon
D. Gelly: *Lester Young* (Tunbridge Wells, England, 1984)

D. George: *The Real Duke Ellington* (London, 1982)
M. Gerow, see P. O. W. Tanner
J. Gerth, see W. Burckhardt
G. Giddins: *Celebrating Bird: the Triumph of Charlie Parker* (New York, 1987)
——: *Rhythm-a-ning: Jazz Tradition and Innovation in the '80s* (New York, and Oxford, England, 1985) [colln of previously pubd articles]
——: *Riding on a Blue Note: Jazz and American Pop* (New York, and Oxford, England, 1981) [colln of previously pubd articles]
G. Giddins, see also C. Friedman
W. G. Gilbert: *Rumbamuziek: volksmuziek van de midden-amerikaansche negers* (The Hague, n.d. [?1947])
W. G. Gilbert and C. Poustochkine: *Jazzmuziek: inleiding tot de volksmuziek der noord-amerikaansche negers* (The Hague, 1939, rev. 2/1948)
D. Gillespie and A. Fraser: *To be, nor not . . . to Bop: Memoirs* (Garden City, NY, 1979; Ger. trans., Vienna, 1984) [autobiography of Dizzy Gillespie]
A. V. Gillet: *Louis A. Mitchell: bio-disco-bibliographie* (Brussels, 1966)
C. Gillett: *The Sound of the City: the Rise of Rock and Roll* (New York, 1970, rev. and enlarged 2/1983)
——: *Making Tracks: Atlantic Records and the Growth of a Multi-billion-dollar Industry* (London, 1975)
F. J. Gillis and J. W. Miner, eds.: *Oh, didn't he Ramble: the Life Story of Lee Collins* (Urbana, IL, Chicago, and London, 1974) [incl. discography]
Giltrap and Dixon: *Kid Ory* (London, n.d. [?1958])
I. Gitler: *Jazz Masters of the Forties* (New York, 1966/*R*1983 with discography)
——: *Swing to Bop: an Oral History of the Transition in Jazz in the 1940s* (New York, and Oxford, England, 1985)
J. Giuffre: *Jazz Phrasing and Interpretation: Aspects of Jazz Performance, Analyzed for the Player . . . a Personal Approach* (New York, 1969)
J. J. Gjedsted: *Montmartre gennem 10 år* [The Montmartre club over ten years] (Copenhagen, 1986)
M. Glaser and S. Grappelli: *Jazz Violin* (New York and elsewhere, 1981) [incl. transcrs.]
R. J. Gleason: *Celebrating the Duke, and Louis, Bessie, Billie, Bird, Carmen, Miles, Dizzy, and other Heroes* (Boston and Toronto, 1975)
R. J. Gleason, ed.: *Jam Session: an Anthology of Jazz* (New York and London, 1958)
J. Godbolt: *All this and Many a Dog: Memoirs of a Loser/Pessimist* (London, 1987)
——: *All this and 10%* (London, 1976)
——: *A History of Jazz in Britain, 1919–50* (London, Melbourne, Australia, and New York, 1984)
C. Goddard: *Jazz away from Home* (London and New York, 1979)
J. Godrich, see R. M. W. Dixon
U. Goeman, see P. Klaasse
R. Goffin: *Aux frontières du jazz* (Paris, 1932)
——: *Jazz: from the Congo to the Metropolitan* (Garden City, NY, 1944/*R*1975, rev. [2]/1946 as *Jazz: from Congo to Swing* [in Eng. trans.]; Fr. orig. pubd as *Histoire du jazz*, Montreal, 1945, rev. [2]/1948 as *Nouvelle histoire du jazz: du Congo au bebop*)
——: *Louis Armstrong: le roi du jazz* (Paris, 1947; Eng. trans., New York, 1947/*R*1977, as *Horn of Plenty: the Story of Louis Armstrong*)
——: *La Nouvelle-Orléans: capitale du jazz* (New York, 1946)
J. Goggin: *Turk Murphy: Just for the Record* (San Leandro, CA, 1982) [incl. discography]
J. Goldberg: *Jazz Masters of the Fifties* (New York and London, 1965/*R*1980)
B. Goldblatt: *Newport Jazz Festival: the Illustrated History* (New York, 1977)
M. Goldstein, see V. Skaarup
[B. Goodman] *Benny, King of Swing: a Pictorial Biography Based on Benny Goodman's Personal Archives* (London and New York, 1979; Ger. trans., Wilhelmshaven, Germany, 1984)
B. Goodman and I. Kolodin: *The Kingdom of Swing* (New York, 1939; Ger. trans. as *Mein Weg zum Jazz: eine Autobiographie*, Zurich, 1961)
M. Gordon: *Live at the Village Vanguard* (New York, 1980)
R. Gordon: *Jazz West Coast: the Los Angeles Jazz Scene of the 1950s* (London and New York, 1986)
W. P. Gottlieb: *The Golden Age of Jazz* (London, Melbourne, Australia, and New York, 1979)
L. Gourse: *Every Day: the Story of Joe Williams* (London, Melbourne, Australia, and New York, 1985) [incl. discography]
——: *Louis' Children: American Jazz Singers* (New York, 1984)
J. de Graef: *Jazz in Belgie: de swingperiode (1935–1947)* (Antwerp, Belgium, 1980)
Les grandes signatures: album photo (Paris, 1987) [special pubn by *Jazz hot*]
A. Granholm: *Finnish Jazz* (Helsinki, 1974, rev. and enlarged by M. Konttinen 2/1982, rev. and enlarged by J.-P. Vuorela 3/1986)
N. Granz: *The Jazz Scene* (New York, 1949)
S. Grappelli, see M. Glaser
B. Grauer, Jr., see O. Keepnews
B. Green: *Drums in my Ears* (New York and London, 1973)
——: *The Reluctant Art: Five Studies in the Growth of Jazz* (London, 1962)
J. Green: *Glenn Miller and the Age of Swing* (London, 1976)
J. P. Green: *Edmund Thornton Jenkins: the Life and Times of an American Black Composer, 1894–1926* (Westport, CT, and London, 1982)
J. P. Green, see also L. Thompson
S. Green, ed.: *Kings of Jazz* (South Brunswick, NJ, and New York, 1978)
M. C. Gridley: *Jazz Styles* (Englewood Cliffs, NJ, 1978, rev. 2/1985 as *Jazz Styles: History and Analysis*, with suppl. *Instructor's Manual and Discography*)
W. Grieder: *Hazy Osterwald Story: Musik ist ein Trumpf* (Zurich, 1961)
N. Griffin: *To be or not to Bop* (New York, 1948)
K. Grime: *Jazz at Ronnie Scott's* (London, 1979)
——: *Jazz Voices* (London, 1983) [incl. interviews]
W. L. Grossman and J. W. Farrell: *The Heart of Jazz* (New York, 1956/*R*1976)
A. Groves: *Bud Powell* (Tunbridge Wells, England, in preparation) [incl. discography]
J. P. Guckin, see F. Kaufman
I. Guillory, see R. Denyer
J. Guinle: *Jazz panorama* (Rio de Janeiro, 1953)
The Guitar Player Book (Saratoga, nr Los Gatos, CA, and New York, 1978, 2/1979) [colln of previously pubd articles]
F. Gulda: *Worte zur Musik* (Munich, 1971)
R. Hadlock: *Jazz Masters of the Twenties* (New York, 1965/*R*1985)
O. Häme: *Rytmin voittokulku* [The triumph of rhythm] (Helsinki, 1949)
C. Hamm, B. Nettl, and R. Byrnside: *Contemporary Music and Music Cultures* (Englewood Cliffs, NJ, 1975)
J. Hammond and I. Townsend: *John Hammond on Record: an Autobiography* (New York, 1977)
D. A. Handy: *The International Sweethearts of Rhythm* (Metuchen, NJ, and London, 1983)
W. C. Handy: *Father of the Blues: an Autobiography*, ed. A. Bontemps (New York, 1941, 4/1970)
C. Hansen, see A. Hodes
J. Hannusch: *I Hear you Knockin': the Sound of New Orleans Rhythm and Blues* (Ville Platte, LA, 1985)
R. Harris: *Jazz* (London, 1952, 5/1957)
S. Harris, see C. E. B. Bernhardt
D. D. Harrison: *Black Pearls: Blues Queens of the 1920s* (New Brunswick, NJ, 1988)
M. Harrison: *Charlie Parker* (London, 1960); repr. in *Kings of Jazz*, ed. S. Green (South Brunswick, NJ, and New York, 1978)
——: *A Jazz Retrospect* (Newton Abbot, England, 1976, rev. 2/1977)
M. Harrison, see also P. Oliver
P. C. Harrison, see C. Stewart
D. Hartmann, see D. Salemann
J. Haskins: *The Cotton Club* (New York, 1977)
——: *Queen of the Blues: a Biography of Dinah Washington* (New York, 1987) [incl. discography]
J. Haskins and K. Benson: *Nat King Cole* (New York, 1984)
J. Haskins, see also Bricktop
J. E. Hasse: *The Creation and Dissemination of Indianapolis Ragtime, 1897–1930* (diss., Indiana U., 1981)
——: *The Works of Hoagy Carmichael* (Cincinnati, 1983)
J. E. Hasse, ed.: *Ragtime: its History, Composers, and Music* (New York and London, 1985)
H. Hawes and D. Asher: *Raise up off me: a Portrait of Hampton Hawes* (New York and Toronto, 1974; Ger. trans. as *Ganz tief Luft holen: Autobiographie eines Jazzmusikers*, Frankfurt am Main, Germany, 1983)
G. Haydon and D. Marks, eds.: *Repercussions: a Celebration of Afro-American Music* (London, 1985)
C. Hayes: *The Dance Band Diary* (Ventnor, England, 1985–)
F. Hedman: *Alice Babs: berättelsen om artisten Alice "Babs" Nilson* [Alice Babs: the story of the artist Alice "Babs" Nilson] (Stockholm, 1975)
A. Heerkens: *Jazz* (Baarn, Netherlands, 1956)
K. Gert zur Heide: *Deep South Piano: the Story of Little Brother Montgomery* (London, 1970)
J. Hélian: *Les grands orchestres de music hall en France* (Paris, 1984)
H. Hellhund: *Cool Jazz: Grundzüge seiner Entstehung und Entwicklung* (Mainz, Germany, 1985)
N. Hellström, ed.: *Jazz: historia, teknik, utövare* (Stockholm, 1940)
T. J. Hennessey: *From Jazz to Swing: Black Jazz Musicians and their Music, 1917–1935* (diss., Northwestern U., 1973)
N. Hentoff: *The Jazz Life* (New York and London, 1961/*R*1975) [incl. previously pubd articles]
——: *John Lewis* (New York, 1960)
N. Hentoff and A. J. McCarthy, eds.: *Jazz: New Perspectives on the History of Jazz by Twelve of the World's Foremost Jazz Critics and Scholars* (New York and Toronto, 1959/*R*1974)
N. Hentoff and R. Sanjek: *Charlie Parker* (New York, 1960) [list of compositions]
N. Hentoff, see also N. Shapiro; D. Stock
D. A. Herfort: *A History of the National Association of Jazz Educators and a Description of its Role in American Music Education, 1968–1978* (diss., U. of Houston, 1979)
H. Herling: *Capt. John Handy: kleine Studie über Leben und Werk sowie seinen Einfluss auf die heutige "New Orleans Revival Jazz"-scene* (Menden, Germany, 1978) [incl. discography]
M. L. Hester: *Going to Kansas City* (Sherman, TX, 1980)

B. Heuvelmans: *De la bamboula au be-bop: esquisse de l'évolution de la musique de jazz* (Paris, 1951)
W. W. Hicks, see D. R. Connor
R. Hilbert, Jr., see S. E. Brown
C. Hillman: *Bunk Johnson* (Tunbridge Wells, England, in preparation) [incl. discography]
R. Himsel: *Bilder av jazz* (Växjö, Sweden, 1983)
M. Hinton and D. Berger: *Bass Lines: the Stories and Photographs of Milt Hinton* (Philadelphia, 1988)
J.-R. Hippenmeyer: *Le jazz en Suisse, 1930–1970* (Yverdon, Switzerland, 1971)
——: *Sidney Bechet* (Geneva, 1980)
A. Z. Hirsch, Jr.: *Black and Tan Fantasy: the Sociology of Jazz Music* (MS, 1946, *NN-Sc*)
T. Hirschmann: *Untersuchungen zu den Kompositionen von Charlie Parker* (diss., U. of Mainz, Germany, 1982)
E. J. E. Hobsbawm, see F. Newton
W. Hobson: *American Jazz Music* (New York, 1939/*R*1976, rev. 2/1941)
A. Hodeir: *Hommes et problèmes du jazz, suivi de La religion du jazz* (Paris, 1954; Eng. trans., rev. Hodeir, as *Jazz: its Evolution and Essence*, New York, 1956/*R*1975)
——: *Introduction à la musique de jazz* (Paris, 1948)
——: *Le jazz, cet inconnu* (Paris, 1945)
——: *Les mondes du jazz* (Paris, 1970; Eng. trans., New York, 1972)
——: *Toward Jazz* (New York, 1962/*R*1976) [in Eng. trans.]
A. Hodes and C. Hansen, eds.: *Selections from the Gutter: Jazz Portraits from "The Jazz Record"* (Berkeley, CA, Los Angeles, and London, 1977)
G. Hoefer, see W. Smith
F. Hoffman: *Henry "Red" Allen in England, 1964, 1966, 1967: an Excerpt out a Future Henry "Red" Allen Bio-disco, 1908–1967* (MS, Berlin, n.d.) [unpubd typescript]
——: *Henry "Red" Allen (Jan. 7th 1980 – Apr. 17th 1967)/J. C. Higginbotham (May 11th 1906 – May 26th 1973): Compiled Negro-press Material about Bands with Henry Red Allen, 1927–1940* (MS, Berlin, 1979, rev. 1982) [unpubd typescript]
——: *Henry "Red" Allen (Jan. 7th 1908 – Apr. 17th 1967)/J. C. Higginbotham (May 11th 1906 – May 26th 1973): Discography, 1927–1968: Excerpt out a Future "Red Allen Bio-disco"* (MS, Berlin, 1982) [unpubd typescript]
B. Holiday and W. Dufty: *Lady Sings the Blues* (Garden City, NY, 1956/*R*1973 with discography by A. J. McCarthy, 1984; Ger. trans., Hamburg, Germany, 1983) [autobiography of Billie Holiday]
L. D. Holmes and J. W. Thomson: *Jazz Greats: Getting Better with Age* (New York, 1986) [colln of interviews]
M. A. Hood and H. N. Flint, eds.: *"Jelly Roll" Morton: the Original Mr. Jazz* (New York, 1975)
R. J. Hopf: *Sidekicks of the Swing Era* (Menden, Germany, 1981)
J. Hornsby, see G. Martin
R. Horricks: *Count Basie and his Orchestra: its Music and its Musicians* (London and New York, 1957)
——: *Dizzy Gillespie and the Be-bop Revolution* (Tunbridge Wells, England, and New York, 1984) [incl. discography by T. Middleton]
——: *Gerry Mulligan's Ark* (London, 1986) [incl. discography by T. Middleton]
——: *Stephane Grappelli, or The Violin with Wings: a Profile* (Tunbridge Wells, England, and New York, 1983) [incl. discography]
——: *Svengali, or The Orchestra Called Gil Evans* (Tunbridge Wells, England, and New York, 1984) [incl. discography by T. Middleton]
R. Horricks and others: *These Jazzmen of our Time* (London, 1959)
R. Horricks, see also A. Morgan
R. Hoskins: *Louis Armstrong: Biography of a Musician* (Los Angeles, 1979) [incl. discography and list of films]
J. A. Howard: *The Improvisational Techniques of Art Tatum* (diss., Case Western Reserve U., 1978)
M. Howe: *Blue Jazz* (Bristol, England, 1934)
F. A. Howlett: *An Introduction to Art Tatum's Performance Approaches: Composition, Improvisation, and Melodic Variation* (diss., Cornell U., 1983)
H. C. Hudson, see D. N. Baker
L. Hughes: *The Big Sea: an Autobiography* (New York, 1945)
——: *Famous Negro Music Makers* (New York, 1955)
——: *The First Book of Jazz* (New York, 1954, rev. 2/1962)
——: *I Wonder as I Wander* (New York, 1964)
L. Hughes and M. Meltzer: *Black Music: a Pictorial History of the Negro in American Entertainment* (Englewood Cliffs, NJ, 1967)
S. Hughes: *Opening Bars* (London, 1946) [autobiography]
——: *Second Movement* (London, 1951) [autobiography]
V. E. Hughes, see M. Kaminsky
G. Hunkel: *Western Swing and Country Jazz: eine Einführung mit Kurzporträts über Bob Wills und Milton Brown* (Menden, Germany, 1983)
H. F. Huon, see D. Ellington
A. Ingram: *Wes Montgomery* (Gateshead, England, 1985) [bio-discography]
A. Jackson: *The World of Big Bands: the Sweet and Swinging Years* (New York, 1977)
A. Jaffe: *Jazz Theory* (Dubuque, IA, 1983)
P. Jalkanen: *Ravintola: ja tanssiorkesterilaitoksen murros Helsingssa 1920–luvulla* [Changes in the dance orchestra in Helsinki in the 1920s] (diss., U. of Helsinki, 1975)
B. James: *Billie Holiday* (Tunbridge Wells, England, 1984)
——: *Bix Beiderbecke* (London, 1959); repr. in *Kings of Jazz*, ed. S. Green (South Brunswick, NJ, and New York, 1978)
——: *Coleman Hawkins* (Tunbridge Wells, England, 1984)
——: *Essays on Jazz* (London, 1961/*R*1985)
M. James: *Dizzy Gillespie* (London, 1959); repr. in *Kings of Jazz*, ed. S. Green (South Brunswick, NJ, and New York, 1978)
——: *Miles Davis* (London, 1961); repr. in *Kings of Jazz*, ed. S. Green (South Brunswick, NJ, and New York, 1978)
——: *Ten Modern Jazzmen: an Appraisal of the Recorded Work of Ten Modern Jazzmen* (London, 1960)
H. Janis, see R. Blesh
D. A. Jasen and T. J. Tichenor: *Rags and Ragtime: a Musical History* (New York, 1978)
Jazz on Television (New York, 1985) [exhibition catalogue of the Museum of Broadcasting]
Jazz sous les pommiers, 83–84: festivals de Coutances (Coutances, France, n.d. [?1985])
D. Jewell: *Duke: a Portrait of Duke Ellington* (London and New York, 1977, 2/1978)
C. Johnson: *Paul Whiteman: a Chronology* (Williamstown, MA, 1977, rev. 2/1979)
J. W. Johnson: *Black Manhattan* (New York, 1930)
C. Jones: *The Bob Crosby Band* (London, 1946)
——: *Jazz in New York* (London, 1944)
——: *J. C. Higginbotham* (London, 1944)
——: *New Orleans and Chicago Jazz* (London, 1944)
L. Jones: *Black Music* (New York, 1967/*R*1980)
——: *Blues People: Negro Music in White America* (New York, 1963)
L. Jones: other works listed under alternative name, Amiri Baraka
Max Jones: *Jazz Photo Album: a History of Jazz in Pictures* (London, 1947)
——: *Talking Jazz* (London, 1987) [colln of previously pubd interviews]
Max Jones and J. Chilton: *Louis: the Louis Armstrong Story, 1900–1971* (London, 1971)
Max Jones and A. McCarthy: *A Tribute to Huddie Ledbetter* (London, 1946)
Max Jones, J. Chilton, and L. Feather: *Salute to Satchmo* (London, 1970)
Max Jones, see also A. McCarthy
T. Jones, see J. Berry
B. Jørgensen: *Leo Mathisen* (Copenhagen, 1962)
E. Jost: *Europas Jazz, 1960–1980* (Frankfurt am Main, Germany, 1987)
——: *Free Jazz* (Graz, Austria, 1974)
——: *Jazzmusiker: Materialen zur Soziologie der afro-amerikanischen Musik* (Frankfurt am Main, Germany, Berlin, and Vienna, 1981)
——: *Sozialgeschichte des Jazz in den USA* (Frankfurt am Main, Germany, 1982)
J. Jungermann: *Ella Fitzgerald: ein Porträt* (Wetzlar, Germany, 1960)
E. J. Kahn: *The Voice* (New York, 1947)
K. Kaisla, see T. Kärki
I. Kamin, see J. Lyons
M. Kaminsky and V. E. Hughes: *My Life in Jazz* (New York, 1963) [autobiography of Max Kaminsky]
T. Kärki and K. Kaisla: *Rytmimusiikki* (Turku, Finland, 1946)
T. Kärki, see also M. Niiniluoto
F. Kaufman and J. P. Guckin: *The African Roots of Jazz* (Los Angeles, 1979)
O. Keepnews and B. Grauer, Jr.: *A Pictorial History of Jazz: People and Places from New Orleans to Modern Jazz* (New York, 1956, rev. 2/1966/*R*1981)
B. D. Kernfeld: *Adderley, Coltrane, and Davis at the Twilight of Bebop: the Search for Melodic Coherence (1958–59)* (diss., Cornell U., 1981)
F. Kerschbaumer: *Miles Davis: stilkritische Untersuchungen zur musikalischen Entwicklung seines Personalstils* (Graz, Austria, 1978) [incl. discography]
R. Kimball and W. Bolcom: *Reminiscing with Sissle and Blake* (New York, 1973)
N. King, see C. Mingus
B. Kinnell, see S. F. Dance
E. Kirkeby, D. P. Schiedt, and S. Traill: *Ain't Misbehavin': the Story of Fats Waller* (London and New York, 1966; Ger. trans., Ravensburg, Germany, 1981)
E. Kjellberg: *Svensk jazzhistoria: en översikt* [Swedish jazz history: an overview] (Stockholm, 1985)
P. Klaasse, M. Gardner, and J. Bernlef: *Jamsession: Portraits of Jazz and Blues Musicians Drawn on the Scene* (Weesp, Netherlands, 1984; Ger. trans., with discography by U. Goeman, Königstein, Germany, 1984)
H. Kleinhout and W. van Eyle: *The Wallace Bishop Story* (Alphen aan de Rijn, Netherlands, 1981)
H. A. Kmen: *Music in New Orleans: the Formative Years, 1791–1841* (Baton Rouge, LA, 1966)
Z. Knauss: *Conversations with Jazz Musicians* (Detroit, 1977)
K. Knox and G. Lindkvist: *Jazz amour affair: en bok om Lars Gullin* (Stockholm, 1986) [incl. discography]
F. W. Koebner: *Jazz und Shimmy: Brevier der neuesten Tänze* (Berlin, 1921)

D. Koechlin: *50 ans de jazz avec Barney Bigard* (n.p. [Darnetal, France], n.d. [1979])
K. Koenig: *Jazz Map of New Orleans* (New Orleans, 1985) [annotated map]
——: *"Just a Closer Walk": the Walker's Guide to Jazz's History in the French Quarter* (New Orleans, 1988)
J. Kofoed, see J. Durante
F. J. Kofsky: *Black Nationalism and the Revolution in Music* (New York, 1970; rev. and enlarged as *Black Nationalism and the Revolution in Music: Social Change and Stylistic Development in the Art of John Coltrane and Others, 1954–1967*, diss., U. of Pittsburgh, 1973)
P. Kohler and K. Schacht: *Die Jazzmusiker: zur Soziolologie einer kreativen Randgruppe* (Freiburg, Germany, 1983)
I. Kolodin, see B. Goodman
B. König, ed.: *Jazzrock: Tendenzen einer modernen Musik* (Reinbek, Germany, 1983)
M. Konttinen, see A. Granholm
B. Korall: *The World's Greatest Jazz Band of Yank Lawson and Bob Haggart* (n.p. [Phoenix, AZ], 1973)
B. Korall, see D. Cerulli
P. Krähenbühl: *Der Jazz und seine Menschen: eine soziologische Studie* (Berne and Munich, 1968)
D. H. Kraner and K. Schulz: *Jazz in Austria: historische Entwicklung und Diskographie des Jazz in Österreich* (Graz, Austria, 1972) [texts in Eng. and Ger.]
E. Kraut: *George Lewis: Streifzug durch ein Musiker-Leben* (Menden, Germany, 1980) [incl. discography]
——: *The Revival: Documents of the American Music Sessions, 1940–45* (Arcegno, nr Ascona, Switzerland, 1986) [exhibition catalogue, Festa New Orleans Music, Ascona; texts in Ger. and It.]
E. Kriss: *Barrelhouse and Boogie Piano* (New York and London, 1974) [incl. discography and transcrs.]
S. M. Kristensen: *Hvad jazz* (Copenhagen, 1938)
——: *Jazz og dens problemer* (Copenhagen, 1946)
L. Kuehl and E. Schokert: *Billie Holiday Remembered* (New York, 1973)
H. Kumpf: *Postserielle Musik und Free Jazz: Wechselwirkungen und Parallelen* (Herrenberg, Germany, 1975, rev. 2/1981)
L. Kunstadt, see S. B. Charters
J. Kuzmich, Jr., and L. Bash: *Complete Guide to Instrumental Jazz Instruction: Techniques for Developing a Successful School Jazz Program* (West Nyack, NY, 1984)
G. E. Lambert: *Duke Ellington* (London, 1959); repr. in *Kings of Jazz*, ed. S. Green (South Brunswick, NJ, and New York, 1978)
——: *Johnny Dodds* (London, 1961); repr. in *Kings of Jazz*, ed. S. Green (South Brunswick, NJ, and New York, 1978)
I. Lang: *Jazz in Perspective: the Background of the Blues* (London and elsewhere, 1947/*R*1976)
H. H. Lange: *Jazz in Deutschland: die deutsche Jazz-Chronik, 1900–1960* (Berlin, 1966)
——: *Loring "Red" Nichols: ein Porträt* (Wetzlar, Germany, 1960)
——: *Nick LaRocca: ein Porträt* (Wetzlar, Germany, 1960)
H. H. Lange, see also H. J. Dietzel
M. Laplace: *Portraits of French Jazz Musicians* (Menden, Germany, 1985)
J. LaPorta: *Developing the School Jazz Ensemble* (Boston, 1965)
——: *A Guide to Improvisation* (Boston, 1968)
P. Larkin: *All what Jazz: a Record Diary, 1961–68* (London and New York, 1970) [colln of previously pubd articles]
S. Larson: *Some Aspects of the Album "Out of the Woods" by the Chamber Ensemble "Oregon"* (diss., U. of Oregon, 1981)
G. Lascelles, see S. Traill
A. Laubich and R. Spencer: *Art Tatum: a Guide to his Recorded Music* (Metuchen, NJ, 1982) [bio-discography]
W. F. Lee: *People in Jazz: Jazz Keyboard Improvisors of the 19th and 20th Centuries* (Hialeah, FL, 1984)
——: *Stan Kenton: Artistry in Rhythm* (Los Angeles, 1980) [incl. discography]
G. Lees and D. DeMicheal, eds.: *Down Beat Jazz Record Reviews* (Chicago, 1957–64) [annual colln of reviews pubd in *DB*, 1956–63]
G. Legrand: *Puissances du jazz* (Paris, 1953)
J.-P. Leloir: *Du jazz plein les yeux* (Cagnes-sur-Mer, France, 1983)
N. Leonard: *Jazz and the White Americans: the Acceptance of a New Art Form* (Chicago, London, and Toronto, 1962)
——: *Jazz: Myth and Religion* (New York, and Oxford, England, 1987)
J. Levey: *Basic Jazz Improvisation* (Delaware Water Gap, PA, 1971)
R. Levin, see P. Rivelli
L. Levine: *Black Culture and Black Consciousness: Afro-American Folk Thought from Slavery to Freedom* (London, Oxford, England, and New York, 1977)
L. H. Levy: *The Formalization of New Orleans Jazz Musicians: a Case Study of Organizational Change* (diss., Virginia Polytechnic Institute and State U., 1976)
H. Lewine, see F. Driggs
V. Lewis and T. Barrow: *Music and Maiden Overs: my Showbusiness Life* (London, 1987) [autobiography of Vic Lewis]
R. Leydi: *Sarah Vaughan* (Milan, 1961)
S. R. Lieb: *Mother of the Blues: a Study of Ma Rainey* (Amherst, MA, 1981) [incl. discography]
D. Liebman and others: *Lookout Farm: a Case Study of Improvisation for Small Jazz Group* (n.p., 1978)
G. Lindkvist, see K. Knox
H.-J. Lindner, see B. Noglik
L. Lindström, see H. Eklund
N. Linehan: *Norm Linehan's Australian Jazz Picture Book* (Salisbury, Australia, 1980)
N. Linehan, ed.: *Bob Barnard, Graeme Bell, Bill Haesler, John Sangster, on the Australian Jazz Convention* (?Melbourne, Australia, 1981)
N. Linehan, see also T. McCardell
O. Lington: *Jazz skal der til* [Jazz is what we need] (Copenhagen, 1941)
A. Little: *From Harlem to the Rhine* (New York, 1936)
J. Litweiler: *The Freedom Principle: Jazz after 1958* (New York, 1984)
G. Lock: *Anthony Braxton: Interviews, Notes and Tours* (in preparation)
A. Lomax: *Mister Jelly Roll: the Fortunes of Jelly Roll Morton, New Orleans Creole and "Inventor of Jazz"* (New York, 1950, 2/1973, Fr. trans., Paris, 1964)
S. Longstreet: *The Real Jazz, Old and New* (Baton Rouge, LA, 1956/R1969)
——: *Sportin' House: a History of the New Orleans Sinners, and the Birth of Jazz* (Los Angeles, 1965)
——: *Storyville to Harlem: 50 Years in the Jazz Scene* (New Brunswick, NJ, and London, 1986) [drawings]
S. Longstreet, see also H. Carmichael
T. Lord: *Clarence Williams* (Chigwell, England, 1976) [bio-discography]
R. E. Lotz: *George F. Hirst* (Menden, Germany, 1982) [incl. discography]
——: *Hot Dance Bands in Germany: a Photo Album*, i: *The Prehistory* (Menden, Germany, 1987); ii: *The 1920s* (Menden, 1982); iii: *The 1930s* (in preparation)
R. E. Lotz and I. Pegg, eds.: *Under the Imperial Carpet: Essays in Black History, 1780–1950* (Crawley, England, 1986)
R. E. Lotz, see also H. J. P. Bergmeier; M. Danzi
R. A. Luckey: *A Study of Lester Young and his Influence on his Contemporaries* (diss., U. of Pittsburgh, 1981)
V. Lupo: *Vocal Groups in Modern Jazz, Vocalese: storia, discografia, biografie* (Ferrara, Italy, 1986)
M. Luzzi: *Charlie Mingus* (Rome, 1983)
——: *Uomini e avanguardie jazz* (Milan, 1980)
J. Lyons and I. Kamin: *Dizzy, Duke, the Count, and me: the Story of the Monterey Jazz Festival* (San Francisco, 1978)
L. Lyons: *The Great Jazz Pianists, Speaking of their Lives and Music* (New York, 1983) [incl. interviews and discographies]
L. Lyons and D. Perlo: *A Guide to the Jazz Masters* (in preparation)
H. Lyttelton: *The Best of Jazz*, i: *Basin Street to Harlem: Jazz Masters and Masterpieces, 1917–1930* (London, 1978), ii: *Enter the Giants, 1931–1944* (London, 1981)
——: *I Play as I Please: the Memoirs of an Old Etonian Trumpeter* (London, 1954)
——: *Second Chorus* (London, 1958) [autobiography]
——: *Take it from the Top: an Autobiographical Scrapbook* (London, 1975)
——: *Why no Beethoven?* (London, 1984)
M. M. McBride, see P. Whiteman
T. McCardell: *Jazz Speaks All Languages*, ed. N. Linehan (?Melbourne, Australia, 1985)
A. McCarthy: *Big Band Jazz* (New York and London, 1974)
——: *Coleman Hawkins* (London, 1963); repr. in *Kings of Jazz*, ed. S. Green (South Brunswick, NJ, and New York, 1978)
——: *The Dance Band Era: the Dancing Decades from Ragtime to Swing, 1910–1950* (London, 1971/*R*1982)
——: *Louis Armstrong* (London, 1960); repr. in *Kings of Jazz*, ed. S. Green (South Brunswick, NJ, and New York, 1978)
——: *The Trumpet in Jazz* (London, 1945)
A. McCarthy, ed.: *Jazzbook, 1947* (London, 1947)
——: *Jazzbook, 1955* (London, 1955)
——: *The PL Jazzbook* (London, 1946)
——: *The PL Yearbook of Jazz, 1946* (London, 1946)
A. McCarthy and Max Jones, eds.: *Piano Jazz* (London, 1945)
A. McCarthy, see also N. Hentoff; B. Holiday; Max Jones
P. S. Machlin: *Stride: the Music of Fats Waller* (Boston and London, 1985)
M. McKee and F. Chisenhall: *Beale Street Black and Blue: Life and Music on Black America's Main Street* (Baton Rouge, LA, and London, 1981)
J. F. McKinney: *The Pedagogy of Lennie Tristano* (diss., Fairleigh Dickinson U., 1978)
M. McPartland: *All in Good Time* (New York, and Oxford, England, 1987) [colln of previously pubd articles; incl. autobiography]
B. McRae: *Dizzy Gillespie* (Tunbridge Wells, England, in preparation) [incl. discography]
——: *The Jazz Cataclysm* (London, South Brunswick, NJ, and New York, 1967/R1985)
——: *The Jazz Handbook* (Harlow, England, 1987)
——: *Miles Davis* (London, 1988) [incl. discography]
——: *Ornette Coleman* (London, in preparation)
P. Maier, see A. Schmitz
L. Malson: *Les maîtres du jazz* (Paris, 1952, rev. 6/1972)

W. Manone and P. Vandervoort: *Trumpet on the Wing* (Garden City, NY, 1948) [autobiography of Wingy Manone]
M. L. Mark: *Contemporary Music Education* (New York and London, 1978, rev. 2/1986)
D. Marks, see G. Haydon
D. M. Marquis: *Finding Buddy Bolden, First Man of Jazz: the Journal of a Search* (Goshen, IN, 1978)
——: *In Search of Buddy Bolden, First Man of Jazz* (Baton Rouge, LA, and London, 1978)
G. Martin and J. Hornsby: *All you Need is Ears* (London, 1979)
H. Martin: *Enjoying Jazz* (New York, 1986)
P. Martin, see B. Crosby
R. J. Martinez, ed.: *Portraits of New Orleans Jazz: its People and Places* (Jefferson, LA, 1971)
B. Martyn, see B. Bigard
B. Matthew: *Trad Mad* (London, 1962)
H. J. Mauerer: *The Pete Johnson Story* (New York, and Frankfurt am Main, Germany, 1965) [incl. discography]
W. Mauro: *Louis Armstrong: il re del jazz* (Milan, 1979)
A. Mazzoletti: *Il jazz in Italia: dalle origini al dopoguerra* (Rome, 1983) [incl. discography]
C. G. Herzog zu Mecklenburg: *Stilformen des Jazz*, i: *Vom Ragtime zum Chicago-Stil* (Vienna, 1973) [incl. discography by M. Scheffner]
——: *Stilformen des modernen Jazz*, [ii]: *Vom Swing zum Free Jazz* (Baden-Baden, Germany, 1979) [incl. discography by M. Scheffner]
C. G. Herzog zu Mecklenburg and W. Scheck: *Die Theorie des Blues in modernen Jazz* (Strasbourg, France, and Baden-Baden, Germany, 1963)
D. D. Megill and R. S. Demory: *Introduction to Jazz History* (Englewood Cliffs, NJ, 1984)
D. W. Megill, see P. O. W. Tanner
J. F. Mehegan: *Contemporary Styles for the Jazz Pianist* (New York, n.d. [?1964–70], 2/n.d. [?1980])
——: *Jazz Improvisation*, i: *Tonal and Rhythmic Principles* (New York, 1959); ii: *Jazz Rhythm and the Improvised Line* (New York, 1962); iii: *Swing and Early Progressive Piano Styles* (New York, 1964); iv: *Contemporary Piano Styles* (New York, 1965)
——: *The Jazz Pianist: Studies in the Art and Practice of Jazz Improvisation* (New York, n.d. [?1960–61])
——: *Styles for the Jazz Pianist* (New York, n.d. [?1962–3])
W. F. Mellers: *Music in a New Found Land: Themes and Developments in the History of American Music* (London, 1964/*R*1975)
G. Melly: *Mellymobile, 1970–1982* (London, 1982) [autobiography]
——: *Owning up* (London, 1965) [autobiography]
——: *Revolt into Style: the Pop Arts in Britain* (London, 1970)
——: *Rum, Bum, and Concertina* (London, 1977)
M. Meltzer, see L. Hughes
R. W. S. Mendl: *The Appeal of Jazz* (London, 1927)
D. Meriwether, Jr.: *The Buddy Rich Orchestra and Small Groups* (Spotswood, NJ, 1974, rev. 2/1984 as *We Don't Play Requests: a Musical Biography/Discography of Buddy Rich*)
R. Meryman: *Louis Armstrong: A Self-Portrait* (New York, 1971) [interview]
M. Mezzrow and B. Wolfe: *Really the Blues* (New York, 1946/*R*1972; Fr. trans. as *La rage de vivre*, Paris, 1950) [autobiography of Mezz Mezzrow]
R. Middleton: *The Rise of Jazz* (Milton Keynes, England, 1979)
T. Middleton, see R. Horricks
H. Miedema: *Jazz Styles and Analysis: Alto Sax* (Chicago, 1975) [125 transcrs. of performances by 103 players]
G. Miller: *Glenn Miller's Method for Orchestral Arranging* (New York, 1943)
M. Miller: *Boogie, Pete & the Senator: Canadian Musicians in Jazz: the Eighties* (Toronto, 1987)
——: *Jazz in Canada: Fourteen Lives* (Toronto, Buffalo, and London, 1982)
P. E. Miller: *Down Beat's Yearbook of Swing* (Chicago, 1939/*R*1978, repr. 1943 as *Miller's Yearbook of Popular Music*)
P. E. Miller, ed.: *Esquire's Jazz Book* (New York, 1944–6) [three vols., pubd annually; abridged P. Miller and R. Venables (London, 1947)]; see also E. Anderson
W. Miller: *Three Brass: Floyd O'Brien, Maxie Kaminsky, Shorty Sherock* (Melbourne, Australia, 1945)
J. W. Miner, see F. J. Gillis
C. Mingus: *Beneath the Underdog*, ed. N. King (New York and London, 1971; Ger. trans. as *Autobiographie*, Hamburg, Germany, 1980, 2/1986)
A. Moller: *Arthur Briggs* (Menden, Germany, 1981)
N. Mongan: *The History of the Guitar in Jazz* (New York, London, and Sydney, 1983) [incl. transcrs. and discography]
E. B. Moogk: *Roll Back the Years: History of Recorded Sound and its Legacy: Genesis to 1930* (Ottawa, 1975)
M. S. Moore: *Yankee Blues: Musical Culture and American Identity* (Bloomington, IN, 1985)
D. L. Moorman: *An Analytic Study of Jazz Improvisation, with Suggestions for Performance* (diss., New York U., 1984)
A. Moré, see Alfredo Papo
A. Morgan: *Count Basie* (Tunbridge Wells, England, 1984)
A. Morgan and R. Horricks: *Gerry Mulligan: a Biography, Appreciation, Record Survey and Discography* (London, 1958)
——: *Modern Jazz: a Survey of Developments since 1939* (London, 1956/*R*1977)
D. Morgenstern: *Jazz People* (New York, 1976) [with photographs by O. Brask]
R. L. Morris: *Wait until Dark: Jazz and the Underworld, 1880–1940* (Bowling Green, OH, 1980)
T. Mortensen: *Miles Davis: den ny jazz* (Copenhagen, 1977)
T. Mosnes: *Jazz i Molde* (Ålesund, Norway, 1980)
R. Mouly: *Sidney Bechet, notre ami* (Paris, 1959)
H. Mückenberger: *Meet me Where they Play the Blues: Jack Teagarden und seine Musik* (Gauting, Germany, 1986)
A. Murray: *Stomping the Blues* (London and New York, 1976)
A. Murray, see also C. Basie
W. Muth: *Ernst Höllerhagen: ein deutscher Jazzmusiker* (Magdeburg, Germany, n.d. [1964])
T. Naitho: *Miles* (Pyworthy, nr Holsworthy, England, 1981) [photographs]
H. Nakadaira: *Jazz Giants of the 60's* (Tokyo, 1981)
C. A. Nanry: *The Occupational Subculture of the Jazz Musician: Myth and Reality* (diss., Rutgers, 1970)
C. Nanry, ed.: *American Music: from Storyville to Woodstock* (New Brunswick, NJ, 1972)
C. Nanry and E. Berger: *The Jazz Text* (New York and elsewhere, 1979)
M. Nasatir, see D. Cerulli
B. Neely, see P. Fountain
D. Nelson: *Jimmy Giuffre: a List of Compositions Licensed by BMI* (New York, 1961)
J. Nesbitt: *Inside Buddy Rich: a Study of the Master Drummer's Style and Technique* (Delevan, NY, 1984)
B. Nettl, see C. Hamm
F. Newton [pseud. of E. J. E. Hobsbawm]: *The Jazz Scene* (London, 1959, New York, 1960/*R*1975; Fr. trans. as *Sociologie du jazz*, Paris, 1966)
M. Niiniluoto: *Toivo Kärki: siks oon ma suruinen* [Toivo Kärki: the reason why I am sad] (Helsinki, 1982)
E. Nisenson: *'Round about Midnight: a Portrait of Miles Davis* (New York, 1982; Ger. trans., Vienna, 1985)
B. Noglik: *Jazzwerkstatt international* (Berlin, 1981, 2/1983)
B. Noglik and H.-J. Lindner: *Jazz im Gespräch* (Berlin, 1978) [colln of interviews]
R. Nolden: *Ella Fitzgerald: ihr Leben, ihre Musik, ihre Schallplatten* (Gauting, Germany, 1986)
D. J. Noll: *Zur Improvisation im deutschen Free Jazz: Untersuchungen zur Ästhetik frei improvisierter Klangflächen* (Hamburg, Germany, 1977)
C. Norman: *Musikant med brutet gehör* [Musician with broken ear] (Stockholm, 1980)
S. J. O'Connell: *Bing: a Voice for All Seasons* (Tralee, Ireland, 1984) [incl. discography]
A. O'Day and G. Eells: *High Times, Hard Times* (New York, 1981) [autobiography of Anita O'Day]
J. Oehlmann, ed.: *Jazzaz: Texte zur Jazzmusik* (Giessen, Germany, 1982)
G. Økland, see O. Angell
P. Oliver: *Bessie Smith* (London, 1959); repr. in *Kings of Jazz*, ed. S. Green (South Brunswick, NJ, and New York, 1978)
——: *Blues Fell this Morning: the Meaning of the Blues* (London, 1960, New York, 1961, repr. 1963 as *The Meaning of the Blues*; Fr. trans. as *Le monde du blues*, Paris, 1962)
——: *Blues off the Record: Thirty Years of Blues Commentary* (Tunbridge Wells, England, and New York, 1984) [colln of previously pubd items]
——: *Conversation with the Blues* (London, 1965)
——: *Savannah Syncopators: African Retentions in the Blues* (London, 1970)
——: *Screening the Blues* (London, 1968, New York, 1970, as *Aspects of the Blues Tradition*)
——: *Songsters and Saints: Vocal Traditions on Race Records* (Cambridge, England, and elsewhere, 1984)
——: *The Story of the Blues* (London, 1969/*R*1982)
P. Oliver, M. Harrison, and W. Bolcom: *The New Grove Gospel, Blues and Jazz* (London and New York, 1986 [*recte* 1987])
B. Olsson: *Memphis Blues and Jug Bands* (London, 1970)
H. O'Neal, see E. Condon
On Stage, Backstage: Montreux Jazz Festival (Lausanne, Switzerland, 1986) [photographs]
J. Orlay: *Jazzdobbal a világ körül* [Around the world with jazz drums] (Budapest, 1943) [autobiography of Chappy]
N. R. Ortiz Oderigo: *Estética del jazz* (Buenos Aires, 1951)
——: *História del jazz* (Buenos Aires, 1952)
——: *Panorama de la música afroamericana* (Buenos Aires, 1944)
——: *Perfiles del jazz* (Buenos Aires, 1955)
H. D. Osgood: *So This is Jazz* (Boston, 1926/*R*1978)
L. Ostransky: *The Anatomy of Jazz* (Seattle, 1960)
——: *Jazz City: the Impact of our Cities on the Development of Jazz* (Englewood Cliffs, NJ, and London, 1978)
——: *Understanding Jazz* (Englewood Cliffs, NJ, 1977)
T. Owens: *Charlie Parker: Techniques of Improvisation* (diss., UCLA, 1974)
——: *Improvisation Techniques of the Modern Jazz Quartet* (thesis, UCLA, 1965)
D. Page: *Drew's Blues: a Sideman's Life with the Big Bands* (Baton Rouge, LA, and London, 1980)

Richard Palmer: *Oscar Peterson* (Tunbridge Wells, England, 1984) [incl. discography]
Robert Palmer: *Deep Blues* (New York and London, 1981)
H. Panassié: *La bataille du jazz* (Paris, 1965)
——: *Cinq mois à New-York* (Paris, 1947)
——: *Douze années de jazz (1927–1938): souvenirs* (Paris, 1946)
——: *Histoire du vrai jazz* (Paris, 1959)
——: *Le jazz hot* (Paris, 1934; Eng. trans., rev. Panassié, London and New York, 1936/*R*1970; Sp. trans., Santiago, 1939)
——: *Jazz panorama* (Paris, 1950)
——: *Louis Armstrong* (Paris, 1947)
——: *Louis Armstrong* (Paris, 1969; Eng. trans., New York, 1971)
——: *Monsieur Jazz* (Paris, 1975)
——: *La musique de jazz et le swing* (Paris, 1943, [2]/1945)
——: *Quand Mezzrow enregistre* (Paris, 1952)
——: *The Real Jazz* (New York and Toronto, 1942 [in Eng. trans.], rev. and enlarged 2/1960/*R*1973 by Panassié; Fr. orig. pubd as *La véritable musique de jazz*, Paris, 1945, rev. and enlarged 2/1952)
A. Papo: *Jazz para cinco instrumentos* (Barcelona, 1975) [with photographs by A. Turbau; text in Sp., Eng., and Fr.]
Alfredo Papo and J. Suñol: *30 anos de jazz: vistos por Aguilar Moré* (Barcelona, 1987) [portraits by A. Moré, with photographs by Anna Papo and J. Suñol; text in Sp., Eng., and Fr.]
C. Parker and F. Paudras: *To Bird with Love* (Antigny, France, 1981) [photographs]
G. Patane: *Be-bop ou pas be-bop? ou A la découverte du jazz* (Geneva, 1951)
J. Patrick, see M. Berger
F. Paudras: *La danse des infidèles: Bud Powell* (Paris, 1986)
F. Paudras, see also C. Parker
A. Pavlow: *The R&B Book: a Disc-history of Rhythm and Blues* (Providence, RI, 1983) [covers the period 1920–*c*1980]
N. W. Pearson, Jr.: *Goin' to Kansas City* (Urbana, IL, and London, 1988)
S. Pease: *Boogie-woogie Piano Styles* (Chicago, 1940, 1943) [incl. transcrs.]
I. Pegg, see R. E. Lotz
A. Pepper and L. Pepper: *Straight Life: the Story of Art Pepper* (New York and London, 1979) [incl. discography by T. Selbert]
J. P. Perhonis: *The Bix Beiderbecke Story: the Jazz Musician in Legend, Fiction, and Fact* (diss., U. of Minnesota, 1978)
D. Perlo, see L. Lyons
R. Pernet: *Jazz in Little Belgium, 1881–1966* (Brussels, 1967)
P. du Peuty, see C. Delaunay
M. Pinfold: *Louis Armstrong* (Tunbridge Wells, England, and New York, 1987) [incl. discography]
M. Pinfold, see also B. Crowther
C. A. Pirie: *Artistry in Kenton: the Bio-discography of Stan Kenton and his Music* (Vienna, 1969, enlarged 3/n.d. [?1972])
S. Placksin: *American Women in Jazz, 1900 to the Present: their Words, Lives, and Music* (New York, 1982; London, 1985, as *Jazzwomen, 1900 to the Present: their Words, Lives, and Music*)
H. Pleasants: *Death of a Music? The Decline of the European Tradition and the Rise of Jazz* (London, 1961)
——: *The Great American Popular Singers* (New York, 1974)
——: *Serious Music, and All that Jazz* (London, 1969)
N. Poindexter: *The Pony Express: Memoirs of a Jazz Musician* (Frankfurt am Main, Germany, 1985)
I. Poledňák, see L. Dorůžka
A. Polillo: *Jazz: la vicenda e i protagonisti della musica afro-americana* (Milan, 1975–6, rev. 2/1983; Ger. trans., Munich and Berlin, 1978)
J. Poling: *Esquire's World of Jazz* (New York, 1962, rev. 2/1975)
L. Porter: *John Coltrane's Music of 1960 through 1967: Jazz Improvisation as Composition* (diss., Brandeis U., 1983)
——: *Lester Young* (Boston and London, 1985)
S. Porto: *Pequeña história do jazz* (Rio de Janeiro, 1953)
C. Poustochkine, see W. G. Gilbert
C. Preiss: *The Steve Lacy Festival Handbook* (New York, 1982) [incl. discography and interview]
D. Preston: *Mood Indigo* (Egham, England, 1946)
S. Price and C. Richmond: *What do they Want? A Jazz Autobiography* (in preparation) [autobiography of Sammy Price; incl. discography by B. Weir]
B. Priestley: *Charlie Parker* (Tunbridge Wells, England, and New York, 1984) [incl. discography]
——: *John Coltrane* (London, 1987) [incl. discography]
——: *Mingus: a Critical Biography* (London, Melbourne, Australia, and New York, 1982)
B. Priestley, see also I. Carr
L. A. Pyke: *Jazz, 1920 to 1927: an Analytical Study* (diss., U. of Iowa, 1962)
R. Radano: *Anthony Braxton and his Two Musical Traditions: the Meeting of Concert Music and Jazz* (diss., U. of Michigan, 1985)
A. Raggenbass and others: *Jazz in Willisau* (Lucerne, Switzerland, 1978)
F. Ramsey, Jr.: *Been Here and Gone* (New Brunswick, NJ, and London, 1960)
——: *Chicago Documentary: Portrait of a Jazz Era* (London, 1944)
——: *Where the Music Started: a Photographic Essay* (New Brunswick, NJ, 1970)
F. Ramsey, Jr., and C. E. Smith, eds.: *Jazzmen: the Story of Hot Jazz Told in the Lives of the Men who Created it* (New York, 1939/*R*1977)
O. Read and W. L. Welch: *From Tin Foil to Stereo: Evolution of the Phonograph* (Indianapolis and New York, 1959/*R*1971, rev. 2/1976)
J. Réda: *L'improviste: une lecture de jazz* (Paris, 1980)
D. Redfern: *David Redfern's Jazz Album* (London, 1980/*R*1982 as *Jazz Portraits*) [photographs]
C. Reiff: *Nights in Birdland: Jazz Photographs, 1954–1960* (New York, 1987)
R. G. Reisner: *Bird: the Legend of Charlie Parker* (New York, 1962/*R*1975)
——: *The Jazz Titans* (Garden City, NY, 1960/*R*1977)
C. Richmond, see S. Price
J. Ridgway: *The Sinatra File* (Birmingham, England, 1977–80)
J. Riedel, see W. J. Schafer
W. Riefler: *Jazz, eine improvisierte Musik: dargestellt an vergleichenden Analysen des St. Louis Blues* (Menden, Germany, 1984)
J. F. Riesco: *El jazz clasico y Johnny Dodds, su rey sin corona* (Santiago, 1972)
T. Riis: *Black Musical Theatre in New York, 1890–1915* (diss., U. of Michigan, 1981)
U. Risak, ed.: *Drittes Jazz im Film Festival: Programmheft zur Veranstaltung* (Vienna, 1985)
G. Riskó: *Bingó, Benkó!* (Budapest, 1985)
D. Ritz, see R. Charles
P. Rivelli and R. Levin, eds.: *Black Giants* (New York and Cleveland, 1970/*R*1980 as *Giants of Black Music*) [colln of previously pubd articles]
J. S. Roberts: *Black Music of Two Worlds* (New York, Washington, and London, 1972)
——: *The Latin Tinge: the Impact of Latin American Music on the United States* (New York, and Oxford, England, 1979)
N. Rockmore, see L. Borenstein
J. Rockwell: *All American Music: Composition in the Late Twentieth Century* (New York, 1983)
——: *Sinatra: an American Classic* (New York, 1984)
C. Roemer, see C. Brandt
A. Roidinger: *Der Elektrobass im Jazz* (Vienna, 1981)
——: *Jazzimprovisation und Pentatonik* (Rottenburg, Baden-Württemberg, Germany, 1984)
——: *Der Kontrabass im Jazz* (Vienna, 1980)
A. Rollini: *Thirty Years with the Big Bands* (London, Urbana, IL, and Chicago, 1987) [autobiography]
B. Rollins, see C. Calloway
E. Ronowski: *Gene Krupa: seine Musik auf Schallplatten, 1927–1973: Biographie und Diskographie* (Dassel, Germany, 1985)
A. Rose: *Eubie Blake* (New York, 1979)
——: *I Remember Jazz: Six Decades among the Great Jazzmen* (Baton Rouge, LA, and London, 1987)
——: *Storyville, New Orleans: being an Authentic, Illustrated Account of the Notorious Red-light District* (University, AL, 1974)
T. Rosenkrantz: *Swing Photo Album* (Copenhagen and London, 1939, rev. 2/1964)
G. S. Rosenthal, ed.: *Jazzways: a Year Book of Hot Music* (Cincinnati, 1946)
A. Ross, see B. Semeonoff
E. R. Routley: *Is Jazz Music Christian?* (London, 1964)
R. Rudorf: *Jazz in der Zone* (Cologne, Germany, and Berlin, 1964)
H. Ruland: *Duke Ellington: sein Leben, seine Musik, seine Schallplatten* (Gauting, Germany, 1983)
R. D. Rusch: *Jazztalk: the Cadence Interviews* (Secaucus, NJ, 1984) [colln of previously pubd interviews]
M. Rusenberg, see R. Dollase
B. Russell, see L. Borenstein
R. Russell: *Bird Lives: the High Life and Hard Times of Charlie "Yardbird" Parker* (New York, 1973; Ger. trans., Vienna, 1985)
——: *Jazz Style in Kansas City and the Southwest* (Berkeley, CA, Los Angeles, and London, 1971/*R*1983, rev. 2/1973)
R. Russell, see also P. Foster
T. Russell: *Blacks, Whites and Blues* (London, 1970)
W. Russo: *Composing for the Jazz Orchestra* (Chicago and London, 1961)
——: *Jazz Composition and Orchestration* (Chicago and London, 1968, rev. 2/1975)
B. Rust: *Brian Rust's Guide to Discography* (Westport, CT, and London, 1980)
——: *The Dance Bands* (London, 1972)
——: *The H.M.V. Studio House Bands, 1912–1939* (Chigwell, England, 1976)
B. Rust, see also W. C. Allen; P. Foster
D. Salemann, D. Hartmann, and M. Vogler: *Edmund Gregory, Sahib Shihab: Solography, Discography, Band Routes, Engagements, in Chronological Order* (Basle, Switzerland, 1986)
——: *Jimmy Heath: Solography, Discography, Band Routes, Engagements, in Chronological Order* (Basle, Switzerland, 1986)
——: *Rudy Williams, 1936–1954: Solography, Discography, Band Routes, Engagements in Chronological Order* (Basle, Switzerland, 1987)
——: *Sonny Criss, 1943–1952: Solography, Discography, Band Routes, Engagements in Chronological Order* (Basle, Switzerland, 1987)
——: *Sonny Stitt: Solography, Discography, Band Routes, Engagements, in Chronological Order* (Basle, Switzerland, 1986)
J. Sallis, ed.: *Jazz Guitars: an Anthology* (New York, 1984)

H. T. Sampson: *Blacks in Black and White: a Source Book on Black Films* (Metuchen, NJ, 1977)
——: *Blacks in Blackface: a Source Book on Early Black Musical Shows* (Metuchen, NJ, 1980)
C. Samuels, see E. Waters
K. Sandegren and others: *Boken om jazz* (Oslo, 1954)
W. Sandner: *Jazz: zur Geschichte und stilistischen Entwicklung afro-amerikanischer Musik* (Laaber, Germany, 1982)
H. Sanford: *Tommy and Jimmy: the Dorsey Years* (New Rochelle, NY, 1972)
R. Sanjek, see N. Hentoff
R. Santelli, see M. Weinberg
W. Sargeant: *Jazz, Hot & Hybrid* (New York, 1938, rev. and enlarged 3/1964/*R*1975 as *Jazz: a History*)
L. Saxon, E. Dreyer, and R. Tallant, eds.: *Gumbo Ya-ya* (Boston, 1945/*R*)
K. Schacht, see P. Kohler
A. Schaeffner, see A. Coeuroy
W. J. Schafer and R. B. Allen: *Brass Bands and New Orleans Jazz* (Baton Rouge, LA, and London, 1977)
W. J. Schafer and J. Riedel: *The Art of Ragtime* (Baton Rouge, LA, 1973)
W. Scheck, see C. G. Herzog zu Mecklenburg
M. Scheffner, see C. G. Herzog zu Mecklenburg
D. Schiedt: *The Jazz State of Indiana* (Pittsboro, nr Lebanon, IN, 1977)
D. Schiedt, see also R. Kirkeby
J. Schiffman: *Harlem Heyday: a Pictorial History of Modern Black Show Business and the Apollo Theatre* (Buffalo, 1984)
——: *Uptown: the Story of Harlem's Apollo Theatre* (New York, 1971)
B. Schiozzi: *Count Basie* (Milan, 1961)
A. Schmitz and P. Maier: *Django Reinhardt: sein Leben, seine Musik, seine Schallplatten* (Gauting, Germany, 1985)
E. Schokert, see L. Kuehl
J. Schoustrup Thomsen: *Erik Moseholm* (Copenhagen, 1962) [incl. discography]
C. Schreiner, ed.: *Jazz aktuell* (Mainz, Germany, 1968)
G. Schuller: *Early Jazz: its Roots and Musical Development* (New York, 1968)
——: *J. J. Johnson: a List of Compositions Licensed by B.M.I.* (New York, 1961)
——: *Musings: the Musical Worlds of Gunther Schuller* (New York, and Oxford, England, 1986) [incl. previously pubd items]
K. Schulz, see D. H. Kraner
D. Schulz-Köhn: *Django Reinhardt: ein Porträt* (Wetzlar, Germany, 1960)
——: *Kleine Geschichte des Jazz* (Gütersloh, Germany, 1963)
——: *Stan Kenton: ein Porträt* (Wetzlar, Germany, 1961)
——: *Wesen und Gestalten der Jazz-Musik* (Kevelaer, Germany, 1951)
I. Schwerké: *Kings Jazz and David/Jazz et David rois* (Paris, 1927, 3/1936 as *Views and Interviews*) [parallel texts in Eng. and Fr.]
J. Scobey: *He Rambled! 'Til Cancer Cut Him Down* (Northridge, CA, 1976) [biography of Bob Scobey]
R. Scott: *Some of my Best Friends are the Blues* (London, 1979) [autobiography of Ronnie Scott]
B. Semeonoff: *Record Collecting: a Guide for Beginners* (Chislehurst, England, 1949, rev. 2/1951) [incl. A. Ross: "Collecting Jazz Records," 90]
J. D. Shacter: *Piano Man: the Story of Ralph Sutton* (Chicago, 1975) [incl. discography]
N. Shapiro and N. Hentoff, eds.: *Hear me Talkin' to ya: the Story of Jazz by the Men who Made it* (New York and London, 1955/*R*1966; Ger. trans. as *Jazz erzählt*, Munich, 1959/*R*1984)
——: *The Jazz Makers* (New York, 1957/*R*1975, 1979 as *The Jazz Makers: Essays on the Greats of Jazz*)
Arnold Shaw: *Honkers and Shouters: the Golden Years of Rhythm and Blues* (New York, 1978)
——: *Sinatra: Twentieth-century Romantic* (New York, 1965)
——: *The Street that Never Slept: New York's Fabled 52nd Street* (New York, 1971/*R*1977 as *52nd Street: the Street of Jazz*)
Artie Shaw: *The Trouble with Cinderella: an Outline of Identity* (New York, 1952/*R*1979) [autobiography]
D. Shepherd and R. F. Slatzer: *Bing Crosby: the Hollow Man* (New York, 1981)
C. Sheridan: *Count Basie: a Bio-discography* (Westport, CT, and London, 1986)
A. Shipton: *Fats Waller* (Tunbridge Wells, England, in preparation)
A. Shipton, see also D. Barker
T. Shoppee, see S. Voce
D. Sickler: *The Artistry of John Coltrane* (New York, 1979)
B. Sidran: *Black Talk* (New York, 1971/*R*1981; Ger. trans., Hofheim, Germany, 1985)
G. T. Simon: *The Big Bands* (New York, 1967, rev. and enlarged 2/1971, rev. 3/1974, 4/1981)
——: *The Feeling of Jazz* (New York, 1961)
——: *Glenn Miller and his Orchestra* (New York, 1974)
——: *Simon Says: the Sights and Sounds of the Swing Era, 1935–1955* (New Rochelle, NY, 1971)
G. T. Simon and others: *The Best of the Music Makers* (Garden City, NY, 1979)
V. Simosko and B. Tepperman: *Eric Dolphy: a Musical Biography and Discography* (Washington, 1974)
C. O. Simpkins: *Coltrane* (New York, 1975)
V. Skaarup and M. Goldstein: *Jazz: dens udvikling, former og udøvere* [Jazz: its development, forms, and creators] (Copenhagen, 1934)
R. F. Slatzer, see D. Shepherd
J. Slawe: *Einführung in die Jazzmusik* (Basle, Switzerland, 1948)
——: *Louis Armstrong: zehn monographische Studien* (Basle, Switzerland, 1953)
A. Smith, see Bricktop
C. E. Smith, see F. Ramsey, Jr.
G. E. Smith: *Homer, Gregory, and Bill Evans? The Theory of Formulaic Composition in the Context of Jazz Piano Improvisation* (diss., Harvard U., 1983)
G. Smith: *Stéphane Grappelli: a Biography* (London, 1987)
W. Smith and G. Hoefer: *Music on my Mind: the Memoirs of an American Pianist* (Garden City, NY, 1964/*R*1975) [autobiography of Willie "the Lion" Smith]
O. Søby: *Jazz kontra europaeisk musikkultur* (Copenhagen, 1935)
A. M. Sonnier, Jr.: *Willie Geary "Bunk" Johnson: the New Iberia Years* (New York, 1977) [incl. discography]
E. Southern: *The Music of Black Americans: a History* (New York and London, 1971, rev. 2/1983)
E. Southern, ed.: *Readings in Black American Music* (New York and Toronto, 1971, rev. 2/1983)
M. Sparke, ed.: *The Great Kenton Arrangers* (Whittier, CA, 1968) [incl. discography]
M. Sparke, see also P. Venudor
R. Spautz: *Django Reinhardt: Mythos und Realität* (Luxembourg, 1983; Fr. trans., Paris, 1984) [incl. discography]
——: *Luxemburgs Pioniere der leichten Muse: eine Porträtsammlung* (Luxembourg, 1983)
R. Spedale, Jr.: *A Guide to Jazz in New Orleans* (New Orleans, 1984)
A. B. Spellman: *Four Lives in the Bebop Business* (New York, 1966/*R*1970 as *Black Music: Four Lives*)
R. Spencer, see A. Laubich
D. D. Spitzer: *Jazzshots: a Photographic Essay* (Miami, 1979)
T. Stahl: *Sun Ra Materialen/Sun Ra Materials* (Freudenberg, nr Siegen, Germany, 1983, rev. and enlarged 2/1987) [texts in Ger. and Eng.; incl. discography]
B. Starr: *I'm in the Groove Man* (Inglewood, CA, 1986)
S. F. Starr: *Red and Hot: the Fate of Jazz in the Soviet Union, 1917–1980* (New York, and Oxford, England, 1983)
T. Stauffer: *Es war und ist ein herrliches Leben* (Berlin, Frankfurt am Main, Germany, and Vienna, 1968) [autobiography of Teddy Stauffer]
M. W. Stearns: *The Story of Jazz* (New York, 1956, rev. and enlarged 2/1958, enlarged 1970; Ger. trans., Munich, 1959; Dan. trans., Copenhagen, 1962; Port. trans., São Paulo, 1964)
M. Stearns and J. Stearns: *Jazz Dance: the Story of American Vernacular Dance* (New York and London, 1968/*R*1979)
R. A. Stebbins: *The Jazz Community: the Sociology of a Musical Subculture* (diss., U. of Minnesota, 1964)
B. Stendahl: *Jazz hot & swing: jazz i Norge, 1920–1940* (Oslo, 1987) [incl. discography by J. Bergh]
C. Stewart and P. C. Harrison: *Chuck Stewart's Jazz Files* (Boston, 1985) [photographs]
M. L. Stewart: *Structural Development in the Jazz Improvisational Technique of Clifford Brown* (diss., U. of Michigan, 1973; pubd in *Jf*, vi–vii (1974–5), 141–273)
R. Stewart: *Jazz Masters of the Thirties* (New York and London, n.d. [?1972])
D. Stewart-Baxter: *Ma Rainey and the Classic Blues Singers* (New York and London, 1970)
D. Stock and N. Hentoff: *Jazz Street* (Garden City, NY, and London, 1960)
T. Stoddard: *Jazz on the Barbary Coast* (Chigwell, England, 1982)
T. Stoddard, see also P. Foster
H. J. Stollenwerk, see R. Dollase
J. A. Stuart [pseud. of D. Tait]: *Call him George* (London, 1961) [biography of George Lewis (i)]
C. J. Stuessy, Jr.: *The Confluence of Jazz and Classical Music from 1950 to 1970* (diss., Eastman School, 1970)
D. G. Such: *Music, Metaphor, and Values among Avant-garde Musicians Living in New York City* (diss., UCLA, 1985)
R. M. Sudhalter, P. R. Evans, and W. Dean-Myatt: *Bix: Man & Legend* (New Rochelle, NY, and London, 1974) [incl. chronology and discography]
T. Sugrue, see E. Condon
M. J. Summerfield: *The Jazz Guitar: its Evolution and its Players* (Gateshead, England, 1978)
J. Suñol, see Alfredo Papo
J. Sypniewski: *Ein Problem der Gegenwartsmusik: Jazz, unter besonderer Berücksichtigung des symphonisches Jazz (George Gershwin)* (diss., U. of Zurich, 1949)
D. von Szadkowski: *Auf schwarzweissen Flügeln: Jazz-Musik, europäische Perspektiven* (Giessen, Germany, 1983)
D. Tait, see J. A. Stuart
R. Tallant, see L. Saxon

P. O. W. Tanner and M. Gerow: *A Study of Jazz* (Dubuque, IA, 1964, rev. 5/1983, rev. 6/1987 with D. W. Megill)
A. Taylor: *Notes and Tones: Musician-to-musician Interviews* (Liège, Belgium, 1977/*R*1982)
B. Taylor: *Jazz Piano: History and Development* (Dubuque, IA, 1982)
F. C. Taylor and G. Cook: *Alberta Hunter: a Celebration in Blues* (New York and elsewhere, 1987)
F. Ténot and P. Carles: *Le jazz* (Paris, 1978)
B. Tepperman, see V. Simosko
J. C. Thomas: *Chasin' the Trane: the Music and Mystique of John Coltrane* (Garden City, NY, 1975)
L. Thompson and J. P. Green: *An Autobiography* (Crawley, England, 1985) [autobiography of Leslie Thompson]
J. W. Thomson, see L. D. Holmes
V. Thomson: *The Musical Scene* (New York, 1945)
L. Thoorens: *Essai sur le jazz* (Liège, Belgium, 1942)
T. J. Tichenor, see D. A. Jasen
F. Tirro: *Jazz: a History* (New York, 1977)
J. Titon: *Early Downhome Blues: a Musical and Cultural Analysis* (Urbana, IL, Chicago, and London, 1977)
R. de Toledano, ed.: *Frontiers of Jazz* (New York, 1947, rev. 2/1962) [colln of previously pubd articles]
E. Townley, see S. Traill
I. Townsend, see J. Hammond
J. Tracy, see L. Feather
S. Traill, ed.: *Concerning Jazz* (London, 1957)
——: *Play that Music: a Guide to Playing Jazz* (London, 1956)
S. Traill and G. Lascelles, eds.: *Just Jazz* (London, 1957–60) [four annual vols.: D. Coller and E. Townley: *Jazz Discography, 1956[–1957]*; F. Dutton and E. Townley: *Jazz Discography, 1958*; G. Cherrington: *Jazz Discography, 1959/60*]
S. Traill, see also E. Kirkeby
D. J. Travis: *An Autobiography of Black Chicago* (Chicago, 1981)
——: *An Autobiography of Black Jazz* (Chicago, 1983) [incl. interviews]
J. de Trazegnies: *Duke Ellington: Harlem Aristocrat of Jazz* (Brussels, 1946)
J. A. Treichel: *Keeper of the Flame: Woody Herman and the Second Herd, 1947–1949* (n.p. [Zephyrhills, FL], 1978) [bio-discography]
W. W. Triggs: *The Great Harry Reser* (London, 1978) [bio-discography]
A. Turbau, see A. Papo
B. Turner: *Hot Air, Cool Music* (London, Melbourne, Australia, and New York, 1984) [autobiography; incl. discography by M. Clutten]
F. Turner: *Remembering Song: Encounters with the New Orleans Jazz Tradition* (New York, 1982)
D. Turrell, see G. Valentin
W. Twittenhoff: *Jugend und Jazz: ein Beitrag zur Klärung* (Mainz, Germany, 1953)
L. Tyrmand: *U brzegów jazzu* [On the side of jazz] (Kraków, Poland, 1957)
B. Ulanov: *Duke Ellington* (New York, 1946/*R*1975)
——: *A Handbook of Jazz* (New York, n.d. [?1957]/*R*1975)
——: *A History of Jazz in America* (New York, 1952/*R*1972; Fr. trans. as *Histoire du jazz*, Paris, 1955)
M. Ullman: *Jazz Lives: Portraits in Words and Pictures* (Washington, 1980)
M. Unterbrink: *Jazz Women at the Keyboard* (Jefferson, NC, and London, 1983)
F. Usinger: *Kleine Biographie des Jazz* (Offenbach am Main, Germany, 1953)
W. W. Vaché, Sr.: *Pee Wee Erwin: this Horn for Hire* (Metuchen, New Jersey, 1987) [incl. discography]
P. Vacher, see J. Darensbourg
G. Valentin and D. Turrell: *And all that Jazz: Copenhagen Jazz Festival* (Copenhagen, 1983) [texts in Dan. and Eng.]
J. Vance: *Fats Waller: his Life and Times* (Chicago, 1977)
P. Vandervoort, see W. Manone
W. van Eyle, see H. Kleinhout
H. Vemane: *Swing et moeurs* (Lille, France, 1943)
R. Venables, see P. E. Miller
P. Venudor and M. Sparke: *The Standard Stan Kenton Directory*, i: *1937–1949* (Amsterdam, 1968)
J. de Vergnies, see E. Bernhard
B. Vian: *Chroniques de jazz* (Paris, 1967) [colln of previously pubd items]
J. Viera: *Der Free Jazz: Formen und Modelle* (Vienna, 1974)
——: *Das Saxophon im Jazz* (Vienna, 1977)
S. Voce: *Woody Herman* (London, 1986) [incl. discography by T. Shoppee]
M. Vogler, see D. Salemann
J. E. Vold, see O. Angell
G. Von Physter, see C. Cons
J.-P. Vuorela, see A. Granholm
T. Waldo: *This is Ragtime* (New York, 1976) [incl. discography]
E. S. Walker: *Don't Jazz, it's Music, or Some Notes on Popular Syncopated Music in England during the 20th Century* (Walsall, England, 1978)
L. Walker: *The Big Band Almanac* (Hollywood, CA, 1978)
——: *The Wonderful Era of the Great Dance Bands* (Berkeley, CA, 1964)
M. Waller and A. Calabrese: *Fats Waller* (New York and London, 1977) [incl. discography and list of compositions]
E. Walles: *Jazzen anfaller* (Stockholm, 1946)
D. Walley: *No Commercial Potential: the Saga of Frank Zappa and the Mothers of Invention* (New York, 1972, 2/1980) [incl. discography]
O. M. Walton: *Music: Black, White and Blue: a Sociological Survey of the Use and Misuse of Afro-American Music* (New York, 1972)
C. Wareing and G. Garlick: *Bugles for Beiderbecke* (London, 1958) [incl. discography]
B. Waters: *The Key to a Jazzy Life* (n.p. [Toulouse, France], n.d. [1985]) [autobiography of Benny Waters]
E. Waters and C. Samuels: *His Eye is on the Sparrow* (New York and London, 1951) [autobiography of Ethel Waters]
E. Waters [and C. Samuels]: *To me it's Wonderful* (New York and elsewhere, 1972) [autobiography of Ethel Waters]
H. J. Waters, Jr.: *Jack Teagarden's Music: his Career and Recordings* (Stanhope, NJ, 1960)
H. Weber and G. Filtgen: *Charles Mingus: sein Leben, seine Musik, seine Schallplatten* (Gauting, Germany, 1984)
D. Webster, see B. Wilber
M. Weinberg and R. Santelli: *The Big Beat: Conversations with Rock's Great Drummers* (Chicago, 1984)
B. Weir, see B. Clayton; S. Price
P. E. Weisenborn, see R. Daschkey
M. Weiss: *Jazz Styles and Analysis: Piano* (Chicago, *c*1982)
W. L. Welch, see O. Read
D. Wells and S. Dance: *The Night People: Reminiscences of a Jazzman* (Boston and London, 1971) [autobiography of Dicky Wells]
B. Westin: *Sag det med musik: Thore Ehrling och hans orkester* [Say it with music: Thore Ehrling and his orchestra] (Stockholm, 1987) [incl. discography]
I. Whitcomb: *After the Ball* (Harmondsworth, nr London, 1972)
A. N. White III: *Andrew's X-rated Band Stories* (Washington, 1984)
——: *Hey Kid! Wanna Buy a Record? A Treatise on Self Production in the Music Business* (Washington, 1982)
J. White: *Billie Holiday* (Tunbridge Wells, England, and New York, 1987) [incl. discography]
P. Whiteman and M. M. McBride: *Jazz* (New York, 1926)
E. Wiedemann: *Jazz i Danmark i tyverne, trediverne og fyrrerne: en musikkulturel undersøgelse* [Jazz in Denmark in the twenties, thirties, and forties: a study of musical culture] (Copenhagen, 1982) [incl. discography]
P. Wiessmüller: *Miles Davis: sein Leben, seine Musik, seine Schallplatten* (Gauting, Germany, 1984)
L. Wigh, ed.: *Jazz på fotografiska: Fotografiska Museet i Moderna Museet 12 april – 3 augusti 1986* (Stockholm, 1986) [catalogue of exhibition at the Fotografiska Museet]
B. Wilber: *Music was not Enough*, ed. D. Webster (London and New York, 1987) [autobiography of Bob Wilber]
R. J. Wilbraham: *Charles Mingus: a Biography and Discography* (London, 1967) [incl. list of compositions]
A. Wilder: *American Popular Song: the Great Innovators, 1900–1950* (London and New York, 1972)
J. Wildman, see B. Benward
E. Willems: *Le jazz et l'oreille musicale: étude psychologique* (Geneva, 1945)
J. K. Williams: *Themes Composed by Jazz Musicians of the Bebop Era: a Study of Harmony, Rhythm, and Melody* (diss., Indiana U., 1982)
Martin Williams: *Jazz Heritage* (New York, and Oxford, England, 1985) [colln of previously pubd articles]
——: *Jazz Masters in Transition, 1957–69* (New York and London, 1970/*R*1980) [colln of previously pubd reviews]
——: *Jazz Masters of New Orleans* (New York and London, 1967/*R*1978)
——: *The Jazz Tradition* (New York, 1970, rev. 2/1983)
——: *Jelly Roll Morton* (London, 1962); repr. in *Kings of Jazz*, ed. S. Green (South Brunswick, NJ, and New York, 1978)
——: *King Oliver* (London, 1960); repr. in *Kings of Jazz*, ed. S. Green (South Brunswick, NJ, and New York, 1978)
Martin Williams, ed.: *The Art of Jazz: Essays on the Nature and Development of Jazz* (New York, 1959/*R*1979 as *The Art of Jazz: Ragtime to Bebop*)
——: *Jazz Panorama* (New York and London, 1962/*R*1979) [colln of previously pubd articles]
——: *The Smithsonian History of Jazz* (in preparation)
Martin Williams, see also A. Francis
Mike Williams: *The Australian Jazz Explosion* (London and elsewhere, 1981)
K. Williamson, ed.: *This is Jazz* (London, 1960)
V. Wilmer: *As Serious as your Life: the Story of the New Jazz* (London, 1977, rev. 1980)
——: *The Face of Black Music* (New York, 1976)
——: *Jazz People* (London, Indianapolis, and New York, 1970/*R*1985)
V. Wilmer, see also C. Fox
E. Wilson: *Sinatra: an Unauthorized Biography* (New York, 1976)
R. Wilson, see D. Chamberlain
J. Woelfer: *Dizzy Gillespie: sein Leben, seine Musik, seine Schallplatten* (Waakirchen, nr Bad Tölz, Germany, 1987)
B. Wolfe, see M. Mezzrow
C. D. Woodson: *Solo Jazz Drumming: an Analytical Study of the Improvisational Techniques of Anthony Williams* (thesis, UCLA, 1973)

L. Wright: *Mr. Jelly Lord* (Chigwell, England, 1980) [bio-discography of Jelly Roll Morton]

L. Wright and others: *Walter C. Allen & Brian A. L. Rust's "King" Oliver* (Chigwell, England, 1987) [bio-discography; completely rev. version of Allen and Rust: *King Joe Oliver* (Belleville, NJ, 1955)]

L. Wright, see also J. R. T. Davies

M. Wyler: *A Glimpse of the Past: an Illustrated History of some Early Record Companies that Made Jazz History* (West Moors, England, 1957)

I. Yeomans, see I. Berg

R. Yockey, see M. Bookspan

A. Young: *Bodies & Souls: Musical Memoirs* (Berkeley, CA, 1981)

——: *Kinds of Blue: Musical Memoirs* (San Francisco, 1984)

D. Zinn: *The Structure & Analysis of the Modern Improvised Line*, i: *Theory* (New York, and Bryn Mawr, PA, 1981)

W. Zinsser: *Willie and Dwike: an American Profile* (New York and Toronto, 1984) [biographies of Willie Ruff and Dwike Mitchell]

M. Zufferey: *Jazz als sozio-politisches Selbstverständnis der Schwarzen in Amerika* (Zurich, 1980; Fr. trans., Sierre, Switzerland, 1980)

M. Zwerin: *Close Enough for Jazz* (London, 1983) [autobiography]

——: *La tristesse de Saint Louis: Swing under the Nazis* (London, Melbourne, Australia, and New York, 1985)

J. Zylber: "40 Jahren Jazz in Polen," *Radar* [Ger. edn], no.3 (Warsaw, 1966), 7

PERIODICALS

c.i. – cumulative index(es)
incorp. – incorporated
irreg. – irregular
s.i. – special issue(s)

Accordion Times & Musical Express [from no.70 (6 Feb 1948) *Musical Express*; from no.269 (7 March 1952) *New Musical Express*] (London, 4 Oct 1946–) weekly; suppl.: *New Musical Express Annual* [sometimes *New Musical Express Xmas Annual*] (1953–) yearly

Aktuality melodie, see *Melodie*

American Jazz (Chilwell, nr Newark-on-Trent, England, 1945–6) 2 nos., irreg.

American Jazz Review (New York, Nov 1944 – ? March 1947) ?3 vols., ?monthly

American Music (Urbana, IL, spr. 1983–) quarterly

American Musician (Cincinnati, Jan 1897 – July 1901) 55 nos., monthly; contd as *International Musician*

And All that Jazz (Kerrville, TX, 1974–) 4 issues yearly

Annual Review of Jazz Studies (New Brunswick, NJ, 1982–) irreg.; contd from *Journal of Jazz Studies*

Anschlaege: Zeitschrift des Archivs für Populäre Musik (Bremen, Germany, ?1978–) quarterly

ASCAP Jazz Notes (New York, Feb 1962 – June 1965) 39 nos., monthly

Australian Jazz Quarterly: a Magazine for the Connoisseur of Hot Music (Melbourne, Australia, May 1946 – April 1957) 31 nos., irreg.

Band Yearbook, see *Billboard Advertising*

Bass World: Annual Journal, see *International Society of Bassists*

The Beat (London, 1947–9) 3 vols.; contd as *The New Beat*

The Beat (Sydney, Sept – Nov 1949) 3 nos., monthly

Beat: the Heart of the Music Scene [from ii/7 (July 1958) *Jazz Beat: the Heart of the Music Scene*] (London, n.d. [1956]/1957 – July 1958) 2 vols., monthly

Be-bop and Beyond (Los Angeles, Jan 1983–) bimonthly, from v/1 (Jan 1987) quarterly

Berlin-Jazz (Berlin, 1955–8) ?4 vols.

Bielefelder Jazzkatalog, see DISCOGRAPHIES, *General*, M. Scheffner

Billboard Advertising [from 1 Nov 1896 *The Billboard*; from 9 Jan 1961 *Billboard: the International Music-record Newsweekly*; from 7 June 1969 *Billboard: the International Music-record-tape Newsweekly*] (Cincinnati, later New York, 1894/5–1971; Los Angeles, 1971–) weekly; song charts; c.i. 1972–3; suppls.: *Billboard: Index of the New York Legitimate Stage* (1931/2–1938/9) yearly; *Band Yearbook* (1939–42) yearly; *Talent and Tunes on Music Machines* (1939–41) yearly; *Who's Who in the World of Music* (1961–) yearly

Black Music (London, 1973–8) 5 vols. (= 52 nos.), monthly; contd as *Black Music and Jazz Review*

Black Music and Jazz Review (London, April 1978 – 1984) 7 vols., monthly; contd from *Black Music*

Black Music Research Journal (Nashville, 1980–82; Nashville and Chicago, 1983–4; Chicago, 1985–) yearly

Black Music Research Newsletter (Carbondale, IL, 1977/8; Nashville, 1978/9–1981/2; Nashville and Chicago, 1983/4–1984; Chicago, 1985–) quarterly, from 1980 half-yearly

The Black Perspective in Music (New York, 1973–) 2 issues yearly; c.i. 1973–82

Blue Rhythm, see *Jazz Notes* (Melbourne)

Blues & Rhythm: the Gospel Truth (London, 1984 – Sept 1986; Cheadle, Greater Manchester, England, 1986–) 10 issues yearly; index of record reviews in nos.1–10 separately pubd (1985)

Blues Notes: erstes deutschsprachiges Blues- & Jazzmagazin (Linz, Austria, 1969–79) 11 vols. (= 37 nos.), irreg.

Blues Unlimited: the Journal of the Blues Appreciation Society [from no.5 (1963) *Blues Unlimited*] (Bexhill-on-Sea, England, April 1963 – Dec 1974/Jan 1975; London, March/April 1975–) 10 issues yearly, from no.102 (June 1973) bimonthly, from no.134 (March/June 1979) half-yearly, from no.146 (aut./win. 1984) irreg.

BMI: the Many Worlds of Music, see *News about BMI Music & Writers*

Brass Bulletin (Switzerland, 1971–) 3 issues yearly, from no.13 (1976) quarterly [in Eng., Fr., and Ger.]

Break Bulletin (Tampere, Finland, 1977–81) quarterly

Bulletin du Hot Club de France, [1st ser.] (Paris, Dec 1940 – June 1945) 43 nos.; [2nd ser.] (Paris, Oct 1945 – n.d.) 3 nos.; 3rd ser. (Montauban, France, Oct 1950 – Sept/Oct 1977; St.-Vrain, nr Corbeil-Essonnes, France, April 1978–) 10 issues yearly

Bulletin Panassié (Paris, Oct–Nov 1947) 2 nos.

Cadence: the American Review of Jazz & Blues (Redwood, nr Watertown, NY, Jan 1976–) monthly

Les cahiers du jazz: revue musicale (Paris, ?Nov 1959 – 1968) 17 nos., irreg.

Catalogo: discos – long play, see DISCOGRAPHIES, *Other listings*

Christensen's Ragtime Review [from ii/6 (May 1916) *Ragtime Review*] (Chicago, Dec 1914 – Jan 1918) 4 vols. (= 33 nos.), monthly

Clef (Santa Monica, CA, March–Sept 1946) 1 vol. (= 7 nos.), monthly

Coda (Toronto, May 1958–) monthly, from vi/6 (Feb 1964) bimonthly, from no.136 (March 1975) irreg., from no.151 (Oct 1976) bimonthly

Collector (Cosenza, Italy, *c*1960–?) irreg. [in Eng. and It.]; s.i. (in place of nos.29–35) pubd as *Collector's Catalog*, ii (Cosenza, 1972)

Collectors Items (Walton-on-Thames, England, Aug 1980–) bimonthly, from no.42 (June 1987) irreg.; c.i. nos.1–12 (1983), nos.13–36 (in preparation)

Contemporary Keyboard [from vii/7 (July 1981) *Keyboard*] (Saratoga, nr Los Gatos, CA, later Cupertino, nr Santa Clara, CA, Sept 1975–) bimonthly, from iii/1 (Jan 1977) monthly

Le courrier du disque microsillon, see DISCOGRAPHIES, *Other listings*

CRC [Collector's Record Club] *Newsletter* [from v/2 (Aug 1979) to v/3 (Sept/Dec 1979) *Jazzology Newsletter*] (Decatur, GA, ?1975–) half-yearly, from v (1979) 3 or 4 issues yearly

Crescendo [from v/9 (April 1967) *Crescendo International*] (London, July 1962 – June/July 1986, Jan 1987–) monthly, from xxii/1 (Oct/Nov 1983) irreg., from xxiv/1 (Jan 1987) monthly

Dallas Jazz News Letter [from i/8 (Dec 1977) *Dallas Jazz News*; from ii/11 (Nov 1978) *Texas Jazz*] (Dallas, May 1977 – Dec 1982) 6 vols. (= ?68 nos.), monthly; contd as *Texas Ragg*

Diapason, see DISCOGRAPHIES, *Other listings*

Different Drummer: the Magazine for Jazz Listeners (Rochester, NY, Sept 1973 – Jan 1975) 1 vol. (= 15 nos.), monthly

Discographical Forum (London, 1960–) bimonthly, from 1972 irreg.

La discographie française, see DISCOGRAPHIES, *Other listings*

La discographie de la France: tous les disques de la quinzaine [by no.88 (15 April 1970) *La discographie de la France: bandes et disques de la quinzaine*] (Paris, March 1966–) fortnightly [contd from suppl. to *Diapason*, see DISCOGRAPHIES, *Other listings*]

Discography (London, Oct 1942 – 1947) fortnightly, from ?May 1944 irreg.; incorp. into *Jazz Music* (1947)

The Discophile: the Magazine for Record Information (London, Aug 1948 – Dec 1958) 61 nos., irreg.; incorp. into *Matrix* (1959)

Discopop '77, see DISCOGRAPHIES, *Other listings*

Disc'ribe (Ann Arbor, MI, 1980–) yearly

Disk in the World (Tokyo, 1980–)

Disques de longue durée, see DISCOGRAPHIES, *Other listings*

Doctor jazz: contactblad voor liefhebbers en versamelaars van classic jazz, blues, en verwante volksmuziek (Eindhoven, Netherlands, Jan 1963 – Sept/Oct 1964; Utrecht, Netherlands, Nov 1964–) bimonthly, from no.82 (1977) quarterly; c.i. nos.11–16 (1965)

Down Beat: the Contemporary Music Magazine (Chicago, 1934–) monthly, from vi/10 (Oct 1939) semimonthly, from xiii/1 (1 Jan 1946) fortnightly, from xxxvii/11 (28 May 1970) monthly or fortnightly, from xlvi/13 (July 1979) monthly; incorp. *Tempo: the Modern Musical Newsmagazine* (?1940); suppl.: *Down Beat Music* [1960–62 *Down Beat's Music*] (1956–) yearly; music suppl. irreg.

Eureka: the Bi-monthly Magazine of New Orleans Jazz (London, Jan/Feb 1960 – Jan/Feb 1961) 2 vols. (= 7 nos.), bimonthly

Fanfare (London, 1943–?1946) ?4 vols., monthly

Federation Jazz (Savannah, GA, Oct 1985 – April 1986) bimonthly

Footnote: Dedicated to New Orleans Music (Cambridge, England, n.d. [Dec 1969] – Feb 1976; Meldreth, nr Cambridge, March 1976 – Oct 1983; Melbourn, nr Cambridge, Nov 1983–) monthly, from ii/4 (April 1971) bimonthly; c.i. 1969–1984/5

Forty-fiver, see DISCOGRAPHIES, *Other listings*

Gene Lees Jazzletter (Ojai, CA, Aug 1981–Dec 1986; Oak View, CA, Jan 1987–) monthly; c.i. 1981–6 yearly, 1987– biennially

The Grackle: Improvised [sometimes *Improvisational*] *Music in Transition* (New York, n.d. [1975]–) irreg.

The Gramophone Long Playing Popular Record Catalogue, see DISCOGRAPHIES, *Other listings*, E. Jackson

Guia de jazz (Buenos Aires, Nov 1984–) bimonthly

Guitar Player: the Magazine for Professional and Amateur Guitarists (San Jose,

CA, later Saratoga, nr Los Gatos, CA, 1967–71; Los Gatos, 1971–) 4 issues yearly, from ii (1968) 6 issues yearly, from iv (1970) 8 issues yearly, from viii (1974) monthly

HCD [Hot Club Dortmund]*-Bulletin* [from 1956 *Westjazz: Jazz-Nachrichten aus Westdeutschland*] (Dortmund, Germany, 1955; Wanne-Eickel, Germany, 1956–?)

Hip: the Jazz Record Digest (Sterling, nr Reston, VA, later McLean, VA, March 1967 – Dec 1971) 10 vols., 12 issues yearly in 2 vols.; contd from *Hip: the Milwaukee Jazz Letter*; contd as *Jazz Digest*

Hip: the Milwaukee Jazz Letter (Milwaukee, Sept 1962 – Jan 1967) 5 vols.; contd as *Hip: the Jazz Record Digest*

H.o.t.: tidsskrift for moderne musik (Copenhagen, 1934/5) 1 vol. (= 12 nos.), monthly

Hot Club Journal (Stuttgart, Germany, 1947/8–1949) 2 vols.

Hot club magazine: revue internationale de jazz (Brussels, Jan 1946 – Aug 1948) 29 nos., monthly; contd from *Jazz* (Brussels); incorp. into *Jazz hot: la revue internationale de la musique de jazz* (Nov 1948)

Hot House (New York, ?1982–) monthly

Hot Jazz (Frankfurt am Main, Germany, 1973–) bimonthly

Hot jazz club (Sastre, Argentina, 1944–) quarterly

Hot News and Rhythm Record Review (London, April – Sept/Oct 1935) 1 vol. (= 6 nos.), monthly; incorp. into *Jazz Music* (1942)

Hot Notes (Waterford, Ireland, March 1946 – spr. 1948) bimonthly

Hot Notes (New York, Jan 1969 – ? March 1975) 7 vols., monthly

Hot Record Society Rag, see *H.R.S. Rag*

Hot-revue: revue mensuelle de jazz-hot (Lausanne, Switzerland, Dec 1945 – May 1947) 2 vols., monthly

H.R.S. [Hot Record Society] *Rag* (New York, July 1938 – March 1941) ?11 nos., irreg., from no.4 (Aug 1940) monthly

IAJRC [International Association of Jazz Record Collectors] *Record* [from ii/1 (Jan 1969) *IAJRC Journal*] (New York, later Indianapolis, 1967–) quarterly, except 1982–3; c.i.

Impetus: New Music [from no.8 (1978) *Impetus*] (London, n.d. [1976]–?) irreg.

L'indépendant du jazz (Paris, 1974–) monthly, 1 issue in 1976, from 1977 quarterly

Intermission (Buena Park, CA, 1968–) monthly

International Association of Jazz Record Collectors Journal, see *IAJRC Record*

Das internationale Podium [iii/4 (April 1954) *Jazz-Podium*; from iii/5 (May 1954) *Das internationale Jazz-Podium*; from iv/1 (Jan 1955) *Jazz Podium*] (Vienna and Munich, 1947 or 1948 – ?Aug 1952; Stuttgart, Munich, and Vienna, ?Sept 1952 – June 1965; Stuttgart and Munich, July 1965 – Feb 1966; Stuttgart, March 1966–) monthly; incorp. *Jazz-Spiegel der Deutschen Jazz-Föderation* (?Sept 1952)

International Musician [from xviii (1919/20) *International Musician: Official Journal of the American Federation of Musicians of the United States & Canada*] (St. Louis, July 1901 – 1922; Newark, NJ, and elsewhere, 1922–75; New York, 1975–) monthly; contd from *American Musician*

International Record News (Imola, Italy, May 1982–) ?irreg. [in Eng.]

International Society of Bassists: Newsletter [each 4th issue *Bass World: Annual Journal*; from ix/1 (aut. 1982) *International Society of Bassists: Journal*] (Cincinnati, aut. 1974–) quarterly, from ix/1 (aut. 1982) 3 issues yearly

Into Jazz (London, Feb–Aug 1974) 1 vol. (= 7 nos.), monthly

Jazz (New York, June 1942 – Dec 1943) 1 vol. (= 10 nos.), irreg.; new ser. (Dec 1944 – Jan 1945) 1 vol. (= 2 nos.), monthly

Jazz (Brussels, March 1945 – Nov 1945) 6 issues (= 13 nos.) bimonthly; contd as *Hot club magazine: revue internationale de jazz*

Jazz [from vi/8 (Aug 1967) *Jazz & Pop*] (New York, Oct 1962 – Sept 1971) 10 vols. (= 95 nos.), monthly

Jazz (Aneby, Sweden, 1965–?) 6 issues yearly

Jazz (Basle, Switzerland, 1982–) bimonthly

Jazz (Budapest, 1986–)

Jazz (Copenhagen), see *Jazzavisen*

Jazz (Chilwell, nr Newark-on-Trent, England), see *Jazz Record*

Jazz: l'actualité intellectuelle (Paris, 1929–30, 1931) 15 nos., monthly

Jazz: the Australasian Contemporary Music Magazine (Sydney, Jan/Feb 1981–) bimonthly, from iv (1984) quarterly, from vi (1986) irreg.

Jazz: list věnovaný jazzu a moderní hudbě [Jazz: jazz and modern music journal] (Prague, 1947–8) 2 vols.

Jazz: miesięcznik ilustrowany (Gdańsk, Poland, 1956–8; Warsaw, 1959–) monthly

Jazz: a Quarterly of American Music (Berkeley, CA, Oct 1958 – win. 1960) 5 nos., irreg.

Jazz: Unterhaltungs- und Informationszeitschrift für Jazz, Blues, Gospel and Spirituals, Rhythm 'n' Blues, Soul [from ?v/1 (Jan/Feb 1978) *Jazz & Classic*] (Muttenz, Switzerland, ?1974–1979) 6 vols. (= ?36 nos.), bimonthly

Jazz & Blues (London, April 1971 – Dec 1973) 3 vols. (= 32 nos.), monthly; contd from *Jazz Monthly*; incorp. into *Jazz Journal* (Jan 1974)

Jazz & Classic, see *Jazz: Unterhaltungs- und Informationszeitschrift . . .*

Jazz & Pop, see *Jazz* (New York)

Jazz at the Pizza Express [from no.29 (Feb 1982) *Jazz Express Incorporating Jazz at the Pizza Express*; from no.50 (March 1984) *Jazz Express*] (London, ?1978–) 11 issues yearly

Jazz at Ronnie Scott's (London, Aug/Sept [1979]–) bimonthly

Jazz Australia (Sydney, 1976–) monthly

Jazzavisen [from i/5 (1934) *Jazz*; from v/1 (1938) *Jazz og film*; from v/7 (1938) *Musik og film*] (Copenhagen, 1934–8) 5 vols., monthly

Jazzband (Buenos Aires, March/April 1972 – Jan/Feb 1974) 6 nos., irreg.

Jazz Beat: the Heart of the Music Scene, see *Beat*

Jazz Beat: the Lively Jazz Magazine [from ii/1 (Jan 1965) *Jazzbeat: the Official Publication of the Jazzbeat Association*] (London, Jan 1964 – Dec 1966) 3 vols., monthly; contd from *Jazz News & Review*, see *Jazz News* (London)

Jazz, Blues and Co. (Paris, 1975–83) 7 vols. (= 64 nos.), irreg.

Jazz-Bulletin [from no.81 (Aug 1960) *Jazz Scene*; from no.93 (May 1961) *Swiss Jazz Notes*] (Basle, Switzerland, 1952–60; Birsfelden, nr Basle, 1960–61; Reinach, nr Basle, Switzerland, 1961–3) 97 nos., 3 issues yearly, from 1953 monthly, later 10 issues yearly, then irreg.; suppl. *Who's Who: Discograph* (1952–6) yearly

Jazz Catalogue, see DISCOGRAPHIES, *General*, G. Cherrington

Jazz CD, Record, Video [1986], see *Swing Journal*

Jazz Circle News (Manchester, England, ?Feb 1978 – Oct 1979) 18 nos., monthly

Der Jazz-Courier, see *Vier Viertel*

Jazz Digest (McLean, VA, Jan/Feb 1972 – June 1974) 3 vols. (= 18 nos.), irreg.; suppl. *Jersey Jazz* (1973); contd from *Hip: the Jazz Record Digest*

Jazz Disco & Video [1984–5], see *Swing Journal*

Jazz Down Under (Sydney, 1975–7) 20 nos., monthly

Jazz Echo: Publication of the International Jazz Federation, see *Swinging Newsletter*

Jazz-Echo: ständige Gondel-Beilage für die Jazzfreunde (Hamburg, Germany, 1949–?1968) monthly; suppl. to *Gondel Magazine*

Jazz Educators Journal, see *National Association of Jazz Educators: Newsletter*

Jazz Express, see *Jazz at the Pizza Express*

Jazzfinder [from ii/1 (Jan 1949) *Playback*] (New Orleans, Jan 1948 – March 1950, Jan–March/April 1952) 4 vols. (= 29 nos.), irreg.

Jazz, Folk & Blues: a Monthly Discographical Listing of Current Record Releases, see *Jazz Monthly*

Jazzforschung/Jazz Research (Graz, Austria, 1969–) yearly

Jazzforum (Vienna, 1955) 1 vol.

Jazz Forum (Warsaw and Vienna, 1967–) bimonthly [2 edns, Eng. (intl edn) and Pol.]

Jazz Forum: Quarterly Review of Jazz and Literature (Fordingbridge, England, May 1946 – July 1947) 5 nos., quarterly

Jazz Freak (Breda, Netherlands, Sept 1973–) bimonthly

Der Jazzfreund (Itzehoe, Germany, 1953–5) 3 vols.; contd as *Mitteilungsblatt der Arbeitsgemeinschaft norddeutscher Jazz-Clubs*

Der Jazzfreund: Mitteilungsblatt für Jazzfreunde in Ost und West (Goseck, nr Halle, Germany, March 1958 – April 1960; Wanne-Eickel, Germany, Sept 1962 – March 1965; Menden, Germany, June 1965–) monthly, from Sept 1962 quarterly

Jazz Guide (London, 1964/5–1965/6) 3 vols., monthly

Jazz Heritage Foundation (Los Angeles, 1980–?) bimonthly

Jazz Home (Frankfurt am Main, Germany, 1949) 1 vol.

Jazz-hot: revue internationale de la musique de jazz, [1st ser.] (Paris, March 1935 – July/Aug 1939) 32 nos., monthly [in Fr. and Eng.]; new ser. as *Jazz hot* (Paris, March 1945–), to Dec 1947 irreg., 1948–76 11 issues yearly, from 1977 9 or 10 issues yearly

Jazz hot: la revue internationale de la musique de jazz (Brussels, 1948–9) 2 vols., monthly; incorp. *Hot club magazine* (Nov 1948)

Jazz Illustrated (London, 1949/50) 1 vol. (= 8 nos.), monthly

Jazz Index: Bibliographie unselbständiger Jazzliteratur/Bibliography of Jazz Literature in Periodicals, see BIBLIOGRAPHIES AND REFERENCE MATERIALS, N. Ruecker

Jazz Information (New York, 8 Sept 1939 – Nov 1941) 2 vols. (51 nos.), weekly, from ii/1 (26 July 1940) fortnightly, later irreg.

Jazzinformation (Copenhagen, 1950) 5 nos.

Jazzinformation: tribune, see *Tribune*

Jazziz (Gainesville, FL, Jan 1984–) bimonthly

Jazz Journal [from vi/2 (Feb 1953) to vi/11 (Nov 1953) *Jazz Journal and Popular Music Review*; incorp. *Jazz & Blues* in xxvii/1 (Jan 1974) to form *Jazz Journal and Jazz and Blues*; from xxvii/11 (Nov 1974) to xxviii/8 (Aug 1975) *Jazz Journal: Incorporating "Jazz and Blues"*; from xxx/5 (May 1977) *Jazz Journal International*] (London, 1948–) monthly

Jazz Journal (Heemstede, Netherlands, Feb 1955 – July 1956) 11 nos., monthly

Jazz Journal (Halle, Germany, 1955–6) 2 vols.

Jazzletter, see *Gene Lees Jazzletter*

Jazz Line (Mineola, NY, 1981–) monthly

Jazzline (Melbourne, Australia, June 1968–) quarterly

Jazz magazine (Buenos Aires, Sept 1945 – ?) monthly, later 4–7 issues yearly

Jazz magazine (Paris, Dec 1954–) monthly

Jazz Magazine (Northport, nr Huntington, NY, sum. 1976 – spr. 1980) 3 vols. (= 14 nos.), quarterly

Jazz Magazine (Chilwell, nr Newark-on-Trent, England), see *Jazz Record*

Jazz moderne (Vienna, 1953/4) 1 vol.

Jazz Monthly (London, March–May 1955; St. Austell, England, June 1955 – Feb 1971) 192 nos., monthly; suppl. *Jazz Records: a Monthly Discographical Listing of Current Jazz Releases* [from at latest Nov 1965 *Jazz, Folk & Blues:*

a Monthly Discographical Listing of Current Record Releases] (England, ? Oct 1962 – Feb 1966); contd as *Jazz & Blues*
Jazz Music: the International Jazz Magazine (London, Oct 1942 – April 1960) 11 vols., bimonthly; incorp. *Hot News and Rhythm Record Review*; incorp. *Jazz Tempo* (London) (1944); incorp. *Discography* (1947); contd as *Jazz Times* (London)
Jazz Music Mirror, see *Music Mirror*
Jazz Music News (London, April–July 1982) 5 nos., monthly, from no.5 semi-monthly
Jazz New England (Andover, MA, Oct 1974 – ? Nov 1975) ?8 nos., irreg.
Jazz News [from vi/44 (7 Nov 1962) *Jazz News & Review*] (London, Nov 1956 – Dec 1963) monthly, from 5 Dec 1958 fortnightly, from iv/7 (25 March 1960) weekly; contd as *Jazz Beat*
Jazz News: Blue Star Revue (Paris, 1948–50) 11 nos., monthly
Jazz News: Ireland's Jazz & Blues Magazine [from no.3 (May/June 1987) *Jazz News*] (Dublin, Dec 1986–) bimonthly
Jazz News: offizielles Organ des Hot Club Zürich (Zurich, Nov 1940 – Jan/Feb 1942) 9 nos. [variously in Eng., Fr., and Ger.]
The Jazz Newsletter (Kerrville, TX, Jan 1984 – April 1986) monthly; contd from *The Jazzologist*
Jazz-note (Lyons, France, 1953) 2 nos., fortnightly
Jazz Notes (Adelaide, Australia, Jan 1941–?) monthly
Jazz Notes [from no.37 (Feb 1944) *Jazz Notes and Blue Rhythm*; from no.60 (Jan 1946) *Jazz Notes*; no.96 (Sept 1949) and no.97 (Oct 1949) *Jazz Notes, Incorporating Hot Notes*] (Melbourne, Australia, Jan 1941 – Oct 1950; July 1960 – Dec 1962) 113 nos., three-weekly, from i/4 (March 1941) monthly [ceased pubn 1950–60]; incorp. *Blue Rhythm* (Feb 1944)
Jazz nu: maandblad voor aktuele geïmproviseerde muziek (Tilburg, Netherlands, Oct 1978 – sum. 1980; Amsterdam, Sept 1980 – aut. 1985; Groningen, Netherlands, Nov 1985–) monthly; contd from *Jazzpress*; c.i. yearly
Jazz nytt (Molde, Norway, 1965–) 5 issues yearly
Jazznytt [from 1967 *Jazznytt från SJR* [Svenska Jazzklubbarnas Riksforbund]] (Stockholm, 1965–) 5 issues yearly, from 1982 bimonthly; contd from *Jazz Times* (Stockholm)
Jazz og film, see *Jazzavisen*
The Jazzologist (Orange, nr Santa Ana, CA, May 1963 – Oct 1972; Kerrville, TX, Nov 1972 – Dec 1983) monthly, from July 1968 5 issues yearly; contd as *The Jazz Newsletter*
Jazzology Newsletter, see *CRC Newsletter*
Jazzophone (Paris, 1978–) quarterly
Jazz Panorama: the Canadian Music Scene (Toronto, Dec 1946 – May 1948) irreg.
Jazz Parade (Adelaide, Australia, Jan 1957–?) monthly
Jazz Podium, see *Das internationale Podium*
Jazz press (Almelo, Netherlands, 17 Sept 1975 – 1 Sept 1978) 54 nos., fortnightly, from no.43 (Sept 1977) monthly; contd as *Jazz nu: maandblad voor aktuele geïmproviseerde muziek*
Jazz Quarterly (Chicago, spr. 1942 – ?1945) ?2 vols. (= ?7 nos.), irreg.
Jazz Rag (Berkeley, CA, ?1979–) monthly
Jazzrealities Magazine (Freiburg, Germany, Aug 1982–) irreg.
Jazz Record [from ?1945 *Jazz*; from Sept 1946 *Jazz Magazine*] (Chilwell, nr Newark-on-Trent, England, ?1939, 1945–6) 3 vols. (= 12 nos.), irreg.
The Jazz Record (New York, Feb 1943 – Nov 1947), 60 nos., monthly
Jazz Record Review [from ii/10 (Nov 1971) *Jazz Review*] (Adelaide, Australia, 1970–?) irreg.
Jazz Records: a Monthly Discographical Listing of Current Jazz Releases, see *Jazz Monthly*
Jazz Records [1975–83], see *Swing Journal*
Jazz Register (San Diego, ?Jan/March 1965 – ? Jan/March 1966) 2 vols. (= 5 nos.), quarterly
Jazz Report (St. Louis, 1953 – mid-1958; Chicago, mid-1958 – May 1960) 8 vols., irreg.; contd as *Jazz Report* (Ventura, CA)
Jazz Report: the Record Collector's Magazine (Ventura, CA, Sept 1960 – ?March 1982) 10 vols., monthly, from iii/3–4 (Jan/Feb 1963) bimonthly, later irreg.; contd from *Jazz Report* (St. Louis, later Chicago)
Jazzreports: organ for "swing fans" i Danmark (Copenhagen, 1941–3) 3 vols.
Jazz Reprints (Portsmouth, England, 1962/3) 1 vol. (= 3 nos.)
Jazz Research, see *Jazzforschung/Jazz Research*
Jazz Review, see *Jazz Record Review*
The Jazz Review (New York, Nov 1958 – Jan 1961) 4 vols. (= 23 nos.), monthly
Jazz Revue (Berlin, 1950–54) 5 vols., monthly; v (1954) incorp. as suppl. in *Vier Viertel*
Jazzrevy (Copenhagen, 1935–6) 2 vols.
Jazzrevy, see *Musikrevue*
Jazz, Rhythm & Blues: schweizerische Jazz-Zeitschrift/Revue suisse de jazz (Zurich, ?1968) 1 vol., monthly
Jazz riffs (Antwerp, Belgium, 1940, 1946–8) 30 nos., monthly
Jazz Scene, see *Jazz-Bulletin*
The Jazz Session (Chicago, Sept 1944 – July 1946) 13 nos., variously monthly and bimonthly
Jazz-Spiegel der Deutschen Jazz-Föderation, see *Das internationale Podium*
Jazz Spotlite News (New York, June 1979 – sum. 1982) 2 vols. (= 10 nos.)
Jazz Statistics (Basle, Switzerland, April 1956 – 1960); ?Birsfelden, nr Basle, 1960–61; Reinach, nr Basle, 1961 – Oct 1963) 29 nos., irreg.
Jazz String Newsletter (Milwaukee, 1982 – July/Sept 1983) quarterly
Jazz Studies (England, ?1964 – March 1971) irreg.; incorp. into *Pieces of Jazz*
Jazz tango [also *Jazz tango dancing*]: *revue internationale de la musique de danse* (Paris, 1930–40) 66 nos., monthly; incorp. into *L'orchestre: organe d'informations musicales* to form *L'orchestre et Jazz tango réunis* (1963–8) bimonthly
Jazz Tempo (London, March 1943 – March 1944) 19 nos., irreg.; incorp. into *Jazz Music* (1944)
Jazz Tempo: Zeitschrift für die Freunde des Jazz (Kassel, Germany, 1951) 1 vol.
Jazzthetik: Zeitschrift für Jazz und Anderes (Münster, Germany, 1987–)
Jazz 360° (Sierre, Switzerland, Oct 1977 – April 1986) 88 nos., monthly
Jazz Times (Stockholm, 1955–1961/2) ?18 nos., irreg.; contd as *Jazznytt*
Jazz Times (London, Sept 1964 – Dec 1971/Jan 1972) monthly; contd from *Jazz Music*
Jazz Times (Washington), see *Sound Exposure*
Jazzways (Cincinnati, 1946) 1 no.
De jazzwereld (The Hague, 1931 – Nov/Dec 1940) 10 vols., monthly
Jazz wereld (Hilversum, Netherlands, July 1965 – May/June 1973) 43 nos., bimonthly; c.i. nos.1–24 pubd in no.25 (Aug/Sept 1969)
Jazz World, see *Swinging Newsletter*
Jazz World Index, see *Swinging Newsletter*
Jersey Jazz (Pluckemin, nr Plainfield, NJ, later Rahway, NJ, later Verona, NJ, 1973–) mostly 10 or 11 issues yearly; i (1973) (= 11 nos.) as suppl. to *Jazz Digest*
Joslin's Jazz Journal (Parsons, KS, Feb 1982–) quarterly
Journal of Jazz Discography (Newport, Gwent, Wales, Nov 1976 – Sept 1979) 5 nos., irreg.
Journal of Jazz Studies: Incorporating Studies in Jazz Discography [from iii/2 (spr. 1976) *Journal of Jazz Studies*] (New Brunswick, NJ, 1973/4–1980/81) half-yearly; contd as *Annual Review of Jazz Studies*
Keyboard, see *Contemporary Keyboard*
Keynote: a Magazine for the Musical Arts (New York, 1977–) monthly
Klacto: Hawaii's Jazz Newsletter (Honolulu, ?March 1980 – ? Jan 1982) ?3 vols. (= ?15 nos.), monthly except July, from i/9 (Nov 1980) bimonthly
Living Blues [from no.21 (1975) *Living Blues: a Journal of the Black American Blues Tradition*] (Chicago, 1970–spr. 1983; University, MS, aut. 1983–) quarterly, from no.19 (Jan/Feb 1975) bimonthly, from no.43 (sum. 1979) quarterly, from no.67 (1985) 5 issues yearly; suppl.: *Living Blues Letter* (Jan 1983 – Dec 1984) monthly; c.i. nos.1–39 pubd in no.40 (1978)
The Long Player, see DISCOGRAPHIES, *Other listings*
Mainstream (Richmond, nr London, England, sum. 1974) 1 no.
Matrix: Jazz Record Research Magazine (Victoria, Australia, July 1954 – Dec 1958; Stoke on Trent, later Madeley, nr Crewe, England, Jan 1959 – Dec 1975) 108 nos., bimonthly, from no.93 (July 1971) irreg.; c.i. 1954–63; incorp. *The Discophile* (1959)
Mecca: the Magazine of Traditional Jazz (New Orleans, 1974) 3 nos., monthly
Melbourne Jazz News (Melbourne, Australia, March 1959–?)
Melodie (Prague, 1963–) monthly; suppl. *Aktuality melodie* (1969–70) fortnightly
Melodie und Rhythmus (Berlin, 1957–) semimonthly, from April 1971 monthly
The Melody Maker and British Metronome [from no.70 (Oct 1931) *The Melody Maker*] (London, Jan 1926 – May 1933) monthly; new ser. as *The Melody Maker* [from no.330 (Oct 1939) to no.965 (15 March 1952) *Melody Maker Incorporating "Rhythm"*; from no.966 (22 March 1952) *Melody Maker*] (London, 27 May 1933–) weekly
Merritt Rag (Hicksville, NY, aut. 1980–) irreg.
Metronome: Modern Music and its Makers [from lxxvi/1 (Jan 1959) to lxxvii/4 (April 1960) *Music USA*] (New York, 1885 – Dec 1961) 77 vols., monthly; suppl.: *Metronome Yearbook* (1950–51, 1953–9) yearly
Micrography: Jazz and Blues on Microgroove (Deventer, Netherlands, n.d. [Dec 1968] – Feb 1971; Alphen aan de Rijn, Netherlands, May 1971 – June 1982; Amsterdam, Feb 1983–) irreg. [in Eng.]; c.i.
Micro surco, see DISCOGRAPHIES, *Other listings*
The Mississippi Rag: the Voice of Traditional Jazz and Ragtime (Minneapolis, Nov 1973–) monthly
Mitteilungsblatt der Arbeitsgemeinschaft norddeutscher Jazz-Clubs (Hamburg, Germany, 1956–?); contd from *Der Jazzfreund* (Itzehoe, Germany)
MM: tidsskrift for rytmisk musik m.m. [from xvii/1 (Jan 1985) *MM: månedsblad for rock og jazz m.m.*; from xvii/9 (Sept 1985) *MM: månedsblad for rock & jazz*] (Copenhagen, ?1969–) 9 issues yearly
Modern Drummer (Clifton, NJ, 1977–) quarterly, from 1979 6 issues yearly, from 1980 9 issues yearly, from 1983 monthly
Music (Brussels, 1924 – Dec 1939) monthly
Music (London, 1951/2–1953/4) 3 vols., monthly; contd as *Music Mirror*
Musica jazz: rassegna mensile di informazione e critica musicale (Milan, 1945–) monthly
Musical Express, see *Accordion Times & Musical Express*
Music and Rhythm (Chicago, Nov 1940 – Aug 1942) 3 vols., irreg.
Music Life (Tokyo, 1950–?) monthly [in Jap.]
Music Master, see DISCOGRAPHIES, *Other listings*
Music Memories [from iii/2 (April 1963) *Music Memories Monthly*; from iii/5 (aut. 1963) *Music Memories Quarterly*; from iii/6 (win. 1963) *Music Mem-*

ories and Jazz Report] (Birmingham, AL, July 1961 – spr. 1965) 4 vols., 6 issues yearly, from iii/2 (April 1963) monthly, from iii/5 (aut. 1963) quarterly
Music Mirror [from iv/11 (Dec 1957) alternate issues entitled *Jazz Music Mirror* and *Pop Music Mirror*] (London, May 1954 – July 1958) 5 vols., monthly, from iv/11 (Dec 1957) fortnightly; contd from *Music* (London)
Music USA (Heemstede, Netherlands, Feb–May 1954) 4 nos., monthly
Music USA, see *Metronome*
Musikjournalen: blad for moderne dansemusikk, see *Norsk jazz*
Musik og film, see *Jazzavisen*
Musikrevue [from 1961, no.5, to 1970 *Jazzrevy*] (Copenhagen, 1954–72) 19 vols., 4 issues yearly
NAJE Educator, see *National Association of Jazz Educators: Newsletter*
Names & Numbers (Amsterdam, April 1985 – Jan 1987) 6 nos., irreg. [in Eng.]
National Association of Jazz Educators: Newsletter [from ii/2 (Dec 1969/Jan 1970) *NAJE Educator*; from xiii/2 (Dec 1980/Jan 1981) *Jazz Educators Journal*] (Manhattan, KS, 1968/9–) irreg., from ii/2 (Dec 1969/Jan 1970) 5 issues yearly, from iv/1 (Oct/Nov 1971) quarterly
The Needle: Record Collectors' Guide (New York, June 1944 – ?Jan 1945) 2 vols. (= 6 or 7 nos.), monthly
The New Beat (London, July 1949 – July 1950) 13 nos., monthly; contd from *The Beat*
New Musical Express, see *Accordion Times & Musical Express*
News: Mitteilungsblatt der BFN Rhythm Clubs, see *News Sheet*
News about BMI Music & Writers [from Nov 1964 *BMI: the Many Worlds of Music*] (New York, 1963–) 10 issues yearly, from 1972 7 issues yearly, from 1973 3–4 issues yearly; suppl.: *Rhythm and Blues* [1943–68] (1969)
News Sheet: Mitteilungsblatt der Anglo-German Swing-Clubs [from 1950/51 *News: Mitteilungsblatt der BFN* [British Forces Network] *Rhythm Clubs*] (Hamburg, Germany, 1949/50–1950/51) 2 vols.
Norsk jazz: ukeavis for jazz og moderne dansemusikk [from iii/4 (1957) *Musikjournalen: blad for moderne dansemusikk*] (Bergen, Norway, 1955–7) 3 vols., irreg.
Not Just Jazz (New York, 1980–) 8 issues yearly, later quarterly
Orchestra World (New York, 1925–?1954) 29 vols., irreg., from iv (1928) 10 issues yearly
L'orchestre et Jazz tango réunis, see *Jazz tango*
Orkester journalen: aktuella nyheter för dansorkestrar [from iv/1 (Jan 1936) *Orkester journalen: tidskrift för modern dansmusik*; from xxi/1 (Jan 1953) *Orkester journalen: tidskrift för jazzmusik*; from li/4 (April 1983) *Orkester journalen: om jazz*] (Stockholm, Nov 1933–) monthly
Philharmonic (Heemstede, Netherlands, Jan 1950 – Dec 1953) 32 nos., monthly
Pickin' the Blues (East Calder, West Lothian, Scotland, n.d. [Jan 1982] – June 1983) 15 nos., 10 issues yearly
Pickup (London, 1946–7) 2 vols., ?monthly
Pieces of Jazz (Canterbury, England, win. 1967 – 1971) 9 nos., irreg.; no.7 (1969) incorp. *Jazz Studies*
Playback, see *Jazzfinder*
Le point du jazz (Brussels, 1969–) irreg.
Pop Music Mirror, see *Music Mirror*
Quarterly Rag, [1st ser.] (Sydney, Oct 1955 – June 1967) 39 nos., 3–4 issues yearly; 2nd ser. (Sydney, April 1976–) quarterly
Radio Free Jazz, see *Sound Exposure*
Ragtimer, see *Ragtime Society Bulletin*
Ragtime Review, see *Christensen's Ragtime Review*
Rag Times (Los Angeles, May 1967–) bimonthly
Ragtime Society Bulletin [from vi (1967) *Ragtimer*] (Weston, Canada, 1962–) bimonthly
The Record Changer (Fairfax, VA, Aug 1942 – Dec 1947; New York, Jan 1948 – 1957) 15 vols. [= 152 nos.], monthly, from xiv/1 (Jan 1955) bimonthly, from xiv/7 (Jan 1956) irreg.
Record Research (New York, Feb 1955–) irreg.; suppl. (June 1955 – Aug 1965), 18 nos., irreg.
Record Review (Los Angeles, 1976 – ? Aug 1984) [trial issue i/A (1976); regular issues from i/1 (1977)] bimonthly
Revista "Long-playing", see DISCOGRAPHIES, *Other listings*
La revue du jazz (Paris, Jan 1949 – March/April 1950) 11 nos.
La revue du jazz: revue trimestrielle d'éducation musicale des orchestres de jazz (Paris, 1937) 1 vol., quarterly
Revue suisse de jazz, see *Jazz, Rhythm & Blues*
Rhythm (London, Sept 1927 – Sept 1939) 13 vols. (144 nos.), monthly; incorp. into *Melody Maker* (Oct 1939)
Rhythm and Blues, see *News about BMI Music & Writers*
Rhythme (Eindhoven, Netherlands, Oct 1949 – Sept 1961) 144 nos., monthly
Rolling Stone (San Francisco, 1967/8–1976/7; New York, 1977/8–) fortnightly
Route (Münster, Germany, 1956/7) 1 vol., quarterly
Rytmi (Helsinki, April 1934 – Dec 1937, Jan 1949 – Dec 1981; Tampere, Finland, Jan 1982–) 3–6 issues yearly, later 10 issues yearly
Sabin's Happenings, see *Sound Exposure*
Sabin's Radio Free Jazz, USA, see *Sound Exposure*
Santandrea catalogo generale, see DISCOGRAPHIES, *Other listings*
Saxophone Sheet [later *Saxophone Journal*] (Medfield, MA, 1976/7–) quarterly
Schlagzeug: das Jazz-Magazin (Berlin, 1956–60) 5 vols., monthly
Schwann: Long Playing Record Catalog, see DISCOGRAPHIES, *Other listings*
The Second Line (New Orleans, April 1950–) 12 issues in pairs yearly, from xxv/[1] (Jan 1971) quarterly
Soul Bag (Levallois-Perret, France, *c*1970–) irreg.
Sound Exposure [from x/? (Oct 1970) *Sabin's Happenings*; from xii/? (May 1972) *Sabin's Radio Free Jazz, USA*; from xv/6 (June 1975) *Radio Free Jazz*; from June 1980 *Jazz Times*] (Washington, ?1961–) irreg., from 1973 monthly
Sounds & Fury (Utica, NY, July 1965 – Aug 1966) 6 nos., bimonthly
The Stars of Jazzette (Versailles, France, Jan 1976 – 1978) 9 nos., irreg. [parallel texts in Eng. and Fr.]
Storyville (London, Oct/Nov 1965 – Oct/Nov 1973; Chigwell, England, Dec 1973/Jan 1974–) bimonthly, from no.128 (Dec 1986/Jan 1987) quarterly
Stuttgarter Brief: Mitteilungsblatt des Clubs der Schlüssel (Stuttgart, Germany, 1951) 1 vol.
Swing (Buenos Aires, Oct 1936–) irreg.
Swing (Auckland, New Zealand, Oct 1941 – Aug 1942) ?11 nos., monthly
Swing: the Guide to Modern Music (New York, April 1938 – 1940) monthly
Swing: officeel orgaan van The Batavia Rhythm Club (Batavia [now Jakarta], Java, 1937–8) monthly
Swing: tidskrift för ungdom, modern musik, sport och dans (Stockholm, Oct 1944 – ? Dec 1945), ?15 nos., monthly
Swing & Sweet from Hollywood and 52nd Street (Amsterdam, Jan–May 1950) 5 nos., monthly
Swinging Newsletter [from no.5 (June 1973) *Swinging Newsletter: Bulletin of the European Jazz Federation*; from ?no.32 (?April 1977) *Swinging Newsletter: Publication of the International Jazz Federation*; from no.39 (Jan 1979) *Jazz Echo: Publication of the International Jazz Federation*; from no.46 (Aug 1981) *Jazz World Index*; from no.59 (1984) *Jazz World*] (Vienna, 1972–7; New York, Dec 1977–) monthly, from ?nos.16–17 (?1975) bimonthly, from ?no.32 (?April 1977) irreg., from no.59 (1984) bimonthly
Swing Journal (Tokyo, 1947–) monthly; s.i. irreg.; discographical suppls.: [*?1974*] *Swing Journal* (1975) yearly; *Jazz Records* [*1975–83*] (?1976–1983) yearly; *Jazz Disco & Video* [*1984–5*] (1984–5) yearly; *Jazz CD, Record, Video* [*1986*] (1987–) yearly [in Jap.]
Swing Music (London, March 1935 – aut. 1936) 2 vols. (= 14 nos.), monthly, from i/8 (1935) bimonthly, from no.14 (1936) quarterly
Swingtime: maandblad voor jazz en blues/Swing Time: revue mensuelle de la musique de jazz (Ruiselede, Belgium, 1950–) monthly [in Dutch and Fr.]
Swiss Jazz Notes, see *Jazz-Bulletin*
Syncopation (Sydney, Dec 1946 – June 1947) 5 nos., irreg.
Syncopa y ritmo: revista de jazz (Buenos Aires, Aug 1934 – Aug 1944) *c*75 nos., monthly
Talent and Tunes on Music Machines, see *Billboard Advertising*
Tanečni hudba a jazz [Dance music and jazz] (Prague, 1960–)
Tempo [later *Tempo and Television*] (Sydney, Sept 1937 – Jan 1960) 22 vols., irreg.
Tempo: the Modern Musical Newsmagazine (Los Angeles, 1933–40) 8 vols., 8–10 issues yearly, from viii/1 (Oct 1939) fortnightly; incorp. into *Down Beat* (?1940)
Texas Jazz, see *Dallas Jazz News Letter*
Texas Ragg (Dallas, Jan–Nov 1983) 11 nos., monthly; contd from *Texas Jazz*, see *Dallas Jazz News Letter*
Tribune: tidsskrift for moderne dansemusik [from no.8 (1946) *Jazzinformation: tribune*] (Copenhagen, 1945–6) 11 nos.
Variety: a Variety Paper for Variety People [from xviii/12 (1910) *Variety*] (New York, 16 Dec 1905–) weekly
Vier Viertel: Musik-Magazin für Schlager-, Film-, Jazz-, und Schallplattenfreunde [subtitle varies: also *Halbmonatsschrift für Musik und Tanz*] (Berlin, 1947–56) 10 vols., 24 issues yearly; suppls. *Jazz Revue* (1954) 1 vol., monthly; *Der Jazz-Courier* (1955–6)
Vintage Jazz Mart (London, Dec 1953–) irreg.
Wavelength (New Orleans, Nov 1980–) monthly
Western Australia's Music Maker (Perth, Australia, Jan 1983–)
Westjazz: Jazz-Nachrichten aus Westdeutschland, see *HCD-Bulletin*
Whiskey, Women, and. . . (Haverhill, MA, ?1971–1972; Boston, 1972–) irreg.
Who's Who: Discograph, see *Jazz-Bulletin*
Who's Who in the World of Music, see *Billboard Advertising*
The Wire [from no.24 (Feb 1986) *Wire*] (London, sum. 1982–) quarterly, from no.8 (Oct 1984) monthly; c.i. nos.1–22 separately pubd

Appendix 2

LIST OF CONTRIBUTORS

Below are listed all signatories of articles in this dictionary. For living contributors, the name is followed by his/her last known place of work or residence. The entries by each are listed after his/her name; where a title is preceded by an asterisk (*), the contributor concerned is a part-author.

Adams, Simon (London) Ardley, Neil; Biscoe, Chris; Cadillac (ii); Charig, Marc; Collier, Graham; Company; Crombie, Tony; European Jazz Quintet; Gare, Lou; Goode, Coleridge; Hunter, Chris; Ind, Peter; Jazz Centre Society; Jenkins, Karl; Laurence, Chris; Lemer, Pete; Le Sage, Bill; London Jazz Composers Orchestra; Marshall, John; Mathewson, Ron; Mosaic (i); Ogun; Pine, Courtney; Ricotti, Frank; Rutherford, Paul; Spontaneous Music Ensemble; Surman, John; Tippetts, Julie; Wachsmann, Phil; Warleigh, Ray; Watts, Trevor

Allen, Richard B. (New Orleans) Jackson, Preston

Ashforth, Alden (Reseda, CA) Barrett, Sweet Emma; *Bigard family; Cagnolatti, Cag; Desvigne, Sidney; Frazier, Cié; Handy, Capt. John; Howard, Kid; Johnson, Bill (i); Lewis, George (i); Pavageau, Alcide "Slow Drag"; Pichon, Fats; Piron, A. J.; Rena, Kid; Robinson, Jim; *Tio family

Ayala, Cristóbal Díaz (Hato Rey Station, PR) Bauzá, Mario; Caunedo, Jesús; Irakere; O'Farrill, Chico; Sandoval, Arturo; Valdés, Chucho

Bacon, Tony (London) *Electric bass guitar; *Guitar

Baggenaes, Roland (Copenhagen) Bailey, Benny; Blackburn, Lou; Clarke–Boland Big Band; Hampton, Slide; Jaspar, Bobby; Lundgaard, Jesper; Martinez, Sabu; Shihab, Sahib; Spaulding, James; Sulieman, Idrees

Barbera, André (Notre Dame, IN) Albany, Joe; Burns, Dave; Christy, June; Coles, Johnny; Connor, Chris; Copeland, Ray; Drew, Kenny; Freeman, Russ; Hardman, Bill; Levy, Lou

Barker, Danny (New Orleans) Hamfat

Barnett, Anthony (Lewes, England) Crouch, Stanley

Barrell, Alan (Cambridge, England) Alcorn, Alvin; Baquet, Achille; Baquet, George; Collins, Lee

Bash, Lee (Louisville, KY) National Association of Jazz Educators

Beck, Frederick A. (Greensboro, NC) Battle, Puddinghead; Brashear, Oscar; Bridgewater, Cecil; Candoli, Conte; Candoli, Pete; Collins, Burt; Dedrick, Rusty; Eardley, Jon; Fagerquist, Don; Harden, Wilbur; Henderson, Eddie; Hillyer, Lonnie; Johnson, Money; Moore, Danny; Owens, Jimmy; Porcino, Al; Rader, Don; Travis, Nick; Wilson, Gerald; Wright family

Bemis, Ed (Hanover, NH) Dearie, Blossom; McRae, Carmen

Bennett, Bill (Palo Alto, CA) Davis, Richard; Dawson, Alan; Taylor, Billy (ii)

Berendt, Joachim E. (Baden Baden, Germany) *Dauner, Wolfgang; *Kühn, Rolf; *Mangelsdorff, Albert

Berger, Edward (Newark, NJ) Carter, Benny; Discography; Edison, Harry; Hammond, John; Institute of Jazz Studies

Bevan, Clifford (Winchester, England) *Cornet; Flugelhorn; Horn; Marimba; Mellophone; Multiphonics; *Mute; Saxhorn; Trombone; Trumpet; Tuba; Vibraphone; Xylophone

Blake, Ran (Boston) Bley, Paul; Monk, Thelonious

Bonoff, Edward L. (New Rochelle, NY) Grimes, Tiny

Boulton, Heidi (Stuttgart, Germany) Beckerhoff, Uli; Doldinger, Klaus; Freund, Joki; Greger, Max; Kriegel, Volker; Mangelsdorff, Emil; Naura, Michael; Rediske, Johannes

Braman, Chuck (Cleveland Heights, OH) Erskine, Peter; Gadd, Steve; Motian, Paul; Muhammad, Idris; Ndugu; Washington, Kenny

Britt, Stan (London) Beck, Gordon; Carr, Ian; Carr, Mike; Clyne, Jeff; Dillard, Bill; Drew, Martin; Gaillard, Slim; Hiseman, Jon; King, Peter; Morgan, Lanny; Morrissey, Dick; Mullen, Jim; Rose, Denis; Thompson, Barbara; Wilkins, Ernie

Brockman, William S. (Madison, NJ) Domanico, Chuck; Friesen, David; Gaskin, Vic; Hughart, Jim; Lee, John; Magnusson, Bob; Moore, Michael; Richmond, Mike; Sproles, Victor; Swartz, Harvie; Warren, Peter

Brodowski, Pawel (Warsaw) Matuszkiewicz, Jerzy; Smietana, Jarosław

Brown, T. Dennis (Amherst, MA) Alvin, Danny; Barcelona, Danny; Bauduc, Ray; Berton, Vic; Crawford, Jimmy; Drootin, Buzzy; Drum set; Fatool, Nick; Feld, Morey; Fields, Kansas; Francis, Panama; Hall, Minor; Hall, Tubby; Johnson, Manzie; Johnson, Walter; Marshall, Kaiser; Morehouse, Chauncey; Rudiments; Sbarbaro, Tony; Spencer, O'Neill; Trappier, Art

Brunner, Gerhard (Vienna) *Gulda, Friedrich

Brylawski, Samuel S. (Washington) *Mercer, Johnny; Robinson, Bill

Budds, Michael J. (Columbia, MO) Hirt, Al; Schifrin, Lalo; Tormé, Mel; Wilson, Nancy

Carner, Gary (Belmont, MA) Alemán, Oscar; Ashby, Irving;

Beck, Joe; Brignola, Nick; Cook, Junior; Davis, Steve; Gales, Larry; Puma, Joe; Williams, Leroy; Wright, Leo

Chilton, John (London) Bailey, Buster; Bostic, Earl; Boswell, Connee; Bradford, Perry; Brown, Pete; Celestin, Papa; Cheatham, Doc; Clayton, Buck; Cole, Cozy; Crosby, Bob; Davison, Wild Bill; Dickenson, Vic; Dutrey, Honore; Foster, Pops; Greer, Sonny; Hackett, Bobby; Hamilton, Jimmy; Harris, Bill (i); Harrison, Jimmy; Hinton, Milt; Jackson, Tony; James, Harry; Laine, Papa Jack; McKinney's Cotton Pickers; Marable, Fate; Mezzrow, Mezz; Morton, Benny; Murphy, Turk; New Orleans Rhythm Kings; Original Dixieland Jazz Band; Page, Hot Lips; Petit, Buddy; Picou, Alphonse; Rollini, Adrian; Shavers, Charlie; Simmen, Johnny; Smith, Jabbo; Smith, Joe; *Tio family; Trumbauer, Frankie

Clergeat, André (Fontenay-aux-Roses, France) Badini, Gérard; Bolling, Claude; Delaunay, Charles; Fol, Hubert; Fol, Raymond; Gilson, Jef; Hodeir, André; Humair, Daniel; Jenny-Clark, Jean-François; Lafitte, Guy; Legrand, Michel; Lockwood, Didier; Louiss, Eddy; Loussier, Jacques; Michelot, Pierre; Panassié, Hugues; Pedersen, Guy; Quintette du Hot Club de France; Reinhardt, Joseph; Renaud, Henri; Romano, Aldo; Saury, Maxim; Silva, Alan; *Solal, Martial; Urtreger, René; Viale, Jean-Louis

Coller, Derek (Sawbridgeworth, England) Collie, Max; Donegan, Lonnie; Fairweather, Al; Halcox, Pat; Lightfoot, Terry; Rimington, Sammy; Smith, Keith; Temperance Seven; Webb, George

Collier, James Lincoln (New York) Armstrong, Louis; Bands; Barnet, Charlie; Bechet, Sidney; Dorsey, Jimmy; Dorsey, Tommy; Grofé, Ferde; *Hall family; Henderson, Fletcher; Higginbotham, J. C.; Holiday, Billie; Jazz (i); Mainstream jazz; Miller, Glenn; Raeburn, Boyd; Tailgate; *Teagarden family; Wells, Dicky

Collins, Catherine (Brookline, MA) Acuña, Alex; Barbieri, Gato; Camero, Candido; Castro-Neves, Oscar; Clarke, Stanley; D'Rivera, Paquito; Farrell, Joe; Gismonti, Egberto; MacDonald, Ralph; Valdez, Carlos "Potato"

Collinson, John (Heathfield, Sussex, England) Blythe, Jimmy; Ewell, Don

Conrad, Gerhard (Menden, Germany) Barrelhouse Jazzband; Behounek, Kamil; Brom, Gustav; Déczi, Ladislav; Dobschinski, Walter; Essen, Reimer von; Habart, Ladislav; Hála, Kamil; Havlik, Ferdinand; Hnilička, Jaromír; Hulan, Ludek; Ježek, Jaroslav; Kavka, Arnošt; Krautgartner, Karel; Ludvik, Emil; Šima, Jan; Smetaček, Pavel; Velebný, Karel; Vlach, Karel

Cook, Eddie (London) Cobb, Arnett; Hucko, Peanuts; Jacquet, Illinois; Jacquet, Russell; Johnson, Budd; Klink, Al; Person, Houston; Tate, Buddy

Cooper, Jeffrey (Ann Arbor, MI) Caceres, Ernie; Douglas, Tommy; Fazola, Irving; Hutchenrider, Clarence; Mince, Johnny; Yaged, Sol

Cooper, Reg (Fareham, England) Chisholm, George; Kral, Irene; Kral, Roy; McCall, Mary Ann; Roche, Betty; Ross, Annie; Sherrill, Joya; Turner, Bruce; Waters, Benny

Cowley, John (Kings Langley, England) *Appleton, Joe; *Blake, Cyril; *Hutchinson, Jiver; *Johnson, Ken "Snake Hips"; *King, Bertie

Crawford, Richard (Ann Arbor, MI) McKenna, Dave

Curry, John (Easthampton, MA) Abdul-Malik, Ahmed; Booker, Walter; Brown, Cameron; Houston, Clint; Lombardi, Clyde; Lucas, Al; Maize, Bob; May, Earl; Merritt, Jymie; Mitchell, Red; Mitchell, Whitey; Parham, Truck; Pemberton, Bill; Raglin, Junior; Ruther, Wyatt; Ware, Wilbur; Warren, Butch; Williams, Buster

Daniel, Oliver (Scarsdale, NY) Overton, Hall

Dapogny, James (Ann Arbor, MI) *Beiderbecke, Bix; Berigan, Bunny; Freeman, Bud; Hines, Earl; Lang, Eddie; Livingston, Fud; Mole, Miff; Nichols, Red; Rushing, Jimmy; Russell, Pee Wee; Schoebel, Elmer; Wallace, Sippie

Darke, Peter Solomon, Reuben; West, Cedric

Davies, Hugh (London) Synthesizer

Dean, Roger T. (Harrow, England) Bailey, Derek; Beckett, Harry; Dickerson, Walt; Guy, Barry; Hampel, Gunter; Kühn, Joachim; Naughton, Bobby

Deffaa, Chip (Glen Rock, NJ) Beckett, Fred; Coker, Henry; Gee, Matthew; Hamilton, Scott; Igoe, Sonny; Johnson, Charlie; Napoleon family; Tarto, Joe; Vaché, Warren; Williams, Johnny

de Ledesma, Charles (London) Bahula, Julian; Dyani, Johnny; Feza, Mongezi; McGregor, Chris; Masekela, Hugh; Miller, Harry; Moholo, Louis; Pukwana, Dudu

DeVeaux, Scott (Charlottesville, VA) Adderley, Nat; Best, Skeeter; Boyd, Nelson; Collins, Rudy; Farmer, Addison; Foster, Frank; Gaskin, Leonard; Green, Freddie; Greenlee, Charles; Guy, Joe; Harris, Joe (ii); McGhee, Howard; Mills, Jackie; Parker, Leo; Potter, Tommy; Rumsey, Howard; Russell, Curly; Sears, Al; Thompson, Sir Charles; Wayne, Chuck

Dibussolo, Frank A. (Philadelphia) Bertoncini, Gene; Szabó, Gábor

Dickow, Robert (Moscow, ID) Barone, Gary; Barone, Mike; Blanchard, Terence; Bryant, Bobby; Ellis, Don; Faddis, Jon; Ferris, Glenn; Harrell, Tom; Henderson, Wayne; Noto, Sam; Sun Ra

Dobbins, Bill (Rochester, NY) Brackeen, JoAnne; *Cole, Nat "King"; Corea, Chick; Flanagan, Tommy; Garland, Red; Hancock, Herbie; Hanna, Roland; Harris, Barry; Hart, Clyde; Hopkins, Claude; Jarrett, Keith; *Jones family; Kelly, Wynton; Peterson, Oscar; Rivers, Sam; Shearing, George; Silver, Horace; Smith, Jimmy; Smith, Willie "the Lion"; Stacy, Jess; Taylor, Cecil; Tyner, McCoy; *Waller, Fats

Doerschuk, Bob (Cupertino, CA) Kirkland, Kenny; Mance, Junior; Marmarosa, Dodo; Miles, Barry; Nock, Mike; Ozone, Makoto; Petrucciani, Michel; Rowles, Jimmie; Strazzeri, Frank; Waldron, Mal; Zeitlin, Denny

Doran, James M. (Pomona, NY) Bowman, Dave; Bushkin, Joe; Calhoun, Eddie; Chittison, Herman "Ivory"; Duncan, Hank; Hill, Alex; Jackson, Cliff; Jaffe, Nat; Johnson, Pete; Jones, Jimmy; Jones, Richard M.; Kerr, Brooks; Richards, Red; Ross, Arnold; Schroeder, Gene; Signorelli, Frank; Simmons, Norman; Weatherford, Teddy; Wein, George; White, Sonny; Williams, Al

Driggs, Frank (New York) Bascomb, Dud; Bascomb, Paul; Blakeney, Andy; Cab Jivers; Chocolate Dandies; Dash, Julian; Douglas, Billy; Gibson, Andy; Holland, Peanuts; Howard, Paul; Jeter–Pillars Orchestra; Jones–Smith, Inc.; Jordan, Louis; Kansas City Rockets; Kansas City Six; Lee, George E.; Lee, Julia; Leonard, Harlan; Lewis, Ed; Lewis, Willie; Little Chicks; McShann, Jay; Millinder, Lucky; Missourians; Palmer, Singleton; Randolph, Irving "Mouse"; Robinson, Prince; Sampson, Edgar; Smith, Tab; Spirits of Rhythm; Stovall, Don; Thomas, Joe (iii); Thomas, Joe (iv); Washington, Jack; Wilson, Dick; Wooding, Sam

Fairweather, Digby (Westcliff-on-Sea, England) Ambrose, Bert; Ash, Vic; Ashton, Bill; Ballamy, Iain; *Barber, Chris; Bates, Django; Chilton, John; Clare, Alan; Coe, Tony; Cohen, Alan; Cotton, Mike; *Dankworth, John; Davies, John R. T.; Downes, Bob; Ellington, Ray; Elsdon, Alan; Fallon, Jack; Fierstone, George; Galbraith, Charlie; Galbraith, Gus; Gay,

Al; *Gibbs, Mike; Graham, Kenny; Greig, Stan; Hawdon, Dickie; Heckstall-Smith, Dick; Heralds of Swing; Hogg, Derek; Hughes, Spike; Hylton, Jack; Ingham, Keith; Jacobson, Pete; Klein, Harry; Korner, Alexis; Lee, Tony; Lemon, Brian; Loose Tubes; Lowther, Henry; *Lyttelton, Humphrey; Montgomery, Marian; Moore, Gerry; Mulligan, Mick; Munn, Billy; Picard, John; Priestley, Brian; *Scott, Ronnie; Seamen, Phil; Smith, Brian; South, Harry; Spring, Brian; Temperley, Joe; Themen, Art; Thompson, Eddie; *Tracey, Stan; Warren, John; *Westbrook, Mike; Whittle, Tommy; Winters, Tiny

Feather, Leonard (Sherman Oaks, CA) *Singing

Ferguson, Jim (Cupertino, CA) Bauer, Billy; Breau, Lenny; Collins, John; Diorio, Joe; *Electric bass guitar; Ellis, Herb; Galbraith, Barry; *Guitar; Hall, Jim; Holdsworth, Allan; Jordan, Stanley; Lagrene, Bireli; Palmier, Remo; Remler, Emily; Reuss, Allan; Roberts, Howard

Fernández, Laureano (Buenos Aires) *Boiarsky, Andrés; *Franzetti, Carlos; *López Fürst, Rubén; *López Ruiz, Jorge; *Navarro, Jorge; *Oliva, Hernán; *Porteña Jazz Band; *Remus, Alfredo; *Saluzzi, Dino; *Sanchez Reinoso, Raúl; *Santa Paula Serenaders; *Trío Argentina; *Villegas, Enrique

Flanagan, David (Ithaca, NY) Asmussen, Svend; Bang, Billy; Byers, Billy; Byrd, Charlie; Carver, Wayman; Dennis, Matt; Finegan, Bill; Garland, Joe; Jackson, Chubby; Jobim, Antonio Carlos; Kincaide, Deane; Lamare, Nappy; Lucie, Lawrence; McIntosh, Tom; Marrero, Lawrence; Mastren, Carmen; Scott, Bud; Steig, Jeremy; White, Michael (i); Zoller, Attila

Fox, Charles (Weymouth, England) *Barber, Chris; *Dankworth, John; *Elizalde, Fred; Foresythe, Reginald; *Gibbs, Mike; *Lyttelton, Humphrey; *Scott, Ronnie; *Tracey, Stan; *Westbrook, Mike

Fredrickson, Scott (Fullerton, CA) Anderson, Ivie; Bey, Andy; Boone, Richard; Bridgewater, Dee Dee; Franks, Michael; Hall, Adelaide; Hibbler, Al; Ward, Helen

Gagnon, Yves (Montreal) *Boland, Francy

Gannon, Robert (Bellefonte, PA) Fox, Charles; Harrison, Max; James, Michael; McRae, Barry; Morgan, Alun; Oliver, Paul; Rust, Brian; Traill, Sinclair; Wilmer, Val

García Brunelli, Omar (Capital Federal, Argentina) *Boiarsky, Andrés; *Franzetti, Carlos; *López Fürst, Rubén; *López Ruiz, Jorge; *Navarro, Jorge; Oliva Hernán; *Porteña Jazz Band; *Remus, Alfredo; *Saluzzi, Dino; *Sanchez Reinoso, Raúl; *Santa Paula Serenaders; *Trío Argentina; *Villegas, Enrique

Gardner, Mark (Faversham, England) Affinity; Argo; Atco; Ava; Bakton; Bee Hive; Bethlehem; Black Jazz; Charlie Parker Records; Christlieb, Pete; Cleveland, Jimmy; Cobblestone; Contact; Contemporary; Criss Cross Jazz; Dauntless; Davis, Charles; Dial; DiNovi, Gene; Discovery; East: West; Epic; Ervin, Booker; ESP-disk; Foster, Gary; Fresh Sounds; Galaxy; GNP; Green, Bennie; Guild; Hayes, Tubby; Hep; Hifijazz; Hogan, G. T.; IAJRC (i); Imperial; Impulse!; Jaro; Jazzline; Jazz West; Jones, Carmell; Jordan, Clifford; Judson; Kahn, Tiny; Klacto; Knepper, Jimmy; Kotick, Teddy; Land, Harold; Little, Wilbur; Macero, Teo; Mariano, Charlie; Metrojazz; Mettome, Doug; Mole; Moody, James; Morrow, George; Musicraft; Onyx (ii); Pacific Jazz; Peacock's Progressive Jazz; Phoenix Jazz; Pleasure, King; Progressive; Regina; Reprise; Revelation; Richardson, Jerome; Rosolino, Frank; Sackville; Scepter; 77; Signal; Spotlite (ii); Storyville (ii); Time (ii); Transition; Turrentine, Tommy; United Artists; Vault; Warwick; Wave; Williamson, Claude; Wilson, Shadow; Workman, Reggie; World Wide; Wyands, Richard; Xanadu

Gariglio, Raymond J. (Wilmington, NC) Arodin, Sidney; Bilk, Acker; Bivona, Gus; Browne, Toby; Bushell, Garvin; Caldwell, Happy; Cless, Rod; D'Amico, Hank; De Faut, Volly; Dixon, Joe; Fountain, Pete; Inge, Edward; Jackson, Rudy; Lytell, Jimmy; McCracken, Bob; Muranyi, Joe; Nelson, Big Eye Louis; Parenti, Tony; Polo, Danny; Rodin, Gil

Gelly, Dave (London) Auld, Georgie; Coker, Jerry; Hafer, Dick; Lanphere, Don; Marsh, Arno; Mosse, Sandy; Steward, Herbie

Gentieu, Norman P. (Philadelphia) Sullivan, Joe; Sutton, Ralph

Gilbert, Mark (London) Berg, Bob; Bruce, Jack; Coxhill, Lol; Crawford, Hank; Dean, Elton; Garrick, Michael; Harris, Eddie; Nicols, Maggie; Osborne, Mike; Oxley, Tony; Parker, Evan; Paz; Prévost, Eddie; Race, Steve; Rendell, Don; Ross, Ronnie; Skidmore, Alan; Soft Machine; Stewart, Louis; Tippett, Keith

Glaser, Matt (Cambridge, MA) Smith, Stuff; South, Eddie; *Violin

Gould, Tony (Melbourne, Australia) Barnard, Bob; Barnard, Len; Biddell, Kerrie; Brown, Brian; Lee, Alan; Monsbourgh, Ade; Sedergreen, Bob; Smith, Frank; Traynor, Frank

Graziano, John (Flushing, NY) Sissle, Noble

Green, Jeffrey P. (Crawley, England) Briggs, Arthur; Jenkins, Edmund Thornton; Jenkins' Orphanage bands; *Johnson, Ken "Snake Hips"; Thompson, Leslie; Wilkins, Dave; Williams, Spencer

Greene, Philip (Hamden, CT) Allison, Mose; Bavan, Yolande; Bishop, Walter, Jr.; Hammer, Jan; Hendricks, Jon; Lambert, Dave; Lambert, Hendricks, and Ross; Mahones, Gildo; Mitchell, Dwike; Ruff, Willie

Gridley, Mark C. (Tiffin, OH) Cherry, Don; Cool jazz; Coryell, Larry; Ferguson, Maynard; Haden, Charlie; Hard bop; Henderson, Joe; Jazz-rock; McLaughlin, John; Mangione, Chuck; Martino, Pat; Turrentine, Stanley; World Saxophone Quartet; Zawinul, Joe

Gronow, Pekka (Helsinki) Aaltonen, Juhani; Aho, Erkki; Ahola, Sylvester; Danielsson, Palle; Donner, Otto; Häme, Olli; Hansen, Ole Kock; Kärki, Toivo; Koivistoinen, Eero; Kukko, Sakari; Laakko, Bruno; Lindström, Erik; Malmstén, Eugen; Paakkunainen, Seppo; Persson, Bent; Pethman, Esa; Pöyry, Pekka; Radiojazzgruppen (ii); Salmi, Klaus; Sarmanto, Heikki; Sarmanto, Pekka; Schwindt, Christian; Stenson, Bobo; Tolonen, Jukka; Vesala, Edward

Gushee, Lawrence (Urbana, IL) New Orleans jazz; Oliver, King; Traditional jazz

Haefliger, Kathleen (New York) Charters, Samuel B.

Harrison, Max (London) Chaloff, Serge; Charles, Teddy; Dameron, Tadd; Desmond, Paul; Haig, Al; Progressive jazz; Russell, Luis; *Solal, Martial; Symphonic jazz; West Coast jazz

Hasse, John Edward (Alexandria, VA) Blesh, Rudi; Carmichael, Hoagy; Parker, Knocky; Robinson, J. Russel; Rose, Wally; Scobey, Bob

Hatch, Marty (Ithaca, NY) Alexandria, Lorez; Brewer, Teresa; Carroll, Joe "Bebop"; Dorough, Bob; Gilberto, Astrud; Gilberto, João; Hartman, Johnny; Jordan, Sheila; Lincoln, Abbey; McFerrin, Bobby

Hazeldine, Mike (Stockport, England) Adde, Leo; Armstrong, Lil; Bean, Floyd; Big Four; Black Bottom Stompers; Blair, Lee; Bland, Jack; Bocage, Peter; Brown, Boyce; Cary, Dick; Chicago Footwarmers; Christian family; Cottrell, Louis, Jr.; Cottrell, Louis, Sr.; Dixie Syncopators; Gowans, Brad; Harlem Blues and Jazz Band; Hayton, Lennie; Hodes, Art; Hot

Five; Jackson, Franz; Jazz Cardinals; Jones and Collins Astoria Hot Eight; Legends of Jazz; Louisiana Five; New Orleans Feetwarmers; New Orleans Wanderers; Original Creole Band; Original New Orleans Jazz Band (i); Original New Orleans Jazz Band (ii); Preservation Hall Jazz Band; Prima, Leon; Prima, Louis; Ragas, Henry; Red Hot Peppers; Red Onion Jazz Babies; Rhythmakers; Robichaux, John; Robichaux, Joseph; Robinson, Fred; Russell, Bill; Spikes' Seven Pods of Pepper; State Street Ramblers; Washboard Rhythm Kings; *Williams, Clarence

Hazell, Ed (Somerville, MA) Arnold, Horacee; Black Artists Group; Blake, Ran; Blythe, Arthur; Bradford, Bobby; Burrell, Dave; Carter, John; Coltrane, Alice; Cooper, Jerome; Cowell, Stanley; Freeman, Chico; Freeman, Von; Greene, Burton; Harris, Beaver; Hill, Andrew; Holland, Dave; Ibrahim, Abdullah; Jackson, Ronald Shannon; Jazz Composer's Orchestra Association; Lyons, Jimmy; McBee, Cecil; McIntyre, Kalaparusha Maurice; Moffett, Charles; Moncur, Grachan, III; Patrick, Pat; Riley, Howard; Smith, Warren (ii); Stevens, John; Stewart, Bob; Wadud, Abdul; White, Andrew; Wilson, Phillip

Henley, Clarrie (Bolton, England) Barnes, John; Bryden, Beryl; Christie, Ian; Christie, Keith; Crimmins, Roy; Disley, Diz; Fairweather, Digby; Felix, Lennie; Gold, Harry; Hastings, Lennie; Hunt, Fred; Melly, George; Moss, Danny; Moule, Ken; Parry, Harry; Semple, Archie; Welsh, Alex; Williams, Roy

Hodeir, André (Garches, France) *Ellington, Duke

Holden, Stephen (New York) Bennett, Tony; Blood, Sweat and Tears

Homzy, Andrew (Montreal) *Boland, Francy

Hosiasson, José (Santiago) Calloway, Cab; Carney, Harry; Ory, Kid; Rich, Buddy; Strayhorn, Billy

Howlett, Felicity (New York) *Tatum, Art

Huesmann, Günther (Cologne, Germany) Auer, Pepsi; Berking, Willy; *Brocksieper, Freddie; De Weille, Benny; Edelhagen, Kurt; Lenz, Günter; Weber, Eberhard; Wehner, Heinz; Weintraub Syncopators

Hultin, Randi (Oslo) Andersen, Arild; Christensen, Jon; Garbarek, Jan; Krog, Karin; Rypdal, Terje; Stubø, Thorgeir

Iannapollo, Robert J. (Rochester, NY) Bennink, Han; Brötzmann, Peter; Christmann, Günter; Dudek, Gerd; Favre, Pierre; Globe Unity Orchestra; Harris, Craig; Jamal, Khan; Kowald, Peter; Lovens, Paul; Niebergall, Buschi; Schoof, Manfred; Sharrock, Sonny; van Hove, Fred

Iwanami, Yozo (Tokyo) Hara, Nobuo; Hino, Motohiko; Hino, Terumasa; Honda, Toshiyuki; Ishikawa, Hisao; Karashima, Fumio; Kawaguchi, George; Kawasaki, Ryo; Kikuchi, Masabumi; Kitamura, Eiji; Maeda, Norio; Masuda, Ichiro; Masuo, Yoshiaki; Matsumoto, Sleepy; Miyama, Toshiyuki; Miyazawa, Akira; Mukai, Shigeharu; Nakamura, Teruo; Ohno, Shunzo; Sakata, Akira; Sato, Masahiko; Shimizu, Jun; Suzuki, Yoshio; Takahashi, Tatsuya; Togashi, Masahiko; Watanabe, Kazumi; Yagi, Masao; Yamashita, Yosuke

Jaffe, Andrew (Conway, MA) Abney, Don; Broadbent, Alan; Byard, Jaki; Costa, Eddie; Davis, Wild Bill; Earland, Charles; Fuller, Gil; Guaraldi, Vince; Guarnieri, Johnny; Heywood, Eddie; Holmes, Groove; Jolly, Pete; Katz, Dick; Kersey, Kenny; Lang, Mike; Lytle, Johnny; McDuff, Brother Jack; Massey, Cal; Matthews, Ronnie; Morris, Marlowe

James, Michael (Pilton, England) Giuffre, Jimmy; Herman, Woody; McPherson, Charles; Marsh, Warne; Mobley, Hank; Morgan, Lee; Reinhardt, Django; Wellins, Bobby

Jeske, Lee (New York) Abrams, Muhal Richard; Adams, Pepper; Benson, George; Bowie, Lester; Farmer, Art; Hutcherson, Bobby; Lateef, Yusef; Laws, Hubert; McLean, Jackie; Marsalis, Wynton; Rudd, Roswell; Thomas, Leone; Winding, Kai

Johnson, Bruce (Kensington, New South Wales, Australia) Acheson, Merv; Bell, Graeme; Bell, Roger; Brokensha, Jack; Coughlan, Frank; Dallwitz, Dave; Daly, Warren; Featherstone, Benny; Munro, Charlie; Pickering, Tom; Price, Ray; Wilson, Ed

Johnson, Carl (Williamstown, MA) Whiteman, Paul

Joly, Marcel (Rymenam, Belgium) Allen, Henry, Sr.; Balliu, Rudy; Barnes, Emile; Barnes, Polo; Boutté, Lillian; Dirty Dozen Brass Band; Foster, Willie; Laine, Alfred "Baby"; McCord, Ted; Mares, Joe; Nelson, George; Parker, Frank; Petit, Joseph; Purnell, Alton; Rena, Joseph; Sayles, George; van Breedam, Camiel; White, Michael (ii)

Kaye, Harold S. (Atlanta) *New Yorkers (i)

Kenney, William H., III (Kent, OH) Condon, Eddie; De Paris, Sidney; De Paris, Wilbur

Kenselaar, Robert (Maplewood, NJ) Redman, Don

Kernfeld, Barry (State College, PA) Accordion; Adderley, Cannonball; Ammons, Gene; Anderson, Andy (i); Art Ensemble of Chicago; Association for the Advancement of Creative Musicians; Ayler, Albert; Balliett, Whitney; Beat; Berger, Karl; Berimbau; *Blues; Blues progression; Bongos; Bossa nova; Braxton, Anthony; Break; Byrd, Donald; Call and response; Carter, Betty; Carter, Ron; Chambers, Paul; Chase; Circular breathing; Clavichord; Coltrane, John; Conga; Cuíca; Davis, Anthony; Davis, Miles; DeFranco, Buddy; Dixon, Bill; Dolphy, Eric; Dorham, Kenny; Du wah; Eckstine, Billy; False fingering; Favors, Malachi; *Festivals; Garrison, Jimmy; Ghost note; Giddins, Gary; Gilmore, John; Gliss; Griffin, Johnny; Half-valve; Hamilton, Chico; Harmolodic theory; Harmonica; Harp (i); Haynes, Roy; Hentoff, Nat; Hubbard, Freddie; Humphrey, Ralph; Improvisation; Jarman, Joseph; Jefferson, Eddie; *Jones family; Jump; Kessel, Barney; Kirk, Roland; *Lacy, Steve; LaFaro, Scott; Lake, Oliver; Latin jazz; Mahavishnu Orchestra; *Mandolin; Manne, Shelly; Mastersounds; Menza, Don; Merrill, Helen; Metcalf, Louis; Mingus, Charles; Mitchell, Billy; Mitchell, Blue; *Mitchell, George; Mitchell, Roscoe; *Montgomery family; Montoliu, Tete; Moore, Brew; Moore, Oscar; Morello, Joe; Mosley, Snub; Moye, Don; Mraz, George; Mundy, Jimmy; Murray, David; Musette; Musso, Vido; Nance, Ray; Neidlinger, Buell; Nelson, Oliver; Newton, James; Nicholas, Big Nick; Nichols, Herbie; Niewood, Gerry; Norvo, Red; O'Day, Anita; Ørsted Pedersen, Niels-Henning; Payne, Cecil; Pearson, Duke; Pege, Aladár; Peiffer, Bernard; Pepper, Art; Persip, Charli; Peterson, Hannibal; Phillips, Flip; Pomeroy, Herb; Ponty, Jean-Luc; Procope, Russell; Pullen, Don; Purim, Flora; Rava, Enrico; *Recording; Redman, Dewey; Reed, Waymon; Rehak, Frank; Revolutionary Ensemble; Ridley, Larry; Ritenour, Lee; Robinson, Janice; Roland, Gene; Rollins, Sonny; Rouse, Charlie; Rushen, Patrice; Sample, Joe; Sanborn, David; Sanders, Pharoah; Scott, Shirley; Scott, Tom; Scott, Tony; Seifert, Zbigniew; Shake; Shaw, Woody; Shepp, Archie; Shoffner, Bob; Shorter, Wayne; Sims, Zoot; *Singing; Sitar; Smith, Leo; Smith, Lonnie Liston; Snowden, Elmer; Soul jazz; Steel drum; Stop-time; Subtone; Suzuki, Isao; Tablā; Terminal vibrato; Thielemans, Toots; Timeless; Timmons, Bobby; Tolliver, Charles; Ulmer, James "Blood"; Urbaniak, Michal; Vasconcelos, Nana; Vaughan, Sarah; Ventura, Charlie; Verve; Vinson, Eddie "Cleanhead"; Violoncello; Vitous, Miroslav; Waits, Freddie; Waits, Tom; Walcott, Collin; Wallington, George; Walton, Cedar; Warren, Earle; Washington, Dinah; Washington, Grover, Jr.; Watanabe, Sadao; Watkins, Julius; Weather Report; Wellstood, Dick; Wess, Frank; Weston, Randy; Wheeler, Kenny; White, Lenny; Woods, Phil; Young, Snooky

Kjellberg, Erik (Uppsala, Sweden) Arnold, Harry; Babs, Alice; Billberg, Rolf; Björksten, Hacke; Brehm, Simon; Domnérus, Arne; Ehrling, Thore; Ellboj, Lulle; Eriksberg, Folke; Görling, Miff; Görling, Zilas; Gullin, Lars; Gustafsson, Rune; Hallberg, Bengt; Hasselgård, Stan; Hedrenius, Gugge; Hülphers, Arne; Jederby, Thore; Johansson, Jan; Kustbandet; Laine, Bob; Larsson, Rolf; Lidström, Jack; Lind, Nisse "Bagarn"; Lind, Ove; Metronome; Nilson, Gunnar; Norin, Carl-Henrik; Norman, Charlie; Österwall, Seymour; Paramountorkestern; Persson, Åke; Redland, Charles; Rena Rama; Riedel, Georg; Rosengren, Bernt; Sandström, Nisse; Sonet; Svenska Hotkvintetten; Svensson, Reinhold; Swanerud, Thore; Thelin, Eje; Theselius, Gösta; Törner, Gösta; Von Eichwald, Håkan; Wallin, Bengt-Arne; Werner, Lasse; Wickman, Putte; Zetterlund, Monica

Knauer, Wolfram (Kiel, Germany) Bartkowski, Czesław; Bliziński, Marek; *Dauner, Wolfgang; Dębski, Krzesimir; Goykovich, Dusko; Haurand, Ali; Herbolzheimer, Peter; Jaremko, Zbigniew; Karolak, Wojciech; Kay, Connie; *Kühn, Rolf; Kulpowicz, Slawomir; Kurylewicz, Andrzej; Majewski, Henryk; Makowicz, Adam; *Mangelsdorff, Albert; Muniak, Janusz; Namysłowski, Zbigniew; Novi Singers; Orchestra U.S.A.; Passport; Pilz, Michel; Rettenbacher, J. A.; Roidinger, Adelhard; Sadowski, Krzysztof; Schlüter, Wolfgang; Schwab, Sigi; Sehring, Rudi; Stefański, Janusz; Suchanek, Bronisław; Szukalski, Tomasz; Trzaskowski, Andrzej; United Jazz and Rock Ensemble; Weiss, Klaus; Wróblewski, Jan; Zadlo, Leszek; Zgraja, Krzysztof

Koch, Lawrence (Pottsville, PA) Albert, Don; Anderson, Ernestine; Archey, Jimmy; Babasin, Harry; Bates family; Bernstein, Artie; Bert, Eddie; Carisi, Johnny; Catlett, Buddy; Chambers, Henderson; Clark, Buddy; Cole, June; Coleman, Earl; Collette, Buddy; Cranshaw, Bob; Creath, Charlie; Crow, Bill; Davis, Eddie "Lockjaw"; Dominique, Natty; Donaldson, Lou; Drew, John; Duvivier, George; Eager, Allen; Enevoldsen, Bob; Fontana, Carl; Fowlkes, Charlie; Gonzales, Babs; Gray, Wardell; Hayes, Clancy; Henry, Ernie; Holley, Major; Howard, Darnell; Hughes, Bill; Jackson, Quentin; Jazztet; Johnson, Keg; Jones, Sam; McEachern, Murray; McFarland, Gary; McRae, Teddy; Mares, Paul; Marshall, Wendell; Matthews, George; Minor, Dan; Morrow, Buddy; Nelson, Dave; Nicholas, Albert; Nicholas, Wooden Joe; Nimitz, Jack; Nuñez, Alcide "Yellow"; Pecora, Santo; Peña, Ralph; Piano; Powell, Seldon; Six, Jack; Stewart, Buddy; Swope, Earl; Taylor, Billy (i); Vinnegar, Leroy; Watson, Leo; White, Harry

Koenig, Karl (Covington, LA) Assunto family; Brown, Tom; Dejan, Harold; Dukes of Dixieland; Johnson, Dink; Kelly, Chris; Perez, Manuel; Stein, Johnny

Kolleritsch, Elisabeth (Graz, Austria) Institut für Jazzforschung

Kramlich, Raymonde S. (San Francisco) *Bailey, Mildred; Swingle Singers

La Barbara, Joan (Pecos, NM) Teitelbaum, Richard

Laird, Paul R. (State College, PA) Antibes–Juan-les-Pins Jazz Festival; Colorado Jazz Party; Festival International de Jazz de Montréal; *Festivals; International Jazz Jamboree Festival; International New Jazz Festival Moers; Jazzfest Berlin; JVC Grande Parade du Jazz Nice; Molde International Jazz Festival; *Monterey Jazz Festival; Montreux International Jazz Festival; New Orleans Jazz and Heritage Festival; *Newport Jazz Festival; North Sea Jazz Festival; Pori Jazz; Sacramento Dixieland Jubilee

Lamb, Andrew (Croydon, England) Noble, Ray

Lambert, Eddie Ashby, Harold; Bell, Aaron; Brown, Lawrence; Carruthers, Jock; Carry, Scoops; Cook, Willie; Cooper, Buster; Davis, Kay; Davis, Lem; Dixon, Eric; Ellington, Mercer; Glenn, Tyree; Goodwin, Henry; Guy, Fred; Hardwick, Otto; Holder, Terrence; Irvis, Charlie; Jefferson, Hilton; Jenkins, Freddie; Johnson, Jimmy; Lamb, John; Maxwell, Jimmy; Mills, Irving; Minerve, Geezil; Oliver, Sy; Powell, Specs; Quebec, Ike; Quinichette, Paul; Scott, Cecil; Smith, John; Stone, Fred; Sweatman, Wilbur; Thomas, Foots; Tizol, Juan; Webb, Speed; Webster, Paul; Whetsol, Artie; White, Rocky; Wiggins, J. J.; Williams, Franc; Wood, Booty; Woodman, Britt; Woodyard, Sam

Laplace, Michel (La Chapelle St. Ursin, France) *Arvanitas, Georges; Barelli, Aimé; Bellest, Christian; Brun, Philippe; Capon, Jean-Charles; Chautemps, Jean-Louis; Chiboust, Noël; Cohanier, Edmond; Combelle, Alix; Cullaz, Pierre; Double Six; Ekyan, André; Fonsèque, Raymond; Gerard, Fred; Gossez, Pierre; Gregor; Guérin, Roger; Jaume, André; Jeanneau, François; Jullien, Ivan; Legrand, Christiane; Le Lann, Eric; Naude, Jean-Claude; Paquinet, André; Paquinet, Guy; Perrin, Mimi; Persiany, André; Portal, Michel; Rostaing, Hubert; Steckar, Marc; Vander, Maurice; Vauchant, Léo; Ventura, Ray; Warlop, Michel; Weiss, René; Wilen, Barney

Larson, Steve (Philadelphia) Bryant, Ray; Bryant, Tommy; Feldman, Victor; Frishberg, Dave; Grusin, Dave; Hawes, Hampton; Lewis, Ramsey; Oregon

Lee, William F., III (Miami) Almeida, Laurindo; Alvarez, Chico; Bernhart, Milt; Childers, Buddy; Cooper, Bob; Holman, Bill; Levy, Hank; Maiden, Willie; Salvador, Sal; Shank, Bud

Levin, Floyd (Studio City, CA) Burrell, Duke

Lindenmaier, H. L. (Freiburg, Germany) Berendt, Joachim-Ernst; *Lacy, Steve

Litchfield, Jack (Toronto) Davidson, Trump; Harrison, Lance; Holmes, Johnny; Hooper, Lou; Jackson, Calvin; McKay, Cliff; Namaro, Jimmy; Niosi, Bert; Norris, Ray; Sutton, Mynie; Thomas, Millard G.; Watson, Gilbert

Lotz, Rainer E. (Bonn) Abbey, Leon; Abriani, John; Andreozzi, Eduardo; Astaire, Fred; *Bacsik, Elek; Barriteau, Carl; Barton, Billy; *Beamter, Jenő; *Benkó, Sandor; Berlin, Ben; Berry's; Bhumibol Adulyadej; Böhler, Fred; Borchard, Eric; Brandt, Helmut; *Brocksieper, Freddie; Brunner, Eddie; Bubbles, John; *Buttola, Ede; Castandet, Sam; Chaix, Henri; *Chappy; Choquart, Loys; Danzi, Mike; De Gregori, Rio; Dies, Werner; Douglas, Louis; Etté, Bernard; *Filu; Flemming, Herb; Freichel, Louis; Fuhs, Julian; Gluskin, Lud; Goldene Sieben; Guarente, Frank; Henkels, Kurt; Heymans, Phyllis; Hirst, George F.; Hohenberger, Kurt; Höllerhagen, Ernst; Hyde, Alex; Kaye, Cab; Kleindin, Teddy; Kok, James; Kőrössy, János; *Kovács, Andor; *Kovács, Gyula; Lanigiros; Laurence, Baby; Léardée, Ernest; McFarlane, Howard; McKenzie, Red; *Martiny, Lajos; Mavounzy, Robert; Maycock, George; Müller, Werner; New Hot Players; *New Yorkers (i); Nicholas Brothers; Notte, Flavius; Osterwald, Hazy; Pitman, Booker; *Ratip, Ahmed; Rosner, Ady; Salnave, Bertin; Siobud, André; Smith, Crickett; Snow, Valaida; Stauffer, Teddy; Stellio, Alexandre; *Szabados, György; *Tabányi, Mihály; Templin, Lutz; Tevelian, Meg; Wick, Joe; Widmann, Kutte; Williams, Rubberlegs

McCord, Kimberly (Denver) Dodgion, Dottie; Dodgion, Jerry; Dudziak, Urszula; Elias, Eliane; Geller, Herb; Geller, Lor-

raine; International Sweethearts of Rhythm; Rully, Aura
Machlin, Paul S. (Waterville, ME) Larkins, Ellis
Malone, Bill C. (New Orleans) Western Swing; Wills, Bob
Mandel, Howard (New York) Air; McCall, Steve; Olu Dara; Threadgill, Henry
Marsh, Dave (New York) Charles, Ray
Matthiessen, Ole (Copenhagen) *Tchicai, John
Mattingly, Rick (Cedar Grove, NJ) Alexander, Mousey; Brice, Percy; Campbell, Jimmy; Capp, Frank; Chambers, Joe; Clark, Bill; Franco, Guilherme; Harewood, Al; Hooper, Stix; Humphries, Lex; Jackson, Oliver; Miles, Butch; Moore, Eddie; Moses, Bob; Mouzon, Alphonse; Peraza, Armando; Purdie, Bernard; Rae, Johnny; Smith, Charlie; Smith, Marvin "Smitty"
Mazzoletti, Adriano (Rome) Alvaro, Romero; Barzizza, Pippo; Basso, Gianni; Cerri, Franco; Cottiglieri, Piero; Cuppini, Gil; Di Ceglie, Cosimo; Galli, Cesare; *Gaslini, Giorgio; Gorni, Kramer; Grasso, Alfio; Masetti, Glauco; Mobiglia, Tullio; Mojoli, Franco; Mussolini, Romano; Nicolosi, Roberto; Roman New Orleans Jazz Band; Rossi, Aldo; Rotondo, Nunzio; Trovajoli, Armando; Valdambrini, Oscar; Volonté, Eraldo; Zuccheri, Luciano
Milkowski, Bill (New York) Beck, Jeff; Bruford, Bill; Carlton, Larry; Catherine, Philip; Di Meola, Al; Evans, Bill (iii); Frisell, Bill; Guerin, John; James, Bob; Liebman, Dave; Miller, Marcus; Rainey, Chuck; Scofield, John; Stern, Mike; Tacuma, Jamaaladeen; Winter, Paul
Miller, Mark (Toronto) Appleyard, Peter; Clarke, Terry; Collier, Ron; Delamont, Gordon; Galloway, Jim; Jones, Oliver; Koffman, Moe; McConnell, Rob; MacPherson, Fraser; Nimmons, Phil; Ranger, Claude; Symonds, Nelson; Thompson, Don; Vogel, Vic
Mongan, Norman (Dublin) Barbour, Dave; Barksdale, Everett; Barnes, George; Bean, Billy; Budimir, Dennis; Collins, Cal; Gourley, Jimmy; Hendrickson, Al; Kress, Carl; Lowe, Mundell; Pisano, John; Raney, Jimmy; Sete, Bola; Shirley, Jimmy; Thomas, René
Monson, Karen McPartland, Marian
Moore, Carman (New York) *Russell, George
Morgan, Paula (Princeton, NJ) Gushee, Lawrence; Morgenstern, Dan; Shaw, Arnold; Williams, Martin
Morgenstern, Dan (Newark, NJ) Berry, Chu; Challis, Bill; Gifford, Gene
Mumma, Gordon (Santa Cruz, CA) *Recording
Murray, Edward (Ithaca, NY) Evans, Bill (ii)
Nemko, Frankie (Venice, CA) Feather, Leonard
Noglik, Bert (Leipzig, Germany) Bauer, Conrad; Dašek, Rudolf; Gumpert, Ulrich; Petrowsky, Ernst-Ludwig; Schlippenbach, Alex; Schweizer, Irène; Sommer, Gunter; Stańko, Tomasz; Stivín, Jiří; *Szabados, György; Union Deutscher Jazzmusiker
Norton, Pauline (Ann Arbor, MI) Black bottom; Charleston
Ojakäär, Walter (Tallinn, USSR) Bril, Igor; Chekasin, Vladimir; Chizhik, Leonid; Ganelin, Vyacheslav; Garanyan, Georgy; Goloshchokin, David; Gol'shteyn, Gennady; Kozlov, Aleksey; Kuryokhin, Sergey; Kuznetsov, Aleksey; Levinovsky, Nikolay; Luk'yanov, German; Lundstrem, Oleg; Mustafa-Zade, Vagif; Nosov, Konstantin; Oganesyan, Tatevik; Pauls, Raimond; Paulus, Tiit; Raubiško, Raymond; Rozenbergs, Gunārs; Saarsalu, Lembit; Tarasov, Vladimir; Tsfasman, Aleksandr; Utyosov, Leonid; Vapirov, Anatoly; Zubov, Aleksey
Oliver, Paul (Woodstock, England) Barrelhouse; *Blues; Boogie-woogie; Cox, Ida; Hokum; Johnson, Lonnie; Jug band; Race record; Rainey, Ma; Smith, Bessie; Smith, Mamie; Smith, Pine Top; Spivey, Victoria; Tharpe, Sister Rosetta; Turner, Joe (ii); Washboard band
Olliver, Guillermo I. (Capital Federal, Argentina) *Ratip, Ahmed
Ostransky, Leroy (Tacoma, WA) Barber, Bill; Brown, Garnett; Butterfield, Don; Cohn, Al; De la Rosa, Frank; Elliott, Don; Grey, Al; Harris, Bill (ii); Horn, Paul; Jones, Quincy; Mann, Herbie; Newman, Joe; Payne, Sonny; Powell, Benny; Redd, Vi; Richards, Emil; Royal, Ernie; Royal, Marshall; Safranski, Eddie; Three Sounds
Owens, Thomas (Torrance, CA) American Jazz Orchestra; Bop; Burrell, Kenny; Byas, Don; Calypso; Christian, Charlie; Cole, Richie; Criss, Sonny; Crusaders; Forms; Gillespie, Dizzy; Gryce, Gigi; Handy, John; Heath family; Jackson, Milt; Jazz at the Philharmonic; L. A. Four; Lewis, John; Modern Jazz Quartet; Navarro, Fats; Poindexter, Pony; Quill, Gene; Samba; Stitt, Sonny; Supersax; V.S.O.P. (i)
Papo, Alfredo (Barcelona) Albalat, Sebastià; Bas, Vlady; Benavent, Carles; Farras, Josep-María; Farreras, Joe; Iturralde, Pedro; Moro, Joe; Puertas, Josep; Regoli, Enrique; Roda, Ricard
Passy, Charles (New York) *Lewis, George (ii)
Patrick, James (Eggertsville, NY) Parker, Charlie; Tinney, Al
Peerless, Brian (London) Beneke, Tex; Benford, Bill; Benford, Tommy; Bernhardt, Clyde; Best, Johnny; Bob Cats; Bonano, Sharkey; Brown, Vernon; Butterfield, Billy; Clambake Seven; Cutshall, Cutty; Elman, Ziggy; Erwin, Pee Wee; Gramercy Five; Haggart, Bob; Hubble, Ed; Humphrey family; Lawson, Yank; McGarity, Lou; Miller, Eddie; Miller, Punch; O'Brien, Floyd; Privin, Bernie; Rosengarden, Bobby; Shu, Eddie; Van Eps, George; World's Greatest Jazz Band
Pennell, Brenda (Cary, NC) Brecker, Mike; Brecker, Randy; Budwig, Monty; De Brest, Spanky; Flory, Med; Kloss, Eric; Mondragon, Joe; Ortega, Tony; Tucker, George; Wright, Gene
Pernet, Robert (Brussels) Aerts, Jos; Bay, Francis; Bee, David; Bistrouille ADO; Bob Shots; Brenders, Stan; Breyre, Jos; Bruder, Rudy; Candrix, Fud; Claes, Johnny; Clark, Gus; Colignon, Raymond "Coco"; Compère, René; Coppieters, Fernand; Coppieters, Francis; Cotton City Jazz Band; De Bie, Ivon; De Boeck, Jeff; De Kers, Robert; Deloof, Gus; Dixie Stompers; Doucet, Clément; Excellos Five; Kluger, Jack; Naret, Bobby; Omer, Jean; Ouwerx, John; Packay, Peter; Pâques, Jean; Pelzer, Jacques; Quersin, Benoit; Remue, Chas; Robert, Jean; Sadi, Fats; Sels, Jack; Van Ha Trio; Viseur, Gus
Phillips, David C. (Reading, England) *Ukulele
Pleasants, Henry (London) *Bailey, Mildred; Crosby, Bing; *Laine, Cleo; Sinatra, Frank; Waters, Ethel
Porter, Lewis (Riverdale, NY) Bassoon; *Bigard family; Blakey, Art; Clarinet; DeJohnette, Jack; Flute; Gordon, Dexter; Hawkins, Coleman; Hodges, Johnny; Johnson, J. J.; *Montgomery family; Oboe; Saxophone; Williams, Tony; Young, Lester
Potter, Jeff (New York) Best, Denzil; Bobo, Willie; Correa, Mayuto; Da Costa, Paulinho; Dahlander, Bert; Deems, Barrett; Dunlop, Frankie; Goodwin, Bill; Johnson, Osie; Kluger, Irv; Landrum, Richard; Levey, Stan; McCurdy, Roy; Mason, Harvey; Narell, Andy; Richmond, Dannie; Riley, Ben; Roker, Mickey; Shaughnessy, Ed; Taylor, Art
Pressing, Jeff (Bundoora, Victoria, Australia) *Bailey, Judy; *Banks, Don; *Buddle, Errol; *Burrows, Don; *Golla, George; *Gould, Tony; *Johnson, Frank; *Lyall, Graeme; *Rohde, Bryce; *Sangster, John; *Speers, Stewie; *Turnbull, Alan

Priestley, Brian (London) Adams, George; Amram, David; Burns, Ralph; Cirillo, Wally; Dennis, Willie; Heath, Ted; Hefti, Neal; Henderson, Horace; Jazz Artists Guild; Johnson, Howard (ii); Jones, Bobby; LaPorta, John; McCarthy, Albert; Mingus Dynasty; Morgan, Frank; New York Jazz Repertory Company; Rugolo, Pete; Sauter, Eddie; Strozier, Frank; Walrath, Jack

Radano, Ronald M. (Madison, WI) Casa Loma Orchestra; Gray, Glen; Hunter, Alberta; Thornhill, Claude

Rattenbury, Ken (Walsall, England) Allan, Jan; Baker, Kenny; Baker, Shorty; Ball, Kenny; California Ramblers; Collins, Shad; Donaldson, Bobby; Ericson, Rolf; Jordan, Taft; Kaminsky, Max; McKinley, Ray; Martin, Sara; Moore, Big Chief; Original Memphis Five; Randall, Freddy; Reece, Dizzy; Roy, Harry; Zurke, Bob

Rhyan, Dianna (Columbus, OH) Caliman, Hadley; Cherico, Gene; Herbert, Gregory; Isaacs, Ike (i); Khan, Steve; Lorber, Jeff; McKusick, Hal; Ore, John; Simpkins, Andy; Watkins, Doug

Richards, Martin (Worcester, England) Turney, Norris

Riis, Thomas (Athens, GA) Theater Owners' Booking Association

Rinzler, Paul (Santa Cruz, CA) Alexander, Monty; *Arvanitas, Georges; Baker, David; Barron, Bill; Barron, Kenny; Beirach, Richard; Bonner, Joe; Bright, Ronnell; Bunch, John; Cables, George; Cameron, Jay; Coker, Dolo; Davis, Walter; De Arango, Bill; Dunbar, Ted; Friedman, Don; Galper, Hal; Gumbs, Onaje Allen; Hakim, Sadik; Hammond, Johnny; Hyman, Dick; Jackson, Michael Gregory; Jordan, Duke; Kuhn, Steve; *Laine, Cleo; Legge, Wade; Longo, Mike; Mabern, Harold; McCandless, Paul; Mainieri, Mike; Malachi, John; Manhattan Transfer; Maria, Tania; Melvoin, Mike; Moore, Glen; Newborn, Calvin; Newborn, Phineas; Parlan, Horace; Patterson, Don; Pizzi, Ray; Powell, Richie; Previn, André; Rare Silk; Schnitter, David; Tompkins, Ross; Tucker, Mickey

Roberts, David Thomas (Littleton, CO) Bloom, Rube; Schutt, Arthur

Roberts, John Storm (Tivoli, NY) Barretto, Ray; Machito; Pozo, Chano; Santamaria, Mongo; Santana, Carlos; Tjader, Cal

Robinson, J. Bradford (Haar, Germany) Abercrombie, John; Akiyoshi, Toshiko; Allen, Henry "Red"; Anderson, Cat; Baker, Chet; Basie, Count; *Beiderbecke, Bix; Bellson, Louie; Blanton, Jimmy; Bley, Carla; Blue note (i); Bolden, Buddy; Brookmeyer, Bob; Brown, Ray; Catlett, Sid; Chicago jazz; Cobham, Billy; Dixieland jazz; Dodds, Baby; Dodds, Johnny; Eldridge, Roy; Evans, Herschel; Farlow, Tal; Fitzgerald, Ella; Free jazz; Garner, Erroll; Getz, Stan; Gonsalves, Paul; Granz, Norman; Grappelli, Stephane; Hampton, Lionel; Humes, Helen; Jarreau, Al; Jones, Jo; Kansas City jazz; Kenton, Stan; Kirby, John; Komeda, Krzysztof; Konitz, Lee; Lunceford, Jimmie; Mulligan, Gerry; Nanton, Tricky Sam; Page, Walter; Pass, Joe; Pastorius, Jaco; Pettiford, Oscar; Pollack, Ben; Powell, Bud; Riff; Rogers, Shorty; Scat singing; Singleton, Zutty; Smith, Willie; Stewart, Rex; Stewart, Slam; Sullivan, Maxine; Swallow, Steve; Swing (i); *Tatum, Art; Territory band; Terry, Clark; Tough, Dave; Towner, Ralph; Trent, Alphonso; Tristano, Lennie; Venuti, Joe; Vocalese; Webb, Chick; Webster, Ben; Williams, Cootie; Williams, Mary Lou; Wilson, Teddy; Yancey, Jimmy

Rockwell, John (New York) Palmer, Robert

Root, Deane L. (Pittsburgh) Vamp

Rouder, Willa (New York) Johnson, James P.

Roy, James G., Jr. (New York) *Russell, George

Russell, Bill (New Orleans) Barbarin family; Braud, Wellman; Brunies family; Butler, Joe; Dutrey, Sam; Hug, Armand; Manetta, Manuel; *Morgan family; Palmer, Roy; Pierce, De De; St. Cyr, Johnny; Simeon, Omer; Thomas, Joe (i); Thompson, Butch; Watkins, Joe; Wiggs, Johnny

Rye, Howard (London) *Appleton, Joe; Baranco, Wilbert; Black Swan; *Blake, Cyril; Booker, Beryl; Brown, Olive; Butler, Billy; Chamblee, Eddie; Craig, Al; Davis, Maxwell; Gary, Shelton; Godley, A. G.; Handy, W. C.; *Hutchinson, Jiver; Johnson, Floyd "Candy"; *King, Bertie; Mitchell, Louis; Profit, Clarence; Queen, Alvin; Silva, Michael; Smith, Carrie; Smith, Clara; Stokes, Irvin; Turner, Charlie; Washington, Buck; Williams, J. Mayo

Santi, Piero (Milan) *Gaslini, Giorgio

Schafer, William J. (Berea, KY) Brass band; Camelia Brass Band; Eagle Band; Eureka Brass Band; Excelsior Brass Band; Imperial Orchestra; Olympia Brass Band; Olympia Orchestra; Onward Brass Band (i); Onward Brass Band (ii); Original Tuxedo Orchestra; Ragtime; Young Tuxedo Brass Band

Scheinin, Richard (Philadelphia) Lee, Jeanne

Schneider, Wayne (Waterville, ME) Anthony, Ray; Bradley, Will; Castle, Lee; Clinton, Larry; Donahue, Sam; Gray, Jerry; Hite, Les; Jones, Isham; May, Billy; Zentner, Si

Schuller, Gunther (Newton Centre, MA) Afro-Cuban jazz; Arrangement; Coleman, Ornette; *Ellington, Duke; Evans, Gil; Jam session; Krupa, Gene; Morton, Jelly Roll; Moten, Bennie; Smith, Buster; Stomp; Third stream; Walking bass

Schulz, Klaus (Vienna) Auer, Vera; Drewo, Karl; George, Fatty; Grah, Bill; *Gulda, Friedrich; Kleinschuster, Erich; Koller, Hans; Landl, Ernst; Vienna Art Orchestra; Winter, Horst

Schwalm, Peter (Basel, Switzerland) Ambrosetti, Franco; Antolini, Charly; Court, Raymond; Eckinger, Isla; Gruntz, George; Klein, Oscar; Moeckel, Thomas; Schmidli, Peter; Schwaller, Roman; Trippel, Fritz

Shaw, Arnold (Las Vegas, NV) Bailey, Pearl

Sheridan, Chris (Berkhamsted, England) Bolton, Dupree; Brooks, Tina; Deuchar, Jimmy; Green, Urbie; Harding, Buster; Harriott, Joe; Henderson, Bill; Johnson, Gus; Jones, Eddie; Jones, Harold; Jones, Rufus; Keane, Shake; Keenan, Norman; Killian, Al; Mitchell, Grover; Most, Sam; Plater, Bobby; *Recording; Rutherford, Rudy; Smith, Jimmie; Taylor, John; Wilder, Joe; Williams, Claude; Winstone, Norma

Shipton, Alyn (Oxford, England) Banjo; Barker, Blue Lu; Barker, Danny; Battle of bands; Celesta; Colar, Kid Sheik; *Cornet; Double bass; Firehouse Five Plus Two; Garland, Ed "Montudi"; *Goodman, Benny; *Hall family; Hall, Al; Harpsichord; Jones, Dill; Kelley, Peck; Keppard, Louis; Kohlman, Freddie; Lafertin, Fapy; Landers, Wes; Lindsay, John; *Mandolin; Martyn, Barry; Miller, Sing; *Mitchell, George; *Morgan family; *Mute; New Black Eagle Jazz Band; Organ; Piccolo bass; Reed organ; Sherman, Herman; Slap-bass; Slap-tonguing; String band; *Teagarden family; Tiple; Trad; *Violin; *Waller, Fats; Waso; Young, Trummy

Simmen, Johnny (Zurich) Alvis, Hayes; Autrey, Herman; Berry, Emmett; Buckner, Teddy; Bunn, Teddy; Carlisle, Una Mae; Coleman, Bill; Kelly, George; Kyle, Billy; Leeman, Cliff; Mills Blue Rhythm Band; Newton, Frankie; Savoy Sultans (i); Savoy Sultans (ii); Shaw, Arvell; Simmons, John; Smith, Russell; Turner, Joe (i); Wettling, George

Simon, Géza Gábor (Budapest) *Bacsik, Elek; *Beamter, Jenő; *Benkó, Sandor; *Buttola, Ede; *Chappy; *Filu; *Kőrössy, János; *Kovács, Andor; *Kovács, Gyula; *Martiny, Lajos; *Szabados, György; *Tabányi, Mihály

Skrimshire, Nevil (Rayleigh, England) Amstell, Billy; Archer, Tony; Babbington, Roy; Baldock, Kenny; Branscombe, Alan; Clare, Kenny; Colyer, Ken; Condon, Les; Dvorak, Jim; Featherstonhaugh, Buddy; Green, Dave; Griffiths, Malcolm; Harvey, Eddie; Hayes, Harry; Heatley, Spike; Kinsey, Tony; Krahmer, Carlo; Laurie, Cy; McQuater, Tommy; Mann, Tony; Mumford, John; Parnell, Jack; Phillips, Sid; Purbrook, Colin; Pyne, Chris; Pyne, Mick; Shaw, Hank; Skidmore, Jimmy; Smith, Betty; Smythe, Pat; Squadronaires; Sunshine, Monty; Williams, John (iii)

Smith, Ernie (New York) Films

Smith, Gregory E. (Boston) Abene, Mike; Clark, Sonny; Dailey, Al; Harris, Gene; Hope, Elmo; Kellaway, Roger; Lawson, Hugh; Mayers, Lloyd; Norris, Walter; Redd, Freddie

Southern, Eileen (Cambridge, MA) Blake, Eubie; Cook, Will Marion; Europe, James Reese

Starkie, Walter *Elizalde, Fred

Strunk, Steven (Washington) Albam, Manny; Berry, Bill; Brown, Marshall; Fischer, Clare; Golson, Benny; Graas, John; Handy, George; Harmony (i); Harris, Little Benny; Hill, Teddy; Hooper, Les; LaBarbera family; Mandel, Johnny; Mello, Mike; Nestico, Sammy; Ogerman, Claus; Paich, Marty; Phillips, Sonny; Richards, Johnny

Such, David G. (Los Angeles) Anderson, Fred; Brown, Marion; Ewart, Douglas; Garnett, Carlos; Hemphill, Julius; Howard, Noah; Lancaster, Byard; Lowe, Frank; McIntyre, Ken; Tyler, Charles

Sudhalter, Richard (New York) Bose, Sterling; Edwards, Eddie; Goldkette, Jean; Klein, Manny; LaRocca, Nick; McPartland, Dick; McPartland, Jimmy; Rollini, Art; Shields family; Wiley, Lee

Tallmadge, William H. (Berea, KY) Watters, Lu

Taylor, J. R. (Washington) Johnson, Bunk; Keppard, Freddie; Kirk, Andy; Miley, Bubber; Roberts, Luckey; Spanier, Muggsy; Teschemacher, Frank; *Williams, Clarence

Thacker, Eric (Leeds, England) Allyn, David; Arnet, Jan; Hot; McVea, Jack

Theroux, Gary (Ossining, NY) Ayers, Roy; Curtis, King; Friedman, David; Gibbs, Terry; Gordon, Joe; Mantler, Mike; Pike, Dave; Sheldon, Jack; Williams, Richard; Young, Larry

Tovey, Michael (Ashbourne, Ireland) Barrelhouse jazz; Burbank, Albert; Casimir, John; Duhé, Lawrence; Hightower, Willie; Hill, Chippie; Jones, Snags; Manone, Wingy; Miles, Lizzie; Montgomery, Little Brother; O'Bryant, Jimmy; Price, Sammy; Roppolo, Leon; Tate, Erskine; Taylor, Jasper; Thomas, Kid; Williams, Pearlis

Tucker, Mark (New York) Allen, Steve; Brown, Les; Jungle music; Lewis, Ted; Mills Brothers; Pastor, Tony; Riddle, Nelson; Schuller, Gunther; Scott, Hazel; Severinsen, Doc; Transcription (i); Washingtonians

Ullman, Michael (Newton, MA) Ali, Rashied; Benjamin, Joe; Blackwell, Ed; Cyrille, Andrew; Daniels, Eddie; Davis, Art; Fields, Herbie; Gomez, Eddie; Graves, Milford; Higgins, Billy; Jones, Philly Joe; Kamuca, Richie; Moreira, Airto; Murray, Sunny; Peacock, Gary; Perkins, Bill

Vaché, Warren, Sr. (Rahway, NJ) Addison, Bernard; Braff, Ruby; Casey, Al; Clooney, Rosemary; Corcoran, Corky; Evans, Doc; Flanigan, Phil; Haymer, Herbie; Jerome, Jerry; Marsala, Joe; Marsala, Marty; Matlock, Matty; *Mercer, Johnny; Most, Abe; Nash, Dick; Nash, Ted; Pettis, Jack; Pizzarelli, Bucky; Pizzarelli, John; Powell, Rudy; Sedric, Gene; Wolverines

Vacher, Peter (Pinner, England) Buckner, Milt; Buckner, Ted; Callender, Red; Claxton, Rozelle; Darensbourg, Joe; Davern, Kenny; Durham, Eddie; Edwards, Teddy; Forrest, Jimmy; Heard, J. C.; Middlebrooks, Wilfred; Smalls, Cliff; Wiggins, Gerry; Woods, Chris

Vanberg, Vidar (Oslo) Bergh, Øivind; Bergheim, Kristian; Big Chief Jazzband; Engstrøm, Kalle; Flagstad, Michael; Greenberg, Rowland; Hauger, Kristian; Iversen, Einar; Johansen, Bjørn; Kapstad, Egil; Normann, Robert; Ottersen, Frank; Sønstevold, Gunnar

Van Eyle, Wim (Sint Maarten, Netherlands) Altena, Maarten; Beck, Pia; Bishop, Wallace; Breuker, Willem; Bunink, Nico; Burton, Ann; Courbois, Pierre; De Graaff, Rein; De Vries, Louis; Dutch Swing College Band; Engels, John; Haverhoek, Henk; Hinze, Chris; Ilcken, Wessel; Jacobs, Pim; Janssen, Guus; Loevendie, Theo; Masman, Theo Uden; Mengelberg, Misha; Meyer, Johnny; Morks, Jan; Noordijk, Piet; Povel, Ferdinand; Ramblers; Reys, Rita; Schilperoort, Peter; See, Cees; Stichting Jazz en Geïmproviseerde Musiek in Nederland; van Dijk, Louis; van Rooyen, Ack; van 't Hof, Jasper; van 't Hoff, Ernst; van Vliet, Toon; Weersma, Melle; Willebrandts, Dick

Van Vorst, Paige (Chicago) Chicago Rhythm Kings; Harlem Hamfats

Vaughn, Genevieve (Waldwick, NJ) Russo, Bill

Velez, Sara (New York) *Monterey Jazz Festival; *Newport Jazz Festival

Vincent, Julian F. V. (Reading, England) Banjulele; *Ukulele

Voigt, John (Allston, MA) Bennett, Max; Betts, Keter; Bond, Jimmy; Counce, Curtis; Crosby, Israel; Egan, Mark; Gilmore, Steve; Grimes, Henry; Haas, Eddie de; Heard, John; Izenzon, David; James, Stafford; Johnson, Reggie; Laird, Rick; McClure, Ron; Nasser, Jamil; Phillips, Barre; Stinson, Albert; Taylor, Gene; Totah, Nobby

Vollmer, Albert (Larchmont, NY) Barefield, Eddie; Purnell, Keg; Ramirez, Ram

Waggoner, Andrew (Syracuse, NY) Brown, Sam; Brown, Sonny; Carvin, Michael; Fuller, Curtis; Green, Grant; Ponder, Jimmy; Vick, Harold

Wang, Richard (Chicago) Brubeck, Dave; *Cole, Nat "King"; *Goodman, Benny; Jamal, Ahmad; Noone, Jimmie; Shaw, Artie

Webster, Derek (Manchester, England) Bechet Legacy; Soprano Summit; Wilber, Bob

Weir, Bob (Cardiff) Cohn, Sonny; Countsmen; Larkin, Milt; Metronome All Stars; Price, Jesse; Saints and Sinners; Williams, Joe; Witherspoon, Jimmy

Whiteoak, John (Bundoora, Victoria, Australia) *Bailey, Judy; *Banks, Don; *Buddle, Errol; *Burrows, Don; *Golla, George; *Gould, Tony; *Johnson, Frank; *Lyall, Graeme; *Rohde, Bryce; *Sangster, John; *Speers, Stewie; *Turnbull, Alan

Wiedemann, Erik (Copenhagen) Axen, Bent; Bonfils, Kjeld; Botchinsky, Allan; Christensen, Bernhard; Clausen, Thomas; Dørge, Pierre; Eiberg, Valdemar; Emborg, Jørgen; Esbensen, Egon; Ewans, Kai; Fabricius-Bjerre, Bent; Foss, Niels; Glindemann, Ib; Hagemann, Henry; Harlem Kiddies; Henriksen, Bruno; Jædig, Bent; Kroner, Erling; Lington, Otto; Mathisen, Leo; Mazur, Marilyn; Mikkelborg, Palle; Moseholm, Erik; Parker, Erik; Radioens Big Band; Radiojazzgruppen (i); Rasmussen, Peter; Riel, Alex; Roger Henrichsen, Børge; Savery, Finn; Skjoldborg, Anker; Stief, Bo; *Tchicai, John; Thilo, Jesper; Tuxen, Erik; Vinding, Mads

Wild, David (Los Angeles) Altschul, Barry; Anderson, Ray; Bartz, Gary; Bluiett, Hamiet; Coleman, George; Curson, Ted; Davis, Nathan; Draper, Ray; Ford, Ricky; Fortune, Sonny; Grossman, Steve; Harper, Billy; Hoggard, Jay; Klemmer,

John; Lawrence, Arnie; Lawrence, Azar; *Lewis, George (ii); Little, Booker; Lloyd, Charles; Marsalis, Branford; Maupin, Bennie; Newman, David "Fathead"; Owens, Charles; Priester, Julian; Robinson, Perry; Simmons, Sonny; Tabackin, Lew; Ward, Carlos

Will, Patrick T. (Goleta, CA) Bernhardt, Warren; Gale, Eric; Gottlieb, Danny; Klugh, Earl; Lee, David; Mays, Lyle; Return to Forever; Sebesky, Don; Spyro Gyra; Steps Ahead

Williams, J. Kent (Greensboro, NC) Bailey, Dave; Bailey, Donald; Brooks, Roy; Bunker, Larry; Butler, Frank; Cobb, Jimmy; Foster, Al; Gladden, Eddie; Hamilton, Jeff; Hanna, Jake; Hart, Billy; Hayes, Louis; La Roca, Pete; Lewis, Mel; McBrowne, Lennie; Morgan, Sonny; Perkins, Walter; Tate, Grady; Thigpen, Ben; Thigpen, Ed

Williams, Martin (Washington) Ammons, Albert; Lewis, Meade "Lux"

Wilmer, Valerie (London) Gaynair, Wilton "Bogey"

Wilson, Clive (New Orleans) *Hall family

Wilson, Olly (Berkeley, CA) Brown, Clifford; Clarke, Kenny; *Jones family; Roach, Max

Witmer, Robert (North York, Canada) Ax; Back; Ballad; Bend; Blow; Bomb; Book; Chops; Comp; Fake book; Fill; Honk; Lead; Lead sheet; Lick; Lip; Notation; Standard

Woolley, Stan (Southport, England) Israels, Chuck; Liston, Melba; McKibbon, Al; Stamm, Marvin; Wallace, Bennie

Worsfold, Sally-Ann (Rayleigh, England) Burch, John; Fawkes, Wally; McNair, Harold; Napper, Kenny; Nichols, Keith; Parker, Johnny; Patterson, Ottilie; Shannon, Terry; Stobart, Kathy; Taylor, Mike; Tompkins, Trevor

Yanow, Scott (Burbank, CA) Berman, Sonny; Castro, Joe; Doggett, Bill; Duke, George; Fuller, Walter; Hawkins, Erskine; Hicks, John; Hurley, Clyde; Jones, Jonah; Jones, Reunald; Lamond, Don; Lawson, Janet; Leviev, Milcho; Lightsey, Kirk; McCann, Les; Maini, Joe; Matthews, Dave; Montrose, Jack; Mullens, Moon; New York Jazz Quartet; Nistico, Sal (ii); Nottingham, Jimmy; Pierce, Nat; Rebillot, Pat; Rodney, Red; Ruiz, Hilton; Sherock, Shorty; Shew, Bobby; Spivak, Charlie; Stoller, Alvin; Sullivan, Ira; Thompson, Lucky; Vance, Dick; Watrous, Bill; Webster, Freddie; West, Doc; Williams, James; Williamson, Stu; Wilson, Jack; Wilson, Phil

Zager, Daniel (Oberlin, OH) Allen, Walter C.; Baraka, Amiri; Dance, Stanley; Dapogny, James; DeMicheal, Don; Gitler, Ira; Gleason, Ralph J.; Hoefer, George; Lyons, Len; Ramsey, Fred; Rusch, Bob; Shapiro, Nat; Simon, George T.; Smith, Charles Edward; Stearns, Marshall W.; Wanzo, Mel

Zieff, Bob (Carlisle, PA) Allen, Ed; Austin, Lovie; Carey, Mutt; Dickerson, Carroll; Dunn, Johnny; Green, Charlie; Jones, Claude; Ladnier, Tommy; Stark, Bobby; Williams, Sandy